The Great Alternative & Indie Discography

Reviews for
Martin C. Strong's

The Great Rock Discography

"Illustrated with some humour and considerable expertise by Harry Horse, it's a killer tome well worth the money that Canongate are asking ... as far as discographical books are concerned, this one can safely be filed under 'unbelievable' " – **Fred Dellar, N.M.E.**

"Exhaustive and refreshingly opinionated" – **The Guardian**

"Strong is rock's Leslie Halliwell" – **Scotland on Sunday**

"The book, which took ten years to compile, is a worthy rival to the Music Master catalogue" – **The Times**

"A labour of love which has produced a monumental chronicle of rock music ... mighty" – **The Herald**

"Far more accurate and comprehensive than many other similar books" – **Time Out**

"Extremely well-presented and more readable than a reference book has any right to be" – **Mojo**

"If you really want to know EVERTHING, you need *The Great Rock Discography*" – **The Sun**

'This is THE rock reference bible" – **What's On**

"A Herculean labour of love ... Strong should provide hours of useful diversions for record collectors" – **Q**

"The last word in rock 'n' roll trainspotting" – **The Guardian**

"An essential tome for music obsessives" – **The Face**

The Great Alternative & Indie Discography

Martin C. Strong

Illustrations by Harry Horse

CANONGATE

First published in Great Britain in 1999 by Canongate Books Ltd,
14 High Street, Edinburgh EH1 1TE

10 9 8 7 6 5 4 3 2 1

British Library Cataloguing-in-Publication Data
A catalogue record for this book is available on request from the British Library

ISBN 0 86241 913 1

Typeset by TexturAL, Edinburgh

Printed and bound by WSOY, Finland

This book is dedicated to . . .

my mother JEAN FOTHERINGHAM
(born: 6th of January 1929,
died of cancer: 31st of August 1985)

Still missing you
and thanks for still
guiding me through all
the hard times.

my dad GERRY/GEOFF STRONG
(born: 28th of July 1930,
died of a heart attack: 20th October 1998)

Will miss you always.
You were also a great friend, inspiration
and someone who could make me laugh.
Hope you're both getting on up there.
If only . . .

Acknowledgements

I'd like to thank the following people who've helped me with this book (i.e. contributors):– BRENDON GRIFFIN, ALAN Y. LAWSON, SUZANNE STRONG, VAN JOHANN, PAUL and NAN McCARTHY, LEIGH HARGREAVES, JEROEN DERUITER, CAROLINE ROBERTSON, and great friends ALLAN and ELAINE BREWSTER, VIC ZDZIEBLO, SANDY and CAROLINE McCRAE, PETER McGUCKIN, DOUGIE NIVEN, MIKEY KINNAIRD, JOHN HILL, BRIAN and MARGARET HUNTER, MICHAEL FLETCHER + SHONA, EILEEN SCOTT-MONCRIEFF, FORREST DUNCAN, TAM MORRISON, LES O'CONNOR (deceased), CHRIS REID (deceased), GEORDIE YOUNG (deceased), DAVIE BLAIR, everyone at Alex SMITH's bar/lounge including the manager ALLAN MANN, pint-pullers ANDY SHERIFF, GEORDIE CUNNINGHAM, CARRIE DRUMMOND, FIONA McNEILL, JENNI DEWAR, COLIN ARMSTRONG and anchor woman CHRISTINE MAIN, regulars PAUL KLEMM, BILL FISHER, JOE SIMPSON, TONY HUGHES, BRIAN LONEY, JOHN McARDLE, BILLY and ANN ROSS, GRANT + CAROL ANN BAILEY, JOCK NEWTON, ELLA CRAWFORD, DAVIE McPHAIT + LIZ RISK, MARTIN 'No.2' McDERMOTT, WATTY MORRISON, SKIN, GORDON GREGG, BARRY MOORE, IRENE WHYTE, big DAVIE, JIM McPHAIL, ALAN windows! 'EGIE', BRIAN + KAREN, DOUGIE AITKEN, DEREK IRVINE, SCOTT CAMERON, along with HAMISH 'the artist', MARTIN KAY, YVONNE TOAL, ANDY RISK, ALEX O'NEILL, BRIAN VAUSE, RUSSELL MAYES, my accountant GRAHAM MINTO, my solicitor RAY MORTON, DAVID BLUE, JOCK HANLON, BOBBY CALLAGHAN, IAN 'HARRY' HARRISON, TOMMY 'The Token' COCHRANE, HUNTER WATT, TED MOCHAR, DAVIE SEATH, HAMISH McLEOD-PRENTICE, ROY JACK, MALCOLM STEWART (of *Jimpress* fanzine), Hebrides guys DAVIE BISSETT, MALCOLM YORK, ANDY SUTHERLAND and JOHN BISSETT, EWAN (of Europa Records, Stirling), the Falkirk Library, The 'Great' NME, Rough Guide, Billboard, Guinness Who's Who/Muze, All Music Guide and Laserlog (for a few catalogue numbers), plus Record Collector for finally reviewing this book (as if!).

A special mention to my daughters SUZANNE (aged 17) and SHIRLEY (aged 19), my grandson IVOR (aged 1 and a half), my granny MACKAY (now aged 92!), my auntie JOYCE, my cousins PAUL, STEPHEN, BRIAN, MAUREEN and KEVIN McELROY (ages not necessary).

I'm "great"-ful to everyone who wrote to me over the last year or so:- JAN KUEHNEMUND (of the US girl band VIXEN; wow! makes you wanna visit the States!), STEFFEN SCHMITT, HOLGER RINGEISEN, a metal fanatic called ROD, KIP HANNAN, ALBRECHT KOENIG, KLAUS HENSEL, DAVID JOHNS, BJ PURDIE, IAN STEWART, JURGEN SCHAFER, PAUL WHITTINGHAM, CHRISTOPH CASSEL, MIKE ALEXANDER, WOLFGANG SCHMIDT, Australian RITA GIACOMELLI, NEIL SANDERS, JAN SCHAEFER, MARTIN NISBET, BOB PARR, RICHARD-MICHAEL KUJAS, ALEXANDER KAROTSCH, NICK MORONEY, RICHARD HENNESSEY, GRAEME LARMOUR, TERRY POULTON, JOEL A. STEIN, TONY McGROGAN, JOHN SIEWERT, RICHARD JONES, GUILLAUME BARREAU-DECHERF, MICHAEL YEATES, BERTHOLD NUCHTER, DOUGLAS A. BROWN, C. BLAIR, STEWART WILLIAMSON, MARK CHAMBERLIN, DAVID CLOUTER, ANDREAS DUDA, STUART MAZDON, SAM VANDIVER, STEVE ALLEN, WOLFGANG NUCHTER, ALEXEI ROUDITCHEV, STEFAN WEBER, STUART CAMERON, CHRIS CLARK, WIM VAN DER MARK, MARK O SULLIVAN, BERNARD PIERRE (Ambassador of Belgium in Prague!), JOHN MACKIE, NIGEL COUZINS, TONY FARNBOROUGH, CHRIS OWEN, JOHN STEEL, GEOFF WHITE, JONATHAN and PAUL COOK, HORST LUEDTKE, FRANZ ZEIDLER, OLIVER SEIDL, AL HOLLYWOOD, ULI SCHMIDT, JOHN GREAVES, J. BENNINK, ANDREAS SCHOLLIG, SCOTT MURPHY (*The Filth And The Fury* fanzine), ALAN SPICER, PETER J. SMITH, AIDAN P. DOWNEY, JORG FOTH, SILVIO HELLEMANN, AXEL DREYER, ALAN OFFICER, DAVE NASH, JAMES MICHAEL CURLAND, ANDY CARR and NICK WALL.

I'd also like to give a special mention to BRENDON, who contributed his spare time collaborating with me on certain areas of the book. He'd like to thank all those who have given him inspiration and/or support:– A big hi! to the usual suspects and a special mention for MICHELLE CHUNG, who I criminally overlooked last time around. Likewise all the good, good people I've met in the last year: HOLLY PETERS, EVA MANZANO CAPEL, GAIL MUIR and associated crew (NEIL, KATE, ALAN, JOHN, etc), SOUL SISTER No.1, NIKKI KING and the last but definitely not least, the ever lovely JENNY McKENZIE.

Preface / Introduction
(The Secret History of The Punk Rock Book)

The GREAT ALTERNATIVE & INDIE DISCOGRAPHY is my 8th book published by Canongate and the third in a series of offshoots which have also included The GREAT PSYCHEDELIC DISCOGRAPHY and The GREAT METAL DISCOGRAPHY.

Believe it or not, I began this "Punk/New Wave" book over 17 years ago in the summer of '82, finally completing it – or I thought I did – 3 years later. The first "neatly written" incarnation went with me to London and was – quite rightly so – rejected by publishers, Salamander, whose managing editor, Ray Bonds, gave me good advice to er . . . think about typing it out. A few years later I tried again and was rejected – by post – several times, each with the same answer. It was then I sold my house and decided to buy a wee computer, although this was yer basic Amstrad steam engine type thing that was only useful as a good print-out machine.

By the early 90's, I took their advice and expanded my discographies to incorporate mainstream ROCK and pre-Punk artists/groups; I liked all types of ROCK, so why not. I think everybody knows the story of me walking into Canongate's offices and quite literally convincing the editors to give it a once over before they knocked it back. They were stunned and almost immediately said yes to the whole project getting underway. The rest is history and I've not got the space (or deadline time) to tell you more. The BOOK OF ROCK DISCOGRAPHIES was going to be published, hooray for MARTIN STRONG; Falkirk would know he wasn't bullshitting after all (another long story!).

Several years and books later (and after the death of my father in October 1998), I decided to restart the "ALTERNATIVE & INDIE" (formerly the "PUNK & NEW WAVE") book. Of course, although many of the acts had been included in the main 4th EDITION (which was published around that time), there were loads – and I mean loads – of groups/artists I had to find out about. I never thought it would take me until the 8th of September (my birthday, incidentally!) to complete the tome; I had virtually let a decade go by without enjoying the more obscure acts of the 80's & 90's. I thought it would contain the same amount of pages as the other two offshoots. I was so wrong, it was double that and I could have split it into two, one catering for Punk/New Wave, the other more laid back 80's/90's Alternative/Indie acts. Could you the public have afforded this? I said Yes, the publisher said No. 700-odd (sometimes very odd!) pages and 1400 acts with over 500 sub-entries to boot and everything you ever wanted to know about each of them.

What a quarter of a century it's been. We've seen music progress even further, new genres and a plethora of varied acts – to say the least – appear on the scene. But when did it all start for me?

My recollections of my "punk" days started when I first heard "ANARCHY IN THE UK" blaring out of a speaker in my local "Brian Findlay's" record store (it's now called Sleeves). My world changed that day. I was 16, I had no job, no prospects but I certainly had an attitude – doesn't everyone at that age! – and after listening to the John Peel show and buying loads of "Punk/New Wave" records over the course of the next year, I was a truly paid up member of the new "safety-pin" brigade. My nights out were spent with me "punk" mates (especially Brian "Butcher" Hunter), walking three miles to "The Nash" (The International in Grangemouth to the unaffiliated!) and pogoing to every Punk song played by the DJ. The local Maniqui night spot in Falkirk was also a fantastic place to be (at the time, that is!), punk/new wave acts such as The JAM, ELVIS COSTELLO, The REZILLOS, The ADVERTS, The ELECTRIC CHAIRS, The BOOMTOWN RATS (I met Sir Bob and Co at the aforementioned record store that afternoon!) and of course The STRANGLERS. The "Thatcher" years were another killer for my job prospects, but as they say, you can't keep a good man down; the story now reverts back to the top of the page!

What's next then?

Should be retirement, as 70-80 hours a week for 17 years is taking its toll on me and I'm currently getting a check-up from the neck-up to see how my brain is working. People think I'm well off or I'm stupid but I think I've been shrewd enough to last this long. Sacrifice is probably the closest word to describe my life. I've nothing left. Ahh! but wait, you never know what's around the corner – INTERNET – novels/plays – money – house – girlfriend – peace at last.

MARTIN STRONG

P.S.– Just another intro of hope for all, I suppose.

How To Read The Book

If you're struggling in any way how to comprehend some of the more complex parts of each discography, here are some examples to make it easier. Read below for around 10 minutes, taking a step at a time. The final lines/examples you see will give you a good guide before you proceed with the actual chronological discographies. However, I think that once you've read your own favourites you'll have a good idea.

GROUP / ARTIST

Formed/Born: Where/When ... biography including style/analysis, songwriters, cover versions, trivia, etc.

Album rating: i.e. rating between 1-10 amalgamated between music press reviews, your letters and my own personal opinion.

SINGER (born; b. day/month/year, town/city, country) – vocals, whatever (ex-GROUP; if any) / **MUSICIAN** (b. BIRTH NAME, 8 Sep'60, Musselburgh, Scotland) – instruments / **OTHER MUSICIANS** – other instruments, vocals, etc.

UK Label US Label

UKdate. (single, ep or album) *(UK cat.no.)* *<US cat.no.>* **THE TITLE** US date
note:- UK label – might be another country's label if not released in UK.
also:- Labels only appear when the group signs to a new one.
note:- UK date – might be foreign, <even American at times>, if not initially issued in Britain.
note:- (UK catalogue number; in curved brackets) <US cat.no.; in angle brackets>
note:- chart positions, UK + US, are in the boxes below labels.
also:- the boxes in the above example have been left blank, thus they did not hit either UK or US charts.
note:- US date after the boxes indicates a variation from its UK counterpart.
also:- Any other info on the right of the boxes (e.g. German) indicates it was not issued in the US.

UKdate. (7") *(UK cat.no.)* **A-SIDE. / B-SIDE** -
US date. (7") *<US cat.no.>* **A-SIDE. / DIFFERENT B-SIDE** -
note:- The two examples above show that the UK + US release did not have an identical A-side & B-side, thus the chart boxes are marked with a – to indicate it was not released in either the UK or the US.

UKdate. (7"/c-s) *(CATNO 1/+C)* **A-SIDE. / B-SIDE** -
note:- above had two formats with the same tracks (i.e. 7"/c-s). However, catalogue numbers will always vary among different formats – often only slightly (e.g. CATNO 1/+C). Each cat.no. would read thus:- (7")=*(CATNO 1)* and (c-s)=*(CATNO 1C)*. To save space the (/) slash comes into effect. The (/) means "or" and in this case it is prefixed with a + sign for the equivalent cassette (c-s).

UKdate. (7"/c-s) *(example same as above)* **SEE ABOVE** -
(12"+=/cd-s+=) *(CATNO 1-12/1-CD)* – Extra tracks.
note:- If there are more formats with extra or different tracks, a new line would be used. Obviously there would also be alternative catalogue numbers utilising the "(/)" as before. Extra tracks would therefore mean the addition of the sign "(+=)" to each format.

UKdate. (lp/c/cd) *(CATNO 200/+MC/CD)* *<US catno 4509>* **ALBUM TITLE**
– Track listing / Track 2 / And so on. *(re-issued = re-iss. A later date, and other 'Label' mentioned, if different from original; new cat.no.) (could be re-iss. many times and if "(+=)" sign occurs there will be extra tracks from the original)* <*could also apply to the US release if in pointed brackets*>
note:- Album above released in 3 formats, thus 3 catalogue numbers are neccessary. The "long-player" lp *(CATNO 200)* is obvious. The "cassette" c = +MC *(CATNO 200MC)* or "compact disc" CD *(CATNO 200CD)*. The US *<cat.no.>* will normally be just one set of numbers (or see further below for other details).

UKdate. (cd/c/lp) *(CD/TC+/CATNO+200)* *<UScatno 4509>* **ALBUM TITLE** US date
note:- This time a prefix is used instead of a suffix, hence the difference before the standard lp catalogue number. For instance, the cd would read as *(CDCATNO 200)*.

Jun 97. (cd/c/lp) *<(5557 49860-2/-4/-1)>* **ALBUM TITLE** 1 1 May97
note:- Some catalogue numbers don't include any letters, but instead consist of a number sequence followed by one digit which universally corresponds with the format (i.e. 2 = cd / 4 = c / 1 = lp).
also:- If the US numbers are identical, there would be no need to list them separately, i.e. *<(the numbers)>*
note:- I've also marked down an actual date of release and its variant in the US (you'll find this fictitious album also hit No.1 in both charts "and ah've no even heard it yet, man!")

— **NEW MUSICIAN/SINGER** (b.whenever, etc.) – instruments (ex-GROUP(s) replaced = repl. DEPARTING MUSICIAN/SINGER, who joined whatever
note:- Above denotes a line-up change.

GROUP or ARTIST with major change of name

note:- above would always be in grey.

UK Label US Label

Jun 97. (cd/c/lp; GROUP or ARTIST with minor change of name) *<(5557 49860)>* **ALBUM TITLE** 1 1 May97

– compilations, etc. –

UKdate. (cd) *compilation Label only; (cat.no.)* **ALBUM TITLE** 100 -
– Track listing would be selective, only included if the release was deemed essential.

RECORD-LABEL ABBREVIATIONS

Nearly all the record-labels have been shown in full, but the following abbreviations have been used:

Amphetam. Reptile – Amphetamine Reptile
Dead Good Dolly Platt. – Dead Good Dolly Platters
EMI Internat. – EMI International
New Europ. Records – New European Records
New U'ground – New Underground
Rough Trade Sing. Club – Rough Trade Singles Club
Sympathy F – Sympathy For The Record Industry
U.A. – United Artists
not iss. – not issued

Formats & Abbreviations

VINYL (black coloured unless stated)

(lp) = The (LONG PLAYER) record ... circular 12" plays at $33^{1/3}$ r.p.m., and has photo or artwork sleeve. Approximate playing time ... 30–50 minutes with average 10 tracks. Introduced in the mid-50's on mono until stereo took over in the mid-60's. Quadrophonic had a spell in the 70's, but only on mainly best-selling lp's, that had been previously released. Because of higher costs to the manufacturer and buyer, the quad sunk around 1978. Also note that around the mid-50's, some albums were released on 10 inch. Note:– average cost to the customer as of August 1999 = £9.00 (new). Collectors can pay anything from £1 to over £500, depending on the quality of the recording. Very scratched records can be worthless, but unplayed mint deletions are worth a small fortune to the right person. Auctions and record fairs can be the place to find that long lost recording that's eluded you. This applies to all other vinyl below.

(d-1p) = The (DOUBLE-LONG PLAYER) record ... as before. Playing time 50–90 minutes on 4 sides, with average 17 tracks. Introduced to rock/pop world in the late 60's, to complement compilations, concept & concert (aka live) albums.[1]
Compilations:– are a selection of greatest hits or rare tracks, demos, etc.
Concepts:– are near-uninterrupted pieces of music, based around a theme.
Note that normal lp's could also be compilations, live or concept. Some record companies through the wishes of their artists, released double lp's at the price of one lp. If not, price new would be around £15.

(t-1p) = The (TRIPLE-LONG PLAYER) record ... as before. Playing time over 100 minutes with normally over 20 tracks. Because of the cost to the consumer, most artists steered clear of this format. Depending on the artwork on the sleeve, these cost over £17.50. (See its replacement, the CD.)

(4-1p-box) = The (BOXED-LONG PLAYER) record (could be between 4 and 10 in each boxed-set). As the triple album would deal with live, concept or compilation side, the boxed-set would be mostly re-issues of all the artist's album material, with probably a bonus lp thrown in, to make it collectable. Could be very pricey, due to lavish outlay in packaging. They cost over £25 new.

(m-lp) = The (MINI-LONG PLAYER) record ... playing time between 20 and 30 minutes and containing on average 7 tracks. Introduced for early 80's independent market, and cost around £5.
= Note:– This could be confused at times with the extended-play 12" single.

(pic-1p) = The (PICTURE DISC-LONG PLAYER) record ... as before but with album artwork/ design on the vinyl grooves. Mainly for the collector because of the slightly inferior sound quality. If unplayed, these can fetch between £10 and £250.

(coloured lp) = The (COLOURED-LONG PLAYER) record; can be in a variety of colours including ... white / blue / red / clear / purple / green / pink / gold / silver.

(red-1p) = The (RED VINYL-LONG PLAYER) record would be an example of this.

(7") = The (7 INCH SINGLE). Arrived in the late 50's, and plays at 45 r.p.m. Before this its equivalent was the 10" on 78 r.p.m. Playing time now averages 4 minutes per side, but during the late 50's up to mid-60's, each side averaged $2^{1/2}$ minutes. Punk rock/new wave in 1977/78 resurrected this idea. In the 80's, some disco releases increased playing time. Another idea that was resurrected in 1977 was the picture sleeve. This had been introduced in the 60's, but mostly only in the States.
Note:– cost in mid-98 was just under £2.50; second-hand rarities can cost between 25p and £200, depending again on their condition. These might also contain limited freebies/gifts (i.e. posters, patches, stickers, badges, etc). Due to the confusion this would cause, I have omitted this information, and kept to the vinyl aspect in this book. Another omission has been DJ promos, demos, acetates, magazine freebies, various artists' compilations, etc. Only official shop releases get a mention.

(7" m) = The (7 INCH MAXI-SINGLE). Named so because of the extra track, mostly on the B-side. Introduced widely during the early 70's; one being ROCKET MAN by ELTON JOHN.

(7" ep) = The (7 INCH EXTENDED PLAY SINGLE). Plays mostly at $33^{1/3}$ r.p.m., with average playing time 10–15 minutes and 4 tracks. Introduced in the late 50's as compilations for people to sample their albums. These had a *title* and were also re-introduced from 1977 onwards, but this time for punk groups' new songs.

(d7") = The (DOUBLE 7 INCH SINGLE). Basically just two singles combined ... 4 tracks. Introduced in the late 70's for the “new wave/romantics”, and would cost slightly more than normal equivalent.

(7" pic-d) = The (7 INCH PICTURE-DISC SINGLE). This was vinyl that had a picture on the grooves, which could be viewed through a see-through plastic cover.

(7" sha-pic-d) = The (7 INCH SHAPED-PICTURE-DISC SINGLE). Vinyl as above but with shape (i.e. gun, mask, group) around the edge of the groove. Awkward because it would not fit into the collector's singles box. Initially limited, and this can still be obtained at record fairs for over £3. Note:– However, in the book the type of shape has not been mentioned, to save space.

(7" coloured) = The (7 INCH COLOURED SINGLE). Vinyl that is not black (i.e. any other colour; red, yellow, etc). Note:– (7" multi) would be a combination of two or more colours (i.e. pink/purple).

1: **Note**:– Interview long players mainly released on 'Babatak' label, have not been included due to the fact this book only gives artists' music discography.

(7" flexi) = The (7 INCH FLEXIBLE SINGLE). One-sided freebies, mostly given away by magazines, at concerts or as mentioned here; free with single or lp. Worth keeping in mint condition and well protected.

(12") = The (12 INCH SINGLE). Plays at 45 r.p.m., and can have extended or extra tracks to its 7" counterpart (+=) or (++=). B-side's playing speed could be at 33 r.p.m. Playing time could be between 8 and 15 minutes. Introduced in 1977 with the advent of new wave and punk. They were again a must for collectors, for the new wave of British heavy metal scene.

(12"ep) = The (12 INCH EXTENDED PLAY SINGLE). Virtually same as above but *titled* like the 7" ep. Playing time over 12 minutes, and could have between 3 and 5 tracks.

(d12") = The (DOUBLE 12 INCH SINGLE). See double 7". Can become very collectable and would cost new as normal 12", £4.50.

(12" pic-d) = The (12 INCH PICTURE-DISC SINGLE). As with 7" equivalent ... see above.

(12" sha-pic-d) = The (12 INCH SHAPED-PICTURE-DISC SINGLE). See above 7" equivalent.

(12" colrd) = The (12 INCH COLOURED SINGLE). Not black vinyl ... see above 7" equivalent.

(10") = The (10 INCH SINGLE). Plays at 45 r.p.m. and, like the 12", can have extra tracks (+=). Very collectable, it surfaced in its newer form around the early 80's, and can be obtained in shops at £4.50. Note:– also (10" ep) / (d10") / (10" coloured) / (10" pic-d) / (10" sha-pic-d).

CASSETTES

(c) = The (CASSETTE) album ... size in case 4 1/2 inches high. Playing-time same as lp album, although after the mid-80's cd revolution, some were released with extra tracks. Introduced in the late 60's, to compete with the much bulkier lp. Until the 80's, most cassettes were lacking in group info, lyric sheets, and freebies. Note:– cost to the consumer as of August 1999 = £8 new. But for a few exceptions, most do not increase in price, and can be bought second-hand or budget-priced for around £5.

(d-c) = The (DOUBLE-CASSETTE) album ... as above, and would hold same tracks as d-lp or even t-1p. Price between £12 and £16.

(c-s) = The (CASSETTE-SINGLE). Now released mostly with same two tracks as 7" equivalent. The other side played the same 2 or 3 tracks. Introduced unsuccessfully in the US around the late 60's. Re-introduced there and in Britain in the mid-80's. In the States, it and its cd counterpart have replaced the charting 7" single for the 90's. Cost new is around £1.50–£2.50, and might well become quite collectable.

(c-ep) = The (CASSETTE-EXTENDED PLAY SINGLE). Same as above but *titled* as 12".

COMPACT DISCS

(cd) = The (COMPACT DISC) album. All 5" circular and mostly silver on its playing side. Perspex casing also includes lyrics & info, etc. Introduced late in 1982, and widely the following year (even earlier for classical music). Initially for top recording artists, but now in 1999 nearly every release is in cd format. Playing time normally over 50 minutes with some containing extra tracks or mixes. Possible playing time is just over 75 minutes. Marketed as unscratchable, although if they go uncleaned, they will stick just as vinyl. Average price (mid-99) is £15, and will become collectable, possibly early in the next century if, like most gloomy predictions, they do not deteriorate with time.

(d-cd) = The (DOUBLE-COMPACT DISC) album ... same as above although very pricey, between £20 and £25.

(cd-s) = The (COMPACT DISC-SINGLE). Mainly all 5" (but some 3" cd-s could only be played with a compatible gadget inside the normal cd player). Playing time over 15 minutes to average 25 minutes, containing 4 or 5 tracks. Introduced in 1986 to compete with the 12" ep or cassette. 99% contained extra tracks to normal formats. Cost new: over £4.50.

(pic-cd-s) = The (PICTURE-COMPACT DISC-SINGLE). Has picture on disc, which gives it its collectability. Also on (pic-cd-ep).

(vid-pic-s) = The (VIDEO-COMPACT DISC-SINGLE). A video cd, which can be played through stereo onto normal compatible TV screen. Very costly procedure, but still might be the format of the future. Promo videos can be seen on pub jukeboxes, which has made redundant the returning Wurlitzer style.

DIGITAL AUDIO TAPE

(dat) = The (DIGITAL AUDIO TAPE) album. Introduced in the mid-80's and, except for Japan and the rich yuppie, are not widely issued. It is a smaller version of the cassette, with the quality of the cd.

Another format (which I have not included) is the CARTRIDGE, which was available at the same time as the cassette. When the cassette finally won the battle in the early 80's, the cartridge became redundant. All car-owners of the world were happy when thieves made them replace the stolen cartridge player with the resurrected cassette. You can still buy these second-hand, but remember you'll have to obtain a second-hand 20-year-old player, with parts possibly not available.

Other abbreviations: repl. = replaced / comp. = compilation / re-iss. = re-issued / re-dist. = re-distributed

A Very Brief History of Alternative & Indie Music

Alternative to what, the casual listener/reader might well ask? Basically, what follows is a selfishly opinionated attempt to summarise the evolution of that music which has (initially) positioned itself outside the mainstream of conventional "pop" music or attempted to redefine musical boundaries. As for "indie", well it certainly doesn't refer to classical sitar music from New Delhi – although Brit Asian bands such as CORNERSHOP do actually draw on this tradition – an illusion that more than a few well-oiled pub dwellers seem to have been labouring under. Of course, most readers will recognise the term as the slang abbreviation for Independently released alternative records (i.e. not issued on a major label).

Let's go back, way back in time, well before Punk Rock first gobbed on a stagnant music scene in the mid 70's. We're talking mid to late 60's here, a time when flower power 'n' peace was the order of the day; not everyone was sold on the hippy trip, though, and, like the proverbial mad scientist beavering away in his lab, a few disparate US-based mavericks were cooking up something dangerously different. In New York, The **VELVET UNDERGROUND** (**LOU REED**, JOHN CALE, STERLING MORRISON, MO TUCKER and NICO) were doing strange things with dark psychedelia and twisted pop while over in sunny L.A., DON VAN VLIET aka **CAPTAIN BEEFHEART & HIS MAGIC BAND** were alchemising a bizarre but effective avant-garde Rhythm & Blues (the rhythm of course, being mangled beyond recognition) cocktail. More importantly though, the former soul stronghold of Detroit (home of 'Tamla Motown') had given birth to both The STOOGES and **MC5**, primal sonic riffmeisters with a penchant for white-noise nihilism and rock'n'roll revolution respectively. The former's **IGGY POP** needs no introduction, a man who has generally come to be regarded as "The Godfather Of Punk", while the latter's WAYNE KRAMER is still motoring 30-odd years on. Last but not least, early 70's cross-dressing 'Stones wannabes, The **NEW YORK DOLLS**, fashioned a make-up smeared blueprint for many a shambolic DIY punk band. For the purposes of this book, the aforementioned innovators get a section all to themselves, the logic being these artists preceded the Punk/New Wave explosion without being an intrinsic part of it; they were all going on or past thirty by the mid-70's, virtual dinosaurs in the eyes of the angry new youth brigade.

Always touted as an English/British phenomenon, the first rumblings of the Punk revolution were actually felt in and around New York where acts like poetess PATTI SMITH, TELEVISION, RICHARD HELL, The HEARTBREAKERS (with ex-NY DOLLS) the RAMONES, TALKING HEADS and BLONDIE were all using the guitar-rock format in exciting new ways and providing an eclectic alternative to the mainstream domination of hard/AOR-rock and watered down disco-pop. Most of these bands were associated with the CBGB's and Max's Kansas City venues which formed the hub (along with Seymour Stein's 'Sire' records) of what was dubbed the "New Wave" scene; even more leftfield confrontational artists like SUICIDE, TEENAGE JESUS & THE JERKS (i.e. LYDIA LUNCH), etc, were getting decent crowds, forming the basis of the short-lived nihilistic "No-Wave" scene that BRIAN ENO documented with his subsequent compilation of the same name. Elsewhere in the USA, there were isolated pockets of punk related activity; in Boston, The MODERN LOVERS (with JONATHAN RICHMAN) had attracted a cult following while the state of Ohio was home to both PERE UBU and DEVO, the former one of the first avant-garde New Wave outfits and the latter a proto-electro quasi-pop band.

If Britain was slower off the mark, it certainly made up for lost time as the full filth and fury of the punk time-bomb hit the musical establishment square on. While the thriving pub-rock scene had created a sympathetic environment with its back to basics R&B ethos, it took maverick fashion guru turned musical opportunist, Malcolm McLaren, to light the touchpaper by dreaming up the concept of the SEX PISTOLS after seeing out the last days of The NEW YORK DOLLS as manager. Rounding up prospective members (STEVE JONES, PAUL COOK, GLEN MATLOCK and carrot-topped frontman, JOHNNY ROTTEN) from regular customers in his Kings Road 'Sex' boutique, he set out to shock the music industry into submission with a sound and image so confrontational that the media couldn't resist demonising them. After a string of riotous gigs including an infamous date at Oxford Street's 100 Club, the punk figureheads transformed the genre into a nationwide phenomenon by signing to 'E.M.I.' and releasing the inflammatory 'ANARCHY IN THE UK' towards the end of 1976. Fed up with a bloodless music scene and a stagnant political climate, the nation's restless youth adopted the record as an anthem and made sure the SEX PISTOLS made the Top 40.

All across the country, safety-pinned, spiky-topped kids were arming themselves with guitars, a couple of chords and an enterprising DIY attitude. The DAMNED had already established themselves as one of first generation's leading lights with the single, 'NEW ROSE'; released on pioneering indie imprint, 'Stiff' (who also boasted "New Wave" acts, ELVIS COSTELLO, IAN DURY, etc, artists who combined the newfound creative freedom and attitude of punk with traditional songwriting) the track was the first bonafide punk song to make it onto vinyl. While Radio One DJ John Peel provided a platform for punk on his night-time show, ALTERNATIVE TV frontman MARK PERRY gave the movement a voice through his influential 'Sniffin Glue' fanzine; and the NME had already championed the new breed with many a cover story. 1977 also proved a pivotal year with The CLASH, The STRANGLERS, The JAM, (Australia's) The SAINTS and the BUZZCOCKS amongst others all releasing seminal 7" singles (with picture covers!) before finally putting together enough material for an LP. After having "celebrated" the Silver Jubilee year by releasing 'GOD SAVE THE QUEEN' (originally released on 'A&M' before the ROTTEN and Co were politely asked to leave), The SEX PISTOLS ended the year by delivering the definitive punk album, appropriately titled 'NEVER MIND THE BOLLOCKS . . . HERE'S . . .'. The record was a massive-selling No.1 success and the face of the music industry changed irreversibly.

The bulk of the charts had now become the domain of New Wave/Punk acts, bands like SIOUXSIE & THE BANSHEES, X-RAY SPEX (a band that were first brought to attention via gigs at the infamous 'Roxy' venue) and MAGAZINE making their name over the course of 1978. Although rumours of punk's death were greatly exaggerated (especially after the following year's messy demise of the 'PISTOLS and the controversial death of their iconic bassman, SID VICIOUS), the initial flash of angry energy had dimmed slightly as the music branched out into more experimental, individualistic and claustrophobic territory.

While second generation punk bands like SHAM 69, UK SUBS, STIFF LITTLE FINGERS and The ANGELIC UPSTARTS (from which was formed the genesis of the much derided "Oi" movement) followed the tried and tested formula, outfits like The FALL, WIRE, the SLITS, The CURE and PUBLIC IMAGE LTD (Johnny Rotten's new band) were heading into the dark uncharted waters of post-punk. And they didn't come much darker than Manchester's JOY DIVISION, a bleak, coldly minimalistic pre-goth band led by the enigmatic IAN CURTIS. After two classic albums ('UNKNOWN PLEASURES' and 'CLOSER') and a hit single 'LOVE WILL TEAR UP APART' in 1980, their career was cut short as the troubled epileptic singer took his own life; the remaining members chose to carry on as NEW ORDER, an equally influential group that laid the foundations for Manchester's alternative dance scene. 'Factory', the label that spawned these two outfits, was arguably one of the most creative imprints of the 1980's, being instrumental in the careers of A CERTAIN RATIO, DURUTTI COLUMN, etc as well as the development of the 'Madchester' indie/dance phenomenon. Liverpool also made itself heard as The TEARDROP EXPLODES (with arch eccentric JULIAN COPE) and ECHO & THE BUNNYMEN (with the moody IAN McCULLOCH) took a post-punk ferry across the Mersey while the "Sound Of Young Scotland" was aired via 'Postcard' acts, ORANGE JUICE, JOSEF K and AZTEC CAMERA alongside future 'Virgin'-signed stadium rockers, SIMPLE MINDS. While Northern Ireland had been getting its 'TEENAGE KICKS' with Power-Pop punks, The UNDERTONES, the Republic produced what would become one of the biggest alternative rock bands in the world, U2.

The independent ethos engendered by the "New Wave" had also given rise to such key labels as 'Rough Trade' (home to electronic experimentalists CABARET VOLTAIRE), 'Mute' and '4 a.d.'. The latter served as a launching pad for proto-Goth act, BAUHAUS and Aussie avant-noise terrorists, The BIRTHDAY PARTY; while the former helped inspire a whole brood of black-clad "gothic" bands led by Leeds' SISTERS OF MERCY, the latter were beloved of the "psychobilly" crew, bequiffed afficionados of a punk/rockabilly hybrid that had its roots back in America with The CRAMPS. Led by the inimitable LUX INTERIOR (an IGGY POP clone if ever there was one!), the latter outfit had actually been loosely associated with the original CBGB's scene. This venue was now the focus for a new breed of US hardcore/avant-punk acts including the hugely influential feedback merchants, SONIC YOUTH. The West Coast mirrored the developments in the Big Apple with a brace of ear-bleeding new talent including the establishment-baiting DEAD KENNEDYS whose JELLO BIAFRA had instigated his own 'Alternative Tentacles' label (later home to Canadians, D.O.A.) full-time after the independent success of two politico-punk classics, 'CALIFORNIA UBER ALLES' and 'HOLIDAY IN CAMBODIA'. California was also the base for 'S.S.T.', a label that spawned a slew of hardcore/alternative bands such as BLACK FLAG, HUSKER DU and The MEAT PUPPETS. The latter band were partly influenced by the desert rock twang of NEIL YOUNG, also a touchstone for the Paisley underground psychedelic/jangle-pop scene that numbered R.E.M., The RAIN PARADE, The DREAM SYNDICATE, GREEN ON RED and The LONG RYDERS.

Back in Britain, The SMITHS were rescuing the term "alternative" from electro-popsters/New Romantics with a highly original sound hinged on JOHNNY MARR's legendary jangling guitar and MORRISSEY's equally legendary miserabilist lyrics/vocals. From the summer of '83 onwards (after the 'HAND IN GLOVE' single), the MORRISSEY-MARR partnership inspired hitherto unseen obsessive fan worship and dominated the Top 20 until it all ended in tears at the end of 1987. The SMITHS aside, the mid-80's indie scene was dominated by Glaswegian Alan McGee's 'Creation', a label that first made its name with the surf-pop/noise feedback kings, The JESUS & MARY CHAIN, before going on to help define the archetypal "indie" band by signing a long list of shambling, jangling guitar outfits such as The PASTELS and PRIMAL SCREAM (also both hailing from north of the border!). The NME-created C-86 scene named after that year's similarly-titled cassette also centered on these types of bands, providing a platform for John Peel Festive 50 favourite, The WEDDING PRESENT.

As the 80's neared their conclusion, more and more indie bands were cross-fertilizing their music with dance rhythms after experiencing the euphoric high of the insurgent acid-house culture and the "first summer of love". The scene coalesced around Manchester where working class heroes The HAPPY MONDAYS were gettin' it on with a sleazy combination of groovy 'Stones rhythms, scratchy funk-guitar and of course SHAUN RYDER's glassy-eyed, fookin' tuneless vocals and x-rated cartoon lyrics. Scottish stalwarts, PRIMAL SCREAM and the "Eezergood" SHAMEN, also saw the strobelight after becoming hooked on London's club scene, BOBBY GILLESPIE and Co finally coming of age in 1991 with the genre-defining 'SCREAMADELICA'. Most legendary of all though were The STONE ROSES, the classic psychedelic guitar-pop of their 1989 eponymous debut album setting them up as one of the most revered bands in Rock history. In the right place at the right time, the beeny-topped 'ROSES were adopted by the indie dance crowd as homecoming Messiahs while their rock/funk crossover classic, 'FOOL'S GOLD', still stands as a benchmark for any aspiring group. Running parallel to "Madchester" was the more exclusively alternative "Shoegazing" scene, so-called because those involved had a tendency to er . . . study their feet while "tripping" the night away to swathes of swirling feedback melodica. Armed with a collection of SPACEMEN 3, MY BLOODY VALENTINE and COCTEAU TWINS (all hugely influential sound pioneers in their own right) albums and EP's, outfits such as RIDE, SLOWDIVE and LUSH enjoyed a brief period of music press acclaim before the genre died a swift death along with the painful last remnants of the "baggy" scene.

Neither of these scenes cut much ice in America where "Grunge" was beginning to ferment in deepest, darkest Seattle via the reborn 'Sub Pop' label. Influenced equally by mid-80's alternative/hardcore punk (i.e. The PIXIES, DINOSAUR JR, etc), 70's heavy-metal and 60's garage, NIRVANA, SOUNDGARDEN and MUDHONEY redefined the whole American music scene, breaking the stranglehold of the cucumber'n'spandex hard-rock brigade and uniting alternative music fans. With precision perfect timing, NIRVANA stormed onto the international stage with the incendiary 'SMELL LIKES TEEN SPIRIT' single and the 'NEVERMIND' album in Autumn '91, paving the way for a plethora of often second-rate imitators. Although the likes of PEARL JAM and their ilk continued to sell million of records, in reality the scene died with the controversial suicide of KURT COBAIN (whose wife, COURTNEY LOVE and her band, HOLE, were the most famous in a long list of femme-punks) in April '94. Yet still the shockwaves continued to be felt in America where an insatiable appetite for everything punk saw the re-issue of obscure 70's/80's UK material and the success of workaday bands like GREEN DAY and OFFSPRING. The success of Grunge also opened up the market for all kinds of previously marginalised sub-genres – i.e. Industrial, a noisy electronic percussion-driven punk-metal style spearheaded by stalwarts from MINISTRY to NINE INCH NAILS.

Of course, Britain could only stomach so many hairy, check-shirted noise merchants and finally re-invented its Rock history with the advent of Brit-pop in the mid-90's. Chief protagonists, BLUR (who had already been once around the "baggy" block) and new lads on the block, OASIS, battled it out in a media-fuelled race to the top spot reminiscent of the BEATLES/ROLLING STONES heyday. By this point the bands had already released their landmark albums, 'PARKLIFE' and 'DEFINITELY MAYBE' respectively, while SUEDE, PULP (JARVIS COCKER's long-standing outfit) and SUPERGRASS all topped the charts with their own brand of alt/indie pop. When the GALLAGHER brothers weren't at each other's throats, they were embroiled in a war of words with DAMON ALBARN, the gossip column overload helping to breathe life into an ailing music industry.

From the early to mid-90's, a number of dance acts had also been absorbed into the alternative mainstream, the likes of The ORB, The CHEMICAL BROTHERS, LEFTFIELD, UNDERWORLD and of course techno-punk guerillas, The PRODIGY, making a name for themselves outside the anonimity of the club scene with shit-kicking live shows. The NME crowd had also embraced the Bristol-based "trip-hop" scene, a hybrid of slow-motion hip-hop and paranoid dub pioneered by MASSIVE ATTACK and developed by PORTISHEAD, TRICKY, et al.

"Lo-Fi" was another buzz word of the era, originally coined for US post-grunge slacker outfits like PAVEMENT, MERCURY REV and SEBADOH, although it has since been used to cover the massive spectrum of experimental knob-twiddling music made by artists as creatively and geographically wide-ranging as TORTOISE and STEREOLAB. In fact, this scene could be taken as a microcosm of the melting pot that constitutes the current alternative landscape, a free-for-all no man's land where diversity is the key word. In the wake of Brit-pop, hardened campaigners, RADIOHEAD, THE VERVE and SPIRITUALIZED (a SPACEMEN 3 offshoot!) all released naval-gazing but groundbreaking career peak albums, while Wales finally put itself on the map with a clutch of eclectic talent (i.e. SUPER FURRY ANIMALS, GORKY'S ZYGOTIC MYNCI, STEREOPHONICS and CATATONIA) to back up the long-running success of The MANIC STREET PREACHERS. Where else could we end but Scotland of course, where arguably the most innovative music is currently being made by the likes of the mighty MOGWAI, Falkirk "bairns" ARAB STRAP and cross-border marauders, The BETA BAND. Amen!

The REBEL MC and BRENDON GRIFFIN

CONTENTS

Iggy POP

Born: JAMES JEWEL OSTERBERG, 21 Apr'47, Ypsilanti, Michigan, USA. The son of an English father and American mother, he joined The IGUANAS as a drummer in 1964. They issued a cover of Bo Diddley's 'MONA', which was limited to 1,000 copies sold at gigs. The following year, he became IGGY POP and joined The PRIME MOVERS with bassist RON ASHETON, although they folded, IGGY subsequently moving to Chicago. In 1967, he returned to Michigan and formed The (PSYCHEDELIC) STOOGES with RON and his drummer brother SCOTT. They were soon joined by DAVE ALEXANDER, IGGY making his celluloid debut in the avant-garde film, 'Francois De Moniere' with girlfriend NICO. In 1968, the band gigged constantly, on one occasion IGGY being charged with indecent exposure. The following year, A&R man Danny Fields, while looking to sign MC5, instead signed The STOOGES to 'Elektra', furnishing them with a $25,000 advance. Their eponymous debut (produced by JOHN CALE – another VELVET UNDERGROUND connection), later proved to be way ahead of its time. Tracks such as 'NO FUN', '1969' and 'I WANNA BE YOUR DOG', were howling proto-punk, garage classics, later covered by The SEX PISTOLS, SISTERS OF MERCY and SID VICIOUS! respectively. The album just failed to secure a Top 100 placing, the second album faring even worse commercially, although it was hailed by the more diserning critics of the day as a seminal work. From the primal nihilism of 'DIRT', to the psychedelic kiss-off, 'I FEEL ALRIGHT (1970)', it seemed, to The STOOGES at least, as if flower-power had never happened. They were subsequently dropped by their label, following drug-related problems and dissension in the ranks. IGGY moved to Florida, becoming a greenkeeper while taking up golf more seriously, a healthier pastime than his penchant for self-mutilation. In 1972, he had a chance meeting with DAVID BOWIE and manager TONY DeFRIES, who persuaded IGGY to reform his STOOGES and sign a MainMan management deal, this in turn leading to a 'C.B.S.' contract. After his/their flawed classic, 'RAW POWER' (not one of BOWIE's best productions), they folded again, citing drugs as the cause. It was, however, even more of an embryonic punk record, the amphetamine rush of 'SEARCH AND DESTROY' highly influential on the "blank generation" that would trade-in their STEELY DAN albums for anything with two chords and a sneering vocal. In 1975, IGGY checked in to a psychiatric institute, weaning himself off heroin. His only true friend, BOWIE, who regularly visited him in hospital, invited him to appear on his 'LOW' album. He signed to 'R.C.A.' (home of BOWIE) in 1977, issuing the BOWIE-produced debut solo album, 'THE IDIOT', which, due to the recent "new wave" explosion, broke him into the UK Top 30 and US Top 75. It contained the first BOWIE/POP collaboration, 'CHINA GIRL', later a smash hit for BOWIE. His second solo release, 'LUST FOR LIFE' (also produced by BOWIE in '77), was another gem, again deservedly reaching the UK Top 30 (the title track was later resurrected in 1996 after appearing on the soundtrack to the cult Scottish movie, 'Trainspotting'). In 1979, IGGY moved to 'Arista' records, shifting through various infamous personnel, although his commercial appeal was on the wane. The first half of the 80's saw IGGY desperately trying to carve out a successful solo career while combating his continuing drug problems. Albums such as, 'SOLDIER' (1980), 'PARTY' (1981) and 'ZOMBIE BIRDHOUSE' (1982) marking the nadir of POP's chequered career. Finally teaming up again with BOWIE for 1986's 'BLAH BLAH BLAH', the proclaimed "Godfather Of Punk" at last gained some belated recognition, his revival of a 1957 Johnny O'Keefe hit, 'REAL WILD CHILD', gaving IGGY his first Top 10 hit (UK). Still with 'A&M' records and adding ex-SEX PISTOLS guitarist STEVE JONES, he consolidated his recovery with 'INSTINCT' (1988). His new lease of life prompted 'Virgin America' to give IGGY (who had recently taking up acting) a new contract, the 1990 set, 'BRICK BY BRICK' featuring the G N' R talents of SLASH and DUFF McKAGAN. To end the year, IGGY showed his caring side by duetting with former punkette, DEBORAH HARRY, on AIDS benefit single, 'WELL DID YOU EVAH!' (a bigger hit for NANCY Sinatra & LEE Hazlewood in 1971). He resurfaced once again in 1993 with 'AMERICAN CAESAR', a length set which contained some of his raunchiest tracks for some time, including 'WILD AMERICA', 'F*****' ALONE' and Richard Berry's 'LOUIE LOUIE'. Busying himself with more film work, he eventually broke his recording silence with an umpteenth album, 'NAUGHTY LITTLE DOGGIE', in 1996. • **IGGY covered;** SOMETHING WILD (John Hiatt) / LIVIN' ON THE EDGE OF THE NIGHT (Rifkin / Rackin) / SEX MACHINE (James Brown). • **Trivia:** In 1987, IGGY made a cameo appearance in the film, 'The Color Of Money'. In 1990, his film & TV work included, 'Cry Baby', 'Shannon's Deal', Tales From The Crypt' & 'Miami Vice'. In 1991, he starred in the opera! 'The Manson Family'.

Album rating: THE STOOGES (*8) / FUN HOUSE (*10) / RAW POWER (*7) / solo:- THE IDIOT (*9) / LUST FOR LIFE (*9) / BLAH-BLAH-BLAH (*7) / INSTINCT (*8) / BRICK BY BRICK (*7) / AMERICAN CAESAR (*6)

STOOGES

IGGY POP – vocals / **RON ASHETON** (b. RONALD RANKLIN ASHETON JR., 17 Jul'48, Washington, D.C.) – guitar / **DAVE ALEXANDER** (b. DAVID MICHAEL ALEXANDER, 3 Jun'47, Ann Arbor) – bass / **SCOTT ASHETON** (b. SCOTT RANDOLPH ASHETON, 16 Aug'49, Washington) – drums

Elektra Elektra

Sep 69. (lp) *<(EKS 74051)>* **THE STOOGES** [ ] [ ] Aug69
– 1969 / I wanna be your dog / We will fall / No fun / Real cool time / Ann / Not right / Little doll. *(re-iss. Mar77; K 42032) <US cd-iss. 1988; 74051-2> (cd-iss. Nov93; 7559 60667-2)*

Oct 69. (7") *<EK 45664>* **I WANNA BE YOUR DOG. / 1969** [-] [ ]

—— added guests **STEVE MACKAY** – saxophone / **BILL CHEATHAM** – 2nd guitar

Dec 70. (lp) *<(EKS 74071)>* **FUN HOUSE** [ ] [ ]
– Down on the street / Loose / T.V. eye / Dirt / I feel alright (1970) / Fun house / L.A. blues. *(re-iss. Mar77; K 42051) <US cd-iss. 1988; 74071-2> (cd-iss. Nov93; 7559 60669-2)*

Dec 70. (7") *<EKM 45695>* **I FEEL ALRIGHT (1970). / DOWN ON THE STREET** [-] [ ]

—— broke-up in 1972. **IGGY** re-formed the group with **SCOTT** and **RON** (now bass)

IGGY AND THE STOOGES

JAMES WILLIAMSON – guitar repl. DAVE (died 10 Feb'75)

C.B.S. Columbia

Jun 73. (lp) *(CBS 65586) <KC 32111>* **RAW POWER** [ ] [ ] May73
– Search and destroy / Gimme danger / Hard to beat * / Penetration / Raw power / I need somebody / Shake appeal / Death trip. *(re-iss. May77 on 'CBS-Embassy'; 31464)*, hit UK No.44, *track repl. by – Your pretty face is going to Hell. *(re-iss. Nov81; CBS 32081) <US cd-iss. 1988 on 'Columbia'; > (UK re-iss. May89 on 'Essential' cd/c/lp; ESS CD/MC/LP 005) (cd-iss. all tracks) (re-iss. May94 & Apr97 on 'Columbia' cd/c; 485176-2/-4) (lp re-iss. Jul98 on 'Simply Vinyl'; SVLP 33)*

Jun 73. (7") *<45877>* **SEARCH AND DESTROY. / PENETRATION** [-] [ ]

—— added **SCOTT THURSTON** – keyboards (on last 1974 tour, before disbanding) The ASHETONS formed The NEW ORDER (US version), with RON moving on to DESTROY ALL MONSTERS who had three 45's for UK label 'Cherry Red' in the late 70's.

– compilations, others, etc. –

1977. (white-d-lp) *Visa; <IMP 1015>* **METALLIC K.O.** [-] [ ]
– Raw power / Head on / Gimme danger / Rich bitch / Cock in my pocket / Louie Louie. *(originally issued 1976 on French 'Skydog'; SGIS 008) (re-iss. May88 as 'METALLIC KO x 2' on 'Skydog' lp/cd; 62232-1/2) (cd-iss. Sep94; same) (re-iss. Sep96 & May98 on 'Dressed To Kill'; DTKLP 001)*

1977. (7"ep) *Bomp; <EP 113>* **I'M SICK OF YOU** [-] [ ]
– I'm sick of you / Tight pants / Scene of the crime.

1977. (7"ep; by IGGY POP & JAMES WILLIAMSON) *Bomp; <EP 114>* **JESUS LOVES THE STOOGES** [-] [ ]
– Jesus loves the Stooges / Consolation prizes / Johanna. *(re-iss. 10"ep.Nov94;)*

1977. (7") *Siamese; <PM 001>* **I GOT A RIGHT. / GIMME SOME SKIN** [-] [ ]
(UK-iss.Dec95 on 'Bomp'; REVENGE 2)

Feb 78. (lp,green-lp; as IGGY POP with JAMES WILLIAMSON) *Radar; (RAD 2) / Bomp; <BLP 4001>* **KILL CITY** [ ] [ ] Nov77
– Sell your love / Kill city / I got nothin' / Beyond the law / Johanna / Night theme / Night theme reprise / Master charge / No sense of crime / Lucky monkeys / Consolation prizes. *(re-iss. ! on 'Elektra';) (cd-iss. Feb89 on 'Line'; LICD 9.00131) (cd-iss. Jan93;) (re-iss. 10"lp Feb95 on 'Bomp'; BLP 4042-10) (cd-iss. ; BCD 4042)*

Apr 78. (7") *Radar; (ADA 4)* **KILL CITY. / I GOT NOTHIN'** [ ] [-]

1978. (7"ep) *Skydog; (SGIS 12)* **(I GOT) NOTHING** [-] [-] France
– I got nothing / Gimme danger / Heavy liquid.

Aug 80. (lp/c) *Elektra; (K/K4 52234) <EF 7095>* **NO FUN** (1969-70 best of THE STOOGES) [ ] [ ]

1983. (lp) *Invasion; <E 1019>* **I GOT A RIGHT** [-] [ ]

1987. (lp) *Revenge; (MIG 2)* **I GOT A RIGHT** [-] [-] France

1987. (7") *Revenge; (SS 1)* **I GOT A RIGHT. / NO SENSE OF CRIME** [-] [-] France

1987. (7") *Revenge; (BF 50) KILL CITY. / I'M SICK OF YOU* [-] [-] France

Dec 87. (lp) *Fan Club; (FC 037)* **RUBBER LEGS** [-] [-] France
– Rubber legs / Open up and bleed / Johanna / Cock in my pocket / Head on the curb / Cry for me. *(free 7")* – GIMME DANGER (live). / I NEED SOMEBODY (live) *(cd-iss. Apr97 on 'Last Call'; 422248)*

1988. (cd-ep) *Revenge; (CAX 1)* **PURE LUST** [-] [-] France
– I got a right / Johanna / Gimme some skin / I got nothing.

1988. (cd-ep) *Revenge; (CAX 2)* **RAW POWER** [-] [-] France
– Raw power / Head on the curb / Purple haze / Waiting for the man.

1988. (12"pink-ep,cd-ep) *Revenge; (CAX 3)* **GIMME DANGER** [-] [-] France
– Gimme danger / Open up and bleed / Heavy liquid / I got nothing / Dynamite boogie.

1988. (7") *Revenge; (SS 6)* **JOHANNA. / PURPLE HAZE** [-] [-] France

Sep 88. (pic-lp; as IGGY & THE STOOGES) *Revenge; (LPMIG 6)* **DEATH TRIP** [-] [-] France

May 88. (cd; as IGGY & THE STOOGES) *Revenge; (HTM 16)* **OPEN UP AND BLEED** [-] [-] France
(re-iss. Feb96 on 'Bomp' cd/lp; BCD/BLP 4051) (cd re-iss. Jul96; 890016)

Dec 88. (lp; as IGGY & THE STOOGES) *Revenge; (MIG 7)* **LIVE AT THE WHISKEY A GO-GO** [ ] [-]
(cd-iss. Nov94 & Feb97; 895104F)

Dec 88. (lp; as IGGY & THE STOOGES) *Electric; (190069)* **RAW STOOGES VOL.1** [-] [-] German

Dec 88. (lp; as IGGY & THE STOOGES) *Electric; (190070)* **RAW STOOGES VOL.2** [-] [-] German

May 92. (cd) *Line; (LICD 921175)* **I'M SICK OF YOU / KILL CITY** [ ] [-]

Jun 94. (cd; IGGY & THE STOOGES) *New Rose; (890028)* **MY GIRL HATES MY HEROIN** [ ] [-]
(re-iss. Feb97 on 'Wrote Music'; 7890028) (re-iss. Sep97 on 'Revenge'; MIG 28)

Jul 94. (cd; IGGY & THE STOOGES) *New Rose; (642100)* **NIGHT OF DESTRUCTION** [ ] [-]
(re-iss. as 6xcd-s-box on 'Wind'; WM 375)

Jul 94. (cd; IGGY & THE STOOGES) *New Rose; (642042)* **TILL THE END OF THE NIGHT** [ ] [-]
(re-iss. Apr97; same) (re-iss. Sep97 on 'Revenge'; MIG 42)

Sep 94. (cd; IGGY & THE STOOGES) *New Rose; (642011)* **LIVE 1971 & EARLY LIVE RARITIES (live)** [ ] [-]
(re-iss. Apr97; same)

Sep 94. (cd; IGGY & THE STOOGES) *New Rose; (895002)* **RAW MIXES VOL.1** [ ] [-]

Sep 94. (cd; IGGY & THE STOOGES) *New Rose; (895003)* **RAW MIXES VOL.2** [ ] [-]

'LUST FOR LIFE'

Sep 94. (cd; IGGY & THE STOOGES) *New Rose; (895004)* **RAW MIXES VOL.3** -
Feb 95. (10"lp/cd) *Bomp; (BLP/BCD 4049)* **ROUGH POWER** -
— Also in France; **THE STOOGES**(12"ep) / **SHE CREATURES OF HOLLYWOOD HILLS**
Jul 96. (cd) *Revenge; (642050)* **WILD ANIMAL (live 1977)** -
Jul 96. (cd) *Revenge; (893334)* **PARIS HIPPODROME 1977 (live)** -
Jul 96. (cd; as IGGY & THE STOOGES) *Trident; (PILOT 008)* **YOUR PRETTY FACE IS GOING TO HELL** -
Mar 97. (cd; IGGY & THE STOOGES) *Bomp; (BCD 4063)* **YEAR OF THE IGUANA** -
Apr 97. (cd; STOOGES) *Arcade; (301563-2)* **THE COMPLETE RAW MIXES** -
Sep 97. (cd/lp; IGGY & THE STOOGES) *Bomp; (BCD/BLP 4069)* **CALIFORNIA BLEEDING** -
Nov 97. (cd) *King Biscuit; (88003)* **KING BISCUIT FLOWER HOUR** -
Mar 98. (cd) *Snapper; (SMMCD 528)* **LIVE IN L.A. 1973 (live)** -
Apr 98. (cd) *King Biscuit; (KBFHCD 001)* **KING BISCUIT PRESENTS . . .** -
May 88. (12"ep; IGGY & THE STOOGES) *Revenge; (CAX 8MAXI)* **I GOT NOTHING. / SEARCH AND DESTROY / COCK IN MY POCKET** -
Jun 98. (lp; IGGY & THE STOOGES) *Get Back; (GET 33LP)* **RUBBER** -

IGGY POP

— had already went solo, augmented by **DAVID BOWIE** – producer, keyboards / **RICKY GARDINER** – guitar / **TONY SALES** – bass / **HUNT SALES** – drums (latter 2; ex-TODD RUNDGREN) / guest **CARLOS ALOMAR** – guitar

R.C.A. R.C.A.

Feb 77. (7") *<10989>* **SISTER MIDNIGHT. / BABY** -
Mar 77. (lp/c) *(PL/PK 12275) <2275>* **THE IDIOT** 30 72
– Sister midnight / Nightclubbing / Fun time / Baby / China girl / Dum dum boys / Tiny girls / Mass production. *(re-iss. Apr90 on 'Virgin' lp/c/cd; OVED/OVEDC/CDOVD 277)*
May 77. (7") *(PB 9093)* **CHINA GIRL. / BABY**
— **STACEY HEYDON** – guitar / **SCOTT THURSTON** – keyboards repl. BOWIE + ALOMAR
Sep 77. (lp/c) *(PL/PK 12488) <2488>* **LUST FOR LIFE** 28
– Lust for life / Some weird sin / The passenger / Tonight / Success / Turn blue / Neighbourhood threat / Fall in love with me. *(re-iss. 1984 lp/c; NL/NK 82488) (re-iss. Apr90 on 'Virgin' lp/c/cd; OVED/OVEDC/CDOVD 278) (lp re-iss. Nov97 on 'Virgin'; LPCENT 40)*
Oct 77. (7") *(PB 9160)* **SUCCESS. / THE PASSENGER**
— **IGGY** retained **THURSTON**, and recruited **SCOTT ASHETON** – drums / **FRED 'SONIC' SMITH** – guitar (ex-MC5) / **GARY RAMUSSEN** – bass (The SALES brothers later to BOWIE's TIN MACHINE)
Apr 78. (7") *(PB 9213)* **I GOT A RIGHT (live). / SIXTEEN (live)**
May 78. (lp/c) *(PL/PK 12796)* **TV EYE (live 1977)**
– T.V. eye / Funtime / Sixteen / I got a right / Lust for life / Dirt / Nightclubbing / I wanna be your dog. *(cd-iss. Jul94 on 'Virgin'; CDOVD 448)*
— **IGGY / THURSTON** now with **JAMES WILLIAMSON** – guitar, producer / **JACKIE CLARKE** – bass (ex-IKE & TINA TURNER) / **KLAUS KREUGER** – drums (ex-TANGERINE DREAM) / **JOHN HORDEN** – saxophone

Arista Arista

Apr 79. (lp/c) *(SPART/TC-SPART 1092) <4237>* **NEW VALUES** 60
– Tell me a story / New values / Girls / I'm bored / Don't look down / The endless sea / Five foot one / How do ya fix a broken part / Angel / Curiosity / African man / Billy is a runaway. *(re-iss. Mar87; 1201144) (re-iss. Oct90 cd/lp; 260/210 997)*
May 79. (7") *(ARIST 255) <0438>* **I'M BORED. / AFRICAN MAN**
Jul 79. (7"/7"pic-d) *(ARIP/+D 274)* **FIVE FOOT ONE. / PRETTY FLAMINGO** -
— **IGGY / KREUGER** recruited **IVAN KRAL** – guitar (ex-PATTI SMITH) / **PAT MORAN** – guitar / **GLEN MATLOCK** – bass (ex-SEX PISTOLS, ex-RICH KIDS) / **BARRY ANDREWS** – keyboards (ex-XTC, ex-LEAGUE OF GENTLEMEN) (THURSTON formed The MOTELS)
Jan 80. (lp/c) *(SPART/TC-SPART 1117) <4259>* **SOLDIER** 62
– Knockin' 'em down (in the city) / I'm a conservative / I snub you / Get up and get out / Ambition / Take care of me / I need more / Loco mosquito / Mr. Dynamite / Play it safe / Dog food. *<US re-iss. Oct87; 201160> (cd-iss. Apr91; 251 160)*
Jan 80. (7") *(ARIST 327)* **LOCO MOSQUITO. / TAKE CARE OF ME** -
— **IGGY / KRAL** now with **ROB DuPREY** – guitar / **MICHAEL PAGE** – bass / **DOUGLAS BROWNE** – drums (BARRY ANDREWS formed SHRIEKBACK)
May 81. (7") *(ARIST 407)* **BANG BANG. / SEA OF LOVE** -
Jun 81. (lp/c) *(SPART/TC-SPART 1158) <9572>* **PARTY**
– Pleasure / Rock and roll party / Eggs on plate / Sincerity / Houston is hot tonight / Pumpin' for Jill / Happy man / Bang bang / Sea of love / Time won't let me. *(re-iss. Jan87 lp/c; 203/403 806) (cd-iss. Sep89 on 'R.C.A.'; 253 806)*
— **IGGY / DuPREY** found new people **CHRIS STEIN** – guitar, producer (ex-BLONDIE) / **CLEM BURKE** – drums (ex-BLONDIE)

Animal-Chrysalis Animal

Aug 82. (7") *(CHFLY 2634)* **RUN LIKE A VILLAIN. / PLATONIC**
Sep 82. (lp/c) *(CHR/ZCHR 1399) <APE 6000>* **ZOMBIE BIRDHOUSE**
– Run like a villain / The villagers / Angry hills / Life of work / The ballad of Cookie McBride / Ordinary bummer / Eat to be eaten / Bulldozer / Platonic / The horse song / Watching the news / Street crazies.
— In 1984, he sang the title song on Alex Cox's movie 'REPO MAN'. For the same director, he appeared in the 1985 film 'SID & NANCY' about SID VICIOUS.
— **IGGY** now with **ERDAL KIZILCAY** – drums, bass, synthesizers / **KEVIN ARMSTRONG** – guitar / **BOWIE + STEVE JONES** (guest writers)

A&M A&M

Sep 86. (7"/12") *(AM/+Y 358) <2874>* **CRY FOR LOVE. / WINNERS & LOSERS**
Oct 86. (lp/c/cd) *<(AMA/AMC/CDA 5145)>* **BLAH-BLAH-BLAH** 43 75
– Real wild child (wild one) / Baby, it can't fail / Shades / Fire girl / Isolation / Cry for love / Blah-blah-blah / Hideaway / Winners and losers. *(cd+=)* – Little Miss Emperor. *(cd re-iss. 1989; 395 145-2) (re-iss. Jun91 cd/c; CD/C+/MID 159)*
Nov 86. (7"/12") *(AM/+Y 368) <2909>* **REAL WILD CHILD (WILD ONE). / LITTLE MISS EMPEROR** 10
Feb 87. (7") *(AM 374)* **SHADES. / BABY IT CAN'T FAIL**
(12"+=) *(AMY 374)* – Cry for love.
Apr 87. (7"/12") *(AM/+Y 392)* **FIRE GIRL. / BLAH-BLAH-BLAH (live)**
Jun 87. (7") *(AM 397)* **ISOLATION. / HIDEAWAY**
(12"+=) *(AMY 397)* – Fire girl (remix).
— IGGY now with **STEVE JONES** – guitar / **PAUL GARRISTO** – drums (ex-PSYCHEDELIC FURS) / **SEAMUS BEAGHEN** – keyboards / **LEIGH FOXX** – bass
Jul 88. (lp/c/cd) *<(AMA/AMC/ADA 5198)>* **INSTINCT** 61
– Cold metal / High on you / Strong girl / Tom tom / Easy rider / Power & freedom / Lowdown / Tuff baby / Squarehead.
Aug 88. (7") *(AM 452)* **COLD METAL. / INSTINCT**
(12"+=/12"pic-d+=) *(AM Y/P 452)* – Tuff baby.
Nov 88. (7") *(AM 475)* **HIGH ON YOU. / SQUAREHEAD**
(12"+=) *(AMY 475)* – Tuff baby (remix).
— **ALVIN GIBBS** – guitar (ex-UK SUBS) repl. STEVE JONES (continued solo) / **ANDY McCOY** – bass (ex-HANOI ROCKS) repl. FOXX (to DEBORAH HARRY)
Nov 88. (lp/c/cd) **LIVE AT THE CHANNEL (live 17.9.88)** -
(UK-iss.May94 on 'New Rose'; 642005) (re-iss. cd Sep97 on 'Revenge'; MIG 40-41)
— now with **SLASH** – guitar / **DUFF McKAGAN** – bass (both of GUNS N' ROSES) / **KENNY ARONOFF** – drums

Virgin America Virgin America

Jan 90. (7"/c-s) *(VUS/+C 18) <VSC 1228>* **LIVIN' ON THE EDGE OF THE NIGHT. / THE PASSENGER** 51
(12"+=/12"pic-d+=/cd-s+=) *(VUS T/TE/CD 18)* – Nightclubbing / China girl.
Jun 90. (7"/c-s) *(VUS/+C 22)* **HOME. / LUST FOR LIFE**
(12"+=/cd-s+=) *(VUS T/CD 22)* – Pussy power / Funtime.
Jul 90. (cd/c/lp) *(CDVUS/VUSMC/VUSLP 19) <91381>* **BRICK BY BRICK** 50 90
– Home / Main street eyes / I won't crap out / Candy / Butt town / The undefeated / Moonlight lady / Something wild / Neon forest / Stormy night / Pussy power / My baby wants to rock & roll / Brick by brick / Livin' on the edge of the night. *(c re-iss. Apr92; OVEDC 426)*
— (below 'A'side featured **KATE PIERSON** – vox (of B-52's)
Oct 90. (7"/c-s) *(VUS/+C 29) <98900>* **CANDY. / PUSSY POWER (acoustic demo)** 67 28
(10"+=/cd-s+=) *(VUS 29)* – My baby wants to rock'n'roll (acoustic demos).
(12"/cd-s) *(VUS T/CD 29)* – ('A'side) / The undefeated / Butt town (acoustic demo).
— Oct 90, IGGY dueted with DEBORAH HARRY on UK Top 50 single 'DID YOU EVAH'; *Chrysalis; CHS 3646)*
— with **LARRY MULLEN** (U2) – drums, percussion / **HAL CRAGIN** – bass / **ERIC SCHERMERHORN** – guitar plus guests **MALCOLM BURN** – guitars, etc
Aug 93. (7"ep/c-ep/12"ep/cd-ep) *(VUS/+C/T/CD 74)* **THE WILD AMERICA EP** 63
– Wild America / Credit card / Come back tomorrow / My angel.
Sep 93. (cd/c/d-lp) *(CDVUS/VUSMC/VUSLP 64)* **AMERICAN CAESAR** 43
– Character / Wild America / Mixin' the colors / Jealousy / Hate / It's our love / Plastic & concrete / F***in' alone / Highway song / Beside you / Sickness / Boogie boy / Perforation / Problems / Social life / Louie Louie / Caesar / Girls of N.Y
May 94. (10"ep) *(VUS A/C 77)* **BESIDE YOU / EVIL CALIFORNIA. / HOME (live) / FUCKIN' ALONE** 47
(cd-ep) *(VUSCD 77)* – ('A'side) / Les amants / Louie Louie (live) / ('A'acoustic).
Feb 96. (cd/c/lp) *(CDVUS/VUSMC/VUSLP 102)* **NAUGHTY LITTLE DOGGIE**
– I wanna live / Pussy walk / Innocent world / Knucklehead / To belong / Keep on believing / Outta my head / Shoeshine girl / Heart is saved / Look away.
— He's soon to be featured in the film 'The Crow II'. Rumours are rife that he will re-form The STOOGES with RON and SCOTT, early in '97.

– compilations, etc. –

May 82. (7") *RCA Gold; (GOLD 549)* **THE PASSENGER. / NIGHTCLUBBING**
Sep 84. (lp/c) *R.C.A.; (PL/PK 84597)* **CHOICE CUTS** -
Apr 88. (cd-ep) *A&M; (AMCD 909)* **COMPACT HITS** -
– Real wild child (the wild one) / Isolation / Cry for love / Shades.
Jan 92. (cd) *Arista; (262 178)* **POP SONGS** -
Jan 93. (3xcd-box) *Virgin; (TPAK 21)* **LUST FOR LIFE / THE IDIOT / BRICK BY BRICK** -
Jun 93. (cd) *Revenge; (642044)* **LIVE NYC RITZ '86 (live)** -
Aug 93. (cd/c) *Revenge; (642/644 050)* **SUCK ON THIS!** -
Aug 95. (cd) *Skydog;* **WE ARE NOT TALKING ABOUT COMMERCIAL SHIT** -
Aug 95. (cd) *Skydog;* **WAKE UP SUCKERS** -
Aug 96. (cd) *M.C.A.; (MCD 84021)* **THE BEST OF IGGY POP LIVE (live)** -
Sep 96. (cd) *Camden RCA; (74321 41503-2)* **POP MUSIC** -
Oct 96. (cd/c/d-lp) *Virgin; (CDVUS/VUSMC/VUSLP 115)* **NUDE & RUDE: THE BEST OF IGGY POP**
Nov 96. (7"colrd/c-s) *Virgin; (VUS/+C 116)* **LUST FOR LIFE / (GET UP I FEEL LIKE BEING A) SEX MACHINE** 26
(cd-s+=) *(VUSCD 116)* – ('A'live) / I wanna be your dog (live).
Dec 96. (cd) *The Network; (3D 013)* **IGGY POP** -
Apr 97. (cd) *Wotre; (642007)* **LIVE IN BERLIN '91** -
Sep 97. (d-cd) *Snapper; (SMDCD 142)* **HEAD ON** -
Nov 97. (cd) *Other People's Music; (OPM 2116CD)* **HEROIN HATES YOU** -
Nov 97. (cd) *Eagle; (EABCD 011)* **THE MASTERS** -
Feb 98. (c-s) *Virgin; (VSC 1689)* **THE PASSENGER /** 22 -
(12"+=/cd-s+=) *(VS T/CDT 1689)* –
Aug 98. (cd) *A&M; (540943-2)* **BLAH BLAH BLAH / INSTINCT** -

NEW YORK DOLLS

Formed: New York City, New York, USA . . . Dec '71 by JOHNNY THUNDERS, DAVID JOHANSEN, BILLY MURCIA, ARTHUR KANE and RICK RIVETS. In March the following year, RIVETS left to form The BRATS, being swiftly replaced by SYLVAIN SYLVAIN. After a promising start as support act on a FACES British tour, the 'DOLLS' first casualty was MURCIA who died on the 6th of November '72 after drowning in his own bath (not, as widely believed, from a drug overdose). With JERRY NOLAN as a replacement, they signed to 'Mercury' in March '73 and promptly began work on an eponymous debut album with TODD RUNDGREN producing. Released in the summer of that year, 'THE NEW YORK DOLLS' was a proto-punk revelation, a way cool schlock of visceral rock'n'roll which combined the more essential moments of MC5, The PRETTY THINGS, PINK FAIRIES and The SHANGRI-LAS. The ROLLING STONES were another obvious reference point, JOHANSEN a dead-ringer for MICK JAGGER in terms of both vocal style and mascara'd looks. Inevitably, then, THUNDERS was the glam-punk KEITH RICHARDS, Glitter Twins to the JAGGERS/RICHARDS Glimmer coupling. The 'DOLLS' trashy transvestite attire also borrowed heavily from the 'STONES (circa '66 'Have You Seen Your Mother . . .'), although being American they'd obviously taken it to almost cartoon-esque proportions. The likes of 'PERSONALITY CRISIS', 'TRASH' and 'JET BOY' were seminal squalls of guitar abuse, making up in attitude what they lacked in musical ability. Although the record had the critics salivating, commercial success wasn't forthcoming and, unhappy with the record's production, the band opted for SHANGRI-LA's producer, GEORGE MORTON to work on 'TOO MUCH TOO SOON' (1974). Though the album had its moments, again the band had been paired with the wrong producer and the music press were emphatically unimpressed. The lukewarm reviews heightened inter-band tension and the 'DOLLS demise was swift and inevitable. Early the following year, Londoner MALCOLM McLAREN made a last-ditch attempt to save the band, revamping their image to no avail. THUNDERS was the first to leave, departing in 1975 to form The HEARTBREAKERS, while JOHANSEN and SYLVAIN subsequently sacked KANE before finally calling it a day the following Christmas. While THUNDERS went on to most acclaim with his HEARTBREAKERS (dying from an overdose on 23rd April '91), JOHANSEN recorded a number of solo albums, 'DAVID JOHANSEN' (1978), 'IN STYLE' (1979) and 'HERE COMES THE NIGHT' (1981) as well as releasing a 1988 set under the pseudonym of BUSTER POINDEXTER. NOLAN also met an untimely death, almost a year on from THUNDERS (14th January, 1992), suffering a fatal stroke while undergoing treatment for meningitis and pneumonia. A pivotal reference point for not only punk, but the US sleaze/glam metal movement of the mid-80's (FASTER PUSSYCAT, L.A. GUNS, GUNS N' ROSES, et al), The NEW YORK DOLLS influence remains hugely disproportionate to their relatively slim legacy. • **Songwriters:** JOHANSEN with THUNDERS or SYLVAIN. Covered PILLS (Bo Diddley) / DON'T START ME TALKIN' (Sonny Boy Williamson) / SHOWDOWN (Archie Bell) / SOMETHIN' ELSE (Eddie Cochran) / etc. • **Trivia:** Two songs 'PERSONALITY CRISIS' & 'WHO ARE THE MYSTERY GIRLS', appeared on the 1977 Various Artists compilation 'NEW WAVE'. **JOHANSEN's filmography:** 'Married To The Mob', 'Scrooged' and 'The Fisher King'.

Album rating: NEW YORK DOLLS (*8) / TOO MUCH TOO SOON (*7)

DAVID JOHANSEN (b. 9 Jan'50, Staten Island, N.Y.) – vocals / **JOHNNY THUNDERS** (b. JOHN GENZALE, 15 Jul'54) – guitar, vocals / **SYLVAIN SYLVAIN** (b. SIL MIZRAHI) – guitar, vocals repl. RICK RIVETS / **ARTHUR KANE** (b. 3 Feb'51) – bass / **JERRY NOLAN** (b. 7 May'51) – drums repl. BILLY MURCIA who died.

Mercury | Mercury

Jul 73. (7") *<73414>* **TRASH. / PERSONALITY CRISIS** [-] [ ]

Aug 73. (lp) *(6338 270) <SRM 675>* **NEW YORK DOLLS** [ ] [ ] Jul73
– Personality crisis / Looking for a kiss / Vietnamese baby / Lonely planet boy / Frankenstein / Trash / Bad girl / Subway train / Pills / Private world / Jet boy. *<US re-iss. 1984; same>*

Nov 73. (7") *(6052 402)* **JET BOY. / VIETNAMESE BABY** [ ] [-]

Jul 74. (lp) *(6338 498) <SRM 1001>* **TOO MUCH TOO SOON** [ ] [ ] May74
– Babylon / Stranded in the jungle / Who are the mystery girls? / (There's gonna be a) Showdown / It's too late / Puss 'n' boots / Chatterbox / Bad detective / Don't start me talkin' / Human being. *<US re-iss. 1984; same>*

Jul 74. (7") *(6052 615) <73478>* **STRANDED IN THE JUNGLE. / WHO ARE THE MYSTERY GIRLS?** [ ] [ ]

Sep 74. (7") *<73615>* **(THERE'S GONNA BE A) SHOWDOWN. / PUSS 'N' BOOTS** [-] [ ]

not iss. | Trash

1974. (fan club-7"ep) *<TR 001>* **LOOKING FOR A KISS (live). / WHO ARE THE MYSTERY GIRLS? (live) / SOMETHIN' ELSE (live)** [-] [ ]

— **PETER JORDAN** – bass (the roadie filled in on stage when KANE was drunk)

— Disbanded mid-1975, after **BOBBY BLAIN** – keyboards repl. CHRIS ROBINSON who had repl. THUNDERS (he formed The HEARTBREAKERS with NOLAN). **TOMMY MACHINE** (was last drummer). The NEW YORK DOLLS reformed again with JOHANSEN and SYLVIAN but only toured until late '76. SYLVIAN later formed The CRIMINALS. DAVID JOHANSEN went solo in 1978.

– compilations, others, etc. –

Jun 77. (7"m) *Mercury; (6160 008)* **JET BOY. / BABYLON / WHO ARE THE MYSTERY GIRLS?** [ ] [-]

Jul 77. (d-lp) *Mercury; (6641 631)* **NEW YORK DOLLS / TOO MUCH TOO SOON** [ ] [-]
(re-iss. Apr86; PRID 12)

Nov 81. (c) *R.O.I.R.; <A 104>* **LIPSTICK KILLERS – MERCER ST. SESSIONS** [-] [ ]
(re-iss. May90 on 'Danceteria' cd/lp; DAN CD/LP 038) (re-iss. cd Feb95 & Jun97 on 'ROIR Europe'; 885615027-2)

Sep 82. (12"ep) *Kamera; (ERA 13-12)* **PERSONALITY CRISIS / LOOKING FOR A KISS. / SUBWAY TRAIN / BAD GIRL** [ ] [-]
(re-iss. Jul90 on 'See For Miles' cd-ep; SEACD 3)

Sep 84. (red-m-lp) *Fan Club; (FC 007)* **RED PATENT LEATHER (rec. 75)** [-] [-] France
– Girls / Downtown / Private love / Personality crisis / Pills / Something else / Daddy rollin' stone / Dizzy Miss Lizzy. *(cd-iss. Oct88; FC 007CD) (UK cd-iss. Feb93 on 'Receiver'+=; RRCD 173) (cd re-iss. Apr97 on 'Last Call'; 42241-2)*

Oct 84. (7"white) *Fan Club; (NYD 1)* **PILLS (live). / DOWN, DOWN, DOWN TOWN (live)** [-] [-] France

1985. (lp) *Mercury; <8260 941>* **NIGHT OF THE LIVING DOLLS** [-] [ ]

Feb 86. (7",12"pic-d,12"red) *Antler; (DOLLS 1)* **PERSONALITY CRISIS. / SUBWAY TRAIN** [ ] [-]

Feb 86. (7",12"pic-d,12"blue) *Antler; (DOLLS 2)* **LOOKING FOR A KISS. / BAD GIRL** [ ] [-]

1986. (lp; one-side by SEX PISTOLS) *Receiver; (RRLP 102)* **AFTER THE STORM** [ ] [-]

Oct 94. (cd) *Mercury; (522 129-2)* **ROCK'N'ROLL** [ ] [ ]

DAVID JOHANSEN

– vocals, keyboards with his group **STATEN ISLAND BOYS: THOMAS TRASK** – guitar / **JOHHNY RAO** – guitar / **BUZZ VERNO** – bass (ex-CHERRY VANILLA) / **FRANKI LA ROCKA** – drums (ex-CHERRY VANILLA)

Blue Sky | Blue Sky

Jul 78. (lp) *(SKY 82335) <34926>* **DAVID JOHANSEN** [ ] [ ] May78
– Funky but chic / Girls / Pain in my heart / Not that much / Donna / Cool metro / I'm a lover / Lonely tenement / Frenchette.

Sep 78. (7") *(BS 6663)* **FUNKY BUT CHIC. / THE ROPE (THE LET GO SONG)** [ ] [ ]

Sep 79. (lp) *(SKY 83745) <JZ 36082>* **IN STYLE** [ ] [ ]
– Melody / She / Big city / She knew she was falling in love / Swaheto woman / Justine / In style / You touched me too / Wreckless crazy / Flamingo road.

Sep 79. (7") *<ZS 92781>* **MELODY. / RECKLESS CRAZY** [-] [ ]

Mar 80. (7"/12") *(SKY/12SKY 8125) <BS 2789>* **SWAHETO WOMAN. / SHE KNEW SHE WAS FALLING IN LOVE** [ ] [ ] Nov79

— with new band **BLONDIE CHAPLIN** – guitar, vocals / **ERNIE BROOKS** – bass / **TOM MANDEL** – organ / **BOBBY BLAIN** – piano / **TONY MACHINE** – drums

Aug 81. (lp) *(SKY 84504) <FZ 36589>* **HERE COMES THE NIGHT** [ ] [ ]
– She loves strangers / Bohemian love pad / You fool me / My obsession / Marquesa de Sade / Here comes the night / Suspicion / Party tonight / Havin' so much fun / Rollin' job / Heart of gold. *(cd-iss. Oct94 on 'Rewind';)*

Sep 81. (7") **HERE COMES THE NIGHT. / SHE LOVES STRANGERS** [-] [ ]

Jun 82. (7") *<ZS 550 3003>* **BOHEMIAN LOVE PAD. / MEDLEY: WE GOTA GET OUT OF THIS PLACE – DON'T BRING ME DOWN (live)** [-] [ ]

1982. (lp) *(ARZ 38004)* **LIVE IT UP** [-] [ ]
(cd-iss. Jan94 on 'Legacy';)

— now with **JOE DELIA** – keyboards / **DAVID NELSON** – guitar / **BRETT CARTWRIGHT** – bass / **DENNIS McDERMOTT** – drums

10-Virgin | Passport

Feb 85. (lp) *(DIX 8) <PB 6043>* **SWEET REVENGE** [ ] [ ] Nov84

Mar 85. (7"/12") *(TEN 46/+12)* **HEAR THE NEWS. / KING OF BABYLON** [ ] [ ]

BUSTER POINDEXTER & HIS BANSHEES OF BLUE

(aka DAVID JOHANSEN)

R.C.A. | R.C.A.

Jun 88. (7"/12") *(PB/PT 49581) <53577R>* **HOT HOT HOT. / CANNIBAL** [ ] [45] Nov87

Jul 88. (lp)(c)(cd) *<6633>* **BUSTER POINDEXTER** [ ] [90] Dec87
– Smack dab in the middle / Bad boy / Hot hot hot / Are you lonely for me baby / Screwy music / Good morning judge / Oh me oh my (I'm a fool for you baby) / Whadaya want? / House of the rising sun / Cannibal / Heart of gold.

Jul 88. (7") *<7638>* **OH ME, OH MY (I'M A FOOL FOR YOU BABY). / CANNIBAL** [-] [ ]

1989. (7") *<8914>* **HEART OF GOLD. / HIT THE ROAD JACK** [-] [ ]

1989. (7") **ALL NIGHT PARTY. / ('A'-hot mix)** [-] [ ]

1989. (7") *<9195 – 2572>* **UNDER THE SEA. / DEBOURGE YOURSELF** [-] [ ]

– compilations, etc. –

Oct 94. (cd) *Sequel-Rhino; (RSFCD 818)* **BUSTER'S HAPPY HOUR** [ ] [-]

MC5

Formed: Detroit, Michigan, USA . . . 1965 by ROB TYNER, FED 'SONIC' SMITH and WAYNE KRAMER. After two limited single releases, MC5 (MOTOR CITY FIVE) signed a contract with 'Elektra' in mid '68, helped by counter-cultural activist and DJ, John Sinclair. In addition to becoming the band's manager, he heavily influenced both their political extremism and warped takes on free jazz improvisation. Reflecting the harsher geographical and economic climate of Detroit, the band espoused revolution and struggle as opposed to the love and peace ethos of the sun-kissed Californian flower children. The riotous proto-punk of their legendary, acid-fuelled live show was captured on the controversial debut, 'KICK OUT THE JAMS'. Recorded in late October '68, it eventually hit the shops in May '69 and while the original uncensored pressings contained the line "Kick Out The Jams, Motherfuckers!", the offending word was later supplanted with the milder "Brothers And Sisters". Unfortunately, this wasn't enough to prevent some record stores from refusing to stock the lp, and after the band explicitly aired their views on one of the aforementioned dealers in a local newspaper, they were duly given the boot by Elektra. Nevertheless, the album reached No.30 in America and although it sounds a bit dated to modern ears, it was way radical for the time, remaining an inspiration to each new generation of noiseniks. After a split with Sinclair, the band signed with Atlantic and began to move away from the overtly subversive nature of their earlier material to a more straightahead rock approach, evidenced on their Jon Landau-produced follow-up album, 'BACK IN THE U.S.A.'. Wired rock'n'roll of an impeccable degree, the record didn't fare well in the laid-back, doped-up climate of the early 70's. An ambitious third album in 1971, 'HIGH TIME', featuring horns and even Salvation Army musicians, still failed to cut any commercial ice and the band split in 1972. KRAMER subsequently spent five years in jail for cocaine dealing before embarking on a low key solo career while former manager, Sinclair, was sentenced to ten years in the early 70's for a minor dope charge, serving only two after appeal. Tragically, ROB TYNER died from a heart attack in 1991 aged only 46. Pioneers in the true sense of the word, the MC5 together with the STOOGES were the first real punk bands, the originators who were never bettered. **Songwriters:** Group compositions, except; I CAN ONLY GIVE YOU EVERYTHING (Them) / TUTTI FRUTTI (Little Richard).

Album rating: KICK OUT THE JAMS (*9) / BACK IN THE USA (*8)

ROB TYNER (b. ROBERT DERMINER, 12 Dec'44) – vocals, harmonica / **WAYNE KRAMER** (b.30 Apr'48) – guitar, vocals, keyboards / **FRED 'SONIC' SMITH** (b. West Virginia) – guitar / **MICHAEL DAVIS** – bass / **DENNIS THOMPSON** – drums

not iss. — A.M.G.

1966. (7") *<AMG 1001>* **I CAN ONLY GIVE YOU EVERYTHING. / I JUST DON'T KNOW** [-] [ ]
(above credited to MOTOR CITY FIVE)

not iss. — A2.

Mar 68. (7") *<A2 333>* **LOOKING AT YOU. / BORDERLINE** [-] [ ]

—— added 6th member **Brother J.C.CRAWFORD** – rapper / narrative

Elektra — Elektra

May 69. (7") *(EKSN 45056) <EK 45648>* **KICK OUT THE JAMS. / MOTOR CITY IS BURNING** [ ] [82] Mar 69

May 69. (lp) *(mono/stereo; EKL/EKS 74042)* **KICK OUT THE JAMS** [ ] [30] Mar 69
– Ramblin' rose / Kick out the jams / Come together / Rocket reducer No.62 (rama lama fa fa) / Borderline / Motor city is burning / I want you right now / Starship. *(re-iss. May77.) (re-iss. +cd.Nov91) (re-iss. cd+c Mar93 on 'Pickwick') (re-iss. cd/c Sep95 on 'Warners')*

Aug 69. (7") *(EKSN 45067)* **RAMBLIN' ROSE. / BORDERLINE** [ ] [-]

Atlantic — Atlantic

Oct 70. (7") *<2678>* **TONIGHT. / LOOKING AT YOU** [-] [ ]

Nov 70. (lp) *(2400 016) <SD 8247>* **BACK IN THE U.S.A.** [ ] [ ] Feb 70
– Tutti frutti / Tonight / Teenage list / Looking at you / Let me try / High school / Call me animal / The American ruse / Shakin' Street / The human being lawnmower / Back in the U.S.A. *(re-iss. Feb77.) (cd-iss. May93 on 'Rhino-Atlantic')*

1970. (7") *<2724>* **SHAKIN' STREET. / THE AMERICAN RUSE** [-] [ ]

Oct 71. (lp) *(2400 123) <SD 8285>* **HIGH TIME** [ ] [ ]
– Sister Anne / Baby won't ya / Miss X / Gotta keep movin' / Future – Now / Poison / Over nnd over / Skunk (sonically speaking). *(cd-iss. May93 on 'Rhino-Atlantic')*

—— (split early '72 when DAVIS departed) THOMPSON, SMITH and DAVIS formed short-lived ASCENSION. FRED SMITH married PATTI SMITH and later formed SONIC'S RENDEZVOUS BAND. TYNER was credited on HOT RODS single, late'77. (see ⇒ EDDIE & THE HOT RODS.

– compilations, etc. –

1969. (7") *A.M.G.; <AMG 1001>* **I CAN ONLY GIVE YOU EVERYTHING. / ONE OF THE GUYS** [-] [ ]

Jul 83. (c) *R.O.I.R.; <A 122>* **BABES IN ARMS** [-] [ ]
(re-iss. Apr90 & Dec92 on 'Danceteria' lp/cd; DAN LP/CD 031)

May 94. (cd) *Receiver; (RRCD 185)* **BLACK TO COMM** [ ] [-]

Oct 94. (10"lp/cd) *Alive; (ALIVE 005/+CD)* **POWER TRIP** [ ] [-]

Nov 94. (cd) *Receiver; (RRCD 193)* **LOOKING AT YOU** [ ] [-]

Feb 95. (10"lp/cd) *Alive; (NER/+CD 2001)* **THE AMERICAN RUSE** [ ] [-]

Mar 95. (10"lp) *Alive; (ALIVE 008)* **ICE PICK SLIM** [ ] [-]
(cd-iss. Feb97; ALIVECD 8)

Sep 95. (10"ep/cd) *Alive; (ALIVE 0010/+CD)* **FRIDAY, THE 13TH** [ ] [-]

Dec 96. (cd) *Dressed To Kill; (DTKLP 002)* **THUNDER EXPRESS – ONE DAY IN THE STUDIO** [ ] [-]

Mar 97. (lp) *Alive; (NER 3008)* **TEENAGE LUST** [ ] [-]

WAYNE KRAMER

—— went solo after spending 5 years in prison for cocaine dealing.

Stiff-Chiswick — not iss.

Oct 77. (7") *(DEA-SUK 1)* **RAMBLIN' ROSE. / GET SOME** [ ] [-]

Radar — not iss.

Jul 79. (7") *(ADA 41)* **THE HARDER THEY COME. / EAST SIDE GIRL** [ ] [-]

not iss. — Pure&Easy

1983. (7") *<PE 017>* **NEGATIVE GIRLS. / STREET WARFARE** [-] [ ]

—— GANG WAR formed in 1980 with **JOHNNY THUNDERS** – vocals

Zodiac — not iss.

1987. (7"ep; WAYNE KRAMER'S GANG WAR) *(800)* **GANG WAR (live at Max's May 1980)** [ ] [-]

May 90. (lp) *(LP 1001)* **GANG WAR** (live/studio) [ ] [-]

—— WAYNE had joined the DEVIANTS in 1984 for their album HUMAN GARBAGE.

Curio — Progressive

1987. (7"; as WAYNE KRAMER'S DEATH TONGUE) **SPIKE HEELS EP** [-] [ ]

—— (WAYNE played late 80's with DAS DAMEN and G.G. ALLIN)

Nov 91. (d-cd/d-lp) *(ITEM 2 CD/LP) <PRO 023>* **DEATH TONGUE** [ ] [ ]
– Take your clothes off / Sike heels / Spend the rent / Negative girls / Death tongue / Leather skull / The scars never show / McArthur Park / Fun in the final days / Who shot you Dutch.

—— In Sep'91, ROB TYNER was found dead after suffering heart attack. He was 46.

—— with on first **KEITH MORRIS, BRETT REED, MATT FREEMAN, DALE CROVER, JOSH FREESE, BRETT GUREWITZ, CHRIS BAGAROZZI**, etc

Epitaph — Epitaph

Jan 95. (cd/c/lp) *<(E 86447-2/-4/-1)>* **THE HARD STUFF** [ ] [ ]
– Crack in the universe / Junkie romance / Bad seed / Poison / Realm of the pirate kings / Incident on Stock Island / Pillar of fire / Hope for sale / Edge of the switchblade / Sharkskin suit.

Feb 96. (cd/lp) *<(86458-2/-1)>* **DANGEROUS MADNESS** [ ] [ ]
– Dangerous madness / Back to DEtroit / Wild America / Something broken in the promised land / Take exit '97 / God's worst nightmare / The boy's got that look in their eyes / Dead man's vest / It's never enough / Rats of illusion / Dead movie stars.

May 97. (cd) *<(6488-2)>* **CITIZEN WAYNE** [ ] [ ]
– Stranger in the house / Back when dogs could talk / Revolution in apt.29 / Down on the ground / Shining Mr. Lincoln's shoes / Dope for democracy / No easy way out / You don't know my name / Count time / Snatched defeat / Doing the work / Farewell to whiskey.

—— MC5 were about to reform with KRAMER, DAVIS + THOMSON

—— next with rhythm **DOUGLAS LUNN + RIC PARNELL**

Nov 98. (cd/lp) *<(86539)>* **LLMF** (Live Like A Motherfucker) [ ] [ ]
– Bad seed / Stranger in the house / It's never enough / Something broken in the promised land / Take your clothes off / Down on the ground / Junkie romance / Poison / Count time / No easy way out / Crack in the universe / So long, Hank / Kick out the jams / Bomb day in Paris.

– others, etc. –

Nov 96. (cd; by WAYNE KRAMER – DENIZ TEK – SCOTT MORGAN) *Alive; <(ALIVE 25)>* **DODGE MAIN** [ ] [ ]
– City slang / 1.94 / Citizen of time / Future – Now / Fire comin' / 100 fools / The harder they come / Over and over / Better than that / I got a right.

VELVET UNDERGROUND

Formed: New York City, New York, USA . . . early 1965, by LOU REED and JOHN CALE, who nearly hit as The PRIMITIVES with the single, 'The Ostrich'. They met modern pop artist, ANDY WARHOL, who invited German chanteuse NICO to join the set-up alongside STERLING MORRISON and MO TUCKER. Early in 1966, they signed to 'MGM-Verve', and soon began work on what was to be their debut album, 'THE VELVET UNDERGROUND AND NICO'. The album was a revelation, strikingly different from the love and peace psychedelia of the day, The VELVETS vision was decidedly darker and more disturbing. Combining sublime melodies and nihilistic noise, it featured eleven superb ahead-of-their-time classics, notably the brutally frank and frenetic 'HEROIN', the S&M 'VENUS IN FURS' and the garage raunch of 'WAITING FOR THE MAN'. It also contained three NICO sung beauties, 'FEMME FATALE', 'ALL TOMORROW'S PARTIES' and 'I'LL BE YOUR MIRROR'. The record only managed a brief stay in the US Top 200, as did the 1967 follow-up, 'WHITE LIGHT, WHITE HEAT', which included the 17-minute white noise freak-out of 'SISTER RAY'. With CALE now out of the picture, the focus fell on REED's songwriting for the self-titled third album. An altogether mellower set of more traditionally structured songs, the highlight was undoubtedly REED's beautiful lullaby, 'PALE BLUE EYES'. The band's last studio album, 'LOADED', was the closest The VELVET UNDERGROUND ever came to mainstream rock and an indicator of the direction REED would take in his solo career. 'SWEET JANE' and 'ROCK 'N' ROLL' marked his creative peak, a final glorious burst of guitar noise before the group disbanded and the myth started to crystallise. And that was that. Except it wasn't, not come 1992 anyway, when many a precious, pasty faced obsessive went even whiter with horror as The VELVET UNDERGROUND reformed. Many more fans, however, eagerly shelled out their hard earned cash for a reunion tour and album as CALE and REED became buddies once more. The live shows were apparently rather joyous and the accompanying vinyl document, 'LIVE MCMXCII' (1993), was an enjoyable romp through all the favourites. After the death of STERLING MORRISON in 1995, however, the prospect of further VELVETS activity looks doubtful. Yet despite the reunion, despite LOU REED's dodgy hairdo, despite everything, The VELVET UNDERGROUND of the 60's remain perenially cool and insidiously influential. Basically, alternative music begins and ends with VU and they have been cited as the inspiration for punk rock. A decade after that, a generation of indie groups (i.e. JESUS & MARY CHAIN, early PRIMAL SCREAM, MY BLOODY VALENTINE, etc.) paid barely disguise homage to their heroes. • **Songwriters:** REED compositions, except some by group. Many rock acts have covered their material, but so far not surprisingly, none have managed to score a major chart hit yet. • **Miscellaneous:** In 1990, REED and CALE re-united on a tribute album to the deceased ANDY WARHOL. NICO had earlier died on the 18th of July '88 after suffering a brain haemorrhage due to a fall from her bike while on holiday in Ibiza. • **Trivia:** The debut lp sleeve, featured a gimmick peeling banana skin sticker. They reformed for a gig in Paris, 15 June 1990. UK's Channel 4, featured a night-long session of all their previous work.

Album rating: THE VELVET UNDERGROUND AND NICO (*10) / WHITE LIGHT – WHITE HEAT (*9) / V.U. (*7) / THE VELVET UNDERGROUND (*7).

LOU REED (b. LOUIS FIRBANK, 2 Mar'44, Long Island, N.Y.) – vocals, guitar (ex-JADES, ex-PRIMITIVES) / **JOHN CALE** (b. 9 Dec'42, Garnant, Wales) – bass, viola, vocals, etc. / **STERLING MORRISON** – guitar / **MAUREEN TUCKER** – drums / plus **NICO** (b. CHRISTA PAFFGEN, 16 Oct'38, Cologne, Germany) – vocals (also – Solo artist)

Verve / Verve

Oct 66. (7") *<10427>* **ALL TOMORROW'S PARTIES. / I'LL BE YOUR MIRROR** [-] [ ]

Dec 66. (7") *<10466>* **SUNDAY MORNING / FEMME FATALE** [-] [ ]

Oct 67. (lp; stereo/mono) *(S+/VLP 9184) <5008>* **THE VELVET UNDERGROUND AND NICO** [ ] [ ] Dec66
– Sunday morning / I'm waiting for the man / Femme fatale / Venus in furs / Run run run / All tomorrow's parties / Heroin / There she goes again / I'll be your mirror / Black angel's death song / European son to Delmore Schwartz. *(re-iss. Oct71 on 'M.G.M.; 2315 056) (re-iss. Aug83 on 'Polydor' lp/c; SPE LP/MC 20) (cd-iss. 1986 on 'Polydor'; 823 290-2) (cd re-iss. May96 on 'Polydor'; 531 250-2)*

— Trimmed to a quartet when NICO preferred the solo life

Jan 68. (7") *<10543>* **WHITE LIGHT – WHITE HEAT. / HERE SHE COMES NOW** [-] [ ]

Mar 68. (7") *<10560>* **I HEARD HER CALL MY NAME. / HERE SHE COMES NOW** [-] [ ]

Jun 68. (lp; stereo/mono) *(S+/VLP 9201) <5046>* **WHITE LIGHT / WHITE HEAT** [ ] [ ] Dec67
– White light – white heat / The gift / Lady Godiva's operation / Here she comes now / I heard her call my name / Sister Ray. *(re-iss. Oct71 on 'MGM Select'; 2353 024) (re-iss. Apr84 on 'Polydor' lp/c; SPE LP/MC 73) (cd-iss. 1986 on 'Polydor'; 825 119-2) (cd re-iss. May96 on 'Polydor'; 531 251-2)*

— **DOUG YULE** – bass, vocals, keyboards, guitar repl. CALE who went solo

M.G.M. / M.G.M.

Apr 69. (lp) *(CS 8108) <4617>* **THE VELVET UNDERGROUND** [ ] [ ] Mar 69
– Candy says . . . / What goes on / Some kinda love / Pale blue eyes / Jesus / Beginning to see the light / I'm set free / That's the story of my life / The murder mystery / Afterhours. *(re-iss. Nov71 on 'MGM Select'; 2353 022) (re-iss. Mar76;) (re-iss. Sep83 on 'Polydor' lp/c; SPE LP/MC 39) <US re-iss. Apr85; 815454> (cd-iss. May96 on 'Polydor'; 531 252-2)*

May 69. (7") *<14057>* **JESUS. / WHAT GOES ON** [-] [ ]

— **BILLY YULE** – drums repl. TUCKER who had a baby. **MO TUCKER** returned in 1970 and BILLY only appeared on MAX's live album (see compilations)

Atlantic / Cotillion

Jan 71. (7") *<44107>* **WHO LOVES THE SUN? / OH! SWEET NUTHIN'** [-] [ ]

Apr 71. (lp) *(2400 111) <9034>* **LOADED** [ ] [ ] Aug70
– Who loves the sun? / Sweet Jane / Rock and roll / Cool it down / New age / Head held high / Lonesone cowboy Bill / I found a reason / Train around the bend / Oh! sweet nuthin'. *(re-iss. 1972 lp/c; K/K4 40113) (cd-iss. Jun88 on 'Warners') (cd-iss. Feb93 on 'Warners') (d-cd-iss. May97 as 'LOADED (THE FULLY LOADED EDITION)' on 'Rhino'+=; 812272563-2)* – (diff.mixes & demos, etc.)

Apr 71. (7") *(2091 008)* **WHO LOVES THE SUN. / SWEET JANE** [ ] [-]

— (Aug70) now with no originals The **YULE's** brought in newcomers **WALTER POWERS** – bass repl. LOU REED who went solo in 1971. (1971) **WILLIE ALEXANDER** – guitar repl. MORRISON who took a doctorate in English. MO TUCKER finally departed to raise her new family and eventually had five children in total, before going solo in 1980.

Polydor / not iss.

Feb 73. (lp) *(2383 180)* **SQUEEZE** [ ] [-]
– Little Jack / Mean old man / She'll make you cry / Wordless / Dopey Joe / Crash / Friends / Jack and Jane / Send no letter / Louise.

— Folded soon after above, DOUG sessioned for ELLIOTT MURPHY and later joined AMERICAN FLYER.

— VELVET UNDERGROUND re-formed in 1993; **REED, CALE, MORRISON & TUCKER**

Sire / Sire

Oct 93. (d-cd/d-c) *(9362 45464-2/-4)* **LIVE MCMXCII (live)** [70] [ ]
– We're gonna have a good time together / Venus in furs / Guess I'm falling in love / After hours / All tomorrow's parties / Some kinda love / I'll be your mirror / Beginning to see the light / The gift / I heard her call my name / Femme fatale / Hey Mr. Rain / Sweet Jane / Velvet nursery rhyme / White light – white heat / I'm sticking with you / Black angel's death song / Rock'n'roll / I can't stand it / I'm waiting for the man / Heroin / Pale blue eyes / Coyote.

Feb 94. (7"/c-s) *(W 0224/+C)* **VENUS IN FURS (live). / I'M WAITING FOR THE MAN (live)** [71] [ ]
(cd-s+=) *(W 0224CD)* – Heroin (live) / Sweet Jane (live).

— On the 30th August 1995, STERLING MORRISON died of lymphoma.

— Group inducted into the Rock'n'roll Hall Of Fame, and performed 'LAST NIGHT I SAID GOODBYE TO A FRIEND', REED's tribute to recently deceased STERLING.

– compilations, others, etc. –

Dec 71. (d-lp) *M.G.M.; (2683 006)* **ANDY WARHOL'S VELVET UNDERGROUND FEATURING NICO** [ ] [-]
– I'm waiting for the man / Candy says / Run, run, run / White light – white heat / All tomorrow's parties / Sunday morning / I heard her call my name / Femme fatale / Heroin / Here she comes now / There she goes again / Sister Ray / Venus in furs / European son / Pale blue eyes / Black angel's death song / Beginning to see the light.

Aug 72. (lp) *Atlantic; (K 30022) / Cotillion; <9500>* **LIVE AT MAX'S KANSAS CITY (live 22 Aug'70)** [ ] [ ] May72
– I'm waiting for the man / Sweet Jane / Lonesome Cowboy Bill / Beginning to see

the light / I'll be your mirror / Pale blue eyes / Sunday morning / New age / Femme fatale / After hours. *(cd-iss. Jun93 on 'Warners'; 7567 90370-2)*

Jun 73. (7"m; as LOU REED & VELVET UNDERGROUND) *M.G.M.; (2006 283)* **CANDY SAYS. / I'M WAITING FOR THE MAN / RUN RUN RUN** [ ] [-]

Aug 73. (7") *Atlantic; (K 10339)* **SWEET JANE (live). / ROCK AND ROLL** (live) [ ] [-]

Oct 73. (lp) *Verve; (2315 258) / Pride; <0022>* **THE VELVET UNDERGROUND AND LOU REED** [ ] [ ]

1974. (lp) *M.G.M.; <4950>* **ARCHETYPES** [-] [ ]

1976. (ltd-7"m) *A.E.B.;* **FOGGY NOTION – INSIDE YOUR HEART. / I'M STICKING WITH YOU / FERRYBOAT BILL** [ ] [-]

Feb 79. (d-lp) *Mercury; (6643 900) <SRM2 7504>* **1969 – THE VELVET UNDERGROUND LIVE (live)** [ ] [ ] Apr74

– I'm waiting for the man / Lisa says / What goes on / Sweet Jane / We're gonna have a real good time together / Femme fatale / New age / Rock and roll / Beginning to see the light / Ocean / Pale blue eyes / Heroin / Some kinda love / Over you / Sweet Bonnie Brown – It's just too much / I'll be your mirror / White light – white heat. *(re-iss. Nov84; PRID 7) (re-iss. 1987; 834 823-1) (re-iss. 1988 as 'VOL.1' & 'VOL.2' cd/c; 834823-2/-4 & 834824-2/-4)*

Nov 80. (d-lp)(d-c) *Polydor; (2664 438)(3578 485)* **GREATEST HITS** [ ] [-]

Oct 82. (12"ep) *Polydor; (POSPX 603)* **HEROIN / VENUS IN FURS. / I'M WAITING FOR THE MAN / RUN RUN RUN** [ ] [-]

Feb 85. (lp/c) *Polydor; (POLD/+C 5167) <823721>* **V.U.** (rare rec.68-69) [47] [85]

– I can't stand it / Stephanie says / She's my best friend / Lisa says / Ocean / Foggy notion / Temptation inside your heart / One of these days / Andy's chest / I'm sticking with you. *(cd-iss. Jun87; 825 092-2)*

May 86. (5xlp-box)(5xcd-box) *Polydor; (VUBOX 1)(815 454-2)* **BOXED SET** [ ] [ ]

– (first 3 albums, plus V.U. & ANOTHER VIEW)

Aug 86. (lp/c/cd) *Polydor; (829 405-1/-4/-2)* **ANOTHER VIEW** [ ] [ ]

– We're gonna have a good time together / I'm gonna move right in / Hey Mr. Rain (version 1) / Ride into the Sun / Coney Island steeplechase / Guess I'm falling in love / Hey Mr. Rain (version 2) / Ferryboat Bill / Rock and roll (original).

Feb 88. (12") *Old Gold; (OG 4049)* **I'M WAITING FOR THE MAN. / HEROIN** [ ] [-]

Mar 88. (12") *Old Gold; (OG 4051)* **VENUS IN FURS. / ALL TOMORROW'S PARTIES** [ ] [-]

Sep 88. (lp) *Plastic Inevitable; <FIRST 1>* **THE VELVET UNDERGROUND ETC.** [-] [ ]

– The ostrich / Cycle Annie / Sneaky Pete / Noise.

Sep 88. (lp) *Plastic Inevitable; <SECOND 1>* **THE VELVET UNDERGROUND AND SO ON** [-] [ ]

– It's alright (the way you live) / I'm not too sorry / Stephanie says.

Oct 89. (lp/c/cd) *Verve; <(841 164-1/-4/-2)>* **THE BEST OF THE VELVET UNDERGROUND (THE WORDS AND MUSIC OF LOU REED)** [ ] [ ]

– I'm waiting for the man / Femme fatale / Run run run / Heroin / All tomorrow's parties / I'll be your mirror / White light – white heat / Stephanie says / What goes on / Beginning to see the light / Pale blue eyes / I can't stand it / Lisa says / Sweet Jane / Rock and roll.

Oct 95. (cd/c) *Global; (RAD CD/MC 21)* **THE BEST OF LOU REED & VELVET UNDERGROUND** [56] [ ]

Oct 95. (4xcd-box) *Polydor; (527887-2)* **PEEL SLOWLY AND SEE** [ ] [-]

— (see also LOU REED discography for other tracks on comps & B's)

— Also tribute albums 'HEAVEN AND HELL' 1, 2 & 3 were isued Oct'90-Feb'92, all on 'Imaginary' records, as was another '15 MINUTES'.

Lou REED

Born: LOUIS FIRBANK, 2 Mar'42, Freeport, Long Island, New York, USA. In 1958, he formed The JADES, who released two REED-penned singles, 'LEAVE HER FOR ME' / 'SO BLUE' and 'LEAVE HER FOR ME' / 'BELINDA' for 'Time' and 'Dot' respectively. Late in '64, he joined the 'Pickwick' stable of writers, achieving a local minor hit when The PRIMITIVES issued his 'The Ostrich' / 'Sneaky Pete' 45. Later in the year, he helped for the seminal VELVET UNDERGROUND. An integral part of the group's songwriting prowess, he departed in September 1970, going solo and signing to 'R.C.A.'. His eponymous 1972 debut (with Richard Robinson on production), scraped into the US Top 200, gaining nothing in renewed respect. Later that year, helped by stablemates DAVID BOWIE and MICK RONSON, he unleashed 'TRANSFORMER', gaving him his first major triumph when it reached the Top 30 on both sides of the Atlantic. It was boosted by 'WALK ON THE WILD SIDE' (a superb Top 20 single), the piano-led melancholy of 'PERFECT DAY', the raw glam of 'VICIOUS' and one-that-got-away 'SATELLITE OF LOVE'. His next album, 'BERLIN' (1973), although unfairly panned by US critics, still managed a Top 10 placing in Britain. On reflection, its subject matter of suicide and child neglect ('THE BED' and 'THE KIDS') didn't help win any new friends and it still stands as one of the most unrelentingly bleak listens in the history of rock. After the claustrophobic confessions of BERLIN, the live 'ROCK 'N' ROLL ANIMAL' (1974) album must have come as something of a relief to R.C.A. A technically faultless back-up band roared through a selection of old VELVETS numbers with REED hollering over the top, and while the set represented something of a concession to commercial credibility (by REED's standards anyway) it captured little of the VELVET UNDERGROUND's subtlety. It also saw REED sinking further into self-parody, hamming up his studied image of sleazy decadence to the max. 'SALLY CAN'T DANCE', released later the same year, was REED in full emotionless flight, an icy collection of biting cyniscism that included the infamous 'ANIMAL LANGUAGE' track. But laughing LOU hadn't played his ace card yet, that musical two fingered salute fell to 1975's 'METAL MACHINE MUSIC', the one everyone talks about but have never had the will or mental endurance to listen to the whole way through. A double album of impenetrable feedback noise interspersed with inhuman screams, hums etc., the record successfully alienated most of REED's long suffering fans amid critical meltdown. In true contrary style, he sashayed sweetly back with the mellow 'CONEY ISLAND BABY' (1976), although the lyrics remained as brutally frank as ever. His first record for 'Arista', 'ROCK 'N' ROLL HEART' (1976) was indeed as vacantly awful as the title suggests, though the punk-inspired 'STREET HASSLE' (1978) showcased a re-energised REED, most impressively on the malicious guitar workout of 'DIRT' and the swaggering title track. After a tedious live album, REED started to show uncharacteristic signs of maturity in both his music and lyrics with 'THE BELLS' (1979) and 'GROWING UP IN PUBLIC' (1980). At the turn of the 80's, he hooked up with former Void-Oid, ROBERT QUINE, a partnership that resulted in one of the most consistent and accomplished sets in REED's solo career, 'THE BLUE MASK'. Newly married and back at his original stable, 'R.C.A.', REED proffered more domestic lyrical fare alongside darker musings. QUINE remained for one more studio album, the similarly focused 'LEGENDARY HEARTS', before breaking ranks. 1984's 'NEW SENSATIONS' was fairly low-key while 'MISTRIAL' (1986) saw REED introduce a few drum machine tracks in typical 80's style. These were competent albums but hardly essential and only the most devout REED believer could've predicted the creative, commercial and critical renaissance that would ensue with 1989's 'NEW YORK' album. A skeletal strum-athon, this was LOU REED in the raw with the sparsest of musical accompaniment. Back on familiar territory, his sardonic tales of the Big Apple's seedier side made for compelling listening. 'SONGS FOR DRELLA' (1990), a collaboration with JOHN CALE, was a heartfelt tribute to ANDY WARHOL, while 'MAGIC AND LOSS' (1992) was a sincere series of stark meditations on life and death. Despite an ill-advised VELVET UNDERGROUND reunion, REED retained critical favour, going on to release another well-received album in 1996, 'SET THE TWILIGHT REELING'. • **Songwriters:** REED compositions except, SEPTEMBER SONG (Kurt Weill) / SOUL MAN (Sam & Dave). In 1979 and 1980, he co-wrote with MICHAEL FORFARA plus other group members. The single, 'CITY LIGHTS', was co-written with NILS LOFGREN. • **Trivia:** Surprisingly in 1973, WALK ON THE WILD SIDE was not banned from airplay. It contained lyrics "giving head", which had been overlooked by unstreet-wise cred. radio producers. LOU has been married twice, first to cocktail waitress, Betty on the 9th of January '73, then to Sylvia Morales on the 14th of February '80. He played guitar and composed four tracks on NICO'S 'Chelsea Girl' lp in 1967. Nine years later he produced NELSON SLATER'S 'Wild Angel' album, also contributing guitar, piano and vocals. In 1979 and 1981 he co-composed with NILS LOFGREN and KISS on their 'NILS' and 'THE ELDER' albums respectively. In the late 80's, he guested for RUBEN BLADES and his old friend MAUREEEN TUCKER. He was also backing vocalist on SIMPLE MINDS' 'This is Your Land' / DION'S 'King of The New York Streets' and TOM TOM CLUB'S version of 'Femme Fatale'.

Album rating: TRANSFORMER (*9) / BERLIN (*7) / RETRO (*8) / THE BLUE MASK (*7) / NEW YORK (*9) / MAGIC AND LOSS (*8) / SONGS FOR DRELLA (*7) / SET THE TWILIGHT REELING (*8)

LOU REED – vocals, guitar (ex-VELVET UNDERGROUND) / with **STEVE HOWE** – guitar / **RICK WAKEMAN** – keyboards (both of YES) / **CLEM CATTINI** – drums (ex-TORNADOES)

R.C.A. R.C.A.

Jun 72. (7") *<0727>* **GOING DOWN. / I CAN'T STAND IT** [-] [ ]

Jul 72. (lp) *(SF 8281) <4701>* **LOU REED** [ ] [ ] Jun72

– I can't stand it / Going down / Walk and talk it / Lisa says / Berlin / I love you / Wild child / Love makes you feel / Ride into the Sun / Ocean.

Aug 72. (7") *(RCA 2240) <0784>* **WALK AND TALK IT. / WILD CHILD** [ ] [ ]

— now with **MICK RONSON** – guitar / **HERBIE FLOWERS + KLAUS VOORMANN** – bass / **JOHN HALSEY + RITCHIE DHARMA + BARRY DE SOUZA** – drums / **RONNIE ROSS** – saxophone / **DAVID BOWIE** – backing vocals, producer

Nov 72. (lp) *(LSP 4807) <4807>* **TRANSFORMER** [13] [29]

– Vicious / Andy's chest / Perfect day / Hangin' round / Walk on the wild side / Make up / Satellite of love / Wagon wheel / New York telephone conversation / I'm so free / Goodnight ladies. *(re-iss. Feb81 lp/c; INT S/K 5061); hit UK No.91) (re-iss. 1984 lp/c; NL/NK 83806) (cd-iss. 1985 + Oct87; PD 83806)*

Nov 72. (7") *(RCA 2303) <0887>* **WALK ON THE WILD SIDE. / PERFECT DAY** [10] [16]

(re-iss. May79 on 'RCA Gold'; GOLD 5)

Feb 73. (7") *<0964>* **SATELLITE OF LOVE. / WALK AND TALK IT** [-] [ ]

Mar 73. (7") *(RCA 2318)* **SATELLITE OF LOVE. / VICIOUS** [ ] [-]

Apr 73. (7") *<0051>* **VICIOUS. / GOODNIGHT LADIES** [-] [ ]

— all new band **DICK WAGNER + STEVE HUNTER** – guitar (both ex-ALICE COOPER) / **STEVE WINWOOD** – keyboards / **JACK BRUCE** – bass / **AYNSLEY DUNBAR** – drums / etc.

Oct 73. (7") *<0172>* **HOW DO YOU THINK IT FEELS. / LADY DAY** [-] [ ]

Oct 73. (lp) *(RS 1002) <0207>* **BERLIN** [7] [98]

– Berlin / Lady day / Men of good fortune / Caroline says I / How do think it feels / Oh Jim / Caroline says II / The kids / The bed / Sad song. *(re-iss. Oct81 lp/c; INT S/K 5150) (re-iss. 1984 lp/c; NL/NK 84388) (cd-iss. Jun86; PD 84388)*

Feb 74. (7") *(APBO 0221)* **CAROLINE SAYS I. / CAROLINE SAYS II** [ ] [-]

— **PRAKASH JOHN** – bass (ex-ALICE COOPER) repl. TONY LEVIN / **JOSEF CHIROWSKY** – keyboards / **WHITNEY GLEN** – drums (ex-ALICE COOPER)

Feb 74. (lp/c) *(APL 1/4 0472) <0472>* **ROCK'N'ROLL ANIMAL (live)** [26] [45]

– (intro) – Sweet Jane / Heroin / White light – white heat / Lady day / Rock and roll. *(re-iss. May81 lp/c; INT S/K 5086) (re-iss. 1984 lp/c; NL/NK 83664) (cd-iss. Jun86; PD 83664)*

Apr 74. (7") *<(APBO 0238)>* **SWEET JANE (live). / LADY DAY (live)** [ ] [ ]

— **MICHAEL FORFARA** – keyboards repl. JOSEF

Aug 74. (7") *<10053>* **SALLY CAN'T DANCE. / VICIOUS** [-] [ ]
Sep 74. (lp/c) *(APL 1/4 <0611>)* **SALLY CAN'T DANCE** [ ] [10]
– Ride Sally ride / Animal language / Baby face / N.Y. stars / Kill your sons / Billy / Sally can't dance / Ennui. *(cd-iss. Mar87; PD 80611) (re-iss. cd Feb89; ND 90308)*
Oct 74. (7") *(RCA 2467) <10081>* **SALLY CAN'T DANCE. / ENNUI** [ ] [ ]
Mar 75. (lp) *(RS 1007) <0959>* **LOU REED LIVE (live)** [ ] [62]
– Walk on the wild side / I'm waiting for the man / Vicious / Oh Jim / Satellite of love / Sad song. *(re-iss. Feb81 lp/c; INT S/K 5071) (cd-iss. Mar87 + Feb90; ND 83752)*

— LOU now used synthesizer only.

Jul 75. (d-lp) *<(CPL2 1101)>* **METAL MACHINE MUSIC – (THE AMINE B RING)** [ ] [ ]
– Metal machine music A1 / A2 / A3 / A4. *(re-iss. Mar91 on 'Great Expectations' cd/d-c/d-lp; PIPD C/M/L 023)*

— Band now featured **MICHAEL SUCHORSKY** – percussion / **BOB KULICK** – guitar / **BRUCE YAW** – bass

Jan 76. (lp/c) *(RS/ 1035) <0915>* **CONEY ISLAND BABY** [52] [41]
– Crazy feeling / Charley's girl / She's my best friend / Kicks / A gift / Oooh baby / Nobody's business / Coney Island baby. *(re-iss. Mar81 lp/c; INT S/K 5082) (re-iss. 1984 lp/c; NL/NK 83807) (cd-iss. Dec86 & Sep89; PD 83807)*
Mar 76. (7") *(RCA 2666) <10573>* **CHARLEY'S GIRL. / NOWHERE AT ALL** [ ] [ ]
May 76. (7") *<10648>* **CRAZY FEELING. / NOWHERE AT ALL** [-] [ ]

Arista Arista

Nov 76. (lp/c) *(ARTY/TC-ARTY 142) <4100>* **ROCK AND ROLL HEART** [ ] [64]
– I believe in love / Banging on my drum / Follow the leader / You wear it so well / Ladies pay / Rock and roll heart / Temporary thing.
Nov 76. (7") *<0215>* **I BELIEVE IN LOVE. / SENSELESSLY CRUEL** [-] [ ]
Apr 77. (7") *(105)* **ROCK AND ROLL HEART. / SENSELESSLY CRUEL** [ ] [-]

— **STUART HEINRICH** – guitar, vocals repl. KULICK / **MARTY FOGEL** – saxophone repl. YAW

Apr 78. (lp/c) *(SPART/TC-SPART 1045) <4169>* **STREET HASSLE** [ ] [89]
– Gimme some good times / Dirt / Street hassle / I wanna be black / Real good time together / Shooting star / Leave me alone / Wait.
Apr 78. (12") **STREET HASSLE. / (same track)** [-] [ ]
Jul 78. (12"ep) *(ARIST12 198)* **STREET HASSLE. / Waiting For The Man + Venus In Furs (by "The VELVET UNDERGROUND")** [ ] [-]

— **ELLARD BOLES** – bass, guitar repl. HEINRICH. (Below released 'RCA' UK)

Mar 79. (d-lp)<red,blue-lp> *(XL 03066) <8502>* **LIVE – TAKE NO PRISONERS (live)** [ ] [ ] Nov78
– Sweet Jane / I wanna be black / Satellite of love / Pale blue eyes / Berlin / I'm waiting for the man / Coney Island baby / Street hassle / Walk on the wild side / Leave me alone.

— **REED** now with **FORFARA, BOLES, SUCHORSKY, FOGEL** and **DON CHERRY** – trumpet

Oct 79. (lp/c) *(SPART/TC-SPART 1093) <4229>* **THE BELLS** [ ] [ ] May 79
– Stupid man / Disco mystic / I want to boogie with you / With you / Looking for love / City lights / All through the night / Families / The bells. *(cd-iss. Aug92; 262 918)*
Jun 79. (7") *<0431>* **CITY LIGHTS. / I WANT TO BOOGIE WITH YOU** [-] [ ]
Oct 79. (7") *(ARIST 308)* **CITY LIGHTS. / SENSELESSLY CRUEL** [ ] [-]

— **CHUCK HAMMER** – synthesizer, guitar repl. FOGEL & CHERRY

May 80. (lp/c) *(SPART/TC-SPART 1131) <9522>* **GROWING UP IN PUBLIC** [ ] [ ]
– How do you speak to an angel / My old man / Keep away / Growing up in public / Standing on ceremony / So alone / Love is here to stay / The power of positive drinking / Smiles / Think it over / Teach the gifted children. *(cd-iss. Aug92; 262 917)*
Jun 80. (7") *<0535>* **THE POWER OF POSITIVE DRINKING. / GROWING UP IN PUBLIC** [-] [ ]

— **ROBERT QUINE** – guitar repl. HAMMER

R.C.A. R.C.A.

Mar 82. (lp/c) *(RCA LP/K 6028) <4221>* **THE BLUE MASK** [ ] [ ] Feb82
– My house / Women / Underneath the bottle / The gun / The blue mask / The gun / The heroine / Waves of fear / The day John Kennedy died / Heavenly arms.
Mar 83. (lp/c) *(RCA LP/K 6071) <4568>* **LEGENDARY HEARTS** [ ] [ ]
– Legendary hearts / Don't talk to me about work / Make up mind / Martial law / The last shot / Turn out the light / ow wow / Betrayed / Bottoming out / Home of the brave / Rooftop garden. *(re-iss. Oct86 lp/c; NL/NK 89843) (re-iss. Apr91 cd/c; ND/NK 89843)*
Apr 83. (7") *<13558>* **MARTIAL LAW. / DON'T TALK TO ME ABOUT WORK** [-] [ ]
Jan 84. (d-lp/c) *(PL/PK 89156)* **LIVE IN ITALY (live)** [ ] [-]
– Sweet Jane / I'm waiting for the man / Martial law / Satellite of love / Kill your sons / Betrayed / Sally can't dance / Waves of fear / Average guy / White light – white heat / Some kinda love / Sister Ray / Walk on the wild side / Heroin / Rock and roll.

— Line-up now **FERNANDO SAUNDERS** – bass, rhythm guitar / **FRED MAHER** – drums / **PETER WOOD** – piano, synthesizer, accordion / **L. SHANKER** – electric violin

Mar 84. (7") *<13841>* **I LOVE YOU SUZANNE. / MY FRIEND GEORGE** [-] [ ]
May 84. (12") *<13849>* **MY RED JOY STICK. / ('A' remix)** [-] [ ]
May 84. (lp/c) *(PL/PK 84998) <4998>* **NEW SENSATIONS** [92] [56]
– I love you, Suzanne / Endlessly jealous / My red joystick / Turn to me / New sensations / Doin' the things that we want to / What becomes a legend most / Fly into the Sun / High in the city / My friend George / Down at the arcade. *(cd-iss. Jul86; PD 84998)*
May 84. (7") *(RCA 417)* **I LOVE YOU, SUZANNE. / VICIOUS** [ ] [-]
(12"+=) *(RCAT 417)* – Walk on the wild side.
Apr 86. (12") *<14427>* **THE ORIGINAL WRAPPER. / (2 'A' versions)** [-] [ ]
Apr 86. (lp/c/cd) *(PL/PK/PD 87190) <7190>* **MISTRIAL** [69] [47]
– Mistrial / No money down / Outside / Don't hurt a woman / Video violence / Spit it out / The original wrapper / Mama's got a lover / I remember you / Tell it to your heart. *(re-iss. Oct88 lp/c/cd; NL/NK/ND 90253)*
Jun 86. (7") *(RCA 501) <14368>* **NO MONEY DOWN. / DON'T HURT A WOMAN** [ ] [ ]
(12"+=) *(RCAT 501) <14388>* – ('A'dub version).
Next from the film 'Soul Man'.

A&M A&M

Jan 87. (7"; LOU REED & SAM MOORE) *(AM 364)* **SOUL MAN. / Sweet Sarah (by 'Tom Scott')** [30] [ ]
<US-12"+=> – My love is chemical.

— new band **MIKE RATHKE** – guitar / **ROB WASSERMAN** – bass / **FRED MAHER** – drums / **MAUREEN TUCKER** – drums on 2 (ex-VELVET UNDERGROUND)

Sire Sire

Jan 89. (lp/c)(cd) *(WX 246/+C)(925 829-2) <25829>* **NEW YORK** [14] [40]
– Romeo had Juliette / Halloween parade / Dirty Blvd. / Endless cycle / There is no time / The last great American whale / Beginning of a great adventure / Busload of faith / Sick of you / Hold on / Good evening Mr. Waldheim / Xmas in February / Strawman / Dime store mystery. *(re-iss. Feb95 cd/c;)*
Feb 89. (7") **ROMEO HAD JULIETTE. / BUSLOAD OF FAITH (live)** [-] [ ]
Feb 89. (7") *(W 7547)* **DIRTY BLVD. / THE LAST GREAT AMERICAN WHALE** [ ] [-]
(12"+=) *(W 7547T)* – The room.
Apr 90. (cd)(lp/c); by LOU REED / JOHN CALE) *(7599 <26140-2>(WX 345/+C)* **SONGS FOR DRELLA** [22] [ ]
– Smalltown / Open house / Style it takes / Work / Trouble with classicists / Starlight / Faces and names / Images / Slip away (a warning) / It wasn't me / I believe / Nobody but you / A dream / Forever changed / Hello it's me. *(re-iss. Feb91 & Jan97; same)*
(above re-united the two VELVET UNDERGROUND members, tributing the recently deceased ANDY WARHOL)

— **MICHAEL BLAIR** – percussion, drums, vocals repl. MAHER

Jan 92. (cd/lp/c) *(7599 <26662-2>)(WX 435/+C)* **MAGIC AND LOSS** [6] [80]
– Dorita – the spirit / What's good – the thesis / Power and glory – the situation / Magician – internally / Sword of Damocles – eternally / Goodby mass – in a chapel bodily termination / Cremation – ashes to ashes / Dreamin' – escape / No chance – regret / Warrior king – revenge / Harry's circumcision – reverie gone astray / Gassed and stoked – loss / Power and glory part II – magic transformation / Magic and loss – the summation. *(cd re-iss. Jan97; same)*
Mar 92. (7"/c-s) **WHAT'S GOOD. / THE ROOM** [ ] [ ]
(12"+=/cd-s+=) – Mary's circumcision / A dream.

— now with just **FERNANDO SAUNDERS** – basses / **TONY 'Thunder' SMITH** – drums / + guest **LAURIE ANDERSON** – backing vocals

WEA Reprise

Feb 96. (cd/c) *<(9362 46159-2/-4)>* **SET THE TWILIGHT REELING** [26] [ ]
– Egg cream / NYC man / Finish line / Trade in / Hang on to your emotions / Sex with your parents (motherfucker) part II (live) / Hooky wooky / The proposition / Adventurer / Riptide / Set the twilight reeling.
May 96. (c-s) *(W 0351C)* **HOOKY WOOKY / ON THE RUN** [ ] [ ]
(cd-s) *(W 0351CD)* – ('A'side) / This magic moment / You'll never know you loved.

– compilations, others, etc. –

Below releases issued on 'RCA' unless mentioned otherwise

Apr 77. (lp/c) *(PL/PK 12001) <2001>* **WALK ON THE WILD SIDE – THE BEST OF LOU REED** [ ] [ ]
(cd-iss. Mar87; PD 83753)
Jan 79. (lp/c) *(NL/NK 42731)* **VICIOUS** [ ] [ ]
Dec 80. (d-lp) *Arista; (DARTY 8)* **ROCK AND ROLL DIARY 1967-1980** [ ] [ ]
(above featured 8 tracks by Velvet Underground)
Aug 81. (7") *RCA Gold; (GOLD 523)* **WALK ON THE WILD SIDE. / VICIOUS** [ ] [-]
(re-iss. Oct86 & Mar89 on 'Old Gold'; OG 9635)
Sep 82. (lp) *(SF 8281)* **I CAN'T STAND IT** [ ] [ ]
Oct 85. (7") *A&M; (AM 283)* **SEPTEMBER SONG. / Oh Heavenly Action (by 'Mark Bingham with Johnny Adams & Aaron Neville')** [ ] [-]
May 86. (c) *(NK 89895)* **MAGIC MOMENTS** [ ] [-]
Sep 86. (lp/c) *Fame; (FA/TC-FA 3164)* **NEW YORK SUPERSTAR** [ ] [-]
Feb 89. (3"cd-ep) *(PD 49453)* **WALK ON THE WILD SIDE / PERFECT DAY / SATELLITE OF LOVE / VICIOUS** [ ] [ ]
Sep 89. (lp/c/cd) *(PL/PK/PD 90389)* **RETRO** [29] [ ]
Walk on the wild side / Satellite of love / I love you Suzanne / Wild child / How do you think it feels / Lady day / Coney Island baby / Sweet Jane (live) / Vicious / Sally can't dance / Berlin / Caroline says II / Kill your sons / White light – white heat (live). *(cd+=)* – I'm waiting for the man (VELVET UNDERGROUND) / Heroin (VELVET UNDERGROUND).
Mar 92. (3xcd/3xc) *(PD/PK 90621)* **BETWEEN THOUGHT AND EXPRESSION** [ ] [ ]

CAPTAIN BEEFHEART AND HIS MAGIC BAND

Formed: Los Angeles, California, USA . . . 1964 by DON VAN VLIET, a child-prodigy sculptor who, between the ages of five and thirteen, had his clay animals featured on a weekly TV show hosted by Portuguese sculptor Augustino Rodriguez. An opportunity to develop his art skills were halted when his parents declined a scholarship on his behalf to study art in Europe, preferring instead to move to Lancaster in the Mojave desert. Here he met FRANK ZAPPA at the local high school, setting up a few local bands while ZAPPA started to write a script for a B-movie 'CAPTAIN BEEFHEART MEETS THE GRUNT PEOPLE'. When FRANK went to Los Angeles to form The MOTHERS OF INVENTION, he adopted the name CAPTAIN BEEFHEART and set about recruiting The MAGIC BAND. They signed to 'A&M' in 1964, releasing their version of BO DIDDLEY's 'DIDDY WAH DIDDY', which sold enough copies to encourage the label to buy studio time for an album. When completed, president Jerry Moss rejected the tapes, citing it too strange and anti-commercial. Undaunted, VAN VLIET and a new set of musicians, including RY COODER, re-recorded most of these masters, the album 'SAFE AS MILK' finally surfacing in 1967 on the 'Buddah' label. This was a masterpiece of its time, full of BEEFHEART on a HOWLIN' WOLF-style trip; the great tracks being 'ELECTRICITY', 'ABBA ZABA', 'AUTUMN CHILD' & 'ZIG ZAG WANDERER'. However, RY COODER departed for more safer pastures when VAN VLIET/BEEFHEART left the stage halfway through their set at the 1967 Monterey Pop Festival, leaving the band to play to a bewildered but carefree hippy audience. BEEFHEART often showed signs of outlandish behaviour which split the band up as much as his personality. Late in 1968, they recorded another album, 'MIRROR MAN', although this was shelved until his popularity had grown in the early 70's. However, one album did appear that year, 'STRICTLY PERSONAL', which BEEFHEART slammed for its radical remix by producer BOB KRASNOW. This riled him so much that he signed a new contract with old friend ZAPPA who gave him complete artistic control on his new 'Straight' label. Having wrote about 30 songs in a day, BEEFHEART took his new bunch of weirdo musicians (ANTENNAE JIMMY SEMENS, DRUMBO, ART TRIPP III, ZOOT HORN ROLLO and THE MASCARA SNAKE) to rehearse in a house which was close-by an old friend JIMMY CARL BLACK (drummer for ZAPPA). They stayed there for a full eight months, only one of them at a time venturing out if the band was in need of food & drink, etc. This was VAN VLIET's tyrannical way of keeping the band tight, so as to establish virtuoso musicianship while he got on with the weird vocals. The resulting album (a double!) 'TROUT MASK REPLICA' was handed to ZAPPA, much to his surprise, after four and a half hours in the studio. When released at the turn of the decade, it was initially given the thumbs down by many critics and fans. Those hardy enough to give it a few tolerant spins, however, were convinced of its genius. The record surprisingly nearly made the UK Top 20, having been played to death on John Peel's radio one night-time show. Its virtual insanity was literally not of this world, utilising the complex structures of jazz legend ORNETTE COLEMAN; the best tracks to break through – to the sane among us, were 'THE BLIMP', 'PENA', 'DALI'S CAR', 'ELLA GURU' & 'OLD FART AT PLAY'. It has since become regarded as a classic, although it should never be played to someone not of your generation. He returned a thank-you to ZAPPA, when he sang a track, 'WILLIE THE WIMP', on his 'Hot Rats' album, although their friendship was fraying with every meeting, two egos too big for one room. In 1970, he settled down to a more conventional avant-garde Delta-blues album 'LICK MY DECALS OFF, BABY' (compared that is, to their last). It was another excellent set; combing through the depths of his unearthly roots to find tracks such as 'DOCTOR DARK', 'I LOVE YOU, YOU BIG DUMMY' and the title track. 1972 saw another great album 'THE SPOTLIGHT KID', featuring the delights of 'CLICK CLACK', 'I'M GONNA BOOGLARIZE YOU BABY' & 'WHEN IT GROWS IT STACKS'. Their next, 'CLEAR SPOT' covered new territory on softer tracks like 'TOO MUCH TIME' & 'MY HEAD IS MY ONLY HOUSE UNLESS IT RAINS', tempting the MAGIC BAND to bail out and form their own outfit, MALLARD. The album did, however, include another powerful BEEFHEART special in the shape of 'BIG EYED BEANS FROM VENUS'. In 1974, with a new line-up, he signed to UK's 'Virgin' label but his work at this point, especially on the albums 'UNCONDITIONALLY GUARENTEED' & 'BLUEJEANS AND MOONBEAMS', was poor. He tried to escape yet another restrictive deal; it was said he would sign anything, and teamed up with his old pal FRANK ZAPPA and The MOTHERS. Their collaboration, 'BONGO FURY', set the ball rolling for a litigation battle between him and Virgin' UK, resulting in another deal!, this time with 'Warner Brothers' for the 1978 album 'SHINY BEAST (BAT CHAIN PULLER)', a marked return to form on some tracks. Virgin won the rights to this album, which gained a UK release in early 1980. Two other records surfaced in the next two years; 'DOC AT RADAR STATION' and the considerably better 'ICE CREAM FOR CROW', the latter containing the excellent title track, his final epitaph. He retired from the music business and set up home with his wife JAN at a trailer park in the Mojave desert. Still an avid sculptor and painter, with the help of fan Julian Schnabel, he began exhibiting his primitive canvases which made him more money than his records ever did. In the mid-80's, a host of young British indie acts including STUMP, McKENZIES, The SHRUBS, etc, took on the mantle of the BEEFHEART sound. Always asked if he would return, BEEFHEART has repeatedly refused to get back on the bandwagon (having fallen into ill-health, both physically and mentally, a return to the recording studio is unlikely to say the least). A remarkable figure of his time, DON VAN VLIET examplified the glory of not worrying about the exploitation of the music industry, only happy with his own, and of course the MAGIC BAND's work. Let's just hope he's around for several more years to enjoy whatever he creates. • **Trivia:** He also covered Jack Nitzsche's 'HARD WORKIN' MAN' on the 1978 film 'Blue Collar', which starred Harvey Keitel.

Album rating: SAFE AS MILK (*9) / TROUT MASK REPLICA (*10 or *2; depending on your taste) / MIRROR MAN (*7) / LICK MY DECALS OFF, BABY (*8) / THE SPOTLIGHT KID (*8) / CLEAR SPOT (*7) / SHINY BEAST (BAT CHAIN PULLER (*6) / DOC AT RADAR STATION (*5) / ICE CREAM FOR CROW (*6)

CAPTAIN BEEFHEART (b. DON VAN VLIET, 15 Jan'41, Glendale, California) – vocals, harmonica, occasional guitar, wind instruments / **ALEX ST. CLAIRE** – guitar / **DOUG MOON** – guitar / **JERRY HANDLEY** – bass / **PAUL BLAKELY** – drums

A&M — A&M

1966. (7") *<794>* **DIDDY WAH DIDDY. / WHO DO YOU THINK YOU'RE FOOLING** [-] [ ]
1966. (7") *<818>* **MOONCHILD. / FRYING PAN** [-] [ ]
1968. (7") *(AMS 726)* **MOONCHILD. / WHO DO YOU THINK YOU'RE FOOLING** [ ] [-]

— **The CAPTAIN** recruited an entire new band . . . **RY COODER** – slide guitar repl. MOON + ST.CLAIRE (they later joined DENNY KING) / **HERB BERMANN** – bass, co-composer repl. HANDLEY / **JOHN FRENCH** (DRUMBO) – drums repl. BLAKELY

Pye International — Kama Sutra

Jan 68. (7") *(7N 25443)* **YELLOW BRICK ROAD. / ABBA ZABA** [ ] [ ]
Feb 68. (lp) *(NPL 28110) <BDS 5001>* **SAFE AS MILK** [ ] [ ] 1967
Surc 'nuff 'n yes I do / Zig zag wanderer / Call on me / Dropout boogie / I'm glad / Electricity / Yellow brick road / Abba zaba / Plastic factory / Where there's woman / Plastic factory / Grown so ugly / Autumn child. *(re-iss. 1968 on 'Marble Arch' 2 tracks less; MAL 1117) (re-iss. 1970 on 'Buddah' stereo; 623 171) (re-iss. Jan82 on 'P.R.T.'; NCP 1004) (re-iss. Jul85 on 'Buddah' lp/c; 252260-1/-4) (cd-iss. May91 on 'Castle'; CLACD 234)*

— **JEFF COTTON** (ANTENNAE JIMMY SEMENS) -guitar repl. COODER who went solo

not iss. — Buddah

1968. (lp) *<BDS 5077>* **MIRROR MAN** (rec.1965) [-] [ ]
– Tarot plane / Kandy korn / 25th century Quaker / Mirror man. *(UK-iss.May71 on 'Buddah'; 2365 002); reached No.49) (re-iss. May82 on 'P.R.T.'; NCP 1006) (re-iss. Apr86 on 'Edsel'; ED 184) (cd-iss. May91 on 'Castle'; CLACD 235)*

Liberty — Blue Thumb

Dec 68. (lp; mono/stereo) *(LBL/LBS 83172) <BTS 1>* **STRICTLY PERSONAL** [ ] [ ]
– Ah feel like acid / Safe as milk / Trust us / Son of Mirror Man – Mere man / On tomorrow / Beatles bones 'n' smokin' stones / Gimme that harp boy /

Kandy korn. *(re-iss. Nov79 lp/c; LBR/TCR 1006) (cd-iss. Aug94 on 'E.M.I.'; CZ 529)*

— **The CAPTAIN** retained **DRUMBO** and **ANTANNAE** plus new members **ZOOT HORN ROLLO** (b.BILL HARKLEROAD) – brass, narrator, guitar, flute / **ROCKETTE NORTON** (b.MARK BOSTON) – bass, narrator repl. HERB / **THE MASCARA SNAKE** (b.VICTOR HAYDEN) – clarinet / guest **DOUG MOON** returned

Straight Straight

Nov 69. (d-lp) *(STS 1053) <RS 2027>* **TROUT MASK REPLICA** 21
– Frownland / The dust blows forward 'n dust blows back / Dachau blues / Ella guru / Hair pie: bake 1 / Moonlight on Vermont / Hair pie: bake 2 / Pena / Well / When big Joan sets up / Fallin' ditch / Sugar 'n spikes / Ant man bee / Pachuco cadaver / Bills corpse / Sweet sweet bulbs / Neon meate dream of an octafish / China pig / My human gets me blues / Dali's car / Orange claw hammer / Wild life / She's too much for my mirror / Hobo chang ba / The blimp (mousetrap replica) / Steal softly thru snow / Old fart at play / Veteran's day poppy. *(re-iss. May75 on 'Reprise'; K 64026) (re-iss. cd Sep94 on 'WEA'; K 927 196-2)*

— **ED MARIMBA** (ART TRIPP) – marimba (ex-MOTHERS OF INVENTION) repl. THE MASCARA SNAKE

Jan 71. (lp) *(STS 1063) <RS 6240>* **LICK MY DECALS OFF, BABY** 20
– Lick my decals off, baby / Doctor Dark / I love you, you big dummy / Peon / Bellerin' plain / Woe-is-uh-me-bop / Japan in a dishpan / I wanna find a woman that'll hold my big toe till I have a go / Petrified forest / One rose that I mean / The Buggy boogie woogie / The Smithsonian Institute blues (or the big dig) / Space-age couple / The clouds are full of wine (not whiskey or rye) / Flash Gordon's ape. *(re-iss. Jul73 on 'Reprise')*

— **THE WINGED EEL FINGERLING** (r.n. ELLIOT INGBER) – guitar, etc. (ex-MOTHERS etc.) repl. SEMENS who had already formed MU

Reprise Reprise

Jan 72. (7") *<1068>* **CLICK CLACK. / I'M GONNA BOOGLARIZE YOU BABY** -

Feb 72. (lp; by CAPTAIN BEEFHEART) *(K 44162) <RS 2050>* **THE SPOTLIGHT KID** 44
– I'm gonna booglarize you baby / White jam / Blabber 'n smoke / When it blows its stacks / Alice in Blunderland / The spotlight kid / Click clack / Grow fins / There ain't no Santa Claus on the evenin' stage / Glider.

— **ROY 'OREJON' ESTRADA** – bass (ex-LITTLE FEAT, ex-MOTHERS OF INVENTION) repl. INGBER. ROCKETTE moved to guitar, and augmented by backing vocals The **BLACKBERRIES / RUSS TITELMAN** – guitar (guested, as he did on "Safe as Milk")

Nov 72. (lp) *(K 54007) <MS 2115>* **CLEAR SPOT**
– Low yo yo stuff / Nowadays a woman's gotta hit a man / Too much time / Circumstances / My head is my only house unless it rains / Sun zoom sparks / Clear spot / Crazy little thing / Long neck bottles / Her eyes are a blue million miles / Big eyed beans from Venus / Golden birdies.

Mar 73. (7") *(K 14233) <1133>* **TOO MUCH TIME. / MY HEAD IS MY ONLY HOUSE UNLESS IT RAINS**

— **ALEX ST.CLAIRE** – guitar returned to repl. ROY. Added **MARK MERCELLO** – keyboards

Virgin Mercury

Apr 74. (lp) *(V 2015) <SRMI 709>* **UNCONDITIONALLY GUARENTEED**
– Upon the my-oh-my / Sugar bowl / New electric ride / Magic be / Happy love song / Full Moon, hot Sun / I got love on my mind / This is the day / Lazy music / Peaches. *(re-iss. Aug82 + Aug85 on 'Fame' lp/c; FA/TCFA 3034) (re-iss. Aug88; OVED 66) (cd-iss. Jun88; CDV 2015)*

Apr 74. (7") *(VS 110)* **UPON THE MY-OH-MY. / MAGIC BE** -

Apr 74. (7") *<73494>* **UPON THE MY-OH-MY. / I GOT LOVE ON MY MIND** -

— **ELLIOT INGBER** – guitar returned to repl. ST.CLAIRE plus session men **MARK GIBBONS, MICHAEL SMOTHERMAN, JIMMY CARAVAN** – all keyboards repl. MARCELLO.

— **DEAN SMITH** – guitar / **BOB WEST** – bass / **GENE PELLO** – drums / **TV GRIMES** – percussion

Nov 74. (lp) *(V 2123)* **BLUEJEANS AND MOONBEAMS**
– Party of special things do / Same old blues / Observatory crest / Pompadour swamp / Captain's holiday / Rock'n'roll's evil doll / Further than we've gone / Twist ah luck / Bluejeans and moonbeams. *(re-iss. Mar84; OVED 19) (cd-iss. Jun88; CDV 2023)*

— Late '75 **BEEFHEART** collaborated with **FRANK ZAPPA** on **"BONGO FURY"** album. This was a near live album with 2 studio tracks.

— His new touring band featured past members **ELLIOT, INGBER** and **JOHN FRENCH** plus **DENNY WHALLEY** – slide guitar / **BRUCE FOWLER** – trombone (both on bongos)

— His '76 band were **DRUMBO, WHALLEY, JEFF MORRIS TEPPER** – guitar, and **JOHN THOMAS** – piano. They recorded first sessions for the next album

— **ERIC DREW FELDMAN** – keyboards, bass repl. THOMAS / **ROBERT WILLIAMS** – drums repl. DRUMBO / **RICHARD REDISS** – slide guitar repl. WHALLEY / **ART TRIPP** – marimba returned from MALLARD. **BRUCE FOWLER** also returned.

Virgin Warners

Feb 80. (lp) *(V 2149) <BSK 3256>* **BAT CHAIN PULLER** (US-title 'SHINY BEAST') 1978
– The floppy boot stomp / Tropical hot dog night / Ice rose / Harry Irene / You know you're a man / Bat chain puller / When I see mommy I feel like a mummy / Owed t'Alex / Candle mambo / Love lies / Suction prints / Apes-ma. *(re-iss. Aug88; OVED 67) (cd-iss. Jun87; CDV 2149)*

— **GARY LUCAS** – guitar repl. REDISS

Virgin Virgin

Aug 80. (lp) *(V 2172)* **DOC AT RADAR STATION**
– Hot head / Ashtray heart / A carrot is as close as a rabbit gets to a diamond / Run paint run run / Sue Egypt / Brickbats / Dirty blue Gene / Best batch yet / Telephone / Flavour bud living / Sheriff of Hong Kong / Making love to a vampire with a monkey on my knee. *(re-iss. Aug88; OVED 68) (cd-iss. Jun88; CDV 2172)*

— The CAPTAIN brought in **HATSIZE SNYDER, CLIFF MARTINEZ, WILLIAMS, LAMBOURNE FOWLER and DRUMBO**

Aug 82. (12") *(VS 534-12) <03190>* **LIGHT REFLECTED OFF THE OCEANS OF THE MOON. / ICE CREAM FOR CROW**

Virgin Epic

Sep 82. (lp) *(V 2237)* **ICE CREAM FOR CROW** 90
– Ice cream for crow / The host, the ghost, the most holy-o / Semi-multi-(coloured) caucasian / Hey Garland, I dig your tweed coat / Evening bell / Cardboard cut-out sundown / The past is sure tense / Ink mathematics / The witch doctor life / "81" poop hatch / The thousand and tenth day of the human totem pole / Skeleton makes good. *(re-iss. Aug88; OVED 121) (cd-iss. Apr88; CDV 2237)*

— He retired from music business to concentrate on painting/sculpting in his recently bought Mojave desert home.

– compilations etc. –

Jul 70. (lp) *Buddah; (2349 002)* **DROPOUT BOOGIE** -
(a re-iss. of "SAFE AS MILK" 2 tracks less)

1975. (lp) *WRMB;* **WHAT'S ALL THIS BOOGA-BOOGA MUSIC (live)** -

Aug 76. (d-lp) *Reprise; (K 84006)* **TWO ORIGINALS OF . . .**
– LICK MY DECALS OFF, BABY / THE SPOTLIGHT KID.

Nov 77. (d-lp/d-c) *Pye; (FILD/ZCFILD 008)* **THE CAPTAIN BEEFHEART FILE** (first 2-lp's) -

1978. (d-lp) *Impossible;* **EASY TEETH** -

Jan 78. (7") *Buddah; (BDS 466)* **SURE 'NUFF 'N' YES I DO. / ELECTRICITY** -

May 78. (7") *M.C.A.; (MCA 366)* **HARD WORKIN' MAN (by Jack Nitzsche featuring Captain Beefheart). / Coke Machine (by Jack Nitzche)** -
Above also features RY COODER – on guitar

1978. (7"pic-ep) *Virgin; (SIXPACK 1)* **SIX-PACK / SIX TRACK** -
– Sugar bowl / Same old blues / Upon the My-Oh-My / Magic be / Rock'n'roll's evil doll / New electric ride.

Jul 83. (10"lp/c) *P.R.T.; (DOW/ZCDOW 15)* **MUSIC IN SEA MINOR** -

Jul 84. (lp/pic-lp) *Design; (PIL/+P 4)* **TOP SECRET** -

Oct 84. (m-lp) *A&M; (AMY 226)* **THE LEGENDARY SESSIONS** -
– Diddy wah diddy / Who do you think you're folling / Moonchild / Frying pan / Here I am, I always am. *(re-iss. Oct86 on 'Edsel'; BLIMP 902) (cd-iss. Mar92; BLIMPCD 902)*

Jun 88. (d-lp)(c)(d-cd) *That's Original; (TFO LP/MC/CD 11)* **SAFE AS MILK / MIRROR MAN** -
(re-iss. d-cd.May91 on 'Castle')

Feb 91. (d-cd) *Reprise; (7599 26249-2)* **THE SPOTLIGHT KID / CLEAR SPOT** -

Jul 91. (cd) *The Collection; (ORO 146)* **ZIG ZAG WANDERER** -

Jun 92. (cd) *Sequel; (NEXCD 215)* **I MAY BE HUNGRY BUT I SURE AIN'T WEIRD – THE ALTERNATIVE CAPTAIN BEEFHEART** -

Jun 93. (cd) *Virgin; (CDVM 9028)* **A CARROT IS AS CLOSE AS A RABBIT GETS TO A DIAMOND** -

Nov 93. (cd) *Movieplay Gold; (MPG 74025)* **LONDON 1974 (live)** -

Jan 98. (cd) *Camden;; (74321 55846-2)* **ELECTRICITY** -

Feb 98. (cd) *Sonic Book; (SB1)* **PEARLS BEFORE SWINE** (poems, etc) -

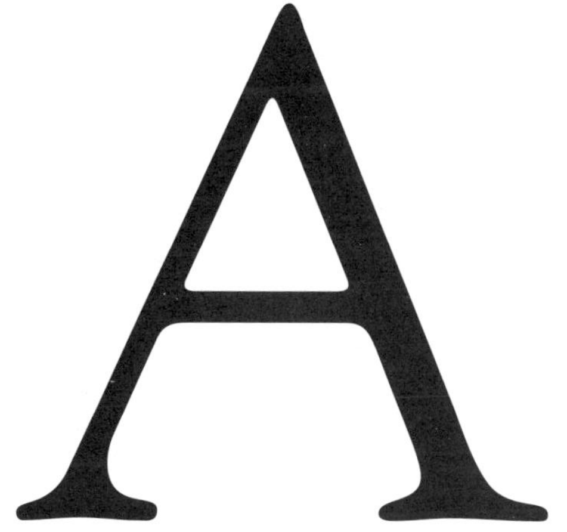

A

Formed: Leeds/Lowestoft, England . . . 1994 by the PERRY brothers, JASON, GILES and ADAM, who duly recruited MARK CHAPMAN and STEVIE SWINDON. Initially VAN HALEN obsessives, they progressed into an alternative heavy/punk fun-rock outfit influenced by JANE'S ADDICTION, GREEN DAY and The MANICS. They formed their own 'Tycoon' label which was adopted by London records, who helped output their well-received debut single 'FIVE IN THE MORNING' in the summer of '96. During the next year, they released three more (including 'No.1', which used lyrics from Billy Joel's 'My Life') and an album 'HOW ACE ARE BUILDINGS', which was given rave reviews in Kerrang! • **Covered:** OWNER OF A LONELY HEART (Yes).

Album rating: HOW ACE ARE BUILDINGS (*6)

JASON PERRY – vocals / **MARK CHAPMAN** – guitar / **GILES PERRY** – keyboards, vocals / **STEVIE SWINDON** – bass, vocals / **ADAM PERRY** – drums

		Tycoon	not iss.
Jul 96.	(7") *(TY 1)* **FIVE IN THE MORNING. /** (cd-s+=) *(TYCD 1)* –		-
Nov 96.	(7") *(TY 2)* **HOUSE UNDER THE GROUND. /** (cd-s+=) *(TYCD 2)* –		-
May 97.	(7") *(TY 3)* **BAD IDEA. / LOOK WHAT YOU MADE ME DO** (cd-s+=) *(TYCD 3)* – 40.		-
Aug 97.	(7") *(TY 4)* **NO. 1. / ALRIGHT** (cd-s+=) *(TYCD 4)* – Ouch! / ('A'version).		-
Sep 97.	(cd/c) *(828 916-2/-4)* **HOW ACE ARE BUILDINGS** – Turn it up / Foghorn / Cheeky monkey / No.1 / Bad idea / Sing-a-long / Winter of '96 / Out of tune / Fistral / House under the ground / Five in the morning / Ender. *(re-iss. Jun98; same)*		

— (summer '97) **DAN CARTER** – bass; repl. SWINDON

Oct 97.	(cd-s) *(COUP 06)* **HOUSE UNDER THE GROUND / (track by Glitterbox)** (above issued on 'Revolution')		-
Jan 98.	(7") *(TY 5)* **FOGHORN. / LAST GIRL** (cd-s+=) *(TYCD 5)* – A demolished house.	63	
Mar 98.	(7") *(TY 6)* **NO.1. / GOOD TIME** (cd-s+=) *(TYCD 6)* – Alright / Saskwatch. (cd-s) *(TYCDP 6)* – ('A'side) / Ouch! / Foghorn.	47	
Jun 98.	(7") *(TY 7)* **SING-A-LONG. / I'M OVER IT** (cd-s+=) *(TYCD 7)* – Callhimin / Photofinger. (cd-s) *(TYCDP 7)* – ('A'side) / Singing out of tune (literally in a castle) / No.1.	57	
Oct 98.	(7") *(TY 8)* **SUMMER ON THE UNDERGROUND. / I CAN'T WAIT UNTIL MORNING** (cd-s+=) *(TYCD 8)* – Owner of a lonely heart.	72	-

ABRASIVE WHEELS

Formed: Leeds, England . . . 1980 by SHONNA (a male!), DAVE, HARRY and RYAN. Late the following year, the lads booted out their anti-military anthem, 'THE ARMY SONG', a pretty much standard blast of 3-chord "oi" with a SHAM 69/COCKNEY REJECTS sing-a-long factor. Initially released on their own eponymous imprint, it was subsequently given a re-issue by 'Riot City' after that label had issued a follow-up EP, 'VICIOUS CIRCLE'. Later in '82, the anarchy-by-numbers continued with the 'BURN THE SCHOOLS' single and their debut album, 'WHEN THE PUNKS GO MARCHING IN'. Smoothing out their rough edges as "oi" rapidly went down the pan, the ABRASIVE WHEELS signed to 'Clay' and speeded up their inevitable decline with an ill-advised cover of Elvis Presley's 'JAILHOUSE ROCK'.

Album rating: WHEN THE PUNKS GO MARCHING IN! (*4) / BLACK LEATHER GIRL (*3)

SHONNA – vocals / **DAVE** – guitar / **HARRY** – bass, vocals / **RYAN** – drums

		Abrasive Wheels	not iss.
Nov 81.	(7"m) *(ABW 1)* **THE ARMY SONG. / JUVENILE / SO SLOW** *(re-iss. Mar82 on 'Riot City' 7"red; RIOT 9)*		-
		Riot City	**not iss.**
Jan 82.	(7"ep) *(RIOT 4)* **VICIOUS CIRCLE EP**		-
Oct 82.	(7"m) *(RIOT 16)* **BURN THE SCHOOLS. / URBAN REBELS / BURN 'EM DOWN**		-
Nov 82.	(lp) *(CITY 001)* **WHEN THE PUNKS GO MARCHING IN** – Vicious circle / 1982 / Danger, danger / BBC / Mayday / Voice of youth / Just another punk band / Gottarun / Burn 'em down / Shout it out / Slaughterhouse / First rule (no rule) / Attack / When the punks go marching in.		-
		Clay	**not iss.**
Jun 83.	(7") *(CLAY 24)* **JAILHOUSE ROCK. / SENIC OCEAN**		-
Nov 83.	(7") *(CLAY 28)* **LAW OF THE JUNGLE. / BANNER OF HOPE**		-

— **NEV** – drums; repl. RYAN

Mar 84.	(lp) *(CLAYLP 9)* **BLACK LEATHER GIRL**		-
Jun 84.	(7") *(CLAY 33)* **THE PRISONER. / CHRISTIANNE** (12"+=) *(12CLAY 33)* – Black leather girl.		-

— disbanded soon after above release

ABSOLUTE GRAY

Formed: Rochester, New York, USA . . . Autumn 1983 by BETH BROWN, MITCH RASOR, PAT THOMAS and MATT KITCHEN. After an initial gig early the following year, they surfaced on vinyl with mini-lp, 'GREEN HOUSE'. Melancholy psychedelic pop-rock, the album was heavily influenced by ECHO & THE BUNNYMEN (although ABSOLUTE GRAY featured haunting female vocals courtesy of BETH BROWN) and included a cracking rendition of the VELVET UNDERGROUND's 'Beginning To See The Light'. The band subsequently signed to 'Midnight' for what might have been their last album, 'WHAT REMAINS', although they re-formed in 1987 with a new line-up, releasing a few more low-key sets.

Album rating: GREEN HOUSE (*6) / WHAT REMAINS (*7)

BETH BROWN – vocals (ex-HIT & RUN) / **MATT KITCHEN** – guitar, viola / **MITCH RASOR** – bass / **PAT THOMAS** – drums

		not iss.	Earring
1984.	(m-lp) **GREEN HOUSE** – Beginning to see the light / More walnuts / etc *<re-iss. 1986 on 'Midnight'; >*	-	
		not iss.	**Midnight**
1986.	(lp) *<MIRLP 125>* **WHAT REMAINS** – My own / Untitled / Bad influence / Umbrella / Perfect life / No man's land / A joke / What remains / Little ditty / Grey farewell.	-	

— now without PAT THOMAS, who went onto release eponymous solo album for the 'Heyday' imprint.

— they were soon down to BROWN & RASOR, when KITCHEN left

1986.	(7"ep) **THE PAINTED POST**	-	
		not iss.	**Greek Di-Di**
1988.	(lp) **A JOURNEY THRU THE PAST** (live compilation)	-	
1989.	(lp) **SAND DOWN THE MOON**	-	

— nothing heard of BETH in the 90's

ACACIA

Formed: England . . . 1993 by ALEXANDER and a former sound engineer for BJORK and SEAL, GUY SIGSWORTH. Augmented by MAURIZIO ANZALONE and TALVIN SINGH (of Italian-Spanish and Kenyan-Indian parentage respectively), they recorded a home-cassette which was only available on mail-order. This highlighted their unique "liquid" ambient tabla sound, much perfected by ALEXANDER's Balinese style of guitar plucking.

Album rating: CRADLE (*6)

ALEXANDER – vocals, guitar / **GUY SIGSWORTH** – sound engineer / with **MAURIZIO ANZALONE** – guitar / **TALVIN SINGH** – percussion

		Alchemy Arts	not iss.
May 94.	(10"ep/cd-ep) *(ALH V/D 001)* **MADDENING SHROUD**		-
Oct 94.	(12") *(ALHV 002)* **THE MORE YOU IGNORE ME. /**		-
		Radarscope	**not iss.**
Jun 96.	(c-s) *(SCANMC 15)* **HATE /** (12"+=/cd-s+=) *(SCAN T/CD 15)* –		-
Sep 96.	(c-s) *(SCANMC 20)* **SWAY /** (12"+=/cd-s+=) *(SCAN T/CD 20)* –		-
		WEA	**WEA**
Oct 97.	(cd) *<(3984 24080-2)>* **CRADLE** – Wired / I'm in love with love / The more you ignore me / Sway / Maddening shroud / Unfulfilled desire / Yellow is the colour of my cowardice / Sympathy / Hate / Boils down to money / Woe woe song / You nothing / Wire.		

A.C. ACOUSTICS

Formed: Glasgow, Scotland . . . 1992 by Kenmore raised songwriter, PAUL CAMPION. Supporting the likes of MAZZY STAR and PJ HARVEY at Glasgow's Barrowlands, the band's initial line-up was completed by ROGER WARD, CAZ RILEY and DAVE GORMLEY. After an infamous gig at Glasgow's Garage supporting hard-core act NO MEANS NO, the boys were snapped up by respected indie label, 'Elemental'. Their early indie-rock sound was crystallised on a handful of inspired, sporadic releases reminiscent of PAVEMENT or MERCURY REV, fuelling expectations for an album of skewed sonic brilliance. The band went to ground for a couple of years, resurfacing late in '96 with a new guitarist MARK RAINE and a single 'STUNT GIRL'. During their hiatus they recorded an album in Wales, which was deemed unacceptable for release. Their debut album proper, 'VICTORY PARTS' finally saw light of day in the summer of '97. In their absence, MOGWAI, URUSEI YATSURA, etc, had already found minor success after taking the lead from AC's early work.

Album rating: VICTORY PARTS (*6)

PAUL CAMPION – vocals / **ROGER WARD** – guitar / **CAZ RILEY** – bass / **DAVE GORMLEY** – drums

El'e'mental Trance

Nov 93. (7") **MV. / SWEATLODGE** [ ] [-]
Apr 94. (m-lp/m-cd) *(ELM 21 MLP/MCD) <31>* **ABLE TREASURY** [ ] [ ] Jan95
– Mother head sander / King Dick / Three / Leather buyer / Fat Abbey / Sister grab operator / Oregon pine washback / M.V. / Sweatlodge.
Nov 94. (12"ep/cd-ep) *(ELM 25 T/CD)* **HAND PASSES PLENTY / + 3** [ ] [-]

—— **MARK RAINE** – guitar; repl. WARD

Nov 96. (7") *(ELM 30S)* **STUNT GIRL. / SHOKA** [ ] [-]
(cd-s+=) *(ELM 30CDS)* – Skeptic wrist eye / Sidenova.
Mar 97. (7") *(ELM 29S)* **I MESSIAH, AM JAILER. / HIGH DIVERS** [ ] [-]
(7") *(ELM 29SX)* – ('A'side) / Violent peep.
(cd-s) *(ELM 29CDS)* – (all 3 tracks).
Jun 97. (cd/lp) *(ELM 31 CD/LP)* **VICTORY PARTS** [ ] [-]
– Hand pressed empty / Stunt girl / Ex quartermaster / Admirals all / Hammerhead / Kill Zane / Fast / Continuity freak / High divers / Absent luck liner / I messiah, am jailer / Can't see anything (red not yellow).

YoYo not iss.

Nov 98. (7"ep/cd-ep) *(YO/+CD 3)* **LIKE RIBBONS / SHE'S WITH STARS** [ ] [-]

ACCELERATORS

Formed: North Carolina, USA . . . early 80's by mainman GERALD DUNCAN (not to be confused with the same named bands from Los Angeles, New Jersey or Liverpool). Recorded with the added expertise of DON DIXON and MITCH EASTER, The ACCELERATORS kickstarted their sporadic career with 'LEAVE MY HEART', an album that contained a power-pop cover of The Box Tops' 'THE LETTER'. Retaining only drummer DOUG WHELCHEL, GERALD enlisted guitarist BRAD RICE, although it would around three to four years before the release of the eponymous follow-up set. Now signed for 'Profile', the band would take a further extended sabbatical before delivering a third and final offering, 'DREAM TRAIN' (1991).

Album rating: LEAVE MY HEART (*5) / THE ACCELERATORS (*5) / DREAM TRAIN (*4)

GERALD DUNCAN – vocals, guitar / **DOUG WHELCHEL** – drums

not iss. Dolphin

1983. (lp) **LEAVE MY HEART** [-] [ ]

—— added **BRAD RICE** – guitar / **MIKE JOHNS** – bass

not iss. Profile

1987. (lp/c/cd) *<PRO/PCT+/1246>* **THE ACCELERATORS** [-] [ ]
– Stayin' up in the city / (Why you) Hang up on me / Two girls in love / Black slacks / Under your wing / Radio / Ohh whee / You're a fool / What is real / Tears / Black and white / Letter.
1991. (cd) *<1404>* **DREAM TRAIN** [-] [ ]

—— looked to have disbanded

A CERTAIN RATIO

Formed: Manchester, England . . . 1977 by JEREMY KERR, PETER TERREL, SIMON TOPPING and MARTIN MOSCROP. One of the original 'Factory' bands, ACR came to shape and influence the nascent Manchester dance scene in much the same way as NEW ORDER, if never gaining even a fraction of the commercial success afforded that band. Signed to the label by head honcho Tony Wilson, the band's debut single, 'ALL NIGHT PARTY', appeared in late '79, closely followed by part-live, cassette only mini-set, 'THE GRAVEYARD AND THE BALLROOM'. By this point the drum machine had been replaced by a real live musician, BOB JOHNSON and ACR began expanding on their early bass-heavy, punk-funk/industrial sound towards an increasingly experimental, heavily rhythmic dance style. Released on 'Factory's Belgian sister label, 'Benelux', ACR's take on the BANBARRA funk classic, 'SHACK UP', suggested the direction the band were headed and following another one-off 12", they issued their first album proper, 'TO EACH', in 1981. With MARTHA TILSON taking over vocal duties and TOPPING moving to percussion, the sound was lent an even greater rhythmic dimension. 1982's 'SEXTET' was a benchmark of the band's early career and incredibly one of their few UK chart entries; an acclaimed collection taking in everything from funk and latin to avant-jazz, the album nevertheless struggled to make the Top 60. By the release of third album, 'I'D LIKE TO SEE YOU AGAIN' (1982), ACR had lost two of its founder mmebers, TOPPING and TERREL, along with TILSON. A new vocalist, CAROL McKENZIE, was recruited for a series of 12" singles, with sax player, TONY QUIGLEY, further enhancing ACR's complex sonic textures. After a final album for 'Factory', 1986's 'FORCE', little was heard from the band – save an Italian 12" and live album on 'Dojo' – as they made the transition from cult indie band to a major label, 'A&M'. 1989's club hit, 'THE BIG E (I WON'T STOP LOVING YOU)', was released at the height of the house craze ACR had helped pioneer, yet both 'GOOD TOGETHER' (1989) and the live 'M.C.R.' failed to make any inroads into the mainstream chart. A subsequent move to dance label, 'Rob's' (set up by former NEW ORDER manager, Rob Gretton) saw future PRIMAL SCREAM collaborator, DENISE JOHNSON, guesting on the 'UP IN DOWNSVILLE' (1992) set, ACR now ploughing the most accessible furrow of their career. In recognition of their far reaching influence on both dance and independent music in general, 'Creation' released remix tribute set, 'LOOKING FOR A CERTAIN RATIO', in 1994, featuring such Manchester luminaries as ELECTRONIC. At various times throughout the 80's, MOSCROP and KERR were part of KALIMA with TONY and ANN QUIGLEY. Although a few albums hit the shops they were best remembered for covering Sarah Vaughan's 'SMILING HOUR' and featuring in the movie, 'Absolute Beginners'. • **Covered:** DON'T YOU WORRY 'BOUT A THING (Stevie Wonder). • **Trivia:** DONALD JOHNSON'S brother, BARRY, was a member of soul/pop outfit SWEET SENSATION. SHAUN RYDER of HAPPY MONDAYS and BARNEY SUMNER of NEW ORDER guested vocals on 1990 ep '4 FOR THE FLOOR'.

Album rating: THE GRAVEYARD AND THE BALLROOM (*6) / TO EACH . . . (*5) / SEXTET (*7) / I'D LIKE TO SEE YOU AGAIN (*4) / FORCE (*6) / THE OLD AND THE NEW compilation (*9) / LIVE IN AMERICA (*4) / GOOD TOGETHER (*5) / MCR (*5) / UP IN DOWNSVILLE (*5) / LOOKING FOR A CERTAIN RATIO remixes (*5) / CHANGE THE STATION (*5)

JEREMY KERR – bass, vocals / **SIMON TOPPING** – vocals, trumpet / **MARTIN MOSCROP** – guitar, vocals / **PETER TERREL** – guitar

Factory Factory

Sep 79. (7"ltd.) *(FAC 5)* **ALL NIGHT PARTY. / THE THIN BOYS** [ ] [-]

—— added **DONALD JOHNSON** – percussion, drums

Jan 80. (c) *(FACT 16C)* **THE GRAVEYARD AND THE BALLROOM** (one-side live) [ ] [-]
– Flight / Faceless / Crippled child / Strain / Do the du (casse) / I feel / The choir / Flight / All night party / The fox / Genotype-phenotype / Oceans / The choir / Suspect. *(re-iss. Nov85; same) (cd-iss. Nov94 on 'Creation Rev-Ola'; CREV 022CD)*
Jul 80. (7") *Factory Benelux; (FAC BN 1-004)* **SHACK UP. / AND THEN AGAIN (live)** [-] [-] Belgian
Nov 80. (12") *(FAC 22)* **BLOWN AWAY. / FLIGHT / AND THEN AGAIN** [ ] [-]
Jan 81. (12"ep) *<FACUS 4>* **SHACK UP / SON AND HEIR. / DO THE DU (casse) / THE FOX** [-] [ ]

—— added **MARTHA TILSON** – vocals (ex-OCCULT CHEMISTRY)

May 81. (lp) *(FACT 35)* **TO EACH . . .** [ ] [-]
– Felch / My spirit / Forced laugh / Choir / Back to the start / The fox / Loss / Oceans / Winter hill. *(cd-iss. Nov94 on 'Creation Rev-Ola'; CREV 023CD)*
Sep 81. (d12") *(FACT 42)* **THE DOUBLE 12"** [-] [-] Italian
– (the EP's FAC 22 + FACUS 4)
Dec 81. (12") *(FAC 52)* **WATERLINE. / FUNAEZEKEA** [ ] [-]
Jan 82. (lp/c) *(FACT 55/+C)* **SEXTET** [53] [-]
– Lucinda / Crystal / Gum / Knife slits water / Skipscada / Day one / Rub down / Rialto / Below the canal. *(cd-iss. Nov94 on 'Creation Rev-Ola'; CREV 024CD)*
Jul 82. (12") *Factory Benelux; (FBN 17)* **GUESS WHO?. / (part Two)** [-] [-] Belgian
Sep 82. (7") *(FAC 62-7)* **KNIFE SLITS WATER. / TUMBA RUMBA** [ ] [-]
(12") *(FAC 62T)* – ('A'side) / Kether-Hot Knives mix-in special.

—— reverted to quintet when MARTHA departed

Nov 82. (lp/c) *(FACT 65/+C)* **I'D LIKE TO SEE YOU AGAIN** [ ] [-]
– I'd like to see you again / Axis / Saturn / Touch / Showcase / Guess who? / Hot knives / Sesano apriti-cordo vada. *(cd-iss. Nov94 on 'Creation Rev-Ola'; CREV 025CD)*

—— **ANDY CONNELL** – keyboards, vocals repl. TERREL / **CAROL McKENZIE** – (guest) vocals; repl. TOPPING who went solo (one 1985 single, 'PROSPECT PARK') before forming T-COY with ex-QUANDO QUANGO member, MIKE PICKERING (later M-PEOPLE)

Sep 83. (12") *(FAC 72)* **I NEED SOMEONE TONIGHT. / DON'T YOU WORRY BOUT A THING** [ ] [-]

—— **TONY QUIGLEY** – sax (also of KALIMA) repl. McKENZIE

Nov 84. (12") *(FAC 112)* **LIFE'S A SCREAM. / THERE'S ONLY THIS** [ ] [-]
Feb 85. (12") *Factory Benelux; (FBN 32)* **BRAZILIA. / BRAZILIA (extended)** [-] [-] Belgian
Jun 85. (12") *(FAC 128)* **WILD PARTY. / SOUNDS LIKE SOMETHING DIRTY** [ ] [-]
(c-s+=) *(FAC 128C)* – Life's a scream (live) / Force (live) / Wild party (live).
Dec 85. (lp/c) *(FACT 135/+C)* **THE OLD AND THE NEW** (best of; remixed) [ ] [ ]
– Flight / Do the du / And then again / The fox / Blown away / Sounds like something dirty / Life's a scream / There's only this / Wild party. *(w/ free 7")(7FAC 135)* – SHACK UP. / THE THIN BOYS *(cd-iss. Nov94 on 'Creation Rev-Ola'; CREV 026CD)*

—— added guests **CORRINE DREWERY** – vocals / **TOM BARRISH** – trombone / **PAUL HARRISON** – bass programmer

Factory not iss.

Sep 86. (12") *(FAC 168)* **MICKEY WAY (THE CANDY BAR). / INSIDE / SI FERMIR OGRIDO** [ ] [-]
Nov 86. (lp/cd)(c) *(FACT/FACD 166)(FACT 166C)* **FORCE** [ ] [-]
– Only together / Bootsy / Fever / Naked and white / Mickey Way (the candy bar) / And then she smiles / Take me down / Anthem. *(c+=)* – Inside / Nostromo a go-go. *(cd++=)* – Si fermir Ogrido. *(cd-iss. Nov94 on 'Creation Rev-Ola'; CREV 027CD)*

Dojo not iss.

Feb 87. (lp/cd) *(DOJO LP/CD 47)* **LIVE IN AMERICA (live 1985)** [ ] [-]
– Sounds like something dirty / The fox / Shack up / Life's a scream / Wild party / Flight / And then again / Touch / Knife slits water / Si fermir Ogrido.

Materiali / not iss.

Jul 87. (12"ep) *(MASO 70004)* **GREETINGS FOUR** [-] [-] Italy
– The runner / Inside / Bootsy.

—— now line-up **KERR, MOSCROP, JOHNSON + QUIGLEY** when CONNELL took guest DREWERY to form SWING OUT SISTER

A&M / not iss.

Jun 89. (7") *(ACR 514)* **THE BIG E (I WON'T STOP LOVING YOU). / LOVE IS THE WAY (instrumental)** [ ] [-]
(12"+=/cd-s+=) *(ACR Y/CD 514)* – Day 2.
Aug 89. (7") *(ACR 517)* **BACKS TO THE WALL. / BE WHAT YOU WANT TO BE** [ ] [-]
(12"+=/cd-s+=) *(ACR Y/CD 517)* – ('A' instrumental).
Sep 89. (lp/c/cd) *(AMA/AMC/CDA 9008)* **GOOD TOGETHER** [ ] [-]
– Your blue eyes / Your little world / The big E / God's own girl / Love is the way / Backs to the wall / River's edge / Every pleasure / Coldest days / Good together / Repercussions / 2000 a.d.
Oct 89. (7") *(ACR 534)* **YOUR BLUE EYES. / THIN GREY LINE** [ ] [-]
(12"+=/cd-s+=) *(ACR Y/CD 534)* – Coldest days.
Feb 90. (7") *(ACR 550)* **GOOD TOGETHER (live). / BE WHAT YOU WANNABE (live)** [ ] [-]
(12"ep+=/cd-ep+=) *(ACR Y/CD 550)* 4 FOR THE FLOOR EP – Spirit dance / Tribeca.
Jun 90. (7") *(ACR 540)* **WON'T STOP LOVING YOU. / THE BIG E** [55] [-]
(7"/c-s) *(ACR R/MC 540)* – ('A'-Bernard Sumner mix) / ('A'-Norman Cook mix).
(12") *(ACRY 540)* – ('A'-Bernard Sumner mix) / Repercussions (live) / Love is the way (instrumental).
(cd-s) *(ACRCD 540)* – (3 tracks above) / ('A'extended).
Jul 90. (cd/c/lp; as ACR) *(397057-2/-4/-1)* **MCR (live)** [ ] [-]
– Spirit dance / Won't stop loving you / B.T.T.W.90 / Be what you wanna be / Good together / Funky Heaven / Tribeca / Repercussions.

—— Promos of 'SHACK UP' were issued in Sep'90; *ACR/+Y 590)*

—— added on guest vocals **DENISE JOHNSON**

Robs Records / not iss.

Jul 91. (7"/ext.12") *(7/12 ROB 2)* **LOOSEN UP YOUR MIND. / THE PLANET** [ ] [-]
(cd-s+=) *(CDROB 2)* – ('A'+'B'versions).
Nov 91. (7") *(7ROB 5)* **27 FOREVER. / ('A'loose mix)** [ ] [-]
(12"+=) *(12ROB 5)* – ('A'instrumental dub).
(cd-s++=) *(CDROB 5)* – ('A'-Higher plane edit).
(12") *(12ROB 5R)* – ('A'-Da Silver mixes; Bubble bath + Soundstation).
Oct 92. (12"ep/cd-ep) *(12/CD ROB 6)* **MELLO (M-People mix) (part 1) / (part 2) / ('A'-Fon mix) / ('A'-Soundstation mix)** [ ] [-]
(12"ep) (12ROB 6) – Mello'd up / Mello dub / 27 forever (testimonial mix) / Mello (303 dub).
Oct 92. (cd/lp) *(CD/L ROB 20)* **UP IN DOWNSVILLE** [ ] [-]
– Manik / Turn me on / Mello / Wonder Y / Up in Downsville (pt.1) / 27 forever / Tekno 4 an answer / Salvador's (fish) / Up in Downsville (pt.2).

ACR

Feb 93. (12"ep/cd-ep) *(12/CD ROB 11)* **TURN ME ON ("O" mix) / ('A'-Tackle mix) / ('A'-Primetime mix) / ('A'-M21 mix)** [ ] [-]
Dec 93. (12") *(12ROB 18)* **TEKNO (Way out west mix). / TEKNO (Lip mix)** [ ] [ ]

Creation / not iss.

May 94. (12"ep)(cd-ep) *(CRE 151T)(CRESCD 151)* **SHACK UP (3 mixes; Wipeout / Radio / Work) / LIFE'S A SCREAM (Shaven not stirred mix)** [ ] [-]
Jul 94. (cd/c/lp)(2x12") *(CRE CD/MC/LP 159)(CRELP 159B)* **LOOKING FOR A CERTAIN RATIO** (remixes) [ ] [-]

Rob's Records / not iss.

Aug 96. (12"/cd-s) *(12/CD ROB 48)* **SOUNDSTATION VOLUME 1** [ ] [-]
Nov 96. (cd) *(CDROB 50)* **CHANGE THE STATION** [ ] [-]
Mar 97. (12") *(12ROB 52)* **SOUNDSTATION VOLUME 2** [ ] [-]

– compilations, others, etc. –

Dec 94. (lp) *Creation Rev-Ola; (CREV 013LP)* **SAMPLER** [ ] [-]

SIR HORATIO

a reggae version and pseudonym for A CERTAIN RATIO
Jan 82. (12") *Rock Steady; (666 MIX 1T)* **ABRACADUBRA. / SOMMADUB** [ ] [-]

SWAMP CHILDREN

MARTIN MOSCROP – percussion, drums / **ANN QUIGLEY** – vocals / **JOHN KIRKHAM** – guitar, percussion / **CLIFF SAFFER** – saxophone, clarinet / **ALAN** – bass

Factory / not iss.

Oct 81. (12"ep) *(FAC 49)* **HONEY** [ ] [-]
– Little voices / Call me honey / Boy.

—— now without ALAN; repl. by **TONY QUIGLEY** – bass, percussion / **CERI EVANS** – keyboards, bass, percussion, vocals
Nov 82. (12") *Factory Benelux; (FACBN 16)* **TASTE WHAT'S RHYTHM. /** [ ] [-]
Jan 83. (lp) *(FACT 70)* **SO HOT** [ ] [-]
– Samba zippy (part 1) / El Figaro / Tender game / Magic / Sunny weather / Samba zippy (part 2) / No sunshine / Spark the flame / Secret whispers.

—— they changed their moniker to . . .

KALIMA

Nov 83. (7"/12") *(FAC 87/+12)* **SMILING HOUR. / FLYAWAY** [ ] [-]

—— now a 4-piece **MARTIN, ANN, TONY + JOHN**

Jul 85. (12"ep) *(FAC 127-12)* **4 SONGS** [ ] [-]
– Land of dreams / Sparkle / So sad / Trickery.

—— added **ANDY CONNELL** – keyboards / **JEREMY KERR** – bass / **CLIFF SAFFER** – saxophone
Apr 86. (12"m) *(FAC 147-12)* **WHISPERED WORDS. / SUGAR 'N' SPICE / IN TIME** [ ] [-]
Jul 86. (lp) *(FACT 155)* **NIGHT TIME SHADOWS** [ ] [-]
– Mystic rhymes / After hours / Green dolphin street / Backwater / In time / Father pants / Start the melody / Token freaky / Love suspended in time.
May 87. (7"/12") *(FAC 187/+12)* **WEIRD FEELINGS. / THE DANCE** [ ] [-]
Apr 88. (lp/c)(cd) *(FACT 206/+C)(FACD 206)* **KALIMA** [ ] [-]
– That twinkle / Casabel / Sad and blue / Over the waves / Now you're mine / The strangest thing / Special way / Autumn leaves (French version) / Julian.
May 89. (cd) *(FACD 219)* **FLYAWAY** (compilation) [ ] [-]
– Samba zippy / Tender games / Smiling hour / Flyaway / Trickery / Land of dreams / Sparkle / Whispered words / Sugar and spice / Mystic rhymes / After hours / Start the melody / Token freaky / Love suspended in time / Weird feelings / The dance.
Jul 90. (12") **SHINE. /** [ ] [-]
Jul 90. (cd/lp) *(FACD/FACT 249)* **FEELING FINE** [ ] [-]
– Shine / A thousand signs / Take it easy / Interstella / Al the way through / Big fat city / The groovy one / Azure / Unreal.

ACETONE

Formed: based- Los Angeles, California, USA . . . 1992 originally as the quartet, SPINOUT, by RICHIE LEE, MARK LIGHTCAP and STEVE HADLEY (the other member departed before they became ACETONE). Having met at the remote Cal Arts establishment, the trio pooled their skills to create a unique desert hybrid of post-grunge'n'funk. Coupled with their well-documented fondness for narcotics and a penchant for hot-rod/surf stylings, the ACETONE sound attracted the attention of Virgin offshoot imprint, 'Hut'. Their 1993 debut, 'CINDY', displayed their kaleidoscopic retro sound in a mainly instrumental setting, although RICHIE's throaty vocals were put to good use on the follow-up. Recorded in Nashville, the mini-set of country covers, 'I GUESS I WOULD' (1995), found them chewing on a more commercially-oriented fix. A tour of America, however, first with Brit-rock brats, The VERVE, and then with manic Mancunians, OASIS, set them back on rock's doomed highway. A year later, ACETONE delivered their second full set, 'IF YOU ONLY KNEW' (1996), although their tenure with 'Hut' was soon to come to an end. Emerging from their twilight world of drugs and booze, the trio released the eponymous 'ACETONE, their first for 'Vapour' and their most high profile outing to date. • **Covers:** (Johnny Horton) / JUANITA (Flying Burrito Brothers) / BORDER LORD (Kris Kristofferson) / DON'T TALK PUT YOUR HEAD ON MY SHOULDER (Beach Boys).

Album rating: CINDY (*7) / I GUESS I WOULD (*5) / IF YOU ONLY KNEW (*5) / ACETONE (*6)

RICHIE LEE – vocals, bass, guitar / **MARK LIGHTCAP** – guitar, vocals / **STEVE HADLEY** – drums, vocals

Hut / Vernon Yard

May 93. (12"ep/cd-ep) *(HUT T/CD 30)* **ACETONE EP** [ ] [ ]
Sep 93. (7") *(HUT 38)* **PINCH. /** [ ] [ ]
(12"+=/cd-s+=) *(HUT T/DG 38)* –
Oct 93. (cd/c/lp) *(CDHUT/HUTMC/HUTLP 13)* <V2/V4 39068> **CINDY** [ ] [ ]
– Come on / Pinch / Sundown / Chills / Endless summer / Intermission / Louise / Don't cry / No need swim / Barefoot on Sunday.
Jan 95. (m-cd/m-lp) *(HUTM CD/LP 21)* **I GUESS I WOULD** [ ] [ ]
– Juanita / The late John Garfield blues / I guess I would / Sometimes you just can't win / All for the love of a girl / How sweet I roamed / Border Lord.
Oct 95. (7") *(HUT 62)* **THE FINAL SAY. / O.I.E.** [ ] [ ]
(cd-s+=) *(HUTCD 62)* – Diamondhead.
Mar 96. (cd) *(CDHUT 31)* **IF YOU ONLY KNEW** [ ] [ ]
– If you only knew / I don't really care / In the light / I've enjoyed as much of this as I can stand / The final say / When you're gone / Hound dog / 99 / What I see / Nothing at all / Always late.

Vapour / Vapor

Mar 98. (cd) *(936246818-2)* **ACETONE** [ ] [ ] Oct97
– Every kiss / All the time / Germs / Might as well / Shobud / All you know / Good life / Dee / Waltz / Another minute / So slow / Chew.

A.C. MARIAS

Formed: London, England . . . early 80's as a vehicle for chanteuse, ANGELA CONWAY. A one-off 45, 'DROP', for WIRE's "new music" showcase imprint, 'Dome' was issued in the summer of '81, before she became part of WIRE's (GILBERT & LEWIS) splinter outfit, DUET EMMO. This collaboration resulted in a sole album for 'Mute', 'OR SO IT SEEMS' (1983), the singer subsequently signing to the label in a solo capacity. Hardly prolific, A.C. MARIAS finally resurfaced in her/their own right towards the end of '86 (during this period she also provided backing vocals for GRAHAM LEWIS's HE SAID project) with a comeback single, 'JUST TALK'. Sticking by musical mentor, BRUCE GILBERT and enlisting alternative stalwarts, ROWLAND S. HOWARD (ex-BIRTHDAY PARTY, now of CRIME & THE CITY SOLUTION) plus BARRY ADAMSON (ex-MAGAZINE and solo artist), she/they released a taster to her long awaited debut album, 'ONE OF OUR GIRLS (HAS GONE MISSING)' (1989). The record's title track was released early the following year, another slice of ethereal gothic weirdness which proved to be her music biz swansong.

Album rating: ONE OF OUR GIRLS (HAS GONE MISSING) (*4)

ANGELA CONWAY – vocals

Dome / not iss.

Jul 81. (7"; as A.C. MARIAS A.C.) *(DOM45 1)* **DROP./ SO** [ ] [-]

— guests included WIRE guys, GILBERT & LEWIS

Mute / not iss.

Oct 86. (7"/12") *(MUTE/12MUTE 50)* **JUST TALK. / JUST TALK (NO TALK)** [ ] [-]
(re-iss. Jun88)

— now w/ **ROWLAND S. HOWARD / BRUCE GILBERT / BARRY ADAMSON**

Jan 88. (7"/12") *(MUTE/12MUTE 70)* **TIME WAS. / SOMETHING** [ ] [-]

Aug 89. (cd/c/lp) *(CD/C+/STUMM 68)* **ONE OF OUR GIRLS (HAS GONE MISSING)** [ ] [-]
– Trilby's couch / Just talk / There's a scent of rain in the air / Our dust / So soon / Give me / To sleep / Looks like / Sometime / One of our girls has gone missing / Time was.

Feb 90. (12"/cd-s) *(12/CD MUTE 105)* **ONE OF OUR GIRL IS MISSING. / TIME WAS** [ ] [-]

— retired from the music biz

ACT (see under ⇒ LEER, Thomas)

A.C. TEMPLE

Formed: Sheffield, England . . . 1985 by PAUL DORRINGTON and JANE BROMLEY. Influenced by the harsh industrial environment of their native city, A.C. TEMPLE alchemised a disturbing percussive cacophony utilising crashing guitars and filtering them through an echo chamber. Similar in spirit to the BIRTHDAY PARTY, JESUS & MARY CHAIN or SONIC YOUTH, the band released their first two albums, 'SONGS OF PRAISE' (1987) and 'BLOWTORCH' (1988) on the independent 'Further' label before signing to influential experimental noise outlet, 'Blast First'. With the addition of TIM BECKHAM and MAT SILCOX, A.C. TEMPLE released a third set, 'SOURPUSS' (1989), although press reaction was lukewarm and the band struggled to scale the heights of labelmates like DINOSAUR JR, etc. Even with the production expertise of BONGWATER's KRAMER, a fourth set, 'BELINDA BACKWARDS' (1991), failed to bring the band any more recognition; DORRINGTON, in turn, defected to The WEDDING PRESENT as the TEMPLE finally crumbled.

Album rating: SOURPUSS (*4)

JANE BROMLEY – vocals / **PAUL DORRINGTON** – guitar

Further / not iss.

Jun 87. (lp) *(FU 001)* **SONG OF PRAISE** [ ] [-]
– Ulterior / Make mine music / A motel in Kansas / Fear no more the heat of the sun / All hail discordia / 90 seconds.

Jul 88. (lp/cd) *(FU 6 LP/CD)* **BLOWTORCH** [ ] [-]
– Mincemeat / Yield / I dream of fraud / American / Weekend / Sheikh / Chinese burn / Shimmer queen / Hank / Armache / Ulterior.

— new **TIM BECKHAM** – guitar / **MAT SILCOX** – drums

Blast First / not iss.

Nov 89. (lp/c/cd) *(BFFP 45/+C/CD)* **SOURPUSS** [ ] [-]
– Sundown pet corner / Miss Sky / Stymied / Mother tongue / Crayola / Devil you know / Horsetrading / A mouthful / Faith in a windsock / Ringpiece / (Dirty) Weekend.

Apr 91. (lp/cd) *(BFFP 63/+CD)* **BELINDA BACKWARDS** [ ] [-]
– Glitterball / Silver swimmer / Half-angel / Come sunrise / Girlseye / Lifesize / Spacebore / Skyhooks / Baby seals / P2.

— disbanded when DORRINGTON joined The WEDDING PRESENT

ACTIFED

Formed: Hounslow, London, England . . . 1981 by WEAZEL, CLINTON GRACE, JOHN BRISTOW and STUART HEMPHILL. A victim of their own hype, ACTIFED graced the front cover of "oi" sympathisers, Sounds (the now defunct weekly NME rival!), before getting any vinyl in the shops! Legal problems over the use of their name (from the pharmaceutical company), etc., etc., plus the instalment of a fresh singer, DAVID ROGERS, held up the recording of their debut EP, 'DAWN OF A LEGION'. Finally surfacing on 'Jungle' in 1983, the EP's indie chart sales benefitted from the production kudos of former GENERATION X man, TONY JAMES. A further latter day punk effort, 'CRUCIFIXION', appeared the following year, although by this point the initial buzz had dimmed down as underground indie fashion diversified into two distinct tribes, "Gothic" and "Anarcho-Punk".

Album rating: the singles, I suppose!

DAVID ROGERS – vocals, lead guitar; repl. WEAZEL / **CLINTON GRACE** – guitar / **JOHN BRISTOW** – bass / **STUART HEMPHILL** – drums

Jungle / not iss.

Aug 83. (12"ep) *(JUNG 7)* **DAWN OF A LEGION EP** [ ] [-]
– Creation / Prophecy / Innocent / Exit.

Jun 84. (12") *(JUNG 11)* **CRUCIFIXION. / BLACK SKINNED BLUE EYED BOYS** [ ] [-]

— split late in 1984, an album of recordings shelved

ACTION PACT

Formed: Essex, England . . . early 80's out of the BAD SAMARITANS by KIM IGOE, DES 'WILD PLANET', JOE FUNGUS and KIM's brother JOHN on vocals. The latter was replaced by female, GEORGE CHEEX, before they actually hit the studio, their debut 7", 'HEATHROW TOUCHDOWN', being a split affair with DEAD MAN SHADOW (a band which JOHN subsequently joined as a guitarist). Following heavy radio support from Radio One DJ, JOHN PEEL, they signed to "oi/punk" specialist, 'Fall Out', issuing the anti glue-sniffing anthem, 'SUICIDE BAG', in the heady summer of '82. With drummer FUNGUS moving out for the gruesomely monikered GRIMLY FIENDISH, the quartet released a third single, 'PEOPLE', prior to a reissue of their most sought after track, 'LONDON BOUNCERS' (originally included on the split debut) and a long awaited debut album, 'MERCURY THEATRE ON THE AIR AGAIN' (1983). A new bass player, THISTLES (the permanent replacement for KIM IGOE, who had been substituted in the meantime by PHIL LANGHAM), featured on a handful of further singles and their vinyl parting shot, 'SURVIVAL OF THE FATTEST' (1984).

Album rating: MERCURY THEATRE – ON THE AIR (*5) / SURVIVAL OF THE FATTEST (*5)

GEORGE CHEEX (b.1966) – vocals; repl. JOHN who joined DEAD MAN'S SHADOW / **DES 'WILD PLANET'** – guitar / **KIM IGOE** – bass / **JOE FUNGUS** – drums

Subversive / not iss.

Nov 81. (7"ep) *(ANARCHO 1)* **HEATHROW TOUCHDOWN EP** [ ] [-]
– London bouncers / All purpose action footwear / DEAD MAN'S SHADOW: Police force / Danger UXB.

Fall Out / not iss.

Aug 82. (7") *(FALL 003)* **SUICIDE BAG. / STANWELL / BLUE BLOOD** [ ] [-]

— **GRIMLY FIENDISH** – drums; repl. FUNGUS

Mar 83. (7") *(FALL 010)* **PEOPLE. / TIMES MUST CHANGE / SIXTIES FLIX** [ ] [-]

Jul 83. (7") *(FALL 016)* **LONDON BOUNCERS. / ALL PURPOSE ACTION FOOTWEAR** [ ] [-]
(12"+=) *(FALL12 016)* –

Sep 83. (lp/c) *(FALL LP/CLP 013)* **MERCURY THEATRE – ON THE AIR** [ ] [-]
– (Drowning out the) Big jets / Fools factions / Things that need . . . / Cowslick blues / Double standards / Losers / London bouncers (bully boy version) / People / Currant bun / Mindless aggression / Blue blood / Protest is alive / Mercury Theatre (on the air again).

— **THISTLES** – bass; repl. PHIL LANGHAM (ex-DARK) who repl. IGOE

Nov 83. (7") *(FALL 019)* **QUESTION OF CHOICE. / HOOK LINE AND SINKER / SUSS OF THE SWISS** [ ] [-]

Aug 84. (7") *(FALL 026)* **YET ANOTHER DOLE QUEUE SONG. / ROCKAWAY BEACH** [ ] [-]
(12"+=) *(FALL12 026)* – 1974 / Rock'n'roll part 2.

Oct 84. (7") *(FALL 029)* **COCKTAIL CREDIBILITY. / CONSUMER MADNESS** [ ] [-]

Nov 84. (lp) *(FALLLP 030)* **SURVIVAL OF THE FATTEST** [ ] [-]
– Open your eyes / Optimism / Keep it tickin' over / Have fun / Up on the heath / Johnny Fontaine / Yet another dole queue song / Cocktail credibility / Who's to blame? / Human beings / Voice in the wilderness.

— split early in 1985

– compilations, etc. –

1997. (cd) *Cleopatra; ()* **THE PUNK SINGLES COLLECTION** [ ] [-]

ADAM & THE ANTS

Formed: London, England . . . April '77 by STUART GODDARD (aka ADAM ANT) along with LESTER SQUARE, ANDY WARREN and PAUL FLANAGAN. Initially a fairly rote punk act with attitude, what got the band noticed was their lurid stage show and penchant for S&M trappings. Derek Jarman was sufficiently enamoured to offer ADAM a part in his controversial punk flick, 'Jubilee' (released Feb '78), a revised ANTS line-up (featuring new members DAVE BARBE and MARK GAUMONT) recording two songs for the soundtrack, 'Plastic Surgery' and 'Deutcher Girls'. Later that year, the group released a one-off debut single for 'Decca', 'YOUNG PARISIANS', before releasing their rated debut album, 'DIRK WEARS WHITE SOX' in late '79. A morose slab of post-punk doom-mongering, the record stood in stark contrast to their later albums by a remodelled ADAM & THE ANTS. The shake-up came courtesy of none other than ex-SEX PISTOLS svengali, MALCOLM McLAREN, who, after dreaming up the flamboyant new image (a surprisingly effective if retrospectively ridiculous Native Indian cum swashbuckling pirates concept), whisked ADAM's band off to become BOW WOW WOW. Virtually written off by his critics, ADAM came swaggering back with a new line-up (MARCO PIRRONI, CHRIS HUGHES aka MERRICK, KEVIN MOONEY and TERRY LEE MIALL), a new sound and a new album (his first for 'C.B.S.'), 'KINGS OF THE WILD FRONTIER' (1980). Taking their cue from the Burundi drummers of Africa, the band had stumbled on a unique musical mutant which combined retro rock'n'roll with pseudo-tribal, dayglo pouting pop; teenyboppers loved it and a string of anthemic singles, 'DOG EAT DOG', 'ANT MUSIC' and the thundering title track all made the UK Top 5. The album itself rode to the top of the charts (even scaping into the US Top 50) and for a brief but warpainted period, Britain was gripped with "Antmania". The sight of the ever photogenic ADAM striding boldly through his video adventures like some dandy Indiana Jones was the stuff of girly fantasy and if you didn't have a white stripe across your nose, well, you could forget about getting lucky at the school disco. ANT was clever enough to slightly tweak his image on the follow-up set, 'PRINCE CHARMING' (1981), this time going for a dashing highwayman cum 18th century courtier get-up. It was even more effective, the group scoring two No.1 singles in quick succession with 'STAND AND DELIVER' and the title track, while 'ANT RAP' made the Top 3. To be fair to the man, he had the good sense to disband ADAM & THE ANTS at the height of their fame, although by carrying on as ADAM ANT in a vaguely similar vein, he was bound to suffer a backlash sooner or later. Retaining sidekick, PIRRONI, ANT's solo career nevertheless got off to an auspicious start with No.1 single, 'GOODY TWO SHOES', while the accompanying album, 'FRIEND OR FOE' (1982) made the Top 5 (and bizarrely the US Top 20). The following three years brought only one major hit in 'PUSS 'N' BOOTS' and after the 'VIVE LE ROCK' (1985) set, ANT took four years off to develop his acting career while PIRRONI joined SPEAR OF DESTINY. By the turn of the decade, the pair were back with an underwhelming new single, 'ROOM AT THE TOP', and album, 'MANNERS & PHYSIQUE', both enjoying a brief stint in the charts but largely ignored as the nation's pop kids raved to acid house. • **Trivia:** He acted in stage production of 'Entertaining Mr. Sloane'. After retiring to the States in 1986 he took parts in 'Slam Dance' film, and 'Equalizer' TV serial.

Album rating: DIRK WEARS WHITE SOX (*6) / KINGS OF THE WILD FRONTIER (*6) / PRINCE CHARMING (*5) / FRIEND OR FOE (*5) / STRIP (*4) / VIVE LE ROCK (*4) / MANNERS AND PHYSIQUE (*4) /WONDERFUL (*5) / HITS (1980-1985) compilation (*6)

ADAM ANT (b. STUART GODDARD, 3 Nov'54) – vocals, guitar / **MATTHEW ASHMAN** (b.'62) – guitar, vocals (ex-KAMERAS) / **ANDY WARREN** (b.'61) – bass, vocals / **DAVE BARBE** (b.'61) – drums (ex-DESOLATION ANGELS)

Decca | not iss.

Oct 78. (7") *(F 13803)* **YOUNG PARISIANS. / LADY** [ ] [-]
(re-act.Dec80; hit No.9)

Do-It | not iss.

Jun 79. (7") *(DUN 8)* **ZEROX. / WHIP IN MY VALISE** [ ] [-]

—— (some copies had B-side playing 'PHYSICAL (YOU'RE SO)')
(re-act.Jan81; hit No.45)

Nov 79. (lp/c) *(RIDE 3/+M)* **DIRK WEARS WHITE SOX** [ ] [-]
– Cartrouble (part 1 & 2) / Digital tenderness / Nine plan failed / Day I met God * / Tabletalk / Cleopatra / Catholic day / Never trust a man (with egg on his face) / Animals and men / Family of noise / The idea. *(re-act.Jan81; hit No.16) (remixed & re-iss. Apr83 on 'C.B.S.' lp/c; CBS/40 25361) (track * replaced by)* – Zerox / Kick! / Whip in my valise. *(cd-iss. Jul95 on 'Columbia'; 480521-2)*

—— **LEIGH GORMAN** – bass (on B-side) repl. WARREN who joined MONOCHROME SET

Feb 80. (7") *(DUN 10)* **CARTROUBLE. / KICK!** [ ] [-]
(re-act.Jan81; hit No.33)

—— (Jan80) until (Mar'80 when ADAM brought in entire new group) **MARCO PIRRONI** (b.27 Apr'59) – guitar, vocals (ex-MODELS) repl. ASHMAN / **MERRICK** (b.CHRIS HUGHES, 3 Mar'54) – drums repl. BARBE / **KEVIN MOONEY** – bass, vocals repl. GORMAN (who with above 2 formed BOW WOW WOW) / added **TERRY LEE MIALL** (b. 8 Nov'58) – 2nd drummer (ex-MODELS)

C.B.S. | Columbia

Jul 80. (7") *(CBS 8877)* **KINGS OF THE WILD FRONTIER. / PRESS DARLINGS** [48] [-]
(re-act.Feb81; hit No.2)

Sep 80. (7") *(CBS 9039)* **DOG EAT DOG. / PHYSICAL (YOU'RE SO)** [4] [-]

Nov 80. (lp/c) *(CBS/40 84549)* <37033> **KINGS OF THE WILD FRONTIER** [1] [44] Feb81
– Dog eat dog / Ant music / Feed me to the lions / Los Rancheros / Ants invasion / Killer in the home / Kings of the wild frontier / The magnificent five / Don't be square (be there) / Jolly Roger / Making history / The human beings. *(cd-iss. Oct93 on 'Sony Europe'; 477902-2)*

Nov 80. (7") *(CBS 9352)* **ANT MUSIC. / FALL IN** [2] [-]

Jan 81. (7")(12") <02042><01061> **ANT MUSIC. / DON'T BE SQUARE (BE THERE)** [-] [ ]

—— **GARY TIBBS** (b.25 Jan'58)- bass (ex-ROXY MUSIC, ex-VIBRATORS) repl. MOONEY

May 81. (7")<US-12"> *(A-1065)* <02193> **STAND AND DELIVER. / BEAT MY GUEST** [1] [ ]

Sep 81. (7") *(A-1408)* **PRINCE CHARMING. / CHRISTIAN D'OR** [1] [-]

Nov 81. (lp/c) *(CBS/40 85268)* <37615> **PRINCE CHARMING** [2] [94]
– Prince Charming / The Scorpios / Picasso visita el Planeta de los Simios / 5 guns west / That voodoo / Stand and deliver / Mile high club / Ant rap / Mowhok / S.E.X. *(re-iss. cd Mar96 on 'Columbia'; 474606-2)*

Dec 81. (7"/7"pic-d) *(A/+11 1738)* **ANT RAP. / FRIENDS** [3] [-]

—— they broke up early '82

ADAM ANT

continued solo augmented by **PIRRONI** and sessioners

C.B.S. | Epic

May 82. (7"/7"pic-d) *(A/+11 2367)* **GOODY TWO SHOES. / RED SCAB** [1] [-]

Sep 82. (7"/7"pic-d) *(A/+11 2736)* **FRIEND OR FOE. / JUANITO THE BANDITO** [9] [-]

Oct 82. (lp/c) *(CBS/40 25040)* <38370> **FRIEND OR FOE** [5] [16]
– Friend or foe / Something girls / Place in the country / Desperate but not serious / Here comes the grump / Hello I love you / Goody two shoes / Crackpot history and the right to lie / Made of money / Cajun twisters / Try this for sighs / A man called Marco. *(cd-iss. Jul96 on 'Columbia'; 484436-2)*

Oct 82. (7") <03367> **GOODY TWO SHOES. / CRACKPOT HISTORY** [-] [12]

Nov 82. (7"/7"pic-d) *(A/+11 2892)* **DESPERATE BUT NOT SERIOUS. / WHY DO GIRLS LOVE HORSES?** [33] [-]

Feb 83. (7") <03688> **DESPERATE BUT NOT SERIOUS. / PLACE IN THE COUNTRY** [-] [66]

Oct 83. (7"/7"pic-d/ext.12") *(A/WA/TA 3614)* <04461> **PUSS 'N' BOOTS. / KISS THE DRUMMER** [5] [ ] May84

Nov 83. (lp/c) *(CBS/40 25705)* <39108> **STRIP** [20] [65]
– Baby let me scream at you / Libertine / Spanish games / Vanity / Puss'n'boots / Playboy / Strip / Montreal / Navel to neck / Amazon. *(cd-iss. Jul84; CD 25705)*

Dec 83. (7"/7"pic-d/ext.12") *(A/WA/TA 3589)* <04337> **STRIP. / YOURS, YOURS, YOURS** [41] [42]

Sep 84. (7"/'A'-Orbit mix-12") *(A/TA 4719)* **APOLLO 9. / B SIDE BABY** [13] [ ]
(12") *(QTA 4719)* – ('A'-Splashdown remix & acappella instrumental).

Jul 85. (7") *(A 6367)* <05574> **VIVE LE ROCK. / GRETA X** [50] [ ]
(12"+=) *(TA 6367)* – ('A'instrumental dub mix).

Sep 85. (lp/c) *(CBS/40 26583)* <40159> **VIVE LE ROCK** [42] [ ]
– Vive le rock / Miss Thing / Razor keen / Rip down / Scorpio rising / Apollo 9 / Hell's eight acres / Mohair lockeroom pin-up boys / No zap / P.O.E. *(c+=)* – Human bondage den. *(cd-iss. 1988+=; CD 26583)* – Apollo 9 (acappella). *(re-iss. cd Mar95 on 'Rewind'; 478504-2)*

—— ADAM retired for 4 years. MARCO joined SPEAR OF DESTINY

ADAM ANT

brought back MARCO to resurrect career.

M.C.A. | M.C.A.

Feb 90. (7"/7"s/c-s) *(MCA/+R/C 1387)* <53679> **ROOM AT THE TOP. / BRUCE LEE** [13] [17]
(cd-s+=/12"+=) *(D+/MCAT 1387)* – ('A'house vocals).
(cd-s+=) *(DMCAX 1387)* – ('A'mixes).

Mar 90. (cd/lp)(c) *(D+/MCG 6068)(MCGC 6068)* <6315> **MANNERS & PHYSICIQUE** [19] [57]
– Room at the top / If you keep on / Can't set rules about love / Bright lights black leather / Young dumb and full of it / Rough stuff / Manners & physicique / U.S.S.A. / Piccadilly / Anger Inc.

Apr 90. (7"/c-s) *(MCA/+C 1404)* **CAN'T SET RULES ABOUT LOVE. / HOW TO STEAL THE WORLD** [47] [ ]
(cd-s+=/12"+=) *(D+/MCAT 1404)* – Brand new torso.
(cd-s++=) *(DMCAP 1404)* – ('A'-lp version).

Jun 90. (7") <79042> **BRIGHT LIGHTS BLACK LEATHER. / ROUGH STUFF** [-] [ ]

—— w/ **PIRRONI** / **BOZ BOORER** – guitars / **BRUCE WITKIN** – bass / **DAVE RUFFY** – drums

E.M.I. | Capitol

Jan 95. (c-s/7") *(TC+/EM 366)* <58239> **WONDERFUL. / GOES AROUND** [32] [39] Mar95
(cd-s+=) *(CDEMS 366)* – Norman / Woman love run through me.
(cd-s) *(CDEM 366)* – ('A'side) / If / Phoenix.

Mar 95. (c-s/7"; withdrawn) *(TC+/EM)* **BEAUTIFUL DREAM. / LET'S HAVE A FIGHT** [ ] [ ]
(cd-s+=; w-drawn) *(CDEMS)* – Billy boy / Wonderful (acoustic).
(cd-s; w-drawn) *(CDEM)* – ('A'side) / Shake your hips / Ant music (acoustic) / ('A'-Lucas master mix).

Apr 95. (cd/c) *(CD/TC EMC 3687)* <30335> **WONDERFUL** [24] [39]
– Won't take that talk / Beautiful dream / Wonderful / 1969 again / Yin & Yang / Image of yourself / Alien / Gotta be a sin / Vampires / Angel / Very long ride. *(cd re-iss. Sep97; same)*

May 95. (c-s) *(TCEM 379)* **GOTTA BE A SIN / DOG EAT DOG (live)** [48] [ ]
(cd-s) *(CDEM 379)* – ('A'side) / Cleopatra (live) / Beat my guest (live) / Red scab (live).
(cd-s) *(CDEMS 379)* – ('A'side) / Desperate but not serious (live) / Car trouble (live) / Physical (you're so) (live).

– compilations, others, etc. –

Feb 82. (7") *E.G.; (EGO 5)* **DEUTCHER GIRLS. / PLASTIC SURGERY** [13] [-]

Mar 82. (7"ep/7"pic-ep) *Do-It; (DUN/+X 20)* **THE B-SIDES** [46] [-]
– Friends / Kick! / Physical (you're so).
(12"ep+=) *(DUNIT 20)* – Cartrouble (pts. 1 & 2).

1982. (7"; as MANEATERS) *E.G.; (EGO 8)* **NINE TO FIVE. / (SUZI PINNS: Jerusalem)** [ ] [-]
(above another from the film 'Jubilee' & featuring TOYAH)

Sep 86. (lp/c) *C.B.S.; (CBS/40 450074-1/-4)* **HITS** [ ] [ ]
– Kings of the wild frontier / Dog eat dog / Ant music / Stand and deliver / Prince Charming / Ant rap / Goody two shoes / Friend or foe / Desperate but not serious / Puss 'n' boots / Strip / Apollo 9 / Vive le rock. *(re-iss. Jul90 & Jul98 on 'Columbia' cd/c; R 450074-2/-4)*

Jan 88. (7") *Old Gold; (OG 9739)* **ANT MUSIC. / STAND AND DELIVER** [ ] [-]

Oct 89. (12"white/12"pic-d) *Damaged Goods; (FNARR/+P 7)* **YOUNG PARISIANS / LADY. / (interview)** [ ] [-]

Nov 90. (7") *Old Gold; (OG 9953)* **PRINCE CHARMING. / GOODY TWO SHOES** [ ] [-]

Feb 91. (cd/c/lp) *Strange Fruit; (SFR CD/MC/LP 115)* **THE PEEL SESSIONS** (early 1979 material) [ ] [-]

Jun 91. (cd/c) *Columbia; (468762-2/-4)* **ANTICS IN THE FORBIDDEN ZONE** [ ] [-]

Aug 93. (cd/c) *Arcade; (ARC 31000 5-2/6-4)* **ANTMUSIC – THE VERY BEST OF ADAM ANT** [6] [-]
(re-iss. Mar94 d-cd+ 'LIVE'; ARC 310000-2); hit No.30)

Oct 94. (cd) *Columbia; (477513-2)* **THE BEST (ADAM ANT)** [ ] [-]

May 95. (cd) *Columbia; (480362-2)* **B SIDES BABIES** [ ] [-]

Barry ADAMSON

Born: 1 Jun'58, Moss Side, Manchester, England. As the bassist of avant-punksters, MAGAZINE, ADAMSON played on such classic albums as 'Real Life' (1978) and 'The Correct Use Of Soap' (1980), before going on to work with ex-BUZZCOCKS man, PETE SHELLEY. This proved to be a short-lived collaboration as ADAMSON was subsequently recruited as one of NICK CAVE's BAD SEEDS. He remained with the ex-BIRTHDAY PARTY man until the late 80's, playing on four albums: 'From Her To Eternity' (1984), 'The Firstborn Is Dead' (1985), 'Kicking Against The Pricks' (1986) and 'Your Funeral . . . My Trial' (1986). An impressive musical CV by anyone's standard and one which ADAMSON put to good use in his first solo venture, 'MOSS SIDE STORY' (1989). With echoes of MAGAZINE's angular noise and The BAD SEEDS' black majesty, the record was conceived as a soundtrack to a would-be movie set in the seedy underbelly of Manchester's crime-ridden Moss Side area. By subverting the classic recipe of cheesy hammond and setting it against both his feel for the avant-garde and the clever use of samples, ADAMSON created a noir collage which proved so effective he subsequently found himself writing and recording bonafide soundtracks to such cult films as 'Gas Food Lodging'. A similarly unsavoury follow-up album proper, 'SOUL MURDER', eventually appeared in 1992 while the following year's 'THE NEGRO INSIDE' explored more accessible and familiar musical territory duly examining ADAMSON's thoughts on cultural identity. 'OEDIPUS SCHMOEDIPUS' (1996) pleased his fans (it featured JARVIS COCKER and NICK CAVE) if not exactly breaking the established mould, ADAMSON remaining the kingpin of his self-created genre while his brooding shadow lurks in the recordings of trip hop artists like PORTISHEAD. The man – who was once labelled "the Ennio Morricone" of the 90's – issued his seventh album, 'AS ABOVE SO BELOW' (1998), another delivery of class. • **Covered:** THESE BOOTS ARE MADE FOR WALKING (Nancy Sinatra).

Album rating: MOSS SIDE STORY (*7) / DELUSION (*5) / SOUL MURDER (*6) / THE NEGRO INSIDE mini (*5) / OEDIPUS SCHMOEDIPUS (*7)

BARRY ADAMSON – bass, keyboards, vocals (ex-MAGAZINE, ex-NICK CAVE & THE BAD SEEDS, ex-IGGY POP)

Mute / Mute-Elektra

1988. (7") *(MUTE 77)* **MAN WITH THE GOLDEN ARM. / BOMBASTO** [ ] [-]
(12"+=/cd-s+=) *(12/CD MUTE 77)* – Fifteen rounds / Suck on the honey of love.

Mar 89. (cd/c/lp) *(CD/C+/STUMM 53) <71420>* **MOSS SIDE STORY** [ ] [ ]
– (The ring's the thing): On the wrong side of relaxation / Under wraps / Central control / Round up the usual suspects / (Real deep cool): Sounds from the big house / Suck on the honey of love / Everything happens to me / The swinging detective / (Final irony): Auto destruction / Intensive care / The most beautiful girl in the world / Free at last / (For your ears only): Alfred Hitchcock presents / Chocolate milkshake / The man with the golden arm.

Oct 89. (12"ep/3"cd-ep) *(12/CD MUTE 97)* **TAMING OF THE SHREWD** [ ] [-]
– Diamonds / Boppin' out / Eternal morning / Splat goes the cat / From Rusholme with love.

Jul 91. (7"; as BARRY ADAMSON, ANITA LANE AND THE THOUGHT SYSTEMS OF LOVE) *(MUTE 119)* **THESE BOOTS ARE MADE FOR WALKING. /** [ ] [-]
(12"+=/cd-s+=) *(12/CD MUTE 119)* –

Aug 91. (cd/c/lp) *(CD/C+/IONIC 004) <61127-2/-4>* **DELUSION** (Original Soundtrack) [ ] [ ]
– Delusion / Crossin' the line / Il soltario / Patti's theme / A settlin' kinda scam / Fish face / Go Johnny / The life we leave behind / An amendment / La cucaracha / Diamonds / George's downfall / Got to bet to win / The track with no name / Patti's theme (Two stage variation) / Death valley junction / These boots are made for walking.
(above released on 'Ionic'/'Mute')

Apr 92. (cd/c/lp) *(<CD/C+/STUMM 105>)* **SOUL MURDER** [ ] [ ]
– Preface / Split / The violation of expectation / Suspicion / A gentle man of colour / Trance of hatred / Checkpoint Charlie / Reverie / Un petit miracle / 007, a fantasy Bond theme / The Adamson family / Cool green world / On the edge of atonement / Epilogue.

Sep 92. (cd-ep) *(CDMUTE 149)* **CINEMA IS KING EP** [ ] [-]

Jun 93. (cd/lp) *(<CD+/STUMM 120>)* **THE NEGRO INSIDE** [ ] [ ] Oct93
– The snowball effect / Dead heat / Dusted / Cold black preach / Je t'aime . . . mon non plus / A perfectly natural union.

Apr 95. (12"ep) *(12MUTE 183)* **MOVIEOLOGY EP** [ ] [ ]

Jul 96. (12"ep/cd-ep) *(12/CD MUTE 188)* **ACHIEVED IN THE VALLEY OF THE DOLLS /** [ ] [-]
(cd-ep) *(LCDMTE 188)* –

Jul 96. (cd/lp) *(CD+/STUMM 134) <69019>* **OEDIPUS SCHMOEDIPUS** [ ] [ ] Aug96
– Set the controls for the heart of the / Something wicked this way comes / Vibes ain't nothin' but the vibes / It's business as usual / Miles / Dirty Barry / In a moment of clarity / Achieved in the valley of the dolls / Vermillion kisses / Big bamboozle / State of contraction / Sweetest embrace / Se the controls again.

May 98. (12"ep/cd-ep) *(12/CD MUTE 188)* **CAN'T GET LOOSE / TROUBLE ASUNDER (ODEIPUS RETURNS). / HEAR THE ANGELS / NAMASTE MPC (END TITLE)** [ ] [-]

Jun 98. (cd/lp) *(CD+/STUMM 161) <69035>* **AS ABOVE SO BELOW** [ ] [ ]
– Can't get loose / What it means / Deja voodoo / Come hell or high water / Jazz devil / Still I rise / Girl / Monkey speaks his mind / Goddess of love / Jesus wept.

Jul 98. (12"ep) *(12MUTE 219)* **WHAT IT MEANS. / ('A'-Skylab plucked chicken mix) / ('A'-Subsonic legacy master mix)** [ ] [-]
cd-s+=) *(CDMUTE 219)* – Akylab a smokin' Japanese were – Chicken in Moss Sid.

Oct 98. (12"/cd-s) *(12/CD MUTE 223)* **JAZZ DEVIL / JAZZ DEVIL (version). / SATURN IN THE SUMMER / JAZZ DEVIL (instrumental)** [ ] [-]

ADD N TO X

Formed: South London, England . . . 1994 by former Radio Prague DJ, BARRY SMITH, alongside ANN SHENTON and STEVEN CLAYTON, taking their puzzling moniker from a mathematical formula. Moog and theremin dole-meisters of the Nth degree, ADD N TO X debuted early in 1996 with 'VERO ELECTRONICS', a strangely strange set of mind-blowing knob twidling. The following year, after inking a deal with 'Satellite', the eardrum-bashing futurists had two NME Singles Of The Week, 'THE BLACK REGENT' and 'KING WASP'. Early in 1998, they established themselves with an innovative electro A-Bomb of sound in their second long-player, 'ON THE WIRES OF OUR NERVES'. Extreme and trailblazing, like STEREOLAB/SUICIDE with a rocket shoved up their rectum, the album's lengthy, disorientated tracks were a prime feature of DJ, Mary Ann Hobbs' Radio One "Breeze Block" show. After turning down the majors, ADD N TO X subsequently signed to semi-seminal indie, 'Mute', their first outing being the wonderful 'LITTLE BLACK ROCKS IN THE SUN'. • **Trivia:** In September of '98, they were probably the first band ever to play underground at a nuclear shelter, the bunker in question being in the rural backwaters of north east Fife near Anstruther.

Album rating: VERO ELECTRONICS (*6) / ON THE WIRES OF OUR NERVES (*8)

BARRY SMITH – synthesizer / **ANN SHENTON** – programming/ **STEVEN CLAYTON** – synthesizer

Blow Up / not iss.

Jan 96. (cd/lp) *(BLOW UP 004 CD/LP)* **VERO ELECTRONICS** [ ] [-]
– Inevitable fast access / A silhouette of a man and a wasp / Meetings in compact boxes / A very uncomfortable status (wet disco) / Inevitable fast access (sleeze) / A very uncomfortable status (mathematical) / Aphine repetition. *(cd re-iss. Aug97; same)*

Satellite / Mute

Jun 97. (12") *(STL 003)* **THE BLACK REGENT. / MURMUR ONE** [ ] [-]

Oct 97. (12") *(STL 007)* **KING WASP./ HIT ME** [ ] [-]

Nov 97. (ltd-12") *(PIAO 10)* **DEMON SEED. / (track by FRIDGE)** [ ] [-]
(above single issued on 'Piao!')

—— added **ROB HALLUM** (of the HIGH LLAMAS)

Feb 98. (cd/d-lp) *(STL 010 CD/LP) <69053>* **ON THE WIRES OF OUR NERVES** [ ] [ ] May98
– We are Add N To X / Murmur one / Sound of accelerating concrete / Gentle Germans / The black regent / Planet Munich / Nevermind / King Wasp / Orgy of Bubastus / Grey body, green gun / On the wires of our nerves / Hit me / Sir Ape.

Mute / Mute

Jul 98. (10"ep/cd-ep) *(10/CD MUTE 219)* **LITTLE BLACK ROCKS IN THE SUN. / VOICES 1-3** [ ] [-]

ADICTS

Formed: Ipswich, England . . . 1978 by MONKEY (aka KEITH WARREN), MELVIN ELLIS, KID DEE (aka (MICHAEL DAVISON) and PETE DAVIDSON, who intentionally incorrectly spelled their group moniker (or did they?). Kitted out in "Clockwork Orange"-style garb, these second wave punks veered on the ridiculous, releasing an EP, 'LUNCH WITH THE ADICTS' and an album, 'SONGS OF PRAISE', in late '81. The following year, The ADICTS supplied their fans with another fix in the shape of the 'VIVA LA REVOLUTION' single. During the course of the following year, they scraped into both the album and singles charts with 'SOUND OF MUSIC' (1982) and 'BAD BOY' respectively. After a very brief spell with 'Warners/Sire' (under the revamped moniker of ADX), the stalwart punks returned with a series of workmanlike efforts which did nothing to create any musical dependence among the record buying public. • **Trivia:** The cover of their demo compilation, 'THIS IS YOUR LIFE', was packaged in a similar "red book" fashion to the famous TV programme.

Album rating: THE VERY BEST OF THE ADICTS compilation (*6)

MONKEY (b. KEITH WARREN) – vocals / **PETE DAVIDSON** – guitar / **MELVIN ELLIS** – bass / **KID DEE** (b. MICHAEL DAVISON) – drums

Dining Out / not iss.

Jun 81. (7"ep) *(TUX 1)* **LUNCH WITH THE ADICTS** [ ] [-]
– This week / Straight jacket / Organised confused / Easy way out.

D.W.E.D. / not iss.

Oct 81. (lp) *(SMT 008)* **SONGS OF PRAISE** [ ] [-]
– England / Just like me / Viva la revolution / Hurt / Tango / Telepathic people / Mary Whitehouse / Distortion / Songs of praise / Sensitive / Dynasty / Get addicted / Calling calling / In the background / Peculiar music / Numbers. *(re-iss. Apr86 yellow-lp/pic-lp on 'Fall Out'; FALLLP 006/+P) (cd-iss. Jan94 on 'Cleopatra'; CLEO 2481CD)*

Fall Out / not iss.

Jul 82. (7") *(FALL 002)* **VIVA LA REVOLUTION. / STEAMROLLER** [ ] [-]

Razor / not iss.

Nov 82. (7") *(RZS 101)* **CHINESE TAKEAWAY. / YOU'LL NEVER WALK ALONE** [ ] [-]

Nov 82. (lp) *(RAZ 2)* **SOUND OF MUSIC** [99] [-]
– How sad / 4321 / Chines takeaway / Johnny was a soldier / Disco / Eyes in the back of your head / Joker in the pack / Lullaby / My baby got run over by a steamroller / A man's gotta do / Let's go / The easy way out / Shake, rattle, bang your head. *(cd-iss. Aug93 on 'Great Expectations'; PIPCD 040) (cd re-iss. an94 on 'Cleopatra'; CLEO 3315CD)*

May 83. (7"/7"pic-d) *(RZS/+P 104)* **BAD BOY. / SHAKE, RATTLE, BANG YOUR HEAD** [75] [-]

Zig Zag / not iss.

1984. (7"; as ADDIX) **TOO BLIND TO SEE. / (NO SUCH THING AS A) BAD BOY** [ ] [-]

ADX

Warners / not iss.

Apr 84. (7") *(W 9298)* **TOKYO. / THE ODD COUPLE** [ ] [-]
(12"+=) *(W 9298T)* – Medley.

Sire / not iss.

May 85. (7") *(U 9070)* **FALLING IN LOVE AGAIN. / COME ALONG** [ ] [-]
(12"+=) *(U 9070T)* – It's a laugh/ Saturday night.

ADICTS

Fall Out / not iss.

Nov 85. (12"ep) *(FALL12 038)* **BAR ROOM BOP EP** [ ] [-]
– Champs Elysees / Sound of music / Who spilt my beer / Cowboys.

Sep 87. (lp) *(FALLLP 042)* **FIFTH OVERTURE** [ ] [-]

Jun 90. (lp/cd) *(FALL LP/CD 046)* **ROCKERS IN ORBIT – LIVE IN ALABAMA (live '88)** [ ] [-]
– Viva la revolution / Let's go / Tango / England / Hurt / Put yourself in my hands / Change / Joker in the pack / Just like me / Rockers in rags / Chinese takeaway / Odd couple / Steam roller / Numbers / Bad boy / Ode to joy. *(cd+=)* – Crazy / Sensitive / Na na na / She's a rocker / Easy way out / Shake rattle bang your head / Get adicted / Straight jacket / Organized confusion / Calling calling / How sad / Viva / Rocking wrecker.

—— Disbanded around late 80's after completing below

—— Reformed in the 90's.

Anagram / not iss.

Sep 93. (cd) *(GRAMM 68)* **27** [ ] [-]
– Angel / Love sucks / Do it / That's happiness / Shangri-la / Football fairy story / Rossini / Breakdown / Give me more / F*** it up / G.I.R.L. / What am I to do / Rockers in rags / Let's dance / 7:27 / Bog / Come out to play (learn to play guitar with monkey & kid / Give me more (reprise) / Just wanna dance with you. *(re-iss. Feb97; same)*

– compilations, etc. –

Jan 85. (lp) *Fall Out; (FALLLP 021)* **THIS IS YOUR LIFE (1978-80)** (demos) [ ] [-]
(re-iss. Sep92 lp/cd; FALL LP/CD 021)

Jul 87. (lp) *Link; (LINKLP 010)* **LIVE AND LOUD!! – THE OFFICIAL BOOTLEG (live)** [ ] [-]

Nov 92. (cd) *Dojo; (DOJOCD 69)* **TOTALLY ADICTED** [ ] [-]
– Viva la revolution / Songs of praise / Get adicted / Sensitive / Just like me / Too young / Chinese takeaway / Joker in the pack / Steamroller / How sad / Let's go / Easy way out / Smart Alex / Troubadour / Tokyo / Crazy / Bad boy / Runaway / Come along / I wanna be sedated / Falling in love again / It's a laugh / Saturday night / Zimbabwe brothers are go.

Aug 93. (cd) *Great Expectations; (PIPCD 041)* **SMART ALEX** [ ] [-]
– Ode to joy / Smart Alex / Troubadour / Tokyo / California / Crazy / Bad boy / Jelly babies / Maybe maybe not / Rocking wrecker / Runaway / You're all fools.

Jun 94. (cd) *Anagram; (CDPUNK 33)* **THE COMPLETE ADICTS SINGLES COLLECTION** [ ] [-]

May 96. (cd) *Dojo; (DOJOCD 263)* **THE BEST OF THE ADICTS** [ ] [-]

Jul 97. (cd) *Cleopatra; (CLP 9963)* **ULTIMATRE ADICTION** [ ] [-]

May 98. (cd) *Captain Oi; (AHOYCD 088)* **SOUND OF MUSIC / SMART ALEX** [ ] [-]

Jun 98. (cd) *Anagram; (CDPUNK 105)* **THE VERY BEST OF THE ADICTS** [ ] [-]
– Easy way out / Straight jacket / Viva la revolution / Steamroller / Songs of praise / England / Get adicted / Chinese takeaway / Joker in the pack / How sad / Let's go / Bad boy / Tokyo / Odd couple / Smart Alex / Troubadour / Runaway / Champ Elysees / Angel / Love sucks.

ADOLESCENTS

Formed: Fullarton, Orange County, California, USA ... 1980 by TONY 'MONTANA' BRANDENBURG and STEVE 'SOTO' RODGERS (ex-AGENT ORANGE), who poached the other three members, FRANK AGNEW, his brother RIKK and CASEY ROYER (latter two also ex-DETOURS) from an embryonic version of SOCIAL DISTORTION. Emerging from the fertile US hardcore scene of the day, The ADOLESCENTS appeared very briefly on the 'Posh Boy' label via the ultra limited gold 7", 'AMOEBA'. Their follow-up single for 'Frontier', 'WELCOME TO REALITY', enjoyed a more conventional pressing as did the accompanying eponymous album in '81. However, this was to be their last set for some time as RIKK pursued a brief solo career, releasing the appropriately titled, 'ALL BY MYSELF' (1982) while simultaneously enjoying stints with CHRISTIAN DEATH and T.S.O.L. During a mid 80's hiatus, The ADOLESCENTS carried on with live work, ALFIE AGNEW filling the shoes of his absent brother. A self-financed comeback album, 'BRATS IN BATTALIONS' (1987), appeared as the hardcore scene was increasingly being influenced by the noisier end of the metal spectrum. It came as little surprise then, when RIKK, STEVE and Co. were snapped up by 'Triple X', who issued two further albums, 'BALBOA FUN*ZONE' (1988) and 'LIVE 1981 AND 1986', the former on European imprint, 'Roadrunner'. Although they subsequently disbanded at the turn of the decade, RIKK's second solo set – released as RIKK AGNEW'S YARD SALE – 'EMOTIONAL VOMIT' (1990) was an ADOLESCENTS album in all but name featuring as it did all three AGNEW siblings. • **Covered:** INSTANT JARMA (John Lennon) / SURF YOGI (Balk-Hardwick) / I GOT A RIGHT (Iggy Pop) / ALL DAY AND ALL OF THE NIGHT (Kinks).

Album rating: ADOLESCENTS (*5) / BRATS IN BATTALIONS (*5) / BALBOA FUN*ZONE (*5)

TONY 'MONTANA' BRANDENBURG – vocals / **RIKK AGNEW** – lead guitar (ex-SOCIAL DISTORTION, ex-DETOURS) / **FRANK AGNEW** – rhythm guitar (ex-SOCIAL DISTORTION) / **STEVE 'SOTO' RODGERS** – bass, vocals (ex-AGENT ORANGE) / **CASEY ROYER** – drums, vocals (ex-SOCIAL DISTORTION, ex-DETOURS)

not iss. / Posh Boy

1980. (ltd-7"gold) *<PBS 6>* **AMOEBA. /** [-] [ ]

not iss. / Frontier

1981. (7"ep) *<FRT 101>* **WELCOME TO REALITY / LOSING BATTLE. / NO WAY / THINGS START MOVING** [-] [ ]

1981. (lp) *<FLP 1003>* **ADOLESCENTS** [-] [ ]
– I hate children / Who is who / Wrecking crew / L.A. girl / Self destruct / Kids of the black hole / No way / Amoeba / Word attack / Rip it up / Democracy / No friends / Creatures. *(UK-iss.Apr88 on 'Weird Systems'; WS 32) (re-iss. Apr92 on 'Frontier' cd/c/lp; 4601-2L/4L/1L) (re-iss. May97 on 'Epitaph' cd/c/lp; E 0102-2/-4/-1)*

—— split soon after above, RIKK AGNEW released a solo album, 'ALL BY MYSELF' for 'Frontier' in 1982. The ADOLESCENTS reunited for live work, FRANK's place was taken by his other brother, **ALFIE AGNEW**

not iss. / S.O.S.

Sep 87. (lp) *<SOS 1001>* **BRATS IN BATTALIONS** [-] [ ]
– Brats in battalions / I love you / The liar / Things start moving / Do the Freddie / Losing battle / House of the rising sun / Peasant song / Skate Babylon / Welcome to reality / Marching with the Reich / I got a right / She wolf. *(UK-iss.1989 on 'Armageddon'; 083604) (cd-iss. 1995 on 'Triple X'; TX 51061CD)*

—— **RIKK + STEVE** recruited new members

Roadrunner / Triple X

Nov 88. (lp/cd) *(RR 9494-1/-2) <51010-1/-2>* **BALBOA FUN*ZONE** [ ] [ ]
– Balboa funzone / Just like before / Instant karma! / Alone against the world / Allen hotel / Frustrated / Genius in pain / It's tattoo time / Til' she comes down / Modern day Napoleon / I'm a victim / Balboa funzone (it's in your touch) / Runaway / She walks alone / Surf Yogi. *(cd-iss. Jul95 on 'Triple X'; TX 51010CD)*

—— disbanded in 1989, although RIKK AGNEW'S YARD SALE (with his brothers) released one album, 'EMOTIONAL VOMIT' for 'Triple X' in 1990.

– others, etc. –

1989. (cd) *Triple X; <51015>* **LIVE 1981 AND 1986 (live)** [-] [ ]
– Amoeba / Who is who / No friends / Welcome to reality / Self destruct / Things start moving / Word attack / Losing battle / I got a right / No way / Liar / Rip it up / L.A. girl / Wrecking crew / Creatures / Kids of the black hole / Peasant song / Do the Eddy / Liar / Who is who / Wrecking crew.

Jan 98. (cd) *Amsterdamned; (51225-2) / Triple X; <51225>* **RETURN TO THE BLACK HOLE (live)** [ ] [ ] Sep97
– No way / Who is who / Word attack / Self destruct / L.A. girl / Brats in battalions / Welcome to reality / Wrecking crew / Do the Eddy / I love you / Losing battle / Creatures / All day and all of the night / Rip it up / Amoeba / Kids of the black hole / I got a right.

ADORABLE

Formed: Coventry, England ... 1991 by Polish-born frontman, PIOTR FIJALKOWSKI, plus ROBERT DILLAN, KEVIN GRITTON and WILL. Signing to 'Creation' records, these ALAN McGEE proteges issued their debut EP, 'SUNSHINE SMILE', in the Spring '92. Taking up where ECHO & THE BUNNYMEN and PSYCHEDELIC FURS left off, ADORABLE fitted nicely into the void previously filled by the "baggy" and "shoegazing" scenes. Although never quite breaking out of the indie chart ghetto, the band followed up a further clutch of singles with a debut album, 'AGAINST PERFECTION' (1993), which scraped into the Top 75. However, after only three years in the indie limelight (and a second album, 'FAKE' – 1994), they disbanded, going out with a damp squib rather than a bang with a gig in Brussels. PIOTR, meanwhile, dreamed of a comeback that would propel him to stardom, although his time leading a synth duo with a female vocalist came to nothing. Late in '96, PIOTR (now PETE), together with his guitar-playing sibling, KRYZ, slowly evolved into a band after finding new recruits, SIMON DUNFORD, BOB BROWN and CHRIS PARSONS. Naming themselves, POLAK, a derogatory term used for a Polish person, PETE and Co. bounced back in 1998 with a cracking pop single, appropriately titled, '2MINUTES45'.

Album rating: AGAINST PERFECTION (*6) / FAKE (*5)

PIOTR FIJALKOWSKI – vocals, guitar / **ROBERT DILLAN** – guitar / **WILL** – bass / **KEVIN GRITTON** – drums

Creation / SBK-Capitol

Apr 92. (7") *(CRE 127) <19780>* **SUNSHINE SMILE. / A TO FADE IN** [ ] [ ]
(12"+=)(cd-s+=) *(CRE 127T)(CRESCD 127)* – Sunburnt.

Jul 92. (7") *(CRE 133)* **I'LL BE YOUR SAINT. / SUMMERSIDE** [ ] [-]
(12"+=)(cd-s+=) *(CRE 133T)(CRESCD 133)* – Self-imperfectionist.

Oct 92. (7") *(CRE 140)* **HOMEBOY. / PILOT** [ ] [-]
(12"+=)(cd-s+=) *(CRE 140T)(CRESCD 140)* – Contented eye.

Jan 93. (12"ep)(cd-ep) *(CRE 153T)(CRESCD 153)* **SISTINE CHAPEL CEILING /** [ ] [-]

Mar 93. (cd/lp)(c) *(CRE CD/LP 138)(C-CRE 138) <81416>* **AGAINST PERFECTION** [70] [ ] May93
– Glorious / Favourite fallen idol / A to fade in / I know you too well / Homeboy / Sistine chapel ceiling / Cut #2 / Crash sight / Still life / Breathless.

Apr 93. (12"ep)(cd-ep) *(CRE 159T)(CRESCD 159)* **FAVOURITE FALLEN IDOL /** [ ] [-]

May 94. (12"ep)(cd-ep) *(CRE 172T)(CRESCD 172)* **KANGAROO COURT. / DINOSAUR NO.3 / BALLROOM** [ ] [-]

Aug 94. (7") *(CRE 177)* **VENDETTA. /** [ ] [-]
(cd-s+=) *(CRESCD 177)* –

Sep 94. (cd/lp)(c) *(CRE CD/LP 165)(C-CRRE 165)* **FAKE** [ ] [-]
– Feed me / Vendetta / Man in a suitcase / Submarine / Lettergo / Kangaroo court / Radio days / Go easy on her / Road movie / Have you seen the light.

POLAK

PETE FIJALKOWSKI – vocals, guitar / **KRYZ FIJALKOWSKI** – guitar (ex-BARDOTS) / **SIMON DUNFORD** – keyboards / **BOB BROWN** – bass / **CHRIS PARSONS** – drums

Generic | not iss.

Jun 98. (cd-s) *(GEN 0245)* **2MINUTES45. /** | | -
Oct 98. (cd-s) *(GEN 0244)* **I'M SICK / I'LL LIE TO YOU / PRIVATE GOD** | | -

ADRENALIN O.D.

Formed: New Jersey, USA . . . Autumn 1981 by PAUL RICHARD, JIM FOSTER, JACK STEEPLES and DAVE SCOTT. Their first effort, the 1983 self-financed mini-set, 'LET'S BARBEQUE WITH . . .', instigated a series of fun hardcore releases with a distinctly adolescent sense of humour. Unlike many bands of their ilk, ADRENALIN O.D. maintained a fairly stable line-up throughout their career, FOSTER's replacement by guitarist BRUCE WINGATE prior to their debut album proper, 'THE WACKY HI-JINKS OF . . .' (1985) the only minor hiccup. Early '87 saw the release of the album, 'HUMUNGOUSFUNGUSAMONGUS', the title a shining example of ADRENALIN O.D.'s boisterous penchant for a play on words. Two further sets were sighted in the shops at the turn of the decade, 'CRUISING WITH ELVIS IN BIGFOOT'S UFO' and 'ISHTAR', although these failed to benefit from a more commercial approach. • **Covered:** WE WILL ROCK YOU + SHEER HEART ATTACK (Queen) / DETROIT ROCK CITY (Kiss).

Album rating: THE WACKY HI-JINKS OF . . . (*5) / HUMUNGOUSFUNGUSAMONGUS (*7) / CRUISING WITH ELVIS IN BIGFOOT'S UFO (*6) / ISHTAR (*3) / THEME FROM AN I (*3) / SITTIN' PRETTY (*4)

PAUL RICHARD – vocals, guitar / **JIM FOSTER** – guitar / **JACK STEEPLES** – bass / **DAVE SCOTT** – drums

Rough Justice | Buy Our Records

1983. (12"ep) **LET'S BARBEQUE WITH ADRENALIN O.D. EP** | - |

—— **BRUCE WINGATE** – guitar; repl. FOSTER

—— **KEITH HARTEL** – bass; repl. STEEPLES

1984. (lp) *<BOR12 002>* **THE WACKY HI-JINKS OF . . .** | - |
– A.O.D. vs Godzilla / Middle aged whore / etc.

1985. (7"ep) **split EP** | - |
– We will rock you / etc.

Jan 87. (lp) *(JUST 5) <BOR12 008>* **HUMUNGOUSFUNGUSAMONGUS** | | Nov86
– A.O.D. vs son of Godzilla / Office building / Tuppe answer / Pope – on a rope / Fishin' musician / Pizza 'n' beer / Bugs / Youth blimp / Commercial cuts / Survive / Masterpiece / Crowd control / Velvet Elvis / F**k the neighbours / Surfin' Jew / Bruce's lament / The nice song.

1988. (10"ep) *(10KORE 105)* **THEME FROM AN IMAGINARY MIDGET WESTERN. / DETROIT ROCK CITY / COFFIN CRUISER** | |

Oct 88. (lp) *(JUST 12M) <BOR 018>* **CRUISING WITH ELVIS IN BIGFOOT'S UFO** | |
– If this is Tuesday . . . it must be Walla-Walla / Bulimic food fight / Swindel / Stew / Second to none / My mother can't drive / Theme from an imaginary midget western / Something about . . . Amy Carter / Flip side unclassified / Baby elephant walk.

Restless | Restless

1990. (cd/c) *<(72380-2/-4)>* **ISHTAR** | |
– My achin' back / Twenty dollar bill / Sheer heart attack / Obvious toupee / Tiny fingers / What a way to go / Big time major love thang / Paul A Roid / All right Tokyo / Joe from Lodi / Dave A Roid / Bad karma merchant.

not iss. | Buy Our Records

1992. (cd) *<BOR 016>* **THEME FROM AN I** | - |

not iss. | Grand Theft Auto

Jan 96. (cd) *<GFA 9>* **SITTIN' PRETTY** | - |
– Status symbol / Hijack / Suburbia / Old people talk loud / Trans am / House husband / Scare tactics / Mischief night / Status symbol / Workd War 4 / Hijack / White hassle / Brady bunch / A.O.D. vs Godzilla / White hassle / Small talk / Going to a funeral / Corporate Disneyland / Trans am (the saga continues) / Sightseeing / Middle-aged whore / World War 4 / Clean and jerk / Sleep / Rah-jah / Rock'n'roll gas station / Paul's not home / Suburbia / Trans am / Going to a funeral / New Years Eve / World War 4 / Midle-aged whore / Clean and jerk / Infiltrate the state / Masterpiece / Status symbol / Velvet Elvis / Crowd control / Rah-jah / Rather be asleep / Sightseeing / We will rock you.

ADULT NET

Formed: Manchester, England . . . late 1984 by native New Yorker, BRIX E. SMITH (aka LAURA ELISE), wife at the time of FALL mainman, MARK E. SMITH. She had joined the aforesaid Mancunian indie outfit as guitarist/co-singer in 1982, forming the ADULT NET as her extracurricular outfit. With help from fellow FALL musicians, MARSHA SCHOFIELD (also once a member of BRIX's former group, BANDA BRATSING) and SIMON ROGERS, the sultry retro-chick made her debut on 'Beggars Banquet' with a cover of the Strawberry Alarm Clock's late 60's US chart-topper, 'INCENSE AND PEPPERMINTS', in April '85. A follow-up single, 'EDIE', dealt with the life of the infamous VELVET UNDERGROUND sidekick/dancer, EDIE SEDGWICK. Two further commercially-orientated 45's appeared in quick succession, the latter of which, 'WAKING UP IN THE SUN', featured a cover of Shangri-la's '(REMEMBER) WALKING IN THE SAND' on its flip side. In a concerted attempt to break into the mainstream, she transformed her ADULT NET into an indie supergroup of sorts with the help of CRAIG GANNON (ex-AZTEC CAMERA), JAMES ELLER (ex-JULIAN COPE) and CLEM BURKE (ex-BLONDIE). Landing a major deal with 'Fontana' late in '88 (along with The FALL), BRIX and Co released a comeback single, 'TAKE ME', although it was to be yuppie violinist, NIGEL KENNEDY, who would accept her offer, not MARK E whom she would subsequently separate from. Having now also split from The FALL, she/ADULT NET had their first taste of chart success when 'WHERE WERE YOU' broke into the Top 75. The accompanying long awaited debut album, 'THE HONEY TANGLE' (1989), failed to give them the expected breakthrough despite being an enjoyable set of dreamy, psychedelic indie-pop. By this point divorced from MARK E. she was a surprise guest on long-running TV show, 'This Is Your Life', as the girlfriend of the aforementioned KENNEDY. The first half of the 90's were something of a musical wilderness, although she subsequently buried the proverbial hatchet with MARK E and rejoined The FALL.

Album rating: THE HONEY TANGLE (*5)

BRIX E. SMITH – vocals, guitar (of The FALL); with **MARSHA SCHOFIELD** – keyboards, vocals / **SIMON ROGERS** – bass (both of FALL)

Beggars Banquet | not iss.

Apr 85. (7"/12") *(BEG 137/+T)* **INCENSE AND PEPPERMINTS. / SEARCHING FOR THE NOW** | | -
Nov 85. (7") *(BEG 148)* **EDIE. / GET AROUND** | | -
(12"+=) *(BEG 148T)* – Phantom power.
Jun 86. (7"/12") *(BEG 164/+T)* **WHITE NIGHT (STARS SAY GO). / NAUGHTY OF ME** | | -
Aug 86. (7"/12") *(BEG 171/+T)* **WAKING UP IN THE SUN. / (REMEMBER) WALKING IN THE SAND** | | -

—— **BRIX** recruited new band; **CRAIG GANNON** – guitar (ex-SMITHS, ex-BLUEBELLS, ex-AZTEC CAMERA, etc.) / **JAMES ELLER** – bass (ex-JULIAN COPE, + of THE THE) / **CLEM BURKE** – drums (ex-BLONDIE, ex-RAMONES) / **CRAIG LEON** – keyboards, producer

Fontana | not iss.

Mar 89. (7") *(BRX 1)* **TAKE ME. / SEA OF RAIN** | | -
(10"blue+=/12"+=/cd-s+=) *(BRX 1-10/12/CD)* – Going nowhere/ Incense and peppermints.
May 89. (7"/10"white) *(BRX 2/+10)* **WHERE WERE YOU. / OVER THE RIVER** | 66 | -
Jul 89. (lp/c/cd) *(838125-1/-4/-2)* **THE HONEY TANGLE** | | -
– Take me / August / Waking up in the Sun / Spin this web / Sad / Where were you / Honey tangle / Tiffany Tuesday / Tomorrow morning daydream / It's the way.
Jul 89. (7"/7"pic-d) *(BRX/+P 3)* **WAKING UP IN THE SUN. / AUGUST** | | -
(12"+=/cd-s+=) *(BRX 3-12/CD)* – (Remember) Walking in the sand.

—— lost her recording contract not long after above, although she found a new beau in NIGEL KENNEDY. She subsequently rejoined The FALL later in the 90's.

ADVENTURES

Formed: London, England . . . early 1984 by songwriters TERRY SHARPE and PAT GRIBBEN, two ex-members of Belfast's pop-punk outfit, The STARJETS. For a few years from 1978, this quartet (with also PAUL BOWEN and SEAN MARTIN) delivered an album and a handful of 45's including near UK Top 50 hit, 'WAR STORIES'. When they split (after a brief stint as TANGO BRIGADE), the pair moved to the capital, forming The ADVENTURES sextet with GRIBBEN's wife EILEEN, their old roadie, 'GERARD 'SPUD' MURPHY, TONY AYRE and PAUL CROWDER. Signed to 'Chrysalis', the group had a few minor pop hits ('ANOTHER SILENT DAY' and 'FEEL THE RAINDROPS'), although their album, 'THEODORE AND FRIENDS' (1984/85), disappointed their growing fanbase. Retiring from the scene for a few years, The ADVENTURES resurfaced on 'Elektra' records early in 1988. Their comeback single, 'BROKEN LAND', with its beautiful harmonies and intelligent lyrics cracked the UK Top 20 with its parent album, 'THE SEA OF LOVE', nearly following the same route. However, they were all but forgotten a few years later when their third set, 'TRADING SECRETS WITH THE MOON' (1990), failed to achieve any degree of success.

Album rating: THEODORE AND FRIENDS (*4) / THE SEA OF LOVE (*5) / TRADING SECRETS WITH THE MOON (*4) / LIONS & TIGERS & BEARS (*3) / Starjets: GOD BLESS THE STARJETS (*5)

STARJETS

TERRY SHARPE – vocals / **LIAM L'ESTRANGE** (b. PAT GRIBBEN) – guitar / **PAUL BOWEN** – bass / **SEAN MARTIN** – drums

Epic | Portrait

Jan 79. (7") *(EPC 6968)* **IT REALLY DOESN'T MATTER. / SCHOOLDAYS** | | -
Mar 79. (7") *(EPC 7123)* **RUN WITH THE PACK. / WATCHOUT** | | -
Jun 79. (d7") *(EPC 7417)* **TEN YEARS. / ONE MORE WORD // ANY DANGER LOVE /** | | -
Jul 79. (lp) *(EPC 83534) <JR 36245>* **GOD BLESS THE STARJETS** <US-title 'STARJETS'> | |
– Schooldays / Any danger love / Ten years / Run with the pack / What a life / Smart boys / It's a shame / I'm so glad / War is over / War stories / Sitting on top of the world.
Aug 79. (7") *(EPC 7770)* **WAR STORIES. / DO THE PUSH** | 51 |
Nov 79. (7") *(EPC 7986) <2-70036>* **SCHOOLDAYS. / WHAT A LIFE** | |
Mar 80. (7") *(EPC 8276)* **SHIRALEO. / STAND BY NINETEEN** | | -

—— split in June 1980

ADVENTURES

TERRY SHARPE – vocals / **PAT GRIBBEN** – guitar / **EILEEN GRIBBEN** – vocals / **GERARD 'SPUD' MURPHY** – guitar / **TONY AYRE** – bass / **PAUL CROWDER** – drums

Chrysalis Chrysalis

Aug 84. (7") *(CHS 2000)* **ANOTHER SILENT DAY. / NOWHERE NEAR ME** 71
(12"+=) *(CHS12 2000)* – ('A'version).
(d7"+=) *(CHSD 2000)* – Token.

Nov 84. (7") *(CHS 2001)* **SEND MY HEART. / THESE CHILDREN** 62
(12"+=) *(CHS12 2001)* – Life during wartime.

Dec 84. (lp/c) *(CHR/ZCHR 1488)* **THEODORE AND FRIENDS** <US-title 'THE ADVENTURES'>
– Always / Feel the raindrops / Send my heart / Don't tell me / Two rivers / Another silent day / When the world turns upside down / Love in chains / Hollywood / These children. *(re-iss. May85; same) (cd-iss. Jun88; CCD 1488)*

Jun 85. (7") *(AD 1)* **FEEL THE RAINDROPS. / NOWHERE NEAR ME** 58
(12"+=) *(ADX 1)* – Tristesse en vitese.

Sep 85. (7") *(ADU 1)* **TWO RIVERS. / LOVE IN CHAINS**
(12"+=) *(ADUX 1)* – Always (live).

Elektra Elektra

Mar 88. (7"/12") *(EKR 69/+T)* <69414> **BROKEN LAND. / DON'T STAND ON ME** 20 95

May 88. (lp/c)(cd) *(EKT 45/+C)(960772-2)* <60772> **THE SEA OF LOVE** 30 Apr88
– Drowning in the sea of love / Broken land / You don't have to cry anymore / The trip to the Bountiful (when the rain comes down) / Heaven knows which way / Hold me now / The sound of summer / When your heart was young / One step from Heaven.

Jun 88. (7") *(EKR 76)* **DROWNING IN THE SEA OF LOVE. / STAY AWAY** 44
(12"+=/cd-s+=) *(EKR 76 T/CD)* – The Curragh of Kildare.

Oct 88. (7") *(EKR 80)* **ONE STEP FROM HEAVEN. / THE TRIP TO THE BOUNTIFUL (WHEN THE RAIN COMES DOWN)**
(12"+=/cd-s+=) *(EKR 80 T/CD)* – Instant karma.

Oct 89. (7") *(EKR 98)* **WASHINGTON DECEASED. / NEVER GONNA CHANGE**
(12"+=/cd-s+=) *(EKR 98 T/CD)* – Heaven knows which way.

Feb 90. (7") *(EKR 106)* **YOUR GREATEST SHADE OF BLUE. / PUT ME TOGETHER AGAIN**
(12"+=/cd-s+=) *(EKR 106 T/CD)* – Break me down.

Mar 90. (lp/c)(cd) *(EKT 63/+C)(<7559 60871-2>)* **TRADING SECRETS WITH THE MOON** 64
– Your greatest shade of blue / Scarlet / Washington deceased / Don't blame it on the moon / Bright new morning / Loves lost town / Desert rose / Hey Magdalene / Sweet burning love / Never gonna change / Put me together again.

—— now without EILEEN and SPUD

Polydor Polydor

Jun 92. (7") *(PO 211)* **RAINING ALL OVER THE WORLD. /** 68
(12"+=/cd-s+=) *(PO Z/CD 211)* –

May 93. (cd/c) *(512858-2/-4)* **LIONS & TIGERS & BEARS**

—— disbanded later in 1993

ADVERTS

Formed: London, England . . . late 1976 by singer TV SMITH and one of punk's first female icons, the sultry GAYE ADVERT. Enlisting HOWARD PICKUP and LAURIE DRIVER, the group gigged constantly at the infamous Covent Garden punk club, The Roxy, appearing on the 1977 compilation, 'Live At The Roxy' with their first recording, 'BORED TEENAGERS'. Subsequently signed for a one-off single deal with 'Stiff' through the help of The DAMNED, the band released the self explanatory 'ONE CHORD WONDERS' in Spring '77. While the track generated some interest, it was the amphetamine rush of 'GARY GILMORE'S EYES' which launched them into the UK Top 20. Based on the request of the notorious death row inmate to have his eyes donated to science, the single predictably caused a minor furore in the tabloid press. Yet despite this publicity and major label muscle courtesy of CBS subsidiary 'Bright', both a third single, 'NO TIME TO BE 21' and debut album, 'CROSSING THE RED SEA WITH THE ADVERTS' (1978) barely scraped into the Top 40. The general concensus was that the band had failed to capture the energy of their live shows in the studio and an increasingly mainstream sound and attitude ensured that 'CAST OF THOUSANDS' (1979) and its attendant singles would sink without trace. Line-up changes dogged the band as they went through a succession of drummers Spinal Tap-style, even recruiting a former MIKE OLDFIELD synth player (TIM CROSS) and blowing the remnants of their fast dissipating street cred. Following the tragic electrocution of manager, Michael Dempsey, TV and GAYE finally threw in the towel in late '79 and embarked on solo projects. SMITH formed TV SMITH'S EXPLORERS before ploughing a singer/songwriter vein, releasing a debut solo effort, 'CHANNEL 5', in 1983. Absent from the music scene for most of the 80's, SMITH re-emerged in 1992 on 'Cooking Vinyl' with 'MARCH OF THE GIANTS'.

Album rating: CROSSING THE RED SEA WITH THE ADVERTS (*7) / CAST OF THOUSANDS (*4)

TV SMITH (b. TIM, Cornwall, England) – vocals / **GAYE ADVERT** – bass (b.29 Aug'56) / **HOWARD PICKUP** – guitar / **LAURIE DRIVER** – drums

Stiff not iss.

Apr 77. (7") *(BUY 13)* **ONE CHORD WONDERS. / QUICKSTEP** –

Anchor not iss.

Aug 77. (7") *(ANC 1043)* **GARY GILMORE'S EYES. / BORED TEENAGERS** 18 –

Oct 77. (7") *(ANC 1047)* **SAFETY IN NUMBERS. / WE WHO WAIT** –

Bright-CBS not iss.

Jan 78. (7") *(BR 1)* **NO TIME TO BE 21. / NEW DAY DAWNING** 38 –

Feb 78. (lp,red-lp) *(BRL 2001)* **CROSSING THE RED SEA WITH THE ADVERTS** 38 –
– One chord wonders / Bored teenagers / New church / On the roof / New boys / Bomb site boy / Mo time to be 21 / Safety in numbers / Drowning men / On wheels / Great British mistake / Gary Gilmore's eyes. *(re-iss. Oct81 & Sep83 [red-lp] on 'Butt'; ALSO 2) (re-iss. Dec88 on 'Bright' cd/lp; CD+/BUL 2)*

—— **JOHN TOWE** – drums (ex-ALTERNATIVE TV, ex-GENERATION X) repl. DRIVER (Spring'78) **ROD LATTER** – drums (ex-MANIACS, ex-RINGS) repl. TOWE

R.C.A. not iss.

Nov 78. (7") *(PB 5128)* **TELEVISION'S OVER. / BACK FROM THE DEAD** –

Jun 79. (7") *(PB 5160)* **MY PLACE. / NEW CHURCH (live)** –

Sep 79. (7") *(PB 5191)* **CAST OF THOUSANDS. / I WILL WALK YOU HOME** –

—— added **TIM CROSS** – keyboards, synthesizers (of MIKE OLDFIELD)

Oct 79. (lp/c) *(PL/PK 25246)* **CAST OF THOUSANDS** –
– Cast of thousands / The adverts / My place / Male assault / Television's over / Fate of criminals / I looked at the Sun / Love songs / I surrender / I will walk you home. *(cd-iss. Feb98 on 'Anagram'; CDPUNK 102)*

—— **PAUL MARTINEZ** repl. HOWARD (he died in 1997) / his brother **RICK** repl. ROD. After manager MICHAEL DEMPSEY was electrocuted to death, TV, GAYE and TIM decided to split late 1979.

– compilations, others, etc. –

May 83. (7"m) *Bright-CBS; (BULB 1)* **GARY GILMORE'S EYES / WE WHO WAIT / NEW DAY DAWNING** –

Oct 87. (12"ep) *Strange Fruit; (SFPS 034)* **THE PEEL SESSIONS (25.4.77)** –
– Quickstep / Gary Gilmore's eyes / Bored teenagers / New boys / One chord wonders.

Nov 90. (cd/c/lp) *Receiver; (RR CD/LC/LP 136)* **LIVE AT THE ROXY (live)** –

Oct 97. (lp) *Get Back; (GET 24)* **WONDERS DON'T CARE** –

Jun 98. (lp) *Get Back; (GET 30)* **THE ADVERTS SINGLES COLLECTION** –

TV SMITH'S EXPLORERS

were formed late 79 by **TV** and **TIM CROSS, JOHN TOWE**, plus **ERIC RUSSELL** – guitar / **COLIN STONER** – bass (ex-DOCTORS OF MADNESS)

—— (Mar'80) **MEL WESSON** repl. CROSS who rejoined MIKE OLDFIELD / **DAVE SINCLAIR** (of LONDON ZOO) repl. TOWE, who later joined UK SUBS

Big Beat not iss.

Nov 80. (7") *(NS 64)* **TOMAHAWK CRUISE. / SEE EUROPE** –
(re-iss. Jan81 on 'Chiswick'; CHIS 140)

Kaleidoscope Epic

Apr 81. (7") *(KRLA 1162)* **THE SERVANT. / LOOKING DOWN ON LONDON** –
(ltd.c-s+=) *(KRLA40 1162)* – Walk in a straight line.

Jun 81. (7") *(KRLA 1359)* **HAVE FUN. / IMAGINATION** –

Jul 81. (lp/c) *(KRL/40 85087)* **THE LAST WORDS OF THE GREAT EXPLORER**
– I live for everything / The servant / Have fun / Walk away / The last words of the great explorer / Imagination / The easy way / The unwelcome guest / The perfect life. *(w/ free 7") (SXPS 119) (c+=)* – WALK IN A STRAIGHT LINE. / WORLD OF MY OWN

Oct 81. (7") *(KRLA 1590)* **THE PERFECT LIFE. / IMAGINATION** –

—— (Oct'81) disbanded

TV SMITH

went solo, recruiting yet again **TIM CROSS** plus **TIM RENWICK** – guitar (ex-MIKE OLDFIELD, ex-SUTHERLAND BROTHERS)

Expulsion not iss.

May 83. (7") *(OUT 2)* **WAR FEVER. / LIES** –

Jun 83. (lp) *(EXIT 4)* **CHANNEL FIVE** –

PRODUCTION HOUSE

were group formed by same line-up above.

Production House not iss.

May 85. (7") *(PH 1)* **COMING ROUND. / WOODPECKER** –

CHEAP

were formed late'86 by **TV** plus **SIMON BUDD** – drums / **ANDY BENNY** – bass (ex-SLEAZE) / **MIK HESLIN** – guitar (ex-CHAOTIC DISCHORD)

Donated a few songs to Various Artists albums before releasing 7" in '89.
MARTIN DENTZ – drums repl. BUDD (in 1988)

Deltic not iss.

May 90. (7") *(DELT 4)* **THIRD TERM. / BURIED BY THE MACHINE** –

TV SMITH

Cooking Vinyl not iss.

Jul 92. (cd/c/lp) *(COOK CD/C/LP 047)* **MARCH OF THE GIANTS** –
– Lion and the lamb / March of the giants / Can't pay won't pay / Atlantic tunnel / Haves and have-nots / Straight and narrow / Free world / Ship in a bottle / Empty wallet / Useless / Runaway train driver / Borderline. *(re-iss. Mar94 cd; same)*

Humbug not iss.

Jun 93. (cd; by T.V. SMITH'S CHEAP) *(BAH 5)* **RIP . . . EVERYTHING MUST GO!** –

– Leisure time / My string will snap / New ways are best / Free world / Silicon Valley holiday / Luxury in exile / Buried by the machine / Ghosts / Ready for the axe to drop / The newshound / Beauty treatment / The Lord's Prayer.

Feb 95. (cd) *(BAH 21)* **THE IMMORTAL RICH** [ ] [-]
– The immortal rich / Living world / Walk the plank / We want the road / High society / Head on! dear! / The day we caught the big fish / Thin green line / Let 'em go / In there / Earth 2.

May 96. (cd-s) *(HUM 8)* **THIN GREEN LINE /** [ ] [-]

AERIAL-M (see under ⇒ SLINT)

AFGHAN WHIGS

Formed: Denver, Colorado, USA . . . Autumn '86, by GREG DULLI and RICK McCOLLUM who met in a prison. The pair moved to Cincinatti, Ohio, after signing for Seattle based indie label 'Sub Pop' in 1989, their independently released debut set, 'BIG TOP HALLOWEEN' (1988), having caused something of a stir with its proto-grunge exhortations. Produced by Seattle maestro, Jack Endino, the album, 'UP IN IT', worked around the same formula, hinting at their wider country and soul influences. After a further set for 'Sub Pop', 'CONGREGATION' (1992), and an EP of soul covers, 'UPTOWN AVONDALE', the group were plucked from the mire of grunge cultdom by 'Elektra' in the major label stampede following NIRVANA's success. A former film student, DULLI cannily negotiated the right to creative control over the band's videos, his acting ambitions duly realised in 1994 when he scored the part of JOHN LENNON in Stuart Sutcliffe's story, 'Backbeat'. The 'WHIGS major label debut, 'GENTLEMEN', pushed all the right critical buttons, fleshing out their grungy noir-soul sound against a typically hard-bitten lyrical background. Although the record surprisingly failed to make the US charts, it scored a Top 60 placing in the UK. DULLI's rendition of Barry White's 'CAN'T GET ENOUGH OF YOUR LOVE', was an indication of where AFGHAN WHIGS were headed with 'BLACK LOVE'. An even more soul-centric offering, the album almost scraped into the British Top 40, the band now signed to 'Mute' (still on 'Elektra' US). 'Columbia' took up the reins for er . . . 1998's '1965', a celebration of rock music's debt to the power of sex. Recorded in New Orleans, the record was hailed as their long promised masterpiece, a writhing, sweaty slab of post-grunge voodoo soul. • **Songwriters:** DULLI, some McCOLLUM except; covers by MY WORLD IS EMPTY WITHOUT YOU (Diana Ross & The Supremes) / (Al Green) / BAND OF GOLD (Freda Payne) / I KEEP COMING BACK (Austell-Graham) / IF I ONLY HAD A HEART (from 'Wizard Of Oz') / CREEP (Radiohead) / LITTLE GIRL BLUE (Hart-Rodgers) / MR. SUPERLOVE (Ass Ponys).

Album rating: BIG TOP HALLOWEEN (*4) / UP IN IT (*6) / CONGREGATION (*7) / GENTLEMEN (*7) / BLACK LOVE (*6) / 1965 (*8)

GREG DULLI – vocals, guitar / **RICK McCOLLUM** – guitar / **JOHN CURLEY** – bass / **STEVE EARLE** – drums

not iss. Ultrasuede

Oct 88. (lp) *<001>* **BIG TOP HALLOWEEN** [-] [ ]
– Here comes Jesus / In my town / Priscilla's wedding day / Push / Scream / But listen / Big top Halloween / Life in a day / Sammy / Doughball / Back o' the line / Greek is extra.

Sub Pop Sub Pop

Aug 89. (7") *<SP 32>* **I AM THE STICKS. / WHITE TRASH PARTY** [-] [ ]

Apr 90. (cd/c/lp/orange-lp) *<SP 60>* **UP IN IT** [-] [ ]
– Retarded / White trash party / Hated / Southpaw / Amphetamines and coffee / Now can we begin / You my flower / Son of the south / I know your secret. *(cd/c+=)* – I am the sticks. *(UK-iss.Aug90 on 'Glitterhouse'; GR 0092) (cd re-iss. Sep98; SPCD 60)*

Oct 90. (7",7"red) *<SP 84>* **SISTER BROTHER. / HEY CUZ** [-] [ ]

Dec 90. (12"ep) *<(SP 4-115)>* **THE RETARD EP** [ ] [ ]
– Retarded / Sister brother / Hey cuz / Turning in two. *(cd-ep May93; SPCD 4-115)*

Jan 92. (lp/cd) *<(SP 183/+CD)>* **CONGREGATION** [ ] [ ]
– Her against me / I'm her slave / Turn on the water / Conjure me / Kiss the floor / Congregation / This is my confession / Dedicate it / The temple / Let me lie to you / Tonight. *(cd re-iss. Sep98; same)*

Jan 92. (12"ep) *<(SP 187)>* **TURN ON THE WATER. / MILES IZ DEAD / DELTA KONG** [ ] [ ]
(cd-ep+=) *(SPCD 187)* – Chalk outline.

May 92. (7"white,7"lavender) *<(SP 142)>* **CONJURE ME. / MY WORLD IS EMPTY WITHOUT YOU** [ ] [ ]
(12"+=)(cd-s+=) *<(SP 42)><(SP 203CD)>* – My flower.

Oct 92. (7"ep) *<(SP 216)>* **UPTOWN AVONDALE EP: BAND OF GOLD. / COME SEE ABOUT ME** [ ] [ ]
(12"+=) *<(SP 215)>* – True love travels on a gravel road / Beware.
(cd-s++=) *<(SP 215CD)>* – Rebirth of the cool.
(above release could have been issued earlier in US, early 1990)

Blast First Elektra

Sep 93. (7") *(BFFP 89)* **GENTLEMEN. / MR. SUPERLOVE** [ ] [ ]
(12"+=/cd-s+=) *(BFFP 89 T/CD)* – The dark end of the street.

Oct 93. (lp/cd) *(BFFP 90/+CD) <7559 61501-2>* **GENTLEMEN** [58] [ ]
– If I were going / Gentlemen / Be sweet / Debonair / When we two parted / Fountain and fairfax / What jail is like / My curse / Now you know / I keep coming back / Brother Woodrow – Closing prayer. *(lp w/free 7"ep)* – ROT. / TONIGHT

—— guests on the album: **HAROLD CHICHESTER** – keyboards / **BARB HUNTER** – cello / **JODY STEPHENS** – vocals / **MARCY MAYS** – vocals

Feb 94. (7"ep/12"ep/cd-ep) *(BFFP 95/+T/CD)* **BROKEN PROMISES EP** [ ] [ ]
– Debonair / My curse / Little girl blue / Ready.
(cd-ep) *(BFFP 95CDL)* – ('A'side) / Rot / I keep coming back / Tonight.

—— In Mar'94, 'MR.SUPERLOVE' was issued on B-side of ASS PONY's single on 'Monocat'.

Aug 94. (7"ep/10"ep/cd-ep) *(BFFP 96/+T/CD) <61708>* **WHAT JAIL IS LIKE EP** (some live) [ ] [ ]
– What jail is like / Mr. Superlove / Dark end of the street / Little girl blue / Gentlemen / Now you know / My world is empty without you.

Mute Elektra

Feb 96. (10"ep/cd-ep) *(10/CD MUTE 128)* **HONKY'S LADDER E.P.** [ ] [ ]
– Honky's ladder / Blame, etc. / If I only had a heart / Creep.

Mar 96. (cd/c/lp) *(CD/C+/STUMM 143) <61896>* **BLACK LOVE** [41] [79]
– Crime scene part one / My enemy / Double day / Blame, etc. / Step into the light / Going to town / Honky's ladder / Night by candlelight / Bulletproof / Summer's kiss / Faded.

Aug 96. (cd-ep) *(CDMUTE 199)* **GOING TO TOWN / GOING TO TOWN – MODERN ROCK LIVE / YOU'VE CHANGED / I WANT TO GO TO SLEEP / MOON RIVER** [ ] [ ]

Columbia Columbia

Oct 98. (7") *(666576-7)* **SOMETHIN' HOT / MISS WORLD** [ ] [ ]
(cd-s+=) *(666576-2)* – Papa was a rascal.

Oct 98. (cd/c) *(491486-2/-4) <69450>* **1965** [ ] [ ]
– Somethin' hot / Crazy / Uptown again / Sweet son of a bitch / 66 / City soleil / John the baptist / Slide song / Neglekted / Omerta / Vampire Lanois.

AFRAID OF MICE

Formed: Liverpool, England . . . late 1978 out of BEANO, by PHILIP FRANZ JONES, the only mainstay of this initially unstable group. Original drummer CLIVE GEE moved over to keyboards with the arrival of TERRY STERLING, the line-up completed by SHAUN McLAUGHLIN who replaced JEFF KELLY. Part of the much lauded Merseyside new wave/alternative scene, AFRAID OF MICE signed to 'Charisma' (home of GENESIS!) and released a series of spiky pop-punk singles between 1981 and '82. However, after the release of their eponymous debut set, the outfit receded back into obscurity as PHIL moved on to form TWO'S COMPANY (a duo that would subsequently evolve into UP AD RUNNING).

Album rating: AFRAID OF MICE (*5)

PHILIP FRANZ JONES – guitar, vocals (ex-NEXT) / **CLIVE GEE** – keyboards / **SAM BREW** – guitar / **SHAUN McLAUGHLIN** – bass; repl. JEFF KELLY / **TERRY STERLING** – drums

Charisma not iss.

Jul 81. (7") *(CB 383)* **I'M ON FIRE. / DOWN IN THE DARK** [ ] [-]

Aug 81. (12"m) *(CB 389)* **INTERCONTINENTAL. / HAVE A NICE DAY / WHAT SHALL WE DO?** [ ] [-]

Oct 81. (7") *(CB 395)* **POPSTAR. / WHAT I WANT** [ ] [-]

Apr 82. (7") *(CB 397)* **TRANSPARENTS. / THAT'S NOT TRUE** [ ] [-]

Aug 82. (7") *(CB 398)* **AT THE CLUB. / I WILL WAIT** [ ] [-]

Sep 82. (lp) *(CAS 1155)* **AFRAID OF MICE** [ ] [-]

—— they continued to work under various guises but finally gave up when PHIL joined forces with ALEX McKECHNIE (ex-MODERN EON) and formed TWO'S A CROWD who subsequently evolved into UP AND RUNNING. In the late 80's two singles were issued, 'JOHNNY AND MARIE' and 'I CAN'T SAY NO', although an 'LIVE AT LIME STREET' never saw light.

AGENT ORANGE

Formed: Fullerton, Orange County, California, USA . . . late 70's by main songwriter, MIKE PALM, alongside STEVE 'SOTO' RODGERS and SCOTT MILLER. Naming themselves after a chemical weapon used in the Vietnam War, the hardcore trio took a similarly vicious approach in their sound. Having featured on disc jockey, Rodney Bingenheimer's (presenter on the KROQ radio station) 'Posh Boy' various artists compilation, 'Rodney On The Roq's' with the track, 'BLOODSTAINS', the band were signed to the Robbie Fields-run label in their own right. A single, 'EVERYTHING TURNS GRAY', was unleashed in '81, the last to feature ADOLESCENTS-bound RODGERS, who was replaced by JAMES LEVESQUE. Later that year, AGENT ORANGE issued their debut album, 'LIVING IN DARKNESS', a more melodic affair that fused punk with early 60's DICK DALE-esque surf. Three more "skate-punk" instrumentals were showcased on 1983's 'BITCHIN' SUMMER', an EP that brought them to the attention of 'Enigma'. Their first release for the label was the 'WHEN YOU LEAST EXPECT IT' EP, a record that contained an unlikely cover of Jefferson Airplane's psychedelic classic, 'SOMEBODY TO LOVE'. A much anticipated second album, 'THIS IS THE VOICE', eventually surfaced in 1986, although another five year hiatus was just around the corner. During this period, they found ex-SOCIAL DISTORTION guy, BRENT LILES, who replaced LEVESQUE on what proved to be their music biz swansong, 'REAL LIVE SOUND', in 1991. • **Covered:** POLICE TRUCK (Dead Kennedys) / PIPELINE (Chantays) / SHAKIN' ALL OVER (Johnny Kidd & The Pirates).

Album rating: THIS IS THE VOICE (*6)

MIKE PALM – vocals, guitar / **STEVE 'SOTO' RODGERS** – bass / **SCOTT MILLER** – drums

not iss. Posh Boy

1981. (7"ep) *<PBS 12>* **EVERYTHING TURNS GRAY. / PIPELINE** [-] [ ]

—— **JAMES LEVESQUE** – bass; repl. RODGERS who joined the ADOLESCENTS

Oct 81. (lp) *<PBS 122>* **LIVING IN DARKNESS** [-] [ ]
– Too young to die / Everything turns gray / Miserlou / The last goodbye / No such thing / A cry for help in a world gone mad / Bloodstains / Living in darkness / Pipeline / Breakdown / Mr. Moto.

1983. (7"ep) *<PBS 103-7>* **BITCHIN' SUMMER EP** [-] [ ]

not iss. Enigma

1984. (12"ep) *<E 1047>* **WHEN YOU LEAST EXPECT IT EP** [-] [ ]
– It's up to me and you / Bite the hand that feeds / Somebody to love / Out of limits. *(UK cd-iss. Feb95 on 'Restless'; 722182)*

1986. (lp) *<971209>* **THIS IS THE VOICE** [-] [ ]
– Voices / It's in your head / Say it isn't true / Fire in the rain / In your dreams tonight / Tearing me apart . . . so strange / Bite the hand that feeds / I kill spies / This is not the end. *(UK cd-iss. Feb95 on 'Restless'; 725402)*

— **BRENT LILES** – bass (ex-SOCIAL DISTORTION) repl. LEVESQUE

Restless Restless

Dec 90. (cd/c) *<72529-2/-4>* **REAL LIVE SOUND (live)** [-] [ ]
– Fire in the rain / Everything turns grey / Tearing me apart / Too young to die / It's in your head / I kill spies / Bite the hand that feeds (part 1) / Somebody to love / No such thing / Say it isn't true / Bloodstains / Pipeline / Last goodbye / Police truck / This is not the end / Shakin' all over. *(UK cd-iss. Feb95; same as US)*

— disbanded around the early 90's; the AGENT ORANGE of the mid 90's who released the 'VIRTUALLY INDESTRUCTABLE ALBUM', were not the same act

AGE OF CHANCE

Formed: Leeds, Yorkshire, England . . . early 80's by STEVE ELVIDGE, NEIL HOWSON, GEOFF TAYLOR and JAN PERRY. Released on their own 'Riot Bible' label, the 'MOTOR CITY' single introduced their grating noise/dance fusion to a jingle-jangle indie scene, the band even securing a place on the infamous C86 compilation with the cacophonous 'FROM NOW ON, THIS WILL BE YOUR GOD'. While the 'BIBLE OF THE BEATS' single was even more dancefloor oriented, AGE OF CHANCE were at their most entertaining interpreting other artists' work; a cover of Prince's 'KISS' (before TOM JONES got hold of it!) set the scene while an alternative-dance trashing of The Trammps' 'DISCO INFERNO' almost cracked the Top 40. Securing a major label deal with 'Virgin', the band made their bid for the big time with the 'ONE THOUSAND YEARS OF TROUBLE' (1987) set. It went nowhere, as did a succession of singles, even vocalist ELVIDGE had bailed out as the more soulful sounding CHARLES HUTCHINSON was drafted in as a replacement. After the disappointing follow-up set, 'MECCA' (1990), AGE OF CHANCE again found themselves minus a frontman as HUTCHINSON departed. While PERRY stepped in temporarily, the band finally took fate into their own hands and killed off AGE OF CHANCE in 1991. ELVIDGE, meanwhile, formed MAD LOVE, before carving out a career as a DJ in his hometown of Leeds.

Album rating: THE TWILIGHT WORLD OF SONIC DISCO 12" (*6) / ONE THOUSAND YEARS OF TROUBLE (*5) / MECCA (*5)

STEVEN ELVIDGE – vocals / **NEIL HOWSON** – guitar / **GEOFF TAYLOR** – bass / **JAN PERRY** – drums

Riot Bible not iss.

Apr 85. (7") *(RIOT 1)* **MOTOR CITY. / EVERLASTING YEAH!** [ ] [-]

Jan 86. (7") *(RIOT 2)* **THE BIBLE OF THE BEATS. / THE LIQUID JUNGLE** [ ] [-]

May 86. (12"ep; pink or yellow) *(BIBLE 001)* **THE TWILIGHT WORLD OF SONIC DISCO** [ ] [-]
– Motor City / Everlasting yeah! / The bible of the beats / The liquid jungle.

Fon-MCA not iss.

Nov 86. (7"orange,7"green,12") *(AGE 5)* **KISS. / CRUSH COLLISION** [50] [-]
(12"+=/d7"+=;-rel.Feb87) *(AGE 5M)* – Disco inferno / Kiss (remix).

Virgin Charisma

May 87. (7") *(VS 962)* **WHO'S AFRAID OF THE BIG BAD NOISE. / BIG BAD RAP** [ ] [-]
(12"+=) *(VS 962-12)* – ('A'-symphony).

Sep 87. (7") *(VS 989)* **DON'T GET MAD GET EVEN. / GETTING MAD (instrumental)** [ ] [-]
(12"+=) *(VS 989-12)* – ('A'mix) / Getting even / ('A'-bonus beats). *(re-iss. Jul88 with extra see below; same)*
(12"+=)(cd-s+=) *(VS 989-12)(CD-EP 7)* – New York's revenge / The beats of New York / NYC versus AOC.

Oct 87. (cd/c/lp) *(CD/TC+/V 2473)* *<90672>* **ONE THOUSAND YEARS OF TROUBLE** [ ] [ ]
– Don't get mad get even / We've got trouble / Ready or not here we come / Shut up and listen / Big bad noise / Take it / This is crush collision / Learn to pay / Hold on.

Jan 88. (7") *(VS 1035)* **TAKE IT. / TAKING TOP DOLLARS** [ ] [-]
(12"+=) *(VST 1035)* – ('A'mix).

— **CHARLES HUTCHISON** – vocals; repl. ELVIDGE

Oct 89. (7") *(VS 1133)* **TIMES UP. / FOUR MORE YEARS: MOTORCADE** [ ] [-]
(12") *(VST 1133)* – Times up: Prove it / ('B'side) / Superpower.
(cd-s) *(VSCD 1133)* – ('A'side) / Times up: Prove it / Superpower / You can run.
(12") *(VSTX 1133)* – (3 versions of the 'A'side).

Jan 90. (7") *(VS 1228)* **HIGHER THAN HEAVEN. / ('A'-green mix)** [ ] [-]
(12") *(VST 1228)* – (3 'A'versions).
(cd-s++=) *(VSCD 1228)* – Snowblind.

Mar 90. (cd/c/lp) *(CD/TC+/V 2561)* *<91366>* **MECCA** [ ] [ ]
– Four more years / Higher than Heaven / Joyride / Refuse to lose / Snowblind / Mecca / Time's up / You can run but you can't hide / Playing with fire / What's happening.

May 90. (7") *(VS 1258)* **PLAYING WITH FIRE. / JOYRIDE** [ ] [-]
(12") *(VST 1258)* – ('A'-playing with house mix) / Times up (pop mix).
(cd-s) *(VSCD 1258)* – (2 'A'versions) / Red alert / Higher than Heaven (mix).
(12") *(VSTX 1258)* – (3 versions of 'A'side).

— disbanded soon after above

AGNOSTIC FRONT

Formed: New York, USA . . . 1983 by frontman ROGER MIRET (a tattooed and pit-bull breeding veggie!) and guitarist VINNIE STIGMA, who completed the line-up with ALEX KINNON, ROB KABULA and LOUIE BEATTO. Initially playing hardcore (the 45, 'UNITED BLOOD' proves the point), the band gradually assumed more of a metallic sheen, releasing 'VICTIM OF PAIN' for the 'Rat Cage' label in '84 before signing with 'Relativity' for the release of 1986's 'CAUSE FOR ALARM'. Their right wing political leanings distanced them even further from NY's punk scene, the uncompromising lyrics complementing the aggressive musical backing. A third set, 'LIBERTY & JUSTICE FOR . . .' was issued the following year, their last vinyl outing for some time. This was due to MIRET's subsequent year and a half incarceration on drugs charges. In 1992 with temporary frontman, ALAN PETERS, they returned from their sabbatical, unleashing the fine 'ONE VOICE' (which also featured new guitarist MATT HENDERSON). However, although MIRET was out of jail, they played their last gig at CBGB's just prior to Xmas that year (an album of the show was issued the following year as 'LAST WARNING'). STIGMA and HENDERSON duly joined MADBALL, a band in the same vein, fronted by MIRET's younger brother, FREDDY CRICIEN.

Album rating: CAUSE FOR ALARM (*6) / LIBERTY AND JUSTICE FOR (*6) / TO BE CONTINUED . . . THE VERY BEST OF . . . compilation (*6)

ROGER MIRET – vocals / **VINNIE STIGMA** – guitar / **ALEX KINNON** – guitar / **ROB KABULA** – bass / **LOUIE BEATTO** (RAYBEEZ) – drums

not iss. unknown

1983. (7") **UNITED BLOOD. /** [-] [ ]

not iss. Rat Cage

1984. (lp) **VICTIM IN PAIN** [-] [ ]
– Victim in pain / Remind them / Blind justice / Last warning / United and strong / Hiding inside / Power / Fascist attitude / Society sucker / Your mistake / With time. *<re-iss. Aug87 on 'Combat'; 88561-8181-1>*

— **ADAM MOOCHIE** – bass repl. ROB + ALEX

Rough Justice Combat

May 86. (lp)<cd> *(JUST 3)* *<88561-3022-2>* **CAUSE FOR ALARM** [ ] [ ]
– The eliminator / Existance of hate / Time will come / Growing concern / Your mistake / Out for blood / Toxic shock / Bomber Zee / Public assistance / Shoot his load. *(cd-iss. Aug87; CDJUST 3)*

— **JIMMY MERRICK** – drums; repl. BEATTO

Oct 87. (cd/lp) *(CD+/JUST 8)* *<970.958>* **LIBERTY & JUSTICE FOR . . .** [ ] [ ]
– Liberty and justice / Crucial moment / Strength / Genesis / Anthem / Another side / Happened yesterday / Lost / Hypocrisy / Crucified / Censored.

— **ALAN PETERS** – vocals; repl. imprisoned MIRET, although the latter still managed to contribute the lyrics. PETERS joined CRAWLPAPPY after its release.

— **MATT HENDERSON** was added

Roadracer Relativity

Jan 92. (cd/lp) *(RO 9222-2/-1)* *<88561-3022-2>* **ONE VOICE** [ ] [ ]
– New Jack / One voice / Infiltrate / The tombs / Your fall / Over the edge / Undertow / Now and then / Crime without sin / Retaliate / Force feed / Bastard. *(re-iss. May95; same)*

— MIRET was now on below album, although they had already disbanded late '92, STIGMA and HENDERSON having moved on to MADBALL (see above).

Jun 93. (cd/lp) *(RO 9078-2/-1)* *<88561-1170-2/-1>* **LAST WARNING (live)** [ ] [ ]
– Undertow / Your mistake – Victim in pain / One voice / Infiltrate – Strength / United blood / Public assistance – Over the edge / Blind justice – Last warning / Crucified / Toxic shock – United and strong / Fascist attitudes / Anthem – The eliminator / No one rules / Final war / Last warning / Traitor / Friend or foe / United blood / Fight / Discriminate me / In control / Crucial changes. *(re-iss. May95; same)*

Epitaph Epitaph

May 98. (cd/lp) *<(E 6536-2/-1)>* **SOMETHING'S GOTTA GIVE** [ ] [ ]
– Something's gotta give / Believe / Gotta go / Before my eyes / No fear / Blinded / Voices / Do or die / My war / Bloodsucker / Blame / Today, tomorrow, forever / Rage / Pauly the dog / Crucified.

Dec 98. (7") *(0414-7)* **PURO DE MADRE. /** [ ] [-]

– compilations, etc. –

1989. (cd) *Combat; <3001>* **LIVE AT CBGB (live)** [-] [ ]

Jul 92. (cd/c/lp) *Rough Justice; (CD/T+/JUST 20M)* **TO BE CONTINUED . . . THE VERY BEST OF AGNOSTIC FRONT** [ ] [-]
– Victim in pain / Your mistake / Hypocrisy / New Jack / Liberty and justice / Time will come / Power / Society sucker / Toxic shock / Public assistance / Blind justice / The eliminator / One voice / Crucified / United and strong / Your mistake / Fascist attitudes (live) / Anthem (live) / Last warning (live).

Jul 95. (cd) *Grand Theft Auto; (GTA 002-R051)* **RAW UNRELEASED** [ ] [ ]

A HOUSE

Formed: Dublin, Ireland . . . 1985 by DAVE COUSE, FEARGAL BUNBURY and MARTIN HEALY (along with additional part-time members, DAVE MORRISSEY, DAVE DAWSON and SUSAN KAVANAGH). Stamped with the characteristically broad-accented bile and wit of lyricist/vocalist COUSE, A HOUSE's highly individual take on Celtic rock was initially picked up on by 'Warners' alternative subsidiary, 'Blanco Y Negro'. The London-based label signed the now Belfast-based band up on the strength of three self-financed singles, issuing their first album, 'ON OUR BIG FAT MERRY GO ROUND', in 1988. Unfortunately, both the debut and its acclaimed follow-up, 'I WANT TOO MUCH' (1990) failed to meet major label sales targets and the band soon found themselves back at square one. All fuel for the fire of COUSE's barbed muse of course, the band trooping on against the odds and inking a subsequently deal with Keith Cullen's hip'n'happening new 'Setanta' label. An EP, 'DOODLE', was closely followed by arguably their most effective – and possibly most controversial – single, 'ENDLESS ART', a strangely hypnotic spoken-word 'list' of history's most famous painters, musicians, writers etc., spliced with a snippet of one of Mozart's symphonies. It certainly stood out from almost any other 'indie' release of the day, perhaps too much; its distinct lack of female achievers, perhaps understandably, riled many women. The band made up for it by cutting a revised version, made up entirely of the fairer sex, prior to the release of their third and most successful album, the EDWYN COLLINS-produced 'I AM THE GREATEST' (1991). Critics suggested that COUSE's edge seemed blunted on 1994's 'WILD EYED AND IGNORANT', a record that failed to build on the artistic and relative commercial feats of its predecessor. Nevertheless, A HOUSE haven't called in the removals people just yet, perhaps a little renovation is all that's needed. • **Covered:** CHILDREN OF THE REVOLUTION (T.Rex) / I FEEL LOVE (Donna Summer) / LOVE SONG (Damned).

Album rating: ON OUR BIG FAT MERRY GO ROUND (*5) / I WANT TOO MUCH (*6) / I AM THE GREATEST (*7) / WIDE EYED AND IGNORANT (*5) / NO MORE APOLOGIES (*5)

DAVE COUSE – vocals, acoustic guitar / **FEARGAL BUNBURY** – guitar / **MARTIN HEALY** – bass / **DERMOT WYLIE** – drums

Rip / not iss.

Mar 87. (7") *(ARIP 1)* **KICK ME AGAIN JESUS. / I WANT YOU** -
(12"+=) *(ARIPT 1)* – When I change.

Jun 87. (7") *(ARIP 2)* **SNOWBALL DOWN. / Y.O.U.** -

Aug 87. (12"ep) *(ARIPT 3)* **KISS ME AGAIN JESUS / I WANT YOU / WHEN I CHANGE. / SNOWBALL DOWN / Y.O.U.** -

Blanco Y Negro / Sire

Nov 87. (7") *(NEG 28)* **HEART HAPPY. / PRETTY SOMETHING** -
(12"+=) *(NEGT 28)* – Oh God I hurt inside.

Jun 88. (7") *(NEG 35)* **CALL ME BLUE. / FREAK OUT** -
(12"+=) *(NEGT 35)* – Michael / Plane or pearl.

Sep 88. (7") *(NEG 38)* **I'LL ALWAYS BE GRATEFUL. / FUNNYMAN** -
(12"+=) *(NEGT 38)* – This child is yours not mine / There's only one thing wrong with the perfect.

Oct 88. (lp/c)(cd) *(BYN/+C 18)(244079-2)* <25821> **ON OUR BIG FAT MERRY-GO-ROUND**
– Call me blue / I'll always be grateful / Don't ever think you're different / Love of the eighties / Love quarry / Stone the crows / I want to kill something / My little greenhouse / That's not the truth / Violent love / Clump of trees. *(cd+=)* – Make hay when the sun shines.

Apr 90. (7") *(NEG 43)* **I THINK I'M GOING MAD. / I WANT TOO MUCH** -
(12"+=/cd-s+=) *(NEG 43 T/CD)* – Why must we argue.

May 90. (cd)(lp/c) *(903171316-2)(BYN/+C 22)* <26204> **I WANT TOO MUCH**
– I want too much / Talking / The patron saint of mediocrity / Shivers up my spine / Marry me / I give you now / Now that I'm sick / I think I'm going mad / Bring down the beast / Manstrong / Keep the homefires burning / You'll cry when I die / Small talk.

Setanta / Radioactive

Nov 90. (12"ep/cd-ep) **DOODLE EP** -
– The last to know / Bugaboo / A minute of your time / Sometimes I feel.

Sep 91. (12"ep) **BINGO SPINSTER EP** -
– Spinster / Easy way out / Senses / There is no time.
(c-ep/cd-ep) – (1st track) / Angeline / I want to be allowed to love you / I'll make it up to you.

Oct 91. (lp/c/cd) *(SET/+C/CD 3)* <RAR/+C/D 10600> **I AM THE GREATEST** Jan92
– I don't care / You're too young / Endless art / Blind faith / Cotton pickers / How strong is love / When I first saw you / I am afraid / Victor / Take it easy on me / Creatures of craze / Slipping away / I wanted to die / I lied / Live life dead die / I am the greatest. *(cd re-iss. Aug92; same)*

Jan 92. (7") **YOU'RE TOO YOUNG. / TAKE IT EASY ON ME** -
(12"ep+=) **ZOP EP** – Serious lovin' / When I first saw you (long).
(cd-ep+=) **ZOP EP** – Baby, you're too much / Our love is good enough.

Jun 92. (7") *(AHOU 1)* **ENDLESS ART. / MORE ENDLESS ART** 46 -
(12"+=/cd-s+=) *(12/CD AHOU 1)* – Freak show / Charity.

Aug 92. (c-s/7") *(TC+/AHOU 2)* **TAKE IT EASY ON ME. / I LOVE YOU** 55 -
(12"+=/cd-s+=) *(12/CD AHOU 2)* – Everything's wrong.
(w /free flexi) – Force fed.

Sep 92. (7"mail-order) *(AHOU 3)* **WHEN I FIRST SAW YOU (live). / I WANT TO KILL SOMETHING / SECOND WIND** - -

Jun 94. (c-s/7") *(TC+/AHOU 4)* **WHY ME. / I HOPE I'M WRONG / MY HEART BLEEDS FOR YOU** 52 -
(10") *(10AHOU 4)* – (first 2 tracks) / Angeline / You think you know.
(cd-s) *(CDAHOU 4)* – (first & third tracks) / I will never forget you / This hurts me.

Jul 94. (cd/c/lp) *(AHOU CD/TC/LP 2)* **WIDE EYED AND IGNORANT** -
– Intro / Here comes the good times / She keeps me humble / Why me / Make me proud / Everything I am / Curious / These things / The comedy is over / The strong & the silent / Big talk / Deadhead / I want to be allowed to love you.

Sep 94. (c-s/7") *(TC+/AHOU 5)* **HERE COME THE GOOD TIMES. / CHILDREN OF THE REVOLUTION / I FEEL LOVE** 37 -
(cd-s+=) *(CDAHOU 5)* – Love song.
(10"/cd-s) *(10/CD AHOUS 5)* – ('A'side) / Everybody needs something / Soon / All I need.

Sep 96. (c-s) **NO MORE APOLOGIES /** -
(cd-s) –

Sep 96. (cd/c) *(SET CD/MC 028)* **NO MORE APOLOGIES** -
– Start / Into the light / Cry easily / No more apologies / My sweet life / Sister's song / Twist and squeeze / Love is . . . / Without dreams / Just because / I can't change / Clothes horse / My mind / Broken / Happy ending.

Feb 97. (cd-ep) *(SETCD 029)* **WITHOUT DREAMS / DAYS LIKE THESE / MY SHELTERED LIFE / JEAN** -

AINTS! (see under ⇒ LAUGHING CLOWNS)

AIRHEAD

Formed: Maidstone, Kent, England . . . 1987 by songwriter MIKE WALLIS and STEVE MARSHALL, who became The APPLES after being joined by the KESTEVEN brothers, BEN and SAM. At the turn of the decade the alternative popsters signed to 'Korova', almost immediately (due to the existence of another similarly monikered outfit) opting for JEFFERSON AIRHEAD. After one LEIGH GORMAN-produced single, 'CONGRATULATIONS' in early '91 and its follow-up, 'SCRAP HAPPY', they inevitably perhaps received objections from the management of 60's stalwarts, JEFFERSON AIRPLANE. They soon put paid to this idea and resumed life simply as AIRHEAD. With this minor controversy over, the lads floated into the lower regions of the UK singles charts with their third attempt, 'FUNNY HOW'. They started 1992 on a high as the single, 'COUNTING SHEEP' and the much delayed accompanying debut album, 'BOING!', both hit the Top 40 (the latter was originally scheduled for release the previous Spring under the shelved 'JEFFERSON AIRHEAD' banner!). This BYRDS meets WONDER STUFF set also contained what turned out to be their final chart entry, 'RIGHT NOW', the band taking off for a last ditch effort, 'THAT'S ENOUGH', on the much smaller 'Mother Tongue' label.

Album rating: BOING! (*5)

MIKE WALLIS – vocals / **STEVE MARSHALL** – keyboards / **BEN KESTEVEN** – bass / **SAM KESTEVEN** – drums

Korova-WEA / WEA

Mar 91. (7"/c-s; as JEFFERSON AIRHEAD) **CONGRATULATIONS. / SOMETHING BLUE** -
(12"+=/cd-s+=) – ('A'demo).

Jun 91. (7"/c-s; as JEFFERSON AIRHEAD) **SCRAP HAPPY /** -
(12"+=/cd-s+=) –

Sep 91. (7"/c-s) *(KOW/+C 47)* **FUNNY HOW. / KEEP THE APPLE** 57 -
(12"+=/cd-s+=) *(KOW T/CD 47)* – ('A'extended).

Dec 91. (7") *(KOW 48)* **COUNTING SHEEP. / TAKE MY TRAIN** 35 -
(12"+=) *(KOWT 48)* – ('A'version).
(cd-s++=) *(KOWCD 48)* – Keep the apple.

Jan 92. (cd)(c/lp) *(9031 74679-2)(CODE/KODE 17)* **BOING!** 29
– Scrap happy / I might fall / Right now / Funny how / Easy / I don't mind / Congratulations / Wish you were here / Isn't it rich? / Everybody needs.

Feb 92. (7"/c-s) *(KOW/+C 49)* **RIGHT NOW. / COUNTING SHEEP** 50 -
(12") *(KOWT 49)* – ('A'side) / The enemy / ('A'demo).
(cd-s+=) *(KOWCD 49)* – Through my window.

— **BEN** also became a member of the POPINJAYS in 1992

Mother Tongue / not iss.

May 93. (10"ep/12"ep/cd-ep) **THAT'S ENOUGH. / THEY DON'T KNOW / SOMEONE SHOULD HAVE TOLD ME** -

AIR MIAMI (see under ⇒ UNREST)

ALABAMA 3

Formed: Brixton, London, England . . . 1996 as a loose collective of ELVIS fans, including Glaswegian, THE VERY REVEREND DR. D.WAYNE LOVE (aka MATTHEW VAUGHAN), LARRY LOVE, MISSISSIPPI GUITAR LOVE, LITTLE BOY DOPE, THE SPIRIT, MOUNTAIN OF LOVE and last but not least CONGAMAN LOVE. They forsook their hard druggin' lifestyle for mock Christian beliefs (and the odd reefer), adopting "red"-neck attitudes via communist country & western acid-house! Kicking up a duststorm with their highly charged debut, 'AIN'T GOIN' TO GOA', the band scored a single of the week in the NME. Late in '97, they scraped into the UK Top 75 with their third single, 'SPEED OF THE SOUND OF LONELINESS' (a JOHN PRINE cover), lifted from their debut album, 'EXILE ON COLDHARBOUR LANE'.

Album rating: EXILE ON COLDHARBOUR LANE (*6)

THE VERY REVEREND DR. D. WAYNE LOVE – vocals / **LARRY LOVE** – vocals / **MISSISSIPPI GUITAR LOVE** – guitar / **THE SPIRIT** – keyboards / **THE MOUNTAIN OF LOVE** – vocals, harmonica / **LITTLE BOY DOPE** – drums / **SIR REAL "CONGAMAN" LOVE** – percussion, acoustic guitar

Elemental / Geffen

Aug 96. (12"/cd-s) *(ELM 40 T/CD)* **AIN'T GOIN' TO GOA. / MAO TSE TUNG SAID** -

— (below featured The STREET ANGELS CHOIR N.Y.C.)

May 97. (12"/cd-s) *(ELM 41 T/CD1)* **WOKE UP THIS MORNING (Chosen one mix) / CONVERTED (Last supper mix). / WOKE UP THIS MORNING (Drillaz In The Church mix) / WOKE UP THIS MORNING (Volume mix)** -
(cd-s) *(ELM 41CD2)* –

Nov 97. (12"/cd-s) *(ELM 42 T/CD1)* **SPEED OF THE SOUND OF LONELINESS. / OLD PURPLE TIN** 72 -
(cd-s) *(ELM 42CD2)* – ('A'mixes).

Nov 97. (cd/lp) *(ELM 40 CD/LP)* <25158> **EXILE ON COLDHARBOUR LANE**
– Converted / Speed of the sound of loneliness / Woke up this morning / U don't dans 2 tekno / Bourgeoise blues / Ain't goin' to Goa / Mao Tse Tung said / Hypo full of love (the 12 step plan) / The old purple tin (9% of pure heaven) / The night we nearly got busted / Sister Rosetta / Peace in the valley.

Mar 98. (12"/cd-s) *(ELM 45 12T/CD2)* **AIN'T GOIN' TO GOA (mixes; radio / Trouser Enthusiast / Motiv8)** 40 -
(cd-s) *(ELM 45CD1)* – ('A'mixes).
Nov 98. (12"/cd-s) *(ELM 51 T/CDS1)* **CONVERTED** -
(cd-s) *(ELM 51CDS2)* –

ALARM

Formed: Rhyl, Wales . . . 1977 as punk band The TOILETS by MIKE PETERS, DAVE SHARP, EDDIE McDONALD and NIGEL TWIST. They became "mod" outfit "17" before the same quartet changed name again to The ALARM in 1981. After one indie 45 on the 'White Cross' label, they signed to Miles Copeland's US based 'I.R.S.' in summer '82. Just over a year later and now living in London, they entered the UK Top 20, not for the last time, with single '68 GUNS'. Compared to The CLASH, but inspired by the earnest passion of U2, the group's music was at odds with the limp synth-pop of the day, attracting fans who were too young to have experienced punk's heyday but still wanted energetic anthems that eschewed clever lyrics for a populist sensibility. Premiered by another banner-waving hit, 'WHERE WERE YOU HIDING WHEN THE STORM BROKE', the debut album, 'DECLARATION', arrived in early '84. Part of a kind of Celtic triumvirate (completed by Ireland's U2 and Scotland's BIG COUNTRY), The ALARM were essentially a rock extension of the folk tradition, their acoustic rendition of mining ballad (previously recorded by PETE SEEGER and The BYRDS amongst others), 'THE BELLS OF RHYMNEY' hardly seeming out of place. As with U2, there was always the possibility of taking things too far down the road of grandiose stadium rock, The ALARM coming perilously close on follow-up set, 'STRENGTH' (1985). Another UK Top 20 hit (it also cracked the US Top 40, where their big sound was much appreciated), the record spawned a futher epic Top 20 single in 'SPIRIT OF '76'. That self-same spirit seemed to be lacking on subsequent releases, although the 'CHANGE' album saw them adopt a more rootsy approach, even looking to their native heritage with the help of a Welsh male choir and The Welsh Symphony Orchestra. Although the band continued to cut little ice with the more snobbish critics, they soldiered on for a final set, 'RAW' (1991), before PETERS embarked on a solo career. • **Songwriters:** McDONALD / PETERS or SHARP / TWIST, except; KNOCKIN' ON HEAVEN'S DOOR (Bob Dylan) / WORKING CLASS HERO + HAPPY XMAS (WAR IS OVER) (John Lennon) / ROCKIN' IN THE FREE WORLD (Neil Young).

Album rating: STANDARDS compilation (*7)

MIKE PETERS (b.25 Jan'59) – vocals, guitar / **DAVE SHARP** (b.28 Jan'59) – guitar / **EDDIE McDONALD** (b. 1 Nov'59) – bass / **NIGEL TWIST** (b. 18 Jul'58) – drums

Vendetta not iss.
Mar 80. (7"; as SEVENTEEN) *(VD 001)* **DON'T LET GO. / BANK HOLIDAY WEEKEND** -

White Cross not iss.
Sep 81. (7") *(W 3-4)* **UNSAFE BUILDINGS. / UP FOR MURDER** -

Illegal not iss.
Oct 82. (7"m) *(ILS 032)* **MARCHING ON. / ACROSS THE BORDER / LIE OF THE LAND** -

I.R.S. I.R.S.
Apr 83. (7") *(PFP 1014)* **THE STAND. / THIRD LIGHT** -
(12") *(PFPX 1014)* – ('A'side) / For freedom / Reason 41.
Jun 83. (7") **THE STAND. / REASON 41** -
Jul 83. (m-lp) *<70504>* **THE ALARM (live)** -
– The stand / Across the border / Marching on / Lie of the land / For freedom.
Sep 83. (7") *(PFP 1023)* **68 GUNS. / (part 2)** 17 -
(w/ free c-s) *(PFPC 1023)* – (see mini-lp for tracks).
(12") *(PFPX 1023)* – ('A'extended) / Thoughts of a young man.
Nov 83. (7") **68 GUNS. / PAVILLION STEPS** -
Jan 84. (7") *(IRS 101)* **WHERE WERE YOU HIDING WHEN THE STORM BROKE? / PAVILLION STEPS** 22
(12"+=) *(IRSX 101)* – What kind of Hell.
Feb 84. (lp/c) *(IRS A/C 7044) <70608>* **DECLARATION** 6 50
– Declaration / Marching on / Where were you hiding when the storm broke? / Third light / 68 guns / We are the light / Shout to the Devil / Blaze of glory / Tell me / The deceiver / The stand (prophecy) / Howling wind. *(cd-iss. Oct88; CDILP 25887) (re-iss. Oct92 on 'A&M' cd/c; CD/C MID 103)*
Mar 84. (7"clear) *(IRS 103)* **THE DECEIVER. / REASON 41** 51
(12"+=) *(IRSX 103)* – Second generation.
(ltd.d7"+=) *(IRSD 103)* – Lie of the land / Legal matter.
May 84. (7") **THE DECEIVER. / SECOND GENERATION** -
Oct 84. (7") *(IRS 114)* **THE CHANT HAS JUST BEGUN. / THE BELLS OF RHYMNEY** 48
(12"+=) *(IRSY 114)* – The stand (extended).
Feb 85. (7"/12") *(ALARM 1/+2)* **ABSOLUTE REALITY. / BLAZE OF GLORY** 35
(ltd.d7"+=) *(ALARMD 1)* – Room at the top / Reason 36.
Sep 85. (7") *(IRM 104) <52736>* **STRENGTH. / MAJORITY** 40 61 Dec85
(12"+=) *(IRT 104)* – ('A'side) / Absolute reality (acoustic).
Oct 85. (lp/c) *(MIRF/+C 1004) <5666>* **STRENGTH** 18 39
– Knife edge / Strength / Dawn chorus / Spirit of '76 / The day the ravens left the tower / Deeside / Father to son / Only the thunder / Walk forever by my side. *(cd-iss. Apr87; DMIRF 1004) (cd re-iss. Jan90 on 'M.C.A.'; DMIRL 1504) (re-iss. Apr92 cd/c; IRLD/IRLC 19006)*
Jan 86. (7") *(IRM 109)* **SPIRIT OF '76. / WHERE WERE YOU HIDING WHEN THE STORM BROKE? (live)** 22
(12"+=) *(IRMT 109)* – Deeside (live).
(d12"++=) *(IRMTD 109)* – Knockin' on Heaven's door (live) / 68 guns (live).
Apr 86. (7"/7"sha-pic-d) *(IRM/+SP 112)* **KNIFE EDGE. / CAROLINE ISENBERG** 43
(12"+=) *(IRMT 112)* – Howling wind / Unbreak the promise.
Sep 87. (7") *(IRM 144) <53219>* **RAIN IN THE SUMMERTIME. / ROSE BEYOND THE WALL** 18 71 Nov87
(12"+=) *(IRMT 144)* – The bells of Rhymney / Time to believe.
(12") *(IRMX 144)* – ('A'-Through the haze mix) / ('A'-Lightning mix).
Nov 87. (lp/c/cd) *(MIRG/MIRGC/DMIRG 1023) <42061>* **EYE OF THE HURRICANE** 23 77
– Rain in the summertime / Newtown Jericho / Hallowed ground / One step closer to home / Shelter / Rescue me / Permanence in change / Presence of love / Only love can set me free / Eye of the hurricane. *(cd re-iss. May90 on 'M.C.A.'; DMIRL 1506)*
Nov 87. (7"/7"blue) *(IRM/+BV 150)* **RESCUE ME. / MY LAND YOUR LAND** 48
(12"+=) *(IRMT 150)* – The Hurricane sessions.
Feb 88. (7"/7"pic-d) *(IRM/+P 155) <53259>* **PRESENCE OF LOVE (LAUGHARNE). / KNIFE EDGE (live)** 44 77
(12"+=) *(IRMT 155)* – This train is bound for glory (live) / Dawn chorus (live).
(cd-s+=) *(DIRM 155)* – Rain in the summertime (Through The Haze mix).
Oct 88. (m-lp/m-c/m-cd) *(MIRM/MIRMC/DMIRM 5001) <39108>* **ELECTRIC FOLKLORE LIVE (live)** 62
– Rescue me / Rain in the summertime / Permanence in change / Strength / Spirit of '76 / Blaze of glory.
Sep 89. (7"/7"s) *(EIRS/+P 123) <73002>* **SOLD ME DOWN THE RIVER. / GWETHOCH FI I YR AFON** 43 50
(10"+=) *(EIRS10 123)* – Firing line.
(12"+=/cd-s+=) *(EIRS T/CD 123)* – Corridors of power.
Sep 89. (lp/c/cd) *(EIRSA X/C/CD 1020) <82018>* **CHANGE** 13 75
– Rivers to cross / A new South Wales / Sold me down the river / The rock / Devolution / Workin' man blues / Love don't come easy / Hard land / Change II / No frontiers / Scarlet / Where a town once stood / Prison without prison bars.
Oct 89. (7"/12") *(EIRS/+T 129)* **A NEW SOUTH WALES. / THE ROCK (long version)** 31
(cd-s+=) *(EIRSCD 129)* – Working class hero.
(10"white++=) *(EIRSTEN 129)* – Rivers to cross (new version).
(7" also in Welsh) *(EIRSB 129)* – HWYLIO DROS Y MOR. / Y GRAIG
Jan 90. (7"/c-s) *(EIRS/+C 134)* **LOVE DON'T COME EASY. / CROESI'R AFON** 48
(12"+=/cd-s+=) *(EIRS T/CD 134)* – No frontiers.
(10"pic-d+=) *(EIRSPD 134)* – Change II.
Oct 90. (7"/12") *(ALARME 2/+T)* **UNSAFE BUILDINGS (1990). / UP FOR MURDER (1990)** 54
(c-s+=/cd-s+=) *(ALARME 2 C/CD)* – Unsafe Buildings (original).
Nov 90. (lp/c/cd) *(EIRSA/+C/CD 1043) <13056>* **STANDARDS** (compilation) 47
– The road / Unsafe buildings / The stand / 68 guns / Where were you hiding when the storm broke? / Absolute reality / Strength / Spirit of '76 / Rain in the summertime / Rescue me / Sold me down the river / A new south Wales / Happy Xmas (war is over). (cd/c+=) – Marching on / Blaze of glory.
Apr 91. (7") *(ALARM 3)* **RAW. / CHANGE 1** 51
(12"+=/cd-s+=) *(ALARM 3 T/CD)* – Devolution / Workin' man's blues.
Apr 91. (lp/c/cd) *(EIRSA/+C/CD 1055) <13087>* **RAW** 33
– Raw / Rockin' in the free world / God save somebody / Moments in time / Hell or high water / Lead me through the darkness / The wind blows away my words / Let the river run its course / Save your crying / Wonderful world.

— in mid '91, MIKE PETERS went solo and the band folded

– compilations, others, etc. –

Apr 88. (cd-ep) *I.R.S.; (AMCD 906)* **COMPACT HITS** -
– 68 guns / Blaze of glory / Shout to the Devil / Where were you hiding when the storm broke?
Apr 98. (cd) *(7243-493751-2)* **THE BEST OF THE ALARM AND MIKE PETERS**
– 68 guns / Spirit of '76 / Down the road / Rain in the summertime / Strength / Breathe / Sold me down the river / New South Wales / 21st century / Stand / Where were you hiding when the storm broke / Majority / Deceiver / Blaze of glory / Walk forever by my side / One step closer to home / No better than this / Presence of love / Absolute reality / Rescue me (tearing the bonds asunder).

MIKE PETERS

Crai not iss.
Jan 94. (c-ep/12"ep/cd-ep) *(CRAI 040 MC/T/CD)* **BACK INTO THE SYSTEM. / 21st CENTURY (demo) / A NEW CHAPTER** -
(cd-ep) *(CRAI 040CDW)* – (Welsh language version).
Apr 94. (c-ep/12"ep/cd-ep) *(CRAI 041 MC/T/CD)* **IT JUST DON'T GET ANY BETTER THAN THIS. / DEVIL'S WORLD / WHITE NOISE** -
Oct 94. (cd/c/2x10"lp; as MIKE PETERS & THE POETS) *(CRAI 042CD/042MC/10-42)* **BREATHE** -
– Poetic justice / All I wanted / If I can't have you / Breathe / Love is a revolution / Who's gonna make the piece / Spiritual / What the world can't give me / Levis & bibles / Beautiful thing / Into the 21st century / This is war / The message / Back into the system * / It just don't get any better than this * / Train a comin' / A new chapter (reprise). *(d-lp += *) (re-iss. Jan95 as Welsh language; CRAICD 047)*

Transatlantic not iss.
Aug 96. (cd) *(TRACD 233)* **FEEL FREE** -
– Shine on (13th dream) / The message / Feel free / All is forgiven / My calling / Regeneration / R.I.P. / What is it for / Psychological combat zone / The love we made / Breathe / Broken silence.
Nov 96. (cd-s) *(TRAX 1033)* **SHINE ON** -
Mar 97. (cd-s) *(TRAX 1038)* **MY CALLING** -

— with **CHRIS LEWIS** – guitars / **RICHARD LLEWELLYN** – bass / **OWEN THOMAS** – drums / **MARK O'GRADY** – electronica

Eagle not iss.
Feb 98. (cd) *(EAGCD 019)* **RISE** -
– In circles / Transcendental / Rise / You are to me / My calling / First light / High on the hill / Ground zero / White noise (part II) / The wasting land / Burnout syndrome.

ALBERTO Y LOST TRIOS PARANOIAS

Formed: Manchester, England . . . 1976 by actors/musicians, C.P. LEE and BRUCE MITCHELL along with a BONZO DOG BAND-like entourage of LES PRIOR, BOB HARDING, JIMMY HIBBERT, TONY BOWERS and SIMON WHITE. Although serious musicians in their own right, The ALBERTO's dealt in scathing parodies of 60's/70's icons; among those unlucky enough to be singled out for treatment on their first two albums, 'ALBERTO Y . . .' (1976) and 'ITALIANS FROM OUTER SPACE' (1977), included LOU REED/V.U. (substituting 'ANADIN' for 'Heroin'; surprisingly effective!) and that portly Greek tent-wearer ('HAPPY TO BE ON – AN ISLAND AWAY FROM DEMIS ROUSSOS'). Moving from 'Transatlantic' records to "new wave" bastion, 'Stiff', for a one-off EP, 'SNUFF ROCK', the band decided to set their satirical sights on the thriving punk and reggae movement. The record fooled many afficionados who believed its A-side (featuring the tracks, 'KILL' and 'GOBBIN' ON LIFE') to be the work of an authentic punk band, its release tied to a London Royal Court Theatre stage play, Sleak', in which ALBERTO and Co. presented the concept of "snuff rock" i.e. faked onstage suicide. Subsequently signing to 'Logo' (home of The TOURISTS), they hit the Top 50 with a STATUS QUO pastiche, 'HEADS DOWN NO NONSENSE MINDLESS BOOGIE', a track taken from their third and final album, 'SKITE' (1978). The aforementioned 'Sleak' subsequently enjoyed another run in the early 80's alongside a further production, 'Never Mind THe Bullocks', although The ALBERTOS were all but finished (bar a one-off reunion 45 in 1982) after the untimely death (from leukaemia) of LES PRIOR on the 31st January, 1980. HIBBERT released a metal-ish solo album, 'HEAVY DUTY', before going on to become the man behind TV cartoon, 'Count Duckula'. C.P. LEE enjoyed live appearances under the guise of LORD BUCKLEY, a spoof show, 'RADIO SWEAT', was released on cassette in '81. The remaining members, BOWERS, HARDING and MITCHELL, made more successful attempts at breaking back into the pop limelight via The MOTHMEN, DURUTTI COLUMN and SIMPLY RED (just BOWERS that is).

Album rating: SNUFF ROCK – THE BEST OF THE ALBERTOS compilation (*7)

C.P. 'Chris' LEE – vocals, guitar / **BOB HARDING** – vocals, guitar, bass / **TONY BOWERS** – guitar, bass / **JIMMY HIBBERT** – vocals / **LES PRYOR** – vocals / **SIMON WHITE** – guitar, steel guitar / **BRUCE MITCHELL** – drums, percussion

Transatlantic / not iss.

Apr 76. (7") *(BIG 541)* **DREAD JAWS. / DE VERSION** [ ] [-]

May 76. (lp) *(TRA 316)* **ALBERTO Y LOST TRIOS PARANOIAS** [ ] [-]
– Torture you / Pavlov / I like gurls / Dread jaws / Follow the guru / Dead meat / Anadin / 6:45 / Jesus wept / Mandrax sunset variations pt.1, pt.2, pt.3.

Jul 77. (lp) *(TRA 349)* **ITALIANS FROM OUTER SPACE** [ ] [-]
– Old Trust / Brrrr / I'll come if you let me / Invocation of the fundamental orrifice of St. Agnes / No change / Peon in the neck / Happy to be on (an island away from Demis Roussos) / Teenager in schtuck / Italians from Outer Space: (a) The ballad of Colonel Callan, (b) A fistfull of spaghetti / Mandrax sunset variations pt.IV / Neville / Breakfast / Wholefood love / Holiday frog / Teenage Paradise / Willie Baxter's blues / It never rains in El Paso / Whispering grass / Death of rock'n'roll.

Stiff / not iss.

Sep 77. (7"ep) *(LAST 2)* **SNUFF ROCK E.P.** [ ] [-]
– Kill / Gobbin' on life / Snuffin' / Snuffin' in a Babylon.

Logo / not iss.

Nov 77. (7"m) *(GO 106)* **OLD TRUST. / NEVILLE / TEENAGER IN SCHTUCK** [ ] [-]

Sep 78. (7") *(GO 323)* **HEADS DOWN NO NONSENSE MINDLESS BOOGIE. / THANK YOU** [47] [-]

Sep 78. (lp) *(1009)* **SKITE** [ ] [-]
– Juan Lopez / Mother Superior / Heads down no nonsense mindless boogie / Where have all the flowers gone / 23 / Peter Parker / Rockin' sav'yer / **** you / Where have all the flowers gone (dub) / Anarchy in the U.K. / God is mad.

Nov 78. (7") *(GO 335)* ****** YOU. / DEAD MEAT (pt.2)** [ ] [-]

Dec 78. (d7") *(GOD 340)* **JUAN LOPEZ. / TEENAGE PARADISE // DEAD MEAT (pt.3)** [ ] [-]

Jul 80. (lp) *(MOGO 4008)* **THE WORST OF THE BERTS** (compilation) [ ] [-]

— Disbanded 1979, PRYOR died of cancer in 1980. HIBBERT made a solo album, 'HEAVY DUTY'. LEE became a music journalist and as LORD BUCKLEY, recorded a live album, 'M'LORDS & LADIES'. BOWERS and HARDING formed indie outfit, The MOTHMEN, who released two sets, 'PAY ATTENTION' and 'ONE BLACK DOT'. MITCHELL, with the aforementioned MOTHMEN, were also part of DURUTTI COLUMN. The ALBERTOS re-formed in 1982 for one-off 45.

New Hormones / not iss.

Dec 82. (7") *(ORG 30)* **CRUISIN' WITH SANTA. /** [ ] [-]

– compilations, etc. –

Apr 91. (cd) *Mau Mau; (MAUCD 604)* **SNUFF ROCK – THE BEST OF THE ALBERTOS** [ ] [-]
– Old Trust / Brrr! / I'll come if you let me / Invocation of the fundamental orrifice of St.Agnes / No change / Peon in the neck / Happy to be on (an island away from Demis Roussos / Teenager in schtuck / Italians from Outer Space: (a) The battle of Colonel Callan, (b) A fistfull of spaghetti / Mandrax variations part IV / Naville breakfast / Whole food love / Holiday frog / Teenage paradise / Willie Baxter's blues / It never rains in El Paso / Whispering grass / Death of rock and roll / Heads down, no nonsense, mindless boogie / Jesus wept / Kill / Gobbin' on life / Snuffin' like that / Snuffin' in a Babylon / 23 / Dead meat / Juan Lopez / Anadin / Pavlov / Anarchy in the UK.

Feb 97. (cd) *Overground; (OVER 56CD)* **RADIO SWEAT** [ ] [-]

ALICE DONUT

Formed: New York, USA . . . mid 80's by singer TOMAS ANTONA, MICHAEL JUNG, RICHARD MARSHALL, TED HOUGHTON, STEPHEN MOSES and DAVE GIFFIN. Described as nasty, horrible Americans, who like nothing better than to outrage people with their crazy lyrics and antics, ALICE DONUT found a natural home at JELLO BIAFRA's 'Alternative Tentacles' label. Fronted by a man who looks like GENESIS P. ORRIDGE (Psychic TV) leaving an Oxfam shop and characterised by a fondness for outlandishly juvenile song titles, ALICE DONUT accumulated a (very!) cult fanbase with releases such as 'DONUT COMES ALIVE' (1988) and 'BUCKETFULLS OF SICKNESS AND HORROR IN AN OTHERWISE MEANINGLESS LIFE' (1989). The lads began the 90's in much the same fashion, spinning their sub-JESUS LIZARD/DEAD KENNEDYS punk squall over a series of critically lambasted sets, their "unique" sense of humour one of their few saving graces. Having bulldozed through Black Sabbath's 'WAR PIGS' on the 'REVENGE FANTASIES OF THE IMPOTENT' album in '91, they virtually demolished The Beatles' 'HELTER SKELTER' on 1994's 'DRY HUMPING THE CASH COW'. The latter remains something of an oddity, featuring as it does a number of bonafide live tracks (at the CBGB's) alongside their best known songs dubbed over with a mock stadium crowd roar. A year later it seemed all over bar the shouting when they delivered their final set, 'PURE ACID PARK'.

Album rating: DRY HUMPING THE CASH COW part compilation (*4)

TOMAS ANTONA – vocals / **MICHAEL JUNG** – guitar, vocals / **RICHARD MARSHALL** – guitar, vocals / **TED HOUGHTON** – bass, vocals / **STEPHEN MOSES** – drums, trombone / **DAVE GIFFIN** – guitar

Alternative Tentacles / Alternative Tentacles

1988. (lp/cd) *<(VIRUS 61/+CD)>* **DONUT COMES ALIVE** [ ] [ ]
– Green meat stew / American lips / etc.

Jul 89. (lp/cd) *<(VIRUS 73/+CD)>* **BUCKETFULLS OF SICKNESS AND HORROR IN AN OTHERWISE MEANINGLESS LIFE** [ ] [ ]
– Lydia's black lung / Testosterone gone wild / Dorothy / Sinead O'Connor on T.V. / Sky of bones / Egg / Consumer decency / My life is a mediocre piece of shit / Incinerator heart / Buckets, pock, fork / Demonologist / Lisa's father.

Aug 90. (7") *<(VIRUS 83)>* **MY BOYFRIEND'S BACK. / DEMONOLOGIST** [ ] [ ]

Sep 90. (lp/cd) *<(VIRUS 82/+CD)>* **MULE** [ ] [ ]
– Mother of Christ / Mrs. Hayes / Roaches in the sink / Crawlpappy / My severed heads / Bottom of the chain / Burlesque / Big ass / Roadkill / Tiny ugly world / J train downtown – A nest of murder cow's placenta to armageddon. *(cd+=)* – My boyfriend's back.

May 91. (lp/cd) *<(VIRUS 91/+CD)>* **REVENGE FANTASIES OF THE IMPOTENT** [ ] [ ]
– Rise to the skin / My best friend's wife / Telebloodprintmeadiadeathwhore / What / Dead river / Sleep / Naked, sharp and perfect / Come up with your hands out / War pigs / Good pasta.

Oct 91. (12"/cd-s) *<(VIRUS 101/+CD)>* **BIGGEST ASS. / BIGGER ASS / BIG ASS (live)** [ ] [ ]

— **SISSI SCHULMEISTER** – bass, vocals; repl. HOUGHTON + GIFFIN

Jul 92. (7") *<(VIRUS 114)>* **MAGDALENE. / ONLY THE GOOD DIE YOUNG** [ ] [ ]
(cd-s+=) *<(VIRUS 114CD)>* –

Sep 92. (lp/cd) *<(VIRUS 115/+CD)>* **THE UNTIDY SUICIDES OF YOUR DEGENERATE CHILDREN** [ ] [ ]

Mar 93. (7") *<(VIRUS 121)>* **MEDICATION. /** [ ] [ ]
(cd-s+=) *<(VIRUS 121CD)>* –

Apr 94. (lp/cd) *<(VIRUS 143/+CD)>* **DRY-HUMPING THE CASH COW** (some live at CBGB's 1993) [ ] [ ]
– Green meat stew / Hose / The tingler / Dorothy / Every body is on sale / My best friend's wife / Mrs. Hayes / The son of a disgruntled x-postal worker reflects on his life while getting stoned in the parking lot of a Winn Dixie listening to Metallica / Dead river / Mother of Christ / Helter skelter / American lips / Egg / Demonologist / Buckets, pock, fork. *(cd re-iss. Nov97; same)*

— In Oct'94, they teamed up with ICE PRINCESS for a single on 'Cargo'; *BEAT 013)*

Nov 94. (7") *<(VIRUS 154)>* **NADINE. / CHICKEN DOOR** [ ] [ ]
(cd-s+=) *<(VIRUS 154CD)>* – Empty streets.

Jul 95. (lp/cd) *<(VIRUS 163/+CD)>* **PURE ACID PARK** [ ] [ ]
– Millenium / Dreaming in Cuban / Freaks in love / Big cars and blow jobs / I walked with a zombie / The senator and the cabin boy / Mummenschantz pachinko / Insane / Shining path / Unspeakable pleasure of being me / Lost in space / Cain. *(cd re-iss. Nov97; same)*

ALIEN SEX FIEND

Formed: London, England . . . 1982 by NIK WADE, a former DEMON PREACHERS member who enlisted the help of his wife, CHRISTINE (aka MRS. FIEND). The aforementioned band released a couple of 45's towards the end of the decade, recording for such established indie imprints as 'Illegal' and 'Small Wonder. Adding DAVID JAMES (aka YAXI HIGHRIZER) and JOHNNY 'HA HA' FRESHWATER, the couple adopted the ALIEN SEX FIEND moniker and secured a residency at the infamous 'Batcave' club. Complete with thick ghoulish make-up, NIK led his band of ALICE COOPER devotees through a regular performance of cabaret goth, recording a live demo cassette 'THE LEWD, THE MAD, THE UGLY & OLD NIK' at their famous haunt. Carving out a deal with Cherry Red subsidiary, 'Anagram', the 'FIENDS released two singles, 'IGNORE THE MACHINE' and 'LIPS CAN'T GO', both highlights of their late 1983 debut set, 'WHO'S BEEN SLEEPING IN MY BRAIN?'. An almost permanent fixture in the indie charts from then on ('ACID BATH' – 1984, etc), the band also became massive in Japan, their third set, 'LIQUID HEAD IN TOKYO – LIVE' (1985) documenting this surprise phenomenon. Subsequently continuing as a trio without JOHNNY, they were finally offered the honour of supporting their schlock-rocker idol, ALICE COOPER, on his 1986 "Nightmare Returns" tour. Having contributed to three further mid-80's sets (' . . . MAXIMUM SECURITY', 'IT – THE ALBUM' and 'HERE CUM GERMS'), YAXI was the next to depart, leaving the husband and wife team to record a one-off single, 'WHERE ARE BATMAN AND ROBIN', as The DYNAMIC DUO. ALIEN SEX FIEND returned to terrorize self-respecting indie fans with the likes of 'ANOTHER PLANET' (1988), 'TOO MUCH ACID?' (1989), although their shift more electronically based territory ALIENated some of their more traditional fans. Later in the 90's, after a couple of patchy sets, including the 'INFERNO' CD-ROM game/album, they initiated their own '13th Moon Records' label. • **Songwriters:** NIK penned most except; SCHOOL'S OUT (Alice Cooper) / I WALK THE LINE (Johnny Cash) / HURRICANE FIGHTER PLANE (Red Crayola) / SILVER MACHINE (Hawkwind).

Album rating: THE SINGLES 1983-1995 compilation (*6)

DEMON PREACHERS

NIK FIEND (b. Wales) – vocals, bass (ex-EARWIGS, ex-MR. & MRS. DEMEANOUR) / (+ 3 others)

Illegal not iss.

1978. (7"m) *(SRTS-CUS 78110)* **ROYAL NORTHERN (N7) / LAUGHING AT ME. / STEAL YOUR LOVE / DEAD END KIDZ** -

Small Wonder not iss.

Aug 78. (7") *(SMALL TEN)* **LITTLE MISS PERFECT. / PERFECT DUB** -

Crypt Music not iss.

1980. (7"; as The DEMONS) *(DEM 1)* **ACTION BY EXAMPLE./ I WISH I WAS A DOG** -

ALIEN SEX FIEND

NIK WADE – vocals, bass / **CHRISTINE WADE** – synthesizers / **DAVID JAMES** (aka YAXI HIGHRIZER) – guitar / **JOHNNY 'HA HA' FRESHWATER** – drums

Anagram not iss.

Aug 83. (7") *(ANA 11)* **IGNORE THE MACHINE. / THE GIRL AT THE END OF MY GUN** -
(12"+=) *(12ANA 11)* – I'm not mad.
(12"+=) *(12ANA 11X)* – Under the thunder.
(re-iss. Mar85 7"pic-d; (PANA 11) – ('A'mix) / ('A'dub version). *(pic-cd-s iss.Sep88; CDANA 11)*

Oct 83. (7") *(ANA 15)* **LIPS CAN'T GO. / DRIVE MY ROCKET (UP URANUS)** -
(12"+=) *(12ANA 15)* – Toytown mix / 30 second coma.

Nov 83. (lp) *(GRAM 10)* **WHO'S BEEN SLEEPING IN MY BRAIN?** -
– I wish I woz a dog / Wild women / I'm not mad / New Christian music / Wigwam wipeout / I'm her Frankenstein / I am a product / Ignore the machine / R.I.P. / Lips can't go / Black rabbit. *(cd-iss. Sep98; CDGRAM 10)*

Feb 84. (7"/7"red) *(ANA 18)* **R.I.P. / NEW CHRISTIAN MUSIC** -
(10"+=/12"+=) *(10/12 ANA 18)* – Crazee.

Aug 84. (7"pic-d/7",7"red) *(P+/ANA 23)* **DEAD AND BURIED. / ATTACK** -
(12"+=) *(12ANA 23)* – Ignore the machine.

Oct 84. (lp/c) *(GRAM/CGRAM 18)* **ACID BATH** -
– In God we trust / Dead and re-buried / Smoke my bones / She's a killer / E.S.T. (trip to the Moon) / Breakdown and cry (lay down and say goodbye) / Hee-haw (here come the bone people) / Attack / Boneshaker baby. *(c+=)* – WHO'S BEEN SLEEPING IN MY BRAIN? *(cd-iss. Jun88 & May93 & Jun97 +=; CDMGRAM 18)* – I am a product (live) / 30 second coma.

Oct 84. (7") *(ANA 25)* **E.S.T. (TRIP TO THE MOON). / BONESHAKER BABY** -
(11"+=) *(11ANA 25)* – I am a product (live).

Jul 85. (m-lp) *(MGRAM 22)* **LIQUID HEAD IN TOKYO (live)** -
– R.I.P. / E.S.T. / Dead and buried / In God we trust / Back to the egg / Attack / Lips can't go / Wild woman. *(cd-iss. Jan97 on 'Summit'; SUMCD 4087)*

— trimmed to a trio, when JOHNNY departed HA HA (it's not funny- ed)

Aug 85. (12"m) *(12ANA 30)* **I'M DOIN' TIME IN A MAXIMUM SECURITY TWILIGHT HOME. / IN AND OUT OF MY MIND / BACKWARD BEAVER** -

Sep 85. (lp) *(GRAM 24)* **(I'M DOIN' TIME IN A) MAXIMUM SECURITY TWILIGHT HOME** -
– I'm doin' time in a maximum security twilight home / Spies / Depravity lane / Seconds to nowhere / The beaver destroys forest / Mine's full of maggots / In and out of my mind / Fly in the ointment / Do you sleep (not of one mind). *(re-iss. Jun88 on 'Antler'; ANT037) (cd-iss. Nov88 & Apr94 as 'THE FIRST ALIEN SEX FIEND CD' =; CDGRAM 25)* – E.S.T. (trip to the Moon) / Boneshaker baby / Ignore the machine / Attack!!!.

Flicknife not iss.

May 86. (7") *(SFLEP 106)* **I WALK THE LINE. / SCHOOL'S OUT** -
(d7"+=/12"+=) *(DL/FL EP 106)* – Here she comes/ Can't stop smoking. *(d7"re-iss. Feb95; SFLEP 106)*

Vat not iss.

Aug 86. (7") **GET INTO IT. / SOMEONE KEEPS ON BUGGIN' ME** -

Anagram not iss.

Oct 86. (7"/12") *(ANA/12ANA 32)* **SMELLS LIKE SHIT. / SOMEOME KEEPS ON BUGGIN' ME** -

Oct 86. (lp/c) *(GRAM/CGRAM 26)* **IT – THE ALBUM** -
– Smells like shit / Manic depression / Believe it or not / Get into it / Wop bop / April showers / Lesson one / Do it right / To be continued . . . *(re-iss. Jun88 on 'Antler' lp/c+=; ANT 048/+C)* – TWILIGHT HOME (lp tracks) *(cd-iss. Dec91 +=; CDGRAM 26)* – Buggin' me / Hurricane fighter pilot / It lives again.

Feb 87. (7") *(ANA 33)* **HURRICANE FIGHTER PLANE. / IT LIVES AGAIN** -
(12"+=) *(12ANA 33)* – ('A'mix).

Jun 87. (7") *(ANA 34)* **THE IMPOSSIBLE MISSION. / MY BRAIN IS IN THE CUPBOARD ABOVE THE KITCHEN SINK** -
(12"+=) *(12ANA 34)* – Put A-Z.

Aug 87. (7") *(ANA 38)* **HERE CUM GERMS. / ('A'-Ravi mix) / ('A'dub)** -
(12"+=) *(12ANA 38)* – Camel camel.

Oct 87. (lp/c) *(GRAM/CGRAM 31)* **HERE CUM GERMS** -
– The mission impossible / Here cum germs (Ravi mix) / Isolation / My brain is in the cupboard above the kitchen / You are soul / Death / Boots on!. *(cd-iss. Jun92 +=; CDGRAM 31)* – Camel, camel / Stuff the turkey / They all call me crazee.

Nov 87. (7",7"red,7"green) *(ANA 40)* **STUFF THE TURKEY. / THEY ALL CALL ME CRAZEE** -

— now as duo when YAXI left

Oct 88. (12"m) *(12ANA 45)* **BUN HO!. / SILVER MACHINE / SATISFACTION** -

Oct 88. (cd/c/lp) *(CD/C+/GRAM 38)* **ANOTHER PLANET** -
– Bun ho! / Everybody's dream / Radiant city / Spot your lucky warts / Sample my sausage / Outer limits / Instant karma sutra / So much to do – So little time / Alien / Wild green fiendly liquid / Nightmare zone / Bun ho (time after time) / Another planet. *(c+=)* – Silver machine / Satisfaction. *(cd re-iss. Jun97; same)*

Mar 89. (7") *(ANA 46)* **HAUNTED HOUSE. / ('A'dub version)** -
(12"+=/cd-s+=) *(12/CD ANA 46)* –

Sep 89. (cd/c/d-lp) *(CD/C+/GRAM 41)* **TOO MUCH ACID? (live)** -
– It lives again / I walk the line / Nightmare zone / Get into it / E.S.T. (trip to the Moon) / So much to do, so little time / Bun ho! / Haunted house / Smells like shit / Hurricane fighter plane / Sample my sausage / Boneshaker baby. *(cd re-iss. May93; same)*

Sep 90. (7") **NOW I'M FEELING ZOMBIEFIED. / ?** -
(12"+=/cd-s+=) –

Oct 90. (cd/c/lp) *(CD/C+/GRAM 46)* **CURSE** -
– Katch 22 / You – Along cums reality – Hubble bubble / Goodbye to space / Now I'm feeling zombiefied / Stress / Blessings of the state / Eat! eat! eat! (an eye for an eye) / Ain't got time to bleed / Bleeding (reprise) / Dalisms / Burger bar baby / I think I . . . Mad daddy drives a UFO / Wuthering wind / Radio Jimi / Hands of the silken / Blessing in disguise.

Mar 92. (cd/c/lp) *(CD/C+/GRAM 51)* **OPEN HEAD SURGERY** -
– Clockwork banana banana – moon / Magic / Class of '69 / Aliensexfiend / Coma / Lickin' ma bone / Stressed out / B-B-Bone boogie.

Feb 93. (cd/c/lp) *(CD/C+/GRAM 60)* **THE ALTERED STATES OF AMERICA** -
– Wild women / Now I'm feeling zombiefied / Class of '69 / Ignore the machine / Magic / Coma / Eat! eat! eat! / R.I.P. (blue crumb truck).

Jul 94. (12") *(MFF 007T)* **INFERNO. /** -
(above issued on 'Cherry Red')

Oct 94. (cd) *(CDGRAM 80) <9529>* **INFERNO**
– Inferno / Human installation / Take off tune / Space 1 / Happy tune / Planet 1 / Human atmosphere / Happy finale / Alien installation / Aromatic tune / Moon toon / Planet 2 / Bad news / Space 2 / Alien atmosphere / Death tune / Sad finale / Moon ton (lunaphases mix) / Planet 2 (together dreamscape mix) / Inferno.

Mar 95. (cd-ep) *(CDGRAM 56)* **INFERNO / INFERNO (Mix) / PLANET 2 / ECHOES** -

13th Moon 13th Moon

Feb 96. (12"/cd-s) *(FULL T/CDS 001)* **EVOLUTION. / ('A'mixes)** -
Mar 97. (cd/d-lp) *(FULL CD/DLP 1301)* **NOCTURNAL EMISSIONS** Nov98
Aug 97. (12") *(FULLT 002R)* **ON A MISSION (remix). /** Oct98
Nov 98. (12") *(FULLT 003R)* **TAROT (7 mix). / ('A'-No.6 mix) / ('A'-POD dub mix)** -

– compilations, etc. –

Mar 88. (cd/c/lp) *Anagram; (CD/C+GRAM 34)* **ALL OUR YESTERDAZE (The Singles Collection 1983-87)** -
– Ignore the machine / Lips can't go / R.I.P. – Blue crumb truck / Dead & buried / E.S.T. – Trip to the Moon / I'm doing time in a maximum security twilight home / I walk the line / Smells like shit / Hurricane fighter pilot. *(cd re-iss. May93; same)*

Mar 88. (12"; as DYNAMIC DUO) *Anagram; (12ANA 42)* **WHERE ARE BATMAN AND ROBIN? / BATMAN THEME** -

Oct 93. (cd/c) *Anagram; (CD/C+/GRAM 69)* **THE LEGENDARY BATCAVE TAPES (live)** -
(cd re-iss. Jun98 as 'BAT CAVE MASTERS' on 'Cleopatra'; CLP 232)

Aug 94. (cd) *Cleopatra; (CLEO 9412-2)* **DRIVE MY ROCKET** -
Jun 95. (cd) *Cleopatra; (CLEO 9508CD)* **I'M HER FRANKENSTEIN** -
Oct 95. (d-cd) *Anagram; (CDGRAM 99)* **THE SINGLES 1983-1995** -
Feb 98. (d-cd) *Snapper; (SMDCD 133)* **WARDANCE OF THE ALIEN SEX FIEND** -

ALL (see under ⇒ DESCENDENTS)

ALL ABOUT EVE

Formed: London, England . . . 1985 by music journalist JULIANNE REGAN and ex-AEMOTTI CRII member TIM BRICHENO. Named after a 1950 Bette Davis film, they released four indie hits on own their 'Eden' records, before landing a contract with 'Mercury' in mid-87. Their major label debut (a re-mix of their second 45, 'IN THE CLOUDS') hit the UK Top 50, and paved the way for late 80's chart status. Touting progressive "acid-folk" "hippy-goth" influenced by early 70's acoustic LED ZEPPELIN or even CURVED AIR (imagary & mysticism), ALL ABOUT EVE were for a brief period in the late 80's, something of an alluring alternative to the disposable pop clogging up the charts. A follow-up single, 'WILD HEARTED WOMAN', made the Top 40, although the band really broke through later that summer with the ethereal 'MARTHA'S HARBOUR', a single which crossed over to rock/pop fans and made the UK Top 10. Its success fuelled further sales of the eponymous debut album which achieved a similar chart position. The tricky momentum of simultaneously balancing a goth/indie and mainstream fanbase came undone with a more morose follow-up album, 'SCARLET AND OTHER STORIES' (1989). Though it made the Top 10, it failed to match the success of its predecessors, the record's downbeat sound possibly attributable to the internal ructions taking place. BRICHENO finally left for The SISTERS OF MERCY in 1990, his replacement being CHURCH-man, MARTY WILLSON-PIPER, initially on a temporary basis and subsequently full-time. Despite being touted as a return to form, 'TOUCHED BY JESUS' (1991) failed to meet commercial expectations and the band split from theie label shortly after. Despite a comeback with a set for 'M.C.A.', 'ULTRAVIOLET', the band finally called it a day in early '93. REGAN subsequently formed HARMONY AMBULANCE (who released a one-off 45 for 'Rough Trade') before going on to work with BERNARD BUTLER and later form MICE. • **Songwriters:** REGAN – lyrics / BRICHENO – music, until his departure, then group compositions. Covered; THE WITCHES' PROMISE (Jethro Tull)? • **Trivia:** 1987 single 'OUR SUMMER' was produced by WAYNE HUSSEY and SIMON HINKLER (of The MISSION). JULIANNE returned the favour by guesting on their 'God's Own Medicine' album. BRICHENO also joined The MISSION for a time, after his relationship with REGAN floundered.

Album rating: ALL ABOUT EVE (*8)

JULIANNE REGAN – vocals, (some) keyboards / **TIMOTHY BRICHENO** (b. 6 Jul'63, Huddersfield, England) – guitar / **ANDY COUSIN** – bass (group augmented by a drum machine)

Eden | not iss.

Jul 85. (12") *(1 EDEN)* **D FOR DESIRE. / DON'T FOLLOW ME (MARCH HARE)** [ ] [-]
Apr 86. (12") *(2 EDEN)* **IN THE CLOUDS. / END OF THE DAY / LOVE LEADS NOWHERE** [ ] [-]
Apr 87. (7") *(EVEN 3)* **OUR SUMMER. / LADY MIDNIGHT** [ ] [-]
(ext.12"+=) *(EVENX 3)* – Shelter from the rain.
Jul 87. (7") *(EVEN 4)* **FLOWERS IN OUR HAIR. / PARADISE** [ ] [-]
(12"+=) *(EVENX 4)* – Devil woman.

—— added **MARK PRICE** – drums

Mercury | Mercury

Oct 87. (7") *(EVEN 5)* **IN THE CLOUDS. / SHE MOVES THROUGH THE FAIR** [47] [-]
(12"+=) *(EVENX 5)* – Calling your name.
Jan 88. (7") *(EVEN 6)* **WILD HEARTED WOMAN. / APPLE TREE MAN** [33] [-]
(c-s+=/12"+=) *(EVEN M/X 6)* – Like Emily.
(12"box++=) *(EVENX 6-22)* – What kind of fool (live).
(cd-s+=) *(EVNCD 6)* – Like Emily / In the clouds.
Feb 88. (lp/c)(cd) *(MERH/+C 119)(<834 260-2>)* **ALL ABOUT EVE** [7] [ ]
– Flowers in our hair / Gypsy dance / In the clouds / Martha's harbour / Every angel / Like Emily / Shelter from the storm / She moves through the fair / Wild hearted woman / Never promise (anyone forever) / What kind of fool. *(c+=/cd+=)* – Apple tree man / In the meadow / Lady Midnight.
Mar 88. (7"/7"g-f) *(EVEN/+G 7)* **EVERY ANGEL. / WILD FLOWERS** [30] [-]
(12"+=) *(EVENX 7)* – Candy tree.
(10"++=)(cd-s++=) *(EVEN 710)(EVNCD 7)* – More than this hour.
Jul 88. (7") *(EVEN 8)* **MARTHA'S HARBOUR. / ANOTHER DOOR** [10] [-]
(12"+=) *(EVENX 8)* – In the meadow (live).
(c-s++=) *(EVENM 8)* – Never promise (anyone forever) (live).
(cd-s+=) *(EVNCD 8)* – She moves through the fair (live) / Wild flowers (live).
(12"+=) *(EVENXB 8)* – In the clouds (live) / Shelter from the rain (live).
Nov 88. (7") *(EVEN 9)* **WHAT KIND OF FOOL. / GOLD AND SILVER** [29] [-]
(12"+=) *(EVENX 9)* – The garden of Jane Delawney.
(12"box++=/cd-s++=) *(EVN XB 9/CD 99)* – ('A'-Autumn rhapsody mix).
(10"+=) *(EVEN 9-10)* – Every angel (live).
Sep 89. (7"/c-s) *(EVEN/EVNMC 10)* **ROAD TO YOUR SOUL. / PIECES OF OUR HEART** [37] [-]
(ext.12"+=)(pic-cd-s+=) *(EVNXP/EVCDX 10)* – Hard Spaniard.
Oct 89. (lp/c/cd) *(<838 965-1/-4/-2>)* **SCARLET AND OTHER STORIES** [9] [ ]
– Road to your soul / Dream now / Gold and silver / Scarlet / December / Blind lemon Sam / More than the blues / Tuesday's child / Pieces of our heart ** / Hard Spaniard * / The empty dancehall / Only one reason / The pearl fisherman. *(c+= *)(cd++= **)*
Dec 89. (7"/c-s) *(EVEN/+MC 11)* **DECEMBER. / DROWNING** [34] [-]
(7"pic-d+=/10"+=) *(EVEN P/B 11)* – Paradise ('89 remix).
(c-s+=/12"+=/cd-s+=) *(EVE MC/NX/NCD 11)* – The witches' promise.
Apr 90. (7"/c-s) *(EVEN/+MC 12)* **SCARLET. / OUR SUMMER (live)** [34] [-]
(12"+=/cd-s+=) *(EVENX/EVNCD 12)* – Candy tree (live) / Tuesday's child (live).

—— (Aug'90) When BRICHENO went off to join SISTERS OF MERCY. **MARTY WILLSON-PIPER** (of The CHURCH) came in temp. at first, then full-time.

Jun 91. (7") *(EVEN 14)* **FAREWELL MR. SORROW. / ELIZABETH OF GLASS** [36] [-]
(12"+=/cd-s+=) *(EVENX/EVNCD 14)* – All the rings round Saturn.

Vertigo | Mercury

Aug 91. (7"/7"pic-d/c-s) *(EVEN/+P/MC 15)* **STRANGE WAY. / DRAWN TO EARTH** [50] [-]
(pic-cd-s+=) *(EVNCD 15)* – Share it with me.
(10"+=) *(EVENB 15)* – Share it with me / Nothing without you.
(12"+=) *(EVENX 15)* – Nothing without you / Light as a feather.
Aug 91. (cd/c/lp) *(<51046-2/-4/-1>)* **TOUCHED BY JESUS** [17] [ ]
– Strange way / Farewell Mr. Sorrow / Wishing the hours away / Touched by Jesus / The dreamer / Share it with me * / Rhythm of life / The mystery we are / Hide child / Ravens / Are you lonely. *(c/cd+= *) (re-iss. Feb93; same)*
Oct 91. (7") *(EVEN 16)* **THE DREAMER (remix). / FRIDA OF BLOOD AND GOLD** [41] [-]
(12"+=) *(EVENX 16)* – Road to Damascus / Strange way (demo).
(cd-s+=) *(EVNCD 16)* – Road to Damascus / ('A'-nightmare mix).

M.C.A. | M.C.A.

Sep 92. (7"ep/c-ep/cd-ep/10"blue-ep) *(MCS/+C/CD/T 1688)* **PHASED EP** [38] [-]
– Phased / Mine / Infrared / Ascent-descent.
Oct 92. (cd/c/lp) *(<MCD/MCC/MCA 10712>)* **ULTRAVIOLET** [46] [ ]
– Phased / Yesterday goodbye / Mine / Freeze / Things he told her / Infrared / I don't know / Dream butcher / Some finer day / Blindfolded visionary / Outside the Sun.
Nov 92. (7"/c-s) *(MCS/+CS 1706)* **SOME FINER DAY. / MOODSWING** [57] [-]
(10"+=/cd-s+=) *(MCS T/CD 1706)* – Dive in.

—— Disbanded early 1993, JULIANNE formed HARMONY AMBULANCE and released one-off 45 for 'Rough Trade'. In 1994, she began working with BERNARD BUTLER (ex-SUEDE), signing solo to 'Permanent' she soon formed her own band, MICE, with past AAE members

– compilations, others, etc. –

Feb 91. (cd-ep) *Mercury; (EVCDX 13)* **THIRTEEN (live)** [ ] [-]
– In the clouds / Never promise (anyone forever) / Scarlet / More than the blues / Road to your soul.
Nov 92. (cd/c/lp) *Vertigo; (514 154-2/-4/-1)* **WINTER WORDS – HITS AND RARITIES** [ ] [-]
(re-iss. Apr95 cd/c; same)
Nov 93. (cd) *Windsong; (WINCD 044)* **BBC RADIO 1 LIVE IN CONCERT – GLASTONBURY FESTIVAL (live)** [ ] [-]

MICE

—— **JULIANNE REGAN** – vocals / with **COUSIN** + **PRICE** and **BIC** – guitar (ex-CARDIACS)

Permanent | Permanent

Nov 95. (7"yellow/c-s) *(7/CA SPERM 30)* **MAT'S PROZAC. / BANG BANG** [ ] [-]
(cd-s+=) *(CDSPERM 30)* – Julie Christie.
Apr 96. (7"/c-s/cd-s) *(7/CA/CD SPERM 31)* **THE MILKMAN (semi-skimmed version) / THE MILKMAN (full-cream version) / MARTIAN MAN / DIE UBERMAUS** [ ] [-]
Jul 96. (7"colrd/c-s) *(7/CA SPERM 033)* **DEAR SIR. / ('A'mix)** [ ] [-]
(cd-s+=) *(CDSPERM 033)* – Pyjamadrama / Tiny window.
Aug 96. (cd/c/lp) *(<PERM CD/MC/LP 035>)* **BECAUSE I CAN** [ ] [ ]
– Mat's prozac / Star / Dear sir / Bang bang / The milkman / Trumpet song / Blue sonic boy / Julie Christie / Miss World / Battersea / Messed up.

G. G. ALLIN

Born: KEVIN ALLIN, c.1960, New Hampshire, USA. The high priest of animalistic, degenerate punk rock, the man used to relieve himself on stage, yes one's AND two's folks (a bit of an asshole, you could say!). Influenced by, and going one (hundred times!) uglier than IGGY POP and MC5, ALLIN went beyond conventional rock'n'roll outrage by indulging in increasingly more explicit acts of on-stage sex, violence, self-mutilation, drug-taking, defecation, masturbation, verbal-abuse and general depravity as his career dragged on. Public enemy No.1, the crazed ALLIN was continually in trouble with the law, the performance (and actual enactment!) of songs such as 'YOU SCUM, EAT MY DIARRHOEA' not exactly the behaviour of an upstanding US citizen. Alternately backed by The JABBERS and The SCUMFUCS, ALLIN recorded a series of sporadic lp's for a number of independent labels, among them 'ALWAYS WAS, IS, AND ALWAYS SHALL BE' (1980), 'EAT MY FUC' (1984) and 'ARTLESS' (1985). In 1987, ALLIN collaborated with 'Homestead' head honcho, GERARD COSLOY (as The HOLY MEN), on an album, 'YOU GIVE LOVE A BAD NAME'. Early in 1990, ALLIN was sent down for four years (Aggravated GBH was the charge), boasting from his Michigan (Jackson State) prison cell that he'd kill himself on stage upon his return to civvie street. In the event, ALLIN died from a drugs overdose (27th June, 1993) having run amok, naked in the street after a New York show, indiscriminately attacking stunned passers-by. He had recently completed sessions with new band, The MURDER JUNKIES, these recordings posthumously released as 'BRUTALITY & BLOODSHED FOR ALL'. ALLIN was recently (late in '98) one of the subjects of a Channel 4 (UK) series documenting the history of subversive performers in rock music.

Album rating: HATED IN THE NATION (*5)

G.G. ALLIN – vocals / **CHRIS CHAOS** – guitar / **ALLEN CHAPPLE** – bass / **STEVE L** (b. Manchester, England) – drums

not iss. | Orange

Sep 80. (lp; as G.G. ALLIN & THE JABBERS) *<ORA-777>* **ALWAYS WAS, IS, AND ALWAYS SHALL BE** [-] [ ]
– Bored to death / Beat, beat, beat / One man army / Assface / Pussy summit meeting / Cheri love affair / Automatic / I need adventure / Don't talk to me / Unpredictable / 1980's rock'n'roll.

—— guests included on next, WAYNE KRAMER + DENNIS THOMPSON (both ex-MC5)

Aug 81. (7"; as G.G. ALLIN & THE JABBERS) *<ORA-69>* **GIMME SOME HEAD. / DEAD OR ALIVE** [-] [ ]
1982. (7"ep) **PUBLIC ANIMAL #1** [-] [ ]
1983. (7"ep) **NO RULES EP** [-] [ ]

—— did a stint with The CEDAR STREET SLUTS

not iss. | Blood

1984. (7"ep) **HARD CANDY COCK EP** [-] [ ]
1984. (lp; as G.G. ALLIN & THE SCUMFUCS) **EAT MY FUC** [-] [ ]
– Hard candy cock / Out for blood / I don't give a shit / Drunk fight and fuck / Convulsions / I wanna fuck your brains out / I'm gonna rape you / Teachers pet / Fuckin' the dog / Cock on the loose / Clit licker / God of fire in Hell / Blow jobs / Live at A7 club in NYC.
1985. (7"ep) **I WANNA FUCK YOUR BRAINS OUT** [-] [ ]

not iss. | Starving Missile – Holy War

1985. (lp; as G.G. ALLIN & THE SCUMFUCS) **G.G. ALLIN & THE SCUMFUCS – ARTLESS** [-] [ ]

— next a collaboration with 'Homestead' boss, **GERARD COSLOY** – guitar / with others **GREG BULLOCK** – guitar / **MIKE KIRKLAND** – bass / **MIKE 'MACHINE GUN' EDISON** – drums

not iss. Homestead

1987. (lp; as G.G. ALLIN & THE HOLY MEN) **YOU GIVE LOVE A BAD NAME** [-] [ ]
– Swank fuckin' / Bloody Mary's bloody cunt / I'm a rapest / Suck dog / Teenage twats / Beer picnic / Stick finger clit / Scars on my body – Scabs on my dick / Garbage dump / Watch me kill the Boston girl / Castration crufixtion / Snakeman's dance / Slaughterhouse deathcamp / Feces and blood / Master daddy / (interview from prison). *(cd-iss. 1992 on 'Awareness'; 4)*

— now with **DORK** – keyboards / **JOHNNY X** – guitar

1988. (lp) **FREAKS, FAGGOTS, DRUNKS & JUNKIES** [-] [ ]
– My revenge / Dope money / Be my fuckin' whore / Suck my ass it smells / Dog shit / Wild riding / Sleeping in my piss / Anti social masterbator / Last in line for the gang bang / Die when you die / Commit suicide / Crash & burn / Outlaw scumfuc / Caroline and Sue / Cunt suckin' cannibal / Family / Young little meat / I wanna kill you / My bloody mutilation. *(cd-iss. 1992 on 'Awareness'; 3)*

not iss. Black & Blue

1988. (7"ep) **LIVE FAST, DIE FAST** [-] [ ]
1989. (lp; G.G. ALLIN & THE JABBERS) **BANNED IN BOSTON** [-] [ ]
1990. (lp) **DOCTRINE OF MAYHEM** [-] [ ]
– Blood for you / Darkness and a bottle to hold / In this room / Sluts in the city / Blood for you / (interview) / Abuse me (I want to die) / I wanna fuck myself / Ass fuckin' butt sucking / You'll never tame me / Torture you / Bite it you scum / Fuck the dead / I wanna piss on you / GG's Xmas song.

— in the early 90's, ALLIN was sentenced to 4 years imprisonment. He maintained he would commit suicide on stage after his release, although he OD'd (heroin & cocaine) after a gig on the toilet (where else!) on the 27th June '93. He left behind (you could say!) some more releases.

Alive Alive

Oct 93. (cd/lp; as G.G. ALLIN & THE MURDER JUNKIES) *<(ALIVE 001 CD/LP)>* **BRUTALITY AND BLOODSHED FOR ALL** [ ] [ ]
– Highest power / Kill thy father, rape thy mother / Anal cunt / Raw, brutal, rough and ready / Shoot, knife, strangle, beat & stab / I kill everything I fuck / Shove thy warrant up your ass / My sadistic killing spree / I'll slice yer fucking throat / Terror in America / Fuck off, we murder / Take aim and fire / Bastard son of a loaded gun / Legalise murder / Brutality and bloodshed for all.

— his last band above incl. **WILLIAM WEBER** – guitar, vocals / **MERLE ALLIN** – bass, vocals / **DINO SEX** – drums

New Rose New Rose

May 94. (cd) *(422008)* <4265> **MURDER JUNKIES** [ ] [ ] Oct94
– Savage blood bath / Murder for the mission-terrorist . . . / Sidewalk walking / I love nothing / Self absorbed / 99 stab wounds – Decapitation ritual / No limits no laws / War in my head – I'm your enemy / Dead fuck / Sister sodomy – Death and defication / Kill, kill, kill / Violence now – Assassinate the . . . / Drink from the pissing snakes mouth / Rape, torture, terminate and fuck / Guns and revolution / Kill the police – Destroy the system / Immortal pieces of me / My prison walls – 206045 / Death before life – Bloody cunt slider / I hate people.

Overground Alive

Dec 95. (cd; as G.G. ALLIN & THE MURDER JUNKIES) *(OVER 43CD) <ALIVE 12>* **TERROR IN AMERICA** [ ] [ ]
– Bite it / Look into my eyes and hate me / Take aim and fire / Outlaw scumfuc / Terror in America / Highest power / Cunt suckin' cannibal / Expose yourself to kids / I'm gonna rape you / Kill the police / Gypsy motherfucker / I live to be hated / Outlaw scumfuc / Fuck authority / I kill everything I fuck / Cunt suckin' cannibal / Highest power / Terror in America / Gypsy motherfucker / Outlaw scumfuc / Be my fuckin' whore / Wendy and Tilla.

– compilations, etc. –

1986. (c) *R.O.I.R.; <A 148>* **HATED IN THE NATION** [ ] [ ]
(cd-iss. Nov94; RE 148CD) (cd re-iss. Jul98; RUSCD 8242)
Nov 87. (lp) *Fan Club; (FC 032)* **DIRTY LOVE SONGS** [ ] [ ]
1989. (cd) *Awareness; <2>* **SUICIDE SESSIONS** [-] [ ]
1993. (cd) *Evergreen; <206045>* **ANTI-SOCIAL PERSONALITY DISORDER: LIVE (live 1989)** [-] [ ]
1990's. (7") *Stilleandacht; (SA 05)* **WATCH ME KILL. /** [-] [ ]
Apr 95. (cd) *Performance; <6>* **WAR IN MY HEAD** [-] [ ]
Jan 96. (cd) *Vinyl Retentive; <4>* **CARNIVAL OF EXCESS** [-] [ ]
Nov 97. (cd) *Mountain; (MCDLP 008)* **TROUBLED TROUBADOUR** [ ] [-]
1998. (cd) *Black & Blue;* **BOOZIN' AND PRANKS (live)** [-] [ ]

Marc ALMOND

Born: PETER MARC ALMOND, 9 Jul'59, Southport, England. Having met DAVE BALL at Leeds Polytechnic, the pair formed SOFT CELL and with the help of visual technician, STEVEN GRIFFITHS, they embarked on studio and live work in 1980 with the 'MUTANT MOMENTS' EP. After appearing on the infamous 'Some Bizzare Album', with cut, 'The Girl With The Patent Leather Face', they secured a bonafide deal with the 'Some Bizzare' label. The following year, after a debut single, 'MEMORABILIA' failed to make an impression, a darkly compelling, electro-fuelled cover of 'TAINTED LOVE' (once the dancefloor domain of disco diva, GLORIA JONES) slipped in to the UK chart, peaking at No.1 for two weeks. To end the year, SOFT CELL cracked the Top 5 with both 'BEDSITTER' and their debut album, 'NON-STOP EROTIC CABARET', an early 80's classic which trawled the depths of ALMOND's black-leather, neon-lit fantasies to a sleazy musical backdrop of low-rent alternative disco. Apart from the aforementioned singles, tracks such as 'YOUTH', 'SEX DWARF', 'SEEDY FILMS', 'CHIPS ON MY SHOULDER' and the forthcoming hit, 'SAY HELLO, WAVE GOODBYE', even found a rampant audience in the gay disco community of New York. The extroverted ALMOND was a figurehead for young homosexuals, although the media were scathing in their criticism of what they saw as the singer's effeminate posturing. Nevertheless, SOFT CELL continued to chalk up the hits, 'TORCH' (an exquisite duet featuring CINDY ECSTACY) narrowly missing No.1, while a revamped dance model of the debut, 'NON-STOP ECSTATIC DANCING', marked time as BALL and ALMOND worked on a follow-up. Early in '83, their second set proper, 'THE ART OF FALLING APART', hit the shops and subsequently the Top 5, the record coming with a free 12" single that saw ALMOND bravely attempting a HENDRIX medley. As the pair increasingly concentrated on separate projects, MARC & THE MAMBAS and DAVE BALL solo, a split seemed imminent; by the release of 'THIS LAST NIGHT . . . IN SODOM' in January '84, SOFT CELL was no more. After many threats of impending retirement, ALMOND was back in his beloved spotlight with the 'VERMIN IN ERMINE' (1984) album, cut with new backing band, The WILLING SINNERS. Developing further as an interpretive balladeer/torch singer with each successive release, ALMOND's mid-late 80's output found him marginalised to cult appeal despite an impressive array of cover material from such luminaries as JACQUES BREL, SCOTT WALKER and JOHNNIE RAY. This approach finally resulted in a massive comeback hit duet with GENE PITNEY, the melodramatic 'SOMETHING'S GOTTEN HOLD OF MY HEART', originally a Top 5 hit in 1967 for the singing/songwriting hearthrob. In the early 90's, SOFT CELL enjoyed a bit of a renaissance, remixed versions of 'SAY HELLO WAVE GOODBYE' and 'TAINTED LOVE' making the charts, while ALMOND scored a surprise Top 20 hit with a dancefloor reworking of Jacques Brel's 'JACKY'. Taken from the album, 'TENEMENT SYMPHONY' (1991), this return to form also numbered future hits, 'MY HAND OVER MY HEART' and 'THE DAYS OF PEARLY SPENCER', the latter another blast from the 60's past and originally a hit for DAVID McWILLIAMS. ALMOND continued to work on various idoisyncratic projects, including a set of old French songs and poems, 'ABSINTHE' (1993). • **Covered:** WHERE DID OUR LOVE GO (Supremes). MARC & THE MAMBAS covered IF YOU GO AWAY + THE BULLS (Jacques Brel) / CAROLINE SAYS (Lou Reed) / TERRAPIN (Syd Barrett) / CATCH A FALLEN STAR (Perry Como). MARC ALMOND solo:- A WOMAN'S STORY (Cher) / A SALTY DOG (Procol Harum) / THE LITTLE WHITE CLOUD THAT CRIED (Johnnie Ray) / THE PLAGUE (Scott Walker). • **Trivia:** In 1983, DAVE BALL scored the music for Tennessee Williams' play 'Suddenly Last Summer'. In mid 1987, ALMOND guested and wrote on SALLY TIMMS' single 'This House Is A House Of Tears'.

Album rating: Soft Cell: NON-STOP EROTIC CABARET (*8) / Soft Cell: MEMORABILIA – THE SINGLES compilation (*8) / Marc And The Mambas: UNTITLED (*8) / Marc Almond: THE SINGLES (1984-1987) compilation (*7)

SOFT CELL

MARC ALMOND – vocals / **DAVE BALL** – keyboards, synthesizers, drum programming

Big Frock not iss.

1980. (7"ep) *(ABF 1)* **MUTANT MOMENTS** [ ] [-]
– Potential / L.O.V.E. feelings / Metro MRX / Frustration.

Some Bizzare Sire

Mar 81. (7") *(HARD 1)* **MEMORABILIA. / A MAN CAN GET LOST** [ ] [-]
(12") *(HARD 12)* – ('A'extended) / Persuasion (extended).
Jul 81. (7") *(BZS 2) <49855>* **TAINTED LOVE. / WHERE DID OUR LOVE GO** [1] [8] Dec81
(12"+=) *(BZS 2-12)* – Tainted dub / Memorabilia.
(re-iss. Jul82; hit 50, re-iss. Jan85; hit 43)
Nov 81. (7"/ext-12") *(BZS 6/+12)* **BEDSITTER. / FACILITY GIRLS** [4] [ ]

— guests **CINDY ECSTACY** – dual vox / **DAVE TOFANI** – sax / **JOHN GATHELL** – trumpet

Dec 81. (lp/c) *(BZ LP/MC 2) <3647>* **NON-STOP EROTIC CABARET** [5] [22] Jan82
– Frustration / Tainted love / Seedy films / Youth / Sex dwarf / Entertain me / Chips on my shoulder / Bedsitter / Secret life / Say hello, wave goodbye. *(re-iss. May90 on 'Vertigo' cd/c/lp; 800 061-2/-4/-1)*
Jan 82. (7"/ext-12") *(BZS 7/+12)* **SAY HELLO, WAVE GOODBYE. / FUN CITY** [3] [ ]
May 82. (7"/ext-12") *(BZS 9/+12)* **TORCH. / INSECURE ME** [2] [ ]

— duo carried on without CINDY, who later formed SIX SEE RED

Jun 82. (m-lp/m-c) *(BZ X/M 1012) <23694>* **NON-STOP ECSTATIC DANCING** [6] [57] Jul82
– Memorabilia / Where did our love go / What! / A man could get lost / Chips on my shoulder * / Sex dwarf. *<US version repl.* with =>* – Insecure . . . me? *(re-iss. Mar92 on 'Mercury' cd/c; 510 295-2/-4)* – (extra tracks).
Aug 82. (7"/ext-12") *(BZS 11/+12)* **WHAT! / . . . SO (remix)** [3] [ ]
Nov 82. (7"/ext-12") *(BZS 16/+12)* **WHERE THE HEART IS. / IT'S A MUG GAME** [21] [ ]
Feb 83. (lp/c) *(BIZL/+C 3) <23769>* **THE ART OF FALLING APART** [5] [84]
– Forever the same / Where the heart is / Numbers / Heat / Kitchen sink drama / Baby doll / Loving you, hating me / The art of falling apart. *(12"ep with above +=)* – MARTIN. / HENDRIX MEDLEY: HEY JOE – PURPLE HAZE – VOODOO CHILE *(re-iss. Nov87; SOD 2) (re-iss. Mar92 on 'Mercury' cd/c; 510 296-2/-4)* – (extra tracks).
Feb 83. (7"/ext-12") *(BZS 16/+12)* **NUMBERS. / BARRIERS** [25] [-]
Apr 83. (7") **HEAT. / IT'S A MUGS GAME** [-] [ ]
Sep 83. (7") *(BZS 20)* **SOUL INSIDE. / YOU ONLY LIVE TWICE** [16] [ ]
(12"+=) *(BZS 20-12)* – Loving you, hating me / 007 theme.
(d7"+=) *(BZS 20-20)* – Loving you, hating me / Her imagination.
Feb 84. (7") *(BZS 22)* **DOWN IN THE SUBWAY. / DISEASE AND DESIRE** [24] [ ]
(ext-12"+=/12"remix+=) *(BZS/+R 22-12)* – Born to lose.
Mar 84. (lp/c) *(BIZL/+C 6)* **THIS LAST NIGHT . . . IN SODOM** [12] [ ]
– Mr. Self destruct / Slave to this / Little rough rhinestone / Meet murder my angel / The best way to kill / L'Esqualita / Down in the subway / Surrender (to a stranger) / Soul inside / Where was your heart (when you needed it most). *(cd-iss. Aug84; 818 436-2)*

— waved goodbye just prior to the above album

– compilations, others, etc. –

1982. (6x12"box) *Some Bizzare; (CELBX 1)* **THE 12" SINGLES** -
Dec 86. (lp/c)(cd) *Some Bizzare; (BZ LP/MC 3)(830 708-2)* **SOFT CELL – THE SINGLES** 58 -
Mar 91. (7"/c-s) *Mercury; (SOF T/MC 1)* **SAY HELLO, WAVE GOODBYE '91. / MEMORABILIA (Grid remix)** 38 -
(12"+=)(cd-s+=) *(SOFT 1-12)(SOFCD 1)* – ('A'-Mendelsohn extended remix).
(cd-s) *(SOFCP 1)* – ('A'side) / Numbers / Torch (12"version).
May 91. (7"/c-s)(12") *Mercury; (SOF T/MC 2)(SOFT 2-12)* **TAINTED LOVE ('91 remix). / ('A'-Original)** 5 -
(cd-s+=) *(SOFCP 2)* – Where did our love go?
(cd-s) *(SOFCD 2)* – Tainted love – Where the heart is / Loving you – hating me / Where the heart is.
May 91. (cd/c/lp) *Mercury; (848 512-2/-4/-1)* **MEMORABILIA – THE SINGLES** 8
– Memorabilia '91 / Tainted love / Bedsitter / Torch / What was the matter with Rachmaninov? / Say hello wave goodbye '91 / Where the heart is / I feel love / Tears run rings / A lover spurned / Something's gotten hold of my heart. *(cd+=)* – (Soul inside / Say hello wave goodbye (12"mix) / Waifs and strays (Grid twilight mix).
Mar 94. (cd/c) *Spectrum; (550 189-2/-4)* **DOWN IN THE SUBWAY** -
Mar 96. (cd) *Some Bizzare; (552 086-2)* **SAY HELLO TO SOFT CELL** -

MARC AND THE MAMBAS

with **ANNIE HOGAN** – piano / **TIM TAYLOR** – bass / **DAVE BALL** – multi instruments
Mar 82. (12"; mail order) *(BZS 5-12)* **FUN CITY. / SLEAZE (TAKE IT, SHAKE IT) / TAKING IT SHAKING IT** - -

— guests on next 2 albums were **GENESIS P. ORRIDGE + MATT JOHNSON**
Oct 82. (lp/c) *(BZA/BZC 13)* **UNTITLED** 42 -
– Untitled / Empty eyes / Angels / Big Louise / Caroline says / Margaret / If you go away. *(free-12"ep with above +=)* – Terrapin / Twilights and lowlifes (street walking soundtrack) / Twilights and lowlifes. *(re-iss. Mar92 on 'Mercury' cd/c; 510 298-2/-4)*
Nov 82. (7";w-drawn) *(BZS 15)* **BIG LOUISE. / EMPTY EYES** - -
(12";w-drawn+=) *(BZS 15-12)* – The dirt behind the neon.
Jun 83. (7") *(BZS 19)* **BLACK HEART. / YOUR AURA** 49 -
(12"+=) *(BZS 19-12)* – Mamba.
Aug 83. (d-lp/c) *(BIZL/+C 4)* **TORMENT AND TOREROS** 28 -
– The animal in you / Narcissus / Gloomy Sunday / Vision / Your love is a lesson / The untouchable one / My little book of sorrows / In my room / First time / The bulls / Boss cat / Intro / Catch a fallen star / Beat out dat rhythm on a drum / A million manias / Torment / Black heart. *(re-iss. Mar92 on 'Mercury' cd/c; 812 872-2/-4) (cd re-iss. Oct97; SBZCD 028CD)*
Nov 83. (12"ep) *(BZS 21-12)* **TORMENT / FIRST TIME. / YOU'LL NEVER SEE ME ON A SUNDAY / MAGAMILLIONMANIA-MULTIMANIAMIX** -

MARC ALMOND

— went solo augmented by **The WILLING SINNERS: ANNIE HOGAN** – piano / **BILLY McGEE** – bass / **RICHARD RILEY** – guitar / **STEPHEN HUMPHRIES** – drums / **MARTIN McCARRICK** – cello
May 84. (7") *(BZS 23)* **THE BOY WHO CAME BACK. / JOEY DEMENTO** 52
(10"/12") *(BZS 23 10/12)* – ('A'-Loud cut) / ('B'extended).
Sep 84. (7") *(BZS 24)* **YOU HAVE. / SPLIT UP** 57
(ext-10"+=) *(BZS 24-10)* – Black mountain blues.
(ext-12"+=) *(BZS 24-12)* – Joey Demento.
Oct 84. (lp/c)(cd) *(BIZL/+C 8)(<822 832-2>)* **VERMINE IN ERMINE** 36
– Shining sinners / Hell was a city / You have / Crime sublime / Gutter hearts / Ugly head / The boy who came back / Solo adultos / Tenderness is a weakness. *(c+=/cd+=)* – Pink shack blues / Split lip / Joey Demento.
Nov 84. (7") *(BZS 25)* **TENDERNESS IS A WEAKNESS. / LOVE FOR SALE** -
(10"+=) *(BZS 25-10)* – Pink shack blues (live) / The heel (live).

— In April '85, he teamed up with BRONSKI BEAT on Top 3 version of 'I FEEL LOVE'. Two months later, he featured anonymously on 12" 'SKIN' as The BURMOE BROTHERS
Aug 85. (7") *(BONK 1)* **STORIES OF JOHNNY. / STORIES OF JOHNNY (with The Westminster City School Choir)** 23 -
(12"+=) *(BONK 1-12)* – Take my heart.
(d7"++=/10"++=) *(BONK 1/+10)* – Blond boy.
Sep 85. (lp/c/cd) *(FAITH/TFTH/CDFTH 1)* **STORIES OF JOHNNY** 22
– Traumas, traumas, traumas / Stories of Johnny / The house is haunted (by the echoes of your last goodbye) / Love letter / The flesh is willing / Always / Contempt / I who never / My candle burns / Love and little white lies. *(c+=/cd+=)* – Take my heart / Blond boy / Stories of Johnny (with The Westminster City School Choir).
Oct 85. (7") *(BONKP 2)* **LOVE LETTER. / LOVE LETTER (with The Westmonster City School Choir)** 68 -
(10"/12") *(BONK 2 10/12)* – ('A'-Special mix) / ('B'side).
Jan 86. (d7") *(GLOW D1)* **THE HOUSE IS HAUNTED (BY THE ECHO OF YOUR LAST GOODBYE). / BROKEN BARRICADES // CARA A CARA (FACE TO FACE). / MEDLEY: (UNCHAIN MY HEART – BLACK HEART – TAKE MY HEART)** 55 -
('A'-Ectoplasm mix-12"+=) *(GLOW 1-12)* – Burning boats.
May 86. (7") *(GLOW 2)* **A WOMAN'S STORY. / FOR ONE MOMENT** 41
(c-ep+=)(10"pic-d-ep+=)(12"ep+=) **SOME SONGS TO TAKE TO THE TOMB EP** *(TGLOW 2-12)(GLOWY 2-10)(GLOW 2-12)* – The heel / A salty dog / The plague / The little white cloud that cried / Just good friends.
Oct 86. (7") *(GLOW 3)* **RUBY RED. / I'M SICK OF YOU TASTING OF SOMEONE ELSE** 47 -
('A'-Arnacoma mix-12"+=) *(GLOW 3-12)* – Broken hearted and beautiful / Jackal jackal (Mustapha Tomb Stone Teeth).
('A'ext.dance mix-12") *(GLOW 3-13)* – ('A'instrumental).
Jan 87. (7") *(GLOW 4)* **MELANCHOLY ROSE. / GYP THE BLOOD** 71 -
(12"+=) *(GLOW 4-12)* – A world full of people / Black lullaby.
(d7+=) *(GLOWD 4)* – Surabaya Johnny / Pirate Jenny.
Mar 87. (lp/c/cd) *(FAITH/TFTH/CDFTH 2)* **MOTHER FIST AND HER FIVE DAUGHTERS** 40
– Mother Fist / There is a bed / Saint Judy / The room below / Angel in her kiss / The hustler / Melancholy rose / Mr. Sad / The sea says / Champ / Ruby red / The river.
Mar 87. (7") *(GLOW 5)* **MOTHER FIST. / TWO SAILORS ON THE BEACH** -
(12"+=) *(GLOW 5-12)* – The hustler.
Nov 87. (lp/c/cd) *(FAITH/TFTH/CDFTH 3)* **THE SINGLES 1984-1987** (compilation)
– The boy who came back / You have / Tenderness is a weakness / Stories of Johnny / Love letters / The house is haunted / A woman's story / Ruby red / Melancholy rose / Mother Fist.

— He was now backed by LA MAGIA. (aka HOGAN, HUMPHRIES + McGEE)

Parlophone Capitol

Aug 88. (7"/7"box) *(R/RX 6186)* <44240> **TEARS RUN RINGS. / EVERYTHING I WANTED LOVE TO BE** 26 67 Jan89
(12"+=/cd-s+=) *(12R/CDR 6186)* – ('A'extended).
('A'-Justin Strauss mix-12"+=) *(12RX 6186)* – ('A'-La Magia dance mix).
Sep 88. (cd/c/lp) *(CD/TC+/PCS 7324)* <91042> **THE STARS WE ARE** 41 Jan89
– The stars we are / These my dreams are true / Bitter sweet / Only the moment / Your kisses burn / Tears run rings / Something's gotten hold of my heart / The sensualist / She took my soul in Instanbul. *(c+=/cd+=)* – The frost comes tomorrow / Kept boy.
Oct 88. (7"/7"g-f/7"clear) *(R/RG/RC 6194)* **BITTER SWEET. / KING OF THE FOOLS** 40 -
(12"+=/12"g-f+=/12"etched+=/'A'-Big Beat mix-12"+=/cd-s+=) *(12R/12RG/12RS/12RX/CDR 6194)* – Tears run rings (Justin Strauss remix).
Jan 89. (7"/7"box; by MARC ALMOND & GENE PITNEY) *(R/RX 6201)* **SOMETHING'S GOTTEN HOLD OF MY HEART. / ('A'-solo version)** 1
(12"+=/12"etched+=/cd-s+=) *(12R/12RS/CDR 6201)* – The frost comes tomorrow.
Mar 89. (7",7"clear) *(R 6210)* **ONLY THE MOMENT. / REAL EVIL** 47 -
(cd-s+=) *(CDR 6210)* – She took my soul in Instanbul (The Blue Mosque mix).
(12"/12"etched) *(12R/+S 6210)* – ('A'-All The Time In The World mix) / She took my soul in Istanbul (The Blue Mosque mix).
Feb 90. (7"/ext-7"square-pic-d/ext-c-s) *(R/RPD/TCR 6229)* **A LOVER SPURNED. / EXOTICA ROSE** 29 -
(12"+=/cd-s+=) *(12R/CDR 6229)* – ('A'version).
May 90. (c-s/7") *(TC+/R 6252)* **THE DESPERATE HOURS. / THE GAMBLER** 45 -
(12"+=/12"clear-pic-d+=/cd-s+=) *(12R/12RPD/CDR 6252)* – ('A'extended Flamenco mix).
Jun 90. (cd/c/lp) *(CD/TC+/PCS 7344)* <94404> **ENCHANTED** 52
– Madame de la luna / Waifs and strays / The desperate hours / Toreador in the rain / Widow weeds / A lover spurned / Death's diary / Sea still sings / Carnival of life / Orpheus in red velvet.
Oct 90. (c-s/7") *(TC+/R 6263)* **WAIFS AND STRAYS. / OLD JACK'S CHARM** -
(12") *(12R 6263)* – (2 'A'-Grid mixes).
(cd-s+=) *(CDR 6263)* – City of nights.

— Wrote w/**DAVE BALL + NORRIS** (The GRID)

W.E.A. Sire

Sep 91. (7"/c-s) *(YZ 610/+C)* **JACKY. / DEEP NIGHT** 17 -
(12"+=) *(YZ 610T)* – ('A'-Alpine dub).
(cd-s+=) *(YZ 610CD)* – A love outgrown.
Oct 91. (cd/c/lp) *(9031 75518-2/-4/-1)* <26764> **TENEMENT SYMPHONY** 39
– Meet me in my dream / Beautiful brutal thing / I've never seen your face / Vaudeville and burlesque / Champagne / Tenement symphony (i) Prelude, (ii) Jacky, (iii) What is love?, (iv) Trois Chansons de Bilitis – extract, (v) The days of Pearly Spencer, (vi) My hand over my heart. *(re-iss. cd Feb95; same)*
Dec 91. (7"/c-s) *(YZ 633/+C)* **MY HAND OVER MY HEART. / DEADLY SERENADE** 33 -
(12"pic-d) *(YZ 633TP)* – ('A'-Grit & Glitter mix) / Money for love (2 versions).
(cd-s) *(YZ 633CD)* – (above 3 tracks) / Night and no morning.
Apr 92. (7"/c-s) *(YZ 638/+C)* **THE DAYS OF PEARLY SPENCER. / BRUISES** 4 -
(cd-s+=) *(YZ 638CD)* – Dancing in a golden cage / Extract from 'Trois Chanson De Bilitis'.

— with **DAVE CLAYTON** – keyboards, musical director / **MARTIN WATKINS** – piano / **ANDY HAMILTON** – saxophone / **MICHELE DREES** – drums, perc. / **CRIS BONACCI** – guitars / **SHIRLEY LEWIS, ANNA ROSS & AILEEN McLAUGHLIN** – b.vox / **TENEMENT SYMPHONY ORCH.**
Mar 93. (7"/c-s) *(YZ 720/+C)* **WHAT MAKES A MAN A MAN (live). / TORCH (live)** 60 -
(cd-s+=) *(YZ 720CD)* – The stars we are (live).
(cd-s) *(YZ 720CDX)* – ('A'side) / Tainted love (live) / Vision (live) / Only the moment (live).
Apr 93. (cd/c/lp) *(4509 92033-2/-4/-1)* <45247> **12 YEARS OF TEARS – LIVE AT THE ROYAL ALBERT HALL (live)** May93
– Tears run rings / Champagne / Bedsitter / Mr. Sad / There is a bed / Youth / If you go away / Jacky / Desperate hours / Waifs and strays / Something's gotten hold of my heart / What makes a man a man / Tainted love / Say hello wave goodbye.

Some Bizzare not iss.

Sep 93. (cd/c/lp) *(SBZ CD/MC/LP 10)* **ABSINTHE: THE FRENCH ALBUM** -
– Undress me / Abel and Cain / Lost Paradise / Secret child / Rue Des Blancs Manteaux / The slave / Remorse of the dead / Incestuous love / A man / My little lovers / In your bed / Yesterday when I was young. *<US cd-iss. 1996 on 'Thirsty Ear'; 57026>*

Mercury Mercury

Apr 95. (c-s) *(MERMC 431)* **ADORED AND EXPLORED / ('A'-original)** 25 -
(cd-s) *(MERCD 431)* – ('A'side) / The user / Loveless world / ('A'-Andy Meecham's Slow Fat dub).

(cd-s) *(MERDD 431)* – ('A'side) / ('A'-Beatmasters 12 take 1) / ('A'-Andy Meecham club mix) / ('A'-X-Press 2 extre,me excess mix).
Jul 95. (c-s) *(MERMC 437)* **THE IDOL / ('A'-Tin Tin Out mix)** 44 -
(cd-s+=) *(MERDD 437)* – ('A'-Idolized mix) / ('A'-Teenage dream mix).
(cd-s) *(MERCD 437)* – ('A'-part 1) / Law of the night / Adored and explored (live) / Bedsitter (live).
Nov 95. (c-s) *(MERMC 450)* **CHILD STAR / EDGE OF HEARTBREAK** 41 -
(cd-ep+=) **CHILD STAR EP** *(MERCD 450)* – Christmas in Vegas / My guardian angel.
(cd-ep) **CHILD STAR EP** *(MERDD 450)* – ('A'side) / We need jealousy (live) / The idol (live) / Out there (live).
Feb 96. (c-s) *(MERMC 444)* **OUT THERE / BRILLIANT CREATURES** -
(cd-s+=) *(MERCD 444)* – Lie (Beatmasters mix) / Lie.
(12") *(MERX 444)* – ('A'mixes:- Tony De Vite parts 1 & 2 / Non Eric / House Of Usher / Valerie Singleton).
Feb 96. (cd/c) *(528 659-2/-4)* **FANTASTIC STAR** 54 -
– Caged / Out there / We need jealousy / Idol (parts 1 & 2) / All gods fall / Baby night eyes / Adored and explored / Child star / Looking for love (in all the wrong places) / Addicted / Edge of heartbreak / Love to die for / Betrayed / On the prowl / Come in sweet assassin / Brilliant creatures / Shining brightly. *(cd re-iss. Sep97; same)*

— In Dec'96, MARC was credited on PJ PROBY minor hit single 'YESTERDAY HAS GONE' on 'EMI Premier' (PRESTC/CDPRES/CDPRESX 13).

Echo Instinct
Nov 98. (7"pic-d) *(ECS 58)* **BLACK KISS. / ('A'-DJ mix)** -
(cd-s) *(ECSCD 58)* – ('A'side) / Satan's child / ('A'live).

– (MARC ALMOND) compilations, etc. –

Dec 89. (lp/c/cd) *Some Bizzare; (BREL/+C/CD 001)* **JAQUES** (most rec.1986) -
– The Devil (okay) / If you need / The lockman / We must look / Alone / I'm coming / Litany for a return / If you go away / The town fell asleep / The bulls / (Never to be) Next / My death.
(above a tribute to Belgian singer, JAQUES BREL)
Sep 92. (cd/c) *Virgin; (CD/TC VM 9010)* **A VIRGIN'S TALE VOL.1 (1985-1988)** -
Sep 92. (cd/c) *Virgin; (CD/TC VM 9011)* **A VIRGIN'S TALE VOL.2 (1988-1991)**
(re-iss. both above Nov92 as d-cd; DCDVM 901 0/1) (both re-iss. Nov97; SBZ 032/033 CD)
Aug 95. (d-cd) *E.M.I.; (CDMATBOX 1)* **TREASURE BOX** -
Sep 97. (cd; MARC ALMOND & FOETUS) *Some Bizarre; (SBZ 022CD)* **VIOLENT SILENCE**
Nov 97. (cd; MARC ALMOND & FOETUS) *Some Bizarre; (SBZ 034CD)* **FLESH VOLCANO / SLUT** -

ALONE AGAIN OR (see under ⇒ SHAMEN)

ALTAMONT (see under ⇒ PORCUPINE TREE)

ALTERED IMAGES

Formed: Glasgow, Scotland . . . 1979 by JOHNNY McELHONE, TONY McDAID and MICHAEL 'TICH' ANDERSON, subsequently recruiting 'Gregory's Girl' bit actress, CLARE GROGAN, as a suitably kinetic frontwoman and second guitarist CAESAR. By mid 1980, they'd secured a support slot with SIOUXSIE & THE BANSHEES and following a promising John Peel session, were duly signed to 'Epic'. Following minor chart succes in early '81 with cult classic, 'DEAD POP STARS', CEASAR was replaced with JIM McINVEN and the band released a second single, 'A DAY'S WAIT', to minimal reaction. It was a case of third time lucky, however, and the celebrations began in earnest with the release of 'HAPPY BIRTHDAY', a song which narrowly missed the top of the UK charts and came to define the band's kaleidoscopic pop sound. Bouncing about like a demented rag doll, GROGAN made for a compelling stage presence, her little-girl-on-helium vocals among the most disinctive in the new wave pack. 'HAPPY BIRTHDAY' the album spawned a further two major hits, namely 'I COULD BE HAPPY' and 'SEE THOSE EYES', although the band's popularity began to dip after the release of a second album, 'PINKY BLUE' (1982). ANDERSON and McINVEN subsequently departed (the latter would later reappear with ambient popsters ONE DOVE), STEPHEN LIRONI brought in as a replacement. A change in direction (or at least an altered image) resulted in a one-off Top 10 hit, 'DON'T TALK TO ME ABOUT LOVE', lifted from the accompanying album, 'BITE' (1983), although with GROGAN increasingly concentrating her full-time efforts on an acting career, the band ground to a halt later that year. While LIRONI went on to form FLESH, McELHONE re-emerged initially with HIPSWAY, then TEXAS. Music wise, GROGAN released a lone 7" single, 'LOVE BOMB' in the mid-80's, later teaming up with LIRONI once more to form UNIVERSAL LOVE SCHOOL. Her cheeky grin can currently be witnessed on cable music channel, VH1, for whom GROGAN works as a presenter. • **Songwriters:** McELHONE and group compositions / GROGAN lyrics. Also covered JEEPSTER (T.Rex) / SONG SUNG BLUE (Neil Diamond) / LITTLE TOWN FLIRT (Del Shannon). • **Trivia:** STEVE SEVERIN (Siouxsie & The Banshees) produced debut 45, and MARTIN RUSHENT the debut album.

Album rating: HAPPY BIRTHDAY (*6) / PINKY BLUE (*5) / BITE (*4) / COLLECTED IMAGES compilation (*6)

CLARE GROGAN (b.Mar'62) – vocals / **JOHNNY McELHONE** – guitar / **TONY McDAID** – bass / **MICHAEL 'Tich' ANDERSON** – drums / **CAESAR** – guitar

Epic Portrait
Feb 81. (7") *(EPCA 1023)* **DEAD POP STARS. / SENTIMENTAL** 67
(c-s+=) *(EPC40A 1023)* – Leave me alone.

— **JIM McINVEN** – guitar (ex-BERLIN BLONDES) repl. CAESAR who joined The WAKE

May 81. (7") *(EPCA 1167)* **A DAY'S WAIT. / WHO CARES?**
Aug 81. (7") *(EPCA 1522)* **HAPPY BIRTHDAY. / SO WE GO WHISPERING** 2
('A'dance mix-12"+=) *(EPCA13 1522)* – Jeepster.
Sep 81. (lp/c) *(EPC/40 84893)* **HAPPY BIRTHDAY** 26
– (intro – Happy birthday) / Love and insects / Real toys / Idols / Legionaire / Faithless / Beckoning strings / Happy birthday / Midnight / A day's wait / Leave me alone / Insects / (outro – Happy birthday). *(re-iss. Sep83 lp/c; EPC/40 32355) (cd-iss. Sep91 & Jun95 on 'Columbia'; 480528-2) (re-iss. May93 on 'Sony Collectors'; 932944-2)*
Nov 81. (7"/7"pic-d) *(EPCA/+11 1834)* **I COULD BE HAPPY. / INSECTS** 7
('A'dance mix-12"+=) *(EPCA13 1834)* – Disco pop stars.
Mar 82. (7"/7"pic-d) *(EPCA/+11 2198)* **SEE THOSE EYES. / HOW ABOUT THAT THEN (I MISSED MY TRAIN)** 11
(12"+=) *(EPCA13 2198)* – ('A'extended).
Apr 82. (lp/c) *(EPC/40 85665)* **PINKY BLUE** 12
– Pinky blue / See those eyes / Forgotten / Little brown head / See you later / Song sung blue / Funny funny me / Think that It might / I could be happy (version) / Jump jump / I could be happy (version) / Goodnight and I wish. *(cd-iss. Mar94 on 'Sony Collectors'; 983227-2)*
May 82. (7",7"pink) *(EPCA 2426)* **PINKY BLUE. / THINK THAT IT MIGHT (dance mix)** 35
(12") *(EPCA13 2426)* – ('A'dance mix) / Jump jump – Think that it might (sequed dance mix).

— **STEPHEN LIRONI** – guitar, drums (ex-RESTRICTED CODE) repl. ANDERSON and McKINVEN The latter reappeared in the early 90s in ONE DOVE. Also used session people including **ANDY HAMILTON** – saxophone

Mar 83. (7"/7"pic-d/ext.12") *(EPCA/WA/EPCA13 3083)* **DON'T TALK TO ME ABOUT LOVE. / LAST GOODBYE** 7
May 83. (7"/ext.12"/7"pic-d/ext.12"pic-d) *(EPCA/TA 3398)(WA/WTA 3398)* **BRING ME CLOSER. / SURPRISE ME** 29
Jun 83. (lp/c) *(EPC/40 25413)* **BITE** 16
– Bring me closer / Another lost look / Love to stay / Now that you're here / Don't talk to me about love / Stand so quiet / Change of heart / Thinking about you. *(c+=)* – Bring me closer (dance mix) / Don't talk to me about love (extended) / Surprise me / I don't want to know / Last goodbye.
Jul 83. (7"/ext.12") *(EPCA/TA 3582)* **LOVE TO STAY. / ANOTHER LOST LOOK (live)** 46
Sep 83. (7") *(EPCA 3735)* **CHANGE OF HEART. / ANOTHER LOST LOOK**
(12"+=) *(TA 3735)* – Happy birthday / I could be happy.

— Had added on summer tour **DAVID WILD** – drums / **JIM PRIME** – keyboards But the inevitable split came late '83. LIRONI formed FLESH and in the mid-90's returned to cult status when he formed The REVOLUTIONARY CORPS OF TEENAGE JESUS (with augmentation from – of all people – SUICIDE's ALAN VEGA). McELHONE formed HIPSWAY and, later in 1989, formed TEXAS.

– compilations, others, etc. –

Mar 83. (7"ep/c-ep) *Epic; (EPCA/+40 2617)* **GREATEST ORIGINAL HITS** -
– Happy birthday / I could be happy / Dead pop stars / A day's wait.
May 84. (lp/c) *Epic; (EPC/40 25973)* **COLLECTED IMAGES**
Jan 87. (7") *Old Gold; (OG 9663)* **HAPPY BIRTHDAY. / I COULD BE HAPPY** -
Jul 96. (cd) *Epic; (484339-2)* **REFLECTED IMAGES (THE BEST OF ALTERED IMAGES)** -

CLARE GROGAN

— revived acting career, noteably in another Bill Forsyth movie 'Comfort And Joy', plus TV parts in 'Red Dwarf' & 'Blott On The Landscape'. Around this period (1986), she also went solo. Now with songwriters **DAVEY HENDERSON** (of WIN) and **HILARY MORRISON** (ex-FLOWERS)

London not iss.
May 87. (7"/12") *(LON/+X 134)* **LOVE BOMB. / I LOVE THE WAY YOU BEG** -

— in 1989 she teamed up with LIRONI again to form UNIVERSAL LOVE SCHOOL

ALTERNATIVE TV

Formed: London, England . . . 1976 by "Sniffin Glue" fanzine editor, MARK PERRY. Completing the initial line-up with ALEX FERGUSSON, TYRONE THOMAS and JOHN TOWE, the band's first recording was given away with an issue of the aforesaid pamphlet in the form of a flexi-disc (the track in question, 'LOVE LIES LIMP' – a subsequent B-side). A debut ATV single proper, 'HOW MUCH LONGER' / 'YOU BASTARD', arrived on the punk scene in late '77 via the local 'Deptford Fun City' indie imprint. A humourously cynical cockney rant against everything and everyone, the track was one of the genre's rawest missives to date and set the tone for what what was to come. In the Spring of '78, PERRY and Co. surprised many commentators by taking a diversion into reggae/dub with the less offensive 'LIFE AFTER LIFE/DUB'. PERRY sought out new personnel in the shape of DENNIS BURNS and CHRIS BENNETT, after his previous backing bailed out for pastures new. This line-up recorded the seminal 'IMAGE HAS CRACKED' (1978) album, a commercially overlooked masterpiece containing such powerhouse gems as 'ACTION TIME VISION', 'VIVA LA ROCK'N'ROLL' and 'SPLITTING IN TWO', while even tackling a Frank Zappa number, 'WHY DON'T YOU DO ME RIGHT' with characteristic sarcasm. Contrary to the last, PERRY ended the year with a defiantly experimental and commercially suicidal follow-up, 'VIBING UP THE SENILE MAN (PART 1)', a difficult, intense and paranoid record which nevertheless yielded up a minimalist treat, 'FACING UP TO THE FACTS'. Its release coincided with a split live set, 'WHAT YOU SEE IS WHAT YOU ARE' with commune-dwelling hippies HERE & NOW, PERRY moving even further left of centre as he attempted to distance himself from the increasingly homogenised punk/new wave industry. ATV delivered a final single before PERRY and BURNS formed The GOOD MISSIONARIES (named after an ATV track) with the former's wife GILLIAN HANNA, releasing one 1979 set, 'FIRE FROM HEAVEN'. Ever industrious, PERRY subsequently juggled a solo venture (one album, 'SNAPPY TURNS') with yet more avant-garde knob-twiddling in the form of The DOOR AND THE WINDOW. However, early in 1981, PERRY, BURNS and the returning ALEX FERGUSSON decided to switch their ATV back on, signing to Miles Copeland's burgeoning 'I.R.S.' label and releasing a one-off album, 'STRANGE KICKS'. Splitting in two once more when FERGUSSON went off to join PSYCHIC TV, PERRY floundered for a spell until he inevitably re-formed his beloved project and continued to sporadically release the odd experimental set.

Album rating: THE IMAGE HAS CRACKED (*9) / VIBING UP THE SENILE MAN (PART ONE) (*4) / STRANGE KICKS (*4) / SPLITTING IN 2 compilation (*8)

MARK PERRY – vocals, guitar / **ALEX FERGUSSON** (b.16 Dec'52, Glasgow) – guitar / **TYRONE THOMAS** – bass / **CHRIS BENNETT** – drums

Deptford Fun City / not iss.

Dec 77. (7") *(DFC 02)* **HOW MUCH LONGER. / YOU BASTARD** [ ] [-]
May 78. (7") *(DFC 04)* **LIFE AFTER LIFE. / LIFE AFTER DUB** [ ] [-]

— FERGUSSON formed CASH PUSSIES. **PERRY** brought in **JOHN TOWE** – drums; repl. BENNETT / **DENNIS BURNS** – bass; repl. THOMAS

Added guests **KIM TURNER** – rhythm guitar / **JOOLS HOLLAND** – piano (on 2)

May 78. (lp) *(DLP 01)* **THE IMAGE HAS CRACKED** [ ] [-]
– Alternatives / Action time vision / Why don't you do me right / Good times / Still life / Viva la rock'n'roll / Nasty little lonely / Red / Splitting in 2.
Jun 78. (7") *(DFC 07)* **ACTION TIME VISION. / ANOTHER COKE** [ ] [-]
Nov 78. (7") *(DFC 06)* **LIFE. / LOVE LIES LIMP** [ ] [-]

— Trim to duo of **PERRY & BURNS** with **GENESIS P.ORRIDGE / MARK LINEHAN** (TOWE joined The ADVERTS)

Dec 78. (lp) *(DLP 03)* **VIBING UP THE SENILE MAN (PART 1)** [ ] [-]
– Release the natives / Serpentine gallery / Poor association / The radio story / Facing up to the facts / The good missionary / Graves of deluxe green / Smile in the day.
Dec 78. (lp; shared with HERE & NOW) *(DLP 02)* **WHAT YOU SEE IS WHAT YOU ARE (live)** [ ] [-]
– Action time lemon / Circles / Fellow sufferer / Splitting in 2.
May 79. (7") *(DFC 10)* **THE FORCE IS BLIND. / LOST IN ROOM** [ ] [-]

GOOD MISSIONARIES

— PERRY and BURNS. MARK's girlfriend **GILLIAN HANNA** – recorder / plus **DAVE GEORGE** – guitar / **HENRY BADOWSKI** – drums

Aug 79. (lp) *(DLP 04)* **FIRE FROM HEAVEN** [ ] [-]
– Another coke / The boby / The force is blind / Thief of fire / The radio story / Strange loons / Fire from Heaven / Release the natives / Fellow sufferer in dub / Bugger the cat.

— without PERRY, released more singles in 1980/81 on 'Unnormality' UK indie label. **VIBING UP THE SENILE WORLD** *(NORM 001)* **DERANGED IN HASTINGS** *(NORM 002)*

MARK PERRY

Mar 80. (7") *(DFC 12)* **WHOLE WORLD'S DOWN ON ME. / I LIVE – HE DIES** [ ] [-]
Jun 80. (lp) *(DLP 06)* **SNAPPY TURNS** [ ] [-]
– Snappy turns / The object is to love / You know / Inside / At war / Death looks down / The game is over / Quagga's last stand.

DOOR AND THE WINDOW

off-shoot band featuring **PERRY, BENDLE and NAG**

N.B. / not iss.

1979. (7"ep) *(NB 3)* **PERMANENT TRANSCIENCE** [ ] [-]
– He feels like a Doris / I like sound / Innocent / Dig / Production line.
1980. (lp) *(NB 5)* **DETAILED TWANG** [ ] [-]
– Dads / Habits / We do scare each other / Order and obey / He feels like a Doris / Part time punks / In the car / Subculture fashion slaves / Sticks and stones / Positive / Why must you build walls around us / Detailed twang.
1980. (c) *(NB 9)* **MUSIC AND MOVEMENT (live)** [ ] [-]

— they made other recordings without PERRY; **FIRST & SECOND ep's**

MARK PERRY & DENNIS BURNS (one-off)

N.B. / not iss.

Mar 80. (7") *(NB 7)* **YOU CRY YOUR TEARS. / MUSIC DEATH?** [ ] [-]

REFLECTIONS

PERRY, BURNS / + NAG (b. LEE) – bass, vocals / **KARL BLAKE** – drums (of-LEMON KITTENS) / **GRANT SHOWBIZ** – bass / others

Cherry Red / not iss.

Nov 81. (lp) *(BRED 22)* **SLUGS AND TOADS** [ ] [-]
– Tightrope walker / Zigzagging / Keep it easy / Toy dog ripped by cat / Demon of my desires / The human touch / The interpreter / Oh baby, look out / I had love in my hands / Clamming up / Nag takes a ride / The parting.

Jan 82. (7") *(CHERRY 33)* **4 COUNTRIES. / THE CORONER AND THE INQUEST** [ ] [-]
Jan 84. (7") *(CHERRY 75)* **SEARCHING. / ('A'remix)** [ ] [-]

ALTERNATIVE TV

— reformed with **PERRY, BURNS** and **FERGUSSON** plus (ex-CASH PUSSIES) / **ALAN GRUNER** – keyboards / **RAY WESTON** – drums

I.R.S. / I.R.S.

Jun 81. (7") *(PFP 1006)* **THE ANCIENT REBELS. / SLEEP IN DUB** [ ] [-]
Jul 81. (lp) *(SP 70023)* **STRANGE KICKS** [ ] [ ]
– The ancient rebels / Strange kicks / Communicate / Mirror boy / Anye is back / My hand is still wet / Fun city / TV operator / There goes my date with Doug / Cold rain / Who are they / Sleep in dub.
Oct 81. (7") *(PFP 1009)* **COMMUNICATE. / OBSESSION** [ ] [-]

— PERRY went into production, and FERGUSSON joined PSYCHIC TV. ATV reformed in 1984 with **PERRY, DAVE GEORGE, PROTAG + NAG**

— by 1985 **MARK and DAVE** were joined by **STEVEN CANDEL** – bass / **ALISON PHILIPS** – drums

Noiseville / not iss.

Feb 86. (12"ep) *(VOO 1T)* **WELCOME TO THE END OF FUN. / ANTI / DEATH TIME** [ ] [-]
Jul 86. (12"ep) *(VOO 2T)* **LOVE / SEX EP** [ ] [-]
– Victory / Repulsion / You never know.

Anagram / not iss.

Aug 87. (12"m) *(ANA 36)* **MY BABY'S LAUGHING (EMPTY SUMMER'S DREAM). / LOOK AT HER EYES / I HAD LOVE IN MY HANDS** [ ] [-]
Nov 87. (lp) *(GRAM 32)* **PEEP SHOW** [ ] [-]
– Chrissie's moom / Let's sleep now / Tumble time / The river / Boy eats girl / My baby's laughing (empty summer dream) / Scandal / White walls / Animal. *(cd-iss. Oct96 on 'Overground'; OVER 54CD)*

— were now **PERRY + JAMES KYLIO**

Chapter 22 / not iss.

Apr 90. (12"ep) *(12CHAP 46)* **THE SOL EP** [ ] [-]
– Everyday / The word / Affecting people / Pain barrier.
Nov 90. (lp) *(CHAPLP 51)* **DRAGON LOVE** [ ] [-]
– Coming of age / Something happened / Last rites / You pushed it a little too far / Captured fantasy / Never gonna give it up / Dragon love / Few feathers fall / (Do you believe) The time / We're through / Don't you leave me.

Overground / Feel Good All Over

1994. (7") <FGAO 6> **BEST WISHES. / WESTERN WORLD** [-] [ ]
Nov 94. (cd) *(OVER 39CD)* <FGAO 16> **MY LIFE AS A CHILD STAR** [ ] [ ] 1995
1995. (7") <FGAO 22> **PURPOSE IN MY LIFE. / COMPANY OF LIES** [-] [ ]

— **MARK** reformed the band with **TYRONE THOMAS, ALEX FERGUSSON**, the latter subsequently being replaced by a guy called CLIVE (1996)

Jan 98. (cd) *(OVER 70CD)* **PUNK LIFE** [ ] [-]

– compilations, others, etc. –

Dec 79. (lp) *Crystal; (CLP 1)* **LIVE AT THE RAT CLUB (live '77)** [ ] [-]
Mar 80. (lp) *Deptford Fun City; (DLP 05)* **ACTION TIME VISION** [ ] [-]
1980. (c; shared with The GOOD MISSIONARIES) *Weird Noise; (WEIRD 001)* **SCARS ON SUNDAY** [ ] [-]
Aug 80. (c; shared with The GOOD MISSIONARIES) *Conventional; (CON 14)* **AN YE AS WELL** [ ] [-]
Feb 89. (lp) *Anagram; (GRAM 40)* **SPLITTING IN 2 – SELECTED VIEWING** [ ] [-]
– Action time vision / Love lies limp / Life / How much longer / Another coke / Still life / You bastard / Nasty little lonely / Why don't you do me right / Facing up to the facts / Lost in room / Force in blind / Splitting in two.
Jul 93. (cd) *Overground; (OVER 29)* **LIVE 1978 (live)** [ ] [-]
Feb 94. (cd) *Anagram; (CDPUNK 24)* **THE IMAGE HAS CRACKED – THE ALTERNATIVE TV COLLECTION** [ ] [-]
(lp-iss.Apr98 on 'Get Back'; GET 26LP)
Oct 95. (cd) *Overground; (OVER 44CD)* **THE RADIO SESSIONS** [ ] [-]
Apr 96. (cd) *Overground; (OVER 49CD)* **THE INDUSTRIAL SESSIONS 1977** [ ] [-]
1996. (cd) *Anagram; (CDMGRAM 102)* **VIBING UP THE SENILE MAN – THE SECOND ATV COLLECTION** [ ] [-]

AMBITIOUS LOVERS (see under ⇒ DNA)

AMELIA (see under TALULAH GOSH)

AMERICAN MUSIC CLUB

Formed: Burbank, California, USA ... 1983 by MARK EITZEL, who had set up home in San Francisco after his Columbus, Ohio band The NAKED SKINNIES broke up in '82; they released one US-only single, 'ALL MY LIFE' / 'THIS IS THE BEAUTIFUL NIGHT' for 'Naked House'; (103457). With a line-up of MARK 'VUDI' PANKLER, DAN PEARSON, BRAD JOHNSON and MATT NORELLI, the AMERICAN MUSIC CLUB cut a debut album, 'RESTLESS STRANGER', for the small 'Grifter' label in 1985, before signing to 'Zippo' for the 'THE ENGINE' (1987). Regularly cited as one of the most criminally undervalued songwriters in the US, EITZEL has captured many a critics hear with his neon-lit meditations on the tragic futulity of human existence and the fleeting consolation of romantic love. Apart from a cult fanbase, however, AMC's appeal never translated to a wider audience, even after the band were picked up by 'Virgin' in the early 90's. By this point, the group had a clutch of austere, country-tinged classics under their belt, namely 'CALIFORNIA', 'UNITED KINGDOM' (1989) and 'EVERCLEAR' (1991), the latter set especially haunting in spite of its more accessible approach. EITZEL's wracked outpourings were often shot through with a kind of outraged desperation, the 'RISE' single, a poignant tribute to a friend who died of AIDS. Also featuring suck bleakly beautiful material as 'SICK OF FOOD', the album saw EITZEL named as Rolling Stone magazine's songwriter of the year in 1991. The acclaim didn't sit particularly well with the AMC frontman, EITZEL, perhaps in response, accentuated the self-mocking tone of his work on the major label debut, 'MERCURY' (1993). Critically acclaimed once again, the album failed to sell, although it did almost scrape into the UK Top 40. It was the same story with 'SAN FRANCISCO' (1994). Parting company with 'Virgin', the band also saw fit to part company with each other, at least they'd given it their best shot. EITZEL remained with the label for a further solo album, '60 WATT SILVER LINING' (1996), another critical success seemingly doomed to obscurity. • **Covered:** CALIFORNIA DREAMIN' (Mamas & The Papas). EITZEL covered THERE IS NO EASY WAY DOWN (Carole King). • **Trivia:** EITZEL also moonlighted with The TOILING MIDGETS (a 5-piece also featuring early 90's AMC newcomer TIM MOONEY; he had always been part of the early 80's combo). They released an album, 'SON' (1993), before signing to 'Reprise' the same year.

Album rating: THE RESTLESS STRANGER (*5) / ENGINE (*6) / CALIFORNIA (*7) / UNITED KINGDOM (*7) / EVERCLEAR (*8) / SAN FRANCISCO (*6) / Mark Eitzel: SONGS OF LOVE: LIVE AT THE BORDERLINE – 1/19/91 (6) / 60 WATT SILVER LINING (*6)

MARK EITZEL (b.30 Jan'59, Walnut Creek, Calif.) – vocals, guitar, keyboards / **MARK "VUDI" PANKLER** (b.22 Sep'52, Chicago, Illinois) – guitar, accordion, bass / **DAN PEARSON** (b.31 May'59, Walnut Creek) – bass, guitar, dulcimer, vocals, etc. / **BRAD JOHNSON** – keyboards / **MATT NORELLI** – drums

not iss. Grifter

Jan 86. (lp) **THE RESTLESS STRANGER** [–]
– $1,000,000 song / Away down my street / Yvonne gets dumped / Ms. Lucky / Point of desire / Goodbye reprise #54 / Tell yourself / When your love is gone / Heavenly smile / Broken glass / Hold on to your love.

— **TOM MALLON** – guitar, drums, vocals / **DAVE SCHEFF** – drums repl. JOHNSON + NORELLI

Zippo Zippo

Oct 87. (lp/cd) *(ZONG/+CD 020)* **ENGINE**
– Big night / Outside this bar / At my mercy / Gary's song / Nightwatchman / Lloyd / Electric light / Mom's TV / Art of love / Asleep / This year.

— now without SCHEFF

Demon Zippo

Oct 88. (lp/cd) *(FIEND/+CD 134)* **CALIFORNIA**
– Firefly / Somewhere / Laughing stock / Lonely / Pale skinny girl / Blue and grey shirt / Bad liquor / Now you're defeated / Jenny / Western sky / Highway 5 / Last harbor. *(cd re-iss. Apr93; FMCD 1)*

— **MIKE SIMMS** – drums; repl. MALLON

Oct 89. (lp/cd) *(FIEND/+CD 151)* **UNITED KINGDOM**
– Here they roll down / Dreamers of the dream / Never mind / United kingdom / Dream is gone / Heaven of your hands / Kathleen / The hula maiden / Animal pen. *(cd+=)* – California (album). *(cd re-iss. Apr93; FMCD 2)*

— added **BRUCE KAPHAN** (b. 7 Jan'55, San Francisco) – pedal steel guitar, keyboards, bass, producer (now full-time)

Alias Alias

Oct 91. (lp/c/cd) *<(A 015/+C/D)>* **EVERCLEAR**
– Why won't you stay / Rise / Miracle on 8th Street / Ex-girlfriend / Crabwalk / The confidential agent / Sick of food / The dead part of you / Royal cafe / What the pillar of salt held up / Jesus' hands.

Nov 91. (cd-s) *(A 014D)* **RISE /**

— **TIM MOONEY** (b. 6 Oct'58, Las Vegas, Nevada) – drums (of TOILING MIDGETS) repl. SIMMS

Virgin Reprise

Mar 93. (cd/c/lp) *(CD/TC+/V 2708)* **MERCURY** [41]
– Gratitude walks / If I had a hammer / Challenger / I've been a mess / Hollywood 4-5-92 / What Godzilla said to God when his name wasn't found in the book of life / Keep me around / Dallas, airports, bodybags / Apology for an accident / Over and done / Johnny Mathis' feet / The hopes and dreams of Heaven's 10,000 whores / More hopes and dreams / Will you find me?

Apr 93. (c-s) *(VSC 1445)* **JOHNNY MATHIS' FEET / WILL YOU FIND ME / THE HOPES AND DREAMS OF HEAVEN'S 10,000** [58]
(cd-s+=) *(VSCDX 1445)* – The amylnitrate dream of Pat Robertson.
(cd-s) *(VSCDT 1445)* – ('A'side) / What Godzilla said to God when his name wasn't found in the book of life / Dallas, airports, bodybags (demo).

Jun 93. (c-ep) *(VSC 1464)* **KEEP ME AROUND / CHALLENGER / IN MY ROLE AS THE MOST HATED SINGER IN THE LOCAL UNDERGROUND MUSIC SCENE / MEMO FROM AQUATIC PARK**
(cd-ep+=) *(VSCDG 1464)* – (no 2nd track) / Walking tune.

Aug 94. (7"/c-s) *(VS/+C 1512)* **WISH THE WORLD AWAY. / I JUST TOOK TWO SLEEPING PILLS AND NOW I'M LIKE A BRIDEGROOM** [46]
(cd-s+=) *(VSCDT 1512)* – The revolving door (demo).
(cd-s) *(VSCDX 1512)* – ('A'side) / The President's test for physical fitness / Cape Canaveral.

Sep 94. (cd/c/lp) *(CD/TC+/V 2752)* **SAN FRANCISCO** [72]
– Fearless / It's your birthday / Can you help me / Love doesn't belong to anyone * / Wish the world away / How many six packs to screw in a light? / Cape Canaveral * / Hello Amsterdam / The revolving door / In the shadow of the valley * / What holds the world together / I broke my promise / The thorn in my side is gone / I'll be gone / Fearless (reprise) * / I just took my two sleeping pills and now I'm like a bridegroom. *(cd+=/c+= *)*

Feb 95. (7"/c-s) *(VS/+C 1523)* **CAN YOU HELP ME. / THE THORN IN MY SIDE IS GONE**
(cd-s+=) *(VSCDT 1523)* – California dreamin' (alt.version).

MARK EITZEL

Demon Alias

Apr 91. (lp/cd) *(FIEND/+CD 213)* **SONGS OF LOVE: LIVE AT THE BORDERLINE 1/19/91 (live)**
– Firefly / Chanel No.5 / Western sky / Blue and grey shirt / Gary's song / Outside this bar / Room above the club / Last harbour / Kathleen / Crabwalk / Jenny / Take courage / Nothing can bring me down.

Virgin Warners

Mar 96. (cd/c/lp) *(CD/TC+/V 2798)* **60 WATT SILVER LINING**
– There is no way down / Sacred heart / Always turn away / Saved / Cleopatra Jones / When my plane finally goes down / Mission rock / Wild sea / Aspirin / Some bartenders have the gift of pardon / Southend on sea / Everything is beautiful.

Warners Warners

Jun 97. (cd) *<(9362 46602-2)>* **WEST** May96
– If you have to ask / Free of harm / Helium / Stunned and frozen / Then it really happens / In your life / Lower Eastside tourist / Three inches of wall / Move myself ahead / Old photographs / Fresh screwdriver / Live or die.

TOILING MIDGETS

TIM MOONEY – drums / **RICKY WILLIAMS** – vocals (ex-SLEEPERS) / **CRAIG GRAY** – guitar (ex-NEGATIVE TREND) / **PAUL HOOD** – guitar / with **JONATHAN HENDRICKSON** – bass

not iss. Rough Trade

Apr 82. (lp) *<ROUGHUS 11>* **SEA OF UNREST** [–]
– Destiny / Trauma girl / Late show / Microage / Wishful thinking / All the girls cry / DJMC / Shooting gallery / Again / Big surprise / Sea of unrest. *<cd-iss. Sep94 on 'Fist Puppet'; 16>*

— **KARL J GOLDRING** – bass; repl. HENDRICKSON

— **MARK EITZEL** – guitar; repl. WILLIAMS

Hut Matador

Jan 93. (12"ep/cd-ep) *(HUT 25 T/CD)* **FAUX PONY. / GOLDEN FROG / MR. FOSTER'S SHOES**

— **LISA DAVIS** – bass; repl. KARL

Jan 93. (cd/lp) *(CDHUT/HUTLP 6) <030>* **SON**
– Faux pony / Fabric / Slaughter on Sumner St. / Mr. Foster's shoes / Process words / Clinging fire – Clams / Third chair / Listen / Chains.

— signed to 'Reprise', although commitments elsewhere led to break-up

A MINOR FOREST

Formed: San Francisco, California, USA . . . 1993 by ERIK HOVERSTON and ANDREE CONNORS. The pair debuted with 'FLEMISH ALTRUISM' (1996), an album characterised by the production work of third and fourth members, STEVE ALBINI and BOB WESTON who also contributed in the songwriting department. Described as beefy-rock with a lo-fi melodic ambience thrown in for good measure (i.e. SLINT, LOW, SHELLAC), the record (released on 'Thrill Jockey' in the US) certainly had a few choice titles. BRIAN PAULSON took over the controls for 1998's 'ININDEPENDANCE', JOHN BENSON filling the shoes of the ever in-demand ALBINI and WESTON.

Album rating: FLEMISH ALTRUISM (CONSTITUENT PARTS 1993-1996) (*6) / ININDEPENDANCE (*6)

ERIK HOVERSTON – vocals, guitar / **ANDREE CONNORS** – drums, vocals / with **STEVE ALBINI + BOB WESTON** augmenting & writing

Divot Divot

Nov 96. (7"split with GAINER) *<(DVT 004)>* **split**

Runt Thrill Jockey

Mar 97. (cd) *(RUNT 27) <THRILL 34CD>* **FLEMISH ALTRUISM (CONSTITUENT PARTS 1993-1996)** Oct96
– But the pants stay on / Bill's mom likes to fuck / Ed is 50 / So Jesus was at the last supper / Jacking off George Lucas / Speed for Gavin / Perform the critical straw transfer / Dainty Jack and his amazing . . . Beef rigger / Loneliest enuretic. *(re-iss. Jul97 on 'Thrill Jockey'; same as US)*

— **JOHN BENSON** – repl. ALBINI + WESTON

Thrill Jockey Thrill Jockey

Aug 98. (d-lp/cd) *<(THRILL 56/+CD)>* **ININDEPENDANCE**
– Dutch fist / Erik's budding romance / Look at that car, it's full of . . . / . . . It's salmon! / Smell of hot / Michael Anthony / Discoler.

AMPS (see under ⇒ BREEDERS)

ANASTASIA SCREAMED

Formed: Boston, Massachusetts, USA . . . 1987 by CHRIS BURDETT and CHRISTOPHER CUGINI, who subsequently added SCOTT LERNER and vocalist ANDY JAGOLINZER. After a few well-received local indie 45's, the band relocated to Nashville after replacing relative newcomers with CHICK GRANING and CHARLIE BOCK. These free-flowing hardcore singles found their way into Europe on import, the band subsequently winning a contract in 1990 with 'Fire' subsidiary outlet, 'Roughneck'. Touring the college circuit with THROWING MUSES (GRANING was to become the beau of TANYA DONELLY), ANASTASIA SCREAMED finally unveiled their debut set, 'LAUGHING DOWN THE LIMEHOUSE', a collection of unclassifiable alternative rock. A second album, 'MOONTIME' (1991), was met with similar press enthusiasm, although ANASTASIA SCREAMED for the last time early the following year. GRANING formed SCARCE in Rhode Island a few years later, although he was subsequently to suffer a brain aneurysm on the 12th June '95 which stopped him recording for some time. Against all the odds however, GRANING recovered suffiently to promote the band's debut long-player, 'DEADSEXY', which saw a release through 'A&M' a month later.

Album rating: LAUGHING DOWN THE LIMEHOUSE (*6) / MOONTIME (*5) / Scarce: RED mini (*5) / DEADSEXY (*6)

ANDY JAGOLINZER (b.11 Jun'69) – vocals / **CHRISTOPHER CUGINI** (b.23 Nov'66) – guitar / **SCOTT LERNER** (b. 3 Mar'66) – bass / **CHRIS BURDETT** (b. 8 Mar'68) – drums

Roughneck Fire

1988. (7") **unknown** –

—— **CHICK GRANING** (b.28 Oct'66, Vancouver, Canada) – vocals; repl. ANDY

—— **CHARLIE BOCK** (b.26 Jan'65, Nashville, USA) – bass; repl. SCOTT

Aug 90. (7") **SAMANTHA BLACK. /** –
(12"+=) –

Sep 90. (cd/lp) *(NECK CD/LP 002)* **LAUGHING DOWN THE LIMEHOUSE** –
– Beautiful / Lime / Disintegration / Yesterday / The skidder & violet / Searcher No.9 (song 16) / Tide / Parts of us / Tricked into feel / Shade / Samantha Black / Notown.

Nov 90. (7") **DISINTIGRATION. /** –
(12"+=)

Mar 91. (12"ep/cd-ep) *(HYPE 008 T/CD)* **15 SECONDS OR 5 DAYS** –

Oct 91. (12"ep/cd-ep) *(HYPE 012 T/CD)* **TORNADO** –

Oct 91. (cd/lp) *(NECK CD/LP 007)* **MOONTIME** –
– Tornado / Out of the light / Stand by / One deep breath / She must / Dead in the grass / Get a load of that machine / 15 seconds or 5 days / Fall to ceiling / Blues (featuring DON BYAS) / Dead ants.

—— split in 1992; GRANING later formed SCARCE

SCARCE

CHICK GRANING – vocals, guitar / **JOYCE RASKIN** – bass / **JOSEPH PROPATIER** – drums

Domino Rockamundo

May 94. (7") *(RUG 13)* **ALL SIDEWAYS. /**

Big Cat Rockamundo

Aug 94. (m-lp/m-cd) *(ABB 75X/+CD)* **RED**

Oct 94. (12"ep/cd-ep) *(ABB 76/+CD)* **ALL SIDEWAYS EP**

Paradox A&M

Apr 95. (7") *(PDOX 003)* **FREAKSHADOW. / THIS TOWN**
(cd-s+=) *(PDOXD 003)* – Salvador Sammy / Bottomfeeder.

Jun 95. (7") *(PDOX 005)* **GLAMOURIZING CIGARETTES. / SUDDEN DOWNTOWN POLO CLUB**
(cd-s+=) *(PDOXD 005)* – Angels from Montgomery / Ashes to ashes.

Jul 95. (cd/c/lp) *(PDOX CD/MC/LP 001)* *<540 358-2/-4/-1>* **DEADSEXY**
– Honeysimple / All sideways / Rains of Kansas / Summertime / Glamourizing cigarettes / Crimea river / Days like this / Sing me Stella / Freakshadow / Salvador Sammy / Days like this / Stella / Glamourising cigarettes / Salvador Sammy / Sense of quickness / Obviously midnight.

—— disbanded some time later due to GRANING's poor health

AND ALSO THE TREES

Formed: Inkberrow, Worcestershire, England . . . 1979 by SIMON HUW-JONES, JO-JUSTIN JONES, STEVEN BURROWS and NICK HAKAS. Finally finding a home with the independent 'Reflex' imprint, the 'TREES released their debut single, 'SHANTELL', towards the end of '83. However, the song wasn't included on the following year's eponymous album, a record showcasing the quartet's alternative-rock. Firmly in the CURE-est tradition, tracks such as 'MIDNIGHT GARDEN', 'THE TENSE THE TEAR' and 'IMPULSE OF MAN', characterised by HUW-JONES' morbid monotone and delivered against a backdrop of spectral, downward spiralling guitars. Rapidly attracting a cult fanbase, AATT issued a further couple of 45's in the shape of 'THE SECRET SEA' and 'A ROOM LIVES IN LUCY', neither featured on the "difficult" second album, 'VIRUS MEADOW' (1986). The band carried on in much the same vein throughout the rest of the 80's without any mainstream success, even attempting a Cat Stevens number, 'LADY D'ARBANVILLE'. Finding more listeners on the continent, they secured a deal with Germany's 'Normal' label in the early 90's, who released 'GREEN IS THE SEA' (1992) and 'THE KLAXON' (1993), before re-issuing their back catalogue on cd.

Album rating: AND ALSO THE TREES (*6) / VIRUS MEADOW (*5)

SIMON HUW-JONES – vocals / **JO-JUSTIN JONES** – guitar / **STEVEN BURROWS** – bass / **NICK HAKAS** – drums

Reflex Troy

Nov 83. (7") *(FS 9)* **SHANTELL. / WALLPAPER DYING** –

Mar 84. (lp) *(LEX 1)* **AND ALSO THE TREES** –
– So this is silence / Talk without words / Midnight garden / The tease the tear / Impulse of man / Shrine / Twilights pool / Out of the moving life of circles. *(cd-iss. Nov88; LEX 1CD) (cd re-iss. Mar94 on 'Normal'; NORMAL 85CD)*

Apr 84. (7") *(RE 3)* **THE SECRET SEA. / SECRECY** –
(12"+=) *(12RE 6)* – There were no bounds / The tease the tear / Midnight garden / Wallpaper dying.

Jan 85. (12"ep) *(12RE 8)* **A ROOM LIVES IN LUCY. / THERE WAS A MAN OF DOUBLE DEED / SCARLET ARCH** –

Jun 86. (lp) *(LEX 6)* **VIRUS MEADOW** –
– Slow pulse boy / Maps in her wrists and arms / The dwelling place / Vincent Crane / Jack / Headless clay woman / Gone . . . like the swallows / Virus meadow. *(cd-iss. Nov88; LEX 6CD) (cd re-iss. Mar94 on 'Normal'; NORMAL 90CD)*

May 87. (cd) *(LEX 7CD)* **A RETROSPECTIVE 1983-1986 (compilation)** –
– Shantell / Talk without words / Shine / Midnight garden / Impulse of man / Twilights pool / A room lives in Lucy / Scarlet arch / Slow pulse boy / Maps in her wrists and arms / The dwelling place / Vincent Crane / Gone like the swallows / Virus meadow.

May 87. (lp) *(LEX 8)* **THE NIGHT OF THE 24th** –
– A room lives in Lucy / Twilight pool / Vincent Crane / Wallpaper dying / Shantell / Gone like the swallows / Headless clay woman / Slow pulse boy / Virus meadow / So this is silence.

Jun 87. (12"m) *(12RE 12)* **THE CRITICAL DISTANCE. / SCYTHE AND SPADE / THE RENEGADE** –

Nov 87. (12"m) *(12RE 13)* **SHALETOWN. / NEEDLE STREET / L'UNICA STRADA** –

May 88. (7") *(RE 014)* **THE HOUSE OF THE HEART. /** –
(12"+=)(cd-s+=) *(12RE 014)(RE 014CD)* –

May 88. (lp/cd) *(LEX 9/+CD)* **THE MILLPOND YEARS** –
– The suffering of the stream / Simple Tom and the ghost of Jenny Bailey / The house of the heart / This ship in trouble / Count Jefferey / Shaletown / The sandstone man / From the silver frost / The millpond years / Needle street / L'unica strada. *(cd re-iss. Mar94 on 'Normal'; NORMAL 100CD)*

Apr 89. (12")(cd-s) *(12RE 15)(RE 015CD)* **LADY D'ARBANVILLE. /** –

Oct 89. (cd)(c/lp) *(LEX 10CD)(MC+/LEX 10)* *<004>* **FAREWELL TO THE SHADE**
– Prince Rupert / Macbeth's head / The Nobody Inn / Belief in the rose / The street organ / Lady D'Arbanville / Misfortunes / The pear tree / Ill omen / The horse fair. *(cd re-iss. Mar94 on 'Normal'; NORMAL 114CD)*

Aug 91. (7") **THE PEAR TREE. / ?** –

Normal not iss.

Jun 92. (cd) *(NORMAL 134CD)* **GREEN IS THE SEA** –

Dec 93. (cd) *(NORMAL 164CD)* **THE KLAXON** –

China not iss.

Aug 96. (cd) *(MEXCD 1)* **ANGELFISH**

– compilations, etc. –

Aug 90. (12"box-set) *Reflex;* **AND ALSO THE TREES 12" BOX SET**

Jun 93. (d-lp/cd) *Normal; (NORMAL 154/+CD)* **FROM HORIZON TO HORIZON (1983 TO 1992)** –

Laurie ANDERSON

Born: 5 Jun'47, Chicago, Illinois, USA. Graduating from Columbia University in the early 70's, she soon became the Mother Superior of the New York art-rock cognescenti, after moving there to sculpture in the mid 70's. In 1977, a debut 45 'IT'S NOT THE BULLET THAT KILLS YOU', saw her turn her talents to music although the single did nothing. Gave up history tuition to concentrate more on performance art and fashion, utilising her weird violin playing to great effect. It wasn't until 1981 that her recording career took off, when a surprise 8-minute nauseating UK hit, 'O SUPERMAN', paved the way for debut 'Warners' album 'BIG SCIENCE'. This highlighted her speech-based, hypnotic minimalism, rounding on such topics as technology, culture and alienation with a wry, unsightful ease. The follow-up, 'MR HEARTBREAK', was a slightly more mainstream effort, due in part to BILL LASWELL's production on a couple of tracks. Two live albums were released during the mid-80's, one of them the latter 'HOME OF THE BRAVE', with its accompanying concert film, was a flop despite garnering critical plaudits at Cannes. 'STRANGE ANGELS' (1989) saw ANDERSON move towards "real" singing and a more melodious approach while 1994's 'BRIGHT RED', co-produced by BRIAN ENO was characterised by a more claustrohobic feel. Another live album and tour cemented her reputation as a witty and succinct cultural commentator, although her recorded output, while often being innovative, sometimes verred too close to theater to warrant repeated listening. • **Trivia:** Her audio-visual concerts, complete with orchestra lasted for around 7 hours. Guests on her '84 lp, were PETER GABRIEL, NILE RODGERS and WILLIAM S. BURROUGHS. She was romantically involved with LOU REED in the early 90's. • **Bibliography:** THE PACKAGE: A MYSTERY (1971) / TRANSPORTATION (1974) / NOTEBOOK (1977) / WORDS IN REVERSE (1979) / HOME OF THE BRAVE (1979) / EMPTY PLACES (1991) / STORIES FROM THE NERVE BIBLE (1994).

Album rating: BIG SCIENCE (*6) / UNITED STATES LIVE (*5) / MISTER HEARTBREAK (*7) / HOME OF THE BRAVE (*6) / STRANGE ANGELS (*7) / BRIGHT RED (*6) / THE UGLY ONE WITH THE JEWELS AND OTHER STORIES (*7)

LAURIE ANDERSON – vocals, multi-instrumentalist (violin / synthesizers)

—— with many on session incl. **DAVID VAN TIEGHEM** – percussion, drums / **ROMA BARAN** – accordian / **BILL OBRECHE** – sax, flute / **CHICK FISHER** – sax, clarinet / **PETER GORDON** – clarinet, sax / etc

not iss. Holly Solomon Gallery

1977. (7"ltd) *<004>* **IT'S NOT THE BULLET THAT KILLS YOU – IT'S THE HOLE** –

not iss. One-Ten

Sep 81. (7") *<OT 005>* **O SUPERMAN. / WALK THE DOG** –

Warners Warners

Oct 81. (7") *(K 17870)* *<49876>* **O SUPERMAN. / WALK THE DOG** 2

Jan 82. (7") *(K 17941)* **BIG SCIENCE. / EXAMPLE 22** –

Apr 82. (lp/c) *(K/K4 57002)* *<3674>* **BIG SCIENCE** 29
– From the air / Big science / Sweaters / Walking and falling / Born, never asked / O Superman (for Massenet) / Example #22 / Let x = x / It tango. *(cd-iss. Apr84; K2 57002)*

Jul 82. (7") *(K 17956)* **LET X = X. / IT TANGO** –
(12"+=) *(K 17956)* – Sweaters.

Feb 84. (lp/c) *(925077-1/-4)* *<25077>* **MISTER HEARTBREAK** 93 60
– Sharkey's day / Language d'amour / Gravity's angel / Kokoku / Excellent birds / Blue lagoon / Sharkey's night. *(cd-iss. Jul84; 925077-2)*

Jan 85. (5-lp-box) *(925192-1)* *<25192>* **UNITED STATES LIVE (live)**
– Say hello / Walk the dog / Violin solo / Closed circuits / For a large and changing

rooms / Pictures of it / The language of the future / Cartoon song / Small voice / Three walking songs / The healing horn / New Jersey turnpike / So happy birthday / English / Dance of electricity / Three songs for paper, film and video / Sax solo / Sax duet / Born, never asked / From the air / Beginning French / O Superman (for Massenet) / Talkshow / Frames for the pictures / Democratic why / Looking for you walking and falling / Private property / Neon duet / Let x = x / The Mailman's nightmare / Difficult listening hour / Language is a virus from Outer Space – (William S. Burroughs) / Reverb / If you can't talk about it, point to it / Violin walk / City song / Finnish farmers / Red map / Hey ah / Bagpipe solo / Steven Weed / Time and a half / Voices on paper / Example #22 / Strike / False documents / New York social life / A curious phenomenon / Yankee see / I dreamed I had to take a test . . . / Running dogs / Four, three, two, one / The big top / It was up in the mountains / Odd objects / Dr. Miller / Big science / Big science (reprise) / Cello solo / It tango / Blue lagoon / Hothead (la langue d'amour) / Stiff neck / Telephone song / Sweaters / We've got four big clocks (and they're all ticking) / Song for two Jims / Over the river / Mach 20 / Rising sun / The visitors / The stranger / Classified / Going somewhere / Fireworks / Dog show / Lighting out for the territories.

Apr 86. (lp/c/cd) *(925400-1/-4/-2) <25400>* **HOME OF THE BRAVE** [ ] [ ]
– Smoke rings / White lily / Late show / Talk normal / Radar / Language is a virus from outer space / Sharkey's night / Credit racket.

May 86. (7"/12") *(W 8701/+T)* **LANGUAGE IS A VIRUS FROM OUTER SPACE (edit). / WHITE LILY** [ ] [-]

Nov 89. (lp/c)(cd) *(WX 258/+C)(K 925900-2) <25900>* **STRANGE ANGELS** [ ] [ ]
– Strange angels / Monkey's paw / Coolsville / Ramon / Babydoll / Beautiful red dress / The day the Devil / The dream before / My eyes / Hiawatha.

Oct 94. (cd/c) *<(9362 45534-2/-4)>* **BRIGHT RED** [ ] [ ]
– Speechless / Bright red / The puppet motel / Speak my language / World without end / Freefall / Muddy river / Beautiful pea green boat / Love among the sailors / Poison / In our sleep / Night in Baghdad / Tightrope / Same time tomorrow.

Mar 95. (cd/c) *<(9362 45347-2/-4)>* **THE UGLY ONE WITH THE JEWELS & OTHER STORIES FROM THE NERVE BIBLE** [ ] [ ]
– The end of the world / The salesman / The night flight from Houston / Word of mouth / The soul is a bird / The ouija board / The ugly one with the jewels / The geographic North Pole / John Lilly / The rotowhirl / On the way to Jerusalem / The Hollywood strangler / Maria Teresa Teresa Maria / Someone else's dream / White lily / The mysterious "J" / The cultural ambassador / Same time tomorrow.

—— disbanded after above

AN EMOTIONAL FISH

Formed: Dublin, Ireland . . . 1988 by GERARD WHELAN, DAVE FREW who teamed up with ENDA WYATT and MARTIN MURPHY after moving back to their native city from London. The 'FISH soon had a healthy buzz surrounding them after early gigs and were one of the lucky bands to be given a break via U2's new 'Mother' label. Following on from the domestic success of debut single, 'CELEBRATE', the chest beating Irish Top 10 anthem was given a full UK release for 'East West'. Radio One (on the strength of a session) subsequently sponsored a UK tour and the group seemed set for the same success as fellow Celts like HOTHOUSE FLOWERS. Things went awry however, as the music press turned on the band amid criticisms of the sponsorship deal and the 1990 eponymous debut album met with some scathing reviews. Basically it was the same critical treatment meted out to patrons U2 i.e. overblown, earnest, pompous etc; in reality, the band's sound was unlikely to accrue as much interest in Britain as it had in their native Ireland. America was kinder to the group but only just; while they failed to reach the stadium rock heights they might've, they did find an audience on the college-rock circuit. 'JUNKPUPPETS' (1993) carried on in much the same vein and attracted much the same criticism, while by the release of 1995's independently issued 'SLOPER', most pundits had lost interest.

Album rating: AN EMOTIONAL FISH (*5) / JUNKPUPPETS (*4) / SLOPER (*4)

GERARD WHELAND (b.14 Jul'64) – vocals / **DAVE FREW** (b.30 Apr'62) – guitar / **ENDA WYATT** (b.13 Jun'60) – bass / **MARTIN MURPHY** (b/. 9 Nov'67) – drums; with guest vox of **JIL TURNER**

East West / Atlantic

Jun 90. (7"/c-s) *(YZ 489/C)* **CELEBRATE. / ANYWAY** [46] [-]
(ext.12"+=) *(YZ 489T)* – Jonathan and Doodle pip.
(cd-s++=) *(YZ 489CD)* – Brick it up (live).

Aug 90. (lp/c/cd) *(WX 359/+C/CD)* **AN EMOTIONAL FISH** [40] [-]
– Celebrate / Grey mother / Blue / Lace Virginia / Julian / All I am / Change / Colours / That demon jive / Brick it up.

Aug 90. (7"/c-s) **LACE VIRGINIA. / MOVE ON** [ ] [-]
(12"+=) – Man's world / The last time.
(cd-s+=) – Talk.

Nov 90. (7"/c-s) **BLUE (new version). / AN OBVIOUS SONG** [ ] [-]
(12"+=/cd-s+=) – The island.

Aug 91. (10"ep/cd-ep) **THE CELEBRATION EP (live)** [ ] [-]
– The island / Mother / Lace Virginia / Celebrate.

Dec 91. (cd-ep) *<PRCD 3828-2>* **LIVE BAIT** [-] [ ]
– Celebrate / Grey matter / Jonathan and doodle pip / All I am (live on KCRW) / Rock and roll / Change.

May 93. (7"/c-s) *(YZ 745/+C)* **RAIN. / CARELESS** [ ] [-]
(10"+=/cd-s+=) *(YZ 745 TE/CD)* – Higher ground.

Jun 93. (cd/c/lp) *(4509 92357-2/-4/-1) <82473>* **JUNKPUPPETS** [ ] [ ]
– Rain / Harmony central / Sister change / If God was a girl / Careless child / Star / Hole in my heaven / Innocence / Half moon / Digging this hole / Yeh yeh yeh.

Blue Music / not iss.

Oct 94. (c-ep/cd-ep) *(WMC/WCD 22)* **TIME IS ON THE WALL EP** [ ] [-]

Dec 94. (c-ep/cd-ep) *(WMC/WCD 24)* **AEROPLANES EP** [ ] [-]

Mar 95. (c-ep/cd-ep) *(WMC/WCD 27)* **SUPERMAN EP** [ ] [-]
– Superman / Happy families / Digging this hole / Dublin (acoustic) / France Carroll (acoustic).

Pure / not iss.

Feb 96. (cd) *(2260)* **SLOPER** [ ] [-]
– Time is on the wall / Summertime / Aeroplanes / Clowns / Other planet girl / Happy families / Mistake factory / Disco Vera / Superman / Dirt / Air / Strange things.

ANGEL CORPUS CHRISTI

Born: San Francisco, California, USA, the mysterious singer/songwriter and accomplished accordion player refusing to reveal her Christian name to the press (her surname is ROSS). Two VERY low-key albums, 'I LOVE NEW YORK' and 'WAKE UP AND CRY', appeared in the mid-80's, although her self-described ' ACCORDION POP VOL.1' didn't surface until the turn of the decade. Despite being influenced by 60's icons such as LOU REED and LEONARD COHEN, both her music and her lyrics are firmly rooted in the present. Her talents were finally recognised by major backed label, 'Almo Sounds', who issued the well-received 'WHITE COURTESY PHONE' in 1995 (incidentally co-written with her guitarist, RICH STIM – add a certain lady, CICCONE, for the 'THREW IT AWAY' track!). Of late, she has collaborated with alternative stalwarts, DEAN WAREHAM (ex-GALAXIE 500) and ALAN VEGA (of SUICIDE) on a cover of Serge Gainsbourg's naughty classic 'JE T'AIME'.

Album rating: WHITE COURTESY PHONE (*6)

ANGEL CORPUS CHRISTI – vocals, accordion

Criminal Damage / Criminal Damage

Aug 85. (lp) *<(CRIMLP 128)>* **I LOVE NEW YORK** [ ] [ ]

Aug 86. (lp) *<(CRIMLP 137)>* **WAKE UP AND CRY** [ ] [ ]

Stim / Stim

May 90. (lp) *<(STIM 001)>* **ACCORDION POP VOL.1** [ ] [ ]

Next Big Thing / Next Big Thing

Sep 90. (lp) *<(NBT 007)>* **THE EIGHTIES** [ ] [ ]

—— now with **NANCY KRAVITZ** – bass / **WINDY WILD** – percussion, drums / **RICH STIM** – guitar / **JOEL 'POPEYE' JONES** – sax / + many guests incl. HERB ALPERT!, CASSELL WEBB, HAL BLAINE + producer CRAIG LEON

Almo Sounds / Almo Sounds

Nov 95. (cd) *(ALMOCD 004) <80000>* **WHITE COURTESY PHONE** [ ] [ ]
– Big black cloud / Threw it away / Homeboy / Candy / Nature girl / Dim the lights / Down / John Cassavetes / Lazy / Fall./ Been there done that / Way out west.

Feb 96. (cd-ep) *(CDXALMOS 018)* **ME AND MY BERETTA / CANDY / I'M 18 / RUFF TUFF CREME PUFF (demo)** [ ] [ ]

Nov 97. (7") *(NBT 4527)* **split with MAGIC DIRT** [ ] [-]
(above on 'Next Big Thing', below on 'Via Satellite')

Mar 98. (7"pink) *(V-SAT 011)* **JE T'AIME – I WANNA BOOGIE WITH YOU. / CHERRE / SURFER GIRL** [ ] [-]
(above A-side credited with DEAN WAREHAM, B-side with ALAN VEGA)

ANGELFISH (see under ⇒ GOODBYE MR. MACKENZIE)

ANGELIC UPSTARTS

Formed: Brockley Whim, South Shields, England . . . 1977 by MENSI along with MOND, RONNIE WOODEN and DECCA. Perhaps unsurprisingly for a northern punk band, The ANGELIC UPSTARTS cited the injustice of the class divide as one of their driving motivations and there was certainly no love lost between them and their more intellectual London-centric cousins. The boys in blue were another sitting target for their righteous anger, an independently released 1978 debut single, 'MURDER OF LIDDLE TOWERS', condemning police brutality and winning them both the patronage of SHAM 69 mainman, JIMMY PURSEY and a deal with 'Warners'. The PURSEY-produced 'TEENAGE WARNING' (1979) was a straightahead three-chord assault on all things right wing, including the creeping plague of racism and the menace of the new Thatcher government. Like fellow working class heroes, SHAM 69, The ANGELIC UPSTARTS were beleaguered by fascist skinheads disrupting their gigs and misinterpreting their political stance. Still, it didn't take a genius to work out which side of the fence MENSI was on from the lyrical content of follow-up set, 'WE GOTTA GET OUT OF THIS PLACE' (1980), another tirade aimed at Britain's would-be oppressors. A switch to 'E.M.I.' at the dawn of the 80's was shortlived as the punk revolution filtered out into the mainstream, the band defiantly carrying on with their collectivist crusade over a series of independently released albums inlcuding 'REASON WHY' (1983) and 'POWER OF THE PRESS' (1986). While their musical palate had broadened to include the use of keyboards etc., the message remained the same, if even more vitriolic than ever. The contentious 'BRIGHTON BOMB' single paid tribute to the IRA's failed attempt at killing the whole Conservative cabinet; after almost a decade of Tory rule, MENSI (who found himself taken up on obscenity charges!) was obviously reaching the end of his tether. Most of the band's fans were also giving up the ghost and in 1986, The ANGELIC UPSTARTS finally called it a day. An ill-advised reformation in 1992 saw the group sign to metal/hardcore specialist, 'Roadrunner', hardly a natural home. The resulting album, 'BOMBED OUT' (1992) was met with little enthusiasm, by either old fans or new. • **Songwriters:** MENSI and MOND, except WE GOTTA GET OUT OF THIS PLACE (Animals) / GREEN FIELDS OF FRANCE (Eric Bogle) / WHITE RIOT (Clash).

Album rating: ANGEL DUST (THE COLLECTED HIGHS) compilation (*5)

MENSI (b.THOMAS MENSFORTH) – vocals / **MOND** (b. COWIE) – guitar / **RONNIE WOODEN** (b. WARRINGTON) – bass; repl. STEVE due to drug problems / **DECCA** (b. TAYLOR) – drums

Dead not iss.

Jun 78. (7") *(IS-AU 1024)* **THE MURDER OF LIDDLE TOWERS. / POLICE OPPRESSION** [ ] [-]
(re-iss. Sep78 on 'Rough Trade/Small Wonder'; RT-SW 001)

Warners not iss.

Apr 79. (7",7"green/12") *(K 17354/+T)* **I'M AN UPSTART. / LEAVE ME ALONE** [31] [-]
Jul 79. (7"/7"red) *(K 17426/+C)* **TEENAGE WARNING. / THE YOUNG ONES** [29] [-]
Aug 79. (lp/c) *(K/K4 56717)* **TEENAGE WARNING** [29] [-]
– Teenage warning / Student power / The yong ones / Never again / We are the people / Liddle Towers / I'm an upstart / Small town, small mind / Youth leader / Do anything / Let's speed / Leave me alone.
Oct 79. (7") *(K 17476)* **NEVER 'AD NOTHING. / NOWHERE LEFT TO HIDE** [52] [-]
Jan 80. (7") *(K 17558)* **OUT OF CONTROL. / SHOTGUN SOLUTION** [58] [-]
Mar 80. (7") *(K 17586)* **WE GOTTA GET OUT OF THIS PLACE. / UNSUNG HEROES PART 2** [65] [-]
Apr 80. (lp/c) *(K/K4 56906)* **WE GOTTA GET OUT OF THIS PLACE** [54] [-]
– Never 'ad nothing / Police oppression / Lonely man of Spandau / Their destiny is coming / Shotgun solution / King Coal / Out of control / Ronnie is a rocker / Listen to the steps / Can't kill a legend / Capital city / We gotta get out of this place.

Zonophone not iss.

Jul 80. (7") *(Z 7)* **LAST NIGHT ANOTHER SOLDIER. / THE MAN WHO CAME IN FROM THE BEANO** [51] [-]
Nov 80. (7") *(Z 12)* **ENGLAND. / STICK'S DIARY** [ ] [-]
Jan 81. (7") *(Z 16)* **KIDS ON THE STREET. / THE SUN NEVER SHINES** [57] [-]
May 81. (7") *(Z 22)* **I UNDERSTAND. / NEVER COME BACK** [ ] [-]
(12"+=) *(12Z 22)* – Heath's lament.
Jun 81. (lp) *(ZONO 104)* **2,000,000 VOICES** [32] [-]
– 2,000,000 voices / Ghost town / You're nicked / England / Heath's lament / Guns for the Afghan rebels / I understand / Mensi's marauders / Mr. Politician / Kids on the street / We're gonna take the world / Last night another soldier / I wish. *(re-iss. May93 & Jan98 on 'Dojo'; DOJOLP 081)*
Sep 81. (lp) *(ZEM 102)* **ANGELIC UPSTARTS LIVE (live)** [27] [-]
– Teenage warning / Never 'ad nothing / Four words / Last night another soldier / Guns for the Afghan rebels / Mr. Politician / Shotgun solution / Pride without prejudice / England / Police oppression / Kids on the street / I understand / You're nicked / 2,000,000 voices / I'm an upstart. *(c+=)* – (free live flexi 7"with above) – THE YOUNG ONES / WHITE RIOT. / WE'RE GONNA TAKE THE WORLD / LEAVE ME ALONE *(cd-iss. Feb94 on 'Dojo'; DOJOCD 169)*
Oct 81. (7") *(Z 25)* **DIFFERENT STROKES. / DIFFERENT DUB** [ ] [-]

—— **TONY FEEDBACK** – bass repl. DECCA who went solo

Mar 82. (7") *(Z 28)* **NEVER SAY DIE. / WE DEFY YOU** [ ] [-]
Apr 82. (lp) *(ZONO 106)* **STILL FROM THE HEART** [ ] [-]
– Never say die / Flames of Brixton / Action man / Wasted (loved by none) / Here comes trouble / Theme for lost souls / I stand accused / Black knights of the 80's / Cry wolf / Soldier. *(cd-iss. Nov93 on 'Dojo'; DOJOCD 144)*

—— (MENSI, MOND and FEEDBACK) were joined by **BRYAN HAYES** – rhythm guitar / **PAUL THOMPSON** – drums

Anagram not iss.

Nov 82. (7"/12") *(ANA/12ANA 3)* **WOMAN IN DISGUISE. / LUST FOR GLORY** [ ] [-]
Mar 83. (7"/12") *(ANA/12ANA 7)* **SOLIDARITY. / FIVE FLEW OVER** [ ] [-]
Jul 83. (7"; w-drawn) *(ANA 12)* **THE BURGLAR. /** [-] [-]

—— next 45 with guest vocalist MAX SPLODGE (ex-SPLODGENESSABOUNDS)

Sep 83. (7") *(ANA 13)* **NOT JUST A NAME. / THE LEECH** [ ] [-]
(12"+=) *(12ANA 13)* – Leave me alone / Liddle Towers.
Dec 83. (lp) *(GRAM 04)* **REASON WHY?** [ ] [-]
– Woman in disguise / Never give up / Waiting, hating / Reason why? / Nobody was saved / Geordie's wife / Loneliness of the long distance runner / 42nd Street / The burglar / Solidarity / As the passion / A young punk / Where we started. *(cd-iss. Nov92; CDGRAM 04) (cd re-iss. Jan97 on 'Summit'; SUMCD 4086)*

Picasso not iss.

Oct 84. (7") *(PIK 001)* **MACHINE GUN KELLY. / PAINT IT IN RED** [ ] [-]
(12"+=) *(PIKT 001)* – There's a drink in it.
Aug 85. (lp) *(PIK 004)* **LAST TANGO IN MOSCOW (live)** [ ] [-]
(re-iss. Feb88 on 'Razor'; RAZ 004) (cd-iss. Nov93 on 'Great Expectations'; PIPCD 047) (cd re-iss. May98 on 'Captain Oi'; AHOYCD 087)
Sep 85. (lp) *(HCLP 002M)* **LIVE IN YUGOSLAVIA (live)** [ ] [-]
– Never ad nothing / Leave me alone / Teenage warning / Solidarity / Last night another soldier / Guns for the Afghan rebels / Machine gun Kelly / Police oppression / Kids on the street / Women in disguise / 2,000,000 voices / One more day / Upstart / Who killed Liddle Towers / White riot. *(re-iss. Feb88 on 'Razor'; RAZM 32) (cd-iss. Aug93 on 'Great Expectations'; PIPCD 048) (cd re-iss. Oct95 on 'Punx'; PUNXCD 2)*

Gas Chameleon

Jun 85. (7") *(GM 1010)* **BRIGHTON BOMB. / SOLDIER** [ ] [-]
(12"+=) *(GM 3010)* – Thin red line.
Jan 86. (m-lp) *(GAS 4012)* **THE POWER OF THE PRESS** [ ] [-]
– I stand accused / Nottingham slag / Joe where are you now? / Empty street / Soldier / Brighton bomb / The power of the press / Stab in the back / Here I come / Thin red line / I'd kill her for six pence / Green fields of France. *(re-iss. Jun90 on 'Streetlink'; CLINK 006)*
1987. (c) *<CHC 8603>* **BRIGHTON BOMB** [-] [ ]

—— disbanded 1986 and little or nothing heard of until 1992

Roadrunner not iss.

May 92. (cd/lp) **BOMBED OUT** [ ] [-]
(re-iss. Aug94 on 'Dojo'; DOJOCD 198)

– compilations, others, etc. –

Apr 81. (c-s) *Warners; (SPZ 2)* **I'M AN UPSTART / NEVER 'AD NOTHING** [ ] [-]
Sep 83. (lp/c) *Anagram; (GRAM/CGRAM 07)* **ANGEL DUST (THE COLLECTED HIGHS)** [ ] [-]
– The murder of Liddel Towers / Police oppression / I'm an upstart / Teenage warning / Never 'ad nothing / Shotgun solution / England / Last night another soldier / 2,000,000 voices / Kids on the street / Never say die / Heath's lament / I understand / Woman's disguise / Solidarity. *(cd-iss. Oct88; CDMGRAM 7)* – REASON WHY. *(cd re-iss. Sep93; same)*
Mar 86. (lp) *Dojo; (DOJOLP 7)* **BOOTLEGS AND RARITIES** [ ] [-]
(cd-iss. Nov93 on 'Great Expectations'; PIPCD 049)
Dec 87. (lp) *Link; (LINKLP 019)* **BLOOD ON THE TERRACES** [ ] [-]
Jul 88. (12"ep) *Skunx; (MENSIX 1)* **ENGLAND'S ALIVE (live)** [ ] [-]
– England / We're gonna take the world / Liddle Towers / The young ones.
Jan 92. (cd) *Streetlink; (AOK 102)* **ALTERNATIVE CHARTBUSTERS** [ ] [-]
Jul 92. (cd) *Streetlink; (STRCD 027)* **GREATEST HITS LIVE (live)** [ ] [-]
(re-iss. Mar93 on 'Dojo'; DOJOCD 127)
Aug 92. (cd) *Soundtrack Music; (SLOGCD 1)* **BLOOD ON THE TERRACES / LOST AND FOUND** [ ] [-]
(re-iss. Feb94 on 'Loma'; LOMACD 11)
Jun 95. (cd) *Anagram; (CDPUNK 59)* **THE INDEPENDENT PUNK SINGLES COLLECTION** [ ] [-]
Dec 97. (cd) *Captain Oi; (AHOYCD 80)* **RARITIES** [ ] [-]

ANGRY SAMOANS

Formed: Van Nuys, Los Angeles, California, USA ... August '78 by 'METAL' MIKE (SAUNDERS), GREGG TURNER, TODD HOMER and BILL VOCKEROTH and P.J. GALLIGAN (the latter was replaced by STEVE DROJENSKY after their first lp). One of the prime movers in the emerging L.A. hardcore scene along with the likes of BLACK FLAG and the CIRCLE JERKS, The ANGRY SAMOANS' first release was an EP, 'INSIDE MY BRAIN'. Transmitted via 'Bad Trip' (the label that is!), their next offering upset radio DJ's & the US music press alike due to the EP's content (i.e. the pseudonym, The QUEER PILLS, the label, 'Homophobic' and the explicit song titles, 'TIME TO F*** and 'THEY SAVED HITLER'S C***'), although subsequent copies were rubber stamped with the ANGRY SAMOANS moniker. Their debut, 'BACK FROM SAMOA' (1982), arrived with a little less controversy, their comic-strip punk rock drawing comparisons to The DICKIES and The RAMONES. However, the 80's proved a fairly barren time on the recording front, their short spell with 'Triple X' resulting in their swansong album, 'LIVE AT RHINO RECORDS' (1990).

Album rating: THE UNBOXED SET compilation (*6)

'METAL' MIKE (SAUNDERS) – vocals, guitar / **GREGG TURNER** – guitar, vocals / **P.J. GALLIGAN** – lead guitar / **TODD HOMER** – bass / **BILL VOCKEROTH** – drums

not iss. Bad Trip

1981. (12"ep) *<BT 201>* **INSIDE MY BRAIN EP** [-] [ ]
– Right side of my mind / Gimme sopor / Hot cars / Inside my brain / You stupid asshole / Get off the air. *(cd-iss. Jul95 on 'Triple X'; TX 51033CD)*

not iss. Homophobic

Feb 82. (7"; as The QUEER PILLS) *<HOMO 02>* **STUPID JERK / TIME TO FUCK. / THE TODD KILLINGS / THEY SAVED HITLER'S COCK** [-] [ ]

not iss. P.V.C.

1982. (lp) *<PVC 8958>* **BACK FROM SAMOA** [-] [ ]
– Gas chamber / The Todd killings / Lights out / My old man's a fatso / Time has come today / They saved Hitler's cock / Homo-sexual / Steak knife / Haiz-man's brain is calling / Tuna taco / Coffin chase / You stupid jerk / Ballad of Jerry Curlan / Not of this earth. *(cd-iss. Jul95 on 'Triple X'; TX 51034CD)*

—— **STEVE DROJENSKY** – guitar; repl. GALLIGAN

1987. (m-lp) **YESTERDAY STARTED TOMORROW** [-] [ ]
– Different world / Electrocution / It's raining today / Unhinged / Psych-out 129 / Somebody to love. *(cd-iss. Jul95 on 'Triple X'+=; TX 51035CD)* – 31 GARBAGE PIT HITS (compilation)
1988. (lp/c/cd) *<PVC/+C/D 8965>* **STP NOT LSD** [-] [ ]
– I lost (my mind) / Wild hog rhyde / Laughing at me / STP not LSD / Staring at the sun / Death of Beewak / Egyptomania / Attack of the mushroom people / Feet on the ground / Garbage pit / (I'll drink to this) Love song / Lost highway. *(cd-iss. Jul95 on 'Triple X'; TX 51036CD)*

not iss. Triple X

1990. (cd) *<51037>* **LIVE AT RHINO RECORDS (live)** [-] [ ]
– Too animalistic / Right side of my mind / Commando / My old man's a fatso / Party games / Todd's not here / You stupid asshole / I'm a pig / I'm in love with your mom.

—— split when 'METAL' MIKE went solo, releasing a mini-cd in 1991

– compilations, etc. –

1987. (lp) *P.V.C.;* **31 GARBAGE PIT HITS** (live & unreleased) [-] [ ]
1990. (lp) *Shakin' Street;* **RETURN TO SAMOA** [-] [ ]
(UK-iss.Jun97 on 'Vermiform'; YUPPY 008CD)
Jul 95. (cd) *Triple X; <(TX 51190CD)>* **THE UNBOXED SET** [ ] [ ]

ANIMALS THAT SWIM

Formed: London, England ... 1992 by self-proclaimed genius/poet, HANK STARRS, alongside his brothers, HUGH and AL BARKER. Releasing two self-financed 45's on 'Beachheads In Space' during the next year ('KING BEER' and 'ROY'), ATS earned column inches in the music press as critics marvelled at their prodigious talent. 'Che' records also took note and issued their third single, the excellent and now very rare '50 DRESSES'. In 1994, they were ensconced in the studio over a six-month period, piecing together the material for their debut album, 'WORKSHY'. 'Alternative Tentacles' subsidiary 'El-e-mental' obviously thought they were industrious enough to make it and released the album later that Autumn. Previewed by the single, 'MADAME YEVONDE', the album was hailed by reviewers who raved over STARRS' melancholy wanderings, his voice reminiscent of

CATHAL COUGHLAN (of FATIMA MANSIONS), MARK GOLDTHORPE (ex-ARTERY) or even JACQUES BREL; CRABTREE's vaguely mariachi-esque trumpet playing also set them apart. Highlights of the album included most of the aforementioned singles, the forthcoming one-that-got-away, 'PINK CARNATIONS' and a tribute to the cult US singer/songwriter, 'VIC' (CHESNUTT). Upon their overdue return in 1996, things seemed to turn pear-shaped as a follow-up set, 'I WAS THE KING, I REALLY WAS THE KING', failed to keep up the impossibly high standards they'd set themselves. • **Songwriters:** STARRS – H.BARKER and some with CRABTREE. • **Trivia:** DEL also moonlights for BARK PSYCHOSIS while ANTHONY does the same for MAMBO TAXI.

Album rating: WORKSHY (*9) / I WAS THE KING, I REALLY WAS THE KING (*8)

HANK STARRS – vocals, drums / **HUGH BARKER** – guitar / **AL BARKER** – guitar, keyboards, vocals / **DEL CRABTREE** – trumpet / **ANTHONY COOTE** – bass

		Beachheads In Space	not iss.
May 92.	(7") *(BIS 1)* **KING BEER. /**	[ ]	[-]
Feb 93.	(7") *(BIS 2)* **ROY. / WEARY MIND**	[ ]	[-]
		Che	Big Bop
Aug 93.	(10"ep) *(che 5)* **50 DRESSES / CHAPEL MARKET. / HOLLOWAY AVIATOR / OREGON STATE FAIR**	[ ]	[-]
		El-e-mental	not iss.
Sep 94.	(7"m/cd-s) *(ELM 23 S/CD)* **MADAME YEVONDE. / ME AND CAPTAIN AMERICA / MAY**	[ ]	[-]
Sep 94.	(cd/lp) *(ELM 24 CD/LP) <510>* **WORKSHY**	[ ]	[ ] 1996

– How to make a chandelier / Smooth steps / Roy / Pink carnations / St. Francis / Action at Tescos / King Beer / Barney / Susie's friends / Madame Yevonde / Vic / Silent film / Stay with me.

— They now have a new drummer **KARL** (in Spring '95)

Mar 95.	(7"ep/cd-ep) *(ELM 26 S/CD)* **PINK CARNATIONS / KANDY KARS. / NEW BOOTS / HARRY DEAN / DEL FRESCO**	[ ]	[-]
Feb 96.	(7") *(ELM 35S)* **THE GREENHOUSE**	[ ]	[-]
	(cd-s+=) *(ELM 35CD)* –		
May 96.	(7") *(ELM 36S)* **FADED GLAMOUR**	[ ]	[-]
	(cd-s+=) *(ELM 36CD)* –		
Jun 96.	(cd/c/lp) *(ELM 37 CD/MC/LP)* **I WAS THE KING, I REALLY WAS THE KING**	[ ]	[-]

ANNIE CHRISTIAN

Formed: Edinburgh, Scotland . . . Spring '97 by main songwriter, LARRY LEAN, CHRIS ADAMS, DAVID HUNTER and ANDREW HASTINGS, all possessing a penchant for PRINCE and the late political comedian, BILL HICKS. Managed by Bruce Findlay (Radio DJ, famous for overseeing SIMPLE MINDS' rise to fame), the quartet delivered their debut, 'LOVE THIS LIFE', early the following year. They fitted neatly into the MANICS / STEREOPHONICS brand of rifferama rock, their gothic lyrics overpowering enough to set them apart. • **Covered:** TRANSMISSION (Joy Division).

Album rating: awaited debut album

LARRY LEAN – vocals, guitar / **CHRIS ADAMS** – guitar / **DAVID HUNTER** – bass / **ANDREW HASTINGS** – drums

		Equipe Ecosse – V2	not iss.
Mar 98.	(7") *(EQE 500139-7)* **LOVE THIS LIFE. / THE SHATTERED BURLESQUE**	[ ]	[-]
	(cd-s+=) *(EQE 500139-3)* –		
May 98.	(7") *(EQE 500190-7)* **SOMEDAY MY PRINCE WILL COME AGAIN. /**	[ ]	[-]
	(cd-s+=) *(EQE 500190-3)* –		
Sep 98.	(7") *(EQE 500253-7)* **THE OTHER WAY. / TRANSMISSION**	[ ]	[-]
	(cd-s+=) *(EQE 500253-3)* –		

ANOTHER PRETTY FACE (see under ⇒ WATERBOYS)

ANOTHER SUNNY DAY

Formed: Penzance, Cornwall, England . . . 1987 as the brain-child of HARVEY WILLIAMS. This singer and multi-instrumentalist packed in a communications engineering course at Plymouth Polytecnic and devoted himself to his music. Having signed a singles deal with indie-pop label, 'Sarah', WILLIAMS' one-man band were initially heard via a flexi-single, 'ANORAK CITY', available free with the 'Are You Scared To Get Happy' fanzine. ANOTHER SUNNY DAY's debut single proper came in the shape of the long-winded 'I'M IN LOVE WITH A GIRL WHO DOESN'T KNOW I EXIST', WILLIAMS strumming along pleasantly enough although the saccharine-sweet vocals leave a bad taste in the ear. He continued in a similarly fey manner over a further clutch of singles, never quite managing to break the 2-minute barrier.

Album rating: none released

HARVEY WILLIAMS – vocals, guitar, bass, keyboards, drums, percussion

		Sarah	not iss.
Apr 88.	(6"flexi) *(SARAH 004)* **ANORAK CITY**	[ ]	[-]
Jun 88.	(7"m) *(SARAH 007)* **I'M IN LOVE WITH A GIRL WHO DOESN'T KNOW I EXIST. / THINGS WILL BE NICE / THE CENTRE OF MY LITTLE WORLD**	[ ]	[-]
May 89.	(7"m) *(SARAH 016)* **WHAT'S HAPPENED. / ?**	[ ]	[-]
1989.	(7"ltd) *(CAFF 7)* **GENETIC ENGINEERING. / KILLOWN TOWERS**	[ ]	[-]
	(above single on 'Caff')		
Nov 89.	(7"m) *(SARAH 022)* **YOU SHOULD ALL BE MURDERED. / ?**	[ ]	[-]
Aug 90.	(7"m) *(SARAH 0??)* **RIO. / THE VERY BEGINNING**	[ ]	[-]

— WILLIAMS disappeared (where is he now?)

Adam ANT (see under ⇒ ADAM AND THE ANTS)

ANTI

Formed: Los Angeles, California, USA . . . early 80's by DANNY PHILLIPS, GARY KAIL (also of MOOD OF DEFIANCE), original vocalist BERT and JOHN McCARTHY. One of the L.A. hardcore scene's most intense acts, ANTI were basically anti-everything, or at least anything conventional (especially war), airing their angry views over a couple of 1982 EP's and a debut album, 'I DON'T WANT TO DIE IN YOUR WAR' (1983). While they kept up the politically correct fury on follow-up set, 'DEFY THE SYSTEM' (1983), new members, STEVE LIND and DOUG CARRION (who replaced McCARTHY and BERT respectively), ensured a more melodic musical approach. KAIL subsequently split the band, taking PHILLIPS with him to his other hardcore project, MOOD OF DEFIANCE. CARRION, meanwhile, found a new lease of life with INCEST CATTLE (the band that is!), ADOLESCENTS and DAG NASTY.

Album rating: I DON'T WANT TO DIE IN YOUR WAR (*4) / DEFY THE SYSTEM (*4)

BERT – vocals / **GAIL KAIL** – guitar (of MOOD OF DEFIANCE) / **DANNY PHILLIPS** – bass / **JOHN McCARTHY** – drums

		not iss.	New U'ground
1982.	(7"ep's) **unknown**	[-]	[ ]
Jan 83.	(lp) *<NU-22>* **I DON'T WANT TO DIE IN YOUR WAR**	[-]	[ ]

– I'm going insane / The cycle / Streets / What do you do / Fight war not wars / Acid test / I don't want to die in your war / New underground / Pushed around / I hate you / Poseur.

— **STEVE LIND** – drums; repl. McCARTHY (he left during sessions)

— **DOUG CARRION** – bass; repl. BERT (DANNY now vocals, guitar)

Dec 83.	(lp) *<NU-77>* **DEFY THE SYSTEM**	[-]	[ ]

– I try / Lies / Your government's caling you / Working in a factory / Map of the star's homes / Your problems / Five downtown / Nothing new / Club me like a baby seal / Backfire bomber / Be free / Over-throw the government / Parents of punks / Repressed aggresion.

— split in 1984, KAIL took PHILLIPS with him to MOOD OF DEFIANCE, while the former moonlighted in many projects. CARRION formed INCEST CATTLE before becoming part of the DESCENDENTS and later DAG NASTY.

ANTIETAM

Formed: based New York, USA . . . 1983 out of Louisville, Kentucky arty power-pop outfit, the BABYLON DANCE BAND. Taking the rather non-descript moniker from a 19th century American civil war battle, this bizarre husband and wife team of TIM HARRIS and TARA KEY enlisted the first in a series of drummers, MICHAEL WEINERT. The influential 'Homestead' delivered their eponymous debut set, a self-indulgent collection which failed to make much of an impact. Borrowing violinist DANNA PENTES from FETCHIN BONES, they added a new dimension to their avant-indie rock, releasing a second album, 'MUSIC FROM ELBA', in '86. Four years elapsed before the group (with new sticksman, CHARLES SCHULTZ) resurfaced from the trenches of obscurity, releasing the IRA KAPLAN and GEORGE HUBLEY (YO LA TENGO)-produced 'BURGOO' (1990) on 'Triple X'. Half a decade later, ANTIETAM were still battling on, although TARA KEY enjoyed some belated recognition with a solo set, 'BOURBON COUNTY' (1993). Around the same time, interest was being shown in her

Album rating: ANTIETAM (*4) / MUSIC FROM ELBA (*4) / BURGOO (*7) / EVERYWHERE OUTSIDE (*5) / ROPE A DOPE (*4) / COMES ALIVE (*4) / Tara Key: BOURBON COUNTY (*6) / EAR AND ECHO (*4) / Babylon Dance Band: BABYLON DANCE BAND (*6)

TARA KEY – vocals, guitar / **TIM HARRIS** – vocals, bass / **MICHAEL WEINERT** – drums

		Homestead	Homestead
Jul 85.	(lp) *<(HMS 025)>* **ANTIETAM**	[ ]	[ ]

— added **DANNA PENTES** – violin (of FETCHIN BONES) – also new drummer

Sep 86.	(7") *<(HMS 059)>* **UNTIL NOW. /**	[ ]	[ ]
Sep 86.	(lp) *<(HMS 068)>* **MUSIC FROM ELBA**	[ ]	[ ]

— **CHARLES SCHULTZ** – drums; repl. last drummer

		Triple X	Triple X
1990.	(cd) *<(TX 51026CD)>* **BURGOO**	[ ]	[ ]
1991.	(cd) *<(TX 51083CD)>* **EVERYWHERE OUTSIDE**	[ ]	[ ]

— **JOSH MADELL** – drums; repl. SCHULTZ

		Homestead	Homestead
Feb 95.	(cd) *<(HMS 2182)>* **ROPE-A-DOPE**	[ ]	[ ]

– Hands down / What she will / Pine / Certain muse / Hardly believe / Graveyard / Rope-a-dope / Leave home / Betwixt / Silver solace.

– compilations, others, etc.

Jul 95.	(cd) *Triple X; <(TX 51112CD)>* **COMES ALIVE**	[ ]	[ ]

TARA KEY

— with **TIM HARRIS, WOLF KNAPP + JOSH MADELL**, etc

Homestead Homestead

Mar 94. (cd) <*(HMS 210-2)*> **BOURBON COUNTY** [ ] [ ] Nov93
– Northern star / Tranquility base / Jack of hearts / Long trail / Seraphim / Bender / V.O.B. / Kali / One spark / I found out / Turbo dog / Need to need / Gypsy village.

May 95. (cd) <*(HMS 222-2)*> **EAR AND ECHO** [ ] [ ] Apr95
– All lit up / Burn / Breakin' in / In absinthe / Left-handed way / Rhythm jester / Lost and found / No reason now / Up and down / Get it straight / No tractor blues.

BABYLON DANCE BAND

TARA KEY + TIM HARRIS (had earlier released a US-only solo)

Matador Matador

May 94. (cd/lp) <*(OLE 033-2/-1)*> **BABYLON DANCE BAND** (rec.early 80's) [ ] [ ]
– When I'm home / Bold beginnings / The reckoning / Shively spleen / My friend Roger / Leave / Resources / See that girl / Jacob's chain / ABC / Golden days / Someday / All radical / Shake!

ANTI-NOWHERE LEAGUE

Formed: Tunbridge Wells, Kent, England . . . 1980 by biker/punks ANIMAL and MAGOO. First came to the attention of the music world, after their gutter-angst cover of Ralph McTell's folkie hit, 'STREET OF LONDON' hit the Top 50 at the end of '81. However, it was 'SO WHAT', the b-side of the record that caused the most controversy, when around 10,000 copies of the 45 were seized by the police under the obscene publications act. Another independent chart-topper followed in the Spring of '82, 'I HATE PEOPLE', a song, like most of the hardcore/oi tracks on their debut album, 'WE ARE THE LEAGUE', offended everybody but the mohawks and skins. The UK Top 30 album (like earlier 45's, also with WINSTON and PJ), was a barrage of foul-mouthed protest 100 mph punk, fusing "oi" with "metal". A very disappointing live set recorded in Yugoslavia was their next delivery, although this was their last show as out and out punks. In the mid 80's, they were back as biker-clad heavies, The LEAGUE and after only one album, 'THE PERFECT CRIME' (1987) they had returned to ground. It was a case of sporadic reunions from then on, until that is, METALLICA covered 'SO WHAT' and thus the reformation in '93.

Album rating: WE ARE . . . THE LEAGUE (*6) / PERFECT CRIME (*4) / LONG LIVE THE LEAGUE – R.I.P. compilation (*6)

ANIMAL (b. NICK KARMER) – vocals / **MAGOO** (b. CHRIS EXALL) – guitar / **WINSTON BLAKE** – bass / **P.J.** – drums

WXYZ not iss.

Nov 81. (7"/12"w-drawn) *(ABCD 1/+T)* **STREETS OF LONDON. / SO WHAT** [48] [-]

Mar 82. (7") *(ABCD 2)* **I HATE . . . PEOPLE. / LET'S BREAK THE LAW** [46] [-]

Apr 82. (lp/c) *(LMNOP/+C 1)* **WE ARE . . .THE LEAGUE** [24] [-]
– We are the league / Animal / Woman / Can't stand rock'n'roll / (We will not) Remember you / Snowman / Streets of London / I hate . . . people / Wreck-a-nowhere / World War III / Nowhere man / Let's break the law. *(lp re-iss. Nov85 on 'I.D.'; NOSE 6) (cd-iss. Oct92 on 'Streetlink'; STRCD 028) (<cd re-iss. Apr93 on 'Dojo'; DOJOCD 128>) (cd re-iss. Sep97 on 'Snapper'; SMMCD 515)*

Jun 82. (7"pic-d) *(ABCD 4)* **WOMAN. / ROCKER** [72] [-]

Nov 82. (7") *(ABCD 6)* **FOR YOU. / THE BALLAD OF J.J. DECAY** [ ] [-]

— added **GILLY** – guitar

I.D. not iss.

Oct 83. (lp) *(NOSE 3)* **LIVE IN YUGOSLAVIA (live)** [88] [-]
– Let's break the law / Streets of London / Let the country feed you / We will survive / I hate . . .people / Snowman / For you / Going down / Woman / Can't stand rock'n'roll / So what / Wreck-a-nowhere / Paint it black / We are the league.

A.B.C. not iss.

Dec 84. (7"/7"pic-d) *(ABCS 004/+P)* **OUT ON THE WASTELAND. / WE WILL SURVIVE** [ ] [-]
(12"+=) *(ABCS 004T)* – Queen and country.

— **MICHAEL BETTELL** – drums repl. P.J.

— also added a keyboard player, before reverting to original name.

G.W.R. G.W.R.

May 87. (lp/c) *(GW LP/TC 12)* <*PAL 1238*> **THE PERFECT CRIME** [ ] [ ]
– Crime / On the waterfront / Branded / I don't believe this is my England / Johannesburg / Shining / Working for the company / System / Curtain.

— disbanded although they re-formed the 1985 line-up in 1992

SPV Pavement

Nov 97. (cd) *(SPV 0845301-2)* <*32286*> **SCUM** [ ] [ ] Aug98
– Fucked up and wasted / Chocolate soldiers / Get ready / Suicide . . . have you tried / Pig iron / Scum / Burn 'em all / Gypsies tramps and thieves / How does it feel? / Great unwashed / . . . Long live punk. *(lp-iss.Nov97 on 'Knock Out'; KOLP 069)*

– compilations, etc. –

Apr 86. (lp) *Dojo; (DOJOLP 15)* **LONG LIVE THE LEAGUE – R.I.P.** [ ] [-]
– For you / We will survive / Out on the wasteland / Queen & country / We are the League / Streets of London / So what / Let's break the law / The ballad of J.J. Decay / Woman / Snowman / Wreck a nowhere / Let the country feed you / Going down / I hate . . . people. *(cd-iss. 1987; DOJOCD 15)*

Feb 89. (d-lp) *I.D.; (NOSE 36)* **WE ARE . . . THE LEAGUE / LIVE IN YUGOSLAVIA** [ ] [-]
(cd-iss. Jan90; CDOSE 36)

Mar 90. (lp) *Link; (LINKLP 120)* **LIVE AND LOUD (live)** [ ] [-]
(cd-iss. Oct90; LINKCD 120)

Oct 92. (cd) *Streetlink; (STRCD 013)* **THE BEST OF THE ANTI-NOWHERE LEAGUE** [ ] [-]
(cd-iss. Mar93 on 'Dojo'; DOJOCD 113) (cd re-iss. Jan94 on 'Cleopatra'; CLEO 07279CD) (re-iss. Apr98 on 'Snapper'; SMMCD 514)

Nov 92. (cd) *Castle; (LOMACD 9)* **THE PERFECT CRIME / LIVE IN YUGOSLAVIA** [ ] [-]

Feb 95. (cd) *Anagram; (CDPUNK 44)* **ANTI-NOWHERE LEAGUE PUNK SINGLES COLLECTION** [ ] [-]

May 96. (cd) *Receiver; (<RRCD 219>)* **THE HORSE IS DEAD (THE ANTI-NOWHERE LEAGUE LIVE)** [ ] [ ]

Nov 96. (7") *Visionary Vinyl; (V 713)* **STREETS OF LONDON. /** [ ] [-]

Jul 98. (cd/lp) *Knock Out; (IRRCD/KOLP 078)* **RETURN TO YUGOSLAVIA** [ ] [-]

— also a various artists compilation 'SO WHAT' was released in 1997

ANTI-PASTI

Formed: Derby, England . . . 1978 as The SCRINCERS by DUGI BELL, EDDIE BARKE and RUSSELL MAW, adopting the ANTI-PASTI moniker following the recruitment of MARTIN ROPER. By the release of a DIY debut EP, 'FOUR SORE POINTS' (1980), the line-up had undergone the first of many changes, STU WINFIELD and STAN SMITH replacing MAW and BARKE. The record nevertheless contained one of their finest moments, the live favourite, 'NO GOVERNMENT', a blistering tirade against Thatcher and her newly elected Tory cronies. With the agenda established, ANTI-PASTI made their first inroads into the newly established independent chart with follow-up single, 'LET THEM FREE', despite more personnel disruption as SMITH and WINFIELD were replaced by KEVIN NIXON and WILL HOON respectively. More recognition followed as the group nearly scraped into the UK Top 30 with debut album, 'THE LAST CALL' (1981) and topped the indie chart with the defiant 'SIX GUNS' single. Despite building up a committed following, however, ANTI-PASTI, along with the likes of ANGELIC UPSTARTS and SHAM 69 were struggling to set themsleves apart from the proliferation of right wing Oi! bands that were splitting punk unity. Although a joint effort with The EXPLOITED, 'DON'T LET 'EM GRIND YOU DOWN', also made No.1 in the indie chart, follow-up album, 'CAUTION TO THE WIND' (1982) saw them lose momentum. Following the departure of original member ROPER, the group struggled on before finally calling it a day in the mid-80's. With an inevitable CD re-issue of their two albums in the mid-90's, the band re-formed for a one-off bout of touring although no new material was forthcoming.

Album rating: THE LAST CALL (*4) / CAUTION IN THE WIND (*3)

MARTIN ROPER – vocals / **DUGI BELL** – guitar / **STU WINFIELD** – bass / **STAN SMITH** – drums

Rondelet not iss.

Nov 80. (7"ep) *(ROUND 2)* **FORE SORE POINTS EP** [ ] [-]
– No government / 1980 / Two years too late / Something new.

— **WILL HOON** – bass; repl. STU

— **KEV NIXON** – drums; repl. STAN

Jan 81. (7",7"red) *(ROUND 5)* **LET THEM FREE. / ANOTHER DEAD SOLDIER** [ ] [-]

Jul 81. (lp/c) *(ABOUT/CARB 5)* **THE LAST CALL** [31] [-]
– No government / Brew your own / Another dead soldier / Call the army (I'm alive) / City below / 24 hours / Night of the war cry / Freedom row / St.George (get's his gun) / The last call / Ain't got me / Truth and justice / Hell / I wanna be your dog. *(cd-iss. Mar95 on 'Anagram'; CDPUNK 48) (re-iss. Oct96 on 'Get Back'; GET 7)*

Oct 81. (7"m) *(ROUND 10)* **SIX GUNS. / NOW'S THE TIME / CALL THE ARMY** [ ] [-]

— Late in '81, they shared a single EP, with EXPLOITED.

May 82. (7") *(ROUND 18)* **EAST TO THE WEST. / BURN IN YOUR OWN FLAMES** [ ] [-]

— added **OLLIE (HOON)** – guitar

Jun 82. (lp/c) *(ABOUT/CARB 7)* **CAUTION IN THE WIND** [ ] [-]
– Caution in the wind / One Friday night / X affair / Get out now / Mr. Mystery / East to the west / See how they run / Hate circulation / Agent ABC / The best of us / Guinea pigs / Beyond belief. *(cd-iss. May95 on 'Anagram'; CDPUNK 53)*

Sep 82. (7") *(ROUND 26)* **CAUTION IN THE WIND. / LAST TRAIN** [ ] [-]

— they split late 1982 and went to the States (ROPER went solo)

– compilations, etc. –

Sep 83. (lp) *Rondelet; (ABOUT 13)* **ANTI-PASTI (SINGLES COLLECTION)** [ ] [-]

Mar 96. (cd) *Dojo; (DOJOCD 230) / Cleopatra; <9686>* **NO GOVERNMENT: THE BEST OF ANTI-PASTI** [ ] [ ] Feb96
– No government / 1980 / Two years too late / Another dead soldier / Hell / Ain't got me / East to west / Burn in your own flames / Caution in the wind / Last train to nowhere / Blind faith / Call the army (I'm alive) / Night of the warcry / Six guns / Now's the time / Brew your own.

Jun 98. (cd) *Cherry Red; (CDPUNK 106)* **THE PUNK SINGLES COLLECTION** [ ] [-]

LINKMEN

— were formed by 2 former ANTI-PASTI's (STU & STAN)?

Kitchenware not iss.

Jun 84. (12"ep) *(SKX 17)* **EVERY INCH A KING / RUIN. / HEAVEN AND BACK AGAIN / JACK BE NIMBLE / STICKS AND STONES** [ ] [-]

Jan 85. (7") *(SK 17)* **EVERY INCH A KING. / MANIC DEPRESSION** [ ] [-]

Spice not iss.

Oct 85. (7") *(HERB 1)* **ILL WIND. / ?**

—— Split when STU formed CLINIC P.

Annie ANXIETY

Born: New York, USA. A member of The ASEXUALS, the singer crossed the water to London in '81 and released a solo single, 'BARBED WIRE HALO', for the 'Crass' label. It would be a few years before she would finally unleash a full set of songs, 'SOUL POSSESSION' (1984), for 'Corpus Christi'. Produced by 'On-U-Sound' man, ADRIAN SHERWOOD, it also featured musicians from The POISON GIRLS and FLUX OF PINK INDIANS. In 1987, she formed ANNIE ANXIETY BANDEZ, although only a solitary set, 'JACKAMO', appeared on Derek Birkett's 'One Little Indian' operation.

Album rating: SOUL POSSESSION (*4) / JACKAMO (*4)

ANNIE ANXIETY – vocals / with **MARTIN FREDERIX** – guitar / **DEREK BIRKETT** – bass / **PENNY RIMBAUD + PRISONER** – drums / **KISHI** – synthesizer, piano / **EVE LIBERTINE** – vocals / **BONJO** – percussion

Crass not iss.

Sep 81. (7") *(321984-3)* **BARBED WIRE HALO. / COULD THIS BE LOVE**

Corpus Christi not iss.

Feb 84. (lp) *(CHRIST ITS 10)* **SOUL POSSESSION**
– Closet love / Third gear / Turkey girl / Burnt offerings / To know evil / Sad shadows / Viet not mine, El Salvador yours / Waiting for the fun.

ANNIE ANXIETY BANDEZ

One Little Indian not iss.

Aug 87. (lp) *(TPLP 4)* **JACKAMO**
– As I lie in your arms / Bastinado / Chasing the dragon down Broadway / Jackamo / Jack yo mama / One mourning / Rise / Hier encore. *(cd-iss. 1989 +=; TPLP 4CD)* – Down by the station / Rise (dub).

Oct 87. (12") *(12TP 6)* **AS I LIE IN YOUR ARMS. / DOWN BY THE STATION / RISE (dub)**

Mar 88. (12"; w-drawn) *(12TP 13)* **HIER ENCORE**

East West not iss.

May 90. (7") *(B 8967)* **SUGAR BOWL. / DIAMONDS MADE OF GLASS**
(12"+=/cd-s+=) *(B 8967 T/C)* –

—— retired from her solo career after above

APARTMENTS

Formed: Brisbane, Australia . . . 1979 by PETER MILTON WALSH and BRUCE CARRICK. They released a one-off, 'HELP', for Australian indie, 'Able' (then also home of The GO-BETWEENS), before breaking up when WALSH joined The LAUGHING CLOWNS with ED KUEPPER (ex-SAINTS). WALSH later re-formed The APARTMENTS in 1984 after a stay in London, gaining support slots to EVERYTHING BUT THE GIRL in the process. With ex-TRIFFIDS steel guitar player GRAHAM LEE in tow, the outfit signed a contract with 'Rough Trade', releasing their long-awaited debut album, 'THE EVENING VISITS . . . AND STAYS FOR YEARS', in 1985. The critics gave it good reviews – especially the French ones – some remarking it was reminiscent of 60's hippie icons, LOVE and TIM BUCKLEY (SERGE GAINSBOURG also comes to mind). Early in 1987, WALSH and Co completed a part soundtrack to the John Hughes film, 'Some Kind Of Wonderful' and shifted stables to 'Glass'. After a lengthy hiatus (at least as far as UK releases were concerned), the group resurfaced in the mid-90's, releasing a series of albums for Australian-based 'Hot'.

Album rating: THE EVENING VISITS . . . AND STAYS FOR YEARS (*7)

PETER MILTON WALSH – vocals, bass / **BRUCE CARRICK** – drums

Able not iss.

Oct 79. (7") *(AB 005)* **HELP. / NOBODY LIKE YOU** Austra

—— split when WALSH joined the LAUGHING CLOWNS

—— He reformed the name, adding **GRAHAM LEE** – steel guitar (ex-TRIFFIDS)

Rough Trade not iss.

Oct 85. (lp) *(ROUGH 88)* **THE EVENING VISITS . . . AND STAYS FOR YEARS**
– Sunset hotel / Mr. Somewhere / What's the morning for? / All the birthdays / Great fool / Speechless with Tuesday / Cannot tell the days apart / Lazarus, Lazarus / The black road shines. *(cd-iss. Jul98 on 'Hot'; HOT 1059CD) <US cd-iss. 1997 on 'Twin/Tone'; 89331>*

Mar 86. (7") *(RT 188)* **ALL I WANTED. / SUNSET HOTEL**
(12"+=) *(RTT 188)* – What's the morning for / The black road shines.

Glass not iss.

May 88. (7") *(GLASS 055)* **THE SHYEST TIME. /**
(12"+=) *(GLASS12 055)* –

—— split once again, although they were by no means finished

Hot Restless

Mar 95. (cd) *(HOT 1050CD) <72955>* **A LIFE FULL OF FAREWELLS**
– Things you'll keep / The failure of love is a brick wall / You became my big excuse / End of some fear / Not every clown can be in the circus / Thank you for making me beg / Paint the days white / She sings to forget you / All the time in the world.

Jun 95. (cd-ep) *(HIT 009)* **LIFE EP**
– Things you'll keep / All you wanted / The shyest time / Make it count.

—— **WALSH** + ATKINSON – guitar, vocals / **KATHY WEMYSS** – string arrangements

Hot Twin/Tone

Mar 97. (cd) *(HOT 1060CD) <89330>* **DRIFT** Austra
– Goodbye train / On every corner / Mad cow / Nothing stops it / Over / Knowing you were loved / Places where the night is long / All his stupid friends / Could I hide here? / What's left of your nerve. *(UK-iss.Jul98; same)*

Jul 97. (cd) *(HOT 1063CD)* **APART**
– Doll hospital / No hurry / Breakdown in Vera Cruz / To live for / Welcome to Walsh world / Your ambulance rides / Friday rich – Saturday poor / World of liars / Place of bones / Cheerleader / Everything is given to be taken away.

Jul 98. (cd) *(HOT 1068CD)* **FETE FORAINE (live)**
– What's the morning for / Knowing you were loved / Not every clown can be in the circus / On rvery corner / Sunset hotel / End of some fear / Thank you for making me beg / Things you'll keep / Paint the days white.

APOLLO XI (see under ⇒ ORB)

A POPULAR HISTORY OF SIGNS

Formed: North London, England . . . 1979 by CHRISTINE ISHERWOOD, LINDSAY SMITH, ANDY SMITH, ANDREW JARMAN and PAUL CLARKE. Described as the worst dressed band in Britain, these industrial new wave politico funksters released a few singles on their own 'Melodia' label, before signing to UK indie, 'Jungle'. There, they made a further series of low key attempts including 'IF SHE WAS A CAR' and 'LADDERJACK', before finally getting around to their debut album, 'COMRADES' (1985). Basically a self-indulgent feast of New York underground rhythms, the band unsurprisingly received the two-fingered salute (not always 'A POPULAR SIGN') from the music press. With A CERTAIN RATIO and a dozen others supplying a tighter sculptured sound, APHOS decided to finish their 7-year career after their third set, 'ENGLAND IN THE RAIN' (1988).

Album rating: COMRADES (*4) / TASTE (*3) / ENGLAND IN THE RAIN (*3)

CHRISTINE ISHERWOOD – vocals / **LINDSAY SMITH** – guitar, keyboards / **ANDY SMITH** – guitar / **ANDREW JARMAN** – bass, keyboards, vocals / **PAUL CLARKE** – drums

Melodia not iss.

Dec 80. (7") *(M 1)* **JUSTICE NOT VENGEANCE. / POSSESSION**

Oct 81. (7") *(M 2)* **CROWDS. / CROSSING THE BORDER**

Oct 82. (7") *(M 4)* **DANCING WITH IDEAS. /**

—— now without ANDY SMITH

Jungle not iss.

Sep 83. (7") *(JUNG 6)* **IF SHE WAS A CAR. / STIGMA / GUERMIC**

Mar 84. (7") *(JUNG 10)* **HOUSE. / LADDERJACK / SINK OR SWIM**

Oct 84. (7") *(JUNG 19)* **BODY AND SOUL. / LENIN**
(12"+=) *(JUNG 19T)* – ('A'version).

Feb 85. (lp) *(FREUD 05)* **COMRADES**

Dec 85. (12"ep) *(WAX 005)* **LADDERJACK / HOUSE. / IF SHE WAS A CAR / STIGMA**
(above issued on 'Wax Trax')

Sep 86. (7") **ART OF PERSUASION. /**

Oct 87. (lp) *(FREUD 17)* **TASTE**

May 88. (lp) *(FREUD 21)* **ENGLAND IN THE RAIN**

—— split some time in 1988

APPLES (IN STEREO)

Formed: Denver, Colorado, USA . . . 1993 initially as The APPLES by singer-songwriter, ROBERT SCHNEIDER who, along with JEFF MANGUM enlisted the help of JIM McINTYRE, HILARIE SIDNEY and ROBERT PARFITT. Part of the 'Elephant 6' musicians collective that also included NEUTRAL MILK HOTEL and OLIVIA TREMOR CONTROL, The APPLES covered poppier territory than their counterparts, debuting with an eponymous EP in '93. What with the surge in popularity for the name APPLES, SCHNEIDER and Co tacked on (IN STEREO) to the end of their moniker to prevent any confusion, showcasing their new name on 1995's 'FUN TRICK NOISEMAKER'. Breezy, bright, wide-eyed and charming, the record was feted by Lo-Fi connoisseurs on both sides of the Atlantic for its melodic simplicity and unpretentious references to US kids TV nostalgia. With MANGUM already uprooting to another part of the country to regroup his NEUTRAL MILK HOTEL, SCHNEIDER took up the reins for a second album proper, 'TONE SOUL EVOLUTION' (1997); the previous year, a compilation set of obscure early material, 'SCIENCE FAIRE', had been heartily received by critics and collectors alike.

Album rating: FUN TRICK NOISEMAKER (*7) / SCIENCE FAIRE compilation (*7) / TONE SOUL EVOLUTION (*6)

ROBERT SCHNEIDER – vocals / **JEFF MANGUM** – guitar (ex-OLIVIA TREMOR CONTROL) / **ROBERT PARFITT** – guitar / **JIM McINTYRE** – bass / **HILARIE SIDNEY** – drums

not iss. SpinART

1993. (7"; as the APPLES) **THE APPLES EP**

—— now without MANGUM who was repl. by **KURT HEASLEY** – guitar

May 95. (lp/cd) *<SPART 42/+CD>* **FUN TRICK NOISEMAKER**
– Narrator / Tidal wave / High tide / Green machine / Winter must be cold / She's just like me – Taking time / Glowworm / Dots 1-2-3 / Lucky charm / Innerspace / Show the world / Love you Alice – D / Pine away. *(UK-iss.Dec96; same as US)*

Nov 96. (lp/cd) *<(SPART 48/+CD)>* **SCIENCE FAIRE** (compilation) Sep96
– Tidal wave / Motorcar / Turncoat Indian / Haley / Not the same / Stop along the way / Running in circles / Hypnotic suggestion / Touch the water / Glowworm / To the love the vibration of the bulb / Time for bed – I know you'd do well / Rocket pad.

Nov 97. (lp/cd) <(SPART 57/+CD)> **TONE SOUL EVOLUTION** [ ] [ ] Sep97
– Seems so / What's the number? / About your fame / Shine a light / Get there fine / Silvery light of a dream / We'll come to be / Tin pan alley / You said that last night / Try to remember / Find our way / Coda.

APPLIANCE

Formed: Exeter-based, England . . . 1997 by JAMES BROOKS, DAVID IRELAND and MICHAEL PARKER. Influenced by TELEVISION and MY BLOODY VALENTINE, the trio issued their post-rock, 'Star Wars'-type trilogy of 10"ers over the course of the next year; the appliance of indie science, you could say!

Album rating: TIME AND SPACE EP (*6)

JAMES BROOKS – vocals, guitar / **MICHAEL PARKER** – bass / **DAVID IRELAND** – drums

		Plastic Cowboy	not iss.
Oct 97.	(10"ep) *(PLASTIC 001)* **INTO YOUR HOME EP** – Organised sound / etc	[ ]	-
		Earworm	not iss.
Mar 98.	(7",7"blue) *(WORM 12)* **OUTER. / REV A**	[ ]	-
		Enraptured	not iss.
Jul 98.	(10"colrd-ep/cd-ep) *(RAPT 20/+CD)* **TIME AND SPACE EP**	[ ]	-

A PRIMARY INDUSTRY (see under ⇒ ULTRAMARINE)

(see under ⇒ ULTRAMARINE)

ARAB STRAP

Formed: Falkirk, Scotland . . . 1995 by AIDAN MOFFAT and MALCOLM MIDDLETON. The former had already given up his day job at the local Sleeves record shop to team up with songwriter, JASON TAYLOR, in the 2-man outfit, BAY. This low-key band (augmented at times by RONNIE YOUNG, WILL HEGGIE – ex-COCTEAU TWINS – and ROSS BALLANY), released a couple of RED HOUSE PAINTERS-esque cd's, namely 'HAPPY BEING DIFFERENT' (1994) and 'ALISON RAE' (1995), the latter including a Lo-Fi cover of Roxy Music's 'IN EVERY DREAM HOME A HEARTACHE' and also coming free with an acoustic cd featuring a version of Nick Drake's 'WHICH WILL'. AIDAN, meanwhile, was plotting his own breakaway group, ARAB STRAP (named after a device used for horse-breeding and better known for something bought from a sex shop), re-establishing a friendship with MALCOLM while writing songs together in the latter's bedroom. A debut ARAB STRAP single, 'THE FIRST BIG WEEKEND', was warmly received by the music press in September '96, critics describing it as "trainspotting for the music world". AIDAN's drug/drink-fuelled life was portrayed in painful detail in a couple of the narrative songs from debut album, 'THE WEEK NEVER STARTS ROUND HERE' (incidentally the rhythm section was completed by GARY MILLER and DAVID GOW). His bittersweet, off-the-cuff, Scots-accented demo-esque sagas of broken romance were squeezed between Lo-Fi mumblings of occasional pure genius. MALCOLM's guitar-plucking, meanwhile, came from the laid back school of cool, often played while literally lying on his back. The album was heralded by many (including John Peel) as the next big thing in exotic sound. It included seminal classics, 'THE CLEARING', 'COMING DOWN', 'I WORK IN A SALOON', 'WASTING' and 'DEEPER'. Their live set (including an early afternoon spot at Scotland's 'T In The Park' that added a host of singalong friends), was a mixture of apathy-in-concrete attitude with most people shouting for their favourite, 'THE FIRST BIG WEEKEND'; the track was subsequently used as the backing (with a new coherent talker!) on the Guinness ad (yes, that one that says about 38 per cent of all strippers were educated in a convent!). A year on, with word of mouth cult status ensured, ARAB STRAP finally achieved minor chart glory when 'THE GIRLS OF SUMMER' EP dented the Top 75. Following on from a double header tour with drinking buddies, MOGWAI, the now bearded AIDAN and Co. delivered a surprise Top 50 hit, 'HERE WE GO' (a double A-side with 'TRIPPY'), one of the many low-rent, x-rated classics on their Top 40 Spring 1998 follow-up, 'PHILOPHOBIA'.

Album rating: THE WEEK NEVER STARTS ROUND HERE (*8) / PHILOPHOBIA (*8)

BAY

AIDAN MOFFAT – vocals / **JASON TAYLOR** – guitar / **RONNIE YOUNG** – guitar / **WILL HEGGIE** – bass (of LOWLIFE, ex-COCTEAU TWINS) / **ROSS BALLANY** – drums

		Noise Annoys	Cargo
Nov 94.	(cd) *(ANANCD 2)* **HAPPY BEING DIFFERENT**	[ ]	[ ]
Oct 95.	(cd) *(ANANCD 6)* **ALISON RAE** – Washington / Pure / Home / Dutch / Siamese / In every dream home a heartache / In Lisa's living room / Ruptured / Are you alone? / A great red shark / Surely someone somewhere. *(w/ free cd)* **ACOUSTIC** – Washington / Pure / Surely someone somewhere / Concrete lions / Spleen / Obligatory / Kate / Four years / Spaniard / Which will.	[ ]	[ ]

ARAB STRAP

AIDAN MOFFAT – vocals, keyboards / **MALCOLM MIDDLETON** – guitar / with mainly **GARY MILLER** – bass / **DAVID GOW** – drums

		Chemikal Underground	Chemikal Underground
Sep 96.	(7") *(CHEM 007)* **THE FIRST BIG WEEKEND. /**	[ ]	-
Nov 96.	(lp/cd) *(<CHEM 010/+CD>)* **THE WEEK NEVER STARTS ROUND HERE** – Coming down / The clearing / Driving / Gourmet / I work in a saloon / Wasting / General plea to a girlfriend / The first big weekend / Kate Moss / Little girls / Phone me tonight / Blood / Deeper.	[ ]	[ ] 1997
Mar 97.	(12"/cd-s) *(CHEM 013/+CD)* **THE CLEARING (guest starring Isobel Campbell & Chris Geddes). / (remixed by Hungry Lions) (remixed by Iain Hanlon & Jonathan Hilditch)**	[ ]	-
Sep 97.	(12"ep/cd-ep) *(CHEM 017/+CD)* **THE GIRLS OF SUMMER E.P.** – Hey! fever / Girls of summer / The beautiful barmaids of Dundee / One day, after school.	74	-
Nov 97.	(7"m) *(LISS 22)* **THE SMELL OF OUTDOOR COOKING. / THEME TUNE / BLACKSTAR** *(above issued 'Lissy's)*	[ ]	-
		Chemikal Underground	Matador
Mar 98.	(10"/cd-s) *(CHEM 20 T/CD)* **HERE WE GO. / TRIPPY**	48	-
Apr 98.	(cd) *(CHEM 21CD)* <315> **PHILOPHOBIA** – Packs of three / Soaps / Here we go / New birds / One day, after school / Islands / The night before the funeral / Not quite a yes / Piglet / Afterwards / My favourite muse / I would've liked me a lot last night / The first time you're unfaithful.	37	[ ] May98
Sep 98.	(7") *(CHEM 27)* **(AFTERNOON) SOAPS. / PHONE ME TOMORROW** (12"+=/cd-s+=) *(CHEM 27 T/CD)* – ('A'side) / Toy fights / Forest hills.	74	-

ARCHERS OF LOAF

Formed: Chapel Hill, North Carolina, USA . . . 1992 by university students ERIC BACHMAN and ERIC JOHNSON (both Asheville born lads) along with MARK PRICE and MATT GENTLING. Following an offer from a local fanzine to record a one-off single, mainman BACHMAN diverted his attention from Chapel Hill punks, SMALL (with whom he was playing at the time) and concentrated on ARCHERS OF LOAF's first recording session. The fruits of their labour emerged in the shape of 'WRONG', a heartfelt blast of grungy, melodic hardcore/punk reeking of adolescent frustration, pent-up emotion and a hip record collection. San Franciscan label, 'Alias', were suitably impressed to offer the band a deal, their first single, 'WEB IN FRONT', appearing in early '93. With its neo lo-fi, angular sound, the ARCHERS were initially compared with PAVEMENT although subsequent releases revealed a band with a wide ranging array of influences inconsistent with an art-rock tag. The much anticipated debut album, 'ICKY METTLE', appeared later that year, confirming the band's credentials and putting the fertile musical breeding ground of Chapel Hill firmly on the map. A John Peel session and a critically acclaimed EP ('ARCHERS OF LOAF VS. THE GREATEST OF ALL TIME') later, the ARCHERS were being pestered by a string of major labels including MADONNA's 'Maverick'. Choosing to remain resolutely independent, the band stuck with 'Alias' and concentrated on writing material for a follow-up album, 'VEE VEE'. Released in 1995 amid much critical praise, thc record displayed a marked leap in songwriting ability and a more considered stylistic approach, further enhancing the band's desirability amongst the record industry big boys. Following the release of a B-sides collection, 'THE SPEED OF CATTLE' (1996), ARCHERS OF LOAF remained with 'Alias' for a third album proper, 'ALL THE NATION'S AIRPORTS' (1996).

Album rating: ICKY METTLE (*7) / VEE VEE (*6) / THE SPEED OF CATTLE compilation (*7) / ALL THE NATION'S AIRPORTS (*6) / Eric Bachman: BARRY BLACK (*5)

ERIC BACHMAN – vocals, guitar (ex-SMALL) / **ERIC JOHNSON** – guitar / **MATT GENTLING** – bass / **MARK PRICE** – drums

not iss. — Stay Free

1992. (7") **WRONG. / SOUTH CAROLINA** [-] [ ]

Alias — Alias

Jul 93. (7") *(A-041S)* **WEB IN FRONT. / BATHROOM** [ ] [ ]
(cd-s+=) *(A-041CD)* – Tatyana.

Sep 93. (lp/c/cd) *(A-049/+C/D)* **ICKY METTLE** [ ] [ ]
– Web in front / Last word / Wrong / You and me / Might / Hate paste / Fat / Plumb line / Learo, you're a hole / Sick file / Toast / Backwash / Slow worm.

Sep 93. (7") *(A-053S)* **WRONG. / (other track by SMALL)** [ ] [ ]

Mar 94. (7") *(A-066S)* **WHAT DID YOU EXPECT? / ETHEL MERMAN** [ ] [ ]
(above on 'Merge') (below on 'Sonic Bubblegum')

1994. (7") **FUNNELHEAD. / (other by The Treepeople)** [-] [ ]

Sep 94. (12"ep/cd-ep) *(A-070/+D)* **ARCHERS OF LOAF VS. THE GREATEST OF ALL TIME** [ ] [ ]
– Audiowhore / Lowest part is free / Freezing point / Revenge / All hail the black market.

Feb 95. (7") *(A-072S)* **HARNESSED IN SLUMS. / DON'T BELIEVE THE GOOD NEWS** [ ] [ ]
(cd-s+=) *(A-072CD)* – Telepathic traffic.

Mar 95. (lp/cd) *(A-064/+D)* **VEE VEE** [ ] [ ]
– Step into the light / Harnessed in slums / Nevermind the enemy / Greatest of all time / Underdogs if Nipomo / Floating friends / 1985 / Fabricoh / Nostalgia / Let the loser melt / Death in the park / Worst has yet to come / Underachievers march and fight song.

Mar 96. (lp/cd) *(A-094/+D)* **THE SPEED OF CATTLE** (compilation) [ ] [ ]
– Wrong / South Carolina / Web in front / Bathroom / Tatyana / What did you expect? / Ethel Merman / Funnelhead / Quinn beast / Telepathic traffic / Don't believe the good news / Smokin pot in the hot city / In the hot city / Mutes in the steeple / Revenge / Bacteria / Freezing point / Powerwalker / Backwash.

Sep 96. (lp/cd) *(A-100/+CD)* **ALL THE NATION'S AIRPORTS** [ ] [ ]
– Strangled by the stereo wire / All the nation's airports / Scenic pastures / Worst defence / Attack of the killer bees / Rental sting / Assassination on Xmas eve / Chumming the ocean / Vocal shrapnel / Bones of her hands / Bumpo / Form & file / Acromegaly / Distance comes in droves / Bombs away.

Sep 96. (7") *(A-103)* **VOCAL SHRAPNEL. / DESTINY** [ ] [ ]

Feb 97. (10"lp)<m-cd) *(A-115)* <60115> **VITUS TINNITUS** [ ] [ ]

ERIC BACHMAN

Alias — Alias

1995. (cd) **BARRY BLACK** [-] [ ]

A.R. KANE

Formed: East London, England . . . 1986 by ALEX AYULI and RUDI TAMBALA. They signed a one-off deal with 'One Little Indian', debuting in the indie charts with the 'WHEN YOU'RE SAD' EP in 1987. Described in the press as a unique fusion of COCTEAU TWINS meeting MILES DAVIS and ROBERT WYATT, their ROBIN GUTHRIE (Cocteau Twins)-produced follow-up, 'LOLITA', came out on '4 a.d.'. This led to a one-off collaboration with the label's COLOUR BOX; M/A/R/R/S. This project soon rose to No.1 simultaneously in the UK pop, dance and indie charts with the techno/dub classic 'PUMP UP THE VOLUME' (by the end of the year, it also hit No.13 in the States). During this fruitful period, they moved to 'Rough Trade', who issued their first long player '69'. This, together with their late 1989 follow-up, 'i', again topped the indie chart, although little was heard of them until they returned in 1994 with the album, 'NEW CLEAR CHILD'.

Album rating: 69 (*8) / i (*8) / NEW CLEAR CHILD (*6)

ALEX AYULI – guitars, etc / **RUDI TAMBALA** – guitars, etc

One Little Indian — not iss.

Feb 87. (12"ep) *(12TP 2)* **WHEN YOU'RE SAD. / WHEN YOU'RE SAD / THE HAUNTING** [ ] [-]
(re-iss. Aug87; same)

4 a.d. — Nesak

Jul 87. (12"ep) *(BAD 704)* <704> **LOLITA. / SADO-MASOCHISM IS A MUST / BUTTERFLY COLLECTOR** [ ] [ ]
(above was to have been issued May87; *12TP 8)*

Rough Trade — Rough Trade

Apr 88. (12"ep) *(RTT 201)* **UP HOME. / BABY MILK SNATCHER / W.O.G.S.** [ ] [-]

Jun 88. (lp/c/cd) *(ROUGH/+C/CD 119)* **69** [ ] [-]
– Crazy blue / Suicide kiss / Baby milk snatcher / Scab / Sulliday / Dizzy / Spermwhale trip over / The sun falls into the sea / The Madonna is with child / Spanish quay (3).

Nov 88. (7") *(RT 231)* **GREEN HAZED DAZE. / IS THIS IT?** [ ] [-]
(12"ep+=) *(RTT 231)* **LOVESICK EP** – Sperm travels like a juggernaut / Is this dub?.

Jul 89. (7"/12"plays-@48rpm) *(RT/+T 239)* **POP. / WHAT'S ALL THIS THEN?** [ ] [-]
(cd-s+=) *(RT 239CD)* – Snow joke.

Oct 89. (d-lp/c/cd) *(ROUGH/+C/CD 139)* **i** [ ] [-]
– Snow joke / Off into space / Hello / Crack up / Yeti / What's all this then? / Honeysuckleswallow / In a circle / Insect love / Miles apart / Sugar wings / Down / And I say / Catch my drift / A love from outer space / Timewind / Conundrum / Long body / Fast kg / Pop / Mars / Spook/ Back home / Super vixens / Sorry / Challenge.

May 90. (m-cd/m-lp) *(RT CD/CMC/D 171)* **REM'I'XES** (6 remixes) [ ] [-]
– Miles apart / Crack up / Crack up (space mix) / Sugarwings / Love from Outer Space / Catch my drift.

not iss. — Luaka Bop-Sire

Jan 92. (cd/c) *<26669-2/-4>* **AMERICANA** (compilation of first 2 albums) [-] [ ]
– Love from Outer Space / Snow joke / Baby milk snatcher / Madonna is with child / In a circle / Miles apart / Green dazed haze / Water / Long body / Up / Supervixens / Spook / Crack up / And I Say / Sperm whale trip over.

Feb 92. (cd-ep) **LOVE FROM OUTER SPACE** [-] [ ]

3rd Stone — 3rd Stone

Oct 94. (cd) *(<STONE 11CD>)* **NEW CLEAR CHILD** [ ] [ ]
– Deep blue breath / Grace / Tiny little drop of perfumed time / Surf motel / Gather / Honey be (for Stella) / Cool as moons / Snow White's world / Pearl / Sea like a child.

— split the following year

ARMOURY SHOW (see under ⇒ SKIDS)

ARNOLD

Formed: London, England . . . early 1996 as PATIO by ROB, PHIL MORRIS (aka CAINEY), MARK SAXBY and PHIL PAYNE. Following the death of vocalist ROB, the remaining members renamed themselves ARNOLD, abandoning their indie guitar pop of old for a darker, more introspective direction. Creation's ALAN McGEE was suitably impressed enough to sign them up, the first fruits of their new deal surfacing as the mini-album, 'THE BARN TAPES', in Spring '97. Always in a scrape or a boxing match of some sort – with the "Blond Fox" CAINEY in the thick of it – ARNOLD were attempting to be the next FACES or BIG STAR. 1998's rustic 'HILLSIDE' album finally saw ARNOLD's sound come together, mainstream success still eluding them despite unanimous critical acclaim from the music press.

Album rating: THE BARN TAPES (*6) / HILLSIDE (*7)

PHIL MORRIS (aka CAINEY) – vocals, drums / **MARK SAXBY** – guitar / **PHIL PAYNE** – bass

Creation — Sony

May 97. (m-cd/10"m-lp) *(CRE CD/LP 218)* **THE BARN TAPES** [ ] [-]
– Float my boat / Calling Ira Jones / Face / Dog on the stairs / Windsor park / Sun / 2 chairs / Medication time.

Aug 97. (7") *(CRE 257)* **TWIST. /** [ ] [-]
(cd-s+=) *(CRESCD 257)* –

Apr 98. (7") *(CRE 287)* **FLEAS DON'T FLY. / BIG BLACK CLOUD** [ ] [-]
(cd-s+=) *(CRESCD 287)* – On the bus.

Jun 98. (7") *(CRE 293)* **FISHSOUNDS. / JOHNNY WAS A DABBLER** [ ] [-]
(cd-s+=) *(CRESCD 293)* –

Jul 98. (cd/lp) *(CRE CD/LP 231/+L)* <69333> **HILLSIDE** [ ] [ ]
– Fleas don't fly / Ira Jones goes to the country / Hillside / Fishsounds / Country biscuit / Windsor park / Curio / Rabbit / Goodbye grey / Face / Rubber duck (parts 1, 2 & 3) / Mickey's mother / Moroccan roll (part 2) / Catherine day.

Sep 98. (7") *(CRE 300)* **WINDSOR PARK. / FLIGHTLESS ROAD** [ ] [-]
(cd-s+=) *(CRESCD 300)* –

ART ATTACKS

Formed: London, England . . . 1977 by 'Sounds' cartoonist extrordinaire, SAVAGE PENCIL (aka EDWIN POUNCEY), who turned his talents to "singing" against a 3-chord punk-rock backdrop provided by STEVE SPEAR, MARION FUDGER and JD HANEY (who replaced WIRE bound, ROBERT GOTOBED). Although they only gigged sporadically, they definitely had their moments, two of which ('Frankenstein's Heartbeat' & 'Animal Bondage') were the only classic punk tracks on that year's otherwise dull Various Artists lp, 'Live At The Vortex'. The ART ATTACKS contributed to yet another V/A compilation, 'Streets', the track in question being 'ARABS IN 'ARRADS', another slice of Dalek-voxed DIY. Appropriately titled, 'I AM A DALEK', became their debut 45 in Spring '78, although the scene had moved on leaps and bounds in such a short time span that their amateurism seemed outdated. They were still flogging a dead horse at the turn of the decade when they issued their wannabe final effort, 'PUNK ROCK STARS'. POUNCEY continued to record occasionally under various pseudonyms while keeping an illustrious career as a cartoonist. As SAVAGE PENCIL, he penned an obscure one-off solo album, 'ANGEL DUST' (1988), the soundtrack to the 'Bikers' movie which did nothing.

Album rating: never released one!

EDWIN POUNCEY – vocals / **STEVE SPEAR** – guitar / **M.S.** (MARION FUDGER) – bass (ex-DERELICTS) / **J.D. HANEY** – drums; repl. ROBERT GOTOBED who joined WIRE

Albatross — not iss.

Apr 78. (7") *(TIT 1)* **I AM A DALEK. / NEUTRON BOMB** [ ] [-]

— had already split. ? replaced HANEY who joined MONOCHROME SET

Fresh — not iss.

Dec 79. (7"m) *(FRESH 3)* **PUNK ROCK STARS. / RAT CITY / FIRST AND LAST** [ ] [-]

TAGMEMICS

were formed by EDWIN or an ex-member.

Index / not iss.

1980. (7"m) *(INDEX 003)* **CHIMNEYS. / (DO THE) BIG BABY / TAKE YOUR BRAIN OUT FOR A WALK** [ ] [-]

SAVAGE PENCIL

Furthur / not iss.

Apr 88. (lp) *(FU 3)* **ANGEL DUST** (music from the movie, Bikers') [ ] [-]

KRAY CHERUBS

formed by EDWIN? or other.

Fierce / not iss.

1988. (7"-1 sided) *(FRIGHT 014)* **NO** [ ] [-]

Snakeskin / not iss.

1989. (7"ltd.) *(SS 002)* **RIOT IN HELL MOM. / "SAUCERMAN":- Motor Drag** [ ] [-]

— Split for final time.

ARTERY

Formed: Sheffield, England . . . 1978, as an outlet for weird, extrovert singer, MARK GOLDTHORPE. Completing the line-up with MICHAEL FIDLER, NEIL MacKENZIE and GARRY WILSON, the band issued their self-financed debut 45, 'MOTHER MOON', prior to the addition of future MISSION-ary, SIMON HINKLER. At the turn of the decade, ARTERY appeared at Leeds Futurama Festival, releasing a long awaited follow-up, 'UNBALANCED', later in 1980. After a further two indie 7"ers, they were signed to the 'Red Flame' imprint through whom they delivered their first album, the DALE GRIFFIN (ex-Mott The Hoople) produced mini-set, 'OCEANS' (1982). With GOLDTHORPE contributing gothic, narrative-esque vocals against a backdrop of dense, mood-shattering post-punk textures, track highlights included the sinister carousel of 'THE CLOWN' and the repetitive bass-plucking of 'INTO THE GARDEN'. The first of many personnel upheavals occured prior to the release of their first full-length effort, 'ONE AFTERNOON IN A HOT-AIR BALLOON' (1983), issued in conjunction with a non-album rendition of Jacques Brel's 'ALABAMA SONG'. In 1984, after relocating business to 'Golden Dawn', ARTERY attempted another moody classic, Leonard Cohen's 'DIAMONDS IN THE MINE', the single/track actually included on that year's lp, 'THE SECOND COMING'. Unfortunately their efforts were in vain, as the extremely shoddy 1986 live set proved that ARTERY's finger was no longer on the proverbial pulse. However, main songwriters, GOLDTHORPE and HINKLER collaborated one last time on 'FLIGHT COMMMANDER SOLITUDE & THE SNAKE' (1986).

Album rating: OCEANS mini (*5) / ONE AFTERNOON IN A HOT-AIR BALLOON (*5) / THE SECOND COMING (*5)

MARK GOLDTHORPE – vocals, guitar / **MICHAEL FIDLER** – guitar, vocals / **NEIL MacKENZIE** – bass / **GARRY WILSON** – drums

Take One / not iss.

Apr 79. (7"m) *(TAKE 1)* **MOTHER MOON. / PRETENDS TO BE / HEINZ** [ ] [-]

— added **SIMON HINKLER** – keyboards (ex-TV PRODUCT)

Aardvark / not iss.

Nov 80. (7") *(STEAL 3)* **UNBALANCED. / THE SLIDE** [ ] [-]
(7"live-ep+=) – PERHAPS / TURTLE. / TOYTOWN / HEINZ

1981. (7") *(AARD 15)* **CARS IN MOTION. / LIFE AND DEATH** [ ] [-]

Armageddon / not iss.

Nov 81. (7") *(AS 026)* **INTO THE GARDEN. / AFTERWARDS** [ ] [-]

Red Flame / not iss.

Aug 82. (7") *(RF 704)* **THE CLOWN 1. / THE CLOWN 2** [ ] [-]

Oct 82. (m-lp) *(RFM 4)* **OCEANS** [ ] [-]
– The ghost of a small tour-boat captain / Into the garden / The clown 1 / Afterwards / The slide / The clown 2 / The sailor situation.

— **JOHN WHITE** – guitar; repl. FIDLER

— **CHRISTOPHER HENDRICK** – bass; repl. MacKENZIE

— added at gigs only **DAVID HINKLER** – keyboards

— now a trio of **GOLDTHORPE, WILSON** + multi-instrumentalist **HENDRICK** (JOHN WHITE formed UV POP himself & SIMON HINKLER produced PULP (not the same as the famous one!)

Nov 83. (lp) *(RF 18)* **ONE AFTERNOON IN A HOT-AIR BALLOON** [ ] [-]
– Perhaps / Being there / Unbalanced / Being there / One afternoon in a hot-air balloon / Song for Lena / Potential silence / Turtle / Butcher's wife / Louise / It's good to be alone.

Nov 83. (12"m) *(RFB 25-12)* **ALABAMA SONG. / SONG FOR LENA / THE DEATH OF PETER X** [ ] [ ]

— **NEIL MacKENZIE** – bass; returned to repl. HENDRICK

— added **MURRAY FENTON** – guitar, organ

Golden Dawn / not iss.

May 84. (12"m) *(GD 12-02)* **A BIG MACHINE. / BRINK OF EXTINCTION / I OPEN MY EYES & WALK** [ ] [-]

Oct 84. (12"ep) *(GD 12-04)* **DIAMONDS IN THE MINE. / LOVE LIKE THE REST / ONEPENNY HORROR SHOW / BUTCHER'S SHOP** [ ] [-]

Nov 84. (lp) *(GDLP 001)* **THE SECOND COMING** [ ] [-]
– The last song / My age, my beast / Diamonds in the mine / The father song / The mother song / Little boy blue / Ringing the bells.

— **TONY PERRIN** – bass, manager (1984 live 5th member) repl. MacKENZIE / added the returning **SIMON HINKLER** – now guitar

Nov 85. (lp) *(GDLP 002)* **NUMBER 4 (live in Amsterdam)** [ ] [-]

— they disbanded in 1985, HINKLER was soon to join The MISSION

– compilations, etc. –

Pleasantly Surprised / not iss.

Apr 89. (c) *(PS 011)* **AFTERWARDS** [ ] [-]

MARK GOLDTHORPE & SIMON HINKLER

Golden Dawn / not iss.

Apr 86. (lp) *(GDLP 003)* **FLIGHT COMMANDER SOLITUDE & THE SNAKE** [ ] [-]
– Monkey men / Message from a dead man / Another wild rose / Hold on tight / Dogs in leather / Serpent / Hidden for days / Shipwreck on the moon / Bad harvest / In late afternoon / Time & again / Wall of eyes.

ART OBJECTS (see under ⇒ BLUE AEROPLANES)

ASH

Formed: Ulster, N.Ireland . . . 1989 by 12-year old,TIM WHEELER and MARK HAMILTON, relocating to Downpatrick, County Down (southern Ireland) a few years later where they officially formed the trio with RICK McMURRAY. ASH's precocious talents were quickly spotted by American record moguls eager for more punk-centric guitar music which would also cross over to the pop market. Though they eventually opted to sign with 'Reprise', the trio had already released their debut set, 'TRAILER' on 'Infectious'. Their starry-eyed, bushy-tailed but ultimately derivative blend of indie punk finally became a part of the pop vocabulary when the catchy 'GIRL FROM MARS' sky-rocketed into the UK Top 20 in summer '95. This was pursued by another Top 20 hit later that year in 'ANGEL INTERCEPTOR'. With the hype machine going into overload, the group hit the UK Top 5 in Spring of the following year with 'GOLDFINGER', the single trailing a No.1 album, '1977' (1996). Apparently a reference to the year 'Star Wars' was released rather than any reference to safety-pins and saliva, the record included all their hit singles to date and confirmed them increasingly melodic approach. Keeping their profile high with festival appearances, the band later added another guitarist, CHARLOTTE HATHERLEY in summer '97. She made her debut on ASH's theme for the much lauded Ewan McGregor/Cameron Diaz film, 'A LIFE LESS ORDINARY', another Top 10 in late '97. While the indie scene continues to cry out for something innovative, it remains difficult to envisage any figureheads less ordinary than ASH (songs!). Surprisingly 'Kerrang!-friendly, the quartet lost a little of their indie cred with the release of their third album proper, 'NU-CLEAR SOUNDS' (1998), a record that quickly vacated the Top 10 with the accompanying single, 'JESUS SAYS', only managing to make a Top 20 placing. • **Songwriters:** WHEELER or w/ HAMILTON except covers; PUNKBOY (Helen Love) / GET READY (Temptations) / DOES YOUR MOTHER KNOW (Abba). • **Trivia:** The cover sleeve of their single, 'KUNG FU', had a photo of French former Man U star footballer, ERIC CANTONA, giving his famous throat and neck tackle on an abusive Crystal Palace supporter in 1995.

Album rating: TRAILER (*7) / 1977 (*9) / LIVE AT THE WIRELESS live official bootleg (*5) / NU-CLEAR SOUNDS (*7)

TIM WHEELER – vocals, guitar / **MARK HAMILTON** – bass / **RICK McMURRAY** – drums

La La Land / not iss.

Feb 94. (7") *(LA LA 001)* **JACK NAMES THE PLANETS. / DON'T KNOW** [ ] [-]

Infectious / Reprise

Aug 94. (7"ep) *(INFECT 13S)* **PETROL. / THE LITTLE POND / A MESSAGE FROM OSCAR WILDE AND PATRICK THE BREWER** [ ] [-]
(cd-s+=) *(INFEVT 13CD)* – Things. *(re-iss. Nov96; same)*

Oct 94. (cd/c/lp) *(INFECT 14CD/MC/LP)* <45985> **TRAILER** [ ] [ ] Oct95
– Season / Message from Oscar Wilde and Patrick the brewer / Jack names the planets / Intense thing / Uncle Pat / Message from Mr. Waterman / Get out / Petrol / Obscure thing. *(lp w/ free 7"yellow) (INFECT 14S)* SILVER SURFER. / JAZZ '59 *<diff.tracks US>*

Oct 94. (7") *(INFECT 16S)* **UNCLE PAT. / DIFFERENT TODAY** [ ] [-]
(cd-s+=) *(INFECT 16CD)* – Hulk Hogan bubble bath. *(re-iss. Nov96; same)*

Mar 95. (7") *(INFECT 21J)* <17706> **KUNG FU. / DAY OF THE TRIFFIDS** 57 [ ] Nov95
(cd-s+=) *(INFECT 21CD)* – Luther Ingo's star cruiser. *(re-iss. Nov96; same)*

Jul 95. (7"/c-s) *(INFECT 24S/24MC)* **GIRL FROM MARS. / CANTINA BAND** 11 [-]
(cd-s+=) *(INFECT 24CD)* – Astral conversations with Toulouse Lautrec. *(re-iss. Nov96; same)*

Sep 95. (7"colrd-various) <G26> **PETROL. / PUNKBOY** [-] [ ]

Oct 95. (7"/c-s/cd-s) *(INFECT 27S/27MC/27CD)* **ANGEL INTERCEPTOR. / 5 A.M. ETERNAL / GIVE ME SOME TRUTH** 14 [-]
(re-iss. cd-s Nov96; same)

Dec 95. (7"red) *(FP 004)* **GET READY. / ZERO ZERO ZERO** [ ] [-]
(above 45 issued on 'Fantastic Plastic')

Apr 96. (7"/c-s) *(INFECT 39 S/MC)* **GOLDFINGER. / I NEED SOMEBODY / SNEAKER** 5 [-]
(cd-s+=) *(INFECT 39CD)* – Get ready. *(re-iss. Nov96; same)*

May 96. (cd/c/lp) *(INFECT 40 CD/MC/LP)* <46191> **1977** 1 [ ]
– Lose control / Goldfinger / Girl from Mars / I'd give you anything / Gone the dream / Kung Fu / Oh yeah / Let it flow / Innocent smile / Angel interceptor / Lost in you / Darkside lightside. *(cd+=hidden track)* – Sick of vomiting.

Jun 96. (7"yellow/c-s) *(INFECT 41 S/MC)* **OH YEAH / T. REX / EVERYWHERE IS ALL AROUND / OH YEAH (quartet version)** 6 [-] (cd-s) *(INFECT 41CD)* – (first 3 tracks) / Does your mother know. *(re-iss. Nov96; same)*

— added **CHARLOTTE HATHERLEY** – guitar

Infectious Imprint

Oct 97. (7"blue/c-s) *(INFECT 50 S/MC)* **A LIFE LESS ORDINARY. / WHERE IS LOVE GOING / WHAT DEANER WAS TALKING ABOUT** 10
(cd-s+=) *(INFECT 50CD)* – Halloween.

Sep 98. (7") *(INFECT 059S)* **JESUS SAYS. / TAKEN OUT** 15
(c-s+=/cd-s+=) *(INFECT 059 MCS/CDS)* – Heroin vodka white noise.
(cd-s) *(INFECT 059CDSX)* – ('A'side) / Radiation / Dancing on the moon.

Oct 98. (cd/c/lp) *(INFECT 060 CD/MC/LP)* <112507> **NU-CLEAR SOUNDS** 7
– Projects / Low ebb / Jesus says / Wild surf / Death trip 21 / Folk song / Numbskull / Burn out / Aphrodite / Fortune teller / I'm gonna fall.

Nov 98. (7") *(INFECT 061S)* **WILD SURF. / STORMY WATERS** 31
(c-s+=/cd-s+=) *(INFECT 061 MCS/CDS)* – When I'm tired.
(cd-s) *(INFECT 061CDSX)* – ('A'side) / Lose control / Gonna do it soon.

— added on tour **DJ DICK KURTAINE** – turntables

– compilations, etc. –

Feb 97. (cd) *Death Star; (DEATH 3)* **LIVE AT THE WIRELESS (live)** -

Daniel ASH (see under ⇒ BAUHAUS)

ASIAN DUB FOUNDATION

Formed: Farringdon, London, England ... 1993 by DR. DAS, PANDIT G and MASTER D, a tutor, an assistant and a student respectively at an inner city community music programme designed for young aspiring Asian musicians/DJ's/MC's/etc. Initially trading as a sound system, ADF began making their own records the following year. Signed to 'Nation' (home of TRANSGLOBAL UNDERGROUND), the trio issued the 'CONSCIOUS' EP prior to adding unorthodox sitar-influenced guitarist, CHANDRASONIC, synth man SUN-J and stage dancer, BUBBLE-E. Taking up the agit-prop, slash'n'burn politico-musical baton from the ailing SENSER, ADF fought off the neo-Nazis with an infammatory combination of Bengali folk, drum'n'bass and punk that strangely and uniquely recalled the spirit of ALTERNATIVE TV's MARK PERRY. In 1995, this radical troupe unleashed their debut long player, 'FACTS AND FICTIONS', a surprising cohesive set given the amount of disparate musical strands running through each track. Amassing a cult following drawn from both the indie and dance communities (much in the same way that The PRODIGY rose to such giddy heights a few years earlier), ADF soon found themselves under the wing of 'London' offshoot, 'FFRR' in 1997. Gaining more column inches and higher chart placings with each successive release via the incendiary singles, 'NAXALITE', 'BUZZIN', 'FREE SATPAL RAM' and 'BLACK WHITE', the long awaited follow-up set, 'RAFI'S REVENGE' (1998) blazed a trail into the UK Top 20. Nominated for a 'Mercury Award', the album didn't win but received some free televised publicity/criticism courtesy of Fantasy Football thingy/ 3 Lions/"comedian", David Baddiel, who obviously prefers the fluffier sounds of the LIGHTNING SEEDS.

Album rating: FACTS AND FICTIONS (*7) / RAFI'S REVENGE (*9)

MASTER D (DEEDER ZAMAN) – rapping / **PANDIT G** (JOHN PANDIT) – turntables, voice / **DR. DAS** (ANIRUDDHA DAS) – bass, programming, voice

Nation not iss.

Aug 94. (12"ep/cd-ep) *(NR 42 T/CD)* **CONSCIOUS EP.** -
– Debris / Tu meri / Jericho / Witness.

— added **CHANDRASONIC (STEVE CHANDRA SAVALE)** – guitar, programming, vocals (ex-HEADSPACE, ex-The HIGHER INTELLIGENCE AGENCY)

— added **SUN-J** (TAILOR) – synths / + dancer **BUBBLE-E**

Apr 95. (12"ep/cd-ep) *(NR 51 T/CD)* **REBEL WARRIOR. / STRONG CULTURE** -

Oct 95. (cd/lp) *(NAT CD/LP 58)* **FACTS AND FICTIONS** -
(cd re-iss. Aug98; NATCDM 058)

May 96. (12"/cd-s) *(NR 61 T/CD)* **CHANGE A GONNA COME. /** -

Damaged Goods not iss.

Jul 97. (7"; split with ATARI TEENAGE RIOT) *(DAMGOOD 132)* **split** -

Sub Rosa not iss.

Jul 97. (12"; split with EUPHONIC) *(QUANTUM 605)* **TRIBUTE: ... SOUND SYSTEM / WAY OF THE EXPLODING FIST** -

— now as ASIANDUBFOUNDATION

FFRR Polygram

Oct 97. (7") *(F 320)* **NAXALITE. / CHARGE** -
(12"+=/cd-s+=) *(FX/FCD 320)* – ('A'+'B'mixes).

Feb 98. (7") *(F 326)* **FREE SATPAL RAM. / TRIBUTE TO JOHN STEPHENS** 56
(12"+=/cd-s+=) *(FX/FCD 326)* –

Apr 98. (12"ep/cd-ep) *(FX/FCD 335)* **BUZZIN' (mixes) / DIGITAL UNDERCLASS** 31
(cd-ep) *(FCDP 335)* – ('A'side) / Free Satpal Ram / Charge / Naxalite.

May 98. (cd/c/d-lp) *(556 006-2/-4/-1)* <556 053> **RAFI'S REVENGE** 20
– Naxalite / Buzzin' / Black white / Assassin / Hypocrite / Charge / Free Satpal Ram / Dub mentality / Culture move / Operation eagle lie / Change / Tribute to John Stevens.

Jun 98. (12"/cd-s) *(FX/FCDP 337)* **BLACK WHITE / BLACK WHITE (maximum roach mix). / NAXALITE (Underdog mix) / NAXALITE (Underdog instrumental)** 52 -

(cd-s) *(FCD 337)* – ('A'side) / Rafi / Assassin (live) / Buzzin' (live).

Sep 98. (12"ep/cd-ep) *(FX/FCD 348)* <570289> **NAXALITE / CULTURE MOVE EP** Nov98
– Naxalite (main mix) / Culture move (pusher sound mix) / Free Satpal Ram (Russell Simmons mix) / Culture move (urban decay mix) / Culture move (silver haze mix).

ASSERT

Formed: Telford, England ... mid 90's by the man 'The Times' described as one of the most subversive men in Britain, the heavily tattooed singer, BRITT. The line-up was completed by three other equally anarcho-socialists, RYAN, JOHNNY SINISTER and SPEN, who reactivated the hardcore/oi/punk/thrash days of yore (ANGELIC UPSTARTS and CONFLICT come to mind). Two EP's unleashed either end of 1997 announced the band's agenda, while the following year's 'MORE THAN A WITNESS' varied little in its approach.

Album rating: MORE THAN A WITNESS (*5)

BRITT – vocals / **RYAN** – guitar / **JOHNNY SINISTER** – bass / **SPEN** – drums

Hideous Eye not iss.

Feb 97. (7"ep) **ASSERT YOURSELF EP** -
– Straight edge / Four legs good (two legs bad) / Assert yourself / Corporate logo strangulation.

Household Name not iss.

Oct 97. (7"ep) *(HAUS 008)* **FOUR FINGERS AND A THUMB FOLD A FIST EP** -
– Something safe in negativity / Violently blue / Assertiveness (should be a way of life) / A collective force.

Jul 98. (cd) *(HAUS 015CD)* **MORE THAN A WITNESS** -

ASSOCIATES

Formed: Dundee, Scotland ... 1979 by BILLY MacKENZIE and ALAN RANKINE, who had worked as a duo in 1976, The ABSORBIC ONES. After a debut single on their own 'Double-Hip' label, they signed to Chris Parry's 'Fiction', a subsidiary of 'Polydor' records. Their glorious debut set, 'THE AFFECTIONATE PUNCH', was followed by a series of highly rated 45's for the independent 'Situation 2' label. In 1982, they enjoyed their first taste of success when stylish 'PARTY FEARS TWO' and 'CLUB COUNTRY' both hit the UK Top 20. Energetic alternative dance rock, featuring high, passionate vocals of MacKENZIE, The ASSOCIATES inimitable, unclassifiable sound enjoyed only a very brief liaison with the pop charts. Now signed to 'Warners', the group's more accessible 'SULK' (1982) album made the UK Top 10, its lavish arrangements, white funk and stirring vocal histrionics going down well amid the craze for all things "New Romantic". Despite this belated recognition, the pair subsequently went their seperate ways, losing their commercial momentum in the process. When they finally got back together in 1984 (with a line-up of STEVE GOULDING, IAN McINTOSH, ROBERT SUAVE and L. HOWARD JONES), MacKENZIE and RANKINE recorded only one further single together, 'THOSE FIRST IMPRESSIONS', before the latter finally bowed out. The remaining members recorded the 'PERHAPS' (1985) album, a relative flop which saw a further set, 'THE GLAMOUR CHASE' shelved and MacKENZIE returned in 1990 with an album on the 'Circa' label, 'WILD AND LONELY', to little reaction. The ASSOCIATES name had seemingly been laid to rest when, a couple of years later, the singer released a solo set, 'OUTERNATIONAL'. The next five years were quiet as MacKENZIE attended to his beloved greyhounds in his native Dundee. The music world was shocked, when, on the 22nd January '97, it was announced that the Scotsman had taken his own life, he'd reportedly been depressed after the death of his mother a little earlier. Ironically, MacKENZIE had signed to the hip 'Nude' label (home of SUEDE), and had been working on new material at the same time of his death. This material was posthumously released as 'BEYOND THE SUN', pundits and public alike mourning the death at 39 of one of music's forgotten geniuses. • **Songwriters:** Lyrics / music by duo (until RANKINE's departure), except BOYS KEEP SWINGING (David Bowie) / LOVE HANGOVER (Diana Ross) / GOD BLESS THE CHILD (Billie Holiday) / HEART OF GLASS (Blondie) / KITES (Simon Dupree & The Big Sound) / GROOVIN' WITH MR. BLOE (Mr. Bloe) / GREEN TAMBOURINE (Lemon Pipers) / I'M GONNA RUN AWAY FROM YOU (Tammi Lynn). • **Trivia:** MacKENZIE featured on B.E.F.'s (HEAVEN 17) single 'IT'S OVER' circa '82.

Album rating: THE AFFECTIONATE PUNCH (*6) / FOURTH DRAWER DOWN (*8) / SULK (*7) / PERHAPS (*5) / WILD AND LONELY (*4) / POPERA: THE SINGLES COLLECTION compilation (*8) / Billy MacKenzie: OUTERNATIONAL (*5) / BEYOND THE SUN (*7)

BILLY MacKENZIE (b.27 Mar'57) – vocals / **ALAN RANKINE** – keyboards, guitar, etc

Double Hip not iss.

Oct 79. (7") *(DHR 1)* **BOYS KEEP SWINGING. / MONA PROPERTY GIRL** -
(re-iss. Dec79 on 'M.C.A.'; MCA 537)

— added **NIGEL GLOCKER** – drums / guest **ROBERT SMITH** – guitar (of-CURE) who replaced unknown guitarist

Fiction not iss.

Aug 80. (7") *(FICS 11)* **THE AFFECTIONATE PUNCH. / YOU WERE YOUNG** -

Aug 80. (lp/c) *(FIX/+C 5)* **THE AFFECTIONATE PUNCH** -
– The affectionate punch / Amused as always / Logan time / Paper house / Trans-

port to Central / A matter of gender / Even dogs in the wild / Would I . . . bounce back / Deeply concerned / A. *(remixed & re-iss. Nov82; FIXD 5) (re-iss. Aug83 on 'Polydor' lp/c; SPE LP/MC 33)*

— **JOHN MURPHY** (b. Australia) – drums repl. GLOCKER (to TOYAH)

Situation 2 | not iss.

Apr 81. (7"/12") *(SIT 1/+12)* **TELL ME EASTER'S ON FRIDAY. / STRAW TOWELS** [ ] [-]
(re-iss. but w-drawn Nov82 on 'Beggars Banquet'; BEG 86)

Jun 81. (7") *(SIT 4)* **Q: QUARTERS. / KISSED** [ ] [-]
(12"+=) *(SIT 4T)* – Q: Quarters (original).

Aug 81. (7"/12") *(SIT 7/+T)* **KITCHEN PERSON. / AN EVEN WHITER CAR** [ ] [-]

Oct 81. (7"/12") *(SIT 10/+T)* **MESSAGE OBLIQUE SPEECH. / BLUE SOAP** [ ] [-]

Nov 81. (7"/12") *(SIT 11/+T)* **WHITE CAR IN GERMANY. / THE ASSOCIATE** [ ] [-]

Jan 82. (lp/c) *(SITU 2/+C)* **FOURTH DRAWER DOWN** [ ] [-]
– White car in Germany / A girl named Property / Kitchen person / Q; quarters / Tell me Easter's on Friday / The associate / Message oblique speech / An even whiter car. *(re-iss. Nov82 on 'Beggars Banquet' lp/c; BEGA/BEGC 43)*

R.S.O. | not iss.

1981. (7"/12"; as 39, LYON STREET) *(RSO/+X 78)* **KITES. / A GIRL NAMED POVERTY** [ ] [-]

— added **MICHAEL DEMPSEY** – bass (of CURE) / **MARTHA LADLY** – backing vocals (ex-MARTHA & THE MUFFINS)

Associates | WEA

Mar 82. (7"/12") *(ASC 1/+T)* **PARTY FEARS TWO. / IT'S BETTER THIS WAY** [9] [ ]

May 82. (7") *(ASC 2)* **CLUB COUNTRY. / IT'S YOU AGAIN** [13] [ ]
(12"+=) *(ASC 2T)* – Ulcragyceptemol.

Jun 82. (lp/c) *(ASCL/ASCC 1)* **SULK** [10] [ ]
– It's better this way / Party fears two / Club country / Love hangover / 18 carat love affair / Arrogance gave him up / No / Skipping / Nothing in something particular / Arrogance gave him up / White car in Germany / Gloomy Sunday / The associate. *(re-iss. Oct82 on 'WEA' lp/c; 240 005-1/-4) (cd-iss. Jul88 on 'WEA'; K 240005-2)*

Jul 82. (7") *(ASC 3)* **18 CARAT LOVE AFFAIR. / LOVE HANGOVER** [21] [ ]
(12"+=) *(ASC 3T)* – Voluntary wishes, swapit production.

— split & reformed 1984 by **MacKENZIE + RANKINE** recruiting **STEVE GOULDING** – drums / **IAN McINTOSH** – rhythm guitar / **ROBERT SUAVE** – bass / **L. HOWARD JONES** – keyboards

WEA | WEA

May 84. (7"/ext.12") *(YZ 6/+T)* **THOSE FIRST IMPRESSIONS. / THIRTEEN FEELINGS** [43] [ ]

— **STEPHEN REID** – guitar; repl. RANKINE who joined PAUL HAIG. He also had a solo career between 1986-87, releasing two albums, 'THE WORLD BEGINS TO LOOK HER AGE' for 'Crepescule' and 'SHE LOVES ME NOT' for 'Virgin'

Aug 84. (7"/ext.12") *(YZ 16/+T)* **WAITING FOR THE LOVE BOAT. / SCHAMP OUT** [53] [ ]

Jan 85. (7"/7"pic-d) *(YZ 28/+P)* **BREAKFAST. / BREAKFAST ALONE** [49] [ ]
(12"+=) *(YZ 28T)* – Kites.

Feb 85. (lp/c) *(WX 9/+C)* **PERHAPS** [23] [ ]
– Those first impressions / Waiting for the love boat / Perhaps / Schampout / Helicopter helicopter / Breakfast / Thirteen feelings / The stranger in your voice / The best of you / Don't give me that I told you so look.

Oct 85. (7") *(YZ 47)* **TAKE ME TO THE GIRL. / PERHAPS** [ ] [-]
(ext.12"+=) *(YZ 47T)* – The girl that took me / ('A'instrumental).
(10"+=) *(YZ 47TE)* – God bless the child (live) / Even dogs in the wild (live) / The boy that Santa Claus forgot (live).

— The above 'A'side was later (in Mar88) covered by group/artist JIH.

— (early 1986) HUGHES and SUAVE joined PETE MURPHY. MacKENZIE now used different session people under The ASSOCIATES

Sep 88. (7") *(YZ 310)* **HEART OF GLASS. / HER ONLY WISH** [56] [ ]
(3"cd-s+=) *(YZ 310CD)* – Breakfast / Those first impressions.
('A'-Auchterhouse mix-12"+=) *(YZ 310T)* – ('A'-Auchterhouse instrumental).
(12"+=) *(YZ 310TX)* – ('A'-Temperamental mix) / Heavens blue.

Nov 88. (w-drawn lp/c)(cd) *(WX 222/+C)(244619-2)* **THE GLAMOUR CHASE** [-] [-]

Jan 89. (w-drawn 7") *(YZ 329)* **COUNTRY BOY. / JUST CAN'T SAY GOODBYE** [-] [-]
(w-drawn 12"+=) *(YZ 329T)* – Heart of glass (dub mix).
(w-drawn 3"cd-s++=) *(YZ 329CD)* – Take me to the girl.

Circa | Charisma

Mar 90. (c/cd/lp) *(CIRC/+D/A 11)* **WILD AND LONELY** [71] [ ]
– Fire to ice / Fever / People we meet / Just can't say goodbye / Calling all around the world / The glamour chase / Where there's love / Something's got to give / Strasbourg Square / Ever since that day / Wild and lonely / Fever in the shadows.

Apr 90. (7"/c-s) *(YR/+C 46)* **FEVER. / FEVER IN THE SHADOWS** [ ] [-]
(12"+=/s12"+=/3"cd-s+=/cd-s+=) *(YR T/TB/CD/CDT 46)* – Groovin' with Mr.Bloe.

Aug 90. (7"/c-s) *(YR/+C 49)* **FIRE TO ICE. / GREEN TAMBOURINE** [ ] [-]
(ext.12"+=) *(YRT 49)* – The glamour chase.
(10"++=/ext.cd-s++=) *(YR TX/CD 49)* – Groovin' with Mr.Bloe.

Sep 90. (12"ep) *<096448>* **FIRE TO ICE (mixes) / GREEN TAMBOURINE** [-] [ ]

Jan 91. (7"/c-s) *(YR/+C 56)* **JUST CAN'T SAY GOODBYE. / ONE TWO THREE** [ ] [-]
(12") *(YRT 56)* – ('A'-Time Unlimited mix) / ('A'-Time Unlimited instrumental) / ('A'-US mix).
(12") *(YRTX 56)* – ('A'-Time Unlimited mix) / ('A'-Time Unlimited instrumental) / ('A'-Karma mix).
(cd-s) *(YRCD 56)* – ('A'side) / ('A'-Time Unlimited piano mix) / ('A'-US version) / I'm gonna run away from you.

BILLY MacKENZIE

Jun 92. (7") *(YR 86)* **BABY. / SACRIFICE AND BE SACRIFICED (CH 8032 mix)** [ ] [-]
(cd-s+=) *(YRCD 86)* – Grooveature (D 1000 mix) / Colours will come (US 60659 mix).
(12") *(YRT 86)* – ('A'side) / Colours will come (Larry Heard remix) / Opal krush / Colours will come (Raw Stylus remix).

Aug 92. (7") *(YR 91)* **COLOURS WILL COME. / OPAL KRUSH** [ ] [-]
(12"+=/cd-s+=) *(YRT/YRCD 91)* – Look what you've done / Feels like the richtergroove.

Sep 92. (c/cd) *(CIRC/+D 22)* **OUTERNATIONAL** [ ] [-]
– Outernational / Feels like the richtergroove / Opal krusch / Colours wil come / Pastime paradise / Groovecture / Sacrifice and be sacrificed / Baby / What made me turn on the lights / Windows cell.

— In Jul'96, BILLY was featured on a single by LOOM, 'ANACOSTIA BAY'.

— Tragically on the 22nd January 1997, BILLY committed suicide in his father's home in Dundee. He had recently signed to 'Nude' records.

Nude | not iss.

Oct 97. (cd) *(NUDE 8CD)* **BEYOND THE SUN** [64] [-]

– (ASSOCIATES) compilations, others, etc. –

Sep 81. (7"/12") *Fiction; (FICS/+X 13)* **A. / WOULD I . . . BOUNCE BACK** [ ] [-]

Nov 82. (7"/12") *Fiction; (FIXS/+X 16)* **A MATTER OF GENDER. / EVEN DOGS IN THE WILD** [ ] [-]

Oct 89. (12"ep/cd-ep) *Strange Fruit; (SFPS/+CD 075))* **THE PEEL SESSIONS** ('82) [ ] [-]
– It's better this way / Nude spoons / Me myself and the tragic story / Natural gender / Ulcragyceptemol.

Jan 91. (cd)(lp/c) *East West; (9031 72414-2)(WX 363/+C)* **POPERA** [ ] [-]
– Party fears two / Club country / 18 Carat love affair / Love hangover / Those first impressions / Waiting for the loveboat / Breakfast / Take me to the girl / Heart of glass / Country boy / The rhythm divine / Waiting for the loveboat (slight return) / Tell me Easter's on Friday / Q; quarters / Kitchen person / Message oblique speech / White car in Germany.

Jan 91. (7"/c-s) *East West; (YZ 534/+C)* **POPERETTA EP: WAITING FOR THE LOVEBOAT (Slight Return). / CLUB COUNTRY CLUB** [ ] [-]
(12"+=/cd-s+=) *(YZ 534 T/CD)* – Waiting for the loveboat (extended voyage) / Club country club (Time Unlimited).

Sep 94. (cd) *Nighttracks; (CDNT 006)* **THE RADIO ONE SESSION** [ ] [-]

ASS PONYS

Formed: Cincinnati, Ohio, USA . . . late 80's by CHUCK CLEAVER, DAN KLEINGERS (both out of LUNCHBUDDIES and a band called GOMEZ), plus JOHN ERHARDT and former LIBERTINES' bassman RANDY CHEEK. After delivering a debut album, 'MR. SUPERLOVE' for the small 'Okra' label at the turn of the decade, the band suffered some setbacks when distributor 'Rough Trade' went under. With a new drummer DAVE MORRISON in tow, the band began work on a follow-up set although this too was subject to delay as the 'PONYS' run of bad form continued. Belated released on Germany's 'Normal' label, the JOHN CURLEY (of AFGHAN WHIGS)-produced 'GRIM' (1992) was a more focused affair than their raw, spasmodic and undisciplined previous effort. Although subsequently signed to 'A&M' (alongside the likes of MONSTER MAGNET), the careworn ASS PONYS have yet to enjoy the privilege of a UK release for their last two albums, 'ELECTRIC ROCK MUSIC' (1994) and 'THE KNOWN UNIVERSE; (1996).

Album rating: MR. SUPERLOVE (*6) / GRIM (*6) / ELECTRIC ROCK MUSIC (*6) / THE KNOWN UNIVERSE (*6)

CHUCK CLEAVER – vocals, guitar (ex-LUNCHBUDDIES, ex-GOMEZ) / **JOHN ERHARDT** – guitar, pedal steel, bass, vocals / **RANDY CHEEK** – bass, guitar, vocals (ex-LIBERTINES) / **DAN KLEINGERS** – percussion, drums (ex-LUNCHBUDDIES, ex-GOMEZ)

not iss. | Okra

Jun 90. (cd) *<9>* **MR. SUPERLOVE** [-] [ ]

— **DAVE MORRISON** – drums, percussion; repl. KLEINGERS (on most)

not iss. | Safe House

Aug 93. (cd) *<SH-2104-2>* **GRIM** [-] [ ]
– Big rock ending / Azalea / It's not happening / No dope no cigarettes / Ballpeen / Not since Superman died / I love Bob / Stupid / Dirty backseat car thing / High Heaven / Julia Pastrana / Disappointed / Her father was a sailor / The big E / Good with guns / California bingo.

A&M | A&M

Nov 94. (cd) *<540270-2>* **ELECTRIC ROCK MUSIC** [-] [ ]
– Grim / Little bastard / Ape hanger / Place out there / Lake Brenda / Wall eyed girl / Live until I die / Peanut '93 / Banlon girl / Gypped / Blushing bride / Earth to grandma / Otter side. *(UK-iss.1997; same as US)*

Mar 95. (7") **LITTLE BASTARD. / YOU, MY FLOWER** [-] [ ]

— **BILL ALLETZHAUSER** repl. ERHARDT

Apr 96. (cd) *<540478>* **THE KNOWN UNIVERSE** [-] [ ]
– Shoe money / Under cedars and stars / God tells me to / Blow Oskar / Cancer show / Dead fly the birds / And she drowned / Redway / French muscleman / It's summer here / John boat / Hagged / Some kind of fun.

Virginia ASTLEY

Born: c.Oct'60, Watford, England. After graduating from the Guildhall School Of Music, she co-founded The RAVISHING BEAUTIES along with NICKY HOLLAND and JOCELYN POOK. At the turn of the decade they provided an unusual backdrop for many alternative-pop hitmakers including ECHO & THE BUNNYMEN, SIOUXSIE & THE BANSHEES and The SKIDS. After augmenting VICTIMS OF PLEASURE on a few rare singles, ASTLEY reconvened with her aforementioned 'BEAUTIES who backed her up on what would have been her debut album, 'SHE STOOD UP AND CRIED' (1981); initially shelved, the record finally appeared three years later as 'PROMISE NOTHING'. In the meantime she moved from 'Crespescule' records to 'Why-Fi', the label delivering two singles, the latter of which, 'LOVE'S A LONELY PLACE TO BE', hit high in the indie charts. 1983 proved to be a minor turning point for her, the angelic soprano signing to 'Rough Trade' for her first full release, 'FROM THE GARDENS WHERE WE FEEL SECURE', a delightfully dreamy collection of drifting neo-chamber music that was unique in the glitzy musical climate of the day. An English blueprint for the more commercial "new age" sounds created by the likes of ENYA later in the decade, VIRGINIA's style was marketed towards the mainstream charts as she signed to 'Elektra'/'WEA' in '85 and released the 'HOPE IN A DARKENED HEART' (1986) set. Augmented by kindred spirit, producer RYUICHI SAKAMOTO (ex-YMO), the album had its moments with the highlight being the single, 'SOME SMALL HOPE', a duet with ex-JAPAN mainman DAVID SYLVIAN. Although ASTLEY continued to maintain a low profile in Britain, she had more success in Japan where she secured a deal with 'Columbia'. To date, the "quiet-pop" queen has released two albums, 'ALL SHALL BE WELL' (1992) and 'HAD I THE HEAVENS' (1996), both finally given a belated British release via 'Rosebud' late '97.

Album rating: FROM GARDENS WHERE WE FEEL SECURE (*6) / HOPE IN A DARKENED HEART (*6)

VICTIMS OF PLEASURE

VIRGINIA ASTLEY – synthesizer / **GEZ PRIOR** – guitar / **KENNY JONES** – bass / **CHRIS WYLES** – drums

P.A.M. — not iss.

1980. (7"m) *(VOP 1)* **WHEN WE'RE YOUNG. / IF I WAS / SPORTING PASTIMES** [ ] [-]

Rialto — not iss.

Nov 81. (7"/12") *(RIA/12RIA 2)* **SLAVE TO FASHION. / ON THE GAME** [ ] [-]

Apr 82. (7") *(RIA 7)* **JACK AND JILL. / RED MOON** [ ] [-]

Oct 82. (7"; w-drawn) *(RIA 11)* **WHEN YOU'RE YOUNG. /** [ ] [-]

VIRGINIA ASTLEY

— - vocals, piano / with **AUDREY RILEY** – cello / **ANNE STEPHENSON** – violin / **JOCELYN POOK** – viola (all ex-RAVISHING BEAUTIES)

Crepescule — not iss.

Nov 81. (lp; w/drawn) *(TWI 050)* **SHE STOOD UP AND CRIED** [-] [-]
(iss.Dec84 as 'PROMISE NOTHING'; TWI 194)

Why-Fi — not iss.

Jan 82. (10"ep) *(WHYD 8)* **4 BAU A QU – WE WILL MEET THEM AGAIN** [ ] [-]
(w/free 7"demos)

Jan 83. (7") *(WFI 001)* **LOVE'S A LONELY PLACE TO BE. / SOARING** [ ] [-]
(12"+=) *(WFIT 001)* – A summer long since passed / It's too hot to sleep.

— now w/guest **JO WELLS** – clarinet (of KISSING THE PINK)

Rough Trade — not iss.

Aug 83. (lp) *(ROUGH 58)* **FROM GARDENS WHERE WE FEEL SECURE** [ ] [-]
– Morning / With my eyes wide open, I'm dreaming / A summer long since passed / From gardens where we feel secure / Hiding in the ha-ha / Afternoon / Out in the lawn I lie in my bed / Too bright for peacocks / Summer of their dreams / When the fields were on fire / It's too hot to sleep. *(cd-iss. Nov97 on 'Rosebud'; RBXCD 1001)*

Mar 85. (12"ep) *(RTT 158)* **MELT THE SNOW. / untitled / untitled** [ ] [-]
(also on 'Happy Valley'; HA 002)

— added brothers **JON + TED**

Elektra — Elektra

Sep 85. (7") *(EKR 21)* **TENDER. / A LONG TIME AGO** [ ] [-]
(ext-12"+=) *(EKR 21T)* – Mindless days / ('A'instrumental).

W.E.A. — W.E.A.

Dec 85. (7") *(YZ 53)* **DARKNESS HAS REACHED ITS END. / THE END OF TIME** [ ] [-]
(12"+=) *(YZ 53T)* – Shadows will fall behind.

Nov 86. (lp)(cd) *(WX 78)(242039-2)* **HOPE IN A DARKENED HEART** [ ] [ ]
– Some small hope / A father / So like Dorian / Darkness has reached its end / I'm sorry / Tree top club / Charm / Love's a lonely place to be / A summer long since passed.

— (below single credited with DAVID SYLVIAN. He and RYUICHI SAKAMOTO on above album)

Feb 87. (7") *(YZ 107)* **SOME SMALL HOPE. / A SUMMER LONG SINCE PASSED** [ ] [ ]
(12"+=) *(YZ 107T)* – So long Dorian (instrumental).

Columbia — not iss.

1992. (cd) **ALL SHALL BE WELL** [-] [-] Japan
– My smallest friend / All shall be well / You take me away / I live for the day / Love's eloquence / Although I know / Martin / Blue sky white sky / How I miss you. *(UK-iss.Nov97 on 'Rosebud'; RBXCD 1002)*

1996. (cd) **HAD I THE HEAVENS** [-] [-] Japan
(UK-iss.Nov97 on 'Rosebud'; RBXCD 1003)

Pete ASTOR (see under ⇒ WEATHER PROPHETS)

ASTROPUPPEES

Formed: Albany, Oregon, USA ... mid 90's by songwriter KELLEY RYAN and her friend MAUREEN SERRAO. A budding songwriter from her earliest adolescent days, RYAN later worked as songwriter for publishing company, 'Bug Music', through who she met her musical partner, SERRAO. Unsurprisingly, RYAN took advantage of her position to secure a recording deal with 'HighTone', seasoned producer, DON DIXON brought in to work with the girls on their debut album, 'YOU WIN THE BRIDE' (1996). Fusing elements of alternative pop with a rootsy singing/songwriting muse, the record featured a cover of Stealer's Wheel's 'STUCK IN THE MIDDLE'.

Album rating: YOU WIN THE BRIDE (*6)

KELLEY RYAN – vocals, guitar, bass, percussion / **MAUREEN SERRAO** – vocals, bass / with a few extras on session

HighTone — HighTone

Dec 96. (cd) *<(8076)>* **YOU WIN THE BRIDE** [ ] [ ] Oct96
– Underdog / Rockets in my head / She can't say no / Dear John / Lower the line / Amanda / Little weekend / Stuck in the middle / Dead around here / Don't be / Problem / It's not me it's her / Love is all that matters / You win the bride.

— strengthened the line-up when the duo went on tour; scheduled '99 set

ATARI TEENAGE RIOT

Formed: West Berlin, Germany ... 1992 by anti-Nazi cyberpunks ALEC EMPIRE, Syrian-born punk goddess HANIN ELIAS and Swiss-born CARL CRACK. With his 'Digital Hardcore' label as the main weapon of attack, EMPIRE has waged war on an what he sees as an increasingly corporate, decadently comotose German dance scene. His self proclaimed 'lo-fi' techno owes more to the headfuck onslaught of radical hardcore punk (like X-RAY SPEX or CRASS) than any regular notion of 'dance' music and ATARI TEENAGE RIOT's staunch anti-nazi, anti-Ecstacy stance has made EMPIRE a spokesman of sorts for the disillusioned Berlin underground scene. After a trio of fearsome albums, 'DELETE YOURSELF' (1995), 'THE FUTURE OF WAR' and the well-received 'BURN, BERLIN, BURN!' (both 1997), they secured support slots with big guns RAGE AGAINST THE MACHINE and WU-TANG CLAN. More recently, the 'RIOT released the 'DESTROY 2,000 YEARS OF CULTURE EP', though presumably EMPIRE'll make an exception for dodgy 70's punk, having already covered the old SHAM 69 chestnut, 'IF THE KIDS ARE UNITED'. In 1998, with a number of solo releases behind him, EMPIRE worked on the JON SPENCER BLUES EXPLOSION while planning ATR's comeback complete with a second female, the German/Japanese, face-painted, NIC ENDO. She also delivered a solo EP in '98, 'WHITE HEAT', a searing, uncompromising, computerised set of five hardcore sounds that became NME's Single Of The Week!

Album rating: DELETE YOURSELF (*7) / THE FUTURE OF WAR (*4) / BURN, BERLIN, BURN (*7) / Alec Empire: LTD EDITIONS 90-94 compilation (*7) / GENERATION STAR WARS (*7) / SQUEEZE THE TRIGGER (*6) / Carl Crack: BLACK ARK (*6)

HANIN ELIAS – vocals / **ALEC EMPIRE** (b. 2 May'72) – programming, shouts / **CARL CRACK** – MC

Force Inc — not iss.

Nov 92. (12") **HUNTING FOR NAZIS. /** [-] [-] German

Raver Dassline — not iss.

Aug 94. (7") *(RB 4)* **RAVER BASHING. /** [ ] [-]

Digital Hardcore — not iss.

Apr 95. (cd/lp) *(DHR CD/LP 001)* **DELETE YOURSELF** [ ] [-]
– Start the riot / Into the death / Raver bashing / Speed / Sex / Midi junkies / Delete yourself you got no chance to wine / Hetzjagd auf nazis / Cyberpunks are dead / Atari teenage riot / The kids are united / Riot 1995.

1996. (cd/lp) **THE DESTROYER** [-] [-] German

Nov 96. (7") *(DHRUS 71)* **DEUTSCHLAND HAS GOTTA DIE. / RIOT 1996** [ ] [-]

Jan 97. (12"ep/cd-ep) *(DHR/+MCD 012)* **SICK TO DEATH EP** [ ] [-]
– Sick to death / We got the fucking power / Waves of disaster.

Mar 97. (cd/d-lp) *(DHR CD/LP 006)* **THE FUTURE OF WAR** [ ] [-]
– Get up while you can / Fuck all / Sick to death / P.R.E.S.S. / Deutschland (has gotta die) / Destroy 2000 years of culture / Not your business / You can't hold us back / The heatwave / Redefine the enemy / Deathstar / The future of war.

Grand Royal — Grand Royal

Jun 97. (12") *(GR 039)* **NOT YOUR BUSINESS. /** [ ] [ ]
(below single on 'Damaged Goods')

Jul 97. (7"; split with ASIAN DUB FOUNDATION) *(DAMGOOD 132)* **split** [ ] [-]

Aug 97. (cd) *(<GR 042>)* **BURN, BERLIN, BURN!** [ ] [ ]
– Start the riot / Fuck all! / Sick to death / Press / Deutschland (has gotta die!) / Destroy 2000 years of culture / Not your business / Heatwave / Atari Teenage Riot / Delete yourself / Into the death / Death star / Speed / Future of war. *(re-iss. Jan98 lp/cd; same)*

— added **NIC ENDO** – programmer

Dec 97. (ltd;12"ep/cd-ep) *(DHR/+MCD 015)* **DESTROY 2000 YEARS OF CULTURE EP** [ ] [-]
– Destroy 2000 years of culture / Paranoid / Destroy 2000 years of culture remix / You can't hold us back.
(above on 'Digital Hardcore')

ALEC EMPIRE

Mille Plateau / Grand Royal

May 94. (cd/lp) *(EFA 00652-2/-6)* **LTD EDITIONS**
Oct 94. (12"ep) *(DHR 4)* **DEATH EP** -
(above issued on 'Digital Hardcore') (below on 'Force Inc.)
Dec 94. (12"ep) *(FIM 71)* **JAGUAR EP** -
Mar 95. (12"; by ALEC EMPIRE & IAN POOLEY) *(MP 3)* **PULSE CODE EP** -
Mar 95. (cd/lp) *(EFA 00661-2/-6)* **GENERATION STAR WARS**
Oct 95. (cd/lp) *(EFA 00688-2/-6)* **LOW ON ICE**
Apr 96. (cd/lp) *(EFA 00673-2/-6)* **HYPERMODERN JAZZ 2000.5**

Digital Hardcore / Grand Royal

Jun 96. (cd/d-lp) *(DHR CD/LP 004)* **THE DESTROYER** -
– Intro / We all die / Suicide / Bang your head / Don't lie white girl / Firebombing / I just wanna destroy / Bonus beats / Nobody gets out alive / My body cannot die / Peak / Heartbeat that isn't there / I don't care what happens / My face would crack / Pleasure is our business / Ending.
1997. (cd) **SQUEEZE THE TRIGGER** -
— not sure of above release, as with CARL CRACK's 'BLACK ARK' set.

ATHLETICO SPIZZ '80 (see under SPIZZ)

ATTILA THE STOCKBROKER

Born: JOHN BAINE, 21 Oct'57, England. After initially training to be a real stockbroker, the lure of the music biz proved too much and BAINE set himself up as performance poet, ATILLA THE STOCKBROKER. After brief stints in obscure punk bands, ENGLISH DISEASE and BRIGHTON RIOT SQUAD, he enjoyed another fleeting position with Belgian band, CONTINGENT (one single released in 1979, 'POLICE CONTROL'). Following a John Peel session, BAINE secured a deal with independent label, 'Cherry Red', who issued a belated debut album, 'RANTING AT THE NATION', in 1983. Described as the alternative LES DAWSON, his ranting was a light refreshment to the "oi" music around him and took up where JOHN COOPER CLARKE left off. Shot through with typically barbed humour, his state-of-the-nation commentaries were well observed if something of an acquired taste. Critical opinion wasn't exactly in his favour and perhaps as a result, ATILLA was increasingly developing the musical aspect of his work. Moving on from the sparse mandolin backing which had accompanied his earlier work, the release of 'SAWDUST AND EMPIRE' (1984) found the man moving in folkier circles alongside the likes of fellow erstwhile punk and general space cadet, JOHN OTWAY. With titles like 'LIBYAN STUDENTS FROM HELL' (1987) and 'SCORNFLAKES' (1988), you know what to expect from this decidedly un-PC performer, you've been warned!

Album rating: RANTING AT THE NATION (*5)

ATTILA THE STOCKBROKER – vocals

No Wonder / not iss.

1981. (7"ep) *(E 1)* **PHAZING OUT CAPITALISM** -

Cherry Red / not iss.

Oct 82. (7"ep) *(CHERRY 46)* **COCKTAILS** -
– Contributory negligence / The night I slept with Seething Wells / Fifth column / The oracle.
Apr 83. (lp) *(ARED 46)* **RANTING AT THE NATION** -
– Away day / I slept with Seething Wells / Albanian football / A bang and a Wimpey / Burn it down / Flappin' in the wind / Contributory negligence / Nigel wants to go to C&A's / The perils of stealing half a bottle of wine / They must be Russians / Russians in the DHSS / Russians in MacDonalds / The oracle / Death in Bromley / Nigel wants to go and see Depeche Mode / Russians at the Henley regatta / Russians on the centre court / Fifth column / The fall of King Zog / Holiday in Albania / England are back (Luxembourg where are you?) / Where are you goin' with that flounder? / Hands off our halibuts / Gentlemen of the wrist / Eros products commercials / The Spencers croft cat (dead cat strat) / A very silly East European propaganda station / The fall of King Zog (reprise).

Anagram / not iss.

Mar 84. (lp) *(GRAM 13)* **SAWDUST & EMPIRE** -
– Sawdust & empire / Boadicea uber alles / Factory gods / March of the levellers / Nigel's revenge / Recession / Diesirae (World War III) / Holiday in Albania / Alone in Sidco / Spare a thought / Midas the ground / Ghosts of the levellers.

Cherry Red / not iss.

Aug 84. (12"ep) *(12CHERRY 82)* **RADIO RAP 1** -
– Let the drain take the strain / Take a leak on a green / (Everytime) I eat vegetables / Vomit on a Viking / I don't talk to pop stars / Love and herpes / Albanian rifle poem / Nigel wants to join the S.A.S. / A letter from Nigel's mum / Russians versus the Tetley bitter man / Poetry requiem.

B.B.C. / not iss.

May 86. (7") **HEROES. (with The ESSEX ARTISTS) / ?** -

Plastic Head / not iss.

Mar 87. (lp) *(PLASLP 009)* **LIBYAN STUDENTS FROM HELL** -
– Libyan students from Hell / I'm so miserable / Airstrip one / The ballad of Comrade Enver / Pedi dies / The rapping mole / Another country / Glenzendes empire / The green fields of France.

Probe Plus / not iss.

Sep 88. (lp) *(PROBE 20)* **SCORNFLAKES** -

Musidisc / not iss.

Apr 91. (cd/c/lp) *(10789-2/-4/-1)* **DONKEY'S YEARS** -

Larrikin / not iss.

Jul 93. (cd/c) *(LRF CD/C 264)* **666: NEIGHBOUR OF THE BEAST** - - Austra

Demi-Monde / not iss.

Aug 96. (cd/c) *(HELMET CD/CAS 1)* **SIEGE OF SHOREHAM**

AU PAIRS

Formed: Birmingham, England . . . 1979 by LESLEY WOODS, PAUL FOAD, JANE MUNRO and PETE HAMMOND. Pointedly political and musically eclectic, the AU PAIRS carried on where the likes of GANG OF FOUR and DELTA 5 left off, spiritually at least. Musically, the group were heavily influenced by the 2-tone scene and its mash-up of ska, reggae and pop (they had supported fellow Brummies, UB40), a healthy dose of quirky bass-led post-punk experimentalism keeping things interesting. In true DIY style, the band initiated their recording career with a self-financed EP, 'YOU', in 1980, following it up with a debut album, 'PLAYING WITH A DIFFERENT SEX' (1981) and a heavy touring schedule. While The AU PAIRS struggled to make any inroads into the mainstream, critics were generally supportive and WOODS' lyrics were often thought provoking in their presentation of a uniquely feminine perspective on gender and sexuality. Although a second album, 'SENSE AND SENSUALITY' (1982) appeared on 'Kamera' records (featuring members of The POP GROUP), it proved to be their epitaph as the band fell apart in 1983 after WOODS missed a gig in Belgium. She subsequently resurfaced fronting all-female band The DARLINGS while FOAD and HAMMOND formed END OF CHAT. • **Songwriters:** Group compositions, except SEX MACHINE (James Brown).

Album rating: PLAYING WITH A DIFFERENT SEX (*8) / SENSE AND SENSUALITY (*5) / LIVE IN BERLIN (*5)

LESLEY WOODS (b.25 Jan'58, Hockley, Essex) – vocals, guitar / **JANE MUNRO** (b. 9 Dec'53) – bass, vocals / **PAUL FOAD** – guitar, vocals / **PETE HAMMOND** – drums

021 / not iss.

1980. (7"m) *(OTO 2)* **YOU. / DOMESTIC DEPARTURE / KERB CRAWLER** -
Nov 80. (7") *(OTO 4)* **IT'S OBVIOUS. / DIET** -

Human / not iss.

Apr 81. (lp) *(HUMAN 1)* **PLAYING WITH A DIFFERENT SEX** 33 -
– We're so cool / Love song / Set-up / Repetition / Headache (for Michelle) / Come again / Armagh / Unfinished business / Dear John / It's obvious. *(cd-iss. Nov92 on 'R.P.M.'+=; RPM 107)* – You / Domestic departure / Kerb crawler / Diet / It's obvious (7"version) / Inconvenience (12"version) / Pretty boys / Headache (for Michelle) (remix).
Jul 81. (7") *(HUM 8)* **INCONVENIENCE. / PRETTY BOYS** -
(12"+=) *(HUM 8-12)* – Heartache (remix).

Kamera / not iss.

Aug 82. (lp) *(KAM 010)* **SENSE AND SENSUALITY** 79 -
– Don't look back / (That's when) It's worth it / Instant touch / Sex without stress / Fiasco / In-tact / Tongue in cheek / Stepping out of line / Shakedown / America. *(cd-iss. Sep93 on 'R.P.M.'; RPM 111)*
— disbanded early '83, FOAD and HAMMOND evolved the band into END OF CHAT with WOODS' replacement GRAHAM HAMILTON

– compilations, etc. –

Aug 83. (lp) *a.k.a.; (AKA 6)* **LIVE IN BERLIN 1981 (live)** -
– Diet / Headache for Michelle / Dear John / Love song / Set up / Inconvenience / Armagh / Repetition / We're so cool / Cum again / Piece of my heart. *(cd-iss. Oct96 on 'Essential'; ESMCD 452)*
Jul 94. (cd) *R.P.M.; (RPM 139CD)* **EQUAL BUT DIFFERENT** -
– Pretty boys / Ideal woman / Come again / Monogamy / It's obvious / Love song / Repetition / Dear John / Set up / Headache / We're so cool / Armagh / Steppin' out / America / Sex without stress / Instinct / Shakedown / The slider / Unfinished business.

AUTEURS

Formed: Southgate, London, England . . . early 1992 by LUKE HAINES (ex-SERVANTS) and girlfriend ALICE READMAN. They quickly signed to 'Fire', soon moving to Virgin off-shoot label, 'Hut', and indie chart surfing with their debut single, 'SOWGIRL' later in the year. Glossy garage indie/punk merchants, fronted by the flamboyant but cynical HAINES, The AUTEURS sound was characterised by the singer's brooding lyrical complexities. The addition of cellist, JAMES BANBURY produced an extra dimension to their standard guitar, bass, drums approach and the debut album's encouragingly critical reception was matched by a UK Top 40 placing for 'NEW WAVE' (1993) and a nomination for the Mercury Music Award. Their third single, 'LENNY VALENTINO', almost scraped into the UK Top 40, the track relating to the debut album sleeve, which depicted Lenny Bruce dressed as Rudolph Valentino. HAINES preoccupations both, another favoured subject of the controversial frontman was the British Class System, 'THE UPPER CLASS' appearing on the follow-up set, 'NOW I'M A COWBOY' (1994). The record secured a Top 30 placing, although the group's critical acclaim continued to outweigh their commercial appeal. A remix set, 'THE AUTEURS VS U-ZIQ' appeared, although it wasn't until 1996 that a long-awaited third album materialised. Produced by STEVE ALBINI, this atmospheric offering combined HAINES' downbeat tales of intrigue with grinding organs, discordant guitars and mournful strings to often hypnotic effect. Despite garnering further plaudits, the record sold poorly and after a clutch of final gigs, HAINES wound the band up, subsequently releasing an album under the moniker of BAADER – MEINHOF (first mentioned on the bleak 'TOMBSTONE' track). In 1998, HAINES teamed up with two former members of BALLOON, JOHN MOORE (ex-EXPRESSWAY) and singer,

SARAH NIXEY, in the more melodic, BLACK BOX RECORDER. Signing a major deal with 'Chrysalis', it didn't look likely that either their singles, 'CHILD PSYCHOLOGY' and 'ENGLAND MADE ME' or the latterly-titled accompanying album, would return the moody HAINES to earlier heights.

Album rating: NEW WAVE (*6) / NOW I'M A COWBOY (*8) / AFTER MURDER PARK (*7) / Baader-Meinhof: BAADER-MEINHOF (*5) / Black Box Recorder: ENGLAND MADE ME (*6)

LUKE HAINES (b. 7 Oct'67, Walton-On-Thames, Surrey, England) – vocals, guitar (ex-SERVANTS) / **ALICE READMAN** (b. 1967, Harrow, England) – bass (ex-SERVANTS) / **GLENN COLLINS** (b. 7 Feb'68, Cheltenham, England) – drums (ex-DOG UNIT, ex-VORT PYLON)

Hut Caroline

Dec 92. (12"ep/cd-ep) *(HUT T/CD)* **SHOWGIRL. / GLAD TO BE GONE / STAYING POWER** [ ] [-]

— added **JAMES BANBURY** – cello

Mar 93. (cd/c/lp) *(CDHUT/HUTMC/HUTLP 7)* <1735> **NEW WAVE** [35] [ ]
– Showgirl / Bailed out / American guitars / Junk shop clothes / Don't trust the stars / Starstruck / How could I be wrong / Housebreaker / Valet parking / Idiot brother / Early years / Home again. *(free 7"w/lp on cd+c+=)* – Untitled.

May 93. (10"ep/12"ep/cd-ep) *(HUT EN/T/CD 28)* **HOW COULD I BE WRONG. / HIGH DIVING HORSES / WEDDING DAY** [ ] [ ]

— **BARNEY CROCKFORD** – drums; repl. COLLINS

Hut Vernon Yard

Nov 93. (7") *(HUT 36)* **LENNY VALENTINO. / DISNEY WORLD** [41] [ ]
(12"/cd-s) *(HUT T/CD 36)* – ('A'side) / Car crazy / Vacant lot / ('A'original mix).

Apr 94. (7") *(HUTG 41)* **CHINESE BAKERY. / ('A'acoustic)** [42] [ ]
(7"/cd-s) *(HUT/+CD 41)* – ('A'side) / Government bookstore / Everything you say will destroy you.
(12") *(HUTDX 41)* – ('A'side) / ('A'acoustic) / Modern history.

May 94. (cd/c/lp) *(CDHUT/HUTMC/HUTLP 16)* <39597> **NOW I'M A COWBOY** [27] [ ]
– Lenny Valentino / Brainchild / I'm a rich man's toy / New French girlfriend / The upper classes / Chinese bakery / A sister like you / Underground movies / Life classes – Life model / Modern history / Daughter of a child. *(lp w /free 1-sided 7") (HUTLPX 16)* – MODERN HISTORY (acoustic).

Nov 94. (m-cd/m-lp) *(DGHUTM/HUTMLP 20)* **THE AUTEURS VS U-ZIQ** (remixes) [ ] [-]
– Lenny Valentino No.3 / Daughter of a child / Chinese bakery / Lenny Valentino No.1 / Lenny Valentino No.2 / Underground movies.

Hut Hut

Dec 95. (7"ep/c-ep/cd-ep) *(HUT/+C/CD 65)* **BACK WITH THE KILLER E.P.** [45] [-]
– Unsolved child murder / Back with the killer again / Former fan / Kenneth Anger's bad dream.

Feb 96. (10"ep/cd-ep) *(<HUT EN/CD 66>)* **LIGHT AIRCRAFT ON FIRE / BUDDHA (demo). / CAR CRASH / X – BOOGIE MAN** [58] [ ]

Mar 96. (cd/c/lp) *(<DGHUT/HUTMC/HUTLP 33>)* **AFTER MURDER PARK** [53] [ ]
– Light aircraft on fire / The child brides / Land lovers / New brat in town / Everything you say will destroy you / Unsolved child murder / Married to a lazy lover / Buddha / Tombstone / Fear of flying / Dead Sea navagators / After Murder Park.

May 96. (10"ep/cd-ep) *(<HUT EN/CD 68>)* **"KID'S ISSUE" EP** [ ] [ ]
– Buddha / A new life a new family / After murder park.

BAADER-MEINHOF

— **HAINES** with others **JAMES BANBURY + ANDY NICE** – cello / **JUSTIN ARMITAGE** – violin / **GARY STRASBOURG** – drums / **KULJIT BHAMRA** – percussion, tabla

Oct 96. (cd/lp) *(<CDHUT/HUTLP 36>)* **BAADER-MEINHOF** [ ] [ ] Feb97
– Baader Meinhof / Meet me at the airport / There's gonna be an accident / Mogadishu / Theme from Burn Warehouse Burn / GSG-29 / . . .It's a moral issue / Back on the farm / Kill Ramirez / Baader Meinhof.

BLACK BOX RECORDER

— **HAINES** with **JOHN MOORE** – guitar (ex-JESUS & MARY CHAIN, ex-EXPRESSWAY, ex-REVOLUTION 9, ex-BALLOON) / **SARAH NIXEY** – vocals (ex-BALLOON)

Chrysalis Chrysalis

May 98. (7") *(CHS 5082)* **CHILD PSYCHOLOGY. / GIRL SINGING IN THE WRECKAGE** [ ] [-]
(cd-s+=) *(CDCHS 5082)* – Seasons in the sun.

Jul 98. (7") *(CHS 5091)* **ENGLAND MADE ME. / LORD LUCAN IS MISSING** [ ] [ ]
(cd-s) *(CDCHS 5091)* – ('A'side) / Factory radio / Child psychology (audio) / Child psychology (video).

Jul 98. (cd/d-lp) *(493907-2/-1)* **ENGLAND MADE ME** [ ] [ ]
– Girl singing in the wreckage / England made me / New baby boom / It's only the end of the world / Ideal home / Child psychology / I C one female / Uptown top ranking / Swinging / Kidnapping an heiress / Hated Sunday.

AVANT GARDENERS

Formed: London, England . . . 1977 by RUSSELL MURCH, MARTIN SAUNDERS, NIGEL RAE and MIKE KELLY. One of the many "New Wave" acts to hitch a ride on the 'Punk' bandwagon via Richard Branson's 'Virgin' records, The AVANT GARDENER (as they were called then) debuted with an eponymous EP later that summer. The green-fingered ones then disappeared from the scene for a few years, returning in 1980 with MURCH as the sole remaining original alongside a new line-up of MIKE ROBERTS, ROB HILL and guest drummers. More popular on the continent, The AVANT GARDENERS found a deal with Italy's 'Appaloosa' imprint and issued their long-awaited debut set, 'DIG IT' (1980), basically re-hashed versions of their early material alongside a Roky Erickson cover, 'TWO HEADED DOG'. The band further pursued their interest in warped 60's psychedelia with their final lp, 'THE CHURCH OF THE INNER COSMOS' (1983/84) their final rake through retro muck before they paved their proverbial way out of the music business.

Album rating: DIG IT (*6) / THE CHURCH OF THE INNER COSMOS (*6)

RUSSELL MURCH – vocals, guitar / **MARTIN SAUNDERS** – guitar / **NIGEL RAE** – bass / **MIKE KELLY** – drums

Virgin not iss.

Aug 77. (7"ep; as The AVANT GARDENER) *(VEP 1003)* **THE AVANT GARDENER EP** [ ] [-]
– Gotta turn back / Back door / Bloodclad boogie / Strange gurl in clothes.

— split for a time, while **MURCH** recruited entirely new musicians **MIKE ROBERTS** – guitar / **ROB HILL** – bass / plus guest drummers **STEVE HARTLEY, ED LEWIS + SID SLATER** (RAE played keyboards)

Appaloosa not iss.

1980. (lp) *(AP 013)* **DIG IT** [-] [-] Italy
– Strange gurl in clothes / Where are my hormones / Gotta turn back / Johnny Cash / Dateless night / Two-headed dog / Bloodclad boogie baby / Never turn your back on a silicon chip.

— the trio also increased guest list including drummers **HARTLEY, STEVE SATURN + MARTIN HUGHES**

Jan 84. (lp) *(AP 027)* **THE CHURCH OF THE INNER COSMOS** [ ] [-]
– Looking for a sun / C.D.C. / Loose in the sky / $30 / Pe 13th son of Rameses / Looking for another sun / Jennifer Jones / The lecture / The force is with you / The kitchen of oblivion.

Speed not iss.

Dec 83. (7"m) *(SPEED 11)* **DEADWOOD STAGE. / JOHN PRIEST / WHERE ARE MY HORMONES** [ ] [-]

— nothing was heard from them after above

AVENGERS

Formed: San Francisco, California, USA . . . 1977 by PENELOPE HOUSTON, DANNY FURIOUS, JONATHAN POSTAL and GREG WESTERMARK (the latter two were subsequently replaced by JIMMY WILSEY, BRAD KENT and GREG INGRAHAM before any recordings). Their debut release was a maxi-single featuring the lead track, 'CAR CRASH', a head-on collision of raw punk and primitive hardcore for the 'Dangerhouse' imprint that made its mark on the fertile San Fran underground scene. Garnering a minor degree of fame by supporting the SEX PISTOLS at their final gig in December '78 at the city's Winterland Ballroom, The AVENGERS subsequently worked with ex-PISTOL, STEVE JONES on a follow-up release, 'THE AMERICAN IN ME' EP. However, the file was closed on the group shortly after, PENELOPE HOUSTON going on to become a singer/songwriter.

Album rating: THE AVENGERS 1977-1979 compilation (*6)

PENELOPE HOUSTON – vocals / **GREG INGRAHAM** – guitar; repl. GREG WESTERMARK / **JIMMY WILSEY** – bass; repl. JONATHAN POSTAL / **DANNY FURIOUS** – drums / added **BRAD KENT** – second guitar

not iss. Dangerhouse

Dec 77. (7"m) *<SFD 400>* **CAR CRASH. / WE ARE THE ONE / I BELIEVE IN ME** [-] [ ]

not iss. White Noise

Jan 79. (7"ep) *<WNR 002>* **THE AMERICAN IN ME / UH-OH. / CORPUS CHRISTI / WHITE NIGGER** [-] [ ]
<re-iss. 1981 with diff.sleeve; same>

— split in 1979, PENELOPE HOUSTON later became a singer/songwriter, releasing one album, 'BIRDBOYS' for 'Subterranean'.

– compilations, etc. –

Aug 86. (cd) *CD Presents; (CD 007)* **THE AVENGERS 1977-1979** [ ] [-]
– We are the one / Car crash / I believe in me / Open your eyes / No martyr / Desperation / Thin white line / Paint it black / The American in me / White nigger / Uh-oh / Second to none / Corpus Christi / Fuck you (live). *(re-iss. Apr90 as 'CADILLACS AND LINCOLNS' on 'Rockhouse'; ROCK 8901)*

A WITNESS

Formed: Stockport, near Manchester, England . . . 1985 by RICK AITKEN, KEITH CURT, VINCE HUNT and ALAN BROWN. Signed to C86 stalwart, 'Ron Johnson', A WITNESS became associated with the NME-created scene after having the track, 'SHARPENED STICKS', featured on the cassette of the same name. The band had already won praise from the same publication for their debut EP, 'LOUDHAILER SONGS'. Trading in the same jerky rhythms and crazed vocals as BEEFHEART, The FALL and The CRAVATS, the band had obviously cocked an ear at some point to new wave pioneers WIRE. A full length album, 'I AM JOHN PANCREAS', appeared in '86 and the group enjoyed a brief period of cult acclaim until the collapse of both the scene which spawned them and the 'Ron Johnson' label itself. Another independent imprint, 'Communion', issued their belated follow-up set, 'SACRED COW HEART' (1988), before the band hooked up with The MEMBRANES' 'Vinyl Drip' label for a final single early in 1990, 'I LOVE YOU MR. DISPOSABLE RAZORS'. Inquisitive readers can sample an overview of A WITNESS's career (which was cut short by RICK's untimely death) via the 'DOUBLE

PEEL SESSIONS' compilation of their recordings with the cult Radio One DJ and indie tastemaker.

Album rating: I AM JOHN'S PANCREAS (*6) / LOUDHAILER SONGS (*5)

KEITH CURTIS – vocals / **RICK AITKEN** (b.18 Aug'56) – guitar / **VINCE HUNT** – bass / **ALAN BROWN** – drums

Ron Johnson | not iss.

Nov 85. (12"ep) *(ZRON 5)* **LOUDHAILER SONGS** [ ] [-]
– Lucky in London / Kitchen sink drama / Regular round / Camera / Drill one.

Oct 86. (lp) *(ZRON 12)* **I AM JOHN PANCREAS** [ ] [-]
– Smelt like a pedestrain / O'Grady's dream / Car skidding / Red snake / Dipping bird / Sharpening sticks / The loudhailer song / Legs be sturdy / 4.49 stool / Hard days love.

May 87. (12"ep) *(exist)* **RED SNAKE. / ?** [ ] [-]

Feb 88. (12"ep) *(ZRON 30)* **RAW PATCH** [ ] [-]

Communion | not iss.

Oct 88. (lp/c) *(COMM 003/+C)* **SACRED COW HEART** [ ] [-]

Vinyl Drip | not iss.

Feb 90. (12"ep) *(SUK 010)* **I LOVE YOU MR. DISPOSABLE RAZOR** [ ] [-]

— had already disbanded in 1989; RICK was to die the same year

– compilations, etc. –

Dec 89. (m-lp/m-cd) *Strange Fruit; (SFPMA/+CD 206)* **THE PEEL SESSIONS** [ ] [-]

AZTEC CAMERA

Formed: East Kilbride, Scotland . . . early 1980 by 15 year-old, RODDY FRAME, who released two independent 45's on ALAN HORNE's now semi-famous 'Postcard' label, before moving on to 'Rough Trade' in 1982. The following year, RODDY and Co. hit the top of the indie charts (reached Top 30 nationally) with debut album, 'HIGH LAND, HARD RAIN', a largely acoustic-based affair combining folkish flights of fancy, Latin/jazz rhythms and an incisive lyrical flair with stunning results. The record's breezy lead track, 'OBLIVIOUS', was re-issued by new label 'Warners' later that year on the back of the album's success, one of the few AZTEC CAMERA singles to break the Top 20. FRAME brought in a new cast of musicians for 1984's MARK KNOPFLER-produced 'KNIFE' set, including seasoned Scots players CRAIG GANNON and MALCOLM ROSS. A more commercial offering, the record almost made the UK hit in 'ALL I NEED IS EVERYTHING'. After a world tour, FRAME laid low for more than two years, penning material for 'LOVE' (1987), the most successful album of his career. Initially something of a non-starter, this over-produced yet affecting album eventually made the Top 10 almost a year after its release following the massive Top 5 success of the plaintive 'SOMEWHERE IN MY HEART' single. Despite courting the pop mainstream, FRAME's subsequent effort, 'STRAY' (1990) veered off into more eclectic territory, the Top 20 hit, 'GOOD MORNING BRITAIN', featuring MICK JONES of BIG AUDIO DYNAMITE / CLASH fame. The 90's, meanwhile, have witnessed FRAME developing his earlier style, especially on the 1995 set, 'FRESTONIA'. Come 1998, the Scots veteran had signed to 'Independiente', releasing a minor hit, 'REASON FOR LIVING' which accompanied the relatively low-key pop-rock album, 'THE NORTH STAR'. • **Covered:** JUMP (Van Halen) / DO I LOVE YOU (Cole Porter) / I THREW IT ALL AWAY (Bob Dylan) / BAD EDUCATION (Blue Orchids) / IF PARADISE WAS HALF AS NICE (Amen Corner). • **Trivia:** In Autumn '83, while in the States supporting ELVIS COSTELLO, he lied about his age (19) to get into the country.

Album rating: HIGH LAND, HARD RAIN (*8) / KNIFE (*6) / LOVE (*5) / STRAY (*6) / DREAMLAND (*6) / FRESTONIA (*5) / Roddy Frame:

RODDY FRAME (b.29 Jan'64) – vocals, acoustic guitar / **DAVE MULHOLLAND** – bass / **CAMPBELL OWENS** – drums (He replaced ALAN WELSH)

Postcard | not iss.

Mar 81. (7") *(81-3)* **JUST LIKE GOLD. / WE COULD SEND LETTERS** [ ] [-]

Jul 81. (7") *(81-8)* **MATTRESS OF WIRE. / LOOK OUTSIDE THE TUNNEL** [ ] [-]

— (mid-'82) added temp. member **BERNIE CLARK** – keyboards / **DAVE RUFFY** – drums (ex-RUTS) repl. MULHOLLAND

Rough Trade | Sire

Aug 82. (7"/7"pic-d) *(RT 112/+P)* **PILLAR TO POST. / QUEEN'S TATTOO** [ ] [-]

Jan 83. (7") *(RT 122)* **OBLIVIOUS. / ORCHARD GIRL** [47] [-]
(12"+=) *(RT 122T)* – Haywire.

Apr 83. (lp) *(ROUGH 47) <23899>* **HIGH LAND, HARD RAIN** [22] [ ] Aug83
– Oblivious / The boy wonders / Walk out to winter / The bugle sounds again / We could send letters / Pillar to post / Release / Lost outside the tunnel / Back on board / Down the dip. *(cd-iss. Feb87 +=; ROUGHCD 47)* – Haywire / Queen's tattoo / Orchard girl. *(re-iss. Sep93 on 'WEA' cd/c; 4509 92849-2/-4)*

May 83. (7"/12") *(RT/+T 132)* **WALK OUT TO WINTER. / SET THE KILLING FREE** [64] [ ]

WEA | Sire

Oct 83. (d7") *(AZTEC 1)* **OBLIVIOUS. / ORCHARD GIRL // WE COULD SEND LETTERS (live). / BACK ON BOARD (live)** [18] [ ]

— **RODDY FRAME** retained **DUFFY** and brought into line-up. **CRAIG GANNON** – bass (ex-BLUEBELLS) repl. OWENS / added **MALCOLM ROSS** – guitar (ex-ORANGE JUICE, ex-JOSEF K) / guest / **GUY FLETCHER** – keyboards

Aug 84. (7") *(AC 1)* **ALL I NEED IS EVERYTHING. / JUMP** [34] [ ]
(12") *(AC 1T)* – ('A'-Latin mix) / Jump (Loaded version).

Sep 84. (lp/c)(cd) *(WX 8/+C)(240 483-2) <25183>* **KNIFE** [14] [ ]
– Still on fire / Just like the U.S.A. / Head is happy (heart's insane) / The back door to Heaven / All I need is everything / Backwards and forwards / Birth of the true / Knife. *(cd-iss. Sep93; same)*

Nov 84. (7"/7"sha-pic-d) *(AC 2/+P)* **STILL ON FIRE. / WALK OUT TO WINTER** [ ] [ ]
(12"+=) *(AC 2T)* – Mattress of wire (live) / The boy wonders (live) / The bugle sounds again (live).

Apr 85. (10"m-lp) *<25285>* **AZTEC CAMERA (live)** [-] [ ]
– Birth of the true / Mattress of wire / Jump / The bugle sounds again / Backwards and forwards.

— **FRAME & DUFFY** plus alongside other session musicians **MARCUS MILLER** – bass / **DAVID FRANK** – keyboards (ex-SYSTEM) / **STEVE JORDAN** – guitar

Sep 87. (7"/ext-12") *(YZ 154/+T)* **DEEP AND WIDE AND TALL. / BAD EDUCATION** [ ] [ ]

Oct 87. (lp/c)(cd) *(WX 128/+C)(242 202-2) <25646>* **LOVE** [10] [ ]
– Deep and wide and tall / How men are / Everybody is a number one / More than a law / Somewhere in my heart / Working in a goldmine / One and one / Paradise / Killermont Street. *(cd-iss. Sep93; same)*

Jan 88. (7") *(YZ 168)* **HOW MEN ARE. / THE RED FLAG** [25] [ ]
(12"+=) *(YZ 168T)* – Killermont Street (live) / Pillar to post (live).
(cd-s+=) *(248 028-2)* – Oblivious / All I need is everything.

Apr 88. (7") *(YZ 181)* **SOMEWHERE IN MY HEART. / EVERYBODY IS A NUMBER ONE '86** [3] [ ]
(12"+=) *(YZ 181T)* – Down the dip / Jump.
(cd-s+=) *(YZ 181CD)* – Walk out to winter / Still on fire.

Jul 88. (7") *(YZ 199)* **WORKING IN A GOLDMINE. / I THREW IT ALL AWAY** [31] [ ]
(12"+=/12"s+=) *(YZ 199 T/W)* – ('A'version).
(cd-s++=) *(YZ 199CD)* – How men are.

Sep 88. (7") *(YZ 154)* **DEEP AND WIDE AND TALL. / BAD EDUCATION** [55] [ ]
(12"+=/cd-s+=) *(YZ 154 T/CD)* – More than a law.

— (live band '88: augmenting **FRAME + DUFFY**) **EDDIE KULAK** – keyboards / **GARY SANFORD** – guitar / **PAUL POWELL** – bass

— (by 1990, **FRAME** had lost **DUFFY**) retained **POWELL** / and new **GARY SANCTUARY** – keyboards / **FRANK TONTOH** – drums / guests **PAUL CARRACK, EDWYN COLLINS, MICKEY GALLAGHER & STEVE SI DELYNK.**

Jun 90. (cd)(lp/c) *(<9031 71694-2>)(WX 350/+C)* **STRAY** [22] [ ]
– Stray / The crying scene / Get outta London / Over my head / How it is / Good morning Britain (featuring MICK JONES) / The gentle kind / Notting Hill blues / Song for a friend. *(re-iss. cd+c Sep93)*

Jun 90. (7") *(YZ 492)* **THE CRYING SCENE. / TRUE COLOURS** [70] [ ]
(12"+=/cd-s+=) *(YZ 492 T/CD)* – Salvation.
(10"+=) *(YZ 492X)* – I threw it all away (live).

Sep 90. (7"/c-s; AZTEC CAMERA and MICK JONES) *(YZ 521/+C)* **GOOD MORNING BRITAIN. / ('A'live version)** [19] [ ]
(12"+=) *(YZ 521T)* – ('A'remix)
(cd-s+=) *(YZ 521CD)* – Consolation prize. (with EDWYN COLLINS)

Jul 92. (7"/c-s) *(YZ 688/+C)* **SPANISH HORSES. / JUST LIKE THE U.S.A. (live)** [52] [ ]
(cd-s) *(YZ 688CD1)* – ('A'side) / Killermont street / Birth of the true / Song for a friend.
(cd-s) *(YZ 688CD2)* – ('A'live version) / Stray (live) / The bugle sounds again (live) / Dolphins (live).

Apr 93. (7"/c-s) *(YZ 740/+C)* **DREAM SWEET DREAMS. / SISTER ANN** [67] [ ]
(cd-s+=) *(YZ 740CD1)* – Good morning Britain (live) / How men are (live).
(cd-s) *(YZ 740CD2)* – ('A'side) / Mattress of wire (live) / Let your love decide (live) / Orchid girl (live).

May 93. (cd/c/lp) *(<4509 92492/-2/-4/-1>)* **DREAMLAND** [21] [ ]
– Birds / Safe in sorrow / Black Lucia / Let your love decide / Spanish horses / Dream sweet dreams / Piano's and clocks / Sister Ann / Vertigo / Valium Summer / Belle of the ball.

Jun 93. (7"/c-s) *(YZ 754/+C)* **BIRDS. / DEEP AND WIDE AND TALL** [ ] [ ]
(cd-s) *(YZ 754CD1)* – ('A'side) / Working in a goldmine / Knife.
(cd-s) *(YZ 754CD2)* – ('A'side) / Somewhere in my heart / Oblivious / Good morning Britain.

WEA | Reprise

Oct 95. (c-s) *(WEA 007C)* **SUN / SUNSET** [ ] [ ]
(cd-s+=) *(WEA 007CD)* – The crying scene (live).
(cd-s) *(WEA 007CDX)* – ('A'side) / We could send letters / Black Lucia / The rainy season.

Nov 95. (cd/c) *(<0630 11929-2/-4>)* **FRESTONIA** [ ] [ ]
– The rainy season / Sun / Crazy / On the avenue / Imperfectly / Debutante / Beautiful girl / Phenomenal world / Method of love / Sunset.

– compilations, etc. –

Sep 90. (7") *Old Gold;* **SOMEWHERE IN MY HEART. / OBLIVIOUS** [ ] [-]

— In Nov'90, 'DO I LOVE YOU?' appeared as the extra track on the 12" & cd-s of a Cole Porter tribute by The POGUES and KIRSTY MacCOLL

Oct 94. (cd) *Windsong; (WHISCD 006)* **LIVE ON THE TEST (live)** [ ] [-]

RODDY FRAME

Independiente | Sony

Sep 98. (c-s) *(ISOM 18MS) <66231A>* **REASON FOR LIVING /** [45] [ ] Nov98
(cd-s) *(ISOM 18CD) <66231B>* –

Sep 98. (cd) *<120123>* **THE NORTH STAR** [55] [ ] Nov98

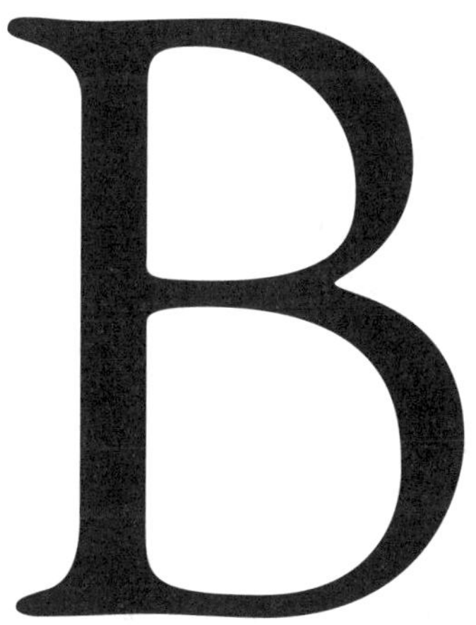

BAADER-MEINHOF (see under ⇒ AUTEURS)

BABES IN TOYLAND

Formed: Minneapolis, Minnesota, USA ... 1987 by KAT BJELLAND, MICHELLE LEON and LORI BARBELO. Signing to influential local label, 'Twintone', the all-girl group released an early proto-grunge classic in the Jack Endino-produced 'SPANKING MACHINE' (1990). Featuring such white hot blasts of feminine subversiveness as 'HE'S MY THING' and 'PAIN IN MY HEART', the album opened the floodgates for a slew of similar angry young women (i.e. L7 and HOLE, whose JENNIFER FINCH and COURTNEY LOVE respectively, LYDIA LUNCH soundalike BJELLAND had previously played with in SUGAR BABY DOLL). Over the course of the next year, they released a mini-album, 'TO MOTHER', replaced MICHELLE with MAUREEN HERMAN and signed to 'Warner Brothers', releasing a second album proper, 'FONTANELLE' in the Spring of '92. Produced by LEE RANALDO of SONIC YOUTH, the record breached the UK Top 30 on the back of rave reviews from both the inkies and the metal press. Following a stop-gap part live set, 'PAINKILLERS', the BABES took a sabbatical, BJELLAND turning up in STUART GRAY (her new husband)'s outfit, LUBRICATED GOAT, while moonlighting with CRUNT. BABES IN TOYLAND returned in 1995 with 'NEMESISTERS', which disappointed many of their more hardcore following by including covers of 'WE ARE FAMILY' (Sister Sledge), 'DEEP SONG' (Billie Holiday) and 'ALL BY MYSELF' (Eric Carmen). • **Other covers:** WATCHING GIRL (Shonen Knife) / THE GIRL CAN'T HELP IT (Little Richard).

Album rating: SPANKING MACHINE (*7) / TO MOTHER (*7) / FONTANELLE (*8) / PAINKILLERS (*5) / NEMESISTERS (*6)

KAT BJELLAND (b. KATHERINE, 9 Dec'63, Woodburn, Oregon) – vocals, guitar / **MICHELLE LEON** – bass / **LORI BARBERO** (b.27 Nov'60) – drums, vocals

not iss. | Treehouse

Jul 89. (7",7"green) *<TR 017>* **DUST CAKE BOY. / SPIT TO SEE THE SHINE** [-] [ ]

not iss. | Sub Pop

Apr 90. (7",7"gold) *<SP 66>* **HOUSE. / ARRIBA** [-] [ ]

Twin Tone | Twin Tone

Jul 90. (cd/lp/mauve-lp) *<TTR 89183-2/-4/-1>* **SPANKING MACHINE** [-] [ ]
– Swamp pussy / He's my thing / Vomit heart / Never / Boto (w)rap / Dogg / Pain in my heart / Lashes / You're right / Dust cake boy / Fork down throat. *(re-iss. +c Dec91 on purple-lp)*

Jun 91. (m-cd/m-c/m-lp) *<(TTR 89208-2/-4/-1)>* **TO MOTHER** [ ] [ ]
– Catatonic / Mad pilot / Primus / Laugh my head off / Spit to see the shine / Pipe / The quiet room.

— (Mar'92) **MAUREEN HERMAN** (b.25 Jul'66, Philadelphia, Pensylvania) – bass (ex-M+M STIGMATA drummer) repl. MICHELLE whose roadie boyfriend John Cole was killed by a burglar

Strange Fruit | not iss.

Mar 92. (cd/10"m-lp) *(SFPMCD/SFPMA 211)* **THE PEEL SESSIONS (live on John Peel show)** [ ] [-]
– Catatonic / Ripe / Primus / Spit to see the shine / Pearl / Dogg / Laugh my head off / Mad pilot.

Southern | Warners

Aug 92. (cd/c/red-lp) *(18501-2/-4/-1) <2-/4-26998>* **FONTANELLE** [24] [ ]
– Bruise violet / Right now / Blue bell / Handsome & Gretel / Blood / Magick flute / Won't tell / The quiet room / Spun / Short song / Jungle train / Pearl / Real eyes / Mother / Gone.

Nov 92. (7"purple) *(18503-7)* **BRUISE VIOLET. / GONE** [ ] [ ]
(12"+=/cd-s+=) *(18503-6/-2)* – Magick flute.

Jun 93. (cd/c/lp) *(18512-2/-4/-1) <45339>* **PAINKILLERS (part live)** [53] [ ]
– He's my thing / Laredo / Istigkeit / Ragweed / Angel hair / Fontanellette (live at CBGB's): Bruise violet – Bluebell – Angel hair – Pearl – Blood – Magick flute – Won't tell – Real eyes – Spun – Mother – Handsome & Gretel.

— KAT married STUART GRAY and sidelined with bands, CRUNT and KATSTU

CRUNT

— **KAT BJELLAND / STUART GRAY** (of LUBRICATED GOAT) + **RUSSELL SIMINIS** (of JON SPENCER BLUES EXPLOSION)

Insipid | Insipid

1993. (7") *(IV-31)* **SWINE. / SEXY** [ ] [ ]

Trance Syndicate | Trance Syndicate

Mar 94. (lp,blue-lp/cd) *<(TR 19/+CD)>* **CRUNT** [ ] [ ] Feb94
– Theme from Crunt / Swine / Black heart / Unglued / Changing my mind / Snap out of it / Sexy / Punishment / Spam / Elephant.

BABES IN TOYLAND

— re-formed (see last line-up)

Reprise | Reprise

Apr 95. (cd/c/lp) *<(9362 45868-2/-4/-1)>* **NEMESISTERS** [ ] [ ]
– Hello / Oh yeah! / Drivin' / Sweet '69 / Surd / 22 / Ariel / Kiler on the road / Middle man / Memory / S.F.W. / All by myself / Deep song / We are family.

May 95. (12"ep/c-ep/cd-ep) *(W 0291 TEX/C/CD)* **SWEET '69 / S.F.W. (live) / SWAMP PUSSY (live)** [ ] [ ]

Sep 95. (c-s/cd-s) *(W 0313 C/CD)* **WE ARE FAMILY (Arthur Baker remix) / ('A'-Ben Grosse remix)** [ ] [ ]
(12"+=) *(W 0313T)* – (2 other Baker & Grosse mixes).

— In 1998, KAT's alternative/metal supergroup rock opera, Songs Of The Witchblade: A Soundtrack To The Comic Books', was released on cd (Dreamworks; DRMD 50102) featuring her alongside PETER STEELE (Type O Negative), BUZZ OSBORNE (Melvins), JIM THIRLWELL (Foetus), among others.

BABYBIRD

Formed: Sheffield, England ... 1988 by Telford born singer STEPHEN JONES. He had been a prolific writer in his bedroom, composing over 400 songs, some of which appeared on five well-received albums between mid-'95 and mid-'96. Each album came with a voting section on which the buyer was asked to write in with their "best of" lists. The top 12 appeared on BABYBIRD's "GREATEST HITS" later in '96, JONES finally coming to prominence that summer as he signed to 'Echo', roped in a full band (JOHN PEDDER, ROBERT GREGORY, LUKE SCOTT and HUW CHADBOURN) and had his first bonafide Top 30 hit with the 'GOODNIGHT' single. BABYBIRD only really took flight with 'YOU'RE GORGEOUS', however, a massive Top 3 hit and a masterstroke of pop genius which managed to weld JONES' wonderfully subversive lyrics to a twinkling, soaring melody and chorus. A simultaneous album, 'UGLY BEAUTIFUL' (1996) made the Top 10, although critics who'd praised his more endearing amateurish early recordings were unsure about this leap into semi-accessible chartbound territory. Nevertheless, a growing army of fans who'd never even heard the other albums (mainly because they were so rare it was impossible to get hold of them!) put a third single, 'CANDY GIRL' into the Top 10. A series of much talked about live appearances emphasized JONES performance-arty background, the singer drawing comparisons with PULP's JARVIS COCKER. Of late, STEPHEN and Co have been back in the public eye, 1998 seeing them hovering around the fringes of the UK Top 30 with a couple of singles and an album, 'THERE'S SOMETHING GOING ON'.

Album rating: I WAS BORN A MAN (*8) / BAD SHAVE (*7) / FATHERHOOD (*6) / THE HAPPIEST MAN ALIVE (*8) / UGLY BEAUTIFUL (*6) / THERE'S SOMETHING GOING ON (*7)

STEPHEN JONES (b.16 Sep'62) – vocals, guitar – with band; **LUKE SCOTT** (b.25 Aug'69) – guitar / HUW CHADBOURN (b. 7 Dec'63) – keyboards / **JOHN PEDDER** (b.29 May'62) – bass / **ROBERT GREGORY** (b. 2 Jan'67) – drums

Baby Bird | not iss.

Jul 95. (cd) *(BABYBIRD 001)* **I WAS BORN A MAN** [ ] [-]
– Blow it to the Moon / Man's tight vest / Lemonade baby / C.F.C. / Cornershop / Kiss your country / Hong Kong blues / Dead bird sings / Baby bird / Farmer / Invisible tune / Alison / Love love love.

Oct 95. (cd/d-lp) *(BABYBIRD CD/LP 002)* **BAD SHAVE** [ ] [-]
– KW Jesus TV roof appeal / Bad jazz / Too handsome to be homeless / Steam train / Bad shave / Oh my God, you're a king / The restaurant is guilty / Valerie / Shop girl / W.B.T. / Hate song / 45 & fat / Sha na na / Bug in a breeze / It's okay / Happy bus / Swinging from tree to tree.

Dec 95. (cd/d-lp) *(BABYBIRD CD/LP 003)* **FATHERHOOD** [ ] [-]
– No children / Cooling towers / Cool and crazy things to do / Bad blood / Neil Armstrong / I was never here / Saturday / Goodnight / I don't want to wake up with you / Iceberg / Aluminium beach / Goddamn it, you're a kid / Daisies / Failed old singer / Fatherhood / Dustbin liner / Not about a girl / Good weather / But love / May me.

Apr 96. (cd/lp) *(BABYBIRD CD/LP 004)* **THE HAPPIEST MAN ALIVE** [ ] [-]
– Razorblade shower / Sundial in a tunnel / Little white man / Halfway up the hill / Horsesugar / Please don't be famous / Louse / Copper feel / Seagullably / Dead in love / Candy girl / Gunfingers / Married / In the country / Planecrash Xmas / This beautiful disease / You'll get a slap / In the morning.

Echo | Atlantic

Jul 96. (7") *(ECS 024)* **GOODNIGHT. / JULY** [28] [ ]
(cd-s+=) *(ECSCD 024)* – Harry and Ida swop teeth.
(cd-s) *(ECSCX 024)* – ('A'side) / Shellfish / Girl with money.

Oct 96. (c-s) *(ECSMC 026)* **YOU'RE GORGEOUS / BEBE LIMONADE** [3] [ ]
(cd-s+=) *(ECSCX 026)* – Ooh yeah / Car crash.
(cd-s) *(ECSCD 026)* – ('A'side) / You're gorgeous too / Honk Kong blues / KW Jesus TV roof appeal.

Oct 96. (cd/c/d-lp) *(ECH CD/MC/LP 011) <83049>* **UGLY BEAUTIFUL** [9] [ ] 1997
– Goodnight / Candy girl / Jesus is my girlfriend / I didn't want to wake you up / Dead bird sings / Atomic soda / You're gorgeous / Bad shave 2 / Cornershop / King Bing / You & me / 45 & fat / Too handsome to be homeless / July / Baby bird.

Jan 97. (c-s) *(ECSMC 031)* **CANDY GIRL / FARMER** [14] [ ]
(cd-s+=) *(ECSCD 031)* – You're gorgeous (BBC session) / Oh what a beautiful day.
(cd-s) *(ECSCX 031)* – ('A'side) / Bad shave (BBC session) / Cooling towers (BBC session) / Amtrack.
Apr 97. (ltd-7"pic-d) *(ECSPD 033)* **CORNERSHOP. / ALUMINIUM** [ ] [-]
May 97. (c-s) *(ECSMC 033)* **CORNERSHOP / HAPPIEST MAN ALIVE** [37] [ ]
(cd-s) *(ECSCD 033)* – ('A'side) / Death of the neighbourhood II / Shop girl / You're gorgeous (original demo – 1991).
(cd-s) *(ECSCX 033)* – ('A'side) / Death of the neighbourhood I / Pretty little graves / Cornershop (original demo – 1987).

— now without HUW who left left early in '98

Echo / Imprint

Apr 98. (7"pic-d) *(ECS 060)* **BAD OLD MAN. /** [31] [ ]
(cd-s+=) *(ECSCD 060)* –
(cd-s) *(ECSCX 060)* –
Aug 98. (7"pic-d) *(ECS 065)* **IF YOU'LL BE MINE. / POOLSIDE** [28] [ ]
(c-s+=/cd-s+=) *(ECS MC/CD 065)* – Worn.
(cd-s) *(ECSCX 065)* – ('A'side) / Memorise / I want nothing.
Aug 98. (cd/c/lp) *(ECH CD/MC/LP 024)* *<111059>* **THERE'S SOMETHING GOING ON** [28] [ ]
– Bad old man / If you'll be mine / Back together / I was never here / First man on the sun / You will always love me / The life / All men are evil / Take me back / It's not funny anymore / There's something going on.

– compilations, etc. –

Aug 97. (cd) *Baby Bird; <60804>* **GREATEST HITS** [-] [ ]
– Goddamn it, you're a kid / Man's tight vest / KW Jesus TV roof appeal / Bad blood / Kiss your country / Hong Kong blues / Razor blade shower / Sha na na / Aluminium beach / Alison / Grandma begs to be 18 again / I was never here / Petrol cigarette / Losing my hair / Saturday / Invisible tune / Failed old singer / Swinging from tree to tree / Anot about a girl / In the morning.

BABY CHAOS

Formed: Stewarton, Strathclyde, Scotland . . . 1992 by school-mates, CHRIS GORDON, GRANT McFARLANE, BOBBY DUNN and DAVEY GREENWOOD. Discovered by former HAPPY MONDAYS manager turned A&R man, Nathan McGough, after an appearance on BBC2's 'Late Show', BABY CHAOS were promptly signed to 'East West' and initiated a series of singles starting with late 1993's 'SPERM'. 'BUZZ', 'GOLDEN TOOTH' and 'HELLO VICTIM' followed over the course of '94, a year which saw them play at the inaugural 'T In The Park' festival in Scotland and culminated in the release of their debut album, 'SAFE SEX, DESIGNER DRUGS & THE DEATH OF ROCK'N'ROLL'. Described as Britain's answer to post-Seattle grunge rock with similarities to The WILDHEARTS and The MANICS, BABY CHAOS nevertheless had trouble with their musical identity; while the likes of Kerrang! tried to claim them for their own they were always more "Wean's Wild" than "Wayne's World". The band returned in the Spring of '96 with a follow-up, 'LOVE YOUR SELF ABUSE', hardly a departure from the debut but worthy of attention nonetheless.

Album rating: SAFE SEX, DESIGNER DRUGS & THE DEATH OF ROCK'N'ROLL (*6) / LOVE YOUR SELF ABUSE (*6)

CHRIS GORDON – vocals, guitar / **GRANT McFARLANE** – guitar / **BOBBY DUNN** – bass / **DAVEY GREENWOOD** – drums

East West / Atlantic

Nov 93. (10"ep/cd-ep) *(YZ 792 TE/CD)* **SPERM. / SUPERPOWERED / TONGUE** [ ] [ ]
Feb 94. (7"/c-s) *(YZ 800/+C)* **BUZZ. / ETHER** [ ] [ ]
(12"+=/cd-s+=) *(YZ 800 T/CD)* – Coming clean.
May 94. (7"ep/12"ep/cd-ep) *(YZ 822/+T/CD)* **GOLDEN TOOTH E.P.** [ ] [ ]
– Golden tooth / Resurrected / No way / The Earth is dying, but never mind.
Oct 94. (7"/c-s) *(YZ 852/+C)* **HELLO VICTIM. / ROTTEN TO THE CORE** [ ] [ ]
(12"+=/cd-s+=) *(YZ 852 T/CD)* – Skinny.
Nov 94. (cd/lp) *(<4509 98052-2/-1>)* **SAFE SEX, DESIGNER DRUGS AND THE DEATH OF ROCK'N'ROLL** [ ] [ ]

— (on tour only) **SIMON 'GEN' MATTHEWS** – drums (of JESUS JONES) repl. GREENWOOD due to nervous exhaustion

Apr 96. (7"/c-s) *(EW 036/+C)* **HELLO. /** [ ] [ ]
(cd-s+=) *(EW 036CD)* –
Apr 96. (cd/c) *(<0630 14610-2/-4>)* **LOVE YOUR SELF ABUSE** [ ] [ ]
– Hello / She's in pain / Mental bruising for beginners / Ignoramus / Sensual art of suffocation / Confessions of a teenage pervert / Penny dropped / Pink / Love your self abuse.
Jun 96. (7"/c-s) *(EW 045/+C)* **IGNORAMUS. / FETCH** [ ] [ ]
(cd-s+=) *(EW 045CD)* – I don't want your friend.

— now without GREENWOOD who had a heart problem (possibly end of band)

BABYLON DANCE BAND (see under ⇒ ANTIETAM)

Eric BACHMAN (see under ⇒ ARCHERS OF LOAF)

BACK TO THE PLANET

Formed: In a ex-dole office squat(!) . . . Peckham, London, England . . . 1989 by FIL (the girl) WALTERS and four self-confessed unwashed and proud-of-it male musicians!; FRAGGLE, GUY McAFFER, CARL HENDRICKSE and HENRY CULLEN. Spaced-out, skanking mainstays of the thriving crusty scene, the group built up a grass roots following through extensive festival touring and gigs in the capital. Following a series of self-financed tapes and a one-off single, 'REVOLUTION OF THOUGHT', the group were picked up by 'London' records subsidiary, 'Parallel'. The 'TEENAGE TURTLES' single followed amid general acclaim and an NME Single Of The Week award, the group's engaging mash-up of pop, metal, phat beats and wigged-out dub seeing them bracketed alongside fellow agitators like SENSER and DUB WAR. A further couple of fine singles, 'PLEASE DON'T FIGHT' and 'DAYDREAM', surprisingly failed to dent the charts and despite a Top 40 placing for debut album, 'MIND AND SOUL COLLABORATORS' later that year, the collective soon found themselves out in the commercial cold. No doubt more comfortable with the DIY ethos of the scene which spawned them, BACK TO THE PLANET resumed their rounds of the festival circuit, finding time to release a follow-up set, 'MESSAGES AFTER THE BLEEP' (1995), on their own 'Arthur Mix' label.

Album rating: MIND AND SOUL COLLABORATORS (*7) / MESSAGES AFTER THE BLEEP (*6)

FIL 'the girl' WALTERS (b.31 Jan'70, Dartford, Kent, England) – vocals / **FRAGGLE** (b. DAVID FLETCHER, 5 Aug'68, Kent) – guitar / **GUY McAFFER** (b.27 May'69) – keyboards / **CARL HENDRICKSE** (b.28 Jan'70, London) – bass / **HENRY CULLEN** (b.10 Oct'69, Lewisham, London) – drums

Arthur Mix / not iss.

1991. (c) *(BTTP 1)* **WARNING THE PUBLIC** [-] [-] mail-o
– Teenage turtles / London City / You're the judge / Starved by ignorance / Misunderstood / Human error / Daydream.
Feb 92. (12") *(12BTTP 2)* **THE REVOLUTION OF THOUGHT. /** [ ] [-]
Aug 92. (c) *(BTTP 3)* **EARZONE FRIENDLY** [-] [-] mail-o
Aug 92. (c) *(BTTP 4)* **LIVE VOL.1 (live)** [-] [-] mail-o

Parallel / not iss.

Apr 93. (c-s) *(LLLCS 3)* **TEENAGE TURTLES / REPRISE** [ ] [-]
(12"+=/cd-s+=) *(LLL X/CD 3)* – ('A'extended).
Jun 93. (c-s/12"/cd-s) *(LLL CS/X/CD 6)* **PLEASE DON'T FIGHT. / MANWOMAN 2000 / ('A'mix)** [ ] [-]
Aug 93. (7"/c-s) *(LLL/+CS 8)* **DAYDREAM. / (2-'A'mixes)** [ ] [-]
(12"/cd-s) *(LLL X/CD 8)* – ('A'side) / Breakin' roots / Takin' time / ('A'mix).

London / not iss.

Sep 93. (cd/c/lp) *(828437-2/-4/-1)* **MIND AND SOUL COLLABORATORS** [32] [ ]
– Please don't fight / Crossed lines / Daydream / Mother / Misunderstood / Starved by ignorance / London City / Teenage turtles / Hard edge few / Sleepless nights.

— dropped by 'London' records for no apparent reason?!

Arthur Mix / not iss.

Mar 95. (12"ep/cd-ep) *(BTTP 006 V/CD)* **A SMALL NUCLEAR DEVICE** [ ] [-]
– Flexing muscle / Immanent deities / Meditational thoughts / Colour sex.
Mar 95. (cd/c/lp) *(BTTP 007 CD/C/V)* **MESSAGES AFTER THE BLEEP!** [ ] [-]
– Tidal motion / Electro rays / Flexing muscles / Immanent deities / Elemental bliss / Never let them / Meditational thoughts / Colour sex / Criminal / Super powers / Under your skin.

— seemed to have ceased from recording duties.

– compilations, etc. –

Jan 95. (c) *Arthur Mix; (BTTP 5)* **A POTTED HISTORY** [-] [-] mail-o
– (1992 cassette tracks +) / The revolution of thought / Go go lemmings / Thoughts in a day / Let our roots breathe / Rub in the cream / Sunshine / Betty Boop / The revolution of thought (dub).

BACKWATER

Formed: Belfast, Northern Ireland . . . 1990 by schoolmates, BARRY PEAK and BOYD LOWE, who gigged sporadically with a conveyer belt of rhythm musicians. Around the mid-90's the line-up finally cemented around RYAN McAULEY and RICHARD BASSETT, the band enjoying inclusion on three various artists EP collections for 'Noisebox' before sharing a single, 'DIDACTIC NO' with fellow indie cohorts, BEAR. Now part of the growing 'Che' indie stable, BACKWATER emerged from relative obscurity early in '96 with their "own" single, 'SUPERCOOL'. The band kept up a heavy touring and recording schedule throughout the year, a debut set, 'ANGELS ARE COOL', finally seeing the light of day towards the end of the year; differentiating between the writing styles of PEAK and LOWE, the album veered from the former's drifting muse to the latter's manic freakouts. However, the loss of BASSETT and subsequently LOWE inevitably slowed down their progress, the releases reduced to a trickle of low-key 7"ers.

Album rating: ANGELS ARE COOL (*6)

BARRY PEAK (b. 7 Jun'74) – vocals, guitar / **BOYD LOWE** (b.1974) – guitar, vocals / **RYAN McAULEY** (b. 4 Oct'72) – bass / **RICHARD BASSETT** – drums

— Jun94-Mar95, they appeared on three various artists cd-ep's (VOL.2, 3 & 4) on 'Noisebox'; *NBX 004 / 006 / 009)*

X-Ten / not iss.

Nov 95. (7") *(X10 03)* **DIDACTIC NO. / (other track by BEAR)** [ ] [-]

Che / Che

Jan 96. (7") *(che 48)* **SUPERCOOL. /** [ ] [-]
Apr 96. (7") *(che 50)* **SHADY. / WORLD FLY PAST** [ ] [-]
(cd-s) *(che 50cd)* – ('A'side) / Single and celibate / My mouth's the Devil / Real happy if it wasn't so damn sad.
Sep 96. (7") *(che 56)* **MEMORY. /** [ ] [-]
(cd-s+=) *(che 56cd)* –
Oct 96. (cd/lp) *(che 57 cd/lp)* **ANGELS ARE COOL** [ ] [-]

— **SEAN ROBINSON** (b. 8 Apr'74) – drums; repl. BASSETT

— now without LOWE who retired to his hobbie

Jan 97. (cd) <62025> **PURE SONIC RAIN** [-] [ ]
Feb 97. (7"tour freebie) *(che 64)* **THINGS LOOK BETTER . . .** [-] [-]
1997. (7") **IN THESE LAST DAYS. /** [ ] [-]
(above issued on 'Gorgonzola', below on 'Fantastic Plastic')
May 98. (cd-ep) *(FP 009)* **EARTHLY FACES IN ALIEN PLACES** [ ] [-]

BAD BRAINS

Formed: Washington DC, USA . . . 1978 by Afro-Americans, H.R., his brother EARL, DR. KNOW and DARRYL JENNIFER. Prior to the advent of the punk rock movement in 1976/77, they had all played together in a jazz fusion outfit, carrying over the jazz dynamic to their frenetic, dub-wise hardcore. Subsequently relocating to New York, the late 70's saw the release of two classic 45's, 'PAY TO CUM' and 'BIG TAKEOVER'. These virtually went unnoticed, the band's UK profile remaining low after being refused work permits to support The DAMNED on a British tour. In 1983, they finally delivered their debut album, 'ROCK FOR LIGHT' (produced by RIC OCASEK of The CARS), a set that featured one side of hardcore and the other reggae. For three years, H.R. went solo, returning to the fold for 1986's 'I AGAINST I', a more metallic affair which anticipated the funk-rock explosion of the late 80's. H.R. (with EARL) subsequently departed to realise his more reggae orientated ambitions, releasing several albums for 'S.S.T.'. The remainder of BAD BRAINS parted company with this label, eventually reactivating the band for touring purposes with the addition of CHUCK MOSELEY (ex-FAITH NO MORE). H.R. and EARL returned to the fold for the 'QUICKNESS' album in 1989, remaining for the live set, 'THE YOUTH ARE GETTING RESTLESS'. Once again, H.R. and EARL decided to take off, their replacements being ISRAEL JOSEPH-I and the returning MACKIE. This line-up was in place for their major label debut for 'Epic', 'RISE' (1993), although incredibly yet again H.R. and EARL were invited back as BAD BRAINS were offered a place on MADONNA's 'Maverick' label. The resulting 1995 album, 'GOD OF LOVE' (again produced by OCASEK) focused more on dub reggae stylings, proving that the band were as open to experimentation as ever. However, during the accompanying tour, the athletic H.R. left the band for good in controversial circumstances, fighting with his fellow musicians and eventually being pulled up on a drugs charge (BAD BRAINS right enough!). • **Songwriters:** H.R. / DR. KNOW / group, except DAY TRIPPER (Beatles) / SHE'S A RAINBOW (Rolling Stones).

Album rating: BAD BRAINS (*7) / ROCK FOR LIGHT (*8) / I AGAINST I (*8) / LIVE (*5) / QUICKNESS (*4) / RISE (*4) / GOD OF LOVE (*6)

H.R. (b. PAUL HUDSON, 11 Feb'56, London, England) – vocals / **DR. KNOW** (b. GARY WAYNE MILLER, 15 Sep'58, Washington) – guitar, keyboards / **DARRYL AARON JENIFER** (b.22 Oct'60, Washington) – bass, vocals / **EARL HUDSON** (b.17 Dec'57, Alabama) – drums, percussion

not iss. / Bad Brains
Jun 80. (7") <BB 001> **PAY TO CUM. / STAY CLOSE TO ME** [-] [ ]

Alternative Tentacles / Alternative Tentacles
Jun 82. (12"ep) *(VIRUS 13)* **THE BAD BRAINS EP** [ ] [ ]
– I luv jah / Sailin' on / Big takeover.

R.O.I.R. / R.O.I.R.
Dec 82. (c) *(A 106)* **BAD BRAINS** [ ] [ ]
– Sailin' on / Don't need it / Attitude / The regulator / Banned in D.C. / Jah calling / Supertouch / FVK / Big take over / Pay to cum / Right brigade / I love I jah / Intro / Leaving Babylon. *(cd-iss. Dec89 as 'ATTITUDE – THE ROIR SESSIONS' on 'We Bite' lp/cd; WB 056/+CD) <US re-iss. Nov89 on 'In-Effect'> (re-iss. cd/c/lp 1991 on 'Dutch East Wax'/ re-iss. lp Mar93) (re-iss. cd Apr96; RUDCD 8223) (lp re-iss. Jul98; RUSLP 8223R)*

Food For Thought / Important
Mar 83. (12"ep) *(YUMT 101)* **I AND I SURVIVE / DESTROY BADYLON EP** [ ] [ ]

Abstract / P.V.C.
Mar 83. (lp) *(ABT 007)* <PVC 8933> **ROCK FOR LIGHT** [ ] [ ]
– Coptic times / Attitude / We will not / Sailin' on / Rally around jah throne / Right brigade / F.V.K. (Fearless Vampire Killers) / Riot squad / The meek shall inherit the Earth / Joshua's song / Banned in D.C. / How low can a punk get / Big takeover / I and I survive / Destroy Babylon / Rock for light / At the movies. *(re-mixed re-iss. Feb91 on 'Caroline' cd/c/lp; CAR CD/MC/LP 4) (re-iss. cd Sep91; same) (cd re-iss. Jun97; CAROLCD 1375)*

S.S.T. / S.S.T.
Feb 87. (lp/c) <(SST 065/+C)> **I AGAINST I** [ ] [ ] Nov86
– Intro / I against I / House of suffering / Re-ignition / Secret '77 / Let me help / She's calling you / Sacred love / Hired gun / Return to Heaven. *(cd-iss. Feb88 & May93; SST 065CD)*

— **CHUCK MOSELEY** – vocals (ex-FAITH NO MORE) repl. H.R.

— **MACKIE JAYSON** (b.27 May'63, New York City) – drums repl. EARL

Nov 88. (lp/c/cd) <(SST 160 LP/C/CD)> **LIVE (live)** [ ] [ ]
– I cried / At the movies / The regulator / Right brigade / I against I / I and I survive / House of suffering / Re-ignition / Sacred love / She's calling you / Coptic times / F.V.K. (Fearless Vampire Killers) / Secret 77 / Day tripper. *(re-iss. May93; same)*

— both **H.R. + EARL** returned

Caroline / Caroline
Jul 89. (lp/c/cd) <(CAR LP/C/CD 4)> **QUICKNESS** [ ] [ ]
– Soul craft / Voyage into infinity / The messengers / With the quickness / Gene machine – Don't bother me / Don't blow bubbles / Sheba / Yout' juice / No conditions / Silent tears / The prophet's eye / Endtro. *(re-iss. cd Sep91; same) (cd re-iss. Jun97; CAROLCD 1375)*

S.S.T. / S.S.T.
Oct 89. (10"m-lp/m-c/m-cd) <SST 228> **SPIRIT ELECTRICITY** [-] [ ]
– Return to Heaven / Let me help / Day tripper / She's a rainbow / Banned in D.C. / Attitude / Youth are getting restless.

— **ISRAEL JOSEPH-I** (b. DEXTER PINTO, 6 Feb'71, Trinidad) – vocals repl. H.R. / **MACKIE** returned EARL

Epic / Epic
Sep 93. (cd/c/lp) <(474265-2/-4/-1)> **RISE** [ ] [ ]
– Rise / Miss Freedom / Unidentified / Love is the answer / Free / Hair / Coming in numbers / Yes jah / Take your time / Peace of mind / Without you / Outro.

— **H.R. + EARL** returned to repl. JOSEPH-I + JAYSON

Maverick / Maverick
May 95. (cd/c) <(9362 45882-2/-4)> **GOD OF LOVE** [ ] [ ]
– Cool mountaineer / Justic keepers / Long time / Rights of a child / God of love / Over the water / Tongue tee tie / Darling I need you / To the heavens / Thank jah / Big fun / How I love thee.

– compilations, etc. –

May 90. (cd/lp) *Caroline; (CARCD/LP 8)* **THE YOUTH ARE GETTING RESTLESS (1987 live)** [ ] [ ]
– I / Rock for light / Right brigade / House of suffering / Day tripper – She's a rainbow / Coptic times / Sacred love / Re-ignition / Let me help / The youth are getting restless / Banned in D.C. / Sailin' on / Fearless vampire killer / At the movies / Revolution / Pay to cum / Big takeover. *(cd re-iss. Jun97; CAROLCD 1617)*
May 92. (d-cd) *Line; (LICD 921176)* **ROCK FOR LIGHT / I AGAINST I** [-] [-] German
Oct 96. (cd/lp) *Caroline; (PCAROL 005CD/LP)* **BLACK DOTS** (rec.1979) [ ] [ ]
– Don't need it / At the Atlantis / Pay to cum / Supertouch – Shitfit / Regulator / You're a migraine / Don't bother me / Banned in D.C. / Why'd you have to go / Man won't annoy ya / Redbone in the city / Black dots / How low can a punk get / Just another damn song / Attitude / Send you no flowers.
Nov 97. (10"ep/cd-ep) *Victory; (VR 064/+CD)* **THE OMEGA SESSIONS** [ ] [ ]
– I against you / Stay close to me / I love jah / At the movies / Attitude.

H.R.

— released some reggae-orientated material (some issued previously on 'Olive Tree' US-only)

S.S.T. / S.S.T.
Mar 88. (lp/c/cd) <(SST 117/+C/CD)> **HUMAN RIGHTS** [ ] [ ]
– My mama / Human rights / I luv King Jah / Now you say / Luv ain't crazy / No return / Don't break / Life after death / Conquering / Judah / Jah like like that / Viva Azania / Acting so bad.
Jun 88. (12") <SST 173> **NOW YOU SAY. /** [-] [ ]
Jun 88. (12") <(SST 177)> **KEEP OUT OF REACH. /** [ ] [ ]
(cd-s iss.Mar89; SSTCD 177)
Jun 88. (12") <(SST 179)> **IT'S ABOUT LUV. /** [ ] [ ]
Jul 88. (c/cd) <(SST 171 C/CD)> **THE H.R. TAPES** (rec.1984-86) [ ] [ ]
– Prelude / Roots / It'll be alright / We're gonna let you – Heaven forbid / Let's have a revolution / Who loves you girl / It's about luv / Happy birthday my son / Free our mind / Keep out of reach / Keep out of reach (dub version) / Power of the trinity.
Sep 89. (lp/c/cd) <(SST 224/+C/CD)> **SINGIN' IN THE HEART** [ ] [ ]
– Fool's gold / Youthman sufferer / Rasta time / Fool's gold (dub) / Singin' in my heart / Don't trust (no shadows after dark) / Treat street / Youthman sufferer (dub).
Apr 90. (lp/c/cd) <(SST 256/+C/CD)> **CHARGE** [ ] [ ]
– Rasta / Just because I'm poor / Dancing souls / Selassie fee / Let luv lead the way / Shame in dem game / While you were sleeping / Charge / Saddest day / It's reggae.
May 93. (lp/c/cd) <(SST 274/+C/CD)> **ROCK OF ENOCH** [ ] [ ]
Aug 98. (cd) *(SST 361CD)* **ANTHOLOGY** (compilation) [ ] [ ]

BADLY DRAWN BOY

Formed: 1997, as a one-man vehicle for the highly charged but eccentric DAMON GOUGH. The Bolton-born (or at least in a village outside it) first initiated his weird brand of gnome-ish psychedelia when he self-financed an EP on his own 'Twisted Nerve' label. 'EP1', in 1997, was quickly pursued by the following year's 'EP2', a contract with 'XL Recordings' (home of The PRODIGY) just around the corner. In the Autumn of '98, his third set, the imaginatively titled 'EP3' hit the shops, this BECK-esque trio of tracks finally making the more diserning music punter sit up and listen. Prior to this, GOUGH had contributed the track, 'Nursery Rhyme', to the acclaimed UNKLE album, 'Psyence Fiction'.

Album rating: the EP3's

DAMON GOUGH – instruments & things

Twisted Nerve / not iss.
1997. (cd-ep) **EP1** [ ] [-]
1998. (cd-ep) **EP2** [ ] [-]

X.L. / not iss.
Oct 98. (cd-ep) **EP3** [ ] [-]
– My friend Cubilas / Kerplunk by candlelight / I need a sign.

— (all his records are very limited affairs)

Henry BADOWSKI

Born: London, England. Having played for a variety of "Conference League" punk outfits in '77, the following year saw BADOWSKI sign for "1st Division/Premier League" punk contenders, CHELSEA. Switching from bass to drums (an unusual occurence during these DIY times!), the man served time with singer, WRECKLESS ERIC before taking up keyboards and vocal duties for KING (no relation to PAUL's 80's outfit!). A one-off project exploring the unlikely link between punk and psychedelia, the band also featured KIM BRADSHAW, DAVE BERK (from JOHNNY MOPED) and CAPTAIN SENSIBLE, the latter soon inviting HENRY to play bass with the new short-lived incarnation of the DAMNED; The DOOMED.

The following year BADOWSKI hooked up with another influential punk, MARK PERRY (ex-ALTERNATIVE TV), requesting his drumming talents in The GOOD MISSIONARIES while he procured some solo studio time and recorded a debut single, 'MAKING LOVE WITH MY WIFE', for 'Deptford Fun City'. Inspired by late 60's idol, SYD BARRETT, the single included BERK, ALEKSANDER KOLKOWSKI (another JOHNNY MOPED sidekick) and CHELSEA's JAMES STEPHENSON. The multi-instrumentalist almost immediately signed to 'A&M' (SQUEEZE had made a similar move a few years previous!), a series of solo flops being succeeded by a full-blown long-player, 'LIFE IS A GRAND' (1981). However, despite some favourable press reaction, HENRY disappeared from view for the rest of the 80's (and the 90's!) . . .. where are you now?

Album rating: LIFE IS A GRAND (*6)

HENRY BADOWSKI – vocals, saxophone, bass, keyboards, percussion / with **JAMES STEPHENSON** – guitar, bass (of CHELSEA) / **ALEKSANDER KOLKOWSKI** – violin (of JOHNNY MOPED) **DAVE BERK** – drums (of JOHNNY MOPED)

Deptford Fun City | not iss.

Jul 79. (7") *(DFC 11)* **MAKING LOVE WITH MY WIFE. / BABY, SIGN HERE WITH ME** [ ] [-]

A&M | not iss.

Sep 79. (7") *(AMS 7478)* **BABY, SIGN HERE WITH ME. / MAKING LOVE WITH MY WIFE** [ ] [-]

Feb 80. (7") *(AMS 7503)* **MY FACE. / FOUR MORE SEASONS** [ ] [-]

— now without BERK

Jun 81. (7") *(AMS 8135)* **HENRY'S IN LOVE. / LAMB TO THE SLAUGHTER** [ ] [-]

Jul 81. (lp) *(AMLH 68527)* **LIFE IS A GRAND** [ ] [ ]
– My face / Henry's in love / Swimming with the fish in the sea / The inside out / Life is a grand / Silver trees / This was meant to be / Anywhere else / Baby, sign here with me / Rampant.

— HENRY retired from the music scene

BAD RELIGION

Formed: Los Angeles, California, USA . . . 1980 by teenagers, GREG GRAFFIN, BRETT GUREWITZ, JAY BENTLEY and JAY LISHROUT. To combat disinterest from major labels, the group initiated their own label, 'Epitaph', which has since become a proverbial pillar of the US hardcore/punk fraternity (i.e. OFFSPRING, etc). After one self-titled EP in '81, they unleashed their cheerily-titled debut, 'HOW COULD HELL BE ANY WORSE'. After they withdrew their next album, 'INTO THE UNKNOWN' from sale, BAD RELIGION disappeared for a long spell in the mid 80's. GRAFFIN returned with a new line-up in '87, numbering GREG HETSON, PETE FINESTONE and TIM GALLEGOS. An album, 'SUFFER' was a triumphant comeback effort, defining the new BAD RELIGION sound, a hybrid of melodic punk and machine-gun metal. In 1989, the band consolidated their newfound cult popularity with the follow-up, 'NO CONTROL', although their early 90's output suffered a slight decline. After 'Epitaph' experienced problems with distribution in '93, they signed to 'Columbia', with the result that they cracked the US Top 100 with their umpteenth album, 'STRANGER THAN FICTION'. Two years later, GUREWITZ having earlier bailed out, they released 'THE GRAY RACE' (produced by RIC OCASEK, ex-CARS), re-establishing them at the forefront of the burgeoning hardcore/metal scene.

Album rating: HOW COULD HELL BE ANY WORSE (*5) / INTO THE UNKNOWN (*7) / BACK TO THE KNOWN (*4) / SUFFER (*7) / NO CONTROL (*8) / AGAINST THE GRAIN (*7) / GENERATOR (*6) / RECIPE FOR HATE (*6) / STRANGER THAN FICTION (*7) / THE GRAY RACE (*6) / ALL AGES compilation (*8)

GREG GRAFFIN – vocals / **BRETT GUREWITZ** – guitar / **JAY BENTLEY** – bass / **JAY LISHROUT** – drums

Epitaph | Epitaph

Sep 81. (m-lp) <*EP1 BRLP 1*> **HOW COULD HELL BE ANY WORSE** [-] [ ]
– Bad religion / Along the way / New leaf / Bad religion / Slaves / Drastic actions.

— **PETE FINESTONE** – drums repl. LISHROUT

— **PAUL DEDONA** – bass + **DAVY GOLDMAN** – drums repl. JAY + PETE

Dec 83. (lp) **INTO THE UNKNOWN** [-] [ ]

— **GRAFFIN** the sole survivor recruited **GREG HETSON** – guitar / **TIM GALLEGOS** – bass / **PETE FINESTONE** – drums (returned) / GUREWITZ joined CIRCLE JERKS

1987. (7"ep) **BACK TO THE KNOWN** [-] [ ]

— **GUREWITZ + BENTLEY** rejoined to repl. GALLEGOS

1988. (lp) <*6404-1*> **SUFFER** [-] [ ]
– You are (the government) / 1000 more fools / How much is enough / When? / Give you nothing / Land of competition / Forbidden beat / Best for you / Suffer / Delirium of disorder / Part II (the numbers game) / What can you do? / Do what you want / Part IV (the index fossil) / Pessimistic lines. *(UK-iss.cd/lp Mar91 & Jun93; same)*

1989. (lp) <*6406-1*> **NO CONTROL** [-] [ ]
– Change of ideas / Big bang / No control / Sometimes it feels like *?%+! / Automatic man / I want to conquer the world / Sanity / Henchman / It must look pretty appealing / You / Progress / I want something more / Anxiety / Billy / The world won't stop without you. *(UK-iss.cd/lp Mar91 & Jun93; same)*

Jan 91. (cd/c/lp) <*(6409-2/-4/-1)*> **AGAINST THE GRAIN** [ ] [ ]
– Modern man / Turn on the light / Get off / Blenderhead / Positive aspect of negative thinking / Anesthesia / Flat Earth Society / Faith alone / Entropy / Against the grain / Operation rescue / God song / 21st century digital boy / Misery and famine / Unacceptable / Quality or quantity / Walk away.

Mar 92. (cd/c/lp) <*(6416-2/-4/-1)*> **GENERATOR** [ ] [ ]
– Generator / Too much to ask / No direction / Tomorrow / Two babies in the dark / Heaven is falling / Atomic garden / Answer / Fertile crescent / Chimaera / Only entertainment.

Jun 93. (cd/c/lp) <*(6420-2/-4/-1)*> **RECIPE FOR HATE** [ ] [ ]
– Recipe for hate / Kerosene / American Jesus / Portrait of authority / Man with a mission / All good soldiers / Watch it die / Struck a nerve / My poor friend me / Lookin' in / Don't pray on me / Modern day catastrophists / Skyscraper / Sheath.

— GUREWITZ retired to spend time with his record label 'Epitaph'.

— line-up:- **GRAFFIN / HETSON / BENTLEY / + BRIAN BAKER** – guitar (ex-MINOR THREAT, ex-DAG NASTY) / **BOBBY SCHAYER** – drums

Plastic Head | Plastic Head

1993. (7") *(MRR 006)* **NOAM. /** [ ] [ ]

Sympathy F | Sympathy F

Aug 94. (7") *(SFTRI 158)* **ATOMIC. /** [ ] [ ]

Aug 94. (7") *(SFTRI 232)* **AMERICAN JESUS. /** [ ] [ ]

Aug 94. (7") *(SFTRI 326)* **STRANGER THAN FICTION. /** [ ] [ ]

Columbia | Atlantic

Sep 94. (cd/c/lp) *(477343-2/-4/-1)* <*82658*> **STRANGER THAN FICTION** [ ] [87]
– Incomplete / Leave mine to me / Stranger than fiction / Tiny voices / The handshake / Better off dead / Infected / Television / Individual / Hooray for me / Slumber / Marked / Inner logic.

Jan 95. (10"pic-d-ep) *(661143-0)* **21st CENTURY (DIGITAL BOY) / AMERICAN JESUS (live). / NO CONTROL (live) / WE'RE ONLY GONNA DIE (live)** [41] [ ]
(c-ep/cd-ep) *(661143-8/-2)* – ('A'side) / Leaders and followers (live) / Mediocrity (live) / American Jesus (live).

Mar 96. (cd/c)(grey-lp) *(493524-2/-4)(483652-0)* **THE GRAY RACE** [ ] [ ]
– The gray race / Them and us / Walk / Parallel / Punk rock songs / Empty causes / Nobody listens / Pity the dead / Spirit shine / Streets of America / Ten in 2010 / Victory / Drunk sincerely come join us / Cease / Punk rock song (German version).

Jun 96. (7") *(6628677-7)* **PUNK ROCK SONG. / CEASE** [ ] [ ]
(cd-s+=) *(6628677-5)* – Leave mine to me (live) / Change of ideas (live).
(cd-s) *(6628677-2)* – ('A'-German version) / The universal cynic / The dodo.
(above was shelved when they decided to do some more German gigs)

Apr 97. (cd/lp) *(486986-2/-1)* <*82870-2/-1*> **TESTED (live)** [ ] [56]

May 98. (cd/c) *(489570-2/-4)* <*83094*> **NO SUBSTANCE** [ ] [78]
– Hear it / Shades of truth / All fantastic images / Biggest killer in American history / No substance / Raise your voice / Sowing the seeds of Utopia / Hippy killers / State of the end of the millenium / Vocacious march of godlines / Mediocre / Victims of the revolution / Strange denial / At the mercy of imbeciles / Same person / In so many ways.

– compilations, etc. –

Nov 91. (cd/c) *Epitaph;* <*(86407-2X/4X)*> **(1980-1985)** [ ] [ ]
– We're all gonna die / Latch key kids / Part III / Faith in God / F*** armageddon . . . this is Hell / Pitty / Into the night / Damned to be free / White trash (2nd generation) / American dream / Eat your dog / Voice of God is government / Oligarchy / Doing time / Politics / Sensory overload / Slaves / Drastic actions / World War III / Yesterday / Frogger. *(w/ free cd)* – HOW COULD HELL BE ANY WORSE

Nov 95. (cd/c/lp) *Epitaph;* <*(86443-2/-4/-1)*> **ALL AGES** (1988-1992 + 2 from '94) [ ] [ ]
– I want to conquer the world / Do what you want / You are (the government) / Modern man / We're only gonna die / Answer / Flat Earth society / Against the grain / Generator / Anesthesia / Suffer / Faith alone / No control / 21st century digital boy / Atomic garden / No direction / Automatic man / Change of ideas / Sanity / Walk away / Best for you / Fuck armageddon . . . this is Hell.

Chris BAILEY (see under ⇒ SAINTS)

BAILTER SPACE

Formed: New Zealand . . . mid-80's, although mainman HAMISH KILGOUR had initiated the trio much earlier as Kiwi-rock pioneers, The GORDONS. Many readers will also recognise KILGOUR as being one of the founding members of another legendary NZ act, The CLEAN, alongside his brother DAVID. BAILTER SPACE originally began as a side project during a lull in CLEAN activities, HAMISH teaming up ALISTER PARKER and JOHN HALVORSEN for what turned out to be an extended career, in NZ terms at least. Who else but that seminal Antipodean indie, 'Flying Nun', would release the first two domestic-only EP's, 1987's 'NELSH' and the following year's 'GRADER SPADER', both records well represented on the first European release, 'TANKER' (1988). Their first album proper, 'THERMOS' (1990), was the last to feature HAMISH, who erm, bailed out for a musical respite before concentrating on the re-formed CLEAN. His replacement, BRENT McLAUGHLIN making his inaugural appearance on 1992's comeback EP, 'THE AIM', also released in the US on 'Matador'. 1993's 'ROBOT WORLD' meanwhile, carried on the band's preoccupation with technology and alienation, although their driving fuzz-garage sound never strayed too far from rock's earthy roots. BAILTER SPACE continued their interstellar musical explorations into the mid-90's, reporting back to Earth with two further sets, 'VORTURU' (1994) and 'WAMMO' (1995). Of late, the trio have concentrated on singles/EP's, two releases surfacing on the 'Turnbuckle' imprint.

Album rating: TANKER (*6) / THERMOS (*6) / ROBOT WORLD (*7) / VORTURU (*6) / WAMMO (*6)

HAMISH KILGOUR – vocals, drums (of The CLEAN) / **ALISTER PARKER** – guitar, vocals / **JOHN HALVORSEN** – bass, vocals

Flying Nun | Matador

1987. (7"ep) **NELSH EP** [-] [-] New Z

1988. (7"ep) **GRADER SPADER EP** [-] [-] New Z

1988. (m-lp) *(FNE 31)* **TANKER** [ ] [-]
– Glass / The "W" song / Grader spader / Titan / Your invisible life / Valve / The today song / Tanker / One more reason. *(re-iss. Aug94 lp/cd; FN/+CD 107)* <*US cd-iss. 1995 on 'Matador'; OLE 136*>

1990. (cd) *(FNCD 142)* **THERMOS** [ ] [-]
(re-iss. Aug94; same) <*US cd-iss. 1995 on 'Matador'; OLE 135*>

— **BRENT McLAUGHLIN** – drums; repl. HAMISH who eventually returned to The CLEAN

Aug 92. (cd-ep) *(FNCD 232)* <*OLE 41*> **THE AIM** [ ] [ ]

— early in 1993, they issued a single for 'Clawfist' UK

Mar 93. (cd) *(FNCD 259)* <*OLE 50*> **ROBOT WORLD** [ ] [ ]
– Begin / Robot world / Morning / Be on time / Fascination / Ore / Get lost / EIP / Orbit / Make remain.

Mar 94. (cd-ep) *(FNCD 284)* <*OLE 72*> **B.E.I.P. E.P.** [ ] [ ] Jan94
– X / Projects / Robot world / EIP.

Apr 94. (lp/cd) *(FN/+CD 295)* <*OLE 93*> **VORTURU** [ ] [ ] May94
– Projects / Process paid / X / Voices / No.2 / I.C.Y. / Dark blue / Shadow / Galaxy / Reactor / Control.

Matador Matador

Jul 95. (7") *(OLE 147-7)* **SPLAT. / AT FIVE WE DRIVE** [ ] [-]
(cd-s+=) *(OLE 147-2)* – Fascination.

Jul 95. (cd/lp) *(<OLE 142-2/-1>)* **WAMMO** [ ] [ ]
– Untied / Splat / At five we drive / Zapped / Colours / Retro / Glimmer / Voltage / D thing / Wammo.

Turnbuckle Turnbuckle

Oct 97. (cd-ep) *(<TB 005CD>)* **THE CAPSUL / ARGONAUT** [ ] [ ]

Aug 98. (cd-ep) *(<TB 012>)* **PHOTON EP** [ ] [ ] May99

BALAAM AND THE ANGEL

Formed: Cannock, Staffordshire, England . . . 1984 by Scottish born brothers JIM, MARK and DES MORRIS. They were encouraged at an early age by their father, who initiated their career by obtaining some cabaret gigs at Motherwell working mens clubs. Along with manager CRAIG JENNINGS, they founded the 'Chapter 22' label and soon found themselves supporting the likes of The CULT. Late in 1985, after releasing three indie hits, they moved onto 'Virgin', their debut for the label, 'SHE KNOWS', breaking them into the Top 75 in March '86. Five months later, the album, 'THE GREATEST STORY EVER TOLD' trod the same post-punk goth path. Two more albums followed until they were dropped by 'Virgin', obviously fans opting for their contemporaries The CULT and SISTERS OF MERCY. They re-emerged in 1990 as the heavier BALAAM, although little happened commercially, MARK nearly joining The CULT that year as the replacement for JAMIE STEWART.

Album rating: THE GREATEST STORY EVER TOLD (*6) / LIVE FREE OR DIE (*7)

MARK MORRIS (b.15 Jan'63, Motherwell) – vocals, bass / **JIM MORRIS** (b.25 Nov'60, Motherwell) – guitar, keyboards, recorder / **DES MORRIS** (b.27 Jun'64, Motherwell) – drums, percussion

Chapter 22 not iss.

Nov 84. (12"ep) *(22-001)* **WORLD OF LIGHT / FOR MORE THAN A DAY. / THE DARKLANDS / A NEW DAWN** [ ] [-]

Mar 85. (12"ep) *(22-002)* **LOVE ME / THE THOUGHT BEHIND IT ALL. / FAMILY AND FRIENDS / 15th FLOOR** [ ] [-]

Sep 85. (7") *(CHAP 3-7)* **DAY AND NIGHT. / ISABELLA'S EYES** [ ] [-]
(12"+=) *(CHAP 3-73)* – Touch / Return again.

Virgin Virgin

Mar 86. (7") *(VS 842)* **SHE KNOWS. / DREAMS WIDE AWAKE** [70] [-]
(d7"+=) *(VSD 842)* – Sister moon / Warm again.
(12"+=) *(VS 842-12)* – 2 into 1 / The darklands.

Jun 86. (7") *(VS 864)* **SLOW DOWN. / WALK AWAY** [ ] [-]
(12"+=) *(VS 864-12)* – Travel on / In the morning.

Aug 86. (lp/c) *(V/TCV 2377)* **THE GREATEST STORY EVER TOLD** [67] [ ]
– New kind of love / Don't look down / She knows / Burn me down / Light of the world / Slow down / The wave / Warm again / Never end / Nothing there at all. *(cd-iss. Jul87+=; CDV 2377)* – Walk away / Day and night. *(re-iss. 1989 lp/c; OVED/+C 250)*

Aug 86. (7") *(VS 890)* **LIGHT OF THE WORLD. / DAY AND NIGHT (live)** [ ] [-]
(12"+–) *(VS 890-12)* – She knows / Love.

Jul 87. (7") *(VS 970)* **(I'LL SHOW YOU) SOMETHING SPECIAL. / I FEEL LOVE** [ ] [-]
(12"+=) *(VS 970-12)* – Let it happen / You took my soul.

Sep 87. (7") *(VS 993)* **I LOVE THE THINGS YOU DO TO ME. / YOU'RE IN THE WAY OF MY DREAMS** [ ] [-]
(12"+=) *(VS 993-12)* – Things you know / As tears go by.

— added **IAN McKEAN** – guitar (ex-20 FLIGHT ROCKERS)

Jul 88. (7") <*99340*< **I LOVE THE THINGS YOU DO TO ME. / WARM AGAIN** [-] [ ]

Jul 88. (lp/c/cd) *(V/TCV/CDV 2476)* <*90869*> **LIVE FREE OR DIE** [ ] [ ] Apr88
– (I'll show you) Something special / I love the things you do to me / Big city fun time girl / On the run / Would I die for you / Live free or die / It goes on / Long time loving you / I won't be afraid / Running out of time. *(c+=)* – I feel love. *(cd++=)* – You took my soul / Let it happen / You're in my way of dreams / As tears go by.

Aug 88. (7") *(VS 1124)* **LIVE FREE OR DIE. / EAGLE** [ ] [-]
(12"+=) *(VST 1124)* – Complete control / ('A'-Texas Redbeard mix).

Sep 89. (7") *(VS 1213)* **I TOOK A LITTLE. / LONG TIME LOVIN' YOU** [ ] [-]
(12"+=/12"pic-d+=) *(VST/VSP 1213)* – Big city fun time girl / Would I die for you.
(12"+=/cd-s+=) *(VSTX/VSCD 1213)* – (remixes).

Nov 89. (lp/c/cd) *(V/TCV/CDV 2598)* **DAYS OF MADNESS** [ ] [ ]
– Don't want your love / I took a little / She really gets to me / Body and soul / Heartbreaker / The tenderloin / Two days of madness / Did you fall (or were you pushed?) / Goodbye forever / I'm the only one / Stop messin' round.

Feb 90. (7") *(VS 1229)* **LITTLE BIT OF LOVE. / DID YOU FALL (OR WERE YOU PUSHED?)** [ ] [-]
(12"+=/cd-s+=) *(VST 1229)* – She really gets to me (acoustic).

— split in the autumn of 1990. Now without McKEAN

Intense not iss.

Oct 91. (m-lp/m-c/m-cd; as BALAAM) *(TENS 001/+MC/CD)* **NO MORE INNOCENCE** [ ] [-]
– Shame on you / Next to me / What love is / She's not you / Mr. Business / Just no good.

— next release took six from last and added five new ones

Bleeding Hearts not iss.

Apr 93. (cd) *(CDBLEED 1)* **PRIME TIME** [ ] [-]
– Shame on you / Prime time / Next to me / What love is / Gathering dust / Eagle / She's not you / Mr. Business / Like a train / Burning / Just no good. *(re-iss. Feb98 on 'Darkend'; DARK 003CD)*

– compilations, etc. –

Oct 86. (lp) *Chapter 22; (CHAPLP 4)* **SUN FAMILY** [ ] [-]

BALANCING ACT

Formed: Los Angeles, California, USA . . . 1984 by singer-songwriter JEFF DAVIS along with WILLIA ARON, STEVE WAGNER and ROBERT BLACKMON. Hardly typical for an 80's L.A. band, this lot attempted to balance the authenticity of traditional roots music with the spontaniety of rock's avant garde. After an obscure debut EP in '86, they laid down tracks with noted producer and former PLIMSOULS leader, PETER CASE, the results surfacing as 'NEW CAMPFIRE SONGS' on 'I.R.S.' subsidiary, 'Primitive Man'. Even featuring a cover of Captain Beefheart's 'ZIG ZAG WANDERER', the mini-set's quirky folk-rock sound was quite unlike anything else around at the time. Two further sets, 'THREE SQUARES AND A ROOF' (1987) and 'CURTAINS' (1988), developed their style without ever threatening the mainstream, the latter produced by ANDY GILL and featuring a cover of Funkadelic's 'CAN YOU GET TO THAT'.

Album rating: NEW CAMPFIRE SONGS (*7) / THREE SQUARES AND A ROOF (*8) / CURTAINS (*7)

JEFF DAVIS – vocals, guitar / **WILLIE ARON** – guitar / **STEVE WAGNER** – bass / **ROBERT BLACKMON** – drums

Illegal I.R.S.

1986. (m-lp/m-c) <*IRS/+C 39097*> **NEW CAMPFIRE SONGS** [-] [ ]
– Wonderful world tonight / Who got the pearls? / Zig zag wanderer / + 3. <*originally issued on 'Type A'*>

Jul 88. (lp/c/cd) *(ILP 023)* <*IRS/+C/D 42082*> **THREE SQUARES AND A ROOF** [ ] [ ] Nov87
– 3 cards / Kicking clouds across the sky / Whiskered wife / Adventure / Ballad of Art Snyder / Red umbrella / Governor of Pedro / Waiting for the mail / Searching for this thing / We're not lost. <*US cd+=*> – (tracks from 'NEW CAMPFIRE SONGS')

Nov 88. (lp/cd) <*IRS/+D 42237*> **CURTAINS** [-] [ ]
– Generator / She doesn't work here / Lost in the mail / Red pants and romance / Dangerous roof / Can you get to that / Understanding furniture / Sleep on the trusty floor / Fishing in your eye / Between two oceans / Learning how to cheat.

Jun 89. (7") *(EIRS 116)* **CAN YOU GET TO THAT. /** [ ] [ ]
(12"+=) *(EIRST 116)* –

— disbanded after above

B.A.L.L.

Formed: New York, USA . . . 1987 by MARK KRAMER, DAVID LICHT, DON FLEMING and JAY SPIEGEL. All had indie rock pedigrees, the former two ex-members of SHOCKABILLY (KRAMER also of BONGWATER and ex-BUTTHOLES), the latter both ex-HALF JAPANESE and VELVET MONKEYS. A twin-drum fuelled precursor to the late 80's grunge explosion, B.A.L.L.'s debut album, 'PERIOD' (ANOTHER AMERICAN LIE)', surfaced on KRAMER's own 'Shimmy Disc' label towards the end of that year. Next up was the following years' 'BIRD' album which parodied the sleeve design of The Beatles' "butcher-cover". The fab-four piss-take continued inside with a mock pastiche of George Harrison's 'CONCERT FOR BANGLA DESH', segueing Ringo Starr's 'IT DON'T COME EASY', Harrison's 'WAH WAH' and T.Rex's 'BUICK MACKANE'. Two further slices of slap-dash irreverence surfaced at the turn of the decade, 'TROUBLE DOLL' (1989) and 'BALL 4 – HARDBALL' (1990), before the culprits chose to take on other projects; KRAMER and LICHT carried on with BONGWATER. FLEMING and SPIEGEL, meanwhile, reunited in The VELVET MONKEYS (their album, 'RAKE' was released by 'Rough Trade' in 1990), at the same time joining DINOSAUR JR for a year before forming GUMBALL. This lot made a series of recordings for UK indie imprints 'Paperhouse' and 'Big Cat' (mainly the albums 'SPECIAL KISS' and 'SUPER TASTY'), before finally going corporate and signing a major deal with 'Columbia' in 1994 who issued third set, 'REVOLUTION ON ICE'. • **Covers:** Gumball: ALL I WANT (Troggs) / WHY DON'T WE DO IT IN THE ROAD (Beatles) / BACK OFF BOOGALOO (Ringo Starr). FLEMING + TOM SMITH; DIZZY (Tommy Roe). • **Trivia:** FLEMING took to production work for TEENAGE FANCLUB ('Bandwagonesque') and FREE KITTEN (the brainchild of KIM GORDON and JULIE CAFRITZ). Another SONIC YOUTH (90's) offshoot, DIM STARS, featured FLEMING alongside THURSTON MOORE, STEVE SHELLEY and Void-Oid legend, RICHARD HELL.

Album rating: BIRD (*7) / BALL 4 – HARDBALL (*6)

DON FLEMING – vocals, lead guitar (ex-HALF JAPANESE, ex-VELVET MONKEYS) / **JAY SPIEGEL** – drums (ex-HALF JAPANESE, ex-VELVET MONKEYS) /

MARK KRAMER – bass, vocals, production (of-BONGWATER, ex-SHOCKABILLY, ex-BUTTHOLE SURFERS) / **DAVID LICHT** – drums (of-BONGWATER, ex-SHOCKABILLY)

Shadowline Shimmy Disc

Feb 88. (lp) *(SR 0388) <SHIMMY 006>* **PERIOD** Nov87
– All I sought is progress / Ballad of Little Richard / King will never die / Favourite day / My TV is broke / Black spring / No song / Skull and cross / Treasure island / St. Vitus dance / In the woods / Theme B.A.L.L.

Jan 89. (lp) *(SD 8803) <SHIMMY 014>* **BIRD**
– When is a man / Bird / If I breakdown / Charm / Love was the end / Long ago / Burning wood / Buick Mackane / Another straight line / It don't come easy / Spit shine / Just like the last time / Wah-wah / Drink it on / Dylan side / Swim this way / Eye / Bangla-Desh / Scene's over / / I could always be with you. *(cd-iss. Nov89 ++; SDE 8907)* – PERIOD

Oct 89. (lp/cd) *(SDE 8909 LP/CD)* **TROUBLE DOLL** (live + studio)
– Should brother kill / Never mant to say / Trouble world / This is war / Little Tex in trouble / Trash man / Trouble momma / I could always be with you / The cracked life of a cracked man / Floers grow on the wall / The French / When is a man / Bird / Charm / My T.V is broke / The king will never die / If I break down / It don't come easy / Love was the end / Just like the last time / Buick McKane. *(cd+=)* – Little Tex's prelude / Reagan's bush is on fire / Amazon / Trouble baby / TX-five / African sunset / Everywhere / Trouble finale.

Mar 90. (cd/lp) *(SDE 9018 CD/LP) <SHIMMY 030>* **BALL 4 – HARDBALL**
– Hard ball / She's always driving / Timmy the toad man / Mary Jane / The road to Heaven / Ball 4 prelude:- Ball 1 – Ball 2 – Ball 3 / Ball 4 R.I.P.

— split when FLEMING and SPIEGEL re-formed The VELVET MONKEYS and joined DINOSAUR JR for a year. Meanwhile KRAMER and LICHT carried on with BONGWATER.

VELVET MONKEYS

— early recordings included a 1982 US-only cassette collaboration with HALF JAPANESE, 'EVERYTHING IS RIGHT' (for 'Monkey Business') and in 1983, 'FUTURE' (for 'Fountain Of Youth'); both gathered together as 'ROTTING CORPSE AU GO-GO' in 1989 for 'Shimmy Disc' <SHIMMY 018>. Others included the cassette 'BIG BIG SUN' for 'K' in 1985

DON FLEMING (as "Rake") / **JAY SPIEGEL** (as "The Rummager") / **MALCOLM RIVIERA** (as "The Assassin") / **THURSTON MOORE** (as "The Action Pussy") / **J. MASCIS** (as "Sweet Dick") / **JULIA CAFRITZ** (as "Miss Sugar Bowl") / **JOHN HAMMILL** (as "Polack Johnny") / **DAISY VON FIRTH** (as "Chickley")

Rough Trade Rough Trade

Oct 90. (lp/c/cd) *(ROUGH/+C/CD 102)* **RAKE**
– We call it rock / She's not a girl / The ballad of 'Rake' / Something's in the air / Velvet monkey theme song / Rock the night / Harmonica hell house / Love to give / 7 angels / Rock party / Velvet monkey (Assassin mix) (theme). *(re-iss. cd Feb95 on 'Danceteria'; DANCD 061)*

GUMBALL

FLEMING + SPIEGEL plus **ERIC VERMILLION**

Paperhouse Primo Scree

Nov 90. (12"ep/cd-ep) *(PAPER 006 T/CD) <SCREE-ONE>* **ALL THE TIME**

Jan 91. (12"ep/cd-ep) *<SCREE-TWO>* **THIS TOWN**

Jun 91. (lp/c/cd) *<SCREE-THREE>* **SPECIAL KISS** <US-title 'GUMBALL'>
– This town / All the time / Window pain / Wake up / Summer days / Yellow pants / Restless / Gone too far / Gettysburg / Alternate feed / You know / Pre / High or low / Gettysburg. *<re-iss. 1991 on 'Caroline'; 2703>*

Sep 91. (12"ep/cd-ep) *(PAPER 012 T/CD)* **LIGHT SHINES THROUGH**

— In Nov'91, DON FLEMING & TOM SMITH (ex-Peach Of Immorality) collaborated on EP 'GIN BLOSSOMS' for 'Seminal Twang'.

— In Mar'92, DON teamed up with RICHARD HELL (---), THURSTON MOORE and STEVE SHELLEY to form DIM STARS, who released eponymous EP for 'Paperhouse'.

not iss. Sony

Nov 92. (cd-ep) *<74754>* **NEW ROSE** –

Big Cat Columbia

Jan 93. (12"ep)(cd-ep) *(ABB 041T)(ABBSCD 041) <74754>* **WISCONSIN HAYRIDE**
– New rose / Tell me have you ever seen me / Butterfly potion / Depression / Awakening.

May 93. (lp/cd) *(ABB 46/+CD) <52023>* **SUPER TASTY**
– Accelerator / Hell of a message / Here it comes again / Tumbling / Marilyn / The damage done / Real gone deal / Thunder / Black payback / No more / Get the cure / Upsetters theme song.

May 93. (12"ep)(cd-ep) *(ABB 048T)(ABBSCD 048)* **ACCELERATOR. / STRAIGHT LINE / CHEW THE CHEW** –

May 93. (cd-ep) *<44K 77138>* **DAMAGE DONE / THUNDER / CHEW THE CHEW / STRAIGHT LINE / UPSETTERS / ACCELLERATOR** –

Columbia Columbia

Sep 94. (cd/c) *<(475927-2/-4)>* **REVOLUTION ON ICE**
– Revolution on the rocks / Free grazin' / With a little rain / Nights on fire / Whatcha gonna do? / Breath away / Gone to the moon / I ain't nothin' / Read the news / The boat race / Trudge / She's as beautiful as a foot.

Edward BALL

Born: 23 Nov'59, Chelsea, London, England. After leaving school, ED and DAN TREACY put together "DIY" punk outfit, TV PERSONALITIES. Late in 1977, they gained national airplay on the John Peel show with a self-financed debut 45, '14TH FLOOR'. Meanwhile, ED initiated his own outfit, O-LEVEL, who, after a number of gigs, released 'EAST SHEEN'. An EP, 'MALCOLM', surfaced later in '78, although it was overshadowed by another TELEVISION PERSONALITIES gem, 'WHERE'S BILL GRUNDY NOW?'. Enjoying a sales boost courtesy of its B-side, 'PART-TIME PUNKS', it sold its limited run of copies in a matter of weeks and the band became overnight underground cult legends dabbling in SYD BARRETT-type psychedelia. In 1979, The O-LEVEL became The TEENAGE FILMSTARS. This outfit released three 45's before ED (still with TVP's) formed retro-mod combo, The TIMES. ED and DAN subsequently initiated the 'Whaam!' label as an outlet for both groups' material while also functioning as a starting point for fellow indie acts, SMALL WORLD, The PASTELS, DOCTOR & THE MEDICS, DIRECT HITS, etc. The TIMES created some fine tunes, including a TEENAGE FILMSTARS re-make of 'I HELPED PATRICK McGOOHAN ESCAPE' (the main actor in cult 60's TV series 'The Prisoner'; "I am not a number!"). ED re-released the debut album, 'POP GOES ART!', for his new 'Art Pop' label in 1983, enjoying something of a mini-cult following. He finally left the TVP's in 1985 and concentrated wholly on The TIMES, the latter outfit signing to Alan McGee's 'Creation' in 1988 and issuing the album, 'BEAT TORTURE'. Although sales were nothing spectacular, Alan McGee kept faith with ED as he ventured into yet more side projects, i.e. LOVE CORPORATION, TEENAGE FILMSTARS (again!), CONSPIRACY OF NOISE. At the same time, EDWARD (as he was now calling himself), attempted to carve out a solo career, a move which brought minor success in 1996 with the single, 'THE MILL HILL SELF HATE CLUB'. In the 90's, he was also involved in The BOO RADLEYS with fellow baldy, SICE, while his solo albums, 'IF A MAN EVER LOVED A WOMAN' (1996) and 'CATHOLIC GUILT' (1997), performed well enough for BALL to retain his informal position on the slimmed-down 'Creation' roster. A fashion-conscious near-genius with a taste for melancholy eccentricity, the man could yet become a smaller version of the Millenium Dome if he continues to elicit regular hype from McGee and the music press. • **Songwriters:** Self-penned except covers; YOU CAN GET IT IF YOU REALLY WANT (Jimmy Cliff) / YOUR GENERATION (Generation X) / NOWHERE TO RUN (hit; Martha & The Vandellas) / MAN FROM UNCLE (Jerry Goldsmith) / BLUE MONDAY (as 'LINDI BLEU') (New Order).

Album rating: IF A MAN EVER LOVED A WOMAN (*6) / CATHOLIC GUILT (*7) / Times: PURE (*7) / Times: PINK BALL, BROWN BALL, RED BALL (*8) / Teenage Filmstars: A DAY IN THE LIFE OF GILBERT & GEORGE (*7)

O-LEVEL

ED BALL – vocals, organ / **JOHN BENNETT** – bass / **GERARD BENNETT** – drums (both also of TELEVISION PERSONALITIES) / **DICK SCULLY** – guitar

Psycho not iss.

Jul 78. (7") *(PSYCH 2)* **EAST SHEEN. / PSEUDO PUNK** –

Kings Road not iss.

Dec 78. (7"ep) *(KR 002)* **THE MALCOLM EP** –
– We love Malcolm / Leave me / Everybody's on Revolver / Stairway to boredom.

— In 1979, ED financed a DRY RIB ep 'THE DRY SEASON' on 'Clockwork'.

TEENAGE FILMSTARS

ED BALL – vocals, organ / **DAN TREACY** – bass (of TELEVISION PERSONALITIES) / **JOE FOSTER** – guitar (of TELEVISION PERSONALITIES) / **PAUL DAMIEN** – drums

Clockwork not iss.

Sep 79. (7") *(COR 002)* **(THERE'S A) CLOUD OVER LIVERPOOL. / SOMETIMES GOOD GUYS DON'T FOLLOW TRENDS** –

Wessex not iss.

Mar 80. (7") *(WEX 275)* **ODD MAN OUT. / I APOLOGISE** –
(re-iss. Jun80 on 'Blueprint'; BLU 2013)

Fab Listen not iss.

Nov 80. (7") *(FL 1)* **I HELPED PATRICK McGOOGHAN ESCAPE. / WE'RE NOT SORRY** –

TIMES

EDWARD BALL – vocals, guitar / **JOHN EAST** – bass, vocals / **PAUL DAMIEN** – drums, vocals

Whaam! not iss.

May 81. (7") *(WHAAM 002)* **RED WITH PURPLE FLASHES. / BIFF! BANG! POW!** –

Jul 82. (lp) *(LP 01)* **POP GOES ART!** –
– Picture gallery / Biff! bang! / It's time / If now is the answer /A New arrangement / Looking through the world through dark glasses / I helped Patrick McGastan escape / Pop goes art! / Miss London / The Sun never sets / This is tomorrow. *(re-iss. Jul83 on 'Art Pop' pic-lp Jul90; ART 20)*

Art Pop not iss.

Jun 82. (7"; as JONI DEE & THE TIMES) *(POP 50)* **HERE COMES THE HOLIDAYS. / THREE CHEERS FOR THE SUN** –

Jul 83. (lp) *(ART 19)* **THIS IS LONDON** –
– This is London / Goodbye Piccadilly / Whatever happened to Thamesboat / Big painting / If only / Goodnight children everywhere / The party / Stranger than fiction / (There's a) Cloud over Liverpool / Will success spoil Frank Summit? / The chimes of Big Ben.

Sep 83. (7") *(POP 49)* **I HELPED PATRICK McGOOGHAN ESCAPE. / THE THEME FROM 'DANGER MAN'** –

Nov 83. (m-lp) *(ARTPOP 1)* **I HELPED PATRICK McGOOGHAN ESCAPE** –
– Big painting / Stranger than fiction / Danger Man theme / I helped Patrick McGooghan escape / All systems go / Up against it.

Jul 84. (7") *(POP 46)* **BOYS BRIGADE. / POWER IS FOREVER** –

Oct 84. (7") *(POP 45)* **BLUE FIRE. / WHERE THE BLUE REIGNS** –

Nov 84. (lp) *(ART 17)* **HELLO EUROPE** –
– Dada Europe (I'm so cut up about you) / Boys brigade / The things we've learnt /

Ra diate / Blue fire / Everything turns to black and white / Where the blue begins / Public reaction killed this cat / Kultureshock.

— Early in 1985 he made another for 'Art Pop!' under EDWARD BALL'S L'ORANGE MECHANIK name; 'SYMPHONY. / INTERMEZZO (SPRECHSTIMME) / SCHERZO'. Four years later an lp was given away free with ED's Edgar Allen Poe poems for 'Creation'.

Mar 85. (m-lp) *(ARTPOP 2)* **BLUE PERIOD** ☐ -
Sep 85. (12"ep) *(POP 43DOZ)* **BOYS ABOUT TOWN EP** ☐ -
– David Jones (is on his way) / Victim 1960 / Up against it / Song for Joe Walton.
Apr 86. (lp) *(ART 16)* **UP AGAINST IT (soundtrack)** ☐ -
– Up against it / Last tango for one / Boy's about town / Gordon into moonlight / W.P.C. Boon / Most modern woman in the world / Jade's revolution / Ladies of the cause / Mutiny in the British Empire / Escape / She's a professional / It's a cabaret time / The way / The wedding song.

Unicorn / not iss.

Apr 86. (7") *(PHZ 1)* **LONDON BOYS. / (WHERE TO GO) WHEN THE SUN GOES DOWN** ☐ -

Fire / not iss.

Oct 86. (7") *(BLAZE 16S)* **TIMES TV. / TRAILER FROM 'ENJOY'** ☐ -
(12"+=) *(BLAZE 16T)* – The policeforce / El Aragma / Pick it up.

Creation / not iss.

Oct 88. (lp/cd) *(CRELP/+CD 038)* **BEAT TORTURE** ☐ -
– God evil / Heaven sent me an angel / I'll be your volunteer / Department store / Love like haze or rain / It had to happen / Chelsea green / How to start your own country // On the peace line / Scarlet and Sapphire / Angel / Volunteer / Country / Love. *(re-iss. May94)*
Oct 89. (lp/cd) *(CRELP/+CD 053)* **E FOR EDWARD** ☐ -
– Manchester / Valvaline / Snow / Catherine Wheel / Crashed on you / Count to five / All your life / French film bleurred / No love on Haight street / Acid Angel of Ecstasy / Gold / Sold / Life.
Feb 90. (7") *(CRE 71)* **MANCHESTER. / LOVE AND TRUTH** ☐ -
(12") *(CRE 71T)* – ('A'side) / Dada won't buy me a Bauhaus / ('A'extended).
(cd-s) *(CRESCD 71)* – ('A'side) / ('A'extended) / Ulysses / Shoom!.
Oct 90. (7") *(CAFF 13)* **EXTASE. / SLEEP (by "BIFF! BANG! POW!")** ☐ -
(above single on 'Caff' label)
Oct 90. (lp/cd) *(CRELP/CD 070)* **ET DIEU CREA LA FEMME** ☐ -
– Septieme ciel / Aurore boreale / Confiance / Chagrin d'amour / Volupte / Baisers voles / Pour Kylie / Sucette / 1990 Annee erotique / Extase.
Mar 91. (lp/cd) *(CRELP/+CD 091)* **PURE** ☐ -
– From Chelsea Green to Brighton Beach / A girl called Mersey / Lindi bleu / From L.A. to Edgbaston / Ours is wonderlove world / Another star in Heaven. *(re-iss Sep 92).*
Apr 92. (lp/cd) *(CRELP/+CD 123)* **AT THE ASTRADOME LUNAVILLE (GOLDEN OLDIES OF THE 1990's)** ☐ -
Jul 92. (7"/c-s) *(CRE/+CS 114)* **LINDI BLEU (version Francais de Blue Monday). / ('A'instrumental)** ☐ -
(12") *(CRE 114T)* – ('A'- Grid & Bandulu mixes; Praise the Lord / Grid World communications / Bandulu smiling mixes).
(cd-s+=) *(CRESCD 114)* – (above 3) / (Brazilian, Japanese, German & Spanish versions).
Apr 93. (lp/cd) *(CRELP/+CD 137)* **ALTERNATIVE COMMERCIAL CROSSOVER** ☐ -
– Obligatory grunge song / Finnegan's break / How honest are Pearl Jam / Sweetest girl / Ballad of Georgie Best / Lindi bleu (praise the lord mix by the GRID) / Palace in the sun / Sorry, I've written a melody / Finnegan's break (corporate rock mix) / Whole world's turning seaface / All I want is you to care.
May 93. (7"; TIMES featuring TIPPA IRIE) *(CRE 158)* **FINNEGAN'S BREAK. / HEARTBROKEN LOST IN BLUE** ☐ -
(12"+=)(cd-s+=) *(CRE 158T)(CRESCD 158)* – Soultight / Come alive.
Jun 93. (12"ep/cd-ep) **BABY GIRL. / THE COLOUR OF MY LOVE / MASH IT UP / PRIMROSE 0822** ☐ -

– (TIMES) compilations, etc. –

May 85. (lp) *Pastell; (POW 3)* **GO! WITH THE TIMES** (rec.1980) - - German
– You can get it / I'm with you / Your generation / Pinstripes / Dressing up for the cameras / Red with purple flashes / The joke's on Zandra / Nowhere to run / No hard feelings / My Andy Warhol poster / Man from Uncle Reflections in an imperfect mirror.
Nov 86. (lp) *Art Pop; (ART 15)* **ENJOY** ☐ -
Jul 91. (lp/cd) *Creation; (CRELP/+CD 073)* **PINK BALL, BROWN BALL, ED BALL** ☐ -
Nov 92. (cd) *Rev-Ola; (CREV 005CD)* **A DAY IN THE LIFE OF GILBERT & GEORGE** (O-LEVEL & TEENAGE FILMSTARS) ☐ -
Nov 93. (cd) *Rev-Ola; (CREV 028CD)* **THIS IS LONDON / HELLO EUROPE** ☐ -
Dec 93. (cd) *Rev-Ola; (CREV 029CD)* **ENJOY / UP AGAINST IT** ☐ -
Apr 94. (cd) *Rev-Ola; (CREV 030CD)* **GO! WITH THE TIMES / POP GOES ART!** ☐ -

— ED BALL was also part of BIFF BANG POW, another 'Creation' outfit and in the 90's joined The BOO RADLEYS

LOVE CORPORATION

aka **ED BALL** solo

Creation / not iss.

Feb 90. (lp/cd) *(CRELP/+CD 056)* **TONES** ☐ -
– Fleshtones / Monumental / Tones of incorporation / World / Palatial.
Apr 90. (7") *(CRE 076)* **PALATIAL. / PALATIAL II** ☐ -
(cd-s+=) *(CRESCD 076)* – Palatial III / (b-side extended).
(12") *(CRE 176T)* – ('A'-Danny Rampling extended remix) / ('A'-II extended).
Feb 91. (lp/cd) *(CRELP/+CD 068)* **LOVERS** ☐ -
– L-O-V-E / Warm / Crystal / Sun / Happy days and lonely nights / Nice / Lovers / Smile.
Mar 91. (12") *(CRE 086T)* **GIME ME SOME LOVE. / ('A'version)** ☐ -
(12") *(CRE 086X)* – ('A'-Andrew Weatherall remix) / Lovers.
Nov 94. (lp/cd) *(CRELP/+CD 116)* **INTELLIGENTSIA** ☐ -

TEENAGE FILMSTARS

— re-united in 1992 for below.

Creation / not iss.

Mar 92. (lp/cd) *(CRELP/+CD 111)* **STAR** ☐ -
– Kiss me / Loving / Inner space / Apple / Flashes / Kaleidoscope / Vibrations / Soulful / Hallucinations / Moon.
Mar 93. (lp/cd) *(CRELP/+CD 141)* **ROCKET CHARMS – SPLASHDOWN AVEC LES TEENAGE FILMSTARS** ☐ -

CONSPIRACY OF NOISE

ED BALL with **PHIL KANE** or **DEAN JONES** – vox (of EXTREME NOISE TERROR)

Creation / not iss.

Oct 93. (lp/cd) *(CRELP/+CD 161)* **CHICKS WITH DICKS AND SPLATTER FLICKS** ☐ -

EDWARD BALL

with ANDY BELL, MARTIN CARR, NICK HEYWARD, SICE IDHAR, TIM BROWN, ALAN McGEE, NOEL JOYCE & THE IAN SHOW ORCHESTRA featuring NAOMI ZOOB

Creation / not iss.

Feb 95. (d-lp/cd) *(CRELP/+CD 183)* **WELCOME TO THE WONDERFUL WORLD OF ED BALL** (compilation) ☐ -
Apr 95. (7") *(CRE 197)* **IF A MAN EVER LOVED A WOMAN. / FIREHORSE BLUES / 12 NOON 28.8.93** ☐ -
(cd-s+=) *(CRESCD 197)* – United States of loneliness.
Jun 95. (cd/lp) *(CRELP/+CD 195)* **IF A MAN EVER LOVED A WOMAN** ☐ -
– It's kinda lonely where I am (acoustic) / Fire horse / If a man ever loved a woman / She's just high maintenance, baby / The Arizona loner / You only miss me when I'm bleeding / The ballad of a lonely man / A ton of blues / You're an idiot babe / It's kinda lonely where I am.
Jun 95. (7") *(CRE 208)* **IT'S KIND OF LONELY WHERE I AM / DOCKLANDS BLUES** ☐ -
(cd-s+=) *(CRESCD 208)* – Bled a river over you / Another member of the Mill Hill Self Hate Club.
Jun 96. (7") *(CRE 233)* **THE MILL HILL SELF HATE CLUB. / WRAPPED UP IN LONESOME BLUES** 57 -
(cd-s+=) *(CRESCD 233)* –
Sep 96. (7"/c-s) *(CRE/+CS 239)* **TRAILBLAZE. / THE OTHER SIDE OF LOVE IS GUILT** ☐ ☐
(cd-s+=) *(CRESCD 239)* – Blues for Brian Wilson.
Feb 97. (7"/c-s) *(CRE/+CS 244)* **LOVE IS BLUE. / WHEN YOU LOSE YOUR LOVER, LEARN TO LOSE** 59 ☐
(cd-s+=) *(CRESCD 244)* – The Mill Hill Self Hate Club (acoustic) / Love is blue (acoustic).
Apr 97. (7") *(CRE 260)* **THE MILL HILL SELF HATE CLUB. / FOR THE SOULS OF DEAD HORSES** ☐ -
(cd-s+=) *(CRESCD 260)* – Ma blues / Never live to love again.
May 97. (cd/lp) *(CRE CD/LP 200)* **CATHOLIC GUILT** ☐ ☐
– The Mill Hill Self Hate Club / Love is blue / Docklands blues / Controversial girlfriend / Hampstead therapist / Tilt / Trailblaze / Never live to love again / This is the story of my love / This is real.

BAMBI SLAM

Formed: South London, England ... April '86 by Lancashire-born ROY FELDON, a multi-musician who was raised in a suburb of Pickering in Toronto, Canada and had once lived in California. Fly-posting an ad at the prestigious Royal Academy, the ambitious RON subsequently found a couple of capable musicians in the shape of drummer NICK MAYNARD and cellist LINDA MELLOR. A series of singles for Mute Subsidiary 'Product Inc.' followed in '87, namely 'BAMP-BAMP', 'DON'T IT MAKE YOU FEEL' and 'HAPPY BIRTHDAY', upbeat ditties fusing elements of PiL and MOTT. With work on a debut album dragging on interminably, FELDON and Co. were shown the door and found themselves temporarily out of contract. Their fairy Godfather arrived in the form of Rough Trade mainman, Geoff Travis, who added them to his Warner Brothers backed offshoot, 'Blanco Y Negro'; by this point, the trio had become a septet with the addition of SAM WILLIAMS, NATALIE McKAY, JULIEN DIGG and AKABU. Originally scheduled for release under the title of 'IS', the eponymous debut set was finally released to minimal interest by BAMBI SLAM's new home late in '88.

Album rating: THE BAMBI SLAM (*6)

ROY FELDON – multi-instruments / **LINDA MELLOR** – cello / **NICK MAYNARD** – drums

Product Inc. / not iss.

Feb 87. (7") *(7PROD 2)* **BAMP-BAMP. / HIT ME WITH YOUR HAIRBRUSH** ☐ -
(12"+=) *(12PROC 2)* – The awful flute song (first half).
May 87. (7") *(7PROD 8)* **DON'T IT MAKE YOU FEEL. /** ☐ -
(12"+=) *(12PROD 8)* –
Jul 87. (7") *(7PROD 13)* **HAPPY BIRTHDAY. / YET ANOTHER** ☐ -
(12"+=) *(12PROD 13)* –
Feb 88. (lp; w-drawn) *(EXPROD 20)* **IS . . .** - -

— trio now augmented by **NATALIE MacKAY** – bass, vocals / **SAM WILLIAMS** – saxophone / **JULIEN DIGG** – congas / **AKABU** – vocals

Blanco Y Negro / not iss.

Sep 88. (7") *(NEG 36)* **LONG TIME COMIN'. / I AND I** ☐ -
(12"+=) *(NEG 36T)* – Shame of the sick / Sad psycho.
Oct 88. (lp/c)(cd) *(BYN/+C 17)(BYN 17CD)* **THE BAMBI SLAM** ☐ -
– Ba ba ba boom / Long time comin' / Now / Outa my head / Thinkin' 'bout chu /

Summer smilin' / Take me with you / I'm left wonderin' / We can't let go our mellowdrama / The awful flute song.

— ROY let his band leave and he subsequently retired from music biz

BANDIT QUEEN

Formed: Manchester, England . . . 1992 by one-time PJ HARVEY-influenced music journo, TRACY GOLDING, along with JANET WOLSTENHOLME and DAVID GALLEY, the trio taking their moniker from a true story (made into a movie) about an Indian woman who becomes an outlaw leader after surviving violence and torture at the hands of her kidnappers. Defiantly feminist, these feisty indie chicks sweetened their bitter rants with a fair dose of pop acumen on their one and only 'Playtime' album, 'HORMONE HOTEL' (1995).

Album rating: HORMONE HOTEL (*6)

Playtime / Mammoth

Apr 93. (10"ep/cd-ep) *(AMUSE 17 T/CD)* **DIRT & SOUL EP** [ ] [-]
– Incredible /
(re-iss. Oct93; same)
Feb 94. (cd-ep) *(AMUSE 22CD)* **SCORCH / FRIDA KAHLO / HIGH HEELS AND PEARLS** [ ] [ ]
Jun 94. (7") *(AMUSE 024)* **QUEEN BEE. /** [ ] [-]
Nov 94. (12"/cd-s) *(AMUSE 25 T/CD)* **MISS DANDYS. / DIRT & SOUL (speed mix) / HOLLYWOOD FAIR** [ ] [-]
(re-iss. May95; same)
Feb 95. (cd/c/lp) *(AMUSE 26 CD/MC/LP)* <130> **HORMONE HOTEL** [ ] [ ]
– Scorch / Back in the belljar / Miss Dandys / Nailbiter / Give it to the dog / Petals and razorblades / Overture for beginners / Big sugar emotional thing / Essence vanilla / Oestrogen / Frida Kahlo / Hormone hotel. *(cd+=)* – Blue black.
Feb 95. (7") *(AMUSE 27)* **GIVE IT TO THE DOG. / FACELIFT** [ ] [-]
(cd-s+=) *(AMUSE 27CD)* – Touchstone.

— subsequently disbanded

BAND OF . . . BLACKY RANCHETTE
(see under ⇒ GIANT SAND)

BAND OF HOLY JOY

Formed: New Cross / Soho, London, England . . . 1984 by JOHNY BROWN. He gathered up a host of friends including BRETT TURNBULL and proceeded to record two privately released cassettes. The following year, they signed to South London indie, 'Flim Flam', who issued their debut single, 'HAD A MOTHER WHO WAS PROUD'. POGUES-like in their make-up and approach, this extended musical family traded in a similar raucous folk sound, although based on European cabaret and influenced by the likes of JACQUES BREL or BERTOLD BRECHT. A mini debut lp, 'THE BIG SHIP SAILS', appeared the following year, while a more stabilised line-up (JOHNY recruiting a whole new cast including ADRIAN BAILEY, BILL LEWINGTON, BIG JOHN, KAREL VAN BERGEN, ALFIE THOMAS and JUB JENKINS) worked on 1987's debut album proper, 'MORE TALES FROM THE CITY'. 'Rough Trade' subsequently signed them and issued two acclaimed sets 'MANIC, MAGIC, MAJESTIC' (1989) and 'POSITIVELY SPOOKED' (1990), before the band clipped their moniker to HOLY JOY.

Album rating: MANIC, MAGIC, MAJESTIC (*8) / POSITIVELY SPOOKED (*8)

JOHNY BROWN – vocals / **BRETT TURNBULL** – vocals / + unknown musicians

Pleasantly Surprised / not iss.

1984. (c) **MORE FAVOURITE FAIRY TALES** [ ] [-]
1985. (c) **INTO THE CITY OF TALES** [ ] [-]

— added **MAXINE** – accordion, vocals

Flim Flam / not iss.

Oct 85. (12"ep) *(HARP 1T)* **HAD A MOTHER WHO WAS PROUD AND LOOK AT ME NOW. / CONSUMPTION / NYLON ROSE / DISGUST** [ ] [-]
May 86. (10"m-lp) *(HARP 1)* **THE BIG SHIP SAILS** [ ] [-]
Oct 86. (7") *(HARP 4)* **WHO SNATCHED MY BABY. /** [ ] [-]
(12"+=) *(HARP 4T)* –

— **JOHNY** recruited new members **ADRIAN BAILEY** – trombone / **BILL LEWINGTON** – drums / **BIG JOHN** – keyboards, banjo / **KAREL VAN BERGEN** – violin / **ALFIE THOMAS** – accordion, keyboards / **JUB JENKINS** –

Apr 87. (7") *(HARP 6)* **ROSEMARY SMITH. /** [ ] [-]
(12"+=) *(HARP 6T)* –
May 87. (lp) *(HARPLP 1)* **MORE TALES FROM THE CITY** [ ] [-]
Dec 87. (lp) *(BYEBYE 1)* **WHEN STARS COME OUT TO PLAY** (compilation) [ ] [-]
– Don't stick knives in the babies' heads / Mad Dot / Janis – this one's for you / Nico – this is the way out / Tide of life / One child / Amsterdam / North Shields / Fishwives / Who snatched the baby / Yo!.

Cause For Concern / not iss.

1988. (lp) *(CFC 003)* **THE DEVIL AND THE DEEP BLUE SEA** [ ] [-]

— **MARK CAVENER** – double bass repl. JUB JENKINS

— with guests **MISS ADELE WINTER + DAVID COULTER**

Rough Trade / not iss.

Sep 88. (7") *(RT 223)* **TACTLESS. /** [ ] [-]
(12"+=) *(RTT 223)* –
Jan 89. (lp/c/cd) *(ROUGH/+C/CD 125)* **MANIC, MAGIC, MAJESTIC** [ ] [-]
– Route to love / Baubles, bangles, emotional tangles / Nightjars / Tactless / You've grown so old in my dreams / Killy car thieves / Bride / Manic, magic, majestic / What the moon saw / Your not singing anymore / Blessed joy.
Nov 89. (12") *(RTT 233)* **EVENING WORLD HOLIDAY SHOW. /** [ ] [-]
Apr 90. (lp/c/cd) *(ROUGH/+C/CD 155)* **POSITIVELY SPOOKED** [ ] [-]
– Real beauty passed through / Evening world holiday show / Because it was never resolved / Unlikely girl / Shadows fall / Bitten lips / Here it comes / Hot little hopes / Freda Cunningham / Torch me / Positively spooked / Look who's changed with the times.
Jun 90. (12"ep/cd-ep) *(RTT 243/+CD)* **REAL BEAUTY PASSED THROUGH. / CHANTAL / LONELY COTTAGE / LONELY COTTAGE (instr.)** [ ] [-]

HOLY JOY

JOHNY, BILL, ADRIAN, ALFIE, BIG JOHN + HOWARD, EMMET, CHESS + CHRIS

Equador / not iss.

Jul 92. (cd/lp) *(EQ CD/LP 004)* **A TRACKSUIT VENDETTA** [ ] [-]
1992. (12"/cd-s) **CLAUDIA DREAMS. /** [ ] [-]

Rough Trade / not iss.

Aug 92. (7") **IT'S LOVEBITE CITY. /** [ ] [-]

— split in 1993, although BROWN and LEWINGTON formed SUPERDRUG in '95.

BAND OF SUSANS

Formed: Buffalo, New York, USA . . . mid 80's by SUSAN STENGER, SUSAN TALLMAN, SUSAN LYALL and Susan.. no, er . . . ROBERT POSS (the latter rejected a vacant position with PiL, formerly filled by KEITH LEVENE). Adding drummer RON SPITZER and signing to indie imprint, 'Further', The BAND OF SUSANS delivered an EP, 'BLESSING AND CURSE', prior to 1988's debut set, 'HOPE AGAINST HOPE'. Retaining their moniker despite losing two of their Susans (TALLMAN and LYALL), songwriters STENGER and POSS – plus SPITZER – recruited PAGE HAMILTON and KAREN HAGLOF, the latter also formerly a member of RHYS CHATHAM (with messrs., SUSAN and ROBERT). This configuration managed to secure a deal with 'Blast First' and complete another sonic guitar frenzy of an album, 'LOVE AGENDA', before the end of the decade. Yet more personnel upheaval dogged the band as they entered the 90's; PAGE exited to form HELMET while HAGLOF's dislike of touring led to her being temporarily substituted by WIRE's BRUCE GILBERT! – on a more permanent basis they were replaced by MARK LONERGAN and ANNE HUSICK. Inking a fresh deal with 'Restless', BOS unleashed two more sets, 'THE WORD AND THE FLESH' (1991) and 'VEIL' (1993), the second of which featured new drummer JOEY KAYE. Subsequently reuniting with 'Blast First', they issued a retrospective of their work to date entitled 'WIRED FOR SOUND', followed a few months later by new material in the shape of 'HERE COMES SUCCESS' (1995). Unfortunately, success is the one thing that has eluded the BAND OF SUSAN and Co. throughout their decade-plus lifespan.

Album rating: HOPE AGAINST HOPE (*7) / LOVE AGENDA (*7) / THE WORD AND THE FLESH (*6) / VEIL (*5) / HERE COMES SUCCESS (*7) / WIRED FOR SOUND: 1986-1993 compilation) (*7)

ROBERT POSS (b.20 Nov'56) – vocals, guitar / **SUSAN STENGER** (b.11 May'55) – bass, vocals / **SUSAN TALLMAN** – guitar / **SUSAN LYALL** – guitar, vocals / **RON SPITZER** – drums / with also **ALVA ROGERS** – backing vocals (on debut)

Further / Further

1987. (12"ep) *(FU 2T)* **BLESSING AND CURSE EP** [ ] [-]
– Hope against hope / You were an optimist / Sometimes / Where have all the flowers gone.
Apr 88. (lp/c/cd) *(FU 005/+C/CD)* **HOPE AGAINST HOPE** [ ] [ ]
– Not even close / Learning to sin / Throne of blood / Elliott Abrahams in Hell / All the wrong reasons / I, the jury / No God / You were an optimist / Ready to bend / Hope against hope.

— **KAREN HAGLOF** – guitar, vocals (ex-RHYS CHATHAM . . .) rcpl. LYALL

— **PAGE HAMILTON** – guitar, vocals; repl. TALLMAN

Blast First / Blast First

Apr 89. (lp/c/cd) <(BFFP 043/+C/CD)> **LOVE AGENDA** [ ] [ ]
– The pursuit of happiness / It's locked away / Birthmark / Tourniquet / Thorn in my side / Sin embargo / Because of you / Hard light / Which dream came true / Child of the Moon / Take the express.

— **MARK LONERGAN** – guitar; repl. PAGE HAMILTON who formed HELMET

— **ANNE HUSICK** – guitar; repl. KAREN (she had been temp. repl. by BRUCE GILBERT of WIRE)

World Service / Restless

Mar 91. (cd/c) <72534-2/-4> **THE WORD AND THE FLESH** [-] [ ]
– Ice age / Now is now / Trouble follows / Plot twist / Estranged / Labor / Sermon on competition (part 2) / Bitter and twisted / Bad timing / Tilt / Silver lining / Guitar trio.
Apr 93. (m-cd/m-cd) *(RTD 1591491-2)* <72722-2/-4> **NOW** [ ] [ ]
– Pearls of wisdom / Following my heart / Trash train / Paint it black / Now is now (remix) / Paint it black (instrumental).

— **JOEY KAYE** – drums; repl. SPITZER

Jun 93. (cd) *(RTD 1571561-2)* <72733-2> **VEIL** [ ] [ ]
– Mood swing / Not in this life / The red and the black / Following my heart / Stained glass / The last temptation of Susan / Truce / Trouble spot / Out of the question / Pearls of wisdom / Troilbinders theme / Blind.

Blast First / World Service

Apr 95. (lp/cd) *(BFFP 114/+CD)* <257> **HERE COMES SUCCESS** [ ] [ ]
– Elizabeth Stride (1843-1888) /

- compilations, etc. -

Feb 94. (cd) *Strange Fruit; (SFRCD 128) / Dutch East India; <8353>*
THE PEEL SESSIONS [ ] [ ]
– I found that essence rare / Throne of blood / Child of the moon / Hope against hope / Which dream came true / Too late.

Jan 95. (lp/cd) *Blast First; <(BFFP 111/+CD)>* **WIRED FOR SOUND: 1986-1993** [ ] [ ]

Honey BANE (see under ⇒ FATAL MICROBES)

Ed BANGER (see under ⇒ NOSEBLEEDS)

BANGLES

Formed: Los Angeles, California, USA . . . 1981 as The BANGS by sisters VICKI and DEBBI PETERSON alongside SUSANNA HOFFS, getting together after the siblings replied to an ad placed by the latter. After a one-off US indie 45, they became The BANGLES, added a bass player, ANNETTE ZILINSKAS and signed to Miles Copeland's 'IRS/Faulty' records in mid '82. An eponymous mini-set showed them to be a feisty garage-pop band whose sound was characterised by the harmonies of the PETERSON sisters and influenced by the likes of LOVE, GRASS ROOTS, The BYRDS, The BEATLES and The GO-GO's, an all-female quartet in the male dominated Paisley Underground. Replacing ZILINSKAS (who subsequently joined BLOOD ON THE SADDLE) with MICKI STEELE, the band secured a major label deal with 'CBS/Columbia' and breached the lower fringes of both the UK and US charts with debut album proper, 'ALL OVER THE PLACE' (1985). Although the rough edges had been smoothed out for public consumption, no hit singles were forthcoming and it would take the masterful pen of PRINCE to furnish the girls with a breakthrough track; 'MANIC MONDAY' was released in early '86, a MAMAS & PAPAS-esque tale of 9 to 5 frustration that quickly captured the popular imagination and climbed into the Top 3 on both sides of the Atlantic. 1986 proved to be The BANGLES' year, a follow-up album, 'DIFFERENT LIGHT', again achieving transatlantic Top 3 status and spawning a further minor hit in the melancholy reading of Jules Shear's 'IF SHE KNEW WHAT SHE WANTS' and a monster US No.1 in 'WALK LIKE AN EGYPTIAN'. To end the year, they were back in the Top 20 with a remix of 'WALKING DOWN YOUR STREET'. While only a solitary flop single, 'FOLLOW', appeared in '87, The BANGLES kickstarted their career in early '88 with a storming cover of Simon & Garfunkel's 'HAZY SHADE OF WINTER', cut for the soundtrack to cult 80's bratpack movie, 'Less Than Zero'. With seemingly no end to their pop ascendancy, The BANGLES again hired outside writers for the slick 'EVERYTHING' (1988), another massive Stateside success which spawned US Top 5, 'IN YOUR ROOM', as well as the band's syrupy calling card, 'ETERNAL FLAME', a transatlantic chart topper in early '89. With sex symbol HOFFS (who sang the latter unaccompanied) increasingly regarded as the band's focal point, tensions eventually split the band in 1990 as their run of hits stuttered to a halt. While HOFFS went on to a marginally succesful solo career, the PETERSONS continued to work on the alternative/pop underground. • **Songwriters:** Mostly HOFFS collaborations, except GOING DOWN TO LIVERPOOL (Kimberley Rew – SOFT BOYS) / WALK LIKE AN EGYPTIAN (Liam Sternberg) / SEPTEMBER GURLS (Alex Chilton). HOFFS solo; BOYS KEEP SWINGING (David Bowie) + UNCONDITIONAL LOVE (Cyndi Lauper). • **Trivia:** SUSANNA HOFFS made film acting debut in 'The Allnighter' released 1987.

Album rating: ALL OVER THE PLACE (*6) / DIFFERENT LIGHT (*5) / EVERYTHING (*4) / GREATEST HITS compilation (*7)

The BANGS

SUSANNA HOFFS (b.17 Jan'57, Newport Beach, Calif.) – vocals, rhythm guitar / **VICKI PETERSON** (b.11 Jan'58) – lead guitar, vocals (ex-The FANS) / **DEBBI PETERSON** (b.22 Aug'61) – drums, vocals (ex-The FANS)

not iss. / Down Kitty

Dec 81. (7") *<BANG 1>* **GETTING OUT OF HAND. / CALL ON ME** [-] [ ]

The BANGLES

— added **ANNETTE ZILINSKAS** – bass

not iss. / Faulty-IRS

Jun 82. (m-lp) **THE BANGLES** [-] [ ]
– How is the air up there? / Mary Street / The real world / Want you / I'm in line.

— **MICKI STEELE** (b.MICHAEL, 2 Jun'54) – bass, vocals (ex-RUNAWAYS, ex-SLOW CHILDREN) repl. ANNETTE who joined BLOOD ON THE SADDLE

C.B.S. / Columbia.

Sep 84. (7") *(A 4527)* **HERO TAKES A FALL. / WHERE WERE YOU WHEN I NEEDED YOU** [ ] [ ]

Mar 85. (lp/c) *(CBS/40 26015) <39220>* **ALL OVER THE PLACE** [86] [80] Jul84
– Hero takes a fall / Live / James / All about you / Dover beach / Tell me / Restless / Going down to Liverpool / He's got a secret / Silent treatment / More than meets the eye. *(re-iss. Oct86 lp/c/cd; 450091-1/-4/-2) (re-iss. Apr93 on 'Columbia' cd/c;)*

Mar 85. (7") *(A 4914)* **GOING DOWN TO LIVERPOOL. / DOVER BEACH** [56] [ ]
(12"+=) – *(TX 4914)* – The real world / I'm in line / How is the air up there?.
(d7"+=) *(DA 4914)* – Hero takes a fall / Where were you when I needed you?.

Jan 86. (7"/7"w-poster) *(A/QA 6796) <05757>* **MANIC MONDAY. / IN A DIFFERENT LIGHT** [2] [2]
(12"+=) *(TX 6796)* – Going down to Liverpool / Dover beach.

Mar 86. (lp/c/cd) *(CBS/40/CD 26659) <40039>* **DIFFERENT LIGHT** [3] [2] Jan86
– Manic Monday / In a different light / Walking down your street / Walk like an Egyptian / Standing in the hallway / Return post / If she knew what she wants / Let it go / September gurls / Angels don't fall in love / September girls / Following / Not like you. *(re-iss. Mar90 cd/c/lp; 46558-2/-4/-1)*

Apr 86. (7"/7"sha-pic-d) *(A/WA 7062) <05886>* **IF SHE KNEW WHAT SHE WANTS. / ANGELS DON'T FALL IN LOVE** [31] [29]
(12"+=) *(TA 7062)* – Manic Monday (extended).
(d7"+=) *(DA 7062)* – Hero takes a fall (remix) / James.

Jul 86. (7") *(A 7255)* **GOING DOWN TO LIVERPOOL. / LET IT GO** [ ] [ ]
(12"+=) *(TA 7255) – Walking down your street – James (live medley).*

Sep 86. (7"/7"w-poster) *(650071-7/-0) <06257>* **WALK LIKE AN EGYPTIAN. / NOT LIKE YOU** [3] [1]
(12"+=) *(650071-6)* – ('A'dub version) / ('A'acappella).
(d7"+=) *(650071-8)* – Manic Monday / In a different light.

Dec 86. (7"/7"g-f/ext.12") *(BANGS/+G/T 1) <06674>* **WALKING DOWN YOUR STREET (remix). / RETURN POST** [16] [11]
(d7"+=) *(BANGS D1)* – Walk like an Egyptian / Not like you.

Apr 87. (7"/7"w-poster) *(BANGS/+Q 2)* **FOLLOWING. / DOVER BEACH** [55] [ ]
(12"+=/d7"+=) *(BANGS T/D 2)* – Bangles hit mix medley (Manic Monday – If she knew what she wants – Walking down your street – Going down to Liverpool – Walk like an Egyptian).

— next 45 was a one-off for movie 'Less Than Zero' on 'Def Jam-CBS' label

Jan 88. (7"/7"pic-d) *(BANGS/+Q 3) <07630>* **HAZY SHADE OF WINTER. / (b-side by "Joan Jett & The Blackhearts")** [11] [2]
(12") *(BANGS T3)* – ('A'-Purple haze mix) / ('A'dub) / ('A'-Shady haze mix).
(cd-s++=) *(BANGS C3)* – (the 4 tracks) / Walk like an Egyptian.

Oct 88. (7"/7"w-poster) *(BANGS/+Q 4) <08090>* **IN YOUR ROOM. / BELL JAR** [35] [5]
(12"+=/12"pic-d+=/cd-s+=) *(BANGS T/P/C 4)* – Hazy shade of winter (remix).

Nov 88. (lp/c/cd) *(462977-1/-4/-2) <44056>* **EVERYTHING** [5] [15]
– In your room / Complicated girl / Bell jar / Something to believe in / Eternal flame / Be with you / Glitter years / I'll set you free / Watching the sky / Some dreams come true / Make a play for her now / Waiting for you / Crash and burn. *(re-iss. Apr93 on 'Columbia' cd/c;)*

Jan 89. (7") *(BANGS R5) <68533>* **ETERNAL FLAME. / WHAT I MEANT TO SAY** [1] [1]
(12"+=/cd-s+=) *(BANGS T/C 5)* – Walk like an Egyptian (dance mix).
(12") *(BANGS Q5)* – ('A'side) / Bangles hitmix.
(c-s) *(BANGS M5)* – ('A'side) / Going down to Liverpool / Hero takes a fall / James.

May 89. (7"/7"sha-pic-d/c-s) *(BANGS/+P/M 6) <68744>* **BE WITH YOU. / LET IT GO** [23] [30]
(12"+=/cd-s+=) *(BANGS T/C 6)* – In your room (extended).
(pic-cd-s+=) *(BANGS D6)* – Manic Monday (extended California mix).

Oct 89. (7") *(BANGS 7)* **I'LL SET YOU FREE. / WATCHING THE SKY** [74] [ ]
(12"+=/cd-s+=) *(BANGS T/C 7)* – Walking down your street (extended).

May 90. (cd/c/lp) *(466769-2/-4/-1) <46125>* **BANGLES' GREATEST HITS** (compilation) [4] [97]
– Hero takes a fall / Going down to Liverpool / Manic Monday / If she knew what she wants / Walk like an Egyptian / Walking down your street / Following / Hazy shade of winter / In your room / Eternal flame / Be with you / I'll set you free / Everything I wanted / Where were you when I needed you. *(re-iss. May95 + Dec95 on 'Columbia' cd/c;)*

May 90. (7") *(BANGS 8)* **WALK LIKE AN EGYPTIAN (remix). / ('A'-Ozymandias remix)** [73] [ ]
(c-s+=/12"+=/cd-s+=) *(BANGS M/T/C 8)* – ('A'extended dance) / ('A'dub) / ('A'acappella).

— In the autumn of 1990, they disbanded

BANNED

Formed: Croydon, nr. London, England . . . in the summer of '77 by drummer/vocalist PAUL SORDID, PETE FRESH, BEN DOVER and TOMMY STEAL (obviously not their real names!). One of the many pub-rock acts (i.e. The MOTORS, etc) to turn punk-rock/new wave, the BANNED self-financed the release of their version of The Syndicate's 1966 US hit, 'LITTLE GIRL'. Two months later in November, 'Harvest' records signed the group to their roster (the label had also recently signed WIRE) and with radio airplay it became a surprise UK Top 40 hit. Their early '78 follow-up, 'HIM OR ME' (another cover; PAUL REVERE & THE RAIDERS the source this time), failed to capture the same fanbase, however and the BANNED er . . . dis-banned-ed.

Album rating: none released!

PAUL SORDID – vocals, drums / **PETE FRESH** – guitar / **BEN DOVER** (b. RICK MANSWORTH) – guitar / **TOMMY STEAL** (b. JOHN THOMAS) – bass

Can't Eat / not iss.

Sep 77. (7") *(EATUP 1)* **LITTLE GIRL. / C.P.G.J.'s** [ ] [-]

Harvest / Harvest

Nov 77. (7") *(HAR 5145)* **LITTLE GIRL. / C.P.G.J.'s** [36] [ ]

Mar 78. (7") *(HAR 5149)* **HIM OR ME. / YOU DIRTY RAT** [ ] [-]

— split sometime in 1978, although they'll no doubt be featuring on an upcoming edition of Mark Lamaar's BBC2 pop quiz show, 'Never Mind The Buzzcocks'.

BARK PSYCHOSIS

Formed: Woodford, East London, England . . . 1988 by former schoolmates GRAHAM SUTTON, JOHN LING and MARK SIMNOTT, whose ambitions to be the next NAPALM DEATH shocked classmates and teachers alike at an end of term free day two years previously. In fact, BARK PSYCHOSIS performed their first gig supporting the aforementioned group's rivals, EXTREME NOISE TERROR. The subsequent exposure led to a deal with indie imprint, 'Cheree', three 45's, 'CLAW HAMMER, 'ALL DIFFERENT THINGS' and 'NOTHING FEELS' being released at the turn of the decade. Taking avant-garde pop extremism to its outer limits, BARK PSYCHOSIS combined elements of shoegazing while drawing inspiration from such leftfield luminaries as SPACEMEN 3, SWANS, JOY DIVISION and latter period TALK TALK! Following the addition of DANIEL GISH (on keyboards) in 1991, the band's next two singles appeared via '3rd Stone', the second of which, 'SCUM' received music press plaudits for its 20 minute-plus sonic textures and hypnotic noise. Moving on up to Virgin subsidiary 'Circa', the band began the arduous task of completing a debut album during which time GISH walked out as inter band tensions reached an all-time high. Early in 1994, preceded by an accompanying single, 'A STREET SCENE', the album, 'HEX' finally hit the shops, although by the time of its release LING had bailed out.

Album rating: HEX (*7)

GRAHAM SUTTON – vocals, samples, etc / **JOHN LING** – bass, samples, etc / **MARK SIMNOTT** – drums

Cheree | not iss.

Aug 89. (7"flexi) *(Cheree 5)* **CLAW HAMMER. / (other side by The FURY THINGS)** –
Apr 90. (12") *(Cheree 6T)* **ALL DIFFERENT THINGS. / BY-BLOW** –
Nov 90. (12") *(Cheree 10T)* **NOTHING FEELS. / I KNOW** –
(cd-s+=) *(Cheree 10CD)* – All different things / By-blow.

— added **DANIEL GISH** – keyboards

3rd Stone | unknown

Apr 92. (12"ep) **MAN MAN. / BLOOD RUSH / TOOLED UP** –
Sep 92. (12"/cd-s; 22 minutes) **SCUM** –

— now without GISH

Circa | Plan 9-Caroline

Jan 94. (10"/cd-s) *(YR A/CD 109)* **A STREET SCENE. / RESERVE SHOT-GUNMAN** –
Feb 94. (cd/c/lp) *(CIR CD/C/CA 29)* <1753> **HEX**
– The loom / A street scene / Absent friend / Big shot / Fingerspit / Eyes and smiles / Pendulum man.
May 94. (12"white/cd-s) *(YR T/CD 117)* **BLUE. / HEX / BIG SHOT** –

— split with LING while the above album was in process of being released, their sawnsong gig coming in April '94

– compilations, etc. –

Jul 94. (cd) *3rd Stone; (STONE 010CD)* **INDEPENDENCY** (early 90's material) –
Mar 94. (cd) *3rd Stone; (STONE 031CD)* **GAME OVER** –
– Blue / Three girl rhumba / I know / All different things / Man man / Bloodrush / A street scene / Murder city / Scum / Pendulum man.

Lou BARLOW (see under ⇒ DINOSAUR JR.)

Richard BARONE (see under ⇒ BONGOS)

BARRACUDAS

Formed: London, England ... Spring 1979 by a cosmopolitan crew of Canadian JEREMY GLUCK, American DAVID BUCKLEY, plus Brits ROBIN WILLS and NICKY TURNER. Like The RAMONES playing The BEACH BOYS garage-style, The BARRACUDAS splashed onto the scene via the independently released 'I WANT MY WOODY BACK'. After inking a major deal with EMI's 'Zonophone' imprint, their second single, 'SUMMER FUN', bit the arse-end of the UK Top 40 in 1980 and was followed by a wave of formulaic retro-surf singles prior to a debut album, 'DROP OUT WITH THE BARRACUDAS', early in '81. As the band progressed to more adventurous sounds, BUCKLEY and TURNER were replaced by JIM DICKSON and TERRY SMITH, while CHRIS WILSON (ex-FLAMIN' GROOVIES) added a new dimension. In 1982, 'Flicknife' (stable of HAWKWIND at the time) issued two limited edition 45's, although they found it difficult to secure a UK album deal. However, they did find an outlet for their material through French label, 'Closer', who issued two albums, 'MEAN TIME' (1983) and 'ENDEVOUR TO PERSEVERE' (1984) prior to their untimely demise late in '84. While GLUCK ventured on a solo sojourn (one album in '87, 'I KNEW BUFFALO BILL'), WILLS formed the FORTUNATE SONS (named after a CREEDENCE CLEARWATER REVIVAL classic), filling in time before a belated BARRACUDAS reunion. The reformation was short-lived however, only a one-off single in 1990 and a solitary album, 'WAIT FOR EVERYTHING' (1992), seeing the light of day. • **Covered:** YOU'RE GONNA MISS ME (13th Floor Elevators) / FORTUNATE SON (Creedence Clearwater Revival) / SEVEN AND SEVEN IS (love) / etc.

Album rating: DROP OUT WITH THE BARRACUDAS (*6) / MEAN TIME (*6)

JEREMY GLUCK – vocals (ex-YOHAWKS) / **ROBIN WILLS** – guitar, vocals (ex-CHRYSLER ET LES NOUSTIQUAIRES, ex-R.A.F.) / **DAVID BUCKLEY** – bass, vocals (ex-SKYSCRAPERS, ex-R.A.F.) / **NICKY TURNER** – drums

Cells | not iss.

Aug 79. (7") *(SELLOUT 1)* **I WANT MY WOODY BACK. / SUBWAY SURFIN'** –

Zonophone | Bomp

Jul 80. (7") *(Z 5)* **SUMMER FUN. / CHEVY BABY** 37 –
Sep 80. (7"m) *(Z 8)* **HIS LAST SUMMER. / BARRACUDA WAVER / SURFERS ARE BACK** –
Nov 80. (7") *(Z 11)* **(I WISH IT COULD BE) 1965 AGAIN. / RENDEZVOUS** –
Jan 81. (7") *(Z 17)* **I CAN'T PRETEND. / THE K.G.B. (MADE A MAN OUT OF ME)** –
Feb 81. (lp/c) *(ZONO/ZC-ZONO 103)* <BLP 4022> **DROP OUT WITH THE BARRACUDAS** Jun82
– I can't pretend / We're living in violent times / Don't let go / Codeine / This ain't my time / I saw my death in a dream last night / Somewhere outside / Summer fun / His last summer / Somebody / Campus tramp / On the strip / California lament / (I wish it could be) 1965 again. *<US cd-iss. Aug88 on 'Voxx'; 200009> (cd-iss. Jun94; VOXXCD 2009)*

— **JIM DICKSON** – bass; repl. BUCKLEY

— **TERRY SMITH** – drums; repl. GRAEME POTTER who repl. TURNER who joined LORDS OF THE NEW CHURCH

— added **CHRIS WILSON** – guitar, vocals (ex-FLAMIN' GROOVIES)

Flicknife | not iss.

Feb 82. (7") *(FLS 207)* **INSIDE MIND. / HOUR OF DEGRADATION** –
May 83. (12"ep) *(FLEP 103)* **HOUSE OF KICKS** –
– House of kicks / Next time around / Dead skin / Takes what.

Closer | not iss.

Mar 83. (lp) *(CL 01)* **MEAN TIME** –
– Grammar of misery / Bad news / I ain't no miracle worker / Be my friend again / Shades of today / Dead skin / Middle class blues / You've come a long way / Ballad of a liar / When I'm gone / Eleventh hour / Hear me calling. *(cd-iss. May95 on 'Mau Mau'; MAUCD 641)*
Feb 84. (7") *(CL 06)* **THEY SAY WE'VE CHANGED. / LAUGHING AT YOU** –
Apr 84. (lp) *(CL 09)* **ENDEAVOUR TO PERSEVERE** –
– Dealing with today / Leaving home again / Song for Lorraine / World turned upside down / See her eyes again / Black snake / The way we've changed / She knows / Man with money / Pieces broken / Losin' steak / Corrine / Barracuda. *(cd-iss. May95 on 'Mau Mau'+=; MAUCD 642)* – Stolen heart (single mix) / Laughing at you.
Aug 84. (7") *(CL7 15)* **STOLEN HEART. / I SEE HER EYES AGAIN** –
(12"+=) *(CL12 15)* – Be my friend again (original demo).

— split in December 1984, although all remained part of the scene. GLUCK and DICKSON became LIFE AHEAD CORPORATION, although they only issued a 12" EP, 'RICH MEN'S BURDEN' on 'Truth' (TRUET 02) in April '85.

JEREMY GLUCK

— solo with various people including on the first NIKKI SUDDEN and ROWLAND S. HOWARD (ex-SWELL MAPS and BIRTHDAY PARTY respectively)

Flicknife | not iss.

Apr 87. (lp/c) *(SHARP/+C 037)* **I KNEW BUFFALO BILL** –
– Looking for a place to fall / Too long / Gone free / Hymn / Time undone / Gallery wharf / Four seasons of trouble / All my secrets.

Tuff Enuff | not iss.

Sep 87. (12"ep) *(TUFFT 01)* **THRILLING TALE OF BUFFALO BILL EP** –
– Thrilling tale of Buffalo Bill / Looking for a place to fall / Time goes faster / One more story.

FORTUNATE SONS

— **ROBIN WILLS** – vocals, guitar / **STEVE LABINSO** – bass, vocals / **LEE ROBINSON** – drums, vocals

Bam Caruso | not iss.

Jun 86. (7") *(NRIC 043)* **SOMETIMES YOU WIN . . . . / ME & MY UNCLE** –
Jun 86. (lp) *(KIRI 050)* **RISING** –
– Sometimes you win . . . / Under the light / Down down / Wastin' time / Just another day / Where we stand / Burning / Rock'n'roll time / All the time in the world / 20th century myth.

— added **CHRIS WILSON** – guitar

Jul 87. (12") *(PABL 087)* **HAMMERHEAD. /** –
Nov 87. (lp) *(KIRI 093)* **KAREZZA** –

BARRACUDAS

— reformed with **GLUCK + WILLS** plus **STEVE ROBINSON** – bass

Brown Buffalo | Sympathy F

Apr 90. (7"colrd; various) **NEXT TIME AROUND. / TAKE WHAT HE WANTS** –
Feb 92. (lp/c/cd) *(SAL/+C/CD 203)* **WAIT FOR EVERYTHING** –

— split for the final time in 1993

– compilations, imports, etc. –

Jun 82. (7"ep) *Voxx-Bomp;* **I CAN'T PRETEND** –
– I can't pretend / Surfers are back / You were on my mind / Surfer Joe.
Oct 83. (lp) *Coyote; (COR 021)* **LIVE 1983 (live)** – – French
– Inside mind / You've come a long way / Violent times / Codeine / Fortunate son / Middle class blues / Hour of degradation / Seven & seven is / Miracle worker / You're gonna miss me.

— above featured **MARK SHEPPARD** (aka EMPIRE) – drums (not SMITH)

Jul 84. (lp) *Coyote; (COR 022)* **THE BIG GAP** (early demos 1978-81) – – French
Apr 85. (m-lp) *Trust; (TRUST 001)* **THE WORLD'S A BURN** –
(re-iss. Dec88 on 'Flicknife'; BLUNT 044)
Jan 90. (lp) *Shakin' Street; (YEAHHUP 006)* **THE GARBAGE DUMP TAPES – THE COMPLETE HOUSE OF KICKS SESSIONS** (remixes and re-recordings of early 80's material) –
Nov 90. (12"ep) *Shakin' Street;* **GRAMMAR OF MISERY** –
– Grammar of misery / Laughing at you / Slow death (live).
Jan 91. (cd) *EMI Capitol;* **THE COMPLETE EMI RECORDINGS** –
(UK-iss.May93 on 'Dojo'; DOJOCD 99)
Feb 93. (cd) *Anagram; (CDGRAM 62)* **TWO SIDES OF A COIN 1979-1984** –

– I want my Woody back / Subway surfin' / Inside mind / Hour of degradation / Next time round / Take what he wants / DEad skin / Two sides of a coin / Kingdom of pain / 20th century myth / The very last day / Wastin' time / Daggers of justice / There's a world out there / Seven and seven is / Codeine / Song for Lorraine / Fortunate son.

May 94. (cd) *New Rose; (899027)* **SURF AND DESTROY** □ –

BASTRO (see under ⇒ SQUIRREL BAIT)

Martyn BATES (see under ⇒ EYELESS IN GAZA)

BATFISH BOYS

Formed: York, England . . . late 1984 by indie-goths, SIMON DETROIT (ex-MARCH VIOLETS) and MARTIN PINK (ex-SKELETAL FAMILY), alongside T.G. ASHTON and JOHEY ELLIOTT. Forming their own 'Batfish' label, they abandoned goth for a more trashabilly-rock/STOOGES sound, releasing their debut 45, 'SWAMP LIQUOR', not long after formation. An album, 'THE GODS HATE KANSAS' (1985), was nothing new in the music stakes, although they were to add a second guitarist, ZERO REK, for a beefed up second single, 'CROCODILE TEARS'. With each successive release they became heavier and heavier and it was no surprise when 'G.W.R.' (home of MOTORHEAD) signed BATFISH (as they were now called) to their roster. An album, 'BATFISH BREW', was released in 1989, although the pain was unbearable by the accompanying 'ANOTHER ONE BITES THE DUST' single.

Album rating: THE GODS HATE KANSAS (*5) / HEAD (*3) / BATFISH BREW (*4)

SIMON D – vocals (ex-MARCH VIOLETS) / **JOHEY ELLIOTT** – guitar / **T.G. ASHTON** – bass / **MARTIN PINK** – drums (ex-SKELETAL FAMILY)

Batfish Inc. not iss.

Apr 85. (7") *(BF 102)* **SWAMP LIQUOR. / HOUND OF DEATH** □ –
(12"+=) *(USS 101)* – Hot dog.

Jul 85. (lp) *(USS 102)* **THE GODS HATE KANSAS** □ –

—— added **ZERO REK** – guitar

May 86. (12"ep) *(USS 105)* **CROCODILE TEARS EP** □ –

Sep 86. (lp) *(USS 106)* **HEAD** □ –

Oct 86. (7") *(USS 107)* **JUSTINE. / AMOEBA ROCK** □ –

—— **BOB + BOMBER** – rhythm; repl. ASHTON + PINK respectively

Mar 87. (7") *(USS 108)* **THE BOMB SONG. /** □ –
(12"+=) *(USS 108-12)* –

G.W.R. not iss.

Jan 88. (7") **PURPLE DUST. /** □ –

Sep 89. (lp/c/cd) *(GW LP/TC/MCD 28)* **BATFISH BREW** □ –

Dec 89. (12"pic-d) *(GWPD 7)* **ANOTHER ONE BITES THE DUST. / THE BOMB SONG (echology mix) / BORN TO BE WILD (live)** □ –

—— disbanded after above

Stiv BATORS (see under ⇒ DEAD BOYS)

BATS

Formed: Christchurch, New Zealand . . . 1983 by former CLEAN member and main songwriter ROBERT SCOTT, along with PAUL KEAN, also from another Kiwi act, TOY LOVE. Adding KAYE WOODWARD and MALCOLM GRANT, The BATS signed to influential NZ label, 'Flying Nun', releasing a debut EP, 'BY NIGHT', the following year. In 1985, a mini-lp, ' . . .THE FIRESIDE', continued in a similar roots pop-rock mould, no doubt confusing any goths who bought it on the strength of their moniker. The following year, The BATS became the first Kiwi act to appear on the UK branch of the aforementioned imprint with the 'MADE UP IN BLUE' EP (they also signed to 'Mammoth' in the States). In the Autumn of '88, The BATS finally released their first full-length set, 'DADDY'S HIGHWAY', a record fusing urban folk-rock, bluegrass and WIRE-esque garage. A two year sabbatical ensued during which time KAYE took maternity leave and KEAN regrouped The CLEAN. After a fine domestic release, 'THE LAW OF THINGS' (1990), The BATS returned to the fray, this time for 'Rough Trade' with 'FEAR OF GOD' (1992). Homing in again on 'Flying Nun', the seasoned indie-pop campaigners issued two further sets, 'SILVERBEET' (1993) and 'COUCHMASTER' (1995), garnering the usual critical acclaim and steady sales.

Album rating: COMPILETELY BATS compilation (*7) / DADDY'S HIGHWAY (*7) / THE LAW OF THINGS (*8) / FEAR OF GOD (*6) / SILVERBEET (*6) / SPILL THE BEANS mini (*4) / COUCHMASTER (*6)

ROBERT SCOTT – guitar, vocals (ex-CLEAN) / **PAUL KEAN** – bass (ex-TOY LOVE) / **KAYE WOODWARD** – vocals, guitar, keyboards / **MALCOLM GRANT** – drums, percussion

Flying Nun Communion

1984. (7"ep) **BY NIGHT EP** – – New Z

1985. (m-lp) **"AND HERE IS 'MUSIC FOR THE FIRESIDE'!"** – – New Z

Oct 86. (12"ep) *(FNUK 001)* **MADE UP IN BLUE EP** – –

1987. (c) **COMPILETELY BATS** (compilation) – – New Z
– (all of the above) *(cd-iss. Dec92; FNCD 143)*

Oct 88. (12"ep) *(FNE 22)* **FOUR SONGS EP** □ –
– North by north (remix) / Straight through my heart / Get fat / Best friend's brain.

Oct 88. (lp/cd) *(FNE 23/+CD)* *<5>* **DADDY'S HIGHWAY** □ □
– Treason / Sir Queen / Round and down / Take it / Tragedy / North by north / Block of wood / Miss these things / Mid city team / Some peace tonight / Had to be you / Daddy's highway / Calm before the storm / Candidate / Mad on you / Trouble in this town / Made up in blue. *<US cd re-iss. 1994 on 'Mammoth'; MR 0071-2>*

—— in 1989, they took a sabbatical while KAYE had a baby and PAUL returned to The CLEAN

1990. (cd) *<15>* **THE LAW OF THINGS** – □ New Z
– The other side of you / The law of things / Never said goodbye / Yawn vibes / Time to get ready / Ten to one / Mastery / I fall away / Cliff edge / Nine days / Bedlam / Smoking her wings. *<US re-iss. 1994 on 'Mammoth'; MR 0072-2>*

Rough Trade Mammoth

Mar 92. (cd/c/lp) *(R 283-2/-4/-1)* *<MR 0040-2/-4>* **FEAR OF GOD** □ □
– Boogey man / The black and the blue / Dancing as the boat goes down / Old ones / Hold all the butter / Fear of God / It's a lie / Straight image / Watch the walls / You know we shouldn't / Jetsam / Looming past.

Flying Nun Mammoth

Sep 93. (cd/c) *(FN CD/MC 260)* *<MR 0051-2/-4>* **SILVERBEET** □ □
– Courage / Sighting the sound / Too much / Slow alight / Valley floor / Love floats two / Green / No time for your kind / Straight on home / Before the day / Stay away / Drive me some boars / Halfway to nowhere.

Oct 93. (cd-ep) *<MR 0052>* **COURAGE / MIND HOW YOU RUN / SLOW ALRIGHT / WIND IS SAD** – □

Jul 94. (m-cd) *<MR 0070-2>* **SPILL THE BEANS EP** – □
– Under the law / Spill the beans / Empty head / Make it clear / Give in to the sands.

Oct 95. (lp/cd) *(FN/+CD 301)* *<MR 0126>* **COUCHMASTER** □ □
– Outside / Afternoon in bed / Around you like snow / Work it out / Train / Land o' lakes / Chain home low / Supernova / Shoeshine / Crow song / Smorgasboard / Knowledge is power / It's happening to you / Lost weekend / For the ride / Out of bounds / Down to me.

BAUHAUS

Formed: Northampton, England . . . late 1978, by PETE MURPHY, DANIEL ASH, DAVID J and KEVIN HASKINS, initially calling themselves BAUHAUS 1919. Obtaining a one-off deal with indie label 'Small Wonder', releasing an 8-minute epic 'BELA LUGOSI'S DEAD', backed with the infamous 'DARK ENTRIES', the latter track subsequently issued as a follow-up 45. A gender-bending but hard-edged collage of glam and punk influences shrouded in gothic horror posturing, BAUHAUS carved out their own inimitable niche in the early 80's post-new wave wasteland. After an album, 'IN THE FLAT FIELD' (1981) and a couple of singles (one a cover of T.Rex's 'TELEGRAM SAM') on '4 a.d.', the band signed to 'Beggars Banquet', scoring a Top 30 hit with their second set, 'MASK' (1981). Featuring the minor hit singles, 'KICK IN THE EYE' and 'THE PASSION OF LOVERS', the album remains their most consistent set. Still, the underground cred was called into question after MURPHY apeared in a TV ad for Maxell tapes later that year. More appropriate, perhaps, was the band's performance of 'BELA LUGOSI'S DEAD' for 1982 vampire film, 'The Hunger' starring the band's boyhood hero, DAVID BOWIE. In fact, it was one of BOWIE's classics, 'ZIGGY STARDUST', that gave BAUHAUS their commercial breakthrough, the single's Top 20 success seeing the accompanying album, THE SKY'S GONE OUT' make the UK Top 5. The droning affectations of 'SHE'S IN PARTIES' remains one of the band's most recognisable tracks while the swan song album, 'BURNING FROM THE INSIDE' (1983), saw BAUHAUS signing off on an unsettling, if creatively high point. MURPHY soon reappeared with MICK KARN of JAPAN in a new outfit, DALI'S CAR, although only one album, 'THE WAKING HOUR', surfaced in '84. The singer went on to release a string of albums, surprising many in Britain when he had a US Top 50 placing with 'DEEP', which contained the 1990 hit, 'CUTS YOU UP'. Meanwhile, the rest were enjoying success as LOVE AND ROCKETS (from earlier incarnation of TONES ON TAILS and DAVID J solo) and this trio also took America by storm having had a Top 3 smash, 'SO ALIVE' in '89. • **Covered:** THIRD UNCLE (Eno) / WAITING FOR THE MAN (Velvet Underground). PETER MURPHY solo, wrote with STREATHAM and covered; FINAL SOLUTION (Pere Ubu) / THE LIGHT POURS OUT OF ME (Magazine) / FUNTIME (Iggy Pop). LOVE AND ROCKETS covered BALL OF CONFUSION (Temptations) / BODY AND SOUL (trad). DAVID J covered 4 HOURS (ClockDva) / SHIP OF FOOLS (John Cale).

Album rating: BAUHAUS 1979-1983 compilation (*9) / NIGHT MUSIC (TONES ON TAIL *6) / LOVE AND ROCKETS (LOVE AND ROCKETS *5)

PETER MURPHY (b.11 Jul'57) – vocals / **DANIEL ASH** (b.31 Jul'57) – guitar, vocals / **DAVID J** (b. HASKINS, 24 Apr'57) – bass, vocals / **KEVIN HASKINS** (b.19 Jul'60) – drums, percussion

Small Wonder not iss.

Aug 79. (12",12"white) *(TEENY 2)* **BELA LUGOSI'S DEAD. / BOYS / DARK ENTRIES** □ –
(re-dist.Mar81 & Mar82; same) (re-iss. Sep86 in various colours; same) (12"pic-d.1987; TEENY 2P) (re-iss. May88 & Jun98, c-s/cd-s; TEENY 2 C/CD)

Axis not iss.

Jan 80. (7") *(AXIS 3)* **DARK ENTRIES. / UNTITLED** □ –
(re-iss. Feb80 on '4.a.d.'; AD 3) (some mispressed on 'Beggars Banquet'; BEG 37)

4.a.d. not iss.

Jun 80. (7") *(AD 7)* **TERROR COUPLE KILL COLONEL. / SCOPES / TERROR COUPLE KILL COLONEL II** □ –

Oct 80. (lp) *(CAD 13)* **IN THE FLAT FIELD** 72 –
– Double dare / In the flat field / A god in an alcove / Dive / Spy in the cab / Small talk stinks / St. Vitus dance / Stigmata martyr / Nerves. *(cd-iss. Apr88 +=; CAD 13CD)* – Untitled.

Oct 80. (7") *(AD 17)* **TELEGRAM SAM. / CROWDS** □ –
(12"+=) *(AD 17T)* – Rosegarden funeral of sores.

Beggars Banquet A&M

Mar 81. (7"/12") *(BEG 54/+T)* **KICK IN THE EYE. / SATORI** 59 –

Jun 81. (7") *(BEG 59)* **THE PASSION OF LOVERS. / 1: 2: 3: 4:** [56] [-]
Oct 81. (lp/c) *(BEGA/BEGC 29)* **MASK** [30] [-]
– Hair of the dog / The passion of lovers / Of lillies and remains / Dancing / Hollow hills / Kick in the eye / Muscle in plastic / In fear of fear / Man with x-ray eyes / Mask. *(re-iss. Feb88 & Jul91 on 'Beggars Banquet-Lowdown' lp/c; BBL/+C 29) (cd-iss. Oct88 & Jul91 +=; BBL 29CD)* – Satori / Harry / Earwax / In fear of dub / Kick in the eye.
Feb 82. (7"ep) *(BEG 74)* **SEARCHING FOR SATORI** [45] [-]
– Kick in the eye / Harry / Earwax.
(12"ep+=) *(BEG 74T)* – In fear of dub.
Jun 82. (7"/7"pic-d) *(BEG 79/+P)* **SPIRIT. / TERROR COUPLE KILL COLONEL (live)** [42] [-]
Sep 82. (7") *(BEG 83)* **ZIGGY STARDUST. / THIRD UNCLE (live)** [15] [-]
(12"+=) *(BEG 83T)* – Party of the first part / Waiting for the man.
Oct 82. (d-lp/d-c) *(BEGA/BEGC 42) / (BEGA/BEGC 38)* <SP 4918>
THE SKY'S GONE OUT / PRESS THE EJECT BUTTON AND GIVE ME THE TAPE (live) [4] [ ]
– Third uncle / Silent hedges / In the night / Swing the heartache / Spirit / The three shadows (parts 1, 2, 3) / Silent hedges / All we ever wanted was everything / Exquisite corpse. *(re-iss. Feb88 & Jul91 on 'Beggars Banquet-Lowdown' lp/c; BBL/+C 42) (cd-iss. Oct88 & Jul91 +=; BBL 42CD)* – Ziggy Stardust / Watch that grandad go / Party of the first part / Spirit (extended). **PRESS THE EJECT BUTTON AND GIVE ME THE TAPE** – In the flat field / Rosegarden funeral of sores / Dancing / Man with the x-ray eyes / Bela Lugosi's dead / Spy in the cab / Kick in the eye / In fear of fear / Hollow hills / Stigmata martyr / Dark entries. *(re-iss. Feb88 & Jul91 on 'Beggars Banquet-Lowdown'; BBL/+C 38) (cd-iss. Oct88 & Jul91 +=; BBL 38CD)* – Terror couple kill colonel / Double dare / Waiting for the man / Hair of the dog / Of lillies and remains. *(free 7"ep with above; BH 1)* – SATORI IN PARIS (live)
Jan 83. (7") *(BEG 88)* **LAGARTIJA NICK. / PARANOIA! PARANOIA!** [44] [-]
(12"+=) *(BEG 88T)* – Watch that grandad go / In the flat field (live).
Mar 83. (7") <2524> **LAGARTIJA NICK. / ZIGGY STARDUST** [-] [ ]
Apr 83. (7"/7"pic-d) *(BEG 91/+P)* **SHE'S IN PARTIES. / DEPARTURE** [26] [ ]
(12"+=) *(BEG 91T)* – Here's the dub.
Jul 83. (lp/c) *(BEGA/BEGC 45)* **BURNING FROM THE INSIDE** [13] [ ]
– She's in parties / Antonin Artaud / King Volcano / Who killed Mr. Moonlight? / Slice of life / Honeymoon croon / Kingdom's coming / Burning from the inside / Hope. *(re-iss. Feb88 & Jul91 on 'Beggars Banquet-Lowdown' lp/c; BBL/+C 45) (cd-iss. Oct88 & Jul91 +=; BBL 45CD)* – Lagartija Nick / Departure / Here's the dub / The sanity assassin.

—— disbanded mid 1983. DAVID J. continued splinter solo venture before forming LOVE AND ROCKETS with DANIEL and KEVIN who had come from own outfit, TONES ON TAIL. MURPHY went solo (see below).

– compilations, others, etc. –

on 'Beggars Banquet' unless mentioned otherwise
Sep 83. (12"ep) *4 a.d.; (BAD 312)* **THE 4.A.D. SINGLES** [ ] [-]
– Dark entries / Terror couple kill colonel / Telegram Sam / Rosegarden full of sores / Crowds.
Oct 83. (12"ep) *(BEG 100E)* **THE SINGLES 1981-83** [52] [-]
– The passion of lovers / Kick in the eye / Spirit / Ziggy Stardust / Lagartija Nick / She's in parties. *(re-iss. Dec88 as 3"pic-cd; BBP 4CD)*
Nov 85. (d-lp/c) *(BEGA/BEGC 64)* **BAUHAUS 1979-1983** [36] [ ]
(d-cd-iss. Feb88; BEG 64CD) (re-iss. d-cd Sep95)
Jul 89. (d-lp/c)(d-cd) *(BEGA/BEGC 103)(BEGA 103CD)* <9804>
SWING THE HEARTACHE (the BBC sessions) [ ] [ ]
(re-iss. 2xcd Sep95; BBL 64 CD1/CD2)

DALI'S CAR

were formed by **PETE MURPHY** – vocals / **MICK KARN** – bass, multi (ex-JAPAN) / **PAUL VINCENT LAWFORD** – rhythms

Paradox | Beggars Banquet

Oct 84. (7"/7"pic-d) *(DOX/+Y 1)* **THE JUDGEMENT IS THE MIRROR. / HIGH PLACES** [66] [-]
(12"+=) *(DOX 1-12)* – Lifelong moment.
Nov 84. (lp/c/cd) *(DOX LP/C/CD 1)* **THE WAKING HOUR** [84] [ ]
– Dali's car / His box / Cornwall stone / Artemis / Create and melt / Moonlife / The judgement is the mirror. *(re-iss. Jan89 on 'Beggars Banquet-Lowdown'; lp/c)(cd; BBL/+C 52)(BBL 52CD)*

PETER MURPHY

went solo, augmented by **JOHN McGEOGH** – guitar / **HOWARD HUGHES** – keyboards / **ROBERT SUAVE** – bass / **STEVE YOUNG** – rhythm prog. / **PLUG** – harmonica

Beggars Banquet | Beggars Banquet

Nov 85. (7") *(BEG 143)* **THE FINAL SOLUTION. / THE ANSWER'S CLEAR** [ ] [ ]
(12"+=) *(BEG 143T)* – ('A'full version).
(12"pic-d+=) *(BEG 143TP)* – ('A'club mix).
Jun 86. (7"/12") *(BEG 162/+T)* **BLUE HEART. / CANVAS BEAUTY** [ ] [ ]
Jul 86. (lp/c) *(BEGA/BEGC 69)* **SHOULD THE WORLD FAIL TO FALL APART** [82] [ ]
– Canvas beauity / The light pours out of me / Confessions / Should the world fail to fall apart / Never man / God . . . sends / Blue heart / The answer is clear / The final solution / Jemal. *(re-iss. Jul88 on 'Beggars Banquet-Lowdown' lp/c)(cd; BBL/+C 69)(BBL 69CD)*
Oct 86. (7") *(BEG 174)* **TALE OF THE TONGUE. / SHOULD THE WORLD FAIL TO FALL APART** [ ] [ ]
(12"+=) *(BEG 174T)* – ('A'-2nd version).

—— **MURPHY** brought in **PAUL STATHAM** – co-composer, keyboards (ex-B-MOVIE) / **EDDIE BRACH** – bass / **PETER BONAS** – guitar / **TERL BRYANT** – drums

Feb 88. (7") *(BEG 207)* **ALL NIGHT LONG. / I'VE GOT A SECRET CAMERA** [ ] [-]
(12"+=) *(BEG 207T)* – Funtime (in cabaret).
Mar 88. (lp/c)(cd) *(BEGA/BEGC 92)(BEGA 92CD)* <7634> **LOVE HYSTERIA** [ ] [ ]
– All night long / His circle and hers meet / Dragnet drag / Socrates the python / Indigo eyes / Time has got nothing to do with it / Blind sublime / My last two weeks / Funtime. *(cd+=)* – I've got a miniature secret camera / Funtime (cabaret mix).
Mar 88. (7") <8670> **ALL NIGHT LONG. / FUNTIME (Cabaret mix)** [-] [ ]
Apr 88. (7"/7"box) *(BEG/+B 210)* **INDIGO EYES. / GOD SENDS (live)** [ ] [ ]
(12"+=) *(BEG 210T)* – Confessions (live).
Jun 88. (7") <8707> **INDIGO EYES. / MY LAST TWO WEEKS** [-] [ ]
Mar 90. (7") *(BEG 237)* <9140> **CUTS YOU UP. / STRANGE KIND OF LOVE** [ ] [55]
(12"+=/cd-s+=) *(BEG 237 T/CD)* – Roll call (reprise).
May 90. (cd)(c/lp) *(BEGA 107CD)(BEGC/BEGA 107)* <9877> **DEEP** [ ] [44]
– Deep ocean vast sea / Crystal waters / Marlene Dietrich's favourite poem / Seven veils / The line between the Devil's teeth (and that which cannot be repeated) / Cuts you up / A strange kind of love / Roll call. *(cd+=)* – Strange kind of love (alt.version).
Apr 92. (7") *(BBQ)* **YOU'RE SO CLOSE. / THE SWEETEST DROP** [ ] [ ]
(12"+=/cd-s+=) *(BBQ)* – Cuts you up (live) / All night long (live).
Apr 92. (cd)(c/lp) *(BEGA 123CD)(BEGC/BEGA 123)* <66007> **HOLY SMOKE** [ ] [ ]
– Keep me from harm / Kill the hate / You're so close / The sweetest drop / Low room / Let me love you / Our secret garden / Dream gone by / Hit song.
Jul 92. (7") *(BBQ)* **HIT SONG. / SEVEN VEILS** [ ] [ ]
(12"+=/cd-s+=) *(BBQ)* – The line between the Devil's teeth (and that which cannot be repeated).
Apr 95. (cd-ep) *(BBQ 52CD)* **THE SCARLET THING IN YOU / CRYSTAL WRISTS / WISH / DRAGNET DRAG (live)** [ ] [ ]
Apr 95. (cd/c) *(BBQ CD/MC 175)* **CASCADE** [ ] [ ]
– Mirror to my woman's mind / Subway / Gliding like a whale / Disappearing / Mercy rain / I'll fall with your knife / Scarlet thing in you / Sails wave goodbye / Wild birds flock to me / Huuvola / Cascade.

TONES ON TAILS

GLEN CAMPLING – vocals, bass, keyboards (roadie of BAUHAUS) / **DANIEL ASH** – guitar, vocals / **KEVIN HASKINS** – drums

4.a.d. | not iss.

Apr 82. (12"ep) *(BAD 203)* **A BIGGER SPLASH / COPPER. / MEANS OF ESCAPE / INSTRUMENTAL** [ ] [-]

Beggars Banquet | not iss.

Sep 82. (12") *(BEG 85T)* **THERE'S ONLY ONE. / NOW WE LUSTRE** [ ] [-]

Situation 2 | not iss.

May 83. (7") *(SIT 21)* **BURNING SKIES. / OK, THIS IS THE POPS** [ ] [-]
(12"+=) *(SIT 21T)* – When you're smiling / You, the night and the music.

—— In 1983, they broke from BAUHAUS. ASH and HASKINS joined The JAZZ BUTCHER. TONES ON TAILS soon re-actified their line-up.

Beggars Banquet | not iss.

Mar 84. (7") *(BEG 106)* **PERFORMANCE. / SHAKES** [ ] [-]
(12"+=) *(BEG 106T)* – ('A'dub version).
Apr 84. (lp/c) *(BEGA/BEGC 51)* **POP** [ ] [ ]
– Performance / War / Lions / Happiness / The never never / Real life / Slender fungus / Movement of fear / Rain. *(re-iss. Oct88 & Jul91 on 'Beggars Banquet-Lowdown' lp/c)(cd; BBL/+C 51)(BBL 51CD) (cd-iss. Oct88 as 'NIGHT MUSIC' +=; BEGA 51CD)* – (rest of material).
May 84. (7") *(BEG 109)* **LIONS. / GO! (LET'S GO TO YA YA'S NOW)** [ ] [-]
(12",12"red) *(BEG 109T)* – ('A'side) / Go! (club mix).
Nov 84. (7"/12"blue) *(BEG 121/+T)* **CHRISTIAN SAYS. / TWIST** [ ] [ ]

—— split from this name

Situation 2 | not iss.

Feb 85. (lp/c) *Situation 2; (SITU/SITC 12)* **TONES ON TAILS** (the singles compilation) [ ] [-]
(re-iss. Oct88 & Jul91 on 'Situation 2-Lowdown' lp/c; SITL/+C 12)

LOVE AND ROCKETS

ASH + HASKINS were joined by **DAVID J.** – vocals, bass, keyboards (also ex-BAUHAUS + a solo artist)

Beggars Banquet | Beggars Banquet

May 85. (7"/12") *(BEG 132/+T)* **BALL OF CONFUSION. / INSIDE THE OUTSIDE** [ ] [ ]
Sep 85. (7"/12") *(BEG 146/+T)* **IF THERE'S A HEAVEN ABOVE. / GOD AND MR. SMITH** [ ] [ ]
Oct 85. (lp/c) *(BEGA/BEGC 66)* <85071> **7th DREAM OF TEENAGE HEAVEN** [ ] [ ]
– If there's a Heaven above / A private future / 7th dream of teenage Heaven / Saudade / Haunted when the minutes drag / The dog-end of a day gone by / The game. *(cd-iss. May86; BEGA 66CD) (re-iss. Jan89 & Jul91 on 'Beggars Banquet-Lowdown' lp/c)(cd+=; BBL/+C 66)(BBL 66CD)* – Ball of confusion (USA mix) / God and Mr. Smith (Mars mix) / If there's a Heaven above (Canadian mix).

Beggars Banquet | Big Time

Jun 86. (12"m) *(BEG 163T)* **KUNDALINI EXPRESS. / LUCIFER SAM / HOLIDAY ON THE MOON** [ ] [ ]
Sep 86. (7"/12") *(BEG 166/+T)* **YIN AND YANG (THE FLOWERPOT MEN). / ANGELS AND DEVILS** [ ] [ ]
Sep 86. (lp/c) *(BEGA/BEGC 74)* <6011> **EXPRESS** [ ] [72]
– Kundalini express / It could be sunshine / Love me / All in my mind / Life in Laralay / Yin and Yang (the flowerpot men) / An American dream / All in my mind (acoustic version). *(cd-iss. Jan88; BEGA 74CD) (re-iss. Jan89 & Jul91 on 'Beggars Banquet-Lowdown' lp/c)(cd; BBL/+C 74)(BEGA 74CD)*
Sep 87. (lp/c)(cd) *(BEGA/BEGC 84)(BEGA 84CD)* <6011> **EARTH, SUN, MOON** [ ] [64]
– The light / Mirror people / Welcome tomorrow / Here on Earth / Lazy / Waiting for the flood / Rainbird / Telephone is empty / Everybody wants to go to Heaven /

The sun / Youth. *(re-iss. Jan89 & Jul91 on 'Beggars Banquet' lp/c)(cd+=; BBL/+C 84)(BBL 84CD)* – Mirror people (slow version).

Oct 87. (7"/12") *(BEG 186/+T)* **THE LIGHT. / MIRROR PEOPLE (slow version)**

Mar 88. (7") *(BEG 209)* **NO NEW TALE TO TELL. / EARTH, SUN, MOON**
(12"+=) *(BEG 209T)* – 7th dream of teenage Heaven.

May 88. (7") *(BEG 213)* **MIRROR PEOPLE. / DAVID LANFAIR**
(12"+=) *(BEG 213T)* – ('A'live version).

Aug 88. (7") *(BEG 217)* **LAZY. / THE DOG-END OF A DAY GONE BY**
(12"+=) *(BEG 217T)* – The purest blue.

Beggars Banquet — R.C.A.

Jan 89. (12"ep) *(BEG 224T)* **MOTORCYCLE / I FEEL SPEED. / BIKE / BIKEDANCE**

Jul 89. (7"/c-s/12") *(BEG 229/+C/T)* <8956> **SO ALIVE. / DREAMTIME** — 3 May89
(cd-s+=) *(BEG 229CD)* – Motorcycle / Bike. *(re-dist.Jan90)*

Sep 89. (lp/c)(cd) *(BEGA/BEGC 99)(BEGA 99CD)* <9715> **LOVE AND ROCKETS** — 14
– **** (Jungle law) / No big deal / The purest blue / Motorcycle / I feel speed / Bound for Hell / The teardrop collector / So alive / Rock and roll Babylon / No words no more.

Oct 89. (7") *(BEG 234)* <9045> **NO BIG DEAL. / NO WORDS NO MORE** — 82 Sep89
(12"+=) *(BEG 234T) - 100 watts of your love.*

Beggars Banquet — Beggars Banquet

Jul 94. (12"/cd-s) *(BBQ 36 T/CD)* **THIS HEAVEN / THIS HEAVEN (Secret Knowledge mix). / THIS HEAVEN (Lost In It) / THIS HEAVEN (Torched mix)**

Sep 94. (12"/cd-s) *(BBQ 42 T/CD)* **BODY AND SOUL. / BODY AND SOUL (Secret Knowledge out of body mix) / BODY AND SOUL (Delta Lady Rebel Trouser mix)**

— above featured **NATACHA ATLAS** – vocals (of TRANS-GLOBAL UNDERGROUND)

Sep 94. (cd/c/d-lp) *(BBQ CD/MC/LP 145)* **HOT TRIP TO HEAVEN**
– Body and soul (parts 1 & 2) / Ugly / Trip and glide / This Heaven / No worries / Hot trip to Heaven / Eclipse / Voodoo baby / Be the revolution / Set me free. *(re-iss. cd Sep95; BBL 145CD)*

Mar 96. (cd-ep; unreleased) *(BBQ 67CD)* **SWEET F.A. / THE GLITTERING DARKNESS / TRIP AND GLIDE / RITUAL RADIO / BAD MONKEY** — -

DANIEL ASH

Beggars Banquet — Beggars Banquet

Jun 91. (cd)(c/lp) *(BEGA 114CD)(BEGA/BEGC 114)* <3014> **COMING DOWN**
– Blue moon / Coming down fast / Walk this way / Closer to you / Day tripper / This love / Blue angel / Me and my shadow / Candy darling / Sweet little liar / Not so fast / Coming down.

— Above features covers DAY TRIPPER (Beatles) / BLUE MOON (Rodgers / Hart) / ME AND MY SHADOW (Al Jolson/+).

Jun 91. (7") **WALK THIS WAY. / HEAVEN IS WAITING** — -
(12") – ('A'side) / ('A'groovy vox) / ('A'groovy guitar).
(cd-s) – (all 4 tracks).

Apr 93. (12"ep/cd-ep) *(BBQ 9 T/CD)* **GET OUT OF CONTROL. / THE HEDONIST / GET OUT OF CONTROL (farewell mixes)**

May 93. (cd/c/lp) *(BBQ CD/MC/LP 129)* **FOOLISH THING DESIRE**
– Here she comes / Foolish thing desire / Bluebird / Dream machine / Get out of control / The void / Roll on / Here she comes again / The hedonist / Higher than this.

DAVID J.

4 a.d. — not iss.

Sep 81. (7"; by DAVID JAY & RENE HACKETT) *(AD 112)* **NOTHING. / ARMOUR** — -

Situation 2 — not iss.

Aug 83. (7") *(SIT 26)* **JOE ORTON'S WEDDING. / THE GOSPEL ACCORDING TO FEAR** — -
(12"+=) *(SIT 26T)* – Requiem for Joe / Point of venture.

Oct 83. (lp) *(SITU 8)* **ETIQUETTE OF VIOLENCE** — -
– The gospel according to fear / I hear only silence now / No one's sending roses / The fugitive / Betrayal / Joe Orton's wedding / The promised land / With the Indians permanent / Say uncle / Disease / Roulette / Saint Jackie. *(re-iss. Oct88 & Jul91 on 'Situation 2-Lowdown' lp/c/cd; SITL 8/+C/CD)*

Glass — not iss.

Nov 83. (7"; as DAVID J. & J. WALKERS) *(GLASS 031)* **THE PROMISED LAND. / SAINT JACKIE** — -
(12"+-) *(GLASS12 031)* – A seducer, a doctor, a card you cannot trust.

Jun 84. (12"ep; by DAVID J. & ALAN MOORE) *(GLASS12 032)* **V FOR VENDETTA** — -
– This vicious cabaret / (AV.T.V. broadcast) / V's theme (intro) / V's theme (outro).

Sep 84. (7"/12") *(GLASS/+12 039)* **I CAN'T SHAKE THIS SHADOW OF FEAR. / WAR GAME** — -

Mar 85. (lp) *(GLALP 010)* **CROCODILE TEARS & THE VELVET COSH** — -
– And the velvet cosh / Crocodile tears / Too clever by half / The first incision / Imitation pearls / Light & shade / Rene / Stop this city / Justine / The ballad of Cain / Vandal & the saint / Boats / Slip the rope / Greener. *(cd-iss. Jun88; GLACD 010)*

Apr 85. (7") *(GLASS 042)* **CROCODILE TEARS & THE VELVET COSH. / ELEGY** — -
(12"+=) *(GLASS12 042)* – Rene.

Jun 85. (12"ep) *(GLAEP 101)* **BLUE MOODS TURNING TAILS** — -
– 4 hours / The conjurors hand / Ship of fools.

Mar 86. (lp/c) *(GLA LP/MC 017)* **DAVID J. ON GLASS** (singles compilation) — -
(cd-iss. Jun88; GLACD 017)

— w/ **MAX KIDER** – guitar / **ANGUS WALLACE + OWEN JONES** – drums / **DAVE ANDERSON** – steel guitar / **ALEX GREEN** – sax / **BEN HEANEY** – violin / **BEN GREENAWAY** percussion / **JANIS ZAKIS** – accordian.

Beggars Banquet — Beggars Banquet

Jun 90. (7") *(BEG 243)* **I'LL BE YOUR CHAUFFEUR. / THE MOON IN THE MAN**
(12"+=) *(BEG 243T)* – ('A'original version).

Jul 90. (cd)(c/lp) *(BEGA 112CD)(BEGA/BEGC 112)* **SONGS FROM ANOTHER SEASON**
– Fingers in the grease / A longer look / Sad side to the sand boy / New woman is an attitude / Sweet ancenthexra / On the outskirts (of a strange dream) / I'll be your chauffeur (original) / The Moon in the man / Little star / Stranded Trans-Atlantic hotel nearly famous blues / The national anthem of nowhere / Nature boy.

not iss. — Arista

Apr 92. (12"ep) <54424> **CANDY ON A CROSS / ANTARTICA STARTS HERE. / MEMPHIS GHOST – ANTARTICA STARTS HERE (reprise)** — -

BAWL

Formed: Dublin, Ireland . . . mid 90's by brothers MARK, DARREN and JASON CULLEN, plus STEPHEN McBRIDE. Surfacing on their own label, 'Dependent', BAWL's first two singles, 'BATHROOM' (STICKY ROCK) and 'GIRLS NIGHT OUT', were released either side of Xmas '95. Ireland's answer to Brit-pop or yet another would-be SMITHS or HOUSEMARTINS successor, the band delivered two further lyrically tongue-in-cheek singles, 'GLEN CAMPBELL NIGHTS' and 'BEYOND SAFE WAYS', the latter of which featured on their debut album, 'YEAR ZERO' (1996).

Album rating: YEAR ZERO (*6)

MARK CULLEN – vocals, guitar / **DARREN CULLEN** – guitar / **STEPHEN McBRIDE** – bass / **JASON CULLEN** – drums

Dependent — not iss.

Nov 95. (7") *(BAWL 001)* **BATHROOM. / KITCH** — -

Jan 96. (7") *(DEPE 002)* **GIRLS NIGHT OUT. / HOW CAN I UPSET YOU** — -
(cd-s+=) *(DEPE 002CD)* – Fat boy.

May 96. (7") *(DEPE 003)* **GLEN CAMPBELL NIGHTS. /** — -
(cd-s+=) *(DEPE 003CD)* –

Aug 96. (7") *(DEPE 004)* **BEYOND SAFE WAYS. / PARALLEL** — -
(cd-s+=) *(DEPE 004CD)* – Perfect hairstyle / Some people need others.

Sep 96. (cd/c/lp) *(DEPA D/M/V 005)* **YEAR ZERO** — -
– Approaching zero / Older and older / My spine hurts / Beyond safe ways / Mistake / Shallow / Sticky rock / Fake it / Ex-boyfriend / Mechanic from Rhyl / Girls = songs / Unfinished / Some people need others / He's all that great about pop.

Dec 96. (7"/c-s) *(DEPS S/M 005)* **STICKY ROCK. / LEVER** — -
(cd-s+=) *(DEPSD 005)* – I go wild.

Feb 97. (7"/c-s) *(DEPS S/M 006)* **HE'S ALL THAT'S GREAT ABOUT POP. / CROCODILES** — -
(cd-s+=) *(DEPSD 006)* – Bones / Some people need others.

BAY (see under ⇒ ARAB STRAP)

BEASTIE BOYS

Formed: Greenwich Village, New York, USA . . . 1981 by ADAM YAUCH and MIKE DIAMOND. They recruited ADAM HOROWITZ to replace two others (KATE SCHELLENBACH and JOHN BERRY), and after two US indie releases they signed to 'Def Jam', the label run by The BEASTIE's friend and sometime DJ, RICK RUBIN. RUBIN paired with the BEASTIE BOYS was a match made in Heaven (or Hell, if you were unfortunate enough to own a Volkswagon) and the debut album 'LICENSED TO ILL' (1986) was the first real attempt to create a white, rock-centric take on of Afro-American Hip Hop. At turns hilarious and exhilirating, RUBIN and the BEASTIE's shared taste in classic metal was evident with samples from the likes of AC/DC and LED ZEPPELIN along with the theme tune from American TV show 'Mr. Ed'. With snotty rapping and riff-heavy rhymes, tracks like 'FIGHT FOR YOUR RIGHT (TO PARTY) and 'NO SLEEP TILL BROOKLYN' stormed the charts on both sides of the Atlantic, 'LICENSED TO ILL' becoming the fastest selling debut in Columbia's history. The record turned the band into a phenomenon and in 1987 they undertook a riotous headlining tour. Courting controversy wherever they played, the band were savaged by the press, a dispute with 'Def Jam' not helping matters any. Despite all the upheaval, by the release of 'PAUL'S BOUTIQUE' in 1989, the group's profile was negligible and the album was more or less passed over. A tragedy, as it remains one of hip hop's lost gems, a widescreen sampladelic collage produced by the ultra-hip DUST BROTHERS (US). Bypassing the obvious guitar riffs for samples of The BEATLES, CURTIS MAYFIELD and PINK FLOYD along with a kaleidoscopic array of cultural debris and hip references, the album was a funky tour de force. After another extended sabbatical during which the group relocated to California, the BEASTIE BOYS returned in 1992 with 'CHECK YOUR HEAD'. Hipness and attitude were still there in abundance but by now, the group were using live instrumentation. Despite veering from all out thrash to supple funk, the record was a success and only the BEASTIE BOYS could get away with a TED NUGENT collaboration ('THE BIZ VS THE NUGE'). 'ILL COMMUNICATION' (1994) developed this strategy to stunning effect. From the irresistable funk of 'SURE SHOT' and 'ROOT DOWN' to the laid back swing of 'GET IT TOGETHER' and 'FLUTE LOOP', this was the group's most mature and accomplished work to date. The hardcore was still there, 'TOUGH GUY' and 'HEART ATTACK MAN' but it was offset by the sombre strings of 'EUGENE'S LAMENT' and the mellow 'RICKY'S THEME'. A double A-side 'GET IT TOGETHER' and the screachingly brilliant 'SABOTAGE' (complete with entertaining cop-pastiche video) quite rightly returning them into the UK Top 20. From the artwork to the meditative feel of the music (well o.k., maybe not the punk numbers) it was no surprise that YAUCH had become a buddhist and the band subsequently played a high profile benefit for the oppressed nation of Tibet. Ever industrious, the group also started their own label and fanzine 'Grand Royal', signing the likes of LUSCIOUS JACKSON and the now "Big In Japan" BIS. • **Songwriters:** Although they released little cover versions, they sampled many songs (see above). In 1992, they covered JIMMY JAMES (Jimi Hendrix) + TIME FOR LIVIN' (Stewart Frontline), also collaborating with NISHITA. • **Trivia:** ADAM HOROWITZ is the son of playwrite ISRAEL. HOROWITZ played a cameo role in TV serial 'The Equalizer' (circa '88).

Album rating: LICENSED TO 'ILL (*8) / PAUL'S BOUTIQUE (*7) / CHECK YOUR HEAD (*7) / ILL: COMMUNICATION (*9)

'MCA' ADAM YAUCH (b. 5 Aug'65, Brooklyn, New York) – vocals / **'MIKE D' MIKE DIAMOND** (b.20 Nov'66, New York) – vocals / **KATE SCHELLENBACH** (b. 5 Jan'66, New York City) – drums / **JOHN BERRY** – guitar

Ratcage Ratcage

Nov 82. (7"ep) *<MOTR 21>* **POLLY WOG STEW EP** [ ] [ ]
– B.E.A.S.T.I.E. boys / Transit cop / Jimi / Holy snappers / Riot fight / Ode to . . . / Michelle's farm / Egg raid on mojo. *(UK-iss.Apr88 12"/c-s; same) (re-iss. 12"ep/c-ep/cd-ep Feb93; same)*

— **KIND AD-ROCK – ADAM HOROWITZ** (b.31 Oct'67, New York City) – vocals, guitar (ex-The YOUNG & THE USELESS) repl.BERRY + SCHELLENBACH (she later joined LUSCIOUS JACKSON)

Aug 83. (7") *<MOTR 26>* **COOKY PUSS. / BEASTIE REVOLUTION** [-] [ ]
(UK-iss.Jan85 + Jul87; MOTR 26 C/CD) (cd-ep-iss.Dec87; same) (re-issues +=) – Bonus batter / Cooky puss (censored version). *(re-iss. 12"ep/c-ep/cd-ep Feb93; same)*

— added guest RICK RUBIN – scratcher, DJ

Def Jam Def Jam

Dec 85. (12"ep; w-drawn) *<002>* **ROCK HARD / BEASTIE GROOVE. / THE PARTY'S GETTING ROUGH / BEASTIE GROOVE (instrumental)** [-] [-]

Jan 86. (7"/12") *(A/TA 6686) <05683>* **SHE'S ON IT. / SLOW AND LOW** [ ] [ ]

May 86. (7"/12") *(A/TA 7055) <05864>* **HOLD IT NOW, HIT IT. / ACAPULCO (Hold it now, hit it acapella)** [ ] [ ]

Sep 86. (7") *(650 114-7)* **SHE'S ON IT. / SLOW AND LOW** [ ] [-]
(12"+=) *(650 114-6)* – Hold it now, hit it.

Nov 86. (7") *(650 169-7) <06341>* **IT'S THE NEW STYLE. / PAUL REVERE** [ ] [-]
(12"+=) *(650 169-6)* – ('A'&'B'instrumentals).
(d12"++=) *(650 169-8)* – Hold it now, hit it / Hold it now, hit it (Acapulco version) / Hold it now, hit it (instrumental).

Nov 86. (lp/c/cd) *(450 062-1/-4/-2) <40238>* **LICENSED TO 'ILL** [7] [1]
– Rhymin and stealin' / The new style / She's crafty / Posse in effect / Slow ride / Girls / (You gotta) Fight for your right (to party) / No sleep till Brooklyn / Paul Revere / Hold it now, hit it / Brass monkey / Slow and low / Time to get ill. *(re-iss. Nov89 on 'Capitol'; 460 949-1) (re-iss. Jun94 cd/c; 460 949-2/-4) (cd-iss. Jul95; 527 351-2)*

Dec 86. (7") *<06595>* **(YOU GOTTA) FIGHT FOR YOUR RIGHT (TO PARTY). / PAUL REVERE** [-] [7]

Feb 87. (7") *(650 418-7)* **(YOU GOTTA) FIGHT FOR YOUR RIGHT (TO PARTY). / TIME TO GET ILL** [11] [-]
(12"+=) *(650 418-6)* – No sleep till Brooklyn.

Apr 87. (7") *<06675>* **NO SLEEP TILL BROOKLYN. / SHE'S CRAFTY** [-] [ ]

May 87. (7"/7"sha-pic-d) *(BEAST/+P 1)* **NO SLEEP TILL BROOKLYN. / POSSE IN EFFECT** [14] [-]
(12"+=) *(BEASTT 1)* – Hold it now, hit it / Brass monkey.

Jul 87. (7"/7"s/7"s) *(BEAST/+B/D 2)* **SHE'S ON IT. / SLOW AND LOW** [10] [-]
(12"+=) *(BEASTT 2)* – Hold it now, hit it.

Sep 87. (7"/7"s/7"s/7"s/10"sha-pic-d) *(BEAST/+P/S/Q/W 3)* **GIRLS. / SHE'S CRAFTY** [34] [-]
(12"+=/12"s+=) *(BEASTT/+Q 3)* – Rock hard.

Mar 88. (7") *<07020>* **BRASS MONKEY. / POSSE IN EFFECT** [-] [48]

— no more RICK RUBIN as DJ

Capitol Capitol

Jul 89. (7") *(CL 540) <44454>* **HEY LADIES. / SHAKE YOUR RUMP** [ ] [36]
(12"ep+=/cd-ep+=) *(12/CD CL 540)* **LOVE AMERICAN STYLE** – 33% God / Dis yourself in '89 (just do it). *(re-iss. Jul98 on 'Grand Royal'; GR 064)*

Jul 89. (cd/c/lp) *(DE/TC+/EST 2102) <91743>* **PAUL'S BOUTIQUE** [44] [14]
– To all the girls / Shake your rump / Johnny Ryall / Egg man / High plains drifter / The sound of science / 3-minute rule / Hey ladies / 5-piece chicken dinner / Looking down the barrel of a gun / Car thief / What comes around / Shadrach / Ask for Janice / B-boy bouillabaisse:- (a) 59 Chrystie Street, (b) Get on the mic, (c) Stop that train, (d) A year and a day, (e) Hello Brooklyn, (f) Dropping names, (g) Lay it on me, (h) Mike on the mic, (i) A.W.O.L.

Aug 89. (12"ep) *<Y 15523>* **AN EXCITING EVENING AT HOME WITH SHADRACH, MESHACH AND ABEDNEGO EP** [-] [ ]
– Shadrach / Caught in the middle of a 3-way mix / And what you give is what you get / Car thief / Some dumb cop gave me two tickets already / Your sister's def.

— Trio now also on instruments; **MCA** – bass / **AD ROCK** – keyboards / **MIKE D** – drums

Apr 92. (c-s/7") *(TC+/CL 653)* **PASS THE MIC. / PROFESSOR BOOTY** [47] [ ]
(etched-12"+=/c-s+=) *(12CL/TCCLX 653)* – Time for livin' / Drunken Praying Mantis style.
(cd-s) *(CDCL 653)* – ('A'side) / Netty's girl / Something's got to give / ('A'-pt.2 – The skills to pay the bills).

May 92. (cd/c/d-lp) *(CD/TC+/EST 2171) <98938>* **CHECK YOUR HEAD** [ ] [10]
– Jimmy James / Funky boss / Pass the mic / Gratitude / Lighten up / Finger lickin' good / So what 'cha want / The biz .vs. the Nuge (with TED NUGENT) / Time for livin' / Something's got to give / The blue nun / Stand together / Pow / The maestro / Groove Holmes / Live at P.J.'s / Mark on the bus / Professor Booty / In 3's / Namaste. *(re-iss. Sep94 on 'Grand Royal'; CDP 798938-2/-4)*

May 92. (12"ep/c-ep/cd-ep) *<Y/4Y/C2 15836>* **JIMMY JAMES / THE MAESTRO / JIMMY JAMES (album version) / BOOMIN' GRANNY / JIMMY JAMES (original) / DRINKIN' WINE** [-] [ ]

Jun 92. (12"ep/12"white-ep/c-ep) *(12CL 665)* **FROZEN METAL HEAD EP** [55] [-]
– Jimmy James / So what'cha want (All the way live freestyle version) / Jimmy James (original) / Drinkin' wine.
(cd-ep) *(CDCL 665)* – The blue nun *[repl. original]*

Jun 92. (cd-ep) *<15847>* **SO WHAT'CHA WANT (3 versions; including pt.2 – The Skills to pay the bills) / GROOVE HOLMES (2 versions)** [-] [93]

Dec 92. (12"ep/cd-ep) *<Y/C2 07777>* **GRATITUDE EP** [-] [ ]
– Gratitude / Stand together (live) / Finger lickin' good (remix) / Gratitude (live) / Honkey rink.

Capitol Grand Royal

May 94. (cd/c/d-lp) *(CD/TC+/EST 2229) <28599>* **ILL: COMMUNICATION** [10] [1]
– Sure shot / Tough guy / Freak freak / Bobo on the corner / Root down / Sabotage / Get it together / Sabrosa / The update / Futterman's rule / Alright hear this / Eugene's lament / Flute loop / Do it / Rick's theme / Heart attack man / The scoop / Shambala / Bodhisattva vow / Transitions. *(lp re-iss. Apr97 on 'Grand Royal'; GR 006LP)*

Jul 94. (c-s/7"green) *(TC+/CL 716)* **GET IT TOGETHER. / SABOTAGE / DOPE LITTLE SONG** [19] [ ]
(10") *(10CL 716)* – (first 2 tracks) / ('A'-Buck Wild remix) / ('A'instrumental).
(cd-s) *(CDCL 716)* – (first 2 tracks) / ('A'-A.B.A. remix) / Resolution time.

Nov 94. (7"maroon) *(CL 726)* **SURE SHOT. / MULLET HEAD / SURE SHOT (Mario mix)** [27] [ ]
(10"+=) *(10CL 726)* – The vibes.
(cd-s+=) *(CDCLS 726)* – Son of neck bone.
(cd-s) *(CDCL 726)* – ('A'mixes:- Pruins – European B-Boy / Nardone / Large Professor / instrumental).

Jun 95. (m-cd/m-c/m-lp) *(CD/TC+/EST 2262) <33603>* **ROOT DOWN EP** (some live) [23] [50]
– Root down (free zone mix) / Root down / Root down (PP balloon mix) / Time to get ill / Heart attack man / The maestro / Sabrosa / Flute loop / Time for livin' / Something's got to give / So what'cha want. *(m-lp-iss.Apr97 on 'Grand Royal'; GR 018)*

Dec 95. (12"ep/cd-ep) *<GR 026/+CD>* **AGLIO E OLIO** (11 minutes of hardcore) [-] [ ]
– Brand new / Deal with me / Believe me / Nervous assistant / Square wave in unison / You catch a bad one / I can't think straight / I want some. *(UK-iss.Mar98; same)*

— added guest co-writers **(MONEY) MARK RAMOS NISHITA** – claviers / **ERIC BOBO** – percussion / **EUGENE GORE** – violin

Mar 96. (cd/c) *(CD/TC EST 2281) <7243 8 33590-2/-4>* **THE IN SOUND FROM WAY OUT!** (instrumental) [45] [45]
– Groove Holmes / Sabrosa / Namaste / Pow / Son of neckbone / In 3's / Eugene's lament / Bobo on the corner / Shambala / Lighten up / Ricky's theme / Transitions / Drinkin' wine.

Jun 98. (c-s) *(TCCL 803) <58705>* **INTERGALACTIC / HAIL SAGAN (Special K)** [5] [28] Jul98
(cd-s+=) *(CDCL 803)* – ('A'-Prisoners Of Technology TMSI remix).
(10") *(10CL 803)* – ('A'side) / ('A'-Prisoners Of . . . remix).

Jul 98. (cd/c/d-lp) *(495723-2/-4/-1) <37716>* **HELLO NASTY** [1] [1]
– Super disco breakin' / The move / Remote control / Song for the man / Just a test / Body movin' / Intergalactic / Sneakin' out of hospital / Putting shame in your game / Flowin' prose / And me / Three MC's and one DJ / Can't, won't, don't stop / Song for Junior / I don't know / The negotiation Limerick file / Electrify / Picture this / Unite / Dedication / Dr. Lee PhD / Instant death.

Oct 98. (cd-s) *(CDCLS 809)* **BODY MOVIN' / (Mickey Finn mix) / DR. LEE phD (dub mix)** [15] [ ]
(cd-s) *(CDCL 809)* – ('A'side) / (Fatboy Slim remix) / (Peanut butter and jelly mix).
(12") *(12CL 809)* – ('A'side) / (Kut Masta Kurt remix) / (Erick Sermon remix) / (instrumental).

– compilations, etc. –

Feb 94. (cd/c) *Honey World; (CD/TC EST 2225) / Grand Royal; <89843>* **SOME OLD BULLSHIT** [ ] [46]
– (compilation of 1st 2 EP's)

BEASTS OF BOURBON (see under ⇒ SCIENTISTS)

BEAT (see under ⇒ NERVES)

BEAT FARMERS

Formed: San Diego, California, USA . . . 1983 by 'COUNTRY' DICK MONTANA, formerly known as DAN McLAIN when he played drums for late 70's/early 80's San Diego new wave act, The PENETRATORS (not to be confused with Washington DC and Syracuse bands of the same name). The latter outfit (completed by GARY HEFFERN – vocals, CHRIS DAVIES – guitar, vocals, CHRIS SULLIVAN – bass, vocals and JIM CALL – synthesizer) issued a couple of singles, 'SENSITIVE BOY / STIMULATION' <World Records; WR 101>, 'UNTAMED YOUTH. / VENGEANCE / BE AMERICAN' <m.r.; DM 51155> and a 12" EP, 'WALK THE BEAT' <E&M; E&M 1>, before they called it a day. Changing personnel and direction completely, the young DICK assembled a band of country-rockers (JERRY RAINEY, BUDDY BLUE and ROLLE DEXTER) who also added offbeat humour by the way of their annual fanzine, 'Beat Farmer's Almanac'. On their well-received 1985 debut set, 'TALES OF THE NEW WEST' (licensed to 'Demon' in the UK), the line-up was boosted by some other ex-new wavees turned country-rockers including CHIP and TONY KINMAN (of RANK & FILE), SID GRIFFIN (LONG RYDERS) and PETER CASE (of The PLIMSOULS). Opportunity subsequently knocked in the shape of 'Curb' ('M.C.A.' in the UK), who released their follow-up set, 'VAN GO' (1986), a record that took them to the frontier of the Top 100. Replacing BUDDY with JOEL HARRIS (a previous part-time member), The BEAT FARMERS ploughed a similar furrow with their third set, 'THE PURSUIT OF HAPPINESS' (1988). A few more US-only sets were harvested at the turn of the decade, although the band's future was thrown into doubt when MONTANA was diagnosed with thyroid cancer. Finally securing a new record contract, The BEAT FARMERS returned in the mid-90's with two more downhome collections, 'VIKING LULLABYS' and 'MANIFOLD'. However, the latter was to be the group's finale with MONTANA finally succuming to his long illness during a live performance on the 8th of November 1995 (a posthumous solo album, 'THE DEVIL LIED TO ME' was isued in '96).

Album rating: TALES OF THE NEW WEST (*6) / GLAD 'N' GREASY mini (*5) / VAN GO (*5) / THE PURSUIT OF HAPPINESS (*5) / POOR & FAMOUS (*3) / LOUD AND PLOWED AND . . . LIVE!! (*7) / BEST OF compilation (*7) / VIKING'S LULLABYS (*4) / MANIFOLD (*4)

'COUNTRY' DICK MONTANA (b. DAN McLAIN, 1955) – vocals, drums, accordion (ex-PENETRATORS) / **JERRY RAINEY** – vocals, guitar / **BUDDY BLUE** – vocals, guitars, etc / **ROLLE DEXTER** – bass

Demon Rhino

Feb 85. (lp) *(FIEND 39)* *<853>* **TALES OF THE NEW WEST**
– Bigger stones / There she goes again / Reason to believe / Lost weekend / California kid / Never goin' back / Goldmine / Showbiz / Lonesome hound / Where do they go? / Selfish heart / Happy boy. *(cd-iss. Sep90 +=; FIENDCD 39)<RNCD 75887>* – GLAD 'N' GREASY (m-lp).

Jul 85. (7") *(D 1031)* **BIGGER STONES. / GOLDMINE**

Apr 86. (m-lp) *(VEX 5)* *<R21Y-70791>* **GLAD 'N' GREASY**
– Powderfinger / Death train / Beat generation / Glad 'n' greasy / Delayed reaction / Big rock candy mountain.

M.C.A. Curb-MCA

Jun 86. (7") *(MCA 1067)* **POWDERFINGER. / BIG UGLY WHEELS**
(12"+=) *(MCAT 1067)* – Come sail at the church.

Jul 86. (lp/c) *(MCF/+C 3326)* *<5759>* **VAN GO**
– Riverside / Deceiver / Powderfinger / Seven year blues / Blue Chevrolet / I want you, too / Road of ruin / Buy me a car / Gun sale at the church / Bigger fool than me / Big ugly wheels.

— **JOEL HARRIS** – vocals, guitar (a 5th member on previous sets); repl. BUDDY who joined The JACKS

R.C.A. Curb-MCA

Jun 88. (lp/c) *(ZL/ZK 71545)* *<5993>* **THE PURSUIT OF HAPPINESS** Aug87
– Hollywood hills / Ridin' / Dark light / Make it last / Key to the world / God is here tonight / Big big man / Elephant day parade / Rosie / Texas / Big river.

1989. (lp/cd) *<MCA/+D 6296>* **POOR & FAMOUS** -
– Socialite / Hideaway / What I mean to say / Wait so long / Wheels / Girl I almost married / If I can hold / King of sleaze / The trouble with you / Time in between.

May 90. (cd) *<D21S-77265>* **LOUD AND PLOWED AND . . . LIVE!~! (live)** -
– Introduction / California kid / Socialite / Texas / Maureen / Revenooer man / Lucille / Happy boy / 20th century man / Blue Chevrolet / Big big man / Ridin' / Hideaway / Selfish heart / Big ugly wheels / Roll another number (for the road) / Hollywood hills / If I were a carpenter / God is here tonight / Riverside / King of sleaze.

— in the early 90's, MONTANA was diagnosed with thyroid cancer which put paid to any BEAT FARMERS studio recordings during that period

Sector 2 Sector 2

Jul 95. (cd) *<(SECTOR2 10013)>* **VIKING LULLABYS** Nov94
– Southern cross / Complicated life / Baby's liquor'd up / Garden / Woo-woo song / Atomic age mutants / Gettin' drunk / Are you drinkin' with me Jesus? / Midnight world / Why should I cry / Pretty woman / Are you gonna love me / Lakeside trailer park.

— with **ROSIE FLORES, DAVE ALVIN, JOHN DOE + MOJO NIXON**

Sector 2 Bar None

Oct 95. (cd) *(SECT 10019)* *<080>* **MANIFOLD** Jan96
– Indigo rider / Rich man's town / Home front, pt.1 / Headed for Texas / Picture of you / Anywhere / I wanted you to know / Home front, pt.2 / Listen to her heart / Hurt by love / Party dolls and wine / It's only cocaine / Green door / Trendy shitbag / Home front, pt.3 / King of the hobos / Tweak twuck / Bum rap / Suddenly a valley / Only whore around.

— tragically, MONTANA died on stage on the 8th of November 1995.

– posthumous releases and others –

Nov 96. (cd; solo 'COUNTRY' DICK MONTANA) *Last Call;* *<(742251-2)>* **THE DEVIL LIED TO ME**

BEAT HAPPENING

Formed: Olympia, Washington, USA . . . 1983 by CALVIN JOHNSON and his band of arty, JONATHAN RICHMAN-influenced alternative popsters. After two self-financed, mail-order cassettes, 'BEAT HAPPENING' (1983) and 'THREE TEA BREAKFAST' (1984), CALVIN and Co (HEATHER LEWIS and BRET LUNSFORD) brought BEAT HAPPENING to the wider indie public via their long-playing eponymous debut for UK's 'Rough Trade' in the mid 80's. Continuing the transatlantic connection, they signed to small Scottish-based label, '53rd & 3rd', unveiling their UK debut 45, 'CRASHING THROUGH EP', early in '88. A further EP, 'POLLY PEREGRIN' (shared with the SCREAMING TREES), was accompanied by a follow-up album, 'JAMBOREE' (1988). Later re-issued by American institution 'Sub Pop', the latter set remains one of their finest achievements featuring the classic 'INDIAN SUMMER' track. Side by side with BEAT HAPPENING, CALVIN was also running his own record label, 'K', releasing songs by the likes of TEENAGE FANCLUB, MELODY DOG, to mention but a few. Following a medicore set for 'Rough Trade', 'BLACK CANDY' (1989), the band (HEATHER was now co-writing a lot of the songs) wound down their career at 'Sub Pop' without pandering to the grunge craze over two final releases, 'DREAMY' (1991) and 'YOU TURN ME ON' (1992).

Album rating: BEAT HAPPENING (*6) / JAMBOREE (*7) / BLACK CANDY (*5) / DREAMY (*7) / YOU TURN ME ON (*8) / 1983-85 compilation (*6)

CALVIN JOHNSON – vocals, guitar / **HEATHER LEWIS + BRET LUNSFORD**

not iss. K

1983. (c-ep) **BEAT HAPPENING** - - mail-o

1984. (c-ep) *<KLP 1C>* **THREE TEA BREAKFAST** - - mail-o
(UK-iss.Mar88; same)

1985. (lp) *<KLP 1>* **BEAT HAPPENING** -
(UK-iss.Nov86 on 'Rough Trade'; ROUGH 105) (re-iss. Apr96 on 'K' cd/lp; KCD/KLP 1)

Jan 88. (7") *<L 26501>* **LOOK AROUND. /** -

53rd & 3rd K

Jan 88. (12"ep) *(AGARR 15T)* **CRASHING THROUGH EP**

Jul 88. (lp/pic-lp) *(AGAS 002/+F)* *<KLP 22>* **JAMBOREE**
– Bewitched / In between / Indian summer / Hangman / Jamboree / Ask me / Crashing through / Catwalk / Drive car girl / Midnight ago-go / The this many boyfriends club. *<US re-iss. Jun90 on 'Sub Pop' cd/c; SP B/A>* *(UK cd-iss. Mar94 on 'Sub Pop'; SP 62B)* *(lp re-iss. Jan95 on 'K'; KLP 22)*

53rd & 3rd Positive

Aug 88. (12"ep) *(AGARR 20T)* *<110>* **POLLY PEREGRIN / TALES OF BRAVE APHRODITE. / (other tracks by SCREAMING TREES)**

1988. (7"flexi) *(ABENDI 001)* **HONEY POT** - -

Rough Trade K

Sep 89. (lp/cd) *(ROUGH/+CD 145)* *<KLP 23>* **BLACK CANDY**
– Other side / Black candy / Knick knack / Pahama party in a haunted hive Gravedigger blues / Cast a shadow / Bonfire / T.V. girl / Playhouse / Ponytail. *<US re-iss. Sep90 on 'Sub Pop; cd/c; SP 78 B/A>*

Sub Pop Sub Pop

Sep 90. (7",7"red) *<SP 74)* **RED HEAD WALKING. / SECRET PICNIC SPOT** -

Mar 91. (lp/c/cd) *<SP/+A/B 98>* **DREAMY** -
– Me untamed / Left behind / Hot chocolate boy / I've lost you / Cry for a shadow / Collide / Nancy sin / Fortune cookie prize / Revolution come and gone / Red head walking.

Oct 92. (cd/lp) *<(SP 207CD/45-207)>* **YOU TURN ME ON**
– Tiger trap / Noise / Pinebox derby / Teenage caveman / Sleep head / You turn me on / Godsend / Hey day / Bury the hammer.

— disbanded early in 1993

– compilations, etc. –

1990. (cd) *K;* **1983-85**
– Our secret / What's important / Down at the sea / I love you / Fourteen / Run down the stairs / Primitives / I spy / Bad seeds / Down at the sea / In my memory / Honey pot / Fall / Youth / Don't mix the colors / Foggy eyes / Bad seeds / I let him get to me / I spy / Run down the stairs / Christmas / Fourteen / Let's kiss / 1,2,3 / In love with you thing / Look around.

BEATNIK FILMSTARS

Formed: Bristol, England . . . late 1990 by ANDREW JARRETT, JOHN AUSTIN, ANDY and IAN – who subsequently became a 5-piece with the addition of co-writer JEZ FRANCIS – having all moved to the city from other parts of the country. Inspired by the likes of the PALE SAINTS, TEENAGE FANCLUB and GALAXIE 500, the BEATNIK FILMSTARS made a concerted effort to musically distance themselves from the prevailing "baggy" and "shoegazing" scenes, setting up their own 'Big Sky' label after intitially being courted by 'Rough Trade'. Low-key rather than Lo-Fi at this stage in their career, the band garnered an initial buzz of acclaim with the eddying guitar soundscapes of vinyl debut, 'MAHARISHI' (1991). After a further couple of 45's, the BEATNIK posse signed a long-term deal with 'La-Di-Da', the indie label finally issuing their first album proper (although it was a singles compilation!), 'LAID BACK AND ENGLISH', in the summer of '94. As the aforementioned FRANCIS began to redirect the band through the increasing influence of his songwriting, The BEATNIK FILMSTARS made more of an impact with a fresh collection, 'ASTRONAUT HOUSE', which included the memorably titled single, 'APATHETIC ENGLISH SWINE'. The latter three releases were licensed to 'Caroline' in the States, the band (whose eclectic style was now more akin to GUIDED BY VOICES) subsequently concentrating on the larger American market; 1997 saw the US-only release (on 'Merge') of 'INHOSPITABLE'.

Album rating: LAID BACK AND ENGLISH compilation (*5) / ASTRONAUT HOUSE (*7) / BEEZER (*5) / ALL POPSTARS ARE TALENTLESS SLAGS mini (*6) / INHOSPITABLE (*6)

ANDREW JARRETT – vocals, guitar / **JOHN AUSTIN** – guitar / **ANDY** – bass / **IAN** – drums

Big Sky not iss.

May 91. (m-lp) **MAHARISHI** -

Mobster not iss.

1992. (7") *<001>* **BIGOT SPONGER HAIRCUT POLICY. /** -

Vinyl Japan / not iss.

Sep 92. (12") *(TASK 12)* **THEMES FROM EVERYONE. /** [ ] [-]

La-Di-Da / Caroline

Jul 93. (12") *(LADIDA 026)* **REVOLT INTO STYLE. /** [ ] [-]
Nov 93. (7") *(LADIDA 029)* **LAP DOG KISS. /** [ ] [-]
Jun 94. (lp/cd) *(LADIDA 027/+CD)* <9400> **LAID BACK AND ENGLISH** (compilation of singles) [ ] [ ]
– Ciao America No.2 / You can't fake sadness / Clean / Kick in the head / Sick / Tearing apart my world / Haircut / Skill / Revolt into style / Follow cats / Missed / Ambulance / Swillyagro / Orange / Band A / Diseaser 399.

— added **JEZ FRANCIS** – guitar, vocals, co-writer

Jul 94. (7") *(LADIDA 036)* **APATHETIC ENGLISH SWINE. / GUM / CLOTHES** [ ] [-]
Sep 94. (cd) *(LADIDA 037)* <9403> **ASTRONAUT HOUSE** [ ] [ ] Apr95
– Fruitmousse / Slag dogs – Disco dogs / Wreck my style / Astronaut house / Kefpler's first law / Apathetic English swine / We don't want to / Protein + / What goes around comes around / New improved formula / Best idea probably / (Beat) Clear (beat) clear (beat) clear / Untitled.

Low / not iss.

1995. (7") <005> **BRIDEGROOMS. /** [ ] [-]

not iss. / Slumberland

1995. (7"ep) <043> **PINK NOIZE EP** [-] [ ]
Feb 96. (cd) <058> **BEEZER** [-] [ ]

not iss. / Scratch

Jun 97. (m-cd) <27> **ALL POPSTARS ARE TALENTLESS SLAGS** [-] [ ]
– Wasted / Pilot Jack Harrison / Faze down face down / 13th annual showdown / Eight dollar haircut / Hopeless will do battle / Tense / I am a pioneer.

not iss. / Merge

Sep 97. (cd) <MRG 125> **INHOSPITABLE** [-] [ ]
– Phone kids / Hep boys / Artist V star / Ransack the misfits / Look up and be amazed / Wrong / Footstands / Buffalo Bill haircut / Atlas / Now I'm a millionaire / 0, minus 16, minus 30 / My incident free life / Geiger water deep / Skiving in mono / Everything is relative – This is a take / Mess / Is this is rad? / Lifestyles of the rich and famous / Fracture / Phone kids (reprise).

BEAT RODEO

Formed: Minneapolis, Minnesota, USA . . . 1981/82 by former SUICIDE COMMANDOS and CRACKERS bassist, STEVE ALMAAS. The former revved-up punk outfit emerged out of the local new wave scene early '77, releasing their debut, 'MAKE A RECORD' (1978) for 'Blank'. After two US-only singles and a posthumous live set of the final outing in November '78, 'THE COMMANDOS COMMIT SUICIDE DANCE CONCERT', the group were no more. In 1981, ALMAAS cut a one-off EP alongside RICHARD BARONE (ex-BONGOS) and producer MITCH EASTER under the BEAT RODEO moniker, subsequently deciding to make the country-rock project a full-time concern albeit with new personnel. With the line-up of BILL SCHUNK, ALLAN GRELLER and PETER MOSER, ALMAAS initiated BEAT RODEO proper with a series of gigs before releasing their DON DIXON-produced debut set, 'STAYING OUT LATE', in 1984 on German imprint 'Zensor'. They subsequently signed a more lucrative deal with Miles Copeland's 'I.R.S.', the label re-issuing the debut in remixed form (courtesy of ALMAAS and DIXON), although by this time GRELLER and MOSER had been substituted by DAN PRATER and LOUIS KING respectively; the latter two made their debut on a couple of new bonus tracks. Produced by another future R.E.M. knob-twiddler (Scott Litt), the follow-up, 'HOME IN THE HEART OF THE BEAT' (1986) – their last – failed to achieve quite the same critical and commercial reaction as their Georgian contemporaries.

Album rating: Suicide Commandos: MAKE A RECORD (*6) / THE COMMANDOS COMMIT SUICIDE DANCE RECORD (*5) / Beat Rodeo: STAYING OUT LATE WITH . . . BEAT RODEO (*4) / HOME IN THE HEART OF THE BEAT (*5)

SUICIDE COMMANDOS

CHRIS OSGOOD – vocals, guitar / **STEVE ALMAAS** – bass, vocals / **DAVE AHL** – drums

not iss. / Au Go Go

1978. (7") **EMISSION CONTROL. / CLICHE OLE / MONSTER** [-] [ ]
1978. (7") **MATCH MISMATCH. / MARK HE'S A TERROR** [-] [ ]

not iss. / Blank

1978. (lp) <002> **MAKE A RECORD** [-] [ ]
– Shock appeal / Attacking the beat / Mosquito crucifixion / Mr. Dr. / Semi-smart / Call of the wild / You can't / I need a torch / Kidnapped / Premature / I don't get it / Real cool / She / Burn it down / Match – Mismatch. *<cd-iss. 1996 on 'Polygram'; 532878>*

not iss. / Twin Tone

1979. (lp) <TTR 7906> **THE COMMANDOS COMMIT SUICIDE DANCE CONCERT (live)** [-] [ ]

— had already split late '78, although ALMAAS initiated another band

Jul 81. (12"ep) <TTR 8122> **SIR CRACKERS** [-] [ ]
– Ultimato / I can't have faith / Light blue dress / Your heart.

— ALMAAS subsequently released an EP in 1981 under the name, BEAT RODEO, augmented by RICHARD BARONE (ex-BONGOS) and MITCH EASTER (of LET'S ACTIVE and the producer). BEAT RODEO were formed in 1982 . . .

BEAT RODEO

STEVE ALMAAS – vocals, guitar / **BILL SCHUNK** (b. Riverhead, New York, USA) – guitar / **ALLAN GRELLER** – bass / **PETER MOSER** – drums

Zensor / not iss.

Jul 84. (lp) *(ZS 11)* **STAYING OUT LATE WITH . . . BEAT RODEO** [-] [-] German
– She's more / Just friends / Heart attack / Who's gonna be around / Pet project / Mistake / Kind that says no / Without you / Not the girl loves me / Only for myself / You're the only reason / Take you home. *(UK-iss.Dec84; ZSUK 01)* *<re-mixed & issued in US on 'I.R.S.' +=; >* – (unknown 2 tracks).

— by this time, GRELLER + MOSER were repl. by **DAN PRATER** – bass, vocals / **LEWIS KING** – drums, percussion (guest on 1986 set, SYD STRAW)

I.R.S. / I.R.S.

Nov 86. (lp/c) *(MIRF/+C 1019)* <5774> **HOME IN THE HEART OF THE BEAT** [ ] [ ]
– Twin hometowns / Everything I'm not / New love / It could happen here / (I have) Everything I need / I'm not afraid (doesn't matter to me) / In the summertime / Home in the heart of the beat / Song for an angry young man / It's been too long / While we're apart.

Feb 87. (12"ep) *(IRMT 131)* **EVERYTHING I'M NOT / NEW LOVE. / TRUE / STILL IN HOLLYWOOD** [ ] [ ]

— split in the late 80's after continuing to tour the States

BECAUSE (see under ⇒ FURNITURE)

BECK

Born: BECK HANSEN, 8 Jul'70, Los Angeles, California, USA. After absorbing the strains of primitive country blues artists like LEADBELLY and MISSISSIPPI JOHN HURT, along with the aural terrorism of hardcore noise, the 17-year old BECK relocated to New York in 1989 to try his hand on the post-punk East Village folk scene. Broke, he retired to L.A., setting himself up in the (now) trendy Silverlake district, playing low key gigs in local coffeehouses. Spotted by 'Bongload' owner TOM ROTHROCK, he was offered some studio time and the resulting sessions produced the 'LOSER' (1993) single. Caned by L.A.'s alternative radio stations, its popularity led to BECK signing with 'Geffen'. 'LOSER' (1994) in its re-issued, major label form went top 20 in both Britain and America, its slow burning hip hop blues turning the rosy cheeked BECK into an overnight slacker anti-hero. The 'MELLOW GOLD' (1994) album went some way towards crystallising BECK's skewed vision of a modern folk music that encapsulated roots blues, hip hop, country, noise-core and psychedelia. While the record went on to sell half a million copies, BECK's unique contract allowed him the option of recording for other labels. 'STEREOPATHIC SOUL MANURE' (1994) was a U.S. only release of rough early material on the small 'Flipside' label, while 'ONE FOOT IN THE GRAVE' (1995) was a mainly acoustic set released on CALVIN JOHNSON's 'K' records, its stark harmonica-driven title track remaining a highlight of the BECK live experience. Any dubious whispers of one-hit wonder were cast aside with the release of 1996's 'ODELAY', a record that topped many end of year polls and turned BECK into the music world's coolest hep cat. Garnering gushing praise from the dance, rock and hip hop communities alike, the album's effortless fusion of disparate styles was breathtaking. The cut'n'paste surrealism of the lyrics flourished imagery of a lucidness to match BOB DYLAN's 60's work and indeed, the gorgeously bittersweet 'JACKASS' used DYLAN's 'IT'S ALL OVER NOW BABY BLUE' as a shimmering harmonic backdrop. The album segued smoothly from distortion and dissonance into downhome steel guitar hoedown, all the while retaining an irresistably funky backbeat. For now, this pop auteur/wunderkid can do no wrong, his live experience is a dayglo potted history of American music and any readers who were lucky enough to catch his glorious set at the Chelmsford V97 festival, will know that BECK doesn't take too kindly to bottle throwing eunuchs! • **Songwriters:** BECK writes most of his material, some with KARL STEPHENSON. 'LOSER' used a sample of DR.JOHN's 'I Walk On Guilded Splinters'. • **Trivia:** The 'Geffen Rarities Vol.1' album of various artists, featured the BECK track, 'Bogusflow'.

Album rating: MELLOW GOLD (*7) / STEREOPATHETIC SOULMANURE (*4) / ONE FOOT IN THE GRAVE (*6) / ODELAY (*9)

BECK – vocals, acoustic guitar with guests **RACHEL HADEN** – drums, vocals / **ANNA WARONKER** – bass, vocals / **PETRA HADEN** – violin, vocals / **MIKE BOITO** – organ / **DAVID HARTE** – drums / **ROB ZABRECKY** – bass

not iss. / Flipside

1992. (ltd-7"blue-ep) <FLIP 46> **TO SEE THAT WOMAN OF MINE / MTV MAKES ME WANNA SMOKE CRACK. / (other side 2 tracks by BEAN)** [-] [ ]

not iss. / Sonic Enemy

Jan 93. (c-ep) <none> **GOLDEN FEELINGS** [-] [ ]

not iss. / Bongload

1993. (ltd-12") <BL 5> **LOSER. / STEAL MY BODY HOME** [-] [ ]
1994. (ltd-7") <BL 11> **STEVE THREW UP. / MUTHERFUCKER / (CUPCAKE)** [-] [ ]
(both above UK-iss.Jan95; same) (cd-s iss.Dec97; BL 11CDS)

not iss. / Fingerpaint

1994. (10"ep) <FP 02> **A WESTERN HARVEST FIELD BY MOONLIGHT** [-] [ ]
<re-iss. Sep95; same> (UK cd-iss. Oct97; same)

Geffen / D.G.C.

Mar 94. (7"/c-s) *<DGC S7-19/CS-12 270>* **LOSER. / ALCOHOL** [-] [10]
(cd-s+=) *<DGCDM-21930>* – Corvette bumper / Soul suckin' jerk (reject) / Fume.
Mar 94. (7"/c-s) *(GFS/+C 67)* **LOSER. / ALCOHOL / FUME** [15] [-]
(cd-s) *(GFSTD 67)* – ('A'side) / Totally confused / Corvette bumper / MTV makes me want to smoke crack.
Mar 94. (cd/c/lp) *(GED/GEC/GEF 24634)* *<DGCD/DGC 24634>* **MELLOW GOLD** [41] [13]
– Loser / Pay no mind (snoozer) / Fuckin with my head (mountain dew rock) / Whiskeyclone, Hotel City 1997 / Soul suckin jerk / Truckdrivin neighbors downstairs (yellow sweat) / Sweat sunshine / Beercan / Steal my body home / Nitemare hippy girl / Motherfuker / Blackhole. *<lp-iss. on 'Bongload'(hidden track cd+=)* – Analog odyssey. *(lp re-iss. Apr97 on 'Bongload'; BL 12>*

May 94. (cd-ep) <*DM-22000*> **BEERCAN / GOT NO MIND / ASSKIZZ POWERGRUDGE (PAYBACK '94) / TOTALLY CONFUSED / SPANKING ROOM / BONUS NOISE** [-] [ ]

May 94. (7"/c-s; w-drawn) *(GFS/+C 73)* **PAY NO MIND (SNOOZER). / SPECIAL PEOPLE** [-] [ ]
(12"+=/cd-s+=)<US cd-ep> *(GFST/+D 73)<GED 21911>* – Trouble all my days / Supergolden (sunchild).

— BECK featured on Various Artists 'Mammoth' EP 'JABBERJAW: GOOD TO THE LAST DROP'. In the same year, with CHRIS BALLEW of The PRESIDENTS . . . and under the moniker of CASPAR AND MOLLUSK, they issued the single, 'TWIG'. He was also featured on below alongside CALVIN JOHNSON – vocals (ex-BEAT HAPPENING), SCOTT PLOUFF – drums / JAMES BERTRAM – bass / +2

not iss. K

Aug 94. (cd/c) <*(KLP 28 CD/C)*> **ONE FOOT IN THE GRAVE** [-] [ ]
– He's a mighty good leader / Sleeping bag / I get lonesome / Burnt orange peel / Cyanide breath mint / See water / Ziplock bag / Hollow log / Forcefield / Fourteen rivers fourteen floods / Asshole / I've seen the land beyond / Outcome / Girl dreams / Painted eyelids / Atmospheric conditions.
(UK-iss.Nov95; lp-iss.Jun97; KLP 28) (re-iss. Oct98; same)

Nov 94. (7",7"brown) <*iPU 45*> **IT'S ALL IN YOUR MIND. / FEATHER IN YOUR CAP / WHISKEY CAN CAN** [-] [ ]

D.G.C. D.G.C.

Jun 96. (c-s) *(GFSC 22156)* **WHERE IT'S AT / WHERE IT'S AT (Mario C & Mickey P remix)** [35] [61]
(cd-s+=)<US cd-ep> *(GFSTD 22156)<DGC CD-22214>* – Bonus beats.
(12"++=)<US 12"ep> *(GFST 22156)<DGC 12-22214>* – ('A'-U.N.K.L.E. remix).

Jun 96. (cd/c; as BECK!) *(GED/GEC 24908) <DGCD/DGC 24823>* **ODELAY** [18] [16]
– Devils haircut / Hotwax / Lord only knows / The new pollution / Derelict / Novacane / Jack-ass / Where it's at / Minus / Sissyneck / Readymade / High 5 (rock the catskills) / Ramshackle / Diskobox. <*lp-iss.Apr97 on 'Bongload'; BL 030LP*>

Nov 96. (7") *(GFSC 22183)* **DEVILS HAIRCUT. / LLOYD PRICE EXPRESS** [22] [94]
(cd-s)<US cd-ep> *(GFSTD 22183)<GED 22175>* – ('A'side) / Dark and lovely (Dust Brothers remix) / American wasteland (Mickey P remix).
<US 12"ep++=> *<DGC 12-22222>* – Lloyd Price express / Clock.
(cd-s) *(GFSXD 22183)* – ('A'side) / ('A'-Noel Gallagher remix) / Groovy Sunday (Mike Simpson remix) / Trouble all my days.

Mar 97. (7") *(GFS 22205)* **THE NEW POLLUTION. / ELECTRIC MUSIC AND SUMMER PEOPLE** [14] [78]
(c-s) *(GFSC 22205)* – ('A'side) / Richard's hairpiece (Aphex Twin remix).
(cd-s)<US cd-ep> *(GFSTD 22205) <GED 22204>* – (all 3 tracks).
(cd-s)<US 12"ep> *(GFSTXD 22205) <DGC12 22300>* – ('A'side) / ('A'-Mario C & Mickey P remix) / Lemonade.
(rel.Europe 12" May97 on 'Play It Again Sam'; 22300)

May 97. (7") *(GFS 22253)* **SISSYNECK. / FEATHER IN YOUR CAP** [30] [ ]
(c-s) *(GFSC 22253)* – ('A'side) / The new pollution (remix by Mickey P).
(cd-s) *(GFSTD 22253)* – (all 3 tracks).

Aug 97. (d7"/cd-ep) *(GFS/+TD 22276) <22303>* **JACK-ASS (Butch Vig mix). / STRANGE INVITATION (orchestral version) / DEVIL GOT MY WOMAN // JACK-ASS (Lowrider mix). / BURRO / BROTHER** [ ] [-]

Aug 97. (12"ep) *<DGC12 22303>* **JACK-ASS / BURRO. / STRANGE INVITATION / BROTHER** [-] [97]

Oct 97. (7"/c-s) *(GFS/+C 22293)* **DEADWEIGHT / ERASE THE SUN** [23] [ ]
(cd-s+=) *(GFSTD 22293)* – SA-5.

Nov 98. (cd/c) *(GED/GEC 25184) <25309>* **MUTATIONS** [24] [13]
– Cold brains / Nobody's fault but my own / Lazy flies / Cancelled chack / We live again / Tropicalia / Dead melodies / Bottle of blues / O Maria / Sing it again / Static / Diamond bollocks / Runners dialed zero. *(lp-iss. on 'Bongload'; BL 39)*

Dec 98. (7"/c-s) *(GFS/+C 22365)* **TROPICALIA. / HALO OF GOLD** [39] [ ]
(cd-s+=) *(GFSTD 22365)* – Black balloon.

– compilations, etc. –

Apr 94. (cd) *Flipside; <FLIP 60>* **STEREOPATHETIC SOULMANURE** (home recordings '88-'93) [-] [ ]
(UK-iss.Dec95 & Nov97; same)

Pete BECKER (see under ⇒ EYELESS IN GAZA)

BEDHEAD

Formed: Dallas, Texas, USA . . . 1991 by songwriters BUBBA KADANE and his brother MATT, the quintet being completed by TENCH COXE, KRIS WHEAT and TRINI MARTINEZ. In 1994, they finally released their debut, 'WHAT FUN LIFE WAS', for The BUTTHOLE SURFERS' label, 'Trance Syndicate'. Slo-core, melancholy psychedelia-influenced rock, similar to LOW and even sleepier than The RED HOUSE PAINTERS, the mysterious BEDHEAD kept such a low profile at this particular time that they were virtually unknown outside America. Two years went by before their 'Rough Trade' follow-up, 'BEHEADED' (1996), gained some belated press recognition having been cited as an inspiration by such alternative luminaries as STEREOLAB. BEDHEAD awakened once more in early '98, the album 'TRANSACTION DE NOVO' seeing them back with 'Trance Syndicate'. • **Covered:** DISORDER (Joy Division) / GOLDEN BROWN (Stranglers).

Album rating: WHAT FUN LIFE WAS (*6) / BEHEADED (*7) / TRANSACTION DE NOVO (*6)

BUBBA KADANE – vocals / **MATT KADANE** – guitar / **TENCH COXE** – guitar / **KRIS WHEAT** – bass / **TRINI MARTINEZ** – drums

Trance Syndicate Trance Syndicate

Apr 94. (lp/cd) <*(TRANCE 21/+CD)*> **WHAT FUN LIFE WAS** [ ] [ ]

Nov 94. (cd-ep) <*(TR 28CD)*> **BEDHEAD E.P.** [ ] [ ]
(12"ep-iss.Nov97; TR 29LP)

Mar 96. (10"ep/cd-ep) <*(TR 42/+CD)*> **THE DARK AGES. / INHUME / ANY LIFE** [ ] [ ]

Rough Trade Mayking

Sep 96. (cd/lp) *(R 405-2/-1)* **BEHEADED** [ ] [ ]
– Beheaded / The rest of the day / Left behind / What's missing / Smoke / Burned out / Roman candle / Withdrew / Felo de sen / Lares and Penatia / Lost me works.

Trance Syndicate Trance Syndicate

Feb 98. (lp/cd) <*(TR 67/+CD)*> **TRANSACTION DE NOVO** [ ] [ ]
– Exhume / More than ever / Parade / Half thought / Extramundane / Forgetting / Lepidoptera / Psychodomatica / Present.

Mar 98. (cd-ep) <*TR 69*> **LEPIDOPTERA /** [-] [ ]

BEDLAM AGO GO

Formed: Leeds, England . . . 1996 by former mental patient (and shaven-headed) LEIGH KELLY, plus other long-term unemployed, PHIL NAYLOR, JOHN LUDMAN and TWILL. In fact, they took their moniker from a Victorian mental hospital, initiating their own label, 'Friendly Fire' and appropriately enough, releasing the x-rated 'PARANOID' as their debut single in Autumn '96. After rounding off the year with a follow-up single, 'NOAH', BEDLAM AGO GO signed big time with 'Sony', treading in the crossover wake of UNDERWORLD's 'Born Slippy' and SENSER with major label debut single, 'FLAT 29' (sampling the VELVETS' 'The Gift'), released in August '97. The following March, the lads unleashed what was to be a minor hit single, 'SEASON No.5', a track that also featured on their impressive, if not pioneering debut album, 'ESTATE STYLE ENTERTAINMENT'. Kicking off with the industrial dub of 'NORTHERN NIGHTS' – based on The Ruts' 'BABYLON'S BURNING' – and bulldozing its way through Gil Scott-Heron's 'Angel Dust' on the track 'AIMY', the record updated ALTERNATIVE TV and similar narrative-friendly punks in aggro-techno stylee while flitting between the dark reggae psychosis of MASSIVE ATTACK.

Album rating: ESTATE STYLE ENTERTAINMENT (*8)

LEIGH KENNY – vocals / **TWILL** – guitars / **JOHN LUDMAN** – bass / **PHIL NAYLOR** – electronics / + later **CHRIS DAWKIN** – guitar

Friendly Fire not iss.

Sep 96. (12") *(FFC 001)* **PARANOID. / JUNCTION 47** [ ] [-]

Dec 96. (12"/cd-s) *(FFC 002 S/CD)* **NOAH. /** [ ] [-]

Sony Soho2 Sony

Sep 97. (12") *(BDLM 1-12)* **FLAT 29. / OVERSEER RECONDITION / GLAMOROUS HOOLIGAN LOFT CONVERSION** [ ] [ ]
(cd-s+=) *(BDLM 1CD)* – Step to the bedlamite.
(cd-s) *(BDLM 1CD2)* – ('A'side) / Paranoid / Noah.

Mar 98. (12"/cd-s) *(BDLM 2 12/CD)* **SEASON NO.5. /** [57] [-]
(cd-s) *(BDLM 2 CD2)* –

Jul 98. (12"/cd-s) *(BDLM 3 12/CD)* **ASYLUM. / ('A'-Deejay Punk-Roc mix) / ('A'-album version)** [ ] [-]

Jul 98. (cd/lp) *(BDLM 4 CD/LP)* **ESTATE STYLE ENTERTAINMENT** [ ] [ ]
– Intro / Northern nights / Aimy / Paranoid / Flat 29 / Demons in the reefa / Heroin / Asylum / Season No.5 / When the penny drops / Meeting of the minds / My so called life (acoustic version).

BEEFEATER

Formed: Washington DC, USA . . . 1984, most members stemming from various local hardcore acts. The line-up consisted of TOMAS SQUIP JONES, DUG E. BIRD, BRUCE TAYLOR and FRED SMITH, breaking the 'Dischord' norm with an experimental hybrid of avant-jazz, dub, metal and of course hardcore. This soundclash was unleashed on two mid 80's albums, 'PLAYS FOR LOVERS' (1985) and 'HOUSE BURNING DOWN', although their lack of success led to a subsequent break-up (JONES and BIRD formed FIDELITY JONES).

Album rating: PLAYS FOR LOVERS (*6) / HOUSE BURNING DOWN (*6)

TOMAS SQUIP JONES – vocals (ex-RED C) / **FRED SMITH** – guitar / **DUG E. BIRD** (b. BIRDZELL) – bass (ex-UNDERGROUND SOLDIER) / **BRUCE TAYLOR** – drums (ex-CLEAR VISION, ex-HATE FROM IGNORANCE, ex-SUBTLE OPPRESION)

Dischord Dischord

1985. (lp) <*(DISCHORD 17)*> **PLAYS FOR LOVERS** [ ] [ ]

1987. (lp) <*(DISCHORD 23)*> **HOUSE BURNING DOWN** [ ] [ ]

— disbanded when JONES and BIRD formed FIDELITY JONES

– compilations, etc. –

May 92. (cd) *Dischord; (DIS 64CD)* **PLAYS FOR LOVERS / HOUSE BURNING DOWN** (above 2 + extra) [ ] [ ]
– Trash funk / Reaganomix / Song for lucky / 4 3 2 1 / Mr. Silverbird / Manic D / Mourning / Satyagraha / Dog day / Red carpet / Assholes / Beefeater / Fred's song / I miss you / Out of the woods / Wars in space / Just things / Bedlam rainforest / Move me strong / One soul down / Ain't got no time / Sinking me / Dover beach / Insurrection chant / 40 sonnets on plants / With you always / Freditude / Live the life / Blind leads blind.

Chris BELL

Born: 12 Jan'51, Memphis, Tennessee, USA. Influenced by classic British pop/rock, BELL began writing and performing while in high school. It was here that he met ALEX CHILTON, his future sparring partner in BIG STAR, one of America's great lost bands and a towering inspiration for countless indie hopefuls. Recorded while BELL was at university – he actually handed the album in for a class project! – '£1 RECORD' (1972) should've been massive but for the well documented disaster with its distribution; while critics reached for the collective thesaurus, 'Stax' subdivision, 'Ardent', proved themselves incapable of handling a white rock act. Devastated by the record's failure, BELL found himself at loggerheads with CHILTON on how best to proceed, finally departing in late '72 and falling into a deep depression which would dog him on and off for the next few years. During that time he briefly reunited with CHILTON and BIG STAR drummer, JODY STEPHENS, cutting a handful of tracks which turned up on BIG STAR's second album, 'RADIO CITY'. Yet such was the tension between the former writing partners that BELL subsequently refused to be credited. Instead, he cut three tracks, 'I GOT KINDA LOST', 'I DON'T KNOW' and the sublime 'I AM THE COSMOS' at 'Shoe' studios in Memphis before his brother, worried about his worsening emotional state, accompanied him to Chateau D'Herouville studios in France. The resulting sessions produced an impressive clutch of tracks which were subsequently mixed by BEATLES engineer, Geoff Emerick and which CHRIS and his brother duly attempted to hawk around the London record companies. Despite considerable interest, no concrete deal was forthcoming and CHRIS eventually resigned himself to working in his family's restaurant business. He nevertheless carried on with his music in his spare time, enthused by the mid-78 "2 on 1" re-issue of '£1 RECORD/RADIO CITY' and the belated release of his own 'I AM THE COSMOS / YOU AND YOUR SISTER' on New York indie label, 'Car'. Tragically, on the 27th of December 1978, BELL died instantly after the car he was driving struck a telegraph pole. Incredibly, BELL's unreleased masters gathered dust until the early 90's when a surge of interest in BIG STAR – due in no small part to the patronage of Scottish artists such as PRIMAL SCREAM and TEENAGE FANCLUB – saw 'Rykodisc' finally releasing the tracks as an album. From its meditative cover shot to the hypnotic beauty of the music contained within, 'I AM THE COSMOS' (1992) finally did the man justice. Worth the asking price alone for the opening salvo of 'I AM THE COSMOS', the LENNON-esque 'BETTER SAVE YOURSELF' and the lovely 'SPEED OF SOUND', the collection highlighted a criminally underrated talent whose inability to secure a recording contract in the 70's remains baffling.

Album rating: I AM THE COSMOS (*8)

CHRIS BELL – vocals, guitar (ex-BOX TOPS, ex-BIG STAR) / with **ALEX CHILTON + BILL CUNNINGHAM**

not iss. | Car

1977. (7") *<CRR 6>* **I AM THE COSMOS. / YOU AND YOUR SISTER** [-] [ ]

— CHRIS had retired a few years previously before the release of the above single. He worked with a new band late in 1978, however tragedy struck (see above). Below was a posthumous release of his 1973 recordings, etc.

— with mainly **KEN WOODLEY** – bass, organ / **RICHARD ROSEBROUGH** – drums

Rykodisc | Rykodisc

Mar 92. (cd/c) *<(RCD/RACS 10222)>* **I AM THE COSMOS** [ ] [ ]
– I am the cosmos / Better save yourself / Speed of sound / Get away / You and your sister / Make a scene / Look up / I got kinda lost / There was a light / Fight at the table / I don't know / Though I know she lies / I am the cosmos (slow version) / You and your sister (country version) / You and your sister (acoustic version).

BELLE AND SEBASTIAN

Formed: Glasgow, Scotland . . . early '96 by ex-choirboy/boxer!, STUART MURDOCH (the main songwriter) and ISOBEL CAMPBELL, who met and recruited additional members STUART DAVID, RICHARD COLBURN, STEVIE JACKSON and CHRIS GEDDES in a local cafe. They borrowed the group name from a popular 70's children's TV series (from France) about a young boy and his Pyrenees mountain dog. Two months into their career, the expanded outfit released a very limited (1000 copies) college financed album, 'TIGERMILK', which gained sufficient airplay on national radio to ensure encroaching cult status. By the end of the year (and now with 7th member, SARAH MARTIN) they had unleashed their debut proper, 'IF YOU'RE FEELING SINISTER', which went on to sell in excess of 15,000 copies and gained much respect from end of the year critic polls. Since then, BELLE AND SEBASTIAN have hit the singles chart three times with a series of highly desirable EP's, culminating with their critically acclaimed Top 40 entry, '3.. 6.. 9 SECONDS OF LIGHT'. The fact that they've scaled such giddy heights of indie stardom with only a minimum of promotion and a handful of gigs speaks volumes for the quality of their vintage twee C-86-esque sound. By late summer '98, expectations for a new album had reached fever pitch, critics unanimously hailing 'THE BOY WITH THE ARAB STRAP' as one of the year's finest (sadly, too late for esteemed Mercury Prize, maybe next year!?) and helped ease it into the Top 20. Their by now trademark combination of fey vocals, killer hooklines and avant-pop experimentalism resulted in some of B&S's most infectious tracks to date. With the spirit of NICK DRAKE ghosting in and out of focus (especially on 'SLEEP THE CLOCK AROUND' and 'A SUMMER WASTING'), this troupe of Glaswegian revivalists succeeded in putting the 60's and 70's through an 80's filter, incredibly coming up with something quintessentially 90's! The unitiated should head straight for the holy trinity of tracks opening side two wherein BELLE & SEBASTIAN do an "ARAB STRAP" so to speak, the "Bairn"-like narrative of 'A SPACE BOY DREAM' complementing the BOLAN-esque stomp of the title track and sandwiching the brassy, BOO RADLEYS (but don't let that put you off!) style 'DIRTY DREAM NUMBER TWO'. Fans eager to get a glimpse of these elusive Scots shysters in the flesh should keep their eyes peeled, actual gigs are woefully few and far between. Extra-curricular activities, meanwhile, included a US 'Sub Pop' 7" from STUART DAVID's spoken word/electro outfit, LOOPER (with also his wife, Wee KARN and his brother, RONNIE BLACK). They would continue as a unit early in 1999, releasing a debut album for 'Jeepster', while ISOBEL's side project, The GENTLE WAVES, also released a long-player on the same label.

Album rating: TIGERMILK (*7) / IF YOU'RE FEELING SINISTER (*8) / THE BOY WITH THE ARAB STRAP (*9)

STUART MURDOCH (b.1967) – vocals, acoustic guitar / **ISOBEL CAMPBELL** – violin / **STEVIE JACKSON** – guitars, vocals / **STUART DAVID** – bass / **RICHARD COLBURN** – drums / **CHRIS GEDDES** – piano

Electric Honey | not iss.

Jun 96. (lp) *(EHRLP 5)* **TIGERMILK** [ ] [-]
– The state I am in / Expectations / She's losing it / You're just a baby / Electronic renaissance / I could be dreaming / We rule the school / My wandering days are over / I don't love anyone / Mary Jo.

— added **SARAH MARTIN** – violin, saxophone / and also extra member **MICK COOKE** – trumpet

Jeepster | Enclave-Capitol

Nov 96. (cd/c/lp) *(JPR CD/MC/LP 001) <56713>* **IF YOU'RE FEELING SINISTER** [ ] [ ] Feb97
– Stars of track and field / Seeing other people / Me and the Major / Like Dylan in the movies / The fox in the snow / Get me away from here, I'm dying / If you're feeling sinister / Mayfly / The boy done wrong again / Judy and the dream of horses.

May 97. (7") *(JPR7 001)* **DOG ON WHEELS. / THE STATE I AM IN (demo)** [59] [-]
(12"+=/cd-s+=) *(JPR 12/CDS 001)* – String bean Jean / Belle & Sebastian.

— guest on below, **MONICA QUEEN** – vocals (of THRUM)

Aug 97. (7") *(JPR7 002)* **LAZY LINE PAINTER JANE. / YOU MADE ME FORGET MY DREAMS** [41] [-]
(12"+=/cd-s+=) *(JPR 12/CDS 002)* – Photo Jenny / A century of Elvis.

Oct 97. (7"ep) *(JPR7 003)* **3.. 6.. 9 SECONDS OF LIGHT EP** [32] [-]
– A century of fakers / Le pastie de la bourgeoisie.
(12"ep+=/cd-ep+=) *(JPR 12/CDS 003)* – Beautiful / Put the book back on the shelf / *(hidden track-)* Songs for children.

— added guest **NEIL ROBERTSON** – bass

Jeepster | Matador

Sep 98. (cd/c) *(JPR CD/MC 003) <311>* **THE BOY WITH THE ARAB STRAP** [12] [ ]
– It could have been a brilliant career / Sleep the clock around / Is it wicked not to care? / Ease your feet in the sea / A summer wasting / Seymour Stein / A space boy dream / Dirty dream number two / The boy with the arab strap / Chickfactor / Simple things / The rollercoaster ride.

Dec 98. (12"ep/cd-ep) *(JPR 12/CDS 009)* **THIS IS JUST A MODERN ROCK SONG / I KNOW WHERE THE SUMMER GOES. / THE GATE / SLOW GRAFFITI** [-] [-] -chart

BELLY

Formed: Providence, Rhode Island, USA . . . late '91 by ex-THROWING MUSES and BREEDERS co-leader TANYA DONELLY. Recruiting brothers, THOMAS and CHRIS GORMAN along with FRED ABONG, DONELLY set her pet project in motion with the 'SLOWDUST' EP in summer '92, BELLY remaining with '4 a.d.' (the label that had been home to both DONELLY's previous outfits). Produced by The PIXIES maestro, Gil Norton, the record introduced BELLY's hypnotic blend of provocative musings and strident, infectious indie-rock, a style which flowered on the follow-up EP, 'GEPETTO' (featuring a cover of The Flying Burrito Brothers' classic 'HOT BURRITO #2') and the hit single 'FEED THE TREE'. The debut album, 'STAR' narrowly missed the UK No.1 spot, DONELLY's little-girl-lost sweetness occasionally transforming into a fearsome howl. Similarly, DONELLY's lyrics were by turns twisted and twee, this delicate balance undoubtedly part of the band's appeal. Despite this incredible start, a second set, the Glyn Johns-produced, 'KING', took off in a rockier direction, losing some of the BELLY mystique in the process. Though the record made the UK Top 10, its relative critical and commercial failure eventually led to DONELLY splitting the group up and heading for a solo career. In 1997, her debut, 'LOVESONGS FOR UNDERDOGS', was released to minimal impact, although it did contain two minor hits, 'PRETTY DEEP' and 'THE BRIGHT LIGHT'. • **Covered:** TRUST IN ME (Sherman – Sherman; for 'Jungle Book') / ARE YOU EXPERIENCED (Jimi Hendrix).

Album rating: STAR (*8) / KING (*7) / Tanya Donelly: LOVESONGS FOR UNDERDOGS (*5)

TANYA DONELLY (b.16 Jul'66, Newport, Rhode Island) – vocals, guitar / **THOMAS GORMAN** (b.20 May'66, Buffalo, N.Y.) – guitar **FRED ABONG** – bass / **CHRIS GORMAN** (b.29 Jul'67, Buffalo) – drums

4 a.d. | Sire

Jun 92. (12"ep/cd-ep) *(BAD 2009/+CD)* **SLOWDUST** [ ] [ ]
– Dusted / Slow dog / Dancing gold / Low red moon.

— **GAIL GREENWOOD** (b.10 Mar'60) – bass repl. FRED

Nov 92. (7") *(AD 2018)* **GEPETTO. / SEXY S** [ ] [ ]

(12"+=/cd-s+=) *(BAD 2018/+CD)* – Hot burrito #1 / Sweet ride.

Jan 93. (7"/c-s) *(AD/+C 3001)* **FEED THE TREE. / DREAM ON ME** 32 -

(12"+=/cd-s+=) *(BAD 3001/+CD)* – Trust in me / Star.

Jan 93. (cd)(lp/c) *(CAD 3002CD)(CAD/+C 3002) <45187>* **STAR** 2 59

– Someone to die for / Angel / Dusted / Every word / Gepetto / Witch / Slow dog / Low red moon / Feed the tree / Full Moon, empty heart / White belly / Untogether / Star / Sad dress / Stay.

Mar 93. (c-ep)(cd-ep) *(BADC 2018)(BADD 2018CD)* **GEPETTO (remix) / IT'S NOT UNUSUAL / STAR (demo)** 49

(12"ep)(cd-ep) *(BADR 2018)(BAD 2018CD)* – ('A'side) / Hot burrito #1 / Sexy S / Sweet ride.

Feb 93. (cd-ep) *<941 547-2>* **LOW RED MOON / ARE YOU EXPERIENCED? / IT'S NOT UNUSUAL (3 mixes) / FULL MOON, EMPTY HEART (3 mixes)** -

Apr 93. (c-s) *<18570>* **FEED THE TREE / STAR** - 95

Jan 95. (7"/c-s) *(AD/+C 5003)* **NOW THEY'LL SLEEP. / THIEF** 28

(12"+=/cd-s+=) *(BAD 5003/+CD)* – Baby's arm / John Dark.

Feb 95. (cd)(lp/c) *(CAD 5004CD)(CAD/+C 5004) <45833>* **KING** 6 57

– Puberty / Seal my fate / Red / Silverfish / Super-connected / The bees / King / Now they'll sleep / Untitled and unsung / Lil' Ennio / Judas my heart.

Jul 95. (7"clear) *(AD 5007)* **SEAL MY FATE. / BROKEN / JUDAS MY HEART (live)** 35

(cd-s) *(BAD 5007CD)* – ('A'-U.S. radio mix) / Spaceman / Diamond rib cage / Think about your troubles.

(cd-s) *(BADD 5007CD)* – ('A'live) / White belly (live) / Untitled and unsung (live) / The bees (live).

— disbanded in July '96.

TANYA DONELLY

— with **DEAN FISHER + WALLY GAGEL** – bass / **RICH GILBERT** – guitars / **STACY JONES** – guitar / + others

4 a.d. Warners

Nov 96. (d7"ep)(cd-ep) *(ADD 6018)(BAD 6018CD)* **SLIDING & DRIVING**

– Bum / Restless / Human / Swoon.

Aug 97. (7") *(AD 7007)* **PRETTY DEEP. / VANILLA (Wally's mix)** 55

(cd-s) *(BAD 7007CD)* – ('A'side) / Spaghetti / Morna.

(cd-s) *(BADD 7007CD)* – ('A'side) / These days / Influenza.

Sep 97. (cd)(lp/c) *(CAD 7008CD)(CAD/+C 7008) <46495>* **LOVESONGS FOR UNDERDOGS**

– Pretty deep / The bright light / Landspeed song / Mysteries of the unexplained / Lantern / Acrobat / Breathe around you / Bum / Clipped / Goat girl / Manna / Swoon.

Nov 97. (7") *(AD 7012)* **THE BRIGHT LIGHT. / THE BRIGHT LIGHT (live)** 64

(cd-s) *(BAD 7012)* – ('A'side) / Bury my heart / How can you sleep.

(cd-s) *(BADD 7012)* – ('A'side) / Life on Sirius / Moon over Boston.

BELOVED

Formed: Camberwell, London, England ... 1983/4 as JOURNEY THROUGH by JON MARSH, GUY GOUSDEN and TIM HARVARD. With the addition of Cambridge graduate STEVE WADDINGTON, the band assumed the BELOVED moniker and began releasing records through their own 'Flim Flam' label. Early efforts at indie psychedelia a la The SHAMEN had developed into a more bass-heavy pop-dance sound by the release of the 'WHERE IT IS' album in 1987 and the band were signed up by 'Warners'. A split in the ranks the following year led to GOUSDEN and HARVARD leaving MARSH and WADDINGTON to lead The BELOVED into the brave new world of the emerging 'house' culture by way of electronic bass and drums as evidenced on their early efforts for the label, 'LOVING FEELING' and 'YOUR LOVE TAKES ME HIGHER'. The blissed out vibe continued with 'THE SUN RISING', a second-summer-of-love-era classic placing a mesmerising female vocal over a near-ambient backing to stunning effect. Unsurprisingly, the track finally broke the band into the UK Top 30 as well as earning them a fair whack in licensing revenue after being used as a musical backdrop to many a TV ad. A kind of pop companion piece to A HOUSE's 'Endless Art', The BELOVED's follow-up single, 'HELLO', was another list of the great and the erm ... not so great (people, that is). Along with a third hit single, a revamped 'YOUR LOVE TAKES ME HIGHER', the track was one of the many highlights of the best selling 'HAPPINESS' (1990) album, an essential document of early 90's dance culture along with PRIMAL SCREAM's 'Screamadelica'. All good things come to an end, though, and with the departure of WADDINGTON to work with STEVE HILLAGE and his SYSTEM 7 project, MARSH recruited his other half, HELENA to work on new material. The resulting 'SWEET HARMONY' single in 1993 proved to be their most commercially successful effort to date, incredibly furnishing The BELOVED with its first UK Top 10 hit. The accompanying album, 'CONSCIENCE' (1993) narrowly missed the top of the charts despite being a less immediate collection. A further couple of minor hits followed before The BELOVED faded from view, their eventual return in 1996 with the 'X' album merely underlining the fact that the group had failed to keep pace with a dance scene continually in flux. • **Songwriters:** MARSH and WADDINGTON (until his departure), except a cover of GIVE IT TO ME (Bam Bam).

Album rating: HAPPINESS (*6) / BLISSED OUT (*5) / CONSCIENCE (*6) / X (*4)

JON MARSH (b.1963) – vocals, guitar / **STEVE WADDINGTON** (b.1958) – guitar, keyboards / **TIM HARVARD** – bass / **GUY GAUSDEN** – drums

Flim Flam not iss.

Apr 86. (12"m) *(HARP 2T)* **A HUNDRED WORDS. / SLOW DANCING / IN TROUBLE AND SHAME** -

Sep 86. (7") *(HARP 3)* **THIS MEANS WAR. / IF ONLY** -

(12") *(HARP 3T)* – ('A'side) / Let it begin / Saints preserve us.

Mar 87. (12"ep) *(HARP 5T)* **HAPPY NOW** -

– Righteous me / A kiss goodbye / If pennies came.

Jul 87. (7"/12") *(HARP 7/+T)* **FOREVER DANCING. / SURPRISE ME** -

(12"+=) *(HARP 7E)* – ('A'remix).

Nov 87. (lp) *(HARPLP 2)* **WHERE IT IS** -

– A hundred words / Slow dancing / In trouble and shame / This means war / If only / Let it begin / Saints preserve us / If pennies came / Righteous me / A kiss goodbye / Surprise me / Forever dancing. *(cd-iss. Jul90; HARPCD 2)*

— (trimmed to duo of **MARSH** and **WADDINGTON** & drum machine)

W.E.A. Atlantic

Oct 88. (7"/12"/cd-s) *(YZ 311/+T/CD)* **LOVING FEELING. / ACID LOVE** -

Jan 89. (7") *(YZ 357)* **YOUR LOVE TAKES ME HIGHER. / PARADISE (MY DARLING, MY ANGEL** -

(12"/cd-s) *(YZ 357 T/CD)* – ('A'&'B'remix).

Oct 89. (7"/c-s/12"pic-d) *(YZ 414/+C/PD) <86126>* **THE SUN RISING. / ('A'instrumental)** 26 Oct90

(12"+=/cd-s+=) *(YZ 414 T/CD)* – (2 extra mixes).

Jan 90. (7"/c-s) *(YZ 426/+C) <86235>* **HELLO. / ('A'-Dolly mix)** 19 Mar90

(12"+=) *(YZ 426T)* – ('A'mix).

(cd-s++=) *(YZ 426CD)* – ('A'extra mix).

Feb 90. (cd/c/lp) *(2292 46253-2/-4/-1) <82047>* **HAPPINESS** 14 Mar90

– Hello / Your love takes me higher / Time after time / Don't you worry / Scarlet beautiful / The sun rising / I love you more / Wake up soon / Up, up and away / Found. *(re-iss. cd/c Feb95; same)*

Mar 90. (7"/c-s) *(YZ 463/+C)* **YOUR LOVE TAKES ME HIGHER. / PABLO** 39 -

(12") *(YZ 463T)* – ('A'side) / ('A'version).

(cd-s++=) *(YZ 463CD)* – (all above tracks).

May 90. (7"/c-s) *(YZ 482/+C) <86184>* **TIME AFTER TIME. / ('A' through the round window mix)** 46

(12"+=) *(YZ 482T)* – ('A'-Muffin mix).

(cd-s+=) *(YZ 482CD)* – ('A'extended mix).

Oct 90. (7"/c-s) *(YZ 541/+C)* **IT'S ALRIGHT NOW. / ('A'instrumental)** 48 -

(12"+=/cd-s+=) *(YZ 541 T/CD)* – ('A'extra mix).

Oct 90. (cd)(lp/c) *(<9031 72907-2>)(WX 383/+C)* **BLISSED OUT** (remixes of last album) 39

– Up, up and away (happy sexy mix) / Wake up soon / Pablo (special K mix) / It's alright now (back to basics) / Hell (honky tonk) / Time after time (muffin mix) / The sun rising / Your love takes me higher. *(re-iss. cd Feb95; same)*

— **HELENA MARSH** – producer, writer (wife of JON) repl. WADDINGTON

East West Atlantic

Jan 93. (7"/c-s) *(YZ 709/+C)* **SWEET HARMONY. / MOTIVATION (Empathised)** 8 -

(12"+=/cd-s+=) *(YZ 709 T/CD)* – (2 'A'mixes).

Feb 93. (cd/c/lp) *(4509 91483-2/-4/-1) <82457>* **CONSCIENCE** 2

– Spirit / Sweet harmony / Outer space girl / Lose yourself in me / Paradise found / You've got me thinking / Celebrate your life / Rock to the rhythm of love / Let the music take you / 1000 years from today / Dream on. *(cd re-iss. Dec96; 4509 91483-2)*

Mar 93. (7"/c-s) *(YZ 738/+C)* **YOU'VE GOT ME THINKING. / CELEBRATE YOUR LIFE (Fit For Life Mix)** 23 -

(12"+=/cd-s+=) *(YZ 738 T/CD)* – ('B'dub mix) / Sweet harmony (club mix).

Aug 93. (7"/c-s) *(YZ 726/+C)* **OUTER SPACE GIRL. / ('A'-Space Hopper mix)** 38 -

(12") *(YZ 726T)* – ('A'-Destination Moon + Organism mixes).

(cd-s++=) *(YZ 726CD)* – ('A'-Space Cadet + Space Dust mixes).

Jan 94. (12") *<85716>* **ROCK TO THE RHYTHM OF LOVE** -

Mar 96. (c-s) *(EW 034C)* **SATELLITE /** 19 -

(cd-s+=) *(EW 034CD)* –

Apr 96. (cd/c/lp) *(0630 13316-2/-4/-1) <82962>* **X** 25 Oct96

– Deliver me / Satellite / Ease the pressure / A dream within a dream / Crystal wave / For your love / Physical love / Missing you / Three steps to Heaven / Spacemen.

May 96. (c-s) *(EW 043C)* **DELIVER ME** -

(cd-s+=) *(EW 043CD)* –

(12"+=) *(EW 043T)* –

Aug 96. (c-s) *(EW 058C)* **EASE THE PRESSURE /** 43 -

(cd-s) *(EW 058CD)* –

(12") *(EW 058T)* –

Aug 97. (12"/cd-s) *(EW 122 T/CD1)* **THE SUN RISING /** 31 -

(cd-s+=) *(EW 122CD2)* –

Aug 97. (cd/c) *(0630 19932-2/-4)* **SINGLE FILE (THE BEST OF THE BELOVED)** (compilation) -

– The sun rising / Sweet harmony / Your love takes me higher / Satellite / Outerspace girl / Time after time / Hello / Ease the pressure / It's alright now / You've got me thinking / Deliver me / Mark's deep house.

BENNET

Formed: Reading, England ... 1993 by JASON APLIN (vocals) and JOHNNY PEER (guitar), who eventually recruited the current line-up of KEVIN MOOREY (drums), ANDY BENNET (bass) and NEIL CURLEY (keyboards). Signing to 'Roadrunner', a label more associated with venom spitting young men with unfeasibly long hair, the NHS-bespectacled BENNET raised the flag for shiny, happy, gawky geek-rock with their late '96 debut album, 'SUPER NATURAL' and the infectious pop parody of 'MUM'S GONE TO ICELAND', a Top 40 hit in early '97. Despite a gruelling trek around the nation's less salubrious music hostelries and another moderately-recieved album in late '97, 'STREET VS SCIENCE', BENNET have yet to attain the lofty commercial heights of their namesake TONY (or, let's face it, even a modicum of his style and sophistication).

Album rating: SUPER NATURAL (*6) / STREET VS SCIENCE (*5)

JASON APLIN – vocals / **JOHNNY PEER** – guitar / **KEVIN MOOREY** – drums / **ANDY BENNET** – bass / **NEIL CURLEY** – keyboards

Roadrunner Roadrunner

Mar 96. (7") *(RR 2316-7)* **IF YOU MET ME THEN YOU'D LIKE ME. / OH YEAH**
(cd-s+=) *(RR 2316-3)* – Back to Americaat Bracknell / Jute's theme.

May 96. (7") *(RR 2306-7)* **COLOSSAL MAN. / BIG FAT WIFE** [ ] [-]
(cd-s+=) *(RR 2306-3)* – Club foot angel / Motorbike.

Aug 96. (7"red/c-s) *(RR 2298-7/-4)* **SOMEONE ALWAYS GETS THERE FIRST. / HELLO WE ARE BENNET** [ ] [-]
(cd-s+=) *(RR 2298-3)* – Charity Dave / Congregation de Freitas.
(re-iss. Apr97; same) – hit UK No.69

Sep 96. (cd/c/lp) *(<RR 8866-2/-4/-1>)* **SUPER NATURAL**
– Norway wife / If you met me, then you'd like me / Only thirty / Jordan Bennet / Cha cha Charlie / I hate my family / Wanker / Colossal man / Young, free & snotty / Sandman / Mum's gone to Iceland / Someone always gets there first / Mockney rebel / Kiss the radio / Never ending blue / Secret track.

Feb 97. (7"/c-s) *(RR 2285-7/-4)* **MUM'S GONE TO ICELAND. / BENNET HAVE LEFT THE BUILDING** [34] [ ]
(cd-s+=) *(RR 2285-3)* – This is a song / Hope you'd like to.

Sep 97. (7"clear) *(RR 2260-7)* **I LIKE ROCK. / TOUCH TOO MUCH**
(cd-s+=) *(RR 2260-3)* – C'mon c'mon / Rock'n'roll all nite.
(cd-s) *(RR 2260-5)* –

Oct 97. (cd/c) *(RR 8761-2/-4)* **STREET VS SCIENCE**

Feb 98. (cd-ep) *(RR 2243-3)* **HORSE'S MOUTH / SELF MURDER / DOGS / A.L.I.E.N.D.I.V.O.R.C.E.**
(cd-ep) *(RR 2243-9)* – ('A'side) / Married with children / Polka / Home karaoke.

BENNY PROFANE (see under ⇒ ROOM)

BENTLEY RHYTHM ACE

Formed: Birmingham, England . . . 1997 by former POP WILL EAT ITSELF man, RICH MARSH plus ex-tarmac layer, MIKE STOKES. Described as the Black Country's answer to The CHEMICAL BROTHERS, the band were the ACE in the pack of Big Beat connoiseurs, 'Skint', their debut single, 'MIDLANDER' becoming a cult classic upon its Spring '97 release. A self-titled debut album followed soon after, BRA motoring their way to the front of the breakbeat pack with a larger than life collection of dayglo dancefloor stompers. Putting the fun back into moody clubland, the band's customised live shows soon became the stuff of legend, the ubiquitous dance tent at summer festivals struggling to contain the group's ever growing fanbase of frugging nutters. With the buzz surrounding the duo almost drowning out the turbo thrum of the BENTLEY roadmaster, it wasn't long before the majors attempted to hitch a ride, 'Parlophone' finally managing to flag them down and tune up sales of the debut with some financial muscle. Late summer also saw the release of 'BENTLEY'S GONNA SORT YOU OUT!', possibly their finest moment to date, a Top 20 hit guaranteed to sort out the real ravers from the posing fakers. With Japanese and American success imminent, it seems only a foolhardy case of road rage can hold back these Brummie chancers from the brink of pop stardom.

Album rating: BENTLEY RHYTHM ACE (*8)

RICH MARSH – keyboards, samples (ex-POP WILL EAT ITSELF) / **MIKE STOKES** – samples, etc

Skint AstralWerks

Sep 96. (12") *(SKINT 13)* **LATE TRAIN TO BENTLEY ON C. /** [ ] [-]

Apr 97. (12"/cd-s) *(SKINT 23/+CD)* **MIDLANDER. /** [ ] [-]

May 97. (cd/d-lp) *(BRASSIC 5 CD/LP)* *<ASW 6223>* **BENTLEY RHYTHM ACE** [40] [ ] Oct97
– Let there be flutes / Midlander (there can only be one . . .) / Why is a frog too..? / Mind that gap / Run on the spot / Bentley's gonna sort you out! / Ragtopskodacarchase / Whoosh / Who put the bom in the bom bom diddleye bom / Spacehopper / Return of the hardcore jumble carbootechnodisco roadshow. *(re-iss. Oct97 on 'Parlophone' cd/c/d-lp; CD/TC+/PCS 7391)*

Parlophone Astralwerks

Aug 97. (12"ep) *(12R 6476)* **BENTLEY'S GONNA SORT YOU OUT! / RUN ON THE SPOT / ON HER MAJESTY'S SECRET WHISTLE / RAGTOPSKODACARCHASE** [17] [ ]
(cd-ep) *(CDR 6476)* – (first 3 tracks) / The spy who loved moose.
(cd-ep) *(CDRS 6476)* – (tracks 1,2 & 4) / Two turntables a powercut and the DJ's gone off.

Heidi BERRY

Born: USA, although she has resided in London since her childhood. Having more than likely been inspired by the vocal dexterity of such female icons as SANDY DENNY, GRACE SLICK and JONI MITCHELL, HEIDI bizarrely enough got her first break on indie-guitar haven, 'Creation', in 1987. Alan McGee and Co. released her first work, the mini-set, 'FIREFLY', an atmospheric, string-cloaked piece of singer-songwriter melancholy which featured the keyboard talent of MARTIN DUFFY. In the Spring of '89 and now accompanied by her brother CHRISTOPHER BERRY and pianist ROCKY HOLMAN, HEIDI delivered her first full-length, 'BELOW THE WAVES', one of the highlights, the austere 'NORTH SHORE TRAIN' previously featured on her label's 99p album sampler 'Doin It For The Kids'. Invited by IVO's '4 a.d.' alternative ensemble, THIS MORTAL COIL, to interpret Rodney Crowell's 'Til I Gain Control Again', BERRY signed a full-time contract with the label around the same time. Augmented by the likes of MARTIN McCARRICK, LAURENCE O'KEEFE, TERRY BICKERS, LOL COXHILL and IAN KEARNEY, she delivered the 'LOVE' album in '91, a record that boasted her version of Bob Mould's 'UP IN THE AIR'. Throughout the 90's, HEIDI continued to plough her own idiosyncratic furrow to critical favour on the likes of 'HEIDI BERRY' (1993) and 'MIRACLE' (1996).

Album rating: FIREFLY (*5) / BELOW THE WAVES (*6) / LOVE (*5) / HEIDI BERRY (*5) / MIRACLE (*6)

HEIDI BERRY – vocals / with **MARTIN DUFFY** – piano (of FELT) / + others

Creation Positive

Sep 87. (m-lp) *(CRELP 023)* **FIREFLY** [ ] [-]

— added **ROCKY HOLMAN** – piano, synthesizer / her brother **CHRISTOPHER BERRY** – acoustic guitar

May 89. (lp/cd) *(CRE LP/CD 048)* *<6063>* **BELOW THE WAVES**
– Ribbons / Below the waves / Little tragedy / Legacy / North shore train / Gather all the hours / River song / All for you / Living memory / ancer / Out of my hands / Firefly / Nobody tells on you / Will it all change / Houses made of wood / Hasten the buds to bloom.

— added guests **MARTIN McCARRICK** (of SIOUXSIE & THE BANSHEES) / **TERRY BICKERS + LAURENCE O'KEEFE** (of LEVITATION) / **IAN KEARNEY** (of BLUE AEROPLANES) / **LOL COXHILL** (solo artist)

4 a.d. 4 a.d.

Aug 91. (cd)(lp/c) *<(CAD 1012CD)>(CAD/+C 1012)* **LOVE**
– Washington Square / Up in the air / Gloria / Great big silver key / Wake / Cradle / Hand over head / Silver buttons / Lonely heart / Bright as day / Lily. *(cd re-iss. Jul98; GAD 1012CD)*

4 a.d. 4ad-Warners

Jun 93. (12"ep/cd-ep) *(BAD 3010/+CD)* **THE MOON AND THE SUN EP** [ ] [-]
– The moon and the sun / Unholy light / Zither song / You upset the grace of living when you lie.

Jul 93. (cd)(lp/c) *(CAD 3009CD)(CAD/+C 3009)* *<45301>* **HEIDI BERRY** [ ] [ ] Jan93
– Mercury / Little fox / The moon and the sun / One-string violin / arling companion / Distant thunder / Heart like a wheel / For the rose / Follow / Ariel / Dawn. *(cd re-iss. Jul98; GAD 3009CD)*

Jul 96. (cd)(lp/c) *(CAD 6011CD)(CAD/+C 6011)* *<46020>* **MIRACLE** [ ] [ ] Sep96
– Mountain / Time / The holy grail / Darkness, darkness / Miracle / Californian / Queen / Only human / Northern country. *(cd re-iss. Jul98; GAD 6011CD)*

Cindy Lee BERRYHILL

Born: San Diego, California, USA. After pursuing theatre studies in L.A., CINDY LEE fell in with the local punk scene and formed her first band, The STOOPIDS (a few recordings do exist on cassette). Subsequently becoming disillusioned with her musical environment, BERRYHILL suffered a nervous breakdown and it was the second half of the decade before she fully recuperated. The stalwart singer-songwriter finally made it onto vinyl via a various artists compilation, 'The Radio Tokyo Tapes, Vol.3', the track in question being 'DAMN, WISH I WAS A MAN'. The latter song featured on her debut solo set, 'WHO'S GONNA SAVE THE WORLD' (1988), a record that gained a release through UK folkie imprint, 'New Routes'. Her LENNY KAYE-produced follow-up, 'NAKED MOVIE STAR' (1989) – on 'Awareness' UK – found her dabbling with jazz styles but failing to convince record buyers. At the turn of the decade, BERRYHILL suffered the loss of all her personal effects when they were stolen en route to her new home in San Diego. A few years later, her career was reactivated following interest from the 'Unique Gravity' stable, her long-awaited third set, 'GARAGE ORCHESTRA' (1994), named after her backing musicians. BERRYHILL suffered further misfortune as her boyfriend was injured in a serious motorbike crash. Although she nursed him through his ordeal, the resilient songstress found time to cut a fourth album, 'STRAIGHT OUTTA MARYSVILLE' (1996), issued via Britain's long-standing independent specialists, 'Demon'. • **Covered:** SEASON OF THE WITCH (Donovan).

Album rating: WHO'S GONNA SAVE THE WORLD? (*7) / NAKED MOVIE STAR (*7) / GARAGE ORCHESTRA (*6) / STRAIGHT OUTTA MARYSVILLE (*6)

CINDY LEE BERRYHILL – vocals, guitars, harmonica / with sessions from BOB LENOX – keyboards / JONES BEACH – guitar / PAUL DUGAN – bass / DEBBIE SPINELLI + CHARLES PERSIP – drums / KWEYAO AGYAPON – percussion

New Routes Rhino

Jun 88. (lp) *(RUE 001)* **WHO'S GONNA SAVE THE WORLD?** [ ] [ ] Nov87

Awareness Rhino

Jul 89. (lp/c/cd) *(AWL/AWT/AWCD 1016)* *<R1/R4/R2 70845>* **NAKED MOVIE STAR**
– Me, Steve, Kirk and Keith / Old trombone routine / Supernatural fact / Indirectly yours / Trump / 12 dollar motel / Turn off the century / What's wrong with me / Yipee / Baby (should I have the baby?).

Sep 89. (7") *(AWP 001)* **ME, STEVE, KIRK AND KEITH. / BABY (SHOULD I HAVE THE BABY?)** [ ] [-]
(12"+=) *(AWPX 001)* –

— In the early 90's, she encountered one ordeal after another (see above)

Unique Gravity Earth Music – Cargo

Jul 95. (cd) *(UGCD 5502)* *<008>* **GARAGE ORCHESTRA** [ ] [ ] Sep94
– Father of the seventh son / I wonder why / Radio astronomy / Gary Handeman / Song for Brian / UFO / Suite / I want stuff / Every someone tonight / The scariest thing in the world / Etude for ph machine. *(re-iss. Apr98; same)*

Demon Cargo

Apr 96. (cd) *(FIENDCD 782)* **STRAIGHT OUTTA MARYSVILLE** [ ] [ ] Mar96
– High jump / Unknown master painter / Diane / Season of the witch / Riddle riddle / Jane and John / The virtues of being apricot / Unwritten love song / Just like

me / Talkin' with a mineral / I'm a tumbleweed / Caravan / Elvis of Marysville / California.

BETA BAND

Formed: London, England . . . 1994 by ex-patriate Scotsman, STEVE MASON, the St. Andrews-born singer meeting up Edinburgh University students, decksman JOHN MacLEAN and drummer ROBIN JONES on a train down to the capital. There they worked at various day jobs while sharing a flat in Shepherd's Bush; Portsmouth-born RICHARD GREENTREE, formerly bassist of SINISTER FOOTWEAR would become part of the zany quartet in early '97 after being introduced through mutual friends, PUSHERMAN. Discovered and subsequently produced by THE VERVE's NICK McCABE, who saw some potential in their psychedelic transcendental dub malarky. A pot-pourri of sound right enough (STONE ROSES or The MOONFLOWERS – remember them? – on a mantric mission!), the lads issued three EP's in the space of a year, 'CHAMPION VERSIONS', 'THE PATTY PATTY SOUND' and the excellent 'LOS AMIGOS DEL BETA BANDIDOS'. By popular demand (the vinyl was changing hands for upwards of £40 a time!) these were soon collected together on one shiny cd/album, simply titled 'THE THREE EP'S'. Lauded by the more discerning factions of the music press (the NME for one!), the bumbling art-rockers (by-passing the fashion stakes completely; safari suits, judo gear and horror of horrors, STEVE's "smart-arse" shell-suit being the disorder of the day) found themselves in the Top 40 by Autumn '98 with a long player that hung together surprisingly well. The sound of "baggy" ten years on, filtered through a kingsized bong, BETA standards such as 'DRY THE RAIN' ("It Will Be Alright"), 'INNER MEET ME', 'SHE'S THE ONE', 'DR. BAKER' and 'NEEDLES IN MY EYES' will surely come to be regarded as underground classics. To end the year, MASON moonlighted as KING BISCUIT TIME, releasing (to coincide with the latest edition of the band's zany in-house comic!) a bizarre EP of spaced-out drum'n'bass, '"SINGS" NELLY FOGGIT'S BLUES IN "ME AND THE PHARAOHS"'. • **Trivia:** They guested on SPIRITUALIZED's 'Abbey Road' EP early '98.

Album rating: THE THREE E.P.'S (*9)

STEVE MASON – vocals, percussion, drums, etc / **JOHN MacLEAN** – turntable, sampling / **RICHARD GREENTREE** – bass (ex-SINISTER FOOTWEAR) / **ROBIN JONES** – drums, percussion

		Regal	not iss.
Jul 97.	(12"ep) *(REG 16)* **CHAMPION VERSIONS** – Dry the rain / I know / B + A / Dogs got a bone.		-
Mar 98.	(2x12"ep/cd-ep) *(REG 18/+CD)* **THE PATTY PATTY SOUND** – Inner meet me / The house song / The monolith / She's the one.		-
Jul 98.	(cd-ep) *(REG 20CD)* **LOS AMIGOS DEL BETA BANDIDOS** – Push it out / It's over / Dr. Baker / Needles in my eyes.		-
Sep 98.	(cd) *(7243 4 97385 2 2)* **THE THREE E.P.'S** (compilation)	35	-

KING BISCUIT TIME

aka **STEVE MASON** – vocals, etc

Dec 98.	(12"ep/cd-ep) *(REG 025/+CD)* **"SINGS" NELLY FOGGIT'S BLUES IN "ME AND THE PHARAOHS"** – Fatheriver / Niggling discrepancy / Little white / Eye o' the dug.		-

BETTER THAN EZRA

Formed: New Orleans, Louisiana, USA . . . 1988 by university pals, KEVIN GRIFFIN (their main songwriter), TOM DRUMMOND and CARY BONNECAZE. Debuting their rather derivative DINOSAUR JR guitar-based sound on a privately distributed cassette at the turn of the decade, the band spent the first half of the 90's rehearsing and touring extensively in their southern domain. In 1993/4, BETTER THAN EZRA self-financed their debut release, 'DELUXE' (on 'Swell'), the album shifting enough copies to attract major label interest. Eventually signing to 'Elektra', the band went back into the studio with producer, Dan Rothchild, the man helping them polish up their aforementioned debut for re-release in '95. Catchy grunge by numbers with a MICHAEL STIPE-esque vocal inflection, the record gradually ascended the US charts helped by the Top 30 success of single, 'GOOD'. The following year, after CARY was replaced by TRAVIS AARON McNABB, the trio returned with a second collection, 'FRICTION BABY', a record that barely reached the shallows of the US chart as the grunge wave subsided. Obviously WEA/Elektra had given up any hope of marketing the band in Britain and like its predecessor, 'HOW DOES YOUR GARDEN GROW?' (1998), was a US-only release.

Album rating: DELUXE (*6) / FRICTION BABY (*4) / HOW DOES YOUR GARDEN GROW? (*3)

KEVIN GRIFFIN – vocals, guitar / **TOM DRUMMOND** – bass / **CARY BONNECAZE** – drums

		WEA Int.	Elektra
May 95.	(cd/c) *<7559 61784-2/-4>* **DELUXE** – In the blood / Good / Southern girl / The killer inside / Rosealia / Cry in the sun / Teenager / Untitled / Summerhouse / Porcelain / Heaven / This time of year / Coyote.		35
—	<above was initially released on their own 'Swell' imprint>		
Jun 95.	(c-s) *<64428>* **GOOD / CIRCLE OF FRIENDS (live)**	-	30
Jun 95.	(c-s) *(EKR 204C)* **GOOD / SUMMERHOUSE** (cd-s+=) *(EKR 204CD)* – Know you better (live) / Circle of friends (live).		-
Nov 95.	(c-s,cd-s) *<64352>* **ROSEALIA / IN THE BLOOD (live)**	-	71
—	**TRAVIS AARON McNABB** – drums; repl. BONNECAZE		
Aug 96.	(cd/c) *<7559 61944-2/-4>* **FRICTION BABY**	-	64
Dec 96.	(c-s,cd-s) *<64228>* **DESPERATELY WANTING / PALACE HOTEL**	-	48
Sep 98.	(cd/c) *<62247>* **HOW DOES YOUR GARDEN GROW?**	-	

BETTIE SERVEERT

Formed: Amsterdam, Netherlands . . . . 1990 by CAROL VAN DIJK, PETER VISSER, HERMAN BUNSKOEKE and BEREND DUBBE. Naming themselves, bizarrely enough, after a caption underneath a photo of Dutch/US tennis player, Bettie Stove (the literal translation is Bettie serves!), BETTIE SERVEERT got their break when US indie 'Matador' copped an earful of the band's demo tape. The label almost immediately issued their debut single, 'TOMBOY', a long-player, 'PALOMINE' (1992), hot on its heels the following month. Licensed in Britain to 4ad's 'Guernica' offshoot, the album's infectious, vaguely 60's indie-rock with a coninental flavour was the toast of critics, even featuring a cover of a Sebadoh number, 'HEALTHY SICK'. Switching to 'Beggars Banquet', the band marked time while in the studio recording their more downbeat follow-up set, 'LAMPREY' (1995), by releasing the title track of their debut early in '94. A few years later, BETTIE SERVEERT failed to resurrect their fading star with third set, 'DUST BUNNIES' (1997), initial interest in the band receding. Of late, the Dutch also-rans were sighted on the 'Brinkman' imprint with the release of 'PLAYS VENUS AND FURS' (1998).

Album rating: PALOMINE (*8) / LAMPREY (*5) / DUST BUNNIES (*6)

CAROL VAN DIJK – vocals, guitar / **PETER VISSER** – guitar / **HERMAN BUNSKOEKE** – bass / **BEREND DUBBE** – drums

		Guernica	Matador
Oct 92.	(cd-ep) **TOMBOY /**	-	
Nov 92.	(cd/c/lp) *(GU 3 CD/C/LP)* **PALOMINE** – Leg / Palomine / Kid's alright / Brain-tag / Tomboy / Under the surface / Balentine / This thing nowhere / Healthy sick / Sundazed to the core / Palomine (small). *(cd re-iss. Jul98; same)*		Jul93
		Beggars Banquet	**Matador**
Feb 94.	(12"/cd-s) *(BBQ 28 T/CD)* **PALOMINE. / SILENT SPRING / SMALL**		
Jan 95.	(10"ep/cd-ep) *(BBQ 46 TT/CD)* **CRUTCHES. / SHADES / ENTIRE RACES**		
Jan 95.	(cd/c/lp) *(BBQ CD/MC/LP 169)* **LAMPREY** *(lp w/free ltd 7")*		
Mar 95.	(7"/c-s) *(BBQ 50/+C)* **RAY, RAY RAIN. / LOOK BACK IN ANGER** (cd-s+=) *(BBQ 50CD)* – What friends?		
Jun 95.	(cd-ep) *(BBQ 58CD)* **SOMETHING SO WILD / TRIGGER CUT / CRUTCHES (BBC session) / STANLEY PARK**		
Feb 97.	(7") *(BBQ 308)* **WHAT FRIENDS. / SPINE** (cd-s+=) *(BBQ 308CD)* – Genuine life form.		
Mar 97.	(cd/c/lp) *(BBQ CD/MC/LP 189)* **DUST BUNNIES** – Geel / Link / Musher / Dust bunnies / What friends / Misery galore / Story in a nutshell / Sugar the pill / Rudder / Pork and beans / Fallen foster / Co-coward / Heaven.		
May 97.	(cd-s) *(BBQ 314CD)* **CO-COWARD / ALMOST MONKEYS**		
		Brinkman	**unknown**
Apr 97.	(7") *(BRTS 65)* **ALL THE OTHER FISH. /**		
Aug 98.	(cd) *(BKMN 74)* **PLAYS VENUS AND FURS**		

BEVIS FROND

Formed: Walthamstow, London, England . . . 1987 by quintessential English eccentric, NICK SALOMAN, who had been part of the duo NICK & DICK, who became ODDSOCKS in 1975. They made one album, 'MEN OF THE MOMENT', for the 'Sweet Folk' label. In 1980, NICK formed the 5-piece, VON TRAPP FAMILY, which made an EP, 'BRAND NEW THRILL'. Two years later, the band became ROOM 13, releasing another single, 'MURDER MYSTERY'. Unfortunately, NICK was seriously injured in a motorcycle accident, using the compensation money to finance his next project, the solo BEVIS FROND. Early in 1987, he was back on vinyl with the 'MIASMA' album, a critically acclaimed, psychedelic guitar-rock feast – with influences ranging from JIMI HENDRIX and CREAM to folky punk – released on his own 'Woronzow' label. Another two albums, 'INNER MARSHLAND', and 'BEVIS THROUGH THE LOOKING GLASS', were issued during that year and several others followed, although he kept a low profile. In the late 80's, he also set up his own underground magazine 'Ptolemaic Terrascope'. In 1990, he recorded a collaboration album, 'MAGIC EYE', with the legendary PINK FAIRIES drummer TWINK. SALOMAN continued to beaver away with at least one album a year, the latest being 1997's 'NORTH CIRCULAR'. • **Covers:** XPRESS MAN (Groundhogs) / POSSESSION (Iron Butterfly) / SUMMER HOLIDAY EP (Cliff & The Shadows) / etc.

Album rating: MIASMA (*8) / A GATHERING OF FRONDS (*7) / NEW RIVER HEAD (*8)

NICK SALOMAN – vocals, guitar / + 4 others

		Woronzow	not iss.
1980.	(7"ep; as VON TRAPP FAMILY) *(WOO 1)* **BRAND NEW THRILL. / DREAMING / NO REFLEXES**		-
—	**SALOMAN** + 2 others		
1982.	(12"; as ROOM 13) *(WOO 2)* **MURDER MYSTERY. / NEED SOME DUB**		-
—	**NICK SALOMAN** – vocals, instruments		

Mar 87. (lp) *(WOO 3)* **MIASMA** [ ] [-]
– Garden gate / She's in love with time / Wild mind / Wild afterthought / Splendid isolation / The Earl of Walthamstow / The Newgate wind / Release yourself / Maybe / Ride the train of thought / Confusion days. *(re-iss. Jul89 on 'Reckless'; RECK 13) (cd-iss. Mar89+=; CDRECK 13)* – Rat in a waistcoat / In another year / Mudman / Now you know / 1970 home improvements.

Aug 87. (lp) *(WOO 4)* **INNER MARSHLAND** [ ] [-]
– Cries from the inner marshland / Termination station grey / Window eye / Once more / Defoliation part one / Reflections in a tall mirror / Hey Mr. Undecided / I've got eyes in the back of my head / Minsmere sphagnum Sienese acid blues / Defoliation part two / I can't get into your scene / Song for the sky / The shrine. *(re-iss. Jul89 on 'Reckless'; RECK 14) (cd-iss. Mar89 +=; CDRECK 14)* – (3 tracks).

Dec 87. (d-lp) *(WOO 5)* **BEVIS THROUGH THE LOOKING GLASS – THE GREAT MAGNET DISASTER** [ ] [-]
– 1970 home improvements / Now you know / The shrine / Rat in a waistcoat / In another year / Express man / Mudman / Song for the sky / Purtle sline / I can't get into your scene / Soot / Die is cast / Alistair Jones. *(re-iss. Dec88 on 'Reckless'; RECKD 9)*

Jun 88. (lp) *(WOO 6)* **ACID JAM** [ ] [-]
– (featured 2 BEVIS tracks).

— BEVIS featured on OUTSKIRTS OF INFINITY lp 'Lord Of The Dark Skies' *WOO 7)*

Aug 88. (lp) *(WOO 8)* **TRIPTYCH** [ ] [-]
– Into the cryptic mist / Debbie's new song for drums / Lights are changing / Gemini machine / Phil exorcises the Daemons / Old man blank / The daily round / Hurt goes on / Corinthian / Nowhere fast / Tangerine infringement beak / Hey Joe / Purtle sline / Soot / Long journey into light. *(re-iss. Mar89 on 'Reckless' cd+=/lp; CD+/RECK 15)* – (3 tracks).

— used occasional musicians; **MARTIN CROWLEY** – drums / **SHAW + GOODWAY**

Reckless Reckless

Jul 89. (cd/lp) *(<CD+/RECK 17>)* **THE AUNTIE WINNIE ALBUM** [ ] [ ]
– Malvolios dream – Journey to Pikes / Foreign laugh / Down again / Will to lose / Repressor / Winters blues / The mizmaze / Close / Without mind / City of the sun. *(cd+=)* – Die is cast / The miskatonic variations.

Feb 90. (cd/lp) *(<CD+/RECK 18>)* **ANY GAS FASTER** [ ] [ ]
– Lord Plentiful reflects / Rejection day (a.m.) / Ear song / This corner of England / Legendary / When you wanted me / Lost rivers / Somewhere else / These dark days / Head on a pole / Your mind's gone grey / Old sea dog / Rejection day (p.m.) / Olde world.

Oct 90. (12"ep) *(RECK 20)* **EAR SONG / OLDE WORLDE. / I'VE GOT EYES IN THE BACK OF MY HEAD (live) / MEDIAEVAL SIENESE ACID BLUES (live) / OLDE WORLDE (live) / RADIO BLOODBEAST (live)** [ ] [-]

Woronzow Reckless

Feb 91. (lp/cd; by BEVIS & TWINK) *(WOO 13)* **MAGIC EYE** [ ] [-]
– Sorrow remembered / Flying igloos / The fairy / She darks the sun / Eclipse / Fractured sky / Black queen / Gryke / Bag drip.

Sep 91. (d-lp/cd) *(WOO 16/+CD) <CDRECK 24>* **NEW RIVER HEAD** [ ] [ ]
– White sun / Drowned / She's entitled to / Waving / New river head / Wild jack hammer / He'd be a diamond / Undertaker / Stain on the sun / Thankless task / Mistatonic variations II / It won't come again / Chinese burn / God speed you to earth.

Dec 91. (7"ep; with PTOLEMAIC TERRASCOPE 8) *(WOO 16 1/2)* **SNOW EP** [ ] [-]

Nov 92. (lp/cd) *(WOO 18/+CD)* **LONDON STONE** [ ] [-]

Feb 93. (lp/cd; as FRED BISON FIVE) *(WOO 19/+CD)* **BEATROOTS** [ ] [-]
(cd+=) – (3 extra tracks).

— In Feb'93, TODD DILLINGHAM & NICK SALOMAN collaborated on a 'Voiceprint' cd, 'ART INTO DUST' (VP 121CD).

Jul 93. (7"ep) *(WOO 20)* **SUMMER HOLIDAY EP** [ ] [-]
– Summer holiday / Big news / Dancing shoes / Round and round.

Oct 93. (d-lp/cd) *(WOO 21/+CD)* **IT JUST IS (live)** [ ] [-]
– Can't stop lying / Time-share heart / Idiot dance / Desperate / What's it all about / Day one / Let me live / Terrible day / Dreamboat sinking / A sorry tale / Human overload / I can't catch up with you / Hit the lights / Everyday sunshine / Not for now / All gone / Time piece / And then?

Jul 94. (7") *(EFA 40304-7)* **LET'S LIVE FOR TODAY. /** [ ] [-]
(above issued on 'Helter Skelter')

Woronzow Imprint

Oct 94. (d-lp/cd) *(WOO 22/+CD) <92422>* **SPRAWL** [ ] [ ] Feb99
– I know we're going / Awake! / Love you more / The puller / Oh Gideon / Right on (hippie dream) / I bought my love a lapdog / New Alexandria / Anodyne – See you.

— live band included; **ANDY WARD** – drums (ex-CAMEL) / **ADRIAN SHAW** – bass / **RIC GUNTHER + MARTIN CROWLEY** occasional drums

Oct 95. (d-lp/cd) *(WOO 26/+CD) <92426>* **SUPERSEEDER** (compilation) [ ] [ ] Feb99
– Superseded / Dolly bug / Stoned train driver / Animal tracks / Jaye / I can't cry / Could be / Flashy / Golden walks of London / House of mountains / The queen of May / Sue me / Loveland / Could you fly higher?

Oct 95. (7") *(DAMGOOD 81)* **DOLLY BUG. / GREEN PARK SATURDAY** [ ] [-]
(above issued on 'Damaged Goods')

Woronzow Flydaddy

Oct 96. (d-lp/cd) *(WOO 28/+CD) <022>* **SON OF WALTER** [ ] [ ]

Apr 97. (7") *(SPAREME 004)* **LITTLE TOWN PIER. /** [ ] [-]
(above on 'Spare Me')

Nov 97. (t-lp/d-cd) *(W 406/+CD) <029>* **NORTH CIRCULAR** [ ] [ ] Feb99
– Stars burn out / Hole song No.2 / Sun room / Eyeshine / He had you / That's why you need us / Where the old boys go / Pips / Blew me out / Love is / Heritage coast / Stay at home girl / Growing up / Wind blew all around me / There's always one / Book / Psychedelic unknowns / You make me feel / Revival / Gold and silver / Her father's daughter / Stoneground head / Timothy's powders / For want of you / Stranger's mirror / Story ends.

– compilations, etc –

May 92. (cd) *Reckless; (CDRECK 25)* **A GATHERING OF FRONDS** [ ] [-]
– Down in the well / Mother dust / Cuvie / Blurred vision / Solar marmalade / Son of many mothers / Hillview (PARTHENOGENTICK BROTHERHOOD) / Bad time / High in a flat / Snow / Express man / African violet / Possession / Visions (through dilated eyes) (VACANT PLOT) / Somewhere else / Alistair Jones.

1990's. (7") *(HELPF 101)* **AFRICAN VIOLET. / The Steppes: History Hates No Man** [ ] [-]

Apr 98. (lp; by DOCTOR FROND) *Magic Gnome; (MG 429932-2)* **DOCTOR FROND** [ ] [-]

B-52's

Formed: Athens, Georgia, USA . . . late '76, by KATE PIERSON, FRED SCHNEIDER, KEITH STRICKLAND, RICKY WILSON and his sister CINDY. After one self-financed 45 sold out its limited 2,000 copies, they drew the attention of Island's Chris Blackwell, who signed them after they played residency at Max's Kansas City late in 1978. They subsequently re-issued their 'ROCK LOBSTER' debut, the single making UK Top 40 lists the following year. Combining a kitsch image and sound which took in everything from rock'n'roll and 60's beat to new wave REZILLOS-style dual harmonies, The B-52's brightened up the increasingly dour late 70's/early 80's punk/pop scene. The marine madness of the classic 'ROCK LOBSTER' eventually made its way into the US charts in early 1980, by which time the eponymous '79 debut album had made UK Top 30. Even JOHN LENNON was a fan, the former BEATLES man surprisingly admitting that The B-52's were one the groups who inspired him to start writing again. A strong follow-up set, 'WILD PLANET' (1980), made the Top 20 in both Britain and America, although critics weren't quite so enamoured with the more mannered 'MESOPOTAMIA' set (1982), produced by DAVID BYRNE of TALKING HEADS. The mid-80's were a bleak time for the band as RICKY finally died from AIDS on the 12th October, 1985, and the group struggled to capture the inspired creativity of their earlier period (fans were content in making 'ROCK LOBSTER' an even bigger UK hit than before). Signing a new deal with 'Reprise', The B-52's reunited their roots on the 'BOUNCING OFF SATELLITES', an album which should have spawned a hit single, 'WIG'. DON WAS / NILE RODGERS-produced 'COSMIC THING' (1989), a remarkable comeback that showcased their alternative dancefloor smash, 'LOVE SHACK', the album becoming their most successful release to date, making the US Top 5. Trimmed to a trio of PIERSON, SCHNEIDER and STRICKLAND following the departure of CINDY in 1992, the group recorded another album in the classic B-52's style, 'GOOD STUFF', before setting to work on the soundtrack for the revamped 'Flintstones' movie. Something of a canny pairing, SCHNEIDER's nasal-voiced nonsense was a perfect backdrop for Fred and family's stone age adventures. • **Songwriters:** All mainly STRICKLAND or group compositions. PLANET CLAIRE (w/ Henry Mancini) • **Trivia:** In 1981, during lay-off, STRICKLAND, PIERSON and CINDY WILSON did one-off Japan venture as "MELON" with group The PLASTICS and ADRIAN BELEW. Late 1990, PIERSON contributed on singles by IGGY POP (Candy) and R.E.M. (Shiny Happy People).

Album rating: DANCE THIS MESS AROUND THE BEST OF THE B-52's compilation (*9)

KATE PIERSON (b.27 Apr'48, Weehawken, N.J.) – vocals, organ, bass / **CINDY WILSON** (b.28 Feb'57) – vocals, percussion, guitar / **RICKY WILSON** (b.19 Mar'53) – guitar / **FRED SCHNEIDER** (III) (b. 1 Jul'56, Newark, N.J.) – vocals, keyboards / **KEITH 'Julian' STRICKLAND** (b.26 Oct'53) – drums

not iss. Boo-Fant

Nov 78. (7") *<DB-52>* **ROCK LOBSTER. / 52 GIRLS** [-] [ ]

Island Warners

Jul 79. (7") *(WIP 6506)* **ROCK LOBSTER. / RUNNING AROUND** [37] [-]

Jul 79. (lp/c) *(WIP/ICT 9580) <3355>* **THE B-52's** [22] [59]
– Planet Claire / 52 girls / Dance this mess around / Rock lobster / Lava / There's a Moon in the sky (called the Moon) / Hero worship / 6060-842 / Downtown. *(lp w/ free 7") (PSR 438)* – ROCK LOBSTER. / 52 GIRLS *(re-iss. May86; same) (cd-iss. Jan87; CID 9580) (re-iss. Jan94 + May94;)*

Sep 79. (7") *(WIP 6527)* **6060-842. / HERO WORSHIP** [ ] [ ]

Nov 79. (7"pic-d/7") *(P+/WIP 6551) <WBS 49212>* **PLANET CLAIRE. / THERE'S A MOON IN THE SKY (CALLED THE MOON)** [ ] [ ] May80

Jan 80. (7") *<WBS 49173>* **ROCK LOBSTER. / 6060-842** [-] [56]

Jul 80. (7") *(WIP 6579)* **GIVE ME BACK MY MAN. / STROBE LIGHT** [61] [-]

Sep 80. (lp/c) *(ILPS/ICT 9622) <BSK 3471>* **WILD PLANET** [18] [18]
– Party out of bounds / Dirty back road / Runnin' around / Give me back my man / Private Idaho / Devil in my car / Quiche Lorraine / Strobe light / 53 miles west of Venus. *(cd-iss. May90; 842436-2)*

Oct 80. (7") *<WBS 49537>* **PRIVATE IDAHO. / PARTY OUT OF BOUNDS** [-] [74]

Nov 80. (7") *(WIP 6685)* **DIRTY BACK ROAD. / STROBE LIGHT** [ ] [-]

Jan 81. (7") *<WBS 49717>* **QUICHE LORRAINE. / LAVA** [-] [ ]

Jul 81. (m-lp/c) *(IPM/ICT 1001) <MINI 3596>* **THE PARTY MIX ALBUM** (remixes) [36] [55]
– Party out of bounds / Private Idaho / Give me back my man / Lava / Dance this mess around / 52 girls. *(cd-iss. May90; 846044-2)*

Aug 81. (7") *(WIP 6727)* **GIVE ME BACK MY MAN (Party mix). / PARTY OUT OF BOUNDS (version)** [ ] [-]

Feb 82. (m-lp/c) *(ISSP/ICT 4006) <3641>* **MESOPOTAMIA** [18] [35]
– Loveland / Deep sleep / Mesopotamia / Cake / Throw that beat in the garbage can / Nip it in the bud. *(cd-iss. May90; 846239-2)*

Mar 82. (7") *<50064>* **DEEP SLEEP. / NIP IT IN THE BUD** [-] [ ]

Jun 82. (7") *<29971>* **MESOPOTAMIA. / THROW THAT BEAT IN THE GARBAGE CAN** [-] [ ]

Apr 83. (7") *(IS 107)* **SONG FOR A FUTURE GENERATION. / ('A'instrumental)** [63] [-]
(12"+=) *(12IS 107)* – Planet Claire.
(d7"++=) *(ISD 107)* – There's a moon in the sky (called the moon).

May 83. (lp/c) *(ILPS 9759) <23819>* **WHAMMY!** [33] [29]
– Legal tender / Whammy kiss / Song for a future generation / Butterbean / Trism /

Queen of Las Vegas / Don't worry / Big bird / Work that skirt. *(cd-iss. May90; 842445-2)*

Jul 83. (7") *<29579>* **LEGAL TENDER. / MOON 83** - 81

Oct 83. (7") *<29561>* **SONG FOR A FUTURE GENERATION. / TREASON** -

— **RICKY** suffering from full blown AIDS, died 12 Oct'85.

May 86. (7"/7"sha-pic-d; rock/planet/lobster) *(BFT+/G/P/L 1)* **ROCK LOBSTER (new version). / PLANET CLAIRE** 12 -
(d7"+=) *(BFTD 1)* – Song for a future generation / 52 girls.
(12"+=) *(12BFT 1)* – Song for a future generation / Give me back my man.

— They carry on, augmented by session man **RALPH CARNEY** – guitar

Jun 87. (7"/7"pic-d) *(BFT/+P 2)* **WIG. / SUMMER OF LOVE**
(c-s+=/12+=) *(BFTD/12BFT 2)* – Song for a future generation.

Jul 87. (lp/c/cd) *(ILPS/ICT/CID 9871) <25504>* **BOUNCING OFF THE SATELLITES** 74 85 Sep86
– Summer of love / Girl from Ipanema goes to Greenland / Housework / Detour thru your mind / Wig / Theme for a nude beach / Ain't it a shame / Juicy jungle / Communicate / She brakes for rainbows. *(cd-iss. May90; 842480-2)*

Sep 87. (7") **SUMMER OF LOVE. / HOUSEWORK** -

— added on tour **PAT IRWIN** – keyboards / **ZACH ALFORD** – drums / **PHILIPPE SASSE** – (studio keyboards) / **SARA LEE** – bass (ex-GANG OF FOUR) (also studio)

Reprise Reprise

Jul 89. (lp/c)(cd) *(WX 283/+C)(925854-2) <25854>* **COSMIC THING** 8 4
– Cosmic thing / Dry country / Deadbeat club / Love shack / Junebug / Roam / Bushfire / Channel Z / Topaz / Follow your blues.

Aug 89. (7") *<22817>* **LOVE SHACK. / CHANNEL Z** - 3

Sep 89. (7") *(W 2831)* **CHANNEL Z (remix). / JUNEBUG** 61 -
(12")(cd-s) *(W 2831 T/CD)* – ('A'-Rock mix) / ('A'side) / ('A'dub mix). *(re-iss. Aug90;)*

Dec 89. (7") *<22667>* **ROAM. / BUSHFIRE** - 3

Feb 90. (7"/7"g-f/7"pic-d/c-s/cd-s) *(W 9917/+X/P/C/CD)* **LOVE SHACK. / PLANET CLAIRE (live) / ROCK LOBSTER (live)** 2 -
(12") *(W 9917T)* – ('A'-Dany Rampling remix) / ('A'-Ben Grosse mix) / ('A'side).

Apr 90. (7") *<19938>* **DEADBEAT CLUB. / PLANET CLAIRE** - 30

May 90. (7"/c-s/cd-s) *(W 9827/+C/CD)* **ROAM. / WHAMMY KISS (live) / DANCE THIS MESS AROUND (live)** 17 -
(12"/12"w-poster) *(W 9827T/+W)* – ('A'-Radio mix) / ('A'remix) / ('A'extended remix).

Sep 90. (7"/c-s) **DEADBEAT CLUB. / LOVE SHACK** -
(12"+=/cd-s+=) – B-52's megamix.

— now trimmed to basic trio of **PIERSON, SCHNEIDER** – vox / + **STRICKLAND** – guitar with guest musicians **IRWIN / ALFORD / LEE /** plus **JEFF PORCARO + STERLING CAMPBELL** – drums / **DAVID McMURRAY** – sax / **JAMIE MULHOBERAC + RICHARD HILTON** – keyboards / **LENNY CASTRO** – percussion / **TRACY WORMWORTH** – bass

Jun 92. (7"/c-s) *(W 0109/+C) <18895>* **GOOD STUFF. / BAD INFLUENCE** 21 28
(12"+=/cd-s+=) *(W 0109 T/CD)* – Return to Dreamland.
(12") *(W 0109TX)* – (4-'A'mixes).

Jul 92. (cd/c/lp) *<(7599 26943-2/-4/-1)>* **GOOD STUFF** 8 16
– Tell it like it t-i-is / Hot pants explosion / Good stuff / Revolution Earth / Dreamland / Is that you Mo-Dean? / The world's green laughter / Vision of a kiss / Breezin' / Bad influence. *(re-iss. Feb95 cd/c;)*

Sep 92. (7"/c-s) *(W 0130/+C)* **TELL IT LIKE IT T-I-IS. / THE WORLD'S GREEN LAUGHTER** 61
(12"/cd-s) *(W 0130 T/CD)* – ('A'-4 other mixes).

Nov 92. (7"/c-s) **IS THAT YOU MO-DEAN?. / ('A'-Moby mix)**
(12"+=/cd-s+=) – ('A'-2 other mixes) / Tell it like it t-i-is.

Feb 93. (7"/c-s) **HOT PANTS EXPLOSION. / LOVE SHACK**
(cd-s+=) – Channel Z / Roam.

— **SCHNEIDER, PIERSON + STRICKLAND**

M.C.A. M.C.A.

Jun 94. (7"/c-s; BC-52's) *(MCS/+CS 1986) <54839>* **(MEET) THE FLINTSTONES. / ('A'-Barney's mix)** 3 33 May94
(cd-s+=) *(MCSTD 1986)* – (2-'A'mixes).
(above from that year's movie, 'The Flintstones')

– compilations, others, etc. –

Jun 90. (cd/c/lp) *Island; (ILPS/ICT/CID 9959)* **DANCE THIS MESS AROUND THE BEST OF THE B-52's** 36 -
– Party out of bounds / Devil in my car / Dirty back road / 6060-842 / Wig / Dance this mess around / Private Idaho / Rock lobster / Strobe light / Give me back my man / Song for a future generation / Planet Claire / 52 girls. *(cd+=)* – (2 extra mixes).

Feb 91. (cd) *Reprise; <26401>* **PARTY MIX! / MESOPOTAMIA** -

Nov 92. (d-cd) *Island; (ITSCD 1)* **THE B-52'S / WILD PLANET** -

Sep 95. (cd) *Spectrum; (551210-2)* **PLANET CLAIRE** -

Jul 98. (cd/c) *Reprise; (9362 46995-2/-4) <46920>* **TIME CAPSULE – SONGS FOR A FUTURE GENERATION** 93 Jun98
– Planet Claire / Rock lobster / Private Idaho / Quiche Lorraine / Mesopotamia / Summer of love / Channel Z / Deadbeat club / Love shack / Roam / Good stuff / Is that you Mo-Dean? / Meet the Flintstones / Debbie / Hallucinating Pluto.

FRED SCHNEIDER

solo, recorded 1984 and written with COTE

— with various session people

Reprise Reprise

May 91. (cd/c/lp) *<(7559 26592-2/-4/-1)>* **FRED SCHNEIDER & THE SHAKE SOCIETY**
– Monster / Out the concrete / Summer in Hell / Orbit / I'm gonna haunt you / It's time to kiss / This planet's a mess / Wave / Boonga (the New Jersey caveman).

Jun 91. (cd-s) *<19262>* **MONSTER /** - 85

— next with **STEVE ALBINI** – producing backing from **DEADLY CUPCAKE, SHADOWY MEN ON A SHADOWY PLANET + SIX FINGER SATELLITE**

WEA WEA

Jun 96. (cd) *<(9362 46215-2)>* **JUST. . .FRED**
– Whip / Helicopter / Sugar in my hog / Bulldozer / Coconut / Center of the universe / Radioactive lady eyeball / Lick / Bad dream / Secret sharer / Stroke of genius.

Jello BIAFRA (see under ⇒ DEAD KENNEDYS)

BIBLE

Formed: Norwich, England . . . 1985 out of Cambridge outfit, The GREAT DIVIDE, by BOO HEWERDINE and KEVIN FLANAGAN. The latter combo released a handful of singles before the duo, along with newcomers TONY SHEPHERD and CLIVE LAWSON formed The BIBLE. A few classy 45's (including the definitive 'GRACELAND' and 'MAHALIA – named after gospel singer, MAHALIA JACKSON) both from the mini-lp, 'WALKING THE GHOST BACK HOME', brought comparisons to The SMITHS. Released on local label, 'Backs', the record caused enough of a stir to see the band – now augmented by NEIL MacCOLL (brother of KIRSTY) and new drummer DAVE LARCOMBE – snapped up by 'Chrysalis'; the label duly re-issued the aforementioned 'GRACELANDS' early in 1987, confident of at least a decent sized hit. It flopped however, and the band retired to work on their first album proper, the STEVE EARLE-produced 'EUREKA' (1988). A collection of soft-ish romantic rock, lying somewhere between contemporaries CHINA CRISIS, DANNY WILSON or The BIG DISH, this UK Top 75 breakthrough surprisingly failed to spawn any hits, at least first time round; 'HONEY BE GOOD' became a belated minor success upon its re-release in summer '89. By this time, HEWERDINE had already found a new musical foil in the shape of Texas troubadour, DARDEN SMITH, the pair collaborating on a one-off album, 'EVIDENCE'. HEWERDINE's solo work – which also included 1992's 'IGNORANCE' – was similarly unsuccessful (although ironically EDDI READER took his 'Patience Of Angels' into the UK Top 40 in 1994) and together with SHEPHERD and LARCOMBE he re-formed The BIBLE. This proved to be short-lived, the band's guiding light taking his songs and releasing them (as 'BAPTISM HOSPITAL') under his own name. • **Songwriters:** HEWERDINE writes most w / SHEPHERD except; ABRAHAM, MARTIN & JOHN (Marvin Gaye) / ON BROADWAY (Drifters).

Album rating: THE BIBLE (*8) / EUREKA (*7) / Boo Hewerdine: BAPTISM HOSPITAL (*6)

GREAT DIVIDE

BOO HEWERDINE (b. MARCUS) – vocals, guitar / **KEVIN FLANAGAN** – saxophone / **+?**

Wimp not iss.

Dec 82. (7") *(WIMP 004)* **WHO BROKE THE LOVE BANK. / BLESS MY SOUL** -

Ensign not iss.

Oct 83. (7") *(ENY 504)* **WHISPERED IN HEAVEN. / SWEAT** -
(12"+=) *(12ENY 504)* –

Apr 84. (7") *(ENY 512)* **MONEY AND TIME. / ANIMATION TIME** -
(12"+=) *(12ENY 512)* –

Blue Murder not iss.

Oct 84. (12"ep) *(BLUE 701)* **IT'S GOT TO BE LOVE / THE DYING ART OF CONVERSATION. / THE TALKING BLUES (LIE FOR YOU, DIE FOR YOU, DO ANYTHING FOR YOU) / I.O.U.T.L.C.** -

BIBLE

— **BOO HEWERDINE + KEVIN FLANAGAN** / plus **TONY SHEPHERD** – keyboards, drums / **CLIVE LAWSON** – bass

Backs not iss.

Mar 86. (m-lp) *(NCHLP 8)* **WALKING THE GHOST BACK HOME** -
– Red flag / Talk to me like Jackie Kennedy / Walking the ghost back home / She's my bible / Mahalia (Newport '58) / Kid Galahad and the chrome kinewa / King Chicago. *(cd-iss. Oct88' NCHCD 8) (cd re-iss. Nov95 on 'Haven'; HAVENCD 4)*

Apr 86. (7") **GRACELAND. / SWEETNESS** -

— **LEROY LENDOR** – bass; repl. LAWSON

Nov 86. (7") *(NCH 011)* **MAHALIA (NEWPORT '58). / SPEND SPEND SPEND** -
(12"+=) *(12NCH 011)* – Sweetness.

— **DAVE LARCOMBE** – drums; repl. FLANAGAN (who was still a future guest)

— added **NEIL MacCOLL** – guitar, mandolin (ex-ROARING BOYS) / guest **CONSTANCE REDGRAVE** – bass

Chrysalis Chrysalis

Feb 87. (7") *(BIB 1)* **GRACELANDS (remix). / GLORY BOUND (live)**
(12"+=) *(BIBX 2)* – High, wide & handsome / The slow drag down (live) / Walking the ghost back home (live).
(d7"+=) *(BIBD 2)* – Mahalia (Newport '58) / Spend spend spend.

— **GREG HAREWOOD** – bass; repl. CONSTANCE

Jan 88. (lp/c/cd) *(CHR/ZCHR/CCD 1646)* **EUREKA** 71
– Skywriting / Honey be good / Skeleton crew / November brides / Cigarette girls / Crystal Palace / The wishing game / Red Hollywood / Tiny lights / Blues shoes stepping. *(re-dist.May88; same) (cd re-iss. Nov95 on 'Haven'; HAVENCD 5)*

Apr 88. (7") *(BIB 2)* **CRYSTAL PALACE. / THE GOLDEN MILE**
(12"+=) *(BIBX 2)* – Bubblehead / The slow drag down.
(cd-s+=) *(BIBCD 2)* – Graceland / Mahalia (Newport '58).

Sep 88. (7") *(BIB 3)* **HONEY BE GOOD. / UP IN SMOKE**
(12"+=) *(BIBX 3)* – Coming of age / White feathers.

(cd-s+=) *(BIBCD 3)* – Glory bound (live) / Abraham, Martin & John.
Apr 89. (7"/c-s) *(BIB/+MC 4)* **GRACELANDS (remix). / GLORY BOUND** 51
(12"+=/cd-s+=) *(BIB X/CD 4)* – Hide, wide & handsome (parts 1 & 2).
Aug 89. (7"/c-s) *(BIB/+MC 5)* **HONEY BE GOOD. / KING CHICAGO** 54
(12"+=) *(BIBX 5)* – Skywriting / Elastic money.
(cd-s+=) *(BIBCD 5)* – Crystal Palace / On Broadway.
Sep 89. (lp/c/cd) *(CHR/ZCHR/CCD 1732)* **THE BEST OF THE BIBLE** (compilation) 67
– Graceland / Crystal Palace / Honey be good / Skeleton crew / Red Hollywood / Abraham, Martin & John / Skywriting / Glory bound / Up in smoke / Blue shoes stepping / Cigarette girls / The golden mile.

BOO HEWERDINE

— with **DARDEN SMITH** who was a troubadour from Austin, Texas. Others on album; **MARTIN LASCELLES** – keyboards / **I.D. FOSTER** – bass / **PAUL PEARCY** – drums / **REESE WYNANS** – keyboards / **SONNY LANDREATH** – guitar / **CHRIS BIRKETT** – percussion / **SYD STRAW** – vocals

Ensign Chrysalis

Jul 89. (7"; BOO HEWERDINE & DARDEN SMITH) *(ENY 625)* **ALL I WANT IS EVERYTHING. / SOUTH BY SOUTH WEST** -
(12"+=/cd-s+=) *(ENY X/CD 625)* – Tell me why.

Chrysalis Compas

Aug 89. (lp/c/cd; BOO HEWERDINE & DARDEN SMITH) *(CHR/ZCHR/CCD 1726) <74232>* **EVIDENCE**
– All I want is everything / Reminds me (a little of you) / These chains / Out of this world / Evidence / Who, what, where and why / Under the darkest Moon / South by south west / The first chill of winter / Love is a strange hotel / Oil on the water / A town called Blue. *(cd re-iss. Nov95 on 'Haven'; HAVENCD 6)*

Ensign Compas

Feb 92. (cd)(c/lp) *(CCD 1930)(Z+/CHEN 24) <74235>* **IGNORANCE**
(re-iss. cd Nov95 on 'Haven')
Mar 92. (12"ep/cd-ep) **HISTORY / LITTLE BITS OF ZERO./ TALK ME DOWN / GHOST OF JOHNNE** -
May 92. (12"ep/cd-ep) *(ENY X/CD 654)* **59 YDS. / LIBERTY HORSES./ GHOST OF SUMMER WALKING / 16 MILES (version)** -

BIBLE

— reformed with **HEWERDINE, SHEPHERD + LARCOMBE**

Blanco Y Negro Discovery

Dec 94. (c-ep/12"ep/cd-ep) *(NEG 78 C/T/CD)* **THE DREAMLIFE E.P.** -
– Mosquito / Firedogs / Explaining love to aliens.

— split just after the above's release. An album, RANDOM ACTS OF KINDNESS' was withdrawn by 'Haven'; *HAVENCD 8)* although HEWERDINE released the songs as his own solo material below . . .

BOO HEWERDINE

— with a plethora of musicians

Nov 95. (c-s) *(NEG 83 C/CD)* **WORLD'S END / ONE SAD COWBOY** -
(cd-s+=) *(NEG 83CDX)* – A mess of blues.
Jan 96. (cd/c) *(0630 12045-2/-4)* **BAPTISM HOSPITAL**
– World's end / Love thieves / Last cigarette / Dreamlife / Joke / Baptism hospital / Song for a friend / Candyfloss / Sycamore fall / Holywater / Junk / Greedy.
Feb 96. (c-s) *(NEG 86C)* **JOKE / AUCTIONEERS** -
(cd-s+=) *(NEG 86CD)* – Black cat / Firedog.
(cd-s) *(NEG 86CDX)* – ('A'side) / Buzz Aldrin / First day in Hell / I miss you.

BIFF BANG POW!

Formed: London, England . . . 1983 by Glaswegian, ALAN McGEE, the boss of up and coming indie imprint, 'Creation'. Named after 60's cult psych-pop combo, The CREATION (who recorded a track, 'BIFF BANG POW!'), the label was to become McGEE's most successful venture into the music business after years of low-key activities on the fledgling indie scene. His first outfit had been the LAUGHING APPLE, who issued a couple of 45's in the early 80's, a trial run for BIFF BANG POW! The latter outfit's debut single, '50 YEARS OF FUN', appeared in '84, the man McGEE subsequently launching the careers of such influential acts as JESUS & MARY CHAIN, PRIMAL SCREAM and of course, OASIS. When he found the time, the flame-haired entrepreneur beavered away at BIFF BANG POW! material. Over the course of nearly a decade, McGEE indulged his love of psychedelia, punk and NEIL YOUNG with such albums as 'PASS THE PAINTBRUSH . . . HONEY!' (1985), 'LOVE IS FOREVER' (1988) and his final studio outing 'ME' (1991). Now a multi-millionaire, McGEE has always had an uncanny ability to spot innovative "indie" rock talent, the success of outfits like RIDE, BOO RADLEYS and initially MY BLOODY VALENTINE allowing him to loyally stand by less profitable artists such as EDWARD BALL.

Album rating: PASS THE PAINTBRUSH . . . HONEY (*6) / THE GIRLS WHO RUNS THE BEAT HOTEL (*6) / OBLIVION (*6) / LOVE IS FOREVER (*6) / SONGS FOR THE SAD EYED GIRL (*6) / ME (*5) / L'AMOUR, DEMURE, STENHOUSEMUIR compilation (*6)

LAUGHING APPLE

ALAN McGEE (b.29 Sep'60, East Kilbride, Scotland) – vocals, guitar / with others unknown

Autonomy not iss.

1981. (7"ep) *(AUT 001)* **HA HA HEE HEE** -
1981. (7") *(AUT 002)* **PARTICIPATE!. / WOULDN'T YOU** -

Essential not iss.

1982. (7") *(ESS 001)* **PRECIOUS FEELING. / CELEBRATION** -

— in 1983, the track, 'WOULDN'T YOU' appeared on a 7"flexi given away free to buyers of the LEGEND's 7" '73 IN '83' on 'Creation' (CRE 001).

BIFF BANG POW!

— **ALAN McGEE** with **DICK GREEN** – guitar / **JOE FOSTER** – bass (aka SLAUGHTER JOE) / **KEN POPPLE** – drums

Creation not iss.

Feb 84. (7") *(CRE 003)* **50 YEARS OF FUN. / THEN WHEN I SCREAM** -
Jun 84. (7") *(CRE 007)* **THERE MUST BE A BETTER LIFE. / THE CHOCOLATE ELEPHANT MAN** -

— **DAVE EVANS** – bass; repl. FOSTER (who continued solo)

— **ANDREW INNES** – guitar, organ (became part-timer)

Feb 85. (lp) *(CRELP 004)* **PASS THE PAINTBRUSH . . . HONEY** -
– There must be a better life / Lost your dreams / Love and hate / The chocolate elephant man / Water bomb / Colin Dobbins / Wouldn't you? / A day out with Jeremy Chester.
Mar 86. (7") *(CRE 024)* **LOVE'S GOING OUT OF FASHION. / IT HAPPENS ALL THE TIME** -
(12"+=) *(CRE 024T)* – Inside the mushroom / In the afternoon.
Nov 86. (7") *(CRE 034)* **SOMEONE STOLE MY WHEELS. / SUNNY DAYS** -
(12"+=) *(CRE 034T)* – It makes you scared.

— below credited the artist/painter, JC BROUCHARD

Feb 87. (7") *(CRE 038)* **THE WHOLE WORLD IS TURNING BROUCHARD. / THE DEATH OF ENGLAND** -
Mar 87. (lp) *(CRELP 015)* **THE GIRL WHO RUNS THE BEAT HOTEL** -
– Someone stole my wheels / Love's going out of fashion / She never understood / He don't need that girl / She shivers inside / The beat hotel / The happiest girl in the world / If I die / Five minutes in the life of Greenwood Goulding / The whole world is turning Brouchard. *(cd/c-iss.May88 +=; CRECD/CCRE 015)* – PASS THE PAINTBRUSH . . . HONEY.
Jun 87. (lp) *(CRELP 020)* **OBLIVION** -
– In a mourning town / There you go again / Seven seconds to Heaven / A girl called destruction / She's got diamonds in her hair / The only colour in the world is love / Baby sister / Then when I scream / I see the sun / I'm still waiting for my time.
Feb 88. (12"ep) *(CRE 051)* **SHE HAUNTS / THE BEAT HOTEL. / SHE PAINTS / IT HAPPENS ALL THE TIME** -
Apr 88. (lp) *(CRELP 029)* **LOVE IS FOREVER** -
– Miss California Toothpaste 1972 / She haunts / Searching for the pavement / She paints / Close / Ice cream machine / Electric sugar child / Dark in mind / Startripper / She went away to love / The beat hotel / It happens all the time.
Jun 89. (lp/cd) *(CRE LP/CD 046)* **THE ACID HOUSE ALBUM** (compilation) -
– I'm still waiting for my time / Love and hate / Someone stole my wheels / Love's going out of fashion / She haunts / 50 years of fun / She paints / She never understood / The beat hotel / In a mourning town / Then when I scream / She's got diamonds in her hair / The girl from Well Lane / There must be a better life.
Jan 90. (cd/c/lp) *(CRECD/CCRE/CRELP 058)* **SONGS FOR THE SAD EYED GIRL** -
– She kills me / The girl from Well Lane / Baby you just don't care / If you don't love me now, you never ever will / Someone to share my life with / Religious / Hug me honey. *(cd+=)* – OBLIVION *(c+=)* – LOVE IS FOREVER
Nov 90. (7") *(CAFF 13)* **SLEEP. / (other by The TIMES)** -
(above issued on 'Caff')
Apr 91. (cd/c/lp) *(CRECD/CCRE/CRELP 071)* **ME** -
– My first friend / Miss you / I'm burned / Song for a nail / She saved me / You just can't buy satisfaction / Sad eyes in velvet / Guilt ridden / Lovers / Baby you just make me strong.
Nov 91. (cd/c/lp) *(CRECD/CCRE/CRELP 099)* **L'AMOUR, DEMURE, STENHOUSEMUIR** (compilation) -
– She haunts / Someone to share my life with / Startripper / There must be a better life / She paints / Ice cream machine / Hug me honey / Miss you / She kills me / I'm waiting for my time / Someone stole my wheels / Song for a nail / Love's going out of fashion / Girl from Well Lane / Baby you just don't care / The chocolate elephant man / Tell Laura I love her / Searching for the pavement.
Feb 92. (cd/lp) *(CRE CD/LP 125)* **DEBASEMENT TAPES** (compilation of out-takes, etc.) -
– Long live Neil Young and all who sail in him / In bed with Paul Weller / It makes you scared / It happens all the time / The death of England / In the afternoon / Sleep / Back to the start / Inside the mushroom / Everybody wants to divorce her.

— McGEE decided to hang up his proverbial boots and sign on OASIS

– compilations, etc. –

Apr 94. (cd) *Tristar;* **BERTULA POP** -

BIG AUDIO DYNAMITE

Formed: London, England . . . 1984 by ex-CLASH guitarist/singer, MICK JONES, who was still under contract with 'C.B.S.' records. Amongst others, namely DAN DONOVAN, LEO WILLIAMS and GREG ROBERTS, he recruited film-maker/friend and non-musician DON LETTS. Although their 1985 debut 45, 'THE BOTTOM LINE', soon became a favourite, it narrowly missed out on a chart placing. However, the follow-up 'E=MC2', gave them a close brush with the Top 10 early the following year, resurrecting sales of the critically acclaimed but commercially disastrous album, 'THIS IS . . .'. Mick's unique punk-ish vocals with the band's sound was not unlike a danceable CLASH. Indeed, the band were attempting to fashion a gleaming new hip-hop/electro/alternative rock hybrid, using the latter day CLASH sound as a springboard. The debut set was at least partially successful in this endeavour, standout cuts being the aforementioned 'E=MC2' and its follow-up Top 30 hit,

'MEDICINE SHOW'. A second set, 'NO.10 UPPING STREET' (1986) was even more ambitious, featuring contributions from JONES's former mucker, JOE STRUMMER. The following two years saw the band struggle as JONES survived a near fatal bout of pneumonia, the albums 'TIGHTEN UP VOL.88' (1988) and 'MEGATOP PHOENIX' (1989) brave attempts at further pushing back the boundaries between different genres, mixing up reggae, hip-hop and even country. However, by the end of the decade, the B.A.D. blueprint was being more successfully and inventively interpretated by a new wave of white kids armed with samples, drum machines and an attitude, enter EMF, JESUS JONES etc. The original line-up split at the turn of the decade although JONES recruited new players for BIG AUDIO DYNAMITE II, namely NICK HAWKINS, GARY STONEAGE and CHRIS KAVANAGH. The revamped B.A.D. recorded a further couple of critically and commercially underwhelming albums, 'KOOL-AID' (1990) and 'THE GLOBE' (1991), DJ ZONKA adding his turntable skills to the latter. Though JONES continued working under the B.A.D. name into the 90's, his output is largely confined to a cult following. • **Songwriters:** Mainly JONES and LETTS, with other members contributing. Covers: DUELLING BANJOS (Arthur Smith's theme from 'Deliverance' Soundtrack) / BATTLE OF NEW ORLEANS (trad). • **Trivia:** In 1991, JONES was credited on AZTEC CAMERA's Top 20 UK hit, 'GOOD MORNING BRITAIN'.

Album rating: THIS IS BIG AUDIO DYNAMITE (*7) / No.10 UPPING STREET (*6) / TIGHTEN UP, VOL.'88 (*4) / MEWGATOP PHOENIX (*5) / THE GLOBE (*6) / HIGHER POWER (*4) / F-PUNK (*4) / GREATEST HITS compilation (*8)

MICK JONES (b.26 Jun'55) – vocals, guitar (ex-CLASH) / **DON LETTS** – effects, keyboards, vocals / **DAN DONOVAN** – keyboards / **LEO WILLIAMS** – bass / **GREG ROBERTS** – drums

C.B.S. Columbia

Sep 85. (7"/12") *(A/TA 6591)* **THE BOTTOM LINE. / B.A.D.**

Nov 85. (lp/c) *(CBS/40 26714) <40220>* **THIS IS BIG AUDIO DYNAMITE** 27
– Medicine show / Sony / E=MC2 / The bottom line / Sudden impact / Stone Thames / B.A.D. / A party. *(cd-iss. Jun86; CD 26714) (re-iss. Nov88 lp/c/cd; 462 999-1/-4/-2)*

Mar 86. (7"/12") *(A/TA 6963)* **E=MC2. / THIS IS BIG AUDIO DYNAMITE** 11
(d12"+=) *(QTA 6963)* – The bottom line (US remix) / B.A.D.

May 86. (7") *(A 7181)* **MEDICINE SHOW. / A PARTY** 29
(12") *(TA 7181)* – ('A'extended) / ('B'dub).
(d12"+=) *(DTA 7181)* – E=MC2 (remix) / Albert Einstein meets the human beatbox.

Oct 86. (7") *(650147-7)* **C'MON EVERY BEATBOX. / BEDROCK CITY** 51
(12"+=) *(650147-8)* – Beatbox's at dawn.
(with free one-sided-12"++=) *(XPR 1320)* – The bottom line (Rick Rubin remix).

Oct 86. (lp/c/cd) *(450137-1/-4/-2) <40445>* **No.10 UPPING STREET** 11
– C'mon every beatbox / Beyond the pale / Limbo the law / Sambadrome / V thirteen / Ticket / Hollywood boulevard / Dial a hitman / Sightsee M.C! *(c+=/cd+=)* – Ice cool killer (dial a hitman-instrumental) / The big V (V thirteen – instrumental). *(re-iss. Oct89 lp/c; 463398-1/-4)*

Feb 87. (7") *(BAD 2)* **V THIRTEEN. / HOLLYWOOD BOULEVARD** 49
(12"+=) *(BADT 2)* – ('B'club).

Jul 87. (12"m) *(BAADT 3)* **SIGHTSEE MC! (radio cut) / ANOTHER ONE RIDES THE BUS / SIGHTSEE MC! / SIGHTSEE - WEST LONDON** -

May 88. (7"/ext-12") *(BAAD/+T 4)* **JUST PLAY MUSIC. / MUCH WORSE** 51
(12"+=/cd-s++) *(BAADQTA/CDBAAD 4)* – ('A'remix).

Jun 88. (lp/c/cd) *(461199-1/-4/-2) <44074>* **TIGHTEN UP VOL.'88** 33
– Rock non stop (all night long) / Other 99 / Funny names / Applecart / Esquerita / Champagne / Mr. Walker said / The battle of All Saints Road, incorporating:- Battle of New Orleans – Duelling banjos / Hip neck and thigh / 2000 shoes / Tighten up vol.88 / Just play music. *(re-iss. Oct94 on 'Columbia' cd/c; 461199-2/-4)*

Jul 88. (7"/7"box) *(BAAD/+B 5)* **OTHER 99. / WHAT HAPPENED TO EDDIE?**
(12"/cd-s) *(BAADT/CDBAAD 5)* – ('A'extended) / Just play music (club mix).

Sep 89. (lp/c/cd) *(465790-1/-4/-2) <45212>* **MEGATOP PHOENIX** 26 85
– Start / Rewind / All mink and no manners / Union, Jack / Contact / Dragon town / Baby don't apologise / Is yours working yet? / Around the girls in 80 ways / James Brown / Everybody needs a holiday / Mick's a hippie burning / House arrest / The green lady / London Bridge / Stalag 123 / End.

Oct 89. (7") *(BAAD 6)* **CONTACT. / IN FULL EFFECT**
(12"+=/cd-s+=) *(BAADT/CDBAAD 6)* – Who beats / If I were John Carpenter.

BIG AUDIO DYNAMITE II

— were formed by **JONES + DONOVAN** (latter left mid'90) **NICK HAWKINS** (b. 3 Feb'65, Luton, England) – guitar / **GARY STONAGE** (b.21 Nov'62, Southampton, England) – bass / **CHRIS KAVANAGH** (b. 4 Jun'64, Woolwich, England) – drums (ex-SIGUE SIGUE SPUTNIK)all repl. others who formed SCREAMING TARGET in 1991

Oct 90. (cd/c/lp) *(467466-2/-4/-1)* **KOOL-AID** 55
– Change of atmosphere / Can't wait / Kickin' in / Innocent child / On one / Kool-aid / In my dreams / When the time comes.

— added **DJ ZONKA** (b. MICHAEL CUSTANCE, 4 Jul'62) – DJ

Columbia Columbia

Jul 91. (cd/c/lp) *(467706-2/-4/-1) <46147>* **THE GLOBE** 63 72
– Rush / Can't wait (live) / I don't know / The globe / Innocent child / Green grass / Kool-aid / In my dreams / When the time comes / The tea party.

Jul 91. (7") *(657588-7) <74149>* **THE GLOBE (remix). / CITY LIGHTS** 76 Jan92
('A'-Danny Rampling remix-12"+=) *(657588-6)* – ('A'dub mix) / ('A'instrumental) / ('A'-Orb ambient mix).
(cd-s+=) *(657588-2)* – ('A'-Danny Rampling dub).

Nov 91. (7"/c-s) *(657640-7/-4) <73987>* **RUSH. / (A3 version)** 32 Sep91
(cd-s+=) *(657640-2)* – City lights (full version).
(12") *(657640-6)* – ('A'side) / ('A'-3 other mixes).

(above A-side was issued Feb'91 on other side of the CLASH single, 'Should I Stay Or Should I Go')

BIG AUDIO

— added **ANDRE SHAPPS** – keyboards

Nov 94. (c-s) *(661018-4)* **LOOKING FOR A SONG / MODERN STONEAGE BLUES** 68
(12"+=/cd-s+=) *(661018-6/-2)* – ('A'-Zonka-Shapps early mix) / ('A'-Zonka-Shapps remix).
(cd-s) *(661018-5)* – ('A'extended) / ('A'-Zonka-Shapps Adventures In Space mix) / Medicine show (live) / Rush (live).

Nov 94. (cd/c/d-lp) *(477239-2/-4/-1)* **HIGHER POWER**
– Got to wake up / Harrow Road / Looking for a song / Some people / Slender Loris / Modern stoneage blues / Melancholy maybe / Over the rise / Why is it? / Moon / Lucan / Light up my life / Hope.

BIG AUDIO DYNAMITE

RadioactiveRadioactive

Jun 95. (c-s) *(RAXC 15)* **I TURNED OUT A PUNK / WHAT ABOUT LOVE**
(cd-s+=) *(RAXTD 15)* – ('A'-Live fast, live fast mix).
(12") *(RAXT 15)* – ('A'side) / (A'-Live fast mix) / ('A'-Live fast instrumental) / ('A'-Feelin' lucky mix).

Jun 95. (cd/c) *(RAD/RAC 11280)* **F-PUNK**

- compilations, etc. -

Nov 88. (d-cd) *C.B.S.; (CDBAD 241)* **THIS IS BIG AUDIO DYNAMITE / No.10 UPPING STREET** -

Sep 95. (cd/c) *Columbia; (481133-2/-4)* **PLANET B.A.D.** -
– The bottom line / E=MC2 / Medicine show / C'mon every beatbox / V thirteen / Sightsee MC! / Just play music / Other 99 / Contact / Free / Rush / The globe / Looking for a song / Harrow road (ska mix) / I turned out a punk.

BIG BLACK

Formed: Evanston, Illinois, USA . . . 1982 by mainman STEVE ALBINI (vocals/guitar). The first official release, 'LUNGS' appeared later that year on local independent label, 'Ruthless', a six-track drum-machine driven EP that announced ALBINI's intent to take punk/hardcore into uncharted territory. Now with an expanded line-up numbering SANTIAGO DURANGO on guitar and JEFF PEZZATI on bass, the BIG BLACK trio unleashed two more 12"ep's/mini-lp's in the mid 80's, 'BULLDOZER' (1983) and 'RACER X' (1985), prior to the seminal 'IL DUCE' single in '86. Replacing PEZZATI with DAVE RILEY (aka LOVERING), they created a minor hardcore classic in 'ATOMIZER' (1986), its bleak examinations of small-town American despair a theme which would be echoed countless times by their grunge/industrial successors. With DURANGO off to study law, MERVIN BELLI came in for the inflammatory titled, 'SONGS ABOUT *!?KING', BIG BLACK giving their all on an album which they knew would be their last. However, they did bow out in uncharacteristic style with a double A-sided 45 covering Cheap Trick's 'HE'S A WHORE' and 'Kraftwerk's 'THE MODEL'. Taking his twisted vision to its warped conclusion, ALBINI formed the controversially named RAPEMAN with two former SCRATCH ACID players, DAVID WM. SIMS and REY WASHAM. It wasn't just the name that provoked outrage, tracks such as 'HATED CHINEE', 'SUPERPUSSY' and 'KIM GORDON'S PANTIES' causing a fuss which possibly contributed to ALBINI abandoning the operation early in '89. Having already turned in classic productions for the likes of The PIXIES ('Surfer Rosa'), ALBINI, along with BUTCH VIG became one of the highest profile and most respected/hard working figures of the grunge era (credits include NIRVANA, TAD, PJ HARVEY, etc). ALBINI also sorted out another side project, SHELLAC, who released two spaced-out, metallic albums, 'AT ACTION PARK' (1994) and 'TERRAFORM' (1998). • **Songwriters:** ALBINI and group compositions except; HEARTBEAT (Wire) / REMA REMA (Rema Rema) / Rapeman: JUST GOT PAID (ZZ Top).

Album rating: ATOMIZER (*7) / SONGS ABOUT *!?KING (*8) / PIGPILE live compilation (*7) / Shellac: AT ACTION PARK (*6) / TERRAFORM (*7)

STEVE ALBINI – vocals, guitar

not iss. Ruthless

1982. (c) *<none>* **BIG BLACK LIVE (live)** -
(UK-iss.Oct89 on 'Blast First' lp/c/cd; BFFP 49/+C/CD)

Nov 82. (12"ep) *<RRBB 02>* **LUNGS** -
– Steelworker / Live in a hole / Dead Billy / I can be killed / Crack / R.I.P. *(UK-iss.Nov92 on 'Touch & Go'; TG 89)*

— added **SANTIAGO DURANGO** – guitar (ex-NAKED RAYGUN, ex-SILVER ABUSE) / **JEFF PEZZATI** – bass (ex-NAKED RAYGUN) / + on session 4th member **PAT BYRNE** – drums

Nov 83. (12"ep) *<RRBB 07>* **BULLDOZER** -
– Cables / Pigeon kill / I'm a mess / Texas / Seth / Jump the climb. *(UK-iss.Nov92 on 'Touch & Go'; TG 90)*

Homestead Homestead

Apr 85. (m-lp) *<(HMS 007)>* **RACER-X** 1984
– Racer-x / Shotgun / The ugly American / Deep six / Sleep! / Big payback. *(re-iss. Nov92 on 'Touch & Go'; TG 91)*

Sep 86. (7") *(HMS 042)* **IL DUCE. / BIG MONEY** 1985
(re-iss. Nov92 on 'Touch & Go'; TG 96)

— **DAVE RILEY** (aka LOVERING) – bass (ex-SAVAGE BELIEFS) repl. PEZZATI / drum machine replaced BYRNE

Sep 86. (lp) *<(HMS 43)>* **ATOMIZER**

– Jordan, Minnesota / Passing complexion / Big money / Kerosene / Bad houses / Kerosene / Fists of love / Stinking drunk / Bazooka Joe / Strange things. *(re-iss. Nov86 on 'Blast First'; BFFP 11) (re-iss. Nov92 on 'Touch & Go' lp/cd; TG 93/+CD)*

Blast First Touch&Go

Jun 87. (12"ep/c-ep) *(BFFP 14/+C)* *<TG 20>* **HEADACHE** 1986
– My disco / Grinder / Ready men / Pete, king of all detectives.
(free 7"w.a./tracks on c-ep) *(TG 21)* – HEARTBEAT. / THINGS TO DO TODAY / I CAN'T BELIEVE *(UK re-iss. Nov92 on 'Touch & Go'; TG 20)*

—— **MELVYN BELLI** – guitar; repl. DURANGO

Jul 87. (lp/c/cd) *(BFFP 19/+C/CD)* *<TG 24/+C/CD>* **SONGS ABOUT *!?KING**
– The power of independent trucking / The model / Bad penny / El doper / Precious thing / Columbian neck-tie / Kitty empire / Ergot / Kashmir S. Pulasiday / Fish fry / Pavement saw / Tiny, the king of the Jews / Bombastic intro. *(re-iss. Nov92 on 'Touch & Go' lp/cd +=; TG 24/+CD)* – He's A Whore.

Aug 87. (7") *(BFFP 24)* *<TG 23>* **HE'S A WHORE. / THE MODEL**
(re-iss. Nov92 on 'Touch & Go'; TG 23)

—— Disbanded in 1988.

– compilations, etc. –

Mar 87. (lp) *Homestead; (HMS 044)* **THE HAMMER PARTY**
– (LUNGS + BULLDOZER) *(re-iss. Nov92 on 'Touch & Go' lp/cd +=; TG 92/+CD)* – RACER-X

Jun 87. (lp) *Not 2; (BUT 1)* **SOUND OF IMPACT (live bootleg)**
(re-iss. 1990)

Jan 88. (cd) *Blast First; (BFFP 23)* **RICH MAN'S EIGHT TRACK TAPE**
– (ATOMIZER + HEADACHE + HEARTBEAT) *(re-iss. Nov92 on 'Touch & Go'; TG 94CD)*

Oct 92. (lp/cd) *Touch & Go; <(TG 81/+CD)>* **PIGPILE (live)**

RAPEMAN

—— were formed by **ALBINI** with **DAVID WM. SIMS** – bass / **REY WASHAM** – drums (both ex-SCRATCH ACID, latter ex-BIG BOYS)

not iss. Fierce

1988. (7") *<none>* **HATED CHINEE. / MARMOSET**

Blast First Touch & Go

Nov 88. (12"ep) *(BFFP 27)* *<TG 34>* **BUDD (live) / SUPERPUSSY (live). / LOG BASS (live) / DUTCH COURAGE**

Dec 88. (lp/c/cd) *(BFFP 33/+C/CD)* *<TG 36/+C/CD>* **TWO NUNS AND BLACK MULE**
– Steak and black onions / Monobrow / Up beat / Cotition ignition mission / Kim Gordon's panties / Hated Chinee / Radar love wizard / Marmoset / Just got paid / Trouser minnow. *(cd+=)* – Budd / Superpussy / Log brass / Dutch courage.

Sub Pop Sub Pop

Aug 89. (7",7"clear) *<(SP 40)>* **INKI'S BUTT CRACK. / SONG NUMBER ONE**

—— Had to split in Feb'89 due to the backlash against group name. SIMS returned to Austin, where he re-united with ex-SCRATCH ACID members to form JESUS LIZARD. They were produced by ALBINI who continued as a producer, noteably for others The PIXIES, The BREEDERS, NIRVANA, WEDDING PRESENT. ALBINI formed below in '93.

SHELLAC

STEVE ALBINI – guitar, vocals / **BOB WESTON** – bass (ex-VOLCANO SONS) / **TODD TRAINER** – drums (ex-RIFLE SPORT, etc)

Touch & Go Touch & Go

1994. (7") **URANUS. /**

1994. (7") **THE ADMIRAL. /**

Sep 94. (7") *<TG 123>* **THE RUDE GESTURE: A PICTORIAL HISTORY. /**

Oct 94. (lp/c/cd) *<(TG 141/+C/CD)>* **AT ACTION PARK**
– My black ass / Pull the cup / Admiral / Crow / Song of the minerals / Minute / Idea of north / Dog and pony show / Boche's dick / Il porno star.

Feb 98. (lp/cd) *<(TG 200/+CD)>* **TERRAFORM**
– Didn't we deserve a look at you the way you really are / This is a picture / Disgrace / Mothpiece / Canada / Rush job / House full of garbage / Copper.

BIG BOYS

Formed: Austin, Texas, USA . . . 1980 by TIM KERR, CHRIS GATES and singer RANDY 'BISCUITS' TURNER. Completing the line-up with drummer STEVE COLLIER, this not entirely serious skate-punk combo delivered their debut EP later that year, a self-financed 4-song collection that included such "playground standard" gems as 'FRAT CARS' and 'MUTANT ROCK'. The following year, they surfaced on a joint live set with fellow Texans, The DICKS, while their first album proper, 'WHERE'S MY TOWEL / INDUSTRY STANDARD', appeared a few months later. In 1983, now with future RAPEMAN (STEVE ALBINI's outfit) drummer, REY WASHAM, they issued what was to be their final outing, 'LULLABIES HELP THE BRAIN GROW'.

Album rating: WHERE'S MY TOWEL – INDUSTRY STANDARD (*5) / LULLABIES HELP THE BRAIN GROW (*6)

RANDY 'BISCUITS' TURNER – vocals / **TIM KERR** – guitar, vocals / **CHRIS GATES** – bass, vocals / **STEVE COLLIER** – drums

not iss. Big Boys

Nov 80. (7"ep) *<BB 42480>* **FRAT CARS / HEARTBEAT. / MOVIES / MUTANT ROCK**

not iss. Rat Race

Jan 81. (lp; one side by the DICKS) **RECORDED LIVE AT RAUL'S CLUB (live)**

not iss. Wasted Talent

Jun 81. (lp) *<JWT 3405>* **WHERE'S MY TOWEL / INDUSTRY STANDARD**

—— **REY WASHAM** – drums; repl. FRED SCHULTZ who repl. COLLIER

not iss. Moment

1982. (lp) *<MOMBB 001>* **FUN, FUN, FUN**

1983. (lp) *<MOMBB 002>* **LULLABIES HELP THE BRAIN GROW**
– Brickwall / Jump the fence / Ambivalence . . . I always jump the fence / Assault / Manipulation / Same old blues / Gator fucking / White nigger / Baby let's play God / We got your money / Lesson / Funk off / I'm sorry / We're not in it to lose / Fight back / Sound on sound.

—— split in 1984, KERR joined JUNKYARD, WASHAM joined SCRATCH ACID

– compilations, etc. –

1984. (lp) *Enigma;* **NO MATTER HOW LONG THE LINE IS AT THE CAFETERIA, THERE'S ALWAYS A SEAT!**

1988. (c) *Unseen Hand; <727-C>* **WRECK COLLECTION**

Aug 93. (cd/c) *Touch & Go; <TG 98 CD/C>* **THE SKINNY ELVIS**
– Frat cars / Heartbeat / Movies / Mutant rock / Detectives / Out of focus / Psycho / Red – Green / In the city / Nightbeat / After 12:00 / Security / T.V. / I don't wanna dance / Identity crisis / Thin line / Advice / Complete control / Work without play / Spit / Act – Reaction / Self contortion / Wise up.

1993. (cd/c) *Touch & Go; <TG 99 CD/C>* **THE FAT ELVIS**
– Nervous / Apolitical / Hollywood swinging / Prison / We got soul / Fun, fun, fun / We got your money / Lesson / Funk off / I'm sorry / We're not in it to lose / Sound on sound / Fight back / Brickwall / Jump the fence / Assault / Manipulation / Same old blues / Gator fuckin' / White nigger / Baby let's play God / No / Narrow view / I do care / Listen / What's the word? / Common beat / No love / Which way to go / Killing time / Work.

1990's. (7") *Plastic Head; (SFLS 010)* **THE DICKS. /**

BIG CAR (see under ⇒ FASTBALL)

BIG CHIEF

Formed: Ann Arbor, Michigan, USA . . . late 80's by singer/growler and head honcho, BARRY HENSSLER, twin-guitarists MARK DANCEY and PHIL DuRR, plus bassist MATT O'BRIEN. Signed to 'Sub Pop', just as grunge was going overground, BIG CHIEF asserted their dominance in the retro stakes with a dirty, leaden guitar sound and a raw soulful edge. Following on from the debut album, 'REPULSION' (1990), the band introduced gritty blues songstress, THORNETTA DAVIS on 1991's 'FACE' outing. She continued to contribute to the BIG CHIEF set-up, advancing to a joint credit on their final 'Sub Pop' set, 'SHOUT OUT (TO THE DUSTHUFFER)', in '94; squeezed inbetween these was 1993's mock soundtrack album, 'MACK AVENUE SKULL GAME'. Contrary as ever, BIG CHIEF brought out 'PLATINUM JIVE' in 1994 (their first for 'Capitol') which was, as they put it, their GREATEST HITS 1969-99 (!) – the first two tracks described the nonsensical proceedings:- 'LION'S MOUTH' from the album, 'Bright Future Behind You', released 1999 and 'TAKEOVER BABY' from the album, 'Titty Twist Whitey', released 1969. Fantasy aside, SCHOOLY D made a guest appearance on the track, 'BONA FIDE'.

Album rating: DRIVE IT OFF compilation (*6) / FACE (*6) / MACK AVENUE SKULLGAME (*6) / SHOUT OUT (TO THE DUSTHUFFER) (*6) / PLATINUM JIVE (*5)

BARRY HENSSLER – vocals / **MARK DANCEY** – guitar / **PHIL DuRR** (b. Germany) – guitar / **MATT O'BRIEN** – bass / **MIKE DANNER** – drums, percussion

Sub Pop Sub Pop

Mar 90. (7"white) *<SP 53>* **BLOWOUT KIT. / CHROME HELMET**

—— added **THORNETTA DAVIS** – vocals

Jul 91. (cd/c) *<SP 147 B/A>* **FACE**
– Fresh vines / Drive it off / Ballad of Dylan Cohl / Desert jam / Honey-legged / 500 reasons / Reduced to tears / Who's gonna do all that / Lie there and be good / Wasted on B.C.

Apr 93. (lp/cd) *<(SP/+CD 89-260)>* **BIG CHIEF BRAND PRODUCT** (compilation)

Aug 93. (7") *<(SP 106-282)* **ONE BORN EVERY MINUTE. / LOT LIZARD**

Sep 93. (lp/cd) *(SP/+CD 109-285)* *<SP 218/+B>* **MACK AVENUE SKULLGAME**
– Skullgame No.3, take 3 / My name is Pimp (Mack's theme) / Let's do it again / One born every minute (Doc's theme) / Sonica / No free love on the street (Sonica's theme) / Soul on a roll / 10 karat pinky ring / Have another glass of brandy, baby / Gairty lounge punk / Cop kisser (Mack fucks up the scene) / If I had a nickel for every dime / Mixed jive / He needs to be dead – Ten easy pieces / Cut to the chase / Meet the man day / O woman (Mack's lament) / Skullgame.

Sep 94. (lp/cd; BIG CHIEF featuring THORNETTA DAVIS) *<(SP/+CD 135-322)>* **SHOUT OUT (TO THE DUSTHUFFER)**

Sympathy F Sympathy F

1994?. (7") *(SFTRI 157)* **STRANGE NOTES. /**

Capitol Capitol

Oct 94. (cd/c) *(CD/TC EST 2239)* *<27302-2/-4>* **PLATINUM JIVE**
– Lion's mouth / Takeover baby / John's scared / M.D. 20-20 / Map of your failure / Bona fide / Armed love / Philly nocturne / Locked out / All downhill from here / The liquor talkin' / Sick to my pants / Your days are numbered / Clown pimp / Simply Barry / Lot lizard.

—— they split some time in the mid 90's

– compilations, etc. –

1991. (cd) *Get Hip; <1004>* **DRIVE IT OFF**

BIG DIPPER (see under ⇒ EMBARRASSMENT)

BIG FLAME

Formed: Manchester, England . . . 1983 by ALAN BROWN, DAVID 'DIL' GREEN and GREG O'KEEFE. Taking up where The POP GROUP or PERE UBU left off, BIG FLAME unleashed their breakneck, psychotic BEEFHEART-like stutters on a number of 45's in the mid 80's for the cult 'Ron Johnson' imprint. A ten-inch compilation EP of the aforementioned tracks, 'TWO KAN GURU', was released in the summer of '86 immediately prior to their best and penultimate workfest, 'CUBIST POP MANIFESTO'. Having taken their chosen sound to its limits, the BIG FLAME finally extinguished itself as ALAN and DIL attempted to make a GREAT LEAP FORWARD. This revamped outfit issued a further couple of forgettable EP's in the latter half of the 80's, later disbanding at the turn of the decade.

Album rating: TWO KAN GURU (*6)

ALAN BROWN – vocals, guitar / **GREG O'KEEFE** – bass / **DAVID 'DIL' GREEN** – drums

Laughing Gun | not iss.

Apr 84. (7"m) *(PLAQUE 001)* **SINK. / THE ILLNESS / SOMETIMES** [ ] [-]

Ron Johnson | not iss.

Mar 85. (7"ep) *(ZRON 3)* **RIGOUR** [ ] [-]
– Debra / Man of few syllables / Sargasso.

Sep 85. (7"ep) *(ZRON 4)* **TOUGH!** [ ] [-]
– Cuba / Where's our Carol / All the Irish.

May 86. (7"m) *(ZRON 7)* **WHY POPSTARS CAN'T DANCE. / !CHANEL SAMBA! / DREAM OF OF A NATION** [ ] [-]

Jul 86. (10"ep) *(RERON 8)* **TWO KAN GURU** [ ] [-]
– Sink / Sometimes / Man of few syllables / Sargasso / Cuba / All the Irish.

Dec 86. (7"pink-ep) *(ZRON 13)* **CUBIST POP MANIFESTO. / (+ 2)** [ ] [-]

Feb 87. (12"ep) *(ZRON 15)* **XPZWRTX** [ ] [-]

— when GREG went off to become MEATMOUTH, **ALAN + DIL** changed their name (see further below)

– compilations, etc. –

Dec 96. (cd) *Drag City; (DC 19)* **RIGOUR** [ ] [ ]

GREAT LEAP FORWARD

— **ALAN + DIL**

Apr 87. (12"ep) *(ZRON 20)* **CONTROLLING THE EDGES OF TONE** [ ] [-]
– Controlling the edges of tone / Let's jive while we're still alive / Hope's not enough son.

Nov 87. (12"ep) *(ZRON 27)* **A PECK ON THE CHEEK A LA POLITIQUE. / PROPPING UP / THE NOISE OF A KING** [ ] [-]

Apr 88. (12"ep) *(ZRON 34)* **WHO WORKS THE WEATHER?** [ ] [-]

Communications Unique | not iss.

Apr 89. (lp) *(CULP 1)* **DON'T BE AFRAID OF CHANGE** (compilation) [ ] [-]
– Bereavement of speech / Hope's not enough son / Let's jive while we're still alive / A peck on the cheek / Who works the weather? / Controlling the edges of tone / Ask your parents / My grandfathers clock / The noise of the king. *(re-iss. Feb90 as 'THE GREAT LEAP FORWARD SEASON 87-88' lp/cd+=; CU 003/004)* – (demos; see above).

Nov 89. (12"ep) *(12CU 002)* **HEART AND SOUL. /** [ ] [-]

— split early in 1990

BIG IN JAPAN

Formed: Liverpool, England . . . 1977 by BILL DRUMMOND, KEVIN WARD and PHIL ALLEN. They completed the line-up with singer JAYNE CASEY, IAN BROUDIE and CLIVE LANGER, who issued a self-titled debut 45 for the 'Eric's' label, run by the local club of the same name; it's b-side was actually recorded by local mates, The YACHTS, under the guise of the CHUDDY NUDDIES. 1978 was a year when they found AMBROSE REYNOLDS, although he was subsequently replaced by HOLLY JOHNSON – yes, another who would make the grade in the 80's! – in time for their second single and final single/EP, 'FROM A TO Z AND NEVER AGAIN'. Released on DRUMMOND's own label, 'Zoo', the record didn't fully prepare listeners for the full-on live show wherein the shaven-headed CASEY would often appear with false electrodes attached to her skull. With all the peronnel comings and goings, it was inevitable that the band would split, nearly all of them finding major fame in one form or another (i.e. DRUMMOND with the KLF, BROUDIE with the LIGHTNING SEEDS and JOHNSON with FRANKIE GOES TO HOLLYWOOD).

Album rating: FROM A TO Z AND NEVER AGAIN EP (*6)

JAYNE CASEY – vocals / **BILL DRUMMOND** – guitar, vocals / **KEVIN WARD** – bass, vocals / **PHIL ALLEN** – drums / **IAN BROUDIE** – guitar / **CLIVE LANGER** – guitar (ex-DEAF SCHOOL)

Eric's | not iss.

Nov 77. (7") *(ERIC'S 0001)* **BIG IN JAPAN. / (CHUDDIE NUDDIES: Do The Chud)** [ ] [-]

— **HOLLY (JOHNSON)** – bass repl. AMBROSE REYNOLDS who joined WALKIE TALKIES, after repl. CLIVE LANGER (to The BOXES)

— **BUDGIE** – drums repl. PHIL ALLEN

Zoo | not iss.

Nov 78. (7"ep) *(CAGE 001)* **FROM A TO Z AND NEVER AGAIN** [ ] [-]
– Nothing special / Cindy & the Barbi dolls / Suicide a go-go / Taxi.

— **DAVE BALFE** – bass repl. STEVE LINDSAY (ex-DEAF SCHOOL) who had repl. HOLLY, who formed HOLLYCAUST and later FRANKIE GOES TO HOLLYWOOD (LINDSAY was later part of The SECRETS, The PLANETS, etc). When BIG IN JAPAN split in 1979, most went onto greater things. JAYNE formed PINK MILITARY / INDUSTRY. After being main part of LORI & THE CHAMELEONS, DRUMMOND and BALFE, went into production. The former managed The TEARDROP EXPLODES and ECHO & THE BUNNYMEN, went solo and formed duo KLF, while the latter joined TEARDROP EXPLODES and later formed 'Food' records; home of EMI subsidised BLUR). BROUDIE formed The ORIGINAL MIRRORS, The CARE, went into production for nearly everybody! and made The LIGHTNING SEEDS a household name. The last member BUDGIE, joined The SLITS and later SIOUXSIE & THE BANSHEES (also The CREATURES). BROUDIE and BUDGIE were also in The SECRETS during late 70's. Phew!

BIKINI KILL

Formed: Olympia, Washington, USA . . . late 1990 by former stripper KATHLEEN HANNA, TOBI VAIL and KATHI WILCOX, who all met at their local Evergreen College and named themselves after their feminist fanzine. The band released a few low-key albums for the 'Kill Rock Stars' label (one produced by IAN MacKAYE of FUGAZI), adamnantly resisting the temptation to sign for a major. Self-styled "Riot-Grrl" spokeswomen and figureheads for a new generation of fearless female punkettes, BIKINI KILL obviously took at least some of their cues from original femme-punks, The SLITS and The RAINCOATS, although musically they combined fragments of SONIC YOUTH and X-RAY SPEX. HANNA was undoubtedly the band's controversial focal point, allegedly appearing T-shirtless on stage in one incident having scrawled "Kill Me" on her chest in lipstick! The feisty frontwoman was also said to have spray-painted "Smells Like Teen Spirit" on KURT COBAIN's house, an action which inspired him to write the legendary song of the same name. In 1993, BIKINI KILL toured and recorded together with UK counterparts, HUGGY BEAR, releasing a split album, 'YEAH YEAH YEAH' (issued by 'Wiiija' in the UK). JOAN JETT produced the subsequent single, 'REBEL GIRL', released around the same time as their first official long-player, appropriately-titled 'PUSSYWHIPPED'. Following the demise of the "Riot Grrl" movement, it was to be two long years before BIKINI KILL re-emerged with what was to be their final statement, 'REJECT ALL AMERICAN' (1996).

Album rating: BIKINI KILL (*6) / PUSSYWHIPPED (*7) REJECT ALL AMERICAN (*6)

KATHLEEN HANNA(-DANDO) (b. 9 Jun'69, Portland, Oregon) – vocals / **KATHI WILCOX** (b.19 Nov'69, Vancouver, Washington) – bass / **TOBI VAIL** (b.20 Jul'69, Auburn, Washington) – drums (ex-SOME VELVET SIDEWALK) / **BILLY BOREDOM** (b. WILLIAM F. KARREN, 10 Mar'65, Memphis, Tenn.) – guitar

not iss. | K

1991. (c) **REVOLUTION GIRL STYLE NOW** [-] [ ]

Kill Rock Stars | Kill Rock Stars

Nov 92. (m-lp) *<(KRS 204)>* **BIKINI KILL** [ ] [ ]
– Double dare ya / Liar / Carnival / Suck my left one / Feels blind / Thurston hearts the who. *<(cd-iss. Mar94 +=; KRS 204CD)>* – YEAH YEAH YEAH

Catcall | Kill Rock Stars

Mar 93. (lp; shared with HUGGY BEAR) *(PUSS 001)* **YEAH YEAH YEAH** [ ] [ ]
– White boy / This is not a test / Don't need you / Jigsaw youth / Resist psychic death / Rebel girl / Outta me.

Wiiija | Kill Rock Stars

Oct 93. (cd/lp) *(WIJ 028 CD/V) <KRS 218>* **PUSSYWHIPPED** [ ] [ ]
– Blood one / Alien she / Magnet / Speed heart / Lil red / Tell me so / Sugar / Star bellied boy / Hamster baby / Rebel girl / Star fish / For Tammy Rae.

1994. (7") **NEW RADION. / REBEL GIRL / DEMIREP** [-] [ ]

1994. (7") **IN ACCORDANCE TO NATURAL LAW. / STRAWBERRY JULIUS / ANTI-PLEASURE DISSERTATION** [-] [ ]

1995. (7") **RAH! RAH! REPLICA. / I HATE FUCKING / I HATE DANGER** [-] [ ]

Kill Rock Stars | Kill Rock Stars

Apr 96. (cd/lp) *<(KRS 260 CD/LP)>* **REJECT ALL AMERICAN** [ ] [ ]
– Statement of vindication / Capri pants / Jet ski / Distinct complicity / False start / R.I.P. / No backrub / Bloody ice cream / For only / Tony Randall / Reject all American / Finale.

— disbanded around Spring '98

– compilations, etc. –

Jun 98. (cd) *Kill Rock Stars; <(KRS 298CD)>* **THE SINGLES** [ ] [ ] May98
– New radio / Rebel girl / DemiRep / In accordance to natural law / Strawberry Julius / Anti-pleasure dissertation / Rah! rah! replica / I like fucking / I hate danger.

BIRDLAND

Formed: near Coventry, Midlands, England . . . 1988 by the VINCE brothers, ROBERT and LEE, who had formerly played with ZODIAC MOTEL. The latter outfit only managed a solitary album, 'THE STORY OF ROLAND FLAGG' and a couple of singles before evolving into BIRDLAND. Late in '88, the bleach-blonde retro rockers – now also numbering GENE KALE and

SID ROGERS – signed to 'Lazy' (once home to The PRIMITIVES), scoring a handful of minor hits, namely 'HOLLOW HEART', 'PARADISE' and 'SLEEP WITH ME'. Late in 1990, they were snapped up by MCA backed 'Radioactive' (US-only) and 'Toshiba' (Japan-only), although this leap to major status failed to live up to the hype. Despite a further couple of hits with 'ROCK'N'ROLL NIGGER' and 'EVERYBODY NEEDS SOMEBODY', they pulled the plug after the relative failure of their eponymous debut album in '91. • **Covers:** ROCK'N'ROLL NIGGER (Patti Smith) / SEE NO EVIL (Television).

Album rating: BIRDLAND (*5)

ZODIAC MOTEL

ROBERT VINCE – vocals / **LEE VINCE** – guitar / **GENE KALE** – drums

Swordfish | not iss.

Feb 87. (lp) *(SWFLP 001)* **THE STORY OF ROLAND FLAGG** – | –
Apr 87. (7") *(SWF 004)* **SUNSHINE MINER. / CRESCENDO** – | –
(12"+=) *(ZOMO 1)* – Inside my mind / Sugarblood.

— did VINCE brothers depart, as RETRO + LIDD were main writers

Aug 87. (12"ep) *(ZOMO 2)* **CRYSTAL INJECTION / (I CAN ONLY GIVE YOU) EVERYTHING. / DESTINY RANCH / STEPHANIE BLUE** | –

BIRDLAND

— added **SID ROGERS** – bass

Lazy | Radioactive

Mar 89. (7") *(LAZY 13)* **HOLLOW HEART. / SUGARBLOOD** 70 | –
(7"ep+=/12"ep+=) **THE BIRDLAND EP** *(LAZY 13 D/T)* – Crystal / Got to get away.
Jun 89. (7") *(LAZY 14)* **PARADISE. / WHITE** 70 | –
(12"ep+=) **EP 2** *(LAZY 14T)* – Rage. *(some with 'Stay')*
Jan 90. (7"ep/12"ep/cd-ep) *(LAZY 17/+T/CD)* **SLEEP WITH ME / WANTED. / HOLLOW HEART (acoustic) / SLEEP WITH ME (acoustic)** 32 | –
Sep 90. (7"ep/12"ep/cd-ep) *(LAZY 20/+T/CD)* **ROCK'N'ROLL NIGGER / FUN FUN FUN. / ROLLER COASTER / PROTECTION** 47 | –
Jan 91. (7") *(LAZY 24)* **EVERYBODY NEEDS SOMEBODY. / DON'T HANG ON** 44 |
(12"+=) *(LAZY 24T)* – Shoot you down (acoustic) / Untitled.
(cd-s+=) *(LAZY 24CD)* – Shoot you down (acoustic) / Twin sons.
(7"ep+=) *(LAZY 24D)* – Twin sons / Exit (acoustic).
Feb 91. (cd/c/lp) *(LAZY 25 CD/MC/LP)* <RAR 10214> **BIRDLAND** 44 |
– Shoot you down / Sleep with me / Don't look back / Wake up dreaming / Letter you know / Rock'n'roll nigger / Everybody needs somebody / Beat me like a star / She belongs to me / Exit. *(cd+=)* – Hollow heart / Crystal / Got to get away.
Jun 91. (m-cd) <*RARDS 54181*> **BIRDLAND** – |
– Sleep with me / Don't hang on / Wanted / White / Protection / Sleep with me (acoustic).

— disbanded soon after being dropped by their record label

BIRDSONGS OF THE MESOZOIC (see under ⇒ MISSION OF BURMA)

BIRTHDAY PARTY (see under ⇒ CAVE, Nick)

BIS

Formed: Glasgow, Scotland . . . late 1994 by teenagers MANDA RIN and brothers SCI-FI STEVEN and JOHN DISKO. Initially gaining exposure through the tight-knit fanzine network, BIS were the first outfit to appear on The DELGADOS' now influential D.I.Y. label, 'Chemikal Underground', the release in question being the 7" maxi, 'DISCO NATION'. In March '96, BIS also became the first bonafide indie band to play live on Top Of The Pops with a track, 'KANDY POP', from their Top 30 EP, 'THE SECRET VAMPIRE SOUNDTRACK'. Their blend of cutesy brat-pop – like ALTERED IMAGES meeting The SLITS – was developed over a further couple of low-key 45's before they finally signed on the dotted line for The BEASTIE BOYS' trendy 'Grand Royal' label (remaining independent in the UK through 'Wiiija') after turning down 50 major imprints. The trio subsequently forsook the unappreciative Britain (where the press was increasingly turning against them after all the hype) to try Japan, where they soon became a top act, shifting 100,000 units of their 1997 debut album, 'THE NEW TRANSISTOR HEROES', in the space of only a few weeks. Returning to UK shores in 1998, they eventually hit the Top 40 again with 'EURODISCO', a taster from the non-charting accompanying album, 'INTENDO'. • **Songwriters:** SCI-FI or group, except THE BOY WITH THE THORN IN HIS SIDE (Smiths).

Album rating: THE NEW TRANSISTOR HEROES (*5) / INTENDO (*5)

MANDA RIN (b. AMANDA MacKINNON, 22 Mar'77) – vocals, keyboards, recorder / **SCI-FI STEVEN** (b. STEVEN CLARK, 20 Mar'76) – vocals, synthesizers / **JOHN DISKO** (b. JOHN CLARK, 21 Aug'78) – guitar

Chemikal Underground | not iss.

Aug 95. (7"m) *(Chem 002)* **DISCO NATION. / PLASTIK PEOPLE / CONSPIRACY A GO-GO** | –
Dec 95. (7"ep; various artists) *(che 47)* **ICKY-POO AIR-RAID** | –
(above issued on 'Che')
Mar 96. (7"ep/cd-ep) *(Chem 003/+cd)* **THE SECRET VAMPIRE SOUNDTRACK** 25 | –
– Kandy pop / Secret vampires / Teen-c power! / Diska.

Teen C | not iss.

Jun 96. (7"m/c-s/cd-s) *(SKETCH 001/+CS/CD)* **BIS VS. THE D.I.Y. CORPS** 45 | –
– This is fake d.i.y. / Burn the suit / Dance to the disco beat.

Southern | K

Jun 96. (7") *(IPU 66)* **KEROLEEN. / ("Heavenly":- Trophy Girlfriend)** |

Wiiija | Grand Royal

Oct 96. (7"ep/c-ep/cd-ep) *(WIJ 55/+MC/CD)* **ATOM POWERED ACTION! EP** 54 | –
– Starbright boy / Wee love / Team theme / Cliquesuck.
Dec 96. (cd-ep) **THIS IOS TEEN-C POWER** – |
– Kill yr boyfriend / School disco / Kandy pop / This is fake D.I.Y. / Burn the suit / Teen-C power.
Mar 97. (7") *(WIJ 67)* **SWEET SHOP AVENGERZ. / I'LL GET YOU BACK** 46 | –
(7") *(WIJ 67X)* – ('A'side) / Rollerblade zero.
(cd-s+=) *(WIJ 67CD)* – Ninja hi skool.
Apr 97. (cd/c/lp) *(WIJ CD/MC/LP 1064)* **THE NEW TRANSISTOR HEROES** 55 |
– Tell it to the kids / Sweet shop avengerz / Starbright boy / Popstar kill / Mr. Important / Antiseptic poetry / Popyura / Skinny tie sensurround / Poster parent / Monstarr / Everybody thinks that they're going to get theirs / Rebel soul / Photo shop / X-defect / Lie detector test / Dinosaur germs.
Apr 97. (7") *(GUIDE 11)* **/ (other by LUGWORM)** | –
(above on 'Guided Missile')
May 97. (7") *(WIJ 69)* **EVERYBODY THINKS THAT THEY'RE GOING TO GET THEIRS. / STATEMENT OF INTENT** 64 |
(7") *(WIJ 69X)* – ('A'side) / Girl star.
(cd-s+=) *(WIJ 69CD)* – Cookie cutter kid.
Nov 98. (c-s) *(WIJ 086C)* **EURODISCO / LIKE ROBOTS** 37 | –
(cd-s+=) *(WIJ 086CD)* – Cinema says.
(7") *(WIJ 086)* – ('A'side) / Stray cat blues.

– compilations, etc. –

Aug 98. (m-cd) *Grand Royal; (7581 480060-2)* <GR 60> **INTENDO** |
(demos & B-sides)
– Grand Royal with cheese / Girl star / Clockwork punk / Famous / Ninja hi skool / Kid cut / Automatic freestyle / I'll get you back / Cookie cutter kid / Grand Royal with cheese.

BISHOPS (see under ⇒ COUNT BISHOPS)

BITCH MAGNET (see under ⇒ SEAM)

BITING TONGUES

Formed: Manchester, England . . . 1980 by main composers GRAHAM MASSEY and HOWARD WALMSLEY. Commissioned to write film soundtracks, the latter duly recruited the aforesaid MASSEY together with KEN HOLLINGS, COLIN SEDDON and EDDIE SHERWOOD. BITING TONGUES' debut release came in the shape of 'DON'T HEAL', released on Beggars Banquet newly formed off-shoot label, 'Situation 2'. A fusion of jazzy punk and danceable soundscapes, the 'TONGUES ouvre was developed over a further clutch of lp's including 'LIBREVILLE' (1984) and 'FEVERHOUSE', the latter for 'Factory' records. Having already lost SHERWOOD (to SIMPLY RED) and HOLLINGS, MASSEY and WALMSLEY recruited PHIL KIRBY and BASIL CLARKE, although both would in turn, go off to follow their own path with YARGO. 1988 saw the release of their pioneering video album, 'WALL OF SURF', although the following year, sessions for a new album, 'RECHARGE' (as yet unreleased), were abandoned when their label, 'Cut Deep', folded. It wasn't long before MASSEY was hitting the proverbial big time with 808 STATE, WALMSLEY working on film projects full-time.

Album rating: DON'T HEAL (*6) / LIBREVILLE (*6) / FEVERHOUSE (*7)

GRAHAM MASSEY (b. 4 Aug'60) – guitar / **HOWARD WALMSLEY** – saxophone / **KEN HOLLINGS** – vocals / **COLIN SEDDON** – bass / **EDDIE SHERWOOD** – drums

Situation 2 | not iss.

Apr 81. (lp) *(SITU 1)* **DON'T HEAL** | –
– Blue traces / Dog face / Heart disease / Or with eyes closed / Stabbing soft ice / You can choke like that / Walkway / Coil / R.R.O.R. / Give diamonds you can't.

New Hormones | not iss.

Dec 81. (c) *(CAT 3)* **LIVE IT** | –

Paragon | not iss.

Apr 84. (lp) *(VIRTUE 1)* **LIBREVILLE** | –
– First use all the G's / Forty four / Smash the strategie hamlets / Live it / The toucanostra / Doctor restore the sight / Dirt for 485 / Air care.

— **BASIL CLARKE** – vocals; repl. HOLLINGS

— **PHIL KIRBY** – drums; repl. SHERWOOD who joined SIMPLY RED

Factory | not iss.

Mar 85. (lp) *(FACT 105)* **FEVERHOUSE (soundtrack)** | –
Oct 85. (12"ep) *(FAC 134)* **TROUBLE HAND / PANORAMA. / MEAT MASK SEPARATIST / BOSS TOYOTA TROUBLE / PROBATE** | –

— were now a duo when BASIL and PHIL formed YARGO

May 87. (12"m) *(FAC 188)* **COMPRESSOR. / BLACK JESUS / BLACK AND WHITE JESUS** | –

Antler | not iss.

Jan 88. (12") *(AN 005)* **EVENING STATE. / EVENING STATE** – | – Belgian

Cut Deep — not iss.

1989. (12"ep) *(CUT 12-004)* **LOVE OUT / LOVE OUT (brainwash mix instrumental). / SURRENDER (mellow mix) / SURRENDER** [ ] [-]

— split in 1989, when MASSEY found 808 STATE. WALMSLEY however carried on with more film soundtracks.

BIVOUAC

Formed: Derby, England . . . early 90's by songwriter PAUL YEADON, along with GRANVILLE MARSDEN and ANTHONY HODKINSON. Straight outta Derby as the US grunge scene exploded in the UK, BIVOUAC may have seemed unlikely candidates for beating the Americans at their own game. Yet by the mid-90's, the band had been signed to 'Geffen', home to NIRVANA amongst others and a far cry from the band's early days co-headlining with JACOB'S MOUSE. Initially securing a deal with Workers Playtime offshoot, 'Elemental', the band issued a debut single/EP, 'A.B.C.', closely following it up with 'SLACK' and 'GOOD DAY SONG'. Whether by accident or design, BIVOUAC sounded like they'd lived in Seattle all their lives, right down to the choppy, buzz-saw guitar riffs and Americanised vocal style. No bad thing at the time of course, as the band secured themselves support slots with such US alt-rock aristocrats as FUGAZI and The JESUS LIZARD. 1993 also saw the release of their debut album, 'TUBER', a major label bidding war ensuing as the big boys vyed for the lads' signatures. Going the whole hog and signing for 'Geffen', the band concentrated their efforts on cracking the American market, KEITH YORK replacing the departing HODKINSON. By the release of 1995's follow-up album, 'FULL SIZE BOY', however, the grunge scene had splintered and BIVOUAC's moment seemed to have passed.

Album rating: TUBER (*7) / FULL SIZE BOY (*7)

PAUL YEADON – vocals, guitar / **GRANVILLE MARSDEN** – bass / **ANTHONY HODKINSON** – drums

El-e-mental — Engine

May 92. (12"ep) *(ELM 002T)* **A.B.C. / FISHES. / STICK STUCK / ME TED AND CHARLES** [ ] [-]

Oct 92. (12"ep/cd-ep) *(ELM 004 T/CD)* **SLACK. / TOWLD / TWO STICKS** [ ] [-]

Jun 93. (c-ep) *<3>* **DERBY & JOAN** (compilation) [-] [ ]

Jun 93. (7") *(ELM 10S)* **GOOD DAY SONG. /** [ ] [ ]
(cd-s+=) *(ELM 10CD)* – Squeaker, Bess, bread, beans and cash / Trepanning.

Jun 93. (cd/c/lp) *(ELM 11 CDX/LP)* **TUBER** [ ] [ ] Mar94
– Good day song / Big question mark / Dragging your weight around / Rue / Deadend friend / Drank / Steel strung / The need / The bell foundry / Bad day song.

Aug 93. (7") *(ELM 12S)* **THE BELL FOUNDRY. / LEAD** [ ] [ ]
(cd-s+=) *(ELM 12CD)* – Saltwater heal.

May 94. (10"ep/7"ep/cd-ep) *(ELM 20/+S/CD)* **MARKED AND TAGGED E.P.** [ ] [ ]
– And then she ate / Spine / Art, science and making things.

— **KEITH YORK** – drums (ex-DOCTOR PHIBES & THE HOUSE OF WAX EQUATIONS) repl. HODKINSON

Geffen — D.G.C.

May 95. (7") *(GFS 89)* **THINKING. /** [ ] [ ]
(cd-s+=) *(GFSTD 89)* –

Jul 95. (7"/c-s) *(GFS/+C 90)* **MONKEY SANCTUARY (CYNIC). / 45 SEATED STANDING NIL** [ ] [ ]
(cd-s+=) *(GFSTD 90)* – Deadend friend.

Jul 95. (cd/c/lp) *(GED/GEC/GEF 24561) <24803>* **FULL SIZE BOY** [ ] [ ]
– Not going back there again / Thinking / Trepanning / Gecko or skink / Monkey sanctuary / My only safe bet / Familiar / Mattress / Bing bong / Lounge lizard / Ray is related to the shark.

— split after the failure of above

BJORK

Born: BJORK GUDMUNDSDOTTIR, 21 Oct'65, Reykjavik, Iceland. Growing up in a creative communal family and something of a child prodigy, the strikingly unique BJORK enjoyed her first taste of the music business at the age of 11 when she impressed her teachers with her rendition of TINA CHARLES' No.1 'I LOVE TO LOVE', who in turn convinced a local radio station to play it. This led to her recording a self-titled album with many of Iceland's top musicians. It also included other covers; YOUR KISS IS SWEET (hit; Syreeta) / ALFUR UT UR HOL (FOOL ON THE HILL; Beatles) / CHRISTOPHER ROBIN (Melanie) / ALTA MIRA (Edgar Winter). BJORK graduated to her first band EXODUS, and in 1981 aged 14, she instigated another; TAPPI TIKARRASS, which meant 'Cork The Bitch's Arse'. In the next two years, the X-RAY SPEX-type outfit completed two albums 'BITID FAST I VITID' and 'MIRANDA'. She subsequently worked with KILLING JOKE theorists, JAZ COLEMAN and YOUTH, who had both fled to the frozen north in fear of a supposed impending apocalypse. In the interim, she guested for free-form jazz-rock duo STIFGRIM, who comprised of comedian/vocalist KRISTINN JON GUDMUNDSSON and guitarist STEINN SKAPTASON. They went down in the record books as one of over a hundred bands who took part in the longest ever continuous live performances (seven weeks!). She then spent two summer seasons playing synthesizer in a covers band named, CACTUS. In 1984, she teamed up with friends EINAR ORN BENEDIKTSSON (he of the legendary, erm, rapping "talent") and SIGTRYGGUR 'SIGGI' BALDERSSON to form KUKL ('Sorcery'), this FALL/BANSHEES influenced lot finding their way into Britain's earlobes (via the 'Crass' label) with two albums 'THE EYE' and 'HOLIDAYS IN EUROPE'. During this mid 80's period, she was also part of ROKHA ROKHA DRUM (as a drummer! and voice). They included lead vocalist JOHNNY TRIUMPH (b. SJON), who collaborated with BJORK's most famous and productive outfit The SUGARCUBES. Hooking up with BRAGI OLAFSSON, THOR ELDON (the father of BJORK's son, Sindri) and EINAR MELLAX, BJORK and Co. formed Iceland's first (and so far only) internationally renowned band. Signed to Derek Birkett's 'One Little Indian', the group had the critics frothing with their debut single, the sublime 'BIRTHDAY'. Like pop music from another planet, the song's reverbating bassline, celestial brass and ethereal production conspired to make this the aural equivalent of a particularly sensual massage. The track also introduced BJORK's inimitable vocals, a perversely melodic combination of wide-eyed child and Icelandic banshee. A further two slices of avant-garde strangeness, 'COLD SWEAT' and 'DEUS' followed into the UK Top 75 before a debut album, 'LIFE'S TOO GOOD', crashed into the Top 20 in Spring '88. An intoxicating blend of jazzy instrumentation, indie stylings and wilful weirdness, the album's success allowed the band to set up their own multi-media enterprise, 'Bad Taste Ltd.' back in Iceland. Though a follow-up, 'HERE TODAY, TOMORROW, NEXT WEEK' (1989) again made the UK Top 20, the critical reception was poor, particular vitriol reserved for EINER's (ORN) jarring vocal exhortations. After extensive touring the band headed back to Iceland to work on various outside jazz-styled projects, BJORK keeping her name in the music press via collaborative work with 808 STATE on their 'Ex:El' album. Then, in late '91, The SUGARCUBES bounced back with the celebratory avant-funk of 'HIT', the band putting in an unforgettable performance on Channel 4's 'The Word'. The accompanying album, 'STICK AROUND FOR JOY' (1992) saw the group back in critical favour, a brassy pot-pourri of spiked melody and faultless instrumental dexterity. To consolidate the new dancefloor-friendly direction, a set of remixes, 'IT'S IT', was released in late '92, coinciding with the voluntary demise of The SUGARCUBES. It had been a short strange trip, but not as strange as BJORK's forthcoming rise to international pop superstardom. While she undoubtedly had a distinctive, beguiling charm, few would've predicted the massive critical and commercial achievements of her solo debut, entitled, er . . . 'DEBUT' actually. Released in summer '93, co-written with ex-SOUL II SOUL/MASSIVE ATTACK guru, NELLEE HOOPER and featuring such underrated talents as TALVIN SINGH and JHELISA ANDERSON, proceedings were dominated by pulsing, house-orientated material, although there was a fair smattering of off-the-wall BJORK oddities. Lauded by the indie and dance press alike, the album's kudos was further boosted by the success of the 'PLAY DEAD' single, a collaboration with soundtrack man, DAVID ARNOLD recorded for the movie, 'Young Americans'. A UK Top 3 success and a Mercury Music Prize nominee, 'DEBUT' turned BJORK into a household name, remixers clamouring to get to grips with her work. A true celebrity hobnobber, BJORK co-wrote the title track to MADONNA's 'Bedtime Stories' set, while 1995's follow-up album, 'POST', saw her working with everyone from TRICKY and SKUNK ANANSIE to The BRODSKY QUARTET and EVELYN GLENNIE! The latter two featured on the experimental/schizophrenic (delete according to taste) Top 5 hit, 'IT'S OH SO QUIET', an, ahem, 'adaptation' of Betty Hutton's 40's big band number which saw BJORK veer wildly from hushed reverence to shouting the rafters down in fine style. The song was characteristic of the album's more fragmented nature, a challenging listen but proof positive that the elfen firebrand wasn't content to rest on her laurels. The following year saw BJORK take up residence in the gossip columns rather than the charts, what with her highly publicised relationship with GOLDIE and her unfortunate fracas with a reporter at Bangkok airport (19th February '96). In September, an obsessed fan from Florida blew his brains out and sent a letter bomb to BJORK. Luckily neighbours contacted police after smelling his decomposed body and the bomb was averted, although unsurprisingly it caused her much distress. The stresses and strains of stardom formed the lyrical backbone for her acclaimed 1997 set, 'HOMOGENIC', a return to more electronic waters that was nevertheless more downbeat than dancefloor. One of the music world's more unpredictable stars, her maverick genius is sorely needed in a chart choked with indie loser clones.

• **Songwriters:** SUGARCUBES – all written by BJORK and EINAR, except TOP OF THE WORLD (Carpenters) / MOTORCYCLE MAMA (Sailcat).

• **Trivia:** BJORK was married to THOR, although after they had a child, he soon married new SUGARCUBE, MAGGI. SIGGI and BRAGI were former brother-in-laws who were married to twin sisters. In 1989, they divorced and moved to Denmark to get married to each other!. The first openly gay marriage in rock/pop history.

Album rating: Tappi Tikarrass: MIRANDA (*4) / Kukl: THE EYE mini (*4) / HOLIDAYS IN EUROPE mini (*4) / Sugarcubes: LIFE'S BEEN GOOD (*9) / STICK AROUND FOR JOY (*8) / HERE TODAY, TOMORROW, NEXT WEEK (*8) / Bjork: DEBUT (*10) / POST (*8) / TELEGRAM remixes (*7) / HOMOGENIC (*7)

BJORK GUDMUNDSDOTTIR

Falkinn — not iss.

Dec 77. (lp/c) *(FA 006/+C)* **BJORK** [-] [-] Icelan

TAPPI TiKARRASS

BJORK – vocals, keyboards, etc / **JAKOB MAGNUSSON** – bass (ex-EXODUS) / etc.

Spor — not iss.

Sep 81. (m-lp) *(SPOR 4)* **BITID FAST I VITID** [-] [-] Icelan

Gramm / not iss.

Aug 83. (lp) *(GRAMM 16)* **MIRANDA** [-] [-] Icelan

KUKL

BJORK – vocals, keyboards / **EINAR ORN BENEDIKTSSON** (b.29 Oct'62, Copenhagen, Denmark) – trumpet, vocals / **SIGTRYGGUR 'Siggi' BALDURSSON** (b. 2 Oct'62, Stavanger, Norway) – drums, percussion / **EINAR MELLAX** – keyboards

Gramm / not iss.

Sep 83. (7") *(GRAMM 17)* **SONGULL. / POKN FYRIR BYRJENDUR** [-] [-] Icelan

Crass / not iss.

Nov 84. (m-lp) *(1984-1)* **THE EYE** [ ] [-]
– Dismembered / Assassin / Anna. *(cd-iss. Mar97; 1984 2CD)*

Mar 86. (m-lp) *(Cat.No.4)* **HOLIDAYS IN EUROPE (THE NAUGHTY NOUGHT)** [ ] [-]

SUGARCUBES

BJORK, EINAR, EINAR + SIGGI recruited **THOR ELDON JONSON** (b. 2 Jun'62, Reykjavik) – guitar / **BRAGI OLAFSSON** (b.11 Aug'62, Reykjavik) – bass

One Little Indian / Elektra

Sep 87. (7") *(7TP 7)* **BIRTHDAY. / BIRTHDAY (Icelandic)** [65] [-]
(12"+=) *(12TP 7)* – Cat (Icelandic).
(cd-s;Dec87;++=) *(7TP 7CD)* – Motorcrash.

Feb 88. (7") *(7TP 9)* **COLD SWEAT. / DRAGON (Icelandic)** [56] [-]
(12"+=) *(12TP 9)* – Traitor (Icelandic).
(12"++=) *(L12TP 9)* – Birthday (demo).
(cd-s+=) *(7TP 9CD)* – Traitor (Icelandic) / Revolution.

Apr 88. (7") *(7TP 10)* **DEUS. / LUFTGITAR (Icelandic) (with JOHNNY TRIUMPH)** [51] [-]
(10"+=/12"+=) *(10TP/12TP 10)* – Organic prankster.
(cd-s+=) *(7TP 10CD)* – Night of steel (Icelandic).

Apr 88. (lp/c/cd/dat) *(TPLP/TPC/TPCD/DTPLP 5)* **LIFE'S TOO GOOD** [14] [54] Jun 88
– Mama / Delicious demon / Birthday / Traitor / Blue eyed pop / Petrol / F***ing in rhythm and sorrow / Cold sweat / Deus / Sick for toys. *(cd+=)* – I want.

May 88. (12"ep)(cd-ep) **COLD SWEAT / COLD SWEAT (meat mix). / BIRTHDAY (Icelandic) / DELICIOUS DEMON / COLD SWEAT (instrumental)** [-] [ ]

— **MARGRET 'Magga' ORNOLFSDOTTIR** (b.21 Nov'67, Reykjavik) – keyboards repl. MELLAX

Sep 88. (7") *(7TP 11)* **BIRTHDAY. / CHRISTMAS (with Jesus & Mary Chain)** [65] [-]
(12")(cd-s) *(12TP 11)(7TP 11CD)* – ('A'side) / Fucking in rhythm and sorrow (live) / Cowboy (live) / Cold sweat (live).
(12")(cd-s) *(12TP 11L)(7TP 11CDL)* – BIRTHDAY CHRISTMAS MIX: – Christmas eve – Christmas day / Christmas present / Petrol (live).
(US-green-ep title 'DELICIOUS DEMONS')

Dec 88. (c-s) **MOTORCRASH (live) / POLO** [-] [ ]
(12"+=)(3"cd-s+=) – Blue eyed pop.

Aug 89. (7"/c-s) *(26 TP7/+C)* **REGINA. / HOT MEAT** [55] [ ]
(7"ep+=) *(26 TP7L)* – Hey / Propeller vs jet.
(12"+=) *(26 TP12)* – Regina (Icelandic).
(cd-s+=) *(26 TP7CD)* – Hey / Regina (Icelandic).
(12") *(26 TP12L)* – ('A'-Propeller mix) / ('A'-Jet mix).

Oct 89. (lp/silver-lp/c)(cd) *(TPLP 15/+SP/C)(TPCD 15)* **HERE TODAY, TOMORROW, NEXT WEEK** [15] [70]
– Tidal wave / Regina / Speed is the key / Dream T.V. / Nail / Pump / Eat the menu / Bee / Dear plastic / Shoot him / Water / Day called Zero / Planet. *(cd+=)* – Hey / Dark disco! / Hot meat.

Feb 90. (7") *(32 TP7)* **PLANET. / PLANET (somersault version)** [ ] [ ]
(12"+=/cd-s+=) *(32 TP 12/7CD)* – Planet (Icelandic) / Cindy.

Dec 91. (7") *(62 TP7)* **HIT. / HIT (instrumental)** [17] [ ]
(12"+=) *(62 TP12)* – Theft.
(cd-s++=) *(62 TP7CD)* – Chihuahua (instrumental).
(12"+=) *(62 TP12L)* – Leash called love.

Feb 92. (lp/c/cd) *(TPLP 30/+C/CD)* **STICK AROUND FOR JOY** [16] [95]
– Gold / Hit / Leash called love / Lucky night / Happy nurse / I'm hungry / Walkabout / Hetero scum / Vitamin / Chihuahua.

Mar 92. (7"/c-s) *(72 TP7/+C)* **WALKABOUT (remix). / STONE DRILL (IN THE ROCK)** [ ] [ ]
(12"+=) *(72 TP12)* – Top of the world (live).
(cd-s++=) *(72 TP7CD)* – Bravo pop.

Aug 92. (12"ep) *(102 TP12)* **VITAMIN REMIXES** [ ] [-]
– ('A'-Babylon's Burnin mix) / ('A'-Earth dub) / ('A'-Laser dub in Hell mix) / ('A'-Decline of Rome part II & III) / ('A'-Meditation mix).
(cd-ep+=) *(102 TP7CD)* – ('A'-E mix).

Sep 92. (c-ep/12"ep/cd-ep) *(104 TP 7C/12/7CD)* **BIRTHDAY REMIX EP** [64] [ ]
– ('A'-Justin Robertson remix) / ('A'-Tommy D. dub mix) / ('A'-Jim & William Reid Christmas Eve mix) / ('A'original) / ('A'-Tommy D. 12" or dub mix) / ('A'-Justin Robertson dub) / ('A'-Jim & William Reid Christmas Day mix) / ('A'demo).
(cd-ep) *(104 TP7CDL)* – Birthday (Justin Robertson edit) / Birthday (Tommy D. edit) / Hit (Tony Humphries mix) / Mama (Mark Saunders mix).

Oct 92. (lp/c/cd/d-cd) *(TPLP 40/+C/CD/CDL)* **IT'S IT** (remixes) [47] [ ]
(cd w/ bonus cd)

— officially disbanded late 1992

– compilations, others, etc. –

all on 'One Little Indian'.

Apr 90. (11x12"box) *(TP BOX 1)* **12.11** (box set) [ ] [-]
Apr 90. (8x7"box) *(TP BOX 2)* **7.8** (box set) [ ] [-]
Apr 90. (6xcd-s-box) *(TP BOX 3)* **CD.6** [ ] [-]
Jul 98. (cd/c/lp) *(TPLP 333 CD/MC/LP)* **THE GREAT CROSSOVER POTENTIAL** [ ] [ ]
– Birthday / Cold sweat / Mama / Motor crash / Deus / Regina / Pump / Planet / Water / Hit / Vitamin / Walkabout / Gold / Chihuahua.

BJORK GUDMUNDSDOTTIR & TRIO GUDMUNDAR INGOLFSSONAR

Smekkleysa / not iss.

Oct 90. (lp/c/cd) *(SM 27/+C/CD)* **GLING-GLO** [-] [-] Icelan

BJORK

— solo, with **MARIUS DE VRIES, PAUL WALLER, MARTIN VIRGO + GARRY HUGHES** – keyboards / **NELLEE HOOPER** (co-writer of some), **LUIS JARDIM** (also bass) + **BRUCE SMITH** – drums, percussion / **JON MALLISON** – guitar / **TALVIN SINGH** – tabla / **CORKI HALE** – harp / **JHELISA ANDERSON** – backing vocals / **OLIVER LAKE, GARY BARNACLE, MIKE MOWER** – brass

One Little Indian / Elektra

Jun 93. (c-s) *(112 TP7C)* **HUMAN BEHAVIOUR / ATLANTIC** [36] [ ]
(12") *(112 TP12)* – ('A'-Underworld mix) / ('A'-Close to human mix) / ('A'-Dom T. mix).
(cd-s) *(112 TP7CD)* – ('A'side) / (above extras) / ('A'-Bassheads edit).

Jul 93. (cd/c/lp) *(TPLP 31 CD/C/L)* **DEBUT** [3] [61]
– Human behaviour / Crying / Venus as a boy / There's more to life than this recorded live at the Milk Bar toilets / Like someone in love / Big time sensuality / One day / Aeroplane / Come to me / Violently happy / The anchor song. *(re-iss. Nov93 cd/c; TPLP 31 CDX/CX)(+=)* – Play dead.

Aug 93. (7"/c-s) *(122 TP7/+C)* **VENUS AS A BOY. / ('A'-Dream mix)** [29] [ ]
(cd-s) *(122 TP7CD)* – ('A'side) / ('A'-Mykaell Riley mix) / There's more to life than this (non toilet mix) / Violently happy.
(cd-s) *(122 TP7CDL)* – ('A'side) / Stigdu mig / Anchor song (Black Dog mix) / I remember you.

— (below single credited with DAVID ARNOLD and from the movie 'Young Americans', released on 'Island' records)

Oct 93. (7"/c-s) *(IS/CIS 573)* **PLAY DEAD. / ('A'-Tim Simenon remix)** [12] [ ]
(12"+=/cd-s+=) *(12IS/CID 573)* – ('A'-Tim Simenon mixes; Orchestral / 12" / Instrumental) / ('A'-Original film mix).

Nov 93. (c-s) *(132 TP7C)* **BIG TIME SENSUALITY / SiDASTA EG** [17] [-]
(cd-s+=) *(132 TP7CD)* – Gloria / Come to me (Black Dog Productions).
(12"/cd-s) *(132 TP 12/7CDL)* – ('A'-Dave Morales def radio mix) / ('A'-Fluke mixes) / ('A'-Justin Robertson – Lionrock Wigout & Prankster's Joyride mix) / ('A'-Dom T. mix).

Jan 94. (c-s) *<64561>* **BIG TIME SENSUALITY / THERE'S MORE TO LIFE THAN THIS** [-] [88]

— In Mar'94, BJORK was accused by SIMON FISHER (LOVEJOY) of not crediting him on 4 of her songs on her 'DEBUT' album.

Mar 94. (c-s) *(142 TP7C)* **VIOLENTLY HAPPY. / ('A'-Fluke mix)** [13] [ ]
(cd-s) *(142 TP7CD)* – ('A'side) / Anchor song (acoustic) / Come to me (acoustic) / Human behavior (acoustic).
(d-cd-s) *(142 TP7CDL)* – ('B'side) / ('A'-5 other mixes).

Sep 94. (cd/c) *(MUM CD/SC 59)* **BEST MIXES FROM THE ALBUM DEBUT (For All The People Who Don't Buy White Labels)** [ ] [-]
(above rel. on 'Mother')

Apr 95. (c-s) *(162 TP7C)* **ARMY OF ME / ('A'-ABA All-Stars mix)** [10] [ ]
(cd-s+=) *(162 TP7CD)* – You've been flirting again / Sweet intuition.
(cd-s+=) *(162 TP7CDL)* – ('A'-Massey mix) / ('A'-featuring SKUNK ANANSIE) / ('A'-ABA All-Stars instrumental).
(cd-s) *(162 TP7)* – ('A'side) / Cover me.

Jun 95. (cd/c/lp) *(TPLP 51 CD/C/L) <612740>* **POST** [2] [32]
– Army of me / Hyper-ballad / The modern things / It's oh so quiet / Enjoy / You've been flirting again / Isobel / Possibly maybe / I miss you / Cover me / Headphones.

Aug 95. (c-s/cd-s) *(172 TP7 C/CD)* **ISOBEL / CHARLENE (Black Dog mix) / I GO HUMBLE / VENUS AS A BOY (harpsicord version)** [23] [ ]
(cd-s) *(172 TP7CDL)* – ('A'side) / ('A'-Goldie mix) / ('A'-Eumir Deodato mix) / ('A'-Siggi mix).

Nov 95. (c-s) *(182 TP7C)* **IT'S OH SO QUIET / YOU'VE BEEN FLIRTING AGAIN (flat is a promise mix)** [4] [ ]
(cd-s+=) *(182 TP7CD)* – Hyper-ballad (Over the edge mix) / Sweet sweet intuition.
(cd-s) *(182 TP7CDL)* – ('A'side) / Hyper-ballad (Girl's blouse mix) / Hyper-ballad (with The Brodsky Quartet) / My spine (featuring Evelyn Glennie).

Feb 96. (c-s) *(192 TP7C)* **HYPER-BALLAD / HYPER-BALLAD (Robin Hood riding through the glen mix)** [8] [ ]
(cd-s+=) *(192 TP7CD)* – ('A'-The stomp remix) / ('A'-Fluke mix) / ('A'-Subtle abuse mix) / ('A'-Tee's freeze mix).
(cd-s) *(192 TP7CDL)* – ('A'side) / Isobel (the Carcass remix) / Cover me (Plaid mix) / ('A'-Towa Tei remix).

Oct 96. (cd-s) *(193 TP7CD)* **POSSIBLY MAYBE (mixes; Lucy / Calcutta Cyber Cafe / Dalas Austin)** [13] [ ]
(cd-s) *(193 TP7CDT)* – ('A'-Calcutta Cyber Cafe dub) / Cover me (Dillinja mix) / One day (Trevor Morais mix) / I miss you (Photek mix).
(cd-s) *(193 TP7CDL)* – ('A'live mix) / Big time sensuality (Plaid remix) / Visur vatnsenda-rosu / Hyper-ballad (live).

Nov 96. (cd/c/lp) *(TPLP 51 CDT/CT/T)* **TELEGRAM** (remixes) [ ] [66] Jan97

Feb 97. (c-s) *(194 TP7C)* **I MISS YOU / I MISS YOU (Photek mix)** [36] [ ]
(cd-s) *(194 TP7CD)* – ('A'side) / ('A'-Dobie part 2) / ('A'Darren Emerson mix) / Karvel (Graham Massey mix).
(cd-s) *(194 TP7CDL)* – ('A'-Dobie part 1) / Hyperballad (LFO) Violently happy (live) / Headphones (Miko Vainio remix).

Sep 97. (cd-s) *(202 TP7CD)* **JOGA (mixes; album / Alec Empire / Alec Empire Digital Hardcore 1 & 2)** [ ] [ ]
(cd-s) *(202 TP7CDL)* – ('A'album mix) / Sod off / Immature (Bjork's version) / So broken.
(cd-s) *(202 TP7CDX)* – (mixes; Howie B. main / String & Vocal / Buzzwater) / All is full of love (original).

Sep 97. (lp/c/cd) *(TPLP 71/+C/CD)* **HOMOGENIC** [4] [28]
– Hunter / Joga / Unravel / Bachelorette / All neon like / 5 years / Immature / Alarm call / Pluto / All is full of love.

Dec 97. (c-s) *(212 TP7C)* **BACHELORETTE / ('A'-Howie "Spread" mix)** 21
(cd-s+=) *(212 TP7CD)* – My snare / Scary.
(12") *(212 TP12P1)* – ('A'-Alec Empire remix) / ('B'side).
(12") *(212 TP12P2)* – ('A'-Mark Bell "Optimism" remix) / ('A'-Mark Bell "Zip" remix).
(cd-s) *(212 TP7CDL)* – (mixes; above + RZA / Grooverider / etc).

— In Aug'98, BJORK collaborated with FUNKSTORUNG on a single, 'ALL IS FULL OF LOVE', released on 'Fat Cat' cd-s; *CDFAT 022)*

Oct 98. (cd-s) *(222 TP7CD)* **HUNTER / ALL IS FULL OF LOVE (In Love With Funkstorung remix) / ('A'-U-Ziq remix)** 44
(cd-s) *(222 TP7CDL)* – ('A'side) / ('A'-State Of Bengal mix) / ('A'-Skothus mix).
(cd-s) *(222 TP7CDX)* – ('A'-Moodswing mix) / So broken (DK Krust remix) / ('A'live).

Nov 98. (cd-s) *(232TP7CD)* **ALARM CALL (mixes; radio / Rhythmic Phonetics / Bjeck)** 33
(cd-s) *(232 TP7CDL)* – (mixes; Potage du jour / French edit / French dub).
(cd-s) *(232 TP7CDX)* – (mixes; Phunk you / Gangsta / Locked).
(12") *(232 TP12P1)* – (mixes; Bjeck [Beck] / Rhythmic Phonetics [Matmos] / Speech therapy [Matmos]).
(12") *(232 TP12P2)* – (mixes; Enough is enough [Mark Bell] / Rise & shine [Mark Bell]) / All is full of love (Mark Bell mix).
(12") *(232 TP12P3)* – (mix; Repossession [DJ Krust] / So broken (DJ Krush mix).
(12") *(232 TP12P4)* – (mixes; Alan Braxe & Ben Diamond [Stardust] / Teesmade dub [Swag] / Alan Braxe & Ben Diamond).
(12") *(232 TP12P5)* – (mixes; Andy Bradford & Mark Bell / album / Snooze button [Dom T] / (Moodswing [Mark Bell]).

– others, etc. –

Aug 96. (12"ltd) *(193 TP12TD)* **POSSIBLY MAYBE (Talvin Singh mix). / I MISS YOU (Dobie mix)** -
Sep 96. (12"ltd) *(193 TP12DM)* **POSSIBLY MAYBE (LFO mix). / ENJOY (Dom T mix)** -
Oct 96. (12"ltd) *(193 TP12PT)* **BIG TIME SENSUALITY (Plaid mix). / ONE DAY (Trevor Morais mix)** -
Jun 97. (12"ltd) *(193 TP12PT)* **BIG TIME SENSUALITY. / ONE DAY** -
Jun 97. (12"ltd) *(193 TP12PD)* **I MISS YOU (Photek mix). / COVER ME (Dillinja mix)** -
Jun 97. (12"ltd) *(193 TP12GH)* **ISOBEL'S LONELY HEART (Goldie remix). / HYPERBALLAD (Robin Hood Riding Through The Glen mix)** -
Jun 97. (12"ltd) *(193 TP12MO)* **POSSIBLY MAYBE (Lucy mix – Mark Bell). / ENJOY (Further Over The Edge mix – Outkast)** -
Jun 97. (12"ltd) *(193 TP12TT)* **HYPERBALLAD (Towa Tei remix). / ENJOY (The Beats mix – Dom T)** -
Aug 98. (12"/cd-s; BJORK & FUNKSTORUNG) *Fat Cat; (12/CD FAT 022)* **ALL IS FULL OF LOVE (mixes)** -

BLACK

Formed: Liverpool, England . . . 1980 by mainman, COLIN VEARNCOMBE. Following the recruitment of a couple of musical partners in crime, BLACK made their live debut as a trio on New Years' Day 1981. The group issued two independent 45's before getting a break in 1984 with 'WEA' subsidiary, 'Eternal', run by WAH! manager, Pete Fulwell. Despite major label backing, both the 'HEY PRESTO' and revamped 'MORE THAN THE SUN' singles failed to garner anything more than cult/critical acclaim and BLACK soon found themselves without a deal. Virtually running the show alone (mainstay DAVE 'DIX' DICKIE was only operating in a part-time capacity), VEARNCOMBE finally found an outlet for the 'WONDEFUL LIFE' single via the tiny 'Ugly Man' label. A brilliantly lugubrious pop ballad with more than a hint of BLACK humour, the track scraped into the UK Top 75 and prompted 'A&M' to sign the outfit for a second crack at mainstream success. Although the first single, 'EVERYTHING'S COMING UP ROSES' made little headway, 'A&M's investment was rewarded when BLACK finally hit the Top 10 in summer '87 with 'SWEETEST SMILE'. A re-issued 'WONDERFUL LIFE' followed into the Top 10 a cuople of months later and a similarly titled debut album made the Top 3 as music lovers clamoured for VEARNCOMBE's soothing balm of intelligent, moodily romantic rock/pop (not unlike early ASSOCIATES or The CHAMELEONS). A follow-up set, 'COMEDY' (1988), made the Top 40 in late '88 although it was obvious BLACK's understated musings weren't quite to the taste of the average chart punter. Guest stars ROBERT PALMER and SAM BROWN were drafted in for cameos on 1991's 'BLACK', VEARNCOMBE's last effort for 'A&M' before heading back to semi-obscurity. No doubt resigned to such a fate anyhow, the BLACK stalwart set up his own label, 'Nero Schwarz', to release 'ARE WE HAVING FUN YET?' (1994), ironically released the same year as 'WONDEFUL LIFE' was trundled out for a third time after being used in a TV ad. • **Songwriters:** VEARNCOMBE with DICKIE on some, until latters departure. Covered SHADES (Iggy Pop – Bowie) / WHOLE WIDE WORLD (Wreckless Eric) / CONTROL (Janet Jackson).

Album rating: WONDERFUL LIFE (*6) / COMEDY (*5)

COLIN VEARNCOMBE (b.26 May'61) – vocals, guitar, keyboards (ex-EPILEPTIC TITS) / **DAVE 'Dix' DICKIE** – keyboards, guitar (ex-LAST CHANT) / **JIMMIE SANGSTER** – bass

Rox / not iss.
Jan 82. (7") *(ROX 17)* **HUMAN FEATURES. / ELECTRIC CHURCH** -

— (Jun'82) trimmed to a duo of **COLIN + DAVE**

W.W.O. / not iss.
Oct 82. (7") *(WW 3)* **MORE THAN THE SUN. / JUMP** -

Eternal / not iss.
Jan 84. (7") *(JF 3)* **HEY PRESTO. / STEPHEN** -
(12"+=) *(JF 3T)* – Liquid dream.

WEA / not iss.
Jan 85. (7") *(BLACK 1)* **MORE THAN THE SUN (remix). / BUTTERFLY MAN** -
(12"+=) *(BLACKT 1)* – I could kill you / Wide mouth / Stephen.

— **BLACK** are virtually **COLIN VEARNCOMBE,** with **DIX** now just the engineer and on part-time keyboard sessions. Other contributions were from **ROY CORKHILL** – fretless bass / **MARTIN GREEN** – saxophone / **JIMMY HUGHES** – drums

Ugly Man / not iss.
Aug 86. (12") *(JACK 001)* **WONDERFUL LIFE. / BIRTHDAY NIGHT** 72 -
(d7"+=) *(JACK 071D)* – Sometimes for the asking / Everything's coming up roses.

A&M / A&M
Apr 87. (7"white) *(AM 388)* *<2995>* **EVERYTHING'S COMING UP ROSES. / RAVEL IN THE RAIN** Nov87
(12"+=) *(AM 388)* – It's not like you Lady Jane.
Jun 87. (7") *(AM 394)* *<1205>* **SWEETEST SMILE. / SIXTEENS** 8 Feb88
(12"+=/cd-s+=) *(AM Y/CD 394)* – Leave yourself alone / Hardly star-crossed lovers.
Aug 87. (7"/c-s) *(AM/+C 402)* *<2969>* **WONDERFUL LIFE. / LIFE CALLS** 8
(12"+=/cd-s+=) *(AM Y/CD 402)* – Had enough / All we need is money.
Sep 87. (lp/c/cd) *(AMA/AMC/CDA 5165)* **WONDERFUL LIFE** 3
– Wonderful life / Everything's coming up roses / Something for the asking / Finder / Paradise / I'm not afraid / I just grew tired / Blue / Just making memories / Sweetest smile. *(c+=)* – Sixteens. *(cd++=)* – Hardly star-crossed lovers / Leave yourself alone / It's not like you Lady Jane / Ravel in the rain. *(re-iss. Aug91 cd/c; CD/C MID 166)*
Oct 87. (7") *(AM 414)* **I'M NOT AFRAID. / HAVE IT YOUR OWN WAY** -
(12"+=) *(AMY 414)* – My love.
Dec 87. (7") *(AM 422)* **PARADISE. / DAGGER REELS** 38
(12"+=/cd-s+=) *(AM Y/CD 422)* – Sometimes for the asking (new version).
Sep 88. (7") *(AM 468)* **THE BIG ONE. / YOU ARE THE ONE** 54 -
(12"+=/cd-s+=) *(AM Y/CD 468)* – Scrapbook.
Oct 88. (lp/c/cd) *(AMA/AMC/CDA 5222)* **COMEDY** 32
– The big one / I can laugh about it now / Whatever people say you are / You're a big girl now / Let me watch you make love / Hey, I was right, you were wrong / All we need is money / You don't always do what's best for you / Now you're gone / No one done nothing. *(cd+=)* – It's not over yet / Paradise lost.
Nov 88. (7") *(AM 480)* **YOU'RE A BIG GIRL NOW. / ENOUGH IS ENOUGH** -
(12"+=/12"pic-d/cd-s+=) *(AMY/AMP/CDEE 480)* – Reunion.
Jan 89. (7") *(AM 491)* **NOW YOU'RE GONE. / ('A'-Mardi Gras version)** 66 -
(12"+=/cd-s+=) *(AMY/CDEE 491)* – Brother o' mine.

— **VEARNCOMBE** retained **GREEN** – (sax, guitar, clarinet) plus **ROY MARTIN** – drums / **BRAD LANG** – bass / **GORDON MORGAN** – guitar / **PETE DAVIS** – keyboards / **STEVE SIDWELL** – trumpet / **LUIS JARDIM** – percussion / **CAMILLA GRICHSEL-VEARNCOMBE** – backing vocals

Apr 91. (7"m) *(AM 780)* **FEEL LIKE CHANGE. / I NEVER WANTED TO WRITE THIS SONG / IT WON'T HELP WHAT'S GOING ON** 56 -
(12"+=/cd-s+=) *(AMY/CDEE 780)* – Wonderful life.
May 91. (cd/c/lp) *(387126-2/-4/-1)* *<75021 5365-2/-4>* **BLACK** 42
– Too many times / Feels like change / Here it comes again / Learning how to hate / Fly up to the Moon / Let's talk about me / Sweet breath of your rapture / Listen / She's my best friend / This is life.
Jun 91. (7"/c-s) *(AM/+C 753)* **HERE IT COMES AGAIN. / EVERY WAKING HOUR** 70 -
(12"+=/cd-s+=) *(AMY/CDEE 753)* – Shades / Wonderful life (88 Christmas recording).
Aug 91. (7"/c-s) **FLY UP TO THE MOON. / YOU LIFT ME UP / WHAT YOU ARE** -
(cd-s+=) – Control.
(cd-s+=) – Whole wide world / Under wraps / What's right is right.
(above featured **SAM BROWN** – vocals)

Nero Schwarz / not iss.
Mar 94. (cd-s) *(CDNERO 1)* **(THAT'S) JUST LIKE LOVE / SURRENDER / PAPER CROWN** -
Apr 94. (cd/c/lp) *(NERO CD/MC/LP 9401)* **ARE WE HAVING FUN YET?** -
– Don't take the silence too hard / Swingtime / Wishing you were here / Leaving song / That's just like love / Ave Lolita / Wish the world awake / Paper crown / Change your mind / To take a piece.

— COLIN disbanded BLACK soon after above

– compilations, others, etc. –

Nov 87. (m-lp/m c) *WEA; (WX 137/+C)* **BLACK** (84-85 material) -
Nov 92. (c-ep/cd-ep) *A&M;* **WONDERFUL LIFE / NOW YOU'RE GONE / YOU'RE A BIG GIRL NOW** -
Feb 94. (7"/c-s) *Polygram TV; (580554-7/-4)* **WONDERFUL LIFE. / SWEETEST SMILE** 42 -
(cd-s+=) *(580555-2)* – The big one / Feel the change.

Frank BLACK (see under ⇒ PIXIES)

BLACK BOX RECORDER (see under ⇒ AUTEURS)

BLACK FLAG

Formed: Hermosa Beach, California, USA . . . 1976 by GREG GINN and CHUCK DUKOWSKI. In 1977, their demo reached local indielabel 'Bomp', who, after over half a year decided not to release BLACK FLAG's debut

45, 'NERVOUS BREAKDOWN'. Instead, GREG and CHUCK, with sound men MUGGER and SPOT, formed their own label, 'S.S.T.' (Solid State Tuners), issuing the aforesaid single in 1978. By the time BLACK FLAG's debut lp, 'DAMAGED', was released in 1981, the group had suffered label difficulties with 'MCA-Unicorn', who didn't like the outrageous content of the tracks. Numerous personnel changes had also occured, mainly the substitution of KEITH MORRIS, with the harder looking and now legendary HENRY ROLLINS. SST took the major label to court and although the pivotal hardcore group won, they had to pay out a 6-figure sum. The influential label went on to help kickstart the careers of many hardcore/alternative acts such as HUSKER DU, MINUTEMEN, DINOSAUR JR, MEAT PUPPETS, etc. Meanwhile, BLACK FLAG (with GINN and ROLLINS at the helm), completed a series of near brilliant albums, ROLLINS even contributing a spoken word side on the half instrumental album, 'FAMILY MAN' (1984), a thing that he would do more when he took off on a successful solo venture that year. GINN and some new cohorts completed two more mid 80's sets, 'IN MY HEAD' and 'WHO'S GOT THE 10 1/2', before he too pursued a solo sojourn, although at first with instrumental punk-jazz fusion, GONE. BLACK FLAG were one of the first US acts to take DIY punk into hardcore, a hybrid sound that would later be revered by metal fans who had picked up on 90's US hardcore/punk groups like BAD RELIGION and OFFSPRING.

Album rating: DAMAGED (*8) / EVERYTHING WENT BLACK (*5) / THE FIRST FOUR YEARS (*7) compilation / MY WAR (*6) / FAMILY MAN (*4) / SLIP IT IN (*5) / LOOSE NUT (*5) / IN MY HEAD (*6) / WHO'S GOT THE 10 1/2 (*6) / WASTED . . . AGAIN (*7)

KEITH MORRIS – vocals / **GREG GINN** (b. 8 Jun'54) – guitar / **CHUCK DUKOWSKI** – bass (ex-WURM) / **BRIAN MIGDOL** – drums

not iss. S.S.T.

Oct 78. (7"ep) *<SST 001>* **NERVOUS BREAKDOWN. / FIX ME / I'VE HAD IT / WASTED** [-] [ ]
<US 10"colrd-ep/12"ep/cd-ep iss.1990; same>

— **CHAVO PEDERAST** (aka RON REYES) – vocals (ex-RED CROSS) repl. KEITH who formed CIRCLE JERKS. **ROBO** – drums repl. MIGDOL

Mar 80. (12"ep) *<SST 003>* **JEALOUS AGAIN / REVENGE. / WHITE MINORITY / NO VALUES / YOU BET WE'VE GOT SOMETHING PERSONAL AGAINST YOU!** [-] [ ]
(UK-iss.Mar83; same) <US 10"colrd-ep/12"ep/cd-ep iss.1990; same>

— **DEZ CADENA** – vocals, guitar (ex-RED CROSS) repl. REYES

Jan 81. (7"ep) *<SST 005>* **SIX PACK. / I'VE HEARD IT ALL BEFORE / AMERICAN WASTE** [-] [ ]
(UK-iss.Dec81 on 'Alternative Tentacles'; VIRUS 9) <US 10"colrd-ep/12"/ep/cd-ep iss.1990; same>

— **HENRY ROLLINS** (b. HENRY GARFIELD, 13 Feb '61, Washington, D.C.) – vocals (ex-SOA) repl. CHUCK who later formed SWA.

— Group now **ROLLINS, GINN, CADENA** (now rhythm guitar only) + **ROBO**

S.S.T. S.S.T.

Nov 81. (lp) *<(SST 007)>* **DAMAGED** [ ] [ ]
– Rise above / Spray paint / Six pack / What I see / TV party / Thirsty and miserable / Police story / Gimmie gimmie gimmie / Depression / Room 13 / Damaged II / No more / Padded cell / Life of pain / Damaged I.

— In the US, 'Posh Boy' issued '79 recording LOUIE LOUIE. / DAMAGED 1 *(PBS 13)* *(This was finally issued 10"coloured 1988 on 'SST' US) (re-iss. cd/c/lp Oct95; same)* LOUIE LOUIE was a KINGSMEN original.

— **BILL STEVENSON** + guest **EMIL** – drums repl. ROBO

1982. (7"ep) *<SST 012>* **TV PARTY. / I'VE GOT TO RUN / MY RULES** [-] [ ]
<US 12"+cd-ep iss.1990; same>

— guest on half **DALE NIXON** – bass (actually GREG under pseudonym) repl. CADENA

Mar 84. (lp) *<(SST 023)>* **MY WAR** [ ] [ ]
– My war / Can't decide / Beat my head agaist the wall / I love you / The swinging man / Forever time / Nothing left inside / Three nights / Scream. *(cd-iss. 1990; SST 023CD) (re-iss. cd/c/lp Oct95; same)*

— added **KIRA ROESSLER** – bass

Sep 84. (lp) *<(SST 026)>* **FAMILY MAN** [ ] [ ]
– Family man / Salt on a slug / The pups are doggin' it / Let your fingers do the walking / Long lost dog of it / I won't stick any of you unless and until I can stick all of you / Hollywood diary / Armageddon man / Account for what? / Shred reading (rattus norvegicus) / No deposit, no return. *(cd-iss. 1990; SST 026CD) (re-iss. cd/c/lp Oct95; same)*

Oct 84. (12") *<(SST1 2001)>* **FAMILY MAN. / I WON'T STICK ANY OF YOU UNLESS AND UNTIL I CAN STICK ALL OF YOU** [ ] [ ]

Dec 84. (lp) *<(SST 029)>* **SLIP IT IN** [ ] [ ]
– Slip it in / Black coffee / Wound up / Rat's eyes / Obliteration / The bars / My ghetto / You're not evil. *(cd-iss. 1990; SST 029CD) (re-iss. cd/c/lp Oct95; same)*

Jan 85. (c) *<(SST 030)>* **LIVE '84 (live)** [ ] [ ]
– The process of weeding out / My ghetto / Jealous again / I love you / Swinging man / Three nights / Nothing left inside / Black coffee. *(cd-iss. 1990; SST 030CD) (re-iss. cd/c/lp Oct95; same)*

Jun 85. (lp) *<(SST 035)>* **LOOSE NUT** [ ] [ ]
– Loose nut / Bastard in love / Annihilate this week / Best one yet / Modern man / This is good / I'm the one / Sinking / Now she's black. *(cd-iss. 1990; SST 035CD) (re-iss. cd/c/lp Oct95; same)*

— trimmed to of **GINN, KIRA + STEVENSON** when ROLLINS went solo

Sep 85. (m-lp) *<(SST 037)>* **THE PROCESS OF WEEDING OUT** [ ] [ ]
– Your last affront / Screw the law / The process of weeding out / Southern rise. *(US 10"colrd/m-cd iss.1990)*

Nov 85. (lp) *<(SST 045)>* **IN MY HEAD** [ ] [ ]
– Paralyzed / The crazy girl / Black love / Retired at 21 / Drinking and driving / White hot / In my head / Society's tease / It's all up to you / You let me down. *(cd-iss. 1990 +=; SST 045CD)* – Out of this world / I can see you. *(cd re-iss. Oct95; same)*

— **ANTHONY MARTINEZ** – drums repl.STEVENSON

May 86. (lp) *<(SST 060)>* **WHO'S GOT THE 10 1/2 (live in Portland 23/8/85)** [ ] [ ]
– I'm the one / Loose nut / Bastard in love / Slip it in / This is good / Gimmie gimmie gimmie / Drinking and driving / Modern man / My war. *(cd-iss. 1990) (re-iss. cd/c/lp Oct95; same) (cd+=)* – Annihilate / Wasted / Sinking / Jam / Louie Louie / Best one yet.

— Had already, earlier in '86. KIRA continued with DOS, alongside MIKE WATT of The MINUTEMEN. GINN teamed up with DUKOWSKI again, and formed instrumental group GONE.

– compilations, others, etc. –

on 'S.S.T.' unless mentioned otherwise

Mar 83. (d-lp) *<(SST 015)>* **EVERYTHING WENT BLACK** (rare 78-81) [ ] [ ]
(re-iss. Oct95 lp/c/cd; SST 015/+C/CD)

1984. (lp) *<SST 021>* **THE FIRST FOUR YEARS** [-] [ ]
(UK-iss.Oct95 lp/c/cd; SST 021/+C/CD)

Dec 87. (lp/c/cd) *<(SST 166/+C/CD)>* **WASTED . . . AGAIN** [ ] [ ]
– Wasted / TV party / Six pack / I don't care / I've had it / Jealous again / Slip it in / Annihilate this week / Loose nut / Gimme gimme / Louie Louie / Drinking and driving. *(re-iss. Oct95; same)*

Jun 93. (12"/c-s/cd-s) *(SST 226/+C/CD)* **I CAN SEE YOU** [ ] [ ]

GONE

— **GREG GINN** – guitar / **ANDREW WEISS** – bass

S.S.T. S.S.T.

Jul 86. (lp) *<(SST 061)>* **LET'S GET REAL, REAL GONE FOR A CHANGE** [ ] [ ]
– Insideous detraction / Get gone / Peter gone / Rosanne / Climbing Rat's wall / Watch the tractor / Last days of being stepped on / CH 69 / Lawndale Rock City / Hypercharge – the wait (the fifth force suite). *(re-iss. May93 cd/c; SST 061 CD/C)*

Jan 87. (lp) *<(SST 086)>* **GONE II – BUT NEVER TOO GONE!** [ ] [ ]
– Jungle law / New vengeance / Unglued / Turned over stone / Drop the hat / Adams / Time of entry / Left holding the bag / GTV / Daisy strut / Cut off / Put it there / Utility hole / Yesterday is teacher / How soon they forget / Cobra XVIII. *(re-iss. May93 cd/c; SST 086 CD/C)*

— In 1993, GREG released 'COLLEGE ROCK' EP as POINDEXTER STEWART

— **GINN** re-formed GONE with **STEVE SHARP** – bass / **GREGORY MOORE** – drums

Jan 94. (lp/cd) *<(SST 300/+CD)>* **THE CRIMINAL MIND** [ ] [ ]
– Poor losers / Punch drunk / Pull it out / Pump room / Snagglepuss / PS was wrong / Off the chains / Smoking gun in Waco / Spankin' plank / Piled one higher / Row nine / Toggle / Big check / Ankle strap / Hand out / Freeny / Unknown calibar.

Apr 94. (12"/cd-s) *<(SST 303)>* **SMOKING GUN IN WACO. /** [ ] [ ]
(re-iss. Feb96; same)

Aug 94. (lp/c/cd) *<(SST 306/+C/CD)>* **ALL THE DIRT THAT'S FIT TO PRINT** [ ] [ ]
– Picket fence asylum / Upward spiral / Mutilated fade / Damage control / Kattiwompus / 39051 / White tail / Crawdad / Meet me in the van / Bosco pit / Huntin w/ a rich man / 4 a.m.

Sep 95. (12") *<(SST 303)>* **DAMAGE CONTROL. / SMOKING GUN (IN WACO)** [ ] [ ]

Apr 96. (cd) *<(SST 313)>* **BEST LEFT UNSAID** [ ] [ ]
– Bicycle riding assassin / My name is on the masthead but . . . / Hotheaded butchers / Closet courtaholic / Stray bullet / We have pigs / Closeted publishers / Second gunman / Bomb plot case / Mother called Ill / Hostile witness.

Jul 98. (cd) *<(SST 344)>* **COUNTRY DUMB** [ ] [ ]
– Dinky cat / (Lost in) Filegate / Big government, small mind / Pentagon expands / Cut your hair, drink Coors / "Punks" in government / Rage against intelligence / Another existential excuse / Paula Jones Clinton / Hip Castro conservative / Woozy news hound / "Punk" and the cash narcotic / Country dumb or city stupid? / Sugar bear.

GREG GINN

— with **GREGORY MOORE** – tom-tom / **DAVID RAVEN** – drums / later added **STEVE SHARP** – bass

Cruz Cruz

Jun 93. (12"/c-s/cd-s) *<(CRZ 028/+C/CD)>* **PAYDAY. / PAYDAY / PIG MF** [ ] [ ]

Jun 93. (lp/c/cd) *<(CRZ 029/+C/CD)>* **GETTING EVEN** [ ] [ ]
– I've changed / Kill burn fluff / You drive me crazy / Pig MF / Hard thing / Payday / Nightmares / Torn / PF flyer / I can't wait / Short fuse / Not that simple / Yes officer / Crawling inside.

Sep 93. (lp/c/cd) *<(CRZ 032/+C/CD)>* **DICK** [ ] [ ]
– Never change baby / I want to believe / You wanted it / I won't give in / Creeps / Strong violent type / Don't tell me / You dirty rat / Disgusting reference / Walking away / Ignorant order / Slow fuse / You're gonna get it.

Mar 94. (12"/cd-s) *(CRZ 033/+CD)* **DON'T TELL ME. /** [ ] [ ]

Aug 94. (lp/c/cd) *<(CRZ 036/+C/CD)>* **LET IT BURN (BECAUSE I DON'T LIVE THERE ANYMORE)** [ ] [ ]
– On a roll / Taking the other side / Lame Hollywood cop / Lame excuses / In your face motherfucker / Hey, stupid face / Venting / Let it burn / Drifting away / Military destroys mind/body / I don't want it / Destroy my mind / Exiled from Lame Street.

BLACK GRAPE

Formed: Manchester, England . . . late 1994 by ex-HAPPY MONDAYS men SHAUN RYDER and BEZ, the line-up completed by KERMIT and JED from The RUTHLESS RAP ASSASSINS, plus a host of extras. SHAUN's brilliant return from oblivion was complete by summer 1995 when the storming 'REVEREND BLACK GRAPE' launched him back into the Top 10. The mouthiest, grooviest low-slung Manc rave-up to grace the charts since the 'MONDAYS peak, the record pointed squarely in the direction where the party was really happening, bypassing completely the tedious Brit-pop posturing. As

Shaun Ryder
BLACK GRAPE

ever, RYDER and entourage were never far from controversy, both the song and video subsequently banned from TV as the Catholic church alleged the lyrics condoned Venezuelan terrorist, Carlos The Jackal (which also angered the New York based ADL – Anti-Defamation League). Another classic single, 'IN THE NAME OF THE FATHER', followed into the Top 10, funk rhythms and a sitar tinged intro previewing the eclecticism of the accomapanying No.1 album, 'IT'S GREAT WHEN YOU'RE STRAIGHT . . . YEAH!'. Its title a reference to RYDER's clean living new ways (his inimitable cut 'n' paste lyrics apparently fuelled solely by Guiness!?), the record was compared favourably against The HAPPY MONDAYS' best work and the second coming-style fuss over RYDER's critical rebirth seemed at least partly justified. Loping through a dayglo musical smarty pack of hip-hop, rock, indie-dance, soul and indeed, anything close to hand, RYDER proved his subversive genius was well intact, while KERMIT's hyperactive rapping assaults were a perfect foil for his stoned immaculate drawl. During this time, they were one of the successes at Hamilton Park's 'T In The Park' 2-day festival (near Glasgow), even though KERMIT broke his leg and had to sit out most of the gig on a speaker! During an eventful 1996 of regular touring and high profile press coverage, BEZ and RYDER finally parted ways, while KERMIT embarked on a side project, MAN MADE, the following year. A follow-up album, 'STUPID, STUPID, STUPID' finally emerged at the end of '97 amid furious interband disputes, claims and counter claims. The feuding saw the band cancel their New Year's Eve show at London's Alexandra Palace and, at the time of writing, the band's future doesn't look entirely certain. • **Songwriters:** SHAUN & KERMIT alongside DANNY SABER, although in October '95, INTASTELLA members MARTIN WRIGHT and MARTIN MITTLER served a writ, claiming they co-wrote with SHAUN on early demos before they departed.

Album rating: IT'S GREAT WHEN YOU'RE STRAIGHT. . . YEAH! (*9) / STUPID, STUPID, STUPID (*7)

SHAUN RYDER (b.23 Aug'62) – vocals (ex-HAPPY MONDAYS) / **BEZ** – dancer (ex-HAPPY MONDAYS) / **KERMIT** (b.PAUL LEVEREDGE) – rapper (ex-RUTHLESS RAP ASSASINS) / **JED BIRTWHISTLE** – rapper (ex-RUTHLESS RAP ASSASSINS) / **WAGS** – guitar (ex-PARIS ANGELS) / **CRAIG GANNON** – guitar (ex-SMITHS) who replaced INTASTELLA guitarists **MARTIN WRIGHT + MARTIN MITTLER**

Radioactive Radioactive

May 95. (c-s) *(RAXC 16)* **REVEREND BLACK GRAPE / STRAIGHT OUT OF TRUMPTON (BASEMENT TAPES)** [9] [ ]
(cd-s+=) *(RAXTD 16)* – ('A'-dark side mix).
(12") *(RAXT 16)* – ('A'side) / ('A'-dub collar mix) / ('A'-dark side mix).

Jul 95. (c-s) *(RAXC 19)* **IN THE NAME OF THE FATHER / LAND OF A THOUSAND KAMA SUTRA BABIES** [8] [ ]
(cd-s+=) *(RAXTD 19)* – ('A'-chopper's mix) / ('A'-chopper's instrumental).
(12") *(RAXT 19)* – ('A'side) / (above 2).

Aug 95. (cd/c/lp) *(<RAD/RAC/RAR 11224>)* **IT'S GREAT WHEN YOU'RE STRAIGHT. . .YEAH** [1] [ ]
– Reverend Black Grape / In the name of the father / Tramazi party / Kelly's heroes / Yeah yeah brother / Big day in the north / Shake well before opening / Shake your money / Little Bob.

Nov 95. (c-s) *(RAXC 22)* **KELLY'S HEROES / ('A'-The Milky Bar Kid mix)** [17] [ ]
(cd-s+=) *(RAXTD 22)* – ('A'-The Archibald mix) / Little Bob (live).
(cd-s) *(RAXXD 22)* – ('A'live) / In the name of the father (live) / Fat neck.

— BEZ quit due to argument with SHAUN over his role in the group.

— On Channel 4's TFI Friday, SHAUN caused more controversy by adding loads of live f words on their version on SEX PISTOLS 'Pretty Vacant'.

May 96. (c-s) *(RAXC 24)* **FAT NECK / PRETTY VACANT (live)** [10] [ ]
(cd-s+=) *(RAXTD 24)* – Yeah yeah brother (Outlaw Josey Wales mix).
(12") *(RAXT 24)* – ('A'-GOLDIE Beat the f*** down mix) / Yeah yeah brother (Clockwork Orange mix) / Yeah yeah brother (Dog day afternoon mix).

Jun 96. (c-s) *(RAXC 25)* **ENGLAND'S IRIE /** [6] [ ]
(cd-s) *(RAXTD 25)* – ('A'side) / ('A'-Pass The Durazac mix) / ('A'-Suedehead dub) / ('A'-Mel's L.A. Irie mix).
(12") *(RAXT 25)* –

— above featured JOE STRUMMER and KEITH ALLEN

— In Oct'96, SHAUN moonlighted with The HEADS (ex-TALKING HEADS) on minor hit single 'Don't Take My Kindness For Weakness'.

Oct 97. (c-s/cd-s) *(RAX C/TD 32)* **GET HIGHER / ('A'mixes)** [24] [ ]
(cd-s) *(RAXXD 32)* – ('A'mixes).

Nov 97. (lp/c/cd) *(<RAR/+C/D 11716>)* **STUPID STUPID STUPID** [11] [ ]
– Get higher / Squeaky / Marbles / Dadi was a badi / Rubber band / Spotlight / Tell me something / Money back guarenteed / Lonely / Words.

Feb 98. (cd-s) *(RAXTD 33)* **MARBLES (remixes by R.I.P. and FABIO PARAS) / MARBLES (demo)** [46] [ ]
(12"+=) *(RAXT 33)* – ('A'-Tricky remix).
(cd-s) *(RAXXD 33)* – ('A'-Tricky remix) / Harry the dog / Get higher (uncensored video on CD-ROM).

BLACK RANDY & THE METRO SQUAD

Formed: Los Angeles, California, USA . . . 1977 by caucasian punk rocker, BLACK RANDY. With a free'n'easy attitude to recruitment, The METRO SQUAD were probably the genuine definition of the punk DIY philosophy and the line-up varied accordingly. Tagged after the punk club of the same name, the 'Dangerhouse' label was home to the band's debut single, 'TROUBLE AT THE CUP', featuring such classic B-side material as 'LONER WITH A BONER' and 'SPERM BANK BABY'. Clearly untroubled by the American work ethic, RANDY and co. released a single a year through '78 and '79 – 'IDI AMIN' and 'I SLEPT IN AN ARCADE' respectively – before bowing out with a solitary album, 'PASS THE DUST, I THINK I'M BOWIE' (1980). No prizes for guessing what the dust in the title referred to, RANDY's alleged fondness for PCP no doubt contributing to the chaos surrounding the band. The 'SQUAD's subsequent demise was followed by RANDY's mysterious death while GARRETT went on to play with The DILS. • **Covered:** GIVE IT UP OR TURNIT A LOOSE + I'M BLACK AND PROUD (James Brown).

Album rating: PASS THE DUST, I THINK I'M BOWIE (*4)

BLACK RANDY – vocals / **DAVID BROWN** – keyboards, vocals / **BOB DEADWYLER** – guitar, vocals / **PAT GARRETT** – bass, guitar, vocals / **KK BARRETT** – guitar / **JOE RAMIREZ** – bass / **TOM HUGHES** – guitar, bass / **JOE NANINI** – drums, percussion

not iss. Dangerhouse

Dec 77. (7"m) *<MO 721>* **TROUBLE AT THE CUP. / LONER WITH A BONER / SPERM BANK BABY** [-] [ ]

1978. (7"ep) *<IDI 722>* **IDI AMIN / I'M BLACK AND PROUD PART 3. / I'M BLACK AND PROUD PART 14 / I WANNA BE A NARK** [-] [ ]

Jul 79. (7") *<KY 724>* **I SLEPT IN AN ARCADE. / GIVE IT UP** [-] [ ]

Jan 80. (lp) *<PCP 725>* **PASS THE DUST, I THINK I'M BOWIE** [-] [ ]
– I slept in an arcade / Marlon Brando / Down at the laundromat / I tell lies every day / San Francisco / Give it up or turn it a loose / Idi Amin / Barefootin' on the wicked picket / Shaft / I wanna be a nark / Sperm bank baby / Tellin' lies / I'm black and proud.

— split early 1980 when RANDY died of drug related causes. PAT GARRETT later joined The DILS. RAMIREZ, BROWN, NANINI + bassist JIMMY LEACH were also part of The EYES, who had a few releases in the late 70's.

BLAGGERS I.T.A.

Formed: London, England . . . early 1992 by frontman MATTY 'BLAG' alongside a cast of equally militant musical comrades. Founded on a staunch anti-fascist platform, BLAGGERS ITA communicated their firmly held beliefs through a frantic musical barrage of punk, ska, hip-hop and reggae. By their own admittance not the greatest of musicians, the band – in the time honoured punk style – made up in attitude what they lacked in ability. After a series of seriously angry releases on their own 'Words Of Warning' label (they'd previously released an album in '89 under the BLAGGERS moniker), the band finally issued their debut album proper, 'UNITED COLOURS OF BLAGGERS ITA', in early '93. With a snowballing reputation earned largely via their blistering live work, the band subsequently found themselves the subject of a major label bidding war. 'Parlophone' eventually secured the band's signatures, a Top 40 hit later that summer with 'STRESSS' suggesting a bright future. Things turned pear-shaped, however, after MATTY was involved in a fight with Melody Maker journalist, Dave Simpson, the altercation a result of revelations regarding the frontman's previous Nazi sympathies. The band were subsequently dropped as the appropriately titled 'BAD KARMA' (1994) album sank without trace. Although they carried on with a series of releases on their own 'Disinformation' label, the posse suffered an irreperable split following the sacking of MATTY in summer '95. • **Covered:** GUNS OF BRIXTON (Clash). • **Trivia:** 'HERE'S JOHNNY' was a dig at Prime Minister of the time JOHN MAJOR.

Album rating: UNITED COLOURS OF BLAGGERS (*6) / BAD KARMA (*5)

MATTY 'BLAG' – vocals / **CHRISTY** – vocals / **CARLOS** – keyboards / **SERIOUS STEVE + JASON** – guitar / **BRENDAN** – trumpet / **OLAF** (b. Germany) – saxophone / **MATT VINYL** – bass (BLAG / BILKO / MINTER / VYNEL / JESTER) surnames; COOK, COUTINHO, HODGES, MOLF, PERRY, ROBERTS, ROBSON.

Oi! not iss.

May 89. (lp; as BLAGGERS) *(OIR 014)* **ON YER TOEZ** [ ] [-]
– On yer toes / Young blaggers / Crazy / Skateboard bop / Weekend warning / Bronco bullfrog / Shaw tailor / Nufting (blagged again) / Jailhouse doors / Freedom fighters / Britains dream / Ireland / Greetings from Ireland / Save your hate / House of the fascist scum / Nice on Blaggers.

Words Of Warning not iss.

Nov 90. (7") **IT'S UP TO YOU. / I WON'T EAT HERE / GET OUTTA HERE** [ ] [-]

Nov 91. (m-lp) *(WOW 019)* **BLAGGERMUFFIN** [ ] [-]
(re-iss. Jun93; same)

Apr 92. (7") *(WOW 22)* **HERE'S JOHNNY. / ?** [ ] [-]
(re-iss. May93; same)

Nov 92. (7") **THE WAY WE OPERATE. / THATCHER CHILLIN'** [ ] [-]
(above released on 'Fluffy Bunny' records)

— now w/out OLAF who returned to his homeland after a racist fracas at a COCK SPARRER gig in December '92.

Jan 93. (cd/lp) *(WOW CD/LP 027)* **UNITED COLOURS OF BLAGGERS** [ ] [-]

Parlophone Parlophone

Jun 93. (7") *(ITA 1)* **STRESSS. / THE WAY TO DIE / WILD SIDE / STRESSS** [56] [ ]
(12"+=/cd-s+=) *(12/CD ITA 1)* – The way to die (extended).

Sep 93. (7"yellow) *(ITAY 2)* **OXYGEN. / U.S.D.** [51] [ ]
(7"green) *(ITAG 2)* – ('A'side) / TEN MEN DEAD
(12") *(12ITA 2)* – ('A'side) / The way we operate in 1993.
(cd-s+=) *(CDITA 2)* – (all 4 tracks)

Dec 93. (7"orange) *(ITAO 3)* **ABANDON SHIP. / HERE'S JOHNNY (live)** [48] [ ]
(7"turquoise) *(ITAT 3)* – ('A'side) / JOSEPHINE BAKER
(cd-s+=) *(CDITA 3)* – Stresss.
(12") *(12ITA 3)* – ('A'side) / Bastard chillin' I (live) / Oxygen (mix) / Abandon ship (mix).

Oct 94. (12") *(12ITA 4)* **MANTRAP. / GUNS OF BRIXTON / ROAD TO BASRA** [ ] [-]

(cd-s) *(CDITA 4)* – (1st 2 tracks) / Pirate shutdown / Shutdown.
Oct 94. (cd/c/lp) *(CD/TC+/PCSD 156)* **BAD KARMA**
– The hits / 1994 / Mantrap / Bad karma / Famine queen / Stresss / Abandon ship / Nation / Garden of love / Slam / Hate generator / Oxygen.

Damaged Goods | not iss.

Jan 95. (7"colrd) *(DAMGOOD 58)* **THRILL HER WITH A GUN. / DIARY THIEF** | -

Disinform-ation | not iss.

May 95. (7"/cd-s) *(BITA 1/+CD)* **RUMBLEFISH. / DEATH BY COOL** | -
Sep 95. (7"/cd-s) *(BITA 2/+CD)* **GUNS OF BRIXTON. /** | -
Sep 95. (cd-ep) *(BITA 3CD)* **I.T.A. SESSIONS** | -

— had already split when MATTY was sacked from the band

Karl BLAKE

Born: c.1958, Australia. Influenced by occult merchants like BLACK SABBATH and inspired by the experimental possibilities opened up by the punk explosion, BLAKE began making his own home spun recordings from 1977 onwards. During this period, the guitarist also initiated The LEMON KITTENS, who, after a solitary RESIDENTS-esque EP, 'SPOONFED AND WRITHING' (which featured a twisted cover of Johnny Kidd's 'SHAKIN' ALL OVER'), invited the equally bizarre multi-instrumentalist DANIELLE DAX into the fold. Based in Richmond, Surrey, the pair worked hard at flouting musical convention over three independently released sets, 'WE BUY A HAMMER FOR DADDY' (1980), 'CAKE FEAST' (1981) and 'THE BIG DENTIST', before DAX ventured solo. BLAKE was also the man behind the obscure GLAND SHROUDS, a series of cassette-only releases appearing on his own label during the early 80's. Slightly higher profile was the SHOCK HEADED PETERS project, a collaboration with DAVE KNIGHT which resulted in only one proper album, 'NOT BORN BEAUTIFUL' (1985). At times dark, rough and nightmarish, the 'PETERS, like most of BLAKE's repertoire, wasn't exactly easy listening. Incredibly, BLAKE would subsequently team up with hard-rock chick, KATERYNA BURBELA (a former guitarist with all-girl trio, ROCK GODDESS!), under the banner of the UNDERNEATH. After only a couple of EP outings, KARL formed the EVIL TWIN (apparently with a guy called DAVE MELLOR!) and augmented MARK PERRY's outfit, ALTERNATIVE TV.

KARL BLAKE – guitar, etc.

Daark Inc. | not iss.

1980. (c) *(D.I. 1)* **TANK DEATH** | -
1981. (c) *(D.I. 2)* **THE NEW POLLUTION** | -

LEMON KITTENS

KARK BLAKE – guitar, etc / **G. THATCHER / M. MERCER**

Step Forward | not iss.

Oct 79. (7"ep) *(SF 10)* **SPOONFED AND WRITHING** | -
– Shakin' all over / This kind of dying / Morbotalk / Whom do I have to ask / Chalet d'amour / . . .Nor a mirror. *(re-iss. Apr96 as cd-ep on 'Biter Of Thorpe; BOT 131-08CD)*

— basically **BLAKE + DANIELLE DAX** – vocals, keyboards, flute / + live **IAN STURGESS** – bass / **PETE FALLOWELL** – drums / briefly joined in the studio **MARK PERRY** – drums (of ALTERNATIVE TV)

United Dairies | not iss.

Aug 80. (lp) *(UD 02)* **WE BUY A HAMMER FOR DADDY** | -
Feb 81. (lp) *(UD 07)* **CAKE FEAST** | -
– Kites / Only a rose / Popsykle.

Illuminated | not iss.

Dec 81. (lp) *(JAMS 131)* **(THOSE THAT BITE THE HAND THAT FEEDS THEM, SOONER OR LATER MUST MEET . . .) THE BIG DENTIST** | -
– They are both dirty / The hospital hurts / Mylmus / The girl / The log and the pin / Nudies.

— They split early in '82, when DANIELLE DAX went solo

GLAND SHROUDS

KARL BLAKE + ?

Daark Inc. | not iss.

1981. (c) *(D.I. 3)* **STAFF IN CONFIDENCE / TOYSHOP UNIVERSAL** | -
1982. (c) *(D.I. 4)* **ANIMAL DANCE** | -
1982. (c) *(D.I. 5)* **YOUR ANIMALS** | -
1983. (c) *(D.I. 6)* **EVERYONE WANTS TO WIN** | -

Detrimental History | not iss.

1980's. (c) *(DHSS 2)* **FERTIVE CHEATS** | -
1980's. (c) *(DHSS 3)* **A TELESCOPE IN THE SKY** | -
1980's. (c) *(DHSS 4)* **MORGUE DREAMS** (as "HOMUNCULUS") | -

— KARL was also behind CHINESE FOUR ABREAST / ORANGE JELLYBABY & SIX WHITE CHOCOLATE MICE / PROBLEM 5.

KARL BLAKE

Glass | not iss.

1983. (lp) *(GLASS 013)* **THE PREHENSILE TAPES** (compilation 1977-81) | -
– Baby's in grey / Switchback / Whistle and weep / Blast the human flower / The waiting list / No limits / People with no shoulders / Dreams of Lichen Tester / A misogyny of song / Love so much like violent death.

SHOCK HEADED PETERS

KARL BLAKE + DAVE KNIGHT

el | not iss.

Sep 84. (7") *(EL 1)* **I, BLOOD BROTHER BE. / TRUTH HAS COME** | -
(12"+=) *(ONET)* – Katabolism / Hate on sight.
May 85. (7") *(EL 3)* **THE KISSING OF GODS. / ALWAYS BE WAITING** | -
(12"+=) *(ELT 3)* – Heartbreak hotel / Mr. Very big.
Jun 85. (lp) *(FIN 1)* **NOT BORN BEAUTIFUL** | -

— next with guest **DAVID CROSS** – violin (ex-KING CRIMSON)

Beach Culture | not iss.

Feb 86. (12"ep) *(3BC)* **LIFE EXTINGUISHER** | -
– Scorch / Life extinguisher / Son of thumbs of a murderer / Win on condition.

— split 1986, and left behind compilations

Nov 87. Produkt Korps; (lp) *(PKLP 0020)* **FEAR ENGINE** | -
Nov 92. Cyclops Prod.; (cd) **SEVERAL HEADED ENEMY** | -

Tak Tak Tak | not iss.

1992. (c) *(TAK 07)* **MANDIBLES** | -
(cd-iss. Apr96 on 'Swordex Hieroglyph Proper'; SHP 616131-01CD)

UNDERNEATH

— **KARL** with **KATERYNA BURBELA** – guitar (ex-ROCK GODDESS)

el | not iss.

Oct 86. (7"ep) *(GPO 17)* **THE IMP OF THE PERSERSE** | -
– Fire / Short term agreement.
(12"ep+=) *(GPO 17T)* – Have I the right? / Black roots: A tribute to Black Sabbath.
May 87. (12"ep) *(ACME 9)* **LUNATIC DAWN OF THE DISMANTLER** | -
– Positive force for good and evil / Thick black angular / Black England / White bomb / No / Tragedy boys and girls / Zophia / Bayonet / Smear / Another death in the family / Psranticide / Partyclens plus / This lady devoid / Hanging / Letter from an institution.

— KARL with DAVE MELLOR formed The EVIL TWIN, while KARL worked with MARK PERRY in ALTERNATIVE TV.

BLAKE BABIES (see under ⇒ HATFIELD, Juliana)

BLAMELESS

Formed: Sheffield, England . . . early 1994 when JASON, MATT and JON bumped into each other after spilling out of the pub at closing time. Almost immediately, the trio became a quartet with the addition of gruff EDDIE VEDDER-esque vocalist, JARED DALEY. While a debut song, 'TOWN CLOWNS' for the 'Rough Trade Singles Club' sparked an A&R stampede for their signatures, the lads honed their craft before opting for 'China' records. After releasing their first single for the label, 'DON'T SAY YOU'RE SORRY', BLAMELESS were spirited away to the States (Boston, exactly!) to cut an album's worth of material. Compared with everyone from The POLICE to PEARL JAM, the quartet previewed their debut long-player with a further couple of singles, both 'MORE THAN I' and a re-issue of 'TOWN CLOWNS' failing to live up to the hype. 'THE SIGNS ARE ALL THERE' (1995), meanwhile, wasn't exactly the career launching pad the band had banked on; although it was re-issued on the back of a belated Top 30 hit, 'BREATHE (A LITTLE DEEPER)', in the Spring of '96, sales figures didn't meet expectations. As usual, long-term development was sacrificed as a young band failed to meet impossibly high standards and of course, the record company was blameless.

JARED DALEY – vocals / **MATT** – guitar / **JASON** – bass **JON** – drums

Album rating: THE SIGNS ARE ALL THERE (*6)

Rough Trade Sing. Club | not iss.

Jan 95. (7") **TOWN CLOWNS. /** | -

China | Atlantic

Mar 95. (7"/c-s/etched-10") *(WOK/+MC/T 2053)* **DON'T SAY YOU'RE SORRY. / SIGNS . . .** | -
(cd-s+=) *(WOKCD 2053)* –
Jul 95. (7"/c-s) *(WOK/+MC 2060)* **MORE THAN I. /** | -
(cd-s+=) *(WOKCD 2060)* –
Oct 95. (7"red) *(WOKMC 2046)* **TOWN CLOWNS. / NEVER BELIEVER** | 56 | -
(cd-s) *(WOKCD 2046)* – ('A'side) / Sympathy / Second hand prima donna / Swing.
(cd-s) *(WOKCDR 2046)* – ('A'side) / Long gone / Are you worried? / Nan.
Oct 95. (cd/c) *(WOL CD/MC 1059)* <82770> **THE SIGNS WERE ALL THERE**
– Town clowns / Don't say you're sorry / Signs . . . / More than I / Digger / Sympathy / What if? / So debonair / Blueprint / News / Made up my mind / Worthless / In leather. *(re-iss. Apr96; same)*
Mar 96. (7") *(WOK 2070)* **BREATHE (A LITTLE DEEPER). /** | 27 | -
(cd-s+=) *(WOKCD 2070)* –
(cd-s) *(WOKCDR 2070)* –
May 96. (7"/c-s) *(WOK/+MC 2077)* **SIGNS . . . /** | 49 | -
(cd-s+=) *(WOKCD 2077)* –

— disbanded after above

BLANKS (see under ⇒ DESTRUCTORS)

BLASTERS

Formed: Downey, Los Angeles, California, USA . . . 1979 by brothers PHIL and DAVE ALVIN alongside JOHN BAZZ and BILL BATEMAN. Taking their name from blues artist Jimmy McCracklin's Blues Blasters, the band traded off the music PHIL and DAVE ALVIN had soaked up in their youth; urban blues, stone country, greasy rockabilly and classic R&B were the base ingredients, the vibrancy of the local punk/hardcore scene the glue binding the whole thing together. Initially erm, blasting out a set comprised largely of cover versions at any establishment that would have them, the band had soon sufficiently honed their skills to undertake a debut album in 1980, 'AMERICAN MUSIC' (released on Ronnie Weiser's 'Rollin Rock' imprint). One of the most sought after artefacts of the early 80's 'cowpunk' scene, this independently released record featured a couple of songs ('MARIE, MARIE' and the title track) which would resurface on their eponymous major label debut for 'Slash/Warners'. Don't let the fact that 'MARIE, MARIE' was covered by SHAKIN' STEVENS put you off, the album (enhanced by saxophonists LEE ALLEN & STEVE BERLIN and pianist GENE TAYLOR) remains a thrilling and satisfying journey through the weatherbeaten terrain of US tradition, as consummate as it is kick-ass. Following a raucous stop-gap live EP, 'OVER THERE: LIVE AT THE VENUE, LONDON' (1982), the band endeavoured to widen their musical horizons with mixed results on 'NON FICTION' (1983). DAVE ALVIN's songwriting (bar John Cougar Mellencamp's 'COLORED LIGHTS) was beginning to outgrow the confines of The BLASTERS's trad-rock format and the subsequent 'HARD LINE' (1985) set would be the last recorded with the original line-up. Following ALVIN's departure, the band limped on for another year before finally splitting early in 1986. This was due to the untimely death (heart attack) of DAVE's replacement, MICHAEL 'HOLLYWOOD FATS' MANN, aged only 32. While PHIL recorded a one-off solo set, 'UNSUNG STORIES', before going back to university, DAVE undertook a more long term solo career, recording a string of albums between 1987 and 1994 as well as scoring the music for a minor budget movie, 'Border Radio'. • **Covers:** REAL ROCK DRIVE (Bill Haley) / BAREFOOT ROCK (Harper-Scott) / I WISH YOU WOULD (Billy Boy Arnold) / CRAZY BABY (Minari-Volz/Wernsman) / NEVER NO MORE BLUES (McWilliams-Rodgers) / BUZZ BUZZ BUZZ (Byrd-Gray) / 21 DAYS IN JAIL (Willie Dixon) / LOVE 24 HOURS A DAY (. . . Jarrett) / SO GLAD (Howlin' Wolf) / ASHAMED OF MYSELF (McCoy-Singleton) / LONE WOLF (Winonie Harris) / etc.

Album rating: AMERICAN MUSIC (*6) / THE BLASTERS (*7) / OVER THERE mini (*5) / NON FICTION (*6) / HARD LINE (*5) / THE BLASTERS COLLECTION compilation (*7)

PHIL ALVIN (b. 6 Mar'53) – guitar, vocals / **DAVE ALVIN** (b.11 Nov'55) – guitar / **JOHN BAZZ** (b. 6 Jul'52) – bass / **BILL BATEMAN** (b. 2 Jul'52, Tyler, Texas) – drums / **GENE TAYLOR** (b. 2 Jul'52, Tyler) – piano / plus **LEE ALLEN + STEVE BERLIN** – saxes

not iss. / Rollin' Rock

1980. (lp) *<none>* **AMERICAN MUSIC** [-] [ ]
– American music / Real rock drive / Barefoot rock / I don't want to / Marie, Marie / I wish you would / She ain't got the beat / Falattop joint / Crazy baby / Never no more blues / Buzz buzz buzz / She's gone away / Barn burning / 21 days in jail / Love 24 hours a day / I feel in love / So glad / Ashamed of myself / Lone wolf. *(UK cd-iss. Oct97 on 'Hightone'; HCD 8086)*

F-Beat / Slash

Jun 82. (lp) *(XXLP 15) <SR 109>* **THE BLASTERS** [ ] [ ] Nov81
– Marie Marie / No other girl / I'm shakin' / Border radio / American music / So long baby goodbye / Hollywood bed / Never no more blues / This is it / Highway 61 / I love you so / Stop the clock.

Jun 82. (7") *(XX 27)* **SO LONG BABY GOODBYE. / AMERICAN MUSIC** [ ] [-]

Nov 82. (7") *(XX 25)* **I'M SHAKIN'. / NO OTHER GIRL** [ ] [-]

WEA / Slash

Jan 83. (lp) *(923735-1) <23735>* **OVER THERE – LIVE AT THE VENUE, LONDON (live)** [ ] [ ] Nov82
– High school confidential / Rock boppin' baby / Keep a knockin' / I don't want to / Go go go / Roll 'em Pete.

Nov 83. (lp) *<23818>* **NON FICTION** [-] [ ]
– Red rose / Barefoot rock / Bus station / One more dance / It must be love / Jubilee train / Long white Cadillac / Fool's paradise / Boomtown / Leaving / Tag along.

— now without STEVE BERLIN who joined LOS LOBOS

Slash / Slash

May 85. (lp/c) *(SLAP/SMAC 5) <25093>* **HARD LINE** [ ] [ ]
– Trouble bound / Just another Sunday / Hey girl / Dark night / Little honey / Samson and Delilah / Colored lights / Help you dream / Common man / Rock and roll will stand.

— split early in 1986 after the death of DAVE's replacement **MICHAEL 'HOLLYWOOD FATS' MANN** – vocals, guitar. DAVE subsequently issued a handful of sets, 'EVERY NIGHT ABOUT THIS TIME' (1987 on 'Demon'), BLUE BLVD. (1991 on 'Hightone'), 'MUSEUM OF HEART' (1993 on 'Hightone'), 'KING OF CALIFORNIA' (1994 on 'Hightone'), 'INTERSTATE CITY' with The GULTY MEN (1996 on 'Hightone'), 'BLACKJACK DAVID; (1998 on 'Hightone') and the 1996 compilation 'ROMEO'S ESCAPE' (on 'Razor & Tie'). He was also a part of The KNITTERS, which was basically the group, X.

– compilations, etc. –

Jan 91. (cd/c) *Slash; <2/4 26451>* **THE BLASTERS COLLECTION** [-] [ ]

PHIL ALVIN

— solo with SUN RA & HIS ARKESTRA plus The DIRTY DOZEN BRASS BAND

Slash / Slash

Sep 86. (lp) *(SLAP 12)* **UNSUNG STORIES** [ ] [ ]
– Somebody stole Gabriel's horn / Next week sometime / The ballad of Smokey Joe / Death in the morning / The old man of the mountain / Dady rollin' stone / Titanic blues / Brother can you spare a dime / Collins' cave / Gangster's blues.

— PHIL took time out of the music business to pursue his maths degree at California State University. In 1994, he reformed The BLASTERS (although credited solo) with **BAZZ**, plus **JAMES INTVELD** – guitar / **JERRY ANGEL** – drums

Hightone / Hightone

Nov 94. (cd/c) *<(HCD/HC 8056)>* **COUNTRY FAIR 2000** [ ] [ ] Oct94
– Country fair / Wreck your V-8 Ford / Blue line / That thing / Turnin' blues into gold / Starlight / Keep in touch / What's the reason I'm not pleasin' / She loves so good / Callin' Corrine / Terror / Oh, doctor / Mr. Satellite man / Low down rhythm / Danny boy's mourning sunset: the old . . .

BLEACH

Formed: Ipswich, England . . . 1989 by songwriting brothers NEIL and NICK SINGLETON together with STEVE SCOTT and frontwoman SALLI CARSON (a former Anglian TV researcher). Released on the 'Way Cool' label in 1990, the 'ECLIPSE' EP (allegedly recorded during an eclipse of the sun!) introduced the BLEACH blueprint of distorted guitars, scattershot drumming and female vocals. Equally at home on the workaday nihilism of 'WIPE IT ALL AWAY' as the moody soundscapes of 'CRIMSON O', CARSON switched easily from in-your-face grrrl to ethereal songstress as conditions demanded. The record won praise from the indie press and BLEACH followed it up with the 'SNAG' EP, another critical favourite that heightened anticipation for a debut album proper. By the release of 'KILLING TIME' in 1992, however, the shoegazing scene – a sound that BLEACH had helped pioneer – was at its peak and BLEACH were ironically overlooked in favour of RIDE, SLOWDIVE, CURVE etc. Now signed to 'Musidisc', the band (complete with the newly shaven-headed CARSON) pushed on with a mini-album, 'HARD', and a second long player, 'FAST', both released in 1993. With US grunge all the rage, even the shoegazing bands had fallen by the wayside and it came as no surprise when BLEACH finally split up later that year.

Album rating: BLEACH SINGLES compilation (*6) / KILLING TIME (*7) / HARD (*4) / FAST (*5)

NEIL SINGLETON (b.14 Sep'65) – guitar / **NICK SINGLETON** (b. 2 Feb'68) – bass / **SALLI CARSON** (b. 6 Oct'66, Yorkshire) – vocals / **STEVE SCOTT** (b.29 Nov'63, Norwich) – drums

Way Cool / Artlos

Oct 90. (12"ep/cd-ep) *(WAY 8/+CD)* **ECLIPSE E.P.** [ ] [ ]
– Decadence / Wipe it away / Crimson 'O'.

Feb 91. (12"ep/cd-ep) **SNAG** [ ] [ ]
– Dipping / etc

Artlos / Artlos

1991. (lp/cd) *(EFA 01826/+CD)* **BLEACH SINGLES** (compilation) [ ] [ ]

Musidisc / Dali-Chameleon

Feb 92. (7") **SHOTGUN. / BONE** [ ] [ ]
(12"+=/cd-s+=) – First and last.

Mar 92. (cd/c/lp) *(10901-2/-4/-1) <61356>* **KILLING TIME** [ ] [ ]
– First / Headless / Push / Paint my face / Friends / Fall / Trip and slide / Shotgun / Surround / Tangle. *(re-iss. Feb93)*

Sep 92. (m-cd/m-lp) *(10964-2/-1)* **HARD** [ ] [ ]
– Fuse / Can / Dead eyes / Hit on me / Baby toes / Fragment.

Jul 93. (cd/lp) *(11032-2/-1)* **FAST** [ ] [ ]

— split some time in '93

BLEED

Formed: London, England . . . 1994 by siblings RITA and NOEL FARRAGHER along with GRAHAM HANKS and ANDREW PARESI (the latter had formerly sessioned for The BLACK VELVET BAND). Forming their own label, the band issued a series of EP's and 7" singles prior to the release of debut album, 'THE GOOD TIMES ARE KILLINMG ME' (1995). One such single, 'IT MAKES MONEY', was the subject of some controversy as the band promoted its anti-porn message by sending an anonymous fax to top shelf magazine, 'Forum'. Despite an unrelentingly grim lyrical slant taking in depression, low self esteem, male violence etc., the album itself was at least partially redeemed by a relatively airy semi-acoustic musical backing and sympathetic PJ HARVEY/KATE BUSH-esque vocals. A sceptical indie press gave the band short thrift, however and a follow-up set, 'ACTION MAN' (1997) surfaced to little interest.

Album rating: THE GOOD TIMES ARE KILLING ME (*5) / ACTION MAN (*5)

RITA FARRAGHER – vocals / **NOEL FARRAGHER** – guitar / **GRAHAM HANKS** – bass / **ANDREW PARESI** – drums

Bleed / not iss.

1992. (12"ep) *(BLEED 1)* **unknown** [ ] [-]

Feb 93. (12"ep) *(BLEED 2)* **LADYKILLER LAUREATE. / SPIT IT OUT / IF I WERE A RICH MAN** [ ] [-]

May 93. (12"ep) *(BLEED 3)* **A TUNE WITH A VIEW. / TAKE BACK THE NIGHT / DON'T YOU JUST LOVE IT?** [ ] [-]

Dec 93. (ltd-7") *(BLEED 4LTD)* **MAD COW DISEASE./** [ ] [-]

Apr 94. (7") *(BLEED 5)* **IT MAKES MONEY. /** [ ] [-]
(cd-s+=) *(BLEED 5CD)* –

Jul 95. (lp/cd) *(BLEED 6/+CD)* **THE GOOD TIMES ARE KILLING ME** -
– No means no / Good times, bad times, mummy and me / Bloodbath / Kiss of death / The art of contradiction / Slaughter / It makes money / God's little angel / Misogynistic baby / Addicted / Cradle.

Jun 97. (cd) *(BLEED 7CD)* **ACTION MAN** -

BLESSED ETHYL

Formed: Malvern, England . . . early '92 by frontwoman SARA DORAN and her partner in crime, guitarist/vocalist DAN BARNES. The pair concocted the idea of forming a band after writing songs together on their second hand Bontempi organ before recruiting the rhythm section of MIKE HARRIS and RICK HUNUBAN. Fired by the suffocating, Tory-infested rural environment of their hometown, BLESSED ETHYL first kicked against the pricks in the summer of '93 with a rabid JOHN ROBB (ex-MEMBRANES)-produced single, 'DOG'. Barking mad but brilliant, the record was backed by a commentary on the infamous Castlemorton rave held in the nearby locale, 'SOMETHING WEIRD', and, like most of their material, sparked on the sexually loaded lyrical jousting between co-wordsmiths, SARA and DAN. Second and third 45's for '2 Damn Loud', 'RAT' and 'TWO MINUTE MIND' (both unleashed in the first half of '94), lived up to their demented bumpkin punk expectations; if you can imagine the REZILLOS picking a fight with PIXIES then you're probably not halfway there. However, just as things looked bright for the band – and ear-shattering for their audience – an 18-month vinyl absence prior to release of a single, 'VERONICA' and accompanying album, 'WELCOME TO THE RODEO' (1995), saw them lose momentum.

Album rating: WELCOME TO THE RODEO (*5)

SARA DORAN – vocals / **DAN BARNES** – vocals, guitar / **MIKE HARRIS** – bass / **RICK HUNUBAN** – drums

2 Damn Loud — not iss.

Aug 93. (7"colrd) *(2DM 03)* **DOG. / SOMETHING WEIRD / CRYSTAL TIPS** -

Jan 94. (7") *(2DM 04)* **RAT. /** -
(cd-s+=) *(2DMCD 04)* –

May 94. (7") *(2DM 05)* **TWO MINUTE MIND. /** -
(12"+=/cd-s+=) *(2DMM T/CD 05)* –

Oct 95. (7") *(2DM 10)* **VERONICA. / FAT STAR** -
(cd-s+=) *(2DMCD 10)* –

Nov 95. (cd/lp) *(2DM CD/LP 12)* **WELCOME TO THE RODEO** -
– Pullman car to Venus / Calico B / Confidential / Another world / Hangin' in the sun / That man / Shooting cowboys / Fat star / Veronica / Rope / Blue movie / Into the sun / Two minute mind.

— disbanded after above

BLIND MELON

Formed: Newport Beach, Los Angeles, California, USA . . . 1989 by West Point, Mississippi born BRAD SMITH and ROGER STEVENS. In the early 90's, they were joined by SHANNON HOON, CHRISTOPHER THORN and a little later, GLEN GRAHAM. After recording a widely circulated demo, the band were eventually picked up by 'Capitol'. While awaiting release of their self-titled debut, SHANNON (cousin of AXL ROSE) guested on the GUNS N' ROSES set, 'Use Your Illusion'. With MTV heralding their excellent 'NO RAIN' track, their debut album finally shot into the US Top 3 in 1993. A laid back 70's/GRATEFUL DEAD influenced affair, alternately jangly and funky, HOON's vocals weren't too dissimilar to AXL's. Following a disapointing second set, 'SOUP' (1995), HOON died of a drug overdose on the 21st October '95.

Album rating: BLIND MELON (*6) / SOUP (*5)

SHANNON HOON (b.RICHARD SHANNON HOON, 26 Sep'67, Lafayette, Indiana) – vocals / **ROGER STEVENS** (b.31 Oct'70, West Point, Mis.) – guitar / **CHRISTOPHER THORN** (b.16 Dec'68, Dover, Pensylvania) – guitar / **BRAD SMITH** (b.29 Sep'68, West Point) – bass / **GLEN GRAHAM** (b. 5 Dec'68, Columbus, Miss.) – drums

Capitol — Capitol

Jun 93. (12"pic-d-ep/12"ep/cd-ep) *(12P/12/CD CL 687)* **TONES OF HOME / NO RAIN (live). / DRIVE (live) / SOAK THE SIN (live)** 62 -

Aug 93. (cd/c) *(CD/TC EST 2188)* *<96585>* **BLIND MELON** 53 3
– Soak the sin / Tones of home / I wonder / Paper scratcher / Dear ol' dad / Change / No rain / Deserted / Sleepy house / Holyman / Seed to a tree / Drive / Time. *(re-dist.Jul94 w/ free cd, hit UK 53)*

Aug 93. (c-s) *<44939>* **NO RAIN / NO RAIN (live) / SOAK THE SIN** - 20

Dec 93. (c-s/7"yellow) *(TC+/CL 699)* **NO RAIN. / NO BIDNESS (live)** 17 -
(12"+=/cd-s+=) *(12/CD CL 699)* – I wonder.
(12"pic-d/pic-cd-s) *(12P/CDP CL 699)* – ('A'live) / Soak the sin / Paper scratcher / Deserted.

Jun 94. (c-s/7"green) *(TC+/CL 717)* **CHANGE. / PAPER SCRATCHER (acoustic)** 35
(12"pic-d/pic-cd-s) *(12/CDS CL 717)* – ('A'side) / No rain (live) / Candy says (live) / Time (live).

Jul 95. (cd-s) *(CDCL 755)* **GALAXIE / WILT / CAR SEAT (GOD'S PRESENTS)** 37
(12"+=) *(12CL 755)* – 2 x 4.
(cd-s) *(CDCLS 755)* – (first 2 tracks) / 2 x 4 / Change.

Aug 95. (cd/c) *(CD/TC EST 2261)* *<28732>* **SOUP** 48 28
– Galaxie / 2 x 4 / Vernie / Skinned / Toes across the floor / Walk / Dumptruck / Car seat (God's presents) / Wilt / The duke / St.Andrew's fall / New life / Mouthful of cavities / Lemonade.

— On October 21st, '95, frontman SHANNON HOON died of drug overdose.

– compilations, etc. –

Feb 97. (cd) *Capitol; (CDEST 2291)* **NICO**
– Pusher / Hell / Soup / No rain / Soul one / John Sinclair / All that I need / Glitch / Life ain't so shitty / Swallowed / Oull / St. Andrew's hall / Letters from a porcupine.

BLINK

Formed: Dublin, Ireland . . . early 90's by DERMOT, ROBBIE, BRIAN and BARRY. Post-baggy musical chameleons, BLINK operate in the DIY spirit of punk with the added help of modern day dance technology. Signed to 'Parlophone', the band debuted with the 'GOING TO NEPAL' in late '93, following it up with 'IT'S NOT MY FAULT' in Spring '94. Produced by indie guru, Gil Norton, and ambient veteran STEVE HILLAGE, 'A MAP OF THE UNIVERSE' (1994) was a debut album which managed to push beyond the realms of bog standard indie-dance fare, pitting DERMOT's JAMES ATKIN (EMF)-style vocals and quirky lyrics against an alternately hypnotic, funky and propulsive musical backdrop. Strangely, even the dramatic synth-string flourish of 'CELLO' failed to crack the charts and BLINK duly called it a day in the mid-90's.

DERMOT – vocals / **ROBBIE** – keyboards / **BRIAN** – bass / **BARRY** – drums

Parlophone — Parlophone

Oct 93. (c-s) **GOING TO NEPAL /** -
(cd-s+=) –

Apr 94. (c-s/7") *(TC+/R 6376)* **IT'S NOT MY FAULT. / ED'S GOT A NEW CAR / SHINY JIM**
(12"+=/cd-s+=) *(12R/CDR 6376)* – Five new friends.

Jul 94. (c-s/7") *(TC+/R 6385)* **HAPPY DAY. / ('A'mix)**
(cd-s+=) *(CDR 6385)* – Everything comes, everything goes / Hank.

Aug 94. (cd/c) *(<CD/TC PCS 7369>)* **A MAP OF THE UNIVERSE**
– It's not my fault / Cello / Happy day / Everything comes everything goes / Show (be precious) / Fundamentally loveable creature / Love me / The greatest trick / Going to Nepal / There's something wrong with Norman's mom / Christmas 22 / Is God really groovy? / Separation.

Oct 94. (c-s) *(TCR 6393)* **CELLO / WONDERFUL SCENE**
(cd-s+=) *(CDRS 6393)* – ('A'ambient mix) / ('A'-Millwall brick mix).
(cd-s) *(CDR 6393)* – ('A'side) / Fundamentally loveable creature (live) / Love me (live) / ('A'live).

Grilled Cheese — not iss.

May 95. (cd) *(GRL 001)* **CHESHIRE CAT** -

Mutant Sound — Mutant Sound

Feb 94. (cd) *(80027)* **BLINK**
– Planet made of rain / Would you kill for love? / Cello / Dead little bird / Luckiest man alive / This one is wild / Girl with the backward skin / Sky land scraper paper fly / Raven / House that illuminates your thoughts / Baby you broke my heart but you . . . / I'm not sorry now / Fundamentally loveable creature.

BLITZ

Formed: New Mills, Derbyshire, England . . . 1978 by CARL, NIDGE, MACKIE and CHARLIE. One of the main players in the second generation "oi" movement, BLITZ made their belated debut (after making an early appearance on the V/A compilation, 'Live At The Roxy') in early '82 with the EP, 'ALL OUT ATTACK'. Anarcho-punk yob anthem, 'SOMEONE'S GONNA DIE TONIGHT', introduced their vicious sound and paved the way for a further couple of indie chartbusters, 'NEVER SURRENDER' and 'WARRIORS'. Incredibly, the band scored a bonafide Top 30 album entry with 'VOICE OF A GENERATION', an ambitiously titled collection that scraped the barrel of punk's aftermath. Thankfully, it was their only chart appearance as the follow-up, 'SECOND EMPIRE JUSTICE' (1983), failed to ignite the same spark as its predecessor. MACKIE and MILLER subsequently formed the short-lived ROSE OF VICTORY, although BLITZ were on the attack once more with a final directionless 45, 'SOLAR'. The turn of the decade saw a brief reformation, an album, 'THE KILLING DREAM' (1990), not exactly hitting any new targets.

Album rating: THE COMPLETE BLITZ SINGLES COLLECTION compilation (*6)

CARL FISHER – vocals / **NIDGE MILLER** – guitar / **MACKIE** (b. NEIL McLENNAN) – bass / **CHARLIE HOWE** – drums

No Future — not iss.

Jan 82. (7"ep) *(OI 1)* **ALL OUT ATTACK** -
– Someone's gonna die / Attack / Fight to live / Revolutions 45.

Mar 82. (7") *(OI 6)* **NEVER SURRENDER. / RAZOR IN THE NIGHT** -

Jul 82. (7") *(OI 16)* **WARRIORS. / YOUTH** -

Oct 82. (lp) *(PUNK 1)* **VOICE OF A GENERATION** 27 -
– We are the boys / Time bomb / Voice of a generation / Bleed / I don't need you / T.O. / Propaganda / Criminal damage / Vicious / Warriors / Nation on fire / Your revolution / Scream / 4.Q. / Escape / Moscow / Closedown. *(cd-iss. Jul89 + May92 on 'Cherry Red'+=; CDPUNK 1)* – Someone's gonna die / Attack / Fight to live / 45 revolutions / Never surrender.

— **TIM HARRIS** – guitar, keyboards repl. NIDGE (briefly)

Future — not iss.

Jan 83. (7") *(FS 1)* **NEW AGE. / FATIGUE** -
(12"+=) *(FSL 1)* – Bleed (remix).

Apr 83. (7") *(FS 3)* **TELECOMMUNICATION. / TELETRON** [ ] [-]
(12"+=) *(12FS 3)* –

May 83. (lp) *(FL-1)* **SECOND EMPIRE JUSTICE** [ ] [-]
– Flowers & fire / Underground / Acolyte / Into the daylight / Telecommunication / White man / For you / Skin / H.M.K. Grey.

— were finally blitzed themselves, when MILLER and MACKIE formed ROSE OF VICTORY. Released one single in July '83 'OVERDRIVE. / SUFFRAGETTE CITY' for 'No Future'; *(OI 24)*.

Oct 83. (7") *(FS 6)* **SOLAR. / HUSK** [ ] [-]
(12") *(12FS 6)* – ('A'extended remix) / ('B'dance mix).

— re-formed in the late 80's, although below release was their last

Skunx | not iss.

Mar 90. (lp) *(SKUNKLP 002)* **THE KILLING DREAM** [ ] [-]
– The killing dream / Overdrive / Intermission 1 / Intermission 2 / Thrown away / Lady Anne / Fade / All you want / Empire fall / Those days / Final hour / Don't care / Walkaway. *(cd-iss. Nov97 on 'Step 1' +=; STEPCD 111)* – RARE INTERVIEWS

– compilations, etc. –

Apr 88. (lp) *Link; (LINKLP 029)* **ALL OUT ATTACK** [ ] [-]
– All out attack / 4.Q. / Time bomb / Criminal damage / Razor in the night / Attack / Escape / Never surrender / Nation on fire / Warriors / Someone's gonna die / 45 revolutions / Fight to live / Youth / I don't need you / Propaganda / Closedown. *(re-iss. May97 on 'Get Back'; GET 14)*

Aug 92. (cd) *Dojo; (DOJOCD 93)* **BLITZED AND ALL OUT ATTACK** [ ] [-]

Mar 93. (cd) *Dojo; (DOJOCD 123)* **THE BEST OF BLITZ** [ ] [-]
(re-iss. Jun98 as 'THE VERY BEST OF BLITZ' on 'Anagram'; CDPUNK 104)

Dec 93. (cd) *Anagram; (CDPUNK 25)* **THE COMPLETE BLITZ SINGLES COLLECTION** [ ] [-]

Nov 94. (12"ep) *Retch; (RR 12003)* **ALL OUT ATTACK EP** [ ] [-]

BLONDE REDHEAD

Formed: based – New York, USA ... 1993 by Japanese-born KAZU MAKINO, who met Italian, jazz-loving, twin brothers AMEDEO and SIMONE PACE. Described as the re-birth of no-wave, they were snapped up by SONIC YOUTH's STEVE SHELLEY for his 'Smells Like' imprint. An eponymous set was subsequently followed up by 1995's 'LA MIA VITA VIOLENTA', the latter taking the sound of SONIC YOUTH and lyrical themes of Catholic/Communist guilt influencd by the homosexual novelist/filmmaker, Pier Paolo Pasolini. A few years later, BLONDE REDHEAD made a shift to 'Touch & Go', the results being the third DIY-sounding set, 'FAKE CAN BE JUST AS GOOD' (1997). The album, 'IN AN EXPRESSION OF THE INEXPRESSIBLE' (co-produced by FUGAZI's GUY PICCIOTTO with JOHN GOODMANSON), was the odd trio's coming of age, a noisy, art-core masterpiece seemingly custom built for a companion piece movie.

Album rating: IN AN EXPRESSION OF THE INEXPRESSIBLE (*7)

KAZU MAKINO – vocals, guitar / **AMEDEO PACE** – vocals, guitars / **SIMONE PACE** – drums, keyboards, programming

Smells Like | Smells Like

Dec 94. (7") <*(SLR 007)*> **VAGUE. /** [ ] [ ] 1995
(UK-iss.Apr97; same as US)

Jan 95. (cd) <*(SLR 011)*> **BLONDE REDHEAD** [ ] [ ] Jan95
– I don't want u / Sciura sciura / Astro boy / Without feathers / Snippet / Mama Etta / Swing pool / Girl boy. *(UK-iss.Sep95; same as US)*

Jun 95. (7") <*(SLR 014)*> **10 FEET HIGH. /** [ ] [ ] 1995
(UK-iss.Apr97; same as US)

Sep 95. (cd) <*SLR 018*> **LA MIA VITA VIOLENTA** [-] [ ]
– (I am taking out my Eurotrash) I ... Violent life / UFO / I am there while you choke on me / Harmony / Down under / Bean / Young Neil / 10 feet high / Jewel.

— added guest **VERN** – bass (of UNWOUND)

Touch & Go | Touch & Go

Mar 97. (7") <*(TG 168)*> **SYMPHONY OF TREBLE. / KASUALITY** [ ] [ ]

Apr 97. (lp/cd) <*(TG 169/+CD)*> **FAKE CAN BE JUST AS GOOD** [ ] [ ]
– Kazuality / Symphony of treble / Water / Ego maniac kid / Bipolar / Pier Paolo / Oh James / Futurism vs. passeism.

Mar 98. (7") *(TG 188)* **SLOGAN. /** [ ] [ ]

Sep 98. (lp/cd) <*(TG 196/+CD)*> **IN AN EXPRESSION OF THE INEXPRESSIBLE** [ ] [ ]
– Luv machine / 10 / Distilled / Missle++ / Futurism vs. passeism / Speed x distance = time / In an expression of the inexpressible / Suimasen / Led Zep / This is for me and I know everyone ... / Justin joyous.

BLOOD ON THE SADDLE

Formed: Los Angeles, California, USA ... Spring '83 by GREG DAVIS, RON BOTELHO and HERMANN SENAC. With the addition of ex-BANGLES bassist turned vocalist ANNETTE ZILINKAS, this critically revered cowpunk act completed their eponymous debut in 1984. It would be two years until their follow-up, 'POISON LOVE', although its lack of promotion was a contributing factor to the band's increasing disillusionment. Despite a third effort, 'FRESH BLOOD' (1987) on the influential American imprint 'S.S.T.', consistently poor sales led to these saddle-sore veterans calling it a day.

Album rating: BLOOD ON THE SADDLE (*6) / POISON LOVE (*5) / FRESH BLOOD (*5)

GREG DAVIS – vocals, guitar, banjo / **ANNETTE ZILINSKAS** – vocals (ex-BANGLES) / **RON BOTELHO** – bass / **HERMANN SENAC** – drums

not iss. | New Alliance

Apr 84. (lp) <*NAR 15*> **BLOOD ON THE SADDLE** [-] [ ]

Gates Of Heaven | Chameleon

Apr 86. (lp) *(PETE 1)* <*CHLP 8601*> **POISON LOVE** [ ] [ ]
– One step away / Police siren / Steal you away / Poison love / I thought I heard some thunder / Johnny's at the fair / A bed of roses / Colt 45 / Promise your heart to me / Down and out / In the pines / A mother's love / Abilene.

New Rose | S.S.T.

1988. (lp/cd) *(ROSE 126/+CD)* <*SST 116*> **FRESH BLOOD** [ ] [ ] 1987
– Born with a hole in my pocket / Help wanted / Always there, never here / Rawhide / Endless highway / Burning sun / Black river / Baptist church blues (1 & 2) / Folsom prison / One step away / In the pines / Police siren / Steal you away / Poison love / A bed of roses / Mother's love / Abilene.

— split later in the year but reformed after 7 year itch

Kill Rock Stars | Kill Rock Stars

Sep 94. (7"ep) *(KRS 235)* **4 SONG 7"** [ ] [ ]
– Please quit calling me from jail / I'm a poor lonesome cowboy / I wanna ramble and roam / Beer drinking man.

BLOOD UNCLES (see under ⇒ EXPLOITED)

BLOW UP

Formed: Brighton, England ... 1986 by NICK ROUGHLEY, who had just departed from 14 ICED BEARS. Completing the line-up with ALAN STIRNER, AZIZ HASHMIX (aye, right!) and CHRIS WINDOW, the jangly, melodic quartet entered the indie scene with two 1987 'Creation' singles, 'GOOD FOR ME' and 'POOL VALLEY'. Becoming more popular in the Netherlands, they released a compilation of these tracks, 'ROLLERCOASTER', having moved to 'Ediesta' then 'Cherry Red' in the process. Two singles, 'FOREVER HOLIDAY' and 'OWN WORLD WAITING', preceded their first album proper, 'IN WATERMELON SUGAR', a somewhat disappointing collection that was more sour than sweet.

Album rating: IN WATERMELON SUGAR (*4) / AMAZON EYEGASM (*4)

NICK ROUGHLEY – vocals (ex-14 ICED BEARS) / **ALAN STIRNER** – guitar / **AZIZ HASHMIX** – bass / **CHRIS WINDOW** – drums

Creation | not iss.

Jun 87. (7") *(CRE 045)* **GOOD FOR ME. / TO YOU** [ ] [-]
(12") *(CRE 045T)* – ('A'side) / 125 / I won't hurt you.

Nov 87. (12") *(CRE 049T)* **POOL VALLEY. / WHEN YOU SMILE / WISH** [ ] [-]

Megadisc | not iss.

Jul 88. (lp) *(MD 7918)* **ROLLERCOASTER** (compilation) [-] [-] Dutch

Ediesta | not iss.

Oct 88. (12") *(CALC 066T)* **FOREVER HOLIDAY. / GOOD FOR NOTHING / TAKE ME AS I WAS** [ ] [-]

— **WILL TAYLOR** (b.23 Aug'68) – bass (ex-14 ICED BEARS) repl. AZIZ

Cherry Red | not iss.

Oct 89. (7") *(CHERRY 103)* **FOREVER HOLIDAY. / HONKER'S CHA-CHA** [ ] [-]
(12"+=) *(12CHERRY 103)* – Lovescene.

Feb 90. (7") *(CHERRY 104)* **OWN WORLD WAITING. / SLIP INTO SOMETHING** [ ] [-]
(12"+=) *(12CHERRY 104)* – Little fool 52 / Gut rot.

Feb 90. (cd/c/lp) *(CDBRED/BREDMC/BRED 85)* **IN WATERMELON SUGAR** [ ] [-]
– Own world waiting / Heaven tonight / Sweet skin / Beauty lies / Forever holiday / Baby superstar / What is in your mind? / I / Todd / Wish. *(cd+=)* – Honker's cha cha / Lovescene / Slip into something / Little fool 52.

Mar 91. (cd/lp) *(CD+/BRED 91)* **AMAZON EYEGASM** [ ] [-]
– Somersault / Fly me across the ocean / World / Thorn of crowns / Caterpillar song / Just sin / She fades away / Different sounding sighs / Across me today.

— disintegrated after above

BLUE AEROPLANES

Formed: Bristol, England ... 1984 out of The ART OBJECTS and EXPLODING SEAGULLS by GERARD LANGLEY, who has subsequently piloted The BLUE AEROPLANES with an extended, revolving cast of musicians over the course of the last decade. While NICK JACOBS, GERARD's brother, JOHN and dancer WOJTEK DMOCHOWSKI remained constants over the course of the band's career, others such as ANGELO BRUSCHINI came and went according to circumstance. In essence LANGLEY's concept, The BLUE AEROPLANES existed initially as a vehicle for combining GERARD's manic beat poetry with experimental, often psychedelic rock/folk. Following a debut album, 'BOP ART' (1984) on the 'Abstract' label, the band signed with 'Fire', where they developed their sound over further albums, 'TOLERANCE' (1986) and 'SPITTING OUT MIRACLES' (1897). With a serrated guitar sound embellished by backing tapes, banjos, mandolin etc., The BLUE AEROPLANES' were nothing if not original although there were discernible BYRDS/FELT traces in their flight path. The late '88 compilation set, 'FRIENDLOVERPLANE', signalled the end of their tenure with 'Fire' and, following an incendiary Christmas gig at Camden's Electric Ballroom, the band were snapped up by 'Ensign'. As the band toured the UK as support to R.E.M. (MICHAEL STIPE guested on that year's album) and grazed the Top 75 with the near radio-friendly rumblings

The publishers apologise for an error in the production of The Great Alternative & Indie Discography that has resulted in the omission of the entry for Blondie which should have appeared on pages 84 and 85. The text for the entry has been reproduced below. We hope that this oversight does not spoil your enjoyment of the book.

BLONDIE

Formed: New York City, New York, USA . . . August 1974 by former Playboy bunny girl, DEBBIE HARRY and boyfriend CHRIS STEIN. Other original members excluding female backing singers were sticksman, BILLY O'CONNOR (soon replaced by CLEM BURKE), bassist FRED SMITH (later of TELEVISION) and guitarist IVAN KRAL (later of PATTI SMITH GROUP). After line-up changes which saw the latter two replaced by GARY VALENTINE and JIMMY DESTRI respectively, the group soon found themselves supporting the likes of punk legend, IGGY POP. Subsequently hooking up with veteran producer, Richard Gottehrer, the group released their debut single, 'X-OFFENDER', on his 'Private Stock' label in late '76. This was followed up with a second track, 'IN THE FLESH', while the eponymous debut hit the shelves later that Spring. Trawling tacky 60's girly pop and sprucing it up with a healthy dose of punk muscle and attitude, BLONDIE laid the foundations for their swoonsomely infectious late 70's/early 80's hits. With HARRY as the peroxide Marilyn Monroe of new wave, BLONDIE almost immediately caught the eye of the UK scene, where a follow-up album, 'PLASTIC LETTERS', made the Top 10 in Spring '78. By this point BLONDIE had signed to 'Chrysalis' (who had reputedly bought the contract out for $500,000 in August of the previous year) and had replaced VALENTINE with FRANK INFANTE. A cover of Randy & The Rainbows 60's nugget, 'DENISE' (aka 'DENIS') almost topped the British charts, while another single pulled from the album, '(I'M ALWAYS TOUCHED BY YOUR) PRESENCE DEAR', made the Top 10. With the subsequent recruitment of bassist NIGEL HARRISON, INFANTE switched to rhythm guitar, the music taking on a whole new dimension with the seminal 'PARALLEL LINES' (1978). Produced by legendary pop picker, MIKE CHAPMAN, the album spawned a UK Top 5 in 'HANGING ON THE TELEPHONE', plus two No.1's with 'SUNDAY GIRL' and 'HEART OF GLASS'. The latter track's throbbing disco feel was further developed on fourth album, 'EAT TO THE BEAT', a set which featured yet another UK chart topper in the moody dancefloor classic, 'ATOMIC' (later famous for providing the aural backdrop to the disco scene in 'Trainspotting'). BLONDIE even teamed up with electro disco guru, GEORGIO MORODER, for 'CALL ME' (recorded for the soundtrack to 'American Gigolo'), the band's second transatlantic No.1. They repeated this feat with 'THE TIDE IS HIGH', a wonderfully dreamy cover of a track originally cut by reggae outfit, The PARAGONS, while also having a bash at hip hop with 'RAPTURE', their fourth US No.1. Both tracks were included on 1980's 'AUTOAMERICAN', an album which suggested BLONDIE were beginning to lose their musical curls. Although 'THE HUNTER' (1982) spawned a further British No.1 in 'ISLAND OF LOST SOULS', the album met with a less than rapturous reception, likewise their final tour. The band finally split in summer '82, STEIN forming his own 'Chrysalis'-backed label, 'Animal', before falling ill the following year. This put HARRY's solo career (begun rather noneventfully with 1981's BERNARD EDWARDS / NILE RODGERS collaborative set, 'KOO KOO') temporarily on the back burner, the singer re-emerging in late '86 with the UK Top 10, 'FRENCH KISSIN' IN THE U.S.A.'. The accompanying album, 'ROCKBIRD' made the Top 40 although 1989's 'DEF, DUMB AND BLONDE' was more successful, its shiny, poppy single 'I WANT THAT MAN' making the UK Top 20. If nothing else, she proved herself an adaptable stylist although much more interesting was a tongue in cheek duet with IGGY POP in 1990, 'WELL, DID YOU EVAH!'. Throughout her career, HARRY had also made the occasional venture into celluloid (see below). • **Songwriters:** Most written by STEIN-HARRY except; HANGING ON THE TELEPHONE (Jack Lee; Nerves) / RING OF FIRE (Johnny Cash) / HEROES (David Bowie). • **Trivia:** DEBBIE HARRY filmography:- UNION CITY (1979) / ROADIE (1980) / VIDEODROME (1982) / HAIRSPRAY (1982) / Broadway play 'TEANECK TANZI: THE VENUS FLYTRAP' (1983), which bombed after one night. She also appeared on 'The Muppet Show' circa 1980.

Album rating: BLONDIE (*6) / PLASTIC LETTERS (*7) / PARALLEL LINES (*8) / EAT TO THE BEAT (*6) / AUTOAMERICAN (*5) / THE BEST OF BLONDIE compilation (*9) / THE HUNTER (*4) / THE COMPLETE PICTURE – THE VERY BEST OF DEBORAH HARRY & BLONDIE compilation (*9) / BLONDE AND BEYOND compilation (*5) / Debbie Harry: KOOKOO (*5) / ROCKBIRD (*6) / DEF, DUMB & BLONDE (*5) / DEBRAVATION (*4)

DEBBIE HARRY (b. DEBORAH, 1 Jul'45, Miami, Florida) – vocals (ex-WIND IN THE WILLOWS) / **CHRIS STEIN** (b. 5 Jan'50, Brooklyn, New York) – guitar / **JIMMY DESTRI** (b.13 Apr'54) – keyboards (ex-KNICKERS) / **GARY VALENTINE** – bass / **CLEM BURKE** (b.CLEMENT, 24 Nov'55) – drums (ex-SWEET REVENGE)

Private Stock | Private Stock

Dec 76. (7") *<PVT 90>* **X OFFENDER. / IN THE SUN** [–] [ ]
Dec 76. (lp) *<PS 2023>* **BLONDIE** [–] [ ]
– X offender / Little girl lies / In the flesh / Look good in blue / In the sun / A shark in jet's clothing / Man overboard / Rip her to shreds / Rifle range / Kung Fu girls / The attack of the giant ants. *<re-iss. Feb77; PVLP 1017> (UK-iss.Dec77 on 'Chrysalis'; CHR 1165)* – (hit UK No.75 in Mar79) *(re-iss. Oct82 on 'Hallmark' lp/c; SHM/HSC 3119) (re-iss. Apr85 on 'M.F.P.' lp/c; MFP 41-5696-1/-4) (cd-iss. Sep94 on 'Chrysalis'; CDCHR 6081)*
Feb 77. (7") *<PVT 105>* **IN THE FLESH. / MAN OVERBOARD** [–] [ ]
May 77. (7") *(PVT 105)* **IN THE FLESH. / X OFFENDER** [ ] [–]

Chrysalis | Chrysalis

Nov 77. (7"m/12"m) *<CHS 2180/+12)* **RIP HER TO SHREDS. / IN THE FLESH / X OFFENDER** [ ] [–]
(re-iss. 12"m Dec81; same)

—— (Oct'77) **FRANK INFANTE** – bass (ex-WORLD WAR III) repl. VALENTINE

Feb 78. (7"m/12"m) *<(CHS 2180/+12)>* **DENIS. / CONTACT IN RED SQUARE / KUNG FU GIRLS** [2] [ ]
(re-iss. 12"white Dec81; same)
Feb 78. (lp/c) *<(CHR/ZCHR 1166)>* **PLASTIC LETTERS** [10] [72] Feb78
– Fan mail / Denis / Bermuda Triangle blues (Flight 45) / Youth nabbed as sniper / Contact in Red Square / (I'm always touched by your) Presence, dear / I'm on E / I didn't have the nerve to say no / Love at the pier / No imagination / Kidnapper / Detroit 442 / Cautious lip. *(cd-iss. Sep94; CDCHR 6085)*
Apr 78. (7"m/12"m) *<(CHS/+12 2217)>* **(I'M ALWAYS TOUCHED BY YOUR) PRESENCE, DEAR. / POET'S PROBLEM / DETROIT 442** [10] [ ]
(re-iss. Dec81; same)

—— (Nov77 on recording of 2nd lp) added **NIGEL HARRISON** – bass (b.24 Apr'51, Stockport, England) now sextet with **INFANTE** – now on rhythm guitar

Aug 78. (7"yellow) *<(CHS 2204)>* **PICTURE THIS. / FADE AWAY (AND RADIATE)** [12] [ ]
Sep 78. (7") *<2251>* **I'M GONNA LOVE YOU TOO. / JUST GO AWAY** [–] [ ]
Sep 78. (lp/c) *<(CHR/ZCHR 1192)>* **PARALLEL LINES** [1] [6]
– Fade away (and radiate) / Hanging on the telephone / One way or another / Picture this / Pretty baby / I know but I don't know / 11:59 / Will anything happen / Sunday girl / Heart of glass / I'm gonna love you too / Just go away. *(re-iss. Nov83 on 'Fame' lp/c; FA/TCFA 3089-1/-4) (re-iss. Jul88 lp/c/cd; CDL/ZCDL/CCD 1192) (re-iss. Dec92 on 'Fame' cd/c; CD/TC FA 3282) (re-iss. Jul94 cd/c; CCD/ZCDL 1192)*
Nov 78. (7") *(CHS 2266)* **HANGING ON THE TELEPHONE. / WILL ANYTHING HAPPEN** [5] [–]
Nov 78. (7") *<CHS 2266>* **HANGING ON THE TELEPHONE / FADE AWAY AND RADIATE** [–] [ ]
Jan 79. (7") *(CHS 2275)* **HEART OF GLASS. / RIFLE RANGE** [1] [–]
(12"+=) – ('A'instrumental). *(re-iss. 12" Dec81; same)*
Feb 79. (7") *<CHS 2275>* **HEART OF GLASS. / 11:59** [–] [1]
May 79. (7") *(CHS 2320)* **SUNDAY GIRL. / I KNOW BUT I DON'T KNOW** [1] [–]
(12"+=) *(CHS/+12 2320)* – ('A' French version).
(re-iss. 12"clear Dec81; same)
May 79. (7") *<CHS 2336>* **ONE WAY OR ANOTHER. / JUST GO AWAY** [–] [24]
Sep 79. (7") *(CHS 2350)* **DREAMING. / SOUND ASLEEP** [2] [–]
Sep 79. (7") *<CHS 2379>* **DREAMING. / LIVING IN THE REAL WORLD** [–] [27]
Oct 79. (lp/c) *<(CHR/ZCHR 1225)>* **EAT TO THE BEAT** [1] [17]
– Dreaming / The hardest part / Union city blue / Shayla / Eat to the beat / Accidents never happen / Die young stay pretty Slow motion / / Atomic / Sound-a-sleep / Victor / Living in the real world. *(cd-iss. Jun87; CPCD 1225) (cd-iss. Nov92; CDCHR 1225)*
Nov 79. (7") *(CHS 2400)* **UNION CITY BLUE. / LIVING IN THE REAL WORLD** [13] [ ]
Jan 80. (7") *<CHS 2408>* **THE HARDEST PART. / SOUND-A-SLEEP** [–] [84]
Feb 80. (7") *<(CHS 2410)>* **ATOMIC. / DIE YOUNG STAY PRETTY** [1] [39] May80
(12"+=) *(CHS12 2410)* – Heroes. *(re-iss. 12" Dec81; same)*
Apr 80. (7") *<(CHS 2414)>* **CALL ME. / ('A'instrumental)** [1] [1] Feb80
(12"+=) *(CHS12 2414)* – ('A'-Spanish version).
Oct 80. (7") *<(CHS 2465)>* **THE TIDE IS HIGH. / SUZIE AND JEFFREY** [1] [1] Nov80
Nov 80. (lp/c) *<(CDL/ZCDL 1290)>* **AUTOAMERICAN** [3] [7]
– Europa / Live it up / Here's looking at you / The tide is high / Angels on the balcony / Go through it / Do the dark / Rapture / Faces / Do the dark / T-Birds / Walk like me / Follow me. *(cd-iss. Sep94; CDCHR 6084)*
Jan 81. (7") *<(CHS 2485)>* **RAPTURE. / WALK LIKE ME** [5] [1]
(12") *(CHS12 2485)* – ('A'side) / Live it up.
Oct 81. (lp/c) *(CDLTV/ZCLTV 1) <1371>* **THE BEST OF BLONDIE** (compilation) [4] [30]
– Denis / The tide is high / In the flesh / Sunday girl / (I'm always touched by your) Presence dear / Dreaming / Hanging on the telephone / Rapture / Picture this / Union city blue / Call me / Atomic / Rip her to shreds / Heart of glass. *(cd iss. Jan88; CCD 1371)*
Apr 82. (7"/7"pic-d) *<(CHS/+P 2608)>* **ISLAND OF LOST SOULS. / DRAGONFLY** [1] [37] May82
May 82. (lp/c/pic-lp) *<(CDL/ZCDL/PCDL 1384)>* **THE HUNTER** [9] [33]
– Orchid club / Island of lost souls / Dragonfly / For your eyes only / The beast / War child / Little Caesar / Danceaway / (Can I) Find the right words (to say) / English boys / The hunter gets captured by the game. *(cd-iss. Sep94; CDCHR 6083)*
Jul 82. (7"/7"pic-d/12") *<(CHS/+P/12 2624)>* **WAR CHILD. / LITTLE CAESAR** [39] [ ]

—— (Aug'82) STEIN formed own 'Animal' label through 'Chrysalis'. CLEM BURKE joins EURYTHMICS and later RAMONES. He also teams up with HARRISON to form CHEQUERED PAST. A solo album HEART ON THE WALL was released by JIMMY DESTRI in 1982 and featured most of BLONDIE. DEBBIE (DEBORAH). HARRY continued solo career.

– compilations, others, etc. –

on 'Chrysalis' unless mentioned otherwise

Dec 82. (d-c) *(2CDP 101)* **EAT TO THE BEAT / AUTOAMERICAN** [ ] [-]
Feb 87. (7") *Old Gold; (OG 9672)* **DENIS. / PICTURE THIS** [ ] [-]
Feb 87. (7") *Old Gold; (OG 9674)* **SUNDAY GIRL. / HANGING ON THE TELEPHONE** [ ] [-]
Feb 87. (7") *Old Gold; (OG 9676)* **CALL ME. / UNION CITY BLUE** [ ] [-]
Feb 87. (7") *Old Gold; (OG 9678)* **HEART OF GLASS. / THE TIDE IS HIGH** [ ] [-]
Feb 87. (7") *Old Gold; (OG 9680)* **DREAMING. / ATOMIC** [ ] [-]
Nov 88. (7") *(CHS 3328)* **DENIS (remix). / RAPTURE (Teddy Riley remix)** [50] [-]
(12"+=/12"pic-d+=/cd-s+=) *(CHS/+12/12P/CD 3328)* – Heart of glass (remix) / Atomic (remix).
Dec 88. (lp/c/cd) *(CJB/ZCJB/CDJB 2)* **ONCE MORE INTO THE BLEACH (GREATEST HITS)** [50] [-]
– Denis / Heart of glass / Call me / Rapture / Rapture (bonus beats) / The tide is high / The jam was moving (DEBBIE HARRY) / In love with love (DEBBIE HARRY) / Rush rush (DEBBIE HARRY) / French kissin' in the U.S.A. (DEBBIE HARRY) / Feel the spin (DEBBIE HARRY) / Backfired (DEBBIE HARRY) / Sunday girl (French version).
Dec 88. (lp/c) *Star; (84026-1/-4)* **BLONDIE HIT COLLECTION** [ ] [-]
Feb 89. (7") *(CHS 3342)* **CALL ME. / CALL ME (version)** [61] [-]
(12"+=/cd-s+=) *(CHS 12/CD 3342)* – Backfired (DEBBIE HARRY).
Mar 91. (cd/c/d-lp) *(CCD/ZCHR/CHR 1817)* **THE COMPLETE PICTURE – THE VERY BEST OF DEBORAH HARRY & BLONDIE** [3] [ ]
– Heart of glass / I want that man / Call me / Sunday girl / French kissin' in the USA / Denis / Rapture / Brite side / (I'm always touched by your) Presence dear / Well, did you evah! / The tide is high / In love with love / Hanging on the telephone / Island of lost souls / Picture this / Dreaming / Sweet and low / Union city blue / Atomic / Rip her to shreds.
Jan 94. (cd/c) *(CD/TC CHR 6063)* **BLONDIE AND BEYOND – RARITIES AND ODDITIES** [ ] [-]
Aug 94. (c-s/12"/cd-s) *(12/ZC/CD CHS 5013)* **ATOMIC (re-mix). / ('A'mixes by Diddy & Alan Thompson)** [19] [-]
(cd-s) *(CDCHSS 5013)* – ('A'side) / Sunday girl (re-mix) / Union City blues (re-mix).
Nov 94. (d-cd) *(CDCHR 6089)* **THE PLATINUM COLLECTION** [ ] [-]
Jun 95. (12") *(12CHS 5023) HEART OF GLASS (re-mix). / CALL ME (re-mix)* [15] [ ]
(c-s) *(CDCHS 5023)* – ('A'side) / Rapture (re-mix) / Atomic (re-mix).
(cd-s+=) *(CDCHSS 5023)* – ('A'mixes).
Jul 95. (cd/c/d-lp) *(CD/TC+/CHR 6105)* **BEAUTIFUL – THE REMIX ALBUM** [25] [-]
Oct 95. (12"blue/cd-s) *(12/CD CHS 5027)* **UNION CITY BLUE (re-mix) / I FEEL LOVE (live)** [31] [-]
(cd-s) *(CDCHSS 5027)* – (other mixes by:- Diddy / The Burger Queens / OPM / Vinny Vero & Jammin' Hot).
Jul 98. (cd/c) *E.M.I.; (494996-2/-4)* **ATOMIC – THE VERY BEST OF** [12] [ ]
Jul 98. (c-s) *E.M.I.; (TCATOM 150)* **ATOMIC (1998 remix)** [ ] [-]
(12"+=/cd-s+=) *(12/CD ATOM 150)* – ('A'mixes).

DEBBIE HARRY

solo, with **NILE RODGERS** and **BERNARD EDWARDS** on production, etc.

Chrysalis Chrysalis

Jul 81. (7"/12") *<(CHS/+12 2526)>* **BACKFIRED. / MILITARY RAP** [32] [43]
Aug 81. (lp/c) *<(CHR/ZCCHR 1347)>* **KOO KOO** [6] [23]
– Jump jump / The jam was moving / Chrome / Under arrest / Inner city spillover / Surrender / Backfired / Now I know you / Military rap / Oasis. *(cd-iss. Sep94; CDCHR 6082)*
Sep 81. (7") *<(CHS 2554)>* **THE JAM WAS MOVING. / CHROME** [ ] [82]
(12"+=) *(CHS12 2554)* – Inner city spillover.

— now worked with various session musicians.

Chrysalis Geffen

Jan 84. (7") **RUSH RUSH. / DANCE DANCE DANCE** [-] [ ]
Jan 84. (7"/12") *(CHS/12CHS 2752)* **RUSH RUSH. / RUSH RUSH (dub)** [ ] [-]
Nov 86. (7") *(CHS 3066)* **FRENCH KISSIN' IN THE U.S.A. / ROCKBIRD** [8] [-]
('A'dance; 12"+=/12"pic-d+=) *(CHS12 3066/+B)* – ('A'dub version).
Nov 86. (7") *<28546>* **FRENCH KISSIN' IN THE U.S.A. / BUCKLE UP** [-] [57]
Nov 86. (lp/c/cd) *(CHR/ZCHR/CCD 1540) <24123>* **ROCKBIRD** [31] [97]
– I want you / French kissin' in the U.S.A. / Buckle up / In love with love / You got me in trouble / Free to fall / Rockbird / Secret life / Beyond the limit. *(cd re-iss. Sep94; CCD 1540)*
Feb 87. (7") *<(CHS 3093)>* **FREE TO FALL. / FEEL THE SPIN** [46] [ ]
(12"+=/12"pic-d+=) *(CHS12 3093/+B)* – Secret life.
(d7"+=) *(CHSD 3093)* – French kissin' in the U.S.A. / Rockbird.
Apr 87. (7") *(CHS 3128)* **IN LOVE WITH LOVE. / FEEL THE SPIN** [45] [-]
(12"+=/12"pic-d+=) *(CHS/+P 12-3128)* – French kissin' in the U.S.A. (French version).
Jun 87. (7") *<28476>* **IN LOVE WITH LOVE. / SECRET LIFE** [-] [70]

DEBORAH HARRY

— with **CHRIS STEIN** – guitar / **LEIGH FOXX** – bass / **TERRY BOZZIO** – drums / **TOMMY PRICE** – drums / **PHIL ASHLEY** – synthesizers / **STEVE GOLDSTEIN** – keyboards, etc.

Chrysalis Sire

Sep 89. (7"/c-s) *(CHS/+MC 3369)* **I WANT THAT MAN. / BIKE BOY** [13] [ ]
(12"pic-d+=/cd-s+=) *(CHS 12P/CD 3369)* – ('A'remix) / ('A'instrumental).
Oct 89. (lp/c/cd) *(CHR/ZCHR/CCD 1650) <25938>* **DEF, DUMB AND BLONDE** [12] [ ]
– I want that man / Lovelight / KIss it better / Bike boy * / Get your way / Maybe for sure / I'll never fall in love / Calmarie / Sweet and low / He is so / Bugeye / Comic books / Brite side / End of the run *. *(cd+=*) (cd re-iss. Sep94; CCD 1650)*
Nov 89. (7"/7"s) *(CHS/+PB 3452)* **BRITE SIDE. / BUGEYE** [59] [ ]
(12"+=/cd-s+=) *(CHS 12/CD 3452)* – In love with love.
('A'remix-cd-s++=) *(CHSCCD 3452)* – French kissin' in the U.S.A.

— Her touring group at time included **STEIN** and **FOXX** plus **SUZY DAVIS** – keyboards / **CARLA OLLA** – rhythm guitar / **JIMMY CLARK** – drums

Mar 90. (7"/7"s) *(CHS/+PB 3491)* **SWEET AND LOW. / LOVELIGHT** [57] [ ]
(12"/12"pic-d/cd-s) *(CHS 12/P12/CD 3491)* – (3-'A'mixes).
May 90. (7") *(CHS 3537)* **MAYBE FOR SURE. / GET YOUR WAY** [ ] [ ]
(12"+=/cd-s+=) *(12/CD CHS 3537)* – ('A'extended).

— below featured on a Cole Porter tribute album, 'Red Hot & Blue'.

Dec 90. (7"/12"; by DEBORAH HARRY & IGGY POP) *(CHS/+12 3646)* **WELL DID YOU EVAH! / (b-side by The Thompson Twins)** [42] [ ]
(cd-s+=) *(CHSCD 3646)* – (track by 'Aztec Camera').
Jun 93. (c-s/7") *(TC+/CHS 4900)* **I CAN SEE CLEARLY. / STANDING IN MY WAY** [23] [ ]
(12"+=/cd-s+=) *(12/CD CHS 4900)* – Atomic / Heart of glass.
(cd-s+=) *(CDCHSS 4900)* – Call me / In love with love.
Jul 93. (cd/c/lp) *(CD/TC+/CHR 6033)* **DEBRAVATION** [24] [ ]
– I can see clearly / Stability / Strike me pink / Rain / Communion / Lip service / Mood ring / Dancing down the moon / Standing in my way / The fugitive / Dog star girl.
Sep 93. (c-s) *(TCCHS 5000)* **STRIKE ME PINK / 8 AND A HALF RHUMBA** [46] [ ]
(cd-s) *(CDCHS 5000)* – Dreaming.
(12"pic-d/cd-s) *(12CHSPD/CDCHSS 5000)* – ('A'side) / Sweet and low / On a breath.

of 'JACKET HANGS', it seemed as if The BLUE AEROPLANES' moment had finally arrived. Their most accessible effort to date, 'SWAGGER' (1990), followed soon after and the band embarked on a hectic touring schedule taking them everywhere from Canada to the Far East. A second single, ' . . .AND STONES', also scraped the charts later that summer, possibly one of their most effective marriages of ringing arpeggios and LANGLEY's slurred, half-spoken style. With an extended line-up including a returning BRUSCHINI, the ELVIS COSTELLO co-produced 'BEATSONGS' arrived in 1991 as the most fully formed and consistently listenable album of the band's chequered career, featuring such spiky, infectious pop gems as 'HUH!' and 'COLOUR ME'. Yet although it became their first and only Top 40 hit, the album surprisingly failed to produce a bonafide single and The BLUE AEROPLANES seemed to have missed the boat (or even the train) yet again. A period of instability ensued as the band transferred to 'Beggars Banquet' and underwent more line-up flux, the resulting 'LIFE MODEL' (1994) set failing to excite critics in quite the same fashion as its predecessor. The BLUE AEROPLANES nevertheless remain something of an institution until their split in late '95, content to release relentlessly experimental material to their adoring fans while being generally ignored by the rock, or even indie mainstream. This despite the promise shown by their final recordings, 'ROUGH MUSIC' (album) and 'SUGARED ALMONDS' (EP). • **Songwriters:** GERARD LANGLEY and JACOBS with other members until latters' departure. Covered; UNSQUARE DANCE (Dave Brubeck) / BAD MOON RISING (Creedence Clearwater Revival) / BREAKING IN MY HEART (Tom Verlaine) / THE BOY IN THE BUBBLE (Paul Simon) / I WANNA BE YOUR LOVER (Bob Dylan) / TOP OF THE POPS (Smithereens).

Album rating: BOP ART (*6) / TOLERANCE (*6) / SPITTING OUT MIRACLES (*6) / SWAGGER (*8) / BEATSONGS (*8) / LIFE MODEL (*5) / ROUGH MUSIC (*5) / FRIENDLOVERPLANE compilation (*7) / FRIENDLOVERPLANE 2 compilation (*6) / HUH! THE BEST OF THE BLUE AEROPLANES compilation (*8)

ART OBJECTS

GERARD LANGLEY – vocals / **JONATHAN KEY** – guitar, synthesizer, vocals / **WILLIAM STAIR** – bass, guitar / **JOHN LANGLEY** – drums, vocals / **ROBIN KEY** – guitar, bass, keyboards / **WOJTEK DMOCHOWSKI** – dance, percussion

Heartbeat not iss.

Oct 80. (7") *(PULSE 10)* **SHOWING OFF TO IMPRESS THE GIRLS. / OUR SILVER SISTER (live)** -

1981. (lp) *(HB 5)* **BAGPIPE MUSIC** -
– Dumbness / Showing off to impress / Conversation / Who switches off the light / Landscape workers / Batpoem / Miraculous birth / 20th century composites / Magog / Passengers of fortune / What am I supposed to do? / Underground market / The paperweight flood.

Fried Egg not iss.

1981. (7"m) *(EGG 007)* **HARD OBJECTS. / BIBLIOTHEQUE / FIT OF PIQUE** -

BLUE AEROPLANES

GERARD LANGLEY – vocals / **NICK JACOBS** – rhythm guitar / **WOJTEK DMOCHOWSKI** – dancer / **with JOHN LANGLEY** – drums / **IAN KEAREY** – bass (of OYSTER BAND), + guests WILLIAM STAIR, J.KEY, R. KEY + MAXIMUM JOY members

Abstract not iss.

Apr 84. (lp) *(ABT 009)* **BOP ART** -
– Control of embassies / Pinkies hit the union / Gunning the works / Owls / Outback jazz / Chelsea wallpaper / Bagpipe music / Built in a day. *(re-iss. Feb89 on 'Party'; PART 001RV)*

— added **ANGELO BRUSCHINI** – guitar, vocals (he was to leave and return soon) / **JOHN STAPLETON** – tapes / **RUTH COCHRANE** – bass, vocals / **DAVE CHAPMAN** – guitar, bass, vocals

Fire Restless

Mar 85. (12"ep) *(FIRE 2)* **ACTION PAINTING / LE PETIT CADEAU DE DON JUAN. / ASH TRAYS FROM MT. ETNA / POLICE (38 DIVINITY)** -

Mar 86. (12"ep) *(FIRE 8)* **LOVER AND CONFIDANTE PLUS OTHER STORIES** -
– Lover and confidante / Who built this station in the Midwest / Breaking in my heart / Weird heart.

Jun 86. (lp) *(FIRELP 3)* **TOLERANCE** -
– Arriving / Journal of an airman / Rare flowers / Warhol's fifteen / 30 love / Lover and confidante / Tolerance / Ups / When the wave comes / Soul (seen and unseen). *(cd-iss. Oct89 & Sep91; FIRECD 3)*

Oct 86. (7") *(BLAZE 12)* **TOLERANCE. / WHEN THE WAVE COMES** -
(12"+=) *(BLAZE 12T)* – Teaching English people through sex and death (remix) / And the couple in the next room / Complete blessing.

— briefly added **CAROLINE HALCROW** – guitar (a member in '87) became CAROLINE TRETTINE and subsequently went solo, releasing one 1990 folk mini-set, 'BE A DEVIL', for 'Utility'; contained KEARNEY + JACOBS

Nov 87. (12"ep) *(BLAZE 23T)* **BURY YOUR LOVE LIKE TREASURE / KING OF THE SOAP BOX / VICE KING'S SON? CONTINUALLY TORN APART** -

Nov 87. (lp) *(FIRELP 10)* *<72254-1/4/-2>* **SPITTING OUT MIRACLES**
– Goats / Cowardice and caprice / Julie / Spitting out miracles / Ceiling roses / In the mystery / Season ticket to a bad place / Bury your love like treasure / Days of 49 / Teaching English through sex and death / Winter sun / What do you mean (what I said) / Do the dead know what time it is? *(free-7"flexi.w/a)* – COWARDICE AND CAPRICE Instrumental) *(cd-iss. Oct89; FIRECD 10) (re-iss. Oct91; FIRE 33/11 010)*

May 88. (12"ep) *(BLAZE 24T)* **VEILS OF COLOUR. / SPITTING OUT MIRACLES (remix) / ARRIVING / BUILT IN A DAY** -

— **RODNEY ALLEN** – vocals, rhythm guitar (ex-PRESS) repl. NICK — **ANDY McCREETH** – bass (ex-PRESS) repl. RUTH

— **GERARD + JOHN LANGLEY, RODNEY, ANDY, WOJTEK** and entourage, added **ALEX LEE** – guitar, keyboards, vocals (now a 7-piece)

Ensign Chrysalis

Jan 90. (7") *(ENY 628)* **JACKET HANGS. / RAZOR WALK** 72 -
(12"+=/cd-s+=) *(ENY X/CD 628)* – Different now / Big sky.

Feb 90. (cd)(c/lp) *(CCD 1752)(Z+/CHEN 13)* **SWAGGER** 54
– Jacket hangs / World view blues / Weightless / . . . and stones / Your ages / Love come around / The applicant / What it is / Anti-pretty / Careful boy / Picture framed / Cat-scan his'try.

May 90. (7"/c-s) *(ENY/+MC 632)* **. . . AND STONES (remix). / ('A' lp version)** 63 -
(12"+=/cd-s+=) *(ENY X/CD 632)* – ('A'vocal) / ('A'-Lovers mix).

Oct 90. (10"ep/12"ep/cd-ep) *(ENY 10/X/CD 636)* **THE LOVED EP** -
– You (are loved) / You're going to need somebody / Sweet Jane / World view blue (acoustic).

— (Jan'91) **PAUL MULREANY** – drums (ex-JAZZ BUTCHER CONSPIRACY) repl. JOHN / **ANGELO BRUSCHINI** – guitar, accordion, vocals (returned from Saudi Arabia) guests on '91 album, **IAN KEAREY** – multi / **ALEX ACUNA** – percussion / **DANNY TIMMS** – keyboards / **DAVID MANSFIELD** – violins, bouzouki / **J.J. KEY** – guitar / **JERRY MAROTTA** – drums / guest **JAZZ BUTCHER** – b.vocals / **ELAINE SUMMERS** – vocals

Jul 91. (7") *(ENY 647)* **YR OWN WORLD. / PONY BOY** -
(12"+=/cd-s+=) *(ENY X/CD 647)* – Mis-firing / Autumn journal XXII.

Aug 91. (cd)(c/lp) *(CCD 1856)(Z+/CHEN 21)* **BEATSONGS** 33
– Huh! / Yr own world / Angel words / Fun / cardboard box / My hurricane / Jack leaves & back spring / Aeroplane blues / Colour me / Streamers / The boy in the bubble / sixth continent.

Oct 91. (7") *(ENY 649)* **THE BOY IN THE BUBBLE. / TALKIN' ON THE OTHER PHONE / DISNEY HEAD** -
(12"+=) *(ENYX 649)* – Huh! (remix).
(cd-s++=) *(ENYCD 649)* – Disneyhead.

— added on tour August '91 **HAZEL KEY** – guitar; repl. injured ROBIN (JJ) and **MARCUS WILLIAMS** – bass (MIGHTY LEMON DROPS) repl. injured ANDY / **SUSIE HUGG** – vocals (of KATYDIDS) repl. HAZEL

— now a 5-piece after ANGELO left in July '92

Beggars Banquet Beggars Banquet

Jan 94. (12"ep/cd-ep) *(BBQ 26 T/CD)* **BROKEN AND MENDED / LOVE IS. / STAR CROSS'D / GET OUT!** -

Mar 94. (cd/c/lp) *(BBQ CD/MC/LP 143)* **LIFE MODEL** 59
– Broken & mended / (I'm a) Smart drug / Ghost-nets / Frightened at night / Daughter movie / Open / Honey I / Vade mecum gunslinger / Mercury (Hold / Protect / Love) / Fragile.

Nov 94. (7") *(BBQ 39)* **THE DETECTIVE SONG. / YOU'RE MINE AND ALWAYS WILL BE: JACK OF ALL HEARTS – JEALOUS TOWN – IT'S ALRIGHT** -
(cd-s+=) *(BBQ 39CD)* – A map below / Top of the pops.

Jan 95. (cd/c/lp) *(BBQ CD/MC/LP 167)* **ROUGH MUSIC**
– Detective song / Sugared almond / Scared / Worry beads / Contact high / A map below / James / Whatever hapened to our golden birds? / Wond'ring wild / Saint me and the Devil / Dark / Secret destination / Dear, though the night is gone.

Mar 95. (cd-ep) *(BBQ 53CD)* **SUGARED ALMONDS EP** -
– Sugared almonds (remix) / Sacred (remix) / Bad moon rising / Broken and mended (live).

— split later in '95

– compilations, others, etc. –

Nov 88. (d-lp/cd) *Fire; (FIRE LP/CD 15) / Restless; <72314>* **FRIENDLOVERPLANE**
– Veils of colour / Complete blessing / Weird heart / Le petit cadeau de Don Juan / Severn beach / Police (36 divinity) / Action painting / Who built this station in the mid west / Old men sleeping on the bowery / 88 out / Ashtrays from Mt.Etna / Gunning the works / King of the soap box / Tolerance / Etiquette! / Continually torn apart / Days of 49 / I wanna be your lover / Warhol's fifteen / Shame / The couple in the next room / Stripped. *(cd+=)* – (4 extra tracks). *(re-iss. Oct91; FIRE 33/11 015)*

Nov 92. (cd/c/lp) *Ensign; (CD/TC+/CHEN 28)* **FRIENDLOVERPLANE 2 (UP IN A DOWNWORLD)** -
– You (are loved) / Pony boy / Different now / World view blue (acoustic version) / . . . .And stones (lovers all around mix) / Razor walk / Growing up, growing down / Autumn journal XV / Here it comes / For Tim Collins / Talkin' on the otherphone / You're going to need somebody / Missy Lane / Stranger / Trouble, tell me I'm alive / Big sky / Mis-firing / Disney head

Apr 88. (12"ep) *Night Tracks; (SFNT 009)* **THE EVENING SHOW SESSIONS** (15.2.87) -
– Cowardice and Caprice / Coats / What do you mean / Shame.

Apr 96. (cd) *Fire; (FIRECD 057)* **FRUIT** (live compilation) -

Aug 96. (12") *Fantastic Plastic; (FP 002)* **UP IN A DOWN WORLD. /** -

Jun 98. (cd) *Reactive; (REMCD 526)* **THE BEST OF WARHOL'S 15** -

Sep 98. (cd) *Chrysalis; (CDCHRM 101)* **HUH! (THE BEST OF THE BLUE AEROPLANES)** -
– Jacket hangs / Huh! / Colour me / Razor walk / Growing up, growing down / Fun / Weightless / . . .And stones / You (are loved) / Jack leaves and back spring / Anti-pretty / Disney head / Yr. own world / What it is / Lovething – Higherthing / Sixth continent.

GERARD LANGLEY & IAN KEAREY

(above with an OYSTER BAND member)

Fire not iss.

Feb 87. (m-lp) *(FIRELP 4)* **SIAMESE BOYFRIENDS** -
– Nicknames / Snow-walking / Joe Taylor's / La marisque / Good weather / Dear through the night has gone / The famous aren't.

BLUE NILE

Formed: Glasgow, Scotland . . . 1981 by songwriter PAUL BUCHANAN, PAUL JOSEPH MOORE and ROBERT BELL. After a debut 45 on 'R.S.O.' (just prior to the label going belly up!), they were offered an unusual record contract by Scottish (East Lothian) label, 'Linn', the hi-fi manufacturer using their tape as a demo and susbsequently being sufficiently impressed to sign the band up for their recently formed music business venture. After an initial single, 'STAY', in Spring '84, the label issued the languerous debut album, 'A WALK ACROSS THE ROOFTOPS'. Garnering gushing reviews, this classic set of understated pop elegance created eough of a buzz for 'Virgin' to take over distribution. Its relatively lowly final chart position of No.80 belied the record's influence and impact, although it would be another five years before a follow-up as the trio locked themselves in the studio and dilligently attempted to create another masterpiece. After a few false starts, they finally emerged in 1989 with 'HATS', a record which arguably topped the debut in the late night sophistication stakes, its moody atmospherics delicately caressed by PAUL BUCHANAN's silky croon (a singer who undoubtedly has the potential of being the next SINATRA). A UK Top 20 hit, the record's success saw The BLUE NILE leave their studio cocoon in the early 90's for a tour of America where they ended up working with such luminaries as ROBBIE ROBERTSON and RICKIE LEE JONES amongst others. Now signed to 'Warners', it looked as if The BLUE NILE were finally destined to leave cultdom behind with a third set, 'PEACE AT LAST' (1996). Another classy effort, again the trio enjoyed critical plaudits and modest chart success while simultaneously failing to corner the wider pop market.

Album rating: A WALK ACROSS THE ROOFTOPS (*8) / HATS (*9) / PEACE AT LAST (*6)

PAUL BUCHANAN – vocals, guitar, synthesizer / **PAUL JOSEPH MOORE** – keyboards, synthesizer, etc. / **ROBERT BELL** – bass, synthesizer, etc.

R.S.O. | not iss.

Oct 81. (7") *(RSO 84)* **I LOVE THIS LIFE. / SECOND ACT** [ ] [-]

— added guests **CALUM MALCOLM** – keyboards, vocals (ex-BADGER, ex-HEADBOYS) / **NIGEL THOMAS** – drums

Linn-Virgin | A&M

Apr 84. (7"/12") *(LKS 1/+12)* **STAY. / SADDLE THE HORSES** [ ] [ ] 1985
(re-iss. Jan89 remixed 7"/12"/d7"+=; same/same/LKSD 1) – Tinseltown in the rain / Heatwave (instrumental).

Apr 84. (lp/c) *(LKH/+C 1)* **A WALK ACROSS THE ROOFTOPS** [80] [ ] 1985
– A walk across the rooftops / Tinseltown in the rain / From rags to riches / Stay / Easter parade / Heatwave / Automobile noise. *(cd-iss. Jan89; LKHCD 1)*

Jul 84. (7") *(LKS 2)* **TINSELTOWN IN THE RAIN. / HEATWAVE (instrumental)** [ ] [-]
('A'ext-12") *(LKS 2-12)* – Regret.

— now a basic trio plus session musicians.

Sep 89. (7") *(LKS 3)* **THE DOWNTOWN LIGHTS. / THE WIRES ARE DOWN** [67] [ ]
(12"+=/3"cd-s+=) *(LKS 3-12/CD3)* – Halfway to Paradise (TV theme).

Oct 89. (lp/c/cd) *(LKH/+C/CD 2) <5284>* **HATS** [12] [ ]
– Over the hillside / The downtown lights / Let's go out tonight / Headlights on the parade / From a late night train / Seven a.m. / Saturday night. *(re-iss. Apr92 on 'Virgin' cd/c; OVED CD/C 391)*

Sep 90. (7"/c-s) *(LKS/+C 4)* **HEADLIGHTS ON THE PARADE (Bob Clearmount mix). / ('A'-lp version)** [72] [ ]
(12"+=/cd-s+=) *(LKS 4-12/CD4)* – Easter parade (with RICKIE LEE JONES).

Jan 91. (7"/c-s) *(LKS/+C 5)* **SATURDAY NIGHT. / ('A'version)** [50] [ ]
(12"+=/cd-s+=) *(LKS 5-12/CD5)* – Seven a.m. (live in the U.S.) / or / Our lives.

Warners | Warners

Jun 96. (cd/c/lp) *(<9362 45848-2/-4/-1>)* **PEACE AT LAST** [13] [ ]
– Happiness / Tomorrow morning / Sentimental man / Love came down / Body and soul / Holy love / Family life / War is love / God bless you kid / Soon.

Sep 96. (c-ep/cd-ep) *(W 0373 C/CD2)* **HAPPINESS / NEW YORK MAN / WISH ME WELL** [ ] [ ]
(cd-ep) *(W 0373CD1)* – ('A'side) / War is love / O Lolita.

BLUE ORCHIDS

Formed: Manchester, England . . .early 80's, by ex-FALL members MARTIN BRAMAH and UNA BAINES. Boasting a line-up completed by RICK GOLDSTRAW, STEVE TOYNE and JOE KIN, this fondly remembered alternative outfit bear inevitable comparison to The FALL, if only for BRAMAH's very MARK E.-esque vocals. Musically there was less resemblance, the emphasis placed on the harmonic discord of the organ pumping away behind the frontman's half-spoken/half-wailing efforts. The group signed to 'Rough Trade' and debuted with the 'DISNEY BOYS' single in late 1980, the first of many rhythm section replacements coming soon after as IAN ROGERS replaced KIN and TOYNE. Early '81 saw the release of a follow-up single, 'WORK', after which the drum stool was again vacated and subsequently filled by TOBY, a veteran of both The NOSEBLEEDS and DURUTTI COLUMN. The BLUE ORCHIDS' debut album, 'THE GREATEST HIT (MONEY MOUNTAIN)' (1982) made for interesting listening; 'SUN CONNECTION' could almost be described as a post-punk DOORS, the record's swirling hammond and angular guitar occasionally throwing up a treat like 'BAD EDUCATION'. After a further EP, 'AGENTS OF CHANGE', later that year, The BLUE ORCHIDS temporarily went to ground as BAINES joined The FATES and settled down to a life of married bliss with BRAMAH. The couple reactivated the band in 1985 for a one-off single, 'SLEEPY TOWN', BRAMAH subsequently forming THIRST with another ex-FALL man, KARL BURNS, along with his wife, CARRIE and the mysterious LEE. This was another one-off project, resulting in a sole EP, 'RIDING THE TIMES', in Autumn '87. BRAMAH later reformed The BLUE ORCHIDS for one last time in the early 90's, featuring a line-up of indie veteran, CRAIG GANNON alongside MARTIN HENNAN and DICK HARRISON. Signed to the established 'Playtime' label, they issued an EP, 'DIAMOND AGE', followed by an album, 'A VIEW FROM THE CITY' (1991). A final EP, 'SECRET CITY', appeared in late '92, the last chapter in The BLUE ORCHIDS' erratic career.

Album rating: THE GREATEST HIT (*7)

MARTIN BRAMAH – vocals, guitar (ex-FALL) / **UNA BAINES** – keyboards (ex-FALL) / RICK GOLDSTRAW – guitar / **STEVE TOYNE** – bass / **JOE KIN** – drums

Rough Trade | not iss.

Nov 80. (7") *(RT 065)* **DISNEY BOYS. / (AFTER) THE FLOOD** [ ] [-]

— **IAN ROGERS** – drums; repl. KIN + TOYNE

Feb 81. (7") *(RT 067)* **WORK. / THE HOUSE THAT FADED OUT** [ ] [-]

— **TOBY** – drums (ex-NOSEBLEEDS, ex-DURUTTI COLUMN) repl. ROGERS

1982. (lp) *(ROUGH 37)* **THE GREATEST HIT (MONEY MOUNTAIN)** [ ] [-]
– Sun connection / Dumb magician / Tighten my belt / A year with no head / Hanging man / Bad education / Wait / No looking back / Low profile / Money mountain.

— **MARK HELLYER** – bass; repl. GOLDSTRAW

Nov 82. (12"ep) *(RTT 117T)* **AGENTS OF CHANGE** [ ] [-]
– Agents of change / Release / Conscience / The long nights out.

— BAZ MURPHY replaced MARK for a time, before he joined CAPTAINS OF INDUSTRY. UNA took time out to join The FATES, and take up married life with BRAMAH. They both reformed BLUE ORCHIDS in 1985 with **NICK MARSHALL** – drums / **MICK** – bass

Racket | not iss.

Jun 85. (12") **SLEEPY TOWN. / THIRST** [ ] [-]

— they disbanded again

THIRST

— were formed by **BRAMAH** and another (ex-FALL) drummer **KARL BURNS** / plus his wife **CARRIE BURNS** – guitar (ex-SEEDS) / **LEE** – bass

Rough Trade | not iss.

Oct 87. (12"ep) *(RTT 206)* **RIDING THE TIMES** [ ] [-]

— They split and BRAHAM re-joined The FALL in 1989, but left 1990. Other group of same name released Oct'89 single 'Devious'.

BLUE ORCHIDS

reformed with **BRAMAH** + **CRAIG GANNON** – guitar (ex-SMITHS, ex-AZTEC CAMERA, ex-BLUEBELLS) / **MARTIN HENNAN** – bass / **DICK HARRISON** – drums

Playtime | not iss.

Mar 91. (12"/cd-s) **DIAMOND AGE. / ?** [ ] [-]

Oct 91. (cd/lp) *(AMUSE 011 CD/LP)* **A VIEW FROM THE CITY** [ ] [-]

Authentic | not iss.

Nov 92. (12"ep) **SECRET CITY** [ ] [-]
– N.Y. gargoyles / Out of sight / Love fiend.

— split for the last time after above

BLUETONES

Formed: Hounslow, London, England . . . 1994 by brothers MARK and SCOTT MORRISS, along with ADAM DEVLIN and ED CHESTERS. An indie band in the classic sense of the term, The BLUETONES stood somewhat apart and aloof from the Brit-pop class of '95. The previous year, they'd contributed the track, 'No.11', (later retitled 'BLUETONIC') to a 'Fierce Panda' compilation EP, 'Return To Splendour', before attracting attention from A&M's 'Superior Quality' label early in 1995. A struttingly assured live proposition, the initial buzz surrounding the band was almost tangible. It came as little surprise when a debut single, 'ARE YOU BLUE OR ARE YOU BLIND?' crashed into the charts at No.31, followed later in the long, hot summer of '95 by Top 20 hit, 'BLUETONIC'. A further series of gigs followed before the band narrowly missed the UK No.1 spot in early '96 with the 'SLIGHT RETURN' single. A classic slice of jangle-pop following the time-honoured lineage of The BYRDS, The SMITHS, The LA's and The STONE ROSES, MORRIS even donned a duffel coat(!) for the video, his nimble footed shuffle and boyish good looks generating talk of another IAN BROWN in the ascendant. The long awaited album, 'EXPECTING TO FLY' was released almost simultaneously, reaching the UK No.1 spot and eventually going platinum. Listeners expecting a series of breezy strumalong's were disappointed; the album's dense, evershifting sound rewarded repeated listening, classic rock references slipping in and out of focus but never revealing themselves fully. The catchy 'CUT SOME RUG' was the next single, making the Top 10 ahead of a new track, 'MARBLEHEAD JOHNSON' later that year.

Album rating: EXPECTING TO FLY (*9) / RETURN TO THE LAST CHANCE SALOON (*6)

MARK MORRISS – vocals / **ADAM DEVLIN** – guitars / **SCOTT MORRISS** – bass, vocals / **ED CHESTERS** – drums, percussion

Superior | Polydor

Feb 95. (7"blue; mail-o) *(TONE 001)* **SLIGHT RETURN. / FOUNTAINHEAD** [-] [-]

Jun 95. (7") *(BLUE 001X)* **ARE YOU BLUE OR ARE YOU BLIND?. / STRING ALONG** [31] [ ]

(12"+=/cd-s+=) *(BLUE 001 T/CD)* – Driftwood.

Oct 95. (7"/c-s) *(BLUE 002 X/MC)* **BLUETONIC. / GLAD TO SEE Y'BACK AGAIN?** 19 –

(12"+=/cd-s+=) *(BLUE 002 T/CD)* – Colorado beetle.

Dec 95. (cd-ep) *<1142>* **BLUETONES COMPANION** - –

– Are you blue or are you blind? / String along / Driftwood / Bluetonic / Colorado beetle / Glad to see y' back again.

Superior A&M

Jan 96. (7"/c-s) *(BLUE 003 X/MC)* **SLIGHT RETURN. / DON'T STAND ME DOWN** 2 –

(cd-s+=) *(BLUE 003CD)* – Nae hair on't.

Feb 96. (cd/c/lp/s-lp) *(BLUECD/BLUEMC/BLUELP/BLUELPX 004) <540475>* **EXPECTING TO FLY** 1 –

– Talking to Clarry / Bluetonic / Cut some rug / Things change / he fountainhead / Carnt be trusted / Slight return / Putting out fires / Vampire / A parting gesture / Time & again.

Apr 96. (7"/c-s) *(BLUE 005 X/MC)* **CUT SOME RUG. / CASTLE ROCK** 7 –

(cd-s+=) *(BLUE 005CD)* – The devil behind my smile.

Sep 96. (7"/c-s) *(BLUE 006 X/MC)* **MARBLEHEAD JOHNSON. / THE SIMPLE THINGS / NIFKIN'S BRIDGE** 7 –

(cd-s+=) *(BLUE 006CD)* – Are you blue or are you blind?

Feb 98. (7"/c-s) *(BLUE X/M 007)* **SOLOMON BITES THE WORM. / I WAS A TEENAGE JESUS** 10 –

(cd-s+=) *(BLUED 007)* – I walked all night.

Mar 98. (cd/c/lp) *(BLUE D/M/V 008) <LC 0485>* **RETURN TO THE LAST CHANCE SALOON** 10 –

– Tone blooze / Unpainted Arizona / Solomon bites the worm / U.T.A. / 4-day weekend / Sleazy bed track / If . . . / The jub-jub bird / Sky will fall / Ames / Down at the reservoir / Heard you were dead / Broken starr. *(hidden track on cd+=)* – Woman done gone left me.

Apr 98. (7"/c-s) *(BLUE X/M 009)* **IF . . . / BLUE SHADOWS** 13 –

(cd-s+=) *(BLUED 009)* – The watchman.

Jul 98. (7"/c-s) *(BLUE X/M 010)* **SLEAZY BED TRACK. / THE BALLAD OF MULDOON** 35 –

(cd-s+=) *(BLUED 010)* – Blue.

BLUMFELD

Formed: Hamburg, Germany . . . 1992 by JOCHEN DISTELMEYER, EIKE BOHLKEN and ANDRE RATTAY. One of the few German guitar-based bands to break through the enduringly untrendy preconceptions held by many UK music journos, BLUMFELD surprisingly sang in their native tongue although their music was inspired by the angular noise of American acts like SONIC YOUTH, BIG BLACK and early PAVEMENT. Distributed in the UK by 'Cargo', 'ISCH MASCHINE' (1994), introduced their heavily politicised, determinedly anti-fascist agenda although obviously German-language night classes were essential for us mono-lingual English speakers. Subsequently signing to 'Big Cat', BLUMFELD confusingly enough released a French titled follow-up set, 'L'ETAT ET MOI' (1995), their overtly intellectual art-rock not exactly going down a storm with the Brit-pop boys of the mid-90's.

Album rating: ISCH MASCHINE (*5) / L'ETAT ET MOI (*5)

JOCHEN DISTELMEYER – vocals, guitar, piano / **EIKE BOHLKEN** – bass, guitar, harmonica / **ANDRE RATTAY** – drums, percussion

Cargo not iss.

Oct 94. (cd) *(2915-2)* **ISCH MASCHINE** – -

Big Cat Big Cat

Feb 95. (7") *(ABB 82S)* **DRAUSSEN AUF KAUTION. / JET SET** – -

Mar 95. (lp/cd) *(<ABB 73/+CD>)* **L'ETAT ET MOI** – –

– Draussen auf kaution / Jet set / 2 oder 3 dinge, die ich von dir weiss / Walkie, talkie / Eine eigene geschichte / Verstarker / Ich – Wie es wirklich war / L'etat et moi (Mein vorgehen in 4, 5 satzen) / Sing sing / Evergreen / Superstarfighter / You make me.

Aug 95. (cd-ep) *(ABB 95)* **VERSTARKER / ANDERES ICH / DER ANGRIFF DER GEGENWART AUF MEINE UBRIGE ZEIT / LANGSAM** – -

BLUR

Formed: Colchester, Essex, England . . . 1989 by DAMON ALBARN, GRAHAM COXON, ALEX JAMES and DAVE ROWNTREE. Initially they went under the moniker of SEYMOUR before opting for The GREAT WHITE HOPES. Finally settling with BLUR, they soon were on the books of David Balfe's 'Food' label, a subsidiary of Parlophone. There, they secured their first UK Top 50 entry with 'SHE'S SO HIGH', an early PINK FLOYD-influenced tune, that rode the coat-tails of the baggy brigade. With the ghost of SYD BARRETT even more pronounced, they created one of the more psychedelic singles of the era in 'THERE'S NO OTHER WAY', the record hitting Top 10 in '91. Another single, 'BANG', preceded their debut album, 'LEISURE', a record that received mixed reviews at the time. Still mainly a singles orientated outfit, they progressed dramatically with the much-improved, 'MODERN LIFE IS RUBBISH' (1993) album, which featured some classy tracks including the hits, 'FOR TOMORROW', 'CHEMICAL WORLD' and 'SUNDAY SUNDAY'. Although they had come on leaps and bounds creatively, this wasn't translated into sales. With the release of 'GIRLS AND BOYS', however, they embarked upon a commercial renaissance that saw the record become their biggest hit to date. It was the opening track on the critically approved 'PARKLIFE' album, which also spawned further hits, 'TO THE END' and the title track (co-sung with actor PHIL DANIELS). By this point they had evolved into a mod-ish indie-pop combo, ALBARN supplying the cockney barra-boy delivery over a musical backdrop that drew from the rich English pop heritage, once the domain of such luminaries as The SMALL FACES and The KINKS. The following year, 1995, saw them win the battle to the coveted No.1 spot with 'COUNTRY HOUSE', beating rivals OASIS who were sharpening their tongues for an onslaught of media slagging. However, BLUR lost ground in the credibility stakes, when their 'GREAT ESCAPE' album failed to impress the critics. OASIS, on the other hand, were scaling new heights with their 2nd album. 1997 marked a slight return to favour, both the single, 'BEETLEBUM', and their eponymous 5th album hitting pole position. With BLUR taking a slight sabbatical from the recording studio, GRAHAM COXON took the opportunity to release a respectable solo effort, 'THE SKY IS TOO HIGH', the BLUR factor and a few good reviews nearly carrying it into the Top 30. • **Covered:** MAGGIE MAY (Rod Stewart) / LAZY SUNDAY (Small Faces). • **Trivia:** DAMON's father, KEITH ALBARN, used to be the manager of 60's rock outfit, The SOFT MACHINE.

Album rating: LEISURE (*6) / MODERN LIFE IS RUBBISH (*8) / PARKLIFE (*9) / THE GREAT ESCAPE (*7) / BLUR (*8)

DAMON ALBARN (b.23 Mar'68, Whitechapel, London) – vocals / **GRAHAM COXON** (b.12 Mar'69, Germany) – guitars / **ALEX JAMES** (b.21 Nov'68, Dorset, England) – bass, vocals / **DAVE ROWNTREE** (b. 8 Apr'63) – drums

Food-EMI S.B.K.

Oct 90. (c-s/7") *(TC+/FOOD 26)* **SHE'S SO HIGH. / I KNOW** 48 -

(12") *(12FOOD 26)* – ('A'-Definitive) / Sing / I know (extended).

(cd-s) *(CDFOOD 26)* – ('A'side) / I know (extended) / Down.

Apr 91. (c-s/7") *(TC+/FOOD 29)* **THERE'S NO OTHER WAY. / INERTIA** 8 -

(ext.12"+=/cd-s+=) *(12/CD FOOD 29)* – Mr.Briggs / I'm all over.

(12") *(12FOODX 20)* – ('A'remix). / Won't do it / Day upon day (live).

Jul 91. (c-s/7") *(TC+/FOOD 31)* **BANG. / LUMINOUS** 24 –

(ext.12"+=) *(12FOOD 31)* – Explain / Uncle Love.

(cd-s+=) *(CDFOOD 31)* – Explain / Beserk.

Aug 91. (cd/c/lp) *(FOOD CD/TC/LP 6) <97880>* **LEISURE** 7 –

– She's so high / Bang / Slow down / Repetition / Bad day / Sing / There's no other way / Fool / Come together / High cool / Birthday / Wear me down.

Dec 91. (c-s,cd-s) *<07374>* **THERE'S NO OTHER WAY / EXPLAIN** - 82

Mar 92. (c-s/7") *(TC+/FOOD 37)* **POPSCENE. / MACE** 32 –

(12"+=) *(12FOOD 37)* – I'm fine / Garden central.

(cd-s+=) *(CDFOOD 37)* – Badgeman Brown.

Apr 93. (c-s) *(TCFOOD 40)* **FOR TOMORROW. / INTO ANOTHER / HANGING OVER** 28 –

(12"+=) *(12FOOD 40)* – Peach.

(cd-s) *(CDFOOD 40)* – ('A'extended) / Peach / Bone bag.

(cd-s) *(CDSFOOD 40)* – ('A'side) / When the cows come home / Beachcoma / For tomorrow (acoustic).

May 93. (cd/c/lp) *(FOOD CD/TC/LP 9) <89442>* **MODERN LIFE IS RUBBISH** 15 –

– For tomorrow / Advert / Colin Zeal / Pressure on Julian / Star shaped / Blue jeans / Chemical world / Sunday Sunday / Oily water / Miss America / Villa Rosie / Coping / Turn it up / Resigned.

Jun 93. (7"red) *(FOODS 45)* **CHEMICAL WORLD. / MAGGIE MAY** 28 –

(12"/cd-s) *(12/CD FOOD 45)* – ('A'side) / Es Schmecht / Young and lovely / My ark.

(cd-s) *(CDFOODS 45)* – ('A'side) / Never clever (live) / Pressure on Julian (live) / Come together (live).

Oct 93. (7"yellow) *(FOODS 46)* **SUNDAY SUNDAY. / TELL ME, TELL ME** 26 –

(12") *(12FOODS 46)* – ('A'side) / Long legged / Mixed up.

(cd-s) *(CDFOODS 46)* – ('A'side) / Dizzy / Fried / Shimmer.

(cd-s) *(CDFOODX 46)* – ('A'side) / Daisy bell / Let's all go The Strand.

Mar 94. (7"/c-s) *(FOODS/TCFOOD 47)* **GIRLS AND BOYS. / MAGPIE / PEOPLE IN EUROPE** 5 -

(cd-s) *(CDFOOD 47)* – ('A'side) / People in Europe / Peter Panic.

(cd-s) *(CDFOODS 47)* – ('A'side) / Magpie / Anniversary waltz.

Apr 94. (cd/c/lp) *(FOOD CD/TC/LP 10) <29194>* **PARKLIFE** 1 – Jun94

– Girls and boys / Tracy Jacks / End of a century / Park life / Bank holiday / Bad head / The debt collector / Far out / To the end / London loves / Trouble in the message centre / Clover over Dover / Magic America / Jubilee / This is a low / Lot 105.

May 94. (c-s) *(TCFOOD 50)* **TO THE END / GIRLS AND BOYS (Pet Shop Boys remix) / THREADNEEDLE STREET** 16 –

(12"/cd-s) *(12/CD FOOD 50)* – (1st 2 tracks; 2 versions of 2nd).

(cd-s) *(CDFOODS 50)* – ('A'side) / Threadneedle Street / Got yer.

(above featured LETITIA of STEREOLAB. Next with actor PHIL DANIELS.

Jun 94. (c-s,cd-s) *<58155>* **GIRLS AND BOYS / GIRLS AND BOYS (Pet Shop Boys radio mix) / MAGGIE MAY** - 59

Aug 94. (c-s/cd-s) *(TC/CDS FOOD 53)* **PARKLIFE. / SUPA SHOPPA / THEME FROM AN IMAGINARY FILM** 10 –

(12") *(12FOOD 53)* – (1st 2 tracks) / To the end (French version).

(cd-s) *(CDFOOD 53)* – (1st track) / Beard / To the end (French version).

Nov 94. (c-s/7") *(TCFOOD/FOODS 56)* **END OF A CENTURY. / RED NECKS** 19 –

(cd-s+=) *(CDFOOD 56)* – Alex's song.

Food Virgin

Aug 95. (c-s/7") *(TC+/FOOD 63)* **COUNTRY HOUSE. / ONE BORN EVERY MINUTE** 1 –

(cd-s+=) *(CDFOOD 63)* – To the end (with FRANCOISE HARDY).

(cd-ep) *(CDFOODS 63)* ('A'live) / Girls and boys (live) / Parklife (live) / For tomorrow (live).

Sep 95. (cd/c/lp) *(FOOD CD/MC/LP 14) <40855>* **THE GREAT ESCAPE** 1 –

– Stereotypes / Country house / Best days / Charmless man / Fade away / Top man / The universal / Mr. Robinson's quango / He thought of cars / It could be you / Ernold Same / Globe alone / Dan Abnormal / Entertain me / Yuko and Hiro.

Nov 95. (c-s) *(TCFOOD 69)* **THE UNIVERSAL / ENTERTAIN ME (the live it! remix)** 5 –

(cd-s+=) *(CDFOODS 69)* – Ultranol / No monsters in me.

(cd-ep) *(CDFOOD 69)* – ('A'live) / Mr. Robinson's quango (live) / It could be you (live) / Stereotypes (live).

Feb 96. (c-s/7") *(TC+/FOOD 73)* **STEREOTYPES. / THE MAN WHO LEFT HIMSELF / TAME** 7 □
(cd-s+=) *(CDFOOD 73)* – Ludwig.
Apr 96. (c-s/7") *(TC+/FOOD 77)* **CHARMLESS MAN. / THE HORRORS** 5 □
(cd-s+=) *(CDFOOD 77)* – A song / St. Louis.

— BLUR were joint winners (with rivals OASIS; NOEL) of the Ivor Novello Award for songwriter of the year.

May 96. (d-cd; ltd on 'EMI Japan') *(TOCP 8400)* **LIVE AT THE BUDOKAN (live)** - -

— ALEX JAMES helped to form one-off indie supergroup ME ME ME alongside JUSTIN WELCH (Elastica –), STEPHEN DUFFY and CHARLIE BLOOR. Had a UK Top 20 hit in Aug'96 with 'HANGING AROUND'.

Food Virgin

Jan 97. (c-s/cd-s/7"red) *(TC/CD+/FOOD 89)* **BEETLEBUM. / ALL YOUR LIFE / A SPELL (FOR MONEY)** 1 □
(cd-s) *(CDFOODS 89)* – ('A'side) / Woodpigeon song / ('A'-Mario Caldato Jr mix) / Dancehall.
Feb 97. (cd/c/lp) *(FOOD CD/TC/LP 19)* **BLUR** 1 61
– Beetlebum / Song 2 / Country sad ballad man / M.O.R. / On your own / Theme from retro / You're so great / Death of a party / Chinese bombs / I'm just a killer for your love / Look inside America / Strange news from another star / Movin' on / Essex dogs.
Apr 97. (c-s) *(TCFOOD 93)* **SONG 2 / GET OUT OF CITIES** 2 □
(cd-s+=) *(CDFOODS 93)* – Polished stone.
(cd-s) *(CDFOOD 93)* – ('A'side) / Bustin' & dronin' / Country sad ballad man (live acoustic).
Jun 97. (7") *(FOOD 98)* **ON YOUR OWN. / POP SCENE (live) / SONG 2 (live)** 5 □
(cd-s+=) *(CDFOOD 98)* – On your own (live).
(cd-s) *(CDFOODS 98)* – ('A'side) / Chinese bombs (live) / Moving on (live) / MOR (live).
Sep 97. (c-s/7"orange) *(TC+/FOOD 107)* **M.O.R. (Alan Moulder road version). / SWALLOWS IN THE HEATWAVE** 15 □
(cd-s+=) *(CDFOOD 107)* – Movin' on (William Orbit mix) / Beetlebum (Moby's minimal house mix).

GRAHAM COXON

Transcopic Caroline

Aug 98. (cd/c) *<7560>* **THE SKY IS TOO HIGH** 31 □
– That's all I wanna do / Where'd you go? / In a salty sea / Day is far too long / R U lonely? / I wish / Hard and slow / Me you, we two / Waiting / Who the fuck? / Morning blues.

BLURT

Formed: London, England . . . 1980 by poet TED MILTON and brother JAKE. Having previously toured his provocative one-man puppet theatre project, 'Mr. Pugh's Blue Show' around Britain and Europe, TED turned his eccentric talents to playing a mean sax and narrating/screaming his way through what could only loosely be described as songs. Along with guitarist PETE CREESE, the trio issued a debut single, 'MY MOTHER WAS A FRIEND OF AN ENEMY OF THE PEOPLE', in summer 1980, following it up with a live album, 'IN BERLIN' (1981), the latter featuring the classic 'PUPPETEERS OF THE WORLD UNITE'. MILTON had already released a solo EP, 'CONFESSIONS OF AN AEROPLANE FARTER'. A debut solo album proper, 'BLURT', appeared on 'Red Flame' in 1982, MILTON subsequently bringing in keyboard player HERMAN MARTIN and moving away from the initial guitar-orientated sound. The frontman's manic lyrical poetry remained the focal point of BLURT throughout the 80's, although the eventual replacement of MILTON's brother by sticksman/violinist, PAUL WIGENS (prior to 1986 album, 'POPPYCOCK'), added a further twist to BLURT's already twisted sound. A gap of three years ensued before 'KENNY ROGERS' GREATEST HIT: TAKE 2' (1989), a live set, 'THE BODY!..' released the same year. Sadly, MILTON hung up his instrument after 1992's 'PAGAN STRINGS', abandoning sax devotees to the mercy of KENNY G and his ilk.

Album rating: IN BERLIN (*7) / BLURT (*5) / POPPYCOCK (*5) / SMOKE TIME (*4) / KENNY ROGERS' GREATEST HIT (*4)

TED MILTON – vocals, saxophone / **PETE CREESE** – guitar, trombone / **JAKE MILTON** – drums, vocals

Test Press not iss.

Aug 80. (7") *(TP 1)* **MY MOTHER WAS A FRIEND OF AN ENEMY OF THE PEOPLE. / GET** □ -

Armageddon Ruby

Feb 81. (lp) *(ARM 6)* **IN BERLIN (live)** □ -
– Cherry blossom polish / My mother was a friend of an enemy of the people / Puppeteers of the world unite / Dyslexia blues / Get / Tube plane / Paranoid blues / Ubu. *(re-iss. Apr84; same)*
Jun 81. (7") *(AS 013)* **THE FISH NEEDS A BIKE. / THIS IS MY ROYAL WEDDING SOUVENIR** □ -

— added **HERMAN MARTIN** – keyboards

Red Flame not iss.

May 82. (m-lp) *(RF 1206)* **BLURT** □ -
– Dog save my sole / Trees / Physical fitness / Empty vessels / Play the game / The ruminanth plinth / Arthur.

— **STEVE EAGLET** – guitar repl. CREESE

Devine not iss.

1984. (lp) **BULLETS FOR YOU** □ -

Embryo not iss.

Jan 85. (7"; as MILTON) *(CELET 2)* **LOVE IS LIKE A VIOLENCE. / NOW THAT STARLINGS** □ -

Another Side not iss.

Apr 85. (lp) *(SIDE 8418)* **WHITE LINE FEVER. / SHARKS OF PARADISE / NOMADS** □ -
Apr 85. (lp) **FRIDAY THE 12th** □ -
– Cherry blossom polish / Deepfrozen heart / Enemy ears / No go dada / Grave spit / Kill time / Dog save my soul / The fish needs a bike / Benighted.

— **PAUL WIGENS** – drums, violin; repl. JAKE

Toeblock not iss.

Jan 86. (12"; as TED MILTON) *(TBL 001)* **ODE: O TO BE SEEN THROUGH YOUR EYES. /** □ -
Apr 86. (lp) *(TBL 002)* **POPPYCOCK** □ -
– Domain of dreams / Down in the Argentine / Men to fly / etc.
Mar 87. (lp/cd) *(TB LP/CD 400307)* **SMOKE TIME** □ -
– Smoke time / Nights before / Bulletproof vest / Aboule ton fric / Through by you / Congregate / The body that they built to fit the car / Schadenfreude / The tree is dead, long live the tree. *(re-iss. 1989 on 'Celluloid' lp/c/cd; MT/+C/CD 013)*
Apr 89. (lp/cd) *(TB LP/CD 666)* **KENNY ROGERS' GREATEST HIT: TAKE 2** □ -
– Shoot & shout / Kenny Rogers' greatest hit / Healthy shadows / Mirador / Am I lonesome tonight / Portage & Main / Sharks of Paradise / Forget about for whom the last bell / Chanson du sang / Nameless / Stroud the town of make-believe / Ubuture / The body that they built to fit the car / O to be seen through your eyes (ode).
Jul 89. (lp/cd) *(EFA 15081/+CD)* **THE BODY! LIVE! (live)** □ -
– They bombed too soon / The body that they built to fit the car / Mickey / Enemy ears / Schadenfraude / Argentine / Nights before / Empty vessels / Poppycock / Jap zero / No there's a thing / Aboulton / Eric / Deep-frozen heart.
(above issued on 'Heute')
Aug 92. (cd) *(TBCD 013)* **PAGAN STRINGS** □ -
(re-iss. Feb97 on 'Spalax'; 14988)

— split after above

BLYTH POWER

Formed: Camden Town, London, England . . . 1984 by Somerset lad, JOSEF PORTA, who had recently departed from Yeovil mob, er . . . called The MOB. This early 80's anarchist punk combo was completed by CURTESS and MARK WHO, a handful of singles (one for 'Crass', 'NO DOVES FLY HERE') and an album, 'LET THE TRIBE INCREASE' (1983), taking a similar line in defiant protest as the likes of CRASS. By 1984, PORTA had begun pursuing a rootsier direction with his new punk/folk outfit, BLYTH POWER (named after a Class 56 diesel engine), lyrically exploring the history of England's working classes from a largely rural perspective and taking in historical oppressors from Oliver Cromwell onwards. The missing link between NEW MODEL ARMY and The LEVELLERS, BLYTH POWER sparked their own mini-musical revolution, debut single 'CHEVY CHASE' sadly not evaluating the career of the latter day comic actor. Several albums later, PORTA and his merry band were commanding a small army of grass roots fans with their poetic evocations of past victories for the common man.

Album rating: The Mob: LET THE TRIBE INCREASE (5) / Blyth Power: A LITTLE TOUCH OF HARRY IN THE MIDDLE OF THE NIGHT cassette (*5) / WICKED WOMEN, WICKED MEN AND WICKET KEEPERS (*5) / THE BARMAN & OTHER STORIES (*5) / ALNWICK AND TYNE (*5) / THE GUNS OF CASTLE CARY (*4) / PASTOR SKULL (*4) / PARADISE RAZED (*4) / OUT FROM UNDER THE KING (*4) / PONT AU-DESSUS DE LA BRUE compilation (*5) / TEN YEARS INSIDE THE HORSE compilation (*6)

The MOB

JOSEF PORTA (b.21 Feb'62, Templecombe, Somerset, England) – drums / **MARK WHO** – vocals, guitar / **CURTESS YOUE** – bass

All The Madmen not iss.

Jan 80. (7") *(MAD 1)* **YOUTH. / CRYING AGAIN** □ -
Dec 80. (7"m) *(MAD 2)* **WITCH HUNT. / SHUFFLING SOUL / WHAT'S GOING ON** □ -
Apr 82. (7") *(321984-7)* **NO DOVES FLY HERE. / I HEAR YOU LAUGHING** □ -
(above issued on the 'Crass' label)
Feb 83. (lp) *(MAD 4)* **LET THE TRIBE INCREASE** □ -
– Another day, another death / Cry of the morning / Dance on (you fool) / Raised in a prison / Slayed / Our life, our world / Gates of Hell / I wish / Never understand / Roger / Witch hunt. *(cd-iss. Oct95 on 'Rugger Bugger' lp/cd+=; SEEP 012/+CD)* – Youth / Crying again / Shuffling souls / No doves fly here / I hear you laughing / The mirror breaks / Stay.
Oct 83. (7") *(MAD 6)* **THE MIRROR BREAKS. / STAY** □ -

Cause For Concern not iss.

Nov 84. (lp/c; shared with APOSTLES) *(CFC 002/015)* **LIVE AT LMC (live)** □ -

– compilations, etc. –

Oct 86. (d7"ep) *All The Madmen; (MAD 13)* **CRYING AGAIN / YOUTH / NO DOVES FLY HERE. / GATES OF HELL / WHAT'S GOING ON** □ -

BLYTH POWER

— **JOSEF PORTA** – vocals / **NEIL** – / **ANDY** – / **CURTESS** – bass / **SARAH LEWINGTON** – backing vocals / **GARY JAMES HATCHER** – drums

96 Tapes not iss.

Mar 85. (c) *(96 15)* **A LITTLE TOUCH OF HARRY IN THE MIDDLE OF THE NIGHT** □ -

All The Madmen / not iss.

Sep 85. (7") *(MAD 9)* **CHEVY CHASE. / PFUCKE MASTICHE ROOM** -

May 86. (7") *(MAD 12)* **JUNCTION SIGNAL. / BIND THEIR KINGS IN CHAINS (& THE NOBLES WITH LINKS OF IRON)** -
(12"+=) *(MADT 12)* – Tribute to Admiral Byng / Pfucke mastiche room.

—— **JOSEF** recruited **MARTIN 'PROTAG' NEISH** + **SIAN JEFFRIES** plus **LIBERTY KROPOTKIN** – drums

Apr 87. (lp) *(MADLP 006)* **WICKED WOMEN, WICKED MEN AND WICKET KEEPERS** -
– Goodbye General / Stand into danger / Bricklayers arms / Smoke from Cromwell's gun / John O'Grant / Hurling time / Probably going to rain / Caligula / Probably won't be easy / Marine's moves / Ixion / Some of Shelley's hang-ups.

Midnight Music / not iss.

May 88. (lp) *(CHIME 0036S)* **THE BARMAN & OTHER STORIES** -

May 88. (12"ep) *(DONG 37)* **UP FROM THE COUNTRY. / A TALE OF A COCK AND A BULL / BLOW THE MAN DOWN** -

Aug 88. (7") *(DONG 38)* **GOODBYE TO ALL THAT. /** -

Jan 89. (lp) *(CHIME 0042S)* **PONT AU-DESSUS DE LA BRUE** (compilation) -

Jan 90. (7") *(DONG 58)* **BETTER TO BAT. /** -

Apr 90. (lp) *(CHIME 0102)* **ALNWICK AND TYNE** -

Oct 91. (lp/cd) *(CHIME 0116/+CD)* **THE GUNS OF CASTLE CARY** -

Downward Spiral / not iss.

1993. (cd) *(DR 002CD)* **PASTOR SKULL** -
– Pastor skull / The man who came in third / Gabriel the angel / In the lines of graves / Breitenfeld / General winter / Sunne in splendour / Stonehaven / Vane tempest / Pandora's people / Stitching in time.

Feb 95. (cd) *(DR 003CD)* **PARADISE RAZED** -

Sep 96. (cd) *(DR 004CD)* **OUT FROM UNDER THE KING** -

– compilations, etc. –

Aug 94. (cd) *Anagram; (CDMGRAM 83)* **TEN YEARS INSIDE THE HORSE** -

B-MOVIE

Formed: Mansfield, Nottinghamshire, England ... 1979 by STEVE HOVINGTON and two former ABORTED members GRAHAM BOFFEY and PAUL STATHAM. Picked up by the local 'Dead Good' label, the band had a couple of tracks, 'REFUGE' and 'MAN ON A THRESHOLD', included on compilation set, 'East'. Adding a new dimension to their doomy guitar jangle with the addition of keyboard player, RICK HOLLIDAY, the band released the 'TAKE THREE' EP in 1980, earning themselves positive column inches in the process. Following a further 6-track EP 'NOWHERE GIRL', the band signed to Stevo's 'Some Bizzare' imprint – he also became their manager – and released the anthemic 'REMEMBRANCE DAY', the track's synth flourishes bizarrely reminiscent of ABBA's 'Gimme A Man After Midnight'(!). Yet it was B-MOVIE's association with the New Romantic scene rather than boy/girl Swedish pop that proved a thorn in their side as they attempted to break beyond the bounds of the indie chart. Major personnel changes resulted in an almost completely different line-up (HOVINGTON, STATHAM and newcomer MARTIN WINTER – RICK HOLLIDAY formed SIX SEE RED) by the release of the band's long awaited debut album, 'FOREVER RUNNING' (1985). Issued by major alternative player, 'Sire', and preceded by a single, 'A LETTER FROM AFAR', the record's release was marred by the band's collapse.

Album rating: FOREVER RUNNING (*5) / THE DEAD GOOD TAPES compilation (*6) / REMEMBRANCE DAY compilation (*6)

STEVE HOVINGTON – vocals, bass / **PAUL STATHAM** – guitar / **RICK HOLLIDAY** – keyboards, bass / **GRAHAM BOFFEY** – drums

Dead Good / not iss.

Jul 80. (7"ep) *(DEAD 9)* **TAKE THREE EP** -
– The soldier stood alone / Drowning man / Soundtrack.

Dec 80. (12"ep) *(BIG DEAD 12)* **NOWHERE GIRL EP** -
– Nowhere girl / This is still life / Institution walls / Aeroplanes and mountains / Left out in the cold / Remembrance day.

Deram / not iss.

Mar 81. (12") *(DMX 437)* **REMEMBRANCE DAY. / INSTITUTION WALLS (remix)** 61 -

Jul 81. (7"/12") *(DM/+X 443)* **MARILYN DREAMS. / FILM MUSIC (Part 1)** -

—— added (on tour only) **LUCIANO CODEMO** then **MIKE PEDHAM** – bass (ex-EVEREST THE HARD WAY)

Some Bizzare / not iss.

Mar 82. (7") *(BZZ 8)* **NOWHERE GIRL. / SCARE SOME LIFE INTO ME** 67 -
(12"+=) *(BZZ 8-12)* – ('A'version).

—— **AL CASH** – drums; repl. ANDY JOHNSON who temp'd for BOFFEY (he became a member of SLAUGHTERHOUSE 5)

—— **MARTIN WINTER** – bass; repl. MARTIN SMEDLEY who repl. PEDHAM

—— (1983) RICK HOLLIDAY left to form SIX SEE RED (and later MCX) with ex-SOFT CELL guest CINDY ECSTASY. One 12" single appeared in Feb'84, 'SHAKE IT RIGHT' / 'BANG 'EM RIGHT' on 'Sire' (SIR 4059T)

Sire / Sire

Jan 84. (7"/ext.12") *(SIR 4058/+T)* **A LETTER FROM AFAR. / NO JOY IN HEAVEN** -

—— trimmed to a trio of **HOVINGTON, STATHAM + WINTER** (CASH left)

—— drumming was supplied by **GRAHAM BROAD + JAMIE LANE**

Sep 85. (7") *(W 8933)* **SWITCH ON SWITCH OFF. / JUST AN ECHO** -
(12"+=) *(W 8933T)* – Forever running.

Oct 85. (lp/c) *(925272-1/-4)* **FOREVER RUNNING**
– Forever running / Heart of gold / My ship of dreams / Just an echo / Remembrance day / Switch on switch off / Blind allegience / Arctic summer / Nowhere girl.

—— split late in '85 when STATHAM joined PETE MURPHY's band. HOVINGTON formed ONE with SARA JANE (ex-BELLE STARS)

– compilations, etc. –

on 'Wax' records unless mentioned otherwise

May 87. (7") *(7WAX 2)* **REMEMBRANCE DAYS. / MARILYN DREAMS** -
(12"+=) *(12WAX 2)* – Nowhere girl.

Mar 88. (lp/cd)(pic-lp) *(WAX LP/CD 1)(WAXLP 1P)* **THE DEAD GOOD TAPES** -

Apr 88. (12",12"pink,12"orange) *(12WAX 3)* **NOWHERE GIRL. / REMEMBRANCE DAY** -

Aug 88. (12"clear/cd-s) *(12/CD WAX 4)* **POLAR OPPOSITES. / TAXI DRIVER** -
(re-iss. Jul89 as 12"pic-d; same)

1991. (lp) *Dead Good; (GOOD 3)* **REMEMBRANCE DAYS** -
– Man on a threshold / Refugee / Drowning man / Soundtrack / Nowhere girl / Institution walls / This still life / Left out in the cold / Remembrance day / Aeroplanes and mountains / Remembrance day (version) / Remembrance day (version). *(with free 7") (CHEAP 1)* – THE FOOL. / SWINGING LIGHTS *(cd-iss. Mar97 on 'Cherry Red'; CDMRED 137)*

BMX BANDITS

Formed: Belshill, nr.Glasgow, Scotland . . .summer 1985 by DUGLAS T. STEWART with future SOUP DRAGONS, SEAN DICKSON and JIM McCULLOCH. In 1986, they released a couple of 45's for Stephen Pastel's '53rd & 3rd' label, notably 'THE DAY BEFORE TOMORROW'. Later that year, DUGLAS was joined by FRANCIS McDONALD, although the pace slowed a little to let DUGLAS get out and support The SHOP ASSISTANTS (he was to mime Klaus Wunderlich on the organ and later host a night-time pop-TV show). In 1989, The BMX BANDITS' return was complete with the release of a debut long-player, 'C86' (1990!). A year later, having signed to Tokyo-based 'Vinyl Japan', DUGLAS and Co (this time around boasting a beefed up sound courtesy of MacDONALD, EUGENE KELLY, GORDON KEEN and JOE McALINDEN) issued a more up to date jangle-pop follow-up, 'STARWARS' (1991). Subsequently signing to 'Creation' (who else!?), the 'BANDITS enjoyed cult success with 'SERIOUS DRUGS' and 'KYLIE'S GOT A CRUSH ON US' (the latter boasting of Miss MINOGUE's surprising patronage!); the latter was also performed by local friends and cohorts, TEENAGE FANCLUB. During the mid-90's, this Bellshill pedal-(steel) powered supergroup delivered a further two sets of pleasant, harmony-fuelled retro-pop in 'GETTIN' DIRTY' (1995) and 'THEME PARK' (1996). • **Songwriters:** DUGLAS, until 1990 when he co-wrote with NORMAN BLAKE. Covered DON'T FIGHT IT, FEEL IT (Primal Scream) / C'EST LA VENT BETTY (Gabriel Yared) / GREEN GROW (Rabbie Burns; trad) / YO YO SONG (trad) / THINKIN' 'BOUT YOU BABY (Beach Boys) / GIRL AT THE BUS STOP (Television Personalities) / COME AND GET IT (Badfinger) / KYLIE'S GOT A CRUSH ON US (melody; Clydesmen) / LIKE A HURRICANE (Neil Young) / NAZI PUNKS FUCK OFF (Dead Kennedys) / CAST A SHADOW (Johnson-Lunsunda-Lewis) / I CAN'T STAY MAD AT YOU (Goffin-King) / THAT SUMMER FEELING (Jonathan Richman) / LITTLE RIVER OF SPRING (Okana-Takano). • **Trivia:** Took their name from children's bike film of the same name. 'KYLIE'S GOT A CRUSH ON US' was tongue-in-cheek humour about that lovely Australian singer!?

Album rating: C86 (*6) / A TOTALLY GROOVY LIVE EXPERIENCE (*5) / STARWARS (*6) / GORDON KEEN AND HIS BMX BANDITS mini (*5) / LIFE GOES ON (*7) / GETTIN' DIRTY (*7) / THEME PARK (*7)

DUGLAS STEWART – vocals / with **SEAN DICKSON** – bass / **JIM McCULLOCH** – guitar (both of SOUP DRAGONS) / **BILLY & WILLIE** (of SHOP ASSISTANTS?)

53rd & 3rd / not iss.

May 86. (7") *(AGARR 3)* **SAD? / E102** -
(12"+=) *(AGARR 3-12)* – The cat from outer space (live) / Strawberry Sunday (live) / Groovy good luck friend (live).

—— now w /out SEAN (B-side only for JIM)

Jan 87. (7") *(AGARR 6)* **WHAT A WONDERFUL WORLD. / THE DAY BEFORE TOMORROW** -
(12"+=) *(AGARR 6-12)* – Johnny Alucard / Sad? / Sandy's wallet.

—— **DUGLAS** w / **FRANCIS McDONALD** – drums (ex-BOY HAIRDRESSERS, ex-PASTELS) / + **GORDON KEEN** – guitar / + **NORMAN BLAKE** – guitar, vocals (of TEENAGE FANCLUB)

Jan 88. (7") *(AGARR 18)* **FIGURE 4. / STARDATE 21.11.70.** -
(12"+=) *(AGARR 18T)* – In her hair / Bette Blue.

—— now w / **NORMAN BLAKE + GERRY** (from TEENAGE FANCLUB)

Click / not iss.

Mar 90. (lp) *(LP 001)* **C86** -
– Right across the street / Top Shop girl / Rimbaud and me / Yo yo song (1969) / Medley: Disco girl – Disco daze and disco knights / Your class / Disco girl II / Whirlpool / C86 / On somedays / But tonight / Let Mother Nature be your guide / Heaven's daughter. *(cd-iss. Nov92 as 'C86 PLUS' on 'Vinyl Japan'+=; ASKCD 19)* – Stardate / Figure 4 / Strawberry sundae / C'est la vent Betty / Thinkin' 'bout you baby / Let Mother Nature be your guide (karaoke mix) / Your class. *(cd re-iss. Jul97 on 'Elefant'; ER 1048)*

Only / not iss.

Dec 90. (cd/lp) *(ONLY CD/LP 007)* **TOTALLY GROOVY LIVE EXPERIENCE (live at Hattonrig Hotel)** -

– Whirlpool / Girl at the bus stop / Your class / In her hair / E102 / Bongo brains / Disco girl / The day before tomorrow / Like a hurricane / Nazi punks fuck off.

— **DUGLAS** now w/ **EUGENE KELLY** (ex-VASELINES, of CAPTAIN AMERICA + EUGENIUS) **+ GORDON KEEN / JOE McALINDEN** – guitar (of GROOVY LITTLE NUMBERS) / **FRANCIS MacDONALD**

Vinyl Japan not iss.

Oct 91. (cd/lp) *(ASK CD/LP 007)* **STARWARS**
– Come clean / Think tank / Smile for me / Green grow / Retitled / Life goes on / The sailor's song (pt.1) / Disguise / Studcats of life / Extraordinary / Do you really love me? / The sailor's song / Stars Wars.

Jan 92. (12"ep/cd-ep) *(TASK 12005/+CD)* **COME CLEAN / LET MOTHER NATURE BE YOUR GUIDE. / RETITLED / ('A'-funky train mix)**

Sunflower not iss.

Aug 92. (red-lp) *(SUN 006)* **GORDON KEEN AND HIS BMX BANDITS**
– Kylie's got a crush on us / Come and get it / Girl at the bus stop / etc.

Creation Tristar

Nov 92. (12"ep)(cd-ep) *(CRE 131T)(CRESCD 131)* **SERIOUS DRUGS / FUNNY FACE. / DON'T FIGHT IT FEEL IT (in concert) / SERIOUS DRUGS (demo)**

Jul 93. (7"/c-s) *(CRE/+CS 154)* **KYLIE'S GOT A CRUSH ON US. / HOLE IN MY HEART**
(12"+=)(cd-s+=) *(CRE 154T)(CRESCD 154)* – Thinkin' 'bout you baby / My generation.

Oct 93. (cd/lp) *(CRE CD/LP 133)* *<67207>* **LIFE GOES ON**
– Little hands / Serious drugs / Space girl / Scar / I'll keep on joking / Hole in my heart / Cast a shadow / Cats and dogs / Your dreams / My friend / It hasn't ended / Intermission (bathing beauties) / Kylie's got a crush on us.

Nov 93. (12"ep)(cd-ep) *(CRE 168T)(CRESCD 168)* **LITTLE HANDS / THE NEXT GIRL. / WITCHI TAI TO (home recording) / BUT TONIGHT (acoustic session)**

Apr 94. (7"ep/cd-ep) *(CRE/+SCD 181)* **SERIOUS DRUGS / LITTLE PONY. / I'LL KEEP ON JOKING / THE SAILOR'S SONG**

Creation Creation

Mar 95. (7") **(CRE 192) GETTIN' DIRTY. / I CAN'T STAY MAD AT YOU**
(cd-s+=) *(CRESCD 192)* – Tiny fingers, tiny toes / This guy's in love with you.

May 95. (cd/lp) *(CRE CD/LP 174)* **GETTIN' DIRTY**
– Gettin' dirty / Hello again / Lost girl / Love, come to me / No future / Konnichiva #2 / On the road to Heaven / Little river of spring.

— (below featured The MORLEY STRING QUARTET; b-side featured DAN PENN)

Aug 95. (7") *(CRE 207)* **LOVE, COME TO ME. / THAT SUMMER FEELING**
(cd-s+=) *(CRESCD 207)* – Come summer / Sunshine day.

Oct 96. (cd) *(CRECD 202)* **THEME PARK**

— Mar'97, they turned up with idol KIM FOWLEY on cd 'HIDDEN AGENDA' on 'Receiver'; *RRCD 231)*

BOB

Formed: North London, England . . . 1986 by RICHARD BLACKBOROW, SIMON ARMSTRONG and JEM MORRIS. After using a drum machine for their debut EP, 'WHAT A PERFORMANCE', they subsequently required the services of a real drummer, GARY CONNORS, his first appearance being on the follow-up, 'KIRSTY'. Fortunate enough to have both records playlisted on John Peel's Radio One show, the lads took advantage of their rising profile by compiling the two EP's on one long-player, 'SWAG SACK' (1988). Soon afterwards, ex-JAMIE WEDNESDAY drummer, DEAN LEGGAT, substituted CONNORS just as the band were in the midst of delivering a further two 45's, 'PRUNE' and 'CONVENIENCE'. An indie pop outfit in the true sense of the word, BOB (whose idea was it to call them that?!) were never likely to stumble upon any great musical innovations although they were slightly influenced by the noisy, groovy psychedelia of the insurgent "baggy" scene. By the release of their fifth single, 'ESMERALDA BROOKLYN', MORRIS made way for STEPHEN HERSOM, the new bassist sticking around for a few more 12" singles and the belated release of their debut album proper, 'LEAVE THE STRAIGHT LIFE BEHIND' (1991). However, fate seemed to be against BOB as the financial collapse of the distribution arm of 'Rough Trade' affected sales, leading to their demise.

Album rating: SWAG SACK (*7) / LEAVE THE STRAIGHT LIFE BEHIND (*7)

RICHARD BLACKBOROW (b.21 Mar'66, Hackney, London) – vocals / **SIMON ARMSTRONG** (b.12 Feb'66, Hull, England) – guitar / **JEM MORRIS** (b. Aberdare, Wales) – bass / + drum machine

Sombrero not iss.

Oct 87. (12"ep) *(SOMBRERO ONE)* **WHAT A PERFORMANCE / DREARY ME. / PIGGERY / MEMORY OF A FREE FESTIVAL**

— **GARY CONNORS** – drums; repl. drum machine

May 88. (12"ep) *(SOMBRERO TWO)* **KIRSTY / THE HIPPY GOES FISHING. / BANWELL BLUES LIKE THESE (No.2) / TIMES LIKE THESE**

Dec 88. (lp) *(SOMBRERO FIVE)* **SWAG SACK**
– Kirsty / Piggery / Smelly summer / Prune / Deary me / The hippy goes fishing / What a performance / Times like these / Memory of a free lunch / Groove / Banwell blues No.2 / So far, so good.

— **DEAN LEGGETT** (b.30 Aug'63) – drums (ex-JAMIE WEDNESDAY) repl. CONNORS

House Of Teeth not iss.

Feb 89. (7"flexi) *(HOT 001)* **PRUNE (YOUR TRUE). / GROOVE / BRIAN WILSON'S BED**

May 89. (7") *(HOT 7-002)* **CONVENIENCE. /**
(12"+=) *(HOT 12-002)* -

— **STEPHEN HERSOM** (b.28 Apr'63, Plaistow, London) – bass (ex-CARETAKER RACE) repl. MORRIS

Oct 89. (12") *(HOT 12-003)* **ESMERALDA BROOKLYN. / I DON'T KNOW**

May 90. (12"ep) *(HOT 12-004)* **STRIDE UP**
– Daymaker / Rain / My blood is drink / + 1.

May 91. (cd/lp) *(HOT CD/LP 13-013)* **LEAVE THE STRAIGHT LIFE BEHIND**

Sep 91. (7") **NOTHING FOR SOMETHING. /**

— they dissolved when the Rough Trade distribution collapsed

BODINES

Formed: Glossop, nr.Manchester, England . . . 1985 by MIKE RYAN, PAUL BROTHERTON, TIM BURTONWOOD and PAUL LILLEY. Heading out of the dole queue and onto the stage, the band (who took their moniker from Beverley Hillbillies character, Jethro Bodine) built up a healthy local following and signed to 'Creation' around the same time as the C86 phenomenon propelled The BODINES and their ilk (PRIMAL SCREAM, The WEDDING PRESENT, BOGSHED, The MIGHTY LEMON DROPS etc.) into the limelight via the infamous tape of the same name. Dreamt up by the NME (who else?), C86 gathered together a clutch of jangly indie hopefuls and created a short-lived and subsequently much derided scene in the process; while most of them aspired to be The BYRDS via The SMITHS, many never made it off the starting blocks, including The BODINES. A shame, as their three 'Creation' singles, 'GOD BLESS', the angst-ridden 'THERESE' (their most enduring, infectious track and their star turn on C86) and 'HEARD IT ALL' displayed definite potential – 'THERESE' introduced new drummer JOHN ROWLAND. While a further brace of singles including a remix of 'THERESE', 'SKANKING QUEENS' and 'SLIP SLIDE' were interspersed by a long overdue, IAN BROUDIE-produced album, 'PLAYED' (1987) on 'Magnet' records, none of their efforts met with much more than critical plaudits from the indie press. The final nail in the coffin was the collapse of their label, the group disappearing from view save a one-off reunion gig at Manchester's Hacienda in 1988.

Album rating: PLAYED (*5)

MIKE RYAN – vocals / **PAUL BROTHERTON** – guitar / **TIM BURTONWOOD** – bass / **PAUL LILLEY** – drums

Creation not iss.

Sep 85. (7") *(CRE 016)* **GOD BLESS. / PARADISE**

— **JOHN ROWLAND** – drums; repl. LILLEY

Feb 86. (7") *(CRE 028)* **THERESE. / I FEEL**
(12"+=) *(CRE 028T)* – Scar tissue.

Aug 86. (7") *(CRE 030)* **HEARD IT ALL. / CLEAR**
(12"+=) *(CRE 030T)* – William Shatner.

Magnet not iss.

Feb 87. (7") *(BOD 1)* **THERESE (wear mix). / HEARD IT ALL**
(ext.12"+=) *(BODT 1)* – ('A'original). *(w/ free 7" CANADIAN BOOTLEG)*

Jun 87. (7"m/12"m) *(BOD/+T 2)* **SKANKIN QUEENS. / 1000 TIMES / MY REMARKABLE MIND**

Aug 87. (lp/c) *(BODL/ZCBOD 2001)* **PLAYED**
– Skankin queens / What you want / Scar tissue / Tall stories / Clear / Untitled / Therese / Slip slide / The back door / William Shatner. *(cd-iss. Apr88; CDBOD 2001)*

Sep 87. (7"/12") *(BOD/+T 3)* **SLIP SLIDE. / NAMING NAMES**

— split but re-formed late '88. **IAN** – bass; repl. BURTONWOOD

— **SPENCER** – drums; repl. ROWLAND who joined RAINKINGS

Play Hard not iss.

Mar 89. (12"m) *(DEC 18)* **DECIDE. / HARD ON / THE GROOVE**

— split again after above

MEDALARK 11

RYAN / + GARETH THOMAS – bass / **ADRIAN DONAHUE** – drums

3 Bass not iss.

May 92. (12"ep) *(3B 1)* **SNAKE**

Creation not iss.

Aug 92. (cd/lp) *(CRE CD/LP 145)* **SHAPED UP, SHIPPED OUT**
(re-iss. Feb94; same)

Oct 92. (12"ep)(cd-ep) *(CRE 132T)(CRESCD 132)* **I CALL YOUR NAME**

Aug 93. (12"ep)(cd-ep) *(CRE 144T)(CRESCD 144)* **SMOKE**

— split soon after above

BOGSHED

Formed: Hebden Bridge, England . . . 1985 as THE AMAZING ROY NORTH PENIS BAND by PHIL HARTLEY, MARK McQUAID, MIKE BRYSON and TRIS KING. Sensibly adopting the marginally less offensive BOGSHED moniker, this absurdly humourous band were signed up by MEMBRANES man, JOHN ROBB, to his fledgling 'Vinyl Drip' label. A debut EP, 'LET THEM EAT BOGSHED', won them the patronage of John Peel who aired a couple of sessions, relaying the patented BOGSHED sound of herky-jerky, knotty rhythms and demented vocals provided by the madcap genius of HARTLEY. 1986 saw the release of the band's debut album, 'STEP ON IT BOGSHED', the group becoming inextricably linked to the much maligned

C86 scene after having a track featured on the NME cassette of the same name. This association proved to be a thorn in the band's side as a fickle music press (in customary style) derided the scene they had helped create, BOGSHED's follow-up set, 'BRUTAL' receiving short thrift from critics. Undeterred, they ploughed on through their own idiosyncratic furrow until finances dictated otherwise. With the indie scene increasingly focusing on US alternative acts towards the end of the 80's, the 'EXCELLENT GIRL' single proved to be BOGSHED's epitaph, the lads finally discovering the luxuries of an inside loo. While KING went on to play with A WITNESS (not criminally though!), HARTLEY attempted a more sedate solo career. • **Trivia:** BRYSON did artwork on all the record sleeves and later went into animation.

Album rating: STEP ON IT BOGSHED (*8) / BRUTAL (*6)

PHIL HARTLEY – vocals / **MARK McQUAID** – guitar / **MIKE BRYSON** – bass / **TRISTIAN KING** – drums

Vinyl Drip | not iss.

Oct 85. (12"ep) *(DRIP 2)* **LET THEM EAT BOGSHED** ☐ -
– Fat lad exam failure / etc.

Shellfish | not iss.

May 86. (7") *(SHELF 1)* **MORNING SIR. /** ☐ -
Aug 86. (lp) *(SHELF 2)* **STEP ON IT BOGSHED** ☐ -
– Jobless youngsters / Tried to hide but forced to howl / The fastest legs / Adventure of dog / Tommy Steele record / etc.
Jan 87. (12"ep) *(SHELF 3)* **TRIED AND TESTED PUBLIC SPEAKER (The Peel Session)** ☐ -
– Champion love shoes / Little grafter / Morning sir / Fastest legs / Adventure of dog / Tried and tested public speaker.
Aug 87. (lp) *(SHELF 4)* **BRUTAL** ☐ -
Nov 87. (7") *(SHELF 6)* **EXCELLENT GIRL. /** ☐ -

— disbanded in 1988 and KING joined JACKDAW WITH CROWBAR then A WITNESS. HARTLEY went solo but after a PEEL session, he gave up.

BOLLOCK BROTHERS

Formed: London, England ... 1980 as a punk satirist outfit headed by chief mouthpiece, JOCK McDONALD. Gathering together fellow jesters, RICHARD COLLINS, KEITH LEWIS, KEITH BRADSHAW, DAVID REAGAN and PAUL SHIRLEY, McDONALD incredibly netted a deal with re-issue specialist, 'Charly', releasing a slew of 12"ers that were generally regarded as being er, bollocks. Their debut long-player, 'THE LAST SUPPER' (1983), contained many of the aforementioned 45's, could possibly be termed piss-tiche, a cross between piss-taking and pastiche. An uninspired run through of the SEX PISTOLS' album 'NEVER MIND THE BOLLOCKS' in its entirety brought cheap publicity for the inclusion of guest vocals by MICHAEL FAGIN, the man infamous for getting past the Buckingham Palace security and into the Queen's bedroom. Excepting the first of many official live bootleg albums, The BOLLOCKS BROTHERS finally released their follow-up set in '85, 'THE FOUR HORSEMEN OF THE APOCALYPSE', McDONALD this time around opting for covers of Alex Harvey's 'FAITH HEALER' and Aphrodite Child's 'SEVENTH SEAL'. Following a one-off cover of Brigette Bardot's 'HARLEY DAVIDSON' on Belgium's top indie 'Play It Again Sam', McDONALD recruited an entire new force to record his next album project, 'THE PROPHECIES OF NOSTRADAMUS' (1988). The SEX PISTOLS connection continued as the singer(!?) managed to rope in ex-PISTOLS (McDONALD was also behind a questionable outfit of the same name!), COOK and JONES alongside guests BILLY IDOL, GEORDIE and YOUTH, on the 'MYTHOLOGY' set in '89. Released under the moniker THE FAMOUS B. BROTHERS, McDONALD's final project was another biblical examination going under the title of 'THE DEAD SEA SCROLLS' (1991).

Album rating: THE LAST SUPPER (*3) / NEVER MIND THE BOLLOCKS '83 (*3) / LIVE PERFORMANCES – THE OFFICIAL BOOTLEG (*2) / 77, 78, 79 compilation (*3) / THE FOUR HORSEMEN OF THE APOCALYPSE (*1) / ROCK'N'ROLL SUICIDE (*2) / LIVE – IN PUBLIC IN PRIVATE (*1) / THE PROPHECIES OF NOSTRADAMUS (*3) / MYTHOLOGY (*3) / THE DEAD SEA SCROLLS (*3) / THE BEST OF THE BOLLOCKS compilation (*3)

JOCK McDONALD – vocals / **RICHARD COLLINS** – guitar, french horn / **KEITH LEWIS** – guitar, violin / **KEITH BRADSHAW** – bass / **DAVID REAGAN** – drums, percussion / **PAUL SHIRLEY** – synthesizer

Charly | not iss.

Jan 81. (12") *(BOLL 1)* **THE BUNKER. / BOOTLEG MAN** ☐ -
(re-iss. Apr83 as 7"; BOLL 4)
Mar 81. (12") *(BOLL 2)* **THE ACT BECAME REAL. / THE ACTORS (DUB-LE)** ☐ -
Oct 82. (12") *(BOLL 3)* **SLOW REMOVAL OF VINCENT VAN GOGH'S LEFT EAR. / ROCK & ROLL PART 2 (1 & 2)** ☐ -
Jan 83. (12") *(BOLL 5)* **HORROR MOVIES. / ENCHANTMENT** ☐ -
Feb 83. (lp) *(BOLL 100)* **THE LAST SUPPER** ☐ -
– Horror movies / Enchantment / Reincarnation of / Save our souls / Face in the mirror / The last supper / The act became real / The gift 2. *(cd-iss. Feb89; CDCHARLY 175) (cd re-iss. Feb97; CDCRH 103)*
Jul 83. (lp) *(BOLL 101)* **NEVER MIND THE BOLLOCKS '83** ☐ -
– Holidays in the sun / Problems / No feelings / God save the Queen / Pretty vacant / Submission / New York / Seventeen / Anarchy in the UK / Liar / Bodies / E.M.I. *(cd-iss. Dec89; CDCHARLY 178) (cd re-iss. Feb97; CDCRH 104)*
Dec 83. (d-lp) *(BOLL 102)* **LIVE PERFORMANCES – THE OFFICIAL BOOTLEG (live)** ☐ -
– Slow removal of Vincent Van Gogh's left ear / Loose / Horror movies / The bunker / The last supper / Reincarnation of / New York / Problems / Holidays in the sun / Vincent / Pretty vacant / God save the Queen. *(cd-iss. Feb89; CDCHARLY 174) (cd re-iss. Feb97; CDCRH 102)*
Aug 84. (12") *(DID 127700)* **PRINCE AND THE SHOWGIRL. / SHOWGIRLS** ☐ -

(above issued on Belgium label, 'Disc')
Jul 85. (lp) *(BOLL 103)* **THE FOUR HORSEMEN OF THE APOCALYPSE** ☐ -
– Legend of the snake / Mistress of the macabre / Woke up this morning found myself dead / Faith healer / King rat / The four horsemen of the apocalypse / Loud, loud, loud / The seventh seal / Return to the Garden of Eden. *(cd-iss. Mar87; CDCHARLY 72) (cd re-iss. Feb97; CDCRH 109)*
Apr 86. (12") *(BOLL 6)* **DRAC'S BACK. / HORROR MOVIES** ☐ -
Oct 86. (12") *(BOLL 7)* **FAITH HEALER. / RETURN TO THE GARDEN OF EDEN** ☐ -
Jan 87. (lp) *(BOLL 104)* **LIVE – IN PUBLIC IN PRIVATE (live)** ☐ -
– Woke up this morning / Drac's back / The four horsemen of the apocalypse / Midnight Moses / Rock and roll / Count Dracula where's yar troosers / King rat / Faith healer. *(cd-iss. Nov89; CDCHARLY 179) (cd re-iss. Feb97; CDCRH 105)*

Play It Again Sam | not iss.

Sep 86. (12") *(BIAS 036)* **HARLEY DAVIDSON. /** ☐ -

— **McDONALD** had now recruited **BORIS DOMMENGET** – guitar / **SERGE FEYS** – keyboards / **SEAN PETTIT** – bass / **PATRIK PATTYN** – drums / **GENEVIEVE FRENCH** – vocals

M.B.C. | not iss.

Jan 88. (lp) *(85-3527)* **THE PROPHECIES OF NOSTRADAMUS** ☐ -
– Magic carpet ride / Calendar of visions / Brigitte Bardot / Ceremony / Heartbreaker / The prophecies of Nostradamus / God created woman / The beast is calling / Harley Davidson.

— **McDONALD** with guests **BILLY IDOL + PAUL YOUNGIE** – vocals / **STEVE JONES + GEORDIE** – guitar / **YOUTH + KEITH BRADSHAW** – bass / **PAUL COOK + PATRICK PATTYN** – drums

Blue Turtle – SPV | not iss.

May 89. (lp)(cd) *(08-3543)(853544)* **MYTHOLOGY** ☐ -
– G.D.M. / Spooky / Beats of love / Dinner with Dracula / My fair daughter / Monster mash / Wiped out / For your blood / Wilde mythology / Legend piano mix.

— **JOCK, RICHARD, BORIS + PATRIK**

S.P.V. | not iss.

Oct 91. (cd/lp; FAMOUS B. BROTHERS) *(084/008 8846-2/-1)* **THE DEAD SEA SCROLLS** ☐ -
– Blood meets flood / Nimrod – Tower of Babel / Abraham – Sodom & Gomorrha / Into the night / Joseph (dream interceptor) / The virgin birth / Revelations of St. John / Babylon the great has fallen / The Dead Sea scrolls / In holiness, in honour.

— finally, McDONALD retired

– compilations, etc. –

Apr 85. (lp) *Mausoleum; (KOMA 788011)* **77, 78, 79** ☐ -
Feb 86. (lp) *Konnexion; (JUNK 788010)* **ROCK'N'ROLL SUICIDE** ☐ -
Jul 93. (cd) *Charly; (CDCRM 1011)* **THE BEST OF THE BOLLOCKS** ☐ -

BOMB PARTY

Formed: Leicester, England . . . early 80's initially as FARMLIFE, by SARAH CORINA, STEVE GERRARD, ANDY 'JESUS' MOSQUERA and MARK THOMPSON. Under this moniker they issued only one single, 'SUSIE'S PARTY', early in '82, although it might have been two but for the abandonment of a follow-up, 'BIG COUNTRY, a year later. BOMB PARTY were a different kind of proposition, taking an anti-American stance while treating us to a molotov cocktail of hardcore grebo gothabilly lying somewhere between The CRAMPS or BAUHAUS. Signing to the up and coming indie-punk label, 'Abstract' early in '85, the band blasted out with the 'RAY GUN' EP. Over the course of the next year, the BOMB PARTY unleashed two more, 'THE NEW MESSIAH' and 'LIFE'S A BITCH', before getting around to delivering their debut album, 'DRUGS' (1986). A slight shake up in the band's personnel resulted in the addition of LESZEK RATAJ and he was in place for their first album for 'Worker's Playtime', 'LIBERACE RISING' (1987). Around the same time, SARAH moonlighted with The JANITORS offshoot outfit, BIG ZAP. Augmented by the girls from VOICE OF THE BEEHIVE, The BOMB PARTY released what was to be their most commercial record to date, a cover of The Archies' 'SUGAR SUGAR'. Issued on Germany's 'Normal' label at the back end of '88, it was trailed by their third album, 'FISH' (1989).

Album rating: DRUGS (*5) / THE LAST SUPPER compilation (*5) / LIBERACE RISING (*5) / FISH (*4) / NATIVITY (*4)

JESUS MOSQUERA (b. ANDY) – vocals / **STEVE GERRARD** – guitar / **SARAH CORINA** – bass / **MARK THOMPSON** – drums

Dining Out | not iss.

Feb 82. (7"; as FARMLIFE) *(TUX 19)* **SUSIE'S PARTY. / SIMPLE MEN** ☐ -

Whaam! | not iss.

Sep 83. (7"; as FARMLIFE) *(WHAAM 13)* **BIG COUNTRY. / (part 2)** - - w/draw

Abstract | not iss.

May 85. (12"ep) *(12ABS 032)* **RAY GUN EP** ☐ -
– Harry the babysitter / Ray gun / Get lost my love / Knocking.
Aug 85. (12"ep) *(12ABS 035)* **THE NEW MESSIAH EP** ☐ -
Dec 85. (7"ep) *(ABS 038)* **LIFE'S A BITCH. / GET SO DOWN / THE NEW MESSIAH** ☐ -
Jun 86. (lp) **DRUGS** ☐ -
– Kill your wife / Don't die Keith / Johnny took her breath away / Jesus was a pinko / Gas / Johnny Nero / Susie's party / Our love is pushing up daisies / Slide / Zombie head / Refugee.
May 87. (lp) *(ABT 016)* **THE LAST SUPPER** (compilation) ☐ -

— added **LESZEK RATAJ** – guitar

Workers Playtime | not iss.

Oct 87. (m-lp) *(PLAYLP 2)* **LIBERACE RISING** ☐ -

– Crawl / Don't talk just kiss / Come on and get closer / Evil eye / El savor del amor / Metropolis.

Dec 87. (7") *(WPCS 1)* **PRETTY FACE. / THESE ARE YOUR RIGHTS / I WANNA BE ABUSED**

Normal not iss.

Oct 88. (7") *(NORMAL 93)* **SUGAR SUGAR. / DO THE RIGHT THING**
(12"+=/cd-s+=) *(NORMAL 93 T/CD)* – Some people settle for less.

May 89. (lp/cd) *(NORMAL 103/+CD)* **FISH**
– Praise the Lord / L.S.D. / Some bodies / Venus in dirt / The last waltz / Do the right thing / Theme from "God Bless America" / Mephistopleles (a million worth of pillion) / Shakespeare / Why don't we talk / Love at any price / The only rule (there is no rule) / Car crash (on the highway of love) / Nobody's.

Artlos not iss.

Apr 91. (lp/cd) *(efa 01819/+CD)* **NATIVITY**

— split soon after above

Beki BONDAGE (see under ⇒ LIGOTAGE)

BONE ORCHARD

Formed: Brighton, England . . . 1983 by female singer CHRISSIE McGEE, MARK HORSE, TROY TYRO, MICK FINCH and PAUL HENDRICKSON. Led by CHRISSIE, a grunting banshee with gothic psychobilly overtones and described by music mags as "Nick Cave with tits~", these post-punk crypt creepers signed to the 'Jungle' label following their fifteen minutes worth of fame on a John Peel session. Hot on the heels of their debut EP 'STUFFED TO THE GILLS', the band made an appearance at that year's Futurama festival, drummer RIM TIM CHEESE subsequently replacing MICK. 'SWALLOWING HAVOC' was the title of their follow-up EP, while BEN TISDALL became their new drummer on 1984's mini-set, 'JACK'. Given short thift by the music press, BONE ORCHARD faded from view following the release of a low-key album, 'PENTHOUSE POULTRY' (1985).

Album rating: JACK (*4) / PENTHOUSE POULTRY (*3)

CHRISSIE McGEE – vocals / **MARK HORSE** – guitar / **TROY TYRO** – guitar / **PAUL HENDRICKSON** – bass / **MICK FINCH** – drums

Jungle not iss.

Nov 83. (12"ep) *(JUNG 8)* **STUFFED TO THE GILLS**
– Fats terminal / Shall I carry the budgie woman? / etc

— **RIM TIM CHEESE** – drums; repl. MICK

Apr 84. (12"ep) *(JUNG 15)* **SWALLOWING HAVOC**

— **BEN TISDALL** – drums; repl. TIM who joined SKELETAL FAMILY

Sep 84. (7") *(JUNG 18)* **JACK. /**

Nov 84. (lp) *(FREUD 06)* **JACK**
– Jack / Lynched / Marianne / Touched / Five days in the neighbourhood / Girl with a gun / Tongue / Scarlett ropes.

— had a new drummer; unknown to repl. BEN

Jun 85. (12"ep) *(JUNG 22T)* **PRINCESS EPILEPSY. / SAME OLD BALL AND CHAIN / YOU DON'T PRESS MY PANTS**

Vax not iss.

Nov 85. (lp) *(VAXLP 1)* **PENTHOUSE POULTRY**

— split some time in the mid 80's

BONGOS

Formed: Hoboken, New Jersey, USA . . . late '79 by RICHARD BARONE, FRANK GIANNINI and ROB NORRIS. Brought to London to feature in special gigs alongside other New York-based outfits BUSH TETRAS, dB's and The FLESHTONES, they signed to UK indie label, 'Fetish' (also home to a number of the more avant-garde new wave groups such as CLOCKDVA; CHARLIE COLLINS made an appearance for them early on). During the early 80's, the label issued a string of singles including debut 'TELEPHONE LENS' (after the release of which JAMES MASTRO joined up as 4th member), along with two mini-sets, 'THE BONGOS' (1981) and 'TIME AND A RIVER' (1982). Guitar-based pop with a twist, The BONGOS were unashamedly retro yet managed to capture the imagination of the post New Wave cognoscenti. After a successful support slot to The B-52's, the quirky quartet signed an American deal with 'R.C.A.', releasing the Richard Gottehrer-produced 'NUMBERS WITH WINGS' EP in '83. A few years later, The BONGOS finally issued their first full-length album (barring compilation, 'DRUMS ALONG THE HUDSON'), 'BEAT HOTEL' (1985), ex-RICHARD HELL & THE VOID-OIDS man, IVAN JULIAN coming in for MASTRO prior to their demise. BARONE later carved out a low-key solo career that took in albums such as 'COOL BLUE HALO' (1989), 'PRIMAL DREAM' (1990), 'CLOUDS OVER EDEN' (1993) and 'BETWEEN HEAVEN AND CELLO' (1994).

Album rating: THE BONGOS mini (*5) / TIME AND A RIVER mini (*6)

RICHARD BARONE (b. 1 Oct'60, Tampa, Florida) – vocals, guitar / **ROB NORRIS** (b. 1 Apr'55, New York City, N.Y.) – bass, vocals / **FRANK GIANNINI** (b. 6 Aug'59, Morristown, N.J.) – drums, vocals / augmented by **COSEY FANNI TUTTI** – concertina (of THROBBING GRISTLE) / **CHARLIE COLLINS** – saxophone (of CLOCKDVA)

Fetish not iss.

Apr 80. (12") *(FET 003)* **TELEPHONE LENS. / GLOW IN THE DARK**

— added **JAMES MASTRO** (b. JAMES MASTRODIMUS, 9 Dec'60, Springfield, Ohio) – guitar, vocals

1981. (m-lp) *(FR 2004)* **THE BONGOS**

May 81. (12") *(FET 005)* **IN THE CONGO. / MAMBO SUN**

Dec 81. (7") *(FET 009)* **THE BULLRUSHES. / AUTOMATIC DOORS**

Feb 82. (m-lp) *(FR 2009)* **TIME AND A RIVER**
– Question ball / Clay midgets / Burning bush / Certain harbours / Speaking sand / Vieo eyes / Zebra club / Three wise men.

Feb 82. (7") *(FE 17)* **ZEBRA CLUB. / CERTAIN HARBOURS**

Apr 82. (7"/12") *(FE/+T 18)* **MAMBO SUN. / HUNTING**

not iss. R.C.A.

1983. (12"ep) **NUMBERS WITH WINGS**

1985. (lp) **BEAT HOTEL**
<cd-iss. Jul92 on 'Razor & Tie'+=; > – NUMBERS WITH WINGS

— **IVAN JULIAN** – guitar (ex-RICHARD HELL) repl. MASTRO who released an album for 'Passport'; 'NUTS AND BOLTS' with RICHARD BARONE. MASTRO later released solo and with STRANGE CAVE plus The HEALTH AND HAPPINESS SHOW.

— disbanded shortly after brief change

– compilations, etc. –

1982. (lp) *P.V.C.;* **DRUMS ALONG THE HUDSON**
– In the Congo / The bullrushes / Clay midgets / Video eyes / Glow in the dark / Telephoto lens / Certain harbours / Speaking sands / Burning bush / Automatic doors hunting / Zebra club / Three wise men / Mambo sun / Question ball. *<cd-iss. 1992 on 'Razor & Tie'; > (UK-iss.Oct94 on 'Line'; LICD 900770)*

RICHARD BARONE

— with main musicians; **NICK CELESTE** – vocals, guitar / **JANE SCARPANTONI** – cello / **VALERIE NARANJO** – percussion

New Rose Passport

Sep 89. (lp/cd) *(ROSE 171/+CD) <PB/+C/+CD 6058>* **COOL BLUE HALO (live)** Nov87
– The bullrushes / I belong to me / The visit / Tangled in your web / Silent symphony / Flew a falcon / Cry baby cry / Sweet blue cage / The man who sold the world / Love is a wind that screams / Numbers with wings. *(also cd on 'Line'; LICD 9.00707)*

M.C.A. M.C.A.

1990. (lp/cd) *(MCA/+D 6370)* **PRIMAL DREAM**
– Where the truth lies / Before you were born / Something happens / River to river / Opposites attracting / I only took what I needed / Mr. Used-To-Be / Native tongue / To the pure . . . / I'll be your mirror / Roman circus.

1990. (cd-ep) **MR. USED-TO-BE (remix) / RIVER TO RIVER (live acoustic) / WHERE THE TRUTH LIES (live acoustic) / MR. USED-TO-BE (extended remix)**

— now with large string ensemble

not iss. Mesa

1993. (cd) *<79060>* **CLOUDS OVER EDEN**
– Within these walls / Paper airplane / Forbidden / Nobody knows me / Clouds over Eden / Waiting for the train / Miss Jean / Beautiful human / Standing in the line / Law of the jungle / Within these walls (reprise).

Line not iss.

Sep 94. (cd) *(LICD 901289)* **BETWEEN HEAVEN AND CELLO**
– Certain harbours / Guinevere / Miss Jean / Before you were born / Forbidden / Beautiful human / Tangled in your web / Numbers with wings / To the pure / Barberella / Ballrooms of Mars / Standing in the line / Under someone's spell.

BONGWATER

Formed: New York, USA . . . 1987 by MARK KRAMER and actress ANN MAGNUSON, who he had met while working in the latter's PULSALLAMA band. KRAMER founded his new indie label, 'Shimmy Disc', releasing the mini-lp, 'BREAKING NO NEW GROUND'. This featured a cover of The MONKEES' 'PORPOISE SONG' and avant-garde guitarist FRED FRITH. The 1988 follow-up, 'DOUBLE BUMMER' featured more inspired covers including GARY GLITTER's 'ROCK & ROLL PART 2', JOHNNY CASH's 'THERE YOU GO' and an outrageous version of LED ZEPPELIN's 'DAZED AND CONFUSED' (re-born/aborted as DAZED AND CHINESE). They satirized many styles and cultures, nobody (even DAVID BOWIE) being safe from their merciless humour. KRAMER moonlighted with other projects, producing just about anyone who was anyone (i.e. GALAXIE 500, URGE OVERKILL and DOGBOWL) from the US indie world, while also finding time to play with B.A.L.L. The albums, 'THE POWER OF PUSSY' (1991) and 'THE BIG SELL-OUT' (1992), showed KRAMER and MAGNUSON at their most wilfully perverse/diverse. The neo-narrative, seductive/soft-core vox of ANN lent a shimmering, psychedelic beauty to proceedings, even on their version of FRED NEIL's 'EVERYBODY'S TALKIN''. Sadly, their partnership came to an abrupt halt, both taking off on solo flights. • **Songwriters:** KRAMER – music / MAGNUSON – lyrics (later a few with HUDSON), except RIDE MY SEE-SAW (Moody Blues) / WE DID IT AGAIN (Soft Machine) / JUST MAY BE THE ONE (Monkees) / SPLASH 1 (13th Floor Elevators) / THE DRUM (Slapp Happy) / KISSES SWEETER THAN WIRE (Newman – Campbell) / BEDAZZLED (from the film) / ONE SO BLACK (Dogbowl) / LOVE YOU TOO + RAIN (Beatles) / REAGANATION (Fugs). • **Trivia:** ANN's acting C.V. included a TV sitcom, 'Anything But Love', and a film, 'Making Mr Right'.

Album rating: BREAKING NO NEW GROUND (*5) / DOUBLE BUMMER (*6) / TOO MUCH SLEEP (*6) / THE POWER OF PUSSY (*7) / THE BIG SELL-OUT (*8)

KRAMER – guitar, other instruments, vocals (of-B.A.L.L., ex-SHOCKABILLY, ex-BUTTHOLE SURFERS) / **ANN MAGNUSON** – vocals / guest **FRED FRITH** – guitar (ex-HENRY COW)

Shimmy Disc Shimmy Disc

Feb 88. (m-lp) *(SHIMMY 002)* **BREAKING NO NEW GROUND** Nov87

– Ride my see-saw / Barely coping / Sticks / U.S.O. / His new look / Julia.

— the duo added **DAVE RICK** – guitar (was part-time) / **DAVID LICHT** – drums, percussion

Feb 89. (lp) *(SDE 8801) (SHIMMY 011)* **DOUBLE BUMMER**
– Lesbians of Russia / Frank / We did it again / Homer / Joy ride / Decadent Iranian country club / David Bowie wants ideas / Rock & roll (part 2) / Just may be the one / There you go / Shark / Jimmy / Crime / Pornography / Dazed and Chinese / Bullaby / So help me God / His old look / Stone / Number / Love you too / Reaganation / Double birth / Bruce / Pool / Rain.

— In 1989, he and JAD FAIR (of HALF JAPANESE) released album 'ROLL OUT THE BARREL' *(SDE 8802)*

Apr 90. (cd/lp) *(SDE 9017/+CD) <SHIMMY 031>* **TOO MUCH SLEEP** Nov89
– The living end / The drum / Mr & Mrs Hell / Too much sleep / Talent is a vampire / Psychedelic sewing room / Slash one / He loved the weather / Teena stays the same / One hand on the road / Khomeini died tonight / One so black / No trespassing.

— Late in 1990, KRAMER collaborated with CARNEY & HILD on 'cd 'HAPPINESS FINALLY CAME TO THEM'. Just earlier, he and REBBY SHARP issued 'IN ONE MOUTH AND OUT THE OTHER' *(SHIMMY 033)*

Feb 91. (lp/cd) *<(SHIMMY 040/+CD)>* **THE POWER OF PUSSY**
– The power of pussy / Great radio / What if? / Kisses sweeter than wine / Chicken pussy / White rental car blues / Nick Cave dolls / Bedazzled / Obscene and pornographic art / Connie / What kind of man reads Playboy / I need a new tape / Women tied up in knots / Junior / Mystery hole / Time is coming / Polar song.

— **RANDOLPH A. HUDSON III** – guitars, devices, repl. DAVE RICK

— **DOGBOWL** also provided live guitar

Mar 92. (lp/cd) *(SDE 9239/+CD) <SHIMMY 050>* **THE BIG SELL-OUT**
– Ye olde backlash / The real thing / Free love messes up my life / You're like me now / I wanna talk about it now / What's big in England now? / Schmoozedance / Celebrity compass / When Johnnie dies / The big sell-out / Over the credit line / Flop sweats / Holding hands / Flute of shame / On the cusp of 1970 / Her litigious nature / Love song / Everybody's talking.

— dropped out of scene man. ANN signed a solo contract with 'Geffen'. This led to a bitter lawsuit, between her and the now solo KRAMER, which led to his label folding.

KRAMER

— in 1992, KRAMER & DAEVID ALLEN (of GONG) released a collaborative work, 'WHO'S AFRAID'.

— with **RANDOLPH HUDSON III** – guitar / **DAVID LICHT** – percussion

Jun 93. (d-cd/d-c/d-lp) *(SHIMMY 055 CD/MC/LP)* **THE GUILT TRIP**
– Overture / Stupid summer / Got what I deserved / Wish I were in Heaven / Not guilty / Wisdom sits / Stubb's hallucination / Drowning heart / Welcome home / Swallow up Jonah / Hello music / Murder of God / You don't know / Wall of sleep / Guilt trip / Wait for the hate / Natasha disappears / Big of you / My friend Daniel / Maximus poems / Seven seizures / Thank you music / Kathleen, I'm sorry / God will see you / I'm your fan / Bosom friend / I love you / Next time, try compassion / Charlotte's brain / Mudd Hutt Four / Well hung jury / Won't get far without me / Ball five / She won't let go / I've seen the end / Coda.

— **BILLY BACON** – percussion, drums; repl. LICHT

Aug 94. (lp/cd) *<(SHIMMY 075/+CD)>* **SECRET OF COMEDY**
– Nine minus seven is two / Midnight / Strings / Secret of philosophy / I can watch / Who are you today? / My rock'n'roll / Secret of the band / Sounds like? / Wishing well / Second coda.

— In May '95, KRAMER collaborated on an album with CARNEY (Ralph) and HILD (David), 'BLACK POWER' (SHIMMY 72 CD/LP)

Mar 97. (cd; KRAMER & DAVID HILD) *<(SHIMMY 087CD)>* **RUBBER HAIR**

— **KRAMER** now with **DENI BONET** – violin, accordion, viola

Tzadik Tzadik

Jan 98. (cd) *<(TZA 7119)>* **LET ME EXPLAIN SOMETHING TO YOU ABOUT ART**
– Umberto D. / Odds against tomorrow / Jupiter and the infinite.

— now with **SEAN EDEN** – guitar (of LUNA) / **DAMON KRUKOWSKI** – drums (ex-GALAXIE 500)

Knitting Factory Knitting Factory

Feb 98. (cd) *<(502)>* **SONGS FROM THE PINK DEATH**
– Funny scene / Buddy Holly will never die / Opium wars have long ceased / Don't come around / Parasite song / Pink death song of love / It never stops being absurd / Eddie called back on the carphone / You've got to hide your love away / Hot dog song / It's alright if she don't love you.

Tracy BONHAM

Born: 1969, Boston, Massachusetts, USA, although her large family relocated to Eugene, Oregon, where she took up violin at an early age. After dropping out of music school, TRACY found herself part of the tight-knit Boston alt-rock scene as she left behind her classical training and took up the guitar. While her live sets got people talking, she cut a debut EP, 'THE LIVERPOOL SESSIONS', for local indie label, 'Cherrydisc'. 'Island' were also sufficiently impressed with the budding singer/songwriter's talent to release the record on the 'Island Red' imprint in late summer '95. The company also signed her up for an album, the resulting 'THE BURDENS OF BEING UPRIGHT' issued in summer '96. While the record made the Top 60 in America, TRACY couldn't quite follow ALANIS MORRISETTE into the UK market, her approach perhaps just a little too abrasive for the Top 40. Favouring the softly softly build-up then all-out screaming assault of grunge, BONHAM nevertheless leavened her autobiographical broadsides with a dose of tongue-in-cheek humour. While comparisons with Boston compadres such as THROWING MUSES, BREEDERS, etc., were predictable, BONHAM showed off her English influences with a cover of PJ Harvey's '50 FT. QUEENIE' on subsequent single, 'MOTHER MOTHER'. • **Covered:** LUST FOR LIFE (Iggy Pop).

Album rating: THE BURDENS OF BEING UPRIGHT (*6)

TRACY BONHAM – vocals, guitar / with session band

Island Red Cherrydisc

Sep 95. (10"ep/cd-ep) *(10IR/CIRD 109) <22810>* **THE LIVERPOOL SESSIONS E.P.**
– Sunshine / Dandelion / 18 heads will roll by / The real / Talk too much / I'm not a waif / Big foot.

Island Island

Jun 96. (cd/c) *<(524 187-2/-4)>* **THE BURDENS OF BEING UPRIGHT** 54
– Mother mother / Navy bean / Tell it to the sky / Kisses / Brain crack / One / One hit wonder / Sharks can't sleep / Bulldog / Every breath / 30 seconds / Real.

Sep 96. (7") *(IS 644)* **MOTHER MOTHER. / 50ft QUEENIE (live)** -
(cd-s+=) *(CID 644)* – Navy bean (live).
(cd-s) *(CIDX 644)* – ('A'side) / Dandelion / 18 heads will roll by.

Nov 96. (7"white) *(IS 651)* **SHARKS CAN'T SLEEP. / I'M NOT A WAIF**
(cd-s+=) *(CID 651)* – Bulldog.
(cd-s) *(CIDX 651)* – ('A'side) / Lust for life / 50ft Queenie (live).

Simon BONNEY (see under ⇒ CRIME & THE CITY SOLUTION)

BOOMTOWN RATS

Formed: Dun Laoghaire (near Dublin), Ireland . . . 1975 by former NME journalist BOB GELDOF, JOHNNIE FINGERS, GERRY COTT, PETE BRIQUETTE, GERRY ROBERTS and SIMON CROWE. Moving to London in late 1976, they signed to the newly formed 'Ensign' records. Though their music was rooted in R&B and they were more of a New Wave outfit than anything, The BOOMTOWN RATS were loosely affiliated with the burgeoning punk scene, at least initially. In the long, hot summer of '77, their debut single, 'LOOKIN' AFTER No.1' made the UK Top 20. This was closely followed by a similarly successful eponymous debut album and a second Top 20 hit, 'MARY OF THE 4th FORM'. With a lean sound lying somewhere between EDDIE & THE HOT RODS and The ROLLING STONES, The BOOMTOWN RATS were also a compelling live proposition, GELDOF's moody charisma helping to give the band a distinct identity. Major success came with 'A TONIC FOR THE TROOPS' (1978), this album spawning a number of hits including their first No.1 in the insistent 'RAT TRAP'. They scored a second number one and a massive worldwide hit with 'I DON'T LIKE MONDAYS', a stunningly effective, piano-driven belter inspired (if that's the appropriate word) by schoolgirl Brenda Spencer, who snipered/shot dead several of her school colleagues. The accompanying album, 'THE ART OF SURFACING' (1979) showed the 'RATS at the peak of their power, although subsequent albums increasingly followed a more mundane pop/rock direction and the band slowly faded from view, finally splitting in 1984. GELDOF's profile remained high, however, the Irishman helping to mastermind the mammoth undertaking that was LIVE AID. He and ULTRAVOX's MIDGE URE, assembled together all the major stars of the time to sing 'DO THEY KNOW IT'S CHRISTMAS', the resulting 45 making millions of pounds/dollars/etc for famine relief in Ethiopia. Not content with this, BOB and MIDGE reunited most of them again for the LIVE AID concert at Wembley Stadium on the 13th of July '85 (this was simultaneously broadcast over the Atlantic at JFK Stadium, Philadephia). At the time, it amassed well over £10m, the money also being spread around other needy charities as well as Ethiopia (the total at the end of 1991 was over £100m). In June 1986, BOB was now Sir BOB GELDOF, after being knighted by the Queen and two months later he married long-time fiancee, PAULA YATES (TV presenter/writer/etc). She gave birth to FIFI TRIXIBELLE and in 1989, their second daughter, PEACHES, was born. During the latter half of a very busy decade for GELDOF, he managed to maintain a solo career, a hit single, 'THIS IS THE WORLD CALLING', was appropriate enough to become a Top 30 hit in 1986, while 1990's 'THE GREAT SONG OF INDIFFERENCE' went one step better. His backing band at the time, The VEGETARIANS OF LOVE, provided the title of the single's folky/cajun parent album, which also sold reasonably well. His last solo album, 'THE HAPPY CLUB' (1992), was something of a disappointment and Sir BOB virtually retired from the studio side of things to run his own Planet 24 company and The Big Breakfast on Channel 4. PAULA was also part of the latter, although by 1995, she had opted to bed MICHAEL HUTCHENCE of INXS, citing BOB as the adulterer. BOB and PAULA were subsequently divorced as the new couple became the media focal point (tragically, this was cut short when MICHAEL took his own life on the 22nd November, 1997 – see INXS). • **Songwriters:** Most written by GELDOF except; BAREFOOTIN' (Robert Parker). GELDOF solo covered SUNNY AFTERNOON (Kinks). • **Trivia:** GELDOF starred in the feature films, 'The Wall' (1982) and 'Number One' (1984).

Album rating: THE BOOMTOWN RATS (*6) / A TONIC FOR THE TROOPS (*5) / THE FINE ART OF SURFACING (*5) / MONDO BONGO (*4) / V DEEP (*4) / IN THE LONG GRASS (*5)

BOB GELDOF (b. 5 Oct'54, Dublin, Ireland) – vocals / **JOHNNIE FINGERS** (b. JOHNNY MOYLETT) – keyboards, vocals / **GERRY COTT** – guitar / **PETE BRIQUETTE** (b. PATRICK CUSACK) – bass / **GERRY ROBERTS** – guitar, vocals / **SIMON CROWE** – drums, vocals

Ensign Mercury

Aug 77. (12"m) *(ENY 4)* **LOOKIN' AFTER No.1. / BORN TO BURN (live) / BAREFOOTIN' (live)** [11] [-]

Sep 77. (lp/c) *(ENVY/ENCAS 1)* *<SRM 1188>* **THE BOOMTOWN RATS** [18] [ ]
– Lookin' after No.1 / Neon heart / Joey's on the street again / Never bite the hand that feeds / Mary of the 4th form / (She gonna) Do you in / Close as you'll ever be / I can make it if you can / Kicks. *(re-iss. Dec83 on 'Mercury' lp/c; PRICE/PRIMC 57)*

Nov 77. (7") *(ENY 9)* **MARY OF THE 4th FORM. / DO THE RAT** [15] [-]

Ensign Columbia

Mar 78. (7") *(ENY 13)* **SHE'S SO MODERN. / LYING AGAIN** [12] [ ]

Jun 78. (7") *(ENY 14)* **LIKE CLOCKWORK. / HOW DO YOU DO?** [6] [ ]

Jul 78. (lp/c) *(ENVY/ENCAS 3)* *<35750>* **A TONIC FOR THE TROOPS** [8] [ ]
– Like clockwork / Blind date / (I never loved) Eva Braun / Living in an island / Don't believe what you read / She's so modern / Me and Howard Hughes / Can't stop * / (Watch out for) The normal people / Rat trap. *<US version repl.* with – Joey> (re-iss. Dec83 on 'Mercury' lp/c; PRICE/PRIMC 58)*

Oct 78. (7") *(ENY 16)* **RAT TRAP. / SO STRANGE** [1] [-]

Nov 78. (7") **RAT TRAP. / DO THE RAT** [-] [ ]

Jul 79. (7") *(ENY 30)* *<11117>* **I DON'T LIKE MONDAYS. / IT'S ALL THE RAGE** [1] [73] Jan80

Oct 79. (lp/c) *(ENROX/ENCAS 11)* *<36248>* **THE FINE ART OF SURFACING** [7] [ ]
– Someone's looking at you / Diamond smiles / Wind chill factor (minus zero) / Having my picture taken / Sleep (Fingers' lullaby) / I don't like Mondays / Nothing happened today / Keep it up / Nice 'n' neat / When the night comes. *(re-iss. Nov84 on 'Mercury' lp/c; PRICE/PRIMC 73)*

Nov 79. (7") *(ENY 33)* **DIAMOND SMILES. / LATE LAST NIGHT** [13] [-]

Jan 80. (7",12") *(ENY 34)* **SOMEONE'S LOOKING AT YOU. / WHEN THE NIGHT COMES** [4] [-]

May 80. (7") *<11248>* **SOMEONE'S LOOKING AT YOU. / I DON'T LIKE MONDAYS (live)** [-] [ ]

Mercury Columbia

Nov 80. (7") *(BONGO 1)* **BANANA REPUBLIC. / MAN AT THE TOP** [3] [-]

Dec 80. (lp/c) *(6359/7150 042)* *<37062>* **MONDO BONGO** [6] [ ]
– Please don't go / The elephant's graveyard (guilty) / Banana republic / Fall down / Hurt hurts / Whitehall 1212 * / Mood mambo / Straight up / This is my room / Another piece of red / Under their thumb . . . is under my thumb / Go man go. *<US version repl. * with – Don't talk to me>*

Jan 81. (7") *(BONGO 2)* **THE ELEPHANT'S GRAVEYARD (GUILTY). / REAL DIFFERENT** [26] [-]

—— (Mar'81) trimmed to a quintet when GERRY COTT left to go solo

Nov 81. (7") *<60512>* **UP ALL NIGHT. / ANOTHER PIECE OF RED** [-] [ ]

Nov 81. (7") *(MER 87)* **NEVER IN A MILLION YEARS. / DON'T TALK TO ME** [62] [-]

Mar 82. (7"/12") *(MER/+X 91)* **HOUSE ON FIRE. / EUROPE LOOKED UGLY** [24] [-]

Mar 82. (lp/c) *(6359/7150 082)* **V DEEP** [64] [ ]
– Never in a million years / The bitter end / Talking in code / He watches it all / Storm breaks / Charmed lives / House on fire / Up all night / Skin on skin / Little death.

Jun 82. (7") *(MER 106)* **CHARMED LIVES. / NO HIDING PLACE** [ ] [-]
(d7"+=) *(MER 106-2)* – Nothing happened today (live) / Storm breaks (instrumental).
(12") *(MERX 106)* – ('A'side) / A storm breaks.

Aug 82. (7") *<03386>* **CHARMED LIVES. / NEVER IN A MILLION YEARS** [-] [ ]

Jan 84. (7") *(MER 154)* **TONIGHT. / PRECIOUS TIME** [73] [-]
(12"+=) *(MERX 154)* – Walking downtown.

May 84. (7") *(MER 163)* **DRAG ME DOWN. / AN ICICLE IN THE SUN** [50] [-]
(12"+=) *(MERX 163)* – Rat trap / She's so modern.

Nov 84. (7"pic-d) *(MER 179)* **DAVE. / HARD TIMES** [ ] [-]
(d7"+=) *(MER 179-2)* – I don't like Mondays / It's all the rage.
(12"+=) *(MERX 179)* – Banana republic (live) / Close as you'll ever be (live).

Dec 84. (lp/c) *(MERL/+C 38)* *<39335>* **IN THE LONG GRASS** [ ] [ ]
– A hold of me / Drag me down / Dave / Over again / Another sad story / Tonight / Hard times / Lucky / Icicle in the Sun / Up or down.

Feb 85. (7") *(MER 184)* **A HOLD OF ME. / NEVER IN A MILLION YEARS** [ ] [-]
(12"+=) *(MERX 184)* – Say hi to Mick.

Mar 85. (7") *<04892>* **ICICLE IN THE SUN. / RAIN** [-] [ ]

Jun 85. (7") *<05590>* **DRAG ME DOWN. / HARD TIMES** [-] [ ]

—— had already split late '84. FINGERS and CROWE formed GUNG HO. BOB GELDOF pieced together BAND/LIVE AID before going solo.

– compilations, others, etc. –

Dec 83. (6x7"box) *Mercury; (none)* **RAT PACK** (6 best of singles pack) [ ] [-]

Jan 88. (7") *Old Gold; (OG 9790)* **I DON'T LIKE MONDAYS. / RAT TRAP** [ ] [-]
Note; below single by BOOMTOWN RATS (also compilation tracks *)

Jun 94. (7"colrd/c-s) *(VER/+MC 87)* **I DON'T LIKE MONDAYS. / BORN TO BURN / DO THE RAT** [38] [ ]
(cd-s) *(MERCD 87)* – ('A'side) / Looking after No.1 / Mary of the 4th form / She's so modern.
(cd-s) *(MERCX 87)* – ('A'side) / Rat trap / Someone's looking at you / Banana republic.

Jul 94. (cd/c) *(522 283-2/-4)* **LOUDMOUTH – THE BEST OF THE BOOMTOWN RATS & BOB GELDOF** (compilation) [10] [ ]
– I don't like Mondays * / This is the world calling / Rat trap * / The great song of indifference / Love or something / Banana republic * / The elephant's graveyard (guilty) * / Someone's looking at you * / She's so modern * / House on fire * / The beat of the night / Diamond smiles * / Like clockwork * / Room 19 (sha la la la lee) / Mary of the 4th form * / Looking after No.1 *. *(* tracks by The BOOMTOWN RATS)*

Clint BOON EXPERIENCE (see under ⇒ INSPIRAL CARPETS)

BOO RADLEYS

Formed: Liverpool, England . . . 1988, by schoolmates SICE and MARTIN CARR. Another friend, TIM BROWN, was invited to join after teaching MARTIN how to play guitar. They took the group name from a weird character in the film, 'To Kill A Mockingbird'. The quartet was complete when they found drummer STEVE HEWITT. They worked hard on the Mersey gig circuit but no major deal was forthcoming. Come 1990, they finally found a home with small indie label, 'Action', who released their debut lp 'ICHABOD AND I'. On its merit, they were invited by the illustrious DJ John Peel to session for Radio 1. This led to a signing for 'Rough Trade', who issued 3 popular EP's between late 1990 & 91. They then moved to 'Creation', their psychedelic, BYRDS-influenced jangle-pop soon making them favourites of the music press (Singles Of The Week, etc). The release of 1992's 'EVERYTHING'S ALRIGHT FOREVER' and the following years' masterful 'GIANT STEPS' album infused their sugary pop with screeching guitars and jagged brass accompaniment. The latter secured them their first Top 20 placing, the tracks 'I HANG SUSPENDED', 'BARNEY (. . . AND ME)' and 'LAZARUS' being effervescent highlights. Early to rise in '95, they scored their first Top 10 hit with 'WAKE UP BOO!', taken from their similarly titled No.1 album. The single was subsequently spoiled after it was played to death as the theme tune for ITV's Breakfast TV. In 1996, SICE (aka EGGMAN) released a patchy solo album, while The BOOS returned with another slice of nostalgic pop, 'C'MON KIDS'. • **Songwriters:** CARR lyrics / group music, except TRUE FAITH (New Order) / ALONE AGAIN OR (Love) / ONE OF US MUST KNOW (Bob Dylan) / THE QUEEN IS DEAD (Smiths). • **Trivia:** MERIEL BARHAM of The PALE SAINTS provided vocals on 2 tracks for GIANT STEPS album. ED BALL (ex-TV PERSONALITIES) often made guest appearances.

Album rating: ICHABOD AND I (*5) / EVERYTHING'S ALRIGHT FOREVER (*7) / GIANT STEPS (*9) / WAKE UP! (*8) / C'MON KIDS (*6) / KINGSIZE (*5) / Eggman: FIRST FRUITS (*5)

SICE (b. SIMON ROWBOTTOM, 18 Jun'69, Wallasey, England) – vocals, guitar / **MARTIN CARR** (b.29 Nov'68, Thurso, Scotland) – guitar / **TIM BROWN** (b.26 Feb'69, Wallasey) – bass / **STEVE DREWITT** (b. Northwich, England) – drums

Action not iss.

Jul 90. (lp) *(TAKE 4)* **ICHABOD AND I** [ ] [-]
– Eleanor everything / Bodenheim Jr. / Catweazle / Sweet salad birth / Hip clown rag / Walking 5th carnival / Kaleidoscope / Happens to us all.

—— **ROB CIEKA** (b. 4 Aug'68, Birmingham, England) – drums repl. DREWITT to BREED

Rough Trade not iss.

Oct 90. (12"ep/cd-ep) *(RTT 241/+CD)* **KALEIDOSCOPE EP** [ ] [-]
– Kaleidoscope / How I feel / Aldous / Swansong.

Apr 91. (12"ep/cd-ep) *(R 201127-10/-13)* **EVERY HEAVEN EP** [ ] [-]
– The finest kiss / Tortoiseshell / Bluebird / Naomi.

Sep 91. (12"ep/cd-ep) *(R 275-0/-3)* **BOO UP! EP (Peel sessions)** [ ] [-]
– Everybird / Sometime soon she said / Foster's van / Song for up!.

Creation Columbia

Feb 92. (12"ep)(cd-ep) *(CRE 128T)(CRESCD 124)* **ADRENALIN EP** [ ] [-]
– Lazy day / Vegas / Feels like tomorrow / Whiplashed.

Mar 92. (cd/c/lp) *(CRE CD/MC/LP 120)* *<52912>* **EVERYTHING'S ALRIGHT FOREVER** [55] [ ] Aug92
– Spaniard / Towards the light / Losing it (song for Abigail) / Memory babe / Skyscraper / I feel nothing / Room at the top / Does this hurt / Sparrow / Smile fades fast / Firesky / Song for the morning to sing / Lazy day / Paradise.

Jun 92. (7") *(CRE 128)* **BOO! FOREVER. / DOES THIS HURT** [67] [-]
(12"+=)(cd-s+=) *(CRE 128T)(CRESCD 128)* – Buffalo Bill / Sunfly II: Walking with the kings.

Nov 92. (7") *(CRE 137)* **LAZARUS. / LET ME BE YOUR FAITH** [76] [-]
(12"+=)(cd-s+=) *(CRE 137T)(CRESCD 137)* – At the sound of speed / Petroleum.

—— added **STEVE KITCHEN** – trumpet, flugel horn / **JACKIE ROY** – clarinet / **LINDSAY JOHNSTON** – cello

Jul 93. (7") *(CRE 147)* **I HANG SUSPENDED. / RODNEY KING (St. Etienne mix)** [77] [-]
(12"+=)(cd-s+=) *(CRE 147T)(CRESCD 147)* – As bound a stomorrow / I will always ask where you have been though I know the answer.

Jul 93. (cd/c/d-lp) *(CRE CD/MC/LP 149)* *<53794>* **GIANT STEPS** [17] [ ] Aug93
– I hang suspended / Upon 9th and Fairchild / Wish I was skinny / Leaves and sand / Butterfly McQueen / Rodney King (song for Lenny Bruce) / Thinking of ways / Barney (. . . and me) / Spun around / If you want it, take it / Best lose the fear / Take the time around / Lazarus / One is for / Run my way runway / I've lost the reason / The white noise revisited. *(cd re-iss. Aug98; same)*

Oct 93. (7"/c-s) *(CRE/+CD 169)* **WISH I WAS SKINNY. / PEACHY KEEN** [75] [-]
(12"+=)(cd-s+=) *(CRE 169T)(CRESCD 169)* – Furthur / Crow eye.

Feb 94. (7"/c-s) *(CRE/+CS 178)* **BARNEY (. . .AND ME). / ZOOM** [48] [-]
(12"+=)(cd-s+=) *(CRE 178T)(CRESCD 178)* – Tortoiseshell / Cracked lips, homesick.

May 94. (7") *(CRE 187)* **LAZARUS. / (I WANNA BE) TOUCHDOWN JESUS** [50] [-]
(12"+=) *(CRE 187T)* – ('A'-Secret Knowledge mix) / ('A'-Ultramarine radio mix).
(cd-s+=) *(CRESCD 187)* – ('A'acoustic) / ('A'-St. Etienne mix).
(cd-s) *(CRESCD 187X)* – ('A'-Secret Knowledge mix) / ('A'-Ultramarine mix) / ('A'-Augustus Pablo mix) / ('A'-12"mix).

Feb 95. (c-s) *(CRECS 191)* **WAKE UP BOO! / JANUS** [9] [-]
(cd-s+=) *(CRESCD 191)* – Blues for George Michael / Friendship song.
(12") *(CRE 191T)* – Wake up Boo!: Music for astronauts / Janus / Blues for George Michael.

(cd-s) *(CRESCD 191X)* – Wake up Boo!: Music for astronauts / . . .And tomorrow the world / The history of Creation parts 17 & 36.

Mar 95. (cd/c/lp) *(CRE CD/MC/LP 179) <67249>* **WAKE UP!** 1 □
– Wake up Boo! / Fairfax scene / It's Lulu / Joel / Find the answer within / Reaching out from here / Martin, Doom! it's 7 o'clock / Stuck on amber / Charles Bukowski is dead / 4am conversation / Twinside / Wilder. *(cd re-iss. Aug98; same)*

May 95. (c-s) *(CRECS 202)* **FIND THE ANSWER WITHIN / DON'T TAKE YOUR GUN TO TOWN** 37 -
(cd-s+=) *(CRESCD 202)* – Wallpaper.
(12"++=) *(CRE 202T)* – The only word I can find / Very together.
(cd-s) *(CRESCD 202X)* – ('A'-High Llamas mix) / The only word I can find / Very together.

Jul 95. (c-s) *(CRECS 211)* **IT'S LULU / THIS IS NOT ABOUT ME** 25 -
(cd-s+=) *(CRESCD 211)* – Reaching out from here (the High Llamas mix / Martin, doom! it's seven o'clock (Stereolab mix).
(cd-s) *(CRESCD 211X)* – ('A'side) / Joel (Justin Warfield mix) / Tambo / Donkey.

Sep 95. (c-s/7") *(C+/CRE 214)* **FROM THE BENCH AT BELVIDERE. / HI FALUTIN'** 24 -
(cd-s+=) *(CRESCD 214)* – Crushed / Nearly almost time.

Creation Mercury

Aug 96. (7") *(CRE 220)* **WHAT'S IN THE BOX? (SEE WHATCHA GOT). / BLOKE IN A DRESS** 25 -
(cd-s+=) *(CRESCD CRESCD 220)* – Flakes / ('A'-Kris Needs mix).
(cd-s) *(CRESCD 220X)* – ('A'side) / Atlantic / The absent boy / Annie and Marnie.

Sep 96. (cd/c)(d-lp) *(CRECD/CCRE 194)(CRELP 194L) <534256>* **C'MON KIDS** 20 □
– C'mon kids / Meltin's worm / Melodies for the deaf / Get on the bus / Everything is sorrow / Bullfrog green / What's in the box? (see whatcha got) / Four saints / New Brighton promenade / Fortunate sons / Shelter / Ride the tiger / One last hurrah. *(lp w/ free 7")* SKYWALKER. / FRENCH CANADIAN BEAN SOUP

Oct 96. (7") *(CRE 236)* **C'MON KIDS. / SPION COP** 18 -
(cd-s+=) *(CRESCD 236)* – Too beautiful / Bullfrog green (ultra living mix).
• (cd-s) *(CRESCD 236X)* – ('A'side) / Nothing to do but scare myself / From the bench at Belvidere (Ultramarine mix) / Fortunate sons (Greg Hunter remix).

Jan 97. (7") *(CRE 248)* **RIDE THE TIGER. / VOTE YOU** 38 -
(cd-s) *(CRESCD 248)* –
(cd-s) *(CRESCD 248X)* –

Creation Creation

Oct 98. (10") *(CRE 299X)* **FREE HUEY. /** 54 -
(cd-s) *(CRESCD 299)* –
(cd-s) *(CRESCD 299X)* –

Oct 98. (cd/d-lp)(c) *(CRE CD/LP 228)(CCRE 228)* **KINGSIZE** 62 -
– Blue room in archway / Old newsstand at Hamilton Square / Free Huey / Monuments for a dead century / Heaven's at the bottom of this glass / Kingsize / High as monkeys / Eurstar / Put your arms around me and tell you love me / Adieu clo clo / Jimmy Webb is God / She is everywhere / Comb your hair / Song for the blueroom / The future is now.

EGGMAN

— i.e. **SICE** with **ROB CIEKA** – drums / **ED BALL** – bass / **SEAN JACKSON** – lead guitar / **TIM BROWN** – piano, etc / others

Creation Tristar

May 96. (7"/c-s) *(CRE/+CS 225)* **NOT BAD ENOUGH. / IDENTIKIT** □ -
(cd-s+=) *(CRESCD 225)* – We won the war.

May 96. (cd/lp)(c) *(CRE CD/LP 201)(CCRE 201) <36910>* **FIRST FRUITS** □ □
– Purple patches / Tomas / That's that then (for now) / Not bad enough / The funeral song / Replace all your lies with truth / Out of my window / Look up / I'll watch your back / First fruits fall.

BOOTH AND THE BAD ANGEL (see under ⇒ JAMES)

BOOTS FOR DANCING

Formed: Edinburgh, Scotland . . . late 1979 by the songwriting pair of DAVE CARSON and GRAHAM HIGH, who enlisted the rhythm section of DOUGIE BARRIE and STUART WRIGHT. Influenced by the quirky/manic dance-punk rhythms of GANG OF FOUR or The POP GROUP, BOOTS FOR DANCING enjoyed a bit of airplay on the John Peel radio one show. The quartet signed to 'Pop Aural' (also the launching pad for The FIRE ENGINES) and released their debut platter, the eponymous 'BOOTS FOR DANCING' single in 1980. They were subsequently dogged by numerous personnel changes initiating with a brief stint from ex-REZILLOS man, ANGEL PATERSON, who left to join TV21 (two drummers/percussionists were introduced, JAMO STEWART and DICKIE FUSCO). HIGH was also to take off, his replacement being another REZILLOS ex, JO CALLIS who was joined by MIKE BARCLAY. After a year long spell without a record, BFD were back with the follow-up, 'RAIN SONG', although this was certainly not as good as their debut. When CALLIS departed to take up a post in the HUMAN LEAGUE, the quintet were to release their third and last effort, 'OOH BOP SH'BAM', before CARSON became the only surviving original, he and BARCLAY having recruited SIMON TEMPLAR (another ex-REZILLOS and SHAKE member) and RONNIE TORRANCE (ex-JOSEF K).

Album rating: never released any

DAVE CARSON – vocals / **GRAHAM HIGH** – guitar / **DOUGIE BARRIE** – bass / **STUART WRIGHT** – drums

Pop Aural not iss.

Apr 80. (12"ep) *(POP 002)* **BOOTS FOR DANCING / PARACHUTE. / GUITARS / GIRL TROUBLE** □ -

— **JAMO STEWART** – drums + **DICKIE FUSCO** – percussion; repl. ANGEL PATERSON (ex-SHAKE, ex-REZILLOS) who repl. WRIGHT

— MIKE BARCLAY – guitar (ex-THURSDAYS) repl. HIGH who joined DELTA 5

— added **JO CALLIS** – guitar, vocals (ex-SHAKE, ex-REZILLOS)

Mar 81. (7") *(POP 006)* **RAIN SONG. / HESITATING** □ -

— trimmed to a quintet when CALLIS left to join HUMAN LEAGUE

Re-Pop X not iss.

Feb 82. (7") *(WAY 100)* **OOH BOP SH'BAM. / MONEY IS THIN ON THE GROUND** □ -

— **SIMON TEMPLAR** (b. BLOOMFIELD) – bass (ex-FLOWERS, ex-SHAKE, ex-REZILLOS) repl. BARRIE

— **RONNIE TORRANCE** – drums (ex-JOSEF K) repl. FUSCO + STEWART (the latter formed The SYNDICATE

— hung up their footwear some time in '82.

BOREDOMS

Formed: Osaka, Japan . . . 1983 by vocalist/frontman, YAMATSUKA EYE and percussionist, TABATA. This pairing released the first BOREDOMS product, the 'ANAL BY ANAL' EP in '85. There was a similarly worrying anal fixation on 'ONAMIE BOMB MEETS THE SEX PISTOLS', a cacophponous blast of musical anarchy akin to a cross between the post-hardcore US noise of JESUS LIZARD and BIG BLACK and the experimental torture of the REVOLUTIONARY PEKING ORCHESTRA. Following TABATA's departure to ZEVI GEVA, YAMATSUKA met HIRA HAYASHI while working in a gay bar, the pair subsequently recruiting second vocalist, TOYOHITO YOSHIKAWA. By the late 80's, the line-up had expanded to include YAMAMOTO, YOSHIMI P-WE and ATARI, the crew finding a natural home at ~KRAMER's 'Shimmy Disc', for 1990's 'SOUL DISCHARGE '89' album. By this point, the band's crazed stage antics (usually resulting in injury for YAMATSUKA) preceded them and partly due to their increasingly infamous reputation, netted a major label deal with 'Reprise'. From the label that once gifted the world FRANK SINATRA came such schizophrenic, subversively unfathomable albums as 'POP TATARI' (1993), 'CHOCOLATE SYNTHESIZER' (1994) and 'SUPER ROOTS VI' (1996), the latter consisting solely of songs titled after cardinal numbers; even the band themselves admit that their lyrics mean absolutely nothing!

Album rating: SOUL DISCHARGE 99 (*6) / CHOCOLATE SYNTHESIZER (*6)

YAMATSUKA EYE – vocals / **TABATA** – percussion

not iss. Reprise

1985. (7"ep) **ANAL BY ANAL EP** - □

1985. (lp) **ONANIE BOMB MEETS THE SEX PISTOLS** - □
– Wipe out shock shoppers / Boredoms vs. SDI / We never sleep / Bite my bollocks / Young assouls / Call me God / No core punk / Lick'n cock boatpeople / Melt down boogie / Feedbackfuck / Anal eater / God from anal / Born to anal. *(cd-iss. Sep94 on 'Earthnoise'; EN 001) <cd-iss. Nov94 on 'Reprise'; 45636>*

— TABATA left to join as ZEVI GEVA guitarist and was repl. by **TOYOHITO YOSHIKAWA** (aka HUMAN RICH VOX Y) – vocals / **HIRA HAYASHI** (aka HYLA Y) – bass, vocals / **YAMAMOTO** (aka YY) – guitar, vocals / **ATARI** (aka GOD MANA) – synthesizer, drums + **YOSHIMI P-WE** – drums, vocals / and 7th member **KING KAZOO EYE** – kazoo, sound effects

Shimmy Disc Shimmy Disc

Aug 90. (lp) *(<SHIMMY 035>)* **SOUL DISCHARGE 99** □ □ Dec89
– Your name is limitless / Bubblepop shot / 52 boredom (club mix) / Sun, gun, run / Z & U & T & A / TV scorpion / Pow wow now / J.B. Dick and Tina Turner pussy / G.I.L. '77 / Jup-na-keeeeeel / Catastro mix '99 / Milky Way / Songs without electric guitars / Hamaiin disco bollocks / Hamaiin disco without bollocks. *(cd-iss. Sep94 on 'Earthnoise'; EN 002)*

not iss. Reprise

1992. (m-cd) **ROOTS** - □

1993. (cd/c) *<45416-2/-4>* **POP TATARI** - □
– Noise Ramones / Nice B-O-R-E guy & Boyoyo touch / Hey bore hey / Bo go / Bore now bore / Okinawa rasta beef (mockin' fuzz 2) / Which dooyoo like / Molecicco / Telehorse Uma / Hoy / Bocabola / Heeba / Poy (mockin' fuzz 1) / Bod / Cheba / Pop tatari / Cory & the mandara suicide pyramid.

Nov 93. (cd) *(AVANT 026)* **WOW 2** □ □
(above released in the UK on 'Avant')

Jun 94. (cd-ep) *<41559>* **SUPER ROOTS** - □
– Pop kiss / Budokan tape try (500 tapes high) / Finger action No.5 / 4 (chocolate *ut) / Pitch at bunch on itch / Machine 3 / Monster Rex & S*und 'a' R*undus / Nuts room / Ear?wig?web? / 96 teenage bondage / Super frake 009.

1994. (cd) *<45814>* **CHOCOLATE SYNTHESIZER** - □
– Acid police / Chocolate synthesizer / Synthesizer guide book on fire / Shock city / Tomato synthesizer / Anarchy in the UKK / Voredoms / B for Boredoms / Ecdoms / Smoke 7 / Turn table Boredoms / I'm not synthesizer (YP?) / Now dom go synthesizer way (why?).

Aug 96. (cd) *<46163>* **SUPER ROOTS VI** - □
– 01 / 0 (X12) / 6 / 2 / 3 / 9 / 4 / 7 / 8 / 5 / 10 / 11 / 12 / 13v / 14 / 15 / 1.

— in 1996, EYE also worked with JOHN ZORN on the album, 'Nani Nani', while moonlighting with other act . . .

not iss. Birdman

Oct 98. (cd) *<19>* **SUPER ARE** - □
– Super you / Super are / Super going / Super coming / Super are you / Super shine.

HANATARASH

Public Bath Public Bath

Jun 97. (cd) *(<PBCD 3>)* **4-AIDSADELIC** □ □

Adrian BORLAND (see under ⇒ SOUND)

BOSS HOG (see under ⇒ PUSSY GALORE)

BOTTLE ROCKETS

Formed: Festus, Missouri, USA . . . early 90's by former UNCLE TUPELO roadie turned singer BRIAN HENNEMAN, along with mates TOM and BOB PARR; TOM RAY and drummer MARK ORTMANN were replacements for the latter after they became The BOTTLE ROCKETS. Just prior to the launch of The BOTTLE ROCKETS, HENNEMAN released a one-off solo single, 'INDIANAPOLIS', augmented by UNCLE TUPELO luminaries JAY FARRAR and JEFF TWEEDY; he actually played on their peerless 'MARCH 16-20' album. Later in 1993, the eponymous 'BOTTLE ROCKETS' was issued on 'East Side Digital', a gritty debut combining the rootsy power of NEIL YOUNG/CRAZY HORSE and LYNYRD SKYNYRD with the hard-bitten lyricism of JOHN PRINE. With the rise and rise of alt-country, HENNEMAN and Co soon found themselves signed to 'Atlantic' (through 'Tag') and had the American critics falling over themselves to praise ERIC AMBEL (DEL LORDS)-produced follow-up set, 'THE BROOKLYN SIDE' (1995). A few years later, The BOTTLE ROCKETS confirmed their position along the cream of the country-rock crop with the release of third set, '24 HOURS A DAY' (1997).

Album rating: BOTTLE ROCKETS (*7) / THE BROOKLYN SIDE (*7) / 24 HOURS A DAY (*5)

BRIAN HENNEMAN

with **JAY FARRAR** – acoustic guitar (ex-UNCLE TUPELO) / **JEFF TWEEDY** – bass, vocals (ex-UNCLE TUPELO) / **MARK ORTMANN** – drums

Rockville Rockville

Mar 93. (7") *<(ROCK 6088-7)>* **INDIANAPOLIS. / GET DOWN, WAVE THAT FLAG**

BOTTLE ROCKETS

BRIAN HENNEMAN – vocals, guitar / **TOM PARR** – guitar / **TOM RAY** – bass; repl. BOB PARR / **MARK ORTMANN** – drums

East Side Digital East Side Digital

Sep 93. (cd) *<ESD 80772>* **BOTTLE ROCKETS** -
– Early in the morning / Gas girl / Trailer mama / Wave that flag / Kerosene / Every kinda everything / Got what I wanted / Manhattan countryside / Rural route / Bad nanney theme / Lonely cowboy. *(UK-iss.Mar96; same)*

East Side Digital Tag-Atlantic

Sep 95. (cd) *<ESD 81002>* **THE BROOKLYN SIDE** -
– Welfare music / Gravity falls / I'll be comin' around / Radar gun / Sunday sport / Pot of gold / 1000 dollar car / Idiots revenge / Young lovers in town / Take me to the bank / Stuck in a rut / I wanna come home now / Queen of the world. *(UK-iss.Mar96; same)*

Aug 97. (cd) *<83015>* **24 HOURS A DAY** -
– Kit Kat clock / When I was dumb / 24 hours a day / Smokin' 100's alone / Slo Toms / Indianolopis / Things you didn't know / One of you / Perfect far away / Waitin' on a train / Dohack Joe / Rich man / Turn for the worse.

– compilations, etc. –

Nov 98. (cd) *Doolittle; <358029>* **LEFT OVERS** -
– Get down river / Dinner train to Dutchtown / Skip's song / Coffee monkey / If walls could talk / Financing his romance / My own Cadillac / Chattanooga.

BOURGIE BOURGIE (see under ⇒ QUINN, Paul)

BOWLFISH

Formed: Harrow, England . . . 1992 by main songwriter STEVE LOWE, plus STEVE GENT and PHIL MARTIN. A mix'n'match power trio featuring a bearded hippy, a babyfaced indie-kid and a bequiffed STRAY CATS fan, BOWLFISH made their vinyl debut in summer '92 with the 'DOGBERRY' single. Released on indie label, 'Roughneck', the track's amphetamnine punk-pop was followed up by the denser, more adventurous guitar textures of 'MRS FRANK' in early '93. A third single, 'TWISTED HIPS', previewed debut album, 'THE BISCUIT' (1993), although a subsequent one-off single (the intriguingly titled 'FACEACHE', which came backed with a cover of Pulp's 'LIPGLOSS') on US indie label, 'Domino', proved to be the BOWLFISH epitaph. Presumably the two STEVE's have returned to their favourite pastime, birdwatching!

Album rating: THE BISCUIT (*4)

STEVE LOWE – vocals, guitar, percussion / **STEVE GENT** – bass, percussion / **PHIL MARTIN** – drums, percussion, vocals

not iss. Twenty

1992. (cd-s) *<3>* **DOGBERRY. / BANG BANG BANG** -

Roughneck not iss.

Jan 93. (10"/cd-s) *(HYPER 020 T/CD)* **MRS. FRANK. /** -
Jun 93. (7") *(HYPE 25)* **TWISTED HIPS. /** -
(cd-s+=) *(HYPE 25CD)* –
Oct 93. (cd/lp) *(NECK CD/LP 13)* **THE BISCUIT** -
– Bubba / Bufflehead / Brigh 'n' sigh / Sultana / Twisted hips / Reggie / Dirty Darren / Brutus.

Domino not iss.

Jun 94. (12"/cd-s) *(RUG 20 T/CD)* **FACEACHE. / JIM DEMON / LIPGLOSS** -

— disbanded later in '94

BOW WOW WOW

Formed: London, England . . . late '79 by extrovert entrepreneur and former SEX PISTOLS mastermind, MALCOLM McLAREN, who cannily matched up ADAM ANT's former backing band of MATTHEW ASHMAN, LEROY GORMAN and DAVE BARBAROSSA with a 14-year old Burmese schoolgirl, ANNABELLA LWIN. He'd apparently recruited her after hearing her sing in a North London launderette. If that sounds like a typically opportunistic McLAREN-esque scenario, then the debut single was straight out of the rock'n'roll swindle handbook; a bouncy little ditty entitled 'C'30, C'60, C'90', the song's calculated celebration of home taping (remember the skull & crossbones?) earned BOW WOW WOW instant infamy and a Top 40 placing. Music wise, the band were touting a suspiciously similar Burundi-drumming guitar-pop style to the revamped ADAM & THE ANTS, adopting a kind of primitive savage image in contrast to ADAM's pirates. McLAREN's next brainwave was for a cassette only EP, 'YOUR CASSETTE PET' (1980), featuring such provocative material as 'SEXY EIFFEL TOWERS'. While LWIN's yelp was perhaps something of an acquired taste there was no doubting her smouldering adolescent appeal and of course it was milked for all it was worth. In a move reminiscent of his 'PISTOLS tactics, McLAREN took the band from 'E.M.I.' to 'R.C.A.' and after a further couple of minor hits, a long awaited debut album, 'SEE JUNGLE! SEE JUNGLE! . . .' was finally unveiled in late '81. Boasting a decidedly risque cover shot of LWIN (then still only 15) er . . . at one with nature (a mock-up of Monet's 'Dejeuner sur l'herbe'), the record was a three-chord teen-frenzy revelling in its own trashiness. Not exactly one-hit wonders, BOW WOW WOW would nevertheless struggle to come up with anything quite as infectious and exuberant as 'GO WILD IN THE COUNTRY', their first and most famous Top 10 hit. With constant hassle from LWIN's mother (who was none too happy about her daughter posing in the curly-headed one's teen mag, 'Chicken'), McLAREN almost replaced her with a certain Lieutenant Lush; perhaps he should've done, Lush later resurfaced as BOY GEORGE in CULTURE CLUB. Save for a last gasp Top 10 hit with a tepid cover of The Strangeloves' 'I WANT CANDY', BOW WOW WOW, meanwhile, were rapidly spiralling into pop oblivion. A follow-up album 'WHEN THE GOING GETS TOUGH, THE TOUGH GET GOING' (1983) was generally ignored amid critical meltdown and the band folded later that year. The backing boys, ASHMAN, GORMAN and BARBAROSSA carried on as CHIEFS OF RELIEF to little avail, while LWIN eventually surfaced in the mid 80's with a couple of flop singles and an album, 'FEVER'. She also had the dubious honour of releasing the first ever mini-disc single, 'CAR SEX', after signing to 'Sony' almost a decade later. • **Covers:** FOOLS RUSH IN (Brook Benton) / FEVER (Peggy Lee).

Album rating: I WANT CANDY compilation (*6)

ANNABELLA LWIN (b.MYANT MYANT AYE, 31 Oct'65, Rangoon, Burma) – vocals / **MATTHEW ASHMAN** – guitar / **LEROY GORMAN** – bass / **DAVE BARBAROSSA** – drums (all 3 men **ex-ADAM & THE ANTS)**

E.M.I. not iss.

Jul 80. (7") *(EMI 5088)* **C'30, C'60, C'90, GO. / SUN, SEA & PIRACY** 34 -
Nov 80. (c-ep) *(WOW 1)* **YOUR CASSETTE PET** 58 -
– Louis Quatorze / Gold he said / Fools rush in / Giant sized baby thing / I want my baby on Mars / Uomo sex al Apache / Sexy Eiffel Towers / Radio G-string. *(cd-iss. Oct93; CDP 827223-2)*
Mar 81. (c-s/7") *(TC+/EMI 5153)* **W.O.R.K. (NO NAH NO NO NO MY DADDY DON'T). / C'30, C'60, C'90, GO . . . ANDA!** 62 -

— added 2 female backing vocalists around 1981

R.C.A. R.C.A.

Jul 81. (7") *(RCA 100)* **PRINCE OF DARKNESS. / ORANG UTAN** 58 -
(12") *(RCAT 100)* – ('A'side) / Sinner! sinner! sinner! (Prince of darkness).
Oct 81. (7"/12") *(RCA/+T 144)* **CHIHUAHUA. / GOLLY! GOLLY! GO BUDDY** 51 -
Oct 81. (lp/c) *(RCA LP/K 3000) <4147>* **SEE JUNGLE! SEE JUNGLE! GO JOIN OUR CRAZY GANG YEAH CITY ALL OVER! GO APE CRAZY!** 26
– Jungle boy / Chihuahua / Sinner! sinner! sinner! (Prince of darkness) / Mickey put it down / (I'm a) T.V. savage / Elimination dancing / Golly! golly! go buddy! / King Kong / Go wild in the country / I am not a know it all / Why are babies so wise? / Orang-utang / Hello, hello daddy (I'll sacrifice you). *(c+=)* – The joy of eating raw flesh. *(re-iss. Jul90 on 'Great Expectations' lp/cd+=; PIP LP/CD 013)* – Orang utan / El boss dicho. *(cd re-iss. Jun97 on 'One Way'; OW 34502)*
Jan 82. (7"/ext.12") *(RCA/+T 175)* **GO WILD IN THE COUNTRY. / EL BOSS DICKO** 7
Apr 82. (7"/ext.12") *(RCA/+T 220)* **SEE JUNGLE (JUNGLE BOY). / T.V. SAVAGE** 45
May 82. (7") *<13204>* **I WANT CANDY. / ELIMINATION DANCING** - 62
May 82. (m-lp) *<4314>* **THE LAST OF THE MOHICANS** - 67
– Cowboy / Louis Quatorze / I want candy / Mile High club.
May 82. (7"etched) *(RCA 238)* **I WANT CANDY** 9 -
(7"+=) *(RCA 238)* – King Kong.
(ext.12"+=) *(RCAT 238)* – Cowboy.
Jul 82. (7") *(RCA 263)* **LOUIS QUATORZE. / THE MILE HIGH CLUB** 66
Feb 83. (7"pic-d) *(RCA 314) <13467>* **DO YOU WANNA HOLD ME? / WHAT'S THE TIME (HEY BUDDY)** 47 77
(12"+=) *(RCAT 314)* – Biological phenomenom.

Feb 83. (lp/c) *(RCA LP/K 6068) <4570>* **WHEN THE GOING GETS TOUGH, THE TOUGH GET GOING** 82
– Aphrodisiac / Do you wanna hold me? / Roustabout / Lonesome tonight / Love me / What's the time (hey buddy) / Mario (your own way to Paradise) / Quiver (arrows in my) / Rikki Dee / Tommy Tucker / Love, peace and harmony. *(re-iss. Nov90 on 'Great Expectations' lp/cd; PIP LP/CD 022) (cd re-iss. Jun97 on 'One Way'; OW 34503)*

— disbanded mid '83 when ANNABELLA opted for a solo career. ASHMAN formed CHIEFS OF RELIEF with ex-SEX PISTOLS. Sadly he was to die on 21st Nov'95 of complications due to his diabetis.

– compilations, others, etc. –

Jul 82. (lp/c) *E.M.I.; (EMC 3416) / R.C.A.; <4375>* **I WANT CANDY** Sep82
– I want Candy / Cowboy / Louis Quatorze / Mile high club / W.O.R.K. (ne no my daddy oh) / Fools rush in / I want my baby on Mars / Gold he said / Sexy Eiffel Towers / Radio G-string / C-30, C-60, C-90, go / Sun, sea & piracy / Uomo sex al apache / Giant sized baby thing / C-30, C-60, C-90, anda (Spanish version). *(re-iss. Nov90 on 'Great Expectations' lp/cd; PIP LP/CD 021)*
Sep 82. (7") *E.M.I.; (EMI 5344)* **FOOLS RUSH IN. / UOMO SEX AL APACHE** -
May 83. (c-ep) *R.C.A.; (RCXK 004)* **I WANT CANDY / SEE JUNGLE (JUNGLE BOY). / GO WILD IN THE COUNTRY / CHIHUAHUA** -
Nov 86. (7") *Old Gold; (OG 9638)* **GO WILD IN THE COUNTRY. / I WANT CANDY** -
Aug 89. (lp/cd) *Receiver; (RR LP/CD 116)* **THE BEST OF BOW WOW WOW** -
(re-iss. Jul93; same)
Jun 94. (cd) *Arista; (74321 21336-2)* **GO WILD – THE BEST OF BOW WOW WOW** -
– I want candy / Go wild in the country / Prince of darkness / Cowboy / Baby, oh no / Do you wanna hold me / Golly! Golly! go buddy / Louis Quatorze / What's the time? (hey buddy) / Joy of eating raw flesh / Elimination dancing / Aphrodisiac / The mile high club / T.V. savage / See jungle (see jungle boy) / Chihuahua (12" version) / Go wild in the country (12"version) / Chihuahua.
Oct 96. (cd) *Camden-RCA; (74321 41967-2)* **APHRODISIAC (THE BEST OF BOW WOW WOW)** -
Feb 97. (cd) *Receiver; (RRCD 233)* **LIVE IN JAPAN (live)** -

BOX

Formed: Sheffield, England . . . 1982 by ex-CLOCKDVA members, PAUL WIDLER, CHARLIE COLLINS and ROGER QUAIL, alongside frontman PETER HOPE and bass player TERRY TODD. Becoming the first band to sign for indie imprint, 'Go! Discs' (later the home of HOUSEMARTINS, PAUL WELLER, etc), The BOX debuted early the following year with a 12" EP, 'NO TIME FOR TALK'. While ADI NEWTON took CLOCKDVA into darker but more popular territories, The BOX opened up further experimental possibilities in the spirit of The POP GROUP or The BIRTHDAY PARTY. Bass-heavy, saxy, discordant and jerkily rhythmic, The BOX's unconventional sound was topped off by HOPE's strangulated larynx, an approach that won them a marginal underground following but next to no mainstream coverage. Their debut album, 'SECRETS OUT' was unveiled in mid '83, tracks such as 'WATER GROWS TEETH', 'OLD STYLE DROP DOWN' and a guest appearance from STEPHEN MALLINDER (of CABARET VOLTAIRE), partly rescuing it from a critical savaging. A second set, 'GREAT MOMENTS IN BIG SLAM', was delivered exactly a year later, although ~'Go! Discs' subsequent move into more commercial indie waters found The BOX on the CABS' 'DoubleVision' label for a swansong live lp, 'MUSCLE OUT' (1985). By this time, HOPE had begun the first of his numerous collaborations, a single with DAVID HARROW entitled 'TOO HOT'. The other half of CABARET VOLTAIRE, RICHARD H. KIRK was next to lend his services, their 'LEATHER HANDS' also surfacing later in '85; they would go on to work with each other on future projects. Early in 1987, the singer showcased a further collaborative sojourn, PETER HOPE & THE JONATHAN S. PODMORE METHOD, with an album, 'DRY HIP ROTATION'; HOPE reunited with saxman, CHARLIE COLLINS to form the short-lived BONE ORCHESTRA. • **Note:** Another outfit (a French one!) used the moniker in the late 80's after this group's demise.

Album rating: SECRETS OUT (*5) / GREAT MOMENTS IN BIG SLAM (*6) / MUSCLE OUT (*4) / Peter Hope & The Jonathan S. Podmore Method: DRY HIP ROTATION (*5)

PETER HOPE – vocals, percussion / **PAUL WIDLER** – guitar (ex-CLOCKDVA) / **CHARLIE COLLINS** – saxophone (ex-CLOCKDVA, ex-BONGOS guest) / **TERRY TODD** – bass / **ROGER QUAIL** – drums (ex-CLOCKDVA)

Go! Discs — not iss.

Jan 83. (12"ep) *(VFM 1)* **NO TIME FOR TALK** -
– Burn down that village / Unstable / Limpopo / Hazard.
May 83. (7") *(VFM 2)* **OLD STYLE DROP DOWN. / MOMENTUM** -
(12"+=) *(VFM 3)* –
Jun 83. (lp) *(VFM 4)* **SECRETS OUT** -
– Water grows teeth / Skin, sweat and rain / Something beginning with "L" / Strike / The hub / Hang your hat on that / I give protection / No sly moon / Slip and slant / Old style drop down / Swing / Out.
Jun 84. (lp/c) *(VFM/ZVFM 5)* **GREAT MOMENTS IN BIG SLAM** -
– Walls come down / Flatstone / Big slam / Stop / Low line / Breaking strain / Small blue car / Still in the woodwork.

DoubleVision — not iss.

Jan 85. (12") *(DVR 10)* **MUSCLE IN. /** -
Aug 85. (lp) *(DVRP 3)* **MUSCLE OUT (live)** -

— disbanded some time in '85 with TERRY joining The IAN ELLIOTT BAND after briefly co-forming WORKFORCE.

PETER HOPE

— worked on a series of collaborative work

Ink — not iss.

Jun 85. (12"ep; as PETER HOPE & DAVID HARROW with PINKIE McCLURE) *(INK12 11)* **TOO HOT. /** -

— in Oct'85, PETER HOPE linked with RICHARD H. KIRK (of CABARET VOLTAIRE) on a 12", 'LEATHER HANDS'

Native — not iss.

Oct 85. (12"; as CHAIN) *(NTV 2)* **BANGING ON THE HOUSE. / CHAINS** -
Feb 87. (7"; by PETER HOPE & THE JONATHAN S. PODMORE METHOD) *(NTV 13)* **KITCHENETTE. / THE UNKNOWN INDUSTRIAL FATALITY** -
(12"+=) *(NTV12 13)* – ('A'version).
Feb 87. (lp; by PETER HOPE & THE JONATHAN S. PODMORE METHOD) *(NTVLP 14)* **DRY HIP ROTATION** -
– Kitchenette / Canal / 217 / Dry bone / Haulage / Dog eared pictures of birdwing cars / Needleheat / Hypnosis / Knife / Scurry bug / The unknown industrial fatality.

— once again, HOPE and KIRK collaborated, this time on the 'HOODOO TALK' (1987) album, which spawned the following year's 'SURGEONS' 12"

— HOPE and COLLINS subsequently reunited in the short-lived, BONE ORCHESTRA

BOY HAIRDRESSERS

(see under ⇒ TEENAGE FANCLUB)

BOYS

Formed: London, England . . . summer 1976 by JOHN PLAIN, KID REID, JACK BLACK and two slightly more experienced musicians MATT DANGERFIELD and Norwegian CASINO STEEL, the latter fresh from The HOLLYWOOD BRATS. After supporting JOHN CALE on his Spring '77 tour, the lads signed to the 'NEMS' label, debuting almost immediately with the single, 'I DON'T CARE'. Power-pop punk sounding like a less abrasive hybrid of BUZZCOCKS and RAMONES, the track didn't chart but seemingly sold well in Scandinavia and Europe. Their second 45, 'FIRST TIME', deserved a better fate, although its inclusion as a highlight of their UK Top 50 eponymous debut album no doubt boosted sales. They couldn't repeat the formula however, and it didn't help when they inaugurated their annual Christmas appearance as The YOBS. After a second long-player, 'ALTERNATIVE CHARTBUSTERS' (1978) failed to make the grade, The BOYS signed to 'Safari', also home of TOYAH whom DANGERFIELD was asked to produce. At the turn of the decade, the improbably named crew released the poorly received 'TO HELL WITH THE BOYS' (1979); presumably this was also what their fans thought as their support dwindled and they faded from view after swansong set, 'BOYS ONLY' (1981). • **Songwriters:** STEEL / DANGERFIELD, except YOU BETTER MOVE ON (Arthur Alexander) / SABRE DANCE (Love Sculpture). • **Question:** What was The BOYS' connection with other late 70's outfits. The ROWDIES and COCKNEY & WESTERNS. Was MATT on production?

Album rating: THE BOYS (*4) / ALTERNATIVE CHARTBUSTERS (*5) / TO HELL WITH THE BOYS (*5) / BOYS ONLY (*4)

MATT DANGERFIELD – vocals, guitar (ex-LONDON SS) / **CASINO STEEL** (b. Norway) – keyboards (ex-LONDON SS, ex-HOLLYWOOD BRATS) / **KID REID** (b. DUNCAN) – vocals, bass / **JOHN PLAIN** (b. Leeds, England) – guitar / **JACK BLACK** – drums

NEMS — not iss.

Apr 77. (7") *(NES 102)* **I DON'T CARE. / SODA PRESSING** -
Jul 77. (7"m) *(NES 111)* **FIRST TIME. / WHATCHA GONNA DO / TURNING GREY** -
Sep 77. (lp) *(NEL 6001)* **THE BOYS** 50 -
– Sick on you / I call your name / Tumble with me / Tonight / I don't care / Soda pressing / No money / First time / Box number / Kiss like a nun / Cop cars / Kep running / Tenement kids / Living in the city.
Dec 77. (7"; as The YOBS) *(NES 114)* **RUN RUDOLPH RUN. / THE WORM SONG** -
Feb 78. (7") *(NES 116)* **BRICKFIELD NIGHTS. / TEACHER'S PET** -
Mar 78. (lp) *(NEL 6015)* **ALTERNATIVE CHARTBUSTERS** -
– Brickfield nights / Usi / Taking on the world / Sway / Do the contract / Heroine / Not ready / Classified Susie / T.C.P. / Neighbourhood brat / Stop stop stop / Backstage pass / Talking / Cast of thousands.

Yob — not iss.

Dec 78. (7"; as The YOBS) *(YOB 79)* **SILENT NIGHT. / STILLE NACHT** -

Safari — not iss.

Nov 79. (7") *(SAFE 21)* **KAMIKAZE. / BAD DAYS** -
Nov 79. (lp) *(1-2 BOYS)* **TO HELL WITH BOYS** -
– Kamikaze / Lonely cowboy / Waiting for the lady / Bad day / Independent girl / You better move on / Sabre dance / Rue Morgue / Terminal love / See ya later / You can't hurt a memory.
Dec 79. (7"; as the YOBS) *(YULE 1)* **RUB-A-DUM-DUM. / ANOTHER CHRISTMAS** -
Jan 80. (7") *(SAFE 23)* **TERMINAL LOVE. / I LOVE ME** -
May 80. (7") *(SAFE 27)* **YOU BETTER MOVE ON. / SCHOOLGIRLS** -

— now without STEEL. (JOHN PLAIN joined LURKERS man PETE STRIDE for an album and single, before returning to the fold)

Sep 80. (7") *(SAFE 31)* **WEEKEND. / COOL** -
Dec 80. (lp; as the YOBS) *(RUDE 1)* **CHRISTMAS ALBUM** (compilation) -
Feb 81. (lp) *(4)* **BOYS ONLY** -

– Weekend / Wrong arm of the law / Poor little rich girl / Monotony / Nothing ventured / Wonderful world / Scrubber / Satisfaction guarenteed / Gabrielle / Miss you / Little white lifeline / Let it rain.

Mar 81. (7") *(SAFE 33)* **LET IT RAIN. / LUCY** [ ] [-]

Fresh not iss.

Jan 82. (7"; as the YOBS) *FRESH 1)* **YOBS ON 45. / THE BALLAD OF WARRINGTON** [ ] [-]

— disbanded after above

BOYS NEXT DOOR (see under ⇒ CAVE, Nick)

B-PEOPLE

Formed: Los Angeles, California, USA ... March 1979 out of various punk outfits by PAT DELANEY (ex-DEADBEATS; one mid'78 EP exists, 'KILL THE HIPPIES' for 'Dangerhouse' IQ 29), ALEX GIBSON, FREDRIK NILSEN and TOM RECCHION (the latter both ex-DOO DOOETTES; some recordings exist from 1976). The early 80's saw B-PEOPLE release their only two EP's, 'YOU AT EIGHT' and the eponymous 'B-PEOPLE', the band's provocatively experimental material later collected together for posterity on the 1986 compilation, 'PETRIFIED CONDITIONS 1979-1981'. Before their split they did manage to appear on V/A compilation, 'Let Them Eat Jellybeans', with the track 'PERSECUTION – THAT'S MY SONG'. MICHAEL GIRA (later SWANS) and PAUL CUTLER were said to have been part of the band prior to their demise.

Album rating: PETRIFIED CONDITIONS 1979-1981 compilation (*6)

PAT DELANEY – synthesizer, saxophone (ex-DEADBEATS) / **ALEX GIBSON** – guitar, vocals / **FREDRIK NILSEN** – bass, vocals, saxophone (ex-DOO DOOETTES) / **TOM RECCHION** – drums (ex-DOO DOOETTES)

not iss. Faulty

May 81. (7"m) <*FP 03*> **YOU AT EIGHT. / WEATHER TO WORRY / M.C.P.D.** [-] [ ]

Feb 82. (12"ep) <*FEP 1300*> **B-PEOPLE** [-] [ ]

— MICHAEL GIRA and PAUL CUTLER could well have been members before they split. In 1984, ALEX GIBSON scored the soundtrack for the film, 'SUBURBIA', which was released by 'Enigma' in the US-only.

– compilations, etc. –

1986. (lp) *Restless;* **PETRIFIED CONDITIONS 1979-1981** [-] [ ]

BRACKET

Formed: Forestville, California, USA ... early 90's (although they had been playing together since their schooldays in the mid 80's) by MARTY GREGORI, LARRY TINNEY, ZACK CHARLOS and RAY CARLOS. After a series of low-key independently released singles, the band finally delivered their debut album for 'Caroline', '924 FORESTVILLE ST.' in 1994. Another Virgin offshoot, 'Hi-Rise' handled them in the UK, the one-time ardent AC/DC fans now trading in a Power-punk sound closer to GREEN DAY. The following year, BRACKET consolidated their rise with a DON FLEMING-produced second set, '4-WHEEL VIBE', a series of previously recorded 45's flooding onto the UK market courtesy of FAT MIKE's (NOFX) 'Fat Wreck Chords'. This label also masterminded their following two sets, 'E IS FOR EVERYTHING' (1996) and 'NOVELTY FOREVER' (1997).

Album rating: 924 FORESTVILLE ST. (*6) / 4-WHEEL VIBE (*6) / E IS FOR EVERYTHING (*5) / NOVELTY FOREVER (*5)

MARTY GREGORI – vocals, guitar / **LARRY TINNEY** – guitar / **ZACK CHARLOS** – bass / **RAY CARLOS** – drums

Hi-Rise Hut

Jan 95. (12"ep) *(FLAT 13)* <*5045*> **PRESENTS . . . "5.35"** [ ] [ ]
– Huge balloon / Why should eye.
(cd-ep+=) *(FLATSCD 13)* – Mother to blame.

Hi-Rise Caroline

Mar 95. (cd/c/lp) *(FLAT CD/MC/LP 15)* <*CAROLCD 1754*> **924 FORESTVILLE ST.** [ ] [ ] 1994
– Get it rite / Dodge ball / Missing link / Sleep / Huge balloon / Stalking stuffer / Why should eye / Warren's song (pt.1) / Warren's song (pt.2) / Can't make me / Skanky love song / J. Weed / Rod's post. *(cd re-iss. Jun97 on 'Caroline'; same as US)*

May 95. (cd/c/lp) *(FLAT CD/MC/LP 17)* <*CAROLCD 1787*> **4-WHEEL VIBE** [ ] [ ]
– Circus act / Cool aid / Happy to be sad / John Wilkes isolation booth / Tractor / Green apples / Closed caption / Trailer park / Fresh air / PC / G-vibe / Warren's song (pt.4) / 2 hotdogs for 99c / The metal one / Pesimist / Lazy / My stepson. *(cd re-iss. Jun97 on 'Caroline'; same as US)*

May 95. (7") <*(FAT 516-7)*> **STINKY FINGERS. /** [ ] [ ]
(above and below issued on 'Fat Wreck Chords')

Oct 95. (7") <*(FAT 530-7)*> **FOR THOSE ABOUT TO MOCK. /** [ ] [ ]

Nov 95. (cd-s) *(FLATSCD 23)* **TRAILER PARK / STYLIN' / WARREN'S SONG PART 5** [ ] [ ]

Nov 96. (cd) <*(FAT 548CD)*> **E IS FOR EVERYTHING** [ ] [ ]
(above and below issued on 'Fat Wreck Chords')

Nov 96. (d7"ep) <*(FAT 549)*> **F IS FOR FAT** [ ] [ ]

Sep 97. (cd) <*FAT 559*> **NOVELTY FOREVER** [-] [ ]
– Last day Sunday / Three gardens / Exit bean / Don't tell Miss Fenley / Sour / Back to Allentown / Little Q & A / One more hangover day / I won't mind / Optimism / Drama queen / Little Q & A.

BRAD

Formed: Seattle, Washington, USA ... 1992 by SHAWN SMITH, who had spread his soulful vocal talent around groups like PIGEONHED and SATCHEL. He teamed up with PEARL JAM guitarist STONE GOSSARD and two others, JEREMY TOBACK and REGAN HAGAR, to complete a debut album, 'SHAME', in 1993. An evocative, free-form affair, the album utilised influences from an eclectic array of musical styles, garnering rave reviews and notching up respectable sales. They returned four years later with the follow-up, 'INTERIORS', SMITH and REGAN having recorded two albums in the interim, 'E.D.C.' and 'FAMILY', both under the moniker of SATCHEL. Meanwhile, PIGEONHED (SMITH and producer, STEVE FISK again) were delivering their second set for 'Sub Pop', 'THE FULL SENTENCE' (1997), having given us an eponymous headtrippin' set in '93.

Album rating: SHAME (*7) / INTERIORS (*6) / Satchel: E.D.C. (*7) / THE FAMILY (*7) / Pigeonhed: PIGEONHED (*6) / THE FULL SENTENCE (*7)

SHAWN SMITH – vocals, piano / **STONE GOSSARD** – guitar (of PEARL JAM) / **JEREMY TOBACK** – bass / **REGAN HAGAR** – drums (of SATCHEL, of MALFUNKSHUN)

Epic Epic

May 93. (cd/c/lp) <*(473596-2/-4/-1)*> **SHAME** [72] [ ]
– Buttercup / My fingers / Nadine / Screen / 20th century / Raise love / Bad for the soul / Down / Rock star / We. *(re-iss. Aug95; same)*

Jun 93. (7") *(659248-7)* **20TH CENTURY. / SKIN** [64] [ ]
(cd-s+=) *(659248-2)* – ('A'mixes).

Jun 97. (cd/c) <*(487921-2/-4)*> **INTERIORS** [ ] [ ]
– Secret girl / The day brings / Lift / I don't know / Upon my shoulders / Sweet Al George / The funeral song / Circle and line / Some never come home / Candles / Those three words.

SATCHEL

SMITH + HAGAR

Epic Epic

Sep 94. (cd/c/lp) <*(477314-2/-4/-1)*> **E.D.C.** [ ] [ ]
– Mr. Brown / Equilibrium / Taste it / Trouble come down / More ways than 3 / Hollywood / O / Mr. Pink / Built 4 it / Mr. Blue / Willow / Roof almighty / Suffering.

Sep 96. (cd/c) <*(484428-2/-4)*> **THE FAMILY** [ ] [ ]
– Isn't that right / Without love / Not too late / Criminal justice / Breathe deep / Time "O" the year / For so long / Some more trouble / Tomorrow / Roll on / Breathe deep (instrumental dub).

PIGEONHED

SHAWN SMITH – vocals, guitars, keyboards, drums / **STEVE FISK** – keyboards, loops, producer

Sub Pop Sub Pop

Jun 93. (7") **AIN'T IT SO. /** [ ] [ ]

Jul 93. (lp/cd) <*(SP/+CD 101/273)*> **PIGEONHED** [ ] [ ]
– Theme from Pigeonhed / Ain't it so / Special way / Her / Lovely lines / Cadillac / Trial by sex / Salome / Brothers / Buzz / Grace. *(cd re-iss. Oct98; SP 224B)*

— next added guests JERRY CANTRELL + KIM THAYIL

Feb 97. (lp/cd) <*(SP/+CD 373)*> **THE FULL SENTENCE** [ ] [ ]
– It's like the man said / The full sentence / Marry me / Keep on keepin' on / Battle flag / Glory bound / Phunpurephun / P-street / Phunpurephun / Who's to blame / 31st of July / More than just a girl / Fire's coming down / For those gone on / Honor. *(cd re-iss. Aug97 on 'Warners'; 9878 70224-2)*

Warners Sub Pop

Jun 97. (cd-s) <*SP 405*> **GLORY BOUND /** [-] [ ]

Oct 97. (12"/cd-s) *(W 0420 T/CD)* **BATTLEFLAG. /** [ ] [ ]

Mar 98. (cd) *(9878 70408-2)* <*SP 408*> **PIGEONHED'S FLASHBULB EMERGENCY** [ ] [ ] Oct97
– Full sentence / Phunperephun / Glory bound / Battle flag / Marry me / It's like the man said / Keep on keepin' on / Marry me / Full sentence.

Billy BRAGG

Born: STEVEN WILLIAM BRAGG, 20 Dec'57, Barking, Essex, England. Inspired by The CLASH, he formed Peterborough-based R&B/punk band, RIFF RAFF, in 1977. After releasing a string of indie 7" singles, (including the wonderfully titled 'I WANNA BE A COSMONAUT'), the band split in 1981, BILLY incredibly going off to join the army. Thankfully, a career in the military wasn't to be though, and he bought himself out after only 90 days. Complete with amplifier and guitar, he busked around Britain, finally furnished with some studio time in 1983 courtesy of 'Charisma' indie subsidiary, 'Utility'. The result was 'LIFE'S A RIOT WITH SPY VS SPY', and with the help and distribution of new label 'Go! Discs', the record finally hit the UK Top 30 in early '84. BRAGG's stark musical backdrop (for the most part, a roughly strummed electric guitar) and even starker vocals, belied a keen sense of melody and passionate, deeply humane lyrics. 'THE MILKMAN OF HUMAN KINDNESS' was a love song of the most compassionate variety which illustrated that BRAGG approached politics from a humanist perspective rather than a soapbox. After seeing firsthand how Thatcher had decimated mining communities, BRAGG's songs became more overtly political. 'BREWING UP WITH BILLY BRAGG' (1984) opened with the fierce 'IT SAYS HERE', but again the most affecting moments were to be found on heartfelt love songs like the wistful 'ST. SWITHIN'S DAY'. It would be another two years before he released a new album, in the interim taking time to make his Top Of The Pops debut and play a lead role in the 'Red Wedge' campaign. A well intentioned but ultimately hopeless initiative to persuade people to vote Labour, BRAGG toured alongside The STYLE COUNCIL, MADNESS, The COMMUNARDS and MORRISSEY. As the Conservatives romped home to another sickening victory, BRAGG licked his wounds and bounced back with a third album, 'TALKING WITH THE TAXMAN ABOUT POETRY' (1986). His most successful and accomplished release to date, the record spawned the classic single, 'LEVI STUBBS' TEARS' as well as the JOHNNY MARR collaboration, 'GREETINGS TO THE NEW BRUNETTE'. And of course, who could argue with the sentiments of 'HELP SAVE THE YOUTH OF AMERICA'?! Not content with saving our Transatlantic cousins, BRAGG also did his bit for kids back in Blighty. Recording a cover of 'SHE'S LEAVING HOME' with CARA TIVEY, BRAGG found himself at No.1 when the song was released as the B-side to WET WET WET's cover of 'WITH A LITTLE HELP FROM MY FRIENDS', the not inconsiderable proceeds going to the Childline charity. BRAGG's next album, 'WORKER'S PLAYTIME' (1988), saw a move away from the sparse accompaniment of old, while lyrically the record focused more on matters of the heart than the ballot box. 'THE INTERNATIONALE' (1990), meanwhile, was BRAGG's most political work to date, with the likes of 'NICARAGUITA' and 'THE RED FLAG'. On 'DON'T TRY THIS AT HOME' (1991), BRAGG enlisted a cast of musicians to flesh out the sound, a tactic that elicited mixed results. His stance with CND and anti-apartheid, anti-poll tax, etc, has often saw him on wrong side of the law. For the 90's it looks as though he will become a bit more cosmopolitan but still ungagged. In 1998, BILLY and the alt-country group WILCO decided to do a tribute album dedicated to their dustbowl hero, WOODY GUTHRIE. 'MERMAID AVENUE' (a street in Coney Island where WOODY lived with his family in the late 40's and early 50's) was the title, the lyrics seemingly found in an attic while messers BRAGG and WILCO set them to tunes. Also noted was the track, 'CALIFORNIA STARS', which featured guest vocals via NATALIE MERCHANT. • **Covered:** WALK AWAY RENEE (Four Tops) / SHE'S LEAVING HOME + REVOLUTION (Beatles) / JEANE (Smiths) / SEVEN AND SEVEN IS (Love) / THERE IS POWER IN A UNION (trad.new words) / THINK AGAIN (Dick Gaughan) / CHILE YOUR WATERS RUN RED THROUGH SOWETO (B.Johnson Reagan) / TRAIN TRAIN (Z.Delfeur) / DOLPHINS (Fred Neil) / EVERYWHERE (Sid Griffin-Greg Trooper) / JERUSALEM (William Blake) / WHEN WILL I SEE YOU AGAIN (Three Degrees) / NEVER HAD NO ONE EVER (Smiths).

Album rating: LIFE'S A RIOT WITH SPY VS. SPY mini (*7) / BREWING UP WITH BILLY BRAGG (*8) / TALKING WITH THE TAXMAN ABOUT POETRY (*8) / WORKERS PLAYTIME (*7) / THE INTERNATIONALE (*5) / DON'T TRY THIS AT HOME (*8) / WILLIAM BLOKE (*7) / BACK TO BASICS compilation (*7)

RIFF RAFF

(BILLY BRAGG – vocals, guitar) and other members

Chiswick / not iss.

May 78. (7"ep) *(SW 34)* **I WANNA BE A COSMONAUT** [ ] [-]
– Cosmonaut / Romford girls / What's the latest? / Sweet as pie.

Geezer / not iss.

Oct 80. (7") *(GZ 1)* **EVERY GIRL AN ENGLISH ROSE. / U SHAPED HOUSE** [ ] [-]
Oct 80. (7") *(GZ 2)* **KITTEN. / FANTOCIDE** [ ] [-]
Oct 80. (7") *(GZ 3)* **LITTLE GIRLS KNOW. / SHE DON'T MATTER** [ ] [-]
Oct 80. (7") *(GZ 4)* **NEW HOME TOWN. / RICHARD** [ ] [-]

BILLY BRAGG

went solo

Utility / not iss.

Jun 83. (m-lp) *(UTIL 1)* **LIFE'S A RIOT WITH SPY VS. SPY** [30] [-]
– The milkman of human kindness / To have and have not / A new England / The man in the iron mask / The busy girl buys beauty / Lover's town revisited / Richard. *(re-iss. Jan84 on 'Go! Discs' lp/c; UTIL/+C 1) (cd-iss. Sep96 on 'Cooking Vinyl'; COOKCD 106)*

—— added for back-up **KENNY CRADDOCK** – organ / **DAVE WOODHEAD** – trumpet

Go! Discs / Elektra

Oct 84. (lp/c) *(A/Z GOLP 4)* **BREWING UP WITH BILLY BRAGG** [16] [-]
– It says here / Love gets dangerous / The myth of trust / From a Vauxhall Velox / The Saturday boy / Island of no return / St. Swithin's Day / Like soldiers do / This guitar says sorry / Strange things happen / A lover sings. *(cd-iss. Sep96 on 'Cooking Vinyl'; COOKCD 107)*
Feb 85. (7") **ST. SWITHIN'S DAY. / A NEW ENGLAND** [-] [-] Euro
Mar 85. (7"ep) *(AGOEP 1)* **BETWEEN THE WARS** [15] [-]
– Between the wars / Which side are you on? / World turned upside down / It says here.
Dec 85. (7"m) *(GOD 8)* **DAYS LIKE THESE. / I DON'T NEED THIS PRESSURE RON / SCHOLARSHIP IS THE ENEMY OF ROMANCE** [43] [-]

—— + guests **JOHNNY MARR** – guitar / **KIRSTY MacCOLL** – b.vocals / **KENNY JONES** – drums, co-producer / **JOHN PORTER** – bass, co-producer / **SIMON MORTEON** – percussion / **BOBBY VALENTINO** – violin

Jun 86. (7"m) *(GOD 12)* **LEVI STUBBS' TEARS. / THINK AGAIN / WALK AWAY RENEE** [29] [-]
(12"+=) *(GODX 12)* – Between the wars (live).
Sep 86. (lp/c) *(A/Z GOLP 6)* **TALKING WITH THE TAXMAN ABOUT POETRY** [8] [ ]
– Greetings to the new brunette / Train train / The marriage / Ideology / Levi Stubbs' tears / Honey, I'm a big boy now / There is power in a union / Help save the youth of America / Wishing the days away / The passion / The warmest room / The home front. *(cd-iss. May87; AGOCD 6) (cd re-iss/Sep96 on 'Cooking Vinyl'; COOKCD 108)*
Nov 86. (7"m) *(GOD 15)* **GREETINGS TO THE NEW BRUNETTE. / DEPORTEES / THE TATLER** [58] [-]
(12"+=) *(GODX 15)* – Jeane / There is power in a union (instrumental).

—— Oct'87, BRAGG is credited with OYSTER BAND backing **LEON ROSSELSON** on his single **BALLAD OF A SPYCATCHER** (Upside Down records)

—— May'88, he's credited with **CARA TIVEY** on 45 **SHE'S LEAVING HOME** the B-side of **WET WET WET** – With A little Help From My Friends. This UK No.1 single issued on 'Childline' gave all proceeds to children's charity, with backing including his usual friends.

Go! Discs / Elektra

May 88. (12"ep/cd-ep) *(A/ZA GOLP 1) <960-787-2>* **HELP SAVE THE YOUTH OF AMERICA (LIVE AND DUBIOUS)** [ ] [ ]
– Help save the youth of America / Think again / Chile your waters run red through Soweto / Days like these (DC mix) / To have and have not / There is power in a union (with The PATTERSONS).
Aug 88. (7"m) *(GOD 23)* **WAITING FOR THE GREAT LEAP FORWARD. / WISHING THE DAYS AWAY / SIN CITY** [52] [ ]
Sep 88. (lp/c/cd) *(AGOLP/ZGOLP/AGOCD 15) <60824>* **WORKER'S PLAYTIME** [17] [ ]
– She's got a brand new spell / Must I paint you a picture / Tender comrade / The price I pay / Little timb-bomb / Rotting on demand / Valentine's day is over / Life with the lions / The only one / The short answer / Waiting for the great leap forward. *(cd re-iss. Sep96 on 'Cooking Vinyl'; COOKCD 109)*
Nov 88. (7") *(GOD 24)* **SHE'S GOT A BRAND NEW SPELL. / MUST I PAINT YOU A PICTURE** [ ] [-]

—— In Jul'89, BRAGG was credited on a NORMAN COOK Top 30 single 'Won't Talk About it'.

May 90. (m-lp/m-c/m-cd; on 'Utility') *(UTIL/+C/CD 011)* **THE INTERNATIONALE** [34] [ ]
– The internationale / I dreamed I saw Phil Ochs last night / The marching song of the convent battalions / Jerusalem / Nicaraguita / The red flag / My youngest son came home today.

—— still holding on to **MARR, MacCOLL, TIVEY** (keyboards) and WOODHEAD plus **WIGGY** – guitar, bass / **J.F.T. HOOD** – drums / **AMANDA VINCENT** – keyboards / etc.

Jun 91. (7") *(GOD 56)* **SEXUALITY. / BAD PENNY** [27] [ ]
(12"+=/cd-s+=) *(GOD X/CD 56)* – (2 'A'mixes).
Aug 91. (7") *(GOD 60)* **YOU WOKE UP MY NEIGHBOURHOOD. / ONTARIO, QUEBEC AND ME** [54] [ ]
(12"+=/cd-s+=) *(GOD X/CD 60)* – Bread and circuses / Heart like a wheel.
(above single 'A'featured **MICHAEL STIPE and PETER BUCK (R.E.M.)** with first 12"extra track with **NATALIE MERCHANT** (10,000 MANIACS) – also backing vocals
Sep 91. (cd/c/d-lp)(8x7"box) *(828279-2/-4/-1)* **DON'T TRY THIS AT HOME** [8] [ ]
– Accident waiting to happen / Moving the goalposts / Everywhere / Cindy of a thousand lives / You woke up my neighbourhood / Trust / God's footballer / The few / Sexuality / Mother of the bride / Tank park salute / Dolphins / North sea bubble / Rumours of war / Wish you were here / Body of water. *(re-iss. Nov93 & Apr98 on 'Cooking Vinyl' lp/c/cd; COOK/+C/CD 062) (cd re-iss. Sep96; COOKCD 110)*
Feb 92. (7"ep) *(GOD 67)* **ACCIDENT WAITING TO HAPPEN (Red Star version) / SULK. / THE WARMEST ROOM (live) / REVOLUTION** [33] [-]
(12"+=/cd-s+=) *(GOD X/CD 67)* – ('A'live version) / Levi Stubbs' tears / Valentine's day is over / North Sea bubble.

Cooking Vinyl / Elektra

Aug 96. (7"/c-s) *(FRY/+C 051)* **UPFIELD / THATCHERITES** [46] [ ]
(cd-s+=) *(FRYCD 051)* – Rule nor reason.
Sep 96. (lp/c/cd) *(COOK/+C/CD 100)* **WILLIAM BLOKE** [16] [ ]
– From red to blue / Upfield / Everybody loves you babe / Sugardaddy / A Pict song / Brickbat / The space race is over / Northern industrial town / The fourteenth of February / King James version / Goalhanger.
May 97. (7") *(FRY 064)* **THE BOY DONE GOOD. / SUGARDADDY** [55] [ ]
(cd-s+=) *(FRYCD 064)* – Just one victory / Qualifications.
(cd-s+=) *(FRYCDX 064)* – Never had no one ever / Run out of reasons.
Jun 97. (cd) *(COOKCD 127)* **BLOKE ON BLOKE** [72] [ ]
– The boy done good / Just one victory / Qualifications / Sugar daddy / Never had no one ever / Run out of seasons / Rule nor reason / Thatcherites.

Elektra / Elektra

Jun 98. (cd/c; BILLY BRAGG & WILCO) *(<7559 62204-2/-4>)* **MERMAID AVENUE** [34] [90]
– Walt Whitman's niece / California stars / Way over yonder in the minor key / Birds and ships / Hoodoo voodoo / She came along to me / At my window sad and lonely / Ingrid Bergman / Christ for President / I guess I planted / One by one / Eisler on the go / Hesitating beauty / Another man's done gone / The unwelcome guest.
Nov 98. (7"/c-s; BILLY BRAGG & WILCO) *(E 3798/+C)* **WAY OVER YONDER IN THE MINOR KEY. / MY THIRTY THOUSAND** [ ] [-]
(cd-s+=) *(E 3798CD)* – Bug-eyed Jim.

– compilations, others, etc. –

May 87. (12"ep) *Strange Fruit; (SFPS 027)* **THE PEEL SESSIONS** [ ] [-]
– A new England / Strange things happen / This guitar says sorry / Love gets dangerous / A13 trunk road to the sea / Fear . . . *(cd-iss. 1988; SFPSCD 027)*
Jun 87. (d-lp/d-c/cd) *Go! Discs; (AGOLP/ZGOLP/AGOCD 8)* **BACK TO BASICS** (best 83-85 material) [37] [-]
(re-iss. Apr98 on 'Cooking Vinyl' d-lp/c/cd; COOK/+C/CD 060)
Feb 92. (cd/c/lp) *Strange Fruit; (SFR CD/MC/LP 117)* **THE PEEL SESSIONS ALBUM** [ ] [-]
(cd with extra tracks)
Nov 93. (d-lp/c/cd) *Cooking Vinyl; (COOK/+C/CD 061)* **VICTIM OF GEOGRAPHY** [ ] [-]
– Greetings to the new brunette / Train train / Marriage / Idealogy / Levi Stubbs' tears / Honey I'm a big boy now / There is a power in a union / Help save the youth of America / Wishing the days away / Passion / The warmest room / Home front / She's got a new spell / Must I paint you a picture / Tender comrade / The price I pay / Little timb bomb / Rotting on demand / Valentine's day is over / Life with

the lions / The only one / Short answer / Waiting for the great leap forward. *(re-iss. Apr98 cd/c; same)*

Brian BRAIN

Born: MARTYN ATKINS, 3 Aug'59, Coventry, Midlands, England. The drummer had cut his teeth in an outfit caled MYND before being snapped up by JOHN LYDON (ex-JOHNNY ROTTEN of the SEX PISTOLS) for his avant-garde punks, PUBLIC IMAGE LTD. While contributing on their live set, 'Paris Au Printemps' in 1980, ATKINS departed only to return the following year. Meanwhile, ATKINS (under the guise of BRIAN BRAIN) issued a handful of releases on the 'Secret' imprint, although these were initially of novelty/experimental value. His backing band at the time consisted of BOBBY SURGEONER and PETE JONES, the latter another to join ATKINS on his second expedition to PiL. Having left PiL for the last time, BRIAN BRAIN delivered a few low key disasters before ATKINS was invited to join KILLING JOKE at the turn of the decade. This led to ATKINS collaborating with a plethora of musicians (including CHRIS CONNELLY) on the PIGFACE project, releasing several dark experimental noise albums in the process. • **Covered:** AT HOME HE'S A TOURIST (Gang Of Four) / CAREERING (PiL).

Album rating: UNEXPECTED NOISES (*4)

MARTYN ATKINS – drums, vocals / **PETE JONES** (b.22 Sep'57) – bass / **BOBBY SURGEONER** – vocals, guitar

Secret / not iss.

Apr 80. (7") *(SHH 101)* **THEY'VE GOT ME IN THE BOTTLE. / I GET PAIN** [ ] [-]

Aug 80. (7") *(SHH 105)* **ANOTHER MILLION MILES. / PERSONALITY COUNTS** [ ] [-]

Nov 80. (lp) *(BRAIN 1)* **UNEXPECTED NOISES** [ ] [-]
– Another million miles / Our man in Hong Kong / I get pain / The hots for you / The asthma game / Brainstorm / Unexpected noises / They've got me in the bottle / Dirty dealing in the lone star state / Turn it into noise / I'm suffocating / Jet boats up the Ganges.

Jan 81. (12"ep) *(12SHH 109)* **CULTURE** [ ] [-]
– Fun people / Working in a farmyard in a white suit / At home he's a tourist / Careering.

Dec 81. (7") *(SHH 119)* **JIVE JIVE. / HELLO TO THE WORKING CLASS** [7-]

Oct 82. (7"/12") *(SHH 142/+12)* **FUNKY ZOO. / FLIES** [ ] [-]

— left PiL and retired for a while. **MARGOT OLAVARRIA** – bass (ex-GO-GO'S) repl. PETE who joined PiL

Wide Angle / not iss.

Jul 86. (7") **FUN WITH MUSIC. /** [ ] [-]

— ATKINS joined KILLING JOKE and then PIGFACE in the 90's

PIGFACE

— **MARTIN ATKINS** with **TRENT REZNOR** (Nine Inch Nails) / **BILL RIEFLIN** (Ministry / Revolting Cocks) / **OGRE** (Skinny Puppy) / **EN ESCH** (K.M.F.D.M.) / **DAVID YOW** (Jesus Lizard) / **CHRIS CONNELLY** (Revolting Cocks / solo) **WILLIAM TUCKER** (Ministry / Scornflakes) / **MATT SCHULTZ** (A.T.G.) / producer **STEVE ALBINI** (ex-Big Black)

Anagram / not iss.

Feb 91. (cd/lp) *(CD+/GRAM 47)* **GUB** [ ] [-]
– Tapeworm / The bushmaster / Cylinder head world / Point blank / Suck / Symphony for taps / The greenhouse / Little sisters / Tailor made / War ich nicht immer ein guter junge? (remix) / Blood and sand / Weightless. *(re-iss. Sep91 on 'Devotion' cd/c/lp; CD/T+/DVN 2) (cd re-iss. Mar96 on 'Invisible'+=; INV 009CD)* – Tonight's the night (little sisters) (remix) / Winnebago induced tapeworm (remix) / Bushmaster bushmaster (remix) / War ich nicht immer.

— **PAUL RAVEN** (Killing Joke) + **PAUL BARKER** (Ministry) + **MARY BYKER** (Gaye Bykers On Acid) repl. ESCH

Devotion / Devotion

Nov 91. (cd/c/d-lp) *(<CD/T+/DVN 3>)* **WELCOME TO MEXICO** [ ] [ ]
– The love serenade (I hate you?) / Blood and sand / Peaking too early (William) / Little sisters / Twice removed / Beneath my feet / Point blank / Stowaway / Suck / Weightless / T.F.W.O. / Lash – Herb – Taxi / Tapeworm / The breakfast conspiracy. *(cd re-iss. Mar96 on 'Invisible'; INV 011CD)*

Oct 92. (cd/c/lp) *(<CD/T+/DVN 18>)* **FOOK** [ ] [ ]
– Alles ist mein / Ten ground & down / Seven words / Insemination / Hips, tits, lips, power / Satellite / I'm still alive / Auto hag / Go / I can do no wrong. *(cd re-iss. Mar96 on 'Invisible'; INV 018CD)*

Nov 93. (d-cd) *(<CDDVN 25>)* **TRUTH WILL OUT / WASHINGMACHINE MOUTH** [ ] [ ]
– TRUTH WILL OUT:- Can you feel pain? / War ich nicht / Point blank / Do no wrong / Weightless / White trash reggae – Pigface in your area / Alle ist mein / Hips tits lips power / 7 words / Henry / Jungle bells / Suck // WASHINGMACHINE MOUTH:- Flowers are evil / Cutting face / Satan on the inside looking in / H.T.L. a) Red around the eye, b) The calm before the storm, c) The return of wet brain 2000 / Cutting face-gas mash mix / Satellite – Needle in the groove / No damage done / Prepare to die go! go! go! / The last word. *(re-iss. Mar96 on 'Invisible'; INV 026CD & INV 021CD)*

Nov 94. (cd) *(<CDDVN 29>)* **NOTES FROM THE UNDERGROUND** [ ] [ ]
– Asshole / Dive bomber / Your own your own / Fuck it up / Hagseed / Chicksaw / Empathy / Magazine / Think / Trivial scene / Slut / Blood / Pain / Psalm springs eternal / Steamroller / Your music is garbage.

Invisible / Invisible

Nov 95. (cd) *(<INV 034CD>)* **FEELS LIKE HEAVEN . . . SOUNDS LIKE SHIT** [ ] [ ]
– (Dialogue) / Think / Steamroller / Hagseed / (Dialogue) / Fuck it up / Chikasaw / Suck / Asphole / Steamroller / Sick asp fuck / (Dialogue) / Empathy / Divebomber / Chikasaw / Chikasaw.

Sep 97. (cd) *<INV 063CD>* **A NEW HIGH IN LOW** [ ] [ ] Aug97
– Radio bagpipe / Kiss king (high high high) / Burundi / Bring unto me / More / Nutopia / Methylated: . . . / Aboriginal / Metal tangerine / First taken third found / Warzone / You know – you know – you know / Howler: an English breakfast / Train / Howler: an English breakfast.

Jun 98. (cd) *<INV 099CD>* **BELOW THE BELT** [ ] [ ]
– Radio bagpipe / Kiss king / Burundi / More / Nutopia / More methylated / Metal tangerine / First taken third found / Burundi / Nutopia / More / Warzone / You know . . .

– compilations, etc. –

Jul 93. (12") *Invisible; (INV 008T)* **SPOON BREAKFAST. /** [ ] [-]

Jul 93. (lp/cd) *Invisible; (INV 012/+2)* **LEAN JUICY PARK** (interviews) [ ] [-]

Aug 93. (12"/c-s; BRIAN BRAIN) *(INV 005 T/C)* **EP** [ ] [ ]

BRAINIAC

Formed: Dayton, Ohio, USA . . . early '92 by TIM TAYLOR and JUAN MONASTERIO as an experimental bedroom project. Fleshing out the line-up with TYLER TRENT and MICHELLE BODINE, the pair began building a fearsome reputation via a serious local gigging schedule. Following the release of a US-only debut single, 'SUPER DUPER SEVEN' on the 'Limited Potential' label and a split 7" with riot-grrrls, BRATMOBILE, the quartet signed to indie label, 'Grass', for a debut album, 'SMACK BUNNY BABY' (1993). Produced by GIRLS AGAINST BOYS bassist, ELI JANNEY, the record was lauded in the underground press for its uncompromising attitude and noisy dissonance, resulting in big money offers which BRAINIAC unceremoniously rejected. Replacing BODINE with JOHN SCHMERSAL, the band remained with 'Grass' for a second album, 'BONSAI SUPERSTAR' (1995), before hitching their wagon to Chicago-based house of noise, 'Touch & Go'. First up for the label was the interestingly titled 'HISSING PRIGS IN STATIC COUTURE', a more experimental outing that once again brought attention from industry big guns. Tragedy struck, however, as TAYLOR was killed in a freak car accident shortly after the completion of Spring '97's 'ELECTRO SHOCK FOR PRESIDENT' EP.

Album rating: SMACK BUNNY BABY (*6) / BONSAI SUPERSTAR (*6) / HISSING PRIGS IN STATIC COUTURE (*6)

TIM TAYLOR (b.1969) – vocals / **MICHELLE BODINE** – guitar / **JUAN MONASTERIO** – bass / **TYLER TRENT** – drums

not iss. / Limited Potential

Sep 92. (7") **SUPER DUPER SEVEN. /** [-] [ ]

not iss. / 12 x 12

1993. (7"; split with BRATMOBILE) [-] [ ]

Grass / Grass

Oct 93. (lp/cd) *<GROW 004-1/-2>* **SMACK BUNNY BABY** [ ] [ ]
– I, fuzzbot / Ride / Smack bunny baby / Martian dance invasion / Cultural zero / Brat girl / Hurting me / I could own you / Anesthetize / Draag / Get away. *(re-iss. Mar95 & Dec95; same)*

Feb 95. (lp/cd) *<GROW 46-1/-2>* **BONSAI SUPERSTAR** [ ] [ ] Nov94
– Hot metal dobermans / Hands of the genius / Fucking with the altimiter / Radio Apeshot / Transmissions after zero / Juicy (on a Cadillac) / Flypaper / Sexual frustration / To the baby-counter / You wrecked my hair / Meathook manicure / Status: Choke / Collide.

— **JON SCHMERSAL** – guitar; repl. MICHELLE

Touch & Go / Touch & Go

Oct 95. (7"ep/cd-ep) *<TG 148/+CD>* **INTERNATIONALE** [ ] [ ]
– Go freaks go / Silver iodine / Simon says.

Mar 96. (lp/cd) *<TG 155/+CD>* **HISSING PRIGS IN STATIC COUTURE** [ ] [ ]
– Indian poker (part 3) / Pussyfootin' / Vincent come on down / This little piggy / Strung / Hot seat can't sit down / Vulgar trade / Beekeepers maxim / Kiss me u jacked up jerk / 70 kg man / Indian poker (part 2) / Nothing ever changes / I am a cracked machine.

Apr 97. (12"ep/cd-ep) *(TG 174/+CD)* **ELECTRO SHOCK FOR PRESIDENT** [ ] [ ]

— tragically, on the 23rd of May '97, TAYLOR died in a car smash

Glenn BRANCA

Born: 1948, Harrisburg, Pennsylvania, USA. He left college in Boston to set up home in New York, where he formed a theatre-no wave outfits, STATIC and The THEORETICAL GIRLS. During the rest of the 70's, he composed and conducted an array of musicians on tour including Y PANTS, KONK, NYC NOISE and LIQUID LIQUID. A few other musicians, LEE RANALDO and THURSTON MOORE, played guitar on his debut 45 'LESSON No.1'. He finally issued his first album 'THE ASCENSION', which was to sell independently around 10,000 copies. BRANCA resurrected the avant-garde in one foul swoop, generating repetitive rhythms from several guitarists, backed with heavy percussion. In 1982, he contributed 'BAD SMELLS' to poet JOHN GIORNO's 'WHO ARE YOU STARING AT?', which also featured experimental dance piece choreographed by TWYLA THARP. He then formed the 'Neutral' label', which after his 'SYMPHONY No.1 (TONAL PLEXUS)' album (recorded July 16-19, 1981); became the platform for RANALDO & MOORE's splinter outfit SONIC YOUTH. In 1986, his film score for PETER GREENAWAY's 'Belly Of An Architect' was rejected in favour of WIM MERTEN's, although several minutes of BRANCA can be heard. In 1989, he was back on record with 'SYMPHONY No.6 (DEVIL CHOIRS AT THE GATES OF HEAVEN)', which added many more guitarists alongside other musicians. He turned up a few times in the 90's, and in February '94, premiered in the UK 'SYMPHONY No.10 FOR MASSED GUITARS'. • **Style:** Moved quickly from minimal symphonic "No Wave", to PHILIP GLASS-like experimental classical music with heavenly crescendos of guitars.

Album rating: THE ASCENSION (*7) / SYMPHONY No.6 (DEVIL CHOIRS AT THE GATES OF HEAVEN) (*7)

THEORETICAL GIRLS

GLENN BRANCA – guitar, vocals / **MARGARET DEWYS** – bass, organ / **JEFFREY LOHN** – keyboards, bass / **WHARTON TIERS** – drums

not iss. Theoretical

Oct 78. (7") *<TR 01>* **U.S. MILLIE. / YOU GOT ME** [-] [ ]

— split early the following year, DEWYS later joined PINK PONG

STATIC

— **BRANCA** with **BARBARA ESS** – bass (ex-DAILY LIFE, ex-Y PANTS, ex-DIS BAND) / **CHRISTINE HAHN** – drums (ex-DAILY LIFE, ex-LUXUS)

Jun 79. (7") *<TR 02>* **MY RELATIONSHIP. / DON'T LET ME STOP YOU** [-] [ ]

— when they split CHRISTINE joined MALARIA

GLENN BRANCA

— with the GUITAR ARMY; **LEE RANALDO, NED SUBLETTE, DAVID ROSENBLOOM** – guitars / **JEFFREY GLENN** – bass / **STEPHAN WISCHERTH** – drums

not iss. 99

Jul 80. (12"ep) *<99-01>* **LESSON No.1 FOR ELECTRIC GUITAR. / DISSONANCE** [-] [ ]

Nov 81. (lp) *<99-001>* **THE ASCENSION** [-] [ ]

— added **THURSTON MOORE** – guitars

not iss. Giornio Poetry Systems

1982. (lp; with JOHN GIORNIO) **WHO ARE YOU STARING AT** [-] [ ]

not iss. ROIR

1983. (lp) *<A 125>* **SYMPHONY No.1 (TONAL PLEXUS)** [-] [ ]
(UK-iss.1988; same) (cd-iss. Nov94 & Aug98; RE 125CD)

— now without RANALDO and MOORE who were sacked when they moonlighted as SONIC YOUTH on his tour

not iss. Neutral

1984. (lp) **SYMPHONY No.3 (GLORIA)** [-] [ ]
(UK-iss.Aug93 on 'Atavistic'; ALP 5CD) (cd-iss. Apr94 on 'Barooni'; DEALP 05)

— now with several guitarists including **ALGIS KIZYS** (of SWANS)

Blast First Blast First

Apr 89. (lp/c/cd) *(BFFP 39/+C/CD)* **SYMPHONY No.6 (DEVIL CHOIRS AT THE GATES OF HEAVEN)** [ ] [ ]
– First movement / Second movement / Third movement / Fourth movement / Fifth movement.

— below with The NEW YORK CHAMBER SINFONIA

Les Disques Du Crepescule Atavistic

Sep 92. (cd) *(TWI 9102)* **THE WORLD TURNED UPSIDE DOWN (A BALLET FOR ORCHESTRA IN 7 MOVEMENTS)** [ ] [ ]

Aug 93. (cd) *(ALP 8CD)* **SYMPHONY No.2 (THE PEAKS OF THE SACRED)** [ ] [ ]

Blast First Blast First

Oct 96. (cd) *(BFFP 106CD)* **SYMPHONIES NO.8 & 10 – THE MYSTERIES** [ ] [ ]
– Symphony No.8 (The mystery): First movement (The passage) – Second movement (Spiritual anarchy) / Symphony No.10 (The mystery part 2): First movement (The final problem) – Second movement (The horror).

– compilations, etc. –

Dec 97. (cd) *Atavistic; (ALP 35CD)* **SELECTION FROM THE SYMPHONIES** [ ] [ ]

Kirk BRANDON'S 10:51 (see under ⇒ SPEAR OF DESTINY)

BRASSY

Formed: Manchester, England . . . early 1994 by US-born singer, MUFFIN SPENCER (her big brother is none other than JON SPENCER of the BLUES EXPLOSION; MUFFIN arrived in England late 80's). On a mission to recreate the sound of her Brit-rock idols The SMITHS (especially MORRISSEY), she enlisted the help of KAREN FROST, STEFAN GORDON and JOHNNY BARRINGTON and after many rehearsals the band were ready to play live. It was the 'Costermonger' label (home of fellow SMITHS-esque fans, GENE) who took the plunge, although their sound was now more akin to that of ELASTICA. A debut 7", 'BOSS', finally hit the shops in early '96, although by the release of a third single, 'SURE THING' (their second was 'STRAIGHTEN OUT'), MUFFIN and Co were possibly too brassic to carry on.

Album rating: never released any

MUFFIN SPENCER (b. New Hampshire, USA) – vocals / **STEFAN GORDON** – guitar / **KAREN FROST** – bass / **JOHNNY BARRINGTON** – drums

Costermonger not iss.

Mar 96. (7") *(COST 007)* **BOSS. / ROUTE OUT** [ ] [-]

Jul 96. (7") *(COST 008)* **STRAIGHTEN OUT. / RIGHT BACK** [ ] [-]
(cd-s+=) *(COST 008CD)* – Boss (remix).

Jul 97. (7") *(COST 010)* **SURE THING. / BOOT DANCING** [ ] [-]
(cd-s+=) *(COST 010CD)* –

— what are they doing and where are they now??

BRATMOBILE

Formed: Olympia, Washington, USA . . . early 90's by ERIN SMITH, ALLISON WOLFE and MOLLY NEUMAN. Having already helped set the Riot Grrrl ball rolling with the 'Girl Germs' fanzine, the trio decided to relay their message through the male-dominated medium of alternative rock. Following an appearance on a 1991 compilation, 'Kill Rock Stars', put together by the 'K' label and a debut live set at Olympia's International Pop Underground convention (run by the ever industrious CALVIN JOHNSON, supremo of aforesaid 'K'), BRATMOBILE released their debut single proper, 'KISS AND RIDE', on 'Homestead' in Summer '93. An inaugural album, 'POTTYMOUTH' (1993) followed on 'Kill Rock Stars'; sassy pop/hardcore/punk with severe attitude in the vein of BIKINI KILL and HUGGY BEAR, the record even featured a tongue-in-cheek cover of the Runaways' CHERRY BOMB. Although HEATHER DUNN subsequently replaced NEUMAN, the band cut only one further recording, 1994's mini-set, 'THE REAL JANELLE'. While a PEEL SESSIONS EP served as a postscript to the band's short-lived career, ERIN and ALISON went on to play together in COLD COLD HEARTS. DUNN, meanwhile, was invited to take part in a reformation of seminal femme post-punks, the RAINCOATS.

Album rating: POTTYMOUTH (*6) / THE REAL JANELLE (*7)

ALLISON WOLFE – vocals / **ERIN SMITH** – guitar, vocals / **MOLLY NEUMAN** – drums, vocals

Homestead Homestead

Jul 93. (7") *<(HMS 178-7)>* **KISS AND RIDE. / NO YOU DON'T / QUEENIE** [ ] [ ]

Kill Rock Stars Kill Rock Stars

Jun 93. (cd/lp) *<KRS 208>* **POTTYMOUTH** [-] [ ]
– Love thing / Stab / Cherry bomb / Throwaway / P.R.D.C.T. / Some special / Fuck yr. fans / Polaroid baby / Panik / Bitch theme / Richard / Cool schmool / Juswanna / Kiss & ride / No you don't / Queenie.

— **HEATHER DUNN** – drums; repl. MOLLY NEUMAN who joined PEECHEES

Aug 94. (m-cd/m-lp) *<(KRS 219 CD/EP)>* **THE REAL JANELLE** [ ] [ ]
– The real Janelle / Brat girl / Yeah, huh? / Die / And I live in a town where the boys amputate their hearts / Where eagles dare.

— when they split, DUNN was to join the the reformed RAINCOATS

– compilations, etc. –

May 94. (cd-ep) *Strange Fruit; (SFPSCD 089) / Dutch East India; <8357>* **PEEL SESSIONS EP** [ ] [ ]
– There's no other way – No you don't / Bitch theme / Make me Miss America / Panik.

BREATHLESS

Formed: London, England . . . 1983 by DOMINIC APPLETON, GARY MURRAY, ARI NEUFELD and MARTYN WATTS. Releasing records on their own 'Tenor Vossa' imprint, BREATHLESS became noted for APPLETON's unique vocal chords. After a few platters, notably the '2 DAYS FROM HEAVEN' 12"ep in 1985, DOMINIC moonlighted in IVO's '4 a.d.' supergroup, THIS MORTAL COIL (three tracks, 'The Jeweller', 'Tarantula' and 'Strength Of Strings' from the album, 'Filigree & Shadow', to be precise). During this period, BREATHLESS released their own debut (named after a Herman Hesse novel), 'THE GLASS BEAD GAME' (1986), a somewhat disappointing effort that was followed a year later by a second, 'THREE TIMES AND WAVING'. In 1989, a further set, 'CHASING PROMISES', was another lacklustre affair, DOMINIC and Co. finally running out of steam late in 1991 after 'BETWEEN HAPPINESS & HEARTACHE'. • **Note:** Not to be confused with a similarly titled band who released 'OH YOU BABE' and another BREATHLESS on 'E.M.I.' who issued 'TWILIGHT ZONE' in '89.

Album rating: THE GLASS BEAD GAME (*4) / THREE TIMES AND WAVING (*4) / CHASING PROMISES (*4) / BETWEEN HAPPINESS & HEARTACHE (*4)

DOMINIC APPLETON – vocals / **GARY MURRAY** – guitar / **ARI NEUFELD** – bass / **MARTYN WATTS** – drums (ex-DANIELLE DAX)

Tenor Vossa not iss.

Apr 84. (7") *(BREATH 1)* **WATERLAND. / SECOND HEAVEN** [ ] [-]

Nov 84. (7") *(BREATH 2)* **AGELESS. /** [ ] [-]

Aug 85. (12"ep) *(BREATH 3)* **2 DAYS FROM HEAVEN** [ ] [-]
– Stone harvest / Pride / Across the water / Like knives.

Jun 86. (lp) *(BREATHLP 4)* **THE GLASS BEAD GAME** [ ] [-]
– Across the water / All my eye and Betty Martin / Count on angels / Monkey talk / Every road leads home / Touchstone / Sense of purpose / See how the land lies.

Nov 86. (12") *(BREATH 5)* **NAILING COLOURS TO THE WHEEL. / BAD BLOOD** [ ] [-]

Nov 87. (lp/c) *(BREATH LP/CAS 6)* **THREE TIMES AND WAVING** [ ] [-]
– Sold down the river / Is it good news today / Three times and waving / Into the fire / Working for space / Waiting on the wire / Pizzy life / Say September sings / Let's make a night of it.

Apr 89. (lp/cd) *(BREATH LP/CD 7)* **CHASING PROMISES**
– Compulsion / Here by chance / Better late than never / Heartburst / Moment by moment / Smash palace / Sometimes on Sunday / Glow.
Oct 89. (12"ep) *(BREATH 8)* **I NEVER KNOW WHERE YOU ARE. / MOMENT BY MOMENT / HEARTBURST**
Jul 90. (7") *(7BREATH 9)* **ALWAYS. / FLOWERS DIE**
(12"+=) *(BREATH 9)* – ('A'extended).
Nov 91. (cd/lp) *(BREATH CD/LP 10)* **BETWEEN HAPPINESS & HEARTACHE**
– I never know where you are / Over and over / Wave after wave / You can call it yours / All that matters now / Clearer than daylight / Flowers die / Help me get over it.
Mar 92. (cd-s) *(BREATHCD 11)* **OVER AND OVER / ALL THAT MATTERS NOW**
Jun 93. (cd-s) *(BREATHCD 12)* **DON'T JUST DISAPPEAR / EVERYTHING I SEE / DON'T JUST DISAPPEAR (mix)**
May 94. (cd) *(BREATHCD 13)* **HEARTBURST** (compilation)
– Don't just disappear (radio edit) / You can call it yours / Never know where you are / All that matters now / Always / Over and over / Waiting on the wire / Wave after wave / Ageless / Pride / All my eye and Betty Martin / Touchstone / Don't just disappear.

— had already disbanded some time in '93

BREEDERS

Formed: Boston, Massachusetts, USA . . . 1989 by TANYA DONELLY (of THROWING MUSES) and KIM DEAL (of The PIXIES) as a side project to their respective musical careers, an opportunity to exercise their frustrated songwriting talent. Recruiting JOSEPHINE WIGGS (of PERFECT DISASTER) on bass and SHANNON DOUGHTY (of the late, great SLINT) on drums, the BREEDERS cut their debut outing, 'POD', in a matter of weeks. Released in May 1990, the album rapidly achieved cult status, even enjoying a hearty endorsement from one KURT COBAIN. Inevitably, the record was compared with The PIXIES by critics although in reality there was little in common between the two bands. Where The PIXIES were enigmatic and frenetic, The BREEDERS were deliberate, dark and intense. While the pace picked up with 'HELLBOUND', tracks like the opener, 'GLORIOUS' and 'IRIS' were more representative of the record as a whole and if their cover of LENNON's 'HAPPINESS IS A WARM GUN' didn't add much to the original, it sounded so BREEDERS-like within the context of the album that they could've conceivably penned it themselves. The group recorded a further EP, 'SAFARI' (1992), with the original line-up before DONELLY went off to work full-time with her own outfit, BELLY. Following The PIXIES' demise later that year, DEAL devoted all her energies to a BREEDERS follow-up album. Enlisting her sister KELLEY in place of the departed DONELLY, the band released the 'CANNONBALL' single in Autumn '93. With its undulating guitar riff and pneumatic rhythm section, the track became an alternative classic, tearing up indie dancefloors across the country. The subsequent album, 'LAST SPLASH', powered into the UK Top 5 upon its release the following month. While much of the set sounded less focused than the debut, it nevertheless contained another stellar guitar pop moment in 'DIVINE HAMMER', also released as a single. Although the album's sales topped the million mark, things have been quiet on The BREEDERS front of late, save for a lone 10" EP in 1994. The following year, (KIM) DEAL did surface in the guise of The AMPS, releasing an album, 'PACER', on '4 a.d.'. • **Songwriters:** KIM DEAL wrote bulk from 1992 onwards. • **Covered:** HAPPINESS IS A WARM GUN (Beatles / George Harrison) / LORD OF THE THIGHS (Aerosmith) / SO SAD ABOUT US (Who). The AMPS covered JUST LIKE A BRIAR (Tasties).

Album rating: POD (*7) / LAST SPLASH (*9) / Amps: PACER (*6)

TANYA DONELLY (b.14 Jul'66, Newport, Rhode Island) – rhythm guitar, vocals (of THROWING MUSES) / **KIM DEAL** (b.10 Jun'61, Dayton, Ohio, USA) – guitar, vocals (of The PIXIES) / **JOSEPHINE WIGGS** (b.26 Feb'65, Letchworth, England) – bass, cello, vocals (of PERFECT DISASTER) / **SHANNON DOUGHTY** (aka MIKE HUNT) (b. BRITT WALFORD, Louisville, Kentucky) – drums (of SLINT) repl. NARCIZO and another from HUMAN SEXUAL RESPONSE

4 a.d. / Elektra

May 90. (cd)(lp/c) *(CAD 0006CD)(CAD/+C 0006)* **POD** — 22
– Glorious / Doe / Happiness is a warm gun / Oh! / Hellbound / When I was a painter / Fortunately gone / Iris / Opened / Only in 3's / Limehouse / Metal man.

— **DONELLY, KIM DEAL, JO WIGGS + JON MATLOCK** (of SPIRITUALIZED)

Apr 92. (12"ep/cd-ep) *(BAD 2003/+CD)* **SAFARI** — 69
– Safari / So sad about us / Do you love me now? / Don't call home.

— now **KIM** her sister **KELLEY DEAL** (b.10 Jun'61, Dayton) – guitar, vocals / **JO WIGGS** – bass, vox / **JIM MacPHERSON** (b.23 Jun'66, Dayton) – drums, vocals (ex-RAGING MANTRAS) / (DONELLY formed BELLY)

Aug 93. (12"ep/cd-ep) *(BAD 3011/+CD)* *<64566>* **CANNONBALL. / CRO-ALOHA / LORD OF THE THIGHS / 900** — 40 — 44 Nov93
Sep 93. (cd)(lp/c) *(CAD 3014CD)(CAD/+C 3014)* *<61508>* **LAST SPLASH** — 5 — 33
– New Year / Cannonball / Invisible man / No aloha / Roi / Do you love me now? / Flipside / I just wanna get along / Mad Lucas / Divine hammer / S.O.S./ Hag / Saints / Drivin' on 9 / Roi (reprise).
Oct 93. (7"clear/c-s) *(AD/+C 3017)* **DIVINE HAMMER. / HOVERIN'** — 59
(10"ep+=)(cd-ep+=) *(BADD 3017)(BAD 3017CD)* – I can't help it (if I'm still in love with you) / Do you love me now Jr (J. Mascis remix).
Jul 94. (10"ep) *(BADD 4012)* **HEAD TO TOE. / SHOCKER IN GLOOMTOWN / FREED PIG** — 68 — -
(cd-ep+=) *(BAD 4014CD)* – Saints.

— new 1997 line-up, includes **KIM DEAL + JIM MacPHERSON** plus **MICHAEL O'DEAN** – guitar / **NATE FARLEY** – guitar / **LOUIS NERMA** – bass / **CARRIE BRADLEY** – violin

AMPS

KIM DEAL / JIM MacPHERSON / NATHAN FARLEY + LUIS LERMA

4 a.d. / 4 a.d.

Oct 95. (12"ep/cd-ep) *(BAD 5015/+CD)* **TIPP CITY / JUST LIKE A BRIAR. / EMPTY GLASSES (Kim's basement 4 track version)** — 61
Oct 95. (cd)(lp/c) *(CAD 5016CD)(CAD/+C 5016)* **PACER** — 60
– Pacer / Tipp city / I am decided / Mom's drunk / Bragging party / Hoverin' / First revival / Full on idle / Breaking the split screen barrier / Empty glasses / She's a girl / Dedicated.

BRICK LAYER CAKE

Formed: Chicago, Illinois, USA . . . early 90's by STEVE ALBINI cohort and SHELLAC drummer, TODD TRAINER, initially as a diversion from his main occupation. Roping in GERARD BOISSY from RIFLE SPORT and producer BRIAN 'EXPENSIVE' PAULSON, TRAINER signed to 'Touch & Go' and released a debut album, 'CALL IT A DAY – EYE FOR AN EYE' (1991). Hypnotic, noisy and occasionally dreamy, the records guitar swirls brought to mind the likes of J&MC and LOOP. A full three years passed before their follow-up, 'TRAGEDY – TRAGEDY' hit the shops, an equally intense offering that would serve as a swansong.

Album rating: CALL IT A DAY – EYE FOR AN EYE (*5) / TRAGEDY – TRAGEDY (*6)

TODD TRAINER – drums (of SHELLAC) / **GERARD BOISSY** (ex-RIFLE SPORT) / **BRIAN 'EXPENSIVE' PAULSON** – producer, etc

Touch & Go / Touch & Go

Nov 91. (lp/cd; BRICK LAYER CAKE featuring TODD TRAINER) *<(TG 75/+CD)>* **CALL IT A DAY / EYE FOR AN EYE**
Oct 94. (lp/cd) *<(TG 127/+CD)>* **TRAGEDY – TRAGEDY**
– Christ / Gone today / Thin ice / Precious / Thirteenth drink / Cold day in Hell / Reach me now / Doomsday / Cakewalkmusic / Elevenovens / Boissy Paulson / Trainer / Icing Inc.

— nothing heard from them after above

BRIDEWELL TAXIS

Formed: Leeds, England . . . 1983 by Leeds United fans and local record shop (Crash & Jumbo) workers, MICK ROBERTS, GLENN SCULLION, CHRIS WALTON, SIMON SCOTT, GARY WILSON and SEAN McELHONE. They turned semi-pro in the 80's having being helped by Al Neville, who set up his own 'Grateful Dead'-like label. Supporting the likes of INSPIRAL CARPETS and sounding a little reminiscent of The HAPPY MONDAYS, the group – armed with some xylophones, etc – released a flexi-disc, 'LIES', before issuing two proper singles at the turn of the decade, 'JUST GOOD FRIENDS' and 'GIVE IN'. 1990 saw two more, 'HONESTY' and 'SPIRIT', although the band suffered a major setback early the following year when frontman ROBERTS was scarred attempting to stop a pub brawl. Back into action, The 'TAXIS released their Chris Nagle-produced version of Blue Oyster Cult's 'DON'T FEAR THE REAPER'. However, with a sharp change of direction (DEACON BLUE were cited), The BRIDEWELLS delivered their debut album proper (a compilation, 'INVISIBLE TO YOU' appeared a year previously), 'CAGE' (1992).

Album rating: INVISIBLE TO YOU compilation (*5) / CAGE (*4)

MICK ROBERTS – vocals / **SEAN McELHONE** – guitar / **GARY WILSON** – keyboards / **CHRIS WALTON** – trombone / **SIMON SCOTT** – bass / **GLENN SCULLION** – drums

Stolen / not iss.

1989. (12"ep) *(BLAG 1)* **JUST GOOD FRIENDS. / WILD BOAR / OBSOLETE** — -
Mar 90. (12"ep) *(BLAG 2)* **GIVE IN. / WHOLE DAMN NATION / IN GOD WE TRUST / PRECIOUS TIME** — -
Aug 90. (12"/cd-s) *(BLAG 3/+CD)* **HONESTY. / SPIRIT** — -
Nov 90. (12") *(BLAG 4)* **SPIRIT. /** — -
May 91. (7"/c-s) *(BLAG 6)* **DON'T FEAR THE REAPER. / FACE IN THE CROWD** — -
(12"+=/cd-s+=) *(BLAG 6 T/CD)* – ('A'-What Horse remix).
Jul 91. (lp/c/cd) *(BLAG 7/+C/CD)* **INVISIBLE TO YOU** (compilation 89-91) — -

BRIDEWELLS

Expression / not iss.

Jul 92. (12"ep/cd-ep) *(EXPEP/+D 1)* **SMILE EP** — -
– Smile I still care / World of lies / Missing link / Return.
Oct 92. (lp/c/cd) *(EXPAL/+MC/CD 14)* **CAGE** — -
– Cage / Devil inside / Way of the world / Girl / Juggler / Smile I still care / Snake eyes / Clear as the day / Paris / Inner city blues / Rachel / Sail the wind.

— split early the following year.

BRIGANDAGE

Formed: Camden, London, England . . . 1982 by MICHELLE, MICK BROWN, and brothers BEN and SCOTT ADDISSON, however, the latter was subsequently replaced by MICHELLE's long-time boyfriend, RICHARD NORTH (also a columnist with the NME). After supporting the likes of The SEX GANG CHILDREN and featuring on the 'Batcave' compilation, BEN departed. Describing themselves as "positive punk" and dressing in leather shock'n'roll goth style fashion, they beat out their hollow drum rhythms around the capital until their dissolution in '85/'86. This wasn't quite the end though as BRIGANDAGE (Mk.II) re-emerged with DAVID EAVES and TIM NUTTAL replacing the ADDISSONS and finally releasing a solitary underwhelming album, 'PRETTY LITTLE THING', in late '86.

Album rating: PRETTY LITTLE THING (*3) / BRIGANDAGE (*3)

MICHELLE (b.1960) – vocals / **DAVID EAVES** – guitar; repl. MICK BROWN / **RICHARD NORTH** – bass; repl. SCOTT ADDISSON / **TIM NUTTAL** – drums; repl. BEN ADDISSON

Gung Ho | not iss.

Nov 86. (lp) *(GHLP 001)* **PRETTY LITTLE THING** [ ] [-]
– I need something pt.1 / etc

— disbanded for the final time during the mid 80's

– compilations, etc. –

May 88. (c) *F.Y.M.; (FYM 1)* **BRIGANDAGE** (live & studio) [ ] [-]
– Hope / Fragile / Wasteland / etc

BRILLIANT CORNERS

Formed: Bristol, England . . . 1983 by DAVEY WOODWARD, who took the name from a Thelonius Monk track. He recruited other likeminded indie minstrels, CHRIS, WINSTON, BOB and DAN, before setting up their own label, 'SS20' and releasing debut single, 'SHE'S GOT FEVER'. After several singles and a few mini-sets, 'GROWING UP ABSURD' (1985) and 'WHAT'S IN A WORD' (1986), went barely noticed, they came up with their finest and most comical three minutes in 'BRIAN RIX' (a parody of the English "King of farce' actor), its video appearance on 'The Tube' – featuring DAVEY running RIX-like around a couch with his trousers around his ankles accompanied by a trumpeter – helping raise the band's profile. The following year, the band initiated another label, 'McQueen', for the release of their first full-length set, 'SOMEBODY UP THERE LIKES ME' (1988). More fun-loving indie fare was to surface in the shape of 'EVERYTHING I EVER WANTED' (compilation 1988), 'JOYRIDE' (1989), 'HOOKED' (1990) and 'A HISTORY OF WHITE TRASH' (1993), although none were given full consideration by the press. • **Note:** The BRILLIANT CORNERS who released 'Two Roads' in '98 were not the same.

Album rating: GROWING UP ABSURD mini (*5) / WHAT'S IN A WORD (*5) / SOMEBODY UP THERE LIKES ME (*7) / EVERYTHING I EVER WANTED compilation (*6) / JOYRIDE (*6) / HOOKED (*6) / CREAMY STUFF compilation (*7) / A HISTORY OF WHITE TRASH (*6)

DAVEY WOODWARD (b.1966) – vocals, guitar / **CHRIS** – bass / **WINSTON** – percussion, vocals / **BOB** – drums / **DAN** – occasional keyboards

SS20 | not iss.

Jan 84. (7") *(SS21)* **SHE'S GOT FEVER. / BLACK WATER** [ ] [-]
Jun 84. (7") *(SS22)* **BIG HIP. / TANGLED UP IN BLUE** [ ] [-]
Oct 84. (12"m) *(SS23T)* **MY BABY'S IN BLACK. / ROPE IN MY HAND / SIXTEEN YEARS** [ ] [-]
Oct 85. (m-lp) *(SS24)* **GROWING UP ABSURD** [ ] [-]
May 86. (7"ep/12"ep) *(SS25/+T)* **FRUIT MACHINE** [ ] [-]
– Meet me on Tuesday / Jim's room / The funniest thing / Everything I ever wanted.
Nov 86. (m-lp) *(SS26)* **WHAT'S IN A WORD** [ ] [-]
(re-iss. Jul88 on 'McQueen'; MCQLP 2)

— added trumpeter

Apr 87. (7") *(SS27)* **BRIAN RIX. / TRUDY IS A SEQUEL** [ ] [-]
Oct 87. (7") *(SS28)* **DELILAH SANDS. / IS THERE ANYBODY HOME?** [ ] [-]
(12"+=) *(SS28T)* – Please please please.

— when DAVEY broke his arm, he was briefly replaced by guitarist **PHIL. ANTHONY FORBES** became guitarist around this time.

McQueen | not iss.

Mar 88. (7") *(MCQ 1)* **TEENAGE. / I DON'T WANT TO TALK TO YOU** [ ] [-]
(12"+=) *(MCQ 1T)* –
Apr 88. (lp/cd) *(MCQ LP/CD 1)* **SOMEBODY UP THERE LIKES ME** [ ] [-]
Oct 88. (7") *(MCQ 2)* **WHY DO YOU HAVE TO GO OUT WITH MEN, WHEN YOU COULD GO OUT WITH ME?. /** [ ] [-]
(12"+=) *(MCQ 2T)* –
Oct 88. (lp/cd) *(MCQ LP/CD 2)* **EVERYTHING I EVER WANTED** (compilation) [ ] [-]
– Rambling Rose / Growing up absurd / One of these days / Meet me on Tuesdays / The funniest thing / Under the bridge / A girl called Property / Southern mystery / Mary / Jim's room / Everything I ever wanted / Trudy is a sequel.
May 89. (lp/cd) *(MCQ LP/CD 4)* **JOYRIDE** [ ] [-]
– You don't know how lucky you are / This girl / Grow cold / I didn't see you / Emily / Nothing / Hemingway's back / Accused by the angels.
Mar 90. (7") *(MCQ 3)* **I LOVE IT, I LOST IT. /** [ ] [-]

— personnel change

Sep 90. (7") *(MCQ 4)* **THE POPE, THE MONKEY AND THE QUEEN. /** [ ] [-]
Oct 90. (cd/lp) *(MCQ CD/LP 5)* **HOOKED** [ ] [-]
Aug 91. (cd/lp) *(MCQ CD/LP 6)* **CREAMY STUFF** (compilation 84-90) [ ] [-]
– She's got fever / angled up in blue / Big hip / My baby's in black / Sixten years / Meet me on Tuesdays / Jim's room / Brian Rix / Trudy is a squeal / Please please please / Delilah sands / Teenage / I don't want to talk to you / Why do you have to go out with him when you could go out with me / Shangri-la / Love it I lost it / The pope, the monkey and the queen / The ghost of a girl.

C.M.P. | not iss.

Mar 93. (cd/lp) *(CMP CD/LP 005)* **A HISTORY OF WHITE TRASH** [ ] [-]

BROADCAST

Formed: Birmingham, England . . . mid-1995 by TRISH KEENAN, ROJ STEVENS, TIM KELTON, JAMES CARGILL and STEVE PERKINS (the latter played drums for COOLER THAN JESUS, a band that included MENSWEAR's SIMON). Openly admitting the heavy influence of Stateside psychedelic 60's outfit, the UNITED STATES OF AMERICA, BROADCAST specialise in retro-futuristic avant-pop constructed from soundtrack samples, slo-mo beats and synth experimentation. Early the following year, the neatly-pressed quintet delivered their first 45, 'ACCIDENTALS', for the tiny limited edition-only label, 'Wurlitzer Jukebox'; today the single is fetching upwards of £50. Subsequently finding a natural home at STEREOLAB's 'Duophonic', BROADCAST released two further rare singles, 'LIVING ROOM' and 'THE BOOK LOVERS' EP, both written unconventionally in waltz-time. Having also contributed the track, 'LIGHTS OUT', to the V/A NME C-96 compilation, the band had their entire recorded output to date collected together on the 'Warp' album, 'WORK AND NON WORK' (1997). • **Trivia:** KEENAN and Co also remixed SAINT ETIENNE's 'Angel' for their recent 'Casino Classics' album.

Album rating: WORK AND NON WORK compilation (*7)

TRISH KEENAN – vocals / **ROJ STEVENS** – keyboards / **TIM KELTON** – guitar / **JAMES CARGILL** – bass / **STEVE PERKINS** – drums (ex-COOLER THAN JESUS)

Wurlitzer Jukebox | not iss.

Jan 96. (7") *(WJ 6)* **ACCIDENTALS. / WE'VE GOT TIME** [ ] [-]

Duophonic | not iss.

May 96. (ltd-7") *(DS45 14)* **LIVING ROOM. / PHANTOM** [ ] [-]
Nov 96. (12"ep/cd-ep) *(DS45/+CD 16)* **THE BOOK LOVERS / MESSAGE FROM HOME. / ACCORDING TO NO PLAN / THE WORLD BACKWARDS** [ ] [-]

Warp | Warp

Jun 97. (cd/c/lp) *(<WARP CD/MC/LP 52>)* **WORK AND NON WORK** (compilation) [ ] [ ]
– Accidentals / The book lovers / Message from home / Phantom / We've got time / Living room / According to no plan / The world backwards / Lights out.

Caspar BROTZMANN

Born: Berlin, Germany . . .. the son of saxophonist, PETER BROTZMANN. A mean guitarist, he formed The CASPAR BROTZMANN MASSAKER in 1987 along with EDUARDO DELGADO and DANNY ARNOLD LOMMEN, releasing a German-only album, 'THE TRIBE', later that year. Influenced by his father's rampant free-jazz and reared on late 60's/early 70's heavy-metal, CASPAR developed a searing, incendiary style that brought comparisons to TONY IOMMI and JIMI HENDRIX. A second domestic release, 'BLACK AXIS' (1989), continued in a similar vein, BROTZMANN's forboding vocals and six-string intensity churned up by the grinding rhythm section of LOPEZ and LOMMEN. The early 90's saw him break away from MASSAKER and release a collaborative set, 'LAST HOME' with his dad, although he and his guitar were back in full swing in 1992 with 'EVENING OF BLACK FOLKLORE'. The man went onto release a few solo albums, 'KOKSOFEN' (1993) and 'HOME' (1995), while further collaborative works, 'MERRY CHRISTMAS' (1994) and 'ZULUTIME' (1996), found him sparring with F.M. EINHEIT (of EINSTURZENDE NEUBAUTEN) and PAGE HAMILTON (of HELMET) respectfully.

Album rating: THE TRIBE mini (*5) / BLACK AXIS (*6) / LAST HOME with Peter Brotzmann (*5) / EVENING OF BLACK FOLKLORE (*7) / KOKSOFEN (*7) / MERRY CHRISTMAS with F.M. Einheit (*5) / HOME (*5) / ZULUTIME with Page Hamilton (*5)

CASPAR BROTZMANN – vocals, guitar / with **EDUARDO DELGADO LOPEZ** – bass / **DANNY ARNOLD LOMMEN** – drums

Zensor | not iss.

1987. (m-lp; by CASPAR BROTZMANN MASSAKER) *(ZS 08)* **THE TRIBE** [-] [-] German
(UK cd-iss. Jul92; ZSCM 08)
Oct 89. (lp; by CASPAR BROTZMANN MASSAKER) *(MARAT 14)* **BLACK AXIS** [-] [-] German
– Die tiere / Hunter song / Bohmen / Mute / Tempelhof / Black axis.

Pathological | not iss.

Jan 91. (lp/c/cd; by CASPAR & PETER BROTZMANN) *(PATH 004/+C/CD)* **LAST HOME** [ ] [-]
– Die, saurier, die / Talk to the canoe driver / Last home / Little mabn in the boat / Doozandazzy / Yazzihamper / Witch Hazel in the dark afternoon.

Our Choice | unknown

Mar 92. (cd/lp) *(RTD 951248-2/-1)* **EVENING OF BLACK FOLKLORE** [ ] [ ]
– Schwarze folklore / Bass totem / Sarah / War horse.

Big Cat | Homestead

Jun 93. (lp/cd; by CASPAR BROTZMANN MASSAKER) *(ABB/+CD 052) <HMS 208>* **KOKSOFEN** [ ] [ ]
– Hymne / Wiege / Kerkersong / Schlaf / Koksofen.

Blast First / Thirsty Ear

May 94. (lp/cd; by F.M. EINHEIT & BROTZMANN) *(BFFP 97/+CD)* **MERRY CHRISTMAS** [ ] [-]

Feb 95. (lp/cd; by CASPAR BROTZMANN MASSAKER) *(BFFP 110/+CD)* <57007> **HOME** [ ] [ ]
– The tribe / Tempelhof / Massader / Hunter song / Bohmen.

Blast First / Rough Trade

Jul 96. (cd; by CASPAR BROTZMANN & PAGE HAMILTON) *(BFFP 129CD)* **ZULUTIME** <US-title 'SUBSONIC 4'> [ ] [ ]
– Zulutime / Head hunter / Hit single / Dream date / Suburban blight / Imbiss.

Ian BROWN (see under ⇒ STONE ROSES)

Steven BROWN (see under ⇒ TUXEDOMOON)

Peter BRUNTNELL

Born: 26 Jan'64, Auckland, New Zealand. The son of a Welsh father who worked for the foreign office, BRUNTNELL was used to moving around during his childhood, living in England and finally Vancouver, Canada where he began his singer-songwriter career. The start of the 90's saw BRUNTNELL leave North America and return to English soil where he formed the short-lived MILKWOOD. Now in his thirties, PETER was subsequently taken under the wing of Pete Smith (who had previously worked in the studio with The POLICE and STING), who secured him a contract with HERB ALPERT and JERRY MOSS's 'Almo Sounds' label (Stateside home of GARBAGE). 1995 saw the release of his debut album, 'CANNIBAL', a country-tinged affair that won praise from the likes of Mojo magazine. Two years on, BRUNTNELL was hailed as one of the best unsung alternative singer-songwriters in Britain with the release of follow-up set, 'CAMELOT IN SMITHEREENS' (1997).

Album rating: CANNIBAL (*6) / CAMELOT IN SMITHEREENS (*7)

PETER BRUNTNELL – vocals, guitar / with his COMBO

Almo Sounds / Almo Sounds

Jul 95. (c-s/cd-s; as PETER BRUNTNELL COMBO) *(MC/CD ALMOS 002)* **I WILL I WON'T / ASTRONAUT** [ ] [ ]
(re-iss. May96; same)

Jan 96. (cd-ep) *(CDALMOS 020)* **ASTRONAUT / BROADWAY / FOOD FOR THE MOON / SHAKE (live)** [ ] [-]

Apr 96. (cd) *(ALMOCD 002)* **CANNIBAL** [ ] [ ] Nov95

May 97. (7") *(7ALM 33)* **HAVE YOU SEEN THAT GIRL AGAIN. /** [ ] [ ]
(cd-s+=) *(CDALM 33)* –

Aug 97. (7"/c-s) *(7/MC ALM 34)* **CAMELOT IN SMITHEREENS. /** [ ] [ ]
(cd-s+=) *(CDALM 34)* –

Sep 97. (cd/c/lp) *(ALM CD/MC/LP 14)* **CAMELOT IN SMITHEREENS** [ ] [ ]

BUBONIQUE (see under ⇒ COUGHLAN, Cathal)

Jeff BUCKLEY

Born: 17 Nov'66, Orange County, California, USA. The offspring of the late, great TIM BUCKLEY, JEFF's chosen career as a musician, singer and songwriter was always destined to bear the heavy burden of his father's unique legacy (note: in this instance JEFF appears out of alphabetical sequence). To his credit, BUCKLEY Jnr. persevered at carving out a distinctive niche in the musical landscape of the early 90's, plugging away on the once legendary Greenwich Village scene of New York. Torch rather than tortured, JEFF utilised his inherited multi-octave vocal chords in ever more impressive and innovative fashion, both in tackling an eclectic variety of cover material (see below) and lavishly dramatic originals. Given his first British break in 1994, via 'LIVE AT THE SIN-E' EP (1992 in America) on the 'Big Cat' label, BUCKLEY was a surprise success at the grunge overload of Reading 1994. Coinciding with his appearance was the release of his major label ('Columbia') debut, 'GRACE', an emotionally raw and occasionally claustrophobic listen that gained almost unanimous praise from UK critics and enjoyed a brief residence in the Top 50. Tracks such as 'SO REAL', 'LAST GOODBYE' and 'DREAM LOVER', suggested a mercurial talent in the ascendant, although the lad had possibly listened to too much LED ZEPPELIN as a youth. Eventually resuming his recording career early in 1997 with TOM VERLAINE (ex-TELEVISION) at the controls, JEFF looked like making a severe dent in the rock mainstream with a follow-up to 'GRACE', although subsequent sessions proved problematic. Fate was to deal a cruel hand when, on the 29th of May '98, JEFF, like his father before him, was cut down in his prime; hardly a typical rock'n'roll death, the young singer was swept away by a powerful current while swimming in Memphis harbor. Exactly a year later, the half-finished project BUCKLEY had been working on at the time of his death was posthumously released as 'SKETCHES FOR MY SWEETHEART THE DRUNK'. A double CD partly curated by his mother, the UK Top 10 set gave an indication as to where JEFF was headed as well as serving as a convincing last word on the career of a man many considered a genius. • **Covers:** JE N'EN CONNAIS PAS LA FIN (Edith Piaf) / THE WAY YOUNG LOVERS DO (Van Morrison) / LILAC WINE (Elkie Brooks) / HALLELUJAH (Leonard Cohen) / KANGA ROO (Big Star) / KICK OUT THE JAMS (MC5) / YARD OF BLONDE GIRLS (Audrey Clark) / BACK IN N.Y.C. (Genesis) / SATISFIED MIND (J.Hayes & J.Rhodes).

Album rating: LIVE AT SIN-E mini (*6) / GRACE (*8) / SKETCHES FOR MY SWEETHEART THE DRUNK (*7)

JEFF BUCKLEY – vocals, guitars, harmonium, organ, dulcimer / with **MICK GRONDAHL** – bass / **MATT JOHNSON** – drums, percussion / plus MICHAEL TIGHE – guitar / **GARLY LUCAS** – magicalguitarness

Big Cat / Big Cat

Apr 94. (m-lp/m-cd) *(ABB 61/+CD)* **LIVE AT SIN-E (live)** [ ] [ ]
– Mojo pin / Eternal life / Je n'en connais pas la fin / The way young lovers do.

Columbia / Columbia

Aug 94. (cd/c/lp) *(475928-2/-4/-1)* <57528> **GRACE** [50] [ ]
– Mojo pin / Grace / Last goodbye / Lilac wine / So real / Hallelujah / Lover, you should've come over / Corpus christi Carol / Eternal life / Dream brother.

May 95. (10"ep/cd-ep) *(662042-0/-2)* **LAST GOODBYE. / LOVER, YOU SHOULD'VE COME OVER (live) / TONGUE (live)** [54] [ ]
(cd-ep) *(662042-5)* – ('A'side) / Dream brother (live) / So real (live).

1996. (m-cd) **LIVE FROM YHE BATACLAN (live)** [-] [ ]

— Sadly, JEFF was to die in a drowning accident on the 29th of May '97 (see biography)

May 98. (d-cd/d-c/d-lp) *(488661-2/-4/-1)* <67228> **SKETCHES FOR MY SWEETHEART THE DRUNK** [7] [64]
– The sky is a landfill / Everybody here wants you / Opened once / Nightmares by the sea / Yard of blonde girls / Witches' rave / Morning theft / Vancouver / You & I // Nightmares by the sea / New Year's prayer / Haven't you heard / I know we could be so happy baby (if we wanted to be) / Murder suicide meteor slave / Back in N.Y.C. / Gunshot glitter *[cd-only]*/ Demon John / Your flesh is so nice / Jewel box / Satisfied mind.

May 98. (cd-ep) *(665791-2)* **EVERYBODY HERE WANTS YOU / THOUSAND FOLD / ETERNAL LIFE / HALLELUJAH** [43] [ ]
(cd-ep) *(665791-5)* – ('A'side) / Lover, you should've come over / Tongue.

BUFFALO TOM

Formed: Boston, Massachusetts, USA . . . 1986 by BILL JANOVITZ, CHRIS COLBOURN and TOM MAGINNIS. Signed to 'S.S.T.', the band debuted in summer '89 with an eponymous album of high octane melodic hardcore. Though drawing countless comparisons with DINOSAUR JR. (J. MASCIS produced them), the group ploughed on, developing their own unique sound and garnering critical praise for the impressive writing talents of JANOVITZ and COLBOURN. Somewhat akin to a grunge hybrid of HUSKER DU and VAN MORRISON, these soulful indie rockers signed to 'Beggars Banquet' subsidiary, 'Situation 2', for their follow-up set, 'BIRD BRAIN'. However, it was with the acclaimed 'LET ME COME OVER' (1992), that BUFFALO TOM's bruised beauty really began to resonate, the classic 'TAILLIGHTS FADE' warranting gushing but deserved praise from the music press. By taking their collective foot off the noise accelerator, the group had given the songs time to catch their breath and enjoy the scenery. This didn't translate into major sales, however, the record stalling just inside the UK Top 50. 'BIG RED LETTER DAY' (1993) went for a slicker sound, this approach paying off as the album became the first BUFFALO TOM record to make the Top 20. Released just prior to the band's 1995 Reading Festival appearance, 'SLEEPY EYED' proved that JANOVITZ and co. have the talent and ability to last the course, their sound noticeably more confident and mature. In fact, JANOVITZ was sufficiently sure of his talents to attempt a solo set in 1996, the rootsy 'LONESOME BILLY'. • **Songwriters:** As said, except SHE BELONGS TO ME (Bob Dylan) / HEAVEN (Psychedelic Furs) / THE SPIDER AND THE FLY (Rolling Stones).

Album rating: LET ME COME OVER (*7) / (BIG RED LETTER DAY) (*7) / SLEEPY EYED (*6) / SMITTEN (*5)

BILL JANOVITZ – vocals, guitar / **CHRIS COLBOURN** – bass / **TOM MAGINNIS** – drums

S.S.T. / S.S.T.

Oct 89. (lp/c/cd) <*(SST/+C/CD 250)*> **BUFFALO TOM** [ ] [ ] Jul89
– Sunflower suit / The plank / Impossible / 500,000 warnings / The bus / Racine / In the attic / Flushing stars / Walk away / Reason why. *(cd re-iss. Apr92 on 'Megadisc'; MDC 7896) (re-iss. Oct92 on 'Beggars Banquet' lp/c/cd+=; BBQ LP/MC/CD 126)* – Blue / Deep in the ground.

Caff / not iss.

Feb 90. (7"ltd) *(CAFF 6)* **ENEMY. / DEEP IN THE GROUND** [ ] [-]

Megadisc / Megadisc

Jun 90. (12"/cd-s) <*(MD/+C 125276)*> **CRAWL. / THE BUS** [ ] [ ]

Situation 2 / Beggars Banquet

Oct 90. (12"ep/cd-ep) **BIRDBRAIN. / REASON WHY (live acoustic) / HEAVEN (live acoustic)** [ ] [ ]

Oct 90. (cd)(c/lp) *(SITU 31CD)(SIT C/U 31)* <2434-2/-4> **BIRDBRAIN** [ ] [ ]
– Birdbrain / Skeleton key / Caress / Guy who is me / Enemy / Crawl / Fortune teller / Baby / Directive / Bleeding heart. *(cd+=)* – Heaven / Reason why (acoustic). *(cd re-iss. Sep95 & Nov97 on 'Beggars Banquet'; BBL 31CD)*

May 91. (12"/cd-s) **FORTUNE TELLER. / WAH WAH** [ ] [-]

Feb 92. (12"ep/cd-ep) **VELVET ROOF / SHE BELONGS TO ME. / CRUTCH / SALLY BROWN** [ ] [-]

Mar 92. (cd)(c/lp) *(SITU 36CD)(SIT C/U 36)* <61105> **LET ME COME OVER** [49] [ ]
– Staples / Taillights fade / Mountains of your head / Mineral / Darry / Larry / Velvet roof / I'm not there / Stymied / Porch light / Frozen lake / Saving grace. (cd+=) – Crutch. *(cd re-iss. Nov97 on 'Beggars Banquet'; BBL 36CD)*

May 92. (10"ep/12"ep/cd-ep) *(SIT 96 TT/T/CD)* **TAILLIGHTS FADE / BIRDBRAIN (live). / LARRY (live) / SKELETON KEY (live)** [ ] [ ]

Beggars Banquet / Beggars Banquet

Oct 92. (7"/7"green) **MINERAL. / SUNFLOWER SUIT** [ ] [ ]
(cd-s+=) – Crawl / The bus.

Sep 93. (cd/c/lp) *(BBQ CD/MC/LP 142)* <92292> **(BIG RED LETTER DAY)** [17] [ ]
– Sodajerk / I'm allowed / Tree house / Would not be denied / Latest monkey / My

responsibility / Dry land / Torch singer / Late at night / Suppose / Anything that way. *(cd re-iss. Nov97; BBL 142CD)*

Sep 93. (12"ep/cd-ep) *(BBQ 20 T/CD)* **SODA JERK / WOULD NOT BE DENIED. / WITCHES / THE WAY BACK**

Nov 93. (7") *(BBQ 25)* **TREE HOUSE. / ANYTHING THAT WAY (acoustic)**
(12"+=/cd-s+=) *(BBQ 25 T/CD)* – Late at night (acoustic).

Beggars Banquet | Atlantic

Apr 94. (12"ep/cd-ep) *(BBQ 30 T/CD)* <95942> **I'M ALLOWED. / FOR ALL TO SEE / BUTTERSCOTCH**

Beggars Banquet | East West

Jun 95. (10"ep/cd-ep) *(BBQ 49 TT/CD)* **SUMMER. / CLOUDS / DOES THIS MEAN YOU'RE NOT MY FRIEND?** | – |

Jul 95. (cd/c/lp) *(BBQ CD/MC/LP 177)* <61782> **SLEEPY EYED** | 31 |
– Tangerine / Summer / Kitchen door / Rules / It's you / When you discover / Sunday night / Your stripes / Sparklers / Clobbered / Sundress / Twenty-points (the ballad of sexual dependency) / Souvenir / Crueler. *(cd re-iss. Nov97; BBL 177CD)*

Nov 95. (7") *(BBQ 64)* **TANGERINE. / BREATH** | – |
(cd-s+=) *(BBQ 64CD)* – The spider and the fly.

Beggars Banquet | Polydor

Sep 98. (7") *(BBQ 329)* **WISER. / CUPID COME** | – |
(cd-s+=) *(BBQ 329CD)* – Hawaiian baby.

Sep 98. (cd/lp) *(BBQ CD/LP 205)* <557867> **SMITTEN**
– Rachael / Postcard / Knot it in / Bible / Scottish windows / White paint morning / Wiser / See to me / Register side / Do you in / Under milkwood / Walking wounded.

BILL JANOVITZ

— with **JOEY BURNS** – upright bass, vocals / **JOHN CONVERTINO** – drums / and guests CRAIG SCHUMACHER, HOWE GELB + NEIL HARRY

Dec 96. (cd/lp) *(BBQ CD/LP 186)* **LONESOME BILLY**
– Girl's club / Think of all / Shoulder / Gaslight / Ghost in my piano / Strangers / My funny valentine / Peninsula / Talking to the Queen / Red balloon.

BUILT TO SPILL

Formed: Boise, Idaho, USA . . . early 90's by songwriter and chief, DOUGH MARTSCH, who had just left TREEPEOPLE. Basically a one-man operation (with bassist BRETT NELSON and drummer RALF in tow), BUILT TO SPILL first emerged in 1993 with the 'ULTIMATE ALTERNATIVE WAVERS' album on 'C/Z' records, MARTSCH subsequently securing a deal with Seattle's 'Up!' label ('City Slang' in the UK and Europe) and releasing the acclaimed 'THERE'S NOTHING WRONG WITH LOVE' in late '94; RALF had now been replaced by ANDY CAPPS. The album's beguiling blend of strident, largely acoustic guitar and strings engendered enough underground support to see BTS secure a series of dates on the following year's Lollapalooza tour (by which point the band's ever varying line-up consisted of MARTSCH, a rhythm section of JAMES BERTRAM and DAVE SCHNEIDER plus cellist JOHN McMAHON, the latter becoming a permanent fixture) as well as a prestigious support slot to the FOO FIGHTERS. In the ensuing A&R melee, 'Warners' won their signatures and bundled them off to the studio to what turned out to be a jinxed third album. Although SCOTT PLOUFF had replaced SCHNEIDER as a permanent sticksman, the sessions didn't exactly go smoothly and after some material was eventually laid down, damage to the tapes forced the trio to begin from scratch. 'Warners' bailed out at this point, the album eventually surfacing in the form of the appropriately titled 'PERFECT FROM NOW ON' (1997) via 'Up!/City Slang'. Embellished by the cello of McMAHON and mellotron of ROBERT ROTH, the album was met with glowing praise from the press, MARTSCH no doubt breathing a sigh of relief to see his work in the shops at last. • **Covered:** BY THE WAY (Heavenly) / SOME THINGS LAST A LONG TIME (Jad Fair & Daniel Johnston).

Album rating: ULTIMATE ALTERNATIVE WAVERS (*6) / THERE'S NOTHING WRONG WITH LOVE (*6) / PERFECT FROM NOW ON (*8)

DOUGH MARTSCH (ex-TREEPEOPLE, ex-HALO BENDERS) – vocals, guitar / **BRETT NELSON** – bass, etc (ex-BUTTERFLY TRAIN) / **RALF** – drums

not iss. | C/Z

1993. (cd) **ULTIMATE ALTERNATIVE WAVERS** | – |
– First song / Three years ago today / Revolution / Shameful dread / Nowhere nothin' fuckup / Get a life / Built to spill / Lie for a lie / Hazy / Built too long (pts.1,2 & 3). *(UK-iss.Jan96 on 'Fire'; FIRECD 51)*

— **ANDY CAPPS** – drums (ex-BUTTERFLY TRAIN) repl. RALF

City Slang | Up!

Sep 95. (7") *(EFA 04962-7)* **CAR. /**
(cd-s+=) *(EFA 04962-2)* –

Oct 95. (cd/lp) *(EFA 049632/-1)* <UP 006> **THERE'S NOTHING WRONG WITH LOVE** | | Nov94
– In the morning / Reasons / Big dipper / Car / Fling / Cleo / Source / Twin falls / Some / Distopian dream girl / Israeli's song / Stab.

Dec 95. (7") *(EFA 04970-7)* **IN THE MORNING. / SO AND SO SO AND SO FROM WHEREVER WHEREVER**
(cd-s+=) *(EFA 04970-2)* – Terrible perfect.

Jan 96. (cd-ep; shared with CAISTIC RESIN) <018> **EP** | – |
– When not being stupid is not enough / One thing / (other two by CAUSTIC RESIN).

— **SCOTT PLOUF** – drums (ex-SPINANES) repl. JAMES DILLON

— added guests **ROBERT ROTH** – mellotron / **JOHN McMAHON** – cello

— abandoned by 'Warners' when master tapes were damaged

Feb 97. (cd/lp) *(EFA 04992-26/08)* <UP 033> **PERFECT FROM NOW ON**
– Randy described eternity / I would hurt a fly / Stop the show / Made up dreams / Velvet waltz / Out of site / Kicked in the sun / Untrustable (part 2).

– compilations, etc. –

May 96. (cd) *K;* <KLP 52CD> **THE NORMAL YEARS**
– So and so so and so wherever / Shortcut / Car / Some things last a long time / Girl / Joyride / Some / Sick and wrong / Still flat / Terrible – Perfect.

1996. (7") *K;* <IPU 89> **BY THE WAY. / Marine Research: SICK & WRONG** | – |

Mark BURGESS (see under ⇒ CHAMELEONS)

J. J. BURNEL (see under ⇒ STRANGLERS)

JAKE BURNS & THE WHEEL (see under ⇒ STIFF LITTLE FINGERS)

BUSH TETRAS

Formed: New York City, New York, USA . . . 1979 by Chicago-born guitarist, PAT PLACE, who, after a musical apprenticeship with JAMES CHANCE's CONTORTIONS, began rehearsals with fellow compadres ADELE BERTEI, JIMMY ULIANO and DEE POP. Retaining only DEE, she formed The BUSH TETRAS, enlisting "No Wave" students, LAURA KENNEDY and CYNTHIA SLEY, former classmates at the Cleveland Institute Of Art. Early in 1980, the 3-girl/1-guy quartet released a debut EP, 'TOO MANY CREEPS', which was issued on the '99' label. Subsequently signed to UK label, 'Fetish' (also home of another American outfit, The BONGOS), they hit the US dance charts late in 1981 with the TOPPER HEADON-produced follow-up, 'RITUALS'. Intentionally amateurish, the band's funky "No Wave" non-conformist jungle-rock was something of an anomaly on the early 80's post-punk scene. A cassette-only album finally reached the shops in 1983; entitled 'WILD THINGS', this was basically a collection of live recordings, the 'TETRAS having already ventured into other projects. Back due to popular demand, the original line-up re-united in 1995 (after having previously got back together for live gigs in '92) to record a one-off set of new material, 'BEAUTY LIES' (1996). • **Covered:** WILD THING (Troggs) / COLD TURKEY (John Lennon). • **Trivia:** SLEY once designed clothes for LYDIA LUNCH (Teenage Jesus) and JUDY NYLON (Snatch).

Album rating: WILD THINGS compilation (*5) / BETTER LATE THAN NEVER compilation (*6) / BOOM IN THE NIGHT compilation (*5) / BEAUTY LIES (*5) / TETRAFIED compilation (*5)

PAT PLACE (b. 1964, Chicago, Illinois) – guitar (ex-JAMES CHANCE & THE CONTORTIONS) / **CYNTHIA SLEY** (b. 3 May'57, Cleveland, Ohio) – vocals, percussion / **LAURA KENNEDY** (b.30 May'57, Cleveland, Ohio) – bass / **DEE POP** (b.14 Mar'56, Queens, N.Y.) – drums

not iss. | 99

Sep 80. (7"ep) <99-02> **TOO MANY CREEPS. / SNAKES CRAWL / YOU TASTE LIKE THE TROPICS** | – |

Fetish | Stiff

May 81. (7") *(FET 007)* **THINGS THAT GO BOOM IN THE NIGHT. / DAS AH RIOT** | | – |

1981. (7"w/drawn) *(FE 15)* **CAN'T BE FUNKY** | – | – |

Dec 81. (12"ep) *(FET 16)* **RITUALS**

R.O.I.R. | R.O.I.R.

Jan 83. (c) <A 119> **WILD THINGS**
– Cowboys in Africa / Making a mistake / Stare / Rituals / Enemies / Wild thing / Boom / Damned / Submerging nations / Too many creeps / Can't be funky / Voodoo / Jaws.

— split; DEE POP formed FLOOR KIS, DEERFRANCE before joining GUN CLUB, etc. SLEY formed MAD ORPHAN (later LOVELIES) with then-husband IVAN JULIAN (ex-RICHARD HELL & THE VOID-OIDS). In the 90's, she was in 1-800-BOXX, before she briefly re-united BUSH TETRAS in 1992 for live gigs.

not iss. | Tim/Kerr

Oct 96. (c-ep) <139> **PAGE 18 /** | – |

not iss. | Polygram

Dec 96. (cd) <830149> **BEAUTY LIES** | – |
– Mr. Love song / Page 18 / Dirty little secret / Beauty lies / Color green / Satan is a bummer / Silver chain / Ballad / Mental mishap / Find a lie / Basement babies / World / World dub.

– compilations, etc. –

1989. (c) *R.O.I.R.;* **BETTER LATE THAN NEVER, 1980-1983** | – |

Feb 96. (cd) *ROIR USA; (RUSCD 8218)* **BOOM IN THE NIGHT**

Apr 97. (cd) *2.13.61.;* **TETRAFIED** (early demos, etc) | – |
– Punch drunk / Fess up / In mind a run / Ah dub / Dub in the night / Funky dub / Cowboys in Africa / Cold turkey / Boom lakka lakka / Make sure / Stare you down / Point that gun / Race for space / Dewback / Juana lagusta / Voodoo.

BUSINESS

Formed: South London, England . . . late 1979 by MICKEY FITZ, STEVE WHALE, STUART WILLIAMS and PRYOR. Described as the SLADE of the "oi" movement, The BUSINESS set up shop on the 'Secret' label, debuting in late '81 with the classic Cock-er-nee gangster anthem, 'HARRY MAY'. Almost immediately throwing away any credibility they might have earned, The BUSINESS went artistically bankrupt with a yuletide cover of Elton John's

'STEP INTO CHRISTMAS', released as part of a V/A EP. The lads' love of glitzy nightlife shone through on 'SMASH THE DISCO', while another proto-TOY DOLLS job, 'DAYO (THE BANANA BOAT SONG)', was thown in for 'bad' measure on the B-side. PRYOR and STUART subsequently clocked out, their replacements, MARK BRENNAN and KEV BOYCE making their inagural appearance on the band's debut lp, 'SUBURBAN REBELS' (1983). Later in the year, the 'OUT OF BUSINESS' EP was shelved and should have contained a cover of Crass' 'DO THEY OWE US A LIVING'. Back in business and on a new label, 'Word Of Warning', the boys returned in 1985 with a single, 'GET OUT OF MY HOUSE'. A cover of Sham 69's 'HURRY UP HARRY', meanwhile, turned up as the extra track on the 12" of the 'DRINKING 'N' DRIVING' single, the accompanying album, 'SATURDAY HEROES' (1986) being released on their own 'Harry May' imprint. Over the course of the next decade or so, The BUSINESS continued to set out their stall for hardcore fans every few years, their most recent album being 1997's 'THE WHOLE TRUTH AND NOTHING BUT THE TRUTH'. • **Note:** Not to be confused with The BUSINESS who released 'GET UP' for 'M.C.A.' early in 1981.

Album rating: SUBURBAN REBELS (*4) / SATURDAY HEROES (*4) / WELCOME TO THE REAL WORLD (*3) / IN AND OUT OF BUSINESS (*3) / THE BEST OF THE BUSINESS compilation (*4) / KEEP THE FAITH (*3) / THE WHOLE TRUTH AND NOTHING BUT THE TRUTH (*4)

MICKEY FITZ (b. MICHAEL FITZSIMONS) – vocals / **STEVE WHALE** (b. STEVE KENT) – guitar / **STUART WILLIAMS** – bass / **PRYOR** – drums

Secret not iss.

Oct 81. (7") *(SHH 123)* **HARRY MAY. / NATIONAL INSURANCE BLACKLIST** ☐ -

Dec 81. (7"ep; various) *(SHH 126)* **STEP INTO CHRISTMAS** ☐ -

Apr 82. (7") *(SHH 132)* **SMASH THE DISCO. / DISCO GIRLS / DAYO (THE BANANA BOAT SONG)** ☐ -

— **KEV BOYCE** – drums; repl. PRYOR

— **MARK BRENNAN** – bass; repl. STUART who joined BANDITS AT 4 O'CLOCK

Mar 83. (lp) *(SEC 11)* **SUBURBAN REBELS** ☐ -
– Get out while you can / Blind justice / Work or riot / The employer's blacklist / Nobody listened / Suburban rebels / Mortgage mentality / Guttersnipe / Real enemy / Another rebel dead / Sabotage the hunt / Harry May / Drinking and driving. *(cd-iss. Sep93 on 'Captain Oi'; AHOYCD 7)*

Dec 83. (12"ep; w-drawn) *(SHH 150)* **OUT OF BUSINESS** - -
– Last train to Clapham Junction / Law and order / Do they owe us a living / Tell us the truth.

Wonderful World Of... not iss.

Aug 85. (12"ep) *(WOW 121)* **GET OUT OF MY HOUSE / ALL OUT TONIGHT. / FOREIGN GIRL / OUTLAW** ☐ -

Sep 85. (lp; shared with LOUD) *(WOWDLP 4)* **THE OFFICIAL BOOTLEG** ☐ -

Diamond not iss.

Dec 85. (7") *(DIA 001)* **DRINKING 'N' DRIVING. / H-BOMB (live)** ☐ -
(12"+=) *(DIA 001T)* – Hurry up Harry / ('A'original).

Harry May not iss.

Jan 86. (lp) *(SE 13)* **SATURDAY HEROES** ☐ -
– Spanish jails / All out tonight / Never been taken / Harder life / Freedom / Frontline / Foreign girl / Shout it out / Nothing can stop us / Saturday heroes / Drinking 'n' driving. *(re-iss. Mar90 on 'Street Link'; LINKLP 115) (re-iss. Feb97 on 'Taang!'; TAANG 122) (cd-iss. Nov97 on 'Captain Oi'+=; AHOYCD 013)* – Hurry up Harry / Get out of my house / Outlaw / Coventry.

Link not iss.

Apr 88. (12"ep) *(LINK12 01)* **DO A RUNNER / COVENTRY. / WELCOME TO THE REAL WORLD / ANYWHERE BUT HERE / ALL OUT / (YOU'RE) GOING DOWN IN HISTORY** ☐ -

Jul 88. (lp) *(LINKLP 035)* **WELCOME TO THE REAL WORLD** ☐ -
– Mouth an' trousers / Do a runner / Ten years / We'll take 'em on / Fear in your heart / Welcome to the real world / Never say never / Hand ball / Living in daydreams / Look at him now / We gotta go / Never say never (reprise) / Coventry / No emotions / Tina Turner / Welcome to the real world (12). *(cd-iss. Apr93 on 'Captain Oi'; AHOYCD 2) (lp re-iss. Feb96 on 'Taang!'; TAANG 123LP)*

1990. (lp) *(LRMO 1)* **IN AND OUT OF BUSINESS** - - mail-o
(cd-iss. Mar98 on 'Mog'; MOGCD 001)

— shut up shop at the turn of the decade (opened up again in '94)

Century Media Century Media

Oct 94. (cd/lp) *(<CM 77083-2/-1>)* **KEEP THE FAITH** ☐ ☐

Taang! Taang!

Feb 96. (7"/cd-s) *(T 114/+CD)* **DEATH II DANCE. /** ☐ ☐

Burning Heart Taang!

Sep 97. (cd/lp) *(BHR 067 CD/LP) <115>* **THE TRUTH, THE WHOLE TRUTH AND NOTHING BUT THE TRUTH** ☐ ☐
– Spirit of the street / Blood ties / The truth, the whole truth and nothing but the truth / One common voice / What's the story / Justice not politics / One thing left to say / Death to dance / No time 4U / S.E. 12 / Crime of the century / Informer / Southgate / Hardcore hooligan.

– compilations, etc. –

Dec 83. (lp) *Syndicate; (SYNLP 2)* **1980-81 OFFICIAL BOOTLEGS** ☐ -
(cd-iss. Mar98 on 'Mog'; MOGCD 002)

1984. (lp) *Syndicate; (SYNLP 6)* **LOUD, PROUD 'N' PUNK, LIVE (live)** ☐ -
(tracks originally from a 'TOTAL NOISE' EP released June '82)

Aug 86. (lp) *Dojo; (DOJOLP 35)* **SINGALONGABUSINESS** ☐ -
– Suburban rebels / Blind justice / Loud, proud & punk / The real enemy / Spanish jails / Product / National insurance blacklist / Get out of my house / Saturday heroes / Out in the cold / Smash the discos / Harry May / Drinking 'n' driving / Hurry up Harry. *(cd-iss. Nov94 on 'Captain Oi'; AHOY 19)*

Feb 92. (cd/c/lp) *Blackout; <BL 009 CD/MC/LP>* **1979-1989** - ☐

Aug 92. (cd) *Street Link; (LINKCD 156)* **THE BEST OF THE BUSINESS** ☐ -
(re-iss. Apr93 on 'Dojo'; DOJOCD 124) (re-iss. Apr98 on 'Snapper'; SMMCD 539)

Aug 94. (cd) *Loma; (LOMACD 32)* **SUBURBAN REBELS / WELCOME TO THE REAL WORLD** ☐ -

Jun 95. (cd) *Anagram; (CDPUNK 57)* **THE COMPLETE BUSINESS SINGLES COLLECTION** ☐ -

Dec 96. (d-lp) *Taang!; (TAANG 124)* **HARRY MAY: THE SINGLES** ☐ -

May 98. (cd) *Step-1; (STEPCD 024)* **SMASH THE DISCOS / LOUD, PROUD AND PUNK** ☐ -

Sep 98. (cd) *PinHead; (PINCD 106)* **THE BUSINESS LIVE (live)** ☐ -

Bernard BUTLER

Born: 1970, Stamford Hill, London, England. Temporarily putting aside his violin and piano, BUTLER took up guitar as a young teenager, idolizing JOHNNY MARR (of The SMITHS) in the mid-80's. In 1989, after an unsuccessful year at London's Queen Mary College, he answered an ad in the NME; it was to join SUEDE. His creative and imaginative songwriting helped the band and their chief wordsmith, BRETT ANDERSON reach the heady heights in the first half of the 90's, although a personality clash with the SUEDE mainman BUTLER's led to him seeking out pastures new in the summer of '94. After a brief spell working with ALL ABOUT EVE singer JULIANNE REGAN, he began putting pen to paper once more in his new London abode (which he shares with wife, Elisa). He provided the song, 'YES', for the up and coming, flashily extravagant soul singer, DAVID McALMONT, thus the partnership McALMONT & BUTLER duly signed to Virgin offshoot, 'Hut'. A terrific follow-up single, 'YOU DO', gave the pair another UK Top 20 hit, while the accompanying album, 'THE SOUND OF. . .' became their swansong in late 1995; unfortunately they just couldn't stop backstabbing each other in the press. BERNARD subsequently worked with BRYAN FERRY, AIMEE MANN, EDWYN COLLINS, EDDI READER, NENEH CHERRY and made a substantial contribution to the BOOTH & THE BAD ANGEL project (aka TIM BOOTH of JAMES and ANGELO "Twin Peaks" BADALAMENTI). The following year (1997), BUTLER signed to 'Creation' and worked on his debut solo album, 'PEOPLE MOVE ON'. Released in the Spring of '98 and containing two Top 30 hits, 'STAY' and 'NOT ALONE', it knocked on the door of the Top 10 after receiving rave reviews. A largely acoustic affair the record saw BUTLER re-invent himself as a tortured balladeer, although the OTT production and ghosts of his more elaborate recent past seemed to haunt him. The esteemed guitarist went on to play the festival circuit, his axework outshining even the great MARR, especially his electric set at 'T In The Park'.

Album rating: PEOPLE MOVE ON (*6)

BERNARD BUTLER – vocals, guitar (ex-SUEDE, ex-McALMONT & BUTLER) / with **MAKOTO SAKAMOTO** – drums / and guests DENISE JOHNSON – backing vocals / NICK WOLLAGE – sax / EDWYN COLLINS – vocals / GEORGE SHILLING – cello / RICHARD BISSILL – French horn / & The Brilliant Strings conducted by BILLY McGEE: GINI BALL, JACKIE NORRIE, MARGARET ROSEBERRY, ANNE WOOD, ANNA HEMERY, SALLY HERBERT + ANNE STEPHENSON – violins / CHRIS PITISILLIDES + ELLEN BLAIR – viola / DINAH BEAMISH + SIAN BELL – cello

Creation Columbia

Jan 98. (7"/c-s) *(CRE/+CS 281)* **STAY. / HOTEL SPLENDID** 12 -
(cd-s+=) *(CRESCD 281)* –

Mar 98. (7"/c-s) *(CRE/+CS 289)* **NOT ALONE. / BYE BYE** 27 -
(cd-s+=) *(CRESCD 289)* –

Apr 98. (cd/lp)(c) *(CRE CD/LP 221)(CCRE 221) <69332>* **PEOPLE MOVE ON** 11 ☐
– Woman I know / You just know / People move on / A change of heart / Autograph / You light the fire / Not alone / When you grow / You've got what it takes / Stay / In vain / I'm tired.

Jun 98. (7"/c-s) *(CRE/+CS 297)* **A CHANGE OF HEART. / MY DOMAIN** 45 ☐
(cd-s+=) *(CRESCD 297)* – More than I thought.

BUTTHOLE SURFERS

Formed: San Antonio, Texas, USA . . . 1980 originally as The ASHTRAY BABY HEELS by ex-accountant GIBBY (son of US children's TV presenter "Mr. Peppermint") and PAUL LEARY, who met at Trinity College, San Antonio. By 1983, they had signed to JELLO BIAFRA's (Dead Kennedys) label, 'Alternative Tentacles'. Around the mid-80's, they gigged heavily in Britain due to lack of Stateside interest, and this, together with radio play from John Peel, helped them make it into the UK indie charts. Heavy psychedelia mixing noise, confusion and futuristic art-punk, the manic GIBBY, (complete with loudspeaker, etc), was always offensive and disturbing while their weird stage act included the nude dancer, KATHLEEN. She covered herself in green jello, while GIBBY simulated sex with her! GIBBY was well-known for other stage antics; pissing in plastic baseball bats ('piss wands') and annointing the audience at the front. There were other obscenities, too rude to print here (no need to mention President Carter's creamy briefcase). In 1987, they unleashed the brilliantly crazed 'LOCUST ABORTION TECHNICIAN', complete with a parody of BLACK SABBATH's 'SWEET LEAF', the humourously titled 'SWEAT LOAF'. Also deep inside its nightmarish musical grooves was their gem, 'TWENTY TWO GOING ON TWENTY THREE', a track that made John Peel's Festive 50. A longer sojourn in Britain culminated in some riotous, oversubscribed London gigs. The follow-up, 'HAIRWAY TO STEVEN' (another piss-take; this time of LED ZEPPELIN – Stairway To Heaven), deliberately left the tracks nameless (instead using obscene looking symbols) as a twisted tribute to ZEPPELIN's "untitled" symbols album. 1990 saw them shift to a more commercial sound with 'PIOUGHD' (which means "pissed-off" in Red Indian), which featured a re-working of DONOVAN's 'HURDY GURDY MAN'. Having signed to 'Capitol' in 1992, they were back to their abrasive sound of old with the JOHN PAUL JONES-produced album, 'INDEPENDENT WORM SALOON'. This, together with their previous effort, had given them their first taste of chart success in Britain, this being well surpassed in 1996 when 'ELECTRICLARRYLAND' hit the US Top 30. It was due, no doubt, to a surprise domestic hit with 'PEPPER', and probably their "fiery" guest appearance on American mock talk show, The LARRY Sanders Show' in '97. • **Songwriters:** GIBBY and co., except AMERICAN WOMAN (Guess Who) / THE ONE I LOVE (R.E.M.). P covered DANCING QUEEN (Abba).

Album rating: BROWN REASONS TO LIVE mini (*6) / PSYCHIC ... POWERLESS ... ANOTHER MAN'S SAC (*7) / REMBRANDT PUSSYHORSE (*7) / LOCUST ABORTION TECHNICIAN (*8) / HAIRWAY TO STEVEN (*7) / DOUBLE LIVE (*4) / PHIOGHD (*6) / INDEPENDENT WORM SALOON (*7) / ELECTRICLARRYLAND (*7)

GIBBY HAYNES (b. GIBSON JEROME HAYNES, 1957) – vocals / **PAUL LEARY** (b.1958) – guitar / **KING COFFEY** – drums repl. ? / **ALAN ?** – bass

Alternative Tentacles / Alternative Tentacles

Apr 84. (m-lp) *(VIRUS 32)* **BUTTHOLE SURFERS** <'BROWN REASONS TO LIVE; US-title> — 1983
– The Shah sleeps in Lee Harvey's grave / Hey / Something / Bar-b-que / Pope / Wichita cathedral / Suicide / The legend of Anus Presley. *(re-iss. Sep93 as 'BROWN REASONS TO LIVE' brown-lp; same)*

Jan 85. (12"ep) *(VIRUS 39)* **LIVE PCPPEP (live)**
– Cowboy Bob / Bar-b-q pope / Dance of the cobras / The Shah sleeps in Lee Harvey's grave / Wichita cathedral / Hey / Something.

— **TERENCE** – bass repl. ALAN (?)

Fundamental / Touch&Go

Apr 85. (7") **LADY SNIFF. /** [-]

Jul 85. (lp) *(SAVE 5)* **PSYCHIC . . . POWERLESS . . . ANOTHER MAN'S SAC**
– Concubine / Eye of the chicken / Dum dum / Woly boly / Negro observer / Butthole surfer / Lady sniff / Cherub / Mexican caravan / Cowboy Bob / Gary Floyd. *(cd-iss. Jan88+=)* – CREAM CORN FROM THE SOCKET OF DAVIS

— **MARK KRAMER** – bass (of SHOCKABILLY) repl. TREVOR who had repl. TERENCE

Oct 85. (12"ep) *(PRAY 69)* **CREAM CORN FROM THE SOCKET OF DAVIS**
– Moving to Florida / Comb – Lou Reed (two parter) / Tornados.

Red Rhino Europe / Touch&Go

Apr 86. (lp) *(RRELP 2)* *<TGLP 8>* **REMBRANDT PUSSYHORSE**
– Creep in the cellar / Sea ferring / American woman / Waiting for Jimmy to kick / Strangers die / Perry / Whirling hall of knives / Mark says alright / In the cellar. *(cd-iss. May88; RRECD 2)*

— **JEFF 'TOOTER' PINKUS** – bass repl. KRAMER who formed BONGWATER

Blast First / Blast First

Mar 87. (lp/c/cd) *(BFFP 15/+C/CD)* **LOCUST ABORTION TECHNICIAN**
– Sweat loaf / Graveyard 1 / Pittsburgh to Lebanon / Weber / Hay / Human cannonball / U.S.S.A. / Theoman / Kintz / Graveyard 2 / 22 going on 23 / The G-men.

— added **THERESA NERVOSA (NAYLOR)** – 2nd drummer / **KATHLEEN** – naked dancer (above with GIBBY, PAUL, COFFEY and PINKUS)

Apr 88. (lp/cd) *(BFFP 29/+CD)* **HAIRWAY TO STEVEN**
– Hairway part 1 / Hairway part 2 / Hairway part 3 / Hairway part 4 / Hairway part 5 / Hairway part 6 / Hairway part 7 / Hairway part 8 / Hairway part 9. *(9 tracks marked rude symbols as titles)*

Aug 89. (12"ep/10"ep/cd-ep) *(BFFP 41/+T/CD)* **WIDOWERMAKER**
– Bong song / 1401 / Booze tobacco / Helicopter.

— now without THERESA

Rough Trade / Rough Trade

Nov 90. (7") *(RT 240)* **THE HURDY GURDY MAN. / BARKING DOGS**
(12"+=/cd-s+=) *(RTT 240/+CD)* – ('A'-Paul Leary remix).

Feb 91. (cd/c/lp) *(R 2081260-2/-4/-1)* *<RTE R2601>* **PIOUGHD** — 68
– Revolution pt.1 & 2 / Lonesome bulldog pt.1 & 2 / The hurdy gurdy man / Golden showers / Lonesome bulldog pt.3 / Blindman / No, I'm iron man / Something / P.S.Y. / Lonesome bulldog pt.IV. *(cd+=)* – Barking dogs. *(cd-iss. Dec 94 on 'Danceteria';)*

— In Apr'92, GIBBY guested for MINISTRY on single 'Jesus Built My Hotrod'.

Capitol / Capitol

Mar 93. (cd/c/lp) *(CD/TC+/EST 2192)* *<98798>* **INDEPENDENT WORM SALOON** — 73
– Who was in my room last night / The wooden song / Tongue / Chewin' George Lucas' chocolate / Goofy's concern / Alcohol / Dog inside your body / Strawberry / Some dispute over T-shirt sales / Dancing fool / You don't know me / The annoying song / Dust devil / Leave me alone / Edgar / The ballad of a naked man / Clean it up.

May 96. (cd/c/d-lp) *(CD/TC+/EST 2285)* *<29842>* **ELECTRICLARRYLAND** — US 31
– Birds / Cough syrup / Pepper / Thermador / Ulcer breakout / Jingle of a dog's collar / TV star / My brother's wife / Ah ha / The Lord is a monkey / Let's talk about cars / L.A. / Space.

Sep 96. (7") *(CL 778)* **PEPPER. / HYBRID** — 59
(cd-s+=) *(CDCL 778)* – Pepper (Butcha' Bros remix) / The Lord is a monkey.

– compilations, others, etc. –

Jun 89. (d-lp/cd) *Latino Bugger; (LBV ?)* **DOUBLE LIVE (live)** [-]

Nov 94. (7"/7"pic-d) *Trance Syndicate; (TR 30/+PD)* **GOOD KING WENCENSLAUS. / THE LORD IS A MONKEY** [-]

Apr 95. (cd) *Trance Syndicate; (TR 35CD)* **THE HOLE TRUTH & NOTHING BUTT!** (early demos) [-]

JACKOFFICERS

off-shoot with **GIBBY, JEFF & KATHLEEN**

Naked Brain / Rough Trade

Dec 90. (lp/c/cd) *(NBX 003/+C/CD)* *<ROUGHUS 100>* **DIGITAL DUMP**
– Love-o-maniac / Time machine pt.1 & 2 / L.A.name peanut butter / Do it / Swingers club / Ventricular retribution / 6 / Don't touch that / An Hawaiian Christmas song / Flush.

PAUL LEARY

Rough Trade / Rough Trade

Apr 91. (cd/c/lp) *<(R 2081263-2/-4/-1)>* **THE HISTORY OF DOGS**
– The birds are dying / Apollo one / Dalhart down the road / How much longer / He's working overtime / Indians storm the government / Is it milky / Too many people / The city / Fine home.

DRAIN

aka **KING COFFEY + DAVID McCREETH** (ex-SQUID)

Trance Syndicate / Trance Syndicate

Apr 91. (7") *<(TR 04)>* **A BLACK FIST. / FLOWER MOUND**

Mar 92. (lp/cd) *<(TR 11/+CD)>* **PICK UP HEAVEN**
– National anthem / Crawfish / Martyr's road / Non compis mentis / Funeral pyre / Ozark monkey chant / Instant hippie / Flower mound / Every secret thing / The ballad of Miss Toni Fisher.

Apr 96. (cd) *<(TR 49CD)>* **OFFSPEED & IN THERE**
– Playground twist / Burma slowdrive / Return to Rosedale / Marrakesh: 3 a.m. / Bunch of guys about to turn blue / Helicopters are burning / Saipan murder mystery / Stop six / Wendy will win / Nitrous shuffle / In the Spring we eat cucumbers / Upright and in love.

P

— formed 1993 by **GIBBY + JOHNNY DEPP** – bass, guitar (yes! the actor & beau of supermodel Kate Moss) / **BILL CARTER** – bass / **SAL JENCO** – drums

Capitol / Capitol

Feb 96. (cd/c/lp) *(CD/TC PCS 7379)* *<7243 8 32942-2/-4/-1>* **P**
– I save cigarette butts / Zing Splash / Michael Stipe / Oklahoma / Dancing queen / Jon Glenn (megamix) / Mr Officer / White man sings the blues / Die Anne / Scrapings from ring / The deal.

BUZZARDS (see under ⇒ LEYTON BUZZARDS)

BUZZCOCKS

Formed: Manchester, England . . . April 1976 by HOWARD DEVOTO and PETE SHELLEY who met at Bolton Institute Of Higher Education. Having recruited STEVE DIGGLE and JOHN MAHER, they played their first gig on the 20th of July '76 supporting the SEX PISTOLS. Early the following year, they released the first ever DIY punk "indie" 45 on 'New Hormones' in the form of the 'SPIRAL SCRATCH' EP. They then suffered a major bust up when frontman DEVOTO departed (to form MAGAZINE), although the rest carried on having signed to 'United Artists' on the strength of featuring on the now famous 'LIVE AT THE ROXY' Various artists compilation (with tracks 'Breakdown' and 'Love Battery'). By this time, SHELLEY had taken over vocal duties, while DIGGLE switched to guitar, having found a new bassist, GARTH SMITH. Early in 1978, they stormed the charts with the brooding love gem, 'WHAT DO I GET', a two-minute rush of bittersweet pop/punk angst which saw SHELLEY emerging as a strong frontman in his own right. The previous year's masterbating classic, 'ORGASM ADDICT', was too frenetic to allow SHELLEY's effeminate romance'n'roll stylings a look-in, although he blossomed on subsequent releases. A debut album, 'ANOTHER MUSIC IN A DIFFERENT KITCHEN' (1978), made the UK Top 20, while another SHELLEY-penned classic, 'EVER FALLEN IN LOVE (WITH SOMEONE YOU SHOULDN'T'VE?)', almost made the Top 10 later that year. With fervent suport from Radio One DJ, John Peel, the band had squarely cornered the more accessible end of the punk market, although the 'LOVE BITES' album marked a move away from the short, sharp melodic shock which had become their trademark as songwriting duties were more democratically distributed. A final clutch of Top 30 hits, 'PROMISES' (their fifth hit in 1978), 'EVERYBODY'S HAPPY NOWADAYS' and 'HARMONY IN MY HEAD', saw the increasing influence of DIGGLE. 1979's 'A DIFFERENT KIND OF TENSION' saw SHELLEY's influence begin to dissipate and the album's mixed reviews signalled the band were running out of creative steam. After 'Liberty' took over their contract in 1980 and a further three 45's flopped, the BUZZCOCKS split, DIGGLE forming FLAG OF CONVENIENCE with MAHER. SHELLEY, meanwhile, went solo, making his debut in 1981 with the 'HOMOSAPIEN' album. Although the album made little commercial headway in Britain, the title track, bizarrely enough, topped the Australian charts. He released another two sets, 'XL-1' (1983) and 'HEAVEN AND THE SEA' (1986) to mild interest; far more newsworthy was the band's reformation in 1990 with a line-up of SHELLEY, DIGGLE, STEVE GARVEY and ex-SMITHS drummer, MIKE JOYCE. A comeback album, 'TRADE TEST TRANSMISSION' (1993) was lapped up by old punks and new converts alike, while a slightly modified line-up undertook a heartily received tour. A live set culled from the dates, 'FRENCH', was released in 1995, while a follow-up album, 'ALL SET' appeared a year later. The band's classic late 70's output remains one of the most influential bodies of work from the punk era, second only to perhaps the SEX PISTOLS. • **Covered:** HERE COMES THE NICE (Small Faces). • **Trivia:** In 1978, SHELLEY produced fun group, ALBERTO Y LOST TRIOS PARANOIAS.

Album rating: ANOTHER MUSIC IN A DIFFERENT KITCHEN (*9) / LOVE BITES (*7) / DIFFERENT KIND OF TENSION (*6) / SINGLES – GOING STEADY compilation (*9) / TRADE TEST TRANSMISSION (*5) / FRENCH (*4) / ALL SET (*5) / Pete Shelley: SKY YEN (*4) / HOMOSAPIEN (*7) / XL-1 (*5) / HEAVEN AND THE SEA (*6)

HOWARD DEVOTO (b.HOWARD TRAFFORD) – vocals / **PETE SHELLEY** (b.PETER McNEISH, 17 Apr'55) – guitar, vocals / **STEVE DIGGLE** – bass, vocals / **JOHN MAHER** – drums

New Hormones | not iss.

Jan 77. (7"ep) *(ORG 1)* **SPIRAL SCRATCH** [ ] [-]
– Breakdown / Times up / Boredom / Friends of mine. *(re-iss. Aug79 credited as "BUZZCOCKS with HOWARD DEVOTO"; same); hit No.31) (re-iss. 1994 on 'Document' 12"ep/cd-ep)*

— (Mar'77) **GARTH SMITH** – bass; repl. DEVOTO who formed MAGAZINE

SHELLEY now lead vocals, guitar / **DIGGLE** switched to guitar, vocals

U.A. | not iss.

Oct 77. (7") *(UP 36316)* **ORGASM ADDICT. / WHATEVER HAPPENED TO . . . ?** [ ] [-]

— **STEVE GARVEY** – bass repl. GARTH (on tour at first)

Jan 78. (7") *(UP 36348)* **WHAT DO I GET?. / OH SHIT** [37] [-]

U.A. | I.R.S.

Mar 78. (lp/c) *(UAG/TCK 30159)* **ANOTHER MUSIC IN A DIFFERENT KITCHEN** [15] [ ]
– Fast cars / No reply / You tear me up / Get on our own / Love battery / 16 / I don't mind / Fiction romance / Autonomy / I need / Moving away from the pulsebeat. *(re-iss. Aug85 on 'Liberty' lp/c; ATAK/TC-ATAK 51) (re-iss. Jun87 on 'Fan Club' blue-lp; FC 021) (re-iss. May88 on 'Fame' lp/c/cd; FA/TC-FA/CD-FA 3199) (re-iss. cd Jul88 on 'E.M.I.'; CDP 790299-2) (cd re-iss. Jul96; PRDFCD 3)*

Apr 78. (7") *(UP 36386)* **I DON'T MIND. / AUTONOMY** [55] [-]

Jul 78. (7") *(UP 36433)* **LOVE YOU MORE. / NOISE ANNOYS** [34] [ ]

Sep 78. (7") *(UP 36455)* **EVER FALLEN IN LOVE (WITH SOMEONE YOU SHOULDN'T'VE?). / JUST LUST** [12] [ ]

Sep 78. (lp/c) *(UAG/TCK 30197)* **LOVE BITES** [13] [ ]
– Real world / Ever fallen in love with someone you shouldn't've / Operator's manuel / Nostalgia / Just lust / Sixteen again / Walking distance / Love is lies / Nothing left / E.S.P. / Late for the train. *(re-iss. Mar87 on 'Fame' lp/c; FA/TC-FA 3174) (re-iss. Jun87 on 'Fan Club' blue-lp; FC 022) (cd-iss. Jul88 on 'Fame'; CD-FA 3174) (cd re-iss. Jul96; PRDFCD 4)*

Nov 78. (7") *(UP 36471)* **PROMISES. / LIPSTICK** [20] [ ]

Mar 79. (7") *(UP 36499)* **EVERYBODY'S HAPPY NOWADAYS. / WHY CAN'T I TOUCH IT?** [29] [ ]

Jul 79. (7") *(UP 36541)* **HARMONY IN MY HEAD. / SOMETHING'S GONE WRONG AGAIN** [32] [-]

Sep 79. (7") *(BP 316)* **YOU SAY YOU DON'T LOVE ME. / RAISON D'ETRE** [ ] [-]

Sep 79. (lp/c) *(UAG/TCK 30260)* <009> **A DIFFERENT KIND OF TENSION** [26] [ ]
– Paradise / Sitting round at home / You say you don't love me / You know you can't help it / Mad mad Judy / Raison d'etre / I don't know what to do with my life / Money / Hollow inside / A different kind of tension / I believe / Radio Nine. *(initial copies cont. previous 45) (re-iss. Jun87 on 'Fan Club' blue-lp; FC 023) (cd-iss. Jul88 on 'E.M.I.'; CZ 93)*

Oct 79. (7") **I BELIEVE. / SOMETHING'S GONE WRONG AGAIN** [-] [ ]

Nov 79. (lp/c) <010> **SINGLES – GOING STEADY** (compilation) [-] [ ]
– Orgasm addict / What do I get / I don't mind / Love you more / Ever fallen in love with someone you shouldn't've / Promises / Everybody's happy nowadays / Harmony in my head / Whatever happened to . . . ? / Oh shit! / Autonomy / Noise annoys / Just luck / Lipstick / Why can't I touch it / Something's gone wrong again. *(UK-iss.Nov81 on 'Liberty' lp/c; LBR/TC-LBR 1043) (re-iss. Aug85 lp/c; ATAK/TC-ATAK 52) (cd-iss. Jun87 + Jun88 on 'E.M.I.'; CDP 746449-2) (re-iss. Sep90 cd/c/lp; CD/TC+/FA 3241)*

Liberty | I.R.S.

Aug 80. (7") *(BP 365)* **WHY SHE'S A GIRL FROM THE CHAINSTORE. / ARE EVERYTHING** [61] [ ]

Oct 80. (7") *(BP 371)* **STRANGE THING. / AIRWAVES DREAM** [ ] [ ]

Nov 80. (7") *(BP 392)* **RUNNING FREE. / WHAT DO YOU KNOW** [ ] [ ]

— (split Feb81) **DIGGLE** went solo and formed FLAG OF CONVENIENCE, with MAHER

PETE SHELLEY

solo, augmented by **STEVE GARVEY** – bass / **JIM RUSSELL** – drums.

Genetic-Island | Arista

Aug 81. (7"/12") *(WIP/12WIP 6720)* **HOMOSAPIEN. / KEAT'S SONG** [ ] [ ]

Sep 81. (lp/c) *(ILPS/ICT 9676)* **HOMOSAPIEN** [ ] [ ] Jun82
– Homosapien / Yesterday's here / I generate a feeling / Keat's song / Qu'est-ce que c'est que ca / I don't know what it is / Guess I must have been in love with myself / Pusher man / Just one of those affairs / It's hard enough knowing. *(re-iss. cd Sep94 on 'Grapevine';)*

Nov 81. (d7"/12") *(U/12 WIP 6740)* **I DON'T KNOW WHAT IT IS. / WITNESS THE CHANGE/ / IN LOVE WITH SOMEBODY ELSE. / MAXINE** [ ] [ ]

Apr 82. (7"/12") *(WIP/12WIP 6720)* **HOMOSAPIEN. / LOVE IN VAIN** [ ] [ ]

— **BARRY ADAMSON** – bass (ex-MAGAZINE, ex-BIRTHDAY PARTY) repl. GARVEY / added **MARTIN RUSHENT** – keyboards, producer

Island | Arista

Feb 83. (7"/12") *(XX/+T 1)* **TELEPHONE OPERATOR. / MANY A TIME** [66] [ ]

Apr 83. (lp) *(XL 1)* **XL-1** [42] [ ] Jul83
– Telephone operator / If you ask me (I won't say no) / What was Heaven? / You better than I know / Twilight / (Millions of people) No one like you / Many a time / I just wanna touch / You and I / XL-1 *. (c+= dub tracks) (track* = only playable on ZX Spectrum computer) *(re-iss. cd Sep94 on 'Grapevine';)*

Immaculate | not iss.

Nov 84. (7") *(IMMAC 1)* **NEVER AGAIN. / ONE ONE ONE** [ ] [-]
(12"+=) *(12IMMAC 1)* – Give it to me.

— **SHELLEY** brought in new **JOHN DOYLE** – drums / **MARK SANDERSON** – bass / **NORMAN FISCHER-JONES** – guitar / **GERARD COOKSON** – keyboards / **JIM GARDNER** – synth.

Mercury | Mercury

Mar 86. (7"/12") *(MER/+X 215)* **WAITING FOR LOVE. / DESIGNER LAMPS** [ ] [ ]

May 86. (7"/12") *(MER/+X 221)* **ON YOUR OWN. / PLEASE FORGIVE ME . . . BUT I CANNOT ENDURE IT ANY LONGER** [ ] [ ]

Jun 86. (lp/c)(cd) *(MERH/+C 90)(830004-2)* **HEAVEN AND THE SEA** [ ] [ ]
– Never again / My dreams / Blue eyes / You can't take that away / No Moon . . . / Waiting for love / On your own / They're coming for you / I surrender / Life without reason / Need a minit.

Aug 86. (7"/12") *(MER/+X 225)* **BLUE EYES. / NELSON'S RIDDLE** [ ] [ ]

Nov 86. (7"/12") *(MER/+X 234)* **I SURRENDER. / I NEED A MINUTE** [ ] [ ]

— In 1988, **SHELLEY** formed **ZIP** with COOKSON and SANDERSON.

– his compilations, others, etc. –

Apr 80. (m-lp) *Groovy; (STP 2)* **SKY YEN** (rec.1974) [ ] [-]

Apr 89. (7"/12") *Immaculate; (IMMAC/12IMMAC 11)* **HOMOSAPIEN. PETE SHELLEY VS. POWER, WONDER AND LOVE / ('A'mix)** [ ] [-]
(3"cd-s+=) *(IMMACD 11)* – ('A'-Icon mix) / ('A'-shower mix).

STEVE DIGGLE

Liberty | not iss.

Feb 81. (7"m) *(BP 389)* **SHUT OUT THE LIGHTS. / 50 YEARS OF COMPARATIVE WEALTH / HERE COMES THE FIRE BRIGADE** [ ] [-]

FLAG OF CONVENIENCE

were formed by **DIGGLE, MAHER + DAVE FARROW** – bass / **D.P.** – keyboards

Sire | not iss.

Sep 82. (7") *(SIR 4057)* **LIFE ON THE TELEPHONE. / THE OTHER MAN'S SIN** [ ] [-]

— **DIGGLE, MAHER + GARY HAMER** – bass / **MARK** – keyboards

Weird Systems | not iss.

Dec 84. (7") **CHANGE. / LONGEST LIFE** [ ] [-]

— **JOHN CAINE** – drums repl. MAHER and MARK

M.C.M. | not iss.

Apr 86. (7") *(MCM 186)* **NEW HOUSE. / KEEP ON PUSHING** [ ] [-]

Flag of Convenience | not iss.

Apr 87. (12") *(FOC 1)* **LAST TRAIN TO SAFETY. / ?** [ ] [-]

M.C.M. | not iss.

Oct 87. (12"ep; as F.O.C.) *(MCM 001)* **SHOULD I EVER GO DEAF / PICTURES IN MY MIND. / THE GREATEST SIN / DROWNED IN YOUR HEARTACHES** [ ] [-]

Aug 88. (12"ep; as F.O.C.) *(MCM 002)* **EXILES / I CAN'T STOP THE WORLD. / SHOT DOWN WITH YOUR GUN / TRAGEDY IN MARKET SQUARE** [ ] [-]

BUZZCOCKS F.O.C.

— **DIGGLE, HAMMER + ANDY COUZENS** – guitar / **CHRIS GOODWIN** – drums

Thin Line | not iss.

Jul 89. (12"/cd-s) *(THIN 003/+CD)* **TOMORROW'S SUNSET. / LIFE WITH THE LIONS / ('A'version)** [ ] [-]

BUZZCOCKS

— re-formed in 1990 **SHELLEY, DIGGLE, GARVEY** and **MIKE JOYCE** – drums (ex-SMITHS) repl. ANDY and CHRIS who formed The HIGH

Planet Pacific | not iss.

Apr 91. (7"ep/12"ep/c-ep/cd-ep) **ALIVE TONIGHT** [ ] [-]
– Alive tonight / Successful street / Serious crime / Last to know.

— **JOHN MAHER** – drums returned to repl. MIKE who joined PIL.

— **TONY BARBER** – bass / **PHIL BARKER** – drums repl.GARVEY and MAHER

Essential | Caroline

May 93. (7") *(ESS 2025)* **INNOCENT. /** [ ] [-]
(12"+=/cd-s+=) *(ESS T/X 2025)* –

Jun 93. (cd/c/lp) *(ESM CD/MC/LP 389)* <1747> **TRADE TEST TRANSMISSION** [ ] [ ]
– Innocent / Smile / Palm of your hand / Last to know / Do it/ Who will help me to forget / Energy / Alive tonight / Inside / Isolation / Never gonna give it up / Crystal night / 369 / Chegga / It's unthinkable / Somewhere. *(reiss.cd Jul96; same)*

Aug 93. (12"/cd-s) **DO IT. / TRASH AWAY / ALL OVER YOU** [ ] [-]

Apr 94. (12"/cd-s) **LIBERTINE ANGEL. / ROLL IT OVER / EXCERPT FROM PRISON RIOT HOSTAGE** [ ] [-]

Dojo | I.R.S.

Nov 95. (cd) *(DOJOCD 237)* <36761> **FRENCH (live in Paris 12th April 1995)** [ ] [ ] Jan96
– I don't mind / Who'll help me to forget / Get on our own / Unthinkable / Strange thing / Energy / Breakdown / Innocent / Roll it over / Why she's a girl from the chainstore / Last to know? / Running free / Libertine angel / Why can't I touch it / Noise annoys / Isolation / Boredom / Do it / Harmony in my head / I believe.

		I.R.S.	I.R.S.
Apr 96.	(cd) *(EIRSCD 1078)* **ALL SET** – Totally from the heart / Without you / Give it to me / Your love / Point of no return / Hold me close / Kiss & tell / What am I supposed to do? / Some kind of wonderful / (What you) Mean to me / Playing for time / Pariah / Back with you.		

– compilations, others, etc. –

Apr 87.	(lp/c) *Weird Systems; (WS 021/+X1)* **TOTAL POP**		-
Jan 88.	(12"ep) *Strange Fruit; (SFPS 044)* **THE PEEL SESSIONS** (7.9.77) – Fast cars / What do I get / Moving away from the pulsebeat.		-
Oct 88.	(c) *R.O.I.R.; (A 158)* **LEST WE FORGET (live)** *(cd-iss. 1990;)*		-
Sep 89.	(lp/cd) *Absolutely Free; (FREE LP/CD 002)* **LIVE AT THE ROXY CLUB, 2 APRIL 1977 (live)** – (cd= 1 extra track) *(re-iss. Jul90 on 'Receiver'; RR CD/LC/LP 131)*		-
Oct 89.	(7"ep/12"ep/cd-ep) *E.M.I.; (EM/12EM/CDEM 104)* **THE FAB FOUR** – Ever fallen in love with someone you shouldn't've / Promises / Everybody's happy nowadays / Harmony in my head.		-
Nov 89.	(4xlp/2xd-c/2xd-cd) *E.M.I.; (LP/TC/CD PROD 1)* **PRODUCT** – (cont. first 3 albums + 1 live and rare) *(re-iss. May95 cd; PRODUCT 1)*		-
Feb 90.	(cd/lp) *Strange Fruit; (SFR CD/LP 104)* **THE PEEL SESSIONS ALBUM**		-
Sep 91.	(cd/c/d-lp) *E.M.I.; (CD/TC+/EM 1421)* **OPERATOR'S MANUEL**		-
May 92.	(cd) *EMI Gold; (CDGOLD 1029)* **ENTERTAINING FRIENDS LIVE (live)**		-
Oct 92.	(cd-s) *Old Gold; (OG 6182)* **EVER FALLEN IN LOVE WITH SOMEONE . . . / WHAT DO I GET / PROMISES**		-
Feb 94.	(cd; STEVE DIGGLE & THE FLAG OF CONVENIENCE) *Anagram; (CDMGRAM 74)* **THE BEST OF . . . THE SECRET PUBLIC YEARS 1981-1989**		-
Apr 94.	(cd) *E.M.I.; (CDPRDT 12)* **ANOTHER MUSIC IN A DIFFERENT KITCHEN / LOVE BITES**		-
1995.	(7") *One Stop Music; (ONE 7001)* **NOISE ANNOYS. / ISOLATION (live)**		-
Jul 95.	(cd) *Dojo; (DLP 2)* **TIME'S UP**		-
Nov 95.	(cd-s) *Old Gold; (12623 6332-2)* **EVER FALLEN IN LOVE WITH SOMEONE YOU SHOULDN'T HAVE FALLEN IN LOVE WITH / PROMISES**		-

STEVE DIGGLE & THE FLAG OF CONVENIENCE

		3:30	not iss.
Nov 93.	(cd-ep) *(330001)* **HEATED AND RISING / OVER AND OUT / TERMINAL / WEDNESDAYS FLOWERS**		-
		Ax-s	not iss.
Oct 95.	(cd) *(AXSO 2CD)* **HERE'S ONE I MADE EARLIER**		-

David BYRNE (see under ⇒ TALKING HEADS)

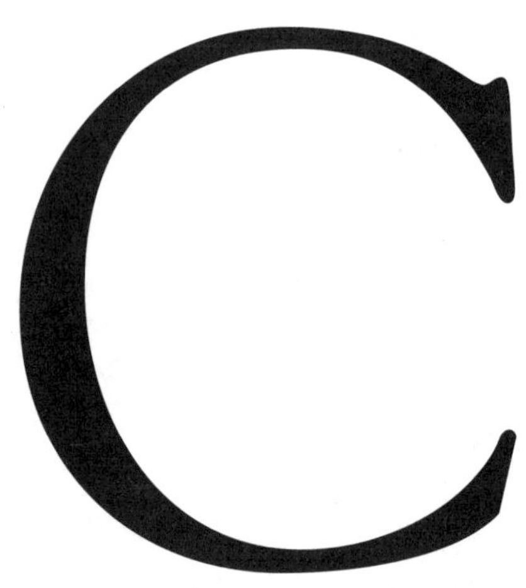

CABARET VOLTAIRE

Formed: Sheffield, England ... 1973 by STEPHEN MALLINDER, RICHARD H. KIRK and CHRIS WATSON, naming themselves after the experimental Parisian Dadaist performances of pre-20's France. A farcical 1975 debut gig saw them using a backing tape of a steamhammer while KIRK played clarinet; his jacket was also covered in fairy lights (!), the whole set up not going down with a rioting audience who proceeded to beat him up! Inspired by the likes of CAN and BRIAN ENO, the CABS contributed two songs (one of them, 'BAADER MEINHOF', was nearly chosen as a debut 45!) to a 1978 various artists double EP, 'A FACTORY SAMPLER', before they signed to Geoff Travis's new independent operation, 'Rough Trade'. Later that year, the trio issued their debut release, 'EXTENDED PLAY', a four track EP that included their industrial mangling of The Velvet Underground's 'HERE SHE COMES NOW'. A classic follow-up, 'NAG NAG NAG', fused electronic sound with the yobbish rush of adrenaline fuelled punk to devastating effect. 1979 also saw the release of their debut long-player, 'MIX-UP', a pivotal experimental affair which, although marking out new territory, was a challenging listen end to end. The early years of the following decade found CABARET VOLTAIRE ploughing their own idiosyncratic furrow over the course of three studio albums (two live events were also issued), namely 'THE VOICE OF AMERICA' (1980), 'RED MECCA' (1981) and '2 X 45' (1982), before WATSON's departure left MALLINDER and KIRK as a duo. In 1983, they were sought out by Virgin off-shoot, 'Some Bizzare', their avant-garde inaccessibility now taking on a more commercial hue with 'THE CRACKDOWN', an album which nearly took them into the UK Top 30. Incorporating elements of Eastern exotica, the record was also more dancefloor friendly than anything they had recorded to date; tracks such as 'JUST FASCINATION', '24-24', 'ANIMATION' and 'WHY KILL TIME (WHEN YOU CAN KILL YOUSELF)', were lent the rhythmic expertise of SOFT CELL's DAVE BALL (later of The GRID). Ironically, the more overtly pop approach of SOFT CELL and their ilk (DEPECHE MODE, HUMAN LEAGUE and OMD) led to the more adventurous CABS being squeezed out the market. They did, however, maintain a loyal if not massive following who stuck by them through a series of lesser mid-80's albums, 'MICRO-PHONIES' (1984), 'THE COVENANT, THE SWORD AND THE ARM OF THE LORD' (1985) and 'CODE' (1987), the latter set their first for 'Parlophone'. Since 1983, both MALLINDER and KIRK had moonlighted in various side projects, the former releasing a solo album, 'POW-WOW', the latter far more prolific in his output with 'BLACK JESUS VOICE' (1986) the pick of the bunch. The late 80's house scene, meanwhile, saw CABARET VOLTAIRE cited as a prominent influence on many of the genre's prime movers; the result was a creative renaissance of sorts which led to a remix by PETE WATERMAN (!) for the 'KEEP ON' single, while house producer, MARSHALL JEFFERSON, took controls on the comeback set, 'GROOVY, LAID BACK AND NASTY' (1990). Despite this uncharacteristic dalliance with the mainstream, the CABS slipped back into semi-obscurity with their former Belgian label, 'Les Disques Du Crepescule' and releasing a handful of low profile sets, 'BODY AND SOUL' (1991), 'PERCUSSION FORCE' (1991), 'INTERNATIONAL LANGUAGE' (1993) and 'THE CONVERSATION' (1994).

Album rating: MIX-UP (*5) / THE VOICE OF AMERICA (*4) / RED MECCA (*7) / 2x45 (*7) / JOHNNY YES NO soundtrack (*3) / THE CRACKDOWN (*8) / MICRO-PHONIES (*6) / DRINKING GASOLINE (*6) / THE COVENANT, THE SWORD & THE ARM (*6) / CODE (*7) / GROOVY, LAIDBACK & NASTY (*6) / THE LIVING LEGENDS compilation (*9) / THE GOLDEN MOMENTS OF CABARET VOLTAIRE compilation (*7) / LISTEN UP WITH CABARET VOLTAIRE compilation (*7) / COLOURS (*5) / PLASTICITY (*5) / Stephen Mallinder: POW WOW (*5) / Richard H.Kirk: BLACK JESUS VOICE (*5)

STEPHEN MALLINDER – vocals, bass, electronics, percussion, trumpet, piano / **RICHARD H. KIRK** – guitar, vocals, synthesizer, bongos, piano / **CHRISTOPHER R. WATSON** – electronics, tapes

(issued cassette 25 copies LIMITED EDITION in 1976 on own label)

Rough Trade | not iss.

Nov 78. (7"ep) *(RT 003)* **EXTENDED PLAY** [ ] [-]
– Talkover / Here she comes now / Do the Mussolini – headkick / The set up.

Jun 79. (7") *(RT 018)* **"NAG NAG NAG." / IS THAT ME (FINDING SOMEONE AT THE DOOR AGAIN)?** [ ] [-]

Oct 79. (lp) *(ROUGH 4)* **MIX-UP** [ ] [-]
– Kurlian photograph / No escape / 4th shot / Heaven and Hell / Eyeless sight (live) / Photophobia / On every other street / Expect nothing / Capsules. *(re-iss. Sep90 on 'Mute' lp/cd; CABS 8/+CD)*

Dec 79. (7") *(RT 035)* **SILENT COMMAND. / The Soundtrack 'CHANCE VERSUS CAUSALITY'** [ ] [-]

— added guest **MARK TATTERSALL** – drums

Jan 80. (lp) *(ROUGH 7)* **LIVE AT THE Y.M.C.A. 27.10.79 (live)** [ ] [-]
– Untitled / On every other street / Nag nag nag / The set up / Havoc / Expect nothing / Here she comes now / No escape / Baader Meinhof. *(re-iss. Jun90 on 'Mute' lp/cd; CABS 4/+CD)*

— now with guests **JOHN CLAYTON** – percussion / **JANE** – tapes

Mar 80. (12"ep) *(RT 038)* **THREE MANTRAS** [ ] [-]
– Eastern mantra / Western mantra. *(re-iss. Jun90 on 'Mute' m-lp/cd; CABS 7/+CD)*

— with guest **HAYDN BOYES-WESTON** – drums (ex-2.3) (also on debut lp)

Jul 80. (lp) *(ROUGH 11)* **THE VOICE OF AMERICA** [ ] [-]
– The voice of America / Damage is done / Partially submerged / Kneel to the boss / Premonition / This is entertainment / If the shadows could march? / Stay out of it / Obsession / News from nowhere / Messages received. *(re-iss. Jun90 on 'Mute' lp/cd; CABS 2/+CD)*

Nov 80. (7") *(RT 060)* **SECONDS TOO LATE. / CONTROL ADDICT** [ ] [-]

Jul 81. (12"ep) *(TWI 018)* **3 CREPUSCULE TRACKS** [-] [-] Belg.
– Sluggin' fer Jesus (Pt.1) / Your agent man / Sluggin' fer Jesus (Pt.2).
(above released on 'Crepuscule')

— **NICK ALLDAY** – drums (ex-GRAPH) repl. HAYDN

Aug 81. (lp) *(ROUGH 27)* **RED MECCA** [ ] [-]
– Touch of evil / Sly doubt / Landslide / A thousand ways / Red mask / Split second feling / Black mask / Spread the virus / A touch of evil (reprise). *(re-iss. Jun90 on 'Mute' lp/cd; CABS 3/+CD)*

Sep 81. (lp) *(COPY 002)* **LIVE AT THE LYCEUM (live)** [ ] [-]
– Taxi music / Seconds too late / Your agent man / Split second feeling / Sluggin' fer Jesus (Pt.1) / Kneel to the bass / Obsession / A thousand ways. *(re-iss. Sep90 on 'Mute' lp/cd; CABS 13/+CD)*

Nov 81. (7") *(RT 095)* **JAZZ THE GLASS. / BURNT TO THE GROUND** [ ] [-]

Dec 81. (12") *(RT 096)* **EDDIE'S OUT. / WALLS OF JERICHO** [ ] [-]
(limited copies contained last 7" free) (below on 'Solidarity')

Mar 82. (12"ep; by PRESSURE COMPANY) *(SOLID 1)* **LIVE IN SHEFFIELD 19th JANUARY 1982 (live)** [ ] [-]
– War of nerves / Wait & shuffle / Get out of my face / Vitrions China (paradox).

— **ALAN FISH** – drums, percussion (of HULA) repl. **ALLDAY /** guest **ERIC RANDOM** – guitar (also a solo artist)

Jun 82. (2x12"lp) *(ROUGH 42)* **2 x 45** [98] [-]
– Breathe deep / Yashar / Protection / War of nerves (T.E.S.) / Wait and shuffle / Get out of my face. *(re-iss. Sep90 on 'Mute' lp/cd; CABS 9/+CD)*

Nov 82. (lp) *(RTD 1)* **HAI! (live)** [-] [-] German
– Walls of Kyoto / 3 days monk / Yashar (version) / Over and over / Diskono / Taxi music (version). *(re-iss. Sep90 on 'Mute' lp/cd; CABS 11/+CD)*

— trimmed to a duo (**MALLINDER + KIRK**) when WATSON departed. Retained **ALAN FISH** and brought in **DAVE BALL** – keyboards (of SOFT CELL)

Feb 83. (12") *(TWI 020)* **FOOLS GAME (SLUGGIN' FER JESUS Pt.3). / GUT LEVEL** [-] [-] Belg.
(above released on 'Crepuscule')

Some Bizzare – Virgin | Virgin

Jul 83. (7") *(CVS 1)* **JUST FASCINATION. / EMPTY WALLS** [ ] [-]
(12") *(CVS 1-12)* – ('A'side) / The crackdown.

Aug 83. (lp/c) *(CV/TCV 1)* **THE CRACKDOWN** [31] [ ]
– 24-24 / In the shadows / Talking time / Animation / Over and over / Just fascination / Why kill time (when you can kill yourself) / Haiti / Crackdown. *(free 12"w/ above + on c+cd)* – MOSCOW / BADGE OF EVIL. / DISKONO / DOUBLE VISION *(cd-iss. 1984; CDCV 1) (re-iss. Aug86 lp/c; OVED/+C 156)*

Nov 83. (lp) *(DVR 1)* **JOHNNY YESNO** (1982 video) [ ] [-]
– Taxi music / Hallucination sequence / DT's / Cold turkey / The quarry (in the wilderness) / Title sequence / Taxi music dub. *(re-iss. Sep90 on 'Mute' lp/cd; CABS 10/+CD)*
(above released on 'DoubleVision')

Dec 83. (7"/ext.12") *(CVS 2/+12)* **THE DREAM TICKET. / SAFETY ZONE** [ ] [ ]

Sep 84. (7"/ext.12") *(CVS 3/+12)* **SENSORIA. / CUT THE DAMN CAMERA** [ ] [ ]

Nov 84. (lp/c/cd) *(CV/TCV/CVCD 2)* **MICRO-PHONIES** [69] [ ]
– Do right / The operative / Digital rasta / Spies in the wires / Theme from Earthshaker / James Brown / Slammer / Blue heat / Sensoria. *(cd+=)* – Blue heat (extended) / Sensoria (extended). *(re-iss. Sep91 on 'Virgin'; cd/c; same)*

Jan 85. (7"/12") *(CVS 4/+12)* **JAMES BROWN. / BAD SELF (part 1)** [ ] [ ]

Jun 85. (2x12"/c) *(CVM/TCVM 1)* **DRINKING GASOLINE** [71] [ ]
– Kino / Sleepwalking / Big funk / Ghost talk. *(re-iss. Sep91 on 'Virgin'; same)*

Sep 85. (7") *(CVS 5)* **I WANT YOU. / DRINK YOUR POISON** [ ] [ ]
(12") *(CVS 5-12)* – ('A'side) / Drink your poison, C.O.M.A.

Oct 85. (lp/c/cd) *(CV/TCV/CDCV 3)* **THE COVENANT, THE SWORD AND THE ARM OF THE LORD** [57] [ ]
– L21st / I want you / Hell's home / Kickback / The arm of the Lord / Warm / Golden halos / Motion rotation / Whip blow / The web. *(cd+=)* – Sleepwalking / Big funk *(re-iss. Sep91 on 'Virgin'; same)*

— guest **DEE BOYLE** – drums (of CHAAK) repl. FISH

DoubleVision | not iss.

Jun 86. (12"ep) *(DVR-DVRP 21)* **THE DRAIN TRAIN** [ ] [-]
– Shakedown (the whole thing) / Menace / Electro-motive.
(w/ free-12") – SHAKEDOWN (The Whole Thing). / SHAKEDOWN (dub).

Parlophone | Capitol

Jul 87. (7") *(R 6157)* **DON'T ARGUE. / DON'T ARGUE (WHO'S ARGUING)** [69] [-]
(12") *(12R 6157)* – ('A'extended) / ('A'-Hate & Destroy mix).

(12") *(12RX 6157)* – ('A'dance mix) / ('A'dub).
Sep 87. (7") *(R 6166)* **HERE TO GO. / HERE TO GO (dub)**
(12") *(12R 6166)* – ('A'extended mix) / ('A'-Space dub mix).
(12") *(12RX 6166)* – ('A'-Linn drum mix) / ('A'-Eleven Eleven mix).
Oct 87. (lp/c/cd) *(PCS/TCPCS/CDPCS 7312)* **CODE**
– Don't argue / Sex, money, freaks / Thank you America / Here to go / Trouble (won't stop) / White car / No one here / Life slips by / Code. (cd+=) – Here to go (little dub) / Hey hey.
Oct 89. (7") *(RS 6227)* **HYPNOTISED (Daniel Miller mix). / ('A'-Gerald's vocal mix)** 66
(12") *(12RS 6227)* – ('A'-Fon Force mix) / ('A'-Fon Force dub) / ('A'-Daniel Miller dub mix) / ('A'-Robert Gordon mix).
(cd-s) *(CDCDR 6227)* – ('A'-Fon Force mix) / ('A'-Gerald's vocal mix).
(12") *(12RX 6227)* – (cd tracks) / ('A'-A Guy Called Gerald's music mix) / ('A'-Western Works mix).
Mar 90. (7") *(R 6250)* **KEEP ON. / KEEP ON (Les dub)** 55
(12") *(12R 6250)* – ('A'-Sweet Exorcist mix) / ('A'-Sleazy Dog mix) / ('A'-Mayday mix).
(cd-s) – ('A'-western works mix) / ('A'club mix).
Jun 90. (cd/c/lp) *(CD/TC+/PCS 7338)* **GROOVY, LAIDBACK AND NASTY**
– Searchin' / Hypnotised / Minute by minute / Runaway / Keep on (I got this feeling) / Magic / Time beats / Easy life. *(free 12"ep w/ above)* **GROOVY, LAIDBACK AND NASTY** (remixes) – Runaway / Magic / Searchin' / Rescue me (city lights) * / Easy life. *(cd+= *)*
Jul 90. (7") *(R 6261)* **EASY LIFE. / ('A'-Robert Gordon mix)** 61
(12") *(12R 6261)* – ('A'side) / Fluid / Positive I.D.
(cd-s) *(CDR 6261)* – ('A'side) / ('A'-Jive Turkey mix) / Fluid.
(12") *(12RX 6261)* – ('A'vocal) / ('A'-Strange mix) / ('A'-Very strange mixes by Robert Gordon and Fon Force).

Crepescule — not iss.

Feb 91. (12") *(TWI 948)* **WHAT IS REAL. / ('A'-Virtual reality mix)** -
(cd-s+=) *(TWI 948-2)* – Legacy of a computer.
Mar 91. (lp/cd) *(TWI 944/+2)* **BODY AND SOUL** -
– No resistance / Shout / Happy / Decoy / Bad chemistry / Vibration / What is real / Western land. *(cd+=)* – What is real (dreamtime mix).
Jul 91. (m-lp/cd) *(TWI 951/+2)* **PERCUSSION FORCE** -
– Don't walk away / Keep on pushin' / Don't walk away (Robert Gordon mix) / Dynamic zone / Jazz the computer (part 1) / Keep on pushin' (version). *(cd+=)* – T.Phunk / Don't walk away (version) / Jazz the computer part 2.

Plastex — Instinct

Oct 91. (m-lp) *(EXL 001)* <93> **COLOURS**
Oct 92. (d-lp/c/cd) *(EXL/+C/CD 003)* <255> **PLASTICITY**
– Low cool / Soul vine (70 billion people) / Resonator /Inside the electronic revolution / From another source / Deep time / Back to Brazilia / Neuron factory / Delmas 19 / Cooled out / Invisible generation / Soulenoid (scream at the right time).
Jun 93. (cd) <264> **INTERNATIONAL LANGUAGE** -
– Everything is true / Radical chic / Taxi mutant / Let it come down / Afterglow / The rest / Millenium / Belly of the beast (back in Babylon) / Other world.

Apollo-R&S — Instinct

Jul 94. (q-lp/d-cd) *(AMB 4934/+CD)* <273> **THE CONVERSATION**
– Exterminating angel (intro) / Brutal but clean / The message / Let's start / Night rider / Night rider / I think / The heat / Harmonic parallel / Project 80 (parts 1-4) / Exterminating angel (outro).

– compilations, others, etc. –

1981. (c) *Industrial; (IRC 35)* **74-76** -
(cd-iss. Jun92 on 'Grey Area-Mute'; CABS 15CD)
Feb 88. (lp/cd) *Crepuscule; (TWI 749/+2)* **8 CREPESCULE TRACKS** - - Belgium
Jul 83. (12") *Factory Benelux; (FBN 25)* **YASHAR (5.00). / YASHAR (7.20)** - - Belgium
Nov 87. (cd) *Rough Trade; (RUFCD 6001)* **THE GOLDEN MOMENTS OF CABARET VOLTAIRE** -
– Do the Mussolini (Head Kick) / Nag nag nag / Photophobia / Expect nothing / Seconds Too late / This is entertainment / Obsession / Sluggin for Jesus / Landslide / Red mask / Get out of my face.
— (below releases on 'Mute' unless otherwise mentioned)
May 90. (cd-ep) *(CABS 1CD)* **"NAG NAG NAG." / YASHAR / YASHAR (John Robie remixes)** -
Jun 90. (lp/c/cd) *(CABS 5/+C/CD)* **LISTEN UP WITH CABARET VOLTAIRE** (rare demos) -
Jun 90. (d-lp/c/cd) *(CABS 6/+C/CD)* **THE LIVING LEGENDS . . . CABARET VOLTAIRE** (the singles)
– Do the Mussolini (head kick) / Talk over / Here she comes now / The set up / Nag, nag, nag / Silent command / Jazz the glass / Walls of Jericho / Seconds too late / Eddie's out / Burnt to the ground / Extract from : Chance Verses Casuality / Control addict / Is that me (finding someone at the door again).
Jun 90. (c) *(CABS 2C)* **LIVE AT THE LYCEUM / THE VOICE OF AMERICA** -
Jun 90. (c) *(CABS 7C)* **THE DRAIN TRAIN / THREE MANTRAS** -
Jun 90. (c) *(CABS 8C)* **MIX-UP / LIVE AT THE Y.M.C.A.** -
Jun 90. (c) *(CABS 10C)* **2 x 45 / JOHNNY YESNO** -
Jun 90. (c) *(CABS 11C)* **HAI! / RED MECCA** -
Apr 92. (12"/cd-s) *Virgin;* **I WANT YOU. / KINO** -
– (Altern 8 remixes / Western re-works '92)
May 92. (d-lp/cd)(c) *Virgin; (CV/+CD 4)(TCV 4)* **TECHNOLOGY** (remixes late 70's & early 80's) -

STEPHEN MALLINDER

Fetish — not iss.

Nov 81. (12") *(FE 12)* **TEMPERATURE DROP. / COOL DOWN** -
(above with DAVE BALL and ROBERT GORDON)
Jan 83. (m-lp) *(FM 2010)* **POW-WOW** -
– Temperature Drop / The Devil In Me / 0.58 / Pow Wow / Three Piece Swing / Cool Down / 1.37 / In Smoke / 1.59 / Length Of Time / Going Out / Del Sol *(re-iss. Oct85 as 'POW-WOW PLUS' on 'DoubleVision'; DVR 16) (cd-iss. Jun92 on 'Grey Area-Mute'; MAL 1CD)*

Parlophone — not iss.

Jun 88. (7"/12"; as LOVE STREET) *(R/12R 6183)* **GALAXY. / COME ON DOWN TO LOVE STREET** -
— LOVE STREET also included **DAVE BALL + RUTH JOY** (of SOFT CELL)

RICHARD H. KIRK

Industrial — not iss.

1981. (c) *(IRC 34)* **DISPOSABLE HALF-TRUTHS** -
– Synesthesia / Outburst / Information therapy / Magic words command / Thermal damage / Plate glass replicas / Insect friends of Allah / Scatalist / False erotic love / L.D. 50 / L.D. 60 / Amnesic disassociation. *(cd-iss. Jun92 on 'Grey Area-Mute'; KIRK 1CD)*

DoubleVision — not iss.

Dec 83. (d-lp) *(DVR 2)* **TIME HIGH FICTION** -
(d-cd-iss. Oct94 on 'Grey Area-Mute'; KIRK 2CD)
Oct 85. (12"; by PETER HOPE & RICHARD H. KIRK) *(DVR 15)* **LEATHER HANDS (master mix). / ('A'radio mix) / ('A'crash mic)** -
(above featured PETER HOPE of The BOX)

Rough Trade — not iss.

Aug 86. (12") *(RTT 199)* **HIPNOTIC. / MARTYRS OF PALESTINE** -
Sep 86. (lp) *(ROUGH 99)* **BLACK JESUS VOICE** -
– Street gang / Hipnotic / Shala / Black Jesus voice / Martyrs of Palestine / This is the H-bomb sound / Short wave. *(cd-iss. Mar95 on 'Grey Area-Mute'; KIEK 3CD)*
Oct 86. (m-lp) *(RTM 189)* **UGLY SPIRIT** -
– The emperor / Confession / Infantile / Frantic machine (part 1 & 2) / Hollywood Babylon / Thai voodoo. *(cassette re-iss. Nov86 of all Sep86 releases) (cd-iss. Mar95 on 'Grey Area-Mute'; KIRK 4CD)*

Native — not iss.

Nov 87. (lp/cd; by RICHARD H. KIRK & PETER HOPE) *(NTV LP/CD 28)* **HOODOO TALK** -
– Intro / Numb skull / N.O. / Cop out / Surgeons / 50 tears / Leather hands / 50 tears (reprise).
Nov 88. (12"ep; by PETER HOPE & RICHARD H. KIRK) *(NTV 36)* **SURGEONS / BEATS. / RESURGENCY / N.O.** -
— SWEET EXORCIST were RICHARD H. KIRK & DJ BARRETT

Warp — not iss.

Feb 90. (12"ep; as SWEET EXORCIST) *(WAP 3)* **TEST ONE** -
– Test 1 / Test 2 / Test 3.
(12"ep+=) *(WAP 3R)* **TEST FOUR** – Test 4 / Test 5 / Test 6.
Dec 90. (12"ep; as SWEET EXORCIST) *(WAP 9)* **CLONK** -
– Clonk / Clonk (Hombase mix) / Clonk (Freebase mix).
(12"ep+=) *(WAP 9R)* **CLONK REMIX** – Per Clonk / Samba / Bonus Samba.
Jan 91. (cd/lp; as SWEET EXORCIST) *(WARP CD/LP 1)* **CLONK'S COMING** -
– Mad Jack / Track Jack / Jack Jack / Trick Jack / Kick Jack / Psych Jack / Clonk's coming. *(cd re-iss. Apr96; same)*

Plastex — not iss.

1991. (12"ep; as SWEET EXORCIST) *(EXL 002)* **POPCONE** -

Network — not iss.

Jan 91. (7"ep; as XON) *(NWKT 17)* **THE MOOD SET** -
— (XON = RICHARD H. KIRK with ROBERT GORDON)

Warp — not iss.

Jan 94. (cd/c/lp) *(WARP CD/MC/LP 19)* **VIRTUAL STATE** -
– November x-ray Mexico / Frequency band / Come / Freezone / Clandestine transmission / The feeling (of warmth and beauty) / Velodrome / Soul catcher / World War Three / Lagoon west.

Sub-Level-Touch — not iss.

Jul 94. (cd/d-lp; as SWEET EXORCIST) *(STO 33.13 CD/LP)* **SPIRIT GUIDE TO LOW TECH** -
– Part of the scene / African / Feel your hands / Nice / We are about to funk / Acid / wing / Jazz / What it is / Scat / Ghettos of the mind.

Beyond — not iss.

Sep 94. (d-cd/q-lp-box) *(RBAD CD/LP 8)* **ELECTRONIC EYE** -

Warp — not iss.

Jul 95. (cd/c/lp) *(WARP CD/MC/LP 32)* **THE NUMBER OF MAGIC** -
– Lost souls on funk / Love is deep / So digital / Indole ring / East of Nina / Atomic / Poets saints revolutionaries / Monochrome dream / The number of magic.

CABLE

Formed: Derby, England . . . 1994 by art-school lads, MATT BAGGULEY, DARIUS HINKS, PETER DARRINGTON and NEIL COOPER. After honing their skills at small venues around the nearby Nottingham locale, they released a couple of early limited edition 7"ers for 'Krunch!', namely 'SALE OF THE CENTURY' and 'OUBLIETTE'. Taking their wired, dischordant indie-rock down south to the capital, CABLE were picked up by 'Infectious', who almost immediately delivered their first widely distributed effort, 'BLINDMAN'. With former MEMBRANES man JOHN ROBB at the production helm, they powered their way into '96 with the release of 'SEVENTY', their fourth single and a highlight of the accompanying debut mini-set, 'DOWN-LIFT THE UP-TRODDEN'. Despite being packaged in BLUESBREAKERS pastiche artwork with sleevenotes depicting the band as modern day blues saviours, the actual sound was closer to a relentless, hard-driving PAVEMENT. Over the course of the next year (by which time COOPER had been replaced by RICHIE MILLS – apparently recruited from an Exchange & Mart ad!), they laid the ground work for their first long-player, 'WHEN ANIMALS ATTACK' (1997), with two singles, 'WHISPER FIRING LINE' and 'BLUEBIRDS ARE BLUE'. The album also installed CABLE in the UK Top 50 for the first time via the single, 'FREEZE THE ATLANTIC', although a further track, 'GOD GAVE ME GRAVITY', failed to spark the same interest. After an electrifying EP, 'LIVE AT THE BRIXTON PRISON', in the tradition of JOHNNY CASH (whose 'RING OF FIRE' they actually covered), CABLE began working with ex-BUGGLES, YES & ASIA man, GEOFF DOWNES. Although a one-one single, 'ARTHUR WALKER', appeared in 1998, fans are currently awaiting new material.

Album rating: DOWN-LIFT THE UP-TRODDEN (*6) / WHEN ANIMALS ATTACK (*6)

MATT BAGGULEY – vocals, guitar / **DARIUS HINKS** – guitar / **PETE DARRINGTON** – bass / **NEIL COOPER** – drums

Krunch! | not iss.

Jan 95. (ltd-7") *(KRUNCH 2)* **SALE OF THE CENTURY. / HYDRA** [ ] [-]
Jun 95. (ltd-7") *(KRUNCH 3)* **OUBLIETTE. /** [ ] [-]

Infectious | not iss.

Sep 95. (7") *(INFECT 25S)* **BLINDMAN. /** [ ] [-]
(cd-s+=) *(INFECT 25CD)* –
Feb 96. (7") *(INFECT 29W)* **SEVENTY. / SPORTS CARS AND DEVIL WORSHIP** [ ] [-]
(cd-s+=) *(INFECT 29CD)* – Dead wood for green.
Mar 96. (m-cd/m-lp) *(INFECT 32 CD/LP)* **DOWN-LIFT THE UP-TRODDEN** [ ] [-]
– New set of bruises / Choice / Blindman / Hydra / Seventy / Murdering spree / Sale of the century / Oubliette.

—— (after above recording) **RICHIE MILLS** – drums; repl. NEIL

Sep 96. (7") *(INFECT 33S)* **WHISPER FIRING LINE. / MURDERING SPREE ELEVATED** [ ] [-]
(cd-s+=) *(INFECT 33CD)* – Can't find my way home.
Apr 97. (7") *(INFECT 36S)* **BLUEBIRDS ARE BLUE. / HORSE DRAWN AND QUARTERED** [ ] [-]
(cd-s+=) *(INFECT 36CD)* – Action replay replay / Clairvoyant.
May 97. (cd/lp) *(INFECT 35 CD/LP)* **WHEN ANIMALS ATTACK** [ ] [-]
– Souvenir / Bluebirds are blue / Signature tune / Freeze the Atlantic / Ultra violet / I'm always right / Colder climate / Whisper firing line / God gave me gravity / From here you can see yourself / Do the tube.
Jun 97. (7") *(INFECT 38S)* **FREEZE THE ATLANTIC. / (WE DID THE MUSIC FOR THE SPRITE AD) BLUES** [44] [-]
(7") *(INFECT 38SX)* – ('A'side) / Ring of fire.
(cd-s) *(INFECT 38CD)* – (all 3 tracks).
Aug 97. (7"m) *(INFECT 45S)* **GOD GAVE ME GRAVITY. / DINKEY / ELECTRO GAZELLE** [ ] [-]
(cd-s+=) *(INFECT 45CD)* – Let's merengue.
Sep 97. (cd-ep) *(INFECT 48CD)* **LIVE AT THE BRIXTON PRISON EP** [ ] [-]
– Ultraviolet / Bluebirds are blue / Ring of fire / Seventy / San Quentin / Oubilette.
Oct 98. (7") *(INFECT 066S)* **ARTHUR WALKER. / VERTIGO** [ ] [-]
(cd-s) *(INFECT 066CDS)* – ('A'side) / Tick tock alarm clock / ('A'-CD-rom video).

CAGNEY & LACEE (see under ⇒ GALAXIE 500)

CAIFANES

Formed: Mexico City, Mexico ... 1986 by SAUL HERNANDEZ, ALEJANDRO MARCOVICH and ALFONSO ANDRE. Influenced by alternative English bands like The CURE and DEPECHE MODE, the CAIFANES added their own sinsiter, ritualistic Latin twist to the genre with 1989's eponymous debut album. Released in the US and Latin America on 'R.C.A.', the record's sales were boosted courtesy of a minor Stateside hit in the cumbia-derived 'LA NEGRA TOMASA'. While the band's lyrics dealt with life's more morbid side, the band were often inaccurately bracketed with the satanic metal movement, a cursory listen to the dark synth-pop/rhythmic exotica combination of 1990's 'EL DIABLITO' dispelling any such charge. Third album, 'EL SILENCIO' (1992), meanwhile, was produced by noted producer ADRIAN BELEW, another compulsive musical hybrid that explored religious, political and spiritual themes. With the belated 90's launch of MTV Latino, the CAIFANES became regular fixtures on screens across South and Central America, confirming their position as alternative Spanish language figureheads with 1994's acclaimed 'MATENME PORQUE DE MUERO'.

Album rating: CAIFANES (*6) / EL DIABLITO (*6) / EL SILENCIO (*6) / MATENME PORQUE DE MUERO (*5)

SAUL HERNANDEZ – vocals / **ALEJANDRO MARCOVICH** – guitar / **ALFONSO ANDRE** – drums / **DIEGO HERRERA** – keyboards, saxophone / **DANIEL FRIEBERG** – synthesizer

not iss. | R.C.A.

1989. (lp/c) *<8548-1/-4>* **CAIFANES** [-] [ ]
– Fuera / Miedo / Aqui no es asi / Ayer me dijo ave / Hasta que dejes de respirar / Avientame / Animal / Quisiera ser alcohol / Pero nunca me cai / Ano del dragon / Lloroma. *<re-iss. 1994 as 'EL NERVIO DEL VOLCAN'; 3381-2>*
1990. (cd/c) *<2218-2/-4>* **EL DIABLITO** [-] [ ]
– Detras de ti / Antes de que nos Olviden / Vida no es eterna / De noche to Dos los Gatos son pardos / Sombras en tiempos perdidos / El negro cosmico / Celula que wxplota / Aqui no pasa nada / Los dioses ocultos / El elefante / Amarrate a una escoba y vuela lijos.

—— **SABO ROMO** – guitar, bass; repl. FREIBERG

Jul 92. (cd/c) *<3381-2/-4>* **EL SILENCIO** [-] [ ]
– Metamorfeame / Nubes / iedra / Tirtuga / Nos vamos juntos / No dejes que . . . / Hasta morir / Debajo de tu piel / Estas dormida / Miercoles de ceniza / El comunicador / Para que no digas que no pienso en ti / Vamos a hacer un silencio / Mariquita.
Feb 94. (cd/c) *<10594-2/-4>* **MATENME PORQUE ME MUERO** [-] [ ]
– Matenme porque me muero / Te estoy mirando / Ni gra tomasa / Cuentame ti vida / Sera por eso? / Viento / Nunca me voy a transformar en ti / perdi mi ojo de venado / Amanece / Bestia humana / Nada.

—— must have disbanded as nothing has been heard from them since

– compilations, etc. –

Jul 97. (d-cd/d-c) *RCA International; <50111-2/-4>* **HISTORIA** [-] [ ]

CAKE

Formed: Sacramento, California, USA . . . 1994 by JOHN McCREA, GREG BROWN, VICTOR DAMIANI, VINCENT DI FIORE and TODD ROPER. Along with fellow mavericks, 311, the success of CAKE has helped resurrect that long-forgotten bastion of southern rock, 'Capricorn' records (once home to the legendary ALLMAN BROTHERS BAND). Don't expect mutton chops and slide guitar though, as CAKE were raised on more eclectic influences, CRACKER and THEY MIGHT BE GIANTS among them. McCREA and BROWN's complex guitar numbers were matched with countrified covers:- MULTIPLY THE HEARTACHES (Kathy Dee) / I WILL SURVIVE (hit; Gloria Gaynor) / PERHAPS, PERHAPS, PERHAPS (Davis-Farres) / SAD SONGS AND WALTZES (Willie Nelson). After a US-only album, 'MOTORCADE OF GENEROSITY' failed to gain much attention in '94/'95, they returned two years later, playing with much fervor on the million seller, 'FASHION NUGGET'. Two semi-classics were subsequently lifted from the record, both 'THE DISTANCE' and 'IT'S COMING DOWN' distinguished from the alternative rock pack by the hazily melancholy trumpet flurries of VINCENT DI FIORE. 1998 saw them break the US Top 40 once again with a further slice of post-ironic US indie, 'PROLONGING THE MAGIC', although their attempts to woo the mainstream were hit and miss.

Album rating: MOTORCADE OF GENEROSITY (*4) / FASHION NUGGET (*6) / PROLONGING THE MAGIC (*6)

JOHN McCREA – vocals, acoustic guitar, organ / **GREG BROWN** – electric guitar, organ / **VICTOR DAMIANI** – bass / **VINCENT DI FIORE** – trumpet, percussion / **TODD ROPER** – drums, percussion

Capricorn | Capricorn

Nov 94. (cd) *<532 506-2>* **MOTORCADE OF GENEROSITY** [-] [ ]
– Comanche / Up so close / Jolene / You part the waters / Jesus wrote a blank cheque / I bombed Korea / Ain't no good / Ruby sees all / Pentagram / Haze of love / Is this love / Rock'n'roll lifestyle / Mr. Mastodon farm. *(UK-iss.Jul97; same)*
Mar 97. (7"/c-s) *(574 220-7/-4)* **THE DISTANCE. /** [22] [ ]
(cd-s) *(574 220-2)* – ('A'side) / Multiply the heartaches / Jolene (live) / It's coming down.
Mar 97. (cd/c) *<(532 857-2/-4)>* **FASHION NUGGET** [53] [36] Sep96
– Frank Sinatra / The distance / Friend is a four letter word / Open book / Daria / Race car ya-yas / I will survive / Stickshifts and safetybelts / Perhaps, perhaps, perhaps / It's coming down / Nugget / She'll come back to me / Italian leather sofa / Sad songs and waltzes. *<clean version Sep97; 534228>*
May 97. (7"/c-s) *(574 470-7/-4)* **I WILL SURVIVE. / RUBY SEES ALL** [29] [-]
(cd-s+=) *(574 470-2)* – Rock'n'roll lifestyle.
Aug 97. (7") *(574 716-7)* **FRANK SINATRA. /** [ ] [-]
(cd-s+=) *(574 717-2)* –
(cd-s) *(574 825-2)* –
Oct 98. (cd) *<(538092-2)>* **PROLONGING THE MAGIC** [ ] [33]
– Satan is my motor / Mexico / Never there / Guitar out the window / You turn the screws / Walk on by / Sheep go to Heaven / When you sleep / Hem of your garment / Alpha beta parking lot / Let me go / Cool blue reason / Where would I be?
Nov 98. (-) *<radio play>* **NEVER THERE** [-] [81]

CAKE LIKE

Formed: New York, USA . . . late 1992 by actress turned amateur guitarist, NINA HELLMAN, together with her equally inexperienced comedienne turned bassist, KERRI KENNEY; she had featured in cable shows, 'Viva Variety' and 'The State'. After a few false starts, the group was completed by mutual acquaintance and drummer JODY SEIFERT, the trio spotted by jazz experimentalist, JOHN ZORN, who, in turn, invited the girls to record on his 'Avant' imprint. The results were released late '94 in the shape of 'DELICIOUS', a spontaneous and cathartic blast of alternative-rock firmly in the NY tradition. Subsequently signing to 'Warners' offshoot, 'Vapor', CAKE LIKE rose to the occasion with follow-up, 'BRUISER QUEEN' (1997).

Album rating: DELICIOUS (*6) / BRUISER QUEEN (*6)

NINA HELLMAN – guitar / **KERRI KENNEY** – vocals, bass / **JODY SEIFERT** – drums

Avant | Avant

Nov 94. (cd) *<(AVANT 029)>* **DELICIOUS** [ ] [ ]

Vapor-Warners | Vapor-Warners

Jun 97. (cd) *<(9362 46601-2)>* **BRUISER QUEEN** [ ] [ ]
– New girl / Wendy / Mr. Fireman / Groovy / Latin lover / Pretty new / Lorraine's car / Franchise / Cancer / American woman / Truck stop hussy / Destroyed.
Jul 97. (cd-s) *(W 0409CD)* **LORRAINE'S CAR / COME AND PLAY** [ ] [-]

CALEXICO (see under ⇒ GIANT SAND)

CALIFONE (see under ⇒ RED RED MEAT)

CALL

Formed: California, USA ... 1980 by songwriting vocalist/guitarist, MICHAEL BEEN, who called up TOM FERRIER, GREG FREEMAN and SCOTT MUSICK. Signed to 'Mercury', The CALL were shouted down by unimpressed critics who questioned their tendency to slide into spiritual pretentiousness while the music itself veered too close to the chest-beating of The ALARM and U2. Although they made their US breakthrough in 1983 with single, 'THE WALLS CAME DOWN', three albums cut between 1982 and 1984 only served to polarise opinion; the second of these, 'MODERN ROMANS' (1983), was notable for the inclusion of guests JIM KERR, PETER GABRIEL and ROBBIE ROBERTSON. In 1985, BEEN (now tackling vocals and bass) and Co, found a new keyboards man, JIMI GOODWIN, to replace the outgoing FREEMAN, this line-up in place for their first 'Elektra' album, 'RECONCILED' (1986). After the relative commercial failure of 1987's 'INTO THE WOODS', The CALL entered a more fruitful era following a move to 'M.C.A.'. Both the single and the album, 'LET THE DAY BEGIN' (1989), captured the public imagination and hovered around the fringes of the singles and albums charts respectively; the memorable title track was also a UK Top 50 hit. Once again they failed to capitalise on the increased interest, 'RED MOON' (1990) – recorded with the help of BONO and T-BONE BURNETT – seeing the sun set on their career despite a number of healthy reviews. • **Trivia:** BEEN released a solo album, 'ON THE VERGE OF A NERVOUS BREAKTHROUGH', although it was only a low key domestic affair.

Album rating: THE CALL (*4) / MODERN ROMANS (*5) / SCENE BEYOND DREAMS (*4) / RECONCILED (*6) / INTO THE WOODS (*5) / LET THE DAY BEGIN (*6) / RED MOON (*5) / THE WALLS CAME DOWN: THE BEST OF THE MERCURY YEARS compilation (*7) / THE BEST OF THE CALL compilation (*7)

MICHAEL BEEN – vocals, guitar, synthesizer / **TOM FERRIER** – guitar, vocals / **GREG FREEMAN** – bass / **SCOTT MUSICK** – drums, percussion

London / Mercury

1982. (lp) *<4037>* **THE CALL** – / –

Jul 83. (7") *(LON 28) <811487>* **THE WALLS CAME DOWN. / UPPERBIRTH** – / 74 Apr83
(12"+=) *(LONX 28)* –

Mercury / Mercury

Sep 83. (lp) *(6337 263) <810307>* **MODERN ROMANS** – / 84 Mar83
– The walls came down / Turn a blind eye / Time of your life / Modern Romans / Back from the front / Destination / Violent times / Face to face / All about you.

1984. (lp/c) *<818793-1/-4>* **SCENE BEYOND DREAMS** – / –

— **JIM GOODWIN** – keyboards; repl. FREEMAN (BEEN now vocals, bass)

Elektra / Elektra

May 86. (7"/12") *(EKR/+T 40) <69546>* **EVERYWHERE I GO. / TORE THE OLD PLACE DOWN**

May 86. (lp/c)(cd) *(EKT 33/+C)(960440-2) <60440>* **RECONCILED** – / 82 Feb86
– Everywhere I go / I still believe (great design) / Blood red (America) / The morning / Tore the whole place down / Oklahoma / With or without reason / Sanctuary / Even now.

— **GREG FREEMAN** – guitar; returned to repl. GOODWIN

Jul 87. (7"/12") *(EKR/+T 60) <69461>* **I DON'T WANNA. / DAY OR NIGHT**

Jul 87. (lp/c/cd) *(960739-1/-4/-2) <60739>* **INTO THE WOODS** – / Jun87
– I don't wanna / In the river / It could have been me / The woods / Day or night / Memory / Too many tears / Expecting / Walk walk.

— **JIM GOODWIN** – keyboards; returned to repl. FREEMAN

M.C.A. / M.C.A.

Aug 89. (7") *(MCA 1362) <53658>* **LET THE DAY BEGIN. / UNCOVERED** 42 / 51 Jul89
(cd-s+=/12"+=) *(D+/MCAT 1362)* –

Oct 89. (lp/c/cd) *(MCG/MCGC/DMCG 6065) <6303>* **LET THE DAY BEGIN** – / 64 Jun89
– Let the day begin / You run / Surrender / When (jive) / Jealousy / Same ol' story / For love / Closer / Communication / Watch / Uncovered.

Jan 90. (7") *(MCA 1390)* **YOU RUN. / WATCH**
(12"+=/cd-s+=/3"cd-s+=) *(MCAT/DMCAT/DMCAX 1390)* –

Nov 90. (cd/c/lp) *<9031 72164-2/-4/-1>* **RED MOON** – / –
– What's happened to you / Red moon / You were there / Floating back / A swim in the ocean / Like you've never been loved / Family / This is your life / The hand that feeds you / What a day.

— **BEEN, FERRIER + MUSICK** re-formed

not iss. / Fingerprint

Nov 97. (cd) *<9701>* **TO HEAVEN AND BACK** – / –
– Soaring bird / Criminal / Love is everywhere / World on fire / Think it over / Musta been outta my mind / All you hold on to / Compromise / Become America / What are you made of / Confession.

– compilations, etc. –

Jun 91. (cd/c) *Mercury; <848741-2/-4>* **THE WALLS CAME DOWN: THE BEST OF THE MERCURY YEARS** – / –
– War weary world / There's a heart here / Doubt / Upperbirth / Flesh and steel / Waiting for the end / Walls come down / Turn a blind eye / Modern Romans / Back from the front / Destination / Violent times / All about you / Scene beyond dreams / Tremble / Delivered / Heavy hand / One life leads to another.

Jul 97. (cd) *Warners; <46488>* **THE BEST OF THE CALL** – / –
– Let the day begin / Everywhere I go / I still believe / I don't wanna / Memory / What's happened to you / You were there / Become America / To feel this way / Us / All you hold on to / We know too much / Walls come down / Uncovered.

CAMBERWELL NOW (see under ⇒ THIS HEAT)

CAMPAG VELOCET

Formed: London, England . . . early '93 by Portsmouth-born schoolfriends ARGE (IAN CATER) and PETE VOSS, the latter deemed a misfit, who actually found out later in life that he had an indentation to the brain (apparently due to a boyhood accident in which he fell out of a loft). Having acquired a home at bassist BARNEY SLATER's Kentish Town (London) pad, the trio began marathon rehearsal sessions, only stopping for the occasional bag of mushrooms (magic they weren't!). Having gone through a plethora of drummers, CAMPAG VELOCET finally recruited LASELLES GORDON and supported other local lads, LO FIDELITY ALLSTARS. They released a couple of singles at the turn of '97, a split affair with the REGULAR FRIES and a highly-rated EP, 'DRENCROM'. Akin to SPACEMEN 3 in bed with PiL and MY BLOODY VALENTINE, their musical soundscapes of repetitive rhythms were on full course for the 'SAUNTRY SLY CHIC' single in April '98.

Album rating: no albums yet, just the EP's

PETE VOSS – vocals / **ARGE** (b. IAN CATER) – guitar / **BARNEY SLATER** – bass / **LASCELLES GORDON** – drums

Fierce Panda / not iss.

Nov 97. (12";split with REGULAR FRIES) *(Ning 41)* **split** / –

Rabid Badger / not iss.

Nov 97. (12"ep) *(Nang 1)* **DRENCROM (VELOCET SYNTHEMESC) EP** / –

Apr 98. (12"ep/cd-ep) *(Nang 3/+CD)* **SAUNTRY SLY CHIC / GAK STACKERS / TV EYE** / –

CAMPER VAN BEETHOVEN

Formed: Redlands / Santa Cruz, California, USA . . . 1983 by DAVE LOWERY and DAVID McDANIELS, who had relocated to college in Santa Cruz. Touted as one of the first real "alternative" acts to come out of America, CAMPER VAN BEETHOVEN were a reaction to the rigid conformity of the all-pervasive Californian hardcore scene, taking it upon themselves to brew up an exotic concoction of avant-folk-pop/cow-punk taking in elements of stone country, reggae, ska and even oompa-jazz. By the release of debut album, 'TELEPHONE FREE LANDSLIDE VICTORY' (1985), the line-up had stabilised around LOWERY, CHRIS MOLLA, VICTOR KRUMMENACHER, GREG LISHER and JONATHAN SEGAL (CHRIS PEDERSON was recruited later), the latter's strident violin flourishes adding the quintessential Eastern European flavour prevalent in much of the band's work. Ranging from the John Peel favourite, 'TAKE THE SKINHEADS BOWLING' to Cossack-style howdown's like 'BALALAIKA GAP' and 'VLADIVOSTOCK' and even an irreverent Black Flag cover, 'WASTED', the record's tongue-in-cheek humour and headlong eclecticism caused a major buzz on the US underground, even prompting R.E.M.'s MICHAEL STIPE to name it as one of his Top 10 albums of the year. A subsequent distribution deal with 'Rough Trade' saw the record gain a UK release yet both Britsh and US sales weren't as high as expected and the group formed their own 'Pitch-A-Tent' label for the release of follow-up double set, 'CAMPER VAN BEETHOVEN II/III' (1986). The latter included one of their most infamous creations, 'ZZ TOP GOES TO EGYPT' alongside another hardcore makeover, Sonic Youth's 'I LOVE HER ALL THE TIME'. An eponymous third album and further couple of EP's, 'GOOD GUYS, BAD GUYS' and 'VAMPIRE CAN MATING OVEN', kept the band's profile high and a subsequent major label bidding war ended in a move to 'Virgin' in 1988. With the luxuries of a decent sized studio budget behind them, CVB made the record they'd probably always wanted to make in 'OUR REVOLUTIONARY SWEETHEART' (1988). Polishing off the rough edges but retaining the spontaneity, this should've been the record to propel them into the indie mainstream. In the event, crossover success proved out of reach and SEGAL bailed out for a solo career. The cracks were beginning to show on what proved to be the band's swansong set, 'KEY LIME PIE' (1990), a final split occuring later that year as PEDERSON, LISHER and KUMMENACHER formed MONKS OF DOOM – releasing one album on 'C/Z', 'INSECT GOD' – and LOWERY eventually forming CRACKER. • **Covers:** PHOTOGRAPH (Ringo Starr) / I'M NOT LIKE EVERYBODY ELSE (Kinks) / INTERSTELLAR OVERDRIVE (Pink Floyd) / PICTURES OF MATCHSTICK MEN (Status Quo). The MONKS OF DOOM covered; WHO ARE THE BRAIN POLICE? (Mothers Of Invention; Frank Zappa).

Album rating: TELEPHONE FREE LANDSCAPE VICTORY (*7) / II & III (*6) / CAMPER VAN BEETHOVEN (*6) / VAMPIRE CAN MATING OVEN mini (*6) / OUR BELOVED REVOLUTIONARY SWEETHEART (*8) / KEY LIME PIE (*7) / CAMPER VANTIQUES compilation (*5)

DAVE LOWERY (b.10 Sep'60, San Antonio, Texas) – vocals, guitar, drums / **JONATHAN SEGAL** (b. 3 Sep'63, Marseilles, France) – keyboards, violin, mandolin, vocals / **GREG LISHER** (b.29 Nov'63, Santa Cruz) – guitar / **VICTOR KRUMMENACHER** (b. 7 Apr'65, Riverside, Calif.) – bass, vocals / **CHRIS MOLLA** – guitar, vocals, drums

Rough Trade / Independents

Apr 86. (lp) *(ROUGH 95) <IP 016>* **TELEPHONE FREE LANDSCAPE VICTORY** / Oct85
– Border ska / The day that Lassie went to the moon / Wasted / Yanqui go home / Oh no! / 9 of disks / Payed vacation: Greece / Where the hell is Bill? / Vladivostock / Skinhead stomp / Tina / Take the skinheads bowling / Mao reminisces about his days / I don't see you / Balalaika gap / Opi rides again – Club Med sucks / Ambiguity song. *<re-iss. 1993 on 'I.R.S.'; X2 13208>*

not iss. / Pitch A Tent

Jan 86. (d-lp) *<PITCH 1>* **CAMPER VAN BEETHOVEN II/III** – /
– Abundance / Cowboys from Hollywood / Sad lovers waltz / Turtlehead / I love her all the time / No flies on us / Down and out / No krugerrands for David / (Don't you go to) Goleta / 4 year plan / (We're a) Bad trip / Circles / Dustpan / Sometimes / Chain of circumstances / ZZ Top goes to Egypt / Cattle (reversed) / From another stone / No more bullshit / Take the skinheads bowling / Epigram No.2 / Cowboys from Hollywood / At Kuda? / Epigram No.1 / Colonel Enrique Adolfo Bermudas.

(UK/German-iss.Nov87 on 'Full Blast'; FBLP 400320) <cd-iss. 1993 on 'I.R.S.'; 13209>

— added **CHRIS PEDERSEN** (b.16 Aug'60, San Diego, Calif.) – drums

— below featured **EUGENE CHADBOURNE** – banjo (of SHOCKABILLY)

Dec 86. (lp) *(ROUGH 109)* *<PITCH 2>* **CAMPER VAN BEETHOVEN** (THE THIRD LP) [ ] [ ] Aug86
– Good guys, bad guys / Jo Stalin's Cadillac / Five sticks / Lulu land / Une fois / We saw Jerry's daughter / Surprise truck / Stairway to Heaven / The history of Utah / Still wishing to course / We love you / Hoe yourself down / Peace & love / Folly / Interstellar overdrive / Shut us down. *<cd-iss. 1993 on 'I.R.S.'; 13210>*

Mar 87. (7"ep/12"ep) *(RT/+T 161)* **TAKE THE SKINHEADS BOWLING** [ ] [ ]

Oct 87. (12"ep) *(RTT 205)* **GOOD GUYS, BAD GUYS EP** [ ] [ ]

— now without MOLLA

Nov 87. (m-lp) *<PITCH 05>* **VAMPIRE CAN MATING OVEN** [-] [ ]
– Opi rides again / Club Med sucks / Oh no / Where the hell is Bill? / etc.

— In Feb 88, they teamed up with EUGENE CHADBOURNE on the lp, 'CAMPER VAN CHADBOURNE', on 'Fundamental' records.

Virgin Virgin

May 88. (cd/c/lp) *(CD/TC+/V 2516)* *<90918>* **OUR BELOVED REVOLUTIONARY SWEETHEART** [ ] [ ]
– Eye of Fatima (pt.1) / Turquoise jewelry / O death / She divines water / Devil song / One of these days / Waka / Change your mind / My path belated / Never go back / Eye of Fatima (pt.2) / Tania / Life is grand / The fool.

Sep 88. (7") *(VS 1122)* **LIFE IS GRAND. / LOVE IS A WEED** [ ] [ ]
(12"+=/cd-s+=) *(VS T/CD 1122)* – Harmony in my head / Wade in the water.

— **MORGAN FICHTER** – violin, vocals; repl. SEGAL who went solo

Virgin America Virgin

Jan 90. (cd/c/lp) *(VUS CD/CM/LP 8)* *<91289>* **KEY LIME PIE** [ ] [ ] Oct89
– Opening theme / Jack Ruby / Sweethearts / When I win the lottery / (I was born in a) Laundromat / Borderline / The light from a cake / June / All her favourite fruit / Interlude / Flowers / The humid press of days / Pictures of matchstick men / Come on darkness.

Jan 90. (7") *(VUS 8)* **PICTURES OF MATCHSTICK MEN. / JACK RUBY** [ ] [ ]
(12"+=) *(VUST 8)* – Closing theme / The humid press of days.

– compilations, etc. –

Mar 93. (cd,c) *I.R.S.; <13211>* **CAMPER VANTIQUES** (B-sides, rarities, etc) [-] [ ]

— disbanded in Spring 1990. LOWERY formed CRACKER, the others formed . . .

MONKS OF DOOM

PEDERSON, LISHER + KRUMMENACHER with also **DAVID IMMERGLUCK** – drums (of OPHELIAS)

not iss. Pitch A Tent

1988. (lp) *<PITCH 6>* **BREAKFAST ON THE BEACH OF DECEPTION** [-] [ ]
<cd-iss. 1990's on 'I.R.S.'; 13213>

not iss. Bated Breath

1991. (cd) *<4>* **MERIDIAN** [-] [ ]

not iss. C/Z

Aug 92. (m-cd) *<CD 047>* **THE INSECT GOD** [-] [ ]

not iss. I.R.S.

1992. (cd/c) *<X2/X4 13163>* **FORGERY** [-] [ ]

Mar 93. (cd) *<X2 13214>* **COSMODEMONIC TELEGRAPH COMPANY** [-] [ ]

CAPTAIN AMERICA (see under ⇒ VASELINES)

(see under ⇒ VASELINES)

CAPTAIN SENSIBLE

Born: RAYMOND BURNS, 23 Apr'55, Balham, South London, England. A founding member of legendary punk band, The DAMNED (along with DAVE VANIAN, BRIAN JAMES and RAT SCABIES), BURNS played bass in the band's initial incarnation (1976-78) before switching to guitar as the outfit re-emerged minus JAMES following a temporary hiatus. One-half of The DAMNED's in-house loony duo alongside SCABIES, BURNS' reputation for high jinks preceded him. Always the most colourful, animated member of The DAMNED, it was perhaps inevitable that sooner or later he'd find an alternative outlet for his manic energy and humour; during the aforementioned lull in DAMNED activities, The CAPTAIN made his first foray into solo waters with the 'JET BOY, JET GIRL' single. By the time he got round to recording a follow-up EP, 'THIS IS YOUR CAPTAIN SPEAKING' (issued on the 'Crass' label) in '81, The DAMNED had released two of the best albums of their career, 'MACHINE GUN ETIQUETTE' (1979) and 'THE BLACK ALBUM' (1980); SENSIBLE played a pivotal role in both and would continue as a full-time member even after his solo career took off big time in '82 as he signed to 'A&M'. With backing from The DOLLY MIXTURES (who'd first worked with him on the 'Crass' EP) and the added talents of ROBYN HITCHCOCK, CAPTAIN SENSIBLE sailed to No.1 in the summer of '82 with a chirpy cockney reading of the Rodgers/Hammerstein 'South Pacific' standard, 'HAPPY TALK'. From punk upstart to dayglo pop star overnight, The CAPTAIN became the acceptable face of rock'n'roll and a favourite fixture of Saturday morning TV. A follow-up single, 'WOT', made the Top 30 although the subsequent debut album, 'WOMEN AND CAPTAIN FIRST' (1982) barely scraped into the Top 75. The following year's 'POWER OF LOVE' album also failed to make much chart headway although it did put SENSIBLE back in the Top 10 with the anti-Falklands War song, 'GLAD IT'S ALL OVER'. 1984's compilation album, 'SENSIBLE SINGLES' smacked of desperation, SENSIBLE's days of pop fame numbered as followed his own eccentric path throughout the remainder of the 80's. 1984 was also the year SENSIBLE finally left The DAMNED, although he continued to help them out on an occasional basis. As well as being a staunch peace campaigner, the CAPTAIN was also a committed vegetarian, releasing the 'WOT, NO MEAT' single in '85 as CAPTAIN SENSIBLE & THE MISSUS (the spouse in question was actually girlfriend and DOLLY MIXTURE, RACHEL BOR). Parting company with 'A&M' in the late 80's, SENSIBLE formed his own label, 'Deltic', for the release of the 1989 double set, 'REVOLUTION NOW'. If his star had faded somewhat, there were still a hardcore of SENSIBLE admirers and ageing DAMNED fans willing to shell out their hard earned cash and the man's career has extended into the 90's via albums such as 'UNIVERSE OF GEOFFREY BROWN' (1993) and 'MEATHEAD' (1995).

Album rating: WOMEN AND CAPTAIN FIRST (*5) / LIVE AT THE MILKY WAY (*6) / MEATHEAD (*6)

CAPTAIN SENSIBLE – vocals, guitar, bass, etc

Dutch Poker not iss.

Jul 78. (7") *(POS 15077)* **JET BOY, JET GIRL. / the Softies: CHILDREN OF THE DAMNED** [ ] [-]
(re-iss. May82 on 'Big Beat' 7"/7"pic-d; NS/+P 77)

— with **DOLLY MIXTURES** – vocals

Crass not iss.

Nov 81. (7"ep) *(321984-5)* **THIS IS YOUR CAPTAIN SPEAKING** [ ] [-]
– The Russians are coming / Oursoles to you / (What d'ya give) The man who's gotten everything.

— retained The DOLLY MIXTURES + enlisted **ROBYN HITCHCOCK** – guitar / **TONY MANSFIELD** – synthesizer, producer / **ROD BOWKETT** – noises

A&M A&M

Jun 82. (7") *(CAP 1)* **HAPPY TALK. / I CAN'T STAND IT** [1] [ ]

Aug 82. (7"/7"pic-d) *(CAP/+P 2)* **WOT. / STRAWBERRY DROSS** [26] [ ]

Sep 82. (lp/c) *(AMLH/CAM 68548)* **WOMEN AND CAPTAIN FIRST** [64] [ ]
– Wot / A nice cup of tea / Brenda (part 1) / Brenda (part 2) / Yanks with guns / Happy talk / Martha the mouth / Nobody's sweetheart / What d'ya give a man who's gotten everything / Who is Melody Lee, Sid? / Gimme a uniform / Croydon.

Oct 82. (7"pic-d) *(CAPP 3)* **CROYDON. / JIMI HENDRIX'S STRAT** [ ] [-]

— next added various session people incl. **DAVE RUFFY** – drums

Jul 83. (7") *(CAP 4)* **STOP THE WORLD. / BACK TO SCHOOL** [ ] [-]

Nov 83. (7") *(CAP 5)* **I'M A SPIDER. / WOMEN SAGA** [ ] [-]

Nov 83. (lp/c) *(AMLX/CXM 68561)* **THE POWER OF LOVE** [ ] [-]
– I'm a spider / I love her / Stop the world / Sir Donald's song / It's hard to believe I'm not / Thanks for the night / Glad it's all over / Royal rave up / Secrets / It would be so nice / The power of love / I love you.

Mar 84. (7"/7"pic-d) *(CAP/+P 6)* **GLAD IT'S ALL OVER. / DAMNED ON 45** [6] [ ]
(12"+=) *(CAPX 6)* – Happy talk.

Jul 84. (7") *(CAP 7)* **THERE ARE MORE SNAKES THAN LADDERS. / THE FOUR MARY'S GO-GO DANCE ALL NIGHT AT THE GROOVY CELLAR** [57] [-]
(12"+=) *(CAPX 7)* – ('A'remix).

Nov 84. (7") *(CAP 8)* **ONE CHRISTMAS CATALOGUE. / RELAX** [ ] [-]
(12"+=) *(CAPY 8)* – Pocketful of dosh / Wendy, where's my snaps?

Dec 84. (lp/c) *(AMA/AMC 5026)* **SENSIBLE SINGLES** (compilation) [ ] [-]
– Happy talk / Wot / It would be so nice / Martha the mouth / Stop the world / Relax / I love her / Glad it's all over / It's hard to believe I'm not / There are more snakes than ladders / I'm a spider / One Christmas catalogue / I love you.

Jul 85. (7"; as CAPTAIN SENSIBLE + THE MISSUS) *(TOUCH 3)* **WOT, NO MEAT? / A MEAT SANDWICH** [ ] [-]
(above was with girlfriend, RACHEL BOR (of DOLLY MIXTURES) / released on 'Animus' imprint) *(re-iss. Nov86; FEEL 3)*

— his backing band now **DAVE BERK** – drums / **CLIVE GATES** – keyboards / **BRIAN KERR** – guitar / **ROBBIE ROMP** – bass

Nov 85. (7") *(AM 290)* **COME ON DOWN. / SHE TAKES ME** [ ] [-]
(12") *(AMY 290)* – ('A'side) / Beggar's can be choosers / Like margarine / The ballad of Sheila and Mark.

Jun 87. (7") *(AM 395)* **REVOLUTION NOW. / COWARD OF TREASON COVE** [ ] [-]
(12"+=) *(AMY395)* – The groove.

Trax not iss.

Apr 88. (7") *(HS 1)* **THE SNOOKER SONG. / MIDNIGHT SMOKE** [ ] [-]

Deltic not iss.

Jun 88. (7") *(DELT 1)* **THE TOYS TAKE OVER. / A SPORTING LIFE** [ ] [-]
(12"+=) *(DELT 1T)* – V.O.A.

Nov 88. (7") **I GET SO EXCITED. / THE DELTIC SUITE** [ ] [-]

Aug 89. (d-lp/c/cd) *(DELT LP/MC/CD 4)* **REVOLUTION NOW** [ ] [-]
– Missing the boat / Smash it up (part 4) / The toys take over / A riot on Eastbourne pier / Wake up (you're only dreaming) / Green light / Lib 2-3 / Revolution now / Phone-in / I get so excited / Vosene. *cd+=)* – The kamikaze millionaire / Exploding heads and teapots / The coward of Treason Cove. *(cd re-iss. 1991 & Jul96 on 'Humbug'; BAH 3) (cd re-iss. Sep98 on 'Blueprint'; BP 293CD)*

Aug 90. (7"; as CAPTAIN SENSIBLE & The BROTHERHOOD OF LIZARDS) *(DELT 5)* **SMASH IT UP (PART 4). / MARKET PLACE** [ ] [-]

Humbug not iss.

Apr 93. (cd/c) *(BAH/+MC 4)* **THE UNIVERSE OF GEOFFREY BROWN** [ ] [-]
– Holiday in my head / Come on Geofrey Brown / Getting to me / Street of shame / Geoff loosens his tie / Home / Govt. Dirty Tricks Dept. WC1 / Life up in the stars / The message / A trip to Cornwall / The universe of Geoffrey Brown. *(cd re-iss. Sep98 on 'Blueprint'; BP 294CD)*

Aug 94. (cd) *(BAH 12)* **LIVE AT THE MILKY WAY (live)** [ ] [-]
– Interstellar overcoat / Jet boy, jet girl / Smash it up / Back to school / Come on Geoffrey Brown / Happy talk / The kamikaze millionaire / Exploding heads &

teapots (past their prime) / Love song / Neat neat neat / New rose / Wot / Lookin' at you / Hey Joe / Glad it's all over.

Dec 94. (c-s/7") *(CA+/HOKEY 1)* **THE HOKEY COKEY. /** 71 -
(cd-s+=) *(CDHOKEY 1)* – ('A'version).
(above issued on 'Have A Nice Day' records)

Sep 95. (d-cd) *(BAH 14)* **MEATHEAD** -

Jun 97. (cd) *(BAH 30)* **A SLICE OF GEOFFREY BROWN** -

– compilations, etc. –

Oct 88. (7") *Old Gold; (OG 9811)* **HAPPY TALK. / GLAD IT'S ALL OVER** -

Jun 97. (d-cd) *Humbug; (BAH 32)* **THE CAPTAIN'S BOX** -

Aug 97. (cd) *Cleopatra; (CLP 0041)* **THE BEST OF CAPTAIN SENSIBLE** -

Mar 98. (cd) *Eagle; (EABCD 101)* **THE MASTERS** -

CARDIACS

Formed: Carshalton, Surrey, England ... 1978 as PHILIP PILF AND THE FILTH by songwriter, TIM SMITH, brother JIM, PETER TAGG and MICK PUGH. Not surprisingly they soon changed their name to CARDIAC ARREST, recruiting COLIN MYERS in the process and releasing a couple of low-key 45's, 'A BUS FOR A BUS ON A BUS' and 'RUNNING IN THE STREET'. With MARK CAWTHRA replacing TAGG, The CARDIACS (as they were now called) began the 80's by self-financing (through their own 'Alphabet' outlet) a series of cassette-only releases, namely 'THE OBVIOUS IDENTITY' (1980), 'TOY WORLD' (1981) and the fan club compilation 'ARCHIVE CARDIACS' (1983). With PUGH and MYERS leaving to join The SOUND, it was down to the SMITH brothers to recruit an entire new line-up. This comprised of SARA SMITH, WILLIAM D. DRAKE, DOMINIC LUCKMAN and TIM QUY, the band's condition remaining stable over the ensuing six years, at least in terms of personnel. A manic rock show parody outfit akin to HALF MAN HALF BISCUIT meeting the BONZOS, The CARDIACS found a sitting duck target in the shape of MORRISSEY, The SMITHS (TIM and JIM, that is!) showering the crowd with flour (as opposed to flowers/gladioli). Musically their ingedients were a more varied, to say the least, chucking in handfuls of off-beat, dated punk, vintage prog-rock and Cockney barrow-boy psychedelia. Virtually ignored by a hostile press, the continued their madcap malarky regardless over an unceasingly prolific release schedule that included fans favourite, 'IS THIS THE LIFE' (apparently loved by DAMON ALBARN), a near chart hit lifted from the equally impressive 'A LITTLE MAN, A HOUSE & THE WHOLE WORLD WINDOW' (1988). A relatively short-lived replacement for the departing trio of QUY, DRAKE and SARA SMITH, was found in the shape of CHRISTIAN 'BIC' HAYES (future LEVITATION), who played on the much loved 1989 album, 'ON LAND AND IN THE SEA'. Proper indie stardom looked to be on the cards with the scheduled 'HEAVEN BORN AND EVER BRIGHT'; in the event, however, a proposed deal with 'Rough Trade' fell through and the album eventually appeared as the 17th(!) release on 'Alphabet'. Despite the continuing media antipathy, TIM SMITH had become a much in-demand producer, working with the likes of EAT, LEVITATION and SIDI BOU SAID, while even BLUR were to sing the band's praises and include them as support act on their landmark Mile End Stadium show. Needless to say, studio activity continued apace with a slew of releases culminating in 1996's 'SING TO GOD' (available as both a double CD and two single discs).

Album rating: ARCHIVE CARDIACS first two cassettes (*6) / THE SEASIDE (*5) / MR & MRS SMITH AND MR DRAKE (*5) / BIG SHIP mini (*5) / RUDE BOOTLEG – LIVE AT READING '86 (*5) / A LITTLE MAN, A HOUSE & THE WHOLE WORLD WINDOW (*7) / CARDIACS LIVE AT THE PARADISO, AMSTERDAM (*5) / ON LAND AND IN THE SEA (*6) / SONGS FOR SHIPS AND IRONS compilation (*7) / HEAVEN BORN AND EVER BRIGHT (*7) / ALL THAT GLITTERS IS A MARE'S NEST (*5) / SING TO GOD double (*6)

CARDIAC ARREST

MICK PUGH (b.21 Sep'58, Kingston, Surrey, England) – vocals / **TIM SMITH** (b. 3 Jul'61) – guitar, vocals / **JIM SMITH** (b.14 Apr'58) – bass / **PETER TAGG** (b. London, England) – drums / **COLVIN MYERS** (b. London) – keyboards

Tortch not iss.

1979. (7"ep) *(TOR 002)* **A BUS FOR A BUS ON A BUS EP** -
– A bus for a bus on a bus / A cake for Bertie's party / Food on the wall.

Another not iss.

1979. (7") *(AN 001)* **RUNNING IN THE STREET. / TV FRIENDS** -

— changed name when another group came out with 'RUNNING IN THE STREET'

CARDIACS

— **MARK CAWTHRA** – drums; repl. TAGG who later formed The TRUDY

Alphabet not iss.

1980. (c) *(none)* **THE OBVIOUS IDENTITY** -

1981. (c) *(none)* **TOY WORLD** -

1983. (c) *(ALPH 000)* **ARCHIVE CARDIACS** -
– (fan club compilation of above 2) *(cd-iss. May95; same)*

— PUGH and MYERS also left to join The SOUND. The SMITH brothers recruited **SARA SMITH** (b.30 Nov'60, Coleford, England) – saxophone / **WILLIAM D. DRAKE** (b. 7 Feb'62, Essex, England) – keyboards / **DOMINIC LUCKMAN** (b.29 Nov'61, Brighton, England) – drums / **TIM QUY** (b.14 Aug'61, Brixton, England) – percussion

1984. (c) *(ALPH 001)* **THE SEASIDE** -
– Jibber and twitch / Gena Lollabridgida / Hello Mr. Sparrow / It's a lovely day / A wooden fish on wheels / Hope day / To go off and things / Ice a spot and a dot on the dog / R.E.S. / To go off and things. *(re-iss. 1990 lp/c/cd; ALPH LP/MC/CD 013) (re-iss. cd May95; ALPHCD 013)*

May 86. (12"ep) *(ALPH 002)* **SEASIDE TREATS EP** -
– The consultants flower garden / Little man and a house / R.E.S. / To go off and things.

1986. (c) *(ALPH 003)* **MR & MRS SMITH AND MR DRAKE** -

Jan 87. (m-lp) *(ALPH 004)* **BIG SHIP** -

1987. (lp/c) *(ALPH 005/MC005)* **RUDE BOOTLEG – LIVE AT READING '86 (live)** -
(cd-iss. May95; ALPHCD 005)

Aug 87. (12"ep) *(ALPH 006)* **THERE'S TOO MANY IRONS IN THE FIRE EP** -
– There's too many irons in the fire / All spectacular / Loose fish scape grace.

Mar 88. (lp/c/cd) *(ALPH/+MC/CD 007)* **A LITTLE MAN, A HOUSE & THE WHOLE WORLD WINDOW** -
– A little man and a house / In a city lining / Is this the life / Interlude / Dive / Icing on the world / The breakfast line / Victory / R.E.S. / The whole world window / Goosegash. *(cd+=)* – Loosefish scape grace / I'm eating in bed / There's too many irons in the fire / All spectacular. *(re-iss. cd May95; same)*

Mar 88. (7"/12") *(ALPH SP/T 008)* **IS THIS THE LIFE. / I'M EATING IN BED** -

Sep 88. (7") *(ALPH 009)* **SUSANNAH'S STILL ALIVE. / BLIND IN SAFETY & LEAFY IN LOVE** -
(12"+=) *(ALPH 009T)* – All his geese are swans.

Oct 88. (lp/cd) *(ALPH LP/CD 010)* **CARDIACS LIVE AT THE PARADISO, AMSTERDAM (live)** -
– The icing on the world / To go off and things / In a city lining / Gina Lollobrigida / There's too many irons in the fire / Tarred and feathered / Goosegash / Loosefish scape grace / Cameras / Is this the life / Big ship. *(cd re-iss. May95; same)*

— **CHRISTIAN 'Bic' HAYES** (b.10 Jun'64, London) – guitar, vocals repl. SARA SMITH, TIM QUY and WILLIAM D. DRAKE

Apr 89. (7") *(ALPH 011)* **BABY HEART DIRT. / I HOLD MY LOVE IN MY ARMS** -
(12"+=) *(ALPH 011T)* – Horsehead / The safety bowl.

Apr 89. (lp/c/cd) *(ALPH LP/MC/CD 012)* **ON LAND AND IN THE SEA** -
– Two bites of cherry / Baby heart dirt / The leader of the starry skies / I hold my love in my arms / The duck and Roger the horse / Arnald / Horsehead / Fast Robert / Mare's nest / The stench of honey / Nuds and spawn / The safety bowl / The everso closely guarded line. *(re-iss. cd May95; same)*

Oct 91. (cd/lp) *(ALPH CD/LP 014)* **SONGS FOR SHIPS AND IRONS** (compilation) -
(re-iss. cd May95; same)

— now without BIC HAYES who joined LEVITATION

Nov 91. (12"ep/cd-ep) *(ALPH 015/+CD)* **DAY IS GONE EP** -
– Day is gone /
(w/ free 7" by SEA NYMPHS – aka TIM & SARA SMITH and DRAKE)

— (below was to have appeared Nov'91)

May 92. (cd/lp) *(ALPH CD/LP 017)* **HEAVEN BORN AND EVER BRIGHT** -
– The alphabet business concern (home of the fadeless splendour) / She is hiding behind the shed / March / Goodbye Grace / Anything I can't eat / Helen and Heaven / Bodysbad / For good and all / Core / Day is gone / Snakes-a-sleepin'. *(re-iss. cd May95; same)*

1993. (cd/lp) *(ALPH CD/LP 018)* **ALL THAT GLITTERS IS A MARE'S NEST** -
(re-iss. cd May95; same)

Apr 95. (cd-ep) *(ORGAN 011CD)* **BELLEYE EP** -
– Belleye / A horse's tail / No gold.
(above issued on 'Organ')

— **BOB POOLE** – keyboards, guitar / **BOB LEITH** – drums; repl. LUCKMAN

Jul 96. (d-cd) *(ALPHCD 022)* **SING TO GOD** -

Jul 96. (cd) *(ALPHCD 023)* **SING TO GOD PART ONE** -

Jul 96. (cd) *(ALPHCD 024)* **SING TO GOD PART TWO** -

Aug 96. (cd-ep) *(ALPHCDS 025)* **MANHOOD / SPINNEY / WHAT PARADISE IS LIKE** -

Nov 96. (cd-ep) *(ALPHCDS 026)* **ODD EVEN /** -

— a TIM SMITH solo album appeared '95/96 and SEA NYMPHS also due

– compilations, etc.

Sep 88. (12"ep) *Nighttracks; (SFNT 013)* **RADIO ONE SESSIONS** (29.11.87) -
– R.E.S. / Buds and spawn / In a city lining / Is this the life / Cameras.

May 95. (cd) *Alphabet; (ALPHCD 000)* **ARCHIVE CARDIACS** -

May 95. (cd) *Alphabet; (ALPHCD 019)* **CARDIACS SAMPLER** -

CARDIGANS

Formed: Jonkoping, Sweden ... October 1992 by songwriters PETER SVENSSON and MAGNUS SVENINGSSON, along with LARS-OLAF JOHANSSON, BENGT LAGERBERG and cutesy bombshell, NINA PERSSON. Despite the fact the band's founding members came from a heavy-metal background, The CARDIGANS' sound leaned more towards fragile, angelic indie-pop drawing on the melodic traditions of fellow Swedes, ABBA and UK pop ironists BEAUTIFUL SOUTH as well as French 60's pop (especially FRANCOISE HARDY's Burt Bacharach period). They initially released an album in Sweden before signing to 'Polydor' UK and in 1995/96, scored minor successes with 'CARNIVAL', 'SICK & TIRED' and 'RISE & SHINE', all stemming from their UK debut album, 'LIFE' (1995). In the late summer of '96, they peaked critically with the starry-eyed 'LOVEFOOL', a near Top 20 hit first time around and an even bigger success upon its re-issue in conjunction with the 'Romeo & Juliet' soundtrack in 1997. The song was a standout track on their acclaimed follow-up set, 'THE FIRST BAND ON THE MOON', although the band no doubt came to regard it as something of an albatross round their necks. Presumably a reaction to being filed under Scando-pop, the more deliberately experimental 'GRAN TURISMO' (1998) saw the band sacrifice some of their charm for instant "alternative" appeal. **• Covered:** SABBATH BLOODY SABBATH + IRON MAN (Black Sabbath) / MR. CROWLEY (Ozzy Osbourne) / BOYS ARE BACK IN TOWN (Thin Lizzy).

Album rating: EMMERDALE (*6) / LIFE (*8) / FIRST BAND ON THE MOON (*7) / GRAN TURISMO (*6)

NINA PERSSON – vocals / **PETER SVENSSON** – guitar / **MAGNUS SVENINGSSON** – bass / **LARS-OLAF JOHANSSON** – keyboards / **BENGT LAGERBERG** – drums, flute

Stockholm / not iss.

May 94. (cd) *(523215-2)* **EMMERDALE** [-] [-] Sweden
– Sick & tired / Black letter day / In the afternoon / Over the water / After all . . . / Cloudy sky / Our space / Rise and shine / Celia inside / Sabbath bloody sabbath / Seems hard / The last song.
(UK-iss.Jan97; same)

Polydor / Minty Fresh

Nov 94. (7"/c-s) *(PO/+CS 336)* **SICK & TIRED. / PLAIN PARADE** [ ] [-]
(cd-s+=) *(PZCD 336)* – Laika / Pooh song.

May 95. (7"/c-s) *(PO/+CS 345)* **CARNIVAL. / MR. CROWLEY** [72] [-]
(cd-s+=) *(PZCD 345)* – Emmerdale.
(re-iss. Nov95, hit No.35; same)

Jun 95. (cd/c/lp) *(523556-2/-4/-1)* *<15>* **LIFE** [58] [ ]
– Carnival / Gordon's garden party / Daddy's car / Sick & tired / Tomorrow / Rise & shine / Beautiful one / Travelling with Charley / Fine / Celia inside / Hey! get out of my way / After all.

Sep 95. (c-s) *(853754-4)* **SICK & TIRED / PLAIN PARADE** [34] [ ]
(cd-s) *(853754-2)* – ('A'side) / Pooh song / The boys are back in town / Carnival (Puck version).

Feb 96. (7"/c-s) *(577824-7/-4)* **RISE & SHINE. / PIKE BUBBLES** [29] [ ]
(cd-s+=) *(577825-2)* – Cocktail party bloody cocktail party.

Stockholm-Polydor / Mercury

Sep 96. (7"/c-s) *(575528-7/-4)* **LOVEFOOL. / NASTY SUNNY BEAM** [21] [ ]
(cd-s+=) *(575595-2)* –

Sep 96. (cd/c/lp) *(<533117-2/-4/-1>)* **FIRST BAND ON THE MOON** [18] [35]
– Your new cuckoo / Been it / Heartbreaker / Happy meal II / Never recover / Step on me / Lovefool / Loser / Iron man / The great divide / Choke.

Nov 96. (7"/c-s) *(575966-7/-4)* **BEEN IT. / LOSERS (FIRST TRY)** [56] [ ]
(cd-s+=) *(575966-2)* – Blah blah blah.

— below was featured on the film 'Romeo & Juliet'

Apr 97. (c-s) *(571050-4)* **LOVEFOOL / RISE & SHINE (live)** [2] [ ]
(cd-s+=) *(571050-2)* – Sick & tired (live) / Carnival (live).
(cd-s) *(571051-2)* – ('A'-Todd Terry remixes).

Aug 97. (7"/c-s) *(571633-7/-4)* **YOUR NEW CUCKOO. /** [35] [ ]
(cd-s+=) *(571633-2)* –

Oct 98. (c-s) *(567988-4)* **MY FAVOURITE GAME /** [14] [ ]
(cd-s+=) *(567989-2)* –
(cd-s) *(567991-2)* – ('A'side) / ('A'-Wubbledub mix) / Love fool (live).

Oct 98. (cd/c) *(<559081-2/-4>)* **GRAN TURISMO** [27] [ ]
– Paralyzed / Erase – Rewind / Explode / Starter / Hanging around / Higher / Marvel hill / My favourite game / Do you believe / Junk of the hearts / Nil.

– compilations, etc. –

May 97. (10xcd-ep-box) *Border; (CARDSIN 1)* **THE COMPLETE SINGLES COLLECTION** [ ] [-]

— there is also a Various Artists tribute album *(TR 012CD)*

CARDINAL (see under ⇒ Davies, Richard)

CARE (see under ⇒ WILD SWANS)

CARETAKER RACE

Formed: East London, England ... 1987 by rock journo and former LOFT guitarist, ANDY STRICKLAND; his former LOFT compadre, PETER ASTOR, found more success with The WEATHER PROPHETS. Recruiting SALLY WARD, HENRY HERSOM and DAVE MEWS, STRICKLAND and his CARETAKER RACE issued a couple of self-financed singles, 'SOMEWHERE ON SEA' and 'ANYWHERE BUT HOME', the leader's strong songwriting skills drawing comparisons to such antipodean critical luminaries as The GO-BETWEENS and The TRIFFIDS. The 'Foundation' label took over the reins in '89, although that year's solitary effort, 'I WISH I'D SAID THAT', was the last to feature HERSOM, who was replaced by ex-FLATMATES keyboard player, JACKIE CARRERA. A fourth single, 'MAN OVERBOARD', was followed by the long-awaited debut set, 'HANGOVER SQUARE' (1990), although STRICKLAND wasn't able to turn press support into sales figures; the split was imminent when SALLY departed for a job in teaching.

Album rating: HANGOVER SQUARE (*5)

ANDY STRICKLAND (b.16 Aug'59, Newport, Isle Of Wight, England) – vocals, guitar (ex-LOFT) / **SALLY WARD** (b.Preston, England) – keyboards / **HENRY HERSOM** – bass / **DAVE MEWS** (b.11 May'59, Epping, Essex, England) – drums

Roustabout / not iss.

Oct 87. (12"ep) *(RST 001T)* **SOMEWHERE ON SEA / ALL LOVE OFFERS. / ANGELA'S BABY / MAN OVERBOARD (demo)** [ ] [-]

Jul 88. (7"promo) *(RST 004)* **ANYWHERE BUT HOME. / GILDA** [ ] [-]
(12"+=) *(RST 004T)* – Things that matter.

Foundation / not iss.

Sep 89. (12"ep) *(TFL 2T)* **I WISH I'D SAID THAT / FIRE IN THE HOLD. / ONE RUNG DOWN / HER SHINING ROOM** [ ] [-]

— **JACKIE CARRERA** (b. 6 Jun'64) – keyboards (ex-FLATMATES) repl. HERSOM who joined the group, BOB

Jun 90. (12"ep) *(TFL 6T)* **MAN OVERBOARD. /** [ ] [-]

Aug 90. (lp/c/cd) *(FOUND 2/+MC/CD)* **HANGOVER SQUARE** [ ] [-]

Nov 90. (12"ep) **TWO STEEL RINGS. /** [ ] [-]

— SALLY WARD departed and was repl. by **ANDREW DEEVEY**

— split some time in 1991

CARPETTES

Formed: Newcastle, England ... 1977 by GEORGE MADDISON, NEIL THOMPSON and KEVIN HEARD, the latter being replaced by TIM WILDER prior to the release of a debut EP, 'RADIO WUNDERBAR'. Released on Walthamstow (London) label, 'Small Wonder' (also home to the CRAVATS), the single did relatively well on the punk/indie circuit, prompting the Geordie youngsters to name their follow-up track, 'SMALL WONDER', in the label's honour. Following in the footsteps of fellow punks The LURKERS, the trio signed to 'Beggars Banquet', although it would be Autumn '79 before their third single, 'I DON'T MEAN IT', hit the shelves. With punk-rock well past its honeymoon period, The CARPETTES didn't fit in with the more experimental musical upholstery of the 'New Wave' scene and the accompanying album, 'FRUSTRATION PARADISE', didn't exactly cut a rug with the critics. A follow-up set, 'FIGHT AMONG YOURSELVES' (1980), followed a similar tack and with the emerging "oi" scene just around the corner, The CARPETTES were rolled up for good.

Album rating: FRUSTRATION PARADISE (*5) / FIGHT AMONGST YOURSELVES (*4)

NEIL THOMPSON – vocals, guitar / **GEORGE MADDISON** – bass / **TIM WILDER** – drums; repl. KEVIN HEARD

Small Wonder / not iss.

Dec 77. (7"ep) *(SMALL 3)* **RADIO WUNDERBAR EP** [ ] [-]
– How about me and you / Help I'm trapped / Radio wunderbar / Cream of youth.

Jul 78. (7") *(SMALL 9)* **SMALL WONDER. / 2 NE 1** [ ] [-]

Beggars Banquet / not iss.

Oct 79. (7") *(BEG 27)* **I DON'T MEAN IT. / EASY WAY OUT** [ ] [-]

Nov 79. (lp) *(BEGA 14)* **FRUSTRATION PARADISE** [ ] [-]
– Frustration Paradise / Reach the bottom / I don't mean it / 3 a.m. / Away from it all / Johnny won't hurt you / Lost love / It don't make sense / A.B.C. / Cruel honesty / How to handle a woman / Indo-China. *(re-iss. 1988;)*

Mar 80. (7") *(BEG 32)* **JOHNNY WON'T HURT YOU. / FRUSTRATION PARADISE** [ ] [-]
(w/ free 7") *(SAM 119)* – TOTAL INSECURITY. / KEYS TO YOUR HEART

Aug 80. (7"m) *(BEG 47)* **NOTHING EVER CHANGES. / YOU NEVER REALISE / FRUSTRATION PARADISE** [ ] [-]

Oct 80. (lp) *(BEGA 21)* **FIGHT AMONGST YOURSELVES** [ ] [-]
– Nothing ever changes / Since you went away / False foundations / Fight amongst yourselves / Dead or alive / If your heart stopped now / Friday night, Saturday morning / The last lone ranger / Youth rebellion / The reason I'm lonely / Total insecurity / Silly games.

Dec 80. (7"m) *(BEG 49)* **THE LAST LONE RANGER. / LOVE SO STRONG / FAN CLUB** [ ] [-]

— disbanded soon after above

Cath CARROLL

Born: 25 Aug'60, Chipping Sodbury, Avon, England; although raised in Greater Manchester. Moving to London and securing a job as a scribe for the NME, CARROLL initially turned her hand to singing as vocalist of the GLASS ANIMALS, then MIAOW alongside STEVE McGUIRE, RON CAINE and CHRIS FENNER. The band's vinyl debut came via a contribution – 'SPORT MOST ROYAL' – to the NME's fabled C86 compilation, a SMITHS-style rockabilly jangle framing CARROLL's fluid, almost DEBBIE HARRY-esque vocals. This was followed up with 'BELLE VUE' (the anti-Thatcher anthem, 'GROCER'S DEVIL DAUGHTER' appearing as an extra track on the 12") and a single for 'Factory', 'WHEN IT ALL COMES DOWN'. Still without an album to their name, the band split after a final single, 'BREAK THE CODE', CARROLL subsequently marrying BIG BLACK guitarist, SANTIAGO DURANGO and going on to pursue a solo career. Sticking with 'Factory', she set to work on a debut album with an exotic cast of musicians including her husband and former BIG BLACK mainman, STEVE ALBINI. Rich in electronically enhanced samba rhythms, 'ENGLAND MADE ME' (1991) illustrated how much CARROLL had been influenced by her time in South America, drawing almost universal praise from the press. Following the collapse of 'Factory', CARROLL cut an album, 'TRUE CRIME MOTEL' (1995) for US indie label, 'Teenbeat', the singer now actually living in Chicago.

Album rating: ENGLAND MADE ME (*6) / TRUE CRIME MOTEL (*5)

MIAOW

CATH CARROLL – vocals, guitar / **CHRIS FENNER** – drums, percussion / **RON CAINE** – bass, guitar / **STEVE McGUIRE** – guitar

Venus — not iss.

Dec 85. (7") *(VENUS 1)* **BELLE VUE. / FATE** [ ] [-]
(12"+=) *(VENUS 1T)* – Grocer's devil daughter.

Factory — not iss.

Feb 87. (7") *(FAC 179)* **WHEN IT ALL COMES DOWN. / DID SHE** [ ] [-]
(12"+=) *(FAC 179T)* – ('A'-Cotechism mix).

— **JOE KORNER** – keyboards; repl. STEVE

Oct 87. (7") *(FAC 189)* **BREAK THE CODE. / STOLEN CARS** [ ] [-]

— disbanded when CATH augmented The HIT PARADE

CATH CARROLL

— with **MARK BRYDON** – guitar (ex-CHAKK) / **SIM LISTER** – sax, drums, keyboards (ex-CHAKK) / **ANTENOR SOARES GANDRA NETO** – guitar / **VINCENTE DA PAULA SILVA** – piano / **OSWALDINHO DA CUICA** – congas / **DIRCEU SIMOES DE MEDEIROS** – drums / **STEVE ALBINI** – guitar / **SANTIAGO DURANGO** – guitar

Factory — not iss.

Jun 91. (lp/c)(cd) *(FACT 210/+C)(FACD 210)* **ENGLAND MADE ME** [ ] [-]
– To close your eyes forever / Unforgettable / Moves like you / Watching you / Beast on the streets / Subtitled / Next time (he's mine) / England made me / Send me over / Train you're on.

— now with new set of musicians

Teenbeat — Teenbeat

May 94. (7") *(TB 137)* **MY COLD HEART. / INTO DAY** [ ] [ ]

Aug 95. (cd/lp) *(<TB 167-2/-1>)* **TRUE CRIMES MOTEL** [ ] [ ]
– Easter bunny song / Into day / True crime motel / Mississippi river factory town / Jimmy's candy / Just once / L'amour c'est ca / Lullaby for a steepleback / Breathe for me.

Sep 95. (cd-s) **BAD STAR / MISSISSIPPI RIVER FACTORY TOWN** [-] [ ]

CARTER THE UNSTOPPABLE SEX MACHINE

Formed: Streatham, South London, England . . . 1988 by FRUITBAT (LES CARTER) and JIM BOB (JIM MORRISON). They had both been in early 80's outfit The BALLPOINTS, and after a lengthy period with real jobs, they formed the group JAMIE WEDNESDAY in 1984; signing to 'Rough Trade' subsidiary label 'Pink', they released two singles before disbanding in early '87. The following year they became CARTER THE UNSTOPPABLE SEX MACHINE, debuting that summer with 'SHELTERED LIFE', railing against shady landlords. It was the first in a memorable, if occasionally grating series of DIY agit-pop/punk singles which characterised an era of British indie music; "baggy" had died a lingering death and "grunge" was lumbering over the horizon, a time when all kinds of sub-standard ephemera made the cover of the NME. CARTER were at least entertaining, an undulatingly melodic follow-up single, 'SHERIFF FATMAN', unlucky not to chart (it later became their first Top 30 hit when re-released in the summer of '91). By this point, CARTER mania had firmly gripped the student nation and you couldn't go to any gig without seeing the ubiquitous '30 SOMETHING' baseball shirt. The 1991 album of the same name followed on from the sample happy drum machine-driven crusty pop of the debut, '101 DAMNATIONS' (1990), and provided a further controversial hit in the anti-army brutality rant, 'BLOODSPORTS FOR ALL'. The chirpy cockney duo (now signed to 'Chrysalis') topped off their annus glorious with a riotous headlining slot at the Reading Festival. There was some grief, however, as the ever vigilant ROLLING STONES legal team made explicit their concern over 'AFTER THE WATERSHED's none too subtle lift from JAGGER and Co.'s 'RUBY TUESDAY'. Following a Christmas re-issue of 'RUBBISH' (featuring one of their inimitable cover versions on the b-side, The Pet Shop Boys' 'RENT' coming in for the CARTER treatment this time around), the group returned in Spring '92 with one of their finest singles, 'THE ONLY LIVING BOY IN NEW CROSS'. A third set, ironically titled '1992 – THE LOVE ALBUM' topped the UK chart, another round of witty punning and HALF MAN HALF BISCUIT style humour. With the advent of American underground domination however, CARTER sounded increasingly tame, subsequent albums 'POST HISTORIC MONSTERS' and 'WORRY BOMB' entering the Top 10 but not hanging around. After a mid-90's split, the band, now signed to indie label, 'Cooking Vinyl', returned in 1997 with the largely ignored 'A WORLD WITHOUT DAVE'. • **Covered:** RANDY SCOUSE GIT (Monkees) / EVERYBODY'S HAPPY NOWADAYS (Buzzcocks) / BEDSITTER (Soft Cell) / THIS IS HOW IT FEELS (Inspiral Carpets) / PANIC (Smiths) / MANNEQUIN (Wire) / KING ROCKER (Generation X) / DOWN IN THE TUBE STATION AT MIDNIGHT (Jam) / ANOTHER BRICK IN THE WALL (Pink Floyd) / THE IMPOSSIBLE DREAM (Mitch Leigh – Joe Darion) / HIT (Sugarcubes) / SPEEED KING (These Animal Men) / SILVER DREAM MACHINE (David Essex). • **Trivia:** Surprisingly it was JONATHAN KING who gave them tabloid exposure in his 'Sun' column.

Album rating: 101 DAMNATIONS (*9) / 30 SOMETHING (*8) / 1992 – THE LOVE ALBUM (*7) / POST-HISTORIC MONSTERS (*8)

JAMIE WEDNESDAY

JIM 'Jim Bob' MORRISON (b.22 Nov'60) – vocals, acoustic guitar / **LES 'Fruitbat' CARTER** (b.12 Feb'58) – bass / **LINDSEY HENRY** – trumpet / **SIMON LOWE** – brass / **DEAS LEGGETT** – drums

Pink — not iss.

Nov 85. (12"ep) *(PINKY 6)* **VOTE FOR LOVE / THE WALL. / WHITE HORSES / BUTTONS AND BOWS** [ ] [-]

May 86. (12"ep) *(PINKY 10)* **WE THREE KINGS OF ORIENT AREN'T. / LAST NIGHT I HAD THE STRANGEST DREAM / I THINK I'LL THROW A PARTY FOR MYSELF** [ ] [-]

— disbanded Feb'87

CARTER THE UNSTOPPABLE SEX MACHINE

— was duo formed by **JIM BOB & FRUITBAT** who now both played guitar with back-up of tape machines & JIM BOB – vocals

Big Cat — not iss.

Aug 88. (12"m) *(BBA 03)* **SHELTERED LIFE. / IS THIS THE ONLY WAY THROUGH TO YOU? / GRANNY FARMING IN THE U.K.** [ ] [-]
(re-iss. Jun94 on 'Southern' cd-ep; 18620-2)

Nov 89. (12"ep) *(ABB 100T)* **SHERIFF FATMAN / R.S.P.C.E.. / TWIN-TUB WITH GUITAR / EVERYBODY'S HAPPY NOWADAYS** [ ] [-]

Jan 90. (lp/c/cd) *(ABB/+C/CD 101)* **101 DAMNATIONS** [ ] [-]
– A perfect day to drop the bomb / Midnight on the murder mile / The road to Domestos / An all-American sport / 24 minutes to Tulsa Hill / Good grief / Charlie Brown / Everytime a churchbell rings / Good grief / Sheriff Fatman / G.I. blues. *(re-dist.Sep91; same); hit No.29)*

May 90. (12"/cd-s) *(ABB 102 T/CD)* **RUBBISH. / RENT / ALTERNATIVE ALF GARNET** [ ] [-]

Oct 90. (export; m-lp/m-cd) *(ABB 103X/+CD)* **HANDBUILT FOR PERVERTS** [-] [-]

Rough Trade — not iss.

Oct 90. (7") *(RT 242)* **ANYTIME, ANYPLACE, ANYWHERE. / RE-EDUCATING RITA** [ ] [-]
(12"+=/cd-s+=) *(RTT 242/+CD)* – Alternative title / Randy sarf git.

Jan 91. (7"/c-s) *(R 2011 268-7/-6)* **BLOODSPORTS FOR ALL. / 2001: A CLOCKWORK ORANGE** [48] [-]
(12"+=/cd-s+=) *(R 2011 268-0/-3)* – Bedsitter.

Feb 91. (cd/c/lp) *(RT 2011 270-2/-4/-1)* **30 SOMETHING** [8] [-]
– Surfin' USM / My second to last will and testament / Anytime anyplace anywhere / Prince in a pauper's grave / Shopper's paradise / Billy's smart circus / Bloodsport for all / Sealed with a Glasgow kiss / Say it with flowers / Falling on a bruise / The final comedown. *<US-iss.Aug91 on 'Chrysalis'; > (re-iss. Jan92 on 'Chrysalis' cd/c/lp; CCD/ZCHR/CHR 1897); hit UK 21) (re-iss. Feb95;)*

Chrysalis — Chrysalis

Jun 91. (7") *(USM 1)* **SHERIFF FATMAN. / R.S.P.C.E.** [23] [ ]
(c-s+=/12"+=/cd-s+=) *(USM X/XMS/CD 1)* – Twin-tub with guitar / Everybody's happy nowadays.

Oct 91. (7"/c-s) *(USM/+XMC 2)* **AFTER THE WATERSHED. / THE 90's REVIVAL / A NATION OF SHOPLIFTERS** [11] [ ]
(12"+=/cd-s+=) *(USM X/CD 2)* – This is how it feels.

Dec 91. (7"/c-s) *(USM/+XMC 3)* **RUBBISH. / ALTERNATIVE ALF GARNET** [14] [ ]
(12"+=/cd-s+=) *(USM X/CD 3)* – Rent.

Apr 92. (7"/c-s/12"/cd-s) *(USM/+XMC/X/CD 4)* **THE ONLY LIVING BOY IN NEW CROSS. / WATCHING THE BIG APPLE TURN / PANIC** [7] [ ]

May 92. (cd/c/lp) *(CCD/ZCHR/CHR 1946)* **1992 – THE LOVE ALBUM** [1] [ ]
– 1993 / Is wrestling fixed? / The only living boy in New Cross / Suppose you gave a funeral and nobody came / England / Do re mi, so far so good / Look mum, no hands / While you were out / Skywest and crooked / The impossible dream. *(re-iss. Mar94 & Feb95 cd/c;)*

Jun 92. (7"/c-s/12"/cd-s) *(USM/+XMC/X/CD 5)* **DO RE MI, SO FAR SO GOOD / MANNEQUIN. / KING ROCKER / DOWN IN THE TUBE-STATION AT MIDNIGHT** [22] [ ]

Nov 92. (7"/c-s/12"/cd-s) *(USM/+XMC/X/CD 6)* **THE IMPOSSIBLE DREAM / TURN ON, TUNE IN AND SWITCH OFF / WHEN THESAURUSES RULED THE WORLD / BRING ON THE GIRLS** [21] [ ]

Aug 93. (7"/c-s) *(USM/+XMC 7)* **LEAN ON ME I WON'T FALL OVER. / HIT** [16] [ ]
(12"+=/cd-s+=) *(12/CD USM 7)* – Always the bridesmaid never the bride.

Sep 93. (cd/c/lp) *(CD/TC+/CHR 7090)* **POST HISTORIC MONSTERS** [5] [ ]
– 2 million years B.C. / The music that nobody likes / Mid day crisis / Cheer up, it might never happen / Stuff the jubilee! / A bachelor for Baden Powell / Spoilsports personality of the year / Suicide isn't painless / Being here / Evil / Sing fat lady sing / Travis / Lean on me I won't fall over / Lenny and Terence / Under the thumb and over the Moon. *(re-iss. Feb95;)*

Oct 93. (7"/c-s) *(USM/+XMC 8)* **LENNY AND TERENCE. / HER SONG** [40] [ ]
(12"+=/cd-s+=) *(12/CD USM 8)* – Commercial fucking suicide (part 1) / Stuff the jubilee (1977).

Mar 94. (c-s/7") *(TC+/USM 10)* **GLAM ROCK COPS. / LEAN ON ME (I WON'T FALL OVER) (by The FAMILY CAT)** [24] [ ]
(12"+=/cd-s+=) *(12USM/CDUSMS 10)* – ('A'-GRID mixes).
(cd-s) *(CDUSM 10)* – ('A'side) / Bloodsports for all (by SULTANS OF PING F.C.) / Lenny and Terence (by BLADE) / Falling on a bruise (by PUBLIC WORKS).

Mar 94. (cd/c/lp) *(CD/TC+/CHR 6069)* **STARRY EYED AND BOLLOCK NAKED (A COLLECTION OF B-SIDES)** (compilation) [22] [ ]
– Is this the only way to get through to you? / Granny farming in the UK / R.S.P.C.E. / Twin tub with guitar / Alternative Alf Garnett / Re educating Rita / 2001: A clockwork orange / The 90's revival / A nation of shoplifters / Watching the big apple turn over / Turn on, tune in and switch off / When Thesauruses ruled the Earth / Bring on the girls! / Always the bridesmaid never the bride / Her song / Commercial f**king suicide / Stuff the jubilee (1977) / Glam rock cops. *(re-iss. Feb95; same)*

— added **WEZ BOYNTON** – drums (ex-RESQUE)

Nov 94. (c-s/7") *(TC+/USM 11)* **LET'S GET TATTOOS. / ESPECIALLY 4 U** [30] [ ]
(cd-s+=) *(CDUSMS 11)* – Speed king / Silver dream machine.
(cd-s) *(CDUSM 11)* – ('A'side) / Turbulence / King for a day.

Jan 95. (c-s/7"colrd) *(TC+/USM 12)* **THE YOUNG OFFENDER'S MUM. / TROUBLE** 34
(cd-s+=) *(CDUSMS 12)* – This one's for me.
(cd-s) *(CDUSM 12)* – ('A'side) / Rubbish (live) / Suicide isn't painless (live) / Falling on a bruise (live).

Feb 95. (cd/c/d-lp) *(CD/TC+/CHR 6096)* **WORRY BOMB** 9
– Cheap'n'cheesy / Airplane food – airplane fest food / The young offender's mum / Gas (man) / The life and soul of the party dies / My defeatest attitude / Worry bomb / Senile delinquent / Me and Mr.Jones / Let's get tattoos / Going straight / God, Saint Peter and the guardian angel / The only looney left in town / Ceasefire. *(d-cd+=) (CDCHRX 6096)* **DOMA SPORTOVA . . . LIVE IN ZAGREB, 20/5/94** – Alternative Alf Garnett / Do re me so far so good / A bachelor pad for Baden Powell / Re-educating Rita / The only living boy in New Cross / Lean on me I won't fall over / Granny farming in the U.K. / Travis / Sing fat lady sing / Lenny and Terence / Commercial fucking suicide part 1.

Sep 95. (c-s/7"red) *(TC+/USM 13)* **BORN ON THE 5th OF NOVEMBER. / D.I.V.O.R.C.E.F.G.** 35
(cd-s) *(CDUSM 13)* – ('A'side) / Tomorrow when you die / The aftertaste of Paradise / Airplane food.

Oct 95. (cd/c/lp) *(CD/TC+/CHR 6110)* **STRAW DONKEY . . .THE SINGLES** (compilation) 37
– A sheltered life / Sheriff Fatman / Rubbish / Antime anyplace anywhere / Bloodsport for all / After the watershed (early learning the hard way) / The only living boy in New Cross / Do re mi, so far so good / The impossible dream / Lean on me (I won't fall over) / Lenny and Terence / Glam rock cops / Let's get tattoos / The young offender's mum / Born on the 5th of November.

— CARTER split for around a year after above

Cooking Vinyl / Cooking Vinyl

Mar 97. (lp/cd) *(<COOK/+CD 120>)* **A WORLD WITHOUT DAVE** 73 Apr97
– Broken down in broken town / A world without Dave / Before the war / Nowhere fast / Johnny Cash / And God created Brixton / Stand up and be counted / Negative equity / Road rage.

True North / True North

Sep 98. (cd) *(<163>)* **I BLAME THE GOVERNMENT**
– Wrong place at the wrong time / 23:59 end of the world / Sunshine / The undertaker and the hippy protest / Sweetheart sugar baby / Growing old disgracefully / The man who bought the world / Winning the war / I blame the government / Citizen's band radio / Psycho Bill / Closedown / Girls can keep a secret.

Peter CASE (see under ⇒ PLIMSOULS)

CASSANDRA COMPLEX

Formed: Leeds, England . . . 1984 by main songwriter, RODNEY ORPHEUS, PAUL DILLON and ANDY BOOTH. In 1985, they issued a self-financed debut single, 'MARCH' (actually released that month), which, after a live cassette, led to a signing for small local independent, 'Rouska'. An electro-industrial art-rock outfit featuring percussive treatments fused with a HAPPY MONDAYS feel, CASSANDRA COMPLEX nevertheless had a tendency to indulge in pseudo-intellectual lyrics. Two subsequent albums, 'GRENADE' (1986) and 'HELLO AMERICA' (1987), helped win them a healthier contract for Belgian-based label, 'Play It Again Sam' in 1987, their slightly contrived sound winning more fans on the continent where they were now living. First up for the label, bar a single 'KILL YOUR CHILDREN', was the live opus, 'FEEL THE WIDTH', which featured a faithful renditions of 'SOMETHING CAME OVER ME' by industrial forebears, Throbbing Gristle and 'GHOST RIDER' by Suicide. In 1988, CASANDRA COMPLEX delivered PAUL and ANDY's swansong, 'THEOMANIA', before RODNEY enlisted an all new cast including JOHN GALVIN and JURGEN JANSEN. Alongside additional members, PATRICK GORDEN and ALAN WILKINSON, the new line-up made its debut on 1989's 'SATAN, BUGS BUNNY AND ME', appropriately covering noneother than the Rolling Stones' 'SYMPATHY FOR THE DEVIL'. The turn of the decade saw GAZ WILSON replacing GALVIN on the 'CYBERPUNX' (1990) set, while prior to their following album, 'WAR AGAINST SLEEP' (1991), WILKINSON and WILSON had made way for VOLKER ZAPHOR ZACHARIAS and the returning ANDY BOOTH. Confusingly enough, the song 'WAR AGAINST SLEEP' actually appeared on 1993's last effort to date, 'SEX & DEATH', a record that also featured another Suicide classic, 'FRANKIE TEARDROP'.

Album rating: GRENADE (*6) / HELLO AMERICA (*6) / FEEL THE WIDTH (*7) / THEOMANIA (*6) / SATAN, BUGS BUNNY AND ME (*6) / CYBERPUNX (*5) / WAR AGAINST SLEEP (*5) / SEX & DEATH (*5)

RODNEY ORPHEUS – vocals / **PAUL DILLON** – keyboards / **ANDY BOOTH** – guitar

Complex / not iss.

Mar 85. (12") *(CXD 001)* **MARCH. / PICKUP (live) / HCOMA** -
Apr 85. (c) *(CXC 004)* **LIVE IN LEATHER** -

Rouska / not iss.

Sep 85. (12") *(COME 2T)* **MOSCOW IDAHO. /** -

— now without DILLON. He was repl. by **JEZ WILLIS** – keyboards, bass / **KEITH LANGLEY** – guitar / **JOHN MARCINI** – sax, bass

Jul 86. (12") *(COME 5T)* **DATA KILL. /** -
Sep 86. (lp/c) *(CXRA/+C 1)* **GRENADE** -
– March 86 / Wonderworld / Presents (come of age) / Pickup / Power / Report from the back / Prairie bitch / Motherad.
(cd-iss. 1987 on 'Play Iy Again Sam'; CXM 1001)

May 87. (lp) *(CXRA 2)* **HELLO AMERICA** -
– Moscow Idaho / Beyond belief / Datakill / Clouds / Fragile / Wintry weather song / David Venus / Three cities. *(cd-iss. May88; CXRA 2CD)*

Play It Again Sam / Play It Again Sam

Oct 87. (7"/12") *(BIAS 064/+T)* **KILL YOUR CHILDREN. /**
Nov 87. (lp/cd) *(BIAS/CDBIAS 068)* **FEEL THE WIDTH (live)**
– Clouds / Wonderworld / Three string blues / Prairie bitch / Data kill / ower / Pickup / Something came over me / Moscow Idaho / March / David Venus / Ghost rider.

— guest **DAVE WILSON** – guitar; repl. WILLIS + LANGLEY

Apr 88. (lp/cd) *(BIAS/CDBIAS 088)* **THEOMANIA** -
– Good John / Oz / Too stupid to sin / Honey trap / One millionth hapy customer / Ground / Second shot / Defcon 1.

— **ORPHEUS** brought in **JOHN GALVIN** – bass, guitar + **JURGEN JANSEN** – keyboards, computer / others **PATRICK GORDEN** – computers, percussion / **ALAN WILKINSON** – sax

Apr 89. (lp/cd) *(BIAS/CDBIAS 118)* **SATAN, BUGS BUNNY, AND ME** -
– What can you say? / E.O.D. / Sympathy for the Devil / Forever / Kill the Christian swine / City of dreams / (In search of) Penny Century.

— **GAZ WILSON** – guitar repl. GALVIN

Jan 90. (lp/cd) *(BIAS 148/+CD)* **CYBERPUNX** -
– Nice work (if you can get it) / Let's go to Europe / Happy days (war is here again) / Jihad girl / Sunshine at midnight / I want you / Sleeper / Nightfall (over E.C.) / Into the heart / I believe in free everything / What turns you on? / Ugly.

Jan 90. (12"/cd-s) *(BIAS 151/+CD)* **FINLAND. /** -
May 90. (12"/cd-s) *(BIAS /+CD)* **NICE WORK** -

— **ANDY BOOTH** returned with new member **VOLKER ZAPHOR ZACHARIAS** – guitar, keyboards; repl. WILSON + WILKINSON

1991. (lp/cd) *(BIAS 195/+CD)* **WAR AGAINST SLEEP** -
– What can I do for you? / Dr. Adder / And you say / Why? / She loves me / Awake all night – When love comes / Tell me / Lullaby for the first born in Outer Space / Lakeside.

Nov 93. (cd) *(BIAS 255CD)* **SEX & DEATH**
– Kneel to the boss / Mouth of Heaven / War against sleep / Come out / Satisfy me / Give me what I need / Devil's advocate / You make me sick / Voices / Realm of the senseless / Frankie Teardrop / In memoriam JC / You still make me sick.

May 94. (cd-s) *(BIAS 258CD)* **GIVE ME WHAT I NEED / ('A'mixes) / YOU STILL MAKE ME FEEL SICK** -

CAST

Formed: Liverpool, England . . . 1994 by ex-LA'S guitarist JOHN POWER, alongside KEITH O'NEIL, LIAM TYSON and PETER WILKINSON. Bassist POWER had become increasingly disillusioned with The LA'S interminable absence from the music scene, taking his future into his own hands and developing his 60's influenced songwriting within a more solid framework. Fortuitously, POWERS' strident, melodic sound was perfectly in tune with the emerging retro fixated Brit-pop sound and, with the influential backing of OASIS, CAST crashed into the Top 20 in the summer of '95 with 'FINETIME'. Surfing on a wave of frothy powerchords and an irrepressibly buoyant melody, 'ALRIGHT' followed soon after, the track becoming something of a theme tune and a definitive highlight of their debut set, 'ALL CHANGE'. Released later that Autumn, the album divided the critics, some raving over its immaculate melodic appeal, some deriding its workmanlike adherance to "classic songwriting". Whatever, there was no doubting POWER's ear for a tune, and the sublime 'SANDSTORM' gave the band a further Top 10 hit in early '96. CAST's solid style inevitably translated well to the live arena and they built up a rabid following of beany-topped fans, the same constituency of check-shirted "lads" who frequented OASIS and OCEAN COLOUR SCENE gigs. In Autumn '96, the group scored their first Top 5 with 'FLYING', a lilting new track which further showcased their mastery of BEATLES-esque pop dynamics. However, the critics were just dying to sink their claws into this resolutely untrendy outfit, with the fine 'MOTHER NATURE CALLS' (1997) unfairly receiving mixed reviews. Detractors rounded on POWER's spiritually-enhanced muse and mystical leanings but there was no arguing with the life-affirming power inherant in songs like 'GLIDING STAR', another Top 10 smash in summer '97. Although the album didn't perhaps cause the stir envisaged, CAST remain one of Britain's more talented indie-type bands with one of the country's most loyal followings.

Album rating: ALL CHANGE (*7) / MOTHER NATURE CALLS (*7)

JOHN POWER – vocals, guitar (ex-LA'S) / **LIAM TYSON** – guitar / **PETER WILKINSON** – bass (ex-SHACK) / **KEITH O'NEIL** – drums

Polydor / Polydor

Jul 95. (7"green/c-s/cd-s) *(579 506-7/-4/-2)* **FINETIME. / BETTER MAN / SATELLITES** 17 -
Sep 95. (7"blue/c-s/cd-s) *(579 926-7/-4/-2)* **ALRIGHT. / FOLLOW ME DOWN / MEET ME** 13 -
Oct 95. (cd/c/d-lp) *(529 312-2/-4/-1)* **ALL CHANGE** 7
– Alright / Promised land / Sandstorm / Mankind / Tell it like it is / Four walls / Finetime / Back of my mind / Walkaway / Reflections / History / Two of a kind.

Jan 96. (7"orange/c-s) *(577 872-7/-4)* **SANDSTORM. / HOURGLASS / BACK OF MY MIND (live)** 8 -
(cd-s+=/tin-cd-s+=) *(577 873/903-2)* – Alright (live).

Mar 96. (7"clear/c-s) *(576 284-7/-4)* **WALKAWAY. / FULFILL / FINETIME (acoustic)** 9 -
(cd-s) *(576 285-2)* – (first 2 tracks) / Mother.

Oct 96. (7"/c-s) *(575 476-7/-4)* **FLYING. / BETWEEN THE EYES / FOR SO LONG** 4 -
(pic-cd-s+=) *(575 477-2)* – Walkaway.

Mar 97. (7"/c-s) *(573 648-7/-4)* **FREE ME. / COME ON EVERYBODY / CANTER** 7 -
(cd-s+=) *(573 649-2)* – ('A'acoustic).
(cd-s) *(573 651-2)* – ('A'side) / Release my soul / Dancing on the flames.

Apr 97. (cd/c/lp) *(537 567-2/-4/-1)* **MOTHER NATURE CALLS** 3
– Free me / On the run / Live the dream / Soul tied / She sun shines / I'm so lonely / The mad hatter / Mirror me / Guiding star / Never gonna tell you what to do (revolution) / Dance of the stars. *(special edition d-cd Nov97; 539681-2)*

Jun 97. (7") *(571 172-7)* **GUIDING STAR. / OUT OF THE BLUE** [9] [-]
(c-s+=) *(571 172-4)* – Keep it alive.
(cd-s+=) *(571 173-2)* – Free me (live) / Mirror me (live).
(cd-s) *(571 295-2)* – ('A'side) / Keep it alive / Redemption song (live) / ('A'acoustic).

Sep 97. (c-s) *(571 500-4)* <6025> **LIVE THE DREAM / HOLD ON / FLOW** [7] [ ] Apr98
(cd-s) *(571 501-2)* – (first 2 tracks) / Effectomatic who / ('A'acoustic).
(cd-s) *(571 685-2)* – (first & third tracks) / On the run.

Nov 97. (c-s) *(569 256-4)* **I'M SO LONELY / THINGS YOU MAKE ME DO / THEME FROM** [14] [-]
(cd-s) *(569 057-2)* – (first 2 tracks) / Never gonna tell you / History.
(cd-s) *(569 059-2)* – (tracks 1 & 3) / History.

CATATONIA

Formed: Cardiff, Wales . . . 1991 by songwriters MARK ROBERTS and PAUL JONES, who had both been part of 'Ankst' label outfit, Y CRYFF (The BODY). Having found OWEN POWELL from The CRUMB BLOWERS and sultry blonde singer, CERYS MATTHEWS, they set about taking their style of Welsh accented hooks to the alternative indie scene. However, things did not get off to a flying start, when the group offended the label's strict Welsh-only language policy and were moved on to another leak-biased label, 'Crai', where they released two singles in 1993/94. In the summer of '94, Geoff Travis's 'Rough Trade Singles Club' label issued 'WHALE', Travis subsequently grabbing them for his 'Blanco Y Negro'. 1996 became a shining year for them with four hit singles and a well-received album, the Stephen Street-produced 'WAY BEYOUND BLUE' denting the Top 40. Much was anticipated for a glorious 1998 after they hit the Top 40 in late '97 with 'I AM THE MOB'. All predictions came true as CERYS and Co. stormed the Top 3 as early as January that year with the X-Files inspired 'MULDER AND SCULLY'. This was only one of the many successes (others being 'ROAD RAGE', 'STRANGE GLUE' and 'GAME ON') taken from their acclaimed chart-topping album, 'INTERNATIONAL VELVET', although indie sex symbol CERYS would also team up with SPACE for the tongue-in-cheek romantic duet, 'The Ballad Of Tom Jones'.

Album rating: THE SUBLIME MAGIC OF CATATONIA European compilation (*7) / WAY BEYOND BLUE (*7) / INTERNATIONAL VELVET (*8)

CERYS MATTHEWS – vocals / **MARK ROBERTS** – guitar / **OWEN POWELL (ex-CRUMB BLOWERS)** – guitar / **PAUL JONES** – bass / **ALED** – drums

Crai / not iss.

Sep 93. (c-ep)(cd-ep) *(C 039L)(CD 039B)* **FOR TINKERBELL EP** [ ] [-]
– For Tinkerbell / New mercurial heights / Dimbran / Sweet Catatonia / Gyda Gwen – New mercurial heights (Welsh mix).

Jun 94. (c-s)(cd-s) *(C 042L)(CD 042B)* **HOOKED. / FALL BESIDE HER / DIFRYCHEULYD (SNAIL AMBITION)** [ ] [-]

Rough Trade Sing. Club / not iss.

Aug 94. (7") *(45rev 33)* **WHALE. / YOU CAN** [ ] [-]

Nursery / not iss.

Feb 95. (7"red) *(NYS 12L)* **BLEED. / THIS BOY CAN'T SWIM** [ ] [-]
(cd-s+=) *(NYSCD 12)* – Painful.

Nov 95. (cd) *(NYSCD 12X)* **THE SUBLIME MAGIC OF CATATONIA** (compilation) [-] [-] Europe
– Bleed / This boy can't swim / Painful / Dream on / Whale / You can / Hooked / Fall beside her / Difrycheulyd (Snail ambition). *(hidden track +=)* – Cariadon ffol.

Blanco Y Negro / Blanco Y Negro

Dec 95. (7"white; mail-o) *(SAM 1746)* **BLOW THE MILLENNIUM BLOW. / BEAUTIFUL SAILOR** [-] [-]

Jan 96. (7"/c-s) *(NEG 85/+C)* **SWEET CATATONIA. / TOURIST** [61] [-]
(cd-s) *(NEG 85CD)* – ('A'side) / Acapulco gold / Cut you inside (demo).

Apr 96. (7"yellow) *(NEGAT 88X)* **LOST CAT. / TO AND FRO** [41] [-]
(c-s/cd-s) *(NEGAT 88 CAS/CD1)* – ('A'side) / All girls are fly / Indigo blind.
(cd-s) *(NEG 88CD2)* – ('A'side) / Sweet Catatonia (live – Mark Radcliffe 1FM session) / Whale (live – Mark Radcliffe 1FM session).

Sep 96. (7") *(NEG 93)* **YOU'VE GOT A LOT TO ANSWER FOR. / DO YOU BELIEVE IN ME?** [35] [-]
(cd-s+=) *(NEG 93CD1)* – Dimbran.
(cd-s) *(NEG 93CD2)* – ('A'side) / You can / All girls are fly.
(c-s) *(NEG 93CAS)* – ('A'side) / Blow the millennium blow (Splott remix).

Sep 96. (cd/c/lp) *(0630 16305-2/-4/-1)* **WAY BEYOND BLUE** [40] [-]
– Lost cat / Sweet Catatonia / Some half baked / Ideal called wonderful / You've got a lot to answer for / Infantile / Dream on. *(lp w/free 7"/cd w/hidden track)* – Gyda Gwen.

Nov 96. (7"red) *(NEG 97)* **BLEED. / DO YOU BELIEVE IN ME? (live – Reading Festival 1FM)** [46] [-]
(cd-s+=) *(NEG 97CD2)* – Bleed (live evening session 1FM).
(cd-s) *(NEG 97CD1)* – ('A'side) / Way beyond blue (live – Mark Radcliffe 1FM session) / Painful (live – Reading Festival 1FM).
(c-s) *(NEG 97CASS)* – ('A'side) / Way beyond blue (live – Mark Radckiffe 1FM session) / Bleed (live – evening session 1FM).

Oct 97. (7"orange/c-s) *(NEG 107/+CASS)* **I AM THE MOB. / JUMP OR BE SANE** [40] [-]
(cd-s+=) *(NEG 107CD)* – My selfish Gene / ('A'-Luca Brasi mix).

Jan 98. (7"blue/c-s) *(NEG 109/+CASS)* **MULDER AND SCULLY. / NO STONE UNTURNED** [3] [-]
(cd-s+=) *(NEG 109CD)* – Mantra for the lost / ('A'-The Ex-files).

Feb 98. (cd/c/lp) *(<3984 20834-2/-4/-1>)* **INTERNATIONAL VELVET** [1] [ ]
– Mulder and Scully / Game on / I am the mob / Road rage / Johnny come lately / Goldfish and paracetamol / International velvet / Why I can't stand one night stands / Part of the furniture / Don't need the sunshine / Strange glue / My selfish gene. *(lp w/ free 12"radio sessions)* – International velvet / No stione unturned / Murder & Scully / Strange glue.

— Feb'98:- CERYS featured on a SPACE hit, 'The Ballad Of Tom Jones'

Apr 98. (7"yellow/c-s) *(NEG 112/+CASS)* **ROAD RAGE. / I'M CURED** [5] [-]
(cd-s+=) *(NEG 112CD)* – Blow the millennium (pt.2) / ('A'-Ghia).

Blanco Y Negro / Imprint

Jul 98. (7"red/c-s) *(NEG 113/+CASS)* **STRANGE GLUE. / THAT'S ALL FOLKS** [11] [ ]
(cd-s+=) *(NEG 113CD)* – Road rage (live).

Oct 98. (7"green/c-s) *(NEG 114/+CASS)* **GAME ON. / STRANGE GLUE (live acoustic)** [33] [-]
(cd-s+=) *(NEG 114CD)* – Mulder and Scully (live in Newport).

CAT HEADS

Formed: San Francisco, California, USA . . . 1985 by MARK ZANANDREA, along with SAM BABBIT, ALAN KORN and MELANIE CLARIN, all seasoned Bay Area alternative writers/musicians. Signing to 'Enigma', the quartet debuted in '87 with 'HUBBA' (produced by RAIN PARADE's MATT PIUCCI), an anarchic ragbag of rootsy retro-rock, punk and off-beat humour. Of their contemporaries, CAMPER VAN BEETHOVEN were closest in spirit and it came as little surprise when the latter outfit's DAVID LOWERY offered his production services for 1988's more focused follow-up, 'SUBMARINE'. The band virtually split in two soon after, only BABBIT and KORN remaining for one further CAT HEADS platter, 'OUR FRISCO' (1989), although (alongside newcomers BARRY HALL and JOHN STUART) MELANIE did make a guest appearance. In the mid-90's, two pairings of the original quartet surfaced, MARK and MELANIE in IT THING while MARK and SAM became the ANDROGYNAUTS; the final CAT HEADS line-up was to re-emerge as the MUDSILLS.

Album rating: HUBBA (*6) / SUBMARINE (*7) / OUR FRISCO (*5)

MARK ZANANDREA – vocals, guitar (ex-LOVE CIRCUS, ex-LEACHES) / **SAM BABBIT** – guitar (ex-OPHELIAS) / **ALAN KORN** – bass (ex-X-TAL) / **MELANIE CLARIN** – drums, vocals (also of DONNER PARTY)

Enigma / Restless

May 87. (lp) *(ENIG 2195-1)* <9-71195> **HUBBA** [ ] [ ]
– Hangin' around / Voyeur in the balcony / I would kill for Suzy / Victim / Final letter / Hubba part 1 / Golden Gate park / Power love and pizza / Need to know / Lego down / Saved by the bottle / New white things / Lullaby.

1988. (lp/c) <72236-1/-4> **SUBMARINE** [-] [ ]
– Little less of me / Apologize / Grass / Hallelujah dance / Alice on the radio / Postcard / Upside down / Sister Tabitha / Juggy saw dust – Gumshoe / Paradise / Bisho / Crash landing.

— **BABBIT + KORN** recruited new members **BARRY HALL** – multi / **JOHN STUART** – drums (of FLYING COLOR) / **MELANIE** (guested) vox (she and MARK became part of IT THING, while the latter re-united with SAM in mid-90's act, ANDROGYNAUTS; SAM and ALAN were now in MUDSILLS)

not iss. / Twitch City

1989. (lp; as ex CAT HEADS) <001> **OUR FRISCO** [-] [ ]

CATHERINE WHEEL

Formed: Great Yarmouth, England . . . April 1990 by ROB DICKINSON and BRIAN FUTTER, completing the line-up with DAVE HAWES and NEIL SIMS and taking their moniker from a type of firework. The quartet recorded a demo on their own 8-track bedroom studio, the results released early the following year by independent imprint, 'Wilde Club', as debut single/EP, 'SHE'S MY FRIEND'. A second rough sounding EP, 'PAINFUL THING', also found its way into the indie charts resulting in them securing a contract with recently re-activated major label, 'Fontana' (recently home to a TEARDROP EXPLODES compilation, who incidentally, CATHERINE WHEEL bear more than a musical passing resemblance to). Becoming an integral part of the early 90's "shoegazing" scene, the CATHERINE WHEEL steadily built up a fanbase through committed gigging and a couple of minor UK hit singles, namely the 7-minute epic, 'BLACK METALLIC' and 'BALLOON'. Both featured on their TIME FRIESE-GREENE (TALK TALK)-produced debut set, 'FERMENT' (early '92), a Top 40 entrant with enough guitar bashing to hint at their future incarnation as a fully-fledged Rock band. In the meantime, ROB and Co finally cracked the Top 40 with 'I WANT TO TOUCH YOU' and subsequently revealed their eclectic musical tastes with a covers EP, running through versions of Scott Walker's '30th CENTURY MAN', Husker Du's 'DON'T WANT TO KNOW IF YOU ARE LONELY' and Mission Of Burma's 'THAT'S WHEN I REACH FOR MY REVOLVER' (they also did a version of Pink Floyd's 'WISH YOU WERE HERE'). 1993 hardly went off with a bang, however, as the GIL NORTON-produced follow-up set, 'CHROME', suffered at the hands of fickle critics, although steadfast fans did push it into the Top 60. Turning their attention to the States, CATHERINE WHEEL began to ferment a heavier, more rhythmic rock sound, finally laying to rest the "shoegazing" soundscapes of old on, er . . . "comeback" album, 'HAPPY DAYS' (1995). Despite featuring a duet, 'JUDY STARING AT THE SUN', with the BREEDERS' leading lady, TANYA DONELLY, the record went down like a damp squib in Britain. Nevertheless, burgeoning Stateside interest led to a deal with 'Chrysalis' and in 1998, they returned with an ever more Kerrang!-friendly sound on their fourth set, ADAM & EVE', a surprise success in the States after a gruelling coast to coast BUSH-like tour.

Album rating: FERMENT (*6) / CHROME (*7) / HAPPY DAYS (*7) / LIKE CATS AND DOGS collection (*5) / ADAM AND EVE (*6)

ROB DICKINSON (b.23 Jul'65, Norwich, England) – vocals, guitar / **BRIAN FUTTER** (b. 7 Dec'65, London) – guitar, vocals / **DAVE HAWES** (b.10 Nov'65) – bass / **NEIL SIMS** (b. 4 Oct'65, Norwich) – percussion, drums

Wilde Club / not iss.

Jan 91. (12"ep) **SHE'S MY FRIEND / UPSIDE DOWN. / WISH / SALT** [ ] [-]
May 91. (12"ep/cd-ep) **PAINFUL THING / SHALLOW / SPIN / I WANT TO TOUCH YOU** [ ] [-]

Fontana / Fontana

Nov 91. (7") *(CW 1)* **BLACK METALLIC. / LET ME DOWN AGAIN** [68] [-]
(12"+=/cd-s+=) *(CW X/CD 1)* – Crawling over me / Saccharin.
Jan 92. (7") *(CW 2)* **BALLOON. / INTRAVENOUS** [59] [ ]
(12"+=/cd-s+=) *(CW X/CD 2)* – Painful thing (live) / Let me down again (live).
Feb 92. (cd/c/lp) *(510903-2/-4/-1)* **FERMENT** [36] [ ]
– Texture / I want to touch you / Black metallic / Indigo is blue / She's my friend / Shallow / Ferment / Flower to hide / Tumbledown / Bill and Ben / Salt. *(incl.free 7"ep)*
Apr 92. (d7"/12"ep/cd-ep) *(CW/+X/CD 3)* **I WANT TO TOUCH YOU. / URSA MAJOR SPACE STATION/ / OUR FRIEND JOEY. / COLLIDEOSCOPE** [35] [ ]
(12") – (first 7") / Half life.
(cd-s) – (first 7") / Wish / Black metallic.
Nov 92. (12"ep/cd-ep) *(CW X/CD 4)* **30th CENTURY MAN. / DON'T WANT TO KNOW IF YOU ARE LONELY / THAT'S WHEN I REACH FOR MY REVOLVER** [47] [ ]

Fontana / Polygram

Jul 93. (7"/c-s) *(CW/+MC 5)* **CRANK. / COME BACK AGAIN** [66] [ ]
(12") *(CWT 5)* – ('A'side) / Black metallic / Painful ting.
(cd-s) *(CWCD 5)* – ('A'side) / La la la-la la / Something strange.
(cd-s) *(CWCDX 5)* – ('A'side) / Pleasure / Tongue twisted.
Sep 93. (7") *(CW 6)* **SHOW ME MARY. / FLOWER TO HIDE (live)** [62] [ ]
(cd-s+=) *(CWCDA 6)* – Car / Girl stand still.
(cd-s) *(CWCDB 6)* – ('A'side) / These four wheels / Smother.
(12") *(CWT 6)* – ('A'side) / High heels / Mouth full of air.
Sep 93. (cd/c/lp) *(<518039-2/-4/-1>)* **CHROME** [58] [ ]
– Kill rhythm / I confess / Crank / Broken head / Pain / Strange fruit / Chrome / The nude / Ursa Major space station / Fripp / Half life / Show me Mary.

— guests on above album:- TIM FRIESE-GREENE and AUDREY RILEY.

Jul 95. (10") *(<CW 7>)* **WAYDOWN. / CRANK / WISH YOU WERE HERE (XFM session)** [67] [ ]
(cd-s) *(CWCD 7)* – ('A'side) / Show me Mary (XFM sessions) / Kill rhythm.
(cd-s) *(CWDD 7)* – ('A'side) / Chrome / Broken head (XFM sessions).
Sep 95. (10"ep) *(CW 8)* **JUDY STARING AT THE SUN / GOD INSIDE MY HEAD. / CRANK (live) / WAYDOWN (live)** [ ] [-]
(cd-ep) *(CWCD 8)* – (first 2 tracks) / Glitter.
(cd-ep) *(CWDD 8)* – (first 2 tracks) / Backwards guitar / Angelo Nero.
(above 'A'side featured TANYA DONELLY of BREEDERS)
Nov 95. (cd/c)(d-lp) *(<514717-2/-4>)(526850-1)* **HAPPY DAYS** [ ] [ ]
– God inside my head / Waydown / Little muscle / Heal / Empty head / Receive / My exhibition / Eat my dust you insensitive fuck / Shocking / Love tips up / Judy staring at the sun / Hole / Fizzy love / Glitter / Kill my soul.

Chrysalis / Polygram

Dec 97. (10"ep) *(10CHS 5071)* **THE DELICIOUS EP** [53] [ ]
– Delicious / Eat my dust you insensitive f**k / Crank (live) / Texture (live).
(cd-ep) *(CDCHS 5071)* – ('A'side) / Future boy / Judy staring at the sun (with TANYA DONELLY) / Heal.
Feb 98. (7"colrd) *(CHS 5077)* **MA SOLITUDA. / KILL RHYTHM (live)** [53] [-]
(cd-s) *(CDCHSS 5077)* – ('A'side) / Delicious / Descending babe / Paranoia.
(cd-s) *(CDCHS 5077)* – ('A'-Tim Friese-Greene mix) / Delicious (live) / Willing to wait / Lucifer.
Apr 98. (7") *(CHS 5086)* **BROKEN NOSE. / LITTLE MUSCLE (live)** [48] [-]
(cd-s) *(CDCHS 5086)* – ('A'side) / Crank (live) / Texture (live) / Black metallic (live).
(cd-s) *(CDCHSS 5086)* – ('A'side) / Flower to hide (live) / Heal (live) / I want to touch you (live).
May 98. (cd/c/d-lp) *(493099-2/-4/-1)* *<534864>* **ADAM AND EVE** [53] [ ] Jul98
– Future boy / Delicious / Broken nose / Phantom of the American mother / Ma solituda / Satellite / Thunderbird / Here comes the fat controller / Goodbye / For dreaming.
Jun 98. (7") *(CHS 5094)* **DELICIOUS. /** [ ] [ ]
(cd-s) *(CDCHS 5094)* –
(cd-s) *(CDCHSS 5094)* –

– compilations, etc. –

Sep 96. (cd) *Polygram; (532456-2)* **LIKE CATS AND DOGS** (B-sides, rarities, etc) [ ] [-]
– Heal 2 / Wish you were here / Mouthful of air / Car / Girl stand still / Saccharine / Backwards guitar / Tongue twisted / These four walls / High heels / Harder than I am / La-la-la.

CAT POWER

Formed: by CHAN MARSHALL (pronounced 'Shan'), a Southern States-born 20-something singer/songwriter trading in gothic-folk music. In 1996, after releasing her demos on two low-key indie label albums, she virtually gave up the ghost, until that is, she was spotted backing LIZ PHAIR at a New York gig by 'Matador' label boss Gerard Cosley and SONIC YOUTH's STEVE SHELLEY. The former subsequently signed her up, the latter, with the addition of guitarist TIM FOLJAHN, became her backing band. The results were soon featured on that year's "comeback" set, 'WHAT WOULD THE COMMUNITY THINK', her recording life back in full swing with a support slot to stablemate, LIZ PHAIR. However, again reluctant to gain any recognition for this fine work, she jumped ship to Australia with SMOG's BILL CALLAHAN. There she was introduced to JIM WHITE and MICK TURNER (both of DIRTY THREE), who helped out on her fourth attempt to break through, 'MOONPIX' (1998). • **Covered:** Y IS HERE (Tom Waits) / S WALKER (TKO Punishment).

Album rating: DEAR SIR (*6) / MYRA LEE (*7) / WHAT WOULD THE COMMUNITY THINK (*8) / MOONPIX (*8)

CHAN MARSHALL (b.1972) – vocals, guitar, piano

not iss. / Runt

Oct 95. (cd) *<006>* **DEAR SIR** [-] [ ]
– 3 times / Rockets / Itchyhead / Y is here / S Walker / Mr. Gallo / No matter / Headlights.

not iss. / Smells Like

Mar 96. (cd) *<019>* **MYRA LEE** [-] [ ]
– Enough / We all die / Great expectations / Top expert / Ice water / Still in love / Rockets / Faces / Fiance / Wealthy man / Not what you want.

— with **TIM FOLJAHN** – guitar (of TWO DOLLAR GUITAR) / **STEVE SHELLEY** – drums (of SONIC YOUTH)

Matador / Matador

Sep 96. (cd/lp) *<(OLE 202-2/-1)>* **WHAT WOULD THE COMMUNITY THINK** [ ] [ ]
– The coat is always on / Enough / Water and air / Bathosphere / The king rides by / Fate of the human carbine / Taking people / They tell me / Nude as the news / What would the community think / Good clean fun / In this hole.
Jan 97. (7") *(OLE 240-7)* **NUDE AS THE NEWS. / SCHIZOPHRENIA'S WEIGHED ME DOWN** [ ] [ ]
(cd-s+=) *(OLE 240-2)* –

— now with **JIM WHITE** – drums / **MICK TURNER** – guitar

Sep 98. (cd/lp) *<(OLE 286-2/-1)>* **MOONPIX** [ ] [ ]
– American flag / He turns down / No sense / Say / Metal heart / Back of your head / Moonshiner / You may know him / Colors and the kids / Cross bones style / Peking saint.

CAUSE FOR ALARM

Formed: New York, USA . . . early 80's by KEITH BURKHARDT, JASON BANKS and JOE ORGERA (drummer unknown). In the old hardcore tradition of fellow NY punk-noise merchants, AGNOSTIC FRONT and CRO-MAGS, the quartet plundered this territory until their untimely demise in '84. A decade later, CFA were once again, this time with a new drummer, RAEPH, and a contract with 'Victory'. An eponymous angst-ridden debut in '95 was quickly pursued by a split set with WARZONE, melodic punk was truly fighting back. A 1997 album, 'CHEATERS AND THE CHEATED', was warmly received, although it was with the following year's 'BENEATH THE WHEEL' that Kerrang! people took note.

Album rating: BENEATH THE WHEEL (*6)

KEITH BURKHARDT – vocals / **JASON BANKS** – guitar / **JOE ORGERA** – bass / **RAEPH** – drums

Victory / Victory

Mar 95. (m-cd) *<(VE 19CD)>* **CAUSE FOR ALARM** (anthology of singles) [ ] [ ] Feb95
– Parasite / Second chance / Time to try / United races / I search of / Poison in the machine / True colors / Stand as one / Time will tell.
Dec 95. (m-cd; split with WARZONE) *<(VR 026)>* **BEYOND BIRTH AND DEATH** [ ] [ ] Oct95
– Reflection / Beyond birth and death / Eyes of war / Prison life / (other tracks by WARZONE).
Apr 97. (lp/cd) *<(VR 049/+CD)>* **CHEATERS AND THE CHEATED** [ ] [ ] Jan97
– Plastic cylinder express / Lies / Shattered faith / Cheaters and the cheated / True believers / Fish on a hook / Still searching / Creation / Eternal life / Quest for reality / Burden.
Oct 97. (d7"ep/c-ep/cd-ep) *<(VR 059/+MC/CD)>* **BIRTH AFTER BIRTH** [ ] [ ] Sep97
– Cold / Birth after birth / Summer on Avenue A / Animal rights / Rite of passage / Killing children.
Sep 98. (lp/cd) *<(VR 088/CD)>* **BENEATH THE WHEEL** [ ] [ ]
– Homeless / Hole we live in / Clear / Cleanser / Put it down / Future war / Rich get richer / Nothing ever dies / Serve / Prabupada.

Nick CAVE

Born: NICHOLAS EDWARD CAVE, 22 Sep'57, Warracknabeal, Australia. He was the main man behind punk/power-pop outfit, The BOYS NEXT DOOR, completing the band with neighbours MICK HARVEY, TRACY PEW and PHIL CALVERT. Formed in Caulfield, Melbourne in late '77, they issued a one-off version of Nancy Sinatra's 'THESE BOOTS WERE MADE FOR WALKING', before they added a fifth member, ROWLAND S. HOWARD. After an album, 'DOOR, DOOR', was released on 'Mushroom' records in 1979, they came to England as The BIRTHDAY PARTY, taking their name from a Harold Pinter play. The band were subsequently snapped up by IVO on the (then) new indie label '4 a.d.', after a recent 'HEE-HAW' EP was given some night time airing by John Peel. About as extreme as any music ever released by the label, The BIRTHDAY PARTY were more a wake than a celebration, albeit one with more than its fair share of black humour. Their first UK album, 'PRAYERS ON FIRE' (1981), featured such enduringly sharp material as 'ZOO MUSIC GIRL', 'CRY', 'CAPERS' and 'NICK THE STRIPPER', although for many obsessive fans and critics alike, 'RELEASE THE BATS' remains the definitive track. Issued in summer '81, the single was a gothic slice of avant-garde that took over the territory once belonging to the likes of PERE UBU and The POP GROUP. Later that year, TRACY PEW was jailed for drunk driving, a revolving cast of BARRY ADAMSON, CHRIS WALSH and HARRY HOWARD deputising for him on tour. Live, The

BIRTHDAY PARTY were even more unhinged than on vinyl, their demented stage show setting them apart from the masses of up and coming goth-rock acts around at the time. While TRACY was behind bars, NICK, ROWLAND and MICK teamed up as The TUFF MONKS with fellow Australians, The GO-BETWEENS on a one-off 45, 'AFTER THE FIREWORKS'. A further album, 'JUNKYARD' (which hit UK Top 75 in 1982), assured The BIRTHDAY PARTY's position as cult favourites among those who favoured black as a fashion statement. Later that year, ROWLAND hooked up with mistress of soft-porn new wave, LYDIA LUNCH, for a cover of Lee Hazlewood & Nancy Sinatra's 'SOME VELVET MORNING', while The BIRTHDAY PARTY were trimmed to a quartet for 'THE BAD SEED' EP. Released in early '83, the set included the incendiary 'SONNY'S BURNING', arguably the group's finest track. Having moved to Berlin to escape the pressures of critical adulation, the party was finally over after the appropriately titled 'MUTINY' EP. CAVE, who at the time also lived in London, played a few low-key gigs in '83 backed by The CAVEMEN who subsequently became The BAD SEEDS. Including a couple of his cronies from the BIRTHDAY PARTY days, MICK HARVEY and BLIXA BARGELD (also a member of cheery industrial types, EINSTURZENDE NEUBAUTEN), the initial line-up also boasted ex-MAGAZINE man, BARRY ADAMSON, who stayed with the band for the first four albums. Released on 'Mute' (whom CAVE was still contracted to), the debut long player, 'FROM HER TO ETERNITY' (1984), introduced CAVE's preoccupation with the ELVIS myth on a cover of 'IN THE GHETTO', an obsession indulged in greater depth on 'THE FIRSTBORN IS DEAD' (1985). The spit and thrash of the BIRTHDAY PARTY had now been replaced with a skeletal, funereal musical backing to accompany CAVE's ominous crooning. Part hellfire preacher, part damned sinner, CAVE's tales of murder most foul and general debauchery were almost always set in a context (real or implied) of Old Testament morality. Yep, this crazy cat's got that old-time religion, his songs steeped in the shadowy blues of the Mississippi Delta and the lure of his namesake, Old Nick himself. While 'KICKING AGAINST THE PRICKS' (1986), an album of covers, saw the likes of 'BLACK BETTY' and 'BY THE TIME I GET TO PHOENIX', falling under CAVE's dark spell like lambs to the slaughter, the singer came into his own on 'YOUR FUNERAL . . . MY TRIAL' later that year. Rich in dark, dense imagery, the compelling narratives of crime and punishment were further developed on 'TENDER PREY' (1988). In the couple of years preceding the next BAD SEEDS release, CAVE published his first novel, 'AND THE ASS SAW THE ANGEL', and appeared in the film, 'GHOSTS OF THE CIVIL DEAD', as well as scoring the soundtrack (along with HARVEY and BARGELD). Largely acoustic, 'THE GOOD SON' (1990) saw CAVE and his BAD SEEDS return in moodily intense style, grandiose string arrangements complimenting CAVE's sombre intonations. 'HENRY'S DREAM' (1992) was somewhat more menacing with the chilling 'JACK THE RIPPER', although 'STRAIGHT TO YOU' found CAVE applying his vocal intensity in lovelorn ballad mode with impressive results. Further musings on the nature of love pervaded 'LET LOVE IN' (1994), although the apocalyptic antipode was back on familiar blood stained ground with 'MURDER BALLADS' a couple of years later. Against a minimal musical backdrop, CAVE recounted tales of a lyrical savagery that made his earlier work read like nursery rhymes. As well as a duet with POLLY HARVEY, the record saw an unlikely, but interesting pairing with KYLIE MINOGUE (!) on 'WHERE THE WILD ROSES GROW'. In comparison, 'THE BOATMAN'S CALL' (1997) was almost evangelical, an opus that seemed to find NICK as at peace with himself and the world as he's ever been. That's not to say this was a happy record, far from it, as CAVE reflected on the redemptive power of love, and the pain of love lost. Mooted by many critics as his best work to date, it was certainly his most accessible and possessed an atmosphere of meditative grace that sets it apart from much of his previous output. In a music world of MTV mediocrity, CAVE's dark, defiantly individual stance is somehow comforting, though you wouldn't necessarily want to meet the man down a dark alley late at night. Later in 1997, CAVE was rumoured to be working on a blues covers album with TIM ROSE, while he was also set to star alongside Ewan Bremner in the film, 'Rhinoceros Hunting In Budapest'. A second volume of 'King Ink' hit the book shops in March '98 although more publicity was generated via the release of a long-overdue NICK CAVE & THE BAD SEEDS best of compilation. • **Covered:** RUNNING SCARED (Roy Orbison) / BLACK BETTY (Ram Jam) / BY THE TIME I GET TO PHOENIX (Jim Webb) / MUDDY WATER (Johnny Rivers) / HEY JOE (Jimi Hendrix) / ALL TOMORROW'S PARTIES (Velvet Underground) / THE CARNIVAL IS OVER (Seekers) / SOMETHING'S GOTTEN HOLD OF MY HEART (Gene Pitney) / HELPLESS (Neil Young) / WHAT A WONDERFUL WORLD (Ray Charles) / etc. mainly from his covers album KICKING AGAINST THE PRICKS.

Album rating: Boys Next Door: DOOR DOOR (*6) / Birthday Party: PRAYERS ON FIRE (*8) / DRUNK ON THE POPE'S BLOOD (*6) / JUNKYARD (*6) / HITS compilation (*8) / Nick Cave & The Bad Seeds: FROM HER TO ETERNITY (*7) / THE FIRSTBORN IS DEAD (*8) / KICKING AGAINST THE PRICKS (*6) / YOUR FUNERAL . . . MY TRIAL (*6) / TENDER PREY (*6) / THE GHOST OF THE CIVIL DEAD soundtrack (*5) / THE GOOD SON (*8) / HENRY'S DREAM (*8) / LIVE SEEDS (*6) / LET LOVE IN (*8) / MURDER BALLADS (*7) / THE BOATMAN'S CALL (*9) / THE BEST OF NICK CAVE & THE BAD SEEDS compilation (*9)

BOYS NEXT DOOR

NICK CAVE – vocals / **MICK HARVEY** (b.29 Sep'58, Rochester, Australia) – guitar / **TRACY PEW** – bass / **PHIL CALVERT** – drums

Suicide · not iss.

May 78. (7") *(103140)* **THESE BOOTS ARE MADE FOR WALKING. / BOY HERO** [-] [- Austra]

— (Dec'78) added **ROWLAND S. HOWARD** (b.24 Oct'59, Melbourne) – guitar (ex-YOUNG CHARLATANS)

Mushroom · not iss.

May 79. (7") *(K 7492)* **SHIVERS. / DIVE POSITION** [-] [- Austra]

May 79. (lp) *(L 36931)* **DOOR, DOOR** [-] [- Austra]
– The nightwatchman / Brave exhibitions / Friends of my world / The voice / Roman Roman / Somebody's watching / After a fashion / Dive position / I mistake myself / Shivers. *(Australian cd-iss. 1987; D 19227) (cd-iss. Mar93 on 'Grey Area-Mute';)*

Missing Link · not iss.

Dec 79. (12"ep) *(MLEP-3)* **HEE-HAW** [-] [- Austra]
– Catholic skin / The red clock / Faint heart / The hair shirt / Death by drowning. *(Australia re-iss. Dec83; credited as BIRTHDAY PARTY; ING 008)*

Feb 80. (7"gig freebie) *(MLS 16)* **HAPPY BIRTHDAY. / THE RIDDLE HOUSE** [-] [- Austra]

BIRTHDAY PARTY

— (same line-up & label)

Jul 80. (7") *(MLS 18)* **MR. CLARINET. / HAPPY BIRTHDAY** [-] [- Austra]

Nov 80. (lp) *(LINK 7)* **THE FIRST ALBUM** (originally credited to BOYS NEXT DOOR) [-] [- Austra]
– The friend catcher / Waving my arms / Catman / The red clock /

— (below Australian releases only are with different label mentioned)

4.a.d. · not iss.

Oct 80. (7"m) *(AD 12)* **THE FRIEND CATCHER. / WAVING MY ARMS / CATMAN** [ ] [-]

Apr 81. (lp) *(CAD 104)* **PRAYERS ON FIRE** [ ] [-]
– Zoo music girl / Cry / Capers / Nick the stripper / Ho-ho / Figure of fun / King Ink / A dead song / Yard / Dull day / Just you and me. *(cd-iss. Apr88+=; CAD 104CD)* – Blundertown / Kathy's kisses.

Jun 81. Missing Link; (12"m) *(MSD 479)* **NICK THE STRIPPER. / BLUNDER TOWN / KATHY'S KISSES** [-] [- Austra]

Aug 81. (7") *(AD 111)* **RELEASE THE BATS. / BLAST OFF** [ ] [-]

Oct 81. (7") *(AD 114)* **MR. CLARINET. / HAPPY BIRTHDAY** [ ] [-]

Feb 82. (m-lp) *(JAD 202)* **DRUNK ON THE POPE'S BLOOD (live)** [ ] [-]
– (Sometimes) Pleasure heads must burn / King Ink / Zoo music girl / Loose / LYDIA LUNCH:- The Agony Is The Ecstasy.

— (Dec81) while **TRACY PEW** was in jail for drunk driving he was replaced on tour only by either BARRY ADAMSON, CHRIS WALSH or **HARRY HOWARD**

May 82. (lp) *(CAD 207)* **JUNKYARD** [73] [-]
– She's hit / Dead Joe / Dim locator / Hamlet (pow-pow-pow) / Several sins / Big-Jesus-trash-can / Kiss me back / 6" gold blade / Kewpie doll / Junkyard. *(cd-iss. Apr88+=; CAD 207CD)* – Dead Joe (version) / Release the bats / Blast off.

— In Sep'82, ROLAND S. HOWARD did duet with LYDIA LUNCH on 12" 'Some Velvet Morning. / I Fell In Love With A Ghost'; *BAD 210)*

Nov 82. Missing Link; (7") *(MLS 32)* **NICK THE STRIPPER. / BLUNDERTOWN** [-] [- Austra]

— Now quartet when **CALVERT** joined **PSYCHEDELIC FURS**. (HARVEY now drums)

Feb 83. (12"ep) *(BAD 301)* **THE BAD SEED** [ ] [-]
– Sonny's burning / Wild world / Fears of gun / Deep in the woods.

— **JEFFREY WEGENER** – drums (ex-LAUGHING CLOWNS) repl. HARVEY Also **BLIXA BARGELD** – guitar (of EINSTURZENDE NEUBAUTEN) repl. absent HOWARD

Mute · not iss.

Nov 83. (12"ep) *(12MUTE 29)* **MUTINY!** [ ] [-]
– Jennifer's veil / Mutiny in Heaven / Swampland / Say a spell.

— Disbanded Autumn 1983. TRACY joined The SAINTS. (He was later to die late '86 of epileptic fit aged 28). ROWLAND HOWARD formed CRIME & THE CITY SOLUTION. NICK CAVE went solo, forming his BAD SEEDS taking with him MICK HARVEY.

– compilations, etc. – (all mostly UK)

on '4 a.d.' unless otherwise stated

Jun 83. (12"ep) *(BAD 307)* **THE BIRTHDAY PARTY EP** [ ] [-]
– Release the bats / Blast off / The friend catcher / Mr. Clarinet / Happy birthday.

Apr 85. (d-lp) *Missing Link; (ING 009)* **IT'S STILL LIVING (live)** [-] [- Austra]

Dec 85. (lp) *Missing Link; (LINK 22)* **A COLLECTION – BEST AND RAREST** [-] [- Austra]

Feb 87. (12"ep) *Strange Fruit; (SFPS 020)* **THE PEEL SESSION** (21.4.81) [ ] [-]
– Release the bats / Rowland around in that stuff / (Sometimes) Pleasure heads must burn / Loose. *(re-iss. Aug88 cd-ep; SFPSCD 020)*

Oct 88. (12"ep/cd-ep) *Strange Fruit; (SFPS/+CD 058)* **THE PEEL SESSIONS** (2.12.81) [ ] [-]
– Big-Jesus-trash-can / She's hit / Bully bones / 6" gold blade.

Aug 89. (cd) *(CAD 301CD)* **MUTINY / THE BAD SEED** [ ] [-]

Aug 89. (cd) *(CAD 307CD)* **HEE-HAW** [ ] [-]
– (contains tracks from THE BIRTHDAY PARTY lp)

Oct 92. (d-lp/cd)(c) *(DAD 2016/+CD)(DADC 2016)* **HITS** [ ] [-]
– The friend catcher / Happy birthday / Mr Clarinet / Nick the stripper / Zoo music girl / King Ink / Release the bats / Blast off / She's hit / 6" Gold blade / Hamlet (pow, pow, pow) / Dead Joe / Junkyard / Big-Jesus-Trash-Can / Wild world / Sonny's burning / Deep in the woods / Swampland / Jennifer's veil / Mutiny in Heaven.

NICK CAVE & THE BAD SEEDS

— **NICK CAVE** – vocals / **MICK HARVEY** – guitar, keyboards / **BLIXA BARGELD** (b.12 Jan'59, Berlin, Germany) – guitar (of EINSTURZENDE NEUBAUTEN) / **BARRY ADAMSON** (b. 1 Jun'58, Manchester, England) – bass, guitar (ex-MAGAZINE, ex-PETE SHELLEY) / **HUGO RACE** – drums

Mute · Restless

Jun 84. (7") *(MUTE 32)* **IN THE GHETTO. / THE MOON IS IN THE GUTTER** [ ] [-]

— added **ANITA LANE** – synthesizers (ex-solo artist)

Jun 84. (lp) *(STUMM 17) <71435>* **FROM HER TO ETERNITY** [40] [ ]
– Avalanche / Cabin fever / Well of misery / From her to eternity / Wings of flies / Saint Huck / A box for black Paul. *(cd-iss. 1987+=; CDSTUMM 17)* – In the ghetto / The Moon is in the gutter / From her to eternity (1987).

— **THOMAS WYDLER** (b. 9 Oct'59, Zurich, Switzerland) – drums (ex-DIE HAUT) repl. HUGO + ANITA

Mute Homestead

Jun 85. (lp/c) *(STUMM/CSTUMM 21) <HMS 026>* **THE FIRSTBORN IS DEAD** [53] [ ]
– Tupelo / Say goodbye to the little girl tree / Train long suffering / Black crow king / Knockin' on Joe / Wanted man / Blind Lemon Jefferson. *(cd-iss. Apr88; CDSTUMM 21)*

Jul 85. (7") *(7MUTE 38)* **TUPELO. / THE SIX STRINGS THAT DREW BLOOD** [ ] [-]

Jun 86. (7") *(7MUTE 47)* **THE SINGER. / RUNNING SCARED** [ ] [-]
(12"+=) *(12MUTE 47)* – Black Betty.

Aug 86. (cd/c/lp) *(CD/C+/STUMM 28) <HMS 065>* **KICKING AGAINST THE PRICKS** [89] [ ]
– Muddy water / I'm gonna kill that woman / Sleeping Annaleah / Long black veil / Hey Joe / The singer / Black Betty * / Running scared * / All tomorrow's parties / By the time I get to Phoenix / The hammer song / Something's gotten hold of my heart / Jesus met the woman at the well / The carnival is over. *(cd+= *)*

Nov 86. (cd/c/lp) *(CD/C+/STUMM 34) <HMS 073>* **YOUR FUNERAL . . . MY TRIAL** [ ] [ ]
– Sad waters / The Carny / Your funeral . . . my trial / Stranger than kindness / Jack's shadow / Hard on for love / She fell away / Long time man. *(cd+=)* – Scum.

— **CAVE** retained **HARVEY, BARGELD** and **WYDLER,** bringing in **ROLAND WOLF** – bass / **KID CONGO POWERS** (b. BRIAN TRISTAN, 27 Mar'61, La Puente, Calif.) – guitar (ex-CRAMPS, ex-GUN CLUB)

Mute Mute-Elektra

May 88. (7") *(MUTE 52)* **THE MERCY SEAT. / NEW DAY** [ ] [-]
(12"+=) *(12MUTE 52)* – ('A'video mix).
(cd-s+=) *(CDMUTE 52)* – From her to eternity (film version) / Tupelo (version).

Sep 88. (cd/c/lp) *(CD/C+STUMM 52) <75401>* **TENDER PREY** [67] [ ]
– The mercy seat / Up jumped the Devil / Deanna / Watching Alice / Mercy / City of refuge / Slowly goes the night / Sunday's slave / Sugar, sugar, sugar / New morning. *(cd+=)* – The mercy seat (video mix). *(free-12"ep.w/above)* **AND THE ASS SAW THE ANGEL** (narration/book) – One Autumn / Animal static / Mah sanctum / Lamentation.

Sep 88. (12") *(12MUTE 86)* **DEANNA. / THE GIRL AT THE BOTTOM OF MY GLASS** [ ] [-]

Mar 89. (cd/c/lp; NICK CAVE – MICK HARVEY – BLIXA BARGELD) *(<CD/C+/IONIC 3>)* **GHOSTS . . . OF THE CIVIL DEAD** (Soundtrack w/ dialogue) [ ] [ ]
– The news / Introduction – A prison in the desert / David Hale – I've been a prison guard since I was 18 years old / Glover – I was 16 when they put me in prison / David Hale – you're danglin' us like a bunch of meat on a hook / Pop mix / Glover – we were united once / David Hale – the day of the murders / Lilly's theme ("A touch of warmth") / Maynard mix / David Hale – what I'm tellin' is the truth / Outro – The free world / Glover – one man released so they can imprison the rest of the world.

— (now a 5-piece, without WOLF)

Mar 90. (12"/cd-s/7") *(12/CD+/MUTE 108)* **THE SHIP SONG. / THE TRAIN SONG** [ ] [-]

Apr 90. (cd/c/lp) *(CD/C+/STUMM 76) <60988>* **THE GOOD SON** [47] [ ] Oct90
– Foi na cruz / The good son / Sorrow's child / The weeping song / The ship song / The hammer song / Lament / The witness song / Lucy. *(w/-7"/cd-s)* **THE MERCY SEAT / CITY OF REFUGE / DEANNA (all acoustic)**

Sep 90. (12"/7") *(12+/MUTE 118)* **THE WEEPING SONG. / COCKS 'N' ASSES** [ ] [-]
(cd-s+=) *(12/CD MUTE 118)* – Helpless / (some with hidden track).

— **CONWAY SAVAGE** (b.27 Jul'60, Foster, Australia) – keyboards + **MARTYN P. CASEY** – 10 Jul'60, Chesterfield, England) – bass (ex-TRIFFIDS) repl. KID CONGO

Mar 92. (7") *(MUTE 140)* **STRAIGHT TO YOU. / JACK THE RIPPER (acoustic)** [68] [-]
(12"+=/cd-s+=) *(12/CD MUTE 140)* – Blue bird.

Apr 92. (cd/c/lp) *(CD/C+/STUMM 92) <61323>* **HENRY'S DREAM** [29] [ ] May92
– Papa won't leave you Henry / I had a dream, Joe / Straight to you / Brother, my cup is empty / Christina the astonishing / When I first came to town / John Finn's wife / Loom of the land / Jack the ripper.

Aug 92. (7") *(LMUTE 147)* **I HAD A DREAM, JOE. / THE GOOD SON (live)** [ ] [-]
(12"/cd-s) *(12/CD MUTE 147)* – ('A'side) / The Carny (live) / The mercy seat (live) / The ship song (live).

Nov 92. (c-s/7"; by NICK CAVE & SHANE MacGOWAN) *(C+/MUTE 151)* **WHAT A WONDERFUL WORLD. / A RAINY NIGHT IN SOHO** [72] [-]
(7") *(MUTE 151D)* – ('A'side / Lucy (by SHANE MacGOWAN).
(12"/cd-s) *(12/CD MUTE 151)* – (all 3 tracks).

Sep 93. (cd) *(CDMUTE 122) <61554>* **LIVE SEEDS (live)** [67] [ ]
– Mercy seat / Deanna / The ship song / Papa won't leave you Henry / Plain gold ring / John Finn's wife / Tupelo / Brother my cup is empty / The weeping song / Jack the ripper / The good son / From her to eternity. *(re-iss. Sep96; LCDSTUMM 122)*

Mar 94. (12/cd-s/7"silver) *(12/CD+/MUTE 160)* **DO YOU LOVE ME? / CASSIEL'S SONG / SAIL AWAY** [68] [-]

Apr 94. (cd/c/lp) *(CD/C+/STUMM 123) <61645>* **LET LOVE IN** [12] [ ]
– Do you love me? / Nobody's baby now / Loverman / Jangling Jack / Red right hand / I let love in / Thirsty dog / Ain't gonna rain anymore / Lay me low / Do you love me? (part 2).

— **JAMES JOHNSON** – guitar (of GALLON DRUNK) repl. on tour only BLIXA

Jul 94. (7"pic-d) *(MUTE 169)* **LOVERMAN. / (I'LL LOVE YOU) TILL THE END OF THE WORLD** [ ] [-]
(12"/cd-s) *(12/CD MUTE 169)* – ('A'side) / B side.

Oct 94. (7"red) *(MUTE 172)* **RED RIGHT HAND. / THAT'S WHAT JAZZ IS TO ME** [ ] [-]
(cd-s+=) *(CDMUTE 172)* – Where the action is.

Oct 95. (c-s/7"; NICK CAVE & THE BAD SEEDS featuring KYLIE MINOGUE) *(C+/MUTE 185)* **WHERE THE WILD ROSES GROW. / THE BALLAD OF ROBERT MOORE & BETTY COLTRANE** [11] [-]
(cd-s+=) *(CDMUTE 185)* – The willow garden.

Feb 96. (cd/c/lp) *(CD/C+/STUMM 138) <46195>* **MURDER BALLADS** [8] [ ]
– Song of joy / Stagger Lee / Henry Lee / Lovely creature / Where the wild roses grow (featuring KYLIE MINOGUE) / The curse of Millhaven / The kindness of strangers / Crow Jane / O'Malley's bar / Death is not the end.

Feb 96. (7"; by NICK CAVE & PJ HARVEY) *(MUTE 189)* **HENRY LEE. / KING KONG KITCHEE KI-MI-O** [36] [-]
(c-s+=/cd-s+=) *(C/CD MUTE 189)* – Knoxville girl.

— <most UK singles were given a US release in 1996>

— JOHNSON was repl. by **JIM SCLAVUNOS + WARREN ELLIS**

Feb 97. (7") *(MUTE 192)* **INTO MY ARMS. / LITTLE EMPTY BOAT** [53] [-]
(cd-s+=) *(CDMUTE 192)* – Right now I'm a-roaming.

Mar 97. (cd/c) *(CD/C+/STUMM 142) <46530>* **THE BOATMAN'S CALL** [22] [ ]
– Into my arms / Lime tree harbour / People ain't no good / Brompton oratory / There is a kingdom / (Are you) The one that I've been waiting for? / Where do we go now but nowhere? / West country girl / Black hair / Idiot prayer / Far from me / Green eyes.

May 97. (7") *(MUTE 206)* **(ARE YOU) THE ONE THAT I'VE BEEN WAITING FOR? / COME INTO MY SLEEP** [67] [-]
(cd-s+=) *(CDMUTE 206)* – Black hair (band version) / Babe, I got you bad.

May 98. (cd/c/d-lp) *(CD/C+/MUTEL 004) <46960>* **THE BEST OF NICK CAVE & THE BAD SEEDS** (compilation) [11] [ ]
– Deanna / Red right hand / Straight to you / Tupelo / Nobody's baby now / Stranger than kindness / Into my arms / (Are you) The one that I've been waiting for? / The Carny / Do you love me? / The mercy seat / Henry Lee (feat. PJ HARVEY) / The weeping song / The ship song / Where the wild roses grow (feat. KYLIE MINOGUE) / For her to eternity. *(special d-cd; LCDMUTEL 004)* **LIVE AT THE ROYAL ALBERT HALL** – Stranger than kindness / The ship song / Let love in / Brompton oratory / Red right hand / Lime tree arbour / The weeping song / Henry Lee / Where the wild roses grow / Deanna / Straight to you / Tupelo / Nobody's baby now / Into my arms / (Are you) The one that I've been waiting for? / The Carny / Do you love me? / The mercy seat / From her to eternity.

C-CAT TRANCE

Formed: Nottingham, England . . . 1983 by JOHN REES LEWIS and NIGEL KINGSTON STONE, actually former members of late 70's/early 80's quintet, MEDIUM MEDIUM. The latter outfit (who also included ANDY RYDER, ALLAN TURTON and soundman, GRAHAM SPINK) appeared on the 'Hicks From The Sticks' V/A compilation (in 1979) and issued a couple of singles plus a solitary album for 'Cherry Red', 'THE GLITTER HOUSE' (1981). LEWIS and STONE had already gone AWOL almost immediately after the album's completion, the pair finally releasing their C-CAT TRANCE debut 12", 'DREAMS OF LIVING', in the Spring of '84. Now into Third World funk, this outfit stuttered commercially and found it hard to claw their way out of the second division indie scene. Three albums (one a year) appeared on Red Flame outlet, 'Ink' between 1985 and 1987, although neither 'KHAMU', 'ZOUAVE' or 'PLAY MASENKO COMBO' made any lasting impression on critic or public. Their most interesting release, 'ISHTA BIL HABUL', arrived in '87, a 12"/single which found C-CAT TRANCE augmented by The St. Louis Symphony Orchestra and conducted by Statkin.

Album rating: Medium Medium: THE GLITTER HOUSE (*5) / C-Cat Trance: KHAMU (*4) / ZOUAVE (*4) / PLAY MASENKO COMBO (*4)

MEDIUM MEDIUM

JOHN LEWIS – saxophones, horns, vocals / **ANDY RYDER** – guitar, vocals / **ALLAN TURTON** – bass / **NIGEL STONE** – drums / **GRAHAM SPINK** – sound

Apt not iss.

Nov 78. (7") *(SAP 01)* **THEM OR US. / FREEZE** [ ] [-]

Cherry Red Cachalot

Feb 81. (7") *(CHERRY 18)* **HUNGRY, SO ANGRY. / NADSAT DREAM** [ ] [-]

Aug 81. (12"ep) *<BIG 1>* **HUNGRY, SO ANGRY / HUNGRY, SO ANGRY (version). / FURTHER THAN FUNK DREAM / NADSAT DREAM** [-] [ ]

Oct 81. (lp) *(BRED 19) <CA 127>* **THE GLITTER HOUSE** [ ] [ ] Nov81
– Hungry, so angry / Serbian village / The glitter house / Guru Maharaja / Further than funk dream / Nice or monsters / That Haiku.

— **STEVE HARVEY** – drums, percussion; repl. STONE (see below)

— **LES BARRETT** – keyboards; repl. SPINK + LEWIS (see below)

— this quartet had a Dutch release, 'LIVE IN HOLLAND', issued in '88

C-CAT TRANCE

— **JOHN REES LEWIS** – saxophone, vocals, etc / **NIGEL KINGSTON STONE** – drums, percussion

Ink not iss.

Mar 84. (12") *(INK12-3)* **DREAMS OF LIVING. / DANGLING ON A STRING** [ ] [-]

Apr 85. (12") *(INK12-6)* **SHE STEALS CARS. / RATTLING GHOSTS** [ ] [-]

May 85. (lp) *(INKLP 6)* **KHAMU** [ ] [-]
(cd-iss. Oct93 as 'LES INVISIBLES'; INKCD 6)

— added 3 members (unknown)

May 86. (12") **SHAKE THE MIND. /** [ ] [-]

Oct 86. (12") *(INK12-23)* **SCREAMING TO BE WITH YOU. /** [ ] [-]
Nov 86. (lp) *(INKLP 20)* **ZOUAVE** [ ] [-]
– Wind howl / Betty / He's crazy / Taksim / Ishta Bil Habul / If you steal / Take me to the beach / You've lost that lovin' feeling / Shake the mind. *(cd-iss. Jun88; INKCD 20)*
Apr 87. (12"ep) *(INK12-27)* **ISHTA BIL HABUL (CREAM GALORE!). / ('A'dance mix) / ('A'edit)** [ ] [-]
Dec 87. (lp) *(INKLP 33)* **PLAY MASENKO COMBO** [ ] [-]
– Dalbouka / They made them up / She ever does / Jamais / I looked for you / Cold / Two words / My tattoo / Railway magazine / Let me sleep / Untitled / Dangling on a string. *(cd-iss. Jun88; INKCD 33)*
Sep 88. (12") *(INK12-35)* **YINNIYA. /** [ ] [-]
— split in the late 80's

CECIL

Formed: Liverpool, England . . . 1993 by ageing teenagers, STE WILLIAMS, ANTONY HUGHES, PATRICK HARRISON, JAY BENNETT and ALLY LAMBERT. After taking part in a 'Battle Of The Bands', competition they found themselves on the roster of EMI's 'Parlophone' imprint. Subsequent tours supporting SKUNK ANANSIE, BLAMELESS and The LEVELLERS, helped raise their profile, although critics found it difficult to pigeonhole the band in either the hard-rock or alternative categories. Fusing crunching, hard-driving riffs with WILLIAMS' emotive vocals, CECIL released a trio of competent if hardly groundbreaking singles prior to their first full set, 'BOMBAR DIDDLAH' (1996). Late the following year, with support from the likes of Kerrang!, the 5-piece scored their first of two minor hits with 'HOSTAGE IN A FROCK', the singer a bit overdressed in the accompanying video. The second of these, 'THE MOST TIRING DAY', previewed the follow-up album, 'SUBTITLES' (1998), although a bonafide breakthrough seemed as distant as ever.

Album rating: BOMBAR DIDDLAH (*5) / SUBTITLES (*5)

STE WILLIAMS – vocals / **ANTONY HUGHES** – guitar / **PATRICK HARRISON** – guitar / **JAY BENNETT** – bass / **ALLY LAMBERT** – drums

Parlophone Parlophone

Oct 95. (7") *(R 6418)* **NO EXCUSES. / UPSIDE DOWN SMILE** [ ] [-]
(cd-s+=) *(CDR 6418)* – Friend (demo).
Mar 96. (7") *(R 6427)* **MY NECK. / WALLOW IN FUSION** [ ] [-]
(cd-s+=) *(CDR 6427)* – Revealing symptom / My piano neck.
Jun 96. (7") *(R 6435)* **MEASURED. / SPIRIT LEVEL** [ ] [-]
(cd-s+=) *(CDR 6435)* – The plastics keep coming.
Nov 96. (cd/c/lp) *(CD/TC+/PCS 7384) <854162>* **BOMBAR DIDDLAH** [ ] [ ] Mar97
– Dream awake / Plastics keep coming / Spirit level / Upside down smile / Fishes / My neck / No excuses / Poshinalagweedy.
May 97. (7") *(R 6467)* **RED WINE AT DEAD TIME. / BOMBAR DIDDLAH** [ ] [-]
(cd-s+=) *(CDR 6467)* – So Long Marianne.
(cd-s) *(CDRS 6467)* – ('A'side) / Look out for my love / Friend.
Oct 97. (7"green) *(R 6471)* **HOSTAGE IN A FROCK. / STUBBORN FEATHER** [68] [-]
(Dave Bascombe mix; cd-s+=) *(CDRS 6471)* – Upside down smile (live).
(cd-s) *(CDR 6471)* – ('A'-Tim Palmer mix) / Antique / Dream awake (live).
Mar 98. (7"colrd) *(R 6490)* **THE MOST TIRING DAY. / SLIPHILLCLIMB** [69] [-]
(cd-s+=) *(CDRS 6490)* – On the inside.
(cd-s) *(CDR 6490)* – ('A'side) / Tinsel scar / When you're in love with a beautiful woman.
Mar 98. (cd/c/lp) *(859821-2/-4/-1)* **SUBTITLES** [ ] [-]
– Larger than a mountain to the ant / Zips for lips / The most tiring day / Red wine at dead time / Fullstop / Acres / Hostage in a frock / Measured / Lovetooth 14 / Charm wrestling / In the day and aged.

CELIBATE RIFLES

Formed: Sydney, Australia . . . 1982 by DAVE MORRIS and KENT STEEDMAN alongside DAMIEN LOVELOCK, PAUL DARROCH and PHIL JACQUET. Following in the musclebound, turbo R&B charged tradition of Aussie punks like RADIO BIRDMAN and The SAINTS, The CELIBATE RIFLES fired their initial vinyl shots on domestic label, 'Hot'. First up was an EP, 'BUT JACQUES, THE FISH?', followed by a debut album, 'SIDEROXYLON' (1983) and an eponymous follow-up in '84. By the release of the band's first UK-available long player, the cheerily titled 'THE TURGID MIASMA OF EXISTENCE' (1986), DARROCH had been killed in a car accident and the record was dedicated to his memory; prior to his untimely death DARROCH had formed EASTERN DARK, who released one obscure EP, 'LONG LIVE THE NEW FLESH'. 'THE TURGID MIASMA . . .' found the 'RIFLES broadening their musical palate while lyrically, an environmento-political bent was increasingly evident alongside the trademark caustic humour. Recorded at New York's infamous CBGB's, 'KISS KISS BANG BANG' was a raucous blast of Sydney's finest live in the raw and served as their first release to be distributed in the USA (on 'Homestead'). Although they also supported their heroes, The RAMONES, on the Stateside jaunt, a hostile reaction from the music press saw them concentrate future efforts on their Antipodean homeland. The latter set gained a UK release on the 'What Goes On' label, also home to their final release of the 80's, the smoking 'ROMAN BEACH PARTY'. By the turn of the decade, JIM LEONE had replaced RUDI (who in turn had previously replaced COUVRET) and PAUL LARSEN came in for the departing JACQUET, the new look rhythm section maintaining the high velocity of old on 1990's uncompromising 'BLIND EAR' album. Their most politically pointed and musically mature work to date, the record was nevertheless their last album to gain a release in America. Punk may have been long dead but the Aussie bruisers were dedicated to guarding the flame, signing a new deal with 'Hot' and continuing to release albums into the 90's, the most recent being 1998's 'ON THE QUIET'. • **Covers:** CITY OF FUN (Only Ones) / BURN MY EYE (Radio Birdman) / DANCING BAREFOOT (Patti Smith) / BABY PLEASE DON'T GO (Big Joe Williams) / 2000 LIGHT YEARS FROM HOME (Rolling Stones) / etc.

Album rating: SIDEROXYLON (*6) / THE CELIBATE RIFLES (*6) / THE TURGID MIASMA OF EXISTENCE (*7) / MINA MINA MINA (*5) / KISS KISS BANG BANG (*5) / ROMAN BEACH PARTY (*7) / BLIND EAR (*7) / HEAVEN ON A STICK (*6) / YIZGARNNOFF (*6) / A SPACEMAN IN A SATIN SUIT (*7) / ON THE QUIET (*5)

DAMIEN LOVELOCK – vocals / **DAVE MORRIS** – guitar / **KENT STEEDMAN** – guitar / **PAUL DARROCH** – bass / **PHIL JACQUET** – drums

Hot not iss.

1983. (12"ep) **BUT JACQUES, THE FISH?** [-] [-] Austra
1983. (lp) *(HOT 1001)* **SIDEROXYLON** [-] [-] Austra
– Killing time / Society / Tick tock / Anthem / Back on the corner / You're gonna cry / Where do I go / Ice blue / Gimme gimme gimme / God squad. *(cd-iss. Feb93; HOR 1001CD)*
Apr 84. (lp) *(HOT 1007)* **THE CELIBATE RIFLES** [-] [-] Austra
– Wild desire / Kiss me deadly / Pretty colours / Back in the red / Darlinghurst confidential / Thank you America / Rainforest / Netherworld / Electric snake river. *(cd-iss. Feb93; HOT 1007CD)*
— **MICHAEL COUVRET** – bass; repl. DARROCH who formed EASTERN DARK (however, he died in a car crash, 1986)
Jun 86. (lp) *(HOT 1024)* **THE TURGID MIASMA OF EXISTENCE** [ ] [-]
(cd-iss. Feb93; HOT 1024CD)

Shigaku not iss.

Apr 87. (7") *(SHIGS 2)* **PRETTY PICTURES. / KENT THEME** [ ] [-]

What Goes On Homestead

Apr 87. (lp) *(GOES ON 8)* **KISS KISS BANG BANG (live at the CGDB's)** [ ] [ ]
– Back in the red / Temper temper / J.N.S. / Pretty colours / Netherworld / Some kinda feeling / New mistakes / Carmine vatelly (N.Y.N.Y.C.) / City of fun / Conflict of instinct / Sometimes / Burn my eye / S.O.S. *(cd-iss. Feb93 on 'Hot'; HOT 1029CD)*
— **RUDI** – bass; repl. COUVRET
Oct 87. (lp) *(HOT 1030)* **ROMAN BEACH PARTY** [ ] [-]
(cd-iss. Feb93; HOT 1030CD)
Jul 88. (7"ep) **DANCING BAREFOOT. /** [ ] [-]
— **JIM LEONE** – bass, percussion, vocals; repl. RUDI
— **PAUL LARSEN** – drums; repl. JACQUET

Rattlesnake True Tone-EMI

Aug 90. (cd) *(RAT 503)* **BLIND EAR** [ ] [ ] Nov89
– Johnny / World keeps turning / Electravision mantra / Dial om / Wonderful life '88 / Sean O'Farrell / Belfast / Cycle / They're killing us all (to make the world safe) / O salvation / Fish and trees. *(re-iss. Oct94 on 'Hot'; HOT 1046CD)*

Hot not iss.

Jul 92. (cd) *(HOT 1038CD)* **HEAVEN ON A STICK** [ ] [ ]
– Light of life / Cold wind / Happy house / Excommunication / S&M TV / Contemplating R.D. Laing (and the bird of paradise) / G.D. absolutely / Dream of night / Groovin' in the land of love / Electric flowers / Compared to what / Outside my window / Wild child. *(re-iss. Aug95; same)*
Aug 93. (cd) *(HOT 1041CD)* **YIZGARNNOFF** [ ] [ ]
– Brickin' around / A word about Jones / Cycle / Downtown (street radio mix) / Johnny / Happy house / Dream of night / Groovin' in the land of love / S&M TV / Electravision mantra / 2000 light years from home / The more things change / Tubular greens / Invisible man / Glasshouse / O salvation / Oceanshore / Baby please don't go. *(re-iss. Aug95; same)*
May 94. (cd) *(HOT 1047CD)* **A SPACEMAN IN A SATIN SUIT** [ ] [ ]
– Spirits / Kev the head / Brickin' around / Living what I dream / City of hope / Seams / Big world / Whatever you want / Kathy says / Diamond sky / Cuttin' it fine / This gift / Let's do it again / A spaceman in a satin suit. *(re-iss. Apr96; same)*
Jul 98. (cd) *(HOT 1067CD)* **ON THE QUIET** [ ] [ ]
– Netherworld / Back on the corner / Sentinel / Electric flowers / This gift / No sign / Electric snake river / Jesus on TV / Boys (what did the detectives say) / Astral wally / Hot generation / Hindu gods of love. *(lp-iss.Mar97 on 'Munster'; MR 115)*

– compilations, etc. –

Jul 85. (lp) *What Goes On; (RIFLE 1)* **QUINTESSENTIALLY YOURS** [ ] [-]
Aug 86. (lp) *What Goes On; (GOES ON 5)* **MINA MINA MINA** [ ] [-]
Dec 90. (cd) *Rattlesnake; (<RAT 504>)* **PLATTERS DU JOUR** [ ] [ ]
– Kent's theme / Let's get married / 24 hours (S.O.S.) / Tubular greens / Pretty pictures / Out in the west again / Summer holiday blues / Merry xmas blues / Wild desire / I'm waiting for the man / Sometimes / E=Mc2 / Six days on the road / Groupie girl / Eddie (acoustic version) / Ice blue / Thank you America / Back in the red / Rain forest / Dancing barefoot / Jesus on TV / The more things change / Junk. *(cd re-iss. Oct94 on 'Hot'; HOT 1033/34CD)*
Jan 94. (cd) *Hot; (HOT 1043CD)* **SOFA** [ ] [ ]
– Killing time / Wild desire / Sometimes / Bill Bonney regrets / Jesus on T.V. / Johnny / Electravision mantra / Wonderful life / More things change / Oceanshore / New mistakes / Back in the red / Ice blue / This week / Netherworld / Glasshouse / Frank Hyde (slight return) / Darlinghurst confidential / Pretty pictures / Gonna cry. *(re-iss. Aug95; same)*
— In 1988, DAMIEN LOVELOCK (with some CELIBATE's and members of the band, The CHURCH – RICHARD PLOOG + PETER KOPPES) released a 'Hot' solo set, 'IT'S A WIG, WIG, WIG, WIG WORLD', while two years later, CRENT (i.e. KENT STEEDMAN + another) issued an eponymous album for 'Waterfront'.

CELL

Formed: Hoboken, New Jersey, USA . . . early 90's by New York underground veterans, JERRY DiRIENZO (ex-VIA), IAN JAMES (ex-FLOWER), DAVID

MOTAMED (ex-DAS DAMEN) and KEITH NEALY (ex-SWINEDIVE). Mates with SONIC YOUTH (KEITH had been a technician for STEVE SHELLEY), CELL used their contacts to secure an initial deal with THURSTON MOORE's 'Ecstatic Peace' label, releasing their debut single, 'NEVER TOO HIGH', in 1991. The SONIC YOUTH connection also helped them net a Stateside deal with the David Geffen Company (DGC), a debut album, 'SLO*BLO', surfacing the following year. Scraping the mutoid sludge from the Grunge barrel, CELL specialised in layers of mesmerising monster riffing with occasional forays into noise abandon, naming their album after a slow action fuse. Following a solitary single in '93, 'CROSS THE RIVER', CELL broke out for one more stab at cult fame, unlocking the door to more mind-numbing guitar abuse via the album, 'LIVING ROOM' (1994).

Album rating: SLO*BLO (*5) / LIVING ROOM (*5)

JERRY DiRIENZO – vocals, guitar (of VIA; w/ THALIA of COME) / **IAN JAMES** – guitar, vocals (of FLOWER) / **DAVID MOTAMED** – bass (of DAS DAMEN) / **KEITH NEALY** – drums (of SWINEDIVE)

not iss. / Ecstatic Peace

1991. (7") *<23>* **NEVER TOO HIGH. /** -

City Slang / D.G.C.

Sep 92. (7"blue) *(EFA 04905-03)* **FALL. / CIRCLES** -
(cd-s+=) *(EFA 04905-45)* –

Oct 92. (lp/c/cd) *(E 04909/+C/CD) <24506>* **SLO*BLO**
– Fall / Wild / Cross the river / Dig deep / Stratosphere / Two / Everything turns / Tundra / Bad day / Hills.

Nov 92. (7") **WILD. / AUF WIEDERSEHEN** -
(above issued on 'Ecstatic Peace/ D.G.C.')

Apr 93. (7"blue) *(EFA 04921-45)* **CROSS THE RIVER. / CHINA LATINA**
(cd-s+=) *(EFA 04921-03)* –

Jan 94. (7") *(EFA 04928-7)* **MILKY. / TWO WEEKS**
(cd-s+=) *(EFA 04928-2)* – Deranged.

Feb 94. (cd/lp) *(EFA 04933-2/-1) <24633>* **LIVING ROOM**
– Milky / China Latina / Sad & beautiful / Goodbye / Chained / Come around / Living room / Fly / Halo / Soft ground / Camera / Blue star.

—— disbanded after above

CHA CHA COHEN

Formed: Austin, Texas . . . 1995 when expatriot Australian singer, JACKIE, met up with two former members of The WEDDING PRESENT, KEITH GREGORY and SIMON SMITH, who actually still reside in Leeds! JACKIE, who had been an integral part of arty-farty rock outfit, The DUSTBALLS, moved to New York where she gained employment working as a casino croupier at a nearby Native American reservation. Writing and posting songs to each other by airmail or E-mail, this unusual band released their debut 7", 'SPARKY'S NOTE', before putting pen to paper for Glasgow's seminal imprint, 'Chemikal Underground'. Three further singles of BLONDIE-esque guitar-pop were delivered between 1996 and late 1998, a promise of an album and UK tour in early '99. If you can imagine CICCONE YOUTH (aka SONIC YOUTH) being backed by a BECK staccato then you have the picture.

Album rating: CHA CHA COHEN (awaiting 1999 release)

JACKIE (b. Sydney, Australia) – vocals, guitar (ex-DUSTBALLS) / **KEITH GREGORY** (b. 2 Jan'63, County Durham) – guitar (ex-WEDDING PRESENT) / **SIMON SMITH** (b. 3 May'65, Lincolnshire) – drums (ex-WEDDING PRESENT)

Hemiola / not iss.

Oct 95. (7") *(HEM 008)* **SPARKY'S NOTE. / SNARES OF URGOIL URMA** -

Chemikal Underground / not iss.

Jul 96. (7"ep) *(chem 005)* **538 EP** -

May 97 (12"ep/cd-ep) *(chem 014/+cd)* **SPOOK ON THE HIGH LAWN. / (mixes)** -

Oct 98. (7") *(chem 031)* **FREON SHORTWAVE. / STREET SOUP** -
(cd-s+=) *(chem 031cd)* – Non-sequitur.

Eugene CHADBOURNE

Born: 4 Jan'54, Mount Vernon, New York, USA. Raised in Boulder, Colorado, the guitarist initially took up journalism before fleeing to Canada to avoid the Vietnam draft. EUGENE returned to New York after the government relaxed their hardline policy, hooking up with avant-garde saxophonist, JOHN ZORN and releasing rare recordings, 'SCHOOL' and '2000 STATUES: THE ENGLISH CHANNEL'. Having been inspired by folk protest icon, PHIL OCHS at an early age, CHADBOURNE developed more wayward tastes as he grew older, getting into classic psychedelia and free-form jazz. He subsequently found a sympathethic musical ally in the form of bassist, MARK KRAMER, the pair instigating SHOCKABILLY in 1982 along with drummer, DAVID LICHT. Signing to UK indie outlet, 'Rough Trade', the madcap trio delivered a series of weird and wonderful releases including their inaugural recording, 'THE DAWN OF SHOCKABILLY EP' and 1983's covers jamboree (see below) 'EARTH VS. SHOCKABILLY'. Three more sets followed over the course of the next two years, namely 'COLOSSEUM' (1984), 'VIETNAM' (1985) and 'HEAVEN' (1985), the latter two issued on 'Fundamental' shortly before their demise. With KRAMER going on to join The BUTTHOLE SURFERS and start up his own 'Shimmy-Disc' label, CHADBOURNE had already prepared for a solo career by releasing a late 1985 set of warped C&W, 'COUNTRY PROTEST', re-activating the radical sentiments previously aired by his hero, OCHS. A series of largely collaborative albums appeared over the latter half of the 80's, notably 'THERE'LL BE NO TEARS TONIGHT' (1987; a 1980 recording with JOHN ZORN), 'VERMIN OF THE BLUES' (1987) with EVAN JOHNS & THE H BOMBS, 'THE LSD C&W' (1987; a turn of the decade recording as The CHADBOURNES) and 'CAMPER VAN CHADBOURNE' (1988), obviously a joint effort with alt-country bumpkins, CAMPER VAN BEETHOVEN. The 90's saw the maverick New Yorker setting up home at JELLO BIAFRA's 'Alternative Tentacles' label and releasing another dual opus with EVAN JOHNS, 'TERROR HAS SOME STRANGE KINFOLK' (1993); fan(s) of BILLY RAY CYRUS should listen out for the pastiche, 'ACHEY RAKEY HEART'. In 1996, the ubiquitous CHADBOURNE collaborated with ex-MOTHERS OF INVENTION drummer, JIMMY CARL BLACK, on an album of ZAPPA and BEEFHEART covers, 'PACHUCO CADAVAR'. • **Covered:** 19th NERVOUS BREAKDOWN (Rolling Stones) / DAY TRIPPER (Beatles) / EIGHT MILES HIGH (Byrds) / I MUST HAVE BEEN BLIND (Tim Buckley) / PEOPLE ARE STRANGE (Doors) / INSTANT KARMA + OH YOKO (John Lennon) / ARE YOU EXPERIENCED + PURPLE HAZE (Jimi Hendrix) / LUCIFER SAM + CAREFUL WITH THAT AXE, EUGENE (Pink Floyd) / etc.

Album rating: Shockabilly: EARTH VS. SHOCKABILLY (*6) / COLOSSEUM (*5) / VIETNAM (*5) / HEAVEN (*5) / Eugene Chadbourne: COUNTRY PROTEST (*5) / CORPSES OF FOREIGN WAR (*5) / THERE'LL BE NO TEARS TONIGHT (*7) / VERMIN OF THE BLUES with Evan Johns & The H-Bombs (*5) / THE LSD C&W (*5) / CAMPER VAN CHADBOURNE (*6) / I'VE BEEN EVERYWHERE (*5) / THE EDDIE CHATTERBOX DOUBLE TRIO LOVE ALBUM (*5) / COUNTRY MUSIC IN THE WORLD OF ISLAM (*5) / EUROPE VAN BEETHOVEN – SINFUNNY (*5) / TERROR HAS SOME STRANGE KINFOLK (*5) / PACHUCO CADAVAR (*6)

SHOCKABILLY

EUGENE CHADBOURNE – vocals, guitar / **MARK KRAMER** – bass / **DAVID LICHT** – drums

Rough Trade / Fundamental

Nov 82. (12"ep) *(RTT 120)* **THE DAWN OF SHOCKABILLY** -

Mar 83. (7") *(RT 127)* **19th NERVOUS BREAKDOWN. / CITY OF CORRUPTION** -

1983. (lp) *(ROUGH 48) <SAVE 17>* **THE DAWN OF EARTH VS. SHOCKABILLY** 1988
– 19th nervous breakdown / Are you experienced? / Psychedelic basement / Big money broad / Tennessee flat top box / City of corruption / People are strange / Day tripper / Purple haze / Wrestling woman / Oh Yoko. *(re-iss. 1988 on 'Shimmy Disc'; SHIMMY 017)*

1983. (12"ep) *(RED 006)* **GREATEST HITS** (compilation) -
– Blue grass breakdown / Burma shave / Voodoo vengeance / People are strange / Wrestling woman / Train.
(above issued on 'Red Music')

Apr 84. (lp) *(ROUGH 68)* **COLOSSEUM** -
– Eight miles high /

Fundamental / Fundamental

Aug 85. (lp) *<(SAVE 001)>* **VIETNAM**
– Pile up all architecture / Born on the bayou / Your U.S.A. and my face / Itan into Tulsa / Vietnam / Flying / Paris / Georgia in a jug / Lucifer Sam / Signed D.C. / Nicaragua.

Nov 85. (lp) *(SAVE 008)* **HEAVEN** -
– Life's a gas / Instant karma /

—— they split in 1985, KRAMER joined BUTTHOLE SURFERS before forming BONGWATER and B.A.L.L.

– compilations, etc. –

1989. (cd) *Shimmy Disc;* **THE GHOST OF SHOCKABILLY** -
– (EARTH VS. SHOCKABILLY + COLOSSEUM)

Jan 90. (cd) *Shimmy Disc; <SHIMMY 026>* **VIETNAM + HEAVEN** -

Feb 90. (cd) *Shimmy Disc; <SHIMMY 027>* **LIVE JUST BEAUTIFUL** -
– Intro / Georgia in a Ju / 8 miles high / Plunger routine / Are you experienced / Burma shave / Rake (birdcage routine) / Outro / Oh Yoko! / Dang me / Lucifer Sam / Nobody's place (dawn of Shockabilly) / Heart full of soul / Good girl's gonna go bad / Psychotic reaction / A hard day's night / Train kept a rollin' / Our daily lead / Byob club / Roman man / Too big for its cage / 8 miles high / Dang me / Secret of the cooler / Hattiesburg, Miss. / You dungeon my brain / Homeward bound / National bummer. *(cd re-iss. 1993; 8914)*

EUGENE CHADBOURNE

—— - guitar, etc

not iss. / Parachute

Sep 79. (c; with JOHN ZORN) *<004-006>* **SCHOOL** -

1983. (c) **CHICKEN ON THE WAY** -

not iss. / Iridescence

1985. (lp) **THE PRESIDENT: HE IS INSANE** -

Fundamental / Fundamental

Nov 85. (lp) *<(SAVE 007)>* **COUNTRY PROTEST**
– Convention of melodies / Melody in C / Always on my mind / I started a joke / The shah sleeps in / Lee Harvey's gone / Waltz across Texas. *(cd-iss. Jul90; SAVE 007CD)*

—— below with **BRIAN RITCHIE** – (of VIOLENT FEMMES)

Jul 86. (lp/c) *<(SAVE/CAVE 010)>* **CORPSES OF FOREIGN WARS**
– Universal soldier / When I'm gone / Fightin' side of me / etc
(cd-iss. Jul90; SAVE 010CD)

Jan 87. (lp) *<(SAVE 016)>* **THERE'LL BE NO TEARS TONIGHT**
(rec.1980)
(cd-iss. Jul90; SAVE 016CD)

Jun 87. (lp) *<(SAVE 018)>* **VERMIN OF THE BLUES** ("EUGENE CHADBOURNE, EVANS JOHNS & THE H BOMBS")
(cd-iss. Jul90; SAVE 018CD)

Jun 87. (d-lp) <*(SAVE 019-020)*> **THE LSD C&W** (recorded 1979-81 as The CHADBOURNES)

Feb 88. (lp; EUGENE CHADBOURNE & CAMPER VAN BEETHOVEN) <*(SAVE 046)*> **CAMPER VAN CHADBOURNE**
– Reason to believe / I talk to the wind / Fayettenam / Evil filthy preacher / Games people play / Zappa medley / Ba-lue bolivar ba-lues are / Boy with the coins / Psychedelic basement / Hum-allah hum-allah / Careful with that axe, Eugene / They can't make it rain bombs. *(cd-iss. Jul90; SAVE 046CD) (cd re-iss. Aug97; HYMN 7)*

Feb 89. (lp/c/cd) <*(SAVE 068/+MC/CD)*> **I'VE BEEN EVERYWHERE**

Feb 89. (lp/c/cd) <*(SAVE 069/+MC/CD)*> **THE EDDIE CHATTERBOX DOUBLE TRIO LOVE ALBUM**
– Sword & shield / Someday / Life x 2 minus 1 / Used record pile / Voodoo vengeance / I must have been blind / Chase the blues away / The river / Blue melody / Strange melody.

May 90. (lp/cd) <*(SAVE 080/+CD)*> **COUNTRY MUSIC IN THE WORLD OF ISLAM**

Sep 90. (d-lp/cd) **EUROPE VAN BEETHOVEN – SINFUNNY (live)** -

EUGENE CHADBOURNE & EVAN JOHNS

Alternative Tentacles | Alternative Tentacles

Jun 93. (lp/cd) <*(VIRUS 19/+CD)*> **TERROR HAS SOME STRANGE KINFOLK**
– Achey rakey heart / Redneck jazz / Sail my ship alone / I gotta pee / I cut the wrong man / George Bush's bones jig / Desert storm chewing gum / Let 'em drink while they're young / Mister Jones / Missing engineer / Killbillies / Got the blues and can't be satisfied / Checkers of blood / There was gloom / Land of used to be / Living in the country.

Jul 93. (7") <*(VIRUS 125)*> **ACHEY RAKEY HEART. /**

EUGENE CHADBOURNE

— (below featured collaboration with ex-FRANK ZAPPA / MOTHERS man)

Fireants | Fireants

Dec 95. (cd; EUGENE CHADBOURNE & JIMMY CARL BLACK) *(1007)* **PACHUCO CADAVAR / JACK & JIM SHOW**

Jul 96. (cd) **JESSE HELMS BUSTED WITH PORNOGRAPHY** -

not iss. | Victo

Feb 97. (cd) <*46*> **PATRIZIO** -

not iss. | Intakt

Mar 97. (cd; by EUGENE CHADBOURNE & HELLINGTON COUNTY) <*052*> **HELLINGTUNES** -

Fundamental | Fundamental

Aug 97. (cd) <*(HYMN 2)*> **LOCKED IN A DUTCH COFFEE SHOP**

not iss. | Rastacan

Aug 98. (cd) <*32*> **VOLUME 2: SOLO ACOUSTIC GUITAR** -

– compilations, others, etc. –

1986. (cd) *RR Records;* **COUNTRY MUSIC OF SOUTH EASTERN AUSTRALIA** -

1986. (cd) *Parachute;* **CALGARY EXILE** -

1987. (cd) *Placebo; (PLCD 5)* **DEAR EUGENE** -
– Ollie's playhouse / How can you kill me / Eight miles high / Women against porno / Purple haze / The plunger / Oh Yoko / Ramblin' man / I must have been blind / Big boys will be little boys / Lucifer Sam / Price of Paradise / In the cemetary / Monk medley / Permanent lonely / Secret of the cooler.

1987. (c) *Parachute;* **MEGADEATH** -

1987. (c) *Parachute;* **THIRD WORLD SUMMIT MEETING** -

1987. (c) *Parachute;* **TUCSON, ARIZONA** -

1988. (c) *Parachute;* **FUCK CHUCK** -

1988. (c) *Parachute;* **WICHITA, KANSAS** -

1993. (cd) *Leo;* **WORMS WITH STRINGS** -

May 95. (cd) *Overtone;* <*001*> **ELECTRIC RAKE CAKE** -

1997. (cd) *Leo; <256>* **INSECT AND WESTERN ATTRACTER** -

Guy CHADWICK (see under ⇒ HOUSE OF LOVE)

Ken CHAMBERS (see under ⇒ MOVING TARGETS)

CHAMELEONS

Formed: Middleton, North Manchester, England … 1981 by MARK BURGESS, DAVE FIELDING and REG SMITHIES. The latter two, with drummer CHRIS SEDDON, had been part of The YEARS, who released one single, 'COME DANCING' / 'RED CHEVY' / 'DON'T LEAVE' on their own 'Tuff Going' label. As The CHAMELEONS, they sent a demo to Radio One DJ, John Peel, who was impressed enough to give them a session, the band's line-up now completed by JOHN LEVER. After a brief, disastrous spell with 'Epic' in 1982, they signed to 'Virgin' subsidiary, 'Statik'. Filling the huge gap left by the demise of TEARDROP EXPLODES, The CHAMELEONS championed a distinctive brand of power rock characterised by subtle shadings of mood and atmosphere. Oft sighted by many as one of the most criminally ignored bands in Manchester's chequered musical history, their acclaimed debut album, 'SCRIPT OF THE BRIDGE' (1983) went largely unnoticed despite glowing reviews for the near hour long set. A record that everyone should have in their collection, it contained the epic 'SECOND SKIN', the best song JULIAN COPE never wrote (and that's high praise indeed!). A belated follow-up, 'WHAT DOES ANYTHING MEAN? BASICALLY' (1985), was almost as strong and, with further critical plaudits, the album made the lower reaches of the chart. Their major break came later in the year, when new manager and 5th member TONY FLETCHER encouraged David Geffen to sign them to his label. Nevertheless, even major label US muscle couldn't help the band break the Top 40, 'SWAMP THING' and 'TEARS' highlights of a slightly patchy set, 'STRANGE TIMES' (1986). More grief was to follow when FLETCHER died of a heart attack the following year, the band finally throwing in the towel soon after. Various spin-off projects (including The SUN AND THE MOON and The REEGS) met with little success outside of their loyal fanbase. • **Songwriters:** All penned by band, except JOHN, I'M ONLY DANCING (Bowie) / TOMORROW NEVER KNOWS (Beatles) / SPLITTING IN TWO (Alternative TV). REEGS covered; SEE MY FRIENDS (Kinks) / As The Three Imaginary Boys; THE LAST TIME (Rolling Stones). MARK BURGESS covered YOU ONLY LIVE TWICE (John Barry) / FACADES (Philip Glass) / SOMETHING FOR THE GIRL WITH EVERYTHING + MOON OVER KENTUCKY (Sparks). • **Trivia:** Nothing whatsoever to do with LORI & THE CHAMELEONS.

Album rating: THE SCRIPT OF THE BRIDGE (*9) / WHAT DOES ANYTHING MEAN? BASICALLY (*6) / STRANGE TIMES (*7) / THE FAN AND THE BELLOWS collection (*6)

MARK 'Birdy' BURGESS – vocals, bass (ex-CLICHES) / **DAVE FIELDING** – guitar, strings (ex-YEARS) / **REG SMITHIES** – guitar (ex-YEARS) / **JOHN LEVER** – drums, percussion (ex-POLITICIANS) repl. BRIAN SCHOFIELD

Epic | not iss.

Mar 82. (7") *(EPCA 2210)* **IN SHREDS. / LESS THAN HUMAN** -

— **JOHN LEVER** was repl. for a year by **MARTIN JACKSON** (ex-MAGAZINE)

Statik | not iss.

Feb 83. (7") *(STAT 20)* **AS HIGH AS YOU CAN GO. / PLEASURE AND PAIN** -
(12"+=) *(STAT 20-12)* – Paper tigers.

Jun 83. (7") *(TAK 6)* **A PERSON ISN'T SAFE ANYWHERE THESE DAYS. / THURSDAY'S CHILD** -
(12"+=) *(TAK 6-12)* – Prisoners of the sun.

Aug 83. (lp,pic-lp/c) *(STAT LP/C 17)* **SCRIPT OF THE BRIDGE** -
– Don't fall / Here today / Monkeyland / Second skin / Up the down escalator / Less than human / Pleasure and pain / Thursday's child / As high as you can go / A person isn't safe anywhere these days / Paper tigers / View from a hill. *(cd+=) –* In shreds / Nostalgia. *(cd-iss. Feb86; SCDT 17) (cd re-iss. Jun89; CDST 017) (cd re-iss. Jul95 on 'Dead Dead Good'; GOODCD 6)*

Nov 83. (7") *(TAK 11)* **UP THE DOWN ESCALATOR. / MONKEYLAND** - - German
(12"+=) *(TAK 11-12)* – Prisoners of the sun.

Feb 85. (7") *(TAK 29)* **IN SHREDS (live). / NOSTALGIA (live)** -
(12"+=) *(TAK 29-12)* – Less than human (live).

— added on stage **ALISTAIR LEWTWAITE** – keyboards, but he was replaced by **ANDY CLEGG** – keyboards (ex-MUSIC FOR ABORIGINES)

May 85. (lp/c) *(STAT LP/C 22)* **WHAT DOES ANYTHING MEAN? BASICALLY** 60 -
– Silence, sea and sky / Perfume garden / Intrigue in Tangiers / Return of the roughnecks / Singing rule Britannia (while the walls close in) / On the beach / Looking inwardly / One flesh / Home is where the heart is / P.S. goodbye. *(cd-iss. Feb86 +=; CDST 22) –* In shreds / Nostalgia. *(cd re-iss. Jul95 on 'Dead Dead Good'; GOODCD 7)*

Aug 85. (7") *(TAK 35)* **SINGING RULE BRITTANIA (WHILE THE WALLS CLOSE IN). / ('A'-Radio 1 version)** -
(12"+=) *(TAK 35-12)* – Pleasure and pain (Radio 1 version).

Geffen | Geffen

Jun 86. (7") *(GEF 4)* **TEARS. / PARADISO**
(w/ free 7") *(SAM 287)* – SWAMP THING. / INSIDE OUT
(12"+=) *(GEF 4T)* – Inside out.

Sep 86. (lp/c) *(924119-1/-4)* **STRANGE TIMES** 44
– Mad Jack / Caution / Soul in isolation / Swamp thing / Time – The end of time / Seriocity / In answer / Childhood / I'll remember / Tears. *(cd-iss. Mar87; 924119-2)* <US-iss.lp w/ free m-lp> – Tears (full arrangement) / Paradiso / Inside out / Ever after / John, I'm only dancing / Tomorrow never knows. *(re-iss. d-cd Jul93; GFLDD 19207)*

Sep 86. (7") *(GEF 10)* **SWAMP THING. / JOHN, I'M ONLY DANCING**
(12"+=) *(GEF 10T)* – Tears (original).

— split late '86, after manager TONY FLETCHER died of a heart attack. MARK and JOHN formed The SUN AND THE MOON with ANDY CLEGG and ANDY WHITAKER. In 1993, MARK BURGESS formed his SONS OF GOD. FIELDING and SMITHIES formed The REEGS in '88.

– compilations, others, etc. –

Mar 86. (ltd-lp) *Hybrid; (CHAMLP 1)* **THE FAN AND THE BELLOWS** (most recorded 1981) -
– The fan and the bellows / Nostalgia / Less than human / In shreds / Prisoners of the Sun / Nostalgia (7" version) / Turn to the vices / Love is / Everyday I'm crucified / Endlessly falling / Nathan's phase. *<US-iss.1989 on 'Caroline'; > (cd-iss. Sep96 on 'Dead Dead Good'; GOODCD 9)*

Oct 90. (cd-ep; w-drawn) *Glass Pyramid; (EMC 1)* **TONY FLETCHER WALKED ON WATER . . . LA LA LA LA LA – LA LA – LA LA** - -
– Is it any wonder / Free for all / The healer / Denims and curls.
(finally issued 1994) (re-iss. May97 on 'Dead Dead Good'; GOOD 39CD)

Oct 90. (cd/lp) *Glass Pyramid; (CD+/EMC 2)* **TRIPPING DOGS** -

Dec 90. (cd/lp) *Strange Fruit; (SFR CD/LP 114)* **PEEL SESSIONS** -

Jun 92. (cd/c/lp) *Illusion; (ILLCD/ILLCASS/ILLUSION 035)* **HERE TODAY . . . GONE TOMORROW** -

Jun 92. (cd/c/lp) *Illusion; (ILLCD/ILLCASS/ILLUSION 036)* **LIVE IN TORONTO (live '87)** -

Jan 93. (cd) *Nightracks; (CDNT 1)* **RADIO 1 EVENING SHOW SESSIONS** -

Feb 93. (pic-cd) *Imaginary; (ILLCD 039P)* **FREE TRADE HALL REHEARSAL (live)** -

May 93. (cd/lp) *Imaginary; (ILLCD/ILLUSION 041)* **DALI'S PICTURE** -
(d-cd; with free-cd 'LIVE IN BERLIN')

Nov 94. (cd) *Bone Idol; (BONE 001L)* **NORTHERN SONGS** □ -
– (includes 'TONY FLETCHER WALKED ON WATER . . . EP')
May 97. (d-cd) *Dead Dead Good; (GOODCD 12X)* **THE RETURN OF THE ROUGHNECKS (THE BEST OF THE CHAMELEONS)** □ -

SUN AND THE MOON

BURGESS + LEVER / + ANDY WHITAKER – keyboards (ex-MUSIC FOR ABORIGINES) / **ANDY CLEGG** – guitar (ex-MUSIC FOR ABORIGINES)

Geffen Geffen

May 88. (lp/c/cd) *(924 182-1/-4/-2) <24182>* **THE SUN AND THE MOON** □ □
– The speed of life / Death of imagination / Peace in our time / A matter of conscience / Dolphin / House on fire / The price of grain / Limbo-land / A picture of England / This passionate breed.
Jun 88. (7") *(GEF 39-7)* **THE SPEED OF LIFE. / DEATH OF IMAGINATION** □ -
(12"+=) *(GEF 39-12)* – The boy who sees everything / I love you, you bastard.

Midnight Music not iss.

Nov 88. (12"ep/cd-ep) *(DONG 44/+CD)* **ALIVE; NOT DEAD EP** □ -
– Adam's song / C'est la vie / Arabs and Americans / Elected.

— In 1991, LEVER, CLEGG + WHITAKER with ATKINSON formed WEAVEWORLD who released a 12"; DAVY JONES. / OUT AND DOWN / PATHETICAL TWAT for 'Sugarpussy'.

MARK BURGESS

Imaginary Pivot

Jul 93. (cd/lp; MARK BURGESS & THE SONS OF GOD) *(ILLCD/ILLUSION 044) <3>* **ZIMA JUNCTION** □ □ May94
– World on fire / Waiting for a friend / Refugees / The great adventure / Beat the boat / When harmony comes / Our soul, dead soul, brother and fool / Happy new life / Up on the hill / Fascades / You only live twice.

Indigo not iss.

Nov 94. (d-cd) *()* **SPRING BLOOMS TRA-LA-LA** □ -

MARK BURGESS & YVES ALTANA

Dead Dead Good not iss.

Aug 95. (7") *(GOOD 32)* **SIN. / HOLLIN HIGH** □ -
(cd-s+=) *(GOOD 32CD)* – Moon over Kentucky.
Sep 95. (7") *(GOOD 33)* **ALWAYS WANT. / STEPHANIE WEAVES** □ -
(cd-s+=) *(GOOD 33CD)* – Something for the girl with everything.
Oct 95. (cd/lp) *(GOOD CD/LP 8)* **PARADYNING** □ -
– Sin / Always went / Adrian be / Silver / Money won't save our soul / You opened my mind (then the acid kicked in) / Inhaling / World without end / Hi Joe / Stop talking.

REEGS

FIELDING + SMITHIES

Imaginary not iss.

Apr 89. (12") *(MIRAGE 006)* **SEE MY FRIENDS. / IS THERE A MOTHER-IN-LAW IN THE CLUB / THIS SAVAGE GARDEN** □ -
Aug 90. (12") *(MIRAGE 012)* **CHORUS OF THE LOST. / POND LIFE / START TO SEE (instrumental)** □ -

— added drum machine + **GARY LAVERY** – vocals

Jul 91. (cd/c/lp) *(ILLCD/ILLCAS/ILLUSION 029)* **RETURN OF THE SEA MONKEYS** □ -
Oct 93. (cd) *(ILLCD 045)* **ROCK THE MAGIC ROCK** □ -
– JJ 180 / The blind denial / Goodbye world / The dream police / The nasty side / The dolphin's enemy / In disbelief / Oil and water / Running to a standstill / The nasty side (instrumental).

Columbus not iss.

Jul 97. (cd-s) *(THEMUS 001)* **AS YOU LEAVE. / JJ 180** □ -
Nov 97. (cd-s) *(THEMUS 002)* **YOU TOLD ME BEFORE. /** □ -

— Split . . . FIELDING became producer notably for The INSPIRAL CARPETS

James CHANCE

Born: JAMES SIEGFRIED, 20 Apr'53, Milwaukee, Wisconsin, USA. Having dropped out of Wisconsin Conservatory music school, JAMES took his saxophone to New York in 1976 and after a short-lived period studying under DAVID MURRAY, he formed The CONTORTIONS (i.e. ADELE BEREI, JODY HARRIS, PAT PLACE, GEORGE SCOTT III and DON CHRISTENSEN). With the city in the grip of punk fever, CHANCE took the opportunity to fuse aggressive nihilism with wildly improvised sax scree and twisted funk rhythms; reputed to be as obsessively meticulous as BEEFHEART during his "Trout Mask Replica" period, CHANCE and his CONTORTIONS' unhinged live shows often degenerated into improvised violence as the man confronted punters indiscriminately. Although they gained infamy in the Big Apple, it wasn't until 1978 that CHANCE and Co reached a wider audience when Avant Garde curator, BRIAN ENO, collected the sounds of various "No Wave" artists (including TEENAGE JESUS & THE JERKS, DNA and MARS) together on the album, 'No New York'; four tracks were featured, namely 'I CAN'T STAND MYSELF', 'JADED', 'DISH IT OUT' and 'FLIP YOUR FACE'. Finally, after nearly three years of aural terrorism, The CONTORTIONS unleashed their one and only studio set, hopefully titled 'BUY' (late '79). By this time, CHANCE had decided to re-invent himself and the band as JAMES WHITE AND THE BLACKS, two albums 'OFF-WHITE' (1980) and 'SAX MANIAC' (1982) offering up a less crazed but still off-beat take on funk and jazz drawing heavily from MACEO PARKER's heyday with JAMES BROWN. In 1980, he also found time to collaborate with ARTO LINDSAY, BRADLEY FIELD and band member, GEORGE SCOTT, on a soundtrack of Diego Cortez's film, 'Grutzi Elvis' (SCOTT was to die of a heroin overdose soon after its release). While The CORTORTIONS were still the subject of a posthumous release schedule, JAMES (WHITE) had already moved to Paris, returning periodically to New York City, mainly to record albums, most noteably 1983's solo effort, 'JAMES WHITE PRESENTS THE FLANING DEMONICS'. In 1987, after spells with trombonist JOSEPH BOWIE (later leader of DEFUNKT) and HENRY THREADGILL (of jazz outfit, AIR), he took on work with The FALSE PROPHETS, his alto sax clearly making the grade on their 'Implosion' set. Of late, CHANCE re-formed his CONTORTIONS, although recordings have been sparse thus far.

Album rating: Contortions: BUY (*7) LIVE IN NEW YORK (*6) / James Chance & The Blacks: OFF-WHITE (*6) / SAX MANIAC (*5) / JAMES WHITE PRESENTS THE FLAMING DELMONICS (*5)

CONTORTIONS

JAMES CHANCE – vocals, saxophone / **ADELE BERTEI** – organ / **JODY HARRIS** – guitar / **PAT PLACE** – slide guitar / **GEORGE SCOTT II** – bass / **DON CHRISTENSEN** – drums

Ze-Island Ze

Oct 79. (12") *<ZEA12 001>* **DESIGNED TO KILL. / THROW ME AWAY** - □
Mar 80. (lp) *(ILPS 7002) <ZEA-33 002>* **BUY** □ □ Nov79
– Designed to kill / My infatuation / I don't want to be happy / Anesthetic / Contort yourself / Throw me away / Roving eye / Twice removed / Bedroom athlete. *(cd-iss. Mar96 on 'Infinite Zero-BMG'; 74321 32757-2)*

JAMES WHITE & THE BLACKS

— virtually the same group members except BERTEI who was retained as guest although she had joined the BLOODS

Ze-Island Ze

May 80. (lp) *(ILPS 7008) <ZEA33 003>* **OFF-WHITE** □ □
– Contort yourself / Stained sheets / Almost black / Heat wave / Almost black / White savages / Off black / White devil / Bleached black. *(cd-iss. Oct95 on 'Infinite Zero-BMG'; 74321 31879-2)*
Aug 80. (12") *<ZE12 006>* **CONTORT YOURSELF. / (TROPICAL) HEATWAVE** - □

— PAT joined BUSH TETRAS, while SCOTT joined LYDIA LUNCH in 8-EYED SPY, before re-grouping with HARRIS and CHRISTENSEN in The RAYBEATS. Meanwhile, JAMES recruited new band; **JERRY ANTONIUS + CHRIS CUNNINGHAM** – guitar / **COLIN WADE** – bass / **RALPH ROLLE** – drums / **CHERIE MARILYN + ROBIN MARLOWE** – vocals / **ROBERT AARON** – tenor sax / **LUTHER THOMAS** – saxes

Chrysalis Animal

Sep 82. (lp) *(CHR 1401)* **SAX MANIAC** □ □
– Irresistable impulse / That old black magic / Disco jaded / Money to burn / Sax maniac / Sax machine / The twitch.

JAMES WHITE

— **RODNEY FORSTALL** – bass; repl. WADE

Ze-Island Ze

1983. (lp) *(ILPS 7023)* **JAMES WHITE PRESENTS THE FLAMING DEMONICS** □ □
– The Devil made me do it / Boulevard of broken dreams / Rantin' & ravin' / The natives are restless / Caravan / It don't mean a thing / Melt yourself down / I danced with a zombie.

– compilations, etc. –

May 80. (lp) *Invisible; (SCOPA 1008)* **LIVE AUX BAINS DOUCHES PARIS (live with new CONTORTIONS)** - - French
– Don't stop till you get enough / I danced with a zombie / My infatuation / I got you (I feel good) / Almost black / King Heroin / Put me back in my cage / Contort yourself.

— above with **GINGER LEE** – vocals / **PATRICK GEOFFROIS + FRED WELLS** – guitar / **AL MacDOWELL** – bass / **RICHARD HARRISON** – drums / **LORENZO WYCHE** – trumpet

1981. (c) *R.O.I.R.;* **LIVE IN NEW YORK (live with The CONTORTIONS)** - □
Apr 91. (lp/c) *R.O.I.R.; <>* **SOUL EXORCISM** (live Amsterdam 1980 with The CONTORTIONS) □ □
Oct 95. (cd) *ROIR USA; (RUSCD 8214)* **LAST CHANCE** □ □

CHANNEL 3

Formed: Cerritos, Los Angeles, California, USA . . . 1980 by MIKE MAGRANN, alongside fellow punk-rock afficionados, KIMM GARDENER, LARRY KELLEY and MIKE BURTON, the latter surviving three other drummers. Having released a solitary EP in Spring '82 for the influential 'Posh Boy' imprint, CHANNEL 3 became one of the few US hardcore acts to sign a UK deal, securing a licensing agreement with 'No Future'. The latter EP was subsequently released a few months later, while the debut album, 'FEAR OF LIFE' (1982), appeared in Britain as 'I'VE GOT A GUN'. Prior to the recording of the follow-up set, 'AFTER THE LIGHTS GO OUT' (1983), JACK DEBAUN replaced BURTON, further personnel reshuffles coming in the shape of GARDENER making way for JAY LANSFORD. His inaugural appearance arrived with the 'AIRBORNE' EP in '84, the former

STEPMOTHERS guitarist sticking around for what was to become their swansong set, 'THE LAST TIME I DRANK' (1985).

Album rating: FEAR OF LIFE – (or)- I'VE GOT A GUN (*4) / AFTER THE LIGHTS GO OUT (*6) / THE LAST TIME I DRANK . . . (*5)

MIKE MAGRANN – vocals, guitar / **KIMM GARDENER** – guitar / **LARRY KELLEY** – bass / **MIKE BURTON** – drums

		No Future	Posh Boy
Jul 82.	(7"ep) *(OI 11)* **I'VE GOT A GUN. / MANZANAR / MANNEQUIN**	[ ]	[ ] May82
Sep 82.	(lp) *(PUNK 2)* **I'VE GOT A GUN** <US-title 'FEAR OF LIFE'>	[ ]	[ ]

(UK)- Fear of life / Out of control / I've got a gun / Wetspots / Accident / You make me feel cheap / You lie / Catholic boy / Waiting in the wings / Strength in numbers / Double standard boys / Life goes on. *(cd-iss. Oct91 on 'Anagram'+=; CDMGRAM 50)* – AFTER THE LIGHTS GO OUT *(cd re-iss. Jun94; CDPUNK 2)*

— **JACK DEBAUN** – drums; repl. BURTON

Aug 83.	(lp) *(PUNK 7)* **AFTER THE LIGHTS GO OUT**	[ ]	[ ]

– What about me? / Separate peace / No love / After the lights go out / Truth and trust / I'll take my chances / All my dreams / Can't afford it / Didn't know / Manzanar / Mannequin. *(cd-iss. Jun93; CDPUNK 7)*

— **JAY LANSFORD** – guitar (ex-STEPMOTHERS) repl. KIMM

		not iss.	Enigma
1984.	(7"ep) **AIRBORNE**	[-]	[ ]
1985.	(lp/c) *<72008-1/-4>* **THE LAST TIME I DRANK . . .**	[-]	[ ]

— split not long after above

– compilations, etc. –

May 94.	(cd) *Lost & Found; (LF 098)* **HOW DO YOU OPEN THE DAMN THING (live)**	[ ]	[ ]
1995.	(cd) *Poshboy; <88156>* **THE SKINHEAD YEARS**	[-]	[ ]

CHAPTERHOUSE

Formed: Reading, England . . . late '87 by ANDREW SHERRIFF, STEPHEN PATMAN, SIMON ROWE, JON CURTIS and ASHLEY BATES. After thoroughly polishing their skills in the studio they toured as a support to SPACEMEN 3, their dense, effects-driven sound subsequently casting them as leading lights of the early 90's "shoegazing" scene. So called due to the scenester's tendency to favour distortion pedals over showmanship, CHAPTERHOUSE (along with LUSH, BLEACH, MOOSE, RIDE etc.) became sitting targets for music press critiscism. Moving to London in 1990, they signed to the newly formed 'Dedicated' label and were initially heralded as indie music's great white hopes following an impressive couple of EP's, 'FREE FALL' and 'SUNBURST', along with the sublime 'PEARL'. With a steadily growing reputation, 1991's debut album, 'WHIRLPOOL', narrowly missed the Top 20 and the band looked set for great things. It all went pear-shaped following an ill-fated attempt to make some headway in the US and with the shoegazing backlash at full strength, a follow-up album, 'BLOOD MUSIC' (1993), was to be the final, ahem . . . chapter in the band's relatively brief career. While the likes of MY BLOODY VALENTINE and RIDE continued to evolve and amass critical aclaim, CHAPTERHOUSE lasted only as long as the scene itself. • **Songwriters:** All SHERRIFF or PATMAN or combined. Covered; RAIN (Beatles) / LADY GODIVA'S OPERATION (Velvet Underground).

Album rating: WHIRLPOOL (*6) / BLOOD MUSIC (*5)

STEPHEN PATMAN (b. 8 Nov'68, Windsor, England) – vocals, guitar / **ANDREW SHERRIFF** (b. 5 May'69, Wokingham, England) – vocals, guitar / **SIMON ROWE** (b.23 Jun'69) – guitar / **ASHLEY BATES** (b. 2 Nov'71) – drums / **RUSSELL BARRETT** (b. 7 Nov'68, Vermont, USA) – bass (ex-BIKINIS) repl. JON CURTIS

		Dedicated	Arista
Aug 90.	(12"ep/cd-ep) *(STONE 001 T/CD)* **FREE FALL**	[ ]	[-]

– Falling down / Need (somebody) / Inside of me / Sixteen years.

Nov 90.	(7") *(STONE 002)* **SOMETHING MORE. / RAIN**	[ ]	[-]

(12"ep+=/cd-ep+=) **SUNBURST EP** *(STONE 002 T/CD)* – Satin safe / Feel the same.

Mar 91.	(7") *(STONE 003)* **PEARL. / COME HEAVEN**	[67]	[-]

(12"+=) *(STONE 003T)* – In my arms.
(cd-s++=) *(STONE 003CD)* – Pearl (edit).

Apr 91.	(cd/c/lp) *(DED CD/MC/LP 001)* **WHIRLPOOL**	[23]	[-]

– Brother / Pearl / Autosleeper / Treasure / Falling down / April / Guilt / If you want me / Something more. *(free-ltd.one-sided-12"w-lp)* – DIE DIE DIE

Oct 91.	(12"ep/cd-ep) *(HOUSE 001/+CD)* **MESMERISE. / PRECIOUS ONE / SUMMER CHILL / THEN WE'LL RISE**	[60]	[-]
Jul 93.	(7"purple) *(HOUSE 003)* **SHE'S A VISION. / DON'T LOOK NOW**	[ ]	[-]

(12"+=) *(HOUSE 003T)* – ('B'-sitar trance mix) / For what it's worth (demo).
(cd-s+=) *(HOUSE 003CD)* – ('B'-sitar trance mix) / Deli (dark jester mix).

Aug 93.	(7") *(HOUSE 004)* **WE ARE THE BEAUTIFUL. / AGE**	[ ]	[-]

(12"colrd+=/cd-s+=) *(HOUSE 004 T/CD)* – Frost.

Sep 93.	(cd/c/lp) *(DED CD/MC/LP 11)* **BLOOD MUSIC**	[ ]	[-]

– Don't look now / There's still life / We are the beautiful / Summer's gone / Everytime / Deli / On the way to fly / She's a vision / Greater power / Confusion trip / Love forever.

Oct 93.	(cd-s) *<2640>* **WE ARE THE BEAUTIFUL / WE ARE (extended)**	[-]	[ ]

— Sank without trace after lukewarm reviews of above album.

Nov 96.	(d-cd) *(DEDCD 025)* **ROWNDERBOWT** (compilation)	[ ]	[-]

— ASHLEY resurfaced in the breakbeat psychedelic duo, CUBA, alongside Canadian CHRISTOPHER ANDREWS. A couple of singles starting with 'CROSS THE LINE' were issued for '4 a.d.' in 1998. Meanwhile, RUSSELL was doing his bit with London 4-piece, INNER SLEEVE and the BIKINIS.

CHARLATANS

Formed: Northwich, Cheshire, England . . . late 1989 by MARTIN BLUNT, ROB COLLINS, JON BROOKES and JON BAKER. They soon found a frontman in singer TIM BURGESS and after a few attempts at getting a record deal, they set up their own 'Dead Dead Good' label. Early in 1990, they scored a massive indie hit with the 'INDIAN ROPE' single. Following the explosion of the "Madchester" scene, the label was taken over by the Beggars Banquet subsidiary, 'Situation 2', for whom they recorded their first Top 10 hit, 'THE ONLY ONE I KNOW'. Another hammond-driven classic, 'THEN', preceded a late summer chart topping debut album, 'SOME FRIENDLY'. A relatively quiet year followed, during which MARTIN BLUNT nearly retired due to severe depression. However, it was actually BAKER who departed after playing at London's Royal Albert Hall. Come 1992, MARK COLLINS was drafted in and things look brighter when the single, 'WEIRDO', gave them another Top 20 hit. Their second album, however, ('BETWEEN 10TH AND 11TH'), was given the thumbs down by the music press, hence its failure to secure a respectable chart placing. This was not the only setback that year, as ROB COLLINS was charged with aiding and abetting an armed robbery. A year later, although maintaining his innocence, he was sentenced to several months in jail, later being released in early 1994 on good behavior. 'CAN'T GET OUT OF BED', saw them return in fine style, and was lifted from the Top 10 album 'UP TO OUR HIPS'. TIM then moonlighted on singles by SAINT ETIENNE and The CHEMICAL BROTHERS, before the group were back to their best on the eponymous 1995 album. From its retro cover art, to the 'Sympathy For The Devil'-style single, 'JUST WHEN YOU'RE THINKIN' THINGS OVER', the album was an obvious homage to The ROLLING STONES. Tragically, on 23rd of July '96, ROB COLLINS was killed when his car spun off a road in Wales. The coroners report concluded that he was the driver and also that he had twice the legal amount of alcohol in his blood. They had just recorded their fifth album, 'TELLIN' STORIES', preceded by their biggest hit singles to date, 'ONE TO ANOTHER' and 'NORTH COUNTRY BOY'. With The CHARLATANS momentum seemingly unstoppable while every other 'baggy' band fell by the wayside, BURGESS and Co celebrated their longevity with a career retrospective, 'MELTING POT' (1998). • **Songwriters:** Group compositions except; I FEEL MUCH BETTER ROLLING OVER (Small Faces). On their eponymous 1995 album, the track 'HERE COMES A SOUL SAVER' featured a guitar riff remarkably similar to that of PINK FLOYD's 'Fearless' (from 'Meddle' 1971).

Album rating: SOME FRIENDLY (*8) / BETWEEN 10th & 11th (*5) / UP TO OUR HIPS (*7) / THE CHARLATANS (*8) / TELLIN' STORIES (*8) / MELTING POT compilation (*8)

TIM BURGESS (b.30 May'68) – vocals (ex-ELECTRIC CRAYONS) repl. BAZ KETTLEY / **ROB COLLINS** (b.23 Feb'63) – organ / **JON BAKER** (b.1969) – guitar / **JON BROOKS** (b.1969) – drums / **MARTIN BLUNT** (b.1965) – bass (ex-MAKIN' TIME, ex-TOO MUCH TEXAS w / TIM)

		Dead Dead Good	not iss.
Feb 90.	(7") *(GOOD ONE SEVEN)* **INDIAN ROPE. / WHO WANTS TO KNOW**	[89]	[-]

(12"+=) *(GOOD ONE TWELVE)* – You can talk to me. *(re-iss. Jul91 12"/cd-s; GOOD 1 T/CD,* hit No.57) *(re-iss. cd-s Oct96)*

		Situation 2	Beggars Banquet
May 90.	(7") *(SIT 70)* **THE ONLY ONE I KNOW. / EVERYTHING CHANGED**	[9]	[ ]

(12"+=) *(SIT 70T)* – Imperial 109.
(cd-s++=) *(SIT 70CD)* – You can talk to me.

Sep 90.	(7"/c-s) *(SIT 74/+C)* **THEN. / TAURUS MOANER**	[12]	[ ]

(12"+=/cd-s+=) *(SIT 74 T/CD)* – ('A'-alternate take) / ('B'instrumental).

Oct 90.	(lp/c/cd/s-lp) *(SITU 30/+MC/CD/R) <2411>* **SOME FRIENDLY**	[1]	[73]

– You're not very well / White shirt / Opportunity / Then / 109 pt.2 / Polar bear / Believe you me / Flower / Sonic / Sproston Green. *(cd+=)* – The only one I know. *(cd re-iss. Sep95 on 'Beggars Banquet'; BBL 30CD)*

Feb 91.	(7"/c-s) *(SIT 76/+CS)* **OVER RISING. / WAY UP THERE**	[15]	[ ]

(12"/c-s+=/cd-s+=) *(SIT 76 T/TC/CD)* – Happen to die / Opportunity Three (re-work).

— **MARK COLLINS** – guitar (ex-CANDLESTICK PARK) repl. BAKER

Oct 91.	(7"/c-s) *(SIT 84/+C)* **ME IN TIME. / OCCUPATION H. MONSTER**	[28]	[ ]

(12"+=/cd-s+=) *(SIT 84 T/CD)* – Subtitle.

Feb 92.	(7"/c-s) *(SIT 88/+C)* **WEIRDO. / THEME FROM 'THE WISH'**	[19]	[ ]

(12"+=/cd-s+=) *(SIT 88 T/CD)* – Sproston Green (U.S. remix) / ('A'-alternate take).

Mar 92.	(lp/c/cd) *(SITU 37/+MC/CD) <61108>* **BETWEEN 10th AND 11th**	[21]	[ ]

– I don't want to see the lights / Ignition / Page one / Tremelo song / The end of everything etc / Subtitle / Can't even be bothered / Weirdo / Chewing gum weekend / (No one) Not even the rain. *(re-iss. cd Sep95 on 'Beggars Banquet'; BBL 37CD)*

Jun 92.	(c-s) *(SIT 97C)* **TREMELO SONG (alternate take) / THEN (live) / CHEWING GUM WEEKEND (live) / TREMELO SONG**	[44]	[ ]

(12") *(SIT 97T)* – Happen to die (unedited) repl. last version.
(cd-s) *(SIT 97CD1)* – ('A'side) / Happen to die (unedited) / Normality swing (demo).
(cd-s) *(SIT 97CD2)* – ('A'live April '92) / Then (live) / Chewing gum weekend (live).

— ROB COLLINS was imprisoned in Sep'93 for taking part in a robbery. (see above) He had already recorded below while awaiting trial, and was free just in time to feature on Top Of The Pops.

Beggars Banquet — Beggars Banquet

Jan 94. (7"/c-s) *(BBQ 27/+C)* **CAN'T GET OUT OF BED. / WITHDRAWN** 24 -
(12"+=/cd-s+=) *(BBQ 27 T/CD)* – Out.

Mar 94. (cd-ep) *(BBQ 31CD)* **I NEVER WANT AN EASY LIFE IF ME AND HE WERE EVER TO GET THERE / ONLY A BOHO / SUBTERRAINEAN / CAN'T GET OUT OF BED (demo)** 38 -

Mar 94. (cd/c/lp) *(BBQ CD/MC/LP 147)* <92352> **UP TO OUR HIPS** 8
– Come in number 21 / I never want an easy life / If me and he were ever to get there / Can't get out of bed / Feel flows / Autograph / Jesus hairdo / Up to our hips / Patrol / Another rider up in flames / Inside – looking out. *(re-iss. cd Sep95; BBL 147CD)*

Jun 94. (c-s) *(BBQ 32C)* **JESUS HAIRDO / PATROL (Dust Brothers mix)** 48 -
(12"+=) *(BBQ 32T)* – Feel flows (the carpet kiss mix).
(cd-s+=) *(BBQ 32CD1)* – Stir it up / Feel flows (Van Basten mix).
(cd-s) *(BBQ 32CD2)* – ('A'side) / I never want an easy life / Another rider up in flames / Up to our hips (BBC Radio 1 live sessions).

Dec 94. (7"/c-s) *(BBQ 44/+C)* **CRASHIN' IN. / BACK ROOM WINDOW** 31 -
(12"+=/cd-s+=) *(BBQ 44 T/CD)* – Green flashing eyes.

May 95. (7"/c-s) *(BBQ 55/+C)* **JUST LOOKIN'. / BULLET COMES** 32 -
(cd-s+=) *(BBQ 55CD)* – Floor nine.

Aug 95. (c-s) *(BBQ 60C)* **JUST WHEN YOU'RE THINKIN' THINGS OVER / FRINCK / YOUR SKIES ARE MINE** 12 -
(cd-s+=) *(BBQ 60CD)* – Chemical risk (toothache remix).
(12") *(BBQ 60T)* – (first 2 tracks) / Chemical risk dub (toothache remix) / Nine acre dust (Dust Brothers mix).

Aug 95. (cd/c/d-lp) *(BBQ CD/MC/LP 174)* <92602> **THE CHARLATANS** 1
– Nine acre court / Feeling holy / Just lookin' / Crashin' in / Bullet comes / Here comes a soul saver / Just when you're thinkin' things over / Tell everyone / Toothache / No fiction / See it through / Thank you. *(d-lp+=)* – Chemical risk (toothache remix).

— On 23rd July '96, ROB COLLINS was killed in a car crash (see above).

Aug 96. (7"/c-s/cd-s) *(BBQ 301/+C/CD)* **ONE TO ANOTHER. / TWO OF US / REPUTATION** 3 -

— **MARTIN DUFFY** – keyboards (of PRIMAL SCREAM) augmented

Beggars Banquet — M.C.A.

Mar 97. (7"/c-s/cd-s) *(BBQ 309/+C/CD)* **NORTH COUNTRY BOY. / AREA 51 / DON'T NEED A GUN** 4 -

Apr 97. (cd/c/lp) *(BBQ CD/MC/LP 190)* <11622> **TELLIN' STORIES** 1
– With no shoes / North country boy / Tellin' stories / One to another / You're a big girl now / How can you leave us / Area 51 / How high / Only teethin' / Get on it / Rob's theme / Two of us / Reputation.

Jun 97. (7"/c-s) *(BBQ 312/+C)* **HOW HIGH. / DOWN WITH THE MOOK** 6 -
(cd-s+=) *(BBQ 312CD)* – Title fight.

Oct 97. (7") *(BBQ 318)* **TELLIN' STORIES. / KEEP IT TO YOURSELF** 16 -
(c-s+=) *(BBQ 318C)* – Thank you (live).
(cd-s++=) *(BBQ 318CD)* – Clean up kid.

— **TONY RODGERS** was now the replacement for ROB

Beggars Banquet — Beggars Banquet

Feb 98. (cd/c/lp) *(BBQ CD/MC/LP 198)* <80198> **MELTING POT** (compilation) 4
– The only one I know / Then / Opportunity three / Over rising / Sproston Green (U.S. version) / Weirdo / Theme from the wish / Patrol (The Chemical Brothers mix) / Can't get out of bed / I never want an easy life if me & he were ever to get there / Jesus hairdo / Crashin' in / Just lookin' / Here comes a soul saver / Just when you're thinkin' things over / One to another / North country boy.

CHAVEZ

Formed: Lower Manhattan, New York, USA . . . 1993 out of the short-lived WIDER by MATT SWEENEY, who enlisted CLAY TARVER (ex-BULLET LAVOLTA), JAMES LO (ex-LIVE SKULL) and DAVEY HOSKINS; the latter was replaced by SCOTT MASCIARELLI after the completion of rough demos. One of the many alt-rock acts to put pen to paper for 'Matador', CHAVEZ's long-playing introduction came with 1995's highly praised 'GONE GLIMMERING', an experimental Lo-Fi effort taking its cue from 70's Krautrock pioneers as well as modern day practitioners such as TORTOISE and SLINT. This was surprisingly critically and musically surpassed the following year with 'RIDE THE FADER', although of late, CHAVEZ have been conspicuous by their absence from the recording scene.

Album rating: GONE GLIMMERING (*7) / RIDE THE FADER (*8)

MATT SWEENEY – vocals, lead guitar (ex-SKUNK) / **CLAY TARVER** – guitar (ex-BULLET LAVOLTA) / **JAMES LO** – drums (ex-LIVE SKULL) / **SCOTT MASCIARELLI** – bass; repl. DAVEY HOSKINS

City Slang — Matador

Sep 94. (7") *(EFA 04944-7)* **REPEAT THE ENDING. / HACK THE SIDES AWAY**

Matador — Matador

Jul 95. (cd/lp) <*(OLE 133-2/-1)*> **GONE GLIMMERING** May95
– Nailed to the blank / Spot / Break up your band / Laugh track / Ghost by the sea / Pentagram ring / In our pools / The flaming gong / Wakeman's air / Relaxed fit.

Oct 95. (cd-ep) <*(OLE 146-2)*> **PENTAGRAM RING / THE NERVE / YOU FADED / HACK THE SIDES AWAY / REPEAT THE ENDING**

Nov 96. (cd/lp) <*(OLE 200-2/-1)*> **RIDE THE FADER**
– Top pocket man / Guard attacks / Unreal is here / New room / Tight around the jaws / Lions / Our boys will shine tonight / Memorize this face / Cold joys / Flight '96 / Ever overpsyched / You must be stopped.

CHELSEA

Formed: London, England . . . October '76 initially as LSD by GENE OCTOBER. He was soon left to take up the reins when other members, BILLY IDOL, TONY JAMES and JOHN TOWE went off to form the more successful GENERATION X. Early the following year, GENE founded CHELSEA along with JAMES STEVENSON, CAREY FORTUNE and SIMON VITESSE, the latter a replacement for short-lived member, HENRY BADOWSKI. Signed to Miles Copeland's new independent imprint, 'Step Forward', CHELSEA released the political protest, 'RIGHT TO WORK' as their debut single in the summer of '77. The people's punks followed up with another anthemic dig at government complacency in the shape of 'HIGH RISE LIVING', a heavy touring schedule taking in the country's more deprived areas as well as the normal city dates. Around this period (Autumn '77), GENE had a bit part in Derek Jarman's controversial punk film, 'Jubilee', alongside the likes of ADAM ANT, TOYAH and WAYNE COUNTY; a couple of CHELSEA songs were to feature on its soundtrack. A new line-up of OCTOBER, STEVENSON, GEOFF MYLES and CHRIS BASHFORD re-emerged in late summer '78 (with 'URBAN KIDS') after a lengthy absence and it was to be a further year before the belated release of their eponymous first album. By this point in time, GENE and Co, had been overtaken by the musical experimentation of their now post-punk peers, the band relegated to the Vauxhall Conference Division of straggling punk diehards. Through varying line-ups, CHELSEA continued to fight the punk wars over the course of the 80's and some of the 90's, GENE's last effort to date being 1995's appropriately titled solo set, 'LIFE AND STRUGGLE'. • **Songwriters:** OCTOBER penned, except STREET FIGHTING MAN (Rolling Stones), and his solo SUFFERING IN THE LAND (Jimmy Cliff). • **Trivia:** In 1985, OCTOBER made an appearance on LWT's rock programme alongside JOOLS HOLLAND and MEAT LOAF!

Album rating: CHELSEA (*4) / ALTERNATIVE HITS compilation (*5) / EVACUATE (*3) / LIVE AND WELL (*4) / JUST FOR THE RECORD compilation (*5) / ROCKS OFF (*3) / UNDERWRAPS (*3) / THE ALTERNATIVE (*3) / TRAITOR'S GATE (*3) / Gene October: LIFE AND STRUGGLE (*3)

GENE OCTOBER – vocals / **JAMES STEVENSON** – lead guitar / **CAREY FORTUNE** – drums / **SIMON VITESSE** – bass; repl. HENRY BADOWSKI who joined WRECKLESS ERIC, The DAMNED, and later HELLIONS, before UK SUBS.

Step Forward — I.R.S.

Jun 77. (7") *(SF 2)* **RIGHT TO WORK. / THE LONER** -

Oct 77. (7") *(SF 5)* **HIGH RISE LIVING. / NO ADMISSION** -

— **OCTOBER + STEVENSON** were joined by **DAVE MARTIN** – guitar / **GEOFF MYLES** – bass / **CHRIS BASHFORD** – drums (CAREY later guested on JJ BURNEL's solo album)

Aug 78. (7") *(SF 8)* **URBAN KIDS. / NO FLOWERS** -

Jul 79. (lp) *(SFLP 2)* **CHELSEA** -
– I'm on fire / Government / Free the fighters / Twelve men / Fool and soldiers / Decide / Your toy / Many rivers / All the downs / Trouble is the day.

Feb 80. (7") *(SF 14)* **NO ONE'S COMING OUTSIDE. / WHAT WOULD YOU DO?** -

Apr 80. (7") *(SF 15)* **LOOK AT THE OUTSIDE. / DON'T GET ME WRONG** -

Jul 80. (7") *(SF 16)* **NO ESCAPE. / DECIDE** -

Nov 80. (lp) *(SFLP 5)* <*SP 70010*> **ALTERNATIVE HITS** <US-title 'NO ESCAPE'> (compilation)
– No escape / Urban kids / No flowers / All the downs / Right to work / Look at the outside / What would you do / No one's coming outside / The loner / Don't get me wrong / Decide / Come on.

— disbanded again when DAVE MARTIN joined PINK MILITARY, and STEVENSON was poached by GENE's favourite group GENERATION X. **OCTOBER** recruited **NIC AUSTIN** – guitar / **LINC** – bass / **STEVE J. JONES** – drums

May 81. (7") *(SF 17)* **ROCKIN' HORSE. / YEARS AWAY** -

Sep 81. (7"m) *(SF 18)* **FREEMANS. / I.D. PARADE / HOW DO YOU KNOW?** -

Nov 81. (7") *(SF 20)* **EVACUATE. / NEW ERA** -

— **SOL MINTZ** – drums; repl. JONES

Mar 82. (7") *(SF 21)* **WAR ACROSS THE NATION. / HIGH RISE LIVING (remix)** -

Apr 82. (lp) *(SFLP 7)* <*SP 70603*> **EVACUATE**
– Evacuate / Looks right / 40 people / Running free / Tribal song / Bodies / City thinking / War across the nation / Last drink / Cover up / How do you know?

Oct 82. (7",7"pic-d) *(SF 22)* **STAND OUT. / LAST DRINK** -

— Disbanded again early in 1983. AUSTIN joined BANDITS AT 4 O'CLOCK, and LINC joined LIGOTAGE.

GENE OCTOBER

Illegal — not iss.

Jan 83. (7") *(ILS 034)* **SUFFERING IN THE LAND. / SUFFERING DUB** -

Slipped Discs — not iss.

Jan 84. (7") *(SPLAT 001)* **DON'T QUIT. / BURNING SOUNDS** -

CHELSEA

— were back for mid-83, with **GENE** plus **PETER DIMMOCK** – bass (ex-CHRON GEN) / **DAVEY JONES** (b. Scotland) – guitar / **GEOFF SEWELL** (or) **COLVILLE** – drums

Picasso — not iss.

May 84. (lp) *(PIK 003)* **LIVE AND WELL (live)** -
(cd-iss. Nov93 on 'Great Expectations'; PIPCD) (cd re-iss. Oct95 on 'Punx'; PUNXCD 1)

— **PHOENIX + TIM BRIFFA** – guitar; repl. DAVEY

Communique not iss.

Jun 85. (7") **VALIUM MOTHER. / ?** [ ] [-]
Aug 85. (lp) **ORIGINAL SINNERS** [ ] [-]
Mar 86. (7") **SHINE THE LIGHT. / BELIEVE ME** [ ] [-]

Jungle not iss.

Nov 86. (lp) *(FREUD 14)* **ROCKS OFF** [ ] [-]
– Fool's Paradise / Revolution No.9 / Hard-up baby / Memory fades / Give me more / Inside out / You and me / Street fighting man / Little princess / Sidewinder.

Chelsea not iss.

May 88. (7") *(CH 001)* **GIVE ME MORE. / SYMPATHY FOR THE DEVIL** [ ] [-]

— next featured **TOPPER HEADON** – drums (ex-CLASH); on 2 tracks.

I.R.S. not iss.

Jun 89. (lp/c/cd) *(EIRSA/+C/CD 1011)* **UNDERWRAPS** [ ] [-]
– Somebody got murdered / Cheat / Give me mercy / Nice girls / No respect / Life of crime / Switchblade / Fool / Time after time / Come on.

Alter-Ego not iss.

Apr 93. (cd) *(ALTGOCD 002)* **THE ALTERNATIVE** [ ] [-]
– The alternative / Weirdos in wonderland / More than a giro / Wasting time / Ever wonder / Where is everything / You can be there too / What's wrong with you / Oh no / Too late / Dreams of dreams / Ode to the travellers. *(re-iss. Oct94 on 'Weser'; WL 24662)*

Weser not iss.

Aug 94. (cd) *(WL 2480-2)* **TRAITORS GATE** [ ] [-]
May 95. (7") *(WL 2482-7)* **WE DARE. /** [ ] [-]

Receiver not iss.

Jul 97. (cd) *(RRCD 242)* **FOOLS AND SOLDIERS** [ ] [-]

– compilations, etc. –

May 85. (lp) *Step Forward; (SFLP 10)* **JUST FOR THE RECORD** [ ] [-]
Sep 88. (lp) *Illegal; (ILP 024)* **BACKTRAX** [ ] [-]
Aug 89. (lp) *Clay; (CLAYLP 101)* **UNRELEASED STUFF** [ ] [-]
– I'm on fire / Come on / No flowers / Urban kids / 12 men / Trouble is the day / Young toy / Decide / Curfew / Look at the outside / Don't get me wrong / Fools and soldiers. *(cd-iss. May93 & Jul94 lp/cd; CLAY/+CD 101)*
Mar 92. (cd) *Released Emotions; (REM 016CD)* **LIVE AT THE MUSIC MACHINE 1978 (live)** [ ] [-]

GENE OCTOBER

Receiver not iss.

Mar 95. (cd) *(RRCD 196)* **LIFE AND STRUGGLE** [ ] [-]
– Born to keep on running / Count to ten / Watch out / Welcome home / Butterfly / Life and struggle / It hurts / I owe you nothing / Big tears / Curfew / Everytime I see you I know I just gotta go.

CHEMICAL BROTHERS

Formed: North London, England . . . 1989 by DJ's ED SIMONS and TOM ROWLANDS. The pair had met at Manchester University, and, discovering a shared love of techno and classic hip hop, they set about creating their own club night, 'NAKED UNDER LEATHER'. The logical next step was to cut their own record and with 'SONG TO THE SIREN', they successfully blended their myriad inluences into an abrasive chunk of freak-beat techno. Wildly impressed, 'Junior Boys Own' maestro ANDY WEATHERALL released the single in early 1993, the more discerning underground D.J.'s of the time caning the track at club nights across the country. The record was credited to The DUST BROTHERS, the name SIMONS and ROWLANDS assumed for their DJ work. Later the same year, they released the '14th Century Sky' EP which included the definitive 'CHEMICAL BEATS'. 'MY MERCURY MOUTH' from the 1994 EP of the same name was equally impressive and by this point the DUST BROTHERS had become one of the hippest name-drops among the dance cognoscenti. Their seminal reworking of SAINT ETIENNE's 'Like a motorway', together with a DJ spot on PRIMAL SCREAM's 1994 tour further increased their profile and it wasn't long before the major record labels came sniffing round. Signing to 'Virgin', they released 'LEAVE HOME' in 1995, following it up with the top ten debut album, 'EXIT PLANET DUST'. The duo were now trading under the moniker of The CHEMICAL BROTHERS following objections from The DUST BROTHERS (U.S), a highly rated hip hop production team (Responsible for the BEASTIE BOYS' classic, 'Paul's Boutique'). For the most part, the debut was an unrelenting, exhilirating, rollercoater ride of breakbeat techno, only letting up on 'ALIVE: ALONE' (featuring a BETH ORTON vocal) and the TIM BURGESS (of CHARLATANS fame) collaboration, 'LIFE IS SWEET'. The 'LOOPS OF FURY EP' was as uncompromising as the title suggests while the 'SETTING SUN' (featuring NOEL GALLAGHER on vocals) single gave the CHEMICALS' their first No.1 later that year. The track featured a 'TOMMORROW NEVER KNOWS'-style rhythm pattern, the folow-up album, 'DIG YOUR OWN HOLE' (1997), similarly psychedelic in its reach. Using samples from 60's theramin pioneers LOTHAR AND THE HAND PEOPLE, and featuring a guest spot from MERCURY REV's JONATHAN DONOHUE, the album was more thrillingly diverse than the debut. With a mind bending live show, universal critical acclaim and even a burgeoning Stateside career, for the moment, The CHEMICAL BROTHERS can do no wrong. • **Songwriters:** ROWLANDS-SIMONS except samples of Blake Baxters 'Brothers Gonna Work It Out' on 'LEAVE HOME'/ Borrowed SWALLOW's; 'Peekaboo' & 'Follow Me Down'.

Album rating: EXIT PLANET DUST (*9) / DIG YOUR OWN HOLE (*9)

DUST BROTHERS

TOM ROWLANDS + ED SIMONS – synthesizers, etc

Junior Boys Own not iss.

1993. (12") *(JBO 10)* **SONG TO THE SIREN. / SONG TO THE SIREN (Sabres Of Paradise mixes)** [ ] [-]
1993. (12"ep) *(COLLECT 004)* **14th CENTURY SKY EP** [ ] [-]
– Chemical beats / One too many mornings / Dope coil / Ref jazz.
(above issued on 'Boys Own')
May 94. (12"ep) *(JBO 20)* **MY MERCURY MOUTH EP** [ ] [-]
– My mercury mouth / If you kling to me I'll kling to you / Dust up beats.

CHEMICAL BROTHERS

TOM ROWLANDS + ED SIMONS with voices by **TIM BURGESS** (CHARLATANS) + **BETH ORTON** (solo artist)

Virgin AstralWerks

Jun 95. (12"/cd-s) *(CHEMS T/D 1) <6167>* **LEAVE HOME (Sabres Of Paradise mix). / LEAVE HOME (Underworld mix) / LET ME IN MATE** [17] [ ] Sep95
(12") *(CHEMSTX 1)* –
Jun 95. (cd/c/d-lp) *(XDUST CD/MC/LP 1) <6157>* **EXIT PLANET DUST** [9] [ ] Aug95
– Leave home / In dust we trust / Song to he siren / Three little birdies down beats / Fuck up beats / Chemical beats / Chico's groove / One too many mornings / Life is sweet / Playground for a wedgeless firm / Alive alone.
Aug 95. (12") *(CHEMSD 2)* **LIFE IS SWEET. / ('A'-Daft Punk remix) / ('A'-remix 1) / ('A'-remix 2)** [25] [-]
(cd-s) *(CHEMSD 2)* – ('A'-remix 1, repl.by) Leave home (terror drums).
(cd-s) *(CHEMSDX 2)* – ('A'remix 1) / If you kling to me I'll klong to you / Chico's groove (mix 2).
Jan 96. (12"ep/cd-ep) *(CHEMS T/D 3) <6174>* **LOOPS OF FURY EP** [13] [ ]
– Chemical beats (Dave Clarke remix) / Loops of fury / (The best part of) Breaking up / Get up on it like this.
Oct 96. (c-s/12"/cd-s) *(CHEMS C/T/D 4) <6187>* **SETTING SUN. / ('A'extended & instrumental mixes) / BUZZ TRACKS** [1] [80] Jan97

— above featured NOEL GALLAGHER (Oasis) on vocals/ co-writer

Mar 97. (12"/cd-s) *(CHEMS T/D 5) <6195>* **BLOCK ROCKIN' BEATS. / PRESCRIPTION BEATS / MORNING LEMON** [1] [ ]
(cd-s) *(CHEMSDX 5)* – ('A'mixes).
Apr 97. (cd/c/d-lp) *(XDUST CD/MC/LP 2) <6180>* **DIG YOUR OWN HOLE** [1] [14]
– Block rockin' beats / Dig your own hole / Elektrobank / Piku / Setting sun / It doesn't matter / Don't stop the rock / Get up on it like this / Lost in the k-hole / Where do I begin / The private psychedelic reel.
Sep 97. (12") *(CHEMST 6) <6204>* **ELEKTROBANK. / NOT ANOTHER DRUGSTORE** [17] [ ]
(cd-s+=) *(CHEMSD 6)* – Don't stop the rock.
(cd-s+=) *(CHEMSDX 6)* – These seats are made for breakin'.
Dec 97. (ltd;12"/cd-s) *(CHEMS T/DX 7)* **THE PRIVATE PSYCHEDELIC REEL. / SETTING SON (version)** [ ] [-]
Sep 98. (cd/c) *<6243>* **BROTHER'S GONNA WORK IT OUT: A DJ REMIX ALBUM** [-] [95]

Vic CHESNUTT

Born: Georgia, Atlanta, USA . . . 1965. Confined to a wheelchair since 1983 after a car crash left him paraplegic, CHESNUTT developed a distinctive singing/songwriting style so popular among fellow musicians that 'Columbia' recently released a tribute album, 'Sweet Relief – Gravity Of The Situation: The Songs Of Vic Chesnutt' (1996). Among the contributors were such luminaries as MADONNA, SMASHING PUMPKINS and R.E.M.; the latter connection had already proved pivotal in the direction of the man's career with MICHAEL STIPE having produced his first two albums, 'LITTLE' (1989) and 'WEST OF ROME' (1991). Critics centred on the bitterness and vivid despair of the lyrics, CHESNUTT trawling the depths of his psyche for 1994's 'DRUNK'. A characteristically semi-detached, ironic delivery leavened the weight of CHESNUTT's burden while by this point, he'd also begun to flesh out the rootsy, acoustic sparseness of his sound, adhering to a more disciplined approach to song structure. The following year's 'IS THE ACTOR HAPPY', meanwhile, found VIC indulging his eccentricity in a concept affair based on the notion of playing live. While 1996 saw his peers paying their dues to his alcohol-sodden muse on the aforementioned tribute album, CHESNUTT himself hooked up with local band WIDESPREAD PANIC for an album, 'NINE HIGH A PALLET', released on the recently revamped 'Capricorn' under the moniker, BRUTE. The rise of the alt-country scene has certainly done CHESNUTT little harm, 'THE SALESMAN & BERNADETTE' (1998) seeing the man working with Nashville revivalists LAMBCHOP and elder stateswoman of country-rock, EMMYLOU HARRIS. Employing a multi-instrumental tapestry including clarinet, euphonium and trumpet, the record offered up positively zestful efforts – lyrics aside of course – like 'UNTIL THE LED' alongside the trademark lugubriousness. • **Covered:** SNOWBLIND FRIEND (Hoyt Axton).

Album rating: LITTLE (*6) / WEST OF ROME (*7) / DRUNK (*8) / IS THE ACTOR HAPPY? (*7) / ABOUT TO CHOKE (*7) / THE SALESMAN & BERNADETTE (*7) / Brute: NINE HIGH A PALLET (*7)

VIC CHESNUTT – vocals, guitar

Texas Hotel Texas Hotel

1989. (lp) *<TXH 020>* **LITTLE** [-] [ ]
– Isadora Duncan / Danny Carlisle / Giupetto / Bakersfield / Mr. Riley / Rabbit fox /

Speed racer / Soft Picasso / Independence day / Stevie Smith. *(UK cd-iss. Feb95 & Jul96; TXH 020-2)*

Jan 92. (cd) *<TXH 021-2>* **WEST OF ROME** [-] [ ]
– Latent blatant / Withering away / Sponge / Where were you / Lucinda Williams / Florida / Stupid preoccupation / Panic / Miss Mary / Steve Willoughby / West of Rome / Big huge valley / Soggy tongues / Fuge. *(UK-iss.Jul94 & Jul96; same)*

Mar 94. (cd/lp) *<(TXH 022-2/-1)>* **DRUNK** [ ] [ ]
– Sleeping man / Bourgeois and biblical / One of many / When I ran off and left her / Dodge / Gluefoot / Drunk / Naughty fatalist / Super Tuesday / Kick my ass. *(re-iss. Jul96; same)*

— now backed by his wife TINA, plus the SCARED SKIFFLE BAND: ALEX McMANUS + JIMMY DAVIDSON and various session people

Apr 95. (cd) *<(TXH 023-2)>* **IS THE ACTOR HAPPY?** [ ] [ ]
– Gravity of the situation / Sad Peter Pan / Strange language / Onion soup / Doubting woman / Wrong piano / Free of hope / Betty lonely / Thumbtack / Thailand / Guilty by association. *(re-iss. Jul96; same)*

— next was a collaboration between VIC and the band WIDESPREAD PANIC

not iss. Capricorn

Jan 96. (cd; as BRUTE) *<42030>* **NINE HIGH ON A PALLET** [-] [ ]
– Westport ferry / Blight / Good morning Mr. Hard on / I ain't crazy enough / Protein drink – Sewing machine / Let's get down to business / George Wallace / PC / Snowblind / Miserable / Bastards in bubbles / Cataclysm.

— now with a session people

P.L.R. Capitol

Nov 96. (cd) *(PLR 005-2) <37556>* **ABOUT TO CHOKE** [ ] [ ]
– Myrtle / New town / Ladle / Tarragon / Swelters / (It's no secret) Satisfaction / Little vacation / Degenerate / Hot seat / Giant sands / Threads / See you around

— augmented by the group **LAMBCHOP** and others inc. guest **EMMYLOU HARRIS**

P.L.R. Polygram

Sep 98. (cd/lp) *(PLR CD/LP 011) <538239>* **THE SALESMAN & BERNADETTE** [ ] [ ] Nov98
– Duty free / Bernadette & her crowd / Replenished / Maiden / Until the led / Scratch, scratch, scratch / Mysterious tunnel / Arthur Murray / Prick / Woodrow Wilson / Parade / Blanket over the head / Square room / Old hotel.

– compilations, etc. –

Jul 94. (cd) *Texas Hotel; (TXH 0213)* **SAMPLER** [ ] [ ]

— a various artists tribute album, 'SWEET RELIEF – GRAVITY OF THE SITUATION: THE SONGS OF VIC CHESNUTT' was released in Aug'96 on 'Columbia'; (484137-2/-4)

CHESTERFIELDS

Formed: Yeovil, England ... summer 1985 by DAVE GOLDSWORTHY, SIMON BARBER, DOMINIC MANNS and BRENDAN HOLDEN. Recalling the heady days of the 'Postcard' era, The CHESTERFIELDS were initially associated with the C-86 scene, showcasing their charming but raw appeal via a debut EP, 'A GUITAR IN YOUR BATH' (hopefully the unplugged version!) on the 'Subway Organisation' label. Two further 45's, 'COMPLETELY AND UTTERLY' and 'ASK JOHNNY DEE', appeared over the course of the next year, although by the release of their summer '87 debut album, 'KETTLE', BRENDAN had been replaced by RODNEY ALLEN. He, in turn, found more fame in the BLUE AEROPLANES, his temp, ANDY STRICKLAND (from the CARETAKER RACE) filling in until the arrival of MARK BARBER. Subsequently initiating their own label, 'Household Name', The CHESTERFIELDS found a sympathetic ally in Radio One DJ, Janice Long, a live session followed by the release of a couple of singles and a follow-up set, 'CROCODILE TEARS' (1988). With GOLDSWORTHY and MANNS now out of the picture, the remaining BARBER brothers persevered, although only one single surfaced before SIMON formed BASINGER.

Album rating: KETTLE (*6) / WESTWARD HO! compilation (*6) / CROCODILE TEARS (*5)

DAVE GOLDSWORTHY – vocals, guitar / **BRENDAN HOLDEN** – guitar / **SIMON BARBER** – bass, vocals / **DOMINIC MANNS** – drums

Subway Org. not iss.

May 86. (7"ep) *(SUBWAY 3)* **A GUITAR IN YOUR BATH** [ ] [-]
– Sweet revenge / What's your perversion / Love mountain / Best of friends.

Nov 86. (7") *(SUBWAY 7)* **COMPLETELY AND UTTERLY. / GIRL ON A BOAT** [ ] [-]

Mar 87. (7") *(SUBWAY 11)* **ASK JOHNNY DEE. / POP ANARCHY!** [ ] [-]

— **RODNEY ALLEN** – guitar; repl. BRENDAN

Jul 87. (lp) *(SUBORG 003)* **KETTLE** [ ] [-]
– Nose out of joint / Ask Johnny Dee / Two girls and a treehouse / Shame about the rain / Everything a boy could ever need / Kiss me stupid / The thumb / Storm Nelson / Holiday yhmn / Oh Mr. Wilson / The boy who sold his suitcase / Completely and utterly. *(cd-iss. Sep93 on 'Vinyl Japan'; ASKCD 030)*

Dec 87. (lp) *(SUBORG 005)* **WESTWARD HO!** (compilation) [ ] [-]
– Sweet revenge / What's your perversion / Love mountain / Best of friends / Completely and utterly / Girl on a boat / Ask Johnny Dee / Pop anarchy!

— temp. **ANDY STRICKLAND** – guitar (of CARETAKER RACE) repl. RODNEY who joined BLUE AEROPLANES

— (Jul'87) **MARK BARBER** – guitar; repl. ANDY

Household Name not iss.

Mar 88. (12") *(HOLD 1T)* **GOODBYE GOODBYE. /** [ ] [-]

Aug 88. (7") *(HOLD 3)* **BLAME. /** [ ] [-]
(12"+=) *(HOLD 3T)* –

Sep 88. (lp/cd) *(HOLD 4 LP/CD)* **CROCODILE TEARS** [ ] [-]
– Lunchtime for the wild youth / Alison wait / When it all comes down / Hopes for Lauren or Joseph / Get some religion / Let it go / Twintown / Goodbye goodbye / Besotted / Blame / Male bimbo / Better smile / Last train to Yeovil / I've got to hand it to you.

— GOLDSWORTHY and MANNS departed later in '88 and although SIMON and MARK carried on with evolving line-up

Apr 89. (12") *(HOLD 5T)* **FOOL IS A MAN. /** [ ] [-]

— split in the summer of '89. SIMON formed BASINGER who issued a few singles, 'SOMETHING' in Apr'92 for 'Wilde Club' and 'HANDSOME / AMERICA' for 'Hair' the following March. MARK joined the Bristol-based GRAPE, who released an album in early '94, 'IN THE FAMILY OF DREAMS' for 'Vinyl Japan' cd/lp; *ASK CD/LP 033)*

– compilations, etc. –

Dec 87. (12"ep) *Night Tracks; (SFNT 003)* **JANICE LONG SESSION** [ ] [-]

May 94. (12"/cd-s) *Vinyl Japan; (TASK/+CD 026)* **DOWN BY THE WISHING POOL. /** [ ] [-]

Aug 94. (cd) *Vinyl Japan; (ASKCD 041)* **FLOOD** [ ] [-]

Jan 95. (7"ep) *Vinyl Japan; (TASKCD 035)* **JOHNNY DEE EP** [ ] [-]
– Open to persuasion / Where's the map / I wanna bang on the drum / Love plays cruel game.

Wild Billy CHILDISH

Born: STEVEN JOHN HAMPER, 1958, Chatham, Kent, England. Having formed the POP RIVETS in 1977 – they only lasted a few years and a couple of albums – he went on to form The MILKSHAKES (subsequently known as THEE MILKSHAKES) with original guitarist, BRUCE BRAND (who was relegated to the drum stool when CHILDISH became 6-string proficient). This psychobilly/garage outfit toured alongside fellow Medway bands, The PRISONERS and The DENTISTS, while BILLY also turned his hand to poetry (his published works are now in double figures, something of an achievement in itself bearing in mind the man's chronic dyslexia!). In the early 80's, The MILKSHAKES released numerous albums, combining a plethora of R&B cover versions somewhat akin to what the COUNT BISHOPS had been doing several years earlier. In 1985, the hard-drinking WILD BILLY formed another outlet for his irrepressible creativity, THEE MIGHTY CAESARS, while also combining a solo career (!). Towards the end of the 80's, he virtually re-formed THEE MILKSHAKES, although this time around they were known as THEE HEADCOATS. In 1990, the group (featuring MICKEY HAMPSHIRE, RUSS WILKINS and BRUCE BRAND) were back on form with the rockin' brilliant third set, 'BEACH BUMS MUST DIE', followed almost immediately by 'HEAVENS TO MURGATROYD . . .' (1991), a set that would find its way on to US grunge bastion 'Sub Pop'. Around the same time, THEE HEADCOATS had the wonderfully amateurish promo for 'MATCHSTICK GIRL' featured on a V/A 'Sub Pop' video collection. While CHILDISH also undertook solo work, he worked with yet another associated project, THEE HEADCOATEES, who initially released the 'SECT' EP on his own 'Hangman's Daughter' imprint. In 1995, CHILDISH finally retired from the biz, celebrating on his way out by inviting all his previous musical incarnations to farewell gigs at London's 'Wild West Rooms'. **• Trivia:** 'A MIGHTY CHILDISH' various artists tribute album was issued late '95 under the title of 'No Hit'; *VEND 007)*

Abbreviated Album rating: I AM THE BILLY CHILDISH (*7) / THEE KNIGHTS OF TRASHE (*6) / Thee Headcoats: BEACH BUMS MUST DIE (*6)

POP RIVETS

WILD BILLY CHILDISH – vocals / **WILL POWER** – guitar, vocals / **BIG RUSS** – bass, vocals / **LI'L RUSS** – drums

Hypocrite not iss.

1979. (7") *(HEP 1)* **POP RIVITS** [ ] [-]
– When I came back / Souvenirs / Glanced the look.

1979. (7") *(HEP 002)* **POP RIVITS. / SULPHATE** [ ] [-]

1979. (d7"ep) *(JIM 1)* **FUN IN THE U.K.** [ ] [-]
– (above tracks)

1979. (lp) *(HIP-O)* **EMPTY SOUNDS FROM ANARCHY RANCH** [ ] [-]
– Hang loose, mongoose / Skip off school / 2 is 2 / The spoken voice / I looked twice / The Pop Rivets mak show / Anarchy ranch / I'm just a satellite for your love / Empty sounds / Return to anarchy ranch . . .

May 80. (lp) *(HIP 007)* **THE POP RIVETS GREATEST HIS** (compilation) [ ] [-]

MILKSHAKES

WILD BILLY CHILDISH – vocals, guitar / **MICK HAMPSHIRE** – guitar, vocals / **MARK GILBERT** – bass / **BRUCE BRAND** – drums

Milkshakes not iss.

1981. (lp) *(MILK-O)* **TALKING 'BOUT MILKSHAKES** [ ] [-]
– She'll be mine / Pretty baby / For she / I wantcha / Rugurge beat / After midnight / Bull's nose / Shed country / Don't love another / Tell me where's that girl / Can'tcha see / Love you the whole night through / There's nothing you can say or do / I say you lie. *(re-iss. Feb86)*

— **LI'L RUSS** – bass (ex-POP RIVETS) repl. MARK

Bilko not iss.

May 82. (7") *(BILK-O)* **PLEASE DON'T TELL MY BABY. / IT'S YOU** [ ] [-]

Big Beat not iss.

Feb 83. (lp) *(NED 4)* **14 RHYTHM AND BEAT GREATS** [ ] [-]
– Seven days / Black sails / Exactly like you / A girl called Mine / Sad girl mambo / I want you / Cadalina / No-one else / I need no-one / You did her wrong / Can you tell me / Red monkey / Take you home tonight / Wo' now.

Upright not iss.

Mar 83. (7") *(UP 6)* **SOLDIERS OF LOVE. / SHIMMY SHIMMY** [ ] [-]

May 83. (lp) *(UPLP 1)* **AFTER SCHOOL SESSION** [ ] [-]
– Shimmy shimmy / I can tell / Tell me child / Goodbye girl / More honey / Soldiers of love / El Salvador / Let's stomp / Hide and scatter / Jaguar / That girl of mine /

You can only lose / Little Minnie / Cadillac. *(re-iss. Jan89 on 'Hangman'; HANG 24LP)*

Wall City — not iss.

Mar 84. (lp) *(EFA 065403)* **THE MILKSHAKES IN GERMANY**

THEE MILKSHAKES

JOHN AGNEW – bass; repl. WILKINS

Milkshakes — not iss.

Mar 84. (lp) *(HARP-O)* **NOTHING CAN STOP THESE MEN**
– You got me girl / Little Bettina / Ida honey (tell me you'll be mine) / She's no good to me / Chatham train / Dull knife / She's just fifteen years / The grim reaper / Everywhere I look / I'm the one for you / That's my revenge / You've been lyin'.

Dec 84. (lp) *(GARB-0)* **THEE KNIGHTS OF TRASHE**
(re-iss. Oct95 on 'Hangman's Daughter'; SCRAG 5LP)

Big Beat — not iss.

Feb 84. (lp) *(WIKM 20)* **20 ROCK & ROLL HITS OF THE 50'S & 60's**
– Hippy hippy shake / Rip it up / I'm gonna sit right down and cry over you / Say mama / Peggy Sue / Jaguar and the thunderbirds / Commanche / I'm talking 'bout you / Sweet little sixteen / Money (that's what I want) / Carol / Boys / Something else / Some other guy / Who do you love / Jezebel / Hidden charms / Little Queenie / Ya ya (twist) / I wanna be your man. *(re-iss. Mar91 cd/lp; CD+/WIKM 20)*

Mar 84. (7"ep) *(NS 94)* **BRAND NEW CADILLAC / COMMANCHE. / JEZEBEL / JAGUAR AND THUNDERBIRD**

Dec 84. (7"ep) *(SW 105)* **THE AMBASSADORS OF LOVE / NO MORE. / GRINGLES AND GROYLES AGAIN / REMARKABLE**

Mar 85. (lp) *(WIK 30)* **THEY CAME, THEY SAW, THEY CONQUERED**
– Bo Diddlius / Did I tell you / Little girl / I'm needing you / Quiet lives / The best things in life / This feeling inside / Wounded Knee / Just like you / Shed country / Thinking 'bout that girl / Gringles and groyles / Mother I want your daughter / How can I love you / Don't destroy me.

Empire — not iss.

Jan 86. (lp) *(MIC 001)* **LAST NIGHT AT THE MIC CLUB (live w/ PRISONERS)**

— WILKINS + BRAND had already joined LEN BRIGHT COMBO, which was fronted by WRECKLESS ERIC.

Aug 86. (7") *(UXF 228)* **LET ME LOVE YOU. / SHE TELLS ME SHE LOVES ME**

Media Burn — not iss.

Nov 86. (d-lp) *(MB 9)* **107 TAPES**
(cd-iss. Feb92 on 'Vinyl Japan'; ASKCD 8)

Hangman — not iss.

Jun 87. (lp) *(HANG 1UP)* **THE MILKSHAKES REVENGE . . . LEGENDARY MISSING LP**
(cd-iss. Sep93 on 'Hand Of Glory'; HOG 001)

Mar 88. (lp) *(HANG 11UP)* **LIVE FROM CHATHAM (live)**

– others, etc. –

Jul 90. (d-cd) *Big Beat; (CDWIKD 939)* **19th NERVOUS SHAKEDOWN**

Sep 92. (lp/cd) *Vinyl Japan; (ASK 10/+CD)* **STILL TALKIN' BOUT**

May 95. (7"ep) *Wonderlamp; (OIL 01)* **BITTE NICHT SPICKEN EP**

Jul 95. (cd/lp) *Hangman's Daughter; (SCRAG 4 CD/LP)* **TALKIN' ABOUT THE MILKSHAKES**

THEE MIGHTY CAESARS

WILD BILLY CHILDISH – vocals, guitar / **GRAHAM DAY** – guitar, vocals (ex-PRISONERS) / +2

Milkshakes — not iss.

Aug 85. (lp) *(NER-O)* **THEE MIGHTY CAESARS**

Big Beat — not iss.

Jan 86. (lp) *(WIK 45)* **BEWARE THE IDES OF MARCH**
– It ain't no sin / You'll be sorry now / Young man afraid of his horses / All of your love / Cyclonic / Little by little / Give it to me / This man's determined / You can't judge a book by the cover / Baby please / Rumble / Roadrunner.

Empire — not iss.

Feb 86. (7") *(LWC 604Q)* **TEN BEARS OF THE COMMANCHES. / BABY WHAT'S WRONG**

Media Burn — not iss.

Feb 86. (12"ep) *(MB 5)* **LITTLE BY LITTLE / THE SWAG. / I WANT WHAT YOU GOT / CYCLONIC**

Ambassador — not iss.

Feb 87. (lp) *(AMBAS 2)* **WISEBLOOD**
– I can't find pleasure / Come into my life / Signals of love / I self destroy / The wiseblood / The Bay of Pigs / The double axe / Tushunka witko / Stay the same / Kinds of women / Signals of love / Slight return / Action time vision. *(re-iss. Jun89 on 'Hangman')*

Big Beat — not iss.

Apr 87. (lp) *(WIK 60)* **LIVE IN ROME (live)**
– Wily coyote / Give it to me / When the night comes / I've got everything indeed / Commanche / Devious means / Little by little / Neat neat neat / The Bay of Pigs / Don't say it's a lie / Too much monkey business / Submission / All of my love / Baby what's wrong.

Hangman — not iss.

Aug 87. (lp) *(HANG 3UP)* **DON'T GIVE ANY DINNER TO HENRY CHINASKI**

Dec 87. (lp) *(HANG 7UP)* **THE PUNK ROCK SHOWCASE**

Milkshakes — not iss.

Feb 89. (lp) *(PLAT-O)* **ACROPOLIS NOW**
– I've got everything indeed / When the night comes / (Miss America) Got to get you outside / Ask the dust / I don't need no baby / Dictator of love / Now I know / I can judge a daughter / Lil' red riding hood / Loathsome n' wild / Despite all this / I feel like giving in / I was led to believe.

Mar 89. (lp) *(APOLL-O)* **THE CAESARS OF TRASH**
– It's you I hate to lose / Don't say it's a lie / Devious means / Not fade away / I've been waiting / Don't break my laws / Man taken from guts / Oh yeah / All night worker / Jack the ripper / True to you / Psycho.

— GRAHAM DAY formed PRIME MOVERS

– compilation, etc. –

Feb 94. (d-cd) *Big Beat; (CDWIKD 124)* **CAESAR'S PLEASURE**

WILD BILLY CHILDISH

Empire — not iss.

Apr 87. (lp) *(LPO 195)* **LAUGHING GRAVY** (w/ BIG RUSS WILKINS)
– Baby what you want me to do / We are what we own / 2 x 7 / Black girl / Little Bettina / Laughing gravy / I need lovin' / Quartet after nine / Gotta get you out of my little head . . . / Bring it on home.

Hangman — not iss.

Jul 87. (lp) *(HANG 2-UP)* **I'VE GOT EVERYTHING I NEED**

Oct 87. (lp; with SEXTON MING) *(HANG 5-UP)* **WHICH DEAD DONKEY DADDY?**
– Muscle horse / Smousgiss / I ain't gonna see Kansas no more / Mi mi and Mi / The cable sausage girls / Major dog be kind to cats / O'Riley / The woods are dangerous / Here on my knee / Sweat and grit with Arnie / Yummy yellow girls / Sons of the desert / Fry-up / The firework man / The caribou of intelligence / Bizzer oxen / The wild breed is here / Dearest.

Jan 88. (lp) *(HANG 9-UP)* **THE 1982 CASSETTES**
– Oh Maude / Col' col' chillen / When I got no one / I hate my little baby / Dog end of a dog end / Tennessee blues / Ammonia '81 / Monkey bissness / Let's make it / Guillotine device / Today's menu / A matter of timing / Evil snake catcher / I'm home grown / Little Queenie.

Feb 88. (lp) *(HANG 10-UP)* **PLUMP PRIZES AND LITTLE GEMS (w/ SEXTON MING)**

Mar 88. (lp) *(HANG 12-UP)* **YPRES 1917 OVERTURE** (w/ SEXTON MING)

Mar 88. (lp) *(HANG 13-UP)* **I REMEMBER . . .**

Jun 88. (lp) *(HANG 16-UP)* **POEMS OF LAUGHTER AND VIOLENCE**
– People don't need oetry / Warts grown like flys / The talking lites / Me 'n' my father / Hawk and spitfire / Heaven she said / In here we believe / The terrible bull / Catastrophy / Mercy.

— (below with The BLACK HEADS)

Jul 88. (lp) *(HANG 21-UP)* **PLAY CAPTAINN CALYPSO'S HOODOO PARTY**
– Rum and coca cola / Under the mango tree / I love Paris / Long tall Shorty / Capt'n Jack is boss / Sen' me to the 'lectric chair / Anarchy in the UK / Three blind mice / Tequila / Yella skinned babies / Dread luck.

Nov 89. (lp) *(HANG 30-UP)* **LONG LEGGED BABY**

— special spoken word on 'Hangman's Daughter

Jun 88. (lp) *(WORDUP 001)* **COMPANIONS IN A DEATH BOAT**

Jun 88. (lp) *(WORDUP 003)* **POEMS FROM THE BARRIER BLOCK**

Jun 88. (lp) *(WORDUP 004)* **POEMS WITHOUT RHYME**

Jun 88. (lp) *(WORDUP 005)* **MONKS WITHOUT GOD**

Jun 88. (lp) *(WORDUP 006)* **CONVERSATIONS WITH DOCTOR X**

Jun 88. (lp) *(WORDUP 007)* **TO THE QUICK**

THEE HEADCOATS

WILD BILLY CHILDISH – vocals, guitar / **MICKEY HAMPSHIRE** – guitar / **RUSS WILKINS** – bass (ex-LEN BRIGHT COMBO) / **BRUCE BRAND** – drums (ex-LEN BRIGHT COMBO)

Hangman's Daughter — not iss.

Jul 89. (lp) *(HANG 29-UP)* **HEADCOATS DOWN**

May 90. (lp) *(HANG 32-UP)* **THE KIDS ARE ALL SQUARE**
– I'm a gamekeeper / Davey Crockett (gabba hey) / Monkey's paw / Meet Jacqueline / Ballad of the fog-bound pinhead / All my feelings denied / Cowboys are square / I can destroy all your love / Poccahontas was her name / Nanook of the north / A town named Squaresville / Karasai.

Crypt — not iss.

1990. (cd/lp) **BEACH BUMS MUST DIE**
(re-iss. cd Apr93; EFA 11563D)

Already — not iss.

Feb 91. (cd/c/lp) **HEAVENS TO MURGATROYD, EVEN IT'S THEE HEADCOATS**
(re-iss. May93 on 'Sub Pop' cd/lp; SP CD6-119/6-117)

Munster — not iss.

Sep 92. (7") *(MR 7037)* **I CAN DESTROY ALL YOUR LOVE. /**

Twist — not iss.

Apr 93. (7") *(TWIST 5)* **BRANDED. / Thee Headcoatees: STRYCHNINE**

Damaged Goods — not iss.

May 93. (7") *(DAMGOOD 17)* **EVERY BIT OF ME. / NEVER TO LOVE AGAIN**

Jul 93. (7") *(DAMGOOD 19)* **WE HATE THE F***ING NME. /**

Mar 94. (7"; with SEXTON MING) *(DAMGOOD 32)* **NO ONE. /**

Feb 95. (7") *(TWIST 17)* **GUN IN MY FATHER'S HAND. / THE DAY I BEAT MY FATHER UP**
(above on 'Twist')

May 95. (7") *(DAMGOOD 62)* **A-Z OF YOUR HEART. /**

May 95. (7") *(DAMGOOD 63)* **JOHNNY JACK. /**

Jun 96. (lp/cd) *(DAMGOOD 96/+CD)* **IN TWEED WE TRUST**

Tom Tom — not iss.

Jul 93. (lp) *(TOM 15)* **THE WURST IS YET TO COME**

Hangman's Daughter — not iss.

Sep 94. (cd/lp) *(SCRAG 2 CD/LP)* **CONUNDRUM**

Sep 96. (cd/lp; by HEADCOAT SECT) *(SCRAG 8 CD/LP)* **DEERSTALKING MEN**

THEE HEADCOATEES

Hangman's Daughter / not iss.

Aug 92. (7"ep) *(LYNCH 001EP)* **SECT EP**

Vinyl Japan / not iss.

Aug 92. (7") *(FAD 1)* **MY BOYFRIEND'S LEARNING KARATE. /**
Aug 92. (cd/lp) *(ASK CD/LP 11)* **HAVE LOVE WILL TRAVEL**
Jan 94. (7"; THEE HEADCOATS) *(PAD 009)* **ACTION TIME VISION. / I WASN'T MADE FOR THIS WORLD**
Dec 93. (7"pic-d) *(DAM 12)* **SANTA CLAUS. /**
(above on 'Damaged Goods' & below single on 'Munster')
Oct 94. (7") *(07768-1)* **GOTTA MOVE. /**
Oct 94. (cd/lp) *(ASK CD/LP 045)* **BALLAD OF THE INSOLENT PUP**
– What once was / This heart / Pretend / Ballad of the insolent pup / You'll be sorry now / All my feelings denied / It's bad / When you stop loving me / Two hearts beating / No respect / Again and again / Now is not the best time / I was led to believe / You'll never do it baby.
Jul 95. (7") *(PAD 018)* **BALLAD OF THE INSOLENT PUP. / SPINELESS LITTLE SHIT**

Sympathy F / Sympathy F

Jul 96. (7") *(SFTRI 332)* **I'M HAPPY. /**

– other HEADCOATS / HEADCOATEES releases

Apr 93. (7") *Twist; (TWIST 5)* **STRYCHNINE. / BRANDED**
Sep 93. (cd) *Damaged Goods; (DAM 9CD)* **THE KIDS ARE ALL SQUARE / GIRLSVILLE**
Mar 94. (lp/cd) *Damaged Goods; (DAMGOOD 30/+CD)* **LIVE IN LONDON (live)**
Dec 95. (lp/cd) *Overground; (OVER 42/+CD)* **SOUND OF THE BASKERVILLES**
Sep 98. (7") *Damaged Goods; (DAMGOOD 155)* **JACKIE CHAN DOES KUNG FU. /**

WILD BILLY CHILDISH

Sub Pop / Sub Pop

Oct 92. (cd/lp; by BILLY CHILDISH & THE BLACKHEADS) *(SP 209CD/47-209)* **THE ORIGINAL CHATHAM JACK**

Damaged Goods / not iss.

Apr 93. (7") *(DAMGOOD 15)* **THE ORIGINAL CHATHAM JACK. / FINE AND MELLOW**
Sep 93. (7") *(TWIST 8)* **WHO DO YOU THINK YOU'RE KIDDING MR. HITLER. /**
(above on 'Twist')
Oct 93. (cd; by BILLY CHILDISH & THE SINGING LOINS) *(DAM 22CD)* **AT THE BRIDGE**
(re-iss. lp Apr94; SCRAG 1UP)

Lissy's / not iss.

Dec 95. (7"; BILLY CHILDISH & THE SINGING LOINS) *(LISS 10)* **THE MAN WITH EYES LIKE LITTLE FISHES. / STUPID SONG**

– others, etc. –

Mar 94. (cd) *Sub Pop; (SP 206B)* **NATIVE AMERICAN SAMPLER**
Apr 94. (lp) *Tom Tom; (TOM 17)* **KITCHEN RECORDINGS**
Sep 94. (cd) *Hangman's Daughter; (SCRAG 3UP)* **CAPTAIN CALYPSO'S HOODOO PARTY / LIVE IN THE NETHERLANDS**
Mar 95. (7"; by THEE BILLY CHILDISH & SEXTON MING) *Hangman's Daughter; (KETCH 5UP)* **GAUD BLESS OLD MITCHELL. /**

CHILLS

Formed: Dunedin, Christchurch, New Zealand . . . October 1980 as a vehicle for singer-songwriter, MARTIN PHILLIPPS. Materialising around the ashes of Kiwi punk band, The SAME, The CHILLS initial line-up featured PHILLIPPS, his sister RACHEL and future VERLAINES musician, JANE TODD. Over the course of the ensuing decade the band would undergo almost continual personnel comings and goings (enough to give Pete Frame – of Rock Family Trees fame – nightmares!), usually from fellow 'Flying Nun' acts like the aforementioned VERLAINES and The CLEAN. One such member was MARTYN BULL, who briefly played with The CHILLS before succumbing to leukaemia in July 1983. The ghostly strains of 'PINK FROST' served as a memorial, the track being one of the most impressive to surface from their string of domestic EP and singles releases throughout the early to mid-80's. In 1985, The CHILLS played a handful of London dates as well as recording a session for John Peel. 'Creation', meanwhile, released a compilation, 'KALEIDOSCOPE WORLD' (1986), featuring the cream of their work to date. Ranging from the atmospheric VELVETS-esque charm of 'SATIN DOLL' to the harmony-driven pop of the title track and moody 'PINK FROST', The CHILLS' sound was characterised by a retro-psych melange of swirling organ, jangling guitars and chugging bass, a recipe also followed by the band's 'Paisley Underground' compatriots in the States. A long awaited debut album proper, the MAYO THOMPSON-produced 'BRAVE WORDS' (1987), was regarded as a half-baked affair by fans and critics alike, PHILLIPPS struggling to realise his unique musical vision over the course of a whole set. Nevertheless, the band secured a major label deal with 'Slash/Warners' and released a more palatable follow-up set, 'SUBMARINE BELLS', at the turn of the decade. Despite a cleaner, more accessible sound, The CHILLS – like most of their NZ brethren – remained an acquired taste, a less than prolific release schedule (1992's 'SOFT BOMB' being last album to date) not helping the transition to a wider market. • **Trivia:** MARTIN played keyboards on The CLEAN's debut Flying Nun 45, 'Tally Ho'.

Album rating: KALEIDOSCOPE WORLD compilation (*8) / BRAVE WORDS (*6) / SUBMARINE BELLS (*7) / SOFT BOMB (*6) / HEAVENLY POP HITS compilation (*7) / SUNBURNT (*5)

MARTIN PHILLIPPS (b. 2 Jul'63) – vocals, guitar / **PETER GUTTERIDGE** (b.19 May'61) – guitar (ex-CLEAN) / **ALAN HAIG** (b. 5 Aug'61) – drums (ex-RED TAPE) / **FRASER BATTS** (b.14 Apr'64) – keyboards, guitar (ex-BORED GAMES) repl. RACHEL PHILLIPPS / **TERRY MOORE** (b.27 Oct'61, England) – bass (ex-BORED GAMES) repl. PETER + JANE DODD

Flying Nun / not iss.

Jan 82. (d12"ep) **DUNEDIN DOUBLE EP** – New Z.
– Satin doll / Kaleidoscope world / (+ 6 other tracks by New Zealand groups The VERLAINES, STONES + The SNEAKY FEELINGS).

— **RACHEL PHILLIPPS** (b.17 Jun'65) – keyboards; returned to replace FRASER

— **MARTYN BULL** (b. 6 Mar'61) – drums; repl. HAIG
May 82. (7"m) **ROLLING MOON. / BITE / FLAME THROWER** – New Z.

— **PETER ALLISON** (b. 7 Jun'60) – keyboards; repl. RACHEL
Jul 82. (7") **PINK FROST. / PURPLE GIRL** – New Z.

— **ALAN HAIG** – drums; returned to repl. MARTYN BULL who died on the 18th July '83 (DAVID GILGOUR was briefly a member)

— **MARTIN KEAN** (b.17 Jun'61) – bass; repl. TERRY
Jan 84. (7") **DOLEDRUMS. / HIDDEN BAY** – New Z.

— **MARTIN PHILLIPS, PETER ALLISON + ALAN HAIG** brought back **TERRY MOORE** – bass, to repl. KEAN
Dec 84. (12"ep) *(COLD 004)* **THE LOST EP** – New Z.
– This is the way / Never never go / Dream by dream. *(UK-iss.Mar86; same)*

Creation / Homestead

Feb 86. (m-lp) *(CRELP 008)* *<HMS 139>* **KALEIDOSCOPE WORLD** (compilation) 1989
– Kaleidoscope world / Satin doll / Frantic drift / Rolling moon / Bite / Flame thrower / Pink frost / Purple girl. *(re-iss. Dec87 on 'Flying Nun'; FNE 13) (w/free 7"ep)* **THE LOST EP** *(cd-iss. Nov92 +=; FNE 13CD)* – This is the way / Never never go / Don't even know her name / Bee bah bee bah bee boe / Whole weird world / Dream by dream / Doledrums / Hidden bay / I love my leather jacket / The great escape.

— **MARTIN PHILLIPS** enlisted an entire new band **CAROLINE EASTHER** (b.30 Nov'58) – drums (ex-VERLAINES) repl. ALAN HAIG / **ANDREW TODD** (b.15 Dec'58) – keyboards, vocals / **JUSTIN HARWOOD** (b. 6 Jul'65) – bass, vocals

Flying Nun / Homestead

Mar 87. (12") *(FNUK 07)* **I LOVE MY LEATHER JACKET. / THE GREAT ESCAPE**
Aug 87. (12") *(FNUK 11T)* **THE HOUSE WITH A HUNDRED ROOMS. / LIVING IN A JUNGLE**
Sep 87. (lp) *(FNUK 12)* *<HMS 103-1>* **BRAVE WORDS**
– Push / Rain / Speak for yourself / Look for the good in others and they'll see the good in you / Wet blanket / Ghosts / Dan Destiny and the Silver Dawn / Night of the chill blue / 16 heart-throbs / Brave words / Dark carnival / Creep. *(cd-iss. Sep89 & Nov92 +=; FNE 12CD)* – Party in my heart / House with a hundred rooms / Living in a jungle.

— **JAMES STEVENSON** (b.17 May'70) – drums; repl. CAROLINE

Slash / Slash

Mar 90. (7") *(LASH 22)* **THE HEAVENLY POP HIT. / WHOLE LOT OF NONE**
(12"+=/cd-s+=) *(LAS HX/CD 22)* – Ways watching / Water wolves.
Mar 90. (cd/c/lp) *(828 191-2/-4/-1)* *<26130-1>* **SUBMARINE BELLS**
– The Heavenly pop hit / Tied up in chain / The oncoming day / Part past part fiction / Singing in my sleep / I soar / Dead web / Familiarity breeds contempt / Don't be a memory / Efforence and deliquence / Sweet times / Submarine bells.

— **GILLIAN DEMPSTER** (b.26 Apr'70) – keyboards; repl. TODD

— **TERRY MOORE** returned to repl. JUSTIN who joined LUNA with former GALAXIE 500 member, DEAN WAREHAM

— **PHILLIPPS + MOORE** recruited **LISA MEDNICK** (b.27 Jun'57, USA) – keyboards / **STEVEN SCHAYER** (b.12 Feb'65, USA) – guitar / **EARL ROBERTSON** (b.15 Apr'62, USA) – bass
Aug 92. (cd/c/lp) *(828 322-2/-4/-1)* *<26787-2/-4/-1>* **SOFT BOMB**
– The male monster from the Id / Background affair / Ocean ocean / Soft bomb / There is no harm in trying / Strange case / Soft bomb II / So long / Song for Randy Newman etc / Sleeping giants / Double summer / Sanctuary / Halo fading / There is no point in trying / Entertainer / Water wolves / Soft bomb III.

— **CRAIG MASON** (b.28 Jul'61) – drums; repl. ROBERTSON

— disbanded when it looked like PHILLIPPS would go solo

– compilations, etc –

Feb 95. (lp/cd) *Flying Nun; (FN/+CD 306)* **HEAVENLY POP HITS**
Sep 96. (cd) *Flying Nun; (FNCD 303)* **SUNBURNT**

CHINA CRISIS

Formed: Kirkby, Merseyside, England . . . late 1979 by GARRY DALY and EDDIE LUNDON. Following an independently released debut single, 'AFRICAN AND WHITE', the group signed to 'Virgin' with an extended line-up of GAZZA JOHNSON, ROBERT LYTHGOE and GARY O'TOOLE beginning work on a debut album, 'DIFFICULT SHAPES & PASSIVE RHYTHMS: SOME PEOPLE THINK IT'S FUN TO ENTERTAIN' (1982). Prior to the record's release the group almost scraped into the UK Top 40 with a re-issued 'AFRICAN . . .', finally cracking the Top 20 early in '83 with 'CHRISTIAN'. Personnel changes subseuqently ensued with KEVIN WILKINSON and BRYAN McNEILL replacing O'TOOLE and LYTHGOE respectively before a further couple of minor hits in 'TRAGEDY AND MYSTERY' and 'WORKING WITH FIRE AND STEEL'. The latter was the title track of the follow-up album, a Top 20 success which spawned the band's biggest hit to date in 'WISHFUL THINKING'. With former STEELY DAN maestro, WALTER BECKER, both guesting and producing, the bulk of 1984 was spent working on 'FLAUNT THE IMPERFECTION'; the STEELY DAN influence had always been present in the band's music, both in their penchant for wordiness and the laid-back late-night feel of their sophisticated pop/rock, BECKER's midas touch ensuring a further two Top 20 singles in 'BLACK MAN RAY' and the jaunty 'KING IN A CATHOLIC STYLE'. Yet CHINA CRISIS really did seem to be facing a problem, if not a crisis, with the poor reception and chart performance of 'WHAT PRICE PARADISE' (1986). Going back to the drawing board and once again roping in BECKER the band eventually re-emerged in 1989 with 'DIARY OF A HOLLOW HORSE', a record which found favour with the critics but failed to resurrect the band's fading career. A split from 'Virgin' and a further lengthy sabbatical took up most of the early 90's, DALY and LUNDON getting back together in '94 and subsequently recording 'ACOUSTICALLY YOURS' (1995), a live, stripped down set of CHINA CRISIS favourites. • **Songwriters:** All written by DALY / LUNDON, until 1985 with JOHNSON. Covered 98.6 (Keith). • **Trivia:** In Jan'85 they were lucky to escape serious injury when their car overturned on icy road. Became first major band to play in Gibraltar early '86.

Album rating: THE CHINA CRISIS COLLECTION compilation (*8) / DIFFICULT SHAPES (*7) / WORKING WITH FIRE AND STEEL (*8) / FLAUNT THE IMPERFECTION (*6)

GARRY DALY (b. 5 May'62) – vocals, keyboards / **EDDIE LUNDON** (b. 9 Jun'62) – guitar, vocals

Inevitable | not iss.

Feb 82. (7") *(INEV 011)* **AFRICAN AND WHITE. / RED SAILS** [ ] [-]
(12"+=) *(INEV 011-12)* – De suspicious.
(re-iss. Jul82, hit No.45)

— added **GAZZA JOHNSON** – bass / **ROBERT LYTHGOE** – keyboards / **GARY O'TOOLE** – drums

Virgin | Warners

Aug 82. (7"/12") *(VS 495/+12)* **SCREAM DOWN AT ME. / CUCUMBER GARDEN** [ ] [-]
Oct 82. (7") *(VS 521)* **NO MORE BLUE HORIZONS. / NO ORDINARY LOVER** [ ] [-]
(12"+=) *(VS 521-12)* – Watching our burning fields.
Nov 82. (lp/c) *(V/TCV 2243)* **DIFFICULT SHAPES & PASSIVE RHYTHMS: SOME PEOPLE THINK IT'S FUN TO ENTERTAIN** [21] [ ]
– Seven sports for all / No more blue horizons / Feel to be driven away / Some people I know to lead fantastic lives / Christian / African and white / Are we a worker / Red sails / You never see it / Temptations big blue eyes / Jean walks in fresh fields. *(re-iss. 1987 lp/c; OVED/+C 173) (cd-iss. Jul87; CDV 2243) (cd re-iss. Mar94;)*
Jan 83. (7") *(VS 562)* **CHRISTIAN. / GOLDEN HANDSHAKE** [12] [ ]
(12"/12"pic-d) *(VS 562-12)* – ('A'side) / Green acre bay / Performing seals.

— **KEVIN WILKINSON** – drums (ex-HOLLY & THE ITALIANS) repl. O'TOOLE

— added guest **BRYAN McNEILL** – keyboards; repl. LYTHGOE

May 83. (7"/12") *(VS 587/+12)* **TRAGEDY AND MYSTERY. / GOLDEN SHAKEDOWN** [46] [ ]
Oct 83. (7") *(VS 620)* **WORKING WITH FIRE AND STEEL. / DOCKLAND** [48] [ ]
(12"+=) *(VS 620-12)* – Forever and I.
Oct 83. (lp/c) *(V/TCV 2286)* **WORKING WITH FIRE AND STEEL** [20] [ ]
– Working with fire and steel / When the piper calls / Hanna Hanna / Animals in jungles / Here comes a raincloud / Wishful thinking / Tragedy and mystery / Papua / The gates of door to door / The soul awakening. *(cd-iss. Sep84; CDV 2286)*
Dec 83. (7"red) *(VS 647)* **WISHFUL THINKING. / THIS OCCUPATION** [9] [ ]
(12"+=) *(VS 647-12)* – Some people I know to lead fantastic lives.
Feb 84. (7") *(VS 665)* **HANNA HANNA. / AFRICAN AND WHITE (live)** [44] [ ]
(12"+=) *(VS 665-12)* – Here comes a raincloud.

— the quartet added guests **WALTER BECKER** – synthesizer, percussion / **NICK MAGNUS** – piano, synthesizer / **TIM RENWICK** – guitars / **STEVE GREGORY** – saxophone

Mar 85. (7"sha-pic-d/12") *(VS 752/+12)* **BLACK MAN RAY. / ANIMALISTICS (A DAY AT THE ZOO)** [14] [ ]
May 85. (lp/c) *(V/TCV 2342)* <25296> **FLAUNT THE IMPERFECTION** [9] [ ]
– The highest high / Strength of character / You did cut me / Black man Ray / Wall of God / Gift of freedom / King in a Catholic style / Bigger the punch I'm feeling / The world spins, I'm part of it / Blue sea. *(cd-iss. 1987; CDV 2342) (re-iss. 1989 lp/c; OVED/+C 272)*
May 85. (7") *(VS 765)* **KING IN A CATHOLIC STYLE (WAKE UP). / BLUE SEA** [19] [ ]
(12"+=) *(VS 765-12)* – ('A'extended).
Aug 85. (7"pic-d) *(VS 799)* **YOU DID CUT ME. / ('A'version)** [54] [ ]
(12"+=) *(VS 799-12)* – Christian.
(d7"++=) *(VSD 799)* – Seven sports for all (live).
Nov 85. (7") *(VS 829)* **THE HIGHEST HIGH. / 96.8** [ ] [ ]
(12"+=) *(VS 829-12)* – Orange mutt mutt dance.

Virgin | A&M

Oct 86. (7") *(VS 898)* **ARIZONA SKY. / TRADING IN GOLD** [47] [ ]
(12"+=) *(VS 898-12)* – ('A'extended).
Nov 86. (lp/c/cd) *(V/TCV/CDV 2410)* <5148> **WHAT PRICE PARADISE** [63] [ ]
– It's everything / Arizona sky / Safe as houses / Worlds apart / Hampton beach / The understudy / Best kept secret / We do the same / June bride / A day's work for a dayo's done. *(cd+=) – Trading in gold. (re-iss. 1989 lp/c; OVED/+C 214) (cd re-iss. Dec96 on 'Virgin-VIP'; CDVIP 167)*
Jan 87. (7") *(VS 926)* **BEST KEPT SECRET. / THE INSTIGATOR** [36] [ ]
(12"+=) *(VS 926-12)* – Little Italy.
(cd-s+=) *(CRIS 926)* – Black man Ray / You did cut me / Arizona sky.
Mar 89. (7") *(VS 1168)* **ST. SAVIOR'S SQUARE. / BACK HOME** [ ] [ ]
(12"+=/3"cd-s+=) *(VS T/CD 1168)* – ('A'version).
May 89. (lp/c/cd) *(V/TCV/CDV 2567)* **DIARY OF A HOLLOW HORSE** [58] [ ]
– St. Savior's Square / Stranger by nature / Sweet charity in adoration / Day after day / Diary of a hollow horse / Red letter day / In northern skies / Singing the praises of finer things / All my prayers / Age old need.
May 89. (7") *(VS 1188)* **RED LETTER DAY. / DIARY OF A HOLLOW HORSE** [ ] [ ]
(7"ep+=/12"+=/3"cd-s+=) *(VS E/T/CDX 1188)* – Strength of character.

— disbanded in 1990, although DALY and LUNDON re-formed in 1994

Stardumb | not iss.

Aug 94. (c-s/12"/cd-s) *(MC7/12/C7 STA 001)* **EVERY DAY THE SAME. / TELL ME WHAT IT IS** [ ] [-]
Aug 94. (cd/c) *(STA CD/MC 001)* **WARPED BY SUCCESS** [ ] [-]
(cd re-iss. Apr98 on 'Rhino'; CP 1003)

Telegraph | not iss.

Sep 95. (cd/c) *(TLG CD/MC 005)* **ACOUSTICALLY YOURS** [ ] [-]
– African and white / No more blue horizons / Wishful thinking / Everyday the same / It's everything / Christian / Good again / Hands on the wheel / Black man Ray / King in a Catholic style / Thank you / Singing the praise of finer things / Working with fire and steel / Diary of a hollow horse.
Apr 96. (cd-s) *(TLGCD 006)* **BLACK MAN RAY /** [ ] [-]

– compilations, etc. –

Jun 88. (3"cd-ep) *Virgin; (CDT 15)* **BLACK MAN RAY / ANIMALISTIC (A DAY AT THE ZOO) / HAMPTON BEACH** [ ] [-]
Nov 88. (7") *Old Gold; (OG 9818)* **CHRISTIAN. / WISHFUL THINKING** [ ] [-]
(re-iss. Feb89 as 12"; OG 4103)
Nov 88. (7") *Old Gold; (OG 9827)* **BLACK MAN RAY. / KING IN A CATHOLIC STYLE (WAKE UP)** [ ] [-]
Aug 90. (cd/c/lp) *Virgin; (CD/TC+/V 2613)* **THE CHINA CRISIS COLLECTION** [32] [ ]
– African and white / No more blue horizons / Christian / Tragedy and mystery / Working with fire and steel / Wishful thinking / Hanna Hanna / Black man Ray / King in a Catholic style / You did cut me / Arizona sky / Best kept secret / It's everything / St.Saviour Square. *(d-cd+=; CDVX 2613)* – Scream down at me / Cucumber garden / A golden handshake for every daughter / Some people I know to lead fantastic lives / The instigator (Italian fuzzbox version) / Little Italy / Greenacre Bay / No ordinary lover / Dockland / Forever and I / Performing seals / This occupation / Watching our burning fields.
Aug 92. (cd/c) *Virgin-V.I.P.; (VVP D/C 117)* **DIARY (A COLLECTION)** [ ] [-]
(re-iss. Nov93 cd/c; CD/TC VIP 109)
May 97. (d-cd) *Snapper; (SMDCD 117)* **WISHING THINKING** [ ] [-]

CHINA DRUM

Formed: Ovingham-Upon-tyne, Northumbria, England . . . 1989 by singing drummer, ADAM and bassist DAVE, along with guitarist, BILL. Paying their dues by gigging hard around the toilet circuit of Northern England, the trio finally got round to self-financing a debut single, 'SIMPLE', in 1993. In addition to their full-on power-punk flurry, the record showcased their "sensitive" side with an acoustic track, 'MEANING'. They also pared things down with 'BISCUIT BARREL', a newly softened-up version of a stompalong live favourite that sat alongside 'GREAT FIRE' on their summer '94 GREEN DAY/THERAPY?-esque EP, the first of two releases for 'Fluffy Bunny'. The following year's 'BARRIER' EP was also released in the States, although most of the material had been previously issued in the UK. A one-off cover of Kate Bush's 'WUTHERING HEIGHTS' (a split 7" with the FLYING MEDALLIONS on 'Fierce Panda') preceded a major record deal with Beggars Banquet off-shoot, 'Mantra', through whom they issued a series of singles: 'FALL INTO PLACE', 'PICTURES', 'CAN'T STOP THESE THINGS' and 'LAST CHANCE'. The latter two scored minor chart placings while their long-awaited debut set, 'GOOSEFAIR' (1996), nearly hit the UK Top 50. Around the same time, the trio toured Bosnia to raise money for charities working in the war-torn region while their aforementioned album elbowed for chart position in America with Stateside competitors like OFFSPRING and GREEN DAY (again!). The challenge from across the water eventually proved too much and despite a further couple of minor hits, CHINA DRUM's second album, 'SELF MADE MANIAC' (1997), failed to impress the public.

Album rating: GOOSEFAIR (*6) / SELF MADE MANIAC (*6)

ADAM – vocals, drums / **DAVE** – bass / **BILL** – guitar

China Drum | Bitzcore

1993. (cd-s) *(CC 193)* <1696> **SIMPLE / ON MY WAY / MEANING (acoustic)** [ ] [ ]

Fluffy Bunny | M.C.A.

Jul 94. (10"ep/cd-ep) *(FLUFF 6/+CD)* **GREAT FIRE / BISCUIT BARREL (acoustic). / MEANING / DOWN BY THE RIVER (live)** [ ] [-]
Mar 95. (10"ep/cd-ep) *(FLUFF 8/+CD)* <11293> **BARRIER EP** [ ] [ ] Jun95
– Barrier / Simple / Biscuit barrel / One way down / Great fire / The meaning.

Fierce Panda | not iss.

Jul 95. (7") *(NING 06)* **WUTHERING HEIGHTS. / (B-side by The Flying Medallions)** [ ] [-]

Mantra | M.C.A.

Sep 95. (10"ep) *(MNT 2TT)* **FALL INTO PLACE /** [ ] [-]
(cd-ep) *(MNT 2CD)* –
Dec 95. (7"green) *(MNT 4)* **PICTURES / LAST CHANCE** [ ] [-]
(cd-s) *(MNT 4CD)* –
Feb 96. (7"/c-s) *(MNT 8/+C)* **CAN'T STOP THESE THINGS. / WUTHERING HEIGHTS** [65] [-]

(cd-s+=) *(MNT 8CD)* – Drown it.
Apr 96. (7"/c-s) *(MNT 10/+C)* **LAST CHANCE. / WALK** 60 -
(cd-s+=) *(MNT 10CD)* – Cut them out / Careful with that chieftain, Adam.
Apr 96. (cd/c/lp) *(MNT CD/MC/LP 1002)* <11438> **GOOSEFAIR** 53
– Can't stop these things / Cloud 9 / Fall into place / Situation / Simple / Biscuit barrel F.M.R. / God bets / Pictures / Find the time / (Had a good idea on) Monday / Last chance / Take it back / The meaning / Better than me.
Jul 96. (7") *(MNT 12)* **WIPEOUT. / BASEBALL IN THE DARK** -
(cd-s+=) *(MNT 12CD)* – Biscuit barrel / Sleazeball (Empirion mix).
Aug 97. (7") *(MNT 21)* **FICTION OF LIFE. / PULL** 65 -
(cd-s+=) *(MNT 21CD)* – Bubblegum buzz / Baseball in the dark (acoustic).
(cd-s) *(MNT 21CD2)* – ('A'side) / Fall at your feet / Jack / Down by the river (acoustic).
Sep 97. (7") *(MNT 22)* **SOMEWHERE ELSE. / LOSER** 74 -
(cd-s+=) *(MNT 22CD)* – Wrong again / Bothered (acoustic).
(cd-s) *(MNT 22CD2)* – ('A'side) / Sleazeball / Don't throw it / ('A'acoustic).
Oct 97. (cd/c/lp) *(MNT CD/MC/LP 1009)* <81009> **SELF MADE MANIAC** Feb98
– One thing / Guilty deafness / Somewhere else / Fiction of life / All I wanna be / Down by the river / Another toy / 60 seconds / Foxhole / Control / Stop it all adding up / Bothered.
Apr 98. (7") *(MNT 30)* **STOP IT ALL ADDING UP. / GUILTY DEAFNESS (live)** -
(cd-s+=) *(MNT 30CD)* – Wipe out (live) / Baseball in the dark (live).

Ted CHIPPINGTON

Born: Stoke-On-Trent, England. Initially one half of local duo, The MISERABLE GITS, TED went solo in 1985, releasing his first EP, 'NON-STOP PARTY HITS OF THE 50's, 60's & 70's', for ROBERT LLOYD's indie imprint, 'Vindaloo'; he had previously supported LLOYD's band The NIGHTINGALES. Comical if not hilarious, TED subsequently crucified a number of classics including The Beatles' 'SHE LOVES YOU', his interpretation accompanied by off-tune organ. Golden oldies were cut into pieces, his deadpan humour wryly pronounced on his debut album, 'MAN IN A SUITCASE' (1986). In July that year, he had his one and only (minor) hit, 'ROCKIN' WITH RITA (HEAD TO TOE)' as part of The VINDALOO SUMMER SPECIAL alongside The NIGHTINGALES and WE'VE GOT A FUZZBOX. The following year, TED enjoyed some daytime radio play from "talkathon" DJ, Steve Wright, for his anti-big head ditty, '(I'M NOT) THE WANDERER' (a wordplay on the DION song). TED subsequently became a guest on a few MEMBRANES records and was last heard trying to get a job on kids TV as a presenter!

Album rating: MAN IN A SUITCASE (*4)

TED CHIPPINGTON – vocals / with NIGHTINGALES group

Vindaloo not iss.
Feb 85. (7"ep) *(UGH 8)* **NON-STOP PARTY HITS OF THE 50's, 60's & 70's** -
Mar 86. (lp) *(YUS 6)* **MAN IN A SUITCASE** -
Apr 86. (7") *(UGH 12)* **SHE LOVES YOU. / ROCKIN' WITH RITA** -
(12"+=) *(UGH 12T)* – Weirdness oh no.
Jul 86. (7"/12"; as VINDALOO SUMMER SPECIAL) *(UGH 13/+T)* **ROCKIN' WITH RITA (HEAD TO TOE). / LET'S SURF** 56 -
Jul 87. (7"/12") *(UGH 15/+T)* **(I'M NOT) THE WANDERER. /** -
Sincere not iss.
Nov 88. (lp) *(SINCERE 001)* **THE REAL TRUTH ABOUT TRUCKING** -
— retired from the music biz

CHIXDIGGIT!

Formed: Calgary, Canada . . . early 90's by school mates MIKE, MARK and KJ (in '93 they added bass player turned drummer, JASON HIRSCH). Initially a ruse to sell T-shirts with the CHIXDIGGIT! moniker, the idea turned into a real band as the lads decided to actually learn to play their instruments. An unusual signing for 'Sub Pop', CHIXDIGGIT! were compared to the RAMONES and modern day pop-punks, GREEN DAY, summer 96's eponymous debut album fitting right in with the prevailing mood of the US alternative scene. The following year, having amicably split from Sub Pop over musical differences, the comic strip punks found a new home at 'Honest Don's' where they unleashed 'BORN ON THE FIRST OF JULY', another happy-go-lucky collection of hook-laden toons.

Album rating: CHIXDIGGIT! (*5) / BORN ON THE FIRST OF JULY (*6)

K.J. JANSEN – vocals, guitar / **MARK O'FLAHERTY** – guitar / **MIKE EGGERMONT** – bass / **JASON HIRSCH** – drums

Sub Pop Sub Pop
Jun 96. (lp/cd) <*(SP/+CD 355)*> **CHIXDIGGIT!** May96
– Dolphins love kids / Great legs / Where's your mom? / Henry Rollins is no fun / I wanna hump you / Song for "R" / Stacked like that / Hemp hemp hooray / 323 / The angriest young men (we're the) / Toilet seat's coming down / Shadow bangers from a shadowy duplex / Van Horne / I drove the coquihalla / (I feel like) Gerry Cleevers . . .
Honest Don's Honest Don's
Nov 97. (7") *(DON 012)* **CHUPA CABRAS. /** -
May 98. (lp/cd) <*(DON 016/+CD)*> **BORN ON THE FIRST OF JULY** Apr98
– Gettin' air / My girl's retro / Sikome beach / Chupacabras / Quit your job / Restaurant / Julianne / 20 times / O-H-I-O / Haven't got time / 2000 flushes / Brunette summer.

CHOIR INVISIBLE

Formed: Pasadena, California, USA . . . late 70's as The FLYBOYS, by THAMES SINCLAIR, SCOTT 'TOWERS' LASKIN, JON BOY CURRIE and DENNY WALSH. After one EP in 1980, 'CRAYON WORLD', WALSH joined The CROWD, his replacement being DANNY BENAIR, a seasoned new waver from The WEIRDOS. They only managed to complete one eponymous set in '81 before DANNY (who subsequently served a stint with The SALVATION ARMY i.e. THREE O'CLOCK) in turn, was substituted by DON DOMINE, although only one EP, 'SEA TO SHINING SEA' was forthcoming before they quietly disappeared.

Album rating: CHOIR INVISIBLE (*4)

JON BOY CURRIE – vocals, guitar / **THAMES SINCLAIR** – guitar, vocals / **SCOTT 'TOWERS' LASKIN** – bass, vocals / **DENNY WALSH** – drums

not iss. Frontier
1980. (m-lp; as FLYBOYS) <*FLP 1001*> **FLYBOYS** -
– Crayon world / Square city / Flyboys.
— **DANNY BENAIR** – drums (ex-QUICK, ex-WEIRDOS) repl. DENNY WALSH who joined The CROWD
1981. (lp) <*FLP 1006*> **CHOIR INVISIBLE** -
— **DON DOMINE** – drums; repl. BENAIR who the SALVATION ARMY group before going on to THREE O'CLOCK
not iss. P.V.C.
1984. (12"ep) **SEA TO SHINING SEA EP** -
— SINCLAIR formed WONDERWALL and CHOIR INVISIBLE split

CHOO CHOO TRAIN (see under ⇒ VELVET CRUSH)

CHRIS & COSEY

Formed: London, England . . . 1981 by former THROBBING GRISTLE members, CHRIS CARTER and COSEY FANNI TUTTI. Just prior to the duo getting together again, CARTER released a solo outing, 'THE SPACE BETWEEN' on cassette (Industrial; IRC 32 – cd-iss. Jan92 on 'Grey Area'; ICC 1CD). The pair's debut album for 'Rough Trade', 'HEARTBEAT' was well received by the underground press, as was their 1982 follow-up, 'TRANCE'. Pioneers of trance-dance musak, CHRIS & COSEY mixed electronic rhythms with dark, subversive undertones that extended the foundations laid by THROBBING GRISTLE. In the Autumn of '83, C&C unveiled their first single, 'OCTOBER (LOVE SONG)', a track that bordered on mainstream Euro-rock territory without losing the sinister edge. A third set, 'SONGS OF LOVE AND LUST' was released simultaneously in late summer '84 with the first batch of material from off-shoot project and label, CTI (CREATIVE TECHNOLOGY INSTITUTE). This included the EP, 'CONSPIRACY INTERNATIONAL' and the lp/video~, 'EUROPEAN RENDEZVOUS'. An unlikely collaboration with top synth popsters, the EURYTHMICS was next on the agenda, the resulting 'SWEET SURPRISE' single nevertheless failing to raise CHRIS & COSEY above cult status. The duo's final album for 'Rough Trade', 'TECHNO PRIMITIV', was issued in early '86, a subsequent move to Belgian label, 'Play It Again Sam' coming about the following year. Several albums appeared over the course of the next half decade, the likes of 1987's 'EXOTICA' to 1992's 'MUSIK FANTASTIQUE!' were more geared towards the continental alternative dance contingent that also included industrial meisters, FRONT 242. The mid-90's, meanwhile, saw CHRIS & COSEY reactivating the dormant CTI via the associated 'Conspiracy' label, a plethora of cd's culminating in 1998's 'POINT SEVEN'.

Album rating: HEARTBEAT (*5) / TRANCE (*8) / SONGS OF LOVE AND LUST (*6) / EUROPEAN RENDEZVOUS (*6) / TECHNO PRIMITIV (*4) / ACTION! (*5) / EXOTICA (*6) / CHRIS & COSEY (*5) / TRUST (*6) / PAGAN TANGO (*6) / MUSIK FANTASTIQUE! (*5) / METAPHYSICAL (*4) / C (*4) / IN CONTINUUM (*5) / SKIMBLE SKAMBLE (*4) / POINT SEVEN (*5)

CHRIS CARTER – synthesizers, electro-percussion / guitar, vocals / **COSEY FANNI TUTTI** – synthesizers, tapes, vocals (with guest on debut before he joined PSYCHIC TV) **ALEX FERGUSSON** – guitar

Rough Trade not iss.
Nov 81. (lp)(c) *(ROUGH 34)(COPY 008)* **HEARTBEAT** -
– Put yourself in Los Angeles / This is me / Voodoo / Moorby / Radio Void / Just like you / Bust stop / Useless information / Moving still / Manic melody / Heartbeat. *(c+=)*– Pressure drop / Tight fit. *(cd-iss. Jul88 on 'Conspiracy'; CTICD 004)*
May 82. (lp) *(ROUGH 44)* **TRANCE** -
– Cowboys in Cuba / Lost / The giants feet / Impulse / Re-education through labour / Secret / Until / The gates of ancient cities. *(cd-iss. Jul88 on 'Conspiracy'; CTICD 005)*
— (In 1982, COSEY FANNI TUTTI released C-30 cassette 'TIME TO TELL' for 'Flow Motion', re-iss. Sep88 on 'Cathexis')
Oct 83. (7"/12") *(RT/+T 078)* **OCTOBER (LOVE SONG). / LITTLE HOUSES** -
Aug 84. (lp) *(ROUGH 64)* **SONGS OF LOVE AND LUST** -
(cd-iss. Jul88 on 'Conspiracy'; CTICD 006)
Sep 84. (7"m) *(CTI 002)* **CONSPIRACY INTERNATIONAL. / THE GIFT OF TONGUES / THE NEED** -
1984. (12"ep) *(CTI 1)* **HAMMER HOUSE EP** -
1984. (12") *(CTI 2)* **GIFT OF TONGUES** -
Oct 84. (lp,video; as CTI) *(DVR 8)* **EUROPEAN RENDEZVOUS** -
(above 4 releases as CTI, the first on label 'International One', the last for 'DoubleVision'). Below featured EURYTHMICS duo.

Feb 85. (12") *(RTT 148)* **SWEET SURPRISE 1 (1984). / SWEET SURPRISE 2 (1985)**

— (CHRIS CARTER released his 2nd lp 'MONDO BEAT'; *(CTILP 3)*

Jan 86. (lp) *(ROUGH 84)* **TECHNO PRIMITIV**
– Hazey daze / Misunderstandings / Morning / Haunted heroes / Stolen kisses / He's an Arabian / Last exit / Do or die / Techno primitiv. *(cd-is.Sep88 on 'Conspiracy'; CTICD 003)*

Licensed — not iss.

Feb 87. (7"ep) *(LD 874)* **TAKE 5**
Apr 87. (lp) *(LD 875)* **ACTION! (live)**
– Akshun / Talk to me / Relay / Send the magick down / Do or die / Love cuts / Shivers / Delerium.

Dragon — not iss.

Jul 87. (lp) *(DRLP 109)* **SWEET SURPRISE**

Play It Again Sam — not iss.

Jul 87. (12") *(BIAS 054)* **OBSESSION. /**
Oct 87. (lp/cd) *(BIAS/CDBIAS 069)* **EXOTICA**
– Confession / Arcade / Exotica / Vengeance / Dancing on your grave / Beatbeatbeat / Dr. John. *(cd+=)* – Sleeping Stephen / Irama.
Jan 88. (12") *(BIAS 075)* **EXOTICA. /**
Jul 88. (12") *(BIAS 105)* **EXOTICA (remix). /**
Aug 88. (lp/c/cd) *(BIAS/+C/CD 108)* **CHRIS & COSEY**
Feb 89. (lp/cd) *(BIAS/CDBIAS 124)* **TRUST**
– Deep velvet / Illusion / The ring / Percusex / Rise / Watching you / Infectus / Trust.
Mar 91. (12") **SYNAESTHESIA. /**
Apr 91. (cd) *(BIAS 179CD)* **PAGAN TANGO**
– In ecstasy / Synaesthesia / I belong to me / Take control / Face to face / Feel to me / Go-go Latino / Pagan tango / Cords of love / Balifigore / Sacred silence.
1991. (7"etched) *(WS7 004)* **PASSION**
(above released on 'World Serpent')
Oct 92. (cd) *(BIAS 221CD)* **MUSIK FANTASTIQUE!**
– Fantastique / Sound of sound / Masqued / Apocalypso / Afrakira / Hidden man / Visions love / Loves lost immortal / Eternal / Never never land / Melancholia.

Conspiracy — not iss.

Oct 96. (cd; as CREATIVE TECHNOLOGY INSTITUTE) *(CTI 93001)* **METAPHYSICAL**
Oct 96. (cd) *(CTI 93002)* **C**
Oct 96. (cd) *(CTI 95003)* **IN CONTINUUM**
Jan 97. (cd) *(CC 1096)* **SKIMBLE SKAMBLE**
Feb 98. (cd) *(CTI 98004)* **POINT SEVEN**
– Alliz / Pausal / Hipspa / Restless / Repose / Daspooki / Reflux / Azimuth / Cell F.

– compilations, etc. –

Sep 89. (cd) *Conspiracy; (CTICD 001)* **COLLECTIV VOL.1**
Sep 89. (cd) *Conspiracy; (CTICD 002)* **COLLECTIV VOL.2 – BEST OF CHRIS & COSEY**
Sep 89. (cd) *Conspiracy; (CTICD 007)* **COLLECTIV VOL.3**
Sep 89. (cd) *Conspiracy; (CTICD 008)* **COLLECTIV VOL.4**
Jul 90. (cd) *Staal Tapes; (STCD 002)* **ALLOTROPY** (rec.1987)

CHRISTIAN DEATH

Formed: Los Angeles, California, USA . . .1979 by ROZZ WILLIAMS, who enlisted the help of former ADOLESCENTS guitarist, RIKK AGNEW, JAMES McGEARLY and GEORGE BELANGER. One of the few, if not the only American post-punk outfits to be influenced by the European "Goth" scene, CHRISTIAN DEATH found it difficult to secure a record deal, although two obscure releases – an EP for 'Bemis Brain' and the album, 'ONLY THEATRE OF PAIN' – did surface in '82. Relocating to the more sympathetic climes of Europe where a French-only mini-set (featuring selected tracks from their first two releases), 'DEATHWISH' (1984) was already available, ROZZ found a new bunch of musical disciples GITANE DEMONE, DAVID GLASS and Australian songwriter, VALOR KAND. This line-up played their inaugural UK gig in mid '84 promoting that year's album, 'CATASTROPHE BALLET', continuing in their established style and examining the interface between religious imagery and erotica. Musically, the band relied on funereal paced doom-metal riffing and sinister synth flourishes, not everyone's cup of tea but sufficiently pompous to attract obsessive post-Goths. KAND's influence was increasingly felt as he established himself as the band's chief singer and songwriter, accusations of blasphemy accompanying ever other release as he persisted in criticising Christ and organised religion in general. With founding member, ROZZ departing after the recording of 1985's Italian-only mini-set, 'THE WIND KISSED PICTURES', CHRISTIAN DEATH became an even more Euro-centric affair, VALOR KAND subsequently recruiting various backing personnel including his brother and mainstay, SVEN. Signing to 'Jungle' records, CHRISTIAN DEATH Mk.II released a solitary 12" in 1986 before finally getting around to completing their first UK-available set for three and a half years, 'THE SCRIPTURES' (1987). The following year, the band released what was possibly their most commercial track to date, 'CHURCH OF NO RETURN', a very SISTERS OF MERCY/MISSION-esque anthem complete with typical goth-diva backing. While their sleeve artwork had always courted controversy, the image of Jesus jacking-up that (un)graced the cover of 1988's 'SEX AND DRUGS AND JESUS CHRIST' surely represented a nadir of bad taste. VALOR and Co continued on their "merry" way into the 90's without ever troubling the cutting edge of the alternative/metal scene, although doubtless they didn't bank on ROZZ returning to the fray with his own version of the original CHRISTIAN DEATH. The two parties battled it out on the record front while the lawyers argued over the finer legal points, while ROZZ simultaneously combined a solo career. Sadly, however, CHRISTIAN DEATH's founder hanged himself at his Hollywood home in April 1998. • **Covered:** KILL YOUR SONS (Velvet Underground).

Album rating: ONLY THEATRE OF PAIN (*6) / CATASTROPHE BALLET (*4) / THE DECOMPOSITION OF VIOLETS (*5) / THE SCRIPTURES (*6) / SEX AND DRUGS AND JESUS CHRIST (*6) / ASHES (*5) / ATROCITIES (*4) / THE WIND KISSED PICTURES (*5) / THE HERETICS ALIVE (*4) / ALL THE LOVE ALL THE HATE (*5) / INSANUS, ULTIO, PRODITIO, MISERICORDIAQUE (*4) / SEXY DEATH GOD (*5) / THE RAGE OF ANGELS (*4) / DEATH IN DETROIT (*4) / JESUS POINTS THE BONE AT YOU compilation (*7) / etc, etc.

ROZZ WILLIAMS – vocals / **RIKK AGNEW** – guitar (ex-ADOLESCENTS) / **JAMES McGEARLY** – bass / **GEORGE BELANGER** – drums

not iss. — Bemis Brain

1982. (12"ep) *<BB 127-128>* **DESPERATE HELL / CAVITY. / SPIRITUAL CRAMP / ROMEO'S DISTRESS / DEATH WISH**

No Future — Frontier

Aug 83. (lp) *(FL 2) <FLP 1997>* **ONLY THEATRE OF PAIN** — Nov82
– Cavity – First communuion / Figurative theatre / Burnt offerings / Mysterium iniquitatis / Dream for mother / Dogs / Stairs – Uncertain journey / Spiritual cramp / Romeo's distress / Resurrection – Sixth communion / Prayer. *(re-iss. Feb85 on 'L'Invitation Au Suicide'; SD 1) (cd-iss. Aug93 on 'Frontier'; FCD 1007)*

L'Invitation Au Suicide — not iss.

Feb 84. (m-lp) *(SD 4)* **DEATHWISH** — France
– Deathwish / Romeo's distress / Dogs / Desperate hell / Spiritual cramp / Cavity. *(re-iss. 1990 on 'Contempo' c/cd; CONTAE/ECD 137) (cd re-iss. May94 on 'Normal'; N 84CD)*

— **ROZZ** relocated group to Europe and recruited new band; **VALOR KAND** (b. Australia) – vocals, guitar / **GITANE DEMONE** – vocals, keyboards / **DAVID GLASS** – drums

May 84. (lp) *(SD 5)* **CATASTROPHE BALLET** — France
– Awake at the wall / Sleepwalk / The drowning / The blue hour / Evening falls / Andro gynous noise hand permeates / Electra descending. *(re-iss. Nov88 on 'Contempo' lp/cd; CONTE/+CD 105) (cd re-iss. Jan96 on 'Normal'; N 181CD)*

R.O.I.R. — R.O.I.R.

Sep 85. (c) *(A 138)* **THE DECOMPOSITION OF VIOLETS**
– Awake at the wall / Sleepwalk / The drowning / Theatre of pain / Cavity / The blue hour / Electra descending / As evening falls / Face / Cervix couch / This glass house / Romeo's distress. *(re-iss. 1991 & Apr98; RUSCD 8240)*

— now without ROZZ, their only remaining founder member

Jungle — not iss.

Feb 86. (12") *(JUNG 24T)* **BELIEVERS OF THE UNPURE. / ?**

— added **JAMES BEAM** – guitar, etc / **SVEN KAND** – flute / **CONSTANCE (KOTA)** – bass

Sep 87. (7"/12") *(JUNG 35/+T)* **SICK OF LOVE. / ?**
Dec 87. (lp/cd) *(FREUD/+CD 18)* **THE SCRIPTURES**
– Prelude / Song of songs / Vanity / Four horsemen / 1983 / Omega dawn / A ringing in their ears / Golden age / Alpha sunset / Split blood / Raw war / Reflections / Jezebel's tribulation / Wraeththu. *(cd re-iss. May94 on 'Normal'; NORMAL 65)*

Normal — not iss.

May 88. (lp/cd) *(NORMAL/+CD 15)* **ASHES** (rec.1985)
– Ashes (part 1 & 2) / When I was bed / Lament (over the shadows) / Face / The luxury of tears / Of the wound. *(cd reiss.May94; same)*
May 88. (lp/cd) *(NORMAL/+CD 18)* **ATROCITIES** (rec.1986)
– Bastinado silhouettes / Foaming dogs with whips sharp teeth / Polished buttons / Pelting cadavernous flesh / Belladonna for you now blue eyes / Shuddering following the slice / Orgasmic flush with scalpelin hand / O the soothing / Is such heedless deliverance / Worship ye nearing quietus. *(cd re-iss. May94; same)*
Aug 88. (lp/cd) *Supporti Fonografici; (SF 003/+CD)* **THE WIND KISSED PICTURES (PAST AND PRESENT)** — Italy
– Believers of the unpure / Ouverture / The wind kisses pictures / The lake of fire / Blast of Bough / Amaterasu / The absolute / Lacrima Christi / Lacrima Christi (Italian version). *(pic-lp Jan92) (cd re-iss. Apr91 Jan96 on 'Normal'; NORMAL 76CD) <US cd-iss. 1990's on 'Dali-Chameleon'; 74789>*

Jungle — not iss.

May 88. (7"/12") *(JUNG 40/+T)* **THE CHURCH OF NO RETURN. /**

— guest **BARRY GALVIN** – guitar, keyboards; repl. BEAM

— guest **JOHANN SCHUMANN** – bass; repl. KOTA

Nov 88. (7"/12") *(JUNG 45/+T)* **WHAT'S THE VERDICT. / THIS IS NOT BLASPHEMY**
Nov 88. (lp/c/cd) *(FREUD/+C/CD 25)* **SEX AND DRUGS AND JESUS CHRIST**
– This is heresy / Jesus where's the sugar / Wretched mankind / Tragedy / The third antichrist / Erection / Ten thousand hundred times / Incendiary lover / Window pain. *(re-iss. Jun91 on 'Normal'; NORMAL 96) (cd re-iss. Oct92; same)*
Jun 89. (7") *(JUNG 50)* **ZERO SEX. / ?**
(12"+=/cd-s+=) *(JUNG 50 T/CD)* –
Jul 89. (lp/c/cd) *(FREUD/+C/CD 29)* **THE HERETICS ALIVE (live)**
– This is heresy / Wretched mankind / Sick of love / The nascent virion / Golden age / Erection / Chimere de.si.de.la / Four horsemen / Church of no return.

— **VALOR + SVEN** brought in new members **NICK THE BASTARD** – guitar, keyboards, bass / **MARK BUCHANAN** – soprano sax / **IAN THOMPSON** – drums

Nov 89. (cd-s) *(JUNG 55CD)* **I HATE YOU / WE FALL LIKE LOVE**
Nov 89. (lp/c/cd) *(FREUD/+C/CD 33)* **ALL THE LOVE ALL THE HATE (PART 1: ALL THE LOVE)**
– Live love together / We fall in love / Love don't let me down / Suivre la trace de quelqu'un / Love is like a (b)itchin' in my heart / I'm using you (for love) / Deviate love / Angel / Woman to Mother Earth.
Nov 89. (lp/c/cd) *(FREUD/+C/CD 34)* **ALL THE LOVE ALL THE HATE (PART 2: ALL THE HATE)**
– Born in a womb, died in a tomb / Baptised in fire / I hate you / Children of the valley / Kneel down / Climate of violence: part 1 – The relinquishment, part 2 – The satanic verses (Rushdie's lament), part 3 – A malice of prejudice / The final solution / Nazi killer / Man to father fire.
Jan 91. (pic-lp/cd) *(FREUD/+CD 48)* **INSANUS, ULTIO, PRODITIO, MISERICORDIAQUE**
– Sevan-us-rex / Malus amor / Tragicus conatus / Infans vexatio / Somnium / Venenum / Mors voluntaria / Vita voluntaria. *(lp-iss.Aug93;)*

Contempo not iss.

Aug 93. (lp) *(CONTE 138)* **LIVE IN HOLLYWOOD (live)**

— line-up now with **VALOR** – vocals, violin, guitar / **CULLEN** – violin, cello / **MATRI** – bass / **STREAMER** – percussion, drums / **MARCEL TRUSSEL** – violin, cello

BulletproofNostradamus

Aug 94. (cd) *(CDVEST 26)* <*1061*> **SEXY DEATH GOD**
– At the threshold / Kingdom of the tainted kiss / Heresy act two / Damn you / Into dust / Eternal love / Serpent's tail / Kingdom of the solemn kiss / Temples of desire / Deeply deeply / Drilling the hole / Upon the sea of blood / Eyelids down / Invitation au suicide.

— **VALOR** now with **FLICK** – guitar / **MATRI** – bass, vocals / **STEVE** – drums

Century Media Century Media

Oct 95. (d-cd) <*(CM 7807)*> **AMEN**
– Prelude / Prologomenon / Nascent virion / Damn you / Into dust / Sick of love / Drilling the hole / Serpent's tail / Wretched mankind / Kingdom of the tainted kiss / Children of the volley / Eternal love / emples of desire / Untitled / Deeply deeply / Androginous noise hand permeates / Invitation au suicide / Zero sex / Heresy act two / Untitled / Sleepwalk / Ashes.

CHRISTIAN DEATH

— original goths re-formed **WILLIAMS + RIKK + FRANK AGNEW** (guitar) + **GEORGE BELANGER** (drums) + **CASEY** (bass)

Triple X Triple X

1994. (cd/c) <*(51164-2/-4)*> **ICONOLOGIA**
– Excommunicamus / Cavity – First communion / Figurative theatre / Cry baby / Dream for mother / Deathwish / Some men – The other / Mysterium iniquitatis / Kill your sons / Stairs (uncertain journey) / Spiritual camp / Ressurection – 6th communion / Sleepwalk / Romeo's distress / Dogs.

— ROZZ committed suicide in Apr'98

– compilations, etc. –

May 88. (lp,pink-lp) *Nostradamus; (NOS 006)* **OFFICIAL ANTHOLOGY OF LIVE BOOTLEGS (live)**
– Awake at the wall / Sleepwalk / Theatre of pain / Cavity (first communion) / The blue hour / When I was bed / Birth / Coming forth by day / This glass house / The drowning / Cervix couch / Figura five theatre / Untitled – (followed by crowd chaos). *(re-iss. Jul91 lp/cd; NOS/CD 1006)*

Mar 92. (lp/c/cd) *Jungle; (FREUD/+C/CD 39)* **JESUS POINTS THE BONE AT YOU** (singles collection from 1986-90)
– Believers of the unpure / After the rain / Sick of love / The loving face / Church of no return / Church of no return (endured version) / What's the verdict / This is heresy / Zero sex / The nascent virion (new version) / We fall in love / I hate you.

Nov 92. (d-cd) *Jungle; (FREUDBX 334)* **LOVE AND HATE**

Jun 93. (lp/cd; by ROZZ WILLIAMS) *Apollyon; (EFA 11906/+CD)* **PATH OF SORROWS**
(cd re-iss. Mar94 on 'Cleopatra'; CLEO 39932)

Dec 93. (cd) *Cleopatra; (CLEO 91092)* **TALES OF INNOCENCE: A CONTINUED ANTHOLOGY**

May 94. (cd) *Cleopatra; (CLEO 81252)* **THE RAGE OF ANGELS**

Jun 94. (cd) *Cleopatra; (CLEO 62082)* **THE DOLL'S THEATRE (live)**

Dec 94. (cd) *Apollo; (APOL 001)* **MANDYLION**

Feb 96. (lp/cd) *Jungle; (FREUD/+CD 053)* **THE PROPHECIES**

Jul 96. (cd) *Cleopatra; (CLEO 9591CD)* **DEATH IN DETROIT** (remixes)

Jun 98. (cd) *Trinity; (TRI 006CD)* **PORNOGRAPHIC MESSIAH**

ROZZ WILLIAMS

Paragoric not iss.

Jun 95. (cd; ROZZ WILLIAMS & GITANE DEMONE) *(PA 014CD)* **DREAM HOME HEARTACHE**
(re-iss. Sep95 on 'Triple X'; TX 51026CD)

Triple X Triple X

Aug 95. (cd; ROZZ WILLIAMS & DAUCUS KAROTA) *(TX 51172CD)* **SHRINE**

Aug 95. (cd; ROZZ WILLIAMS & HELTIR) *(TX 51187CD)* **NEUE SACH LICH KEIT**

Nov 95. (cd) *(TX 512002CD)* **THE WHORE'S MOUTH**

CHROME

Formed: San Francisco, California, USA . . . 1975 by DAMON EDGE, JOHN LAMBDIN and GARY SPAIN. CHROME interpreted the wigged-out psychedelic heritage of their hometown in bizarre sequences of sci-fi obsessed mechanical noise and their two late 70's albums, 'ALIEN SOUNDTRACKS' and 'HALF MACHINE LIP MOVES' were a significant influence on the industrial and grunge scenes of the 80's and 90's. The wonderfully named HELIOS CREED (having joined their ranks by the release of the former) steered the band towards their experimental techno-goth sound. Signing to British indie, 'Beggars Banquet', the group were reduced to the duo of EDGE and CREED and subsequently moved to a more technology-based style. HELIOS departed in 1983, going on to record a string of suitably nasty grunge albums for the American 'Amphetamine Reptile' label. Meanwhile, DAMON EDGE, along with various collaborators maintained a highly prolific recording schedule under the CHROME moniker, releasing more than 20 albums. • **Songwriters:** EDGE mainly, with others contributing.

Album rating: ALIEN SOUNDTRACKS (*6) / HALF MACHINE LIP MOVES (*6)

DAMON EDGE – vocals, guitar, keyboards, drums, Moog / **JOHN LAMBDIN** – guitar / **GARY SPAIN** – bass, violin

not iss. Siren

Feb 77. (lp) <*DE 1000*> **THE VISITATION**
– How many years too soon / Raider / Return to Zanzibar / Caroline / Riding you / Kinky lover / Sun control / My time to live / Memory chords over the body.

— **HELIOS CREED** – guitar, vocals repl. LAMBDIN

Feb 78. (lp) <*DE 2200*> **ALIEN SOUNDTRACKS**
– Chromosome damage / The monitors / All data lost / S.S. Lygni / Nova feedback / Pygmies in Zee Park / Slip it to the android / Pharoah chromium / St. 31 / Re pt.II.

Beggars Banquet Siren

Mar 80. (lp) *(BEGA 15)* **RED EXPOSURE** 1979
– New age / Rm 10 / Eyes on Mars / Jonestown / Animal / Static gravity / Eyes in the center / Electric chair / Night of the Earth / Isolation.

Apr 80. (7") *(BEG 36)* **NEW AGE. / INFORMATION** 1979

— now down to duo **DAMON EDGE + HELIOS CREED**

Aug 80. (lp) *(BEGA 18)* <*DE 333*> **HALF MACHINE LIP MOVES** 1979
– TV as eyes / Zombie warfare (can't let you down) / March of the Chrome police (a cold clamey bombing) / You've been duplicated / Mondo anthem / Half machine lip moves / Abstract nympho / Turned around / Zero time / Creature eternal / Critical mass. <*cd-iss. 1990's on 'Dossier'; 2607496*>

Red-Siren Siren

May 80. (12"ep) *(RS 12007)* **READ ONLY MEMORY** 1979
– You can't see them – They can't touch you / Inacontract / Read only memory / In front of the crowd / I am the jaw.

— added **JOHN STENCH** – drums + **HILARY STENCH** – bass

Don't Fall Don't Fall

Jan 81. (12"ep) *(Y 3)* **INWORLDS. / DANGER ZONE / IN A DREAM**

Jun 81. (lp) *(X 6)* **BLOOD ON THE MOON**
– The need / Inner vacuum / Perfumed metal / Planet strike / The strangers / Insect human / Out of reach / Brain on scan / Blood on the Moon. *(re-iss. Apr87 on 'Dossier'; DOSSIER 001)*

— added guest **FABIENNE SHINE** – vocals

Apr 82. (7") *(Z 17)* **FIREBOMB. / SHADOW OF A THOUSAND YEARS**

Apr 82. (lp) *(X 18)* **3RD FROM THE SUN**
– Firebomb / Future ghosts / Armageddon / Heartbeat / Off the line / 3rd from the Sun / Shadows of a thousand years.

not iss. Expanded

1983. (lp) <*EX 40*> **NO HUMANS ALLOWED**
– Danger zone / The manifestation (of the idea) / In a dream / Information / Read only memory.

— added guest **BETSY HILL** – vocals

Mosquito not iss.

1983. (lp) *(MOS 001)* **RAINING MILK** France
– Wings born in the night / Tribes (ultra) / Gehenna to Canaan / La legende des sentences du futur / Beacons to the eye / Raining milk / Anorexic sacrifice / Gehenna lion.

— HELIOS CREED went on to sign for 'Subterranean', releasing two albums, 'X-RATED FAIRY TALES' and 'SUPERIOR CATHOLIC FINGER' in 1985 and 1986 respectively. 'Amphetamine Reptile' also issued three sets, 'THE LAST LAUGH' (1989), 'BOXING THE CLOWN' (1990) and 'KISS TO THE BRAIN' (1992). Later albums included 'NUGG THE TRANSPORT' and 'CHROMAGNUM MAN' for 'Dossier' and 'ACTIVATED CONDITION' for 'Man's Ruin' (1998).

DAMON EDGE / CHROME

— with **FABIENNE SHINE** – vocals / **REMY DeVILLA** – guitar / **RENAUD THOREZ** – bass / **PATRICK IMBERT** – drums

1984. (lp) *(MOS 003)* <*260 5318*> **INTO THE EYES OF THE ZOMBIE KING** France
– And then the red sun / You can't do anything / Walking and looking for you / Into the eyes of the Zombie King / Trip the switch / It wasn't real / Humans in the rain / Don't move like that. *(UK-iss.Apr87 on 'Dossier'; ST 7513)* <*US-iss.Aug88 on 'Dossier'; DCD 9004*>

DAMON EDGE

New Rose not iss.

Mar 85. (7") *(NEW 51)* **I'M A GENTLEMAN. /**

Mar 85. (lp) *(ROSE 51)* **ALLIANCE** France

Jun 85. (lp) *(ROSE 64)* **THE WIND IS TALKING** France

Jun 86. (lp) *(ROSE 90)* **GRAND VISIONS** France

Dosier not iss.

1987. (lp) **THE RURREAL ROCK**

CHROME

DAMON EDGE + FABIENNE etc.

Dossier Dossier

Apr 86. (lp) *(ST 7503)* **ANOTHER WORLD**
– If you come around / I found out today / Our good dreams / Stranger from another world / Moon glow / The sky said / Loving lovely lover.

Feb 87. (lp) *(ST 7527)* **DREAMING IN SEQUENCE**
– Everyone's the same / Seeing everything / Touching you / Windows in the wind / The Venusian dance / White magic / Love to my rock (cause of me) / She is here.

Apr 87. (lp) *(ST 3004)* **THE LYON CONCERT (live)**
– We are connected / Sanity / As we stand here in time / March of the rubber people / Ghosts of the long forgotten future / Version 2 (Raining milk) / The service improves / Frankenstein's party.

Oct 87. (lp) *(DOSSIER 002)* **THE CHRONICLES**
– The chronicles of the sacrifice / The chronicles of the tribes / The chronicles of the open door / The chronicles of born in the night.

Jul 88. (lp) *(ST 003)* **THE CHRONICLES II**
– The chronicles of the beacons / The chronicles of Gehenna / The chronicles of Canaan. *(cd-iss. Jun89 'CHRONICLES I & II'; 260 7499)*

Feb 89. (lp) *(EFA 5853)* **ALIEN SOUNDTRACKS**

Sep 89. (lp) *(EFA 5859)* **LIVE IN GERMANY (live)**

Sep 90. (cd/lp) **LIQUID FOREST**

Feb 91. (cd/lp) **MISSION OF THE ENTRANCED**

Jul 94. (cd) *(EFA 06456-2)* **THE CLAIRAUDIENT SYNDROME**

Feb 95. (cd) *(EFA 08461-2)* **CHROME SAMPLER VOL.1 (HAVING A WONDERFUL TIME WITH THE TRIPODS)**

Mar 95. (cd) *(EFA 08462-2)* **HAVING A WONDERFUL TIME IN THE JUICE BOX** [ ] [-]

Consolidated unknown

May 95. (cd-s) *(CSD 22003)* **BUMPER /** [ ] [-]
Sep 95. (12") *(CSD 22006)* **I WANT YOU. /** [ ] [-]

Mans Ruin unknown

Sep 96. (10") *(MR 035)* **CHROME EP** [ ] [ ]
Feb 98. (cd) *(MR 061CD)* **TIDAL FORCES** [ ] [ ]

– compilations, others, etc. –

Jun 89. (cd) *Dossier; (260 7490CD)* **BLOOD ON THE MOON / ETERNITY** [ ] [ ]
Jun 89. (cd) *Dossier; (260 7709CD)* **THE LYON CONCERT / ANOTHER WORLD** [ ] [ ]
Aug 95. (cd) *Cleopatra; (CLEO 9533-2)* **3RD FROM THE SUN / INTO THE EYES OF THE ZOMBIE KING** [ ] [-]
Jan 98. (cd) *Cleopatra; (CLP 0080-2)* **RETRO TRANSMISSION** [ ] [-]

CHRON GEN

Formed: Hitchin, Herts, England . . . early 1978 out of the CONDEMNED by schoolmates, GLYNN BARBER and JOHN JOHNSON, the pair drafting in ADAM, who was in turn replaced by PETE DIMMOCK while adding JON THURLOW in the process. CHRON GEN (actually short for CHRONIC GENERATION) really got off the ground in 1981 with an EP, 'PUPPETS OF WAR', followed a few months later by a solitary 45 for 'Step Forward' (then home of CHELSEA, CORTINAS and The FALL!), 'REALITY'. Translating the early spirit of '77 into the yobbish charge of "oi", the band won column inches in the pages of Sounds and toured with the likes of The EXPLOITED. Also in common with the latter band, CHRON GEN signed to the 'Secret' label for a cover of The New York Dolls' 'JET BOY, JET GIRL'. In March '82, they had their one and only chart entry with debut album, 'CHRONIC GENERATION' (containing a savaging of Smokie's 'LIVING NEXT DOOR TO ALICE'), although this would be the last recording to feature THURLOW as guitarist, FLOYD filled his shoes. With DIMMOCK bailing out to join CHELSEA, the band virtually fell apart, only to resurface once more for a low-key comeback set, 'NOWHERE TO RUN', in '85.

Album rating: CHRONIC GENERATION (*5) / NOWHERE TO RUN (*3) / THE BEST OF CHRON GEN compilation (*5)

GLYNN BARBER – vocals, guitar / **JON THURLOW** – rhythm guitar / **PETE DIMMOCK** – bass / **JOHN JOHNSON** – drums

Gargoyle not iss.

Jun 81. (7"ep) *(GRGL 780)* **PUPPETS OF WAR EP** [ ] [-]
– Puppets of war / Lies / Mindless few / Chronic generation. *(re-iss. Sep81 by 'Fresh'; FRESH 36)*

Step Forward not iss.

Sep 81. (7") *(SF 19)* **REALITY. / SUBWAY SADIST** [ ] [-]

Secret not iss.

Feb 82. (7"m) *(SHH 129)* **JET BOY, JET GIRL. / ABORTIONS / SUBWAY SADIST** [ ] [-]
Mar 82. (lp) *(SEC 3)* **CHRONIC GENERATION** [53] [-]
– Lies / Jet boy, jet girl / Hounds of the night / L.S.D. / You make me spew / Chronic generation / Mindless / You'll never change me / Rocka'Bill / Friends tell me lies / Reality / Living next door to Alice. *(with free live-7")* – LIVING NEXT DOOR TO ALICE. / RIPPER / PUPPETS OF WAR *(re-iss. Jul86 as 'CHRON GEN' on 'Razor'; RAZS 20) (re-iss. Feb97 on 'Get Back'; GET 9)*

— **FLOYD** – guitar; repl. THURLOW

Oct 82. (7"m) *(SHH 139)* **OUTLAW. / BEHIND CLOSED DOORS / DISCO** [ ] [-]

— DIMMOCK joined CHELSEA before moving to BANDITS AT 4 O'CLOCK

Picasso not iss.

Sep 85. (lp) *(PIK 002)* **NOWHERE TO RUN** [ ] [-]

— split for the final time in the mid 80's

– compilations, etc. –

1982. (c) *Chaos; (004)* **APOCALYPSE LIVE TOUR '81 (live)** *(lp-is.Apr84; APOCA 1)* [ ] [-]
Nov 94. (cd) *Captain Oi; (AHOY 18)* **THE BEST OF CHRON GEN** [ ] [-]
Oct 95. (cd) *Punx; (PUNXCD 3)* **LIVE AT THE WALDORF IN SAN FRANCISCO (live)** [ ] [-]

CHRYSANTHEMUMS (see under ⇒ DEEP FREEZE MICE)

CHUMBAWAMBA

Formed: Burnley /Barnsley, Yorkshire, England . . . 1980 by vegan sextet, ALICE NUTTER, BOFF, LOU, MAVIS, HARRY and DANBERT NOBACON, who shacked up in a Leeds commune. In 1982, they appeared as SKIN DISEASE on a single 'BACK ON THE STREETS', and toured as CHUMBAWAMBA a year later with CRASS, while releasing three cassettes independently. In 1985/86, they caused a little controversy by issuing records arguing the merits of the BAND/LIVE AID charity causes. Needless to say, these were banned from radio airplay. More publicity surrounded them around this time, when they poured red paint over The CLASH, after the one-time punks arrived in Leeds for their 'Busking Britain Tour'. 1987's 'NEVER MIND THE BALLOTS: HERE'S THE REST OF YOUR LIFE', meanwhile, berated all arties in the forthcoming general election although obviously the Tories came in for the most disdain, 'MR HESELTINE MEETS HIS PUBLIC'. The same year, CHUMBAWAMBA railed against against tabloid hypocrisy when they released 'LET IT BE' under the moniker of SCAB AID. Perhaps as a reaction to yet another Conservative victory, the band released an album of traditional folk protest songs, 'ENGLISH REBEL SONGS 1381-1914' (1988), their MADDY PRIOR (Steeleye Span) meets CRASS sound rising with ease to the challenge. Discovering the subversive possibilities in the emerging rave culture, the band turned in the dancefloor-friendly 'SLAP!' in summer 1990, although it took a pair-up with agit-hip hopper's CREDIT TO THE NATION for CHUMBAWAMBA to finally get their message across to a wider audience. Now signed to 'One Little Indian', the track in question, 'ENOUGH IS ENOUGH', gave the band a minor UK chart hit. Its call to challenge the rise of right-wing activism was echoed in a similarly successful follow-up, 'TIMEBOMB'. The attendant album, 'ANARCHY', made the British Top 30. Unimaginable ten years earlier, the once crustie band signed to conglomerate, 'E.M.I.' in the mid-90's, obviously deciding to subvert the pop world from within (a likely story!). Not only did they come pretty damn close with the annoyingly infectious 'TUBTHUMPING' (a No.2 UK hit!), but they broke the normally impenetrable American market. The accompanying album, 'TUBTHUMPER' (1997) made the US Top 5 (having earlier made UK Top 20), proving that patience is a virtue, even for those committed to radical social change. Love them or loathe them (and there's never usually any waverers!), CHUMBAWAMBA are not something of an institution, their newfound pop/MTV-friendly sound ushering in a new era of chart topping protest, possibly . . . • **Songwriters:** Group, except some traditional Hungarian folk tunes. Also sampled JOHN LENNON (Imagine), ELVIS, ALTERNATIVE TV, GANG OF FOUR, CRASS, FALL, X-RAY SPEX, STIFF LITTLE FINGERS, DAGMAR KRAUSE and GERSHWIN!. The lp tracks on 'ENGLISH REBEL SONGS' were all traditional. Covered on 'JESUS H CHRIST'; ALRIGHT NOW (Free) / MONEY, MONEY, MONEY (Abba) / SOLID GOLD EASY ACTION (T.Rex) / HEY YOU GET OFF MY CLOUD (Rolling Stones) / STAIRWAY TO HEAVEN (Led Zeppelin) / BIGMOUTH STRIKES AGAIN (Smiths) / I SHOULD BE SO LUCKY (Kylie Minogue) / MANNEQUIN (Wire) / HUNCHBACK OF NOTRE DAME (Frantic Elevators; Mick Hucknall). • **Trivia:** In 1982, track 'THREE YEARS LATER' appeared on 'Crass' label album 'BULLSHIT DETECTOR 2'. ALICE NUTTER was named after a 17th century witch. DANBERT NOBACON released a single before he joined them, which featured a picture of his utensil on the cover!. 'NEVER SAY DI' single (proceeds to charity) was surprisingly in support of Princess Diana, as they were anti-royalists. 'BEHAVE!' was a tribute ha!, about 'The Hit Man And Her' (aka PETE WATERMAN & MICHAELA).

Album rating: PICTURES OF STARVING CHILDREN SELL RECORDS (*7) / SHHH (*8) / ANARCHY (*9) / TUBTHUMPER (*5)

ALICE NUTTER – vocals / **BOFF** (b. BILLY McCOID) – guitar, vocals, clarinet / **LOU** (b. LOUISE MARY WATTS) – vocals, guitar / **MAVIS DILLAN** – bass, trumpet, French horn / **HARRY** (b. DARREN HAMMER) drums / **DANBERT NOBACON** (b. ALAN WHALEY) – vocals / with **SIMON COMMONKNOWLEDGE** – keyboards, accordion, piano

— (released 3 cassettes before the mid-80's)

Agit Prop not iss.

Sep 85. (7"ep) *(AGIT 001)* **REVOLUTION** [ ] [-]
Apr 86. (7") *(AGIT 002)* **WE ARE THE WORLD. / A STATE OF MIND** [ ] [-]
In '86, they issued DESTROY FASCISM as The ANTIDOTE; alongside The EX
Oct 86. (lp) *(PROP 001)* **PICTURES OF STARVING CHILDREN SELL RECORDS** [ ] [-]
– (prologue) / How to get your band on television / British colonialism and the BBC – Flickering pictures hypnotise / Commercial break / Unilever / More whitewashing / . . . An interlude. Beginning to take it back / Dutiful servants and political masters / Coca- colanisation / . . . And in a nutshell "food aid is our most powerful weapon" / Invasion.
Jul 87. (lp) *(PROP 002)* **NEVER MIND THE BALLOTS: HERE'S THE REST OF YOUR LIFE** [ ] [-]
– Always tell the voter what the voter wants to hear / Come on baby (let's do the revolution) / The wasteland / Today's sermon / Ah-men / Mr. Heseltine meets his public / The candidates find common ground / Here's the rest of your life.

— Under the name SCAB AID, they issued 'Let It Be' on the 'Scum' label.

Jul 88. (7") *(AGIT 003)* **FIGHT THE ALTON BILL. / SMASH CLAUSE 28** [ ] [-]
Oct 88. (10"lp) *(PROP 003)* **ENGLISH REBEL SONGS 1381-1914** [ ] [-]
– The Cutty wren / The diggers song / Colliers march / The triumph of General Ludd / Chartist anthem / Song of the times / Smashing of the van / World turned upside down / Poverty knock / Idris strike song / Hanging on the old barbed wire / The Cutty wren (reprise). *(re-iss. Feb93 lp/cd; PROP 3/+CD) (re-iss. Feb95 on 'One Little Indian' lp/c/cd; TPLP 64/+C/CD) <US cd-iss. Jun98 on 'Imprint'; 8769>*

— In Dec'89; they appeared on 'Agit Prop' Various Artists (SPORTCHESTRA) lp '101 SONGS ABOUT SPORT' *PROP 004)*. Another Various 'THIS SPORTING LIFE' was iss.Aug'90.

— added **DUNST** (b. DUNSTON BRUCE) – vocals, percussion, soprano sax / **COBIE** – live sound / + others

Jul 90. (cd/lp) *(CD+/PROP 7)* **SLAP!** [ ] [-]
– Ulrike / Tiananmen Square / Cartrouble / Chase PC's flee attack by own dog / Rubens has been shot! / I never gave up: Rappoport's testament / Slap! / That's how grateful we are / Meinhof. *(re-iss. Feb95 on 'One Little Indian' lp/c/cd; TPLP 65/+C/CD)*

— In Mar'91, CHUMBAWAMBA AND OTHER SUBVERSIVES released 7"; GREATEST HITS for 'Peasant Revolt'. At the same time ALICE and LOUISE (I think?) as The PASSION KILLERS released mail-order EP 'FOUR WAR IS SHIT SONGS' featuring tracks 'Shipbuilding', 'Reuters' + 2 for 'Rugger Bugger' records.

— added **MATTY** (MC FUSION) – vocals (of CREDIT TO THE NATION) / **NEIL FERGUSON** – guitar, keyboards / **GEOFF SLAPHEAD** – fiddle / **HOWARD STOREY** – vocals

Jan 92. (7") **I NEVER GAVE UP: RAPPOPORT'S TESTAMENT. / LAUGHING**
(12") – ('A'-Rondo mix) / ('A'-Cass mix).
(cd-s) – (all 4 tracks). *(re-iss. Jul94 on 'Southern' 12"/cd-s; 18521-1/-2)*

Jun 92. (cd/c/lp) *(CD/TC+/PROP 11)* **SHHH** -
– Shhh / Big mouth strikes again / Nothing that's new / Behave! / Snip snip snip / Look! no strings! / Happiness is just a chant away / Pop star kidnap / Sometimes plunder / You can't trust anyone nowadays / Stitch that. *(re-iss. Nov94 & Sep97 on 'Southern' cd/c/lp; 18515-2/-4/-1)*

Jul 92. (7") **NEVER SAY DI. / FOR THE LOVE OF A PRINCESS** -

Nov 92. (12"/cd-s) *(AGIT 666/+CD)* **SOMEONE'S ALWAYS TELLING YOU HOW TO BEHAVE! / (2-'A'mixes by PAPA BRITTLE)** -

Dec 92. (cd/c/lp) **JESUS H CHRIST**
– Alright now / Money, money, money / Solid gold easy action / Silly love songs / Hey you get off my cloud / Stairway to Heaven / Bigmouth strikes again / I should be so lucky.

One Little Indian E.M.I.

Sep 93. (12"ep/c-ep/cd-ep; CHUMBAWAMBA & CREDIT TO THE NATION) *(79 TP 7C/12/7CD)* **ENOUGH IS ENOUGH. / HEAR NO BULLSHIT (on fire mix) / THE DAY THE NAZI DIED (1993 mix)** 56 -

Nov 93. (12"ep/c-ep/cd-ep) *(89 TP 12/7C/7CD)* **TIMEBOMB. / TECHNO THE BOMB / THE WORLD TURNED UPSIDE DOWN** 59 -

May 94. (lp/c/cd) *(TPLP 46/+C/CD)* *<40903>* **ANARCHY** 29 Jun98
– Give the anarchist a cigarette / Timebomb / Homophobia / On being pushed / Heaven – Hell / Love me / Georgina / Doh! / Blackpool rock / This year's thing / Mouthful of shit / Never do what you are told / Bad dog / Enough is enough / Rage.

May 94. (12"ep/c-ep/cd-ep) *(119 TP 12/7C/7CD)* **HOMOPHOBIA (with The SISTERS OF PERPETUAL INDULGENCE). / MORALITY PLAY IN THREE ACTS / ('A'acappella mix) / SONG FOR DEREK JARMEN**
(cd-ep) *(119 TP7CDL)* – ('A'side) / Enough is enough (w / CREDIT TO THE NATION) / The day the Nazi died (w / CREDIT TO THE NATION) / Morality play in three acts.

Mar 95. (lp/c/cd) *(TPLP 56/+C/CD)* **SHOWBUSINESS! CHUMBAWAMBA LIVE (live)** -
– Never do what you are told / I never gave up / Give the anarchist a cigarette / Heaven-Hell / That's how grateful we are / Homophobia / Morality play in three acts / Bad dog / Enough is enough / Mouthful of shit / The day the Nazi died / Time bomb (Jimmy Echo vocal) / Slag aid.

Oct 95. (7"/c-s) *(139 TP7/+C)* **UGH! YOUR UGLY HOUSES! / THIS GIRL** -
(cd-s+=) *(139 TPCD)* – Mannequin / Hunchback of Notre Dame.

Oct 95. (d-lp/c/d-cd) *(TPLP 66/+C/CD)* **SWINGIN' WITH RAYMOND** 70
– This girl / Never let go / Just look at me now / Not the girl I used to be / The morning after (the night before) / Love can knock you over / All mixed up / This dress kills / Salome (let's twist again) / Oxymoron / Waiting, shouting / Hey you! outside now! / Ugh! your ugly houses.

E.M.I. Republic

Aug 97. (c-s) *(TCEM 486)* *<56146>* **TUBTHUMPING / (Buttthumping mix) / (Danny Boy mix)** 2 6
(cd-s+=) *(CDEM 486)* – ('A'-Mawr mix: Pablo & Lawrie) / ('A'-Timeshard mix) / ('A'-Gunshot mix).
(7"red) *(EM 486)* – ('A'side) / Farewell to the Crown (featuring The OYSTER BAND) / Football song ("Shit ground, no fans").

Sep 97. (cd/c) *(CD/TC EMC 3773)* *<53099>* **TUBTHUMPER** 19 3
– Tubthumping / Amnesia / Drip drip drip / Big issue / Good ship lifestyle / One by one / Outsider / Creepy crawling / Mary Mary / Small town / I want more / Scapegoat. *(re-iss. Jun98 cd+=/c+=; 495238-2/-4)* – Top of the world (ole, ole, ole).

Jan 98. (c-s) *(TCEM 498)* **AMNESIA / AMNESIA (Zion Train 359 Amherst Road mix) / TUBTHUMPING (Escape From New York mix)** 10
(cd-s) *(CDEM 498)* – (first 2 tracks) / ('A'-Done Lying Down mix) / ('A'-Jimmy Echo version) / ('A'-Decontrol mix).
(cd-s) *(CDEMS 498)* – (first & third tracks) / Tubthumping (original) / Tubthumping (Tin Tin Out mix).

May 98. (c-s) *(TCEM 511)* **TOP OF THE WORLD (OLE, OLE, OLE) / I'M A WINNER BABY / STRIKE! (Barnsley 3, Man Utd 2 mix)** 21 -
(cd-s) *(CDEM 511)* – (first 2 tracks) / The best is yet to come (acoustic) / The best is yet to come.

– compilations, others, etc. –

Feb 92. (lp/cd) *Agit Prop; (PROP 4)* **FIRST 2** -
– (as said 1st 2 albums, originally Aug89 as '100 SONGS ABOUT SPORT'; *PROP 004) (re-iss. Feb95 on 'One Little Indian' d-lp/c/cd; TPLP 63/+C/CD)*

Apr 96. (cd+book) *One Little Indian; (EYE 1)* **PORTRAITS OF ANARCHISTS** -

DANBERT NOBACON

Rugger Bugger not iss.

Mar 98. (cd) *(SEEP 16CD)* **THE UNFAIRYTALE** -

CHUNK (see under ⇒ SUPERCHUNK)

CHURCH

Formed: Sydney, Australia . . . 1980 by English-born STEVE KILBEY along with PETER KOPPES, MARTY WILLSON-PIPER and NICK WARD. Initially signing to the Aussie arm of 'Parlophone', the quartet garnered much homeland acclaim for their jangling 60's-rooted New Wave sound as heard on their debut album, 'OF SKIN & HEART' (1981); but for a few tracklisting differences, this was virtually re-released in its entirety by 'Carrere' ('Capitol' in the US) as an eponymous set the following Spring. By this point, RICHARD PLOOG had taken the place of WARD, the drummer making his debut on the follow-up album, 'THE BLURRED CRUSADE', later that year. Breaking away from the trademark BOWIE meets RICHARD BUTLER (PSYCHEDELIC FURS) vocal style and Paisley psyche meandering over the course of three mid 80's albums ('SEANCE', 'REMOTE LUXURY' and 'HEYDAY'), KILBEY and his disciples finally broke into the mainstream after signing worldwide to 'Arista'. 1988 saw a US Top 30 single, 'UNDER THE MILKY WAY', taken from a top-selling accompanying Woody Watchel-produced album, 'STARFISH', the band also taking the opportunity to branch out in their own right with individual solo projects. Although not nearly as successful, two early 90's albums, 'GOLD AFTERNOON FIX' (1990) and 'PRIEST = AURA' (1992) found The CHURCH sticking faithfully to their wordy, atmospheric soundscapes in the face of the grunge revolution. Having already lost PLOOG in '91, KILBEY and WILLSON-PIPER became the sole founding members following the subsequent departure of KOPPES. Augmented by a cast of session players, the pair recorded the self-indulgent 'SOMETIME ANYWHERE' (1994), making no concessions to commerciality and subsequently finding themselves minus a deal. Having previously cut an eponymous album in 1991 as JACK FROST (with ex-GO-BETWEENS mainman, GRANT McLENNAN), KILBEY again took on the JF mantle for 1996's 'SNOW JOB'; KILBEY had also previously sidelined with DONETTE THAYER (of GAME THEORY), releasing two albums as HEX. Moving back to the independent sector, The CHURCH followed their spiritual bent with two further albums, 'MAGICIAN AMONG THE SPIRITS' (1997) and 'HOLOGRAM OF BAAL' (1998).

Album rating: OF SKIN AND HEART or THE CHURCH (*7) / THE BLURRED CRUSADE (*6) / SEANCE (*6) / REMOTE LUXURY (*7) / HEYDAY (*7) / STARFISH (*7) / GOLD AFTERNOON FIX (*6) / PRIEST: AURA (*4) / SOMETIME ANYWHERE (*5) / CONCEPTION compilation (*7) / QUICK SMOKE AT POTS compilation (*6)

STEVE KILBEY (b.13 Sep'60, Welwyn Garden City, England) – vocals, bass, occasional keyboards / **PETER KOPPES** (b.1959) – guitar / **MARTY WILLSON-PIPER** (b. 7 May'59, Stockport, England) – guitar / **NICK WARD** – drums, percussion

Parlophone not iss.

1981. (7") *(A367)* **SHE NEVER SAID. / IN A HEARTBEAT** - - Aust.

1981. (lp) *(PCS 07583)* **OF SKINS AND HEART** - - Aust.
– For a moment we're strangers / Chrome injury / Unguarded moment / Memories in future tense / Bel-Air / Is this where you live / She never said / Fighter pilot * / Korean war * / Don't open the door to strangers. *(UK-iss.Sep87 on 'Arista'+=*)* / Too fast for you / Tear it all away / Sisters.

1981. (d7") *(A536-A525)* **TWO FAST FOR YOU. / SISTERS / / TEAR IT ALL AWAY. / YOU'VE GOT TO GO / FRAULEIN** - - Aust.

Carrere Capitol

Mar 82. (7") *(CAR 212)* **UNGUARDED MOMENT. / BUSDRIVER**

Mar 82. (lp) *(CAL 130)* *<ST 12193>* **THE CHURCH**
– (same as 'OF SKINS AND HEART' except 'Tear it all away' repl. * above) *(re-iss. Apr85; same) (cd-iss. May88; CDCAL 130)*

Sep 82. (7") *(CAR 247)* **ALMOST WITH YOU. / LIFE SPEEDS UP**

— **RICHARD PLOOG** (b.1959) – drums (on most tracks) repl. WARD

Oct 82. (lp) *(CAL 140)* **THE BLURRED CRUSADE** -
– Almost with you / When you were mine / Field of Mars / An interlude / Secret corners / Just for you / A fire burns / To be in your eyes / You Took / Don't look back. *(re-iss. Mar85; same) (cd-iss. Aug88; CDCAL 140)*

Nov 82. (7"m) *(CAR 257)* **UNGUARDED MOMENT. / INTERLUDE / GOLDEN DAWN**
(10"ep+=) *(CAREP 257)* – Sisters.

Mar 83. (7") *(CHURCH R5A)* **A DIFFERENT MAN. / I AM A ROCK** -
(12"ep+=) *(CHURCH 5)* **SING SONGS** – Ancient history / Night is very soft / In this room. *(released on 'Capitol')*

Carrere Arista

May 84. (lp)<cd> *(CAL 201)* *<ARCD 8565>* **SEANCE**
– Fly / One day / Electric / It's no reason / Travel by thought / Disappear? / Electric lash / Now I wonder why / Dropping names / It doesn't change. *(re-iss. May85; same)*

Jun 84. (7") *(CAR 336)* **IT'S NO REASON. / SOMEONE SPECIAL**
(12"+=) *(CART 336)* – Autumn soon.

Feb 85. (lp) *(CAL 213)* **REMOTE LUXURY**
– Constant in opal / Violet town / No explanation / 10,000 miles / Maybe these boys / Into my hands / A month of Sundays / Volumes / Shadow cabinet / Remote luxury. *(re-iss. Mar89 on 'Arista' lp/c/cd; 209/409/259 649)*

— (note: they were still signed to 'Parlophone' Australia)

E.M.I. Warners

Feb 86. (7") **COLUMBUS. / AS YOU WILL** -

May 86. (7") *(EMI 5557)* **TANTALIZED. / THE VIEW.**
(12"+=) *(EMI12 5557)* – As you will.

Jun 86. (lp/c/cd) *(EMC/TCEMC/CDEMC 3508)* *<25370>* **HEYDAY**
– Myrrh / Tristesse / Already yesterday / Columbus / Happy hunting ground / Tantalized / Disenchanted / Night of light / Youth worshipper / Roman. *(c-s+=/cd-s+=)* – As you will / The view. *(cd re-iss. Oct97 on 'Axis'; 746256-2)*

Parlophone Warners

Sep 86. (7") *(R 6139)* **DISENCHANTED. / TRANCE ENDING**
(12"+=) *(12R 6139)* – You've got to go.

Arista Arista

Feb 88. (7") *(109 778)* *<9637>* **UNDER THE MILKY WAY. / MUSK** 24
(12"+=/cd-s+=) *(609/659 778)* – Warm spell.

Mar 88. (lp/c/cd) *(208/408/258 895)* *<8521>* **STARFISH** 41
– Destination / Under the Milky Way / Blood money / Lost / North, south, east and west / Spark / Antenna / Reptile / A new season / Hotel womb. *(free 12"w/ lp)* **ANNA MIRANDA / MUSK. / PERFECT CHILD / FROZEN AND DISTANT / TEXAS MOON**

Mar 90. (cd/c/lp) *(260/410/210 541)* *<8579>* **GOLD AFTERNOON FIX** 66
– Pharaoh / Metropolis / Terra Nova Cain / City / Russian Autumn heart / Essence / You're still beautiful / Disappointment / Transient / Fading away / Grind. *(cd+=)* – Monday morning / Laughing.
Apr 90. (7") *(113 086)* **METROPOLIS. / MONDAY MORNING**
(12"+=/cd-s+=) *(613/663 086)* – Much too much.
Jun 90. (cd-ep) **RUSSIAN AUTUMN HEART / HUNTER / FEAST / DESERT / RIDE INTO THE SUNSET** -

— **JAY DEE DAUGHERTY** (b.22 Mar'56, Santa Barbara, Calif.) – drums (ex-PATTI SMITH GROUP) repl. PLOOG / **WILLSON-PIPER** joined ALL ABOUT EVE in 1990.

Mar 92. (cd/c/lp) *(262/412/212 643)* *<18683>* **PRIEST = AURA**
– Aura / Ripple / Paradox / Lustre / Swan lake / Feel Mistress / Kings / Dome / Witch hunt / The disillusionist / Old flame / Chaos / Film.

— now a basic duo of **KILBEY + WILLSON-PIPER** plus **TIM POWELL** – drums / **LINDA NEIL** – violin / **SANDY CHICK** – female voice / **CAROL BROCA-WANDER** – French female voice / **BORIS GOUDENOV** – drumloops / **DARREN RYAN** – loops, + drums on 1

May 94. (d-cd/c/lp) *(<07822 18727-2/-4/-1>)* **SOMETIME ANYWHERE**
– Days of the dead / Lost my touch / Loveblind / My little problem / The maven / Angelica / Lullaby / Eastern / Two places at once / Business woman / Authority / Fly home / The dead man's dream. *(d-cd+=)* – Drought / The time being / Leave your clothes on / Cut in two / The myths you made / Freeze to burn / Macabre tavern.

Festival / Deep Karma

Feb 97. (cd) *(D 31562)* **MAGICIAN AMONG THE SPIRITS**
– Welcome / Comedown / Ritz / Grandoise / Ladyboy / It could be anyone / Further adventures of the time being / Romany caravan / Magician among the spirits / Afterimage.
Aug 98. (cd-s) *(D 1742)* **LOUISIANA / ANYWAY / LIZARD**
Aug 98. (d-cd) *(D 31886)* **HOLOGRAM OF BAAL**
– Anaesthesia / Richochet / Louisiana / Great machine / No certainty attached / Tranquility / Buffalo / This is it / Another Earth / Glow worm / Bastard universe / Movements.

– compilations, others, etc. –

Apr 88. (lp/c/cd) *Carrere; (CAL/CAC/CDCAL 229)* **CONCEPTION** -
– When you were mine / Chrome injury / A different man / To be in your eyes / Is this where you live / Unguarded moment / Just for you / Memories and future tense / Almost with you / You took.
May 88. (7") *Carrere; (CAR 425)* **UNGUARDED MOMENT. / BEL-AIR** -
(12") *(CART 425)* – ('A'side) / Temperature drop / Downtown / Winterland.
Jan 95. (cd) *Raven; (cd) (RVCD 43)* **ALMOST YESTERDAY 1981-1990** - -
1996. (cd) *Mushroom;* **QUICK SMOKE AT POTS** - - Austra

STEVE KILBEY

— solo, with brother **RUSSELL** and fiancee **KARIN JANSSON**

E.M.I. / not iss.

1986. (7"m) *(A 1516)* **ASPHALT EDEN. / NEVER COME BACK / SHELL** - - Austra
(re-iss. 1987 on 'Red Eye'; RED 13)

Enigma / Rykodisc

Aug 87. (lp/cd) *(3297-1/-2)* *<73207>* **UNEARTHED**
– Out of this world / Guilty / Pretty ugly, pretty sad / Swampdrome / Judgement day / Rising son / Tyrant / Transference / My birthday the moon festival / Design error / Nothing inside / Other time / Heliopolis / Famine.

Red Eye / Rykodisc

Nov 87. (lp)<cd> *(REDLP 2)* *<RCD 90043>* **EARTHED** (instrumental) - - Austra
– The dawn poems / Dreambeings / Memory / The white plague / A love letter from Sydney / City of women / Carthage / Hotel / The empire mourns her sun without tears / Cornucopia / Aphrodite / Sad little piano piece / The reality generators malfunctioned / Napoleon's army, Christmas eve, outside Moscow / Atlantis / Pan / The woman who was married to love / Agog / Earthed. *(cd-iss. Mar94 on 'Rykodisc';)*
1988. (7") *(RED 14)* **FIREMAN. / FORGETFULNESS / NONAPOLOGY** - - Austra
1989. (m-lp) *(RED 15)* **THE SLOW CRACK** - - Austra
– Fireman / Woman with reason / A favourite pack of lies / Something that means something / Ariel sings / A minute without you / Surrealist woman blues.
1989. (12"ep) *(RED 19)* **TRANSACTIONS** - - Austra
– Transaction / Consider yourself conquered / Song of Solomon / Starling St. *<US-iss.1990 on 'Rough Trade' lp/c/cd+=; ROUGHUS 70/+C/CD>* – TRANSACTIONS
1990. (d-lp) **REMINDLESSNESS** - - Austra

Red Eye / Sony

1991. (cd-ep) **NARCOSIS** -

Vicious Sloth / unknown

Jun 97. (cd; by STEVE & RUSSELL KILBEY) *(VSC 004)* **GILT TRIP** -
Jun 97. (cd) *(VSC 005)* **NARCOSIS PLUS** -

HEX

KILBEY + DONETTE THAYER (of GAME THEORY)

Demon / Rykodisc

Mar 90. (lp/cd) *(FIEND/+CD 156)* *<10184>* **HEX** Nov89
– Diviner / Hermaphrodite / Ethereal message / Mercury towers / Out of the pink / Fire island / In the net / Silvermine / Elizabeth Green / An arrangement.

— added **JIM McGRATH** – percussion

Feb 91. (lp/cd) *<10186>* **VAST HALOS** Nov90
– Monarch / Shelter / March / Centaur / Antelope / Hollywood in winter / Orpheus circuit / Aquamarine / Hell / Vast halos.

— a different HEX released stuff for the 'Ninja Tune' label

JACK FROST

— formed by **STEVE KILBEY + GRANT McLENNAN** (ex-GO-BETWEENS) with **RUSSELL KILBEY** – keyboards, vocals

Arista / not iss.

Mar 91. (cd/c/lp) *(261/411/211 354)* **JACK FROST** -
– Every hour God sends / Birdowner (as seen on TV) / Civil war lament / Geneva 4 a.m. / Trapeze boy / Providence / Thought I was over you / Threshold / Number eleven / Didn't know where I was / Rauble / Everything takes forever. *(cd+=)*– Even as we speak.

Beggars Banquet / Beggars Banquet

Apr 96. (cd) *(BEGL 183CD)* *<80183>* **SNOW JOB** Aug96
– Jack Frost blues / Aviatrix / Running from the body / Shakedown / You don't know / Weightless and wild / Pony express / Cousin – Angel / Little song / Empire / Angela Carter / Haze / Dry dock.

PETER KOPPES

— solo, featuring his wife **MELODY, KILBEY + PLOOG**

1984. (7") *E.M.I.; (A 1249)* **LOVE CAN'T IMAGINE. / SHOW ME THAT** - - Austra
1987. (12") *Session; (SREP 001)* **WHEN REASON FORBIDS** - - Austra
May 88. (lp) *Session; (SRLP 002) / Rykodisc; <RLP 20046>* **MANCHILD & MYTH**
– Take a vow / These three things / The wise and the wicked / What's the matter? / Quest / Comes as no surprise / Opus / Sahara / The Colosseum / A drink from the cup / Into the bright light / Let you walk away / Our love. *(cd-iss. Mar94 on 'Rykodisc'; RCD 20046)*
1989. (lp) *T.V.T.; <TVT 2460>* **FROM THE WELL** -
Jan 98. (cd) *Worldwater; (WW 1)* **WATER RITES** -
Jan 98. (cd) *Immersion; (IMM 001CD)* **LOVE ERA / IRONY** -

MARTY WILLSON-PIPER

Chase / not iss.

1987. (lp) *(451038)* **IN REFLECTION** - - Austra

Survival / Rykodisc

1988. (7") *(652891.7)* **SHE'S KING. / FRIGHTENED JUST BECAUSE OF YOU** - - Austra
1988. (lp) *(462450.1)* *<RLP 0042>* **ART ATTACK** -
(<cd-iss. Mar94 on 'Rykodisc'; RCD 10042>)

Borderline / Rykodisc

1989. (lp) *(BL 001)* *<RLP 10114>* **RHYME** -
– St. Germain / Melancholy girl / Questions without answers / Melody of the rain / Idiots / Forever (with BOBBY WOMACK) / Say / Time is imaginary / How can I help it / Melancholy god / To where I am now / Cascade. *(<cd-iss. Mar94 on 'Rykodisc'; RCD 10114>)*

Rykodisc / Rykodisc

Jul 92. (cd-s) *<(RCD 51025)>* **I CAN'T CRY / LUSCIOUS GHOST**
Jul 92. (cd) *<(RCD 10197)>* **SPIRIT LEVEL**
– I can't cry / Will I start to bleed / Turn away to the stars / Luscious ghost / Scandivanian stare / Can't ever risk an openess with you / Even though you are my friend / Adelle Yvonne / The saddest house in Stockholm / Kiss you to death / Melts my heart.

CIBO MATTO

Formed: New York City, New York, USA . . . 1994 out of LEITOH LYCHEE (aka "Frozen Lychee Nut") by Japanese-born females, MIHO HATORI and YUKA HONDA, the latter an ex-member of the BROOKLYN FUNK ESSENTIALS, the former from Tokyo rap act, KIMIDORI. Translated from the Italian as "food madness", CIBO MATTO became the toast of NY trendies as they gigged around the capital, the hype generated seeing the duo sign to 'Warners' after a couple of independent singles. Early in '96, the girls unleashed their debut album, 'VIVA! LA WOMAN', wherein music was truly the food of love as HATORI and HONDA paid tribute to culinary delights in cryptic franglais against a colourful, often surreal trip-hop/indie collage of beats and samples. • **Covered:** BLACK HOLE SUN (Soundgarden) / AGUAS DE MARCO (Antonio Carlos Jobim) / SING THIS ALL TOGETHER (Rolling Stones).

Album rating: VIVA! LA WOMAN (*7) / SUPER RELAX mini (*6)

MIHO HATORI – vocals / **YUKA HONDA** – keyboards, programmer / **RUSSELL SIMINS** – drums (of JON SPENCER BLUES EXPLOSION) guests

not iss. / El Diablo

1995. (7") **BIRTHDAY CAKE. /** -
1995. (7") **KNOW YOUR CHICKEN. /** -
1996. (cd-ep) **CIBO MATTO EP** -
– Know your chicken / Black hole sun / etc

Warners / Warners

Mar 96. (cd/c/lp) *<(9362 45989-2/-4/-1)>* **VIVA! LA WOMAN** Jan96
– Apple / Beef jerky / Sugar water / White pepper ice cream / Birthday cake / Know your chicken / Theme / The candy man / Le pain perdu / Artichoke.
Jul 96. (c-s) *(W 0356C)* **KNOW YOUR CHICKEN. / ('A'mix)** -
(cd-s+=) *(W 0356CD)* – ('A'mixes).
Jan 97. (12"ep/cd-ep) *<(I-/2-46478)>* **SUPER RELAX EP**
– Sugar water (Morricone mix) / Sugar water (Morricone version) / Spoon / BBQ / Aguas de Marco / Sing this all together / Sugar water / Crumbs / Sugar water (Morricone extended).

CINDYTALK

Formed: London, England . . . 1984 as studio outfit by vocalist, GORDON SHARPE and guitarist, DAVID CLANCY, both ex-members of young Edinburgh punk outfit, The FREEZE. After only a few independently released singles (namely 'IN COLOUR' and 'CELEBRATION'), they broke up with SHARPE subsequently lending his services to '4 a.d.' conglomerate, THIS MORTAL COIL. Around the same time (1984), he and CLANCY (alongside JOHN BYRNE and KINNISON) resurfaced with a brand new venture, CINDYTALK, a debut album, 'CAMOUFLAGE HEART', being poorly received by critics and public alike due to its impenetrable CLOCKDVA-esque experimentation. However, SHARPE did return to the studio after a three year absence, completing the much improved follow-up double-set, 'IN THIS WORLD' (1988). ALIK and DEBBIE WRIGHT had now taken the place of CLANCY and KINNISON, the new line-up contributing to a refined ambient atmospheric sound incorporating SHARPE's distinctive harsh vocal incantations. An album in 1991, 'THE WIND IS STRONG' was another marked progression, although this in turn was surpassed with the long awaited 1996 effort, 'WAPPINSCHAW'. The album was a return to his Scottish roots and featured readings by long-time SNP affiliated novelist, Alisdair Gray, while references were made to outsider heroes like Sitting Bull and Wolfe Tone among others. • **Songwriters:** SHARPE except traditional, 'HUSH'.

Album rating: CAMOUFLAGE HEART (*2) / IN THIS WORLD (*5) / THE WIND IS STRONG (*5) / WAPPINSCHAW (*6)

FREEZE

GORDON SHARPE – vocals / **DAVID CLANCY** – guitar, vocals / **KEITH GRANT** – bass, vocals / **GRAEME RADIN** – drums

A1 — not iss.

Aug 79. (7"ep) *(A 11)* **IN COLOUR**
– Paranoia / For J.P.'s / Psychodalek nightmares.

Apr 80. (7") *(A 11 S1)* **CELEBRATION. / CROSS-OVER**

— split in 1981. A few years later, SHARPE guested for 4ad conglomerate THIS MORTAL COIL. He provided vox for the track 'KANGAROO' (a cover taken from BIG STAR) on album 'It'll End In Tears'.

CINDYTALK

GORDON SHARPE – vocals, piano / **DAVID CLANCY** – guitar / **JOHN BYRNE** – bass / **KINNISON** – drums

Midnight Music — not iss.

Sep 84. (lp) *(CHIME 00.065)* **CAMOUFLAGE HEART**
– It's luxury / Instinct (backtosense) / Under glass / Memories of skin and snow / The spirit behind the circus dream / The ghost never smiles / A second breath / Everybody is Christ / Disintigrate . . . *(cd-iss. 1988; CHIME 006CD) (cd re-iss. Oct96 on 'Touch'; TOUCH 3CD)*

— **SHARPE** with **BYRNE** – instruments / **ALIK WRIGHT** – instruments / **DEBBIE WRIGHT** – vocals, instruments

Mar 88. (d-lp/cd) *(CHIME 027/028CD)* **IN THIS WORLD**
– In this world / Janey's love / Gift of a knife / Playtime / The room of delight / Touched / Circle of shit / My sun / The beginning of wisdom / No serenade / Sight after sight / Angels of ghosts / Through water / Cherish / Homeless / Still whisper / In this world. *(cd re-iss. Oct96 on 'Touch'; TOUCH 2CD)*

Jan 91. (lp/c/cd) *(CHIME 103/+CC/CD)* **THE WIND IS STRONG**
– Landing / First sight / To the room / Waiting / Through flowers / Second sight / Through the forest / Arrival / Is there a room for hire / Choked I / Choked II / Dream ritual / Fuck you Mrs. Grimace / On snow moor / Angel wings.

Jan 94. (12"/cd-s) *(DONG 76/+CD)* **SECRETS & FALLING**

Touch — not iss.

Oct 96. (7") *(FEEL 001)* **PRINCE OF LIES. / MUSTER**
(cd-s) *(TOUCHED 1)* –

Oct 96. (lp/cd) *(TOUCH/+CD 1)* **WAPPINSCHAW**
– A song of changes / Empty hand / Return to pain / Wheesht / Snow kisses / Secrets and falling / Disappear / Traum lose nacht / And now in sunshine / Prince of lies / Hush.

CINERAMA (see under ⇒ WEDDING PRESENT)

CIRCLE JERKS

Formed: Los Angeles, California, USA . . . 1980 by former BLACK FLAG frontman, KEITH MORRIS along with ex-REDD KROSS guitarist, GREG HUTSON, who recruited ROGER ROGERSON and LUCKY LEHRER. Holed up in their Hawthorne, California garage, they set the tone for the rest of their career by recording their debut album, 'GROUP SEX' (1981), a frenetic burst of primal hardcore and adolescent humour. After appearing in that year's docu-film 'Decline Of Western Civilization', the guys were brought to the attention of POLICE manager, Miles Copeland, his 'Faulty' label (licensed to 'Step Forward' in the UK) issuing the follow-up 'WILD IN THE STREETS' (1982). By this point, ex-DOA drummer, CHUCK BISCUITS replaced LEHRER; he was in turn replaced by JOHN INGRAM prior to the mini compilation album, 'GOLDEN SHOWER OF HITS', featuring the title track medley of crooning standards by PAUL ANKA, BACHARACH & DAVID, etc. Other notable tracks included 'COUP D'ETAT' and 'WHEN THE SHIT HITS THE FAN', both surprise inclusions on the soundtrack to cult 1984 movie, 'Repo Man'. Like many of their hardcore/punk peers, The CIRCLE JERKS changed direction into heavy TWISTED SISTER/DICTATORS-like metal as the thrash and speed scene began to gather momentum in the mid to late 80's. With ZANDER SCHLOSS and KEITH CLARK now coming in as the new rhythm section, the 'JERKS made two further albums, 'WONDERFUL' (1985) and 'VI' (1987) for metal labels 'Combat' and 'Roadrunner' respectively. While they continued to tour the States, they virtually abandoned studio work, that is, until 1995's major label debut, 'ODDITIES, ABNORMALITIES AND CURIOSITIES', infamous for its cover of the Soft Boys' 'I WANNA DESTROY YOU' featuring pop starlet DEBBIE GIBSON on lead vocals.

Album rating: GROUP SEX (*6) / WILD IN THE STREETS (*7) / GOLDEN SHOWER OF HITS compilation (*8) / WONDERFUL (*3) / VI (*6) / ODDITIES, ABNORMALITIES AND CURIOSITIES (*4)

KEITH MORRIS – vocals (ex-BLACK FLAG) / **GREG HUTSON** – guitar (ex-RED CROSS) / **ROGER ROGERSON** (b. DOWDING) – bass / **LUCKY LEHRER** – drums

not iss. — Frontier

Feb 81. (lp) *<FLP 1002>* **GROUP SEX**
– Deny everything / I just want some skank / Beverly Hills / Operation / Back against the wall / Wasted / Behind the door / World up my ass / Paid vacation / Don't care / Live fast die young / What's your problem / Group sex / Red tape. *(UK-iss.Aug88 on 'Weird Systems' lp/cd; WS 031/+YZ) (re-iss. May92 cd/c/lp; 4600-2L/4L/1L) (cd re-iss. Aug92 & Apr97 +=; FCD 1002)* – WILD IN THE STREETS *(re-iss. Jun97 cd/c/lp; 0101-2/-4/-1)*

— **CHUCK BISCUITS** – drums (ex-DOA) repl. LEHRER

Step Forward — Faulty

Jul 82. (lp) *(SFLP 8) <COPE 3>* **WILD IN THE STREETS**
– Wild in the streets / Leave me alone / Stars and stripes / 86' D (good as gone) / Meet the press / Trapped / Murder the disturbed / Letter bomb / Question authority / Defamation innuendo / Moral majority / Forced labor / Political Stu / Just like me / Put a little love in your heart. *(re-iss. May92 on 'Frontier' cd/c/lp; 4617-2L/4L/1L) (re-iss. Jun97 on 'Frontier' cd/c/lp; 0105-2/-4/-1)*

— **JOHN INGRAM** – drums repl. BISCUITS who later joined DANZIG

not iss. — Allegience

1983. (lp) *<72874>* **GOLDEN SHOWER OF HITS**
– In your eyes / Parade of the horribles / Under the gun / When the shit hits the fan / Bad words / Red blanket room / High price on our heads / Coup d'etat / Product of my environment / Rats of reality / Junk mail / Golden shower of hits.

— **ZANDER 'Snake' SCHLOSS** – bass repl. ROGERSON

— **KEITH 'Adolph' CLARK** – drums repl. INGRAM

Rough Justice — Combat

Dec 85. (lp) *(JUST 1) <8048>* **WONDERFUL**
– Wonderful / Firebaugh / Making the bombs / Mrs. Jones / Dude / American heavy metal weekend / I & I / Crowd / Killing for Jesus / Karma stew / 15 minutes / Rook house / Another broken heart for Snake.

Roadrunner — Combat

Nov 87. (lp) *(RR 9584)* **VI**
– Beat me senseless / Patty's killing me / Casualty vampire / Tell me why / Protection / I'm alive / Status clinger / Living / American way / Fortunate son / Love kills / All wound up / I don't. *(cd-iss. Mar90 on 'Roadracer'; RO 9584-2)*

— now without ZANDER who joined The WEIRDOS and JOE STRUMMER (ex-Clash). The CIRCLE JERKS subsequently split until 1995

not iss. — Mercury

Jun 95. (cd/c/lp) **ODDITIES, ABNORMALITIES AND CURIOSITIES**

– compilations, etc. –

1992. (cd) **GIG (live)**

CIRCUS LUPUS

Formed: Washington DC, USA . . . early 90's by CHRIS THOMPSON, CHRIS HAMELY, SETH LORINCZI and ARIKA CASEBOLT. Not typical of the standard 'Dischord' fare, to whom they were signed, CIRCUS LUPUS first made their mark in Spring '92 with the 'SUPER GENIUS' set. Produced by ELI JANNEY (of GIRLS AGAINST BOYS fame), the record found favour with the US college circuit, although it would be the JOAN JETT-produced single, 'POPMAN', that defined their musical independence. The following year, they roped in producer, Don Zientara, who worked on the band's second and final long-player, 'SOLID BRASS'.

Album rating: SUPER GENIUS (*5) / SOLID BRASS (*5)

CHRIS THOMPSON – vocals / **CHRIS HAMELY** – guitar / **SETH LORINCZI** – bass, guitar / **ARIKA CASEBOLT** – drums

Dischord — Dischord

May 92. (cd/c/lp) *<(DIS 63 CD/C/V)>* **SUPER GENIUS**
– Unrequited / Cyclone Billy / Pacifier / Breaking point / Straight through the heart / Marbles / Mean hot & blessed / Cat kicking jerk / Blue baby / Amish blessing / Pulp.

Sep 92. (7") *<(DIS 73V)>* **POPMAN. / PRESSURE POINT**

Mar 93. (7"; shared with CRAIN) *(CPS 3)* **CIRCUS LUPUS & CRAIN E.P.**
(above issued on 'Compulsive')

Jul 93. (cd/c/lp) *<(DIS 79 CD/C/V)>* **SOLID BRASS**
– Turn right circle / 7 x 4 x 1 / I always thought you were an asshole / And you won / New cop car / Texas minute / Deviant gesture catalog / Takes about an hour: Epilepsy / Pop man / Heather / Pressure point. *(cd+/c+=)* – Popman (version).

— disbanded after above

CITIZEN FISH (see under ⇒ SUBHUMANS)

CITIZENS' UTILITIES

Formed: Seattle, Washington, USA . . . mid 90's by JOSHUA MEDARIS, BILL HERZOG, CHAD SHAVER and ERIKE AKRE, all four sharing vocal duties on their post-grunge, roots-rock debut, 'LOST AND FLOUNDERED' (1996). An unlikely signing to 'Mute', CITIZENS' UTILITIES were yet another band to take their inspiration from the country-flavoured sonic alchemy of NEIL YOUNG & CRAZY HORSE. Produced by STEVE BERLIN (ex-LOS LOBOS), it was given another chance in Britain the following year under the title of 'NO MORE MEDICINE'.

Album rating: LOST AND FLOUNDERED (*5) / NO MORE MEDICINE (*5)

BILL HERZOG (b. 5 Jul'67) – vocals, bass / **JOSHUA MEDARIS** (b.15 Oct'65) – vocals, guitar / **CHAD SHAVER** – guitar, vocals / **ERIKE AKRE** (b.11 Jun'70) – drums, vocals

Mute / Mute America

Nov 96. (cd) *(CDSTUMM 135)* <9014> **LOST AND FLOUNDERED** ☐ ☐ May96
– She taught me everything there is to know about poultry / Call it your own / Anderson / Northern lights / Heave away / Bottleneck / Anytime – Anywhere / Parts per million / Lunger / They had no peers (up to here) / Idaho / Remnant king / When the heater's on / No more medicine. *(re-iss. Sep97 as 'NO MORE MEDICINE'; CDSTUMM 166)*

CIV

Formed: New York, USA . . . 1993 out of GORILLA BISCUITS – a band of several years who released two albums in the late 80's – by frontman, ANTHONY CIVARELLI (proprietor of a tattoo parlour in Long Island), ARTHUR and SAMMY. Recruiting former OUTFACE member, CHARLIE, CIV (pronounced 'Sieve') began making a name for themselves around the city prior to the release of their debut album, 'SET YOUR GOALS' (1995). Produced by CIVARELLI's former QUICKSAND mucker, WALTER SCHREIFELS (who would also contribute songs), the record showcased the band's hardcore rockabilly behind the frontman's straight-talking streetwise lyrics. The band were also infamous for wearing garish lame suits on stage, the sharp image doing them no harm in securing a record deal with Atlantic subsidiary, 'Lava'. An enhanced version of their first set added a handful of previously unreleased tracks, the major label backing making sure both the album and re-issued single, CAN'T WAIT ONE MORE MINUTE', reached a wider audience. However, it would be three years before a bonafide follow-up, 'THIRTEEN DAY GETAWAY' (1998), featuring an unlikely cover of the Small Faces' 'ITCHYCOO PARK'.

Album rating: SET YOUR GOALS (*7) / THIRTEEN DAY GETAWAY (*6)

GORILLA BISCUITS

CIV (b. ANTHONY CIVARELLI) – vocals / **WALLY** – guitar / **ARTHUR** – bass / **LUTHER CAMPBELL** – drums

We Bite / Revelation

1988. (lp/c/cd) <REV 4 1/4/2> **GORILLA BISCUITS** [-] ☐
– High hopes / Big mouth / No reason why / Gm2 / Hold your ground / Breaking free / Finish what you started / Sitting aroiund at home / Gorilla biscuits / Short end of the stick / Hold your ground 1 / Gm2 1.

—— added **ALEX** – guitar

Nov 89. (lp/c/cd) *(086-103)* <REV 12 1/4/2> **START TODAY** ☐ ☐
– New direction / Stand still / Degradation / Good intentions / Forgotten / The things we say / Start today / Two sides / First failure / Competition / Time flies / Cats and dogs.

—— ARTHUR subsequently joined TOKEN ENTRY before reunited with CIV

CIV

—— **CIV** – vocals / **CHARLIE** – guitar (ex-OUTFACE) / **ARTHUR** – bass / **SAMMY** – drums (ex-YOUTH OF TODAY, ex-SHELTER)

Revelation / not iss.

Apr 95. (lp) *(REV 041LP)* **SET YOUR GOALS** ☐ [-]
– Set your goals / Do something / Social climber / Don't gotta prove it / Soundtrack for violence / Et tu brute? / Gang opinion / So far, so good . . . so what? / Trust slips through your hands.

May 95. (7") *(REV 41)* **ALL TWISTED. / PUNK HAIRCUTS** ☐ [-]
(cd-s+=) *(REV 41-2)* – Can't wait one more minute.

Lava – Atlantic / Lava – Atlantic

Oct 95. (cd/c) <(7567 92603-2/-4)> **SET YOUR GOALS** ☐ ☐
– Set your goals / So far, so good . . . so what / State of grace / Can't wait one more minute / Trust slips through your hands / Gang opinion / Choices made / Solid bond / Marching goals / United kids / Soundtrack for violence / Boring summer / Et tu brute? / All twisted / Don't got to prove it.

Dec 95. (7"/c-s) *(A 8154/+C)* **CAN'T WAIT ONE MORE MINUTE. / GLUE** ☐ ☐
(cd-s+=) *(A 8154CD)* –

Jan 96. (cd-s) *(A 8127C)* **CHOICES MADE / UNITED TRACKS – SOUNDTRACK FOR VIOLENCE** ☐ [-]
(cd-s+=) *(A 8127CD)* – ('A'side) / Trust slips through your hands (live) / Can't wait one more minute (live) / Don't got to prove it (live).

Apr 96. (7"/c-s) *(A 5682/+C)* **SO FAR, SO GOOD . . .SO WHAT. / CHOICES MADE** ☐ ☐
(cd-s+=) *(A 5682CD)* – Soundtrack for violence / United kids / All twisted.

Aug 96. (7") *(REV 55)* **SOCIAL CLIMBER. / SAUSAGES?** ☐ [-]
(above issued on 'Revelation') (below issued on 'Some Record')

Apr 98. (7") *(SOM 05)* **SECONDHAND SUPERSTAR. /** ☐ [-]

Aug 98. (cd) <(7567 83073-2)> **THIRTEEN DAY GETAWAY** ☐ ☐
– Secondhand superstar / Big girl / Itchycoo park / Haven't been myself in a while / Everyday / Shout it / Owner's manual / Something special / Using something else / It's not your fault / Living life / Ordinary / Little men.

Anne CLARK

Born: Croydon, London, England. An up and coming poet of the early 80's, ANNE issued her debut, German-only album 'THE SITTING ROOM' in 1982, a set that featured fellow wordsmith, PATRIK FITZGERALD as well as keyboard accompaniment from DOMINIC APPLETON (of BREATHLESS). Subsequently signing to 'Red Flame', CLARK enlisted the help of VINI REILLY (of DURUTTI COLUMN) and DAVID HARROW to augment her on her second set, 'CHANGING PLACES' (1983). Combining her poetic works with other more conventional songs, she went on to record for the Red Flame offshoot imprint, 'Ink', where she worked with the RAVISHING BEAUTIES (i.e. VIRGINIA ASTLEY, etc) on a mini-set, 'JOINED UP WRITING' (1984). With her haunting, emotive alternative-pop finaly getting noticed by the major labels, CLARK moved up to Virgin offshoot, '10' for further sets, the JOHN FOXX-produced 'PRESSURE POINTS' (1985), 'HOPELESS CASES' (1987) and 'R.S.V.P.' (1988). More popular on the continent (especially Germany and Norway), the sultry blonde singer/poetess continued to record into the 90's without ever rising above cult status in her home country. Nevertheless she did form writing and musical partnerships with English peers, EYELESS IN GAZA and ANDY BELL (ex-RIDE), while also taking on covers of 60's standards, 'IF I COULD' and 'THE WINDMILLS OF YOUR MIND'.

Album rating: THE SITTING ROOM (*5) / CHANGING PLACES (*5) / JOINED UP WRITING mini (*4) / PRESSURE POINTS (*5) / HOPELESS CASES (*5) / R.S.V.P. (*4) / AN ORDINARY LIFE compilation (*6) / UNSTILL LIFE (*5) / PSYCHOMETRY (*4) / THE LAW IS AN ANAGRAM OF WEALTH (*4) / TO LOVE AND BE LOVED (*5) / THE NINETIES compilation (*5)

ANNE CLARK – vocals, keyboards / with **DOMINIC APPLETON** – keyboards / **ANDREA LASCHETTI** – keyboards / **PATRIK FITZGERALD** – piano / **GARY MUNDY** – guitar, synthesizer, vocals

unknown / not iss.

1982. (lp) *(206865)* **THE SITTING ROOM** [-] [-] German
– The sitting room / Swimming / An ordinary life / Shades / Short story / The power game / All we have to be thankful for.

—— now augmented by **DAVID HARROW** – keyboards / **VINI REILLY** – guitar (of DURUTTI COLUMN)

Red Flame / not iss.

Aug 83. (lp) *(RF 22)* **CHANGING PLACES** ☐ [-]
– Contact / Sleeper in Metropolis / Poem for a nuclear romance / Wallies / Lovers audition / Poets turmoil No.364 / Echoes remain forever / All night party / Pandora's box / Feel / The last emotion.

—— now with **HARROW** / + **VIRGINIA ASTLEY** – keyboards, vocals / **JO WELLS** – keyboards, vocals, clarinet / **ANNE STEPHENSON** – violin / **NICK PRETZEL** – drums, electro-percussion / **NICK COOK** – vocals

Ink / not iss.

Sep 84. (m-lp) *(MINK 5)* **JOINED UP WRITING** ☐ [-]
– Nothing at all / Weltschmerz / Killing time / True love tales / Self destruct / Our darkness.

Nov 84. (12") *(INK12-5)* **OUR DARKNESS. / THE SITTING ROOM / THE SITTING ROOM (LATER ON)** ☐ [-]

Jun 85. (12") *(INK12-13)* **SLEEPER IN METROPLOIS (extended). / SELF DESTRUCT** ☐ [-]

—— next with **ASTLEY, HARROW + CHARLIE MORGAN** – drums

10-Virgin / not iss.

Jul 85. (7") *(TEN 79)* **HEAVEN. / BURSTING** ☐ [-]

Nov 85. (lp/c) *(XID/CXID 18)* **PRESSURE POINTS** ☐ [-]
– Heaven / Red sands / Alarm call / Tide / The interruption / The power game / World without warning / Bursting / Lovers retreat. *(cd iss. Aug86; DIXCD 8)*

Feb 87. (lp/c/cd) *(DIX/CDIX/DIXCD 48)* **HOPELESS CASES** ☐ [-]
– Poem without words 1 – The 3rd meeting / Homecoming / Up / Cane Hill / This must be the verse / Now will you be good? / Hope road / Armchair theatre / Leaving / Poem without words 2 – Journey by night.

Apr 87. (7") *(TEN 167)* **HOPE ROAD (A-Z ROUTE). / POEM WITHOUT WORDS 1 – THE 3rd MEETING** ☐ [-]
(12"+=) *(TENT 167)* – Heaven (live).

—— her live band were:- **MORGAN** / + **GORDON REANEY** – guitar, vocals / **RICK KENTON** – keyboards, bass / **NED MORANT** – percussion

May 88. (lp/c/cd) *(DIX/CDIX/DIXCD 72)* **R.S.V.P. (live)** ☐ [-]
– Up / Homecoming / Red sands / The power game / Cane hill / Leaving / Heaven / The last emotion / Killing time / Wallies / Our darkness / Now will you be good? / This is the verse / Sleeper in Metropolis.

—— retained **MORGAN** and enlisted several musicians

S.P.V. / not iss.

1991. (cd) *(SPV 084-88362)* **UNSTILL LIFE** [-] [-] German
– The moment / Sognsvann / The spiining turning of the summer earth / Ice, moving (instrumental) / White silence / Makes me feel at ease / Empty me / Nida / Counter act / Abuse / Silent prayer / Closed circuit.

1993. (cd) *(SPV 084-89282)* **PSYCHOMETRY** [-] [-] German

1994. (cd) *(SPV 084-92702)* **THE LAW IS AN ANAGRAM OF WEALTH** [-] [-] German

Oct 95. (cd) *(SPV 085-89542)* **TO LOVE AND BE LOVED** ☐ [-]
– Dream made real / Mundesley beach / Letter of tanks to a friend / Healing / Acropolis / Key / Painting / Athens / Virtuality / Elegy for a lost summer.

– compilations, others, etc. –

Sep 85. (12") *Ink; (INK12-16)* **WALLIES. /** ☐ [-]

Mar 86. (12") *Ink; (INK12-18)* **TRUE LOVE TALES. /** ☐ [-]

Aug 88. (cd) *Ink; (INKCD 001)* **TRILOGY** ☐ [-]

– (CHANGING PLACES / THE SITTING ROOM / JOINED UP WRITING).

Nov 90. (cd/c/lp) *Great Expectations; (PIP CD/MC/LP 017)* **AN ORDINARY LIFE** ☐ -
– Sleeper in Metropolis / Self destruct / Wallies / True love tales / Our darkness / The sitting room / All night party / Echoes remain forever (with BOBBY WOMACK) / An ordinary life / Shades / Killing time / Our darkness (alt.mix) / Weltschmerz / Nothing at all / Our darkness (12"mix).

Feb 97. (cd) *S.P.V.; (SPV 085-44632)* **THE NINETIES (A FINE COLLECTION)** ☐ -
– Abuse / Counter act / Empty me / If I could / Windmills of your mind / Haunted road / Fragility / Seize the vivid sky / Elegy for a lost summer / Echoes remain forever / Dream made real / Letter of thanks to a friend / Our darkness / Sleeper in Metropolis.

John Cooper CLARKE

Born: 25 Jan'49, Salford, Manchester, England. After beginning his career in the city's folk clubs, where he met and subsequently hooked up with RICK GOLDSTRAW and his band The FERRETS, self-styled "punk poet" CLARKE signed to the independent 'Rabid' label, releasing his debut EP, 'INNOCENTS', in 1977. Recited in a heavy Manc accent, CLARKE's pulverising but witty and often hilarious verbal assaults saw him adopted by the embryonic punk scene, his uncompromising attitude and disregard for standard poetry mores drawing comparisons with the 50's Beats and influencing such early 80's wordsmiths as ATILLA THE STOCKBROKER and SEETHING WELLS. After touring with BE-BOP DELUXE in 1978, CLARKE secured a deal with 'Epic' and released a debut album, 'DISGUISE IN LOVE' (1978). Produced by BILL NELSON and with musical backing from The INVISIBLE GIRLS, the record kicked off with 'I DON'T WANT TO BE NICE', a tongue-in-cheek rant for the teenager in all of us. It also featured '(I MARRIED A) MONSTER FROM OUTER SPACE', a comment on racial prejudice via a highly amusing tale of intergalactic love as well as masturbation ode, 'READERS WIVES', set of course, to a mellow piano groove. He scored his first and only Top 40 single with 'GIMMIX!' early the following year, yet CLARKE wasn't so popular with music critics who saw him as an extension of the emerging alternative comedy scene. Live work was certainly his forte, CLARKE releasing his first live set, 'WALKING BACK TO HAPPINESS' later that summer, the record boasting one of his most vicious broadsides, 'TWAT', apparently dedicated to leading Tarzan Tory, Michael Heseltine. In 1980, the quick-fire Bard Of Broadsides toured with reggae poet LINTON KWESI JOHNSON and appeared in The Poetry Olympics at Westminster Abbey. That year's, 'SNAP, CRACKLE & BOP', was an altogether more accomplished collection, drawing praise for such gritty pieces as 'BEASLEY STREET'. While the album made the UK Top 30, CLARKE's career subsequently went into decline with third and final studio set, 'ZIP STYLE METHOD' (1982) issued to a muted response. The poet succumbed to drug abuse as the decade wore on, co-habiting with fellow addict NICO. Overcoming his problems, the 90's found CLARKE once again venturing onto the stage although new material has yet to surface. • **Trivia:** Late in 1982, his docu-film, 'TEN YEARS IN AN OPEN NECKED SHIRT' (based on his book of the same name), was seen on UK-TV Channel 4.

Album rating: ME AND MY BIG MOUTH compilation (*7)

JOHN COOPER CLARKE – words, vocals / with The INVISIBLE GIRLS: **MARTIN HANNETT** – bass, producer / **PAUL BURGESS** – drums / **JOHN SCOTT** – guitar / **LYN OAKLEY** – guitar / guest **PETE SHELLEY** – guitar (of BUZZCOCKS) / **STEVE HOPKINS** – keyboards

Rabid not iss.

Oct 77. (7"ep) *(TOSH 103)* **INNOCENTS** ☐ -
– Psycle sluts (part 1 & 2) / Innocents / Suspended sentence. *(re-Sep82; same)*

—— solo with backing musicians, (INVISIBLE GIRLS)

Epic not iss.

Aug 78. (7") *(EPC 6541)* **POST-WAR GLAMOUR GIRLS. / KUNG FU INTERNATIONAL (live)** ☐ -

Oct 78. (lp) *(EPC 83132)* **DISGUISE IN LOVE** ☐ -
– I don't want to be nice / Psycle sluts 1 & 2 / (I've got a brand new) Tracksuit / Teenage werewolf / Readers wives / Post war glamour girl / (I married a) Monster from Outer Space / Salome Maloney / Health fanatic / Strange bed fellows / Valley of the lost women. *(cd-iss. Jun95; 480530-2)*

Feb 79. (7"/7"sha-orange-d) *(EPC/+12 7009)* **GIMMIX! (PLAY LOUD). / I MARRIED A MONSTER FROM OUTER SPACE (third version)** 39 -

Jun 79. (10"clear-lp) *(JCC 1)* **WALKING BACK TO HAPPINESS** ☐ -
– Gaberdine Angus / Majorca / Bronze adonis / Twat / The pest / Who stole the marble index / Gimmix! (play loud) / Nothing / Spilt beans.

Oct 79. (7") *(EPC 7982)* **SPLAT. / TWAT. / SLEEPWALK** ☐ -
(above 'A'side was double grooved to play 2 tracks)

Apr 80. (lp) *(EPC 84083)* **SNAP, CRACKLE & BOP** 26 -
– Evidently Chickentown / Conditional discharge / Sleepwalk / 23rd / Beasley Street / 36 hours / Belladonna / The it man / Limbo / A distant relation. *(cd-iss. Sep94; 477380-2)*

May 80. (7") *(EPC 8655)* **THE IT MAN. / 36 HOURS** ☐ -

May 81. (lp) *(EPC 84979)* **ME AND MY BIG MOUTH** (compilation) ☐ -
– I married a monster from Outer Space / I don't want to be nice / Valley of the lost women / 36 hours / The it man / Kung Fu international / Twat / Majorca / Bronze Adonis / Gimmix! (play loud) / Beasley Street.

Apr 82. (7") *(EPC 2077)* **THE DAY MY PAD WENT MAD. / A DISTANT RELATION** ☐ -

May 82. (lp) *(EPC 85667)* **ZIP STYLE METHOD** 97 -
– Midnight shift / The new assassin / Face behind the scream / I travel in biscuits / The day the world stood still / A heart disease called love / The ghost of Al Capone / Ninety degrees in the shade / The day my pad went mad / I wanna be yours / Drive she said / Night people.

Jun 82. (7") *(EPC 2521)* **NIGHT PEOPLE. / FACE BEHIND THE SCREAM** ☐ -

—— He retired from recording, but still recited occasionally. He lived with American girlfriend/singer NICO until her death on 18th July 1988. He went into TV-advertisements for Sugar Puffs, etc.

– compilations, others, etc –

Jul 80. (lp) *Rabid; (NOZE 1)* **OU EST LA MAISON DE FROMAGE?** ☐ -
– The serial (part 1) / Letter to Fiesta / Film extra's extra / Majorca / Action man / Kung Fu international / Sperm test / Missing persons / Spilt beans / Dumb row laughs / Bunch of twigs / Trains / The cycle accident / Gimmix / Reader's wives / Ten years in an open neck shirt (part 1) / Nothing / I married a monster from outer space / Ten years in an open neck shirt (part 2) / Daily express (you never see a nipple in) / Ten years in an open neck shirt (part 3) / Salome Malone / Psycle sluts (part 1). *(re-iss. Mar89 on 'Receiver'; RRLP 110) (cd-iss. Nov96; RRCD 110)*

CLASH

Formed: London, England ... early '76, by MICK JONES, PAUL SIMONON, JOE STRUMMER (ex-101'ers) and TERRY CHIMES (future PIL member, KEITH LEVENE, also had a brief spell). After a riotous tour supporting the SEX PISTOLS, their manager, BERNIE RHODES, attained a deal with major label big boys 'C.B.S.' in early '77 and subsequently unleashed the two minute classic, 'WHITE RIOT'. A driving chantalong stomp, the record smashed into the UK Top 40 and announced the arrival of a band whose influence and impact was second only to the 'PISTOLS. In contrast to LYDON and Co., The CLASH manipulated the energy of punk as a means of political protest and musical experimentation. 'THE CLASH' (1977) was a blinding statement of intent, a finely balanced masterwork of infectious hooklines and raging conviction. 'I'M SO BORED WITH THE U.S.A.' and 'CAREER OPPORTUNITIES' railed against inertia, while a cover of Junior Murvin's 'POLICE AND THIEVES' was the first of many sporadic forays into dub reggae. The album went Top 20, lauded by many critics as the definitive punk set, while a further two classic singles (not on the album), 'CLASH CITY ROCKERS' and 'WHITE MAN IN HAMMERSMITH PALAIS' made the Top 40 (the latter addressing the issue of racism, a subject never far from the band's agenda). CBS (and no doubt the band themselves) were keen to break America, subsequently enlisting the production services of BLUE OYSTER CULT guru, SANDY PERLMAN for follow-up set, 'GIVE 'EM ENOUGH ROPE' (1978). The album's more rockest, less frenetic approach met with some criticism and despite the label's best efforts, the record just failed to crack the American Top 100. It had, however, made No.2 in Britain and spawned the band's first Top 20 hit in 'TOMMY GUN'. The CLASH subsequently set out to tour the States, while British fans lapped up 'THE COST OF LIVING' EP and its incendiary cover of Sonny Curtis's 'I FOUGHT THE LAW'. Finally, in late '79, The CLASH delivered their marathon masterwork, 'LONDON CALLING'. Overseen by seasoned producer, Guy Stevens, the double set showed The CLASH at an assured creative peak, from the anthemic echo of the title track to the brooding 'GUNS OF BRIXTON'. A UK Top 10'er, it finally cracked the States (Top 30), its universal acclaim spurred them onto ever more ambitious endeavours. After the plangent dub of the 'BANKROBBER' and 'THE CALL-UP' singles, the band unleashed the sprawling, triple vinyl set, 'SANDINISTA!' in December 1980. The record's wildly experimental material met with critical pasting, the bulk of the album's tracks failing to withstand repeated listening. Its relatively poor sales (still at single vinyl price!) forced a back to basics rethink for 'COMBAT ROCK' (1982). Although the record was a healthy seller, it sounded laboured; ironically, it became The CLASH's biggest selling album in America, where the 'ROCK THE CASBAH' single made the Top 10. Drummer TOPPER HEADON was already long gone by this point and was replaced by CHIMES, who had left after the 1977 debut; JONES too, was kicked out the following year. The band stumbled on for a further album, 'CUT THE CRAP' in 1985, before finally disbanding the following month. While JONES enjoyed mid-80's success with BIG AUDIO DYNAMITE, STRUMMER embarked on a low key solo career before working with his pal SHANE MacGOWAN in The POGUES. The CLASH fever gripped the nation again in 1991 when 'SHOULD I STAY OR SHOULD I GO' (a Top 20 hit in 1983), hit the top of the charts after being used in a Levi jeans advert (what else!?). A best of double set, 'THE STORY OF THE CLASH VOL.1', flew off the shelves and rumours were rife of a CLASH reunion (unceremoniously quashed by STRUMMER). • **Songwriters:** Either STRUMMER / – JONES until 1980 group penned, except PRESSURE DROP (Maytals) / POLICE ON MY BACK (Equals) / ARMAGIDEON TIME (Willie Williams) / JUNCO PARTNER + ENGLISH CIVIL WAR (unknown trad) / EVERY LITTLE BIT HURTS (Ed Cobb) / BRAND NEW CADILLAC (Vince Taylor). • **Trivia:** Early in 1980, the band featured live in the docu-film 'Rude Boy' about a fictionalised CLASH roadie. JOE STRUMMER went into acting 1986 (Straight To Hell) / 1989 (Lost In Space).

Album rating: THE CLASH (*10) / GIVE 'EM ENOUGH ROPE (*8) / LONDON CALLING (*9) / SANDINISTA! (*7) / COMBAT ROCK (*6) / CUT THE CRAP (*4) / THE STORY OF THE CLASH, VOL.1 compilation (*9) / CLASH ON BROADWAY (*7) / SUPER BLACK MARKET CLASH (*7)

JOE STRUMMER (b. JOHN GRAHAM MELLOR, 21 Aug'52, Ankara, Turkey / raised London) – vocals, guitar (ex-101'ers) / **PAUL SIMONON** (b.15 Dec'55, Brixton, England) – bass, vocals / **MICK JONES** (b. MICHAEL JONES, 26 Jun'55) – guitar, vocals / **TORY CRIMES** (b. TERRY CHIMES, 25 Jan'55) – drums

C.B.S. Epic

Mar 77. (7") *(S-CBS 5058)* **WHITE RIOT. / 1977** 38 -

Apr 77. (lp/c) *(CBS/40 82000)* **THE CLASH** 12 -
– Janie Jones / Remote control / I'm so bored with the U.S.A. / White riot / Hate and war / What's my name / Deny / London's burning / Career oportunities / Cheat / Protex blue / Police and thieves / 48 hours / Garage land. *<US-iss.Aug79 on 'Epic'; 36060> (tracks differed & contained free 7")* – GROOVY TIMES. / GATES OF THE WEST *(this lp version UK-iss.Jan91 on cd) (re-iss. Nov82 lp/c; CBS/40 32232) (cd-iss. Apr89 on 'Columbia'; CD 32232) (cd re-iss. Aug91 on 'Columbia'; 468783-2)*

—— (Jan'77) (NICKY) **TOPPER HEADON** (b.30 May'55, Bromley, Kent, England) – drums; repl. CHIMES who later joined COWBOYS INTERNATIONAL and GENERATION X

May 77. (7") *(S-CBS 5293)* **REMOTE CONTROL. / LONDON'S BURNING (live)** -

Sep 77. (7") *(S-CBS 5664)* **COMPLETE CONTROL. / THE CITY OF THE DEAD** 28 -

Feb 78. (7") *(S-CBS 5834)* **CLASH CITY ROCKERS. / JAIL GUITAR DOORS** 35 -

Jun 78. (7") *(S-CBS 6383)* **(WHITE MAN) IN HAMMERSMITH PALAIS. / THE PRISONER** 32 -

Nov 78. (lp/c) *(CBS/40 82431)* *<35543>* **GIVE 'EM ENOUGH ROPE** 2 Feb79
– Safe European home / English civil war / Tommy gun / Julie's been working for the drug squad / Guns on the roof / Drug-stabbing time / Stay free / Cheapstakes / All the young punks (new boots and contracts). *(re-iss. 1984 lp/c; CBS/40 32444) (cd-iss. Jan91; CD 32444)*

Nov 78. (7") *(S-CBS 6788)* **TOMMY GUN. / 1, 2, CRUSH ON YOU** 19 -

Feb 79. (7") *(S-CBS 7082)* **ENGLISH CIVIL WAR. / PRESSURE DROP** 25 -

May 79. (7"ep) *(S-CBS 7324)* **THE COST OF LIVING** 22 -
– I fought the law / Groovy times / Gates of the west / Capital radio.

Jul 79. (7") *<50738>* **I FOUGHT THE LAW. / (WHITE MAN) IN HAMMERSMITH PALAIS** -

—— added on tour MICKEY GALLAGHER – keyboards (ex-IAN DURY)

Dec 79. (7") *(S-CBS 8087)* **LONDON CALLING. / ARMAGIDEON TIME** 11 -
(12"+=) *(CBS12 8087)* – Justice tonight (version) / Kick it over (version).

Dec 79. (d-lp/c) *(CLASH/+C 3)* *<36328>* **LONDON CALLING** 9 27 Jan80
– London calling / Brand new Cadillac / Jimmy Jazz / Hateful / Rudie can't fail / Wrong 'em boyo / Death or glory / Koka Kola / The card cheat / Spanish bombs / The right profile / Lost in the supermarket / The guns of Brixton / Lover's rock / Four horsemen / I'm not down / Revolution rock / Train in vain. *(re-iss. Feb88 on 'Columbia' d-lp/c; 460114-1/-4) (cd-iss. Apr89 on 'Columbia'; 460114-2)*

Mar 80. (7") *<50851>* **TRAIN IN VAIN (STAND BY ME). / LONDON CALLING** - 27

Aug 80. (7") *(S-CBS 8323)* **BANKROBBER. / Mickey Dread: ROCKERS GALORE . . . UK TOUR** 12 -

Nov 80. (7") *(S-CBS 9339)* **THE CALL-UP. / STOP THE WORLD** 40 -

Nov 80. (10"m-lp) *<36846>* **BLACK MARKET CLASH** - 74
– Time is tight / Capital radio / Bankrobber / Pressure drop / The prisoner / City of the dead / Justice tonight – kick it over (version). *(UK-iss.Sep91 on 'Columbia' cd/c; 468763-2/-4)*

Dec 80. (t-lp/d-c) *(CBS/40 FSLN 1)* *<37037>* **SANDINISTA!** 19 24
– The magnificent seven / Hitsville U.K. / Junco partner / Ivan meets G.I. Joe / The leader / Something about England / Rebel waltz / Look here / The crooked beat / Somebody got murdered / One more time / One more dub / Lightning strikes (not once but twice) / Up in Heaven (not only here) / Corner soul / Let's go crazy / If music could talk / The sound of the sinners / Police on my back / Midnight log / The equaliser / The call up / Washington bullets / Broadway / Lose this skin / Charlie don't surf / Mensforth Hill / Junkie slip / Kingston advice / The street parade / Version city / Living in fame / Silicone on sapphire / Version pardner / Career opportunites (version) / Shepherds delight. *(d-cd-iss. Apr89 on 'Columbia'; 463364-2)*

Jan 81. (7") *(S-CBS 9480)* **HITSVILLE U.K. / RADIO ONE** 56 -

Feb 81. (7") *<51013>* **HITSVILLE U.K. / POLICE ON MY BACK** -

Apr 81. (12"ep) *<02036>* **THE CALL-UP / THE COOL-OUT. / THE MAGNIFICENT SEVEN / THE MAGNIFICENT DANCE** -

Apr 81. (7"/12") *(A/+12 1133)* **THE MAGNIFICENT SEVEN. / THE MAGNIFICENT DANCE** 34 -

Nov 81. (7") *(A 1797)* **THIS IS RADIO CLASH. / RADIO CLASH** 47 -
(12"+=) *(A12 1797)* – Outside broadcast / Radio 5.

—— **TERRY CHIMES** returned to repl. HEADON who later went solo (signed to 'Mercury', released a couple of singles – 'DRUMMIN' MAN', LEAVE IT TO LUCK' and 'I'LL GIVE YOU EVERYTHING' – all from the 1986 album, 'WAKING UP', which featured 60's soul singer, JIMMY HELMS)

Apr 82. (7") *(A 2309)* **KNOW YOUR RIGHTS. / FIRST NIGHT BACK IN LONDON** 43 -

May 82. (lp/c) *(CBS/40 FMLN 2)* *<37689>* **COMBAT ROCK** 2 7
– Know your rights / Car jamming / Should I stay or should I go / Rock the Casbah / Red angel dragnet / Straight to Hell / Overpowered by funk / Atom tan / Sean Flynn / Ghetto defendant / Inoculated city / Death is a star. *(re-iss. Nov86 lp/c; CBS/40 32787) (cd-iss. Jan91 on 'Columbia'; CD 32787)*

May 82. (7") *<03006>* **SHOULD I STAY OR SHOULD I GO. / INNOCULATED CITY** -

Jun 82. (7"/7"pic-d) *(A/+11 2479)* *<03245>* **ROCK THE CASBAH. / LONG TIME JERK** 30 8 Sep82
(12") *(A12 2479)* – ('A'side) / Mustapha dance.

Jul 82. (7") *<03061>* **SHOULD I STAY OR SHOULD I GO. / FIRST NIGHT BACK IN LONDON** - 45

Sep 82. (7"/7"pic-d/12") *(A/+11/12 2646)* **SHOULD I STAY OR SHOULD I GO. / STRAIGHT TO HELL** 17 -

Feb 83. (7") *<03547>* **SHOULD I STAY OR SHOULD I GO? / COOL CONFUSION** - 50

—— (Feb83-Jan84) **STRUMMER & SIMONON** brought in new musicians **PETE HOWARD** – drums (ex-COLD FISH),repl. CHIMES who later joined HANOI ROCKS / **NICK SHEPHERD** – guitar (ex-CORTINAS) + **VINCE WHITE** – guitar; repl. JONES who formed BIG AUDIO DYNAMITE

Sep 85. (7") *(A 6122)* **THIS IS ENGLAND. / DO IT NOW** 24 -
(12"+=) *(A12 6122)* – Sex mad roar.

Nov 85. (lp/c) *(CBS/40 26601)* *<40017>* **CUT THE CRAP** 16 88
– Dictator / Dirty punk / We are The Clash / Are you red.. Y / Cool under heat / Movers and shakers / This is England / Three card trick / Play to win / Fingerpoppin' / North and south / Life is wild. *(cd-iss. Apr89 on 'Columbia'; CD 465110-2) (cd-iss. Dec92 on 'Columbia';)*

—— disbanded Dec'85 and STRUMMER went solo (see below). SHEPHERD formed HEAD. In the early 90's, SIMONON formed HAVANA 3 A.M. who comprised NIGEL DIXON (ex-WHIRLWIND), GARY MYRICK and TRAVIS WILLIAMS. Signing to 'I.R.S.', they released only one 50's style eponymous rock album in 1991 before splitting their quiffs.

– compilations, others, etc. –

on 'C.B.S.' unless mentioned otherwise

Nov 82. (c-ep) *(A40 2907)* **COMPLETE CONTROL / LONDON CALLING / BANKROBBER / CLASH CITY ROCKERS** -

Sep 86. (c-ep) *(450 123-4)* **THE 12" TAPE** -
– London calling / The magnificent dance / This is Radio Clash / Rock the Casbah / This is England. *(cd-iss. Nov92 on 'Columbia'; 450123-2)*

Mar 88. (7") *(CLASH 1)* **I FOUGHT THE LAW. / THE CITY OF THE DEAD / 1977** 29 -
(12"+=/cd-s+=) *(CLASH T/C 1)* – Police on my back / 48 hours.

Mar 88. (d-lp/c/cd) *(460244-1/-4/-2)* *<44035>* **THE STORY OF THE CLASH** 7
– The magnificent seven / Rock the Casbah / This is Radio Clash / Should I stay or should I go / Straight to Hell / Armagideon time / Clampdown / Train in vain / Guns of Brixton / I fought the law / Somebody got murdered / Lost in the supermarket / Bank robber / White man in Hammersmith Palais / London's burning / Janie Jones / Tommy gun / Complete control / Capital radio / White riot / Career opportunities / Clash city rockers / Safe European home / Stay free / London calling / Spanish bombs / English civil war / Police and thieves. *(re-iss. Mar91 as THE STORY OF THE CLASH VOL.1, on 'Columbia'; same)* – (hit UK 13) *(re-iss. Oct95 on 'Columbia'; same)*

Apr 88. (7"/7"box) *(CLASH/+B 2)* **LONDON CALLING. / BRAND NEW CADILLAC** 46
(12"+=) *(CLASHT 2)* – Rudie can't fail.
(cd-s+=) *(CLASHC 2)* – The street parade.

Jul 90. (7"/c-s) *(656072-7/-4)* **RETURN TO BRIXTON (remix). / ('A'-SW2 mix)** 57 -
(12"+=/cd-s+=) *(656072-6/-2)* – The guns of Brixton.

Feb 91. (7"/c-s) *Columbia; (656667-7/-4)* **SHOULD I STAY OR SHOULD I GO. / B.A.D. II: Rush** 1
(12"+=/cd-s+=) *(656667-6/-2)* – ('B'dance mix) / Protex blue.
(cd-s) *(656667-5)* – ('A'side) / London calling / Train in vain / I fought the law.

Apr 91. (7"/c-s) *Columbia; (656814-7/-4)* **ROCK THE CASBAH. / MUSTAPHA DANCE** 15
(12"+=/cd-s+=) *(656814-6/-2)* – The magnificent dance / This is Radio Clash.
(cd-s) *(656814-5)* – ('A'side) / Tommy gun / (White man) In Hammersmith Palais / Straight to Hell.

Jun 91. (7"/c-s) *Columbia; (656946-7/-4)* **LONDON CALLING. / BRAND NEW CADILLAC** 64
(12"+=) *(656946-6)* – Return to Brixton (remix).
(cd-s++=) *(656946-2)* – The call-up.

Oct 91. (7"/c-s) *Columbia; (656-7/-4)* **TRAIN IN VAIN (STAND BY ME). / THE RIGHT PROFILE** -
(cd-s+=) *(656-2)* – Groovy times / Gates to the west.
(pic-cd-s+=) *(656-5)* – ('A'remix) / Death or glory.

Nov 91. (cd/c) *Columbia; (468946-2/-4)* **THE SINGLES COLLECTION** 68

Nov 93. (cd) *Columbia; (474546-2)* **SUPER BLACK MARKET CLASH** -

May 94. (3xcd-box/3xc-box) *Columbia; (469308-2/-4)* **ON BROADWAY**

—— The CLASH also appeared under different guises for singles below

May 83. (12"; FUTURA 2000 with The Clash) *Celluloid; (CYZ 104)* **ESCAPADES OF FUTURA 2000** -

Dec 83. (7"; JANIE JONES & THE LASH) *Big Beat; (NS 91)* **HOUSE OF THE JU-JU QUEEN. / SEX MACHINE** -

—— They can also be heard on TYMON DOGG's 45; 'Lose This Skin' (May80)

JOE STRUMMER

C.B.S. Epic

Oct 86. (7"/12") *(A/TA 7244)* **LOVE KILLS. / DUM DUM CLUB** 69 -

Virgin Virgin

Feb 88. (cd/c/lp) *(CD/TC+/V 2497)* **WALKER (Soundtrack)**
– Filibustero / Omotepe / Sandstorm / Machete / Viperland / Nica libre / Latin romance / The brooding side of madness / Tennessee rain / Smash everything / Tropic of no return / The unknown immortal / Musket waltz.

Epic Epic

Jun 88. (7"/7"s) *(TRASH/+P 1)* **TRASH CITY. / THEME FROM A PERMANENT RECORD** -
(12"+=/pic-cd-s+=) *(TRASH T/C 1)* – Nerfititi rock.

—— STRUMMER was augmented by new band **JACK IRONS** – drums (of RED HOT CHILI PEPPERS) **ZANDON SCHLOSS** – guitar (ex-CIRCLE JERKS) / **RONNIE MARSHALL** – bass (of TONE LOC)

Aug 89. (7"/c-s) *(STRUM/+M 1)* **GANGSTERVILLE. / JEWELLERS AND BUMS** -
(7"ep+=) *(STRUME 1)* – Passport to Detroit / Punk rock blues.
(12"+=/cd-s+=) *(STRUM T/C 1)* – Don't tango with my django.

Sep 89. (lp/c/cd) *(465347-1/-4/-2)* **EARTHQUAKE WEATHER** 58
– Gangsterville / King of the bayou / Island hopping / Slant six / Dizzy's goatee / Shouting street / Boogie with your children / Leopardskin limousines / Sikorsky parts / Jewellers and bums / Highway on zero street / Ride your donkey / Passport to Detroit / Sleepwalk.

Oct 89. (7") *(STRUM 2)* **ISLAND HOPPING. / CHOLO VEST**
(12"+=/cd-s+=/7"ep+=) *(STRUM T/C/E 2)* – Mango street / Baby o' boogie.

—— STRUMMER joined The POGUES on tour, deputising when SHANE McGOWAN was under the bottle. At the start of 1992, he had begun writing with them, so who knows? At least it will quell the dogged persistent rumours of a CLASH reformation.

CLAW HAMMER

Formed: Long Beach, California, USA . . . mid 80's by former PONTIAC BROTHERS frontman, JON WAHL, along with ROB WALTHER and RICK SORTWELL. Strangely enough, CLAW HAMMER debuted on vinyl in Australia, the 'POOR ROBERT' EP hitting the shops at the turn of the decade. Pounding out a deal with the incredibly prolific US imprint, 'Sympathy For The Record Industry', the trio delivered their eponymous debut set in 1990, featuring weird and wonderful versions of Gordon Lightfoot's 'SUNDOWN', Pere Ubu's 'FINAL SOLUTION' and Hampton-Kelling's 'HEY OLD LADY AND BERT'S SONG'. A creative, punk-like update of QUICKSILVER MESSENGER SERVICE, WAHL, WALTHER and newcomers CHRIS BAGAROZZI and BOB LEE armed themselves with the CLAW HAMMER sound and set about deconstructing DEVO's 'Q: ARE WE NOT MEN, A: WE ARE DEVO' in its entirety. Around the same time they issued a covers EP, 'DOUBLE PACK WHACK ATTACK'; artists chosen this time were Patti Smith, Eno, Pere Ubu and Devo again(!), while original material surfaced on the early '92 album, 'RAMWHALE'. At this junction of the band's career, WAHL also moonlighted with the RED AUNTS as BAGAROZZI augmented DOWN BY LAW. Picked up by BRETT GUREWITZ's 'Epitaph' label, CLAW HAMMER released the acclaimed 'PABLUM' (1993), in turn attracting the attentions of big wigs 'Interscope'. A couple of years in the making, 1995's major label debut, 'THANK THE HOLDER UPPERS', was as uncompromising as ever, while 1997's JIM DICKINSON-produced, 'HOLD YOUR TONGUE AND SAY APPLE', revelled in its hard-nosed Memphis sleaze/punk.

Album rating: CLAW HAMMER (*5) / Q: ARE WE NOT MEN? – A: WE ARE DEVO (*4) / RAMWHALE (*5) / PABLUM (*6) / THANK THE HOLDER UPPERS (*6) / HOLD YOUR TONGUE AND SAY APPLE (*5)

JON WAHL – vocals, guitar (ex-PONTIAC BROTHERS) / **ROB WALTHER** – bass / **RICK SORTWELL** – drums

Grown Up Wrong / not iss.

1989. (12"ep) **POOR ROBERT EP** - / - Austra

Sympathy F / Sympathy F

Oct 89. (7"ep) *<SFTRI 37>* **F.U.B.A.R.** -
Mar 90. (cd/lp) *<SFTRI 57>* **CLAWHAMMER** -
– Shell shocked / Warm Spring night / Brother Brick says / Drop II / Sundown / Hey old lady and Bert's song / Papa's got us all tied in knots / Mr. Pizzazz / Petri dish / Poor Robert / Three fifteen / Final solution / Candle opera / Drop. *(UK-iss.1993; same as US)*

— **CHRIS BAGAROZZI** – guitar + **BOB LEE** – drums; repl. SORTWELL

1991. (cd-ep) **DOUBLE PACK WHACK ATTACK** -
Oct 91. (lp) *<SFTRI 119>* **Q: ARE WE NOT MEN? A: WE ARE DEVO (the DEVO album live in studio)** -
Jan 92. (cd) *<SFTRI 120>* **RAMWHALE** -
– Naked / Succotash / Maheney bus ride / Beat rice / Sticky thing / Crave / People in my peephole / Three fifteen / Don't walk away / Stough.
1993. (7") *<SFTRI 229>* **MALTHUSIAN BLUES. / THE DAY OF THE TRIFFIDS** -

Epitaph / Epitaph

Apr 93. (cd/c/lp) *<(86425 CD/MC/LP)>* **PABLUM**
– Vigil smile / William Tell / Montezuma's hands / Speak softly / Nick / Nut powder / Shitting gold bricks / Malthusian blues / Pablum of my mind.

Interscope / Interscope

May 95. (cd/c) *<92515>* **THANK THE HOLDER UPPERS** -
– Superthings / When Dan's in town / Sweaty palms / Five filths dead / Bums on the flow / Hollow legs / Bedside coffee table roses / Blind pig / Each hit / Lazy brains / Ol' factory blues – Nose hair.
Apr 97. (cd) *<90105>* **HOLD YOUR TONGUE (AND SAY APPLE)** -
– The day it rained pigeon shit / Valley so high / Black eyed blues / Queen's lead helmet / Sugar breath / Gnashville / Hind sight / Ass kisser's union / Water / Air plant / Formaldehyde / Caravan.

Medfly / Medfly

Jun 97. (12") *<(MEDFLY 001)>* **KILOWATT. / FLYSPRAY**
Feb 98. (12") *<(12MED 003)>* **PEOPLE LOVE. /**

– compilations, etc. –

Aug 96. (m-cd) *Sympathy For The Record Industry; (SFTRI 447CD)* **SCUSE THE EXCURSION**
– (the EP's above)

Adam CLAYTON & Larry MULLEN (see under ⇒ U2)

CLEAN

Formed: Dunedin, New Zealand . . . 1978 by DAVID KILGOUR, his brother HAMISH and PETER GUTTERIDGE. While the KILGOURS subsequently relocated to Auckland, GUTTERIDGE had already departed (he soon joined The CHILLS), the band were put on hold until DAVID met ROBERT SCOTT back in Dunedin. Eventually joined by HAMISH, the trio recorded a seminal debut single, 'TALLY HO', on the 'Flying Nun' label. Set up by a fan primarily to release the track, the imprint rapidly became an NZ institution. The fact that The CLEAN were the first band to grace the label is a mark of their influence and, along with The CHILLS, KILGOUR & Co.'s organ-heavy garage-pop sound (memorably described as SONIC YOUTH conducting a choir of page boys) helped launch and inspire a scene that is still thriving today. For all that, The CLEAN's career was relatively brief, the band only releasing a further two mini-sets, 'BOODLE, BOODLE, BOODLE' and 'GREAT SOUNDS GREAT. . .' over the following two years before splitting. The former even breached the NZ Top 5 (!) despite the miniscule recording budget, a mark of the band's musical resourcefulness and instinct for quirky but effective pop. Following the departure of DAVID, SCOTT formed his own outfit, The BATS, although the KILGOUR brothers soon reunited under the banner of The GREAT UNWASHED, GUTTERIDGE returing to the fold as the line-up came full circle. Yet the new material was rootsier than The CLEAN (collected on album 'CLEAN OUT OF OUR MINDS'), bassist ROSS HUMPHRIES was brought in to allow a twin guitar format courtesy of KILGOUR and GUTTERIDGE. This proved to be another short-live venture, however, HAMISH later forming BAILTER SPACE with ALISTER PARKER and JOHN HALVORSEN while GUTTERIDGE formed the J&MC-esque RED SNAPPER. To the delight of many British fans, the KILGOUR brothers and ROBERT SCOTT reformed The CLEAN in 1988 and perfomed in London, a recording of the gig at Fulham's Greyhound venue released in Spring '89 as an EP, 'IN'N'NER LIVE'. The record's positive reception led to the band undertaking a full world tour and, at long last, recording a full length album. The resulting 'VEHICLE' (1990) was a more straightforwardly conventional affair lacking the inspired rough edge of old but making up for it with a sterling set of indie pop songs. With HAMISH concentrating on BAILTER SPACE for most of the early 90's, it was 1995 before a further CLEAN album surfaced, 'MODERN ROCK' being their last effort to date.

Album rating: COMPILATION collection (*7) / ODDITIES collection (*6) / ODDITIES 2 collection (*6) / VEHICLE (*6) / MODERN ROCK (*5) / UNKNOWN COUNTRY (*5)

DAVID KILGOUR (b. 6 Sep'61) – vocals, guitar / **HAMISH KILGOUR** – drums / **ROBERT SCOTT** – bass; repl. PETER GUTTERIDGE who joined The CHILLS / guest on debut **MARTIN PHILLIPPS** (b. 2 Jul'63) – keyboards (of The CHILLS)

Flying Nun / not iss.

Feb 81. (7") *(FN 001)* **TALLY HO! / PLATYPUS** - / - New Z.
1981. (m-lp) **BOODLE BOODLE BOODLE** - / - New Z.
1982. (m-lp) **"GREAT SOUNDS GREAT, GOOD SOUNDS GOOD, SO-SO SOUNDS SO-SO, BAD SOUNDS BAD, ROTTEN SOUNDS ROTTEN" WITH THE CLEAN** - / - New Z.

— split when SCOTT formed The BATS and **PETER GUTTERIDGE** was drafted in as the group changed their moniker in 1983

GREAT UNWASHED

Lambs To The Slaughter / not iss.

Sep 86. (7") *(LTS 3)* **YELLOW RAIN. / FIRE BURNS** -

— PETER left to form SNAPPER, while HAMISH former BAILTER SPACE with former members of The GORDONS

CLEAN

— re-formed in July 1988, **ROBERT SCOTT** (of The BATS) returned

Flying Nun / not iss.

Apr 89. (12"ep) *(FNE 029)* **IN'N'NER LIVE (live at Fulham Greyhound '88)** -
– Flowers / Point that thing somewhere else / Whatever I do is right.

Rough Trade / Rough Trade

Feb 90. (lp/c/cd) *(ROUGH/+C/CD 143)* **VEHICLE**
– Draw(in)g to a (w)hole / I wait around / Bye bye / The blue / Dunes / Someone / Home / Diamond shine / Getting to you / Big soft punch / Big cat / I can see / Gem. *(cd re-iss. Jun95 on 'Flying Nun'; FNCD 147)*

Flying Nun / Summershine

Feb 95. (lp/cd) *(FN/+CD 292) <19007>* **MODERN ROCK** Oct95
– Starting point / Outside the cage / Linger longer / Wake up in the morning / 2 reasons / Safe in the rain / Secret place / Something I need / Different world / Stomp the guru / Too much violence / Phluke / Do your thing / Ginger ale. *(cd re-iss. Sep98; same)*
Nov 96. (cd) *(FNCD 349)* **UNKNOWN COUNTRY** -
– Wipe me, I'm lucky / Champagne and misery / Changing your head / Balkans / Clutch / Franz Kafka at the zoo / Whisk / Indigo blue / Chumpy / Get the liquid / Happy lil fella / Tweezer / Rope / Twist top / Cooking water / Valley cab / Walk walk / Balkans.

— HAMISH seems to be concentrating more on BAILTER SPACE

– compilations, etc. –

on 'Flying Nun' unless mentioned otherwise

1986. (m-lp) **LIVE DEAD CLEAN (live)** - / - New Z.
May 87. (lp) *(FNUK 3) <HMS 114>* **COMPILATION** 1995
– Billy two / At the bottom / Tally ho / Anything could happen / Point that thing somewhere else / Flowers / Fish / Beatnik / Getting older / Slug song / Oddity / Whatever / Whatever I do (wherever I go). *(cd-iss. Nov88; FNE 3CD) (re-iss. Apr93 on 'Homestead'; HMS 114) (cd re-iss. Jun95; FNCD 154)*
Jan 88. (c) *(ODD 001)* **ODDITIES** -
(cd-iss. Jun95; FNCD 223) <US-iss.cd 1995; 9901>
Jun 95. (cd) *(FNCD 208)* **GREAT UNWASHED**

— HAMISH had already formed own outfit, BAILTER SPACE

DAVID KILGOUR

— with his backing group, STEPHEN

Oct 94. (lp/cd) *(FN/+CD 282)* **SUGAR MOUTH**
Dec 95. (lp/cd) *Ajax; (<AJAX 040/+CD>)* **FIRST STEPS AND FALSE STARTS** (compilation) Sep95
– Bootlegger / November / Tape machine / Shine all night / This chord / Scene two / Another echo downer / Way down / Here come the cars / Wooden floor / Untitled / Pop song / Landed / Dirty hallway / Ditch / September / Slow wind / Gone Mekico again / Wait at your door / Bucket of you.

Sep 97. (cd) *(FN 397)* **DAVID KILGOUR & HEAVY EIGHTS**
– Round the bend / Off my mind / Chop me in half / Locked in blue / Brown man / Seemingly Stranded / Wave boarder / My one / Hey you / Maybe / Diggin' for gold / Thumbaline.

CLEANERS FROM VENUS

Formed: Colchester, England . . . 1980 by MARTIN NEWELL and LOL ELLIOTT, GILES SMITH replacing the latter in 1983 after a few (very) limited cassettes ('BLOW AWAY YOUR TROUBLES', 'ON ANY NORMAL MONDAY' and 'IN THE GOLDEN AUTUMN') were distributed by mail order. Although these were of varying amateur quality, they charted the development of NEWELL's 60's influenced songwriting style and often surreal sense of humour, earning him a reputation as the 80's equivalent of SYD BARRETT or RAY DAVIES. With newcomer GILES on board, the CLEANERS polished off two further cassettes, 'UNDER WARTIME CONDITIONS' (1984) and the much loved, 'LIVING WITH VICTORIA GREY' (1986). The following year, the duo (and guests) issued their first lp proper, 'GOING TO ENGLAND', fans unhappy with the slick production sheen that marred revamped versions of tracks from its predecessor. However, they found a willing audience in Germany where their final two 'R.C.A.' issued albums, 'TOWN AND COUNTRY' (1988) and 'NUMBER 13' (1990) hit the shops. In Britain meanwhile, The CLEANERS were signed to Captain Sensible's 'Deltic' imprint for the former and 'Man At The Off License' for the latter. After the duo's final split, GILES went on to write a novel, 'Lost In Music', promoting this in 1995 by co-guesting (with noneother than myself, MC STRONG) at a poncey book launch in Edinburgh. NEWELL, meanwhile, released a few solo sets (including one with the help of ANDY PARTRIDGE, 'THE GREATEST LIVING ENGLISHMAN') and later formed The BROTHERHOOD OF LIZARDS before becoming a scruffy "rock poet", writing his own novel, 'I Hank Marvinned'.

Album rating: BLOW AWAY YOUR TROUBLES (*4) / ON ANY NORMAL MONDAY (*5) / IN THE GOLDEN AUTUMN (*6) / UNDER WARTIME CONDITIONS (*5) / LIVING WITH VICTORIA GREY (*6) / GOING TO ENGLAND (*4) / TOWN AND COUNTRY (*7) / NUMBER 13 (*7) / Martin Newell: THE GREATEST LIVING ENGLISHMAN (*7) / THE OFF WHITE ALBUM (*5)

MARTIN NEWELL – vocals, guitar / **LOL ELLIOTT** – drums

no label — not iss.

1981. (c) *(none)* **BLOW AWAY YOUR TROUBLES** — - — - mail-o
1982. (c) *(none)* **ON ANY NORMAL MONDAY** — - — - mail-o
1983. (c) *(none)* **IN THE GOLDEN AUTUMN** — - — - mail-o

—— **GILES SMITH** – piano, vocals / (plus several guests on each album) repl. LOL

Tao — not iss.

Jul 84. (c) *(none)* **UNDER WARTIME CONDITIONS** — -
– Summer in a small town / Johnny the moondog is dead / Hand of stone / Drowning butterflies / Radio seven / Fracas on West Street / Lukewarm lovesong / A blue wave / Song for Syd Barrett / The Winter Palace. *(lp-iss.1986 on 'Acid Tapes';)*

no label — not iss.

1986. (c) *(none)* **LIVING WITH VICTORIA GREY** — - — - mail-o

Ammunition — not iss.

Feb 87. (lp) *(CLEANLP 1)* **GOING TO ENGLAND** — -
– Julie Profumo / Living with Victria Grey / Clara Bow / Follow the plough / Armistica day / What's going on in your heart / Girl on a swing / A mercury girl / Ilya Kuryakin looked at me / You must be out of my mind.
Mar 87. (12") *(JANGLE 1T)* **ILYA KURYAKIN LOOKED AT ME. /** — -
Jun 87. (12") *(JANGLE 2T)* **LIVING WITH VICTORIA GREY. /** — -

Deltic — R.C.A.

Oct 88. (lp/c) *(DELT LP/MC 1)* **TOWN AND COUNTRY**
– Let's get married / Blue swan / The beat generation and me / Felicity / Mad March hare / Tenpenny Hill / Dizzy girl / Denmark Street / I was a teenage idol dancer / I wasn't drinking / Cardboard town / The last club in the world.

Man At The Off License — not iss.

Jun 90. (lp) **NUMBER 13** — -

—— disbanded after above.

– compilations, etc. –

Mar 93. (7") *Singles Only; (SOL 237)* **SONG FOR SYD BARRETT. /** — -
Jul 93. (cd) *Tangerine; (TANGCD 3)* **THE GOLDEN CLEANERS** — -
Oct 95. (cd) *Tangerine; (TANGCD 014)* **BACK FROM THE CLEANERS** — -

MARTIN NEWELL

Humbug — Pipeline

Nov 93. (cd/d-cd; by MARTIN NEWELL & ANDY PARTRIDGE)
(BAH 10/+X) **THE GREATEST LIVING ENGLISHMAN**
– Goodbye dreaming fields / Before the hurricane / We'll build a house / The greatest living Englishman / She rings the changes / Home Counties boy / A street called Prospect / Christmas in suburbia / Straight to you, boy / The jangling man / The green-gold girl of the summer. *(lp-iss.Jul97 on 'Jar Music'; JAR 005)*
Aug 95. (cd-ep) *(HUM 001)* **LET'S KIOSK!** — -
– The jangling man / Former phonebox vandal / Wunderbarmaid / I will haunt your room.
Apr 96. (cd) *(BAH 25)* **THE OFF WHITE ALBUM** — -
(lp-iss.Jul97 on 'Jar Music'; JAR 010)

– compilations, etc. –

Sep 97. (d-cd+cd-ep) *Humbug; (BAH 33)* **MARTIN NEWELL'S BOX OF OLD HUMBUG** — -
– (THE GREATEST LIVING ENGLISHMAN + THE OFF WHITE ALBUM + LET'S KIOSK!)

CLINIC

Formed: Crosby, Liverpool, England . . . 1997 initially as mid-90's indie act, PURE MORNING, by the surgical crew of ADE, HEARTLEY, BRIAN and CARL. This quartet released a couple of singles in 1994, before being snapped up by 'Radarscope'. However, after only three more 7"ers and an album, '2 INCH HELIUM BUDDHA', the outfit ground to a halt in '96. Subsequently opening new doors for themselves as CLINIC, they delivered three singles on their own imprint, 'Aladdin's Cave Of Golf', starting with that Autumn's quirky and weirdly-titled, 'IPC SUB-EDITORS DICTATE OUR YOUTH'. 1998's 'MONKEY ON YOUR BACK', was a second attempt at experimentation, their landscape soundings the toast of Glastonbury; they were actually voted the festival's Best New Band. A third effort, 'CEMENT MIXER', showed CLINIC at their eclectic best, breaking free from the usual indie-rock tags.

Album rating: Pure Morning: 2 INCH HELIUM BUDDHA (*5)

PURE MORNING

—— (see below for line-up)

Kool Tone — not iss.

Mar 94. (7") *(KT 002)* **I DON'T WANT YOU AROUND. /** — -

Amulet — not iss.

Oct 94. (7") *(AMULET 01)* **SICK PROFIT. /** — -

Radarscope — not iss.

Apr 95. (7") *(SCAN 01)* **ALL THE GUESTS SMILE SO SWEETLY. /** — -
(cd-s+=) *(SCANCS 01)* –
Feb 96. (7") *(SCAN 12)* **SCUM. /** — -
(cd-s+=) *(SCANCS 12)* –
Apr 96. (7") *(SCAN 16)* **DINKY. /** — -
(cd-s+=) *(SCANCS 16)* –
Jun 96. (cd/lp) *(SCAN CD/LP)* **2 INCH HELIUM BUDDHA** — -
Jul 96. (7") *(SCAN 22)* **FOXHOLE. / IPC** — -
(cd-s+=) *(SCANCS 22)* – The gardener.

CLINIC

ADE BLACKBURN – vocals / **HEARTLEY** – keyboards, guitar / **BRIAN** – bass / **CARL TURNEY** – drums

Aladdin's Cave Of Golf — not iss.

Sep 97. (7") *(GOLF 001)* **IPC SUB EDITORS DICTATE OUR YOUTH. /** — -
Mar 98. (7") *(GOLF 002)* **MONKEY ON YOUR BACK. /** — -
(cd-s+=) *(GOLFCD 002)* –
Aug 98. (7") *(GOLF 003-7)* **CEMENT MIXER. /** — -
(cd-s+=) *(GOLFCD 003)* –

CLOCKDVA

Formed: Sheffield, England . . . 1979 by ADI NEWTON, former frontman of The FUTURE (which subsequently became The HUMAN LEAGUE). With a line-up featuring NEWTON, CHARLIE COLLINS, ROGER QUAIL, STEVEN 'JUDD' TURNER and DAVID J. HAMMOND, the outfit released a debut cassette-only affair, 'WHITE SOULS IN BLACK SUITS' (1980) on THROBBING GRISTLE's 'Industrial' label. Lead track, 'CONSENT', was an early classic, an experimental soundclash of avant-garde chaos and dirty industrial funk which had a spiritual cousin in The POP GROUP amongst others. COLLINS' searing, freeform sax work, in particular, would become a distinguishing feature of the CLOCKDVA experience while NEWTON's vocal was pitched somewhere between IGGY POP and IAN CURTIS, even if he did occasionally sound like he'd been force-fed a diet of red-hot gravel. PAUL WILDER subsequently replaced HAMMOND for the release of a follow-up set, 'THIRST' on the small 'Fetish' label, another helping of atmospheric, vaguely gothic jazz-art complete with squealing clarinet, sax, chunky bass and unsettling vocals. A period of upheaval ensued as TURNER met an early death, ADI the only surviving founder member as the rest of the band departed to form The BOX. Hooking up with former SIOUXSIE & THE BANSHEES man, JOHN VALENTINE-CARRUTHERS, alongside new recruits PAUL BROWSE and NICK SANDERSON, NEWTON carried on the CLOCKDVA name and signed to 'Polydor' in 1982. By all accounts, the resulting 'ADVANTAGE' (1983) album should have given ADI his first taste of success, featuring as it did such enduring tracks as 'BEAUTIFUL LOSERS' (a sound from which MATT JOHNSON possibly drew inpiration for his 'Infected' album masterpiece). It wasn't to be though and CLOCKDVA fell apart in early '84, NEWTON subsequently forming The ANTI-GROUP alongside MARK HOLMES, BRDL HIRDEN D.F. D'SILVA, D.A. HEPPENSTAU and ROBERT E.BAKER. This project further served as a vehicle for NEWTON's experimental research (particularly with regards to film; NEWTON's idea of creating a complete audiovisual live experience was later echoed by The SHAMEN), his interest in the interface between technology and human evolution becoming apparent on albums such as 'DIGITARIA' (1987) and 'AUDIOPHILE' (1988). When CLOCKDVA eventually reappeared in the late 80's (with a line-up of NEWTON, BROWSE and DENNIS), a series of singles on Chicago's 'Wax Trax' label suggested an entirely different musical proposition from the group's original incarnation. Obviously influenced by the burgeoning underground dance culture, NEWTON was now creating music of a decidedly electro/techno minimilist hue albeit in the context of his evolutionary philosophy; most of the CLOCKDVA releases forthhence came with a NEWTON essay on the possibilities of sound, consciousness etc., namechecking figures as diverse as Greek scribe, Homer, and arch occultist, Aliester Crowley. Subsequent albums on the 'Contempo' label such as 'MAN AMPLIFIED' (1992) and the belated 'DIGITAL SOUNDTRACKS' (1993) traded in a more refined electronica. NEWTON even released a CD/Book in late '93, the self explanatory 'VIRTUAL REALITY HANDBOOK', possibly for the benefit of old-timer CLOCKDVA fans who didn't have a clue what he was going on about anymore! • **Covered:** BLACK ANGEL'S DEATH SONG (Velvet Underground).

Album rating: WHITE SOULS IN BLACK SUITS (*5) / THIRST (*8) / ADVANTAGE (*9) / BURIED DREAMS (*5) / TRANSITIONAL VOICES (*5) / MAN AMPLIFIED (*5) / DIGITAL SOUNDTRACK (*5) / SIGN (*6) / BLACK WORDS ON WHITE PAPER (*5) / VIRTUAL REALITY HANDBOOK (*5) / 150 EROTIC CALIBRATIONS (*5) / ETERNITY compilation (*7) / Anti-Group: AUDIOPHILE (*5)

ADI NEWTON (b. ADOLPHUS NEWTON) – vocals, clarinet, synths (ex-FUTURE) / **CHARLIE COLLINS** – saxophone, flute, percussion, etc. / **ROGER QUAIL** – drums, perc. / **STEVEN 'Judd' TURNER** – bass, treated guitar / **DAVID J.HAMMOND** – guitar; repl. TYNE

Industrial not iss.

Oct 80. (c) *(IRC 31)* **WHITE SOULS IN BLACK SUITS** [ ] [-]
– Consent / Discontentment 1 & 2 / Still – Silent / Non / Relentless / Contradict / Anti-chance (soundtrack; keyboards assemble themselves at dawn). *(lp-iss.1983; IRLP 31) (re-iss. Jun92 on 'Contempo' cd/c/lp; CONTECD/CONTAPE/CONTE 157)*

— **PAUL WIDLER** – guitar; repl. HAMMOND

Fetish not iss.

Jan 81. (lp) *(FR 2002)* **THIRST** [ ] [-]
– Uncertain / Sensorium / White cell / Piano pain / Blue tone / North loop / 4 hours / Moments / Impressions of African winter. *(re-iss. Nov85 on 'Doublevision'; DVR 19) (cd-iss. Jan95 on 'Contempo'+=; CONTECD 192)* – 4 hours (original single edit) / Sensorium (original single edit).

May 81. (7") *(FET 008)* **4 HOURS (re-mixed). / SENSORIUM** [ ] [-]
(re-iss. Nov85 on 'Doublevision'; DVR 18)

— **ADI** was sole survivor when JUDD died. The others formed The BOX. He recruited **JOHN VALENTINE-CARRUTHERS** – guitar, bass (ex-SIOUXSIE & BANSHEES) / **PAUL BROWSE** – saxophone / **NICK SANDERSON** – drums

Polydor M.C.A.

May 82. (7"ep/12"ep) *(POSP/+X 437)* **PASSION STILL AFLAME** [ ] [-]
– Son of sons / Theme from I.M.D. / Don't (It's taboo) / Noises in limbo.

Nov 82. (7"; as DVA) *(POSP 499)* **HIGH HOLLY DISCO MASS. / THE VOICE THAT SPEAKS FROM WITHIN (TRIUMPH OVER WILL) (part 1)** [ ] [-]

— added **DEAN DENNIS** – bass

Apr 83. (7"/12") *(POSP/+X 578)* **RESISTANCE. / THE SECRET LIFE OF THE BIG BLACKSUIT** [ ] [-]

May 83. (lp/c) *(POLS/+C 1082)* **ADVANTAGE** [ ] [ ]
– Tortured heroine / Beautiful losers / Resistance / Eternity in Paris / The secret life of the big black suit / Breakdown / Dark encounter / Poem. *(re-iss. Jun89 on 'Interfish' lp/cd; EFA 1706/+CD)*

Aug 83. (7"/12") *(POSP/+X 627)* **BREAKDOWN. / BLACK ANGEL'S DEATH SONG** [ ] [-]

— disbanded early '84. CARRUTHERS rejoined SIOUXSIE & THE BANSHEES, while SANDERSON and DENNIS joined JEFFREY LEE PIERCE solo

ANTI-GROUP

— were formed by **ADOLPHUS NEWTON** with **MARK HOLMES** – guitar / **D.F. D'SILVA** – saxophone / **BRDL HIRDEN** – bass / **D.A. HEPPENSTAU** – keyboards, computers / **ROBERT E. BAKER** – engineer

Sweatbox not iss.

Oct 85. (12") *(SOX 09)* **HA. / ZULU** [ ] [-]

Feb 87. (m-lp) *(SOX 010)* **ShT** [ ] [-]
– Shgl / Sunset eyes through water / Po Ema / Further and evident meanings / Morpheus baby / New upheaval.

Apr 87. (lp/cd) *(SOX/SACD 012)* **DIGITARIA** [ ] [-]
(re-iss. cd Sep94 on 'Audioglobe')

Jul 87. (7") *(OX 011)* **BIG SEX. / THE OCEAN** [ ] [-]
(12"+=) *(SOX 011)* – ('A'version).

Jul 87. (m-lp) **LIVE IN BERLIN (live)** [ ] [-]
(above album was released Sep85 as 'THE DELIVERY' on 'Atonal Berlin' Germany.)

Feb 88. (lp) *(SAX 030)* **AUDIOPHILE** [ ] [-]
(re-iss. cd Sep94 on 'Audioglobe')

Side Effects not iss.

Jul 88. (lp) *(SER 12)* **TEST TONES** [ ] [-]

CLOCKDVA

— re-formed with **NEWTON, BROWSE & DENNIS**

Interfisch Wax Trax

Nov 88. (12") *(EFA 1701)* *<WAX 068>* **THE HACKER. / THE CONNECTION MACHINE** [ ] [ ]
(cd-s+=) *(EFA 1701CD)* – The hacker (hacked version).
(re-iss. Jun92 on 'Contempo'; 188MX + 189MX)

Jan 89. (12") *(EFA 1708)* *<WAX 9071>* **THE ACT. / SONOLOGY OF SEX** [ ] [ ]
(cd-s+=) *(EFA 1708CD)* – React / React II.
(re-iss. Jun92 on 'Contempo'; TEMPO 187MX)

Jun 89. (12"ep) *(EFA 1713)* *<WAX 9105>* **SOUND MIRROR EP** [ ] [ ] 1990
– Sound mirror (programme 5) / Sound mirror (programme 5) / The sonology of sex (le comtesse de sang).
(re-iss. Jun92 on 'Contempo'; TEMPO 190MX)

Jul 89. (lp/cd) *(EFA 1717)* **BURIED DREAMS** [ ] [ ]
– Buried dreams / Hide / Sound mirror / Velvet realm / The reign / The act / The hacker / The connection machine / The sonology of sex.

Amphetamine not iss.

Jan 91. (lp) *(EFA 01718)* **TRANSITIONAL VOICES** [ ] [-]

Contempo not iss.

Dec 91. (12"ep) *(TEMPO 173MX)* **FINAL PROGRAM EP** [ ] [-]

Mar 92. (lp/cd) *(CONTE/+CD 182)* **MAN AMPLIFIED** [ ] [-]
– Man-amplifiers / Techno geist / Axiomatic and heuristic / NYC overload / Transitional voices / Fractalize / Bitstream / Final program. *(cd+=)* – Dark attractor / Memories of sound.

Nov 92. (cd-ep/w-book) *(DUCA 172CDS)* **BLACK WORDS ON WHITE PAPER EP / 7DC / OTTO M** [ ] [-]
(cd-iss. Sep93 +=) (DD 172CD) – Alien tapes / 1.23.

Feb 93. (cd/lp) *(CONTECD 217)* **DIGITAL SOUNDTRACKS** [ ] [-]
– The sensual engine / Cycom / Sound sweep / The operators / E-wave / The inversion / Diminishing point / Stations of the mind. *(cd+=)* – The presence / Chemicals / Delta machines / Stills of emotion.

— **ADI NEWTON + ROBERT E. BAKER**

Sep 93. (12") *(TEMPO 183T)* **BITSTREAM / VIRTUAL FLESH. / BITSTREAM (2 mixes)** [ ] [-]
(cd-ep+=_ *(TEMPO 183CD)* – (3 other 'A'versions).

Sep 93. (cd/c/lp) *(CONTECD/CONTAPE/CONTE 225)* **SIGN** [ ] [-]
– Signal / Voice recognition test / The obsession intensifies / Two souls / Re-entry / Pool of shades / Return to blue / Eternity / Sign.

Sep 93. (12"/cd-s) *(TEMPO 224 T/CD)* **VOICE RECOGNITION TEST** [ ] [-]
– Voice recognition test / Cypher / De-cyphered.

Nov 93. (cd-book) **VIRTUAL REALITY HANDBOOK** [ ] [-]

Jul 94. (cd-ep) *(TEMP 266CDS)* **ETERNITY** [ ] [-]

Audioglobe not iss.

Sep 94. (cd) **150 EROTIC CALIBRATIONS** [ ] [-]

– compilations, etc. –

Sep 94. (d-cd) *Hyperium; (HY 39100)* **ETERNITY** [ ] [-]

Jan 95. (cd) *Audioglobe; (WHIP 003)* **THE COLLECTIVE** [ ] [-]

CLOSE LOBSTERS

Formed: Johnstone, Scotland ... 1985 by ANDY BURNETT, his brother BOB BURNETT, TOM DONNELLY, STUART McFADYEN and GRAHAM WILKINTON. These quirky but easy-going jingle-janglers got their break via the NME C86 tape (to which they contributed 'FIRESTATION TOWERS'), subsequently netting a deal with 'Fire' and releasing 'I'M GOING TO HEAVEN TO SEE IF IT RAINS' as their debut single in Autumn '86. Support slots to the likes of the JESUS & MARY CHAIN helped raise their profile while a follow-up single, 'NEVER SEEN BEFORE', confirmed their indie credentials and paved the way for an endearingly titled debut album, 'FOXHEADS STALK THIS LAND' (1987). Vaguely akin to a Caledonian version of The WEDDING PRESENT (especially in vocal terms), The CLOSE LOBSTERS were also – along with DAVID GEDGE & Co. – beloved of the US college circuit and even undertook a spot of transatlantic touring to promote follow-up album, 'HEADACHE RHETORIC' (1989). The strain of such a venture proved too much, however and the band fell apart at the turn of the decade, uniting briefly in 1991 for live work only. WEDDING PRESENT subsequently covered their 'LET'S MAKE SOME PLANS' on a B-side.

Album rating: FOXHEADS STALK THIS LAND (*6) / HEADACHE RHETORIC (*6)

ANDY BURNETT (b.11 Feb'65) – vocals / **TOM DONNELLY** (b.29 Aug'62) – guitar / **GRAHAM WILKINTON** (b.22 Aug'65) / **BOB BURNETT** (b.11 Sep'62) – bass / **STUART McFADYEN** (b.26 Sep'65, Paisley, Scotland) – drums

Fire not iss.

Oct 86. (7") *(BLAZE 15)* **I'M GOING TO HEAVEN TO SEE IF IT RAINS. / PATHETIK TRIVIA** [ ] [-]
(12"+=) *(BLAZE 15T)* – Boys and girls.

Apr 87. (7") *(BLAZE 20)* **NEVER SEEN BEFORE. / PIMPS** [ ] [-]
(12"+=) *(BLAZE 20T)* – Firestation towers / Wide waterway.

— **PAUL BENNETT** – bass; repl. BOB

Oct 87. (lp) *(FIRE 9)* **FOXHEADS STALK THIS LAND** [ ] [-]
– Just too bloody stupid / Sewer pipe dream / I kiss the flower in bloom / Pathetique / A prophecy / In spite of these times / Foxheads / I take bribes / Pimps / Mother of God. *(cd-iss. Mar88; FIRECD 9) (re-iss. Apr89 c/cd; D4/D2 73333)*

Nov 87. (12"m) *(BLAZE 22T)* **LET'S MAKE SOME PLANS. / IN SPITE OF THESE TIMES / GET WHAT THEY DESERVE** [ ] [-]

Aug 88. (7") *(BLAZE 25)* **WHAT IS THERE TO SMILE ABOUT. / LOOPHOLES** [ ] [-]
(12"+=) *(BLAZE 25T)* – From this day on / The skyscrapers of St.Hirin.
(cd-s++=) *(BLAZE 25CD)* – Violently pretty face.

Mar 89. (7") *(BLAZE 34S)* **NATURE THING. /** [ ] [-]
(12"+=/cd-s+=) *(BLAZE 34 T/CD)* –

Mar 89. (lp/c/cd) *(FIRE LP/MC/CD 17)* **HEADACHE RHETORIC** [ ] [-]
– Lovely little swan / Gunpowderkeg / Nature thing / My days are numbered / Gutache / Got apprehension / Words on power / Skyscrapers / Knee trembler. *(c+=/cd+=)* – FOXHEADS STALK THIS LAND

Caff not iss.

1989. (ltd-7") *(CAFF 4)* **JUST TOO BLOODY STUPID. / ALL THE LITTLE BOYS AND GIRLS I KNEW** [ ] [-]

— split for two years, although a return to the live circuit was brief

– compilations, etc. –

Apr 88. (12"ep) *Night Tracks; (SFNT 008)* **EVENING SHOW SESSIONS** (29.6.86) [ ] [-]

COAL PORTERS (see under ⇒ LONG RYDERS)

COCKNEY REJECTS

Formed: London, England . . . 1978, by JEFFERSON TURNER, VINCE RIORDAN, KEITH WARRINGTON and ex-amateur boxer MIKE GEGGUS. After a one-off single in '79, 'FLARES 'N' SLIPPERS' for the indie label 'Small Wonder', they caught the attention of SHAM 69's JIMMY PURSEY. They immediately signed to 'E.M.I.', subsequently enjoying two minor hits, 'I'M NOT A FOOL' and 'BADMAN'. Akin to a more primitive SHAM 69 and taking on that band's rowdy mantle, the average COCKNEY REJECTS gig attracting the less desirable element of the right-wing political spectrum (i.e. NF skinheads and the like). The band were obviously pivotal in the burgeoning "oi" (new punk) movement, their predictable, cartoon-like pro-British (actually pro-South of the Watford Gap) football yob anthems giving an airing on their prophetically-titled first lp, 'GREATEST HITS VOLUME 1'. The album secured them Top 30 success, as did their successive sets, 'VOLUME 2' and the live 'VOLUME 3'. One of their hit singles, 'I'M FOREVER BLOWING BUBBLES', had always been a favourite terrace chant for West Ham United supporters, of which the band could count themselves members. The COCKNEY REJECTS live experience never reached the States, due to the country's crazy work permit rule that didn't allow in musicians without proven musical ability (NEW MODEL ARMY later suffered the same fate). In 1984, casting off the cockney prefix, The REJECTS astonishingly turned their backs on the "oi" scene, opting instead for a full-blown heavy metal approach, hinted at on their previous CR release, 'THE WILD ONES'. Now signed to the 'Heavy Metal' label, the band unleashed their 'ROCK THE WILD SIDE' set, although after one further single they broke up. In 1989, The COCKNEY REJECTS reformed for one more studio outing, 'LETHAL', an unremarkable swansong that soon found its way into the bargain bins. • **Songwriters:** All group compositions, except MOTORHEAD (Motorhead) / MAYBE IT'S BECAUSE I'M A LONDONER (. . . Gregg) / TILL THE END OF THE DAY (Kinks) / BLOCKBUSTER (Sweet) / etc.

Album rating: THE BEST OF THE COCKNEY REJECTS (*5)

JEFFERSON TURNER – vocals / **MICK GEGGUS** – guitar, vocals / **VINCE RIORDAN** – bass, vocals / **KEITH WARRINGTON** – drums

Small Wonder — not iss.

Jul 79. (7"m) *(SMALL 19)* **FLARES 'N' SLIPPERS. / POLICE CAR / I WANNA BE A STAR** [ ] [-]

E.M.I. — not iss.

Nov 79. (7") *(EMI 5008)* **I'M NOT A FOOL. / EAST END** [65] [-]
Feb 80. (7") *(EMI 5035)* **BAD MAN. / THE NEW SONG** [65] [-]

Zonophone — not iss.

Mar 80. (lp/c) *(ZONO/TC-ZONO 101)* **GREATEST HITS VOL.1** [22] [-]
– I'm not a fool / Headbanger / Bad man / Fighting in the street / Here they come again / Join the Rejects / East End / The new song / Police car / Someone like you / (They're gonna) Put me away / Are you ready to rock / Where the hell is Babylon?. *(cd-iss. Mar94 on 'Dojo'+=; DOJOCD 136)* – Shitter / I'm forever blowing bubbles / West Side boys.
Apr 80. (7"yellow) *(Z 2)* **THE GREATEST COCKNEY RIPOFF. / HATE OF THE CITY** [21] [-]
May 80. (7") *(Z 4)* **I'M FOREVER BLOWING BUBBLES. / WEST SIDE BOYS** [35] [-]
Jul 80. (7") *(Z 6)* **WE CAN DO ANYTHING. / 15 NIGHTS** [ ] [-]
Oct 80. (7") *(Z 10)* **WE ARE THE FIRM. / WAR ON THE TERRACES** [ ] [-]
Oct 80. (lp/c) *(ZONO/TC-ZONO 102)* **GREATEST HITS VOL.2** [23] [-]
– War on the terraces / In the underworld / Oi, oi, oi / Hate of the city / With the boys / Urban guerilla / The rocker / The greatest Cockney rip-off / Sitting in a cell / On the waterfront / We can do anything / It's alright / Subculture / Blockbuster. *(cd-iss. Mar94 on 'Dojo'+=; DOJOCD 138)* – 15 nights / We are the firm.
Mar 81. (7"m) *(Z 20)* **EASY LIFE. / MOTORHEAD / HANG 'EM HIGH** [ ] [-]
Apr 81. (lp) *(ZEM 101)* **GREATEST HITS VOL.3 (LIVE AND LOUD) (live)** [27] [-]
– The rocker / Bad man / I'm not a fool / On the waterfront / On the run / Hate of the city / Easy life / War on the terraces / Fighting in the streets / Greatest Cockney rip-off / Join the Rejects / Police car / East End / Motorhead / Hang 'em high. *(re-iss. Dec87 as 'LIVE AND LOUD' on 'Link'; LINKLP 09) (cd-iss. Nov94 on 'Dojo'; DOJOCD 168)*
Jun 81. (7") *(Z 21)* **ON THE STREETS AGAIN. / LONDON** [ ] [-]
Jul 81. (lp) *(ZONO 105)* **POWER AND THE GLORY** [ ] [-]
– Power and the glory / Because I'm in love / On the run / Lumon / Friends / Van bollocks / Teenage fantasy / It's over / On the streets again / B.Y.C. / The greatest story ever told. *(cd-iss. Nov94 on 'Dojo'; DOJOCD 174)*

A.K.A. — not iss.

Nov 82. (lp) *(AKA 1)* **THE WILD ONES** [ ] [-]
– Way of the rocker / City of lights / Rock'n'roll dream / Till the end of the day / Some play dirty / Satellite city / Let me rock you / Victim of the cheap wine / Hell's a long way to go / Heat of the night.
Nov 82. (7") *(AKS 102)* **TILL THE END OF THE DAY. / ROCK & ROLL DREAM** [ ] [-]

Heavy Metal — not iss.

Nov 84. (lp/c; as The REJECTS) *(HMR LP/MC 22)* **ROCK THE WILD SIDE** [ ] [-]
– I ain't nothin' / I saw the light / Back to the start / I can't forget / Quiet storm / Feeling my way / Leave it / Fourth summer / Jog on.

FM Revolver — not iss.

Mar 85. (7"; as The REJECTS) *(VHF 7)* **BACK TO THE START. / LEAVE IT** [ ] [-]

—— disbanded 1985. All retired to other work. Re-formed in 1990.

Neat — not iss.

Jul 90. (lp/cd) *(NEAT/+CD 1049)* **LETHAL** [ ] [-]
– Bad man down / Penitentiary / Struttin' my stuff / Lethal weapon / Rough diamond / Go get it / Down'n'out / One way ticket / Once a rocker / Take me higher. *(cd+=)* – Down the line / Mean city / See you later. *(re-iss. Dec95; same)*

– compilations, others, etc. –

Aug 85. (lp) *Wonderful World; (WOWLP 2)* **UNHEARD REJECTS 1979-1981** [ ] [-]
(cd-iss. Mar95 on 'Step 1'+=;) – FLARES 'N' SLIPPERS
Aug 86. (lp) *Dojo; (DOJOLP 32)* **WE ARE THE FIRM** [ ] [-]
May 93. (cd) *Dojo; (DOJOCD 82)* **THE BEST OF THE COCKNEY REJECTS** [ ] [-]
– Flares 'n' slippers / Police car / I'm not a fool / East end / Bad man / Headbanger / Join the rejects / Where the hell is Babylon / War on the terraces / Oi oi oi / Hate of the city / Rocker / The greatest Cockney rip-off / We can do anything / We are the firm / I'm forever blowing bubbles / Here we go again / Motorhead (live) / Easy life (live) / On the streets again / Power and the glory / Teenage fantasy.
Nov 94. (cd) *Loma; (LOMACD 38)* **THE WILD ONES / LETHAL** [ ] [-]
Mar 97. (cd) *Anagram; (CDPUNK 90)* **THE PUNK SINGLES COLLECTION** [ ] [-]

COCTEAU TWINS

Formed: Grangemouth, Scotland . . . late 1981 when the (then) trio of ELIZABETH FRASER, ROBIN GUTHRIE and WILL HEGGIE visited London to hand DJ John Peel a demo tape. He booked them for sessions on his Radio One night time show and they subsequently signed to IVO WATT-RUSSELL's indie label, '4 a.d.'. The COCTEAUS' debut offering, 'GARLANDS', was hastily recorded, hitting the shops just over a week later and giving a hint of things to come with an interesting fusion of monochromatic rhythms, textured guitar distortion and sampling technology. Resisting many offers from the majors, they were back in the studio again for 1983's 'LULLABIES' EP and 'HEAD OVER HEELS' album. A mesmerising collage of irridescent guitar soundscapes and sheets of feedback perforated with FRASER's unintelligible but highly emotive warbling, the latter record was a blueprint for the best of The COCTEAU TWINS work. After a support slot to OMD, WILL HEGGIE departed, making the long trip back north to set up his own outfit, LOWLIFE. Around the same time ROBIN and LIZ hit No.1 in the indie charts when guesting for 'IVO/4 a.d.' ensemble, THIS MORTAL COIL on 'SONG TO THE SIREN'; it was mistakenly thought by many to be a COCTEAU TWINS off-shoot, rather than IVO's project. That idea was laid to rest after the album, 'IT'LL END IN TEARS', was issued in '84. Meanwhile, The COCTEAU TWINS were back with another blissed out masterpiece, 'TREASURE', introducing newcomer, SIMON RAYMONDE on bass and seeing LIZ explore hitherto uncharted vocal territory in a fascinating, enigmatic and occasionally unsettling language that communicated everything and nothing. It also marked their first taste of Top 30 success although they surpassed this with 1986's more inscrutably minimalist Top 10 effort, 'VICTORIALAND'. An abortive film project collaboration with HAROLD BUDD was issued at the end of the year as they headed towards an increasingly "New Age"-style sound. Two more classics, 'BLUE BELL KNOLL' and 'HEAVEN OR LAS VEGAS' were released over the next half decade, both finding a home in the US charts for 'Capitol' records. In 1992, they finally succumbed to signing for 'Fontana' in the UK, leading to a comeback album, 'FOUR CALENDAR CAFE' in '93. Many longtime fans were disappointed with what was surely the duo's most accessible, grounded album to date yet devoid of much of the mystery that made their earlier work so alluring. The following year saw LIZ guest on FUTURE SOUND OF LONDON's ambient venture, 'Lifeforms'; she would subsequently go on to perform on MASSIVE ATTACK's 'Teardrops' single in '98. After another 3-year hiatus, FRAZER and GUTHRIE returned with 'MILK AND KISSES', a typically COCTEAU-esque affair that moved some critics to suggest the band were treading water. • **Trivia:** ROBIN has produced many '4.a.d.' outfits in addition to The GUN CLUB (1987). An item for some time, LIZ and ROBIN became parents in 1989. Early in 1991, LIZ was surprisingly but not undeservedly nominated for Best Female Vocalist at the 'Brit' awards.

Album rating: GARLANDS (*7) / HEAD OVER HEELS (*8) / TREASURE (*9) / VICTORIALAND (*8) / THE MOON AND THE MELODIES with Harold Budd (*5) / THE PINK OPAQUE compilation (*8) / BLUE BELL KNOLL (*7) / HEAVEN OR LAS VEGAS (*7) / FOUR CALENDAR CAFE (*6) / MILK AND KISSES (*7)

ELIZABETH FRASER (b.29 Aug'63) – vocals / **ROBIN GUTHRIE** (b. 4 Jan'62) – guitar, drum programming, keyboards / **WILL HEGGIE** – bass

4 a.d. — not iss.

Jul 82. (lp) *(CAD 211)* **GARLANDS** [ ] [-]
– Blood bitch / Wax and wane / But I'm not / Blind dumb deaf / Grail overfloweth / Shallow than halo / The hollow men / Garlands. *(c-iss.Apr84 +=; CADC 211)* – Dear heart / Blind dumb deaf / Hearsay please / Hazel. *(cd-iss. 1986 ++=; CAD 211CD)* – Speak no evil / Perhaps some other acorn. *<US cd-iss. 1991 on 'Alliance'; 96415>*
Sep 82. (12"ep) *(BAD 213)* **LULLABIES** [ ] [-]
– It's all but an ark lark / Alas dies laughing / Feathers-Oar-Blades.
Mar 83. (7") *(AD 303)* **PEPPERMINT PIG. / LAUGH LINES** [ ] [-]
(12"+=) *(BAD 303)* – Hazel.

—— Trimmed to a duo when HEGGIE left to form LOWLIFE

Oct 83. (lp) *(CAD 313)* **HEAD OVER HEELS** [51] [-]
– When mama was moth / Sugar hiccup / In our anglehood / Glass candle grenades / Multifoiled / In the gold dust rush / The tinderbox (of a heart) / My love paramour / Musette and drums / Five ten fiftyfold. *(c-iss.Apr84 +=; CADC 313) (cd-iss. 1986 +=; CAD 313CD)* – SUNBURST AND SNOWBLIND EP *<US cd-iss. 1991 on 'Alliance'; 96416>*

Oct 83. (12"ep) *(BAD 314)* **SUNBURST AND SNOWBLIND** [ ] [-]
– Sugar hiccup / From the flagstones / Because of whirl-Jack / Hitherto.

—— added **SIMON RAYMONDE** (b. 3 Apr'62, London, England) – bass, keyboards, guitar (ex-DROWNING CRAZE)

Apr 84. (7") *(AD 405)* **PEARLY DEWDROPS DROP. / PEPPER-TREE** [29] [-]
(12"+=) *(BAD 405)* – The spangle maker.

Nov 84. (lp/c) *(CAD/+C 412)* **TREASURE** [29] [-]
– Ivo / Lorelei / Beatrix / Persephone / Pandora – for Cindy / Amelia / Aloysius / Cicely / Otterley / Donimo. *(cd-iss. 1986; CAD 412CD) <US cd-iss. 1991 on 'Alliance'; 96418>*

Mar 85. (7") *(AD 501)* **AIKEA-GUINEA. / KOOKABURRA** [41] [-]
(12"+=) *(BAD 501)* – Rococo / Quiquose.

Nov 85. (12"ep) *(BAD 510)* **TINY DYNAMITE** [52] [-]
– Pink orange red / Ribbed and veined / Sultitan Itan / Plain tiger.

Nov 85. (12"ep) *(BAD 511)* **ECHOES IN A SHALLOW BAY** [65] [-]
– Great spangled fritillary / Melonella / Pale clouded white / Eggs and their shells *(cd-iss. Oct86 +=; BAD 510/511)* – TINY DYNAMITE

—— **RICHARD THOMAS** – saxophone, bass (of DIF JUZ) repl. SIMON who fell ill

Apr 86. (lp/c)(cd) *(CAD/+C 602)(CAD 602CD)* **VICTORIALAND** [10] [ ]
– Lazy calm / Fluffy tufts / Throughout the dark months of April and May / Whales tales / Oomingmak / Little Spacey / Feet-like fins / How to bring a blush to the snow / The thinner the air. *<US cd-iss. 1991 on 'Alliance'; 96417>*

—— **SIMON RAYMONDE** returned repl.temp. RICHARD (back to DIF JUZ)

Oct 86. (7") *(AD 610)* **LOVE'S EASY TEARS. / THOSE EYES, THAT MOUTH** [53] [-]
(12"+=) *(BAD 610)* – Sigh's smell of farewell.

—— next was a one-off collaboration with label new signing **HAROLD BUDD** – piano

4 a.d. Relativity

Nov 86. (lp/c)(cd; by HAROLD BUDD, ELIZABETH FRASER, ROBIN GUTHRIE, SIMON RAYMONDE) *(CAD/+C 611)(CAD 611CD) <8143>* **THE MOON AND THE MELODIES** [46] [ ]
– Sea, swallow me / Memory gongs / Why do you love me? / Eyes are mosaics / She will destroy you / The ghost has no home / Bloody and blunt / Ooze out and away, one how.

4 a.d. Capitol

Sep 88. (lp/c/dat)(cd) *(CAD/+C/T 807)(CAD 807CD) <90892>* **BLUE BELL KNOLL** [15] [ ]
– Blue bell knoll / Athol-brose / Carolyn's fingers / For Phoebe still a baby / The itchy glowbo blow / Cico buff / Suckling the mender / Spooning good singing gum / A kissed out red floatboat / Ella megablast burls forever.

Oct 88. (7") **CAROLYN'S FINGERS. / BLUE BELL KNOLL** [-] [ ]

—— In Apr'90, LIZ was heard on Ian McCulloch's (ex-ECHO & THE BUNNYMEN) 'Candleland' single.

Aug 90. (7"/c-s) *(AD 0011/+C)* **ICEBLINK LUCK. / MIZAKE THE MIZAN** [38] [-]
(12"+=/cd-s+=) *(AD 0011 T/CD)* – Watchiar.

Sep 90. (cd)(lp/c) *(CAD 0012CD)(CAD/+C 0012) <C2/C1/C4 93669>* **HEAVEN OR LAS VEGAS** [7] [99]
– Cherry coloured funk / Pitch the baby / Iceblink luck / Fifty-fifty clown / Heaven or Las Vegas / I wear your ring / Fotzepolitic / Wolf in the breast / Road, river and rail / Frou-frou foxes in midsummer fires.

—— on U.S. tour, augmented by **MITSUO TATE + BEN BLAKEMAN** – guitars

Fontana Capitol

Sep 93. (7"/c-s) *(CT/+C 1)* **EVANGELINE. / MUD AND LARK** [34] [-]
(12"pic-d+=/cd-s+=) *(CT X/CD 1)* – Summer-blink.

Oct 93. (cd/c/lp) *(518259-2/-4/-1) <C2/C4/C1 99375>* **FOUR CALENDAR CAFE** [13] [78]
– Know who you are ate every age / Evangeline / Blue beard / Theft and wandering around lost / Oil of angels / Squeeze-wax / My truth / Essence / Summerhead / Pur.

Dec 93. (cd-s) *(COCCD 1)* **WINTER WONDERLAND. / FROSTY THE SNOWMAN** [58] [-]
(above festive tracks, deleted after a week in UK Top 60)

Feb 94. (7"/c-s) *(CT/+C 2)* **BLUEBEARD. / THREE SWEPT** [33] [ ]
(12"+=) *(CTX 2)* – Ice-pulse.
(cd-s++=) *(CTCD 2)* – ('A'acoustic).

Sep 95. (7"/7"/cd-ep) *(CCT/CTT/CTCD 3) <30548>* **TWINLIGHTS** [59] [ ] Dec95
– Rilkean heart / Golden-vein // Pink orange red / Half-gifts.

Oct 95. (12"ep/cd-ep) *(CT X/CD 4) <36240>* **OTHERNESS** (An Ambient EP) [59] [ ] Dec95
– Feet like fins / Seekers who are lovers / Violaine / Cherry coloured funk.

Mar 96. (cd-ep) *(CTCD 5)* **TISHBITE / PRIMITIVE HEART / FLOCK OF SOUL** [34] [-]
(12"ep/cd-ep) *(CT X/DDD 5)* – (title track) / Round / An Elan.

Apr 96. (cd/c/lp) *(514 501-2/4/-1) <37049-2/-4/-1>* **MILK & KISSES** [17] [99]
– Violaine / Serpent skirt / Tishbite / Half-gifts / Calfskin smack / Rilkean heart / Ups / Eperdu / Treasure hiding / Seekers who are lovers. *(also ltd.cd; 532 363-2)*

Jul 96. (12") *(CTX 6)* **VIOLAINE. / ALICE** [56] [-]
(cd-s+=) *(CTDD 6)* – Circling girl.
(cd-s) *(CTCD 6)* – ('A'side) / Tranquil eye / Smile.

– compilations, others, etc. –

Dec 85. (cd) *4 a.d.; (CAD 513CD) / Relativity; <ENC 8040>* **THE PINK OPAQUE** [ ] [ ] Sep85
– The spangle maker / Millimillenary / Wax and wane / Hitherto / Pearly-dewdrops' drops (12" Version) / From the flagstones / Aikea-Guinea / Lorelei / Pepper-tree / Musette and drums.

Nov 91. (10xcd-ep-box) *Capitol; (CTBOX 1)* **THE SINGLES COLLECTION** [ ] [-]
– (above featured previous 9 singles + new 1) (sold separately Mar92)

CODEINE

Formed: based- New York, USA . . . early 90's by STEVE IMMERWAHR, JOHN ENGLE and CHRIS BROKAW, the latter subsequently joining COME and replaced by MATTHEW McGUIGAN. Named after a brand of painkiller, CODEINE specialise in painfully slow, lingering songs which make the shoegazing bands of the early 90's seem positively animated. Signed to 'Sub Pop', the trio debuted in 1992 with mini-set, 'BARELY REAL', its slo-mo textures, languid vocals and general air of solemnity ranging through mogodon riffing, semi-acoustic strumming and with 'W.' (even the song titles were minimalist!) even stark piano, to strangely hypnotic effect. The following year saw the release of a full length debut album, 'THE WHITE BIRCH', prompting more superlatives from the critics and ensuring a cult following. Not music to play before a night out! • **Covered:** PROMISE OF LOVE (Emexco/Pale Pachyderm).

Album rating: FRIGID STARS (*6) / BARLEY REAL mini (*5) / THE WHITE BIRCH (*6)

STEPHEN IMMERWAHR – vocals, bass / **JOHN ENGLE** – guitar / **DOUGLAS SCHARIN** – drums; repl. JOSH who had briefly depped for CHRIS BROKAW (who joined COME as a guitarist)

Sub Pop Sub Pop

Aug 90. (lp/c/cd) *<sp 107/+A/B>* **FRIGID STARS** [-] [ ]
– D / Gravel bed / Pickup song / New year's / Second chance / Cave-in / Cigarette machine / Old things / 3 angels / Pea.

Nov 92. (m-lp/m-cd) *<(sp/+cd 51-213)>* **BARELY REAL** [ ] [ ]
– Realize / Jr / Barely real / Hard to find / W. / Promise of love.

May 93. (7") *(WH-MARCH)* **IDES. / Cocktails: Working Holiday** [ ] [ ]
(above issued on 'Simple Machines')

—— added guest guitarist **DAVID GRUBBS** (on below)

Nov 93. (7") *<(sp 117-295)>* **TOM. /** [ ] [ ]

May 94. (lp/cd) *(sp/+cd 118-299)* **THE WHITE BIRCH** [ ] [ ]
– Sea / Loss leader / Vacancy / Kitchen light / Washed up / Tom / Ides / Wird / Smoking room.

—— **MATTHEWS McGUIGAN** – drums; repl. SCHARIN

—— split later in '94

COIL

Formed: London, England . . . 1983 by JOHN BALANCE and PETER 'SLEAZY' CHRISTOPHERSON. The latter had been a graphic designer for Hypnosis (album sleeves for PINK FLOYD and LED ZEPPELIN) in the 70's, before becoming part of THROBBING GRISTLE and later co-founder of PSYCHIC TV (with TG mainman, GENESIS P. ORRIDGE). PETER had just departed from the latter to become a pop video maker but chose to return to the studio in 1984 to record with BALANCE, cutting the 17-minute single, 'HOW TO DESTROY ANGELS'. Soon after its release, they found CLINT RUIN (aka JIM 'FOETUS' THIRLWELL), who produced their debut album 'SCATOLOGY', aided by the expanded line-up of STEPHEN E. THROWER, GAVIN FRIDAY (Virgin Prunes) and ALEX FERGUSSON. Ritualistic industrial experimentation incorporating arcane sexual ambience, one of the record's highlights was the subsequent single, 'PANIC', backed by a cover of Gloria Jones' 'TAINTED LOVE' (more recently covered by SOFT CELL). In fact, they used MARC ALMOND on an accompanying video, which was widely banned. During this time, they had also worked with gay film-maker, Derek Jarman on soundtrack, 'The Angel Conversation'. In 1986, COIL shared a billing with BOYD RICE (NON) on the album, 'NIGHTMARE CULTURE'. STEPHEN was now a full-time member, working on two further 1986 releases, the 'THE ANAL STAIRCASE' EP and 'HORSE ROTORVATOR' album. The following year, the group worked on Clive Barker's soundtrack for the horror movie, 'HELLRAISER', releasing the out-takes as a 10" EP, 'THE CONSEQUENCES OF RAISING HELL'. BALANCE, SLEAZY and Co incorporated OTTO AVERY into the line-up for 'GOLD IS THE METAL' album, although little was heard from them until a compilation was released in 1990. In 1994, the veteran experimentalists were snapped up by TRENT REZNOR, who signed them to his new 'Eksaton' label, the group's sound having evolved into a darker edged techno/industrial sound; 1998's 'TIME MACHINE' showed how far they had come since their early 80's inception. • **Songwriters:** BALANCE – CHRISTOPHERSON, except WHO BY FIRE (Leonard Cohen). • **Note:** Not to be confused with late 70's COIL, who released the 'MOTOR INDUSTRY' single.

Album rating: SCATOLOGY (*6) / HORSE ROTORVATOR (*6) / THE CONSEQUENCES OF RAISING HELL (*8) / GOLD IS THE METAL (*6) / UNNATURAL HISTORY compilation (*6) / LOVE'S SECRET DOMAIN (*7) / BACKWARDS (*6) / BLACK LIGHT DISTRICT (*5) / TIME MACHINES (*5)

JOHN BALANCE – guitar, bass, vocals, piano (also of CURRENT 93) / **PETER 'SLEAZY' CHRISTOPHERSON** – drum programming (ex-PSYCHIC TV, ex-THROBBING GRISTLE)

Himalaya not iss.

Jun 84. (12"one-sided) *(LAY 005)* **HOW TO DESTROY ANGELS** [ ] [-]
(cd-iss. 1988+=; LAY 005CD) – Absolute elsewhere. *(cd re-iss. Oct96 on 'Threshold House'=; LOCICD 5)* – The sleeper / Remotely / The sleeper II / Tectonic plates / Dismal orb.

—— added guests **STEPHEN E. THROWER** – clarinet, percussion (of POSSESSION) / **ALEX FERGUSSON** – guitar (of PSYCHIC TV) / **GAVIN FRIDAY** – vocals (of VIRGIN PRUNES) / **CLINT RUIN** – synthesizers

Force & Form/K422 not iss.

Feb 85. (lp) *(FKK 1)* **SCATOLOGY** [ ] [-]
– Ubu noir / Panic / At the heart of it all / Tenderness of wolves / The spoiler / Clap / Aqua regis / Restless day / Solar lodge / The S.W.B.P. / Godhead = deadhead / Cathedral in flames. *(cd-iss. Dec88; FKK 001CD)(+=)* – Tainted love.

May 85. (12",12"red) *(FFK 512)* **PANIC. / TAINTED LOVE / AQUA REGIS** [ ] [-]

— In 1986, shared billing with BOYD RICE on album 'NIGHTMARE CULTURE'.

— added **STEPHEN E. THROWER** – wind, percussion

Dec 86. (12"ep,12"clear-ep) *(ROTA 121)* **THE ANAL STAIRCASE. / BLOOD FROM THE AIR / RAVENOUS** ☐ -

Jan 87. (lp) *(ROTA 1)* **HORSE ROTORVATOR** ☐ -
– The anal staircase / Slur / Babylero / Ostia / Herald / Penetralia / Circles of mania / Blood from the air / Who by fire / The golden section / The first five minutes after death. *(cd-iss. Jan88; ROTA 1CD)(+=)* – Ravenous.

Solar Lodge / Torso

Jan 88. (lp) *(SL 1)* **MUSIC FOR COMMERCIALS** ☐ -

Jun 88. (10"m-lp; some colrd) *(COIL 001)* **THE CONSEQUENCES OF RAISING HELL** ☐ -
– Hellraiser theme / The hellbound heart / Box theme / No new world / Attack of the Sennapods / Main title. *(re-iss. as 'HELLRAISER' Feb89 c/cd; COIL C/CD 001)(+=)* – MUSIC FOR COMMERCIALS

— added **OTTO AVERY**

Threshold House / Torso

Sep 88. (lp,red-lp,clear-lp/cd) *(LOCI/+CD 1)* **GOLD IS THE METAL** ☐ -
– The last rites of spring / Paradisiac / Thump / For us they will / The broken wheel / Boy in a suitcase / Golden hole / Cardinal points / Red slur / . . .Of free enterprise / Aqua regalia / Metal in the head / Either his, or yours / Chickenskin / Soundtrap / The first five minutes after violent death. *(cd+=)* – The wheal / Hellraiser. *(lp's w/ free 7")* – THE WHEEL. / THE WHEAL *(re-iss. 1990 on 'Normal' lp/cd; NORMAL/+CD 77) (lp w/ free 7")* – THE WHEEL. / KEEL HAULER *(re-iss. cd May94 on 'Normal'; same) (cd re-iss. Oct96; same)*

1990. (7") *(SX 002)* **WRONG EYE. / SCOPE** ☐ -
(above issued on 'Shock')

Dec 90. (12") *(LOCI 3)* **WINDOWPANE. / WINDOWPANE** ☐ -

Torso / Wax Trax!

May 91. (lp/cd) *(TORSO/+CD 181)* <WAXCD 7143> **LOVE'S SECRET DOMAIN** ☐ ☐ 1989
– Disco hospital / Teenage lightning / Things happen / The snow / Dark river / Where even the darkness / Something to see / Windowpane / Further back and faster / Lorca not Orca / Love's secret domain.

Aug 91. (12"ep/cd-ep) *(TORSO/+CD 180)* **THE SNOW REMIXES** ☐ -
– (6 remixes from last album by JACK DANGERS + DREW McDOWELL)

1992. (7") **AIRBORNE BELLS. / IS SUICIDE A SOLUTION** ☐ -

— above issued on 'Clawfist'

Nov 92. (cd) *(LOCICD 4)* **STOLEN AND CONTAMINATED KISSES** ☐ -
(cont. 'HOW TO DESTROY ANGELS') (cd re-iss. Oct96; same)

1994. (12"blue) *(LOCIS 1)* **THEMES FROM BLUE 1. / THEMES FROM BLUE 2** ☐ -

Eskaton / Nothing

1994. (12") *(ESKATON 001)* **NASA ARAB. / FIRST DARK RIDE** ☐ -

1994. (12") *(ESKATON 002)* **BEAUTIFUL CATASTROPHE** ☐ -
– Protection / Glimpse / Crawling sirit / PHILM #1.

1995. (10"ep,10"clear-ep; by COIL & ELPH) *(ESKATON 003)* **PHILM. / STATIC ELECTRICIAN / RED SCRATCH** ☐ -

1995. (cd/lp; as ELpH) *(ESKATON 006/007)* **WORSHIP THE GLITCH** ☐ -

Oct 96. (cd/d-lp) *(ESKATON 008/009)* **BLACK LIGHT DISTRICT** ☐ -

Jan 98. (cd) *(ESKATON 010)* **TIME MACHINES** ☐ ☐
– Telepathine / DOET-Hectate / 5 MeO DMT / Dimethylamino / Psilocybin.

– compilations, etc. –

Dec 89. (cd) *Threshold House; (LOCICD 2)* **UNNATURAL HISTORY** ☐ -

1995. (d-cd) *Eskaton;* **THE SOUND OF MUSIC** (film music) ☐ -

Oct 96. (cd) *Threshold House; (LOCICD 6)* **ANGELIC CONVERSATION** ☐ -

Oct 96. (cd) *Threshold House; (LOCICD 7)* **WINDOWPANE / THE SNOW** ☐ -

Oct 96. (cd) *Threshold House; (LOCICD 10)* **UNNATURAL HISTORY VOL.2** ☐ -

Apr 97. (cd) *Threshold House; (LOCICD 12)* **UNNATURAL HISTORY VOL.3 (JOYFUL PARTICIPATION IN THE SORROWS OF THE WORLD)** ☐ -
– First dark ride / Baby food / Music for commercials / Panic / Neither his nor yours / Feeder / Wrong eye / Meaning what exactly / Scope / Lost rivers Of London.

Oct 97. (cd; COIL & ZOSKIA) *Threshold House; (LOCICD 13) / Imprint;* <84870> **TRANSPARENT** ☐ ☐ Feb99
– Sicktone / Baptism of fire / Rape / Poisons / Truth / Sewn open / Silence et secrecy / Here to here (double headed secret) / Stealing the words / On balance.

COLD WATER FLAT

Formed: Amherst, Massachusetts, USA . . . 1990 by PAUL JANOWITZ, TED SILVA and PAUL HARDING. Following in the grand tradition of Boston guitar acts, COLD WATER FLAT combined noise, melody, experimentation and hooklines in equal measure. While they also boasted the talents of BILL JANOWITZ' brother, PAUL, most commentators agreed that debut album, 'LISTEN' (1993), was impressive enough to withstand the inevitable BUFFALO TOM comparisons. Released in the UK on the tiny 'Bittersweet' label, the record was accompanied by a split single with SLEEPYHEAD, 'LOST AND LAZY'. Having accrued a fair number of respectable support slots and a growing press reputation, the band signed to Boston's influential 'Fort Apache' label, handled by 'M.C.A.' First up was 'MAGNETIC NORTH POLE', a rolling, soaring, bruising epic akin to a Stateside MANIC STREET PREACHERS with the obligatory grunge factor intact. Confusingly enough, the lads decided to release their follow-up set as an eponymous affair, hitting the shops a month after the single in Spring '95.

Album rating: LISTEN (*6) / COLD WATER FLAT (*6)

PAUL JANOWITZ – vocals, guitar / **TED SILVA** – bass / **PAUL HARDING** – drums

Bittersweet / Sonic Bubblegum

Aug 93. (cd) *(BITTERSWEET 002)* <SB 9> **LISTEN** ☐ ☐

Aug 93. (7") *(BITTERSWEET 003)* **LOST AND LONELY. / Sleepyhead: Gingerbread House** ☐ -

Fort Apache – MCA / Fort Apache – MCA

Feb 95. (7"/c-s) *(FAS/+C 1)* **MAGNETIC NORTH POLE. /** ☐ ☐
(cd-s+=) *(FASTD 1)* –

Mar 95. (cd/c) <(MCD/MCC 11210)> **COLD WATER FLAT** ☐ ☐
– Virus road / Kings of the underground / Numb / Magnetic North Pole / Mistaken / Beautiful / Rescue lights / It's over / All I had / She is / Hold my head.

— disbanded soon after above

COLENSO PARADE

Formed: Belfast, N.Ireland . . . 1984 by LINDA CLANDINNING, NEIL LAWSON, JACKIE FORGIE, ROBERT WAKEMAN and frontman, OSCAR. Setting up their own label, COLENSO PARADE released their debut single, 'STANDING UP', showcasing their CHAMELEONS-esque sound complete with elastic bass riffs. Relocating to London the following year, they replaced FORGIE with Englishman, TERRY BICKERS, the guitarist making his first appearance on the single, 'DOWN BY THE BORDER'. Subsequently signing for manager, Dave Bedford's 'Fire' records, the group released their third single, 'HALLELUJAH CHORUS', previewing their long-awaited debut album, 'GLENTORRAN', in the Autumn of '86. However, by the time of the album's release, BICKERS had chose to join the more ambitious HOUSE OF LOVE, his replacement being JOHN WATT. Further personnel shuffles saw drummer OWEN HOWELL substitute WAKEMAN (who would later throw in his lot with SALAD), a parting single, 'FONTANA EYES' rewarding them with a bit of belated recognition before a proposed major label deal collapsed and the band finally split; OSCAR would later turn down an offer to replace IAN McCULLOCH in ECHO & THE BUNNYMEN.

Album rating: GLENTORRAN (*5)

OSCAR – vocals / **LINDA CLANDINNING** – keyboards / **JACKIE FORGIE** – guitar / **NEIL LAWSON** – bass / **ROBERT WAKEMAN** – drums

Goliath / not iss.

Sep 84. (7") *(SLING 01)* **STANDING UP. / SMOKEY FINGERED REMINDER** ☐ -

— **TERRY BICKERS** – guitar repl. FORGIE

Apr 85. (12"m) *(SLING 02)* **DOWN BY THE BORDER. / SEE RED / BORDER MIXES** ☐ -

Fire / not iss.

Jan 86. (12"ep) *(FIRE 7)* **HALLELUJAH CHORUS / THE PERFECT ADOPTERS. / TOO LATE FOR ANYTHING / SACRED LOVER** ☐ -

Aug 86. (lp) *(FIRELP 6)* **GLENTORRAN** ☐ -

— **JOHN WATT** – guitar repl. BICKERS who joined HOUSE OF LOVE. He was later to front LEVITATION

— **OWEN HOWELL** – drums (ex-BIG SELF) repl. WAKEMAN who later re-surfaced in SALAD

Oct 86. (7") *(BLAZE 11)* **FONTANA EYES. / HERE COMES THE NIGHT** ☐ -
(12"+=) *(BLAZE 11T)* – Anything / Our man in Havana.

— split soon after above and OSCAR declined an offer to take over IAN McCULLOCH's job in ECHO & THE BUNNYMEN.

COLLAPSED LUNG

Formed: Harlow, Middlesex, England . . . 1992 by sampler/sometime rapper ANTHONY CHAPMAN and metal guitarist STEVE HARCOURT, the group completed with the addition of Asian rapper NIHIL (MC KRAYZEE A) six months later. This oddball trio were the first act to sign for 'Deceptive' (more famously home to ELASTICA), releasing a series of EP's through '93/'94 beginning with 'THUNDERSLEY INVACAR'. Taking the BEASTIE BOYS/BECK route to mutant rap city via Seattle, COLLAPSED LUNG emerged from the tunnel and onto the pitch with their 1995 debut set, 'JACKPOT GOALIE'. This featured the original version of 'EAT MY GOAL', the funky football terracing anthem subsequently adopted as the theme for Coca Cola's Euro '96 TV ad campaign. Unfortunately the track's near Top 30 success (actually a double-A with 'LONDON TONIGHT') was to become an albatross around the trio's neck; although the accompanying 1996 album, 'COOLER', failed to shift sufficient units, people went out and bought the single all over again when it was re-released for the '98 World Cup.

Album rating: JACKPOT GOALIE (*6) / COOLER (*6)

NIHIL (MC KRAYZEE A) – rapper / **ANTHONY CHAPMAN** – samples, vocals / **STEVE HARCOURT** – guitar

Deceptive / not iss.

Jul 93. (10"ep/cd-ep) *(BLUFF 001/+CD)* **THUNDERSLEY INVACAR / ROTASTAK. / PITCH FORK / THUNDERSLEY INVACAR (butt naked mix)** ☐ -

Sep 93. (12"ep/cd-ep) *(BLUFF 002/+CD)* **CHAINSAW WEDGIE / FIRST & SIXTH. / BARF-O-RAMA / FIRST & SIXTH (scatter mix)** ☐ -

May 94. (12"ep/cd-ep) *(BLUFF 005/+CD)* **DOWN WITH THE PLAID FAD (large). / SPINNING DOWN / HEADGAMES / DOWN WITH THE PLAID (XX large)** ☐ -

Sep 94. (7") *(BLUFF 009)* **DIS MX. / SOMETHING ORDINARY** [ ] [-]
(12"+=/cd-s+=) *(BLUFF 009 T/CD)* – ('A'-Organ-ized mix by Inspiral Carpets) / ('A'-Abdul Van Halen mix by Fun-Da-Mental).
Apr 95. (cd/lp) *(BLUFF 015 CD/LP)* **JACKPOT GOALIE** [ ] [-]
– Maclife intro / Maclife / Down with the plaid fad / Eat my goal / Interactive / I may not know the score but . . . / Something ordinary / Burn rubber soul / Filthy's fix / Dis MX / Begrudgit / Slack agenda.
May 95. (12"ep/cd-ep) *(BLUFF 016 T/CD)* **INTERACTIVE / LUNGIST MASSIVE. / INTERACTIVE (1440 BPS mix) / INTERACTIVE (Edward Stonelayne mix)** [ ] [-]
Dec 95. (7"one-sided) *(BLUFF 018)* **CONNECTION** [ ] [-]
Dec 95. (12") *(COUP 002)* **MACLIFE. / Soul Coughing: SUGAR FREE JAZZ** [ ] [-]
(above issued on 'Jealous')
Jun 96. (12"ep/cd-ep) *(BLUFF 029 T/CD)* **LONDON TONIGHT / EAT MY GOAL. / LONDON TONIGHT (Fila Brazilillia mix) / EAT MY GOAL (Euro '96 mix) / EAT MY GOAL (synchromesh terror on the terrace mix)** [31] [-]
Jun 96. (cd/cd/c/lp) *(BLUFF 031 CDS/CD/MC/LP)* **COOLER** [ ] [-]
– London tonight / Lungs collapse / Ballad night / Sense / Codename: Omega / One foot up the rude ladder / Board game / 25 years / Casino kisschase / TV is life Elvis. *(d-cd+=)* – Connection / Eat my goal / Codename: Omega (instrumental) / Ballad night (instrumental) / Lungs collapse (instrumental) / Casino kisschase (instrumental).
Sep 96. (12"ep/cd-ep) *(BLUFF 034 T/CD)* **BOARD GAME / BOARD GAME (Ballistic Brothers mix). / BALLAD NIGHT / BOARD GAME (Avenue A mix)** [ ] [-]
Mar 97. (12"ep) *(BLUFF 040T)* **BALLAD NIGHT (DJ Solo mix) / BALLAD NIGHT (Scissor mix). / BALLAD NIGHT (Lunatic Calm) / BALLAD NIGHT (A Sherman & Mr Moses mix)** [ ] [-]
May 98. (c-s/12"/cd-s) *(BLUFF 060 MC/T/CD)* **EAT MY GOAL (mixes: original / Mardi Gras / Jackpot Goalie / Synchromesh Terror On The Terraces / Black Cats / Instrumental)** [18] [-]

Edwyn COLLINS

Born: 23 Aug'59, Edinburgh, Scotland. COLLINS formed ORANGE JUICE in Glasgow, Scotland ... 1977 initially as the NU-SONICS with JAMES KIRK, STEPHEN DALY and ALAN DUNCAN, who was subsequently replaced by DAVID McCLYMONT. In 1979, ORANGE JUICE signed to local indie label 'Postcard', the hub of the burgeoning Glasgow indie scene masterminded by ALAN HORNE. In contrast to the post-punk miserabilism coming out of England, ORANGE JUICE were purveyors of studiedly naive, wide-eyed indie pop as best sampled on the brace of early 45's, 'FALLING AND LAUGHING', 'BLUE BOY', 'SIMPLY THRILLED HONEY' and 'POOR OLD SOUL' (later collected on 1993's retrospective, 'THE HEATHER'S ON FIRE'). They subsequently signed to 'Polydor' in 1981, releasing a debut album, 'YOU CAN'T HIDE YOUR LOVE FOREVER', early the following year. Though some of their die-hard fans inevitably accused them of selling out, the set almost made the UK Top 20, its charming guitar pop augering well for the future. The band suffered internal ruction soon after the album's release, however, MALCOLM ROSS and ZEKE MANYIKA replacing KIRK and DALY respectively. The Nigerian-born MANYIKA injected a newfound rhythmic thrust into the follow-up album, 'RIP IT UP' (1982), the clipped funk of the title track providing the band with their only Top 40 hit, albeit a sizeable one. Despite this belated success, further tensions reduced the band to a duo of COLLINS and MANYIKA who recorded an impressive mini-set, 'TEXAS FEVER' (1984) under the production auspices of reggae veteran, DENNIS BOVELL. Later that year, saw the release of swansong set, 'THE ORANGE JUICE – THE THIRD ALBUM', a far more introspective affair which found COLLINS at a low ebb. The singer had already released a cover of The Velvet Underground's 'PALE BLUE EYES', with PAUL QUINN and subsequently embarked on a solo career which remained low key for the ensuing decade. Initially signed to ALAN McGEE's "side" label, 'Elevation', his first two solo singles flopped and as the label went belly-up, COLLINS opted for 'Demon' records. He finally issued a long-awaited album, 'HOPE AND DESPAIR' in summer '89. An eclectic, rootsy affair borne of COLLINS' troubled wilderness years, the record was hailed by the same critics who so vehemently supported ORANGE JUICE. Yet despite the praise, it seemed COLLINS was destined for cult appeal; a second 'Demon' set, 'HELLBENT ON COMPROMISE' (1990) failed to lift his profile and COLLINS went to ground. Well, not completely, the singer honing his production skills for indie outfits such as A HOUSE and The ROCKINGBIRDS. The throaty-voxed singer finally re-emerged in 1994 with 'GORGEOUS GEORGE', the record he'd been threatening to make for years. Recorded on classic studio equipment, the record's organic feel coupled with COLLIN's mordant cynicism and razor sharp songwriting resulted in a massive worldwide hit, 'A GIRL LIKE YOU'. With its crunching, NEIL YOUNG-like riffing and infectious delivery, the record was initially in Europe and Australia before eventually hitting the Top 5 in the UK a year on. Though 1997's 'THE MAGIC PIPER' (from the album 'I'M NOT FOLLOWING YOU') didn't quite match this commercial feat, COLLINS remains one of Scotland's most accomplished songwriters with a reliable line in caustic wit. • **Songwriters:** ORANGE JUICE: most written by COLLINS, some with MANYIKA. Note that KIRK was the writer of FELICITY, and ROSS provided PUNCH DRUNK. They covered L.O.V.E. (Al Green), while COLLINS solo tried his hand at MY GIRL HAS GONE (Smokey Robinson) + TIME OF THE PREACHER (Willie Nelson) / WON'T TURN BACK (Vic Godard).

Album rating: Orange Juice: YOU CAN'T HIDE YOUR LOVE FOREVER (*7) / RIP IT UP (*6) / TEXAS FEVER mini (*5) / THE ORANGE JUICE (*5) / THE ESTEEMED ORANGE JUICE (THE VERY BEST OF ORANGE JUICE) compilation (*9) / Edwyn Collins: HOPE AND DESPAIR (*6) / HELLBENT ON COMPROMISE (*6) / GORGEOUS GEORGE (*8) / I'M NOT FOLLOWING YOU (*6)

ORANGE JUICE

EDWYN COLLINS – vocals, guitar, occasional violin / **JAMES KIRK** – guitar, vocals / **DAVID McCLYMONT** – bass, synths; repl. ALAN DUNCAN / **STEPHEN DALY** – drums

Postcard / not iss.

Feb 80. (7") *(80-1)* **FALLING AND LAUGHING. / MOSCOW** [ ] [-]
(free 7"flexi) *(LYN 7609)* – FELICITY (live).
Aug 80. (7") *(80-2)* **BLUE BOY. / LOVE SICK** [ ] [-]
Dec 80. (7") *(80-6)* **SIMPLY THRILLED HONEY. / BREAKFAST TIME** [ ] [-]
Mar 81. (7") *(81-2)* **POOR OLD SOUL. / (part 2)** [ ] [-]

Polydor / Polydor

Oct 81. (7") *(POSP 357)* **L.O.V.E. LOVE. / INTUITION TOLD ME PT.2** [65] [-]
(12"+=) *(POSPX 357)* – Moscow.
Jan 82. (7") *(POSP 386)* **FELICITY. / IN A NUTSHELL** [63] [-]
(12"+=) *(POSPX 386)* – You old eccentric.
Feb 82. (lp/c) *(POLS/+C 1057)* **YOU CAN'T HIDE YOUR LOVE FOREVER** [21] [ ]
– Falling and laughing / Untitled melody / Wan light / Tender object / Dying day / L.O.V.E. love / Intuition told me (part 1) / Upwards and onwards / Satellite city / Three cheers for our side / Consolation prize / Felicity / In a nutshell.

— **MALCOLM ROSS** – guitar (ex-JOSEF K) + **ZEKE MANYIKA** (b. Nigeria) – percussion, vocals, synths; repl. KIRK DALY who subsequently formed MEMPHIS, releasing only one single for 'Swamplands', 'YOU SUPPLY THE ROSES', early 1985

Jul 82. (7"/10") *(POSP/+T 470)* **TWO HEARTS TOGETHER. / HOKOYO** [60] [-]
Oct 82. (7") *(POSP 522)* **I CAN'T HELP MYSELF. / TONGUES BEGIN TO WAG** [42] [ ]
(12"+=) *(POSPX 522)* – Barbeque.
Nov 82. (lp/c) *(POLS/+C 1076)* **RIP IT UP** [39] [ ]
– Rip it up / Breakfast time / A million pleading faces / Mud in your eye / Turn away / I can't help myself / Flesh of my flesh / Louise Louise / Hokoyo / Tenter hook. *(cd-iss. Jul89; 839768-2)*
Feb 83. (7") *(POSP 547)* **RIP IT UP (remix). / SNAKE CHARMER** [8] [ ]
(some w/ live c-s+=) – The Felicity Flexi Session: The formative years – Simply thrilled honey / Botswana / Time to develop / Blue boy.
(d7"+=) *(POSPD 547)* – Sad lament / Lovesick.
(12") *(POSPX 547)* – ('A'side) / Sad lament / ('A'long version).
May 83. (7"/7"pic-d/ext.12") *(OJ/OJP/OJX 4)* **FLESH OF MY FLESH. / LORD JOHN WHITE AND THE BOTTLENECK TRAIN** [41] [ ]

— basically now a duo of **COLLINS + MANYIKA** with session people replacing ROSS (who joined AZTEC CAMERA) and McCLYMONT (to The MOODISTS)

Feb 84. (7") *(OJ 5)* **BRIDGE. / OUT FOR THE COUNT** [67] [ ]
(free 7"flexi w/ above) *(JUICE 1)* – Poor old soul (live).
(12"+=) *(OJX 5)* – ('A'-Summer '83 mix).
Feb 84. (m-lp/c) *(OJM LP/MC 1)* **TEXAS FEVER** [34] [ ]
– A sad lament / Craziest feeling / A place in my heart / The day I went down to Texas / Punch drunk / Bridge.
Apr 84. (7") *(OJ 6)* **WHAT PRESENCE?!. / A PLACE IN MY HEART (dub)** [47] [ ]
(free c-s w/ above) *(OJC 6)* – In a nutshell (live) / Simply thrilled honey (live) / Dying day (live).
(12"+=) *(OJX 6)* – ('A'extended).
Oct 84. (7") *(OJ 7)* **LEAN PERIOD. / BURY MY HEAD IN MY HANDS** [74] [ ]
(free 7"flexi w/ above) *(JUICE 3)* – Rip it up / What presence?!.
(12"+=) *(OJX 7)* – ('A'extended).
Nov 84. (lp/c) *(OJ LP/MC 1)* **THE ORANGE JUICE – THE THIRD ALBUM** [ ] [ ]
– Get while the goings good / Salmon fishing in New York / I guess I'm just a little sensitive / Burning desire / The artisan / Lean period / What presence?! / Out for the count / All that mattered / Seacharger. *(re-iss. Aug86 lp/c; SPE LP/MC 102) (c+=remixes)* – I can't help myself / Rip it up / Love struck / Flesh of my flesh / Out for the count / What presence?! / Lean period.

— Disbanded after above album. MANYIKA went solo, as did EDWYN COLLINS. He had already in Aug'84 hit UK 72 with PAUL QUINN on 7"/12" 'PALE BLUES EYES' (a Velvet Underground cover) released on 'Swamplands'.

– compilations, etc. –

Jul 85. (lp/c) *Polydor; (OJ LP/MC 3)* **IN A NUTSHELL** [ ] [-]
(w/free 7"flexi) – FELICITY.
Jan 91. (cd/c) *Polydor; (847 727-2/-4)* **THE ORANGE JUICE / YOU CAN'T HIDE YOUR LOVE FOREVER** [ ] [-]
Jul 92. (cd) *Polydor; (513618)* **THE VERY BEST OF ORANGE JUICE (THE ESTEEMED ORANGE JUICE)** [ ] [ ] Oct95
– Falling and laughing / Consolation prize (live) / Old encentric / L.O.V.E. love / Felicity / In a nutshell / Rip it up / I can't help myself / Flesh of my flesh / Tenterhook / Bridge / The day I went down to Texas / Punch drunk / A place in my heart / A sad lament / Lean period / I guess I'm just a little too sensitive / The artisans / Salmon fishing in New York / What presence?! / Out for the count. *(re-iss. cd Sep95; same)* – (extra track).
Jul 92. (lp/c/cd) *Postcard; (DUBH 922/+MC/CD)* **OSTRICH CHURCHYARD (live in Glasgow)** [ ] [-]
(cd re-iss. Oct95; DUBH 954CD)
May 93. (7") *Postcard; (DUBH 934)* **BLUEBOY. / LOVESICK** [ ] [-]
(cd-s+=) *(DUBH 934CD)* – Poor old soul (French version) / Poor old soul (instrumental).
Jul 93. (lp/cd) *Postcard; (DUBH 932/+CD)* **THE HEATHER'S ON FIRE** [ ] [-]
– Falling and laughing / Moscow / Moscow Olympics / Blue boy / Love sick / Simply thrilled honey / Breakfast time / Poor old soul / Poor old soul pt.2 / Felicity / Upwards and onwards / Dying day / Holiday hymn. *(re-iss. cd Oct95; DUBH 955CD)*

EDWYN COLLINS

solo, with **DENNIS BOVELL, MALCOLM ROSS, ALEX GRAY + CHRIS TAYLOR**

Elevation / not iss.

May 87. (7") *(ACID 4)* **DON'T SHILLY SHALLY. / IF EVER YOU'RE READY** [ ] [-]
(12"+=) *(ACID 4T)* – Queer fish.

Elevation / not iss.

Nov 87. (7") *(ACID 6)* **MY BELOVED GIRL. / CLOUDS (FOGGING UP MY MIND)** [ ] [-]
(12"+=) *(ACID 6T)* – My (long time) beloved girl.
(7"box+=) *(ACID 6B)* – 50 shades of blue (acoustic) / What's the big idea.

— now with **BERNARD CLARKE** – keyboards / **DENNIS BOVELL** – bass / **DAVE RUFFY** – drums

Demon / not iss.

Jun 89. (lp/c/cd) *(FIEND/+C/CD 144)* **HOPE AND DESPAIR** [ ] [-]
– Coffee table song / 50 shades of blue / You're better than you know / Pushing it to the back of my mind / The wheels of love / Darling, they want it all / The beginning of the end / The measure of the man / Testing time / Let me put my arms around you / The wide eyed child in me / Ghost of a chance. *(c+=/cd+=)* – If ever you're ready. *(re-iss. cd Sep95)*

Jul 89. (7") *(D 1064)* **THE COFFEE TABLE SONG. / JUDAS IN BLUE JEANS** [ ] [-]
(12"+=) *(D 1064T)* – Out there.

Oct 89. (7") *(D 1065)* **50 SHADES OF BLUE (new mix). / IF EVER YOU'RE READY** [ ] [-]
(12") *(D 1065T)* – ('A'extended) / Kindred spirit / Just call her name / Ain't that always the way.
(cd-s) *(D 1065CD)* – ('A'side) / Judas in blue jeans / Kindred spirit / Just call her name.

Oct 90. (lp/c/cd) *(FIEND/+C/CD 195)* **HELLBENT ON COMPROMISE** [ ] [-]
– Means to an end / You poor deluded fool / It might as well be you / Take care of yourself / Graciously / Someone else besides / My girl has gone / Everything and more / What's the big idea? / Hellbent medley:- Time of the preacher – Long time gone. *(re-iss. cd Oct95; same)*

— now with **STEVEN SKINNER** – guitar / **PHIL THORNALLEY** – bass / **PAUL COOK** – drums

Setanta / Bar None

Aug 94. (cd/c/lp) *(SET CD/MC/LP 014) <058>* **GEORGEOUS GEORGE** [ ] [ ] Sep95
– The campaign for real rock / A girl like you / Low expectations / Out of this world / If you could love me / North of Heaven / Georgeous George / It's right in front of you / Make me feel again / You got it all / Subsidence / Occupy your mind. *(re-iss. Jul95, hit UK No.8)*

Oct 94. (c-ep) *(ZOP 001C)* **EXPRESSLY EP** [42] [-]
– A girl like you / A girl like you (Macrame remix by Youth).
(cd-ep+=) *(ZOP 001CD1)* – Out of this world (I hear a new world) (St.Etienne remix) / Occupy your mind.
(cd-ep) *(ZOP 001CD2)* – ('A'side) / Don't shilly shally (Spotters'86 demo) / Something's brewing / Bring it on back.

Mar 95. (12"ep) *(ZOP 002CD1)* **IF YOU COULD LOVE ME (radio edit). / IN A BROKEN DREAM / INSIDER DEALING / ('A'-MC Esher mix)** [ ] [ ]
(cd-ep) *(ZOP 002CD1)* – (first 3 tracks) / Hope and despair.
(cd-ep) *(ZOP 002CD2)* – ('A'side) / If ever you're ready / Come to your senses / A girl like you (the Victoria Spaceman mix).

Jun 95. (7") *(ZOP 0037)* **A GIRL LIKE YOU. / YOU'RE ON YOUR OWN** [4] [-]
(c-s+=) *(ZOP 003C)* – If you could love me (acoustic version).
(cd-s++=) *(ZOP 003CD)* – Don't shilly shally (Spotters '86 demo).

Oct 95. (c-s) *<58-1234>* **A GIRL LIKE YOU / IF YOU COULD LOVE ME** [-] [32]
(above used on the film 'Empire Records')

Feb 96. (c-s) *(ZOP 004C)* **KEEP ON BURNING / IF YOU COULD LOVE ME (IN TIME AND SPACE)** [45] [-]
(cd-s+=) *(ZOP 004CD1)* – Lava lamp / The campaign for real rock.
(cd-s) *(ZOP 004CD2)* – Won't turn back / You've grown a beard / A girl like you (live) / White room.

Setanta / Sony

Jul 97. (12") *(SET 041T)* **THE MAGIC PIPER. / A GIRL LIKE YOU (Makrame mix) / WELWYN GARDEN CITY** [32] [-]
(cd-s) *(SETCDA 041)* – ('A'side) / More than you bargained for / Red menace / It takes a little time.
(cd-s) *(SETCDB 041)* – ('A'side) / Who is it? / Who is it? (halterbacked by the Victorian spaceman / Welwyn Garden City.

Sep 97. (cd/c/lp) *(SET CD/MC/LP 039) <68716>* **I'M NOT FOLLOWING YOU** [55] [ ] Oct97
– It's a steal / The magic piper (of love) / Seventies night / No one waved goodbye / Downer / Keep on burning / Running away with myself / Country rock / For the rest of my life / Superficial cat / Adidas world / I'm not following you.

Oct 97. (7") *(SET 045)* **ADIDAS WORLD. / HIGH FASHION** [71] [-]
(cd-s+=) *(SETCDA 045)* – Mr. Bojangles / Talking 'bout the times.
(cd-s) *(SETCDB 045)* – ('A'side) / Episode 3 / Episode 5 / Episode 10 (no, no, no Adidas – Adilated by . . .).

Nov 97. (d12") *(ZOPPR 005)* **I HEAR A NEW WORLD (mixes; Red Snapper / Deadly Avenger Supershine / Red Snapper vocal / DOWNER (James Lavelle mix) // The magic piper (the Wiseguys sniper mix) / Adidas world (adilated br Sebastian Lawsely) / Downer (James Lavelle vocal)** [ ] [-]

COLORBLIND JAMES EXPERIENCE

Formed: Rochester, New York, USA . . . 1987 by COLORBLIND JAMES alongside PHILIP MARSHALL, BERNIE HEVERON and JIM McAVANEY. Initially given British exposure via John Peel Radio One airplay for the classic 'CONSIDERING A MOVE TO MEMPHIS' (which featured in the man's Festive 50), COLORBLIND JAMES and his pardners could be experienced in full on the eponymous debut album. Released on NYC indie label, 'Earring', in 1988, the record could only really be described as geek-hillbilly with elements of folk, MOSE ALLISON-style jazz-blues and rockabilly played out awkwardly against often hilariously dry lyrics (check out 'FIRST DAY OF SPRING'). There was even an attempt at student-polka on the awful 'WHY'D THE BOY THROW THE CLOCK OUT THE WINDOW', a track that would've fitted perfectly over an early episode of 'The Young Ones'. By the release of 1989's 'WHY SHOULD I STAND UP?' (released by 'Cooking Vinyl' in the UK), HEVRERON had departed while JOHN EBERT, KEN FRANK and DAVE McINTYRE added a whole new dimension to the band's sound with such diverse instrumentation as violin, tuba, clarinet, sax etc. 1990's 'STRANGE SOUNDS FROM THE BASEMENT', meanwhile, saw the band metamorphosise into COLORBLIND JAMES AND THE DEATH VALLEY BOYS, a more seriously rootsy proposition cutting to the heart of America's damned soul.

Album rating: THE COLORBLIND JAMES EXPERIENCE (*7) / WHY SHOULD I STAND UP (*6) / STRANGE SOUNDS FROM THE BASEMENT (*5)

COLORBLIND JAMES – vocals, rhythm guitar, vibraphone / **PHILLIP MARSHALL** – lead guitar, vocals / **BERNIE HEVERON** – upright bass, vocals / **JIM McAVANEY** – drums

Fundamental / Earring

May 88. (lp/cd) *(SAVE 050/+CD)* **COLORBLIND JAMES EXPERIENCE** [ ] [ ] 1987
– Why'd the boy throw the clock out the window? / The German girls / A diferent Bob / First day of Spring / Walking my camel home / Gravel road / Considering a move to Memphis / Fledgling circus / Dance critters / Great Northwest.

Oct 88. (12") *(PRAY 009)* **DANCE CRITTERS (remix). / YOU NEED SOMEBODY ON YOUR SIDE** [ ] [ ]

— HEVERON was repl. by **KEN FRANK** – bass, violin, vocals / **JOHN EBERT** – trombone, tuba, vocals / **DAVE McINTYRE** – clarinet, saxophone, vocals

Cooking Vinyl / Gold Castle

Oct 89. (lp/c/cd) *(COOK/+C/CD 028) <D2/D4 71356>* **WHY SHOULD I STAND UP?** [ ] [ ]
– Why should I stand up? / She'll break yours too / Buster Cornelius / Polka girl / Ride aboard / I'm a sailor / That's entertainment / He must have been quite a guy / Wedding at Cana / Rocking as fast as I can / Hi-fi alphabet / If nobody loves you in Heaven. *(re-iss. Nov93 cd/c; same)*

Feb 90. (7") *(FRY 015)* **THAT'S ENTERTAINMENT. /** [ ] [ ]
(12"+=) *(FRY 015T)* –

Nov 90. (cd/c/lp; by COLORBLIND JAMES & THE DEATH VALLEY BOYS) *(COOK/+C/CD 042)* **STRANGE SOUNDS FROM THE BASEMENT** [ ] [-]
– Ribbon cutting time / Don't be so hard on yourself / Acorn girl / I think I know what you mean / Cloorblind's night out / Oh come now / Sidewalk sale / Strange sounds from the basement / Jesus at the still / O Sylvia / Two headed girl / Not for sale / Call me sometime. *(re-iss. Nov93 cd/c; same)*

— disappeared after above

– compilations, etc. –

Oct 89. (12"ep/cd-ep) *Strange Fruit; (SFPS/+CD 076) / Dutch East India; <8311>* **PEEL SESSIONS** [ ] [ ]
– Polka girl / Hey Bernadette / Havoc theme / Wedding at Canaan.

Oct 95. (cd) *Red House; (RHRCD 52)* **SOLID! BEHIND THE TIMES** [ ] [-]

COMBUSTIBLE EDISON

Formed: Providence, Rhode Island . . . 1992 out of 80's alt-rock group, CHRISTMAS, by LIZ COX (who subsequently adopted the name of MISS LILY BANQUETTE) and MICHAEL CUDAHY (aka THE MILLIONAIRE). Although they'd been around the indie block a few times, it was 1989 before CHRISTMAS released an album, 'ULTRA PROPHETS OF THE PSYKICK REVOLUTION'. THE MILLIONAIRE then took off for Las Vegas, forming the TIKI WONDER HOUR soon after, a sizeable lounge act ensemble that toured the small cabaret circuit and became skint in the process (thus his ironic name). Inspired by the experience nevertheless, THE MILLIONAIRE returned to team up with LIZ as COMBUSTIBLE EDISON, the line-up completed by his brother, NICK CUDAHY, PETER DIXON and AARON OPEENHEIMER. Taking their cue from Mexican lounge muso, JUAN GURELA ESQUIBEL, they served their music with a jazzy swing and a cool alternative twist, eccentrically kitted out 40's/50's movie style in tuxedos. One of Sub Pop's less predictable signings, COMBUSTIBLE EDISON laid down their new style on debut album, 'I, SWINGER' (1994), their own compositions lounging easily with their cover of Julie London's 'CRY ME A RIVER'. A couple of years went by before the release of their follow-up, 'SCHIZOPHONIC!' (1996), during which time the easy listening revival was at its peak.

Album rating: I, SWINGER (*7) / SCHIZOPHONIC! (*5) / THE IMPOSSIBLE WORLD (*6)

CHRISTMAS

— (see below for most members)

I.R.S. I.R.S.

Jun 89. (lp/c/cd) *(EIRSA/+C/CD 1012)* **ULTRA PROPHETS OF THE PSYKICK REVOLUTION**

1990. (7") **STUPID KIDS. /** -

COMBUSTIBLE EDISON

MISS LILY BANQUETTE (b. LIZ COX) – vocals / **THE MILLIONAIRE** (b. MICHAEL CUDAHY) – vocals / **PETER DIXON** – hi-fi organ / **NICK CADAHY** – double bass / **AARON OPPENHEIMER** – vibraphone

Domino Sub Pop

Feb 94. (7") *(RUG 10)* **BLUE LIGHT. / SUMMER SAMBA**
(cd-s+=) *(RUG 10CD)* – (+2).

City Slang Sub Pop

Mar 94. (cd/lp) *(EFA 04934-2/-1)* <*SP 244CD*> **I, SWINGER**
– Cadillac / The Millionaire's holiday / Breakfast at Denny's / Intermission / Cry me a river / Impact! / Guadaloupe / Carnival of souls / The veldt / Surabaya Johnny / Spy vs. spy / Theme from "The Tiki Wonder Hour".

Feb 96. (cd/lp) *(RTD 3460002-2/-1)* <*SP 313*> **SCHIZOPHONIC!**
– Alright, already / Bluebeard / Checkered flag / One eyed monkey / Solid state / Yeux sans visage / "52" / Short double latte / Mudhead / Morticia / Objet d'amour / Corner table / Lonelyville.

Mar 96. (7") *(RTD 3460001-7)* **SHORT DOUBLE LATTE. /**
(cd-s+=) *(RTD 3460001-3)* –

Jun 96. (12"/cd-s) *(RTD 3460003-0/-3)* **BLUEBEARD. / ('A'mixes)**

Oct 98. (cd) <*SP 431*> **THE IMPOSSIBLE WORLD**
– Utopia / Call of the space siren / Laura's aura / 20th century / Cat o' nine tails / Pink victim / Dior / Hot and bothered / Mr. Pushin came to shore / Seduction / Tickled to death / Garden of earthly delights / Utopia (reprise).

COME

Formed: Boston, Massachusetts, USA – based . . .. 1989 by former LIVE SKULL mainwoman, THALIA ZEDEK, along with former CODEINE man, CHRIS BROKAW and a rhythm section of ARTHUR JOHNSON and SEAN O'BRIEN. Quite possibly the most convincing exponent of brooding feminine intensity since PATTI SMITH (an obvious influence alongside HOLE's COURTNEY LOVE), ZEDEK first stamped her tortured personality over the emerging grunge scene in summer '91 with the 'CAR' single. Hailed by the critics, the track introduced the trademark COME sound, crushing fragments of SONIC YOUTH, NIRVANA and even BLACK SABBATH into painful emotional wounds. A follow-up single, 'FAST PISS BLUES', further raised expectations for debut album, 'ELEVEN: ELEVEN' (1992) and cemented COME's growing reputation as true guardian's of the blues' dark flame. The album itself was met with almost universal acclaim, from the broken-down desolation of 'SUBMERGE' onwards a seriously heavy going trip through COME's often despairing world. Switching from 'Matador' to 'Beggars Banquet', they previewed follow-up set, 'DON'T ASK, DON'T TELL' (1994), with the slo-mo frustration of 'WRONG SIDE', a flavour of the album's mogadon-pace vegetation. Some fresh blood was injected with 1996's 'NEAR LIFE EXPERIENCE' album, however, O'BRIEN and JOHNSON replaced initially by BUNDY K BROWN and MAC McNEILLY and then TARA JANE O'NEILL and KEVIN COULTAS. Guests BETH HEINBERG and ED YAZIJIAN's piano and violin flourishes also added a bit of melancholy colour and subtlety to proceedings. Around the same time the band also backed STEVE WYNN on his solo set, 'Melting In The Dark', while BUNDY and BROKAW hooked up with each other once more as part of the acclaimed PULLMAN project. COME returned in 1998 with another new rhythm section, WINSTON BRAMEN and DANIEL COUGHLIN taking the band back to basics on 'GENTLY DOWN THE STREAM'. • **Covered:** I GOT THE BLUES (Rolling Stones).

Album rating: ELEVEN: ELEVEN (*6) / DON'T ASK, DON'T TELL (*7) / NEAR LIFE EXPERIENCE (*7) / GENTLY DOWN THE STREAM (*6)

THALIA ZEDEK – vocals, guitar, harmonica (ex-LIVE SKULL) / **CHRIS BROKAW** – guitar, vocals, keyboards (ex-CODEINE) / **ARTHUR JOHNSON** – drums (ex-BAR B Q KILLERS) / **SEAN O'BRIEN** – bass (ex-KILKENNY CATS)

Glitterhouse unknown

Aug 91. (7"white) **CAR. / LAST MISTAKE** -

Apr 92. (12"ep/cd-ep) **CAR. / LAST MISTAKE / SUBMERGE** -

Placebo Matador

Nov 92. (lp/cd) *(PILL A/CD 1)* <*OLE 45*> **ELEVEN: ELEVEN**
– Submerge / Dead Molly / Brand new vein / Off to one side / Bell / William / Sad eyes / Power failure / Orbit. *(cd+=)* – Car / Last mistake.

Jan 93. (10"m) *(PILL 3)* <*OLE 27*> **FAST PISS BLUES. / I GOT THE BLUES / BRAND NEW VEIN** Nov92

Beggars Banquet Matador

Apr 94. (7"/12"/cd-s) *(BBQ 34/+T/CD)* <*OLE 86*> **WRONG SIDE. / LOIN OF THE SURF / SVK**

Sep 94. (cd/c/lp) *(BBQ CD/MC/LP 160)* <*OLE 108*> **DON'T ASK, DON'T TELL**
– Finish line / Mercury falls / Yr reign / Poison / Let's get lost / String / German song / In-Out / Wrong side / Arrive.

Feb 95. (10"ep/cd-ep) *(BBQ 48 TT/CD)* **STRING / WHO JUMPED ON MY GRAVE. / GERMAN SONG / ANGELHEAD** -

— **THALIA + CHRIS** were joined by **BUNDY K BROWN** – bass (ex-ELEVENTH DREAM DAY) / **MAC McNEILLY** – drums (then) **TARA JANE O'NEIL** – bass / **KEVIN COULTAS** – drums / guests **BETH HEINBERG** – piano / **ED YAZIJIAN** – violin

Domino Matador

Apr 96. (cd-s) *(RUG 43CD)* **SECRET NUMBER / PRIZE / HURRICANE II** -

May 96. (cd/lp) *(WIG CD/LP 25)* <*OLE 192*> **NEAR LIFE EXPERIENCE**
– Hurricane / Weak as the moon / Secret number / Bitten / Shoot me first / Walk on's / Half life / Slow-eyed.

— around this period, they worked with STEVE WYNN (ex-DREAM SYNDICATE) on his 1996 set, 'Melting In The Dark'.

— BUNDY became part of DIRECTIONS IN MUSIC and side-project, PULLMAN, the latter also featuring BROKAW

— **ZEDEK + BROKAW** recruited **WINSTON BRAMEN** – bass / **DANIEL COUGHLIN** – drums, percussion

Feb 98. (cd/lp) *(WIG CD/LP 43)* <*OLE 254*> **GENTLY DOWN THE STREAM**
– One piece / Recidivist / Stomp / Sorry too late / Saints around my neck / Silk city / Middle of nowhere / The fade-outs / A jam blues / New coat / The former model / March.

– compilations, etc. –

1990's. (lp) *Come;* <*88203*> **RAMPTON** -
– Submerge / Dead Molly / Brand new vein / Off to one side / Bell / William / Sad eyes / Power failure / Orbit / Fast piss blues / I got the blues.

COMET GAIN

Formed: London, England . . . 1993 by songwriter DAVID CHRISTIAN and singer SARAH BLEACH, along with SAM, JAX (a female) and PHIL. Starting out as the 'Riot Grrrl' movement was in full swing, COMET GAIN released a series of amateurish but promising singles before signing to 'Wiiija' in late '94. The following Spring, the shambolic, twee but charming punksters released their debut album, 'CASINO CLASSICS', surprisingly finding favour with the American underground elite (i.e. JON SPENCER, THURSTON MOORE of SONIC YOUTH, etc). A string of EP's/singles (including an appearance on NME's C-96 cassette) kept their profile fairly high before the release of a much anticipated 1997 follow-up set, 'MAGNETIC POETRY' (entitled 'SNEAKY' in the States).

Album rating: CASINO CLASSICS (*6) / MAGNETIC POETRY (*6)

SARAH BLEACH – vocals / **DAVID CHRISTIAN** – guitar / **SAM** – guitar / **JAX** – keyboards, bass / **PHIL** – drums

Soul Static Sound not iss.

Sep 94. (7") *(SOUL 5)* **HOLLOWAY SWEETHEARTS. /** -

Wiiija Beggars Banquet

Mar 95. (7"one-sided) *(LTD 003)* **A MILLION AND NINE** -

Apr 95. (cd/lp) *(WIJ 042 CD/V)* **CASINO CLASSICS** -
– Footstompers / A million and nine / Turnpike county blue / Last night / Original arrogance / Another girl / Music upstairs / Villain / Stay with me / Charlie / Just seventeen / Ghost of the Roman Empire / Intergalactic starbed / Chevron action flash.

Oct 95. (7"ep/cd-ep) *(WIJ 046 V/CD)* **THE "GETTIN' READY" EP** -
– Baby's alright / The shining path / Charlie / White noise.

Apr 96. (7"ep/cd-ep) *(WIJ 050 V/CD)* **SAY YES TO INTERNATIONAL SOCIALISM EP** -
– Hideaway / Say yes / California / Sunsets at her window.

Feb 97. (7") *(WIJ 66)* **STRENGTH. / FILM BY KENNETH ANGER** -
(cd-s+=) *(WIJ 66CD)* – Letting go.

Oct 97. (cd/lp) *(WIJ CD/LP 1054)* <*85009*> **MAGNETIC POETRY** <US-title 'SNEAKY'>
– Strength / Raspberries / Language of the spy / Steps to the sea / (These are the dreams of the) Working girl / Pier Angeli / Pussycat / Tighten up / Say yes / Film by Kenneth Anger / Sunsets at her window / Shining path.

Mei Me not iss.

Jun 98. (7") *(MEI 001)* **JACK NANCE HAIR. /** -

Kill Rock Stars not iss.

Dec 98. (7") *(KRS 323)* **IF I HAD A SOUL. /** -

COMING UP ROSES (see under ⇒ DOLLY MIXTURE)

COMPULSION

Formed: King's Cross, North London . . . early 1992 by Irish exiles JOSEPHMARY, GARRET LEE, SID RAINEY and JAN-WILLEM ALKEMA, all veterans of the alternative music scene. JOSEPHMARY and LEE, as members of THEE AMAZING COLOSSAL MEN, had even been signed to 'Virgin' at one point although the deal fell through and the band split halfway through the recording of their second album. COMPULSION had no such headaches, forming their own label, 'Fabulon', after a year of twiddling their thumbs and fruitlessly seeking out pub gigs. An eponymous debut EP arrived in early '93, taking no prisoners with a razorwire guitar attack and vicious, strangulated vocals. The lyrical themes were equally uncompromising, the NIRVANA-esque 'RAPEJACKET' putting forward the idea that everyone is raped by life's hardships in one way or another. 'NINE FOURTH', meanwhile, recalled with disgust yet another Conservative electoral victory. With airplay from Radio One DJ, Mark Goodier, and support form the music press, COMPULSION already had a healthy buzz going by the release of follow-up EP, 'CASSEROLE'. Tours with CREDIT TO THE NATION and SHED SEVEN as well as an appearance at that year's Phoenix festival prompted interest from 'One Little Indian', through whom they released mini-set, 'SAFETY' and full-length debut album, 'COMFORTER' (1994). Drawing praise from both the indie and rock communities, the album carried on where the EP's left off, mixing sonic guitar barrages with more melancholy reflections and combining bitter realism with flights of surreal fancy and black humour. The record even nudged into the Top 60 although spin-off single, 'BASKETCASE', failed to chart. After a prolonged absence, COMPULSION returned in 1996 with follow-up album, 'THE FUTURE IS MEDIUM', apparently recorded in one session.

Album rating: COMFORTER (*6) / THE FUTURE IS MEDIUM (*6)

JOSEPHMARY – vocals / **GARRET LEE** – guitar / **SID RAINEY** – bass / **JAN-WILLEM ALKEMA** (b. Holland) – drums

Fabulon / not iss.

Feb 93. (12"ep) *(FLON 12-01)* **COMPULSION EP** -
– Find time / Rapejacket / Easterman / Ninefourth / Purring not laughing / Accident ahead.

Apr 93. (12"ep) *(FLON 12-02)* **CASSEROLE EP** -
– Yabba yabba yes yes yes / Crying / How do I breathe? / Here comes Ambrose Beasley / Security.

One Little Indian / Elektra

Oct 93. (m-lp/m-c/m-cd) *(TPLP 49M/+C/CD)* **SAFETY**

Mar 94. (cd-ep) *<66228>* **BOOGIE WOOGIE** -
– Accident ahead / Ninefourth / Yabba yabba yes yes yes / Why do we care? / Find time.

One Little Indian / Interscope

Mar 94. (lp/c/cd) *(TPLP 59/+C/CD) <92456>* **COMFORTER** 59 Jun94
– Rapejacket / Basketcase / Mall monarchy / Ariadne / Late again / Air-raid for the neighbours / Yancy Dangerfield's delusions / Lovers / I am John's brain / Bad cooking / Dick, Dale, Rick and Ricky / Domestique / Oh my fool life / Jean could be wrong. *(cd+=)***EPs** – COMPULSION + CASSEROLE

Jun 94. (c-s) *(95 TP7C)* **BASKETCASE /** -
(12"+=/cd-s+=) *(95 TP12/TP7CD)* –

Feb 96. (7") *(105 TP7)* **QUESTION TIME FOR THE PROLES. / SPOTLIGHT INTO SPACE** -
(cd-s) *(105 TP7CD)* – ('A'side) / Millions / Drop / Burst.

May 96. (lp/c/cd) *(TPLP 79/+C/CD)* **THE FUTURE IS MEDIUM** -

Jun 96. (7"/c-s) *(115 TP7/+C)* **JUVENILE SCENE DETECTIVE. /** -
(cd-s+=) *(115 TP7CD)* –

Nail Imports / not iss.

Jul 96. (cd-ep) **ACID WAVES 2** -

COMSAT ANGELS

Formed: Sheffield, England ... 1978 as RADIO EARTH by STEPHEN FELLOWS, MIK GLAISHER, ANDY PEAKE and KEVIN BACON. Following the release of a self-financed debut EP, 'THE RED PLANET', this doomy new wave quartet were one of the many such outfits signed to 'Polydor' at the dawn of the 80's. 'WAITING FOR A MIRACLE' (1980) was a promising debut showcasing the band's dark, synth-laced pop/rock sound and boasting one of their most enduring tracks, the infectious 'INDEPENDENCE DAY'. By the release of the following year's 'SLEEP NO MORE' opus, the group had adopted an even gloomier, almost gothic sound taking a leaf out of JOY DIVISION's book with a brooding bass rumble and funereal vocals, even if the likes of 'BE BRAVE' could still conceivably have been a Top 10 hit. 'FICTION' (1982) was another worthwhile release, the opening 'AFTER THE RAIN' moving across similarly intense synth-pop territory as that year's SIMPLE MIND's masterpiece, 'New Gold Dream', while the anthemic wail of 'JU JU MONEY' became a live favourite. Yet while the band could cut it with the best of the post-punk pack, chart success remained tantalisingly out of reach and The COMSAT's soon found themsleves label-less. A testament to their undoubted potential, the group were picked up by a further two major record companies, first 'Jive/CBS' – where they released 'LAND' (1983) and 'SEVEN DAY WEEKEND' (1985) – then 'Island', who rather unadvisedly hooked them up with ROBERT PALMER (in a production capacity) on the 'CHASING SHADOWS' (1987) album. The band's run of bad luck continued as they were faced with the threat of legal action by American communications conglomorate, 'Com Sat' and subsequently forced to trade under the clipped moniker of CS ANGELS. In Britain, meanwhile, they also changed name to the DREAM COMMAND (initially the HEADHUNTERS), a tactic which failed to turn around their ailing fortunes. The group eventually re-emerged in 1992 under their original name (although BACON had briefly bailed out), releasing 'MY MIND'S EYE' on 'Thunderbird'. By the release of 1995's 'THE GLAMOUR', BACON was off the menu for good, his replacements being SIMON ANDERSON and TERRY TODD.

Album rating: WAITING FOR A MIRACLE (*8) / SLEEP NO MORE (*6) / FICTION (*6) / LAND (*6) / 7 DAY WEEKEND (*5) / CHASING SHADOWS (*5) / MY MIND'S EYE (*5) / THE GLAMOUR (*5) / Dream Command: FIRE ON THE MOON (*5)

STEVEN FELLOWS – vocals, guitar / **ANDY PEAKE** – keyboards, synthesizers / **KEVIN BACON** – bass / **MIC GLAISHER** – drums

Junta / not iss.

Mar 79. (red-7"m) *(JUNTA 1)* **RED PLANET. / I GET EXCITED / SPECIMEN No.2** -

Polydor / not iss.

May 80. (7"m) *(2059 227)* **TOTAL WAR. / WAITING FOR A MIRACLE / HOME ON THE RANGE** -

Jul 80. (7") *(2059 257)* **INDEPENDENCE DAY. / WE WERE** -

Sep 80. (lp) *(2383 578)* **WAITING FOR A MIRACLE** -
– Missing in action / Baby / Independence day / Waiting for a miracle / Total war / On the beach / Monkey pilot / Real story / Map of the world / Postcard. *(cd-iss. Jan96 on 'R.P.M.'; RPM 155)*

Mar 81. (7") *(POSP 242)* **EYE OF THE LENS. / AT SEA** -
(d12"+=) *(POSPX 242)* – Another world / Gone.

Aug 81. (lp/c) *(POLS/+C 1038)* **SLEEP NO MORE** 51 -
– Eye dance / Slep no more / Be brave / Gone / Dark parade / Diagram / Restless / Goat of the west / Light years / Our secret. *(cd-iss. Jan96 on 'R.P.M.'; RPM 156)*

Oct 81. (d7") *(POSP 359)* **DO THE EMPTY HOUSE. / NOW I KNOW // RED PLANET REVISITED** -

May 82. (7") *(POSP 432)* **IT'S HISTORY. / ZINGER** -

Aug 82. (lp/c) *(POLS/+C 1075)* **FICTION** 94 -
– After the rain / Zinger / Now I know / Not a word / Ju ju money / More / Pictures / Birdman / Don' t look now / What else. *(cd-iss. Jan96 on 'R.P.M.'; RPM 157)*

Oct 82. (7") *(POSP 513)* **AFTER THE RAIN. / PRIVATE PARTY** -

Jive / Jive-Novus

Jul 83. (7") *(JIVE 46)* **WILL YOU STAY TONIGHT. / SHINING HOUR** -
(12"+=) *(JIVET 46)* – A world away.

Sep 83. (lp/c) *(HIP/+C 8) <JL8/JC8 8184>* **LAND** 91
– Will you stay tonight / Alicia (can you hear me) / A world away / Independence day / Nature trails / Mister memory / Island heart / I know that feeling / As above so below.

Oct 83. (7"/12") *(JIVE/+T 51)* **ISLAND HEART. / SCISSORS AND STONES** -

Jan 84. (7") *(JIVE 54)* **INDEPENDENCE DAY. / MISTER MEMORY** 71 -
(12"+=) *(JIVET 54)* – Intelligence.
(d7"+=/d12"+=) *(JIVE/+T 54)* – Total war / After the rain.

May 84. (7") *(JIVE 65)* **YOU MOVE ME. / ESCAPE FROM WILLESDEN** -
(12") *(JIVET 65)* – ('A'side) / Land / Eye of the lens (live).

Sep 84. (7") *(JIVE 73)* **DAY ONE. / WILL YOU STAY TONIGHT** -
(12"+=) *(JIVET 73)* – Independence day.

— added guest **PAUL ROBERTSON** – keyboards

Aug 85. (7") *(JIVE 87)* **I'M FALLING. / NEW HEART AND MIND** -
(12"blue+=) *(JIVET 87)* – ('A'extended).

Sep 85. (lp/c) *(HIP/+C 29) <JL8 8279>* **7 DAY WEEKEND**
– Day one / You're the heroine / High tide / New heart and hand / Still it's not enough / Believe it / Forever young / You move me / I'm falling / Close your eyes.

Oct 85. (7") *(JIVE 111)* **FOREVER YOUNG. / STILL IT'S NOT ENOUGH** -
(12"+=) *(JIVET 111)* – Sign.

— reverted to original quartet, when ROBERTSON departed

Island / not iss.

Jan 87. (lp/cd) *(ILPS/CID 9855)* **CHASING SHADOWS** -
– The thought that counts / The cutting edge / Under the influence / Carried away / You'll never know / Lost continent / Flying dreams / Pray for rain.

Feb 87. (7") *(IS 312)* **THE CUTTING EDGE. / SOMETHING'S GOT TO GIVE** -
(12"+=) *(12IS 312)* – Our secret.
(live-12"+=) *(ISB 312)* – Flying dreams.

— changed their moniker and were without BACON

1990. (cd/lp; as DREAM COMMAND) *<846216-2/-1>* **FIRE ON THE MOON** -
– Celestine / Whirlwind / Sleep walking / Reach for me / Ice sculpture / Venus hunter / Phantom power / Transport of delight / She's invisible / Mercury.

— original COMSAT ANGELS line-up re-formed in 1992 (with BACON again). They signed to 'Crisis' (Benelux) & 'Normal' (Germany). FELLOWS had recently written several songs for the HARBOUR KINGS. They had emerged in 1990 as The HEADHUNTERS until this fell through.

Thunderbird / Caroline

Jun 92. (7") *(CSA7 001)* **DRIVING. / THERE IS NO ENEMY** -
(12"+=/cd-s+=) *(CSA 001 T/CD)* – My mind's eye / Driving (mix).

Sep 92. (cd/lp) *(CSA 101/201) <1891>* **MY MIND'S EYE** Sep93
– Driving / Beautiful monster / Shiva descending / My mind's eye / I came from the sun / Field of tall flowers / Always hear / Route 666 / Mystery plane / And all the stars. *(cd re-iss. Aug98; CSAM 101)*

Jul 93. (7") *(CSA7 003)* **FIELD OF TALL FLOWERS (remix). / STORM OF CHANGE** -
(12"+=/cd-s+=) *(CSA 003 T/CD)* – Too much time / ('A'acoustic).

1993. (cd-ep) **SHIVA DESCENDING / MAFONIA / JU-JU MONEY / GOAT OF THE WEST** - - German

— now without BACON who was repl. by **SIMON ANDERSON** – guitar / **TERRY TODD** – bass

Jun 95. (cd) *(CSA 103)* **THE GLAMOUR** -
– Psychedelic dungeon / The glamour / Audrey in denim / Oblivion / Web of sound / Breaker / SS100X / Sailor / Demon lover / Pacific ocean blues / Anjelica / Valley of the Nile / Spaced.

– compilations, etc. –

Apr 84. (lp) *Polydor; (810735)* **ENZ** - - Dutch
– Independence day / Do the empty house / Total war / It's history / Another world / Eye of the lens / At sea / Mass / Home on the range / After the rain.

Nov 92. (cd) *R.P.M.; (RPM 106)* **TIME CONSIDERED (BBC sessions 1979-1984)** -
– At sea / Eye of the lens / Total war / Real story / Waiting for a miracle / Ju ju money / Independence day / Eye dance / Gone / Dark parade / Our secret / Now I know / Citadel / High tide / Mister memory / Island heart / You move me / Nature trails.

Jul 94. (cd) *R.P.M.; (RPM 123)* **UNRAVELLED – THE DUTCH RADIO SESSIONS** -
– After the rain / Beautiful monster / The cuting edge / Field of all flowers / SS 100X / Our secret / Always near / Eye of the lens / Storm of change / Audrey in denim / Citadel.

CONCRETE BLONDE

Formed: Boston, Massachusetts, USA . . . 1982 initially as DREAM 6, by JOHNETTE NAPOLITANO and JIM MANKEY. After almost five years of plugging away with no recorded output to show save a one-off French-released EP, the duo renamed themselves (a suggestion from R.E.M.'s MICHAEL STIPE) and signed to Miles Copeland's 'I.R.S.' records. Completing the line-up with HARRY RUSHAKOFF, the band released their eponymous debut album in early '87, a feisty if unremarkable punky pop-metal affair that highlighted focal point female, JOHNETTE. Follow-up set, 'FREE' (1989), meanwhile, found PAUL THOMPSON replacing RUSHAKOFF on the drum stool and NAPOLITANO concentrating solely on singing following the introduction of bassist, ALAN BLOCH. Yet it wasn't until 1990's more polished 'BLOODLETTING' that CONCRETE BLONDE achieved some belated chart success, the album scraping into the US Top 50 and spawning a Top 20 hit single, 'JOEY' (sadly not a cover of the BOB DYLAN classic). With the songwriting quality much improved and NAPOLITANO putting in an impressive, emotive vocal performance, it looked as if the band might just break into the glossy MTV big league. Yet '92's 'WALKING IN LONDON' (inspired by a recent relocation to the capital) only just managed to scrape into the Top 75 and despite its exotic explorations of hispanic music and culture, 'MEXICAN MOON' (1994), like most of the band's work, didn't quite hold together as a complete album. Their first and only set for 'Capitol', the record saw CONCRETE BLONDE finally wind up their near decade long career as JOHNETTE formed PRETTY TWISTED. She was also to surface the following year as the interestingly named VOWEL MOVEMENT with ex-HOLLY & THE ITALIANS frontwoman, HOLLY BETH VINCENT. Signed to 'Mammoth', the pair released their eponymous debut in Spring '95. • **Songwriters:** NAPOLITANO or with MANKEY penned, except IT'S ONLY MONEY (Thin Lizzy) / I WANT YOU + SIMPLE TWIST OF FATE (Bob Dylan) / LITTLE WING (Jimi Hendrix) / RUN RUN RUN (Velvet Underground) / IT'S A MAN'S WORLD (James Brown) / GHOST OF A LADIES MAN + EVERYBODY KNOWS (Leonard Cohen) / THE SHIP SONG (Nick Cave) / MERCEDEZ BENZ (Janis Joplin) / DEPORTEE (Arlo Guthrie) / CAMINANDO (Ruben Blades).

Album rating: CONCRETE BLONDE (*5) / FREE (*5) / BLOODLETTING (*7) / WALKING IN LONDON (*6) / MEXICAN MOON (*6) / RECOLLECTION: BEST OF compilation (*7) / CONCRETE BLONDE Y LOS ILLEGALS (*5)

JOHNETTE NAPOLITANO (b.22 Sep'57, Hollywood, Calif.) – vocals, bass / **JIM MANKEY** (b.23 May'55, Pennsylvania) – guitar (ex-SPARKS) / **HARRY RUSHAKOFF** (b.17 Nov'59) – drums

I.R.S. | I.R.S.

1987. (7") **STILL IN HOLLYWOOD. / COLD PART OF YOU** [-] [ ]

Feb 87. (12"ep) *(IRMT 131)* **TRUE. / STILL IN HOLLYWOOD / Beat Rodeo: EVERYTHING I'M NOT / NEW LOVE** [ ] [-]

Feb 87. (lp/c) *(MIRF/+C 1018)* <5835> **CONCRETE BLONDE** [ ] [96]
– True / Your haunted head / Dance along the edge / Still in Hollywood / Song for Kim (she said) / Over your shoulder / Little sister / Make me cry / Cold part of you / True II (instrumental).

May 87. (7") *(IRM 136)* **TRUE. / TRUE II (instrumental)** [ ] [ ]
(12"+=) *(IRMT 136)* – I'll chew you up, and spit you out.

Jul 87. (7") **DANCE ALONG THE EDGE. / MAKE ME CRY** [-] [ ]

—— **PAUL THOMPSON** – drums; repl. RUSHAKOFF

—— added **ALAN BLOCH** – bass (JOHNETTE now vocals only)

Apr 89. (7") *(EIRS 105)* **HAPPY BIRTHDAY. / RUN RUN RUN** [ ] [ ]
(12"+=/cd-s+=) *(EIRS T/CD 105)* – Free.

May 89. (lp/c/cd) *(EIRSA/+C/CD 1004)* <82001> **FREE** [ ] [ ] Apr89
– God is a bullet / Run run run / It's only money / Help me / Sun / Roses grow / Scene of a perfect crime / Happy birthday / Little conversations / Carry me away. *(cd+=)* – Free.

Jul 89. (7") *(EIRS 121)* **GOD IS A BULLET. / FREE** [ ] [ ]
(12"+=) *(EIRST 121)* – Little wing.

—— now without BLOCH

Jun 90. (lp/c/cd) *(EIRSA/+C/CD 1028)* <82083> **BLOODLETTING** [ ] [49] May90
– Bloodletting (the vampire song) / The sky is a poisonous garden / Caroline / Darkening of the light / I don't need a hero / Days and days / The beast / Joey / Lullabye / Tomorrow, Wendy.

Aug 90. (7") *(EIRS 143)* <73014> **JOEY. / I WANT YOU** [ ] [19]
(12"+=/cd-s+=) *(12/CD EIRS 143)* – I don't need a hero.

Feb 91. (c-s/cd-s) **CAROLINE /** [-] [ ]

—— **RUSHAKOFF** returned to repl. THOMPSON

Mar 92. (7") **GHOST OF A TEXAS LADIES' MAN. / EVERYBODY KNOWS** [ ] [ ]
(cd-s+=) – Bloodletting (the vampire song) (extended) / The ship song.

Mar 92. (cd/c/lp) *(EIRS CD/TC/LP 1061)* <13137> **WALKING IN LONDON** [ ] [73]
– Ghost of a Texas ladies' man / Walking in London / Les couers jumeaux / Woman to woman / Why don't you see me / City screaming / Someday / I wanna be your friend again / . . .Long time gone / It's a man's world.

Jul 92. (7"/c-s) **SOMEDAY. / PROBABLY HILL** [ ] [ ]
(cd-s+=) – 100 games of solitaire / Les couers jumeaux.
(cd-s) – ('A'side) / Joey / Happy birthday / Still in Hollywood.

—— added the returning **THOMPSON**

Capitol | Capitol

Feb 94. (cd/c) *(CD/TC EST 2224)* <81129> **MEXICAN MOON** [ ] [67] Oct93
– Jenny I need / Mexican moon / Head it up / Jonestown / Rain / I call it love / Jesus forgive me (for the things I'm about to sing) / When you smile / Close to home / One of my kind / End of the line / (Love is a) Blind ambition / Bajo la lune Mexicana.

Mar 94. (cd-s) <58120> **MEXICAN MOON** [-] [ ]

—— split in 1994 when JOHNETTE formed PRETTY & TWISTED. They released an eponymous debut mid '95 for 'Warners' and she was also part of VOWEL MOVEMENT

—— **JOHNETTE + MANKEY +** the group LOS ILLEGALS: **WILLIAM P. REYES** – percussion, drums, etc.

not iss. | Ark 21

May 97. (cd) *<10005C>* **CONCRETE BLONDE Y LOS ILLEGALS** [-] [ ]
– Caminando / Viva la vida / Llorona / Echoes / Despierta / Another hundred years of solitude / Maria Ele (letter from L.A.) / Ode to Rosa Lopez / Xick vs. the Migra zombies / Deportee.

– compilations, etc. –

Nov 94. (cd/c) *Capitol; <X2+/29128>* **STILL IN HOLLYWOOD** [-] [ ]
– It'll chew you up and spit you out / Everybody knows / Free / God is a bullet / Probably will / Mandocello / The ship song / Joey / Little wing / Roses grow / Sky is a poisonous garden / Bloodletting (the vampire song) / Simple twist of fate / 100 games of solitaire / Tomorrow, Wendy.

Apr 96. (cd) *I.R.S.; (EIRSCD 1077)* <37072> **RECOLLECTION: BEST OF** [ ] [ ] Feb96
– God is a bullet / Tomorrow, Wendy / Joey / Scene of a perfect crime / Someday? / Ghost of a Texas ladies man / Dance along the edge / Bloodletting (the vampire song) / Happy birthday / Caroline / Cold part of town / Walking in London / Heal it up / Everybody knows / True / Mexican moon / Still in Hollywood / Mercedez Benz.

VOWEL MOVEMENT

JOHNETTE NAPOLITANO – vocals, bass / **HOLLY BETH VINCENT** – vocals, guitar (ex-HOLLY & THE ITALIANS)

Mammoth | Mammoth

May 95. <(MR 106-2)> **VOWEL MOVEMENT** [ ] [ ]
– Dinosaur / Hitchhiker / Frank / When we collide / I don't wanna / Las Vegas / Death of a surfer / Vowel movement (A-E-I-O-U) / OhOhOh / Jackie baby / Gecko / Jesus / Tiny music / Jackie baby.

CONFLICT

Formed: Eltham, England . . . 1979 by COLIN JERWOOD, JOHN CLIFFORD, GRAHAM and KEN. Debut EP, 'THE HOUSE THAT MAN BUILT', was unleashed by the 'Crass' label in 1982 although the bulk of their output surfaced on their own 'Mortarhate' imprint. CONFLICT's first bonafide long player came in the shape of 1982's 'IT'S TIME TO SEE WHO'S WHO', a savage set of hardcore/Oi!-style punk which substituted any discernible tune ('YOUNG PARASITES' being the exception) for a barrage of abuse aimed mainly at centralised Government but also taking in meat eaters, the media, fame-hungry musicians and big business. 1983's 'SERENADE IS DEAD' single was the first release on their own label, the band adamnantly standing by their anarchist agenda over subsequent albums 'INCREASE THE PRESSURE' (1984) and 'THE UNGOVERNABLE FORCE' (1985). Floating member STEVE IGNORANT was drafted in after JERWOOD was assaulted in a pub fight in his home town, the former CRASS man helping out on 1987's 'TURNING REBELLION INTO MONEY' and staying for last gasp albums, 'THE FINAL CONFLICT' (1988) and 'AGAINST ALL ODDS' (1989). As with many bands of their ilk, the message usually took precedent over the music, CONFLICT's hardline stance over a wide range of political issues often seeing them in direct confrontation with the authorities. After an uncharacteristic silence of almost four years, the band attended to unfinished business with 1993's 'CONCLUSION', reworking their debut album the following year and releasing the defiant 'WE WON'T TAKE NO MORE' in 1995.

Album rating: IT'S TIME TO SEE WHO'S WHO (*4) / INCREASE THE PRESSURE (*5) / THE UNGOVERNABLE FORCE (*5) / ONLY STUPID BASTARDS USE EMI (*4) / STANDARD ISSUE compilation (*6) / TURNING REBELLION INTO MONEY (*4) / THE FINAL CONFLICT (*4) / AGAINST ALL ODDS (*4) / CONCLUSION (*4)

COLIN JERWOOD (b. 6 May'62) – vocals / **GRAHAM** – guitar / **JOHN CLIFFORD** – bass / **KEN** – drums

Crass | not iss.

May 82. (7"ep) *(221984-1)* **THE HOUSE THAT MAN BUILT** [ ] [-]
– Conflict / Wargames / I've had enough / Blind attack.

—— above with **PAULINE BECK** – vocals

Xntrix | not iss.

Oct 82. (7"ep) *(XN 2001)* **LIVE AT THE CENTRE IBERICO (live)** [ ] [-]
– Kings + punks / Meat means murder / Exploitation / Bullshit broadcast / Vietnam serenade / No island of dreams. *(re-iss. 1987 on 'Mortarhate'; MORT 7)*

—— **PACO** – drums + **PAUL FRYDAY** – visuals, tapes repl. KEN

—— **STEVE IGNORANT** – guitar (of CRASS) repl. GRAHAM

Corpus Christi | not iss.

Dec 82. (lp) *(CHRIST IT'S 3)* **IT'S TIME TO SEE WHO'S WHO** [ ] [-]
– Young parasites / Kids and punks / Meat means murder / No island of dreams / Great what? / The guilt & the glory / 1824 overture / Bullshit broadcast / One nation under the bomb / Blind attack / Vietnam serenade / Blood morons / Exploitation / Crazy governments.

Aug 83. (7") *(CHRIST IT'S 4)* **A NATION OF ANIMAL LOVERS. / LIBERATE** [ ] [-]

—— STEVE returned to CRASS

Mortarhate | not iss.

Nov 83. (7"ep) *(MORT 001)* **SERENADE IS DEAD** [ ] [-]

Jun 84. (lp) *(MORT 006)* **INCREASE THE PRESSURE** [ ] [-]
(re-iss. Dec96 lp/cd; MORT/+CD 006)

Mar 85. (7") *(MORT 008)* **THIS IS NOT ENOUGH. /** [ ] [-]

Oct 85. (7") *(MORT 015)* **THE BATTLE CONTINUES. / (same track)** [ ] [-]
(re-iss. May94; same)

Aug 86. (lp) *(MORT 020)* **THE UNGOVERNABLE FORCE** [ ] [-]
– You cannot win / The ungovernable farce / A piss in the ocean / Crass / Custom rock / 1986 the battle continues / Mental mania / The ungovernable force / They said that / Force or service / The arrest / Statement / The day before / This is the A.L.F. / To be continued. *(re-iss. Dec96 lp/cd; MORT/+CD 020)*

Nov 86. (12") *(MORT 22)* **THE FINAL CONFLICT** [ ] [-]

— **STEVE** returned when JERWOOD was assaulted in a pub fight.

Jun 87. (d-lp/c) *(MORT/+C 030)* **TURNING REBELLION INTO MONEY (live)** [ ] [-]
– Banned in the UK / The piss in the ocean / Increased pressure / Serenade is dead / They said that / From protest to resistance / Big hand / G song / I ain't thick it's a trick / So what / Punk is dead / Rival tribal / Statement. *(re-iss. Dec96 lp/cd; MORT/+CD 030)*

May 88. (lp) *(FUND 1)* **FROM PROTEST TO RESISTANCE** [-] [-] mail-o

Jul 88. (lp/c) *(MORT/+C 040)* **STANDARD ISSUE** (compilation) [ ] [-]
– Conflict / The guilt and the glory / From protest to resistence – Tough s*** Mickey / Reality whitewash / Whichever way you want it / The serenade is dead – The positive junk – The system maintains / This is not enough – Neither is this / Mighty and superior – To whom it may concern. *(re-iss. Dec96 cd/c; MORT CD/C 040) (c+=)* – INCREASE THE PRESSURE

Nov 88. (lp) *(MORT 050)* **THE FINAL CONFLICT** [ ] [-]
– Countdown to confrontation / Let the battle commence / I heard a rumour / The cord is cut / Barricades and broken dreams / Do you get the picture / The 'A' team / These things take time / Radio trash / The final conflict. *(re-iss. Dec96 lp/cd; MORT/+CD 050)*

Jul 89. (lp/c) *(MORT/+C 060)* **AGAINST ALL ODDS** [ ] [-]
– Against all odds / Slaughter of innocence / Assured mutual destruction / The greatest show on Earth / A message to who / A state of mind. *(re-iss. May98 lp/cd; MORT LP/CD 060)*

— split but re-formed in 1993 on same label

Mortarhate Cleopatra

Oct 93. (7") *(MORT 080)* **THESE COLOURS DON'T RUN. /** [ ] [-]
(cd-s+=) *(MORT 080CD)* –

Nov 93. (cd/lp) *(MORT CD/LP 100) <9486>* **CONCLUSION** [ ] [ ] May94
– To live on in hearts / The right to reply / Someday soon / No more excuses / A declaration of independence / The institute of dreams / Climbing the stairs / A question of priorities / Is never to die. *(cd+=)* – These colours don't run.

Apr 94. (cd/lp) *(MORT CD/LP 110)* **IT'S TIME TO SEE WHO'S WHO NOW** (re-workings) [ ] [-]
– Berkshire c*** / No island of dreams / Conflict / Great what? / The guilt and the glory / One nation under a bomb / Blind attack / Vietnam serenade / Blood morons / Exploitation / Meat means murder / Whichever way you want it.

Jul 95. (cd; by CONFLICT & FRIENDS) *(MORJCD 150)* **WE WON'T TAKE NO MORE** [ ] [-]

Jan 96. (cd/lp) *(MORT CD/LP 170)* **STANDARD ISSUE 2** (1988-1994) [ ] [-]

– compilations, others, etc. –

Oct 87. (12") *Konnexion; (KOMA 788029)* **FROM PROTEST TO RESISTANCE** [ ] [-]

May 88. (lp) *Model Army; (THIS NOT 599)* **ONLY STUPID BASTARDS USE EMI** [ ] [-]
(cd-iss. Jan95 on 'Mortarhate'; MORTCD 130)

1990's. (lp) *Corpus Christi; (CHRIST 16)* **HOUSE THAT MAN BUILT / TO A NATION OF ANIMAL LOVERS** [ ] [-]

Jul 94. (cd) *Cleopatra; (<CLEO 1023CD>)* **DEPLOYING ALL MEANS NECESSARY** [ ] [ ] Oct93

Feb 97. (cd/lp) *Mortarhate; (MORT CD/LP 120)* **IN THE VENUE** [ ] [-]

CONNELLS

Formed: Raleigh, North Carolina, USA . . . Spring '84 by brothers MIKE and DAVID CONNELL, the initial line-up completed by DOUG MacMILLAN and JOHN SCHULTZ. Following the replacement of the latter by PEELE WIMBERLEY and the subsequent addition of fifth member, GEORGE HUNTLEY, the band cut a demo that eventually found its way to re-issue specialist, 'Demon', who funded the recording of a debut mini-set, 'DARKER DAYS' (1985). Issued in the States on the 'Black Park' label, the record was an unremarkable but promising showcase for the band's rootsy indie-pop, suggesting the considerable influence of R.E.M. even at this early stage. Appropriately enough, they subsequently secured the services of producer Mitch Easter for 1987's 'BOYLAN HEIGHTS', an interesting fusion of Irish folk influences and BYRDS-style jangle. The CONNELLS continued to develop their winsome alt-folk pop/rock over the course of the late 80's and into the 90's with albums, 'FUN & GAMES' (1989) and 'ONE SIMPLE WORD' (1990), although it would be a further five years before they re-emerged with their one and only hit to date, '74-75'. Newly signed to 'London' in Europe, the band struck lucky as MTV picked up on the lovelorn but catchy folk-pop lament and made sure they cracked the UK Top 20. Originally released in America in 1993, the accompanying 'RING' album made the UK Top 40 although it failed to spawn any more hit singles save a re-issue of the aforementioned hit in early '96. • **Songwriters:** Initially MIKE CONNELL on most. Some by MacMILLAN or HUNTLEY. Covered LIVING IN THE PAST (Jethro Tull).

Album rating: DARKER DAYS (*5) / BOYLAN HEIGHTS (*7) / FUN & GAMES (*4) / ONE SIMPLE WORD (*7) / RING (*6) / WEIRD FOOD & DEVASTATION (*5)

MIKE CONNELL – guitar, vocals / **DAVID CONNELL** – bass / **DOUG MacMILLAN** – vocals, guitar / **PEELE WIMBERLEY** – drums, percussion; repl. JOHN SCHULTZ / added (Mar'85) **GEORGE HUNTLEY** – guitar, vocals, mandolin

Demon Black Park

Nov 85. (m-lp) *(VEX 1) <BPR 001>* **DARKER DAYS** [ ] [ ]
– Darker days / Much easier / 1934 / Brighter worlds / In my head / Hats off / Holding pattern / Seven / Unspoken words.

Nov 86. (12"ep) *<BPR 002>* **HATS OFF E.P.** [-] [ ]

Demon TVT

Oct 87. (lp/c/cd) *<TVT 2540-1/-4/-2>* **BOYLAN HEIGHTS** [-] [ ]
– Scooty's lament / Choose a side / Try / Just like us / If it crumbles / Pawns / Over there / Elegance / Home today / OT^2 (instrumental) I suppose.

Oct 89. (lp/cd) *(FIEND/+CD 153) <TVT 2550-1/-4/-2>* **FUN AND GAMES** [ ] [ ]
– Something to say / Fun and games / Sal / Upside down / Fine tuning / Motel / Hey wow / Ten pins / Inside my head / Uninspired / Sat nite (USA) / Lay me down. *(cd+=)* – Fine tuning.

Nov 90. (lp/cd) *<TVT 2580-1/-2>* **ONE SIMPLE WORD** [-] [ ]
– Stone cold yesterday / Speak to me / All sinks in / Get a gun / What do you want? / Set the stage / One simple word / Another souvenir / Link / The joke / Too gone / Waiting my turn / Take a bow.

— added **STEVE POTAK** – piano, organ, keyboards

London TVT

Nov 94. (cd-ep) *<TVT 2593>* **NEW BOY** [-] [ ]
– New boy / Logan street / Wonder why / Living in the past / Fun and games / New boy.

Jul 95. (7") *(LON 369)* **'74-'75. / NEW BOY** [14] [-]
(cd-s+=) *(LONCD 369)* – Logan Street / Fun and games.

Aug 95. (cd/c) *(828 660-2/-4) <TVT 2590-2/-4>* **RING** [36] [ ] 1994
– Slackjawed / Carry my picture / '74-'75 / Doin' you / Find out / Eyes on the ground / Spiral / Hey you / New boy / Disappointed / Burden / Any day now / Running Mary. *(UK-iss.+=)* – Logan Street / Wonder why / Living in the past.

Feb 96. (7") *(LON 413)* **'74-'75. / NEW BOY** [21] [-]
(cd-s+=) *(LONCD 413)* – Logan Street / Fun and games.

Aug 96. (cd) *<TVT 9010>* **WEIRD FOOD & DEVASTATION** [-] [ ]
– Maybe / Start / Fifth fret / Just like that / Adjective song / Any / Hang on / Back to blue / Smoke / Pretty rough / Let it go / Friendly time / Too high / On your honor.

May 98. (cd) *<TVT 9030>* **STILL LIFE** [-] [ ]
– Dull, brown and grey / Leper / Bruised / Curly's train / Gauntlet / Glade / Soul reactor / Still life / Crown / Circlin' / Gonna take a lie / Queen of charades / Pedro says.

Chris CONNELLY

Born: Edinburgh, Scotland. The one-time mainman of FINITRIBE and a stalwart of The REVOLTING COCKS, he left the latter band for solo pastures in 1991. Enlisting the help of friends, musicians and co-writers, MARTIN ATKINS, CHRIS BRUCE, WILLIAM TUCKER and STUART ZECHMAN, he began work on his debut UK solo outing ('WHIPLASH BOYCHILD' had already been released by 'Wax Trax!' in the States), 'PHENOBARB BAMBALAM' (1992). The record saw CONNELLY shift dramatically from his dance/industrial roots, the Scotsman – whose girlfriend had just recently committed suicide – adopting a different persona (i.e. SCOTT WALKER, BOWIE!, etc) on each track although the cover of Tom Verlaine's 'SOUVENIR FROM A DREAM', added little to the original. 'WHIPLASH BOYCHILD' was issued officially in Britain a few months later while CONNELLY moonlighted with KILLING JOKE off-shoot industrial metal-rap outfit, MURDER INC. Now living in America, CONNELLY delivered two futher US-only albums, 'SHIPWRECK' (1994) and 'THE ULTIMATE SEASIDE COMPANION' (1997).

Album rating: PHENOBARB BAMBALAM (*6) / WHIPLASH BOYCHILD (*5) / SHIPWRECK (*5) / THE ULTIMATE SEASIDE COMPANION (*5)

CHRIS CONNELLY – vocals, pianoforte, keyboards, tapes / **CHRIS BRUCE** – guitars / **MARTIN ATKINS** – drums, percussion / **STUART ZECHMAN** – bass / **WILLIAM TUCKER** – guitar, tapes

Devotion Wax Trax!

Aug 92. (12"/cd-s) *(12/CD DVN 108) <9190>* **COME DOWN HERE. /** [ ] [ ] Jun92

Sep 92. (cd/c/lp) *(CD/T+/DVN 13) <WAX 7189>* **PHENOBARB BAMBALAM** [ ] [ ]
– The whistle blower / July / Souvenir from a dream / Come down here / Too good to be true / Heartburn / No lesser of two evils / Ignition times four / Dirtbox Tennessee / Heartburn (twister mix).

Oct 92. (cd/c/lp) *(CD/T+/DVN 14) <WAXCD 7134>* **WHIPLASH BOYCHILD** [ ] [ ] Nov91
– Daredevil / Ghost of a saint / This edge of midnight / The last of joy / The amorous Humphrey Plugg / Stowaway / The hawk, the butcher, the killer of beauties / The game is all yours / Confessions of the highest bidder / Stowaway (Daydream mix).

— retained **TUCKER + BRUCE**

not iss. TVT

1994. (cd/c) *<TVT 7214 CD/C>* **SHIPWRECK** [-] [ ]
– Candyman collapse / Spoonfed celeste / What's left but solid gold? / Detestimony III / Anyones' mistake / Drench / Early nighters (for River Phoenix) / Swimming / Model murmur / Meridian afterburn / Shipwreck.

not iss. Hit It!

Oct 97. (cd) *<22>* **THE ULTIMATE SEASIDE COMPANION** [-] [ ]
– Fortune / Mississippi palisades / My east is your west / Stray / Empty Sam / No more changing of the guard / Island head / Toledo steel / Caravan / To play a slow game / The ultimate seaside companion / Fortune II.

MURDER INC.

CONNELLY – vocals / **GEORDIE WALKER** – guitar (ex-KILLING JOKE) / **PAUL RAVEN** – bass (ex-KILLING JOKE) / **JOHN BECHDEL** – guitar, keyboards / **MARTIN ATKINS** (ex-PUBLIC IMAGE LTD) + **PAUL FERGUSON** – drums (ex-KILLING JOKE)

Devotion Touch & Go

May 92. (cd/c/lp) *(CD/T+/DVN 9) <TG 13>* **MURDER INC.** [ ] [ ]
– Supergrass / Murder Inc. / Mania / Hole in the wall / Uninvited guest / Gambit / Red black / Last of the urgents / Mrs. Whiskey name. *(re-iss. Feb94 on 'Invisible' lp/cd; INV 016/+CD)*

Jun 92. (12"ep/cd-ep) *(12/CD DVN 106)* **CORPUSCLE EP** [ ] [ ]
(c-ep-iss.Jul93 on 'Invisible'; INV 016CS)

Invisible Invisible

Jun 93. (12"ltd.) *(INV 014)* **MANIA** [ ] [ ]

CONTORTIONS (see under ⇒ CHANCE, James)

Julian COPE

Born: 21 Oct'57, Bargeld, Wales although he was raised in Liverpool, England. His first foray into the music business was with CRUCIAL THREE, alongside IAN McCULLOCH and PETE WYLIE. In the Autumn of '78 he formed The TEARDROP EXPLODES, originally named A SHALLOW MADNESS with MICK FINKLER and PAUL SIMPSON. In late '78 a deal was inked with local UK indie label, 'Zoo', and after three critically acclaimed singles, they transferred to the major label, 'Mercury,' in July 1980. They scored their first hit with 'WHEN I DREAM', from the classic album, Top 30 'KILIMANJARO'. Early in 1981, they cashed-in when 'REWARD' delivered them a Top tenner. 'TREASON', the next 45, didn't emulate this feat, although it still managed a Top 20 placing. Their second album, 'WILDER' was another commercial success, although it lacked the bite of its predecessor. A few minor hits followed over the next year and a bit, but it was clear JULIAN was gearing up for a solo career. Remaining with 'Mercury' records, he released two albums in 1984, 'WORLD SHUT YOUR MOUTH' and 'FRIED', both receiving a lukewarm response from the music press. He then signed for 'Island' in 1985, leaving behind the unissued (until 1990) 'SKELLINGTON' lp. Around the same time he suffered a marriage break-up and drug problems, although he re-married in 1986. Re-emerging triumphantly in 1986, he scored with the Top 20 hit 45, 'WORLD SHUT YOUR MOUTH' (curiously enough, the song wasn't included on the 1984 album of the same name). The single was a taster for the following year's comeback album 'SAINT JULIAN', a record which almost gave him his first solo top ten hit. A disappointing pop album, 'MY NATION UNDERGROUND', lent his street cred a bitter blow and he retreated somewhat with two (meant for mail-order) 1990 albums 'SKELLINGTON' & 'DROOLIAN'. He returned in fine fashion a year later with the splendid double, 'PEGGY SUICIDE', a record that targeted pollution and even the dreadful Tory poll tax (something he protested against vehemently). In 1992, he brought back his old influences (CAN, FAUST, "Kraut-rock") with 'JEHOVAKILL'. Creatively, the album was an admirable effort although it bombed both commercially and critically. This was his last for Island, who dropped him unceremoniously after he recorded the 'RITE' cd-album for German release. In 1994, he signed with 'Echo' and returned with two mediocre and great albums respectively; 'AUTOGEDDON' & '20 MOTHERS' (1995). • **Style:** Keyboard-biased (TEARDROP EXPLODES) were mostly influenced by 60's pop psychedelia, sounding like a modern, post-new wave SCOTT WALKER. On-stage like antics cutting his stomach (IGGY POP-like) in, and singing perched on a high pole in, saw him develop a weird new character. Often he perfomed through his alter-ego (SQWUBBSY a seven foot giant) at work. • **Songwriters:** COPE penned except; READ IT IN BOOKS (co-with; Ian McCulloch). He wrote all material, except NON-ALIGNMENT PACT (Pere Ubu) / BOOKS (Teardrop Explodes). • **Trivia:** The album DROOLIAN, was released as part of a campaign to free from jail ROKY ERICKSON (ex-13th FLOOR ELEVATORS). In '90, COPE took part in the Anti-Poll tax march from Brixton to Trafalgar Square.

Album rating: Teardrop Explodes: KILIMANJARO (*9) / WILDER (*7) / EVERYBODY WANTS TO SHAG THE TEARDROP EXPLODES postumous (*7) / PIANO early (*4) / Julian Cope: WORLD SHUT YOUR MOUTH (*7) / FRIED (*7) / SAINT JULIAN (*7) / MY NATION UNDERGROUND (*8) / SKELLINGTON (*7) / DROOLIAN (*7) / PEGGY SUICIDE (*8) / JEHOVAHKILL (*5) / AUTOGEDDON (*6) / 20 MOTHERS (*8) / FLOORED GENIUS: THE BEST OF JULIAN COPE & THE TEARDROP EXPLODES 1979-1991 compilation (*8) / FLOORED GENIUS, VOL.2 (1983-91) compilation (*7)

TEARDROP EXPLODES

JULIAN COPE (b.21 Oct'57, Bargoed, Wales) – vocals, bass / **PAUL SIMPSON** – keyboards / **MICK FINKLER** – guitar / **GARY DWYER** – drums

Zoo | not iss.

Feb 79. (7"m) *(CAGE 003)* **SLEEPING GAS. / CAMERA CAMERA / KIRBY WORKERS' DREAM FADES** | | -

— **GERARD QUINN** – keyboards repl. SIMPSON who formed The WILD SWANS

May 79. (7") *(CAGE 005)* **BOUNCING BABIES. / ALL I AM IS LOVING YOU** | | -

— **DAVID BALFE** – keyboards (ex-LORI & THE CHAMELEONS, ex-BIG IN JAPAN, ex-THOSE NAUGHTY LUMPS) repl. QUINN who joined The WILD SWANS

Mar 80. (7") *(CAGE 008)* **TREASON (IT'S JUST A STORY). / READ IT IN BOOKS** | | -

— **ALAN GILL** – guitar (ex-DALEK I) repl. FINKLER now (COPE, DWYER, BALFE + GILL)

Mercury | Mercury

Sep 80. (7") *(TEAR 1)* **WHEN I DREAM. / KILIMANJARO** | 47 |

Oct 80. (lp) *(6359 035) <4016>* **KILIMANJARO** | 24 |
– Ha, ha, I'm drowning / Sleeping gas / Treason (it's just a story) / Second head / Poppies in the field / Went crazy / Brave boys keep their promises / Bouncing babies / Books / Thief of Baghdad / When I dream. *(re-iss. Mar81 lp/c +=; 6359/7150 035)* – Reward. *(re-iss. Jul84 lp/c; PRICE/PRIMC 59) (re-iss. May89 lp/c/cd; 836 897-1/-4/-2)*

— (below trumpet by RAY MARTINEZ)

Jan 81. (7") *(TEAR 2)* **REWARD. / STRANGE HOUSE IN THE SNOW** | 6 |

Apr 81. (7") *(TEAR 3)* **TREASON (IT'S JUST A STORY). / USE ME** | 18 |
(12"+=) *(TEAR 3-12)* – Traison (c'est juste une histoire).

Jun 81. (7") *(TEAR 4)* **POPPIES IN THE FIELD. / HA HA I'M DROWNING** | |
(d7"+=) *(TEAR 44)* – Bouncing babies / Read it in books.

— **TROY TATE** – guitar, vocals (ex-INDEX, ex-SHAKE) repl. GILL

Sep 81. (7") *(TEAR 5)* **PASSIONATE FRIEND. / CHRIST VS. WARHOL** | 25 |

— on session/gigs **ALFIE ALGIUS** (b.Malta) – bass / **JEFF HAMMER** – keyboards

Nov 81. (lp/c) *(6359/7150 056) <4035>* **WILDER** | 29 |
– Bent out of shape / Tiny children / The culture bunker / Falling down around me / Passionate friend / Colours fly away / Pure joy / Seven views of Jerusalem / The great dominions / Like Leila Khaled said / . . .And the fighting takes over. *(re-iss. Jun87 lp/c; PRICE/PRIMC 112) (re-iss. May89 lp/c/cd; 836 896-1/-4/-2)*

Nov 81. (7") *(TEAR 6)* **COLOURS FLY AWAY. / WINDOW SHOPPING FOR A NEW CROWN OF THORNS** | 54 |
(12"+=) *(TEAR 6-12)* – East of the equator.

— **DAVID BALFE** returned

— **RON FRANCOIS** – bass (ex-SINCEROS) repl. guests

Jun 82. (7"/7"g-f) *(TEAR 7/+G)* **TINY CHILDREN. / RACHEL BUILT A STEAMBOAT** | 44 |
(12"+=) *(TEAR 7-12)* – Sleeping gas (live).

— now trio of **COPE, DWYER + BALFE** plus session man **FRANCOIS**

— TROY TATE went solo and joined FASHION

Mar 83. (7") *(TEAR 8)* **YOU DISAPPEAR FROM VIEW. / SUFFOCATE** | 41 |
(d7"+=/12"+=) *(TEAR 88/8-12)* – Soft enough for you / Ouch monkey's / The in-psychlopedia.

— Disbanded early '83. BALFE went into producing films and music. JULIAN COPE went solo augmented by DWYER.

– compilations, others, etc. –

Jun 85. (7") *Mercury; (TEAR 9)* **REWARD (remix). / TREASON (IT'S JUST A STORY)** | | -
(12"+=) *(TEAR 9-12)* – Strange house in the snow / Use me.

Jan 90. (7") *Fontana; (DROP 1)* **SERIOUS DANGER. / SLEEPING GAS** | | -
(12"+=)(c-s+=/cd-s+=) *(DROP 1-12)(DRO MC/CD 1)* – Seven views of Jerusalem.

Mar 90. (cd/c/lp) *Fontana; (842 439-2/-4/-1)* **EVERYBODY WANTS TO SHAG THE TEARDROP EXPLODES** (long lost 3rd album) | 72 | -
– Ouch monkey's / Serious danger / Metranil Vavin / Count to ten and run forever / In-psychlopaedia / Soft enough for you / You disappear from view / The challenger / Not only my friend / Sex / Terrorist / Strange house in the snow.

Apr 90. (7") *Fontana; (DROP 2)* **COUNT TO TEN AND RUN FOR COVER. / REWARD** | | -
(12"+=)(cd-s+=) *(DROP 2-12)(DROCD 2)* – Poppies / Khaled said.

Jan 91. (cd/c/lp) *Document; (DCD/DMC/DLP 004)* **PIANO** | | -
– (early 'Zoo' material)

JULIAN COPE

with **GARY DWYER** / **STEVE CREASE + ANDREW EDGE** – drums / **STEPHEN LOWELL** – lead guitar / **RON FRANCOIS** – bass / **KATE ST. JOHN** – oboe

Mercury | Mercury

Nov 83. (7") *(COPE 1)* **SUNSHINE PLAYROOM. / HEY HIGH CLASS BUTCHER** | 64 |
(12"+=) *(COPE 1-12)* – Wreck my car / Eat the poor.

Feb 84. (lp/c) *(MERL/+C 37)* **WORLD SHUT YOUR MOUTH** | 40 |
– Bandy's first jump / Metranil Vavin / Strasbourg / An elegant chaos / Quizmaster / Kolly Kibber's birthday / Sunshine playroom / Head hang low / Pussy face / The greatness and perfection of love / Lunatic and fire pistol. *(cd-iss. 1986; 818 365-2)*

Mar 84. (7") *(MER 155)* **THE GREATNESS AND PERFECTION OF LOVE. / 24a VELOCITY CRESCENT** | 52 |
(12"+=) *(MERX 155)* – Pussyface.

Nov 84. (lp/c) *(MERL/+C 48)* **FRIED** | 87 |
– Reynard the fox / Bill Drummond said / Laughing boy / Me singing / Sunspots / Me singing / Bloody Assizes / Search party / O king of chaos / Holy love / Torpedo. *(cd-iss. 1986; 822 832-2)*

Feb 85. (7") *(MER 182)* **SUNSPOTS. / I WENT ON A CHOURNEY** | |
(d7"+=) *(MER 182-2)* – Mik mak mok / Land of fear.

— **COPE** recruited Americans **DONALD ROSS SKINNER** – guitar / **JAMES ELLER** – bass / **DOUBLE DE HARRISON** – keyboards / **CHRIS WHITTEN** – drums

Island | Island

Sep 86. (7") *(IS 290) <99479>* **WORLD SHUT YOUR MOUTH. / UMPTEENTH UNNATURAL BLUES** | 19 | 84 Feb87
(d7"+=) *(ISB 290)* – ('A'-Trouble Funk remix) / Transportation.
(c-s+=) *(CIS 290)* – I've got levitation / Non-alignment pact.
(12"++=) *(12IS 290)* – (all extra above).

Jan 87. (7") *(IS 305)* **TRAMPOLENE. / DISASTER** | |
(7"ep+=/12"ep+=) *(ISW/12IS 305)* – Mock Turtle / Warwick the kingmaker.

Feb 87. (m-lp) *<90560>* **JULIAN COPE** | - |
– World shut your mouth / Transportation / Umpteenth unnatural blues / Non-alignment pact / I've got levitation.

Mar 87. (lp/c/cd) *(ILPS/ICT/CID 9861) <90571>* **SAINT JULIAN** | 11 |
– Trampolene / Shot down / Eve's volcano (covered in sin) / Spacehopper / Planet ride / Trampolene / World shut your mouth / Saint Julian / Pulsar NX / Space hopper / Screaming secrets / A crack in the clouds. *(re-iss. Aug91 cd)(c; IMCD 137)(ICM 2023)*

Apr 87. (7") *(IS 318)* **EVE'S VOLCANO (COVERED IN SIN). / ALMOST BEAUTIFUL CHILD** | |
(12"+=) *(12IS 318)* – Pulsar NX (live) / Shot down (live).
(12"+=) *(12ISX 318)* – Spacehopper – Annexe / ('B'side; pt.II).
(cd-s++=) *(CID 318)* – (all 3 extra above).

— **DAVE PALMER** – drums (studio) / **MIKE JOYCE** – drums (tour) repl. WHITTEN / added **RON FAIR** – keyboards / **ROOSTER COSBY** – percussion, some drums

Sep 88. (7") *(IS 380)* **CHARLOTTE ANNE. / CHRISTMAS MOURNING** | 35 |

(12"+=/12"pic-d+=/pic-cd-s+=) *(12IS/12ISP/CIDP 380)* – Books / A question of temptation.

Oct 88. (lp/c/cd) *(ILPS/ICT/CID 9918) <91025>* **MY NATION UNDERGROUND** 42 □
– 5 o'clock world / Vegetation / Charlotte Anne / My nation underground / China doll / Someone like me / Easter everywhere / I'm not losing sleep / The great white hoax. *(re-iss. Aug91 cd)(c; IMCD 138)(ICM 9918)*

Nov 88. (7") *(IS 399)* **5 O'CLOCK WORLD. / S.P.Q.R.** 42 □
(10"+=/12"+=/pic-cd-s+=) *(10IS/12IS/CIDP 399)* – Reynard in Tokyo (extended live).

Jun 89. (7") *(IS 406)* **CHINA DOLL. / CRAZY FARM ANIMAL** 53 □
(10"+=/10"pic-d+=/12"+=) *(10IS/10ISP/12IS 406)* – Desi.
(cd-s++=) *(CID 406)* – Rail on.

— **COPE** retained **SKINNER & COSBY** plus **J.D. HASSINGER** – drums / **TIM** – keyboards / **BRAN** – bass (both of Guernsey)

Jan 91. (7"/c-s) *(IS/CIS 483)* **BEAUTIFUL LOVE. / PORT OF SAINTS** 32 □
(12"+=/cd-s+=) *(12IS/CID 483)* – Love L.U.V. / Unisex cathedral.
(12"pink+=) *(12ISX 483)* – Love L.U.V. / Dragonfly.

Mar 91. (cd/c/d-lp) *(CID/ICT/ILPSD 9977) <848338-2/-4>* **PEGGY SUICIDE** 23 □
– Pristeen / Double vegetation / East easy rider / Promised land / Hanging out & hung up on the line / Safesurfer / If you loved me at all / Drive, she said / Soldier blue / You . . . / Not raving but drowning / Head / Leperskin / Beautiful love / Uptight / Western Front 1992 CE / Hung up & hanging out to dry / The American Lite / Las Vegas basement. *(cd re-iss. Aug94; IMCD 188)*

Apr 91. (7"/c-s) *(IS/CIS 492)* **EAST EASY RIDER. / BUTTERFLY E** 51 □
(12"+=/cd-s+=) *(12IS/CID 492)* – Almost live / Little donkey.
(12"pic-d+=) *(12ISX 492)* – Easty Risin' / Ravebury stones.

Jul 91. (7"/c-s) *(IS/CIS 497)* **HEAD. / BAGGED - OUT KEN** 57 □
(12"+=/cd-s+=) *(12IS/CID 497)* – Straw dogs / Animals at all.

Oct 92. (7"/c-s) *(IS/CIS 545)* **FEAR LOVES THE SPACE. / SIZEWELL B.** 42 □
(12"pic-d+=) *(12ISX 545)* – I have always been here before / Gogmagog.

Oct 92. (cd/c/d-lp) *(<514052-2/-4/-1>)* **JEHOVAHKILL** 20 □ Dec92
– Soul desert / No harder shoulder to cry on / Akhenaten / The mystery trend / Upwards at 45° / Cut my friends down / Necropolis / Slow rider / Gimme back my flag / Poet is priest / Julian H Cope / The subtle energies commission / Fa-fa-fa-fine / Fear loves this place / Peggy Suicide is missing. *(cd re-iss. Aug94; IMCD 189)*

— Next was last in the 90's album trilogy about pollution. Its theme this time was the car, (coincidentally he had just passed his driving test). It featured usual musicians.

Echo American

Jul 94. (cd/c/lp) *(ECH CD/MC/LP 001) <45705>* **AUTOGEDDON** 16 □ Aug94
– Autogeddon blues / Madmax / Don't call me Mark Chapman / I gotta walk / Ain't no gettin' round gettin' round / Paranormal in the West Country (medley): i) Paranormal pt.1, ii) Archdrude's roadtrip. iii) Kar-ma-kanik / Ain't but the one way / S.t.a.r.c.a.r.

Aug 95. (7"yellow/c-s) *(ECS/+MC 11)* **TRY TRY TRY. / WESSEXY** 24 -
(cd-s+=) *(ECSCD 11)* – Baby, let's play vet / Don't jump me, mother.

Aug 95. (cd/c/d-lp) *(ECH CD/MC/LP 005)* **20 MOTHERS** 20 -
– Wheelbarrow man / I wandered lonely as a child / Try try try / Stone circles 'n' you / Queen – Mother / I'm your daddy / Highway to the sun / 1995 / By the light of the Silbury moon / Adam and Eve hit the road / Just like Pooh Bear / Girl-call / Greedhead detector / Don't take roots / Senile get / The lonely guy / Cryingbabiessleeplessnights / Leli B. / Road of dreams / When I walk through the land of fear.

Echo Cooking Vinyl

Jul 96. (7"white-ep/cd-ep) *(ECS/+CDX 022)* **I COME FROM ANOTHER PLANET, BABY. / HOW DO I UNDERSTAND MY MOTORMAN? / IF I COULD DO IT ALL OVER AGAIN, I'D DO IT OVER YOU** 34 -
(cd-s) *(ECSCD 022)* – Ambulance: Weesex post-ambient therapy.

Sep 96. (7"white) *(ECS 025)* **PLANETARY SIT-IN. / CUMMER IN SUMMERTIME / TORCH** 34 -
(cd-s) *(ECSCX 025)* – ('A'-Radio sit-in mixes).

Oct 96. (cd/c/lp) *(ECH CD/MC/LP 12) <9007>* **INTERPRETER** 39 □ Feb97
– I come from another planet, baby / I've got my TV and my pills / Planetary sit-in / Since I lost my head, it's awl-right / Cheap new age fix / Battle for the trees / Arthur / Spacerock with me / Re-directed male / Maid of constant sorrow / Loveboat / Dust.

– compilations, others, etc. –

Feb 85. (7"; as RABBI JOSEPH GORDON) *Bam Caruso; (NRICO 30)* **COMPETITION. / BELIEF IN HIM** □ -

May 90. (cd/lp) *Copeco-Zippo; (JUCD/JULP 89)* **SKELLINGTON** (1985 lost lp) □ -
– Doomed / Beaver / Me & Jimmy Jones / Robert Mitchum / Out of my mind on dope and speed / Don't crash here / Everything playing at once / Little donkey / Great white wonder / Incredibly ugly girl / No how, no why, no way, no where, no when / Comin' soon.

Jul 90. (cd/lp) *Mofo-Zippo; (MOFOCO CD/LP 90)* **DROOLIAN** □ -

Jul 92. (c-s/7") *Island; (C+/IS 534)* **WORLD SHUT YOUR MOUTH (remix). / DOOMED** 44 □
(12"+=/cd-s+=) *(12/CD IS 534)* – Reynard the fox / The elevators / Levitation.

Aug 92. (cd/c/d-lp) *Island; (CID/ICT/ILPSD 8000)* **FLOORED GENIUS – THE BEST OF JULIAN COPE AND THE TEARDROP EXPLODES 1981-1991** 22 □
– Reward / Treason / Sleeping gas / Bouncing babies / Passionate friend / The great dominions (; all TEARDROP EXPLODES) / The greatness & perfection of love / An elegant chaos / Sunspots / Reynard the fox / World shut your mouth / Trampolene / Spacehopper / Charlotte Anne / China doll / Out of my mind on dope & speed / Jellypop perky Jean / Beautiful love / East easy rider / Safesurfer.

Nov 92. (d-cd) *Island; (ITSCD 11)* **SAINT JULIAN / MY NATION UNDERGROUND** □ -

Nov 93. (cd/lp) *Night Tracks; (CD/LP NT 003)* **BEST OF THE BBC SESSIONS 1983-91 (FLOORED GENIUS VOL.2)** □ -

Jun 97. (cd) *Island; (IMCD 251)* **THE FOLLOWERS OF SAINT JULIAN** □ -

COP SHOOT COP

Formed: Brooklyn, New York, USA . . . summer '88 by singer/bassist JACK NATZ, second bassist TOD A, DAVE QUIMET, PHIL PULEO and sampler JAMES COLEMAN. Operating from the same seething well of unrelenting negativity as NY "No Wave" pioneers like DNA and MARS, COP SHOOT COP set out to create hateful R&R noise in the most uncompromising, unlistener- friendly style they could muster. Utilising a rhythmic, guitarless sound driven by two bass players, the band made their debut in 1988 with the mini-set, 'HEADKICK FACSIMILE'. Also released on the 'Supernatural Organization' imprint was their 1990 follow-up, 'CONSUMER REVOLT', subsequently unveiled in the UK a few years later on 'Big Cat'. By this time, CSC had already showcased their anti-pop racket on 'WHITE*NOISE' (1991), although surprisingly, given their militant opposition to corporate culture, the band signed a major label deal with 'Interscope'. First up was an EP, 'SUCK CITY', followed by by the slightly more consumer friendly 'ASK QUESTIONS LATER' (1993), an album that found the noisemeisters allowing their claustrophobic sound more room to breathe. Similarly, 1994's 'RELEASE' was easier on the ear with repeated listening, although as far as NY underground kudos is concerned, COP SHOOT COP still take no prisoners.

Album rating: HEADKICK FACSIMILE mini (*4) / CONSUMER REVOLT (*4) / WHITE-NOISE (*5) / ASK QUESTIONS LATER (*7) / RELEASE (*6)

JACK NATZ – vocals, bass / **TOD A.** – bass, vocals / **DAVE QUIMET** – samples / **PHIL PULEO** – drums, metal / **FILER** (aka JAMES COLEMAN) – samples

not iss. Supernatural Organization

1988. (m-lp) **HEADKICK FACSIMILE** - □

Feb 90. (lp) **CONSUMER REVOLT** - □
– Lo. Com. denom / She's like a shot / Waiting for the punchline / Disconnected 666 / Smash retro / Burn your bridges / Consume / Fire in the hole / Pity the bastard / Down come the Mickey / Hurt me baby / System test / Eggs for rib. *(UK + re-iss. Apr92 on 'Big Cat' lp/c/cd; ABB 33/+C/CD)*

Big Cat Big Cat

Oct 91. (lp/c/cd) *<(ABB 29/+C/CD)>* **WHITE*NOISE** □ □
– Discount rebellion / Traitor – Martyr / Coldest day of the year / Feel good / Relief / Empires collapse / Corporate protopop / Heads I win, tails you lose / Chameleon man / Where's the money? / If tomorrow ever comes / Hung again.

Big Cat Interscope

Aug 92. (12"ep/cd-ep) *(ABB 39 T/SCD) <96116>* **SUCK CITY EP** □ □ Nov92
– Nowhere / Days will pass / We shall be changed / Suck city (here we come).

Apr 93. (d-lp/d-cd) *(ABB 45/+CD) <92250>* **ASK QUESTIONS LATER** □ □ Mar93
– Surprise, surprise / Room 429 / No where / Migration / Cut to the chase / $10 bill / Seattle / Furnace / Israeli dig / Cause and effect / Got no soul / Everybody loves you / All the clocks are broken.

Jun 93. (12"green-ep/cd-ep) *(ABB 53 T/SCD)* **$10 BILL. / CAUSE AND EFFECT / SEATTLE** □ □

Dec 93. (12"ep/cd-ep) *(ABB 54 T/SCD)* **ROOM 429 E.P.** □ -
– Room 429 / Ambulance song / Fragment / Shine on Elizabeth (live).

Aug 94. (12"/cd-s) *(ABB 68 T/SCD)* **TWO AT A TIME. /** □ -

Sep 94. (lp/cd) *(ABB 69/+CD) <92424>* **RELEASE** □ □
– Interference / It only hurts when I breathe / Last legs / Two at a time / Slackjaw / Lullaby / Any day now / Swimming in circles / Turning inside out / Ambulance song / Suckerpunch / Divorce / Money drunk.

Jan 95. (12"ep/cd-ep) *(ABB 78 T/SCD)* **ANY DAY NOW / NEW GOD. / QUEEN OF SHINBONE ALLEY / TRANSMISSION** □ -

Submission not iss.

Jul 96. (7"/cd-s; with MEATHEAD) *(SUCK 3/+CD)* **KILL A COP FOR CHRIST AND BRING US HIS HEAD** □ -

— split later in '96

CORNELIUS

Born: KEIGO OYAMADA, 27 Jan'69, Setagaya-ku, Tokyo, Japan. After beginning his career in a Japanese teen band, FLIPPER'S GUITAR, CORNELIUS (who took his nom de plume from a character in the cult film, 'The Planet Of The Apes') branched out into the world of production/remix work (his credits include PIZZICATO 5 and MONEY MARK) while running his own label, 'Trattoria'. Inevitably, this jack of all trades also released his own solo work augmented by his ever-faithful sidekick, BRYAN, who functions as his personal translator as well as being a DJ and lyricist. Having achieved near superstar status in Japan, CORNELIUS turned his attention to Western shores signing to 'Matador'. Early in '98, the first fruits of his labour emerged in the shape of the 'FREE FALL' single, while the follow-up single, 'CHAPTER 8 . . .' was another to be taken from his debut set, 'FANTASMA'. Pilfering from various eras of pop culture, the "monkey" man from the East created a vertible cornucopia of bleeps, tunes and samples; the duo themselves describe their sound as akin to a hard/loungecore MICHAEL JACKSON.

Album rating: FANTASMA (*6)

CORNELIUS – vocals, guitar, bass, drums / **BRYAN** – lyrics

— released 3 albums in his home country in the mid 90's

Matador Matador

Mar 98. (7") *(OLE 308-7)* **FREE FALL. / CLASH** □ -
(cd-s+=) *(OLE 308-2)* – Brand new season / Typewriter lesson.

May 98. (7") *(OLE 319-7)* **CHAPTER 8-SEASHORE AND HORIZON. / COUNT FIVE OR SIX** □ -
(cd-s+=) *(OLE 319-2)* – Micro Disneycal world tour / Fantasma spot.

Jun 98. (cd/lp) *(<OLE 3002/-1>)* **FANTASMA** □ □
– Mic check / Micro Disneycal world tour / New music machine / Clash / Count five or six / Magoo opening / Star fruits surf rider / Chapter 8-Seashore and horizon / Free fall / 2010 / God only knows / Thank you for the music / Fantasma.

Oct 98. (12"/cd-s) *(OLE 320-1/-2)* **STAR FRUITS SURF RIDER / STAR FRUITS BLUE (Damon Albarn mix)** -
(cd-s) *(OLE 320-4)* – ('A'side) / Ball in kick off / Star fruits green.

CORNERSHOP

Formed: Preston, England . . . 1987, evolving from GENERAL HAVOC by Asian songwriting brothers, TJINDER and AVTAR SINGH. They first came to attention of the music press late in 1992, when they publicly derided MORRISSEY for his alleged racist leanings. Already signed to the up and coming 'Wiiija' label, they delivered their debut EP, 'IN THE DAYS OF FORD CORTINA', in a blaze of publicity. Described as JESUS & MARY CHAIN with sitars, the unconventional Sikh/ white thrash fusion was entertaining if hardly professional. Inevitably the initial press hype soon backfired on them, although they struggled on through a clutch of patchy albums including 'HOLD ON IT HURTS' (1994) and 'WOMAN'S GOTTA HAVE IT' (1995). Major alterations were subsequently carried out on the 'SHOP, after which TJINDER re-opened for business in 1997 with the sonic nirvana of 'WHEN I WAS BORN FOR THE 7th TIME'. A surprise Top 40 success, well worthy of merit with its consumate blend of hip hop, Indian folk, country and indie funk, the album spawned the classic 'BRIMFUL OF ASHA' (a ltd-edition original release, it went on to hit the top of the charts in early '98). The record also featured a suitably exotic version of The BEATLES' 'NORWEGIAN WOOD (THIS BIRD HAS FLOWN)', while 'CANDYMAN' took elements from LARRY CORYELL's 'The Opening'.

Album rating: WHEN I WAS BORN FOR THE 7th TIME (*9)

TJINDER SINGH (b. 8 Feb'68, New Cross, Wolverhampton, England) – guitar / **AVTAR SINGH** (b.11 May'65, Punjab, India) – bass, vocals / **DAVID CHAMBERS** (b.1969, Lincoln, England) – drums / **ANTHONY SAFFERY** – sitar / **NEIL MILNER** – tapes

Chapati Heat / not iss.

Dec 91. (7"ep; as the GENERAL HAVOC) *(BIRD 1)* **FAST JASPAL EP** -
– Moonshine / Vacuum cleaner / Another cup of tea, Arch Deacon?

— **BEN AYRES** (b. BENEDICT, 30 Apr'68, St John's, Canada) – guitar, vocals; repl. ANTHONY + NEIL

Wiiija / Merge

Jan 93. (7"ep; some colrd) *(WIJ 019V)* **IN THE DAYS OF FORD CORTINA EP** -
– Waterlogged / Moonshine / Kawasaki (more heat than chapati) / Hanif Kureishi scene.

Apr 93. (10"ep) *(WIJ 22V)* **LOCK STOCK & DOUBLE-BARREL** -
– England's dreaming / Trip easy / Summer fun in a beat up Datsun / Breaking every rule language English.
(cd-ep+=) *(WIJ 22CD)* – (hidden track).

Jul 93. (m-cd) *(WAKEUP 001)* **ELVIS SEX-CHANGE** -
– (above 2 EP's)

Jan 94. (7"ep/cd-ep) *(WIJ 29 V/CD)* **READERS' WIVES EP** -
– Readers' wives / Inside Rani (short version) / Tandoori chicken.

Jan 94. (cd/c/lp) *(WIJ 030 CD/C/V)* <74> **HOLD ON IT HURTS** Jan95
– Jason Donovan – Tessa Sanderson / Kalluri's radio / Readers' wives / Change / Inside Rani (long version) / Born disco; died heavy metal / Counteraction / Where d'u get your information / Tera mera pyar / You always said my language would get me into trouble. *(lp w/ free 7")* – BORN DISCO; DIED HEAVY METAL (disco mix). / ENGLAND'S DREAMING

Mar 94. (7"ep/cd-ep) *(WIJ 033 V/CD)* **BORN DISCO; DIED HEAVY METAL. / THE SAFETY OF OBJECTS / REHOUSED** -

Apr 94. (7") *(XPI 24)* **SEETAR MAN. / (track by Blood Sausage)** -
(above issued on 'Clawfist')

— CHAMBERS departed before below album

Wiiija / Luaka Bop – Warners

Apr 95. (7"etched) *(LTD 004)* **6 A.M. JULLANDAR SHERE** -

May 95. (cd/lp) *(WIJ 045 CD/V)* <46018> **WOMAN'S GOTTA HAVE IT**
– 6 a.m. Jullandar shere / Hong Kong book of Kung Fu / Roof rack / My dancing days are done / Call all destroyer / Camp orange / Never leave yourself (vocal overload mix) / Jamsimran king / Wog / Looking for a way in / 7.20 a.m. Jullander shere.

Aug 95. (7") *(CIP 101)* **MY DANCING DAYS ARE DONE. / Prohibition: I AM NOT A FISH** - - French
(above issued on French label, 'Bruit Distordu')

Feb 96. (12"ep/cd-ep) *(WIJ 048 V/CD)* **6 A.M. JULLANDAR SHERE: The Grid & Star Liner mixes** -
– (Jeh Jeh mix) / (All Fetters Loose mix) / (original).

— AVTAR departed around 1995/96, leaving **TJINDER + BEN** to recruit **PETER BENGRY** – percussion / **ANTHONY SAFFREY** – sitar, harmonium, keyboards (returned) / **NICK SIMMS** – drums, tambourine

Jun 96. (12"ep) *(WIJ 049V)* **W.O.G. – THE U.S. WESTERN ORIENTAL MIXES** -
– (original) / (Freaky's) / (Witchman's Assimilation) / Freaky's Acid DJ) / (Witchman's extended beats).

Dec 96. (12"etched) *(ROOT 011)* **BUTTER THE SOUL** -
(above released on 'Art Bus')

Jun 97. (7") *(WIJ 70)* **GOOD SHIPS. / FUNKY DAYS ARE BACK AGAIN** -
(12"+=/cd-s+=) *(WIJ 70 T/CD)* – ('A'-Intro – instrumental / 'B'extended beats mix).

Aug 97. (7") *(WIJ 75)* **BRIMFUL OF ASHA. / EASY WINNERS (part 1)** 60
(cd-s+=) *(WIJ 75CD)* – Rehoused / ('A'mix).
(cd-s) *(WIJ 75CDX)* – ('A'remixes; Sofa Surfers / Mucho Macho).

Sep 97. (cd/c/d-lp) *(WIJ CD/MC/LP 1065)* <46576> **WHEN I WAS BORN FOR THE 7th TIME** 17
– Sleep on the left side / Brimful of Asha / Butter the soul / Chocolat / We're in yr corner / Funky days are back again / What is happening? / When the light appears boy / Coming up / Good shit / Good to be on the road back home again / It's Indian tobacco my friend / Candyman / State troopers / Norwegian wood (this bird has flown).

Nov 97. (12"etched) *(ROOT 014T)* **BRIMFUL OF ASHA (Norman Cook remix)** -

Feb 98. (7"/c-s) *(WIJ 81/+MC)* **BRIMFUL OF ASHA. / ('A'-Norman Cook remix)** 1
(12"+=) *(ROOT 014T)* – ('A'-Norman Cook extended).
(cd-s++=) *(WIJ 81CD)* – U47S.

May 98. (c-s) *(WIJ 80C)* <44524> **SLEEP ON THE LEFT SIDE / ('A'-Les Rhythms Digitales mix)** 23
(12"+=/cd-s+=) *(WIJ 80 T/CD)* – ('A'-Ashley Beadle mix) / ('A'-Ashley Beadle extended).

— also released a couple of 12"singles as CLINTON:- 'JAM JAR' (1994) and 'SUPERLOOSE!' twice (1995 & 1997).

Nov 98. (12"ltd) *(WIJ 093T)* **CANDYMAN (mixes; Rob Swift vocal & instrumental / Schizoid Man / Uptight Vienna)** -

Hugh CORNWALL (see under ⇒ STRANGLERS)

CORTINAS

Formed: London, England . . . early 1977 by fresh-faced R&B fans, JEREMY VALENTINE, NICK SHEPHERD, MIKE FEWINGS, DEXTER DALWOOD and DANIEL SWAN. Inspired by the onset of punk, the lads were the first act to release a single on 'Step Forward', 'FASCIST DICTATOR' drawing an imaginary line between The JAM, DR. FEELGOOD and SLAUGHTER & THE DOGS. A late '77 follow-up, 'DEFIANT POSE', packed a harder punch although in retrospect both the "sick" cover art and naive lyrics seem faintly ridiculous. Riotous gigs and a healthy major label deal with 'C.B.S.' saw the band dilute the punk influence on the disappointing debut album, 'TRUE ROMANCES' (1978), although cheeky tracks such as 'ASK MR. WAVERLY' (a subsequent B-side which should have been an A-side) and 'I TRUST VALERIE SINGLETON' (a clean living 'Blue Peter' children's TV presenter!) rescued it from bland oblivion. Not surprisingly, The CORTINAS consigned themselves to the scrapheap soon after, their career skidding to a halt after the belated 7" release of album opener, 'HEARTACHE'. The only member to enjoy his 15 minutes worth of fame was guitarist NICK SHEPHERD who became part of The CLASH prior to their mid-80's demise.

Album rating: TRUE ROMANCES (*4)

JEREMY VALENTINE – vocals / **MIKE FEWINGS** – lead guitar / **NICK SHEPPARD** – guitar / **DEXTER DALWOOD** – bass / **DANIEL SWAN** – drums

Step Forward / not iss.

Jun 77. (7") *(SF 1)* **FASCIST DICTATOR. / TELEVISION FAMILIES** -

Dec 77. (7",12") *(SF 6)* **DEFIANT POSE. / INDEPENDENCE** -

C.B.S. / not iss.

Apr 78. (lp) *(CBS 82831)* **TRUE ROMANCES** -
– Heartache / Ask Mr. Waverly / Radio rape / Broken not twisted / I don't really want to get involved / Have it with you / Tribe of the city / I trust Valerie Singleton / Further education / Youth club dance / First I look at the purse / I'll keep my distance / Take that light away.

Nov 78. (7") *(CBS 6759)* **HEARTACHE. / ASK MR. WAVERLY** -

— disbanded late '78, FEWINGS joined ESSENTIAL BOP, SHEPPARD later joined The CLASH after a two-year spell with the SPICS.

Elvis COSTELLO

Born: DECLAN McMANUS, 25 Aug'55, Liverpool, England. The son of a jazz bandleader, he grew up listening to the sounds of the day; the BEATLES (he was a member of their fanclub), the KINKS, the WHO and the sounds of Motown were all to instil in him a love of rock'n'roll and help shape his own musical style. Dividing his time between playing clubs at night and working as a computer operator during working hours (the strain on his eyes leading to the wearing of his now trademark glasses), he subsequently moved to London in 1974 to become frontman and songwriter for a country-rock group called Flip City. Flogging his demos far and wide, the newly formed 'Stiff' label duly took on his talent, McMANUS changing his name to ELVIS COSTELLO; 'Elvis', a challenge to the rock establishment, and 'Costello', his mother's maiden name. While at Stiff he met his long time collaborators NICK LOWE and Jake Rivera, who would in turn become producer and manager to COSTELLO. His first album was recorded in 24 hours, backed by CLOVER, a country and western bar band with a certain HUEY LEWIS at the helm (although he did not participate in the sessions). After little success with the first two singles, 'ALISON' and 'LESS THAN ZERO', the man resorted to playing outside a CBS Records international convention taking place at the Hilton in London. Although arrested, the stunt worked, and in '77 his first album, 'MY AIM IS TRUE' was released by 'Columbia' (US), stand out tracks including the aforementioned singles and 'WATCHING THE DETECTIVES'. Produced by LOWE, the record was hailed as one of the finest debuts in rock history, blending the Stiff sound of punk and new wave with COSTELLO's cynical observations on life. Voted Album of the Year in Rolling Stone's annual poll, COSTELLO toured the States with his newly assembled backing band, The ATTRACTIONS. America got its first taste of COSTELLO's independent stance when his appearance on Saturday Night Live turned into a scathing attack on the media. His next two albums, 'THIS YEARS MODEL' and

'ARMED FORCES' (originally titled Emotional Fascism) were to prove an artistic peak, as well as being commercially successful, the latter charting in the Top 10. Released in 1980, 'GET HAPPY' abandoned the new wave sound for a more 60's Motown approach. With 20 songs on the original LP (and 10 more on the CD reissue), it proved COSTELLO was in prime songwriting mode, the record swiftly followed by his fifth set, 'TRUST' (1981), sounding as captivating and twisted as its predecessor was fast and loose. In between these two sets was the Nashville covers album, 'ALMOST BLUE' more a curiosity than a stand out success. 'IMPERIAL BEDROOM', released in '82, is often cited as COSTELLO's best album, and was produced by the Beatles engineer, Geoff Emerick (who would later go on to produce the '96 effort 'ALL THIS USELESS BEAUTY'). Not surprisingly then, it was compared to the masterpieces of the BEATLES and the BEACH BOYS, and included such fan favourites as 'MAN OUT OF TIME' and 'THE LONG HONEYMOON'. 'PUNCH THE CLOCK', released in '83, and featuring CHET BAKER on the track 'SHIPBUILDING', was less ambitious than the previous album, while 'GOODBYE CRUEL WORLD', released the following year, was his worst record by some margin, starting out as an attempt at folk-rock, but ending up as an example of the '80s sound gone wrong. By this time, a split had developed between COSTELLO and the ATTRACTIONS, and 'KING OF AMERICA' was the penultimate album recorded with this combination until 'BRUTAL YOUTH' in '94. With backing from The CONFEDERATES and co-production by T-BONE BURNETT, it featured a mixture of country and folk with a fair splattering of rockabilly with varied success. 'BLOOD AND CHOCOLATE' (1986) was notable both for the return of NICK LOWE as producer and the man's splitfrom the ATTRACTIONS. With LOWE at the helm, the record was far removed from his '84 effort, featuring a nastier, meatier version of 'THIS YEARS MODEL' plus 'POISONED ROSE', the latter track boasting the bass playing of the legendary jazz bassist RAY BROWN. Subsequently signing to 'Warner Brothers', his first release was the darkly comic and commercially successful 'SPIKE' (1989), its considerable sales due largely to the hit single, 'VERONICA', although it also featured songs of genuine outrage such as 'TRAMP THE DIRT DOWN' and 'LET HIM DANGLE'. The next few years saw COSTELLO become more adventurous in an attempt to break away from the past, symbolised by a change of image. 'MIGHTY LIKE A ROSE' remains arguably his most underrated album, while the follow up, 'THE JULIET LETTERS' (featuring The Brodsky Quartet), mixed pop with chamber music to commercial failure but critical praise. 'BRUTAL YOUTH' in '94 saw the reunion of COSTELLO and the ATTRACTIONS (dubbed the Distractions) and included one of the most beautiful recordings of his career in 'ROCKING HORSE ROAD', while the follow up, 'ALL THIS USELESS BEAUTY', was the ATTRACTIONS swansong and inexplicably a commercial failure. Collaborations outside of his albums for 'Columbia' and 'Warners' are numerous, COSTELLO winning a BAFTA with RICHARD HARVEY for the soundtrack to 'G.B.H.' and also recently contributing the track, 'MY MOOD SWINGS' to the Coen Brothers latest film, 'The Big Lebowski'. Perhaps the most intriguing partnership never to see the light of day, save for three releases as obscure B-Sides, was his collaboration with country legend, GEORGE JONES, singing 'non-country' songs such as Hoagy Carmichael's 'MY RESISTANCE IS LOW' and Bruce Springsteen's 'BRILLIANT SURPRISE'. A collaboration was released at the back end of '98 featuring an album's worth of COSTELLO and BURT BACHARACH material, 'PAINTED FROM MEMORY', together again after the magnificent 'God Give Me Strength' (which was originally recorded on the 'Grace Of My Heart' soundtrack). Released recently, a tribute album of COSTELLO's songs by the likes of JOHNNY CASH, JUNE TABOR, NICK LOWE and ROBERT WYATT demonstrate both the man's musical versatility and the songwriting skills which have made him such an integral part of the last two decades of popular music. • **Songwriters:** All penned by COSTELLO, bar NEAT NEAT NEAT (Damned) / I CAN'T STAND UP FOR FALLING DOWN (Sam & Dave) / SWEET DREAMS (Patsy Cline) / A GOOD YEAR FOR THE ROSES (Jerry Chestnut) / DON'T LET ME BE MISUNDERSTOOD (Nina Simone) / I WANNA BE LOVED (Farnell Jenkins) / THE UGLY THINGS (Nick Lowe) / YOU'RE NO GOOD (Swinging Blue Jeans) / FULL FORCE GALE (Van Morrison) / YOU'VE GOT TO HIDE YOUR LOVE AWAY (Beatles) / STEP INSIDE LOVE (Cilla Black) / STICKS & STONES (Ray Charles) / FROM HEAD TO TOE (Smokey Robinson) / CONGRATULATIONS (Paul Simon) / STRANGE (Screaming Jay Hawkins) / HIDDEN CHARMS (Willie Dixon) / REMOVE THIS DOUBT (Supremes) / I THREW IT ALL AWAY (Bob Dylan) / LEAVE MY KITTEN ALONE (Little Willie John) / EVERYBODY'S CRYIN' MERCY (Mose Allison) / I'VE BEEN WRONG BEFORE (Randy Newman) / BAMA LAMA BAMA LOO (Little Richard) / MUST YOU THROW DIRT IN MY FACE (Louvin Bros.) / POURING WATER ON A DROWNING MAN (James Carr) / THE VERY THOUGHT OF YOU (Ray Noble) / PAYDAY (Jesse Winchester) / PLEASE STAY (Bacharach-David) / RUNNING OUT OF FOOLS (Jerry Ragavoy) / DAYS (Kinks) / etc. • **Trivia:** He has also produced The SPECIALS (1979) / SQUEEZE (1981) / POGUES (1985) retaining a latter acquaintance in CAIT O'RIORDON, whom he married on 16 May'86.

Album rating: MY AIM IS TRUE (*9) / THIS YEAR'S MODEL (*9) / ARMED FORCES (*9) / GET HAPPY!! (*8) / TRUST (*8) / ALMOST BLUE (*5) / IMPERIAL BEDROOM (*8) / PUNCH THE CLOCK (*7) / GOODBYE CRUEL WORLD (*5) / KING OF AMERICA (*7) / BLOOD AND CHOCOLATE (*7) / SPIKE (*5) / MIGHTY LIKE A ROSE (*5) / THE JULIET LETTERS with Brodsky Quartet (*5) / BRUTAL YOUTH (*6) / KOJAK VARIETY (*4) / ALL THIS USELESS BEAUTY (*5) / PAINTED FROM MEMORY with Burt Bacharach (*5) / OUT OF OUR IDIOT collection (*5) / THE VERY BEST OF ELVIS COSTELLO & THE ATTRACTIONS compilation (*8)

ELVIS COSTELLO

(solo) – vocals, guitar with backing band The **SHAMROCKS,** (alias CLOVER) / **JOHN McFEE** – guitar / **ALEX CALL** – guitar, vocals / **SEAN HOPPER** – keyboards / **JOHN CIAMBOTTI** – bass / **MICHAEL SHINE** – drums

		Stiff	Columbia
Mar 77.	(7") *(BUY 11)* **LESS THAN ZERO. / RADIO SWEETHEART**		-
May 77.	(7") *(BUY 14)* **ALISON. / WELCOME TO THE WORKING WEEK**		
Jun 77.	(7") *<3-10641>* **ALISON. / MIRACLE MAN**	-	
Jul 77.	(7") *(BUY 15)* **(THE ANGELS WANNA WEAR MY) RED SHOES. / MYSTERY DANCE**		-
Jul 77.	(lp/c) *(SEEZ/ZSEEZ 3) <JC 35037>* **MY AIM IS TRUE**	14	32 Nov77

– Welcome to the working week / Miracle man / No dancing / Blame it on Cain / Alison / Sneaky feelings / (The angels wanna wear my) Red shoes / Less than zero / Mystery dance / Pay it back / I'm not angry / Waiting for the end of the world. *<re-iss. US Mar78 +=> (AL 35037>* – Watching the detectives. *(re-iss. Jul86 on 'Imp' lp/c/cd; FIEND/+CASS/CD 13) (re-iss. cd Mar93 w/ extra tracks on 'Demon'; DPAM 1)*

ELVIS COSTELLO & THE ATTRACTIONS

— **STEVE NIEVE** (b.NASON)– keyboards repl. HOPPER to HUEY LEWIS & THE NEWS **BRUCE THOMAS** – bass, vocals (ex-QUIVER)repl. CIAMBOTTI, CALL + McFEE / **PETE THOMAS** (b.9 Aug'54, Sheffield, England)– drums (ex-CILLI WILLI, ex-WILKO JOHNSON)repl. SHINE

Oct 77.	(7"m) *(BUY 20)* **WATCHING THE DETECTIVES. / BLAME IT ON CAIN (live) / MYSTERY DANCE (live)**	15	-
Nov 77.	(7" *<3-10705>* **WATCHING THE DETECTIVES. / ALISON**	-	

Radar Columbia

Mar 78. (7") *(ADA 3)* **(I DON'T WANT TO GO TO) CHELSEA. / YOU BELONG TO ME** 16 -

Mar 78. (lp/c) *(XX LP/C 11) <35331>* **THIS YEAR'S MODEL** 4 30
– No action / This year's girl / The beat / Pump it up / Little Triggers / You belong to me / Hand in hand / (I don't want to go to) Chelsea * / Lip service / Living in Paradise / Lipstick vogue / Night rally *. *(free-7"w/ above) (SAM 83)* – STRANGER IN THE HOUSE. / NEAT NEAT NEAT *<tracks * repl. by 'Radio Radio' on US version> (re-iss. May80 on 'F-Beat'; XXLP 4) (re-iss. Apr84 on 'Imp'; FIEND/+CASS 18) (cd-iss. Jan86; FIENDCD 18) (re-iss. cd Mar93 on 'Demon' w/ extra tracks; DPAM 2)*

May 78. (7") *(ADA 10)* **PUMP IT UP. / BIG TEARS** 24 -

Jul 78. (7") *<3-10762>* **THIS YEAR'S GIRL. / BIG TEARS** - ☐

Oct 78. (7") *(ADA 24)* **RADIO RADIO. / TINY STEPS** 29 ☐

Jan 79. (lp/c) *(RAD/RAC 14) <35709>* **ARMED FORCES** 2 10
– Senior service / Oliver's army / Big boys / Green shirt / Party girl / Goon squad / Busy bodies / Sunday's best * / Moods for moderns / Chemistry class / Two little Hitlers / Accidents will happen. *(free 7"w/ above) (SAM 90) <AE 71171>* LIVE AT HOLLYWOOD HIGH EP:- Accidents Will Happen / Alison / Watching The Detectives. *<track * repl. by '(What's So Funny 'Bout) Peace, Love And Understanding' on US version> (re-iss. May80 on 'F-Beat'; XXLP 5) (re-iss. Apr84 on 'Imp' lp/c; FIEND/+CASS 21) (cd-iss. Jan86; FIENDCD 21) (re-iss. cd Mar93 on 'Demon' w/ extra tracks; DPAM 3)*

Feb 79. (7") *(ADA 31)* **OLIVER'S ARMY. / MY FUNNY VALENTINE** 2 ☐

May 79. (7"m) *(ADA 35)* **ACCIDENTS WILL HAPPEN. / TALKING IN THE DARK / WEDNESDAY WEEK** 28 ☐

ELVIS COSTELLO

solo, but still used ATTRACTIONS

F-Beat Columbia

Feb 80. (7") *(XX 1)* **I CAN'T STAND UP FOR FALLING DOWN. / GIRLS TALK** 4 ☐

Feb 80. (lp/c) *(XX LP/C 1) <36347>* **GET HAPPY!!** 2 11
– Love for tender / Opportunity / The imposter / Secondary modern / King Horse / Possession / Man called Uncle / Clowntime is over / New Amsterdam / High fidelity / I can't stand up for falling down / Black and white world / Five years in reverse / B movie / Motel matches / Human touch / Beaten to the punch / Temptation / I stand accused / Riot act. *(re-iss. Apr84 on 'Imp' lp/c; FIEND/+CASS 24) (cd-iss. Jan86; FIENDCD 24) (re-iss. cd May94 on 'Demon' w/ extra tracks; DPAM 5)*

Apr 80. (7") *(XX 3)* **HIGH FIDELITY. / GETTING MIGHTY CROWDED** 30 ☐
(12"+=) *(XX 3T)* – Clowntime is over (version 2).

Jun 80. (7") *(XX5)* **NEW AMSTERDAM. / DR. LUTHER'S ASSISTANT** 36 ☐
(7"ep+=) *(XX 5E)* – Ghost train / Just a memory.

ELVIS COSTELLO & THE ATTRACTIONS

(same line-up)

Dec 80. (7"m) *(XX 12)* **CLUBLAND. / CLEAN MONEY / HOOVER FACTORY** 60 ☐

Jan 81. (lp/c) *(XX LP/C 11) <37051>* **TRUST** 9 28
– Clubland / Lovers walk / You'll never be a man / Pretty words / Strict time / Luxembourg / Watch your step / New lace sleeves / From a whisper to a scream / Different finger / White knuckles / Shot with his own gun / Fish'n'chip paper / Big sister's clothes. *(re-iss. Apr84 on 'Imp'; lp/c; FIEND/+CASS 30) (cd-iss. Jan86; FIENDCD 30) (re-iss. cd May94 on 'Demon' w/ extra tracks; DPAM 6)*

Feb 81. (7") *(XX 14)* **FROM A WHISPER TO A SCREAM. / LUXEMBOURG** ☐ ☐

Sep 81. (7") *(XX 17)* **GOOD YEAR FOR THE ROSES. / YOUR ANGEL STEPS OUT OF HEAVEN** 6 ☐

Oct 81. (lp/c) *(XX LP/C 13) <37562>* **ALMOST BLUE** 7 50
– Why don't you love me (like you used to do) / Sweet dreams / Sucess / I'm your toy / Tonight the bottle let me down / Brown to blue / Good year for the roses / Sittin' and thinkin' / Colour of the blues / Too far gone / Honey hush / How much I lied. *(re-iss. Apr84 on 'Imp' lp/c; FIEND/+CASS 33) (cd-iss. Jan86; FIENDCD 33) (re-iss. cd Oct94 on 'Demon' w/extra tracks; DPAM 7)*

Dec 81. (7") *(XX 19)* **SWEET DREAMS. / PSYCHO (live)** 42 ☐

Apr 82. (7"m) *(XX 21)* **I'M YOUR TOY (live). / CRY CRY CRY / WONDERING** 51 ☐
(12"ep) *(XX 21T)* – ('A'side) / My shoes keep walking back to you / Blues keep calling / Honky tonk girl. (w/ The ROYAL PHILHARMONIC)

Jun 82. (7"m) *(XX 26)* **YOU LITTLE FOOL. / BIG SISTER / THE STAMPING GROUND (The Emotional Toothpaste)** 52 ☐

Jul 82. (lp/c) *(XX LP/C 17) <38157>* **IMPERIAL BEDROOM** 6 30
– Beyond belief / Tears before bedtime / Shabby doll / The long honeymoon / Man out of time / Almost blue / . . .And in every home / The loved ones / Human hands / Kid about it / Little savage / Boy with a problem / Pidgin English / You little fool / Town cryer. *(re-iss. Apr84 on 'Imp' lp/c; FIEND/+CASS 36) (cd-iss. Jan86; FIENDCD 36) (re-iss. cd Oct94 on 'Demon' w/ extra tracks; DPAM 8)*

Jul 82. (7") *(XX 28)* **MAN OUT OF TIME. / TOWN CRYER (alt.take)** 58 -

Jul 82. (7") *<CNR 03269>* **MAN OUT OF TIME. / (one-side)** - ☐
(12"+=) *(XX 28T)* – Imperial bedroom.

Sep 82. (7") *(XX 30)* **FROM HEAD TO TOE. / THE WORLD OF BROKEN HEARTS** 43 ☐

—— (below from the film 'Party Party' and released on 'A&M')

Nov 82. (7") *(AMS 8267)* **PARTY PARTY. / IMPERIAL BEDROOM** 48 ☐

—— (below ELVIS as "The IMPOSTER" and issued on 'Imp-Demon')

May 83. (7") *(IMP 001)* **PILLS AND SOAP. / ('A'extended)** 16 ☐

Jul 83. (7") *(XX 32) <04045>* **EVERYDAY I WRITE THE BOOK. / HEATHEN TOWN** 28 36
(12"+=) *(XX 32T) <44-04115>* – Night time.

Jul 83. (lp/c) *(XX LP/C 19) <38897>* **PUNCH THE CLOCK** 3 24
– Let them all talk / Everyday I write the book / The greatest thing / The element within her / Love went mad / Shipbuilding / T.K.O. (boxing day) / Charm school / The invisible man / Mouth almighty / King of thieves / Pills and soap / The world and his wife. *(re-iss. Sep84 lp/c/cd; ZL/ZK/ZD 70026) (re-iss. Jan88 on 'Demon' lp/c/cd; FIEND/+CASS/CD 72) (re-iss. cd Feb95 on 'Demon' w/ extra tracks; DPAM 9)*

Sep 83. (7"/ext.12") *(XX 33/+T) <04266>* **LET THEM ALL TALK. / KEEP IT CONFIDENTIAL** 59 ☐

—— (below also as "The IMPOSTER" and issued on 'Imp')

Apr 84. (7") *(TRUCE 1)* **PEACE IN OUR TIME. / WITHERED AND DEAD** 48 ☐

Jun 84. (7") *(XX 35) <05625>* **I WANNA BE LOVED. / TURNING THE TOWN RED** 25 ☐
(12"+=) *(XX 35T)* – ('A'extended smoochy'n'runny mix).
(12"+=) *(XX 35Z)* – ('A'discotheque version).

Jun 84. (lp/c) *(ZL/ZK 70317) <39429>* **GOODBYE CRUEL WORLD** 10 35
– The only flame in town / Room with no number / Inch by inch / Worthless thing / Love field / I wanna be loved / The comedians / Joe Porterhouse / Sour milk cow blues / The great unknown / The deportees club / Peace in our time. *(cd-iss. Mar86; ZD 70317) (re-iss. Jan88 on 'Demon' lp/c/cd; FIEND/+CASS/CD 75) (re-iss. cd Feb95 on 'Demon' w/extra tracks; DPAM 10)*

Aug 84. (7"/'A'disco-12") *(XX 37/+T) <04502>* **THE ONLY FLAME IN TOWN. / THE COMEDIANS** 71 56 Jul84
('A'disco-12"+=) *(XX 37Z) <44-05081>* – Pump it up (1984 dance mix).

—— (In May'85, guested on JOHN HIATT single 'Living A Little')

—— (below as The COWARD BROTHERS (w/ T-BONE BURNETT) + issued on 'Imp')

Jul 85. (7") *(IMP 006)* **THE PEOPLE'S LIMOUSINE. / THEY'LL NEVER TAKE THEIR LOVE FROM ME** ☐ ☐

The COSTELLO SHOW

featuring The ATTRACTIONS and The CONFEDERATES
added **JAMES BURTON** – guitar / **MITCHELL FROOM** – keyboards / **JERRY SCHEFF** – bass / **JIM KELTNER** – drums / **RON TUTT** – drums (i.e.The CONFEDERATES)

F-Beat Columbia

Jan 86. (7") *(ZB 40555) <05809>* **DON'T LET ME BE MISUNDERSTOOD. / BABY'S GOT A BRAND NEW HAIRDO** 33 ☐
(12"+=) *(ZT 40556)* – Get yourself another fool.

Feb 86. (lp/c/cd) *(ZL/ZK/ZD 70946) <40173>* **KING OF AMERICA** 11 39
– Brilliant mistake / Loveable / Our little angel / Don't let me be misunderstood / Glitter gulch / Indoor fireworks / Little palaces / I'll wear it proudly / American without tears / Eisenhower blues / Poisoned rose / The big light / Jack of all parades / Suit of lights / Sleep of the just. *(re-iss. Jan88 on 'Demon' lp/c/cd; FIEND/+CASS/CD 78) (re-iss. Jul95 on 'Demon' cd/d-lp; DPAM/+LP 11) (cd w/ bonus cd of 'LIVE ON BROADWAY' EP)*

ELVIS COSTELLO & THE ATTRACTIONS

(ELVIS, BRUCE, STEVE & PETE) plus guest **NICK LOWE** – guitar

Imp-Demon Columbia

Aug 86. (7") *(IMP 007) <06326>* **TOKYO STORM WARNING. / (part 2)** 73 ☐
(12"+=) *(IMP 007T)* – Black sails in the sunset.

Sep 86. (lp/c/cd) *(FIEND/+CASS/CD 80) <40518>* **BLOOD AND CHOCOLATE** 16 84
– Uncomplicated / I hope you're happy now / Tokyo storm warning / Home is anywhere you hang your head / I want you / Honey are you straight or are you blind? / Blue chair / Battered old bird / Crimes of Paris / Poor Napoleon / Next time around. *(re-iss. cd Sep95 on 'Demon'; DPAM 12) (cd w/ bonus interview disc)*

Nov 86. (7") *(IMP 008)* **I WANT YOU. / (part 2)** ☐ ☐
(12"+=) *(IMP 008T)* – I hope you say you're happy.

Demon Columbia

Jan 87. (7") *(D 1047)* **BLUE CHAIR. / AMERICA WITHOUT TEARS NO.2 (Twilight version)** ☐ ☐
(12"+=) *(D 1047T)* – Shoes without heels.

May 87. (7"/12") *(D 1052/+T)* **A TOWN CALLED BIG NOTHING. / RETURN TO BIG NOTHING** ☐ -
(above as "McMANUS GANG" featuring SY RICHARDSON)

ELVIS COSTELLO

solo, with mostly **FROOM, KELTNER, PETE THOMAS** (2), **MICHAEL BLAIR** – percussion / **MARC RIBOT** – guitar / **JERRY MAROTTA** – drums / **PAUL McCARTNEY, ROGER McGUINN, CAIT O'RIORDAN, T-BONE BURNETT, CHRISSIE HYNDE** on 1 or 2, plus The DIRTY DOZEN BRASS BAND (GREGORY DAVIS, EFREM TOWNS, ROGER LEWIS, KEVIN HARRIS, KIRK JOSEPH, C. JOSEPH, plus loads more)

Warners Warners

Feb 89. (lp/c)(cd) *(WX 238/+C)(925848-2) <25848>* **SPIKE** 5 32
– . . . This town . . . / Let him dangle / Deep dark truthful mirror / Veronica / God's comic / Chewing gum / Tramp the dirt town / Stalin Malone / Satellite / Pads, paws and claws / Baby plays around / Miss Macbeth / Any king's shilling / Coal train robbers * / Last boat leaving. *(cd.+= *) (re-iss. cd Nov93;)* – (w/ extra tracks).

Feb 89. (7") *(W 7558) <22981>* **VERONICA. / YOU'RE NO GOOD** 31 19
(12"+=/12"poster+=/cd-s+=/pic-cd-s) *(W 7558 T/TW/CD/CDX)* – The room nobody lives in / Coal train robberies.

May 89. (7"ep/10"ep) *(W 2949/+TE)* **BABY PLAYS AROUND / POISONED ROSE. / ALMOST BLUE / MY FUNNY VALENTINE** 65 ☐
(c-ep/12"ep/cd-ep) *(W 2949 C/T/CD)* – (2nd track repl. by) Point of no return.

Apr 91. (7"/c-s) *(W 0025/+C)* **THE OTHER SIDE OF SUMMER. / COULDN'T CALL IT UNEXPECTED £4** 43 ☐
(12"+=/cd-s+=) *(W 0025 T/CD)* – The ugly things.

May 91. (lp/c/cd) *(WX 419/+C/CD) <26575>* **MIGHTY LIKE A ROSE** 5 55
– The other side of summer / How to be dumb / All grown up / Invasion hit parade / Harpers bizarre / Hurry down doomsday (the bugs are taking over) / After the fall / Georgie and her rival / So like Candy / Interlude: Couldn't call it unexpected £2 / Playboy to a man / Sweet pear / Broken / Couldn't call it unexpected £4. *(re-iss. cd Feb95; 7599 26675-2)*

Oct 91. (7"/c-s) **SO LIKE CANDY. / VERONICA (demo)** ☐ ☐
(12"+=/cd-s+=) – Couldn't call it unexpected (live) / Hurry down doomsday (the blues are taking over).

—— In 1992, he wrote material for WENDY JAMES (Transvision Vamp)

ELVIS COSTELLO / THE BRODSKY QUARTET

with **MICHAEL THOMAS + IAN BELTON** – violins / **PAUL CASSIDY** – viola / **JACQUELINE THOMAS** – violincello (all co-wrote music with him)

Jan 93. (cd/c) *(<9362 45180-2/-4>)* **THE JULIET LETTERS** [18] [ ]
– Deliver us / For other eyes / Swine / Expert rites / Dead letter / I almost had a weakness / Why? / Who do you think you are? / Taking my life in your hands / This offer is unrepeatable / Dear sweet filthy world / The letter home / Jacksons, Monk and Rowe / This sad burlesque / Romeo's seance / I thought I'd write to Juliet / Last post / The first to leave / Damnation's cellar / The birds will still be singing.

Feb 93. (c-s) *(W 0159)* **JACKSONS, MONK AND ROWE / THIS SAD BURLESQUE** [ ] [-]
(cd-s+=) *(W 0159CDX)* – (interviews).

Elvis COSTELLO

Mar 94. (7"/c-s) *(W 0234/+C)* **SULKY GIRL. / A DRUNKEN MAN'S PRAISE OF SOBRIETY** [22] [ ]
(cd-s+=) *(W 0234CD)* – Idiophone / ('A'album version).

Mar 94. (cd/c) *(<9362 45535-2/-4>)* **BRUTAL YOUTH** [2] [34]
– Pony St. / Kinder murder / 13 steps lead down / This is Hell / Clown strike / You tripped at every step / Still too soon to know / 20% amnesia / Sulky girl / London's brilliant parade / My science fiction twin / Rocking horse road / Just about glad / All the rage / Favourite hour.

Apr 94. (7"/c-s) *(W 0245/+C)* **13 STEPS LEAD DOWN. / DO YOU KNOW WHAT I'M SAYING?** [59] [ ]
(cd-s) *(W 0245CD)* – ('A'side) / Puppet girl / Basement kiss / We despise you.

Jul 94. (7"/c-s) *(W 0251/+C)* **YOU TRIPPED AT EVERY STEP. / YOU'VE GOT TO HIDE YOUR LOVE AWAY** [ ] [ ]
(cd-s+=) *(W 0251CD)* – Step inside love / Sticks & stones.

Nov 94. (c-s) *(W 0270C)* **LONDON'S BRILLIANT PARADE / LONDON'S BRILLIANT** [48] [ ]
(12"+=) *(W 0270T)* – My resistance is low / Congratulations.
(cd-s) *(W 270CD1)* – ('A'side) / Sweet dreams / The loved ones / From head to toe.
(cd-s) *(W 270CD2)* – ('A'side) / New Amsterdam / Beyond belief / Shipbuilding.

May 95. (cd/c) *(<9362 45903-2/-4>)* **KOJAK VARIETY** [21] [ ]
– Strange / Hidden charms / Remove this doubt / I threw it all way / Leave my kitten alone / Everybody's cryin' mercy / I've been wrong before / Bama lama bama loo / Must you throw dirt in my face / Pouring water on a drowning man / The very thought of you / Payday / Please stay / Running out of fools / Days.

ELVIS COSTELLO & THE ATTRACTIONS

Apr 96. (c-s) *(W 0348C)* **IT'S TIME / LIFE SHRINKS** [58] [ ]
(cd-s+=) *(W 0348CD)* – Brilliant disguise.

May 96. (cd/c) *(<9362 46198-2/-4>)* **ALL THIS USELESS BEAUTY** [28] [53]
– The other end of the telescope / Little atoms / All this useless beauty / Complicated shadows / Why can't a man stand alone / Distorted angel / Shallow grave / Poor fractured atlas.

Jul 96. (cd-s) *(W 0364CD)* **LITTLE ATOMS / WHY CAN'T A MAN STAND ALONE / ALMOST IDEAL EYES / JUST ABOUT GLAD** [ ] [ ]

Jul 96. (cd-s) *(W 0365CD)* **THE OTHER END OF THE TELESCOPE / ALMOST IDEAL EYES / BASEMENT KISS (live) / COMPLICATED SHADOWS (demo)** [ ] [ ]

Jul 96. (cd-s) *(W 0366CD)* **DISTORTED ANGEL / ALMOST IDEAL EYES / LITTLE ATOMS (DJ Food mix) / Lush: ALL THIS USELESS BEAUTY** [ ] [ ]

Jul 96. (cd-s) *(W 0367CD)* **ALL THIS USELESS BEAUTY / ALMOST IDEAL EYES / Sleeper: THE OTHER END OF THE TELESCOPE / DISTORTED ANGEL (Tricky mix)** [ ] [ ]

Mercury Mercury

Sep 98. (cd/c; ELVIS COSTELLO with BURT BACHARACH) *(<538002-2/-4>)* **PAINTED FROM MEMORY** [32] [78]
– In the darkest place / Toledo / I still have that other girl / This house is empty now / Tears at the birthday party / Such unlikely lovers / My thief / Long division / Painted from memory / Sweetest punch / What's her name today? / God give me strength.

– compilations, others, etc. –

Mar 80. (c) *F-Beat; (XXC 6)* **TEN BLOODY MARY'S & TEN HOW'S YOUR FATHERS** [ ] [-]
(re-iss. Apr84 on 'Imp' lp/c; FIEND/+CASS 27) (cd-iss. Jan86; FIENDCD 27) (re-iss. cd Mar93; FIENDCD 27X)

Oct 80. (lp) *Columbia; <JC 36839>* **TAKING LIBERTIES** [-] [28]

Apr 85. (lp/c/cd) *Telstar; (STAR/STAC/TCD 2247)* **THE BEST OF ELVIS COSTELLO – THE MAN** [8] [-]
– Watching the detectives / Oliver's army / Alison / Accidents will happen / Pump it up / High fidelity / Pills and soap (THE IMPOSTER) / (I don't want to go to) Chelsea / New lace sleeves / A good year for the roses / I can't stand up for falling down / Clubland / Beyond belief / New Amsterdam / Green shirt / Everyday I write the book / I wanna be loved / Shipbuilding (THE IMPOSTER). *(re-iss. May86 on 'Imp' lp/c/cd; FIEND/+CASS/CD 52) (re-iss. cd Mar93 on 'Demon'; FIENDCD 52X)*

Apr 85. (7",7"green) *F-Beat; (ZB 40086)* **GREEN SHIRT. / BEYOND BELIEF** [68] [-]
(12"+=,12"green+=) *(ZT 40086)* – ('A'extended).
(d7"+=) *(ZB 40085-7)* – Oliver's army / A good year for the roses.
(Nov85; d7"+=) *(same)* – The people's limousine / They'll never take her love away from me.

Nov 85. (12"ep) *Stiff; (BUYIT 239)* **WATCHING THE DETECTIVES / RADIO SWEETHEART. / LESS THAN ZERO / ALISON** [ ] [-]

Oct 87. (lp/c/cd; VARIOUS ARTISTS) *Demon; (FIEND/+CASS/CD 67)* **OUT OF OUR IDIOT** [ ] [-]
(re-iss. cd Mar93; FIENDCD 67X)

Oct 89. (d-lp/c/cd/dat) *Demon; (D-)FIEND CASS/CD/DAT 160)* **GIRLS, GIRLS, GIRLS** [67] [-]

Nov 89. (c) *Demon; (FIENDCASS 161)* **GIRLS, GIRLS, GIRLS VOL. 2** [ ] [-]

Nov 93. (4xcd-box) *Demon; (DPAM BOX1)* **THE FIRST 2 1/2 YEARS** [ ] [-]

Nov 94. (cd/c/lp) *Demon; (DMAM CD/MC/LP 13) / Rykodisc;* **THE VERY BEST OF ELVIS COSTELLO** [57] [ ]

— The first 4 singles were also re-issued together around 1980 and could be found on 'Stiff' 10-pack Nos.11-20).

— The ATTRACTIONS released two singles and an album (Aug80) 'MAD ABOUT THE WRONG BOY' on 'F-Beat'.

ELVIS COSTELLO & RICHARD HARVEY

Demon not iss.

Jul 91. (cd/lp) *(DSCD/DSLP 4)* **G.B.H. (TV Soundtrack)** [ ] [-]

ELVIS COSTELLO & BILL FRISELL

Warners Nonesuch

Aug 95. (cd) *(<9362 46073-2>)* **DEEP DEAD BLUE** [ ] [ ] Nov95
– Weird nightmare / Love field / Shamed into love / Gigi / Poor Napoleon / Baby plays around / Deep dead blue.

Cathal COUGHLAN

Born: Cork, Ireland. Together with SEAN O'HAGAN, COUGHLAN made his first real steps into the music industry with alternative/indie outfit, MICRODISNEY. After trying out various stylistic combinations, the songwriting partners decided upon the tried and tested drums, bass, guitar, keyboards format and enlisted MICK LYNCH and ROB MacKAHEY to help them record a debut single, 'HELICOPTER OF THE HOLY GHOST'. Issued on indie label, 'Kabuki', and included – along with follow-up, 'FICTION LAND' and other early recordings – on the unambiguously titled '82-84: WE HATE YOU SOUTH AFRICAN BASTARDS' (1984), the track introduced MICRODISNEY's patented brand of laid-back but thought provoking sophisti-rock. Subsequently relocating to London, COUGHLAN and O'HAGAN recruited a new rhythm section in ED FLESH and TOM FENNER, securing a deal with 'Rough Trade'. The resulting 'EVERYBODY IS FANTASTIC' (1984) album revealed a more readily audible COUGHLAN and a talent for melodic subversiveness not too far removed from The SMITHS. An increasingly scathing lyrical commentator, COUGHLAN put in another sterling performance on the more accessible follow-up set, 'THE CLOCK COMES DOWN THE STAIRS' (1985), growing interest in MICRODISNEY's offbeat style leading to a deal courtesy of 'Virgin'. With STEVE PREGNANT replacing FLESH and JAMES COMPTON added on keyboards, their tenure in major label land got off to a promising start in early '87 as the 'TOWN TO TOWN' single almost threatened the Top 40. Sales wise, the accompanying album, 'CROOKED MILE' (1987) didn't live up to expectations despite continuing critical praise, COUGHLAN upping the lyrical ante with the band's final effort, '39 MINUTES'. Featuring 'SINGER'S HAMPSTEAD HOME', his infamous take on the fading fortunes of labelmate, BOY GEORGE, the album nevertheless proved to be MICRODISNEY's parting shot as COUGHLAN and O'HAGAN went their separate ways. While the former went on to air his lyrical bile in uncompromising fashion with FATIMA MANSIONS, the latter indulged his penchant for classic US West Coast pop with The HIGH LLAMAS. With a line-up comprising COUGHLAN, ANDREAS 'GRIMMO' O'GRUNIA, HUGH BUNKER, NICHOLAS ALLUM and ZAK WOOLHOUSE, FATIMA MANSIONS named themselves after a deprived Dublin housing scheme and proceeded to function as a sounding board for COUGHLAN's increasingly unrestrained muse. Debut album, 'AGAINST NATURE' (1989) revealed an equally unrestrained musical backing as COUGHLAN – with the help of O'GRUNIA's scathing guitar outbursts – marked his departure from the conventional rock/pop approach of MICRODISNEY. The singer's most savage political diatribe to date came in the shape of follow-up single, 'BLUES FOR CEAUSESCU', while 'VIVA DEAD PONIES' (1990) had critics falling over themselves to praise its breadth of musical vision, funereal humour and razor-sharp commentaries. Recorded on the back of a series of lone acoustic gigs, 'BERTIE'S BROCHURES' (1991) was a pared-down mini-set featuring covers of Richard Thompson's 'GREAT VALERIO', Scott Walker's 'LONG ABOUT NOW' and a gleeful brutalisation of R.E.M's 'SHINY HAPPY PEOPLE', the title track skirting around one of COUGHLAN's favourite topics, the relationship between Britain and Ireland. 1992, meanwhile, proved a vintage year as FATIMA MANSIONS witnessed their first chart action with the 'VALHALLA AVENUE' album (Top 60) and COUGHLAN used a U2 support slot in Milan to demonstrate exactly what he thought of the Pope. They also found themselves in the Top 10 singles chart, by default rather than design as another lesson in pop deconstruction – Bryan Adams' nauseating 'EVERYTHING I DO' knocked into shape this time around – found its way onto the B-side of 'Suicide Is Painless', MANIC STREET PREACHERS style. While 1993 saw the release of a compilation set, 'COME BACK MY CHILDREN', COUGHLAN busied himself with his side project, BUBONIQUE, working with comedian SEAN HUGHES (now a regular feature of BBC2's 'Never Mind The Buzzcocks') on the brilliantly titled '20 GOLDEN SHOWERS' (1993). His prolific output continued with a 1994 FATIMA MANSIONS album, 'LOST IN THE FORMER WEST' and a 1995 BUBONIQUE follow-up, 'TRANCE ARSE VOLUME 3'. Giving the 'MANSIONS a break in the mid-90's, the irrepressible Irishman turned his attention towards a solo career proper with the almost RADIOHEAD-like 'UNBROKEN ONES' single and 'THE GRAND NECROPOLITAN' album. One of the most undervalued songwriters in rock, COUGHLAN seems destined for eternal cultdom. • **FATIMA MANSIONS covered:** STIGMATA (Ministry) / LONG ABOUT NOW + NITE FLIGHTS (Scott Walker) / THE GREAT VALERIO (Richard Thompson) / PAPER THIN HOTEL (Leonard

Cohen) / SHINY HAPPY PEOPLE (R.E.M.) / EVERYTHING I DO (Bryan Adams).

Album rating: Microdisney: EVERYBODY IS FANTASTIC (*5) / 82-84: WE HATE YOU SOUTH AFRICAN BASTARDS mini-compilation (*6) / THE CLOCK COMES DOWN THE STAIRS (*6) / CROOKED MILE (*5) / 39 MINUTES (*5) / BIG SLEEPING HOUSE ... FINEST MOMENTS compilation (*7) / Fatima Mansions: AGAINST NATURE (*6) / VIVA DEAD PONIES (*7) / BERTIE'S BROCHURE mini (*7) / VALHALLA AVENUE (*8) / COME BACK MY CHILDREN compilation (*7) / LOST IN THE FORMER WEST (*6) / Cathal Coughlan: THE GRAND NECROPOLITAN (*6)

MICRODISNEY

CATHAL COUGHLAN – vocals, keyboards / **SEAN O'HAGAN** – guitar, vocals, harmonica / **MICK LYNCH** – bass, vocals / **ROB MacKAHEY** – drums

Kabuki not iss.

Sep 82. (7") *(KAMD 2)* **HELICOPTER OF THE HOLY GHOST. / HELLO RASCALS** ☐ -

May 83. (7") *(KAMD 4)* **FICTION LAND. / PINK SKINNED MAN** ☐ -

— **ED FLESH** – bass; repl. LYNCH who formed STUMP

— **TOM FENNER** – drums, percussion; repl. MacKAHEY who formed STUMP

Rough Trade not iss.

May 84. (lp) *(ROUGH 75)* **EVERBODY IS FANTASTIC** ☐ -
– Idea / A few kisses / Escalator in the rain / Dolly / Dreaming drains / I'll be a gentleman / Moon / Sun / Sleepless / Come on over and cry / This liberal love / Before famine / Everybody is dead. *(cd-iss. May96 on 'Creation Rev-Ola'; CREV 40CD)*

Jun 84. (7") *(RT 135)* **DOLLY. / THIS LIBERAL LOVE** ☐ -
(12"+=) *(RTT 135)* – Everbody Is Dead / Dear Rosemary.

Mar 85. (12"ep) *(RTT 175)* **MICRODISNEY IN THE WORLD** ☐ -
– In the world / Loftholdingswood / Teddy dogs / 464.

Sep 85. (7") *(RT 185)* **BIRTHDAY GIRL. / HARMONY TUNES** ☐ -
(12"+=) *(RTT 185)* – Money for the trams.

Oct 85. (lp) *(ROUGH 85)* **THE CLOCK COMES DOWN THE STAIRS** ☐ -
– Horse overboard / Birthday girl / Past / Humane / Are you happy? / Genius / Begging bowl / A friend with a big mouth / Goodbye it's 1987 / And. *(cd-iss. May96 on 'Creation Rev-Ola'; CREV 41CD)*

— **STEVE PREGNANT** – bass; repl. ED

— also added **JAMES COMPTON** – keyboards (to **COUGHLAN, O'HAGAN, FENNER**)

Virgin not iss.

Jan 87. (7") *(VS 927)* **TOWN TO TOWN. / LITTLE TOWN IN IRELAND** 55 -
(12"+=) *(VS 927-12)* – Genius / Bullwhip road.
(d7") *(VSD 927)* **'PEEL SESSIONS' EP:** – Begging bowl / Loftholdingswood / Horse overboard.

Jan 87. (cd/c/lp) *(CD/TC+/V 2415)* **CROOKED MILE** ☐ -
– Town to town / Angels / Our children / Mrs. Simpson / Hey hey Sam / Give me all your clothes / Armadillo man / Bullwhip road / And he descended into Hell / Rack / Big sleeping house / People just want to dream.

— **CRAZY JOHNNY NANCY** – bass; repl. STEVE

Oct 87. (7") *(VS 1014)* **SINGER'S HAMPSTEAD HOME. / SHE ONLY GAVE INTO ANGER** ☐ -
(12"+=) *(VST 1014)* – Brother Olaf.

Feb 88. (7") *(VS 1044)* **GALE FORCE WIND. / I CAN'T SAY NO (Betty Lou version)** ☐ -
(c-s+=) *(VSTC 1044)* – Irish nationl anthem / Say "no I can't".
(12+=) *(VST 1044)* – No, I can't say (thank you for speaking to me Mustapha) / Can't I say no (Hackney aid).
(cd-s+=) *(VSCD 1044)* – ('A'-version) / Town to town.

Mar 88. (cd/c/lp) *(CD/TC+/V 2505)* **39 MINUTES** ☐ -
– Singer's Hampstead home / High and dry / Send Herman home / Ambulance for one / Soul boy / Back to the old town / United colours / Gale force wind / Herr direktor / Bluerings.

— (split around Spring '88). SEAN O'HAGAN formed the TWILIGHT before going solo in 1989 (later he forrmed the HIGH LLAMAS).

– compilations, etc. –

Oct 84. (m-lp) *Rough Trade; (RTM 155)* **82-84: WE HATE YOU SOUTH AFRICAN BASTARDS!** ☐ -
– Helicopter of the holy ghost / Michael Murphy / Love your enemies / Fiction land / Pink skinned man / Patrick Moore says you can't sleep here / Hello rascals / Pretoria quickstep.

Dec 89. (lp/c/cd) *Strange Fruit; (SFR LP/MC/CD 105)* **DOUBLE PEEL SESSIONS** ☐ -
(re-iss. Nov94; same)

Mar 95. (cd) *Virgin; (CDOVD 452)* **BIG SLEEPING HOUSE . . . FINEST MOMENTS (A COLLECTION OF CHOICE CUTS)** ☐ -
– Horse overboard / Loftholdingswood / Singer's Hampstead home / She only gave into her anger / Gale force wind / I can't say no (Betty Lou version) / Angels / Mrs. Simpson / Armadillo man / And he descended into Hell / Rack / Big sleeping house / Back to the old town / Send Herman home / Town to town / Begging bowl.

May 96. (cd) *Creation Rev-Ola; (CREV 42CD)* **LOVE YOUR ENEMIES** ☐ -

FATIMA MANSIONS

CATHAL COUGHLAN – vocals, keyboards, composer with **ANDREAS 'GRIMMO' O'GRUNIA** – guitar / **ZAK** – keyboards / **HUGH BUNKER** – bass / **NICHOLAS TIOMPAN ALLUM** – drums, wind

Kitchenware not iss.

Nov 89. (lp/cd) *(KW LP/CD 11)* **AGAINST NATURE** ☐ -
– Only losers take the bus / The day I lost everything / Wilderness on time / You won't get me here / 13th century boy / Bishop of Babel / Valley of the dead ass / Big madness – Monday club Carol.

Feb 90. (12"m) *(SKX 43)* **ONLY LOSERS TAKE THE BUS. / ('A'version) / WHAT?** ☐ -

Jun 90. (7") *(SK 45)* **BLUES FOR CEAUSESCU. / 13th CENTURY BOY** ☐ -
(12"+=/cd-s+=) *(SK X/CD 45)* – Suicide bridge.

Sep 90. (lp/c/cd) **VIVA DEAD PONIES** ☐ -
– Angel's delight / Concrete block / Mr. Bailey / The door-to-door inspector / Start the week / You're a rose / Legoland 3 / Thursday / Ceausescu flashback / Broken radio No.1 / Look what I stole for us darling / Farewell Ontario / The white knuckle express / Chemical cosh / Tima Mansio speaks / A pack of lies / Viva dead ponies / More smack vicar. *(re-iss. Mar91 on 'Radioactive' lp/c/cd; RAR/+C/D 10242) (re-iss. Sep94 cd/c; KWL CD/MC 19262)*

Feb 91. (12"ep) *(SK 50)* **HIVE / STIGMATA. / CHEMICAL COSH / THE HOLY MUGGER** ☐ -

Apr 91. (7"/c-s) *(SK/+C 53)* **YOU'RE A ROSE. / BLUES FOR CEAUSESCU** ☐ -
(cd-s+=) *(SKXD 53)* – Against nature.
(12"+=) *(SKX 53)* – Only losers take the bus.

Oct 91. (m-cd/m-lp) *(KW CD/LP 16)* **BERTIE'S BROCHURES** (acoustic) ☐ -
– Behind the man / Bertie's brochures / Long about now / The great Valerio / Shiny happy people / VN (apology) / Mario Vargas Yoni / Smiling. *(re-iss. Sep94 cd/c; KWL CD/MC 19257)*

— **DUKE O MALAITHE** – keyboards; repl. ZAK

Kitchenware not iss.

Apr 92. (12"m) *(SKX 56)* **EVIL MAN. / THE SCARECROW / EVIL MAN II** 59 -
(12"m) *(SKXD 56)* – EVIL MAN I & II / Blues for Ceausescu (mix) / Chemical cosh.
(d-cd-s) *(SKXXD 56)* – EVIL MAN I & II / Only losers take the bus (dump the dead) / Hive.

May 92. (cd/c/lp) *(KW CD/MC/LP 18)* **VALHALLA AVENUE** 52 -
– Evil man / Something bad / Valhalla avenue / 1000% / North Atlantic wind / Purple window / Go home bible Mike / Perfumes of Paradise / Greyhair / C7 – breakfast with Bandog / Ray of hope, hope of rape / Be dead. *(re-iss. Sep94 cd/c; KWL CD/MC 19258)*

Jul 92. (12"m) *(SK 59)* **1,000 %. / HIVE (live) / 1,000,000%** 61 -
(cd-s) *(SKXD 59)* – Paper thin hotel *[repl. 'Hive']*
(cd-s) *(SKXXD 59)* – Angel's delight *[repl. '1,000,000']*
(cd-s) *(SKZD 59)* – ('A'side) / Behind the Moon (live) / Evil man (live) / White knuckles express (live).

— Sep'92, covered a version of Bryan Adams' 'EVERYTHING I DO' on B-side of MANIC STREET PREACHERS UK Top 10 hit version of 'Suicide Is Painless'

Feb 93. (cd/c) *(CGCC/+D 001)* **COME BACK MY CHILDREN** (compilation) ☐ -
– Only losers take the bus / The day I lost everything / Wilderness on time / You won't get me home / 13th century you / Bishop of Babel / Valley of the dead cars / Big madness / What? / Blues for Ceausescu / On Suicide Bridge / Hive / The holy mugger / Stigmata / Lady Godiva's operation.

Jul 94. (7"/c-s) *(SK/+MC 67)* **THE LOYALISER. / GARY NUMAN'S PORSCHE / ARNIE'S FIVE** 58 -
(12"+=/cd-s+=) *(SK X/CD 67)* – Into thinner air with the loyaliser.

Sep 94. (cd/c/colrd-lp) *(KW CD/MC/LP 25)* **LOST IN THE FORMER WEST** ☐ -
– Belong nowhere / The loyaliser / Popemobile to Paraguay / Walk yr. way / Brunceling's song / Lost in the former west / Nite flights / Your world customer / Sunken cities / Brain blister / A walk in the woods / Humiliate me.

Oct 94. (c-s) *(SKMC 68)* **NITE FLIGHTS / IGNORANCE IS PISS** ☐ -
(10"/cd-s) *(SK T/CD 68)* – ('A'side) / As I washed the blood off / Diamonds, fur coat, champagne / It's so cold . . . I think.

BUBONIQUE

CATHAL's alter-ego featuring Irish comedian **SEAN HUGHES**

Kitchenware not iss.

Mar 92. (12") *(SKX 52)* **SCREW. / MONOGAMY I'M GOING TO KICK YOUR HEAD IN** ☐ -

Nov 92. (12") *(SKX 54)* **SUMMER THE FIRST TIME. / FREE CHARLES MANSON** ☐ -

Apr 93. (cd) *(KWCD 24)* **20 GOLDEN SHOWERS** ☐ -
– Summer the first time / Think you're cool / Play that funky music / Cop lover / Cod-sucker blues / My baby gave me rabies / Release the bats / Elvis '93 / Chicken arse (theme) / Iron child / Yoda lady / Anytime anyplace it's ok / 2 J.G. / Stock Hausen and Waterman / East sheep station / Love me deadly kiss me Headley / DLT 666 no idea / The bubonique America Top 10 / Frank is Frank / Jellypop porky Jean / Dildo neighbour / Love camp 7 / Nation of Bubonique / Closedown.

Sep 95. (cd) *(KWCD 28)* **TRANCE ARSE VOLUME 3** ☐ -
– You can't fool the dead / Cod is love / The pianna / Truck Turner / The sermon / Freestyle masterclass 1; Sawing / Talkin' about talkin' about / Freebird / I've always liked hunting / Oi copper / Return of the nice age / What's e saying / Hey, handsome / Industrial woman / Rainbow buffalo cornwoman / Freestyle masterclass; Drilling / Q magazine / Kind of pue / 'George' aid suite / Abbabortion / Swan of Newcastle.

CATHAL COUGHLAN

— **CATHAL COUGHLAN** – vocals, keyboards

Kitchenware not iss.

May 96. (7") *(SK 69)* **UNBROKEN ONES. / ON THE PARISH** ☐ -

Jul 96. (cd) *(KWCD 29)* **THE GRAND NECROPOLITAN** ☐ -
– This building / Unbroken ones / On the parish / New "Royal" / Eerin go braghag / We are the sinister world / Government Big lukewarm / Straying away / Irrational falsifier / Two grotesques, embracing / Angry white snail / Free and worthless / Garrai na muic / Last lamplight / The grand necropolitan promenade / Waiting for wood, captain.

COUNT BISHOPS

Formed: London, England . . . mid 70's by MIKE SPENCER, JOHNNY GUITAR, ZENON DE FLEUR HEROWSKI, STEVE LEWINS and PAUL BALBI. One of the bigger attractions on the pub-rock scene just as punk was waiting in the wings, the COUNT BISHOPS specialised in a similar vein of revved-up R&B to the likes of DR. FEELGOOD and the 101'ERS. Signed to the influential rock'n'roll revival label, 'Chiswick', the band made their vinyl debut in late '75 with the 'SPEEDBALL' EP and although this featured SPENCER's vocals, the singer was quickly deposed by the sandpaper-throated DAVE TICE. Despite their promising start, 1976 was a quiet year on the recording front with a sole single release, 'TRAIN TRAIN', The COUNT BISHOPS' eponymous debut album finally unveiled in 1977. While paling next to the white-hot nihilism of that summer's punk crop, the record was an invigorating listen nonetheless, footstomping its way through a set of trad 60's influenced R&B that included covers of The Kinks' 'I NEED YOU', The Standells' 'GOOD GUYS DON'T WEAR WHITE' and Chuck Berry's 'DOWN THE ROAD APIECE'. Following the release of a Dutch-only live set, 'GOOD GEAR' (1977), the band re-emerged the following year as The BISHOPS, new bassist PAT McMULLEN having replaced LEWINS. A single, 'I TAKE WHAT I WANT', was withdrawn although a live set recorded at London's Roundhouse surfaced in April. Later that summer, a further single, 'MR. JONES' was withdrawn, replaced on the 'Chiswick' release schedule by 'I WANT CANDY'. These minor niggles were put in perspective the following year as ZENON suffered a fatal heart attack after a car crash, effectively bringing a premature end to the band's career; the poorly received 'CROSS CUT' (1979) proved a less than thrilling swansong, JOHNNY GUITAR going on to better things in DR. FEELGOOD. • **Covered:** SOMEBODY'S GONNA GET THEIR HEAD KICKED IN TONIGHT (Fleetwood Mac).

Album rating: THE COUNT BISHOPS (*7) / THE BISHOPS LIVE AT THE ROUNDHOUSE (*5) / THE BEST OF THE COUNT BISHOPS compilation (*7)

MIKE SPENCER (b. Brooklyn, New York, USA) – vocals / **JOHNNY GUITAR** – guitar / **ZENON DE FLEUR HEROWSKI** – guitar, vocals / **STEVE LEWINS** – bass / **PAUL BALBI** – drums

Chiswick — not iss.

Nov 75. (7"ep) *(SW 1)* **SPEEDBALL**
– Route 66 / I ain't got you / Beautiful Delilah / Teenage letter.

— **DAVID TICE** – vocals, harmonica; repl. SPENCER

Aug 76. (7") *(NS 5)* **TRAIN TRAIN. / TAKING IT EASY**

Apr 77. (7") *(NS 12)* **BABY YOU'RE WRONG. / STAY FREE**

Apr 77. (lp) *(WIK 1)* **THE COUNT BISHIPS**
– I need you / Stay free / Down in the bottom / Talk to you / Shake your money maker / Down the road apiece / Baby you're wrong / Don't start crying now / Someone's got my number / Sometimes, good guys don't wear white / You're in the way / Taste and try. *(re-iss. 1979; CWK 3006)*

Dynamo — not iss.

1977. (lp) *(DYR33 001)* **GOOD GEAR** — Dutch
– Don't start cryin' now / Shake / Walkin' the dog / Somebody / Candy / Wang dang doodle / Dear dad / Confessin' the blues / Little by little / Carol / Johnny B. Goode / Dust my blues / Shake your money maker. *(French-rel.May84 on 'Lolita'; LOLITA 5014)*

BISHOPS

— **PAT McMULLEN** – bass; repl. LEWINS

Chiswick — not iss.

Mar 78. (7"; w-drawn) *(NS 33)* **I TAKE WHAT I WANT. / NO LIES**

Apr 78. (10"m-lp) *(CH 7)* **THE BISHOPS LIVE AT THE ROUNDHOUSE (live)**
– Too much too soon / Till the end of the day / Taking it easy / Somebody's gonna get their head kicked in tonight / Sometimes, good guys don't wear white / Don't start me talking / Baby you're wrong / I don't like it / I want Candy. *(re-iss. 1979; CWM 2001)*

Jun 78. (7"; w-drawn) *(NS 35)* **MR. JONES / HUMAN BEAN. / ROUTE 66 / TOO MUCH TOO SOON**
(re-iss. Mar79; CHIS 111)

Jun 78. (7") *(NS 37)* **I WANT CANDY. / SEE THAT WOMAN**
(re-iss. 1979, 6"/10"; NS 37-6/-10) (re-iss. 1979 as 6"; CHIS 101-6)

— after a car crash, DE FLEUR died of heart attack on 17th March 1979

Jun 79. (lp) *(CWK 3009)* **CROSS CUT**
– I take what I want / Could you would you / What's your number / Your daddy don't mind / Good times / Too much too soon / Rolling man / I want Candy / Somebody's gonna get their head kicked in tonight / Hands on the wheel / Don't start me talkin' / These arms of mine / No lies / Mr. Jones.

— **CHARLIE MORGAN** – drums; repl. BALBI, although they split due to DE FLEUR's death. JOHNNY GUITAR subsequently joined DR. FEELGOOD

- compilations, etc. -

Aug 95. (cd; as The BISHOPS) *Chiswick; (CDWIKD 150)* **THE BEST OF THE BISHOPS**
– Train train / Baby you're wrong / Stay free / I want Candy / I take what I want / Mr. Jones / I need you / Down in the bottom / You're in my way / Talk to you / Taste and try / Someone's got my number / Good times / Your daddy won't mind / What's your number / Till the end of the day / These arms of mine / Rolling man / Paul's blues / No lies / Too much, too soon / Sometimes good guys don't wear white / Don't start me talkin' / Somebody's gonna get their head kicked in tonight / I don't like it / Route 66 / Train train.

Nov 95. (cd) *Chiswick; (CDWIKM 161)* **SPEEDBALL + 11**

Wayne/Jayne COUNTY

Born: WAYNE COUNTY, c.1950, Georgia, Atlanta, USA. WAYNE left for New York in 1968 where he appeared in a female role alongside PATTI SMITH in an off-Broadway production of 'Femme Fatale' before tackling the role of Florence Nightingale in 'World'. In 1970, the actor/singer encountered ANDY WARHOL, who cast him in his stage show, 'Pork'; the review subsequently arrived in England, impressing DAVID BOWIE and inspiring him to sign COUNTY to his 'Mainman' publishing company. By this point he was already a fully fledged transvestite and began singing in New York band, QUEEN ELIZABETH; their drummer, JERRY NOLAN, was soon to join other cross-dressers, The NEW YORK DOLLS. In 1973, WAYNE found new sidemen, The BACKSTREET BOYS, although BOWIE's manager, Tony DeFries dropped him from Mainman's bulging roster (ooer!). A further setback came a few years later when 'E.S.P.' (former stable of The FUGS) delayed issue of his new group's proposed album, citing it as unsuitable for release, probably due to the fact that it included future singles, 'FUCK OFF' and 'STUCK ON YOU'; it was said the master tapes were lost in an accidental fire. In 1976, the group appeared at Max's Kansas City where three tracks (including one named after the venue itself) were cut for a V/A compilation, John Peel subsequently airing the songs on his night time Radio One show. With punk rock and new wave now dominating the music scene, COUNTY was becoming more accepted and after an infamous gig at another great club, CBGB's (in 1977), Miles Copeland of 'Illegal' records (who had already snapped up brother, STEWART COPELAND and his band The POLICE), signed up the gender-bending punk and his backing band, The ELECTRIC CHAIRS. Based in the less conservative land of Britain, they released their eponymous debut EP which included the tracks 'STUCK ON YOU', 'PARANOIA PARADISE' and The Rolling Stones' 'THE LAST TIME'. Later that year, WAYNE and Co flitted to 'Safari' records (run by DEEP PURPLE's management team), although their controversial second 45, 'FUCK OFF', saw the label issuing it under the pseudonymous guise of the 'Sweet F.A.' imprint. Around the same time, The ELECTRIC CHAIRS re-hashed 'PARANOIA PARADISE' on the punk movie, 'Jubilee', WAYNE kitted out in his trademark blonde wig, pink mini and fish-net stockings. If they were ever to have had a chance to have a hit single, it was surely with 'EDDIE & SHEENA', although its commercial sheen alienated many harder core punks. Hot on the record's heels was the group's eponymous debut album, full of second and occasionally first division sleazy punk rock. WAYNE COUNTY was subsequently given priority billing on their second set that year, 'STORM THE GATES OF HEAVEN' (featuring The Electric Prunes' 'I HAD TOO MUCH TO DREAM LAST NIGHT'), yet The ELECTRIC CHAIRS found it hard to make the big time. Released on either side of the decade, albums 'THINGS YOUR MOTHER NEVER TOLD YOU' (1979) and the live 'ROCK'N'ROLL RESURRECTION' (1980) represented The 'CHAIRS' final sitting as the band had already split. WAYNE was now taking hormone treatment to become his alter-ego, JAYNE, full-time although she never went through with the final operation. After spells in Berlin, JAYNE relocated to London where she released a comeback album, 'PRIVATE OYSTER' (1986); US title 'AMERIKAN CLEOPATRA'. She continues to release the "odd" single and album, although her solo career has been sporadic. WAYNE/JAYNE was the shock formula transvestite turned transexual whose no-holds barred NEW YORK DOLLS meets DUSTY SPRINGFIELD punk'n'roll never survived the "so-called" death of punk rock when the 'PISTOLS split. Her autobiography, 'Man Enough To Be A Woman: The Trials And Tribulations Of An Underground Cult Figure, Wayne County', was published in 1995 and obviously paints a fuller portrait of a bizarre life.

Album rating: THE ELECTRIC CHAIRS (*6) / STORM THE GATES OF HEAVEN (*6) / THINGS YOUR MOTHER NEVER TOLD YOU (*4) / ROCK'N'ROLL RESURRECTION (*5) / THE BEST OF THE ELECTRIC CHAIRS compilation (*7) / ROCK'N'ROLL CLEOPATRA compilation (*7) / PRIVATE OYSTER (*4) / GODDESS OF WET DREAMS (*4) / DEVIATION (*4) /

WAYNE COUNTY & THE BACKSTREET BOYS

WAYNE – vocals with **GREG VAN COOK** – guitar / + 3

not iss. — Max's Kan.

1976. (7"m) *<MAX 1213>* **MAX'S KANSAS CITY 1976. / FLIP YOUR WIG / CREAM IN MY JEANS**

— all above tracks also on US various artists lp 'MAX'S KANSAS CITY', released 1976 on 'Ram'; *1213) (re-iss. Mar78 as 'NEW YORK NEW WAVE, MAX'S KANSAS CITY' on 'C.B.S.'; CBS 82670)*

ELECTRIC CHAIRS

WAYNE + GREG added **VAL HALLER** – bass / **J.J. JOHNSON** – drums

Illegal — not iss.

Jul 77. (7"ep) *(IL 002)* **THE ELECTRIC CHAIRS EP**
– Stuck on you / Paranoia Paradise / The last time.

Sweet F.A. — not iss.

Nov 77. (7") *(WC 1)* **FUCK OFF. / ON THE CREST**

— guest on below **JOOLS HOLLAND** – piano (of SQUEEZE)

Safari — not iss.

Feb 78. (7") *(SAFE 1)* **EDDIE & SHEENA. / ROCK'N'ROLL CLEOPATRA**

Feb 78. (lp) *(LONG 1)* **THE ELECTRIC CHAIRS**
– Eddie & Sheena / Bad in bed / Hot blood / Worry wart / Twenty eight Model 'T' / Out of control / On the crest / Nazca / Big black window / Max's / Toilet love / Rock & roll resurrection.

May 78. (7";w-drawn) *(SAFE 6)* **I HAD TOO MUCH TO DREAM LAST NIGHT. / FUCK OFF**

WAYNE COUNTY AND THE ELECTRIC CHAIRS

— added **HENRY PADOVANI** – guitar (ex-POLICE)

Jun 78. (7"gold+grey-ep) *(WC 2)* **BLATANTLY OFFENZIVE EP** [ ] [-]
– Fuck off / Night time / Toilet love / Mean muthafuckin' man.

— **ELIOT MICHAELS** – guitar repl. COOK who joined The VIBRATORS

Aug 78. (7") *(SAFE 9)* **TRYING TO GET ON THE RADIO. / EVIL MINDED MOMMA** [ ] [-]

Aug 78. (lp-grey+multi) *(GOOD 1)* **STORM THE GATES OF HEAVEN** [ ] [-]
– Storm the gates of Heaven / Cry of angels / Speed demon / Mr. Normal / Man enough to be a woman / Trying to get on the radio / I had too much to dream last night / Tomorrow is another day.

— above album featured MORGAN FISHER keyboards and DARRYL WAY violin

May 79. (lp) *(GOOD 2)* **THINGS YOUR MOTHER NEVER TOLD YOU** [ ] [-]
– Wonder woman / Wall city girl / Boy with the stolen face / Un-con-troll-able / Things / Berlin / C3 / Midnight pal / Waiting for the marines / Think straight.

— producer & synth-man on above; DAVID CUNNINGHAM (FLYING LIZARDS)

Jun 79. (7") *(SAFE 13)* **BERLIN. / WAITING FOR THE MARINES** [ ] [-]
(ext.12"pink+=) *(SAFELS 13)* – Midnight pal.

Nov 79. (7") *(SAFE 18)* **SO MANY WAYS. / J'ATTENDS LES MARINES** [ ] [-]

— **WAYNE + ELIOT** went back to the States and found new members; **PETER JORDAN** – bass / **SAMMY MINELLI** – drums (they replaced HALLER and JOHNSON who joined FLYING LIZARDS after above ELECTRIC CHAIRS credited recording without WAYNE!)

May 80. (lp; as JAYNE COUNTY) *(LIVE 1)* **ROCK'N'ROLL RESURRECTION (live final gig)** [ ] [-]
– Night time / Rock'n'roll Cleopatra / Are you a boy / Bad in bed / Hanky panky / Rock'n'roll resurrection / Fucked by the Devil / Cream in my jeans / Stuck on you / Fuck off.

— had already disbanded his/her group at the end of '79. He/she went to Berlin, before relocating to London, England and going solo

JAYNE COUNTY

w/ 1985 band JC5; **MICK ROBINSON** – guitar / STUART 'Dick' CLARKE – lead guitar / **SNIDE** – bass / **BASIL CREECE** – drums

Heighway R — not iss.

May 86. (7") *(SAD 002)* **SAN FRANCISCO. / WHEN QUEENS COLLIDE (part 1)** [ ] [-]

Revolver — not iss.

Oct 86. (lp) *(REVLP 86)* **PRIVATE OYSTER** [ ] [-]
– Private oyster / Man enough to be a woman / Fun in America / I feel in love with a Russian soldier / Bad in bed / Are you a boy or are you a girl? / When queens collide (part 1) / Double shot / Xerox that man / That Lady Dye twist / Love lives on lies. *(re-iss. Feb87 as 'AMERIKAN CLEOPATRA' for 'Konnexion'; KOMA 788016)*

Jungle — not iss.

Jul 89. (7"ep) *(FREUD 27)* **BETTY GRABLE'S LEGS** [ ] [-]

Jul 89. (7") *(JUNG 49)* **TIME MACHINE. / TAKE A DETOUR** [ ] [-]

not iss. — E.S.P.

Oct 93. (cd) *<ESP 2002-2>* **GODDESS OF WET DREAMS** [-] [ ]

Thunderbird — not iss.

Jun 95. (cd) *(CSA 105)* **DEVIATION** [ ] [-]

– compilations, etc. –

Feb 79. (7") *Illegal; (IL 005)* **THUNDER WHEN SHE WALKS. / WHAT YOU GOT** [ ] [-]

1981. (lp) *Safari; (NEN 1)* **THE BEST OF THE ELECTRIC CHAIRS** [ ] [-]

Jun 83. (7"pic-d) *Safari; (WCP 3)* **FUCK OFF. / TOILET LOVE** [ ] [-]

Dec 93. (cd) *RPM; (RPM 119)* **ROCK'N'ROLL CLEOPATRA – THE ESSENTIAL . . . VOLUME 1** [ ] [-]

Jul 95. (cd) *RPM; (RPM 145)* **LET YOUR BACKBONE SLIP! – THE ESSENTIAL . . . VOLUME 2** [ ] [-]

COWBOY JUNKIES

Formed: Toronto, Canada . . . 1985 by MICHAEL TIMMINS, with younger brother PETER and sister MARGO; all inviting ALAN ANTON to the fold. In the late 70's and early 80's, MICHAEL had been in groups, HUNGER PROJECT and GERMINAL, before moving to New York and London in the process. In the mid-80's, The COWBOY JUNKIES recorded a debut lp, 'WHITES OFF EARTH NOW!!' in their garage, releasing it on their own Canadian indie label 'Latent'. By 1988, they were on the roster of 'R.C.A.', with 'Cooking Vinyl' licensing them in UK. That year's album, 'THE TRINITY SESSION' was famously cut in a Toronto Church with the most basic of recording equipment. Despite this, or more likely because of it, the album remains 'JUNKIES most enduring effort/ Proving that at its heart, real country music really is a religious experience, the band drifted grace through perceptive covers and original material alike. Whether investing in Hank Williams' 'I'M SO LONESOME I COULD CRY' and Patsy Cline's 'WALKIN' AFTER MIDNIGHT' with latter day angst or re-inventing Lou Reed's 'SWEET JANE' with a langueous pignancy, The COWBOY JUNKIES melancholic, minimalistic take on Americana was hypnotic and groundbreaking. Though they initially appealed to the college market, the group successfully crossed over with follow-up set, 'THE CAUTION HORSES' (1990). A slightly more robust album, it included one of the group's most affecting originals to date 'CAUSE CHEAP IS HOW I FEEL', while they even managed to transform NEIL YOUNG's classic 'POWDERFINGER', into a spectral lament. 'BLACK EYED MAN' (1992) was even better, JOHN PRINE and the late, lamented TOWNES VAN ZANDT guesting on an album which mined a rawer country seam. The record also marked the peak of their commercial success, the band playing a prestigious gig at London's Royal Albert Hall. Since then, the band have lost their momentum somewhat, despite a further couple of critically acclaimed albums, 'PALE SUN, CRESCENT MOON' (1993) and 'LAY IT DOWN' (1996). The latter marked their debut for 'Geffen', their tenure with 'R.C.A.' ending in the mid-90's. • **Songwriters:** MICHAEL wrote & produced most songs, except other covers BLUE MOON (hit; Elvis Presley) / SHINING MOON (Lightning Hopkins) / STATE TROOPER (Bruce Springsteen) / ME AND THE DEVIL + CROSSROADS (Robert Johnson) / DECORATION DAY + I'LL NEVER GET OUT OF THESE BLUES ALIVE + FORGIVE ME (John Lee Hooker) / BABY PLEASE DON'T GO (Bukka White) / COWBOY JUNKIES LAMENT + TO LIVE IS TO FLY (Townes Van Zandt) / IF YOU'VE GOTTA GO, GO NOW (Bob Dylan) / LOST MY DRIVING WHEEL (Wiffen) / THE POST (Dinosaur Jr).

Album rating: WHITES OFF EARTH NOW!! (*6) / THE TRINITY SESSION (*7) / THE CAUTION HORSES (*5) / BLACK EYED MAN (*6) / PALE SUN, CRESCENT MOON (*7) / 200 MORE MILES live 1985-1994 (*5) / LAY IT DOWN (*5) / MILES FROM OUR HOME (*5) / STUDIO compilation (*6)

MICHAEL TIMMINS (b.21 Apr'59, Montreal, Canada) – guitar / **MARGO TIMMINS** (b.27 Jun'61, Montreal) – vocals / **PETER TIMMINS** (b.29 Oct'65, Montreal) – drums / **ALAN ANTON** (b. ALAN ALIZOJVODIC, 22 Jun'59, Montreal) – bass

not iss. — Latent

Nov 86. (lp) **WHITES OFF EARTH NOW!!** [-] [ ] Canada
– Shining moon / State trooper / Me and the Devil / Decoration day / Baby please don't go / I'll never get out of these blues alive / Take me / Forgive me / Crossroads. *(UK-iss.Feb91 on 'R.C.A.' cd/c/lp; PD/PK/PL 82380)*

Cooking Vinyl — R.C.A.

Mar 89. (7") *(FRY 008)* **SWEET JANE. / 200 MORE MILES** [ ] [ ] Nov88
(12"+=) *(FRY 008T)* – Postcard blues.

Mar 89. (lp/c/cd) *(COOK/+C/CD 011) <8568>* **THE TRINITY SESSION** [ ] [26] Oct88
– Mining for gold / Misguided angel / Blue moon revisited (a song for Elvis) / I don't get in / I'm so lonesome I could cry / To love is to bury / 200 more miles / Dreaming my dreams with you / Working on a building / Sweet Jane / Postcard blues / Walking after midnight. *(cd re-iss. Feb94; 74321 18356-2)*

May 89. (7") **MISGUIDED ANGEL. / POSTCARD BLUES** [-] [ ]

Jul 89. (7") *(FRY 011)* **BLUE MOON REVISITED (SONG FOR ELVIS). / TO LOVE IS TO BURY** [ ] [ ]
(12"+=/cd-s+=) *(FRY 011 T/CD)* – ('A'live version).
(10") *(FRY 011X)* – ('A'side) / You won't be loved again / Shining moon / Walking after midnight.

R.C.A. — R.C.A.

Feb 90. (7") *(PB 49301)* **SUN COMES UP, IT'S TUESDAY MORNING. / WITCHES** [ ] [ ]
(12"+=) *(PT 49302)* – Powderfinger.
(cd-s++=) *(PD 49302)* – Misguided angel.
(c-s+=) *(PK 49302)* – Dead flowers.

Mar 90. (cd/c/lp) *(PD/PK/PL 90450) <2058>* **THE CAUTION HORSES** [33] [47]
– Sun comes up, it's Tuesday morning / 'Cause cheap is how I feel / Thirty summers / Mariner's song / Powderfinger / Where are you tonight / Witches / Rock and bird / Escape is so easy / You will be loved again. *(cd re-iss. Feb94; 74321 18537-2)*

Jun 90. (7") **'CAUSE CHEAP IS HOW I FEEL. / THIRTY SUMMERS** [ ] [ ]
(12"+=/cd-s+=) – Declaration day / State trooper / Take me.

Sep 90. (c-s) **ROCK AND BIRD /** [-] [ ]

Jan 92. (cd-ep) **SOUTHERN RAIN / MURDER, TONIGHT, IN THE TRAILER PARK / LOST MY DRIVING WHEEL / IF YOU'VE GOTTA GO, GO NOW** [ ] [ ]

Feb 92. (cd/c/lp) *(PD/PK/PL 90620) <61049>* **BLACK EYED MAN** [21] [76]
– Southern rain / Oregon hill / This street, that man, this life / A horse in the country / If you were the woman and I was the man / Murder, tonight, in the trailer park / Black eyed man / Winter's song / The last spike / Cowboy Junkies lament / Townes' blues / To live is to fly. *(w/ free cd-ep)* – DEAD FLOWERS / CAPTAIN KIDD / TAKE ME / 'CAUSE CHEAP IS HOW I FEEL *(cd re-iss. Jun96; 74321 36913-2)*

Mar 92. (7") **A HORSE IN THE COUNTRY. / OREGON HILL** [ ] [ ]
(cd-s+=) – Five room love story

Nov 93. (cd/c) *<(74321 16808-2/-4)>* **PALE SUN, CRESCENT MOON** [ ] [ ]
– Crescent moon / First recollection / Ring on the sill / Anniversary song / White sail / Seven years / Pale Sun / The post / Cold tea blues / Hard to explain / Hunted / Floorboard blues. *(cd re-iss. Jun96; same)*

Feb 96. (d-cd) *<(74321 29643-2)>* **200 MORE MILES (live)** [ ] [ ]
– Blue moon revisited (a song for Elvis) / 200 more miles / Me and the Devil / State trooper / Sun comes up, it's Tuesday morning / Oregon hill / Where are you tonight / 'Cause cheap is how I feel / Floorboard blues / Murder tonight in the trailer park / Sweet Jane / If you were the woman and I was the man / Pale sun / Hunted / Lost mny driving wheel / Forgive me / Misguided angel / I'm so lonesome I could cry / Walking after midnight.

Geffen — Geffen

Mar 96. (c-s) *(GFSC 22117)* **A COMMON DISASTER / COME CALLING (HER SONG)** [ ] [-]
(cd-s+=) *(GFSTD 22117)* – In the long run.

May 96. (cd/c) *<(GED/GEC 24952)>* **LAY IT DOWN** [ ] [55] Mar96
– Something more besides you / A common disaster / Lay it down / Hold on to me / Come calling (his song) / Just want to see / Lonely sinking feeling / Angel mine / Bea's song (river song trilogy: part II) / Musical key / Speaking confidentially / Come calling (her song) / Now I know.

Aug 96. (cd-s) *(GED 2216-2)* **ANGEL MINE /** [ ] [ ]

Sep 98. (cd/c) *<(GED/GEC 25201)>* **MILES FROM OUR HOME** [ ] [98] Jul98

– compilations, etc. –

Feb 98. (cd) *R.C.A.; (07863 67412-2)* **STUDIO** (selected studio recordings 1986-1995) [ ] [ ]
– Shining moon / Misguided angel / Blue moon revisited (a song for Elvis) / Sweet Jane / Sun comes up, it's Tuesday morning / 'Cause cheap is how I feel / Powderfinger / Southern rain / A horse in the country / This street, that man, this life / Anniversary song / Ring on the sill / A common disaster / Lost my driving wheel.

Graham COXON (see under ⇒ BLUR)

CRACKER

Formed: Redlands, California, USA . . . 1990 by DAVID LOWERY and DAVE LOVERING (former members of top cult US acts). While LOVERING had been a sidekick for FRANK BLACK in The PIXIES, LOWERY had been in CAMPER VAN BEETHOVEN, who were known for releasing a string of albums for 'Rough Trade' in the 80's and the classic track 'TAKE THE SKINHEADS BOWLING'. Alternately acoustic laid-back/hard rockin' grunge cowpunks fusing TOM PETTY or IAN HUNTER like songs with twanging country rock, CRACKER emerged in 1992 with the tongue in cheek, 'TEEN ANGST (WHAT THE WORLD NEEDS NOW)'. This was swiftly followed up with an impressive eponymous debut set. Though not a straight grunge act by any means, the band nevertheless appealed to a similar college crowd and a follow-up set, 'KEROSENE HAT' (1994) spawned a grunge mini-anthem in 'LOW'. The album itself sold close to a half million copies, a more experimental outing that saw them cover The Grateful Dead's 'LOSER'. A third set, 'THE GOLDEN AGE' (1996) meanwhile, saw LOVERING getting back to his roots in line with the burgeoning "No Depression" alternative country scene. Another US-only release, 'GENTLEMEN'S BLUES', was released in September '98 to a lukewarm critical reception. • **Covered:** WITHERING AWAY (Vic Chesnutt).

Album rating: CRACKER (*7) / KEROSENE HAT (*8) / THE GOLDEN AGE (*5) / GENTLEMEN'S BLUES (*5)

DAVID LOWERY (b.10 Sep'60, San Antonio, Texas) – vocals, guitars (ex-CAMPER VAN BEETHOVEN) / **JOHNNY HICKMAN** – guitar, vocals / **BOB RUPE** (b.16 Sep'56, Michigan) – bass (ex-SILOS) / **DAVE LOVERING** (b. 6 Dec'61, Boston, Mass.) – drums (ex-PIXIES)

		Virgin America	Virgin
Mar 92.	(7") **TEEN ANGST (WHAT THE WORLD NEEDS NOW). / CAN I TAKE MY GUN TO HEAVEN**	☐	☐
	(12"+=) – China. (cd-s++=) – ('A'version).		
Apr 92.	(cd/c/lp) *(CDVUS/VUSMC/VUSLP 48) <91816-2/-4>* **CRACKER**	☐	☐
	– Teen angst (what the world needs now) / Happy birthday to me / This is Cracker soul / I see the light / St. Cajetan / Mr. Wrong / Someday / Can I take my gun to Heaven / Satify you / Another song about the rain / Don't f*** me up (with peace and love) / Dr. Bernice.		
—	**DAVEY FARAGHER** – bass, vocals; repl. RUPE		
—	**MICHAEL URBANO** – drums; repl. LOVERING		
Mar 94.	(c-s) *<38427>* **LOW / NOSTALGIA**	-	64
May 94.	(7"/c-s) *(VUS/+C 80)* **LOW. / TEEN ANGST (WHAT THE WORLD NEEDS NOW)**	43	-
	(cd-s) *(VUSDG 80)* – ('A'side) / I ride my bike / Sunday train / Whole lotta trouble. (10"colrd) *(VUSA 80)* – ('A'side) / River Euphrates / Euro-trash girl / Bad vibes everybody. *(re-iss. Nov94; same)* – (hit UK No.54)		
Jun 94.	(cd/c) *(CDVUS/VUSMC 67) <39012>* **KEROSENE HAT**	44	59 Sep93
	– Low / Movie star / Get off this / Kerosene hat / Take me down to the infirmary / Nostalgia / Sweet potato / Sick of goodbyes / I want everything / Lonesome Johnny blues / Let's go for a ride / Loser. *(cd+=)* – No songs: Eurotrash girl + I ride my bike / Hi-desert biker meth lab. *(c+=)* – No songs; Euro-trash girl + I ride my bike / Kerosene hat (acoustic).		
Jul 94.	(c-ep/cd-ep) *(VUSC/+D 83)* **GET OFF THIS / HAPPY BIRTHDAY TO ME / CHINA / DR. BERNICE**	41	☐
	(cd-ep) *(VUSDG 83)* – ('A'side) / Fucking up (live) / Blue Danube / Don't fuck me up (with peace and love). (10"ep) *(VUSA 83)* – ('A'side) / Steve's hornpipe / Mr. Wrong / I want everything (acoustic).		
Apr 96.	(cd/c) *<41498>* **THE GOLDEN AGE**	-	83
	– I hate my generation / I'm a little rocket ship / Big dipper / Nothing to believe in / The golden age / 1000 flower power maximum / Dixie Babylon / I can't forget you / Sweet thistle pie / Useless stuff / How can I live without you / Bicycle Spaniard.		
Sep 98.	(cd/c) *<46263>* **GENTLEMAN'S BLUES**	-	☐
	– Good life / Seven days / Star / James river / My life is totally boring without you / Been around the world / World is mine / Lullabye / Waiting for you girl / Trails and tribulations / Wild one / Gentlemen's blues / I want out of the circus / Wedding day / Hallelujah.		

Sarah CRACKNELL (see under ⇒ SAINT ETIENNE)

CRAMPS

Formed: New York City, New York, USA . . . 1975 by LUX INTERIOR and POISON IVY, who recruited fellow weirdos BRYAN GREGORY and PAM 'BALAM' GREGORY (the latter was replaced by MIRIAM LINNA, who in turn was superseded by NICK KNOX). The trashiest, sleaziest 50's throwbacks to ever besmirch the good name of rock'n'roll, The CRAMPS took the genre's inherit debauchery to its thrilling (and often hilarious) conclusion. Crawling from the mire of CBGB's punk scene like the proverbial Swamp Thing in one of their baloved B-movies, The CRAMPS started as they meant to go on, initiating their vinyl career in 1978 with an obscure cover, 'THE WAY I WALK'. The singles was backed with a riotous mangling of The Trashmen's 'SURFIN' BIRD', as close to a theme tune as the band came. A follow-up, 'HUMAN FLY', introduced LUX's impressive capacity for disturbing accurate

animal (and insect!) noises, its voodoo surf twang and creeping tempo scarier than the frontman's skintight leotard. Subsequently signed to Miles Copeland's 'I.R.S.' label, The CRAMPS set up shop in Sun Studios, Memphis (where else?!) with producer ALEX CHILTON at the production helm, working on the material for their acclaimed debut set, 'SONGS THE LORD TAUGHT US' (1980). Featuring such bad taste gems as 'GARBAGEMAN' (more animal noises!), 'I WAS A TEENAGE WEREWOLF' and 'STRYCHNINE', the record further boosted the band's cult following. The departure of GREGORY after the 'DRUG TRAIN' single was the first in a long series of line-up changes through which IVY (the sexiest thing in stockings!) and INTERIOR were the only constants. With KID CONGO POWERS as a replacement, the band cut the less convincing 'PSYCHEDELIC JUNGLE' (1981), their final release for Copeland who they later sued. A short spell with the French 'New Rose' label and then 'Big Beat' saw the release of the live mini 'SMELL OF FEMALE' (1983). This went at least some way to capturing the cheap thrills of a CRAMPS gig, though readers are advised to experience the real thing; if the primeval spirit of raw rock'n'roll doesn't move you, then the sight of a grown man in a leather thong and and high heels just might! INTERIOR had always modelled himself on a kind of ELVIS-from-the-crypt and in 1986, The CRAMPS met their maker, so to speak, on the classic 'A DATE WITH ELVIS'. The likes of 'THE HOT PEARL SNATCH', 'CAN YOUR PUSSY DO THE DOG?' and 'WHAT'S INSIDE A GIRL?', need to further explanation save that THE KING was no doubt turning in his grave. Though this marked a creative and commercial peak of sorts, The CRAMPS continued to think up the best song titles in the Western World over a string of late 80's/90's albums, including 'STAY SICK' (1990), 'LOOK MOM, NO HEAD' (1991; essential if only for the IGGY POP collaboration, 'MINISKIRT BLUES'), 'FLAME JOB' (1994) and 'BIG BEAT FROM BADSVILLE' (1997). Though they've hardly pushed back the boundaries of music, The CRAMPS are arguably even more essential now than in their heyday, if only to remind he current crop of indie dullards what it REALLY means to play "The Devil's Music". • **Songwriters:** Most written by LUX and IVY except SURFIN' BIRD (Trashmen) / FEVER (Little Willie John) / THE WAY I WALK (Robert Gordon) / GREEN DOOR (Jim Lowe) / JAILHOUSE ROCK (Elvis Presley) / MULESKINNER BLUES (Fendermen) / PSYCHOTIC REACTION (Count Five) / LONESOME TOWN (Ricky Nelson) / HARD WORKIN' MAN (Jack Nitzche) / HITSVILLE 29 B.C. (Turnbow) / WHEN I GET THE BLUES (Larry Mize) / HOW COME YOU DO ME? (. . .Joiner) / STRANGE LOVE (. . .West) / BLUES BLUES BLUES (. . .Thompson) / TRAPPED LOVE (Kohler-Fana) / SINNERS (. . .Aldrich) / ROUTE 66 (. . . Troup) / etc. • **Trivia:** Their fan club was surprisingly based in Grangemouth, Scotland (wee Marty fi the Nash ran it!)

Album rating: SONGS THE LORD TAUGHT US (*7) / PSYCHEDELIC JUNGLE (*7) / OFF THE BONE compilation (*8) / SMELL OF FEMALE (*6) / A DATE WITH ELVIS (*7) / STAY SICK (*6) / LOOK MOM, NO HEAD! (*5) / FLAMEJOB (*6) / BIG BEAT FROM BADSVILLE (*5)

LUX INTERIOR (b. ERICK LEE PURKHISER, 1948, Akron, Ohio) – vocals / **POISON IVY RORSCHACH** (b. KIRSTY MARLANA WALLACE, 1954, Sacramento, Calif.) – guitar / **BRYAN GREGORY** (b. Detroit, Mich.) – guitar / **NICK KNOX** (b. NICHOLAS

STEPHANOFF) – drums repl. MIRIAM LINNA who had repl. PAM 'BALAM' GREGORY

not iss. Vengeance

Apr 78. (7") *<666>* **THE WAY I WALK. / SURFIN' BIRD** [-] [ ]
Nov 78. (7") *<668>* **HUMAN FLY. / DOMINO** [-] [ ]

Illegal I.R.S.

Jun 79. (12"ep) *(ILS 12-013)* **GRAVEST HITS** [ ] [-]
– Human fly / The way I walk / Domino / Surfin' bird / Lonesome town. *(re-iss. Sep82 – 7"blue-ep / re-iss. Mar83- 7"red-ep; same)*
Mar 80. (7") *(ILS 0017)* **FEVER. / GARBAGEMAN** [ ] [-]
Apr 80. (lp) *(ILP 005) <SP 007>* **SONGS THE LORD TAUGHT US** [ ] [ ]
– TV set / Rock on the Moon / Garbageman / I was a teenage werewolf / Sunglasses after dark / The mad daddy / Mystery plane / Zombie dance / What's behind the mask / Strychnine / I'm cramped / Tear it up / Fever. *(re-iss. Feb90;)*
May 80. (7") *<IR 9014>* **DRUG TRAIN. / GARAGEMAN** [-] [ ]
Jul 80. (7"m) *(ILS 021)* **DRUG TRAIN. / LOVE ME / I CAN HARDLY STAND IT** [ ] [-]

— **KID CONGO POWERS** (b. BRIAN TRISTAN, 27 Mar'61, La Puente, Calif.) – guitar; repl. JULIEN BOND, who had repl. GREGORY for two months mid 1980.

I.R.S. I.R.S.

May 81. (7"yellow) *(PFS 1003) <IR 9021>* **GOO GOO MUCK. / SHE SAID** [ ] [ ] Aug81
May 81. (lp) *<(SP 70016)>* **PSYCHEDELIC JUNGLE** [ ] [ ] Jul81
– Green fuzz / Goo goo muck / Rockin' bones / Voodoo idol / Primitive / Caveman / The crusher / Don't eat stuff off the sidewalk / Can't find my mind / Jungle hop / The natives are restless / Under the wires / Beautiful gardens / Green door.
Oct 81. (12"m) *(PFSX 1008)* **THE CRUSHER. / SAVE IT / NEW KIND OF KICK** [ ] [-]

— (LUX, IVY & NICK were joined by **IKE KNOX** (Nick's cousin) – guitar; repl. KID CONGO who returned to GUN CLUB (appeared on live tracks 83-84)

Big Beat not iss.

Nov 83. (red-m-lp) *(NED 6)* **SMELL OF FEMALE (live)** [74] [-]
– Faster pussycat / I ain't nuthin' but a gorehound / Psychotic reaction / The most exhalted potentate of love / You got good taste / Call of the wig hat. *(pic-lp Jun84; NEDP 6) (re-iss. Feb91 cd+=/c+=; CDWIKM/WIKMC 95)* – Beautiful gardens / She said / Surfin' dead.

— (signed to below label in France)

New Rose New Rose

Mar 84. (7"/7"pic-d) *(NEW 28/+P)* **FASTER PUSSYCAT. / YOU GOT GOOD TASTE** [-] [-] French
Mar 84. (7"colrd;various) *(NEW 33)* **I AIN'T NUTHIN' BUT A GOREHOUND. / WEEKEND ON MARS** [-] [-] French

— **CANDY FUR** (DEL-MAR) – guitar; repl. IKE

Big Beat not iss.

Nov 85. (7"orange) *(NS 110)* **CAN YOUR PUSSY DO THE DOG? / BLUE MOON BABY** [68] [-]
(12"blue+=) *(NST 110)* – Georgia Lee Brown.
Feb 86. (blue-lp/c/cd) *(WIKA/WIKC/CDWIK 46)* **A DATE WITH ELVIS** [34] [-]
– How far can too far go / The hot pearl snatch / People ain't too good / What's inside a girl? / Can your pussy do the dog? / Kizmiaz / Cornfed dames / Chicken / (Hot pool of) Woman need / Aloha from Hell / It's just that song. *<US-iss.1994 on 'Capitol'; 73579>*
May 86. (7") *(NS 115)* **WHAT'S INSIDE A GIRL? / GET OFF THE ROAD** [ ] [-]
(12"+=) *(NST 115)* – Give me a woman.
(Mar87; cd-s++=) *(CRAMP 1)* – Scene / Heart of darkness.

Enigma Enigma

Jan 90. (7"/7"sha-pic-d/c-s) *(ENV/+PD/TC 17)* **BIKINI GIRLS WITH MACHINE GUNS. / JACKYARD BACKOFF** [35] [ ]
(12"+=/cd-s+=) *(12ENV/ENVCD 17)* – Her love rubbed off.
Feb 90. (cd/c/lp) *(CDENV/TCENV/ENVLP 1001) <73543>* **STAY SICK** [62] [ ]
– Bop pills / Goddam rock'n'roll / Bikini girls with machine guns / All women are bad / Creature from the black leather lagoon / Shortenini' bread / Daisy's up your butterfly / Everything goes / Journey to the centre of a girl / Mama oo pow pow / Saddle up a buzz buzz / Muleskinner blues. *(cd+=)* – Her love rubbed off. *(pic-lp Nov90; ENVLPPD 101) (re-iss. Feb94 cd/lp; CD+/WIKD 126)*
Apr 90. (7"/c-s) *(ENV/+TC 19)* **ALL WOMEN ARE BAD. / TEENAGE RAGE (live)** [ ] [-]
(12"+=/12"pic-d+=/cd-s+=) *(12ENV/12ENVPD/ENVCD 19)* – King of the drapes (live) / High school hellcats (live).
Aug 90. (7") **CREATURES FROM THE BLACK LEATHER LAGOON. / JAILHOUSE ROCK** [ ] [-]
(12"+=/cd-s+=) – Beat out my love.

— **LUX & IVY** were joined by **SLIM CHANCE** – guitar (ex-PANTHER BURNS) / **JIM SCLAVUNOS** – drums

Big Beat Restless

Sep 91. (7") *(NST 135)* **EYEBALL IN MY MARTINI. / WILDER WILDER FASTER FASTER** [ ] [-]
(12"+=/cd-s+=) *(12/CD NST 135)* – Wilder wilder faster faster.
Sep 91. (cd/c/lp) *(CDWIK/WIKDC/WIKAD 101) <72586>* **LOOK MOM, NO HEAD!** [ ] [ ]
– Dames, booze, chains and boots / Two headed sex change / Blow up your mind / Hard workin' man / Miniskirt blues / Alligator stomp / I wanna get in your pants Bend over, I'll drive / Don't get funny with me / Eyeball in my Martini / Hipsville 29 B.C. / When I get the blues (the strangeness in me). *(also pic-lp/pic-cd; WIKDP/CDWIKD 101)*

— **NICKY ALEXANDER** – drums (ex-WEIRDOS); repl. JIM

Sep 92. (cd-ep) *(CDNST 136)* **BLUES FIX EP** [ ] [-]
– Hard workin' man / It's mighty crazy / Jelly roll rock / Shombalor.

— **HARRY DRUMDINI** – drums; repl. NICKY

Creation Medicine – Warners

Oct 94. (7") *(CRE 180)* **ULTRA TWIST! / CONFESSIONS OF A PSYCHO CAT** [ ] [-]
(12"+=)(cd-s+=) *(CRE 180T)(CRESCD 180)* – No club love wolf.
Oct 94. (cd/c/lp) *(CRECD/C-CRE/CRELP 170) <24592>* **FLAMEJOB** [ ] [ ]
– Mean machine / Ultra twist / Let's get f*cked up / Nest of the cuckoo bird / I'm customized / Sado country auto show / Naked girl falling down the stairs / How come you do me? / Inside out and upside down (with you) / Trapped love / Swing the big eyed rabbit / Strange love / Blues blues blues / Sinners / Route 66 (get your kicks on).
Feb 95. (7") *(CRE 196)* **NAKED GIRL FALLING DOWN THE STAIRS. / LET'S GET F*CKED UP** [ ] [-]
(cd-s+=) *9CRESCD 196)* – Surfin' bird.

Epitaph Epitaph

Oct 97. (cd/c/lp) *<(6516-2/-4/-1)>* **BIG BEAT FROM BADSVILLE** [ ] [ ]
– Cramp stomp / God monster / It thing hard on / Like a bad girl should / Sheena's in a goth gang / Queen of pain / Monkey with your tail / Devil behind that bush / Super goo / Hypno sex ray / Burn she devil, burn / Wet nightmare / Badass bug / Haulass hyena.
Dec 97. (7") *(6527-7)* **LIKE A BAD GIRL SHOULD. / WET NIGHTMARE** [ ] [-]
(cd-s+=) *(6527-2)* – I walked all night.

– compilations, others, etc. –

May 83. (lp) *Illegal; (ILP 012) / I.R.S.; <SP 70042>* **OFF THE BONE** [44] [ ] Feb84
<US-title 'BAD MUSIC FOR BAD PEOPLE'>
– Human fly / The way I walk / Domino / Surfin' bird / Lonesome town / Garbageman / Fever / Drug train / Love me / I can't hardly stand it / Goo goo muck / She said / The crusher / Save it / New kind of kick. *(cd-iss. Jan87; ILPCD 012) (cd re-iss. 1992 on 'Castle'+=;)* – Uranium Rock / Good taste (live)
1984. (4x7"box) *New Rose;* **I AIN'T NUTHIN' BUT A GOREHOUND. / WEEKEND ON MARS // FASTER PUSSYCAT. / YOU GOT GOOD TASTE // CALL OF THE WIG HAT. / THE MOST EXHALTED POTENTATE OF LOVE // PSYCHOTIC REACTION. / (one sided)** [-] [-] French
(all 4 either blue/white/black/green)
May 86. (7") *New Rose; (NEW 71)* **KIZMIAZ. / GET OFF THE ROAD** [-] [-]
(12"+=) *(NEW 70)* – Give me a woman.
Nov 87. (lp) *Vengeance;* **ROCKIN' AND REELIN' IN AUCKLAND, NEW ZEALAND (live)** [-] [ ]
(UK cd-iss. Sep94 on 'Big Beat'; CDWIKD 132)

CRANBERRIES

Formed: Limerick, Ireland ... 1990 initially as covers band The CRANBERRY SAW US (corny, or what!) by brothers NOEL and MIKE HOGAN, plus FERGAL LAWLER. The inclusion of singer DOLORES O'RIORDAN, saw the release the following year of an independent single, 'UNCERTAIN'. The quartet returned to the studio late in '91, subsequently resurfacing on the 'Island' label with 'DREAMS', 'LINGER' and 'PUT ME DOWN'. These tracks were featured on 1993's glorious debut album, 'EVERYBODY ELSE IS DOING IT, SO WHY CAN'T WE', which went on to sell a million in America (a year later it went platinum in Britain). An indie style major outfit, initially described as The Irish SUNDAYS, The CRANBERRIES were distinguished by DOLORES' heavily accented vocals, endearing naive and girlish one minute, howling banshee-style the next. An acquired taste, definitely, but one which millions seemingly, erm, acquired, drawn in no doubt by their canny way with a romantic Celtic melody. After their slow beginnings, The CRANBERRIES were now hot property, the UK music press finally recognised their unique talent. Confusingly for newly acquainted fans, a follow-up album, 'NO NEED TO ARGUE' hit the shops the same year ('94), previewed by the grunge like 'ZOMBIE', a "loud" single (in every sense of the word), it made the UK Top 20. Incredibly, the track became a massive international hit for rave outfit, AMY, who took it back into the UK Top 20 in 1995. A third set, 'TO THE FAITHFUL DEPARTED' (1996) saw the band enlisting gloss-rock producer, Bruce Fairbairn, in what was surely a move to further dominate the American market. Songs about Bosnia, John Lennon etc, didn't detract it from cleaning up commercially once more, although most critics were unimpressed. • **Songwriters:** DOLORES / N HOGAN, except (THEY LONG TO BE) CLOSE TO YOU (Carpenters). • **Trivia:** They supported MOOSE in the summer of '91, DOLORES guesting on their 1992 album, 'XYZ'.

Album rating: EVERYBODY ELSE IS DOING IT, SO WHY CAN'T WE (*8) / NO NEED TO ARGUE (*6) / TO THE FAITHFUL DEPARTED (*4)

DOLORES O'RIORDAN (b. 6 Sep'71) – vocals, acoustic guitar / **NOEL HOGAN** (b.25 Dec'71) – guitar / **MIKE HOGAN** (b.29 Apr'73) – bass / **FERGAL LAWLER** (b. 4 Mar'71) – drums

Xerica not iss.

Oct 91. (12"ep) *(XER 14T)* **UNCERTAIN / NOTHING LEFT AT ALL. / PATHETIC SENSES / THEM** [ ] [-]

Island Island

Sep 92. (7") *(IS 548)* **DREAMS. / WHAT YOU WERE** [ ] [-]
(12"+=/cd-s+=) *(12IS/CID 548)* – Liar.
Feb 93. (c-s/7") *(C+/IS 556)* **LINGER. / REASON** [74] [-]
(12"/cd-s) *(12IS/CID 556)* – ('A'side) / How (radical mix).
Mar 93. (cd/c/lp) *(CID/ICT/ILPS 8003) <514156>* **EVERYBODY ELSE IS DOING IT, SO WHY CAN'T WE?** [64] [18]
– I still do / Dreams / Sunday / Pretty / Waltzing black / Not sorry / Linger / Wanted / Still can't . . . / I will always / How / Put me down. *(re-dist.Nov93; same) (re-iss. Mar94, hit UK No.1)*
Oct 93. (c-s) *<862800>* **LINGER / HOW** [-] [8]
Jan 94. (c-s/7") *(C+/IS 559)* **LINGER. / PRETTY (live)** [14] [-]
(10"+=/cd-s+=) *(10IS/CID 559)* – Waltzing black (live) / I still do (live).
Apr 94. (c-s/7") *(C+/IS 594) <864436>* **DREAMS. / WHAT YOU WERE** [27] [42] Mar94
(cd-s+=) *(CID 594)* – Liar.
(cd-s) *(CIDX 594)* – ('A'live) / Liar (live) / Not sorry (live) / Wanted (live).

— Jun'94; DOLORES featured on JAH WOBBLE's hit 'The Sun Does Rise'.

Sep 94. (c-s/7") *(C+/IS 600)* **ZOMBIE. / AWAY** [14] [-]

(cd-s+=) *(CID 600)* – I don't need.
(cd-s) *(CIDX 600)* – ('A'extended) / Waltzing black (live) / Linger (live).
Oct 94. (cd/c/lp) *(CIS/ICT/ILPS 8029)* <524050> **NO NEED TO ARGUE** [2] [6]
– Ode to my family / I can't be with you / 21 / Zombie / Empty / Everything I said / The icicle melts / Disappointment / Ridiculous thoughts / Dreaming my dreams / Yeats' grave / Daffodil lament / No need to argue.
Nov 94. (c-s/7") *(C+/IS 601)* **ODE TO MY FAMILY. / SO COLD IN IRELAND** [29] [-]
(cd-s+=) *(CID 601)* – No need to argue / Dreaming my dreams.
(cd-s) *(CIDX 601)* – ('A'live) / Dreams (live) / Ridiculous thoughts (live) / Zombie (live).
Feb 95. (c-s/7") *(C+/IS 605)* **I CAN'T BE WITH YOU. / (THEY LONG TO BE) CLOSE TO YOU** [23] [-]
(cd-s+=) *(CID 605)* – Empty (BBC session).
(cd-s) *(CIDX 605)* – ('A'-BBC session) / Zombie (acoustic) / Daffodil lament (live).
Jul 95. (c-s/7") *(C+/IS 616)* **RIDICULOUS THOUGHTS. / LINGER** [20] [-]
(cd-s+=) *(CID 616)* – Twenty one (live) / Ridiculous thoughts (live).
Apr 96. (c-s) *(CIS 633)* **SALVATION / I'M STILL REMEMBERING** [13] [-]
(cd-s+=) *(CID 633)* – I just shot John Lennon.
May 96. (cd/c/colrd-lp) *(CID/ICT/ILPS 8048)* <524234> **TO THE FAITHFUL DEPARTED** [2] [4]
– Hollywood / Salvation / When you're gone / Free to decide / War child / Forever yellow skies / The rebels / I just shot John Lennon / Electric blue / I'm still remembering / Will you remember? / Joe / Bosnia.
Jul 96. (c-s) *(CIS 637)* **FREE TO DECIDE / CORDELL** [33] [-]
(cd-s+=) *(CID 637)* – The picture I view.
(cd-s) *(CIDX 637)* – ('A'side) / Salvation (live) / Bosnia.
Nov 96. (c-s) <854802> **FREE TO DECIDE / WHEN YOU'RE GONE** [-] [22]

– compilations, etc. –

Nov 95. (d-cd) **EVERYBODY ELSE IS DOING IT, SO WHY CAN'T WE? / NO NEED TO ARGUE** [ ] [ ]

CRANES

Formed: Portsmouth, England . . . 1986 by the sister and brother team of ALISON and JIM SHAW. Their first foray into the music business was the self-financed and distributed cassette, 'FUSE', a primitive blueprint of the distinctive gothic minimalism which formed the bulk of their early EP's. In addition to contributing tracks to various compilation albums, the group issued a debut mini-set, 'SELF NON SELF', on the small 'Bite Back!' label in 1989 before signing with the 'BMG' subsidiary, 'Dedicated', in the early 90's. Briefly lumped in with the shoegazing scene of the time, in reality The CRANES were a far more complex and disturbing listen; over the course of four EP's, 'INESCAPABLE', 'ESPERO', 'ADORATION' and 'TOMORROW'S TEARS', the group (now augmented by MARK FRANCOME and MATT HOPE) developed an alternately bleakly beautiful/menacingly claustrophobic sound highlighting ALISON's vocal fusion of LYDIA LUNCH and CLARE GROGAN and feeding off the same celestial energy supply as The COCTEAU TWINS. A debut album proper, 'WINGS OF JOY', appeared in 1991 to general critical acclaim; the band did have their detractors of course, such extreme music drawing extreme opinions. Goth-pop stalwarts, The CURE, were impressed enough to invite the band on tour, the influence of ROBERT SMITH and Co apparent on Top 40 follow-up album, 'FOREVER' (1993). Inevitably, subsequent set 'LOVED' (1994) followed in an increasingly easier-on-the-ear vein, yet despite continuing cult appeal, The CRANES failed to make any inroads to chart success with the likes of 'LA TRAGEDIE D'ORESTES' (1996) and 'POPULATION FOUR' (1997).

Album rating: SELF NON SELF mini (*4) / WINGS OF JOY (*7) / FOREVER (*8) / LOVED (*6) / LA TRAGEDIE D'ORESTES ET ELECTRA (*5) / POPULATION 4 (*4)

ALISON SHAW – vocals / **MARK FRANCOME** – guitar / **MATT COPE** – guitar / **JIM SHAW** – drums

Bite Back / not iss.

May 89. (m-lp) *(BB 017)* **SELF NON SELF** [ ] [-]
– One from the slum / Beach mover / Joy lies within / Focus breathe / Heaven or bliss / Fuse / Reach / Nothing in the middle nothing at the end. *(m-cd-iss. Nov92 on 'Dedicated'+=; DEDCD 006)* – (2 extra). <*US cd-iss. Nov97 on 'Dedicated'; 44016*>

Dedicated / Dedicated-R.C.A.

Aug 90. (12"ep) *(CRANE 001T)* **INESCAPABLE EP** [ ] [-]
– Inescapable / Give / Dada 331 / Inescapable II.
Nov 90. (12"ep/cd-ep) *(CRANE 002 T/CD)* **ESPERO EP** [ ] [-]
– I hope / EG shining / Cha cha esqueta.
May 91. (12"/cd-s) *(CRANE 003 T/CD)* **BRIGHTER. / ADORATION** [ ] [-]
Sep 91. (12"ep/cd-ep) *(CRANE 004 T/CD)* **TOMORROW'S TEARS / CASA BLANCA. / SIXTH OF MAY / DREAMLESS** [ ] [-]
Sep 91. (cd/c/lp) *(DED CD/MC/LP 003)* <3007> **WINGS OF JOY** [52] [ ] Nov91
– Watersong / Thursday / Living and breathing / Leaves of summer / Starblood / Wish / Tomorrow's tears / Beautiful sadness / Hopes are high / Adoration. *(cd+=)* – Sixth of May. *(re-iss. Nov92; same)* – (w/ free 5"cd-s) *(CRANE 005CD)*
Mar 93. (12"ep/cd-ep) *(CRANE 006 T/CD)* **ADRIFT. / EVERYWHERE / UNDERWATER** [ ] [ ]
May 93. (cd/c/lp) *(DED CD/MC/LP 009)* <66212> **FOREVER** [40] [ ]
– Everywhere / Cloudless / Jewel / Far away / Adrift / Clear / Sun and sky / And ever / Golden / Rainbows.
Sep 93. (7") *(CRANE 007)* **JEWEL (remix). / CLEAR (scalpicin mix)** [29] [ ]
(7") *(CRANE 007-2)* – ('A'side) / Cloudless (Thai mix).
(7") *(CRANE 007-3)* – ('A'side) / Love her to Heaven (II).
(cd-ep) *(CRANE 007CD)* – (all 4 tracks).

Dedicated / Arista

Aug 94. (7"m) *(CRANE 008)* **SHINING ROAD. / LILIES / SEPTEMBER** [57] [-]
(cd-s+=) *(CRANE 008CD)* – Green song 7.
(7"m) *(CRANE 008-2)* – ('A'-Braver mix) / Lilies (Flood mix) / Don't close your eyes.
Sep 94. (cd/c/lp) *(DED CD/MC/LP 016)* <18769> **LOVED** [ ] [ ] Oct94
– Shining road / Pale blue sky / Reverie / Lillies / Are you gone? / Loved / Beautiful friend / Bewildered / Gone this far / Paris and Rome.
May 96. (ltd-cd) *(DEDCD 024)* <44003> **LA TRAGEDIE D'ORESTES ET ELECTRA** [ ] [ ] Oct96
Feb 97. (cd/c) *(DED CD/MC 026)* <44005> **POPULATION 4** [ ] [ ]
– Tangled up / Fourteen / Breeze / Can't get free / Stalk / Sweet unknown / Angel bell / On top of the world / Brazil / Let go / To be / Lemon tree.
May 97. (cd-ep) *(CRANE 10CD)* **CAN'T GET FREE / PERFECT WORLD / LEMON TREE / TRUMPET SONG (Pier scene from 'Scarborough Ahoy!')** [ ] [-]

– compilations, etc. –

Sep 97. (d-cd) *Dedicated; (DEDCD 035)* <44019> **EP COLLECTION VOL.1 & 2** [ ] [ ]

CRASH (see under ⇒ ULTRA VIVID SCENE)

CRASH TEST DUMMIES

Formed: Winnepeg, Canada . . . mid-late 80's by songwriter BRAD ROBERTS and his younger brother, DAN. Initially a barroom-playing outfit, BRAD took a back seat on the singing front, thinking his voice was unsuitable for the cover versions the band played in their performance repertoire. However, on the advice of his singing tutor, who told him he was a competant bass-baritone, BRAD took up the front role once again. In the early 90's, with the recruitment of a more settled line-up (i.e. ELLEN REID, MICHEL DORGE and BENJAMIN DARVILL), BRAD and the group signed to 'Arista'. Combining his work by day as a literature/philosophy student, BRAD developed into the complete wordsmith, his ability to compose strange storytelling now ready to be heard on record. Initially released in Canada only, the low-key, lo-fi album, 'THE GHOSTS THAT HAUNT ME' (boasting their US Hot 100 breakthrough single, 'SUPERMAN'S SONG'), finally cracked platinum sales and made inroads across the American border. The record impressed former TALKING HEADS man, JERRY HARRISON, who subsequently took over production on their follow-up set, 'GOD SHUFFLED HIS FEET' (1993/94). Full of wit and deep insight into offbeat life, the long-player soon took off, helped no doubt by "alternative rock" favourite and Top 5 single, 'MMM MMM MMM MMM' (their only classic – so far!). Had the group peaked too soon? It was clear that the answer was, well, MMMM, yes, when their third album, 'A WORM'S LIFE' (1996), failed to win over any new fanbase. • **Covered:** ALL YOU PRETTY GIRLS (Xtc).

Album rating: GOD SHUFFLED HIS FEET (*6)

BRAD ROBERTS – vocals, guitars / **ELLEN REID** – keyboards, accordion / **BENJAMIN DARVILL** – mandolin, harmonicas / **DAN ROBERTS** – bass / **MITCH DORGE** – drums, percussion

Arista / Arista

Sep 91. (c-s/cd-s) <12339> **SUPERMAN'S SONG / THE VOYAGE** [ ] [56]
Oct 91. (cd/c) *(261/411 521)* <*ARCD/AC 8677*> **THE GHOSTS THAT HAUNT ME** [ ] [ ]
– Winter song / Comin' back soon (the bereft man's song) / Superman's song / The country life / Here on Earth (I'll have my cake) / The ghosts that haunt me / Thick-necked man / Androgynous / The voyage / At my funeral. *(re-iss. Oct95 cd/c; 74321 20152-2/-4)*

R.C.A. / Arista

Jan 94. (c-s) <12654> **MMM MMM MMM MMM. / SUPERMAN'S SONG** [-] [4]
Apr 94. (7"/c-s/cd-s) *(74321 20151-7/-4/-2)* **MMM MMM MMM MMM. / HERE I STAND BEFORE ME (live)** [2] [-]
(cd-s+=) *(74321 20676-2)* – Superman's song (live).
May 94. (cd/c) *(74321 20152-2/-4)* <16531> **GOD SHUFFLED HIS FEET** [2] [9] Feb94
– God shuffled his feet / Afternoons & coffeespoons / Mmm mmm mmm mmm / In the days of the caveman / Swimming in your ocean / Here I stand before me / I think I'll disappear now / How does a duck know? / When I go out with artists / The psychic / Two knights and maidens / Untitled.
Jun 94. (7"/c-s) *(74321 21962-7/-4)* **AFTERNOONS & COFFEESPOONS. / IN THE DAYS OF THE CAVEMAN (live)** [23] [-]
(cd-s+=) *(74321 21962-2)* – The ghosts that haunt me / Androgynous (live).
(cd-s) *(74321 21963-2)* – ('A'side) / Mmm mmm mmm mmm (live) / God shuffled his feet (live).
Jun 94. (c-s) <12706> **AFTERNOONS & COFFEESPOONS / MMM MMM MMM (live)** [-] [66]
Oct 94. (7"/c-s/cd-s) *(74321 23808-7/-4/-2)* **GOD SHUFFLED HIS FEET. / AFTERNOONS & COFFEESPOONS (live)** [ ] [-]
(cd-s+=) *(74321 23809-2)* – Winter song / Mmm mmm mmm mmm.
—— below featured vocals by ELLEN REID
Apr 95. (c-s) *(74321 27676-4)* <64262> **THE BALLAD OF PETER PUMPKINHEAD / GOD SHUFFLED HIS FEET** [30] [ ] Jan95
(cd-s+=) *(74321 27676-2)* – Afternoons and coffeespoons (live) / Swimming in your ocean.
(cd-s) *(74321 27677-2)* – ('A'side) / Afternoons and coffeespoons (live) / When I go out with artists (live) / Swimming in your ocean (live).
Oct 96. (c-s) *(74321 40200-4)* **HE LIKED TO FEEL IT / ('A'mix)** [ ] [-]
(cd-s) *(74321 40200-2)* – ('A'side) / Afternoons and coffeespoons / Swimming in your ocean.
Oct 96. (cd/c) *(74321 40201-2/-4)* <39779> **A WORM'S LIFE** [ ] [78]

– Overachievers / He liked to feel it / A worm's life / Our driver gestures / My enemies / There are many dangers / I'm outlived by that thing / All of this ugly / An old scab / My own sunrise / I'm a dog / Swatting flies.

CRASS

Formed: North Weald, Essex, England . . . 1978 by commune dwellers STEVE IGNORANT and PENNY RIMBAUD. With a line-up completed by PHIL FREE, JOY DE VIVRE, N.A. PALMER, PETE WRIGHT and MICK G., the pseudonymous crew unleashed the first instalment of their anarchist manifesto in late '78 on indie label, 'Small Wonder'. 'THE FEEDING OF THE FIVE THOUSAND' EP introduced the raging punk blitzkreig of CRASS in full flow, an "Oi!-Guv" cockney vocal raging over military-style drumming and shouting down religion and "the system" in all its multifarious guises. Forming their own label (an operation which subsequently released material by a range of protest bands including POISON GIRLS, CONFLICT and RUDIMENTARY PENI) was the logical next step for such an avowedly anti-establishment operation and Autumn '79 saw the release of 'STATIONS OF THE CRASS', a (part-live) double album's worth of bile directed at all the usual subjects and some surprising ones (i.e. The CLASH in 'WHITE PUNKS ON HOPE'), even taking a pot shot at media outrage over Myra Hindley on 'MOTHER EARTH'. Two politically incendiary 45's appeared in the early 80's, the first, 'BLOODY REVOLUTIONS' was a shared affair with The POISON GIRLS, while the peerless epic, 'NAGASAKI NIGHTMARE', represented the pinnacle of punk outrage. The CRASS line-up fluctuated according to whoever was living with them at the time, the band's democratic approach seeing EVE and PENNY take on the vocal chores for feminist tract, 'PENIS ENVY' (1981). Not a band to do things by halves, CRASS released their second double set with 'CHRIST THE ALBUM' (1983), a record that saw them widen their musical horizons and intersperse songs with spoken word poetry. If the band were straying too far into neo-hippy territory for some fans comfort, there was no doubting the strength of feeling behind 'HOW DOES IT FEEL (TO BE THE MOTHER OF 1000 DEAD)?', directed squarely at Margaret Thatcher and taking her to task over the Falklands conflict. As the war raged, CRASS had tapes confiscated by the government and found themselves charged under The Obscene Publications Act. Not surprisingly, no records were ever given a release outside the UK! The album that had spawned such apparently dangerous fare ('SHEEP FARMING IN THE FALKLANDS' being another sarcastic classic) was 'YES SIR, I WILL' (1983), an even more experimental set that divided opinion. It also proved to be the band's swansong, and, staying true to their original vow of breaking up in early '84 (which was the meltdown year according to George Orwell) following a final single, 'YOU'RE ALREADY DEAD'. While EVE and PENNY worked together on a set of poetry, 'ACTS OF LOVE' (1986), IGNORANT subsequently joined fellow anarchists CONFLICT, for whom he'd previously deputised in the past.

Album rating: THE FEEDING OF THE FIVE THOUSAND (*8) / STATIONS OF THE CRASS (*6) / PENIS ENVY (*6) / CHRIST THE ALBUM (*5) / YES SIR, I WILL (*4) / BEST BEFORE 1984 compilation (*7)

EVE LIBERTINE – vocals / **JOY DE VIVRE** – vocals / **STEVE IGNORANT** – vocals / **PHIL FREE** – lead guitar / **N.A. PALMER** – guitar, vocals / **PENNY RIMBAUD** – drums / **PETE WRIGHT** – bass / **MICK G.** (DUFFIELD) – flute, film-maker /

Small Wonder | not iss.

Dec 78. (12"ep) *(WEENY 2)* **THE FEEDING OF THE FIVE THOUSAND** [ ] [-]
– Asylum / Do they owe us a living? / End result / They've got a bomb / Punk is dead / Reject of society / General Bacardi / Banned from The Roxy's / G's song / Fight war, not wars / Women / Sucks / You pay / Angels / What a shame / So what / Well? . . .do they. *(re-iss. Nov80 & Oct81 & Dec87 as 'FEEDING OF THE 5,000 EP (2nd SITTING)' on 'Crass'; 621984) (cd-iss. Oct90 +=; 621984CD)* – Reality asylum.

Crass | not iss.

May 79. (7") *(521984-1)* **REALITY ASYLUM. / SHAVED WOMAN** [ ] [-]
(re-iss. Dec80; CRASS 19454U)

Sep 79. (d-lp) *(CRASS 521984)* **STATIONS OF THE CRASS** [ ] [-]
– Mother Earth / White punks on hope / You've got big hands / Darling / System / Big man, big M.A.N. / Hurry up Garry / Fun going on / Crutch of society / Heard too much about / Chairman of the bored / Tired / Walls / Uptight citizen / Time out / The gasman cometh / Democrats / Contaminational power / I ain't thick it's just a trick. // live:- System / Big man, big M.A.N. / Banned from the Roxy / Hurry up Garry / Time out / They've got a bomb / Fight war, not wars / Women / Shaved women / You pay / Heard too much about / Angels / What a shame / So what / G's song / Do they owe us a living? / Punk is dead. *(re-iss. Oct81 & Dec87; same) (cd-iss. Oct90; 521984CD)*

May 80. (7") *(421984-1)* **BLOODY REVOLUTIONS. / Poison Girls: PERSONS UNKNOWN** [ ] [-]
(re-iss. Dec80 as above on 'Crass/Xntrix' joint label outing)

Feb 81. (7") *(421984-5)* **NAGASAKI NIGHTMARE. / BIG A LITTLE A** [ ] [-]

Oct 81. (lp) *(CRASS 321984-1)* **PENIS ENVY** [ ] [-]
– Bat a motel / Systematic death / Poison in a pretty pill / What the fuck / Where next Columbus / Berkertex bribe / Smother love / Health surface / Dry weather. *(re-iss. Dec87 lp/c; CRASS 321984-1/-4) (cd-iss. Oct90; 321984CD)*

Dec 81. (7") *(COLD TURKEY 1)* **MERRY CRASSMAS. / MERRY CRASSMAS – HAVE FUN** [ ] [-]

Aug 82. (7"promo+flexi) *(421984-6)* **RIVAL TRIBAL REBEL REVEL> / BULLY BOYS GO OUT FIGHTING** [-] [-]

Aug 82. (d-lp) *(BOLLOX 2U2)* **CHRIST THE ALBUM (some live)** [26] [-]
– Have a nice day / Mother love / Nineteen eighty bore / I know there is love / Beg your pardon / Birth control 'n' rock'n'roll / Reality white-wash / It's the greatest working class rip-off / Deadhead / You can be who / Buy no pay as you go / Rival tribal revel rebel part 2 / Bumhooler / Sentiment / Major General despair / Banned from the Roxy / The sound of one hand / Punk is dead / Nagasaki nightmare / Bat a motel blues / Berkertex bribe / Fold it in half / Big hands / Heart-throb of the mortuary / Bumhooler / Big A little A / First woman / Arlington 73 / Bomb plus bomb tape / Contaminational power / I ain't thick / G's song / Securicor / I can't stand it / Shaved women / A part of life / Do they owe us a living? / So what / Salt'n'pepper. *(cd-iss. Oct90; BOLLOX 2U2CD)*

Oct 82. (7") *(221984-6)* **HOW DOES IT FEEL (TO BE THE MOTHER OF 1000 DEAD?). / THE IMMORTAL DEATH / DON'T TELL ME YOU CARE** [ ] [-]

May 83. (lp) *(121984-2)* **YES SIR, I WILL** [ ] [-]
– Yes sir, I will / The pig's head controversy – the aesthetics of anarchy. *(cd-iss. Oct90; 121984-2CD)*

May 83. (7") *(121984-3)* **SHEEP FARMING IN THE FALKLANDS. / GOTCHA! (live)** [ ] [-]
(free-7"brown+=) *(121984-4)* **WHO DUNNIT? / WHO DUNNIT (part 2)**

Jan 84. (7") *(CATNO 4)* **YOU'RE ALREADY DEAD. / DON'T GET CAUGHT / NAGASAKI IS YESTERDAY'S DOG END** [ ] [-]

— broke up 1984. STEVE joined CONFLICT

— note: all albums were issued by CRASS in the States around mid-90's

– compilations, others, etc. –

Jul 86. (d-lp) *Crass; (CATNO 5)* **BEST BEFORE 1984** [ ] [-]
– Intro / Do they owe us a living? / Major general despair / Angela Rippon / Reality asylum / Shaved women / Bloody revolutions / Nagasaki nightmare / Big a little a / Rival tribal rebel revel – Sheep farming in the Falklands (Flexidisc version) / How does it feel / The immortal death / Don't tell me that you care / Sheep farming in the Falklands / Gotcha / Nagasaki is yesterdays dogend / Don't get caught / Smash the mac / Do they owe us a living? (live) *(cd-iss. Oct90; CRASS 5CD)*

Nov 86. (12") *Crass; (CATNO 6)* **TEN NOTES ON A SUMMER'S DAY. / (instrumental mix)** [ ] [-]
(re-iss. Aug98, 12"/cd-s; CATNO 6/+CD)

Dec 93. (cd) *Pomona; (ONA 002CD)* **YOU'LL RUIN IT FOR EVERYONE (live '81)** [ ] [-]

– others, solo, etc. –

on 'Crass; unless mentioned otherwise

May 81. (7"white-flexi; by JOY DE VIVRE) *(CRASS ENVY 1)* **OUR WEDDING** [ ] [-]

Jun 85. (lp; by EVE LIBERTINE) *(1984-4)* **ACT OF LOVE** [ ] [-]
– (short poems written 1968-73 by Joy's deceased friend, WALLY HOPE) *(re-iss. Oct95; same)*

Jul 92. (cd/lp; by PENNY RIMBAUD) **CHRIST'S REALITY ASYLUM** (spoken word) [ ] [-]

Nov 92. (cd; by EVE LIBERTINE) *Red Herring; (RH 2CD)* **SKATING** [ ] [-]

CRAVATS (see under ⇒ VERY THINGS)

CRAWLING CHAOS

Formed: Rotherham, England . . . 1979 by drummer EDDIE FENN and a handful of mystery sidemen. One of the many acts to sign for Tony Wilson's stable of diverse alt/indie acts, 'Factory', CRAWLING CHAOS delivered their debut single, 'SEX MACHINE' (no, nothing to do with the JAMES BROWN classic!), a noisy non-formulaic affair that unsurprisingly went nowhere. Switching to the Belgian ('Benelux') arm of the label, the group released their debut set, 'THE GAS CHAIR' (1981), a very disappointing collection of FAUST-inspired punk chants, screeching organs and sex-obsessed lyrics; the porny cartoon sleevework probably didn't help its sales. FENN took off to join MARC RILEY & THE CREEPERS (and TOOLS YOU CAN TRUST) and subsequently became a producer of obscure acts like WATERFOOT DANDY and IMPLIES CONSENT. Meanwhile, CRAWLING CHAOS returned on their own 'Foetus' label in the mid-80's with two contrasting sets, 'C' (anti-Commercial in the extreme) and 'WAQQAZ', a surprisingly bright and intelligent avant-garde collection of part instrumentals. Tracks like 'TROUTY HOBIN' – although having a dangerously similar intro to The SPECIALS' 'International Jet Set' – and 'COMRADE DOLPHIN' were stand-out pieces.

Album rating: THE GAS CHAIR (*3) / 'C' (*2) / WAQQAZ (*5)

EDDIE FENN – drums, guitar / with

Factory | not iss.

Jun 80. (7") *(FAC 17)* **SEX MACHINE. / BERLIN** [ ] [-]

Factory Benelux | not iss.

1981. (lp) *(FACBN 6)* **THE GAS CHAIR** [-] [-] Belgian
– Macabre royale / Creamo coyl / Left hand path / Guinness / Arabesque / Harry / Disierta membra / Canadian Pacific / Breaking down.

— FENN joined TOOLS YOU CAN TRUST and MARC RILEY (was he still a member?)

Foetus | not iss.

Mar 84. (lp) *(FOETUS 3)* **'C'** [ ] [-]

Waqqaz | not iss.

Apr 85. (lp) *(WAQQAZ 001)* **WAQQAZ** [ ] [-]
– Remocarpet / The white Sybil / Yoni Suchon / Comrade dolphin / Trouty Hobin / Oh blast / Reg vase / Net Wilf / Bosumptasi.

— split from the music scene after above

CRAZYHEAD

Formed: Leicester, England . . . 1986 by (IAN) ANDERSON, KEV REVERB, FAST DICK, PORK BEAST and ex-DOCTOR & THE MEDICS drummer, VOM. Lumped in with the media created "Grebo" scene along with POP WILL EAT ITSELF, GAYE BYKERS ON ACID and the early WONDER STUFF,

CRAZYHEAD signed to EMI offshoot, 'Food', debuting the following year with the 12"er, 'WHAT GIVES YOU THE IDEA YOU'RE SO AMAZING BABY?'. Over the course of the next year or so, the grimy 5-piece released a string of singles, the last of which, 'RAGS', accompanied the 'DESERT ORCHID' album in Autumn '88. Moving upstairs to 'Parlophone', CRAZYHEAD scored their second minor hit single, 'HAVE LOVE, WILL TRAVEL', having previously entered the charts with 'TIME HAS TAKEN ITS TOLL ON YOU'. In March 1990, having played Romania, CRAZYHEAD were the only Western outfit to appear at Namibia's Independence Festival in front of 50,000 people. After failing to cross over into the alternative mainstream, the group were consigned to 'Revolver' where they released their PAT COLLIER-produced follow-up set, 'SOME KIND OF FEVER' (1990).

Album rating: DESERT ORCHID (*6) / SOME KIND OF FEVER (*4) / LIVE IN MEMPHIS (*3)

(IAN) ANDERSON – vocals / **KEV REVERB** (b. KEVIN BAYLISS) – guitar, piano, sitar / **FAST DICK** (b. RICHARD BELL) – guitar / **PORK BEAST** (b. ALEX PEACH) – bass / **VOM** (b. ROB MORRIS) – drums, percussion (ex-DOCTOR & THE MEDICS)

Food | EMI America

Mar 87. (12"ep) *(SNAK 8)* **WHAT GIVES YOU THE IDEA YOU'RE SO AMAZING BABY? / OUT ON A LIMB / SNAKE EYES** [ ] [-]

Jul 87. (7") *(FOOD 10)* **BABY TURPENTINE. / THAT KIND OF LOVE** [ ] [-]
(12"+=) *(SNAK 10)* – Bang bang / That sinking feeling.

Jun 88. (7") *(FOOD 12)* **TIME HAS TAKEN ITS TOLL ON YOU. / DOWN** [65] [-]
(ext-12"+=) *(12FOOD 12)* – The ballad of Baby Turpentine.
(10"+=) *(10FOOD 12)* – Here comes Johnny.
(cd-s+=) *(CDFOOD 12)* – Bang bang.

Sep 88. (7") *(FOOD 14)* **RAGS. / RUB THE BUDDHA** [ ] [-]
(12"+=) *(12FOOD 14)* – Screaming apple.
(12"++=/cd-s++=) *(12FOODS/CDFOOD 14)* – Fortune teller.

Oct 88. (lp/c/cd) *(FOOD LP/TC/CD 1)* *<E1/E4 91035>* **DESERT ORCHID** [ ] [ ]
– In the sun / Jack the scissorman / Time has taken its toll on you / Have love, will travel / What gives you the idea you're so amazing baby? / I don't want that kind of love / Dragon city / Buy a gun / Rags / Tower of fire / Cardinal Phink. *(c+=)* – Bang bang. *(cd++=)* – Out on a limb / Down / Time has taken its toll on you (extended). *(cd re-iss. Mar89 on 'Parlophone'; CDP 791035-2)*

Parlophone | not iss.

Feb 89. (7"ep/12"ep) *(SGE/12SGE 2025)* **HAVE LOVE, WILL TRAVEL EP** [68] [-]
– Have love will travel / Out on a limb (live) / Baby Turpentine (live) / Snake eyes (live).
(cd-ep++=) *(CDSGE 2025)* – Here comes Johnny (live).

— In Dec'89, CRAZYHEAD also covered Diesel Park West's 'LIKE PRINCES DO' on the Various Artists 'THE FOOD CHRISTMAS EP', which hit No.63.

Revolver | not iss.

Aug 90. (7") **EVERYTHING'S ALRIGHT. /** [ ] [-]

Nov 90. (cd/c/lp) *(REV XD/MC/LP 162)* **SOME KIND OF FEVER** [ ] [-]
– Big sister / Above these things / Everything's alright / Magic eye / I can do anything / Movie theme / Talk about you / Rome / Night train / Some kinda fever.

— disbanded for the rest of the 90's

– compilations, etc. –

Jan 89. (12"ep/cd-ep) *Strange Fruit; (SFNT/+CD 018)* **NIGHT TRACKS** [ ] [-]

Sep 95. (cd) *Pearls From The Past; <BOE 3>* **GRIND (live in Memphis)** [-] [ ]

CREATURES (see under ⇒ SIOUXSIE & THE BANSHEES)

CREEPER LAGOON

Formed: San Francisco, California, USA . . . 1997 by a multi-instrumentalist going under the unlikely name of SHARKY LAGUANA. After virtually giving up looking for work all over the States, the singer/guitarist turned busker spent some months fasting in a Santa Cruz monastery. He thought his luck had changed when an eccentric Bostonian person wanted to become his manager. However, this was curtailed when his condo was burnt to the ground by fire-raising squatters below him; he was subsequently awarded a surprise 5-figure sum due to landlord negligence – no fire alarm! Enjoying his newfound wealth while also buying up recording equipment, SHARKY made friends with his new lodger/squatter, IAN SELCHICK, and together they formed CREEPER LAGOON. Recruiting the rhythm section of GEOFFREY CHISHOLM and DAVID KOSTINER, they gained support from production giants, The DUST BROTHERS, the pair helping create their well-received debut set (musically akin to a more upbeat PAVEMENT), 'I BECOME SMALL AND GO' (1998).

Album rating: I BECOME SMALL AND GO (*7)

SHARKY LAGUANA – vocals, guitar / **IAN SELCHICK** – guitar / **GEOFFREY CHISHOLM** – bass / **DAVID KOSTINER** – drums

not iss. | Dogday

Dec 97. (m-cd) *<3500>* **CREEPER LAGOON** [-] [ ]
– Dear deadly / Sylvia / Drop your head / Empty ships / Second chance. *(UK-iss.Oct98 on 'Shifty Disco'; DISCO 9809)*

Polydor | Nicklebag

Nov 98. (cd) *(559323-2)* *<6>* **I BECOME SMALL AND GO** [ ] [ ] May98
– Wonderful love / Tracy / Empty ships / Dreaming again / Prison mix / Sylvia / Dear deadly / Black hole / Drink and drive / Second chance / He made us all blind.

CREEPERS (see under ⇒ RILEY, Marc)

Marshall CRENSHAW

Born: 11 Nov'53, Detroit, Michigan, USA. After cutting his teeth in a number of local bands, CRENSHAW took a rather unusual route into the music industry by starring in the Broadway Fab Four tribute, 'Beatlemania'. Subsequently securing a contract with 'Warners', the singer/songwriter released an eponmyous debut album in 1982, delighting Stateside critics with his 50's/60's-derived rock'n'roll power-pop. Moulded in the tradition of BUDDY HOLLY, BOBBY FULLER and The BEATLES, this lovingly crafted collection of hook-laden three minute mini-classics made the US Top 50 but surprisingly spawned only one Top 40 hit single, 'SOMEDAY, SOMEWAY' (the B-side, 'MY FAVOURITE WASTE OF TIME', was later a one hit wonder for mid-80's hearthrob, OWEN PAUL!). Undeterred, the man enlisted English alternative guru, Steve Lilywhite, to produce follow-up set, 'FIELD DAY' (1983), a less immediate album that obscured CRENSHAW's naturally ebullient sound but did showcase his fast developing songwriting talent on preview single, 'WHENEVER YOU'RE ON MY MIND'. 1985's T-BONE BURNETT-produced 'DOWNTOWN', by comparison, was a more straightforward set driven by the single, 'WILD ONE (NO.5)'. Yet CRENSHAW remained a cult attraction and despite acting roles in 'Peggy Sue Got Married' and 'La Bamba', subsequent albums, 'MARY JEAN AND 9 OTHERS' (1987) and 'GOOD EVENING' (1989) didn't exactly raise his profile. An inevitable split with 'Warners' at the turn of the decade led him to record a solitary album for 'M.C.A.', 'LIFE'S TOO SHORT' (1991) before signing to US re-issue specialist, 'Razor & Tie' ('Grapevine' in the UK) for a live set, 'MY TRUCK IS MY HOME' (1994). A tireless jack-of-all-trades, CRENSHAW had also been involved in writing a movie encyclopedia as well as contributing to various tribute albums. His first studio album in five years, the eagerly anticipated 'MIRACLE OF SILENCE' was released in 1996.

Album rating: MARSHALL CRENSHAW (*8) / FIELD DAY (*7) / DOWNTOWN (*7) / MARY JEAN & 9 OTHERS (*5) / GOOD EVENING (*5) / LIFE'S TOO SHORT (*6) / LIVE: MY TRUCK IS MY HOME live collection (*5) / MIRACLE OF SILENCE (*5)

MARSHALL CRENSHAW – vocals, guitar / **CHRIS DONATO** – bass, vocals / **ROBERT CRENSHAW** – drums, vocals

Warners | Warners

Jun 82. (lp/c) *(K 57010)* *<3673>* **MARSHALL CRENSHAW** [ ] [50] May82
– There she goes again / Someday, someway / Girls . . . / I'll do anything / Rockin' around in N.Y.C. / The usual thing / She can't dance / Cynical girl / Mary Anne / Soldier of love / Not for me / Brand new lover. *(cd-iss. Jan93; 7599 23673-2)*

Jun 82. (7") *<29974>* **SOMEDAY, SOMEWAY. / YOU'RE MY FAVOURITE WASTE OF TIME** [-] [36]

Jul 82. (7") *(K 17971)* **CYNICAL GIRL. / RAVE ON – SOMEBODY LIKE YOU** [ ] [ ]

Sep 82. (7") *(K 17995)* **SOMEDAY, SOMEWAY. / THE USUAL THING** [ ] [ ]

Jun 83. (7") *(W 9630)* **WHENEVER YOU'RE ON MY MIND. / JUNGLE ROCK** [ ] [ ]
(12"+=) *(W 9630T)* – Somebody like you.

Jul 83. (lp/c) *(923873-1/-4)* *<23873>* **FIELD DAY** [ ] [52] Jun83
– Whenever you're on my mind / Our town / One more reason / Try / One day with you / For her love / Monday morning rock / All I know right now / What time is it? / Hold it.

Mar 84. (12"ep) *(W 0187T)* **OUR TOWN / FOR HER LOVE. / LITTLE SISTER / MONDAY MORNING ROCK** [ ] [ ]

Nov 85. (lp/c) *(925319-1/-4)* *<25319>* **DOWNTOWN** [ ] [ ] Oct85
– Little wild one (No.5) / Yvonne / Blues is king / Terrifying love / Like a vague memory / Distance between / (We're gonna) Shake up their minds / I'm sorry (but so is Brenda Lee) / Lesson number one.

Nov 85. (7") **LITTLE WILD ONE (NO.5). / LIKE A VAGUE MEMORY** [ ] [ ]

Feb 86. (7") *(W 8786)* **DISTANCE BETWEEN. / SOMEDAY, SOMEWAY** [ ] [ ]
(12"+=) *(W 8786T)* – There she goes again / Little wild one (No.5).

Jun 87. (lp/c) *(925583-1/-4)* *<25583>* **MARY JEAN AND 9 OTHERS** [ ] [ ]
– This is easy / A hundred others / Calling out for love (at crying time) / Wild abandon / This street / Somebody crying / Mary Jean / Steel strings / Till that moment / They never will know.

— now with various people KENNY ARONOFF, GRAHAM MABY, DAVID LINDLEY, etc

Jul 89. (lp/c/cd) *(K 925908-1/-4/-2)* *<25908>* **GOOD EVENING (live)** [ ] [ ]
– You should've been there / Valerie / She hates to go home / Someplace where love can't find me / Radio girl / On the run / Live it up / Some hearts / Whatever way the wind blows / Let her dance.

Jul 89. (7") **WHATEVER THE WIND BLOWS. /** [ ] [ ]

— with other session people incl. ARONOFF

M.C.A. | M.C.A.

May 91. (lp/c/cd) *(MCA/+C/D 10223)* **LIFE'S TOO SHORT** [ ] [ ]
– Better back off / Don't disappear now / Fantastic planet of love / Delilah / Face of fashion / Stop doing that / Walkin' around / Starting tomorrow / Everything's the truth / Somewhere down the line.

Grapevine | Razor & Tie

Sep 94. (cd) **LIVE: MY TRUCK IS MY HOME (live 1982-1994)** [-] [ ]

Jun 97. (cd) *(GRACD 231)* **MIRACLE OF SILENCE** [ ] [ ] Jul96

– others, etc. –

May 83. (7"/12") *Albion; (ION/12ION 1029)* **SOMETHING'S GONNA HAPPEN. / SHE CAN'T DANCE** [ ] [-]

CRIME

Formed: San Francisco, California, USA . . . 1976 . . . by FRANKIE FIX, JOHNNY STRIKE, RON THE RIPPER GRECO and RICKY JAMES. Possibly holding the crown of being the first US punk act to release a single, the self-financed double A-side, 'HOT WIRE MY HEART' and 'BABY YOU'RE SO REPULSIVE', appeared as CRIME's debut at the tail end of '76. By the following year's 'MURDER BY GUITAR', The STOOGES influenced crew were minus RICKY who joined FLIPPER and was superseded by BRITTLEY BLACK. He in turn was replaced by the brilliantly named HANK RANK, who stayed around between early '78 and mid '79, studio takes subsequently released as a bootleg, 'SAN FRANCISCO'S DOOMED'. Featuring two raw sessions (the first of which was produced by Elliott Mazer, who'd previously worked on Neil Young's 'Harvest'!), the album included such choice cuts as 'PISS ON YOUR DOG' (not advice that Great British dog trainer, Mrs. Woodhouse would have given readily!). After a brief stint with The FLAMIN' GROOVIES, BLACK was back on the drum stool for one last 7" effort in 1980, 'MASERATI'.

Album rating: SAN FRANCISCO'S DOOMED posthumous bootleg (*4)

JOHNNY STRIKE – vocals, guitar / **FRANKIE FIX** – guitar / **RON THE RIPPER GRECO** – bass (ex-CHOSEN FEW, aka FLAMIN' GROOVIES) / **RICKY JAMES** – drums

not iss. Crime

Dec 76. (7") **HOT WIRE MY HEART. / BABY YOU'RE SO REPULSIVE** [-] [ ]

— **BRITTLEY BLACK** – drums; repl. RICKY who joined FLIPPER

Dec 77. (7") **MURDER BY GUITAR. / FRUSTRATION** [-] [ ]

— **HANK RANK** – drums; repl. BLACK who briefly joined FLAMIN' GROOVIES before moving to DEATH (he rejoined for below)

not iss. B Square

1980. (7") **MASERATI. / GANGSTER FUNK** [-] [ ]

— split in 1980, STRIKE formed REV, while RANK formed OTHER MUSIC. A bootleg, 'SAN FRANCISCO'S DOOMED' appeared in 1983 on US 'Solar Lodge'.

– compilations, etc. –

Feb 94. (cd) *Overground; (OVER 33CD)* **SAN FRANCISCO'S DOOMED** [ ] [-]

CRIME & THE CITY SOLUTION

Formed: Melbourne . . . 1978 by Australian vocalist, SIMON BONNEY, although it wouldn't be until 1984 and the demise of The BIRTHDAY PARTY that the band would arrive fully formed with the latter act's remnants, MICK HARVEY and ROWLAND S. HOWARD, making up the numbers alongside ROWLAND's brother HARRY and BONNEY's wife and future songwriting partner, BRONWYN ADAMS. After a debut EP for 'Mute', 'THE DANGLING MAN', ex-SWELL MAPS drummer, EPIC SOUNDTRACKS was drafted in to complete a mini-album's worth of material, 'JUST SOUTH OF HEAVEN' (1985). Conjuring up an ambitious cinematic sound rooted in voodoo blues, the group's material was often compared to the atmospheric soundtrack mastery of ENNIO MORRICONE, BONNEY's brooding whiskey-throated vocals similar to JIM MORRISON or DAVID McCOMB. This unique chemistry was showcased on 1986's first full album, 'ROOM OF LIGHTS', an acclaimed set which featured 'SIX BELLS CHIME'; the track was subsequently performed by the band in Wim Wenders' cult film, 'Wings Of Desire', while they also contributed a track, 'THE ADVERSARY' to the filmaker's 'Until The End Of The World'. By the time of its premiere, ROWLAND, HARRY and EPIC had struck out on their own to form THESE IMMORTAL SOULS, leaving behind SIMON, BRONWYN and MICK (the latter also moonlighted with NICK CAVE & THE BAD SEEDS) to rebuild the group in Berlin with the help of new members, ALEXANDER HACKE (ex-EINSTURZENDE NEUBAUTEN), CHRISLO HASS (ex-DAF) and PHIL CALVERT (ex-PSYCHEDELIC FURS). This line-up worked on the underrated classic, 'SHINE' (1988), a moody masterpiece highlighting BRONWYN's violin and replacing the blues feel with a more abstract folky sound. 'THE BRIDE SHIP' (1989) meanwhile, saw THOMAS STERN come in for CALVERT, a record based around the theme of emigration that included a revamped version of 'THE DANGLING MAN'. The band's studio swansong set, 'PARADISE DISCOTHEQUE' (1990), was also a pseudo concept affair, with a song cycle based on the collapse of the Nicolae Ceaucescu dynasty in Romania. While HARVEY joined The BAD SEEDS full-time, SIMON developed a rootsier country feel for his debut solo album, 'FOREVER', a record that also featured his wife and an array of session people including J.D. FOSTER. A further four years went by before the release of a follow-up set, 'EVERYMAN' (1996); influenced by his permanent move to the States and evoking that nation's wide open spaces, the record moved even further into classic country.

Album rating: JUST SOUTH OF HEAVEN (*6) / ROOM OF LIGHTS (*8) / SHINE (*8) / THE BRIDE SHIP (*6) / PARADISE DISCOTHEQUE (*5) / THE ADVERSARY – LIVE (*5) / Simon Bonney: FOREVER (*6) / EVERYMAN (*5)

SIMON BONNEY (b. Tasmania, Australasia) – vocals, guitar / **ROWLAND S. HOWARD** – guitar, keyboards (ex-BIRTHDAY PARTY) / **HARRY HOWARD** – bass / **MICK HARVEY** – keyboards, guitar, percussion (ex-BIRTHDAY PARTY) / **BRONWYN ADAMS** – violin

Mute Mute

Jun 85. (12"ep) *(12MUTE 36)* **THE DANGLING MAN** [ ] [-]

— added **EPIC SOUNDTRACKS** – drums (ex-SWELL MAPS)

Sep 85. (m-lp) *(STUMM 22) <71248>* **JUST SOUTH OF HEAVEN** [ ] [ ]

May 86. (12"ep) *(12STUMM 46)* **THE KENTUCKY CLICK / ADVENTURE. / IT TAKES TWO TO BURN** [ ] [-]

Oct 86. (lp) *(STUMM 36) <71329>* **ROOM OF LIGHTS** [ ] [ ]
– Right man wrong man / No money no honey / Hey sin killer / Six bells chime / Adventure / Untouchable / The brother song / Her room of lights. *(cd-iss. 1988+=; CDSTUMM 36)* – Rose blue / The coal train / Five stone walls / The wailing wall / Trouble come this morning / The dangling man.

— split temporary when ROWLAND, HARRY + EPIC formed THESE IMMORTAL SOULS

— **SIMON, BRONWYN + MICK** re-united with **ALEXANDER HACKE** – guitar (ex-EINSTURZENDE NEUBAUTEN) / **CHRISLO HAAS** – synthesizers (ex-DEUTSCH AMERIKANISCHE FREUNDSCHAFT) / **PHIL CALVERT** – drums (ex-BIRTHDAY PARTY, ex-PSYCHEDELIC FURS)

Apr 88. (12") *(12MUTE 76)* **ON EVERY TRAIN (GRAIN WILL BEAR GRAIN). / ALL MUST BE LOVE** [ ] [-]

Apr 88. (cd/lp) *(CD+/STUMM 59) <71402>* **SHINE** [ ] [ ]
– All must be love / Fray so slow / Angel / On every train (grain will bear grain) / Hunter / Steal to the sea / Home is far from here. *(cd+=)* – On every train (extended) / All must be love (early version).

— **THOMAS STERN** – drums repl. CALVERT

Mar 89. (12"/cd-s) *(12/CD MUTE 94)* **THE SHADOW OF NO MAN. /** [ ] [-]

Apr 89. (cd/c/lp) *(CD/C+/STUMM 65) <71422>* **THE BRIDE SHIP** [ ] [ ]
– The shadow of no man / The greater head / Stone / The dangling man / Keepsake / The bride ship / Free world / New world / Three-Four / The bride ship.

Mute Mute-Elektra

Aug 90. (12") **I HAVE A GUN. / MOTHERLESS CHILD** [ ] [-]

Sep 90. (cd/c/lp) *(CD/C+/STUMM 78) <60990-2>* **PARADISE DISCOTHEQUE** [ ] [ ]
– I have the gun / The sky persuaders / The dolphins and the sharks / The Sun before the darkness / Motherless child / The last dictator I-IV.

Feb 91. (10"ep/cd-ep) *(10/CD MUTE 127)* **THE DOLPHINS AND THE SHARKS (instrumental) / THE SUN BEFORE THE DARKNESS. / ON EVERY TRAIN / THE BRIDE SHIP** [ ] [-]

Oct 93. (cd) *(CDSTUMM 110)* **ADVERSARY LIVE (live)** [ ] [-]

SIMON BONNEY

— with **BRONWYN** – violin, backing vox / **J.D. FOSTER** – guitars, mandolin / **JON-DEE GRAHAM** – steel guitar / **REINHOLD REIL** – keyboards / **GREGORY BOAZ** – bass / **HANS BEHRENDT** – percussion / **ARCHIE FRANCIS** – drums / **BIFF BAREFOOT SANDERS** – drums / **SALLY NORVELL, JAYNE KLIMEK, NIKKO WEIDEMANN + CARLA BOZULICH** – b.vocals

Mute Mute-Elektra

May 92. (12"/cd-s) *(12/CD MUTE 141)* **THERE CAN ONLY BE ONE. / ('A'mixes) / THE SUN DON'T SHINE** [ ] [-]

Jun 92. (cd/lp) *(CD+/STUMM 99) <61328>* **FOREVER** [ ] [ ]
– Ravenswood / Forever / A part of you / Like Caesar needs a Brutus / Saw you falling / Someone loves you / There can only be one / Now that she's gone / The sun don't shine / Ravenswood (reprise).

— next also with **J.D. FOSTER**

May 96. (cd-ep) *(CDMUTE 167)* **DON'T WALK AWAY FROM LOVE / ALL GOD'S CHILDREN / FOREVER / EVERYMAN** [ ] [-]

May 96. (cd) *(CDSTUMM 114) <60114>* **EVERYMAN** [ ] [ ]

CRISIS (see under ⇒ DEATH IN JUNE)

CRISPY AMBULANCE

Formed: Manchester, England . . . 1978 by ALAN HEMPSALL, ROBERT DAVENPORT, KEITH DARBYSHIRE and GARY MADELEY. Bass-heavy miserabilists in the classic Mancunian mould, CRISPY AMBULANCE released their debut single, 'FROM THE CRADLE TO THE GRAVE' on their own 'Aural Assault' label in 1980. A chugging dirge with HEMPSALL sounding as if he was singing from the bottom of a particularly deep well (after a particularly heavy dose of mogodon), the track established the group as one of Manchester's most promising acts alongside kindred spirits, JOY DIVISION (HEMPSALL even stood in for doomed frontman, IAN CURTIS, after he'd suffered an epileptic fit). One fan was JOY DIVISION manager, Rob Gretton, who secured the band a contract with 'Factory'. The first release to appear on the label proper was the 10" single, 'UNSIGHTLY AND SERENE', a similarly experimental effort with HEMPSALL adopting a more throaty punk-style growl alongside his trademark doom mongering. Previous to this the 'LIVE ON A HOT AUGUST NIGHT' 12" (featuring the classic 'THE PRESENCE') appeared on Belgium's 'Factory Benelux', a (relatively!) more accessible offering and a primer for the band's one and only album, 'THE PLATEAU PHASE' (1982). With the addition of understated keyboard and the use of even more repetitive rhythms, the effect was akin to a kind of goth psychedelia that bizarrely enough recalled HAWKWIND at their jamming best. With CRISPY AMBULANCE finally crashing soon after the album's release, however, the band were destined for obscure cultdom. They did subsequently reform as RAM RAM KINO, releasing a solitary single on arch weirdo GENESIS P.ORRIDGE's 'Temple' imprint in the mid-80's. Very underrated at the time, CRISPY AMBULANCE have since attained cult status, although some at the NME made them out to be one of worst 'Factory' groups ever!- listen again lads, eh! • **Songwriters:** Group compositions except UNITED (Throbbing Gristle).

Album rating: THE PLATEAU PHASE (*9) / LIVE ON A HOT AUGUST NIGHT 12" (*9) / FIN (*6)

ALAN HEMPSALL – vocals, synthesizer / **ROBERT DAVENPORT** – guitar / **KEITH DARBYSHIRE** – bass, synthesizer / **GARY MADELEY** – drums

Aural Assault / not iss.

Mar 80. (7") *(AAR 001)* **FROM THE CRADLE TO THE GRAVE. / FOUR MINUTES FROM THE FRONT LINE**

Factory Benelux / not iss.

Mar 81. (12"ep) *(facbn 4)* **LIVE ON A HOT AUGUST NIGHT (live)**
– The presence / Concorde square.

Jun 81. (10") *Factory; (fac 32)* **UNSIGHTLY AND SERENE**
– Deaf / Not what I expected.

Feb 82. (lp) *(facbn 12)* **THE PLATEAU PHASE**
– Are you ready? / Travel time / The force and the wisdom / The wind season / Death from above / We move through the plateau phase / Chill / Bardo plane / Federation / Simon's ghost. *(cd-iss. Jun90;)*

Mar 84. (12") *(fbn 18)* **SEXUS. / BLACK DETAIL-LIFE IS KNIFE**

— Split after above, although they soon evolved into RAM RAM KINO

- compilations etc. -

Nov 83. (ltd-c) *C.A. Tapes; (CSBT 5-2)* **BLUE AND YELLOW (OF THE YACHT CLUB)** (rare, sessions & live)
– Motorway boys / Suzie's in fragments / This perfect day / No surrender / (interview #1) / Opening theme / The presence / A sense of reason / Concorde Square / The Eastern Bloc / 3 minutes from the frontline / From the cradle to the grave / (interview #2) / Deaf / New violence / Come on / October 31st / Egypt / (interview #3) / Rain without clouds / The presence / Feedback pease / Drug user, drug pusher.

Nov 83. (ltd-c) *C.A. Tapes; (CSBT 5-3)* **OPEN, GATES OF FIRE** (live late '81 – mid '82)
– United / Chill / I talking – you talking / Federation / Travel time / Say shake (hip wind up) / Cult / Green light – white shirt (Deaf) / Brutal / The plateau phase / Choral / Nightfall ends the ceasefire / The poison.

Aug 85. (lp) *Les Tempes Modernes; (LTMV:X)* **FIN (live)**
– Rain forest / United / Choral / Green light – white shirt (aka Deaf) / Brutal / The plateau phase / Nightfall ends the ceasefire / Bardo plane / At the sounding of the Klaxon / Chill. *(cd-iss. 1989 +=; LTMCD 2302)* – Lucifer rising / Black death / From the cradle to the grave / Four minutes from the frontline.

RAM RAM KINO

reformed original CRISPYS with added members

Temple / not iss.

Dec 85. (12"ep) *(TOPY 006)* **ADVANTAGE – TANTRIC ROUTINES 1-4 / (Basket mix) / (Into The Bush mix) / (Special mix) / (other mix)**

CROCKETTS

Formed: Aberystwyth, Wales ... early 1996 by local college teenagers, OWEN CASH, Irish-born DAVEY MacMANUS, DAN BOONE and RICH TURPIN. A mischievous Celtic-punk outfit lying somewhere between RAMONES or The CLASH, The CROCKETTS unleashed their own self-financed mini-set, 'FROG ON A STICK' (1997), before they were snapped up by Virgin V2 offshoot, 'Blue Dog', after being spotted at Dublin's In The City festival. First up for label was the EP, 'HELLO AND GOOD MORNING'; released in September '97, it was pure unadulterated punk-pop that even The SULTANS OF PING would have been proud of. A series of singles preceded their debut album, 'WE MAY BE SKINNY & WIREY' (1998), an appropriate title as the lads had about as much meat on them as a vegetarian barbeque. • **Covered:** RHINESTONE COWBOY (Glen Campbell).

Album rating: WE MAY BE SKINNY & WIREY (*7)

DAVEY MacMANUS – vocals, guitar / **DAN BOONE** – guitar / **RICH TURPIN** – bass / **OWEN CASH** – drums

Crocketts / not iss.

1997. (m-lp) **FROG ON A STICK**

Blue Dog – V2 / Imprint

Sep 97. (10"ep/cd-ep) *(BDG 500035-8/-3)* **HELLO AND GOOD MORNING EP**
– Will you still care / Cars and footballs / etc.

Mar 98. (7"/cd-s) *(BDG 500156-7/-3)* **LOVED YA ONCE. /**

May 98. (7"/cd-s) *(BDG 500159-7/-3)* **FLOWER GIRL. /**

Sep 98. (cd/lp) *(BDG 100241-2/-1)* <120290> **WE MAY BE SKINNY & WIREY** Nov98

Oct 98. (7"blue/cd-s) *(BDG 500252-7/-3)* **EXPLAIN. / RHINESTONE COWBOY / INSIDE HEAD ON**

CROWD

Formed: Huntington Beach, California, USA . . . late 70's by JIM 'TRASH' DECKER, his brother JAY DECKER, JAMES KAA and BARRY CUDA. Untypical of the harsher hardcore scene around them, The CROWD decked themselves out in bright coloured beach attire, their noisy surf punk-pop never really being taken seriously outside their Californian locality. The only product to emerge during their brief lifespan was a solitary 1980 album, 'A WORLD APART', although following their demise a few members became SEXTET.

Album rating: A WORLD APART (*4)

JIM 'TRASH' DECKER – vocals / **JAMES KAA** – guitar / **TRACY** – guitar / **JAY DECKER** – bass / **BARRY CUDA** – drums

— the tracks, 'SUZY IS A SURF ROCKER', 'LIVING IN MADRID', 'TRIX ARE FOR KIDS', 'MODERN MACHINE' and 'NEW CREW' all featured on 'Posh Boy' various artists album, 'Beach Blvd.' <PBS 102> in 1979.

— added **TRACY** – guitar

— the track, 'RIGHT TIME', appeared on 'Posh Boy' various artists collection, 'Rodney On The Rock' <PBS 106> in 1980

— **DENNIS WALSH** – drums, percussion (ex-FLYBOYS) repl. BARRY + TRACY

not iss. / Posh Boy

Jan 81. (lp/c) <PBS/PBC 108> **A WORLD APART**
– As you were / Can't talk / Desmond and Kathy / He / Melody hill / On my own / Pleasure seeker / Right time / Something said / What's in a name.

— split some time in '81, some joining SEXTET

CROWSDELL

Formed: Jacksonville, Florida, USA ... 1990 by bassist, PAUL CROWSDELL and singer/guitarist SHANNON WRIGHT, the pair adding drummer, LAURIE WALL shortly afterwards. This two-girl/one-guy PAVEMENT-esque outfit chose the name of the former, although embarrassment led to the man adopting the new surname of HOWELL. Out of the savings from a recent bereavement, PAUL sent a number of demo tapes to various labels around the States, although it would be North Carolina's 'Jettison' imprint (run by Todd Goss) who would take CROWSDELL under their wing. In 1993, two singles, 'LICKETY SPLIT' and 'MEANY', appeared, although it was a third for 'Figurehead', 'DARREN', that would get the attention of UK label, 'Big Cat'. Radio One DJ, John Peel, was an early admirer of their work, while PAVEMENT's STEVE MALKMUS (who else!) took up the chance to produce their debut album, 'DREAMETTE'. Released during a well-received Lollapalooza tour in Spring '95, its melodic alt-country-esque guitar-rock saddled with SHANNON's tales of heartfelt woe endeared them to fans from all walks of life. It took two long years until the release of a follow-up, 'WITHIN THE CURVE OF AN ARM' (1997), another charming slice of indie rock/pop that improved with every listen.

Album rating: DREAMETTE (*6) / WITHIN THE CURVE OF AN ARM (*6)

SHANNON WRIGHT – vocals, guitar / **PAUL HOWELL** (b. PAUL VAN CROWSDELL) – bass / **LAURIE WALL** – drums

not iss. / Jettison

1993. (7") **LICKETY SPLIT. /**

1993. (7") **MEANY. /**

not iss. / Figurehead

Nov 94. (7") **DARREN. /**

Big Cat / not iss.

Feb 95. (7") *(ABB 80S)* **SUGAR-COATED. / TRUNK**

Apr 95. (lp/cd) *(ABB 83/+CD)* **DREAMETTE**

Sep 95. (12"ep/cd-ep) *(ABB 94 T/CD)* **THE END OF ANOTHER SUMMER EP**

Apr 97. (7") *(ABB 124S)* **POPSICK. /**
(cd-s+=) *(ABB 124CD)* –

Jun 97. (lp/cd) *(ABB 125/+CD)* **WITHIN THE CURVE OF AN ARM**
– Popsick / Five stars / Mooncalf / Lurking in sagas / You want me dead / Floridian lamb / W.C. Haley / Pharmaceutical fingers / Patches / Sunny sparkle / Cut and paste / Wake the lass / Foul.

Aug 97. (cd-s) *(ABB 127SCD)* **LURKING IN SAGAS /**

CRUCIFUCKS (see under ⇒ LOUDSPEAKER)

CRUNT (see under ⇒ BABES IN TOYLAND)

CUBAN HEELS

Formed: Glasgow, Scotland . . . late 1977 by ex-JOHNNY & THE SELF-ABUSERS (the embryonic SIMPLE MINDS) singer, JOHN MILARKY. While JIM KERR & Co. went on to explore experimental post-punk territory, The CUBAN HEELS kicked up a more straightforward blend of new-wave power-pop and 60's retro sounds. After debuting with a charged-up cover of Petula Clark's 'DOWNTOWN' in Spring '78 on the tiny 'Housewife's Choice' label, the group underwent a shift in personnel as NICK CLARKE replaced ARMOUR and ALI McKENZIE replaced DUNCAN. A further two singles, 'LITTLE GIRL' and 'WALK ON WATER', appeared on their own 'Greville' and 'Cuba Libre' labels respectively, ushering in a major label deal with 'Virgin'. Released in Spring '81, the CUBAN HEELS' first single for the label, 'SWEET CHARITY', sounded like The B-52's FRED SCHNEIDER fronting a poppier SKIDS, a band with whom The 'HEELS were comparable in image terms as well as musical. Frantic follow-up single, 'MY COLOURS FLY', previewed the band's long awaited debut album, 'WORK OUR WAY TO HEAVEN' (1981). With a muted response from both press and punters alike, the band released a last gasp remake of 'WALK ON WATER' before calling it a day the following year. • **Covered:** MATTHEW AND SON (Cat Stevens)

Album rating: WORK OUR WAY TO HEAVEN (*4)

JOHN MILARKY – vocals / **LAURIE CUFFE** – guitar / **PAUL ARMOUR** – bass / **DAVIE DUNCAN** – drums

Housewife's Choice / not iss.

Apr 78. (7") *(JW 1-2)* **DOWNTOWN. / DO THE SMOKE WALK**

— **NICK CLARK** – bass; repl. ARMOUR

— **ALI MacKENZIE** – drums; repl. DUNCAN

Greville / not iss.

Aug 80. (7") *(GR 1)* **LITTLE GIRL. / FAST LIVING FRIEND** [ ] [-]

Cuba Libre / not iss.

Jan 81. (7") *(DRINK 1)* **WALK ON WATER. / TAKE A LOOK** [ ] [-]

Virgin / not iss.

May 81. (7") *(VS 413)* **SWEET CHARITY. / PAY AS YOU GO** [ ] [-]

Aug 81. (7") *(VS 439)* **MY COLOURS FLY. / CUBA LIBRE** [ ] [-]

Oct 81. (lp) *(V 2210)* **WORK OUR WAY TO HEAVEN** [ ] [-]
– Liberty hall / Move up a grade / A matter of time / Homes for heroes / The old school song / Walk on water / Hard times / Coming up for air / Work our way to Heaven / My colours fly.

Nov 81. (7") *(VS 440)* **WALK ON WATER. / HARD TIMES** [ ] [-]
(with free 7"flexi) – Matthew and son.

— split some time in 1982

CUD

Formed Leeds, England . . . 1987 by CARL PUTTNAM, MIKE DUNPHY, WILLIAM POTTER and STEVE 'CUD' GOODWIN. Apparently initiated after the lads found an abandoned set of drums in a skip, CUD soon built up a local following almost as fanatical as fellow indie stragglers The WEDDING PRESENT, on whose label, 'Reception', they issued their earliest recordings. Something of an acquired taste, CUD's er . . . distinctive appeal was best witnessed in the live arena, while the 'Imaginary' label released their first two studio sets, 'WHEN IN ROME, KILL ME' (1989) and 'LEGGY MAMBO' (1990). The latter record found PUTTNAM and co. taking their musical abilities slightly more seriously and with a number of minor hit singles under their belt, the band soon found themselves with a major label deal courtesy of 'A&M'. The first fruits of this unlikely partnership emerged in the shape of the 'ASQUARIUS' (1992) album, an acclaimed set which nevertheless failed to catch on with the more straightahead pop punters. Just as well, perhaps, as the band were beginning to show worrying signs of going all sensible on us by the release of 1994's 'SHOWBIZ' set. • **Songwriters:** Group compositions, except YOU SEXY THING (Hot Chocolate) / LIVING IN THE PAST (Jethro Tull) / PRICE OF LOVE (Everly Brothers) / DOWN DOWN (Status Quo).

Album rating: WHEN IN ROME, KILL ME (*5) / LEGGY MAMBO (*7) / ASQUARIUS (*6) / SHOWBIZ (*5)

CARL PUTTNAM (b.1967, Ilford, Essex) – vocals / **MIKE DUNPHY** (b.1967, Northumberland, England) – guitar, keyboards / **WILLIAM POTTER** (b.1968, Derby, England) – bass / **STEVE GOODWIN** (b.1967, Croydon, Surrey, England) – drums

Reception / not iss.

Oct 87. (12"ep) *(REC 007)* **YOU'RE THE BOSS / MIND THE GAP. / VAN VAN VAN / YOU'RE THE BOSS (Out To Lunch mix)** [ ] [-]

Ediesta / not iss.

Apr 88. (12"ep) *(CALC 049)* **UNDER MY HAT. / PUNISHMENT-REWARD RELATIONSHIP / ART!** [ ] [-]

Dug-Nightime / not iss.

Sep 88. (12"ep) *(DUGNI 001T)* **SLACK TIME. / I'VE HAD IT WITH BLONDES / MAKE NO BONES** [ ] [-]

Imaginary / not iss.

Apr 89. (7") *(MIRAGE 007)* **LOLA. / THE DAY CRIME PAID** [ ] [-]

Jun 89. (lp)(cd) *(ILLUSION 5)(ILLCD 500)* **WHEN IN ROME, KILL ME** [ ] [-]
– When in Rome, kill me: (i) When in Rome, kill me (ii) Only a prawn in Whitby (iii) Bibi couldn't see (iv) Strange kind of love (v) Push and shove / (vi) The day crime paid (vii) When in Rome, kill me again / I've had it with blondes / Van van van / Vocally speaking / Wobbly jelly / Alison springs / Epicurean's answer.

Sep 89. (12"ep) *(MIRAGE 010)* **ONLY A PRAWN IN WHITBY / (other version) / LIVING IN THE PAST / EVERYBODY WORKS SO HARD** [ ] [-]

May 90. (7"one-sided-ltd.) *(MIRAGE 018)* **HEYWIRE** [ ] [-]
(12"+=/cd-s+=) *(MIRAGE 018 T/CD)* – Purple love baloon / Possession.

Sep 90. (7") *(MIRAGE 021S)* **ROBINSON CRUSOE. / PLANTATION ISLAND** [86] [-]
(cd-s+=) *(MIRACD 021)* – L.O.P.H.E. / ('A'-Friday mix).

Oct 90. (cd/c/lp) *(ILLCD/ILLC/ILLUSION 021)* **LEGGY MAMBO** [ ] [-]
– Now / Heart / Hey, boots / Love in a hollow tree / Love mandarin / Not exactly D L E R C / Robinson Crusoe / Eau water / Carl's 115th coach trip nightmare / Magic / Syrup and sour grapes / Brain on a slow train.

Mar 91. (7") *(MIRAGE 027)* **MAGIC (Farsley mix). / MAGIC (Stockport mix)** [80] [-]
(12"+=/cd-s+=) *(MIRAGE 027T)(MIRACD 027)* – Marjorie / Beyond hair.

A&M / A&M

Oct 91. (d7"ep/12"ep/cd-ep) *(AM B/X/CD 829)* **OH NO WON'T DO / ARIEL. / PROCESSION / PRICE OF LOVE** [49] [-]

Nov 91. (cd-ep) *<5380>* **"THE CUD BAND" EP** [-] [ ]
– Magic / Robinson Crusoe / Now / Hey, Boots / Magic.

Mar 92. (7") *(AM 857)* **THROUGH THE ROOF. / UNDOUBTABLY THOMAS** [44] [-]
(12"+=/cd-s+=) *(AM X/CD 857)* – Prime cut.

May 92. (7"/7"pic-d) *(AM/+P 871)* **RICH AND STRANGE. / LOVE MANDARIN (acoustic)** [24] [-]
(12"/cd-s) *(AM X/CD 871)* – ('A'side) / Do it again / A song called that.

Jun 92. (cd/c/lp) *(395 390-2/-4/-1)* **ASQUARIUS** [30] [-]
– Rich and strange / Easy / Sometimes rightly sometimes wrongly / Spanish love story / Magic / Alex / Beyond hair / Pink flamingo / Possession / Through the roof / Soul food / Once again / No smoking. *(re-iss. cd May95; same)*

Jul 92. (7"pic-d/c-s) *(AM 0024/+C)* **PURPLE LOVE BALLOON. / SPANISH LOVE SONG (acoustic)** [27] [-]
(12"pic-d/cd-s) *(AM 0024 T/CD)* – ('A'side) / ('A'-Killer rabbit mix-omatosis) / ('A'-US mix) / Remember what it is that your love.

Oct 92. (7"/c-s) *(AM 0081/+C)* **ONCE AGAIN. / DAY BY DAY** [45] [-]
(12"+=/cd-s+=) *(AM 0081 T/CD)* – Eau water (acoustic) / Soul food (acoustic).

Jan 94. (7"/c-s) *(580 517-7/-4)* **NEUROTICA. / MIDNIGHT RIDE** [37] [-]
(cd-s) *(580 517-2)* – ('A'side) / Juicy eurela / 1.W.G.S. / Brand name skin.
(12"++=) *(580 517-1)* – Neurotica (remix).

Mar 94. (7"/c-s) *(580 546-7/-4)* **STICKS AND STONES. / SKI BUM** [68] [-]
(12"+=) *(580 547-1)* – My need to hurry.
(cd-s) *(580 547-2)* – ('A'side) / Down the plug / My keyhole don't keep secrets anymore.

Apr 94. (cd/c/lp) *(540 211-2/-4/-1)* **SHOWBIZ** [46] [-]
– Somebody snatched my action / E.S.P. / Waving and drowning / Sticks and stones / Mystery deepens / Slip away / One giant love / I reek of chic / Not necessarily evil / You lead me / Tourniquet / Neurotica. *(re-is.cd May95)*

Aug 94. (c-s/cd-s) *(580 729-4/-2)* **ONE GIANT LOVE / LOOK ON UP AT THE BOTTOM / FIND IT** [52] [-]
(12") *(580 729-1)* – ('A'side) / Robinson Crusoe (live) / Strange kind of love (live) / Purple love balloon (live).
(cd-s) *(580 731-2)* – ('A'live) / Slip away (live) / Magic (live) / Neurotica (live).

— split early the following year

– compilations, others, etc. –

Jan 88. (12"ep) *Strange Fruit; (SFPS 045)* **THE PEEL SESSIONS** (16.6.87) [ ] [-]
– Mind the gap / You're the boss / Don't bank on it / You sexy thing.

Jul 90. (cd/c/lp) *Imaginary; (ILLCD/ILLC/ILLUSION 013))* **ELVIS BELT** (1989-1991) [ ] [-]

CUDDLY TOYS

Formed: Ireland-based . . . 1977 out of the ill-advisedly monikered RAPED, by SEAN PURCELL, TONY BAGGETT, FAEBHEAN KWEST, PADDY PHIELD and BILLY SURGEONER. This bunch of peroxide blonde BOWIE-cloning glam-punks released a couple of singles in 1978, 'PRETTY PAEDOPHILES' and 'CHEAP NIGHT OUT', although none were taken seriously by the press. 1980 saw a much needed change of group name to CUDDLY TOYS, their cheap electro-pop never making any inroads commercially. By this point, SURGEONER was replaced by ALIG FODDER and NICKY BROCKWAY, their debut album, 'GUILLOTINE THEATRE', duly issued by RAPED's old label, 'Parole', in 1980. After a few singles ('MADMEN' and 'ASTRAL JOE') found few buyers, TERRY NOAKES and ROBERT BARKER were subsequently drafted in to supersede FAEBHEAN and PADDY, the new line-up completing only one single, 'SOMEONE'S CRYING', before further personnel troubles ensued; S. PAUL WILSON and DAVID KOVACEVIC would come in for BAGGETT, FODDER and BROCKWAY. The second album, 'TRIALS AND CROSSES' (1982), was given short thrift by most critics resulting in the disbandment of the group shortly afterwards.

Album rating: GUILLOTINE THEATRE (*5) / TRIALS AND CROSSES (*5) / Raped: PHILES AND SMILES (*3) / THE COMPLETE RAPED COLLECTION (*4)

RAPED

SEAN PURCELL – vocals / **FAEBHEAN KWEST** – guitar / **BILLY SURGEONER** – keyboards / **TONY BAGGETT** – bass / **PADDY PHIELD** – drums

Parole / not iss.

Jan 78. (7"ep) *(KNIT 1)* **PRETTY PAEDOPHILES** [ ] [-]
– Moving target / Raped / Escalator hater / Normal.

Nov 78. (7") *(PURL 1)* **CHEAP NIGHT OUT. / FOREPLAY PLAYGROUND** [ ] [-]

CUDDLY TOYS

— **ALIG FODDER + NICKY BROCKWAY** – keyboards; repl. BILLY

Fresh / not iss.

Apr 80. (lp) *(FRESHLP 1)* **GUILLOTINE THEATRE** [ ] [-]
– Introvenus / Brain saviour / Join the girls / Wolf / Madman / Universe / Astral Joe / My commando / Full circle / Alien / Guillotine theatre / Time warp.

Jul 80. (7") *(FRESH 10 – PURL 7)* **MADMAN. / JOIN THE GIRLS** [ ] [-]

Nov 80. (7") *(FRESH 20)* **ASTRAL JOE. / SLOW DOWN** [ ] [-]

— **TERRY NOAKES** – guitar; repl. FAEBHEAN

— **ROBERT BARKER** – drums; repl. PADDY

Feb 81. (7") *(FRESH 25)* **SOMEONE'S CRYING. / BRING ON THE RAVERS** [ ] [-]
(12") *(FRESH 25-12)* – ('A'side) / Dancing glass (instrumental) / Slide / Broken mirrors.

— **S. PAUL WILSON** – bass; repl. BAGGETT

— **DAVID KOVACEVIC** – keyboards; repl. FODDER + BROCKWAY

Feb 82. (7") *(FRESH 39)* **IT'S A SHAME. / FALL DOWN** [ ] [-]

Feb 82. (lp) *(FRESHLP 6)* **TRIALS AND CROSSES** [ ] [-]
– It's a shame / Trials and crosses / Action / Colombine's song / Fall down / One close step / Normandy nightfall / Lo and behold / Malice thru the looking glass . . . Pierrot Lunaire.

— disbanded some time in '82

– compilations, etc. –

1984. (lp; as RAPED) *Iguana; (PILLAGED 1)* **PHILES AND SMILES** [ ] [-]

Jul 94. (cd; as RAPED) *Anagram; (CDPUNK 35)* **THE COMPLETE RAPED COLLECTION** [ ] [-]

CUL DE SAC

Formed: Chicago, Illinois, USA . . . 1990 by GLENN JONES (not the gospel/R&B solo artist), ROBIN AMOS and CHRIS GUTTMACHER. Located squarely at the avant-garde end of the alternative rock avenue, CUL DE SAC made their vinyl debut in 1992 with a limited edition UK-only 7" single, 'SAKHALIN', followed closely by a debut album, 'ECIM' (1992). Throwing together disparate strands of world music, 60's/70's psychedelic experimentalism and rootsy folk, the band were augmented in their ambitious endeavours by bass player, CHRIS FUJIWARA, steel guitarist/violinist, ED YAZIJIAN, effects man, PHIL MILSTEIN and guest vocalist, DREDD FOOLE. A series of singles on various obscure indie labels appeared over the next few years while a belated follow-up album, 'I DON'T WANT TO GO TO BED', surfaced in summer '95; a double set released on 'Flying Nun', the record was a ramshackle collection of largely instrumental workouts that steadfastly defied pigeonholing. Following the replacement of GUTTMACHER with JOHN PROUDMAN, the quartet worked with veteran roots man, JOHN FAHEY, on third album, 'CHINA GATE' (1996).

Album rating: ECIM (*5) / I DON'T WANT TO GO TO BED (*7) / CHINA GATE (*6)

GLENN JONES – guitar / **ROBIN AMOS** – multi (ex-GIRLS) / **CHRIS GUTTMACHER** – drums (of BULLET LAVOLTA) / added 4th member **CHRIS FUJIWARA** – bass / plus **ED YAZIJIAN** – steel guitar, violin / **PHIL MILSTEIN** – sampler / guest **DREDD FOOLE** – vocals

Shock / not iss.

1992. (7"ltd) *(SX 017)* **SAKHALIN. / CANT** – -

Pell / Northeastern

Oct 92. (lp/cd) *(PELL 11/12) <5503>* **ECIM** – Nov93
– Death kit train / The moon scolds the morning star / Stranger at Coney Island / Homunculus / The Portland cement factory at Monolith, California / Nico's dream / The invisible worm / Song to the siren / Electar / Lauren's blues.

— now without ED who joined KUSTOMIZED

not iss. / Nuf Sed

Jan 93. (7") **DOLDRUMS. /** -

not iss. / Lunar Rotation

1994. (7") **FRANKIE MACHINE. /** -

not iss. / New World Of Sound

1994. (7") **MILK DEVIL. /** -

Flying Nun / Thirsty Ear

Jun 95. (d-lp/cd) *(FN/+CD 330) <57029>* **I DON'T WANT TO GO TO BED** (compilation) – 1997
– Abandoned hospital / Doldrums / Graveyard for robots / The fraud of satisfaction / Roses in the wallpaper / This is the metal that do not born / Lover Hat, Massachusetts / The Kim Parker report / Count Donut / For seasickness / Lully's gangrene.

— **JOHN PROUDMAN** – drums; repl. GUTTMACHER

Jun 96. (cd) *(FNCD 376) <57023>* **CHINA GATE** – May96
– China gate / Sakhalin / Nepenthe / Doldrums / James Coburn / Virgin among cannibals / . . . His teeth got lost in the . . . / Hemispheric events command / Fourth eye / Colomber / China gate / Utopia Pkwy.

Earworm / not iss.

Dev 98. (7") *(WORM 39)* **THE PORTLAND CEMENT FACTORY AT MONOLITH, CALIFORNIA. / HAGSTROM** – -

CULTURE SHOCK (see under ⇒ SUBHUMANS)

David CUNNINGHAM (see under ⇒ FLYING LIZARDS)

CUPOL (see under ⇒ WIRE)

CURE

Formed: Crawley, Sussex, England . . . 1976 initially as The EASY CURE by ROBERT SMITH, LAWRENCE TOLHURST and MICHAEL DEMPSEY. In 1978, following a brief liaison with the small 'Hansa' label the previous year, the band recorded a one-off '45, 'KILLING AN ARAB', for indie operation, 'Small Wonder'. Although actually inspired by classic Albert Camus novel, 'The Outsider', the track was met with its fair share of controversy upon its early '79 re-release by Chris Parry's new 'Fiction' imprint. A subsequent debut album, 'THREE IMAGINARY BOYS' (1979) remains among The CURE's finest work, their strangely accessible post-punk snippets lent an air of suppressed melancholy by SMITH's plangent whine. The record almost scraped into the Top 40, while the pop brilliance of accompanying single, 'BOYS DON'T CRY', saw The CURE lauded as one of the UK's most promising young bands. With SIMON GALLUP replacing DEMPSEY (who joined The ASSOCIATES), the group again drew critical plaudits for the insidious 'JUMPING SOMEONE ELSE'S TRAIN'. A track railing against fashion victims, The CURE carved out their own solitary path over the course of the next three albums. Claustrophobic is normally the favoured critical bon mot in getting to grips with The CURE's sound and few would argue that the spiralling disorientation of 'A FOREST' was easy listening. SMITH and CO.'s first Top 40 hit, the track previewed follow-up set, 'SEVENTEEN SECONDS' (1980), an album which took them into the UK Top 20 despite its gloomy sound. Revered by the more pasty faced among the group's fanbase, 'FAITH' (1981) and 'PORNOGRAPHY' (1982) ploughed a similarly grim furrow, although the latter set went Top 10. Internal feuding subsequently led to the departure of GALLUP, SMITH and TOLHURST taking charge and effecting a bit of a stylistic departure on the more flippantly pop-friendly 'LET'S GO TO BED' (not before you take that eyeliner off, BOB) single. Finally, in summer of the following year, The CURE scored a long awaited breakthrough hit with 'THE WALK', the track narrowly missing the Top 10. Nevertheless, SMITH was simultaneously busying himself with SIOUXSIE AND THE BANSHEES, contributing guitar to their Top 5 cover of The Beatles' 'Dear Prudence' and playing on the 'Hyaena' album as well as hooking up with BANSHEES man, STEVE SEVERIN, for side project, The GLOVE. Meanwhile, the flouncing 'LOVECATS' single introduced the group to a whole new audience, a song with an alarmingly high irritabilty factor that still gets played to death by radio. With SMITH back on board in a full-time capacity by Spring '84, The CURE again managed to take their skewered pop vision into the pop charts with 'THE CATERPILLAR', a track lifted from bizarre new album, 'THE TOP' (1984). More line-up changes occurred prior to the recording of the band's breakthrough set, 'HEAD ON THE DOOR' (1985), including the return of SIMON GALLUP. Trailed by the classic 'IN BETWEEN DAYS', the record spawned a further major hit in the glockenspiel weirdness of 'CLOSE TO ME', its breathy claustrophobia segueing into a sassy, brassy finale. The track was also accompanied by a celebrated video (directed by long standing associate Tim Pope), featuring the whole band, erm, playing inside a wardrobe (honestly!). A subsequent two year lull was punctuated by an impressive singles retrospective, 'STANDING ON A BEACH' (1986), before the band returned with the sprawling 'KISS ME, KISS ME KISS ME' (1987) double set. Hardly an easy ride, the record showcased the many strange faces of The CURE and more, incredibly making the US Top 40 where they'd slowly been building up a cult following. This time around there was no stellar pop to liven up the Stock, Aitken & Waterman-clogged Top 10 although the record did spawn a trio of minor hits in 'WHY CAN'T I BE YOU', 'CATCH' and 'JUST LIKE HEAVEN'. The latter track was later privy to a genius fuzz-pop mangling courtesy of DINOSAUR JR., an interpretation that reportedly impressed SMITH no end. The CURE were now a formidable commercial proposition on both sides of the Atlantic, which probably explains why the ponderous 'DISINTEGRATION' (1989) album made the UK Top 3 and the 'LOVESONG' single almost topped the American Hot 100. The turn of the decade saw major upheaval as TOLHURST finally bailed out after clashing with SMITH, a pared down line up of SMITH, GALLUP, PORL THOMPSON, BORIS WILLIAMS and PERRY BAMONTE seeing the group through most of the following decade. A remix album, 'MIXED UP', appeared in 1990, its sensual dancefloor appeal illustrating just how adaptable the band's music was, bearing in mind that SMITH and Co. were sometimes dismissed as whimsical, goth-pop throwbacks. New material finally arrived in Spring '92 with the 'WISH' album, the huge hit 'FRIDAY I'M IN LOVE' following in their occasional tradition of jangling dreaminess. The album itself became The CURE's first UK No.1, missing the top of the American charts by a whisker; the band were now sufficiently world dominating that they could almost get away with two double live albums, 'SHOW' amd 'PARIS', released simultaneously in late '93. The remainder of the decade saw the band's profile at its lowest since their shadowy beginnings, a low-key 1996 set, 'WILD MOOD SWINGS' their sole studio output in almost five years. • **Songwriters:** Group compositions, except covers of FOXY LADY + PURPLE HAZE (Jimi Hendrix), HELLO I LOVE YOU (Doors). • **Trivia:** SMITH married childhood sweetheart Mary Poole on the 13th of August '88.

Album rating: THREE IMAGINARY BOYS (*8) / BOYS DON'T CRY exploitation (*7) / SEVENTEEN SECONDS (*6) / FAITH (*6) / PORNOGRAPHY (*6) / JAPANESE WHISPERS mini (*6) / THE TOP (*7) / CONCERT: LIVE (*5) / THE HEAD ON THE DOOR (*7) / STANDING ON THE BEACH / STARING AT THE SEA: THE SINGLES compilation (*9) / KISS ME, KISS ME, KISS ME (*7) / DISINTEGRATION (*8) / MIXED UP (*4) / WISH (*6) / PARIS (*4) / SHOW (*4) / WILD MOOD SWINGS (*5) / GALORE – THE SINGLES 1987-1997 compilation (*6)

ROBERT SMITH (b.21 Apr'59, Blackpool, England) – vocals, lead guitar / **LAWRENCE TOLHURST** (b. 3 Feb'59) – drums, keyboards / **MICHAEL DEMPSEY** – bass

Small Wonder / not iss.

Aug 78. (7") *(SMALL 11)* **KILLING AN ARAB. / 10.15 SATURDAY NIGHT** – -

Fiction / not iss.

Jan 79. (7") *(FICS 001)* **KILLING AN ARAB. / 10.15 SATURDAY NIGHT** – -

May 79. (lp/c) *(FIX/+C 1)* **THREE IMAGINARY BOYS** 44 -
– 10.15 Saturday night / Accuracy / Grinding halt / Another day / Object / Subway song / Foxy lady / Meat hook / So what / Fire in Cairo / It's not you / Three imaginary boys. *(cd-iss. Apr90; 827 686-2)*

May 79. (7") *(FICS 002)* **BOYS DON'T CRY. / PLASTIC PASSION** – -

— **SIMON GALLUP** (b. 1 Jun'60, Surrey, England) – bass, keyboards (ex-MAG-SPYS, ex-LOCKJAW) repl. DEMPSEY who joined The ASSOCIATES

Oct 79. (7") *(FICS 005)* **JUMPING SOMEONE ELSE'S TRAIN. / I'M COLD** – -

— added **MATHIEU HARTLEY** – keyboards, synthesizers

Nov 79. (7") *(FICS 006)* **I'M A CULT HERO (as "CULT HERO"). / I DIG YOU** – -

— (on above they backed FRANK BELL)

Mar 80. (7"/ext.12") *(FICS/+X 10)* **A FOREST. / ANOTHER JOURNEY BY TRAIN** 31 -

Apr 80. (lp/c) *(FIX/+C 004)* **SEVENTEEN SECONDS** 20 -
– A reflection / Play for today / Secrets / In your house / Three . . . / The final sound / A forest / M / At night / Seventen seconds. *(cd-iss. Jan86; 825 354-2)*

— reverted to trio of **SMITH, TOLHURST & GALLUP** when HARTLEY left to form CRY.

Mar 81. (7"/ext.12") *(FICS/+X 12)* **PRIMARY. / DESCENT** 43 -

Fiction P.V.C.

Apr 81. (lp/c) *(FIX/+C 6) <2383 605>* **FAITH** [14] [ ]
– The holy hour / Primary / Other voices / All cats are grey / The funeral party / Doubt / The drowning man / Faith. *(cd-iss. Jan86; 827 687-2) (c+=)* **CARNAGE VISORS** (film soundtrack)

Oct 81. (7") *(FICS 14)* **CHARLOTTE SOMETIMES. / SPLINTERED IN HER HEAD** [44] [-]
(12"+=) *(FICSX 14)* – Faith (live).

Fiction A&M

Apr 82. (lp/c) *(FIX D/C 7) <4902>* **PORNOGRAPHY** [8] [ ]
– One hundred years / A short term effect / The hanging garden / Siamese twins / The figurehead / A strange day / Cold / Pornography. *(cd-iss. Jan86; 827 688-2)*

Jul 82. (7") *(FICS 15)* **THE HANGING GARDEN. / KILLING AN ARAB (live)** [34] [-]
(d7"+=) *(FICG 15)* – One hundred years (live) / A forest (live).

— **STEVE GOULDING** – bass repl. GALLUP who later joined FOOLS DANCE. (LOL now keyboards)

Nov 82. (7"/ext.12") *(FICS/+X 17)* **LET'S GO TO BED. / JUST ONE KISS** [44] [-]

— trimmed to duo of **SMITH + TOLHURST**

Jul 83. (7"/7"pic-d) *(FICS/+P 18)* **THE WALK. / THE DREAM** [12] [-]
(12"+=) *(FICXT 18) <23928>* – The upstairs room / Lament.
(free 12"w/ free 12") *(FICSX 17)* – Let's go to bed / Just one kiss.

— added **PHIL THORNALLEY** – bass / **ANDY ANDERSON-drums** (ex-BRILLIANT)

Oct 83. (7"/7"pic-d) *(FICS/+P 19)* **THE LOVECATS. / SPEAK MY LANGUAGE** [7] [-]
(ext.12"+=) *(FICSX 19)* – Mr. Pink eyes.

Dec 83. (m-lp/c) *(FIXM/+C 8) <25076>* **JAPANESE WHISPERS** [26] [ ]
– Let's go to bed / The dream / Just one kiss / The upstair's room / The walk / Speak my language / Lament / The lovecats. *(cd-iss. Apr87; 817 470-2)*

Mar 84. (7"/7"pic-d) *(FICS/+P 20)* **THE CATERPILLAR. / HAPPY THE MAN** [14] [-]
(12"+=) *(FICSX 20)* – Throw your foot.

Apr 84. (lp/c)(cd) *(FIXS/+C 9)(821 136-2) <25086>* **THE TOP** [10] [ ]
– Shake dog shake / Birdmad girl / Wailing wall / Give me it / Dressing up / The caterpillar / Piggy in the mirror / The empty world / Bananafishbones / The top.

— added **PORL THOMPSON** (b.8 Nov'57, London, England) – guitar, saxophone, keyboards (a member in '77)

Oct 84. (lp/d-c)(cd) *(FIXH/+C 10)(823 682-2)* **CONCERT – THE CURE LIVE (live)** [26] [-]
– Shake dog shake / Primary / Charlotte sometimes / The hanging garden / Give me it / The walk / One hundred years / A forest / 10.15 Saturday night / Killing an Arab. *(d-c+=)* **CURIOSITY: CURE ANOMALIES 1977-1984** – Heroin face / Boys don't cry / Subway song / At night / In your house / The drowning man / Other voices / The funeral party / All mine / Forever.

— **SIMON GALLUP** returned to repl. PORL. **BORIS WILLIAMS** (b.24 Apr'57, Versailles, France) – drums (ex-THOMPSON TWINS) repl. ANDERSON who joined JEFFREY LEE PIERCE (of The GUN CLUB)

Fiction Elektra

Jul 85. (7") *(FICS 22)* **IN BETWEEN DAYS. / EXPLODING BODY** [15] [-]
(12"+=) *(FICSX 22)* – A few hours after this.

Aug 85. (lp/c)(cd) *(FIXH/+C 11)(827 231-2) <60435>* **THE HEAD ON THE DOOR** [7] [59]
– In between days / Kyoto song / The blood / Six different ways / Push / The baby screams / Close to me / A night like this / Screw / Sinking.

Sep 85. (7"/7"poster) *(FICS/+G 23)* **CLOSE TO ME (remix). / A MAN INSIDE MY MOUTH** [24] [-]
(12"+=) *(FICSX 23)* – Stop dead.
(10"++=) *(FICST 23)* – New day.

Jan 86. (7") *<69604>* **IN BETWEEN DAYS. / STOP DEAD** [-] [99]

Mar 86. (7") *<69551>* **CLOSE TO ME. / SINKING** [-] [ ]

Apr 86. (7") *(FICS 24)* **BOYS DON'T CRY (new mix). / PILLBOX BLUES** [22] [-]
(club-12"+=) *(FICSX 24)* – Do the Hansa.

Apr 87. (7"/ext.12") *(FICS/+X 25) <69474>* **WHY CAN'T I BE YOU? / A JAPANESE DREAM** [21] [54] Jun87
(d7"+=) *(FIGSG 25)* – Six different ways (live) / Push (live).

May 87. (d-lp/c)(cd) *(FIXH/+C 13)(832 130-2) <60737>* **KISS ME KISS ME KISS ME** [6] [35]
– The kiss / Catch / Torture / If only tonight we could sleep / Why can't I be you? / How beautiful you are / Snakepit / Hey you / Just like heaven / All I want / Hot hot hot!!! / One more time / Like cockatoos / Icing sugar / The perfect girl / A thousand hours / Shiver and shake / Fight. *(pic-lp.Dec87; FIXP 13) (free-ltd.12"orange / or green,w/cd) – A Japanese dream / Breathe / Chain of flowers / Sugar girl / Snow in summer / Icing sugar (remix).*

— added on tour **ROBERT O'CONNELL** – keyboards (ex-PSYCHEDELIC FURS)

Jul 87. (7"/7"clear) *(FICS/+P 26)* **CATCH. / BREATHE** [27] [ ]
(c-s+=/12"+=) *(FICS C/X 26)* – A chain of flowers.
(7"ep+=) *(FICSE 26)* – Kyoto song (live) / A night like this (live).

Oct 87. (7",7"white/7"pic-d) *(FICS/+P 27)* **JUST LIKE HEAVEN. / SNOW IN SUMMER** [29] [-]
(12"+=/cd-s+=) *(FICSX/FIXCD 27)* – Sugar girl.

Oct 87. (7") *<69443>* **JUST LIKE HEAVEN. / BREATHE** [-] [40]

Feb 88. (12"/cd-s) *(FICSX/FIXCD 28) <69424>* **HOT HOT HOT!!! (extended remix). / HOT HOT HOT!!! (remix) / HEY YOU!!! (extended remix)** [45] [65]

Apr 89. (7"/7"gf/7"clear) *(FICS/+G/P 29)* **LULLABY (remix). / BABBLE** [5] [-]
(ext.12"+=/ext.12"pink+=) *(FIC SX/VX 29)* – Out of mind. (3"cd-s++=) *(FICCD 29)* – ('A'extended).

May 89. (lp/c)(cd) *(FIXH/+C 14)(839 353-2) <60855>* **DISINTEGRATION** [3] [12]
– Plainsong / Pictures of you / Closedown / Lovesong / Lullaby / Fascination street / Prayers for rain / The same deep water as you / Disintegration / Untitled. *(cd+=)* – Last dance / Homesick. *(pic-lp Apr90; FIXHP 14)*

May 89. (7") *<69300>* **FASCINATION STREET. / BABBLE** [-] [46]

Aug 89. (7"/7"box/c-s) *(FIC S/SG/CD 30) <69280>* **LOVESONG. / 2 LATE** [18] [2]
(ext.12"+=) *(FICSX 30)* – Fear of ghosts.
(cd-s++=)(cd-vid++=) *(FICCD 30)(081398-2)* – ('A'-12"mix).

Nov 89. (c-s) *<69249>* **LULLABY / HOMESICK** [-] [74]

— (Mar'89) reverted to a quintet when TOLHURST left **SMITH, GALLUP, THOMPSON, WILLIAMS + PERRY BAMONTE** (b. 6 Sep'60, London, England) – keyboards

Mar 90. (7"/7"green/c-s) *(FIC A/PA/CA 34)* **PICTURES OF YOU (remix). /** [24] [71]
(ext.12"+=/ext.12"green+=/cd-s+=) *(FICXA/FIXPA/FICDA 34)* – Fascination Street (live).
(7"/7"purple/c-s) *(FIC B/PB/CB 34) <64974>* – PICTURES OF YOU (remix). / PRAYERS FOR RAIN (live)
(12"+=/12"purple+=/cd-s+=) *(FICXB/FIXPB/FICDB 34)* – Disintigration (live).

— (W.H. Smith's released ENTREAT (May90) a live EP, which featured the 5 tracks +=) – Closedown / Homesick / Untitled.

Sep 90. (7"/c-s) *(FIC S/CS 35)* **NEVER ENOUGH. / HAROLD AND JOE** [13] [72] Oct90
(12"+=/cd-s+=/pic-cd-s+=) *(FICSX/FICCD/FICDP 35)* – Let's go to bed (milk mix).

Oct 90. (7"/c-s) *(FIC S/CS 36) <64911>* **CLOSE TO ME (closet remix). / JUST LIKE HEAVEN (dizzy mix)** [13] [97] Jan91
(12"+=/cd-s+=) *(FIC SX/CD 36)* – Primary (red mix).
(cd-s+=) *(FICDR 36)* – Why can't I be you? (extended).

Nov 90. (cd)(d-lp/c) *(847 009-2)(FIXH/+C 18) <60978>* **MIXED UP** (remix album) [8] [14]
– Lullaby (extended mix) / Close to me (closer mix) / Fascination Street (extended mix) / The walk (everything mix) / Lovesong (extended mix) / A forest (tree mix) / Pictures of you (extended dub mix) / Hot hot hot!!! (extended mix) / The caterpillar (flicker mix) / Inbetween days (shiver mix) / Never enough (big mix).

Apr 91. (cd)(lp/c) *(843 359-2)(FIXH/+C 17)* **ENTREAT (live)** [10] [ ]
– (finally nationally released; see above)

Mar 92. (7"/c-s) *(FIC S/CS 39) <64766>* **HIGH. / THIS TWILIGHT GARDEN** [8] [42]
('A'-Higher mix-12"+=) *(FICSX 39)* – Play.
(cd-s+=) *(FICCD 39)* – (all above).

Apr 92. (12"clear) *(FICSX 41)* **HIGH (trip mix). / OPEN (fix mix)** [44] [43]
(cd-s) *(FICCD 41)* – (see last cd-s for 4 tracks).

Apr 92. (cd)(d-lp/c) *(513 261-2)(FIXH/+C 20) <61309>* **WISH** [1] [2]
– Open / High / Apart / From the edge of the deep green sea / Wendy time / Doing the unstuck / Friday I'm in love / Trust / A letter to Elise / Cut / To wish impossible things / End.

May 92. (7"/c-s) *(FIC S/CS 42) <64742>* **FRIDAY I'M IN LOVE. / HALO** [6] [18]
('A'-Strangelove mix-12"colrd+=) *(FICSX 42)* – Scared as you.
(cd-s+=) *(FICCD 42)* – (all above).

Oct 92. (7"/c-s) *(FIC S/CS 46)* **A LETTER TO ELISE. / THE BIG HAND** [28] [ ]
(Blue mix-12"+=) *(FICSX 46)* – A foolish arrangement.
(cd-s+) *(FICCD 46)* – (all above).

Sep 93. (d-cd/d-c/d-lp) *(FIX CD/MC/LP 25) <61551>* **SHOW (live)** [29] [42]
– Tape / Open / High / Pictures of you / Lullaby / Just like Heaven / Fascination Street / A night like this / Trust / Doing the unstuck / The walk / Let's go to bed / Friday I'm in love / In between days / From the edge of the deep green sea / Never enough / Cut / End.

— PORL departed after the above.

Oct 93. (cd/c/d-lp) *(FIX CD/MC/LP 26) <61552>* **PARIS (live)** [56] [ ]
– The figurehead / One hundred years / At night / Play for today / Apart / In your house / Lovesong / Catch / A letter to Elise / Dressing up / Charlotte sometimes / Close to me.

Apr 96. (c-s) *(576468-4)* **THE 13TH (swing radio mix) / IT USED TO BE ME** [15] [-]
(cd-s+=) *(576469-2)* – ('A'-Killer bee mix).
(cd-s) *(576493-2)* – ('A'-Two chord cool mix) / Ocean / Adonais.

Apr 96. (c-s) *<64292>* **THE 13TH / ADONAIS** [-] [44]

May 96. (cd/c/lp) *(FIX CD/MC/LP 28) <61744>* **WILD MOOD SWINGS** [9] [12]
– Want / Club America / This is a lie / The 13th / Strange attraction / Mint car / Jupiter crash / Round & round & round / Gone! / Numb / Trap / Treasure / Bare.

Jun 96. (c-s) *(FICCS 52) <64275>* **MINT CAR / HOME** [31] [58]
(cd-s+=) *(FICCD 52)* – ('A'-buskers mix).
(cd-s) *(FISCD 52)* – ('A'-electric mix) / Waiting / A pink dream.

Nov 96. (c-s) *(FICCS 53)* **GONE! / THIS IS A LIE (ambient mix)** [60] [ ]
(cd-s+=) *(FICD 53)* – Strange attraction (strange mix) / The 13th (feels good mix).

Nov 97. (cd/c/lp) *(FIX CD/MC/LP 30)* **GALORE – THE SINGLES 1987-1997** (compilation) [37] [32]
– Why can't I be you / Catch / Just like Heaven / Hot, hot, hot / Lullaby / Fascination Street / Love song / Pictures of you / Never enough / Close to me / High / Friday I'm in love / Letter to Elise / The 13th / Mint car / Strange attraction / Gone / Wrong number.

Nov 97. (c-s) *(FICMC 54)* **WRONG NUMBER /** [62] [ ]
(cd-s+=) *(FICD 54)* –
(12") *(FICSX 54)* –

– compilations, etc. –

Aug 83. (lp/c) *Fiction; (SPE LP/MC 26) / P.V.C.; <7916>* **BOYS DON'T CRY** [71] [ ] Aug80
– Boys don't cry / Plastic passion / 10.15 Saturday night / Accuracy / Object * / Jumping someone else's train / Subway song / Killing an Arab / Fire in Cairo / Another day / Grinding halt / World war * / Three imaginary boys. *(cd-iss. Nov86; 815 011-2) (w/ out tracks * +=)* – So what.

May 86. (7") *P.V.C.;* **BOYS DON'T CRY. / LET'S GO TO BED** [-] [ ]

May 86. (lp/d-c)(cd) *Fiction; (FIXH/+C 12)(829 239-2) / Elektra; <60477>* **STANDING ON THE BEACH** ('A'45's) / **STARING AT THE SEA** ('B'45's) [4] [48]
– Killing an Arab / Boys don't cry / Jumping someone else's train / A forest / Primary / Charlotte sometimes / The hanging garden / Let's go to bed / The walk / The lovecats / The caterpillar / In between days / Close to me. *(cd+=)* – 10.15 Saturday night / Play for today / Other voices / A night like this. *(re-iss. Feb91; same)*

May 88. (12"ep/cd-ep) *Strange Fruit; (SFPS/+CD 050)* **PEEL SESSIONS** ☐ -
– Killing an Arab / Boys don't cry / 10:15 Saturday night / Fire in Cairo.
Oct 88. (vid-cd) *Fiction; (080184-2)* **WHY CAN'T I BE YOU (video) / JAPANESE DREAM / HEY YOU / WHY CAN'T I BE YOU** ☐ -
Oct 88. (vid-cd) *Fiction; (080182-2)* **IN BETWEEN DAYS (video) / SIX DIFFERENT WAYS (live) / PUSH (live)** ☐ -
Oct 88. (vid-cd) *Fiction; (080186-2)* **CATCH (video) / CATCH / BREATHE / A CHAIN OF FLOWERS / ICING SUGAR (new mix)** ☐ -

CURRENT 93

Formed: London, England ... 1983 initially as an offshoot group by 23 SKIDOO members, DAVID TIBET and FRITZ HAAMAN, along with JOHN BALANCE (ex-PSYCHIC TV and a member of COIL) and former members of CRISIS (an outfit who subsequently evolved into DEATH IN JUNE). Obscure but nevertheless influential early players in the UK experimental industrial scene, CURRENT 93 set out combining medieval style choral chants with unsettling samples and hypnotic electronic percussion on albums such as 'WE SEE THE DECAY OF THE ANGEL THE MARCH' (1985) and 'IN MENSTRUAL NIGHT' (1986). Recording alternately for the tiny 'Laylah' and 'Maldorer' labels at a prolific rate throughout the latter half of the 80's, TIBET worked with whoever was available at the time (STEVEN STAPLETON of NURSE WITH WOUND, HILMAR ORN HILMARSON of PSYCHIC TV and ROSE McDOWELL, ex-STRAWBERRY SWITCHBLADE(!), among others), gradually evolving a stark folky sound no less spookier than his earliest work. Come the turn of the decade, CURRENT 93 (and all who sailed with her) began a new chapter in their career via the newly established 'Durtro' imprint, releasing new vinyl-only material as well re-issuing their rare and extremely collectable 80's work on CD.

Album rating: WE SEE THE DECAY OF THE ANGEL THE MARCH (*4) / IN MENSTRUAL NIGHT (*4) / DOGS BLOOD RISING (*4) / IMPERIUM (*4) / NIGHTMARE CULTURE with Sickness Of Snake (*4) / CHRIST AND THE PALE QUEEN (*4) / CURRENT 93 PRESENT C.R. LAMA – TANTRIC NYING MA CHANT OF TIBET (*3) / EARTH COVERS EARTH mini (*3) / DAWN (*3) / SWASTIKAS FOR NOBODY (*4) / LIVE AT BAR MALDORER with Nurse With Wound (*4) / ISLAND (*3) / THUNDER PERFECT MIND (*3) / OF RUINE, OR SOME BLAZING STARRE (*3) / ALL THE PRETTY LITTLE HORSES (*3) / THE CERNE BOX SET with others (*4)

DAVID TIBET – vocals (ex-23 SKIDOO) / **FRITZ HAAMAN** – drums, percussion (of 23 SKIDOO) / **JOHN BALANCE** – instruments (of COIL, ex-THROBBING GRISTLE, ex-PSYCHIC TV)

Benelux | not iss.

Feb 85. (lp) **WE SEE THE DECAY OF THE ANGEL THE MARCH** - | - Belgian

United Dairies | not iss.

May 86. (pic-lp) *(UDO 22M)* **IN MENSTRUAL NIGHT** ☐ -
– Sucking up souls / To feed the moon / etc.
(re-iss. lp Mar88; UD 022) (cd-iss. Oct94 on 'Durtro'+=; 020CD) – Killykillkilly (a fire sermon).

Laylah | not iss.

Apr 86. (12") *(LAY 001)* **LASHTAL** ☐ -
Apr 86. (12"ep) *(LAY 004)* **NATURE UNVEILED** ☐ -
(re-iss. 1990 on 'Maldorer'; MAL 123)
Apr 86. (lp) *(LAY 008)* **DOGS BLOOD RISING** ☐ -
(cd-iss. Oct88; LAY 008CD) (cd re-iss. Aug95 on 'Durtro'+=; 027CD)– Dogs blood rising.
Apr 88. (d-lp) *(LAY 014)* **NIGHTMARE CULTURE** (w/ SICKNESS OF SNAKE) ☐ -
– Killykillkilly (a fire sermon) / etc.
Jul 88. (12") *(LAY 018)* **HAPPY BIRTHDAY PIGFACE CHRISTUS** ☐ -
Feb 89. (lp/cd) *(LAY 020/+C)* **SWASTIKAS FOR NOBODY** ☐ -
– Benediction / Blessing / North / Black Sun bloody Moon / Oh coal blacksmith / Panzer rune / Black flowers please / The final church / The summer of love / The nobody / Beausoleil / Scarlet woman / The stair song / Angel / Since yesterday / Valediction / Malediction.

Maldorer | not iss.

Aug 87. (lp) *(MAL 777)* **IMPERIUM** ☐ -
Oct 87. (12") *(MAL 108)* **CROWLEYMASS. / CHRISTMASSACRE / CROWLEYMASS (mix mix mix)** ☐ -
Mar 88. (12") *(MAL 088)* **RED FACE OF GOD. / THE BREATH AND THE PAIN OF GOD** ☐ -
Mar 88. (lp) *(MAL 666)* **CHRIST AND THE PALE QUEEN** ☐ -
Oct 88. (lp) *(MAL 111)* **CURRENT 93 PRESENT C.R. LAMA – TANTRIC NYING MA CHANT OF TIBET** ☐ -
1989. (lp) *(MAL 093)* **DAWN** ☐ -

Yangki | not iss.

Jul 88. (7") *(002)* **FAITHS FAVOURITES (with NURSE WITH WOUND). / BALLAD OF THE PALE GIRL** ☐ -

United Dairies | not iss.

Oct 88. (m-lp) *(UD 029)* **EARTH COVERS EARTH** ☐ -

—— early '89, they were credited on lp '93 DEAD SUN WHEELS' with DEATH IN JUNE.

Harbinger | not iss.

1990. (7") *(001)* **NO HIDING FROM THE BLACKBIRD. / (NURSE WITH WOUND: Burial of the stoned sardine)** ☐ -

Shock | not iss.

1990. (7") *(SX 003)* **SHE IS DEAD AND ALL FALL DOWN. / GOD HAS THREE FACES AND WOOD HAS NO NAME** ☐ -

—— In 1990, they shared an lp (some coloured) '1888' with DEATH IN JUNE

—— TIBET subsequently added **MICHAEL CASHMORE** – guitar

United Durtro | not iss.

Dec 89. (lp) *(DURTRO 001)* **LIVE AT BAR MALDORER** (first rel.1985 with NURSE WITH WOUND) ☐ -
Dec 90. (12") *(DURTRO 004)* **LOONEY RUNES** ☐ -
1992. (lp) *(DURTRO 006)* **ISLAND** ☐ -
1992. (d-lp) *(DURTRO 011)* **THUNDER PERFECT MIND** ☐ -
1994. (lp-blue) *(DURTRO 018)* **OF RUINE, OR SOME BLAZING STARRE** ☐ -
1994. (12"red) *(DURTRO 019)* **LUCIFER OVER LONDON** ☐ -
1995. (12",cd-s) *(DURTRO 025)* **TAMLIN. / HOW THE GREAT SATANIC GLORY FADED** ☐ -
Feb 96. (lp-clear) *(DURTRO 026)* **ALL THE PRETTY LITTLE HORSES** ☐ -
1997. (12"clear) *(DURTRO 028)* **WHERE THE LONG SHADOWS FALL** ☐ -
Oct 96. (cd) *(DURTRO 031)* **STARRES MARCHING SADLY HOME** ☐ -

– others, compilations, etc

on 'Cerne' unless mentioned otherwise

1990. (7"gig freebie) *(004)* **THIS AIN'T THE SUMMER OF LOVE (live with SOL INVICTUS)** ☐ -
1990. (3xlp-box) *(1-2-3)* **THE CERNE BOX SET** ☐ -
– HORSE lp / plus others by NURSE WITH WOUND + SOL INVICTUS)

CURVE

Formed: London, England ... 1991 by TONI HALLIDAY and her songwriting partner DEAN GARCIA. They had previously been part of the group STATE OF PLAY (one album 'BALANCING THE SCALES' in '86), before TONI ventured solo and released her sole 1989 album, 'HEARTS AND HANDSHAKES'. As CURVE, the pair broke through commercially, DAVE STEWART helping them delelop a much more modern approach on his 'Anxious' label (GARCIA was a friend of DAVE's since playing on EURYTHMICS' albums 'Touch' and 'Be Yourself Tonight'). A pseudo-punk gothic rock act, the sultry dark identity and distinctive vox of TONI combined ideally with the dreamy guitar-playing of DEAN, CURVE's line-up being completed by guitarist CHRIS SHEEHAN and drummer MONTI. The band debuted with 'THE BLINDFOLD EP' in March '91, just as the "shoegazing" scene was reaching its zenith. A kind of palefaced, quasi-industrial cousin to MY BLOODY VALENTINE, the band initially had many critics eating out of their hand. A further two EP's, 'FROZEN' and 'CHERRY' made the Top 40, while in early '92, CURVE cracked the Top 30 with the dark, sexy, 'FAIT ACCOMPLI' single, their finest three minutes. The following month saw the rtelease of a debut set, 'DOPPELGANGER', which met with mixed reviews and suggested that the CURVE sound wore thin over the course of a whole album. A further EP, 'BLACKERTHREETRACKER', and a follow-up album, 'CUCKOO' (1993) saw CURVE lose their creative and commercial momentum, eventually splitting amicably in 1994 when GARCIA decided to devote more time to his family. HALLIDAY's profile remained fairly high with a guest vocal on the hauntingly brilliant LEFTFIELD track, 'ORIGINAL', before CURVE finally made a comeback in 1997 (now signed to 'Universal') with the 'CHINESE BURN' single. • **Covered:** I FEEL LOVE (Donna Summer). • **Trivia:** TONI sang backing vox on ROBERT PLANT'S 'Shaken Not Stirred' and RECOIL's 'Bloodline' albums.

Album rating: DOPPELGANGER (*7) / CUCKOO (*6) / COME CLEAN (*4) / State Of Play: BALANCING THE SCALES (*4) / Toni Halliday: HEARTS AND HANDSHAKES (*4)

STATE OF PLAY

TONI HALLIDAY (b.1965, Sunderland, England) – vocals (ex-UNCLES) / **DEAN GARCIA** (half Hawaiian, lives Kentish Town) – bass / **ROMO / BAVIN**

Virgin | not iss.

Apr 86. (7") *(VS 850)* **NATURAL COLOURS. / LOST SOULS** ☐ -
(12"+=) *(VS 850-12)* – ('A'extended).
Jun 86. (7") *(VS 873)* **ROCKABYE BABY. / METROPOLIS** ☐ -
(12"+=) *(VS 873-12)* – ('A'extended).
Jul 86. (cd/c/lp) *(CD/TC+V 2382)* **BALANCING THE SCALES** ☐ -
– Naked as the day you were born / Natural colour (remix) / Rockabye baby / Workman / Human kind / Winds of change / We go under / Take me to the king / Lost souls. *(c+=)* – The trout / Strange air. *(cd++=)* – Rescue.

TONI HALLIDAY

Anxious | W.T.G.

Apr 88. (7") *(ANX 003)* **WEEKDAY. / TOP OF THE TREE** ☐ -
(12"+=) *(ANXT 003)* – ('A'extended).
(cd-s++=) *(ANXCD 003)* – Get out of the rain.
Jul 88. (7") *(ANX 005)* **LOVE ATTRACTION. / CHILD** ☐ -
(12"+=) *(ANXT 005)* – ('A'-Sub culture mix).
(cd-s++=) *(ANXCD 005)* – ('A'instrumental).
Mar 89. (7") *(ANX 010)* **TIME TURNS AROUND. / DULL MAN** ☐ -
(12"+=/cd-s+=) *(ANX T/CD 010)* – ('A'-Euro Tech mix).
Jul 89. (lp/c/cd) *(ZL/ZK/ZD 71680)* <45251> **HEARTS AND HANDSHAKES** ☐ ☐
– Time turns around / Cut up / Love attraction / Make a wish / Welcome to Heaven / Ode to Anna / Woman in mind / Weekday / I want more / Tales of tomorrow / The price you have to pay / Hearts and handshakes. (cd+=) – Dull man / Child.
Jul 89. (7") *(ANX 013)* **WOMAN IN MIND. / CHEMICAL COMEDOWN** ☐ ☐
(Thicker versions; 12"+=/cd-s+=) *(ANX T/CD 013)* – ('A'live).

CURVE

(HALLIDAY & GARCIA) with **CHRIS SHEEHAN** – guitar / **MONTI** – drums

Anxious | Charisma

Mar 91. (7"ep/12"ep/cd-ep) *(ANX/+T/CD 27)* **THE BLINDFOLD EP** [68] [-]
– Ten little girls / I speak your every word / Blindfold / No escape from Heaven.

May 91. (7"/c-s) *(ANX/+C 30)* **COAST IS CLEAR. / FROZEN** [34] [-]
(12"+=/cd-s+=) **THE FROZEN EP** *(ANX T/CD 30)* – The colour hours / Zoo.

Oct 91. (7"/c-s) *(ANX/+C 35)* **CLIPPED. / DIE LIKE A DOG** [36] [-]
(12"+=/cd-s+=) **THE CHERRY EP** *(ANX T/CD 35)* – Galaxy / Cherry.

Feb 92. (7"/c-s) *(ANX/+C 36)* **FAIT ACCOMPLI. / ARMS OUT** [22] [ ]
(12"+=/cd-s+=) *(ANX T/CD 36)* – Sigh.
(12") *(ANXTX 36)* – ('A'extended) / Coast is clear (live) / Die like a dog (live).

Mar 92. (cd/c/lp) *(ANX CD/MC/LP 77)* *<92108>* **DOPPELGANGER** [11] [ ]
– Already yours / Horror head / Wish you dead / Doppelganger / Lillies dying / Ice that melts the tips / Split into fractions / Think & act / Fait accompli / Sandpit.

— **DEBBIE SMITH + ALEX** – guitar; repl. CHRIS

Jul 92. (7"/c-s) *(ANX/+C 38)* **HORROR HEAD. / MISSION FROM GOD** [31] [-]
(12"+=/cd-s+=) *(ANX T/CD 38)* – Today is not the day / Falling free.

Jun 93. (cd/c/lp) *(ANX CD/MC/LP 80)* **RADIO SESSIONS** [72] [-]
– Ten little girls / No escape from Heaven / The colour hurts / The coast is clear / Die like a dog / Horror head / Arms out / Split into fractions.

— with **MONTI** – ever faithful drummer / and guest **SALLY HERBERT** – violin

Aug 93. (12"ep/c-ep/cd-ep) *(ANX T/C/CD 42)* **BLACKERTHREETRACKER EP** [39] [-]
– Missing link / On the wheel / Triumph.
(cd-ep) *(ANXCDX 42)* – Missing link (screaming bird mix) / Rising (mix) / Half the time (mix).

Sep 93. (cd/c/lp) *(ANX CD/MC/LP 81)* *<39061>* **CUCKOO** [29] [ ]
– Missing link / Crystal / Men are from Mars woman from Venus / All of one / Unreadable communication / Turkey crossing / Super blaster / Left of mother / Sweetest pie / Cuckoo.

— split in July '94 although they re-formed in '96.

FatLip | not iss.

Sep 96. (7") *(LIP 001)* **PINK GIRL WITH THE BLUES. / RECOVERY** [ ] [-]
(cd-s+=) *(LIPCD 001)* – Black Delilah.

— In Nov'97, TONI HALLIDAY featured on PAUL VAN DYK's minor UK hit single 'Words'.

Universal | Universal

Dec 97. (12"/cd-s) *(UMT/UMD 80423)* **CHINESE BURN (mixes; Steve Osborne / Paul Van Dyk / Lunatic Calm / Witchman's Eye Of The Storm / Headcase Medipac / ROBBING CHARITY / COME CLEAN** [ ] [ ]

May 98. (12"/cd-s) *(UMT/UMD 80489)* **COMING UP ROSES. /** [51] [ ]
(cd-s) *(UMDX 80489)* –

May 98. (cd) *(<UMD 80475>)* **COME CLEAN** [ ] [ ]
– Chinese burn / Coming up roses / Something familiar / Dog bone / Alligators getting up / Dirty high / Killer baby / Sweetback / Forgotten sanity / Cotton candy / Beyond reach / Come clean / Recovery.

CYCLEFLY

Formed: Aghada, Ireland ... 1997 by brothers DECLAN and CIERAN O'SHEA, who teamed up with the French/Italian band, SEVENTEEN (soon to be DOGABONE), an outfit that numbered NONO PRESTA, CHRISTIAN MONTAGNE and JEAN MICHEL CAVALLO. The story goes that the latter trio saw the wild DECLAN singing in his local pub and remembering his antics, decided to get in touch with him and his brother. Unfortunately, this took a little more time than anticipated as the pair were helping to build rollercoasters at Disneyland, Paris! Although their sound called to mind such alt-rock luminaries as JANE'S ADDICTION, PLACEBO and KYUSS, DECLAN's orange PVC attire might challenge more conservative audiences outside the bohemian confines of London or Paris. Finding a sympathetic home at the appropriately named 'RadioActive' label, CYCLEFLY took wing to the States in the Spring of '98. There, they worked with TOOL producer, SYLVIA MASSEY on their forthcoming debut 'Universal' album. Meanwhile, 'CRAWL DOWN' was awarded Kerrang! single of the week later that November.

Album rating: awaiting debut album

DECLAN O'SHEA (b.18 May'72) – vocals / **CIERAN O'SHEA** – guitar / **NONO PESTA** – guitar / **CHRISTIAN MONTAGNE** – bass / **JEAN MICHEL CAVALLO** – drums

RadioActive | Universe

Mar 98. (ltd-cd-s) *(demo)* **SUMP / EVERGREEN** [-] [-]

Nov 98. (cd-ep) *(RAXTD 35)* **CRAWL DOWN / SELOTAPE / STAR** [ ] [-]

CYNICS

Formed: Pittsburgh, Pennsylvania, USA ... early 1984 by MARK KERESMAN, GREGG KOSTELICH, BILL VON HAGEN and PAM. KOSTELICH set up his own 'Get Hip' label for the release of the band's debut single, '69', follow-up, 'PAINTED MY HEART', issued a year later. 1985 also saw the arrival of vocalist MICHAEL KASTELIC, a replacement for the departing KERESMAN who would become a stalwart throughout the band's changing fortunes and ever evolving personnel situation. Sticksman, TOM HAHN, was also in place for 1986's debut album, 'BLUE TRAIN STATION', an impressive set that drew on the garage tradition of the late 60's yet flitted between different genres with confident ease. 1988's 'TWELVE FLIGHTS UP', meanwhile, was the first and only CYNICS product to gain a UK issue (through the 'Resonance' label) while MIKE MICHALSKI had replaced PAM by the release of 1989's 'ROCK'N'ROLL'. A one-off 7" on 'Sympathy For The Record Industry' found the band entering the 90's in style and paying homage to their heroes with covers of The Heartbreakers' 'BORN TO LOSE' and T.REX's 'BUICK MACKANE'. The 'Get Hip' label was also reactivated for a string of albums in the early 90's, the most recent being 1994's 'GET OUR WAY'. • **Note:** Not to be confused with an Alaskan band who released an EP in 1980, 'Beat The Cynics'; two out of the four tracks, 'Rock Apocalypse' & 'Fools In Hell', issued in the UK on 'Stickfoot' 1984.

Album rating: BLUE TRAIN STATION (*5) / TWELVE FLIGHTS UP (*6) / ROCK AND ROLL (*5)

MARK KERESMAN – vocals / **GREGG KOSTELICH** – guitar (ex-JETSONS, ex-PROTOTYPE) / **PAM** – bass / **BILL VON HAGEN** – drums

not iss. | Get Hip

Jul 84. (7") **69. /** [-] [ ]

— added an unknown musician

1985. (7") **PAINTED MY HEART. /** [-] [ ]

— **MICHAEL KASTELIC** – vocals (ex-WAKE – US, ex-BOAT PEOPLE, ex-DUB SEX, ex-24 MINUTES) repl. KERESMAN

— **TOM HAHN** – drums (ex-WAKE – US, ex-PROTOTYPE) repl. HAGEN

1986. (7") **NO PLACE TO HIDE. /** [-] [ ]

1986. (lp) **BLUE TRAIN STATION** [-] [ ]
<re-iss. 1990 as 'BLUE TRAIN SESSIONS' on 'Skyclad'; 2>

Resonance | Get Hip

Apr 88. (lp) *(R 3388-13)* **TWELVE FLIGHTS UP** [ ] [ ]
<re-iss. 1990 as 'SIXTEEN FLIGHTS UP' on 'Skyclad'; 5>

— **MIKE MICHALSKI** – bass (ex-HALF LIFE, ex-HERETICS) repl. PAM

not iss. | Skyclad

1989. (lp) *<25>* **ROCK AND ROLL** [-] [ ]

not iss. | Impossible

1991. (lp) *<017>* **STRANDED IN MADRID (live)** [-] [ ]

not iss. | 1+2 Japan

1992. (cd) *(015)* **CYNICISM** [-] [-] Japan

not iss. | Sympathy F

1990's. (7") *<SFTRI 099>* **BUICK MACKANE. / BORN TO LOSE** [-] [ ]

not iss. | Get Hip

1992. (lp) *<GH 1002>* **VPRO RADIO BROADCAST (live in the Netherlands)** [-] [ ]

1993. (cd) *<GH 1008CD>* **LEARN TO LOSE** [-] [ ]

1994. (cd) *<GH 1014CD>* **NO SIESTA TONITE (live)** [-] [ ]

1994. (7") *<GH 129>* **I DON'T NEED YOU. / GIRL< YOU'RE ON MY MIND** [-] [ ]

1994. (cd) *<GH 1030CD>* **GET OUR WAY** [-] [ ]

1994. (7") *<GH 141>* **RIGHT HERE WITH YOU. / LEARN TO LOSE** [-] [ ]

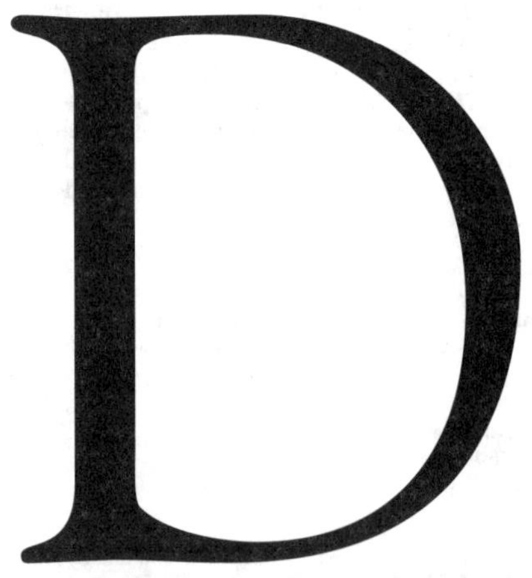

D.A.F.

Formed: Dusseldorf, Germany . . . 1979 as DEUTSCH AMERIKANISCHE FREUDSCHAFT by ROBERT GORL, who took the name from local posters depicting rosy German-US relations. Along with CHRISLO HAAS, MICHAEL KEHMER and WOLFGANG SPELMANS, he recorded a debut album, 'PRODUKT' (1979), for the domestic market before signing to DANIEL MILLER's newly formed 'Mute' label. Following the replacement of KEHMER with GABI DELGADO-(LOPEZ), recording sessions resulted in 1980's 'DIE KLEINEN UND DE BOSEN' ('The Small And The Evil'), the record's teutonic experimentation following in the footsteps of sonic terrorists, SUICIDE, while also tracing the Kraut-rock lineage of forebears such as CAN and KRAFTWERK. Enjoying support from both John Peel and the underground club scene, DAF (now a duo of GORL and DELGADO) subsequently signed to 'Virgin', releasing a further three groundbreaking albums, 'ALLES IST GUT' (1981), 'GOLD UND LIEBE' (1981) and 'FUR IMMER' (1982). Yet DELGADO-LOPEZ's insistence on singing in German undoubtedly restricted their appeal, labelmates DEPECHE MODE going on to massive success while DAF's pioneering electro sounds and sexual claustrophopia were more influential on up and coming acts like FRONT 242 and NITZER EBB. Splitting in late '82, DELGADO-LOPEZ and GORL both recorded solo sets, 'MISTRESS' (1983) and 'NIGHT FULL OF TENSION' (1984) respectively. A brief mid-80's reformation led to a German-only album, '1st STEP TO HEAVEN' (1986), via 'Arista', while GORL re-emerged almost a decade later on German techno label, 'Disko B', releasing a couple of 12" singles and an album, 'THERAPIE' (1994). • **Trivia:** In 1981, DAF guested on the EURYTHMICS debut album, 'In The Garden'. ANNIE LENNOX returned the favour by contributing backing vox to GORL's 'DARLING DON'T LEAVE ME' single.

Album rating: EIN PRODUKT DER DEUTSCH AMERIKANISCHE FREUDSCHAFT (*3) / DIE KLEINEN UND DIE BOSEN (*4) / ALLES IST GUT (*6) / GOLD UND LIEBE (*5) / FUR IMMER (*5) / D.A.F. compilation (*7) / 1st STEP TO HEAVEN (*5) / Robert Gorl: NIGHT FULL OF TENSION (*5) / Gabi Delgado: MISTRESS (*5)

DEUTSCHE AMERIKANISCHE FREUNDSCHAFT

ROBERT GORL – synthesizers, drums / **CHRISLO HAAS** – synthesizers, saxophone, bass / **WOLFGANG SPELMANS** – guitar / **MICHAEL KEHMER** – bass

Warning | not iss.

Nov 79. (lp) *(WR 001)* **EIN PRODUKT DER DEUTSCH AMERIKANISCHE FREUNDSCHAFT** - | - German
– (no song-titles).

— **GABI DELGADO**-(LOPEZ) – vocals (ex-MITTAGSPAUSE); repl. KEHMER

Mute | not iss.

Mar 80. (7") *(MUTE 005)* **KEBAB TRAUME. / GEWALT (VIOLENCE)** -

Aug 80. (lp) *(STUMM 1)* **DIE KLEINEN UND DIE BOSEN** -
– Osten wahrt am langsten / Essen dann schlafen / Co co Pino / Kinderfunk / Nachtarbeit / Ich gebe dir ein Stuck von mir / Die Panne / Gewalt / Gib's mir / Auf wiedersehen / Das ist Liebe / Was ist eine Weele / Anzufassen und anzufassen / Volkstanz / Die lustigen Stiefel / Die kleinen und die Bosen / Ich bin die fesche Lola / El Basilon / Y la gracia. *(cd-iss. Nov92; CDSTUMM 1)*

Oct 80. (7") *(MUTE 011)* **DER RAUBER UND DER PRINZ. / TANZ MIT MIR** -

— trimmed to a duo **DELGADO + GORL** when CHRISLO HAAS left, later joining CRIME & THE CITY SOLUTION (SPELMANS also departed)

Virgin | not iss.

Mar 81. (lp) *(V 2202)* **ALLES IST GUT** -
– Ich und die Wirklichkeit (Me and reality) / Als wars das letzte mal (As if it were the last time) / Verlier nicht den Kopf (Don't loose your head) / Alle gegen all (Everybody fights everybody) / Alles ist gut (Everything is good) / Sato-sato / Der Mussolini (The Mussolini) / Rote Lippen (Red lips) / Mein Herz macht bum (My heart goes boom) / Der rauber und der Prinz (The robber and the Prince). *(re-iss. Mar84; OVED 59) (cd-iss. 1987; CDV 2202)*

May 81. (12") *(VS 418-12)* **DER MUSSOLINI. / DER RAUBER UND DER PRINZ** -

Nov 81. (12") *(VS 448-12)* **GOLDENES SPIELZEUG. / EL QUE** -

Nov 81. (lp) *(V 2218)* **GOLD UND LIEBE** -
– Ich will / Muskel / Absolute Korperkontrolle / Verschwende deine Jugend / Greif nach den Sternen / Liebe auf den ersten Blick / El Que / Sex unter wasser / Was ziehst du an heute nacht / Ich will / Sex unter wasser / Goldenes Spielzeug. *(re-iss. Aug88; OVED 81) (cd-iss. Apr88 w/extra B-sides)*

Feb 82. (12") *(VS 481-12)* **SEX UNTER WASSER. / KNOCHEN AUF KNOCHEN**

Sep 82. (12") **VERLIEB DICH IN MICH. / EIN BISSCHEN KRIEG** -

Oct 82. (lp) *(V 2239)* **FUR IMMER** -
– Kebab traume / Prinzessin / Die Lippe / Verehrt euren Haaarschnitt / Wer schon sein will muss leiden / Im Dschungel der Liebe / Ein bisschen Krieg / Die Gotter sind weiss / Verlieb dich in mich / Geheimnis. *(re-iss. Aug88 lp/c; OVED/+C 82) (cd-iss. Apr88; CDV 2239)*

— split late '82

GABI DELGADO

— went solo with **RAOUL WALTON, STEPHAN WITTNER + EDWARD LOPEZ**

Mar 83. (7"/12") *(VS 579/+12)* **HISTORY OF A KISS. / SEX GODDESS** -

Mar 83. (lp) *(V 2266)* **MISTRESS** -
– Sex goddess / History of a kiss / Amor / Young lions / Victims / Mistress.. *(re-iss. Aug88; OVED 93)*

Jul 83. (12") *(VS 608-12)* **AMOR. / SEX AND SOUL** -

ROBERT GORL

Mute | Elektra

Mar 83. (7") *(7MUTE 27)* **MIT DIR (WITH YOU). / BERUHRT VERFUHT** -

Feb 84. (7"/12") *(7/12 MUTE 31)* **DARLING DON'T LEAVE ME. / IST WEIDER DA**

Mar 84. (lp/c) *(STUMM/CSTUMM 16)* **NIGHT FULL OF TENSION**
– Playtime / I love me / Charlie Cat / Gewinnen wir die beste der Frauen / Queen King / Love in mind / Darling don't leave me / Wind in hair. *(c+=)* – Mit dir (extended) / Beruhrt verfuhrt (remix) / Darling don't leave me (extended) / Ist wieder da / Eckhardt's party.

D.A.F.

— **DELGADO + GORL** reformed

Illuminated | not iss.

Aug 85. (12") *(ILL 62-12)* **ABSOLUTE BODY CONTROL. / 1ST TRIP TO HEAVEN** -

Nov 85. (7"/12") *(LEV/12LEV 65)* **BROTHERS (Robert's mix). / BROTHERS (Gabi's mix)** -

Ariola | not iss.

Jan 86. (lp/c/cd) *(207/407/257 435)* **1ST STEP TO HEAVEN** - | - German
– Voulez vous coucher avec moi (part 1) / Pure joy / Blond hair, dark brown hair / Sex up / Absolute body control / Voulez vous coucher avec moi (part 2) / Crazy crazy / Brothers (opium mix) / 1st step to Heaven (mix).

— split again, although this was for the final time

– compilations etc. –

May 84. (c) *Music For Midgets; (MFM 40)* **LIVE IN BERLIN 1980 (live)** -

Jun 88. (cd/c/lp) *Virgin; (CD/TC+/V 2533)* **D.A.F. – THE BEST OF . . .** -
– Verschwende deine Jugend / Der Mussolini (remix) / Mein Herz macht bum / El que / Ich und die Wirklichkeit / Die gotter sind weiss / Der Rauber und der Prinz / Liebe auf der ersten Blick (remix) / Im Dschungel der Liebe / Prinzessin / Greif nach den Sternen / Kebab traume / Die Lippe / Als wars das letzte mal.

Nov 98. (12"ep) *Grey Area; (12DAF 123)* **DER MUSSOLINI / ALLE GEGEN ALLE. / VERSCHWENDE DEINE JUGEND / KEBAB TRAUME / CO CO PINO** -

ROBERT GORL

Disko B | not iss.

May 93. (7") *(15538)* **PSYCHO SAFE. /** -

Aug 94. (2x12") *(EFA 12283-1)* **THERAPIE** -

Feb 95. (12") *(EFA 122736)* **HAPPY GATHERING. /** -

Mar 96. (cd/lp; ROBERT GORL & PETE NAMLOCK) *(PK 08109/08110)* **ELEKTRO** -
(above issued on 'Fax' records)

May 96. (12") *(EFA12 2896)* **YIP YAP. /** -

Sep 96. (cd/lp) *(EFA 12292-2/-6)* **WATCH THE REAL COPYCAT** -

Jul 98. (2x12") *(EFAMS 29468)* **SEX DROPS EP** -

DAINTEES (see under ⇒ STEPHENSON, Martin)

DAISY CHAINSAW

Formed: London, England . . . early 90's by KATIE JANE GARSIDE, main songwriter CRISPIN GREY, RICHARD ADAMS and VINCE JOHNSON. A one-hit indie wonder if there ever was one, DAISY CHAINSAW were famous for about five minutes in 1992 after hitting the UK Top 30 with grunge-pop ditty, 'LOVE YOUR MONEY'. The lead track of their independently released 'LOVESICKPLEASURE' EP, the song centred around GARSIDE's kooky delivery; dressed like a Dickensian beggar girl, her combination of wide-eyed innocence and ragged rebellion stirred up controversy in much the same way as BOW WOW WOW had done a decade earlier. Unfortunately, unlike Malcolm McLaren's former proteges, they only had the one gimmick as 'One Little Indian' (the band subsequently snubbed MADONNA's 'Maverick' label) found out when debut album, 'ELEVENTEEN' (1992), didn't exactly set the charts alight. Any hopes of further success were extinguished with GARSIDE's subsequent departure, due to press furore surrounding alleged revelations of childhood sexual abuse. The remaining trio re-emerging to a predictably hostile reception with 1994's 'THEY KNOW NOT WHAT THEY DO'. • **Trivia:** A single, 'PIPACHI' (CRISPIN's dogs name), was withdrawn from sale in March 1992.

Album rating: ELEVENTEEN (*5) / FOR THEY KNOW NOT WHAT THEY DO (*3)

KATIE JANE GARSIDE – vocals / **CRISPIN GRAY** (b. JOHN ORION) – guitar / **RICHARD ADAMS** – bass / **VINCE JOHNSON** (b. Toronto, Canada) – drums

Deva A&M

Jan 92. (7"/c-s/12"/cd-s) *(DEVA 001/+C/T/CD) <75021-2403-2>* **LOVE YOUR MONEY. / LOVESICK PLEASURE** 26 Mar92
(above originally issued on 'Deva' only Nov91; same)

One Little Indian A&M

Mar 92. (7"/c-s) *(82 TP7/+C)* **PINK FLOWER. / ROOM 11** 65 -
(12"+=/cd-s+=) *(82 TP12/TP7CD)* – All the kids agree.

Sep 92. (cd/c) *(TPLP 100 CD/C) <314-540031-2/-4>* **ELEVENTEEN** 62 Oct92
– I feel insane / You may be my friend / Dog with sharper teeth / Hope your dreams come true / Natural man / Love your money / Lovely ugly brutal world / Use me use you / The future free / Pink-flower / Waiting for the wolves / Everything is weird.

Nov 92. (12"ep/cd-ep) *(92 TP12/TP7CD)* **HOPE YOUR DREAMS COME TRUE. / PROPELLOR PUNCH / QUEUE FOR TRANSATLANTIC ALIEN** -

— now without GARSIDE, She was repl. by **BELINDA LEITH** – vocals

Mar 94. (7") *(100 TP7)* **LOVE ME FOREVER. / DIAMOND OF THE DESERT** -

Apr 94. (7") *(110 TP7)* **THE FUTURE TREE. / ZEBRA HEAD** -

Jun 94. (cd/c) *(TPLP 111 CD/C)* **FOR THEY KNOW NOT WHAT THEY DO**
– The future tree / Belittled and beaten down / Sleeping with Heaven / Love me forever / Candyfloss / Life tomorrow / Zebra head / Unit shifter / Diamond of the desert / Mosquito / Greatest God's divine / Voice of a generation / Looking for an angel.

Fluffy Bunny not iss.

Jun 95. (cd-s) *(SPLIT 1CD)* **YOU'RE GRUESOME** -

— never reunited for any other recordings

DALEK I LOVE YOU

Formed: Liverpool, England . . . late 1977 out of punk act, RADIO BLANK, by ALAN GILL and DAVID BALFE. Adding DAVE HUGHES and CHRIS 'TEEPEE' SHAW (MARTIN COOPER also p/t sax), the band signed to 'Vertigo' and released a debut single, 'FREEDOM FIGHTERS', in Spring '79. A well received slice of drum-machine backed experimental proto-electro pop, the track was followed by 'THE WORLD' later that year. The turn of the decade found the band setting up their own label, 'Back Door', initiating proceedings with an eponymous single in Spring 1980. The latter was backed with what was arguably the scousers' finest three minutes, 'EIGHT TRACK', an ice cool serving of indie electronica which was also one of the highlights on debut album, 'KUM'PAS (COMPASS)' (1980). A Top 60 success, the record cemented the band's reputation as more musically adventurous cousins to local lads, The TEARDROP EXPLODES. Subsequently reduced to what was basically ALAN GILL's one-man operation (BALFE having joined BIG IN JAPAN), only one further single, 'HEARTBEAT', was released in early '81 before GILL joined the aforementioned TEARDROP EXPLODES for a year. Furnished with a deal courtesy of 'Korova', he re-emerged under the DALEK I LOVE YOU banner in summer '82 with a new single, 'HOLIDAY IN DISNEYLAND'. Another extended gap followed, however, prior to the release of the singles, 'AMBITION', 'HORRORSCOPE' and a belated follow-up album, 'DALEK I LOVE YOU' (1983). Despite the ensuing critical acclaim, commercial success achieved by peers such as OMD seemed as far away as ever and GILL concentrated his efforts on writing the soundtrack to cult mid-80's movie, 'Letter To Brezhnev'. GILL also formed the small 'Bopadub' label, home to a final DALEK I LOVE YOU (cassette-only) album, 'NAIVE' (1985).

Album rating: KUM'PAS (*6) / DALEK I LOVE YOU (*5)

ALAN GILL – vocals, guitar, synthesizer / **DAVID BALFE** – bass, vocals, synthesizer (left before any releases) / **DAVE HUGHES** – keyboards, synthesizer (ex-SECRETS) / **CHRIS 'TEEPEE' SHAW** – synthesizer, bass / guest **MARTIN COOPER** – saxophone

Vertigo not iss.

May 79. (7") *(DALEK 1)* **FREEDOM FIGHTERS. / TWO CHAMELEONS** -

Sep 79. (7") *(DALEK 2)* **THE WORLD. / WE'RE ALL ACTORS** -

— now without BALFE who joined BIG IN JAPAN

Back Door not iss.

Apr 80. (7") *(CLOSE 1)* **DALEK I LOVE YOU. / EIGHT TRACK** -

May 80. (12"ep; as DALEK I) *(DOOR 5)* **DALEK I LOVE YOU (DESTINY). / HAPPY / THIS IS MY UNIFORM** -

— guests were **DAVID BATES + HUGH JONES + CHRIS HUGHES + KEN PEERS**

Jun 80. (lp; as DALEK I) *(OPEN 1)* **KUM'PAS (COMPASS)** 54 -
– The world / 8 track / Destiny (Dalek I love you) / A suicide / The kiss / Trapped / Two chameleons / Freedom fighters / You really got me / Mad * / Good times * / We're all actors / Heat / Missing 15 minutes. *(re-iss. Apr89 on 'Fontana' lp/c/cd; 836894-1/-4/-2)* – (omits 2 tracks =*).

— now basically just **ALAN GILL** when DAVE HUGHES joined OMD

Feb 81. (7") *(DOOR 10)* **HEARTBEAT. / ASTRONAUTS HAVE LANDED ON THE MOON** -

— GILL joined The TEARDROP EXPLODES for around a year

Korova not iss.

Jul 82. (7"/12") *(KOW 25/+T)* **HOLIDAY IN DISNEYLAND. / MARKS AND LICENSES**

Sep 83. (7"/12") *(KOW 29/+T)* **AMBITION. / (I AM) HOT PERSON** -

Nov 83. (7") *(KOW 31)* **HORRORSCOPE. / THESE WALLS WE BUILD** -
(12"+=) *(KOW 31T)* – Heap big pow wow / The angel and the clown.

Nov 83. (lp/c) *(KODE/CODE 7)* **DALEK I LOVE YOU** -
– Holiday in Disneyland / Horrorscope / Health and happiness / Mouse that roared / Dad on fire / Ambition / Lust / 12 hours of blues / Sons of Sahara / Africa express.

— ALAN GILL was commissioned to write the soundtrack for the movie, 'Letter To Brezhnev', released in 1985 he briefly re-formed DALEK I and made one rare cassette-lp, 'NAIVE' for 'Bopadub'.

DALI'S CAR (see under ⇒ BAUHAUS)

Cindy DALL

Born: CYNTHIA DALL, Sacramento, California, USA. Relocating to San Francisco, she hooked up with arch miserablilist, BILL CALLAHAN, as a collaborator in his otherwise solo venture, SMOG. Inking a deal with 'Drag City' ('Domino' – also current home of SMOG), DALL released a mysterious solo album in 1996. Scaling new heights in underground anonymity/modesty, the album came without any artist credits, nor was it graced with a title. Nevertheless, this particular toy story had a happy endng as critics generally gave DALL's obscurely minimalist creations the thumbs up.

Album rating: UNTITLED debut (*6)

CINDY DALL – vocals, guitars / with **JIM O'ROURKE** – piano, guitar, etc (of TORTOISE) / **RIAN MURPHY + TOM MALLON** – drums

Domino Drag City

Mar 96. (cd/lp) *(WIG CD/LP 23) <DR 73>* **UNTITLED**
– Christmas (California) / Berlin, 1945 / Lion becomes dragon / Holland / Bright night / For Tiara / Grey and castles / Aaron Matthew.

DAMNED

Formed: London, England . . . May 1976 by BRIAN JAMES and RAT SCABIES who soon found The CAPTAIN and former undertaker, DAVE VANIAN. Signed to new UK indie label, 'Stiff', by JAKE RIVERA, they released the classic track, 'NEW ROSE', produced by stablemate, NICK LOWE. The DAMNED became the first "New Wave Punks" to release and chart with an album, namely the enduring 'DAMNED DAMNED DAMNED' (1977). One of the classic punk debuts, the album pogo'd and and thrashed its way through a frenetic set of three-chord wonders, LOWE's garden shed production underlining the riotous pandemonium. The band had also broken into the Top 40, although ironically enough, prolonged chart success would come later in the 80's when The DAMNED had changed almost beyond recognition. Live, the band were also one of the major attractions on the London scene; with VANIAN's proto-goth affectations, SENSIBLE's beret-topped antics and SCABIES' demented drummer persona all competing against each other, The DAMNED were indeed a motley crew. Their musical assault was bolstered later that year by a second guitarist, LU EDMONDS, who debuted on the flaccid 'MUSIC FOR PLEASURE' (1977). The album was universally derided and SCABIES soon left for pastures new. Although future CULTURE CLUB man, JOHN MOSS was drafted in briefly as a replacement, the band splintered early the following year. After a period of solo work, VANIAN, SENSIBLE and SCABIES regrouped as The DAMNED early in '79 and emerged rejuvenated into the UK Top 20 via the impressive 'LOVE SONG'. With ALGY WARD completing the line-up, the band scored a second chart hit with 'SMASH IT UP', releasing their lauded 'MACHINE GUN ETIQUETTE' album later that year. Sure, they were still as swift and deadly as the title might suggest, but somehow they'd acquired a mastery of pop dynamics; a third single, 'I JUST CAN'T BE HAPPY TODAY', was the closest they'd yet came to a rock solid tune. PAUL GRAY replaced WARD for 1980's 'UNTITLED (THE BLACK ALBUM)', an even more surprising, ambitious double set which flew in the face of punk convention with its rampant experimentalism. The poppy 'STRAWBERRIES' (1982) marked the last stand of CAPTAIN SENSIBLE, who'd scored with the annoying 'HAPPY TALK' earlier that summer, the first fuits of his solo deal with 'A&M'. VANIAN and SCABIES lumbered on with new members ROMAN JUGG and BRYAN GUNN, suprisingly enough enjoying major chart success with a string of overtly commercial, pseudo goth rockers, the biggest of which, a cover of BARRY RYAN's 'ELOISE' made the Top 3. 'PHANTASMAGORIA' (1985) became their biggest selling album to date, catering to a whole new generation of fans. Most critics were agreed, however, that it paled in comparison to their earlier work, the DAMNED finally fading in the late 80's. For any interested parties, the band periodically get together with an amorphous line-up for all-dayer's and one-off gigs; old punks never die, they just tour with The DAMNED. • **Songwriters:** Most written by JAMES, until he left, when group took over. Covered:- HELP! (Beatles) / I FEEL ALRIGHT (Stooges / Iggy Pop) / JET BOY JET GIRL (New York Dolls) / CITADEL (Rolling Stones) / ELOISE (Paul & Barry Ryan) / WHITE RABBIT (Jefferson Airplane) / ALONE AGAIN OR (Love) / WILD THING (Troggs) / LET THERE BE RATS (aka DRUMS) (Sandy Nelson). • **Trivia:** NICK MASON (Pink Floyd drummer) produced disappointing 2nd album MUSIC FOR PLEASURE.

CAPTAIN SENSIBLE had UK-No.1 in 1982 with (Rogers-Hammerstein's) HAPPY TALK, and although briefly, became a top disco/pop act abroad.

Album rating: DAMNED DAMNED DAMNED (*8) / MUSIC FOR PLEASURE (*5) / MACHINE GUN ETIQUETTE (*7) / BLACK ALBUM (*6) / BEST OF THE DAMNED compilation (*8) / STRAWBERRIES (*5) / PHANTASMAGORIA (*5) / ANYTHING (*3) THE LIGHT AT THE END OF THE TUNNEL compilation (*7) / FINAL DAMNATION (*4)

DAVE VANIAN (b. DAVE LETTS) – vocals / **BRIAN JAMES** (b. BRIAN ROBERTSON) – guitar (ex-LONDON S.S.) / **CAPTAIN SENSIBLE** (b. RAY BURNS, 23 Apr'55) – bass, vocals / **RAT SCABIES** (b. CHRIS MILLER, 30 Jul'57) – drums (ex-LONDON S.S.)

Stiff | Frontier

Nov 76. (7") *(BUY 6)* **NEW ROSE. / HELP!** [ ] [-]

Feb 77. (7") *(BUY 10)* **NEAT NEAT NEAT. / STAB YOR BACK / SINGALONGASCABIES** [ ] [-]

Feb 77. (lp) *(SEEZ 1)* **DAMNED DAMNED DAMNED** [36] [ ] Apr77
– Neat neat neat / Fan club / I fall / Born to kill / Stab yor back / Feel the pain / New rose / Fish / See her tonite / 1 of the 2 / So messed up / I feel alright. *(re-iss. Apr87 on 'Demon' lp/c/cd; FIEND/+CASS/CD 91) (pic-lp 1988; PFIEND 91)*

— added (ROBERT) **LU EDMUNDS** – guitar

Sep 77. (7") *(BUY 18)* **PROBLEM CHILD. / YOU TAKE MY MONEY** [ ] [-]

Nov 77. (lp) *(SEEZ 5)* **MUSIC FOR PLEASURE** [ ] [ ]
– Problem child / Don't cry wolf / One way love / Politics / Stretcher case / Idiot box / You take my money / Alone / Your eyes / Creep (you can't fool me) / You know. *(re-iss. Apr88 on 'Demon' lp/c/cd; FIEND/+CASS/CD 108)*

Dec 77. (7",7"purple) *(BUY 24)* **DON'T CRY WOLF. / ONE WAY LOVE** [ ] [-]

— **DAVE BERK** – drums (ex-JOHNNY MOPED) repl. SCABIES who formed various bands

— **JOHN MOSS** – drums replaced BERK. They split Feb 78. VANIAN joined DOCTORS OF MADNESS. SENSIBLE formed SOFTIES then KING. EDMUNDS & MOSS formed THE EDGE. MOSS later joined ADAM & THE ANTS then CULTURE CLUB. EDMUNDS became part of ATHLETICO SPIZZ 80, The MEKONS, SHRIEKBACK, PIL. etc. BRIAN JAMES formed TANZ DER YOUTH, who released one single, 'I'M SORRY I'M SORRY' for 'Radar', before going solo the following year (1979) to issue his version of 'AIN'T THAT A SHAME'. He subsequently formed another punk supergroup, The HELLIONS, issuing one 1981 single for 'Illegal', 'WHY WHY WHY', before he jointly formed The LORDS OF THE NEW CHURCH. The DAMNED re-formed in Autumn '78 as The **DOOMED** with LEMMY of MOTORHEAD on bass. (1 gig) **HENRY BADOWSKI** – bass (ex-CHELSEA) replaced LEMMY. The group reverted to name The **DAMNED** with originals VANIAN, SENSIBLE (now guitar & keyboards) and **SCABIES**

— **ALGY WARD** – bass (ex-SAINTS) replaced BADOWSKI who went solo

Chiswick | Roadrunner

Apr 79. (7",7"red) *(CHIS 112)* **LOVE SONG. / NOISE NOISE NOISE / SUICIDE** [20] [-]
(re-iss. 7"blue Feb82 on 'Big Beat'; NS 75)

Oct 79. (7") *(CHIS 116)* **SMASH IT UP. / BURGLAR** [35] [-]
(re-iss. 7"red Mar82 on 'Big Beat'; NS 76)

Nov 79. (lp) *(CWK 3011)* **MACHINE GUN ETIQUETTE** [31] [ ] Dec79
– Love song / Machine gun etiquette / I just can't be happy today / Melody Lee / Anti-Pope / These hands / Plan 9 channel 7 / Noise noise noise / Looking at you / Smash it up (parts 1 & 2). *(re-iss. Jun85 on 'Ace' lp/c; DAM/+MC 3) (cd-iss. 1986 +=; CDWIK 905)* – Ballroom blitz / Suicide / Rabid (over you) / White rabbit.

Nov 79. (7") *(CHIS 120)* **I JUST CAN'T BE HAPPY TODAY. / BALLROOM BLITZ / TURKEY SONG** [46] [-]

— **PAUL GRAY** – bass, vocals (ex-EDDIE AND THE HOT RODS) repl. WARD who formed TANK

Jun 80. (7";w-drawn) *(CHIS 130)* **WHITE RABBIT. / RABID (OVER YOU) / SEAGULLS** [ ] [-]

Sep 80. (7"m/12"m) *(CHIS/+12 135)* **THE HISTORY OF THE WORLD (part 1). / I BELIEVE THE IMPOSSIBLE / SUGAR AND SPITE** [ ] [-]

Nov 80. (d-lp) *(CWK 3015)* **UNTITLED** (THE BLACK ALBUM) (1/2 studio, 1/4 live, 1/4 concept) [29] [-]
– Wait for the blackout / Lively arts / Silly kids games / Drinking about my baby / Hit and miss / Doctor Jekyll and Mr. Hyde / 13th floor vendetta / Twisted nerve / Sick of this and that / History of the world (part 1) / Therapy // Curtain call / live side:- Love song / Second time around / Smash it up (parts 1 & 2) / New rose / I just can't be happy today / Plan 9 Channel 7. *(re-iss. Aug82 on 'Ace' as one-lp/d-c; DAM/+MC 3) (c-iss.Jun85; TCWIK 3015) (cd-iss. Mar90; CDWIK 906)* – (omits live tracks)

Nov 80. (7"m) *(CHIS 139)* **THERE AINT NO SANITY CLAUS. / HIT OR MISS / LOOKING AT YOU (live)** [ ] [-]

N.E.M.S. | not iss.

Nov 81. (d7"ep) *(TRY 1)* **FRIDAY THE 13th** [50] [-]
– Disco man / The limit club / Citadel / Billy bad breaks.

Bronze | not iss.

Jul 82. (7"m/7"pic-d) *(BRO/+P 149)* **LOVELY MONEY. / LOVELY MONEY (disco) / I THINK I'M WONDERFUL** [42] [-]

Sep 82. (7"ep) *(BRO 156)* **DOZEN GIRLS. / TAKE THAT / MINE'S A LARGE ONE, LANDLORD / TORTURE ME** [ ] [-]

Oct 82. (lp/c) *(BRON 542)* **STRAWBERRIES** [15] [-]
– Ignite / Generals / Stranger on the town / Dozen girls / The dog / Gun fury / Pleasure and the pain / Life goes on / Bad time for Bonzo / Under the floor again / Don't bother me. *(re-iss. Mar86 on 'Legacy' red-lp/c; LLM/+K 3000) (re-iss. Dec86 on 'Dojo' lp/cd; DOJO LP/CD 46) (cd re-iss. Nov92 on 'Dojo'; DOJOCD 46) (cd-iss. Apr94 on 'Cleopatra'; CLEO 1029-2) (cd re-iss. Mar97 on 'Essential'; ESMCD 473)*

Nov 82. (7"m) *(BRO 159)* **GENERALS. / DISGUISE / CITADEL ZOMBIES** [ ] [-]

Damned | not iss.

Nov 83. (pic-lp/lp) *(P+/DAMU 2)* **LIVE IN NEWCASTLE (live)** [-] [-] mail-o
(cd-iss. Jan94 on 'Receiver'; RRCD 181)

Plus One | not iss.

May 84. (7"colrd/7"pic-d) *(DAMNED 1/+P)* **THANKS FOR THE NIGHT. / NASTY** [ ] [-]
(re-iss. 12"-ltd.1985 +=; DAMNED 1T) – Do the blitz.

— **VANIAN** and **SCABIES** recruited new guys **ROMAN JUGG** – guitar, keyboards / who replaced the CAPTAIN who carried on with solo career. **BRYN GUNN** – bass repl. GRAY

M.C.A. | Off Beat

Mar 85. (7"/7"pic-d/'A'-Spic'n'Spec mix-12") *(GRIM/+P/T 1)* **GRIMLY FIENDISH. / EDWARD THE BEAR** [21] [-]
(12"white+=) *(GRIMX 1)* – ('A'-Bad Trip mix).

Jun 85. (7") *(GRIM 2)* **SHADOW OF LOVE. / NIGHTSHIFT** [25] [ ]
('A'-Ten Inches Of Hell mix-10"+=) *(GRIMX 2)* – Would you.
(12"+=) *(GRIMT 2)* – Would you.
(d7"+=) *(GRIMY 2)* – Let there be Rats / Wiped out.

Jul 85. (lp/c/pic-lp/white-lp/blue-lp) *(MCF/+C/P/W/B 3275)* **PHANTASMAGORIA** [11] [ ]
– Street of dreams / Shadow of love / There'll come a day / Sanctum sanctorium / Is it a dream / Grimly fiendish / Edward the bear / The eighth day / Trojans. *(free 7" w.a.)* I JUST CAN'T BE HAPPY TODAY *(re-iss. 1986; same)* – (contains free 12"blue ELOISE) *(cd-iss. Aug89; DMCL 1887)*

Sep 85. (7") *(GRIM 3)* **IS IT A DREAM (Wild West End mix) / STREET OF DREAMS (live)** [34] [ ]
(12"+=) *(GRIMT 3)* – Curtain call (live) / Pretty vacant (live) / Wild thing (live).

Jan 86. (7") *(GRIM 4)* **ELOISE. / TEMPTATION** [3] [ ]
(12"blue+=/'A'-No Sleep Until Wednesday mix-12") *(GRIM T/X 4)* – Beat girl.

Nov 86. (7") *(GRIM 5)* **ANYTHING. / THE YEAR OF THE JACKAL** [32] [ ]
(10"blue+=,10"yellow+=) *(GRIMX 5)* – ('A'mixes).
(12"+=) *(GRIMT 5)* – Thanks for the night.

Nov 86. (lp/c/cd) *(MCG/MCGC/DMCG 6015)* <5966> **ANYTHING** [40] [ ]
– Anything / Alone again or / The portrait / Restless / In dulce decorum / Gigolo / The girl goes down / Tightrope walk / Psychomania.

Feb 87. (7"colrd/12"clear) *(GRIM/+T 6)* **GIGOLO. / THE PORTRAIT** [29] [-]

Apr 87. (7") *(GRIM 7)* **ALONE AGAIN OR. / IN DULCE DECORUM** [27] [-]
(12"+=) *(GRIMT 7)* – Psychomania.
(d7"++=) *(DGRIM 7)* – Eloise.

Nov 87. (7") *(GRIM 8)* **IN DULCE DECORUM. / PSYCHOMANIA** [72] [-]
(12"+=) *(GRIMT 8)* – ('A'dub).

— disbanded in the late 80's, although re-union gigs were forthcoming

Essential | Restless

Aug 89. (green-lp) *(ESCLP 008)* <72385> **FINAL DAMNATION** (live '88 reunion) [ ] [ ]
– See her tonite / Neat neat neat / Born to kill / I fall / Fan club / Fish / Help / New rose / I feel alright / I just can't be happy today / Wait for the blackout / Melody Lee / Noise noise noise / Love song / Smash it up (parts 1 & 2) / Looking at you / The last time. *(cd-iss. Apr94 on 'Castle'; CLACD 338)*

– compilations, etc. –

1981. (4x7"box) *Stiff; (GRAB 2)* **FOUR PACK** [ ] [-]
– (NEW ROSE / NEAT NEAT NEAT / PROBLEM CHILD / DON'T CRY WOLF)

Nov 81. (lp/c) *Ace; (DAM/+C 1)* **THE BEST OF THE DAMNED** [43] [-]
– New rose / Neat neat neat / I just can't be happy today / Jet boy jet girl / Hit or miss / There ain't no sanity claus / Smash it up (parts 1 & 2) / Plan 9 channel 7 / Rabid (over you) / Wait for the blackout / History of the world (part 1). *(cd-iss. Oct87; CDDAM 1)*

May 82. (7"/7"pic-d) *Big Beat; (NS/+P 77)* **WAIT FOR THE BLACKOUT. / Captain Sensible & The Softies: JET BOY, JET GIRL** [ ] [-]

Oct 82. (7"green) *Big Beat; (NS 80)* **LIVELY ARTS. / TEENAGE DREAM** [ ] [-]
(10"+=) *(NST 80)* – I'm so bored.

Nov 82. (lp) *Ace; (NED 1)* **LIVE SHEPPERTON 1980 (live)** [ ] [-]
– Love song / Second time around / I just can't be happy today / Melody Lee / Help / Neat neat neat / Looking at you / Smash it up (parts 1 & 2) / New rose / Plan 9 channel 7. *(also iss.Nov82 on 'Big Beat'; WIKM 27) (c-iss.Jun85; WIKC 27) (cd-iss. Jun88; CDWIKM 27)*

Nov 85. (12"ep) *Stiff; (BUYIT 238)* **NEW ROSE / NEAT NEAT NEAT. / STRETCHER CASE / SICK OF BEING SICK** [ ] [-]

Jan 86. (lp/c/cd) *Dojo; (DOJO LP/TC/CD 21)* **DAMNED BUT NOT FORGOTTEN** [ ] [-]
(cd re-iss. Nov92; same) (cd re-iss. Feb97 on 'Essential'; ESMCD 472)

Jun 86. (12"ep) *Strange Fruit; (SFPS 002)* **THE PEEL SESSIONS** (10.5.77) [ ] [-]
– Sick of being sick / Stretcher case / Feel the pain / Fan club. *(c-ep.1987; SFPSC 002) (cd-ep.May88; SFPSCD 002)*

Jul 86. (blue-m-lp) *Stiff; (GET 4)* **THE CAPTAIN'S BIRTHDAY PARTY – LIVE AT THE ROUNDHOUSE** [ ] [-]
(cd-iss. Nov91 on 'Demon'; VEXCD 7)

Jul 87. (12"ep) *Strange Fruit; (SFPS 040)* **THE PEEL SESSIONS (30.11.76)** [ ] [-]
– Stab yor back / Neat neat neat / New rose / So messed up / I fall.

Oct 87. (cd/lp) *I.D.; (C+/NOSE 18)* **MINDLESS, DIRECTIONLESS, ENEMY (live)** [ ] [-]
(re-iss. Jun89 cd/c/lp; CDOSE/KOSE/NOSE 18X)

Dec 87. (d-lp) *M.C.A.; (MCSP 312)* **THE LIGHT AT THE END OF THE TUNNEL** [87] [-]

Jun 88. (lp/c) *Big Beat; (WIK/+C 80)* **THE LONG LOST WEEKEND: BEST OF VOL.1/2** [ ] [-]

1990. (cd) *Marble Arch; (cd)* **THE DAMNED LIVE (live)** [ ] [-]

Dec 90. (cd/c/d-lp) *Castle; (CCS CD/MC/LP 278)* **THE COLLECTION** [ ] [-]

Jan 91. (12"blue-ep) *Deltic; (DELT 7T)* **FUN FACTORY ('82). / Captain Sensible: FREEDOM / PASTIES / A RIOT ON EASTBOURNE PIER** [ ] [-]

Jun 91. (cd/colrd-lp) *Receiver; (RR CD/LP 159)* **BALLROOM BLITZ – LIVE AT THE LYCEUM (live)** [ ] [-]

Dec 91. (cd) *Dojo; (DOJOCD 65)* **TOTALLY DAMNED (live + rare)** [ ] [-]

Jan 92. (cd) *Street Link; (AOK 101)* **ALTERNATIVE CHARTBUSTERS** [ ] [-]

Feb 92. (clear-lp) *Receiver; (RRLP 159)* **LIVE AT THE LYCEUM (live)** [ ] [-]

Aug 92. (cd) *Connoisseur; (VSOPCD 174)* **THE MCA SINGLES A'S & B'S** [ ] [-]
Sep 92. (cd) *Demon; (VEXCD 12)* **SKIP OFF SCHOOL TO SEE THE DAMNED (THE STIFF SINGLES A'S & B'S)** [ ] [-]
May 93. (cd) *Receiver; (RRCD 179)* **SCHOOL BULLIES** [ ] [-]
Jul 93. (cd) *Success; (550 747-2)* **THE DAMNED: FROM THE BEGINNING** [ ] [-]
Nov 93. (cd) *Strange Fruit; (SFRSCD 070)* **SESSIONS OF THE DAMNED** [ ] [-]
Jun 94. (cd/c) *M.C.I.; (MUS CD/MC 017)* **ETERNALLY DAMNED – THE VERY BEST OF THE DAMNED** [ ] [-]
Dec 94. (cd) *Cleopatra; (CLEO 7139-2)* **TALES FROM THE DAMNED** [ ] [-]
May 95. (cd) *Spectrum; (550 747-2)* **FROM THE BEGINNING** [ ] [-]
Sep 95. (cd/c) *Emporio; (EMPR CD/MC 592)* **NOISE – THE BEST OF: LIVE** [ ] [-]
Jun 96. (cd) *Nighttracks; (CDNT 011)* **RADIO 1 SESSIONS** [ ] [-]
Oct 96. (cd) *Cleopatra; (CLP 9804)* **FIENDISH SHADOWS** [ ] [-]
Feb 97. (3xcd-box) *Demon; (FBOOK 14)* **NEAT NEAT NEAT** [ ] [-]
Mar 97. (cd) *Cleopatra; (CLP 9960)* **THE CHAOS YEARS** [ ] [-]
Apr 97. (cd/c) *The Record Label; (MOCDR/MOMC 1)* **I'M ALRIGHT JACK AND THE BEANSTALK** [ ] [-]
May 97. (d-cd) *Snapper; (SMDCD 143)* **BORN TO KILL** [ ] [-]
Jun 97. (lp) *Cleopatra; (CLP 9782)* **SHUT IT** [ ] [-]
Nov 97. (7") *Skinnies Cut; (AVL 1077)* **PROKOFIEV. /** [ ] [-]
Nov 97. (7") *Marble Orchard; (MOS 2)* **TOUR SINGLE. /** [ ] [-]
Oct 98. (7") *M Tragedy; (MT 418)* **PRETTY VACANT. / DISCO MAN** [ ] [-]

DAVE VANIAN & THE PHANTOM CHORDS

Camden Town | not iss.

Dec 92. (7") **TOWN WITHOUT PITY. /** [ ] [-]

Big Beat | not iss.

Mar 95. (cd) *(CDWIKD 140)* **BIG BEAT PRESENTS . . .** [ ] [-]
– Voodoo doll / Screamin' kid / Big town / This house is haunted / You and I / Whiskey and me / Fever in my blood / Frenzy / Shooting Jones / Jezebel / Tonight we ride / Johnny Guitar / Chase the wild wind / Swamp thing.

DAMON & NAOMI (see under ⇒ GALAXIE 500)

DANCE HALL CRASHERS

Formed: Berkeley, California . . . 1989 initially as a moonlighting project for OPERATION IVY's TIM ARMSTRONG and MATT FREEMAN, before the skank-punk pair became RANCID. The following year, the remaining members eventually numbered girl vocalists ELYSE ROGERS and KARINA DENIKE, plus MIKEY WEISS and brothers JASON and GAVIN HAMMON. They released two albums of nauseatingly twee ska-pop that rekindled awful memories of that early 80's genre, although their third set, 'LOCKJAW' (1995), was certainly beefed up a bit. However, in 1998, they returned to their SELECTER and BELLE STARS (!) sound on their ska-tastrophic set, 'HONEY, I'M HOMELY', urrgh.

Album rating: LOCKJAW (*5)

ELYSE ROGERS – vocals / **KARINA DENIKE** – vocals / **JASON HAMMON** – guitar / (2 others) repl. OPERATION IVY members (see above)

Moon | Moon

Feb 91. (lp) *<MRE 024>* **DANCE HALL CRASHERS** [ ] [ ]
– Pick up lines / Blind leading the blind / My problem / Time to ease up / Street sweeper / State of mind / Keep on running / Java junkie / Old and grey / Babushka / Truth hurts / Better than anything / DHC.

— split a few years between late 1990 and 1992

— **JOEL WING** – bass / **JASON BERMAK** – keyboards, saxophone ; were members around this time but were repl. by **MIKEY WEISS** – bass / **GAVIN HAMMON** drums

— **SCOTT GOODELL** – guitar; repl. brief member GRANT McINTYRE

Aug 95. (cd) *<11326>* **LOCKJAW** [-] [ ]
– Shelley / Don't wanna behave / Queen for a day / Flyin' / Good for nothin' / Buried alive / Sticky / Too late / Go / Enough / Pictures / Day job / So sue us / We owe.

510-MCA | 510-MCA

Jul 98. (cd,c) *<MCAD 11676>* **HONEY, I'M HOMELY!** [ ] [ ] Sep97
– Lost again / Will tomorrow ever come / All mine / Salted / Next to you / I want it all / Elvis and me / Whiskey and gin / Cold shower / Last laugh / Mr. Blue / Stand by / Truth about me / Big mouth / Over again.

Sep 98. (m-cd) *<MCAD 11845>* **BLUE PLATE SPECIAL** [-] [ ]
– She's trying / Lady Luck / All mine / Truly comfortable / Shelley / I did it for the toys.

- compilations, etc. -

Dec 96. (cd/c/lp) *Honest Don's Hardly; <(DON 002/+MC/LP)>* **OLD RECORD** (singles from 1993) [ ] [ ] Nov96
– Othello / Nuisance / North Pole / He wants me back / My problem / Blind leading the blind / Pick up lines / Street sweeper / State of mind / Keep on running / Java junkie / Old and grey / Babuashka / Truth hurts / Better than anything / Skinhead BBQ / Fight all night / DHC.

DANCING DID

Formed: Evesham, Worcestershire, England . . . 1980 by TIM HARRISON, along with MARTYN DORMER, (trainee shepherd!) ROGER SMITH and CHRIS HOUGHTON. Taking their name from an antiquated term for travelling gypsies, the band set out to combine their love of rock/punk with the folk traditions of the English countryside. Setting up shop with their own 'Fruit & Veg' label, the lads released an eponymous debut single in October '79. Although not a novelty band in any sense of the term, DANCING DID were blessed with an often surreal sense of humour as heard on follow-up single, 'THE HAUNTED TEAROOMS'. A one-off 7" release, 'THE LOST PLATOON', followed on 'Stiff', while 1982 saw the release of a single, 'GREEN MAN AND THE MARCH OF THE BUNGALOWS' and debut album, 'AND DID THOSE FEET', their first effort for new label, 'Kamera'. Unsurprisingly perhaps, in an era more attuned to legwarmers and make-up, the band's pastoral Edwardian rockabilly didn't attract much more than a cult fanbase and after a further two 1983 singles, 'BADGER BOYS' and 'SIX WORD HEX', the various members went on to plough their own individual furrows.

Album rating: AND DID THOSE FEET (*5)

TIM HARRISON – vocals / **MARTYN DORMER** (b. 1957) – lead guitar, synthesizer / **ROGER SMITH** – bass / **CHRIS HOUGHTON** – drums

Fruit & Veg | not iss.

Oct 79. (7") *(F&V 1)* **DANCING DID. / LORRY PIRATES** [ ] [-]
1980. (7") *(F&V 2)* **THE HAUNTED TEAROOMS. / SQUASHED THINGS ON THE ROAD** [ ] [-]

Stiff | not iss.

Nov 81. (7") *(BUY 136)* **THE LOST PLATOON. / THE HUMAN CHICKEN** [ ] [-]

Kamera | not iss.

May 82. (7") *(ERA 008)* **GREEN MAN AND THE MARCH OF THE BUNGALOWS. /** [ ] [-]
Nov 82. (lp) *(KAM 009)* **AND DID THOSE FEET** [ ] [-]
Feb 83. (7") *(ERA 17)* **BADGER BOYS. / THE DAY THE WORLD ENDED IN CHELTENHAM** [ ] [-]
May 83. (7") **SIX WORD HEX. / HOUSE ON THE EDGE OF THE WOOD** [ ] [-]

— split and all went back to their day jobs

DANNY & DUSTY (see under ⇒ GREEN ON RED)

DANSE SOCIETY

Formed: Barnsley, England . . . early 80's as DANSE CRAZY by STEVE RAWLINGS, PAUL NASH, PAUL GILMARTIN and LYNDON SCARFE. Emerging from the ashes of Y? and LIPS-X, the group gained valuable exposure following a performance at the second Futurama Festival in Leeds. By the release of a limited edition debut single, 'THE CLOCK', on their own 'Society' label in summer '81, the band had changed their name and added bass player TIM WRIGHT. Following a further couple of singles on their manager's 'Pax' label, DANSE SOCIETY partially justified the hype surrounding them with the mini-set, 'SEDUCTION'. Part post-punk, part proto-goth, the outfit's dark synth swirls, pounding bass and brooding IAN CURTIS-esque vocals combined to striking effect on 'WAKE UP', the lead track on 'HEAVEN IS WAITING' (1984). The first fruits of their new deal with 'Arista', the album heralded a more immediately accessible, atmospheric style and even included a languid cover of The Rolling Stones' trippy classic, '2000 LIGHT YEARS FROM HOME'. With favourable critical reaction and continued support from DJ John Peel, the future looked bright; it wasn't to be, though, as internal ructions saw SCARFE replaced by DAVID WHITAKER and legal arguments with 'Arista' delayed the release of new material. Fans were less than impressed when they eventually resurfaced in '85 with the Stock, Aitken & Waterman-produced 'SAY IT AGAIN'. Such a sudden stylistic departure proved disastrous, however, and the band's second album was shelved by their record company. A split inevitably followed soon after, RAWLINGS following a more commercial path with SOCIETY while the rest of the band ploughed on in vain as JOHNNY IN THE CLOUDS.

Album rating: HEAVEN IS WAITING (*7) / SEDUCTION (*6)

STEVE RAWLINGS – vocals (ex-Y?) / **PAUL NASH** – lead guitar (ex-Y?) / **LYNDON SCARFE** – keyboards (ex-LIPS-X) / **PAUL GILMARTIN** – drums (ex-LIPS-X) / **PATRIC HERTZ** – guitar / **PAUL HAMPSHIRE** – bass

I.F.K. | not iss.

1981. (7") *(SOC 3-81)* **THE CLOCK. / CONTINENT** [ ] [-]
(re-iss. Jul83 on 'IFK-Society'; SOC 2)

Pax | not iss.

Aug 81. (12"ep) *(PAX 2)* **THERE IS NO SHAME IN DEATH. / DOLPHINS / THESE FRAYED EDGES** [ ] [-]
(re-iss. Jul83 on 'Society' blue-vinyl; SOC 12-1)

— **TIM WRIGHT** – bass; repl. HAMPSHIRE and PATRIC who joined 4 BE 2

Mar 82. (7") *(SOX 5)* **WOMAN'S OWN. / WE'RE SO HAPPY** [ ] [-]
(12"+=) *(POX 5)* – Belief / Continent.
(re-iss. Jul83 on 'Society'; SOC 12-3)

Society | not iss.

Aug 82. (m-lp) *(SOC 882)* **SEDUCTION** [ ] [-]
– Godsend / My heart / Falling apart / Danse – Mmove / Ambition / In Heaven
(re-dist.Apr84 on 'Society-Arista'; same)

Feb 83. (7") *(SOC 4)* **SOMEWHERE. / HIDE** [ ] [-]
(12"+=) *(SOC 12-4)* – The theme.

Society-Arista | not iss.

Aug 83. (7"/12") *(SOC/+12 5)* **WAKE UP. / SEDUCTION** [61] [-]
Oct 83. (7"pic-d) *(SOC 6)* **HEAVEN IS WAITING. / LIZARD MAN** [60] [-]
(12"+=) *(SOC12 6)* – ('A'extended).
Feb 84. (lp/c) *(205/405 972)* **HEAVEN IS WAITING** [39] [-]
– Come inside / Wake up / Angel / Where are you now / Red light (shine) / Heaven

is waiting / The hurt / 2000 light years from home / Valliant to vile / The night.
(re-iss. Jun91 on 'Great Expectations' cd/c/lp; PIP CD/MC/LP 024)

Mar 84. (7") *(SOC 7)* **2,000 LIGHT YEARS FROM HOME. / SEEN THE LIGHT** [ ] [-]
(12"light blue+=) *(SOC12 7)* – Angel (dub).
(d7"+=) *(SOC 7-7)* – Sway / Endless.

—— **DAVID WHITAKER** – keyboards (ex-MUSIC FOR PLEASURE) repl. LYNDON

Jul 85. (7") *(SOC 8)* **SAY IT AGAIN. / FADE AWAY (SHE'S IN MY DREAMS)** [ ] [-]
(12"+=) *(SOC12 8)* – ('A'extended).
(d12"+=) *(SOC22 8)* – Sensimilia / Treat me right.

Feb 86. (7") *(SOC 9)* **HOLD ON (TO WHAT YOU'VE GOT). / DANSE: MOVE** [ ] [-]
(12"+=) *(SOC12 9)* – Heaven is waiting / ('A'dance mix).
(c-s+=) *(SOCCS 9)* – ('A'dance) / 2,000 light years from home / Wake up.

—— (STEVE RAWLINGS solo); others formed JOHNNY IN THE CLOUDS

Aug 86. (lp; as DANSE SOCIETY INTERNATIONAL) *(SOC 886)* **LOOKING THROUGH** [ ] [-]
– Looking through / All I want / Institution / Don't stop now / Sunset gun / Runaway / House of love / Midnight land.

Big Life — not iss.

Aug 87. (7"/12"; as SOCIETY) *(BLR 001/+T)* **SATURN GIRL. / LOVE IT** [ ] [-]
(c-s) *(BLR 1TCC)* (2 'B'versions).

—— RAWLINGS retired from the music biz

DARKSIDE

Formed: Rugby, England . . . late '89 by ex-SPACEMEN 3 members, PETE (BASSMAN) BAINES and STEWART (ROSCO) ROSSWELL. Signing to 'Situation 2', they debuted the following Spring with an EP, 'HIGH RISE LOVE'. Later that year, an album 'ALL THAT NOISE' hit the indie charts, its heavily 60's influenced sound a grab-bag of references taking in everything from The BYRDS and CREEDENCE CLEARWATER REVIVAL to DOORS-style ambience. Unsurprisingly, the spectre of SPACEMEN 3 also hung heavy in the air although BAINES' droning, SUICIDE-influenced vocals tended to grate over the course of a whole album. A mail order-only long player, 'PSYCHEDELIZE SUBURBIA', was made available through the band's own 'Acid Ray' records in 1991 while a follow-up debut album proper, 'MELOMANIA', followed in early '92. Again, The DARKSIDE explored the 60's in enjoyable enough garage fashion without managing to nail down a memorable sound of their own. Faced with critical and commercial indifference, the band finally called it a day after a final single, 'LUNAR SURF EXPERIMENT', in summer '93. • **Covers:** BRIGHT LIGHTS BIG CITY (Jimmy Reed).

Album rating: ALL THAT NOISE (*6) / MELOMANIA (*6)

PETE (BASSMAN) BAINES – vocals, bass (ex-SPACEMEN 3) / **STEWART (ROSCO) ROSSWELL** – keyboards (ex-SPACEMEN 3) / KEVIN COWAN – guitar / **CRAIG WAGSTAFF** – drums (joined 1991)

Situation 2 — Beggars Banquet – RCA

Apr 90. (12"ep) *(SIT 068T)* **HIGH RISE LOVE. / THE KILLING TIME / CAN'T THINK STRAIGHT** [ ] [-]

Aug 90. (12"/cd-s) *(SIT 72 T/CD)* **WAITING FOR THE ANGELS. / SWEET VIBRATIONS** [ ] [-]

Nov 90. (lp/c)(cd/pic-lp) *(SIT U/C 29)(SITU 29 CD/P)* *<3029>* **ALL THAT NOISE** [ ] [ ]
– Guitar voodoo / Found love / She don't come / Good for me / Love in a burning universe / All that noise / Spend some time / Don't stop the rain / Soul deep / Waiting for the angels.

1991. (lp; mail-order) *(DARK 2)* **PSYCHEDELIZE SUBURBIA** [-] [-]
(above and below on 'Acid Ray' records)

Nov 91. (12"ep/cd-ep) *(DARK 3)* **ALWAYS PLEASURE** [ ] [-]

Jan 92. (lp/c)(cd/pic-lp) *(SIT U/C 34)(SITU 34 CD/P)* *<61121>* **MELOMANIA** [ ] [ ]
– Always pleasure / Feeling flow / Tornado / This mystic morning / Someday / Are you for real / 24 hours / Cry for me / Rise.

Jun 92. (12"ep/cd-ep) *(SIT 95 T/CD)* **MAYHEM TO MEDIATE** [ ] [-]
– Straightest shot / This time is mine / Heart of the sun / This mystic morning (remix) / This mystic morning (instrumental dub) / Cry for me (remix).

Bomp — Bomp

Jul 93. (7") *(BMP 141)* **LUNAR SURF EXPERIMENT** [ ] [-]

—— split after above

DARK STAR (see under ⇒ LEVITATION)

DARLING BUDS

Formed: Cardiff, Wales . . . 1986 by ANDREA LEWIS and HARLEY FARR, who subsequently recruited CHRIS McDONAGH and BLOSS before relocating to Gwent, Wales. Fronted by blonde bombshell, Andrea, the band's feisty brand of indie pop/punk was first given an airing on a self-financed debut single, 'IF I SAID'. Subsequently signing with Doncaster based indie label, 'Native', the band released a string of 7"ers which won the favour of Radio One stalwart, John Peel. Playlisted almost nightly, the 'BUDS were soon snapped up by 'Epic', scoring a Top 50 hit with major label debut single, 'BURST'. 'HIT THE GROUND' performed even better, taking the band into the Top 30. While comparisons with BLONDIE may have been a mite too generous, the band notched up a deserved Top 30 placing for debut album, 'POP SAID' (1989). A more accurate comparison was The PRIMITIVES, a group who also arrived in a flurry of hype and acclaim only to fall from the media spotlight almost as quickly as they'd appeared. The signs weren't good for The DARLING BUDS as a further two singles, 'LET'S GO ROUND THERE' and 'YOU'VE GOT TO CHOOSE', scraped into the Top 50. Following the replacement of BLOSS with JIMMY HUGHES, they returned in 1990 with a more streamlined cutesy sound, notching up a minor hit with 'TINY MACHINE'. Another two singles and an accomanying album, 'CRAWDADDY' (1990), failed to chart, however, and The DARLING BUDS looked set for music business oblivion. Major label muscle made little difference as summer 1992's 'SURE THING' became their final (Top 75) hit and the 'EROTICA' (1992) album stiffed completely. As the record competed forlornly with MADONNA's opus of the same name, The DARLING BUDS split later that year. • **Songwriters:** ANDREA lyrics / HARLEY music.

Album rating: POP SAID (*6) / CRAWDADDY (*5) / EROTICA (*5) / SHAME ON YOU compilation (*6)

ANDREA LEWIS (b.25 Mar'67) – vocals / **HARLEY FARR** (b. 4 Jul'64, Singapore) – guitar / **CHRIS McDONOGH** (b. 6 Mar'62, Newport, Wales) – bass / **BLOSS** – drums

Darling Buds — not iss.

Feb 87. (7") *(DAR 1)* **IF I SAID. / JUST TO BE SEEN** [ ] [-]

Native — not iss.

Mar 88. (7") *(NTV 21)* **SHAME ON YOU. / VALENTINE** [ ] [-]
(12"+=) *(12NTV 21)* – That's the reason.

Jun 88. (7") *(NTV 32)* **THINK OF ME. / THAT'S THE REASON** [ ] [-]

Jun 88. (7") *(NTV 33)* **IT'S ALL UP TO YOU. / SPIN** [ ] [-]
(ltd-7"+=) *(NTV 33L)* – Think of me.
(12"+=) *(12NTV 33)* –

Epic — Columbia

Sep 88. (7"/7"g-f/7"box) *(BLOND/+Q/B 1)* **BURST. / BIG HEAD** [50] [-]
(12"+=/cd-s+=) *(BLOND T/C 1)* – Shame on you (psychedelic version).

Dec 88. (7"/7"g-f) *(BLOND/+Q 2)* **HIT THE GROUND. / PRETTY GIRL** [27] [-]
(10"+=/12"+=/cd-s+=) *(BLOND X/T/C 2)* – ('A'version) / If I said.

Jan 89. (lp/c/cd) *(462894-1/-4/-2)* *<45208>* **POP SAID** [23] [ ]
– Hit the ground / Burst / Uptight / The other night / Big head / Let's go round there / She's not crying / Shame on you / You've got to choose / Spin / When it feels good / The things we do for love.

Mar 89. (7"/7"yellow) *(BLOND/+V 3)* **LET'S GO ROUND THERE. / TURN YOU ON** [49] [-]
(12"+=/12"g-f+=cd-s+=) *(BLOND T/Q/C 3)* – Different daze.
(7"ep++=) *(BLONDE 3)* – It's all up to you.

Jun 89. (7"/7"g-f/c-s) *(BLOND/+G/M 4)* **YOU'VE GOT TO CHOOSE. / MARY'S GO TO GO** [45] [-]
(12"+=/cd-s+=) *(BLOND T/C 4)* – I'll never stop.

—— **JIMMY HUGHES** (b. Liverpool, England) – drums (ex-BLACK) repl. BLOSS

May 90. (7"/7"box/c-s) *(BLOND/+B/M 5)* **TINY MACHINE. / SUGAR CITY** [60] [-]
(12"+=/cd-s+=) *(BLOND T/C 5)* – Me satisfied?

Aug 90. (7") *(BLOND 6)* **CRYSTAL CLEAR. / TINY MACHINE** [ ] [-]
(12"+=) *(BLONDT 6)* – ('A'version).
(cd-s+=) *(BLONDC 6)* – Tripped up.

Sep 90. (c-s) **CRYSTAL CLEAR / YOU WON'T MAKE ME DIE** [-] [ ]

Sep 90. (cd/c/lp) *(467012-2/-4/-1)* *<46816>* **CRAWDADDY** [ ] [ ]
– It makes no difference / Tiny machine / Crystal clear / Do you have to break my heart / You won't make me die / A little bit of Heaven / Fall / Honey suckle / So close / The end of the beginning.

Feb 91. (7"/c-s) *(BLOND/+M 7)* **IT MAKES NO DIFFERENCE. / OFF MY MIND** [ ] [-]
(12"+=/cd-s+=) *(BLOND T/C 7)* – Love and death / If.

Epic — Chaos

Aug 92. (7"/c-s) *(658215-7/-4)* **SURE THING. / BABYHEAD** [71] [-]
(12"+=/cd-s+=) *(658215-6/-2)* – Suffer / What goes around (or)

Sep 92. (cd/c/lp) *(472151 2/ 4/ 1)* *<OK/OT+/52913>* **EROTICA** [ ] [ ]
– One thing leads to another / Sure thing / Off my mind / Gently fall / Please yourself / Angels fallen / Isolation / Long day in the universe / Wave / If.

Sep 92. (cd-ep) **SURE THING / BABYHEAD / SUFFER / PLEASE YOURSELF** [-] [ ]

—— split later in 1992

– compilations, etc. –

1989. (7"flexi) *Flexi; (FLX 448)* **VALENTINE (live). / THAT'S THE REASON (live)** [-] [-] fanclub

Sep 90. (cd/c/lp) *Native; (NTV CD/C/LP 44)* **SHAME ON YOU** [ ] [-]

Dec 90. (3x7"box) *Native; (NTV 52)* **SHAME ON YOU. / VALENTINE // IT'S ALL UP TO YOU. / SPIN // THINK OF ME. / THAT'S THE REASON** [ ] [-]

DARYLL-ANN

Formed: based- Amsterdam, Netherlands . . . 1993 by male guitarist and co-songwriter ANNE SOLDAAT, COEM PAULUSMA (subsequently replaced by his brother, JELLE) ANNE SOLDAAT, bassist JEROEN VOS and singer COEM PAULUSMA. The latter (who subsequently became a biologist!) was actually replaced by his twin brother and soon-to-be co-writer, JELLE PAULUSMA, while their original drummer was given the boot in favour of JEROEN KLEIJN. Allegedly taking their name from a character in US police show, 'Hill Street Blues', this bunch of retro indie-rockers began to achieve some recognition after moving to Dutch capital, Amsterdam, in 1993. Subsequently signed to 'Virgin' subsidiary, 'Hut', on the strength of a cassette demo tape, the band released a riff-tastic debut EP, 'I COULD NEVER LOVE

YOU' in early '94. It seemed the improbably named DARYLL-ANN were as keen on American music culture as they were on the country's infamous TV programming, a definite TELEVISON (as in the band) influence at work, at least in PAULUSMA's guitar playing. As for his vocals, they came across like a Euro/US version of BRETT ANDERSON's inimitable nasal affectations. A debut mini-album, 'SEABORNE WEST' finally surfaced in 1995, among its varied delights a tongue-in-cheek version of Carly Simon's 'YOU'RE SO VAIN' (also released as a single). Having toured alongside labelmate giants, The SMASHING PUMPKINS and THE VERVE, they disappeared, becoming one of the many forgotten "retro-rock" alternative acts. • **More covers:** THIRTEEN (Big Star) / HOT SMOKE IN SASAFRASS (Prince – Cox).

Album rating: SEABORNE WEST (*6)

JELLE PAULUSMA – vocals, guitar; repl. COEM PAULUSMA / **ANNE SOLDAAT** – guitar, vocals / **JEROEN VOS** – bass / **JEROEN KLEIJN** – drums; repl. unknown original

Hut Caroline

Feb 94. (7") *(HUT 40)* **I COULD NEVER LOVE YOU. / MY LAST CALL** -
(12"+=/cd-s+=) *(HUT T/DG 40)* – Friends / She is, I'm not.

May 94. (12"ep/c-ep/cd-ep) *(HUT TM/CM/DM 44)* **COME AROUND EP**
– Come around / Doll / Shamrock / Good thing / Mirror mind / Ocean girl.

Mar 95. (7") *(HUT 52)* **STAY. / THIRTEEN** -
(12"+=/cd-s+=) *(HUT T/DG 52)* – Hot smoke in sasafrass.

Mar 95. (cd/c/lp) *(CDHUT/HUTMC/HUTLP 26)* **SEABORNE WEST**
– Stay / Low light / The doctor & I / Sheila / All right / Holida why / You're so vain / Birthmark / Boy you were / Liquid / H.P. confirm.

Jun 95. (7") *(HUT 58)* **YOU'RE SO VAIN. / FRIENDS** -
(cd-s+=) *(HUTDG 58)* – The doctor & I.

DAS DAMEN

Formed: New York – from Arizona – USA . . . mid 80's by JIM WALTERS, ALEX TOTINO, PHIL LEOPOLD VON TRAPP and LYLE HYSEN. After an initial eponymous release on 'Ecstatic Peace', they signed to 'SST', former home of HUSKER DU, MEAT PUPPETS and fIREHOSE. In 1987, they unleashed the sublime 'JUPITER EYE' album, a record of quasi-hardcore that touched on garage psychedelia. This sound was even more pronounced on the follow-up album, 'TRISKAIDEKAPHOBE' and the EP 'MARSHMALLOW CONSPIRACY'. On the latter, the band ploughed through a manic re-working of The BEATLES' 'MAGICAL MYSTERY TOUR. However, this was their last decent effort before signing to 'What Goes On', followed by 'City Slang' in the early 90's.

Album rating: JUPITER EYE (*6) / TRISKAIDEKAPHOBE (*6)

JIM WALTERS – vocals, guitar / **ALEX TOTINO** – guitar, vocals / **PHIL LEOPOLD VON TRAPP** – bass, vocals / **LYLE HYSEN** – drums, electronics

not iss. Ecstatic Peace

1986. (lp) *<004>* **DAS DAMEN** -
– Tsava / Trick question / Slave bird / House of mirrors / How do you measure / Behind my eyes. *<US re-iss. 1988 on 'SST' lp/c; SST 040/+C)*

S.S.T. S.S.T.

1987. (lp/c) *<(SST 095/+C)>* **JUPITER EYE**
– Gray isn't black / Quarter after eight / Trap door / Where they all went / Name your poison / Impasse / Raindance / Do / Girl with the hair.

Aug 88. (lp) *<(SST 190)>* **TRISKAIDEKAPHOBE**
– Spiderbirds / Reverse into tomorrow / Pendant / Seven / Five five five / Firejoke / Bug / Siren plugs / Up for the ride / Ruby Woodpecker / Candy korn.

Dec 88. (m-lp/c/cd) *<(SST/+C/CD 218)>* **MARSHMALLOW CONSPIRACY EP**

Wahat Goes On Twin/Tone

1989. (cd) *<89170>* **MOUSETRAP** -
– Noon daylight / Mirror leaks / Twenty four to zero / Somewhere, sometime / Demagnetized / Hey, angel / Sad mile / Please, please me / Click!

1989. (7") *(GOES ON 16)* **NOON DAYLIGHT. / GIVE ME EVERYTHING**

— **DAVID MOTAMED** – bass; repl. VON TRAPP

City Slang Sub Pop

Jul 91. (m-cd) *(SLANG 10)* *<SP 111B>* **HIGH ANXIETY**
– The promise / Chaindrive (a slight return) / The outsider / Thrilled to the marrow / Silence.

— disbanded after above; DAVID joined CELL

DAVID DEVANT & HIS SPIRIT WIFE

Formed: London, England . . . mid-90's by frontman THE VESSEL (Mr. GEORGESON to his bank manager!), plus his entertaining live crew, PROFESSOR RIMSCHOTT, THE COLONEL, ICE MAN, COCKY YOUNG 'UN and ex-MONOCHROME SET guitarist, FOZ. Two independently released singles appeared in 1995, namely 'PIMLICO' and the carrot-top baiting 'GINGER', the latter an audience participating highlight of the group's outrageous live set. Having signed to 'Rhythm King', the band went through a lean 1996 as three singles in a row failed to chart, although it would be the aforementioned 'GINGER' that would finally see him haunt the Top 60. A follow-up, 'THIS IS FOR REAL' and an accompanying debut album, 'WORK, LOVELIFE, MISCELLANEOUS' (1997), also made the charts, an only partially successful attempt to translate THE VESSEL's BOWIE-esque theatrics and performance art onto vinyl. Highlights included 'GINGER', 'LIE DETECTOR', 'MISCELLANEOUS' and 'THE LAST EVER POP SONG', all enjoyably comical glammed-up cabaret pastiches which no doubt had the real DAVID DEVANT (a Victorian-era magician apparently!) turning in his grave.

Album rating: WORK, LOVELIFE, MISCELLANEOUS (*5)

THE VESSEL (b . . . . GEORGESON) – vocals / **FOZ** (b. FOSTER) – guitar (ex-MONOCHROME SET) / **. . . CARLOW** – bass / **. . . EGERTON** – drums

Humbug not iss.

Aug 95. (7"/cd-s) *(HUM/+CD 4)* **PIMLICO. /** -

Nov 95. (cd-s; as DAVID DEVANT) *(HUM 10)* **GINGER** -

Rhythm King not iss.

Aug 96. (7") *(KIND 1V)* **COOKIE. /** -
(cd-s+=) *(KIND 1CD)* –

Nov 96. (7") *(KIND 2VL)* **LIE DETECTOR. /** -

Nov 96. (7") *(KIND 3VL)* **MISCELLANEOUS. /** -

Mar 97. (7"/c-s) *(KIND 4 VLE/C)* **GINGER. / SLIP IT TO ME (live)** 54 -
(cd-s+=) *(KIND 4CD)* – Life on the crescent (session).

Jun 97. (7") *(KIND 5V)* **THIS IS FOR REAL. /** 61 -
(cd-s) *(KIND 5CD)* – ('A'side) / Everything fits into place / Why can't someone else.
(cd-s) *(KIND 5CDX)* – ('A'side) / Ghost in my house (live) / Pimlico (live).

Jun 97. (cd/c/lp) *(KIND CD/MC/LP 1)* **WORK, LOVELIFE, MISCELLANEOUS** 70 -
– Ginger / Miscellaneous / Lie detector / The lasty ever love song / I think about you / Parallel universe / Re-invent the wheel / This is for real / I'm not even going to try / Light on the surface / Goodnight. *(lp w/ free 7") –*

Oct 97. (7") *(KIND 6VLE)* **LIE DETECTOR (Dave Eringa mix). / WHO WE ARE (alternative vocal)** -
(cd-s+=) *(KIND 6CD)* – This is for real (mix).
(cd-s) *(KIND 6CDX)* – ('A'side) / Black & white (mix) / This is for real (mix).

Richard DAVIES

Born: Sydney, Australia . . . 1964. DAVIES took up songwriting while at university, forming his first professional band, The MOLES, in the late 80's with fellow disaffected law students. Despite claiming not to even like each other, the band managed to release two EP's and a debut album, 'UNTUNE THE SKY' (1992), before upping sticks and moving to London together in 1993 in the hope that they'd find a more appreciative audience for their wildly experimental, off-kilter garage retro-pop. While the UK indie press were sympathetic, however, The MOLES split soon after and although a final album, 'INSTINCT' appeared on US label, 'Flydaddy' ('Fire' in the UK) in 1994, it was a DAVIES solo effort in all but name. A move to the US (more specifically Boston, Massachusetts) saw DAVIES hooking up with San Franciscan music student, ERIC MATTHEWS, after the pair had listened to each other's recent demo tapes. In 1993, The CARDINAL released their 'TOY BELL' EP although it was 1995's eponymous debut album that had the critics raving. With MATTHEWS' sublime brass and string arrangements complementing DAVIES' songwriting verve, they had fashioned a work of baroque pop glory that harked back to the late 60's without sounding derivative. Yet despite the acclaim, internal tension led to an early split with both MATTHEWS and DAVIES going on to release solo material. Despite being so short-lived, the influence of The CARDINAL was writ large over DAVIES' solo debut, 'THERE'S NEVER BEEN A CROWD LIKE THIS', released on 'Flydaddy' in 1996. Two years later, DAVIES was back with another work of flawed genuis, 'TELEGRAPH', having toured with spiritual compadres, The FLAMING LIPS, as his backing band. • **Covered:** CARDINAL covered SINGING TO THE SUNSHINE (US-band; Mortimer).

Album rating: Moles: UNTUNE THE SKY (*6) / INSTINCT (*6) / Cardinal: CARDINAL (*7) / Richard Davies: THERE'S NEVER BEEN A CROWD LIKE THIS (*7) / TELEGRAPH (*7)

The MOLES

RICHARD DAVIS (b.1964) – vocals, flute, guitar / with **ARTHUR BEECHCROFT** – keyboards / **OLIVER STRAUCH** – bass / **HAMISH KILGOUR** – drums (of CLEAN) / +1

Fire Seaside

Dec 90. (m-lp) **UNTUNE THE SKY**

Dec 91. (m-lp) **TENDRILS AND PARACETAMOL** -

not iss. R.I.P.

Jan 92. (cd) *<10>* **UNTUNE THE SKY** -
– Bury me happy / Tendrils and paracetamol / This is a hapy garden / Breathe me in / Lonely hearts get what they deserve / Crown souls / Rebecca / Europe by car / Curdle / Wires / Nailing Jesus to the cross.

1993. (d7"ep) **DOUBLE SINGLE** -

Fire Flydaddy

Oct 94. (cd) *(FIRECD 42)* *<003>* **INSTINCT**
– Minor royal march / Eros lunch (1963) / Already in black / Instinct / Cars for Kings Cross / Cassie peek / Raymond, did you see the red queen? / Treble metal / The crasher.

— split when DAVIES formed The CARDINAL with ERIC MATTHEWS

CARDINAL

RICHARD DAVIES – guitar, vocals / **ERIC MATTHEWS** (b.12 Jan'69, Oregon) – vocals, guitars, trumpet, bass, piano / **TONY LASH** – percussion, drums, production

Flydaddy Flydaddy

Jan 95. (7") *<(FLY 001-7)>* **TOY BELL. /**

Dedicated Flydaddy

Feb 95. (cd) *(DED CD/LP 018)* <*FLY 004*> **CARDINAL**
– If you believe in Christmas trees / Last poems / Bog mine / You've lost me there / Public melody #1 / Dream figure / Tough guy tactics / Angel darling / Singing to the sunshine / Silver machines.

Jun 95. (cd-s) **DREAM FIGURE. /** [-]

RICHARD DAVIES

Flydaddy Flydaddy

Mar 96. (cd/lp) <*(FLY 016-2/-1)*> **THERE'S NEVER BEEN A CROWD LIKE THIS**
– Transcontinental / Sign up maybe for being / 6/4 on / Chips Rafferty / Why not bomb the movies? / Jubilee / In between moods / Hard river / Topple into my fantasy / Showtime.

Blue Rose Flydaddy

Apr 96. (cd-ep) *(BRRC 1004-2)* **CHIPS RAFFERTY / 6/4 ON / IN BETWEEN MOODS / CARS FOR KINGS CROSS / ALREADY IN BLACK**

— with **RONALD JONES** – guitars, etc (of FLAMING LIPS)

Mar 98. (cd/lp) *(BRRC 100115-2/-1)* <*FLY 025*> **TELEGRAPH**
– Cantina / Surface of the sun / Confederate cheerio call / Papillon / Crystal clear / Eye camera / Close to the storyline / Main street electrical parade / Evergreen / Days to remember.

Apr 98. (7") *(BRRC 500144-7)* **CANTINA. /**
(cd-s+=) *(BRRC 500144-3)* –

DAWN OF THE REPLICANTS

Formed: Galashiels, Scotland . . . 1996 by Teeside-raised singer-songwriter, PAUL VICKERS along with guitarist, ROGER SIMIAN, the latter spending the bulk of his student loan on a mail-order debut EP, 'SO FAR SO SPITFIRE' (recorded as The REPLICANTS). Available from early '97, the record's R.E.M.-esque lead track, 'COCAINE ON THE CATWALK', was given airplay by both John Peel and Mark Radcliffe, selling out its initial 500 copies almost immediately. Expanding the line-up with addition of former schoolmates, DONALD KYTE, MIKE SMALL and GRANT PRINGLE, The DAWN OF THE REPLICANTS released a second single, 'HOGWASH FARM' on their 'dumbSULK trigg-er' imprint and after interest from the likes of 'Che', 'Too Pure' and 'Chemikal Underground', they opted to sign on the dotted line for Warner Brothers subsidiary 'East West'. Their major label tenure got off to a prolific start with the release of three EP's (namely 'VIOLENT SUNDAYS', 'ALL THAT CHEYENNE CABOODLE' and 'RHINO DAYS') in the latter half of '97, the lead tracks being re-recorded versions of 'COCAINE ON THE CATWALK', 'LISA BOX' and the brand new 'RADARS' respectively. With music press acclaim steadily growing, the Borders lads notched up their first chart entry with the morbidly infectious 'CANDLEFIRE', a song that invoked the ghosts of early 80's Liverpool (i.e. IAN McCULLOCH, JULIAN COPE and The ROOM's DAVE JACKSON). The heavy release schedule continued unabated with the much anticipated Top 75 debut set, 'ONE HEAD, TWO ARMS, TWO LEGS' (1998), a pot-pourri of wilful experimentation and contrasting styles that collected together all of the aforementioned tracks side by side with fresh material such as 'WINDY MILLER' (Trumpton revisited REPLICANTS style), the U2 goes Lo-Fi 'SO SLEEPY' and the lyrically enigmatic (not for the first time) 'SGT GROWLEY'. • **Covered:** BALLAD OF A THIN MAN (Bob Dylan).

Album rating: DAWN OF THE REPLICANTS (*8)

PAUL VICKERS – vocals, synthesizer / **ROGER SIMIAN** – guitar, keyboards, vocals

dumbSULK trigg-er not iss.

Jan 97. (7"ep; as The REPLICANTS) *(DST 7-1)* **SO FAR SO SPITFIRE EP** [-] [-] mail-o
– Cocaine on the catwalk / Digging bear / Lisa box / Bizarre concoction.

— added **DONALD KYTE** – bass, guitar / **MIKE SMALL** – guitar, keyboards, vocals / **GRANT PRINGLE** – drums, keyboards, vocals

Jun 97. (10") *(SAM 2063)* **HOGWASH FARM. / CHAOS IN AN INKWELL** [-]

East West not iss.

Aug 97. (d7"ep/cd-ep) *(EW 115/+CD)* **VIOLENT SUNDAYS E.P.** [-]
– Cocaine on the catwalk (re-recording) / Non capisco / Only small birds do / Beyond the nest.

Sep 97. (d7"ep/cd-ep) *(EW 125/+CD)* **ALL THAT CHEYENNE CABOODLE E.P.** [-]
– Lisa box (re-recording) / Diggin' bear (re-recording) / Will you ever phone? / Skullcrusher.

Nov 97. (d7"ep/cd-ep) *(EW 134/+CD)* **RHINO RAYS E.P.** [-]
– Radars / Bionic stardust / The wrong turnstile / Seasick odyssey.

Jan 98. (10") *(EW 147 TE/CD1)* **CANDLE FIRE. / SKULLCRUSHER (David Holmes & Tim Goldsworthy remix)** [52] [-]
(cd-s+=) *(EW 147CD1)* – Leaving so soon?
(cd-s) *(EW 147CD2)* – ('A'side) / Leaving iota / Chesty Morgan.

Feb 98. (cd/c/lp) *(0630 19600-2/-4/-1)* **ONE HEAD, TWO ARMS, TWO LEGS** [62] [-]
– Cocaine on the catwalk / Candle fire / Ten sea birds / Lisa box / Return of the board game / Windy Miller / Radars / So sleepy / Let them eat coal / Sgt Growley / Hogwash farm / Sleepy spiders / Float on a raft / Mary Louise / Fatal firework.

Mar 98. (7"ep/cd-ep) *(EW 157/+CD)* **HOGWASH FARM (THE DIESEL HANDS E.P.)** [65] [-]
– Hogwash farm (re-built) / Night train to Lichtenstein / The duchess of Surin / Crow valley.

Jun 98. (12"ep/cd-ep) *(EW 166 T/CD)* **I SMELL VOODOO E.P.** [-]
– Mary Louise / Ballad of a thin man / Myrhh tingle / Dual converter.

Aug 98. (7"/cd-s) *(NING 59/+CD)* **BORN IN BASKETS. / Inner Sleeve: Come Alive** [-]
(above 'GOING DOWN THE TUBES WITH . . . single was on 'Fierce Panda')

Danielle DAX

Born: Southend, England. Following a one-off gig at Reading University as a member of AMY TURTLE & THE CROSSROADS, DAX made her first real foray into the music world alongside KARL BLAKE in his band The LEMON KITTENS. This partnership resulted in two avant-pop albums, 'WE BUY A HAMMER FOR DADDY' (1980) and 'THE BIG DENTIST' (1982), setting the scene for DAX's subsequent solo career. Things got off to an interesting start with 'POP EYES' (1983; complete with gruesome sleeve artwork), wherein the pseudo-goth goddess treated listeners to her ethnic multi-instrumental skills and ear for the bizarre. A detour into acting – a bit part (all her bits in fact!) in Neil Jordan's 'The Company Of Wolves' – was followed by 1984's well received mini-set, 'JESUS EGG THAT WEPT'. The latter featured a one-off collaboration with BLAKE, 'OSTRICH', oft cited as one of her best tracks. It also kickstarted a renewed enthusiasm for live work as DAX recruited a backing band and began building up her profile in tandem with a series of singles on her own 'Awesome' label. Eventually coming to the attention of US alternative bigwig, Seymour Stein (after an appearance at Boston's New Music Seminar), DAX netted a major league deal with his 'Sire' label and proceeded to record the 'DARK ADAPTED EYE' (1988) album. Despite such increasingly accessible material as the DAX-goes-BILLY IDOL 'WHITE KNUCKLE RIDE', crossover success remained surprisingly out of reach. An ill-advised cover of The Beatles' 'TOMORROW NEVER KNOWS' seemed desperate and as the accompanying Stephen Street-produced album, 'BLAST THE HUMAN FLOWER' (1990) sank without trace, DAX returned to her independent roots. Setting up her own 'Biter Of Thorpe' (eh?!) label, the lady re-issued titles from her back catalogue although new material has been thin on the ground. • **Trivia:** Initially a painter/artist, she designed many album covers, including that of LEAGUE OF GENTLEMEN (a ROBERT FRIPP sideline).

Album rating: POP EYES (*6) / THE JESUS EGG THAT WEPT (*6) / INKY BLOATERS (*6) / DARK ADAPTED EYE (*5) / BLAST THE HUMAN FLOWER (*5) / COMATOSE NON-REACTION: THE THWARTED POP CAREER OF . . . compilation (*6)

DANIELLE DAX – vocals, instruments

Initial not iss.

Jun 83. (m-lp) *(IRC 009)* **POP EYES** [-]
– Bed caves / Tower of lies / Here comes the harvest burns / Kernow / Numb companions / Everyone squeak quietly / etc *(re-iss. Apr85 on 'Awesome'; AOR 2) (cd-iss. Dec92 on 'Reckless';) (m-cd re-iss. Oct96 on 'Biter Of Thorpe'; BOT131 01CD)*

— now with **DAVE KNIGHT** – guitar, keyboards, percussion (of SHOCK HEADED PETERS) / **STEVE REEVES** – guitars / **IAN STURGESS** – bass, guitar / **MARTIN WATTS** – drums

Awesome Rough Trade

Oct 84. (m-lp) *(AOR 1)* **THE JESUS EGG THAT WEPT** [-]
– Hammerheads / Ostrich / Pariah / Evil-honky stomp / Fortune cheats / etc *(m-cd-iss. Oct96 on 'Biter Of Thorpe' BOT131 02CD)*

— she continued to work with **KNIGHT + STURGESS**

Oct 85. (7") *(AOR 3)* **YUMMER YUMMER MAN. / BAD MISS "M"** [-]
(12"+=) *(AOR 3T)* – Fizzing human bomb.

Sep 86. (7") *(AOR 6)* **WHERE THE FLIES ARE. / UP IN ARMS** [-]
(12"+=) *(AOR 6T)* – When I was young.

May 87. (lp/c)(cd) *(AOR 13/+CS)(AORCD 13)* **INKY BLOATERS** [-]
– Flashback / Funtime / Inky bloaters / Sleep has no property / Bad Miss "M" / Big hollow man / Brimstone in a barren land / Where the flies are / Born to be bad / Fizzing human bomb. *(cd re-iss. Oct96 on 'Biter Of Thorpe'; BOT131 04CD)*

Jun 87. (7") *(AOR 10)* **BIG HOLLOW MAN. / MUZZLES** [-]
(12"+=) *(AOR 10T)* – The passing of the third floor back.

Apr 88. (7") *(AOR 12)* **CAT-HOUSE. / TOUCH PIGGY'S EYES** [-]
(12"+=) *(AOR 12T)* – House-cat.

Jan 89. (lp/c/cd) <*CD 1290*> **DARK ADAPTED EYE** [-]
– Cat-house / Big hollow man / White knuckle ride / When I was young / Yummer yummer man / Fizzing human bomb / Whistling for his love / Inky bloaters / Brimstone in a barren land / Bad Miss "M" / Touch Piggy's eyes / House-cat / Bed caves / Slep has no property.

Apr 89. (7") *(AOR 23)* **WHITE KNUCKLE RIDE. / WHISTLING FOR HIS LOVE**
(12"+=) *(AOR 23T)* – Cold sweat.

Sire Sire

Oct 90. (7"/c-s) *(921773-7/-4)* **TOMORROW NEVER KNOWS. / KING CRACK** [-]
(12"+=/cd-s+=) *(921773-6/-2)* – (3-'A'mixes).

Jan 91. (cd/c/lp) *(<7599 26126-2/-4/-1>)* **BLAST THE HUMAN FLOWER**
– The I.D. parade / Tomorrow never knows / Big blue bayou / King Crack / Daisy / Dead man's chill / The living and the stubborn / Jehovah's precious stone / 16 candles.

— nothing heard of her recently until . . . below

— now with **DAVID KNIGHT** – keyboards, electronics

Biter Of Thorpe not iss.

Oct 96. (d-cd) *(BOT131 06CD)* **COMATOSE NON-REACTION: THE THWARTED POP CAREER OF DANIELLE DAX** (compilation) [-]

Oct 96. (7"ep/cd-ep) *(BOT131 07/+CDEP)* **TIMBER TONGUE EP** [-]
– Toygit / E.V.I.L. T / Timber tongue / Uru eu wau wau.

– compilations, etc. –

Feb 88. (12"ep) *Nighttracks; (SFNT 006)* **THE EVENING SHOW SESSIONS** (1.12.85) [ ] [-]
– Fizzing human bomb / Pariah / Ostrich / Numb companions.

dB's

Formed: Winston-Salem, North Carolina, USA . . . 1978 by CHRIS STAMEY (ex-RITTENHOUSE SQUARE) and fellow ex-SNEAKERS, WILL RIGBY and GENE HOLDER. Under this moniker, they released two singles between 1976-77 for STAMEY's 'Car' label while the band also featured MITCH EASTER (later a producer and leader of LET'S ACTIVE). A posthumous SNEAKERS ep, 'IN THE RED', surfaced a year later, while a compilation, 'RACKET', was finally put together in the early 90's. In 1977, meanwhile, STAMEY issued a solo 45, 'SUMMER SUN' for the legendary US 'Ork' label, before returning to 'Car' as leader of the dB's. STAMEY had already moved to New York City by this point, playing with ALEX CHILTON (ex-BOX TOPS, ex-BIG STAR) and undertaking a one-off stint with RICHARD LLOYD (of TELEVISION). A debut single, 'IF AND WHEN' (as CHRIS STAMEY & THE dB's) backed with 'I THOUGHT (YOU WANTED TO KNOW)' arrived in mid-'78 and although shunned by every major record company in the States, they found a UK home with 'Albion', who released a string of singles and two BEATLES-esque albums, 'STANDS FOR DECIBELS' (1981) and 'REPERCUSSION' (1982). Like the considerably more successful LENNON and McCARTNEY songwriting partnership before them, STAMEY and HOLSAPPLE acted as foils for each others respective styles; while the former concerned himself with highly melodic but often off-beat pop and psychedelia, the latter's rootsy approach helped to anchor the sound. However, the pairing was severed when STAMEY upped sticks for a solo career in 1983, HOLSAPPLE recruiting bass player, RICK WAGNER, while the band signed for 'Bearsville'. Unfortunately, the band were dogged by legal problems following the death of label boss, Albert Grossman, the subsequent album, 'LIKE THIS' (1984), was bogged down in the ensuing confusion despite being a spirited set of earthier country-orientated sounds. Following an absence of three years, HOLSAPPLE and Co, emerged with their long-awaited comeback album, 'THE SOUND OF MUSIC' (1987), after inking a new deal with 'I.R.S.' and supporting new labelmates, R.E.M.; HOLSAPPLE would subsequently guest for STIPE and Co, guesting on their 'Out Of Time' classic in 1991. The dB's continued to work together well into the 90's, although it would only be HOLSAPPLE and RIGBY who would feature on 1994's umpteenth comeback set, 'PARIS AVENUE'.

Album rating: STANDS FOR DECIBELS (*8) / REPERCUSSION (*7) / LIKE THIS (*5) / THE SOUND OF MUSIC (*5) / RIDE THE WILD TOM (*4) / PARIS AVENUE (*5)

CHRIS STAMEY (b. 6 Dec'54, Chapel Hill, N. Carolina) – vocals, guitar / after debut 45; **PETER HOLSAPPLE** (b.19 Feb'56, Greenwich, Connecticut) – guitar, organ, vocals / **GENE HOLDER** (b.10 Jul'54, Pennsylvania) – bass / **WILL RIGBY** (b.17 Mar'56) – drums

not iss. Car

Jul 78. (7") **I THOUGHT (YOU WANTED TO KNOW). / IF AND WHEN** [-] [ ]

not iss. Shake

1980. (7") *<SHK 100>* **BLACK AND WHITE. / SOUL KISS (part one & two)** [-] [ ]

Albion not iss.

Dec 80. (7") *(ION 1005)* **DYNAMITE. / FIGHT** [ ] [-]
Mar 81. (7") *(ION 1010)* **BIG BROWN EYES. / BABY TALK** [ ] [-]
Apr 81. (lp/c) *(ALB/+C 105)* **STANDS FOR DECIBELS** [ ] [-]
– Black and white / Dynamite / She's not worried / The fight / Espionage / Tearjerkin' / Cycles per second / Bad reputation / Big brown eyes / I'm in love / Moving in your slee / Judy. *(re-iss. Oct87 on 'Line'; ALLP 400009)*
May 81. (7") *(ION 1013)* **JUDY. / CYCLES PER SECOND** [ ] [-]
Nov 81. (7") *(ION 1024)* **AMPLIFIER. / ASK FOR JILL** [ ] [-]
(w/ free 7") **UPS AND DOWNS. / WE WERE HAPPY THERE**
Feb 82. (7") *(ION 1030)* **NEVERLAND. / Ph FACTOR** [ ] [-]
Jun 82. (lp/c) *(ALB/+C 109)* **REPERCUSSIONS** [ ] [-]
– Happenstance / We were happy there / Living a lie / From a window to a screen / Ask for Jill / Amplifier / Neverland / Storm warning / Ups and downs / Nothing is wrong / In Spain / I feel good. *(re-iss. Oct87 on 'Line'; ALLP 400032)*
Jun 82. (7") *(ION 1034)* **LIVING A LIE. / IN SPAIN** [ ] [-]

—— **RICK WAGNER** – bass (HOLDER now guitar) repl. STAMEY (to solo)

not iss. Bearsville

1984. (lp) *<24516>* **LIKE THIS** [-] [ ]
– Love is for lovers / She got soul / Spitting in the wind / Lonely is not cool / Amplifier / A spy in the house of love / Rendezvous / New gun in town / On the battlefront / White train / Darby Hall. *(re-iss. Jun88 on 'Rhino' lp/cd; RN LP/CD 70891)*

—— split for a while in 1984. WILL RIGBY released solo album 'SIDEKICK PHENOMENON' for US 'Egon'.

—— **JEFF BENINATO** – bass; repl. WAGNER

IRS-MCA I.R.S.

Nov 87. (lp/c) *(MIRF/+C 1031) <42055>* **THE SOUND OF MUSIC** [ ] [ ]
– Never say when / Change with the changing times / Molly says / Bonneville / Any old thing / Think too hard / Working for somebody else / Never before and never again / A better place / Looked at the sun too long / Today could be the day.

—— In 1991 for below label, PETER HOLSAPPLE and CHRIS STAMEY released album 'MAVERICKS'. *It featured HOLDER, MICHAEL BLAIR and JANE SCARPENTONI.*

—— new dB's; **ERIC PETERSON** – guitar + **HAROLD KELT** – keyboards repl. HOLDER who became a producer for WYGALS and his own band The INDIVIDUALS

Special Delivery Rhino

Nov 94. (cd) *<(RSACD 805)>* **RIDE THE WILD TOM TOM** [ ] [ ] Aug93
– We should be in bed / Everytime anytime / Let's live for today / Little hands / You got it wrong / Tell me two times / Nothing is wrong / Purple hose / Ash / I read New York rocker / Walking the ceiling (it's good to be alive) / Baby talk / Dynamite (original) / Soul kiss (part one) / Bad reputation / Modern boys and girls / What about the cat / What's the matter with me? / The fight / She's green, I'm blue / If and when / Soul kiss (part two) / The death of rock / Purple hose (light return) / Hardcore Judy / A spy in the house of love.

Monkey Hill Monkey Hill

Apr 95. (cd) *<(MON 6122)>* **PARIS AVENUE** [ ] [ ] Oct94
– Morning bugle / Ride the roller coaster / Lines and dots / Huey, Dewey, and "Louie, Louie" / Girlfriend / Baldhead baby / Window on the world / I can't look her in the eye / Barometers, thermometers / Running over / This is where I belong / We gold / Visible man.

—— disbanded and PETER featured with The CONTINENTAL DRIFTERS on self-titled album (& same label) with new wife SUSAN COWSILL (ex-COWSILLS)

– compilations, etc. –

Aug 86. (lp) *Dojo; (DOJOLP 33)* **AMPLIFIER** [ ] [-]
– Nothing is wrong / Neverland / In Spain / Happenstance / Living a lie / From a window to a scream / Ask for Jill / Amplifier / Bad reputation / Big brown eyes / Moving in your sleep / Black and white / I feel good Toady / Ups and downs.
Apr 92. (d-cd) *Line;* **STANDS FOR DECIBELS / REPERCUSSION** [ ] [-]

DEAD BOYS

Formed: Cleveland, Ohio, USA ... mid '76 by CHEETAH CHROME and JOHNNY BLITZ, both ex-ROCKET FROM THE TOMBS (same band as DAVID THOMAS and PETER LAUGHNER of PERE UBU), who relocated to New York with frontman STIV BATORS (also a short-lived RFTT member), JIMMY ZERO and JEFF MAGNUM. Under The DEAD BOYS moniker, they played the infamous CBGB's, a nightclub owned at the time by their manager, Hilly Kristal. America's answer to The DAMNED, they signed to 'Sire' in 1977, finally unleashing their brash HEARTBREAKERS meets STOOGES debut set, 'YOUNG, LOUD & SNOTTY'. Featuring at least two seminal punk classics in 'SONIC REDUCER' and 'ALL THIS AND MORE' (also available on the V/A album, 'New Wave'), it sold moderately enough to make the US Top 200 for a month. The FELIX PAPPALARDI-produced follow-up, 'WE HAVE COME FOR YOUR CHILDREN' (1978), was everything that punk's critics railed against (i.e. brutally nihilistic, musically limited and sheer bloodied minded), although it did feature 'AIN'T IT FUN' (later covered by GUNS 'N ROSES) and was also graced by the presence of two RAMONES, JOEY and DEE DEE. The DEAD BOYS were finally laid to rest when STIV went solo in 1979, recording a handful of singles (including a version of The Choirs' 'IT'S COLD OUTSIDE') and an album for Greg Shaw's 'Bomp', 'DISCONNECTED' (1980). After putting in a brief stint as an actor in John Waters' 'Polyester', BATORS teamed up with ex-SHAM 69 Brits, DAVE TREGANNA, DAVE PARSONS and MARK GOLDSTEIN to form the short-lived WANDERERS. A solitary album, 'THE ONLY LOVERS LEFT ALIVE' (1981), appeared on UK 'Polydor', before he and TREGANNA hooked up with old DAMNED friend, BRIAN JAMES as The LORDS OF THE NEW CHURCH. With ex-BARRACUDAS drummer NICKY TURNER in tow, the punk supergroup were inaugurated via a live gig in Paris towards the end of 1981. Signed to Miles Copeland's 'Illegal/I.R.S.' imprint, the LORDS delivered their first vinyl sermon in the shape of an eponymous 1982 debut album, a lacklustre sub-metal affair dabbling in pseudo gothic imagery and religious doom-mongering. This set the tone for the remainder of the band's career, two further studio albums, 'IS NOTHING SACRED?' (1983) and 'METHOD TO OUR MADNESS' (1984) hardly adding to their legacy; bizarrely enough, ex-MANFRED MANN'S EARTH BAND keyboard player/bassist, MATT IRVING joined for the latter. As the band's studio output dwindled to almost nothing, BATORS finally sacked his whole band in 1989 and took flight to London where he gathered together a bunch of old punk friends (DEE DEE RAMONE, NEIL X and JOHNNY THUNDERS) for a one-off gig billed as 'Return Of The Living Boys'. Although this loose aggregation actually laid down around half a dozen studio tracks, BATORS was to die in his sleep on the 4th of June, 1990, after he was run over by an automobile in Paris the previous day.

Album rating: YOUNG, LOUD & SNOTTY (*7) / WE HAVE COME FOR YOUR CHILDREN (*5) / Stiv Bators: DISCONNECTED (*5) / Lords Of The New Church: LORDS OF THE NEW CHURCH (*5) / IS NOTHING SACRED? (*4) / THE METHODS TO OUR MADNESS (*4) / KILLER LORDS compilation (*5) / LIVE AT THE SPIT (*3)

STIV BATORS (b. STEVEN BATOR, 22 Oct'56, Cleveland) – vocals / **CHEETAH CROME** (b. GENE CONNOR) – guitar, vocals / **JIMMY ZERO** – guitar / **JEFF MAGNUM** – bass / **JOHNNY BLITZ** – drums

Sire Sire

Oct 77. (lp) *(9103 329) <SR 6038>* **YOUNG, LOUD & SNOTTY** [ ] [ ]
– Ain't nothin' to do / All this and more / Caught with the meat in your mouth / Down in flames / Hey little girl / High tension wire / I need lunch / Not anymore / Sonic reducer / What love is.
Dec 77. (7"m)(12"m) *(SRE 1004)(6078 609)* **SONIC REDUCER. / LITTLE GIRL / DOWN IN FLAMES** [ ] [ ]
Aug 78. (7"m) *(SRE 1029)* **TELL ME. / NOT ANYMORE / AIN'T NOTHIN' TO DO**
Aug 78. (lp) *<(SRK 6054)>* **WE HAVE COME FOR YOUR CHILDREN** [ ] [ ] Jun78
– Third generation nation / I won't look back / Catholic boy / Flame thrower love / Son of Sam / Tell me / Big city / Calling on you / Dead and alive / Ain't it fun.

— now without MAGNUM, they disbanded in 1979. BATORS went solo.

– compilations, etc. –

May 81. (lp) *Bomp; (BLP 4017)* **NIGHT OF THE LIVING DEAD BOYS (live)**
– Detention home / Caught with the meat in your mouth / All this and more / 3rd generation nation / Tell me / Catholic boy / Won't look back / Ain't it fun / What love is / Ain't nothin' to do / Need lunch / Sonic reducer / Route 66 / Hang on Sloopy / It's all over now / Ain't it fun / Sonic reducer. *(cd-iss. Apr94; BCD 4017) (lp re-iss. Jul97; same)*

1989. (lp/cd) *Bomp; <BLP/BCD 4064>* **YOUNGER, LOUDER AND SNOTTIER**
(UK-iss.Jul97; same)

Nov 97. (cd/lp) *Bacchus Archives; (BA 1121 CD/LP)* **TWISTIN' ON THE DEVIL'S FORK**

Aug 98. (d-cd) *Bomp; (BCD 4066)* **ALL THIS AND MORE**

STIV BATORS

— with band; **GEORGE HARRISON** – guitar (no not that one!) / **FRANK SELICH** – bass / **DAVID QUINTON** – drums

London Bomp

Sep 79. (7") *(HLZ 10575) <BMP 124>* **IT'S COLD OUTSIDE. / THE LAST YEAR**

Bomp Bomp

May 80. (7") *<BMP 128>* **NOT THAT WAY ANYMORE. / CIRCUMSTANTIAL EVIDENCE**

May 80. (lp) *<BLP 4015>* **DISCONNECTED**
– Evil boy / Bad luck charm / A million miles away / Make up your mind / Swingin' a g-go / Too much to dream / Ready anytime / The last year / I wanna forget you (just the way you are). *(re-iss. Oct87 on 'Line' lp/cd; LILP4/LICD9 00174) (cd re-iss. Feb94; BCD 4043)*

1980. (12"ep) *<BEP 1202>* **TOO MUCH TO DREAM. / MAKE UP YOUR MIND**

— In Aug'87, BATORS released mini-lp, 'HAVE LOVE WILL TRAVEL' *BMP 12-136*

— BATORS joined The WANDERERS (with ex-SHAM 69 members). They released a few singles and an album in 1981; 'THE ONLY LOVERS LEFT ALIVE'. He then was part of punk supergroup . . .

LORDS OF THE NEW CHURCH

STIV BATOR plus **BRIAN JAMES** – guitar, vocals (ex-DAMNED, ex-TANZ DER YOUTH, ex-HELLIONS) / **DAVE TREGANNA** – bass, vocals (ex-WANDERERS, ex-SHAM 69) / **NICKY TURNER** – drums (ex-BARRACUDAS)

Illegal I.R.S.

Apr 82. (7") *(ILS 0028)* **NEW CHURCH. / LIVIN' ON LIVIN'**

Jul 82. (7") *(ILS 0030)* **OPEN YOUR EYES. / GIRLS GIRLS GIRLS**

Jul 82. (lp) *(ILP 009)* **LORDS OF THE NEW CHURCH**
– New church / Russian roulette / Question of temperature / Eat your heart out / Portobello / Open your eyes / Livin' on livin' / Li'l boys play with dolls / Apocalypso / Holy war. *(cd-iss. Apr87; ILPCD 009)*

Nov 82. (7"/7"pic-d) *(ILS/+P 0033)* **RUSSIAN ROULETTE. / YOUNG DON'T CRY**

I.R.S. I.R.S.

Jun 83. (7") *(PFP 1015)* **LIVE FOR TODAY. / OPENING**

Aug 83. (lp/c) *(SP/CS 70039)* **IS NOTHING SACRED?**
– Dance with me / Bad timing / Johnny too bad / Don't worry children / The night is calling / Black – white girl / Goin' downtown / Tales of two cities / World without end / Partners in crime / Live for today.

Sep 83. (7"/12"colrd-pic-d) *(PFP/PFSX 1022)* **DANCE WITH ME. / I'M NOT RUNNING HARD ENUFF**

— added guest **MATT IRVING** – bass, keyboards (ex-MANFRED MANN'S EARTH BAND)

Oct 84. (7") *(IRS 113)* **M STYLE. / SORRY FOR THE MAN**
(d7"+=) *(IRSY 113)* – Dance with me / I'm not running hard enuff.

Nov 84. (lp) *(IRSA 7049)* **THE METHOD TO OUR MADNESS**
– Method to my madness / I never believed / Pretty baby scream / Fresh flesh / When blood runs cold / M style / The seducer / Kiss of death / Do what thou wilt / My kingdom come.

Illegal not iss.

Apr 85. (7"pic-d) *(LORDSP 1)* **LIKE A VIRGIN. / METHOD TO MY MADNESS**
(12"+=) *(LORDS 1)* – Gun called Justice.

Nov 85. (lp/c) **KILLER LORDS** (compilation)
– Dance with me / Hey tonight / Russian roulette / M style / Lord's prayer / Live for today / Method to my madness / Open your eyes / I never believed / Black girl – white girl / New church / Like a virgin. *(re-iss. Aug90 cd/lp; ILP 016)*

— trimmed to quartet again, when IRVING joined PAUL YOUNG BAND

BondageInt not iss.

Aug 87. (7") *(B 11)* **REAL BAD TIME. / THINGS GO BAD**

New Rose not iss.

Sep 87. (7"/12") *(B 100-1/-2)* **PSYCHO SEX. /**

Illegal not iss.

May 88. (lp/c) *(ILP/+C 021)* **LIVE AT THE SPIT (live)**
– Method to my madness / Partners in crime / Kiss of death / Bad timing / Dance with me / M style / Livin' on livin' / The seducer / Open your eyes / Gun caled Justice / When blood runs cold / Pretty baby scream / Live for today / Holy war / Black girl – white girl / New church. *(w/ free 45)* – Gun called Justice / Johnny too bad / Light and shade / All or nothing.
(re-iss. Aug90 cd; ILPCD 021)

Perfect B. not iss.

May 89. (d-lp; as STIV BATORS & HIS EVIL BOYS) *(PB 003)* **SCENE OF THE CRIME (live at the Limelight 1985)** German
– Introduction / Evil boy / It's cold outside / Have love, will travel / Not that way anymore / The last year / Story in your eyes / It's trash / Ready to snap / Do you believe in magic / Dreams & desires / Sonic reducer / 3rd generation nation.

— split, when BATORS sacked the rest, because they were going to sack him. He started to work with ex-members of SIGUE SIGUE SPUTNIK and HANOI ROCKS, but he died in his sleep in 1990 after being knocked down by a car in Paris.

– STIV BATORS compilations, others, etc. –

May 94. (cd) *New Rose; (64200-2)* **THE DEAD BOYS**

Apr 98. (cd) *Bond Age; (BRCD 96129)* **THE LAST RACE**

DEAD CAN DANCE

Formed: Melbourne, Australia . . . 1981 by multi-instrumentalist, BRENDAN PERRY and vocalist, LISA GERRARD, both of Anglo-Irish parentage. After initially immersing himself in the punk scene, PERRY turned became increasingly intrigued by the possibilities offered by electronic music, subsequently hooking up with GERRARD and two other early members, PAUL ERIKSON and SIMON MONROE. With a solitary homeland recording (very limited for 'Fast Forward' cassette mag) to their name, PERRY and GERRARD decided to take DEAD CAN DANCE to London where they fitted in perfectly among the avant-garde hopefuls at up and coming indie label, '4 a.d.'. At pains to point out that their name symbolised the energy inherent in apparently lifeless matter rather than the goth connotations many assumed, DEAD CAN DANCE were soon mesmerising critics and fans alike with their otherworldly synthesis of classical, ethnic and electronic music. An eponymous debut album emerged in 1984 and although its noisy dissonance only hinted at the sculpted aesthetics to come, highlights included 'A PASSAGE IN TIME', 'THE TRIAL' and 'THE FATAL IMPACT'. However, with a costly 15-piece ensemble in tow, they only selected a few venues for concerts and never toured consistently. 1985's 'SPLEEN AND IDEAL' was a more atmospheric, darkly intoxicating affair, introducing more varied instrumental textures and the wailing Middle Eastern, OFRA HAZA-style vocals of GERRARD on such compulsive tracks as 'THE CARDINAL SIN', 'MESMERISM' and every monk's favourite, 'DE PROFUNDIS (OUT OF THE DEPTHS OF SORROW)'. 'WITHIN THE REALM OF A DYING SUN' (1987) moved towards classical territory with a cast of violin, viola, etc, while 'SERPENT'S EGG' (1988) tackled medieval folk styles of Eastern Europe. PERRY and GERRARD moved even further into the past (or rather brought the past into the future) with their exploration of Renaissance era music – both spiritual and secular – on 1990's 'AION'. The early 90's found PERRY and GERRARD working on a variety of side projects including scoring music for a production of 'Oedipus Rex' and the soundtrack to the movie, 'Baraka'. DEAD CAN DANCE briefly emerged from the realm of cult obscurity and into the Top 50 (also hovered under the US Top 100) in 1993 with their seventh album, 'INTO THE LABYRINTH'. LISA went on to released a few solo outings, one under the pseudonym of ELIJAH'S MANTLE, while DEAD CAN DANCE managed to capture the mystical allure of their studio work on live set, 'TOWARD THE WITHIN' (1994). With 1995's 'SPIRITCHASER', DEAD CAN DANCE nearly cracked the UK Top 40 while making the US Top 75, a mark of burgeoning popular appeal for a band who are already almost universally respected among fellow artists across the musical spectrum. Of late, DEAD CAN DANCE have been keeping uncharacteristically quiet, although LISA GERRARD released a collaborative set with PETER BOURKE (of SOMA) entitled 'DUALITY' (1998). • **Songwriters:** GERRARD / PERRY (some w/ others and some trad folk samples). • **Trivia:** They also can be heard on '4 a.d.' amalgam THIS MORTAL COIL and also featured two tracks on various lp, 'Lonely As An Eyesore'.

Album rating: DEAD CAN DANCE (*7) / SPLEEN AND IDEAL (*6) / WITHIN THE REALM OF A DYING SUN (*8) / THE SERPENT'S EGG (*7) / AION (*8) / A PASSAGE IN TIME compilation (*8) / INTO THE LABYRINTH (*7) / TOWARD THE WITHIN (*6) / SPIRITCHASER (*6) / Lisa Gerrard: THE MIRROR POOL (*6) / Lisa Gerrard & Peter Bourke: DUALITY (*6)

BRENDAN PERRY – multi-instrumentalist, vocals / **LISA GERRARD** – vocals, percussion / **PETER ULRICH** – percussion, drums, tapes with **JAMES PINKER** – timpani, mixer / **SIMON RODGER** – trombone; plus **MARTIN McCARRICK + GUY FERGUSON** – cello / **CAROLYN LOSTIN** – violin / **RICHARD AVISON** – trombone / **TONY AYERS** – timpani / **ANDREW NUTTER** – soprano vox

4 a.d. Rough Trade

Feb 84. (lp) *(CAD 404)* **DEAD CAN DANCE**
– A passage in time / Threshold / The trial / Frontier / Ocean / Fortune / East of Eden / The fatal impact / Wild in the woods / Musical eternal. *(cd-iss. Feb87; CAD 404CD)* – (includes below EP). *<US-iss.1994 on '4 a.d.-Reprise' cd,c; 45546>*

Sep 84. (12"ep) *(BAD 408)* **THE GARDEN OF ARCANE DELIGHTS**
– Carnival of light / The arcane / Flowers of the sea / In power we entrust the love advocated.

Nov 85. (lp/c)(cd) *(CAD/+C 512)(CAD 512CD)* **SPLEEN AND IDEAL**
– De profounds (out of the depths of sorrow) / Ascension / Circumradiant dawn / The cardinal sin / Mesmerism / Enigma of the absolute / Advent / Avatar / Indoctrination. *(cd+=)* – This tide / A design for living. *<US-iss.1994 on '4 a.d.-Reprise' cd,c; 45547>*

— now a basic duo of **BRENDAN + LISA** when ULRICH departed (SIMON + JAMES formed HEAVENLY BODIES). Retained **FERGUSON + AVISON** and recruited **ALISON HARLING + EMLYN SINGLETON** – violin / **PIERO GASPARINI** – viola / **TONY GAMMAGE + MARK GERRARD** (bother) – trumpet / **RUTH WATSON** – oboe, bass trombone / **JOHN + PETER SINGLETON** – trombone / **ANDREW CAXTON** – tuba, bass trombone

Jul 87. (lp/c)(cd) *(CAD/+C 705)(CAD 705CD)* **WITHIN THE REALM OF A DYING SUN**
– Dawn of the Iconoclast / In the wake of adversity / New age / Summoning of the muse / Anywhere out of the world / Cantara / Windfall / Xavier / Persephone (the gathering of flowers). *<US-iss.1994 on '4 a.d.-Reprise' cd,c; 45577>*

— **LISA + BRENDAN** brought in **DAVID NAVARRO SUST** (retained **ALISON + TONY**), new **REBECCA JACKSON** – violin / **SARAH BUCKLEY + ANDREW BEESLEY** – violas

Oct 88. (lp/c)(cd) *(CAD/+C 808)(CAD 808CD)* **THE SERPENT'S EGG** [ ] [-]
– The host of Seraphim / Orbis de Ignis / Severance / Chant of the Paladin / The writing on my father's hand / Echolalia / In the kingdom of the blind, the one-eyed are kings / Song of Sophia / Mother tongue / Ullysses. *<US-ss.1994 on '4 a.d.-Reprise' cd,c; 45576>*

Jul 90. (cd)(lp/c) *(CAD 0007CD)(CAD/+C 0007)* **AION** [ ] [-]
– The arrival and the reunion / Saltarello / Mephisto / The song of the Sibyl / Fortune presents gifts not according to the book / As the bell rings the maypole spins / The end of the words / Black sun / Wilderness / The promised womb / The garden of Zephirus / Radharc. *<US-iss.1994 on '4 a.d.-Reprise' cd,c; 45575>*

Sep 93. (cd)(c)(d-lp) *(CAD 3013CD)(CADC 3013)(DAD 3013) <45384>*
INTO THE LABYRINTH [47] [ ]
– Yulunga (spirit dance) / The ubiquitous Mr. Lovegrove / The wind that shakes the barley / The carnival is over / Ariadne / Saldek / Towards the within / Tell me about the forest (you once called home) / The spider's Stratagem / Emmeleia / How fortunate the man with none. *(d-lp+=)* – Bird / Spirit.

Oct 94. (cd)(d-lp/c) *(DAD 4015CD)(DAD/+C 4015) <45769>* **TOWARD THE WITHIN** [ ] [ ]
– Rakim / Persian love song / Desert song / Yulunga (spirit dance) / Piece for solo flute / The wind that shakes the barley / I am stretched on your grave / I can see now / American dreaming / Cantara / Oman / Song of the Sibyl / Tristan / Sanveen / Don't fade away.

Jun 96. (c/cd)(d-lp) *(CAD 6008/+CD)(DAD 6008) <46230>*
SPIRITCHASER [43] [75]
– Nierika / Song of the stars / Indus / Song of the dispossessed / Dedicaci outr / The snake and the Moon / Song of the Nile / Devorzhum.

– compilations, etc. –

Oct 91. (cd)(c) *4 a.d.; (CAD 1010CD)(CADC 1010) / Rykodisc; <RCD2/RACS 0215>* **A PASSAGE IN TIME** (part compilation) [ ] [ ]
– Salterello / Song of Sophia / Ullyses / Cantara / The garden of Zephirus / Enigma of the absolute / Wilderness / The host of Seraphim / Anywhere out of the world / The writing on my father's hand / Severance / The song of the Sibyl (traditional version; Catalan 16th Century) / Fortune presents gifts not according to the book / In the kingdom of the blind the one-eyed are kings / Bird / Spirit.

Dec 91. (cd) *Emperion; (IMP 008)* **THE HIDDEN TREASURES** (out-takes, live, rare) [ ] [-]
– Awakening / Reached from above / In power we entrust the love advocated / To the shore / Alone / Pray for dawn / Lartomento / The night we were lost / Lyndra / Isabella / Tune for Sheba / Cyndrill / The serpent's army / They don't even cry / Eyeless in Gaza / The endless longing of sea doves.

LISA GERRARD

— with The VICTORIAN PHILHARMONIC ORCHESTRA. She had worked on the scores for 'Oedipus Rex' and 'Baraku', while sidelining with ELIJAH'S MANTLE.

Aug 95. (cd)(c) *(CAD 5009CD)(CADC 5009) <45916>* **THE MIRROR POOL** [ ] [ ]
– Violina: The last embrace / La Bas: Song of the drowned / Persian love song: The silver gun / Sanvean: I am your shadow / The rite / Ajhon / Glorafin / Majhnavea's music box / Largo / Werd / Laurelei / Celon / Ventelas / Swans / Nilleshna / Gloradin. *(cd re-iss. Jul98; GAD 5009CD)*

— next a collaboration with **PETER BOURKE** (of SOMA)

Apr 98. (cd; by LISA GERRARD & PETER BOURKE) *(CAD 8004CD) <46854>* **DUALITY** [ ] [ ]
– Shadow magnet / Tempest / Forest veil / The comforter / The unfolding / Pilgrimage of lost children / The human game / The circulation of shadows / Sacrifice / Nadir (synchronicity).

DEAD FAMOUS PEOPLE

Formed: New Zealand . . . 1986 by DONNA SAVAGE, BIDDY LEYLAND, WENDY KJESTRUP, JENNY RENALS and ROBIN TEARLE. However, after minor homeland hits for who else, the 'Flying Nun' imprint, the 5-piece moved shop to England signing with 'Utility' (once home of BILLY BRAGG).

Album rating: ARRIVING LATE IN TORN AND FILTHY JEANS mini (*6)

DONNA SAVAGE – vocals / **BIDDY LEYLAND** – keyboards / **WENDY KJESTRUP** – guitar / **JENNY RENALS** – bass / **GILL MOON** – drums; repl. ROBIN TEARLE (partly on below set)

Utility — not iss.

Jul 89. (m-lp/m-cd) *(UTIL 007/+CD)* **ARRIVING LATE IN TORN AND FILTHY JEANS** [ ] [-]
– The girl with an attitude problem / Postcard from Paradise / evil child / Barlow's house / Traitor to the cause / Take your leather jacket off.

— split in the summer of 1990, SAVAGE almost immediately guesting for SAINT ETIENNE on their version of The Field Mice's 'LET'S KISS AND MAKE UP'. She subsequently went solo, as did LEYLAND, returning to New Zealand in the process.

– compilations, etc. –

Jun 94. (cd) *La-Di-Da; (LADIDA 016CD)* **ALL HAIL THE DAFFODIL** [ ] [-]

DEAD KENNEDYS

Formed: San Francisco, California, USA . . . early 1978 by JELLO BIAFRA and EAST BAY RAY, who recruited KLAUS FLOURIDE, TED and briefly, the mysterious 6025. Inspired by British punk rock, BIAFRA formed The DEAD KENNEDYS primarily as a vehicle for his raging, razor-sharp satire of America and everything it stood for. Public enemy #1 from the off, major labels steered well clear of the band, BIAFRA and Co. subsequently forming their own label, the legendary 'Alternative Tentacles', releasing 'CALIFORNIA UBER ALLES' as their debut 45 in late '79. A scathing critique of California governor, Jerry Brown, the record introduced the singer's near-hysterical vocal undulations set against a pulverising punk/hardcore musical backdrop. Released on the independent 'Fast' imprint in Britain, the record's initial batch of copies selling like proverbial hotcakes. The 1980 follow-up, 'HOLIDAY IN CAMBODIA' (released on Miles Copeland's 'Faulty' label; 'Cherry Red' in the UK) remains The DEAD KENNEDYS' most viciously realised moment, a dark, twisting diatribe on American middle-class liberal trendies. Later in the year, the group kept up their aural assault with a debut album, 'FRESH FRUIT FOR ROTTING VEGETABLES', an unexpected Top 40 entry in the seemingly "Punk Is Dead" Britain, which contained the aforesaid 45's plus perennial favourites, 'LET'S LYNCH THE LANDLORD', 'DRUG ME' and the forthcoming UK hit, 'KILL THE POOR'. The record also offered a glimpse of BIAFRA's reassuringly twisted sense of humour in such surreal cuts as 'STEALING PEOPLE'S MAIL' and 'VIVA LAS VEGAS' (the latter was a hit for Elvis!). In 1981, drummer D.H. PELIGRO replaced TED, making his debut on the bluntly-titled 'TOO DRUNK TO FUCK', the only UK Top 40 charting single in musical history (up to that point!) to utilise the "f***" word. Once again mocking the inherent hypocrisy of corporate America, The DEAD KENNEDYS released a frenetic 10" mini-set, 'IN GOD WE TRUST INC.' (1981), highlights being the self-explanatory 'NAZI PUNKS FUCK OFF' (a US-only single) and a deadpan version of 'RAWHIDE'. The band then took a brief hiatus, busying themselves with an 'Alternative Tentacles' compilation of promising unsigned American bands, entitled 'Let Them Eat Jellybeans'. That same year (1982), the group released their second album proper, 'PLASTIC SURGERY DISASTERS'; issued on 'Statik' in the UK, it featured the singles 'BLEED FOR ME' and 'HALLOWEEN'. Spending the ensuing few years touring, the band resurfaced in 1985 with 'FRANKENCHRIST', an album that finally saw BIAFRA's upstanding enemies closing in (ie. the PMRC, the US government, etc) due to the album's free "penis landscape" poster by Swiss artist H.R. Giger. Although BIAFRA and Co. (including some senior label staff) were tried in court for distributing harmful material to minors (a revised obscenity law), the case was subsequently thrown out after a hung jury. Nevertheless, the cost of the trial effectively put the band out of business, The DEAD KENNEDYS poignantly-titled finale, 'BEDTIME FOR DEMOCRACY' being issued late in 1986. Although KLAUS and RAY followed low-key solo careers, the ever-prolific BIAFRA vociferously protested against his treatment on spoken-word sets, 'NO MORE COCOONS' (1987) and 'THE HIGH PRIEST OF HARMFUL MATTER' (1989). He subsequently collaborated with a wide range of hardcore/industrial acts such as D.O.A., NO MEANS NO and TUMOR CIRCUS, although it was with LARD (a project with MINISTRY mainmen, AL JOURGENSEN and PAUL BARKER) that BIAFRA really came into his own. A late 80's mini-set, 'THE POWER OF LARD' preceded a full-length album, 'THE LAST TEMPTATION OF LARD', a minor UK hit early in 1990. This demented set included such hilarious BIAFRA monologues as 'CAN GOD FILL TEETH?' and even a rendition of Napolean XIV's 'THEY'RE COMING TO TAKE ME AWAY'. In 1994, he hooked up with another likeminded soul in hillbilly punk, MOJO NIXON, releasing one album, 'PRAIRIE HOME INVASION' (the title possibly a parody of an ICE-T album). BIAFRA continues to work at 'Alternative Tentacles', supplying the country with suitably deranged hardcore and occasionally taking time out for other projects, most recently a second LARD set, 'PURE CHEWING SATISFACTION' (1997). • **Trivia:** In 1979, BIAFRA stood in the elections for Mayor of San Francisco (he came 4th!).

Album rating: FRESH FRUIT FOR ROTTING VEGETABLES (*9) / IN GOD WE TRUST INC. mini (*5) / PLASTIC SURGERY DISASTERS (*6) / FRANKENCHRIST (*6) / BEDTIME FOR DEMOCRACY (*5) / GIVE ME CONVENIENCE OR GIVE ME DEATH compilation (*8) / Jello Biafra: NO MORE COCOONS spoken (*5) / HIGH PRIEST OF HARMFUL MATTER spoken (*5) / THE LAST TEMPTATION OF LARD with Lard (*6) / THE LAST SCREAM OF THE MISSING NEIGHBORS with D.O.A. (*6) / THE SKY IS FALLING AND I WANT MY MOMMY with No Means No (*5) / I BLOW MINDS FOR A LIVING (*6) / HIGH VOLTAGE CONSPIRACY FOR RADICAL FREEDOM with Tumor Circus (*5) / PRAIRIE HOME INVASION with Mojo Nixon (*6) / BEYOND THE VALLEY OF THE GIFT POLICE (*5) / PURE CHEWING SATISFACTION with Lard (*5)

JELLO BIAFRA (b. ERIC BOUCHER, 17 Jun'58, Boulder, Colorado) – vocals / **EAST BAY RAY** (b. RAY GLASSER, Castro Valley, California) – guitar, (synthesisers-later 80's) / **KLAUS FLUORIDE** (b. Detroit, Michigan) – bass, vocals / **BRUCE SLESINGER** (aka TED) – drums

Fast — Alternative Tentacles

Oct 79. (7") *(FAST 12) <AT 95-41>* **CALIFORNIA UBER ALLES. / MAN WITH THE DOGS** [ ] [ ]

Cherry Red — Faulty-IRS

Jun 80. (7")12" *(CHERRY/12CHERRY 13) <IR 9016>* **HOLIDAY IN CAMBODIA. / POLICE TRUCK** [ ] [ ]
(re-iss. 7"/cd-s Jun88 & Mar95; same)

Sep 80. (lp) *(B-RED 10) <SP 70014>* **FRESH FRUIT FOR ROTTING VEGETABLES** [33] [ ] Nov80
– Kill the poor / Forward to death / When ya get drafted / Let's lynch the landlord / Drug me / Your emotions / Chemical warfare / Calilfornia uber alles / I kill children / Stealing people's mail / Funland at the beach / Ill in my head / Holiday in Cambodia / Viva Las Vegas. *(cd-iss. Nov87 & Mar95; CDBRED 10)*

Oct 80. (7") *(CHERRY 16)* **KILL THE POOR. / IN SIGHT** [49] [-]
(re-iss. Nov87 & Mar95; CDCHERRY 16)

— **D.H. PELIGRO** (b. DARREN, East St.Louis, Illinois) – drums; repl. BRUCE/TED

Cherry Red | Alternative Tentacles

May 81. (7"/12") *(CHERRY/12CHERRY 24)* <*VIRUS 2*> **TOO DRUNK TO FUCK. / THE PREY** [36] [ ]
(re-iss. May88 & Mar95 cd-s; CDCHERRY 24)

Statik | Alternative Tentacles

Nov 81. (10"ep) *(STATEP 2)* <*VIRUS 5*> **IN GOD WE TRUST INC.** [ ] [ ]
– Religious vomit / Moral majority / Kepone factory / Dog bite / Nazi punks fuck off / We've got a bigger problem now / Rawhide. <*US c-ep+=; VIRUS 5C*> – Too drunk to fuck / The prey / Holiday in Cambodia. *(re-iss. Jun92 cd-ep; STATEP 2CD)*

Dec 81. (7") <*VIRUS 6*> **NAZI PUNKS FUCK OFF. / MORAL MAJORITY** [-] [ ]

Jul 82. (7"/12") *(STAT/+12 22)* <*VIRUS 23*> **BLEED FOR ME. / LIFE SENTENCE** [ ] [ ]
(cd-s Jun92; STAT 22CD)

Nov 82. (lp) *(STATLP 11)* **PLASTIC SURGERY DISASTERS** [ ] [-]
– Government flu / Terminal preppie / Trust your mechanic / Well paid scientist / Buzzbomb / Forest fire / Halloween / Winnebago warrior / Riot / Bleed for me / I am the owl / Dead end / Moon over Marin. *(re-iss. Oct85; same) (cd-iss. Nov86 & Jun92 +=; same)* – IN GOD WE TRUST INC. (ep)

Nov 82. (7"/12") *(STAT/+12 27)* <*VIRUS 28*> **HALLOWEEN. / SATURDAY NIGHT HOLOCAUST** [ ] [ ]
(cd-s Jun92; STAT 27CD)

—— meanwhile KLAUS and EAST BAY released solo singles (see below)

Alternative Tentacles | Alternative Tentacles

May 82. (12"; KLAUS FLUORIDE) <*(VIRUS 12)*> **SHORTNING BREAD. / DROWNING COWBOY** [ ] [ ]

Jun 84. (7"; EAST BAY RAY) <*(VIRUS 34)*> **TROUBLE IN TOWN. / POISON HEART** [ ] [ ]
(12 re-iss. Apr89 on 'New Rose' France; GMO 40)

Aug 84. (12"ep; KLAUS FLUORIDE) **CHA CHA CHA WITH MR. FLUORIDE** [ ] [-]
– Ghost riders / etc.

Dec 85. (lp) <*(VIRUS 45)*> **FRANKENCHRIST** [ ] [ ]
– Soup is good food / Hellnation / This could be anywhere (this could be everywhere) / A growing boy needs his lunch / Chicken farm / Macho-rama (invasion of the beef-patrol) / Goons of Hazzard / At my job / M.T.V. – Get off the air / Stars and stripes of corruption. *(cd-iss. 1986; VIRUS 45CD)*

Dec 86. (lp/c/cd) <*(VIRUS 50/+C/CD)*> **BEDTIME FOR DEMOCRACY** [ ] [ ]
– Take this job and shove it / Hop with the jet set / Dear Abby / Rambozo the clown / Fleshdunce / The great wall / Shrink / Triumph of the swill / I spy / Macho insecurity / Cesspools in Eden / One-way ticket to Pluto / Do the slag / Gone with the wind / A commercial / Anarchy for sale / Chickenshit conformist / Where do ya draw the line / Potshot heard round the world / D.M.S.O. / Lie detector.

—— split Dec '86 when RAY departed (he subsequently turned up in SKRAPYARD). KLAUS FLUORIDE went solo, releasing albums 'BECAUSE I SAY SO' (1988) and 'THE LIGHT IS FLICKERING' (1991) and forming acoustic outfit FIVE YEAR PLAN

– compilations, etc. –

on 'Alternative Tentacles' unless mentioned otherwise

Jun 87. (lp/cd) <*(VIRUS 57/+CD)*> **GIVE ME CONVENIENCE OR GIVE ME DEATH** [84] [ ]
– Police truck / Too drunk to f*** / California uber alles / Man with the dogs / In sight / Life sentence / A child and his lawnmower / Holiday in Cambodia / Night of the living rednecks / I fought the law / Saturday night holocaust / Pull my strings / Short songs / Straight A's / Kinky sex makes the world go round / The prey. *(cd+=/free flexi-disc)* – BUZZBOMB FROM PASADENA

Jun 93. (7"ep) *Subterranean; (SUB 24)* **NAZI PUNKS **** OFF / ARYANISMS. / ('A'live) / CONTEMPTUOUS** [ ] [-]
(re-iss. Dec97; same)

JELLO BIAFRA

Nov 87. (lp) <*(VIRUS 59)*> **NO MORE COCOONS** (spoken word) [ ] [ ]
(cd-iss. Mar93; VIRUS 59CD)

Jul 89. (d-lp) <*(VIRUS 66)*> **HIGH PRIEST OF HARMFUL MATTER (TALES OF THE TRIALS, LIVE)** (spoken word) [ ] [ ]
(cd-iss. Mar93; VIRUS 66CD)

LARD

BIAFRA, AL JOURGENSEN + PAUL BARKER (Ministry) / **JEFF WARD** – drums

Nov 89. (12"ep/c-ep/cd-ep) <*(VIRUS 72 T/C/CD)*> **THE POWER OF LARD / HELL FUDGE. / TIME TO MELT (31 mins.)** [ ] [ ]

Jul 90. (lp/cd) <*(VIRUS 84/+CD)*> **THE LAST TEMPTATION OF LARD** [69] [ ]
– Forkboy / Pineapple face / Hate, spawn and die / Drug raid at 4a.m. / Can God fill teeth? / Bozo skeleton / Sylvestre Matuschka / They're coming to take me away / I am your clock.

JELLO BIAFRA & D.O.A.

—— w/ **JOE KEITHLEY + CHRIS PROHOM** – guitar, vocals / **BRIAN GOBLE** – bass, vocals / **JON CARD** – drums

May 90. (lp/c/cd) <*(VIRUS 78/+C/CD)*> **THE LAST SCREAM OF THE MISSING NEIGHBORS** [ ] [ ]
– That's progress / Attack of the peacekeepers / Wish I was in El Salvador / Power is boring / We gotta get out of this place / Full metal jackoff.

JELLO BIAFRA & NO MEANS NO

with **TIPPER GORE BOB WRIGHT** – guitar / **JOHN WRIGHT** – drums / **JON CARD** – percussion

Mar 91. (lp/c/cd) <*(VIRUS 85/+C/CD)*> **THE SKY IS FALLING AND I WANT MY MOMMY** [ ] [ ]
– The sky is falling and I want my mommy (falling space junk) / Jesus was a terrorist / Bruce's diary / Sad / Ride the flume / Chew / Sparks in the Gene pool / The myth is real – let's eat.

JELLO BIAFRA

Jun 91. (d-lp/c/cd) <*(VIRUS 94/+C/CD)*> **I BLOW MINDS FOR A LIVING** [ ] [ ]
– Pledge of allegience / Talk on censorship – let us prey / Die for oil, sucker – higher octane version / I was a teenage pacifist / If voting changed anything . . . / Running for mayor / Grow more pot / Lost orgasm / Talk on censorship-Better living through new world orders + Fear of a free planet.

TUMOR CIRCUS

—— **DARREN MOR-X / DALE FLAT-UM + MIKE MDRASKOID** (of STEEL POLE BATH TUB) / **KING GRONG CHARLIE (TOLNAY)** (of LUBRICATED GOAT) + **J. BIAFRA**

Nov 91. (lp/c/cd) <*(VIRUS 087/+C/CD)*> **TUMOR CIRCUS – HIGH VOLTAGE CONSPIRACY FOR RADICAL FREEDOM** [ ] [ ]
– Hazing for success / Human cyst / The man with the corkscrew eyes / Fireball / Calcutta a-go-go / Turn off the respirator. (cd+=) Swine flu / Take me back or I'll drown our dog / Meathook up my rectum.

Feb 92. (7") <*(VIRUS 102)*> **MEATHOOK UP MY RECTUM. / (etched side)** [ ] [ ]
(12"+=/cd-s+=) <*(VIRUS 102 T/CD)*> – Take me back or I'll drown the dog / Swine flu / Fireball.

JELLO BIAFRA & MOJO NIXON

Nov 93. (7") *(VIRUS 136)* **WILL THE FETUS BE ABORTED? / THE LOST WORLD** [ ] [-]
(cd-s+=) *(VIRUS 136CD)* – Drinkin' with Jesus / Achey raky heart.

Feb 94. (lp/cd) <*(VIRUS 137/+CD)*> **PRAIRIE HOME INVASION** [ ] [ ]
– Buy my snake oil / Where are we gonna work (when the trees are gone) / Convoy in the sky / Atomic power / Are you drinkin' with me Jesus / Love me, I'm a liberal / Burgers of wrath / Nostalgia for an angel that never existed / Hammer chicken plant disaster / Mascot mania / Let's go burn de Nashville down / Will the fetus be aborted? / Plastic Jesus.

JELLO BIAFRA

Oct 94. (d-lp) <*(VIRUS 150)*> **BEYOND THE VALLEY OF THE GIFT POLICE** (spoken word) [ ] [-]
– Message to our sponsor / Experts / Ban everything / I have a dream / Talk on censorship / What we are not being told / President McMuffin tightens the belt / Talk on censorship / What we are not being told / In the belly of the wrong beast / Talk on censorship / Eric meets the moose diarrhea / Virturcrats unreality.

LARD

—— see last line-up + add **BILL RIEFLIN** – drums

May 97. (lp/c/cd) <*(VIRUS 199/+MC/CD)*> **PURE CHEWING SATISFACTION** [ ] [ ]
– War pimp renaissance / I wanna be a drug sniffing dog / Moths / Generation execute / Faith hope and treachery / Peeling back the foreskin of liberty / Mangoat / Sidewinder.

DEAD MILKMEN

Formed: Philadelphia, Pennsylvania, USA ... 1983 by RODNEY AMADEUS ANONYMOUS, JOE JACK TALCUM, DAVE BLOOD and DEAN CLEAN. Signed to 'Enigma', this bunch of punkoid piss-takers debuted with 1985's 'BIG LIZARD IN MY BACKYARD' album, no target too soft for their patented brand of adolescent high school humour. 'EAT YOUR PAISLEY!' continued in similar style the following year, the band's natural college campus fanbase lapping up the trashy likes of 'WHERE THE TARANTULA LIVES' and 'SWAMPLAND OF DESIRE'. Following the replacement of TALCUM and BLOOD with JASPER THREAD and LORD MANIAC respectively, the band offered up another trawl through the more satire-friendly aspects of American culture in the shape of 1987's 'BUCKY FELLINI'. Come the turn of the decade, The DEAD MILKMEN were still showing little sign of growing up with 'METAPHYSICAL GRAFITTI' (1990), featuring BUTTHOLE SURFER, GIBBY HAYNES on the YES-baiting 'ANDERSON, WALKMAN, BUTTHOLES and HOW!'.

Album rating: BIG LIZARD IN MY BACKYARD (*7) / EAT YOUR PAISLEY! (*6) / BUCKY FELLINI (*7) / BEELZEBUBBA (*5) / METAPHYSICAL GRAFITTI (*4) / SOUL ROTATION (*3) / NOT RICHARD, BUT DICK (*4) / CHAOS RULES – LIVE AT THE TROCADERO (*4) / STONEY'S EXTRA STOUT (PIG) (*4)

RODNEY AMADEUS ANONYMOUS – vocals / **JOE JACK TALCUM** – guitar, vocals / **DAVE BLOOD** – bass / **DEAN CLEAN** – drums

Enigma | Enigma

1985. (lp/c/cd) <*97-105-1/-4/-2*> **BIG LIZARD IN MY BACKYARD** [-] [ ]
– Tiny town / Beach song / Plum dumb / Swordfish / V.F.W. / Rastabilly / Serrated edge / Lucky / Big lizard / Gorilla girl / Bitchin' Camaro / Filet of sole / Spit sink / Violent school / Takin' retards to the zoo / Junkie / Right wing oigeons / Dean's dream / Laundromat song / Nutrition / Tugena. *(UK cd-iss. Mar98 on 'Restless'; 720542)*

Nov 86. (lp/c/cd) *(2131-1)* <*97-131-1/-4/-2*> **EAT YOUR PAISLEY!** [ ] [ ] Aug86
– Where the tarantula lives / Air crash museum / KK suck 2 / Fifty things / Happy is / Beach party Vietnam / I hear your name / Two feet off the ground / The thing that only eats hippies / Sic days / Swampland of desire / Take me apart / Moron / The fez / Vince Lombardi service center.

—— **JASPER THREAD** – guitar; repl. JOE JACK TALCUM

— **LORD MANIAC** – bass; repl. DAVE BLOOD

Oct 87. (lp) *(3260-1) <73260>* **BUCKY FELLINI** [ ] [ ] Jul87
– The pit / Take me to the specialist / I am the walrus / Watching Scotty die / Going to Graceland / Big time operator / Instant club hit (you'll dance to anything) / The badger song / Tacoland / City of mud / Rocketship / Nitro burning funny cars / Surfin' cow (theme from 'Bloody Orgy Of The Atomic Fern') / Jellyfish heaven.

Nov 87. (cd-ep) *<72231-2>* **INSTANT CLUB HIT (YOU'LL DANCE TO ANYTHING) / ('A'edit) / BONER BEATS / ASK ME TO DANCE / TUGENA / VINCE LOMBARDI SERVICE CENTER** [-] [ ]

Enigma-Virgin Enigma

Dec 88. (lp/c/cd) *(ENVLP/TCENV/CDENV 514) <73351>* **BEELZEBUBBA** [ ] [ ]
– Brat in the frat / RC's mom / Stuart / I walk the thinnest line / Sri Lanka sex hotel / Bad party / Punk rock girl / Bleach boys / My many smells / Smokin' banana peels / The guitar song / Born to love volcanos / Everybody's got nice stuff but me / I against Osbourne / Howard beware / Ringo buys a rifle / Life is shit.

Feb 89. (7") *(ENV 8)* **PUNK ROCK GIRL. / RINGO BUYS A RIFLE** [ ] [ ]
(12"+=) *(ENVT 8)* – Life is shit.

Restless Enigma

Sep 90. (cd/c/lp) *(LS 93591) <D21S-73564-2/-4/-1>* **METAPHYSICAL GRAFFITI** [ ] [ ] Apr90
– Beige sunshine / Do the brown nose / Methodist coloring book / Part 3 / I tripped over the ottoman / The big sleazy / If you love somebody, set them on fire / Dollar signs in their eyes / In praise of Sha Na Na / Epic tales of adventure / I hate you, I love you / Now everybody's me / Little man in my head / Anderson, Walkman, Buttholes and How!

Jan 91. (cd-ep) *<72546>* **SMOKIN' BANANA PEELS (5 versions) / DEPRESSION DAY DINNER / PUKING SONG / I HATE MYSELF / GIRL HUNT / DEATH'S ALRIGHT WITH ME** [-] [ ]

not iss. Hollywood

Apr 92. (cd/c) *<61294-2/-4>* **SOUL ROTATION** [-] [ ]
Nov 92. (m-cd/m-c) *<61409-2/-4>* **IF I HAD A GUN** [-] [ ]
Oct 93. (cd/c) *<61564-2/-4>* **NOT RICHARD, BUT DICK** [-] [ ]

not iss. Restless

Nov 94. (cd,c) *<72793>* **CHAOS RULES: LIVE AT THE TROCADERO (live)** [-] [ ]
– Tiny town / I walk the thinnest line / Smokin' banana peels / Surfin' cow / Bitchin' Camaro / Where the taratula lives / Nutrition / Big lizard / The thing that only eats hippies / I hate you, I love you / Lucky / V.F.W. / Rock girl / Rastabilly / Stuart / Right wing pigeons / Tacoland / Laundromat song / Swordfish.

Nov 95. (cd,c) *<72798>* **STONEY'S EXTRA STOUT (PIG)** [-] [ ]
– Peter Bazooka / Train I ride / Girl with the strong arm / I'm flying away / Helicopter interiors / Blues song / The man who rides the bus / Don't deny your inner child / When I get to Heaven / I can't stay awake / Crystalline / Chaos theory / Khrissy / Like to be alone / Big deal.

— they split some time in '96

– compilations, etc. –

Nov 97. (cd) *Restless; <72945>* **DEATH RIDES A PALE COW: THE ULTIMATE COLLECTION** [-] [ ]
– Milkmen stomp / Tiny town / Big lizard / Bitchin' Camaro / Nutrition / Dean's dream / Beach party Vietnam / The thing that only eats hippies / Big time operator / Instant club hit / Surfin' cow / Labor day / I walk the thinnest line / Stuart / Punk rock girl / Smokin' banana peels / Life is shit / If you love someone set them on fire / Peter Bazooka / Girl with the strong arm / Big deal / Blues song.

Nov 98. (m-cd) *BMG Special; <44841>* **CREAM OF THE CROP: THE BEST OF THE DEAD MILKMEN** [-] [ ]
– Bitchin' Camaro / Punk rock girl / The thing that only eats hippies / Surfin' cow / Instant club hit (you'll dance to anything) / Smokin' banana peels / Stuart / Beach song / Dean's dream / Laundromat song.

DEAF SCHOOL

Formed: Liverpool, England . . .early 1974 by large ensemble; BETTE BRIGHT, CLIFF HANGER, MR.AVERAGE, Rev. MAX RIPPLE, TIM WHITTAKER, ERIC SHARK, ENRICO CADILAC, IAN RITCHIE, MIKE EVANS, ROY HOLDER, ANN BRIGHT and HAZEL BARTRAM. The latter 4 departed before they were joined by PAUL PILNICK and this bunch won the prestigious at the time Melody Maker Rock Contest award, which led to a contract from 'Warners'. Their "New Wave" sound of Vaudevillian rock was highly popular for a time when punk rock and diversified fashions was the rage. Three albums were released, before all took off for greater pastures. BETTE BRIGHT cameod in the SEX PISTOLS film 'The Great Rock'n'roll Swindle' and 3 years later in 1981 married MADNESS singer SUGGS. In 1988, BRIGHT, LANGER, LINDSAY, CADILLAC, SHARK and RIPPLE re-united for 5 sell-out concersts, to celebrate 10 years of separation. • **Songwriters:** LANGER / BRIGHT / ALLEN etc. • **Trivia:** Some members played for PORTSMOUTH SINFONIA ORCHESTRA on various intentional out-of-tune performances.

ENRICO CADILLAC (b. STEVE ALLEN) – vocals / **BETTE BRIGHT** (b. ANN MARTIN, Whitstable, Kent) – vocals / **ERIC SHARK** (b. THOMAS DAVIS) – vocals / **CLIFF HANGER** (b. CLIVE LANGER) – guitar, piano, vocals / **The Rev. MAX RIPPLE** (b. JOHN WOOD) – keyboards, accordion / MR. AVERAGE (b. STEVE LINDSAY) – bass, piano, vocals / **IAN RITCHIE** – sax / **TIM WHITTAKER** – drums / **PAUL PILNICK** – guitar (ex-STEALER'S WHEEL)

Warners Warners

Aug 76. (lp) *(K 56280)* **SECOND HONEYMOON** [ ] [-]
– What a way to end it all / Where's the weekend / Cocktails at 8 / Bigger splash / Knock knock knocking / 2nd honeymoon / Get set ready go / Nearly moonlit night motel / Room service / Hi Jo hi / Snapshots / Final act.

Sep 76. (7") *(K 16812)* **WHAT A WAY TO END IT ALL. / NEARLY MOONLIT NIGHT MOTEL** [ ] [-]

— now without PILNICK who had already left mid-76.

Feb 77. (7") *(K 16870)* **TAXI. / LAST NIGHT** [ ] [-]
Mar 77. (lp) *(K 56364)* **DON'T STOP THE WORLD** [ ] [-]
– Don't stop the world / What a jerk / Darling / Everything for the dancer / Capaldi's cafe / Hypertension / It's a boy's world / End / Operator.

1977. (d-lp) *<2LS 3011>* **DON'T STOP THE WORLD / SECOND HONEYMOON** [-] [ ]
Jan 78. (7") *(K 17087)* **ALL QUEUED UP. / GOLDEN SHOWERS** [ ] [-]
Feb 78. (lp) *(K 56450) <3169>* **ENGLISH BOYS, WORKING GIRLS** [ ] [ ]
– Working girls / Golden showers / Thunder and lightning / What a week / Refugee / Ronny Zamora / English boys (with guns) / All queued up / I wanna be your boy / Morning after / Fire / O blow.

Feb 78. (7") *(K 17100)* **THUNDER AND LIGHTNING. / WORKING GIRLS** [ ] [-]

— Disbanded in Apr'78. STEVE ALLEN formed The ORIGINAL MIRRORS. WHITTAKER joined LORI & THE CHAMELEONS, before BIG IN JAPAN then PINK MILITARY. LINDSAY also joined BIG IN JAPAN and later The SECRETS then The PLANETS. RITCHIE went to JANE AIRE & THE BELVEDERES. BETTE BRIGHT went solo as did renowned producer to be CLIVE LANGER.

– compilations, others, etc. –

Dec 88. (lp) *Demon; (FIEND 135)* **SECOND COMING** [ ] [-]
– What a way to end it all / Shake some action / Hi Jo hi / Nearly moonlit night motel / Taxi / Ronny Zamora / Thunder and lightning / Blue velvet / Princess princess / I wanna be your boy / Lines / Capaldi's cafe / 2nd honeymoon / Final act. *(cd-iss. Jan91; FIENDCD 135)*

Kelley DEAL 6000

Formed: Minneapolis, Minnesota, USA . . . April '95 by floating member of The BREEDERS and twin-sister of the more famous KIM, KELLEY DEAL. A one-time computer systems analyst, KELLEY subsequently threw herself head first into the rock'n'roll lifestyle with The BREEDERS. Things came to a head in late '94 after that year's Lollapolooza tour when she was arrested for possession of heroin in her hometown of Dayton, Ohio. Recovering from her addiction via a court enforced period in a rehab unit in St.Paul's, Minnesota, she returned to the studio. Originally working under the moniker of SOLID STATE, the vocalist/guitarist initiated a writing partnership with JESSE COLIN ROSS and DAVE SHOUSE (of The GRIFTERS), the results surfacing as the debut KELLEY DEAL 6000 album, 'GO TO THE SUGAR ALTAR'. By the time of its release in late '95 on her own 'Nice Record Label', the trio had become a quintet with the addition of MARTY NEDICH and NICK HOOK, although ROSS would subsequently be replaced by STEVE SALETT. Life affirming alt-rock epistles from the mind of an ex-junkie were the order of the day, European-based label, 'Play It Again Sam', sufficiently impressed to offer a new deal for '97's 'BOOM~! BOOM! BOOM!'. In the meantime, her label was working on a scheduled album by The FROGS.

Album rating: GO TO THE SUGAR ALTAR (*6) / BOOM! BOOM! BOOM! (*5)

KELLEY DEAL (b.10 Jun'61, Dayton, Ohio, USA) – vocals, guitar (ex-BREEDERS) / **MARTY NEDICH** – bass / **NICK HOOK** – drums / also with **JESSE COLIN ROSS + DAVE SHOUSE** (of The GRIFTERS)

Bittersweet Nice Record Label

Jul 96. (cd) *(BIT 007CD) <6001>* **GO TO THE SUGAR ALTAR** [ ] [ ] Dec95
– Canyon / How about hero / Dammit / Sugar / Hundred tires / Head of the cult / Nice / Trixie delicious / Marooned / Tick tock / Mr. Goodnight. *<re-iss. 1997 on 'New West'; 36856>*

Nov 96. (cd-s) *(BIT 008)* **CANYON** [ ] [ ]

— **STEVE SALETT** – drums; repl. ROSS who suffered drug problems

Play It Again Sam Nice Record Label

Oct 97. (cd-s) *(BIAS 354CD)* **BRILLO HUNT. / MY BOYFRIEND DIED** [ ] [ ]
Nov 97. (cd) *(BIAS 361CD) <6002>* **BOOM! BOOM! BOOM!** [ ] [ ] Aug97
– Brillo hunt / Shag / My boyfriend died / Baby I'm king / When he calls me kitten / Box / Stripper / Where did the home team go / Total war / Scary / Future boy / Drum solo / Skylark / Confidence girl / Get the writing off my back.

DEATH IN JUNE

Formed: Guildford & Woking, Surrey, England . . . 1981 out of CRISIS by DOUG PEARCE and TONY WAKEFORD. The latter post-punk combo released only three singles and a solitary album, 'HYMNS OF FAITH' (1980), before PEARCE and WAKEFORD teamed up with PATRICK LEAGAS and CHRIS JENNER. Signed to 'New European Records', DEATH IN JUNE released their debut EP in early 82; heavy goths in the mould of SISTERS OF MERCY or early DANSE SOCIETY, the band followed up with a debut album, 'THE GUILTY HAVE NO PRIDE' (1983). What set them apart from their peers was their use of militaristic electronic/percussive rhythms, although their sound did hint at influences as diverse as JOY DIVISION and SOFT CELL. Following WAKEFORD's departure to SOL INVICTUS, DIJ recruited RICHARD BUTLER, releasing follow-up set, 'BURIAL', in 1984. The more heavily electronic 'NADA' (1985), meanwhile, threw a bit of footstomping flamenco (incredibly calling to mind Miles Davis' 'SKETCHES OF SPAIN'!) into the mix with 'THE HONOUR OF SILENCE', while 'THE CALLING' could've been SPANDAU BALLET had they grown up in Sheffield! Like many "goth" bands, however, DEATH IN JUNE were something of an acquired taste, the doom-lord vocals and OTT arrangements occasionally descending into pretentiousness. While the band's prolific release schedule continued through the 80's and 90's on albums such as 'BROWN BOOK' – prior to which, DAVID TIBET replaced JENNER – 'WALL OF SACRIFICE' (1988) and 'ROSE CLOUDS OF HOLOCAUST' (1993), they failed to attract much more than the barest of cult underground publicity.

Album rating: THE GUILTY HAVE NO PRIDE (*6) / BURIAL (*5) / NADA (*5) / THE WORLD THAT SUMMER (*5) / BROWN BOOK (*4) / WALL OF SACRIFICE (*4) / BUT WHAT ENDS WHEN THE SYMBOLS SHATTER (*4) / ROSE CLOUDS OF HOLOCAUST (*4) / SOMETHING IS COMING (*4) / Crisis: WE ARE ALL JEWS AND GERMANS compilation (*5)

CRISIS

DOUGLAS P.(EARCE) – rhythm guitar, vocals / **TONY WAKEFORD** – bass, vocals / **PHRAZER** – vocals / **LESTER JONES** – lead guitar, vocals / **THE CLEANER / INSECT ROBIN** – drums

Peckham Action / not iss.

Feb 79. (7"ep) *(NOTH 1)* **PC 1984. / HOLOCAUST / NO TOWN HALL** ☐ [-]

Ardkor / not iss.

Dec 79. (7") *(CRI 002)* **UK '78. / WHITE YOUTH** ☐ [-]
May 80. (m-lp) *(CRI 003)* **HYMNS OF FAITH** ☐ [-]
– On TV / Laughing / Back in the USSR / Afraid / Frustration / Red brigades / Kanada kommando.
Nov 81. (7"m) *(CRI 004)* **ALIENATION. / BRUKWOOD HOSPITAL** ☐ [-]

— last line-up **DEXTER** – vocals; repl. PHRAZER

— **LUKE RENDALL** – drums; repl. THE CLEANER

- compilations, etc -

Aug 82. (12"ep) *Crisis; (NOTH 1)* **HOLOCAUST UK EP** ☐ [-]
Aug 84. (lp) *Bulleon; (BULP 4)* **ARMED TO THE TEETH** ☐ [-]
Mar 97. (cd) *Crisis; (CR 16)* **WE ARE ALL JEWS AND GERMANS** (all material) ☐ [-]

DEATH IN JUNE

TONY WAKEFORD – keyboards, bass / **DOUGLAS P** – guitar / **PATRICK LEAGAS** – drums / **CHRIS JENNER** – visuals

N.E.R. / not iss.

Feb 82. (12"ep) *(SA 29634)* **HEAVEN ST. / WE DRIVE EAST / IN THE NIGHT TIME** ☐ [-]
(re-iss. Jan84 7"/12"; first 2 tracks only on 7")
Nov 82. (7") *(SA 30634)* **STATE LAUGHTER. / HOLY WATER** ☐ [-]
Jun 83. (lp) *(NER 6)* **THE GUILTY HAVE NO PRIDE** ☐ [-]
– Till the living flesh is burned / All alone in her nirvana / State laughter / Nothing changes / Nation / Heaven street mk II / The guilty have no pride. *(re-iss. 1985; BADVC 3) (cd-iss. Dec90;)*

— **RICHARD BUTLER** – keyboards; repl. WAKEFORD who joined SOL INVICTUS

Apr 84. (lp) *(UBADVC 4)* **BURIAL** ☐ [-]
– Death of the west / Fields / Nirvana / Sons of Europe / Black radio / Till the living flesh is burned / All done in her nirvana / Fields / We drive east / Heaven street. *(re-iss. Dec90 colrd-lp/cd;)*
Aug 84. (12"ep) *(12BADVC 6)* **THE CALLING. / SHE SAID DESTROY / DOUBT NOTHING** ☐ [-]
Feb 85. (lp,pic-lp) *(BADVC 13)* **NADA!** ☐ [-]
– The honour of silence / The calling (mk.II) / Leper lord / Rain of despair / Foretold / Behind the rose (fields of rape) / She said destroy / Carousel / C'est un reve / Crush my love.
Mar 85. (12"m) *(BADVC 69)* **BORN AGAIN. / THE CALLING (Mk.II) / CAROUSEL (Bolt mix)** ☐ [-]
(re-iss. Oct88 on 'Cenaz' 12"pic-d; CENAZ 09)
Nov 85. (7") *(BADVC 73)* **COME BEFORE CHRIST AND MURDER LOVE. / ('A'instrumental)** ☐ [-]
(12") *(12BADVC 73)* – ('A'side) / Torture by roses.

— **DAVID TIBET** – vocals (ex-23 SKIDOO, ex-PSYCHIC TV) repl. JENNER

Apr 86. (lp) *(BADVC 726)* **LESSON 1: MISANTHROPY** ☐ [-]
Jun 86. (d-lp) *(BADVC 9)* **THE WORLD THAT SUMMER** ☐ [-]
– Rule again / Break the black ice / Rocking horse night / Blood victory / Blood of winter / Hidden among the leaves / Torture by roses / Come before Christ and murder love / Love murder / Death of a man / Reprise #1 / Reprise #2 / Reprise #3. *(cd-iss. Dec90;)*
May 87. (10"ep) *(BADVC 10)* **TO DROWN A ROSE. / EUROPA: THE GATES OF HEAVEN / ZIMMERIT** ☐ [-]
Oct 87. (lp) *(BADVC 11)* **BROWN BOOK** ☐ [-]
1988. (lp) *(BADVC 88)* **WALL OF SACRIFICE** ☐ [-]
(cd-iss. Jan90; BADVCCD 88)
Jan 89. (m-lp) *(BADVC 93)* **93 DEAD SUN WHEELS** (with CURRENT 93) ☐ [-]
Feb 92. (12"pic-d-ep) *(BADVC 8)* **CATHEDRAL OF TEARS** ☐ [-]
1993. (lp/cd) *(BADVC/+CD 36)* **BUT WHAT ENDS WHEN THE SYMBOLS SHATTER** ☐ [-]
– Death is the martyr of beauty / He's disabled / Mourner's bench / Because of him / Daedalus rising / Little black angel / Golden wedding of sorrow / Giddy edge of light / Ku ku ku / This is not Paradise / Hollows of devotion / But what ends when the symbols shatter. *(cd re-iss. Oct97; same)*
1993. (lp/cd) *(BADVC/+CD 38)* **ROSE CLOUDS OF HOLOCAUST** ☐ [-]
– Lord winter / God's golden sperm / Omen filled season / Symbols of the sun / Jerusalem / Black / Luther's army / 13 years of carrion / Accidental protege / Rose clouds of holocaust / Lifebooks. *(re-iss. Oct97; same)*
1994. (12"ep) *(BADVC 63)* **PARADISE RISING** ☐ [-]
1994. (d-cd) *(BADVCCD 96)* **SOMETHING IS COMING (live)** ☐ [-]
– Death is the martyr of beauty / Hullo angel / Giddy giddy carousel / Hollows of devotion / Rocking horse night / He's disabled / Fall apart / Heaven Street / Break the black ice / Leper lord / Golden wedding of sorrow / Torture by roses / Little black angel / But what ends when the symbols shatter / Fields of rape / Ku ku ku / Giddy giddy carousel / Runes and men / Golden wedding of sorrow / Death is the martyr of beauty. *(re-iss. Oct97; same)*
(re-iss. 1996 d-lp; BADVC 96)

Twilight Command / not iss.

1994. (7"ep) *(NERO 1)* **SUNDOGS** ☐ [-]
– Rose clouds of holocaust / 13 years of Clarion.

- compilations, etc. -

Sep 87. (lp) *Eyas Media; (EYAS 011)* **OH, HOW WE LAUGHED** ☐ [-]
– Knives / Nirvana / Heaven Street / Nothing changes / Nation / Holy water / State laughter / In the nightime / We drive east / How we laughed. *(cd-iss. Oct89; EYAS 1030) (re-iss. cd Aug93 on 'Trevor'; CDOS 1)*
Feb 89. (cd) *N.E.R.; (BADVCCD 007)* **THE CORN YEARS** ☐ [-]
– Helligel / Torture by roses / Love murder / Zimmerit / We are the lust / To drown a rose / Break the black ice / Behind the rose (frields of rape) / Punishment initiation / Rocking horse night / Break the black ice (instrumental) / Runes and men / Rule again / Hail the white grain / Blood of winter / Fog of the world / Europa / Gates of Heaven / Come before Christ and murder love. *(re-iss. Oct97; same)*
1992. (red-lp) *Leprosy; (LEPER 2)* **NIGHT AND FOG** ☐ [-]
1995. (7"box/10"box/12"box/cd-s-box) *N.E.R.;* **BLACK WHOLE OF LOVE** ☐ [-]

DEATH IN VEGAS

Formed: London, England . . . mid 90's by the production duo of RICHARD FEARLESS and STEVE HELLIER. By the time DIV came to release distorted breakbeat singles like 'OPIUM SHUFFLE' (as DEAD ELVIS) and 'DIRT', FEARLESS was already a respected DJ at the capital's superhip Heavenly Social club (where The Chemical Brothers also made their name). After the underground success of their early releases, DIV became much in demand remixers for major labels desperate for a bit of street cred. After the techno-noir of their acclaimed debut album, 'DEAD ELVIS', the re-issues of 'DIRT' and 'ROCCO' managed Top 75 placings. Just prior to these, they had covered a BEAT hit, 'TWIST AND CRAWL', which featured RANKING ROGER.

Album rating: DEAD ELVIS (*8)

RICHARD FEARLESS – DJ, samples / **STEVE HELLIER** – producer / with guest **ANDY VISSER** – flute, sax (also on album)

Concrete / Time Bomb

May 95. (12"; as DEAD ELVIS) *(HARD 6)* **OPIUM SHUFFLE. /** ☐ [-]

— with guests **ANTHONY ANDERSON** – guitar / **MAT FLINT** – bass (both also on album)

Nov 95. (10") *(HARD 8-10)* **REMATERIALISED. /** ☐ [-]

— bass by **NICK 'AVIN IT** (also on album)

May 96. (10"/12"/cd-s) *(HARD 9-10/-12/-CD)* **DIRT. /** ☐ [-]
Oct 96. (12"/cd-s) *(HARD 14-12/-CD)* **ROCCO. /** ☐ [-]
Feb 97. (12"/cd-s) *(HARD 23-12/-CD)* **REKKIT. /** ☐ [-]
(12") *(HARD 23-12X)* – Death by a thousand cuts (remixes by Two Lone Swordsmen).

— other guests **SELAH** – vocals / **SEAMUS BEAGHAN** – hammond organ / **TIM WELLER** – drums / **JONATHAN HAINES** – strings / **PAUL RUTHERFORD** – trombone

Mar 97. (cd/d-lp) *(HARD 22 LPCD/LP12) <43511>* **DEAD ELVIS** [52] ☐
– All that glitters / Opium shuffle / GBH / Dirt / Rocco / Rekkit / I spy / Amber / Rematerialised / 68 balcony / Sly.
Apr 97. (12"/cd-s) *(HARD 26-12/-CD)* **TWIST AND CRAWL (featuring RANKING ROGER). / OPIUM SHUFFLE (Monkey Mafia mix)** ☐ [-]
Jul 97. (12"/cd-s) *(HARD 27-12/-CD)* **DIRT. /** [61] [-]
Oct 97. (12"/cd-s) *(HARD 29-12/-CD)* **ROCCO. /** [51] ☐
(cd-s) *(HARD 29CDX)* –

DECORATORS

Formed: Manchester, England . . . 1980 by MICHAEL BEVAN, JOHN GILANI, STEVE SANDOR, JOE SAX and ALAN BOROUGHS. Moving to a communal London residence, the flatmates released a couple of singles on the 'New Hormones' imprint (debut, 'PENDULUM AND SWING' on offshoot, 'Red'), before nearly getting their big break from Island's Andrew Lauder. Unfortunately, he was to be snapped up by 'Demon' records and the now six-piece (with the addition of PETE SAUNDERS) found a home at 'Red Flame'. This is where they were to remain ('Virgin' in France), releasing two patchy, brassy MAGAZINE-esque sets, 'TABLETS' (1982) and the mini 'REBEL SONGS' (1983).

Album rating: TABLETS (*5) / REBEL SONGS (*4)

MICHAEL BEVAN – vocals, guitar / **JOHN GILANI** – guitar / **PETE SAUNDERS** – keyboards / **JOE SAX** – saxophone / **STEVE SANDOR** – bass / **ALAN BOROUGHS** – drums

Red / not iss.

Mar 81. (7") *(RS 009)* **PENDULUM AND SWING. / RENDEZVOUS / STRANGE ONE** ☐ [-]

New Hormones / not iss.

Jul 81. (7") *(ORG 5)* **TWILIGHT VIEW. / REFLECTIONS** ☐ [-]

— added **PETE SAUNDERS** – keyboards

Red Flame / not iss.

Jun 82. (7"/12") *(RF7/RF12 05)* **STRANGE ONE. / TABLETS** ☐ [-]
Jul 82. (lp) *(RF 1)* **TABLETS** ☐ [-]
– Strange one / We know it / Hidden hands / Headlights / Absent friends / Red sky over Wembley / American ways / Half world / Without you / We know it (part 2) / Curious.

Dec 83. (m-lp) *(RFM 208)* **REBEL SONGS** ☐ [-]

— disbanded some time the following year

DEEP FREEZE MICE

Formed: Leicester, England . . . 1979 by pop maverick ALAN JENKINS. Forming his own label, 'Mole Embalming', as a means of operating outwith the demands of the mainstream alternative scene, JENKINS – along with musical sidekicks SHERREE LAWRENCE and GRAHAM SUMMERS (MICHAEL BUNNAGE was a part-timer until 1980) – released the first DEEP FREEZE MICE album in 1979. Entitiled 'MY GERANIUMS ARE BULLETPROOF', the record introduced the band's patented brand of psychedelic whimsy, often compared to SYD BARRETT, etc., but in reality more like HALF MAN HALF BISCUIT minus the fun. JENKINS' twee, Herbert-style vocals and off-kilter sense of humour (check out 'I VOTE CONSERVATIVE (BECAUSE I LOVE YOU)' and 'I MET A MAN WHO SPOKE LIKE AN UCCA FORM') can definitely be something of an acquired taste, while side-long slabs of tripped-out indulgence like the 26 minute 'THE OCTAGONAL RABBIT SURPLUS' are recommended only for the most iron-willed of old hippies. Still, if you didn't actually get past the first track, you could always amuse yourself with the chocolate mousse recipe on the lp's back cover. The sleeve also featured the adage, "If it's worth doing, it's worth overdoing". Quite. JENKINS maintained an impressively prolific release schedule throughout the 80's, releasing such inimitably titled albums as 'I LOVE YOU LITTLE BOBO WITH YOUR DELICATE GOLDEN LIONS' (1984) – the first release for the 'Cordella' label – 'WAR, FAMINE, DEATH, PESTILENCE AND MISS TIMBERLAKE' (1986) and 'THE TENDER YELLOW PONIES OF INSOMNIA' (1989). Under the guise of The CHRYSANTHEMUMS, JENKINS also released a trio of albums, namely 'IS THAT A FISH ON YOUR SHOULDER, OR ARE YOU JUST PLEASED TO SEE ME?' (1987), 'LITTLE FLECKS OF FOAM AROUND BARKING' (1988) and a wholesale reinvention of The ZOMBIES' 'ODYSSEY AND ORACLE' album. • **Trivia:** In 1990, JENKINS privately published a booklet about the music business, 'HOW TO BE IN A POP GROUP'.

Album rating: MY GERANIUMS ARE BULLETPROOF (*6) / TEENAGE HEAD IN MY REFRIGERATOR (*6) / THE GATES OF LUNCH (*6) / SAW A RANCH HOUSE BURNING LAST NIGHT (*5) / I LOVE YOU LITTLE BOBO . . . (*6) / WAR, FAMINE, DEATH, PESTILENCE AND MISS TIMBERLAKE (*5) / THE TENDER YELLOW PONIES OF INSOMNIA (*5)

ALAN JENKINS (b.16 Mar'59, Dudley, England) – guitar, clarinet, bass / **SHERREE LAWRENCE** (b.24 May'59, Rushden, England) – pianos, etc / p/t until follow-up lp- **MICHAEL BUNNAGE** (b.21 Dec'58, Romford, England) – bass, vocals (of STATICS) / **GRAHAM SUMMERS** (b.30 Jul'58, Wellingborough, England) – drums (of STATICS)

Mole Embalming — not iss.

1979. (lp) *(MOLE 1)* **MY GERANIUMS ARE BULLETPROOF** ☐ [-]
– Minstrel radio yoghurt / I vote Conservative / Emile Zola / Phylis is a protozoon actually / Embalming fluid fucha / I met a man who spoke like an UCCA form / The octagonal rabbit surplus. *(re-iss. May88)*

1981. (lp) *(MOLE 2)* **TEENAGE HEAD IN MY REFRIGERATOR** ☐ [-]
– I like digestive biscuits in my coffee / Dz / The letter song / My geraniums are bulletproof / Peter Smith is a banana / Hegel's brain / Esther / Vera / God / Path to you / Dictatorship of the proletariat / Teenage head. *(re-iss. Jul88) (cassette 'HEGEL'S BRAIN'; MOLE C2)*

1982. (lp) *(MOLE 3)* **THE GATES OF LUNCH** ☐ [-]
– A red light for the greens / You might need me and this Winchester Curly / A ten legged beast / Fishing / I lay a green egg, it explodes on Tuesday / Bottles / The gates of lunch / Bottles – reprise / Brain dead baby / Godzilla loves me, I'm an ash-tray. *(re-iss. May88)*

Oct 83. (lp) *(MOLE 4)* **SAW A RANCH HOUSE BURNING LAST NIGHT** ☐ [-]
– Under the cafe table / Down to a proton / The new emotional twist / Kiwis come in close / You took the blue one / You think I'm a car / Eat molten death / Hitler's knees / Funny monsters / Matter over mind / The damage / Ammonia suction / Everlasting lollipop / Sagittarians / Saw a ranch house burning last night.

— **PETER GREGORY** – drums repl. SUMMERS

Cordelia — not iss.

1984. (lp) *(ERICAT 001)* **I LOVE YOU LITTLE BOBO WITH YOUR DELICATE GOLDEN LIONS** ☐ [-]
(d-cd-iss. Jul97 on 'Jar'; JAR 011)

1985. (12"ep) *(ERICAT 002)* **THESE FLOORS ARE SMOOTH** ☐ [-]

1985. (12"ep) *(ERICAT 004)* **HANG ON CONSTANCE LET ME HEAR THE NEWS** ☐ [-]

1986. (lp) *(ERICAT)* **WAR, FAMINE, DEATH, PESTILENCE AND MISS TIMBERLAKE** ☐ [-]

1987. (12"ep) *(ERICAT 013)* **RAIN IS WHEN THE EARTH IS TELEVISION** ☐ [-]

1988. (12"ep) *(ERICAT 016)* **NEURON MUSIC** ☐ [-]

Jul 89. (lp) *(ERICAT 027)* **THE TENDER YELLOW PONIES OF INSOMNIA** ☐ [-]

– compilations, etc. –

Mar 89. (lp) *Logical Fish; (LOGICAL FISH 1)* **LIVE IN SWITZERLAND (live)** ☐ [-]

CHRYSANTHEMUMS

— **ALAN JENKINS** – vocals, multi

Egg Plant — not iss.

Mar 87. (7") *(ONE EGG)* **MOUTH PAIN. /** ☐ [-]

Aug 87. (lp) *(TWO EGGS)* **IS THAT A FISH ON YOUR SHOULDER, OR ARE YOU JUST PLEASED TO SEE ME?** ☐ [-]

Apr 88. (12") *(THREE EGGS)* **THE 4 X's SESSIONS** ☐ [-]

1988. (d-lp) *(FOUR EGGS)* **LITTLE FLECKS OF FOAM AROUND BARKING** ☐ [-]

1989. (12") *(FIVE EGGS)* **(LIKE INDUSTRIOUS ELVES) WE STOPPED (live at the London Paladium)** ☐ [-]

May 89. (cd) *(SIX EGGS)* **ODYSSEY AND ORACLE** ☐ [-]
– Care of cell 44 / A rose for Emily / Maybe after he's gone / Beechwood park / Brief candles / Hung up on a dream / Changes / I want her she wants me / This will be our year / Butchers tale (Western Front 1914) / Friends of mine / Time of the season. *(re-iss. May91 on 'Madagascar' lp/cd; MAD 014/+CD)*

Jar Music — not iss.

Oct 97. (cd) *(JAR 007)* **GO GERMANY / INSEKT INSEKT** ☐ [-]

Orgone — not iss.

Nov 97. (cd) *(RG 001)* **BABY'S HEAD** ☐ [-]

JODY AND THE CREAMS

Cordelia — not iss.

May 90. (lp) *(ERICAT 028)* **A BIG DOG** ☐ [-]

Martin DEGVILLE (see under ⇒ SIGUE SIGUE SPUTNIK)

DELAKOTA

Formed: London, England . . . early 1998 by former SENSELESS THINGS drummer, CASS BROWNE, and his pal, DES MURPHY. The duo promptly undertook an eclectic mission to rekindle the spirit of the ROLLING STONES, SLY STONE, STONE ROSES or in fact anything "stoned". The lads were lucky enough to be premiered live on Newsnight to an estimated TV audience of a couple of million! Yes that's right, BBC2's late-night programme hosted by the man politicians fear the most, Jeremy Paxman, invited the duo/band to play a few tracks while "The Pax" grilled Radio One DJ, STEVE LAMACQ and Creation boss, ALAN McGEE on the merits of modern pop/rock music. On the strength of this and a white-label demo of 'CINCINNATI', they signed to the 'Go! Beat' imprint. The pair issued their first official single, 'BROTHERS', a riffing punk/rap tune that crashed into the proverbial eardrums of the indie fraternity. The follow-up, 'THE ROCK', changed direction and vibe, something DELAKOTA would attempt with each successive single. A Top 60 breakthrough, the song was similarly followed by a new version of 'C'MON CINCINNATI', taken from that September's most promising album release, 'ONE LOVE' (1998).

Album rating: ONE LOVE (*8)

CASS BROWNE – vocals, guitar (ex-SENSELESS THINGS) / **DES MURPHY** – samples, turntable

Go! Beat — Go! Beat

1998. (12"/cd-s; w-drawn) **BROTHERS. /** ☐ [-]

Jul 98. (12"/cd-s) *(GOB X/CD 10)* **THE ROCK** 60 [-]

Sep 98. (7"; DELAKOTA featuring ROSE SMITH) *(GOB 11)* **C'MON CINCINNATI. /** 55 [-]
(12"+=/cd-s+=) *(GOB X/CD 11)* –
(above was originally released as a/their white-label 12")

Sep 98. (cd/c/lp) *(557861-2/-4/-1)* <11> **ONE LOVE** 58 ☐ Nov98
– C'mon Cincinatti / I thought I caught / Too tough / 555 / Rock / Stealy / Brothers / On the trail / Metallic blue / Hook, line and sinker / End of line / Show me the door.

DEL FUEGOS

Formed: Boston, Massachusetts, USA . . . 1983 by brothers DAN and WARREN ZANES, who completed the line-up with TOM LLOYD and BRENT WOODY GIESSMANN. Drawing influences from R.E.M., The EVERLY BROTHERS and classic R&B, this harmony-happy country rock outfit signed to the alternative/roots label, 'Slash', releasing their debut set, 'THE LONGEST DAY', in 1984. Cult 70's man, MITCHELL FROOM, produced and played on their 1985 follow-up set, 'BOSTON, MASS.', a record that bubbled under the US Top 100 for a number of weeks. By the release of 1987's 'STAND UP', however, the band's overtly commercial sound had begun to grate with critics and a major breakthrough seemed even less likely. Taking time out for a rethink, the band resufaced at the turn of the decade minus WARREN ZANES and GIESSMANN, ADAM ROTH and JOE DONNELLY their respective replacements for 'SMOKING IN THE FIELDS' (1990). The group's first effort for new label, 'R.C.A.', the album was given a rootsier feel with the addition of ex-J GEILS BAND mouth organist, MAGIC DICK. Yet despite a more positive critical reaction, the band was to subsequently split in the early 90's, DAN ZANES later recording a domestic 1995 solo set, 'COOL DOWN TIME' with the help of FROOM and TCHAD BLAKE (the set included a cover of Mose Allison's 'IF YOU LIVE').

Album rating: THE LONGEST DAY (*7) / BOSTON, MASS. (*7) / STAND UP (*5) / SMOKING IN THE FIELDS (*6)

DAN ZANES – vocals, guitar / **WARREN ZANES** – guitar / **TOM LLOYD** – bass, vocals / **BRENT WOODY GIESSMANN** – drums

Rough Trade — Slash

Dec 84. (lp) *(ROUGH 79)* **THE LONGEST DAY** ☐ ☐
– Nervous and shakey / Backseat nothing / I should be the one / Missing you / The one / Anything you want / When the news is on / The longest day / Out for a ride / Mary don't change / Have you forgotten / Call my name. *(re-iss. Jan87 on 'Slash' lp/c; SLM P/C 14)*

Slash Slash

Oct 85. (lp/c) *(SLA P/C 9)* <25339> **BOSTON, MASS.**
– Don't run wild / Hand in hand / I still want you / Sound of our town / Fade to blue / It's alright / Hold us down / Night on the town / Shame / Coupe DeVille.

Feb 86. (7") *(LASH 6)* <28822> **I STILL WANT YOU. / DON'T RUN WILD** — 87
(12"+=) *(LASHX 6)* – Missing you.

Mar 87. (lp/c) *(SLA P/C 20)* <25540> **STAND UP**
– Wear it like a cape / New old world / Names names / Long slide (for an out) / He had a lot to drink today / A town called love / I can't take this place / News from nowhere / Scratching at your door / I'll sleep with you (cha cha d'amour).

— **ADAM ROTH** – guitar; repl. WARREN

— **JOE DONNELLY** – drums; repl. WOODY

— guest on below **MAGIC DICK** – mouth harp (of J.GEILS BAND)

R.C.A. R.C.A.

May 90. (cd/c/lp) *(PD/PK/PD 90422)* <9860> **SMOKING IN THE FIELDS** — Oct89
– Move with me sister / Down in Allen's mills / I'm inside you / Headlights / Breakaway / Dreams of you / The offer / Part of this earth / Stand by me / Lost weekend / No no never / Friends again.

— split in the early 90's. In 1995, DAN ZANES returned with a solo US-only album, 'COOL DOWN TIME' for 'Private' records.

Gabi DELGADO (see under ⇒ D.A.F.)

DELGADOS

Formed: Glasgow, Scotland . . . late 1994 by ex-university graduates, ALUN WOODWARD, EMMA POLLOCK, STEWART HENDERSON and PAUL SAVAGE. Not only did they kickstart Scotland's flagging (nae, virtually dead) indie scene, they done it by initiated their own imprint, 'Chemikal Underground'. The label's debut, 'MONICA WEBSTER', was greatly received by the music press and of course, who else? DJ John Peel, their angular guitar reminiscent of PAVEMENT, although ALUN and EMMA's twee vocal touches called to mind BELLE & SEBASTIAN. Single after single continued to impress until the excellent debut album, 'DOMESTIQUES', surfaced in late '96. Their "difficult" second album, 'PELOTON' (1998), managed to crack the UK Top 60, spurred on by indie hits, 'PULL THE WIRES FROM THE WALL' and 'THE WEAKER ARGUMENT DEFEATS THE STRONGER'. Where would ARAB STRAP, MOGWAI and now majors-tempted BIS be without the DELGADOS and their seminal label?! • **Covers:** THE DIRGE (New Bad Things) / SACRE CHARLEMAGNE (France Gall) / A VERY CELLULAR SONG (Incredible String Band).

Album rating: DOMESTIQUES (*8) / PELOTON (*8)

ALUN WOODWARD – vocals, guitar / **EMMA POLLOCK** – vocals, guitar / **STEWART HENDERSON** – bass / **PAUL SAVAGE** – drums

Chemikal Underground not iss.

Jul 95. (7") *(chem 001)* **MONICA WEBSTER. / BRAND NEW CAR** — -

Aug 95. (7"ep/cd-ep) *(SCAN/+CS 07)* **THE LAZERWALKER EP** — -
(above issued on 'Radarscope') (below on 'Che')

Dec 95. (7"; various artists) *<che 47>* — -

Mar 96. (7"ep/cd-ep) *(chem 004/+cd)* **CINECENTRE. / THIRTEEN GLIDING PRICES / MULE EMULATOR** — -

Aug 96. (7"ep/cd-ep) *(chem 006/+cd)* **UNDER CANVAS / EEN TELF. / BEAR CLUB / STRATHCONA** — -

Oct 96. (7"ep/cd-ep) *(chem 008/+cd)* **SUCROSE. / EUROSPRINT / THE DIRGE** — -

Nov 96. (lp/cd) *(chem 010/+CD)* **DOMESTIQUES** — -

1996. (ltd-7") *(HISS 4)* **LIQUIDATION GIRL. / (other track by Van Impe)** — -
(above issued on 'Boa' / below release on 'Lissy's)

Jun 97. (7") *(LISS 20)* **SACRE CHARLEMAGNE. / (other by The NEW BAD THINGS)** — -

Mar 98. (7") *(chem 022)* **EVERYTHING GOES AROUND THE WATER / BLACKPOOL** — -
(cd-s+=) *(chem 022cd)* – The drowned and the saved.

May 98. (7") *(chem 023)* **PULL THE WIRES FROM THE WALL. / MAURON CHANSON** — 69 -
(cd-s+=) *(chem 023cd)* – Mark the day.

Jun 98. (cd) *(chem 024cd)* **PELOTON** — 56 -
– Everything goes around the water / The arcane model / The actress / Clarinet / Pull the wires from the wall / Repeat failure / And so the talking stopped / Don't stop / Blackpool / Russian orthodox / The weaker argument defeats the stronger.

Sep 98. (7") *(chem 029)* **THE WEAKER ARGUMENT DEFEATS THE STRONGER. / A VERY CELLULAR SONG** — -
(cd-s+=) *(chem 029cd)* – The actress – Irian Jaya remix.

– compilations, etc. –

Sep 97. (cd) *Strange Fruit; (SFRSCD 037)* **BBC SESSIONS** — -
– Primary alternative / I've only just started to breathe / Lazerwalker / Indian fables / Under canvas under wraps / Sucrose / Teen elf / Thirteen gliding principles / Friendly conventions / Tempered not tamed / Falling and landing.

DELICATESSEN

Formed: Leicester, England . . . early 90's by mainman NEIL CARLILL, plus CRAIG BROWN, WILL FOSTER and STUART DAYMEN. Named after the infamous French film of the same name, this bunch of innovative indie guitar merchants made their debut on 'Big Life'-offshoot, 'Starfish', with the 'INVITING BOTH SISTERS OUT TO DINNER' single in autumn '94. The impressive 'C.F. KANE' followed in early '95, a nod to their cinematic influences against a suprisingly effective musical backdrop of blackboard-scraping guitar crescendos and aching melody. With a soundtrack to a BBC short film, 'George And Ramona', already under their belts, the band issued their debut album, 'SKIN TOUCHING WATER', later in '95. Unfortunately, DELICATESSEN's wilful experimentalism didn't really figure on the more musically conservative Brit-pop agenda of the day, 1996's follow-up set, 'HUSTLE INTO BED', meeting a similarly overlooked fate.

Album rating: SKIN TOUCHING WATER (*6) / HUSTLE INTO BED (*6) / THERE'S NO CONFUSING SOME PEOPLE (*6)

NEIL CARLILL (b. 1966) – vocals / **CRAIG BROWN** (b. 1973) – guitar, flute / **WILL FOSTER** (b.1973) – bass, keyboards, acoustic guitar / **STUART DAYMEN** (b. 1972) – drums, percussion

Starfish not iss.

Oct 94. (7") *(STF 1)* **INVITING BOTH SISTERS OUT TO DINNER. /** — -
(cd-s+=) *(STFC 1)* –

Apr 95. (10"/cd-s) *(STF T/D 2)* **C.F. KANE. / MICE HAIR / EMBALMING THE DEAD ENTERTAINER** — -

May 95. (cd/lp) *(STF CD/LP 001)* **SKIN TOUCHING WATER** — -
– I'm just alive / C.F. Kane / Zebra – Monkey – Liar / Red, blue and green / Watercress / Classic adventure / Appeased / Chomsky / You cut my throat, I'll cut yours / Sick of flying saucers / Smiling you're stupid / Inviting both sisters out to dinner / Advice / Love's liquid / Froth / If she was anybody else.

Jul 95. (7") *(STF 3)* **I'M JUST ALIVE. /** — -
(cd-s+=) *(STFD 3)* –

Aug 96. (7") *(STF 4)* **MONKEY SUIT. /** — -
(cd-s+=; w/free video) *(STFD 4)* –

Aug 96. (cd/c/lp) *(STF CD/MC/LP 2)* **HUSTLE INTO BED** — -

— added 5th member **JON WOOD** – violin

Viper not iss.

Feb 98. (cd) *(VIP 002CD)* **THERE'S NO CONFUSING SOME PEOPLE** — -
– Another meal turns up / Lightbulbs and moths / Various pets / Psycho / He killed himself in 1980 / Boy dough / Cruel country / Priest in half / Sweet.

— NEIL and WILL jointly formed indie supergroup, LODGER, with a member of POWDER and SUPERGRASS!

DEL-LORDS

Formed: The Bronx, New York, USA . . . by ex-DICTATORS guitarist/frontman, SCOTT KEMPNER (alias TOP TEN) and ERIC 'ROSCOE' AMBEL alongside the rhythm section of MANNY CAIATI and FRANK FUNARO. Issued on 'Demon' in the UK and 'Enigma' in the States, 'FRONTIER DAYS' (1985) was a promising debut album, dealing in no frills, blue collar rock'n'roll in the time honoured US tradition, even throwing in a cover of Alfred Reed's depression era classic, 'HOW CAN A POOR MAN STAND SUCH TIMES AND LIVE' (previously covered in blistering style by RY COODER on his 1971 debut album). Subsequently signing a one-off deal with 'E.M.I.', the band used rootsier material for 1986's 'JOHNNY COMES MARCHING HOME', covering similar, if rockier terrain to STEVE EARLE. A more long term deal with 'Enigma', meanwhile, saw the band's most accessible, melodic release to date in the shape of 'BASED ON A TRUE STORY' (1988). attendant singles such as the breezily infectious 'CHEYENNE' aiming straight for the heart of the pop charts but surprisingly falling flat. Returning to the vigour of old for swansong set, 'LOVERS WHO WANDER' (1990), the band bowed out with their heads held high, AMBEL headed for solo pastures and session land.

Album rating: FRONTIER DAYS (*5) / JOHNNY COMES MARCHING HOME (*5) / BASED ON A TRUE STORY (*5) / HOWLIN' AT THE HALLOWEEN MOON (*4) / LOVERS WHO WANDER (*5) / Eric Ambel: ROSCOE'S GANG (*5)

SCOTT KEMPNER – vocals, guitar (ex-DICTATORS) / **ERIC 'ROSCOE' AMBEL** – lead guitar, some vocals / **MANNY CAIATI** – bass, vocals / **FRANK FUNARO** – drums, vocals

Demon Enigma

Jul 85. (lp) *(FIEND 53)* <17133> **FRONTIER DAYS** — Feb85
– How can a poor man stand such times and live / Get tough / Livin' on love / Double life / I play the drums / Burning in the flame of love / Pledge of love / Shame on you / Mercenary / Feel like going home.

EMI America Capitol

May 86. (7") *(EA 215)* **SOLDIER'S HOME. / NO WAITRESS NO MORE**

May 86. (lp/c) *(AML/TC-AML 3103)* <ST 17183> **JOHNNY COMES MARCHING HOME**
– Heaven / Love lies dying / Drug deal / Soldier's home / St. Jake / Dream come true / True love / Everlovin' / Against my will / No waitress no more.

Enigma-Virgin Enigma

Sep 88. (lp/c/cd) *(ENVLP/TCENV/CDENV 508)* <73326> **BASED ON A TRUE STORY**
– Crawl in bed / Judas kiss / Ashes to ashes / I'm gonna be around / Poem of the river / The cool and the crazy / Cheyenne / A lover's prayer / Whole lotta nothin' goin' on / River of justice.

Oct 88. (7") *(ENV 3)* **JUDAS KISS. / WHOLE LOTTA NOTHIN' GOIN' ON**

Apr 89. (7") *(ENV 10)* **CHEYENNE. / RIVER OF JUSTICE**
(12"+=) *(ENVT 10)* – Hand to mouth.

Jul 89. (7") *(ENV 14)* **POEM OF THE RIVER. / GET TOUGH**
(12"+=/cd-s+=) *(ENV T/CD 14)* – No waitress no more.

Jan 90. (m-cd) *(FIENDCD 162)* <772317-2> **LIVE – HOWLIN' AT THE HALLOWEEN MOON (live)**

– True love / Jumpin' at the night / Wastin' time talkin' / The cool 'n' the crazy / Judas kiss / I play the drums / Tallahassee lassie.
(above issued on 'Demon' in the UK)

1990. (cd) *<73361>* **LOVERS WHO WANDER**
– Touch one heart / You and I / I need love / Love on fire / About you / Learn to let go / I stand in your light / Kiss away / Hellbent / Rockabye / Stay with me / The wild boys / A lifetime of trouble.

— split when AMBEL took off for a solo venture. He had previously (in 1988) released his first, 'ROSCOE'S GANG'.

DELTA 5

Formed: Leeds, England . . . 1979 by JULZ SALE, ROS ALLEN, ALAN RIGGS, BETHAN PETERS and SIMON (the latter being replaced by KELVIN KNIGHT). This politicised femme-punk outfit cut a handful of singles for 'Rough Trade' beginning with 'MIND YOUR OWN BUSINESS' the same year. Propelled by a twin-bass funk groove behind a defiant female vocal, the record was repetitive, insidious and highly addictive, bringing enthusiasm from John Peel and drawing comparisons with post-punk experimentalists GANG OF FOUR. 1980 saw the release of another critically acclaimed single, 'YOU', along with a couple of Peel sessions for Radio One before the band took off for a US tour. Upon their return, DELTA 5 issued their third and final independent single, the double A-side 'TRY' and 'COLOUR', before securing a major label deal with Charisma subsidiary, 'Pre'. Boasting a polished-up sound with additional brass and keyboards, reviewers were sceptical and gave the debut album, 'SEE THE WHIRL' (1981) a thumbs down. By this point, SALE and PETERS were the only remaining original members (with newcomer, JACKI) and the group struggled to make any headway in the increasingly airbrushed alternative scene. With only one album to their name the band split (their record label also going under) although their influence has always been in inverse proportion to their recorded output.

Album rating: SEE THE WHIRL (*4)

JULZ SALE – vocals, guitar / **ALAN RIGGS** – guitar / **ROS ALLEN** – bass, vocals (ex-MEKONS) / **BETHAN PETERS** – bass, vocals / **KELVIN KNIGHT** – drums repl. SIMON

Rough Trade | not iss.

Oct 79. (7") *(RT 031)* **MIND YOUR OWN BUSINESS. / NOW THAT YOU'VE GONE**
May 80. (7") *(RT 041)* **YOU. / ANTICIPATION**
Nov 80. (7") *(RT 061)* **TRY. / COLOUR**

— **JULZ + ALAN** with different line-up **JACKI** (BETHAN joined FUN BOY THREE)

Pre | not iss.

Jun 81. (7") *(PRE 16)* **SHADOW. / THE LEAVING**
Jul 81. (lp/c) *(PREX/PRICS 6)* **SEE THE WHIRL**
– Innocenti / Final scene / Circuit / Open life / Trail / Shadow / Delta 5 / Anticipation / Journey / Make up / Triangle / Waiting / Telephone / Different fun.
Jan 82. (7") *(PRE 24)* **POWERLINES. / THE HEART IS A LONELY PLACE TO BE**

— split soon after above, JACKI formed The DELTONES

DEMENTED ARE GO

Formed: Cardiff, Wales . . . mid 80's by MARK PHILLIPS, brothers DICK and ANT THOMAS. Replacing DICK with LEX LUTHER and adding bass player GRAHAM GRANT, they acquired support slots to The DAMNED and KING KURT, their punkabilly racket falling somewhere in between. Around the same period, DEMENTED ARE GO released their first single for 'I.D.' records, 'HOLY HACK JACK', which was accompanied by the album, 'IN SICKNESS AND IN HEALTH' (1986). All done in the worst possible taste (as Kenny Everett might have said!), this lot came up with some of the most gruesomely sick titles every laid down on vinyl over the course of the ensuing decade, i.e. '(I WAS BORN ON A) BUSTED HYMEN', 'BRAIN DAMAGE CHILE (SLIGHT RETARD)' 'CLITORIS BITE BOOGIE' and 'LOVE SEEPS LIKE A FESTERING SORE'. Toning down the gratuitous schlock factor just a tad, the maniac street preachers rounded off nearly ten years at the bottom with 1993's swampong, 'TANGENITAL MADNESS'.

Album rating: IN SICKNESS AND IN HEALTH (*4) / SICK, SICK, SICK (*4)

MARK PHILLIPS – vocals / **LEX LUTHER** – guitar; repl. DICK THOMAS / **GRAHAM GRANT** – bass / **ANT THOMAS** – drums

I.D. | not iss.

Jul 86. (12"m) *(EYET 8)* **HOLY HACK JACK. / RUBBER BUCCANEER / DON'T GO IN THE WOODS**
Aug 86. (lp) *(NOSE 9)* **IN SICKNESS AND IN HEALTH**
– Be bop a lula / Pervy in the park / (I was born on a) Busted hymen / Holy Hack Jack / Frenzied beat / Pickled and preserved / Crazy horses / Transvestite blues / Rubber buccanerr / Vibrate / Rubber love / Nuke mutants / PVC chair / Don't go in the woods.
Oct 87. (lp) *(NOSE 15)* **SICK, SICK, SICK**
– Vibrate / Human slug / Cast iron arm / PVC chair / Rubber buccaneer / Pervy in the park / Rubber love / Holy hack Jack. *(cd-iss. Jun94 on 'Dojo'+=; DOJOCD 23)* – (tracks by SKITZO & COFFIN NAILS).
Jul 88. (lp) *(NOSE 21)* **KICKED OUT OF HELL**
– Satan's rejects / Human slug / Cripple in the woods / Decomposition / Cast iron arm / Call of the wired / Rubber plimsouls / Shadow crypt / Surf ride to oblivion / Old black Joe / Sick spasmoid / Vietnam / Jet tone boogie.

Link | not iss.

May 89. (lp) *(LINKLP 084)* **THE DAY THE EARTH SPAT BLOOD**
– Country woman / Brain damaged Chile (slight retard) / One sharp knife / Flight 103 / Termite man / Skitzoid brain / Life's a bitch / Now she's dead. *(cd-iss. Jun98 on 'Raucous'; RAUCD 035)*
Mar 90. (lp) *(LINKLP 116)* **LIVE 'N' ROCKIN' (live)**

Fury | not iss.

Mar 91. (cd) *(FCD 3016)* **ORGASMIC NIGHTMARE**
– Orgasmic nightmare / Beast in the cellar / House of blood / Now she's dead / Clitoris bite boogie / Love is like electrocution / Who put grandma under the stairs / Love seeps like a festering sore / Night life / Anal wonderland / Demon angel / Straight jacket / Rubber rock / One sharp knife / Cast iron arm / Marijuana / Satan's reject. *(re-iss. May95 on 'Fury'; FCD 3016)*

Nervous | not iss.

Jun 93. (cd/lp) *(DAG CD/LP 001)* **TANGENITAL MADNESS**
– Intro / Brand new corpse / Mongoloid / Gambling queen / Dream space baby / Zombie stalk / Queen of disease / Where you gonna go / Fairies at the bottom of my garden / Aces high / Thrill killers / Up from the skies / Got good lovin' / The chase. *(cd re-iss. May95 on 'Damaged Goods'; DAGCD 1)*

– compilations, etc. –

Dec 91. (cd) *Streetlink; (STRCD 025)* **THE BEST OF DEMENTED ARE GO**
– Pervy in the park / Busted hymen / Holy hack Jack / Pickled and preserved / Transvestite blues / PVC chair / Nuke mutants / Satan's rejects / Cripple in the woods / Call of the wired / Surf ride to oblivion / Shadow crypt / Human slug / Sick spasmoid / Country woman / One sharp knife / Brain damaged Chile / Flight 103. *(re-iss. May93 on 'Dojo'; DOJOCD 125) (re-iss. Nov97 as 'SATAN'S REJECTS – THE BEST OF . . .' on 'Anagram'; CDMPSYCHO 19)*
Mar 93. (cd) *Loma; (LOMACD 15)* **IN SICKNESS AND IN HEALTH / KICKED OUT OF HELL**
Jun 93. (cd) *Loma; (LOMACD 22)* **THE DAY THE EARTH SPAT BLOOD / GO GO DEMENTED**
Jun 94. (cd) *Dojo; (DOJOCD 23)* **LIVE AT THE KLUB FOOT, APRIL '87 (live)**
Jun 94. (cd) *Tombstone; (TBCD 2019)* **LIVE IN JAPAN (live)**
May 96. (cd) *Receiver; (RRCD 218)* **WHO PUT GRANDMA UNDER THE STAIRS (live)**

DENISON / KIMBALL TRIO (see under ⇒ JESUS LIZARD)

DENTISTS

Formed: Chatham, Kent, England . . . 1983 by BOB COLLINS, along with MICK MURPHY, MARK MATTHEW and IAN SMITH. Trading in quintessential indie-pop bearing comparison to The HOUSEMARTINS, The SMITHS and occasionally even The PIXIES, The DENTISTS debuted with the 'STRAWBERRIES ARE GROWING IN MY GARDEN' single in early '85, followed by similarly fruity EP, 'YOU AND YOUR BLOODY ORANGES'. By this point SMITH had been replaced by ALUN GWYNNE JONES, the latter replaced in turn by ROB L GRIGG the following year as the band released their well received 'DOWN AND OUT IN PARIS AND CHATHAM' EP. 1987 saw the release of a second four tracker, 'WRITHING ON THE SHAGPILE', while a follow-up album, 'BEER BOTTLE AND BANNISTER SYMPHPONIE', appeared on the 'Antler' label in 1988. The turn of the decade finally saw the band receiving some long overdue press interest with the 'HEADS AND HOW TO READ THEM' (1990) set, a more enthusiastic response from the American alternative market resulting in college radio airplay for tracks culled from the 'DRESSED' (1992) and 'POWDERED LOBSTER FIASCO' (1993) albums and an eventual major label deal with the 'East West' subsidiary of 'Atlantic' records. The resulting long player, 'BEHIND THE DOOR I KEEP THE UNIVERSE' (1994) kept up their penchant for long winded titles and delivered another fix of airy, spirited guitar pop, MURPHY's strangely feminine, vaguely PAUL HEATON-esque vocals floating over the jingle jangle chords on a carpet of ba-ba-ba backing vocals.

Album rating: SOME PEOPLE . . . (*5) / BEER BOTTLE AND BANNISTER SYMPHONIES (*5) / HEADS AND HOW TO READ THEM (*5) / DRESSED compilation (*6) / POWDERED LOBSTER FIASCO (*5)

MICK MURPHY (b. 8 Oct'63, Bexley, Kent) – vocals, guitar / **BOB COLLINS** (b.12 Jun'65, Gillingham, Kent) – guitar, vocals / **MARK MATTHEWS** (b.15 May'65, Farnborough, Hampshire, England) – bass, vocals / **IAN SMITH** – drums

Spruck | not iss.

Apr 85. (lp) *(SPR 001)* **SOME PEOPLE ON THE PITCH THINK IT'S ALL OVER . . . IT IS NOW**
Jun 85. (7"m) *(SP 003)* **STRAWBERRIES ARE GROWING IN MY GARDEN (AND IT'S WINTERTIME). / BURNING THE THOUGHTS FROM MY SKIN / DOREEN**
(re-iss. Nov86; same)
Nov 85. (12"ep) *(SP 004)* **YOU AND YOUR BLOODY ORANGES**
Jun 86. (12"ep) *(SP 006)* **DOWN AND OUT IN PARIS AND CHATHAM**

— **ALUN GWYNNE-JONES** (b. 3 Feb'66) – drums; repl. SMITH

Tambourine | not iss.

Jun 87. (12"ep) *(URINE 3)* **WRITHING ON THE SHAGPILE / JUST LIKE OLIVER REED. / A STRANGE WAY TO GO ABOUT THINGS / CALM YOU DOWN / THE TURQUISE CASTLE**

Antler | not iss.

Feb 88. (lp) *(ANT 072)* **BEER BOTTLE & BANNISTER SYMPHONIES**
– Writhing on the shagpile / You took me by surprise / A strange way to go about things / She dazzled me with Basil / Dawn overdone / I had an excellent dream / Strawberries are growing in my garden (and it's wintertime) / The turquoise castle / Calm you down / Chainsaw the horses / Peppermint dreams / Just like Oliver Reed.
Apr 88. (12") *(ANT 077)* **THE FUN HAS ARRIVED. / ?**

— **ROB L GRIGG** (b.28 Jul'68, Canterbury, Kent) – drums; repl. JONES

Integrity | Caroline

Jan 91. (7") **BEAUTIFUL DAY. /**
Jan 91. (cd/lp) *<90014>* **HEADS AND HOW TO READ THEM**

1991. (7") **HOUSE THE SIZE OF MARS. /** [ ] [-]

not iss. — Independent Project

1991. (10"lp) *<36>* **NAKED** [-] [ ]

1992. (7") **HEAR NO EVIL. / ?** [-] [ ]

Me Two — Homestead

Aug 92. (cd) *(ME 2001) <HMS 180>* **DRESSED** (compilation) [ ] [ ]
– Strawberries are growing in my garden (and it's wintertime) / She dazzled me with Basil / I had an excellent dream / A strange way to go about things / Chainsaw the horse / Peppermint dreams / Just like Oliver Reed / The turquoise castle / I can see your house from up here / Pailino / Dawn overdone / Writhing on the shagpile / Flowers around me / I'm not the Devil / Tony Bastable v John Noakes / You make me say it somehow / Mary won't come out to play / Kinder still / The little engineers set / Tangerine / The arrow points to the spot / One of our psychedelic beakers is missing.

Jan 93. (7") *<HMS 187>* **SEE NO EVIL. / SPEAK NO EVIL** [-] [ ]

not iss. — Bus Stop

1993. (7") *<026>* **OUTSIDE YOUR INSIDE. / ALL COMING DOWN** [-] [ ]

not iss. — Independent Project

1993. (7") *<041>* **CHARMS AND THE GIRL. / LEAVE ME ALIVE** [-] [ ]

Ball Product – Creation — Homestead

Jul 93. (cd) *(SHED 002CD) <HMS 203>* **THE POWDERED LOBSTER FIASCO** [ ] [ ]
– Pocket of silver / Charms and the girls / Outside your inside / Box of sun / Beautiful day / I can see your house from up here / We thought we'd gone to Heaven / Leave me alive / All coming down / Snapdragon.

East West — Atlantic

Mar 94. (cd/c) *(<7567 92288-2/-4>)* **BEHIND THE DOOR I KEEP THE UNIVERSE** [ ] [ ] Jan94
– This is not my flag / Space man / Sorry is not enough / In orbit / Faces on stone / A smile like oil on water / Tremendous many / Gas / Brittle sin and flowers / Apple beast / Water for a man on fire / The waiter.

not iss. — Elektra

Apr 95. (cd) *<61767>* **DEEP SIX** [-] [ ]
– Shining like a star / Slither / Weirdo (at 25,000 miles per hour) / My heart is like a town you moved / Kick start my body / Apetite / Hedonist / Not coming back / Agony in twelve fits / Whole world explode / Gradual / Good riddance / Orange gold / Electric train of thought.

DEPARTMENT S

Formed: London, England . . . 1980 out of the ashes of ska-punk outfit, GUNS FOR HIRE, by p/t 'Face' journo, VAUGHAN TOULOUSE, MICHAEL D. HERBAGE and TONY LORDAN. With the addition of EDDIE ROXY and MIKE HASLER, GFH issued one 1980 single, 'I'M GONNA ROUGH MY GIRLFRIEND'S BOYFRIEND UP TONIGHT', before metamorphosising into DEPARTMENT S. Taking the moniker from a cult 60's TV series and replacing MIKE and EDDIE with STUART MIZON and MARK TAYLOR, the group had a surprise near Top 30 hit courtesy of 'Demon' the following year with 'IS VIC THERE?'. A cool slice of catchy alternative pop, the single was backed with 'SOLID GOLD EASY ACTION', NOT actually a cover of the T.REX classic. Signing to 'Stiff' (through whom 'VIC' was given a US release), they scored a further minor hit, 'GOING LEFT RIGHT', although their chart luck ran out with 'I WANT'. With a proposed album subsequently shelved, DEPARTMENT S was permanently filed away, although TOULOUSE would later resurface as a solo artist while working for PAUL WELLER's STYLE COUNCIL. Sadly, the singer was to die of AIDS in August 1991 after suffering a long related illness.

Album rating: IS VIC THERE? compilation (*4)

VAUGHAN TOULOUSE (b. VAUGHAN COTILLARD, 30 Jul'59, St.Helier, Jersey, Channel Islands) – vovals / **MICHAEL D. HERBAGE** – guitar / **TONY LORDAN** – bass / **EDDIE ROXY** (b. EDWARD LLOYD BARNES) – keyboards / **MIKE HASLER** – drums (ex-INVADERS; aka MADNESS)

Korova — not iss.

1980. (7"; as GUNS FOR HIRE) *(KOW 6)* **I'M GONNA ROUGH MY GIRLFRIEND'S BOYFRIEND UP TONIGHT. / I'M FAMOUS NOW** [ ] [-]

—— **MARK TAYLOR** – synthesizer, keyboards; repl. EDDIE

—— **STUART MIZON** – drums; repl. MIKE

Demon — not iss.

Mar 81. (7") *(D 1003)* **IS VIC THERE? / SOLID GOLD EASY ACTION** [22] [-]

Stiff — Stiff

Jun 81. (7") *<TEES7 02>* **IS VIC THERE? (remixed). / PUT ALL THE CROSSES IN THE RIGHT BOXES** [-] [ ]

Jun 81. (7") *(BUY 118)* **GOING LEFT RIGHT. / SHE'S EXPECTING YOU** [55] [-]
(12"+=) *(BUY-IT 18)* – Is Vic there? (French version).

Oct 81. (7") *(BUY 128)* **I WANT. / MONTE CARLO** [ ] [-]
(12"+=) *(SBUY 128)* – Put all the crosses in the right boxes.

—— split after they flopped again and an album was shelved. VAUGHAN TOULOUSE worked as a DJ (MAIN T) before going solo and releasing a one-off summer '85 single, 'CRUISIN' THE SERPENTINE'. This was issued by PAUL WELLER's 'Respond' label, being at the same time part of the STYLE COUNCIL miner's charity outfit, COUNCIL COLLECTIVE.

– compilations, etc. –

Mar 93. (cd) *Mau Mau; (MAUCD 633)* **IS VIC THERE?** [ ] [-]
– Of all the lost followers / Just pretend / Romany blood / I want / Fighting Irish / Is Vic there? / Going left right / Age concern / Somewhere between Heaven & Tesco's / Whatever happened to the blues / Ode to Koln / Clap now / Monte Carlo or bust / Put all the crosses in the right boxes / Is Vic there? (French version) / Is Vic there? (Italian version) / She's expecting you / Solid gold easy action.

DEPECHE MODE

Formed: Basildon, Essex, England . . . 1976 by VINCE CLARKE, MARTIN GORE and ANDY FLETCHER while still at school. The line-up was completed by frontman DAVE GAHAN, and by 1980 they had adopted the DEPECHE MODE moniker, immersing themselves in the London 'New Romantic' scene which spawned the likes of SPANDAU BALLET and VISAGE. After gigging around the capital and having a track, 'PHOTOGRAPHIC', included on the 'Some Bizzare Album' various artists collection, the band were picked up by the fledgling 'Mute' label. While their debut single, 'DREAMING OF ME', scraped the lower regions of the chart in 1981, a follow-up, 'NEW LIFE', almost made the Top 10. Dominated by synthesizers and drum machines, yet retaining a keen sense of melody, the band initially took their cue from KRAFTWERK. As evidenced on their insanely catchy Top 10 breakthrough, 'JUST CAN'T GET ENOUGH' (the first of 24 consecutive Top 30 hits), their lyrics weren't quite as enigmatic as their Teutonic heroes, although they improved with time. The success of the single (which no doubt still gets played ten times a night in French discos!) paved the way for the debut album, 'SPEAK AND SPELL' (1981), a promising collection of catchy synth-pop fare which made the UK Top 10. Chief songwriter VINCE CLARKE quit shortly after, going on to pastures new with YAZOO and then ERASURE, GORE taking up the pensmith chores for the follow-up album, 'A BROKEN FRAME' (1982). Shortly after its release, ALAN WILDER, who had previously toured with the band, was recruited as a full time replacement for CLARKE. Like its predecessor, 'CONSTRUCTION TIME AGAIN' (1983) failed to make any significant leap forward from the debut, musically at least, although it did contain the classic 'EVERYTHING COUNTS', GAHAN's voice summoning up as much portentous doom as he could muster. While the 'PEOPLE ARE PEOPLE' single gave the band valuable exposure in America, their real breakthrough came with 1984's 'SOME GREAT REWARD'. Featuring the likes of 'BLASPHEMOUS RUMOURS' and 'MASTER AND SERVANT', the album was palpably darker, the music more satisfyingly varied. 'BLACK CELEBRATION' (1986) was deliberately darker still, much of the material creeping along at a funereal pace. 'MUSIC FOR THE MASSES' (1987) was the band's biggest Stateside success to date, the material for the live album, '101' (1989) coming from the American leg of their 1988 sell-out world tour. 'VIOLATOR' (1990) was heralded as DEPECHE MODE's best work since 'SOME GREAT REWARD', spawning two of their better singles in 'PERSONAL JESUS' and the uncharacteristically emotional 'ENJOY THE SILENCE'. Never the warmest sounding band, with 'SONGS OF FAITH AND DEVOTION' (1993) their clinical sound was softened somewhat with a move towards more rock-centric territory. That's not to say the music was soft, at least not on the single, 'I FEEL YOU', a dirty great guitar riff grinding away relentlessly. Elsewhere, the album had something of a transcendent, redemptive quality about it on such powerful tracks as 'MERCY IN YOU' and 'ONE CARESS'. The record gave the band their first No.1, UK and US, although some longtime fans were understandably miffed at the band's new direction. • **Covered:** ROUTE 66 (Chuck Berry). • **Trivia:** MARTIN GORE's solo album contained six cover versions incl. NEVER TURN YOUR BACK ON MOTHER EARTH (Sparks). He later covered Leonard Cohen's COMING BACK TO YOU.

Album rating: SPEAK & SPELL (*6) / A BROKEN FRAME (*6) / CONSTRUCTION TIME AGAIN (*7) / SOME GREAT REWARD (*7) / THE SINGLES 1981-1985 compilation (*9) / BLACK CELEBRATION (*8) / MUSIC FOR THE MASSES (*7) / 101 (*5) / VIOLATOR (*7) / SONGS OF FAITH & DEVOTION (*7) / SONGS OF LOVE & DEVOTION LIVE (*3) / ULTRA (*6) / THE SINGLES 86>98 compilation (*7)

VINCE CLARKE (b. 3 Jul'60, South Woodford, England) – keyboards, synthesiser / **DAVID GAHAN** (b. 9 May'62, Epping, England) – vocals / **MARTIN GORE** (b.23 Jul'61) – keyboards, synthesizer, vocals / **ANDY FLETCHER** (b. 8 Jul'61, Nottingham, England) – guitar, synthesiser, drum machine

Mute — Sire

Mar 81. (7") *(MUTE 013)* **DREAMING OF ME. / ICE MACHINE** [57] [ ]

Jun 81. (7") *(MUTE 014)* **NEW LIFE. / SHOUT!** [11] [ ]
(12") *(12MUTE 014)* – ('A'extended) / ('B'-Rio mix).

Sep 81. (7") *(MUTE 016)* **JUST CAN'T GET ENOUGH. / ANY SECOND NOW** [8] [-]
(12") *(12MUTE 016)* – ('A'-Schizo mix) / ('B'-altered).

Oct 81. (lp/c) *(STUMM/CSTUMM 5) <3642>* **SPEAK & SPELL** [10] [ ]
– New life / Just can't get enough / I sometimes I wish I was dead / Puppets / Boys say go / No disco / What's your name / Photographic / Tora! Tora! Tora! / Big Muff / Any second now. *(cd-iss. Apr88 +=; CDSTUMM 5)* – Dreaming of me / New life (extended) / Shout! (Rio mix) / Any second now (altered mix).

Nov 81. (7") **JUST CAN'T GET ENOUGH. / TORA! TORA! TORA!** [-] [ ]

—— **ALAN WILDER** (b. 1 Jun'59, London, England) – electronics (ex-HITMEN) repl. VINCE who formed YAZOO

Jan 82. (7"/ext.12") *(MUTE/12MUTE 018)* **SEE YOU. / NOW, THIS IS FUN** [6] [ ] Aug82

Apr 82. (7") *(MUTE 022)* **THE MEANING OF LOVE. / OBERKORN (IT'S A SMALL TOWN)** [12] [ ]
(12") *(12MUTE 022)* – ('A'extended) / ('B'-Fairly odd mix).

Aug 82. (7") *(7BONG 1)* **LEAVE IN SILENCE. / EXCERPT FROM MY SECRET GARDEN** [18] [ ]
(ext.12"+=) *(12BONG 1)* – ('A'quieter version).

Sep 82. (lp/c) *(STUMM/CSTUMM 9) <23751>* **A BROKEN FRAME** [8] [ ]

– Leave in silence / My secret garden / Monument / Nothing to fear / See you / Satellite / The meaning of love / A photograph of you / Shouldn't have done that / The sun and the rainfall. *(cd-iss. Jul88; CDSTUMM 13)*

Feb 83. (7"/ext.12") *(7/12 BONG 2)* **GET THE BALANCE RIGHT. / THE GREAT OUTDOORS** [13] [ ]
(12") *(L12BONG 2)* – ('A'side) / My secret garden (live) / See you (live) / Satellite (live) / Tora! Tora! Tora! (live).

Jul 83. (7") *(7BONG 3)* **EVERYTHING COUNTS. / WORK HARD** [6] [ ]
(12") *(12BONG 3)* – ('A'-larger amounts) / ('B'-East End mix).
(12") *(L12BONG 3)* – ('A'side) / Boys say go (live) / New life (live) / Nothing to fear (live) / The meaning of love (live).

Aug 83. (lp/c) *(STUMM/CSTUMM 13)* **CONSTRUCTION TIME AGAIN** [6] [-]
– Love in itself / More than a party / Pipeline / Everything counts / Two minute warning / Shame / The landscape is changing / Told you so / And then . . . *(cd-iss. Jul88; CDSTUMM 13)*

Sep 83. (7") *(BONG 4)* **LOVE IN ITSELF. / FOOLS** [21] [ ]
(12") *(12BONG 4)* – Love in itself (3) / (4) / Fools (bigger).
(12") *(L12BONG 4)* – ('A'side) / Just can't get enough (live) / Photograph (live) / A photograph of you (live) / Shout! (live).

Mar 84. (7") *(7BONG 5)* *<29221>* **PEOPLE ARE PEOPLE. / IN YOUR MEMORY** [4] [13] May85
(12"+=) *(L12BONG 5)* – ('A'-On-U-Sound remix).
(12") *(12BONG 5)* – ('A'different mix) / ('B'-Slik mix).

Jul 84. (lp) *<25124>* **PEOPLE ARE PEOPLE** [-] [71]
– People are people / Everything counts / Get the balance right / Love in itself / Now this is fun / Leave in silence / Told you so / Work hard.

Aug 84. (7") *(7BONG 6)* *<28918>* **MASTER AND SERVANT. / SET ME FREE (RENOVATE ME)** [9] [ ] Aug85
('A'-Slavery whip mix-12"+=) *(12BONG 6)* – ('A'voxless).
('A'-On-U-Sound mix-12"+=) *(L12BONG 6)* – Are people people?.

Sep 84. (lp/c) *(STUMM/CSTUMM 19)* *<25194>* **SOME GREAT REWARD** [5] [51] Jan85
– Something to do / Lie to me / People are people / It doesn't matter / Stories of old / Somebody / Master and servant / If you want to / Blasphemous rumours. *(cd-iss. Sep87; CDSTUMM 19)*

Nov 84. (7") *(7BONG 7)* **BLASPHEMOUS RUMOURS. / SOMEBODY** [16] [ ]
(7"ep+=) *(7BONG 7E)* – Told you so (live) / Everything counts (live).
(12"+=) *(12BONG 7)* – Ice machine / Two minute warning / Everything counts (live).

May 85. (7"/remix-12") *(7/12 BONG 8)* **SHAKE THE DISEASE. / FLEXIBLE** [18] [ ]
(12") *(L12BONG 8)* – Edit the shake / Master and servant (live) / Flexible (deportation mix) / Something to do (metal mix).

Sep 85. (7"/remix-12") *(7/12 BONG 9)* **IT'S CALLED A HEART. / FLY ON THE WINDSCREEN** [18] [ ]
(ext.d12"+=) *(D12BONG 9)* – ('A'-slow mix) / ('A'-death mix).

Oct 85. (lp/c) *(MUTEL/CMUTEL 1)* *<25346>* **THE SINGLES 1981-1985** (compilation) <US-title 'CATCHING UP WITH DEPECHE MODE'> [6] [ ]
– People are people / Master and servant / It's called a heart / Just can't get enough / See you / Shake the disease / Everything counts / New life / Blasphemous rumours / Leave in silence / Get the balance right / Love in itself / Dreaming of me. *(c+=)* – (2 extra). *(cd-iss. Sep87; CDMUTEL 1)*

Feb 86. (7") *(7BONG 10)* **STRIPPED. / BUT NOT TONIGHT** [15] [ ]
(ext.12"+=) *(12BONG 10)* – Breathing in fumes / Fly on the windscreen (quiet mix) / Black day.

Mar 86. (lp/c) *(STUMM/CSTUMM 26)* *<25429>* **BLACK CELEBRATION** [4] [90]
– Black celebration / Fly on the windscreen – final / A question of lust / Sometimes / It doesn't matter two / A question of time / Stripped / Here is the house / World full of nothing / Dressed in black / New dress. *(cd-iss. Sep87+=; CDSTUMM 26)* – But not tonight / Breathing in fumes / Black day.

Apr 86. (7") *(7BONG 11)* **A QUESTION OF LUST. / CHRISTMAS ISLAND** [28] [ ]
(free c-s. w/7") *(CBONG 11)* – ('A'-Flood mix) / If you want (live) / Shame (live) / Blasphemous rumours (live).
(ext.12"+=) *(12BONG 11)* – It doesn't matter (instrumental) / People are people (live) / A question of lust (minimal).

Aug 86. (7") *(7BONG 12)* **A QUESTION OF TIME. / BLACK CELEBRATION** [17] [ ]
(ext.12"+=) *(12BONG 12)* – Stripped (live) / Something to do (live).
(12") *(L12BONG 12)* – ('A'-Newtown mix) / ('A'live) / ('B'-Black tulip mix) / More than a party (live).

Apr 87. (7") *(7BONG 13)* *<28366>* **STRANGELOVE. / PIMPF** [16] [76]
('A'-Maximix-12"+=) *(12BONG 13)* – ('A'Midimix).
(cd-s++=) *(CDBONG 13)* – Agent orange.
('A'-Blind mix-12"+=) *(L12BONG 13)* – ('A'-Pain mix) / Agent orange.

Aug 87. (7") *(7BONG 14)* *<28189>* **NEVER LET ME DOWN AGAIN. / PLEASURE, LITTLE PLEASURE** [22] [63]
(12"/c-s) *(12/C BONG 14)* – ('A'-split mix) / ('B'-glitter mix) / ('A'-aggro mix).
(cd-s++=) *(CDBONG 14)* – To have and to hold (Spanish taster).
(12") *(L12BONG 14)* – ('A'-Tsangarides mix) / ('B'-join mix) / To have and to hold (Spanish taster).

Sep 87. (cd/d-c/lp,clear-lp) *(CD/C+/STUMM 47)* *<25614>* **MUSIC FOR THE MASSES** [10] [35]
– Never let me down again / The things you said / Strangelove / Sacred / Little 15 / Behind the wheel / I want you now / To have to hold / Nothing / Pimpf. *(cd+=)* – Agent orange / Never let me down again (aggro mix) / To have and to hold (Spanish) / Pleasure the treasure (glitter mix). *(d-c+=)* – BLACK CELEBRATION (album)

Dec 87. (7") *(7BONG 15)* *<27991>* **BEHIND THE WHEEL. / ROUTE 66** [21] [61]
(c-s+=/cd-s+=) *(C/CD BONG 15)* – ('A'-Shep Pettibone mix) / ('A'-lp version).
(12") *(12BONG 15)* – ('A'-Shep Pettibone mix) / ('B'-Beatmasters mix).
(12") *(L12BONG 15)* – ('A'-Beatmasters mix) / ('B'-Casualty mix).

May 88. (7"import) *(LITTLE 15)* **LITTLE 15. /** [60] [ ]

Sep 88. (7") *<27777>* **STRANGELOVE. / NOTHING** [-] [50]

Feb 89. (7") *(7BONG 16)* **EVERYTHING COUNTS (live). / NOTHING (live)** [22] [ ]
(12"+=/cd-s+=) *(12/CD BONG 16)* – Sacred (live) / A question of lust (live).
(remix-cd-s) *(CDLBONG 16)* – Strangelove (remix).
(3"cd-s) *(LCDBONG 16)* – ('A'-Tim Simenon & M. Saunders remix) / ('B'-Justin Strauss remix) / Strangelove (Tim Simenon & M. Saunders remix).
(12") *(L12BONG 16)* **- ('A'-Bomb The Bass mix) / ('B'-Hijack mix).**
(10") *(10BONG 16)* – ('A'-Absolute mix) / ('B'-US mix) / ('A'-1983 mix).

Mar 89. (d-cd/d-c/d-lp) *(CD/C+/STUMM 101)* *<25853>* **101 (live)** [5] [45]
– Pimpf / Behind the wheel / Strangelove / Sacred * / Something to do / Blasphemous rumours / Stripped / Somebody / Things you said / Black generation / Shake the disease / Nothing * / Pleasure little treasure / People are people / A question of time / Never let me down again / A question of lust * / Master and servant / Just can't get enough / Everything counts *. *(c+=*/cd+=*)*

Aug 89. (7")<US-c-s> *(BONG 17)* *<19941>* **PERSONAL JESUS. / DANGEROUS** [13] [28] Nov89
(7"g-f+=/12"+=/c-s+=/cd-s+=) *(G/12/C/CD BONG 17)* – ('A'acoustic mix).
('A'pump mix-3"cd-s) *(LCDBONG 17)* – ('A'-Telephone stomp mix).

Feb 90. (c-s/7") *(C+/BONG 18)* *<19885>* **ENJOY THE SILENCE. / MEMPHISTO** [6] [8] Mar90
(cd-s+=) *(LCDBONG 18)* – ('A'-Bassline):- Bassline / Harmonium / Rikki Tick Tick / Memphesto.
(etched-12"/3"cd-s) *(XL12/XLCD BONG 18)* – ('A'-The quad: Final mix).

Mar 90. (cd/c/lp) *(CD/C+/STUMM 64)* *<26081>* **VIOLATOR** [2] [7]
– World in my eyes / Sweetest perfection / Personal Jesus / Halo / Waiting for the night / Enjoy the silence / Policy of truth / Blue dress / Clean.

May 90. (c-s/7") *(C+/BONG 19)* *<19842>* **POLICY OF TRUTH. / KALEID (remix)** [16] [15] Aug90
('A'-Trancentral mix; 12"+=/cd-s+=) *(LCDBONG 19)* – ('A'-Pavlov's dub mix).

Sep 90. (12"/cd-s/7") *(12/CD+/BONG 20)* *<19580>* **WORLD IN MY EYES. / HAPPIEST GIRL / SEA OF SIN** [17] [52] Nov90
(12") *(L12BONG 20)* – (first 2 tracks) / ('A'remix).
(c-s+=)(cd-s+=) *(CDLBONG 20)* – Meaning of love / Somebody.

Feb 93. (c-s/7") *(C+/BONG 21)* *<18600>* **I FEEL YOU. / ONE CARESS** [8] [37]
(12"+=)(cd-s+=) *(12/CD BONG 21)* – ('A'-Throb mix) / ('A'-Babylon mix).
(12"/cd-s) *(12L/CDL BONG 21)* – ('A'side) / ('A'swamp mix) / ('A'-Renegade Soundwave mix) / ('A'-Helmut mix).

Mar 93. (cd/c/lp) *(CD/C+/STUMM 106)* *<45243>* **SONGS OF FAITH AND DEVOTION** [1] [1]
– I feel you / Walking in my shoes / Condemnation / Mercy in you / Judas / In your room / Get right with me / Rush / One caress / Higher love. *(live version of album iss.Dec93; same)*

May 93. (7"/c-s) *(7/C BONG 22)* *<18506>* **WALKING IN MY SHOES. / MY JOY** [14] [69]
(12"+=/cd-s+=) *(12/CD BONG 22)* – ('A'-Grungy Gonads mix).
(ext;12"/cd-s) *(L12/LCD BONG 22)* – ('A'-Random Carpet mix) / ('A'-Anandamidic mix) / ('A'-Mark Stent 12" Ambient Whale mix).

Sep 93. (7"/c-s) *(7/C BONG 23)* **CONDEMNATION. / DEATH'S DOOR (jazz mix)** [9] [ ]
(cd-s+=) *(CDBONG 23)* – Rush (spiritual mix) / Rush (amylnitrate mix).
(12"+=) *(12BONG 23)* – Rush (mixes).
(12"/cd-s) *(L12/LCD 23)* – ('A'live) / Personal Jesus (live) / Enjoy the silence (live) / Halo (live).

Dec 93. (cd) *<45505>* **SONGS OF FAITH AND DEVOTION – LIVE (live)** [-] [ ]

Jan 94. (c-s) *(CBONG 24)* **IN YOUR ROOM (Zephyr mix) / HIGHER LOVE (Adrenaline mix)** [8] [ ]
('A'-Jeep Rock mix; cd-s+=) *(XLCDBONG 24)* – ('A'-Apex mix).
(12"++=) *(12BONG 24)* – ('A'-extended Zephyr mix).
(cd-s) *(CDBONG 24)* – ('A'-Zephyr mix) / ('A'extended Zephyr mix) / Never let me down again / Death's door.
(cd-s) *(LCDBONG 24)* – ('A'side) / Policy of truth / World in my eyes / Fly on the windscreen (final).
(12"++=) *(L12BONG 24)* – Never let me down again / Death's door.

— ANDREW FLETCHER departed to take over groups' business affairs.

— On the 17th August '95, GAHAN was thought by the music press, to have attempted suicide by cutting at his wrists after his wife left him. His record company however said this had been an accident and was over-hyped by the media. GAHAN is currently being treated for his drug problems and has been charged by US police for similar offences.

Feb 97. (cd-s) *(12BONG 25)* **BARREL OF A GUN / PAINKILLER / ('A'-Underworld soft mix) / ('A'-One Inch Punch mix)** [4] [47]
(12") *(L12BONG 25)* – ('A'-One Inch Punch mix) / ('A'-United mix) / Painkiller (Plastikman mix) / Painkiller.
(cd-s) *(LCDBONG 25)* – ('A'-Underworld hard mix) / ('A'-United mix) / Painkiller (Plastikman mix).
(12") *(12BONG 25)* – ('A'-Underworld hard mix) / ('A'-3 Phase mix) / ('A'-One Inch Punch mix) / ('A'-United mix).

Apr 97. (c-s) *(CBONG 26)* **IT'S NO GOOD / SLOWBLOW** [5] [38]
(cd-s+=) *(CDBONG 26)* – ('A'-Bass bounce mix) / ('A'-Speedy J mix).
('A'-Hardfloor mix; cd-s+=) *(LCDBONG 26)* – ('A'-Andrea Parker mix) / ('A'-Motor bass mix).
(12") *(12BONG 26)* – ('A'-Hardfloor mix) / ('A'-Speedy J mix) / ('A'-Motor bass mix) / ('A'-Andrea Parker mix) / ('A'-Dom T mix).

Apr 97. (cd/c/lp) *(CD/C+/Stumm 148)* *<46522>* **ULTRA** [1] [5]
– Barrel of a gun / The love thieves / Home / It's no good / Uselink / Useless / Sister of night / Jazz thieves / Freestate / The bottom line / Insight.

Jun 97. (c-s) *(CBONG 27)* **HOME / IT'S NO GOOD** [23] [88] Nov97
('A'-Grantby mix; cd-s+=) *(LCDBONG 27)* – ('A'-Jedi Knights remix: Drowning in time) / Barrel of a gun.
(12") *(12BONG 27)* – ('A'-Jedi Knights remix: Drowning in time) / ('A'-Grantby mix) / ('A'-Air around the golf remix) / ('A'-LFO mix).
(cd-s) *(CDBONG 27)* – ('A'side) / ('A'-LFO mix) / ('A'-The Noodles and the damage done mix).

Oct 97. (cd-s) *(CDBONG 28)* **USELESS / ('A'-Escape From Wherever parts 1&2) / ('A'-Cosmic Blues mix) / BARREL OF A GUN (video)** [28] [ ]
(12") *(12BONG 28)* – ('A'-The Kruder & Dorfmeister session) / ('A'-CJ Bolland funky sub mix) / ('A'-Air 20 mix).
(cd-s) *(LCDBONG 28)* – ('A'-CJ Bolland ultrasonar mix) / ('A'-The Kruder & Dorfmaister session) / ('A'live) / It's no good (CD-rom).

Sep 98. (cd-s) *(CDBONG 29)* *<44546>* **ONLY WHEN I LOSE MYSELF / SURRENDER / HEADSTAR** [17] [61]
(12"/cd-s) *(12/LCD BONG 29)* – ('A'-Subsonic legacy remix) / ('A'-Dan The Automator remix) / Headstar (Luke Slater remix).
(12") *(L12BONG 29)* – ('A'remixes) / Painkiller / Surrender.
(cd-s+=) *(XLCDBONG 29)* – World in my eyes.

Sep 98. (d-cd/c/3x12") *(CD/C+/MUTEL 5)* *<47110>* **THE SINGLES 86>98** (compilation) [5] [38] Oct98
– Stripped / A question of lust / A question of time / Strangelove / Never let me down again / Behind the wheel / Personal Jesus / Enjoy the silence / Policy of truth / World in my eyes / I feel you / Walking in my shoes / Condemnation / In your room / Barrel of a gun / It's no good / Home / Useless / Only when I lose myself / Little 15 / Everything counts (live).

- compilations, others -

on 'Mute' unless otherwise mentioned

Nov 91. (6xcd-ep-box) *(DMBX 1CD)* **SINGLES BOX SET** [-]
Nov 91. (6xcd-ep-box) *(DMBX 2CD)* **SINGLES BOX SET** [-]
Nov 91. (6xcd-ep-box) *(DMBX 3CD)* **SINGLES BOX SET** [-]

MARTIN L. GORE

Mute Sire

Jun 89. (m-cd/m-c/m-lp) *(CD/C+/STUMM 67)* *<25980>* **COUNTERFEIT** [51]
– Smile in the crowd / Never turn your back on Mother Earth / Gone / Motherless child / Compulsion / In a manner of speaking.

DESCENDENTS

Formed: South Bay, California, USA . . . early 80's by FRANK NAVETTA, TONY LOMBARDO and BILL STEVENSON. Following the releaase of debut single, 'RIDE THE WILD', the band recruited the short-lived CECILIA as lead vocalist, her tenure lasting only six months. A more permanent replacement was found in MILO AUCKERMAN, who made his debut on 1981's seminal 'FAT' EP, a warpspeed blast of angst-ridden but self-deprecatingly humerous hardcore that took in such favoured teenage obsessions as junk food and parent hating. The following year's debut album, 'MILO GOES TO COLLEGE', is widely regarded as a milestone of the genre, its blitzkreig hardcore bop equal parts hormonal fury, pop genius and teenage humour, bypassing much of the macho posturing favoured by the DESCENDENTS' peers. MILO did indeed go to college, however, while NAVETTA and STEVENSON also departed, the former replaced by RAY COOPER upon MILO's return and the band's re-emergence in the mid-80's. 'I DON'T WANT TO GROW UP' (1985) was the sound of a band in transition, the full pelt chaos of old making way for a more streamlined power-pop/punk direction. With DOUG CARRION coming in for the outgoing LOMBARDO, subsequent albums put the emphasis on louder, heavier guitars and pop hooks while the band's last remaining founder member, MILO, left prior to 1989's swansong, 'HALLRAKER'. His short-lived replacement, SMALLEY, was also a member of the band, ALL, who, along with BILL STEVENSON, KARL ALVEREZ and STEPHEN EGERTON, carried the DESCENDENTS' patented brand of fun-time punk-pop into the 90's on such albums as 'ALLROY SEZ . . .' (1988), 'ALLROY'S REVENGE' (1990) and 'ALLROY SAVES' (1990), all released on 'Cruz' records. The band took on even more of a DESCENDENTS hue in the early 90's with the addition of TONY LOMBARDO, subsequently signing with hardcore stalwart, 'Epitaph', for 1988's 'MASS NERDER' set. With a whole new generation of bands (i.e. GREEN DAY, OFFSPRING etc.) citing the DESCENDENTS as a guiding influence, the original L.A. ne'er do wells were persuaded to reform in the mid-90's, releasing an album, 'EVERYTHING SUCKS' (1996) and a string of singles for who else but 'Epitaph'.

Album rating: MILO GOES TO COLLEGE (*6) / BONUS FAT compilation (*5) / I DON'T WANT TO GROW UP (*6) / ENJOY (*5) / ALL (*6) / LIVEAGE (*5) / HALLRAKER (*4) / SOMERY compilation (*7) / EVERYTHING SUCKS (*6) / All: ALLROY SEZ (*6) / ALLROY'S REVENGE (*6) / TRAILBLAZER (*6) / ALLROY SAVES (*6) / BREAKING THINGS (*5) / PUMMEL (*5)

MILO AUCKERMAN – vocals / **FRANK NAVETTA** – guitar / **TONY LOMBARDO** – bass / **BILL STEVENSON** – drums

not iss. A.O.M.

1979. (7") **RIDE THE WILD. / IT'S A HECTIC WORLD** [-]
1980. (7") *<AOM 445>* **UNNATIONAL ANTHEM. / FACELIFT** [-]

not iss. New Alliance

1981. (7"ep) *<NAR 005>* **FAT EP** [-]
– My dad sucks / Mr. Bass / I like food / Hey hey / Der weinerschnitzel. *(UK-iss.Mar89 on 'S.S.T.' 12"ep/c-ep/cd-ep; SST 212/+C/CD)*

1982. (lp) *<NAR 012>* **MILO GOES TO COLLEGE** [-]
– My age / I wanna be a bear / I'm not a loser / Parents / Tonyage / M 16 / I'm not a punk / Catalina / Suburban home / Statue of liberty / Kabuki girl / Marriage / Hope / Bikage / Jean is dead. *(re-iss. Nov87 & May93 on 'SST' lp/cd; SST 142/+CD)*

— **RAY COOPER** – guitar; repl. NAVETTA (BILL joined BLACK FLAG and NIG HEIST)

1985. (lp) **I DON'T WANT TO GROW UP** [-]
– Descendents / I don't want to grow up / Pervert / Rockstar / No FB / Can't go back / GCF / My world / Theme / Silly girl / In love this way / Christmas vacation / Good good things / Ace. *(re-iss. Nov87 & Nov90 on 'SST' lp/c/cd; SST 143/+C/CD)*

1985. (m-lp) **BONUS FAT** (compilation) [-]
– My dad sucks / Mr. Bass / I like food / Hey hey / Wienerschnitzel / Global probing / Ride the wild / It's a hectic world. *(re-iss. Nov87 on 'SST' lp/cd; SST 144/+CD) (cd re-iss. May93; same)*

— **DOUG CARRION** – bass (ex-ANTI, ex-INCEST CATTLE) repl. LOMBARDO

1986. (m-lp) **ENJOY** [-]
– Enjoy / Floater / 50-50 / Sausage / Barnacle / Loaf / Carbunkle / Choda / Half pipe / Cable service / Lockout. *(re-iss. Sep90 on 'SST' lp/c/cd; SST 242/+C/CD)*

S.S.T. S.S.T.

Jun 87. (lp/c/cd) *<(SST 112/+C/CD)>* **ALL**
– All / Coolidge / No all / Van / Carneage / Impressions / Iceman / Uranus / Jealous of the world / Clean sheets / Pep talk / All-o-gistics / Schizophrenia. *(cd re-iss. May93; same)*

Feb 88. (lp/c/cd) *<(SST 163/+C/CD)>* **LIVEAGE (live)**
– All / I'm not a loser / Silly girl / I wanna be a bear / Coolidge / Wienerschnitzel / I don't want to grow up / Kids / Wendy / Get the time / Descendents / Sour grapes / All-o-gistics / My age / My dad sucks / Van / Suburban home / Hope / Clean sheets / Pervert.

— **DAVE SMALLEY** – vocals (ex-DYS, ex-DAG NASTY) repl. MILO

Feb 89. (lp/c/cd) *<(SST 205/+C/CD)>* **HALLRAKER (live)**
– Global probing / My world / Hurtin' crue / Hey hey / Kabuki girl – All / Pep talk / Jealous of the world / Christmas vacation / I like food / Iceman / Good good things / Cheer / Rockstar / No FB / Cameage. *(re-iss. May93 cd/c; SST 205 CD/C)*

- compilations, etc. -

Nov 87. (lp/c/cd) *S.S.T.; <(SST 145/+C/CD)>* **TWO THINGS AT ONCE** – (MILO GOES TO COLLEGE / BONUS FAT)

Sep 90. (d-lp/c/cd) *S.S.T.; <(SST 259/+C/CD)>* **SOMERY**
(re-iss. May93 & Sep95; same)

ALL

— had already been formed by **BILL STEVENSON** – drums / **DAVE SMALLEY** – vocals / **KARL ALVEREZ** – bass / **STEPHEN EGERTON** – guitar

Cruz Cruz-SST

Jan 88. (lp/c/cd) *<(CRZ 001/+CA/CD)>* **ALLROY SEZ . . .**
– Pretty little girl / Hooidge / Sex in the way / Alfredo's / Sugar and spice / Allthymn / Just perfect / Paper tiger / Auto wreck / A muse / Don Quixote. *(UK-iss.Jan90; same) (re-iss. Sep95; same)*

— **SCOTT REYNOLDS** – vocals; repl. SMALLEY

Jan 90. (12"ep/c-ep/cd-ep) *<(CRZ 004/+C/CD)>* **ALLROY FOR PREZ** 1988
– Just perfect / Skin deep / Wrong again / I hate to love / Wishing well / Son-o-qua / Postage / Daveage.

Jan 90. (7") *(CRZ 005/+C)* **SHE'S MY EX. / CRAZY?** 1989
(re-iss. 10"ep; CRZ 703) (re-iss. Jun96; same)

Jan 90. (lp/c/cd) *<(CRZ 006/+C/CD)>* **ALLROY'S REVENGE** 1989
– Gnutheme / Fool / Check / Scary sad / Man-o-steel / Box / Copping Z / Hot rod Lincoln / She's my ex / Bubblegum / Mary / Net / No traffic / Carnage.

Jun 90. (lp/c/cd) *<(CRZ 010/+C/CD)>* **TRAILBLAZER (live)**
– Carnage / Fool / Box / Skin deep / Just perfect / Postage / Copping Z / She's my ex / Man-o-steel / Paper tiger / Sex in the way / Check one / Hate to love / Gnutheme.

Oct 90. (lp/c/cd) *<(CRZ 011/+C/CD)>* **ALLROY SAVES**
– Educated idiot / Just like them / Prison / Just living / Freaky / Frog / Simple things / Cyclops / Ratchet / Sum / Crawdad / Explorator.

May 93. (lp/c/cd; as TONYALL) *<(CRZ 016/+C/CD)>* **NEW GIRL, OLD STORY** 1992

— above added **TONY LOMBARDO** – bass (ex-DESCENDENTS)

May 93. (12"ep/c-ep/cd-ep) *<(CRZ 022/+C/CD)>* **PERCOLATOR** May92
– Charligan / Nothin' / Dot / Nobody's / Wonder / Minute / Birds / Empty / Mo. 63 / Egg timer / Gnugear (hot) / Hotplate / Hey bug / Breathe. *(re-iss. Sep95; same)*

May 93. (12"ep/c-ep/cd-ep) *<(CRZ 024/+C/CD)>* **DOT. / A BOY NAMED SUE / CAN'T SAY** 1992

Aug 93. (10"ep/cd-ep) *<(CRZ 030/+CD)>* **SHREEN. / ORIGINAL ME / CRUCIFIED**

Sep 93. (lp/c/cd) *<(CRZ 031/+C/CD)>* **BREATHING THINGS**
– Original me / Right / Shreen / 'Cause / Bail / Excuses / Strip bar / Horizontal / Guilty / Birthday I.O.U. / Rosco / Stick / Crucified / Politics.

Feb 94. (10"ep/cd-ep) *<(CRZ 033/+CD)>* **GUILTY. / ALL'S FAIR / MAN'S WORLD**

not iss. Interscope

1995. (cd) *<92528>* **PUMMEL** [-]
– Self-righteous / Million bucks / Uncle critic / Miranda / Not easy / Long distance / Stalker / Button it / This world / Gettin' there / Breakin' up / On foot / Broken / Hetero / Black sky.

Epitaph Epitaph

May 98. (cd/c/lp) *<(6531-2/-4/-1)>* **MASS NERDER**
– World's on heroin / I'll get there / Life on the road / Fairweather friend / Perfection / Greedy / Until I say so / Think the world / Honey peeps / Refrain / Silly me / Romantic junkie / Vida blue / Until then / Good as my word / Silence.

DESCENDENTS

— re-formed **STEVENSON, LOMBARDO** / + **KARL ALVAREZ** – bass / **BILL STEVENSON** – drums, co-producer

Epitaph Epitaph

Sep 96. (cd/c/lp) *<(6481-2/-4/-1)>* **EVERYTHING SUCKS**
– Everything sux / I'm the one / Coffee mug / Rotting out / Sick-o-me / Caught / When I get old / Doghouse / She loves me / Hateful notebook / We / Eunuch boy / This place / I won't let me / Thank you.

Jan 97. (7"colrd-ep/cd-ep) *(6490-7/-2)* **I'M THE ONE / EVERYTHING SUX. / LUCKY / SHATTERED MILO**

Jun 97. (7"ep/cd-ep) *(6506-7/-2)* **WHEN I GET OLD. / GOTTA / SICK-O-ME** [-]

Sessions unknown

Jun 97. (7") *(7SMS 12)* **GRAND THEME. / GOTTA**

DESPERATE BICYCLES

Formed: New Cross, London, England . . . March 1977 by DANNY WIGLEY (a man who later bravely attempted to rehabilitate the Rolf Harris-endorsed stylophone!), along with NICKY STEPHENS, ROGER STEPHENS and

DAVE PAPWORTH. In a similar makeshift DIY-punk mould to the SWELL MAPS or SPIZZ, The DESPERATE BICYCLES released a handful of 45's throughout '77 and '78 on their own 'Refill' imprint. All limited edition affairs, the likes of 'SMOKESCREEN', 'THE MEDIUM WAS TEDIUM', the 'NEW CROSS NEW CROSS' EP and 'OCCUPIED TERRITORY' were successful without ever raising them above cult status. By the release of their debut album, 'REMORSE CODE' (1980), DANNY and NICKY were the only remaining members from the original line-up, DAN ELECTRO and JEFF TITLEY having replaced the rhythm section; after one final single, 'GRIEF IS VERY PERSONAL', WIGLEY and Co got on their bikes for good.

Album rating: REMORSE CODE (*6)

DANNY WIGLEY – vocals (later added stylophone!) / **NICKY STEPHENS** – organ / **ROGER STEPHENS** – bass / **DAVE PAPWORTH** – drums

Refill / not iss.

Aug 77. (7") *(RR 1)* **SMOKESCREEN. / HANDLEBARS** ☐ -

Feb 78. (7") *(RR 2)* **THE MEDIUM WAS TEDIUM. / DON'T BACK THE FRONT** ☐ -

May 78. (7"ep) *(RR 3)* **NEW CROSS NEW CROSS** ☐ -
– Holidays / The housewife song / Cars / (I make the) Product / Paradise lost / Advice on arrest.

Jul 78. (7") *(RR 4)* **OCCUPIED TERRITORY. / SKILL** ☐ -

— **DANNY + NICKY** (now on bass) recruited **DAN ELECTRO** – guitar / **JEFF TITLEY** – drums

Feb 80. (lp) *(RR 6)* **REMORSE CODE** ☐ -
– I am nine / Walking the talking channel / A can of lemonade / Pretty little analyse / Acting / It's somebody's birthday today / Sarcasm / Trendy feelings / Natural history / Blasting radio.

Mar 80. (7") *(RR 7)* **GRIEF IS VERY PERSONAL. / OBSTRUCTION / CONUNDRUM** ☐ -

— disbanded after above

DESTROY ALL MONSTERS

Formed: Detroit, Michigan, USA . . . 1973 by former model and visual artist NIAGARA, who was to be joined by veterans of the garage-punk era MIKE DAVIS (ex-MC5) and RON ASHETON (ex-STOOGES). In 1977, they played a handful of experimental gigs by which time the line-up had expanded to include LARRY and BEN MILLER. The following year, DESTROY ALL MONSTERS released a debut single, 'BORED', a record licensed to UK indie label, 'Cherry Red'. Punk-ish rock'n'roll characterised by NIAGARA's sexual monotone, the band's sound was developed over a further couple of singles, namely 'MEET THE CREEPER' and 'NOBODY KNOWS'. A disappointing tour of Britain led to them disbanding a year later, although two further US-only EP's did surface around the turn of the decade.

Album rating: BORED compilation (*7)

NIAGARA (b. LYNN ROVNER) – vocals, violin / **RON ASHETON** – guitar (ex-STOOGES) repl. CARY LOREN / **LARRY MILLER** – guitar repl. MIKE KELLY / **MIKE DAVIS** – bass (ex-MC5) / **RON KING** – drums repl. JIM SHAW / **BEN MILLER** – saxophone

Cherry Red / Idibi

Jan 79. (7"red) *(CHERRY 3)* **BORED. / YOU'RE GONNA DIE** ☐ ☐ 1978

Jun 79. (7") *(CHERRY 7)* **MEET THE CREEPER. / NOVEMBER 22nd, 1963** ☐ ☐ 1978

Sep 79. (7") *(CHERRY 9)* **NOBODY KNOWS. / WHAT DO I GET** ☐ -

not iss. / Black Hole

1979. (7"ep) *<18551>* **LIVE (live)** - ☐
– Assassination photograph / Dream snug / Destroy all monsters / There is no end.

1980. (7"ep) **BLACK OUT IN THE CITY** - ☐
– No change / Switch the topic / Time bomb 1977.

— disbanded; ASHETON formed NEW RACE

- compilations, etc. -

1989. (lp) *Fan Club; (FC 050)* **LIVE (live)** ☐ -
– Anyone can fuck her / Bored / Party girl / Fast city / Go away / Having it all / Boots / Little boyfriend / November 22nd, 1963 / Right stuff / Ground zero.

1989. (cd) *Revenge; (MIG 11)* **NOVEMBER 22nd, 1963 - SINGLES AND RARITIES** ☐ -
– Bored / You're gonna die / Meet the creeper / November 22nd, 1963 / Jesus is a shotgun / Nobody knows / What do I get / These boots are made for walking / Anybody can / Party girl / A/D (angel in the daytime, Devil at night.

Oct 91. (cd) *Cherry Red; (CDMRED 94)* **BORED** ☐ -
– Bored / You're gonna die / November 22nd 1963 / Meet the creeper / Nobody knows / What do I get? / Goin' to lose. *(re-iss. Apr97; same)*

Oct 96. (cd) *Sympathy For The Record Industry; (SFTRI 444)* **SILVER WEDDING** ☐ -

Apr 98. (lp) *Get Back; (GET 31LP)* **AMAZING . . .** ☐ -

DESTRUCTORS

Formed: Peterborough, England . . . 1977 by ALAN ADAMS and PHIL ATTERSON, although they soon adopted The BLANKS moniker upon entering the studio. Notorious for their controversial one and only single, 'THE NORTHERN RIPPER' (released at the same time as the Yorkshire Ripper was on the loose), the punk outfit later resurrected The DESTRUCTORS name. However, it would be only singer turned bass player, ADAMS, who would remain in the line-up, ATTERSON departing after the recruitment of frontman NEIL SINGLETON, DAVE ITHERMEE (who replaced ANDY JACKSON and GRAHAM BUTTS. Well-meaning but cliched political punk, The DESTRUCTORS sound was first heard on the 1982 EP, 'SENSELESS VIOLENCE'. A series of anti-everything EP's were released at regular intervals, culminating in the debut long-player, 'BOMB HANOI, BOMB SAIGON, BOMB DISNEYLAND' (1984).

Album rating: BOMB HANOI, BOMB SAIGON, BOMB DISNEYLAND (*3)

BLANKS

ALAN ADAMS – vocals / **PHIL ATTERSON** – guitar / **ANDY JACKSON** – rhythm guitar, bass; repl. DIP / **ANDY BUTLER** – drums

Void / not iss.

1979. (7") *(SRTS 79-CUS-560)* **THE NORTHERN RIPPER. / UNDERSTAND / BREAK DOWN** ☐ -

DESTRUCTORS

— **ALAN ADAMS** – (now) bass / **NEIL SINGLETON** – vocals / **ANDY McDONALD** – drums / **DAVE ITHERMEE** – rhythm guitar; repl. JACKSON / **GRAHAM BUTTS** – lead guitar; repl. DAVE (diff.)

Paperback / not iss.

Apr 82. (7"ep) *(BOOK 2)* **SENSELESS VIOLENCE EP** ☐ -
– Meaningless names / AK 47 / Police state / Dachau / Death squad.

Carnage / not iss.

Jul 82. (7"ep) *(KILL 2)* **RELIGION THERE IS NO RELIGION EP** ☐ -
– Religion / Soldier boy / Agent orange / Corpse gas.

Illuminated / not iss.

Oct 82. (7"ep) *(ILL 14)* **JAILBAIT EP** ☐ -
– Jailbait / Kalgsnocov / Sewage worker / Image.

Apr 83. (7"ep) *(ILL 19)* **FORCES OF LAW EP** ☐ -
– Forces of law / Wild thing / Neutron bomb.

Criminal Damage / not iss.

Nov 83. (12"ep) *(CRI12 104)* **CRY HAVOC AND UNLEASH THE DOGS** ☐ -

Feb 84. (7"ep; as DESTRUCTORS V) *(CRI 108)* **TV EYE** ☐ -
– TV eye / The fatal kiss / Love like glass.

Carnage Benelux / not iss.

Aug 84. (lp) *(KILL 666)* **BOMB HANOI, BOMB SAIGON, BOMB DISNEYLAND** ☐ -
– Northern Ripper / Orders / Class war / Breakdown / Overdose / Jailbait / Cocieties morons / Superstars / Control / Prostitute / Son of Sam / Hillside strangler / Sewage worker / Born too late / Urban terrorist / Deathsquad 2 / Out of control / Modern medicine.

— split in 1984

- compilations, etc. -

1980's. (lp) *Radical Change; (RCLP 2)* **ARMAGEDDON IN ACTION** ☐ -
– Soldier boy / AK 47 / Neutron bomb / Bullshit / European sacrifice / Urban terrorist / Forces of law / Duty unto death / Electronic church / Khmer rouge boogie / Nerve gas / Death squad / Wild thing / Northern ripper / Dachau.

dEUS

Formed: Antwerp, Belgium . . . 1991 by TOM BARMAN alongside RUDY TROUVE, KLAUS JANZOONS, JULLE DE BORGHER and STEF CARLENS. Beginning life as a VIOLENT FEMMES / VELVET UNDERGROUND covers outfit, this experimental art-rock collective were picked up by 'Island' in 1994, initially making an impact via their appearance at that year's Glastonbury festival. A UK debut single, 'SUDS AND SODA' (they had issued 'ZEA' in Belgium), was closely followed by 'VIA', TOM WAITS and CAPTAIN BEEFHEART being the most commonly cited reference points – in fact the latter's right hand man, ERIC DREW FELDMAN produced them. Open-ended in the established tradition of late 60's/early 70's Euro-rock yet pregnant with the potential to be as abrasive as early BIG BLACK or even BLACK FLAG, dEUS' avant-garde pop polarised opinion; you either loved it or hated it. Certainly more challenging than many of the identikit grunge albums doing the rounds at the time, 'WORST CASE SCENARIO' (1994) focused the band's wayward muse into a listenable whole; it also proved that there was more to Belgian music than plastic Europap passed off as "techno". dEUS released a follow-up set, 'IN A BAR, UNDER THE SEA' (1996), an album that contained their only Top 50 single to date, 'LITTLE ARITHMETICS'. • **Songwriters:** Group (BARMAN (words) / CARLENS some with SERGEY) or (TROUVE + JANZOONS with VERMEERSCH + VERVLOESEM) except a sample of FRANK ZAPPA on their 1994 album. In 1996, BARMAN, CARLENS and WARD became the writers.

Album rating: MY SISTER IS MY CLOCK (*6) / WORST CASE SCENARIO (*8) / IN A BAR, UNDER THE SEA (*7)

TOM BARMAN – vocals / **KLAUS JANZOONS** – violin / **RUDY TROUVE** – guitar / **JULLE DE BORGHER** – drums / **STEF KAMIL CARLENS** – bass

own label / not iss.

1993. (cd-ep) **ZEA EP** - - Belgian

Island / Polygram

Jul 94. (7") *(IS 598)* **SUDS AND SODA. / SECRET HELL** ☐ -
(12"+=/cd-s+=) *(12IS/CID 598)* – Texan coffee / It. furniture in the far west.

Sep 94. (7") *(IS 599)* **VIA. / VIOLINS AND HAPPY ENDINGS** ☐ -
(12"+=/cd-s+=) *(12IS/CID 599)* – Great American nude (strip mix) / Niche.

Oct 94. (cd/c/lp) *(CID/ICT/ILPS 8028) <524045>* **WORST CASE SCENARIO** ☐ ☐ Feb95
– Intro / Suds and soda / W.C.S. / Jigsaw you / Morticiahair / Via / Right as rain /

Mute / Let's get lost / Hotel lounge (be the death of me) / Shake you up / Great American nude / Secret hell / Dive bomb djingle.

Jan 95. (c-s/7") *(C+/IS 603)* **HOTEL LOUNGE (BE THE DEATH OF ME). / JIGSAW YOU (live)** [55] [-]
(cd-s+=/cd-s+=) *(CID/+X 603)* – Whose Vegas (is it anyway).

Jan 95. (cd) *(IMCD 8031)* **MY SISTER IS MY CLOCK** [-] [-] mail-o
– Middlewave / Almost white / Health insurance / Little ghost / How to row a cat / Only a colour to her / Sick sugar / Sweetness / Horror party jokes / Void / Sans titre pour sira / Glovesong / Lorre in the forest.

—— **CRAIG WARD** (b. Scotland) – guitar repl. TROUVE who formed KISS MY JAZZ

Jul 96. (7"/10") *(IS/10IS 630)* **THEME FROM TURNPIKE. / OVERFLOW / MY LITTLE CONTESSA** [68] [ ]
(cd-s+=) *(CID 630)* – Worried about Satan.

Oct 96. (c-s/7"pic-d) *(C+/IS 643)* **LITTLE ARITHMETICS. / MY WIFE JAN** [44] [-]
(cd-s+=) *(CID 643-854 719-2)* – The tugboat / Everything is the same (except no one believes me).

Nov 96. (cd/c/lp) *(CID/ICT/ILPS 8052) <524296>* **IN A BAR, UNDER THE SEA** [ ] [ ] Mar97
– I don't mind whatever happens / Fell off the floor, man / Opening night / Theme from Turnpike / Little arithmetics / Gimme the heat / Serpentine / Shocking lack thereof / Supermarketsong / Memory of a festival / Guilty pleasures / Nine threads / Disappointed in the sun / Roses / Wake me up before I sleep.

Mar 97. (7"pic-d) *(IS 645)* **ROSES. / I SUFFER ROCK** [56] [-]
(cd-s+=) *(CID 645)* – Nine threads (demo) / Difficult day
(cd-s) *(CIDX 645)* – ('A'-Vermeersch version) / Via (live) / Hotel lounge (be the death of me) (live) / Jigsaw you (live).

Sep 97. (c-s/7"pic-d) *(C+/IS 663)* **LITTLE ARITHMETICS. / FELL OFF THE FLOOR, MAN (Dust Brothers edit)** [ ] [-]
(cd-s+=) *(CID 663)* – Me & your mother / Disappointed in the sun.

DEUTSCHE AMERIKANISCHE FREUNDSCHAFT (see under ⇒ D.A.F.)

Willy DeVILLE (see under ⇒ MINK DeVILLE)

DEVINE & STATTON (see under ⇒ LUDUS)

DEVO

Formed: Akron, Ohio, USA . . . 1972 by two sets of brothers, MARK and BOB MOTHERSBAUGH together with GERALD and BOB CASALE (drummer, ALAN MYERS completed the line-up). From the early 70's, they had been known as The DE-EVOLUTION BAND, before sensibly abbreviating the name to DEVO. This bunch of lab-coated weirdos (taking up The RESIDENTS terminally skewed vision) issued two obscure 45's on their own indie label, 'Booji Boy', which were heavily imported into Britain through leading indie outlet, 'Stiff,' late in 1977. Early the following year, both the double A-sided 'MONGOLOID' / 'JOCKO HOMO' and a hilarious electro-fied rendition of The Rolling Stones' '(I CAN'T GET NO) SATISFACTION', were repressed due to popular demand, the singles subsequently becoming minor chart entries. After a third classic, 'BE STIFF' also hit UK Top 75, the flowerpot-headed, potato-faced futurists secured a deal with 'Virgin' ('Warners' in the US) and continued to inject a quirky humour into the po-faced New Wave movement with a fourth hit, 'COME BACK JONEE'. A debut album, inspiringly titled 'Q: ARE WE NOT MEN? A: WE ARE DEVO!' (produced by BRIAN ENO, who else!?), was released a month later to a confused but appreciative audience who helped propel the record into the Top 20 (Top 100 US). However, their follow-up set, 'DUTY NOW FOR THE FUTURE' (1979), suffered a slight backlash, the novelty wearing thin without the impact of a hit single. 1980's 'FREEDOM OF CHOICE' would have suffered a similar fate, but for a freak US Top 20 single, 'WHIP IT'. The rest of their 80's output lacked their early wit, although America embraced such albums as 'DEV-O LIVE' (1981), 'NEW TRADITIONALISTS' (1981), 'OH NO, IT'S DEVO' (1982) and 'SHOUT' (1984). Having disbanded in the middle of the decade, DEVO (with new drummer, DAVID KENDRICK) reformed in 1988, signing to 'Enigma' and releasing one non-event of an album after another. Their days of inspired innovation now behind them, the legacy of DEVO was nevertheless plundered to unusual effect when SOUNDGARDEN, SUPERCHUNK and even ROBERT PALMER!!! covered their 1980 classic, 'GIRL U WANT'. • **Songwriters:** GERALD and MARK wrote most of material, SECRET AGENT MAN (Johnny Rivers) / ARE U EXPERIENCED (Jimi Hendrix) / WORKING IN A COALMINE (Lee Dorsey). • **Trivia:** In 1982, DEVO had contributed services to choreographer TONI BASIL on her debut solo album 'WORD OF MOUTH'. In the late 70's, MARK had appeared on HUGH CORNWALL (of The STRANGLERS) and ROBERT WILLIAMS collaboration 'Nosferatu'.

Album rating: Q: ARE WE NOT MEN? A: WE ARE DEVO! (*8) / DUTY NOW FOR THE FUTURE (*7) / FREEDOM OF CHOICE (*7) / DEV-O LIVE mini (*2) / NEW TRADITIONALISTS (*6) / OH NO! IT'S DEVO (*6) / SHOUT (*4) / E-Z LISTENING DISC collection (*4) / TOTAL DEVO (*4) / NOW IT CAN BE TOLD (DEVO AT THE PALACE 12/9/88) live (*5) / SMOOTH NOODLE MAPS (*4) / HARDCORE DEVO, VOL.1 compilation (*6) / THE GREATEST HITS compilation (*7) / HARDCORE DEVO, VOL.2 compilation (*5) / DEVO LIVE: THE MONGOLOID YEARS compilation (*4) / HOT POTATOES: THE BEST OF DEVO compilation (*8)

BOB MOTHERSBAUGH – vocals, guitar / **MARK MOTHERSBAUGH** – keyboards, synthesizers / **BOB CASALE** – guitar / **JERRY CASALE** – bass, vocals / **ALAN MYERS** – drums repl. JIM MOTHERSBAUGH

Stiff / Booji Boy

Feb 78. (7") *(DEV 1) <7033-14>* **MONGOLOID. / JOCKO HOMO** [62] [ ] 1977

Apr 78. (7")(12") *(DEV 2)(BOY 1)* **(I CAN'T GET ME NO) SATISFACTION. / SLOPPY (I SAW MY BABY GETTING)** [41] [ ] 1977
<re-iss. 1978 on 'Bomp'; 72843>

Stiff / not iss.

Jul 78. (7"clear,7"lemon) *(BOY 2)* **BE STIFF. / SOCIAL FOOLS** [71] [-]

Virgin / Warners

Aug 78. (7"grey) *(VS 223)* **COME BACK JONEE. / SOCIAL FOOLS** [60] [-]

Sep 78. (lp/c) *(V/TCV 2106) <3239>* **Q: ARE WE NOT MEN? A: WE ARE DEVO!** [12] [78]
– Uncontrollable urge / (I can't get no) Satisfaction / Praying hands / Space junk / Mongoloid / Jocko homo / Too much paranoias / Gut feeling – (slap your mammy) / Come back Jonee / Sloppy (I saw my baby getting) / Shrivel-up. *(w/free flexi-7"; VDJ 27) (pic-lp; VP 2106) (re-iss. Mar84 lp/c; OVED/+C 37)*

Jan 79. (7") *<WB 8745>* **COME BACK JONEE. / PRAYING HANDS** [-] [ ]

Jun 79. (7") *(VS 265)* **THE DAY MY BABY GAVE ME A SURPRIZE. / PENETRATION IN THE CENTREFOLD** [ ] [-]

Jun 79. (lp/c) *(V/TCV 2125) <3337>* **DUTY NOW FOR THE FUTURE** [49] [73]
– Devo corporate anthem / Clockout / Timing X / Wiggly world / Blockhead / Strange pursuit / S.I.B. (Swelling Itching Brain) / Triumph of the will / The day my baby gave me a surprize / Pink pussycat / Secret agent man / Smart patrol – Mr. DNA / Red eye. *(re-iss. Mar84 lp/c; OVED/+C 38)*

Jul 79. (7") *<WBS 49028>* **SECRET AGENT MAN. / RED EYE EXPRESS** [-] [ ]

Aug 79. (7") *(VS 280)* **SECRET AGENT MAN. / SOO BAWLS** [ ] [-]

May 80. (7") *(VS 350)* **GIRL U WANT. / TURN AROUND** [ ] [-]

May 80. (lp/c) *(V/TCV 2162) <3435>* **FREEDOM OF CHOICE** [47] [22]
– Girl u want / It's not right / Whip it / Snowball / Ton o' luv / Freedom of choice / Gates of steel / Cold war / Don't you know / That's Pep! / Mr. B's ballroom / Planet Earth. *(re-iss. Mar84 lp/c; OVED/+C 39)*

Jul 80. (7") *<WBS 49524>* **GIRL U WANT. / MR. B'S BALLROOM** [-] [ ]

Aug 80. (7") *<WBS 49550>* **WHIP IT. / TURN AROUND** [-] [14]

Nov 80. (7") *(VS 383)* **WHIP IT. / SNOWBALL** [51] [-]
(12"+=) *(VS 383-12)* – Gates of steel.

Nov 80. (7") *<WBS 49621>* **FREEDOM OF CHOICE. / SNOWBALL** [-] [ ]

Mar 81. (7") *<WBS 49711>* **GATES OF STEEL. / BE STIFF (live)** [-] [ ]

May 81. (m-lp/m-c) *(OVED 1) <3548>* **DEV-O LIVE (live)** [ ] [49] Apr81
– Freedom of choice (theme song) / Whip it / Girl u want / Gates of steel / Be stiff / Planet Earth.

Jun 81. (7") *<WBS >* **THROUGH BEING COOL. / GOING UNDER** [-] [ ]

Aug 81. (7") *(VS 450)* **THROUGH BEING COOL. / RACE OF DOOM** [ ] [-]

Aug 81. (lp/c) *(V/TCV 2191) <3595>* **NEW TRADITIONALISTS** [50] [24]
– Through being cool / Jerkin' back 'n' forth / Pity you / Soft things / Going under / Race of doom / Love without anger / The super thing / Beautiful world / Enough said. *(re-iss. Aug87 lp/c; OVED/+C 73)*

Aug 81. (7") *<WBS 47204>* **WORKING IN A COALMINE. / PLANET EARTH** [-] [ ]
<above issued on 'Full Moon' US>

Oct 81. (7") *(VS 457)* **WORKING IN A COALMINE. / ENOUGH SAID** [ ] [-]

Oct 81. (7") *<WBS 49834>* **BEAUTIFUL WORLD. / ENOUGH SAID** [-] [ ]

Jan 82. (7") *(VS 470)* **BEAUTIFUL WORLD. / THE SUPER THING** [ ] [-]

Mar 82. (7") *<WBS 50010>* **JERKIN' BACK 'N' FORTH. / MECHA MANIA BOY** [-] [ ]

Oct 82. (7")<US-7"/12"> *(VS 536) <WBS 29931/29906>* **PEEK-A-BOO. / FIND OUT** [ ] [ ]

Oct 82. (lp/c) *(V/TCV 2241) <23741>* **OH NO! IT'S DEVO!** [ ] [47]
– Time out for fun / Peek-a-boo / Out of synch / Explosions / That's good / Patterns / Big mess / Speed racer / What I must do / I desire / Deep sleep. *(re-iss. Aug88 lp/c; OVED/+C 122)*

Jan 83. (7") *<WBS 29811>* **THAT'S GOOD. / WHAT MUST I DO** [-] [ ]

Jun 83. (7"/12") *(MCA/+T 822) <52215>* **THEME FROM DOCTOR DETROIT. / (track by James Brown)** [ ] [59] May83
(above issued on 'M.C.A.' UK / 'Backstreet' US>

Warners / Warners

Oct 84. (7") *<29133>* **ARE YOU EXPERIENCED?. / GROWING PAINS** [-] [ ]

Oct 84. (lp/c) *(925 097-1/-4) <25097>* **SHOUT!** [ ] [83]
– Shout / The satisfied mind / Don't rescue me / The 4th dimension / C'mon / Here to go / Jurisdiction of love / Puppet boy / Please please / Are you experienced?

Mar 85. (7") *(W 9119)* **SHOUT. / C'MON** [ ] [-]
(d7"+=) *(W 9119F)* – Mongoloid / Jocko homo.

—— **DAVID KENDRICK** – drums; repl. MYERS

Enigma / Enigma

Jul 88. (lp/c/cd) *(ENVLP/TCENV/CDENV 503) <73303>* **TOTAL DEVO** [ ] [ ] Jun88
– Baby doll / Disco dancer / Some things never change / Plain truth / Happy guy / Don't be cruel / I'd cry if you died / Agitated / Man turned inside out / Blow up. *(cd re-iss. Mar95 on 'Restless'; 72756-2)*

Jul 89. (3 sided-lp/cd) *(ENVLP/CDENV 532)* **NOW IT CAN BE TOLD (DEVO AT THE PALACE 12/9/88) (live)** [ ] [ ]
(cd re-iss. Mar95 on 'Restless';)

Oct 90. (7") **POST-POST MODERN MAN. / WHIP IT (live)** [ ] [ ]
(12"+=) – ('A'-Ultra post mix).
(cd-s++=) – Baby doll (mix).

Oct 90. (cd/c/lp) *(CDENV/TVENV/ENVLP 1006) <73526>* **SMOOTH NOODLE MAPS** [ ] [ ] Jun90
– Stuck in a loop / Post-post modern man / When we do it / Spin the wheel / Morning dew / A chance is gonna cum / The big picture / Pink jazz trancers / Devo has feelings too / Jimmy / Danghaus. *(re-iss. cd Mar95 on 'Restless'; 72757-2)*

– compilations, etc. –

Jan 79. (m-lp) *Stiff; (ODD 1)* **BE STIFF** (first 3 singles) [ ] [-]

May 83. (12"ep) *Virgin; (VS 594-12)* **COME BACK JONEE. / WHIP IT / + 2** [ ] [-]

Aug 87. (cd) *Warners;* **E-Z LISTENING DISC** [-] [ ]
(UK-iss.Nov91 on 'Rykodisc'; RACD 0031)

Oct 90. (cd) *Fan Club; / Rykodisc; <RCD/RLP 10188>* **HARDCORE DEVO, VOL.1** (demos 74-77) [ ] [ ] Aug90

(re-iss. c Mar94 on 'New Rose'; 422105)

Dec 90. (cd) *Warners;* **THE GREATEST HITS** [-] [ ]

Dec 90. (cd) *Warners;* **THE REST: GREATEST MISSES** [-] [ ]

Dec 91. (cd) *Rykodisc; <(RCD 20208)>* **HARDCORE DEVO, VOL.2: 1974-1977** [ ] [ ] Aug91
(re-iss. c Mar94; RACS 0208)

Oct 92. (cd) *Rykodisc; <(RCD 20209)>* **DEVO LIVE: THE MONGOLOID YEARS (live)** [ ] [ ]

Jun 93. (cd) *Virgin; (CDV 2106)* **Q: ARE WE NOT MEN? A: WE ARE DEVO / DEV-O LIVE** [ ] [ ]

Jun 93. (cd) *Virgin; (CDV 2125)* **DUTY NOW FOR THE FUTURE / NEW TRADITIONALISTS** [ ] [ ]

Jun 93. (cd) *Virgin; (CDV 2241)* **OH NO! IT'S DEVO / FREEDOM OF CHOICE** [ ] [ ]

Sep 93. (cd/c) *Virgin; (CDVM/TCVM 9016)* **HOT POTATOES: THE BEST OF DEVO** [ ] [ ]
– Jocko homo / Mongoloid / Satisfaction (I can't get me no) / Whip it / Girl u want / Freedom of choice / Peek-a-boo / Thru being cool / That's good / Working in a coalmine / Devo corporate anthem / Be stiff / Gates of steel / Come back Jonee / Secret agent man / The day my baby gave me a surprise / Beautiful world / Big mess / Whip it (HMS & M remix).

Oct 94. (3xcd-box) *Virgin; (TPAK 38)* **THE COMPACT COLLECTION** [ ] [ ]
– (Q: ARE WE NOT MEN / DUTY NOW FOR THE FUTURE / OH NO IT'S DEVO!)

Aug 96. (cd-rom) *Discovery;* **ADVENTURES OF SMART PATROL** [-] [ ]

Howard DEVOTO (see under ⇒ MAGAZINE)

DHARMA BUMS

Formed: Portland, Oregon, USA . . . 1987 by JEREMY WILSON, ERIC LOVRE, JIM TALSTRA and JOHN MOEN. Yet another band to have been influenced by the colourful Paisley underground scene of the early 80's (RAIN PARADE, DREAM SYNDICATE, etc), The DHARMA BUMS (named after a Jack Kerouac book) signed to established US indie retro label, 'Frontier', releasing debut album 'HAYWIRE' around the start of '89. A follow-up set, 'BLISS' (1991), fared better critically although that didn't prevent them from splitting after a final lp offering, 'WELCOME' (1992). • **Note:** Watch out for a similarly named dance band who released EP's for 'B.M.G.'.

Album rating: HAYWIRE (*4) / BLISS (*6) / WELCOME (*4)

JEREMY WILSON (b. 1969) – vocals / **ERIC LOVRE** – guitar, vocals / **JOHN MOEN** – drums, vocals / **JIM TALSTRA** – bass

Diabalo Frontier

Mar 89. (lp) *(SORC 5) <4620>* **HAYWIRE** [ ] [ ]
– Timeyard / Boots of leather / Cruel acres / Over the rainbow / Under / Walking stick / Mutiny / Hope of the hour / Jet pilot / Dropping out / Farmyard / Flowers / Haywire.

Frontier Frontier

May 91. (cd/c/lp) *<(4625 2L/4L/1L)>* **BLISS** [ ] [ ]
– Pumpkinhead / Higher / Plunger / Far from gone / 20,000 tears / Stayed up late / Time together / Pigweeds / B-sting / You've see fire / This honourable flame (dues enim rorem) / Gold / A place to be.

Apr 92. (cd/c/lp) *<(34636-2/-4/-1)>* **WELCOME** [ ] [ ] Dec91

May 92. (7") *(34676-7)* **GIVIN' IN. /** [ ] [ ]

—— split some time in 1992

DIAGRAM BROS (see under ⇒ DISLOCATION DANCE)

DICKIES

Formed: San Fernando Valley, California, USA . . . 1977 by CHUCK WAGON, STAN LEE, BILLY CLUB, LEONARD PHILLIPS and KARLOS KABALLERO. Forebears to the likes of GREEN DAY and a poppier prototype of English cover fiends, SNUFF, the DICKIES initially made a name for themselves on the L.A. punk scene through their rabid, tongue-in-cheek versions of rock's sacred cows. Signed to 'A&M', the band's eponymous debut three-tracker surfaced in Spring '78, leading with a frantic reading of Black Sabbath's 'PARANOID'. This was subsequently released as a single in its own right, followed up by a trashing of the Barry McGuire protest classic, 'EVE OF DESTRUCTION'. Christmas '78, meanwhile, saw what else but a rendition of 'SILENT NIGHT', DICKIES style (backed with a none too quiet cover of Simon & Garfunkel's 'SOUNDS OF SILENCE'), a track that gave them an early Top 50 hit. While not featured on debut album, 'THE INCREDIBLE SHRINKING DICKIES' (1979), early '79's version of The Moody Blues' 'NIGHTS IN WHITE SATIN' was a stage favourite and a hit second time around later that year. The DICKIES' defining moment, however, came with their punked-up pilgrimage to classic 70's kids TV, a cover of the theme tune to 'Banana Splits'. A Top 10 UK hit, it cemented the band's reputation as a punk novelty act although the DICKIES' self-penned good-time three-chord anthems won them respect among the safety-pin crew on both sides of the Atlantic. A prolific year came to a close with the release of a follow-up album, 'DAWN OF THE DICKIES', again drawing inspiration from B-movies and assorted American cultural debris. Sadly, CHUCK committed suicide in summer '81, effectively halting the band's career. Although 1983's 'STUKAS OVERT DISNEYLAND' comprised of recordings made before CHUCK's death, the band didn't re-emerge with new material until the late 80's. With a line-up of PHILLIPS, LEE, LORENZO BUNHE, JEROME ANGEL, ENOCH HAIN and CLIFF MARTINEZ, the DICKIES inked a deal with 'Enigma' and released the 'KILLER KLOWNS FROM OUTER SPACE' EP in late '88. An album, 'SECOND COMING', followed in '89, replete with the usual helping of cover versions including Gene Pitney's 'TOWN WITHOUT PITY'. The early 90's saw future SMASHING PUMPKINS keyboard player, JONATHON MELVOIN, come on board while a new deal with L.A.'s 'Triple X' label was inaugurated with 'ROADKILL' (1993). Come 1998, the DICKIES were still chasing their proverbial tail with 'DOGS FROM THE HARE THAT BIT US', basically a covers set ripping into Iron Butterfly's 'UNCONSCIOUS POWER', 'Uriah Heep's 'EASY LIVIN', Beatles' 'THERE'S A PLACE', etc.

Album rating: THE INCREDIBLE SHRINKING DICKIES (*7) / DAWN OF THE DICKIES (*7)/ STUKAS OVER DISNEYLAND (*6) / WE AREN'T THE WORLD (*5) / SECOND COMING (*4) / GREAT DICTATIONS (THE DEFINITIVE DICKIES COLLECTION) compilation (*6) / IDJIT SAVANT (*5) / DOGS FROM THE HARE THAT BIT US (*5)

LEONARD GRAVES PHILLIPS – vocals, keyboards / **STAN LEE** (b.24 Sep'56) – guitar, vocals / **CHUCK WAGON** (b. BOB DAVIS) – keyboards, guitar / **BILLY CLUB** – bass, vocals / **KARLOS KABALLERO** – drums

A&M A&M

May 78. (12"m) *<12-008>* **THE DICKIES** [-] [ ]
– Paranoid / Hideous / You drive me ape (you big gorilla).

Jun 78. (7",7"clear) *(AMS 7368)* **PARANOID. / I'M OK, YOU'RE OK** [ ] [ ]
(re-iss. Jul79; same) – hit UK No.45

Aug 78. (7",7"pink) *(AMS 7373)* **EVE OF DESTRUCTION. / DOGGIE DO** [ ] [-]

Oct 78. (7",7"white) *(AMS 7391)* **GIVE IT BACK. / YOU DRIVE ME APE (YOU BIG GORILLA)** [ ] [-]

Dec 78. (7",7"white) *(AMS 7403)* **SILENT NIGHT. / THE SOUNDS OF SILENCE** [47] [-]

Jan 79. (7") *<2225>* **NIGHTS IN WHITE SATIN. / MANNY, MOE & JACK** [-] [ ]

Feb 79. (lp,yellow-lp,blue-lp,orange-lp) *(AMLE 64742)* **THE INCREDIBLE SHRINKING DICKIES** [ ] [ ]
– Give it back / Poodle party / Paranoid / She / Shadow man / Mental ward / Eve of destruction / You drive me ape (you big gorilla) / Waterslide / Walk like an egg / Curb job / Shake and bake / Rondo.

Apr 79. (7",7"clear) *(AMS 7431)* **BANANA SPLITS (TRA LA LA SONG). / HIDEOUS / GOT IT AT THE STORE** [7] [-]

May 79. (7") *<2241>* **BANANA SPLITS (TRA LA LA SONG). / THE SOUNDS OF SILENCE** [-] [ ]

Jun 79. (7",7"purple; by CHUCK WAGON) *(AMS 7450)* **ROCK'N'ROLL WON'T GO AWAY. / THE SPY IN MY FACE** [ ] [-]

Aug 79. (7"white) *(AMS 7469)* **NIGHTS IN WHITE SATIN. / WATERSLIDE** [39] [ ]

Oct 79. (lp,blue-lp) *(AMLH 68510)* **DAWN OF THE DICKIES** [ ] [ ]
– Where did his eye go / Fan mail / Manny, Moe & Jack / Infedil zombie / I'm a chollo / Nights in white satin / (I'm stuck in a pagoda) With Tricia Toyota / I've got a splitting headache / Attack of the mole men / She loves me not.

Nov 79. (7") *(AMS 7491)* **MANNY, MOE & JACK. / SHE LOVES ME NOT** [ ] [-]

Jan 80. (7"red) *(AMS 7504)* **FAN MAIL. / (I'M STUCK IN A PAGODA) WITH TRICIA TOYOTA** [ ] [-]

Jul 80. (7"yellow) *(AMS 7544)* **GIGANTOR. / BOWLING WITH BEDROCK BARNEY** [ ] [-]

—— CHUCK WAGON committed suicide in June '81 as the band continued in a lower profile (below recordings between 1980-83 with CHUCK)

—— other people used incl. **SCOTT SINDON + STEVE HUFSTETER** – guitar / **LORENZO BUHNE** – bass / **JEROME ANGEL** – drums, percussion

not iss. P.V.C.

1983. (lp) *<6903>* **STUKAS OVER DISNEYLAND** [-] [ ]
– Rosemary / She's a hunch back / Out of sight, out of mind / Communication breakdown / Pretty please me / Wagon train / If Stuart could talk / Stukas over Disneyland. *(UK cd-iss. Jul95 on 'Restless'; 772247-2) (re-iss. Jul98 on 'Overground' 10"lp/cd; OVER 76/+CD)*

—— **PHILLIPS, LEE, ANGEL + BUHNE** plus newcomers **ENOCH HAIN** – guitar / **CLIFF MARTINEZ** – drums

Enigma-Virgin Enigma

Nov 88. (12"ep) *<D2 73322>* **KILLER KLOWNS FROM OUTER SPACE** [-] [ ]
– Killer klowns / Booby trap / Jim Bowie / Magoomba / Eep oop ork (uh uh). *(UK cd-iss. Jul95 on 'Restless'; 772554-2)*

May 89. (lp/c/cd) *(ENVLP/TCENV/CDENV 526) <73289>* **SECOND COMING** [ ] [ ] Feb89
– Hair / Monster island / Town without pity / Cross-eyed Tammy / Going homo / Dummy up / Booby trap / Magoomba / Caligula / I'm Stan / Monkey see, monkey do. *(cd re-iss. Jul95 on 'Restless'; 772553-2)*

Overground unknown

Jul 90. (7"white,7"mauve,7"blue) *(OVER 12)* **JUST SAY YES. / AYATOLLAH YOU SO** [ ] [-]

Oct 90. (7"flexi-tour) *(OVER 17)* **ROADKILL** [ ] [-]

Receiver not iss.

Apr 91. (cd/c/lp) *(RR CD/LC/LP 137)* **LIVE IN LONDON – LOCKED 'N' LOADED 1990 (live)** [ ] [-]
– Attack of the killer clowns from Outer Space / Eve of destruction / Nights in white satin / Pretty please me / You drive me ape (you big gorilla) / Give it back / Just say yes / (Stuck in a pagoda) With Tricia Toyota / Curb job / Cross-eyed Tammy / Going homo / She's a hunch back / If Stuart could talk / Manny, Moe & Jack / Paranoid / Gigantor / Communication breakdown / Banana splits / Fan mail.

—— now with **JONATHAN MELVOIN** – keyboards (of SMASHING PUMPKINS)

Triple X Relativity

May 93. (m-cd) *<(TX 51149CD)>* **ROADKILL** [ ] [ ]

Sep 94. (cd/c) *<(51168-2/-4)>* **IDJIT SAVANT** [ ] [ ] Jan95
– Welcome to the diamond mine / Golden boys / Pretty ballerina / Elevator / Oh baby / Make it so / I'm on crack / I'm stuck in a condo (with Marlon Brando) /

Zeppelina / Roadkill / Just say yes / House of Raoul / Song of the dawn. *(cd re-iss. Mar95 on 'Golf'; CDHOLE 002)*

1995. (7") *(HOLE 008)* **MAKE IT SO. / OH BABY** [ ] [-]
(above issued on 'Golf' records)

Jun 98. (lp/cd) *<(TX 51232/+CD)>* **DOGS FROM THE HARE THAT BIT US** [ ] [ ]
– Intro / Solitary confinement / Easy livin' / Unconscious power / There's a place / Nobody but me / Can't let go / Let me out / Epistle to Dippy.

- compilations, etc. -

Apr 86. (c) *R.O.I.R.; <A 140>* **WE AREN'T THE WORLD (live '78-'85)** [-] [ ]
(cd-iss. Nov94; RE 140CD)

Mar 89. (lp/c/cd) *A&M; (CDA/AMC/AMA 5236)* **GREAT DICTATIONS (THE DEFINITIVE DICKIES COLLECTION)** [ ] [-]
– Hideous / You drive me ape (you big gorilla) / Give it back / Paranoid / I'm ok, you're ok / Got it at the store / The sounds of silence / Banana splits (tra la la song) / Nights in white satin / (Stuck in a pagoda) With Tricia Toyota / Manny, Moe & Jack / Fan mail / Attack of the mole men / Gigantor / Eve of destruction / Silent night.

DICKS (see under ⇒ SISTER DOUBLE HAPPINESS)

DICTATORS

Formed: The Bronx, New York, USA . . . 1974 by ROSS THE BOSS FUNICELLO, MARK "The Animal" MENDOZA, main songwriter ADNY (ANDY) SHERNOFF, SCOTT KEMPNER and STU BOY KING, who were soon joined by "Handsome" DICK MANITOBA. Exploding onto the embryonic NY punk scene at the same time as bands like The RAMONES and The HEARTBREAKERS, the group harnessed the energy of garage-rock to a raucous pre-MOTORHEAD metallic bludgeon. Signed to the 'Epic' label, they nevertheless delivered a rather poorly-received debut album in 1975, 'GO GIRL CRAZY!', which included a few covers including Sonny & Cher's 'I GOT YOU BABE'. 'Asylum' subsequently took up the reins, releasing the much-improved 'MANIFEST DESTINY' (1977), a hard-rocking set that featured their version of Iggy (Pop) & The Stooges' 'SEARCH & DESTROY' (one of the first ever tracks to be released on the 12" format). The single, which also featured new drummer RITCHIE TEETER, surprisingly hit the UK Top 50, although a third album, 'BLOOD BROTHERS' failed to garner any wider support from the evolving punk scene, The DICTATORS also misunderstood by purist metal fans. ROSS THE BOSS and MENDOZA finally found some degree of recognition with MANOWAR and TWISTED SISTER respectively.

Album rating: GO GIRL CRAZY (*7) / MANIFEST DESTINY (*6) / BLOODBROTHERS (*6) / FUCK 'EM IF THEY CAN'T TAKE A JOKE (*6)

'HANDSOME' DICK MANITOBA (b. RICHARD BLUM, 29 Jan'54) – vocals / **ROSS THE BOSS FUNICELLO** (b. 3 Jan'54) – guitar, vocals / **ADNY SHERNOFF** (b. ANDY, 19 Apr'52) – vocals, bass / **SCOTT KEMPNER** (b. 6 Feb'54) – guitar, vocals / **STU BOY KING** – drums, percussion

Epic Epic

Dec 75. (lp) *(EPC 80767) <33348>* **GO GIRL CRAZY!** [ ] [ ]
– The next big thing / I got you babe / Back to Africa / Master race rock / Teengenerate / California sun / Two tub man / Weekend / (I live for) Cars and girls. *(cd-iss. Jul93 on 'Sony Europe';)*

— **RITCHIE TEETER** (b.16 Mar'51, Long Island, N.Y.) – drums repl. STU / added **MARK MENDOZA** (b.13 Jul'56, Long Island) – bass

Asylum Asylum

Jun 77. (7") *<45420>* **DISEASE. / HEY BOYS** [-] [ ]

Jun 77. (lp) *(K 53061) <7E 1109>* **MANIFEST DESTINY** [ ] [ ]
– Exposed / Heartache / Sleepin' with the T.V. on / Disease / Hey boys / Steppin' out / Science gone too far! / Young, fast, scientific / Search & destroy.

Aug 77. (7") *<45470>* **SLEEPIN' WITH THE T.V. ON. / SCIENCE GONE TOO FAR** [-] [ ]

Sep 77. (7"/12") *(K 13091/+T)* **SEARCH & DESTROY. / SLEEPIN' WITH THE T.V. ON** [49] [ ]

— now without MENDOZA who later joined TWISTED SISTER

Aug 78. (lp) *(K 53083) <147>* **BLOODBROTHERS** [ ] [ ]
– Faster & louder / Baby let's twist / No tomorrow / The Minnesota strip / Stay with me / I stand tall / Borneo Jimmy / What is it / Slow death.

Aug 78. (7") *<45523>* **I STAND TALL. / TOO MUCH FUN** [-] [ ]

not iss. PrdTempore

1980. (lp) *<10017>* **DICTATORS** [-] [ ]
– The next big thing / Disease / Hey boys / Two tub man / The moon upstairs / Weekend / New York, New York / I stand tall / Slow death.

— disbanded 1980. ROSS formed SHAKIN' STREET and later MANOWAR. DICK and SHERNOFF later formed MANITOBA'S WILD KINGDOM. In 1990, they were joined by FUNICELLO. In 1994, he, MANITOBA, KEMPNER (ex-DEL-LORDS), SHERNOFF and FRANK FUNARO – drums, reformed The DICTATORS

- compilations, others, etc. -

1981. (c) *R.O.I.R.; <A 102>* **FUCK 'EM IF THEY CAN'T TAKE A JOKE** [-] [ ]
(cd-iss. Feb95 on 'Danceteria'; DANCD 052)

Jan 97. (cd-s) *White Jazz; (JAZZ 003CD)* **I AM RIGHT** [ ] [-]

Nov 97. (7"; split with The NOMADS) *Next Big Thing; (NBT 4527)* [ ] [-]

— (there is also two tribute albums out there on 'Roto' RTI 205/206)

DIE CHEERLEADER

Formed: London, England . . . early 90's by RITA BLAZYCA, SAM IRELAND, DEBBIE QUARGNOLO and ANDY SEMPLE. A dominantly female outfit, DIE CHEERLEADER served up a cocktail of spiky indie-metal with lashings of girlie angst. Three promising EP's were released in the space of a year between '92-'93, the tracks collected on their debut album, 'FILTH BY ASSOCIATION' (1993). One particularly high profile fan was HENRY ROLLINS who signed them up to his American publishing company and subsequently helped secure a deal with 'London' records. The US-only HENRY ROLLINS-produced release, 'SON OF FILTH' (1995), again featured some of their early work, although there was some new material on offer.

Album rating: FILTH BY ASSOCIATION (*5)

SAM IRELAND – vocals / **RITA BLAZYCA** – guitar / **DEBBIE QUARGNOLO** – bass / **ANDY SEMPLE** – drums

Abstract not iss.

Oct 92. (12"ep) *(12ABS 097)* **D.C. EP** [ ] [-]

Feb 93. (12"ep/cd-ep) *(12ABS/ABSCD 098)* **SATURATION EP** [ ] [-]

Jun 93. (7") *(ABS 099)* **CHRIST WITH TEETH. / REMEMBER ZELDA** [ ] [-]
(12"ep+=/cd-s+=) **69 HAYLOFT ACTION E.P.** *(12ABS/CDABS 099)* – Massive tangled muscle / Disease or accident / Smothered.

Oct 93. (cd/lp) *(ABT 097 CD/LP)* **FILTH BY ASSOCIATION**
(compilation) [ ] [-]

not iss. Human Pitbull – London

1995. (cd) *<828591-2>* **SON OF FILTH** [-] [ ]
– Massive tangled muscle / Pigskin parade / Saturation / Smothered / Chokecherry / Starsucker / A case of bad face / Remember Zelda / Disease or accident / Washington D.C.

— disbanded after above

DIESEL PARK WEST

Formed: Leicester, England . . . 1987 by JOHN BUTLER, RICK WILSON, RICH BARTON, GEOFF BEAVAN and DAVE ANDERSON. Signed to the 'Food' label, this bunch of West Coast influenced indie-rockers enjoyed almost immediate critical acclaim with their debut single, 'WHEN THE HOODOO COMES' and album, 'SHAKESPEARE, ALABAMA' (1989). Songwriting craftsmanship of the highest quality, the record's freewheeling trip down rock's lost highway had reviewers reaching for the superlatives while the public remained strangely indifferent. Perhaps the timing was just unlucky, after all the age of 'baggy' was stumbling over the horizon and DPW's classic approach wasn't exactly tailored to the zeitgeist. In fact the band's highest chart placing to date came with the FOOD CHRISTMAS EP, on which they offered up a cover of JESUS JONES' indie-dance stalwart, 'INFO FREAKO'. 1990 saw the release of a B-sides set, 'FLIPPED', prior to a follow-up set, 'DECENCY' (1992). Unfortunately that "difficult" second album proved to be just that and the group came under flak for a flat production, the songwriting failing to reach the standards set with the debut. DIESEL PARK WEST's association with 'Food' came to a less than happy end following a similarly unsuccessful series of covers EP's and the band subsequently signed with veteran adult-rock label, 'Demon', for third set, 'DIESEL PARK WEST VERSUS THE CORPORATE WALTZ' (no prizes for guessing what the title referred to). With IAN MICHIE replacing BEAVAN, the band switched label yet again, this time to 'Permanent' for their fourth album, 'FREAKGENE' (1995). A belated return to form just when it looked as if they'd finally run out of steam, the album proved that DIESEL PARK WEST can still fire on all cylinders when they feel like it, even if their sales figures could do with a turbo boost. • **Covered:** LAZY ME (Moby Grape) / FIND SOMEBODY (Rascals) / MEMO FROM TURNER (Mick Jagger) / NO FACE NO NAME NO NUMBER (Traffic) / MR. SOUL + HUNG UPSIDE DOWN (Buffalo Springfield) / GOD ONLY KNOWS (Beach Boys) / etc.

Album rating: LEFT HAND BAND – THE BEAT OF . . . compilation (*7)

JOHN BUTLER – vocals / **RICK WILSON** – guitar / **RICHARD BARTON** – guitar / **GEOFF BEAVAN** – bass / **DAVID ANDERSON** – drums

Food EMI America

Jul 87. (7") *(FOOD 11)* **WHEN THE HOODOO COMES. / ABOVE THESE THINGS** [ ] [-]
(12"+=) *(SNAK 11)* – The girl with the name.

Oct 88. (7") *(FOOD 15)* **JACKIE'S STILL SAD. / WHAT ABOUT US** [ ] [-]
(12"+=) *(12FOOD 15)* – Friends and enemies / Wings of delight.
(cd-s+=) *(CDFOOD 15)* – Each little happy.

Jan 89. (7") *(FOOD 17)* **ALL THE MYTH'S ON SUNDAY. / BENT, SHATTERED AND BLUE** [66] [-]
(12"+=) *(12FOOD 17)* – Memo from Turner.
(cd-s+=) *(CDFOOD 17)* – The girl with the name.

Feb 89. (lp/c/cd) *(FOOD LP/TC/CD 2) <91689>* **SHAKESPEARE, ALABAMA** [55] [ ]
– Like princes do / All the myths on Sunday / Bell of hope / Out of nowhere / The waking hour / When the hoodoo comes / Opportunity crazy / Here I stand / Jackie's still sad / A house divided. *(cd+=)* – Don't be scared of the night / What about us.

Mar 89. (7") *(FOOD 19)* **LIKE PRINCES DO. / WINGS OF DELIGHT** [58] [-]
(10"+=/12"+=) *(10FOODG/12FOOD 19)* – Endless chains / Don't be scared of the night.
(cd-s+=) *(CDFOOD 19)* – Endless chains / Above these things.

Jul 89. (c-s/7") *(TC+/FOOD 20)* **THE HOODOO EP** [62] [-]
– When the hoodoo comes / It makes no exception at all / Fine Lily fine / Mr. Soul (live).

(12"ep/12"pic-d-ep) *(12FOOD/+P 20)* – (first 2 tracks) / How strong love is / Lazy me (San Francisco mix).
(cd-ep) *(CDFOOD 20)* – (first 2 tracks) / How strong love is / Jingle jangle.

—— In Nov'89, they featured in The Top 30 on a 'Food' Christmas Various Artists EP, doing a version of 'INFO FREAKO

Aug 90. (cd/c/lp) **FLIPPED** (compilation of B-sides & demos) | | -

—— In Aug'91, 'BOY ON TOP OF THE NEWS' was withdrawn

Jan 92. (7") *(FOOD 35)* **FALL TO LOVE. / LET'S TALK AMERICA** | 48 | -
(10"+=) *(10FOOD 35)* – Hung upside down / King Fluid.
(cd-s+=) *(CDFOOD 35)* – Hung upside down / The ballad of Claudia Ray.
(cd-s+=) *(CDFOODS 35)* – All the myths on Sunday / When the hoodoo comes.

Feb 92. (cd/c/lp) *(FOOD CD/TC/LP 7)* **DECENCY** | 57 | -
– While the world cries decency / Walk with the mountain / Fall to love / Boy on top of the news / Souklee in the afterglow / Fine Lily fine / I want no mystery / Till the moon struck two / Hot summer water / Safe life, safe times / Clutching at love.

Mar 92. (7") *(FOOD 36)* **BOY ON TOP OF THE NEWS. / MAYBE EASTERN ZONE** | 58 | -
(10"+=) *(10FOOD 36)* – Hey grandma.
(cd-s+=) *(CDFOOD 36)* – ('A'side) / Hey grandma / Like princes do / A house divided (original).

Aug 92. (7") *(FOOD 39)* **GOD ONLY KNOWS. /** | 57 | -
(cd-s+=) *(CDFOOD 39)* –

Demon | not iss.

May 93. (7") *(DERV 1)* **SIX DAYS TO JUJU. /** | | -
(12"+=/cd-s+=) *(DERV 1 T/CD)* –

Jun 93. (lp/c/cd) *(FIEND/+CASS/CD 747)* **DIESEL PARK WEST VERSUS THE CORPORATE WALTZ** | | -
– Here on the hill / Six days to Juju / The cat's still scratching / Doesn't Candy look good / You killed Sugar Ray / Vanity / Where will the birds sing? / Wonderful (I believe I'm loving you) / Good time liberation blues / Silver girl / Old man's bluff / Hey Holly / The corporate waltz.

Aug 93. (c-s/cd-s) *(DERV 2 MC/CD)* **CAT'S STILL SCRATCHING /** | | -

—— **IAN MICHIE** – bass; repl. BEAVAN

Permanent | not iss.

Apr 95. (cd-s) *(CDSPERM 22)* **NATURAL THINGS / HOOCHIE / SIGMUND SAYS / BLOODY AS FUR** | | -

Apr 95. (cd/c) *(PERM CD/MC 29)* **FREAKGENE** | | -

—— split some time later in '95

Thunderbird | not iss.

Sep 98. (7") *(CSA7 008)* **LOVE IT. / ALL YOUR BIRTHDAYS** | | -
(cd-s+=) *(CSA 008)* – Going going gone.

Oct 98. (cd) *(CSA 115LE)* **HIP REPLACEMENT** | | -
– Suck to live / Bloody as fur / All your birthdays / What are you dreaming now / Here come the refugees / The bridge / Briefly when Mary was young / Love it / Alexander shut up / Siegmund says / Everything works both ways / Last of the silent friends.

– compilations, etc. –

Sep 98. (cd) *EMI Gold; (CDCHRM 105)* **LEFT HAND BAND (THE VERY BEST OF DIESEL PARK WEST)** | | -
– All the myths on Sunday / Here I stand / Jackie's still sad / When the hoodoo comes / Fall to love / Boy on top of the news / Bell of hope / I want no mystery / Fine Lily fine / The girl with the name / Like princes do / King Fluid / Let's talk American / Heathen a go-go / Above these things / While the world cries decency.

DIFFORD & TILBROOK (see under ⇒ SQUEEZE)

DIF JUZ

Formed: London, England . . . 1980 out of the ashes of LONDON PRIDE, by brothers DAVID and ALAN CURTIS, plus GARY BROMLEY and RICHARD THOMAS. Signed to the fledgling '4 a.d.' imprint early the following year, DIF JUZ began their recording career with two EP's in quick succession, namely 'HU/RE/MI/CS' and 'VIBRATING AIR'. Hardly your average post-punk outfit, the quartet delivered a type of sax-happy jazz-rock vaguely reminiscent of SOFT MACHINE / KING CRIMSON. Following a couple of low-key mini-sets, the first of which being 'WHO SAYS SO' (for 'Red Flame'), they were lured back to their original label, also home to the COCTEAU TWINS. In fact it was the husband and wife core of the latter act that augmented DIF JUZ on their debut album proper, 'EXTRACTIONS' (1985), ROBIN GUTHRIE producing and ELIZABETH FRASER contributing vocals on one track. Following a dismal remix album of early material, 'OUT OF THE TREES' (1986), the band went their separate ways, RICHARD THOMAS taking up an invitation to temporarily deputise for the unwell SIMON RAYMONDE in the COCTEAU TWINS.

Album rating: EXTRACTIONS (*6)

DAVID CURTIS – guitar / **ALAN CURTIS** – guitar / **GARY BROMLEY** – bass / **RICHARD THOMAS** – drums, saxophone

4 a.d. | not iss.

Jul 81. (12"ep) *(BAD 109)* **HU/RE/MI/CS** | | -
– Parts 1-4:- Hu / Re / Mi / Cs.

Oct 81. (12"ep) *(BAD 116)* **VIBRATING AIR** | | -
– Heset / Diselt / Gunet / Soarn.

Red Flame | not iss.

Aug 83. (m-lp) *(RFM 24)* **WHO SAYS SO** | | -
– Roy's tray / So shy / Song with no name (pt.2) / Tabla piece / Swan-2 / Pass it on Charlie / Channel / The dub song.

Pleasantly Surprised | not iss.

Feb 85. (c) *(PS 9)* **TIME CLOCK TURNS BACK** | | -

4 a.d. | not iss.

Aug 85. (lp) *(CAD 505)* **EXTRACTIONS** | | -
– Crosswinds / A starting point / Silver passage / The last day / Love insane / Marooned / Two fine days / Echo wreck / Twin and earth. *(cd-iss. Feb87 +=; CAD 505CD)*– VIBRATING AIR (EP). *(cd re-iss. Jul98; GAD 505CD)*

—— guest on below **SCOTT HODGES** – trombone (ex-DEAD CAN DANCE)

Nov 86. (m-lp) *(MAD 612)* **OUT OF THE TREES** (remixes of old tracks) | | -

—— THOMAS having guested for The COCTEAU TWINS, joined the JESUS & MARY CHAIN before moving onto BUTTERFLY CHILD. DAVID joined WOLFGANG PRESS, while he and his NY bound brother were part of THIS MORTAL COIL.

Ani DiFRANCO

Born: 23 Sep'70, Buffalo, New York, USA. Having learned to sing and play guitar at an early age, DiFRANCO began playing professionally after a move to the centre of New York. As fiercely independent and enterprising as she was talented, DiFRANCO set up her own 'Righteous Babe' imprint for the release of her eponymous debut album. Issued in 1990 as an American-only release, the album had originally been on sale at live shows before demand soon outstripped supply and necessitated a larger operation. Featuring the cream of the apparently massive catalogue of songs she'd built up throughout her teens, the record's intimate acoustic confessionals went down a storm with both militant lesbians and straight down the line folk/rock fans. Openly bisexual herself, the tattooed, pierced and shaven-headed DiFRANCO steadily built up a diehard following of kindred spirits through a punishing tour schedule. 1991's 'NOT SO SOFT' was another bare bones acoustic affair dealing in heartfelt sexual politics although it wasn't until the release of the more instrumentally rich 'IMPERFECTLY' (1992) and 'PUDDLE DIVE' (1993), that DiFRANCO began to draw attention from major labels. Standing by her DIY ethos, she released her most widely acknowledged album to date in 'OUT OF RANGE' (1994). Again embellishing her rhythmic acoustic guitar playing with eclectic instrumental textures, the record set the scene for her breakthrough opus, 'NOT A PRETTY GIRL'. With girl power very much on the agenda in the mid-90's, DiFRANCO finally gained recognition as one of America's foremost female commentators alongside the likes of LIZ PHAIR, HEATHER NOVA, etc. The one-woman powerhouse also finally clinched a UK deal with 'Cooking Vinyl', while 1996's acclaimed 'DILATE' gave DiFRANCO her first Top 100 US chart placing. Following on from 1997's well received double set, 'LIVING IN CLIP', she scored her biggest success to date with near Top 20 US album, 'LITTLE PLASTIC CASTLES' (1998).

Album rating: ANI DiFRANCO (*6) / NOT SO SOFT (*6) / IMPERFECTLY (*7) / PUDDLE DIVE (*7) / LIKE I SAID – SONGS 1990-1991 compilation (*7) / OUT OF RANGE (*7) / NOT A PRETTY GIRL (*8) / DILATE (*7) / MORE JOY, LESS SHAME (*5) / LIVING IN CLIP (*8) / LITTLE PLASTIC CASTLE (*7)

ANI DiFRANCO – vocals, guitar

Haven | Righteous Babe

Nov 89. (cd) *<RBR 001CD>* **ANI DiFRANCO** | - |
– Both hands / Talk to me now / Slant / Work you way out / Dog coffee / Lost woman song / Pale purple / Rush hour / Fire door / The story / Every angle / Out of habit / Letting the telephone ring / Egos like hairdos. *(UK-iss.Jul95; same) (re-iss. Jun97 on 'Cooking Vinyl'; COOKCD 112)*

1991. (cd) *<RBR 002CD>* **NOT SO SOFT** | - |
– Anticipate / Rockabye / She says / Make me stay / On every corner / Small world / Not so soft / Roll with it / Itch / Gratitude / Whole night / The next big thing / Brief bus stop / Looking at the holes. *(UK-iss.Sep97 on 'Cooking Vinyl'; COOKCD 133)*

1992. (cd) *<RBD 003CD>* **IMPERFECTLY** | - |
– What if no one's watching / Fixing her hair / In or out / Every state line / Circle of light / If it isn't her / Good, bad, ugly / I'm no heroine / Coming up / Make them apologize / Waiting song / Served faithfully / Imperfectly. *(UK-iss.Jul95; same)*

Jul 93. (cd/c) *(HAVEN CD/MC 002) <RBR 004 CD/C>* **PUDDLE DIVE** | |
– Names and dates and times / Anyday / 4th of July / Willing to fight / Egos like hairdos / Back around / Blood in the boardroom / Born a lion / My IQ / Used to you / Pick yer nose / God's country. *(re-iss. Jan95; same)*

Jul 94. (cd) *<(RBR 005CD)>* **LIKE I SAID: SONGS 1990-1991** (re-recorded early tracks) | |
– Anticipate / Rockabye / Not so soft / Roll with it / Work your way out / Fire door / Gratitude / Whole night / Both hands / She says / Rush hour / Out of habit / Lost woman song / Talk to me now / Slant.

Haven | Righteous Babe

Jan 95. (cd/c) *(HAVEN CD/MC 3) <RBR 006CD>* **OUT OF RANGE** | | Jul94
– Buildings and bridges / Out of range / Letter to a John / Hell yeah / How have you been / Overlap / Face up and sing / Falling is like this / Out of range / You had time / If he tries anything / Diner.

Righteous Babe | Righteous Babe

Nov 95. (cd) *<(RBR 007CD)>* **NOT A PRETTY GIRL** | | Jul95
– Worthy / Tiptoe / Cradle and all / Shy / Sorry I am / Light of some kind / Not a pretty girl / Million you never made / Hour follows hour / 32 flavors / Asking too much / This bouquet / Crime for crime. *(UK-iss.Jan97 on 'Cooking Vinyl'; COOKCD 113)*

Cooking Vinyl | Righteous Babe

Jul 96. (cd) *(COOKCD 103) <RBR 008CD>* **DILATE** | | 87 May96
– Untouchable face / Outta me, onto you / Superhero / Dilate / Amazing grace / Napoleon / Shameless / Done wrong / Going down / Adam and Eve / Joyful girl.

Jan 97. (cd-s) *(FRYCD 049)* **OUTTA ME ONTO YOU / SHY** | |

Apr 97. (cd; UTAH PHILLIPS & ANI DiFRANCO) *(COOKCD 124) <RBR 009CD>* **THE PAST DIDN'T GO ANYWHERE** | |
– Bridges / Nevada City, California /Korea / Anarchy / Candidacy / Bum on the road / Enormously wealthy / Mess with people / Natural resources / Heroes / Half a ghost town / Holding on.

Dec 96. (m-cd) *(COOKCD 119)* *<RBR 010CD>* **MORE JOY, LESS SHAME**
– Joyful girl / Joyful girl / Joyful girl / Joyful girl / Shameless / Both hands.

Jun 97. (d-cd) *(COOKCD 122)* *<RBR 011CD>* **LIVING IN CLIP (live)** Apr97
– Whatever / Wherever / Gravel / Willing to fight / Shy / Joyful girl / Hide and seek / Napoleon / I'm no heroine / Amazing grace / Anitipate / Tiptoe / Sorry I am / Diner – Slant / 32 flavors / Out of range / Untouchable face / Shameless / Distracted / Adam and Eve / Fire door / Both hands / Out of habit / Every state line / Not so soft / Travel tips / Wrong with me / In or out / We're all gonna blow / Letter to a John / Overleaf.

Feb 98. (cd) *(COOKCD 140)* *<RBR 012CD>* **LITTLE PLASTIC CASTLE** 22
– Little plastic castle / Fuel / Gravel / As is / Two little girls / Deep dish / Loom / Pixie / Swan dive / Glass house / Independence day / Pulse.

– compilations, etc. –

Nov 94. (cd) *Tradition & Moderne; (T&M 105)* **WOMEN IN (E)MOTION FESTIVAL** -
<US-iss.Jun98 on 'Imprint'; 28376>

DIG

Formed: San Diego, California, USA . . . early '91 by songwriter SCOTT HACKWITH, a man known for his inspirational vocal style. With guitarists DIX DENNEY, JON MORRIS, bassist PHIL FRIEDMANN and drummer MATT TECU, completing the line-up, these hard driving alt-rockers debuted in Spring '93 with the blistering 'RUNT' EP. Subsequently picked up by the 'Radioactive' label, they released a follow-up single, 'BELIEVE', almost a year on, followed closely by an eponymous debut album. Having already spent a month in the US Top 200 the previous summer, the album was met with a generally positive critical response in the UK where its warped take on US rock history was applauded. After a further two singles, 'I'LL STAY HIGH' and 'UNLUCKY FRIEND', the band laid low for nigh on two years before surfacing with the US-only 'DEFENDERS OF THE FAITH' (1996). • **Covered:** FEARLESS (Pink Floyd). • **Note:** There was also an Australian band going by the name d.i.g.

Album rating: DIG (*6) / DEFENDERS OF THE FAITH (*5)

SCOTT HACKWITH – vocals / **JON MORRIS** – guitar / **JOHNNY CORNWALL** – guitar / **PHIL FRIEDMANN** – bass / **MATT TECU** – drums

Radioactive Wasteland

Apr 93. (12"ep/cd-ep) *(RAXT/+D 005)* *<10781>* **RUNT EP** Jun92
– I'll stay high / Groundhead / We don't care / Mothership.

— **JOHNNY CORNWALL** – guitar; repl. DENNEY

— **ANTHONY SMEDILE** – drums; repl. TECU

Radioactive Radioactive

Mar 94. (7"/c-s) *(RAX/+C 1968)* **BELIEVE. / CONVERSATION / FEARLESS** -
(cd-s+=) *(RAXTD 1968)* – ('A'version).

Apr 94. (lp/c/cd) *<(RAR/+C/D 10916)>* **DIG** Aug93
– Unlucky friend / Let me know / Green room / Conversation / Decide / Anymore / Believe / Ride the wave / Tight brain / Feet don't touch the ground / I'll stay high / Fuck you.

Aug 94. (7"/c-s) *(RAX/+C 10)* **I'LL STAY HIGH. / KING OF MY WORLD** -
(cd-s+=) *(RAXTD 10)* – On the inside.

Dec 94. (7") *(RAX 12)* **UNLUCKY FRIEND. /**
(cd-s+=) *(RAXTD 12)* –
(cd-s) *(RAXXD 12)* –

not iss. M.C.A.

Jul 96. (cd,c) *<11401>* **DEFENDERS OF THE FAITH** -
– Opus / Whose side you on? / Detune / Songs for liars / Little pill / Stop holding your breath / E.I.O. / Modo elevator / Electric cord / Watt socket / White sabbath / Bashing in your head.

— about to release an album in '99, 'LIFE LIKE'

DIGGERS

Formed: Methil, East Fife, Scotland . . . early 90's by ALAN MOFFAT and CHRIS MIEZITIS. After fruitlessly attempting to ply their classic indie-guitar wares around the less than sympathetic environs of Methil, Leven and surrounding Fife backwaters, the duo relocated to Glasgow where their approach was more in tune with the prevailing 'Bellshill Sound'. Completing the line-up with JOHN ESLICK and HANK ROSS, the band received encouraging support prior to a hiccup in their career as the former was laid off for six months following a car accident. By this time, the quartet had issued an eponymous EP on their own label. Subsequently signed to 'Creation', The DIGGERS took more than three years to come up with a debut album, 'MOUNT EVEREST'. Finally surfacing in 1997, the record revealed no great surprises soundwise with an archetypal 'Creation' indie sound vaguely akin to The BLUETONES if not quite so assured, commentators drawing on the ever reliable BEATLES for comparisons.

Album rating: MOUNT EVEREST (*6)

ALAN MOFFAT – vocals, bass / **CHRIS MEIZITIS** – vocals, rhythm guitar / **JOHN ESLICK** – lead guitar / **HANK ROSS** – drums

Death Becomes Me not iss.

Jul 94. (12"ep) *(CS 103)* **DIGGERS E.P.** -

Creation Creation

Aug 96. (7") *(CRE 226)* **PEACE OF MIND. / GET IT** -
(cd-s+=) *(CRESCD 226)* – Tangled web.

Oct 96. (7"/c-s) *(CRE/+CS 234)* **NOBODY'S FOOL. / LIFE'S ALL WAYS** -
(cd-s+=) *(CRESCD 234)* – Here and there.

Feb 97. (7"/c-s) *(CRE/+CS 259)* **O.K. ALRIGHT. / ON THE LINE** -
(cd-s+=) *(CRESCD 259)* – Holiday Inn.

Mar 97. (cd/lp) *(<CRE CD/LP 193>)* **MOUNT EVEREST**
– Circles / Peace of mind / Waking up / Nobody's fool / Come on easy / Downbeat / East coast / O.K. alright / Hormonious / Passport to Rec / They said I'd know / Up against it.

Steve DIGGLE (see under ⇒ BUZZCOCKS)

DILS

Formed: San Diego, California, USA . . . 1977, by brothers CHIP and TONY KINMAN, who recruited drummer ENDRE ALQUOVER. This seminal punk act released two much sought after 45's, 'I HATE THE RICH' and 'CLASS WAR', before a succession of drummers passed through their ranks. In 1980, The DILS issued their finale in the shape of the 'MADE IN CANADA' EP, the KINMAN siblings changing direction and moniker completely for the 80's. Enlisting the help of ALEJANDRO ESCOVEDO and subsequently SLIM EVANS, the new RANK & FILE set up home in New York. The KINMAN brothers were well versed in the application of razor sharp attitude; combining this with a rootsy, gritty country sound, they almost singlehandedly initiated the ubiquitous cowpunk genre of the early-mid 80's. Signed to 'Slash', a label which became synonymous with the scene, the group released their debut album, 'SUNDOWN', in 1982 to widespread critical acclaim; The EVERLY BROTHERS later covered one of the stand-out tracks, 'AMANDA RUTH'. Lacing poppy melodies and clear-eyed harmonies with darker lyrical and musical hues, the band were unfortunately never fully accepted by either the punk or the country fraternity. A subsequent split led to the departure of both EVANS and ESCOVEDO, the KINMANS heading to Austin, Texas, where they cut a further couple of albums, 'LONG GONE DEAD' (1984) and 'RANK AND FILE' (1987) to minimal interest. ESCOVEDO meanwhile, formed the TRUE BELIEVERS with his brother JAVIER before going on to a solo career in the 90's. Eventually dissolving RANK AND FILE, the KINMANS formed BLACKBIRD, an experimental project combining elements from the burgeoning industrial scene with their trademark alt-country sound.

Album rating: LIVE: DILS (*6) / Rank & File: SUNDOWN (*5) / LONG GONE DEAD (*5) / RANK AND FILE (*4)

DILS

CHIP KINMAN (b. 4 Oct'57, Edenton, North Carolina) – vocals, guitar / **TONY KINMAN** (b. 3 Apr'56, Quantico, Virginia) – bass, vocals / **ENDRE ALQUOVER** – drums

not iss. What

Sep 77. (7") *<WHAT 02>* **I HATE THE RICH. / YOU'RE NOT BLANK** -

not iss. Dangerhouse

Dec 77. (7") *<SLA 268>* **198 SECONDS OF THE DILS** -
– Class war / Mr. Big.

— **RAND McNALLY** (aka ZIPPY PINHEAD) – drums (ex-DOA) repl. JOHN SILVERS, who repl. ALQUOVER

not iss. Rogelletti

Apr 80. (d7"ep) *<RR 001>* **MADE IN CANADA** -
– Sound of the rain / Not worth it / Red rockers.

— split when the brothers formed RANK & FILE. McNALLY formed LOS POPULAROS

– compilations, etc. –

Aug 87. (lp) *Triple XXX; <(51003-1)>* **LIVE: DILS (live)**

1990. (lp) *Lost;* **THE DILS (live)** -
(UK cd-iss. 1992 on 'Damaged Goods'; 8)

RANK & FILE

CHIP KINMAN – guitar, vocals / **TONY KINMAN** – bass, vocals / **ALEJANDRO ESCOVEDO** (b.10 Jan'51, San Antonio, Texas) – vocals, guitar (ex-NUNS, ex-JUDY NYLON)

not iss. Jackalope

1981. (7") **LUCKY DAY. / AMANDA RUTH** -

— added **SLIM EVANS** (b. JIM) – drums

Rough Trade Slash

Jan 84. (lp) *(ROUGH 67)* *<23833>* **SUNDOWN** Apr83
– Amanda Ruth / (Glad I'm) Not in love / Rank and file / The conductor wore black / Sundown / I went walking / Lucky day / I don't go out much anymore / Coyote. *(re-iss. Jan87 on 'Slash' lp/c; SLMP/SLMC 18)*

— **KINMAN's** recruited session people **STAN LYNCH** – drums, percussion (of TOM PETTY & THE HEARTBREAKERS) / **RICHARD GREENE** – fiddle / **JEFF ROSS** – guitar / **PETER GRANT** – guitar, steel guitar, banjo / **BILL MEYERS** – woodwind

— ESCOVEDO joined The TRUE BELIEVERS before going solo

Slash Slash

Jun 84. (7") *(LASH 2)* **RANK & FILE. / AMANDA RUTH**
(12"+=) *(LASHX 2)* – I'm an old man.

Jul 84. (lp) *(SLAP 2)* **LONG GONE DEAD**
– Long gone dead / I'm an old man / Sound of the rain / Hot wind / Tell her I love her / Saddest girl in the world / Timeless love / John Brown / Last night I dreamed / It don't matter.

not iss. Rhino

1987. (cd) *<RNCD 70830>* **RANK AND FILE** -
– Black book / One big thing / Golden age / Rbt / Pistol dawn / Sweet life / Good times / Oh! that girl / Unlucky in love / Love house.

— split after above and the KINMAN's formed BLACKBIRD who released three self-titled sets.

DIM STARS (see under ⇒ HELL, Richard)

DINOSAUR JR.

Formed: Amherst, Massachusetts, USA . . . 1983 by J. MASCIS. Initially recording hardcore punk under the DEEP WOUND moniker, the band recruited PATRICK MURPHY and metamorphosised into DINOSAUR. Their self-titled debut album appeared in 1985, a raw blueprint for their distinctive candy-coated noise rock that was good enough to secure an American tour support slot with SONIC YOUTH. After protestations from aging West Coast rockers DINOSAUR, J.MASCIS' crew added the JR. to part of their name. Subsequently recording one album for 'SST', 'YOU'RE LIVING ALL OVER ME' (1987), the band further developed their melodic distortion although it was the 'FREAK SCENE' (1988) single, their debut for 'Blast First', which saw DINOSAUR JR. pressed to the cardigan-clad bosoms of the nations pre-baggy indie kids. A wildly exhilirating piece of pristine pop replete with copious amounts of intoxicating noise pollution, MASCIS' go-on-impress-me vocals epitomised the word slacker when that dubious cliche was still gestating in some hack's subconscious. The follow-up album, 'BUG' (1988) was arguably the band's finest moment, perfectly crafted pop spiked with scathing slivers of guitar squall. BARLOW departed soon after the album's release, going off to form SEBADOH while MASCIS' mob came up with a wonderfully skewed cover of The CURE's 'JUST LIKE HEAVEN'. DON FLEMING (of GUMBALL fame) and JAY SPIEGEL featured on DINOSAUR JR.'s major label debut for 'WEA' subsidiary 'Blanco Y Negro', 'THE WAGON' (1991). Another slice of cascading noise-pop, the single raised expectations for the follow-up album 'GREEN MIND' (1991). More or less a MASCIS solo album, it failed to live up to its promise although by the release of 1993's 'WHERE YOU BEEN', MASCIS had found a permanent bassist in MIKE JOHNSON. Their most successful album to date, DINOSAUR JR. at last reaped some rewards from the grunge scene they'd played a major role in creating. With both JOHNSON and MASCIS releasing solo albums in 1996, DINOSAUR JR. have been conspicuous by their absence of late. • **Songwriters:** MASCIS wrote all, except LOTTA LOVE (Neil Young) / QUICKSAND (David Bowie) / I FEEL A WHOLE LOT BETTER (Byrds) / GOIN' BLIND (Kiss) / HOT BURRITO 2 (Gram Parsons). J. MASCIS solo:- EVERY MOTHER'S SON (Lynyrd Skynyrd) / THE BOY WITH THE THORN IN HIS SIDE (Smiths) / ON THE RUN (Wipers) / ANTICIPATION (Carly Simon). MIKE JOHNSON solo:- SECOND LOVERS SONG (Lynyrd Skynyrd) / LOVE AND OTHER CRIMES (Lee Hazlewood) / IF YOU'RE GONE (Gene Clark). • **Trivia:** In Jun'91, MASCIS moonlighted as a drummer with Boston satanic hard-core group UPSIDE DOWN CROSS, who made one self-titled album Autumn '91 on 'Taang!'. He also wrote songs and made a cameo appearance in the 1992 film, 'Gas, Food, Lodging'.

Album rating: DINOSAUR (*6) / YOU'RE LIVING ALL OVER ME mini (*7) / BUG (*8) / GREEN MIND (*7) / WHERE YOU BEEN (*8) / WITHOUT A SOUND (*5) / HAND IT OVER (*7) / J. Mascis: MARTIN AND ME (*6) / Mike Johnson: YEAR OF MONDAYS (*5)

LOU BARLOW (b.17 Jul'66, Northampton, Mass.) – guitar / **J. MASCIS** (b. JOSEPH, 10 Dec'65) – drums / **CHARLIE NAKAJIMA** – vox / **SCOTT HELLAND** – bass

not iss. Radiobeat

Dec 83. (7"ep; as DEEP WOUND) *<RB 002>* **I SAW IT** [-] [ ]
– I saw it / Sisters / In my room / Don't need / Lou's anxiety song / Video prick / Sick of fun / Deep wound / Dead babies.

— **J. MASCIS** – vocals, guitar, percussion / **LOU BARLOW** – bass, ukelele, vocals / added **MURPH** (b. EMMETT "PATRICK" MURPHY, 21 Dec'64) – drums (ex-ALL WHITE JURY)

not iss. Homestead

Jun 85. (lp; as DINOSAUR) *<HMS 015>* **DINOSAUR** [-] [ ]
– Forget the swan / Cats in a bowl / The leper / Does it float / Pointless / Repulsion / Gargoyle / Several lips / Mountain man / Quest / Bulbs of passion.

Mar 86. (7"; as DINOSAUR) *<HMS 032>* **REPULSION. / BULBS OF PASSION** [-] [ ]
(UK-iss.Apr97; same)

S.S.T. S.S.T.

Mar 87. (12"ep) *<SST 152>* **DINOSAUR JR.** [-] [ ]
– Little fury things / In a jar / Show me the way. *(cd-ep iss.Dec88; SSTCD 152)*

Jul 87. (m-lp/c) *<(SST/+C 130)>* **YOU'RE LIVING ALL OVER ME** [ ] [ ]
– Little fury things / Kracked / Sludgefeast / The lung / Raisans / Tarpit / In a jar / Lose / Poledo / Show me the way. *(cd-iss. Oct95; same)*

Blast First S.S.T.

Sep 88. (7") *(BFFP 30)* **FREAK SCENE. / KEEP THE GLOVE** [ ] [ ]
(US-iss.7",7"green; SST 220)

Oct 88. (lp/c/cd) *(BFFP 31/+C/CD) <SST/+C/CD 216>* **BUG** [ ] [ ]
– Freak scene / No bones / They always come / Yeah we know / Let it ride / Pond song / Budge / The post / Don't.

— **DONNA BIDDELL** – bass (ex-SCREAMING TREES) repl. BARLOW who formed SEBADOH

Apr 89. (7"/etched-12"/cd-s) *(BFFP 47 S/T/CD) <SST 244>* **JUST LIKE HEAVEN. / THROW DOWN / CHUNKS (A Last Rights Tune)** [78] [ ] Feb 90
(US version 12"ep+=/c-ep+=/cd-ep+=) (SST/+C/CD 244) – Freak scene / Keep the glove.

— DONNA left and was repl. by **DON FLEMING** – guitar + **JAY SPIEGEL** – drums (both B.A.L.L.)

Glitterhouse Sub Pop

Jun 90. (7"/7"white) *(GR 0097) <SP 68>* **THE WAGON. / BETTER THAN GONE** [ ] [ ]

— In Oct 90, J.MASCIS and other ex-DINOSAUR JR member FLEMING + SPIEGEL, made an album 'RAKE' as VELVET MONKEYS (aka B.A.L.L. + friends).

Blanco Y Negro Sire

Jan 91. (7"/c-s) *(NEG 48/+C)* **THE WAGON. / THE LITTLE BABY** [49] [-]
(12"+=/cd-s+=) *(NEG 48 T/CD)* – Pebbles + weeds / Quicksand.

Feb 91. (lp/c/cd) *(BYN 24/+C/CD) <26479>* **GREEN MIND** [36] [ ]
– The wagon / Puke + cry / Blowing it / I live for that look / Flying cloud / How'd you pin that one on me / Water / Muck / Thumb / Green mind.

Aug 91. (7"/c-s) *(NEG 52/+C)* **WHATEVER'S COOL WITH ME. / SIDEWAYS** [ ] [-]
(12"+=/cd-s+=) *(NEG 52 T/CD)* – Thumb (live) / Keep the glove (live).

— **MASCIS + MURPH** introduced new member **MIKE JOHNSON** (b.27 Aug'65, Grant's Pass, Oregon, USA) – bass (ex-MARK LANEGAN, ex-GEORGE LANE, ex-SNAKEPIT)

Nov 92. (7") *(NEG 60)* **GET ME. / HOT BURRITO #2** [44] [-]
(c-s+=/12"+=/cd-s+=) *(NEG 60 C/T/CD)* – Qwest (live).

Jan 93. (7") *(NEG 61)* **START CHOPPIN'. / TURNIP FARM** [20] [-]
(10"+=/12"+=/cd-s+=) *(NEG 61 TEP/T/CD)* – Forget it.

Feb 93. (lp/c/cd) *(BYN 28/+C/CD) <45108>* **WHERE YOU BEEN?** [10] [50]
– Out there / Start choppin' / What else is new? / On the way / Not the same / Get me / Drawerings / Hide / Goin' home / I ain't sayin'.

Jun 93. (7"/c-s/12") *(NEG 63/+C/T)* **OUT THERE. / KEEBLIN' (live) / KRACKED (live)** [44] [ ]
(10"+=) *(NEG 63TE)* – Post.
(cd-s++=) *(NEG 63CD)* – Quest (live).
(cd-s) *(NEG 63CDX)* – ('A'side) / Get me / Severed lips / Thumb (radio sessions).

— now without MURPH

Aug 94. (7"/c-s) *(NEG 74/+C)* **FEEL THE PAIN. / GET OUT OF THIS** [25] [ ]
(10"etched+=/cd-s+=) *(NEG 74 TE/CD)* – Repulsion (acoustic).

Sep 94. (cd/c/lp) *(4509 96933-2/-4/-1) <45719>* **WITHOUT A SOUND** [24] [44]
– Feel the pain / I don't think so / Yeah right / Outta hand / Grab it / Even you / Mind glow / Get out of this / On the brink / Seemed like the thing to do / Over your shoulder.

Feb 95. (7"green/c-s) *(NEG 77 X/C)* **I DON'T THINK SO. / GET ME (live)** [67] [ ]
(cd-s+=) *(NEG 77CD)* – What else is new? / Sludge.

Mar 97. (c-s/12"/cd-s) *(NEG 103 C/T/CD)* **TAKE A RUN AT THE SUN. / DON'T YOU THINK IT'S TIME / THE PICKLE SONG** [53] [ ]

Mar 97. (cd/c/lp) *(0630 18312-2/-4/-1) <46506>* **HAND IT OVER** [ ] [ ]
– Take a run at the sun / Never bought it / Nothin's goin' on / I'm insane / Can't we move this alone / Sure not over you / Loaded / Mick / I know yer insane / Gettin' rough / Gotta know.

Trade 2 not iss.

Sep 97. (7") *(TRDSC 009)* **I'M INSANE. / I MISUNDERSTOOD** [ ] [-]

– compilations, etc. –

1990. (10"m-lp) *S.S.T.; (SST 275)* **FOSSILS** [-] [ ]

MIKE JOHNSON

— with **BARRETT MARTIN, AL LARSEN + DAVID KRUEGER**

not iss. Up

Nov 94. (cd) *<8>* **WHERE AM I?** [-] [ ]
– Overland – Turn back alone / Save today / Separation / Untitled / Second lovers song / Down the line / Love and other crimes / See through / If you're gone / Carry on / 100% off / Atrophy.

— now with his wife **LESLIE HARDY** – bass (of JUNED, who he produced) / **J. MASCIS, BARRETT MARTIN + MARK LANEGAN**

Atlantic Atlantic

Apr 96. (cd/c) *<(7567 92669-2/-4)>* **YEAR OF MONDAYS** [ ] [ ] Feb96
– Where am I? / One way out / The way it will be – Too far / Another side / Circle / Eclipse / Left in the dark / Hold the reins / Say it's so / Overdrive.

— now with **KRUEGER, JOHN ATKINS, ELI BRADEN, DAN PETERS, TIFFANY ANDERS, CLAUDIA GROOM + BRETT ARNOLD**

not iss. Up

Aug 98. (cd) *<UP 057>* **I FEEL ALRIGHT** [-] [ ]
– All there is / Turn around / I don't love you / Minor aversion / Not over yet / Leaving Greensleeves / I've got to have you / One liner / Message to pretty / Impatient and unwilling / Performer / Tradewinds.

J. MASCIS

WEA Warners

May 96. (cd/c) *<(46177)>* **MARTIN + ME** [ ] [ ] Apr96
– Thumb / So what else is new / Get me / Blowin' it / Repulsion / Goin' home / The boy with the thorn in his side / Not you again / On the run / Keeblin / Flying cloud / Anticipation / Drawerings / Every mother's son.

DIRTY THREE

Formed: Melbourne, Australia . . . 1992, by WARREN ELLIS, MICK TURNER and JIM WHITE, all already established in various bands including FUNGUS BRAINS, BLACKEYED SUSAN, BUSLOAD OF FAITH and VENOM P. STINGER. The instrumental trio played bars and clubs mainly as a side project to the aforementioned outfits and eventually their impressive tightknit musical gymnastics won them favour among the Australian press. A demo tape eventually worked its way across the globe to a small Boston indie, 'Poon Village', who subsequently issued the mini-set as 'SAD AND DANGEROUS' late in '94. This helped them secure support slots to

PAVEMENT on their North American tour, which, in turn, spurred promoters to book them for that year's 'Lollapalooza' festival. NICK CAVE had been a celebrity fan for over a year now and he proved it by accompanying The DIRTY THREE on piano while they performed Carl Dreyer's silent movie, 'The Passion Of Joan Of Arc', at London's National Film Theatre. The punk crooner also collaborated with the trio on an 'X-Files' TV soundtrack album entitled 'Song In The Key Of X', while ELLIS and CAVE later co-wrote a song for the latter's soap-ish (so pure) pop buddy, KYLIE MINOGUE. On the vinyl front, the DIRTY THREE were establishing themselves with each release. Signing to 'Big Cat' records ('Touch & Go' in the US), they issued two sets, 'THE DIRTY THREE' (1995) and 'HORSE STORIES' (1996). Squeezed inbetween these well-received gems was a collaboration with WILL OLDHAM on his 'Arise Therefore' (PALACE) album. A couple of years passed until the release of their STEVE ALBINI-produced 1998 set, 'OCEAN SONGS' (on SIMON RAYMONDE's new imprint, 'Bella Union'), was heralded as their finest hour yet. Around the same time, both TURNER and WHITE augmented CAT POWER on her 'MOONPIX' set. • **Covered:** KIM'S DIRT (Kim Salmon).

Album rating: SAD AND DANGEROUS (*5) / THE DIRTY THREE (*6) / HORSE STORIES (*6) / OCEAN SONGS (*7)

WARREN ELLIS – electric violin, piano-accordion, etc / **MICK TURNER** – guitar (ex-MOODISTS) / **JIM WHITE** – drums, percussion

not iss. — Poon Village

Dec 94. (cd) <27> **SAD AND DANGEROUS** –
– Kim's dirt / Killy Kundane / Jaguar / Devil in the hole / Jim's dog / Short break / Turk reprise / You were a bum deal / Warren's waltz / Turk.
(UK-iss.Apr96 on 'Big Cat' lp/cd; ABB 107/+CD)

Big Cat — Touch & Go

Aug 95. (lp/cd) *(ABB 93/+CD)* <*TG 147/+CD*> **THE DIRTY THREE**
– Indian love song / Better go home now / Odd couple / Kim's dirt / Everything's fucked / Last night / Dirty equation.

Sep 96. (lp/cd) *(ABB 115/+CD)* <*TG 165/+CD*> **HORSE STORIES**
– 1000 miles / Sues last ride / Hope / I remember a time when once you loved / At the bar / Red / Warren's lament / Horse / I knew it would come to this.

Bella Union — Touch & Go

Mar 98. (cd) *(BELLACD 003)* <*TG 193*> **OCEAN SONGS**
– Sirena / Restless waves / Distant shore / Authentic celestial music / Backwards voyager / Last horse on the sand / Sea above, sky below / Black tide / Deep waters / Ends of the earth. *(re-iss. Sep98; same)*

Sep 98. (7") *(NAR 001)* **A STRANGE HOLIDAY. / (other track by SCENIC)** –
(above issued on 'Narwhal')

Nov 98. (cd) *(BELLACD 006)* **UFKUKO**
– To aster / Mihelkos arm / Cast adrift / Three wheels / Wish I could.

DISCHARGE

Formed: Birmingham, England . . . late 1978 by CAL (KELVIN MORRIS), BONES (TONY ROBERTS), RAINY WAINWRIGHT and original drummer TEZ, who was replaced by BAMBI then GARRY MALONEY. Signing to the newly-formed Stoke-On-Trent based indie label, 'Clay', they initiated their bruising musical assault with the release of the debut EP, 'REALITIES OF WAR' in 1980. Aggressively anti-war and pro-vegetarian, they were unfairly branded as one of the many up and coming "oi" bands by the now defunct Sounds music magazine (notably journalist and future Sun critic, Gary Bushell, who hated them profusely). They nevertheless marched on in their own inimitable style, releasing a series of deliberately inexpensive EP's upon which they innovated the incomprehensible "death-grunt", later adopted by mid 80's grindcore outfits like NAPALM DEATH, EXTREME NOISE TERROR, etc. By mid '81, they progressed to the 12 inch format, releasing an EP, 'WHY', another barrage of sound that did well in the indie charts. This minor success was consolidated when the group had their first real chart hit, 'NEVER AGAIN' denting the Top 75 for 3 weeks (the DHSS had previously fined them for collecting dole money while on tour, perhaps the time had come to sign off?!). Further recognition followed when their 1982 debut album, 'HEAR NOTHING, SEE NOTHING, SAY NOTHING' scraped into the Top 40. Bassist BROKEN BONES subsequently left the band to explore a punk/metal fusion with a solo career, POOCH PURTILL taking his place in time for a disappointing semi-live set, 'NEVER AGAIN' (1983). DISCHARGE concentrated on single/EP's over the next few years, the album, 'GRAVE NEW WORLD' breaking the sequence in 1986. However, frontman CAL was to leave the following year, his replacement coming in the shape of ROB BERKELEY, although no new material was forthcoming. In the early 90's, DISCHARGE were back once more, CAL back in the fold with other members ANDY GREEN, ANTHONY MORGAN and GARRY MALONEY. Embracing the metal genre more explicitly than ever before, the emerged with the album, 'MASSACRE DIVINE' (1991), followed two years later by 'SHOOTIN' UP THE WORLD'.

Album rating: HEAR NOTHING, SEE NOTHING, SAY NOTHING (*7) / NEVER AGAIN (*5) / GRAVE NEW WORLD (*6) / DISCHARGE 1980-1986 compilation (*6) / THE NIGHTMARE CONTINUES comilation (*6)

CAL (b. KELVIN MORRIS) – vocals / **BONES** (b. ANTHONY ROBERTS) – guitar (gutarist changed often) / **RAINY WAINWRIGHT** – bass / **GARRY MALONEY** – drums

Clay — not iss.

Apr 80. (7"ep) *(CLAY 1)* **REALITIES OF WAR / THEY DECLARE IT / BUT AFTER THE GIG / SOCIETY'S VICTIM** –
(re-iss. Feb87; same)

Jul 80. (7"ep) *(CLAY 3)* **FIGHT BACK / WAR'S NO FAIRY TALE / ALWAYS RESTRICTIONS / YOU TAKE PART IN CREATING THIS SYSTEM / RELIGIOUS INSTIGATES** –

Dec 80. (7"ep) *(CLAY 5)* **DECONTROL / IT'S NO TV SKETCH / TOMORROW BELONGS TO US** –

May 81. (12"ep) *(PLATE 2)* **WHY** –
– Visions of war / Does the system work / A look at tomorrow / Why / Maimed and slaughtered / Mania for conquest / Ain't no feeble bastard / Is this to be / Massacre of innocents (air attack). *(re-iss. Jan90 & Apr93 lp/cd+=; PLATE 002/+CD)* – State violence – state control / Doomsday. *(cd re-iss. Aug98 on 'Receiver'; RRCD 259)*

Oct 81. (7") *(CLAY 6)* **NEVER AGAIN. / DEATH DEALERS / TWO MONSTROUS NUCLEAR STOCK-PILES** 64 –

May 82. (lp) *(CLAYLP 3)* **HEAR NOTHING, SEE NOTHING, SAY NOTHING** 40 –
– Hear nothing, see nothing, say nothing / The nightmare continues / The final blood bath / Protest and survive / I won't subscribe / Drunk with power / Meanwhile / A hell on earth / Cries of help / The possibility of life's destruction / Q – and children?, A – and children / The blood runs red / Free speech for the dumb / The end. *(re-iss. Jan90 & Mar95 lp/cd; CLAY LP/CD 3) (cd re-iss. May98 on 'Receiver'; RRCD 255)*

Oct 82. (7") *(CLAY 14)* **STATE VIOLENCE – STATE CONTROL. / DOOMSDAY** –

—— (Nov'82) **POOCH PURTILL** – guitar repl. BONES who formed BROKEN BONES

Feb 83. (red-lp) *(CLAYLP 12)* **NEVER AGAIN (1/2 live)** –
– Warning / Never again / Hear nothing, see nothing, say nothing / The nightmare continues / The final bloodbath / Drunk with power / Where there's a will / Anger burning / Two monstrous nuclear stockpiles / The price of silence / Protest and survive / Born to die in the gutter / Doomsday / The more I see / State violence – state control / Decontrol / In defence of our future. *(re-iss. Jan90 lp/cd; CLAY LP/CD 12) (cd re-iss. Jul98 on 'Receiver'; RRCD 256)*

Mar 83. (7") *(CLAY 29)* **PRIDE OF SILENCE. / BORN TO DIE IN THE GUTTER** –

Sep 83. (12"ep) *(PLATE 5)* **WARNING – H.M. GOVERNMENT: WARNING / WHERE THERE'S A WILL / IN DEFENCE OF OUR FUTURE / ANGER BURNING** –

May 84. (7"/ext.12") *(CLAY/12CLAY 34)* **THE MORE I SEE. / PROTEST AND SURVIVE** –

May 85. (7") *(CLAY 43)* **IGNORANCE. / NO COMPROMISE** –
(12"+=) *(12CLAY 43)* – ('A'extended).

Jul 86. (lp) *(CLAYLP 19)* **GRAVE NEW WORLD** –
– Grave new world / In love believe / DTY/AYF / Time is kind / We dare speak (a moment only) / Sleep in hope / The downward spiral

—— (Feb'87) **ROB BERKELEY** – guitar; repl. CAL

—— (note:- DAVE ELLESMERE an early member later joined FLUX and DR.& CRIPPENS)

—— **DISCHARGE** reformed 1991, with **CAL** and long-standing **GERRY MALONEY** – drums Newcomers were **ANTHONY MORGAN** – bass / **ANDY GREEN** – guitar

Nov 91. (lp/c/cd) *(CLAY/+MC/CD 110)* **MASSACRE DIVINE** –
– City of fear / F.E.D. / Lost tribe rising / Challenge the terrior / White knuckle ride / New age / Terror police / Kiss tomorrow goodbye / Sexplosion / Dying time / E 2.30 / F.E.D. (F2 mix) / Terror police (F2 mix).

Oct 93. (cd) *(CLAYCD 118)* **SHOOTIN' UP THE WORLD** –
– Manson child / Lost in you / Shootin' up the world / Psycho active / Leaders – Deceivers / Fantasy overload / Down and dirty / Never came to care / Real life snuff / Exiled in Hell / Manson's child (reprise).

—— a tribute album, 'DISCHARGED' was issued by 'Rhythm Vicar' in 1992 and included tracks by EXTREME NOISE TERROR, CONCRETE SOX, etc

– compilations etc. –

on 'Clay' unless mentioned otherwise

Jul 87. (lp) *(CLAYLP 24)* **DISCHARGE THE SINGLES COLLECTION 1980-1986** –
(cd-iss. Aug95; same)

Feb 90. (lp/cd) *(CLAY/+CD 103)* **LIVE AT CITY GARDEN NEW JERSEY (live)** –

Mar 91. (lp/c/cd) *(CLAY/+MC/CD 107)* **THE NIGHTMARE CONTINUES (live)** –

Nov 92. (7") *Finn; (FINNRECC 006)* **EXCREMENT OF WAR. /** –

Jan 94. (lp/c/cd) *Nuclear Blast; (NB/+MC/CD 085)* **SEEING, FEELING, BLEEDING** –

Jun 94. (d-cd-box) *(CLAYCD 113)* **PROTEST & SURVIVE** –
(re-iss. May97 on 'Snapper'; SMDCD 131)

Jul 95. (cd) *(CLAYCD 120)* **THE SINGLES COLLECTION** –

DISLOCATION DANCE

Formed: Manchester, England . . . December 1978 by frontman IAN RUNACRES, trumpeter ANDY DIAGRAM (also of The DIAGRAM BROS), bassist PAUL EMMERSON and drummer DICK HARRISON. Issued on The BUZZCOCKS' 'New Hormones' label, 1980's eponymous debut EP introduced the band's GANG OF FOUR-esque sound although it would be almost a year before a follow-up four-tracker, 'SLIP THAT DISC' (1981). A full length album, 'MUSIC MUSIC' (1981) appeared a few months later, its sound embellished by new vocalist KATH WAY. A further series of singles followed over the next two years as the band emphasised the more free-floating, easy-jazz/pop elements of their sound, culminating in 1984's 'MIDNIGHT SHIFT' album. Reflecting this change, the latter set featured HERBIE RYAN guesting on sax, the man subsequently becoming a full-time member along with new recruit, Rochdale-born singer SONJA CLEGG. Her tenure was short-lived, however as the band split following a final single in late '85, 'WHAT'S GOING ON'. The track also featured a briefly returning DIAGRAM who had left a few years previous for The PALE FOUNTAINS, the man also having recorded material – including an album, 'SOME MARVELS OF MODERN SCIENCE' – in the early 80's as a member of The DIAGRAM BROTHERS.

Album rating: MUSIC MUSIC (*5) / MIDNIGHT SHIFT (*4)

IAN RUNACRES – vocals, guitar / **ANDY DIAGRAM** – trumpet, vocals (also of the DIAGRAM BROS) / **PAUL EMMERSON** – bass / **DICK HARRISON** – drums

New Hormones / not iss.

Sep 80. (7"ep) *(ORG 7)* **DISLOCATION DANCE** [ ] [-]
– It's so difficult / Familiar view / Birthday outlook / Perfectly in control.

Jul 81. (12"ep) *(ORG 10)* **SLIP THAT DISC EP** [ ] [-]
– Spare concern / We can work it out / I'll see it / It's all . . . panic!

—— added **KATH WAY** – vocals

Oct 81. (lp) *(ORG 15)* **MUSIC MUSIC** [ ] [-]
Jun 82. (7") *(ORG 19)* **ROSEMARY. / SHAKE** [ ] [-]
Oct 82. (7") *(ORG 22)* **YOU'LL NEVER KNOW. / YOU CAN TELL** [ ] [-]

—— now without ANDY DIAGRAM who joined The PALE FOUNTAINS

The Music Label / not iss.

May 83. (7") *(TML45 01)* **VIOLETTE. / SAN MICHELLE** [ ] [-]

Rough Trade / not iss.

Oct 83. (12"m) *(RTT 142)* **SHOW ME. / WE CAN WORK IT OUT / VENDETTA** [ ] [-]
Aug 84. (lp) *(ROUGH 63)* **MIDNIGHT SHIFT** [ ] [-]
– Show me / I'm doing fine / Here comes love / Remind me / Tyrannes of fun / Open cages / Baby blue / With a reason / Mr. Zak / Bottle of red wine / Midnight shift / San Michelle.

—— **SONJA CLEGG** – vocals; repl. KATH

—— **DIAGRAM** returned as the group added **HERBIE RYAN** – sax (who appeared on the last album)

Slipped Discs / not iss.

Dec 85. (12") *(SLIP12 1)* **WHAT'S GOING ON. /** [ ] [-]

—— split the following year with SONJA (augmented by IAN) going solo releasing the album, 'SOUL PRECIOUS' for 'Bop Cassettes' in '87. DIAGRAM rejoined The PALE FOUNTAINS and later teamed up with the band, JAMES.

DIAGRAM BROS

ANDY DIAGRAM – bass / **FRASER DIAGRAM** – vocals, guitar / **LAWRENCE DIAGRAM** – guitar / **SIMON DIAGRAM** – drums

Construct / not iss.

Oct 80. (7") *(CON 1)* **WE ARE ALL ANIMALS. / THERE IS NO SHOWER / I WOULD LOVE TO LIVE IN PRISON** [ ] [-]

New Hormones / not iss.

Apr 81. (7") *(ORG 9)* **BRICKS. / POSTAL BARGAINS** [ ] [-]
Nov 81. (lp) *(ORG 17)* **SOME MARVELS OF MODERN SCIENCE** [ ] [-]
May 82. (10"ep) **DISCORDS** [ ] [-]

DISORDER

Formed: Bristol, England . . . 1980 by STEVE ALLEN, DEAN CURTIS, MICK and a drummer named VIRUS. Another one of the "Punk's Not Dead" crew, DISORDER showcased their nihilistic, barely listenable yob-noise on the following year's debut EP, 'THE COMPLETE DISORDER'. Rejected by their local 'Riot City' label, the band were forced to self-finance all their releases and concentrated on EP's for the first three years of their career. During this period the one-chord wonder Mohawk-punks suffered an almost constant personnel turnover, the most serious of which occurred when BOOBS (their roadie!) substituted frontman DEAN. In the summer of '84, DISORDER finally delivered a debut LP, 'UNDER THE SCALPEL BLADE', the first in a series of occasional album releases that would be coveted by hardcore fans and ignored by everyone else. With the mid-90's going through a mini-punk renaissance, DISORDER were surprisingly still causing a musical breach of the peace via 1998's 'SLICED PUNX ON MEATHOOKS'.

Album rating: UNDER THE SCALPEL BLADE (*3) / LIVE IN OSLO (*3) / ONE DAY SON ALL THIS WILL BE YOURS shared with Kaska Process (*3) / VIOLENT WORLD (*4) / THE COMPLETE DISORDER compilation (*5)

DEAN CURTIS – vocals / **STEVE ALLEN** – guitar / **MICK** – bass / **VIRUS** – drums

Disorder / not iss.

Jun 81. (7"ep) *(ORDER 1)* **THE COMPLETE DISORDER EP** [ ] [-]
– Today's world / Violent crime / Complete disorder / Insane youth.

—— **STEVE ROBINSON** – bass; repl. MICK

Dec 81. (7"ep) *(ORDER 2)* **DISTORTION TO DEAFNESS / MORE THAN FIGHTS / DAILY LIFE / YOU'VE GOT TO BE SOMEONE** [ ] [-]

—— **TAFF** – bass (ex-X-CERTS REVIEW) repl. ROBINSON

—— **BOOBS** – vocals (their roadie) repl. DEAN

Sep 82. (12"ep) *(12ORDER 3)* **PERDITION** [ ] [-]

—— **GLENN** – drums (ex-DEAD POPSTARS) repl. VIRUS

Mar 83. (7"ep) *(ORDER 4)* **MENTAL DISORDER** [ ] [-]
Jun 84. (lp) *(AARGH 1)* **UNDER THE SCALPEL BLADE** [ ] [-]
– Driller killer / Education // Security guard / The g-song / Transparency / Victim of the NHS / Bent edge / The rhino song / God nose / Overproduction / Other side of the fence / Fuck your nationality / Men make frontiers / Prisoner of conscience / After.

Nov 85. (lp) *(AARGH 2)* **LIVE IN OSLO (live)** [ ] [-]
– Complete disorder / Daily life / More than fights / Remembrance day / Maternal obsession / Bent edge / Provocated wars / God nose / Education / Driller killer / Prisoners of conscience / Stagnation / Life / Rampton / After / Fuck your nationality / Out of order / Rhino song.

Nov 86. (m-lp; shared with KASKA PROCESS) *(AARGH 3)* **ONE DAY SON, ALL THIS WILL BE YOURS** [ ] [-]
– Double standards / Be bad be glad / Marriage story / Love and flowers / Togetherness.

Oct 89. (lp) *(AARGH 4)* **VIOLENT WORLD** [ ] [-]
– Driller killer / Into / Every ate seconds / Another fight another gig / Gods are born in the U.S.A. / I don't like war / Joleen / Fur Elise / Health hazard (live) / Todays world (live) / Violent world / Dope not Pope / Distortion till U vmoit / Take what you need.

—— split after above, although they did surface again from time to time

Desperate Attempt / not iss.

Nov 94. (lp/cd; with MUSHROOM ATTACK) *(DAR 010/+CD)* **MASTERS OF THE GLUENIVERSE** [ ] [-]

Anagram / not iss.

Feb 98. (cd) *(CDMGRAM 118)* **SLICED PUNX ON MEATHOOKS** [ ] [-]
– Fight the right / Fast food / Free society / Therefore we shout / Giro song / Boring / Insane war / Coz of death / Tied down / Pass the gluebag (to the right hand side) / To be continued / Intro / Army of aggressors / Warfear / Drop the bomb / Rumours and lies / Brutal attack / Anti-social reject / Jack hammer / Fight the right / Fuck your nationality.

Position Chrome / not iss.

Sep 98. (2x12") *(EFA 060816)* **GLOBAL DISORDER EP** [ ] [-]

– compilations, etc. –

Jan 84. (12"ep) *Disorder; (12ORDER 5)* **THE SINGLES COLLECTION** [ ] [-]
Dec 91. (cd) *Anagram; (CDPUNK 46)* **THE COMPLETE DISORDER** [ ] [-]
– Today's world / Violent crime / Dirorder / Insane youth / You've got to be someone / More than fights / Daily life / RAmpton / Provocated war / Bullshit everyone / 3 blind mice / Buy I gurt pint / Stagnation / Life / Out of order / Condemned / Media / Suicide children / Preachers / Remembrance day. *(re-iss. Oct96; same) (lp-iss.Oct98 on 'Get Back'; GET 37LP)*

Nov 93. (cd) *Anagram; (CDPUNK 19)* **UNDER THE SCALPEL BLADE / ONE DAY SON ALL THIS WILL BE YOURS** [ ] [-]
Oct 94. (cd) *Anagram; (CDPUNK 39)* **LIVE IN OSLO / VIOLENT WORLD** [ ] [-]
Jul 96. (cd) *Cleopatra; (<CLEO 9704CD>)* **DRILLER KILLER COLLECTION** [ ] [ ]
– Driller killer / Prisoners of conscience / Remembrance day / Complete disorder / Rampton / I don't like war / Out of order / Double standards / Love & flowers / Togetherness & unity / More than fights / Provocated wars / Life / Education / Bent edge / God nose / The other side of the fence / Security guard / Transparency.

Feb 97. (cd) *Anagram; (CDPUNK 88)* **REST HOME FOR SENILE OLD PUNK** [ ] [-]
Oct 98. (cd) *Anagram; (CDPUNK 109)* **THE BEST OF DISORDER** [ ] [-]

DISTRACTIONS

Formed: Manchester, England . . . late 1977 by students MIKE FINNEY and STEVE PERRIN-BROWN, who had played several live gigs in the previous two years with the rhythm section of LAWRENCE TICKLE and TONY TRAP. These originals were replaced by ADRIAN WRIGHT, PIP NICHOLLS and ALEC SIDEBOTTOM (former drummer with 60's combo, The PURPLE GANG), after their jubilee year resurrection. During a hectic touring schedule supporting the likes of MAGAZINE, The BUZZCOCKS and just about every Mancunian New Wave act around at the time, The DISTRACTIONS signed a one-off deal with 'T.J.M.' and unveiled their debut EP, 'YOU'RE NOT GOING OUT DRESSED LIKE THAT', early in '79. That year also saw the lads sign another one-off contract, this time to Tony Wilson's 'Factory', the results coming in the shape of the strongly melodic double-header, 'TIME GOES BY SO SLOW' / 'PILLOW TALK'. At the turn of the decade, The DISTRACTIONS' critical stock had risen to the extent that 'Island' offered them an album deal. Preceded by a re-recorded 'IT DOESN'T BOTHER ME' (originally from the debut EP) and a re-vamped version of (Eden Kane's 1964 Top 10 hit) 'BOYS CRY', 'NOBODY'S PERFECT' (1980) was surprisingly disappointing. One further single for the independent 'That' outlet, 'AND THEN THERE'S', surfaced the following year, singer JULIE FINNEY replacing PERRIN-BROWN before their attention was diverted to other activities.

Album rating: NOBODY'S PERFECT (*4)

MIKE FINNEY – vocals / **STEVE PERRIN-BROWN** – guitar / **ADRIAN WRIGHT** – guitar / **PIP NICHOLLS** – bass / **ALEC SIDEBOTTOM** – drums (ex-PURPLE GANG)

T.J.M. / not iss.

Mar 79. (7"ep) *(TJM 2)* **YOU'RE NOT GOING OUT DRESSED LIKE THAT EP** [ ] [-]
– It doesn't bother me / Waiting for the rain / Do the.

Factory / not iss.

Sep 79. (7") *(FAC 12)* **TIME GOES BY SO SLOW. / PILLOW FIGHT** [ ] [-]

Island / not iss.

Jan 80. (7") *(WIP 6533)* **IT DOESN'T BOTHER ME. / ONE WAY LOVE** [ ] [-]
Apr 80. (7") *(WIP 6568)* **BOYS CRY. / PARACETAMOL PARALYSIS** [ ] [-]
May 80. (lp) *(ILPS 9604)* **NOBODY'S PERFECT** [ ] [-]
– Waiting for Lorraine / Something for the weekend / Boys cry / Sick and tired / Leave you to dream / Louise / Paracetamol paralysis / Fantasy / Nothing / Wonder girl / Untitled / Still it doesn't ring / Looking for a ghost / Valerie.

Sep 80. (7") *(WIP 6650)* **SOMETHING FOR THE WEEKEND. / WHAT'S THE USE** [ ] [-]

That / not iss.

Apr 81. (7"ep) *(THAT 1)* **AND THEN THERE'S / 24 HOURS. / GHOST OF A CHANCE / LOVE IS NOT FOR ME** [ ] [-]

— **JULIE FINNEY** – vocals; repl. PERRIN-BROWN

— changed their moniker to FIRST CIRCLE, although there were no records

DIVINE COMEDY

Formed: Londonderry, Northern Ireland ... 1990 by bishop's son, NEIL HANNON, JOHN McCULLAGH and KEVIN TRAYNOR. Moving across the water to London, the three signed to maverick indie label, 'Setanta', releasing a SEAN O'NEILL (That Petrol Emotion)-produced debut, 'FANFARE FOR THE COMIC MUSE' (1990). A mini-set, it was followed by two further EP's, before the extroverted HANNON took over the reins as McCULLAGH and TRAYNOR bailed out. Free to pursue his own eccentric muse, HANNON steered The DIVINE COMEDY away from trad indie-rock towards a more self-consciously cultured approach which suggested the influence of everyone from SCOTT WALKER to JARVIS COCKER, in a cod-romantic ANDREW LLOYD-WEBBER-esque fashion of course! His first step towards educating the alternative pop scene came in the shape of 1993's 'LIBERATION' album, his debonair charisma in full effect on tracks such as 'EUROPOP', 'BERNICE BOBS HER HAIR' and 'I WAS BORN YESTERDAY'. His next set of songs, 'PROMENADE' (1994), was a loose concept affair and featured the Irish comedian, SEAN HUGHES, who provided verbal support on the track, 'THE BOOKLOVERS'. The name, DIVINE COMEDY, came to the attention of 'Father Ted' loving music fans after the instrumental, 'SONGS OF LOVE', was used as the theme tune to the popular Channel 4 programme. HANNON also co-wrote another ditty for the second series of the show; the downright silly 'My Beautiful Horse' was the singing priests' (Ted and Dougal) entry for the Eurovision Song Contest!!! In 1996, HANNON (together with his new DIVINE COMEDY recruits) released his most perfectly conceived pop masterpiece to date in 'CASANOVA', the Roger Moore of rock crooning his way through a dapper set of richly orchestrated diamonds. Duly encrusted into the Top 50, the album contained such memorably tongue-in-cheek hits as 'SOMETHING FOR THE WEEKEND', 'BECOMING MORE LIKE ALFIE' and 'THE FROG PRINCESS'. Now a firm critical fave, The DIVINE COMEDY (well, HANNON) had two more Top 20 successes with 'A SHORT ALBUM ABOUT LOVE' (a mini-set) and 'EVERYBODY KNOWS (EXCEPT YOU)' (a single). • **Covered:** THERE IS A LIGHT THAT NEVER GOES OUT (Smiths).

Album rating: FANFARE FOR THE COMIC MUSE mini (*4) / LIBERATION (*6) / PROMENADE (*7) / CASANOVA (*8) / A SHORT ALBUM ABOUT LOVE (*7) / FIN DE SIECLE (*7)

NEIL HANNON (b. 7 Nov'70) – vocals, guitar, bass, piano, etc. / **JOHN McCULLAGH** – bass, vocals / **KEVIN TRAYNOR** – drums

Setanta | Setanta

Aug 90. (m-cd/m-lp) *(SET CDM/LPM 002)* **FANFARE FOR THE COMIC MUSE** [ ] [-]
– Ignorance is bliss / Indian rain / Bleak landscape / Tailspin / Rise and fall / Logic vs. emotion / Secret garden.

Nov 91. (12"ep) *(SET 008)* **TIMEWATCH. / JERUSALEM / THE RISE AND FALL** [ ] [-]

Feb 92. (12"ep) *(SET 011)* **EUROPOP EP** [ ] [-]
– New wave / Intifada / Monitor.
(cd-ep+=) *(SET 011CD)* – Timewatch / Jerusalem / The rise and fall.

— now **HANNON** solo after the other two departed

Jul 93. (7"ep) *(CAO 008)* **LUCY. / THE POP SINGER'S FEAR OF THE POLLEN COUNT / I WAS BORN YESTERDAY** [ ] [-]

Aug 93. (cd/c/lp) *(SET CD/MC/LP 011)* **LIBERATION** [ ] [-]
– Festive road / Death of a supernaturalist / Bernice bobs her hair / I was born yesterday / Your daddy's car / Europop / Timewatching / The singer's fear of the pollen count / Queen of the south / Victoria Falls / Three sisters / Europe by train / Lucy. *(re-iss. Aug96; same)*

Oct 93. (7"pic-d-ep) *(DC 001)* **INDULGENCE No.1** [ ] [-]
– Untitled melody / Hate my way / Europe by train.

Mar 94. (cd/c/lp) *(SET CD/MC/LP 013)* **PROMENADE** [ ] [-]
– Bath / Going downhill / The booklovers / A seafood song / Geronimo / Don't look down / When the lights go out all over Europe / The summerhouse / Neptune's daughter / A drinking song / Ten seconds to midnight / Tonight we fly. *(re-iss. Aug96 & Aug97; same)*

Aug 94. (7"ep) *(DC 002)* **INDULGENCE No.2** [ ] [-]
– A drinking song / Tonight we fly (live) / When the lights go out all over Europe.

— now one-man band **NEIL HANNON** and a large ensemble of musicians including main band; **STUART 'PINKIE' BATES** – hammond organ / **JOBY TALBOT** – piano, arranger / **IVOR TALBOT** – guitar / **BRYAN MILLS** – bass / **MIGUEL 'MIGGY' BARRADAS** – drums

Apr 96. (cd/c/lp) *(SET CD/MC/LP 025)* *<36863>* **CASANOVA** [48] [ ]
– Something for the weekend / Becoming more like Alfie / Middle-class heroes / In & out of Paris & London / Charge / Songs of love / The frog princess / A woman of the world / Through a long & sleepless night / Theme from Casanova / The dogs & the horses.

— <above issued on 'Tristar' in the US>

Jun 96. (c-s) *(SETMC 026)* **SOMETHING FOR THE WEEKEND / SONGS OF LOVE (theme from 'Father Ted')** [14] [-]
(cd-s+=) *(SETCD 026)* – Birds of Paradise farm / Love is lighter than air.

Aug 96. (7"/c-s) *(SET/+MC 027)* **BECOMING MORE LIKE ALFIE. / YOUR DADDY'S CAR (live)** [27] [-]
(cd-s+=) *(SETCD 027)* – Untitled melody (acoustic) / The dogs & the horses (acoustic).

Nov 96. (c-s) *(SETMC 032)* **THE FROG PRINCESS / MOTORWAY TO DAMASCUS** [15] [-]
(cd-s+=) *(SETCD 032)* – A woman of the world / Lucy (demo).
(cd-s) *(SETCDL 032)* – ('A'side) / Something before the weekend / Neptune's daughter / Tonight we fly.

Feb 97. (m-cd/m-c) *(<SET CD/MC 036>)* **A SHORT ALBUM ABOUT LOVE** [13] [ ]
– In pursuit of happiness / Everybody knows (except you) / Someone / If . . . / If I were you (I'd be through with me) / Timewatching / I'm all you need.

Mar 97. (cd-ep) *(SETCDA 038)* **EVERYBODY KNOWS (EXCEPT YOU) / MAKE IT EASY ON YOURSELF (live) / A DRINKING SONG (live) / SOMETHING FOR THE WEEKEND (live)** [14] [ ]
(cd-ep) *(SETCDB 038)* – ('A'side) / Johnny Mathis' feet (live) / Your daddy's car (live) / Europe by train (live).
(cd-ep) *(SETCDC 038)* – ('A'side) / Bath (live) / Tonight we fly (live) / Middle class heroes (live).

— In April '98, The DIVINE COMEDY were part of a NOEL COWARD tribute album in which a single, 'I'VE BEEN TO A MARVELLOUS PARTY' was taken. It hit No.28 and was backed with a Shola Ama & Craig Armstrong track

— added **ROB FARRER** – percussion

Setanta | Imprint

Aug 98. (cd/c) *(SET CD/MC 057)* *<111813>* **FIN DE SIECLE** [9] [ ] Dec98
– Generation sex / Thrillseeker / Commuter love / Sweden / Eric the gardener / National express / Life on Earth / The certainty of chance / Here comes the flood / Sunrise. *(also ltd-cd; SETCDL 057)*

Sep 98. (7") *(SET 050)* **GENERATION SEX. / POSTCARD TO ROSIE** [19] [ ] Nov98
(cd-s) *(SETCDA 050)* *<114195>* – ('A'side) / London Irish / Time lapse.
(cd-s) *(SETCDB 050)* *<114197>* – ('A'side) / Chasing sheep is best left to shepherds / Little acts of kindness.

Setanta | Setanta

Nov 98. (c-s) *(SETMC 067)* **THE CERTAINTY OF CHANCE / MARYLAND ELECTRIC RAINSTORM** [49] [ ] Mar99
(cd-s) *(<SETCDA 067>)* – ('A'side) / Last stand in Metroland / Miranda.
(cd-s) *(<SETCDB 067>)* – ('A'side) / Dead only quickly / Knowing the ropes.

DIVINE HORSEMEN (see under ⇒ FLESHEATERS)

DIVINYLS

Formed: Sydney, Australia ... 1980 by co-songwriters, former teenage busker CHRISSIE AMPHLETT and MARK McENTEE, who met at a church choir night. Yet far from being acoustic-strumming Christian evangelists, The DIVINYLS (who also numbered BJARRE OHLIN, RICK GROSSMAN and RICHARD HARVEY) were a provocative musical proposition based around the pair's sleazy pop/rock and AMPHLETT's nymphette image. Featuring several songs from the film of the same name (which co-starred AMPHLETT), the domestic 'MONKEY GRIP' EP served as the band's debut release in 1982. A handful of tracks formed the basis for a debut album proper the following year, 'DESPERATE' (1983) being the first fruits of the band's newly inked worldwide 'Chrysalis' deal. Despite success at home, The DIVINYLS found it difficult to break into either the US or UK markets although they did score a minor American hit single with 'PLEASURE AND PAIN' in 1986. Culled from follow-up set, 'WHAT A LIFE~!', the track was to be the group's last taste of chart action for five years. Dropped by their label following the release of 1988's 'TEMPERAMENTAL', the core duo of AMPHLETT and McENTEE decamped to Europe and revised their strategy. Eventually re-emerging in the early 90's with a new deal (courtesy of 'Virgin') and eponymous album, The DIVINYLS finally hit big with breathy, infectious female masturbation ode, 'I TOUCH MYSELF', entering both the UK and US Top 10. Unfortunately the predictions of pop stardom proved premature as the band struggled to come up with a follow-up and subsequently fell back into obscurity. • **Songwriters:** AMPHLETT + McENTEE except LOVE IS THE DRUG (Roxy Music) / WILD THING (Troggs) / TO SIR WITH LOVE (Black-London) / etc.

Album rating: DESPERATE (*6) / WHAT A LIFE! (*5) / THE ESSENTIAL DIVINYLS COLLECTION compilation (*7) / TEMPERAMENTAL (*4) / DIVINYLS (*5) /

CHRISTINA AMPHLETT (b.25 Oct'60, Geelong, Victoria, Australia) – vocals / **MARK McENTEE** (b.16 Jul'61, Perth, Australia) – guitar / **BJARNE OHLIN** – guitar, keyboards / **JEREMY PAUL** – bass / **RICHARD HARVEY** – drums

WEA | not iss.

Feb 82. (m-lp) **MONKEY GRIP EP** [-] [-] Austra
– Boys in town / Only lonely / Elsie.

— **RICK GROSSMAN** – bass repl. JEREMY PAUL

Chrysalis | Chrysalis

Apr 83. (lp/c) *(<CHR/ZCHR 1404>)* **DESPERATE** [ ] [ ]
– Boys in town / Only lonely / Science friction / Siren song / Elsie / Only you / Ring me up / Victoria / Take a chance / I'll make you happy.

May 83. (7") *(CHR 2673)* **SCIENCE FRICTION. / TAKE A CHANCE** [ ] [ ]
(12"+=) *(CHR12 2673)* – Motion.

Jan 86. (lp/c) *(<CHR/ZCHR 1511>)* **WHAT A LIFE!** [ ] [91] Nov85
– Guillotine day / Pleasure and pain / Don't you go walking / Good die young / Sleeping beauty / Motion / In my life / Casual encounter / Heart telegraph.

Jan 86. (7") *<42916>* **PLEASURE AND PAIN. / HEART TELEGRAPH** [-] [76]

— **TIM MILLIKAN** – bass / **WARREN McLEAN** – drums repl. OHLIN, GROSSMAN + HARVEY (GROSSMAN joined HOODOO GURUS)

Jun 88. (7") *(CHS 3241)* **BACK TO THE WALL. /** [ ] [ ]
(12"+=) *(CHS12 3241)* –

Jul 88. (lp/c) *(<CHR/ZCHR 1627>)* **TEMPERAMENTAL** [ ] [ ]
– Temperamental / Back to the wall / Hey little boy / Punxie / Dance of love / Better days / Dirty love / Because / Fighting / Run-a-way train.

— **RANDY JACKSON** – bass / **CHARLEY DRAYTON** – drums repl. MILLIKAN + McLEAN

Virgin America / Virgin

Feb 91. (cd/c/lp) *(CDVUS/TCVUS/VUSLP 30)* <91397> **DIVINYLS** 59 15
– Make out alright / I touch myself / Lay your body down / Love school / Bless my soul (it's rock-n-roll) / If love was a gun / Need a lover / Follow through / Cafe interlude / Ballet / I'm on your side.

Apr 91. (7"/7"pic-d) *(VUS/+P 36)* <98873> **I TOUCH MYSELF. / FOLLOW THROUGH** 10 4 Feb91
(12"+=/cd-s+=) *(12/CD VUS 36)* – ('A'-alternative mix).

Aug 91. (7") *(1638)* **MAKE OUT ALRIGHT. / NEED A LOVER**
(12"+=/cd-s+=) *(1638)* – I touch myself (live).

—— split after above failure although they did return in the mid 90's after the song, 'SEX WILL KEEP US TOGETHER', featured on TV show 'Melrose Place'.

not iss. / R.C.A.

Nov 96. (cd) <5534-2> **UNDERWORLD** -
– Hard on me / Sex will keep us together / I'm jealous / For a good time / Open windows / Bleed / Underworld / Human on the inside / Come down to earth / Spook / Sorry / Heart of steel / Save me / Black magic.

– compilations, etc. –

Sep 91. (cd/c/lp) *Chrysalis; (CD/Z+/CHR 1846)* **THE ESSENTIAL DIVINYLS COLLECTION**
– Pleasure and pain / Temperamental / Back to the wall / Only lonely / Don't you go walking / Boys in town / Hey little boy / Science fiction / Sleeping beauty / I'll make you happy. *(c+=)* – Better days / Heart telegraph / Dirty love. *(cd++=)* – Punxsie / Hey little boy / Casual encounter.

Jan 94. (cd) *Alex;* <4195> **THE COLLECTION** -
– Ain't gonna eat out my heart / Lay your body down / Make out alright / To sir with love / If love was a gun / I touch myself / Need a lover / Wild thing / Temperamental / Love is the drug / Bless my soul (it's rock'n'roll) / I'm on your side / Pleasure and pain / Love school.

Nov 97. (cd) *Raven;* <67> **MAKE YOU HAPPY 1981-1993: Hits, Rarities & Essential Moments of an Incendiary Australian Band** -
– Boys in town / Girlfriends / Only lonely / Science fiction / Siren (never let you go) / I'll make you happy / 9.50 / Pleasure and pain / The good die young / Sleeping beauty / Hey little boy / Back to the wall / Temperamental / I touch myself / Love school / I'm on your side / Wild thing / Ain't gonna eat out my heart / Love is the drug / Love in motion.

Don DIXON

Born: North Carolina, USA. Having cut his teeth on the local music scene during the 70's, DIXON became more famous for producing the work of other acts (R.E.M., MARSHALL CRENSHAW, GUADALCANAL DIARY, SMITHEREENS, LET'S ACTIVE and his wife, MARTI JONES) during the 80's. Nevertheless he was also a recording artist in his own right, making his solo debut in 1985 with the wryly titled 'MOST OF THE GIRLS LIKE TO DANCE BUT ONLY SOME OF THE BOYS DO'. This was a collection of demos and rough sketches that DIXON had gathered over the previous four years which, having been issued on 'Enigma' and having put in a two months spell in the Top 200, even found an audience in the UK through 'Demon' records; the label was also home to NICK LOWE, a favoured comparison for many critics. Like LOWE, DIXON moved with a sly ease through the spectrum of popular musical styles, excelling himself on follow-up set, 'ROMEO AT JUILLIARD' (1987), a record featuring MARTI and another top producer, MITCH EASTER. His live work was documented on the pared down 'CHI-TOWN BUDGET SHOW' (1988), a fine example of the art of the singer-songwriter. The bolshier 'EEE' (1989) found DIXON flirting with a more readily accessible sound although his barbed lyrical viewpoint remained intact. He subsequently laid low on the solo front for the first half of the 90's, finally returning to the fray with an album, 'ROMANTIC DEPRESSIVE' (1995) for American roots label, 'Sugar Hill'.

Album rating: MOST OF THE GIRLS LIKE TO DANCE BUT ONLY SOME OF THE BOYS DO (*6) / ROMEO AT JUILLIARD (*7) / CHI-TOWN BUDGET SHOW (*6) / EEE (*6) / ROMANTIC DEPRESSIVE (*5)

DON DIXON – vocals, guitar, bass, keyboards / with session people incl. MITCH EASTER

Demon / Enigma

Nov 85. (lp/c/cd) *(FIEND/+CASS/CD 60)* <73239> **MOST OF THE GIRLS LIKE TO DANCE BUT ONLY SOME OF THE BOYS LIKE TO**
– Praying mantis / (You're a) Big girl now / Skin deep / Eyes on fire / Girls L.T.D. / Swallowing pride / Just rites / Wake up / Talk to me / / Pocket / Ice on the river / Renaissance eyes / Fighting for my life / Southside girl.

1987. (cd) <73243> **ROMEO AT JUILLIARD** -
– Borrowed time / Your sister told me / Heart in a box / Cool / Romeo / Million angels sigh / Helen / Swallowing pride / February ingenue / Cat out of the bag / Jean Harlow's return.

1988. (cd) <772296-2> **CHI-TOWN BUDGET SHOW (live)** -
– Heart in a box / Borrowed time / Your sister told me / Girls L.T.D. / February ingenue / Skin deep / Renaissance eyes / Southside girl / Cat out of the bag / Praying mantis.

1989. (cd) <773356-2> **EEE** -
– Oh cheap chatter / Silent screen / Love gets strange / I can hear the river / Dark end of the street / Gimme little sign / One lovely question / Calling out for love / Bad reputation / Roots of truth / Sweet surrender.

Sugar Hill / Sugar Hill

Jul 95. (cd/c) <(SH CD/C 5501)> **ROMANTIC DEPRESSIVE** Mar95
– Righteous side of love / Giving up the ghost / I should know better / Angel angel / Everytime I think of home / What you saw / Peace for the last time / Good golly Svengali / 25,000 days / Lottery of lives / Never slow down.

– compilations, etc. –

Feb 92. (cd) *Mau Mau; (MAUCD 616)* **(IF) I'M A HAM, WELL YOU'RE A SAUSAGE . . . COLLECTION** -
– Don Dixon (age 8) and his sister Ann / Praying mantis / Southside girl / Just rites / Girls L.T.D. / Borrowed time / Your sister told me / Heart in a box / Renaissance eyes (live) / Teenage suicide / Million angels sigh / Oh cheap chatter / I can hear the river / Gimme little sign / Calling out for love / Bad reputation / Sweet surrender / Don Dixon (age 8) and his sister Susan.

DNA

Formed: New York City, New York, USA . . . 1977 by ARTO LINDSAY, who had been brought up in a Brazilian village by his missionary father. In 1975, he arrived in the Big Apple where he initially worked for the 'Village Voice' newspaper. Having nearly joined the band, MARS (for whom he'd later write lyrics) as a drummer, ARTO chose to form his own trio together with ROBIN CRUTCHFIELD and Japanese drummer, IKUE ILE MORI. In 1978, DNA released their debut 45, 'LITTLE ANTS', before contributing four tracks to the BRIAN ENO-produced V/A album, 'No New York' (along with the aforementioned MARS, James Chance's CONTORTIONS and Lydia Lunch's TEENAGE JESUS & THE JERKS). TIM WRIGHT subsequently replaced CRUTCHFIELD and in 1981 a 10-minute EP of six songs, 'A TASTE OF DNA', showcased the man's experimental "No Wave", highlighting his untuned staccato guitar. ARTO had already moonlighted with JOHN LURIE's "fake-jazz" group, The LOUNGE LIZARDS, his unique style an integral part of their eponymous debut set in '81. That year too, MORI surprisingly surfaced as a cellist, violist and violinist on MARS' 'John Gavanti', while WRIGHT played bass on BRIAN ENO & DAVID BYRNE's 'My Life In The Bush Of Ghosts'. Inevitably, DNA had already reached the end of its natural lifespan, ARTO going on to work with the likes of JAMES CHANCE, The GOLDEN PALOMINOS and poet, JOHN GIORNO, on his 1984 album, 'Better An Old Demon Than A New God'. With PETER SCHERER on keyboards, ARTO LINDSAY & The AMBITIOUS LOVERS were formed the following year, the ever adventurous guitarist striving to incorporate the complex rhythms of his beloved Brazil into 1985's 'ENVY'. The AMBITIOUS LOVERS returned in 1988 with an all-star cast of hip New Yorkers including VERNON REID (of LIVING COLOR), JOHN ZORN, BILL FRISELL and the aforementioned LURIE, these multi-talented musicians playing on their only album for 'Virgin', 'GREED' (1988). After becoming the curator of 'The Kitchen' (New York's foremost meeting place for the experimentally inclined) 'LUST' continued LINDSAY's search for an immaculate marriage of sonic chaos and exotic South American funk. In 1992, he formed ARTO with likeminded veterans, BERNIE WORRELL, MARC RIBOT and MELVIN GIBBS, although it would be in a solo capacity that LINDSAY would release his next album, an eponymous set for 'Knitting Factory'. The following year, the enigmatic guitarist delivered two albums for 'Bar None', 'O CORPO SUTIL (THE SUBTLE BODY)' and 'MUNDO CIVILIZADO', the latter covered work by AL GREEN, PRINCE and SANTANA.

Album rating: A TASTE OF DNA mini (*7) / Ambitious Lovers: ENVY (*6) / GREED (*6) / LUST (*6) / Arto Lindsay: ARTO LINDSAY (*6) / O CORPO SUTIL (THE SUBTLE BODY) (*6)

ARTO LINDSAY (b.28 May'53, Richmond, Virginia) – vocals, guitar / **IKUE ILE MORI** (b.17 Dec'53, Tokyo, Japan) – drums / **ROBIN CRUTCHFIELD** – keyboards

not iss. / Lust/Unlust

Dec 78. (7") <11-CAN 234> **LITTLE ANTS. / YOU AND YOU** -

not iss. / DNA

1980. (7") <DNA 1> **DO THE SHOPPING. / ZOO TANGO** -

—— **TIM WRIGHT** – bass, guitar (ex-PERE UBU) repl. CRUTCHFIELD who formed DARK DAY

Rough Trade / American Clave

Aug 81. (12"ep) *(RT 086)* <AMCL 1003EP> **A TASTE OF DNA** May81
– New fast / 5:30 / Blondie red head / 32123 / New life / Lying on the sofa of life.

—— TIM formed HOME & GARDEN

– compilations, etc. –

Aug 93. (cd) *Avant; (AVANT 006)* **DNA** (live at CBGB's June '82) -

ARTO LINDSAY and The AMBITIOUS LOVERS

ARTO LINDSAY with **PETER SCHERER** – keyboards / **TONI NOGUEIRA / CLAUDIO SILVA / REINALDO FERNANDES / M.E. MILLER**

EditionsEG / EG

Feb 85. (lp) *(EGED 39)* **ENVY**
– Cross your legs / Trouble maker / Pagode Americano / Nothings monstered / Crowning roar / Too many mansions / Let's be adult / Venus lost her shirt / Badu / Dora / Beberibe / Locus coruleus. *(cd-iss. Jan87; CDEGED 39) (re-iss. cd Jul96 on 'Virgin'; CDOVD 469)*

AMBITIOUS LOVERS

LINDSAY + SCHERER plus others **VERNON REID** – guitar, vocals / **JOHN ZORN + JOHN LURIE** – saxophone / **BILL FRISELL** – guitar / **NANA VASCONCELOS** – percussion / **MELVIN GIBBS** – bass / **JOEY BARON** – drums / **JILL JAFFE** – violin / **D.K. DYSON + GAIL LOU** – vocals

Virgin / Virgin

Oct 88. (7") *(VS 1128)* **LOVE OVERLAP. / IT ONLY HAS TO HAPPEN ONCE**

(12"+=) *(VST 1128)* – ('A'-Stretched out long mix) / ('A'-Stuck in love mix).

Nov 88. (lp/c/cd) *(V/TCV/CDV 2545) <90903>* **GREED**
– Copy me / Privacy / Caso / King / Omotesando / Too far / Love overlap / Admit it / Steel wool / Para nao contrariar voce / Quasi you / It only has to happen once / Hot stuff. *(re-iss. cd Jul96; same)*

— duo with **GIBBS, RIBOT, VASCONCELOS** plus **TONY LEWIS** – drums / **LORELEI McBROOM** – vocals

Elektra Elektra

Jan 91. (12"ep) *(66583)* **PONTA DE LANCA AFRICANO EP**

Apr 91. (cd/c) *<(7559 60981-2/-4)>* **LUST**
– Lust / It's gonna rain / Tuck it in / Ponta de lanca Africano umbabarauma / Monster / Villain / Half out of it / Slippery / Make it easy / More light / E preciso perdoar.

ARTO LINDSAY

— with **MELVIN GIBBS** – bass (of ROLLINS BAND) / **DOUGIE BOWNE** – drumsb(ex-LOUNGE LIZARDS)

Knitting Factory Knitting Factory

Apr 95. (cd) *<(KFWCD 164)>* **ARTO LINDSAY: AGGREGATES 1-26**
– Be great / Recognize / In love / GTR drums #2 / Stitches / Imbue / Tap GTR / Tap / Absurd children / Noise / Flag of friendship / Venus / Looks like you / Flourish / Awfully short / Voice & lips / GTR bass / Founder / Two / 3 / Four / Bag pipes / Drug finger / GTR drums #1 / Head in a paper bag / Very good.

— now with a plethora of session people incl. RYUICHI SAKAMOTO

Rykodisc Bar None

Aug 96. (cd) *(RCD 10369) <078>* **O CORPO SUTIL (THE SUBTLE BODY)**
– Four skies / Child prodigy / Anima animale / Este seu olhar / My mind is going / Enxugar / No meu sotaque / Unbearable / Nobody in bed / Astronauts / Sovereign.

Dec 96. (cd) *<082>* **MUNDO CIVILIZADO**
– Complicity / Q samba / Simply beautiful / Mundo civilizado / Titled / Horizontal / Mar de Gavea / Ibassai / Pleasure / Erotic city / Clown.

GramaVision GramaVision

Dec 97. (cd) *<(GLP 79519)>* **HYPER CIVILIZADO** (remixes)
– Mundo civilizado / Complicity / Q samba / Q samba / Mundo civilizado / Complicity / Omulu / Complicity.

Mar 98. (cd) *<102>* **NOON CHILL**
– Noon chill / Whirlwind / Simply are / Blue eye shadow / Mulata fuzarqueira / Ridiculously deep / Anything / Gods are weak / Take my place / Daily life / Light moves away / Why compare / Reentry / Auguri.

D.O.A.

Formed: Vancouver, Canada ...1978 with an initial line-up of JOEY 'SHITHEAD' KEITHLEY, RANDY RAMPAGE and CHUCK BISCUITS, their moniker an acronym for DEAD ON ARRIVAL. The name reflected their no-messing approach, D.O.A.'s unceasingly radical stance and uncompromising musical approach doing much to shape the early 80's American hardcore scene. Following a clutch of early 7"/12" EP's and an album 'HARDCORE '81', the group signed to JELLO BIAFRA's 'Alternative Tentacles' and released the influential 'POSITIVELY D.O.A.' EP, such raging political barbs as 'FUCKED UP RONNIE' underlining the band's agit-punk approach. The lean three-chord attack which formed the basis of much of their material was much in evidence on 1984's top compilation 'BLOODIED BUT UNBOWED'. This included the 'WAR ON 45' EP, which introduced new members DAVE GREGG (actually around since 1980), GREGG JAMES and BRIAN GOBLE, recruited as replacements for RAMPAGE and BISCUITS, the latter moving on to CIRCLE JERKS, then BLACK FLAG and later DANZIG. These punk lumberjacks of the North American scene finally released an album's worth of new material, 'LET'S WRECK THE PARTY' in 1985, a set that saw the band's deceptively simple approach reach fruition. JAMES subsequently departed, JON CARD taking up the post prior to the release of their next hardcore delivery, 'TRUE (NORTH) STRONG AND FREE' (1987). More personnel changes were to follow, when DAVE GREGG split to form GROOVAHOLICS, CHRIS PROHOM coming in for the 1990 album, 'MURDER'. This was released around the same time as a collaboration set with JELLO BIAFRA (ex-DEAD KENNEDYS) entitled 'LAST SCREAM OF THE MISSING NEIGHBOURS'. The band stuck by their hardcore principles into the 90's with albums like 'TALK – ACTION = 0' (1991, '13 FLAVOURS OF DOOM' (1992) and 'LOGGERHEADS' (1993), the latter two finding D.O.A. back with the 'Alternative Tentacles'. • **Covers:** WE GOTTA GET OUT OF THIS PLACE (Animals) / FOLSOM PRISON BLUES (Johnny Cash) / COMMUNICATION BREAKDOWN (Led Zeppelin).

Album rating: HARDCORE '81 (*6) / BLOODED BUT UNBOWED compilation (*8) / LET'S WRECK THE PARTY (*7) / TRUE (NORTH) STRONG AND FREE (*5) / MURDER (*6) / TALK – ACTION = 0 (*6) / 13 FLAVOURS OF DOOM (*6) / LOGGERHEADS (*5)

JOEY "SHITHEAD" KEITHLEY – vocals, guitar / **RANDY RAMPAGE** – bass / **CHUCK BISCUITS** – drums

not iss. Sudden Death

May 78. (7"ep) *<SD 001>* **DISCO SUCKS EP**
– Royal police / Woke up screaming / Disco sucks / Nazi training camp. *(re-iss. Apr79 on 'Quintessence'; QEP 002)*

not iss. Quintessence

1978. (7") *<QS 102>* **THE PRISONER. / 13**

1979. (12"ep) **TRIUMPH OF THE IGNOROIDS EP**
– Nazi training camp / Want some bondage / Let's fuck / Rich bitch.

Dec 79. (7") *<QD 206>* **WHATCHA GONNA DO?. / WORLD WAR 3**

not iss. Friends

Sep 80. (7"ep) *<FR 003>* **SOMETHING BETTER CHANGE EP**

Jun 81. (lp) *<FR 010>* **HARDCORE '81**

not iss. Sudden Death

1983. (7") *<SD 003>* **BURN IT DOWN. / FUCK YOU**

1983. (7") *(SD 004>* **GENERAL STRIKE. / THAT'S LIFE**

Alternative Tentacles Alternative Tentacles

Jan 82. (7"ep) *<(VIRUS 7)>* **POSITIVELY D.O.A.**
– Fucked up Ronnie / World War Three / The enemy / My old man's a bum / New wave sucks. *(re-iss. Jul93' same)*

— **KEITHLEY** was now joined by **DAVE GREGG** – guitar, vocals / **GREGG JAMES** – drums / **BRIAN "SUNNY BOY ROY" GOBLE** – bass, vocals (they repl. RAMPAGE + BISCUITS; latter to CIRCLE JERKS, BLACK FLAG then DANZIG)

Nov 82. (7"ep) *<(VIRUS 24)>* **WAR ON 45**
– America the beautiful / Unknown / Rich bitch / Let's fuck war / I hate you / War in the east / Class war.

Feb 84. (lp) *<(VIRUS 31)>* **BLOODED BUT UNBOWED** (compilation 1978-83)
– Liar for hire / Fuck you / The prisoner / I'm right, you're wrong / Smash the state / Slumlord / New age / I don't give a shit / Waiting for you / Whatcha gonna do / World War 3 / 2 + 2 / The enemy / Fucked up Ronnie / Woke up screaming / 001 Loser's club / 13 / Get out of my life / D.O.A. *(cd-iss. Mar92 w/ 'WAR ON 45' on 'Restless'; LS 91852)*

Dec 84. (12"ep) *<(VIRUS 42)>* **DON'T TURN YER BACK (ON DESPERATE TIMES)** (The John Peel session)
– General strike / Race riot / A season in Hell / Burn it down.

Sep 85. (lp) *<(VIRUS 44)>* **LET'S WRECK THE PARTY**
– Our world / Dangerman / Race riot / Singin' in the rain / Dance o'death / General strike / Let's wreck the party / Shout out / Murder in Hollywood / The warrior ain't no more / No way out / Trial by media.

— split for a while, reformed in '87

— **JON CARD** – drums (ex-PERSONALITY CRISIS, ex-SNFU) repl. JAMES

not iss. Profile

Mar 87. (cd) *<1228>* **TRUE (NORTH) STRONG AND FREE**

— **CHRIS PROHOM** – guitar (ex-RED TIDE) repl. GREGG

not iss. Philo

1988. (m-lp) *<9000>* **ORNAMENT OF HOPE**

1988. (m-lp) *<9004>* **ANCIENT BEAUTY**

Restless Restless

Mar 90. (cd/lp) *<(72376-2/-4)>* **MURDER**
– We know what you you want / Guns, booze & sex / Boomtown / Afrikana security / Waiting for you / No productivity / The agony and the ecstasy / The midnight special / Bananaland / The warrior lives again / Concrete beach / Suicidal. *(re-iss. cd Jul95; same)*

— In May'90, teamed up w/ JELLO BIAFRA (ex-DEAD KENNEDYS) to release 'Alternative Tentacles' album 'LAST SCREAM OF THE MISSING NEIGHBORS' (Soundtrack to 'Terminal City Ricochet')

Dec 91. (cd/lp) *<(72506-2/-1)>* **TALK – ACTION = 0**
– America the beautiful / 13 / Burn it down / Murder in Hollywood / Lumberjack city / Waiting for you (part 2) / F*** you / Woke up screaming / Liar for hire / 2 + 2 / Let's wreck the party / The prisoner / Do or die / F*** that shit / General strike / Race riot. *(re-iss. cd Jul95; same)*

Alternative Tentacles Alternative Tentacles

Feb 92. (cd) *<(VIRUS 106CD)>* **THE DAWNING OF A NEW ERROR** (compilation of EP's, etc.)

Oct 92. (lp/c/cd) *<(VIRUS 117/+MC/CD)>* **13 FLAVOURS OF DOOM**
– Already dead / Death machine / Bombs away / The living dead / I played the fool / Too f***in' heavy / Hole in the sky / Hey sister / Use your raincoat / Legalized theft / Rosemary's baby / Beatin' rock'n'roll to death / Time of illusion. *(c+=/cd+=)* – Phantom zone.

Mar 93. (7") *<(VIRUS 120)>* **IT'S NOT UNUSUAL . . . BUT IT'S UGLY!. / DEAD MEN TELL NO TALES**
(cd-s) *<(VIRUS 120CD)>* – ('A'side) / Blue to brown / Help me get out of here / Runaway world.

Oct 93. (lp/c/cd) *<(VIRUS 130/+MC/CD)>* **LOGGERHEADS**
– Logjam / I see you cross / You little weiner / Overpowering urges / That turbulent uneasy feeling / The only green thing / Overtime / Cocktail time in Hell / Cut and dried / Burning in anger / Liberation and execution / Witch hunt / Knots / I can't take much more. *(c+=/cd+=)* – Fulsom prison dirge.

Oct 93. (7") *<(VIRUS 131)>* **THE ONLY THING GREEN. / FOLSOM PRISON BLUES**
(above a benefit single for the "Friends Of Clayoquot Sound" to save the region of Tofino, British Columbia, Canada from commercial logging)

Jan 94. (7") *<(VIRUS 133)>* **DISCO SUCKS. /**

Essential Noise Essential Noise

Dec 96. (cd) *<(35299-2)>* **THE BLACK SPOT** Oct95
– Blind men / Kill ya later / Order / Marijuana motherfuckers / You're playing for your body now / Worries / Road hill / Get away / More / Je declare / Big guys like D.O.A. / I know who you are / 1 bound for glory / Unchained melody / Cut time / Running out of time.

Earache not iss.

Jan 97. (cd; various artists) *(MOSH 164CD)* **NEW YORK CITY SPEEDCORE**
– Total annihilation / Ya mutha / Brooklyn mob / NYC speedcore / Wanna be a gangsta / Zu leiten / Uncle Bill's message / Pound down on your brain / Kill / Uncle Bill's message / Minute madness / Extreme gangsta / Our father / Our father / Ya mutha III / Noize core / I'll give you hard / Ya mutha II / You're dead / This is D.O.A.

– compilations, etc. –

Mar 98. (cd) *Golf; (CDHOLE 015)* **THE LOST TAPES**

May 98. (cd) *Golf; (CDHOLE 014)* **A FESTIVAL OF ATHEISTS**

DOCTOR & THE MEDICS

Formed: London, England ... 1981 by THE DOCTOR (aka CLIVE JACKSON), a six and a half foot Welshman, along with STEVE McGUIRE, RICHIE SEARLE and VOM. The following summer, this gaggle of pseudo hippies debuted with 'THE DRUIDS ARE HERE' single, subsequently signing to Miles Copeland's 'Illegal' for 1985's 'THE HAPPY BUT TWISTED' EP. Moving upstairs to Copeland's 'I.R.S.', the MEDICS had another flop 45 with 'THE MIRACLE OF THE AGE', later that year. Adding The ANADIN BROTHERS (actually COLLETTE and WENDI), they blew their hippie kudos (the lads once supported HAWKWIND at Stonehenge!) by becoming overnight sensations. The definition of a one-hit wonder, DOCTOR and his MEDICS briefly dominated the No.1 spot in 1986 with their grungy pop/rock makeover of uber-hippie Norman Greenbaum's 'SPIRIT IN THE SKY'. Looking like HAYSI FANTAYZEE after a bad acid trip, this bunch of fun-loving psychedelic revivalists provided a brief respite from po-faced synth outfits and jingle jangle indie bands with a song that's still guaranteed to fill the floor at student discos to this day. Qualified as he was in the art of music therapy, the good doctor could do nothing to prevent a subsequent relapse in the band's chart health; follow-up singles, 'BURN' and 'WATERLOO' (featuring WIZZARD man, ROY WOOD) barely scraped the Top 40 even if the debut album, 'LAUGING AT THE PIECES' (1986) made the Top 30 and shifted a few copies on the back of the No.1 single. Successive attempts by their label to resuscitate DOCTOR & THE MEDICS' ailing career met with a blank screen and following the failure of both 'KEEP THINKING IT'S THURSDAY' (1987) and 'THE ADVENTURES OF BODICEA AND THE BEETLE' (1993), the patient was pronounced officially dead, commercially at least. • **Covered:** SILVER MACHINE (Hawkwind) / GOOD GOLLY MISS MOLLY (Little Richard) / WATERLOO (Abba) / DRIVE, HE SAID (Stan Ridgway)

Album rating: LAUGHING AT THE PIECES (*4) / I KEEP THINKING IT'S TUESDAY (*3)

THE DOCTOR (b. CLIVE JACKSON) – vocals / **STEVE McGUIRE** – guitar / **RICHIE SEARLE** – bass / **VOM** (b. ROB MORRIS) – drums

Whaam | not iss.

Aug 82. (7") *(WHAAM 6)* **THE DRUIDS ARE HERE. / THE GOATS ARE TRYING TO KILL ME** | | -

Illegal | not iss.

May 85. (12"ep) *(MEDICS 1T)* **HAPPY BUT TWISTED EP** | | -
– Round and round / Auntie Evil's dormatory / Mole catcher / Silver machine.

I.R.S. | I.R.S.

Nov 85. (7") *(IRM 106)* **THE MIRACLE OF THE AGE. / I DON'T WANT TO BE ALONE** | | -

— added **ANADIN BROS** – (COLLETTE + WENDI) – backing vocals

Apr 86. (7") *(IRM 113)* <52880> **SPIRIT IN THE SKY. / LAUGHING AT THE PIECES** | 1 | 69 Aug86
(12"+=) *(IRMT 113)* – Love, peace and bananas (live) / Fried egg bad Monday (live) / Good golly Miss Molly (live).

Jun 86. (lp/pic-lp/c)(cd) *(MIRG/+C/D 1010)(DMIRG 1010)* <5797> **LAUGHING AT THE PIECES** | 25 |
– No one loves you when you've got no shoes / Kettle on a long chain / Come on call me / Watermelon runaway / Fried egg bad Monday / Spirit in the sky / Lucky Lord Jim / Moon song / Barbara can't dance / Smallness of the mustard pot.

Jul 86. (7") *(IRM 119)* **BURN. / CAPTAIN FREEZE** | 29 |
(12"+=) *(IRM 119T)* – Love, peace and bananas / Paranoid.

Nov 86. (7") *(IRM 125)* **WATERLOO. / DAMAGED BRAINS** | 45 |
(12"+=) *(IRMT 125)* – Stare crazy / Nothing.

— now without VOM who joined CRAZYHEAD

May 87. (12"ep) *(MEDICT 2)* **TWO PIECES OF CLOTH CAREFULLY STITCHED TOGETHER EP** | | -
– Sound of chains / Perfect world / Silver king / Age of gold.
(above was issued as another one-off for 'Illegal')

Aug 87. (7") *(IRM 139)* **MORE. / PRETTY LITTLE HENRY** | | -

Sep 87. (lp/c/cd) *(MIRF/MIRFC/DMIRF 1024)* **I KEEP THINKING IT'S TUESDAY** | |
– Drive, he said / Wild flowers / Gorilla / Jack of Kent / When the hammer comes down / Sea of stone / More / Madman of Bernarae / I keep thinking it's Tuesday / Love and everything you eat / I wanna choke on your love / Age of gold. *(c+=/cd+=)* – Stare crazy.

Feb 88. (7") *(IRM 154)* **DRIVE, HE SAID. / RIDE IN THE BEETLE (live)** | | -
(12"+=) *(IRMT 154)* – Medics mega hits mega mix.

— disbanded for a spell, although still played live, etc.

Dojo | not iss.

Nov 92. (cd) *(DOJOCD 78)* **THE ADVENTURES OF BOADACEA AND THE BEETLE (live 1992)** | | -
– Introduction of the sad Og / Love, peace and bananas / I do it because it makes my hair grow / Dogstar 2001 (a space rarity) / Terrified / Fried egg bad Monday / Instant Heaven / Stare crazy / Black and blue / Ride in the Beetle / Spirit in the sky / No one loves you when you've got no shoes.

Madman | not iss.

May 96. (cd) *(MAMA 005)* **INSTANT HEAVEN** | | -

DOCTORS OF MADNESS

Formed: London, England ... mid-70's by RICHARD 'KID' STRANGE, COLIN 'STONER' BROWN, PETER DILEMMA and URBAN BLITZ. Signed to 'Polydor', this oddball group made their debut in 1976 with the album, 'LATE NIGHT MOVIES, ALL NIGHT BRAINSTORMS', an amalgam of spaced-out ballads and full throttle fiddle-enhanced avant-rock. Vaguely associated with the emerging punk scene (vocalist STRANGE could snarl with the best of them when he felt like it), The DOCTORS released a follow-up set, 'FIGMENTS OF EMANCIPATION' later the same year. A new wave QUEEN might be the best way to describe this lot, favouring as they did overblown violin flourishes (similar to ULTRAVOX!) and ambitious arrangements. The initial burst of creativity dissipated and 1977's recorded output amounted to a solitary single, 'BULLETIN', predictably their most punk-like recording to date. A third album, 'SONS OF SURVIVAL', finally arrived the following year to general public apathy, the band unable to compete in the musically fertile wake of punk and its aftershocks. The record proved to be their epitaph although STRANGE pursued a solo career, recording for both 'Cherry Red' and 'Virgin'.

Album rating: 1975-1978 REVISIONISM compilation (*6)

RICHARD 'KID' STRANGE – vocals, guitar, keyboards, percussion / **URBAN BLITZ** – guitar, violin / **COLIN 'STONER' BROWN** – bass, vocals, percussion / **PETER DILEMMA** – drums, percussion, vocals

Polydor | U.A.

Mar 76. (lp) *(2383 378)* **LATE NIGHT MOVIES ALL NIGHT BRAINSTORMS** | | -
– Waiting / Afterglow / Mitzi's cure / I think we're alone / The noises of the evening / Billy watch out / B-movie bedtime / Mainlines.

Sep 76. (lp) *(2383 403)* **FIGMENTS OF EMANCIPATION** | | -
– Brothers / Suicide city / Perfect pest / Marie and Joe / In camera / Doctors of madness / Out.

Aug 77. (7") *(2058 921)* **BULLETIN. / WAITING** | | -

Mar 78. (7") *(2059 009)* **SONS OF SURVIVAL. / OUT** | | -

Apr 78. (lp) *(2383 472)* **SONS OF SURVIVAL** | | -
– 50's kids / Into the strange / No limits / Bulletin / Network / Sons of survival / Back from the dead / Triple vision / Kiss goodbye tomorrow / Cool.

May 78. (lp) <871> **DOCTORS OF MADNESS** | - |

— Disbanded after ex-DAMNED vocalist DAVE VANIAN repl. STRANGE on brief tour. STONER later joined The ADVERTS.

- compilations, etc. -

Jul 81. (lp) *Polydor; (2478 146)* **1975-1978 REVISIONISM** | | -
– Mainlines / Prologue / Waiting / B-movie bedtime / Triple vision / In camera / Network / Sons of survival / Marie and Joe / Mitzi's cure / Afterglow / Bullitin / Mainlines.

RICHARD STRANGE

— solo with **STEVE BOLTON + ANGUS McLEAN** – guitar / **PETE O'SULLIVAN** – bass / **MARTIN GRIFFIN** – drums / **DAVE WINTHROP** – saxophone (on lp)

Cherry Red | P.V.C.

Jan 80. (7") *(CHERRY 10)* **INTERNATIONAL LANGUAGE. / KISS GOODBYE TOMORROW** | | -

Nov 80. (lp) <7917> **THE LIVE RISE OF RICHARD STRANGE** (live 24/6/80) | - |
– The phenomenal rise of Richard Strange / On top of the world / I make plans / The hero runs away / International language / Replay / Gutter press / I won't run away.

Virgin | not iss.

Apr 81. (7"/12") *(VS 419/+12)* **INTERNATIONAL LANGUAGE. / GOD IS SCIENCE** | | -

May 81. (lp) *(V 2203)* **THE PHENOMENAL RISE OF RICHARD STRANGE** | | -
– The phenomenal rise of Richard Strange / On top of the world / Hearts and minds / Magic man / Gutter press / International language / Who cries for me / Premonition / The road to the room / I won't run away.

Jun 81. (7") *(VS 431)* **THE PHENOMENAL RISE OF RICHARD STRANGE. / ON TOP OF THE WORLD** | | -

Albion | not iss.

May 83. (12") *(SLAM 1)* **NEXT. /** | | -

RICHARD STRANGE & The ENGINE ROOM

— with **JULIE HEPBURN + RENE EYRE**

Arista | Arista

Sep 84. (7"/12"; as The ENGINE ROOM) *(ARIST/+12 587)* **WILD TIMES. / I LOVE HER (SHE'S POISON)** | | -

Mar 85. (7"/7"pic-d; as The ENGINE ROOM) *(ARIST/+P 593)* **YOUR KISS IS A WEAPON. / FALL OF THE HOUSE OF USHER** | | -
(12"+=) *(ARIST 12593)* – ('A'extended).

Nightshift | not iss.

Jul 88. (lp) *(NISHI 205)* **GOING-GONE** | | -
– Damascus / The lion's den / Banco celestial / Dominoes / The fall of the House Of Usher / Fear is the engine / Wounded / Love scare / Pride, time & inspiration / Pioneering surgery.

Dec 88. (12"ep) *(NISHI 206T)* **DAMASCUS** | | -
– Damascus / Haj caravan / Damascus (alt.version) / Pioneering surgery.

EFA | not iss.

1989. (lp) *(2606.143)* **THE REST IS SILENCE** | - | - German
– Low life / God help the wealthy man / Endless winter / Waterlillies / Wake up, America / Inch' Allah / Down comes the hammer / The ghost of Brian Jones.

— RICHARD retired from the music business in the 90's

DODGY

Formed: Hounslow, London, England ... early 1990 by NIGEL CLARK, ANDY MILLER and MATTHEW PRIEST. With DJ, CHRIS SLADE, they set up The Dodgy Club in a London bar, where they cultivated a grassroots fanbase over the course of the summer. Just over a year later, DODGY embarked upon their first national jaunt, christened the 'Word Of Mouth' tour in recognition of its unconventional nature; their fans had to phone up prospective promoters and venues to find out where they were playing (well dodgy!). After initial 7" singles on their own 'Bostin' label, they were snapped up by 'A&M', the major releasing two quickfire follow-ups in Spring '93, 'WATER UNDER THE BRIDGE' and 'LOVEBIRDS', the latter a Top 75 entry. The TURTLES to Oasis's BEATLES, DODGY's hazy shade of peace-pipe pop also incorporated the songwriting quality of SQUEEZE or CROWDED HOUSE. 'THE DODGY ALBUM' bounced onto the shelves that summer, although their spliff-friendly spirituality wasn't an immediate success and charming singles such as 'I NEED ANOTHER' and 'HOMEGROWN' went virtually unnoticed. A year later, DODGY's camper van sound made inroads into the Top 50; two hit singles, 'MELODIES HAUNT YOU' and the evocative 'STAYING OUT FOR THE SUMMER' preceded a second set, 'HOMEGROWN', although the critics remained unconvinced. 'SO LET ME GO FAR' and 'MAKING THE MOST OF' both broke their Top 30 duck and were followed by a re-issue of 'STAYING OUT FOR THE SUMMER', actually released in the summer this time around and a deserved Top 20 smash as Brit-pop gripped the nation. Now summer festival specialists, DODGY had finally found their sunkissed niche and a third album, 'FREE PEACE SWEET' (1996) was released to critical acclaim and major Top 10 success; the record also spawned four Top 20 singles, the pick of the bunch being the Top 5, 'GOOD ENOUGH'. • **Covered:** I CAN'T MAKE IT (Small Faces) / REVOLUTION (Beatles).

Album rating: THE DODGY ALBUM (*7) / HOMEGROWN (*6) / FREE PEACE SWEET (*8) / ACE A'S AND KILLER B'S compilation (*7)

NIGEL CLARK – vocals, bass, guitars / **ANDY MILLER** – lead guitar, vocals / **MATTHEW PRIEST** – drums, vocals, percussion

Bostin / not iss.

Sep 91. (7") *(BTN 001)* **SUMMER FAYRE. / ST. LUCIA** [ ] [-]
Nov 91. (7") *(BTN 002)* **EAST WAY. / SEEMS LIKE A BAD DAY** [ ] [-]
(cd-s+=) *(BTN 002CD)* – Groove song (St. Lucia demo) / See the way.
Apr 92. (7"black & white) *(BTN 003)* **THE BLACK AND WHITE SINGLE:- black side: WORTH THE BLOOD. / white side: THE ELEPHANT** [ ] [-]
(12"black & white+=) *(BTN 003X)* – Worth the blood (full).
(cd-s++=) *(BTN 003CDS)* – The D-Club versions; See the way / Jungle dark dance bath / Elevators goin' up / 4am nocturnal / Watch the sun go down.

— added 4th member **CHRIS SLADE** – DJ, keyboards

A&M / A&M

Mar 93. (7"/c-s) *(AM/+MC 196)* **WATER UNDER THE BRIDGE. / IT'S BEEN SO LONG** [ ] [-]
(12"+=/cd-s+=) *(AM Y/CD 196)* – She wants my loving / Valuable fool.
Apr 93. (7"/c-s) *(AM/+MC 0177)* **LOVEBIRDS. / BIG BROWN MOON** [65] [-]
(12"+=/cd-s+=) *(AM Y/CD 0177)* – Sylvia's bedroom / Smashed up in a flat.
Jun 93. (cd/c/lp) *(<540 082-2/-4/-1>)* **THE DODGY ALBUM** [75] [ ]
– Water under the bridge / I need another / Lovebirds / Satisfied / Grand old English oak tree / Stand by yourself / As my time goes by / Never again / Cold tea / We're not going to take this anymore.
Jun 93. (7"mustard-ep/c-ep) *(580 317-7/-4)* **I NEED ANOTHER. / IF I FALL / HENDRE DHU** [67] [-]
(12"ep+=/cd-ep+=) *(580 317-1/-2)* – Never again (campfire version).
Oct 93. (7"ep/c-ep) *(580 414-7/-4)* **HOMEGROWN E.P.** [ ] [-]
– Don't go back (to the beaten track) / Home grown / Let's wait till we get there.
(10"ep+=/cd-ep+=) *(580 415-0/-2)* –

— now without CHRIS and back to trio

Jul 94. (7"ep/c-ep) *(580 676-7/-4)* **THE MELOD-E.P.: MELODIES HAUNT YOU. / THE SNAKE** [53] [-]
(12"+=) *(580 676-1)* – Don't go back (to the beaten track).
(cd-s++=) *(580 676-2)* – Summer fayre. *(re-iss. Jul97; same)*
Sep 94. (7"blue/c-s) *(580 788-7/-4)* **STAYING OUT FOR THE SUMMER. / LOVEBIRDS (original)** [38] [-]
(cd-s+=) *(580 797-2)* – As time goes by (demo) / Back to life.
(cd-s) *(580 789-2)* – ('A'side) / A summer's day in mid-January / Don't you think / Colour me with paints. *(re-iss. Jul97; same)*
Oct 94. (cd/c/lp) *(<540 282-2/-4/-1>)* **HOMEGROWN** [43] [ ]
– Staying out for the summer / Melodies haunt you / So let me go far / Crossroads / One day / We are together / Whole lot easier / Making the most of / Waiting for the day / What have I done wrong? / Grassman. *(re-iss. Jun95, hit No.28)*
Dec 94. (c-s) *(580 903-4)* **SO LET ME GO FAR / DON'T GET LOW, DON'T LET GO (U.K. R.I.P.)** [30] [-]
(12"+=/cd-s+=) *(580 905-1/-2)* – So let me Wobble Jah / The elephant (the Balaphon-a-bing bong immigrant mix).
(cd-s) *(580 903-2)* – ('A'side) / I need another (live) / Satisfied (live) / Melodies haunt you (live). *(re-iss. Jul97; same)*
(above featured JAH WOBBLE – bass) (below featured The KICK HORNS)
Feb 95. (7"pic-d/c-s) *(580 986-7/-4)* **MAKING THE MOST OF. / FAISONS AU MIEUX (YES, IT'S IN FRENCH)** [22] [-]
(cd-s+=) *(580 987-2)* – The Ludlow sessions part 1: Spent all my time running / All the time in the world.
(cd-s) *(580 989-2)* – ('A'extended) / The Ludlow sessions part 2: Watch out watcha doin' / This is ours / (Get off your) High horse. *(re-iss. Jul97; same)*
Jun 95. (c-s) *(581 092-4)* **STAYING OUT FOR THE SUMMER (mixed up in 95) / SATISFIED (live)** [19] [-]
(cd-s) *(581 093-2)* – ('A'side) / (Your love keeps lifting me) Higher and higher / Crossroads (live) / Melodies haunt you (live).
(cd-s) *(581 095-2)* – ('A'side) / Waiting for the day (live) / One day (live) / (Get off your) High horse (live). *(re-iss. Jul97; same)*

— now with guest (4th member) **RICHARD PAYNE** – keyboards

May 96. (7"white/c-s) *(581 624-7/-4)* **IN A ROOM. / OUTCLUBBING** [12] [-]
(cd-s) *(581 625-2)* – ('A'side) / Self doubt / Long life (acoustic) / Jungle UK (no rest in peace). *(re-iss. Jul97; same)*
Jun 96. (cd/c/lp) *(<540 573-2/-4/-1>)* **FREE PEACE SWEET** [7] [ ]
– Intro / In a room / Trust in time / You've gotta look up / If you're thinking of me / Good enough / Ain't no longer asking / Found you / One of those rivers / Prey for drinking / Jack the lad / Long life / U.K.R.I.P. / Homegrown.
Jul 96. (7"/c-s) *(581 814-7/-4)* **GOOD ENOUGH. / NUTTERS** [4] [-]
(cd-s+=) *(581 815-2)* – Speaking in tongues / Lovebirds on Katovit. *(re-iss. Jul97; same)*
Nov 96. (7"/c-s) *(581 998-7/-4)* **IF YOU'RE THINKING OF ME. / IN A ROOM (acoustic)** [11] [-]
(cd-s) *(581 998-2)* – ('A'side) / Pebblemilljam / Forever remain / Good enough (version). *(re-iss. Jul97; same)*
Mar 97. (7"/c-s) *(582 132-7/-4)* **FOUND YOU. / STAND BY YOURSELF** [19] [-]
(cd-s) *(582 133-2)* – ('A'side) / I can't make it / Revolution.

Polygram / Polygram

Sep 98. (c-s) *(MERMC 512) <582737>* **EVERY SINGLE DAY / THE BRIDGE / MOSTAR KEEP SHINING** [32] [ ] Nov98
(cd-s) *(MERCD 512)* – (first two tracks) / Look up.
(cd-s) *(MERDD 512)* – (first & third tracks) / Staying out for the summer.
Oct 98. (cd/c) *(<541 018-2/-4>)* **ACE A'S AND KILLER B'S** (compilation) [55] [ ] Nov98
– Every single day / Staying out for the summer (summer 95) / Water under the bridge / Good enough / Melodies haunt you / Big brown moon / Found you / Self doubt / In a room / Making the most of / If you're thinking of me / Lovebirds / (Get off your) High horse / So let me go far / Grassman / Ain't no longer asking / The elephant. *(<also d-cd; 541 019-2>)*

John DOE (see under ⇒ X)

DOG FACED HERMANS

Formed: Edinburgh, Scotland ... 1986 by ANDY, MARION, COLIN and WILF. One of the weirdest and most experimental bands to come out of the capital, the DOG FACED HERMANS initially delivered their CHUMBAWAMBA-esque anarchist message via a single on their own 'Demon Radge' imprint. They subsequently appeared on the 'Alternative Tentacles' V/A album, 'Censorship Sucks' (a tribute set to raise funds for Jello Biafra's court case) while also releasing a trio of 45's for 'Calculus'. Towards the end of the decade, a debut LP, 'EVERYDAY TIME BOMB' finally appeared on 'Vinyl Drip', the 'HERMANS trading in the 'Burgh for the more liberal climes of Amsterdam. Finding a sympathetic Dutch recording home at 'Konkurrel' (in-house label of The EX), they released two sets, 'MENTAL BLOCKS FOR ALL AGES' (1991) and 'HUM OF LIFE' (1993), the last of which featured a cover of 8-Eyed Spy/Lydia Lunch's 'LOVE SPLIT WITH BLOOD'. Renewing their relationship with San Francisco's 'Alternative Tentacles', DOG FACED HERMANS completed a further two sets of socially aware, post-feminist avant-punk in the shape of 'BUMP & SWING' (1994) and 'THOSE DEEP BUDS' (1994).

Album rating: EVERYDAY TIME BOMB (*5) / MENTAL BLOCKS FOR ALL AGES (*5) / HUM OF LIFE (*5) / BUMP & SWING (*5) / THOSE DEEP BUDS (*4)

MARION – vocals, trumpet, bells / **ANDY** – guitar / **COLIN** – bass / **WILF** – drums, percussion / **GERT-JAN** – live sound

Demon Radge / not iss.

Feb 87. (7") *(RADGE 1)* **UNBEND. /** [ ] [-]

Calculus / not iss.

Mar 88. (12"ep) *(KIT 001)* **HUMANS FLY** [ ] [-]
Sep 88. (7") *(KIT 002)* **NO PARTISAN. / ?** [ ] [-]
Sep 88. (7") *(KIT 003)* **BELLA – CIAO. / MISS O'GRADY** [ ] [-]

Vinyl Drip / not iss.

Jun 89. (lp) *(SUK 007)* **EVERYDAY TIME BOMB** [ ] [-]

Konkurrel / A Bomb

Nov 91. (lp/cd) *(K 139/+CD)* **MENTAL BLOCKS FOR ALL AGES** [ ] [-]
Mar 93. (lp/cd) *(K 147/+CD)* **HUM OF LIFE** [ ] [-]
– Jan 9 / Viva / Hook and the wire / How we connect / Love split with blood / Wings / White Indians / Hear the dogs / Love is the heart of everything / Madame la mer / Peace warriors.

Compulsive / not iss.

Mar 93. (7") *(CPS 2)* **PEACE WARRIORS. / (track by Jonestown)** [ ] [-]

Konkurrel / Alternative Tentacles

Jun 94. (cd) *(K 153CD) <VIRUS 159CD>* **BUMP & SWING** [ ] [ ] Feb95
– Hear the dogs / Peace warriors / Viva / Love is the heart of everything / Transformation / Keep your laws – Off my body / Jan 9 / Human spark / Love split with blood / Fortune / The bride has feet of clay.
Oct 94. (lp/cd) *(K 155/+CD) <VIRUS 151/+CD>* **THOSE DEEP BUDS** [ ] [ ]
– Blessed are the follies / Volkswagen / Keep your laws – Off my body / Lie and swell / H tribe / Human spark / Les femmes et les filles vont danser / Virginia fur / Calley / Dream forever.

— disbanded some time in '95

DOGSTAR

Formed: Los Angeles, California, USA ... 1993 by actor/Hollywood heart-throb turned bass player, KEANU REEVES, actor/drummer ROB MAILHOUSE, ex-NUNS frontman/songwriter, BRET DOMROSE and GREGG MILLER, the latter leaving after playing a handful of gigs. Apparently formed out of a chance meeting in a supermarket rather than being a planned strategy for KEANU to move into music, the DOGSTAR trio played their inaugural gigs as low-key affairs in local bars. Selling out an American tour almost immediately on the strength of KEANU's sex appeal/fame factor, it was obvious the band's music was always going to take a back seat to the sensationalism. Eventually signing with RCA outlet, 'Zoo', DOGSTAR debuted with the 'QUATTRO FORMAGGI' EP in summer '96, coinciding with a UK tour that took in Scotland's 'T In The Park'. A few months later, the trio released their one and only album, 'OUR LITTLE VISIONARY', a run-of-the-mill sub-Grunge affair that contained an ill-advised cover of Badfinger's 'NO MATTER WHAT'. • **KEANU's filmography:** included 'River's Edge' and 'Bill And Ted's Big Adventure' to mention but a few. • **Note:** Another DOGSTAR released an EP, 'ILLUMINATI FABRICATION', for 'La La Land', in 1994.

Album rating: OUR LITTLE VISIONARY (*5)

BRET DOMROSE – vocals, guitar (ex-NUNS) / **KEANU REEVES** (b.1965) – bass, vocals / **BOB MAILHOUSE** – drums

		American	Zoo
Jul 96.	(c-ep/cd-ep) *(74321 40142-4/-2) <11128>* **QUATTRO FORMAGGI EP**		
	– Honest anyway / Behind her / Return / 32 stories.		
Sep 96.	(cd) *<11133>* **OUR LITTLE VISIONARY**	-	
	– Forgive / Our little visionary / No matter what / Breathe tonight / Nobody home / History light / Honest anyway / And I pray / Enchanted / Bleeding soul / Goodbye / Denial.		

DOLL

Formed: London, England ... October '77 by MARION VALENTINE, ADONIS YIANNI, his brother CHRISTOPHER YIANNI and MARIO WATTS. Bandwagoneers with a catchy line in disposable New Wave punk, The DOLL almost immediately signed to 'Beggars Banquet' (home of The LURKERS and TUBEWAY ARMY), through whom they released their pop-friendly debut 45, 'DON'T TANGO ON MY HEART'. A fusion of The REZILLOS and BLONDIE, the track failed to ignite public interest, although follow-up single, 'DESIRE ME', cracked the Top 30 and saw the leopard-skin clad MARION and Co pout their stuff on Top Of The Pops. With MARION receiving all the press attention, internal tensions came to a head and caused a sizeable split in the ranks; with only CHRISTOS and VALENTINE remaining, new members DENNIS HAINES, JAMIE WEST-ORAM and PAUL TURNER were recruited. After nearly a year's lay off, the band returned to find themselves shunned by fans and critics alike as they attempted to hit the singles chart again via 'CINDERELLA WITH A HUSKY VOICE'. The accompanying debut album, 'LISTEN TO THE SILENCE' (1979) suffered a similar fate as the record buying public took their advice all too literally; The DOLL wound up proceedings shortly after.

Album rating: LISTEN TO THE SILENCE (*3)

MARION VALENTINE (b.1952, Brighton, England) – vocals, rhythm guitar / **ADONIS YIANNI** (b.10 Oct'57) – keyboards / **CHRISTOPHER YIANNI** (b. CHRISTOS, 6 Sep'54) – bass / **MARIO WATTS** (b.1958) – drums

		Beggars Banquet	not iss.
Jan 78.	(7") *(BEG 4)* **DON'T TANGO ON MY HEART. / TRASH**		-
Dec 78.	(7"/ext.12") *(BEG 11/+T)* **DESIRE ME. / T.V. ADDICT**	28	-
	(with free 7") *(SAM 93)* **BURNING UP LIKE A FIRE. / DESIRE ME**		
——	**MARION + CHRISTOS** enlisted **DENNIS HAINES** – keyboards / **JAMIE WEST-ORAM** – lead guitar / **PAUL TURNER** – drums		
Oct 79.	(7") *(BEG 26)* **CINDERELLA WITH A HUSKY VOICE. / BECAUSE NOW**		-
Oct 79.	(lp) *(BEGA 12)* **LISTEN TO THE SILENCE**		-
	– The one kiss / Zero heroes / Ce soir, Cheri / Cinderella with a husky voice / Memories / You used to be my hero / True love / Frozen fire / Carmina / Listen to the silence / Something rare, something beautiful.		
Jan 80.	(7") *(BEG 31)* **YOU USED TO BE MY HERO. / ZERO HEROES**		-
Apr 80.	(7") *(BEG 38)* **BURNING UP LIKE A FIRE. / FROZEN FIRE**		-
——	split in the Spring of 1980, MARION retired after songwriting failed		
——	JAMIE WEST-ORAM went on to be successful with The FIXX		

DOLL BY DOLL

Formed: London, England . . . 1977 by Fife-born JACKIE LEVEN, although it would be a few years later that the band – which also comprised JO SHAW, ROBIN SPREAFICO and DAVID McINTOSH – would make their mark. LEVEN had previously cut his teeth as a singer/songwriter performing under the assumed name of JOHN ST. FIELD, gigging with the likes of MAN until the onset of punk rock captured his imagination and inspired him to form a band. DOLL BY DOLL emerged in punk's wake after signing to Warner Brothers off-shoot, 'Automatic', releasing a debut album, 'REMEMBER', early in 1979. Having replaced SPEARFICO with TONY WAITE, DBD issued a second album that year, 'GYPSY BLOOD', LEVEN's Celtic fringe lyrics and stirring vocals sitting rather uneasily beside the band's elaborate rock arrangements. An unusual signing to pop label, 'Magnet', the quartet delivered two further sets, 'DOLL BY DOLL' (1981) and 'GRAND PASSION' (1982), the latter seeing LEVEN employ a new band including co-vocalist, HELEN TURNER and an array of rock establishment veterans, i.e. DAVE GILMOUR and MEL COLLINS. The following year, LEVEN disbanded the group for a solo deal with 'Charisma', although only two flop singles were forthcoming. Things went horribly wrong as the singer found himself the victim of a street attack in London, amongst other injuries suffering damage to his larynx; it went from bad to worse as LEVEN fell into a spiral of heroin abuse. He nevertheless managed to turn things around, curing himself (with help from his wife, Carol) and setting up a support network, C.O.R.E., for fellow drug addicts. During this period in the musical wilderness, he did actually manage a few gigs with ex-SEX PISTOLS and RICH KIDS bass player, GLEN MATLOCK, as the short-lived C.B.I (CONCRETE BULLETPROOF INVISIBLE). In 1994, LEVEN finally emerged as a fully-fledged solo artist, signed to roots label 'Cooking Vinyl'. Recorded in Scotland and released only north of the border, the mini-set, 'SONGS FROM THE ARGYLL CYCLE', re-introduced LEVEN as a folk-rock artist leaving behind all traces of his punk days amid lyrical images of windswept Highland scenes. LEVEN has since released several more sets in a similar vein while working with American poet, ROBERT BLY and fellow ex-punk Fifer, RICHARD JOBSON.

Album rating: REMEMBER (*6) / GYPSY BLOOD (*7) / DOLL BY DOLL (*5) / GRAND PASSION (*4) / Jackie Leven: SONGS FROM THE ARGYLL CYCLE (*6) / THE MYSTERY OF LOVE IS GREATER THAN THE MYSTERY OF DEATH (*7) / THE FORBIDDEN SONGS OF THE DYING WEST (*7) / FAIRY TALES FOR HARD MEN (*6) / CONTROL (*5)

JACKIE LEVEN (b. Fife, Scotland) – vocals (later added guitar) / **JO SHAW** – guitar, vocals / **ROBIN SPREAFICO** – bass, vocals / **DAVID McINTOSH** – drums, vocals

		Automatic-Warners	not iss.
Mar 79.	(7") *(K 17330)* **THE PALACE OF LOVE. / FOUNTAIN IS RED, FOUNTAIN IS WHITE**		
Mar 79.	(lp/c) *(K/K4 56618)* **REMEMBER**		-
	– Butcher boy / Chances / Sleeping partners / More than human / Lose myself / Janice / The palace of love.		
——	**TONY WAITE** – bass, vocals; repl. ROBIN		
Oct 79.	(lp) *(K 56755)* **GYPSY BLOOD**		-
	– Teenage lightning / Gypsy blood / Strip show / The human face / Hey sweetheart / Binary fiction / Hell games / Forbidden worlds / Highland rain / Endgame / When a man dies.		
Nov 79.	(7") *(K 17496)* **TEENAGE LIGHTNING. / ONE TWO BLUES**		-
Jan 80.	(7") *(K 17559)* **GYPSY BLOOD. / LOVE MYSELF**		-
		Magnet	Magnet
May 81.	(7") *(MAG 188)* **MAIN TRAVELLED ROADS. / BE MY FRIEND**		-
May 81.	(lp/c) *(MAGL/ZCMAG 5039)* **DOLL BY DOLL**		-
	– Figure it out / Carita / Soon new life / Main travelled roads / Those in peril / I never saw the movie / The perfect romance / Fantastic sensation / The street I love / Be my friend / Up / A bright green field.		
Aug 81.	(7") *(MAG 195)* **CARITA. / MURDER ON THE HIGHWAY**		-
	(12"+=) *(12MAG 195)* – An honest woman.		
——	**LEVEN** recruited an entire new line-up **HELEN TURNER** – vocals, keyboards / **TOM NORDON** – vocals, guitar, bass / plus a plethora of famous people in session incl. DAVE GILMOUR, MEL COLLINS, JON FIELD, GRAHAM BROAD, TIM CROSS + MAGGIE RILEY		
Aug 82.	(7") *(MAG 229)* **UNDER MY THUMB. / ETERNAL**		-
Sep 82.	(lp/c) *(MAGL/ZCMAG 5057)* **GRAND PASSION**		-
	– Strong hands / Under my thumb / Dancing shoes / Cool skies / Eternal / onely kind of show / Natural / Grand passion / City of light / Dawn of the rain girls / Boxers hit harder when women are around / So long kid.		
——	subsequently split when LEVEN went solo		

JACKIE LEVEN

		Charisma	not iss.
Aug 83.	(7") *(JACK 1)* **LOVE IS SHINING DOWN ON ME. / GREAT SPIRIT CALLS**		-
Jul 84.	(7") *(JACK 2)* **UPTOWN. / TROPIC OF COOL**		-
	(12"+=) *(JACK 2-12)* – Beautiful train.		
——	JACKIE was attacked in a London street and suffered severe larynx problems which stopped him singing for a long spell. In March '88, he and GLEN MATLOCK surfaced as CONCRETE BULLETPROOF INVISIBLE, releasing the single, 'BIG TEARS', for 'Radioactive'. JACKIE was again a solo artist in the mid 90's		
		Cooking Vinyl	not iss.
Mar 94.	(m-cd) *(COOKCD 065)* **SONGS FROM THE ARGYLL CYCLE**	-	- Scot
	– Stranger on the square / Walking in Argyll / Honeymoon hill / Looking for love / Grievin' at the mish nish / Ballad of a simple heart / As we sailed into Skibbereen / Some ancient misty morning / History of rain / Gylen Gylen / Fly / Crazy song. *(full UK-iss.Apr96; COOKCD 101)*		
Jul 94.	(d-lp/c/cd) *(COOK/+C/CD 064)* **THE MYSTERY OF LOVE IS GREATER THAN THE MYSTERY OF DEATH**		-
	– Clay jugg / Shadow in my eyes / Call mother a lonely field / The crazy song / Farm boy / The garden / Snow in Central Park / Looking for love / Heartsick land / Gylen Gylen / I say a little prayer / Bars of Dundee. *(d-lp+=)* – Donna Karan / Ballad of a simple heart / Stranger on the square / Horseshoe and jug / Mary Jone's dog / So my soul can sing. *(also iss.Sep94 cd+=; COOKCDS 064)* **THE RIGHT TO REMAIN SILENT** (with ROBERT BLY & JAMES HALLAWELL)		
Jan 95.	(cd-s) *(FRY 036)* **I SAY A LITTLE PRAYER /**		-
Sep 95.	(d-lp/c/cd) *(COOK/+C/CD 090)* **THE FORBIDDEN SONGS OF THE DYING WEST**		-
	– Young male suicide blessed by invisible woman / Some ancient misty morning / Working alone – A blessing / Leven's lament / Marble city bar / The wanderer / Exultation / Men in prison / Birds leave shadows / Stornoway girl / Silver roof / Lammermuir hills / Come back early or never of come / By the sign of the sheltered star / The scene that haunts my memory / My Lord, what a morning. *(d-lp+=)* – Exultation.		
Apr 97.	(d-lp/cd) *(COOK/+CD 115)* **FAIRY TALES FOR HARD MEN**		-
	– Boy trapped in a man / Desolation blues / Extremely violent man / Old West African song / aint Judas / Poortoun / Fear of woman / Walled covers of Ravenscraig / Sad Polish song / Sexual danger / Jim o' Windygates / Mad as the mist and snow / Kirkconnell flow / Listening to crows pray / Sir Patrick Spens . . . / Sunflower / Torture blues / Story which could be true / Scotland the brave.		
Sep 97.	(cd) *(COOKCD 131)* **CONTROL** (rec.1971)		-
	– Soft lowland tongue / Raerona / Mansion tension / Dog star / Ruins / I'm always a Prinlaws boy / Problem / Dune voices / Sleeping in bracken.		

DOLLY MIXTURE

Formed: Cambridge, England . . . late 70's by all-girl trio of DEBSEY WYKES, RACHEL BOR and HESTER SMITH. More famous for having backed CAPTAIN SENSIBLE on a couple of his solo singles (including his No.1 smash, 'Happy Talk'), the DOLLY MIXTURE sweetened up the post-New Wave scene with their charmingly eccentric brand of girly pop-punk. Although they made a major label debut in 1980 with the single, 'BABY IT'S YOU' (a Shirelles cover), the trio subsequently disowned the track and complained they were being misrepresented by the company. Finding a more sympathetic home at PAUL WELLER's 'Respond' imprint, the girls released a further two 45's over the course of the early 80's. With all-female acts such as The MO-DETTES, The RAINCOATS and The MARINE GIRLS also making waves, DOLLY MIXTURE were primed for the top with an overload of media coverage and attendant expectation. After being out of the limelight for a while, the trio surprisingly returned with a self-financed double-set of home recordings released under the spartan title of 'DEMONSTRATION TAPES' (1983). Although virtually ignored at the time, the album was later re-issued by pop curator, BOB STANLEY (of SAINT ETIENNE). After their mid-80's demise, DEBSEY and HESTER re-united in a one-album project, COMING UP ROSES.

Album rating: DEMONSTRATION TAPES (*6) / Coming Up Roses: I SAID BALLROOM (*5)

RACHEL BOR (b.16 May'63, Wales) – vocals, guitar, cello / **DEBSEY WYKES** (b.21 Dec'60, London, England) – vocals, bass / **HESTER SMITH** (b.28 Oct'60, West Africa) – drums

Chrysalis / not iss.

Sep 80. (7") *(CHS 2459)* **BABY IT'S YOU. / NEW LOOK AWAY** [ ] [-]

Respond / not iss.

Nov 81. (7") *(RESP 1)* **BEEN TEEN. / HONKY HONDA AND ERNIE BALL** [ ] [-]

Mar 82. (7") *(RESP 4)* **EVERYTHING AND MORE. / YOU & ME ON THE SEASHORE** [ ] [-]

— joined up as backing singers with CAPTAIN SENSIBLE

Dead Good Dolly Platt. / not iss.

Dec 83. (d-lp) *(GOOD 1)* **DEMONSTRATION TAPES** (demos) [ ] [-]
– Dream come true / Ernie Ball / He's so frisky / The didn't song / Will he kiss me tonight / Miss Candy twist / Shonay Shonay / How come you're such a hit with the boys, Jane? / Side street walker / Treasure hunt / Never let it go / Angel treads / Welcome to the perfect day / Step close now / Stareaway / In your eyes / Understanding / Never mind Sundays / Spend your wishes / Day by day / Wave away / Sorry to leave you / Winter seems fine / Grass is greener / Round the corner / Remember this / Whistling in the dark. *(cd-iss. Mar96 on 'Royal Mint'; RM 001CD)*

Jan 84. (7") *(DMS 1)* **REMEMBER THIS. / LISTENING PLEASURE** [ ] [-]

Cordelia / not iss.

May 86. (7"ep) **THE FIRESIDE EP** [ ] [-]

— split in 1986 when RACHEL remained with CAPTAIN SENSIBLE and his band

COMING UP ROSES

— **DEBSEY + HESTER** with **NICKY BRODIE** – vocals, percussion (ex-SHILLELAGH SISTERS) / **PATRICIA O'FLYNN** – saxophone (ex-SHILLELAGH SISTERS) / **LEIGH LUSCIOUS** – guitar / **CLAIRE KENNY** – bass (ex-AMAZULU)

— (1987) **SOPHIE CHERRY** – bass; repl. CLAIRE

— (1989) **DEBSEY, HESTER + NICKY** recruited a new line-up of **TONY WATTS** – lead guitar / **MIDUS** – bass / **JANE KEAY** – saxophone (past members were also featured on the album)

Utility / not iss.

Jul 89. (m-lp/m-cd) *(UTIL 005/+CD)* **I SAID BALLROOM** [ ] [-]
– Remember my name / I could fly / I don't know what it is / Black jean boy / I could have been your girlfriend (if you'd asked me to) / You kill me.

— split early in 1991

DOME (see under ⇒ WIRE)

Tanya DONELLY (see under ⇒ BELLY)

DONNAS

Formed: USA . . . 1996 by DONNA A, DONNA R, DONNA F and DONNA C. Retreading the blitzkrieg bop pioneered by the RAMONES twenty years earlier, the four Donnas came on like a latter day RUNAWAYS minus the pop glamour. Unrelenting punk-rock with a capital P, the girls' eponymous debut album surfaced on the tiny 'Superteem' imprint in '97, a frantic document of teen rebellion revelling in the usual US high school cliches. Subsequently becoming part of the 'Lookout' stable (which launched GREEN DAY and others), The DONNAS toured the States and Japan promoting a follow-up set, 'AMERICAN TEENAGE ROCK'N'ROLL' (1998). • **Covered:** DRIVE IN (Beach Boys) / DA DOO RON RON (Crystals).

Album rating: THE DONNAS (*5) / AMERICAN TEENAGE ROCK'N'ROLL MACHINE (*6)

DONNA A. – vocals / **DONNA R.** – guitar / **DONNA F.** – bass / **DONNA C.** – drums

not iss. / Superteem

1997. (lp) **THE DONNAS** [-] [ ]
– Hey, I'm gonna be your girl / Let's go Mano! / Teenage runaway / Lana and Stevie / I'm gonna make him mine (tonight) / Huff all night / I don't wanna go / We don't go / Friday fun / Everybody's smoking cheeba / Get rid of that girl / Drive in / Do you wanna go out with me / Rock'n'roll boy / High school yum yum / A boy like you / Let's rab. *<cd-iss. Aug98 on 'Lookout'+=singles tracks; LK 201CD>* – Let's go Mano! / Last chance dance / I wanna be a unabomber / Da doo ron ron / I don't wanna go to school / I don't wanna rock'n'roll tonight.

Lookout / Lookout

Jan 98. (7") *<(LK 196)>* **ROCK'N'ROLL MACHINE. / SPEEDIN' BACK TO MY BABY** [ ] [ ]

Feb 98. (cd/lp) *<(LK 191 CD/LP)>* **AMERICAN TEENAGE ROCK'N'ROLL MACHINE** [ ] [ ] Jan98
– Rock'n'roll machine / You make me hot / Checkin' it out / Gimmie my radio / Outta my mind / Looking for blood / Leather on leather / Wanna get some stuff / Speed demon / Shake in the action.

DONNER PARTY

Formed: San Francisco, California, USA . . . 1986 by singer-songwriter, SAM COOMES, who enlisted the aid of CAT HEADS drummer/singer, MELANIE CLARIN and bassist REINHOLD JOHNSON. Debuting with the eponymous 'THE DONNER PARTY' in '87 on their own 'Cryptovision' label, the trio garnered immediate underground acclaim for their wilfully amateurish and eccentric alt-pop folk, COOMES' vocals consistently drawing comparisons to the likes of JONATHAN RICHMAN and JAD FAIR. Spotted by CAMPER VAN BEETHOVEN man, DAVID LOWERY, the group signed to his 'Pitch A Tent' label where they re-issued their debut. This marked the end of the first chapter in the band's career as COOMES teamed up with ELLIOTT SMITH to form HEATMISER. This kept him occupied until the mid-90's when he briefly dusted down The DONNER PARTY for a comeback album, 'FOOD FOR THOUGHT' (1995); SAM is now the mainman behind QUASI.

Album rating: THE DONNER PARTY (*6) / FOOD FOR THOUGHT (*5)

SAM COOMES – vocals, guitar / **REINHOLD JOHNSON** – bass / **MELANIE CLARIN** – drums (of CAT HEADS)

not iss. / Cryptovision

1987. (lp) *<1400>* **THE DONNER PARTY** [-] [ ]
<re-iss. 1988 on 'Pitch-A-Tent'; 11>

— COOMES teamed up ELLIOTT SMITH in his band, HEATMISER, before briefly re-uniting the band

not iss. / Infamous

Jan 95. (cd) *<1332>* **FOOD FOR THOUGHT** [-] [ ]

— COOMES subsequently formed MOTORGOAT then QUASI

DOOR AND THE WINDOW (see under ⇒ ALTERNATIVE TV)

DOROTHY (see under ⇒ RAINCOATS)

DOS (see under ⇒ MINUTEMEN)

DOWN BY LAW

Formed: Los Angeles, California, USA . . . early 90's by seasoned hardcore belter, DAVE SMALLEY. Finding a home at BRETT GUREWITZ's (BAD RELIGION) 'Epitaph' stable, they unleashed the take-no-prisoners punk-metal assault of their eponymous debut. They carried on in much the same vein with a fairly prolific recording schedule over the first half of the 90's. The line-up evolved into a more stabalized affair, SMALLEY emlisting the help of SAM WILLIAMS, ANGRY JOHN and DANNY WESTMAN. Their mid 90's period was overshadowed by lablemates OFFSPRING, although they did manage to squeeze out some competent hardcore on the albums, 'ALL SCRATCHED UP!' (1996) and 'LAST OF THE SHARPSHOOTERS' (1997).

Album rating: DOWN BY LAW (*5) / PUNKROCKACADEMYFIGHTSONG (*5)

DAVE SMALLEY – vocals (ex-DYS, ex-ALL, ex-DAG NASTY) / + members of CHEMICAL PEOPLE + CLAW HAMMER:- **CHRIS BAGAROZZI** – guitar / **DAVE NAZ** – drums / **ED URIK** – bass, vocals

Epitaph / Epitaph

Jul 91. (cd/lp) *<(E 86411-2/-1)>* **DOWN BY LAW** [ ] [ ]

Oct 92. (cd/c/lp) *<(E 86419-2/-4/-1)>* **BLUE** [ ] [ ]
– Last brigade / Looking for something / Break the wall / At home in the wasteland / Rain / Turn away / Air conditioner / Greenest field / Straw / Finally here / Our own way / Dead end. *<actually a re-issue of their eponymous set in '91>*

— **SMALLEY** recruited **MARK PHILIPS** – guitar / **PAT HOED** – bass / **COLIN SEARS** – drums

Aug 93. (cd) *<(LF 064CD)>* **SPLIT** (with GIGANTOR) [ ] [ ] Jun95
(above cd issued on German 'Lost & Found' label)

— **SMALLEY** with **SAM WILLIAMS** (b.Tampa Bay, Florida) – guitar (ex-SLAP OF REALITY, ex-BALANCE) / **ANGRY JOHN** – bass (ex-CLAY IDOLS, ex-LEONARDS) / **DANNY WESTMAN** – drums (ex-SPINDLE, ex-FLORECENE)

Jul 94. (cd/c/lp) *<(86431-2/-4/-1)>* **PUNKROCKACADEMYFIGHTSONG** [ ] [ ]
– Punk won / Hit or miss / Flower tattoo / Sympathy for the world / 500 miles / Brief Tommy / Bright green globe / Minn same / Drummin' Dave / Hunter up / Punk as funk / 1944 / The king and I / Haircut / Chocolate jerk / Sam I / Heroes & hooligans / Soldier boy / Goodnight song / Sam II.

Nov 95. (7"/cd-s) *(WOOS 9 S/CDS)* **500 MILES. /** [ ] [ ]
(above released on 'Out Of Step')

Mar 96. (cd/c/lp) *<(86456-2/-4/-1)>* **ALL SCRATCHED UP!** [ ] [ ]
– Independence day / Cheap thrill / All American / Hell song / True believers / Giving it all away / Gruesome Gary / Radio ragga / Attention: anyone / Superman / Post office lament / Ivory girl / No has beens / Kevin's song / True music / Far and away / Punks and drunks.

Oct 96. (7"ep) *(BEP 930715)* **YELLOW RAT BASTARD**
(above issued on 'Break Even Point')
Aug 97. (cd/c/lp) *<(6501-2/-4/-1)>* **LAST OF THE SHARPSHOOTERS**
– USA today / No equalizer / Call to arms / Gun of '96 / Get out / Burning heart / Question marks and periods / Urban napalm / DJG / Concrete times / No one gets away / The last goodbye / Factory day / Cool crowd / Self destruction.
Sep 97. (7"m) *(SDR 005)* **NO EQUALIZER. / CONCRETE TIMES / SUPERFUCKED**
(above issued on 'Suspect Device')
Nov 97. (7") *(6523-7)* **QUESTION MARKS AND PERIODS. / THE SUPERHEROES**
(cd-s+=) *(6523-2)* – Self-destruction.

DOWNY MILDEW

Formed: Los Angeles, California, USA . . . mid 80's by main songwriter, CHARLIE BALDONADO, part co-writer, JENNY HOMER, NANCY McCOY and MIKE MARASSE. Initially signed to US indie label, 'Texas Hotel', the band debuted in 1986 with an eponymous 12" EP. Rooted in breezy West Coast 60's pop and psychedelia but delivered with an alternative edge, the DOWNY MILDEW sound was fairly typical of the era's loose Paisley Underground scene although the contrasting writing styles of BALDONADO and HOMER marked them out from the pack. A debut album, 'BROOMTREE', appeared in 1987, its folky pop sensibilities drawing comparisons with 10,000 MANIACS. Featuring new drummer JOHN HOFER and violinist, SALVADOR GARZA, follow-up set, 'MINCING STEPS' (1988), fleshed out the sound with atmospheric string flourishes while maintaining the songwriting flair. Replacing HOFER with ROB JACOBS and moving to Windham Hill's 'High Street' offshoot for 1992's Mitchell Froom-produced 'AN ONCOMING TRAIN', the band continued to prefect their retro sound while 1994's 'SLOW SKY' saw JANINE COOPER coming in for the pregnant McCOY.

Album rating: BROOMTREE (*6) / MINCING STEPS (*6) / AN ONCOMING TRAIN (*7) / SLOW SKY (*5)

JENNY HOMER – vocals, guitar / **CHARLIE BALDONADO** – guitar, vocals / **NANCY McCOY** – bass / **MIKE MARASSE** – drums

Glass / Texas Hotel

1986. (12"ep) **DOWNY MILDEW**
– Experience in the far south west / Drive / Purple parlor / Bad dream.
May 87. (lp) *(GLALP 025)* **BROOMTREE**
– The frown song / The kitchen / Sally (part 3) / Good dream / Hollow girl / Ocean motor kid / Burnt bridges / That's enough of that / Sally (part 2) / Everybody's gone. *<re-iss. 1993 on 'High Street' cd+=/c+=; 10319-2/-4>* – DOWNY MILDEW EP

— **JOHN HOFER** – drums; repl. JACOBS

1988. (lp) *<10>* **MINCING STEPS**
– Offering / Turning yourself around / Tangled ladders / Six flights / Floorboard / Big surprise / Misfortune / Inside her house / Flower song / All is not well in this house. *<cd-iss. 1993 on 'High Street'; 10320>*

— **ROB JACOBS** – drums; repl. HOFER

— added **SALVADOR GARZA** – strings

not iss. / High Street

1992. (cd-s) **ELEVATOR**
1992. (cd/c) *<10313-2/-4>* **AN ONCOMING TRAIN**
– An oncoming train / Borrowed chant / Trading jewels / Elevator / Twice told tale / Six months is a long time / Seconds protest / Melissa, I know the difference / Sleep! / Child.

— **JANINE COOPER** – bass (ex-PET CLARK) repl. NANCY

Mar 94. (cd/c) *<10321-2/-4>* **SLOW SKY**
– Your blue eye / Left foot down / Release / Polka-dot-scarved woman / Girls by the lake / Liar needs a good memory / That he wrote / Them that dream / Machine / Sidewinding home / Don't change your mind / I remember yesterday.

— disbanded the following year

– others, etc. –

1992. (cd) *Windham Hill; <19207>* **ELEVATOR**

DRAIN (see under ⇒ BUTTHOLE SURFERS)

DREAM SYNDICATE

Formed: Los Angeles, California, USA 1981 by STEVE WYNN and KENDRA SMITH. The former had previously cut his teeth with SID GRIFFIN in an embryonic LONG RYDERS. They soon completed the line-up with KARL PRECODA and DENNIS DUCK. After an untitled mini-lp back home, they caught the interest of UK indie, 'Rough Trade', in 1983, who released their debut full-length album 'THE DAYS OF WINE AND ROSES'. Cut from a distinctly rougher-hewn cloth than most of the band's 'Paisley Underground' contemporaries, the album's dark intensity caused enough of a stir to eventually get them snapped up by 'A&M'. By the release of their major label debut, 'MEDICINE SHOW' (1984), KENDRA SMITH had been replaced by DAVE PROVOST. Although more mainstream than its predecessor, the album still showed the ragged influence of NEIL YOUNG and THE VELVET UNDERGROUND and while it didn't accrue the success it was probably due, its critical acclaim paved the way for other majors to give them a shot at the big league. After a final album for 'A&M', the compilation of early live material, 'IT'S NOT THE NEW DREAM SYNDICATE ALBUM' (1985), the band released their next studio offering on 'Chrysalis', 1986's 'OUT OF THE GREY'. Despite the more commercial, straight ahead rock sound of the record, success continued to elude the band and they split in early 1989 after releasing a final well-recieved album for 'Enigma', 'GHOST STORIES'. • **Songwriters:** Most written by WYNN, except covers CINNAMON GIRL (Neil Young) / MR. SOUL (Buffalo Springfield). WYNN covered KOOL THING (Sonic Youth) / BOY IN THE BUBBLE (Paul Simon) / GUTTERBALL mainly WYNN with HARVEY or McCARTHY. • **Trivia:** Early '85, STEVE WYNN was also in DANNY & DUSTY duo alongside old cohort DAN STUART (of GREEN ON RED).

Album rating: THE DAYS OF WINE AND ROSES (*7) / THE MEDICINE SHOW (*7) / THIS IS NOT THE NEW DREAM SYNDICATE ALBUM (*4) / OUT OF THE GREY (*6) / 50 IN A 25 ZONE (*4) / GHOST STORIES (*5) / LIVE AT RAJI'S (*7) / TELL ME WHEN IT'S OVER: THE BEST OF DREAM SYNDICATE compilation (*8) / Steve Wynn: KEROSENE MAN (*6) / DAZZLING DISPLAY (*6) / TAKE YOUR FLUNKY AND DANGLE (*5) / FLUORESCENT (*5) / MELTING IN THE DARK (*6)

STEVE 'DUSTY' WYNN (b.21 Feb'60, Santa Monica, Calif.) – vocals / **KARL PRECODA** (b.1961) – guitar / **DENNIS DUCK** (b.25 Mar'53) – drums / **KENDRA SMITH** (b.14 Mar'60, San Diego, Calif.) – bass / guest on below; **TOM ZVONCHECK** – keyboards

not iss. / Down There

Dec 82. (m-lp) *<VEX 10>* **THE DREAM SYNDICATE**
– Sure thing / Some kinda itch / That's what you always say / When you smile. *(UK-iss.Jun85 on 'Zippo'; ZANE 001) (cd-iss. Aug92; VEXCD 10)*

Rough Trade / Ruby

Nov 83. (lp) *(ROUGH 53)* **THE DAYS OF WINE AND ROSES**
– Tell me when it's over / Definitely clean / That's what you always say / Then she remembers / Halloween / When you smile / Until lately / Too little, too late / The days of wine and roses. *(re-iss. Jan87 on 'Slash'; 23844-1) (cd-iss. Jan95 on 'Normal'; NORMAL 176CD)*
Dec 83. (12"ep) *(RTT 121)* **TELL ME WHEN IT'S OVER. / SOME KINDA ITCH (live) / MR. SOUL (live) / SURE THING (live)**

— **DAVE PROVOST** – bass repl. KENDRA (she joined RAINY DAY then OPAL) (appeared on live album early '84) and later went solo

A&M / A&M

Jun 84. (lp/c) *(AMLX/CXM 64990)* **MEDICINE SHOW**
– Still holding on to you / Daddy's girl / Burn / Armed with an empty gun / Bullet with my name on it / The medicine show / John Coltrane stereo blues / Merrittville.
Feb 85. (lp) *(AMLH 12511)* **IT'S NOT THE NEW DREAM SYNDICATE ALBUM (live)**
– Tell me when it's over / Bullet with my name on it / Armed with an empty gun / The medicine show / John Coltrane stereo blues.

— added **PAUL B. CUTLER** (b. 5 Aug'54, Phoenix, Arizona) – lead guitar + **MARK WALTON** (b. 9 Aug'59, Fairfield, Calif.) – bass, repl. PRECODA + PROVOST

Chrysalis / Big Time

Jun 86. (lp/c) *(CHR/ZCHR 1539)* **OUT OF THE GREY**
– Out of the grey / Forest for the trees / 50 in a 25 zone / Boston / Slide away / Dying embers / Now I ride alone / Dancing blind / You can't forget. *(cd-iss. 1987; CCD 1539) (re-iss. Oct87 on 'Big Time' lp/c; ZL/ZK 71457X)*
Sep 87. (12"ep) *(ZT 41420)* **50 IN A 25 ZONE. / DRINKING PROBLEM / BLOOD MONEY / THE LONELY BULL**

— now quartet (**WYNN, CUTLER, PROVOST + DUCK**) when PREGODA departed

Enigma-Virgin / Enigma

Sep 88. (lp/c/cd) *(ENVLP/TCENV/CDENV 506) <73341-1/-4/-2>* **GHOST STORIES**
– The side I'll never show / My old haunts / Loving the sinner, hating the sin / Whatever you please / Weathered and torn / See that my grave is kept clean / I have faith / Some place better than this / Black / When the curtain calls. *(cd re-iss. Sep95 on 'Restless'; 72758-2)*
Nov 88. (7") *(ENV 6)* **I HAVE FAITH. / NOW I RIDE ALONE**
(12"+=) *(ENVT 6)* – I ain't living long like this.

— split early 1989, when WYNN decided to venture solo.

— He released a number of albums, the first two being 'KERSOSENE MAN' and 'DAZZLING DISPLAY'. He also formed GUTTERBALL with Long Ryder; STEPHEN McCARTHY.

– compilations etc. –

Jun 89. (lp/cd) *Enigma-Virgin; (ENVLP/CDENV 531) / Restless; <72293-2>* **LIVE AT RAJI'S (live in Hollywood January '85)**
– Still holding on to you / Forest for the trees / Until lately / That's what you always say / Burn / Merritville / The days of wine and roses / The medicine show / Halloween / Boston / John Coltrane stereo blues. *(re-iss. Jun90 on 'Demon' lp/cd; DFIEND/FIENDCD 176)*
Sep 89. (lp) *Another Cowboy; (ANOTHER 1)* **IT'S TOO LATE TO STOP NOW**
Apr 90. (d-lp/cd) *Demon; (FIEND/+CD 170)* **LIVE AT RAJI'S / GHOST STORIES**
Jun 92. (cd) *Rhino;* **TELL ME WHEN IT'S OVER: THE BEST OF DREAM SYNDICATE**
Nov 93. (cd) *Normal; (NORMAL 156CD)* **THE LOST TAPES 1985-1988**

STEVE WYNN

World Service / Rhino

May 90. (lp/c/cd) *(SERV 011/+MC/CD) <8122 70969-2>* **KEROSENE MAN** Apr90
– Tears won't help / Carolyn / The blue drifter / Younger / Under the weather / Here on Earth as well / Something to remember me by / Killing time / Conspiracy of the heart / Kerosene man / Anthem. *(cd re-iss. Feb93 on 'Rhino'; same as US)*
1991. (cd-ep) **KEROSENE MAN EP**
– Kerosene man / Something to remember me by / Boy in the bubble / Kool thing / etc.

Rhino Rhino

Dec 91. (cd-ep) **DRAG** [-] [ ]

Mar 93. (cd) <*8122 02832-2*> **DAZZLING DISPLAY** [ ] [ ] Nov91
– Drag / Tuesday / When she comes around / A dazzling display / Halo / Dandy in disguise / Grace / As it should be / Bonnie and Clyde / 405 / Close your eyes / Light of hope.

— next with an array of backing musos including JOHN WESLEY HARDING

Brake Out Mute

Nov 94. (cd) *(OUT 1162) <61652>* **FLUORESCENT** [ ] [ ] Mar94
– Follow me / Collision course / Carelessly / Carry a torch / Open the door / Older / Layer by layer / That's why I wear black / Wedding bells / The sun rises in the west / Look both ways / Never ending rain.

— next with the group, COME

Brake Out Zero Hour

Jul 96. (cd) *(OUT 1242) <ZEROCD 1160>* **MELTING IN THE DARK** [ ] [ ]
– Why / Sheeley's blues / What we call love / Drizzle / Angels / Epilogue / Silence is our only friend / Stare it down / Smooth / For all I care / The way you punish me / Down / Melting in the dark.

Zero Hour Zero Hour

Sep 97. (cd) <*(ZEROCD 2160)*> **SWEETNESS AND LIGHT** [ ] [ ]
– Silver lining / Black magic / Sweetness and light / This strange effect / This deadly game / How's my little girl / Ghosts / Blood from a stone / In love with everyone / Great divide / That's the way love is / If my life was an open book.

– his compilations, etc. –

Nov 94. (cd) *Return To Sender; <(RTS 13)>* **TAKE YOUR FLUNKY AND DANGLE** (unisuued material rec.1987-1993) [ ] [ ] Nov93
– Animation / Gospel #1 / How's my little girl / Counting the days / The subject was roses / Closer / Woodshed blues / Boxing song / AA / Gospel #2 / It only comes out at night.

GUTTERBALL

STEVE WYNN – vocals, guitar / **BRYAN HARVEY** – guitar, vocals (ex-HOUSE OF FREAKS) / **STEPHEN McCARTHY** – guitar, vocals (ex-LONG RYDERS) / **JOHNNY HOTT** – drums, vocals (ex-HOUSE OF FREAKS) / **BOB RUPE** – bass, vocals (ex-SILOS)

Brake Out Mute

Jan 94. (cd) *(OUT 113-2) <61510>* **GUTTERBALL** [ ] [ ] Jun93
– Trial separation blues / Top of the hill / Lester Young / Motorcycle boy / One by one / When you make up your mind / Think it over / Falling from the sky / Please don't hold back / The preacher and the prostitute / Patent leather shoes / Blessing in disguise.

— **ARMISTEAD WELLFORD** – bass, vocals; repl. RUPE

Brake Out Brake Out

Apr 95. (cd/lp) <*(OUT 119-2/-1)*> **WEASEL** [ ] [ ]
– Transparency / Your best friend / Black and gold / Is there something I should know? / Hesitation / The firefly / Sugar fix / Maria / One-eyed dog / Tarzana, pt.2 / Angelene / California / Everything / Over 40 / Mickey's big mouth.

– compilations, etc. –

Aug 95. (cd) *Return To Sender; <(RTS 17)>* **TURNYOR HEDINKOV** [ ] [ ]

DRIVE LIKE JEHU (see under ⇒ ROCKET FROM THE CRYPT)

DRONES

Formed: Manchester, England ... late 1976 by M.J. DRONE, GUS GANGRENE, STEVE 'WHISPER' CUNDALL and PETE PURFECT. Bonafide DIY three chord wonders, The DRONES were there at punk's inception; while their fuzzy guitar anthems mightn't have been in the same league as The SEX PISTOLS or even The DAMNED, the pogo-tastic likes of 'BONE IDOL' and 'LOOKALIKES' were loud, dumb and a hell of a lot more fun than the latest REO SPEEDWAGON offering. Making their vinyl debut on the 'Ohm' label in 1977 with the 'TEMPTATIONS OF A WHITE COLLAR WORKER' EP, the band followed up with the aforementioned 'BONE IDOL' (a double A-side with 'I JUST WANNA BE MYSELF') on their self-financed 'Valer' imprint later that year. The DRONES' one and only album, 'FURTHER TEMPTATIONS', also surfaced late in 1977, their two-minute formula not exactly suited to a long playing format (probably in the same way as The SUBURBAN STUDS and The LURKERS). Prior to their inevitable demise im the early 80's, they did manage to have material included on two various artists compilations – the 'Beggars Banquet' compilation, 'Streets' and live punk effort, 'Short Circuit: Live At The Electric Circus' – as well as releasing a final single, 'CAN'T SEE' on the 'Fabulous' label.

Album rating: FURTHER TEMPTATIONS (*5)

M.J. DRONE – vocals, rhythm guitar / **GUS GANGRENE** (b. CALLENDAR) – lead guitar, vocals / **WHISPER** (b. STEVE CUNDELL) – bass / **PETE PURFECT** (b. LAMBERT) – drums

O.H.M.S. not iss.

May 77. (7"ep) *(GOOD MIX 1)* **TEMPTATIONS OF A WHITE COLLAR WORKER** [ ] [-]
– Lookalikes / Corgi crap / Hard on me / You'll lose.

Valer not iss.

Oct 77. (7") *(VRS 1)* **BONE IDOL. / I JUST WANNA BE MYSELF** [ ] [-]

Dec 77. (lp) *(VRLP 1)* **FURTHER TEMPTATIONS** [ ] [-]
– Persecution complex / Bone idol / Movement / Be my baby / Corgi crap / Lookalikes / The underdog / No more time / City drones / I just wanna be myself / Lift off the bans. *(cd-iss. Oct93 on 'Anagram'+=; CDPUNK 20)* – TEMPTATIONS OF A WHITE COLLAR WORKER (tracks) / (other 2 singles).

Jan 78. (12"; w-drawn) *(VRSP 1)* **BE MY BABY. / LIFT OFF THE BANS** [ ] [-]

— continued to work sporadically until final single below

Fabulous not iss.

Mar 80. (7") *(JC 4)* **CAN'T SEE. / FOOLED TODAY** [ ] [-]

DROOGS

Formed: Los Angeles, California, USA ... 1972 by vocalist RIC ALBIN, guitarist ROGER CLAY, bassist PAUL MOTTER and drummer KYLE RAVEN. The latter two were replaced during the next decade by a long list of rhythm players, finally stabilising with DAVID PROVOST and JON GERLACH respectively. Produced by EARLE MANKEY (ex-SPARKS), their first albums, 'STONE COLD WORLD' (1984) and 'KINGDOM DAY' (1987), established the band on the fringe of the Paisley underground scene alongside the likes of The DREAM SYNDICATE and GREEN ON RED, who occasionally augmented their studio efforts. They subsequently signed to German outlet, 'Music Maniac', the albums 'MAD DOG DREAMS' (1990), 'LIVE IN EUROPE' and 'GUERILLA LOVE-IN' (1991) surfacing at the turn of the decade.

Album rating: STONE COLD WORLD (*6) / KINGDOM DAY (*5) / MAD DOG DREAMS (*6) / GUERILLA LOVE-IN (*5) / ANTHOLOGY compilation (*6)

RIC ALBIN – vocals / **ROGER CLAY** – guitar, vocals / **PAUL MOTTER** – bass / **KYLE RAVEN** – drums

— MOTTER was subsequently repl. by **KEVIN McMANUS, BOB KASEY, TOM MUSICK + JOEY HOEY**, while RAVEN was repl. by **ADRIAN FOLTZ + STEVE HAVITOY**

— (released 6 very rare 45's in this time; see anthology)

not iss. Stapled Chin Music

1980. (c) **MEMORIAL** [-] [ ]

— **DAVID PROVOST** – bass; repl. last bass man

— **JON GERLACH** – drums; repl. last drummer

not iss. Plug-n-socket

1983. (12"ep) **HEADS EXAMINED EP** [-] [ ]

Spindrift Passport

May 86. (lp) *(SPIN 117) <6919>* **STONE COLD WORLD** [ ] [ ] 1984
– Change is gonna come / Set my love on you / For these remaining days / Stone cold world / Mr. Right / From another side / He's waitin' (live) / Only game in town (soundtrack version). *(German-iss.Feb92 on 'Music Maniac' cd+=/lp+=; MM CD/LP 034)* – KINGDOM DAY

not iss. PVC

1987. (lp/c/cd) <*PVC/+C/CD 8956*> **KINGDOM DAY** [-] [ ]
– Stranger in the rain / Quarry street / Call off your dogs / Jack of all trades / Kingdom day / Webster field / Collector's item / When angels fall / Countdown to zero. *(German-iss.1989 on 'Music Maniac'; MMLP 011)*

Music Maniac not iss.

Dec 87. (lp/cd) *(MM LP/CD 005)* **ANTHOLOGY** (compilation of all their early singles) [-] [-] German
– He's waitin' / Light bulb blues / Set my love on you / I'm not like everybody else / Ahead of my time / Get away / Overnight success / Last laugh / As much as I want / Off the hook / Only game in town / Garden of my mind.

— **BRIAN HUDSON** – drums; repl. GERLACH

Aug 90. (lp) *(MMLP 026)* **MAD DOG DREAMS** [-] [ ] German
– Paper dolls / We all fall down / Zero house / Reach the dawn / Devil left to pay / I want something / Echo of an empty heart / Wings of mercury / Mad dog dreams. *<issued in the States as 'WANT EVERYTHING' on 'Skyclad'; 75>*

Dec 90. (m-lp) *(MMLP 037)* **LIVE IN EUROPE 1990 (live)** [-] [-] German
– Contdown to zero / Long dark night / Paper dolls / Jack of trades / 98 steps / Zero house.

— **TY RIO** – drums; repl. HUDSON

Nov 91. (lp) *(MMLP 041)* **GUERILLA LOVE-IN** [-] [-] German
– Maria / Cruel highway / Other end of town / Smoke and mirrors / Saints of Mexico / Tempt me / Morning dew / Long dark night / Close to the sun / County line (instrumental).

— disbanded in 1992

DROPKICK MURPHYS

Formed: Boston, Massachusetts, USA ... 1996 by Irish-American guys, MIKE McCOGLAN, KEN CASEY, RICK BARTON and MATT KELLY. Hellraising pub-brawling punk rockers, their sound was STIFF LITTLE FINGERS shaken-not-stirred with the more traditional POGUES – adding bagpipes for good measure (a double of course!). Touring with The MIGHTY MIGHTY BOSSTONES, they duly signed to TIM ARMSTRONG's (of RANCID) label, 'Hellcat'. The 'MURPHY's finally fought their way out of the studio, the results being the highly entertaining, 'DO OR DIE', in 1998.

Album rating: DO OR DIE (*6)

MIKE McCOGLAN – vocals / **KEN CASEY** – bass, vocals / **RICK BARTON** – guitar, vocals / **MATT KELLY** – drums

Flat Flat

Mar 97. (7") *(U 44257M)* **split with The DUCKY BOYS** [ ] [ ]

Gimmie My Money not iss.

Jul 97. (7") *(GMM 124)* **TATTOOS AND SCALLY CAPS. /** [ ] [ ]

Epitaph Hellcat

Mar 98. (cd/c/lp) <*(80407-2/-4/-1)*> **DO OR DIE** [ ] [ ]
– Cadence to arms / Do or die / Get up / Never alone / Caught in a jar / Memories remain / Road of the righteous / Far away coast / Fighstarter Karanke / Barroom hero / 3rd man in / Tenant enemy #1 / Finnegan's wake / Noble / Boys in the docks / Skinhead on the MTBA.

— **AL BARR** (b. Scotland) – vocals (ex-BRUISERS) repl. McCOGLAN

Cyclone Cyclone

Mar 98. (m-cd) *(CYCD 105)* **BOYS ON THE DOCKS** ☐ ☐ Jul98
– Boys on the docks / Never alone / In the streets of Boston / Caps and bottles / Euro trash / Front seat.

Hellcat-TKO Hellcat-TKO

Sep 98. (d7") *(TKOROUND 005)* **split with ANTI HEROES** ☐ ☐
Oct 98. (7"ep) *(TKOROUND 014)* **CURSE OF A FALLEN SOUL / GOING STRONG. / THE LEGEND OF FINN MacCUMHALL / ON THE ATTACK** ☐ ☐

Knock Out Knock Out

Dec 98. (7") *(KOEP 082)* **WATCH YOUR BACK. / Weirdoz: Oxymoron** ☐ ☐
Dec 98. (7") *(KOEP 083)* **CURSE OF THE FALLEN SOUL. / YOU'RE A REBEL** ☐ ☐

– compilations, etc. –

Sep 98. (cd) *Sidekicks; (JABSCO 017CD)* **THE EARLY YEARS – UNDERPAID & OUT OF TUNE** ☐ ☐

DROP NINETEENS

Formed: Boston, Massachusetts, USA . . . 1991 by former classmates GREG ACKELL and CHRIS ROOF, who subsequently added STEVE ZIMMERMAN, MOTOHIRO YASUE and PAULA KELLEY. Securing a UK deal via 'Virgin'-offshoot, 'Hut', DROP NINETEENS debuted in 1992 with the tongue-in-cheek 'WINONA' single. The attendant album, 'DELAWARE' (1992), followed in the grand tradition of schizophrenic Bostonian alternative guitar acts, sugary harmonies (courtesy of PAULA), a smattering of MY BLOODY VALENTINE-style noise and SONIC YOUTH/PIXIES guitar mangling thrown in for good measure. The record also included a cover of Madonna's 'ANGEL' alongside their own 'MY AQUARIUM' – the accompanying 'YOUR AQUARIUM' EP carried a appalling version of 'MANDY' (yes, once sung by Mr. MANILOW himself!). Well timed as they were to fit in with the prevailing grunge craze, the band nevertheless struggled to make significant headway in the UK market. Dramatic personnel changes (only ACKELL and ZIMMERMAN remained having replaced the others with JUSTIN CROSBY, MEGAN GILBERT and PETE KOSPLIN) preceded the follow-up album, 'NATIONAL COMA' (1993), which fell on similarly deaf ears despite some positive critical noises.

Album rating: DELAWARE (*5) / NATIONAL COMA (*5)

GREG ACKELL – vocals, guitar / **MOTOHIRO YASUE** – guitar / **PAULA KELLEY** – vocals, guitar / **STEVE ZIMMERMAN** – bass, vocals / **CHRIS ROOF** – drums

Hut Caroline

Jul 92. (12") *(HUT 019T)* **WINONA. /** ☐ -
Jul 92. (cd/c/lp) *(CDHUT/HUTMC/HUTLP 4) <CAROL 1723-2/-4>* **DELAWARE** ☐ ☐
– Delaware / Ease it Halen / Winona / Kick the tragedy / Baby wonder's gone / Happen / Reber-rymemberer / Angel / My aquarium. *(cd+=)* – Fish dream.
Oct 92. (10"ep/cd-ep) *(HUT EN/CD 22) <1469>* **YOUR AQUARIUM E.P.** ☐ ☐
– My aquarium (second time around) / Mandy / Nausea / Movie.

— **MEGAN GILBERT** – guitar, vocals; repl. YASUE

— **JUSTIN CROSBY** – guitar; repl. KELLEY

— **PETE KOSPLIN** – drums; repl. ROOF

Oct 93. (7") *(HUT 39)* **LIMP. /** ☐ ☐ Jul94
(12"+=/cd-s+=) *(HUT T/CD 39)* –
Oct 93. (cd/c/lp) *(CDHUT/HUTMC/HUTLP 14) <CAROL 1943-2/-4>* **NATIONAL COMA** ☐ ☐
– Limp / All swimmers are brothers / Skull / Cuban / Rot winter / Martini love / 7-8 / Franco inferno / My hotel deb / Moses Brown / Superfeed / The dead / Royal.

— split soon after above

DR. REMIX . . . (see under ⇒ METAL URBAIN)

DRUGSTORE

Formed: London, England . . . 1992 by Brazilian-born ISOBEL MONTEIRO and L.A. exile, MIKE CHYLINSKI. After trying in vain to find a suitable vocalist, MONTEIRO decided to take on the role herself, developing her earthy purr over a couple of early singles. The first of these, 'ALIVE', appeared on the band's own 'Honey' label while 'MODERN PLEASURE' was released as part of the 'Rough Trade' Singles Club series, the attendant press buzz leading to a deal with 'Go! Discs'. Recruiting third member, DARON ROBINSON, the band began work on an eponymous debut album which eventually surfaced in Spring '95, alternating pockets of brooding melody with squalling sheets of feedback in trademark DRUGSTORE fashion. The VELVET UNDERGROUND and MAZZY STAR were the most common reference points, MONTEIRO's tales of life's harsher lessons delivered in darkly seductive style. Although they didn't exactly have the standard Brit-pop credentials, the band were awarded an NME Single Of The Week award for accompanying single, 'SOLITARY PARTY GROOVER', while the album itself made the Top 40. A further single, 'FADER' made the Top 75 although the 'INJECTION' EP failed to chart. A move to 'Roadrunner' rejuvenated their fortunes, the 'EL PRESIDENT' single (featuring a guest vocal spot for THOM YORKE) denting the UK Top 20 in Spring '98. The long-awaited follow-up album, 'WHITE MAGIC FOR LOVERS' (1998), meanwhile, may have hit the Top 50 but failed to win over many new fans. • **Songwriters:** MONTEIRO main writer/ some with group except SHE DON'T USE JELLY (Flaming Lips) / TEENAGE KICKS (Undertones).

Album rating: DRUGSTORE (*6) / WHITE MAGIC FOR LOVERS (*5)

ISOBEL MONTEIRO – vocals, bass / **DARON ROBINSON** – guitar, vocals / **MIKE CHYLINSKI** – drums

Honey not iss.

Nov 93. (ltd-7") *(HON 1)* **ALIVE. / GRAVITY** ☐ -

Rough Trade Sing. Club not iss.

1994. (ltd-7") **MODERN PLEASURE. /** ☐ -

Honey – London Go! Discs – London

Sep 94. (7") *(HON 3)* **STARCROSSED. / ACCELERATE** ☐ -
(10"+=/cd-s+=) *(HON T/CD 3)* – Fader.
Jan 95. (7") *(HON 4)* **NECTARINE. / ANAESTHASIA** ☐ -
(10"+=/cd-s+=) *(HON T/CD 4)* – She don't use jelly.
Mar 95. (7") *(HON 6)* **SOLITARY PARTY GROOVER. / ELECTRIC LIGHT / STARCROSSED (demo)** ☐ -
(12"/cd-s) *(HON X/CD 6)* – (first 2 tracks) / Get inside my head / Spacegirl.
Apr 95. (cd/c/lp) *(<828556-2/-4/-1>)* **DRUGSTORE** 31 ☐
– Speaker 12 / Favourite sinner / Alive / Solitary party groover / If / Devil / Saturday sunset / Fader / Super glider / Baby astrolab / Gravity / Nectarine / Accelerate. *(lp w/free 7", cd w/free cd-s)* – SOLITARY PARTY GROOVER (acoustic). / BABY ASTROLAB (acoustic)
May 95. (7") *(HON 7)* **FADER. / REBOUND / UNDER THE MOON** 72 -
(12"/cd-s) *(HON X/CD 7)* – ('A'side) / French devil / Slide / Sugar sugar.
Oct 95. (7"ep/cd-ep) *(HON 8/+CD)* **INJECTION / HEART OF HONEY. / SHE DON'T USE JELLY (electric version) / GRAVITY (Terry Edwards mix)** ☐ -
Nov 96. (7"/c-s) *(HON/+MC 10)* **MONDO CANE. / NO MORE TEARS** ☐ -
(cd-s+=) *(HONCD 10)* – Adventures of Isabel / What every girl should know.

— added **IAN BURDGE** – cello

Roadrunner Roadrunner

Apr 98. (7") *(RR 2236-7)* **EL PRESIDENT /** 20 ☐
(cd-s+=) *(RR 2236-3)* –
(cd-s) *(RR 2236-9)* –
May 98. (cd/c/lp) *(<RR 8711-2/-4/-1>)* **WHITE MAGIC FOR LOVERS** 45 ☐ Jun98
– Say hello / Mondo cane / El president / Sober / I know I could / Spacegirl / Never come down / Song for Pessoa / I don't wanna be here without you / White magic for lovers / Tips for travelling / The funeral (but most of all).

Roadrunner Imprint

Jun 98. (7"colrd) *(RR 2230-7) <9013>* **SOBER. / WAIT** 68 ☐ Jan99
(cd-s+=) *(RR 2230-3)* – Offside.
(cd-s) *(RR 2230-9)* – ('A'side) / Cover me / The funeral (demo).
Sep 98. (cd-s) *(RR 2224-3)* **SAY HELLO / EL PRESIDENT (Portuguese version) / PRINCESS AND THE BEAST** ☐ -

Bill DRUMMOND (see under ⇒ KLF)

DUBSTAR

Formed: Newcastle, England . . . 1994 by ex-JOANS members; CHRIS WILKIE and STEVE HILLIER, who soon recruited singer, SARAH BLACKWOOD. With help from manager Graham Robinson, DUBSTAR secured a deal with Parlophone outlet 'Food' (home to BLUR). In June 1995, they had first chart appearance with 'STARS' and grew to be an alternative pop favourite of '95. Dreamy experimental Euro-pop lying somewhere between SAINT ETIENNE and The PET SHOP BOYS, the band's debut STEPHEN HAGUE-produced album, 'DISGRACEFUL' (1995), also displayed a talent for biting lyrical realism, this winning combination at its most bittersweet on the Top 20 hit, 'NOT SO MANIC NOW'. A re-issued 'STARS' followed it into the charts soon after, while 'ELEVATOR SONG' made the Top 30. A second album, 'GOODBYE' (1997), was much in the same formula and spawned a further two hits, 'NO MORE TALK' and 'CATHEDRAL PARK'.

Album rating: DISGRACEFUL (*6) / GOODBYE (*5)

SARAH BLACKWOOD – vocals / **CHRIS WILKIE** – guitar / **STEVE HILLIER** – programmer

Food Polygram

Jun 95. (c-s) *(TCFOOD 61)* **STARS / ('A'mix)** 40 -
(cd-s) *(CDFOOD 61)* – ('A'mix).
Sep 95. (c-s) *(TCFOOD 67)* **ANYWHERE / DON'T BLAME ME** 37 -
(12"+=/cd-s+=) *(12/CD FOOD 67)* – ('A'mixes).
Oct 95. (cd/c) *(CD/TC FOOD 13)* **DISGRACEFUL** 33 -
– Stars / Anywhere / Just a girl she said / Elevator song / The day I see you again / Week in week out / Not so manic now / Popdorian / Not once, not ever / St. Swithin's Day / Disgraceful. *(re-iss. Jul96 with free remixes cd; FOODCOR 13)*
Dec 95. (c-s) *(TCFOOD 71)* **NOT SO MANIC NOW / IF IT ISN'T YOU** 18 -
(12"+=/cd-s+=) *(12/CD FOOD 71)* – Song No.9 / Certain sadness.
Mar 96. (c-s) *(TCFOOD 75)* **STARS / ('A'side)** 15 -
(cd-s) *(CDFOODS 75)* – ('A'side) / Excuse me father / Starfish / Bow wow now (we know).
Jul 96. (c-s) *(TCFOOD 80)* **ELEVATOR SONG /** 25 -
(cd-s) *(CDFOOD 80)* –
(12") *(12FOOD 80)* –
Jul 97. (c-s/cd-s) *(TC/CD FOOD 96)* **NO MORE TALK / UNCHAINED MONOLOGUE / LA BOHEME / GOODBYE** 20 -
(cd-s) *(CDFOODS 96)* – ('A'side) / Stars (acoustic) / Elevator song (acoustic) / Not once not ever (acoustic).
Sep 97. (c-s) *(TCFOOD 104)* **CATHEDRAL PARK / CATHEDRAL PARK (Dirty Rotten Scoundrels mix) / NO MORE TALK (Jamie Myerson breakout mix)** 41 -

(cd-s+=) *(CDFOOD 104)* – ('A'-Environmental Science mix pt.1).
(cd-s) *(CDFOODS 104)* – ('A'side) / Let down / This is my home / In my defence.
Sep 97. (cd/c) *(CD/TC FOOD 23) <537961>* **GOODBYE** 18
– I will be your girlfriend / Inside / No more talk / Polestar / Say the worst thing first / Cathedral park / It's over / View from here / My start in Wallsend / It's clear / Ghost / Can't tell me / Wearchest / When you say goodbye / Let's go.
Jan 98. (c-ep/cd-ep) *(TCFOOD/CDFOODS 108)* **I WILL BE YOUR GIRLFRIEND / STARS / NOT SO MANIC NOW / ANYWHERE** 28 -
(cd-s) *(CDFOOD 108)* – ('A'mixes by Dillon & Dickins / Deadly Avenger / Sol Brothers / SDS Inc. and Steve Hillier).

DUET EMMO (see under ⇒ WIRE)

Stephen DUFFY

Born: Birmingham, England . . . 1961. A founding member of DURAN DURAN, DUFFY left after six months i.e. before the hits and the attendant cash began rolling in. He was at least partly compensated (after a brief spell with The HAWKS) by solo success in the mid-80's, his club hit from two years previous, 'KISS ME', remixed and re-issued under the moniker of STEPHEN 'TIN TIN' DUFFY. It duly made the UK Top 5, while the attendant album, 'THE UPS AND DOWNS OF . . .' made the Top 40. Subsequent legal problems over the 'TIN TIN' part of his name led to DUFFY going back to the drawing board and resurfacing in 1987 with a new outfit, The LILAC TIME. Comprised of DUFFY, his brother NICK, MICHAEL GIRI and MICKY HARRIS, the group named themselves after a line in a NICK DRAKE song and traded in a suitably pastoral, acoustic 60's pop sound first aired on the independently released, eponymous debut. 'Phonogram' were impressed enough to sign the band and re-issue the debut, DUFFY amassing further critical plaudits but similarly poor sales with follow-up set, 'PARADISE CIRCUS' (1989). Despite the production clout of John Leckie, 1990's 'AND LOVE FOR ALL' again failed to kickstart the band's career and resulted in a move to 'Creation'. Lost amid the baggy debris and shoegazing feedback, 'ASTRONAUTS' (1991) was another non-starter; it also marked the end of the band's patience and in 1992 The LILAC TIME officially split. DUFFY kept a fairly profile, only a guest spot for SAINT ETIENNE indicating that he still had a finger in the music business pie. Come the mid-90's, the veteran popster had formed the band DUFFY along with US indie-strummers, VELVET CRUSH, signing to 'RCA'-offshoot, 'Indolent', and releasing an eponymous, MITCH EASTER-produced debut. A soothing tonic for Brit-pop overload, the record was generally regarded by longtime DUFFY observers as one of his finest efforts to date, combining as it did the man's charming way with a lyric and the subtle guitar interplay of the VELVET boys. Following another three year fallow period, DUFFY surpringly re-emerged on the contemporary folk label, 'Cooking Vinyl', with 'I LOVE MY FRIENDS' (1998).

Album rating: DUFFY (*6) / Lilac Time: THE LILAC TIME (*6) / PARADISE CIRCUS (*7) / AND LOVE FOR ALL (*6) / ASTRONAUTS (*7)

HAWKS

Five Believers / not iss.

1981. (7") *(FB 001)* **WORDS OF HOPE. / SENSE OF ENDING** -

TIN TIN

STEPHEN 'TIN TIN' DUFFY – vocals (ex-HAWKS, ex-DURAN DURAN)

W.E.A. / not iss.

Oct 82. (7") *(TIN 1)* **KISS ME. / LOVE'S DUET** -
(12") *(TIN 1T)* – ('A'dub) / ('B'dub).
Jun 83. (7") *(X 9763)* **HOLD IT. / BLOWING KISSES** 55 -
(ext-d12"+=) *(X 9763T)* – ('A'instrumental) / Kiss me (US remix) / Love's duet / Kiss me (instrumental).
Mar 84. (12"m) *(X 9823T)* **KISS ME (US remix). / KISS ME (instrumental) / LOVE'S DUET** -

STEPHEN 'TIN TIN' DUFFY

10-Virgin / not iss.

Oct 84. (7"/12") *(TEN 28/+12)* **SHE MAKES ME QUIVER. / PUSH IT** -
Feb 85. (7"/7"pic-d)(12") *(TIN/+P 2)(TIN 2-12)* **KISS ME (1985). / IN THIS TWILIGHT** 4 -
(d7"+=/d12"+=) *(TING 2/+12)* – Kiss me (1983) / Holes in my shoes.
Apr 85. (lp/c/cd) *(DIX/CDIX/DIXCD 5)* **THE UPS AND DOWNS** 35 -
– Kiss me / She makes me quiver / A masterpiece / The darkest blues / But is it art? / Wednesday Jones / Icing on the cake / Be there / Believe in me / The world at large alone. *(re-iss. Jun88 lp/c; XID/CXID 5)*
May 85. (7"/ext-12") *(TIN 3/+12)* **ICING ON THE CAKE. / BROKEN HOME** 14 -
(d7"+=) *(TING 3)* – Hold it / She makes me quiver.
(d12"++=) *(TING 3-12)* – ('A'extended).
Aug 85. (7"/12") *(TIN 4/+T)* **UNKISS THAT KISS. / DONE FOR** -
Feb 86. (7") *(TEN 91)* **I LOVE YOU. / LOVE IS DRIVING ME INSANE** -
(w-drawn;12"+=) *(TEN 91-12)* – ('A'version).

— now with **SANDII** – vocals (ex-SANDII & THE SUNSETZ)

Apr 86. (7"; STEPHEN DUFFY & SANDII) *(TEN 105)* **SOMETHING SPECIAL. / THE DISENCHANTED** -
(12"+=) *(TENT 105)* – Cocksure.
May 86. (lp/c/cd) *(XID/CXID/XIDCD 12)* **BECAUSE WE LOVE YOU** -
– Something special / A lot of ink / Sunday supplement / When you go to bed / Why shouldn't I / Unkiss that kiss / I love you / Love station / We'll never argue / Julie Christie.
Aug 86. (d7"/d12"/d10") *(TEN 5/+12/10)* **I LOVE YOU. / WEDNESDAY JONES** -

– compilations, etc. –

May 89. (7") *Old Gold; (OG 4121)* **KISS ME. / ICING ON THE CAKE** -

LILAC TIME

STEPHEN DUFFY – vocals, instruments / **SAGAT GUIREY** – guitar / **MICKY HARRIS** – bass / **MICHAEL GIRI** – drums, percussion / **NICK DUFFY** – bouziki

Swordfish / not iss.

Feb 88. (7") *(LILAC 1)* **RETURN TO YESTERDAY. / TRUMPETS FROM MONTPARNASSE** -
(12"+=) *(12LILAC 1)* – Railway bazar / Reunion ball.

Fontana / Mercury

May 88. (7") *(LILAC 2)* **RETURN TO YESTERDAY. / GONE FOR A BURTON** -
(12"+=)(cd-s+=) *(LILAC 2-12)(LILCD 2)* – Rooftrees / Reunion ball.
Jun 88. (lp/c)(cd) *(SF LP/MC 006)(834 835-2) <836744-1/-4/-2>* **THE LILAC TIME**
– Black velvet / Rockland / Return to yesterday / Love becomes a savage / You've got to love / Together / Too sooner late than better / The road to happiness / Trumpets from Montparnasse. *(was to have been released on 'Swordfish' lp/cd; SWF LP/CD 6)*
Aug 88. (7") *(LILAC 3)* **YOU'VE GOT TO LOVE. / RAILWAY BAZAAR** -
(12"+=)(cd-s+=) *(LILAC 3-12)(LILCD 3)* – Trumpets from Montparnasse.
Nov 88. (7") *(LILAC 4)* **BLACK VELVET. / BLACK DAWN** -
(12"+=) *(LILAC 4-12)* – Tiger tea.
(cd-s++=) *(LILCD 4)* – Street corner.
Jul 89. (7"/c-s) *(LIL AC/MC 5)* **AMERICAN EYES. / WORLD IN HER ARMS** -
(12"+=) *(LILAC 5-12)* – Crossing the line.
(cd-s++=) *(LILCD 5)* – Shepherd's plaid.
Sep 89. (7") *(LILAC 6)* **THE DAYS OF THE WEEK. / THE QUEEN OF THE HEARTLESS** -
(12"+=)(cd-s+=) *(LILAC 6-12)(LILCD 6)* – Spin a cavalu.
Oct 89. (lp/c/cd) *(838 641-1/-4/-2)* **PARADISE CIRCUS** -
– American eyes / The lost girl in the midnight sun / If the stars shine tonight / The beauty in your body / The days of the week / She still loves you / Paradise Circus / The girl who waves at traffic / The last to know / Father mother wife and child / The rollercoaster song / Work for the weekend / Twilight beer hall.
Nov 89. (7") *(LIL AC/MC 7)* **THE GIRL WHO WAVES AT TRAINS. / IF THE STARS SHINE TONIGHT (acoustic)** -
(12"+=) *(LILAC 7-12)* – Ounce of nails.
(cd-s++=) *(LILCD 7)* – American eyes (acoustic).
Apr 90. (7") *(LILAC 8)* **ALL FOR LOVE & LOVE FOR ALL. / BED OF ROSES** -
(12"+=)(cd-s+=) *(LILAC 8-12)(LILCD 8)* – Rubovia / Night mail dirty armour.
May 90. (7"/c-s; w-drawn) *(LIL AC/MC 9)* **THE LAUNDRY. / ONLY PASSING THROUGH** -
(12"+=) *(LILAC 9-12)* – Hurricaned rice.
(cd-s++=) *(LILCD 9)* – Oeil biques a bacs.
Jul 90. (7") *(LILAC 10)* **IT'LL END IN TEARS. / JUKE WRITTEN ON THE FENCE** -
(12"+=)(cd-s+=) *(LILAC 10-12)(LILCD 10)* – Cover.
Sep 90. (cd/c/lp) *(846 190-2/-4/-1)* **& LOVE FOR ALL** -
– Fields / All for love & love for all / Let our land be the one / I went to the dance / Wait and see / Honest to God / The laundry / Paper boat / Skabackililio / It'll end in tears (I won't cry) / Trinity / And on we go. *(cd/c +free m-lp+=)* **RETURN 1 (GREATEST HITS)** – Black velvet / Return to yesterday / The beauty in your body / Together / The days of the week / American eyes / If the stars shine tonight / The girl who waves at trains.

Caff / not iss.

Sep 90. (7") *(CAFF 12)* **MADRESFIELD. / BIRD ON THE WIRE** -

Creation / not iss.

May 91. (7") *(CRE 104)* **DREAMING. / THE DARKNESS OF HER EYES** -
(12"+=) *(CRE 104T)* – ('A'version).
(cd-s++=) *(CRE 104CD)* – The rain falls deepest on the shortest haircut.
Aug 91. (cd/c/lp) *(CRE CD/MC/LP 098)* **ASTRONAUTS** -
– In Iverna gardens / Hats off here comes the girl / Fortunes / A taste for honey / Grey skies and work things / Finistere / Dreaming / The whisper of your mind / The darkness of her eyes / Sunshine's daughter / North Kensington / Madresfield.

— split after above's release but re-formed early '92

DUFFY

— with session people incl. NIGEL KENNEDY (!)

Parlophone / Parlophone

Apr 93. (c-s/7"; STEPHEN DUFFY) *(TC+/R 6339)* **NATALIE. / A MAN WITHOUT A STAR** -
(cd-s+=) *(CDR 6339)* – An angel gets his wings / C'est la vie, c'est la Guerre.
May 93. (cd/c/lp; STEPHEN DUFFY) *(CD/TC+/PCS 7361) <1423-2>* **MUSIC IN COLOURS**
– It sparkles / Transitoire / Natalie / Transitoire II / She wants to share her magic / Transitoire III / Music in colours / Galaxy / Transitoire IV / Totem / Transitoire V / Holte and hotel / Transitoire VI / Charlotte's conversation / Transitoire VII / Fall from the sky. *(cd re-iss. Jun98 on 'E.M.I.'; 789420-2)*

— recruited members of VELVET CRUSH:- **PAUL CHASTAIN, JEFFREY BORCHARDT + RIC MENCK**

Indolent / Indolent

Jun 95. (7") *(DUFF 001)* **LONDON GIRLS. / YOU, ME & GOD / THE WAITRESS'S STORY** -
(cd-s+=) *(DUFF 001CD)* – The girl of the year.
Jul 95. (7"/c-s) *(DUFF 002/+MC)* **SUGAR HIGH. / TEMPES FUGIT / A VISION OF BLISS** -

(cd-s+=) *(DUFF 002CD)* – The sugar on the pill.
Aug 95. (cd/c/lp; as DUFFY) *(DUFF CD/MC/LP 003)* <21113-2>
DUFFY
– London girls / Sugar high / She freak / Needle mythology / Child is waiting / Kids on every corner / Ghetto child / Starfit / Mr. 20th century man / Rachel / Smitten.
Oct 95. (7"/c-s) *(DUFF 004/+MC)* **STARFIT. /** -
(cd-s+=) *(DUFF 004CD)* –
Jan 96. (7"/c-s) *(DUFF 005/+MC)* **NEEDLE MYTHOLOGY. / SUGAR HIGH (slow version)** -
(cd-s+=) *(DUFF 005CD)* – Twenty three / The world records her every thought.
Aug 97. (cd-s) *(DUFF 006CD1)* **17 / MAO BADGE / COMEDOWN / HEY KAT** -
(cd-s) *(DUFF 006CD2)* – ('A'side) / House of flowers / Barbarellas / Hanging around.
(cd-s) *(DUFF 006CD3)* – ('A'side) / Holding hands with Grace / In the evening of her day / Darling who can't wait to taste you.

— now without VELVET CRUSH who had their own album to do

Cooking Vinyl / not iss.

Apr 98. (cd-ep) *(FRYCD 068)* **17 / MAO BRIDGE / IN THE EVENING OF HER DAY / BARBARELLAS** -
Apr 98. (cd) *(COOKCD 144)* **I LOVE MY FRIENDS** -
– Tune in / Eucharist / 17 / Lover's beware / You are / Deal / She belongs to all / Autopsy / What if I fell in love with you / Something good / Twenty three / Postcard / One day one of these fucks will change your lives.
Jul 98. (cd-ep) *(FRYCD 073)* **YOU ARE / HOLDING HANDS WITH GRACE / COMEDOWN** -

DUKES OF STRATOSPHEAR (see under ⇒ XTC)

DURUTTI COLUMN

Formed: Manchester, England . . . early 1978 by VINI REILLY, CHRIS JOYCE and DAVE ROWBOTHAM. That year, they signed to TONY WILSON's indie label, 'Factory', although they dramatically split in mid-'79 leaving skinny VINI to pick up the pieces. Taking their name from the 1930's art-terrorists, Situationiste Internationale, and given free time by label boss, WILSON, under the wing of producer MARTIN HANNETT, the guitarist finally came up with DURUTTI's debut 'THE RETURN OF . . .' (1980). This was a brilliant introduction to his minimalist yet picturesque guitar improvisations, although his gimmick sandpaper sleeve was not exactly the toast of the record retailers who had to protect the rest of their stock from its glassy debris. He subsequently supported on tour fellow Mancunian, JOHN COOPER CLARKE, PAULINE MURRAY and even JOHN MARTYN, while recording the follow-up, 'L.C.' (1981), another masterpiece that fused light jazz into barren but dreamy landscapes. However, not for the first time, ill-health was to dog VINI, and it took a few years to record 'ANOTHER SETTING' (1983). All the above albums featured eccentric percussionist BRUCE MITCHELL, he of former parody-rock outfit, ALBERTOS Y LOST TRIOS PARANOIAS, the man becoming a stalwart on all VINI/DURUTTI's further work. In 1986, VINI took a trip to California, where he invited punkette, DEBI DIAMOND, to sing on a version of JEFFERSON AIRPLANE's 'White Rabbit'. After the release of the 1987 album, 'GUITAR AND OTHER MACHINES', REILLY was invited by old fellow NOSEBLEEDS chum, MORRISSEY, to play guitar pieces on his 1988 solo debut, 'VIVA HATE'. In 1990, DURUTTI COLUMN returned in fine style with 'OBEY THE TIME', although this was the last for Factory, as the label went bankrupt in '92. Under the control of 'Polygram', the imprint was once again under way in 1994 as 'Factory Too', and a happier VINI unleashed another textured beauty, 'SEX AND DEATH'. • **Songwriters:** All composed by REILLY, except cover; I GET ALONG WITHOUT YOU VERY WELL (Hoagy Carmichael). • **Note:** On the 8th of November '91, original member, DAVE ROWBOTHAM, was axed to death.

Album rating: THE RETURN OF (*9) / VALUABLE PASSAGES (*8) / L.C. (*7) / DOMO ARIGATO (*7) / SEX AND DEATH (*7) / VINI REILLY (*7)

VINI REILLY (b. Aug'53) – guitar (ex-NOSEBLEEDS, ex-V2) / **DAVE ROWBOTHAM** – guitar / **CHRIS JOYCE** – drums / **BRUCE MITCHELL** – percussion / also **TONY BOWERS** – bass / **PHIL RAINFORD** – vocals (left Jul78)

— recorded for Various Artists EP – A FACTORY SAMPLER. Split mid'79, DAVE, CHRIS and TONY joined The MOTHMEN. **VINI REILLY** now brought in **MARTIN HANNETT** – switches, producer (ex-INVISIBLE GIRLS (JOHN COOPER CLARKE) with **PETER CROOKS** – bass / **TOBY** (b.PHILIP TOMANOV) – drums / **GAMMER** – melody

Factory / not iss.

Feb 80. (lp) *(FACT 14)* **THE RETURN OF THE DURUTTI COLUMN** -
– Sketch for Summer / Requiem for a father / Katherine / Conduct / Beginning / Jazz / Sketch for winter / Collette / In "D". *(w/ free testcard flexi by MARTIN HANNETT)* **FIRST ASPECT OF THE SAME THING. / SECOND ASPECT OF THE SAME THING** *(re-iss. Jul80 lp/c; FACT 14/+C)*

— **VINI** on his own, featured **PHIL RAYNHAM** – vocals
Nov 80. (12") *Factory Benelux; (FACBN 2)* **LIPS THAT WOULD KISS (FORM PRAYERS TO BROKEN STONE). / MADELEINE** - - Belgium
(re-iss. Mar81; FACBN 2-005) (re-iss. cd-ep Mar91; FBN 2CD)
Mar 81. (7"ltd) *Sordide Sentimentale; (SS 45-005)* **ENIGMA. / DANNY** - - Italy

— now just a duo when **VINI** – guitars, now on extra vocals & keyboards / added **BRUCE MITCHELL** – percussion (ex-ALBERTOS Y LOST TRIOS PARANOIAS)
Sep 81. (lp/c) *(FACT 44/+C)* **LC** -
– Sketch for dawn 1 / ~Portrait for Frazier / Jacqueline / Messidor / Sketch for dawn 2 / Never known / The act committed / Detail for Paul / The missing boy / The sweet cheat gone.

— VINI now completely solo
1982. (7"ltd) *Factory Benelux; (FBN 100)* **FOR PATTI. / WEARINESS AND FEVER** - - Belgium
Mar 82. (12"ep) *Factory Benelux; (FBN 10)* **DEUX TRIANGLES** - - Belgium
– Favourite painting / Zinni / Piece for out of tune grand piano.

— added guests **LINDSAY WILSON** – vocals / **MAUNAGH FLEMING** – cor anglais
Aug 82. (7") *(FAC 64)* **I GET ALONG WITHOUT YOU VERY WELL. / PRAYER** -

— **VINI** now augmented by **MERVYN FLETCHER** – saxophone / **TONY BOWERS** – bass / **CHRIS JOYCE** – drums / **TIM KELLETT** – trumpet (all ex-MOTHMEN)
Aug 83. (lp/c) *(FACT 74/+C)* **ANOTHER SETTING** -
– Prayer / Bordeaux / The beggar / The response / For a western / Francesca / Smile in the crowd / Dream of a child / Spent time / You've heard it before / Second family.

— **VINI** retained **MERVYN** and **TIM.** (TONY & CHRIS later joined SIMPLY RED with TIM). **BRUCE MITCHELL** rejoined (he had always been part of live set-up) / **MAUNAGH FLEMING** rejoined with new guests **CAROLINE LAVELLE** – cello / **RICHARD HENRY** – trombone / **BLAINE REININGER** – viola/violin (of TUXEDO MOON)
Dec 84. (lp/c) *(FACT 84/+C)* **WITHOUT MERCY** -
– Face 1 / Face 2.

— Now just basically **VINI** with **BRUCE** with old friends augmenting
Mar 85. (12"ep) *(FAC 114)* **SAY WHAT YOU MEAN, MEAN WHAT YOU SAY** -
– Goodbye / The room / E.E. / A little mercy / Silence / Hello.
Aug 85. (video-cd) *(FACD 144)* **DOMO ARIGATO (live Japan)** -
– Sketch for Summer / Mercy theme / Sketch for dawn / E.E. / Little mercy / Jacqueline / Dream of a child / Mercy dance / The room / Blind elevator girl / Tomorrow / Belgian friends / Missing boy / Self-portrait / (audience noise).
Mar 86. (7") *Factory Benelux; (FBN 51)* **TOMORROW. / TOMORROW (live)** - - Belgium
(12"+=) *(FBN 51)* – All that love and maths can do.
Mar 86. (lp)(cd) *(FBN 36)(FACD 154)* **CIRCUSES AND BREAD** -
– Pauline / Tomorrow / Dance 2 / For Hilary / Street fight / Royal infirmary / Black horses / Dance 1 / Blind elevator girl – Osaka. *(cd+=)* – (last 45). *(cd-iss. Nov93 on 'Crepescule';)*

— **VINI** with **MITCHELL, KELLETT, JOHN METCALFE**
Oct 86. (12") *Materiali Sonori; (MASO 70003)* **GREETINGS THREE** - - Italy
– Florence sunset / All that love and maths can do / San Giovanni dawn / For friends in Italy.
Aug 87. (12"ep; w/ DEBI DIAMOND) *(FAC 184)* **THE CITY OF OUR LADY** -
– Our lady of the angels / White rabbit* / Catos con guantes.
Dec 87. (cd-ep) *(FACD 194)* **OUR LADY OF THE ANGELS / CATOS CON GUANTAS / WHEN THE WORLD (Newson mix)** -

— **VINI + BRUCE** were joined by guests **TIM KELLETT** (of SIMPLY RED) (1 track.) / **STANTON MIRANDA** – vocals (solo artist – 2 tracks.) **POL** – vocals (3 tracks.) / **STEPHEN STREET** – bass (1 track.) **JOHN METCALFE** – viola (1 track.) / **ROB GREY** – mouth organ
Nov 87. (lp/cd)(c/dat) *(FAC T/D 204)(FACT 204 C/D)* **THE GUITAR AND OTHER MACHINES** -
– When the world / Arpeggiator / What is it to me (woman) / U.S.P. / Red shoes / Jongleur grey / Bordeaux sequence / Miss Haynes / Don't think you're funny / English tradition landscape / Pol in 'B'. *(cd+=)* – Dream topping / You won't feel out of place / 28 Oldham Street.
Dec 87. (7"flexi) *(FAC 214)* **THE GUITAR AND OTHER MARKETING DEVICES** -
– Jongleur grey / Bordeaux sequence / English landscape tradition / U.S.P.

— added **ROBERT NEWTON** plus **DV8 PHYSICAL THEATRE**
Apr 88. (cd-s-video) *(FACDV 194)* **WHEN THE WORLD (soundtrack) / WHEN THE WORLD (lp) / FINAL CUT / WHEN THE WORLD (video)** -
Dec 88. (3"cd-ep) *(FACD 234)* **WOMAD LIVE (live)** -
– Otis / English landscape tradition / Finding the sea / Bordeaux.
Mar 89. (lp/cd)(dat) *(FAC T/CD 244)(FACT 244D)* **VINI REILLY**
– Homage to Catalonea / Opera II / People's pleasure park / Pol in G / Love no more / Opera I / Finding the sea / Otis / They work every day / Requiem again / My country. *(lp w/ free 7" with MORRISSEY) (FAC 244+)* – I KNOW VERY WELL HOW I GOT MY NOTE WRONG *(cd w/ free 3"cd-ep) (FAC 244+)* – (above) / Red square / William B.

— Included sampled voices of OTIS REDDING, ANNIE LENNOX and TRACY CHAPMAN. **VINI** added **PAUL MILLER**
Dec 90. (cd/lp)(c/dat) *(FAC D/T 274)(FACT 274 C/D)* **OBEY THE TIME**
– Vino della casa Bianco / Fridays / Home / Art and freight / Spanish reggae / Neon / The warmest rain / Contra-indications / Vino della casa rosso.
Feb 91. (12"ep/cd-ep) *(FAC/+D 284)* **THE TOGETHER MIX. / CONTRA INDICATIONS (version) / FRIDAYS (up-person mix)** -
Jun 91. (cd)(lp) *Materiali Sonori, (CDMASO 90024)(33-065)* **DRY** - - Italy
– Dry / Paradise passage road / Rope around my neck / Short / Boat people / Boat people / Our lady / Grade 2 duet / Octaves / Out of the blue / Otis / English language tradition / Finding the sea / Bordeaux / Beggar. *(cd+=)* – WOMAD LIVE (tracks).

— **VINI, BRUCE** w / guests **PETER HOOK** – bass (of NEW ORDER) + **MARTIN JACKSON** – keyboards (ex/of-SWING OUT SISTER)

Factory Too / not iss.

Nov 94. (cd) *(FACD 201)* **SEX AND DEATH** -
– Anthony / The rest of my life / For Colette / The next time / Beautiful lies / My irasable friend / Believe in me / Fermina / Where I should be / Fado / Madre mio / Blue period.

Les Disques Du Crepescule / not iss.

May 96. (cd) *(TWI 9762)* **FIDELITY** -

– compilations, etc. –

Jun 83. (lp) *V.U.; (VINI 1)* **LIVE AT THE VENUE (live VINI & BRUCE)** [ ] [-]
– Sketch for summer / Conduct / Never known / Jacqueline / Party / etc.

Dec 85. (lp) *Fundacao Atlantica; (1652071)* **AMIGOS EM PORTUGAL / DEDICATIONS FOR JACQUELINE** [-] [-] Portu
– Friends in Portugal / Small girl by a pool / Crumpled dress / Sara and Tristana / Nighttime Estoril / Lisbon / To end with / Wheels turning / Favourite descending intervals / Saudade / Games of rhythm / Lies of mercy.

Dec 86. (lp/cd)(d-c) *Factory; (FAC T/D 164)(FACT 164C)* **VALUABLE PASSAGES** [ ] [-]
– Sketch for summer / Conduct / Sketch for winter / Lips that would kiss / Belgian friends / Danny / Piece for out-of-tune piano / Never know / Jacqueline / Missing boy / Prayer / Spent time / Without mercy stanzas 2-8 & 12-15 / Room / Blind elevator girl / Tomorrow / LFO MOD.

Nov 87. (c) *R.O.I.R.; (A-152)* **THE DURUTTI COLUMN LIVE AT THE BOTTOM LINE, NEW YORK (live)** [ ] [-]
(re-iss. May93 & Feb95 cd/c; A-152 CD/C)

Mar 88. (4xcd-box) *Factory; (FACD 224)* **THE DURUTTI COLUMN – THE FIRST FOUR ALBUMS** [ ] [-]

Dec 89. (ltd-cd) *Spore; (CD 1)* **THE SPORADIC RECORDINGS** [ ] [-]

Sep 94. (cd) *Materiali Sonori; (90037)* **RED SHOES** [ ] [-]

Ian DURY

Born: 12 May'42, Upminster, Essex, England. At age seven he became partially crippled from contracting polio. In 1970, he was employed as a teacher / lecturer at Canterbury College. The following year, he formed KILBURN & THE HIGH ROADS, who embarked on pub/college circuit in London. After 1 album in the mid-70's and many line-up changes, they disbanded, leaving DURY and manager DAVE ROBINSON to create solo deal for the singer. Signing to Jake Riviera's new indie label, 'Stiff', he soon raced up album charts in 1977 with the new wave favourite 'NEW BOOTS AND PANTIES!!!'. DURY's articulate patter and intelligent lyrics fused well with funky/jerky group backing which alternated between rock'n'roll and disco. He also developed many areas of Cockney rhyme-slang into rude but clever lyrics. The album made the UK Top 5, preceded by the brilliant 'SEX AND DRUGS AND ROCK AND ROLL', DURY's typically wry comment on the excesses of the music business. The following year, the singer's cast of sidemen became The BLOCKHEADS, the line-up of CHAZ JANKEL, NORMAN WATT-ROY, CHARLEY CHARLES, MICKEY GALLAGHER, JOHN TURNBULL and DAVY PAYNE playing on DURY's first hit single, 'WHAT A WASTE'. However, it was the follow-up, 'HIT ME WITH YOUR RHYTHM STICK' which really earned DURY a smutty place in the annals of pop history, its half-spoken narrative style breaking into a gloriously demented chorus. The track sat astride the UK singles chart for a few weeks, while the attendant album, 'DO IT YOURSELF' (1979) made No.2. The DURY/JANKEL writing partnership was to end soon after, however, the latter embarking on solo work and freeing up a position for ex-DR. FEELGOOD guitarist, WILKO JOHNSON. The resulting album, 'LAUGHTER' (1980), met with limited success, prompting a musical Spring clean from DURY; signing to 'Polydor', securing the esteemed services of SLY & ROBBIE and reuniting with JANKEL, the cheeky cockney released the acclaimed 'LORD UPMINSTER'. Commercial success continued to elude him, however, and DURY semi-retired in the mid-80's following the '4,000 WEEKS HOLIDAY' (1984) opus. He eventually resurfaced in 1989 with the 'APPLES' soundtrack, although he proved his inimitable sense of humour hadn't deserted him on 1992's 'THE BUS DRIVERS PRAYER & OTHER STORIES'. • **Songwriters:** DURY – words / JANKEL – music, until his departure from The BLOCKHEADS. • **Trivia:** After he semi-retired in the mid-80's, he started an acting career in films:- NUMBER ONE (1985) / PIRATES (1986) / HEARTS OF FIRE (1987), and TV plays:- KING OF THE GHETTOS (1986) / TALK OF THE DEVIL (1986) / NIGHT MOVES (1987). His other work on TV was mainly for commercials, etc.

Album rating: NEW BOOTS AND PANTIES!! (*8) / DO IT YOURSELF (*7) / LAUGHTER (*6) / JUKEBOX DURY compilation (*6) / LORD UPMINSTER (*6) / 400 WEEKS HOLIDAY (*5) / SEX AND DRUGS AND ROCK AND ROLL compilation (*7) / APPLES (*5) / THE BUS DRIVER'S PRAYER AND OTHER STORIES (*6) / Mr LOVE PANTS (*6)

KILBURN & THE HIGH ROADS

IAN DURY – vocals / **KEITH LUCAS** – guitar / **DAVEY PAYNE** – sax / **CHARLIE SINCLAIR** – bass repl. HUMPHREY OCEAN who had repl. CHARLIE HART / **LOUIS LAROSE** then **GEORGE BUTLER** – drums

— Early 1974, recorded lp for 'Raft', which was shelved after 'Warners' took over label. It was later issued by them in Oct'78 as 'WOTABUNCH', after DURY was top of the charts.

— (mid-74) **DAVID ROHOMAN** – drums repl. BUTLER / **ROD MELVIN** – piano repl. HARDY

Dawn / not iss.

Nov 74. (7") *(DNS 1090)* **ROUGH KIDS. / BILLY BENTLEY** [ ] [-]

Feb 75. (7") *(DNS 1102)* **CRIPPLED WITH NERVES. / HUFFETY PUFF** [ ] [-]

Jun 75. (lp) *(DNLS 3065)* **HANDSOME** [ ] [-]
– The roadette song / Pam's mood / Crippled with nerves / Broken skin / Upminster kid / Patience / Father / Thank you mum / Rough kids / The badger and the rabbit / The mumble rumble and the cocktail rock / The call up. *(re-iss. Nov85 on 'Flashback' lp/c; FBLP/ZCFBL 8094)*

— Disbanded mid-75, although IAN gigged at times with a new line-up as IAN DURY & THE KILBURNS. KEITH LUCAS was later to become NICK CASH and form 999. There were also other KILBURN material re-released after DURY's success.

1977. (lp) *Warners; (K 56513)* **WOTABUNCH** [ ] [-]

Sep 78. (7") *Warners; (K 17225)* **BENTLEY. / PAM'S MOODS** [ ] [-]

Jul 83. (lp/c) *P.R.T.; (DOW/ZCDOW 17)* **UPMINSTER KIDS** [ ] [-]

IAN DURY

— - vocals solo with **CHAZ JANKEL** – guitar, keyboards (ex-BYZANTIUM) plus session men that became The BLOCKHEADS (see below)

Stiff / Stiff

Aug 77. (7",7"orange) *(BUY 17)* **SEX AND DRUGS AND ROCK AND ROLL. / RAZZLE IN MY POCKET** [ ] [-]

Sep 77. (lp/gold-lp/c) *(SEEZ/SEEZG/ZSEEZ 4) <0002>* **NEW BOOTS AND PANTIES!!!** [5] [ ] Apr78
– Sweet Gene Vincent / ake up and make love with me / I'm partial to your abracadabra / My old man / Billericay Dickie / Clevor Trever / If I was with a woman / Plainstow Patricia / Blockheads / Blackmail man. *(re-iss. Sep86 on 'Demon' lp/c/cd+=; FIEND/+CASS/CD 63)* – (interview). *(re-iss. cd May95 on 'Disky';) (cd re-iss. Aug98 on 'Hit'; AHLCD 57)*

Nov 77. (7") *(BUY 23)* **SWEET GENE VINCENT. / YOU'RE MORE THAN FAIR** [ ] [-]

IAN DURY AND THE BLOCKHEADS

— with **JANKEL** plus **NORMAN WATT-ROY** – bass (ex-LOVING AWARENESS, ex-GLENCOE) / **CHARLEY CHARLES** – drums (ex-LOVING AWARENESS, ex-GLENCOE) / **MICKEY GALLAGHER** – keyboards (ex-LOVING AWARENESS, ex-FRAMPTON'S CAMEL) / **JOHN TURNBULL** – guitar (ex-LOVING AWARENESS) / **DAVEY PAYNE** – saxophone (ex-WRECKLESS ERIC)

Apr 78. (7"/12") *(BUY 27/+12)* **WHAT A WASTE. / WAKE UP AND MAKE LOVE WITH ME** [11] [ ]

Nov 78. (7"; as IAN & THE BLOCKHEADS) *(BUY 38)* **HIT ME WITH YOUR RHYTHM STICK. / THERE AIN'T HALF BEEN SOME CLEVER BASTARDS** [1] [ ]

May 79. (lp/c) *(SEEZ/ZSEEZ 14) <36104>* **DO IT YOURSELF** [2] [ ] Jul79
– Inbetweenies / Quiet / Don't ask me / Sink my boats / Waiting for your taxi / This is what we find / Uneasy sunny hotsy totsy / Mischief / Dance of the screamers / Lullaby for Francies. *(re-iss. Feb90 on 'Demon' lp/c/cd; FIEND/+CASS/CD 133) (re-iss. cd May95 on 'Disky';) (cd re-iss. Aug98 on 'Hit'; AHLCD 58)*

Jul 79. (7") *(BUY 50)* **REASONS TO CHEERFUL (pt.3). / COMMON AS MUCK** [3] [ ]

Aug 80. (7") *(BUY 90)* **I WANT TO BE STRAIGHT. / THAT'S NOT ALL HE WANTS** [22] [ ]

— **WILKO JOHNSON** – guitar (ex-DR. FEELGOOD, solo artist) repl. JANKEL who went solo

Oct 80. (7") *(BUY 100)* **SUEPERMAN'S BIG SISTER. / F***ING ADA** [51] [ ]
(12"+=) *(BUYIT 100)* – You'll see glimpses.

Nov 80. (lp/c) *(SEEZ/ZSEEZ 30) <36998>* **LAUGHTER** [48] [ ] Jan81
– Sueperman's big sister / Pardon / Delusions of grandeur / Yes and no (Paula) / Dance of the crackpots / Over the points / (Take your elbow out of the soup you're sitting on the chicken) / Uncoolohol / Hey, hey, take me away / Manic depression / Oh, Mr. Peanut / F***ing Ada. *(cd-iss. May95 on 'Disky';) (cd re-iss. Aug98 on 'Hit'; AHLCD 59)*

— IAN DURY now brought in the services of rhythm boys **SLY & ROBBIE** plus **JANKEL + TYRONE DOWNIE** – keyboards

Polydor Polydor

Aug 81. (7"/12") *(POSP/+X 285)* **SPASTICUS AUSTICIOUS. / ('A'instrumental)**

Sep 81. (lp/c) *(POLD/+C 5042) <16337>* **LORD UPMINSTER** 53
– Funky disco pops / Red letter / Girls watching / Wait for me / The body song / Lonely town / Trust is a must / Spasticus austicious. *(re-iss. Dec89 on 'Great Expectations' lp/cd; PIP LP/CD 005)*

IAN DURY & THE MUSIC STUDENTS

— with many musicians including **JANKEL, PAYNE + RAY COOPER**

Nov 83. (7"/12") *(POSP/+C 646)* **REALLY GLAD YOU CAME. / INSPIRATION**

Jan 84. (lp/c) *(POLD/+C 5112)* **4,000 WEEKS HOLIDAY** 54 -
– (You're my) Inspiration / Friends / Tell your daddy / Peter the painter / Ban the bomb / Percy the poet / Very personal / Take me to the cleaners / The man with no face / Really glad you came. *(re-iss. Dec89 on 'Great Expectations' lp/cd; PIP LP/CD 004)*

Feb 84. (7") *(POSP 673)* **VERY PERSONAL. / BAN THE BOMB**
(12"+=) *(POSPX 673)* – The sky's the limit.

IAN DURY

— solo, with **PAYNE, GALLAGHER, COOPER** plus **STEVE WHITE** – drums / **MICHAEL McEVOY** – bass, synth / **MERLIN RHYS-JONES** – guitar / **FRANCES RUFELLE** – vocals / etc.

E.M.I. not iss.

Oct 89. (7"/7"pic-d) *(EMI/+P 5534)* **PROFOUNDLY IN LOVE WITH PANDORA. / EUGENIUS (YOU'RE A GENIUS)** 45 -
(above from the TV series, 'Adrian Mole')

WEA WEA

Oct 89. (7") *(YZ 437)* **APPLES. / BYLINE BROWN** -

Oct 89. (lp/c)(cd) *(WX 326/+C)(246355-2)* **APPLES** (soundtrack)
– Apples / Love is all / Byline Browne / Bit of kit / Game on / Looking for Harry / England's glory / Bus driver's prayer / P.C. Honey / The right people / All those who say okay / Riding the outskirts of fantasy.

— In Sep'90 he reformed IAN DURY & THE BLOCKHEADS for two reunion gigs

IAN DURY

Demon not iss.

Apr 91. (lp/cd) *(FIEND/+CD 777)* **WARTS 'N' AUDIENCE (live 22 December 1990)** -
– Wake up / Clever Trevor / Billericay Dickie / Quiet / My old man / Spasticus autisticus / Plaistow Patricia / Clever bastards / Sweet Gene Vincent / What a waste / Hit me with your rhythm stick / Blockheads. *(cd+=)* – If I was with a woman.

Nov 92. (cd/c) *(FIEND CD/CASS 702)* **THE BUS DRIVERS PRAYER & OTHER STORIES** -
– That's enough of that / Bill Haley's last words / Poor Joey / Quick quick slow / Fly in the ointment / O'Donegal / Poo-poo in the prawn / Ave a word / London talking / D'orine the cow / Your horoscope / No such thing as love / Two old dogs without a name / Bus driver's prayer.

IAN DURY & THE BLOCKHEADS

— with **CHAZ JANKEL, MICKEY GALLAGHER, DAVEY PAYNE, JOHN TURNBULL, NORMAN WATT-ROY, STEVEN MONTI** (drums) / **The BREEZEBLOCKS** – backing vocals

Ronnie Harris unknown

Jun 98. (cd) *(DUR 1)* **Mr LOVE PANTS** 57
– Jack shit George / The passing show / You're my baby / Honeysuckle highway / Itinerant / Geraldine / Cacka boom / Bed 'o' roses No.9 / Heavy living / Mash it up Harry.

– compilations etc. –

Nov 81. (lp/c) *Stiff; (SEEZ/ZSEEZ 41)* **JUKE BOX DURY** -
(re-iss. Sep82 as 'GREATEST HITS' on 'Fame' lp/c; FA/TC-FA 3031)

May 85. (7") *Stiff; (BUY 214)* **HIT ME WITH YOUR RHYTHM STICK (Paul Hardcastle mix). / SEX AND DRUGS AND ROCK AND ROLL** 55 -
(12"+=) *(BUYIT 214)* – Reasons to be cheerful / Wake up and make love to me (Paul Hardcastle mix).

Apr 87. (lp/c/cd) *Demon; (FIEND/+CASS/CD 69)* **SEX AND DRUGS AND ROCK AND ROLL** -
– Hit me with your rhythm stick / I want to be straight / There ain't half been some clever bastards / What a waste! / Common as muck / Reasons to be cheerful (pt.3) / Sex and drugs and rock and roll / Sueperman's big sister / Razzle in my pocket / You're more than fair / Inbetweenies / You'll see glimpses.

Jul 91. (7"/c-s) *Flying; (FLYR 1/+C)* **HIT ME WITH YOUR RHYTHM STICK '91 (The Flying Remix Version) / HIT ME WITH YOUR RHYTHM STICK** 73 -
(12"+=/cd-s+=) *(FLYR 1 T/CD)* – ('A'mix).

Aug 91. (3xcd-box) *Demon; (IAN 1)* **IAN DURY & THE BLOCKHEADS** -
– (NEW BOOTS AND PANTIES / DO IT YOURSELF / SEX AND DRUGS AND ROCK AND ROLL)

Aug 96. (cd) *Disky; (DC 88975-2)* **THE BEST OF IAN DURY** -

— The BLOCKHEADS also released their own singles and lp early 80's.

DUST BROTHERS
(see under ⇒ CHEMICAL BROTHERS)

DUST JUNKYS

Formed: Manchester, England . . . 1994 by NICKY LOCKETT aka former rapper, MC TUNES (see 808 STATE, who he performed with regularily). This collaboration resulted in two major Top 20 UK hits in 1990, 'THE ONLY RHYME THAT BITES' and 'TUNES THAT SPLIT THE ATOM' followed by a Top 30 album, 'THE NORTH AT ITS HEIGHT'. The DUST JUNKYS (who included SAM BROX, GANIYU GASPER, STEVE O'JAY, MYKEY WILSON and 6th member PAUL BILLINGTON) heralded the reappearance of LOCKETT after 5 years in the wilderness. With a brief to take hip hop into the live environment and infuse it with the raw excitement of rock, The DJ's kicked up something of a storm with their second 45, 'LIVING IN THE POCKET OF A DRUG QUEEN', a record that drew comparisons with the early BEASTIE BOYS. Although this didn't chart, it was a case of third time lucky with '(NONSTOPOPERATION)' ramraiding the Top 50.

Album rating: DONE AND . . . DUSTED (*7)

NICKY LOCKETT (b.1970) – vocals / **SAM BROX** (b.1976) – guitar / **STEVE OJ (OLIVER JONES)** (b.1965) – bass / **GANIYU PIERRE GASPER** (b.1974) – DJ / **MYKEY LAWRENCE** (b.1960) – drums / plus 6th member **PAUL BILLINGER** – programmer

Polydor Polydor

Nov 96. (7"ep/c-ep/cd-ep) *(1 DUST 7/MC/CD)* **THE FEVER EP** -
– Fever / Nothing personal / Get the funk off.

Aug 97. (7") *(571260-7)* **LIVING IN THE POCKET OF A DRUG QUEEN. /**
(cd-s) *(571261-2)* – ('A'-Fun Lovin' Criminals remixes).
(cd-s) *(571263-2)* –

Nov 97. (7") *(571972-7)* **(NONSTOPOPERATION). /** 47
(12"+=/cd-s+=) *(571973-1/-2)* –

Feb 98. (12"/cd-s) *(569489-1/-2)* **WHAT TIME IS IT? / ('A'-Morcheeba mix) / ('A'-Kid Loops mix)** 39
(cd-s) *(569491-2)* –

Mar 98. (cd/c/lp) *(557043-2/-4/-1)* **DONE AND . . . DUSTED** 35
– Nothin' personal / What time is it? / Fever / Middle man / Non stop operation / Movin' on / Daddy / Here I am / Remember / Living in the pocket of a drug queen / Get the funk up / Wasting hard time.

May 98. (cd-ep) *(569909-2)* **NOTHIN' PERSONAL. / WHAT TIME IS IT? (early version) / TAKE THE STRAIN / TICKET TO THE MOON** 62
(cd-ep) *(569911-2)* – ('A'live) / Fever (stoned in Amsterdam) / Remember (stoned in Amsterdam) / Movin' on (live).
(12") *(569911-1)* – ('A'-Hooligan riot mix) / ('A'-Dylan ryhmes mix) / ('A'-Headrillaz mix).

DWARVES

Formed: Chicago, Illinois, USA . . . 1985 out of The SUBURBAN NIGHTMARE (one album, 'A HARD DAY'S NIGHTMARE' for 'Midnight') by SIGH MOAN, SALT PETER, JULIUS SEIZURE, PETE VIETNAMACHEQUE and WHITE SLAMBEAU. Following in the filth encrusted wake of GG ALLIN, this grossly offensive hardcore punk outfit make local bad boys The JESUS LIZARD look like HANSON! Debuting in 1986 with 'HORROR STORIES', the pseudonymous jokers caused outrage wherever they deemed to inflict their music on the local populace, indulging freely in such time honoured rock'n'roll pastimes as self-mutilation, on-stage sex and hard drugs. After a second set, 'TOOLIN' FOR A WARM TEABAG' (1988), SALT PETER recruited an entire new band of merry pranksters in the shape of guitarist, HEWHOCANNOTBENAMED, BLAG DAHLIA and VADGE MOORE (although it was unclear if they were in fact the same people; the band were infamous for their hoaxes, read on . . .), The DWARVES career reaching a climax of sorts with their outrageously titled 'Sub Pop' debut, 'BLOOD GUTS & PUSSY' (1990) – featuring an equally disgusting sleeve pic that again found them coming under severe flak from feminists. After a further two albums, 'THANK HEAVEN FOR LITTLE GIRLS' (1991) and 'SUGAR FIX' (1993), the grunge bastion finally cracked when the band falsely announced the death of HEWHOCANNOTBENAMED. Just when parents were breathing a sigh of relief, the dreaded DWARVES re-emerged in 1997 with a belated sixth album, 'THE DWARVES ARE YOUNG AND GOOD LOOKING' (on 'Epitaph'); if you believe that you'll believe anything!

Album rating: HORROR STORIES (*5) / TOOLIN' FOR A WARM TEABAG (*3) / BLOOD GUTS AND PUSSY (*7) / THANK HEAVEN FOR LITTLE GIRLS (*5) / SUGAR FIX (*5) / THE DWARVES ARE YOUNG AND GOOD LOOKING (*4)

SIGH MOAN – vocals / **SALT PETER** – bass / **JULIUS SEIZURE** – guitar, vocals / **PETE VIETNAMACHEQUE** – keyboards / **WHITE SLAMBEAU** – drums

not iss. Voxx

Aug 86. (lp) *<VOXX 200037>* **HORROR STORIES** -
– In & out / Oozie / Don't love me / Monday blues / Mind expanders / I'm a living sickness / College town / Be a caveman / Get outta my life / Sometimes gay boys don't wear pink / Stop & listen / Love gestapo. *(UK cd-iss. Dec90 & Jul92; VOXXCD 2037)*

not iss. Ubik

Sep 88. (7") *(CRASH 001)* **LICK IT. / ?** -

not iss. Nasty Gash

Dec 88. (lp) **TOOLIN' FOR A WARM TEABAG** -

— **SALT PETER** recruited **BLAG DAHLIA** – vocals / **HEWHOCANNOTBENAMED** – guitar / **VADGE MOORE** – drums

Sub Pop Sub Pop

Apr 90. (7",7"white) *<(SP 50)>* **SHE'S DEAD. / FUCKHEAD**

Jul 90. (lp,red-lp,pic-lp/c/cd) *<(SP 67/+A/B)>* **BLOOD, GUTS AND PUSSY**

– Back seat of my car / Detention girl / Let's fuck / Drug store / Skin poppin' slut / Fuck you up and get high / Insect whore / Flesh tantrum / SFVD / What hit you / Astro boy / Motherfucker / Fuckhead. *(cd/c+=)* – (5 tracks).

Oct 90. (7",7"purple) *<(SP 81)>* **DRUG STORE / MOTHERFUCKER. / ASTRO BOY / DETENTION GIRL**

1991. (12"ep) **LUCIFER'S CRANK EP**

— <above issued on 'No.6'>

Feb 92. (lp/cd) *<(SP 166/+CD)>* **THANK HEAVENS FOR LITTLE GIRLS**
– Fuck 'em all / Anybody but me / Blood brothers revenge / Three seconds / Dairy queen / Fuck around / Lucky tonight / Blag the ripper / Satan / Speed demon / Who's fucking who.

Jun 93. (12"ep)(cd-ep) *<(SP 83-254)><(SPCD 63-230)>* **ANYBODY OUT THERE**

Jul 93. (lp/cd) *<(SP/+CD 76-243)>* **SUGAR FIX**
– Anybody out there / Evil primeval / Reputation / Lies / Saturday night / New Orleans / Action man / Smack city / Cain novacaine / Underworld / Wish that I was dead.

Jan 94. (c-ep/cd-ep) *<SP 183>* **UNDERWORLD. / LIES / DOWN BY THE RIVER**

— was NICK OLIVERI (REX EVERYTHING) (ex-KYUSS) a member at this point?

Sympathy F — not iss.

1990's. (7") *(SFTRI 132)* **I WANNA KILL YOUR . . . /**

not iss. — Man's Ruin

1990's. (7") *<MR 005>* **DRUG STORE – DAIRY QUEEN. / GOODNIGHT TACOMA / RADIO 2**

Mar 97. (7") *<MR 051>* **WE MUST HAVE BLOOD. / SURFING THE INTERCOURSE BARN**

Epitaph — Theologian

Nov 97. (cd/c/lp) *(6512-2/-4/-1) <53>* **THE DWARVES ARE YOUNG AND GOOD LOOKING** Mar97
– Unrepentent / We must have blood / I will deny / Demonica / Everybodies girl / Throw that world away / Ballad of Vadge Moore / One time only / Pimp / Crucifixion is now / You gotta burn.

DYLANS

Formed: Sheffield, England . . . early 1990 by COLIN GREGORY, JIM RODGER and ANDY CURTIS. Adding QUENTIN JENNINGS and GARRY JONES, the hopelessly retro 60's-styled outfit cashed in on the "baggy" scene with a major label deal courtesy of 'R.C.A.'. However after only one flop single and the recruitment of CURTIS's replacement, ANDY COOK, the harmony-laden band were relegated to Beggars Banquet offshoot, 'Situation 2'. Now officially a bonafide indie band, The DYLANS released a further couple of BEATLES-tinged singles prior to the Stephen Street-produced eponymous debut album. Internal tensions subsequently led to further changes, JONES and JENNINGS making way for newcomers CRAIG SCOTT and IKE GLOVER respectively. A long-awaited second album, 'SPIRIT FINGER' (1994), was virtually ignored with the music scene favouring more up to date sounds.

Album rating: THE DYLANS (*6) / SPIRIT FINGER (*5)

COLIN GREGORY – vocals, bass / **ANDY CURTIS** – guitar / **JIM RODGER** – guitar / **QUENTIN JENNINGS** – keyboards / **GARRY JONES** – drums

R.C.A. — not iss.

Jan 91. (7") *(RCA 2806)* **GODLIKE. /**
(cd-s+=) *(RCACD 2806)* –

— **ANDY COOK** – guitar; repl. CURTIS

Situation 2 — Beggars Banquet

May 91. (7") *(SIT 78)* **LEMON AFTERNOON. / MY HANDS ARE TIED**
(cd-s+=) *(SITU 78CD)* – ('A'&'B'-different versions).

Aug 91. (7") *(SIT 81)* **PLANET LOVE. /**
(cd-s+=) *(SITU 81CD)* –

Oct 91. (lp/cd) *(SITU 33/+CD) <61054-2/-4>* **THE DYLANS**
– She drops bombs / Planet love / I hope the weather stays fine / Sad rush on Sunday / No coming down / Mine / Particle ride / Ocean wide / Godlike / Mary Quant in blue / Love to / Indian sun.

May 92. (7") *(SIT 90)* **MARY QUANT IN BLUE. / I HOPE THE WEATHER STAYS FINE (remix)**
(12"ep+=/cd-ep+=) **QUANT E.P.** *(SIT 90 T/CD)* – You won't last long without me / Deluxe reverse (submarine mix II).

— **CRAIG SCOTT** – drums; repl. JONES

— **IKE GLOVER** – keyboards; repl. JENNINGS

Beggars Banquet — Atlantic

Nov 93. (12"/cd-s) *(BBQ 22 T/CD)* **GRUNGE / WISEBIRD. / PARTIAL RANCH / NERVE HUTCH**

Mar 94. (12"/cd-s) *(BBQ 29 T/CD)* **I'LL BE BACK TO HAUNT YOU. /**

Apr 94. (cd) *(BBQCD 144) <92341>* **SPIRIT FINGER**
– Grudge / Children of the flame / Kill rave / Just one big plastic hassle / Hell no / Smarter than you / I'll be back to haunt you / Wise bird / Live in the know / How little you know / Get it together / Two tomorrows.

— disappeared after their lack of success

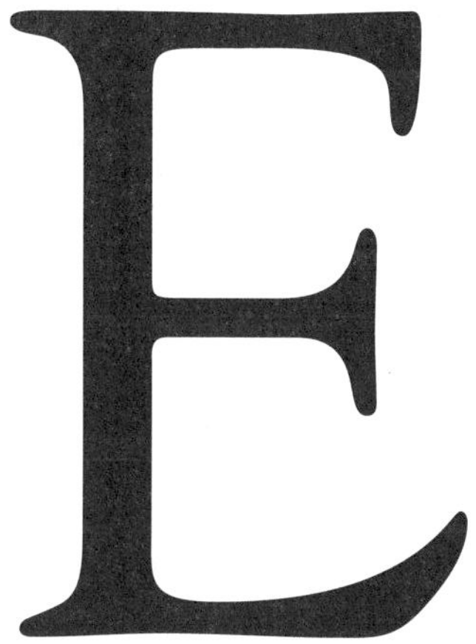

EARL BRUTUS

Formed: London, England . . . 1992 by ex-WORLD OF TWIST keyboard-player, NICK ANDERSON, JAMIE FRY (none other than the brother of ABC's MARTIN FRY), ROB MARCHE and GORDON KING. An unlikely but surprisingly effective combination of KILLING JOKE/FALL-like intensity and GLITTER BAND stomp!, EARL BRUTUS self-financed a debut single, 'LIFE'S TOO LONG', on their own 'Icerink' label. After a long-awaited follow-up in '95!, 'BONJOUR MONSIEUR' (for the 'Royal Mint' imprint), they almost immediately signed to Radio One/Music Week journo, Steve Lamacq's 'Deceptive' label and proceeded to churn out a series of sleazy singles prior to their debut album, 'YOUR MAJESTY . . . WE ARE HERE' (1996). The EARL's bolstered their claim to indie high society by being tipped for the top by none other than soft-porn mag, Club International (don't ask me how I found this out!?). Moving on to 'Fruition' records, the band treated their ever-growing cult following with a further string of near excellent singles beginning late in '97 with 'THE S.A.S. AND THE GLAM THAT GOES WITH IT'. It was a highlight from the following year's much talked about second long-player, 'TONIGHT YOU ARE THE SPECIAL ONE'.

Album rating: YOUR MAJESTY . . . WE ARE HERE (*8) / TONIGHT YOU ARE THE SPECIAL ONE (*7)

NICK SANDERSON – vocals, keyboards (ex-WORLD OF TWIST) / **JAMIE FRY** – keyboards, vocals / **ROB MARCHE** – guitar / **GORDON KING** – keyboards, drum machine

Icerink not iss.

Jun 93. (12"/cd-s) *(DAVO 7 12/CD)* **LIFE'S TOO LONG. /** -

Royal Mint not iss.

Sep 95. (7") *(MINT 001)* **BONJOUR MONSIEUR. / ON ME, NOT IN ME** -

Deceptive not iss.

Dec 95. (7"etched) *(BLUFF 020)* **SINGLE SEATER XMAS** -

Mar 96. (7"m) *(BLUFF 025)* **NAVYHEAD. / NORTH SEA BASTARD / 48 TRASH** -
(cd-s+=) *(BLUFF 025CD)* – Navyhead (Union Street).

Jun 96. (7"m) *(BLUFF 030)* **LIFE'S TOO LONG. / MOTOROLA / I LOVE EARL BRUTUS** -
(cd-s+=) *(BLUFF 030CD)* – Life's too long (Flash Vs Tarkus).

Sep 96. (7"m/cd-s) *(BLUFF 032/+CD)* **I'M NEW. / LIKE QUEER DAVID / MONDO ROTUNDA** -

Sep 96. (cd/lp) *(BLUFF 036 CD/LP)* **YOUR MAJESTY . . . WE ARE HERE** -
– Navyhead / I'm new / Male milk / On me, not in me / Don't leave me behind mate / Thelmex / Black speedway / Motorola / Shrunken head / Curtsy / Blind date / Life's too long / Karl Brutus / Singer seater Xmas.

Mar 97. (7"one-sided) *(BLUFF 039)* **PURCHASING POWER** -

Fruition not iss.

Oct 97. (7"clear) *(FRU 5)* **THE S.A.S. AND THE GLAM THAT GOES WITH IT. / MIDLAND RED** -
(cd-s+=) *(FRUCD 5)* – The Scottish.

Jan 98. (7") *(FRU 6)* **COME TASTE MY MIND. / SUPERSTAR** -
(cd-s+=) *(FRUCD 6)* – Nice man in a bubble / William.

May 98. (7") *(FRU 7)* **UNIVERSAL PLAN. / GYPSY CAMP BATTLE** -
(cd-s+=) *(FRUCD 7)* – TV tower / Bonjour monsieur.
(cd-s) *(FRUDX 7)* – ('A'live) / The S.A.S. and the glam that goes with it (live) / Come taste my mind (live) / Nicotine stains (live).

Jun 98. (cd/lp) *(FRU CD/LP 1003)* **TONIGHT YOU ARE THE SPECIAL ONE** -
– The S.A.S. and the glam that goes with it / Universal plan / God let me be kind (bitterfeld) / Midland red / Come taste my mind / Second class war / Your majesty, we are here / Don't die Jim / 99p (take me away) / East / Edelweiss (blown away) / Male wife.

EASTERHOUSE

Formed: Manchester, England . . . mid-80's by brothers ANDY (the lyricist) and IVOR PERRY, the initial line-up completed by PETER VANDEN, GARY ROSTOCK and MIKE MURRAY. Naming themselves after Glasgow's most infamous housing scheme, the band espoused a defiant left-wing philosophy against an atmospheric, finely textured alternative rock/pop backdrop. Hardly unique during the 80's, yet EASTERHOUSE were more convincing than most, winning over cynical critics and enjoying the patronage of MORRISSEY amongst others. Signed to 'Rough Trade', the band laid out their manifesto in impressive style with 1986's revered 'CONTENDERS' album. Despite the subsequent widespread acclaim, internal ructions led to IVOR departing to form his own outfit, The CRADLE. By the late 80's, ANDY had recruited a whole new cast of musicians – namely NEIL TAYLOR, LANCE SABIN, DAVID VERNER and co-producer STEVE LOVELL. The resultant follow-up set, 'WAITING FOR THE RED BIRD' (1989) strayed too far into chest-beating SIMPLE MINDS territory for many tastes yet the political commitment was as heartfelt as ever. The attendant single, 'COME OUT FIGHTING', had hit written all over it, quite why it wasn't remains a mystery. Moreover, in contrast to many of the far left doom-mongers, PERRY's vision was a generally positive one as outlined on the likes of 'HOPE AND GLORY'. The interest just wasn't there, however and EASTERHOUSE were soon confined to the more obscure annals of Manchester's musical history.

Album rating: CONTENDERS (*8) / WAITING FOR THE REDBIRD (*7)

ANDY PERRY – vocals / **IVOR PERRY** – guitar / **PETER VANDEN** – bass / **GARY ROSTOCK** – drums; repl. drum machine

Easterhouse not iss.

Mar 85. (12"ep) *(EIREX 1)* **IN OUR OWN HANDS** -
– Coming up for air / Endless march / Man alive / One more time.

—— added **MIKE MURRAY** – rhythm guitar

Rough Trade Columbia

Jan 86. (7") *(RT 164)* **WHISTLING IN THE DARK. / AIN'T THAT ALWAYS THE WAY** -
(12"+=) *(RTT 164)* – Confrontation.

Mar 86. (7") *(RT 174)* **INSPIRATION. / JOHNNY I HARDLY KNEW YOU** -
(12"+=) *(RTT 174)* – Easter rising / Nineteen sixty nine.

Jun 86. (lp/c) *(ROUGH/+C 94)* *<CK 40469>* **CONTENDERS**
– Out on your own / Whistling in the dark / Nineteen sixty nine / Cargo of souls / Lenin in Zurich / Get back to Russia / To live like this / The boy can sing / Estates. *(lp w/ free 7")* **GET BACK TO RUSSIA** *(RDJ 94) (cd-iss. May87; ROUGHCD 94)* *(+=)* – Inspiration / Johnny I hardly knew you / Easter rising.

—— They split after an argument. IVOR joined The CRADLE.

—— **ANDY** retained group name and completed line-up by bringing in **NEIL TAYLOR** – lead guitar / **DAVE VERNER** – drums / **STEVE LOVELL** – bass / **LANCE SABIN** – rhythm guitar

Feb 89. (7") *(RT 204)* *<68552>* **COME OUT FIGHTING. / NEW WORLD IN THE MORNING** 82
(12"+=/cd-s+=) *(RTT/CDRT 204)* –

Mar 89. (lp/c/cd) *(ROUGH/+C/CD 124)* *<CK/PCT 44467>* **WAITING FOR THE REDBIRD**
– Waiting for the redbird / You're gonna miss it (when it's gone) / Stay with me (death on the dole) / Come out fighting / America / Hope and glory / Say yes / This country / Sweatshop.

May 89. (7") **YOU'RE GONNA MISS IT (WHEN IT'S GONE). /** -
(12"+=/cd-s+=) –

—— disbanded after above

EAST RIVER PIPE

Formed: Astoria, New York, USA . . . 1989 as the musical alias of FM CORNOG. A hard luck story to beat most hard luck stories, FRED's (as he was then known) hard-bitten adventures were the stuff of scriptwriters' dreams. Born and raised in Suffolk, Virginia and Summit, New Jersey respectively, the self-effacing CORNOG went through numerous menial jobs before succumbing to alcoholism and eventual homelessness. Attracted by the lure of a new start in the Big Apple, the budding singer-songwriter gravitated towards New York where he eked out an existence as a street/subway busker. His fortunes changed however, when his "guardian angel", BARBARA POWERS fell in love, first with his music and then the man himself. She subsequently moved him in to her Queen's, NY apartment, where she provided him with a basic home studio while also taking on the task of publicising and distributing his recordings. So named because FM equated his artistic output with the shit coming out of an NY sewer, EAST RIVER PIPE officially came into existence with the mail-order only demo cassettes, 'POINT OF NO MEMORY' (1990) and 'I USED TO BE A KID COLGATE' (1991). Released on his/her own imprint, 'Hell Gate', these caught the attention of UK indie, 'Sarah', who duly issued his debut 7", 'HELMET ON' in Spring '93. A surprise Melody Maker single of the week, it helped boost ERP's obscure profile for future releases, 'SHE'S A REAL GOOD TIME' and the mini-set, 'GOODBYE CALIFORNIA' (1993). Now on the up and up, CORNOG also found a wider outlet for his records in America, 'Merge' handling the Stateside release of the acclaimed 'POOR FRICKY' (1994) a year after it appeared on UK shelves. Compared to everyone from LOU REED, BIG STAR and ELLIOTT SMITH to ROBERT FORSTER and BILL CALLAHAN, there was no mistaking the Lo-Fi heritage of FRED's one-man band although his surprisingly upbeat style set him apart. Resurfacing in '96 on the 'Shinkansen' label (UK only), EAST RIVER PIPE stuck to his trademark down-at-heel charm for that year's 'MEL' album; sewer(ly) one day his talents will be more widely acknowledged.

Album rating: GOODBYE CALIFORNIA mini (*6) / POOR FRICKY (*7) / EVEN

THE SUN WAS AFRAID (*5) / MEL (*7) / SHINING HOURS IN A CAN compilation (*5)

FM CORNOG – vocals, guitar / with a drum machine

Sarah | not iss.

May 93. (7") *(SARAH 075)* **HELMET ON. / HAPPYTOWN** [ ] [-]
(cd-s+=) *(SARAH 075CD)* – Axl or Iggy.

Jun 93. (7") *(SARAH 078)* **SHE'S A REAL GOOD TIME. / MY LIFE IS WRONG** [ ] [-]
(cd-s+=) *(SARAH 078CD)* – Times Square go-go boy.

Sep 93. (m-lp/m-cd) *(SARAH 405/+CD)* **GOODBYE CALIFORNIA** [ ] [-]
– Firing room / Silhouette town / Dogman / When will your friends all disappear? / Bernie Shaw / Psychic whore / 40 miles / Make a deal with the city.

Oct 94. (7") *<MRG 076>* **BRING ON THE LOSER. / FAN THE FLAME / SLEEPING WITH TALLBOY** [-] [ ]

Nov 94. (cd) *(SARAH 621CD)* *<MRG 081>* **POOR FRICKY** [ ] [ ] Jan95
– Bring on the loser / Metal detector / Here we go / Put-down / Superstar in France / Keep all your windows tight tonight / Ah dictaphone / Walking the dog / Marty / Crawl away / Hey, where's your girl? / Powerful man / When the ground walks away.

May 95. (10"m-lp/m-cd) *(SARAH 407/+CD)* **EVEN THE SUN WAS AFRAID** [ ] [-]
– Here we go / Marty / Sleeping with tallboy / Hide my life away from you / Fan the flame / When the ground walks away / Powerful man / Fan the flames.

Jul 96. (7") *<MRG 110>* **KILL THE ACTION. /** [-] [ ]

Shinkansen | Merge

Nov 96. (7") *(SHINKANSEN 6)* **MIRACLELAND. / KING OF NOTHING EVER / MINDCRACKER** [ ] [-]

Dec 96. (cd) *(SHINKANSEN 7CD)* *<MRG 111>* **MEL** [ ] [ ]
– The club isn't open / I am a small mistake / Spotlight / Beautiful worn-out love / New York crown / Kill the action / We're going to nowhere / Lonely line away / The prettiest whore / Guilty as charged / Take back the days / Life is born today.

– compilations, etc. –

1994. (cd) *Ajax; <041>* **SHINING HOURS IN A CAN** (early material) [-] [ ]
– Make a deal with the city / My life is wrong / Helmet on / Happytown / Axl or Iggy / Psychic whore / Firing room / Silhouette town / Dogman / When will your friends all disappear? / Bernie Shaw / 40 miles / Times Square go-go boy / She's a real good time / Woody's car.

EASY

Formed: Jonkoping, Sweden . . . 1990 by JOHAN HOLMLUND, TOMMY ERICSON, TOMMY JONSSON, RIKARD JORMIN and ANDERS PETERSSON. After recording a demo directly from their first live gig in 1989, the band were unexpectedly snapped up by the UK branch of New York noise specialists, 'Blast First'. Routinely mentioned in the same breath as JESUS & MARY CHAIN, EASY combined caterwauling guitar abuse, pockets of low-rent melody and a curiously Swedish self-deprecating charm, winning over British audiences on their support dates with The CHARLATANS. Debut album, 'MAGIC SEED' (1990), had already given indie fans a taste of what to expect, the band's No.1 rule of not taking themselves too seriously paying off in the UK but affording them a cautious reaction at home where critics were reportedly suspicious of their Blighty success. They subsequently split after a brief association with 'Snap'.

Album rating: MAGIC SEED (*6)

JOHAN HOLMLUND (b.13 Jul'65) – vocals / **TOMMY ERICSSON** (b.23 Mar'66, Umea, Sweden) – guitar / **ANDERS PETERSSON** (b.12 Nov'65) – guitar, keyboards / **RIKARD JORMIN** (b. 2 Aug'65) – bass / **TOMMY JONSSON** (b.15 Jun'66, Vasterik, Sweden) – drums

Blast First | Mute

Oct 90. (lp/c/cd) *(BFFP 57/+C/CD)* *<61125-1/-4/-2>* **MAGIC SEED** [ ] [ ]
– He brings the honey / Cloud chamber / Horoscope / Dam sugar / On a sunny day / Land diving / Between John and Yoko / #25 / Pleasure cruise / Magic seed.

Jan 91. (cd-ep) *(BFFP 61CD)* **HE BRINGS THE HONEY** [ ] [-]

Jun 91. (cd-ep) *(BFFP 65CD)* **HOROSCOPE** [ ] [-]

Snap | not iss.

Aug 93. (cd-ep) *(SNAPC 012)* **NEVER SEEN A STAR / REACH OUT, YVONNE / NEW SPRING** [ ] [-]

Apr 94. (12") *(SNAPT 023)* **LISTEN TO THE BELLS. /** [ ] [-]

May 94. (cd-s) *(SNAPC 021)* **IN BLACK AND WHITE / SAY GOODBYE TO HOLLYWOOD** [ ] [-]

— disbanded when little interest was shown to them

EAT

Formed: Bath, Avon, England . . . 1986 by ANGE DOLITTLE, brothers PAUL and MAX NOBEL, TIM SEWELL and PETE HOWARD. Relocating to the King's Cross area of North London, the band immersed themsleves in the squat culture and warehouse party scene of the late 80's. Securing a deal with Polydor offshoot, 'Fiction', they released the 'AUTOGIFT' EP in early '89. This was closely followed by a debut album, 'SELL ME A GOD' (1989), the mutant grebo-funk/blues contained within confirming the band's position as spiritual southern cousins of Midlands wide boys POP WILL EAT ITSELF and The WONDER STUFF. DOLITTLE's offbeat, often half-spoken commentaries on life in the Big Smoke and other random subjects were powered along by blasting harmonicas, burbling bass and apparently whatever noise came to hand; not exactly easy listening but fun if you're in the mood. Despite positive reviews and the radio support of John Peel, however, inter-band instability led to the departure of the NOBEL brothers (both would go on to form UV RAY) and the end of EAT's first incarnation. DOLITTLE would subsequently re-form the band in 1991 with a line-up of SEWELL and HOWARD together with new members MAZ LAVILLA and JEM MOORSHEAD. A 1992 EP, 'GOLDEN EGG' (produced by TIM SMITH of The CARDIACS and CHRIS KIMSEY), was followed by a long awaited second album, 'EPICURE' (1993), a record which failed to significantly expand their fanbase despite critical praise. Inevitably, EAT splintered once more with DOLITTLE teaming up with ex-WONDER STUFF personnel to form WEKNOWHEREYOULIVE in the mid-90's. • **Songwriters:** PAUL NOBLE until his departure, then group. Covered; SUMMER IN THE CITY (Lovin' Spoonful) / ON THE ROAD AGAIN (Canned Heat).

Album rating: SELL ME A GOD (*8) / EPICURE (*6)

ANGE DOLITTLE – vocals, (later added guitar) / **PAUL NOBLE** – guitar, percussion, vocals / **TIM SEWELL** – bass, synth, vocals / **PETE HOWARD** – drums, percussion / **MAX NOBLE** – guitar, percussion

Fiction | not iss.

Jan 89. (7"ep/12"ep/cd-ep) *(WAN/+TX/CD 100)* **THE AUTOGIFT EP** [ ] [-]
– Skin / Swampadelia / Red Moon.

May 89. (7"ep/12"ep/cd-ep) *(CIF/+X/CD 1)* **THE PLASTIC BAG EP** [ ] [-]
– Plastic bag / Baby boom / Mr. & Mrs. Smack / Little country.

Aug 89. (7") *(CIF 2)* **SUMMER IN THE CITY. / TWO NATIONS** [ ] [-]
(12"+=/cd-s+=) *(CIF/+X/CD 2)* – Gyrate (extended Jib mix).

Sep 89. (lp/c/cd) *(838 944-1/-4/-2)* **SELL ME A GOD** [ ] [-]
– Tombstone / Electric city / Fatman / Stories / Walking man / Skin / Red moon * / Insect head / Body bag / Things I need / Judgement train / Gyrate * / Summer in the city * / Mr. & Mrs. Smack. *(cd+= */c+= *)*

Nov 89. (7") *(FICS 32)* **TOMBSTONE. / SQUAT** [ ] [-]
(12"+=/cd-s+=) *(FICS X/CD 32)* – ('A'-Beyond the groove mix).

— MAX had already departed having formed WE ARE PLABS

Non-Fiction | not iss.

Sep 90. (7") **PSYCHO COUCH. / ALIEN DETECTOR** [ ] [-]
(cd-s+=) – ('A'extended mixes).
(12") – ('A'extended mixes).

— PETE HOWARD departed late 1990 and was repl. by **DANIEL NEWMAN**. PETE returned by mid-1991. PAUL formed UV RAY with brother and early EAT (then WE ARE PLEBS) member MAX NOBLE. (UV RAY other member PAUL O'NEILL – vocals, guitar)

— Meanwhile mid'91 EAT re-formed and brought in **JEM MOORSHEAD** – guitar (ex-FLICK SPATULA) / **MAZ LaVILLA** – guitar

Fiction | November

Jun 92. (7"ep/12"ep/cd-ep) *(FIC/+X/CD 38)* **THE GOLDEN EGG EP** [ ] [-]
– Golden egg / Bellytown / Streets are full / Double bubble.
(12"ep+=) *(FIXT 38)* – Tombstone (live).

Oct 92. (7") **SHAME. / KNOCK ME DOWN** [ ] [-]
(12"+=/cd-s+=) – On The road again / Out of line.

May 93. (7"ep/12"ep/cd-ep) *(FICS/+X/CD 48)* **BLEED ME WHITE. / HADDLYANNDAN / ICE POND** [73] [-]
(cd-ep) *(FICCD 48)* – ('A'side) / How does it feel / Late gain.

Jun 93. (cd/c/lp) *(519 103-2/4/-1)* *<NRD/NRC 1105>* **EPICURE** [ ] [ ] Feb94
– Belly town / Shame / First time love song / Tranquilizer / Golden egg / Bottle blue / Fecund / Baby in flares / Fist / Bleed me white / Out people / Epicure.

— split when DOLITTLE joined WONDER STUFF splinter WEKNOWWHEREYOULIVE

EATER

Formed: London, England . . . late 1976 by ANDY BLADE, BRIAN CHEVETTE, IAN WOODGATE and 15 year-old DEE GENERATE. Signed to DIY label 'The Label', which released in March '77 the debut 45 'OUTSIDE VIEW'. Around this time their songs '15' and 'DON'T NEED IT' were used on the live various artists album 'LIVE AT THE ROXY'. Their debut album finally saw light at the end of that punk year. • **Style:** Basic boy-ish punk rock, showing not every band had talent. • **Songwriters:** except; JEEPSTER (T.Rex).

Album rating: THE HISTORY OF EATER VOL.1 compilation (*5)

ANDY BLADE – vocals / **BRIAN CHEVETTE** – guitar / **IAN WOODGATE** – bass / **DEE GENERATE** (b. PHIL ROWLANDS) – drums

The Label | not iss.

Mar 77. (7") *(TLR 001)* **OUTSIDE VIEW. / YOU** [ ] [-]

Jun 77. (7") *(TLR 003)* **THINKIN' OF THE USA. / SPACE DREAMIN' / MICHAEL'S MONETARY SYSTEM** [ ] [-]

Oct 77. (7"/12") *(TLR 004/+12)* **LOCK IT UP. / JEEPSTER** [ ] [-]

Jan 78. (lp) *(TLRLP 001)* **THE ALBUM** [ ] [-]
– You / Public toys / Room for one / Lock it up / Sweet Jane / 15 / I don't need it / Ann / Get raped / Space dreaming / Queen bitch / My business / Waiting for the man / No more / No brains / Peace and luv (H-bomb).

Sep 78. (7"white-ep/12"white-ep) *(TLR 007/+12)* **GET YOUR YO-YO'S OUT (live)** [ ] [-]
– Debutantes ball / No more / Thinkin' of the USA / Holland.

Nov 78. (7") *(TLR 009)* **WHAT SHE WANTS SHE NEEDS. / REACHING FOR THE SKY** [ ] [-]

— they split early next year. ANDY BLADE owned the group name and recruited BILLY DUFFY, BOB GURNEY and DAVID JOHNSON. In 1980, BLADE released a solo single 'BREAK THE NEWS' for 'SMS'; *SMS 001)*. He later formed The ROYTERS, while ROWLAND joined SLAUGHTER & THE DOGS, after a spell in RADIO SWEETHEARTS.

– compilations, etc. –

Feb 85. (colrd-lp) *De Lorean; (EAT 1)* **THE HISTORY OF EATER** [ ] [-]
(above w/ free 7"; EAT FREEBIE 1)

Apr 93. (cd/lp) *Anagram; (CD+/PUNK 10)* **THE COMPLEAT EATER** [ ] [-]

– (THE ALBUM tracks) / *(cd+=)* – Outside view / Thinking of the U.S.A. / Michaels monetary system / She's wearing green / Notebook / Jeepster / Debutantes ball / Holland / What she wants she needs / Reach for the sky / Point of view / Typewriter babies.

1993. (cd) *Creative Man; <CMCD 024>* **ALL OF EATER** [-] [ ]

ANDY BLADE

Creative Man | Creative Man

May 95. (cd) *(<CMCD 007>)* **FROM THE PLANET POP TO THE MENTAL SHOP** [ ] [-]
– Big bad world / The church bell / Three weeks / Playtime / Creature / The big plan / Beautiful failure / Speed of life / Sad / All I want from you / All of the girls / Horsefly / Heart / The girl who forgets everything / The amazing adventures / Without using hands / Wednesday Jones / The effervescing elephant / Face the window / Speed of life jazz.

Apr 96. (cd-s) *(CMCDS 24)* **JUNKIE SHOOTING STAR /** [ ] [-]

EAT STATIC (see under ⇒ OZRIC TENTACLES)

ECHO & THE BUNNYMEN

Formed: Liverpool, England . . . Autumn 1978 by IAN McCULLOCH, WILL SERGEANT and LES PATTINSON. McCULLOCH had once been in The CRUCIAL THREE alongside future stars, JULIAN COPE and PETE WYLIE, the former two starting up another low key act, A SHALLOW MADNESS, together writing 'READ IT IN BOOKS' (the b-side of E&TB's debut single, 'PICTURES ON MY WALL'). The BUNNYMEN, complete with drum machine ECHO, released the aforementioned 45 as a one-off for the local 'Zoo' label, before signing to 'WEA/Warners' subsidiary, 'Korova', late in '79. By the following year, they'd had a Top 20 album, 'CROCODILES', and were soon breaking into the singles chart with 'RESCUE'. Overtly melancholy and DOORS-influenced, their material contained a fresher up-tempo feel which combined powerful melodrama and McCULLOCH's ego-fuelled attitude. From 1981-84, their albums 'HEAVEN UP HERE', 'PORCUPINE' and 'OCEAN RAIN', solidified a Merseyside revival that even crossed successfully over the Atlantic. They split after their last gig on the 26th April '88, and it surprised everyone, not least the solo bound McCULLOCH (he had issued a single in '84, Kurt Weill's 'SEPTEMBER SONG'), when The BUNNYMEN decided to carry on without him. However, in June '89, PETE DE FREITAS was tragically killed in a motorcycle accident. In the early 90's, The BUNNYMEN (SERGEANT, PATTINSON, plus NOEL BURKE – vocals, JACK BROCKMAN – keyboards and DAMON REECE – drums) struggled without their moody frontman. A disappointing album, 'REVERBERATION' (1990), did little to excite the public, the group forming their own 'Euphoric' label after 'Korova/WEA' dropped them. McCULLOCH meanwhile, had been continuing his search for glory, releasing two albums, the Top 20 'CANDLELAND' (1989) and the Top 50, 'MYSTERIO' (1992), the last of which was poorly received. Late in '94, McCULLOCH and SERGEANT were back with a new rock-driven tour de force, ELECTRAFIXION, their sole album, 'BURNED' (1995), was well received by the music press, went Top 40 and enjoyed moderate sales. There was considerably more media interest over the reformation of the original ECHO & THE BUNNYMEN line-up in 1997. A strong comeback single, 'NOTHING LASTS FOREVER', and album, 'EVERGREEN', both made the UK Top 10, while the band proved they could still cut it live with a tour and a series of summer festival appearances. • **Songwriters:** Mainly group compositions, except covers PEOPLE ARE STRANGE (Doors) / PAINT IT BLACK (Rolling Stones) / ALL YOU NEED IS LOVE (Beatles) / FRICTION (Television) / RUN RUN RUN (Velvet Underground) / SHIP OF FOOLS (John Cale). McCULLOCH covered: RETURN TO SENDER (hit; Elvis Presley) / LOVER, LOVER, LOVER (Leonard Cohen). • **Trivia:** DAVE BALFE (of DALEK I LOVE YOU) played keyboards on their first JOHN PEEL session in August 1979.

Album rating: CROCODILES (*9) / HEAVEN UP HERE (*9) / PORCUPINE (*7) / OCEAN RAIN (*7) / SONGS TO LEARN AND SING compilation (*9) / ECHO & THE BUNNYMEN (*5) / REVERBERATION (*3) / EVERGREEN (*7) / Ian McCulloch: CANDLELAND (*6) / MYSTERIO (*5) / Electrafixion: BURNED (*6)

IAN McCULLOCH (b. 5 May'59) – vocals, guitar (ex-CRUCIAL THREE) **WILL SERGEANT** (b.12 Apr'58) – lead guitar / **LES PATTINSON** (b.18 Apr'58) – bass (& 'ECHO' a drum machine)

Zoo | not iss.

Mar 79. (7") *(CAGE 004)* **PICTURES ON MY WALL. / READ IT IN BOOKS** [ ] [-]
(re-iss. Mar91 on 'Document' 12"/cd-s; DC 3/+CD)

— **PETE DE FREITAS** (b. 2 Aug'61, Port Of Spain, Trinidad) – drums repl. 'ECHO'

Korova | Sire

Apr 80. (7") *(KOW 1)* **RESCUE. / SIMPLE STUFF** [62] [-]
(12"+=) *(KOW 1T)* – Pride.

Jul 80. (lp/c) *(KODE/CODE 1) <6096>* **CROCODILES** [17] [ ]
– Going up / Stars are stars / Pride / Monkeys / Crocodiles / Rescue / Villier's terrace / Pictures on my wall / All that jazz / Happy death men. *(re-iss. Nov80 w/ free 7"; SAM 128)* DO IT CLEAN. / READ IT IN BOOKS *(re-iss. 1989 on 'WEA' lp/c/cd; same/same/2423162)*

Sep 80. (7") *(KOW 11)* **THE PUPPET. / DO IT CLEAN** [ ] [ ]

Apr 81. (12"ep)(c-ep) *(ECHOZ 1)(ECHO 1M)* **SHINE SO HARD (live)** [37] [-]
– Crocodiles / Zimbo / Over the wall / All that jazz.

May 81. (lp/c) *(KODE/CODE 3) <3569>* **HEAVEN UP HERE** [10] [ ]
– Show of strength / With a hip / Over the wall / It was a pleasure / A promise / Heaven up here / The disease / All my colours / No dark things / Turquoise days / All I want. *(cd-iss. Jul88 on 'WEA'; 2432173)*

Jul 81. (7"/12") *(KOW 15/+T)* **A PROMISE. / BROKE MY NECK** [49] [-]

May 82. (7") *(KOW 24)* **THE BACK OF LOVE. / THE SUBJECT** [19] [-]
(12"+=) *(KOW 24T)* – Fuel.

Jan 83. (7") *(KOW 26)* **THE CUTTER. / WAY OUT AND UP WE GO** [8] [-]
(w/ free c-ep+=) *(KOW 26C)* – The cutter / Villier's terrace / Ashes to ashes (stars are stars) / Monkeys / Read it in books.
(12"+=) *(KOW 26T)* – Zimbo (live).

Jan 83. (lp/c) *(KODE/CODE 6) <23770>* **PORCUPINE** [2] [ ]
– The cutter / The back of love / My white devil / Clay / Porcupine / Heads will roll / Ripeness / Higher hell / Gods will be gods / In bluer skies. *(free ltd.c-ep w/ above lp)* – 'JOHN PEEL SESSIONS' *(re-iss. Jul88 on 'WEA' lp/c/cd; same/same/K 400 272)*

Feb 83. (7") **THE CUTTER. / GODS WILL BE GODS** [-] [ ]

Jul 83. (7") *(KOW 28)* **NEVER STOP. / HEADS WILL ROLL** [15] [-]

(12"+=) *(KOW 28T)* – ('A'-Discotheque) / ('B'-Summer version) / The original cutter (A drop in the ocean).

Jan 84. (7") *(KOW 32)* **THE KILLING MOON. / DO IT CLEAN** [9] [-]
(12"+=) *(KOW 32T)* – ('A'-All night version).

Jan 84. (m-lp) *<23987>* **ECHO AND THE BUNNYMEN** [-] [ ]
– Back of love / Never stop / Rescue / The cutter / Do it clean.

Apr 84. (lp/c)(cd) *(KODE/CODE 8)(K 240388-2) <25084>* **OCEAN RAIN** [4] [87] Jun84
– Silver / Nocturnal me / Crystal days / The yo yo man / Thorn of crowns / The killing moon / Seven seas / My kingdom / Ocean rain.

Apr 84. (7") *(KOW 34)* **SILVER. / ANGELS AND DEVILS** [30] [-]
(12"+=) *(KOW 34T)* – Silver (Tidal wave).

Jun 84. (7") *(KOW 35)* **SEVEN SEAS. / ALL YOU NEED IS LOVE** [16] [-]
(12"+=/d7"+=) *(KOW 35 T/F)* – The killing Moon / Stars are stars (acoustic) / Villier's terrace (acoustic).

Oct 85. (7"/7"pic-d) *(KOW 43/+P)* **BRING ON THE DANCING HORSES. / OVER MY SHOULDER** [21] [-]
(ext.12"+=) *(KOW 43T)* – Beds, bugs and ballyhoo.
(d7"+=) *(KOW 43F)* – Villier's terrace / Monkeys.

Nov 85. (lp/c)(pic-lp)(cd) *(KODE/CODE 13)(KODE 13P)(240 767-2) <25360>* **SONGS TO LEARN AND SING** (compilation) [6] [ ]
– Rescue / The puppet / Do it clean / The promise / The back of love / The cutter / Never stop / The killing moon / Silver / Seven seas / Bring on the dancing horses. *(c+=/cd+=)* – Pride / Simple stuff / Read it in books / Angels and devils. *(free ltd.c-s w/ same extra tracks)*

— (Feb86) temp. **MARK FOX** – drums (ex-HAIRCUT 100) repl. DE FREITAS until return Sep'86.

WEA Sire

Jun 87. (7") *(YZ 134)* **THE GAME. / SHIP OF FOOLS** [28] [-]
(12"+=/12"w poster+=) *(YZ 134T/+W)* – Lost and found.

Jul 87. (lp/c)(cd) *(WX 108/+C)(242 137-2) <25597>* **ECHO AND THE BUNNYMEN** [4] [51]
– The game / Over you / Bedbugs and ballyhoo / All in your mind / Bombers bay / Lips like sugar / Lost and found / New direction / Blue blue ocean / Satellite / All my life. *(re-iss. cd Nov94)*

Jul 87. (7"/7"gf/7"box) *(YZ 144/+V/B)* **LIPS LIKE SUGAR. / ROLLERCOASTER** [36] [-]
(12"+=) *(YZ 144T/+X)* – People are strange.

Feb 88. (7"/c-s) *(YZ 175/+C)* **PEOPLE ARE STRANGE. / RUN RUN RUN (live)** [29] [-]
(12"+=) *(YZ 175T)* – Paint it black / Friction. *(re-iss. Feb91 7"/c-s; YZ 567/+C /12"/cd-s; YZ 567 T/CD)* – hit UK No.34)

— They split some unofficial time in '88. Re-formed after McCULLOCH went solo. PETE DE FREITAS joined SEX GODS. He died in motorcycle accident 14 Jun '89.

— **SERGEANT** and **PATTINSON** reformed group early 1990, with newcomers **NOEL BURKE** (b.Belfast, N.Ireland) – vocals (ex-St.VITAS DANCE) / **JACK BROCKMAN** – keyboards / **DAMON REECE** – drums

Korova Sire

Oct 90. (7"/c-s) *(9031 72796-7/-4)* **ENLIGHTEN ME. / LADY, DON'T FALL BACKWARDS** [ ] [ ]
(12"+=/cd-s+=) *(9031 72796-1/-2)* – ('A'extended).

Nov 90. (cd)(c/lp) *(9031 72553-2)(CODE/KODE 14) <26388>* **REVERBERATION** [ ] [ ] Dec90
– Freaks dwell / Cut and dried / Revilement / Flaming red / Salvatore / Fine thing / Gone, gone, gone / Enlighten me / King of your castle / Senseless / Thick skinned world. *(cd+=)* – False goodbyes.

Euphoric not iss.

Oct 91. (12"ep/cd-ep) *(E 001 T/CDS)* **PROVE ME WRONG. / FINE THING / REVERBERATION** [ ] [-]

Mar 92. (12"/cd-s) **INSIDE ME, INSIDE YOU. / WIGGED OUT WORLD** [ ] [-]

— The BUNNYMEN disbanded soon after the above and LES joined TERRY HALL'S backing group.

WILL SERGEANT

WEA not iss.

Jul 82. (7") *(K 19238)* **FAVOURITE BRANCHES. / (b-side by Ravi Shankar & Bill Lovelady)** [ ] [-]

92 Happy Customers not iss.

Mar 83. (lp) *(HAPLP 1)* **THEMES FOR "GRIND"** [ ] [-]
– Grind starts the generator / The wheel turns / The small screen flickers. *(cd-iss. Jan98 +=; HAPSCD 1)* – Theme / Favourite branches / Aquarius dub.

Ochre not iss.

1995. (7"orange) *(OCH 003)* **COSMOS. / VENUS IN FLARES** [ ] [-]

Ian McCULLOCH

IAN McCULLOCH – vocals while still a member of The BUNNYMEN

Korova not iss.

Nov 84. (7"/10") *(KOW 40/+L)* **SEPTEMBER SONG. / COCKLES & MUSSELS** [51] [-]
(12"+=) *(KOW 40T)* – ('A'extended).

— Now solo his back-up came from **RAY SHULMAN** – keyboards, programmer, bass, producer / plus guests **MICHAEL JOBSON** – bass / **BORIS WILLIAMS** – drums / **OLLE REMO** – drum programmer / **LIZ FRASER** – vox (of COCTEAU TWINS)

WEA Sire

Aug 89. (7"/7"box/c-s) *(YZ 417/+B/C)* **PROUD TO FALL. / POTS OF GOLD** [51] [-]
(12") *(YZ 417T)* – ('A'extended) / ('A'side) / The dead end.
(cd-s) *(YZ 417CD)* – (above 3 tracks) / ('A'version).
(12") *(YZ 417TX)* – ('A'side / Everything is real / The circle game.

Sep 89. (lp/c)(cd) *(WX 303/+C)(2292 46225-2) <26012>* **CANDLELAND** [18] [ ]
– The flickering wall / The white hotel / Proud to fall / The cape / Candleland / Horse's head / Faith and healing / I know you well / In bloom / Start again.

Nov 89. (7"/c-s) *(YZ 436/+C)* **FAITH AND HEALING (remix). / TOAD** [ ] [-]
('A'mix-12"+=) *(YZ 436T)* – Fear of the known.
(cd-s++=) *(YZ 436CD)* – Rocket ship.
(12") *(YZ 436TX)* – ('A'side) / Fear of the known / Rocket ship.

Apr 90. (7"/c-s) *(YZ 436/+C)* **CANDLELAND (THE SECOND COMING). / THE WORLD IS FLAT** [75] [-]
(12"+=/12"gf+=/cd-s+=) *(YZ 452 T/TG/CD)* – Big days / Wassailing in the night.

— His backing band from late '89, were The PRODIGAL SONS; **MIKE MOONEY** – guitar / **JOHN McEVOY** – guitar, keyboards / **EDGAR SUMMERTIME** – bass / **STEVE HUMPHRIES** – drums

East West Warners

Feb 92. (7"/c-s) *(YZ 643/+C)* **LOVER, LOVER, LOVER. / WHITE HOTEL (acoustic) / THE GROUND BELOW** [47] [-]
('A'-Indian Dawn remix-12"+=/cd-s+=) *(YZ 643T)* – Vibor blue (acoustic).

Apr 92. (lp/c)(cd) *(WX 453/+C)(<9031 76264-2>)* **MYSTERIO** [46] [ ]
– Mayreal world / Close your eyes / Dug for love / Honeydrip / Damnation / Lover, lover, lover / Webbed / Pomegranate / Vibor blue / Heaven's gate / In my head.

Apr 92. (7"/c-s) *(YZ 660/+C)* **DUG FOR LOVE. / POMMEGRANITE (live)** [ ] [-]
(12"+=)(cd-s+=) *(YZ 660 T/CD)* – Do it clean (live) / In my head (live).

ELECTRAFIXION

— **IAN McCULLOCH** – vocals, guitar / **WILL SERGEANT** – guitar / **LEON DE SYLVA** – bass / **TONY McGUIGAN** – drums

WEA Warners

Nov 94. (c-ep/12"ep/cd-ep) *(YZ 865 C/T/CD)* **THE ZEPHYR EP** [47] [-]
– Zephyr / Burned / Mirrorball / Rain on me.

Sep 95. (7"red/c-s) *(YZ 977 X/C)* **LOWDOWN. / HOLY GRAIL** [54] [-]
(cd-s+=) *(YZ 977CD)* – Land of the dying sun / Razors edge.

Sep 95. (cd/c) *(0630 11248-2/-4) <61793>* **BURNED** [38] [ ] Oct95
– Feel my pulse / Sister pain / Lowdown / Timebomb / Zephyr / Never / Too far gone / Mirrorball / Who's been sleeping in my head? / Hit by something / Bed of nails.

Oct 95. (c-s) *(WEA 022C)* **NEVER / NOT OF THIS WORLD** [58] [-]
(cd-s+=) *(WEA 022CD)* – Subway train / Lowdown (rest of the trash mix).
(cd-s) *(WEA 022CDX)* – ('A'side) / Lowdown / Work it on out / Never (Utah Saints blizzard on mix) / Sister pain.

Mar 96. (cd-ep) *(WEA 037CD1)* **SISTER PAIN / FEEL MY PULSE / ZEPHYR / LOWDOWN (live)** [27] [-]
(cd-ep) *(WEA 037CD2)* – ('A'side) / Burned / Loose (live) / Who's been sleeping in my head (acoustic).
(cd-ep) *(WEA 037CD3)* – ('A'live) / Holy grail (live) / Never (live) / Too far gone (live).

— the last set-up issued a very limited gold-7" in Sep'97, 'BASEBALL BILL' released on 'Phree' (PHREE 1)

ECHO & THE BUNNYMEN

— the original trio (**McCULLOCH, SEARGEANT + PATTINSON**) re-formed

London Polygram

Jun 97. (7") *(LON 396)* **NOTHING LASTS FOREVER. / WATCHTOWER** [8] [-]
(cd-s+=) *(LONCD 396)* – Polly / Colour me in.
(cd-s) *(LONCDP 396)* – ('A'side) / Antelope / Hurracaine / Jonny.

Jul 97. (cd/c/lp) *(<828905-2/-4/-1>)* **EVERGREEN** [8] [ ]
– Don't let it get you down / In my time / I want to be there (when you come) / Evergreen / I'll fly tonight / Nothing lasts forever / Baseball Bill / Altamont / Just a touch away / Empire state halo / Too young to kneel / Forgiven. *(d-cd-iss. Nov97; 828980-2)*

— The above album will no doubt be of little interest to Glastonbury organiser/farmer MICHAEL EAVIS, who was a little perturbed when McCULLOCH slagged his much-loved festival. ('EVERMUD' might have been a more appropriate title)

Aug 97. (7") *(LON 399)* **I WANT TO BE THERE (WHEN YOU COME). /** [30] [-]
(cd-s+=) *(LONCD 399)* –
(cd-s) *(LOCDP 399)* –

Oct 97. (7") *(LON 406)* **DON'T LET IT GET YOU DOWN. / OVER THE WALL** [50] [-]
(cd-s+=) *(LONCD 406)* – Back of love.
(cd-s) *(LONCDP 406)* – ('A'side) / Rescue / Altamont.

— In Jun'98, McCULLOCH provided ENGLAND UNITED with their World Cup song, '(HOW DOES IT FEEL TO BE) ON TOP OF THE WORLD' which hit Top 10.

– compilations, others, etc. –

Nov 88. (12"ep/cd-ep) *Strange Fruit; (SFPS/+CD 060)* **THE PEEL SESSIONS** (15.8.79) [ ] [-]
– Read it in books / Stars are stars / I bagsy yours / Villier's terrace. *(re-iss. cd-ep Dec94; same)*

Jul 90. (7") *Old Gold; (OG 9939)* **THE KILLING MOON. / SEVEN SEAS** [ ] [-]

Jul 90. (7") *Old Gold; (OG 9941)* **THE CUTTER. / THE BACK OF LOVE** [ ] [-]

Nov 91. (cd/lp) *Windsong; (WIN CD/LP 006)* **BBC RADIO 1 LIVE IN CONCERT (live)** [ ] [-]

Mar 93. (cd/c) *Pickwick-WEA; (4509-91886-2/-4)* **THE CUTTER** [ ] [-]
(re-iss. Sep95 on 'Warners'; same)

Jun 97. (cd/c) *W.E.A.; (0630 19103-2/-4)* **BALLYHOO – THE BEST OF ECHO & THE BUNNYMEN** [59] [-]
– Rescue / Do it clean / Villier's terrace / All that jazz / Over the wall / A promise / The disease / The back of love / The cutter / Never stop / The killing moon / Silver / Seven seas / Bring on the dancing horses / People are strange / The game / Lips like sugar / Bedbugs & ballyhoo.

ECHOBELLY

Formed: London, England ... 1992 by Anglo-Asian, SONYA AURORA MADAN, alongside co-writer and guitarist, GLENN JOHANSSON, ALEX KEYSER and ANDY HENDERSON. With MADAN's BLONDIE-esque vocals set to a SMITHS-style musical backdrop, ECHOBELLY were one of Brit-pop's early leading lights, debuting in late '93 with the 'BELLYACHE' EP. Adding former CURVE guitar abuser, DEBBIE SMITH (who had initially filled in for the injured JOHANSSON on a tour of the States with MORRISSEY, one of their biggest fans apparently!) and signing to the independent 'Fauve' label, the band released a debut album, 'EVERYONE'S GOT ONE' (as in EGO), in summer '94. Its jagged indie pop and intelligent, aware lyrics drew considerable critical acclaim and, combining studied cool with a vaguely PC agenda, MADAN became something of a female figurehead for the genre along with LOUISE WENER (SLEEPER) and JUSTINE FRISCHMANN (ELASTICA). A Top 10 UK hit, the album's success spurred them on to greater things as the Britpop phenomena reached its zenith in the summer of '95. That year's follow-up set, 'ON', was a bigger budget affair which nevertheless still managed to capture ECHOBELLY's abrasive immediacy, the record making the UK Top 5. The songwriting was as caustic as ever, singles 'KING OF THE KERB' and 'DARK THERAPY', making the Top 30. By the release of 1997's 'LUSTRA', however, the Britpop bubble had long since burst and, along with acts such as SLEEPER, ECHOBELLY seemed to be at the sharp end of the backlash.

Album rating: EVERYONE'S GOT ONE (*6) / ON (*5) / LUSTRA (*4)

SONYA AURORA MADAN – vocals / **GLENN JOHANSSON** – guitar / **ALEX KEYSER** – bass, piano / **ANDY HENDERSON** – drums

Pandemonium | not iss.

Nov 93. (12"ep/cd-ep) *(PANN/+CD 001)* **BELLYACHE** [ ] [-]
– Give her a gun / Call me names / England swings.

Jan 94. (12"ep/cd-ep) *(PANN/+CD 002)* **BELLYACHE / SLEEPING HITLER. / GIVE HER A GUN / I DON'T BELONG HERE** [ ] [-]
(re-iss. May94; PANN/+CD 003)

Fauve-Epic | Epic

Mar 94. (7"/c-s) *(FAUV 001/+C)* **INSOMNIAC. / TALENT** [47] [-]
(12"+=) *(FAUV 001T)* – ('A'mix).
(cd-s++=) *(FAUV 001CD)* – Centipede.

—— added **DEBBIE SMITH** – guitar noise

Jun 94. (7"/c-s) *(FAUV 002/+C)* **I CAN'T IMAGINE THE WORLD WITHOUT ME. / VENUS WHEEL** [39] [-]
(12"+=/cd-s+=) *(FAUV 002 T/CD)* – Sober.

Aug 94. (cd/c/lp) *(FAUV 3 CD/C/LPS) <66775>* **EVERYONE'S GOT ONE** [8] [ ] Oct94
– Today tomorrow sometime never / Father, ruler, king, computer / Give her a gun / I can't imagine the world without me / Bellyache / Taste of you / Insomniac / Call me names / Close ... but / Cold feet warm heart / Scream.

Oct 94. (7"/c-s/12") *(FAUV 004/+C/T)* **CLOSE ... BUT. / SO LA DI DA** [59] [-]
(cd-s+=) *(FAUV 004CD)* – I can't image the world without me (live) / Cold feet warm heart (live).

Fauve-Epic | Work-Columbia

Aug 95. (c-s) *(FAUV 5C)* **GREAT THINGS / HERE COMES THE SCENE** [13] [-]
(cd-s+=) *(FAUV 5CD)* – God's guest list / On turn off.
(cd-s) *(FAUV 5CDX)* – ('A'side) / On turn on / Bunty / One after 5 a.m.

Sep 95. (cd/c/lp) *(FAUV 6 CD/C/LP) <67368>* **ON** [4] [ ] Oct95
– Oar fiction / King of the kerb / Great things / Natural animal / Go away / Pantyhose and roses / Something hot in a cold country / Four letter word / Nobody like you / In the year / Dark therapy / Worms an angels.

Oct 95. (c-s) *(FAUV 7C)* **KING OF THE KERB / CAR FICTION (French)** [25] [-]
(cd-s+=) *(FAUV 7CD)* – On turn on (acoustic) / Natural animal (acoustic).
(cd-s) *(FAUV 7CDX)* – ('A'live) / I can't imagine the world without me (live) / Insomniac (live) / Great things (live).

Feb 96. (7"blue-ep/c-ep/cd-ep) *(FAUV 8/+C/CD)* **DARK THERAPY / WE KNOW BETTER. / ATOM / ALOHA LOLITA** [20] [-]

—— (Aug'95) **JAMES HARRIS** – bass; repl. KEYSER

Epic | Epic

Aug 97. (c-s/cd-s) *(664815-4/-2)* **THE WORLD IS FLAT / HOLDING THE WIRE / THE WORLD IS FLAT (mix)** [31] [-]
(cd-s+=) *(664815-5)* – Drive myself distracted / Falling flame.

Oct 97. (c-s) *(665245-4)* **HERE COMES THE BIG RUSH / MOUTH ALMIGHTY** [56] [-]
(cd-s+=) *(665245-2)* – Tesh.
(cd-s) *(665245-5)* – ('A'mixes).

Nov 97. (cd/c) *(<488967-2/-4>)* **LUSTRA** [47] [ ]
– Bulldog baby / I'm not a saint / Here comes the big rush / Iris art / The world is flat / Everyone knows better / Wired on / O / Bleed / Paradise / Angel B / Lustra.

EDDIE & THE HOT RODS

Formed: Canvey Island, Essex, England ... 1975 by DAVE HIGGS, alongside former amateur boxer turned singer, BARRIE MASTERS, STEVE NICOLS, PETE WALL and ROB STEEL (the latter pair soon to be replaced by schoolboy, PAUL GRAY and harmonica player, LEW LEWIS). After ripping up the tarmac on the thriving London pub-rock circuit, manager/producer/lyricist, ED HOLLIS, secured them a deal with 'Island'. With precision timing, EDDIE & Co emerged as a catalyst for the nascent punk scene, just edging out ahead of R&B contemporaries (e.g. DR. FEELGOOD and The COUNT BISHOPS) with a raw, rasping three-chord blast more attuned to the intensity of early WHO. Sandwiched between the release of their first two singles, 'WRITING ON THE WALL' and 'WOOLY BULLY' (a Sam The Sham & The Pharaohs cover), was an infamous gig at the Marquee where unknown support act, SEX PISTOLS, made their mark in more ways than one. In fact the 'HOT RODS' subsequent EP was recorded at the same venue, featuring garage/R&B standards, 'GET OUT OF DENVER' (Bob Seger) and '96 TEARS' (? & The Mysterians) together with a medley of 'GLORIA'-'SATISFACTION' (Them – Rolling Stones). The first punk-affiliated record to make the Top 50, the EP's success was improved upon in October that year when the 'TEENAGE DEPRESSION' single made the Top 40. A debut album of the same name also charted, an R&R (i.e. Rough'n'Ready rather than Rock'n'Roll) powerhouse that nevertheless didn't entirely succeed in capturing the spark of their live set. Having already sacked LEW LEWIS prior to the aforementioned 'PISTOLS gig, the group's sound was fuel-injected by the addition of second guitarist, GRAEME DOUGLAS (ex-KURSAAL FLYERS), his introduction coinciding with the release of another Top 50 hit, 'I MIGHT BE LYING'. The latter actually co-wrote what would become the band's biggest hit and signature tune, 'DO ANYTHING YOU WANNA DO'; suspiciously reminiscent of Springsteen's 'Born To Run', this tough-talking power-pop belter became a massive summer '77 hit, giving The RODS (a one-off pseudonym) their only Top 10 hit. That year's album, 'LIFE ON THE LINE', also made it into the UK Top 30, although the band's increasingly sanitised sound and image alienated the spiky-top, safety-pin punk brigade who'd previously lent them their support. While the album spawned a last-ditch Top 40 hit, 'QUIT THIS TOWN', 1979's subsequent 'THRILLER' set was a let down and their last effort for 'Island'. Surprisingly, it would be 'E.M.I.' who'd come to their rescue, although they no doubt regretted their investment as three singles crashed along with a 1981 album, 'FISH 'N' CHIPS', unhealthy listening at its greasiest. The group disbanded shortly after, MASTERS going on to front The INMATES, although he would sporadically re-group EDDIE & THE HOT RODS to minimal interest throughout the 80's and 90's. • **Songwriters:** Group with HOLLIS lyrics, except covers of THE KIDS ARE ALRIGHT (Who) / YOU BETTER RUN (Rascals) / etc. • **Miscellaneous:** One-time member LEW LEWIS was jailed for 7 years in 1987, due to his part in a P.O. robbery.

Album rating: TEENAGE DEPRESSION (*6) / LIFE ON THE LINE (*7) / THRILLER (*4) / FISH 'N' CHIPS (*3) / ONE STORY TOWN mini (*3) / GASOLINE DAYS (*3)

BARRIE MASTERS – vocals / **DAVE HIGGS** – guitar / **PAUL GRAY** – bass / **STEVE NICOL** – drums / plus **LEW LEWIS** – mouth harp

Island | not iss.

Jan 76. (7") *(WIP 6270)* **WRITING ON THE WALL. / CRUISIN' (IN THE LINCOLN)** [ ] [-]

—— now without LEW LEWIS who was sacked due to unruly behavior

Jun 76. (7") *(WIP 6306)* **WOOLY BULLY. / HORSEPLAY (WEARY OF THE SCHMALTZ)** [ ] [-]

Aug 76. (7"ep) *(IEP 2)* **LIVE AT THE MARQUEE (live)** [43] [-]
– 96 tears / Get out of Denver / Medley: Gloria – Satisfaction.

Oct 76. (7") *(WIP 6354)* **TEENAGE DEPRESSION. / SHAKE** [35] [-]

Dec 76. (lp) *(WIP 6354)* **TEENAGE DEPRESSION** [43] [-]
– Teenage depression / The kids are alright / Why can't it be / Horseplay (weary of the Schmatlz) / On the run / Show me / Been so long / Shake / All I need is money / Double checkin' woman. *(cd-iss. May98 on 'Edsel'; EDCD 563)*

—— added **GRAEME DOUGLAS** – guitar (ex-KURSAAL FLYERS)

Apr 77. (7") *(WIP 6388)* **I MIGHT BE LYING. / IGNORE THEM** [44] [-]

Jun 77. (7"ep,12"ep) *(IEP 5)* **AT THE SPEED OF SOUND (live)** [ ] [-]
– Hard driving man / Horseplay / Double checkin' woman / All I need is money.

Aug 77. (7"/12"; as The RODS) *(WIP/12WIP 6401) <IS 091>* **DO ANYTHING YOU WANNA DO. / SCHOOLGIRL LOVE** [9] [-]

Nov 77. (lp) *(ILPS 9509)* **LIFE ON THE LINE** [27] [-]
– Do anything you wanna do / Beginning of the end / Quit this town / (I don't know) what's really going on / We sing the cross / Life on the line / Telephone girl / Ignore them (still life) / (And) don't believe your eyes.

Dec 77. (7"; as ROB TYNER & THE HOT RODS) *(WIP 6418)* **'TIL THE NIGHT IS GONE (LET'S ROCK) . / FLIPSIDE ROCK** [ ] [-]
(above was with the former MC5 on vocals & guitar)

Jan 78. (7") *(WIP 6411)* **QUIT THIS TOWN. / DISTORTION MAY BE EXPECTED** [36] [-]

Mar 78. (7") *(WIP 6438)* **LIFE ON THE LINE. / DO ANYTHING YOU WANNA DO (live)** [ ] [-]
(12"+=) *(12WIP 6438)* – (I don't know) What's really going on (live) / Why can't it be (live).

Oct 78. (7") *(WIP 6464)* **MEDIA MESSIAHS. / HORROR THROUGH THE STRAIGHTNESS** [ ] [-]

Mar 79. (7") *(WIP 6474)* **POWER AND THE GLORY. / HIGHLANDS ONE, HOPEFULS TWO** [ ] [-]

Mar 79. (lp) *(ILPS 9563)* **THRILLER** [50] [-]
– Power and the glory / Media Messiahs / Circles / Take it or leave it / Echoes / Out to lunch / Strangled on the payphone / Breathless / He does it with mirrors / Living dangerously.

E.M.I. | not iss.

Mar 80. (7") *(EMI 5052)* **AT NIGHT. / YOU BETTER RUN / LOOKING AROUND** [ ] [-]

—— now quartet of **MASTERS, HIGGS, DOUGLAS / + T.C.** – bass, (GRAY joined DAMNED)

Nov 80. (7") *(EMI 5110)* **WIDE EYED KIDS. / LEAVE US ALONE** [ ] [-]

—— guests **RUFUS JENKINS** – accordion / **AL KOOPER** – keyboards, guitar, vocals

Apr 81. (7") *(EMI 5160)* **FARTHER ON DOWN THE ROAD. / FISH 'N' CHIPS** [ ] [-]

Apr 81. (lp) *(EMC 3344)* **FISH 'N' CHIPS** [ ] [-]
– Fish 'n' chips (pt.1 & 2) / This is today / Time wont let me / Farther on down the road (you will accompany me) / Wide eyed kids / You better run / Another party / Unfinished business / Call it quits / We want more.

— split '81, BARRIE MASTERS joined The INMATES until he and *NICOL* re-formed **EDDIE & THE HOTRODS** '84 with **WARREN KENNEDY** – guitar / **TONY CRANNEY** – bass

Waterfront / not iss.

Feb 85. (7") *(WFS 9)* **FOUGHT FOR YOU. / HEY TONIGHT** [ ] [-]
Sep 85. (m-lp) *(WF 023)* **ONE STORY TOWN (live)** [ ] [-]

— split finally '85. recent recruit, TEX AXILE, later joined TRANSVISION VAMP. **MASTERS, NICOL, HIGGS + GRAY** re-formed EDDIE & THE HOT RODS in the mid 90's / **MICK RODGERS** (ex-MANFRED MANN'S EARTH BAND) repl. GORDON RUSSELL who repl. STEVE WALWYN

Creative Man / not iss.

Apr 96. (cd) *(CMCD 008)* **GASOLINE DAYS** [ ] [-]

- compilations, others, etc. -

Aug 92. (cd) *Street Link; (LINKCD 157)* **CURSE OF THE HOT RODS** [ ] [-]
(re-iss. Jun93 on 'Dojo'; DOJOCD 142)
Sep 93. (cd) *Receiver; (<RRCD 177>)* **LIVE & RARE (live)** [ ] [ ]
Feb 94. (cd) *Dojo; (DOJOCD 173)* **TIES THAT BIND** [ ] [-]
Jul 94. (cd) *Windsong; (WINCD 062)* **BBC RADIO 1 LIVE IN CONCERT (live)** [ ] [-]
Aug 94. (cd) *Island; (IMCD 156) <61292>* **THE END OF THE BEGINNING – THE BEST OF EDDIE & THE HOT RODS** [ ] [ ]
– Do anything you wanna do / Quit this town / Telephone girl / Teenage depression / The kids are alright (live) / Get out of Denver (live) / 'Til the night is gone (let's rock) / Schoolgirl love / Hard drivin' man (live) / On the run (live) / The power and the glory / Ignore them / Still life / Life on the line / Circles / Take it or leave it / Echoes / We sing the cross / The beginning of the end / Gloria (live) / (I can't get no) Satisfaction.
Jan 95. (cd) *Loma; (LOMACD 44)* **CURSE OF THE HOT RODS / TIES THAT BIND** [ ] [-]
Mar 96. (cd) *Skydog; (622412)* **GET YOUR BALLS OFF** [ ] [-]
Aug 96. (cd) *Anagram; (CDMGRAM 108)* **DOING ANYTHING THEY WANNA DO . . .** [ ] [-]

The EDGE (see under ⇒ U2)

Damon EDGE (see under ⇒ CHROME)

ED GEIN'S CAR

Formed: New York, USA . . . 1982 by ERIC HEDIN and TIM CARROLL who found SCOTT WEISS and filled the drumstool with a succession of temp sticksmen. Poo-pooing the po-faced sincerity of the hardcore scene, the smart-arsed quartet joked their way onto vinyl with 1984's debut single, 'BRAIN DEAD', following it up with a full-length album, 'MAKING DICK DANCE' (1985). Blessed/cursed with the same un-PC adolescent humour as The BEASTIE BOYS would later make their name with, ED GEIN'S CAR were a regular fixture at the infamous CBGB's where their sarcastic stage antics went down a storm; the highlights of this period were captured for posterity on the swansong 1987 set, 'YOU LIGHT UP MY LIVER'. The same year saw WEISS continue his bad taste comedy crusade with the short-lived IRON PROSTATE.

Album rating: MAKING DICK DANCE (*5) / YOU LIGHT UP MY LIVER (*6)

ERIC HEDIN – guitar / **TIM CARROLL** – bass / **SCOTT WEISS** – vocals

not iss. / Ed Gein's Car

1984. (7") **BRAIN DEAD. /** [-] [ ]
1985. (lp) **MAKING DICK DANCE** [-] [ ]

not iss. / Celluloid

1987. (lp/cd) *<97295-1/-2>* **YOU LIGHT UP MY LIVER (live at CBGB'S 1986)** [-] [ ]
– R.A.P.E. / My choice / Too old to die young / Take me to the petting zoo / Middle (r)age / My life's a game / Selby / Last caress / A girl just like you / Anette / Boo fuckin' hoo / Bars and brick / Surf Nazis / We're not you're world / Brain dead baby / Wait till your father gets home / Progress.

— disbanded after above

EELS

Formed: Los Angeles, California, USA . . . 1995 by E (MATT EMERSON), who had previously released two solo albums under this rather minimalist moniker (only in America). Hooking up with fellow slippery characters TOMMY WALTER and BUTCH NORTON, they set free their electric debut album, 'BEAUTIFUL FREAK'. Lyrically grim, The EELS packaged their tales of dysfunctional Americana in deceptively effervescent indie melodies, the UK Top 10 singles 'NOVOCAINE FOR THE SOUL' and 'SUSAN'S HOUSE' being prime examples of post-NIRVANA lo-fi rock. 1998's 'ELECTRO-SHOCK BLUES' was a more private and personal exploration of life's darker side, E exorcising the demons of his sister's suicide and his mother's death from cancer. • **Songwriters:** Most songs by E, some with JIM JACOBSEN, JIM WEATHERLY, MARK GOLDENBERG, JON BRION or JILL SOBULE.

Album rating: E: A MAN CALLED E (*7) / BROKEN TOY SHOP (*5) / Eels: BEAUTIFUL FREAK (*7) / ELECTRO-SHOCK BLUES (*6)

(E)

E (b. MATT EMERSON, Virginia, USA) – vocals, piano, multi

not iss. / Polydor

Dec 91. (cd-s) *<CDP 654>* **HELLO CRUEL WORLD** [-] [ ]
Feb 92. (cd/c) *<511570-2/-4>* **A MAN CALLED (E)** [-] [ ]
– Hello cruel world / Fitting in with the misfits / Are you and me gonna happen / Looking out the window with a blue / Nowheresville / Symphony for toy piano in G minor / Mockingbird Franklin / I've been kicked around / Pray / E's tune / You'll be the scarecrow.

— now with various personnel incl. **PARTHENON HUXLEY + SEAB COLEMAN**

Dec 93. (cd/c) *<519976-2/-4>* **BROKEN TOY SHOP** [-] [ ]
– Shine it all on / Standing at the gate / The only thing I care about / Manchester girl / L.A. river / Most unpleasant man / Mass / Tomorrow I'll be nine / The day I wrote you off / Someone to break the spell / She loves a puppet / My old raincoat / Permanent broken heart / Eight lives left.
Dec 93. (cd-ep) *<SACD 772>* **NOT FOR AIRPLAY** [-] [ ]
– Shine it all on / L.A. river / Tomorrow I'll be nine / Everything's gonna be cool this summer.

EELS

— **E** with **TOMMY WALTER** – bass, vocals / **BUTCH NORTON** – drums, vocals

Dreamworks / Dreamworks

Feb 97. (cd/c) *<(DRD/DRC 50001)>* **BEAUTIFUL FREAK** [5] [ ] Aug96
– Novocaine for the soul / Susan's house / Rags to rags / Beautiful freak / Not ready yet / My beloved monster / Flower / Guest list / Mental / Spunky / Your lucky day in Hell / Manchild.
Feb 97. (7"/c-s) *(DRM S/C 22174)* **NOVOCAINE FOR THE SOUL. / GUEST LIST** [10] [-]
(cd-s+=) *(DRMCD 22174)* – Fucker / My beloved monster (live).
May 97. (7"/c-s) *(DRM S/C 22238)* **SUSAN'S HOUSE. /** [9] [-]
(cd-s+=) *(DRMCD 22238)* –
Sep 97. (7"/c-s) *(DRM S/C 22277)* **YOUR LUCKY DAY IN HELL. /** [35] [-]
(cd-s+=) *(DRMCD 22277)* –
Sep 98. (7"/c-s) *(DRM S/C 22346) <5112>* **LAST STOP: THIS TOWN. / ('A'mix)** [23] [ ]
(cd-s+=) *(DRMCD 22346)* – ('A'mix).
Sep 98. (cd/c) *<(DRD/DRC 50052)>* **ELECTRO-SHOCK BLUES** [12] [ ]
– Elizabeth on the bathroom floor / Going to your funeral part 1 / Cancer for the cure / My descent into madness / 3 speed / Hospital food / Electro-shock blues / Efils' god / Going to your funeral part II / Last stop: this town / Baby genius / Climbing to the moon / Ant farm / Dead of winter / The medication is wearing off / P.S. you rock my world.
Nov 98. (7"/c-s) *(DRM S/C 22373)* **CANCER FOR THE CURE. / EVERYTHING'S GONNA BE COOL THIS XMAS** [60] [ ]
(cd-s+=) *(DRMCD 22373)* – Exodus III.

EGGMAN (see under ⇒ BOO RADLEYS)

EGGS

Formed: Arlington, Richmond, Virginia, USA . . . 1990 by ANDREW BEAUJAN and a cast of players including GRENADINE trombonist, ROB CHRISTIANSEN, who was introduced to ANDREW through mutual acquaintance, MARK ROBINSON (of UNREST, GRENADINE and boss of the 'Teenbeat' imprint). Signed to the latter label, the loose aggregate debuted with the 'BRUISER' set in early '92, an adventurous record that took indie guitar-pop as a canvas and adorned it with everything from Latin-styled pop to off-kilter brass flourishes behind BEAUJAN's parched vocals. Having already poached a series of drummers from local peers, the band's backbeat quandry began resembling a SPINAL TAP-style scenario as they went through more sticksmen than a Welsh colliery marching band. The following year, the basic trio of BEAUJAN, CHRISTIANSEN and new bassist EVAN SHURAK issued a rare UK single, 'THE GOVERNMENT ADMINISTRATOR', while also winning over fans and artists alike via their slot on the Lollapalooza tour. Recorded at the American University in Virginia (where ROB slogs away at his day job), an exhaustive second album, 'TEENBEAT 96 EXPLODER' (1994) made little compromise to commercial considerations with a near 20-track marathon of skewed pop. After the EGGS went sunny side up, CHRISTIANSEN formed his own outfit, VIVA SATELLITE!, the albums 'NISHMA' and 'EXTRA EYE' coming out in '96 and '97 respectively.

Album rating: BRUISER (*7) / TEENBEAT 96 EXPLODER (*7) / HOW DO YOU LIKE YOUR LOBSTER compilation (*6)

ANDREW BEAUJAN – guitar, vocals / **JONATHON RICKMAN** – guitar, vocals / **DAVE PARK** – bass / **MARIANNE McGEE** – French horn / with 5th member **ROB CHRISTIANSEN** – trombone, guitar (of GRENADINE)

Teenbeat / Teenbeat

Jan 92. (cd/lp) *<TEENBEAT 76 CD/V>* **BRUISER** [-] [ ]
(UK-iss.Sep94; same)
1993. (7") **THE GOVERNMENT ADMINISTRATOR. /** [ ] [ ]
May 93. (7") *(WH-APRIL)* **ROLL AWAY THE STONE. / Johnny Cohen & The Shoetrees: Xmas Trees Everywhere** [ ] [ ]
(above issued on 'Simple Machines')

— **ANDREW + ROB** recruited **EVAN SHURAK** – bass; to repl. PARK

Feb 94. (cd/c/lp) *<(TEENBEAT 96 CD/C/LP)>* **EGGS TEENBEAT 96 EXPLODER** [ ] [ ]
– Eggs Teenbeat 96 exploder, let's go! / Why am I so tired all the time? / Er in go bragh / Music without keys No.3 / Ampallang / Side division / March of the triumphant elephants / Claire's snakes / Pit with spikes / Evanston, Il. / Willow, willow / Eggs TNBT 96 XPLDR How're you doing? / Side division / Minestrone / Saturday's cool / Maureen's beans / Conchita / Side division / Oblivist part 3 /

Rollercoaster / Music without keys No.7 / Salsa garden / Eggs Teenbeat 96 exploder bye bye!

Oct 94. (7") <(TEENBEAT 136)> **GENETIC ENGINEERING. /**

Jul 95. (cd) <(TB 156CD)> **HOW DO YOU LIKE YOUR LOBSTER?** (compilation of early singles)

— when they broke-up (sorry!), CHRISTIANSEN formed . . .

VIVA SATELLITE!

— with **IAN JONES** – guitars + **PAIGE SMITH** – vocals

Jan 96. (cd) <TB 186> **NISHMA** [-]

— added **DAN MORRISSEY** – guitar, keyboards, vocals

Oct 97. (cd) <(TB 246)> **EXTRA EYE** Sep97
– Theme / Landing song / Dwight, the crude, but loveable, . . . / Bridget and her editor / Meeting I / Meeting II / Secret wedding plans / Three's company / Halted at the altar / Paranoid / Coda / Theme electronique.

18 WHEELER

Formed: Glasgow, Scotland . . . early 90's by SEAN JACKSON, NEIL HALLIDAY, ALAN HAKE and DAVID KEENAN. A Glasgow band in the firmly established mould and a prime contender for Alan McGee's Creation offshoot label, 'August', 18 WHEELER emerged in 1993 with an eponymous EP prior to the cutesy indie-pop of the 'NATURE GIRL' single. This was followed by the country-ish 'SUNCRUSH', the DINOSAUR JR.-esque guitar squall of 'KUM BACK' and the TEENAGE FANCLUB impression, 'THE REVEALER', prior to the release of debut album, 'TWIN ACTION' in 1994. A trainee TEENAGE FANCLUB wouldn't be such a bad description for this lot in fact, preoccupied as they are with airy harmonies, sugary melodies and a fixation for the classic American triple-B i.e. The BYRDS, The BEACH BOYS and BIG STAR (plus the obligatory GRAM PARSONS factor, the lads even including what is presumably a tribute track, 'GRAM'). No bad thing if you're after a pleasant listen – and 'PROCK SHAKE' really hits the mark – but hardly a contender for a Mercury music prize. With the addition of extra guitarist STEVE HADDOW, follow-up set, 'FORMANKA' (1995), was grungier and relatively more adventurous, even employing strings on the moody instrumental title track. Still, by this point 18 WHEELER had been well and truly eclipsed at 'Creation' by a certain OASIS, the same Manc hopefuls that had supported them only a few years ago in Glasgow! Seemingly destined to forever linger in the Caledonian margins along with The PASTELS, WHITEOUT, The GYRES etc. etc., 18 WHEELER need a tank of rocket fuel if they're to have any hope of breaking through.

Album rating: TWIN ACTION (4) / FORMANKA (*5) / YEAR ZERO (*5)

SEAN JACKSON – vocals, guitar, bass, piano / **ALAN HAKE** – bass, vocals, guitar, Moog / **NEIL HALLIDAY** – percussion, vocals, guitars, synth / **DAVID KEENAN** – was an early member, before he formed the TELSTAR PONIES

August-Creation / not iss.

May 93. (12"ep/cd-ep) (CAUG 005 T/CD) **18 WHEELER EP** [-]

Sep 93. (12"ep/cd-ep) (CAUG 006 T/CD) **NATURE GIRL. / PILLOW FIGHT / GOLDEN CANDLES** [-]

Dec 93. (12"ep/cd-ep) (CAUG 010 T/CD) **SUNCRUSH / YER EYES. / FALLING OUT OF LOVE / SOME THINGS LAST A LONG TIME** [-]

Creation / not iss.

May 94. (7") (CRE 148) **KUM BACK. /** [-]
(cd-s+=) (CRESCD 148) –

Jul 94. (7") (CRE 188) **THE REVEALER. /** [-]
(cd-s+=) (CRESCD 188) –

Jul 94. (cd/c/lp) (CRECD/CCRE/CRELP 164) **TWIN ACTION** [-]
– Sweet tooth / Nature girl / Kum back / Golden candles / The revealer / Honey mink / Gram / Prock shake / Hotel 167 / Suncrush / Frosty hands / Life is strange / I won't let you down / Wet dream.

— added **STEVEN HADDOW** – guitar (was backing vocalist on debut)

Apr 95. (7") (CRE 198) **BODDHA. / FORMANKA** [-]
(cd-s+=) (CRESCD 198) –

May 95. (cd/lp) (CRE CD/LP 181) **FORMANKA** [-]
– Boddha / Drought / Steel guitars / Cartoon / The bottle / Formanka / Winter grrrl / Pretty ugly / The track / John the revelator. *(free cd/lp w/ above) (CRED CD/LP 181L)* –

Jun 95. (7") (CRE 209) **STEEL GUITARS. / SOUNDS** [-]
(cd-s+=) (CRESCD 209) –

Aug 96. (12") (CRE 219T) **THE HOURS AND THE TIMES / ('A'-Ultra Living mix). / BEYOND THE VALLEY OF THE HOURS AND THE TIMES / ('A'-the A&R guys mix – Danny Saber)** [-]
(cd-s) (CRESCD 219) –

Sep 96. (c-s) (CRECD 232) **CRABS / ('A'mix)** [-]
(12"+=)(cd-s+=) (CRE 232T)(CRESCD 232) – ('A'mixes).

Nov 96. (12") (CRE 241T) **PROZAC BEATS. /** [-]
(cd-s+=) (CRESCD 241) –

Mar 97. (12") (CRE 249T) **STAY / STAY (Strange L'Escargot mix). / STAY (Big Kahuna mix) / STAY (Dr. Rockit mix)** 59 [-]
(cd-s) (CRESCD 249) –
(cd-s) (CRESCD 249X) –

Mar 97. (cd/lp) (CRE CD/LP 192) **YEAR ZERO** [-]

Apr 97. (c-s) (CRECS 255) **GREASE / THE BALLAD OF PAUL VERLAINE** [-]
(cd-s) (CRESCD 255) –
(12") (CRE 255T) –

8 EYED SPY (see under ⇒ LUNCH, Lydia)

8 STOREY WINDOW

Formed: London, England . . . early 90's by Boston-born CHRIS CONKLIN, a British resident since 1987. He initially employed his songwriting skills in SPINNING JENNY before hooking up with ex-JANE POW drummer, ANDY CRISP and bassist STEVE GEORGE. Following a couple of EP's in 1992 (the second of which opened with 'I THOUGHT YOU TOLD ME EVERYTHING'), the trio supported LEVITATION, the TERRY BICKERS connection serving them well a year on as the feted guitarist played and co-produced on their 1994 eponymous debut album for 'Ultimate'. By this point in time, STEVE had been substituted by JOHN LODGEPATCH, the aforementioned 'I THOUGHT . . .' one of the record's melancholy high spots alongside the accompanying single, 'I WILL'. Lyrically downbeat but occasionally vertigo-inducing in a NIRVANA-esque kind of way, 8 STOREY WINDOW couldn't quite elevate themselves to the dizzying heights reached by KURT COBAIN and Co.

Album rating: 8 STOREY WINDOW (*5)

CHRIS CONKLIN – vocals, guitar, keyboards (ex-SPINNING JENNY) / **ANDY CRISP** – drums, vocals, keyboards (ex-JANE POW) / **STEVE GEORGE** – bass

Mad Minute / not iss.

May 92. (12"ep) (MADMIN 001) **E.P.** [-]

Sep 92. (12"ep) (MADMIN 003) **E.P. 2** [-]
– I thought you told me everything / etc

— **CONKLIN + CRISP** added **JOHN LODGEPATCH** – bass / **TERRY BICKERS** – guitar (of LEVITATION) / **STEVE TOTERDELL** – backing vocals

Ultimate / Atlantic

Feb 94. (7") (Topp 020) **I WILL. /** [-]
(12"+=/cd-s+=) (Topp 020 T/CD) –

Apr 94. (cd/c/lp) (Topp CD/MC/LP 006) <4077> **8 STOREY WINDOW** Oct95
– I will / Close to the sky / Screaming waterfalls / I thought you told me everything / Next to nothing / Already gone / What you like / Flower hill / Laughing at yourself.

Nov 94. (7"red) (Topd 030) **WHAT YOU LIKE. / IT'S BEEN DONE** [-]
(cd-s+=) (Topp 030cd) – We took a long step years ago.

Mar 95. (7") (Topp 032) **I WILL. /** [-]
(cd-s+=) (Topp 032cd) –

— disbanded soon after above

EINSTURZENDE NEUBAUTEN

Formed: Berlin, Germany . . . 1st April 1980, when this arty industrial conglomerate played their first live gig. They issued a few singles for Germany's 'Zick Zack', before unleashing 'KOLLAPS' at the end of '81. A few more arrived (signed to UK label 'Some Bizzare'), before they settled with the line-up of BLIXA BARGELD, N.U. UNRUH, MUFTI and new mid-80's members ALEX HACKE and MARC CHUNG. By this time, most of them were finding moonlighting work, mainly BARGELD who had joined NICK CAVE & THE BAD SEEDS. Others HACKE joined CRIME & THE CITY SOLUTION, while FM EINHEIT went solo (backed by STEIN ('STONE') for the early 90's. EINSTURZENDE NEUBAUTEN subsequently released the album, 'STEIN', in 1990 and three years later, 'PROMETHEUS LEAR', although they always intending to split during this period. Pioneers of experimental industrial power-metal, picking up any object to make a barrage of sound (i.e. power tools, metal piping, large hammers, steel girders and the more dangerous metal cutters. The band were prone to just basically strip to the waist, wear hard hats and get on with the job. If you can't catch them live, put your radio on to a German station while walking past a dockyard, a precursor to NINE INCH NAILS. • **Songwriters:** Group. • **Trivia:** BARGELD featured alongside The BAD SEEDS in the 1988 Wim Wenders film 'Angels Uber Berlin'.

Album rating: KOLLAPS (*4) / PORTRAIT OF PATIENT O.T. (*5) / STRATEGIES AGAINST ARCHITECTURE compilation (*6) / 2x4 (*5) / HALBER MENSCHE (*5) / HANS DER LUEGE (*4) / STRATEGIES AGAINST ARCHITECTURE, VOL.2 compilation (*7) / TABULA RASA (*7) / ENDE NEU (*5)

BLIXA BARGELD (b.12 Jan'59) – vocals, guitar, percussion / **N.U. UNRUH** (b. ANDREW, 9 Jun'57, New York City) – vocals, bass, percussion / **BEATE BARTEL** – also industrial percussion / **GODRUN GUT** – industrial percussion / soon added **ALEXANDER VAN BORSIG** – percussion

Mongam / not iss.

Nov 80. (7") (005) **FUR DEN UNTERGANG. / STAHLVERSION** [-] [-] German

— **(STUART) MUFTI** (aka F.M. EINHEIT) (b.18 Dec'58, Dortmund, Germany) – industrial percussion (ex-ABWARTS) repl. BARTEL and GUT, who formed MANIA D and MATADOR

Zick Zack / not iss.

Aug 81. (d7"ep) (ZZ 40) **DURSTIGES TIER** [-] [-] German
– Kalte sterne / Aufrecht gehen / Erlicher stein & pygmaen / Schwarz.

— above featured BIRTHDAY PARTY and LYDIA LUNCH

Dec 81. (lp) (ZZ 65) **KOLLAPS** [-] [-] German
– Kollaps / Sehnsucht / Vorm krieg / Hirnsaege / Abstieg & zerfall / Helga / Tanz debil / Steh auf Berlin / Negativ nein / U-haft muzak / Draussen ist feindlich / Horen mit schmerzen / Jet'm. *(re-iss. Dec88 lp/cd; EFA 2517/+CD) (UK-iss.Oct96 on 'Strange Ways' cd/lp; INDIGO 2517-2/-1) (cd re-iss. Mar98 on 'Spalax'; 14537)*

— added **MARC CHUNG** (b. 3 Jun'57, Leeds, England) – bass (ex-ABWARTS)

Some Bizarre / Ze-PVC

Nov 83. (lp) *(SBVART 2)* *<PVC 9902>* **PORTRAIT OF PATIENT O.T.**
– Vanadium-I-Ching / Hospitalistische kinder-engel der vernichtung / Abfackeln / Neun arme / Herde / Merle / Zeichnungen des patienten O.T. / Finger und zaehne / Falschgeld / Styropor / Armenia / Die genaue zeit. *<cd-iss. 1195 on 'Thirsty Ear'; 57011>*

— added **ALEXANDER HACKE** (b.11 Oct'65) – guitar, electronics

Mar 85. (12") *(BART 12)* **YU-GUNG. / SEELEBRENNT / SAND** -

Oct 85. (lp) *(BART 331)* **HALBER MENSCH** (HALF MEN) -
– Halber mensch / Yu-gung (futter mein ego) / Trinklied / Z.N.S. / Seelebrennt / Sehnsucht / Der tod ist ein dandy / Letztes biest / Das schaben / Sand. *(cd-iss. Jan87; BART 331CD) (re-iss. Oct96 on 'Strange Ways'; INDIGO 26141) <cd-iss. 1995 on'Thirst EAr'; TE 57010>*

Jul 87. (lp/c/cd) *(BART 332/+C/CD)* **FUNF AUF DER NACH OBEN OFFENEN RICHTERSKALA** (means 'FIVE ON THE OPEN-ENDED RICHTER SCALE') -
– Zerstorte zell / Morning dew / Ich bin's / Modimidofraso / Zwolf stadte / Keine schonheit ohne gefahr / Kein bestandteil sein. *<cd-iss. 1995 on 'Thirsty Ear'; TE 57016>*

Some Bizarre / Rough Trade

Sep 89. (lp/c/cd) *(BART 333/+C/CD)* *<ROUGHUS 71/+C/CD>* **HANS DER LUEGE**
– Prolog / Feurio / Ein stuhl in der Holle / Haus der luge / Epilog / Fiat lux / Maifestspiele / Himlego / Schwindel / Der kuss. *<cd re-iss. 1995 on 'Thirsty Ear'; TE 57017>*

Beton-Mute / Mute-Elektra

Jan 93. (12"ep/cd-ep) *(BETON 205/+CD)* *<61509>* **INTERIM**
– Interimlovers / Salamandrina / 3 thoughts / Ring my bell / Rausch – Die interimsliebenden.

Feb 93. (lp/c/cd) *(BETON 106/+MC/CD)* *<61458>* **TABULA RASA**
– Die interimsliebenden / Zebulon / Blume / 12305 (te nacht) / Sie / Wuste / Headcleaner.

Apr 93. (lp/cd) *(BETON 206/+CD)* **MALADICTION** -
– Blume (French version) / Blume (English version) / Blume (Japanese version) / Ubique media version / 3 thoughts / Ein gansz kleines loch in einem / Diapositiv / Ring my bell.

Rough Trade / Revolver

Mar 94. (cd) *(1971208)* *<1208-2>* **HEINER MULLER: HAMLETMASCHINE**
– Soll ich / Weils brauch ist ein stuck eisen stecken in / Das nachste Fleisch oder ins uberachste / Mich dran zu halten weil die welt sich dreht / Herr brich mir das Genick im sturz von einer / Bierbank. *<re-iss. 1996 on 'Grey Area-Ego'; EGO 111>*

Ego-Grey Area / Elektra

Feb 96. (cd) *(EGO 501)* *<69021>* **FAUSTMUSIK** May96
– Tische / Monolog / Besetzt / Burokratie / Burleske / Walpurgisnachtfestchen / Orchestrion / Still am abend / Letztes bild.

— next featured JON SPENCER + ALEC EMPIRE (+ now without CHUNG)

Jul 96. (cd-ep) *(BETON 503CD)* *<EGO 503>* **STELLA MARIS (mixes)**

Beton-Mute / Beton-Mute

Jul 96. (lp/cd) *(<BETON 504/+CD>)* **ENDE NEU**
– Was ist ist (What is it) / Stella maris / Die explosion im festspielhaus / Installation No.1 / Nnnaaammm / Ende neu (Ending new) / The garden / Der schacht von babel (shaft of . . .).

Jul 97. (12"ep) *(<BETON 601>)* **THE DARK WELCOME / SIDE GRINDER. / AMBIENT GUILLOTONE / STRAIGHT TO THE PLAIN**
(cd-ep) *(<BETON 601CD>)* – Nnnaaammm remixes (by DARKUS) / (Trilogy & Side Grinder).

Sep 97. (d-lp/cd) *(BETON 602/+CD)* **ENDE NEU REMIXED** -

– compilations, etc

Jan 84. (lp) *Mute; (Stumm 14) / Homestead; <HMS 063>* **80-83 STRATEGIES AGAINST ARCHITECTURE**
– Tanz debil / Schmerzen hoeren / Mikroben / Krieg in den staedten / Zum tier machen / Draussen ist feindlich / Stahlversion / Schwarz / Negativ nein / Kalte sterne / Spaltung / U-haft muzak / Gestohlenes band (ORF) / Schwarz (mutiert). *(cd-iss. Apr88 + Nov92; CDStumm 14) <US cd-iss. 1995 on 'Elektra'; 61677>*

Dec 84. (c) *R.O.I.R.; (<A 133>)* **2 x 4**
– Fleisch "Blutihaut" knochen / Sehnsucht (nie mehr) / Womb / Krach der schlegenden herzen / Armenisch bitter / Zum tier machen / Sehnsucht (still stehend) / Durstige tiere. *(cd-iss. Nov97; RUSCD 8235)*

May 91. (d-cd/d-c) *Mute; / Mute-Elektra; <61100-2/-4>* **STRATEGIES AGAINST ARCHITECTURE II**
– Abfackeln! / Partynummer (live) / Z.N.S. / Die elektrik (Merle) / Intermezzo – Yu-gung (live) / Seelebrennt / Blutvergiftung / Sand / Kangolicht / Armenia (live) / Ein stuhl in der holle / Vanadium I-Ching / Leid und elend (live) / DNS wasserturm / Armenia II (live) / Fackeln! / Ich bin's / Hirnlego / Wardrobe / Bildbeschreibung / Haus der luege (live) / Jordache / Kein bestandteil sein (alternative ending).

Dec 94. (3xcd-box) *Beton-Mute; (BETONBOX 1)* **TRI SET** -

Mark EITZEL (see under ⇒ AMERICAN MUSIC CLUB)

EJECTED

Formed: Dagenham, Essex, England . . . late '81 by ex-DAWN PATROL (who issued a solitary eponymous 12" EP) members BIG JIM BROOKS and GARY SANDBROOK, along with drummer PAUL GRIFFITHS. Another second division "oi/punk" band signed to 'Riot City', The EJECTED nevertheless debuted on vinyl that year via a 'Secret' V/A compilation, 'Carry On Oi'. The following year, the Essex lads released an EP in their own right, 'HAVE YOU GOT 10p?', proof that two-bit bands were ten a penny in the early 80's. Around six months later the trio issued a second EP, 'NOISE FOR THE BOYS', closely pursued by an ambitiously titled debut album, 'A TOUCH OF CLASS' (1983). Such nauseating nationalist yob mentality numbers as 'YOUNG TRIBES OF ENGLAND', 'ENGLAND AIN'T DEAD' and 'GANG WARFARE' just about summed this band up and made sure they were ignored by the more discerning music papers. They finally pressed the eject button in '84 after a final an"oi"ing album, 'THE SPIRIT OF REBELLION'.

Album rating: A TOUCH OF CLASS (*3) / THE SPIRIT OF REBELLION (*3)

BIG JIM BROOKS – vocals, guitar / **GARY SANDBROOK** – bass, vocals / **PAUL GRIFFITHS** – drums, vocals

Riot City / not iss.

Sep 82. (7"ep) *(RIOT 14)* **HAVE YOU GOT 10p?** -
– Have you got 10p? / Class of '82 / One of the boys.

Feb 83. (7"ep) *(RIOT 19)* **NOISE FOR THE BOYS** -
– Fast 'n' loud / Don't care / What happened in Brighton.

May 83. (lp) *(CITY 003)* **A TOUCH OF CLASS** -
– Young tribes of England / Fast 'n' loud / Gang warfare / Class of '82 / England ain't dead / Carnival / Football song / Man of war / Fifteen / Have you got 10p? / Mr. Muggins / East End kids / I'm gonna get me a gun / Dressed to kill / Karnal dub / The sky's in love. *(cd-iss. Jul98 on 'Captain Oi'+=; AHOYCD 024)* – HAVE YOU GOT 10p? + NOISE FOR THE BOYS (EP tracks).

Dec 83. (7"ep) *(RIOT 28)* **PRESS THE BUTTON** -
– Russians / 24 years / In the city.

Aug 84. (lp) *(CITY 007)* **THE SPIRIT OF REBELLION** -

— disbanded after above album

ELASTICA

Formed: London, England . . . October '92 by JUSTINE FRISCHMANN, who had been an embryonic member of SUEDE, with then boyfriend, BRETT ANDERSON. Signing for the new 'Deceptive' label in 1993, JUSTINE and Co. (namely DONNA MATTHEWS, ANNIE HOLLAND and JUSTIN WELSH) collected critical acclaim from the music press for their debut 45, 'STUTTER'. Their (early '94) follow-up, 'LINE UP', gave them a UK Top 20 and made American labels take note. 'Geffen' soon took up the option for worldwide sales as all awaited 1995's tip for the top and their first album. New wave of the new wave featuring fuzzgun WIRE-like guitars, their blatant plagiarism didn't go without notice when they had to settle out of court with WIRE for the use of 'Three Girl Rhumba' riff on the 'CONNECTION' hit. Soon after this, The STRANGLERS were paid out of court for 'No More Heroes'-esque backing on another hit, 'WAKING UP' (however bassist, JEAN-JAQUES BURNEL, is said to be a great fan). Finally released in Spring '95, their eponymous debut album went straight into the UK charts at No.1, ELASTICA's spkiy, punk-inspired sound the toast of Brit-pop's golden year with FRISCHMANN as the scene's uncrowned ice queen. Although HOLLAND departed in summer '95, it was almost a year before replacements were found in SHEILA CHIPPERFIELD conspicuous by their absence from the recording front, FRISCHMANN subsequently refusing any more press interviews following the media circussurrounding her relationship with BLUR frontman, DAMON ALBARN. The only action from the ELASTICA camp of late was the ME ME ME project (featuring STEPHEN DUFFY, Blur's ALEX JAMES and CHARLIE BLOOR) who scored a UK Top 20 hit in summer '96 with 'HANGING AROUND'. • **Songwriters:** FRISCHMANN lyrics / group compositions. • **Trivia:** DAMON ALBARN (as DAN ABNORMAL – anagram) played keyboards on their debut album and featured with them on Top Of The Pops.

Album rating: ELASTICA (*8)

JUSTINE FRISCHMANN (b.1968, Twickenham) – vocals, rhythm guitar (ex-SUEDE) / **DONNA MATTHEWS** (b. Newport, Wales) – vocals, guitar / **ANNIE HOLLAND** (b. Brighton, England) – bass / **JUSTIN WELCH** (b. Nuneaton, England) – drums (ex-SUEDE)

Deceptive / Sub Pop

Oct 93. (7") *(BLUFF 003)* *<SB 275>* **STUTTER. / PUSSYCAT** Aug94

Jan 94. (7") *(BLUFF 004)* **LINE UP. / VASELINE** 20
(12"+=/cd-s+=) *(BLUFF 004 T/CD)* – Rockunroll / Annie (both John Peel sessions).

Deceptive / D.G.C.

Oct 94. (7"/c-s) *(BLUFF 010/+C)* **CONNECTION. / SEE THAT ANIMAL** 17 -
(12"+=/cd-s+=) *(BLUFF 010 T/CD)* – Blue (demo) / Spastica.

Feb 95. (7"/c-s) *(BLUFF 011/+C)* **WAKING UP. / GLORIA** 13
(12"+=/cd-s+=) *(BLUFF 011 T/CD)* – Car wash / Brighton rock.

Mar 95. (cd/c/lp) *(BLUFF 014 CD/C/LP)* *<24728>* **ELASTICA** 1 66
– Line up / Annie / Connection / Car song / Smile / Hold me now / S.O.F.T. / Indian song / Blue / All-nighter / Waking up / 2:1 / Vaseline / Never here / Stutter.

Mar 95. (c-s) *<19385>* **CONNECTION / GLORIA** - 53

— In Jul'95, they guested on 'Sub Pop' 4x7"box-set 'HELTER SHELTER'.

Jun 95. (10"gold-ep/cd-ep) *<DGC 10/CD 22001>* **STUTTER / ROCKUNROLL. / 2:1 (1 F.M. evening session) / ANNIE (John Peel session)** - 67

— ANNIE departed in August '95, and was replaced nearly a year later by **SHEILA CHIPPERFIELD** – bass / **DAVID BUSH** – keyboards (ex-FALL)

ME ME ME

JUSTIN WELCH + ALEX JAMES (Blur), STEPHEN DUFFY + CHARLIE BLOOR

Indolent / not iss.

Aug 96. (c-s/cd-s) *(DUFF 005 C/CD)* **HANGING AROUND / HOLLYWOOD WIVES / TABITHA'S ISLAND** 19 -

ELECTRAFIXION (see under ⇒ ECHO & THE BUNNYMEN)

(see under ⇒ ECHO & THE BUNNYMEN)

ELECTRIC CHAIRS (see under ⇒ COUNTY, Wayne/Jayne)

ELECTRIC EELS

Formed: Cleveland, Ohio, USA . . . 1973 by JOHN MORTON, DAVID E (McMANUS), BRIAN McMAHON and PAUL MAROTTA. They played regularly at a pub owned by JAMIE LYONS (ex-MUSIC EXPLOSION), until, that is, their experimentations went too far after adding industrial and garden equipment. This, together with MORTON's GBH-attitude to the rest of the band led to MAROTTA moving on despite this line-up supporting ROCKET FROM THE TOMBS and the MIRRORS late in '74. The 'EELS soon found a drummer (their first!), NICK KNOX, although this new incarnation was also short-lived as the group split in May '75 after a bust-up on stage. KNOX subsequently joined The CRAMPS, while the remaining quartet (MAROTTA was back in the fold) added ANTON FIER and two former MIRRORS members, JIM JONES and JAIME KLIMEK. By the following year, this group (briefly called MEN FROM U.N.C.L.E.) had evolved into The STYRENES, although only KLIMEK, MAROTTA and FIER were mainstays (MORTON and JONES guested on the odd show). With punk/new wave and avant-garde (fellow Clevelanders, PERE UBU, the prime example) getting a fair crack of the whip in 1978, UK indie imprint 'Rough Trade' decided to issue a posthumous ELECTRIC EELS single, 'AGITATED', as The STYRENES carried on in similarly uncompromising fashion. The latter outfit relocated to New York upon their mid 90's reformation; two albums of note were delivered by 1998 and a handful of rare dates on UK shores heralded their return. • **Note:** There was an unconnected English band called The ELECTRIC EELS, who released a few singles on 'Slippery Discs & Rocket'.

Album rating: HAVING A PHILOSOPHICAL INVESTIGATION posthumous (*6)

JOHN MORTON – vocals, guitar / **DAVID E (McMANUS)** – clarinet, vocals (ex-EX-BLANK-EX) / **BRIAN McMAHON** – guitar / **PAUL MAROTTA** – guitar / added **NICK KNOX** – drums

Rough Trade | not iss.

Jan 79. (7"; as DIE ELECTRIC EELS) *(RT 008)* **AGITATED. / CYCLOTRON** [ ] [-]
(above actually recorded early 1975 with stated line-up)

—— McMANUS subsequently formed the COOL MARRIAGE COUNSELORS, while KNOX joined The CRAMPS. The ELECTRIC EELS briefly reformed adding **ANTON FIER**, who soon joined The FEELIES, The LOUNGE LIZARDS and then PERE UBU (**JIM JONES** also connected to both). Another to be added was **JAIME 'George' KLIMEK** – guitar (he and MAROTTA evolved into the STYRENES)

not iss. | Mustard

Oct 81. (7") *<MUST 107>* **SPIN AGE BLASTERS. / BUNNIES (live)** [-] [ ]

– other posthumous releases, etc. –

1989. (lp) *Tinnitus;* **HAVING A PHILOSOPHICAL INVESTIGATION WITH THE ELECTRIC EELS** (final session in '75) [-] [ ]
– Agitated / Cyclotron / Refrigerator / Tidal wave / Anxiety / Natural situation / Cold meat / Cyclotron (giganto) / Sewercide / Jaguar ride / You're full of shit / No nonsense / Accident / Bunnies / Cards and fleurs / As if I cared / Spin age blasters. *<cd-iss. 1991 as 'GOD SAYS FUCK YOU' on 'Homestead'+=; HMS 174-2>* – (see above).

STYRENES

MAROTTA, KLIMEK + FIER plus part-timers, **MIKE ANTLE** – bass / **TOMMY AMATO** – drums / **PETE HASKINS** – sax / **DAVE FRANDUTO** – guitar / **DAVE KLAMUT** – drums / **PETE HASKINS + PHIL CAPONE** – sax / **TOM KIRSCHNER + ALBERT DENNIS + JOHN ZIMMERMAN** – bass / also with vocalist/collaboration BOBBY MYERS

not iss. | Mustard

Sep 75. (7") *<MM-101>* **DRANO IN YOUR VEINS. / CIRCUS HIGHLIGHTS** [-] [ ]
Sep 77. (7"m) *<MM-103>* **JAGUAR RIDE. / EVERYTHING NEAR ME / I SAW YOU** [-] [ ]
Apr 81. (lp) *<MRDS-4001>* **GIRL CRAZY** [-] [ ]
Oct 81. (7"m) *<MUST-108>* **JENNIFER GYMSHORTS. / EXASPERATION / NO DEPOSIT NO RETURN** [-] [ ]

—— split, but reformed 7 then another 7 years later! (inbetween this, they issued the very low-key, 'A MONSTER AND THE DEVIL')

not iss. | Homestead

1991. (cd) *<HMS 173>* **IT'S ARTASTIC!: CLEVELAND '75 TO '79** (compilation) [-] [ ]
– Drano in your veins / Circus highlights / Radial arms saws / Just walking / Jaguar ride / Everything near me / I saw you / Social whirlpool / As if I cared / Leave the girls / Inside of here / Outer limits / Electricity / Cheap and vulgar / Brian's song / Where the girls are / Tom's problem / Drano in your veins / Opus XII / It's artastic.

—— **MIKE HUDSON** – vocals / **PAUL MAROTTA** – piano / **AL MARGOLIS** – drums / **JAMIE KLIMEK** – guitar / **TOM KIRSCHNER** – bass

Drag City | Drag City

Dec 96. (12"ep) *<DC 108>* **ONE FANZINE READER WRITES EP** [ ] [ ] Feb99

Scat | Scat

Apr 98. (cd) *<SCAT 63CD>* **WE CARE, SO YOU DON'T HAVE TO** [ ] [ ]

Overground | not iss.

Mar 98. (cd; by ELECTRIC EELS) *<OVER 71CD>* **THEIR ORGANIC MAJESTY'S REQUEST** [ ] [ ]

—— **DAVID LICHT** – drums (ex-SHOCKABILLY) + PAUL LAURENCE; repl. MARGOLIS

Sep 98. (cd) *<OVER 74CD>* **ALL THE WRONG PEOPLE ARE DYING** [ ] [-]
– One fanzine reader writes / East side story / Memory of you / Two up two down / Last hot day / Opus 12 / All the wrong people are dying / True confessions / Back in Hell / Jetsam.

ELECTRIC SOUND OF JOY

Formed: East Midlands, England . . . 1996 by frontman, GREG KURCEWICZ and musicians, DAN HAYHURST, BEN RODGERS, SCOTT NICHOLAS and JOHN REVILL. In the Spring of '98, after two 'Earworm' 45's shifted their limited edition copies, the 5-piece were the talk of A&R men vying for their signatures. However, conflict and pressure led to GREG bailing out leaving behind the remaining four to create a new CLUSTER-esque sound of pop/rock electronica. A third single, 'FOOD OF THE RANGE', was released on the new 'Foundry' imprint in the Autumn of '98, the majors having lost interest for the time being.

Album rating: awaiting debut album

GREG KURCEWICZ – vocals / **BEN RODGERS** – keyboards / **SCOTT NICHOLAS** – guitar / **DAN HAYHURST** – bass / **JOHN REVILL** – drums

Earworm | not iss.

Jul 97. (7") *(WORM 5)* **TOTAL TURN. /** [ ] [-]
Sep 97. (7") *(WORM 9)* **PLAY AWAY. / BUILDING BLOCKS** [ ] [-]

—— now without GREG

Foundry | not iss.

Oct 98. (12"ep) *(FR 001T)* **FOOD OF THE RANGE /** [ ] [-]

ELECTRONIC (see under ⇒ NEW ORDER)

ELEVENTH DREAM DAY

Formed: Chicago, Illinois, USA . . . 1983 by RICK RIZZO and JANET BEVERIDGE BEAN. The couple met at Lexington University, discovering a shared musical appreciation of NEIL YOUNG and raw punk. Subsequently relocating to Chicago, they initiated ELEVENTH DREAM DAY with the addition of SHU SHABAT (soon replaced by DOUG McCOMB) and BAIRD FIGI, gigging hard prior to the release of their eponymous 1987 mini-set on the small 'Amoeba' label. 1988 saw RIZZO and BEAN tying the knot while a DIY debut album proper, 'PRAIRIE SCHOOL FREAKOUT', was sufficiently impressive to secure a major label deal with 'Atlantic'. 1989's 'BEET' was a tentative step up to the glare of major label exposure, the band's incisive rootsiness betraying traces of YOUNG, DINOSAUR JR., The PIXIES etc., while carving out their own emotionally charged alt-rock niche. 'LIVED TO TELL' (1991), meanwhile, fulfilled at least some of EDD's promise although it somehow missed out on the buzz surrounding a re-energised alternative scene ripe for the picking. Similarly, the failure of the admittedly more subdued 'EL MOODIO' was equally perplexing, the band unceremoniously shunted from the Atlantic roster and moving on to 'City Slang' ('Thrill Jockey' in the US) for the JOHN McENTIRE-produced 'URSA MAJOR'. Ironically, it would be his moonlighting work in TORTOISE (alongside McENTIRE) and PULLMAN that would bring McCOMB most recognition. In fact, by the release of the latter outfit's critically acclaimed 'Turnstyles And Junkpiles', EDD had already signed off with a final set, 'EIGHTH'. BEAN also attracted more column inches in her own right as a founding member of FREAKWATER, a country/folk roots outfit comprising BEAN, CATHERINE ANN IRWIN and DAVE GAY. Initiated in the late 80's just as ELEVENTH DREAM DAY were being groomed for the big time, the project was EDD's alter ego, dealing in the kind of skeletal, down-to-the-wire country that CMTV wouldn't touch with a bargepole (and that can't be a bad thing!). Following 1989's eponmyous debut and 1991's 'DANCING UNDERWATER', the group also signed up to 'City Slang'/'Thril Jockey', releasing 'FEELS LIKE THE THIRD TIME' in 1995. With the rise and rise of the US alt-country scene, FREAKWATER attracted increasing attention throughout the 90's, albums such as 'OLD PAINT' (1995) and 'SPRINGTIME' (1998) actually garnering more attention in Europe than the States despite their high lonesome sounds. Be warned, though, FREAKWATER may be on an alternative label but their desperately mournful country is as about as authentic as it comes and in reality, this lot have more in common with GILLIAN WELCH than with WILCO. • **Songwriters:** RIZZO or BEAN or FIGI (until latter's departure). FREAKWATER covered OUT OF THIS WORLD (Loudon Wainwright III) / PUT MY LITTLE SHOES + LITTLE BLACK TRAIN (Woody Guthrie) / PALE HORSE (Bailes-Stagg) / YOU'VE NEVER BEEN THIS FAR BEFORE (Twitty) / AMELIA EARHART (McEnry) / YOU MAKE LOVE (Lowe) / MY ONE DESIRE (Burnette) / BURYING GERALDINE (Garrison) / etc. • **Trivia:** RIZZO and BEAN guested on TARA KEY's band's ANTIETAM album, 'Bourbon Country'.

Album rating: PRAIRIE SCHOOL FREAKOUT (*6) / BEET (*6) / LIVED TO TELL (*7) / EL MOODIO (*7) / URSA MAJOR (*6) / EIGHTH (*7) / Freakwater: FREAKWATER mini (*5) / DANCING UNDER WATER (*8) / FEELS LIKE THE THIRD TIME (*6) / OLD PAINT (*7) / SPRINGTIME (*6)

RICK RIZZO (b. 4 Jul'57) – vocals, guitar, harmonica / **JANET BEVERIDGE BEAN** (b.10 Feb'64, Louisville, Kentucky) – drums, vocals / **DOUG McCOMB** (b. 9 Jan'62) – bass repl. SHU SHABAT / **BAIRD FIGI** – guitar

New Rose | Amoeba

1987. (m-lp) **ELEVENTH DREAM DAY** [-] [ ]
– Walking through the barrel of a gun / Vein of gold / Not the ballad of a girl / Liz Beth / The arsonist / Cascade. *(re-iss. Oct89 on 'Fan Club'; FC 056)*

May 89. (lp/cd) *(ROSE 159/CD)* <*003*> **PRAIRIE SCHOOL FREAKOUT** [ ] [ ] Nov88
– Watching the candles burn / Sweet smell / Coercion / Driving song / Tarantula / Among the pines / Through my mouth / Beach miner / Death of Albert C. Sampson / Life on a string / Tenth leaving train. *(cd re-iss. May94; 422128)*

East West | Atlantic

Mar 90. (cd/c/lp) <*(7567 82053-2/-4/-1)*> **BEET** [ ] [ ] Nov89
– Between here and there / Testify / Baghdad's last ride / Awake I lie / Road that never winds / Axle / Michael Dunne / Bomb the Mars Hotel / Teenage pin queen / Love to hate to love / Go (slight return). *(cd+=)* – Seiche.

Jun 91. (cd/c/lp) <*(7567 82179-2/-4/-1)*> **LIVED TO TELL** [ ] [ ] Jan91
– Rose of Jericho / Dream of a sleeping sheep / I could be lost / It's not my world / You know what it is / Frozen mile / Strung up and/or out / North of wasteland / It's all a game / Trouble / There's this thing / Daedalus / Angels spread your wings.

—— (early '91) **MATTHEW "WINK" O'BANNON** (b.22 Jul'56) – guitar repl. FIGI

City Slang | Atlantic

Oct 92. (12"ep/cd-ep) *(EFA 04904/+CD)* **TWO SWEETIES EP** [ ] [-]
Dec 92. (12"ep/cd-ep) *(EFA 0409040-2/-3)* **MAKING LIKE A RUG EP** [ ] [-]
Apr 93. (cd/c) <*(7567 82480-2/-4)*> **EL MOODIO** [ ] [ ]
– Makin' like a rug / Figure it out / After this time is gone / Murder / Honeyslide / That's the point / Motherland / Raft / Bend bridge / Rubber band.

—— now aided by the production of JOHN McENTIRE (of TORTOISE) + now without WINK (JANET BEAN more into FREAKWATER)

City Slang | Atavistic

Sep 94. (7") *(EFA 04941-7)* **ORANGE MOON. / I GOT A THING . . .** [ ] [-]
Jan 95. (cd/lp) *(EFA 04943-2/-1)* <*13*> **URSA MAJOR** [ ] [ ] Dec94

—— McCOMBS still in this operative, although he concentrated more on his other co-project, TORTOISE. O'BANNON departed to form BODECO.

City Slang | Thrill Jockey

Feb 97. (cd) *(EFA 94989-2)* <*THRILL 37*> **EIGHTH** [ ] [ ]
– For a king / Writes a letter home / Two smart cookies / Insomnia / View from the rim / April / Motion sickness / The last call.

—— looked to have split, when McCOMBS helped to initiate yet another offshoot outfit, PULLMAN.

FREAKWATER

JANET BEAN – guitar + **CATHERINE ANN IRWIN** – guitar, vocals / **DAVE GAY** – upright bass with **JOHN RICE** – fiddle, mandolin, pedal steel guitar

not iss. | Amoeba

1989. (m-lp) **FREAKWATER** [-] [ ]
1991. (cd) <*9*> **DANCING UNDERWATER** [-] [ ]
<(UK + re-iss. May97 on 'Thrill Jockey' lp/cd; THRILL 040/+CD)>

City Slang | Thrill Jockey

Nov 93. (cd/lp) *(EFA 04920-2/-1)* <*THRILL 010CD*> **FEELS LIKE THE THIRD TIME** [ ] [ ] May93
– My old drunk friend / Put my little shoes / Crazy man / Pale horse / You make me / You've never been this far before / Dream girl / Sleeping on hold / Amelia Earhart / Are you ready / Lullaby. *(cd re-iss. Feb98 on 'Thrill Jockey'; same US)*

Oct 95. (cd/lp) *(EFA 04965-2/-1)* <*THRILL 022/+CD*> **OLD PAINT** [ ] [ ]
– Gravity / Smoking daddy / Gone to stay / Little black train / Waitress song / My one desire / White rose / Out of this world / Kentucky house / Hero – Heroine / Ugly man / Burying Geraldine. *(cd re-iss. Apr98 on 'Thrill Jockey'; same US)*

Thrill Jockey | Thrill Jockey

Feb 98. (cd) <*(THRILL 047CD)*> **SPRINGTIME** [ ] [ ] Jan98
– Picture in my mind / Louisville lip / Twisted wire / Washed in the blood / Binding twine / One big union / Harlan / Jesus year / Scamp / Lorraine / Slowride / Heaven / Flat hand.

EMBARRASSMENT

Formed: Wichita, Kansas, USA . . . 1979 by JOHN NICHOLS, BILL GOFFRIER, RON KLAUS and BRENT GIESSMANN. Taking their cue from the best of British and American punk but fashioning their own distinctive brand of edgy alternative rock, the band's sound was characterised by GOFFRIER's elaborate guitar work while the lyrics displayed a talent for wry observation. After debuting in summer 1980 with the caustic 'PATIO SET' single, they released an eponymous EP the following year, accruing much underground acclaim for their cutting lyrical portraits and original style. Label hopping once more, they cut a sawnsong mini-set, 'DEATH TRAVELS WEST' (1983), a pseudo-concept affair. And that was that, save for a posthumously issued eponymous album combining new and previously available material. While GIESSMANN joined the DEL FUEGOS, GOFFRIER formed BIG DIPPER with GARY WELEIK, STEVE MICHENER and JEFF OLIPHANT, releasing a series of albums on 'Homestead', 'BOO-BOO', 'CRAPS' and 'HEAVENS'. Come the late 80's, EMBARRASSMENT re-formed on a part-time basis, eventually getting round to recording a one-off US-only album, 'GOD HELP US', for the 'Bar/None' label in 1990. With continuing interest in the band, the latter label released a thorough EMBARRASSMENT retrospective in 1995 entitled 'HEYDAY'. • **Covered:** DON'T STOP TILL YOU GET ENOUGH (Michael Jackson) / IMMIGRANT SONG (Led Zeppelin).

Album rating: GOD HELP US (*7) / HEYDAY 1979-1983 compilation (*8)

JOHN NICHOLS – vocals, keyboards / **BILL GOFFRIER** – guitar, vocals / **RON KLAUS** – bass / **BRENT GIESSMANN** – drums

not iss. | Big Time

Jul 80. (7") <*BT 001*> **PATIO SET. / SEX DRIVE** [-] [ ]

not iss. | Cynykyl

1981. (12"ep) **THE EMBARRASSMENT EP** [-] [ ]
– Don't choose the wrong song / Wellsville / Celebrity art party / Elizabeth Montgomery's face / I'm a Don Juan.

not iss. | Fresh Sounds

1983. (m-lp) <*FS 204*> **DEATH TRAVELS WEST** [-] [ ]
– Careen / Viewmaster / Drive me to the park / Lewis and Clark / D-rings / Chapter 12 / Hip and well read.

—— disbanded after above. GIESSMAN joined the DEL FUEGOS

BIG DIPPER

—— were formed by **BILL GOFFRIER** – vocals / **GARY WELEIK** – guitar (ex-VOLCANO SONS) / **STEVE MICHENER** – bass (ex-VOLCANO SONS) / **JEFF OLIPHANT** – drums (ex-DUMPTRUCK)

Demon | Homestead

Apr 87. (m-lp) <*HMS 077*> **BOO-BOO** [-] [ ]
– Faith healer / San Quentin, CA / What's in Sam Hill? / Wrong in the charts / Ancers / Loch Ness monster.

Oct 88. (lp/cd) *(FIEND/+CD 132)* <*HMS 122/+CD*> **CRAPS** [ ] [ ] Sep88
– Meet the witch / Ron Klaus wrecked his house / The insane girl Semjase / Stardom because / Bonnie / Hey! Mr. Lincoln / The bells of love / A song to be beautiful.

Feb 89. (lp) *(FIEND 136)* <*HMS 086*> **HEAVENS** [ ] [ ] Dec87
– She's fetching / Man o' war / Easter eve / Humanson / Lunar module / All going out together / Younger bums / When men were trains / Wet weekend / Mr. Woods.

not iss. | Epic

1990. (lp/cd) <*E/EK 46063*> **SLAM** [-] [ ]
Love barge / The bond / Another life / Slam / Bony knees of nothing / Baby blue / Picnic / The monsters of jazz / Impossible things / Blood pact / Father's day / Baby doll / Life inside the cemetery / All the way from Memphis.

—— split soon after above, although EMBARRASSMENT (original line-up) attempted once more (this time as a sideline)

EMBARRASSMENT

not iss. | Bar/None

1990. (cd/c/lp) <*72635-2/-4/-1*> **GOD HELP US** [-] [ ]
– Train of thought / Beautiful day / After the disco / Lifespan / Horror of the fire / Podmen / Albert / Burning love / Sex drive / . . . Train reprise / Vision of '61.

– compilations, etc. –

1984. (c) *Fresh Sounds;* **RETROSPECTIVE** [-] [ ]
1987. (lp) *Time To Develop;* **THE EMBARRASSMENT** [-] [ ]
Oct 95. (d-cd) *Bar None;* <*59*> **HEYDAY 1979-1983** [-] [ ]
– Sex drive / Patio set / Celebrity art party / Elizabeth's Montgomery's face / (I'm a) Don Juan / Don't choose the wrong song / Wellsville / Two cars / Carreen / Viewmaster / Drive me to the park / Lewis & Clark / D-rings / Chapter 12 / Hip and well read / Death travels west / Rhythm line / Picture women / Special eyes / Jazzface / Age five / Woods of love / Out of town / Berliner's night out / After the disco / Dress like a man / Two-week vacation / The man with the special eyes / Lifespan / Sound of wasps / Can't forget / Sexy singer girl / Sex drive – Pants down – Gibberish / Dino in the Congo / Godfrey Harold Hardy / D-rings / Chapter 12 / Jazzface / Don't stop till you get enough / Casual man / Immigrant song / She's one of the other kind.

EMBRACE

Formed: Bradford/Huddersfield, England . . . 1993 by Irish-ancestry songwriting brothers, DANNY (lyrics) and RICK McNAMARA (the music), who enlisted the rhythm team of STEVE FIRTH and MIKE KEATON. After the stunning OASIS-esque grandeur of the early '97 debut, 'ALL YOU GOOD GOOD PEOPLE', for the 'Fierce Panda' set-up, they signed to Virgin offshoot, 'Hut'. The band made an immediate impact on the singles chart with the EP, 'FIREWORKS', increasing their chart exposure with the summer '97 follow-up, 'ONE BIG FAMILY'. However, the pop nation finally clutched them to their proverbial bosom with the re-issue of 'ALL YOU GOOD GOOD PEOPLE', which cracked the Top 10 in the Autumn. The following year, the much vaunted songwriting siblings scored a further two Top 10 hits, 'COME BACK TO WHAT YOU KNOW' and 'MY WEAKNESS IS NONE OF YOUR BUSINESS', both taken from their chart-topping debut album, 'THE GOOD WILL OUT'.

Album rating: THE GOOD WILL OUT (*8)

DANNY McNAMARA – vocals / **RICK McNAMARA** – guitar / **STEVE FIRTH** – bass / **MIKE KEATON** – drums

Fierce Panda | not iss.

Feb 97. (ltd-7") *(NING 29)* **ALL YOU GOOD GOOD PEOPLE. /** [ ] [-]

Hut | Geffen

May 97. (c-ep/12"ep/cd-ep) *(HUT C/T/CD 84)* **FIREWORKS EP** [34] [-]
– The last gas / Now you're nobody / Blind / Fireworks. *(12"ep re-iss. Nov98; same)*

Jul 97. (c-ep/12"ep/cd-ep) *(HUT C/T/CD 86)* **ONE BIG FAMILY EP** [21] [-]
– One big family / Dry kids / You've only got to stop to get better / Butter wouldn't melt. *(12"ep re-iss. Nov98; same)*

Oct 97. (c-ep/12"ep/cd-ep) *(HUT C/T/DX 90)* **ALL YOU GOOD GOOD PEOPLE EP** [8] [-]
– All you good good people (extended) / You won't amount to anything – this time / The way I do / Free ride. *(12"ep re-iss. Nov98; same)*
(cd-ep) *(HUTCD 90)* – ('A'radio edit) / One big family (Perfecto mix) / ('A'-Fierce Panda version) / ('A'-orchestral mix).

May 98. (c-s) *(HUTC 93)* <*95132*> **COME BACK TO WHAT YOU KNOW / LOVE IS BACK** [6] [ ] Jul98
(12"+=/cd-s+=) *(HUT T/DX 93)* – If you feel like a sinner / Perfect way.
(cd-s) *(HUTCDX 93)* – ('A'side) / Butter wouldn't melt (live) / Dry kids (live) / ('A'orchestral).

Jun 98. (cd/c/d-lp) *(CDHUT/HUTMC/HUTDLP 46)* <*25165*> **THE GOOD WILL OUT** [1] [ ] Jul98
– Intro / All you good good people / My weakness is none of your business / Come

back to what you know / One big family / Higher sights / Retread / I want the world / You've got to say yes / Fireworks / The last gas / That's all changed forever / Now you're nobody / The good will out.

Aug 98. (7") *(HUT 103)* **MY WEAKNESS IS NONE OF YOUR BUSINESS. / FEELINGS I THOUGHT YOU SHARED** [9] [-]
(c-s+=/cd-s+=) *(HUT C/CD 103)* – Don't turn your back on love.
(cd-s) *(HUTDX 103)* – ('A'live) / Higher sights (live) / Retread (live). *(12"ep re-iss. Nov98; HUTT 103)*

Nov 98. (12"ep) *(HUTT 107)* **THE GOOD WILL OUT** [ ] [-]

EMF

Formed: Cinderford / Forest of Dean, Gloucestershire, England . . .late '89 by Oxford graduate IAN DENCH and JAMES ATKIN, DERRY BROWNSON, ZAC FOLEY, MARK DE CLOEDT and scratcher/DJ, MILF. After their 4th gig, they were spotted by ABBO (from former goth punks, UK DECAY) and his girlfriend, LINDA, who helped get them signed to 'E.M.I.' subsidiary, 'Parlophone' in March '90. Late that year, their debut single, 'UNBELIEVABLE', broke into the UK Top 3 and early the following year, they set about taking both sides of the Atlantic by storm. Similar in style, to say, JESUS JONES, or an uptempo DEPECHE MODE, EMF's brattish blend of indie dance and funky pop saw them hailed as the great white hopes of British music for as long as it took their teenybop fanbase to find someone new (i.e. not that long!). ATKIN's posh-accented whine was a bit much to take over the stretch of a whole album, although, spurred by the success of further singles, 'I BELIEVE' and 'CHILDREN', 'SCHUBERT DIP' (1991) was one of the year's biggest selling sets; it even did well in American where 'UNBELIEVABLE' had topped the charts. Touted as spearheading a second "British Invasion" along with JESUS JONES and Co., EMF's assault soon surrendered to the machinations of the music business as follow-up album, 'STIGMA' (1992) saw them making an ill-advised attempt at big boys' rock. Its heavier approach only succeeded in alienating their original fanbase, the band's apparent attempt to lighten up their image with a VIC REEVES and BOB MORTIMER collaboration (a Top 3 cover of The Monkees 'I'M A BELIEVER') not enough to prevent 'CHA CHA CHA' from virtually stiffing. Subsequently dropped by their label, EMF faced the inevitable and jacked it in. However, the story didn't quite finish there as DENCH resurfaced a few years later with his new trio, WHISTLER. • **Covered:** LOW SPARK OF THE HIGH HEELED BOYS (Traffic) / SHADDAP YOU, FACE (Joe Dolce) / I'M A BELIEVER (Monkees) / STRANGE BREW (Cream). • **Trivia:** EMF was rumoured to stand for ECSTASY MOTHER FUCKERS, but later claimed to be EPSOM MAD FUNKERS.

Album rating: SCHUBERT DIP (*5) / STIGMA (*7) / CHA CHA CHA (*4)

JAMES ATKIN (b.28 Mar'67) – vocals / **IAN DENCH** (b. 7 Aug'64) – guitar, keyboards (ex-APPLE MOSAIC) / **DERRY BROWNSON** (b. DERRAN, 10 Nov'70) – samples, percussion (ex-LAC's) / **ZAC FOLEY** (b. ZACHARY, 9 Dec'70) – bass (ex-IUC's) / **MARK DE CLOEDT** (b.26 Jun'67) – drums (ex-ZU) / plus **MILF** – DJ scratcher

Parlophone E.M.I.

Oct 90. (c-s/7") *(TC+/R 6273)* **UNBELIEVABLE. / EMF (live)** [3] [-]
(12"+=/cd-s+=) *(12R/CDR 6273)* – ('A'-Cin City sex mix).

Jan 91. (c-s/7") *(TC+/R 6279)* **I BELIEVE. / WHEN YOU'RE MINE** [6] [-]
(12"+=/cd-s+=) *(12R/CDR 6279)* – Unbelievable (funk mix).

Mar 91. (c-s) *<50350>* **UNBELIEVABLE / ('A'-Cin City Sex mix)** [-] [1]

Apr 91. (c-s/7") *(TC+/R 6288)* **CHILDREN. / STRANGE BREW (live remix)** [19] [ ]
(12"+=) *(12R 6288)* – Children (mix).
(cd-s++=) *(CDR 6288)* – Children – Battle for the minds of North Amerika.
(7"ep+=) *(RX 6288)* – (live versions).

May 91. (cd/c/lp) *(CD/TC+/PCS 7353) <96238>* **SCHUBERT DIP** [3] [12]
– Children / Long summer days / When you're mine / Travelling not running / I believe / Unbelievable / Girl of an age / Admit it / Lies / Long time. *(re-iss. Mar94 cd/c; same)*

Aug 91. (c-s/7") *(TC+/R 6295)* **LIES. / HEAD THE BALL** [28] [-]
(12"+=/cd-s+=) *(12R/CDR 6295)* – ('A'mix).

Sep 91. (c-s) *<50363>* **LIES / STRANGE BREW (live)** [-] [18]

Apr 92. (7"ep) *(SGE 2026)* **UNEXPLAINED** [18] [-]
– Getting through / Far from me / The same.
(12"ep+=/cd-ep+=) *(12/CD SGE 2026)* – Search and destroy.

Sep 92. (c-s/7") *(TC+/R 6321)* **THEY'RE HERE. / PHANTASMAGORIC** [29] [-]
(12"+=) *(12R 6321)* – ('A'remix).
(cd-s+=) *(CDR 6321)* – Low spark of the high heeled boys.

Sep 92. (cd/c/lp) *(CD/TC+/PCSD 122) <80348>* **STIGMA** [19] [ ]
– They're here / Arizona / It's you that leaves me dry / Never know / Blue highs / Inside / Getting through / She bleeds / Dog / The light that burns twice as bright . . .

Nov 92. (c-s/7") *(TC+/R 6327)* **IT'S YOU. / DOF (Foetus mix)** [23] [-]
(cd-s+=) *(CDR 6327)* – (2 other 'A'-Butch Vig mixes).
(cd-ep) *(CDRS 6327)* – It's you (Orbital mix) / The light that burns twice as bright . . . (mix) / They're here (mix).

Parlophone Parlophone

Feb 95. (c-s) *(TCR 6401)* **PERFECT DAY / ANGEL** [27] [-]
(cd-s+=) *(CDR 6401)* – I won't give into you / Kill for you (lo-fi mix).
(12"+=) *(12R 6401)* – ('A'-Temple of boom remix) / ('A'-Chris & James epic).
(cd-s) *(CDRS 6401)* – ('A'side) / ('A'-Chris & James mix) / ('A'-Black One mix) / ('A'-Toytown mix).

Mar 95. (cd/c) *(<CD/TC PCSD 165>)* **CHA CHA CHA** [30] [ ]
– Perfect day / La plage / The day I was born / Secrets / Shining / Bring me down / Skin / Slouch / Bleeding you dry / Patterns / When will you come / West of the Cox / Ballad o' the bishop / Glass smash Jack.

Apr 95. (c-s) *(TCR 6407)* **BLEEDING YOU DRY / TOO MUCH / EASY / PERFECT DAY (acoustic)** [ ] [-]
(cd-s) *(CDRS 6407)* – (first 3 tracks) / Shining (acoustic).
(cd-s) *(CDR 6407)* – ('A'side) / I pushed the boat out so far it sank / Patterns (acoustic).

Jun 95. (c-s/7"; EMF and REEVES & MORTIMER) *(TC+/R 6412)* **I'M A BELIEVER. / AT LEAST WE'VE GOT OUR GUITARS** [3] [-]
(cd-s) *(CDR 6412)* – ('A'side) / At this stage I couldn't say / ('A'-Unbelievable mix) / La plage (mix).

Oct 95. (c-s) *(TCR 6416)* **AFRO KING / UNBELIEVABLE** [51] [-]
(cd-s+=) *(CDR 6416)* – Children / I believe.
(cd-s) *(CDRS 6416)* – ('A'side) / Too much / Easy / Bring me down.

—— split not long after the relative failure of the above single. DENCH returned in 1998 with a new outfit (see further below)

– compilations, etc. –

1998. (cd,c; shared with JESUS JONES) *EMI Capitol special; <19641>* **BACK 2 BACK** [-] [ ]

WHISTLER

IAN DENCH – vocals, acoustic guitar / **KERRY SHAW** – vocals / **JAMES TOPHAM** – strings (ex-BRIAN ENO)

Wiiija not iss.

May 98. (7") *(WIJ 084)* **RARE AMERICAN SHOES. / THINGS YOU NEVER SAY** [ ] [-]
(cd-s+=) *(WIJ 084CD)* – Thinking it's over.

Sep 98. (7") *(WIJ 091)* **IF I GIVE YOU A SMILE. / GOT WHAT YOU WANTED** [ ] [-]
(cd-s+=) *(WIJ 091CD)* – Song about you.

Alec EMPIRE (see under ⇒ ATARI TEENAGE RIOT)

ENGLISH DOGS (see under ⇒ JANUS STARK)

Jeremy ENIGK (see under ⇒ SUNNY DAY REAL ESTATE)

EPILEPTICS / LICKS (see under ⇒ FLUX OF PINK INDIANS)

ERIC'S TRIP

Formed: Moncton, New Brunswick, Canada . . . 1990 by JULIE DOIRON-CLAYTOR, CHRIS THOMPSON, RICK WHITE and MARK GAUDET, all veterans of the Canadian indie scene. Despite naming themselves after a SONIC YOUTH track, the quartet traded in a slightly more melodic style of Lo-Fi punk/indie-pop than the NY noisesters, showcasing their sound on a series of early cassette demos and mini-sets over the period 1990-92. A surprise signing to 'Sub Pop', the band released a preliminary single, 'SONGS ABOUT CHRIS', for the label in Spring '93, interspersing a debut album proper, 'LOVE TARA' with a further mini-set ('PETER') and 12" EP ('PORTHOLE TO DIMENTIA') for different labels. The prolific release schedule continued the following year with yet another EP, 'THE GORDON STREET HAUNTING' and a full length album, 'FOREVER AGAIN', the latter a marathon near-20 song affair revelling in a characteristically amateurish but often head spinningly addictive brand of noise-pop. Yet with such a limited musical scope, it came as little surprise when the band finally split with the various members going on to different projects on the local underground scene.

Album rating: PETER mini (*6) / LOVE TARA (*6) / FOREVER AGAIN (*7) / PURPLE BLUE (*5)

JULIE DOIRON-CLAYTOR – vocals, bass / **CHRIS THOMPSON** – guitar / **RICK WHITE** – guitar, vocals / **MARK GAUDET** – drums

not iss. unknown

1990. (c) **ERIC'S TRIP** [-] [ ]
1991. (c) **CATERPILLARS** [-] [ ]
1991. (c) **DROWNING** [-] [ ]
1992. (m-lp) **WARM GIRL** [-] [ ]
1992. (m-lp) **BELONG** [-] [ ]

Sub Pop Sub Pop

May 93. (7") *<SP 87-258>* **SONGS ABOUT CHRIS. /** [ ] [-]
(cd-s+=) *<SPCD 87-258>* –

Jun 93. (m-lp/m-cd) *(SP/+CD 102-274) <2>* **PETER** [ ] [ ]

<above issued on 'Murder Camp' US> <below issued on 'Sappy'>

Aug 93. (12"ep) **PORTHOLE TO DIMENTIA** [-] [ ]

Nov 93. (lp/c/cd) *(SP/+MC/CD 115-293) <SP 234-?/A/B>* **LOVE TARA** [ ] [ ] Jun93
– Behind the garage / Anything you want / Stove / Follow / Secret for Julie / Belly / Sunlight / June / To know them / Spring / Frame / May 11 / My room / Blinded / Allergic to love.

Jun 94. (7"ep) *<SP 266>* **THE GORDON STREET HAUNTING EP** [ ] [ ]

Oct 94. (lp/cd) *(SP/+CD 136-336) <SP/+CD 268>* **FOREVER AGAIN** [ ] [ ]
– New love / This way out / About you / Girlfriend / Always there / Stupidest thing / December '93 / Thoroughly / My bed is red / View master / Cloudy / My chest is empty / Run away / Waiting all day / Let go / Hate song / Feeling around / Forever again.

Feb 96. (lp/cd) *<SP/+CD 333>* **PURPLE BLUE** [ ] [ ]
– Introduction into the . . . (pts.1-4) / Hourly / Sixteen hours / Universe / Eyes shut / Alone and annoyed / Lighthouse / Spaceship opening / Universal dawn / One floor below / Now a friend / Soon, coming closer / Not yours / Sun coming up / Beach.

—— split after above DOIRON-CLAYTOR formed BROKEN GIRL, GAUDET re-joined PURPLE KNIGHT, WHITE formed ELEVATOR TO HELL and THOMPSON to MOONSOCKET

– compilations, etc. –

Oct 97. (cd) *Sonic Unyon; <017>* **LONG DAY'S RIDE** (early material) [-] [ ]

ESSENTIAL LOGIC (see under ⇒ LOGIC, Lora)

ETHER

Formed: Blackwood, Wales . . . early 1996 by songwriter RORY MEREDITH, plus BRETT SAWMY and GARETH DRISCOLL. Allegedly hard-drinking lads to a tee, they were rumoured to have come to blows with the Chippendales, amid tales of general hotel debauchery. It was only a matter of time before they were signed to a major, 'Parlophone' picking them up after an indie debut on 'Regal'. However chart success eluded them, despite the soulful indie-pop of their 1997 singles 'IF YOU REALLY WANT TO KNOW' and 'SHE COULD FLY'. • **Note:** An entirely different ETHER (i.e. AMELIA NILES FAIRWEATHER and SEBASTIAN ARCHER) had a few albums between 1993-1998.

Album rating: STRANGE (*6)

RORY MEREDITH – vocals, guitar / **GARETH DRISCOLL** – vocals, bass / **BRETT SAWMY** – drums

Regal – not iss.

Oct 96. (7") *(REG 12)* **HE SAY YEAH. /** [ ] [-]
(cd-s+=) *(REG 12CD)* –

Parlophone – not iss.

Jun 97. (c-s/7") *(TC+/R 6468)* **IF YOU REALLY WANT TO KNOW. / JULIE** [ ] [-]
(cd-s+=) *(CDR 6468)* – Rome yo-yo.
Oct 97. (c-s/7") *(TC+/R 6481)* **SHE COULD FLY. / BATHROOM** [ ] [-]
(cd-s+=) *(CDR 6481)* – Now I'm ready.
Mar 98. (c-s) *(TCR 6491)* **WATCHING YOU / STRANGE (acoustic) / PROMISE THE EARTH** [74] [-]
(cd-s) *(CDR 6491)* – (first two tracks) / Dogs life.
(cd-s) *(CDRS 6491)* – (first & third tracks) / He say yeah (demo).
Jun 98. (7") *(R 6496)* **BEST FRIEND. / GETTING OFF ON T.V.** [ ] [-]
(cd-s+=) *(CDR 6496)* – One good reason.
Jul 98. (cd/c) *(4 94182-2/-4)* **STRANGE** [ ] [-]
– She could fly / Watching you / I love her anyway / He say yeah / Wasting time / When she woke / Best friend / If you really want to know / The world that she sees / Roadworks / Without you / Strange.

ETON CROP

Formed: Kuderstaadt, Amsterdam, Netherlands . . . 1983 by songwriter CORNE BOS, plus ERWIN BLOM, PETER VERSCHUEREN, PETER DE KWAASTENIET and SUSIE HONEYMAN. Following a Dutch-only debut 12", 'TIMMY BARKER IS A COWARD', The ETON CROP made their UK debut with 'GAY BOYS ON THE BATTLEFIELD', John Peel lending his vocal support and inviting them on to his Radio One show for a session (subsequently issued on the 'Strange Fruit' imprint). One of the tracks, 'IT'S MY DOG, MAESTRO', served as the title of their inaugural long-player, a surprisingly English sounding (especially the atonal vocals) indie-rock affair lumberingly reminiscent of MARC RILEY & THE CREEPERS or The WEDDING PRESENT. Later that year (1986), the band continued minus HONEYMAN (who later turned up with The MEKONS), signing to 'Ediesta' and releasing mini-set, 'YES PLEASE, BOB'. ETON CROP's final term report came in the shape of a swan song full-set, 'AND THE UNDERWATER MUSIC GOES ON' (1987), basically nothing to write home about you could say.

Album rating: IT'S MY DOG, MAESTRO (*5) / YES PLEASE, BOB mini (*4) / AND THE UNDERWATER MUSIC GOES ON (*4)

CORNE BOS – bass / **ERWIN BLOM** – guitar / **PETER VERSCHUEREN** – keyboards / **PETER DE KWAASTENIET** – guitar / **SUSIE HONEYMAN** – violin / **MICHAEL HARDING** – trumpet / **FRANZ VREEKE + LEONIEKE DAALDER** – backing vocals

unknown – not iss.

1983. (12") **TIMMY BARKER IS A COWARD. /** [-] [-] Dutch

Bigger Bank – not iss.

May 84. (12"ep) *(BALANCE 1)* **GAY BOYS ON THE BATTLEFIELD. / ROGER TROUDMAN / WE DIDN'T SAY ANYTHING** [ ] [-]

—— **ED SEROOS** – drums; repl. HONEYMAN, HARDING + 2 backers

Grunt Grunt A Go Go – not iss.

Jan 86. (lp) *(ggagg 2)* **IT'S MY DOG, MAESTRO** [ ] [-]
– It's my dog maestro / Loads of beer / Mind manipulation / Wart on a wanker's hand / You won't get me out in the rain / Get something for doing nothing / Live aid / Boy meets tractor / Harry Nelson Pillsbury / I only want to talk about the weather / Rocking the chessboard.

Ediesta – not iss.

Nov 86. (12") *(CALC 12)* **YES PLEASE, BOB. /** [ ] [-]
Dec 86. (m-lp) *(CALCMLP 13)* **YES PLEASE, BOB** [ ] [-]
Apr 87. (12") *(CALC 20)* **A BUNDLE OF BUCKS FOR A DEAD DOG IS A BARGAIN. /** [ ] [-]
Dec 87. (lp) *(CALCLP 33)* **AND THE UNDERWATER MUSIC GOES ON** [ ] [-]

—— split some time in 1988

– compilations, etc. –

Nov 88. (12"ep) *Strange Fruit; (SFPS 063)* **THE PEEL SESSIONS** (1.10.85) [ ] [-]
– Cocacolanization / It's my dog maestro / You won't get me out in the rain / Harry Nelson Pillsbury.

EUGENIUS (see under ⇒ VASELINES)

EVERCLEAR

Formed: Portland, Oregon, USA . . . 1991 by former teenage junkie, ART ALEXAKIS (he gave up alcohol, drugs and nicotine in June '84). Coming from a broken home, he was also dogged by the drug deaths of his girlfriend and older brother, George. Another founder member, CRAIG MONTOYA (other two, STEVEN BIRCH and SCOTT CUTHBERT) helped produce their debut indie album, 'WORLD OF NOISE', in 1994 and after rave reviews they were whisked away by 'Capitol' A&R man PERRY WATTS-RUSSELL. It was alleged that they released from the indie, only when the gun-totting ALEXAKIS convinced the boss to let them go. By Spring '96 (and now with GREG EKLUND who had replaced CUTHBERT and BIRCH), their second album, 'SPARKLE AND FADE', had climbed into the US Top 30, a stylish anti-drug affair, it was described as ELVIS COSTELLO fused with LED ZEPPELIN, HUSKER DU or NIRVANA! ALEXAKIS and Co. returned in 1998 with a third set proper (the previous year's 'WHITE TRASH HELL' consisted of outtakes), 'SO MUCH FOR THE AFTERGLOW', the US Top 40 album almost spawning another UK Top 40 single, 'EVERYTHING TO EVERYONE'. • **Trivia:** The cover of the 1996 album featured snapshots of the trio as young children.

Album rating: WORLD OF NOISE (*8) / SPARKLE AND FADE (*7) / SO MUCH FOR THE AFTERGLOW (*6)

ART ALEXAKIS (b.12 Apr'62) – vocals, guitar / **STEVEN BIRCH** – guitar / **CRAIG MONTOYA** (b.14 Sep'70) – bass, vocals / **SCOTT CUTHBERT** – drums, vocals

Fire – Tim/Kerr

Feb 95. (cd/lp) *(FIRE CD/LP 46)* *<TK 59>* **WORLD OF NOISE** [ ] [ ] Nov93
– Your genius hands / Sick & tired / Laughing world / Fire maple song / Pennsylvania is . . . / Nervous and weird / Malevolent / Sparkle / Trust fund / Loser makes good / Invisible / Evergleam. *<US re-iss. Nov94 on 'Capitol' cd/c; 30562-2/-4>*

Fire – Capitol

Feb 95. (cd-s) *(BLAZE 77CD)* *<58255>* **FIRE MAPLE SONG /** [ ] [ ] Nov94

—— **GREG EKLUND** (b.18 Apr'70) – drums, vocals; repl. CUTHBERT + BIRCH

Nov 95. (cd-ep) *<23261-2>* **HEROIN GIRL / ANNABELLA'S SONG / NAHALEM / AMERICAN GIRL** [-] [ ]

Capitol – Capitol

Mar 96. (cd/c/lp) *(CD/TC+/EST 2257)* *<30929>* **SPARKLE AND FADE** [ ] [25] May95
– Electra made me blind / Heroin girl / You make me feel like a whore / Santa Monica / Summerland / Strawberry / Heartspark dollar / The twistinside / Her brand new skin / Nehalem / Queen of the air / Pale green stars / Chemical smile / My sexual life. *(d-cd=Jun98) (CDESTX 2257)* – (other tracks).
Apr 96. (cd-ep) *<58538>* **HEARTSPARK DOLLARSIGN / HEROIN GIRL / HAPPY HOUR / SIN CITY** [-] [85]
May 96. (7"clear) *(CL 773)* **HEARTSPARK DOLLARSIGN. / LOSER MAKES GOOD (live)** [48] [-]
(cd-s+=) *(CDCL 773)* – Sparkle (live).
(cd-s) *(CDCLS 773)* – ('A'side) / Pennsylvania is (live) / Nervous & weird (live).
Aug 96. (7") *(CL 775)* **SANTA MONICA (WATCH THE WORLD DIE). / AMERICAN GIRL** [40] [ ] Feb96
(cd-s+=) *(CDCL 775)* – Strawberry / Fire maple song.
(cd-s) *(CDCLS 775)* – ('A'side) / Heroin girl / Summerland / Sin city.

—— added **CHRIS BIRCH** – guitar

Mar 98. (cd/c) *<(36503-2/-4/-1)>* **SO MUCH FOR THE AFTERGLOW** [63] [33] Nov97
– So much for the afterglow / Everything to everyone / Ataraxia / Normal like you / I will buy you a new life / Father of mine / One hit wonder / El distorto de melodica / Amphetamine / White men in black suits / Sunflower / Why don't I believe in God / Like a California king.
Apr 98. (7") *(CL 799)* **EVERYTHING TO EVERYONE. / OUR LIPS ARE SEALED** [41] [ ]
(cd-s+=) *(CDCL 799)* – What do I get / ('A'-CD-Rom video).
(cd-s) *(CDCLS 799)* – ('A'side) / Walk don't run / Search and destroy / Santa Monica heroin (CD-Rom video).

not iss. – E.M.I.

Jul 98. (cd-s) *<85592>* **I WILL BUY YOU A NEW LIFE** [-] [ ]
Nov 98. (cd-s) *<86181>* **FATHER OF MINE** [-] [77]

– compilations, etc. –

Apr 97. (cd) *Fire; (MCD 45)* **WHITE TRASH HELL** [ ] [-]
Aug 95. (cd) *Imprint; <97633>* **LIVE FROM TORONTO (live)** [-] [ ]

EVERYTHING BUT THE GIRL

Formed: Hull, England . . . mid 1982 by ex-Hull university graduates TRACEY THORN (ex-MARINE GIRLS) and BEN WATT. They both had recorded solo efforts ('A DISTANT SHORE' and 'NORTH MARINE DRIVE' respectfully) for indie label 'Cherry Red', before venturing onto 'WEA' (in 1983) subsidiary 'Blanco Y Negro' (run by Geoff Travis & Mike Alway). They almost immediately struck gold, with 'EACH AND EVERY ONE' (1984), making the UK Top 30, while its parent album, 'EDEN', hit the Top 20. A publicly shy, melancholy duo, EBTG blended together light jazz, folk and agitpop, their influences ranging from COLE PORTER to the modern day

JOHN MARTYN. The following years' 'LOVE NOT MONEY', however, was a more conventional indie affair which breached the UK Top 10, although the band went for an orchestrated country sound on 'BABY THE STARS SHINE BRIGHT' (1986), having been influenced by America's grassroots music scene while touring there. Thus far, EBTG's career had been grounded in album sales, their loyal student following ensuring a respectable placing for each successive release; no one really expected their tender cover of Danny Whitten's heartbreaking 'I DON'T WANT TO TALK ABOUT IT' to make the Top 3 in summer '88. The attendant album, 'IDLEWILD' (1988), considered by many to be their finest hour, made the Top 20, although no further singles were forthcoming. Employing yet another ensemble of classy musicians, the band cut the more overtly jazzy 'THE LANGUAGE OF LIFE' (1990) at the turn of the decade. The early 90's saw the pair scoring with covers of The Everly Brothers' 'LOVE IS STRANGE' and Simon & Garfunkel's 'THE ONLY LIVING BOY IN NEW YORK', although WATT was still recovering from a rare, life threatening illness (something he later documented in his book). THORN, meanwhile, found a perfect vehicle for her languerous vocal stylings with trip hop pioneers, MASSIVE ATTACK, the singer's contribution resulting in two of the best songs on their 1994 set, 'Protection' i.e. 'Better Things' and the title track. With contributions from such stalwarts as RICHARD THOMPSON, DAVE MATTACKS and the ubiquitous DANNY THOMPSON, 'AMPLIFIED HEART' (1994) was a return to form, showing the duo more willing to experiment with sound and atmosphere. One of the album's tracks, 'MISSING', was given an unlikely remix by house DJ, TODD TERRY; the result was a stunning combination of dancefloor dynamics and raw emotion which captured the imagination of record buyers around the world in late '95 (also a transatlantic Top 5). Suddenly, EBTG were big news, a hip name to drop in dance circles; the following year's 'WALKING WOUNDED' album took the logical next step and paired the duo's stripped down melancholy with cutting edge drum 'n' bass textures. Critically acclaimed by both dance critics and the mainstream rock media, the record became one the biggest selling EBTG albums to date, spawning two Top 10 singles in 'WRONG' and the title track. Where the duo go from here is anybody's guess, an album with WU TANG CLAN perhaps?!! • **Songwriters:** Most written by duo or individually, except the covers; NIGHT AND DAY (Cole Porter) / KID (Pretenders) / ALFIE (hit; Cilla Black) / DOWNTOWN TRAIN (Tom Waits) / I FALL TO PIECES (Patsy Cline) / TAKE ME (Womack And Womack) / ON MY MIND (?) / NO PLACE LIKE HOME (from 'Wizard Of Oz') / LOVE IS STRANGE (Everly Brothers) / TOUGHER THAN THE REST (Bruce Springsteen) / TIME AFTER TIME (Cyndi Lauper) / ALISON (Elvis Costello) / MY HEAD IS MY ONLY HOUSE UNLESS IT RAINS (Captain Beefheart) / THESE DAYS (Jackson Browne) / CORCOVADO (Antonio Carlos Jobim) / SINGLE contains a sample of Tim Buckley's (SONG TO THE SIREN). TRACEY THORN solo:- FEMME FATALE (Velvet Underground). • **Trivia:** EVERYTHING BUT THE GIRL was the name of a local second hand store in Hull.

Album rating: HOME MOVIES compilation (*7)

TRACEY THORN

Cherry Red — not iss.

Aug 82. (m-lp) *(MRED 35)* **A DISTANT SHORE** [ ] [-]
– Smalltown girl / Simply couldn't care / Seascape / Femme fatale / Dreamy / Plain sailing / New opened eyes / Too happy. *(cd-iss. Jun87 + Aug93; MRED 35CD)*

Dec 82. (7") *(CHERRY 53)* **PLAIN SAILING. / GOODBYE JOE** [ ] [-]

BEN WATT

Cherry Red — not iss.

Jun 81. (7"m) *(CHERRY 25)* **CANT. / AUBADE / TOWER OF SILENCE** [ ] [-]

Apr 82. (12"ep; by BEN WATT & ROBERT WYATT) *(12CHERRY 36)* **SUMMER INTO WINTER** [ ] [-]
– Walter and John / Aquamarine / Slipping slowly / Another conversation with myself / A girl in winter.

Feb 83. (7") *(CHERRY 55)* **SOME THINGS DON'T MATTER. / ON BOX HILL** [ ] [-]

Feb 83. (lp) *(BRED 40)* **NORTH MARINE DRIVE** [ ] [-]
– On Box hill / Some things don't matter / Lucky one / Empty bottles / North Marine Drive / Waiting like mad / Thirst for knowledge / Long time no sea / You're gonna make me lonesome when you go. *(cd-iss. Jun87 + Jul93 w/ SUMMER INTO WINTER EP; BRED 40CD)*

EVERYTHING BUT THE GIRL

TRACEY THORN (b.26 Sep'62) – vocals, guitar / **BEN WATT** (b. 6 Dec'62, London, England) – vocals, guitar, piano

Jun 82. (7"m) *(CHERRY 37)* **NIGHT AND DAY. / FEELING DIZZY / ON MY MIND** [ ] [-]
(12"-iss.Dec85; 12CHERRY 37) (cd-s-iss.Mar89; CDCHERRY 37) (re-iss. Jul93)

— with **SIMON BOOTH** – guitar (of WORKING WEEK, ex-WEEKEND) / **CHUCHO MERCHAN** – double bass / **CHARLES HAYWARD** – drums / **BOSCO DE OLIVEIRA** – percuss / **PETER KING** – alto saxophone / **NIGEL NASH** – tenor saxophone / **DICK PEARCE** – flugel trumpet

Blanco Y Negro — Sire

Apr 84. (7") *(NEG 1)* **EACH AND EVERY ONE. / LAUGH YOU OUT THE HOUSE** [28] [-]
(12"+=) *(NEG 1T)* – Never could have been worse.

Jun 84. (lp/c)(cd) *(BYN/+C 2)(<240-395-2>)* **EDEN** [14] [ ]
– Each and every one / Bittersweet / Tender blue / Another bridge / The spice of life / The dustbowl / Crabwalk / Even so / Frost and fire / Fascination / I must confess / Soft touch. *(US-title 'EVERYTHING BUT THE GIRL'; 7599-25212-1>*

Jul 84. (7") *(NEG 3)* **MINE. / EASY AS SIN** [58] [-]
(12"+=) *(NEG 3T)* – Gun cupboard love.

Sep 84. (7") *(NEG 6)* **NATIVE LAND. / RIVERBED DRY** [73] [-]
(12"+=) *(NEG 6T)* – Don't you go.
(12"++=) *(NEG 6TX)* – Easy as sin / Gun cupboard love.

— now with **NEIL SCOTT** – guitars / **PHIL MOXHAM** – bass (ex-The GIST ex-YOUNG MARBLE GIANTS) / **JUNE MILES KINGSTON** – drums, vocals (ex-MODETTES, ex-FUN BOY THREE) and the wind section

Mar 85. (7") *(NEG 7)* **WHEN ALL'S WELL. / HEAVEN HELP ME** [ ] [-]
(12"+=) *(NEG 7T)* – Kid.

Apr 85. (lp/c)(cd) *(BYN 3/+C)(<240-657-2>)* **LOVE NOT MONEY** [10] [ ]
– When all's well / Ugly little dreams / Shoot me down / Are you trying to be funny / Sean / Ballad of the times / Anytown / This love (not for sale) / Trouble and strife / Angel. *(c+=)* – Heaven help me / Kid.

May 85. (7"m) *(NEG 15)* **ANGEL. / PIGEONS IN THE ATTIC ROOM / CHARMLESS, CALLOW WAYS** [ ] [-]
(12"+=) *(NEG 15T)* – Easy as sin.

— now **BEN + TRACEY** used new session people below plus an orchestra **CARA TIVEY** – keyboards / **MICKEY HARRIS** – bass / **PETER KING** – alto sax / **ROBERT PETERS** – drums (ex-DANGEROUS GIRLS)

Jul 86 (7") *(NEG 21)* **COME ON HOME. / DRAINING THE BAR** [44] [-]
(12"+=) *(NEG 21T)* – I fall to pieces.

Aug 86. (lp/c)(cd) *(BYN/+C 9)(<240-966-2>)* **BABY, THE STARS SHINE BRIGHT** [22] [ ]
– Come on home / Don't leave me behind / A country mile / Cross my heart / Don't let the teardrops rust your shining heart / Careless / Sugar Finney / Come hell or high water / Fighting talk / Little Hitler.

Sep 86. (7") *(NEG 23)* **DON'T LEAVE ME BEHIND. / ALFIE** [72] [-]
(12"+=) *(NEG 23T)* – Where's the playground, Susie?.
(d7"+=) *(NEG 23F)* – Come on home (acoustic) / Always on my mind (live).

Feb 87. (7") **DON'T LEAVE ME BEHIND. / DRAINING THE BAR** [-] [ ]

— **BEN and TRACEY** now with **PETER KING / IAN FRASER** – tenor saxophone / **STEVE PEARCE** – bass / **JAMES McMILLAN** – trumpet / **DAMON BUTCHER** – piano, synth.

Feb 88. (7") *(NEG 30)* **THESE EARLY DAYS. / DYED IN THE GRAIN** [75] [-]
(12"+=) *(NEG 30T)* – No place like home.
(12"ep+=/3"cd-ep+=) *(NEG 30TX)* – ('A'original demo) / Another day another dollar.

Mar 88. (lp/c)(cd) *(BYN/+C 14)(<242-288-2>)* **IDLEWILD** [13] [ ]
– Love is here where I live / These early days / I always was your girl / Oxford Street / The night I heard Caruso sing / Goodbye Sunday / Shadow on a harvest moon / Blue moon rose / Tears all over town / Lonesome for a place I know / Apron strings. *(re-iss. Jul88, hit UK No.21- lp/c/cd; BYN/+C 16)(243-840-2) (+=)* – I don't want to talk about it. *(re-iss. 2nd version cd Nov94)*

Mar 88. (7") *(NEG 33)* **I ALWAYS WAS YOUR GIRL. / HANG OUT THE FLAGS** [ ] [-]
(12"+=) *(NEG 33T)* – Home from home.
(3"cd-s++=) *(NEG 33CD)* – Almost blue.

Jun 88. (7") *(NEG 34)* **I DON'T WANT TO TALK ABOUT IT. / OXFORD STREET** [3] [ ]
(12"+=) *(NEG 34T)* – ('A'instrumental) / Shadow on a harvest moon.
(3"cd-s+=) *(NEG 34CD)* – ('A'instrumental) / Come on home.

Sep 88. (7") *(NEG 37)* **LOVE IS HERE WHERE I LIVE. / LIVING ON HONEYCOMB** [ ] [-]
(12"+=) *(NEG 37T)* – How about me?.
(3"cd-s++=) *(NEG 37CD)* – Each and every one.

Dec 88. (7") *(NEG 39)* **THESE EARLY DAYS (Dave Bascombe remix). / DYED IN THE GRAIN** [ ] [-]
(12"+=) *(NEG 39T)* – No place like home.
(3"cd-s++=) *(NEG 39CD)* – Another day another dollar.

— duo now with **OMAR HAKIM** – drums / **JOHN PATITUCCI** – bass / **LARRY WILLIAMS** – synth, piano / **LENNY CASTRO** – percussion / **MICHAEL LANDAU** – guitar / etc.

Blanco Y Negro — Atlantic

Jan 90. (7"/c-s) *(NEG 40/+C)* **DRIVING. / ME AND BOBBY D** [54] [-]
(12"+=/cd-s+=) *(NEG 40 T/CD)* – Downtown train / ('A'extended).
(ext.12"gf+=) *(NEG 40TG)* – Easy as sin / I don't want to talk about it.

Feb 90. (cd)(lp/c) *(246-260-2)(BYN/+C 21) <82057>* **THE LANGUAGE OF LIFE** [10] [77]
– Driving / Get back together / Meet me in the morning / Take me / Me and Bobby D / The language of life / Imagining America / My baby don't love me / Letting love go / The road. *(re-iss. cd Feb95)*

Mar 90. (7"/c-s) *(NEG 44/+C)* **TAKE ME. / DRIVING (acoustic)** [ ] [-]
(12"+=/cd-s+=) *(NEG 44 T/CD)* – ('A'-Hamblin remix).

— now with **GEOFF GISCOYNE and STEVE PEARCE** – bass / **DICK OATTS** – saxophone / **RALPH SALMINS** – drums, percussion

Aug 91. (7"/c-s) *(NEG 51/+C)* **OLD FRIENDS. / APRON STRINGS (live)** [ ] [-]
(12"+=) *(NEG 51T)* – Politics aside (instrumental).
(cd-s+=) *(NEG 51CD)* – Back to the old house (live).

Sep 91. (cd)(lp/c) *(9031-75308-2)(BYN/+C 25)* **WORLDWIDE** [29] [ ]
– Old friends / Understanding / You lift me up / Talk to me like the sea / British summertime / Twin cities / Frozen river / One place / Politics aside / Boxing and pop music / Feel alright. *(re-iss. cd Feb92 +=; 9031-76583-2)* – Love is strange.

Nov 91. (7"/c-s) *(NEG 53/+C)* **TWIN CITIES (Wildwood remix). / MEET ME IN THE MORNING (live)** [ ] [-]
(12"+=) *(NEG 53T)* – ('A'-The green plains a cappella mix). (cd-s++=) *(NEG 53CD)* – Mine.

Feb 92. (7"ep/c-ep/12"ep/cd-ep) *(NEG 54/+C/T/CD)* **COVERS EP** [13] [-]
– Love is strange / Tougher than the rest / Time after time / Alison.
(above issued in the US as 'ACOUSTIC' w/ extra; *7567-82395-2>*

Apr 93. (7"ep/c-ep/12"ep/cd-ep) *(NEG 62/+C/T/CD)* **THE ONLY LIVING BOY IN NEW YORK EP** [42] [-]
– The only living boy in New York / Gabriel / Birds / Horses in the room.

May 93. (cd)(lp/c) *(4509-92319-2)(BYN/+C 29)* **HOME MOVIES – THE BEST OF EVERYTHING BUT THE GIRL** (compilation) [5] [ ]
– Each and every one / Another bridge / Fascination / Native land / Come on home / Cross my heart / Apron strings / I don't want to talk about it / The night I heard

Caruso sing / Driving / Imagining America / Understanding / Twin cities / Love is strange / I didn't know I was looking for love / The only living boy in New York.

Jun 93. (7"ep/c-ep/cd-ep) *(NEG 64/+C/CD)* **I DIDN'T KNOW I WAS LOOKING FOR LOVE EP** 72 -
– I didn't know I was looking for love / My head is my only house unless it rains / Political science / A piece of my mind.

— with **DAVE MATTACKS** – drums / **DANNY THOMPSON** – double bass (both ex-FAIRPORT CONVENTION) / **MARTIN DITCHAM** – percussion / (guests) **RICHARD THOMPSON** – guitar / **PETER KING** – alto sax / **KATE ST.JOHN** – cor anglais

May 94. (7"ep/c-ep/cd-ep) *(NEG 69/+C/CD)* **THE ROLLERCOASTER EP** 65 -
– Rollercoaster / Straight back to you / Lights of Te Touan / I didn't know I was looking for love (demo).

Jun 94. (cd/c) *(4509-96482-2/-4) <82605>* **AMPLIFIED HEART** 20 46
– Rollercoaster / Troubled mind / I don't understand anything / Walking to you / Get me / Missing / Two star / We walk the same line / 25th December / Disenchanted. *(re-iss. Nov95; 0603-10453-2)*

Aug 94. (c-ep/cd-ep) *(NEG 71 C/CD1)* **MISSING – THE LIVE EP** 69 -
– Missing / Each and every one (live) / I don't want to talk about it (live) / These days (live).
(12"ep/cd-ep) *(NEG 71 T/CD2)* **THE (FULL) REMIX EP** – ('A'side) / ('A'-Chris & James remix) / ('A'-Little Joey remix) / ('A'-Ultramarine remix).

Oct 95. (c-s) *(NEG 84C) <87124>* **MISSING (Todd Terry club mix) / ('A'-Amplified Heart album mix)** 3 2 Jul95
(cd-s+=) *(NEG 84CD)* – ('A'-radio edit) / ('A'-Rockin' blue mix) / ('A' Chris & James full on club mix) / ('A'-Todd Terry's piece).
(12") *(NEG 84T)* – (all above except 'B'side).

Virgin Atlantic

Apr 96. (c-s) *(VSC 1577)* **WALKING WOUNDED /** 6 -
(cd-s) *(VSCDT 1577)* –
(12") *(VST 1577)* –

May 96. (cd/c/lp) *(CD/TC+/V 2803) <82912>* **WALKING WOUNDED** 4 37
– Before today / Wrong / Single / The heart remains a child / Walking wounded / Flipside / Big deal / Mirrorball / Good cop bad cop / Wrong (Todd Terry remix) / Walking wounded (Omni Trio remix).

Jun 96. (c-s) *(VSC 1589) <87059>* **WRONG / ('A'mix)** 8 68 May96
(cd-s+=) *(VSCDT 1589)* – ('A'mix).
(12") *(VST 1589)* – ('A'mixes)

Sep 96. (c-s) *(VSC 1600)* **SINGLE / CORCOVADO** 20 -
(cd-s+=) *(VSCDT 1600)* – ('A'-Photek remix) / ('A'-Brad Wood Memphis remix).
(12"+=) *(VST 1600)* – (above except 'Corcovado') / Wrong (Todd Terry remix).

Feb 97. (c-s) *(VSC 1624)* **BEFORE TODAY /** 25 -
(cd-s+=) *(VSCDT 1624)* –

— in Sep'98, EBTG were credited on the DEEP DISH hit single, 'The Future Of The Future (Stay Gold)'.

– compilations, etc. –

Oct 96. (cd/c) *Blanco Y Negro; (0630 16637-2/-4)* **THE BEST OF EVERYTHING BUT THE GIRL** 23

Nov 96. (c-s) *Blanco Y Negro; (NEG 99C)* **DRIVING (remix) /** 36 -
(cd-s) *(NEG 99CD1)* –
(cd-s) *(NEG 99CD2)* –

EVIL SUPERSTARS

Formed: Antwerp, Belgium . . . 1993 by former school mates, MAURO PAWLOWSKI, TIM VANHAMEL, MARC REQUILE, BART VANDEBROEK and DAVE SCHROYEN. One of a growing number of North European bands to make inroads into the influential British market, the 'SUPERSTARS debuted late in 1995 with the EP, 'HAIRFACTS'. Presumably the band were also capable of breaking an ill wind with the best of them, given the title of their follow-up single, 'SATAN IS IN MY ASS'. (F)Art-rockers on a mission to twist our minds with their sexy, sleazy sounds (think of GIRLS AGAINST BOYS meeting The FLAMING LIPS influenced by Euro-rock), the evil ones finally delivered the surprisingly titled 'LOVE IS OKAY' (1996). The group subsequently released a couple of stop gap singles prior to the issue of a second set, 'BOOGIE CHILDREN-R-US' (1998), proving boys and their toys can never be parted.

Album rating: LOVE IS OKAY (*5) / BOOGIE CHILDREN-R-US (*6)

MAURO PAWLOWSKI – vocals, guitar / **TIM VANHAMEL** – guitar / **MARC REQUILE** – keyboards / **BART VANDEBROEK** – bass / **DAVE SCHROYEN** – drums

Paradox not iss.

Nov 95. (7"ep) *(PDOX 007)* **HAIRFACTS EP** -
– Must be mystery puke / Stay angry / (Nothing but a) Sluthead / Nice feelings now.

Feb 96. (7") *(PDOX 009)* **SATAN IS IN MY ASS. / SCRATCH** -
(cd-s+=) *(PDOXD 009)* – Worse than Kafka / Fucking love.

Feb 96. (cd/lp) *(PDOX CD/LP 002)* **LOVE IS OKAY** -
– No more bad people / Power of Haha / Go home for lunch / Parasol / Your dump or mine / Rocking all over / Pantomiming with her parents / Oh funlump / We need your head / 1,000,000 demons can't be wrong / Satan is in my ass / Death by summer. *(cd+=)* – Miss your disease.

Jun 96. (7") *(PDOX 010)* **PANTOMIMING WITH HER PARENTS. / HOLY PEOPLE'S BONER** -
(cd-s+=) *(PDOXD 010)* – March of the losers' families / A higher ugliness.

Mar 97. (7"ep/cd-ep) *(PDOX/+D 016)* **REMIX APOCALYPSE EP** -
– I will always remember last / It's a sad sad planet / Darkage disco / Waiting for Elvis.

Mar 98. (7") *(PDOX 017)* **B.A.B.Y. / X-MASLESS FOREVER / (WE WANT) THE NEW PAIN** -
(cd-s+=) *(PDOXD 017)* – Failure machine.

May 98. (7") *(PDOX 019)* **IT'S A SAD SAD PLANET. / GOOD NEWS FOR WOMEN** -
(cd-s+=) *(PDOXD 019)* – Years of science.

Jun 98. (cd/lp) *(PDOX 018 CD/LP)* **BOOGIE CHILDREN-R-US** -
– B.A.B.Y. / If you cry (I'll go to hell) / I've been wrong before / Can't seem to fuck things up / Gimme animal rights / Just a princess / Oh girl / It's a sad sad planet / Holy spirit come home / First comes farewell / Song off the record / My little dead one / Laserblack / Love happened.

the EX

Formed: Amsterdam, Netherlands . . . 1977 by G.W. SOK and TERRIE HESSELS. Over the years, the EX brought in a sizeable cast of musicians and singers to compliment each release. The first of these, 'DISTURBING DOMESTIC PEACE' (1980), found its way to British shores via import where it was playlisted by Radio One DJ, John Peel. This agit-prop punk collective were finally let loose on a UK label in 1984 courtesy of a shared EP, 'RED DANCE PACKAGE' with ALERTA. A brief stint on the 'Ron Johnson' imprint (with the double 7" EP, 'THE SPANISH REVOLUTION – 1936'), paved the way for the EX to set up their own self-titled indie late in 1987. Always ready to experiment with various musical genres, the left-wing musical activists subsequently worked with SONIC YOUTH's LEE RANALDO and THURSTON MOORE, while on 1990's 'DEAD FISH' set, they were produced by JON LANGFORD of The MEKONS. That year's 'STONE STAMPERS SONG' was adapted from composer, KURT TUCHOLSKY, the band also working with avant-garde violinist, TOM CORA on subsequent collaborative albums, 'SCRABBLING AT THE DOCK' (1991) and 'SHRUG THEIR SHOULDERS' (1993).

Album rating: DISTURBING DOMESTIC PEACE (*5) / HISTORY IS WHAT'S HAPPENING (*5) / TUMULT (*5) / BLUEPRINTS FOR A BLACKOUT (*5) / POKKEHERRIE (*6) / THE SPANISH REVOLUTION 1936 double-7"EP (*7) / TOO MANY COWBOYS (*5) / HANDS UP YOU'RE FREE (*5) / AURAL GUERILLA (*5) / JOGGERS AND SMOGGERS (*4) / DEAD FISH (*4) / SCRABBLING AT THE LOCK (*5) / SHRUG THEIR SHOULDERS (*4) / MUDBIRD SHIVERS (*4) / INSTANT (*5)

G.W. SOK – vocals / **TERRIE HESSELS** – guitar / **BASZ** – bass / **OME GUERT** – drums

Verrecords not iss.

1980. (7"ep) *(EX 001)* **ALL CORPSES SMELL THE SAME EP** - - Dutch

1980. (7"flexi) *(EX 002)* **NEW HORIZONS IN RETAILING** - - Dutch

1980. (lp) *(EX 005)* **DISTURBING DOMESTIC PEACE** - - Dutch
– The sky is blue again / Map / Outlook-army / Sucking pig / Sense of tumour / Meanwhile / Rules / Squatalong / Warning-shot / New wars / Introduction / Human car / Punk / Horse. *(with free live-7") (UK cd-iss. Jun94 on 'Konkurrent'; EX 004-005D)*

Apr 81. (7") *(EX 006)* **WAR IS OVER (WEAPONS FOR EL SALVADOR). / DUST / NEW WARS II** - - Dutch

Jun 81. (7"flexi) *(EX 007)* **CONSTITUTIONAL STATE** - - Dutch

— **WIM** – drums; repl. OME

More DPM not iss.

1982. (lp) **HISTORY IS WHAT'S HAPPENING** - Dutch
– Six of one and half a dozen of the other / Barricades / Life line / Machinery / E.M. why / Moving pictures / Shoes / Watch-dogs / Dutch disease / Blessed box at the back-seat / Who pays / Strong & muscled / Grey / Equals only / H'wood – W'ton / Sports / $ / Pep talk / Attacked / 148.

— over the next decade or so, **G.W. SOK + HESSELS** added **KARTIN BORNFELD + SABIEN WITTEMAN** – drums / **JOS KLEY** – vocals / **JOKE LAARMAN + LUC KLASSEN** – bass / **DOLF PLANTEYDT + TOM GREENE** – guitar / **WINEKE T. HART** – violin / **KEES VANDEN HAAK** – saxophone

Sneeleeer not iss.

Jun 83. (7"ep) **GONNA ROB THE SPERMBANK** - - Dutch
– Soldier toy / etc.

C.N.T. not iss.

Feb 84. (12"ep) *(CNT 017)* **RED DANCE PACKAGE** (shared w/ ALERTA) -
– EX:- Crap rap / Long live the aged / ALERTA:- Perk avenue / Violet days.

V.G.Z. not iss.

Feb 84. (7"box) *(EX 010-013)* **DIGNITY OF LABOUR** -
– Sucked out Cnucked out (parts 1-8). *(cd-iss. Aug95 on 'Konkurrent'; EX 010-013D)*

F.A.I. not iss.

Nov 83. (lp) *(EX 014)* **TUMULT** - - Dutch
– Bouquet of barbed wire / Fear / Hunt the hunters / Survival of the fattest / Red musak / Happy thoughts / Well-known soldier / Black and white statements / Squat! / Same old news / F.U.N.E.I.D.Y. / O.S.L. (new schvienhunt league) / Island race. *(UK-iss.May93 on 'Konkurrent'; EX 14D) <US cd-iss. 1994 on 'Fist Puppet'; 19>*

Pig Brother not iss.

Apr 84. (lp) *(EX 019)* **BLUEPRINTS FOR A BLACKOUT** -
– Streetcars named DEsire – Animal harmonies / Blueprints for a blackout / Rabble with a cause / Requiem for a rip-off / Pleased to meet you / Goodbuy to you / Swim / Boo hoo / U.S. hole / (Not) 2B continued / Grimm stories / Plague to survive / Rise of the Dutch republic / Kidnap connection / Fire and ice / Jack Frost is innocent / Love you till eh / Food on 45 / Scrub that scum. *(cd-iss. May93 on 'Konkurrel-Ex'; EX 19D) <US cd-iss. 1994 on 'Fist Puppet'; 13>*

Pockabilly not iss.

Nov 85. (d-lp) *(EX 024)* **POKKEHERRIE** -
(cd-iss. Aug95 on 'Konkurrel'; EX 024D)

Ron Johnson not iss.

Jul 86. (d7"ep) *(ZRON 11)* **THE SPANISH REVOLUTION – 1936** -
– They shall not pass / Al Carmela / People again / E tron Bundano. *(re-iss. Jan89 & Nov97 on 'Ex'; EX 028-029)*

Mordam not iss.

Jul 87. (d-lp) *(5)* **TOO MANY COWBOYS** -
– Red and black / White shirts / Adversity / People again / Knock / Hands up! you're free / Ignorance / Butter or bombs / Dumbo / How can one sell the air / Business as usual / Olympigs / Choice / Job / Stupid / Oops / No fear / Vivisection / Piece of paper / They shal not pass. *<US cd-iss. 1994 on 'Fist Puppet'; 19>*

Red not iss.

1987. (c) **LIVE IN WROCLAW (live)** - - Dutch

Ex Homestead

Apr 88. (lp) *(EX 035) <HMS 116>* **HANDS UP! YOU'RE FREE** (compilation of John Peel sessions) Sep88

Jul 88. (lp) *(EX 036) <HMS 115>* **AURAL GUERRILLA**
<cd-iss. 1994 on 'Fist Puppet'; 21>

Ex / Fist Puppet

Oct 89. (lp/cd) *(EX 040/041) <05>* **JOGGERS & SMOGGERS** 1990
– Humm (the full house mumble) / At the gate / Pigs and scales / Coughing / Morning star / The wall has ears / Invitation to the dance / Tightly stretched / Ask the prisoner / To be clear / Gentlemen / Make that call / Buzzword medley / Shopping street / Crackle engines vrop vrop / Greetings from Urbania / Wired / Got everything? / Waarom niet / Courtyard / Burst! crack! split! / Brickbat / Hieronymus / Nosey Parker / People who venture / Watch the driver / Let's get sceptical / Tin gods / State of freedom / Provisionally untitled / Kachun-K pschuh / Early bird's worm / Catkin / Upstairs with Picasso.

May 90. (7") *(EX 043)* **STONE STAMPERS SONG. /** -

Jun 90. (12"ep) *(EX 044)* **DEAD FISH EP** -

— In 1990, the EX also collaborated with the DOG FACED HERMANS on a cassette-only release, 'TREAT'.

Mar 91. (7") *(EX)* **SLIMY TOAD JAKE'S CAFE. /** -

Mar 92. (lp/cd; The EX / TOM CORA) *(EX 051/+CD)* **SCRABBLING AT THE LOCK** -

— above was a collaboration with violin player **TOM CORA**

May 92. (7") **THIS SONG IS IN ENGLISH. /** -
(above issued on 'Palber')

Jul 92. (12") *(EX 066)* **EUROCONFUSION. /** -

Sep 93. (cd; The EX / TOM CORA) *(EX 57CD)* **SHRUG THEIR SHOULDERS** -
(re-iss. Feb94 as 'AND THE WEATHERMEN SHRUG THEIR SHOULDERS' on 'Fist Puppet'; 15)

Aug 95. (cd) *(EX 060D)* **MUDBIRD SHIVERS** -

Nov 95. (d-cd; The EX & GUESTS) *(EX 063-064D)* **INSTANT** -

Touch & Go / Touch & Go

Oct 98. (cd) *(<TG 198>)* **STARTERS ALTERNATORS**
– Frenzy / Let's panic later / I.O.U. (nought) / Art of losing / It's a sin / Two struck by the moon / Mother / Bee coz / Lump sum insomnia / Wildebeast / Nem ugy van most.

– others, etc. –

Aug 95. (12"ep) *Moonroof; <50015>* **WE MUST GO FREE** -

EXPERIMENTAL AUDIO RESEARCH

Formed: London, England . . . 1992 by indie noisesters, SONIC BOOM (PETE KEMBER of SPECTRUM), KEVIN SHIELDS (of MY BLOODY VALENTINE) and EDDIE PROVOST (of AMM). EAR as they were known for short, were primarily concerned with exploring the boundaries where stark ambience meets uncompromising guitar manipulation/noise, making their first lunar mission via a US-only debut CD-album, 'MESMERISED' (1994). Reflecting his love collectable vinyl, SONIC BOOM decided to release a 5" single, 'POCKET SYMPHONY' a few months later. Subsequently securing a UK deal with 'Big Cat', EAR finally got round to issuing their first studio venture (actually recorded during their formative year), 'BEYOND THE PALE', in 1996. Over the course of the ensuing two years or so, the group were surprisingly prolific, completing a trio of long-players, 'PHENOMENA 256' (1996), 'THE KONER EXPERIMENT' (1997) and 'MILLENNIUM MUSIC' (1998) for three separate labels. Of late, the avant-garde troupe (who had now lost SHIELDS and MARTIN) introduced a revolutionary technique called "circuit bending" on their sixth album, 'DATA RAPE' (1998).

Album rating: MESMERISED (*5) / BEYOND THE PALE (*6) / PHENOMENA 256 (*5) / THE KONER EXPERIMENT (*4) / MILLENNIUM MUSIC (*6) / DATA RAPE (*6)

SONIC BOOM – effects, etc (PETE KEMBER of SPECTRUM) / **KEVIN SHIELDS** – guitar (of MY BLOODY VALENTINE) / **EDDIE PREVOST** – percussion (of A.M.M.) / **KEVIN MARTIN** – sax, effects (of GOD)

not iss. / Sympathy F

Jun 94. (cd) *<SFTRI 279>* **MESMERISED** -
– D.M.T. symphony (overture to an . . .) / Mesmerise 4901 / California nocturne / Guitar feedback manipulation.

Oct 94. (5") **POCKET SYMPHONY** -

Big Cat / EAR

Jun 96. (lp/cd) *(ABB 96/+CD) <96>* **BEYOND THE PALE** (rec.1992) Feb96
– Beyond the pale / Calm before / In the cold light of day / Calm beyond / Dusk / The circle is blue.

not iss. / Man's Ruin

Sep 96. (10"; as EAR) *<MR 001>* **DELTA 6 (HYDROPHONIC)** -

Space Age / Sympathy F

Sep 96. (d-lp/cd) *(ORBIT 005/+CD) <SFTRI 459>* **PHENOMENA 256**
– Delta (hydrophonic) / Space themes, pt.1 & 2 (tribute to . . .) / Sub aqua (left channel) – Tidal (centre channel) / Ring modulator / Phenomena 256 (3 piece suite) / Spacestation / Mood for a summer sundown. *(re-iss. Apr98; same)*

Mille Plateau / Space Age

Mar 97. (cd/lp) *(<EFA 00666-2/-1>)* **THE KONER EXPERIMENT**

Via Satellite / Via Satellite

May 97. (7"split) *(<VSAT 006>)* **SPUTNIK. / Thurston Moore & Don Fleming: TELSTAR**

— now **SONIC BOOM, EDDIE PREVOST, PETE BASSMAN (BAIN) + TOM PRENTICE**

Atavistic / Atavistic

Jan 98. (d-lp;3-sided/cd) *(<ALP 72/+CD>)* **MILLENIUM MUSIC**
– Delysid / Digitana / Enigma code.

Space Age / Space Age

Jul 98. (cd/d-lp) *<(ORBIT 013 CD/LP)>* **DATA RAPE**

Earworm / not iss.

Aug 98. (7",7"clear) *(WORM 22)* **INTERLUDE. / TRANSISTOR MUSIC** -

Ochre / Ochre

Sep 98. (10"ep) *<(OCH 025)>* **DEATH OF A ROBOT**

Earworm / not iss.

Nov 98. (7"one-sided) *(WORM 35)* **DATA RAPE (part 9)** -

EXPLODING WHITE MICE

Formed: Adelaide, Australia . . . January 1985 by PAUL GILCHRIST, JEFF STEPHENS and GILES BARROW, the trio subsequently being joined by ANDY McQUEEN and CRAIG RODDA (the latter replaced by DAVID BUNNEY during initial recordings). Taking their musical cue from such veteran US punk icons as MC5, The STOOGES and the RAMONES, The EXPLODING WHITE MICE played muscular trash-rock in the best Australian tradition, debuting with that year's 'A NEST OF VIPERS', a mini-set of half covers/half original material that was given a UK release the following year. Preceding the HAPPY MONDAYS by a few years, the EWM dusted down John Kongos' 'HE'S GONNA STEP ON YOU AGAIN' for release as a single. In 1988, they delivered their first full-set, 'BRUTE FORCE & IGNORANCE', JACK JACOMOS subsequently coming in for BARROW shortly after. Despite a limited audience in the homeland and virtually no interest in Britain, the 'MICE received a sympathetic reaction in Germany where they released two further sets, an eponymous(e) partly live affair in 1990 and 'COLLATERAL DAMAGE' in '92.

Album rating: A NEST OF VIPERS (*5) / BRUTE FORCE & IGNORANCE (*6) / EXPLODING WHITE MICE (*6) / COLLATERAL DAMAGE (*5)

PAUL GILCHRIST – vocals / **JEFF STEPHENS** – guitar, vocals / **GILES BARROW** – guitar, vocals / **ANDY McQUEEN** – bass, vocals / **DAVID BUNNEY** – drums; repl. RODDA

Big Time / not iss.

May 86. (m-lp) *(BTA 010)* **A NEST OF VIPERS** -
– Burning red / Bad little woman / Let the kids dance / Pipeline / Your claws / Dangerous. *(Australian-release 1985 on 'Greasy Pop'; GPR 115) (German-iss.1987 on 'Normal'+=; 87)* – He's gonna step on you again / Blaze of glory.

1986. (7") **HE'S GONNA STEP ON YOU AGAIN. / BLAZE OF GLORY** - - Austra

Festival / not iss.

1988. (lp) **BRUTE FORCE & IGNORANCE** - - Austra
– Fear (late at night) / Goodbye gravity / Worry about nothing / Verbal abuse / The wheel / Surfing in a dust storm / Breakdown No.2 / Bury me / Uninvited / Sea of justice / Hit in the face / When I get off / Without warning. *(German-iss.+=; 88)* – A NEST OF VIPERS

— **JACK JACOMOS** – guitar; repl. BARROW

Normal / not iss.

Jul 90. (lp/cd) *(NORMAL 119/+CD)* **EXPLODING WHITE MICE** (some live) -
– Sleepwalk / Intuition / Real tough guy / Do the crunch / You're losing me / I just want my fun / Misunderstood / Ain't it sad / Verbal abuse / Meet the creeper / Univited / Bangkok / King of the surf / Dangerous / First time is the best time. *(cd+=)* – Do the crunch.

— now a trio of **STEPHENS, McQUEEN + BUNNEY**

1992. (lp/cd) *(NORMAL 144/+CD)* **COLLATERAL DAMAGE** - - German
– And stay out / Enemies / In your eyes / Imaginary world / Human garbage / Frozen alive / Shadow in the sky / Everybody's waiting / Empty T.V. / This is the news / When she walks / Falling on all sides / Tooth and nail / Hate mail.

— split after above

EXPLOITED

Formed: East Kilbride, Scotland . . . 1979 by 'BIG JOHN' DUNCAN, WATTIE BUCHAN, GARY McCORMICK AND DRU STIX. Subsequently moving to the capital, they issued three independently released maxi-singles in 1980, 'ARMY LIFE', 'EXPLOITED BARMY ARMY' and 'EXTRACTS FROM AN EDINBURGH NITE CLUB EP', a barrage of three-chord 100 mph punk/oi anthems with BUCHAN spitting out raging anti-establishment diatribes (Maggie Thatcher was a favourite lyrical punchbag). In 1981, after a minor hit, 'DOGS OF WAR' (on 'Secret' records), they unleashed a whole album's worth of two-minute wonders, 'PUNK'S NOT DEAD' (a battlecry of the dyed mohawk hairdo brigade!) which incredibly hit the Top 20. It was quickly pursued by 'DEAD CITIES' (a near Top 30 hit), an abysmal live set, a shared EP with fellow oi-stars ANTI-PASTI, and a Top 50 hit single, 'ATTACK'. A second album proper, 'TROOPS OF TOMORROW' (1982) followed their debut into the Top 20, featuring their infamous tribute to punk's greatest dead hero, 'SID VICIOUS WAS INNOCENT'. When BIG JOHN left at the end of '82 (he formed The BLOOD UNCLES before joining GOODBYE MR MACKENZIE!), the rot set in after the Falklands Conflict-inspired set, 'LET'S START A WAR (SAID MAGGIE ONE DAY)' (1983). A further series of personnel changes marred their subsequent releases, 'HORROR EPICS' in '85 relying on substandard heavy metal to get their still raging points across. WATTIE and his ever changing cast of ageing punk/metal diehards continued, if intermittently, to release predictable albums, while former member BIG JOHN found brief fame when he deputised in 1993 for an A.W.O.L. KURT COBAIN in NIRVANA.

Album rating: PUNK'S NOT DEAD (*5) / ON STAGE (*3) / TROOPS OF TOMORROW (*5) / LET'S START A WAR (SAID MAGGIE ONE DAY) (*5) / HORROR EPICS (*5) / DEATH BEFORE DISHONOUR (*4) / THE MASSACRE (*4) / BEAT THE BASTARDS (*3) / THE SINGLES COLLECTION compilation (*6)

WATTIE BUCHAN – vocals / **'BIG JOHN' DUNCAN** – guitar, vocals / **GARY McCORMICK** – bass, vocals (ex-JOSEF K) / **DRU STIX** (b. DREW CAMPBELL) – drums, vocals

Exploited not iss.

Aug 80. (7"m) *(EXP 001)* **ARMY LIFE. / FUCK THE MODS / CRASHED OUT** [ ] [-]
(re-iss. May81 on 'Secret'; SHH 112)

Nov 80. (7"m) *(EXP 002)* **EXPLOITED BARMY ARMY. / I BELIEVE IN ANARCHY / WHAT YOU WANNA DO?** [ ] [-]
(re-iss. May81 on 'Secret'; SHH 113)

1981. (7"ep) *(EXP 003)* **EXTRACTS FROM EDINBURGH NITE CLUB (live)** [ ] [-]

Secret not iss.

Apr 81. (7") *(SHH 110)* **DOGS OF WAR. / BLOWN TO BITS (live)** [63] [-]

May 81. (lp) *(EXP 1001)* **PUNK'S NOT DEAD** [20] [-]
– Punk's not dead / Mucky pup / Exploited barmy army / S.P.G. / Cop cars / Free flight / Army life (Pt.2) / Dole q / Out of control / Ripper / Blown to bits / Son of a copper / Sex and violence / Royalty / I believe in anarchy. *(re-iss. Feb89 on 'Link'; LINK 065) (cd-iss. Oct92 on 'Streetlink'; STRCD 006) (cd re-iss. Mar93 on 'Dojo'; DOJOCD 106) (re-iss. Mar98 on 'Harry May'; MAYLP 701) (cd re-iss. Aug98 on 'Snapper'; SMMCD 530)*
(above released on 'Exploited' records)

Oct 81. (7"m) *(SHH 120)* **DEAD CITIES. / HITLER'S IN THE CHARTS AGAIN / CLASS WAR** [31] [-]

Superville not iss.

Nov 81. (lp) *(EXP 1002)* **EXPLOITED LIVE-ON STAGE (live)** [52] [-]
– Cop cars / Crashed out / Dole Q / Dogs of war / Army life / Out of control / Ripper / F*** the mods / Exploited barmy army / Royalty / Sex & violence / Punks not dead / I believe in anarchy. *(re-iss. 1987 on 'Dojo' lp/c; DOJO LP/TC 9) <US cd-iss. Oct92 on 'Continium'; 10001-2>*

Nov 81. (12"ep; shared with ANTI-PASTI) *(EXP 1003)* **DON'T LET 'EM GRIND YOU DOWN** [70] [-]

Secret not iss.

Apr 82. (7") *(SHH 130)* **ATTACK. / ALTERNATIVES** [50] [-]

Jun 82. (lp) *(SEC 8)* **TROOPS OF TOMORROW** [17] [-]
– Jimmy Boyle / Daily news / Disorder / Alternatives (remix) / Germs / Rapist / UK '82 / War / Troops of tomorrow / Sid Vicious was innocent / They won't stop / So tragic. *(re-iss. Feb89 on 'Link'; LINK 066) (cd-iss. Oct92 on 'Streetlink'; STRCD 007) (cd re-iss. Mar93 on 'Dojo'; DOJOCD 107) (re-iss. Mar98 on 'Harry May'; MAYLP 702) (cd re-iss. Aug98 on 'Snapper'; SMMCD 529)*

Oct 82. (7") *(SHH 140)* **COMPUTERS DON'T BLUNDER. / ADDICTION** [ ] [-]

— **BILLY DUNN** – guitar (ex-SKROTEEZ) repl. BIG JOHN who formed BLOOD UNCLES with JON CARMICHAEL (ex-TWEETS; yes! 'The Birdie Song' disaster!) and COLIN McGUIRE. They issued a few singles and an album for 'Virgin', 'LIBERTINE' (1987), before BIG JOHN joined GOODBYE MR MACKENZIE

Blurg-Pax not iss.

Oct 83. (7"m) *(PAX 15)* **RIVAL LEADERS. / ARMY STYLE / SINGALONGABUSHELL** [ ] [-]

Pax Combat

Dec 83. (lp) *(PAX 18)* **LET'S START A WAR (SAID MAGGIE ONE DAY)** [ ] [ ]
– Let's start a war / Insanity / Safe below / Eyes of the vulture / Should we can't we / Rival leaders (remix) / God save the Queen / Psycho / Kidology / False hopes / Another day to go nowhere / Wankers. *(re-iss. 1987 on 'Dojo' lp/c; DOJO LP/TC 10) (cd-iss. Mar94 on 'Dojo'; DOJOCD 010) (cd re-iss. Aug98 on 'Snapper'; SMMCD 531)*

— **DEPTFORD JOHN** repl. WAYNE / **MAD MICK** repl. EGGHEAD / **also with WATTIE, KARL, WILLIE BUCHAN** – drums / **CAPTAIN SCARLETT** – guitar

— McCORMICK formed ZULU SYNDICATE, while STIX struggled with a drug addiction and then was sentenced to seven years for armed robbery.

Konnexion not iss.

Mar 85. (lp/c) *(KOMA/AMOK 788012)* **HORROR EPICS** [ ] [-]
– Horror epics / Don't forget the chaos / Law and order / I hate you / No more idols / Maggie / Dangerous vision / Down below / Treat you like shit / Forty odd years ago / My life. *(re-iss. Aug86 on 'Dojo' lp/c; DOJO LP/TC 37) (cd-iss. Mar94; DOJOCD 184) (cd re-iss. Aug98 on 'Snapper'; SMMCD 532)*

Rough Justice not iss.

Apr 86. (12"ep) *(12KORE 102)* **JESUS IS DEAD / POLITICIANS. / DRUG SQUAD / PRIVACY INVASION** [ ] [-]

Nov 88. (12"ep) *(12KORE 103)* **WAR NOW. / UNITED CHAOS AND ANARCHY / SEXUAL FAVOURS** [ ] [-]

Aug 89. (lp/cd) *(JUST/+CD 6)* **DEATH BEFORE DISHONOUR** [ ] [-]
– Anti UK / Power struggle / Scaling the Derry wall / Barry Prossitt / Don't really care / No forgiveness / Death before dishonour / Adding to their fears / Police informer / Drive me insane / Pulling us down / Sexual favours. *(cd+=)* – Drug squad man / Privacy invasion / Jesus is dead / Politicians / War now / United chaos and anarchy / Sexual favours (dub version).

— **WATTIE** – vocals / **SMEGS** – bass, vocals / **GOGS** – guitar / **TONY** – drums

Sep 90. (cd/c/lp) *(CD/T+/JUST 15)* **THE MASSCRE** [ ] [-]
– The massacre / Sick bastard / Porno slut / Now I'm dead / Boys in blue / Dog soldier / Don't pay the poll tax / F. . . religion / About to die / Blown out of the city / Police shit / Stop the slaughter.

— new line-up mid-90's; **WATTIE** – vocals / **ARTHUR** – guitar / **BILLY** – bass / **WULLIE** – drums

Mar 96. (cd/c/lp) *(CD/T+/JUST 22)* **BEAT THE BASTARDS** [ ] [-]
– Beat the bastards / Affected by them / Law for the rich / System fucked up / They lie / If you're sad / Fightback / Massacre of innocents / Police TV / Sea of blood / Dont blame me / 15 years / Serial killer.

– compilations, etc. –

Dec 84. (lp) *Dojo; (DOJOLP 1)* **TOTALLY EXPLOITED** [ ] [-]
– Punk's not dead / Army life / F**k a mod / Barmy army / Dogs of war / Dead cities / Sex and violence / Yops / Daily news / Dole Q / Believe in anarchy / God save the Queen / Psycho / Blown to bits / Insanity / S.P.G. / Jimmy Boyle / U.S.A. / Attack / Rival leaders. *(re-iss. Apr86 lp/c/cd; DOJO LP/TC/CD 1)*

Jan 85. (c) *Chaos; (APOCA 2)* **LIVE ON THE APOCALYPSE TOUR '81 (live)** [ ] [-]
(lp-iss.Feb87; APOCA 2)

Feb 86. (lp) *Suck; (SDLP 2)* **LIVE AT THE WHITEHOUSE (live)** [ ] [-]

Aug 86. (12"ep) *Archive 4; (TOF 107)* **DEAD CITIES / PUNK'S NOT DEAD. / ARMY LIFE / EXPLOITED BARMY LIFE** [ ] [-]

Mar 87. (lp) *Snow; (WAT 1)* **INNER CITY DECAY** [ ] [-]

Dec 87. (lp) *Link; (LINKLP 018)* **LIVE AND LOUD (live)** [ ] [-]
(cd-iss. Oct93; LINKCD 018) (cd re-iss. Apr96 on 'Anagram'; CDPUNK 18)

Jul 88. (12"ep) *Skunx; (EXPX 1)* **PUNK'S ALIVE** [ ] [-]
– Alternative / Let's start a war / Horror epics / Troops of tomorrow / Dogs of war.

1989. (d-lp) *Roadrunner; (RR 4965-1)* **PUNK'S NOT DEAD / TROOPS OF TOMORROW** [ ] [-]

1989. (lp) *Grand Slam; <SLAM 7>* **LIVE, LEWD, LUST (live)** [-] [ ]

Dec 91. (cd) *Streetlink; (STRCD 018)* **THE SINGLES COLLECTION** [ ] [-]
(re-iss. Apr93 & Jan98 on 'Dojo'; DOJOCD 118)

Feb 94. (cd) *Loma; (LOMACD 2)* **LIVE ON STAGE 1981 / LIVE AT THE WHITEHOUSE 1985** [ ] [-]

Feb 94. (cd) *Loma; (LOMACD 3)* **LET'S START A WAR . . . / HORROR EPICS** [ ] [-]

Mar 94. (cd) *Dojo; (DOJOCD 20109)* **LIVE IN JAPAN (live)** [ ] [-]

Apr 94. (cd) *Cleopatra; (CLEO 5000CD)* **THE SINGLES** [ ] [-]

Sep 97. (d-cd) *Snapper; (SMDCD 136)* **TOTALLY EXPLOITED / LIVE IN JAPAN** [ ] [-]

EYELESS IN GAZA

Formed: based- London, England . . . early 80's by MARTYN BATES and PETE BECKER. Taking their moniker from the Aldous Huxley novel of the same name, EYELESS IN GAZA signed to independent label, 'Cherry Red', releasing their debut album, 'PHOTOGRAPHS AS MEMORIES', in 1981. Definitely something of an acquired taste, the duo's wailing, often unintelligible vocals and repetitive, minimalist musical constructs nevertheless attracted a cult following among the post-punk fraternity. Whether utilising pulsing electronics or a more conventional alternative rock format, the material was consistently experimental and its creators nothing if not prolific; a follow-up set, 'CAUGHT IN FLUX' appeared later in '81 while the Norwegian-only set, 'PALE HANDS I LOVED SO WELL', followed in '82. The former featured some brooding avant-pop numbers, namely 'SKELETAL FRAMEWORK', 'SCALE AMISS' and 'ROSE PETAL KNOT', the record buyer also treated to a free 12" EP which included arguably their finest moment, 'STILL AIR'. A further two sets, 'DRUMMING THE BEATING HEART' and 'RUST RED SEPTEMBER' were released over the course of the next year before the group took an extended sabbatical from the recording front. During this period, EIG managed to squeeze out two 45's, the darkly romantic 'SUNBURSTS IN' and 'WELCOME NOW', the latter featuring guest drummer DAVE RUFFY (of AZTEC CAMERA). They returned in 1986 with JOBY PALMER, the new sticksman making his debut on 'BACK FROM THE RAINS'. Following the addition of singer, ELIZABETH S., EYELESS IN GAZA resurfaced as a trio in 1993 with the 'FABULOUS LIBRARY' album, subsequently touring with performance poet, ANNE CLARK. Duly signed to Belgian label, 'Antler', the cream of the band's 'Cherry Red' recordings were released as 'ORANGE ICE AND WAX CRAYONS' in 1992. The previous decade has also seen BATES juggling a prolific solo career with several albums – beginning with the 1982 mini-set, 'LETTERS WRITTEN' – under his belt. In the early 90's he teamed up with ex-PRIMITIVES member STEVE DULLAHAN to form short-lived project, HUNGRY I, the duo covering R.E.M.'s 'TWO STEPS FORWARD', in '91.

Album rating: PHOTOGRAPHS AS MEMORIES (*7) / CAUGHT IN FLUX (*7) / RUST RED SEPTEMBER (*6) / BACK FROM THE RAINS (*5) / VOICES: THE BEST OF EYELESS IN GAZA compilation (*7)

MARTYN BATES – vocals, keyboards, synthesizers / **PETE BECKER** – vocals, synths

Ambivalent Scale not iss.

May 80. (7"m) *(ASR 2)* **KODAK GHOSTS RUN AMOK. / CHINA BLUE VISION / THE FEELING'S MUTUAL** [ ] [-]

Cherry Red not iss.

Feb 81. (lp) *(BRED 13)* **PHOTOGRAPHS AS MEMORIES** [ ] [-]
– Seven years / Fixation / A keepsake / Looking daggers / From A to B / Clear cut apparently / Speech rapid fire / John of Patmos / Knives replace air / Faceless / In your painting / A keepsake / Whitewash / No noise.

Apr 81. (7"m) *(CHERRY 20)* **INVISIBILITY. / THREE KITTENS / PLAGUE OF YEARS** [ ] [-]

Sep 81. (lp) *(BRED 18)* **CAUGHT IN FLUX** [ ] [-]
– Sixth sense / Point you / Voice from the tracks / Scale amiss / The decoration / Continual / Soul on thin ice / Rose petal knot / Skeletal framework / See red / Half light / Every which way. *(w/ free 12"ep)* **THE EYES OF BEAUTIFUL LOSERS** – Still air / Out from the day-to-day / Keynote inertia. *(cd-iss. Sep97; CDMRED 145)*

Nov 81. (7"ep) *(CHERRY 31)* **OTHERS / JANE DANCING. / EVER PRESENT / AVENUE OF TREES** [ ] [-]

Sep 82. (lp) *(BRED 36)* **DRUMMING THE BEATING HEART** [ ] [-]
– Transcience blues / Ill wind blows / One by one / Picture the day / Dreaming at rain / Veil like calm / Throw a shadow / Pencil sketch / At arms length / Lights of April / Before you go. *(cd-iss. Mar96 +=; CDMRED 127)* – PALE HANDS I LOVED SO WELL

Oct 82. (7") *(CHERRY 47)* **VEIL LIKE CALM. / TAKING STEPS** [ ] [-]

May 83. (7"/12") *(CHERRY/12CHERRY 63)* **NEW RISEN. / BRIGHT PLAY OF EYES** [ ] [-]

Jun 83. (lp/c) *(BRED/CBRED 50)* **RUST RED SEPTEMBER** [ ] [-]
– Changing stations / Pearl and pale / New risen / September hills / Taking steps / Only whispers / Leaves are dancing / No perfect stranger / Corner of dusk / Bright plays of eyes / Stealing Autumn. *(c+=)* – Steven / Sun-like-gold / To Elizabeth S. / Lilt of music / Inky blue sky / Tell. *(cd-iss. Jun96 +=; CDMRED 111)*

— next with guest **MARK ROWS** – trumpet

Jun 84. (7") *(CHERRY 74)* **SUNBURSTS IN. / LILT OF MUSIC**
(12"+=) *(12CHERRY 74)* – Inky blue sky / Tell.

Apr 85. (lp) *(U 004)* **PALE HANDS I LOVED SO WELL** — Norway
– Tall and white nettles / Warm breath soft and slow / Blue distance / Sher cliffs / Falling leaf – Fading flower / Goodbye to summer / Lies of love / To Ellen / Pale saints / Letter to she / Light sliding / Big clipper ship.
(above lp rec.1982 released on 'Uniton')

— next with guest **DAVE RUFFY** – drums (of AZTEC CAMERA)

Sep 85. (7") *(CHERRY 92)* **WELCOME NOW. / SWEET LIFE LONGER**
(12"+=) *(12CHERRY 92)* – New love here.

— added **JOBY PALMER** – drums (ex-SINATRAS, ex-IN EMBRACE) + guest **ELIZABETH S** – backing vocals

Jul 86. (12") *(12CHERRY 93)* **BACK FROM THE RAINS. / KISS THE RAIN GOODBYE**

Jul 86. (lp/c) *(BRED/CBRED 69)* **BACK FROM THE RAINS**
– Between these dreams / Twilight / Back from the rains / Lie still, sleep long / Catch me / Evening music / She moved through the fair / Sweet life longer / Welcome now / Your rich sky / Flight of swallows / My last, lost melody. *(cd-iss. Jul89 +=; CDBRED 69)* – New risen / Bright play of eyes / Scent on evening air / Drumming the beating heart.

— split but re-formed in the early 90's

— added **ELIZABETH S** – vocals

Orchid / not iss.

1993. (cd) **FABULOUS LIBRARY** — Europe

— reverted back to a duo

Ambivalent Scale / not iss.

1994. (cd) *(ASCALE 018CD)* **MYSTERY SEAS**
1995. (cd) *(ASCALE 020CD)* **BITTER APPLES**
Oct 96. (cd) *(ASCALER 021)* **ALL UNDER THE LEAVES**

– compilations, etc. –

Feb 87. (lp/c) *Cherry Red; (BRED/CBRED 73)* **KODAK GHOSTS RUN AMOK**
– Kodak ghosts run amok / Invisibility / No noise / Others / Pencil sketch / Veil like calm / Bright play of eyes / New risen / No perfect stranger / Sunbursts in / Welcome now / New love here / Back from the rains. *(c+=)* – CAUGHT IN FLUX

Jan 90. (cd) *Integrity; (IR 006CD) / S.P.V.; <840357>* **TRANSCIENCE IN BLUE**
– Lilt of music / Transcience blues / Sixth sense / Stealing Autumn / Inky blue sky / Evening music / Still air / Sweet life longer / Tell / Blue distance / Scent on evening air / Every which way / Bright play of eyes / Lights of April / Drumming the beating heart.

Dec 92. (lp) *Document; (DLP 005)* **ORANGE ICE & WAX CRAYONS**
(unreleased material)

Oct 93. (cd) *Cherry Red; (CDBRED 104)* **VOICE – THE BEST OF EYELESS IN GAZA**
– Kodak ghosts run amok / No noise / Seven years / From A to B / Speech rapid fire / Invisibility / Others / Rose petal knot / Out from the day-to-day / Transcience blues / Picture the day / Two / Veil like calm / One by one / Pencil sketch / Through east fields / Changing stations / Corner of dusk / Drumming the beating heart / New risen / Sunbursts in / Welcome now / Back from the rains / Lilt of music / Evening music / Between these dreams. *(re-iss. Jun96; same)*

MARTYN BATES

Cherry Red / not iss.

Oct 82. (m-lp) *(TRED 38)* **LETTERS WRITTEN**
– Morning singing / Cut like sunset / In June / Call of birds / Mirrored in me / After taste of old / Jagged tears of words / Letters from yesterday / Overflowing look / Hungry like sharp desire. *(cd-iss. Oct96 +=; CDMRED 134)*– RETURN OF THE QUIET

Oct 87. (7") *(CHERRY 99)* **THE LOOK OF LOVE. / ADAM AND EVE AND PINCH ME**
(12"+=) *(12CHERRY 99)* – May the 3rd.

Nov 87. (lp) *(BRED 81)* **RETURN OF THE QUIET**

Integrity / S.P.V.

Jan 89. (lp) *(IR 002)* **LOVE SMASHED ON A ROCK**
(cd-iss. Jan90; IR 002CD)

Apr 89. (12") *(IR 004)* **YOU SO SECRET. / ?**

Feb 90. (cd) *(IR 005CD) <3242>* **LETTERS TO A SCATTERED FAMILY**
– On the day you climb down / Snow races / City / Little days / Your jewelled footsteps / For love / Shuttered nights / First and last / February / This one return / I'll wrap your hopes.

Integrity / Antler Subway – Caroline

Oct 90. (lp/cd) *(IR 011/+CD) <011>* **STARS COME TREMBLING**

Sub Rosa / Sub Rosa

Oct 94. (cd) *(<SR 81CD>)* **CHAMBER MUSIC I**

Feb 96. (cd) *(<SR 91CD>)* **CHAMBER MUSIC II**
– Be not sad / In the dark pine wood / His love / He who hath glory lost / His companion / Of that so sweet imprisonment / This heart / Between kiss and kiss / Silently she's coming / On the drappled glass / Lightly come or lightly go / Thou leanest to the shell of the night / At ghosting hour / Though I thy mithridates were / Gentle lady, do not sing / Dear heart / Love came to us / O, it was out by Donnycarney / Bat / The rain has fallen / Now o now / The wind is whistling / Sleep now / Unquiet / All day I hear the noise of waters / I hear an army / Fluttering whips.

Ambilavent Scale / not iss.

Apr 97. (ASR 022) **IMAGINATION FEELS LIKE POISON**
– Mock sun / I can't look for you / Bones of your face / Years of salt / I forget you / God on the tree / Full sail / Flanaghan / Fully bright / Mystery seas / This wayward love / Fantacinni playground / Ellen Massey / Letters to a scattered family / Silvery images / No one spoke / Mountain tomb.

HUNGRY I

— **MARTYN BATES + STEVE DULLAHAN** (ex-PRIMITIVES)

Nursery / not iss.

Jun 91. (12"ep) **THE FALLING ORCHARD. / (+3)**
Nov 91. (12"ep) **SECOND STEP. / TWO STEPS FORWARD**

PETE BECKER

Ambivalent Scale / not iss.

1981. (lp) **BY TRAIN TO COAST**

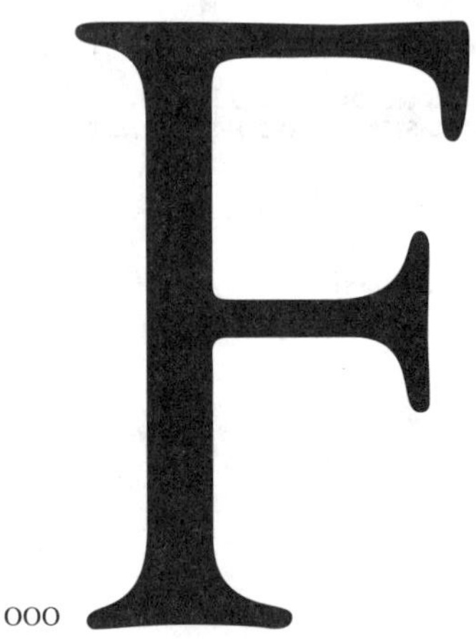

OOO

FABULOUS

Formed: London, England . . . 1991 by NME journalist turned frontman, SIMON DUDFIELD, alongside NME photographers, MARTIN GOODACRE and RUSSEL UNDERWOOD, the line-up being completed by the rhythm section of RONNIE and HODGE. Managed by their assistant editor, James Brown (although they were sadly lacking in the soul/charisma factor defined by his namesake!), the lads certainly weren't short of publicity/hype potential although they did resort to SEX PISTOLS/MALCOLM McLAREN-style tactics to get attention (i.e. stealing a carpet from the offices of 'E.M.I.'). If that wasn't enough to prove their punk-rock credentials, they underlined their rebel status by securing the services of PETE WATERMAN on their second single, 'PERSONALITY RECESSION'. They had already issued their debut, 'DESTINED TO BE FREE', on the fledgling 'Heavenly' label in late '91, a supposed reaction to the drug euphoria of the rave/baggy generation. It would be a further eighteen months or so before the release of the aforementioned follow-up, a third single, 'DEAD FRIENDS', all but sealing their less than fabulous career later that year. Maybe they shouldn't have given up their day jobs. Ah! music journalists . . . who loves them?

Album rating: never released any

SIMON DUDFIELD – vocals / **MARTIN GOODACRE** – guitar / **RUSSEL UNDERWOOD** – guitar / **RONNIE** – bass / **HODGE** – drums

Heavenly — not iss.

Nov 91. (ltd-7") **DESTINED TO BE FREE. / THERE'S A RIOT GOIN' ON (INSIDE HER PRETTY HEAD)** [ ] [-]

Kinglake — not iss.

Jun 93. (12") *(SE 17)* **PERSONALITY RECESSION. /** [ ] [-]
Nov 93. (7"ep) *(KLR 002)* **DEAD FRIENDS EP** [ ] [-]

— disbanded in 1994

FAD GADGET

Formed: London, England . . . late 70's by Irish-born FRANK TOVEY. Basically a vehicle for TOVEY's twisted electronica and performance art (he was known for plucking his pubic hair out on stage, possibly due to a tarred and feathered photo shoot!), FAD GADGET was the first group to sign to the 'Mute' label, releasing a debut single, 'BACK TO NATURE', in late '79. This was followed by 'RICKY'S HAND' and a debut album, 'FIRESIDE FAVOURITES' (1980), for which he enlisted the help of 'Mute' mainman, DANIEL MILLER along with ERIC RADCLIFFE, PAUL WAUCLAIRE, NICHOLAS CASH and JOHN FRYER. Hardly the stuff of Perry Como-style cosiness, the record married repetitive, often jarring synth rhythms to lyrics exploring life's darker, seedier side, occasionally letting it . . . er, all hang out as on the tortured fade-out of 'COITUS INTERRUPTUS'. Retaining FRYER and recruiting a new cast of collaborators including ROBERT GOTOBED of WIRE, TOVEY concocted an even more uncompromising electronic brew on follow-up set, 'INCONTINENT' (1981). The funereal 'SATURDAY NIGHT SPECIAL' (sadly/thankfully not a cover of the LYNYRD SKYNYRD chestnut! delete as appropriate) was released as a single in early '82, a third album, 'UNDER THE FLAG', appearing later that year. Dealing with the Falklands conflict, the likes of 'SCAPEGOAT' bore more than a passing resemblance to the territory later covered by labelmates DEPECHE MODE. Following 1984's 'GAG', TOVEY ditched the FAD GADGET moniker and, hooking up with American, BOYD RICE. cut a disappointing collaborative effort, 'EASY LISTENING FOR THE HARD OF HEARING' (1984). Two years on, 'SNAKES AND LADDERS' marked TOVEY's solo debut proper, the synth veteran increasingly couching his work in a more rock orientated context. TOVEY made an even more radical departure from his early work with 1989's folky 'TYRANNY AND THE HIRED HAND', subsequently teaming up with The PYROS, for 'GRAND UNION' (1991) and 'WORRIED MEN IN SECONDHAND SUITS' (1992).

Album rating: FIRESIDE FAVOURITES (*5) / INCONTINENT (*6) / UNDER THE FLAG (*6) / GAG (*6) / THE FAD GADGET SINGLES compilation (*6) / Frank Tovey: SNAKES AND LADDERS (*6) / CIVILIAN (*5) / TYRANNY AND THE HIRED HAND (*5) / GRAND UNION (*5) / WORRIED MEN AND SECOND HAND SUITS (*5)

FRANK TOVEY (b.Donegal, Ireland) – vocals, synthesizers, flute / **ERIC RADCLIFFE** – keyboards, guitar / **JOHN FRYER** – guitar, percussion / **PAUL WAUCLAIRE** – bass / **NICHOLAS CASH** – drums, percussion (ex-PRAG VEC) / **DANIEL MILLER** – drums, programming (ex-NORMAL)

Mute — not iss.

Oct 79. (7") *(MUTE 002)* **BACK TO NATURE. / THE BOX** [ ] [-]
Mar 80. (7") *(MUTE 006)* **RICKY'S HAND. / HANDSHAKE** [ ] [-]
Sep 80. (7") *(MUTE 009)* **INSECTICIDE. / FIRESIDE FAVOURITES** [ ] [-]
Sep 80. (lp) *(STUMM 3)* **FIRESIDE FAVOURITES** [ ] [-]
– Pedestraian / State of the nation / Salt Lake City Sunday / The box / Fireside favourites / Coitus interruptus / Newsreel / Insecticide / Arch of the aorta. *(re-iss. cd Jun91; CDSTUMM 3)*
Mar 81. (7") *(MUTE 012)* **MAKE ROOM. / LADY SHAVE** [ ] [-]

— **PETER BAHNER** – bass, guitar (ex-SKI PATROL); repl. WAUCLAIRE

— guests included **ROBERT GOTOBED** – drums (of WIRE) / **DAVID SIMMONDS** – keyboards / **BARBARA (BIJI) FRONT + ANNE CLIFT** – backing vocals

Dec 81. (lp/c) *(STUMM/CSTUMM 6)* **INCONTINENT** [ ] [-]
– Saturday night special / Incontinent / Blind eyes / Swallow it / King of the flies / Innocent bystanders / Diminished responsibility / Manual dexterity. *(cd-iss. Jun91 +=; CDSTUMM 6)* – Plain clothes.
Jan 82. (7") *(MUTE 017)* **SATURDAY NIGHT SPECIAL. / SWALLOW IT (live)** [ ] [-]
Apr 82. (7"/12") *(MUTE/12MUTE 021)* **KING OF THE FLIES. / PLAIN CLOTHES** [ ] [-]

— **DAVID SIMMONDS** now replaced RADCLIFFE who joined The ASSEMBLY

Sep 82. (7"/12") *(MUTE/12MUTE 024)* **LIFE ON THE LINE. / 4M** [ ] [-]
Sep 82. (lp/c) *(STUMM/CSTUMM 8)* **UNDER THE FLAG** [ ] [-]
– Under the flag I / Scapegoat / Love parasite / Plainsong / Wheels of fortune / Life on the line IV / The sheep look up / Cipher / For whom the bells toll / Under the flag II. *(cd-iss. Jun91; CDSTUMM 8)*
Jan 83. (7"/12") *(MUTE/12MUTE 026)* **FOR WHOM THE BELLS TOLL. / LOVE PARASITE** [ ] [-]

— **TOVEY, SIMMONDS, CASH, FRONT** added **JONI SACKETT** – backing vocals / **DAVID ROGERS** + guest **ROWLAND HOWARD** – drums

Oct 83. (7") *(7MUTE 028)* **I DISCOVER LOVE. / LEMMINGS ON LOVER'S ROCK** [ ] [-]
(12"+=) *(12MUTE 028)* – Lemming's storm.
Jan 84. (7"/12") *(7/12 MUTE 30)* **COLLAPSING NEW PEOPLE. / SPOIL THE CHILD** [ ] [-]
Feb 84. (lp/c) *(STUMM/CSTUMM 15)* **GAG** [ ] [-]
– Ideal world / Collapsing new people / I discover love / Jump / Sleep / One man's meat / Spoil the child / Stand up / Speak to me – Breathe in the air / The ring (hypnotic seduction of Dale) / Ad nauseam. *(cd-iss. Jun91; CDSTUMM 15)*
May 84. (7") *(7MUTE 033)* **ONE MAN'S MEAT. / SLEEP** [ ] [-]
(12"+=) *(12MUTE 033)* – Ideal world.

BOYD RICE & FRANK TOVEY

— collaboration rec. 1981 with **RICE** – synthesizers (solo artist)

Nov 84. (lp) *(STUMM 20)* **EASY LISTENING FOR THE HARD OF HEARING** [ ] [-]
(cd-iss. May96; CDSTUMM 20)

FRANK TOVEY

with **SIMMONDS / E.C. RADCLIFFE / CASH / ROGERS / GUY EVANS** – vibes

Aug 85. (7"/12") *(7/12 MUTE 39)* **LUXURY. / BED OF NAILS** [ ] [-]
Apr 86. (7") *(7MUTE 44)* **LUDDITE JOE. / CLEAN THIS ACT UP** [ ] [-]
(12"+=) *(12MUTE 44)* – Small world.
May 86. (cd/c/lp) *(CD/C+/STUMM 23)* **SNAKES AND LADDERS** [ ] [-]
– The cutting edge / Snakes and ladders / Shot in the dark / Concrete / Collapsing new people / Luxury / Small world / Luddite Joe / Megalomaniac. *(cd+=)* – Coitus interruptus / The sheep look up / Ideal world.

— now w/ **MARK JEFFERY** – drums, co-producer / **RICO CONNING** – instruments

Apr 88. (7"/12") *(7/12 MUTE 79)* **BRIDGE STREET SHUFFLE. / BRACE OF SHAKES** [ ] [-]
Jun 88. (cd/lp) *(CD+/STUMM 56)* **CIVILIAN** [ ] [-]
– New Jerusalem / Ultramarine / From the city to the Isle Of Dogs / Bridge St reet shuffle / The brotherhood / Diana / Unknown civilian / Desperate Dan.

— added **DAVID ASH** – guitars, piano / **PAUL RODDEN** – banjo / **NETO VAAANDRAGER** – fiddle, violin / **JEAN-MARIE CARROLL** – acoustic guitar, mandolin, etc / **MOLLY McANALLY BURKE** – banjo, guitar, vocals

Jul 89. (12"/cd-s) *(12/CD MUTE 100)* **SAM HALL. / RICKY'S HAND** [ ] [-]
Aug 89. (cd/c/lp) *(CD/C+/STUMM 73)* **TYRANNY AND THE HIRED HAND** [ ] [-]
– '31 depression blues / Hard times in the cotton mill / John Henry – Let your hammer ring / The Blantyre explosion / Money cravin' folks / All I got's gone / Midwife song / Sam Hall / Dark as a dungeon / Men of good fortune / Sixteen tons / North country blues / Buffalo skinners / Black lung song / Pastures of plenty / Joe Hill.

FRANK TOVEY & THE PYROS

with **PAUL RODDEN** – banjo, guitar / **JOHN CUTLIFFE** – banjo, guitar; plus **STEVE SMITH** – organ / **CHARLIE LLEWELLYN** – drums, percussion / **TRACEY BOOTH** – bodhran / **ELLIOT CARNEGIE** – harp / **TOZIE LYNCH** – bones

Apr 91. (7") **THE LIBERTY TREE. /** [ ] [-]
(12"+=/cd-s+=) –
May 91. (cd/c/lp) *(CD/C+/STUMM 84)* **GRAND UNION** [ ] [-]
– Bad day in Bow Creek / When the victim takes the tyrants place / Passing through / Bethnal Green tube disaster / Cities of the plain / Fallen angel / I.K.B. (R.I.P.) / The liberty tree / One November morning / The great attractor.

Oct 92. (cd/lp) *(CD+/STUMM 107)* **WORRIED MEN IN SECOND HAND SUITS** [ ] [-]
– Chasing the blues away / All that is mine / Just like other men / Only doing your job / Hey bailiff / Crow's nest blues / Opportunity's knocking / The hermit of Hermes Point / You won't get that from me / Doing time / Worried man.

– compilations, etc. –

Nov 86. (cd/c/lp; as FRANK TOVEY) *(CD/C+/STUMM 37)* **THE FAD GADGET SINGLES** [ ] [-]
– Back to nature / The box / Ricky's hand / Fireside favourites / Lady shave / Saturday night special / King of the flies / Life on the line / For whom the bells toll / I discover love / Collapsing new people. *(cd+=)* – Insecticide / 4M / Love parasite / One man's meat.

Th' FAITH HEALERS

Formed: Camden, London, England . . . late 80's by ROXANNE STEPHEN and TOM CULLINAN, who expanded the line-up with BEN HOPKIN and JOE DILWORTH (the latter also drummer with STEREOLAB). Along with STEREOLAB and PJ HARVEY, Th' FAITH HEALERS were one of the first bands on the roster of the (then) new indie label, 'Too Pure' (run by Richard Roberts and Paul Cox), for whom they released their debut EP, 'POP SONG', in 1990. Several further EP's hit the shops during the next couple of years, a debut album proper (not counting compilation, 'L') was finally released under the title of 'LIDO' in 1992. Well received by the music press for its repetitive, experimental lurch'n'roll (drifting between STEREOLAB and HAWKWIND!), the record saw th' 'HEALERS fashioning their own unique hybrid of post-modern nostalgic rock. Yet the group would only complete one further set, 'IMAGINARY FRIEND' (1993), bowing out the following year with a shared single, 'S.O.S.' flipped with MAMBO TAXI. Main songwriter, CULLINAN subsequently re-surfaced with a new band, QUICKSPACE SUPERSPORT, although the line-up went through an initial period of instability before stabilising around SEAN NEWSHAM, WENDY HARPER, MAX CORRADI and BARRY STILLWELL after the release of a debut single in early '95. Although CULLINAN initiated his own 'Kitty Kitty Corporation' imprint, the band also recorded for 'Love Train' and 'Domino', the nouveau Kraut-rockers quickly dropping the sporty side of their moniker with the release of an eponymous set in '96. Over the course of the next two years (and now with a new line-up of CULLINAN, NEWSHAM, NINA PASCALE, PAUL SHILTON and CHIN), two further albums hit the shops, the singles compilation 'SUPO SPOT' (1997) and 'PRECIOUS FALLING' (1998). • **Covered:** MOTHER SKY (Can) / etc. • **Trivia:** ROXANNE guested on MOOSE's 'XYZ' album in 1992.

Album rating: 'L' compilation (*6) / LIDO (*7) / IMAGINARY FRIEND (*5) / Quickspace: QUICKSPACE (*6) / SUPO SPOT compilation (*6) / PRECIOUS FALLING (*6)

ROXANNE STEPHEN – vocals / **TOM CULLINAN** – guitar / **BEN HOPKIN** – bass / **JOE DILWORTH** – drums (also of STEREOLAB)

Too Pure / Elektra

Jul 90. (12"ep) *(PURE 2)* **POP SONG. / DELORES / SLAG** [ ] [-]
Feb 91. (12"ep) *(PURE 3)* **A PICTURE OF HEALTH** [ ] [-]
– Gorgeous blue flower in my garden / Not a God / God.
Jan 92. (12"ep) *(PURE 6)* **IN LOVE** [ ] [-]
– Reptile smile / Super / Lovely.
Jun 92. (lp/cd) *(PURE/+CD 12) <61425>* **LIDO** [ ] [ ]
– This time / Word of advice / Hippy hole / Don't Jones me / Love song / Mother sky / It's easy being you / Spin half.
Oct 92. (12"ep/cd-ep) *(PURE/+CD 15)* **MR. LITANSKI** [ ] [-]
– Oh baby / Moona-Inna-Joona / My loser / Reptile smile.
Feb 93. (cd-ep) *(PURECD 18) <66327>* **DON'T JONES ME / GORGEOUS BLUE FLOWER / OH BABY / MY LOSER** [ ] [ ]
Oct 93. (lp/cd) *(PURE/+CD 27) <61585>* **IMAGINARY FRIEND** [ ] [ ] Jan94
– Sparkingly chime / Heart fog / See-saw / Kevin / The people / Curly lips / Everything, all at once forever / Run out groove.

Clawfist / not iss.

Mar 94. (7") *(XPIG 23)* **S.O.S. / ('B'side by Mambo Taxi)** [ ] [-]
—— split soon after above

– compilations, etc. –

Apr 92. (cd) *Too Pure; (31023) / Warners; <43019>* **'L'** (singles compilation) [ ] [ ] Jul95

QUICKSPACE SUPERSPORT

—— **TOM CULLINAN** – vocals, guitar / **SEAN NEWSHAM** – bass / **WENDY HARPER** – vocals, guitar / **BARRY STILLWELL** – keyboards / **MAX CORRADI** – drums

Kitty Kitty Corporation / not iss.

Feb 95. (7") *(CHOOSY 001)* **QUICKSPACE HAPPY SONG (NO.1). / UNIQUE SLIPPY** [ ] [-]

Love Train / not iss.

Aug 95. (7") *(PUBE 04)* **FOUND A WAY. / DO IT MY OWN WAY** [ ] [-]

Domino / not iss.

Oct 95. (12"ep/cd-ep) *(RUG 40 T/CD)* **SUPERPLUS EP** [ ] [-]
– Proplus / Scubaplus / Standard 8.

Kitty Kitty Corporation / not iss.

Apr 96. (7") *(CHOOSY 004)* **FRIEND. / WHERE HAVE ALL THE GOOD TIMES GONE** [ ] [-]
—— **NINA PASCALE** – vocals, guitar; repl. WENDY
Jun 96. (cd-ep) *(CHOOSY 005)* **RISE EP** [ ] [-]
– Rise / Docile / Riseteen sixtynine.

QUICKSPACE

—— **CULLINAN + NEWSHAM + PASCALE** recruited **PAUL SHILTON** – keyboards / **CHIN** – drums

Kitty Kitty Corporation / Slash

Nov 96. (lp/cd) *(CHOOSY 006/+CD) <422-828-924>* **QUICKSPACE** [ ] [ ] Nov97
– Swisher / Song for someone / Quasi-pfaff / Mousetail * / Winona / Docile one / Docile two. *<US repl.* with>* – Rise / Friend.
Jun 97. (lp/cd) *(CHOOSY 008/+CD)* **SUPO SPOT** (compilation of early singles) [ ] [-]
– Happy song No.1 / Unique slippy / Extra plus / Found a way / Do it my own way / Whiff and spoof song / Exemplary swishy / Friend / Where have all the good times gone / Song for NME.
1997. (7") *(182)* **AMIGO. / RISE** [ ] [-]
(above issued on 'Elefant')
Nov 97. (12"ep/cd-ep) *(CHOOSY 010/+CD)* **THE PRECIOUS MOUNTAIN EP** [ ] [-]
– Precious mountain / You used my death as a pretext to go running / Ennio's blues.
May 98. (7") *(CHOOSY 011)* **HADID. / QUEEN OF THE DOWNS** [ ] [-]
Jul 98. (7"ep/cd-ep) *(CHOOSY 014/+CD)* **PRECIOUS LITTLE EP** [ ] [-]
– Quickspace happy song (No.2) / Ming / Hadid / Queen of the downs.
Aug 98. (cd) *(CHOOSY 013CD)* **PRECIOUS FALLING** [ ] [-]
– Death + Annie / Take away / Mouse / 7 like that / Quickspace happy song #2 / Hadid / Melo / Minors / Cola Lola / Obvious / Walk me home / Mountain waltz / Goodbye precious mountain.

FAITH OVER REASON

Formed: Croydon, Surrey, England . . . early 1990 by MOIRA LAMBERT, who recruited BILL LLOYD, SIMON ROOTS and MARK WILSHER. Signed to 'Big Cat', the band released their eponymous debut EP in summer 1990, showcasing LAMBERT's emotive vocals (which graced the original 1990 version of ST. ETIENNE's 'Only Love Can Break Your Heart') and even attempting a version of Nick Drake's sublime 'NORTHERN SKY'. A second EP, 'BILLY BLUES', and an album of demos, 'EYES WIDE SMILE' (1991) followed before the band was put on ice as LAMBERT began a college course. With the addition of TEBO STEELE (as a replacement for ROOTS), a revamped FAITH OVER REASON re-emerged in summer '94 with a belated third EP, 'BLIND'. STEELE had already began to carve himself out a role as chief songwriter and the guitarist ended up penning most of the material on debut album, 'EASY' (1994). Produced by STEPHEN MALKMUS (mainman with labelmates, PAVEMENT), the album was met with mixed reviews as many critics bemoaned the fact that STEELE's guitar was often pushed way too far up in the mix, negating the vocal atmospherics provided by LAMBERT. Despite subsequent high profile support gigs with the likes of PAVEMENT and JEFF BUCKLEY, the musical differences eventually led to a split in the ranks, STEELE, LLOYD and WILSHER forming SOUP while LAMBERT carried on under the FAITH OVER REASON banner; although she later employed the services of former SUNDAYS sticksman, PATCH, no new material has been forthcoming.

Album rating: EYES WIDE SMILE (*5) / EASY (*5)

MOIRA LAMBERT (b.13 Oct'70, Chichester, England) – vocals, acoustic guitar / **SIMON ROOTS** (b. 1 Sep'70) – guitar / **BILL LLOYD** (b.17 Mar'71, London) – bass, keyboards / **MARK WILSHER** (b. 1 May'70) – drums

Big Cat / not iss.

Jul 90. (12"ep) *(ABB 17T)* **FAITH OVER REASON EP** [ ] [-]
– Believing in me / Northern sky / Fallen / Evangeline.
Aug 91. (12"ep/cd-ep) *(ABB 23 T/SCD)* **BILLY BLUES EP** [ ] [-]
– Billy Blue / Move closer / High in the sun / Ice queen.
Sep 91. (lp/cd) *(ABB/+CD 27X)* **EYES WIDE SMILE** (demos) [ ] [-]
– Lullabye (mother love) / Sofya / So free / Northern sky / Song for Jessica / Evangeline / Not so / Eyes wide smile / Fallen.
—— (late '91) **TEBO STEELE** – guitar; repl. ROOTS
Jul 94. (12"ep/cd-ep) *(ABB 58 T/SCD)* **BLIND EP** [ ] [-]
Aug 94. (lp/cd) *(ABB 63/+CD)* **EASY** [ ] [-]
—— LAMBERT was left holding the group name and although she recruited PATCH from The SUNDAYS, the outfit subsequently vanished after releasing nothing. The rest formed SOUP, who did likewise.

Tav FALCO

Born: raised- Arkansas, USA . . . moved to Memphis, Tennessee where he subsequently formed The PANTHER BURNS in the early 80's alongside former BOX TOPS and BIG STAR guru ALEX CHILTON. Signed to 'Rough Trade', the band (completed by JIM DUCKWORTH and RONALD MILLER) made their debut in late '81 with a cover of Johnny Burnette's 'TRAIN KEPT A ROLLIN'. An album's worth of "Wreck-abilly"-style dixie blues, 'BEHIND THE MAGNOLIA CURTAIN', followed a couple of months later, CHILTON employing his not inconsiderable production experience. A parting of the ways was imminent however, the latter going solo and being replaced by JIM SCLAVUNOS prior to the recording of 1982's 'BLOW YOUR TOP' EP. DUCKWORTH was the next to leave, his departure to The GUN CLUB resulting in a three year sabbatical for TAV. In 1985, CHILTON accompanied TAV FALCO'S PANTHER BURNS (as they were now called) to Sam Philips' Memphis studio, recording a comeback mini-set for the French-based 'New

Rose' label, 'SUGAR DITCH REVISITED'. They continued to release the odd EP until 1987's covers album, 'THE WORLD WE KNEW', FALCO renowned for his wild interpretations of blues & R&B standards; the man was to issue a similar collection in the shape of 'RETURN OF THE BLUE PANTHER' (1990). The turn of the decade saw TAV strike out on his own for the 'LIFE SENTENCE' (1991) album although CHILTON and DICKINSON were present in a guest capacity.

Album rating: BEHIND THE MAGNOLIA CURTAIN (*5) / SUGAR DITCH REVISTED mini (*4) / THE WORLD WE KNEW (*4) / RED DEVIL (*4) / MIDNIGHT IN MEMPHIS (*5) / RETURN OF THE BLUE PANTHER (*4) / LIFE SENTENCE (*4) / SHADOW DANCER (*4) / LOVE'S LAST WARNING (THE BEST OF TAV FALCO'S PANTHER BURNS) compilation (*6)

PANTHER BURNS

TAV FALCO – vocals, guitar / **'LX' ALEX CHILTON** – guitar, drums, producer (ex-BIG STAR, ex-BOX TOPS) / **JIM DUCKWORTH** – guitar, drums / **RONALD MILLER** – bass

Rough Trade Rough Trade

Oct 81. (7") *(RT 077)* **TRAIN KEPT A ROLLIN'. / RED HEADED WOMAN** ☐ ☐

Dec 81. (lp) *(ROUGH 32)* <ROUGH-US 16> **BEHIND THE MAGNOLIA CURTAIN** ☐ ☐
– Come on little mama / She's the one that got it / Hey high school baby / Brazil / You're undecided / Ooee baby / River of love / Snake drive / Blind man / Where the Rio de Rosa flows / Snatch it back / Bourgeois blues / St. Louis blues / Moving on down the line. *(re-iss. Aug87 by TAV FALCO'S PANTHER BURNS on 'Fan Club' lp/cd; FC 029/+CD) (cd re-iss. May94 on 'New Rose'; 422135)*

— **JIM SCLAVUNOS** – percussion, vocals; repl. CHILTON who went solo again

Nov 82. (12"ep) *(RT 114T)* **BLOW YOUR TOP** ☐ -
– I'm on this rocket / Pantherman / Love is my business / Bertha Lou.

— they split for a couple of years, DUCKWORTH joined The GUN CLUB

TAV FALCO PANTHER BURNS

New Rose New Rose

Nov 85. (m-lp) *(ROSE 73)* **SUGAR DITCH REVISITED** ☐ ☐
– Lonely avenue / Money talks / Working on a building / Arkansas stomp / White silver sands / Time, the go-go queen. *(cd-iss. May94; 422137)*

Feb 86. (7"ep) **WARRIOR SAM EP** ☐ -
(above issued on 'Criminal Damage')

Sep 86. (7"ep) **SHAKE RAG EP** - - French
– Oh, how she dances / Drifting heart / Poor man / Little puppies and one old shaggy hound.

Mar 87. (7"ep) *(NEW 86)* **DROP YOUR MASK EP** ☐ -
– Tram / Ode to Shetar / Ditch digging / She's the one to blame.

Jun 87. (lp/c/cd) *(ROSE 113/+C/CD)* **THE WORLD WE KNEW** ☐ ☐
– Do the robot / She's a bad motorcycle / Pass the hatchet / I'm doubtful of your love / etc *(cd+=)* – SHAKE RAG EP *(cd re-iss. May94; 422140)*

Mar 88. (lp/cd) *(ROSE 140/+CD)* **RED DEVIL** ☐ ☐
– Oh, how she dances / Drifting heart / Poor man / Little puppies and one old shaggy hound / Tram / Ode to Shetar / Ditch digging / She's the one to blame. *(also iss.as 7"box; NR 335) (cd+=)* – SUGAR DITCH

Aug 89. (lp/cd) *(ROSE 185/+CD)* **MIDNIGHT IN MEMPHIS (live 10th Anniversary)** ☐ ☐
– Oh, how she dances / Bertha Lou / Shade tree mechanic / With your love / Jungle rock / It's only make believe / Big road blues / Goldfinger / She's the one that's got it / Memphis beat / Love whip / The world we knew / Ditch diggin' / Girl after girl / Do the robot / Same thing. *(cd re-iss. May94; 422141)*

Jul 90. (lp/cd) *(ROSE 215/+CD)* **RETURN OF THE BLUE PANTHER** (covers) ☐ ☐
– Mala femmina / You believe everyone but me / I'm movin' on / Knot in my pocket / I got a woman / Rock me baby / Surfside date / I got love if you want it / Girls on fire: a movie theme / Love whip / Fun mob / Mala femmina. *<US cd-iss. 1994 on 'Triple X'; 51051>*

— now with a host of guests including CHILTON + DICKINSON

1991. (cd) *(ROSE 264CD)* **LIFE SENTENCE** ☐ -
– My mind was messed up at the time / Torture / Vampire from Havana / Make me know you're mine / Go on home / Auto sapien / Guarda che luna / Oh, girls, girls / (I'm gonna) Dig myself a hole / Sent up / What's wrong / Why was I born / Only the lonely. *(re-iss. May94; 422136) <US-iss.1994 on 'Triple X'; 51095>*

Intercord Upstart

Feb 96. (cd) *(IRS 993513CD)* <017> **SHADOW DANCER** ☐ ☐ Nov95
– Invocation of the shadow dancer / Funnel of love / Sway / Love's last warning / Lotus blossom / Cuando vedrai la mia raggazza / Born to cry / I'll take care of you / Have I the right / Music maestro please / Guarda che luna / Born too late / Shadow dancer. *(cd re-iss. Nov96 on 'Last Call'; 422246-2)*

Sympathy F Sympathy F

Sep 96. (lp/cd) *<(SFTRI 460/+CD)>* **DISAPPEARING ANGELS** ☐ ☐

– compilations, etc. –

Aug 86. (c) *Frenzi; (C 37)* **NOW** ☐ -
(re-iss. 1988 on 'NBTFZ'; NBTFZ 001)

Oct 92. (lp/cd) *Marilyn; (FM 1011/+CD)* **UNRELEASED SESSIONS** ☐ -

Apr 94. (cd) *Marilyn; (USMCD 1026)* **DEEP IN THE SHADOWS** ☐ -

Nov 96. (cd) *Last Call; (422088)* **LOVE'S LAST WARNING (THE BEST OF TAV FALCO'S PANTHER BURNS)** ☐ ☐

Mar 97. (cd) *Munster; (MRCD 111)* **SHADOW ANGELS AND DISAPPEARING DANCERS** ☐ ☐

FALL

Formed: Salford, Manchester, England . . . late '76 by vocalist MARK E. SMITH, guitarist MARTIN BRAMAH and bassist TONY FRIEL. Completing the line-up with UNA BAINES (electric piano) and KARL BURNS (drums), the unusual punk band completed a 1977 session for Radio One's John Peel show, before signing to indie outlet, 'Step Forward'. In summer of the following year, The FALL released their debut, the 'BINGO-MASTERS BREAK-OUT! EP'. Sharp-witted right from the outset, the shrieking MARK E traversed the minefield of punk sterotypes, the last track, 'REPETITION' a slow teaser to the other quickfire numbers, 'PSYCHO MAFIA' and 'BINGO-MASTER'. The first of many personnel changes was to occur soon after, MARC RILEY and YVONNE PAWLETT coming in for the departing FRIEL (to The PASSAGE) and BAINES (to The BLUE ORCHIDS) respectively. A weird, disappointing follow-up, 'IT'S THE NEW THING' was thankfully not on their glorious Bob Sergeant-produced debut album, 'LIVE AT THE WITCH TRIALS'. Unleashed to an ever-changing alternative rock audience (who were probably now holding down office jobs while daydreaming of their pogoing dancefloor days of yore!?), the studio set (recorded in two days) packed a lyrical angst not heard since the days of The VELVET UNDERGROUND (one of MARK E's inspirators). Quirky punk tracks such as 'FUTURES AND PASTS' and 'REBELLIOUS JUKEBOX' fitted in nicely with longer excursions into experimentation, 'FRIGHTENED' and 'MUSIC SCENE', making this a classic debut worthy of more listeners. MARK E was now in full control after the remaining founding members, BRAMAH and BURNS bailed out (also joining BLUE ORCHIDS and The PASSAGE) to be subsequently replaced by STEVE HANLEY and MIKE LEIGH respectively. What came next was a piece of punk rock genius, the single 'ROWCHE RUMBLE' ditching conventional rhythms in mindblowing style. PAWLETT left the band soon after and was replaced by guitarist, CRAIG SCANLON, just in time for yet another masterful set that year, 'DRAGNET' (1979). A darker, even more experimental affair, MARK E's twisted tales of life's stranger characters were summed up best on tracks such as 'MUZOREWI'S DAUGHTER', 'A FIGURE WALKS', 'SPECTRE VS. RECTOR' and the "rockabilly" 'PSYKICK DANCEHALL'. The FALL kickstarted the 80's in fine fashion with another punkabilly classic, 'FIERY JACK', an ever better version appearing on 'THE FALL LIVE – TOTALE'S TURNS', their first for 'Rough Trade' a couple of months later. With PAUL HANLEY taking over the vacant drum stool, Mark and Co. delivered two more classic 45's, 'HOW I WROTE ELASTIC MAN' and 'TOTALLY WIRED', their third studio set, 'GROTESQUE (AFTER THE GRAMME)', being released later in 1980. An impressive if not brilliant album, it featured such acidic, "Manc-abilly" screechers, 'THE CONTAINER DRIVERS', 'PAY YOUR RATES' and 'NEW FACE IN HELL', the kazoo backing provided by the group's manager and MARK E's girlfriend, KAY CARROLL. Next up was another unusual concept, the 10" mini-set that was 'SLATES' (1981), a patchy affair that nevertheless contained another gem, 'AN OLDER LOVER ETC'. With founder member KARL BURNS (the second drummer! and extra keyboard player) now back in tow, The FALL signed to 'Kamera', releasing another diamond of a single, 'LIE DREAM OF A CASINO SOUL' (backed by 'FANTASTIC LIFE' on the B-side; like all 45's at this time, not from the accompanying album). They finally found some degree of commercial success when 1982's 'HEX ENDUCTION HOUR' broke silently into the Top 75. Recorded in Iceland, it was sixty minutes of lyrical abandon, excellent songs, however confusing, came in the shape of 'THE CLASSICAL', 'WHO MAKES THE NAZIS?', 'HIP PRIEST' and their most commercial tune to date, 'JAW-BONE AND THE AIR-RIFLE'. Later that year, the most prolific band on earth issued yet another long-player, 'ROOM TO LIVE', a more self-indulgent delivery that disappointed their growing college/uni fanbase. In 1983, they lost the talents of MARC RILEY, who formed his own outfit, The CREEPERS (another great band!), KAY also leaving after she split (not for the first time!) with the grumpy one. Returning to 'Rough Trade', The FALL excelled once more with two splendid singles, 'THE MAN WHOSE HEAD EXPANDED' and 'KICKER CONSPIRACY', before MARK E's new Californian girlfriend, BRIX, came into the fold. She immediately made her mark, augmenting on vocals, playing guitar and co-writing a few numbers on The FALL's late 1983 album, 'PERVERTED BY LANGUAGE'. This set was another to whet the appetite of the faithful (and another illustrious indie chart topper), MARK's mental execution of tracks like 'EAT Y'SELF FITTER' and 'TEMPO HOUSE' the pick of a bizarre bunch. Advancing to 'Beggars Banquet', MARK E, BRIX E and Co. delivered a couple of odd pop singles in the shape of 'OH BROTHER' and 'C.R.E.E.P.', the records not featuring on their forthcoming eighth set, 'THE WONDERFUL AND FRIGHTENING WORLD OF . . .' (1984). Their buoyant rockabilly was back in full flow on two numbers, 'LAY OF THE LAND' and '2 x 4', while GAVIN FRIDAY of The VIRGIN PRUNES guested on a couple of tracks. A month later, a 12"ep, 'CALL FOR ESCAPE ROUTE', saw The FALL experimenting once more, although this was their last with PAUL HANLEY, who was superceded by the numerous talents of SIMON ROGERS (he had been a member of panpipes afficionados, INCANTATION!). With STEVE HANLEY on summer vacation in 1985, the band released the disappointing 'COULDN'T GET AHEAD' single, its flipside containing their first cover, Gene Vincent's 'ROLLIN DANY'. STEVE was back in time to record their most accessible recording to date, 'THIS NATION'S SAVING GRACE' (1985). Regarded as their best work since their debut, the UK Top 60 album housed the excellent 'PAINTWORK', 'MY NEW HOUSE' and 'I AM DAMO SUZUKI', the latter track MARK E's tribute (sort of!) to the CAN singer. BURNS jumped ship after the obligatory set of singles, SIMON WOOLSTENCROFT taking his place for The FALL's first hit (well, No.75), a cover version of The Other Half's 'MR. PHARMACIST'. This seemed to pay off commercially, especially when the accompanying (for once) 'BEND SINISTER' album

reached the dizzy heights of the Top 40 in 1986. Another minor hit 45, 'HEY! LUCIANI' (Top 60 this time), preceded the following year's Top 30 embarassment coming in the shape of R. Dean Taylor's 'THERE'S A GHOST IN MY HOUSE'. Some time later in 1987, BRIX brought in her old friend, MARSHA SCHOFIELD (both were in BANDA DRATSING together), the keyboard player and vocalist arriving in time for two more hits, 'HIT THE NORTH' and 'VICTORIA' (the latter from the pen of Ray Davies). Now without SIMON, who stayed on as their producer, MARK E and Co. hit the charts (Top 20!) with 'THE FRENZ EXPERIMENT' (1988), a confused set that nevertheless contained one standout song, 'CARRY BAG MAN'. Having also been a friend of ballet dancer, MICHAEL CLARK (who used FALL tapes as his backing soundtrack), MARK E and The FALL collaborated with the bare-arsed performer on the band's next ambitious concept, 'I AM KURIOUS ORANJ' (1988). It was indeed, curious, although the Top 60 album did have its moments, especially in 'CAB IT UP!' and a tongue-in-cheek rendition of William Blake's 'JERUSALEM' (segued with the 'DOG IS LIFE' poem). A concert set, 'SEMINAL LIVE' (1989) filled in time during which MARK and BRIX split up, the blonde (who had initiated her own band, ADULT NET, some time ago) eventually becoming the girlfriend of posh/cockney (you choose) classical violinist, NIGEL KENNEDY; he had previously guested on an earlier FALL album (she stunned many after appearing on 'This Is Your Life', which looked back over NIGEL's short career). BRAMAH was now back in the fold, enrolling in time for their umpteenth long-player, 'EXTRICATE' (1990), their first album jointly controlled by the group's new imprint, 'Cog Sinister' and major 'Fontana' label. Premiered by a hit version of Cold Cut's 'TELEPHONE THING', the cynical but accessible set featured other acidic attacks, 'SING! HARPY', 'THE LITTLEST REBEL' and two more obscure covers, 'POPCORN DOUBLE FEATURE' (Searchers) and 'BLACK MONK THEME' (Monks). MARK then trimmed the band down to a quartet, retaining only CRAIG, STEVE and JOHN to record an excellent SID VICIOUS-esque version of Big Bopper's 'WHITE LIGHTNING'. This minor hit was followed by a uncharacteristic flop, 'HIGH TENSION LINE', although both tracks appeared on the follow-up album, 'SHIFT-WORK' (1991), which added a fifth member, violinist KENNY BRADY. Split into two, titled sides, the UK Top 20 record was highlighted by two more excellent pieces of wordplay, 'EDINBURGH MAN' (still makes me sad) and their umpteenth rockabilly delivery, 'A LOT OF WIND' (as in, you talk ...). BRADY was let go soon after, DAVID BUSH coming in as a more permanent fixture on their next set, 'CODE: SELFISH' (1992). The album disappointed many of the faithful, although some FALL diehards regard it as one of the best (I'm in the former, I'm afraid), its re-working of Hank Williams' 'JUST WAITING' not the MARK E of old, although the hit single, 'FREE RANGE' gets back to grips. Moving to 'Permanent' records (not the most appropriate label title for them), MARK and the lads released their biggest seller to date, 'THE INFOTAINMENT SCAN', which went Top 10 in 1993. Short of a classic MARK E song, it collected together another bunch of covers, this time in the shape of Sister Sledge's 'LOST IN MUSIC', S. Bent's (who?!) 'I'M GOING TO SPAIN' and Lee Perry's 'WHY ARE PEOPLE GRUDGEFUL?' (a Top 50 hit). For many, The FALL "lost it" from then on, their formula of sticking several good (not brilliant) songs together with a few obscure covers saw their fanbase dwindle dramatically. Early in '94, a collaboration between MARK and The INSPIRAL CARPETS on the brilliant 'I WANT YOU' single gave him another hit, the mainman subsequently being invited to do similar things for other acts (notably, COLD CUT and DOSE). The return of KARL BURNS for the disappointing 'MIDDLE CLASS REVOLT' (Top 50, 1994) and BRIX for the bittersweet 'CEREBRAL CAUSTIC' (Top 75, 1995), did little to rectify this change in commercial climate. Now signed to 'Jet' records (once home to ELO!), they added JULIA NAGLE and a few guest members to the fold for their next effort, 'THE LIGHT USER SYNDROME' (1996), gaining some critical respect once again, as well as brief chart action. Who knows where The FALL are going, hopefully the clue's not in their moniker as they've produced a wealth of fantastic alternative rock over the last twenty years. Come on MARK E. • **Other covers:** A DAY IN THE LIFE (Beatles) / LEGEND OF XANADU (Dave Dee, Beaky, Mick and Tich) / SHUT UP! (Monks) / JUNK MAN (McFree) / WAR (Slapp Happy) / I'M NOT SATISFIED (Frank Zappa) / JUST WAITING (Hank Williams) / ROADHOUSE (John Barry) / STAY AWAY (OLD WHITE TRAIN) (Johnny Paycheck) / LAST CHANCE TO TURN AROUND (hit; Gene Pitney) / JUNGLE ROCK (Hank Mizell). • **Trivia:** MARK E. featured on TACKHEAD b-side of 'Dangerous Sex' in mid 1990, alongside ADRIAN SHERWOOD and GARY CLAIL. Just previous to this, he had a solo track 'ERROR-ORROR I' for the Various Artists compilation 'HOME'.

Album rating: LIVE AT THE WITCH TRIALS (*9) / DRAGNET (*8) / THE FALL LIVE (*6) / GROTESQUE (AFTER THE GRAMME) (*7) / SLATES (*6) / HEX ENDUCTION HOUR (*7) / ROOM TO LIVE (*6) / PERVERTED BY LANGUAGE (*7) / THE WONDERFUL AND FRIGHTENING WORLD OF . . . (*7) / THIS NATION'S SAVING GRACE (*8) / BEND SINISTER (*7) / THE FRENZ EXPERIMENT (*6) / I AM KURIOUS, ORANJ (*7) / SEMINAL LIVE (*4) / EXTRICATE (*8) / SHIFT-WORK (*8) / CODE: SELFISH (*7) / THE INFOTAINMENT SCAN (*7) / MIDDLE CLASS REVOLT (*6) / CELEBRAL CAUSTIC (*6) / THE TWENTY-SEVEN POINTS (*5) / THE LIGHT USER SYNDROME (*7) / LEVITATE (*6) / 458489 A-SIDES compilation (*8) / 458489 B-SIDES compilation (*7)

MARK E. SMITH (b. MARK EDWARD SMITH, 5 Mar'57) – vocals / **TONY FRIEL** – bass / **MARTIN BRAMAH** – guitar / **UNA BAINES** – electric piano / **KARL BURNS** – drums

Step Forward | I.R.S.

Jun 78. (7"ep) *(SF 7)* **BINGO-MASTERS BREAK-OUT!** [ ] [-]
– Psycho Mafia / Bingo-Master / Repitition.

— **MARC RILEY** – bass repl. (ERIC and JOHNNIE BROWN) who had repl. FRIEL (He formed The PASSAGE) / **YVONNE PAWLETT** – keyboards repl. BAINES who formed BLUE ORCHIDS

Nov 78. (7") *(SF 9)* **IT'S THE NEW THING. / VARIOUS TIMES** [ ] [-]

Jan 79. (lp) *(SFLP 1)* *<SP 003>* **LIVE AT THE WITCH TRIALS** [ ] [ ]
– Frightened / Crap rap 2 – Like to blow / Rebellious jukebox / No Xmas for John Quays / Mother-sister! / Industrial estate / Underground medecin / Two steps back / Live at the Witch Trials / Futures and pasts / Music scene. *(cd-iss. Jun97 on 'Cog Sinister – Voiceprint'; COGVP 103CD) <US cd-iss. 1997 on 'Resurgent'; 4107>*

— **MARK E.** (now sole founder), **RILEY** (now guitar) and **PAWLETT** recruited **STEVE HANLEY** (b.20 May'59, Dublin, Ireland) – bass repl. BRAMAH who also joined BLUE ORCHIDS / **MIKE LEIGH** – drums repl. BURNS who also joined The PASSAGE and P.I.L.

Jul 79. (7") *(SF 11)* **ROWCHE RUMBLE. / IN MY AREA** [ ] [-]

— **CRAIG SCANLON** (b. 7 Dec'60) – guitar (RILEY now guitar, keyboards) repl. PAWLETT

Oct 79. (lp) *(SFLP 4)* **DRAGNET** [ ] [-]
– Psykick dancehall / A figure walks / Printhead / Dice man / Before the Moon falls / Your heart out / Muzorewi's daughter / Flat of angles / Choc-stock / Spectre vs. rector / Put away. *(re-iss. Dec90 lp/cd; SFAL/SPLPCD 4)*

Jan 80. (7") *(SF 13)* **FIERY JACK. / SECOND DARK AGE / PSYKICK DANCEHALL II** [ ] [-]

Rough Trade | not iss.

May 80. (lp) *(ROUGH 10)* **THE FALL LIVE – TOTALE'S TURNS (IT'S NOW OR NEVER) (live)** [ ] [-]
– (intro) – Fiery Jack / Rowche rumble / Muzorewi's daughter / In my area / Choc-stock / Spectre vs. rector 2 / Cary Grant's wedding / That man / New puritan / No Xmas for John Quays. *(cd-iss. Nov92 on 'Dojo'; DOJOCD 83)*

— **PAUL HANLEY** – drums repl. LEIGH

Jun 80. (7") *(RT 048)* **HOW I WROTE ELASTIC MAN. / CITY HOBGOBLINS** [ ] [-]

Sep 80. (7") *(RT 056)* **TOTALLY WIRED. / PUTTA BLOCK** [ ] [-]

— **KAY CARROLL** their manager augmented p/t on backing vocals, kazoo

Nov 80. (lp) *(ROUGH 18)* **GROTESQUE (AFTER THE GRAMME)** [ ] [ ]
– Pay your rates / English scheme / New face in Hell / C'n'c Smithering / The container drivers / Impression of J. Temperance / In the park / W.M.C. – Blob 59 / Gramme Friday / The N.W.R.A. *(<cd-iss. Sep93 on 'Castle'; CLACD 391>) (cd re-iss. Jun98 on 'Essential'; ESMCD 640)*

Apr 81. (10"m-lp) *(RT 071)* **SLATES** [ ] [-]
– Middle mass / An older lover etc. / Prole art threat / Fit and working again / Slates, slags, etc. / Leave the capitol.

— **KARL BURNS** – drums returned now alongside **SMITH, RILEY, SCANLON, S and P HANLEY**

Kamera not iss.

Nov 81. (7") *(ERA 001)* **LIE DREAM OF A CASINO SOUL. / FANTASTIC LIFE** [ ] [-]

Mar 82. (lp) *(KAM 005)* **HEX ENDUCTION HOUR** [71] [-]
– The classical / Jaw-bone and the air-rifle / Hip priest / Fortress – Deer park / Mere psued mag. ed / Winter / Winter 2 / Just step s'ways / Who makes the Nazis? / Iceland / And this day. *(re-iss. 1987 on 'Line'; LILP 400126) (<cd-iss. Sep89 & Mar98 ; LICD 900126>)*

Apr 82. (7") *(ERA 004)* **LOOK KNOW. / I'M INTO C.B.** [ ] [-]

Nov 82. (lp) *(KAM)* **ROOM TO LIVE** [ ] [-]
– Joker hysterical face / Marquee cha-cha / Hard life in the country / Room to live / Detective instinct / Solicitor in studio / Papal visit. *(re-iss. Oct87 on 'Line'; LILP 400109) (cd-iss. Apr98 on 'Cog Sinister'; COGVP 105CD) <US cd-iss. 1998 on 'Resurgent'; 4257>*

— reverted to quintet when RILEY left to form MARC RILEY & THE CREEPERS (note that their manager and p/t member KAY CARROLL also departed)

Rough Trade not iss.

Jun 83. (7") *(RT 133)* **THE MAN WHOSE HEAD EXPANDED. / LUDD GANG** [ ] [-]

Oct 83. (d7") *(RT 143)* **KICKER CONSPIRACY. // WINGS / CONTAINER DRIVERS (live) / NEW PURITANS (live)** [ ] [-]

— added **LAURA-ELISE** (now BRIX E. SMITH) (b. California, USA) – guitar, vocals (ex-BANDA DRATSING) P. HANLEY added keyboards and BURNS added lead bass to their repertoire

Dec 83. (lp/c) *(ROUGH/+C 62)* **PERVERTED BY LANGUAGE** [ ] [-]
– Eat y'self fitter / Neighbourhood of infinity / Garden / Hotel Bloedel / I feel voxish / Tempo house / Hexen definitive / Strife knot. *(re-iss. Oct87 on 'Line'; LILP 400116) (cd-iss. Sep89+=; LICD 900116)* – Oh! brother / God-box / C.R.E.E.P. / Pat-trip dispenser. *(<cd re-iss. Sep93 on 'Castle'; CLACD 392>) (cd re-iss. Feb98 on 'Cog Sinister – Voiceprint'; COGVP 104CD) (cd re-iss. Jun98 on 'Essential'; ESMCD 639)*

Beggars Banquet Beggars Banquet

Jun 84. (7") *(BEG 110)* **OH BROTHER. / GOD-BOX** [ ] [-]
(12"+=) *(BEG 110T)* – ('A'instrumental).

Aug 84. (7") *(BEG 116)* **C.R.E.E.P. / PAT-TRIP DISPENSER** [ ] [-]
(12"green+=/12"s) *(BEG 116T/+P)* – ('A'extended).

— added **GAVIN FRIDAY** – some vocals (of VIRGIN PRUNES) (on next 2 releases)

Sep 84. (lp/c) *(<BEGA/+C 58>)* **THE WONDERFUL AND FRIGHTENING WORLD OF . . .** [62] [ ]
– Lay of the land / 2 x 4 / Copped it / Elves / Slang king / Bug day / Stephen song / Craigness / Disney's dream debased. *(re-iss. Jul88 on 'Beggars Banquet' lp/c)(cd+=; BBL/+C 58)(BBL 58CD)* – Oh! brother / Draygo's guilt / God-box / Clear off! / C.R.E.E.P. / Pat-trip dispenser / No bulbs.

Oct 84. (12"ep) *(BEG 120E)* **CALL FOR ESCAPE ROUTE** [ ] [-]
– Draygo's Guilt / No bulbs / Clear Off!.
(with free-7") **NO BULBS 3. / SLANG KING**

— **SIMON ROGERS** – bass, keyboards repl. P. HANLEY (he cont. with KISS THE BLADE) (GAVIN returned to VIRGIN PRUNES and S. HANLEY took a holiday)

Jul 85. (7") *(BEG 134)* **COULDN'T GET AHEAD. / ROLLIN' DANY** [ ] [ ]
(12"+=) *(BEG 134T)* – Petty (thief) lout.

— **STEVE HANLEY** returned to join **MARK E., BRIX, CRAIG, KARL and SIMON**

Sep 85. (lp/c)(cd) *(<BEGA/BEGC 47)(BEGA 67CD>)* **THIS NATION'S SAVING GRACE** [54] [ ]
– Mansion / Bombast / Barmy / What you need / Spoilt Victorian child / L.A. / Out of the quantifier / My new house / Paintwork / I am Damo Suzuki / To nkroachment: yarbles. *(re-iss. Feb90 lp/c)(cd+=; BBL/+C 67)(BBL 67CD)* – Vixen / Couldn't get ahead / Pretty (thief) lout / Rollin' Dany / Cruiser's creek.

Oct 85. (7") *(BEG 150)* **CRUISER'S CREEK. / L.A.** [ ] [-]
(12"+=) *(BEG 150T)* – Vixen.

Jul 86. (7") *(BEG 165)* **LIVING TOO LATE. / HOT AFTER-SHAVE BOP** [ ] [-]
(12"+=) *(BEG 165T)* – Living too long.

— **JOHN SIMON WOOLSTENCROFT** (b.19 Jan'63, Altringham, England) – drums (ex-WEEDS) repl. BURNS who formed THIRST

Sep 86. (7") *(BEG 168)* **MR. PHARMICIST. / LUCIFER OVER LANCASHIRE** [75] [ ]
(12"+=) *(BEG 168T)* – Auto-tech pilot.

Oct 86. (lp/c)(cd) *(<BEGA/BEGC 75)(BEGA 75CD>)* **BEND SINISTER** [36] [ ]
– R.O.D. / Dktr. Faustus / Shoulder pads #1 / Mr. Pharmicist / Gross chapel – British grenadiers / U.S. 80's-90's / Terry Waite sez / Bournemouth runner / Riddler / Shoulder pads #2. *(cd-iss. Jan88 +=)* – Living too late / Auto-tech pilot.

Nov 86. (7") *(BEGA 176)* **HEY! LUCIANI. / ENTITLED** [59] [ ]
(12"+=) *(BEG 176T)* – Shoulder pads.

Apr 87. (7") *(BEG 187)* **THERE'S A GHOST IN MY HOUSE. / HAF FOUND, BORMAN** [30] [ ]
(12"+=/c-s+=) *(BEG 187 T/C)* – Sleepdebt / Snatches / Mark'll sink us.

— added **MARSHA SCHOFIELD** (b.1963, Brooklyn, N.Y.) – keyboards, vocals of ADULT NET, (ex BANDA DRATSING)

Oct 87. (7"/7"pic-d) *(BEG 200/+P)* **HIT THE NORTH. / (part 2)** [57] [ ]
(12"+=) *(BEG 200T)* – Australians in Europe.
(cd-s+=) *BEG 200C)* – Northerns in Europe / (Hit the north versions).

— reverted back to sextet of **MARK E., BRIX, CRAIG, JOHN S., STEVE** and **MARSHA** when **SIMON** became their producer & studio guitarist only

Jan 88. (7") *(BEG 206)* **VICTORIA. / TUFF LIFE BOOGIE** [35] [ ]
(12"+=) *(BEG 206T)* – Guest informant / Twister.

Mar 88. (lp/c)(cd) *(BEGA/BEGC 91)(BEGA 91CD) <6987>* **THE FRENZ EXPERIMENT** [19] [ ]
– Frenz / Carry bag man / Get a hotel / Victoria / Athlete cured / In these times / The steak place / Bremen nacht / Guest informant (excerpt) / Oswald defence lawyer. *(c/cd+=)*– Tuff life boogie / Guest informant / Twister / There's a ghost in my house / Hit the north (part 1).

Oct 88. (lp/c)(cd) *(BEGA/BEGC 96)(BEGA 96CD) <9582>* **I AM KURIOUS, ORANJ** [54] [ ]
– New big prinz / Overture from 'I Am Curious, Orange' / Dog is life – Jerusalem / Wrong place, right time / Guide me soft * / C.D. win fall 2088 ad / Yes, o yes / Van plague? / Bad news girl / Cab it up! / Last nacht * / Big new priest *. *(c+=/cd+= *)*

Nov 88. (d7"ep/d3"cd-ep) *(FALL 2 B/CD)* **JERUSALEM / ACID PRIEST 2088. / BIG NEW PRINZ / WRONG PLACE, RIGHT TIME** [59] [-]

Jun 89. (7") *(BEG 226)* **CAB IT UP. / DEAD BEAT DESCENDENT (out take from ballet** [ ] [-]
(12"+=) *(BEG 226T)* – Kurious oranj (live) / Hit the north (live).

Beggars Banquet – Lowdown not iss.

Jun 89. (lp/c)(cd) *(BBL/+C 102)(BBL 102CD) <9807>* **SEMINAL LIVE (some studio)** [40] [-]
– Dead beat descendant / Pinball machine / H.O.W. / Squid law / Mollusc in Tyrol / 2 x 4 / Elf prefix – L.A. / Victoria / Pay your rates / Cruiser's creek. *(c+=/cd+=)* – Kurious oranj / Hit the north / In these times / Frenz.

— **MARTIN BRAMAH** – guitar returned to repl. BRIX E. who continued with ADULT NET.

Cog Sinister-Fontana Fontana

Jan 90. (7"/c-s) *(SIN/+MC 4)* **TELEPHONE THING. / BRITISH PEOPLE IN HOT WEATHER** [58] [-]
(12"+=)(cd-s+=) *(SIN 4-12)(SINCD 4)* – Telephone (dub).

Feb 90. (cd/c/lp) *(<842204-2/-4/-1>)* **EXTRICATE** [31] [ ]
– Sing! Harpy / I'm Frank / Bill is dead / Black monk theme part 1 / Popcorn double feature / Telephone thing / Hilary / Chicago, now! / The littlest rebel / British people in hot weather / And therein. (c+cd+=) – Arms control poseur / Black monk theme part II / Extricate.

Mar 90. (7"/c-s) *(SIN/+MC 5)* **POPCORN DOUBLE FEATURE. / BUTTERFLIES 4 BRAINS** [ ] [-]
(12"+=) *(SIN 5-12)* – Arms control poseur.
(cd-s+=) *(SINCD 5)* – Zandra / Black monk theme part II.

— trimmed to basic quartet of **MARK E, CRAIG, STEVE and JOHN.**

Aug 90. (7") *(SIN 6)* **WHITE LIGHTNING. / BLOOD OUTTA STONE** [56] [-]
(12"+=) *(SINR 6-12)* – Zagreb.
(12"ep+=)(cd-ep+=) **THE DREDGER EP** *(SIN 6-12)(SINCD 6)* – Life just bounces.

Dec 90. (7") *(SIN 7)* **HIGH TENSION LINE. / XMAS WITH SIMON** [ ] [-]
(12"+=)(cd-s+=) *(SIN 7-12)(SINCD 7)* – Don't take the pizza.

— added guest **KENNY BRADY** – violin

Apr 91. (cd/c/lp) *(<848594-2/-4/-1>)* **SHIFT-WORK** [17] [ ]
– EARTH'S IMPOSSIBLE DAY :- So what about it? / Idiot joy showland / Edinburgh man / Pittsville direkt / The book of lies / High tension line / The war against intelligence/ / NOTEBOOKS OUT PLAGIARISTS :-Shift-work / You haven't found it yet / The mixer / White lightning / A lot of wind / Rose / Sinister waltz.

— **DAVID BUSH** (b. 4 Jun'59, Taplow, England) – keyboards, machines repl. BRADY

Mar 92. (7") *(SINS 8)* **FREE RANGE. / EVERYTHING HURTZ** [40] [-]
(12"+=)(pic-cd-s+=) *(SIN 8-12)(SINCD 8)* – Dangerous / Return.

Mar 92. (cd/c/lp) *(<512162-2/-4/-1>)* **CODE: SELFISH** [21] [ ]
– The Birmingham school of business school / Free range / Return / Time enough at last / Everything hurtz / Immorality / Two-face! / Just waiting / So-called dangerous / Gentlemen's agreement / Married, 2 kids / Crew filth. *(cd re-iss. Aug93)*

Jun 92. (12"ep)(cd-ep) *(SIN 9-12)(SINCD 9)* **ED'S BABE / PUMPKIN HEAD XSCAPES / THE KNIGHT, THE DEVIL AND DEATH / ARID'S AL'S DREAM / FREE RANGER** [ ] [-]

Permanent Matador

Apr 93. (7") *(SPERM 9) <54>* **WHY ARE PEOPLE GRUDGEFUL? / GLAM-RACKET** [43] [ ]
(12"+=/cd-s+=) *(12/CD SPERM 9)* – The Re-Mixer / Lost In Music

Apr 93. (cd/c/lp) *(PERM CD/MC/LP 12) <92263>* **THE INFOTAINMENT SCAN** [9] [ ] May93
– Ladybird (green grass) / Lost in music / Glam-racket / I'm going to Spain / It's a curse / Paranoia man in cheap sh*t room / Service / The league of bald-headed men / A past gone mad / Light fireworks / League Moon monkey mix. *(cd+=)* – Why are people grudgeful?

— added the returning **KARL BURNS** – percussion(now 6-piece yet again)

Dec 93. (d-cd-ep/d12"ep) *(CD/12 SPERM 13)* **BEHIND THE COUNTER EP** [75] [-]
– Behind the counter / War / M5 / Happy holiday / Cab driver / (1).

— Feb 94; MARK guested for INSPIRAL CARPETS on their single 'I Want You'.

Apr 94. (10"clear-ep/12"ep/cd-ep) *(10/12/CD SPERM 14) <94>* **15 WAYS. / HEY! STUDENT / THE $500 BOTTLE OF WINE** [65] [ ]

May 94. (cd/c/lp) *(PERM CD/MC/LP 18) <95>* **MIDDLE CLASS REVOLT (aka THE VAPOURISATION OF REALITY** [48] [ ]
– 15 ways / The reckoning / Behind the counter / M5#1 / Surmount all obstacles / Middle class revolt! / You're not up to much / Symbol of Mordgan / Hey! student / Junk man / The $500 bottle of wine / City dweller / War / Shut up!.

— added on tour the returning **BRIX SMITH**– guitar, vocals

Permanent Permanent

Feb 95. (cd/c/lp) *(<PERM CD/MC/LP 30>)* **CEREBRAL CAUSTIC** [67] [ ] May95
– The joke / Don't call me darling / Rainmaster / Feeling numb / Pearl city / Life just bounces / I'm not satisfied / The aphid / Bonkers in Phoenix / One day / North west fashion show / Pine leaves.

Aug 95. (d-cd/d-c/d-lp) *(<PERM CD/MC/LP 36>)* **THE TWENTY-SEVEN POINTS (live)** [ ] [ ] Sep95
– Mollusc in Tyrol / Return / Lady bird (green grass) / Idiot – Walk-out / Ten points / Idiot – Walk-out / Big new prinz / Intro: Roadhouse / The joke / ME's jokes – The

British people in hot weather / Free range / Hi-tension line / The league of the bald headed men / Glam racket: Star / Lost in music / Mr. Pharmacist / Cloud of black / Paranoia man in cheap shit room / Bounces / Outro / Passable / Glasgow advice / Middle class revolt: Simon, Dave and John / Bill is dead / Strychnine / War! / Noel's chemical effluence / Three points – Up too much.

— added **JULIA NAGLE** – keyboards, guitar / + 7th & 8th members **LUCY RIMMER** – vocals / **MIKE BENNETT** – vocals, co-producer (to MARK E., BRIX, SIMON, STEPHEN + KARL)

Jet Jet

Feb 96. (12"ep/c-ep/cd-ep) *(JET/+MC/SCD 500)* **THE CHISELERS / CHILINIST. / INTERLUDE / CHILINISM** 60 -

— MARK E. worked with DOSE on their single 'PLUG MYSELF IN', released on Pete Waterman's new label 'Coliseum'!

Jun 96. (cd/c/lp) *(<JET CD/MC/LP 1012>)* **THE LIGHT USER SYNDROME** 54
– D.I.Y. meat / Das vulture ans ein nutter-wain / He Pep! / Hostile / Stay away (old white train) / Spinetrak / Interlude – Chilinism / Powder keg / Oleano / Cheetham Hill / The Coliseum / Last chance to turn around / The ballard of J. Drummer / Oxymoron / Secession man.

Artful Artful

Feb 98. (10"ep/cd-ep) *(10/CD ARTFUL 1)* **MASQUERADE. /** 69 -
(cd-ep) *(CXARTFUL 001)* –

Feb 98. (cd/c/lp) *(<ARTFUL CD/MC/LP 9>)* **LEVITATE**
– Ten houses of Eve / Masquerade / Hurricane Edward / I'm a mummy / Quartet of Doc Shanley / Jap kid / 4 1/2 inch / Spencer must die / Jungle rock / Ol' gang / Tragic days / I come and stand at your door / Levitate / Everybody but myself.

– compilations, etc. –

Sep 81. (lp) *Step Forward; (ROUGH 18)* **77-EARLY YEARS-79** -

Mar 82. (c) *Chaos; (LIVE 006)* **LIVE AT ACKLAM HALL, LONDON 1980** -
(cd-iss. Jan96 as 'THE LEGENDARY CHAOS TAPES'; SAR 1005) (cd re-iss. Jul97 on 'Cog Sinister – Voiceprint'; COGVP 101CD)

Nov 82. (lp) *Cottage;* **A PART OF AMERICA THEREIN** -

Nov 83. (7") *Kamera; (KAM 014)* **MARQUEE CHA-CHA. / ROOM TO LIVE / / (PAPAL VISIT original b-side)** -

Mar 85. (lp/c) *Situation 2; (SIT U/C 13)* **HIP PRIESTS AND KAMERADS** (81-82 material) -
(c+=) – (has 4 extra tracks) (cd-iss. Mar88+= same 4; SITU 13CD) (re-iss. 1988 on 'Situation 2-Lowdown' lp/c)(cd+=; SITL/+C 13)(SITU 13CD) (cd re-iss. Sep95 on 'Beggars Banquet')

May 87. (12"ep/c-ep) *Strange Fruit; (<SFPF/SFPSC 028>)* **THE PEEL SESSIONS** (28.11.78) 1991
– Put away / No Xmas for John Quay / Like to blow / Mess of my.

Nov 87. (cd/c/lp) *Cog Sinister; (CD/C+/COG 1)* **IN PALACE OF SWORDS REVERSED (80-83)** -

Sep 90. (cd)(lp/c) *Beggars Banquet; (BEGA 111CD)(BEGA/+C 111)* *<2430>* **458489** ('A'sides; 1984-89) 47
– Oh! brother / C.R.E.E.P. / No bulbs 3 / Rollin' Dany / Couldn't get ahead / Cruiser's creek / L.A. / Living too late / Hit the north (part 1) / Mr. Pharmacist / Hey! Luciani / There's a ghost in my house / Victoria / Big new prinz / Wrong place, right time No.2 / Jerusalem / Dead beat descendant. // God-box / Pat-trip dispenser / Slang king 2 / Draygo's guilt / Clear off! / No bulbs / Petty thief lout / Vixen / Hot aftershave bop / Living too long / Lucifer over Lancashire / Auto tech pilot / Entitled / Shoulder pads £1 / Sleep debt snatches / Mark'll sink us / Haf found Bormann / Australians in Europe / Northerns in Europe / Hit the north (part 2) / Guest informant / Tuff life boogie / Twister / Acid priest 2088 / Cab it up. *<US cd re-iss. 1994 on 'Atlantic'; 92380>*

Dec 90. (cd)(d-lp/c) *Beggars Banquet; (BEGA 116CD)(BEGA/+C 116)* *<2430>* **458489** (B'sides; 1984-89)
– God-box / Pat-trip dispenser / Slang king 2 / Draygo's guilt / Clear off! / No bulbs / Petty thief lout / Vixen / Hot aftershave bop / Living too long / Lucifer over Lancashire / Auto tech pilot / Entitled / Shoulder pads £1 / Sleep debt snatches / Mark'll sink us / Haf found Bormann / Australians in Europe / Northerns in Europe / Hit the north (part 2) / Guest informant / Tuff life boogie / Twister / Acid priest 2088 / Cab it up. *(cd+=)* – Bremen nache run out / Mark'll sink us (live) / Kurious oranj. *<US cd re-iss. 1994 on 'Atlantic'; 92474>*

Mar 93. (7"ep/cd-ep) *Strange Fruit; (SFPS/SFPCD 087) / Dutch East India; <8355>* **KIMBLE**
– Kimble / C'n'c hassle schmuk / Spoilt Victorian child / Words of expectation.

Apr 93. (cd) *Castle; (CCSCD 365)* **THE COLLECTION** -

Aug 93. (m-cd) *Windsong; (WINCD 038) / Griffin; <404>* **BBC RADIO 1 LIVE IN CONCERT** -

Feb 94. (cd) *Loma; (LOMACD 10)* **SLATES / PART OF AMERICA IN THERIN 1981** -

Aug 94. (cd) *Matador; <62>* **THE LEAGUE OF BALD HEADED MEN** -

Feb 96. (cd) *Receiver; (<RRCD 209>)* **SINISTER WALTZ**

Apr 96. (cd) *Receiver; (<RRCD 211>)* **FIEND WITH A VIOLIN**

Apr 96. (cd/lp) *Receiver; (<RRCD/RRLP 213>)* **OSWALD DEFENCE LAWYER**

Oct 96. (3xcd-box) *Receiver; (<RRXCD 506>)* **THE OTHER SIDE OF THE FALL** (above 3 albums)

Apr 97. (d-cd) *Cog Sinister – Voiceprint; (COGVP 102CD)* **FALL IN A HOLE** -
(was originally a New Zealand release on 'Flying Nun') (re-iss. Nov97 on 'Resurgence'; RSG 4016)

Jun 97. (d-cd) *Snapper; (<SMDCD 132>)* **THE LESS YOU LOOK THE MORE YOU FIND**

Aug 97. (cd) *Receiver; (RRCD 239)* **15 WAYS TO LEAVE YOUR MAN (live)** -

Nov 97. (cd) *Receiver; (<RRCD 246>)* **OXYMORON**

Nov 97. (cd) *Rialto; (<RMCD 214>)* **THE FALL ARCHIVES**

Dec 97. (cd) *Receiver; (<RRCD 247>)* **CHEETHAM HILL**

Mar 98. (cd) *Strange Fruit; (SFRSCD 048)* **THE PEEL SESSIONS** -

Mar 98. (cd) *Castle; (CCSCD 823)* **SMILE . . . IT'S THE BEST OF THE FALL** -

Apr 98. (cd) *Cog Sinister – Voiceprint; (COGVP 108CD)* **LIVE ON AIR IN MELBOURNE 1982 (live)** -

Jun 98. (cd) *M.C.I.; (MCCD 350)* **NORTHERN ATTITUDE** -

Jun 98. (cd) *Artful; (ARTFULCD 3)* **IN THE CITY (live in Manchester 1995)**

Aug 98. (cd) *Cog Sinister – Voiceprint; (COGVP 111CD)* **LIVE VARIOUS YEARS (live)** -

FALSE PROPHETS

Formed: New York City, New York, USA . . . June 1980 by frontman STEPHAN IELPI, who surrounded himself with like-minded hardcore punks, PETER CAMPBELL, STEVE WISHNIA and MATTY SUPERTY. One of the first wave US hardcore acts, the FALSE PROPHETS eschewed the hard-man approach favoured by BLACK FLAG etc, choosing instead an intellectually-based manifesto that sought to oppose injustice in all its multifarious guises. Yet like many bands of their ilk, the line-up was in almost constant flux and by the mid-80's – by which point the band's vinyl output amounted to a solitary 7" single, 'BLIND OBEDIENCE' – IELPI was the only remaining founder member (newcomers being DEBRA DeSALVO, STEVEN TAYLOR, NICK MARDEN and BILLY ATWELL III). Securing a deal with the San Francisco-based 'Alternative Tentacles' label, the band re-emerged in 1986 with a long awaited eponymous debut album. This was followed up by 'IMPLOSION' just over a year later although a second extended sabbatical from the recording front meant that fans had to wait until 1990 for further new material. Featuring brass courtesy of new addition JAMES WHITE, 'INVISIBLE PEOPLE' was a much more adventurous affair combining the adrenaline rush of hardcore with the visceral thrill of Latin rhythms.

Album rating: FALSE PROPHETS (*5) / IMPLOSION (*5) / INVISIBLE PEOPLE (*6)

STEPHAN IELPI – vocals / **PETER CAMPBELL** – guitar / **STEVE WISHNIA** – bass / **MATTY SUPERTY** – drums

not iss. Worn Out Brothers

1981. (7") *<WOB 001>* **BLIND OBEDIENCE. / OVERKILL / ROYAL SLIME** -

— **IELPI** was the solo survivor, the quartet having involved others **DEBRA DE SALVO** – guitar, vocals / **STEVEN TAYLOR** – guitar, vocals / **NICK MARDEN** – bass, vocals / **BILLY ATWELL III** – drums, vocals

Alternative Tentacles Alternative Tentacles

Jul 86. (lp) *<(VIRUS 48)>* **FALSE PROPHETS**

Sep 87. (lp) *<(VIRUS 58)>* **IMPLOSION**

— added **JAMES WHITE** – horns (ex-CONTORTIONS)

— **BENJAMIN ORICK** – drums; repl. ATTWELL

Konkurrel Patois

1990. (m-lp) **INVISIBLE PEOPLE**
– Never again, again / Plenty of death for all / Shadow government / Invisible people / No deposit, no return / Limit of the limitless.

— folded in the early 90's after a decade as a unit

FAMILY CAT

Formed: Yeovil, Somerset, England . . . 1988 by PAUL FREDERICK, STEPHEN JELBERT, TIM McVEY, JOHN GRAVES and KEVIN DOWNING. Despite the rather naff moniker, The FAMILY CAT became early 90's critical favourites if never quite managing to convince record buyers. Signed to indie label, 'Bad Girl', in 1989, the group scored an NME Single Of The Week with their debut single, 'TOM VERLAINE' – a thrilling tribute to the much revered TELEVISION guitar guru – but a rush-released mini-set, 'TELL 'EM WE'RE SURFIN' (1989) failed to translate the power of their live work and the band were left facing the frustration which would dog them throughout their career. Following a further two singles, 'REMEMBER WHAT IT IS THAT YOU LOVE' and 'A PLACE WITH A NAME' (they had recently moved to London), the band moved on to 'Dedicated', finally proving what they were made of with a show stopping display of six string manipulation at the 1991 Reading Festival. The subsequent single, 'COLOUR ME GREY' featured none other than a young PJ HARVEY on backing vocals and consolidated their return to form, setting the scene for an impressive second album, 'FURTHEST FROM THE SUN' (1992). Yet despite gushing praise for the sterling, star spangled guitar melodies on offer, indie fans voted with their feet and once again, The FAMILY CAT were left in the commercial doghouse. The advent of grunge and the resulting focus on all things American only served to further marginalise the band and when a similarly obscure fate befell another fine, if more resigned third effort, 'MAGIC HAPPENS' (1994), these West Country stalwarts eventually returned to their proverbial baskets.
• **Covered:** BUS STOP (Hollies) / I MUST HAVE BEEN BLIND (Tim Buckley) / LEAN ON ME (I WON'T FALL OVER) (Carter The Unstoppable Sex Machine).

Album rating: TELL 'EM WE'RE SURFIN' mini (*6) / FURTHEST FROM THE SUN (*7) / MAGIC HAPPENS (*8)

PAUL FREDERICK – vocals, guitar / **STEPHEN JELBERT** – lead guitar / **TIM McVAY** – rhythm guitar / **JOHN GRAVES** – bass / **KEVIN DOWNING** – drums

Bad Girl not iss.

Jul 89. (7"flexi) *(BGRIFC 01)* **TOM VERLAINE (demo version)** -
(12"ep+=) *(BGRLT 01)* – Gabriel's wings / Octopus.

Sep 89. (m-lp) *(BGRMLP 001)* **TELL 'EM WE'RE SURFIN'** -
– Albert Hoffman's bike / Final mistake / Sandbag your heart / Slept in clothes /

From the city to the sea / Taken by surprise / Endless cigarette / Gabriel's wings. *(cd-iss. Mar90; BGRLCD 001)*

May 90. (7") *(BGRL 003S)* **REMEMBER WHAT IT IS THAT YOU LOVE. / PUSH COMES TO SHOVE** -
(12"+=/cd-s+=) *(BGRL 003 T/SCD)* – ('A'extended).

Aug 90. (12"ep/cd-ep) **A PLACE WITH NO NAME. / CONCRETE / PASSAWAY / THEME FROM THE FAMILY CAT** -

Sep 91. (12"ep/cd-ep) *(BGRL 009 T/SCD)* **COLOUR ME GREY. / I MUST HAVE BEEN BLIND / GREAT UGLY PLACE** -
(above featured POLLY JEAN HARVEY on vocals)

—— (below deleted in one day and issued on 'Clawfist')

Dec 91. (7"ep/12"ep/cd-ep) **JESUS CHRIST. / CHILL OUT YE MERRY GENTLEMEN / CHRIST JESUS / JESUS KARAOKE CHRIST (instrumental)** -

Dedicated Dedicated

May 92. (7") *(FCUK 001)* **STREAMROLLER (pt.1). / STEAMROLLER (pt.2)** -
(12"+=/cd-s+=) *(FCUK 001 T/CD)* – What we talk about when we talk about love / Across the universe.

Jun 92. (cd/c/lp) *(DED CD/MC/LP 007)* <66041> **FURTHEST FROM THE SUN** 55 Jan93
– Too many late nights / Colour me grey / Prog one / Furthest from the sun / Steamroller / Keep it to yourself / With a war / River of diamonds / Gameshow / Fire music. *(with free ltd-7"/cd+=)* – Kolombus / Montague Terrace (in blue).

Sep 92. (12"ep/cd-ep) *(FCUK 002 T/CD)* **RIVER OF DIAMONDS (re-navigated). / SANDBAG YOUR HEART (re-bagged) / TOM VERLAINE (re-bereted)** -
(12"with free ltd-7") – Tom Verlaine.

Aug 93. (7"purple) *(FCUK 003)* **AIRPLANE GARDENS. / ATMOSPHERIC ROAD** 69 -
(12"+=/cd-s+=) *(FCUK 003 T/CD)* – Amazing hangover.

Oct 93. (7") *(FCUK 004)* **SPRINGING THE ATOM. / PROG 4** -
(12"+=/cd-s+=) *(FCUK 004 T/CD)* – Happy to be here.

Dedicated-RCA R.C.A.

May 94. (7"clear/c-s) *(74321 20843-7/-4)* **WONDERFUL EXCUSE. / UNWIELDY WORLD** 48 -
(cd-s+=) *(74321 20843-2)* – Sign of the blood cell / Propeller blades.
(12") *(74321 20843-1)* – ('A'side) / Counting crosses (acoustic) / Gameshow (acoustic) / ('A'-acoustic).

May 94. (cd/c/lp) *(<74321 20466-2/-4/-1>)* **MAGIC HAPPENS** Feb95
– Wonderful excuse / Amazing hangover / Move over I'll drive / Your secrets will stay mine / Airplane gardens / Gone, so long / Hamlet for now / Goldenbook / Rockbreaking / Springing the atom / Blood orange / Nowhere to go but down.

Jul 94. (7"green-ep/c-ep) *(74321 22007-7/-4)* **GOLDENBOOK EP** 42 -
– Goldenbook / Bring me the head of Michael Portillo / Springing the atom (acoustic) / River of diamonds (acoustic).
(7"gold-ep) *(74321 22007-)* – (1st track) / Goldenboot / Old faithful.
(cd-s) *(74321 22007-2)* – (1st track) / Blood orange (acoustic) / Gone to Heaven.

—— split towards the end of '94

FAMILY FODDER

Formed: London, England . . . late 70's as a large unit of singers and musicians numbering main songwriter DOMINIQUE PEARCE, other conspirator ALIG LEVILLIAN, plus IAN HILL, FELIX FRIEDOROWICZ, MICK HOBBS, MARTIN FREDERICK, CHARLES BULLEN, RICK WILSON and JUDY CARTER. Weird and musically directionless, this percussion-heavy avant-pop ensemble made their official debut late in '79 with the single, 'PLAYING GOLF (WHILE MY FLESH CRAWLS)', although a pseudonymous EP, 'TE DEUM', was issued around the same time under the guise of FRANK SUMATRA AND THE MOB. A series of singles/EP's followed in quick succession, 'WARM', 'SUNDAY GIRLS' 12"ep, BLONDIE ode, 'DEBBIE HARRY' and DOMINIQUE's pouting French-language showcase, 'SAVOIR FAIRE'. FAMILY FODDER delivered their first full-length baby in the shape of 'MONKEY BANANA KITCHEN' (1981), a shambolic ragbag of competing sounds and influences that made few concessions to chart-friendly accessibility. By the following year, only ALIG, IAN and BAZ remained from the original line-up while new members LYNNE ALICE and GRAHAM PAINTING were found. A switch of labels from 'Fresh' to 'Jungle' led to the subsequent release of a disappointing but appropriately titled second set, 'ALL STYLES' (1983), the group signing off with a 'GREATEST HITS' collection a year later.

Album rating: MONKEY BANANA KITCHEN (*5) / ALL STYLES (*3) / GREATEST HITS compilation (*6)

DOMINIQUE PEARCE – vocals / **IAN HILL** – vocals, percussion / **ALIG LEVILLIAN** – guitars, keyboards, saxophone, vocals / **FELIX FRIEDOROWICZ** – keyboards, bassoon, violin / **MICK HOBBS** – bass, organ / **MARTIN FREDERICK** – bass, vocals / **CHARLES BULLEN** – drums, guitar, viola, vocals / **RICK WILSON** – drums, vocals / **MIKE** – guitar / **JUDY CARTER** – backing vocals / **MARK DOFFMAN** – drums / **BAZZ SMITH** – drums / **JAN BEETLESTONE** – backing vocals

Small Wonder not iss.

Oct 79. (12"ep; as FRANK SUMATRA AND THE MOB) *(TEENY 1)* **TE DEUM** -
– The story so far / Telstar 176 all out: W/Indies 180 for 3 declared / Tedium – the blues.

Parole not iss.

Oct 79. (7") *(PURL 4)* **PLAYING GOLF (WHILE MY FLESH CRAWLS). / MY BABY TAKES VALIUM** -
(re-iss. Apr81 on 'Fresh'; FRESH 1)

Jan 80. (7") *(PURL 6)* **WARM. / DESIRE** -
(re-iss. Apr81 on 'Fresh'; FRESH 8)

Fresh not iss.

Apr 80. (12"ep) *(FRESH 9)* **SUNDAY GIRLS EP**
– Sunday girl 1 / Mine and Billy's head / Disco purge / Good times underwater / No man's land / Accapulco / Street credibility / Kisses / Grand merchant loup / Ragged wolf of my passions / Blue girls / Sunday girl 2.

Jul 80. (7") *(FRESH 15)* **DEBBIE HARRY. / (version)** -

Oct 80. (7") *(FRESH 22)* **SAVOIR FAIRE. / CARNAL KNOWLEDGE** -

Apr 81. (lp) *(FRESHLP 3)* **MONKEY BANANA KITCHEN** -
– Darling / Symbols / Savoir faire / Cold wars / Monkey / Wrong / Organ grinder / Love song / Bass adds bass / Philosophy / Cerf volant / Banana.

Jul 81. (7") *(FRESH 32)* **FILM MUSIC. / ROOM** -

—— now without MIKE

Sep 81. (12"ep) *(FRESH 37-12)* **SCHIZOPHRENIA PARTY** -
– Dinosaur sex / Emergency / Dazomo / Silence / Tea with Dolly / Better lies.

May 82. (7") *(FRESH 42)* **THE BIG DIG. / PLANT LIFE** -

—— remaining members **ALIG, IAN + BAZ** recruited **LYNNE ALICE** – guitar, vocals / **GRAHAM PAINTING** – keyboards, bass

Jungle not iss.

Nov 82. (7") *(JUNG 4)* **CORAL. / FRUSTRATION** -

May 83. (d-lp) *(FREUD 02)* **ALL STYLES** -
– Disarm completely / Winter song / Malfunction / Ecstasy harmony / Falling in love again / Mack the knife / Windmills of your mind.

Crammed Discs not iss.

Sep 83. (7") *(CRAM 245-7)* **SAVOIR FAIRE. / I'LL BE YOURS** -

Sep 84. (lp) *(CRAM 016)* **GREATEST HITS** (compilation) -
– Playing golf (while my flesh crawls) / Film music / Debbie Harry / Savoir faire / Der Leiermann / Cerf volant / No fear no sorrow / Kisses / Love song / Warm / Fragments / One person per suit.

—— disbanded before above was released

FANATICS (see under ⇒ OCEAN COLOUR SCENE)

FARM

Formed: Liverpool, England . . . early '83 by PETE HOOTEN and STEVE GRIMES. They appeared on BBC2 TV's 'Oxford Road Show' where they met MADNESS frontman, SUGGS McPHERSON, who subsequently produced their 1984 debut 45, 'HEARTS AND MINDS'. The group struggled early on and ultimately suffered tragedy when drummer, ANDY McVANN, died in a car crash late in '86. Replacing him initially with MICK HANRATTY and later ROY BOULTER (KEITH MULLEN and CARL HUNTER also replaced MELVIN and PHILIP respectively), the group ploughed on, moving away from their overtly political, brassy DEXYS/REDSKINS fixation and adopting an ill-advised synth orientated sound with the addition of keyboard player, BEN LEACH. The resulting single, 'BODY AND SOUL', was another flop and the band decided drastic measures were needed; initiating their own label, 'Produce', and securing the services of house guru TERRY FARLEY, they score a sizeable club hit (and a Top 60 chart placing) with a dancefloor friendly makeover of The Monkees' 'ALL TOGETHER NOW'. Finally, everything clicked into place; The FARM found themselves at the epicentre of the indie/dance "baggy" scene in 1990 with the unstoppable momentum of 'GROOVY TRAIN' and penned one of the scene's anthems in 'ALL TOGETHER NOW', both becoming massive UK Top 10 hits (even heartthrob, Mike Dixon – from scouse soap, Brookside, was seen sporting a FARM T-shirt!). By the release of a belated debut album proper, 'SPARTACUS', the following year, the scene was fading fast; hardly the most glamourous band in the world, The FARM had always been a favourite target for music press jibes and the continual criticism certainly didn't help reverse the band's swift fall from grace. Though the album had gone straight in at No.1, surplus copies were to be found propping up record store bargain bins for the next three years. Despite a new deal with 'Sony' and a further UK Top 20 hit (an awful cover of The Human League's 'DON'T YOU WANT ME'), the insipid songwriting on 'LOVE SEE NO COLOUR' (1992) saw the album sink without trace. Even a third-time-lucky deal with 'Sire' couldn't halt the decline and the band after the failure of 1994's 'HULLABALOO' (which contained another cover, The Flamin' Groovies 'SHAKE SOME ACTION'). • **Miscellaneous:** In 1990, their live technician RAY TOOMEY, was jailed for 30 months for his part in the Risley Remand Centre rooftop protest.

Album rating: SPARTACUS (*6) / LOVE SEE NO COLOUR (*5) / HULLABALOO (*4) / PASTURES OLD AND NEW early compilation (*5)

PETE HOOTEN (b.28 Sep'62) – vocals / **STEVE GRIMES** (b. 4 Jun'62) – guitar / **JOHN MELVIN** – guitar / **PHILIP STRONGMAN** – bass / **ANDY McVANN** – drums / plus **TONY EVANS** – trombone / **GEORGE MAHER** – trumpet / **STEVE 'SNOWY' LEVY** – saxophone / **and occasional live JOE MUSKER** – percussion

Skysaw not iss.

Nov 84. (12"ep) *(END 1)* **HEARTS AND MINDS. / ('A'dub version) / INFORMATION MAN / SAME OLD STORY** -

Admiralty not iss.

Nov 85. (7") *(PRA 1)* **STEPS OF EMOTION. / MEMORIES** -
(12") *(PRAT 1)* – ('A'side) / Power over me / No man's land / Better / Living for tomorrow.

Fire not iss.

Sep 86. (7") *(BLAZE 13)* **SOME PEOPLE. / STANDING TOGETHER** -
(12"+=) *(BLAZE 13T)* – Sign of the times / The Moroccan.

Oct 86. (lp) *(REFIRE 3)* **PASTURES OLD AND NEW** (compilation of sessions) -
– Hearts and minds / Information man / Same old story / Hearts and minds (dub) / Steps of emotion / Power over me / No man's land / Better / Worn out sayings / Some people / Little ol' wine drinker me. *(re-iss. Aug89;)*

—— (early '87) **MICK HANRATTY** – drums (on tour) repl. ANDY McVANN who died in a crash Dec86. Late 1987; **ROY BOULTER** (b. 2 Jul'64) – drums repl. HANRATTY and the horn section / **KEITH MULLEN** (DR. KEITH LOVE) (b.Bootle) – guitar repl. MELVIN / **CARL HUNTER** (b.14 Apr'65, Bootle, England) – bass repl. PHILLIP

— (early '89) **HOOTEN, GRIMES, HUNTER, MULLEN + BOULTER** added **BEN LEACH** (b. 2 May'69) – keyboards

Foresight | not iss.

Jul 89. (7") *(FR 2301)* **BODY AND SOUL. / COLONELS** [ ] [-]
(12") *(FR 2301-12)* – ('A'side) / Colonels and heroes / Stuck on you.

Produce | Sire

Apr 90. (7"/ext.12") *(MILK 101/+T)* **STEPPING STONE (ghost dance mix). / FAMILY OF MAN** [58] [-]
Sep 90. (7"/c-s) *(MILK 102/+C)* **GROOVY TRAIN. / ('A'-3:30 a.m. mix)** [6] [-]
(ext.12"+=)(cd-s+=) *(MILK 102T)(CDMILK 102)* – ('A'-Bootle mix).

— (below featured PETE WYLIE; WAH!)

Nov 90. (7"/c-s) *(MILK 103/+C)* **ALL TOGETHER NOW. / ('A'-Terry Farley mix)** [4] [ ]
(12"+=)(cd-s+=) *(MILK 103T)(CDMILK 103)* – ('A'-Rocky & Diesel mix).

— added guest backing vocalist **PAULA DAVID**

Mar 91. (cd/c/lp) *(MILK CD/MC/LP 1)* <26600> **SPARTACUS** [1] [ ] Apr91
– Hearts and minds / How long / Sweet inspiration / Groovy train / Higher and higher / Don't let me down / Family of man / Tell the story / Very emotional / All together now. *(initial copies, incl.free remix lp)*
Apr 91. (7"/c-s) *(MILK 104/+C)* **DON'T LET ME DOWN. / ('A' Terry Farley mix)** [36] [-]
(12"+=)(cd-s+=) *(MILK 104T)(CDMILK 104)* – ('A'-Rocky & Diesel mix).
Aug 91. (7"/c-s) *(MILK 105/+C)* **MIND. / STEPPING STONE** [31] [-]
(12"+=)(cd-s+=) *(MILK 105T)(CDMILK 105)* – ('A'new mix).
Sep 91. (c-s) *<19209>* **GROOVY TRAIN / STEPPING STONE** [-] [41]
Dec 91. (7"/c-s) *(MILK 106/+C)* **LOVE SEE NO COLOUR (Suggs mix). / ('A' Noel Watson mix)** [58] [-]
(d12"+=)(cd-s+=) *(MILK 106T)(CDMILK 106)* – (6 other remixes).

— In October 1991, KEITH MULLEN was attacked and stabbed needing over 80 stitches. 'ALL TOGETHER NOW' is used by The Labour Party in their General election campaign.

End Product-Sony | Sire

Jun 92. (7"/c-s) *(658 468-7/-4)* **RISING SUN. / CREEPERS** [48] [-]
(12"+=/cd-s+=) *(658 468-6/-2)* – ('A'-Mark Saunders mix) / ('A'-Steve Spiro mix).
Oct 92. (7"/c-s) *(658 468-7/-4)* **DON'T YOU WANT ME. / OBVIOUSLY** [18] [-]
(cd-s+=) *(658 468-6/-2)* – Groovy train (US mix).
Nov 92. (cd/c/lp) *(472 029-2/-4/-1)* <26959> **LOVE SEE NO COLOUR** [ ] [ ]
– Rising sun / Hard times / Words of wisdom / Mind / Been a long time / Don't you want me / Rain / Good morning sinners / Love see no colour / Suzy Boo.
Dec 92. (7"/c-s) *(658 868-7/-4)* **LOVE SEE NO COLOUR. / ALL TOGETHER NOW** [35] [-]
(12"+=) *(658 868-6)* – Anytown / (other 'A'side).
(cd-s) *(658 868-2)* – ('A'side) / ('A'original) / Rain / Don't you want me (mixes).

Produce | not iss.

Feb 93. (5x12"box)(cd-box-ep) **STEPPING STONE. / ALL TOGETHER NOW (mix)/ / GROOVY TRAIN. / (mix)/ / ALL TOGETHER NOW. / (mix)/ / MIND. / (mix)/ / DON'T LET ME DOWN. / (mix)** [ ] [-]

Warners | Sire

Jul 94. (7"/c-s) *(W 0256/+C)* **MESSIAH. / ONE MORE FOOL** [ ] [-]
(cd-s+=) *(W 0256CD)* – Somewhere (acoustic) / Love made up my mind.
Aug 94. (cd/c) *(<9362 45588-2/-4>)* **HULLABALOO** [ ] [ ] May94
– Messiah / Shake some action / Comfort / The man who cried / Hateful / Golden vision / To the ages / All American world / Distant voices / Echoes.

— split after failure of above album

– compilations, etc. –

May 98. (cd) *Essential; (ESS 595)* **THE BEST OF THE FARM** [ ] [-]

FARMER'S BOYS

Formed: Norwich, England . . . early 80's by BAZ, FROG, MARK and ANDY (the latter being replaced by STAN). Straight outta Norwich in the wake of The HIGSONS, this bunch of straw-chewing, fun loving bumpkins made their vinyl debut in Spring '82 with 'I THINK WE NEED HELP'. This was followed with a further two equally impressive, independently released singles, 'WHATEVER IS HE LIKE' and 'MORE THAN A DREAM'. Akin to ORANGE JUICE with a brass section or a more soulful proto-HOUSEMARTINS, 'E.M.I.' deemed the latter track sufficiently chartworthy to re-issue it in early '83. Perhaps it was also EMI's idea to release 'MUCK IT OUT' in the hope of a WURZELS-style novelty hit, the record scraping into the Top 50. The lilting 'FOR YOU' was also a minor hit, previewing their debut album, 'GET OUT AMD WALK' (1983). While a geeky, happy-go-lucky charm characterised the bulk of their work, BAZ's DAVID BYRNE/MORRISSEY/EDWYN COLLINS vocal hybrid began to wear over the course of an album; even so, the record surely deserved more than its lowly Top 50 placing. Although EMI ultimately failed in their bid to make The FARMERS BOYS the toast of city and country alike, a further two minor hits, 'PHEW WOW' and 'I BUILT THE WORLD', along with a follow-up album, 'I BUILT THE WORLD (WITH THESE HANDS)' (1985) surfaced before the lads went on to pastures new; while FROG joined locals The HIGSONS, BAZ and MARK joined the short-lived AVONS.

Album rating: GET OUT AND WALK (*4) / WITH THESE HANDS (*4)

BAZ – vocals / **FROG** – keyboards, guitar, synth-drums / **STAN** – guitar; repl. ANDY who joined SERIOUS DRINKING / **MARK** – bass

Waap | not iss.

Apr 82. (7") *(WAAP 3)* **I THINK WE NEED HELP. / SQUIT** [ ] [-]
(12"+=) *(12WAAP 3)* – More quit / Squittest.

Backs | not iss.

Jul 82. (7") *(NCH 001)* **WHATEVER IS HE LIKE. / I LACK CONCENTRATION** [ ] [-]
Dec 82. (7") *(NCH 003)* **MORE THAN A DREAM. / COUNTRY LINE** [ ] [-]

E.M.I. | unknown

Jan 83. (7") *(EMI 5367)* **MORE THAN A DREAM. / COUNTRY LINE** [ ] [-]
Mar 83. (7"pic-d/12") *(EMIP/12EMI 5380)* **MUCK IT OUT. / FUNKY COMBINE JOHN** [48] [-]
Jul 83. (7") *(EMI 5401)* **FOR YOU. / T.O.S.D.** [66] [-]
(d7"+=) *(EMID 5401)* – demos:- Muck it out / Drinking and dressing up / Something I ate / I don't know why.
Oct 83. (lp) *(EMC 107799-1)* **GET OUT AND WALK** [49] [-]
– Matter of fact / Probably one of the best investments I ever made / More than a dream / Woke up this morning / The way you made me cry / A promise you can't keep / Soft drink / Wailing wall / For you / Torn in two / Who needs it. *(with free 7"ep)* – PROBABLY ONE OF THE BEST INVESTMENTS I EVER MADE / SOFT DRINK. / FOR YOU / MUCK IT OUT
Apr 84. (7"/12") *(FAB/12FAB 1)* **APPARENTLY. / UNCLE FREDDIE** [ ] [-]
Jul 84. (7"/7"pic-d) *(FAB/+P 2)* **IN THE COUNTRY. / MAMA NEVER TOLD ME** [44] [-]
(12"+=) *(12FAB 4)* – Matter of fact.
Oct 84. (7") *(FAB 3)* **PHEW WOW. / PORTRAIT OF A LEGEND (part 1)** [59] [-]
(12"+=) *(12FAB 3)* – ('A'&'B'extended).
Feb 85. (7") *(FAB 4)* **I BUILT THE WORLD. / SOMETIMES** [ ] [-]
(12"+=) *(12FAB 4)* – Probably one of the best investments I ever made / Sport for all.
Mar 85. (lp/c) *(FBLP/TC-FBLP 2)* **I BUILT THE WORLD (WITH THESE HANDS)** [ ] [-]
– In the country / I built the world / Sport for all / Art gallery / Something from nothing / Phew wow / All of a sudden / Heartache / Walkabout / Whatever is he like.

— they split just after the above was finally released. FROG joined The HIGSONS. BAZ and MARK joined the AVONS who ad two releases for 'Letharge', the lp 'THREE RIVERS REACH' and the 12" 'DIRTY AND CONTROVERSIAL'.

FASHION

Formed: Birmingham, England . . . 1977 by LUKE, JOHN MULLIGAN and DIK DAVIS. A bizarre hybrid of arty post-punk/neo new romantic synth experimentation and Brummie reggae influences, FASHION kickstarted their career via their own label, 'Fashion Music' (distributed by Miles Copeland's 'Faulty' products). Influenced by the likes of ROXY MUSIC, BOWIE and BE-BOP DELUXE, the band were actually more palatable than the aforementioned description might suggest, their debut album, 'PRODUCT PERFECT', possessing a certain mutoid attraction and period fascination (especially for LUKE's brilliantly affected vocals). Prior to 1980's 'SILVER BLADE' single, however, the tonsil-distorting frontman was replaced with DEE HARRIS, the band subsequently adding MARTIN RECCI, MARTIN STOKER and TONY before securing a major label deal with 'Arista'. Following a hiatus of more than a year, FASHION broke the silence with 'MOVE ON', sporting a radically different sound closer to a discofied SIMPLE MINDS with CHIC-slapping bass. Aiming straight at the heart of the electro/dance-pop crossover market, the new-look FASHION were certainly willing to change with the times, earning themselves a UK Top 50 hit with the funky 'STREETPLAYER – MECHANIK' in early '82. Both tracks – along with third single, 'SOMETHING IN YOUR PICTURE' – were featured on the long awaited second album, 'FABRIQUE', later that summer. Despite making the UK Top 10, the album surprisingly failed to provide FASHION with that all important breakthrough single and following a final minor hit, 'LOVE SHADOW', their fortunes faded. Former TEARDROP EXPLODES man, TROY TATE, was briefly installed as frontman before making way for Fife lad, ALAN DARBY, the latter spearheading the band's comeback attempt in 1984. Armed with a new deal courtesy of 'Epic', an increasingly threadbare FASHION scored a minor Top 75 hit with both the single, 'EYE TALK' and album, 'TWILIGHT OF IDOLS' (1984), before finally stepping off the music business catwalk for good later that year. • **Songwriters:** MULLIGAN-DAVIS wrote most of the songs. • **Trivia:** MULLIGAN also made videos for The STRANGLERS.

Album rating: PRODUCT PERFECT (*6) / FABRIQUE (*5) / TWILIGHT OF IDOLS (*4) / THE HEIGHT OF FASHION compilation (*5)

LUKE – vocals, guitar / **JOHN MULLIGAN** – bass, synthesizers, vocals / **DIK** (DAVIS)– percussion, vocals

Fashion Music | I.R.S.

Nov 78. (7") *(FM 001)* **STEADY EDDIE STEADY. / KILLING TIME** [ ] [-]
Jan 79. (lp) *(FML 1)* *<SP 002>* **PRODUCT PERFECT** [ ] [ ] Sep79
– Product perfect / Red, green and gold / Citinite / Fashion / Don't touch me / Bike boys / Big John / The innocent.
Jun 79. (7") *(FM 002)* **CITINITE. / WASTELIFE** [ ] [-]
Sep 79. (7") *<IR 9502>* **THE INNOCENT. / RED, GREEN AND GOLD / SODIUM PENTHATOL NEGATIVE** [-] [ ]

— **DEE HARRIS** (b.DAVE) – vocals, guitar; repl. LUKE to France

Mar 80. (7") *(FM 003)* **SILVER BLADES. / SILVER BLADES (A DEEPER CUT)** [ ] [-]

— added **MARTIN RECCI** – bass, vocals 1980 had also saw them extended to sextet with **MARTIN STOKER** – drums / **TONY** – vox (ex-NEON HEARTS)before reverting to quartet

Arista Arista

Nov 81. (7") *(ARIST 440)* **MOVE ON. / MUTANT DANCE MOVE** [ ] [-]
(12") *(ARIST12 440)* – ('A'-audio extra).

Feb 82. (7"/12") *(ARIST/+12 456)* **STREETPLAYER – MECHANIK. / ('A'version)** [46] [-]

May 82. (7") *(ARIST 472)* **SOMETING IN YOUR PICTURE. / ('A'-alt.version)** [ ] [-]
(12"+=) *(ARIST12 472)* – Motor drive / Smokey dialogue.

Jun 82. (lp/c) *(SPART/TCART 1185)* *<6604>* **FABRIQUE** [10] [ ]
– Move on / Streetplayer – mechanik / Dressed to kill / Do you wanna make love / It's alright / Slow blue / Whitestuff / You only left your picture / Something in your picture / Love shadow.

Aug 82. (7") *(ARIST 483)* **LOVE SHADOW. / LET'S PLAY DIRTY** [51] [-]
(12"+=) *(ARIST12 483)* – Let's play dirty (centrefold).

— (Oct'82) **TROY TATE** – vocals, guitar (ex-TEARDROP EXPLODES) repl. DEE HARRIS who formed ZEE with RICHARD WRIGHT (of Pink Floyd)

— (1983) **ALAN DARBY** (b.1952, Dunfermline, Scotland) – vocals, guitar (ex-CADO BELLE) repl. TATE who continued solo. (others still in band:- **MULLIGAN, DAVIES + RECCI**).

Epic Epic

Jan 84. (7"/12") *(A/TA 4106)* **EYE TALK. / SLOW DOWN** [69] [-]

Apr 84. (7"/12") *(A/TA 4327)* **DREAMING. / WHITE LINE FEVER** [ ] [-]

May 84. (lp/c) *(EPC/+40 25909)* *<39427>* **TWILIGHT OF IDOLS** [69] [ ]
– Eye talk / Dreaming / Hit girl / Trader / Too much too soon / Slow down / Hurricane / You in the night / Twilight of idols / Delirious. *(c+=)* – (alternate mixes).

Jun 84. (7") *(A 4502)* **YOU IN THE NIGHT. / YAMASHATA THEME** [ ] [-]
(c-s+=) *(CA 4502)* – Hurricane
(d7"++=) *(DA 4502)* – White stuff.

— split 1984, DARBY went on to session for BONNIE TYLER, PAUL YOUNG and ROBERT PALMER

– compilations, others, etc. –

Apr 90. (cd/c) *Arista; (260/410 626)* **THE HEIGHT OF FASHION** [ ] [-]
– (virtually 'FABRIQUE' re-issued with extra tracks).

FASTBALL

Formed: Austin, Texas, USA . . . 1995 by former punks, MILES ZUNIGA, JOEY SHUFFIELD and TONY SCALZO. The former two had been members of the short-lived alt-rock act, BIG CAR, who only managed one album, 'NORMAL', for the 'Giant' label in '92. After performing under the moniker MAGENTO U.S.A., the scuzzy country-pop merchants, FASTBALL's first album, 'MAKE YOUR MAMA PROUD', hit the bargain bins in '96. A second long-player, 'ALL THE PAIN MONEY CAN BUY' (1998) was a much zanier affair and surprised many by hitting the US Top 30, helped by the fact, 'THE WAY' (imagine ABBA's 'Fernando' backwoods style), received an MTV playlisting and later became a minor UK hit.

Album rating: MAKE YOUR MAMA PROUD (*5) / ALL THE PAIN MONEY CAN BUY (*5)

BIG CAR

MILES ZUNIGA – vocals, guitar / **JOEY SHUFFIELD** – drums / + 2

Giant-RCA Giant-RCA

May 92. (cd/c) *<(7599 24443-2/-4)>* **NORMAL** [ ] [ ]
– Tunnel of love / Rosalita / Venus / Get started / Mad all the world / Amazing contradictions / Cats / Day by day / Shut up / Easy street.

FASTBALL

— **ZUNIGA + SHUFFIELD** added **TONY SCALZO** – vocals, bass

Polydor Hollywood

Apr 96. (cd/c) *<162045-2/-4>* **MAKE YOUR MAMA PROUD** [-] [ ]
– Human torch / She come 'round / Make your mama proud / Back door / Are you ready for the fastball? / Nothing / Boomerang / Eater / Knock it down / Lender / Altamont / Emily / Seattle / Telephone calls.

Sep 98. (7"/c-s) *(569946-7/-4)* **THE WAY. / ARE YOU READY FOR THE FALLOUT** [21] [-]
(cd-s+=) *(569947-2)* – Freeloader Freddy.

Oct 98. (cd) *<(162130-2)>* **ALL THE PAIN MONEY CAN BUY** [ ] [29] Mar98
– The way / Fire escape / Better than it was / Which way to the top? / Sooner or later / Warm fuzzy feeling / Slow drag / G.O.D. (Good Old Days) / Charlie, the methadone man / Out of my head / Damaged goods / Nowhere road / Sweetwater, Texas.

Dec 98. (cd-s) *<567951>* **FIRE ESCAPE** [-] [86]

FASTBACKS

Formed: Seattle, Washington, USA . . . 1980 by guitarist/vocalist LULU GARGUILO, bassist/vocalist KIM WARNICK, guitarist KURT BLOCH and drummer DUFF McKAGAN. This basic power-pop act delivered one single ('IT'S YOUR BIRTHDAY') in the early 80's before McKAGAN was whisked off to play guitar for seminal grunge act, 10 MINUTE WARNING. He more famously took up the bass for metal superstars, GUNS N' ROSES and stayed with them until he reformed 10MW in 1997. Meanwhile, The FASTBACKS replaced DUFF with RICHARD STUVERUD in '81, releasing a second effort (an unknown EP) the following year. They split not long after, although the Bristol imprint, 'Subway', released some new work in 1988/89, most notably the album, ' . . . AND HIS ORCHESTRA'. LULU, KIM, KURT and an ever changing drummer continued to surface now and then in the early 90's and in 1992 they signed to the seminal 'Sub Pop' label, releasing three worthy albums, 'THE QUESTION IS NO' (1992), 'ZUCKER' (1993) and 'ANSWER THE PHONE, DUMMY' (1994). • **Covered:** EYES OF A CHILD (John Lodge) / SPACE STATION No.5 (Montrose) / SIGN OF THE TIMES (. . .Hatch) / RAMBLIN' ROSE (MC5). • **Trivia:** Said to be EDDIE VEDDER's fave band.

Album rating: FASTBACKS AND HIS ORCHESTRA (*6) / VERY VERY POWERFUL MOTOR (*5) / ZUCKER (*7) / THE QUESTION IS NO (*5) / ANSWER THE PHONE, DUMMY (*5) / NEW MANSIONS IN SOUND (*6)

LULU GARGUILO – vocals, guitar / **KIM WARNICK** – vocals, bass / **KURT BLOCH** – guitar / **DUFF McKAGAN** (b. MICHAEL) – drums

not iss. No Threes

Jun 81. (7") *<N3-005>* **IT'S YOUR BIRTHDAY. / YOU CAN'T BE HAPPY** [-] [ ]

— **RICHARD STUVERUD** – drums, repl. McKAGAN (see above)

Apr 82. (12"ep) *<N3-006>* **FASTBACKS EP** [-] [ ]

— split but reformed in the late 80's

Subway not iss.

Oct 88. (7") *(SUBWAY 24)* **IN THE WINTER. / DREAM** [ ] [-]

Jun 89. (7") *(SUBWAY 26)* **WRONG WRONG WRONG. /** [ ] [-]

Jul 89. (lp) *(SUBORG 008)* **. . .AND HIS ORCHESTRA** [ ] [-]
– Seven days / The light's on you / If you tried / Don't cry for me / In the winter / Wrong, wrong, wrong / K street / You will be the one / Call it what you want / Set me free / I need some help / Midnight confessions / See and say / Only at night / What will they all say? / In America / No lethal hope / Fast enough / Wait! / Whenever I'm walking. *(cd-iss. Feb95 on 'Pop Llama'; PLCD 803)*

Blaster Blaster

Sep 90. (lp) *(BLATLP 001)* **VERY VERY POWERFUL MOTOR** [ ] [ ]
– In the summer / Apologies / Trouble sleeping / Better than before / What to expect / Dirk's car jam / Says who / Last night I had a dream I could fly / I won't regret / I guess / I'll be okay. *(UK-iss.Feb95 on 'Pop Llama'; PLCD 011)*

1991. (lp) *(BLATLP 003)* **NEVER FAILS . . . NEVER WORKS** [ ] [ ]
– In America / No lethal hope / Fast enough / Wait / Whenever I'm walking / Only at night / What will they all say? / Midnight confessions / See and say / It's your birthday / You can't be happy / Was late. *(re-iss. Nov93; same)*

Sub Pop Sub Pop

Jun 92. (cd) *<(SP 146B)>* **THE QUESTION IS NO** [-] [ ]
(UK-iss.Mar94; same)

Jan 93. (lp/cd) *<(SP 231/+CD)>* **ZUCKER** [ ] [ ]
– Believe me never / Gone to the moon / Hung on a bad peg / Under the old lightbulb / Never heard of him / When I'm old / All about nothing / Bill challenger / Parts / A kind of game / They don't care / Please read me / Save room for me / That was.

Mar 93. (7") *<(SP 69-236)>* **GONE TO THE MOON. / GO ALL THE WAY** [ ] [ ]
(12"+=/cd-s+=) *<(SP/+CD 68-235)>* – Right thing / Fanfare.

Sep 94. (7") *(MR 705-7)* **WAIT IT OUT. / THE JESTER** [ ] [ ]
(above issued on 'Munster')

Nov 94. (lp/c/cd) *<(SP/+MC/CD 259)>* **ANSWER THE PHONE, DUMMY** [ ] [ ] Oct94
– Waste of time / On the wall / Went for a swim / Old address of the unknown / Back to nowhere / BRD "coated" / I found the star / And you / On your hands / I'm cold / Think / In the observatory / Trumpets are loud / Meet the author / Future right.

May 96. (10"m-lp/m-cd) *<(MR 087/+CD)>* **ALONE IN A FURNITURE WAREHOUSE SCARING YOU AWAY LIKE A HOTEL MATTRESS** [ ] [ ]
– No information / Ladders / Buried treasure was crap / Wait it out / Alone in a furniture warehouse / Eyes of a child / All in order / Sign of the times.
(above issued on 'Munster')

Jun 96. (cd) *<(SPCD 357)>* **NEW MANSIONS IN SOUND** [ ] [ ]
– Fortunes misery / Which has not been written / No information / I know / Weather perfectly clear / 555 (part one) / 555 (part two) / Stay at home / Bitter drink / Just say / Banner year / Is it familiar? Space station No.5 / Find your way / Girl's eyes.

not iss. Pop Llama

Feb 98. (cd) *<6>* **WIN LOSE OR BOTH** [-] [ ]
– No music played / So wrong / Book of revelation / Used to belong / In the winter / On your hands / I know / I'm cold / Banneryear / 555 (part 2) / Gone to the moon / Always tomorrow / Ramblin' Rose.

– compilations, etc. –

Apr 92. (lp/cd) *Lost & Found; <(LF 016/+CD)>* **IN AMERICA** [ ] [ ]

1994. (cd) *Lucky; <3>* **BIKE TOY CLOCK GIFT** [-] [ ]

Aug 96. (cd) *Lance Rock; <24>* **HERE THEY ARE** (live at the Crocodile Cafe) [-] [ ]
– Out of the charts / Run no more / Hung on a bad peg / The light's on you / On the wall / Went for a swim / Old address of the unknown / Under the old lightbulb / I'm cold / In the observatory / On your hands / They don't care / Save room for me / Rat race.

FATAL MICROBES

Formed: London, England . . . 1978 by 14 year-old singing schoolgirl, DONNA 'HONEY' BANE, DEREK HADLEY and KEITH HUDSON. Augmented by relative veteran, PETE FENDER (of The POISON GIRLS), the young band were invited to share an EP with the latter's outfit. HONEY, however, had been AWOL from a detention centre at the time of the recording. Released via 'Small Wonder' early in '79, the two tracks, 'VIOLENCE GROWS' and 'BEAUTIFUL PICTURES', were also issued in 7" format later that year. The English answer to LYDIA LUNCH (Teenage Jesus) or JUDY NYLON (Snatch), the peroxide-pink HONEY and her glass-shattering shriek was best sampled on the couch-punk plea for public transport peace of mind, 'VIOLENCE GROWS'. However, the band took a backseat when HONEY opted for a solo career, releasing a self-financed single, 'GUILTY', in late 1980. Early the following year, she signed to EMI subsidiary, 'Zonophone' (COCKNEY REJECTS were among her labelmates!), attempts to transform her into a pouting teen-pop starlet initially paying off as 'TURN ME ON TURN

ME OFF' hit the UK Top 40. With her DIY/punk beginnings now just a vague memory, BANE had one more feeble stab at the charts with a cover of the Supremes' 'BABY LOVE'. Three further singles flopped unceremoniously, although she did revisit her radical past one more time on a late 1981 EP, 'YOU CAN BE YOU', mates CRASS (whose label the single also appeared on) backing her as the pseudonymous KEBABS. Prior to the final demise of her short-lived career, HONEY turned her talents to acting and starred in the controversial Mai Zettering film, 'Scrubbers'.

Album rating: still awaiting a comprehensive retrospective

HONEY BANE (b. DONNA BANE) – vocals / **PETE FENDER** – guitar (of POISON GIRLS) / **KEITH HUDSON** – bass / **DEREK HADLEY** – drums

Small Wonder | not iss.

Mar 79. (12"ep) *(WEENY 3)* **FATAL MICROBES MEET THE POISON GIRLS** [ ] [-]
– Violence grows / Beautiful pictures / (POISON GIRLS:- Close shop / Piano lessons).

Nov 79. (7"m) *(SMALL 20)* **VIOLENCE GROWS. / BEAUTIFUL PICTURES / CRY BABY** [ ] [-]

— **DANNY TRICKETT + DAVE MALTBEY** – guitar repl. PETE

— disbanded in 1980

HONEY BANE

Honey Bane | not iss.

Dec 80. (7") *(HB 946)* **GUILTY. / GUILTY (dub)** [ ] [-]

Zonophone | not iss.

Jan 81. (d7") *(Z 15)* **TURN ME ON TURN ME OFF. / IN DREAMS // T'AIN'T NOBODYS BUSINESS / NEGATIVE EXPOSURE** [37] [-]

Mar 81. (7") *(Z 19)* **BABY LOVE. / MASS PRODUCTION** [58] [-]

Jun 81. (7") *(Z 23)* **JIMMY (LISTEN TO ME). / NEGATIVE EXPOSURE** [ ] [-]

Oct 81. (7"m; DONNA & KEBABS) *(Crass; 521984-1)* **YOU CAN BE YOU** [ ] [-]
– Girl on the run / Porno grows / Boring conversations.

Jun 82. (7") *(Z 32)* **I WISH IT COULD BE ME. / CHILDHOOD PRINCE** [ ] [-]

Feb 83. (7") *(Z 36)* **DIZZY DREAMERS. / ONGOING SITUATION** [ ] [-]

— her last 45 was credited to "HONEY BANE & JONATHAN MOORE"

FATIMA MANSIONS (see under ⇒ COUGHLAN, Cathal)

FEAR

Formed: San Francisco, California, USA . . . 1978 by LEE VING, PHILO CRAMER, DERF SCRATCH and SPIT STIX. One of the first bands to emerge from the US West Coast punk/proto-hardcore scene, The FEAR had already become infamous for their raucous stage show by the time they made their vinyl debut on the soundtrack (released in the States on 'Slash') to Penelope Spheeris' acclaimed punkumentary, 'Decline Of Western Civilization'. Subsequently signing a full deal with 'Slash', these defiantly un-PC reprobates eventually issued a single in their own right via 1982's 'THE RECORD', a mini-set rammed with brief bursts of full-throttle hardcore-punk that even stretched to a fine trashing of The Animals' 'WE GOT TO GET OUT OF THIS PLACE'. By the time of the record's release, STIX had already been replaced by JOHNNY BACKBEAT while a certain FLEA (of subsequent hyperactive CHILI PEPPERS fame) honed his bass playing on 1983's yuletide extravaganza, the 'FUCK CHRISTMAS' EP. With FLEA going on to better things, ex-DICKIES sticksman, LORENZO, was in place for 1985's 'MORE BEER' album, FEAR's first release for new label, 'Restless'. Save for a 1991 live album, the ensuing decade saw FEAR keep a low profile, most fans having long forgotten about them by the release of 1995's belated 'HAVE ANOTHER BEER WITH FEAR'.

Album rating: THE RECORD (*6) / MORE BEER (*4) / LIVE . . . FOR THE RECORD (*4) / HAVE ANOTHER BEER WITH FEAR (*4)

LEE VING – vocals, guitar, harmonica / **PHILO CRAMER** – guitar / **DERF SCRATCH** – bass / **SPIT STIX** – drums

not iss. | Slash

Feb 82. (m-lp) *<SR 111>* **THE RECORD** [-] [ ]
– Let's have a war / Beef bologna / Camarillo / I don't care about you / New York's alright if you like.., / Gimme some action / Foreign policy / We destroy the family / I love living in the city / Disconnected / We got to get out of this place / Fresh fresh / Getting the brush / No more nothing. *<cd-iss. 1990 on 'Warners'; 828806>*

— STIX had already been repl. by **JOHNNY BACKBEAT** – drums

— **FLEA** – bass; repl. SCRATCH

1983. (7"ep) **FUCK CHRISTMAS EP** [-] [ ]

— **LORENZO** – bass (ex-DICKIES) repl. FLEA who joined RED HOT CHILI PEPPERS

Restless | Restless

1985. (lp) *<772039-1>* **MORE BEER** [-] [ ]
– Mouth don't stop (the trouble with . . .) / Responsibility / More beer / Hey / I am a doctor / Have a beer with fear / Bomb the Russians / Welcome to the dust ward / Null detector / Waiting for the meat / I love iving in the city / Now you're dead. *(UK cd-iss. Jul95; same as US)*

— **SPIT STIX** was back in the fray after joining NINA HAGEN

Oct 91. (cd) *<772391-2>* **LIVE . . . FOR THE RECORD (live)** [-] [ ]
– Null detector / I love livin' in the city / New York's all right / Beef bologna / More beer / What are friends for / Welcome to the dust war / I am a doctor / We gotta get out of this place / F*** Christmas / Responsibility / Hey / Waiting for the meat / Camarillo / Foreign policy / Give me some action / We destroy the destroy / I don't care about you / Let's have a war. *(re-iss. Jul95; same)*

— had already gave up the ghost . . . until . . .

Sector 2 | Sector 2

Jan 96. (cd) *<SECT2 10020>* **HAVE ANOTHER BEER WITH FEAR** [ ] [ ] Oct95
– Back into battle again / Demons stickin' pitchforks in my . . . / Ugly as you / Bad day / Everybody needs to believe in something / Chaos / U.S.A. / Legalize drugs / Drink some beer / Fuck you let's rodeo / Honor and obey / Meat and potatoes / Beer fight / Untermenschen / Publuc hangings / Free beer. *(cd re-iss. Jun98 on 'Fear'; HR 005-2)*

– compilations, etc. –

Mar 95. (cd) *Solar; <1003>* **AS FAR AS THE I CAN C** [-] [ ]

FEELIES

Formed: Hoboken, New Jersey, USA . . . late 1977 by songwriter, GLENN MERCER and BILL MILLION, who completed the line-up with KEITH CLAYTON and VINNIE DeNUNZIO. They emerged from the garage and played the CBGB's in the late 70's, leading to a one-off single, 'RAISED EYEBROWS', for the UK label, 'Rough Trade'. Early the following decade, with ANTON FIER replacing DeNUNZIO, The FEELIES unleashed their debut album, 'CRAZY RHYTHMS' (1980), a TALKING HEADS meets VELVET UNDERGROUND affair combining sparse two-chord harmonies and jerky pop energy. Issued for another Brit imprint, 'Stiff' and despite critical acclaim, it failed to generate much interest, the band's reluctance to publicise with a tour not helping any. The FEELIES generally lackadaisical attitude towards self promotion subsequently led to their 5-album contract being torn up and the members went off into various side projects, only surfacing occasionally to play on holiday weekends. This hiatus resulted in MERCER and MILLION joining old high school mates, The TRYPES, who released the 1984 EP, 'THE EXPLORERS HOLD' on the FEELIES' new label, 'Coyote'. In 1983, they found fellow songwriter, DAVID WECKERMAN (of YUNG WU), who helped them write the score for the film 'Smithereens'. The following year, the pair featured as The WILLIES in Jonathan Demme's film, 'Something Wild', covering 'I'M A BELIEVER', 'FAME' and 'BEFORE THE NEXT TEARDROP FALLS'. In 1986, PETER BUCK heard they were back together, the ubiquitous R.E.M. man offering to produce their comeback album, 'THE GOOD EARTH'. To many fans and critics alike, it was certainly worth the six year wait, the reaction even spurring them on to a tour of Europe early the following year. In 1988, The FEELIES finally signed to a major ('A&M') and hit the lower regions of the US chart with their third album, 'ONLY LIFE'. The group recorded one further set before MERCER and WECKERMAN took off, the pair later surfacing as WAKE OOLOO. • **Covered:** EVERYBODY'S GOT SOMETHING TO HIDE + SHE SAID SHE SAID (Beatles) / SEDAN DELIVERY (Neil Young) / EGYPTIAN REGGAE (Jonathan Richman) / WAKE OOLOO:- SO WANT TO BE A ROCK'N'ROLL STAR (Byrds).

Album rating: CRAZY RHYTHMS (*8) / THE GOOD EARTH (*7) / ONLY LIFE (*7) / TIME FOR A WITNESS (*4)

GLEN MERCER – vocals, guitar, drums / **BILL MILLION** – percussion, guitar, vocals / **KEITH CLAYTON** – bass, drums, vocals / **VINNIE DeNUNZIO** – drums

Rough Trade | not iss.

Sep 79. (7") *(RT 24)* **RAISED EYEBROWS. / FA CE-LA** [ ] [-]

— **ANTON FIER** – drums, repl. VINNIE who later formed CERTAIN GENERALS after a spell with RICHARD LLOYD / added guests **ARTHUR ADAMS + ROLAND BAUTISTA** – guitars

Stiff | not iss.

Jan 80. (7";w-drawn) *(BUY 65)* **EVERYBODY'S GOT SOMETHING TO HIDE. / ORIGINAL LOVE** [-] [-]

Jan 80. (lp/c) *(SEEZ/ZSEEZ 20)* **CRAZY RHYTHMS** [ ] [-]
– The boy with the perpetual nervousness / Fa ce-la / Loveless love / Forces at work / Original love / Everybody's got something to hide / Moscow nights / Raised eyebrows / Crazy rhythms. *(re-iss. Nov87 on 'Line' lp/cd; XILP4/LICD9 00168) <US-iss.1991 on 'A&M' cd/c; 75021-5319-2/-4>*

— rested/split for a time, when ANTON joined PERE UBU

— **GLENN, BILL, KEITH / + STANLEY DEMESKI** – drums / **DAVE WECKERMAN** – percussion

Rough Trade | Twin-Tone / Coyote

Sep 86. (lp) *(ROUGH 104) <TTC 8673>* **THE GOOD EARTH** [ ] [ ]
– On the roof / The high road / The last round up / Slipping (into something) / When company comes / She said, she said / Let's go / Two rooms / The good earth / Tomorrow today / Slow down / Sedan delivery. *(cd-iss. Nov87 on 'Line'; LICD 900428)*

Nov 86. (12"ep) *(RTT 180)* **NO ONE KNOWS EP** [ ] [-]
– The high road / She said she said / Slipping (into something) / Sedan delivery.

— **BRENDA SAUTER** – bass, vocals (ex-TRYPES) repl. CLAYTON

A&M | Coyote-A&M

Apr 89. (lp/c/cd) *<AMA/AMC/CDA 5214>* **ONLY LIFE** [ ] [ ] Nov88
– It's only life / Too much / Deep fascination / Higher ground / The undertow / For a while / The final word / Too far gone / Away / What goes on.

Mar 91. (cd/lp) *(<75021 5344-2/-1>)* **TIME FOR A WITNESS** [ ] [ ]
– Waiting / Time for a witness / Sooner or later / Find a way / Decide / Doin' it again / Invitation / For now / What she said / Real cool time.

Jan 93. (cd-s) *<CD 17675>* **HIGHER GROUND / EGYPTIAN REGGAE / EVERYBODY'S GOT SOMETHING TO HIDE EXCEPT ME AND MY MONKEY** [-] [ ]

— disbanded in 1992. STANLEY joined LUNA 2 with former GALAXIE 500 member

DEAN WAREHAM. SAUTER joined SPEED THE PLOUGH and later WILD CARNATION

YUNG WU

— **WECKERMAN** (lead vox), **MERCER, MILLION + SAUTER** recruited for this offshoot **JOHN BAUMGARTNER** – keyboards (ex-TRYPES)

not iss. Coyote

Oct 87. (lp/c) *<TTC 87119/+C>* **SHORE LEAVE** [-] [ ]
– Shore leave / Empty pool / Aspiration / Spinning / Big day / Eternal ice / Strange little man / Return to Zion / Child of the moon / Powderfinger / Modern farmer.

WAKE OOLOO

MERCER + WECKERMAN + RUSS GAMBINO – keyboards / **TROY MEISS** – bass

Houses In Motion Pravda

Dec 94. (cd/c) *(EFA 26207-2) <PR 6349-2/-4>* **HEAR NO EVIL** [ ] [ ]
– Time to go / Another song / Forty days / Rise / Nobody heard / Knocking on ever door / From afar / Effax / Grams of sand / Any Mindy.

— **JOHN DEAN** – bass; repl. MEISS

Jun 95. (cd) *(EFA 06197-2) <6356>* **WHAT ABOUT IT** [ ] [ ]
– Don't look now / Beautiful feeling / Anything / Too long gone / Age of reason / Fun to be happy / It's forgotten / Common sense / Nature of the beast / Hard to find / Down that road / Monday morning.

Konkurrent Pravda

Sep 96. (cd) *(K 171CD) <6362>* **STOP THE RIDE** [ ] [ ] Jul96
– Too many times / In the way / Stiff / Stop the ride / Like yesterday / Get caught up / Alive and waiting / Every other one / Final warning / Maybe next time / So you want to be a rock'n'roll star.

John FELICE & THE LOWDOWNS (see under ⇒ REAL KIDS)

FELT

Formed: Birmingham, England ... 1979 by LAWRENCE HAYWARD. Following glowing reviews for a self-produced single, 'INDEX', HAYWARD recruited a full band – MAURICE DEEBANK, GARY AINGE and NICK GILBERT (who issued a solo single, 'NEWTRITION' / 'BLIMP' under The VERSATILE NEWTS moniker on 'Shanghai' in 1980) – in an attempt to realise his dreams of pop stardom. Signed to 'Cherry Red', the first chapter in the FELT story began with a series of early 80's singles (including the sublime 'PENELOPE TREE') and a couple of mini-sets, 'CRUMBLING THE ANTISEPTIC BEAUTY' (1982) and 'THE SPLENDOUR OF FEAR' (1984). Characterised by DEEBANK's resonating guitar sound – an often romantic combination of TOM VERLAINE, The BYRDS and Spanish classical – these early recordings alternated between atmospheric instrumentals and moody HAYWARD vocal cuts. With a highly affected singing style lying somewhere between LLOYD COLE and JARVIS COCKER (although these two were undoubtedly influenced by him rather than the other way around), HAYWARD wasn't the greatest of vocalists in a technical sense yet the combination of his voice and the dreamy backing created music of a strange beauty. He was also something of a demanding boss and by the release of a first album, 'THE STRANGE IDOLS PATTERN AND OTHER SHORT STORIES' (1984), the band had already gone through two bassists with a line-up constantly on the brink of collapse. It was into this precarious situation that hammond player, MARTIN DUFFY entered in the mid-80's as the band began work on 'IGNITE THE SEVEN CANNONS' (1985) with ROBIN GUTHRIE at the production helm. The accompanying single, 'PRIMITIVE PAINTERS', featured fellow COCTEAU TWINS, LIZ FRASER, on vocals, a sterling slice of swirling psychedelia which remains one of the band's few near misses with actual chart action. Despite the permanent departure of DEEBANK in 1985, the band continued to reap critical acclaim with the likes of 'FOREVER BREATHES THE LONELY WORD' (1986), their fourth album proper and their second for new label 'Creation'. While FELT were clearly capable of penning melodies with chart-hit written all over them, HAYWARD's penchant for willfully obscure lyrical fare and song titles significantly reduced their chances of commercial success. Releasing an album – 'TRAIN ABOVE THE CITY' (1988) – consisting solely of Fender Rhodes piano instrumentals wasn't exactly a shrewd move either, although by this point LAWRENCE had obviously resigned himself to eternal cultdom. The following year FELT bowed out with 'ME AND A MONKEY ON THE MOON' (1989), perhaps the most accessible album of their decade-long recording career. While MARTIN DUFFY joined PRIMAL SCREAM's rock'n'roll circus, LAWRENCE eventually resurfaced with DENIM, a self-consciously ironic glitter-pop revivalist project. Recorded with bonafide glam musos from the 70's, 'BACK IN DENIM' was released by the trendy 'Boy's Own' label in '92, the music press briefly reprising LAWRENCE for a new generation of indie kids. Issued at the height of the Britpop phenomenon, follow-up set, 'DENIM ON ICE' (1996) was given scant media attention compared to the column inches devoted to the likes of PULP, an irony that HAYWARD would no doubt savour.

Album rating: CRUMBLING THE ANTISEPTIC BEAUTY mini (*6) / THE SPLENDOUR OF FEAR (*6) / THE STRANGE IDOLS PATTERN AND OTHER SHORT STORIES (*7) / IGNITE THE SEVEN CANNONS (*7) / LET THE SNAKES CRINKLE THEIR HEADS TO DEATH (*6) / FOREVER BREATES THE LONELY WORD (*7) / POEM OF THE RIVER mini (*6) / THE PICTORIAL JACKSON REVIEW (*6) / TRAIN ABOVE THE CITY (*6) / ME AND A MONKEY ON THE MOON (*5) / ABSOLUTE CLASSIC MASTERPIECES compilation (*8) / BUBBLEGUM PERFUME compilation (*6) / Denim: BACK IN DENIM (*7)

LAWRENCE HAYWARD – guitar, vocals

Shanghai not iss.

Sep 79. (7") *(SRTS 79-CUS 321)* **INDEX. / BREAK IT** [ ] [-]

— added **MAURICE DEEBANK** – guitar / **GARY AINGE** – drums / **NICK GILBERT** – bass

Cherry Red not iss.

Jul 81. (7") *(CHERRY 26)* **SOMETHING SENDS ME TO SLEEP. / RED INDIANS / SOMETHING SENDS ME TO SLEEP (version)** [ ] [-]
Feb 82. (m-lp) *(MRED 25)* **CRUMBLING THE ANTISEPTIC BEAUTY** [ ] [-]
– Birdmen / Cathedral / I worship the sun / Templeroy / Fortune / Evergreen dazed. *(cd-iss. w/ next album Sep86; MREDCD 25)*

— NICK GILBERT decided to leave. Also DEEBANK left for a short while

Sep 82. (7") *(CHERRY 45)* **MY FACE IS ON FIRE. / TRAILS OF COLOUR DISSOLVE** [ ] [-]

— added **MICK LLOYD** – bass and the returning **DEEBANK**

Jun 83. (7") *(CHERRY 59)* **PENELOPE TREE. / A PREACHER IN NEW ENGLAND** [ ] [-]
(12"+=) *(12CHERRY 59)* – Now summer's spread its wings again.
Feb 84. (m-lp/c) *(MRED/CRED 57)* **THE SPLENDOUR OF FEAR** [ ] [-]
– The stagnant pool / Red Indians / The world is as soft as lace / Mexican bandits / The optimist and the poet / Preacher in New England.
Mar 84. (7") *(CHERRY 78)* **MEXICAN BANDITS. / THE WORLD IS AS SOFT AS LACE** [ ] [-]
Jul 84. (7") *(CHERRY 81)* **SUNLIGHT BATHED THE GOLDEN GLOW. / FORTUNE** [ ] [-]
(12"+=) *(12CHERRY 81)* – Sunlight strings.
Oct 84. (lp) *(BRED 63)* **THE STRANGE IDOLS PATTERN AND OTHER SHORT STORIES** [ ] [-]
– Roman litter / Sempiternal darkness / Spanish Louise / Vasco da Gama / Sunlight bathed the golden glow / Crucifix heaven / Whirlpool vision of shame / Dismantled King is off the throne / Imprint / Crystal ball. *(cd-iss. Feb93; CDBRED 63)*

— **MARTIN DUFFY** – organ repl. LLOYD (below b-side was above line-up) / **MARCO THOMAS** – bass guested with **ELIZABETH FRAZER** – vocals (COCTEAU TWINS) ROBIN GUTHRIE of The COCTEAUS produced 1985 material.

Aug 85. (12") *(12CHERRY 89)* **PRIMITIVE PAINTERS. / CATHEDRAL (rec.'84)** [ ] [-]
(pic-cd-s iss.Aug88; CDCHERRY 89)

— Band consisted of interchanging lead guitarists LAWRENCE and MAURICE, MARTIN and LIZ on some vocals, MARCO on nearly all bass, plus GARY – drums

Sep 85. (lp) *(BRED 65)* **IGNITE THE SEVEN CANNONS** [ ] [-]
– My darkest light will shine / The day the rain came down / Scarlet servants / I don't know which way to turn / Serpent shade / Primitive painters / Elegance of an only dream / Black ship in the harbour / Textile ranch / Caspian see / Southern state tapestry. (c+=) – (incl.previous lp). *(cd-iss. Jul89 with last album' BREDCD 65) (re-iss. cd May96; CDBRED 65)*

— guest **TONY WILLE** – guitar repl. MAURICE DEEBANK (MARCO now full member)

Creation not iss.

May 86. (7") *(CRE 027)* **BALLAD OF THE BAND. / I DIDN'T MEAN TO HURT YOU** [ ] [-]
(12"+=) *(CRE 027T)* – Candles in a church / Ferdinand Magellan.
Jun 86. (lp) *(CRELP 009)* **LET THE SNAKES CRINKLE THEIR HEADS TO DEATH** [ ] [-]
– Song for William S. Harvey / Ancient city where I lived / The seventeenth century / The palace / Indian scriptures / The Nazca plain / Voyage to illumination / Jewel sky / Viking dress / Sapphire mansions. *(cd-iss. Mar91 & May94; CRECD 009)*

— **TONY WILLE** – guitars guested again

Sep 86. (7") *(CRE 032)* **RAIN OF CRYSTAL SPIRES. / I WILL DIE WITH MY HEAD IN FLAMES** [ ] [-]
(12"+=) *(CRE 032T)* – Gather up your wings and fly / Sandman's on the rise again.
Oct 86. (lp/c) *(CRELP 011/+C)* **FOREVER BREATHES THE LONELY WORD** [ ] [-]
– Down but not yet out / Hours of darkness have changed my mind / All the people I like are those that are dead / Grey streets / Gather up your wings and fly / Rain of crystal spires / A wave crashed on rocks / September lady. *(c+=)* – (includes previous lp). *(cd-iss. Oct90; CRECD 011)*

— added 6th guest member **NEIL SCOTT** – Fender jazzmaster retained guest **TONY WILLE** to augment **LAWRENCE, GARY, MARTIN** and **MARCO**

Jun 87. (m-lp) *(CRELP 017)* **POEM OF THE RIVER** [ ] [-]
– Declaration / She lives by the castle / Riding on the equator / Stained glass windows in the sky / Dark red birds / Silver plane. *(cd-iss. Mar91 & May94; CRECD 017)*

— **FELT** are **LAWRENCE, MARTIN DUFFY, MARCO THOMAS, GARY AINGE** but album features 1. LAWRENCE with guest **RICHARD THOMAS** – soprano saxophone (of DIF JUZ) 2. DUFFY – solo / 3. LAWRENCE – solo guitar / 4. LAWRENCE with **MICK TRAVIS** – bass 5. LAWRENCE, DUFFY and TRAVIS – instrumental

Jul 87. (12"ep) *(CRE 048T)* **THE FINAL RESTING PLACE OF THE ARK / AUTUMN. / FIRE CIRCLE / THERE'S NO SUCH THING AS VICTORY / BURIED WILD BLIND** [ ] [-]

— added **MICK BUND** – bass (MARCO now lead guitar & LAWRENCE added organ)

May 88. (lp) *(CRELP 030)* **THE PICTORIAL JACKSON REVIEW** [ ] [-]
– Apple boutique / Ivory past / Christopher St. / Bitter end / Until the fools get wise / How spook got her man / Don't die on my doorstep / Under a pale light / Sending lady Lord / The darkest ending.

— Next album was down to just DUFFY and AINGE. Others were rested

Aug 88. (lp) *(CRELP 035)* **TRAIN ABOVE THE CITY** [ ] [-]
– On Weegee's sidewalk / Train above the city / Run Chico run / Press softly on the brakes Holly / Seahorses on Broadway / Spectral morning / Book of swords / Teargardens. *(cd-iss. Oct88, with last album; CRELP 035CD)*

— Full group again, + **ROSE McDOWELL** – vocals (ex-STRAWBERRY SWITCHBLADE)

Oct 88. (7") *(CRE 060)* **SPACE BLUES. / TUESDAYS SECRET** [ ] [-]
(12"+=) *(CRE 060T)* – Be still / Female star.

— **JOHN MOHAN** – guitar (ex-SERVANTS) repl. ROSE who was only guest.

El / not iss.

Oct 89. (7"free-flexi) *(GPO F44)* **GET OUT OF MY MIRROR** - -
Nov 89. (lp/cd) *(ACME/+CD 24)* **ME AND A MONKEY ON THE MOON** -
– I can't make love to you anymore / Mobile shack / Free / Budgie jacket / Carton sky / New day dawning / Down an August path / Never let you go / She deals in crosses / Get out of my mirror. *(cd re-iss. Oct96; same)*

— They split late 1989 having been together for 10 years. LAWRENCE moved to New York, having flitted to Brighton a year earlier. DUFFY joined PRIMAL SCREAM.

– compilations, etc. –

Sep 87. (lp/c/cd) *Cherry Red; (BRED/CBRED/BREDCD 79)* **GOLDMINE THRASH** -
(c+=) – (includes 7 extra tracks).
Jun 90. (cd/c/lp) *Creation; (CRE CD/MC/LP 069)* **BUBBLEGUM PERFUME** -
– I will die with my head in flames / Stained glass windows in the sky / I Didn't mean to hurt you / Space blues / Autumn / Be still / There's no such thing as victory / Magellan / The final resting of the ark / Sandman's on the rise again / Don't die on my doorstep / A wave crashed on rocks / Book of swords / Declaration / Gather up your wings and fly / The darkest ending / Bitter end / Rain of crystal spires / Voyage of illumination / Ballad of the band.
Mar 92. (12"ep/cd-ep) *Cherry Red; (12/CD CHERRY 124)* **PRIMITIVE PAINTERS / DISMANTLED KING IS OFF THE THRONE. / SUNLIGHT BATHED THE GOLDEN GLOW** -
Apr 92. (cd) *Cherry Red; (CDBRED 97)* **ABSOLUTE CLASSIC MASTERPIECES** -
– Primitive painters / The day the rain came down / My darkest light will shine / Textile ranch / Sunlight bathed the golden glow / Crystal ball / Dismantled king is off the throne / Fortune / Dance of deliverance / The stagnant pool / Red Indians / The world is as soft as lace / Penelope Tree / Trails of colour dissolve / Evergreen dazed / Templeroy / Something sends me to sleep / Index *(re-iss. Oct96; same)*
Jun 93. (4xcd-ep-box) *Cherry Red; (FELT BOX 1)* **THE FELT BOX SET** -
Sep 93. (d-cd) *Creation; (CRECD 150)* **ABSOLUTE CLASSIC MASTERPIECES VOL.2** -
May 96. (cd) *Cherry Red; (CDBRED 72)* **CRUMBLING THE ANTISEPTIC BEAUTY / THE PLEANDOUR OF FEAR** -

DENIM

— were formed by **LAWRENCE** – vocals, guitar, keyboards with **SIOBHAN** – bass / **GERRY SHEPHERD** – drums (ex-GLITTER BAND)

Boys Own / not iss.

Nov 92. (cd/c/lp) *(82849-2/-4/-1)* **BACK IN DENIM** -
– Back in denim / Fish and chips / Bubble head / Middle of the road / The Osmonds / I saw the glitter on your face / American rock / Livin' on the streets / Here is my song for Europe / I'm against the eighties.
Jan 93. (7"/c-s) *(BOI/+CS 12)* **MIDDLE OF THE ROAD. / APE HANGERS** -
(12"+=/cd-s+=) *(BOI X/CD 12)* – Robin's nest / The great grape ape hangers.

Echo / not iss.

Feb 96. (cd/c/lp) *(ECH CD/MC/LP 008)* **DENIM ON ICE** -
– Great pub rock revival / It fell off the back of a lorry / Romeo Jones in love again / Bumburger / Supermodels / Shut up Sidney / Mrs. Mills / Best song in the world / Synthesizers in the rain / Job centre / Council house / Glue and smack / Jane Suck in '77 / Grandad's false teeth / Silly rabbit / Don't bite too much out of the apple / Myriad of hoops / Denim on ice.
Feb 96. (7"/c-s) *(ECS/+MC 017)* **IT FELL OFF THE BACK OF A LORRY. / I WILL CRY AT CHRISTMAS** -
(cd-s+=) *(ECSCD 017)* – Snake bite / Internet curtains.

EMI Disc / not iss.

Aug 97. (c-s/7") *(TC+/DISC 009)* **SUMMER SMASH. / SUN'S OUT** -
(cd-s+=) *(CDDISC 009)* – Seaside shuffle / ("a'-Denim mix).

MAURICE DEEBANK

— also released a solo album while a FELT member. Augmented by **JOHN A. RIVERS** – producer, keyboards, percussion / **DA'AVE ELSON** – bass

Cherry Red / not iss.

Aug 84. (m-lp) *(MRED 61)* **INNER THOUGHT ZONE** -
– The watery song / Four corners of the Earth / Study No.1 / Golden hills / Silver mountain of Paradise Square / So serene. *(cd-iss. Nov92 +=; CDMRED 61)* – Dance of deliverance / Pavanne / A tale from Seriabins lonely trail / Meastoso con anima.

FIAT LUX

Formed: Wakefield, Yorkshire, England . . . mid '82 by drama college students STEVE WRIGHT and DAVID P. CRICKMORE, who were initially blessed with the patronage of BILL NELSON (ex-BE-BOP DELUXE and boss of his own independent label, 'Cocteau'). He, in turn, introduced his younger brother, IAN NELSON, a session sax/keyboard player who was invited to become a permanent fixture following the release of the FIAT LUX debut single, 'FEELS LIKE WINTER AGAIN'. Healthy reviews and a minor industry buzz led to a deal with 'Polydor', the band raising their profile with support dates to the likes of HOWARD JONES. A string of singles were issued over the next year, 'PHOTOGRAPHY', 'SECRETS' and 'BLUE EMOTION' (the latter two scraping into the lower regions of the chart) collected together on 1984's mini-set, 'HIRED HISTORY'. Subsequent single releases, 'HOUSE OF THORNS' and 'SOLITARY LOVERS' crashed, however, FIAT LUX finally consigned to the synth-pop scrapheap following the departure of first CRICKMORE and then NELSON.

Album rating: HIRED HISTORY (*5)

STEVE WRIGHT (b. SEBASTIAN BARBARO) – vocals / **DAVID P. CRICKMORE** – guitar, bass, keyboards / **IAN NELSON** – keyboards, saxophone

Cocteau / not iss.

Nov 82. (7") *(COQ 9)* **FEELS LIKE WINTER AGAIN. / THIS ILLNESS** -
(re-iss. Mar85; same)

— added on tour **STEVE SMITH** – bass / **RAY MARTINEZ** – drums

Polydor / not iss.

Aug 83. (7") *(FIAT 1)* **PHOTOGRAPHY. / AQUA VITAE** -
(12"+=) *(FIATX 1)* – ('A'extended).
Jan 84. (7") *(FIAT 2)* **SECRETS. / COMFORTABLE LIFE** 65 -
(12"+=) *(FIATX 2)* – Aqua vitae.
Mar 84. (7") *(FIAT 3)* **BLUE EMOTION. / SLEEPLESS NIGHTMARE** 59 -
(7"box+=/12"+=) *(FIAT B/T 3)* – ('A'version).
Aug 84. (m-lp/m-c) *(821 637-1/-4)* **HIRED HISTORY** -
– Blue emotion / Secrets / Photography / Sleepless nightmare / Aqua vitae / Comfortable life.
Sep 84. (7") *(FIAT 4)* **HOUSE OF THORNS. / THREE'S COMPANY** -
(12"+=) *(FIATX 4)* – Sally, free and easy.
Jan 85. (7") *(FIAT 5)* **SOLITARY LOVERS. / NO MORE PROUD** -
(12"+=) *(FIATX 5)* – ('A'extended).

— trimmed a duo when CRICKMORE departed, and when IAN joined his solo brother the group were finished

FIELD MICE

Formed: Mitcham, South London, England . . . 1987 by ROBERT WRATTEN and MARK DOBSON, who recruited HARVEY WILLIAMS after relocating to Bristol and signing with the local 'Sarah' label. The FIELD MICE fast gained a reputation for being the ultimate in "indie tweeness" with their label and nearly every band subsequently signed to it derided by the music press in the same sneering manner. Nevertheless, the indie establishment disdain was matched by an equally intense adoration from their sizeable fan base who snapped up a string of pastoral, largely acoustic singles and EP's including 'SENSITIVE', 'IF YOU NEED SOMEONE' and 'I CAN SEE MYSELF ALONE FOREVER'. The turn of the decade saw the group fleshing out their sound with the addition of ANNEMARI DAVIES and MICHAEL HISCOCK, the more sonically adventurous 'SKYWRITING' (1990) mini-set still failing to convince the band's critics. Even a sterling cover of the band's 'KISS & MAKE UP' by the soon-to-be-suffocatingly-trendy SAINT ETIENNE didn't reverse the band's image problem and after a further handful of singles and a belated full length album, 'FOR KEEPS' (1991) the FIELD MICE went to ground for good.

Album rating: SNOWBALL mini (*5) / SKYWRITING (*6) / FOR KEEPS (*6) / COASTAL compilation (*6)

ROBERT WRATTEN (b. 5 Aug'66, Carshalton, Surrey, England) – vocals / **MARK DOBSON** (b.27 Apr'65, Hartlepool, England) – drums / **HARVEY WILLIAMS** (b.31 Dec'65, Cornwall, England) – guitar (ex-ANOTHER SUNNY DAY)

Sarah / not iss.

Nov 88. (7"ep) *(SARAH 012)* **EMMA'S HOUSE / WHEN YOU SLEEP. / FABULOUS FRIEND / THE LAST LETTER** -
Feb 89. (7") *(SARAH 018)* **SENSITIVE. /** -
Oct 89. (10"m-lp) *(SARAH 402)* **SNOWBALL** -
Jan 90. (7") *(SARAH 024)* **IF YOU NEED SOMEONE. /** -
(12"ep+=) **AUTUMN STORE PART ONE – EP** – Anyone else isn't you / Bleak.
Feb 90. (7"one-sided) *(CAFF 2)* **I CAN SEE MYSELF ALONE FOREVER / EVERYTHING ABOUT YO U** -
(above on 'Caff' records)

— added **ANNEMARI DAVIES** (b. 9 Feb'71, Oxfordshire, England) – guitar, keyboards / **MICHAEL HISCOCK** (b.24 Feb'66, Carshalton) – bass

Jul 90. (m lp) *(SARAH 601)* **SKYWRITING** -
– Canada / Clearer / It isn't forever / Below the stars / Humblebee / Triangle.
Sep 90. (10"ep) *(SARAH 038)* **SO SAID KAY EP** -
Mar 91. (7") **SEPTEMBER'S NOT SO FAR AWAY. /** -
Aug 91. (lp/c/cd) *(SARAH 606/+C/CD)* **COASTAL** (compilation) -
– September's not so far away / So said Kay / The last letter / Sensitive / This is not wrong / If you need someone / Anyone else isn't you / Couldn't feel safer / Let's kiss and make up / Below the stars / Quicksilver / When morning comes to town / It isn't forever / Between hello and goodbye.
Sep 91. (7") **MISSING THE MOON. /** -
Oct 91. (lp/cd) *(SARAH 607/+CD)* **FOR KEEPS** -
– Five movements / Star of David / Coach station reunion / This is not here / Of the perfect kind / Tilting at windmill / Think of these things / Willow / And before the first kiss / Freezing point.

— split late 1991

– compilations, etc. –

1998. (cd) *Shinkansen; <8>* **WHERE'D YOU LEARN TO KISS THAT WAY?** -

FIELDS OF THE NEPHILIM

Formed: Stevenage, Hertfordshire, England . . . 1985 by CARL McCOY, TONY PETTITT, PETER YATES and brothers PAUL and NOD WRIGHT. Eternally popular among flour-faced goths and much ridiculed by the indie/rock press, FIELDS OF THE NEPHILIM were a sort of poorer cousin to darklords, SISTERS OF MERCY and The MISSION. Unlike those two bands, however, The 'NEPHILIM were never likely to cross over for mainstream rock consumption, if only for their steadfast adherence to goth cliches. To be fair, they did have a slightly different slant, at least image wise, kitted out in a kind of faux-Western garb, stetsons and all (black of course). Following on from an independently released debut EP, 'BURNING THE FIELDS', the band signed to Beggars Banquet subsidiary, 'Situation Two' and unveiled their debut album, 'DAWNRAZOR'. OTT apocalyptic vocals and anthemic guitar doom was the order of the day, 'PREACHER MAN' becoming the band's calling card despite boasting a hilariously amateurish video. Attracting a fanatical fanbase, the band even managed to crack the UK Top 20 with the more accomplished follow-up set, 'THE NEPHILIM' (1988) and topped the indie charts with the 'MOONCHILD' single. Yet time honoured "musical differences" would eventually prove the straw that broke the bat's back, third set 'ELYZIUM' (1990) displaying a much more toned down approach in contrast to its predecessor. It was the last album McCOY would record with the band, bailing out in 1991 and taking the name with him while his former pardners in musical crime carried on under the name RUBICON. • **Songwriters:** Group compositions except; IN EVERY DREAM HOME A HEARTACHE (Roxy Music).

Album rating: DAWNRAZOR (*6) / THE NEPHILIM (*6) / ELYZIUM (*4) / EARTH INFERNO (*5) / REVELATIONS compilation (*6)

CARL McCOY – vocals / **PAUL WRIGHT** – guitar / **PETER YATES** – guitar / **TONY PETTITT** – bass / **NOD WRIGHT** – drums

Tower / not iss.

Aug 85. (12"ep) *(N 1)* **BURNING THE FIELDS** [ ] [-]
– Back in the Gehenna / Trees come down / Dark cell / Laura. *(re-iss. Jul87 on 'Jungle'; JUNG 28T)*

Situation 2 / Beggars Banquet

Aug 86. (12"m) *(SIT 42T)* **POWER. / SECRETS / THE TOWER** [ ] [-]
(above 2 re-iss. cd Dec91 as 'LAURA' on 'Contempo'; CONTECD 196)

Mar 87. (7") *(SIT 46)* **PREACHER MAN. / LAURA II** [ ] [-]
(12"+=) *(SIT 46T)* – ('A'-Contaminated version).

May 87. (lp/c)(cd) *(SIT UP/CP 18)(SITU 18CD) <6599>* **DAWNRAZOR** [62] [ ]
– Intro (The harmonica man) / Slow kill / Volcane (Mr. Jealousy has returned) / Vet for the insane / Dust / Reanimator / Dawnrazor / The sequel. *(c+=)* – Preacher man / Power. *(cd++=)* – Laura II / Secrets / The Tower. *(re-iss. 1988 lp/c/cd; SITL/+C 18/+CD) (cd-iss. Sep95 on 'Beggars Banquet-Lowdown'; BBL 18CD)*

Oct 87. (7") *(SIT 48)* **BLUE WATER. / IN EVERY DREAM HOME A HEARTACHE** [75] [-]
(12") *(SIT 48T)* – ('A'-Electrostatic mix) / ('A'-Hot wire version).

May 88. (7") *(SIT 52)* **MOONCHILD (first seal). / SHIVA** [28] [-]
(12"+=) *(SIT 52T)* – ('A'-Longevity version).
(12"+=) *(SIT 52TR)* – Power (live) / Vet for the insane (live).

Sep 88. (lp/c)(cd) *(SIT U/C 22)(SITU 22CD) <8511>* **THE NEPHILIM** [14] [ ]
– Endemoniada / The watchman / Phobia / Moonchild / Chord of souls / Shiva / Celebrate / Love under will / Last exit for the lost. *(re-iss. Jun89 as 2x12"; SITU 22L) (cd re-iss. Sep95 on 'Beggars Banquet-Lowdown'; BBL 22CD)*

May 89. (7"/12") *(SIT 57/+T)* **PSYCHONAUT (Lib.II). / CELEBRATE (second seal)** [35] [-]
(cd-s+=) *(SIT 57CD)* – Psychonaut (Lib.IV).
(12") *(SIT 57T)* – Psychonaut (Lib.III) / Psychonaut (Lib.I) / Psychonaut (Lib.IV).

Beggars Banquet / Polydor

Jul 90. (7") *(BEG 244)* **FOR HER LIGHT. / SUBMISSION** [54] [-]
(12"+=/cd-s+=) *(BEG 244 T/CD)* – ('A'&'B'extended).

Sep 90. (cd)(c/lp) *(BEGA 115CD)(BEGC/BEGA 115) <849488>* **ELIZIUM** [22] [ ]
– (Dead but dreaming) For her light (At the gates of silent memory) Paradise regained / Submission / Sumerland (what dreams may come) / Wail of summer / And there will your heart be also. *(re-iss. cd Sep95 on 'Beggars Banquet-Lowdown'; BBL 115CD)*

Nov 90. (7") *(BEG 250)* **SUMERLAND (DREAMED). / THE WATCHMAN (live)** [37] [-]
(12"+=/cd-s+=) *(BEG 250 T/CD)* – Blue water (live) / Phobia (live).

—— In 1990, for live work they added **PAUL CHOWSER** – keyboards

Mar 91. (cd)(c/d-lp) *(BEGA 120CD)(BEGC/BEGA 120)* **EARTH INFERNO (live)** [39] [-]
– Intro (Dead but dreaming) For her light (at the gates of silent memory) Paradise regained / Moonchild / Submission / Preacher man / Love under will / Sumerland / Last exit for the lost / Psychonaut / Dawnrazor. *(cd re-iss. Sep95 on 'Beggars Banquet-Lowdown'; BBL 120CD)*

—— CARL McCOY departed Oct'91

- compilations, etc. -

Aug 88. (m-lp) *Supporti Fonograph; (SF 008)* **RETURN TO GEHENNA** [ ] [-]
– Power (new version) / Laura (new version) / Secrets / The tower / Returning to Gehenna new version). *(cd-ep iss.Nov93; SF 008CV)*

Jun 92. (cd) *Windsong; (<WINCD 023>)* **BBC RADIO 1 IN CONCERT (live)** [ ] [ ] 1993

Jul 93. (cd)(c/lp) *Beggars Banquet; (BEGA 137CD)(BEGC/BEGA 137) / Atlantic; <82475>* **REVELATIONS** [ ] [ ] 1994
– Moonchild / Chord of souls / Last exit for the lost / Preacher man / Love under will / Power / Psychonaut lib III / For her light / Blue water / Vet for the insane / The watchman / Dawnrazor. *(cd-iss. Sep95 on 'Beggars Banquet-Lowdown'; BBL 137CD)*

Dec 93. (cd) *Nostradamus; (MOO 1CD)* **BURNING THE FIELDS** [ ] [-]

RUBICON

—— (aka FIELDS OF THE NEPHILIM)

—— with new vocalist **ANDY DELANEY** replacing McCOY

Beggars Banquet / Atlantic

Aug 92. (12"ep/cd-ep) *(BBQ T/CD)* **WATCH WITHOUT PAIN. / WATCH WITHOUT PAIN (full version) / KILLING TIME (demo version)** [ ] [-]

Oct 92. (12"ep/cd-ep) *(BBQ 4 T/CD)* **CRAZED. / CHAINS ARE GONE / BRAVE HEARTS (CELLAR TAPE)** [ ] [-]

Oct 92. (cd/c/lp) *(BBQ CD/MC/LP 128) <92495>* **WHAT STARTS, ENDS** [ ] [ ]
– Before my eyes / Crazed / Watch without pain / Brave hearts / Killing time / Inside your head / Unspoken / Hand for you / Rivers / What starts, ends. *(re-iss. Apr93 cd/c; same)*

Mar 93. (12"ep/cd-ep) *(BBQ 10 TP/CD)* **BEFORE MY EYES / STANDING ALONE. / ON YOUR SIDE / HARD FOR YOU** [ ] [-]

Apr 95. (cd-ep) *(BBQ 47CD)* **INSATIABLE / BURY MY GOLD / PRIME** [ ] [-]

Apr 95. (cd/c/lp) *(BBQ CD/MC/LP 170)* **ROOM 101** [ ] [-]
– Ageless / Rest a while / Doubt all / Insatiable / Cut down / On your side / This drenching night / Bury my gold / Empty hands / Eat with me.

NEPHILIM

—— **McCOY + PAUL MILES** – guitar / **CIAN HOUCHIN** – bass, programming / **SIMON RIPPIN** – drums

Beggars Banquet / Beggars Banquet

Mar 96. (12"ep/cd-ep) *(BEG 265 T/CD)* **PENETRATION. / XODUS / 24th MOMENT** [ ] [-]

Mar 96. (cd)(c/lp) *(BEGA 172CD)(BEGC/BEGA 172) <80172>* **ZOON** [ ] [ ] Oct96
– Still life / Xodus / Shine / Penetration / Melt (the catching of the butterfly) / Venus decomposing / Pazuzu (black rain) / Zoon / Zoon / Coma. *<US re-iss. 1997 on 'Metal Blade'; 14116>*

54-40

Formed: Vancouver, British Columbia, Canada ... 1981 by BRAD MERRITT, NEIL OSBOURNE and DARRYL NEUDORF, who took their unusual moniker from an historical "Fifty-Four Forty Or Fight" campaign to alter the border between Canada and the USA. Adding PHIL COMPARELLI in '84, this hard-gigging unit released a domestic debut album, 'SET THE FIRE' the same year, drawing favourable comparisons to up and coming rootsy alt-rock outfit, R.E.M. Prior to a worldwide signing with major label, 'Reprise', 54-40 replaced NEUDORF with drummer MATT JOHNSON (not that one!) and it was this line-up who surfaced from the studio with their well-received eponymous album in '86. Over the course of the next few years, the quartet released two further sets, 'SHOW ME' (1987) and 'FIGHT FOR LOVE', both respectable offerings which nevertheless failed to build on standards they had set. A move to 'Columbia' for 1992's 'DEAR DEAR' could have conceivably introduced the band to a wider audience although in the event they subsequently found themselves without an American label. Finding a sympathetic home at Sony's 'Tristar', 54-40 released another set of sturdy, all-rounder alternative-rock/pop in '94's 'SMILIN' BUDDHA CABARET', displaying the inevitable traces of post-Grunge fallout. • **Trivia:** 'I GO BLIND' was later covered by HOOTIE & THE BLOWFISH; pocket money for OSBORNE and Co, perhaps.

Album rating: SET THE FIRE (*4) / 54-40 (*7) / SHOW ME (*6) / FIGHT FOR LOVE (*5) / DEAR DEAR (*4) / SMILIN' BUDDHA CABARET (*5)

NEIL OSBOURNE – vocals, guitar / **PHIL COMPARELLI** – guitar, steel guitar, vocals / **BRAD MERRITT** – bass / **DARRYL NEUDORF** – drums

not iss. / Mo-Da-Mu

1984. (lp) *<MDM 8>* **SET THE FIRE** [-] [-] Canada
– Set the fire / A big idea / Around the bend / One place set / What to do now / Lost my hand / Sound of truth / Broken pieces.

—— **MATT JOHNSON** – drums; repl. NEUDORF

Warners / Reprise

1986. (lp/c) *<1-/4-25440>* **54-40** [-] [ ]
– Baby ran / I wanna know / I go blind / Being fooled / Take my hand / Grace and beauty / Me island / Holy cow / Alcohol heart /

Dec 87. (lp/c) *<(925572-1/-4)>* **SHOW ME** [ ] [ ]
– One day in your life / Get back down / Walk in line / Standing in the way / Everyday / What's in a name / One gun / Come here / All the love is gone / Show me.

Mar 89. (lp/c/cd) *<925961-1/-4/-2>* **FIGHT FOR LOVE** [-] [ ]
– Here in my house / Kissfolk / Over my head / Miss you / Baby have some faith / Fight for love / Laughing / Walk talk madly / Where is my heart / Journey.

not iss. / Columbia

1992. (cd) *<5440>* **DEAR DEAR** [-] [ ]
– She la / Music man / Nice to luv you / Lovers and losers / We are, we pretend / Apollo and me / Faithful / Inside the horn / You don't get away (that easy) / Book / Dear dear.

not iss. / TriStar-Sony

1994. (cd,c) *<67200>* **SMILIN' BUDDHA CABARET** [-] [ ]
– Blame your parents / Radio luv song / Assoholic / Daisy / Once a killer / Punk grass / Lucy / Beyond the outsider / Don't listen to that / Ocean pearl / Higher / Friends end / What Buddy was / Save yourself.

- compilations, etc. -

1998. (cd) *Columbia; <80336>* **SINCE WHEN** [-] [ ]

FILTER

Formed: Cleveland, Ohio, USA ... 1995 by RICHARD PATRICK and BRIAN LIESEGANG (once both of NINE INCH NAILS). With the addition of GENO LENARDO, FRANK CAVANAGH and MATT WALKER, the group scraped into the lower regions of the US chart with their debut album,

'SHORT BUS' (1995). A basement industrial outfit utilising dense Euro-rock sounds, the group eventually secured some widespread exposure when they hit the UK Top 40 via a collaboration with The CRYSTAL METHOD, '(CAN'T YOU) TRIP LIKE I DO', featured on the soundtrack to 'The Spawn'. • **Note:** Don't get confused with the house/club act, FILTER, who released a single, 'RUNNING AWAY', in '97.

Album rating: SHORT BUS (*8)

RICHARD PATRICK (b.1967) – vocals, guitar, bass / **BRIAN LIESEGANG** (b.1970) – keyboards, drums / with **KEVIN HANLEY** – guitars / **SCOTT KERN + MIKE PEFFER** – drums

Warners Reprise

May 95. (cd/c) <(9362 45864-2/-4)> **SHORT BUS** 59
– Hey man, nice shot / Dose / Under / Spent / Take another / Stuck in here / It's over / Gerbil / White like that / Consider this / So cool.

— basic duo now with **GENO LENARDO** – guitar / **FRANK CAVANAGH** – bass / **MATT WALKER** – drums

Aug 95. (12"/cd-s) *(W 0299 T/CD1)* <43531> **HEY MAN NICE SHOT (sober mix) / ('A'-1/2oz mix) / ('A'-1/4lb mix) / ('A'-Big Mac mix)** 76 Jul95
(cd-s) *(W 0299 CD2)* <43531> – ('A'-Bud gets the lead out mix) / ('A'-Sawed off edit) / ('A'-Nickel bag mix) / White like that.
(re-iss. May96; same)

Nov 95. (cd-s) **DOSE** -

— WALKER joined the SMASHING PUMPKINS in '96

— In Sep'97, FILTER & The CRYSTAL METHOD hit UK Top 40 with '(CAN'T YOU) TRIP LIKE I DO' from the film 'The Spawn'.

FINGERPRINTZ

Formed: London, England ... 1978 by Scots-born JIMMIE O'NEILL alongside CHA BURNZ, KENNY ALTON and BOB SHILLING. One of the earliest bands to translate the energy and anger of punk into a more accessible New Wave style, The FINGERPRINTZ were an obvious choice for 'Virgin' who released their debut single, 'DANCING WITH MYSELF', in early '79. A further two singles, 'WHO'S YOUR FRIEND' and 'TOUGH LUCK', preceded their first long player, 'THE VERY DAB', at the tail end of the year, a musically upbeat album that nevertheless concentrated on the lyrical preoccupations that would come to dominate the post-punk era, i.e. alienation, paranoia, urban decay etc. Produced by ex-DUCKS DELUXE man, NICK GARVEY, 'DISTINGUISHING MARKS' (1980) carried on in a similar, if more streamlined vein while 1981's 'BEAT NOIR' was an ambitious attempt to combine the rhythmic drive of funk with new wave pop sensiblilites. Yet like their predecessors, none of the album's three singles made any commercial impact, FINGERPRINTZ finally marking their books after the last of these, 'THE BEAT ESCAPE'. After another aborted project, INTRO (with JACQUI BROOKS), O'NEILL went on to greater recognition if not acclaim with The SILENCERS.

Album rating: THE VERY DAB (*6) / DISTINGUISHING MARKS (*5) / BEAT NOIR (*5)

JIMMIE O'NEIL – vocals, guitar / **CHA BURNZ** – guitar, vocals / **KENNY ALTON** – bass, vocals / **BOB SHILLING** – drums

Virgin not iss.

Jan 79. (7") *(VS 235)* **DANCING WITH MYSELF. / SEAN'S NEW SHOES** -
(12"+=) *(VS 235-12)* – Sync unit.
Mar 79. (d7"blue) *(VS 252)* **WHO'S YOUR FRIEND. / DO YOU WANT TO KNOW A SECRET / / NERVZ. / NIGHT NURSE** -
Aug 79. (7") *(VS 278)* **TOUGH LUCK. / DETONATOR** -
Oct 79. (lp) *(V 2119)* **THE VERY DAB** -
– Tough luck / Temperamental / Close circuit connection / Beam me up Scotty / Punchy Judy / On the hop / Fingerprintz / Hey Mr.Smith / Wet job / Invisible seams.
Jul 80. (7") *(VS 358)* **BULLET PROOF HEART. / HIDE AND SEEK** -
Aug 80. (lp) *(V 2170)* **DISTINGUISHING MARKS** -
– Yes eyes / Houdini love / Criminal mind / Bullet proof heart / Remorse code / Amnesia / Ringing tone / Radiation / Jabs / Hide and seek.
Oct 80. (7") *(VS 375)* **HOUDINI LOVE. / ALL ABOUT YOU** -

— **BOGDAN WIEZLING** – drums, percussion; repl. SHILLING

May 81. (7") *(VS 420)* **SHADOWED. / MADAME X** -
Jun 81. (lp) *(V 2201)* **BEAT NOIR** -
– The beat escape / The chase / Cat walk / Changing / Get civilised / Shadowed / Touch sense / Echo head / Going going gone / Famous last words.
Jul 81. (7") *(VS 432)* **BOHEMIAN DANCE. / COFFEE & SCREAMS** -
Oct 81. (7") *(VS 452)* **THE BEAT ESCAPE. / DISORIENT EXPRESS** -
(12") *(VS 452-12)* – ('A'side) / Catwalk.

— disbanded after above single. JIMMIE O'NEIL + JACQUI BROOKS formed INTRO who recorded one 'M.C.A.' single in '83, 'LOST WITHOUT YOUR LOVE'. JIMMIE subsequently formed The SILENCERS

FINITRIBE

Formed: Edinburgh, Scotland ... 1984 by CHRIS CONNELLY, JOHN VICKI and DAVID MILLAR. Initially a conventional post-punk guitar outfit, the band released a debut EP, 'CURLING & STRETCHING' on their own 'Finiflex' label in summer '84, graduating to a John Peel session before rethinking their whole approach in the mid-80's. Tired of the conventional drums, bass, guitar set-up, they acquired a sampler and began experimenting with electronic music. The result was 'LET THE TRIBE GROW', an EP released on the 'Cathexis' label and featuring 'DE TESTIMONY', a seminal dancefloor anthem for the original Balearic/Acid House generation. Subsequently hooking up with Chicago industrial label, 'Wax Trax', the FINI's released a further couple of 12" singles, 'I WANT MORE' and 'MAKE IT INTERNAL', raising their profile in the States but failing to advance their cause at home. A disastrous tour in early '88 led to the departure of three members – including CONNELLY, who went on to join The REVOLTING COCKS – and a parting of the ways with 'Wax Trax'. This in turn resulted in a resurrection of the 'Finiflex' label for a long awaited debut album, 'NOISE, LUST & FUN' (1988), featuring contributions from such minor luminaries as LITTLE ANNIE, WILF PLUM (of DOG FACED HERMANS) and JESS HOPKINS. A series of remix EP's proved their dancefloor credentials while a deal with 'One Little Indian' ran into controversy almost immediately with the 'ANIMAL FARM' EP. Subverting the nursery rhyme 'Old MacDonald', for the purposes of berating the similarly titled hamburger outlet, FINITRIBE (as they were now known) offered up a flavour of the anti-consumerist stance prevalent on new album, 'GROSSING 10K' (1989). The subsequent threat of legal action wasn't exactly helped by a "Fuck Off McDonalds" poster campaign, the group running into similar trouble in 1991 with the '101' single, released as FINITRIBE 101 and drawing the wrath of ELECTRIBE 101. The latter effort was culled from 1992's 'AN UNEXPECTED GROOVY TREAT', the FINIS' most accessible, successful album to date and home of groovy near-hit, 'FOREVERGREEN'. The same period also the development of the 'Finiflex' label and in-house production team with releases by the likes of JUSTIN ROBERTSON, EGE BAM YASI and even SPARKS, the group co-ordinating releases from their dockside studio in Leith. A deal with 'Ffrr' gave the operation more commercial viability and even led to a Top 75 FINITRIBE hit single with 1994's 'BRAND NEW' EP. Yet by early '97, MILLER and longstanding member PINSKI were in the process of splitting from founder FINI, VICKI, the slimmed down FINITRIBE now operating from a bedroom studio after the pressures of running 'Finiflex' became too much. The duo subseqently set up a new label, 'UGT', continuing to indulge in side projects such as GEKO. With rumours of a harder edged, more organic sound in the pipeline, the FINITRIBE are currently working on new material with the likes of PAUL HAIG, CHRIS CONNELLY and KATE MORRISON. • **Trivia:** Their group name derives from 'Finny Tribe', the collective name for the fish species known to the Rosicruscians in Ireland.

Album rating: NOISE, LUST AND FUN (*7) / GROSSING 10k (*6) / AN UNEXPECTED GROOVY TREAT (*8) / SHEIGRA (*6)

CHRIS CONNELLY / JOHN VICKI (b. 6 Nov '65) / **DAVID MILLER** (b. 20 Jul '62, Moffat, Scotland) / + 3 others.

Finiflex not iss.

Jun 84. (12"ep) *(LT 1001)* **CURLING & STRETCHING EP** -
(re-iss. 1988; FT 001)

Cathexis not iss.

Oct 86. (12"ep) *(CRF 611)* **LET THE TRIBE GROW** -
– De testimony (collapsing edit) / Throttle hearts (rising mix) / Adults absolved / Monimail. *(re-iss. Oct88 on 'Finiflex';)*
1980's? (lp) **YOU BET WE'VE GOT** (compilation) -

Wax Trax Wax Trax

Oct 87. (12"ep) *(WAKUK 027)* **I WANT MORE / IDIOT STRENGTH. / I WANT MORE (row, row, row the mix)**

— 5-piece **CHRIS CONNELLY, JOHN VICKI, PHILIP PINSKY, SIMON McGOWAN + DAVID MILLER**

Feb 88. (12"ep) *(WAXUK 028)* **MAKE IT INTERNAL (integrity mix) / LITTLE VISITORS. / MAKE IT INTERNAL (here we go round the mulberry mix)** Nov90

— CONNELLY joined The REVOLTING COCKS in 1988 before embarking on solo career

Finiflex not iss.

Oct 88. (12"ep) *(FT 002)* **DE TESTIMONY EP** -
– The batter mix / Micromix / Pick'n'mix.
Nov 88. (12"ep) *(FT 003)* **ZULUS EP** -
– The crunchy mix / The rhythmix / Noise (pick'n'mix).
Nov 88. (lp) *(FTLP 001)* **NOISE, LUST & FUN** -
– Electrolux / Disturb / Swans / Finis / Throttlehearts / Zulus / Fluke / Electrolux / Swans / Disturb / Ultra. *(cd-iss. Oct89 on 'One Little Indian'; TPLP 21CD)*
Dec 88. (12"ep) *(FT 004)* **ELECT-ROLUX EP** -
– Electrolux (pick'n'mix) / Electrolux (minimix) / Disturb (cement mix).

One Little Indian Rough Trade

Nov 89. (12"ep) *(31 TP12)* **ANIMAL FARM EP** -
Chicken mix / Ouch ya go (ouchtakes) / Monkey mix / Animal farm (meatymix).
Dec 89. (lp/c/cd) *(TPLP 24/+MC/CD)* **GROSSING 10K**
– Eyeball / Instant access / An Earth creature / Whale of a tail / Ask a silly question / Monster in the house / Asstrax / 3 AAA's / Put your trunk in it / Built in monster / Animal farm / Ouch ya go.
Mar 90. (12"ep) *(38 TP12)* **MONSTER IN THE HOUSE EP**
– Monster club / Monster in the wireless / Eyeball / Built in monsters

— trimmed to a trio of **VICKI, PINSKY + MILLER** when CONNELLY took off to go solo (having already joined REVOLTING COCKS)

Jul 91. (7"/cd-s; as FINITRIBE 101) *(54 TP7/+CD)* **101. / SONIC SHUFFLE (mixed by Andy Weatherall)**
(12") *(54 TP12L)* – 101 (mixed by Graham Massey of 808 State).
Nov 91. (12"/cd-s) *(64 TP 12/7CD)* **ACE LOVE DEUCE (Steve Osbourne mix). / ('A'-Justin Robertson mix)** -
Jun 92. (12") *(74 TP12F)* **FOREVERGREEN (mixes)** 51 -
(12") *(74 TP12J)* – (2 Justin Robertson mixes)
(12") *(74 12TPY)* – ('A'-Youth mixes) / ('A'-Andy Weatherall mix).
(cd-s) *(74 TP7CD)* – (all mixes).
Sep 92. (lp/c/cd) *(TPLP 34/+C/CD)* <52846> **AN UNEXPECTED GROOVY TREAT** Feb93
– Forevergreen / 101 (sonic shuffle edit) / Come and get it / Mellowman / Yer

crazy / Forevergreen (the lunar eclipse mix) / Bagomatix II (there can only be one) / Ace love deuce (remix Justin Robertson) / Hypnopaedia / Glisten / An unexpected groovy treat / Forevergreen (forevermost excellent) / Ace love deuce (remix Steve Osborne) / Forevergreen (foreverdreaming).

Ffrr-London / London

Nov 94. (12"ep/c-ep/cd-ep) *(FX/FCS/FCD 247)* **BRAND NEW EP** [69] [-]
– Tip top tune / Tip top.
(12") *(FXX 247)* – (remixes).

Mar 95. (c-s) *(FCS 258)* **LOVE ABOVE / ('A'-Sheigra 5 mix)** [ ] [ ]
(12"+=) *(FX 258)* – ('A'-Cheeky Vee half mix) / ('A'-Analogue mix).
(cd-s++=) *(FCD 258)* – ('A'-original mix).

Apr 95. (d-cd/c/d-lp) *(828 615-2/-4/-1)* **SHEIGRA** [ ] [ ]
– Dark / Sunshine / Brand new (tip-top tune) / Mushroom shaped / Sheigra 5 / Truth / Catch the whistle / We have come / Mesmerise / Off on a slow one / Love above (Analogue mix).

Aura Surround Sounds / not iss.

Jun 96. (12"/cd-s) *(SUCD/SUSSX 33)* **SQUELCH (mixes)** [ ] [-]
(12") *(SUSSY 33)* – ('A'mixes).

Infectious / not iss.

Aug 97. (12") *(INFECT 42T)* **FLYING PEPPERS. / WALTZER / FRANTIC** [ ] [-]
(12") *(INFECT 42TX)* – ('A'mixes).

Feb 98. (12") *(INFECT 51T)* **FRANTIC / SCISSORKICKS GETS LAID. / ('A'-Microspeech mix) / ('A'-Cut La Roc mix).**
(cd-s+=) *(INFECT 51CD)* – ('A'-A1 People mix) / Witchman live jam.

Mar 98. (cd/lp) *(INFECT 43 CD/LP)* **SLEAZY LISTENING** [ ] [-]
– Sleazy rider / Mind my make up / Frantic / Chiller / Waltzer / Flying peppers / Electrician / Bells / Shining / Oxbow incident / Theme.

Mar 98. (12"/cd-s) *(INFECT 54 T/CD)* **MIND MY MAKE UP (mixes; original / Dust Junky's / Dope Smugglax O.D. dub / Diminished Responsibility / De Composed bass / Mid My B-Cup)** [ ] [-]

FIRE ENGINES

Formed: Edinburgh, Scotland . . . 1979 out of The DIRTY REDS by DAVEY HENDERSON, MURRAY SLADE, GRAHAM MAIN and RUSSELL BURN. Taking their name from a particularly psychotic 13th FLOOR ELEVATORS track, The FIRE ENGINES caused a minor furore at the dawn of the 80's with their trashy, discordant punk-funk din, as heard on debut single, 'GET UP AND USE ME'. The combination of the POP GROUP/GANG OF FOUR-style rhythmic guitar mangling and HENDERSON's demented vocal was enough to get the music press foaming at the mouth, a largely instrumental, self-financed mini-set, 'LUBRICATE YOUR LIVING ROOM' (1981) working out their frustrations over seven breakneck tracks. Picked up by Bob Last's 'Pop Aural' label, the band came close to a conventional song structure with the infectious 'CANDY SKIN' single, HENDERSON's erm, "unique" vocal talents pushed centre stage. Acclaimed by the press and a sizeable indie hit, the band pushed the boat out for follow-up, 'BIG GOLD DREAM', even employing female backing vocals in a last gasp effort for pop stardom. It wasn't to be and the FIRE ENGINES were soon parked in the station for good, RUSSELL forming the short-lived EVEREST THE HARD WAY with IAN STODDART and future ALTERED IMAGES man, STEPHEN LIRONI. He then enjoyed a further spell with The DIRTY REDS before resurfacing in the mid-80's with HENDERSON and STODDART as sophisticated soul/funk-pop outfit, WIN. Signed to Alan Horne's new 'Swamplands' label, they released two singles, 'UNAMERICAN BROADCASTING' and the anthemic 'YOU'VE GOT THE POWER' (later gaining belated exposure as the musical backdrop for a McEwan's lager TV ad), before the label was taken over by 'London' records. The major label backing led to a Top 60 placing for their debut album, 'UH! TEARS BABY (A TRASH ICON)' (1987), new members MANNY SCHONIVVA, WILLIE PERRY and SIMON SMEETON coming in as the band switched to 'Virgin'. Despite continuing critical acclaim and enthusuastic support from the press, a follow-up set, 'FREAKY TRIGGER' (1989) did nothing and WIN called it a day in 1989. While STODDART went on to play with semi-legendary Edinburgh funksters, CAPTAIN SHIFTY, SCHONIWA hooked up with dance act, YO YO HONEY and RUSSELL recorded as PIE FINGER. HENDERSON went on to create quirky pop material as NECTARINE No.9, signing to the reactivated 'Postcard' label and releasing a debut album, 'A SEA WITH THREE STARS' (1993). A series of EP's followed – including a collaborative effort with PAUL QUINN and Caledonian performance poet, JOCK SCOTT – prior to '95's 'SAINT JACK' album.
• **Songwriters:** All written by HENDERSON, except FASCIST GROOVE (Heaven 17). NECTARINE No.9 covered INSIDE OF YOUR HEART (Velvet Underground) / FROWNLAND (Captain Beefheart) / PULL MY DAISY (Ginsberg-Kerouac).

Album rating: FOND compilation (*9) / Win: UH! TEARS BABY WIN (*7) / FREAKY TRIGGER (*6) / Nectarine No.9: A SEA WITH THREE STARS (*5) / SAINT JACK (*6) / FRIED FOR BLUE MATERIAL (*6)

DAVEY HENDERSON – vocals, guitar (ex-DIRTY REDS) / **MURRAY SLADE** – guitar / **GRAHAM MAIN** – bass / **RUSSELL BURN** – drums

Codex / not iss.

Dec 80. (7") *(CDX 1)* **GET UP AND USE ME. / EVERYTHING'S ROSES** [ ] [-]

Accessory / Fast

Jan 81. (m-lp) *(ACC 001)* <FPA 002> **LUBRICATE YOUR LIVING ROOM** <US title 'AUFGELADEN UND BEREIT FUR ACTION UNDER SPASS'> [ ] [ ] Aug81
– Plastic gift / Get up and use me / Hungry beat / Lubricate your living room pt.1 & 2 / New thing in the cartons / Sympathetic anaesthetic / Discord.

Pop Aural / not iss.

May 81. (7") *(POP 010)* **CANDY SKIN. / MEAT WHIPLASH** [ ] [-]

—— added guests **SIMON BEST** – keyboards / **HI-RAY** (b. HILARY MORRISON) – vocals (of FLOWERS) / **KAREN BROWN** – b. vocals

Nov 81. (7") *(POP 013)* **BIG GOLD DREAM. / SYMPATHETIC ANAESTHETIC** [ ] [-]
(12"+=) *(POP 013-12)* – New thing in cartons.

—— folded on the last day of '81. DAVEY and HILARY formed HEARTBEAT. (1 track on NME-c)

– compilations, etc. –

Aug 92. (lp) *Creation Rev-Ola; (CREV 001LP)* **FOND** [ ] [-]
– (contained all their work)

EVEREST THE HARD WAY

—— were formed by **RUSSELL** with others **IAN STODDART** – bass / **STEPHEN LIRONI** – guitar, keyboards (later ALTERED IMAGES)

Do-It / not iss.

Apr 82. (7"/12") **TIGHTROPE. / WHEN YOU'RE YOUNG** [ ] [-]

split later that year. RUSSELL joined DIRTY REDS before forming below

WIN

DAVEY HENDERSON – vocals, guitar / **RUSSELL BURN** – drums / **IAN STODDART** – bass

Swamplands / not iss.

Mar 85. (7"/12") *(SW/+X 5)* **UNAMERICAN BROADCASTING (pt.1). / UNAMERICAN BROADCASTING (pt.2)** [ ] [-]

Jun 85. (7"/s7") *(SWP/+P 8)* **YOU'VE GOT THE POWER. / IN HEAVEN (LADY IN THE RADIATOR SONG)** [ ] [-]
(12"/s12") *(SWX/+X 8)* – ('A'side) / Unamerican broadcasting (pt.1 & 2).
(d7") *(SWDX 8)* – (all 4 tracks).

London / not iss.

Mar 86. (7") *(LON 85)* **SHAMPOO TEARS. / EMPTY HOLSTERS** [ ] [-]
(12"+=) *(LONX 85)* – The slider / ('A'-dub version).

Mar 87. (7") *(LON 128)* **SUPER POPOID GROVE. / BABY CUTTING** [63] [-]
(12"+=) *(LONX 128)* – You've got the power.
(d7"++=) *(LONG 128)* – In Heaven (the lady in the radiator song).

Apr 87. (lp/c)(cd) *(LON LP/C 31) (828 047-2)* **UH! TEARS BABY (A TRASH ICON)** [51] [-]
– Super popoid groove / Shampoo tears / Binding love spell / Unamerican broadcasting / Hollywood Baby too / Empty holsters / You've got the power / Charms of powerful trouble / It may be a beautiful sky tonight but it's only a shelter for a world at risk / Charms (reprise) / Baby cutting. *(c+cd+=)* – Shampoo tears (extended) / You've got the power (extended).

—— added **MANNY SCHONIVVA** – guitar / **WILLIE PERRY** – keyboards / **SIMON SMEETON** – guitar (appeared on last album alongside EMANUEL SHONIWA)

Virgin / not iss.

Nov 88. (7") *(VS 1121)* **WHAT'LL YOU DO TILL SUNDAY, BABY. / TRIGGER HAPPY** [ ] [-]
(12"+=) *(VST 1121)* – ('A'-Johnson's Baby mix).
(cd-s++=) *(VSCD 1121)* – Peace on egg.

Jan 89. (7") *(VS 1157)* **LOVE UNITS. / SCARY SCARY** [ ] [-]
(12"+=) *(VST 1157)* – ('A'-12"mix).
(cd-s++=) *(VSCD 1157)* – Pull my daisy.

Mar 89. (cd/c/lp) *(CD/TC+/V 2571)* **FREAKY TRIGGER** [ ] [-]
– What'll you do til' Sunday baby / Taboo / Love units / Rainbow / Truckee river / How do you do / What's love if you can kill for chocolate / Mind the gravy / Dusty heartfelt / We can cover up the "C". *(c+=/cd+=)* – Love units (12"mix) / What's love if you can kill for chocolate (12"mix).

May 89. (7") *(VS 1178)* **DUSTY HEARTFELT. / PEACE ON EGG** [ ] [-]
(12"+=/3"cd-s+=) *(VST/VSCD 1178)* – ('A'version).

—— disbanded late 1989, and HENDERSON went on to form . . .

NECTARINE No.9

—— **HENDERSON, SIMON SMEETON + IAIN HOLFORD** with also **JOCK SCOTT**

Postcard / Shake . . .

Feb 93. (lp/cd) *(DUBH 931/+CD)* **A SEA WITH THREE STARS** [ ] [-]
– Pop's love thing / She's a nicer word to sing / The holes of Corpus Christi / Beautiful car / 22 blue / Peanut brain / Smiths new automatic / A sea with three stars / The No. you mean / Don't worry babe, you're not the only one awake / Trace nine / Chocolate swastika.

Oct 93. (cd-ep) **UNLOADED FOR YOU** [ ] [-]
– Pop's new thing / Chocolate swastika / Going off someone / Don't worry babe you're not the only one awake.

Apr 94. (cd-ep) *(CDNT 004)* **GUITAR THIEVES** [ ] [-]
– Frownland / Pull my daisy / Inside of your heart / +.
(above issued on 'Night Tracks')

Jun 95. (cd-ep; PAUL QUINN / NECTARINE No.9 / JOCK SCOTT) *(DUBH 952CD)* **PREGNANT WITH POSSIBILITIES EP** [ ] [-]
– Tiger tiger / Will I ever be inside of you / Just another f***ed-up little druggy on the scene / Grunge girl groan.

Jul 95. (cd) *(DUBH 951CD)* <223> **SAINT JACK** [ ] [ ] Feb96
– Saint Jack / Curdled fragments / Fading memory babe / Can't scratch out / This arsehole's been burned too many times before / It's not my baby putting me down / My trapped lightning / Just another f***ed-up little druggy on the scene / Couldn't phone potatoes / Dead horse a rum / Firecrackers / Unloaded for you / Clipped wings and power stings / Tape your head on.

Jul 95. (cd-ep) *(SALD 214)* **NIAGARA FALLS** [-] [ ]
(UK-iss.Jun98; same)

Sano / not iss.

Apr 97. (cd-s/7"; as JOCK SCOT & THE NECTARINE NO.9) *(ST/+7 1876)* **TAPE YOUR HEAD ON. /** [ ] [-]

Creeping Bent / not iss.

Mar 98. (7") *(bent 033)* **PORT OF MARS. / Alan Vega & The Revolutionary Corps: WHO CARES WHO DIES** [ ] [-]

Apr 98. (cd) *(bent 035cd)* **FRIED FOR BLUE MATERIAL** [ ] [-]
– Stacey Keach dada message bag / Strychnine vinagarette / Adidas Frances Bacon / Walter Travis / Central deli Davis Jr. / Boneless chops / Starthing / Friends of the cult sixties pop / Burnt nylon carseat cover flavour / Fuzzy dice mahlersdog / Port of Mars / South of an imaginary line / Subtitles for the blind drunk / Soon to over / Michaelangelo.

Sano / not iss.

May 98. (7") *(ST 71879)* **ADIDAS FRANCIS BACON. /** [ ] [-]

fIREHOSE (see under ⇒ MINUTEMEN)

FIRE PARTY

Formed: Washington DC, USA . . . 1986 by the all-girl foursome of AMY PICKERING, NATALIE AVERY, KATE SAMWORTH and NICKY THOMAS. Charged up by European support slots to SCREAM then THAT PETROL EMOTION, FIRE PARTY unleashed their eponymous debut mini-set in 1988 for 'Dischord' (base of FUGAZI). The album showed an astonishingly fresh grunge sound fusing elements of NIRVANA, WIRE and SONIC YOUTH, although the following year's, 'NEW ORLEANS OPERA', lacked the debut's bite and the girls split.

Album rating: FIRE PARTY (*6) / NEW ORLEANS OPERA (*4)

AMY PICKERING – vocals / **NATALIE AVERY** – guitar / **KATE SAMWORTH** – bass / **NICKY THOMAS** – drums

Dischord / Dischord

May 88. (m-lp) *<(DISCHORD 28)>* **FIRE PARTY** [ ] [ ]

Oct 89. (m-lp/m-c) *<(DISCHORD 37/+C)>* **NEW ORLEANS OPERA** [ ] [ ]

—— fizzled out after above

- compilations, etc. -

Oct 96. (cd) *Dischord; <DIS 103>* **FIRE PARTY** (first two sets) [-] [ ]
– Jerk / Basis / Cake / Drowning intentions / Walls of mind / Engine / Pilate / Make it quick / Bite / First course / Gethsemane / Prisoner / Fire / Only nine mottos / New Orleans opera / Basis / Are you on? / How to / Stray bullet.

FISCHER-Z

Formed: London, England . . . 1978 by JOHN WATTS, along with STEVE SKOLNIK, DAVID GRAHAM and STEVE LIDDLE. Signed to 'United Artists', this frantic, edgy, guitar/keyboards-dominated New Wave outfit made their vinyl debut in September '78 with the 'WAX DOLLS' single, following it up early in 1979 with 'REMEMBER RUSSIA'. The quartet finally dented the lower regions of the chart later that Spring with 'THE WORKER', all three singles featuring on the attendant debut album, 'WORD SALAD' (1979). As the 70's turned into the 80's, FISCHER-Z scored a further (very) minor hit with 'SO LONG' although that would be the sum total of their success and a follow-up album, 'GOING DEAF FOR A LIVING' (1980) failed to chart. Moving to 'Liberty', the group released one more single, 'LIMBO', before being reduced to a trio following the departure of SKOLNIK. 1981 saw the release of their third and final album, 'RED SKIES OVER PARADISE', the band finally calling it a day after a final, charmingly titled single, 'WRISTCUTTER'S LULLABY'. WATTS (whose yelping prog-rock vocals were something of an acquired taste) subsequently embarked on a similarly commercially fruitless solo career, inking a deal with 'E.M.I.' and releasing two albums in two years, 'ONE MORE TWIST' (1982) and 'THE ICEBERG MODEL' (1983). Incredibly, perhaps, 'Arista' decided to sign up a reformed 'FISCHER-Z' in the late 80's, obviously hoping to succeed where their rivals had earlier failed. Having recruited a new line-up of IAN PORTER, DENIS HAINES, ALAN MORRISON, JENNIE CRUSE and STEVE KELLNER, WATTS proceeded to record a comeback album, 'REVEAL' (1988), before going on to record a German-only follow-up, 'FISH'S HEAD' for the affiliated 'Ariola' label. Mainstream recognition remained as far off as ever and although WATTS carried on with the band into the 90's, nothing more was heard from them after a proposed 1995 set, 'STREAM', was cancelled.

Album rating: WORD SALAD (*5) / GOING DEAF FOR A LIVING (*4) / RED SKIES OVER PARADISE (*4) / REVEAL (*4) / FISH'S HEAD (*4) / DESTINATION PARADISE (*4) / KAMIKAZE SHIRT (*4) / John Watts: ONE MORE TWIST (*5) / THE ICEBERG MODEL (*5)

JOHN WATTS – vocals, guitar, keyboards / **STEVE SKOLNIK** – keyboards / **DAVID GRAHAM** – bass / **STEVE LIDDLE** – drums, percussion

U.A. / U.A.

Sep 78. (7") *(UP 36478)* **WAX DOLLS. / ANGRY BRIGADE** [ ] [-]

Feb 79. (7") *(UP 36486)* **REMEMBER RUSSIA. / BIGGER SLICE NOW** [ ] [-]

May 79. (7") *(UP 36509)* **THE WORKER. / KITTEN CURRY** [53] [-]

Jun 79. (lp) *(UAG 20232)* **WORD SALAD** [66] [ ]
– Pretty paracetamol / Acrobats / The worker / Spiders / Remember Russia / The French let her / Lies / Wax dolls / Headlines / Nice to know / Billy and the motorway police / Lemmings. *(cd-iss. Nov87; CDP 746684-2)*

Aug 79. (7") *(BP 305)* **FIRST IMPRESSIONS. / HIGH WIRE WORKER** [ ] [-]

Apr 80. (7") *(BP 342)* **SO LONG. / HIDING** [72] [-]

May 80. (lp) *(UAG 30295)* **GOING DEAF FOR A LIVING** [ ] [ ]
– Room service / So long / Crazy girl / No right / Going deaf for a living / Pick up, slip up / The crank / Haters / Four minutes in Durham (with you) / Limbo. *(cd-iss. Nov87; CDP 746685-2)*

Liberty / Liberty

Sep 80. (7") *(BP 360)* **LIMBO. / THE RAT MAN** [ ] [-]

—— now a trio when SKOLNIK departed

Mar 81. (7") *(BP 387)* **MARLIESE. / RIGHT HAND MEN** [ ] [-]

Apr 81. (lp) *(LBG 30326)* **RED SKIES OVER PARADISE** [ ] [ ]
– Berlin / Marliese / Red skies over Paradise / In England / You'll never find Brian here / Battalions of strangers / Song and dance brigade / The writer / Bathroom scenario / Wristcutter's lullaby / Cruise missiles / Luton to Lisbon / Multinationals bite. *(cd-iss. Nov87; CDP 746683-2)*

May 81. (7") *(BP 398)* **WRISTCUTTER'S LULLABY. / YOU'LL NEVER FIND BRIAN HERE** [ ] [-]

—— disbanded after above

JOHN WATTS

—— now solo / with **DAVE PURDYE** – bass / **DEREK BALLARD** – drums

E.M.I. / unknown

Oct 81. (7") *(EMI 5239)* **SPEAKING IN A DIFFERENT LANGUAGE. / HOLIDAY IN FRANCE** [ ] [-]

Mar 82. (7") *(EMI 5266) ONE VOICE. / HOLIDAY IN FRANCE* [ ] [-]

Apr 82. (lp) *(EMC 3402)* **ONE MORE TWIST** [ ] [-]
– One voice / Lagonda lifestyle / Watching you / Carousel / That's not enough for me / I know it now / Victims of fashion / Speaking in a different language / Involuntary movement / Relax.

Jun 82. (7") *(EMI 5298)* **YOUR FAULT. / SARAWEGO** [ ] [-]

—— now without BALLARD who was repl. by session people **DICK ADLAND** – drums / **ROSA B.** – violin, vocals / **DENIS HAINES** – keyboards / **BRIAN BRUMMIT + MICK DONNELY + JIM PATERSON + PAUL SPEARE** – wind instruments

Jan 83. (7") *(EMI 5361)* **I SMELT THE ROSRES (IN THE UNDERGROUND). / I NEED ACTION** [ ] [-]

Mar 83. (lp) *(EMC 3427)* **THE ICEBERG MODEL** [ ] [-]
– Interference / Man in someone else's skin / I smelt roses (in the underground) / I was in love with you / Money and power / The prisoner's dilemma / Mayday mayday / Menargerie makers / A face to remember / The iceberg model.

May 83. (7") *(EMI 5387)* **MAYDAY MAYDAY. / TURN THE LIGHT ON** [ ] [-]

FISCHER-Z

—— **WATTS + / IAN PORTER** – bass, keyboards, electric drums / **DENIS HAINES** – keyboards / **ALAN MORRISON** – guitar / **JENNIE CRUSE** – vocals / **STEVE KELLNER** – drums

Arista / Arista

Feb 88. (7"/12") *(109/609 396)* **THE PERFECT DAY. / MARGUERITE** [ ] [ ]

Mar 88. (lp/c/cd) *(208/408/258 620)* **REVEAL** [ ] [ ]
– The perfect day / Leave it to the businessmen to die young / I can't wait that long / Tallulah tomorrow / Realistic man / Fighting back the tears / Big drum / Heartbeat / It takes love / So far.

Apr 88. (7"/12") *(109/609 704)* **BIG DRUM. / THE CAMERA (live)** [ ] [-]

—— now without MORRISON + HAINES

Jun 89. (7") *(112 301)* **SAY NO. / PSYCHOJAZZ SHUFFLE** [ ] [-]
(12"+=/cd-s+=) *(612/662 301)* – ('A'extended).

Ariola / not iss.

Jul 89. (lp/cd) *(209/259 772)* **FISH'S HEAD** [-] [-] German
– Say no / Masquerade / It could be you / Sticky business / Huba / Oh mother / Just words / It's only a hurricane / She said / Ho ho ho.

Marque / not iss.

Oct 90. (7") **SAUSAGES AND TEARS. /** [ ] [-]

Welfare / not iss.

Nov 92. (cd) *(WELFD 3)* **DESTINATION PARADISE** [ ] [-]
– Destination Paradise / Will you be there / Tightrope / Say when / Caruso / Marguerite Yourcenar / Saturday night / Mockingbird again / Still in flames / Time for Rita / Of all the / Count to ten / So hard / Further from love.

Apr 94. (cd) *(WELFD 6)* **KAMIKAZE SHIRT** [ ] [-]
– The peaches and cream / Killing time / Marlon / And this we call crime / Kamikaze shirt / Polythene / Human beings / Stripper in the mirror / Stars / Blue anenome / Radio K.I.L.L.

—— an album, 'STREAM' (WELFD 8), was cancelled in 1995

- compilations, etc. -

May 90. (cd/c/lp) *E.M.I.; (CDP 794132-2/-4/-1)* **GOING RED FOR A SALAD (THE UA YEARS 1979-1982)** [ ] [-]
– So long / Acrobats / The worker / Wax dolls / Remember Russia / Going deaf for a living / Room service / Pretty paracetamol / Marliese / You'll never find Brian here / Berlin / Battalions of strangers / Bathroom scenario / Wristcutter's lullaby / Crazy girl. *(cd+=)* – One voice / Involuntary movement / Mayday mayday / I smelt roses (in the underground).

Jun 95. (cd) *Welfare; (WELFD 7)* **STILL IN FLAMES (THE BEST OF FISCHER-Z)** [ ] [-]

Feb 98. (cd) *Disky; (DC 882812)* **THE WORKER** [ ] [-]

FISHBONE

Formed: Los Angeles, California, USA . . . 1980 by school friends ANGELO MOORE, KENDALL JONES, WALTER KIBBY, CHRIS DOWD, JOHN NORWOOD FISHER, PHILIP 'FISH' FISHER and CHARLIE DOWN. Fusing a variety of music styles including funk, jazz, ska and hard rock, FISHBONE initially showcased their eclectic and energetic stylee on stage supporting the likes of the DEAD KENNEDYS (one gig resulted in

NORWOOD getting stabbed!). Influenced by BAD BRAINS, SEX PISTOLS and DUKE ELLINGTON!, these sets were noted for the wacky rooster-haired ANGELO playing saxophone while doing backflips (later in their career he was to play completely naked although at times his sax hid his essentials). Helped along by the production of DAVID KAHANE, their self-titled debut mini-lp for 'Columbia' in 1985 should have brought them commercial fruits, similar groups such as LIVING COLOUR and RED HOT CHILI PEPPERS were gaining much wider attention. 'IN YOUR FACE' (1986) was next up, an improvement on their first effort, it nevertheless failed to achieve its goal. In the Autumn of '88, their third set, 'TRUTH AND SOUL' dented the US Top 200. Two classy singles were lifted from it, their version of Curtis Mayfield's 'FREDDIE'S DEAD' and 'MA & PA', the latter backed incidentally by another risque gem, 'BONIN' IN THE BONEYARD'. After concentrating on getting their manic message to the world on stage, FISHBONE returned with a new guitarist, JOHN BIGHAM, who played on their long-awaited follow-up, 'THE REALITY OF MY SURROUNDINGS' (1991). This SLY STONE-influenced set finally awoke the buying public and gave them a US Top 50 placing, the track 'EVERYDAY SUNSHINE' one of its highlights. However, the band were blighted when the bible-thumping KENDALL took off to join a religious cult, all the members were subsequently in court having tried to kidnap him from his new found "family". The impetus was certainly lost on their next album, the strangely titled 'GIVE A MONKEY A BRAIN AND HE'LL SWEAR HE'S THE CENTRE OF THE UNIVERSE' (1993), although they did have a minor UK hit with 'SWIM'. It took them three years to get back in the studio, although the resulting album, 'CHIM CHIM'S BADASS REVENGE' (1996) was over indulgent and disappointing. • **Trivia:** FISHBONE have also appeared in the films 'Back To The Beach', 'Tape Heads', 'Far Out, Man' and 'I'm Gonna Git You'.

Album rating: FISHBONE (*6) / IN YOUR FACE (*7) / TRUTH AND SOUL (*7) / THE REALITY OF MY SURROUNDINGS (*8) / GIVE A MONKEY A BRAIN AND HE'LL SWEAR HE'S THE CENTER OF THE UNIVERSE (*4) / CHIM CHIM'S BAD ASS REVENGE (*4) / FISHBONE 101: NUTTASAURUSMEG FOSSIL FUELIN part compilation (*7)

ANGELO MOORE (b. 5 Nov'65) – vocals, saxophone / **KENDALL JONES** – guitar, vocals / **WALTER A. KIBBY II** (b.13 Nov'64) – vocals / **JOHN NORWOOD FISHER** (b. 9 Dec'65) – bass, vocals / **CHRIS 'MAVERICK MEAT' DOWD** (b.20 Sep'65) – trombone, keyboards / **PHILIP 'FISH' FISHER** – drums, percussion / **CHARLIE DOWN** – guitars

C.B.S. Columbia

Sep 85. (lp/c) *(CBS/40 20529)* *<40032>* **FISHBONE** [ ] [ ]
– Ugly / Another generation / ? (Modern industry) / Party at Ground Zero / V.T.T.L.O.T.F.D.G.F. / Lyin' ass bitch.

Sep 85. (7") *<04922>* **MUSIC INDUSTRY. / V.T.T.L.O.T.F.D.G.F.** [-] [ ]

Sep 85. (7"/12") *(A/TA 6544)* **PARTY AT GROUND ZERO. / V.T.T.L.O.T.F.D.G.F.** [ ] [ ]

Nov 86. (cd/c/lp) *<CK/BCT+/40333>* **IN YOUR FACE** [-] [ ]
– When problems arise / A selection / Cholly / I wish I had a date / Movement in the light / Give it up / In the air / Turn the other way / Knock it / "Simon says" The kingpin / Post cold war politics / It's a wonderful life (gonna have a good time) / Slick Nick, you devil you / Iration / Just call me Scrooge.

Nov 87. (12"ep) **IT'S A WONDERFUL LIFE EP** [-] [ ]

Epic Epic

Sep 88. (7") *(FSH 1)* **FREDDIE'S DEAD. / IT'S A WONDERFUL LIFE (GONNA HAVE A GOOD TIME)** [ ] [-]
(12"+=/12"pic-d+=) *(FSH T/P 1)* – ('A'versions).
(cd-s++=) *(CDFSH 1)* – I like to hide behind my glasses.

Oct 88. (lp/c/cd) *(461173-1/-4/-2)* *<40891>* **TRUTH AND SOUL** [ ] [ ] Sep88
– Freddie's dead / Ma and pa / Mighty long way / Pouring rain / Deep inside / Question of life / Bonin' in the boneyard / One day / Subliminal fascism / Slow bus movin' (Howard beach party) / Ghetto soundwave / Change.

Jan 89. (7") *<08500>* **FREDDIE'S DEAD. / QUESTION OF LIFE** [-] [ ]

Mar 89. (7"/7"pic-d) *(FSH/+P 2)* **MA AND PA. / BONIN' IN THE BONEYARD** [ ] [ ]
(12"+=) *(FSHT 2)* – I like to hide behind my glasses.
(cd-s++=) *(CPFSH 2)* – In the name of swing.

— **'BIG' JOHN BIGHAM** – guitar; repl. DOWN

Columbia Columbia

Apr 91. (c-ep) *<73549>* **NEW AND IMPROVED BONIN' / IN THE NAME OF SWING / LOVE AND BULLSHIT / HIDE BEHIND MY GLASSES / BONIN' IN THE JUNGLE** [-] [ ]

Jun 91. (cd/c/lp) *(467615-2/-4/-1)* *<46142>* **THE REALITY OF MY SURROUNDINGS** [75] [49] Apr91
– Fight the youth / If I were a . . . I'd / So many millions / Asswhippin' / Housework / Deathmarch / Behavoir control technician / If I were a . . . I'd / Pressure / Junkies prayer / Prayer to the junkiemaker / Everyday sunshine / If I were a . . . I'd / Naz-tee may'en / Babyhead / If I were a . . . I'd / Those days are gone / Sunless Saturday.

Jun 91. (cd-ep) *<73668>* **SUNLESS SATURDAY / UNDERSTAND ME / FIGHT SWA SKA** [-] [ ]

Nov 91. (c-ep) *<73859>* **EVERYDAY SUNSHINE / SO MANY MILLIONS / PRAYING TO THE JUNKIEMAKER / BEHAVIOR CONTROL TECHNICIAN** [-] [ ]

Jul 92. (7") *(658193-7)* **EVERYDAY SUNSHINE. / FIGHT THE YOUTH** [60] [-]
(12"+=/cd-s+=) *(658193-6/-2)* – Fight the youth (extended) / Freddie's dead (Zeoniq mix).

— now without KENDALL who joined a religious cult!

Jun 93. (cd/c/lp) *(473875-2/-4/-1)* *<52764>* **GIVE A MONKEY A BRAIN AND HE'LL SWEAR HE'S THE CENTRE OF THE UNIVERSE** [ ] [99] May93
– Swim / Servitude / Black flowers / Unyielding conditioning / Properties of propaganda (f**k this shit on up) / The warmth of your breath / Lemon meringue / They all have abandoned their hopes / End the reign / Drunk skitzo / No fear / Nutt megalomaniac.

Aug 93. (12"/cd-s) *(659625-6/-2)* **SWIM. / ('A'-ofishal extended) / ('A'-JB dub) / ('A'stroke mix)** [54] [ ]

not iss. Rowdy-Arista

Apr 96. (cd) *<37010>* **CHIM CHIM'S BADASS REVENGE** [-] [ ]
– Alcoholic / In the cube / Sourpuss / Psychologically overcast / Beergut / Love . . . hate / Nutmeg / Monkey Dick / Pre nut / Rock star / Chim Chim's badass revenge.

– compilations, etc. –

Sep 96. (d-cd) *Sony; <65009>* **FISHBONE 101: NUTTASAURUSMEG FOSSIL FUELIN** (hits & rarities) [-] [ ]

Patrik FITZGERALD

Born: 1958, Bow, East London, England. Inspired by the energy and anti-establishment stance of punk, FITZGERALD attempted to carve out a niche as the genre's acoustic troubadour and often found himself on the receiving end of skinhead intolerance as a result. Signed to the independent 'Small Wonder' label, the singer-songwriter made his debut with the acclaimed 'SAFETY-PIN STUCK IN MY HEART' EP, following it up with another four-tracker, 'BACKSTREET BOYS', the latter's title track a comment on mob violence. Following cult acclaim for these early releases, FITZGERALD recorded a 17-track debut album, GRUBBY STORIES (1979), wherein his alternately affecting and ironic, cockney-intoned tales (highlights being 'LITTLE FISHES' and 'NO FUN FOOTBALL') were augmented by BUZZCOCKS sticksman JOHN MAHER and PENETRATION bass player ROBERT BLAMIRE. Subsequent efforts such as 'GIFTS AND TELEGRAMS' (1982) – now on 'Red Flame' – and 'DRIFTING TOWARDS VIOLENCE' (1984) met with little interest, however, and by the mid-80's, the man had left the music business completely. The following decade saw PATRIK the bard return for some sporadic performances, although no studio material was forthcoming.

Album rating: THE VERY BEST OF . . . compilation (*6)

PATRIK FITZGERALD – vocals, acoustic guitar

Small Wonder not iss.

Dec 77. (7"ep) *(SMALL 4)* **SAFETY-PIN STUCK IN MY HEART** [ ] [-]
– Banging and shouting / Safety-pin stuck in my heart / Work, rest, play, reggae / Set we free / Optimism / Reject.

Jul 78. (7"ep) *(SMALL 6)* **THE BACKSTREET BOYS** [ ] [-]
– Buy me, sell me / The little dippers / Trendy / The backstreet boys.

Oct 78. (12"ep) *(WEENY ONE)* **THE PARANOID WARD / THE BEDROOM TAPES** [ ] [-]
– Babysitter / Irrelevant battles / Cruelist crime / The paranoid ward / The bingo crowd / Ragged generation for real / Live out my stars / George / Live at the top. *(re-iss. Dec78 as 7"ep 'THE PARANOID WARD'; first 5 tracks only)*

— added band; **ROBERT BLAMIRE** – bass (of PENETRATION) / **JOHN MAHER** – drums (of BUZZCOCKS) / **PETER WILSON** – guitar, keyboards, producer

Polydor not iss.

Mar 79. (7") *(2059 091)* **ALL SEWN UP. / HAMMERSMITH ODEONS** [ ] [-]

Apr 79. (lp) *(2383 533)* **GRUBBY STORIES** [ ] [-]
– As ugly as you / Nothing to do / All my friends are dead now / Adopted girl / Don't tell me because I'm young / When I get famous / Little fishes / Lover's pact / All the years of trying / But not anymore / Suicidal wreck / My secret life / Conventions of life / Parent games / No fun football / Make it safe / Your hero.

Jun 79. (7"m) *(2059 135)* **IMPROVE MYSELF. / BINGO CROWD / MY NEW FAMILY** [ ] [-]

— toured with **COLIN PEACOCK** – guitar / **CHARLIE FRANCIS** – bass / **RAB FAE BEITH** – drums

— completely solo again. RAB joined The WALL and CHARLIE joined TOYAH

Red Flame not iss.

Sep 82. (7") *(RF 708)* **PERSONAL LOSS. / STRAIGHT BOY** [ ] [-]

Nov 82. (lp) *(RF 8)* **GIFTS AND TELEGRAMS** [ ] [-]
– One little soldier / Exist / Personal loss / Travel through a dark though scented county / Grey echoes / World is getting better / Solve / My death / Work / Gifts and telegrams / Punch / Island of lost souls.

Himalaya not iss.

Feb 84. (lp) *(HIM 009)* **DRIFTING TOWARDS SILENCE** [ ] [-]

Final Solution not iss.

Apr 84. (7"ep) *(FSEP 001)* **TONIGHT EP** [ ] [-]

— now with **PETER McDONNELL** – keyboards / **ALISDAIR ROBERTS** – bass / **GILLY JARMAN** – drums

Red Flame not iss.

Jun 86. (7") **TUNISIAN TWIST** [ ] [-]

— retired from music scene and went to work as a waiter in the House Of Commons. He went to live in Normandy, France, until his return in the early 90's to try his hand at acting.

– compilations, etc. –

Apr 94. (cd) *Anagram; (CDPUNK 31)* **SAFETY PIN STUCK IN MY HEART – THE VERY BEST OF PATRIK FITZGERALD** [ ] [-]
– Banging and shouting / Safety pin stuck in my heart / Work rest play reggae / Set we free / Optimism reject / Buy me sell me / The little dippers / Trendy / Backstreet boys / Babysitter / Irrelevant battles / Cruelist crime / The paranoid ward / The bingo crowd (instrumental) / Life at the top / Ragged generation for real / Live out my stars / George / All sewn up (demo) / Improve myself (new version) / Tonight / Mr. & Mrs. / Animal mentality / A superbeing / Waiting for the final cue / Without sex / Pop star pop star.

FIVE GO DOWN TO THE SEA

Formed: Cork, Ireland . . . 1982, taking their moniker from the series of

Enid Blyton's children's books. Comprising of vocalist MICK DONNELLY, RICKY, SMELLY, STACK and UNA, the group debuted with a 1983 EP, 'KNOT A FISH'. A year later, and moving from 'Kabuki' records (home of MICRODISNEY) to UK indie imprint, 'Abstract', the FIVE issued their follow-up, 'THE GLEE CLUB'. Incorporating a type of PERE UBU, avant-garde art jazz style, they found favour with 'Creation' boss, ALAN McGEE, who subsequently issued what was to become their third and final effort, the 'HAWKING' EP. The latter contained the controversial and much criticised 'SINGING IN BRAILLE'. DONNELLY went on to form the group, BEETHOVEN, although his choice of moniker proved foolhardy as there was of course a classical bod already in the public domain. Sadly, just like his new outfit's namesake before him, he passed away in 1989.

Album rating: never released any

MICK DONNELLY – vocals / **RICKY** – / **SMELLY** – / **STACK** – / **UNA** –

Kabuki | not iss.

Mar 83. (7"ep) *(KAFIVE 5)* **KNOT A FISH** [ ] [-]
– Fishes for compliments / Elephants for fun and profit / Why wait until April / There's a fish on top of Sharden swears he's Elvis.

Abstract | not iss.

Sep 84. (12"ep) *(12ABS 027)* **THE GLEE CLUB** [ ] [-]
– Jumping Joey / Often / What happened to your leg? / Boon for travellists.

— new drummer on next EP

Creation | not iss.

Sep 85. (12"ep) *(CRE 021T)* **HAWKING EP** [ ] [-]
– Singing in braille / Aunt Nelly / Silk brain worm / Women.

— never went down to the sea again

FIVE THIRTY

Formed: Reading, England . . . 1985 by TARA MILTON and PAUL BASSETT, who released their first single, 'CATCHER IN THE RYE' not long after leaving school. However little was heard of them until 1990, when they moved to North London, drummer PHIL HOPPER being added to the all-male trio in the process. Signed to 'East West' and managed by ALAN McGEE of Creation records, FIVE THIRTY finally issued their follow-up 45, 'ABSTAIN', an adrenaline fuelled neo-Mod affair that was hardly in keeping with the blissed out spirit of the times. It was also their first of four minor hits, all taken from their one and only full-length set, 'BED' (1991), an impressive debut that brought comparisons with The JAM. A couple of years too early for the Brit-pop retro-revival, FIVE THIRTY were a talented band out of time, PHIL hastening their inevitable demise by taking up acting; TARA would subsequently form The NUBILES while PAUL joined ORANGE DELUXE. • **Songwriters:** MILTON – BASSETT except COME TOGETHER (Beatles).

Album rating: BED (*7)

TARA MILTON – vocals, bass / **PAUL BASSETT** – vocals, guitar

Other | not iss.

Oct 85. (12"ep) *(12OTH 2)* **CATCHER IN THE RYE / WEIGHT OF THE WORLD. / MOOD SUITE / SUBURBAN TOWN** [ ] [-]

— added **PHIL HOPPER** – drums

East West | Atco

Jul 90. (7") *(YZ 530)* **ABSTAIN. /** [75] [-]
(12"+=/cd-s+=) *(YZ T/CD 530)* –

Nov 90. (7") *(YZ)* **AIR CONDITIONED NIGHTMARE. /** [ ] [-]
(12"+=/cd-s+=) *(YZ T/CD)* –

May 91. (7") *(YZ 577)* **13th DISCIPLE. / HATE MALE** [67] [-]
(12"+=/cd-s+=) *(YZ T/CD 577)* – Out to get in / Come together.

Jul 91. (7") *(YZ 594)* **SUPER NOVA. / STILL LIFE** [75] [-]
(12"+=/cd-s+=) *(YZ T/CD 594)* – Something's got to give.

Aug 91. (cd)(lp/c) *(9031 75304-2)(WX 530/+C)* <91757> **BED** [57] [ ]
– Supernova / Psycho cupid / Junk male / 13th disciple / Strange kind of urgency / You / Songs and paintings / Womb with a view / Automations / Wrapped in blue. *(cd+=/c+=)* – Abstain / Catcher in the rye.

Oct 91. (7"m) *(YZ 624)* **YOU. / SLOWTRAIN INTO THE OCEAN / CUDDLY RUG** [72] [-]
(c-ep+=/12"ep/cd-ep+=) *(YZ C/T/CD 624)* –

— virtually disappeared for a while after HOOPER became an actor. BASSETT resurfaced in ORANGE DELUXE, while MILTON formed The NUBILES

FIZZBOMBS (see under ⇒ JESSE GARON & THE DESPERADOES)

FLAG OF CONVENIENCE / F.O.C. (see under ⇒ BUZZCOCKS)

FLAMING LIPS

Formed: Oklahoma City, Oklahoma, USA . . . 1983 by the COYNE brothers WAYNE and MARK, who reputedly stole instruments from a church hall to get their act off the ground. After a rare and weird EP in 1985, MARK left brother WAYNE to recruit new members for the 'Enigma' album, 'HEAR IT IS'. Their next, 'OH MY GAWD!!!', in '87, saw them strike with many poetic assaults, including the near 10-minute track 'ONE MILLION BILLIONTH OF A MILLISECOND ON A SUNDAY MORNING'. Their reputation grew, with wild, climactic live appearances, highlighting albums 'TELEPATHIC SURGERY' and 'IN A PRIEST-DRIVEN AMBULANCE (WITH SILVER SUNSHINE STARES)'. Phew!!!. Signed to 'Warners' in 1992, and between appearing at the Reading Festival, they released 'HIT TO DEATH IN THE MAJOR HEAD' and the US No.108 (!) album 'TRANSMISSIONS FROM THE SATELLITE HEART'. By the mid-90's, they had secured weirdo posterity, after giving birth to the drug-orientated, narrative track, 'WATERBUG'. Their avant-garde psychedelic (BARRETT / FLOYD) approach was now well behind them, their barrage of sound, once described as The JESUS & MARY CHAIN meeting BLACK FLAG or The DEAD KENNEDYS, took a sharp detour and ended up, well, er . . . anywhere really. • **Songwriters:** Group except; SUMMERTIME BLUES (Eddie Cochran) / WHAT'S SO FUNNY 'BOUT PEACE, LOVE & UNDERSTANDING (Brinsley Schwarz) / THAN YOU (Led Zeppelin) / DEATH VALLEY '69 (Sonic Youth & Lydia Lunch) / STRYCHNINE (Sonics) / AFTER THE GOLD RUSH (Neil Young) / ALL THAT JAZZ + HAPPY DEATH MEN (Echo & The Bunnymen) / WHAT A WONDERFUL WORLD (Nat King Cole) / ICE DRUMMER (Suicide) / CHOSEN ONE + LITTLE DRUMMERBOY (Smog).

Album rating: HEAR IT IS (*5) / OH MY GAWD!!! . . . THE FLAMING LIPS (*7) / TELEPATHIC SURGERY (*5) / IN A PRIEST-DRIVEN AMBULANCE (*6) / HIT TO DEATH IN THE FUTURE HEAD (*6) / TRANSMISSIONS FROM THE SATELLITE HEART (*8) / CLOUDS TASTE METALLIC (*7)

MARK COYNE – vocals / **WAYNE COYNE** – guitar / **MICHAEL IVINS** – bass / **RICHARD ENGLISH** – drums

not iss. | Lovely Sorts Of Death

1985. (7"green-ep) <L-19679> **THE FLAMING LIPS E.P.** [ ] [ ]
– Bag full of thoughts / Out for a walk / Garden of eyes – Forever is a long time / Scratching the door / My own planet. *(re-iss. 1986 red-ep; same) (re-iss. 1987 on 'Pink Dust' 7"ep/c-ep; 731881-1/-4)*

— **WAYNE** now on vox, when MARK departed

Enigma | Restless

Nov 86. (white-lp,lp/c/cd) *(72173-1/-4/-2)* **HEAR IT IS** [ ] [ ]
– With you / Unplugged / Trains, brains and rain / Jesus shootin' heroin / Just like before / She is death / Charles Manson blues / Man from Pakistan / Godzilla flick / Staring at sound – With you. *(cd+=)* – Bag full of thoughts / Out for a walk / Garden of eyes – Forever is a long time / Scratching the door / My own planet / Summertime blues.

Nov 87. (clear-lp,lp/c/cd) <72207-1/-4/-2> **OH MY GAWD!!! . . . THE FLAMING LIPS** [-] [ ]
– Can't exist / Can't stop the spring / Ceiling is bending / Everything's explodin' / Love yer brain / Maximum dream for Evil Knievel / Ode to CC / One million billionth / Prescription: Overkill / Thank.

Feb 89. (lp/c/cd) *(ENVLP/TCENV/CDENV 523)* <72350-1/-4/-2> **TELEPATHIC SURGERY** [ ] [ ]
– Drug machine / Michael time to wake up / Miracle on 42nd Street / UFO story / Shaved gorilla / Begs and achin' / Right now / Hare Krishna stomp wagon / Chrome plated suicide / Redneck school of technology / Spontaneous combustion of John / The last drop of morning dew.

— **JONATHAN PONEMANN** – guitar + **JOHN DONAHUE** – guitar

City Slang | Sub Pop

Jun 89. (7"m) *(EFA 40153)* <SP-28> **DRUG MACHINE / STRYCHNINE. / (WHAT'S SO FUNNY ABOUT) PEACE, LOVE AND UNDERSTANDING** [ ] [ ] Jan89

— **NATHAN ROBERTS** – drums repl. ENGLISH

City Slang | Atavistic

Jan 91. (12"ep) *(EFA 04063-05)* **UNCONSCIOUSLY SCREAMIN' EP** [ ] [ ]
– Unconsciously screamin' / Lucifer rising / Ma, I didn't notice / Let me be it.

City Slang | Restless

Feb 91. (pink-lp,lp/c/cd) *(SLANG 005/+C/CD)* <72359> **IN A PRIEST-DRIVEN AMBULANCE (WITH SILVER SUNSHINE STARES)** [ ] [ ] Sep90
– Shine on sweet Jesus – Jesus song No.5 / Unconsciously screamin' / Rainin' babies / Take me ta Mars / Five stop Mother Superior rain / Stand in line / God walks among us now / Jesus song No.6 / There you are / Jesus song No.7 / Mountain song / What a wonderful world. *(cd re-iss. Sep96 on 'Restless'; 72359-2)*

Warners | Warners

Jul 92. (cd-ep) <40244> **. . . WASTIN' PIGS IS STILL RADICAL** [-] [ ]
– Talkin' 'bout the smiling deathporn immorality blues (everyone wants to live forever) / All that jazz – Happy death men / Jets (Cupid's kiss vs. the psyche of death).

Aug 92. (cd/c/lp) <(7599 26838-2/-4/-1)> **HIT TO DEATH IN THE MAJOR HEAD** [ ] [ ]
– Talkin' about the smiling deathporn immorality blues (everyone wants to live forever) / Hit me like you did the first time / The Sun / Felt good to burn / Gingerale afternoon (the astrology of a Saturday) / Halloween on the Barbary Coast / The magician vs. the headache / You have to be joking (autopsy of the Devil's brain) / Frogs / Hold your head. *(re-iss. Apr95; same)*

— **RONALD JONES** – guitar repl. JOHN who joined MERCURY REV

— **STEVEN DROZD** – drums repl. NATHAN

Jun 93. (cd/c/lp) <(9362 45334-2/-4/-1)> **TRANSMISSIONS FROM THE SATELLITE HEART** [ ] [ ]
– Turn it on / Pilot can at the queer of God / Oh my pregnant head (labia in the sunlight) / She don't use jelly / Chewin' the apple of your eye / Superhumans / Be my head / Moth in the incubator / Plastic Jesus / When yer twenty-two / Slow nerve action.

Aug 94. (7"/c-s) *(W 0246/+C)* <18131> **SHE DON'T USE JELLY. / TURN IT ON (bluegrass version)** [ ] [55] Nov94
(cd-s+=) *(WO 246CD)* – Translucent egg.
(cd-s) *(WO 246CDX)* – ('A'side) / The process / Moth in the incubator.

Apr 95. (cd-s) <43509> **TURN IT ON** [-] [ ]

Jul 95. (m-cd) <45748> **PROVIDING NEEDLES FOR YOUR BALLOONS** [-] [ ]
– Bad days / Jets part 2 (my two days as an ambulance driver) / Ice drummer / Put the waterbug in the policeman's ear / Chewin the apple of yer ear / Chosen one / Little drummerboy / Slow nerve action.

Sep 95. (cd/c) <(9362 45911-2/-4)> **CLOUDS TASTE METALLIC**
– The abandoned hospital ship / Psychiatric explorations of the fetus with needles / Placebo headwood / This here giraffe / Brainville / Guy who lost a headache and accidentally saves the world / When you smile / Kim's watermelon gun / They punctured my yolk / Lightning strikes the postman / Christmas at the zoo / Evil will prevail / Bad days (aurally excited version).

Dec 95. (c-s) *(W 0322C)* **BAD DAYS / GIRL WITH HAIR LIKE AN EXPLOSION** [-]
(cd-s+=) *(W 0322CD)* – She don't use jelly / Giraffe (demo).
(cd-s) *(W 0322CDX)* – ('A'side) / Ice drummer / When you smiled I lost my only idea / Put the water bug in the policeman's ear.

Mar 96. (cd-s) *(W 0335CD)* **THIS HERE GIRAFFE / JETS pt.2 (MY TWO DAYS AS AN AMBULANCE DRIVER) / LIFE ON MARS** 72 [-]
(c-s/cd-s) *(W 0335 C/CDX)* – ('A'side) / The sun / Hit me like you did the first time.

—— above was the first ever shaped cd single.

Aug 96. (3D-cd-s) *(W 0370CD)* **BRAINVILLE / EVIL WILL PREVAIL (live) / WATERBUG (live)** [-]
(c-s/cd-s) *(W 0370 C/CDX)* – ('A'side) / Brainville (live) / Raindrops keep falling on my head.

Oct 97. (4xcd-box) <(46804)> **ZAIREEKA**
– Okay I'll admit that I really don't care / Riding to work in the year 2025 (your invisible now) / Thirty-five thousand feet of despair / Machine in India / The train runs over the camel but is . . . / How will we know? (futuristic crashendos) / March of the rotten vegetables / Big ol' bug is the new baby now.
(above was an unusual concept in that you needed 4 separate CD players to hear the simultaneous recordings at its full potential)

– compilations, etc. –

Sep 98. (cd) *Restless;* <72963> **A COLLECTION OF SONGS REPRESENTING AN ENTHUSIASM FOR RECORDING . . . BY AMATEURS** (1984-1990) [-]
– Bag full of thoughts / Jesus shootin' heroin / One million billionth / Chrome plated suicide / Michael time to wake up / Hell's angels cracker factory / Unconsciously screamin' / God walks among us now / Stychnini – Peace, love and understanding / Death valley '69 / Thank you / Ma, I didn't notice / After the gold rush / I want to kill my brother: The cymbal.

FLAMINGOES

Formed: Hitchin, Hertfordshire, England . . . Spring 1993 by identical twin brothers, JUDE and JAMES COOK, who completed the line-up with off-kilter drummer KEVIN. Taking flight to the capital, the lads won a talent competition run by DJ, Gary Crowley, stirring up even more publicity when they played the celebrated New Art Riot gig alongside THESE ANIMAL MEN and S*M*A*S*H towards the end of the year. The following February, The FLAMINGOES unleashed their vinyl debut in the shape of 7" single, 'THE CHOSEN FEW', already being tipped for the top by such unlikely organs as the News Of The World. Yet another band harking back to the year of 1977 when The CLASH and The JAM ruled the pop charts, the feathered ones had no reservations about airing their suitability to wipe the floor with the New Wave of neo-Mod Brit-pop acts. Signed to 'Pandemonium', the trio released the 'TEENAGE EMERGENCY' EP (the title track having already netted them the aforementioned award) and a further single, 'DISAPPOINTED', both highlights from their forthcoming debut album, 'PLASTIC JEWELS' (1995). However, just as things looked promising for the hell-raising lads, they rather mysteriously disappeared from view. • **Note:** Not to be confused with another outfit of the same name who had a few singles released on dance label, Rob's, either end of '93.

Album rating: PLASTIC JEWELS (*6)

JUDE COOK (b.1970) – vocals, guitar / **JAMES COOK** (b.1970) – bass, vocals / **KEVIN** – drums

La La Land — not iss.

Feb 94. (7") *(LALA 002)* **THE CHOSEN FEW. /** [-]

Pandemonium — not iss.

Jul 94. (12"ep/cd-ep) *(PANN/+CD 005)* **TEENAGE EMERGENCY** [-]
– Teenage emergency / Running away / Six burning seven / Everyone makes mistakes.

Oct 94. (7") *(PANN 006)* **DISAPPOINTED. / DISTORT** [-]
(cd-s+=) *(PANNCD 006)* – London's laughing.

Feb 95. (cd/c/lp) *(PANN CD/MC/LP 007)* **PLASTIC JEWELS** [-]
– Disappointed / Teenage emergency / Safe / Try it on / Absent fathers, violent sons / Winter / Scenester / The chosen few / Unstable / Suicide bridge / Last of the big spenders / It's been a thrill.

Mar 95. (12"ep/cd-ep) *(PANN/+CD 008)* **SCENESTER. / SUBURBAN SINNERS / TOUGH AGAIN** [-]

—— split after above single

FLAMING STARS

Formed: Camden, London, England . . . late 1994 out of the EARLS OF SUAVE (who released one single, 'IN MY DREAMS') by vocalist/keyboard player MAX DECHARNE (previously the drummer with GALLON DRUNK), drummer JOE WHITNEY, bassist PAUL DEMPSEY and guitarist JOHNNY JOHNSON (the latter two from THEE HEADCOATS and the STINGRAYS). Taking their moniker from an ELVIS PRESLEY movie and adding a fifth member, guitarist MARK HOSKING, the group embarked on a series of dates while also featuring on Radio One sessions including the obligatory John Peel and Mark Radcliffe shows. The FLAMING STARS remained on the EARLS' label, 'Vinyl Japan', several singles/EP's over the course of '95/'96 leading up to the drink-soaked vignettes of debut album, 'SONGS FROM THE BAR ROOM FLOOR' (1996). Two further sets were released the following year, namely 'BRING ME THE REST OF ALFREDO GARCIA' and 'SELL YOUR SOUL TO THE FLAMING STARS'.

Album rating: SONGS FROM THE BAR ROOM FLOOR (*6) / BRING ME THE REST OF ALFREDO GARCIA (*6) / SELL YOUR SOUL TO THE FLAMING STARS (*6)

MAX DECHARNE – vocals, keyboards (ex-GALLON DRUNK) / **JOHNNY JOHNSON** – guitar (ex-THEE HEADCOATS, ex-STINGRAYS) / **PAUL DEMPSEY** – bass (ex-THEE HEADCOATS, ex-STINGRAYS) / **JOE WHITNEY** – drums

Vinyl Japan — Vinyl Japan

Apr 94. (7"; as EARLS OF SUAVE) *(PAD 016)* **IN MY DREAMS. / SOMEBODY BUY ME A DRINK** [-]

—— added **MARK HOSKING** – guitar

Mar 95. (7"ep)(cd-ep) *(PAD 023)(TASKCD 049)* **HOSPITAL, HEAVEN OR HELL EP** [-]
– Kiss tomorrow goodbye / Davy Jones' locker / Like trash / Revenge.

Jul 95. (7") *(PAD 028)* **THE FACE ON THE BAR ROOM FLOOR. / GET CARTER** [-]

Dec 95. (7"ep)(cd-ep) *(PAD 030)(TASKCD 054)* **MONEY TO BURN EP** [-]
– Money to burn / Bandit country / A hell of a woman / New shade of black.

May 96. (7"ep)(cd-ep) *(PAD 031)(TASKCD 056)* **DOWNHILL WITHOUT BRAKES EP** [-]
– Downhill without brakes / Broken heart / Eat your heart out / Burnt out wreck of a man.

Jun 96. (cd/lp) *(ASK CD/LP 062)* **SONGS FROM THE BAR ROOM FLOOR** [-]
– The face on the bar room floor / Forget my name / You can lie / Who's out there? / Burnt out wreck of a man / Bring me the rest of Alfredo Garcia / Kiss tomorrow goodbye / The ballad of the walking wounded / Downhill without brakes / Theme from dog instruction / Back of my mind / Down to you / Oncoming train / Tubs twist / Like trash / 3 a.m. on the bar room floor.

Nov 96. (7") *(PAD 34)* **TEN FEET TALL. / SPAGHETTI JUNCTION** [-]

Mar 97. (cd) *(ASKCD 067)* **BRING ME THE REST OF ALFREDO GARCIA** [-]

Apr 97. (7") *(PAD 035)* **BURY MY HEART AT PIER 13. / DOWN TO YOU** [-]

Oct 97. (cd) *(<ASKCD 076>)* **SELL YOUR SOUL TO THE FLAMING STARS** Mar99
– Sweet smell of success / Blood money / London after midnight / The street that never closes / I remembered to forget to remember / New hope for the dead / Find yourself another drunk / Don't need the sunshine / What you want / Just too bad / Don't mean a thing if you haven't got the king / Better than that / The day the Earth caught fire.

Apr 98. (7"ep/cd-ep) *(PAD/TASKCD 59)* **SWEET SMELL OF SUCCESS EP** [-]
– Sweet smell of success / The day the Earth caught fire / Never missed you tonight / A place in the sun.

FLATMATES

Formed: Bristol, England . . . mid 1985 by head of the household, MARTIN WHITEHEAD – the mastermind of up and coming indie label, 'Subway Organization' – together with fellow residents DEBBIE HAYNES, SARAH FLETCHER (who replaced KATH BEACH) and ROCKER. Joining the so-called jingle-jangle "anorak brigade" alongside The RAZORCUTS, etc, they fused BUZZCOCKS with The SHANGRI-LA'S on a series of mid-late 80's singles beginning with 'I COULD BE IN HEAVEN' in late '86. Flat harmony proved a problem throughout their sporadic recording career, members coming and going as they pleased (i.e. before the 3rd 45, JOEL O'BIERNE taking up ROCKER's empty room and on the group's final outing, 'HEAVEN KNOWS', SARAH handing over her lease to JACKIE CARRERA). Still without an album to their name, The FLATMATES temporarily moved out of the music biz in 1989, WHITEHEAD and relative newcomer TIM RIPPINGTON coming to blows on stage. For anyone who missed the singles first time round, the retrospective 'LOVE AND DEATH' album collected all their material in one package.

Album rating: LOVE AND DEATH (1986-1989) compilation (*6)

MARTIN WHITEHEAD – guitar / **DEBBIE HAYNES** – vocals / **SARAH FLETCHER** – bass; repl. KATH BEACH / **ROCKER** – drums

Subway Org — not iss.

Oct 86. (7") *(SUBWAY 6)* **I COULD BE IN HEAVEN. / TELL ME WHY / SO IN LOVE WITH YOU** [-]

Apr 87. (7") *(SUBWAY 9)* **HAPPY ALL THE TIME. /** [-]
(12"+=) *(SUBWAY 9T)* – (4 extra).

—— **JOEL O'BIERNE** – drums; repl. ROCKER who joined The ROSEHIPS

Nov 87. (7") *(SUBWAY 14)* **YOU'RE GONNA CRY. /** [-]
(12"+=) *(SUBWAY 14T)* –

—— added **TIM RIPPINGTON** – guitar, keyboards

Mar 88. (7") *(SUBWAY 17)* **SHIMMER. / ON MY MIND / BAD** [-]
(12"+=) *(SUBWAY 17T)* – If not for you.

—— **JACKIE CARRERA** – bass; repl. SARAH

Sep 88. (7") *(SUBWAY 21)* **HEAVEN KNOWS. /** [-]
(12"+=/cd-s+=) *(SUBWAY 21 T/CD)* –

—— split late in '88 after a fight with WHITEHEAD and RIPPINGTON. CARRERA joined The CARETAKER RACE, while WHITEHEAD and O'BIERNE formed the SWEET YOUNG THINGS

– compilations, etc. –

May 88. (12"ep) *Night Tracks; (SFNT 011)* **JANICE LONG SESSIONS** (1.3.87) [ ] [-]

Feb 90. (lp/cd) *Subway; (SUBORG 14/+CD)* **LOVE AND DEATH (1986-1989)** [ ] [-]
– I could be in Heaven / Tell me why / I don't care / Life of crime / On my mind / So in love with you / Happy all the time / You're gonna cry / Shimmer / Heaven knows / Don't say it? / Is it me? / Thinking of you / Love cuts / My empty head / This thing called love / Never coming down / Turning you blue / When I'm with you.

FLESH EATERS

Formed: Los Angeles, California, USA ... 1977 by CHRIS 'D' DESJARDINS, who has been the only constant fixture in the band's line-up over its decade and a half lifespan. A cast of DAVE ALVIN, JOHN DOE, BILL BATEMAN, DON BONEBRAKE and STEVE BERLIN were present on their debut album, 'NO QUESTIONS ASKED', at the turn of the decade, although the revolving door personnel policy led them on to better things. CHRIS D and Co delivered a series of average post-punk albums that verged on alternative heavy-metal, although lack of interest led the singer to change direction in the mid 80's via the rootsier DIVINE HORSEMEN. While their music might have less intense, a sinister lyrical edge was never far from the surface, 'S.S.T.' albums such as 'DEVIL'S RIVER' (1986) and 'SNAKE HANDLER' (1987) finding DESJARDINS splitting the vocals with his partner, JULIE C(HRISTENSEN). Towards the end of the decade, CHRIS D founded yet another vehicle for his dark talent, issuing 'I PASS FOR HUMAN' as STONE BY STONE in 1989. The 90's, meanwhile, saw The FLESH EATERS return with a convincing comeback album, 'DRAGSTRIP RIOT' (1991), although the following year's 'SEX DIARY OF MR VAMPIRE' would be their final offering.

Album rating: NO QUESTIONS ASKED (*6) / A MINUTE TO PRAY, A SECOND TO DIE (*6) / FOREVER CAME TODAY (*6) / DRAGSTRIP RIOT (*5) / SEX DIARY OF MR VAMPIRE (*5) / GREATEST HITS – DESTROYED BY FIRE compilation (*6) / PREHISTORIC FITS compilation (*6) / Divine Horsemen: TIME STANDS STILL (*5) / DEVIL'S RIVER (*5) / SNAKE HANDLER (*5) / Stone By Stone: I PASS FOR HUMAN (*5)

CHRIS 'D' DESJARDINS – vocals / **DAVE ALVIN** – guitar / **JOHN DOE** – bass / **BILL BATEMAN** – drums / **DON BONEBRAKE** – marimbas, percussion / **STEVE BERLIN** – saxophone

not iss. | Upsetter

1980. (lp) *<UPCD 34>* **NO QUESTIONS ASKED** [-] [ ]

Initial | Ruby

Sep 81. (lp) *(IRC 007) <JRR 101>* **A MINUTE TO PRAY, A SECOND TO DIE** [ ] [ ]
– Digging my grave / Pray til you sweat / River of fever / Satan's stomp / See you in the boneyard / So long / Cyrano de Berger's back / Divine horsemen.

— **DON KIRK** – guitar; repl. ALVIN who was already part of The BASTERS / **ROBYN JAMESON** – bass; repl. DOE + BONEBRAKE who were part of X / **CHRIS WAHL** – drums; repl. BATEMAN (also of BLASTERS)

1982. (lp) **FOREVER CAME TODAY** [-] [ ]
– My life to live / A minute to pray, a second to die / Secret life / Shallow water / The rosy hours / The wedding dice / Hand of glory / Drag my name in the mud / Because of you / Tightrope of fire.

1983. (lp) **A HARD ROAD TO FOLLOW** [-] [ ]

— split after above

DIVINE HORSEMEN

CHRIS D – vocals / members of BLASTERS, X and GUN CLUB

not iss. | Enigma

1984. (lp) **TIME STANDS STILL** [-] [ ]

— added **JULIE C** (b. CHRISTENSEN) – vocals

New Rose | S.S.T.

Nov 86. (12"ep) *(NEW 87) <SST 090>* **MIDDLE OF THE NIGHT** [ ] [ ]

Dec 86. (lp/cd) *(ROSE 102/+CD) <SST 091/+CD>* **DEVIL'S RIVER** [ ] [ ]
(re-iss. May93 on 'S.S.T.' lp/cd; same as US)

— now with **PETE ANDRUS** – guitar

Oct 87. (lp/cd) *(ROSE 134/+CD) <SST 140/+CD>* **SNAKE HANDLER** [ ] [ ]
– Snake handler / Kiss tomorrow goodbye / Stone by stone (fire is my home) / Curse of the crying woman / Someone like you / Fire kiss / What is red / The blind leading the blind / That's no way to live / Superlungs / Frankie Silver / Past all dishonour / Sanctuary. *(re-iss. May93 on 'S.S.T.' lp/cd; same as US)*

1988. (12"ep) *(NEW 110) <SST 176>* **HANDFUL OF SAND** [ ] [ ]

— broke up the partnership, although CHRIS D formed below solo project with **JOHN NAPIER, ERIC MARTIN + CHRIS HASKETT**

Jul 89. (lp/c/cd; as STONE BY STONE with CHRIS D) *<(SST 247/+C/CD)>* **I PASS FOR HUMAN** [ ] [ ]

FLESH EATERS

— reformed with of course **CHRIS D** at the helm / + **WAYNE JAMES** – guitar / **GLENN HAYS** – bass / **RAY TORRES** – drums, percussion / **TERRI LAIRD** – backing vocals

S.S.T. | S.S.T.

Nov 90. (lp/c/cd) *<(SST 264/+C/CD)>* **PREHISTORIC FITS** (compilation) [ ] [ ]
(re-iss. May93; same)

Mar 91. (d-lp/c/cd) *<(SST 273/+C/CD)>* **DRAGSTRIP RIOT** [ ] [ ]
– Tomorrow never comes / Youngest profession / Soul kiss / Dragstrip riot / Bedful of knives / My baby's done her best / Sugarhead and panther breath / Out of nowhere / Dove's blood ink / Take my hand / Agony shorthand / Agony sorehead / The moon upstairs / Slipped, tripped, fell in love / Fur magnet. *(re-iss. May93; same)*

— **CHRISTIAN FREE** – drums, percussion; repl. TORRES

May 93. (cd/c) *<(SST 292 CD/C)>* **THE SEX DIARY OF MR. VAMPIRE** [ ] [ ] Nov92
– Death installment plan / Cemetery without crosses / Better tomorrow / Soft knife and a brick pillow / Covert counter-insurgency man / Five dolls for an August moon / I love you so / Car named Ego / Diary of a psycho / Diamond in my eye / Eyes of lightning / Kill, baby, kill.

Dec 92. (12"ep/cd-ep) *<SST/+CD 297>* **CRUCIFIED LOVERS IN WOMAN HELL** [-] [ ]

— disbanded after above

– compilations, etc. –

May 87. (lp) *Fan Club; (FC 025) / S.S.T.; <SST 094>* **DESTROYED BY FIRE – GREATEST HITS** [ ] [ ] 1986
– See you in the boneyard / Cyrano / Dominoes / Impossible crime / Secret life / Hard road to follow / The wedding dice / Pony dress / We'll never die / Digging my grave / Lake of burning fire. *(re-iss. May93 on 'S.S.T.'; same as US)*

Mar 89. (lp) *Homestead; <(HMS 124-1)>* **LIVE (live 1979-83)** [ ] [ ]
– Version nation / Digging my grave / So long / Divine horsemen / Cinderella / A minute to pray, a second to die / Because of you / My destiny / Poison arrow / My life to live / I take what I want / Shallow water / Buried treasure / Digging my grave.

FLESH FOR LULU

Formed: Brixton, London, England . . . early 80's by NICK MARSH and JAMES MITCHELL along with GLEN BISHOP and ex-WASTED YOUTH member ROCCO BARKER. Signed to 'Polydor', the band released their debut single, 'ROMAN CANDLE', in late '83, following it up with the infectious 'SUBTERRANEANS' and 'RESTLESS' in summer '84. After the release of an eponymous debut album later that year, BISHOP was replaced by KEVIN MILLS while keyboard player, DEREK GREENING completed the line-up. While the record lacked any coherent musical direction (although there was a loose strand of flashy garage rock akin to IGGY POP, LOU REED or GENERATION X), there were some interesting ideas and it's a fair bet that The PIXIES copped an earful of the distinctive guitar sound. The record's commercial failure led to the end of their major label deal and the band released the decidedly more lo-fi 'BLUE SISTERS SWING' mini-set on the small 'Hybrid' imprint. Generating more publicity for its controversial cover (two nuns locked in an embrace) than its musical content, FLESH FOR LULU recorded their most accessible material to date in the shape of the 'BIG FUN CITY' (1985) album. Kicking off with the singalong 'BABY HURRICANE', the record displayed a quantum leap in confidence, from the itchy funk-rock of 'CAT BURGLER' to the TOM PETTY-esque 'LET GO'. Moving on to 'Beggars Banquet', the band moved in an increasingly commercial direction with subsequent albums, 'LONG LIVE THE NEW FLESH' (1987) and 'PLASTIC FANTASTIC' (1990), their efforts unfortunately not reciprocated in sales terms. Dropped again, the band finally threw in the towel in the early 90's.

Album rating: FLESH FOR LULU (*6) / BLUE SISTERS SWING mini (*5) / BIG FUN CITY (*6) / LONG LIVE THE NEW FLESH (*5) / PLASTIC FANTASTIC (*5)

NICK MARSH – vocals, guitar / **ROCCO BARKER** – guitar, vocals (ex-WASTED YOUTH) / **POPE GLEN BISHOP** – bass / **JAMES MITCHELL** – drums

Polydor | not iss.

Nov 83. (7") *(POSP 653)* **ROMAN CANDLE./ COMING DOWN** [ ] [-]
(12"+=) *(POSPX 653)* – Lame train/ The power of suggestion.

May 84. (7") *(FFL 1)* **SUBTERRANEANS. / WHY ME?** [ ] [-]
(12"+=) *(FFLX 1)* – Gurl at the bar.
(d7"+=) *(FFLD 1)* – Endless sleep / Ten foot tall.

Aug 84. (7"/12") *(FFL/+X 2)* **RESTLESS. / CAT BURGLAR** [ ] [-]
(d7"+=) *(POSP 653)* – Roman candle / Coming down.

Oct 84. (lp) *(POLD 5165)* **FLESH FOR LULU** [ ] [-]
– Restless / Dog dog dog / Hyena / Coming down / Jigsaw puzzle / Subterraneans / Brainburst (darling disarray) / Peace and love / So strong / Heavy heavy angel.

— **KEVIN MILLS** – bass (ex-SPECIMEN) repl.BISHOP who joined UNDER TWO FLAGS. added **DEREK GREENING** – keyboards

Hybrid | not iss.

May 85. (m-lp) *(RIB 3)* **BLUE SISTERS SWING** [ ] [-]
– Seven hail Marys / Death shall come / I may have said you're beautiful, but you know I'm just a liar / Who's in danger / Black tattoo.

Statik | not iss.

Oct 85. (7") *(TAK 37)* **BABY HURRICANE. / ANTI-SOCIAL** [ ] [-]
(12"+=) *(TAK 37-12)* – 1970 (I feel alright).

Oct 85. (lp/c) *(STAT LP/C 28)* **BIG FUN CITY** [ ] [-]
– Baby Hurricane / Cat burglar / Let go! / Vaguely human / Rent boy / Golden handshake girl / In your smile / Blue / Laundromat kat / Just one second. *(cd-iss. Dec86, += w/last lp tracks; CDST 28)*

Beggars Banquet | Capitol

Nov 86. (7") *(BEG 177)* **IDOL. / SLEEPING DOGS** [ ] [-]
(12"+=) *(BEG 177T)* – Life of crime / Spaceball ricochet.

Mar 87. (7") *(BEG 184)* **SIAMESE TWIST. / THE DUMBEST THING** [ ] [-]
(c-s+=/12"+=) *(BEG 184 C/T)* – Blue sky / Idol.

May 87. (lp/cd)(c) *(BEGA 82/+CD)(BEGC 82) <48217>* **LONG LIVE THE NEW FLESH** [ ] [ ]
– Lucky day / Postcards from Paradise / Hammer of love / Siamese twist / Sooner or later / Good for you / Crash / Way to go / Sleeping dogs / Dream on cowboy. *(re-iss. Feb90 & Jul91 lp/c/cd; BBL/+C 82/+CD)*

Jul 87. (7") *(BEG 193)* **POSTCARDS FROM PARADISE. / I'M NOT LIKE EVERYBODY ELSE** [ ] [-]
(12"+=) *(BEG 193T)* – Sometimes good guys don't wear white.

Oct 88. (7") *(BEG 221)* **I GO CRAZY. / CRASH** [ ] [-]
(12"+=) *(BEG 221T)* – Baby, baby, baby, baby, baby.

— **MIKE STEED** – bass + **HANS PERRSON** – drums; repl. MILLS + MITCHELL

Jan 90. (7") *(BEG 240)* **TIME AND SPACE. /** [ ] [-]
(12"+=/cd-s+=) *(BEG 240 T/CD)* –

Feb 90. (lp/cd)(c) *(BEGA 100/+CD)(BEGC 100) <90232>* **PLASTIC FANTASTIC** [ ] [ ] Sep89
– Decline and fall / House of cards / Time and space / Every little word / Slowdown / Highwire / Slide / Day one / Choosing you / Stupid on the street / Avenue / Plastic fantastic.

— **DEL STRANGE FISH** – guitar, keyboards; repl. GREENING

— disbanded when their label dropped them

FLESHTONES

Formed: Queens, New York, USA . . . 1976 by KEITH STRENG, PETER ZAREMBA and JAN MAREK PAKULSKI; BILL MILHIZER subsequently coming in for the departing LENNY CALDERONE. Like most bands of the era, they started out by playing at both the legendary CBGB's and Max's Kansas City venues. A debut single, 'AMERICAN BEAT', was issued in 1979, leading to a contract with Miles Copeland's 'I.R.S.' the following year. Meanwhile, a UK package tour alongside the dB'S and the BUSH TETRAS introduced British audiences to the band's punk/garage revivalist sound complete with melodic fuzz guitar and Farfisa organ. After a few singles were issued, The FLESHTONES finally released their debut album, 'ROMAN GODS' (1982), translating at least some of their live chemistry to vinyl. Adding GORDON SPAETH, they unleashed a second collection of bad-assed rock'n'roll in the shape of the slightly superior 'HEXBREAKER!' (1983). A further personnel change was effected when PAKULSKI was replaced by ROBERT BURKE WARREN, the latter sticking around for two more albums, 'LIVE IN PARIS' (1985) and 'THE FLESHTONES VS REALITY' (1987). The new bassist on the Spanish-only 'SOUL MADRID' was FRED SMITH, although he in turn made way for ANDY SHERNOFF then KEN FOX. Throughout the 90's they have continued to unearth the occasional long-player, 'MORE THAN SKIN DEEP' (1998), their first for their new label, 'Epitaph'. • **Covered:** ROCKET USA (Suicide) / medleys by Kingsmen, etc. • **Trivia:** The guest on the 'BLAST OFF!' album was ALAN VEGA (of Suicide).

Album rating: ROMAN GODS (*7) / HEXBREAKE~R! (*8) / FLESHTONES VS REALITY (*6) / BEAUTIFUL LIGHT (*5) / LABORATORY OF SOUND (*5)

PETER ZAREMBA (b.16 Sep'54) – vocals, keyboards, harmonica / **KEITH STRENG** (b.18 Sep'55) – guitar, vocals / **JAN MAREK PAKULSKI** (b.22 Aug'56, Lewiston, Maine) – bass, vocals / **BILL MILHIZER** (b.21 Sep'49, Troy, N.Y.) – drums (ex-HARRY TOLEDO, ex-ACTION COMBO) repl. LENNY CALDERONE in 1979

not iss. / Red Star

1979. (7") *<RSS 1>* **AMERICAN BEAT. / CRITICAL LIST** [-] [ ]

I.R.S. / I.R.S.

Aug 80. (12"ep) *<SP 70402>* **UP-FRONT** [-] [ ]
– The girl from Baltimore / Cold cold shoes / Feel the heat / Play with fire / Theme from 'The Vindicators'.

May 81. (7") *(PFP 1004)* **GIRL FROM BALTIMORE. / FEEL THE HEAT** [ ] [-]

Jun 81. (7") *<IR 9024>* **THE WORLD HAS CHANGED. / ALL AROUND THE WORLD** [-] [ ]

Feb 82. (lp) *<(SP 70018)>* **ROMAN GODS** [ ] [ ]
– The dreg / I've gotta change my life / Stop fooling around / Hope come back / The world has changed / R-I-G-H-T-S / Let's see the sun / Shadow line / Chinese kitchen / Ride your pony / Roman gods.

Mar 82. (7") *<(PFP 1012)>* **SHADOW LINE. / ALL AROUND THE WORLD** [ ] [ ]

— added **GORDON SPAETH** (b.21 Sep'50, New York City) – organ, saxophone, harmonica

Jul 83. (7") *(PFP 1018)* **RIGHT SIDE OF A GOOD THING. / (LEGEND OF A) WHEELMAN** [ ] [-]

Aug 83. (lp) *<(SP 70605)>* **HEXBREAKER!** [ ] [ ]
– Deep in my heart / What's so new (about you) / Screaming skull / (Legend of a) Wheelman / New scene / Hexbreaker / Right side of a good thing / Brainstorm / This house is empty / Want / Burning hell.

Nov 83. (7") *(PFP 1024)* **SCREAMING SKULL. / BURNING HELL** [ ] [-]

1985. (lp) *<IRS 5627>* **SPEED CONNECTION: THE FINAL CHAPTER** [-] [ ]
– Hide and seek / Watch this / Kingsmen like medley: Trouble – Haunted / Return to the haunted house / Hope come back / B.Y.O.B. / One more time / Dreg / Extended super rock medley: Stop . . . / When the night falls / Wind out / La reprise.

— **ROBERT BURKE WARREN** (b.29 Mar'65, Quantico, Virginia) – bass repl. PAKULSKI

1985. (lp) *(D 26412)* **LIVE IN PARIS** (live) [-] [-] German
– Hide and seek / Watch this / Kingsmen like medley: Trouble – Haunted castle – Twelve month later / Return to the haunted house / Let's see the sun / Hope come back / B.Y.O.B. / This house is empty / Last chance / Super rock medley: Theme from "The Vindicators" – Hexbreaker – Roman gods / I'm back / La la la la.

Emergo / Emergo

Mar 87. (cd/lp) *(EM 34+/9634)* **THE FLESHTONES VS REALITY** [ ] [ ]
– Another direction / Way up here / Way down south / Treat her like a lady / Too late to run / The return of the leather kings / Jump back / Our own time / Whatever makes you happy / Mirror, mirror / The end of the track / Nothing's gonna bring me.

— Mar 88, 'New Rose' released various artists lp 'FLESHTONES PRESENT TIME BOMB'; *(ROSE 137)*

— **FRED SMITH** – bass repl. WARREN

Impossible / not iss.

1989. (lp) **SOUL MADRID** [-] [-] Spain

— **ANDY SHERNOFF** (b.19 Apr'52, Bronx, N.Y.) – bass repl. SMITH

— (1990) **KEN FOX** (b.19 Feb'65, Toronto, Canada) – bass repl. SHERNOFF

Big Beat / Naked Language

May 91. (cd/c) *(CDWIK/WIKC 99) <NAK 6101CD>* **POWERSTANCE!** [ ] [ ]
– Armed and dangerous (remix) / I'm still thirsty / Waiting for a message / Let it rip / 3 fevers / Living legends / I can breathe / Mod teepee / House of rock / Irresistible / Candy ass.

Naked Language / Naked Language

Feb 94. (cd/c) *(NAK 6116 CD/MC)* **BEAUTIFUL LIGHT** [ ] [ ]
– Mushroom cloud / Take a walk with the Fleshtones / Beautiful light / Big heart / Not everybody's Jesus / Whistling past the grave / Outcast / D.T. shadows / Pickin' pickin' / Pocketful of change / Push on thru' / Worried boy blues.

Musidisc / Ichiban

Oct 95. (cd/c) *(11854-2/-4) <24861-2/-4>* **LABORATORY OF SOUND** [ ] [ ]
– Let's go / High on drugs / Sands of our lives / Nostradamus Jr. / The sweetest thing / Hold on / Accelerated emotion / Train of thought / One step less / A motor needs gas / Psychedelic swamp / Fading away / We'll never forget.

Epitaph / Ichiban

Jan 98. (m-cd/m-lp) *(6529-2/-1) <24940>* **MORE THAN SKIN DEEP** [ ] [ ]
– I'm not a sissy / Laugh it off / My love machine / I wanna feel something now / Gentlemen's twist / Smash crash / Dig in / Blow job / God damn it / Dance with the ghoulman / Anywhere you go / Medley: My kinda lovin' – The . . . / Better days.

– compilations, etc. –

Feb 82. (c) *R.O.I.R.; <(A 107)>* **BLAST OFF!** (rec.1978) [ ] [ ]
– Soul struttin' / American beat / Cara-Lin / Shadow line / Comin' in-dead stick / Rocket U.S.A. / Atom spies / B.Y.O.B. / The way I feel / Watch Junior go! / Judy / Critical list / Rockin' this joint. *(cd-iss. May90 on 'Danceteria'; DANCD 039) (cd re-iss. Jul97; RE 107CD)*

1989. (cd/c) *I.R.S.; <44797-0057-2/-4>* **LIVING LEGENDS SERIES** [-] [ ]

1994. (cd) *Impossible;* **THE ANGRY YEARS** [-] [-] Spain
(UK-iss.Mar99 on 'Amsterdamned'; 2)

Jul 97. (cd) *Essential; (ESMCD 573)* **FLESHTONES** [ ] [-]

LOVE DELEGATION

PETER ZAREMBA with

not iss. / Moving Target

1986. (lp) **SPREAD THE WORD** [-] [ ]

Musidisc / Ichiban

Apr 90. (cd/c/lp) *(10490-2/-4/-1)* **DELEGATION** [ ] [ ]

FULL-TIME MEN

KEITH STRENG and FLESHTONES + PETER BUCK (of R.E.M.)

Homestead / Twin/Tone–Coyote

Oct 86. (12"ep) *(SHIF 1T) <TTC 8562>* **FAST IS MY NAME** [ ] [ ] 1985

New Rose / Coyote

1988. (lp) *(ROSE 149)* **YOUR FACE MY FIST** [ ] [ ]

FLINCH

Formed: Camberwell, London, England . . . 1993 by cutesy female singer GROG, along with guitarist PAUL and ex-CARDIACS drummer DOMINIC LUCKMAN. After the release of two independent singles, 'A DUMMY TO LOVE' and 'ORDINARY (THIS CAN'T BE), FLINCH took the honours at the 1994 'In The City' best new band contest, winning a healthy 4-figure sum in the process. Disregarding the ensuing A&R stampede, the trio opted to sign a one-off singles deal with 'Clawfist' (then home of GALLON DRUNK) and proceeded to document their distaste of music industry fashion boffins with the track 'FAKING IT'. Perhaps it was this unwillingness to sell their image that ultimately saw them fall by the wayside, although another factor was undoubtedly the decidely non-Brit pop nature of their music, GROG and her mates bailing out after only two further singles for '~dilo!'.

Album rating: none were released

GROG – vocals / **PAUL** – guitar (ex-SCREEMING CUSTARD) / **DOMINIC LUCKMAN** (b.29 Nov'60, Brighton, England) – drums (ex-CARDIACS)

New Ground / not iss.

Aug 93. (12"ep) *(NG 001T)* **A DUMMY TO LOVE EP** [ ] [-]

Dental / not iss.

May 94. (7") *(7DENT 5)* **ORDINARY (THIS CAN'T BE). /** [ ] [-]

Clawfist / not iss.

Oct 94. (7") **FAKING IT. /** [ ] [-]

!dilo! / not iss.

Feb 95. (7") *(DO 002)* **JAMIE D. / SALT** [ ] [-]
(cd-s+=) *(DI 002CD)* – ('A'instrumental).

May 95. (7") *(DI 003)* **SKIN DEEP. / SPOONZ** [ ] [-]
(cd-s+=) *(DI 003CD)* – Faking / Jamie D.

— looked to have disbanded since nothing has been heard of them

FLIPPER

Formed: San Francisco, California, USA . . . 1979 out of NEGATIVE TREND by WILL SHATTER and STEVE DePACE. Following the departure of the latter act's original singer, ROZZ, the pair recruited RICKIE WILLIAMS, who in turn thought up the FLIPPER moniker. He was soon replaced himself with the wonderfully named BRUCE LOOSE alongside fourth member, TED FALCONI, the raggedy-assed punk renegades attracting a cult following in the Bay Area with their painfully slow, monolithically rhythmic noise-grind. Signed to the newly inaugurated 'Subterranean', the FLIPPER crew made their vinyl debut with a track on the 1979 label sampler, 'SF Underground', while they also popped up on a local v/a album, 'Live At Target'. A belated debut single, 'LOVE CANAL', eventually appeared in 1980 on the tiny 'Thermidor' label while a first single for 'Subterranean', the marathon one (two at a push!) chord screamathon, 'SEX BOMB BABY', previewed the definitive debut set, 'ALBUM-GENERIC FLIPPER' (1982). Seemingly dredged up from the blackest studio murk, this lumbering, deceptively basic collection of inspired hardcore sloppiness set the scene for all manner of SF weirdness to come (i.e. PRIMUS etc.), its malign influence winding its way right up the coast to Seattle where the likes of TAD and NIRVANA would later incorporate at least the spirit of FLIPPER into their work. Yet by the release of the cleaned-up but demented follow-up, 'GONE FISHIN' (1984), FLIPPER had done just that, posthumous live releases following in the shape of 'BLOWING CHUNKS' (1984) and double set, 'PUBLIC FLIPPER LTD.' (1987). Tragically, any possiblilites of a full reunion were cut short when WILL SHATTER died of an accidental heroin overdose in late '87. Nevertheless, the patronage of many leading figures in the 90's grunge scene (and KURT COBAIN in particular) led to a belated re-formation with new member, JOHN DOUGHERTY. A surprise signing to Rick Rubin's 'Def American' label, the band were afloat once again with comeback album, 'AMERICAN GRAFISHY' (1993). Despite being given a cautious thumbs up by FLIPPER commentators, many mourned the noisy abandon of old as it became clear the guys had actually been practicing in their absence! • **Songwriters:** SHATTER – LOOSE.

Album rating: GENERIC FLIPPER (*8) / GONE FISHIN' (*7) / BLOW'N'CHUNKS: LIVE (*4) / PUBLIC FLIPPER LIMITED (*5) / SEX BOMB BABY (*6) / AMERICAN GRAFISHY (*4)

WILL SHATTER (b. RUSSELL WILKINSON, 1956) – vocals, bass (ex-NEGATIVE TREND) / **TED FALCONI** (b. LAURENCE FALCONI, 2 Sep'47, Bryn Mawr, Penns.) – guitar (ex-RAD COMMAND) / **BRUCE LOOSE** (b. BRUCE CALDERWOOD, 6 Jun'59, Fresno, Calif.) – bass, vocals / **STEVE DePACE** (b.29 Jan'57) – drums

not iss. / Thermidor

1980. (7") *<T 1>* **LOVE CANAL. / HA HA HA** [–] [ ]
<re-iss. 1981 on 'Subterranean'; SUB 7> (UK-iss.Jan82 on 'Alternative Tentacles'; VIRUS 8)

Alternative Tentacles / Subterranean

Apr 82. (7"red) *(VIRUS 18) <SUB 23>* **SEX BOMB. / BRAINWASH** [ ] [ ] Nov81
Apr 82. (lp) *<SUB 25>* **ALBUM-GENERIC FLIPPER** [–] [ ]
– Ever / Life is cheap / Shed no tears / (I saw you) Shine / Way of the world / Life / Nothing / Living for the depression / Sex bomb. *(UK-iss.Aug93 on 'Def American' cd/lp; DAB CD/LP 3)*
1984. (lp) **GONE FISHIN'** [–] [ ]
(UK-iss.Mar87 on 'Fundamental'; SAVE 017)

— On the 9th Dec'87, SHATTER died of an accidental heroin overdose. They decided to split, although they re-formed early '91 with new member **JOHN DOUGHERTY** (b.20 Apr'61, Oakland, Calif.) – bass

American / American

Jun 93. (cd/lp) *(DABCD/LP 1) <45120>* **AMERICAN GRAFISHY** [ ] [ ] Jan93
– Someday / Flipper twist / May the truth be known / We're not crazy / Fucked up once again / Exist or else / Distant illusion / Telephone / It pays to know / Full speed ahead.

Fuel / unknown

Mar 98. (12"ep/cd-ep) *(FUEL 004/+CD)* **TWISTED EP** [ ] [ ]

– compilations, etc. –

Feb 84. (c) *R.O.I.R.; <A 126>* **BLOW'N CHUNKS (live)** [–] [ ]
– Way of the world / The light, the sound, the rhythm, the . . . / Shed no tears / Love canal / Ha ha ha / In your arms / Life is cheap / In life my friend / Get away. *(UK cd-iss. Nov94; RE 126CD)*
Feb 87. (d-lp) *Fundamental; (SAVE 015/016) / Subterranean;* **PUBLIC FLIPPER LTD. (live 1980-82)** [ ] [ ] Nov86
– Nuru nuru / Hard cold world / I'm fighting / The game's gotta price / Love canal / Oh oh ay oh / We don't understand / If I can be drunk / Sex bomb / Brainwash / Shy / Southern California / Life / The whel / Flipper blues.
1988. (lp) *Subterranean; <SAVE 059>* **SEX BOMB BABY** [–] [ ]
– Sex bomb / Love canal / Ha ha ha / Sacrifice / Falling / Ever get away / Earthworm / The games got a price / The old lady who swallowed a fly / Brainwash / Lowrider / End the game. *(UK cd-iss. Oct95 on 'Infinite Zero-BMG'; 74321 29898-2)*
Jul 97. (cd) *Overground; (OVER 63CD)* **LIVE AT CBGB'S 1983 (live)** [ ] [–]

FLOAT UP CP (see under ⇒ RIP, RIG + PANIC)

FLOWERED UP

Formed: London, England . . . mid 1989 by LIAM MAHER, who recruited younger brother JOE along with TIM DORNEY, JOHN TUVEY and MICK LEADER. Touted as the cheeky-cockney answer to the scally charm of Manchester's HAPPY MONDAYS, FLOWERED UP lurched onto the "baggy" scene of summer 1990 in a blaze of hype with their debut single, 'IT'S ON'. Released by the fledgling 'Heavenly' label, the single grazed the Top 60 as the indie-dance craze reached its zenith, FLOWERED UP subsequently taking their already semi-legendary live show – complete with BEZ-style dancer/mascot, BARRY MOONCULT – on the road. Seemingly primed for big things, the group ran into problems following Heavenly's distribution deal with 'London', although by the release of their third single, 'TAKE IT' (co-written with JOE STRUMMER), they were in the Top 40. While the much anticipated debut album, 'A LIFE WITH BRIAN', was subsequently held up, the record eventually surfaced in Spring '91, breaking the UK Top 30 and receiving glowing praise for its good-natured vignettes of London bad boys living the high life. Eventually released in Spring '92 as part of a new deal with 'Columbia' following 'London's decision not to handle it, 'WEEKENDER' proved to be both FLOWERED UP's defining moment and their premature epitaph. A twelve minute-plus celebration of ectasy culture hedonism, the single has since become regarded as one of the movement's most accurate portrayals and was even the basis for an accompanying short film. Despite the track's critical acclaim and Top 20 success, FLOWERED UP's precarious existence ceased the following year, their penultimate effort a cover of Right Said Fred's 'DON'T TALK JUST KISS', recorded for a 'Heavenly' charity EP. Mysteriously, FLOWERED UP resurfaced for a further one-off single in 1994, 'A BETTER LIFE', before permanently going to ground. • **Trivia:** Their flowery dancer, BARRY MOONCULT covered The Troggs' 'WILD THING'.

Album rating: A LIFE WITH BRIAN (*6)

LIAM MAHER – vocals / **TIM DORNEY** – keyboards (repl. SIMON, who formed SLY & LOVECHILD) / **JOE MAHER** – guitar / **JOHN TUVEY** – drums (repl. other JOHN) / **ANDY JACKSON** – bass

Heavenly / not iss.

Jul 90. (7") *(HVN 3)* **IT'S ON. / IT'S ON – SONIA** [54] [–]
(12") *(12HVN 3)* – ('A'side) / It's bloody on (it's on mix) / It's still on (dub).
(10"etched) *(10HVN 3)* – IT'S ON – FEEL PAIN
(cd-s) *(CDHVN 3)* – ('A'side) / It's on and on (not much like the Happy Mondays mix) / It's on John.
Nov 90. (12"/cd-s) *(12/CD HVN 7)* **PHOBIA (extended). / FLAPPING / PHOBIA (paranoid mix)** [75] [–]
(re-iss. May91 as 7"; *HVN 7)* – (1st two tracks only).

London / London

Apr 91. (7"/c-s) *(FUP 1/+C)* **TAKE IT. / I'LL BE YOUR DOG** [34] [–]
(12"+=) *(FUP 1T)* – Phobia (live).
(cd-s+=) *(FUP 1CD)* – ('A'mixes).
Aug 91. (7"/c-s) *(FUP 2/+C)* **IT'S ON (re-recorded). / EGG RUSH (vox ANNA HAIGH)** [38] [–]
(12"+=/cd-s+=) *(FUP 2 T/CD)* – Take it (live).
Aug 91. (cd/c/lp) *(<828 244-2/-4/-1>)* **A LIFE WITH BRIAN** [23] [ ]
– Sunshine / Take it / Mr. Happy reveller / Hysterically blue / It's on / Silver plan / Phobia / Egg rush / Doris . . . is a little bit partial / Crackerjack.

— **MICKEY LEADER** – bass; repl. ANDY

Heavenly / Columbia

Apr 92. (12"one-sided/cd-s) *(HVN 16/+CD)* **WEEKENDER** [20] [–]
(12") *(HVN 16X)* – WEATHERALL'S WEEKENDER (Andy Weatherall remix).
In Oct'92, they did a version of RIGHT SAID FRED's 'DON'T TALK JUST KISS' on an 'Heavenly' artists EP. Proceeds were given to the Terence Higgins trust. Other tracks 'DEEPLY DIPPY' (Rockingbirds) + 'I'M TOO SEXY' (St.Etienne). Disbanded sometime in 1993, MAHER went back to work as a cassette/bootleg seller in Camden market.
Jul 94. (12") *(HVN 38)* **A BETTER LIFE. / ('A'mixes)** [ ] [–]

— after FLOWERED UP officially split, DORNEY helped form REPUBLICA

FLOWERPOT MEN

Formed: London, England . . . 1983 by ADAM PETERS and BEN WATKINS, the latter also being a member of EMPTY QUARTER (with ex-KILLING JOKE bassman, YOUTH); this outfit released two albums, 'YOUTH' (1984) and 'DELIRIUM' (1986). Meanwhile, The FLOWERPOT MEN (of course, nothing whatsoever to do with the one-off hitmakers who had a 1967 smash, 'Let's Go To San Francisco') surfaced late in 1984 with 'JO'S SO MEAN', a gutsy gothic SUICIDE-esque dance attempt, knob-twiddled by STEVE SEVERIN (of SIOUXSIE & THE BANSHEES). A long-awaited follow-up (also recorded at the Greenhouse studios, no less!), a cover of Dr.John's 'WALK ON GILDED SPLINTERS', came out approximately a year later, although it was clear both BEN and ADAM had other outside interests; BEN with EMPTY QUARTER and ADAM with The TRIFFIDS (he had also guested for ECHO & THE BUNNYMEN on 'Ocean Rain'). A third and final 45, 'ALLIGATOR BAIT', was issued early in '87, although the pair did re-form in the guise of SUNSONIC, a disco-fied techno outfit fused with ambient ethnic "rain forest" elements (one album in 1991, 'MELTING DOWN ON MOTOR ANGEL', was titled after a FLOWERPOT MEN track!).

Album rating: Sunsonic: MELTING DOWN ON MOTOR ANGEL (*6)

BEN WATKINS – / **ADAM PETERS** –

Compost / not iss.

Nov 84. (12") *(COMPOST 01)* **JO'S SO MEAN. / UG / RAPIDS** [ ] [–]
Oct 85. (7") *(COMPOST7 02)* **WALK ON GILDED SPLINTERS. / MELTING DOWN ON MOTOR ANGEL** [ ] [–]
Feb 87. (7"m) *(COMPOST 03)* **ALLIGATOR BAIT. / DJANGO / WATCHING THE PHAROAHS / SHARPEN MY HEART** [ ] [–]

— when they split, they resurfaced once more as SUNSONIC

– compilations, etc. –

Jan 88. (12"ep) *Night Tracks; (SFNT 7)* **THE EVENING SHOW SESSIONS** (9.12.86) [ ] [–]

SUNSONIC

Polydor / not iss.

Apr 90. (7"/c-s) *(PO/+CS 76)* **A KIND OF LOVING. / INNOCENT MAN** [ ] [–]
(12"+=/cd-s+=) *(PZ/+CD 76)* –
Jul 90. (7"/c-s) *(PO/+CS 92)* **ROLL MY BODY. / ROLLING JOE** [ ] [–]
(12"+=/cd-s+=) *(PZ/+CD 92)* – ('A'version).
Feb 91. (cd/c/lp) *(843538-2/-4/-1)* **MELTING DOWN ON MOTOR ANGEL** [ ] [–]

— not sure of their whereabouts after this point

FLOWERS

Formed: Edinburgh, Scotland . . . 1978 by HILARY MORRISON, SIMON BEST, ANDY COPELAND and FRASER SUTHERLAND. The quartet initially bloomed on Bob Last's 'EARCOM 1' 12"ep (a various artists collection), performing two numbers, 'CRIMINAL WASTE' and 'AFTER DARK', the second of which became a B-side of their 1979 debut single for 'Pop Aural', 'CONFESSIONS'. Lying somewhere between DELTA 5 and stablemates The FIRE ENGINES, The FLOWERS completed only one more bop-friendly indie single, 'THE BALLAD OF MISS DEMEANOR', before calling it a day in 1980.

Album rating: never released any

HILARY (MORRISON) – vocals / **ANDY COPELAND** – guitar / **FRASER SUTHERLAND** – bass / **SIMON BEST** – drums

Pop Aural / not iss.

Dec 79. (7") *(POP 001)* **CONFESSIONS. / (LIFE) AFTER DARK** [ ] [-]

May 80. (7") *(POP 003)* **THE BALLAD OF MISS DEMEANOR. / FOOD / TEAR ALONG** [ ] [-]

— after their split, FRASER joined SO YOU THINK YOU'RE A COWBOY issuing one 'Cheatin' Heart' single in 1984, 'DON'T NEED YOU'; he subsequently joined the group, The SYNDICATE, while HILARY (HI RAY) joined HEARTBEAT with an ex-FIRE ENGINE (a band SIMON also made guest appearances for)

Gary FLOYD (see under ⇒ SISTER DOUBLE HAPPINESS)

FLUFFY

Formed: London, England . . . 1994 by AMANDA E. ROOTES, BRIDGET JONES, ANGIE ADAMS and PANDORA ORMSBY-GORE, the latter making way for new bassist HELEN STORES. The latest bunch of tough-nut girlies to pick up guitars and take on the boys at their own game, FLUFFY were initially accused of being talentless posh birds on the musical make. Dressing down in provocative mini-skirted Grunge chic, the lassies had NME journos frothing at the mouth, especially when they proved their working class credentials. Taking their musical cue from ELASTICA, HOLE or even the GERMS, the feisty punkettes released their debut single, 'HYPERSONIC', in the Autumn of '95. With the hype machine still in overdrive, they released a second single, 'HUSBAND', scraping into the Top 60 the following February; the label, 'Tim/Kerr' subsequently issued it in America, where the girls recorded the '5 LIVE' EP shortly after. Landing themselves a lucrative contract with 'Virgin', they finally made it onto Top Of The Pops with single, 'NOTHING', a minor hit which previewed the accompanying debut album, 'BLACK EYE' (1996). Despite featuring a guest spot from the FOO FIGHTERS' PAT SMEAR, the record failed to live up to the publicity they'd already generated and a final flop single, 'I WANNA BE YOUR LUSH', FLUFFY became yesterday's bunnies. • **Covered:** I'M A BOY (Who).

Album rating: BLACK EYE (*6)

AMANDA E. ROOTES – vocals, guitar / **BRIDGET JONES** – guitar / **HELEN STORES** – bass; who repl. PANDORA ORMSBY-GORE / **ANGIE ADAMS** – drums

Parkway / Tim/Kerr

Sep 95. (7") *(PARK 003)* **HYPERSONIC. / CROSSDRESSER** [ ] [-]
(cd-s+=) *(PARK 003CD)* – Psychofudge.

Feb 96. (7") *(PARK 006)* *<135>* **HUSBAND. / DENY EVERYTHING** [58] [ ] May96
(cd-s+=) *(PARK 006CD)* – Cheap.

Enclave / not iss.

Jul 96. (10"ep/cd-ep) *(58571-1/-2)* **5 LIVE (live in New York)** [ ] [-]
– I wanna be your lush / Deny everything / Psychofudge / Bed of vomit / Scream.

Virgin / Capitol

Sep 96. (7") *(VS 1614)* **NOTHING. / SCREAM (live)** [52] [-]
(cd-s+=) *(VSCDT 1614)* – Laphog.
(7") *(VSX 1614)* – ('A'side) / I'm a boy.

Oct 96. (cd/c) *(CDV/TCV 2817)* *<53020>* **BLACK EYE** [ ] [ ]
– Nothing / Hypersonic / Black eye / Scream / I wanna be your lush / Crossdresser / Psychofudge / Too famous / Technicolour yawn / Cosmetic dog / Crawl / Husband / Dirty old bird / Cheap. *(lp on 'Enclave'; ENC 53020-1)*

Jun 97. (7") *(VS 1631)* **I WANNA BE YOUR LUSH. / BED OF VOMIT (live)** [ ] [-]
(cd-s) *(VSCDT 1631)* – ('A'side) / Reanimator / ('A'live).
(cd-s) *(VSCDX 1631)* – ('A'side) / Sick things / Deny everything.

FLUID

Formed: Denver, Colorado, USA . . . 1986 by JOHN "JR" ROBINSON, JAMES CLOWER, RICK KULWICKI, MATT BISCHOFF and GARRETT SHAVLIK. Yet another outfit to base their sound on the proto-punk blueprint of The STOOGES and MC5, the FLUID first made it on to vinyl via a self-financed album, 'PUNCH N JUDY' (1986). Picked up by the fledgling 'Sub Pop' label, the grungey retro-rockers subsequently toured with labelmates, TAD, while promoting their second set, 'CLEAR BLACK PAPER' (1988); issued in the UK a year later as 'FREAK MAGNET'. 'ROADMOUTH' (1989) was another transitional set, honing their chops for 1990's mini-album, 'GLUE'. Next on the agenda was a shared 7" with the soon-to-be massive NIRVANA, the FLUID's 'CANDY' back to back with COBAIN and Co's cover of The VASELINES 'Molly's Lips'. One of the original Grunge pioneers, the FLUID had evaporated by the time the Seattle scene realy took off, ROBINSON, CLOWER, etc (having now signed to 'Hollywood') quitting while on top after recording the best album of their career, 'PURPLEMETALFLAKEMUSIC'.

Album rating: PUNCH N JUDY (*4) / CLEAR BLACK PAPER (*5) / ROADMOUTH (*5) / GLUE mini (*6) / PURPLEMETALFLAKEMUSIC (*7)

JOHN "JR" ROBINSON – vocals / **JAMES CLOWER** – guitar / **RICK KULWICKI** – guitar / **MATT BISCHOFF** – bass / **GARRETT SHAVLIK** – drums, vocals

not iss. / Rayon

1986. (lp) **PUNCH N JUDY** [-] [ ]

Glitterhouse / Sub Pop

May 88. (lp/c) *<SP 16/+A>* **CLEAR BLACK PAPER** [-] [ ]
(UK-iss.May89 as 'FREAK MAGNET'; efa 4476)

Oct 89. (lp/cd) *(efa 4489)* *<SP 36/+B>* **ROADMOUTH** [ ] [ ] Jun89
– Hooked / Human mill / Big brother / Girl bomb / Leave it / Fools rule / Cop a plea / Ode to Miss Lodge / Twisted & pissed / Is it day / What man / Saccharin rejection.

Mar 90. (7"orange,7"yellow) *<SP 57>* **TIN TOP TOY. / TOMORROW** [-] [ ]

Apr 90. (m-lp/m-c/m-cd) *<SP 64/+B/A>* **GLUE** [-] [ ]
– Our love will still be there / Black glove / Closet case / Candy / Pretty mouse / Wasted time. *<cd+=/c+=>* – ROADMOUTH

Jan 91. (7"/7"green) *<SP 97>* **CANDY (live). / (B-side by Nirvana)** [-] [ ]

not iss. / Hollywood

Apr 93. (c/cd) *<1+/61445>* **PURPLEMETALFLAKEMUSIC** [-] [ ]
My kind / One eye out / She don't understand / 7/14 / Pill / Wasn't my idea / On my feet / Lies / Mister Blameshifter / Said that I'm through / Change / Hand in hand.

— disbanded some time in 1993; SHAVLIK formed SPELL.

FLUX OF PINK INDIANS

Formed: Bishop Stortford, England . . . 1978 as The EPILEPTICS by DEREK BIRKETT and COLIN LATTER. Unsurprisingly, complaints from The British Epilepsy Association led to them changing their moniker to EPI-X or The LICKS. It would be the latter incarnation under which their debut EP, '1970s' would surface at the turn of the decade. An EPILEPTICS single, meanwhile, 'LAST BUS TO DEBDEN', surfaced a few years later although its release was overshadowed by the new line-up of FLUX OF PINK INDIANS, who unleashed the 'NEU SMELL' EP (featuring the definitive 'TUBE DISASTERS'); the record was actually issued by the in-house label of fellow anarcho subversives, CRASS, with whom FOPI had recently supported on tour. In 1982, they set up their own independent label, 'Spiderleg', notching up a small victory in early 1983 with the non-tunes and militant politicism of debut album, 'STRIVE TO SURVIVE'. Eighteen months later, a follow-up, the uncompromising troopers issued what must surely be a contender for the most bluntly (to put it lightly!) titled album in the history of rock, 'THE FUCKING CUNTS TREAT US LIKE PRICKS'. Predictably, this piece of fractured, barely listenable noise caused uproar among retailers such as HMV who immediately banned it. The Eastern Bloc record shop in Manchester was even charged for daring to display the album sleeve, seeing their stock seized by the Greater Manchester police under the obscene articles for publication law. 1987's more subdued 'UNCARVED BLOCK', meanwhile, was released on BIRKETT's new label project, 'One Little Indian', replacing the seething mess of noise with a caustic brand of free-funk influenced by the likes of ACR and 23 SKIDOO and produced by dubmeister, ADRIAN SHERWOOD. BIRKETT's label went on to become one of the main players in the indie scene, signing The SUGARCUBES, The HEART THROBS and The SHAMEN while 1990 saw the man return in his own right with new project, HOTALACIO. • **Songwriters:** BIRKETT (+ COLIN).

Album rating: STRIVE TO SURVIVE (*7) / THE FUCKING CUNTS . . . (*2) / UNCARVED BLOCK (*6)

LICKS

COLIN 'Colsk The Terrible' LATTER – vocals / **KEVIN HUNTER** – guitar / **DEREK BIRKETT** (b.18 Feb'61, London, England) – bass / **MARTIN WILSON** – drums

Stormbeat / not iss.

Nov 79. (7"ep) *(BEAT 8)* **1970'S E.P.** [ ] [-]
– 1970's have been made in Japan / System rejects / Hitler's still a Nazi / War crimes. *(re-iss. Jan82 by EPILEPTICS on 'Spiderleg'; SDL 1)*

EPILEPTICS

(same line-up)

Spiderleg / not iss.

Oct 81. (7"ep) *(SDL 2)* **LAST BUS TO DEBDEN** [ ] [-]
– Tube disasters / Two years too late / Target on my back / What've you got.

FLUX OF PINK INDIANS

COLIN + DEREK / + ANDY – guitar / **SID ATTION** (b.18 Apr'60, Sutton Coalfield, England) – drums

Crass / not iss.

Oct 81. (7"ep) *(321984-2)* **NEU SMELL EP** [ ] [-]
– Neu smell / Tube disasters / Poem: Sick butchers / Background of malfunction. *(re-iss. Aug87 on 'One Little Indian' 12"ep; 12T PEP 1)*

— **DAVE 'BAMBI'** – drums (ex-DISCHARGE) repl. SID who joined RUBELLA BALLET / **SIMON** – guitar repl. ANDY repl. NEIL PINCHER

— **KEVIN HUNTER + MARTIN WILSON** returned to repl. SIMON + BAMBI who went back to INSANE

Spiderleg | not iss.

Jan 83. (lp) *(SDL 8)* **STRIVE TO SURVIVE CAUSING THE LEAST SUFFERING POSSIBLE** 79 | -
– Song for them / Charity hilarity / Some of us scream, some of us shout / Take heed / TV dinners / Tapioca surprise / Progress / They lie, we die / Blinded by justice / Myxamatosis / Is there anybody there? / The fun is over. *(re-iss. Jun87 on 'One Little Indian'; TPLP 2) (cd-iss. Jun88; TPLP 2CD)*

Sep 84. (d-lp) *(SDL 13)* **THE FUCKING CUNTS TREAT US LIKE PRICKS** | -
– Punk / Mind fuckers fucking minds / Hard sell / Love song / Mickey Tuneoil / Desire / Blood lust rite / The Falklands war / Punk / Life we make / Trouble at the heart / The sun / Shadow of abuse / Very funny / Cure for the coprlite. *(re-iss. Jun87 on 'One Little Indian'; TPLP 3) (cd-iss. Jan89; TPLP 3CD) (+=)* – TAKING A LIBERTY EP

FLUX

Mar 85. (7"ep) *(SDL 16)* **TAKING A LIBERTY EP** | -
– Taking a liberty / Pass me another issue / For the love of beauty.

One Little Indian | not iss.

Jan 87. (lp) *(TP 1)* **UNCARVED BLOCK** | -
– Value of nothing / Youthful immortal / Just is / Children who know / Back word / Footprints in the snow / Nothing is not done / The stonecutter. *(re-press.Aug87; TPLP 1) (cd-iss. Jun88; TPLP 1CD)*

Mar 87. (12") *(12TP 6)* **NEU SMELL. / TAKING A LIBERTY** | -

May 87. (12") *(12TP 9)* **VISION. /** | -

– compilations, etc. –

Nov 97. (lp/cd) *Overground; (OVER 67/+CD)* **NOT SO BRAVE** | -

HOTALACIO

BIRKETT / TIM KELLY / COAL (ex-FLUX) / **LYDIE** (b. France) – drums / **KEITH LeBLANC** – producer (of TACKHEAD)

Big Kiss | not iss.

Mar 90. (7") **TALKIN' OUT THE SIDE OF YOUR NECK** | -

Sep 90. (lp) *(KISS 5)* **SURVEILLANCE** | -
– Talkin' out the side of your neck / Take me for a ride / How ya livin / Bass hell / Why d'ya lie? / Big boss boys / Don't kick me / Why July / Imagination / Deconstruction.

— DEREK now concentrated on his record company

FLYING COLOR

Formed: San Francisco, California, USA ... 1984 by DALE DUNCAN, HECTOR PENALOSA, RICHARD CHASE and JOHN STUART. Stemming from various Bay Area outfits, FLYING COLOR were heavily influenced by their harmonious West Coast forebears and traded in a similar, if less adventurous rootsy jangle to Georgia's R.E.M. A one-off 7" single, 'DEAR FRIEND', was their sole output in '85, prolific they weren't as it would take a further two years for the band to release their eponymous debut album. Drawing comparisons with The BEATLES with regard to their interchangeable songwriting abilities and pristine melodies, FLYING COLOR had recorded a minor gem. Unfortunately, they didn't stick around long enough to reap the rewards, CHRIS VON SNEIDERN coming in briefly for CHASE before their early demise. In 1996, a CD-issue of the aforementioned album rekindled interest, inspiring DUNCAN, STUART and VON SNEIDERN to re-form.

Album rating: FLYING COLOR (*7)

DALE DUNCAN – guitar (ex-LOVE CIRCUS) / **RICHARD CHASE** – guitar / **HECTOR PENALOSA** – bass (ex-ZEROS) / **JOHN STUART** – drums

Sound & Shigaku | Sound & Shigaku

1987. (7") *<(SHIGS 1)>* **DEAR FRIEND. / LOOK MY WAY** | 1985

not iss. | Frontier

Sep 87. (lp) *<FLP 1022>* **FLYING COLOR** - |

— **CHRIS VON SNEIDERN** – guitar; repl. CHASE

— disbanded in 1990 (all went on own projects) but re-formed in '96

FLYING LIZARDS

Formed: based – Kent, England ... 1978 by Irish-born DAVID CUNNINGHAM, a former art college graduate and conceptual artist who had issued a solo album, 'GREY SCALE'. Subsequently discovering monotone chanteuse, DEBORAH EVANS and pianist/keyboardist, JULIAN MARSHALL, CUNNINGHAM signed to 'Virgin' and recorded a DIY cover of Eddie Cochran's 'SUMMERTIME BLUES' on a basic tape recorder for a sum total of £6 (!). Barrett Strong's 'MONEY' was next up for the minimalist, monochromatic treatment, the bizarre but catchy results hooking a UK Top 5 placing in late summer '79 before going on to storm the US Top 50 later that year! Early 1980's self-penned follow-up, 'T.V.', stalled outside the Top 40 and although an eponyous debut album made the Top 60, a cover of Curtis Mayfield's 'MOVE ON UP' (featuring the debut of new vocalist, PATTI PALLADIN) failed to chart. A further couple of original singles followed before CUNNINGHAM added sticksman, JJ JOHNSON and recorded 'THE FOURTH WALL' (1981) with the help of such alternative luminaries as ROBERT FRIPP and GARETH SAGER. After taking a few years out to concentrate on production work, CUNNINGHAM returned in summer '84 with a savage reading of James Brown's 'SEX MACHINE'. Too much to take for some fans, the single sold poorly, as did a follow-up version of Larry Williams' 'DIZZY MISS LIZZY' and a wholesale covers set, 'TOP TEN' (1984). CUNNINGHAM made a belated comeback in the mid-90's with a series of solo and collaborative albums, the last of which, 'ARTIFICIAL HOMELAND' (1988), saw him working with ANGELA JAEGAR. • **TOP TEN covers:** TUTTI FRUTTI (Little Richard) / PURPLE HAZE (Jimi Hendrix Experience) / GREAT BALLS OF FIRE + WHOLE LOTTA SHAKIN' GOIN' ON (Jerry Lee Lewis) / WHAT'S NEW PUSSYCAT? (hit; Tom Jones) / THEN HE KISSED ME (Crystals) / SUZANNE (Leonard Cohen) / DIZZY MISS LIZZY (Larry Williams) / TEARS (Bobby Vinton).

Album rating: THE FLYING LIZARDS (*5) / THE FOURTH WALL (*4) / TOP TEN (*2)

DAVID CUNNINGHAM – synthesizer, electronics, keyboards, guitar / **DEBORAH EVANS** – vocals / **JULIAN MARSHALL** – piano, keyboards

Virgin | Virgin

Oct 78. (7") *(VS 230)* **SUMMERTIME BLUES. / ALL GUITARS** | -

Aug 79. (7") *(VS 276) <67003>* **MONEY. / MONEY (instrumental)** 5 | 50 Nov79

— added **STEVE BERESFORD** – keyboards, bass, guitar

Jan 80. (7") *(VS 325)* **T.V. / TUBE** 43 |

Feb 80. (lp) *(V 2150) <13137>* **THE FLYING LIZARDS** 60 | 99
– Der song Von Mandelay / Her story / T.V. / Russia / Summertime blues / Money / The flood / Trouble / Events during flood / The window.

— **PATTI PALLADIN** – vocals (ex-SNATCH) repl. DEBORAH

Oct 80. (7") *(VS 381)* **MOVE ON UP. / PORTUGAL** | -

Jan 81. (7") *(VS 392)* **HANDS 2 TAKE. / CONTINUITY** | -

May 81. (7") *(VS 421)* **LOVERS AND OTHER STRANGERS. / WIND** | -

— added **JJ JOHNSON** – drums (ex-ELECTRIC CHAIRS)

— guests incl. ROBERT FRIPP, GARETH SAGER + PETER GORDON

Jun 81. (lp) *(V 2190)* **THE FOURTH WALL** | -
– Lovers and other strangers / Glide spin / In my lifetime / Cirrus / A-train / New voice / Hands 2 take / On age / Steam away / Move on up / Another story / Lost and found.

— **CUNNINGHAM** returned after a few years on the production front

— others:- **BERESFORD, MARSHALL, GORDON + / SALLY** – vocals / **JOHN GREAVES** – bass / **ELIZABETH PERRY + ALEX BALANESCH** – strings

Statik | not iss.

Jul 84. (7") *(TAK 19)* **SEX MACHINE. / FLESH AND STEEL** | -
(12"+=) *(TAK 19-12)* – Machine sex.

Oct 84. (7") *(TAK 25)* **DIZZY MISS LIZZY. / DIZZY** | -
(12"+=) *(TAK 25-12)* – ('A'extended).

Nov 84. (lp/c) *(STAT LP/C 20)* **TOP TEN** | -
– Tutti frutti / Sex machine / What's new pussycat? / Whole lotta shakin' goin' on / Purple haze / Great balls of fire / Dizzy Miss Lizzy / Suzanne / Then he kissed me / Tears. *(cd-iss. Dec86; CDST 20)*

— folded after the above dive bombed

– compilations, etc. –

Nov 88. (7") *Old Gold; (OG 9828)* **MONEY. / T.V.** | -

DAVID CUNNINGHAM

— with **STEPHEN REYNOLDS** – glockenspiel, keyboards / **ALAN HUDSON** – bass / **DEREK ROBERTS** – piano, percussion / **MICHAEL DOHERTY** – percussion

Piano | not iss.

1979. (lp) *(PIANO 001)* **GREY SCALE** | -
– Error system (Bagfgab) / Error system (C pulse solo recording) / Error system (C pulse group recording) / Error system (E based group recording) / Error system (Efga) / Ecuador / Water systemised / Venezuela I / Guitar systemised / Venezuela II / Bolivia.

Made To Measure | Made To Measure

Apr 95. (cd) *(<MTM 31>)* **WATER** |
– Stars / Next day / Once removed / Fourth sea / White, blue and grey / Shade creek / Short winter's day / Blue river / Beneath the vines / Yellow river / Low sun / Only shadows / Liquid hand / Dark ocean / Same day. *(re-iss. Jun96; same)*

Piano | Resurgent

Jul 96. (cd; PETER GORDON & DAVID CUNNINGHAM) *(PIANO 504)* **THE YELLOW BOX** | -

Jul 96. (cd) *(PIANO 505) <4003>* **VOICEWORKS** | Nov97
– Siren sign / Engine window / Magic words / At one remove / Engine definite / Not speech / Masks and voices / Mass / Canta / Collective / Resolution / Black air tower / Belgrano / True air / Idiolect / Invisible.
(above was originally a 1992 Japanese-only set, 'VOICES')

Aug 98. (cd; DAVID CUNNINGHAM & ANGELA JAEGAR) *(PIANO 509) <4293>* **ARTIFICIAL HOMELAND** |
– Silver thread / Artificial homeland / Beyond that star / Wood and glass / Fortuna / Turning left / Made of sand / Unlock the hills / Blue gold seven / Forsythia / Hot day / Time can make a difference / Radioloop / River west.

FLYING SAUCER ATTACK

Formed: Bristol, England ... 1992 by DAVE PEARCE and RACHEL BROOK, who had just dropped out of LYNDA'S STRANGE VACATION. The duo's initial releases consisted of limited singles for the 'Heartbeat' imprint, the first of these, 'SOARING HIGH' appearing in '93. Specialising in arty Lo-Fi psychedelia, FSA were influenced by everything from SYD BARRETT, SPACEMEN 3 and ambient Krautrockers such as CAN and POPOL VUH to JOHN COLTRANE-esque experimental jazz. In 1994, the pair signed to 'Domino' ('Drag City' in the States), debuting later in the year with the single 'LAND BEYOND THE SUN'. Around the same time, they played their first live gigs, augmented by ex-LYNDA'S STRANGE VACATION members, MATT ELLIOT and KATE WRIGHT; the former worked under the THIRD EYE FOUNDATION banner, releasing 'SEMTEX' in '96, while he, RACHEL and KATE had surfaced as MOVIETONE. By this point, FSA had already released two compilation sets, 'DISTANCE' (1994) and 'CHORUS' (1995) issued either side of a follow-up album proper, 'FURTHER' (1995). Continuing with their idiosyncratic aural experimentation, PEARCE and BROOK released a further batch of 45's, while recording another album, 'NEW LANDS' (1997). • **Songwriters:** PEARCE or duo, except OUTDOOR MINER (Wire) / THE DROWNERS (Suede).

Album rating: FLYING SAUCER ATTACK (*7) / DISTANCE compilation (*8) / FURTHER (*7) / CHORUS compilation (*7) / NEW LANDS (*6)

DAVE PEARCE – slide guitar, etc / **RACHEL BROOK** – vocals, multi

Heartbeat VHF

Mar 93. (ltd-7") *(FSA 6)* **SOARING HIGH. / STANDING STONE** [ ] [-]
Jun 93. (ltd-7") *(FSA 61)* **WISH. / OCEANS** [ ] [-]
Nov 93. (lp) *(FSA 62)* *<VHF 11CD>* **FLYING SAUCER ATTACK** [ ] [ ] Aug94
– My dreaming hill / A silent tide / Moonset / Make my dream / Wish / Popol Vuh 2 / The drowners / Popol Vuh 1 / Still / The season is ours.
(cd-iss. Aug94 & Nov95 & Dec96 on 'V.H.F.'; same as US)

—— added **MATT ELLIOT + KATE WRIGHT**

Domino VHF

Oct 94. (ltd-7"/7") *(RUG 23/+X)* **LAND BEYOND THE SUN. / EVERYWHERE WAS EVERYTHING** [ ] [-]
Oct 94. (cd/lp) *(WIG CD/LP 12)* *<VHF 14CD>* **DISTANCE** (singles compilation) [ ] [ ]
– Oceans / Standing stone / Crystal shade / Instrumental wish / Distance / November mist / Soaring high / Oceans 2.

Planet not iss.

Apr 95. (ltd-7") *(PUNK 008)* **BEACH RED LULLABY. / SECOND HOUR** [ ] [-]

Domino Drag City

Apr 95. (cd/lp) *(WIG CD/LP 20)* *<DC 69>* **FURTHER** [ ] [ ]
– Rainstorm blues / In the light of time / Come and close my eyes / For silence / Still point / Here I am / To the shore / She is the daylight.
Sep 95. (7") *(RUG 41)* **OUTDOOR MINER. / PSYCHIC DRIVING** [ ] [-]
(cd-s+=) *(RUG 41CD)* – Land beyond the sun / Everywhere was everything.
Nov 95. (cd/lp) *(WIG CD/LP 22)* *<DC 87CD>* **CHORUS** (compilation of singles & sessions) [ ] [-]
– Feedback song / Light in the evening / Popol Vuh III / Always / Feedback song (demo) / Second hour / Beach red lullaby / There but not there / February 8th / There dub.
Nov 96. (cd-s)<12"> *(RUG 48CD)* *<DC 109>* **SALLY FREE AND EASY / THREE SEAS** [ ] [ ]
Dec 96. (m-cd) *<DC 117>* **DISTANT STATION** [-] [ ]
– Part one / Part two.
Jan 97. (12"ep/cd-ep) *(<VHF 26/+CD>)* **GOODBYE EP** [ ] [ ]
– Goodbye / And goodbye / Whole day.
(above issued on 'VHF') <below on 'Enraptured'>
1997. (7") **AT NIGHT. / FROM HERE TO NOW OTHERWISE** [-] [ ]
Sep 97. (7") *(RUG 57)* **COMING HOME. / HOPE** [ ] [ ]
Oct 97. (cd/lp) *(WIG CD/LP 38)* *<DC 137>* **NEW LANDS** [ ] [ ]
– Past / Present / Up in her eyes / Respect / Night falls / Whole day song / Sea / Forever.

FLYS

Formed: Coventry, England . . . 1976 out of MIDNIGHT CIRCUS by NEIL O'CONNOR, DAVID FREEMAN, JOE HUGHES and relative newcomer PETE KING. Inspired by punk's DIY ethic, the band issued 'BUNCH OF FIVE' as a debut EP on their own 'Zama' label in 1977. The ominous mob-chorus strains of 'LOVE AND A MOLOTOV COCKTAIL' attracted the attentions of 'E.M.I.', who subsequently signed the band and issued the track as a single in its own right in early '78. Despite the ensuing buzz, The FLYS failed to land a chart placing, another couple of singles and a debut album, 'WAKIKI BEACH REFUGEES' (1978) making little commercial headway despite strong critical support. Nevertheless, 'E.M.I.' stayed behind them for a further string of singles and a follow-up album, 'OWN' (1979) before the band moved along the corridor to 'Parlophone' for early 1980's 'FOUR FROM THE SQUARE' EP and a swansong single, 'WHAT WILL MOTHER SAY?'. Their continuing chart drought combined with internal pressures to hasten the FLYS' inevitable demise, NEIL going on to work with his more famous sister, HAZEL. DAVID FREEMAN and JOE HUGHES, meanwhile, formed The LOVER SPEAKS, a mid-late 80's act discovered by DAVE STEWART of The EURYTHMICS and signed to 'A&M'. Despite an initial Top 60 hit in summer '86 with 'NO MORE "I LOVE YOU'S" (later covered by ANNIE LENNOX) the group's eponymous album failed to chart.

Album rating: WAIKIKI BEACH REFUGEES (*5) / OWN (*5) / THE FLYS compilation (*6)

NEIL O'CONNOR – vocals, guitar, keyboards / **DAVID FREEMAN** – guitar, vocals / **JOE HUGHES** – bass / **PETE KING** – drums / **LYN DOBSON** – saxophone

Zama not iss.

1977. (7"ep) *(ZA 10EP)* **BUNCH OF FIVE** [ ] [-]
– Can I crash here? / Civilization / Love and a molotov cocktail / E.C.4.

—— **GRAHAM DEACON** – drums (ex-SNIPS, ex-FRANKIE MILLER, ex-JOHN ENTWISTLE'S OX) repl. KING who joined AFTER THE FIRE (later died)

E.M.I. not iss.

Jan 78. (7"m) *(EMI 2747)* **LOVE AND A MOLOTOV COCKTAIL. / CAN I CRASH HERE? / CIVILIZATION** [ ] [-]
May 78. (7") *(EMI 2795)* **FUN CITY. / E.C.4** [ ] [-]
Oct 78. (7"/7"yellow) *(EMI/+Y 2867)* **WAIKIKI BEACH REFUGEES. / WE DON'T MIND THE RAVE** [ ] [-]
Nov 78. (lp) *(EMC 3249)* **WAIKIKI BEACH REFUGEES** [ ] [-]
– We don't mind the rave / Oh Beverley / She's the one / Some kind of girl / Looking for new hearts / Monsoon sky / Wakiki beach refugees / I don't know / Dark nights / Fun city / Don't moonlight on me / Saturday sunrise.
Jan 79. (7") *(EMI 2907)* **OH BEVERLEY. / DON'T MOONLIGHT ON ME** [ ] [-]
Apr 79. (7") *(EMI 2936)* **NAME DROPPING. / FLY V FLY** [ ] [-]
Jul 79. (7") *(EMI 2976)* **WE ARE THE LUCKY ONES. / LIVING IN THE STICKS** [ ] [-]
Oct 79. (lp) *(EMC 3316)* **OWN** [ ] [-]
– Energy boy / Let's drive / Fascinate me / Taking to the world / 16 down / Fortunes / Night creatures / When 2 & 5 make 9 / Undercover agent zero / Cheap days / Walking the streets / Through the windscreen / Freezing / Frenzy is 23.

Parlophone not iss.

Feb 80. (7"ep) *(R 6030)* **FOUR FROM THE SQUARE EP** [ ] [-]
– 16 down / Night creatures / Lois Lane / Today belongs to me.
Apr 80. (7") *(R 6036)* **WHAT WILL MOTHER SAY? / UNDERCOVER AGENT ZERO** [ ] [-]

—— disbanded 1980 when NEIL joined his sister HAZEL O'CONNOR's group. FREEMAN, meanwhile briefly went solo while reuniting with HUGHES in The LOVER SPEAKS

- compilations, etc. -

Jan 91. (lp/cd) *See For Miles; (SEE/+CD 304)* **THE FLYS BUZZ BACK** [ ] [-]
(re-iss. Apr93; same)

LOVER SPEAKS

—— **DAVID FREEMAN** – vocals / **JOE HUGHES** – instruments

A&M A&M

Jul 86. (7") *(AM 326)* **NO MORE "I LOVE YOU'S". / THIS CAN'T GO ON** [58] [ ]
(12"+=) *(AMY 326)* – Of tears.
Sep 86. (7") *(AM 347)* **TREMBLE DANCING. / STILL FAKING THIS ART OF LOVE** [ ] [-]
(12"+=) *(AMY 347)* – This could be the night / It's your life.
Oct 86. (7") *(AM 361)* **EVERY LOVER'S SIGN. / ('A'dub)** [ ] [-]
(12"+=) *(AMY 361)* – ('A'extended).
1986. (lp/c/cd) *(AMA/AMC/CDA 5127)* **THE LOVER SPEAKS** [ ] [ ]
– Every lover's sign / No more "I Love You's" / Never to forget you / Face me and smile / Absent one / Love is: "I Gave You Everything" / This can't go on / Still faking this art of love / Tremble dancing / Of tears. *(cd re-iss. Apr95; 395127-2)*
Feb 87. (7") *(AM 378)* **I CLOSE MY EYES AND COUNT TO TEN. / NEVER FORGET YOU** [ ] [-]
(12"+=) *(AMY 378)* – ('A'extended).
Mar 88. (7") *(AM 438)* **NO MORE "I LOVE YOU'S". / TREMBLE DANCING** [ ] [-]
(12"+=/cd-s+=) *(AMY/CD 438)* – Every lover's sign / I close my eyes and count to ten.

FOETUS

Formed: London, England . . . 1980 as a vehicle for Australian emigre and all round musical extremist JIM THIRLWELL (once a guest for PRAG VEC in '79). Despite being released under various FOET-al incarnations (i.e FOETUS UBER FRISCO, YOU'VE GOT FOETUS ON YOUR BREATH, FOETUS Inc., THE FOETUS ALL-NUDE REVUE etc.), almost all THIRLWELL's excursions have a common trait of ear grinding nihilism, all done in the best possible taste of course and not without a scraping of black-(board, as in nails) humour. After failing to secure a deal, JIM boy started up his own label, 'Self Immolation', releasing his first abortive attempts at industrial noise via 'OKFM' (1981; as FOETUS UNDER GLASS) and as the inimitable YOU'VE GOT FOETUS ON YOUR BREATH, 'DEAF' (1981) and 'ACHE' (1982). One his few early admirers was 'Some Bizzare' head honcho, STEVO, who was sufficiently impressed to offer added financial backing for 1984's 'HOLE' album. Released under the guise of SCRAPING FOETUS OFF THE WHEEL, the record saw THIRLWELL adopt the persona of CLINT RUIN – a parody of bloated rock star excess – for a "musical" blitzkreig skewering snippets of film dialogue, WWII chaos and assorted surreal/apocalyptic samples with sheets of clattering metallic noise, distorted guitar and pulverising percussion. Under the guise of RUIN, THIRLWELL also played a handful of anarchic shows with NICK CAVE, MARC ALMOND and LYDIA LUNCH as The IMMACULATE CONSUMPTIVE. The mid-80's proved a busy time as the growing cult of FOETUS found THIRLWELL working his black magic alongside everyone from the VIRGIN PRUNES to ORANGE JUICE (!), even finding time for a follow-up SCRAPING . . . record, 'NAIL' (1985). Subsequently relocating to noise mecca New York, he formed WISEBLOOD with SWANS man, ROLI MOSSIMANN, pooling their capacity for ear-bleeding noise on 1986's 'DIRTDISH'. While still beavering away at his own work – including FOETUS INTERRUPTUS' 'THAW' (1988) – and composing soundtracks for NY avant-garde filmaker, Richard Kern (he also co-starred with LYDIA LUNCH in a famous "blow your mind if it's under your belt" scene from one of Kern's sex flicks, 'Right Side Of My Brain') – THIRLWELL's pioneering influence could be heard in the work of up and coming industrial acts such as MINISTRY, REVOLTING COCKS, NINE INCH NAILS etc. Ironically, these were the very bands who took the genre to the masses in the early to mid-90's, THIRLWELL having to content himself with releases on indie label 'Big Cat'. 1995's 'GASH' found him in as lyrically and musically uncompromising form as ever, putting the boot in to such time honoured targets as religion and white Western smugness to a musical backdrop embellished with the alternately screaming/grooving brass of The HERESY HORNS. • **Covered:** LITTLE JOHNNY JEWEL (Television) / I AM THE WALRUS (Beatles) / SONIC REDUCER (Dead Boys) / ELECTED (Alice Cooper) / HELLO THERE (. . .Nielsen).

Album rating: DEAF (*6) / ACHE (*6) / HOLE (*8) / NAIL (*6) / BEDROCK mini (*5) / THAW (*6) / SINK compilation (*6) / RIFE (*5) / QUILOMBO (*5) / MALE (*5) / GONDWANALAND (*5) / GASH (*7) / BOIL (*6) / YORK (*5) / NULL AND VOID (*5) / Wiseblood: DIRTDISH (*6) / PEDDLE TO THE METAL (*5)

JIM FOETUS – synthesizers, keyboards

Self Immolation / not iss.

Jan 81. (7"; as FOETUS UNDER GLASS) *(WOMB S201)* **OKFM. / SPITE YOUR FACE** -

Apr 81. (7"; as YOU'VE GOT FOETUS ON YOUR BREATH) *(WOMB ALL007)* **WASH IT ALL OFF. / 333** -

Sep 81. (lp; as YOU'VE GOT FOETUS ON YOUR BREATH) *(OYBL-1)* **DEAF** -
– New York or bust / Is that a line / Why can't it happen to me / I am surrounded by incompetence / What have you been doing / Today I started slogging again / Harold McMillan / Thank heavens for push button phones / Flashback / Negative energy. *(cd-iss. Mar98 by FOETUS on 'Thirsty Ear'; THI 57034-2)*

Jan 82. (7"; as PHILIP & HIS FOETUS VIBRATIONS) *(WOMB KX 07)* **TELL ME, WHAT IS THE BANE OF YOUR LIFE. / MOTHER I'VE KILLED THE CAT** -

Apr 82. (12"m; as FOETUS UBER FRISCO) *(WOMB 125-SUSC 12)* **CUSTOM BUILT FOR CAPITALISM. / 1.0.4.5. / BIRTHDAY** -

Aug 82. (lp; as YOU'VE GOT FOETUS ON YOUR BREATH) *(OYBL-2)* **ACHE** -
– Dying with my boots on / J.Q. murder / Gums bleed / Mark of the ostracizor / Exit the man with nine lives / Get out of my house / Wholesome town / Whole wheat rolls / Kid hate kid / Instead . . . I became anenome. *(cd-iss. Mar98 by FOETUS on 'Thirsty Ear'; THI 57035-2)*

Sep 84. (lp; as SCRAPING FOETUS OFF THE WHEEL) *(WOMB FDL 3)* **HOLE** -
– I'll meet you in Poland baby / Hot horse / Sickman / Suck this, sickman, eat hot led . . . he's grinding-shaking-daning dead / Street of shame / Satan place / White knuckles / Water torture / Cold day in Hell. *(cd-iss. Jan89; WOMB FDL 3CD)*

Oct 84. (12"; as FOETUS ART TERRORISM) *(WOMB FAT 11.12)* **CALAMITY CRUSH. / CATASTROPHE CRUNCH** -

Feb 85. (12"; as YOU'VE GOT FOETUS ON YOUR BREATH) *(FGH 12.8)* **WASH IT ALL OFF. / TODAY I STARTED SLOGGING AGAIN** -

Mar 85. (12"; as FOETUS UBER FRISCO) *(WOMB UNC 7.12)* **FINELY HONED MACHINE. / SICK MINUTES** -

Oct 85. (lp/c; as SCRAPING FOETUS OFF THE WHEEL) *(WOMBFIP/WOMBCFIP 4)* **NAIL** -
– Theme from pigdom come / The throne of agony / Pigswill / Descent into the inferno / Enter the exterminator / DI-1-9026 / The overture from pigdom come / Private war / Anything. *(cd-iss. Apr86; WOMBCDFIP 4)*

Nov 85. (box for lp's; as FOETUS) *(FOE 1)* **THE FOETUS OF EXCELLENCE** - -

Jun 87. (m-lp; as The FOETUS ALL NUDE REVUE) *(WOMBFAN 13)* **BEDROCK** -
– Diabolus in musica / Shut / Rattlesnake insurance / Bedrock ship.

Oct 87. (12"; as SCRAPING FOETUS OFF THE WHEEL) *(WOMD PIG 12.1)* **RAMROD. / BOXHEAD / SMUT** -

—— below was a collaboration with MARC ALMOND

Feb 88. (12"; as FLESH VOLCANO) *(SLUT 001)* **SLUT. / THE UNIVERSAL CESSPOOL / BRUISIN' CHAIN** -

Sep 88. (lp/c/cd; as FOETUS INTERRUPTUS) *(WOMBFIP 5/+C/CD)* **THAW** -
– Don't hide it provide it / Asbestos / Fin / English faggot – Nothin man / Hauss-on-fah / Fratricide pastorale / Dipsomaniac / Barbedwire tumbleweed / Chingada / Prayer for my death. <*US cd-iss. 1995 on 'Thirsty Ear'; THI 57013*>

—— toured with **NORMAN WESTBERG** – guitar / **AL KYZYS** – bass / **BOB BERT** – drums / **NAINZ WATTS** – guitar, effects

Oct 88. (12"; as CLINT RUIN & LYDIA LUNCH) *(WSP 14)* **STINKFIST. / THE MELTDOWN ORATORIO 1,2,3 / SON OF STINK** -

Big Cat / Wax Trax!

Apr 90. (d-lp/c/cd; as FOETUS INC) *(WOMBINC 6/+C/CD)* <*WAX 7110*> **SINK** (compilation)
– Bedrock / Ramrod / Boxhead / Lilith / Shut / Diabolus in musica / Smut / Sick minutes / Rattlesnake insurance / Himmelfahrtstransport – Primordial industry / Spit on the griddle / Anxiety attack / Baphomet / Dead Christian / Halo flamin lead / OKFM / Catastrophe crunch / Wash it all off / Slog / Calamity crush. *(w/ free booklet 'THE FOETUS OF EXCELLENCE 2')*

May 90. (12")(cd-s; as FOETUS INC) *(ABB 16T)(ABBCD 16)* **BUTTERFLY POTION. / FREE JAMES BROWN**

Rifle / not iss.

Dec 90. (d-lp; as FOETUS CORRUPTUS) *(RIFLE 1)* **RIFE** -
– Fin / Honey I'm home / The dipsomatic kiss / English faggot / Grab yr ankles / Slut / A prayer for my death / Chingada / Hate feeler / The fudge punch / Clothes hoist / Private war – Anything (viva). *(re-iss. pic-d-lp Jul91; RIFLEPIC 001) (d-cd-iss. Dec94 & Jun96; RIFLECD 001)*

Big Cat / Atavistic

Nov 91. (cd; as STEROID MAXIMUS) *(ABBCD 028)* **QUILOMBO** -
– Life in the greenhouse effect / The Heidnik manoeuvre / No joy in Pudville / Fighteous / Big Hedda meets little Napoleon / Quilombo / Phantom miscarriage / Ogro / The smother brother / Transcendental moonshine.

Mar 92. (d-cd/d-c; as FOETUS IN EXCELSIS CORRUPTUS) *(ABB 31-2/+C)* <*24*> **MALE** Jan94
– Free James Brown / Fin / Hot horse / English faggot / Faith healer / Honey I'm home / Butterfly potion / I'll meet you in Poland / Anything (viva) / Death rape 2000 / Puppet dude / Stumbo / Someone drowned in my pool / Behemoth / Salvation.

Nov 92. (cd; as STEROID MAXIMUS) *(ABBCD 037)* **GONDWANALAND** -
– Quilombo / Radio Raheem / The Trojan hearse (1st movement) / The auctioneer of souls (2nd movement) / Crawling Goliath (3rd movement) / Erupture (4th movement) / Life in the greenhouse effect / I will love you always (wild Irish rose) / Destino matar / Cross double cross / Volgarity / Ol (kwik lube) / Powerhouse / Homeo.

—— with **TOD ASHLEY** – bass / **VINNIE SIGNORELLI** – drums / **MARC RIBOT** – guitar / **STEVE BERNSTEIN** – trumpet / etc

Aug 94. (7"pic-d; as FOETUS & CHROME CRANKS) *(PCP 011-7)* **VICE SQUAD DICK. / LITTLE JOHNNY JEWEL** -
(cd-s+=) *(PCP 011-2)* – Outside of time.
(above issued on 'PCP')

Big Cat / Columbia

May 95. (cd) *(ABB 88CD)* <*66461*> **GASH**
– Mortgage / Mighty Whity / Friend or foe / Hammer falls / Downfall / Take it outside godboy / Verklemmt / They are not so true / Slung / Steal your life away / Mutapump / See ya later.

Oct 95. (12"ep/cd-ep) *(ABB 87 T/CD)* **NULL EP** -

Big Cat / Cleopatra

Aug 96. (cd) *(ABB 119CD)* <*9789*> **BOIL (live)**
– Take it outside Godboy / Clothes hoist / Verklemmt / I'll meet you in Poland baby / I am the walrus / They are not so true / Hot horse / Mortgage / Mighty whity / Elected / Sonic reducer / Hello there.

Oct 97. (cd) *(ABB 149CD)* <*9931*> **NULL AND VOID** Feb97
– Verklemmt / Be thankful / Verklemmt / Butter / Into the light / Verklemmt / Friend or foe / Incesticide / See Dick run / Flux / Friend or foe / Iris evergreen.

Big Cat / Thirsty Ear

Oct 97. (cd; as the FOETUS symphony orchestra featuring Lydia Lunch) *(ABB 148XCD)* <*57031*> **YORK** Mar97
– Black adonis / Crumpled city / Puddlin' doorway / Egomaniacs with insecurity problems / Arschficken.

WISEBLOOD

CLINT RUIN + ROLI MOSIMANN

Some Bizzare/K422 / Wax Trax!

May 85. (12") *(WISE 1-12)* **MOTORSLUG. / DEATH RAPE 2000** Oct90

Nov 86. (12") *(WISE 2-12)* **STUMBO (remix). / SOMEONE DROWNED IN MY POOL** -

Nov 86. (lp/c) *(WISE/+C 003)* **DIRTDISH** -
– Prime Gonzola / O-O (where evil dwells) / Stumbo / Someone drowned in my pool / Godbrain / The fudge punch. *(cd-iss. May89; WISECD 3)(+=)* – Stumbo (extended) / Motorslug / Death race 2000. <*US cd-iss. 1995 on 'Thirsty Ear'; 57015*>

Big Cat / Big Cat

Nov 91. (m-lp/cd) *(ABB/+CD 030X)* **PEDAL TO THE METAL** -
– Stop trying to tie me / Hey bop a ree bop / Grease nipples / Pedal to the metal.

Ben FOLDS FIVE

Formed: Chapel Hill, USA . . . 1994 by songwriter/singer/pianist BEN FOLDS, bassist ROBERT SLEDGE and drummer DARREN JESSEE. Taking his cue from the likes of SUPERTRAMP and RANDY NEWMAN, self-confessed rather uncool fellow FOLDS eventually formed his unconventional guitarless, lo-fi piano combo after years of dallying with classical orchestras. Putting a new slant on nerd-rock, FOLDS' inspired ivory bashing/tinkling tales of life's losers won him a cult following upon the release of his self-titled debut album in Spring '96. Further exposure came with a slot on the Lollapolooza touring festival later that summer, FOLDS gaining a reputation for instrument (piano) abuse not seen since JIMI HENDRIX shagged his axe and set it on fire. Surprisingly then, perhaps, the band's early '97 follow-up, 'WHATEVER AND EVER AMEN' was a more laid back affair, albeit with a darkly caustic undercurrent, the likes of 'SONG FOR THE DUMPED' and 'ONE ANGRY DWARF AND 200 SOLEMN FACES' not without a hint of bitterness. • **Covered:** CHAMPAGNE SUPERNOVA (Oasis) / SHE DON'T USE JELLY (Flaming Lips).

Album rating: BEN FOLDS FIVE (*8) / WHATEVER AND EVER AMEN (*7)

BEN FOLDS – piano / **ROBERT SLEDGE** – bass / **DARREN JESSEE** – drums

Caroline / Passenger

Apr 96. (cd/c/lp) *(CAROL 002 CD/MC/LP)* <*9501*> **BEN FOLDS FIVE** Aug95
– Jackson cannery / Philosophy / Julianne / Where's summer B.? / Alice Childress / Underground / Sports & wine / Uncle Walter / Best imitation of myself / Video / The last polka / Boxing. *(cd re-iss. Oct96 on 'Epic'; 7243.8.41629-2/-4)*

Caroline / Alex

Apr 96. (7") *(7CAR 002)* <*5620*> **UNDERGROUND. / JACKSON CANNERY (live) / ('A'live)** May96
(cd-s) *(CDCAR 002)* – ('A'side) / Sports & wine / Boxing.

Jun 96. (7"/c-s) *(7/MC CAR 005)* <*5673*> **WHERE'S SUMMER B. / TOM AND MARY (live)**
(cd-s+=) *(CDCAR 005)* – Emaline (live).

Sep 96. (7") *(7CAR 008)* **UNDERGROUND. / SATAN IS MY MASTER** 37 -
(cd-s+=) *(CDCAR 008)* – Video (live).
(cd-s) *(CDCAR 008X)* – ('A'side) / Jackson Cannery.

Epic / Sony

Feb 97. (7") *(664230-7)* **BATTLE OF WHO COULD CARE LESS. / CHAMPAGNE SUPERNOVA (live)** 26 -
(cd-s+=) *(664230-2)* – Theme from Dr. Pyser.
(cd-s) *(664230-5)* – ('A'side) / Hava nagila / For those of ya'll who wear fannie packs.

Mar 97. (cd/c/lp) *(486698-2/-4/-1)* <*67762*> **WHATEVER AND EVER AMEN** 30 42
– One angry dwarf and 200 solemn faces / Fair / Brick / Song for the dumped / Selfless, cold and composed / Kate / Smoke / Cigarette / Steven's last night in town / Battle of who could care less / Missing the war / Evaporated.

May 97. (cd-s) *(664536-2)* **KATE / BAD IDEA / FOR ALL THE PRETTY PEOPLE** 39 -
(cd-s) *(664536-5)* – ('A'side) / Mitchell Lane / All shook up.

Jan 98. (cd) <*(CAR 7554)*> **NAKED BABY PHOTOS** (rare & live) [65] [94]
– Eddie Walker / Jackson Cannery / Emaline / Alice Childress / Dick Holster / Tom and Mary / For those of y'all who wear fannie packs / Bad idea / Underground / Ultimate sacrifice / Satan is my master / Julianne / Song for the dumped / Philosophy / Twin falls / Boxing.
(above also issued on 'Caroline' in the UK & US) <below on 'Alex' US>
Apr 98. (c-s) *(665661-4)* <*6019*> **BRICK / SMOKE (live)** [26] [ ]
(cd-s+=) *(665661-2)* – Song for the dumped (Japanese version).
(cd-s) *(665661-5)* – ('A'side) / Missing the war (live) / She don't jelly.

FOLK DEVILS (see under ⇒ LOWERY, Ian)

FOLK IMPLOSION (see under ⇒ SEBADOH)

FOO FIGHTERS

Formed: Seattle, Washington, USA . . . April/May '94, after the death of KURT COBAIN (Nirvana), by drummer turned singer/guitarist DAVE GROHL. He subsequently brought in COBAIN stand-in, PAT SMEAR, along with NATE MANDEL and WILLIAM GOLDSMITH, taking the group name from the mysterious lights reported by pilots during World War II. Continuing the UFO concept, the group founded their own 'Roswell' label, (funded by 'Capitol') and debuted in the summer of '95 with UK Top 5 single, 'THIS IS A CALL'. More harmonic and positively life-affirming than NIRVANA (comparisons were inevitable), The FOO FIGHTERS' offered up one of the most exciting debuts of the year; while the lyrics may have been somewhat cryptic, the obvious grunge influences were tempered with an infectious, pop-hardcore rush that was impossible to resist. The album sold well on both sides of the Atlantic, with GROHL & Co. heading out on a successful series of festival dates. Work on the Gil Norton-produced follow-up, 'THE COLOUR AND THE SHAPE', got off to a difficult start with initial sessions in Seattle being scrapped. Further problems arose with the departure of sticksman GOLDSMITH halfway through recording, although GROHL subsequently completed the drum parts and the record was finally released in Spring '97 to rave reviews. Outpacing even the debut, The FOO FIGHTERS had come on leaps and bounds in the songwriting department, their rich post-grunge tapestry markedly more diverse. With good old romantic love as the driving theme of the record, the likes of the heart-rending (UK Top 20) 'EVERLONG' took starry-eyed, melodic distortion-pop to new (neck) hair-raising limits (complete with 'Evil Dead'-style video for that true-love atmosphere!) while more mellow musings like 'WALKING AFTER YOU' and 'DOLL' suggested GROHL was gaining enough confidence in his writing to chill out and reflect rather than continually going for the jugular. The group's growing self-belief was confirmed by some storming festival sets, while the album later came out top in rock 'bible', 'Kerrang!'s yearly critic's poll. • **Covers:** OZONE (Kiss) / GAS CHAMBER (Angry Samoans) / BAKER STREET (Gerry Rafferty). • **Trivia:** GREG DULLI (Afghan Whigs) played guitar on 'X-static'.

Album rating: FOO FIGHTERS (*8) / THE COLOUR AND THE SHAPE (*9)

DAVE GROHL (b.14 Jan'69, Warren, Ohio) – vocals, guitar / **PAT SMEAR** – guitar (ex-GERMS) / **NATE MANDEL** – bass / **WILLIAM GOLDSMITH** – drums (both of SUNNY DAY REAL ESTATE)

Roswell Roswell

Jun 95. (7") *(CL 753)* **THIS IS A CALL. / WINNEBAGO** [5] [-]
(12"+=/cd-s+=) *(12/CD CL 753)* – Podunk.
Jun 95. (cd/c/lp) *(CD/TC+/EST 2266)* <*34027*> **FOO FIGHTERS** [3] [23]
– This is a call / I'll stick around / Big me / Alone + easy target / Good grief / Floaty / Weenie beenie / Oh, George / For all the cows / X-static / Wattershed / Exhausted.
Sep 95. (c-s/7"red) *(TC+/CL 757)* **I'LL STICK AROUND. / HOW I MISS YOU** [18] [-]
(12"+=/cd-s+=) *(12/CD CL 757)* – Ozone.
Nov 95. (c-s/7"blue) *(TC+/CL 762)* **FOR ALL THE COWS. / WATTERSHED (live)** [28] [-]
(cd-s+=) *(CDCL 762)* – ('A'live at Reading).
Mar 96. (c-s/7"white) *(TC+CL 768)* **BIG ME. / FLOATY / GAS CHAMBER** [19] [-]
(cd-s+=) *(CDCL 768)* – Alone + easy target.

— **TAYLOR HAWKINS** – drums (of-ALANIS MORISSETTE) repl. GOLDSMITH

Apr 97. (7"/cd-s) *(CL/CDCLS 788)* **MONKEY WRENCH. / UP IN ARMS (slow version) / THE COLOUR & THE SHAPE** [12] [-]
(cd-s) *(CDCL 788)* – ('A'side) / Down in the park / See you (acoustic).
May 97. (cd/c/lp) *(CD/TC+/EST 2295)* <*58530*> **THE COLOUR & THE SHAPE** [3] [10]
– Doll / Monkey wrench / Hey Johnny Park / My poor brain / Wind up / Up in arms / My hero / See you / Enough space / February stars / Everlong / Walking after you / New way home.
Aug 97. (7"blue) *(CL 792)* **EVERLONG. / DRIVE ME WILD** [18] [-]
(cd-s+=) *(CDCL 792)* – See you (live).
(cd-s) *(CDCLS 792)* – ('A'side) / Requiem / I'll stick around (live).
Jan 98. (7"red) *(CL 796)* **MY HERO. / DEAR LOVER** [21] [-]
(cd-s+=) *(CDCL 796)* – Baker Street. *(with enhanced cd+=)* – Everlong / Monkey wrench (video).
Aug 98. (7"/c-s/cd-s) *(E 4100/+C/CD)* **WALKING AFTER YOU. / Ween: Beacon Light** [20] [-]
(above issued on 'East West')

FOR SQUIRRELS

Formed: Gainsville, Florida, USA . . . early 1993 by JON FRANCIS VIGLIATURA IV, BILL WHITE, TRAVIS MICHAEL TOOKE and JAY RUSSELL. These ill-fated alt-rockers already had two independently released mini-sets ('BAYPATH RD.' and 'PLYMOUTH') under their belts and were on the verge of making their major label debut when two of the band members, JACK and BILL, were fatally injured in a car smash on the 8th of September 1995 . The aforementioned album, 'EXAMPLE', was issued on '550/Epic' the following month and spent a respectable four weeks in the Top 200. Although RUSSELL's replacement, JACK GREIGO was also seriously injured, he and TOOKE decided to carry on playing, completing the devastated line-up with the addition of new bass player, ANDY LORD.

Album rating: EXAMPLE (*6)

JON FRANCIS VIGLIATURA IV – vocals / **BILL WHITE** – guitar / **TRAVIS MICHAEL TOOKE** – guitar / **JAY RUSSELL** – drums

not iss. unknown

Feb 94. (m-cd) **BAYPATH RD.** [-] [ ]
Dec 94. (cd-ep) **PLYMOUTH EP** [-] [ ]

— **JACK GREIGO** – drums; repl. RUSSELL

— On the 8th of September 1995, VIGLIATURA and WHITE were killed in an automobile accident in which GREIGO also suffered a broken back

not iss. 550 – Epic

Oct 95. (cd/c) <*67150-2/-4*> **EXAMPLE** [-] [ ]
– 8:02 PM / Orangeworker / Superstar / Mighty K.C. /Under Smithville / Long live the king / The immortal dog and pony show / Stark pretty / Disenchanted / Eskimo sandune.

— although the remaining two carried on after above disaster (added **ANDY LORD** – bass); no further recordings were forthcoming

Robert FORSTER (see under ⇒ GO-BETWEENS)

FORTUNATE SONS (see under ⇒ BARRACUDAS)

FOUNTAINS OF WAYNE

Formed: New York City, New York, USA . . . 1995 by songwriting team of ADAM SCHLESINGER and CHRIS COLLINGWOOD, who met at Williams College in Massachusetts in 1987. ADAM, also of the revered outfit IVY, helped form the 'Scratchie' label with D'ARCY of The SMASHING PUMPKINS, the former having already recorded under the moniker of PINNWHEEL alongside CHRIS. Other moonlighting shenanigans included penning 'THAT THING YOU DO' for mock outfit The WONDERS, which featured in the movie of the same name starring Tom Hanks. FOW signed to 'Atlantic' in '96 and achieved some degree of success with debut single, 'RADIATION VIBE', a taste of retro 60's BEACH BOYS-esque pop with an edgy 90's slant. Their eponymous debut followed later that summer, a fine collection of power-pop akin to a heavier LEMONHEADS.

Album rating: FOUNTAINS OF WAYNE (*7)

ADAM SCHLESINGER (b.1968) – vocals, guitars / **CHRIS COLLINGWOOD** (b.1968) – vocals, guitar / live work:- **JODY PORTER** – bass (ex-BELLTOWER) / **BRIAN YOUNG** – drums (of The POSIES)

Atlantic Atlantic

Mar 97. (7"/c-s) *(A 5626/+C)* **RADIATION VIBE. / KARPET KING** 32 -
(cd-s+=) *(A 5626CD)* – Janice's party / Imperial.

Apr 97. (7"/c-s) *(A 5612/+C)* **SINK TO THE BOTTOM. / CAN'T GET IT OUT OF MY HEAD** -
(cd-s+=) *(A 5612CD)* –

May 97. (cd/c) *<(7567 92725-2/-4)>* **FOUNTAINS OF WAYNE** 67
– Radiation vibe / Sink to the bottom / Joe Rey / She's got a problem / Survival car / Barbara H / Sick day / I've got a flair / Leave the biker / You curse all girls / Please don't rock me tonight / Everything's ruined.

Jul 97. (7"/c-s) *(AT 0004/+C)* **SURVIVAL CAR. / COMEDIAN** 53 -
(cd-s+=) *(AT 004CD)* – I want you around.

Oct 97. (7"/c-s) *(AT 0016/+C)* **BARBARA H. / PLACES** -
(cd-s+=) *(AT 0016CD)* – She's got a problem (live).

Dec 97. (7"/c-s/cd-s) *(AT 0020/+C/CD)* **I WANT AN ALIEN FOR CHRISTMAS. / MAN IN THE SANTA SUIT** 36

4-SKINS

Formed: Southall, London, England . . . early 80's by er, 4 SKINS (i.e. four skinheads), namely PANTHER, HOXTON TOM and JOHNNY JACOBS together with a mysterious sticksman. This cheesily monikered bunch of Oi! upstarts followed in the wake of working class hero punk acts like SHAM 69, combining a seething but simplistic lyrical manifesto and punk-by-numbers riffs with an archetypal boot-boy image. After a one-off debut single, 'ONE LAW FOR THEM', on the tiny 'Clockwork Fun' label, the band signed to "Oi!" sanctuary, 'Secret', where they released a second single, 'YESTERDAY'S HEROES' (initially withdrawn) and a part-live debut album, 'THE GOOD, THE BAD AND THE 4-SKINS' (1982). More line-up changes followed as TOM recruited PAUL SWAIN on guitar, the new look 4 SKINS subsequently cutting a pseudonymous one-off single as The PLASTIC GANGSTERS in Spring '83. Later that year came the cringeingly titled 'A FISTFUL OF . . . 4-SKINS' album, their parting shot save for a live album, 'FROM CHAOS TO 1984'. • **Covered:** MERRY XMAS EVERYBODY (Slade). • **Note:** Not to be confused with another turn of the decade hardcore outfit from New York.

Album rating: THE GOOD, THE BAD AND THE 4-SKINS (*4) / A FISTFUL OF 4-SKINS (*3) / FROM CHAOS TO 1984 (*3) / THE BEST OF THE 4 SKINS compilation (*4)

PANTHER – vocals / **HOXTON TOM** – bass, vocals / **JOHNNY JACOBS** – guitar, vocals / – drums

Clockwork Fun not iss.

Jul 81. (7") *(CF 101)* **ONE LAW FOR THEM. / BRAVE NEW WORLD** -

Secret not iss.

Oct 81. (7"; w-drawn) *(SHH 118)* **YESTERDAY'S HEROES. / ONE LAW FOR THEM** -

Dec 81. (7"m) *(SHH 125)* **YESTERDAY'S HEROES. / JUSTICE / GET OUT OF MY LIFE** -

Apr 82. (lp) *(SEC 4)* **THE GOOD, THE BAD AND THE 4-SKINS** (some live) 80 -
– Plastic gangster / Jealousy / Yesterday's heroes / Justice / Jack the lad / Remembrance day / Manifesto / Wonderful world / Sorry / Evil / I don't wanna die / A.C.A.B. / Chaos / One law for them. *(cd-iss. Jul93 & Mar98 on 'Captain Oi'; AHOYCD 3)*

— (mid '82) **TOM** recruited **PAUL SWAIN** – guitar; repl. JACOBS

Oct 82. (7") *(SHH 141)* **LOW LIFE. / BREAD OR BLOOD** -

Apr 83. (7"; as PLASTIC GANGSTERS) *(SHH 144)* **PLASTIC GANGSTERS. / SRETSGNAG CITSALP** - - promo

Syndicate not iss.

Oct 83. (lp) *(SYN 1)* **A FISTFUL OF . . . 4-SKINS** -
– Five more years / Waiting for a friend / Johnny go home / The gambler / I'll stick to my guns / On file / Forgotten hero / Spy from Alaska / H.M.P. / No excuse / Betrayed / City boy / New war / One the streets / Saturday. *(cd-iss. Nov93 & May98 on 'Captain Oi'; AHOYCD 8)*

Jun 84. (lp) *(SYNLP 5)* **FROM CHAOS TO 1984 (live)** -

— above was HOXTON and Co's final release; might re-form or will he?

– compilations, etc. –

on 'Street Link' unless mentioned otherwise

Feb 87. (lp) *(LINKLP 02)* **WONDERFUL WORLD OF 4 SKINS** -
(cd-iss. May98 on 'Step 1'; STEPCD 027)

Sep 87. (lp) *(LINKLP 15)* **A FEW 4 SKINS MORE, VOL.1** -
(cd-iss. Oct92; LINKCD 15)

Dec 87. (lp) *(LINKLP 21)* **A FEW 4 SKINS MORE, VOL.2** -
(cd-iss. Feb98 on 'Step 1'; STEPCD 016)

Jun 89. (lp) *(LINKLP 90)* **LIVE AND LOUD! (live)** -

Aug 92. (cd) *LINKCD 154)* **THE BEST OF THE 4-SKINS** -
– One law for them / Yesterday's heroes / Clockwork skinhead / Brave new world / Chaos / Wonderful world / Evil / Sorry / 1984 / A.C.A.B. / I don't wanna die / Plastic gangsters / Yesterday's heroes (7"version) / Get out of my life / Justice / Jack the lad / Low life / Bread or blood / Seems to me / Norman / On the streets / Five more years / Betrayed / Saturday (live) / Dambusters. *(<re-iss. Jun93/Oct94 on 'Dojo'; DOJOCD 140>) (lp re-iss. Mar98 on 'Harry May'; MAYLP 705)*

Nov 97. (cd) *CanCan; (CANCAN 006CD)* **ONE LAW FOR THEM** -

Jul 98. (cd) *Pinhead; (PINCD 102)* **SINGALONG-A-4-SKINS** -

14 ICED BEARS

Formed: Brighton, England . . . 1985 by ROB SEKULA, NICK EMERY and ALAN WHITE. This initial line-up only lasted for a short time as WHITE was replaced with DOMINIC MINQUES and KEVIN CANHAM, prior to their debut EP, which led with the track, 'INSIDE'. Line-up changes continued to dog the band to the extent that by the time they'd got round to recording a debut album, SEKULA was the only remaining founder member (joined at this point by WILL TAYLOR and GRAHAM DURRANT). Released on 'Sarah' records in 1988, the eponymous set moved away from the amateurish jangle of their early singles to a more focused retro sound. After a further series of singles and a contribution (a near comotose reading of 'Grease' classic, 'SUMMER NIGHTS') to anti-Poll Tax compilation, 'Alvin Lives In Leeds', the band released a belated follow-up set, 'WONDER' (1991). Characterised by spiralling guitars and a psuedo-psychedelic eastern feel, the record was well timed to coincide with the interest in all things "Shoegazing" yet failed to attract anything more than the usual minimal press coverage.

Album rating: 14 ICED BEARS (*4) / PRECISION compilation (*5) / WONDER (*5)

ROB SEKULA (b.12 Dec'63, Camberwell, Surrey, England) – vocals, guitar / **DOMINQUE MINQUES** – bass; repl. ALAN WHITE who formed PLEASURE SPLINTERS / **NICK EMERY** – drums / **KEVIN CANHAM** (b.10 Oct'64, Aldershot, England) – guitar

Frank not iss.

Nov 86. (12"ep) *(COPPOLA 101)* **INSIDE. / BLUESUIT / CUT** -

— added **NICK ROUGHLEY** – keyboards

Feb 87. (12"ep) *(CAPRA 202)* **LIKE A DOLPHIN / BALLOON SONG. / TRAIN SONG / LIE TO CHOOSE** -

— now without ROUGHLEY who joined BLOW UP

Penetration not iss.

1987. (7"flexi) *(001)* **LIE TO CHOOSE. / (other track by Splendour In The Grass)** -

— **STEVE ORMSBY** – bass; repl. MINQUES

— **BILL COX** – drums; repl. EMERY

Sarah not iss.

Apr 88. (7"m) *(SARAH 005)* **COME GET ME. / UNHAPPY DAYS / SURE TO SEE** -

— **SEKULA + CANHAM** then recruited newcomers **WILL TAYLOR** (b.23 Aug'68) – bass / **GRAHAM DURRANT** (b.10 Oct'63, Camberwell) – drums

Thunderball not iss.

Nov 88. (lp) *(TBLP 001)* **14 ICED BEARS** -

Apr 89. (7"; w-drawn) *(7TBL 2)* **MOTHER SLEEP. /** -

Nov 89. (7") *(7TBL 5)* **WORLD I LOVE. /** -

Mar 90. (lp) *(TBLP 002)* **PRECISION** (compilation) -

— **TIM WHITE** (b.30 Mar'67, Essex, England) – bass; repl. TAYLOR who also joined BLOW UP

1990's. (ltd-7"ep) *(Surfacer 002)* **FALLING BACKWARDS / WORLD I LOVE. / (other tracks by Crocodile Ride)** -

Borderline not iss.

1991. (12"m) *(BORD12 001)* **HOLD ON. / SUMMER NIGHTS / IN THE MORNING** -

1991. (cd; as FOURTEEN ICED BEARS) *(BORD 002)* **WONDER** -
– Hold on / Heaven star / Smooth in the sun / These are the things / When it comes / Rare (like you are) / Love on a sugar mountain / Eyes / RED NOW.

— **ROB COLLEY** (b.27 Jun'63) – bass (ex-WHIRL) repl. TIM WHITE

— they finally split for good after above

John FOXX

Born: DENNIS LEIGH, Chorley, Lancashire, England. After dramatically leaving new wave oufit, ULTRAVOX! (who subsequently split for a time after his departure in March '79), he concentrated on a solo career. The "quiet man" (nicknamed as such from a past ULTRAVOX number) created a new label, 'Metal Beat' (through 'Virgin'), releasing his debut 45, 'UNDERPASS', which nearly cracked the UK Top 30 early in 1980. A compulsive, brooding slice of proto-electro, the single's minor chart success helped push the accompanying debut album, METAMATIC' into the Top 20. Although his previous act, ULTRAVOX, were doing a lot better commercially with new frontman, MIDGE URE ('Vienna', etc.), FOXX's cult following ensured Top 30 placing for subsequent sets, 'THE GARDEN' (1981) and 'THE GOLDEN SECTION' (1983). Finally, after the commercially disappointing 'IN MYSTERIOUS WAYS' (1985), the "mannequin of rock" who made the KRAFTWERK look energetic in comparison, retired from the music business, working on his book, 'The Quiet Man' (what else!?). Surprisingly, he was back early in 1997 with two simultaneously released sets of new ambient/electro-type material, 'CATHEDRAL OCEANS' and 'SHIFTING CITY' (the latter with LOUIS GORDON).

Album rating: METAMATIC (*7) / ASSEMBLY compilation (*7)

JOHN FOXX – vocals, synthesizers, guitar, drum machine (ex-ULTRAVOX!) with **JOHN BARKER** – synth-drums / **JAKE DURANT** – bass / **ED CASE** – drums *(on 2nd lp)*

Virgin not iss.

Jan 80. (7") *(VS 318)* **UNDERPASS. / FILM 1** 31 -

Jan 80. (lp/c) *(V/TCV 2146)* **METAMATIC** 18 -
– Plaza / He's a liquid / Underpass / Metal beat / No one driving / A new kind of man / Blurred girl / 030 / Tidal wave / Touch and go. *(re-iss. Mar84 lp/c; (OVED/+C 46) (cd-iss. Apr93; CDV 2146)*

Mar 80. (d7") *(VS 338)* **NO ONE DRIVING. / GLIMMER / / MR. NO. / THIS CITY** 32 -

Jul 80. (7"pic-d) *(VS 360)* **BURNING CAR. / 20th CENTURY** 35 -

Oct 80. (7") *(VS 382)* **MILES AWAY. / A LONG TIME** [51] [-]

—— **ROBIN SIMON** – guitar + **JO DWORNIAK** – bass repl. BARKER

Aug 81. (7") *(VS 393)* **EUROPE AFTER THE RAIN. / THIS JUNGLE** [40] [-]

Sep 81. (lp/c) *(V/TCV 2194)* **THE GARDEN** [24] [-]
– Europe after the rain / Systems of romance / When I was a man and you were a woman / Dancing like a gun / Pater noster / Night suit / You were there / Fusion – Fission / Walk away / The garden. *(re-iss. Mar84 lp/c; OVED/+C 47) (cd-iss. Apr93; CDV 2194)*

Oct 81. (7") *(VS 459)* **DANCING LIKE A GUN. / SWIMMER 2** [ ] [-]
(12"+=) *(VS 459-12)* – Swimmer 1.

—— **PAUL WICKENS** (WIX) – drums, keyboards repl. DURANT

Jul 82. (7"pic-d) *(VS 543)* **ENDLESSLY. / YOUNG MAN** [66] [-]
(d7"++=) *(VSY 543)* – Dance with me / A kind of love.

Aug 83. (7") *(VS 615)* **YOUR DRESS. / WOMAN OF THE STAIRWAY** [61] [-]
(12"+=) *(VS 615-12)* – The Garden.
(d7"+=) *(VSY 615)* Lifting sky / Annexe.

Oct 83. (lp/c) *(V/TCV 2233)* **THE GOLDEN SECTION** [27] [-]
– My wild love / Someone / Your dress / Running across thin ice with tigers / Sitting at the edge of the world / Endlessly / Ghosts on water / Like a miracle / The hidden man / Twilight's last gleaming. *(c+=)* – Woman on the stairway / Young man / Dance with me / Wing and a wind / Lifting sky / Annexe. *(re-iss. Aug88 lp/c; OVED/+C 120)*

Oct 83. (7"sha-pic-d) *(VSP 645)* **LIKE A MIRACLE. / WING AND A WIND** [ ] [-]
(12"+=) *(VS 645-12)* – ('A'extended).

Jun 85. (7"/12") *(VS 771/+12)* **THE STARS ON FIRE. / WHAT KIND OF GIRL** [ ] [-]
(free 7"with the 7")

Sep 85. (lp/c) *(V/TCV 2355)* **IN MYSTERIOUS WAYS** [85] [-]
– The stars on fire / Lose all sense of time / Shine on / Enter the angel / In mysterious ways / What kind of girl / This side of Paradise / Stepping softly / Enter the angel 2 / Morning glory. *(cd-iss. Jul87; CDV 2355) (re-iss. Aug88 lp/c; OVED/+C 189)*

Sep 85. (7"/12") *(VS 814/+12)* **ENTER THE ANGEL. / STAIRWAY** [ ] [-]

—— FOXX retired from music biz, until he astonishing released two sets in 1997

Metamatic not iss.

Mar 97. (cd) *(META 001)* **CATHEDRAL OCEANS** [ ] [-]
– Cathedral oceans / City as memory / Summer rooms / Geometry and coincidence / If only . . . / Shifting perspective / Floating islands / Infinite in all directions / Avenham collanade / Sunset rising / Invisible architecture.

Mar 97. (cd; JOHN FOXX & LOUIS GORDON) *(META 002)* **SHIFTING CITY** [ ] [-]
– Crash / Noise / Here we go / Shadow man / Through my shadow / Forgotten years / Everyone / Shifting city / Concrete / Bulletproof / Invisible / Ocean we can breathe.

– compilations, etc. –

1988. (cd) *Virgin; (COMCD 6)* **ASSEMBLY** [ ] [-]
– A new kind of man / Underpass / Burning car / This city / Twilight's last gleaming / Ghosts on water / This jungle / Endlessly / Someone / Sitting at the edge of the world / In mysterious ways / Morning glory / Europe after the rain / Systems of romance / Walk away / When I was a man and you were a woman / Pater noster / The garden. *(re-iss. Jun92; CDVM 9002)*

Roddy FRAME (see under ⇒ AZTEC CAMERA)

FRANK & WALTERS

Formed: Cork, Ireland . . . 1990 by young brothers PAUL and NIALL LINEHAM plus neighbour ASHLEY KEATING. Signed to the Celtic-friendly 'Setanta' label, the trio debuted their charmingly eccentric musical wares on 1991's 'THE FRANK AND WALTERS EP', 'Father Ted'-style power pop vignettes of everyday rural Irish life in stark contrast to the grunge/baggy dominated indie scene of the day. A follow-up EP, 'THE FRANK AND WALTERS 2', offered up more of the same and boasted the infamous 'FASHION CRISIS HITS NEW YORK' – although by this point the lads had moved to home of the Wombles, Wimbledon! – forever the band's defining moment and the track which saw them adopted as a kind of mascot by the indie press. A move to London and subsequent switch to 'Go! Discs' saw the lads hit the UK Top 50 for the first time with the EDWYN COLLINS-produced 'HAPPY BUSMAN' EP, the ex-ORANGE JUICE man also overseeing their much anticipated 'TRAINS, BOATS AND PLANES' (1992) debut album. With many previously available tracks, the record wasn't exactly essential listening and only scraped into the Top 40; stretching the FRANK & WALTERS concept over a whole album was probably too much too soon. Yet help was at hand courtesy of twee master, IAN BROUDIE (of The LIGHTNING SEEDS), who remixed 'AFTER ALL' and turned it into a near Top 10 hit. But even BROUDIE's deft touch couldn't secure a Top 40 placing for a revamped 'FASHION CRISIS . . . ', as the band were looking increasingly bereft of original ideas and wearing thin the patience of a fickle music press. Returning homewards to think again was probably the best option although their long awaited return found them back with 'Setanta', the label issuing a disappointing follow-up album, 'THE GRAND PARADE' (1997). Nothing has been heard from them since, rumours that they're currently holed up on Craggy Island remain unconfirmed . . . • **Songwriters:** Group except; FUNKY COLD MEDINA (Tone Loc) / I'M A BELIEVER (The Monkees) / LOVE IS IN THE AIR (John Paul Jones) / CEMETERY GATES (Smiths).

Album rating: TRAINS, BOATS AND PLANES (*6) / THE GRAND PARADE (*4)

PAUL LINEHAM – vocals, bass / **NIALL LINEHAM** – guitar / **ASHLEY KEATING** – drums

Setanta not iss.

Aug 91. (12"ep) **THE FRANK AND WALTERS EP** [ ] [-]
– Walter's trip / Frank's night / Michael / Never ending staircase.

Sep 91. (12"ep) **THE FRANK AND WALTERS 2** [ ] [-]
– Fashion crisis hits New York / Rasputin / Daisy chain / Angela Cray. *(cd-ep+= EP1;)*

Go! Discs London

Mar 92. (7"/c-s) *(HOO/+MC 2)* **HAPPY BUSMAN. / THE WORLD CARRIES ON** [49] [-]
(12"ep+=/cd-ep+=) **EP 3** *(HOO X/CD 2)* – Humphrey / If you're still waiting.

Sep 92. (7"/c-s) *(HOO/+MC 3)* **THIS IS NOT A SONG. / DAVY CHASE** [46] [-]
(12"+=/cd-s+=) *(HOO X/CD 3)* – Lawrence Olivier / Happy busman (live).

Oct 92. (cd/c/lp) *(828402-2/-4/-1) <162-351005-2/-4>* **TRAINS, BOATS AND PLANES** [36] [ ]
– This is not a song / Walter's trip / Trainspotters / After all / Happy busman / Fashion crisis hits New York / Daisy chain / John and Sue / Bake us a song / Time / High is low. *(re-iss. Jul93; same)*

Dec 92. (c-s) *(HOOMC 4)* **AFTER ALL / THE DAY BEFORE THE WORLD ENDED** [11] [-]
(cd-s+=) *(HOOCD 4)* – The turquoise gardens.
(12"++=) *(HOOX 4)* – Funky cold Medina.
(cd-s) *(HOCCD 4)* – ('A'side) / Funky cold Medina / Love is in the air / I'm a believer.

Apr 93. (7"ep/c-ep/cd-ep) *(HOO/+MC/CD 5)* **FASHION CRISIS HITS NEW YORK / TIME (R.T.E.session). / NEVER ENDING STAIRCASE / FRANK'S RIGHT** [42] [ ]
(cd-s) *(HOACD 5)* – ('A'original) / Rasputin / Daisy chain / Angela Cray.

Jul 96. (7"/c-s) *(HOO/+MC 6)* **INDIAN OCEAN. / PATHWAYS** [ ] [-]
(cd-s+=) *(HOOCD 6)* – You can't take too much notice / Restraint.

Aug 96. (7"/c-s; w-drawn) *(HOO/+MC 7)* **COLOURS. / SURRENDER 2 WIN** [ ] [-]
(cd-s+=) *(HOOCD 7)* – Last train home / You asked me.

Setanta Go! Discs

Mar 97. (cd-s) *(SETCD 051)* **COLOURS / SURRENDER 2 WIN / YOU ASKED ME** [ ] [-]

Jun 97. (cd) *(SETCD 054) <828823>* **GRAND PARADE** [ ] [ ]
– Colours / Indian Ocean / Little dolls / Russian ship / I suppose / Saturday night / How can I exist / Mrs. Xavier / Have you ever / Tony Cochran / Landslide / Lately.

Jun 97. (c-s/cd-s) *(SET MC/CDA 055)* **HOW CAN I EXIST / LAST TRAIN HOME / FAST ANTHONY** [ ] [-]
(cd-s) *(SETCDB 055)* – ('A'side) / Indian Ocean (acoustic) / Little dolls.

not iss. Tristar

Jul 97. (cd-ep) *<36457>* **INDIAN OCEAN / RESTRAINT / PATHWAYS / LAST TRAIN HOME / FAST ANTHONY / LITTLE DOLLS** [-] [ ]

—— disbanded after above

FRANK CHICKENS

Formed: London, England . . . 1982 by KAZUKO HOHKI and KAZUMI TAGUCHI (augmented by NORIKO IWATSUBO until late 1983), who met while helping out at the Japanese/American Toy Theatre. They first got their recording break when BILL NELSON invited them to sing on his 'Invisibility Exhibition' early in '83, the girls receiving publicity through a wacky promotional appearance on Channel 4's (then) flagship pop show, 'The Tube'. While their work may have benefitted from the attendant novelty factor, The FRANK CHICKENS were nevertheless attempting to present a more positive, proto girl-power portrait of the Japanese female (i.e. their first 45, 'WE ARE NINJA' (NOT GEISHA)'). With the support of airplay from John Peel, the pigeon-English funsters became a mid-80's cult phenomenom, the independent 'Kaz' label unleashing their long-playing debut album, 'WE ARE . . .', in 1984. Three years on, KAZUKO and KAZUMI launched their own 'Flying Lecords' rabel (sorry, label!), releasing a follow-up set, 'GET CHICKENIZED', before helping to introduce the Karaoke craze to Britain via their own zany celebrity-singing TV show. In the 90's, the 'CHICKENS scratched a living around the capital's cabaret circuit, their only recording venture being 1996's 'YUKASITA UNDERFLOOR'.

Album rating: WE ARE FRANK CHICKENS (*6) / GET CHICKENIZED (*5)

KAZUKO HOHKI – vocals / **KAZUMI TAGUCHI** – vocals / with a plethora of session people including STEVE BERESFORD, DAVID TOOP, LOL COXHILL, ELIZABETH PERRY, ANNIE WHITEHEAD, ROBERT PIA, BOSCO DeOLIVERA, TONY COE, ALEX BALANESCU + CLIVE BELL

Kaz not iss.

Jan 84. (7") *(KAZ 10)* **WE ARE NINJA (NOT GEISHA). / FUJIYAMA MAMA** [ ] [-]
(12"+=) *(KAZT 10)* – Shellfish bamboo.

Oct 84. (lp) *(KAZLP 2)* **WE ARE FRANK CHICKENS** [ ] [-]
– Cheeba cheeba chimpira / Mothra / Green banana / Madam fatal / We are Ninja (not Geisha) / Yellow detective / Shellfish bamboo / Nichon fatal / Pikadon / We are Frank Chickens / Sake ballad. *(c-iss.Feb89; KAZMC 2) (cd-iss. Jul89; KAZCD 2)*

Oct 85. (7") *(KAZ 20)* **BLUE CANARY / WE ARE FRANK CHICKENS** [ ] [-]
(12"+=) *(KAZT 20)* – China night / Japanese rumba.

Flying Lecords Flying Lecords

Aug 87. (7") *(SIZZLE 1)* **YELLOW TOAST. /** [ ] [-]
(12"+=) *(SIZZLE 1-12)* –

Oct 87. (lp/cd) *(<STIR/+D 1>)* **GET CHICKENIZED** [ ] [ ]
– We say you say / Sacred marriage / Street angels, Tokyo / Two little ladies / Solid life / Japanese girl / Island inside island / Young summer / Chicken ondo / Yellow toast. *(cd re-iss. Aug98 on 'Resurgence'; RES 136CD)*

—— the duo were augmented by musicians CLIVE BELL + JUSTIN ADAMS

Dec 88. (lp/c/cd) *(<STIR/+C/D 2>)* **CLUB MONKEY** [ ] [ ]
– Club Monkey / Waiting for a dog / Burn that body / Revolution / Night drain / Feed me / Jackie Chan / Shaken by God's hand / M.Y.T.H. / Hey dead / Club Monkey reprise. *(cd re-iss. Aug98 on 'Resurgence'; RES 137CD)*

Jun 89. (7") *(SIZZLE 2)* **DO THE KARAOKE. /** [ ] [-]

— **ATSUKO KAMURA** – vocals; repl. TAGUCHI

Creative Man | not iss.

Jun 96. (cd) *(CMCD 009)* **YUKASITA UNDERFLOOR** [ ] [-]

John FRANKOVIC (see under ⇒ PLASTICLAND)

FRAZIER CHORUS

Formed: Brighton, England . . . mid 80's as PLOP by songwriter/vocalist/pianist, TIM FREEMAN, with others MICHELE ALLARDYCE, KATE HOLMES and CHRIS TAPLIN. Initially signed to '4 a.d.', FRAZIER CHORUS unveiled their deliciously different amalgam of dreamy instrumental textures, infectious pop hooks and whispered vocals with the 'SLOPPY HEART' single. Moving on to 'Virgin', the quartet released their widely acclaimed but criminally overlooked debut album, 'SUE' (1989), critics salivating over such subtle, knowing snippets of domestic drama as 'KITCHEN' and 'TYPICAL', both tracks coming within shouting (make that whispering) distance of the Top 40. And therein lay the problem with this band, close but no cigar led to a change in musical direction as they embraced the all-pervasive dance culture. With ALLARDYCE departing midway through sessions for follow-up set, 'RAY' (1991), the group were reduced to a trio by the time of the album's release, its more dance-orientated feel dividing reviewers and fans. Yet major chart success still proved elusive and even a revamped version of the near-classic, 'CLOUD 8', failed to penetrate the Top 40, the group finally going their separate ways after a further couple of minor hits and a disappointing follow-up set, 'RAY' (1991). It took four years for FRAZIER CHORUS (now reduced to TIM and KATE – CHRIS formed dance-pop outfit ESPIRITU) to resurface, the duo finally emerging in summer '95 with 'WIDE AWAKE'.

Album rating: SUE (*6) / "RAY" (*4) / WIDE AWAKE (*5)

TIM FREEMAN – vocals / **KATE HOLMES** – flute / **MICHELE ALLARDYCE** – percussion / **CHRIS TAPLIN** – clarinet, keyboards

4 a.d. | not iss.

Oct 87. (12") *(BAD 708)* **SLOPPY HEART. / TYPICAL** [ ] [-]

Virgin | Atlantic

Jan 89. (7") *(VS 1145)* **DREAM KITCHEN. / DOWN** [57] [-]
(12"+=/3"cd-s+=) *(VS T/CD 1145)* – Little chef.

Mar 89. (7") *(VS 1174)* **TYPICAL. / STRING** [53] [-]
(10"+=/12"+=/3"cd-s+=) *(VS /T/CD 1174)* – Born with a headcase.

May 89. (cd/c/lp) *(CD/TC+/V 2578)* **SUE** [56] [-]
– Dream kitchen / Storm / Forty winks / Ha-ha happiness / Sloppy heart / Living room / Sugar high / Forgetful / Typical / Skihead. *(cd+=)* – Little chef.

Jun 89. (7") *(VS 1192)* **SLOPPY HEART. / ANARCHY IN THE UK** [73] [-]
(12"+=) *(VST 1192)* – Spoonhead.
(12"+=) *(VSTX 1192)* – Living room (demo) / 40 winks (demo).
(3"cd-s+=) *(VSCD 1192)* – Typical / Storm.

May 90. (7") *(VS 1252)* *<96378>* **CLOUD 8. / LE CHANGE EST MAGNIFIQUE** [52] [ ] Apr91
(12"+=/cd-s+=) *(VS T/CD 1252)* –

Aug 90. (7") *(VS 1284)* **NOTHING. / ?** [51] [-]
(12"+=/cd-s+=) *(VS T/CD 1284)* –

Feb 91. (7"/c-s) *(VS/+SC 1330)* **WALKING ON AIR. / ?** [60] [-]
(12"+=/cd-s+=) *(VS T/CD 1330)* –

Mar 91. (cd/c/lp) *(CD/TC+/VFC 2654)* *<91641>* **"RAY"** [66] [ ]

— ALLARDYCE departed during recording of above

— were now basically **TIM + KATE** who tried their luck in the States. TAPLIN formed ESPIRITU in 1992 with VANESSA QUINENES.

Pinkerton | Pure

Jul 95. (cd) *(PINKCD 1)* *<642310>* **WIDE AWAKE** [ ] [ ] Jun96
– Wide awake / If the weather was up to me / Bye-bye little bird / Driving / Here we are / Next to on-one / Funny thing / Take us away / Lie, mimic and mime / Sound asleep / Thankyou.

Aug 96. (cd-s) *<642311>* **DRIVING** [-] [ ]

FREAKWATER (see under ⇒ ELEVENTH DREAM DAY)

FREAKY REALISTIC

Formed: Peckham, London . . . 1991 by singer-songwriter JUSTIN ANDERSON and Texan rapper, MICHAEL LORD (cx-NASTY GROOVE). Hooking up with foxy Japanese voclaist, AKI OMORI, the pair set out to realise their 70's inspired, space-themed, genre blurring musical vision. Armed with only synths, samplers and toy rayguns, the trio beamed up a series of funky singles for 'Polydor' over the course of '92/'93, beginning with underground club favourite, 'SOMETHING NEW'. This was quickly followed by 'COSMIC LOVE VIBES', while 'KOOCHIE RYDER' and 'LEONARD NIMOY' were minor chart hits. DEE-LITE had already covered similar territory much more successfully however and by the release of FREAKY REALISTIC's debut album, 'FREALISM' (1993), the dayglo hippie-indie-pop that had characterised the charts of the early 90's had already began to dissipate.

Album rating: FREALISM (*5)

JUSTIN ANDERSON – songwriting/vocals / **AKI OMORI** – vocals / **MICHAEL LORD** – rapper/vocals

Polydor | not iss.

1992. (7") **SOMETHING NEW. /** [ ] [-]
(12"+=/cd-s+=) –

1992. (7") **COSMIC LOVE VIBES. /** [ ] [-]
(12"+=/cd-s+=) –

Mar 93. (7"/c-s) *(FRE AL/CS 2)* **KOOCHIE RYDER. /** [52] [-]
(12"+=/cd-s+=) *(FRE AX/CD 2)* –
(cd-s) *(FREDD 2)* –

Jun 93. (7"/c-s) *(FRE AL/CS 3)* **LEONARD NIMOY. /** [71] [-]
(12"+=/cd-s+=) *(FRE AX/CD 3)* –

Oct 93. (cd/d-lp) *(517 919-2/-1)* **FREALISM** [ ] [-]
– Frealism / Something new – Cosmic love blues / Koochie ryder / Love that loves / Leonard Nimoy / Reach / Salivate special / Trickle in / Imaginary pavillions / Make it happen / Sooner / Most / This is Freaky Realistic / Reprise – Frealism.

— when MICHAEL departed nothing more was heard from the outfit

FREE KITTEN (see under ⇒ SONIC YOUTH)

FREEZE (see under ⇒ CINDYTALK)

FRENTE!

Formed: Melbourne, Australia . . . early 90's by songwriters, ANGIE HART and SIMON AUSTIN alongside TIM O'CONNOR and ALISTAIR BARDEN (although MARK PICTON replaced the latter after a few singles). FRENTE! (Spanish for "front") were one of the more interesting musical exports to arrive from down under, eschewing the usual rock/pop predictability for a more experimental folky pop sound. Following a debut EP, 'LABOUR OF LOVE' on 'Flying Nun' subsidiary, 'White', the band signed to 'Mushroom' and issued their debut set, 'MARVIN THE ALBUM', in Spring '94. A focal point was undoubtedly the blonde-bobbed HART, an Antipodean hybrid of The CARDIGANS' NINA PERSSON, DUBSTAR's SARAH BLACKWOOD and SUZANNE VEGA, singing her cryptic, world-weary lyrics against a skeletal backing of often acoustic guitar, piano, rhythm section and sound effects. The record's cover of New Order's 'BIZARRE LOVE TRIANGLE' subsequently entered the US Top 50 although strangely, FRENTE! struggled to make any headway in Britain. Augmented by CAMERON McVEY (BOOGA BEAR) and STEVE GRIPA HOPWOOD, FRENTE!'s 1996 follow-up set, 'SHAPE', was another fine effort, again dominated by HART's haunting vocals. The album also featured possibly their most experimental track to date, 'SIT ON MY HANDS', uncannily reminiscent of territory once explored by The BEATLES on the likes of 'Sgt. Peppers' and 'Abbey Road'. • **Covered:** HERE YOU COME AGAIN (Mann-Weil) / SOMETHIN' STUPID (hit; Frank & Nancy Sinatra) / BLUE (Joni Mitchell)

Album rating: MARVIN THE ALBUM (*5) / SHAPE (*6)

ANGIE HART (b.1971) – vocals / **SIMON AUSTIN** (b.1966) – guitars, piano, vocals / **TIM O'CONNOR** – bass / **ALISTAIR BARDEN** – drums, percussion

Thumbprint | not iss.

1991. (7"ep/c-ep/cd-ep) *(WHI 003/002/001)* **WHIRLED** [ ] [-]
– Labour of love / etc. *(UK-iss.Oct93; same)*

Mushroom | Alex

1992. (cd-ep) *(D 11125)* **CLUNK** [ ] [-]

1993. (cd-ep) *(D 11352)* *<4831>* **NO TIME / THINKING DARLING / BLUE / NO TIME / FACE LIKE A SPIDER** [ ] [ ] Nov94

1994. (cd-ep) *(D 11608)* **LONELY / EXPLODE / GET REAL** [ ] [-]

Mushroom | Mammoth

1994. (m-cd) *<MR 056>* **LABOUR OF LOVE** [-] [ ]
– Labour of love / Testimony / Not given lightly / Paper, bullets, walls / Risk / Bizarre love triangle / Oh brilliance.

Apr 94. (7"ep/c-ep/cd-ep) *(S/C/D 12063)* **ACCIDENTLY KELLY STREET / MANY WINGS / HERE YOU COME AGAIN / SOMETHIN' STUPID** [ ] [-]

May 94. (cd/c) *(TVD/TVC 93367)* *<92300>* **MARVIN THE ALBUM** [ ] [75]
– Girl / Accidently Kelly Street / Most Beautiful / No time / Cuscatlan / Pretty friend / Lonely / Reflect / Explode / See – Believe / Labour of love / Ordinary angels / Dangerous.

Aug 94. (7"/7"colrd/c-s) *(S/SR/C 11839)* *<98274>* **BIZARRE LOVE TRIANGLE. / TESTIMONY** [ ] [49] Apr94
(cd-s+=) *(D 11839)* – Risk

Feb 95. (7"clear-ep/cd-ep) *(SP/D 11968)* **ORDINARY ANGELS – THE EP** [ ] [-]

— **BILL McDONALD** – bass, guitar; repl. O'CONNOR

Jul 96. (7"/7"pic-d) *(S/SX 2001)* **HORRIBLE. /** [ ] [-]
(cd-s+=) *(D 2001)* –

Sep 96. (7"blue) *(S 1451)* **WHAT'S COME OVER ME. / I MISS YOU** [ ] [-]
(cd-s+=) *(DX 1451)* – Ruby's arms.
(cd-s) *(D 1451)* – ('A'mixes) / A real miracle.

Oct 96. (cd/c/lp) *(D/C/L 93429)* *<980123>* **SHAPE** [ ] [ ] Jul96
– Sit on my hands / Horrible / Goodbye goodguy / Burning girl / Clue / Harm / Air / Jungle / So mad / Safe from you / The destroyer / What's come over me / Calmly.

FRENZAL RHOMB

Formed: Sydney, Australia . . . 1993 by purple dreadlocked singer, JASON WHALLEY and cohorts, LEX FELTHAM and BENJAMIN COSTELLO (the latter was replaced by LINDSAY McDOUGAL), while third drummer in succession, GORDY FOREMAN superseded KARL and NAT. Leaders of the Australian contingent of the largely US-based Ska-punk movement (which included OFFSPRING, RANCID, etc), FRENZAL RHOMB spluttered into life with an Australian-only, self-financed debut long-player, 'COUGHING UP A STORM' (1995). With the subsequent patronage of NOFX's FAT MIKE, the group began building up a profile outside their homeland, securing a Stateside release on 'What Are Records' for their follow-up, 'NOT SO TOUGH NOW' (1996/97). The band went on to preview tracks from third set, 'MEET THE FAMILY' (1998) on the highly publicised Vans Warped Tour, taking in both Australia and America.

Album rating: COUGHING UP A STORM (*5) / NOT SO TOUGH NOW (*5) / MEET THE FAMILY (*5)

JASON WHALLEY – vocals / **LINDSAY McDOUGAL** – guitar; repl. BENJAMIN COSTELLO / **LEX FLETHAM** – bass / **GORDY FOREMAN** – drums; repl. KARL then NAT

Shagpile / not iss.

1995. (lp) **COUGHING UP A STORM** [-] Austra
<US-iss.Oct97 as 'ONCE A JOLLY SWAGMAN ALWAYS A JOLLY SWAGMAN' on 'Liberation'; 37807>

Fat Wreck Chords / What Are Records?

Sep 95. (7"ep) *(FAT 529-7)* **4 LITRES EP**
Aug 97. (cd) *<69993>* **NOT SO TOUGH NOW** [-]
Jun 98. (cd) *<69994>* **MEET THE FAMILY** [-]
– Mum changed the locks / Mr. Charisma / There's your dad / Racist / Ship of beers / Be still my beating off / I hate my brain / The ballad of Tim Webster / U.S. anus / Constable care / (That's) Just not legal / Hakimastita / Genital are funny / All your friends / Beaded curtains (part 2) / Beaded curtains (part 3) / Guns don't kill ducklings (ducklings do) / You can't move into my house.

FRESHIES

Formed: Manchester, England . . . mid-70's by sole conspirator, CHRIS SIEVEY. The man had previously reputedly barged his way into London's Abbey Road studios, demanding the listening attention of the engineers, secretaries or indeed anyone who happened to be there at the time. Having literally suffered a catalogue of record company rejection notices, SIEVEY finally formed his own label ('Razz') and proceeded to release a plethora of DIY cassettes over the period 1975 to 1985. However, SIEVEY and his FRESHIES would make their mark via the 7" market, the man's eccentric humour landing him a belated radio hit with 'I'M IN LOVE WITH THE GIRL ON THE MANCHESTER VIRGIN MEGASTORE CHECKOUT DESK', 'M.C.A.' picking it up in early '81 and making it a minor hit. A further series of chart attempts failed to make the grade, although 'I CAN'T GET BOUNCING BABIES BY THE TEARDROP EXPLODES' was just as bizarrely memorable. The mid-80's found SIEVEY re-inventing himself as FRANK SIDEBOTTOM, a decidedly childish alter-ego that recalled the freaky anonymity of The RESIDENTS minus the surreal humour. His tongue-in-cheek tributes to KYLIE MINOGUE, QUEEN, etc, consigned him to children's TV land, adult programmers (save some mad Manchester shows with 'Factory boss', Tony Wilson!) giving him a body swerve.

Album rating: THE VERY VERY BEST OF THE FRESHIES compilation (*6)

CHRIS SIEVEY – vocals / with various musicians including **MARTIN JACKSON + BILLY DUFFY** (before they made their name)

Razz / not iss.

Feb 78. (7"ep) *(RAZZXEP 1)* **WASHED UP / MOON MIDSUMMER. / Chris Sievey: BAISER / TWO OF THE SAME GIRL** [-]

—— now with **BARRY SPENCER** – guitar, vocals / **EDDIE CARTER** – guitar, vocals / **BOB DIXON** – drums

Nov 78. (7"ep) *(RAZZXEP 2)* **STRAIGHT IN AT NO.2** [-]
– Johnny Radar / U-boat / Skid room / Last.

—— now with **BARRY SPENCER** – guitar / **RICK SARKO** – bass (ex-ED BANGER & THE NOSEBLEEDS) / **MIKE DOHERTY** – drums (ex-SMIRKS)

Jul 79. (7"; as CHRIS SIEVEY) *(TOSH 109)* **BAISER. / LAST** [-]
(above issued on 'Rabid') *(re-iss. Sep80 as 'SKIP THE FIGHT'. / 'JIM BAISER' on 'Razz'; RAZZ 9)*
Nov 79. (7"ep) *(RAZZ 3)* **THE MEN FROM BANANA ISLAND WHOSE STUPID IDEAS NEVER CAUGHT ON IN THE WESTERN WORLD AS WE KNOW IT** [-]
– Amoco Cadiz / Children of the world / Octopus.
Mar 80. (mag+7") *(RAZZ 4)* **MY TAPE'S GONE. / MOON MIDSUMMER** [-]
May 80. (7") *(RAZZ 5)* **WE'RE LIKE YOU. / Chris Sievey: HEY** [-]
Aug 80. (7") *(RAZZ 6)* **YELLOW SPOT. / IF IT'S NEWS** [-]
Sep 80. (7") *(RAZZ 7)* **NO MONEY. / OH GIRL** [-]
Sep 80. (7"ep; as FRESHIES with CHRIS SIEVEY) *(RAZZ 8)* **RED INDIAN MUSIC** [-]
– Sue of the Sioux / Riding out to Devil's Ridge / Return of Sue of the Sioux.
Oct 80. (7") *(RAZZ 11)* **I'M IN LOVE WITH THE GIRL ON THE MANCHESTER VIRGIN MEGASTORE CHECKOUT DESK. / SINGALONG VERSION** [-]
(also radio bleeped out "Virgin" version; RAZZ 12) (re-iss. Jan81 on 'M.C.A.'; MCA 670) – hit No.54 in UK charts.

—— early in 1981, CHRIS + BARRY augmented JILTED JOHN in his new band, GOING RED?; one single 'SOME BOYS'.

M.C.A. / not iss.

Mar 81. (7") *(MCA 693)* **WRAP UP THE ROCKETS. / IT'S GONNA GET BETTER** [-]
(remixed; c-s+=/12"+=) *(MCA S/T 693)* – Tell her I'm ill.
Jun 81. (7") *(MCA 725)* **I CAN'T GET BOUNCING BABIES BY THE TEARDROP EXPLODES. / TELL HER I'M ILL** [-]

CV / not iss.

1981. (7") *(CVS 1)* **IF YOU REALLY LOVE ME, BUY ME A SHIRT. / I AM A WALRUS** [-]

Razz – Pinnacle / not iss.

Oct 81. (7") *(RP 8)* **DANCIN' DOCTORS. / ONE TO ONE** [-]

Stiff / not iss.

Aug 82. (7") *(BUY 158)* **FASTEN YOUR SEAT BELYS. / BEST WE CAN DO** [-]

—— had already decided to abandon The FRESHIES

E.M.I. / not iss.

Jun 83. (c-s/7") *(TC+/EMI 5398)* **CAMOUFLAGE / (ZX 81 programme "CAMOUFLAGE"). / FLYING TRAIN / F.T.** [-]

—— (also issued on 'Random; *RND 1)*

– others, unofficial specials, etc. –

1975. (c; CHRIS SIEVEY) *Hey Boss; (none)* **GIRL IN MY BLUE JEANS** [-]
1976. (c; CHRIS SIEVEY) *Razz; (RAZZCS-1)* **ALL SLEEPS SECRETS** [-]
1979. (c) *Razz; (RAZZCS-2)* **MANCHESTER PLAYS** [-]
1979. (c) *Razz; (RAZZCS-3)* **SING THE GIRLS FROM BANANA ISLAND . . .** [-]
1980. (c) *Razz; (RAZZCS-4)* **ROUGH AND READY** [-]
1981. (c) *Razz; (RAZZCS-5)* **LONDON PLAYS** [-]
1981. (12"white label) *(HANNA 1)* **VIRGIN MEGASTORE / WRAP UP THE ROCKETS. / BUY ME A SHIRT / TELL HER I'M ILL / FRANK TALKS TO CHRIS (conversation)** [-] [-]
1985. (c,lp) *E.T.S.; (1)* **JOHNNY RADAR STORY** [-]
1985. (c) *E.T.S., (3)* **EARLY RAZZ** [-]
1985. (c) *E.T.S.; (4)* **STUDIO OUT-TAKES** [-]
1986. (lp) *Cordelia; (ERICAT 015)* **CHRIS SIEVEY'S BIG RECORD** *(w/ free 7"; TOSH 109)* – BAISER. / LAST [-]
Apr 96. (cd) *Cherry Red; (CDMRED 129)* **THE VERY VERY BEST OF THE FRESHIES** [-]

FRANK SIDEBOTTOM

Regal Zonophone / not iss.

Aug 85. (7") *(Z 39)* **POPULAR MEDLEY** [-]
– Bohemian rhapsody / Anarchy in the UK / Every breath you take / Material boy / God save the queen.
Nov 85. (7"ep) *(Z 40)* **OH BLIMEY IT'S CHRISTMAS:- OLIVER'S ARMY - CHRISTMAS IN AUSTRALIA - IN THE SUMMERTIME - OLD LANG ZINE - LIFE IN A NORTHERN TOWN** [-]
(12"+=) *(12Z 40)* – Greengrocer on the corner.
Jul 86. (7"/7"pic-d) *(Z/+P 41)* **I'M THE URBAN SPACEMAN. / OH SUPERMUM** [-]
(12"+=) *(12Z 41)* – Sci-fi medley: Space is ace – Robot Frank – Fireball ZL5 – Life on Mars – Close encounters of the third kind.

In Tape / not iss.

Dec 86. (7") *(IT 041)* **CHRISTMAS IS REALLY FANTASTIC. / O COME ALL YE FAITHFUL (ADESTE FIDELIS) / I WISH IT COULD BE CHRISTMAS EVERDAY** [-]
(12"+=) *(ITT 041)* – Xmas medley: Twist 'n' shout – The benefit of Mr. Kyte – Flying – It was nearly 20 years ago today – Mull of Timperley.
Jul 87. (12"ep) *(ITT 045)* **SALUTES THE MAGIC OF FREDDIE MERCURY & K MINOGUE** [-]
– I should be so lucky – Love poem for Kylie – Radio Ga Ga – Save me – We will rock you – Frank Gordon – Queen (hip hop disco mix) – Everybody sings Queen – I am the champion.
Nov 87. (7"ep/12"ep) *(IT/+T 048)* **TIMPERLEY SUNSET** [-]
– Born in Timperley / Anarchy in Timperley / Timperley sunset / Wild thing in Timperley / Next train to Timperley / Oh Timperley / Surfin' Timperley.
Sep 88. (lp) *(IT 058)* **5.9.88** [-]
Sep 88. (c) *(IT 060)* **13.9.88** [-]
Oct 88. (cd) *(ITCD 063)* **11.10.88** [-]
Jul 90. (10"m-lp) *(IT 069-10)* **MEDIUM PLAY** [-]

—— continued to work on mainly children's TV

– compilations, etc. –

Apr 97. (cd) *Cherry Red; (CDMRED 143)* **FRANK SIDEBOTTOM'S ABC AND D** (all his singles) [-]

FREUR (see under ⇒ UNDERWORLD)

FRIDGE

Formed: Putney, London, England . . . 1995 by former classmates, KIERAN HEBDEN, ADEM ILHAN and SAM JEFFERS. Lucky enough to sign a deal almost immediately with Trevor Jackson's 'Output', FRIDGE dished out their first vinyl helping in the shape of 7", 'LOJEN', followed closely by debut album (a double!), 'CEEFAX' (1997). Obviously turned on by the ever expanding list of outfits experimenting in the post-rock grey area of indie electronica, FRIDGE clearly liked to chill out to ambient noodling in the vein of TORTOISE and ROME. A busy year for the cool teenagers, they would go on to deliver another two singles, the radio-friendly 'ANGLEPOISED' and a shared effort with ADD N TO X. Precociously prolific, the FRIDGE boys passed their critical exams with early 1998's 'SEMAPHORE', a brooding, intoxicating series of undulating anti-rock frequencies that endeared them to more discerning indie fans. A neat overview of the band's career trajectory was presented later that year with the 'SEVEN'S AND TWELVE'S' singles compilation.

Album rating: CEEFAX (*5) / SEMAPHORE (*7) / SEVEN'S AND TWELVE'S compilation (*7)

KIERAN HEBDEN – guitar, etc / **ADEM ILHAN** – bass, etc / **SAM JEFFERS** – drums, etc

Output not iss.

Jan 97. (7") *(OPR 5)* **LOJEN. / MORE EDH4800 (PHASE SHIFTER)**

Mar 97. (d-lp/cd) *(OPR 6/+CD)* **CEEFAX**
– EDH / Helicopter / Tricity / More EDH4800 / Jazz loop / Robots in disguise / EDH2 / Oracle / EDH 3 / Zed ex ay-ti-wan. *(re-iss. Jul98; same)*

Sep 97. (12") *(OPR 9)* **ANGLEPOISED. /**

— In Nov'97, they shared a ltd-12" on 'Piao!' with ADD N TO X

Feb 98. (7"ep/12"ep) *(OPR 11/+T)* **LIGN EP**
– Lign / For force / Must be magic / Sequoia / Traps / Fisa.

Feb 98. (d-lp/cd) *(OPR 12/+CD)* **SEMAPHORE**
– Cassette / Furniture boy / Slow / Motorbuss / Teletexed / Chroma / Low fat diet / Swerve and spin / Curdle / Lign / Stamper / There is no try / Michael Knight.

May 98. (7") *(22)* **INDEGUISE. /**
(above issued on 'Soul Static')

Aug 98. (12"w/7") *(OPR 15)* **ORKO. / DISTANCE // IT'S ALL ON / JESSICA**

Oct 98. (cd) *(OPR 19)* **SEVEN'S AND TWELVE'S** (compilation)

FRONTLINE ASSEMBLY

Formed: Vancouver, Canada . . .1986 by RHYS FULBER and Austrian-born BILL LEEB, the latter having cut his teeth as a pseudonymous member (WILLIAM SCHROEDER) of fellow industrialists, SKINNY PUPPY. Initially augmented by MICHAEL BALCH, the duo issued their self-titled debut set in 1987 (released outside the UK as 'THE INITIAL COMMAND'), inaugurating a highly prolific release schedule that saw them deliver two more albums, 'STATE OF MIND' and 'CORROSION', in as many months. As the mushrooming techno scene began cross-filtering with the harder-edged industrial sound, FRONTLINE ASSEMBLY set to constructing a more alternative dance-floor orientated approach on the 'GASHED SENSES' album. Subsequently becoming part of the bulging 'Wax Trax!' stable (also home to CLOCKDVA, MINISTRY and REVOLTING COCKS), the duo (now without BALCH) entered the 90's with the 'CAUSTIC GRIP' album. Following their dalliance with hypno-trance music, the stripped down FRONTLINE ASSEMBLY beefed up their sound with guitars on 1994's 'MILLENNIUM'. By 1997, LEEB was the sole remaining founder member after FULBER departed, his replacement, CHRIS PETERSON making his first appearance on 1998's '[FLA]VOUR OF THE WEAK'.

Album rating: THE INITIAL COMMAND (*4) / STATE OF MIND (*5) / CORROSION (*5) / DISORDER (*5) / CONVERGENCE (*5) / GASHED SENSES AND CROSSFIRE (*5) / CAUSTIC GRIP (*4) / TACTICAL NEURAL IMPLANT (*4) / THE BLADE (*4) / MILLENNIUM (*5) / HARD WIRED (*5) / LIVE WIRED (*4) / [FLA]VOUR OF THE WEAK (*5)

BILL LEEB – electronics (ex-SKINNY PUPPY) / **RHYS FULBER** – electronics / early member **MICHAEL BALCH** – synths

Dossier not iss.

Nov 87. (lp) *(ST 7547)* **FRONTLINE ASSEMBLY**
(cd-iss. Jun96 on 'Westcom'; 0864319-2)

K.K. not iss.

Dec 87. (lp/cd) *(KK 001/006CD)* **INITIAL COMMAND**
– Complexity / Intelligence dream / State / Insanity lurks nearby / Casualties / Ausgang zum Himmel / Nine times / Black march / No control / Slaughterhouse. *(re-iss. Feb92 on 'R.O.I.R.' lp/cd; KK 001/006CD) (cd re-iss. Jun93 on 'Third Mind'; TM 9175> (re-iss. Sep97 on 'Zoth Ommog'; ZOT 189CD)*

Dossier not iss.

Jan 88. (cd) *(DCD 9005)* **STATE OF MIND**
– First reprisal / Consequence / Burnt soul / Testimony / Landslide / Terminal power / Malignant fracture / Eastern voices / Resistance / Sustain upright / No tomorrow / And they shall bow. *(cd-iss. 1992 on 'Third Mind'; TM 9176-2)*

Third Mind Wax Trax!

Feb 88. (lp) *(TMLP 21)* <*WAX 038*> **CORROSION**
– Lurid sensation / Right hand of Heaven / Concussion / On the cross / Conflict / Controversy / Dark dreams / The wrack (part 2).

Jun 88. (m-lp) *(TMLP 24)* <*WAX 041*> **DISORDER**

Sep 88. (cd-ep) *(TMCD 002)* **CONVERGENCE / ON THE CROSS / COLLISION OF DEMONIC / RIGHT HAND OF HEAVEN**

Oct 88. (lp) *(TM 002)* <*WAX 048*> **CONVERGENCE**
– Lurid sensation / Obsession / Controversy / Right hand of Heaven / Conflict / Solitude of confinement / Body count / Die-sect / Headcase fargone / Collision / Concusion / On the cross / Dark dreams / The wrack (part 1). *(cd-iss. Oct92; TM 9114-2)*

Nov 88. (12"ep/3"cd-ep) *(TMS/TMCD 11)* **DIGITAL TENSION DEMENTIA**

May 89. (lp/cd) *(TMLP/TMCD 031)* <*WAX/+CD 7075*> **GASHED SENSES AND CROSSFIRE**
– No limit / Antisocial / Hypocrisy / Shutdown / Prayer / Digital tension dementia / Big money / Bloodsport / Foolsgame / Sedation. *(re-iss. cd Oct92; TM 9115-2)*

Jun 89. (12"ep/cd-ep) *(TMS/TMCD 43)* **NO LIMIT (damaged goods mix) / ('A'mixes)**

Third Mind Wax Trax!

Jun 90. (12"ep/cd-ep) *(TMS/+CD 052)* <*8637*> **ICEOLATE. / MENTAL DISTORTION**

Jul 90. (lp/cd) *(TM LP/CD 50)* <*WAX/+CD 7146*> **CAUSTIC GRIP**
– Resist / Victim / Overkill / Forge / Provision / Force fed / Iceolate / Threshold / Mental distortion / The chair. *(re-iss. cd Oct92; TM 9116-2)*

Feb 91. (12"ep/cd-ep) *(TMS/+CD 065)* <*8147*> **VIRUS**

— in Feb'92 as INTERMIX, they issued 'INTERMIX' instrumental cd.

— now with guests PAUL KENDALL and MARK STAGE

Third Mind Third Mind

Apr 92. (12"ep/cd-ep) *(<TM 2402/+CD)* **MINDPHASER / MINDPHASER / TOXIC / MUTILATE**

Apr 92. (cd/c) *(<TM 9118-2/-4>)* **TACTICAL NEURAL IMPLANT** May92
– Final impact / The blade / Mindphaser / Remorse / Bio-mechanic / Outcast / Gun / Lifeline.

Oct 92. (cd) *(TM 9119-2)* **THE BLADE**
– The blade (technohead) / Re-animate / Target / The blade (worldwide mix) / The blade (progress mix) / Heatwave / Laughing pain / The blade (blindfold).

Nov 92. (m-cd) <*TM 2392*> **THE BLADE**
– The blade (mix) / The blade (mix) / Re-animate / Laughing pain.

Roadrunner Roadrunner

Sep 94. (12"ep/cd-ep) *(<RR 2370-6/-3>)* **MILLENIUM EP**
– Millennium (100 years of decay) / Millennium / Transtime / Millennium (edit).

Oct 94. (cd) *(<RR 9019-2>)* **MILLENIUM**
– Vigilante / Millennium / Liquid separation / Search and destroy / Surface patterns / Victim of a criminal / Division of a criminal / This faith / Plasma Springs / Sex offender.

Jan 95. (cd-s) <*RR 2349*> **SURFACE PATTERNS (mixes)**

Off Beat Metropolis

Oct 95. (cd-ep) *(05522303)* <*14*> **CIRCUITRY / CIRCUITRY / EPIDEMIC / CIRCUITRY**
(cd-ep) *(05622300)* – (other 'A'mixes).

Nov 95. (cd) *(08522292CD)* <*15*> **HARD WIRED**
– Neologic spasm / Rebirth / Circuitry / Mortal / Modus operandi / Transparent species / Barcode / Condemned / Infra red combat.

Apr 96. (cd-s) *(05622423)* <*20*> **PLASTICITY / REPLICANT / PLASTICITY (alternative mix)**

Oct 96. (d-cd) *(088-43262CD)* <*26*> **LIVE WIRED (live)**
– Mortal / Vigilante / Circuitry / Bio-mechanic / Resist / Surface patterns / Plasticity / Modus operandi / Liquid seperation / Gun / Overkill / Millennium / Condemned / Mindphaser / Neologic spasm / Body count:- Mortal – Vigilante – Circuitry – Bio-mechanic – Iceolate – Resist – Surface patterns – Millennium – Gun – Modus operandi – Virus – Liquid separation – The blade – Overkill – Millennium – Laughing pain – Mindphaser – Body count – Plasticity.

— **CHRIS PETERSON** – electronics (p/t member) repl. FULBER who concentrated on production work

Nov 97. (cd-ep) <*MET 073*> **COLOMBIAN NECKTIE / DEADLOCK / ELECTROCUTION / COLOMBIA NECKTIE (extended)**
(re-iss. Feb98 on 'Westcom;; 05643783)

Feb 98. (cd) *(085-4379-2)* <*77*> **[FLA]VOUR OF THE WEAK** Jan98
– Corruption / Sado-masochist / Autoerotic / Colombian neck tie / Evil playground / Comatose / Life = Leben / Predator.

Aug 98. (d-cd) <*103*> **RE-WIND** (remixes by BILL LEEB and others)
– Predator / Aftermath / Electrocution / Life / Oblivion / Colombian necktie (loosed lips) / Comatose / Comatose / Predator / Evil playground / Life = Leben / Comatose / Comatose nacktie / Auto-erotic.

Nov 98. (cd-s) *(SPV 05643863)* <*86*> **COMATOSE (Valium 15mg) / COMATOSE / OBLIVION / COMATOSE (Prozac 75mg)** Jul98

– compilation, etc. –

Dec 93. (cd) *Dossier; (EFA 08451CD) / Cleopatra;* <*9410*> **TOTAL TERROR 1**

Dec 93. (cd) *Dossier; (EFA 08452CD) / Cleopatra;* <*9411*> **TOTAL TERROR 2** Jul94

Jan 96. (cd) *Westcom; (08422332CD) / Cleopatra;* <*9656*> **CORRODED DISORDER: THE COLLECTION** Nov95

Oct 97. (cd) *Roadrunner;* <*(RR 8790-2)*> **RECLAIMATION**

Sep 88. (cd) *Roadrunner; (<RR 8703>)* **MONUMENT** (1989-1993)

FRONT 242

Formed: Belgium ... 1981 by DANIEL B., recruiting JEAN-LUC DE MEYER and PATRICK CODENYS shortly after. Pioneers of the 80's Belgian 'New Beat' scene, the band's avant-garde industrial dance was shaped by its founders' design background; a cut 'n' paste collage of sound that incorporated loops, samples and repetitive, minimal rythms. While their initial recordings were vaguely similar to the synth hits of early 80's British acts, by the release of 'OFFICIAL VERSION' (1987), the band were well on the way to crystallising their dark JOY DIVISION/TEST DEPT. fusion. With an ever expanding cult following and increasing critical acclaim, along with the underground success of the 'HEADHUNTER (V1.0)' single, FRONT 242 finally dented the lower regions of the UK charts with 'TYRANNY FOR YOU' (1991). The album was preceeded by the doom-laden electro of the 'TRAGEDY FOR YOU' single, proffering a slightly more sinister take on the indie-dance sound of the day. As well as influencing the likes of MINISTRY and NINE INCH NAILS, FRONT 242 were favourites with Braintree's finest, The PRODIGY, who worked their voodoo magic on the 'RELIGION' single in 1993. The band were given another boost later that summer when they were invited to play on the American Lollapalooza Tour. • **Songwriters:** DANIEL and PATRICK. • **Trivia:** JEAN-LUC and RICHARD were also part of REVOLTING COCKS with AL JOURGENSEN of MINISTRY.

Album rating: BACK CATALOGUE compilation (*6) / OFFICIAL VERSION (*8) / FRONT BY FRONT (*8) / TYRANNY FOR YOU (*7) / 06:21:03:11 UP EVIL (*6) / 05:22:09:12 OFF (*6) / MUT@GE MIX@GE (*6)

DANIEL B. PROTHESE – keyboards / **RICHARD K. 23** – vocals, drum programmes / **JEAN-LUC DE MEYER** – vocals, drum machine / **PATRICK CODENYS** – keyboards

New Dance not iss.

Nov 81. (7") *(ND 002)* **PRINCIPLES. / BODY TO BODY**

May 82. (7") *(ND 005)* **U-MEN. / ETHICS**
(12"of above 4 tracks; issued Jan86; ND 009) (cd-ep Oct88; ND 009CD)

— DANIEL B. had now departed in 1984

Himalaya not iss.

Feb 86. (7"/12") *(OPS/12OPA 13)* **NO SHUFFLE. / BODY TO BODY**

— below releases on 'Mask' were issued much earlier in Belgium

Mask / not iss.

Nov 86. (lp) *(MK 001/+MC)* **GEOGRAPHY (1981-83)** –
– Operating tracks / With your cries / Art & strategy / Geography II / U-men / Dialogues / Least inkling / G.V.D.T. / Geography I / Black, white blues / Kinetics / Kampfbereit. *(cd-iss. 1988; CDMK 1) (cd-iss. Jun92 +=; MK 001CD)* – Rthics / Principles / Body to body.

Nov 86. (lp/c) *(MK 002)* **NO COMMENT (1984-85)** –
– Commando (mix) / S.Fr. no menklatura (pt.1 & 2) / Deceit / Lonely day / No shuffle / Special forces (demo). *(cd-iss. Jan87 on 'Mask'; CDMK 2) (cd-iss. Jun92 +=; MK 002CD)* – See the futire (live) / In November (live) / Special forces (demo) / Body to body.

Nov 86. (12"ep) *(MK 003)* **ENDLESS RIDDANCE** –
– Take one / Controversy / Between / Sample D. *(cd-ep.Aug88; MK 003CD)*

Nov 86. (12"ep) *(MK 004)* **POLITICS OF PRESSURE** –
– Commando (remix) / No shuffle / Don't crash / Funkahdafi.

Red Rhino Europe / Epic

Nov 86. (7"/ext.12") *(RRE/+T 003)* **INTERCEPTION: QUITE UNUSUAL. / AGGRESIVA** –
(cd-ep.Aug88; RRET 003CD)

Jan 87. (cd) *(RRECD 004)* **BACK CATALOGUE** (compilation 1982-85) –
(re-iss. Jun92 +=; RRE 004CD) – (extra tracks).

Jun 87. (lp/c/cd) *(RRE LP/MC/CD 005) <52405>* **OFFICIAL VERSION**
– What you have is what you get / Re-run / Television station / Aggressive due / Masterhits 1 & 2 / Slaughter / Quite unusual / Red team / Aggressive angst. *(cd re-iss. Jun92 +=; RRE 005CD)* – Quite unusual / Aggresiva / Masterblaster / Hypnomix.

Nov 87. (12"ep) *(WAX 036)* **MASTER HIT (pt.1 masterblaster mix). / MASTER HIT (pt.2 hypno mix) / MASTER HIT (pt.3 lp edited version)** –
(above on 'Waxtrax') (re-iss. Jan90 on 'Red Rhino Europe' 12"ep/c-ep/cd-ep; RRE T/C/CD 009)

Sep 88. (7"/12") *(RRE/+T 006)* **HEADHUNTER (V1.0). / WELCOME TO PARADISE (V1.0)** –
(cd-s+=) *(RRECD 006)* – Headhunter (V2.0).

Oct 88. (lp/c/cd) *(RRE LP/MC/CD 007) <52406>* **FRONT BY FRONT**
– Until death (do us part) / Circling overland / Im rhythmus bleiben / Felines / First in – first out / Blend the strengths / Headhunter V 3.0 / Work 01 / Terminal state. *(cd re-iss. Jun92 +=; RRE 007CD)* – Welcome to paradise / Head hunter / Never stop! / Work 242 N.off is N.off / Agony (until death) / Never stop! / Work 242.

Mar 89. (7") *(RRE 008)* **NEVER STOP (V1.1). / WORK 242** –
(12"+=/3"cd-s+=) *(RRE T/CD 008)* – Never stop (V1.0) / Work 242 N.off is N.off / Agony (until death).

— RICHARD was now only a live performer

Red Rhino Europe / Epic

Oct 90. (7") *(RRE 10)* **TRAGEDY FOR YOU. / ('A'short version)** –
(12"/cd-s) *(RRE T/CD 10)* – ('A'side) / ('A'long version) / ('A'slow-mo mix).
(12"/cd-s) *(RRE TX/CDX 10)* – ('A'neurodancer mix) / ('A'instrumental) / Trigger 3.

Jan 91. (cd/c/lp) *(RRE CD/MC/LP 11) <46998>* **TYRANNY FOR YOU** 49 95
– Sacrifice / Rhythm of time / Moldavia / Trigger 2 (anatomy of a shot) / Gripped by fear / Tragedy for you / The untold / Neurobashing / Leitmotiv 136 / Soul manager.

1991. (12") *<73767>* **RHYTHM OF TIME (Anti-G mix) / ('A'-Victor The Cleaner mix)** –

Apr 93. (12"ep/cd-ep) *(RRE 16 T/CD)* **RELIGION (7"mix) / RELIGION (pussy whipped mix) / RELIGION (the Prodigy bass under siege mix) / RELIGION (bitch slapper mix) / RELIGION (the Prodigy trance U down mix)** 46
(12"ep/cd-ep) *(RRE 16 R/CDR)* – Crapage (never hurry a Murray mix) / Crapage (the turd mix) / Religion (lovelace a go-go mix).
(cd-ep re-iss. Dec93; RRECDX 16)

May 93. (lp/c/cd) *(RRE 21/+MC/CD) <53433>* **06:21:03:11 UP EVIL** 44
– Crapage / Waste / Skin / Motion / Religion / Stratoscape / Hymn / Fuel / Melt / Flag / Mutilate. *(cd+=)* – (S)Crapage / Religion (pussy whipped mix).

Sep 93. (lp/c/cd) *(RRE 22/+MC/CD) <53902>* **05:22:09:12 OFF** 46
– Animal – Cage – Gate – Guide / Modern angel / Junkdrome / Serial killers don't kill their girlfriend / Skin – Fur coat / Genecide / Crushed / Offend / Animal zoo / Serial killers don't kill their boyfriend / Happiness – More angels / Crushed – Obscene / Melt – Again / Speed angels.

Nov 93. (12") *(RRE 18T)* **ANIMAL. / ('A'version)**

Nov 93. (m-cd) *(RRE 18CD)* **ANGELS VERSUS ANIMALS** (re-workings) –
– Animal (radio) / Angel (wipe out) / Serial killers don't kill their dog either / Modern angel (KMFDM remix) / Animal (extended) / Break me / Der verfluchte engel / L'ange modern / Born to breathe.

Mar 96. (12") *(RRE 20T)* **HAPPINESS (dance mix by UNDERWORLD). / RELIGION (trance u down mix by THE PRODIGY) / RHYTHM OF LIFE (victor the cleaner mix by THE ORB)**

Mar 96. (cd) *(RRE 20CD)* **MUT@GE.MIX@GE** –
– Rhythm of time / Happiness / Gripped by fear / Crapage / Junkdrome / Religion / Break me / Dancesoundtrackmusic.

Zoth Ommog / Metropolis

Jul 98. (d-lp/cd) *<ZOT 242/+CD> <MET 100>* **RE-BOOT: LIVE '98 (live)**
– Happiness / Master hit / Moldavia / Melt / Soul manager / No shuffle / In rhythmus bleiben / Crapage / Body to body / Religion / Headhunter / Welcome to Paradise / First in first out / Punish your machine.

Dec 98. (cd) *<MET 121>* **HEADHUNTER (17 various mixes)** –

– compilations, others, etc. –

Dec 92. (cd) *Guzzi; (GUZZ 1888)* **LIVE TARGET (live)** –

Nov 94. (cd) *Play It Again Sam; (<BIAS 242CD>)* **LIVE CODE 6413356-424225**
– Der verfluchte engel / Motion / Masterhit / Flag / Tragedy for you / Im rhythmus bleiben / Skin / Headhunter / Welcome to Paradise / Crapage / Soul manager / Punish your machine / Religion.

FUGAZI

Formed: Arlington, Virginia, USA . . . 1987 by IAN MacKAYE (now of Washington DC), who had the previous year featured on an album by EMBRACE (not the more recent outfit!). MacKAYE and drummer JEFF NELSON subsequently founded the 'Dischord' label, a bedrock of the Washington DC hardcore scene and an outlet for the pair's new band, MINOR THREAT. Completing the line-up with LYLE PRESLAR and BRIAN BAKER, this highly influential outfit releasing two singles in 1981, before they added STEVE HANSEN to boost their minimalist sound on the album, 'OUT OF STEP' (1983). A further album, the eponymous 'MINOR THREAT', contained the track 'STRAIGHT EDGE', a term which would be adopted by a generation of fans who followed MacKAYE and Co.'s example of abstinence and individual responsibility. Following their split, mainman MacKAYE formed FUGAZI, sharing vocal and songwriting duties with GUY PICCOTTO (ex-leader of RITES OF SPRING and INSURRECTION – the latter outfit having released a self-titled effort for 'Peaceville'). With the FUGAZI line-up crystallising around BRENDAN CANTY and JOE LALLY, they released two HENRY ROLLINS-produced mini-sets, the eponymous 'FUGAZI' and 'MARGIN WALKER' (1989), before fully realising their aggressively economical sound on the acclaimed 'REPEATER' (1990) album. Bringing to mind the once wilfully obscure vocals of DAVID THOMAS (PERE UBU) backed by the hardcore of NO MEANS NO, FUGAZI delivered a fourth set, 'STEADY DIET OF NOTHING' (1991), their perseverance paying off with a minor placing in the UK charts. Two years later, 'IN ON THE KILLTAKER' scored a deserved UK Top 30 and dominated the indie charts for months; despite persistent major label interest, FUGAZI have admirably refused to play the corporate game (how many bands can you say that about?). The mid 90's saw the release of the last FUGAZI album to date, 'RED MEDICINE', taking the staunchly independent hardcore crusaders into previously uncharted territory, i.e. the UK Top 20 (appropriately enough, the commercial behemoth that is the American music industry has so far prohibited the band's domestic success). • **Covered:** 12XU (Wire). • **Trivia:** MacKAYE produced the early '89 BEEFEATER single, 'House Burning Down'.

Album rating: 13 SONGS compilation (*8) / REPEATER (*8) / STEADY DIET OF NOTHING (*7) / IN ON THE KILLTAKER (*7) / RED MEDICINE (*6) / END HITS (*6) / Minor Threat: COMPLETE DISCOGRAPHY compilation (*8)

MINOR THREAT

IAN MacKAYE (b.1963) – vocals, guitar / **LYLE PRESLAR** – guitar / **BRIAN BAKER** – bass (ex-GOVERNMENT ISSUE) / **JEFF NELSON** – drums

Dischord / Dischord

Jun 81. (7"ep) *<Dischord 3>* **MINOR THREAT EP** –

Dec 81. (7",7"red) *<Dischord 5-Limp 41>* **IN MY EYES** –

— added **STEVE HANSEN** – bass (BAKER now on second guitar)

1983. (lp/c) *<(DISCHORD 10/+C)>* **OUT OF STEP**
– Betray / It follows / Think again / Look back and laugh / Sob story / No reason / Little friend / Out of step / Stand up / 12XU.

1984. (lp/c) *<(DISCHORD 12/+C)>* **MINOR THREAT**
– Filler / I don't wanna hear it / Seeing red / Straight edge / Small man, big mouth / Screaming at a wall / Bottled violence / Minor threat / In my eyes / Out of step (with the world) / Guilty of being white / Steppin' stone.

Aug 85. (7"ep) *<(DISCHORD 15)>* **SALAD DAYS / GOOD GUYS. / STUMPED / CASHING IN**

Mar 90. (cd) *<(DISCHORD 40)>* **COMPLETE DISCOGRAPHY** (compilation)

FUGAZI

IAN MacKAYE – vocals, guitar (ex-MINOR THREAT, ex-TEEN IDES, ex-EMBRACE) / **GUY PICCIOTTO** (b.1966) – vocals (ex-INSURRECTION, ex-RITES OF SPRING, ex-ONE LAST WISH) / **JOE LALLY** (b.1964, Rockville, Maryland) – bass / **BRENDAN CANTY** (b.1967) – drums

Dischord / Dischord

Dec 88. (m-lp/m-c) *<(DISCHORD 30/+C)>* **FUGAZI**
– Waiting room / Bulldog front / Bad mouth / Burning / Give me the cure / Suggestion / Glue man. *(re-iss. Apr98; same)*

Jul 89. (m-lp/m-c) *<(DISCHORD 35/+C)>* **MARGIN WALKER**
– Margin walker / And the same / Burning too / Provisional / Lockdown / Promises. *(cd-iss. Oct89 as '13 SONGS'+=; DIS 36)* – FUGAZI *(re-iss. Apr98; same)*

Feb 90. (7",7"green) *<(DISCHORD 43)>* **JOE #1. / BREAK IN / SONG #1**

Mar 90. (lp/c/cd) *<(DISCHORD 44/+C/CD)>* **REPEATER**
– Turnover / Repeater / Brendan /1 / Merchandise / Blueprint / Sieve-fisted grind / Greed / Two beats off / Styrofoam / Reprovisional / Shut the door. *(cd+=)* – Song #1 / Joe /1 / Break in. *(re-iss. Apr98; same)*

Aug 91. (lp/c/cd) *<(DISCHORD 60/+C/CD)>* **STEADY DIET OF NOTHING** 63
– Exit only / Reclamation / Nice new outfits / Stacks / Latin roots / Steady diet / Long division / Runaway return / Polish / Dear justice letter / K.Y.E.O. *(re-iss. Apr98; same)*

Jun 93. (m-lp/c/m-cd) *<(DIS 70/+C/D)>* **IN ON THE KILLTAKER** 24
– Facet squared / Public witness program / Returning the screw / Smallpox champion / Rend it / 23 beats off / Sweet and low / Cassavetes / Great cop / Walken's syndrome / Instrument / Last chance for a slow dance. *(re-iss. Apr98; same)*

May 95. (lp/cd) *(DIS 90/+CD) <EFA 17990-2>* **RED MEDICINE** 18
– Do you like me / Bed for the scraping / Latest disgrace / Birthday pony / Forensic scene / Combination lock / Fell, destroyed / By you / Version / Target / Back to base / Downed city / Long distance runner. *(re-iss. Apr98; same)*

— FUGAZI were put in backburner until their return below

Apr 98. (cd/c/lp) *<(DIS 110 CD/C/V)>* **END HITS** 47

– Break / Place position / Recap modotti / No surprise / Five corporations / Caustic acrostic / Closed captioned / Floating boy / Foreman's dog / Arpeggiation / Guilford fall / Pink frosty / F/D.

FULL TIME MEN (see under ⇒ FLESHTONES)

FU MANCHU

Formed: San Clemente, California, USA . . . late 80's by main songwriter SCOTT HILL, plus RUBEN ROMANO, MARK ABSHIRE and CHIVENS (the latter replaced by SCOTT VOTAW before any recordings). Fusing their blend of noisy garage metal (STOOGES to BLUE CHEER to MONSTER MAGNET), they initially released records for 'Bongload' (home of BECK!) before signing to 'Mammoth'. Their second album, 'IN SEARCH OF . . .' (1996), showed them taking a retro fixation to a wider market, the following year's limited edition cover of Blue Oyster Cult's 'GODZILLA', giving them Kerrang! cred. WHITE ZOMBIE's Y YUENGER produced their most recent material. • **Covers:** NOTHING DONE (. . . Barile).

Album rating: IN SEARCH OF . . . (*7) / THE ACTION IS GO (*7)

SCOTT HILL – vocals, guitar / **SCOTT VOTAW** – lead guitar / **MARK ABSHIRE** – bass / **RUBEN ROMANO** – drums, vocals

not iss. | Elastic

Dec 91. (7"ep) <*ELS* > **SENIORITIS / PINBUSTER. / EL DON / SIMCO** [-] [ ]

May 92. (7") <*ELS 005*> **PICK-UP SUMMER. / VANKHANA (ROLLIN' ROOMS)** [-] [ ]
(UK-iss.Oct96; same)

— now without VOTAW

Nov 92. (7"m) <*ELS 007*> **DON'T BOTHER KNOCKIN' (IF THIS VAN'S ROCKIN'). / SPACE SUCKER / OJO ROJO** [-] [ ]
(UK-iss.Oct96; same)

Bongload | Bongload

1994. (cd) <*BL 10*> **NO ONE RIDES FOR FREE** [-] [ ]
– Time to fly / Ojo rojo / Show and shine / Mega-bumpers / Free and easy (summer girls) / Superbird / Shine it on / Snakebellies. *(UK-iss.Feb97; same)*

— added **EDDIE GLASS** – lead guitar

Mar 95. (cd/lp) <*(BL 19 CD/LP)*> **DAREDEVIL** [ ] [ ] Jan95
– Trapeze freak / Tilt / Gathering speed / Coyote duster / Travel agent / Sleestak / Space farm / Lug / Egor / Wurkin' / Push button magic. *(re-iss. Feb97; same)*

— **BRAD DAVIS** – bass; repl. ABSHIRE who formed NEBULA

— **BRANT BJORK** – drums (ex-KYUSS) repl. ROMANO (also to NEBULA)

Mammoth | Mammoth

Mar 96. (cd/lp) <*(MR 0134-2/-1)*> **IN SEARCH OF . . .** [ ] [ ]
– Regal begal / Missing link / Asphalt risin' / Neptune's convoy / Redline / Cyclone launch / Strato-streak / Solid hex / The falcon has landed / Seahag / The bargain / Supershooter.

May 96. (7"red) *(MR 139-7)* **ASPHALT RISIN'. / CHEVY VAN** [ ] [ ]

Aug 96. (7"white) *(MR 157-7)* **MISSING LINK. / OJO ROJO** [ ] [-]

— produced by JOSH HOMME (of KYUSS, QUEENS OF THE STONE AGE)

— (below on 'Man's Ruin')

Apr 97. (10"green-ep) *(<MR 048>)* **GODZILLA. / MODULE OVERLOAD / LIVING LEGEND** [ ] [ ]

— **BOB BALCH** – guitars; repl. GLASS

Feb 98. (cd-ep) **EVIL EYE / MODULE OVERLOAD / SWAMI'S LAST COMMAND** [ ] [ ]

Mar 98. (7"; split with FATSO JETSON) *(SMS 14)* **JAILBREAK** [ ] [-]
(above issued on the 'Sessions' label)

Mar 98. (cd) *(557070-2)* <*3549 80173-2*> **THE ACTION IS GO** [ ] [ ] Nov97
– Evil eye / Urethene / Action is go / Burning road / Guardrail / Anodizer / Trackside hoax / Unknown world / Laserblast! / Hogwash / Grendel, snowman / Strolling astronomer / Saturn III / Nothing done.

Sep 98. (7") *(567750-7)* **JAILBREAK. / URETHANE** [ ] [ ]
(cd-s+=) *(567686-2)* – Coyote duster.

– compilations, etc. –

Nov 98. (cd/lp) *Elastic; (ELS 001 Cd/LP)* **RETURN TO EARTH 91-93** [ ] [ ] May97
– (the early singles)

FUN LOVIN' CRIMINALS

Formed: Manhattan, New York, USA . . . 1993 by former marine HUEY (of Puerto-Rican/Irish decent), FAST and STEVE. This hard-bitten NY rap-rock posse, took on the mantle of early BEASTIE BOYS, fusing it together with "acid"-ic jazz and the mandatory drug references. The slow-rollin' CHEECH & CHONG-ish 'SCOOBY SNACKS' and 'SMOKE 'EM', were highlights from their much touted debut album, 'COME FIND YOURSELF'. Initally unleashed in '96, it was virtually ignored in the States, although it created quite a stir in Britain almost a year on, when 'SCOOBY SNACKS' (sampling MOVEMENT OF FEAR by Tones On Tails!), 'THE FUN LOVIN' CRIMINAL' and 'THE KING OF NEW YORK' all had Top 30 success. In the summer of '97, they played major festivals including Scotland's 'T In The Park'. • **Songwriters:** Group, except WE HAVE ALL THE TIME IN THE WORLD (Hal David & John Barry) / I'M NOT IN LOVE (10cc). Sampled LYNYRD SKYNYRD's 'Freebird' on 'BOMBIN' THE L' and the soundtracks from QUENTIN TARANTINO's 'Reservoir Dogs' & 'Pulp Fiction' on 'SCOOBY SNACKS'. 'KING OF NEW YORK' used pieces of 'Insensatez' (Ray Brown Trio) & 'Also Sprach Zarathestra' (Deodato). • **Trivia:** In '97, FAST was quick off the mark in the romance stakes, netting REPUBLICA babe, SAFFRON.

Album rating: COME FIND YOURSELF (*8) / 100% COLOMBIAN (*7)

HUEY – vocals, guitar / **FAST** – bass, keyboards, trumpet / **STEVE** – drums

not iss. | Silver Spotlight

Nov 95. (cd-ep) <*36515*> **ORIGINAL SOUNDTRACK FOR HI-FI LIVING** [-] [ ]
– Passive – Aggressive / Blues for suckers / I can't get with that / Coney Island girl.

Chrysalis | Capitol

Jun 96. (7") *(CHS 5031)* **THE GRAVE AND THE CONSTANT. / BOMBIN' THE L / BLUES FOR SUCKERS** [72] [-]
(12"+=/cd-s+=) *(12/CD CHS 5031)* – King of New York.

Jul 96. (cd/c/lp) *(CD/TC+/CHR 6113)* <*35703*> **COME FIND YOURSELF** [7] [ ] Feb96
– The fun lovin' criminal / Passive – Aggressive / The grave and the constant / Scooby snacks / Smoke 'em / Bombin' the L / I can't get with that / King of New York / We have all the time in the world / Bear hug / Come find yourself / Crime and punishment / Methadonia / I can't get with that (schmoove version) / Coney Island girl.

Aug 96. (7") *(CHS 5034)* **SCOOBY SNACKS. / I'LL BE SEEING YOU** [22] [-]
(cd-s) *(CDCHS 5034)* – ('A'side) / Smoke 'em (live) / Come find yourself (live) / I can't get with that (live).
(cd-s) *(CDCHSS 5034)* – ('A'mixes).

Nov 96. (7"pic-d) *(CHSPD 5040)* <*58581*> **THE FUN LOVIN' CRIMINAL. / COME FIND YOURSELF (live BBC session)** [26] [ ] Feb97
(cd-s+=) *(CDCHSS 5040)* – ('A'-Hee Haw version) / The grave and the constant (Stephen Lironi 12"mix).
(cd-s) *(CDCHS 5040)* – ('A'side) / The grave and the constant (live) / Coney Island girl (live) / Scooby snacks.

Mar 97. (7"colrd) *(CHS 5049)* **KING OF NEW YORK. / SCOOBY SNACKS (Schmoove version)** [28] [-]
(cd-s+=) *(CDCHS 5049)* – ('A'-Jack Dangers complex mix).
(cd-s) *(CDCHSS 5049)* – ('A'side) / ('A'-Jack Dangers complex mix) / Blues for suckers / ('A'instrumental).

Jun 97. (7"m) *(CHS 5060)* **SCOOBY SNACKS. / I'M NOT IN LOVE / CONEY ISLAND GIRL (Schmoove version)** [12] [-]
(cd-ep) *(CDCHS 5060)* – (first 2 tracks) / Scooby snacks (live) / I can't get with that (live).
(cd-ep) *(CDCHSS 5060)* – (2nd & 3rd tracks) / Scooby snacks (Schmoove version) / Bombin the L (Schmoove version).

Chrysalis | Virgin

Aug 98. (c-s/cd-s) *(TC/CD CHS 5096)* **LOVE UNLIMITED / SHINING STAR / 10th STREET** [18] [-]
(cd-s) *(CDCHSS 5096)* – ('A'side) / ('A'mix) / ('A'instrumental).

Aug 98. (cd-s) 97463> **100% COLOMBIAN (mixes)** [-] [ ]

Aug 98. (cd/c/lp) *(497056-2/-4/-1)* <*23140*> **100% COLOMBIAN** [3] [ ]
– Up on the hill / Love unlimited / The view belongs to everyone / Korean bodega / Back on the block / 10th street / Sugar / South side / We are all very worried about you / All for self / All my time is gone / Big night out / Mini bar blues.

Oct 98. (c-s/cd-s) *(TC/CD CHS 5101)* **BIG NIGHT OUT / SUMMER WIND (with IAN McCULLOCH) / LOVE UNLIMITED** [29] [-]
(cd-s) *(CDCHSS 5101)* – ('A'side) / We are all very worried about you / My D (slight return).

FURNITURE

Formed: London, England . . . 1981 by JIM IRVIN, TIM WHELAN and HAMMY LEE. Following the release of a mini-set, 'WHEN THE BOOM WAS ON' (1983) on their own label ('The Guy From Paraguay'), the band signed to the small 'Survival' imprint as the ranks swelled with the arrival of MAYA GILDER and SALLY STILL. A further series of singles followed, collected together on a Japan-only long player, 'THE LOVEMONGERS'. The band's mid-80's signing to 'Stiff' looked set to thrust them into the limelight as the stark but casual pop genius of the 'BRILLIANT MIND' single saw FURNITURE narrowly miss the UK Top 20. Disaster struck, however, as 'Stiff' went into liquidation and a follow-up single – a revamped version of 'LOVE YOUR SHOES' – fell by the wayside. The attendant album, 'THE WRONG PEOPLE' (1986) fared little better as 'Z.T.T.' took up the reins and deleted the record after pressing an initial 30,000 copies. An extended bout of legal jousting ensued with FURNITURE eventually extricating themselves from the label and signing to 'Arista'. The resulting 'FOOD, SEX AND PARANOIA' (1989) album brought further critical praise although by this point the momentum from their earlier success had long since dissipated, strained record company relations developing yet again as the record sank without trace. The subsequent departure of GILDER was followed by a wholesale split in the early 90's with IRVIN and STILL both diversifying into music journalism while WHELAN and LEE formed TRANSGLOBAL UNDERGROUND. Victims of bad timing and even worse luck, FURNITURE were one of the 80's hidden gems, their off-beat charm fairly represented by 1991's compilation, 'SHE GETS OUT THE SCRAPBOOK'.

Album rating: SHE GETS OUT THE SCRAPBOOK compilation (*6)

JIM IRVIN (b.20 Jul'59, Chiswick, London) **- vocals / TIM WHELAN** (b.15 Sep'58) – guitar / **HAMMY LEE** (b. HAMILTON, 7 Sep'58) – drums

Guy From Paraguay | not iss.

Oct 80. (7") *(PARA 1)* **SHAKING STORY. / TAKE A WALK DOWN TOWN** [ ] [-]

— added **MAYA GILDER** (b.25 Apr'64, Poonak, India) – keyboards / **SALLY STILL** (b. 5 Feb'64) – bass

Survival not iss.

Aug 83. (m-lp) *(4C 1)* **WHEN THE BOOM WAS ON** [ ] [-]
Apr 84. (7") *(SUR 023)* **DANCING THE HARD BARGAIN. / ROBERT NIGHTMAN'S STORY** [ ] [-]
(12"+=) *(SUR12 023)* – ('A'extended).
Sep 84. (7"/12") *(SUR/+12 028)* **YOUR BRILLIANT MIND. / ROBERT NIGHTMAN'S STORY** [ ] [-]

Premonition not iss.

Nov 84. (7") *(PREM 2)* **LOVE YOUR SHOES. / THROW AWAY THE SCRIPTS** [ ] [-]
(12"+=) *(12PREM 2)* – Escape into my arms.
Jun 85. (12"ep) *(PREM 3)* **I CAN'T CRACK. / SWITCH OFF / PAUSE / BROKEN MY ARMS (mix)** [ ] [-]
Jan 86. (7") *(PREM 5)* **THE LOVE MONGERS. / TALKING KITTENS** [ ] [-]
(12"+=) *(12PREM 5)* – I can't crack.
Feb 86. (lp; cancelled) *(PREM 6)* **LOVEMONGERS** [-] [-]

Stiff not iss.

May 86. (7"/12") *(BUY/+IT 251)* **BRILLIANT MIND. / TO GUS** [21] [-]
Oct 86. (7") *(BUY 254)* **LOVE YOUR SHOES. / TURNSPEED** [ ] [-]
(12"+=) *(BUYIT 254)* – Me and you and the name.
Nov 86. (lp/c) *(SEEZ/ZSEEZ 64)* **THE WRONG PEOPLE** [ ] [-]
– I miss you / She gets out the scrapbook / Pierre's fight / Brilliant mind / Make believe I'm in / Love your shoes / Shake like Judy says / Let me feel your pulse / The sound of the bell / Escape into my arms / Answer the door.

Arista not iss.

Sep 89. (7") *(112 648)* **SLOW MOTION KISSES. / FORTY HOURS IN A DAY** [ ] [-]
(12"+=/cd-s+=) *(612/662 648)* – Brlliant mind / She gets out the scrapbook.
Feb 90. (cd/c/lp) *(260/410/210 377)* **FOOD, SEX AND PARANOIA** [ ] [-]
– One step behind you / Slow motion kisses / A taste of you / Swing tender / Plot to kiss what was / On a slow fuse / Song for a Doberman / Subway to the beach / Love me / Friend of a friend / Hard to say.
Feb 90. (7") *(112 844)* **ONE STEP BEHIND YOU. / IT CONTINUES** [ ] [-]
(12"+=) *(612 844)* – ('A'extended club mix).
(cd-s++=) *(662 844)* – International people.

— disillusioned by the music industry, they split Autumn 1990. IRVIN and STILL became journalists for The Melody Maker. GILDER went on to be part of the BBC, while LEE and WHELAN formed TRANSGLOBAL UNDERGROUND

– compilations, etc. –

Aug 91. (12") *Survival; (SURT 53)* **BRILLIANT MIND. /** [ ] [-]
Sep 91. (cd/c/lp) *Survival; (SUR CD/C/LP 013)* **SHE GETS OUT THE SCRAPBOOK – THE BEST OF FURNITURE** [ ] [-]
– Brilliant mind / Make believe I'm him / Forever / Song for a Doberman / Dancing the hard bargain / Love your shoes / Robert Nightman's story / Slow motion kisses / I miss you / How I've come to hate the moon / Bullet / Turnupspeed / One step behind you / She gets out the scrapbook.

BECAUSE

— **IRWIN** duo with **COLIN INGHAM** – piano

Haven not iss.

May 92. (cd/c/lp) *(HAVEN CD/MC/LP 1)* **MAD, SCARED, DUMB AND GORGEOUS** [ ] [-]
– Orientation / Her rhythm and her blues / A glass room / Song of all things / Archaeology / Love is coming / Stolen / Feast of Stephen / You don't forget / Mad scared dumb and gorgeous.

— IRWIN has since become editor for 'Mojo' magazine

FUTURE BIBLE HEROES
(see under ⇒ MAGNETIC FIELDS)

FUTURE SOUND OF LONDON

Formed: London, England . . . 1991 initially as HUMANOID by Manchester dance duo of GARY COCKBAIN and BRIAN DOUGANS, who created one of the all-time great acid-house records with the 1988 UK Top 20 hit, 'STAKKER HUMANOID'. This outfit spawned other projects; SEMI REAL, YAGE, METROPOLIS + ART SCIENCE TECHNOLOGY before 'Virgin' signed the duo as FUTURE SOUND OF LONDON in 1991. Early the following year, their fourth effort, the seminal 'PAPUA NEW GUINEA', was very reminiscent of ENO & DAVID BYRNE's proto-ambient work, although it possessed an overtly commercial appeal. 'LIFEFORMS', in 1994, was a 90 minute gothic soundscape epic which careered into the Top 10 and featured a guest vocal spot from LIZ FRASER (Cocteau Twins). To complete the year, they conducted a pioneering experiment by playing gigs down a ISDN line, issuing the results as a cd-album. In 1996, prior to the 'DEAD CITIES' double-album, they returned to the singles charts with the moody classic, 'MY KINGDOM'. • **Songwriters:** DOUGANS / COCKBAIN except FLAK; co-written w / ROBERT FRIPP plus WILLIAMS / GROSSART / THOMPSON / NIGHTINGALE. OMNIPRESENCE co-wriiten with KLAUS SCHULZE. MY KINGDOM sampled VANGELIS & ENNIO MORRICONE. • **Trivia:** Augmented on NOMAD's single 'Your Love Has Lifted Me', SYLVIAN-FRIPP's album 'Darshan' and APOLLO 440's 'Liquid Cool'.

Album rating: ACCELERATOR (*7) / ISDN (*7) / LIFEFORMS (*8) / DEAD CITIES (*7)

HUMANOID

GARRY COCKBAIN (b. Bedford, England) – keyboards / **BRIAN DOUGANS** (b.Scotland) – keyboards

Westside not iss.

Oct 88. (7") *(WSR 7)* **STAKKER HUMANOID. / (part 2)** [6] [-]
(12"+=/3"cd-s+=) *(WSR T/CD 12)* – ('A'-Omen mix).
(re-iss. 8 mixes Jul92 on 'Jumpin' & Pumpin' 12"ep/cd-ep; 12/CD TOT 27); hit No.40 (note 7"+c-s+cd-s; original part 2 was repl. by 'A'-Smart Systems remix)
Apr 89. (7") *(WSR 14)* **SLAM. / BASS INVADERS** [54] [-]
(12"+=/cd-s+=) *(WSR T/CD 14)* – ('A'dub mix) / ('A'-hip house).

Humanoid not iss.

Aug 89. (7"; HUMANOID featuring SHARON BENSON) *(HUM 1)* **TONIGHT. / ('A'mix)** [ ] [-]
(12"+=/cd-s+=) *(HUM/+T/CD 1)* – (3-'A'mixes).
Oct 89. (lp/c/cd) *(HUMAN/ZCHUM/CDHUM 1989)* **GLOBAL** [ ] [-]
Apr 90. (12"ep) *(HUMT 2)* **THE DEEP (3 mixes). / CRY BABY** [ ] [-]

Debut not iss.

1990. (12"; as ART SCIENCE TECHNOLOGY) *(DEBTX 3100)* **A.S.T. / ESUS FLOW** [ ] [-]

FUTURE SOUND OF LONDON

— same line-up as above.

Jumpin' & Pumpin' not iss.

1991. (12"ep) *(12TOT 11)* **PULSE EP** [ ] [-]
– Bring on the pulse / In the mind of a child / Hardhead / Pulse state.
1991. (12"ep) *(12TOT 15)* **PRINCIPLES OF MOTION EP** [ ] [-]
1991. (12"ep) *(12TOT 16)* **PULSE 3 EP** [ ] [-]
– Tingler / Owl / Bite the bullet / Calcium.
Feb 92. (12"ep) *(TOT 17)* **PAPUA NEW GUINEA (Dali mix) / ('A'-Dumb child of a Q mix) / ('A'-Qube mix)** [22] [ ]
(12"ep/c-ep/cd-ep) *(12/TC/CD TOT 17)* – (the remixes by Andy Weatherall & Graham Massey). *(re-iss. May95 12"cd-s; 12TOT/CDSTOT 17) (12" re-issjun97; 12TOT 17R)*
1992. (12"ep) *(12TOT 18)* **SMART SYSTEMS EP** [ ] [-]
1992. (12") *(12TOT 2S)* **PULSE 4** [ ] [-]
– I'm not gonna let you do it / The creator / Shrink / 18 space virus.
Jun 92. (cd/c/lp) *(CD/MC/LP TOT 2)* **ACCELERATOR** [75] [-]
– Expander / Stolen documents / While others cry / Calcium / It's not my problem / Papau New Guinea / Moscow / 1 in 8 / Pulse state / Central industrial. *(cd re-iss. Aug94 +=; CDTOT 2R)* – Expander (remix) / Moscow (remix).

— above featured **BASIL CLARKE** – vocals (ex-YARGO)

1992. (12"ep) **EXPANDER (remix). / MOSCOW (remix) / CENTRAL INDUSTRIAL (remix)** [ ] [ ]
(cd-ep+=) *– ('A'radio remix). (re-iss. Jul94 12"/cd-s; 12/CDS TOT 37); hit UK 72)*

Quigly not iss.

Jun 93. (lp/c; as AMORPHOUS ANDROGYNOUS) *(LP/TC EBV 1)* **TALES OF EPHIDRINA** [ ] [-]
– Swab / Mountain goat / In mind / Ephidrina / Auto pimp / Pod room / Fat cat.
Aug 93. (12"ep/cd-ep; as AMORPHOUS ANDRONGYNOUS) **ENVIRONMENTS** [ ] [-]

Virgin Astralwerks

Oct 93. (12"/c-s) *(VS T/C 1478)* **CASCADE. / ('A'-parts 2-5)** [27] [-]
(cd-s+=) *(VSCDT 1478)* – ('A'-short form mix).
May 94. (d-cd/c/d-lp) *(CD/TC+/V 2722)* **LIFEFORMS** [6] [-]
– Cascade / Ill flower / Flak / Bird wings / Dead skin cells / Lifeforms / Eggshell / Among myselves / / Domain / Spineless jelly / Interstat / Vertical pig / Cerebral / Life form ends / Vit / Omnipresence / Room 208 / Elaborate burn / Little brother.
Aug 94. (7"/c-s) *(VS P/C 1484)* **LIFEFORMS. / ('A'alternative mix)** [14] [-]
(12"+=/cd-s+=) *(VS/+T/CDT 1484)* – ('A'-paths 1-7).
(above featured LIZ FRASER (of COCTEAU TWINS) on vocals)
Dec 94. (cd/c/d-lp) *(CD/TC+/VX 2755)* **I.S.D.N.** [62] [-]
– Just a f***in' idiot / Far out son of lung and the ramblings of a madman / Appendage / Slider / Smokin' Japanese babe / You're creeping me out / Eyes-pop-skin explodes everybody's dead / It's my mind that works / Dirty shadows / Tired of bugs / Egypt / Are they fighting us? / Hot knives. *(re-iss. Jun95 with 3 new remixed tracks, hit No.44)*

— (In 1994, they were also at times, abbreviated to F.S.O.L.)

May 95. (12"ep/c-ep/cd-ep) *(VS T/C/CDT 1540)* **FAR OUT SON OF LUNG AND THE RAMBLINGS OF A MADMAN. / SNAKE HIPS / SMOKIN' JAPANESE BABE / AMOEBA** [22] [-]
Oct 96. (12") *(VST 1605)* **MY KINGDOM (parts 1-4)** [13] [ ]
(c-s+=/cd-s+=) *(VS C/CDT 1605)* – (part 5).
Oct 96. (cd/c) *(CD/TC+/V 2814)* **DEAD CITIES** [26] [-]
– Herd killing / Dead cities / Her face forms in summertime / We have explosive / Everyone in the world is doing something without me / My kingdom / Max / Antique toy / Quagmire / In a state of permanent abyss / Glass / Yage / Vit drowning / Through your gills I breathe / First death in the family. *(d-cd-iss. ; CDVX 2814)*
Apr 97. (12"/cd-s) *(VST/VSCDT 1616)* **WE HAVE EXPLOSIVE. / ('A'mix)** [12] [-]
(cd-s) *(VSCDX 1616)* – ('A'mixes).

FUXA

Formed: Detroit, Michigan, USA . . . 1995 by former WINDY & CARL member, RANDALL NIEMAN who teamed up with RYAN ANDERSON (ex-ASHA VIDA). Having both set up independent labels ('Mind Expansion', 'An I', etc), NIEMAN and ANDERSON collaborated on a series of 7" singles/EP's, the cream of these collected on 1996's debut set, '3 FIELD ROTATION'. Very much in the retro space-rock tradition, FUXA were orbiting a vintage musical world of analogue Moog synths, Hammond, etc, lying somewhere between SPACEMEN 3 and HAWKWIND. Later in the year, fresh material surfaced in the shape of 'VERY WELL ORGANIZED', the pair taking a smoother flightpath into trance-inducing spacey ambience.

Album rating: 3 FIELD ROTATION (*5) / VERY WELL ORGANIZED (*7)

RANDALL NIEMAN – guitar, Moog synth, samples (ex-WINDY & CARL) / **RYAN ANDERSON** – drums, Moog, bass / with also **ERIK MORRISON + JESSE PERCIVAL**

An I | An I – Mind Expansion

Sep 96. (cd/lp) <(IRE 101-2/-1)> **3 FIELD ROTATION** (compilation of three 7"EP's + two new) Jan96
– " / 100 white envelopes / Tokearian parade / Main sequence diffusion – Photon – Lojolla / Subway short – Free your soul – First abductions / Dreamlanding / The anvil / (+2).

Mar 97. (cd/3x12") <(IRE 106-2/-2)> **VERY WELL ORGANIZED** Nov96
– At your leisure / Latitude – Longitude / Unexplained transmission repair / Witness to natural invention / 3 cp / Pangaea / Outer drive / Pleasant orbitings / Homonym hymn / Unified frequency.

not iss. | Darla

Nov 97. (cd-ep) <033> **VENOY EP** -

—— (split a single with the group, BRIGHT, also on 'Darla')

Mind Expansion | Mind Expansion

May 98. (cd-ep) <(ME 024)> **ACCRETION** May98

FUZZTONES

Formed: New York, USA . . . 1982 out of TINA PEEL, by RUDI PROTRUDI and DEB O'NAIR. In the closing years of the 70's, the aforementioned punk band (with rhythm section, JIM NASTICS and JACKSON PLUGS) released one self-financed US 7", 'FIFI GOES POP' / 'WEEKEND GEEK' and an EP, 'PYJAMA PARTY', before contributing to a string of various artists collections. With a line-up completed by ELAN PORTNOY, MICHAEL JAY and IRA ELLIOT (who replaced initial stickman, MICHAEL PHILLIPS), The FUZZTONES made their UK vinyl debut in late '84 with the live set, 'LEAVE YOUR MIND AT HOME'. While they shared a similar trash aesthetic as fellow Americans, The CRAMPS, the group were more obsessed with garage-psych freakouts than 50's R'n'R and blues, as reflected in their choice of cover material. Follow-up studio set, 'LYSERGIC EMANATIONS', (1984) offered up more chemically enhanced nuggets although save for a further couple of singles, The FUZZTONES were put on hold in the mid-80's as RUDI, MICHAEL and MIKE CZEKAJ worked on an instrumental project, 'DRIVE IT HOME' (released in 1988 under the moniker of LINK PROTRUDI & THE JAYMEN). New FUZZTONES material eventually appeared in 1989 in the shape of the 'IN HEAT' album on Beggars Banquet offshoot, 'Situation 2', although PROTRUDI subsequently recruited an all-new line-up (featuring CZEKAJ, PHIL ARRIAGADA, RAHUL SARIPUTRA and even former LOVE genius, ARTHUR LEE in a guest capacity) for 1991's 'BRAINDROPS' album on the aptly titled 'Music Maniac' label. While PROTRUDI & Co. finally called a halt to proceedings the following year, the mysterious LINK PROTRUDI & THE JAYMEN reappeared with an EP in '97. • **Covers:** HIGHWAY 69 (Bob Dylan) / YOU'RE GONNA MISS ME (13th Floor Elevators) / PSYCHOTIC REACTION (Count Five) / 7 AND 7 IS (Love) / MY LITTLE RED BOOK (Bacharach-David) / HELLO I LOVE YOU (Doors) / 99th FLOOR (Moving Sidewalks) / JACK THE RIPPER (Screamin' Lord Sutch) / I CAN'T CONTROL MYSELF (Troggs) / etc.

Album rating: LEAVE YOUR MIND AT HOME (*4) / LYSERGIC EMANATIONS (*6) / LIVE IN EUROPE (*5) / CREATURES THAT TIME FORGOT (*5) / IN HEAT (*3) / BRAINDROPS (*4) / FLASHBACKS compilation (*6)

RUDI PROTRUDI – vocals, guitar (ex-TINA PEEL, ex-DEVIL DOGS) / **DEB O'NAIR** – organ (ex-TINA PEEL) / **ELAN PORTNOY** – guitar / **MICHAEL JAY** – bass / **IRA ELLIOT** – drums; repl. MICHAEL PHILLIPS

Midnight Int. | not iss.

Nov 84. (m-lp) *(MIRLP 105)* **LEAVE YOUR MIND AT HOME (live)** -
Voices green and purple / Blackout at Cretely / No friend of mind / We're pretty quick / Flash on you / The bag I'm in / You burn me up and down.

A.B.C. | Pink Dust

Mar 85. (lp) *(ABCLP 4)* <72123> **LYSERGIC EMANATIONS**
– 1-2-5 / Gotta get some / Journey to tyme / Ward 81 / Radar eyes / Cinderella / Highway 69 / Just once / Living sickness / She's wicked. *(pic-lp Sep88; ABCLP 4P) (re-iss. Feb91 on 'Music Maniac' lp/cd+=; MM LP/CD 036)* – (next singles).

Jul 85. (7") *(ABCS 006)* **SHE'S WICKED. / EPITAPH FOR A HEAD** -
(12"+=) *(ABCS 006T)* – Bad news travels fast.

Jul 86. (12"ep) *(ABCS 011T)* **BAD NEWS TRAVELS FAST / GREEN SLIME. / STRYCHNINE / AS TIME'S GONE** -

Music Maniac | not iss.

Mar 87. (lp) *(MM 006)* **LIVE IN EUROPE (live)**
– Bad little woman / Blues theme / Cellar dwellar / Love at psychedelic velocity / 1523 Blair / Run chicken run / 13 women / 7 and 7 is / Gotta get some / Journey to tyme / Human fly / Psychotic reaction / I'm loose.

Jan 88. (lp; as LINK PROTRUDI & THE JAYMEN) *(MMLP 009)* **DRIVE IT HOME** -
– Avalanche / Backfire / Chicken choke / The stroll / Slinky / Mr. Guitar / Commanche / No stopping / Orbit / Rawhide / Bodacious / Hanky panky / Psyclone / Bandito / Chaquita / Rumble. *(re-iss. Oct97 on 'Skoda'; 006)*

—— above was instrumental featuring **RUDI, MICHAEL + MIKE CZEKAJ**

Apr 88. (12"ep) *(MM 013S)* **NINE MONTHS LATER / GIRL YOU CAPTIVATE ME. / CHEYENNE RIDER / GREATEST LOVE IN THE WORLD** -
(re-iss. Sep89 on 'Situation 2' 7"ep/10"ep/12"ep; SIT 061/+P/T)

Feb 89. (lp) *(MMLP 020)* **CREATURES THAT TIME FORGOT** (compilation) -
– 99th floor / Riot on Sunset Strip / Don't do it some more / Shooz wicked / The thing / Fabian lips / Brand new man / Action woman / Green slime / Bad news travels fast / Ward 81 / The witch.

Situation 2 | Beggars Banquet

Jun 89. (7") *(SIT 058)* **HURT ON HOLD. / JACK THE RIPPER** -
(12"+=) *(SIT 058T)* – I can't control myself.

Jun 89. (lp/c/cd) *(SITU/+C/CD 23)* <9808-1/-4/-2> **IN HEAT**
– In heat / Cheyenne rider / Black box / It came in the mail / Heathen set / What you don't know / Nine months later / Everything you got / Shame on you / Me Tarzan, you Jane / Hurt on hold / Charlotte's remains.

Mar 90. (12"ep/cd-ep) *(SIT 069 T/CD)* **ACTION EP** -
– Action speaks louder than words / (+3)

—— **PROTRUDI** enlisted an entire new band **CHRIS HARLOCK** – bass / **"MAD" MIKE CZEKAJ** – drums (ex-LINK PROTRUDI & THE JAYMEN) / with back-up **PHIL ARRIAGADA** – guitar / **RAHUL SARIPUTRA** – sitar / + guest vocalists **ARTHUR LEE, SEAN BONNIWELL + JACQUI LYNN**

Music Maniac | not iss.

Nov 91. (cd/lp) *(MM CD/LP 044)* **BRAINDROPS** -
– Third times the charm / Skeleton farm / Romilar D / Fear / Rise / Ghost clinic / 7 and 7 is / Look for the question mark / I looked at you / The people in me / All the kings horses / Blackout.

—— split at the end of the year

– compilations, etc. –

1994. (cd) *Music Maniac;* <MM 052> **LYSERGIC EJACULATIONS, LIVE IN EUROPE 1991 (live)** -

Nov 97. (cd)(d-lp) *Sundazed;* <(SC 11045)>*(LP 5044)* **FLASHBACKS**
– 1-2-5 / Nine months later / Heathen set / I never knew / Bad news travels fast / Charlotte's remains / Ward 81 / Strychnine / In heat / All the kings horses / Rise / Down on the street / Look for the question mark / She's my witch / Blue's theme / Blood from a stone / Hurt on hold / Romilar D / I'm the wolfman / She's wicked / Cinderella.

Sep 98. (7") *Sundazed; (SEP 139)* **ONE GIRL MAN. / I'M GONNA MAKE YOU MINE / YOU MUST BE A WITCH**

FUZZY

Formed: Boston, Massachusetts, USA . . . early 90's by HILKEN MANCINI, CHRIS TAPPIN and WINSTON BRAMAN. Boosted by the addition of LEMONHEADS drummer, DAVE RYAN – who'd come on board after checking out the band at the LEMONHEADS' studio – FUZZY secured a series of dates backing DINOSAUR JR. As it turned out, RYAN was absent with touring commitments to his other band, fill-in sticksman, "TOM THE MONK", proving a less than suitable replacement as TAPPIN and BRAMAN came to the brink of onstage fisticuffs. Help came in the unlikely form of SOUL ASYLUM man, DAVE PIRNER, the band's reputation saved from ruin before they'd even released their eponymous debut album. The accompanying single, 'FLASHLIGHT', narrowly missed an NME Single Of The Week award, while FUZZY's femme spangle-pop secured them a place – with indie ballad, 'CHRISTMAS' – on 'Fierce Panda's girl-powered Various Artists EP, 'FROM GREER TO ETERNITY'. In 1996, they moved on up to 'East West' (through 'Tag' records) and delivered a follow-up, 'ELECTRIC JUICES'.

Album rating: FUZZY (*6) / ELECTRIC JUICES (*7)

HILKEN MANCINI – vocals / **CHRIS TAPPIN** – vocals, guitar / **WINSTON BRAMAN** – bass / **DAVID RYAN** – drums (of LEMONHEADS)

Seed | Seed

Jun 94. (7"m) *(SEED 009)* **FLASHLIGHT. / THURBER / COUNTRY SONG**

Jul 94. (cd/lp) <(14254-2/-1)> **FUZZY**
– Flashlight / Bill / Postcard / Now I know / 4 wheel friend / Almond / Lemon ring / Rock song / Intro / Sports / Severe / Got it / Surfing / Girlfriend.

Apr 95. (7") *(SEED 011)* **LEMON RIND. / CHRISTMAS** -
(cd-s+=) *(SEEDCD 011)* – Thurber.

East West | Tag-Atlantic

May 96. (cd/c) <(7567 92626-2/-4)> **ELECTRIC JUICES**
– Glad again / Drag / Throw me a bone / Girl don't tell me / Miss the mark / Sleeper / Flavor / It started today / One request / Someday / Pop a dime / Uncut / Christmas.

—— about to release a third set in '99

GADGETS (see under ⇒ THE THE)

Diamanda GALAS

Born: 29 Aug'55, San Diego, California, USA – although raised by Greek parents. A classically trained opera singer, GALAS' occult banshee glass-shattering vocal style (using a multi-mic stage set-up!) was supposedly based on the Schrei (shriek) opera of German expressionism. Finding a sympathetic home at 'Y Records' (home of PIGBAG), she made her UK vinyl debut with the characteristically intense 'LITANIES DU SATAN' (1982). In 1984 a German-only eponymous set – containing two more lengthy tales of historical human suffering – became her second release before she subsequently signed to UK's large independent, 'Mute'. GALAS' third set, 'THE DIVINE PUNISHMENT' (1986), was another morally challenging listen, the first of a trilogy, 'Masque Of The Red Death', written as a reaction to the spread of AIDS (her brother had recently died from the disease). Part two of the series, 'SAINT OF THE PIT', was premiered at Austria's ARS Electronica Festival on the 23rd June, 1986 and released on vinyl later that November. The final instalment, meanwhile, was unveiled two years later as 'YOU MUST BE CERTAIN OF THE DEVIL', GALAS also working with MAYO THOMPSON and SIMON TURNER on the scores for controversial films, 'Caravaggio' and 'The Last Days Of England'. The following decade saw the uncompromising tonsil-rupturing lady of avant-rock art deliver a further string of shock-goth albums with her trademark dark religious overtones and song titles that any black/death-metal group would DIE! for. Reportedly a good friend of ex-LED ZEPPELIN duo, PAGE and PLANT, GALAS also collaborated with JOHN PAUL JONES on a 1994 set, 'THE SPORTING LIFE'. • **Covered:** MY LOVE WILL NEVER DIE + INSANE ASYLUM (Willie Dixon) / I PUT A SPELL ON YOU (Screamin' Jay Hawkins) / REAP WHAT YOU SOW (Mike Bloomfield – Nick Gravenites) / WERE YOU THERE WHEN THEY CRUCIFIED MY LORD (Roy Acuff) / GLOOMY SUNDAY (Carter-Javor-Seress) / DARK END OF THE STREET (Moman-Penn) / IRON LADY (Phil Ochs) / THE THRILL IS GONE (BB King) / MY WORLD IS EMPTY WITHOUT YOU (hit; Supremes) / I'M GONNA LIVE THE LIFE (Lee Dosey) / 25 MINUTES TO GO (Shel Silverstein) / DEATH LETTER (. . . House) / KEIGOME KEIGOME (Gatsos-Xarhakos) / + a number of traditional work-outs LET MY PEOPLE GO + BALM IN GILEAD – SWING LOW, SWEET CHARIOT + SEE THAT MY GRAVE IS KEEP CLEAN.

Album rating: LITANIES DU SATAN (*4) / DIAMANDA GALAS (*6) / THE DIVINE PUNISHMENT (*5) / SAINT OF THE PIT (*5) / YOU MUST BE CERTAIN OF THE DEVIL (*5) / PLAGUE MASS (*5) / THE SINGER (*5) / VENA CAVA (*5) / THE SPORTING LIFE (*5) / SCHREI X LIVE (*5)

DIAMANDA GALAS – vocaaarrgghhls!!!

Y — not iss.

Mar 82. (lp) *(Y 18)* **LITANIES DU SATAN** ☐ [-]
– Litanies of Satan / Wild women with steak knives (the homocidal love song for solo scream). *(re-iss. Apr89 on 'Fine Line' lp/cd; ISO/CDIS 001) <US-iss.1989 on 'Restless-Mute' lp/c/cd; 71419-1/-4/-2>*

Metalanguage — not iss.

Oct 84. (lp) **DIAMANDA GALAS** [-] [-] German

Mute — Restless

Jul 86. (lp) *(STUMM 27)* **THE DIVINE PUNISHMENT** ☐ [-]
<US-iss.1989 on 'Restless-Mute'; 71417>

Nov 86. (lp) *(STUMM 33)* **SAINT OF THE PIT** ☐ [-]
– La trezieme revient / E-eaoyme / L'heautontimoroumenos / Artemis / Cris d'aveugle. *(cd-iss. Apr88 +=; CDSTUMM 33) <US-iss.1989 on 'Restless-Mute' 71418>*

Apr 88. (12") *(12MUTE 75)* **DOUBLE-BARREL PRAYER. / MALADICTION / DOUBLE-BARREL PRAYER** ☐ [-]

Jun 88. (cd/lp) *(CD+/STUMM 46) <71403>* **YOU MUST BE CERTAIN OF THE DEVIL** ☐ ☐
– Swing low, sweet chariot / Double-barrel prayer / Let's not chat about despair / Birds of death / You must be certain of the Devil / Let my people go / Malediction / The Lord is my shepherd.

Mute — Mute

Apr 91. (cd/lp) *(CD+/STUMM 83) <61034>* **PLAGUE MASS (1984 – END OF THE EPIDEMIC) (live)** ☐ ☐
– Were you a witness / This is the law of the plague / I wake up and see the face of the Devil / Confessional (give me sodomy or give me death) / How shall our judgement be carried out upon the wicked / Let us praise the masters of slow death / Consecration / Sono L'Antichristo / Cris D'Aveugle: Blind man's cry / Let my people go.

Apr 92. (cd/lp) *(CD+/STUMM 103) <61278>* **THE SINGER (live)** ☐ ☐
– My love will never die / Reap what you sow / Were you there when they crucified my Lord? / Gloomy Sunday / Balm in Gilead – Swing low, sweet chariot / Insane asylum / I put a spell on you / Let my people go / See that my grave is kept clean / Judgement day.

Sep 93. (cd/lp) *(CD+/STUMM 119) <61459>* **VENA CAVA** ☐ ☐
– Vena Cava (parts 1-?).

Aug 94. (cd-s; DIAMANDA GALAS & JOHN PAUL JONES) *(CDMUTE 171) <60171>* **DO YOU TAKE THIS MAN? / HEX / DO YOU TAKE THIS MAN?** ☐ ☐

Sep 94. (cd/lp; DIAMANDA GALAS & JOHN PAUL JONES) *(CD+/STUMM 127) <61672>* **THE SPORTING LIFE** ☐ ☐
– Skotoseme / Do you take this man? / Dark end of the street / You're mine / Tony / Devil's rodeo / The sporting life / Baby's insane / Last man down / Hex.

Sep 96. (cd) *<(CDSTUMM 146)>* **SCHERI X LIVE / SCHERI 27** ☐ ☐
– Do room / I-I am – Dreams / M dis I / O.P.M. / Abasement / Headbox / Cunt / Hepar / Coitum / Vein / M dis II / Smell / Hee shock die // Do room / II / M dis I / O.P.M. / Headbox / Cunt / Hepar / Vein / M dis II / Smell / Hee shock die.

Mute — Asphodel

May 98. (cd/d-lp) *(CD+/STUMM 163) <984>* **MALEDICTION AND PRAYER (live)** ☐ ☐
– Iron lady / The thrill is gone / My world is empty without you / Abel et Cain / Death letter / Supplica a mia madre / Insane asylum / Si la muerte / 25 minutes to go / Keigome keigome / I'm gonna live the life / Gloomy Sunday.

– compilations, etc. –

Dec 88. (cd) *Mute; (GALAS 001)* **MASQUE OF THE RED DEATH TRILOGY** ☐ ☐
– (THE DIVINE PUNISHMENT / SAINT OF THE PIT / YOU MUST BE CERTAIN OF THE DEVIL)

GALAXIE 500

Formed: Boston, Massachusetts, USA . . . mid-80's by ex-Harvard College student, DEAN WAREHAM, along with NAOMI YANG and DAMON KRUKOWSKI. The trio soon relocated to New York where they met KRAMER (ex-BUTTHOLE SURFER and Shimmy Disc label boss), who produced their 1987 album, 'TODAY'. Two years later, they signed to 'Rough Trade' and with KRAMER at the controls yet again, unleashed their flawed epic, 'ON FIRE' (1989). Lo-Fi anti-rock psychedelia reminiscent of JONATHAN RICHMAN being backed by The VELVET UNDERGROUND, the album's minimalist appeal subsequently gained the band many fans in the UK, although their homebase critics lambasted WAREHAM's limited vocals at every opportunity. He and the other two (DAMON & NAOMI) went their separate ways early in 1991 after their third album, 'THIS IS OUR MUSIC' (1990), failed to cut much critical ice. WAREHAM went on to produce his mates, MERCURY REV ('Car Wash Hair' EP), before becoming part of 'Elektra'-signed indie supergroup, LUNA. After a patchy, unsettling debut, 'LUNAPARK' (1992), his band – who comprised JUSTIN HARWOOD (ex-CHILLS) ans STANLEY DEMESKI (ex-FEELIES) – made good with the more enchanting 1994 follow-up, 'BEWITCHED', a record which enticed veteran VELVET UNDERGROUND guitarist, STERLING MORRISON, out of retirement. Another famous guest was TOM VERLAINE (ex-TELEVISION), a major influence on the band's sound (similar to GALAXIE 500, although a little lighter and jazzier) alongside LOU REED. A further two albums, 'PENTHOUSE' (1995) and 'PUP TENT' (1997), also pleased the faithful, STEREOLAB's LAETITIA SADIER guesting on the former. Meanwhile, DAMON & NAOMI (also known as PIERRE ETOILE around the early 90's) remained with KRAMER, the man producing their 1992 debut album, 'MORE SAD HITS'. As well as helping out on two mid-90's albums, 'NO EXCESS IS ABSURD' and 'WILL THEY TURN YOU ON OR WILL THEY TURN ON YOU', with their friends (WAYNE ROGERS and KATE BIGGAR) in retro-psychedelic outfit, MAGIC HOUR, D&N released a follow-up 'Sub Pop' album, 'THE WONDROUS WORLD OF . . .' (1995). It would be a few more years before a third long-player, 'PLAYBACK SINGERS', appeared on 'Rykodisc' in 1998. • **Songwriters:** Group, except CHEESE AND ONIONS (Rutles) / VICTORY GARDEN (Red Crayola) / LISTEN, THE SNOW IS FALLING (Yoko Ono) / DON'T LET OUR YOUTH GO TO WASTE (Jonathan Richman) / HERE SHE COMES NOW (Velvet Underground) / CEREMONY (New Order) / ISN'T IT A PITY (George Harrison). LUNA covered INDIAN SUMMER (Beat Happening) / RIDE INTO THE SUN (Velvet Underground) / THAT'S WHAT YOU ALWAYS SAY (Dream Syndicate) / SEASON OF THE WITCH (Donovan) / OUTDOOR MINER (Wire) / NO REGRETS (Tom Rush) / THANK YOU FOR SENDING ME AN ANGEL (Talking Heads) / IN THE FLESH (Blondie). CAGNEY & LACEE covered BORDERLINE (Madonna) / BE MINE (Martin Rev) / LOVIN' YOU (Minnie Riperton) / SIX FEET OF CHAIN + BY THE WAY (Lee Hazlewood) / THE LAST GOODBYE (Marty Robbins) / GREYHOUND GOIN' SOMEWHERE (Lee Dorsey) / FOR THE SAKE OF THE CHILDREN (Baskin-Reicheg) / MEMPHIS (Otis Blackwell) / I'M NOT SAYIN' (Gordon Lightfoot). MAGIC HOUR covered AMERICA (Traffic Sound). DAMON & NAOMI covered: TRANSLUCENT CARRIAGES (with Tom Rapp) / LIFE

WILL PASS YOU BY (Chris Darrow) / WHISPERING PINES (Band) / WHO AM I? (. . . McDonald).

Album rating: TODAY (*8) / ON FIRE (*7) / THIS IS OUR MUSIC (*8) / GALAXIE 500 boxed compilation (*8) / COPENHAGEN live (*5) / Luna: LUNAPARK (*6) / BEWITCHED (*8) / PENTHOUSE (*7) / PUP TENT (*6) / Damon & Naomi: MORE SAD SONGS (*6) / THE WONDROUS WORLD OF . . . (*6) / PLAYBACK SINGERS (*6) / Cagney & Lacee: SIX FEET OF CHAIN (*5) / Magic Hour: NO EXCESS IS ABSURD (*6) / WILL THEY TURN YOU ON OR WILL THEY TURN ON YOU (*6)

(MICHAEL) DEAN WAREHAM (b. 1 Aug'63, Wellington, New Zealand) – vocals, guitar / **NAOMI YANG** (b.15 Sep'64) – bass, vocals / **DAMON KRUKOWSKI** (b. 6 Sep'63) – drums, percussion

not iss. Aurora

May 88. (7",7"blue) <*AU 001*> **TUGBOAT. / KING OF SPAIN**

Feb 89. (lp) <*AU 002*> **TODAY**
– Flowers / Pictures / Parking lot / Don't let our youth go to waste / Temperature's rising / Oblivious / It's getting late / Instrumental / Tugboat. *(UK-iss.Sep89 on 'Schemer' lp/cd+=; 8905/+CD)* – King of Spain / Crazy. *(UK re-iss. Oct89 on 'Shimmy Disc' cd/lp; SDE 8908/+LP) (UK re-iss. Sep91 on 'Rough Trade' lp/c/cd; ROUGH/+C/CD 266) (cd re-iss. Apr97 on 'Rykodisc'+=; RCD 10356)* – King of Spain.

Rough Trade Rough Trade

Oct 89. (lp/c/cd) *(ROUGH/+C/CD 146)* <*ROUGHUS 74/+C/CD*> **ON FIRE**
– Blue thunder / Tell me / Snowstorm / Strange / When will you come home / Decomposing trees / Another day / Leave the planet / Plastic bird / Isn't it a pity. *(re-iss. Sep91 w/cd-ep+=; ROUGH 146L)* – Blue thunder / Victory garden / Ceremony / Cold night. *(cd re-iss. Apr97 on 'Rykodisc'+=; RCD 10357)*

Feb 90. (12"ep/cd-ep) *(RTT 246/+CD)* **BLUE THUNDER / VICTORY GARDEN. / CEREMONY / COLD NIGHT**

Jun 90. (7"ltd) *(CAFF 8)* **RAIN (live). / DON'T LET OUR YOUTH GO TO WASTE (live)**
(above 45 on 'Caff' records)

Sep 90. (12"/cd-s) *(RTT 249/+CD) / Gasatanka; <6083>* **FOURTH OF JULY. / HERE SHE COMES NOW**

Oct 90. (lp/c/cd) *(ROUGH/+C/CD 156)* <*ROUGHUS 86/+C/CD*> **THIS IS OUR MUSIC**
– Fourth of July / Hearing voices / Spook / Summertime / Way up high / Listen, the snow is falling / Sorry / Melt away / King of Spain, part two. *(other cd-iss. ; CDR 156L) (cd re-iss. Apr97 on 'Rykodisc'+=; RCD 10358)* – Here she comes now.

— In Spring '91, DEAN WAREHAM departed to work on solo project and guest for MERCURY REV. DAMON & NAOMI became PIERRE ETOILE and went into studio with Boston various musicians.

– compilations, etc. –

on 'Rykodisc' unless mentioned otherwise

Sep 96. (4xcd-box) <*(RCD 10355)*> **GALAXIE 500**
– (TODAY / ON FIRE / THIS IS OUR MUSIC / UNCOLLECTED).

Apr 97. (cd) <*(RCD 10363)*> **COPENHAGEN**
– Decomposing trees / Fourth of July / Summertime / Sorry / When will you come home / Spook / Listen, the snow is falling / Here she comes now / Don't let our youth go to waste.

Sep 98. (cd) <*(RCD 10445)*> **THE PORTABLE GALAXIE 500**

DEAN WAREHAM

— augmented by JUSTIN HARWOOD (Chills), JIMMY CHAMBERS (Mercury Rev) + BYRON GUTHRIE (Ultra Vivid Scene)

Mint Tea not iss.

Feb 92. (12"/cd-s) *(MINT 6 T/CD)* **ANESTHESIA. / I CAN'T WAIT / TOMATO PEOPLE**

LUNA

— **DEAN WAREHAM** – vocals, guitar / **JUSTIN HARWOOD** – bass (ex-CHILLS) / **STANLEY DEMESKI** – drums (ex-FEELIES)

Rough Trade Rough Trade

Jan 92. (12"ep/cd-ep) *(R 2973/+CD)* **INDIAN SUMMER / EGG NOG. / RIDE INTO THE SUN / THAT'S WHAT YOU ALWAYS SAY**

Elektra Elektra

Aug 92. (12"ep/cd-ep) *(EKR 169 T/CD)* **SMILE / SLASH YOUR TIRES. / HEY SISTER (demo) / ROLLERCOASTER**

Mar 93. (c-ep/cd-ep) <*61472-4/-4*> **SLIDE EP**
– Slide / Indian summer / Ride into the sun / That's what you always say / Hey sister / Rollercoaster.

Aug 92. (cd/c/lp) <*(7559 61360-2/-4/-1)*> **LUNAPARK**
– Slide / Anaesthesia / Slash your tires / Crazy people / Time / Smile / I can't wait / Hey sister / I want everything / Time to quit / Goodbye / We're both confused.

Mar 94. (cd/c) <*(7559 61617-2/-4)*> **BEWITCHED**
– California (all the way) / Tiger Lily / Friendly advice / Bewitched / This time around / Great Jones Street / Going home / Into the fold / I know you tried / Sleeping pill.

— added **SEAN EDEN** – guitar

Beggars Banquet Elektra

Apr 95. (12"ep/cd-ep) *(BBQ 56 T/CD)* **BONNIE AND CLYDE EP**
– Bonnie and Clyde (The Bonnie Parker version) / Chinatown / Thankyou for sending me an angel / Bonnie and Cylde (The Clyde Barrow version).

— above w/ guest LAETITIA SADLER – vocals (of STEREOLAB)

Aug 95. (cd/c/lp) *(BBQ CD/MC/LP 178)* <*61807*> **PENTHOUSE**
– Chinatown / Sideshow by the seashore / Moon palace / Double feature / 23 minutes in Brussels / Lost in space / Rhythm king / Kalanazoo / Hedgehog / Freakin' and peakin' / Bonnie and Clyde (The Clyde Barrow version).

Nov 95. (7") *(BBQ 59)* **HEDGEHOG. / 23 MINUTES IN BRUSSELS / NO REGRETS**
(cd-s+=) *(BBQ 59CD)* – Happy New Year.

— **LEE WALL** – drums; repl. DEMESKI

Mar 96. (cd-ep) <*KAR 036-2*> **LUNA EP**
– Sideshow by the seashore / Thankyou for sending me an angel / The moviegoer / It's bringing you down / The enabler / No regrets.
<above issued on 'No.6'>

Sep 96. (10"ep/cd-ep) *(BBQ 302 TT/CD)* **SEASON OF THE WITCH / INDIAN SUMMER. / LOST IN SPACE / 23 MINUTES IN BRUSSELS**

Apr 97. (ltd.7") *(TRDSC 005)* **IN THE FLESH. / EARLY MORNING**
(above on 'Trade 2') <below on 'Radiation'>

Jun 97. (7"colrd) <*RARE 027*> **OUTDOOR MINER. / ROLL IN THE SAND**

Jun 97. (7") *(BBQ 313)* **IHOP. / WORDS WITHOUT WRINKLES**
(cd-s+=) *(BBQ 313CD)* – Fuzzy wuzzy.

Jul 97. (cd/c/lp) *(BBQ CD/MC/LP 194)* <*62055*> **PUP TENT**
– IHOP / Beautiful view / Pup tent / Bobby Peru / Beggar's bliss / Tracey I love you / Whispers / City kitty / Creeps / Fuzzy wuzzy.

Sep 97. (7"clear) *(BBQ 319)* **BOBBY PERU. / BOB LA FLAMBEUR / DANCE WITH ME**
(cd-s) *(BBQ 319CD)* – (first 2 tracks) / In the flesh / Beggar's bliss (demo).

Jul 98. (cd-ep) *(BBQ 322CD)* **BEAUTIFUL VIEW / BOBBY PERU (US radio edit) / CALIFORNIA ALL THE WAY**

1998. (7") <*RS 004*> **DANCE WITH ME. / (other side by WAKE OOLOO)**

— <above on 'Rocker! Supernova'> <below on 'Sub Pop'>

1998. (7"yellow) <*SP 438*> **EVERYBODY'S TALKIN'. / FUZZY WUZZY (demo)**

CAGNEY & LACEE

— aka **WAREHAM** and his wife **CLAUDIA SILVER**

Earworm No.6

1995. (7") <*KAR 034*> **TIME. / BY THE WAY (I STILL LOVE YOU)**

Mar 97. (cd) <*KAR 041-2*> **SIX FEET OF CHAIN**
– Be mine / Lovin' you / Six feet of chain / The last goodbye / By the way / Greyhound goin' somewhere / For the sake of the children / Memphis / I'm not sayin'.

Nov 98. (one-sided-7"white) *(WORMSS 3)* **BORDERLINE / ORANGE**

DAMON & NAOMI

Rough Trade Rough Trade

Jul 91. (12"ep/cd-ep; as PIERRE ETOILE) *(R 272-0/-3)* **IN THE SUN. / NINETEEN SIXTY-NINE / THIS CAR CLIMBED MT. WASHINGTON**
(re-iss. Jun97 on 'Elefant'; ER 306)

Shimmy Disc Shimmy Disc

Nov 92. (lp/c/cd) <*(SHIMMY 058/+MC/CD)*> **MORE SAD HITS**
– E.T.A. / Little red record co. / Information age / Laika / This car climbed Mt. Washington / Astrafiammante / Boston's daily temperature / (Scene change) / Sir Thomas and Sir Robert / Once more / This changing world / Memories. *<(cd re-iss. Oct98 on 'Rykodisc'; RCD 10439)>*

Sub Pop Sub Pop

Nov 95. (lp/cd) *(SP 322/+B)* **THE WONDROUS WORLD OF DAMON & NAOMI**
– In the morning / New historicism / Tour of the world / Forgot to get high / Pyewacket / Life will pass you by / Who am I? / New York City / Pandora's box / How long / Whispering blues.
<(cd re-iss. Oct98 on 'Rykodisc'; RCD 10440)>

— DAMON & NAOMI joined up with MAGIC HOUR (see further below)

Earworm Earworm

Aug 97. (7") *(WORM 3)* **THE NAVIGATOR. / AWAKE IN A MUDDLE**

Rykodisc Sub Pop

Apr 98. (cd) *(RCD 10438)* <*SP 425*> **PLAYBACK SINGERS**
– Turn of the century / Eye of the storm / In the sun / Navigator / I'm yours / Kinetoscope / Awake in a muddle / We're not there / Translucent carriages.

MAGIC HOUR

— **WAYNE ROGERS** – vocals (from TWISTED VILLAGE & CRYSTALIZED MOVEMENTS stable) / **KATE BIGGAR / DAMON KRUKOWSKI / NAOMI YANG**

Che Twisted Village

Dec 93. (7") <*TW 1028*> **HEADS DOWN. / (part 2)**

Sep 94. (10"ep) *(che 18)* **AFTER TOMORROW. / WORLD OF ONE / PERMANENT GREEN LIGHT**

Oct 94. (cd/lp) *(che 20 cd/lp)* <*TW 1031*> **NO EXCESS IS ABSURD**
– Isn't a way / Always leaving never / Sally free and easy / After tomorrow / Lower / World of one / The last mistake / Heads down #2.

May 95. (7") *(che 29)* **I HAD A THOUGHT. / AMERICA**

Jun 95. (cd/lp) *(che 30 cd/lp)* <*TW 1035*> **WILL THEY TURN YOU ON OR WILL THEY TURN ON YOU**

Dec 96. (cd) <*TW 1039*> **SECSESSION96**
– Sunset one / Rosebud / Sunrise / Sunset two.

GALLON DRUNK

Formed: Turnpike Lane, London, England . . . 1990 by JAMES JOHNSTON and MIKE DELANIAN along with ex-EARLS OF SUAVE man, MAX DECHARNE and early drummer NICK COOMBE. Replacing the latter with maestro of the maracas, JOEY BYFIELD, GALLON DRUNK swaggered onto an indie stage dominated by the fag-end of the baggy scene and limp-wristed shoegazers; pausing only to grease back their quiffs and dust down their vintage suits, JOHNSTON & Co. proceeded to unleash the most violent, paranoid, unholy racket this side of The BIRTHDAY PARTY. After a clutch of early singles on their manager's 'Massive' label, the band signed to London indie, 'Clawfist'. Rolling in on a crescendo of distorted bass and exploding in a howl of organ abuse and clenched-teeth threats, 'SOME FOOLS MESS' was quintessential GALLON DRUNK (if you only ever buy one GALLON DRUNK record etc . . ..). It was also a much heralded NME Single Of The Week, paving the way for a debut album, 'YOU, THE NIGHT AND THE MUSIC' (1992). When this lot weren't spitting out their trademark cocktail of twisted blues/R&B, New Orleans voodoo and amphetamine fuelled rockabilly (LINK WRAY comes to mind), they were partial to a bit of low-rent lounge crooning; ok, JOHNSTON was never going to be NEIL DIAMOND and they never pulled it off with quite the same panache as The TINDERSTICKS but covers of Lee Hazelwood's 'LOOK AT THAT WOMAN' and Neil Sedaka's 'SOLITAIRE' remain compulsive listening. These tasty nuggets can be found hiding on the B-side of the searing 'BEDLAM' single, TERRY EDWARDS' baritone sax adding depth to what was basically a sharpened-up, groovier take on 'SOME FOOLS . . .'. The best track by some measure on 'FROM THE HEART OF THE TOWN' (1992), it only served to underline the impression that they couldn't quite keep the pedal to the metal over a whole album. Still, GALLON DRUNK cruising was infinitely preferable to the bloodless indie pap of the day and grimy Big Smoke sketches like 'ARLINGTON ROAD' made a mockery of BLUR's subsequent oi! guv! pastiche. A mark of the man's underrated talents, JOHNSTON was signed up for touring duties with NICK CAVE during the BAD SEED's Lollapalooza '94 jaunt, no doubt a more entertaining proposition than GALLON DRUNK's disastrous gig at Glasgow's King Tut's the previous year (when some f***wit in the audience persisted in pulling the leads and caused JOHNSTON to storm off after about two songs). 1994 also saw JOHNSTON and EDWARDS cut the musical accompaniment for a spoken word album ('DORA SAUREZ') by crime writer, Derek Raymond while GALLON DRUNK the band eventually emerged from the pub in 1995 with an EP, 'THE TRAITOR'S GATE'. By this point the line-up was JOHNSTON, DELANIAN, BYFIELD alongside newcomers IAN WATSON, ANDY DEWER and IAN WHITE, this combination working on the long awaited third set, 'IN THE LONG STILL NIGHT'. Released on 'City Slang' in '96, the record revealed a more sober GALLON DRUNK; while the songwriting was probably stronger – highlights being the storming lead track, 'TWO CLEAR EYES' and the celluloid funk-noir of ~'THE BIG PAYOFF', gone was the gloriously filthy sound, JOHNSTON's mumbled menace and the delirious sense of impending chaos that characterised the band's early work. Despite overwhelmingly positive reviews, a subsequent decision that GALLON DRUNK had reached its ultimate conclusion led to the band's official dissolution in '97. Of late, JOHNSTON has found a new outlet for his manic energy, linking up with EDWARDS to form J.J. STONE, who stormed the alternative dancefloors in 1998 (con)fusing unlikely elements of SPIRITUALIZED and QUINCY JONES. • **Songwriters:** Group penned except; SOLITAIRE (Andy Williams) / LOOK AT THAT WOMAN (Lee Hazlewood) / RUBY (Silver Apples). • **Trivia:** JOE BYFIELD had brief spell with MY BLOODY VALENTINE, and drummer MAX DECHARNE also played keyboards with The PYROS (FRANK TOVEY's outfit!).

Album rating: YOU, THE NIGHT AND THE MUSIC (*6) / FROM THE HEART OF TOWN (*7) / TONITE . . . THE SINGLES BAR compilation (*7) / IN THE LONG STILL NIGHT (*7)

JAMES JOHNSTON – vocals, guitar, organ / **MIKE DELANIAN** – bass / **NICK COOMBE** – drums

Gallon Drunk | not iss.

May 90. (ltd.7") **SNAKEPIT. / PLEASE GIVE ME SOMETHING** [ ] [-]
added p/t GARY BONNEYFACE – maracas

Clawfist | Rykodisc

Nov 90. (7") *(HUNKA LURVE 1)* **RUBY. / US AND COUSIN EMMY** [ ] [-]

— **MAX DECHARNE** – drums / **JOE BYFIELD** – maracas; repl. NICK + GARY

Mar 91. (7") **DRAGGIN' ALONG. / MISERLOU** [ ] [-]
Jul 91. (7") **THE LAST GASP. / THE WHIRLPOOL** [ ] [-]
Oct 91. (7"ep/12"ep/cd-ep) *(HUNKA/+12/CD 006)* **SOME FOOLS MESS. / ROLLING HOME / MAY THE EARTH OPEN HERE** [ ] [-]
Feb 92. (cd/lp) *(HUNKA CDL/LP 001)* *<RCD/RCS 10258>* **YOU, THE NIGHT . . . AND THE MUSIC (GALLON DRUNK)** [ ] [ ] Sep92
– Rev up, T.P.A. / Some fool's mess / Just one more / Two wings mambo / You, the night and the music / Gallon Drunk / Night tide / Eye of the storm / Thundering away.
Jul 92. (cd/lp) *(HUNKA CDL/LP 002)* *<RCD/RCS 10257>* **TONITE . . . THE SINGLES BAR** (compilation) [ ] [ ]
– The last grasp (safety) / Rolling home / Snakepit / Miserlou / Ruby / Draggin' along / May the Earth open here / Please give me something / The whirlpool / Gallon drunk.
Oct 92. (7") *(HUNKA 011)* **BEDLAM. / LOOK AT THAT WOMAN** [ ] [-]
(12"+=/cd-s+=) *(HUNKA/+12/CD 011)* – Solitaire.

— recruited **TERRY EDWARDS** – saxophone, organ, trumpet, harmonica (ex-HIGSONS, solo artist)

Clawfist | Sire

Apr 93. (cd/lp) *(HUNKA CD/LP 005)* *<25269>* **FROM THE HEART OF TOWN** [67] [ ]
– Jake on the make / Arlington Road / Not before time / Keep moving on / Bedlam / You should be ashamed / End of the line / Loving alone / Push the boat out / Paying for pleasure. *(w/free 20 minute live cd/lp)* **LIVE AT MADISON SQUARE GARDENS)**
May 93. (12"ep/cd-ep) *(HUNKA 018/+CD)* **YOU SHOULD BE ASHAMED. / THE AMSTERDAM RUN / SILVER WINGS** [ ] [-]
Oct 93. (7"ltd) *(XPIG 21)* **KNOWN NOT WANTED. / (b-side by Tindersticks)** [ ] [-]

Blue Eyed Dog | not iss.

Dec 93. (10"; with BARRY ADAMSON) **SAVAGE SOUNDTRACKS FOR SWINGING LOVERS** [ ] [-]

— **IAN WHITE** – drums; repl. MAX who formed FLAMING STARS as frontman

— added on some tracks **IAN R. WATSON** – guitar, trumpet + **ANDY DEWAR** – percussion

Gallon Drunk | not iss.

Dec 95. (cd-ep) *(GDR 001)* **TRAITOR'S GATE** [ ] [-]

City Slang | City Slang

Sep 96. (cd/lp) *(<EFA 04982-2/-1>)* **IN THE LONG STILL NIGHT** [ ] [ ]
– Two clear eyes / Up on fire / It's all mine / Eternal tide / The road ahead / The big payoff / Take this poison / Some cast fire / Geraldine / Get ready . . . To love somebody / In the long still night.
Sep 96. (7") *(EFA 04985-7)* **TWO CLEAR EYES. / MR SLINKY'S** [ ] [-]
(cd-s+=) *(EFA 04985-2)* – Fade away / My spent love.
Mar 97. (7") *(EFA 04986-7)* **TO LOVE SOMEBODY. / COME UNTO ME** [ ] [-]
(cd-s+=) *(EFA 04986-2)* – The shakedown / Heaven holds all of my treasures.

— split some time in 1997

– compilations, others, etc. –

Nov 92. (cd/lp; shared with BREED) *Clawfist; / Dutch East India; <8414>* **CLAWFIST – THE PEEL SESSIONS** [ ] [-]
– Ruby / Some fool's mess / Drag '91 / Two wings mambo.

J.J. STONE

— aka **JAMES JOHNSTON** with **IAN WHITE** + **TERRY EDWARDS**

Itchy Teeth | unknown

Aug 98. (12"/cd-s) *(ITCHY 12/CD 001)* **HURRICANE. / (mixes by Psychedelia Smith & PK)** [ ] [-]

GAME THEORY

Formed: Sacramento, California, USA . . . 1982 by main songwriter, SCOTT MILLER, along with NANCY BECKER, FRED JUHOS and MICHAEL IRWIN. MILLER had previously been part of ALTERNATIVE LEARNING, which numbered NANCY's brother JOZEF BECKER (later of TRUE WEST and THIN WHITE ROPE). Their extremely limited 1982 debut album, 'BLAZE OF GLORY', led MICHAEL QUERCIO (of THREE O'CLOCK) to produce a 1983 EP, 'DISTORTION'. Knob-twiddling was subsequently taken over by MITCH EASTER (button pusher for R.E.M. and dB's) on 1985's 'REAL NIGHT TIME', an album indebted to the ghost of BIG STAR and which established them as yet another contender in the Paisley underground power-pop stakes. Their next effort, 'THE BIG SHOT CHRONICLES' (1986), was surprisingly passed over by the buying public and throughout the remainder of the 80's the band were sadly content to tread water. In the early 90's, MILLER was back again with a new outfit, The LOUD FAMILY, a band who had completed four albums by 1996. • **Covered:** YOU CAN'T HAVE ME (Big Star) / I WANT TO HOLD YOUR HAND (Beatles) / COULDN'T I JUST TELL YOU (Todd Rundgren).

Album rating: BLAZE OF GLORY (*4) / REAL NIGHTTIME (*6) / THE BIG SHOT CHRONICLES (*7) / LOLITA NATION (*7) / TWO STEPS FROM THE MIDDLE AGES (*4) / TINKER TO EVERS TO CHANCE (SELECTED HIGHLIGHTS 1982-1989) compilation (*8) / Loud Family: PLANTS AND BIRDS AND ROCKS AND THINGS (*7) / SLOUCHING TOWARDS LIVERPOOL mini (*6) / TAPE OF ONLY LINDA (*6) / INTERBABE CONCERN (*6)

SCOTT MILLER – vocals, guitar, synthesizers / **NANCY BECKER** – keyboards / **FRED JUHOS** – bass, vocals / **MICHAEL IRWIN** – drums

not iss. | Rational

1982. (lp) *<ION 003>* **BLAZE OF GLORY** [-] [ ]
– Something to show / Tin scarecrow / White blues / Date with an angel / Mary Magdalene / The young drug / Bad year at the U.C.L.A. / All I want is everything / Stupid heart / Sleeping through Heaven / It gives me chills / T.G.A.R.T.G. / Dead center / Penny, things won't / Metal and glass exact / Selfish again / Life in July.
1983. (12"ep) *<ONA 004>* **POINTED ACCOUNTS OF PEOPLE YOU KNOW** [-] [ ]
– Penny / Metal and glass exact / Selfish again / I wanna get hit by a car / Life in July / 37th day.
1984. (12"ep) *<RGP 8405>* **DISTORTION** [-] [ ]
– Shark pretty / Nine lives to Rigel 5 / The Red Baron / Kid Convenience / Too late for tears.
1984. (lp) **DEAD CENTER** [-] [-] French
– (compilation of 2 ep's above; issued on 'Lolita').

Enigma | Enigma

1985. (lp) *<72002-1>* **REAL NIGHTTIME** [-] [ ]
– Here comes everybody / 24 / Waltz the halls always / I mean it this time / Friend of the family / If and when it all falls apart / Curse of the frontierland / Rayon Drive / She'll be a verb / Real nighttime / You can't have me / I turned her away / Any other hand / I want to hold your hand / Couldn't I just tell you. *(UK cd-iss. Feb94 on 'Alias'; A 047D)*

— **DONNETTE THAYER** – guitar, vocals, piano (ex-VEIL) + **GIL RAY** – drums, repl. JUHOS

Nov 86. (lp) *<(3210-1)>* **THE BIG SHOT CHRONICLES** [ ] [ ]
– Here it is tomorrow / Where you going Northern / I've tried subtlety / rica's word / Make any vows / Regenisraen / Crash into June / Book of millionaires / The only lesson learned / Too closely / Never mind / Like a girl Jesus / Girl W / A guitar / Come home with me / Seattle / Linus and Lucy / Faithless. *(cd-iss. Feb94 on 'Alias'; A 046D)*
Dec 87. (lp) *<(3280-1/-2)>* **LOLITA NATION** [ ] [ ]
– What's the frequency / Not because you can / Shard / Go ahead, you're dying to / Dripping with looks / Exactly what we don't want to hear / We love you Carol and Alison / The waist and the knees / Nothing new / The world's easiest job / Look away / Slip / The real Sheila.

— **SHELLEY LA FRENIERE** – vocals, keyboards, repl. NANCY

— **GILLAUME GASSAUN** – bass, repl. IRWIN

Oct 88. (cd/c/lp) *(CD/TC+/ENV 507)* *<73350-1>* **TWO STEPS FROM THE MIDDLE AGES**
– Room for one more, honey / What the whole world wants / Picture of agreeability / Amelia have you lost / Rolling with the moody girls / Wyoming / In a Delorean / You drive / Leilan / Wish I could stand or have / Don't entertain me twice / Throwing the election / Initations week.

— **MILLER + RAY** (now guitar, keyboards) were joined by **QUERCIO + BECKER** (of THIN WHITE ROPE). THAYER went onto HEX with CHURCH singer STEVE KILBEY.

— This line-up only lasted until the early 90's, when even MILLER left to form own outfit The LOUD FAMILY.

– compilations, etc. –

Mar 90. (cd) *Enigma;* *<D21S-75351-2>* **TINKER TO EVERS TO CHANCE (SELECTED HIGHLIGHTS 1982-1989)**
– Beach state rocking / Band year at UCLA / Sleeping through Heaven / Something to show / Penny, things won't / Metal and glass exact / Shark pretty / Nine lives to Rigel 5 / The Red Baron / Curse of the frontier land / I turned her away / Regenisraen / Erica's word / Crash into June / Like a girl Jesus / We love you, Carol and Alison / The real Sheila / Together now, very minor / Room for one more, honey / Leilani / Throwing the election.

Feb 94. (cd) *Alias;* *<(A 048CD)>* **DISTORTION OF GLORY** (the debut EP and the EP)

LOUD FAMILY

SCOTT MILLER – vocals, guitar, etc / with others unknown

Alias Alias

Feb 93. (lp/cd) *<(A 033/+D)>* **PLANTS AND BIRDS AND THINGS** Oct92
– He do the police in different voices / Sword swallower / Aerodeleria / Self righteous boy reduced to tears / Jimmy still comes around / Take me down (too halloo) / Don't thank me all at once / Idiot son / Some grand vision of motives and irony / Spot the set-up / Inverness / Rosy overdrive / Slit my wrists / Isaac's law / The second grade applauds / Last honest face / Even you / Ballad of how you can all shut up / Give in world.

Sep 93. (7") *<(A 043S)>* **TAKE ME DOWN. / THE COME ON**

Dec 93. (m-lp/m-cd) *<(A 055/+D)>* **SLOUCHING TOWARDS LIVERPOOL**
– Take me down / The come on / Back of a car / Slit my wrists (live) / Aerodeliri (live) / Erica's word (live in studio).

Jan 95. (lp/cd) *<(A 060/+D)>* **THE TAPE OF ONLY LINDA** Oct94
– Soul drain / My superior / Marcia and Etrusca / Hyde Street virgins / Baby hard-to-be-around / It just wouldn't be Christmas / Better nature / Still its own reward / For beginners only / Ballet hetero.

Aug 96. (cd) *<(A 098D)>* **INTERBABE CONCERN** Jul96
– Sodium laureth sulfate / North San Bruno dishonor trip / Don't respond, she can tell / I'm not really a spring / Rise of the chokehold princess / Such little non-believers / Softest hip of her baby tongue / Screwed over by stylist introverts / Top dollar survivalist hardware / Not expecting both contempo and classique / I no longer fear the headlines / Hot rox avec lying sweet talk / Uncle Lucky / Just gone / Asleep and awake on the man's freeway / Where they go back to school but get depressed / Where they sell antique food / Where the flood waters soak their belongings / Where they walk over Saint Therese.

GANG GREEN

Formed: Boston, Massachusetts, USA . . . 1982 by main songwriter CHRIS DOHERTY, who was sole survivor by 1985, when he recruited FRITZ ERICKSON (who replaced CHUCK STILPHEN), JOE GITTLEMAN and BRIAN BERTZGER. After securing the honour of being the first band to release a record on the influential indie label, 'Taang!', GANG GREEN delivered their debut album, 'ANOTHER WASTED NIGHT' (1986). Firmly committed to drinking beer and riding their skateboards, the group's ramshackle line in thrash/funcore drew in fans from both sides of the metal/punk divide. Ex-DRI man, JOSH PAPP, was recruited to replace GITTLEMAN, the sticksman debuting on the band's first release for 'Roadrunner', 'YOU GOT IT' (1987). GANG GREEN were at their best when wielding their cutting brand of subversive humour, in full effect with the VAN HALEN send-up, 'I81B4U' (1988). Another "hilarious" album title was unearthed on 'OLDER . . . BUDWEISER' (1989), although GANG GREEN proved they were anything but with their terminally adolescent musical antics. A final live set, 'CAN'T LIVE WITHOUT IT', signalled the end of the line, the corpse of GANG GREEN left to rot in the annals of hardcore history. • **Covered:** SUSPECT DEVICE (Stiff Little Fingers).

Album rating: ANOTHER WASTED NIGHT (*5) / YOU GOT IT (*5) / I81B4U mini (*6) / OLDER . . . (BUDWEISER) (*4) / CAN'T LIVE WITHOUT IT (*4) / KING OF BANDS compilation (*5)

CHRIS DOHERTY – vocals, guitar / **FRITZ ERICKSON** – guitar; repl. CHUCK STILPHEN / **JOE GITTLEMAN** – bass / **BRIAN BERTZGER** – drums

not iss. Deluxe

1986. (12"ep) **DRUNK AND DISORDERLY, BOSTON MA** -

Funhouse Taang!

1987. (12"ep) *<TAANG! 1>* **P.M.R.C. SUCKS** -

Oct 87. (lp) *(FH 12-002)* *<856418>* **ANOTHER WASTED NIGHT** 1986
– Another wasted night / Skate to Hell / Last chance / Alcohol / Have fun / 19th hole / Skate hate / Let's drink some beer / Protect and serve / Another bomb / Voices carry / Sold out Alabama. *(re-iss. May89; 086 401)* *(cd-iss. Jan90; FH 039)* *(re-iss. Nov92 & Aug97 on 'Taang!' lp/cd; TAANG 131 LP/CD)*

— **JOSH PAPP** – bass (ex-DRI), repl. JOE

Roadrunner Roadrunner

Nov 87. (lp) *<(RR 9591-1)>* **YOU GOT IT**
– Haunted house / We'll give it to you / Sheetrock / Ballerina massacre / Born to rock / Bomb / L.S.D.B. / Whoever said / Party with the Devil / Some things / The climb / Sick sex six. *(re-iss. 1989 cd/c; RR 9591-2/-4)*

Jul 88. (12") *<(RR 24631)>* **LIVING LOVING MAID. /**

Jan 89. (m-lp/m-c/m-cd) *<(RR 9500-1/-4/-2)>* **I81B4U**
– Bartender / Lost chapter / Rent / Put her on top / Cum in u.

Sep 89. (lp/c/cd) *(EM 9464-1/-4/-2)* **OLDER . . . (BUDWEISER)**
– Church of fun / Just one bullet / We can go / Tear down the walls / Flight 911 / Bedroom of doom / Casio jungle / Why should you care / I'm still young / The ballad. (above was co-issued with 'Emergo')

Jul 90. (cd/lp) *<(RR 9380-2/-1)>* **CAN'T LIVE WITHOUT IT (live at the Marquee)**
– Let's drink some beer / Bartender / Lost chapter / We'll give it to you / We can go / Have fun / Last chance / Just one bullet / Born to rock / Rabies / Voices carry / Sold out / Bedroom of doom / Bomb / Alcohol.

Nov 91. (cd/c/lp) *<(RR 9254-2/-4/-1)>* **KING OF BANDS** (compilation)
– Thunder / Alcohol / We'll give it to you / Bartender / Ballad / Fuck in A / Just one bullet / Another wasted night / Put her on top / Church of fun / Rub it in your face.

— disbanded late in 1991 when DOHERTY quit to raise his family; he subsequently re-formed the group in '97 with **GUSTAFSON, SWEET + MARK WEISS**

Taang! Taang!

Aug 97. (12"/cd-s) *<(TAANG 133/+CD)>* **BACK AND CRACKED**

Oct 97. (lp/c/cd) *<(TAANG 135/+MC/CD)>* **ANOTHER CASE OF BREWTALITY**
– Eviction party / Wash the blood / Break the bottle / Hole (in the road) / Death of the party / I missed it / Beach whistle / Don't you know / Tricked into bed . . . again / Denied / This job sucks / Out on the couch / Weekend millionaire / I'll woryy about it Monday / Time to pay / Say good buy / Livin' in oblivion / Accidental overdose / 6,000 crucified slaves / Suspect device / Penalty box / To the point / Here to saty.

– compilations, etc. –

Sep 97. (cd) *Taang!;* *<1>* **PRE SCHOOL** -
– Sold out / Terrorize / Snob / Lie lie / Don't know / Rabies / Narrow mind / Kill a Commie / Have fun / Selfish.

GANG OF FOUR

Formed: Leeds, England . . . 1977 by journalist ANDY GILL, JON KING, DAVE ALLEN and HUGO BURNHAM. After releasing a debut EP, 'DAMAGED GOODS' for Bob Last's 'Fast' label, they signed to 'E.M.I.' in late '78. Their debut 45 for the label, 'AT HOME HE'S A TOURIST', hit the Top 60 and should have reached a lt higher but for a BBC ban due to the use of the word 'Rubbers' (i.e. contraceptives) in the lyrics. In Autumn '79, their debut album 'ENTERTAINMENT' hit the Top 50, a startling showcase for the band's adrenaline fuelled post-punk sound, GILL's rifling staccato guitar slicing through the twisted funk rhythms. Lyrically, they were also pretty incendiary, although their radical political agenda rarely descended into heavy handed preaching or took precedence over the music. It would be another couple of years before they released a follow-up, 'SOLID GOLD' (1981) mixing down GILL's patented feedback assault and coming in for some critical stick. Although he played on the landmark 'TO HELL WITH POVERTY' single (released in summer '81), ALLEN subsequently left the band to form his own outfit, SHRIEKBACK, his replacement being SARA LEE. Thereafter, the band favoured a more conventional approach, 'SONGS OF THE FREE' (1982) notable for its barbed comments on the Falklands war, 'CALL ME UP' and 'I LOVE A MAN IN UNIFORM (another single blacklisted by Radio 1). Following the departure of BURNHAM, they moved further towards a slick funk/Philly sound with 'HARD' (1983), employing a cast of studio professionals and female backing singers. With diminishing artistic and commercial returns, the band finally split in mid-'84 following the release of live set, 'AT THE PALACE' (1984). While GILL subsequently relocated to America and concentrated on production work, renewed interest in the band towards the end of the decade saw a GANG OF FOUR reformation, although GILL and KING were the only original members involved in the project. The result was a one-off album for 'Polydor', 'MALL' (1991), the label soon losing interest after it failed to sell; there was more grief for them the following year when, despite their best efforts in supplying the soundtrack for the Labour Party's 1992 campaign, the Tories romped home yet again. The duo initiated yet another reincarnation of the band in 1995 for the 'SHRINKWRAPPED' set, although sales were again disappointing. • **Songwriters:** Penned by KING / ALLEN / GILL, until ALLEN departed. Covered SOUL REBEL (Bob Marley).

Album rating: ENTERTAINMENT (*7) / SOLID GOLD (*6) / SONGS OF THE FREE (*6) / HARD (*5) / AT THE PALACE (*3) / A BRIEF HISTORY OF THE 20TH CENTURY compilation (*8) / MALL (*4) / SHRINKWRAPPED (*5)

JON KING (b. 8 Jun'55, London) – vocals, melodica / **ANDY GILL** (b. 1 Jan'56, Manchester) – guitar / **DAVE ALLEN** (b.23 Dec'55, Cumbria) – bass / **HUGO BURNHAM** (b.25 Mar'56, London) – drums

Fast not iss.

Oct 78. (7"m) *(FAST 5)* **DAMAGED GOODS. / LOVE LIKE ANTHRAX / ARMALITE RIFLE** -

E.M.I. Warners

Mar 79. (7") *(EMI 2956)* **AT HOME HE'S A TOURIST. / IT'S HER FACTORY** 58 -

Sep 79. (lp/c) *(EMC/TC-EMC 3313)* *<BSK 3446>* **ENTERTAINMENT** 45
– Ether / Natural's not in it / Not great men / Damaged goods / Return the gift / Guns before butter / I found that essence rare / Glass / Contract / At home he's a tourist / 5-45 / Anthrax. *(re-iss. 1985 lp/c; ATAK/TC-ATAK 41)* *(cd-iss. Feb95; CZ 541)* *<cd-iss. 1995 on 'Infinite Zero'+=; 14502-2>* – YELLOW EP

Regal Zonophone not iss.

Apr 80. (7") *(Z 1)* **OUTSIDE THE TRAINS DON'T RUN ON TIME. / HE'D SEND IN THE ARMY** -

Regal Zonophone / Warners

Oct 80. (12"ep) *<MINI 3494>* **OUTSIDE THE TRAINS DON'T RUN ON TIME / HE'D SEND IN THE ARMY. / IT'S HER FACTORY / ARMALITE RIFLE** [-] [ ]
Mar 81. (7"/12") *(EMI/12EMI 5146)* **WHAT WE ALL WANT. / HISTORY'S BUNK** [ ] [-]
Mar 81. (lp/c) *(EMC/TC-EMC 3364) <BSK 3565>* **SOLID GOLD** [52] [ ]
– Paralysed / What we all want / If I could keep it for myself / Outside the trains don't run on time / Why theory? / Cheeseburger / The republic / In the ditch / A hole in the wallet / He'd send in the army.
May 81. (7") *(EMI 5177)* **CHEESEBURGER. / PARALYSED** [ ] [-]

— (tour) **BUSTA CHERRY JONES** – bass (ex-SHARKS) repl. ALLEN (to SHRIEKBACK)

Jul 81. (7"/12") *(EMI/12EMI 5193)* **TO HELL WITH POVERTY. / CAPITAL (IT FAILS US NOW)** [ ] [-]
Feb 82. (m-lp) *<MINI 3646>* **ANOTHER DAY / ANOTHER DOLLAR** [-] [ ]
– To hell with poverty / What we all want / Cheeseburger / Capital (it fails us now) / History's bunk!

— **SARA LEE** – bass, vocals (ex-JANE AIRE, ex-ROBERT FRIPP) repl. BUSTA

Apr 82. (7"/12") *(EMI/12EMI 5299)* **I LOVE A MAN IN A UNIFORM. / WORLD AT FAULT** [65] [-]
May 82. (lp/c) *(EMC/TCEMC 3412) <23683>* **SONGS OF THE FREE** [61] [ ]
– Call me up / I love a man in a uniform / Muscle for brains / It is not enough / Life, it's a shame / I will be a good boy / History of the world / We live as we dream, alone / Of the instant.
Jun 82. (7") *<29921>* **I LOVE A MAN IN A UNIFORM. / I WILL A GOOD BOY** [-] [ ]
(12"+=) *<29907>* – ('A'extended).
Jul 82. (7") *(EMI 5320)* **CALL ME UP. / I WILL BE A GOOD BOY** [ ] [-]

— (**KING, GILL + BURNHAM** were joined by) **JON ASTROP / CHUCK KIRKPATRICK + JOHN SOMBATERO** – bass repl. SARA / added backing singers **ALFA ANDERSON** and **BRENDA WHITE**

Aug 83. (7"/12") *(EMI/12EMI 5418)* **IS IT LOVE. / MAN WITH A GOOD CAR** [ ] [-]
Sep 83. (lp/c) *(EMC 165219-1/-4) <23936>* **HARD** [ ] [ ]
– Is it love / I fled / Silver lining / Woman town / A man with a good car / It don't matter / Arabic / A piece of my heart / Independence.
Sep 83. (7") *<29449>* **IS IT LOVE. / ARABIC** [-] [ ]
Nov 83. (7") *(EMI 5440)* **SILVER LINING. / INDEPENDENCE** [ ] [-]

— **STEVE GOULDING** – drums (ex-RUMOUR) repl. BURNHAM who joined ILLUSTRATED MAN

Mercury / not iss.

Oct 84. (12"m) *(GANG 12)* **I WILL BE A GOOD BOY (live). / IS IT LOVE (live) / CALL ME UP (live)** [ ] [-]
Nov 84. (lp/c) *(MERL/+C 51)* **AT THE PALACE (live)** [ ] [-]
– We live as we dream, alone / History is not made by great men / Silver lining / The history of the world / I love a man in uniform / Paralysed / Is it love / Damaged goods / At home he's a tourist / To hell with poverty. *(c+=)* – I will be a good boy / Call me up.

— (split mid-84) **JON** later formed KING BUTCHER

ANDY GILL

— finally went solo

Survival / not iss.

Aug 87. (12") *(SUR12 039)* **DISPOSSESSION. / GENUINE** [ ] [-]

GANG OF FOUR

— reformed 1990 (**JON KING + ALAN GILL**) added **HIROMI + STAN LOUBIERES**

Scarlett / not iss.

Jun 90. (7") **MONEY TALKS (The Money mix). / USE THE COLOUR FROM THE TUBE** [ ] [-]
(12") – ('A'side) / ('A'dub version).
(cd-s) – ('A'extended) / (above 3 tracks).

Polydor / Polydor

May 91. (cd/c/lp) *<849 124-2/-4/-1>* **MALL** [-] [ ]
– Cadillac / Motel / Satellite / F.M.U.S.A. / Don't fix what ain't broke / Impossible / Money talks / Soul rebel / Hiromi & Stan talk / Colour from the tube / Hey yeah / Everybody wants to come / World falls apart.
Aug 91. (12") *(P2 152DJ)* **CADILLAC. / MOTEL / FAVOURITES** [ ] [-]

— disbanded again when their record label dropped them. GILL then supplied the soundtrack in 1992 for the Labour Party's unsuccessful general election campaign. Re-formed again in 1994.

— **GILL + KING + STEVE MONTI** (ex-CURVE) + **PHIL BUTCHER** (ex-IGGY POP)

When! / not iss.

Aug 95. (7"/c-s) *(WEN 7/M 1002)* **TATTOO. / BANNED WORDS / COP GOES HOME** [ ] [-]
(cd-s+=) *(WENX 1002)* – ('A'-Quiet guy mix).
Sep 95. (cd/c) *(WEN CD/MC 003)* **SHRINKWRAPPED** [ ] [-]
– Tattoo / Sleepwalker / I parade myself / Unburden / Better him than me / Something 99 / Showtime, valentine / Unburden, unbound / The dark side / I absolve you / Shrinkwrapped.

– compilations etc. –

Oct 86. (12"ep) *Strange Fruit; (SFPS 008)* **THE PEEL SESSIONS** (16.1.89) [ ] [-]
– I found that essence rare / Return the gift / 5-45 / At home he's a tourist. *(c-ep.iss.Jun87; SFPSC 008)*
May 90. (lp/c/cd) *Strange Fruit; (SFR LP/C/CD 107) / Dutch East India; <8101>* **THE PEEL SESSIONS (COMPLETE SESSIONS 1979-81)** [ ] [ ]
Mar 90. (cd)(c/lp) *Greenlight – Capitol; (CDP 795051-2)(TC+/GO 2028)* **YOU CATCH UP WITH HISTORY (1978-1983)** [ ] [-]
Nov 90. (cd/c/lp) *E.M.I.; (CD/TC+/EMC 3583) / Warners: <26448>* **A BRIEF HISTORY OF THE 20th CENTURY** [ ] [ ] Dec90
– At home he's a tourist / Damaged goods / Natural's not in it / Not great men / Anthrax / Return the gift / It's her factory / What we all want (live) / Paralysed / A hole in the wallet / Cheeseburger / To hell with poverty / Capital (it fails us now) / Call me up / I will be a good boy / History of the world / I love a man in a uniform / Is it love / Woman town / We live as we dream, alone. (c+cd.+=) – (4 tracks)
Jan 91. (7"ep/c-ep/12"ep/cd-ep) *E.M.I.; (EMS/TCEM/12EM/CDEM 172)* **TO HELL WITH POVERTY (the loaded edit) / ('A'-original version). / CHEESEBURGER (live) / CALL ME UP** [ ] [-]
Oct 95. (cd) *Warners; <43035>* **SOLID GOLD / ANOTHER DAY – ANOTHER DOLLAR** [-] [ ]
Nov 98. (d-cd) *Rhino; <RCD 75479>* **100 FLOWERS BLOOM** (rare tracks) [-] [ ]

GARBAGE

Formed: Madison, Wisconsin, USA … 1994 by BUTCH VIG, DUKE ERIKSON and STEVE MARKER, out of the ashes of FIRE TOWN and SPOONER. BUTCH's latter ham-pop/rock act, had been on the go since early 1978 and released their debut ep 'CRUEL SCHOOL' a year later <Boat; SP 4001>. Another soon followed, 'WHERE YOU GONNA RUN?' <Boat; SP 3001>, before an album, 'EVERY CORNER DANCE' surfaced in '82; <Mountain Railroad; HR 8005>. BUTCH then set up his own studio and produced KILLDOZER, before giving SPOONER another outing with the album 'WILDEST DREAMS' <Boat; SP 1004>. In 1986, their final flop 45, 'MEAN OLD WORLD' <Boat; SP 1018>, made BUTCH form FIRE TOWN, with old buddy STEVE MARKER and co-songwriter DOUG ERIKSON. A few singles, 'CARRY THE TORCH' <7-89242> and 'RAIN ON YOU' <7-89204>, appeared from the 'Atlantic' stable alongside albums 'IN THE HEART OF THE HEART COUNTRY' <Boat; 1013 / re-iss. Atlantic; 81754> & 'THE GOOD LIFE' cd/lp; <781945-2/-1>. In 1989/90, BUTCH re-formed with the original line-up of SPOONER; DUKE ERIKSON, DAVE BENTON, JEFF WALKER and JOEL TAPPERO, to release one-off comeback cd 'THE FUGITIVE DANCE' <Dali-Chameleon; 89026>. He was then to find fame in production work for greats like NIRVANA, SONIC YOUTH, SMASHING PUMPKINS, NINE INCH NAILS and U2, before coming across Edinburgh born vixen SHIRLEY MANSON fronting the band ANGELFISH on MTV. The new-look GARBAGE contributed the electro-goth of 'VOW' to a 'Volume' various artists compilation and this ended up as their limited edition debut 45 in 1995. By that years' summer, they had signed to Geffen's 'Almo Sounds' (UK 'Mushroom') records, which helped them break into the UK Top 50 with 'SUBHUMAN'. Success finally came with the 'ONLY HAPPY WHEN IT RAINS' single, a grungey, more tuneful affair that retained the goth overtones, MANSON weaving her deep throat vocals around the melody like a spider's web. She was an obvious focal point for the group; on their Top Of The Pops debut the singer made like a brooding, 90's incarnation of CHRISSIE HYNDE while the rest of the band remained comfortably anonymous in uniform black. The eponymous debut album, released later that year, was a mixed bag of styles that worked fairly effectively. Subsequent single, 'QUEER', kind of summed up the GARBAGE ethos, a deceptively poppy number featuring a MANSON vocal positively dripping with loathing, self or otherwise. GARBAGE continued their rise to the top of the pile with a UK chart-topping second set, 'VERSION 2.0', masterfully treading the finest of lines between alternative credibility and outright mainstream success; the hits kept on coming with 'PUSH IT', 'I THINK I'M PARANOID' and 'SPECIAL' all making the UK Top 20. • **Covered:** KISS MY ASS (Vic Chesnutt) / sampled the CLASH's 'Train In Vain' on 'STUPID GIRL'.

Album rating: GARBAGE (*8) / VERSION 2.0 (*7)

SHIRLEY MANSON (b. Edinburgh, Scotland) – vocals, guitar (ex-GOODBYE MR MACKENZIE) / **STEVE MARKER** – guitar, samples, loops / DUKE ERIKSON (b. DOUG) – guitar, keyboards, bass / **BUTCH VIG** (b. BRYAN VIG, Viroqua, Wisconsin) – drums, loops, efx

Discordant / AlmoSounds

Mar 95. (7") *(CORD 001) <89000>* **VOW. / VOW (Torn Apart version)** [ ] [97] Jul95

Mushroom / AlmoSounds

Aug 95. (s7"/7") *(SX/S 1138) <89001>* **SUBHUMAN. / £1 CRUSH** [50] [ ]
(cd-s+=) *(D 1138)* – Vow.
Sep 95. (7"/c-s/cd-s) *(SX/C/D 1199) <89002>* **ONLY HAPPY WHEN IT RAINS. / GIRL DON'T COME / SLEEP** [29] [55] Feb96
Oct 95. (cd/c/2x45rpm-lp/6x7"box) *(D/C/L/LX 31450) <80004>* **GARBAGE** [6] [20] Aug95
– Supervixen / Queer / Only happy when it rains / As Heaven is wide / Not my idea / A stroke of luck / Vow / Stupid girl / Dog new tricks / My lover's box / Fix me now / Milk.

— on above **MIKE KASHAN** – bass / **PAULI RYAN** – percussion

Nov 95. (7") *(SX 1237) <89003>* **QUEER. / QUEER (Adrian Sherwood remix)** [13] [ ] Mar96
(silver-cd-s) *(D 1237)* – ('A'side) / Trip my wire / ('A'-The very queer dub-bin mix) / ('A'-The most beautiful girl in town mix).
(gold-cd-s) *(DX 1237)* – ('A'side) / Butterfly collector / ('A'-Rabbit in the Moon remix) / ('A'-Danny Saber remix).
Mar 96. (7") *(SX 1271)* **STUPID GIRL. / DOG NEW TRICKS (pal mix)** [4] [-]
(red-cd-s+=) *(D 1271)* – Driving lesson / ('A'-Red Snapper mix).
(blue-cd-s) *(DX 1271)* – ('A'side) / Alien sex fiend / ('A'-Dreadzone dub) / ('A'-Dreadzone vox).
Jul 96. (c-s) *<89004>* **STUPID GIRL / DRIVING LESSON** [-] [24]
Nov 96. (7") *(SX 1494) <89007>* **MILK (The wicked mix). / MILK (the Tricky remix)** [10] [ ]

(cd-s) *(D 1494)* – Milk (the wicked mix featuring TRICKY) / ('A'-Goldie's completely trashed remix) / ('A'-original version) / Stupid girl (Tees radio mix by TODD TERRY).
(cd-s) *(DX 1494)* – Milk (the wicked mix featuring TRICKY) / ('A'-Massive Attack classic remix) / ('A'-Rabbit in the moon udder remix) / Stupid girl (the Danny Saber remix).

May 98. (c-s) *(MUSH 28MCS)* <89014> **PUSH IT / LICK THE PAVEMENT** [9] [52]
(cd-s+=) *(MUSH 28CDS)* – ('A'-Boom Boom Satellites remix).
(3"cd-s) *(MUSH 28CDSX)* – ('A'side) / Thirteen.

May 98. (cd/c/lp) *(74321 55410-2/-4/-1)* <80018> **VERSION 2.0** [1] [13]
– Temptation waits / I think I'm paranoid / When I grow up / Medication / Special / Hammering in my head / Push it / The trick is to keep breathing / Dumb / Sleep together / Wicked ways / You look so fine.

Jul 98. (c-s) *(MUSH 35MCS)* <40035> **I THINK I'M PARANOID / DEADWOOD** [9] [ ]
(cd-s+=) *(MUSH 35CDS)* – Afterglow.
(cd-s) *(MUSH 35CDX)* – ('A'side) / ('A'extended) / ('A'-Purity mix).
(3"cd-ep+=) *(MUSH 35CDXXX)* – (all of the above).

Oct 98. (c-s) *(MUSH 39C)* <827> **SPECIAL / THIRTEEN X FOREVER** [15] [ ] Nov98
(cd-s+=) *(MUSH 39CDS)* – ('A'-Brothers In Rhythm mix).
(cd-s) *(MUSH 39CDSX)* – ('A'side) / Medication (acoustic) / Push it (Victor Calderone remix).
(3"cd-s) *(MUSH 39CDSXXX)* – (all 5 above).

Nick GARVEY (see under ⇒ MOTORS)

GASTR DEL SOL (see under ⇒ SQUIRREL BAIT)

GAYE BYKERS ON ACID

Formed: Leicester, England . . . mid 80's by IAN GARFIELD HOXLEY (aka MARY MARY or MARY GOLIGHTLY) and TONE, along with KEVIN HYDE, ROBBER, and subsequently DJ, WILLIAM SAMUEL RONALD MONROE. A bizarre troupe of dayglo, grebo pseudo-bikers led by the cross-dressing, MARY MARY, GBOA made their album debut in 1987 with the 'Virgin' album (who else!), 'DRILL YOUR OWN HOLE'. Fans had to do just that as the record came minus a centre-punch, rendering it impossible to play. Though some might argue that was actually a blessing in disguise, the band atracted a cult following, gaining coverage mainly in the indie press. After a further major label set, 'STEWED TO THE GILLS' (1989), the band subsequently completed the independently issued 'GROOVEDIVESOAPDISH' the same year, before starting up their own label, 'Naked Brain'. The group folded after a few albums, various members going on new projects, most notably MARY MARY, who surfaced in industrial "supergroup", PIGFACE, before co-forming HYPERHEAD. • **Trivia:** The band were at times complemented/augmented on stage by "drag-queen" DJ, ROCKET RONNIE, winner of 'The Alternative Miss Universe'.

Album rating: DRILL YOUR OWN HOLE (*6) / STEWED TO THE GILLS (*5)

MARY MARY (b. IAN GARFIELD HOXLEY) – vocals / **TONE** (b. RICHARD ANTHONY HORSFALL) – guitar / **ROBBER** (b. IAN MICHAEL REYNOLDS) – bass / **KEVIN HYDE** (aka DR. JECKYL) – drums / plus **ROCKET RONNIE** (b. WILLIAM SAMUEL RONALD MONROE) – DJ

In-Tape / not iss.

Nov 86. (7"/12") *(IT/+TI 040)* **EVERYTHING'S GROOVY. / T.V. CABBAGE** [ ] [–]

May 87. (7") *(IT 046)* **NOSEDIVE KARMA. / DON'T BE HUMAN ERIC** [ ] [–]
(10"+=) *(IT 46-10)* – Golf trek.
(12"+=) *(ITTO 46)* – Delirium.

Virgin / Caroline

Oct 87. (7") *(VS 1008)* **GIT DOWN (SHAKE YOUR THANG). / TOLCHOCKED BY KENNY PRIDE** [54] [–]
(12"+=/12"s+=) *(VS T/X 1008)* – Go go in out, in out Garotschka.

Nov 87. (cd/c/lp) *(CD/TC+/V 2478)* <CAROL 1347> **DRILL YOUR OWN HOLE** [95] [ ]
– Motorvate / Call me a liar / All hung up / Zen express / World War 7 blues / Git down / After suck there's blow / So far out / Drive-in salvation / T.V. cabbage.

Dec 87. (7") *(VS 1027)* **ALL HUNG UP. / AFTERNOON TEA WITH DAVE GREENFIELD** [ ] [–]
(12"+=/12"pic-d+=) *(VS T/X 1027)* – ('A'-Rough Rider mix) / ('A'-Reprisal mix).

Jan 89. (7") *(VS 1165)* **HOT THING. / RAD DUDE** [ ] [–]
(10"+=/12"+=) *(VSA/VST 1165)* – After there's blow there's suck.

Feb 89. (cd/c/lp) *(CD/TC+/V 2579)* <CAROL 1376> **STEWED TO THE GILLS** [ ] [ ]
– It is are you? / Better of dead / M.A.D. / Hot thing / Testicle of God (and was it good) / Ill / Mass gyrate / Harmonious murder / Shoulders / Hair of dog / Rad dude / Teeth / Floydrix / Bedlam a g-go / Fairway to Heaven / It is are you? (concept reprise).

Naked Brain / not iss.

Mar 90. (lp/c) *(NBX 001/+MC)* **CANCER PLANET MISSION** [ ] [–]
– Welcome cancer planet mission / Face at the window / Hope ans psyche / Satyr naked / Catalytic converter / Advertise / Alive oh! / Mr. Muggeridge / Got is the kink / Demon seed / Bleed / Candle / Insomnia / Heavenly body. *(cd-iss. Oct90; NBXCD 001)*

Dec 90. (lp/c/cd; as PFX) *(NBX 2/+C/CD)* **PERNICIOUS NONSENSE** [ ] [–]

— when they split during this period, KEVIN formed G.R.O.W.T.H. with JEFF from The JANITORS. TONE formed The CAMP COLLECTION with BRAD BRADBURY.

– compilations, etc. –

Jan 89. (12"ep) *Nighttracks; (SFNT 010)* **THE JANICE LONG SESSIONS** [ ] [–]

Nov 89. (m-lp/c/cd) *Dry Communications; (MLP/DRY/DRYCD 002)* **GROOVEDIVESOAPDISH** [ ] [–]

Apr 93. (cd/lp) *Receiver; (<RRCD/RRLP 160>)* **G.B.O.A.** [ ] [ ] May99
– Killer teens in New Orleans / S.P.A.C.E. / Radiation / John Wayne's a fag / Iguana trifle / What happened to Malcolm / Disinformation rise & shine / T.V. cabbage / Face at the window / Don't be human Eric – Let's be frank / Delirium / Everythings groovy baby.

May 93. (cd) *Receiver; (<RRCD 162>)* **FROM THE TOMB OF THE NEAR LEGENDARY** [ ] [ ] Dec94
– Watch that roundabout Ben / Shit happens / Killer teens in New Orleans (a joy toy remix) / Why? / Space cadet / Nero fiddles / Animal farm / No justice, just us / S.P.A.C.E. (a joy toy remix).

GBH

Formed: Stoke-On-Trent, England . . . 1980 as CHARGED GBH, by CAL, JOCK, ROSS and WILF. Taking their name from the criminal offence GBH (Grevious Bodily Harm), these uncompromising Mohican-sporting oi/punks followed in the mould of EXPLOITED, BLITZ or DISCHARGE, releasing the violent debut EP, 'LEATHER BRISTLES . . .' in 1981. A year later, after a minor hit single, 'NO SURVIVORS', they found themselves smashing into the UK Top 20 with debut album, 'CITY BABY ATTACKED BY RATS'. Brutally basic three-chord punk assaults bolstered with a metallic edge and mob-rule vocals, the record was in tune with the prevailing zeitgeist, although they never again matched this success as the scene gave way for NWOBHM and proto-thrash acts. As the 80's wore on, GBH subsequently turned their backs on the punk/hardcore movement, taking an overtly metallic/speed approach on albums such as 'A FRIDGE TOO FAR' (1989) and 'FROM HERE TO REALITY' (1990).

Album rating: CITY BABY ATTACKED BY RATS (*6)

CAL (b. COLIN ABRAHALL) – vocals / **JOCK BLYTH** – guitar / **ROSS LOMAS** – bass / **WILF WILLIAMS** – drums

Clay / not iss.

Aug 81. (12"ep) *(PLATE 3)* **LEATHER BRISTLES, STUDS AND ACNE** [ ] [–]
– Race against time / Knife edge / Lycanthropy / Necrophilia / State executioner / D.O.A. / Generals / Freaks. *(re-iss. May90 lp/c/cd; PLATE/+MC/CD 3)*

Jan 82. (7"m) *(CLAY 8)* **NO SURVIVORS. / SELF DESTRUCT / BIG WOMEN** [63] [–]

Jun 82. (7"m) *(CLAY 11)* **SICK BOY. / SLIT YOUR OWN THROAT / AM I DEAD YET?** [ ] [–]

Aug 82. (lp/c; as CHARGE GBH) *(CLAY/+MC 4)* **CITY BABY ATTACKED BY RATS** [17] [–]
– City baby attacked by rats / The prayer of a realist / Passenger on the menu / Heavy discipline / Boston babies / Bellend bop / Time bomb / Sick boy / Willie Whitelaw's willie / No survivors / Self destruct / Big women / Slit your own throat. *(re-iss. Jul90 cd/c/lp; CLAY CD/MC/LP 4) (cd re-iss. Jul98 on 'Receiver'; RRCD 257) <US-iss.1990 on 'Combat'; 8217>*

Nov 82. (7"/7"pic-d) *(CLAY 16/+P)* **GIVE ME FIRE. / MANTRAP** [69] [–]

Dec 82. (lp) **LIVE AT THE CITY GARDEN (live)** [ ] [–]

Apr 83. (7") *(CLAY 22)* **CATCH 23. / HELLHOLE** [ ] [–]

Dec 83. (lp/c) *(CLAY/+MC 8)* **CITY BABYS REVENGE** [ ] [–]
– Diplomatic immunity / Drugs party in 526 / See the man run / Vietnames blues / Womb with a view / The forbidden zone / Valley of death / City babies revenge / Pins and needles / Christianised cannibals / Faster faster / High octane fuel / I feel alright / Skanga (herby weed). *(re-iss. May90 cd/c/lp; CLAY CD/MC/LP 8) <US-iss.1990 on 'Combat' lp,cd; 8004> (cd re-iss. Aug98 on 'Receiver'; RRCD 258)*

Aug 84. (7") *(CLAY 36)* **DO WHAT YOU DO. / FOUR MEN** [ ] [–]
(12"+=) *(12CLAY 36)* – Children of dust.

Rough Justice / Combat

Feb 86. (lp/c) *(JUST/TJUST 2)* <8067> **MIDNIGHT MADNESS AND BEYOND . . .** [ ] [ ]
– Limpwristed / Future fugitives / Too much / Iroquis / Guns and guitars / Horror story / Midnight madness / Chance for living / Seed of madness / Sam is your leader / How come? / Blood. *(cd-iss. Aug87; CDJUST 2)*

Sep 86. (12"ep) *(12KORE 101)* **OH NO IT'S GBH AGAIN** [ ] [–]
– [then take from below]

Jul 87. (lp) *(JUST 7)* **NO NEED TO PANIC** [ ] [–]
– Transylvanian perfume / Hearing screams (for the last time) / To unerstand / Makin' whips / I shot the marshall / Electricity through space / Hit the deck / Rumblin' underground / Desperate times / Gunning for the president / Avenues and alleyways / Unanswered prayers. *(cd-iss. 1989+=; CDJUST 7)* – OH NO IT'S GBH AGAIN / WOT A BARGAIN

Mar 88. (12"ep) *(12KORE 104)* <8232> **WOT A BARGIN** [ ] [ ]

— **KAI LUIGI REDER** – drums; repl. WILF

Mar 89. (cd/c/lp) *(CD/T+/JUST 13)* **A FRIDGE TOO FAR** [ ] [–]
– Pass the axe / Captain Chaos / Go home / Checkin' out / See you bleed / When will it end? / A fridge too far / Fist of regret / Needle in the haystack / Twenty floors below / Nocturnal journal / Crossfire.

Rough Justice / Restless

Oct 90. (cd/c/lp) *(CD/T+/JUST 16)* <72525-2/-4> **FROM HERE TO REALITY** [ ] [ ]
– New decade / Trust me, I'm a doctor / B.M.T. / Mass production / The old school of self destruction / You don't do enough / From here to reality / Dirty too long / Destroy / Just in time for the epilogue / Don't leave your honey down the pits / Moonshine song. *(cd re-iss. Oct96 on 'Powerage'; PRAGE 007CD)*

— **ANTHONY MORGAN** – bass; repl. ROSS

Oct 92. (c/lp) *(T+/JUST 21)* <11015> **CHURCH OF THE TRULY WARPED** [ ] [ ] 1993
– Pure greed / Not enough hate / Leather coffin / Candy man / Lords of discipline / Where the wild things are / Church of the truly warped / Back / I

need energy / Evil ever / All for the cause. *(cd-iss. Oct96 on 'Powerage'; PRAGE 008CD)*

— **JOSEPH MONTANARO** – drums; repl. KAI

We Bite | Triple X

Sep 96. (cd) *(WB 1151CD) <TX 51211>* **PUNK JUNKIES** [ ] Jun97
– Intro / Junkies / Impounded / Harmony / Tokyo after dark / Shakin' hands with the machine / Don't drag me down / Break the chains / Kangaroo court / Stormchaser / Hole / Damn good time / Cryin (on the hard shoulder) / Civilized / Lowering the standard / Enzo / Outro.

– compilations, etc. –

on 'Clay' unless mentioned otherwise

1982. (lp) *(CLAYLP 5)* **LEATHER, BRISTLES, NO SURVIVORS AND SICK BOYS** [ ] [-]
– Race against time / Knife edge / Lycanthropy / Necrophilia / State executioner / Dead on arrival / Generals / No survivors / Self destruct / Big women / Slit your own throat / Sick boy / Am I dead yet / Freak. *(re-iss. Jul90 cd/c/lp; CLAY CD/MC/LP 5) <US-iss.1990 on 'Combat'; 8218>*

Jul 86. (lp/cd) *(CLAY LP/CD 21) / Combat; <8216>* **THE CLAY YEARS 1981-84** [ ] 1990
(re-iss. cd Jul92; same)

Aug 89. (lp/cd) *(CLAY LP/CD 102)* **NO SURVIVORS** [ ] [-]

1989. (c) *Roadrunner; (RR 49643)* **CITY BABY ATTACKED BY RATS / LEATHER BRISTLES etc** [ ] [-]

1989. (cd) *Roadrunner; (RR 349678)* **ATTACK AND REVENGE** [ ] [-]

Apr 90. (lp/c/cd) *(<CLAY/+MC/CD 106>)* **DIPLOMATIC IMMUNITY** [ ] [ ]
– No survivors / Self destruct / Give me fire / Catch 23 / City baby attacked by rats / Time bomb / Maniac / I am the hunted / Sick boy / Boston babies / I feel alright / Slut / Diplomatic immunity / Pins and needles / Faster faster / City babies revenge / Necrophilia / Generals / Womb with a view / Christianised cannibals / Four men.

Jul 93. (d-cd) *(<CLAYDCD 112>)* **CHAGED G.B.H.: THE CLAY RECORDINGS** [ ] [ ]

Oct 93. (cd) *Dojo; (DOJOCD 112) / Creative Man; <5>* **LIVE IN JAPAN (live)** [ ] Oct94

May 95. (cd) *Clay; (<CLAYCD 119>)* **THE CLAY PUNK SINGLES COLLECTION** [ ] [ ]

Jun 96. (cd) *Cleopatra; <9744>* **GBH CELEBRITY LIVE STYLE (live)** [-] [ ]

Sep 96. (cd) *Anagram; (CDPUNK 82)* **LIVE IN LOS ANGELES (live)** [ ] [-]

GEE MR. TRACY

Formed: Norwich, England . . . 1984 by TOM 'BRICK' SMITH and former TESTCARD-F member, VINCE ROGERS. Taking their moniker from a catchphrase used (by the character, Brains) on children's cult TV programme, 'Thunderbirds', GEE MR. TRACY embarked in their crusade to amuse (just slightly!) the indie-pop world. Their simple electronic ditties matched the the cronic lyrics of the bespectacled BRICK, his off-the-wall humour only matched by The VERY THINGS or even ALEXEI SAYLE. Surfacing on local label, 'Backs', GEE MR TRACY unleashed 'SHOOT THE SHERBET HERBERT' (1985) to an unwitting public, a mini-set that featured their most outrageously mad track, 'THE DAY THE SHOES BIT BACK' (quite literally barking!). The quartet (the other gruesome twosome being REBECCA SLATER and er, ANT) carried on regardless but finally hit a "Brick" wall after the release of their second mini-set, 'HARMONY! RHAPSODY! DESTINY!' (1986).

Album rating: SHOOT THE SHERBET HERBERT (*4) / HARMONY! RHAPSODY! DESTINY! (*3)

TESTCARD-F

VINCE ROGERS – keyboards / with a female vocalist + two others

Backs | not iss.

Apr 83. (7") *(NCH 004)* **BANDWAGON TANGO. / UNFAMILIAR ROOM** [ ] [-]

Mar 84. (7") *(NCH 010)* **THE THIRD STROKE. / IF ONLY IT WASN'T** [ ] [-]

GEE MR. TRACY

— **TOM 'BRICK' SMITH** – vocals, trumpet / **VINCE ROGERS** – keyboards / **REBECCA SLATER** – vocals / **ANT** – backing vocals

Backs | not iss.

Mar 85. (7"m) *(NCH 102)* **YOU MAKE MY HOUSE SHINE. / GO SCUBA / FOR MY HONEY** [ ] [-]

May 85. (m-lp) *(NCHMLP 5)* **SHOOT THE SHERBERT HERBERT** [ ] [-]
– The day the shoes bit back / Ooh bop sh'bam / Sorrowful / You make my house shine / When I lost my baby.

Jul 85. (7") *(NCH 103)* **I WISH THE WHOLE DAMN WORLD WAS IN A BOTTLE. / HONEY, I'M OUT OF MY TREE** [ ] [-]

Feb 86. (7") *(NCH 106)* **LAVA MAN. / MR. UNLUCKY** [ ] [-]

Jun 86. (7") *(NCH 108)* **PERMANENT SWOON. / I FELL THROUGH THE FLOOR** [ ] [-]

Oct 86. (m-lp) *(NCHMLP 11)* **HARMONY! RHAPSODY! DESTINY!** [ ] [-]
– Permanent swoon / Lava man / etc

— the fun was over after above

Howe GELB (see under ⇒ GIANT SAND)

GENE

Formed: Watford, England . . . Summer 1993 by MARTIN ROSSITER and three ex-members of GO HOLE and then SP!N (STEVE MASON, MATT WINGLEY (JAMES) and KEVIN MILES). SP!N were indie raves (mixing style of STONE ROSES and JIMI HENDRIX) for three years from 1988, before (on the 23rd March '91) a motorway accident left them shattered and unable to continue as a group for some time. Their tour manager, their soundman and their bassman, JOHN MASON (STEVE's older brother) were all seriously injured, with the latter having to be replaced by KEVIN MILES. In 1992, they found ROSSITER from gay disco group, DROP, finally debuting with 'FOR THE DEAD' in the Spring of '94. Both they and their label, 'Costermonger', were then picked up by 'Polydor', who issued Top 60 single, 'BE MY LIGHT, BE MY GUIDE'. Another couple of singles, 'SLEEP WELL TONIGHT' and 'HAUNTED BY YOU' followed, before the band finally released their debut album, 'OLYMPIAN' in Spring '95. With ROSSITER's effete tales of bedsit angst, alienation and despair and SMITHS-style musical approach, GENE polarized opinion. Fans found much to savour in the record's grooves, the vitality of singles giving way to a more reflective, downbeat ambience that characterised much of the album. It went Top 10 in the UK, spawning further singles with the title track and the re-released, 'FOR THE DEAD'. The latter was accompanied by an odds and sods compilation, 'TO SEE THE LIGHTS' (The SMITHS did the same a decade earlier), while a follow-up set proper, 'DRAWN TO THE DEEP END', hit the shelves about a year later. • **Songwriters:** Group penned except DON'T LET ME DOWN (Beatles) / I SAY A LITTLE PRAYER (Burt Bacharach) / WASTELANDS (Jam) / NIGHTSWIMMING (R.E.M.).

Album rating: Sp!n: IN MOTION (*5) / Gene: OLYMPIAN (*7) / TO SEE THE LIGHTS (*6) / DRAWN TO THE DEEP END (*6)

GO HOLE

LEE CLARKE (b.20 Jan'63, Cleethorpes, England) – vocals, guitar / **STEVE MASON** (b.17 Apr'71, Pontypridd, Wales) – guitar / **JOHN MASON** (b. 8 Aug'67, Bristol, England) – bass / **MATT WINGLEY** (b. MATT JAMES, 20 Sep'65) – drums

Big Pot | not iss.

Aug 87. (7") *(GONE 1)* **FLIGHT OF ANGELS. / SPANISH FLY** [ ] [-]

SP!N

Foundation | not iss.

Aug 90. (12"ep) **SCRATCHES IN THE SAND. / SHAFTED / EAST** [ ] [-]
(cd-ep+=) – ('A'radio edit).

Feb 91. (12"ep) **LET'S PRETEND / (part 2). / MANIFESTO OF LOVE / LET'S PRETEND (JIMI'S DEAD)** [ ] [-]
(cd-ep+=) – ('A'radio edit).

Jul 91. (lp/c/cd) *(FOUND 3/+MC/CD)* **IN MOTION** [ ] [-]
– Many sides of you / Let's pretend / Everything / Ask me / Shafted / Sweet / Colour of your eyes / Mary / Scratches (in the sand) / Sister Pearl.

— **KEV MILES** – bass repl. JOHN who after transit accident left and travelled around the country and then France as a bohemian poet.

Nov 91. (12"ep/cd-ep) **HOT BLOOD** [ ] [-]
– Fifteen minutes / I'm getting out / Landslide / You're my worst nightmare.

— **MARTIN T. FALLS** (b.15 May'70, Cardiff, Wales) – vocals repl. LEE

— disbanded 1992 after new member bailed out.

GENE

MARTIN ROSSITER (b.1970, Cardiff, Wales) – vocals, keyboards / **STEVE MASON** – guitars / **KEVIN MILES** – bass / **MATT JAMES** – drums, percussion

Costermonger-Polydor | Polydor

Apr 94. (7") *(COST 1)* **FOR THE DEAD. / CHILD'S BODY** [76] [-]

Aug 94. (7") *(COST 2)* **BE MY LIGHT, BE MY GUIDE. / THIS IS NOT A CRIME** [54] [-]
(cd-s+=) *(COST 2CD)* – I can't help myself.

Oct 94. (7"/c-s/cd-s) *(COST 3/+MC/+CD)* **SLEEP WELL TONIGHT. / SICK, SOBER AND SORRY / HER FIFTEEN YEARS** [36] [-]

Feb 95. (7"/c-s/cd-s) *(COST 4/+MC/+CD)* **HAUNTED BY YOU. / DO YOU WANT TO HEAR IT FROM ME / HOW MUCH FOR LOVE** [32] [ ]

Mar 95. (cd/c/lp) *(GENE 1CD/1MC/1LP) <52-7662>* **OLYMPIAN** [8] [ ] Jun95
– Haunted by you / Your love, it lies / Truth, rest your head / A car that sped / Left-handed / London, can you wait? / To the city / Still can't find he phone / Sleep well tonight / Olympian / We'll find our own way.

Jun 95. (7"blue) *(SP 294)* **BE MY LIGHT, BE MY GUIDE. / I CAN'T HELP MYSELF** [ ] [ ]
(above on 'Sub Pop' UK & feat. on 'HELTER SHELTER' box-set)

Jul 95. (7"/c-s) *(COST 5/+MC)* **OLYMPIAN. / I CAN'T DECIDE IF SHE REALLY LOVES ME / TO SEE THE LIGHTS** [18] [-]
(cd-s+=) (COST 5CD) – Don't let me down.

Nov 95. (m-cd) *<31457 9247-2>* **GENE** [-] [ ]
– Sleep well tonight / I can't help myself / This is not my crime / Child's body / The olympian.

Jan 96. (7") *(7COST 6A)* **FOR THE DEAD (version). / CHILD'S BODY** [14] [-]
(7"+=/c-s+=) *(COST 6/+MC)* – Sick, sober & sorry (live).
(cd-s) *(COST 6CD)* – ('A'side) / Sick, sober & sorry (live) / Truth rest your head (live).

Jan 96. (cd/c/d-lp) *(GENE 2LP/2MC/2CD) <8249>* **TO SEE THE LIGHTS** (compilation of rare, live & bootleg material) [11] [ ]
– Be my light, be my guide / Sick, sober & sorry / Her fifteen years / Haunted by you (live – Helter Skelter) / I can't decide if she really loves me / To see the lights / I can't help myself / A car that sped (Radio 1 session) / For the dead (version) / Sleep well tonight (live – Forum) / How much for love / London, can you wait? (Radio 1 session) / Child's body / Don't let me down (Radio 1 session) / I say a little prayer (live – Glastonbury) / Do you want to hear it from me / This is not my crime / Olympian (live – Forum) / Child's body (live – Forum).

		Polydor	A&M
Oct 96.	(7"/c-s) *(575689-7/-4)* **FIGHTING FIT. / DRAWN TO THE DEEP END**	22	-
	(cd-s+=) *(575689-2)* – Autumn stone.		
Jan 97.	(7"/c-s) *(COS TS/MC 10)* **WE COULD BE KINGS. / DOLCE / GABBANA OR NOWT**	17	-
	(cd-s+=) *(COSCD 10)* – Wastelands.		
Feb 97.	(cd/c/d-lp) *(GENE CD/M/L 3)* <537104> **DRAWN TO THE DEEP END**	8	Mar97
	– New amusements / Fighting fit / Where are they now? / Speak to me someone / We could be kings / Whi I was born / Long sleeves for the summer / Save me, I'm yours / Voice of the father / Accidental / I love you, what are you? / Sub rosa.		
May 97.	(7") *(COSTS 11)* **WHERE ARE THEY NOW? / CAST OUT IN THE SEVENTIES**	22	-
	(cd-s+=) *(COSCD 11)* – Nightswimming.		
	(cd-ep) **LIVE AT THE ROYAL ALBERT HALL EP** *(COSDD 11)* – ('A') / Save me, I'm yours / Voice of the father / Sub Rosa.		
Jul 97.	(7"/c-s) *(COS ST/MC 12)* **SPEAK TO ME SOMEONE. / AS THE BRUISES FADE**	30	-
	(cd-s) *(COSCD 12)* – ('A'side) / Ship song / Drawn to the deep end.		
	(cd-s) *(COSDD 12)* – ('A'side) / New amusements / The olympian.		

– compilations, etc.

1996.	(cd) *Hispanolo; <040>* **IF THE DRESS FITS: THE UNOFFICIAL COMPILATION**	-	

GENE LOVES JEZEBEL

Formed: Porthcawl, Wales . . . 1981 by identical twins JAY and MICHAEL ASTON, a rhythm section of STEVE MARSHALL and DICK HAWKINS completing the line-up. Relocating to London, the group signed to the 'Situation 2' label and made their vinyl debut in Spring '82 with the 'SHAVING MY NECK' single. Bass-heavy tribal repetition and proto-goth posturing – albeit with a sense of humour – was the order of the day, the tortuous 'MACHISMO' showing the band at their most unlistenably experimental. While the twins formed the core of the outfit, a succession of people came and went as needed; future ALL ABOUT EVE frontwoman, JULIENNE REGAN, was a brief member while old school pal IAN HUDSON joined up prior to the recording of debut album, 'PROMISE' (1983). Promoted by the singles 'SCREAMING (FOR EMMALENE)' and 'BRUISES', the record's tarted-up goth grooves (well, image-wise anyway!) won them support from the likes of John Peel. The following year the band travelled to the States where they subsequently enjoyed greater success and even secured a contract with 'Geffen' in the mid-80's (funnily enough, The ASTONS' vocal bleatings could possibly, at a pinch, be described as a gothic AXL ROSE!). Back in Britain, meanwhile, more personnel upheaval saw PETER RIZZO and MARCUS GILVEAR take up the rhythm section reins for follow-up album, 'IMMIGRANT' (1985). A considerably more commercial and accessible affair, some tracks (eg. 'WORTH WAITING FOR') were even reminiscent of U2 in an ECHO & THE BUNNYMEN kinda way!? After a further US jaunt that resulted in the departure of HUDSON and recruitment of punk stalwart, JAMES STEVENSON, the 'JEZEBELS finally scraped the UK Top 75 in Spring '86 with 'THE SWEETEST THING' single. 'HEARTACHE' achieved a similar feat later that summer while a third set, 'DISCOVER' (1986) made the Top 40. The subsequent recruitment of ex-SPEAR OF DESTINY man, CHRIS BELL, preceded further minor hit singles and a fourth album, 'THE HOUSE OF DOLLS'. The turn of the decade brought major upheaval as MICHAEL ASTON emigrated to America and left his twin brother to take up the reins. Ironically enough, the subsequent single, 'JEALOUS' proved their biggest US hit, preceding the 'KISS OF LIFE' (1990) album. After a break of three years, GENE LOVES JEZEBEL resurfaced with yet another line-up – JAY ASTON, RIZZO, STEVENSON and ROBERT ADAM – and a new record deal with 'Savage-Arista'. The resulting album, 'HEAVENLY BODIES' (1993) failed to re-ignite their career and group subsequently split as STEVENSON defected to The CULT. The mid-90's saw another reformation with ASTON, STEVENSON and RIZZO, a live set, 'IN THE AFTERGLOW' (1995) appearing on the independent 'Pink Gun' label.

Album rating: PROMISE (*6) / DISCOVER (*5)

MICHAEL ASTON (b. 4 May'61) – vocals / **JAY ASTON** (b.JOHN) – guitar, vocals / **STEVE MARSHALL** – bass / **DICK HAWKINS** – drums

		Situation 2	Relativity
May 82.	(7") *(SIT 18)* **SHAVING MY NECK. / SUN AND INSANITY**		-
	(12"+=) *(SIT 18T)* – Machismo / Glad to be alive.		
—	guests were **STEVE GOULDING** – saxophone / **JOHN MURPHY** – drums (ex-SPK, ex-ASSOCIATES)		
Apr 83.	(7") *(SIT 20)* **SCREAMING (FOR EMMALENE). / SO YOUNG (HEAVE HARD HEAVE HO)**		-
	(12"+=) *(SIT 20T)* – No voodoo dollies.		
—	on tour they used **JULIENNE REGAN** – bass (future ALL ABOUT EVE) / **ALBIO DE LUCA** – guitar (future FURYO)		
Jul 83.	(7") *(SIT 24)* **BRUISES. / PUNCH DRUNK**		-
	(12"+=) *(SIT 24T)* – Brando bruises.		
Oct 83.	(lp) *(SITU 7)* **PROMISE**		-
	– Screaming (for Emmalene) / Bread from Heaven / Wraps and arms / Upstairs / Psychological problems / Scheming / Influenza / Punch drunk. *(re-iss. 1988 on 'Situation 2-Lowdown' lp/cd; SITL 7/+CD)* *<US-iss.1987 on 'Geffen'; 24165>*		
Mar 84.	(7") *(SIT 31)* **INFLUENZA (RELAPSE). / WALKING IN THE PARK**		-
	(12"+=) *(SIT 31T)* – Stephen.		
May 84.	(7") *(SIT 35)* **SHAME (WHOLE HEART BOWL). / THIN THINGS**		-
	(12"+=) *(SIT 35T)* – Gorgeous.		
—	The **ASTON's** brought in **PETER RIZZO** – bass repl. MARSHALL / **MARCUS GILVEAR** – drums (ex-KLAXON 5) repl. HAWKINS who joined SKELETAL FAMILY. / added **I.C. HUDSON** – guitar (who had joined on earlier tours)		
May 85.	(7") *(SIT 36)* **COW. / ONE SOMEONE**		-
	(12") *(SIT 36T)* – ('A'extended) / Weep for her (cow).		
Jun 85.	(lp/c) *(SITU/SITC 14)* **IMMIGRANT**		-
	– Worth waiting for / Shame / Stephen / The rhino plasty / Cow / Cole Porter / Always a flame / The immigrant / Deep south whale. *(cd-iss. Jan88; SITU 14CD) (re-iss. 1988 on 'Situation 2-Lowdown' lp/cd; SITL 14/+CD)*		
—	**JAMES STEVENSON** – guitar (ex-CHELSEA, ex-GENERATION X) repl. HUDSON		
Nov 85.	(7") *(SIT 41)* **DESIRE. / FLAME (Steve Hurley mix)**		
	(12"+=) *(SIT 41T)* – The immigrant.		
Dec 85.	(12"ep) *<8075>* **DESIRE EP**	-	
	– Desire / Worth waiting for / Cow / Desire / Flame.		

		Beggars Banquet	Geffen
Mar 86.	(7") *(BEG 156)* **THE SWEETEST THING. / PSYCHO II**	75	
	(12"+=) *(BEG 156T)* – Sweetest Jezebel.		
Jun 86.	(7") *(BEG 161)* **HEARTACHE. / BEYOND DOUBT**	71	
	(12"+=) *(BEG 161T)* – Heartache I / Deli babies.		
Jul 86.	(lp/cd)(c) *(BEGA 73/+CD)(BEGC 73)* *<24118>* **DISCOVER**	32	
	– Heartache / Over the rooftops / Kick / White horse / Wait and see / Desire / Beyond doubt / The sweetest thing / Maid of Sker / Brand new moon. *(free-lp w/a)* **GLAD TO BE ALIVE (live)** – Upstairs / Over the rooftops / The rhino plasty / Worth waiting for / Cow / The immigrant / Brittle punches / Pop tarantula.		
Oct 86.	(7") *(BEG 173)* **DESIRE (COME AND GET IT). / SAPPHIRE SCAVENGER**		
	(12"+=) *(BEG 173T)* – New horizons / Message.		
	(c-s+=) *(BEG 173C)* – ('A'-US mix) / Message.		
—	**CHRIS BELL** – drums (ex-SPEAR OF DESTINY, ex-THOMPSON TWINS, ex-SPECIMEN) repl. GILVEAR (he went to the States)		
Aug 87.	(d7"/d12") *(BEG 192 D/TD)* **THE MOTION OF LOVE. / A FRESH SLICE // BUGG'S BRUISES. / VAGABOND (A NEW ADVENTURE)**	56	-
Oct 87.	(lp/cd)(c) *(BEGA 87/+CD)(BEGC 87)* *<24171>* **THE HOUSE OF DOLLS**	81	
	– Gorgeous / The motion of love / Set me free / Suspicion / Every door / 20 killer hurts / Treasure / Message / Drowning crazy / Up there.		
Nov 87.	(7"/7"g-f) *(BEG 202/+S)* **GORGEOUS. / SOMEONE ON THE 6TH FLOOR (AT THE JEZEBEL PALACE)**	68	
	(12"+=/cd-s+=) *(BEG 202 T/CD)* – Suspicion / The motion of love / (Jezebel mixes).		
Jan 88.	(7"/12";w-drawn) *(BEG 212/+T)* **EVERY DOOR. /**		-
Jan 88.	(7") *<28183>* **THE MOTION OF LOVE. / BUGG'S BRUISES**	-	87
Apr 88.	(7") **SUSPICION. / DROWNING CRAZY**	-	
—	(mid'89) **JAY** now sole survivor, when twin emigrated to the US He brought in **RISINGHAM & RIZZO**		
Jun 90.	(7") *(BEG 236)* *<19688>* **JEALOUS. / LAST YEAR**		68
	(12"+=/cd-s+=) *(BEG 236 T/CD)* – While you were there.		
Jul 90.	(lp/cd)(c) *(BEGA 109/+CD)(BEGC 109)* *<24260>* **KISS OF LIFE**		
	– Jealous / It'll end in tears / Kiss of life / Why can't I / Syzygy / Walk away / Tangled up in you / Two shadows / Evening star / I die for you.		
Dec 90.	(12"ep/cd-ep) **TANGLED UP IN YOU**		
	– Tangled up in you / Suspicion / Heartache / Stephen.		
—	line-up; **JAY ASHTON / RIZZO / STEVENSON + ROBERT ADAM**		
—	MICHAEL ASTON would released a solo set in '95, 'WHY ME WHY THIS WHY NOW' for 'Triple X'		

		Savage-Arista	not iss.
May 93.	(7"/c-s) *(74321 13152-7/-4)* **JOSEPHINA. / TOMORROW COLOURS**		-
	(cd-s+=) *(74321 13152-2)* – ('A'extended).		
Jun 93.	(cd/c) *(74785 50210-2/-4)* **HEAVENLY BODIES**		-
	– American dreamer / Wild horse / Josephina / Any anxious colour / Break the chain / Down in a lonely place / Sweet sweet rain / Rosary / Heavenly bodies / Voice in the dark.		
—	Split for a while when JAMES STEVENSON was poached by The CULT.		
—	re-formed yet again with **ASHTON / STEVENSON + RIZZO**		

		Pink Gun	not iss.
Nov 95.	(d-cd) *(PINKGCD 1)* **IN THE AFTERGLOW (live)**		-
	– Gorgeous / The sweetest thing / Bugg's bruises / Coal porter / Set me free / Suspicion / Over the rooftops / Stephen / Every door / Heartache / The motion of love / 20 killer hurts / Desire / American dreamer / Sweet sweet rain / Suspicion / Wild horse / Any anxious colour / Why can't I / Kiss of life / Evening star / 20 killer hurts / Jealous / Josephina / Always a flame / Desire.		

– compilations, etc. –

Sep 95.	(cd) *Avalanche; <21>* **SOME OF THE BEST OF GENE LOVES JEZEBEL: FROM THE MOUTHS OF BABES**	-	
	– Desire (come and get it) / Heartache / Jealous / Twenty killer hurts / Kiss of life / Suspicion / Upstairs / No sweat / Beyond dobt / Bread from Heaven / Body of soul.		
Oct 98.	(cd) *Cleopatra; <377>* **DESIRE: GREATEST HITS REMIXED**	-	

GENERATION X (see under ⇒ IDOL, Billy)

GENERATION X

Formed: London, England . . . 1976 by aspiring young punk, BILLY IDOL, alongside BOB ANDREWS and ex-CHELSEA members, TONY JAMES and JOHN TOWE (the latter was soon replaced by former SUBWAY SECT man, MARK LAFF). Though they attracted a loyal fanbase, GENERATION X were never considered a dyed-in-the-wool punk band per se, their more commercial, hook-filled power pop at odds with the genre's inherent nihilism. Signed to 'Chrysalis', the band hit the Top 40 with their first single, 'YOUR GENERATION', following it up with 'WILD YOUTH' and 'READY STEADY GO', the latter track a decidedly un-punk 60's tribute. An eponymous debut album hit the Top 30 in Spring '78, while the band's sound grew increasingly commercial on successive albums, 'VALLEY OF THE DOLLS' (1979; produced by IAN HUNTER) and 'KISS ME DEADLY' (1981; released under the slightly clipped moniker of GEN X). Following their split in '81, JAMES later formed SIGUE SIGUE SPUTNIK, while the bleached-blond IDOL was free to pursue his barely concealed desire for pop stardom. Relocating to New York, he met manager, Bill Aucoin and producer, Keith Forsey, recruiting guitarist STEVE STEVENS and cutting a cover of Tommy James & The Shondells' 'MONY MONY' (along with a few other tracks – including the GENERATION X song, 'DANCING WITH MYSELF' – it formed part of a US-only mini-set, 'DON'T STOP'). • **Covers:** GIMME SOME TRUTH (John Lennon) / SHAKIN' ALL OVER (Johnny Kidd).

Album rating: GENERATION X (*6) / VALLEY OF THE DOLLS (*5) / KISS ME DEADLY (*5) / PERFECT HITS compilation (*7)

BILLY IDOL (b. WILLIAM BROAD, 30 Nov'55, Stanmore, Middlesex, England) – vocals (ex-CHELSEA, ex-INFANTS) / **BOB 'Derwood' ANDREWS** – guitar / **TONY JAMES** – bass, vocals (ex-CHELSEA, ex-INFANTS) / **MARK LAFF** – drums (ex-SUBWAY SECT) repl. JOHN TOWE (ex-CHELSEA, ex-INFANTS) who joined ALTERNATIVE TV then ADVERTS, etc

		Chrysalis	Chrysalis
Sep 77.	(7") *(CHS 2165)* **YOUR GENERATION. / DAY BY DAY**	36	
Dec 77.	(7") *(CHS 2189)* **WILD YOUTH. / WILD DUB** *(some copies were mispressed with b-side 'NO NO NO')*		
Mar 78.	(7") *(CHS 2207)* **READY STEADY GO. / NO NO NO**	47	
Mar 78.	(lp/c) *(CHR/ZCHR 1169)* **GENERATION X** – From the heart / One hundred punks / Listen / Ready steady go / Kleenex / Promises promises / Day by day / The invisible man / Kiss me deadly / Too personal / Youth, youth, youth. *(cd-iss. Jan86; CCD 1169) (re-iss. cd Mar94; CD25CR 14) (cd re-iss. Jul96 on 'EMI Gold'; CDGOLD 1039)*	29	
Jan 79.	(7",7"red,7"pink,7"orange,7"yellow) *(CHS 2261)* **KING ROCKER. / GIMME SOME TRUTH**	11	
Jan 79.	(lp/c) *(CHR/ZCHR 1193)* **VALLEY OF THE DOLLS** – Running with the boss sound / Night of the Cadillacs / Paradise west / Friday's angels / King rocker / Valley of the dolls / English dream / Love like fire / Paradise west / The prime of Kenny Silvers. *(cd-iss. Jan86; CCD 1193)*	51	
Mar 79.	(7",7"brown) *(CHS 2310)* **VALLEY OF THE DOLLS. / SHAKIN' ALL OVER**	23	
Jun 79.	(7",7"pink) *(CHS 2330)* **FRIDAY'S ANGELS. / TRYING FOR KICKS / THIS HEAT**	62	

— **TERRY CHIMES** – drums (ex-CLASH, ex-COWBOYS INTERNATIONAL) repl. LAFF / **JAMES STEPHENSON** – guitar (ex-CHELSEA) repl. 'DERWOOD' (later to WESTWORLD)

GEN X

Sep 80.	(7") *(CHS 2444)* **DANCING WITH MYSELF. / UGLY RASH** (12"+=) *(CHS12 2444)* – Loopy dub / What do you want	62	
Jan 81.	(lp/c) *(CHR/ZCHR 1327)* **KISS ME DEADLY** – Dancing with myself / Untouchables / Happy people / Heaven's inside / Triumph / Revenge / Stars look down / What do you want / Oh mother. *(cd-iss. Jan86; CCD 1327)*		
Jan 81.	(7"ep,7"clear-ep/12"ep) *(CHS/+12 2488)* **DANCING WITH MYSELF / UNTOUCHABLES. / KING ROCKER / ROCK ON**	60	

— split early '81, when BILLY went solo. CHIMES rejoined The CLASH, TONY JAMES later formed SIGUE SIGUE SPUTNIK. STEPHENSON later joined GENE LOVES JEZEBEL, then The CULT.

– compilations, etc. –

on 'Chrysalis' unless otherwise mentioned

Nov 85.	(lp/c) *(CHM/ZCHM 1521)* **THE BEST OF GENERATION X**		
Feb 87.	(7") *Old Gold; (OG 9693)* **KING ROCKER. / VALLEY OF THE DOLLS**		-
Jun 87.	(lp) *M.B.C.; (JOCKLP 9)* **THE ORIGINAL GENERATION X**		-
Jun 88.	(lp) *M.B.C.; (JOCKLP 11)* **GENERATION X LIVE (live)**		-
Oct 91.	(cd/c/lp) *(CCD/ZCHR/CHR 1854)* **PERFECT HITS (1975-81)** – Dancing with myself / Your generation / Ready steady go / The untouchables / Day by day / Wild youth / Wild dub / One hundred punks / King rocker / Kiss me deadly / Gimme some truth / New order / English dream / Triumph / Youth, youth, youth.		

GENEVA

Formed: Aberdeen, Scotland ... late 1992 (briefly as SUNFISH) by DOUGLAS CASKIE, STEVEN DORA, STUART EVANS, KEITH GRAHAM and ex-journalist ANDREW MONTGOMERY (with The Sunday Post!). Eventually after only a few gigs, they were spotted by 'Nude' records (home to the likes of SUEDE), where they released their stunning debut, 'NO ONE SPEAKS', which bubbled under the Top 30 singles chart late '96. Around the same time, they secured a support slot on a BLUETONES' tour, exposing the angelic, high-pitched vox of MONTGOMERY, a hybrid of BILLY MacKENZIE, THOM YORKE, IAN ASTBURY or even, God forbid, an 80's style alternative rock version of MORTEN HARKET! During the first half of '97, the singles, 'INTO THE BLUE' and 'TRANQUILIZER', both went Top 30 and featured on their soaringly spiritual Top 20 album, 'FURTHER'. • **Songwriters:** Most by DORA and MONTGOMERY, a few by MONTGOMERY, GRAHAM and one with EVANS.

Album rating: FURTHER (*8)

ANDREW MONTGOMERY – vocals / **STEVEN DORA** – guitar / **STUART EVANS** – guitar / **KEITH GRAHAM** – bass / **DOUGLAS CASKIE** – drums

		Nude	Sony
Oct 96.	(7"/c-s) *(NUD 22 S/MC)* **NO ONE SPEAKS. /** (cd-s) *(NUD 22CD)* –	32	-
Jan 97.	(7"/c-s) *(NUD 25 S/MC) <78594>* **INTO THE BLUE. / AT THE CORE** (cd-s) *(NUD 25CD)* – ('A'side) / Riverwatching / Land's End.	26	Jun97
May 97.	(7"/c-s) *(NUD 28 S/MC)* **TRANQUILLIZER. / DRIFTWOOD** (cd-s) *(NUD 28CD1)* – ('A'side) / Dead giveaway / Strung out on you. (cd-s) *(NUD 28CD2)* – ('A'side) / Michaelmas / Compulsive love disorder.	24	-
Jun 97.	(cd/c/lp) *(NUDE 7 CD/MC/LP) <68156>* **FURTHER** – Temporary wings / Into the blue / The god of sleep / Best regrets / Tranquillizer / Further / No one speaks / Worry beads / Fall apart button / Wearing off / Nature's whore / In the years remaining.	20	Aug97
Aug 97.	(7") *(NUD 31S)* **BEST REGRETS. / SELF BELIEF** (cd-s) *(NUD 31CD1)* – ('A'side) / Feel the joy / Raymond Chandler. (cd-s) *(NUD 31CD2)* – ('A'side) / Last orders / The god of sleep (demo).	38	-

GERALDINE FIBBERS

Formed: Los Angeles, California, USA ... 1992 by former ETHYL MEATPLOW and NEON VEIN singer, CARLA BOZULICH (real name!), who enlisted DANIEL KEENAN, WILLIAM TUTTON, JESSY GREENE and KEVIN FITZGERALD. Making a departure from her noisy industrial early work, CARLA used the GERALDINE FIBBERS as a vehicle to explore the common ground between American roots music and stark, blues-influenced punk. Signed to the local 'Sympathy For The Record Industry' label, the 'FIBBERS made their debut in 1993 with the 'DRAGON LADY' single, previewing their heavily country influenced mini-set, 'GET THEE GONE' (1994). Subsequently signing to 'Virgin', CARLA and Co delivered their first album proper, 'LOST SOMEWHERE BETWEEN THE EARTH AND MY HOME' in 1995, revamping some of their earlier tracks and drawing comparisons with long-lost cowpunkers, X. A few years later, NELS CLINE was drafted in for the departing KEENAN and GREENE, the resulting 'BUTCH' (1997) featuring a more robust guitar-rock sound and even attempting a cover of Can's 'YOU DOO RIGHT'. • **Covered:** JOLENE (Dolly Parton) / BLUE CROSS (... Hansen) / GRAND TOUR (Richey-Taylor-Wilson) / FANCY (Bobbie Gentry) / HANDS ON THE WHEEL (Rainravens) / IF DRINKIN' DON'T KILL ME (Beresford-Sanders) / KISS OF FIRE (Allen-Hill).

Album rating: GET THEE GONE mini (*5) / LOST SOMEWHERE BETWEEN THE EARTH AND MY HOME (*6) / BUTCH (*6)

CARLA BOZULICH – vocals, guitar / **DANIEL KEENAN** – lead guitar, vocals / **JESSY GREENE** – violin, viola, vocals / **WILLIAM TUTTON** – double bass, vocals / **KEVIN FITZGERALD** – drums, vocals

		not iss.	Sympathy F
1993.	(7") *<SFTRI 384>* **DRAGON LADY. / BIRTHDAY BOY**	-	
1994.	(m-cd) **GET THEE GONE** – Get thee gone / Jolene / Marmalade / Outside of town / Blue cross / Mary / Grand tour / Fancy / They suck / She's a dog / Pills / Smaller song / Hands on the wheel / If drinkin' don't kill me / Kiss of fire / Grand tour. *<re-iss. Feb97 as 'WHAT PART OF "GET THEE GONE" DON'T YOU UNDERSTAND?'+=; SFTRI 481>* – (extra tracks incl. in above).	-	

		Hut	Virgin
Jan 95.	(7") *(HUT 49)* **MARMALADE. / GET THEE GONE**		-
Jan 95.	(m-cd) *(DGHUTM 22)* **THE GERALDINE FIBBERS** – Marmalade / Get thee gone / Grand tour / Outside of town / They suck / Fancy / Blue cross.		-
Jul 95.	(cd/c) *(CDHUT/HUTMC 28) <40602>* **LOST SOMEWHERE BETWEEN THE EARTH AND MY HOME** – Lilybelle / The small song / Marmalade / Dragon lady / A song about walls / House is falling / Outside of town / The French song / Dusted / Richard / Blast off baby / Get thee gone.		
Aug 95.	(7") *(HUT 60)* **DRAGON LADY. / BITTER HONEY** (cd-s+=) *(HUTCD 60)* – Birthday boy.		-

— **NELS CLINE** – guitar; repl. KEENAN + GREENE

		Virgin	Virgin
Oct 97.	(cd) *(CDVUS 133) <4419>* **BUTCH** – California fluffy / Toy box / I killed the cuckoo / Trashman in furs / Swim back to me / Seven or in 10 / Claudine / Folks like me / Pet angel / Butch / Arrow to my drunken eye / You doo right / The dwarf song / Heliotrope.		Jul97

Lisa GERMANO

Born: 1958, Mishawaka, Indiana, USA. Having learned the piano at an early age, LISA later landed the job of backing violinist with both JOHN MELLENCAMP and BOB SEGER. Working on her own material in her spare time, she continued to earn a living as a session musician for the likes of IGGY POP before self-financing her debut album, 'ON THE WAY DOWN FROM MOON PALACE' (1991). A stark departure from her work with MELLENCAMP, the record was characterised by a dark atmospheric sensitivity that drifted between dreamlike reverie and unsettling intimation, although her folky roots were never far from the surface. 'Capitol' obviously noted her potential, signing her up for 1993's eponymous follow-up wherein LISA exercised her darkest demons but failed to connect with mainstream record buyers. Released in Britain as 'HAPPINESS' for IVO's '4 a.d.', the record was more warmly received by UK listeners eager for female singer-songwriter angst. 1994's 'GEEK THE GIRL', meanwhile, was a pseudo-concept affair charting the emotional and sexual development of an adolescent girl against a more musically adventurous backdrop. Of late, the moody chanteuse has been as prolific as ever, working with GIANT SAND mainman, HOWE GELB as OP8 and releasing two further sets, 'EXCERPTS FROM A LOVE CIRCUS' (1996) and 'SLIDE' (1998).

Album rating: ON THE WAY DOWN FROM MOON PALACE (*5) / LISA GERMANO – HAPPINESS (*6) / GEEK THE GIRL (*6) / EXCERPTS FROM A LOVE CIRCUS (*7)

LISA GERMANO – vocals, piano, violin, etc / with **KENNY ARONOFF** – drums

not iss. Major Bill

1991. (cd/c) *<CAROL 191-2/-4>* **ON THE WAY DOWN FROM MOON PALACE** [-] [ ]

— added a plethora of session people

not iss. Capitol

Jul 93. (cd) *<45593>* **LISA GERMANO** [-] [ ]
– Bad attitude / Destroy the flower / Puppet / Everyone's victim / Energy / Cowboy / Happiness / The Earth / Around the world / Sycophant / Miamo-tutti / The dresses song / The darkest night of all. *(UK-iss.Apr94 as 'HAPPINESS' on '4 a.d.' lp/c)(cd; CAD 4005/+CD)(CADC 4005) (cd re-iss. Jul98 +=; GAD 4005CD)* – INCONSIDERATE BITCH

4 a.d. 4 a.d.

Jan 94. (m-cd) *<74005>* **INCONSIDERATE BITCH** [-] [ ]
– Energy / Puppet / Sychopant / Late night.

Oct 94. (cd) *(CAD 4017CD)* **GEEK THE GIRL** [ ] [ ]
– My secret reason / Trouble / Geek the girl / Just geek / Cry wolf / . . . A psychopath / Sexy little girl princess / Phantom love / Cancer of everything / A guy like you / . . .Of love and colours / Stars. *(cd re-iss. Jul98; GAD 4017CD)*

Aug 96. (7") *(AD 6019)* **SMALL HEADS. / FUN, FUN FOR EVERYONE (acoustic)** [ ] [-]
(cd-s+=) *(BAD 6019CD)* **Tom, Dick and Harry / Messages from Sophia (instrumental).**

Sep 96. (lp/cd) *(CAD 6012/+CD) <46217>* **EXCERPTS FROM A LOVE CIRCUS** [ ] [ ]
– Baby on a plane / A beautiful schizophrenic "Where's Miamo-Tutti? – interlude / I love a snot / Forget it, it's a mystery / Victoria's secret (Just a bad dream – interlude) / We suck / Lovesick / Singing to the birds / Messages from Sophia (There's more Kitties in the world than Miamo-Tutti – interlude) / Big, big world. *(cd re-iss. Jul98; GAD 6012CD)*

Sep 97. (12") *<8>* **LOVESICK** [-] [ ]

— <above was issued in US on 'Output'>

— In June '97, LISA subsequently teamed up with GIANT SAND who had become OP8. They released a one-off set, 'SLUSH'.

Jul 98. (cd) *<78014>* **SLIDE** [-] [ ]
– Way below the radio / No color here / Tomorrowing / Electrified / Slide / If I think of love / Crash / Wood floors / Turning into Betty / Guillotine / Reptile.

GERMS

Formed: Los Angeles, California, USA . . . April '77 by DARBY CRASH, PAT SMEAR, LORNA DOOM and BELINDA CARLISLE. The latter soon departed before groundbreaking debut 45, 'FORMING' (she later helped to form The GO-GO'S). The GERMS signed to the (then) indie, 'Slash', finally issuing a debut album, 'GI', in '79, this highly influential (KURT COBAIN was a massive fan!) outfit doing more than their fair share to define the boundaries of American punk/hardcore. In keeping with their incendiary nature, the band burned out in early 1980, only to reform approximately a year later. This incarnation was even more short-lived, CRASH dying of a heroin overdose a week after their reunion on the 12th July '80, aged only 22. Pioneers of hardcore punk, The GERMS made way for The DEAD KENNEDYS, BLACK FLAG and a host of grunge devotees including NIRVANA, HOLE, etc. • **Covered:** ROUND AND ROUND (Chuck Berry). • **Trivia:** They were given tribute from many of the aforementioned bands on 1996 album, 'GERMS (TRIBUTE) – A SMALL CIRCLE OF FRIENDS' on 'Grass Grow' label; (10042). In March '95, PAT SMEAR, now a member of DAVE GROHL's post-Nirvana outfit, FOO FIGHTERS, was part of HOLEZ (aka COURTNEY LOVE, PATTY & ERIC) on their 7" tribute to The GERMS, 'CIRCLE 1' (released by 'Dutch East India'; (9037-7); The B-side was by MONKEYWRENCH)

Album rating: GI (*8)

DARBY CRASH (b. JAN PAUL BEAHM) – vocals / **PAT SMEAR** – guitar / **LORNA DOOM** – bass / **D.J. BONEBRAKE** (b. DON BOLES) – drums repl. BELINDA CARLISLE who later joined GO-GO'S and is currently top solo chanteuse

not iss. What?

Nov 77. (7") *(WHAT 01)* **FORMING. / SEX BOY (live)** [-] [ ]

not iss. Slash Scam

Nov 78. (7"m) *<101>* **LEXICON DEVIL. / CIRCLE ONE / NO GOD** [-] [ ]

— **DON BOLLES** – drums (of 45 GRAVE) repl. BONEBRAKE who joined X

Nov 80. (lp) *<SR 103>* **GI** (rec.1979) [-] [ ]
<US re-iss. 1990's on 'Warners'; 23932>

— split early in 1980, but featured on various artists lp 'THE DECLINE' for 'Slash'; <SR 105>. Had to split once more, when on 6th December '80, CRASH died of heroin overdose.

Sep 81. (12"ep) *<SREP 108>* **WHAT WE DO IS SECRET** [-] [ ]
– Round and round / Lexicon devil / Circle one / Caught in my eye / No god / The other newest one / My love.

— PAT SMEAR later went solo.

– compilations, etc. –

May 83. (c) *R.O.I.R.; <A 108>* **GERMICIDE – LIVE AT THE WHISKY (live)** [-] [ ]
– Forming / Sex boy / Victim / Street dreams / Let's pretend / Get a grip / Suicide machine / Sugar sugar / Teenage clone (wild baby) / Grand old flag. *(cd-iss. Nov94; RE 108CD)*

1985. (lp) *Gasatanka;* **LET THE CIRCLE BE UNBROKEN** [-] [ ]

1985. (lp) *Ghost O' Darb;* **LION'S SHARE** [-] [ ]

1986. (lp) *X.E.S.;* **ROCK N' RULE** [-] [ ]

Apr 93. (7") *Rockville; (ROCK 6094)* **COMMUNIST EYES. /** [ ] [-]

Aug 93. (cd) *Slash; <45239-2>* **GERMS (M.I.A.) THE COMPLETE ANTHOLOGY** [-] [ ]
– Forming / Sexboy / Lexicon devil / Circle one / No God / What we do is secret / Communist eyes / Land of treason / Richie Dagger's crime / Strange notes / American leather / Lexicon devil / Manimal / Our way / We must bleed / Media blitz / Other newest one / Let's pretend / Dragon lady / Slave / Shut down (annihilation man) / Caught in my eye / Round and round / My tunnel / Throw it away / Not all right / No I hear the laughter / Going down / Lion's share / Forming 2.

Jan 94. (cd) *Cleopatra; <(CLEO 3731CD)>* **MEDIA BLITZ** [ ] [ ] Jun93

1990's. (cd-ep) *Munster; <MR 25>* **CAT'S CLAUSE** [-] [ ]

PAT SMEAR

— with **WALTER SPENCER** – bass / **GARY JACOBY** – drums / **MICHELE GREGG** – voices

S.S.T. S.S.T.

May 93. (cd/c) *<(SST 294 CD/C)>* **SO YOU FELL IN LOVE WITH A MUSICIAN** [ ] [ ] Nov92
– I'll find you / Lulu Belle / Creep street / Holy Bulsara / Ever alone with thee / All my cheating / Innocent X / Cold towne / Yummy yuck / Love your friends / Lazy.

— joined NIRVANA in 1993 and helped form FOO FIGHTERS with DAVE GROHL

Lisa GERRARD (see under ⇒ DEAD CAN DANCE)

GHOST DANCE

Formed: Leeds, England . . . 1985 by GARY MARX and ANNE-MARIE (NOVAK), both card-carrying goths with a top pedigree:- the former ex-SISTYERS OF MERCY, the latter ex-SKELETAL FAMILY. Completing the line-up with a rhythm section of ETCH and PANDORA (actually a drum machine!), the group debuted on their own imprint, 'Karbon', the single, 'RIVER OF NO RETURN' selling well enough in Spring '86 to reach the higher rungs of the indie chart. A further handful of 45's haunted the shops over the course of the following year, collected together at the tail end of '87 as 'GATHERING DUST'. With the recruitment of second guitarist, RICHARD STEEL, the band signed a major record deal with 'Chrysalis', the resulting single, 'DOWN TO THE WIRE' (a minor UK hit) and album, 'STOP THE WORLD' (1989), treading an uncomfortable line between commerciality and underground credibility. While contemporaries such as the SISTERS, the MISSION and ALL ABOUT EVE, all found a way to combine artistic integrity and chart success, GHOST DANCE could only walk in their shadow, finding themselves unceremoniously dropped by their label midway through a European tour. The final nail in their proverbial coffin came early 1990 as ETCH signed up with rivals, The MISSION. • **Songwriters:** MARX except BOTH ENDS BURNING (Roxy Music) / HEART FULL OF SOUL (Yardbirds) / RADAR LOVE (Golden Earring) / CAN THE CAN (Suzi Quatro) / etc.

Album rating: GATHERING DUST compilation (*6) / STOP THE WORLD (*5)

ANNE-MARIE (NOVAK) – vocals (ex-SKELETAL FAMILY) / **GARY MARX** – guitar (ex-SISTERS OF MERCY) / **ETCH** – bass (ex-CITRON GIRLS) / drum machine PANDORA

Karbon not iss.

Apr 86. (12"ep) *(KAR 602T)* **RIVER OF NO RETURN. / YESTERDAY AGAIN / BOTH ENDS BURNING** [ ] [-]

Jul 86. (12") *(KAR 606T)* **HEART FULL OF SOUL. / RADAR LOVE** [ ] [-]

Oct 86. (7") *(KAR 604)* **THE GRIP OF LOVE. / WHERE SPIRITS FLY** [ ] [-]
(12") *(KAR 604T)* – ('A'-Bombay mix) / Last train / A deeper blue / ('A'-Cheaper blues version).

— **JOHN GRANT** – drums repl. drum machine

— extra guitar players on tour **STEVE SMITH + PAUL SOUTHERN**

Jul 87. (12"ep) *(KAR 608T)* **A WORD TO THE WISE** [ ] [-]
– When I call / Fools gold / One light / Holding on.

Dec 87. (lp) *(KARXL 303)* **GATHERING DUST** [ ] [-]
– (compilation of early singles)

— added **RICHARD STEEL** – guitar

Chrysalis Chrysalis

Jun 89. (7") *(CHS/+MC 3376)* **DOWN TO THE WIRE. / BLOOD STILL FLOWS** [66] [ ]
(12"+=) *(CHS12 3376)* – Mirror blind / Dr. Love.
(cd-s+=) *(CHSCD 3376)* – The grip of love (live) / Last train (live) / Celebrate (live).

Sep 89. (lp/c/cd) *(CHR/ZCHR/CCD 1706)* **STOP THE WORLD** [ ] [ ]
– Down to the wire / Celebrate / Walk in my shadow / Cinder road / I will wait / Stop the world / Falling again / Heaven and beyond / The love I need / Spin the wheel. *(c+=/cd+=)* – Stop the world (live) / The love I need (live) / Fools gold (live) / Turn to me (live).

Sep 89. (7"/c-s) *(CHS/+MC 3402)* **CELEBRATE. /** [ ] [ ]
(12"+=/cd-s+=) *(CHS 12/CD 3402)* –

— split early 1990 and ETCH joined The MISSION, then LOUD

GIANT SAND

Formed: Tucson, Arizona ... 1980 as GIANT SANDWORMS by singer-songwriter/multi-instrumentalist, HOWE GELB along with RAINER PTACEK, DAVE SEGER and BILLY SED. The original line-up recorded two EP's preceding a temporary relocation to New York. By the time they'd returned to Arizona, SEGER had departed for fellow desert-rockers NAKED PREY and had been replaced by SCOTT GERBER. A further EP followed before GELB sacked the whole band and basically operated GIANT SAND as a solo venture, using varying personnel according to the project in hand. The first such project was the 'VALLEY OF RAIN' (1986) album, utilising GERBER, NAKED PREY's TOM LARKINS and GREEN ON RED man, CHRIS CACAVAS. Released on 'Zippo' (the Clapham, London based record shop/label who were also instrumental in kickstarting the careers of GREEN ON RED and The LONG RYDERS), the record showcased GELB's brand of breakneck roots-rock and guitar manipulation/abuse (notably on 'BLACK VENETIAN BLIND') framing a vocal style lying somewhere between a preacher-like NEIL YOUNG exhortation and a LOU REED drawl. As prolific as he was restless, GELB filtered his acutely observed, sun-scorched vignettes through side projects such as THE BAND OF BLANKY RANCHETTE and bonafide solo ventures like 1991's 'DREADED BROWN RECLUSE'. GIANT SAND recordings continued to come thick and fast, 1986 seeing the release of a second album, 'BALLAD OF A THIN LINE MAN' (the last to feature GERBER, who went on to form LOS CRUZOS with fomer GS sticksman SED), while the blistering 'STORM' and the more composed 'LOVE SONGS' both surfaced in 1988. Augmented by drummer JOHN CONVERTINO, 'LONG STEM RANT' was released at the turn of the decade while a link-up with EVAN DANDO resulted in touring emsemble, FRUIT CHILD LARGE. On the recording front, the Arizonian enigma continued to impress the critics and his cult following with a further series of GIANT SAND albums on various labels including 'RAMP' (1991), 'CENTER OF THE UNIVERSE' (1992) and 'STROMAUSFALL' (1994). Around the same time, GELB issued his third solo set, 'GLUM' (1994), later returning to the studio with his GIANT SAND cohorts to record 'BACKYARD BARBEQUE BROADCAST' (1996). Of late, HOWIE has been working with LISA GERMANO under the guise of OP8, releasing the 'SLUSH' (1997) album on Richard Branson's 'V2' imprint. CONVERTINO and other GELB/'SAND sidekick, JERRY BURNS, subsequently hooked up to form minimalist alt-country outfit, CALEXICO, releasing the 'SPOKE' album in '97 and a critically acclaimed follow-up, 'THE BLACK LIGHT', in '98. • **Songwriters:** GELB except ALL ALONG THE WATCHTOWER (Bob Dylan) / THE DOCK OF THE BAY (Otis Redding) + a THIN LIZZY tribute medley. OP8 covered SAND (Lee Hazlewood) / LOST IN SPACE (. . . Burns) / ROUND AND ROUND (Neil Young).

Album rating: VALLEY OF RAIN (*7) / BALLAD OF A THIN LINE MAN (*6) / STORM (*6) / THE LOVE SONGS LP (*6) / LONG STEM RANT (*6) / RAMP (*6) / GIANT SONGS compilation (*7) / GIANT SONGS 2 compilation (*6) / Howie Gelb: GLUM (*5) / DREADED BROWN RECLUSE (*5) / OP8: SLUSH (*6)

GIANT SANDWORMS

HOWE GELB – vocals, guitar, bass, keyboards / **RAINER PTACEK** – guitar / **BILLY SED** – drums

not iss. Boneless

1980. (7"ep) **WILL WALLOW AND ROAM AFTER THE RUIN** -

— added **DAVE SEGER** – bass

New Rose not iss.

1985. (7"ep) *(NEW 72)* **VALLEY OF RAIN** - French

— **SCOTT GERBER** – bass, vocals repl. SEGER who joined NAKED PREY

One Big Guitar not iss.

Dec 85. (7") *(OBG 001)* **DON'T TURN AWAY. / LONGSLEEVES**

GIANT SAND

— **GELB + GERBER** brought in **TOM LARKINS** – drums (of NAKED PREY) / **WINSTON A. WATSON** – drums / guest **CHRIS CACAVAS** – piano (on 1) (of GREEN ON RED)

Zippo not iss.

May 86. (lp/c) *(ZONG/+CASS 008)* **VALLEY OF RAIN** -
– Down on town / Love's no answer / Black venetian blind / Curse of a thousand flames / Artists / Man of want / Valley of rain / Tumble and tear / October anywhere / Barrio / Death, dying and channel 5 / Torture of love. *(cd-iss. Jul90; ZONGCD 008)*

— GELB added girlfriend **PAULA BROWN** – bass, guitar

Sep 86. (lp) *(ZONG 13)* **BALLAD OF A THIN LINE MAN** -
– Thin line man / All along the watchtower / Graveyard / Body of water / Last legs / You can't put your arms around a memory / A hard man to get to know / Who am I / The chill outside / Desperate man. *(cd-iss. Jul90; ZONGCD 013)*

— now without GERBER who joined SIDEWINDERS and eventually LOS CRUZOS

Demon Homestead

Mar 88. (7") **UNEVEN LIGHT OF DAY. /** -
Apr 88. (lp/cd) *(FIEND/+CD 115)* **STORM** -
– Uneven light of day / Town where no town belongs / Back to black and grey / Bigger than that / Right makes right / Three 6ixes / Big rock / The replacement / Storm / War is a big word / Town with little or no pity / The weight. *(cd re-iss. Sep90; same)*

Dec 88. (lp/cd) *(FIEND/+CD 129)* <HMS 129> **THE LOVE SONGS**
– Wearing the robes of bible black / One man's woman / No man's land / Mad dog a man / Fingernail moon, barracuda and me / Mountain of love / Almost the politician's wife / The doors / Love like a train / Is that all there is? *(cd re-iss. Sep90; same)*

Jan 90. (lp/cd) *(FIEND/+CD 164)* <HMS 148> **LONG STEM RANT**
– Unfinished love / Sandman / Bloodstone / Searchlight / Smash jazz / Sucker in a cage / Patsy does Dylan / Its long / Bout now / Lag craw loving cup / Paved road to Berlin / Anthem / Picture shows / Drum & guitar / Get to leave. *(cd+=)* – Searchlight cha cha / Return of the big red guitar / Stuck dog / Real gone blue guitar / The jig "zup". *(re-iss. Jun93 on 'Homestead' cd/lp; same)*

Demon Restless

Nov 90. (lp/cd) *(FIEND/+CD 204)* <72595> **SWERVE**
– Trickle down system / Dream stay / Former version of ourselves / Angels at night / Can't find love / Swerver / Sisters and brothers / Swerving / Every grain of sand. *(cd+=)* – Some kind of / Swervette / Final swerve.

— HOWE + PAULA brought in **JERRY BURNS** – bass, vocals / **JOHN CONVERTINO** – drums / **INDIOSA PATSY JEAN** – vocals

Rough Trade Restless

Nov 91. (cd/c/lp) *(R 276-2/-4/-1)* <72599> **RAMP**
– Romance of falling / Warm storm / Wonder / Welcome to my world /-Anti-shadow / Jazzer snipe / Shadow to you / Z.Z. quicker foot / Neon filler / Seldom matters / Resolver / Nowhere. *(cd+=/c+=)* – Always horses coming / Patsy's blues.

Brake Out Restless

Nov 92. (cd) *(OUT 1092)* <72731> **CENTER OF THE UNIVERSE** Aug92
– Seeded ('tween bone and bark) / Pathfinder / Center of the universe / Off ramp man / Year of the dog / Live to tell / Thrust / Loretta and the insect world / Sonic drive in / Milkshake girl / Stuck / Thing like that / Return to fodder / Unwed and well sped / Solomon's ride. *(hidden track+=)*

Feb 93. (7") *(PELL 027)* **SOLOMON'S RIDE. /**
(above issued on 'Capella')

1994. (cd) <72746> **PURGE & SLOUCH** -
– Slander / Bender / Swamp thing / Santana, Castanada and you / Blue lit rope / Overture, pt.1 / Rice road rumba / Corridor / Slice and dice blues / High lonesome curl / New carjack city blues / Owed ode / Overture, pt.2 / Here on the planet / Elevator music / Song for the accountants / The dock of the bay / Tripping moon / Thin Lizzy tribute / Bed of nails / Dance of Cicadas.

— **MARK WALTON** – bass (ex-DREAM SYNDICATE) repl. BURNS (although BURNS was later to return)

— **NEIL HARRY** – pedal steel guitar repl. PATSY

Return To Sender Return To Sender

Nov 94. (cd) *(RTSCD 7)* **STROMAUSFALL** -

not iss. Imago

1995. (cd/c) <21037-2/-4> **GLUM** -

Enemy Enemy

Dec 95. (cd/lp) *(OUT 122-2/-1)* **GOODS AND SERVICES** -

Koch Int. Koch Int.

Apr 96. (m-cd) <(7914-2)> **BACKYARD BARBEQUE BROADCAST**
– BBQ suite / Mope a long / Lean / Get to leave / Lester lampshade / Blue waltz.

— added **LISA GERMANO** – vocals, instruments (solo artist)

V2 Thirsty Ear

Jun 97. (cd; as OP8 & LISA GERMANO) *(VVR 100033-2)* <57030> **SLUSH** Feb97
– Sand / Lost in space / If I think of love / Leather / It's a rainbow / OP8 / Cracklin' water / Never see it coming / Tom, Dick and Harry / The Devil loves L.A. / Round and round.

– compilations, etc. –

1989. (cd) *Homestead;* <HMS 134> **GIANT SANDWICH** -
– Wishing well / Tumble 'n' tear / Reptilian / Hard man to get to know / Black venetian blind / Thin line man / Artists / What you hate / October anywhere / Black venetian blind (page 1) / Code of the road / Underground train / Spinning room waltz / Accordion to Howe / Badlands / Up on the hill / Heartland.

Jul 89. (cd) *Demon; (GSCD 1)* **GIANT SONGS: THE BEST OF GIANT SAND** -
– Down on town / Love's no answer / Curse of a thousand flames / Valley of rain / Barrio / Thin line man / Graveyard / Body of water / Heartland / Moon over Memphis / Underground train / Uneven light of day / Bigger than that / Big rock / Wearing the robes of bible black / One man's woman / No man's land / Finger nail moon, barracuda and me / Mountain of love.

Aug 95. (cd) *Demon;* <(GSCD 2)> **GIANT SONGS 2 – THE BEST OF GIANT SAND VOLUME TWO**
– Can't find love / Get to leave / Town with little or no pity / Dreamville New Mexico / October anywhere / Almost the politician's wife / Badlands / Trickle down system / Love like a train / Sage advice / Sisters and brothers / Sandman / Death dying and channel 5 / Who am I? / Sucker in a cage / Christmas everyday (maybe it'll help).

Jun 97. (cd) *Diablo;* <831> **BALLAD OF A THIN LINE MAN + VALLEY OF RAIN** -

BAND OF . . .BLACKY RANCHETTE

HOWE GELB + a plethora of musicians

Zippo Black Sand

Oct 86. (lp) *(ZONG 014)* **HEARTLAND**
– Heartland / Moon over Memphis / All done in / Badlands / Roof's on fire / Underground train / Nowhere / Steadfast / One way ticket / Changing heart. *(rel.1985 on 'New Rose' in France)*

Demon Demon

May 90. (lp/cd) *(FIEND/+CD 181)* <72742> **SAGE ADVICE**
– Loving cup / Burning desire / Trouble man / Dreamville, New Mexico / Indiosa / Wild dog waltz / Sage advice / Outside an angel's reach / Shards of time / Still too far / Blanket of stars / You are my sunshine. *(cd+=)* – HEARTLAND (7 tracks).

HOWE GELB

— with members of GIANT SAND recorded in last 5 years

Houses In Motion Restless

Oct 93. (cd) *(HIM 8907)* <72743> **DREADED BROWN RECLUSE**
– Spirit lie / Picture shows / Loretta & the insect world / Actually faxing Sophia / Cello in the city / Still too far / Warm storm / Always horses coming / Vigdis / Vienna two-step throw-away / Bible black, book II / Brown recluse / Wild dog waltz / Blanket for Tina / Victoria Wisp.

V2 V2

Aug 98. (cd) <27028> **HISSER**

CALEXICO

— aka the moonlighting **JERRY BURNS + JOHN COVERTINO**, who incidentally play a type of desert "new country" rock (duo with **BRIDGET KEATING** – violin)

Quarter Stick Quarter Stick

Sep 97. (cd) <(QS 51CD)> **SPOKE** Aug97
– Low expectations / Mind the gap / Mazurra / Sanchez / Haul / Slag / Paper route / Glimpse / Navy cut / Spokes / Scout / Point Vicente / Wash / Ice cream jeep / Windjammer / Mazurka / Removed / Hitch / Stinging nettle.

All City Quarter Stick

Oct 97. (7") *(ALLCITY 2)* **LACQUER. / DRAPE**

City Slang Quarter Stick

Oct 98. (cd/d-lp) *(efa 08707-2/-1)* <QS 54CD> **THE BLACK LIGHT** May98
– Gypsy's curse / Fake fur / Ride (part II) / Where water flows / The black light / Sideshow / Chach / Missing / Minas de cobre (for better metal) / Over your shoulder / Vinegaroon / Trigger / Sprawl / Stray / Old man waltz / Bloodflow / Frontera.

Oct 98. (cd-s) *(08713-2)* **STRAY / LACQUER / DRAPE** –

GIFT (see under ⇒ POISON IDEA)

GIGOLO AUNTS

Formed: Potsdam, New York, USA . . . 1981 as SNIPER by DAVE GIBBS, brothers PHIL and STEVE HURLEY and PHIL BROUWER. After running a gamut of different monikers (including MARAUDER and ROSETTA STONE), the lads settled on the GIGOLO AUNTS following a suggestion by GIBBS' father who'd conceivably heard the SYD BARRETT track of the same name. Now basing themselves in Boston, Massachusetts, the power-pop quartet set to work on their debut album, 'EVERYBODY HAPPY' (1988). Inactive for the next few years, GIBBS guested for the VELVET CRUSH on a 1992 British tour in the interim, a chance meeting with 'Creation' supremo ALAN McGEE leading to a UK deal (with 'Fire') for the GIGOLO AUNTS. A trio of BYRDS-esque power-pop singles surfaced over the course of the next year, 'COPE', 'GUN' and 'MRS. WASHINGTON', all three featuring on their long-awaited second album, 'FLIPPIN' OUT' (1993); amid encouraging reviews and a considerable degree of hype, the 'AUNTS were taken on by 'R.C.A.' in the States, where the album was released the following Spring. One of the album's stand-out tracks, 'WHERE I FIND MY HEAVEN', saw the band achieve a modicum of belated fame after it was used in the film, 'Dumb And Dumber', although its subsequent Top 30 status in the UK (Spring '95) came after BBC2 adopted the song as the theme tune to sit-com, 'Game On'. Names such as The ICICLE WORKS, CROWDED HOUSE, the RASPBERRIES and BIG STAR continually cropped up in reviews, the good-time harmony merchants (DAVE and PHIL) even turning down a chance to play in the much-publicised 1993 re-formation of the latter outfit. Surprisingly, the GIGOLO AUNTS have been conspicuous by their absence from the music scene of the mid to late 90's, only a mini-cd, 'LEARN TO PLAY GUITAR', emerging in 1997. • **Covered:** ASK (Smiths) / CAN YOU GET TO THAT (Funkadelic) / FLIPPIN' OUT (V. Casey) / WINDSOR DAM (Big Dipper) / SERIOUS DRUGS (BMX Bandits).

Album rating: EVERYBODY HAPPY (*5) / FLIPPIN' OUT (*8) / LEARN TO PLAY GUITAR (*5)

DAVE GIBBS – vocals, guitar / **PHIL HURLEY** – guitar / **STEVE HURLEY** – bass / **PAUL BROUWER** – drums

not iss. Twin Tone – Coyote

1988. (lp) <TTC 88146> **EVERYBODY HAPPY** –
– Summertime evening / Avalanche / Slipping away / Marble statue / Outside inside / Her face contorted / I can see / Coming clean / People walk up / Not for me / Holy Toledo / Is everybody happy?

Fire R.C.A.

Oct 92. (7") *(BLAZE 58)* **COPE. / BLOOM** –
(cd-s+=) *(BLAZE 58CD)* –

Mar 93. (7") *(BLAZE 61)* **GUN. / TAKE ME ON** –
(cd-s+=) *(BLAZE 61CD)* – Sled / Walk among us.

Aug 93. (7") *(7SM 001)* **MRS. WASHINGTON. / SERIOUS DRUGS** –

Oct 93. (cd/c/lp) *(FIRE CD/MC/LP 35)* <66392-2/-4/-1> **FLIPPIN' OUT** Apr94
– Cope / Where I find my Heaven / Lullaby / Easy reader / Figurine / Mrs. Washington / Bloom / Gun / Pin cushion / Flippin' out. *(re-iss. May95 +=; same)* – FULL-ON BLOOM

Jan 94. (cd-s) **WHERE I FIND MY HEAVEN. / THAT'S O.K.** –

Apr 94. (7"/c-s) *(BLAZE 68/+MC)* **MRS. WASHINGTON. / SERIOUS DRUGS** 74
(12"/cd-s) *(BLAZE 68 T/CD)* – ('A'side) / Can you get to that / Windsor dam / Supernova crush.

Fire Alias

May 94. (cd-ep) *(mail-order)* <60051> **FULL-ON BLOOM** – Jul93
– Bloom / Serious drugs / That's O.K. / Little Carl / Walk among us / Take me on.

Apr 95. (7"/c-s) *(BLAZE 87/+MC)* **WHERE I FIND MY HEAVEN (remix). / RIDE ON BABY RIDE ON (acoustic)** 29
(cd-s+=) *(BLAZE 87CD)* – Lemon peeler / Serious drugs.

— **FRED ELTRINGHAM** – drums; repl. BROUWER

Wicked Disc Wicked Disc

Sep 97. (m-cd) <(WIC 1007)> **LEARN TO PLAY GUITAR** Feb97
– Kinda girl / Wishing you the worst / Sway / Slow / Rocking chair / The sun will rise again.

– compilations, etc. –

Jun 98. (cd) *Reactive; (REMCD 528) / Nectar; <549>* **WHERE I FIND MY HEAVEN (THE BEST OF THE GIGOLO AUNTS)** 1997

GILBERT & LEWIS (see under ⇒ WIRE)

Andy GILL (see under ⇒ GANG OF FOUR)

GIN BLOSSOMS

Formed: Tempe, Arizona, USA . . . early 90's by ROBIN WILSON, JESSE VALENZUELA, DOUG HOPKINS, BILL LEEN and PHILIP RHODES. In 1992, they signed to 'A&M', who issued their JOHN HAMPTON (ex-REPLACEMENTS)-produced debut album, the college radio countryish-rock of 'NEW MISERABLE EXPERIENCE'. Although slow to get off the mark, the record soon shot into the Stateside Top 30, helped by two memorable major hit singles in 1993; 'HEY JEALOUSY' and 'FOUND OUT ABOUT YOU'. However, the resigned melancholy of much of the band's material was to take on a tragic resonance when the 32 year-old HOPKINS committed suicide on the 5th of December '93. However, the group persevered and found a new guitarist, SCOTT JOHNSON, who finally made his debbut of early '96's comeback, 'CONGRATULATIONS . . . I'M SORRY'. This US Top 10 album featured their biggest selling single to date, 'TIL I HEAR IT FROM YOU'. • **Songwriters:** Mostly HOPKINS or VALENZUELA / WILSON; except CHRISTINE SIXTEEN (Kiss).

Album rating: NEW MISERABLE EXPERIENCE (*6) / CONGRATULATIONS . . . I'M SORRY (*5)

ROBIN WILSON – vocals, acoustic guitar / **JESSE VALENZUELA** – guitar, vocals / **DOUG HOPKINS** – guitars / **BILL LEEN** – bass / **PHILLIP RHODES** – drums, percussion

Fontana A&M

Jul 92. (12"ep/cd-ep) **UP & CRUMBLING** –

Jul 93. (c-s) <0242> **HEY JEALOUSY / 29** – 25

Aug 93. (c-ep/cd-ep) *(GIN MC/CD 1)* **HEY JEALOUSY / KELI RICHARDS / COLD RIVER DICK / KRISTINE IRENE** –

Sep 93. (cd/c) *(395403-2/-4)* <5403> **NEW MISERABLE EXPERIENCE** 30 Aug92
– Lost horizons / Hey jealousy / Mrs. Rita / Until I fall away / Hold me down / Cajun song / Hands are tied / Found out about you / Allison Road / 29 / Pieces of the night / Cheatin'. *(re-dist.Feb94 hit UK No.53)*

Oct 93. (c-s/12"colrd/cd-s) *(GIN MC/T/CD 2)* **MRS. RITA. / SOUL DEEP / HEART AWAY** –

Nov 93. (c-s) <0418> **FOUND OUT ABOUT YOU / HANDS ARE TIED** – 25

Jan 94. (7"ep/c-ep) *(GIN/+MC 3)* **HEY JEALOUSY / COLD RIVER DICK. / KRISTINE IRENE / KELI RICHARDS** 24 –
(cd-ep) *(GINCD 3)* – ('A'side) / Cajun song / Just south of nowhere / Angels tonight.
(9"ep) *(GIN 3-12)* – ('A'side) / Keli Richards / Cajun song.

Apr 94. (7"/c-s) *(GIN/+MC 4)* **FOUND OUT ABOUT YOU. / HEY JEALOUSY (live)** 40 –
(cd-s+=) *(GINCD 4)* – Hands are tied (live) / 29 (live) / Fulsome Prison (live).
(cd-s+=) *(GINCX 4)* – Hold me down (live) / Mrs. Rita (live).

— **SCOTT JOHNSON** – guitars; repl. HOPKINS who killed himself on the 5th December '93

A&M A&M

Jan 96. (c-s,cd-s) <1380> **TIL I HEAR IT FROM YOU / FOLLOW YOU DOWN** – 9 11

Jan 96. (c-ep/cd-ep) *(581 227-4/-2)* **TIL I HEAR IT FROM YOU / SEEING STARS / IDIOT SUMMER / HANDS ARE TIED** 39 –

Feb 96. (cd/c) *(540 470-2/-4)* <0470> **CONGRATULATIONS . . . I'M SORRY** 42 10
– Day job / Highwire / Follow you down / Not only dumb / As long as it matters / Perfectly still / My car / Virginia / Whitewash / I can't figure you out / Memphis time / Competition smile / Til I hear it from you.

Apr 96. (c-ep/cd-ep) *(581 507-4/-2)* **FOLLOW YOU DOWN** –
(cd-ep) *(581 551-2)* –

Jul 96. (c-s,cd-s) <1672> **AS LONG AS IT MATTERS / ALLISON ROAD (live)** – 75

Aug 96. (c-ep/cd-ep) *(581 843-4/-2)* **AS LONG AS IT MATTERS / FOLLOW YOU DOWN / MEMPHIS TIME (live) / MRS. RITA (live)** –

GINGER (see under ⇒ GRAPES OF WRATH)

Greg GINN / GONE (see under ⇒ BLACK FLAG)

Michael GIRA (see under ⇒ SWANS)

GIRLS AGAINST BOYS

Formed: Washington DC, USA . . . 1988 out of LUNCHMEAT, then SOULSIDE (2/3 albums for 'Dischord') by SCOTT McCLOUD, ALEXIS FLEISIG and JOHNNY TEMPLE. ELI JANNEY, who had been the latter act's soundman joined as the band evolved into GIRLS AGAINST BOYS (drummer BRENDAN CANTY was also part of the part-time band before he joined FUGAZI, while AMY PICKERING was also involved). Their brand of hardcore industrial rock was first sampled on the 'Adult Swim' debut, 'NINETIES Vs. EIGHTIES' (1990), although it was their second set a few years later, 'TROPIC OF SCORPIO', that tested the waters. SCOTT subsequently moved to New York to try out film school, the others joining as they signed with 'Touch & Go'. Three albums of considerable European success were delivered during the mid 90's, 'VENUS LUXURE NO 1 BABY' (1993), 'CRUISE YOURSELF' (1994) and 'HOUSE OF GVSB' (1996), before their bass-heavy gutter sound was wanted by major 'Geffen'. In 1998, the 'BOYS were on the threshold of mini-stardom with their sixth set, 'FREAK*ON*ICA', an album full of sexual sleaze and of course, noise. • **Covered:** SHE'S LOST CONTROL (Joy Division).

Album rating: HOUSE OF GVSB (*7) / FREAK*ON*ICA (*7)

SOULSIDE

SCOTT McCLOUD (b.1968) – vocals, guitar / **JOHNNY TEMPLE** (b.1968) – bass / **ALEXIS FLEISIG** (b.1967) – drums

Dischord Dischord

Aug 88. (lp) <(DISCHORD 29)> **TRIGGER**
Jun 89. (7") <(DISCHORD 34)> **BASS. / 103**
Jan 90. (m-lp) <(DISCHORD 38)> **HOT BODI-GRAM**
Feb 91. (cd) <(DISCHORD 51)> **SOON COME HAPPY** (compilation of all work)
– Baby / Trigger / Name is mind / Problems faced with traveling / War / K.T.T.K. / Pocket hurts / Forgiveness / Bass / 103 / The other side / God city / What / Punch the geek / Clifton wall / New slow fucky / Pembroke / Hate music / New fast fucky / Kill / Bad show / Love supreme / Crazy.

(Dec87 on first three US releases)

— had already evolved into . . .

GIRLS AGAINST BOYS

McCLOUD, TEMPLE, FLEISIG + ELI JANNEY (b.1967) – sampler bass (keyboards) / plus **AMY PICKERING** (angel vocals) + **BRENDAN CANTY** (drums, organ) also on debut, CANTY joined FUGAZI

Adult Swim Adult Swim

Nov 90. (m-cd) <AS 3CD> **NINETIES vs. EIGHTIES** -
– Stay in the car / Jamie / Kitty-yo / Move / Angels / Skind.
Jun 92. (cd/c/lp) <(AS 4 CD/C/V)> **TROPIC OF SCORPIO**

Touch & Go Touch & Go

May 93. (7") <(TG 115)> **BULLETPROOF CUPID. /**
Jun 93. (lp/c/cd) <(TG 117/+C/CD)> **VENUS LUXURE NO.1 BABY**
– In like Flynn / Go be delighted / Rockets are red / Satin down / Let me come back / Learned it / et down / Bullet proof Cupid / Seven seas / Billy's one stop / Bug house.
May 94. (7") <(TG 129)> **SEXY SAM. / I'M FROM FRANCE**
(cd-s+=) <(TG 129CD)> – Stay in the car / My night of pleasure / Rockets are red.
Sep 94. (7") <(TG 137)> **I DON'T GOT A PLACE. /**
Oct 94. (lp/c/cd) <(TG 134/+C/CD)> **CRUISE YOURSELF**
Feb 95. (cd-ep) <(TG 140CD)> **KILL THE SEXPLAYER / SEXY SAM (live) / LEARNED IT (live) / LET ME COME BACK (live)**
Sep 95. (7"white/cd-s) (HUT 61/+CD) **SHE'S LOST CONTROL. / Miranda: LOVE WILL TEAR US APART**
(above issued on 'Hut')
Feb 96. (7"etched) <(TG 160)> **SUPER-FIRE**
(10"+=) <(TG 160-10)> – Viva Roma Star / Cashmachine.
(cd-s+=) <(TG 160CD)> – If glamour is dead / Cashmachine.
Mar 96. (lp/c/cd) <(TG 149/+C/CD)> **HOUSE OF GVSB**
– Super-fire / Click click / Crash 17 (X-rated car) / Disco six six six / Life in pink / The kinda mzk you like / Vera Cruz / Another drone in my head / Cashmachine / Wilmington / Zodiac love team. *(re-iss. Jun98; same)*
Nov 96. (cd-ep) <(TG 166CD)> **DISCO SIX SIX SIX / DISTRACTED (RVS7) / DO IT LIKE DIAMONDS / BLACK LEATHER / KEEP YER PANTS ON**

Radiopaque Radiopaque

Mar 97. (cd; shared with GUIDED BY VOICES) <(RR 13CD)> **8 ROUNDS** Jul97

Geffen Geffen

May 98. (cd/d-lp) <(GED/GEF 25156)> **FREAK*ON*ICA**
– Park avenue / Pleasurized / Psycho-future / Black hole / Roxy / One firecracker / Speedway / Exorcisto / Vogue thing / Push the fader / Exile / Cowboy's orbit.
Jun 98. (7"/cd-s) (GFS/+TD 22335) **PARK AVENUE. / AMERICAN WHITE DWARF (Miami Bassomatic remix) / EPR**
Dec 98. (7") (AKR 07) **ROXY (WHATEVER). /** -
(above issued on 'Akashic')

GIRLS AT OUR BEST

Formed: Leeds, England . . . 1979 out of S.O.S./BUTTERFLIES by JUDY 'JO' EVANS and three guys, JAMES 'JEZ' ALAN, GERARD 'TERRY' SWIFT and CHRIS OLDROYD. GAOB self-financed their debut single, 'GETTING NOWHERE FAST', the following Spring, a song which remains one of the band's finest three minutes and was later covered by Leeds' finest, The WEDDING PRESENT. A follow-up single, 'POLITICS', meanwhile, appeared on 'Rough Trade' later in 1980, their blend of RAINCOATS meets Baroque'n'roll one of the more interesting fusions of the post-punk era. JO's unique MADDY PRIOR-esque choral phrasing was meticulously enunciated in her characteristically Anglicised but off-key fashion, digging away at men in general on such proto-'Girl Power' ditties as 'FAST BOYFRIENDS'. The latter track actually previewed the group's one and only long-player, 'PLEASURE' (1981), a surprisingly impressive set of classy nursery rhyme punk which found a cult audience and a UK Top 60 placing; DARREN CARL HARPER had replaced OLDROYD by this point. Unfortunately, after a double-header, 'HEAVEN' / '£600,000' (both taken from the album), failed to hit the charts, they disbanded in the summer of '82, JEZ subsequently joined SEXBEAT (and later TALL BOYS). • **Trivia:** JUDY EVANS guested on THOMAS DOLBY's 1982 album, 'The Golden Age Of The Wireless'.

Album rating: PLEASURE (*8)

JUDY 'JO' EVANS – vocals / **JAMES 'JEZ' ALAN** – guitar / **GERARD 'TERRY' SWIFT** – bass / **CHRIS OLDROYD** – drums

Record not iss.

Apr 80. (7") (RR 001) **GETTING NOWHERE FAST. / WARM GIRLS** -

Rough Trade Rough Trade

Nov 80. (7") (RT 055) <RR 2> **POLITICS. / IT'S FASHION**

— **DARREN CARL HARPER** – drums; repl. OLDROYD (to MUSIC FOR PLEASURE)

Happy Birthday not iss.

Jun 81. (7") (UR 4) **GO FOR GOLD. / I'M BEAUTIFUL NOW** -

— **ROD JOHNSON** – drums; repl. HARPER (shared duties on album), guests incl. **THOMAS DOLBY** – synthesizer / **ALAN WAKEMAN** – clarinet / **DAVE FISHER** – piano

Oct 81. (lp) (RULP 1) **PLEASURE** 60 -
– Fast boyfriends / £600,000 / Pleasure / China blue / Heaven / I'm beautiful now / She's flipped / Waterbed babies / This train / Too big for your boots / Fun-city teenagers / Goodbye to that jazz. *(cd-iss. Oct94 on 'Vinyl Japan'; ASKCD 047)*
Oct 81. (7") (UR 6) **FAST BOYFRIENDS. / THIS TRAIN** -

God not iss.

May 82. (7") (GOD 1) **HEAVEN. / £600,000** -

— split 1982; JAMES ALAN joined SEXBEAT, and after only one single, 'PUMP', he joined The TALL BOYS

– compilations, etc. –

May 87. (12"ep) *Strange Fruit; (SFPS 029)* **THE PEEL SESSIONS (17.2.81)** -
– China blue / This train / Getting nowhere fast / Warm girls.

GIST (see under ⇒ YOUNG MARBLE GIANTS)

GLAND SHROUDS (see under ⇒ BLAKE, Karl)

GLAXO BABIES

Formed: Bristol, England . . . late 1977 by songwriter ROB CHAPMAN and DAN CATSIS (who also later moonlighted with The POP GROUP), the subsequent line-up also including TONY WRAFTER, TOMMY NICHOLS and the twin-drumming of GEOFF ALSOPP and CHARLES LLEWELLYN. Signing to Cherry Red subsidiary, 'Heartbeat', the freaky sextet issued their first John Peel Sessions in the shape of the 12"ep, 'THIS IS YOUR LIFE'. Later in 1979, a follow-up release, 'CHRISTINE KEELER', showed signs of danceability not unlike politico-punksters GANG OF FOUR and The MEKONS. The dawn of the 80's saw the release of their debut album, 'NINE MONTHS TO THE DISCO', recorded without lead singer, CHAPMAN and drummer, ALSOPP, the former having been replaced by a guy called AYLETT. Confusingly enough, a further album, 'PUT ME ON THE GUEST LIST', was released five months later although the recording stemmed from '78/'79. However, The GLAXO BABIES were forced to abandon the name after objections from the pharmaceutical company, Glaxo. In 1981, CATSIS, WRAFTER and LLEWELLYN adopted a new moniker, MAXIMUM JOY (after a GB track, 'MAXIMUM SEXUAL JOY'), taking on newcomers JANINE RAINFORTH and JOHN WADDINGTON (the latter ex-POP GROUP). Remaining with the GLAXO's last label, 'Y Records' (also home to SLITS and PIGBAG), MJ delivered a handful of 45's, the last of which, 'DO IT TODAY' (co-issued with 'Phonogram'), was aimed at the dance market. A disastrous attempt at a long-player, 'STATION MXJY' (co-produced by ADRIAN SHERWOOD), followed in 1982 and after an excursion into dance/DENNIS BOVELL-treated funk with a cover of Timmy Thomas' 'WHY CAN'T WE LIVE TOGETHER', the band finally split.

Album rating: NINE MONTHS TO THE DISCO (*4) / PUT ME ON THE GUEST LIST compilation (*5) / Maximum Joy: STATION MXJY (*3)

ROB CHAPMAN – vocals / **DAN CATSIS** – guitar, vocals / **TONY WRAFTER** – saxophone / **TOMMY NICHOLS** – bass, vocals / **GEOFF ALSOPP** – drums / **CHARLES LLEWELLYN** – drums

Heartbeat not iss.

Mar 79. (12"ep) (12PULSE 3) **THIS IS YOUR LIFE** -
– This is your life / Stay awake / Because of you / Who killed Bruce Lee.
Aug 79. (7") (PULSE 5) **CHRISTINE KEELER. / NOVA BOSSANOVA** -

— **AYLETT** – vocals; repl. CHAPMAN + ALSOPP

Apr 80. (lp) (HB 2) **NINE MONTHS TO THE DISCO** -
– Maximum sexual joy / This is your vendetta / Seven days / Electric church / Nine months to the disco / Promised land / The tea master and the assassin / Free dem cells / Dinosaur disco meets the swampstomp / Conscience / Slim / Shake.
Jun 80. (7") (PULSE 8) **SHAKE THE FOUNDATIONS. / SHE WENT TO PIECES (live)** -
Sep 80. (lp) (HB 3) **PUT ME ON THE GUEST LIST** (rec.1978-79 w/orig.line-up) -
– Avoiding the issue / Because of you / This is your life / Police state / Who killed Bruce Lee / Stay awake / She went to pieces / Burning / Flesh / Puppet patrol.

— **JONES** – saxophone; repl. WRAFTER

Y not iss.

Dec 80. (7"ep) (Y 6) **LIMITED ENTERTAINMENT** -
– There'll be no room for you in the shelter / Permission to be wrong / Limited entertainment / Dahij.

— altered their group moniker to . . .

MAXIMUM JOY

— **CATSIS, LLEWELLYN + WRAFTER** recruited **JANINE RAINFORTH** – vocals, clarinet / **JOHN WADDINGTON** – guitar, vocals (ex-POP GROUP)

Y Records 99 Records

Oct 81. (7"/12") *(Y 11/+T) <99 08EP>* **STRETCH. / SILENT STREET**
Feb 82. (7"/12") *(Y 15/+T)* **WHITE AND GREEN PLACE. / BUILDING BRIDGES** -

— **KEV EVANS** – bass, piano, vocals; repl. CATSIS

Jul 82. (7"/12") *(Y 26/+T)* **IN THE AIR. / SIMMER TIL DONE** -
Jul 82. (7") *(CLUB 1)* **DO IT TODAY. / TOUCHDOWN** -
(above was co-issued with 'Phonogram')
Oct 82. (lp) *(Y 28LP)* **STATION MXJY** -
– Dancing on my boomerang / Do it today / Let it take you there / Searching for a feeling / Where's Pete / Temple bomb twist / Mouse an' me / All wrapped up.

— **CATSIS** rejoined repl. EVANS

— guests on below were **PETA** – vocals / **DENNIS BOVELL** – production, vocals / **NELLY** – percussion

Garage not iss.

Apr 83. (7"/12") *(GAR 1/+12)* **WHY CAN'T WE LIVE TOGETHER. / MAN OF TRIBES** -

— disbanded after the commercial failure of above

GLITTERBOX

Formed: London, England ... late 1993 by JONNY GREEN, MILES HESELTINE and MARK SERVAS, who met at a college in Norwich, deciding there and then to start a band without the knowledge of how to play an instrument (who said punk was dead!). Early the following year, the three recruited TONY HOLLAND and subsequently played a disastrous solitary gig at a pub in London before retreating to their day jobs. Resurfacing with some of their own material early in '95, JONNY, MILES and TONY came up with the group name, SHE, eventually coaxing MARK to return from his new home in Barcelona. Annoyed by UK record labels who could not pigeonhole them between rock and indie, they sent demos to the States, the result being that A&R men quickly flew over to size them up; 'Atlantic' won the battle. However, luck was not on their side, when, in 1996, 'Death Row' all-female R&B act, SHE, threatened legal action (sleeping and fishes are two words that come to mind!?). Having already finished off the recording of their debut album, the release was delayed while the band came up with a new moniker, GLITTERBOX. However, yet more problems ensued as JONNY was hit by a throat virus which kept him out of the game for half a year. In August '97, the quartet finally released a single, 'YOU CAN'T LIVE ON MARS', its lack of appeal seeing the band downshift to Atlantic's subsidiary, 'Radar' for subsequent releases. Early the following year, the first of these, 'SCARED OF ALL THE WORLD', hit the shops and another, 'HOUDINI' preceded the long-awaited and nearly cancelled album, 'TIED AND TANGLED'. This was an overdue piece of Britrock-pop taking a whole list of influences including The MANICS, AFGHAN WHIGS and even TALKING HEADS!

Album rating: TIED & TANGLED (*7)

JONNY GREEN – vocals, guitar / **MILES HESELTINE** – guitar, vocals / **TONY HOLLAND** – bass / **MARK SERVAS** – drums

Atlantic Atlantic

Aug 97. (7") *(AT 005)* **YOU CAN'T LIVE ON MARS. / MOTORCYCLE SONG**
(cd-s+=) *(AT 005CD)* – Roller skates.

Radar Atlantic

Feb 98. (7") *(SCAN 28)* **SCARED OF ALL THE WORLD. / I'M YOUR MONSTER** -
(cd-s+=) *(SCANCS 28)* – Your ghost.
Apr 98. (7") *(SCAN 29)* **HOUDINI. / SUNK** -
(cd-s) *(SCANCS 29)* – ('A'side) / Still breathing / Illuminate you / Promises.
May 98. (cd) *(SCANCD 30) <83021>* **TIED & TANGLED** Oct97
– Houdini / Scared of all the world / Woody Allen / Superman / I can wait / You can't live on Mars / Jesus song / Summer song / Step inside / Sit back and watch her fly / Tonight to Hell.

GLOVE (see under ⇒ SIOUXSIE AND THE BANSHEES)

Jeremy GLUCK (see under ⇒ BARRACUDAS)

GO-BETWEENS

Formed: Brisbane, Australia ... 1978 by ROBERT FORSTER (guitar, vocals) and GRANT McLENNAN (vocals, lead guitar, bass) with DENNIS CANTWELL on drums. After a debut Australian-only 7" single, 'LEE REMICK', CANTWELL was replaced with TIM MUSTAFA while organist MALCOLM KELLY was brought in briefly for the early classic, 'PEOPLE SAY', the band's second and final domestic release (were also on the books of 'Beserkley' UK for a few months). Finally settling with LINDY MORRISON on drums, The GO-BETWEENS recorded two singles for seminal Scottish indie label, 'Postcard', before settling in London and signing with 'Rough Trade'. Their debut, 'SEND ME A LULLABY' (1982), drew comparisons with The TALKING HEADS, although their root influences remained the classic songwriting of BOB DYLAN and The VELVET UNDERGROUND. Following the addition of ROBERT VICKERS on bass, allowing McLENNAN to switch to guitar, 'BEFORE HOLLYWOOD' (1983) was a marked improvement. The twin songwriting and singing strength of McLENNAN and FORSTER was developing apace, the former's 'CATTLE AND CANE' a yearning, melancholy highlight. Rave reviews abounded and the band were soon signed to the Warner Brothers-affiliated 'Sire' label. 'SPRING HILL FAIR' (1984) marked the GO-BETWEENS major label debut, their swooning melodies enhanced by a superior production on classics like 'BACHELOR KISSES'. Again the band were heralded by the press and adored by a cult following yet a commercial breakthrough proved elusive. The group switched labels yet again (moving to 'Beggar's Banquet') for 'LIBERTY BELLE AND THE BLACK DIAMOND EXPRESS' (1986), the band's most accesible, and probably finest effort of their career; it remains a mystery why the lush guitar-pop of 'SPRING RAIN' failed to breach the charts. With the addition of AMANDA BROWN (guitar, violin, oboe, keyboards), the band cut the more ambitious 'TALLULAH' (1987) and despite a couple of strong singles, were still confined to the indie margins. Understandably, the group were miffed at their lack of any real success and '16 LOVERS LANE' (1988), another sterling set of consummate, painstakingly crafted songs, proved to be their final effort. The record reached a lowly No.81 on the UK chart, The GO-BETWEENS finally going their own way with McLENNAN and FORSTER both embarking on solo careers. FORSTER's 1991 debut, 'DANGER IN THE PAST' was a fine effort, its sound not much of a departure from the later GO-BETWEENS albums. 'CALLING FROM A COUNTRY PHONE' (1993) was rootsier, employing such traditional instrumentation as banjo and mandolin. McLENNAN initially worked on the more avant-garde project, JACK FROST, with STEVE KILBEY of The CHURCH, before releasing 'WATERSHED' in 1991 as G.W. McLENNAN. Another two fine albums followed with 'FIREBOY' (1993) and 'HORSEBREAKER STAR' (1994), FORSTER releasing an album of covers the same year, 'I HAD A NEW YORK GIRLFRIEND'. • **Songwriters:** All compositions by FORSTER and McLENNAN, with LINDY MORRISON contributing some. McLENNAN covered BALLAD OF EASY RIDER (Byrds). FORSTER covered; NATURE'S WAY (Spirit) / BROKEN HEARTED PEOPLE (. . .Clarke) / ECHO BEACH (Martha & The Muffins) / TELL ME THAT IT ISN'T TRUE (Bob Dylan) / 2541 (Bob Mould) / ANYTIME (. . . Nelson) / LOCKED AWAY (Richards-Jordan) / LOOK OUT HERE COMES TOMORROW (Neil Diamond) / ALONE (Kelly-Steinberg) / BIRD (. . .Hansoms) / FRISCO DEPOT (. . . Newbury) / 3 A.M. (Anderson-Todd). • **Trivia:** In 1991, FORSTER and McLENNAN did support slot to LLOYD COLE on a Toronto gig, which prompted GO-BETWEENS reformation rumours.

Album rating: SEND ME A LULLABY (*7) / BEFORE HOLLYWOOD (*8) / SPRING HILL FAIR (*7) / LIBERTY BELLE AND THE BLACK DIAMOND EXPRESS (*7) / TALULAH (*7) / 16 LOVERS LANE (*8) / THE GO-BETWEENS 1979-1990 compilation (*9) / Robert Forster: DANGER IN THE PAST (*6) / CALLING FROM A COUNTRY PHONE (*6) / I HAD A NEW YORK GIRLFRIEND (*5) / WARM NIGHTS (*5) / G.W. McLennan: WATERSHED (*7) / FIREBOY (*6) / HORSEBREAKER STAR (*7) / IN YOUR BRIGHT RAY (*6)

GRANT McLENNAN (b.12 Feb'58, Rock Hampton, Australia) – vocals, lead guitar, bass / **ROB FORSTER** (b.29 Jun'57) – guitar, vocals / **DENNIS CANTWELL** – drums

Abel not iss.

Oct 78. (7") *(AB 001)* **LEE REMICK. / KAREN** - - Austra

— added **TIM MUSTAFA** – drums + **MALCOLM KELLY** – organ to repl. CANTWELL

Oct 79. (7") *(AB 004)* **PEOPLE SAY. / DON'T LET HIM COME BACK** - - Austra
(above released UK Nov86 as 12"ep on 'Situation 2'; *SIT 44T)*

— **LINDY MORRISON** (b. 2 Nov'51) – drums (ex-ZERO) repl. TIM + MALCOLM

Postcard not iss.

Nov 80. (7") *(80-4)* **I NEED TWO HEADS. / STOP BEFORE YOU SAY IT** -
Jul 81. (7") *(81-9)* **YOUR TURN, MY TURN. / WORLD WEARY** -
(possibly not issued in UK, released on their Australian label, 'Missing Link'; MISS 29)

Rough Trade not iss.

Jun 82. (lp) *(ROUGH 45)* **SEND ME A LULLABY** -
– Your turn, my turn / One thing can hold us / Eight pictures / People know / The girls have moved / Midnight to neon / Ride / Caress / All about strength / Hold your horses / It could be anyone / Arrow in a bow. *<US cd-iss. 1990 on 'Beggars Banquet'; 92702>*
Jul 82. (7") *(RT 108)* **HAMMER THE HAMMER. / BY CHANCE** -

— added **ROBERT VICKERS** (b.25 Nov'59) – bass

Feb 83. (7") *(RT 124)* **CATTLE AND CANE. / HEAVEN SAYS** -
Sep 83. (lp) *(ROUGH 54)* **BEFORE HOLLYWOOD** -
– A bad debt follows you / Two steps step out / Before Hollywood / Dusty in here / Ask / Cattle and cane / By chance / As long as that / On my block / That way. *(cd-iss. Jun90; LCD 54) <US cd-iss. 1990 on 'Beggars Banquet'; 92703>*
Oct 83. (7") *(RT 114)* **MAN O' SAND TO GIRL O' SEA. / THIS GIRL BLACK GIRL** -

Sire not iss.

Jul 84. (7") *(W 9211)* **PART COMPANY. / JUST A KING IN MIRRORS** -
(12"+=) *(W 9211T)* – Newton told me.
Sep 84. (lp) *(925 179-1)* **SPRING HILL FAIR** -
– Bachelor kisses / Five words / The old way out / You've never lived / Part company / Slow slow music / Draining the pool for you / River of money / Unkind and unwise / Man o' sand girl o' sea. *<US cd-iss. 1990 on 'Beggars Banquet'; 82003>*
Sep 84. (7") *(W 9156)* **BACHELOR KISSES. / RARE BREED** -
(12"+=) *(W 9156T)* – Unkind and unwise (instrumental).

Beggars Banquet / Big Time

Feb 86. (7") *(BEG 155)* **SPRING RAIN. / LIFE AT HAND** -
(12"+=) *(BEG 155T)* – Little Joe.

Mar 86. (lp/c) *(BEGA/BEGC 72)* *<6010>* **LIBERTY BELLE AND THE BLACK DIAMOND EXPRESS**
– Spring rain / The ghost and the black hat / The wrong road / To reach me / Twin layers of lightning / In the core of the flame / Head full of steam / Palm Sunday (on board the S.S.Within) / Apology accepted. *(re-iss. Feb89 on 'Beggars Banquet-Lowdown' lp/c)(cd; BBL/+C 72)(BBL 72CD)*

May 86. (7") *(BEG 159)* **HEAD FULL OF STEAM. / DON'T LET HIM COME BACK** -
(12"+=) *(BEG 159T)* – The wrong road.

— added **AMANDA BROWN** (b.17 Nov'65) – keyboards, violin, guitar, oboe

Feb 87. (7") *(BEG 183)* **RIGHT HERE. / WHEN PEOPLE ARE DEAD** -
(12"+=) *(BEG 183T)* – Don't call me gone.
(d7"++=) *(BEG 183D)* – A little romance (live).

May 87. (7") *(BEG 190)* **CUT IT OUT. / TIME IN DESERT** -
(12"+=) *(BEG 190T)* – Doo wop in "A".

Jun 87. (lp/c)(cd) *(BEGA/BEGC 81)(BEGA 81CD)* *<6042>* **TALLULAH** 91
– Right here / You tell me / Someone else's wife / I just get caught out / Cut it out / The house that Jack Kerouac built / Bye bye pride / Spirit of a vampyre / The Clarke sisters / Hope then strife. *(re-iss. Feb90 on 'Beggars Banquet-Lowdown' cd)(c/lp; BEGA 81CD)(BEGC/BEGA 81)*

Aug 87. (7"/12") *(BEG 194/+T)* **BYE BYE PRIDE. / THE HOUSE THAT JACK KEROUAC BUILT** -

— **JOHN WILSTEED** (b.13 Feb'57) – bass repl. VICKERS

Beggars Banquet / Capitol

Jul 88. (7") *(BEG 218)* *<4BX 44262>* **STREETS OF YOUR TOWN. / WAIT UNTIL JUNE**
(12"+=) *(BEG 218T)* – Casanova's last words.
(cd-s++=) *(BEG 218CD)* – Spring rain / Right here.

Aug 88. (lp/c)(cd) *(BEGA/BEGC 95)(BEGA 95CD)* *<91230>* **16 LOVERS LANE** 81
– Love goes on / Quiet heart / Love is a sign / You can't say no forever / The Devil's eye / Streets of your town / Clouds / Was there anything I could do? / I'm alright / Dive for your memory.

Oct 88. (7") *(BEG 219)* **WAS THERE ANYTHING I COULD DO. / ROCK'N'ROLL FRIEND** -
(12"+=) *(BEG 219T)* – Mexican postcard.
(cd-s++=) *(BEG 219CD)* – Bye bye pride.

— Split on the day we moved into the 90's. FORSTER and McLENNAN went solo. The latter also being part of JACK FROST with STEVE KILBEY of The CHURCH. AMANDA formed CLEOPATRA WONG.

– compilations, others, etc. –

1982. (lp) *Man Made;* **VERY QUICK ON THE EYE – BRISBANE 1981 (demo)** -

1985. (lp) *P.V.C.; <PVC 8942>* **METAL AND SHELLS** -

Oct 89. (12"ep/cd-ep) *Strange Fruit; (SFPS/+CD 074) / Dutch East India; <8339>* **THE PEEL SESSIONS** 1991
– The power that I have now / Second hand furniture / Fire woods / Rare breed.

Mar 90. (cd)(c/d-lp) *Beggars Banquet; (BEGA 104CD)(BEGC/BEGA 104) / Capitol; <94681>* **THE GO-BETWEENS 1979-1990**
– Hammer the hammer / I need two heads / Cattle and cane / When people are dead / Man o' sand to girl o' sea / Bachelor kisses / People say / Draining the pool for you / World weary / Spring rain / Rock and roll friend / Dusty in here / The Clarke sisters / Right here / Second-hand furniture / Bye bye pride / This girl, black girl / The house that Jack Kerouac built / Don't call me gone / Streets of our own town / Love is a sign / You won't find it again. *(c+=/d-lp+=)* – Karen / 8 pictures / The sound of rain / The wrong road / Mexican postcard.

ROBERT FORSTER

— (solo, with MICK HARVEY – producer)

Beggars Banquet / Beggars Banquet

Sep 90. (7") **BABY STONES. /** -
(12"+=/cd-s+=) -

Oct 90. (cd)(c/lp) *(BEGA 113CD)(BEGA/BEGC 113)* *<3028>* **DANGER IN THE PAST**
– Baby stones / The river people / Leave here satisfied / Heart out to tender / Is this what you call change / Dear black dream / Danger in the past / I've been looking for somebody / Justice.

Apr 93. (cd/c) *(BBQ CD/MC 127)* **CALLING FROM A COUNTRY PHONE** -
– Atlanta lie low / 121 / The circle / Falling star / I want to be quiet / Cats life / Girl to a world / Drop / Beyond their law / Forever & time. *(cd re-iss. Sep95 on 'Beggars Banquet-Lowdown'; BBL 127CD)*

— with **JOHN KEANE** – guitars, banjos, keyboards, bass, etc / **JOEL MORRIS** – drums / **STEVE VENZ** – bass / **ANDY CARLSON** – guitars, mandolin / **TIM WHITE & BILL HOLMES** – porga & piano / **DWIGHT MANNING** – oboe / **SYD STRAW** – backing vocals

Beggars Banquet / Atlantic

Jul 94. (cd-ep) *(BBQ 38CD)* **25-41 / 3 a.m. / FREDDIE FENDER / DANGER IN THE PAST (live)** -

Aug 94. (cd/c) *(BBQ CD/MC 161)* *<92482>* **I HAD A NEW YORK GIRLFRIEND**
– Nature's way / Broken hearted people / Echo beach / Tell me that it isn't true / 2541 / Anytime / Locked away / Look out loves comes tomorrow / Alone / Bird / Frisco depot / 3 a.m.

Beggars Banquet / Beggars Banquet

Jul 96. (cd-ep) *(BEG 300CD)* **CRYIN' LOVE** -

Aug 96. (cd)(lp) *(BEGL 185CD)(BEGA 185)* *<80185>* **WARM NIGHTS** Sep96
– I can do / Warn nights / Cryin' love / Snake skin lady / Loneliness / Jug of wine / Fortress / Rock-n-roll friend / On a street corner / I'll jump.

G.W. McLENNAN

Beggars Banquet / Beggars Banquet

Mar 91. (12"ep)(cd-ep) **WHEN WORD GETS AROUND / BLACK MULE / SHE'S SO STRANGE / THE MAN WHO DIED IN RAPTURE** -

May 91. (7") **EASY COME EASY GO. / MAKING IT RIGHT FOR HER** -
(12"+=)(cd-s+=) – Stones for you.

Jun 91. (cd)(c/lp) *(BEGACD 118)(BEG/BEGC 118)* **WATERSHED** -
– When word gets around / Haven't I been a fool / Haunted house / Stones for you / Easy come easy go / Black mule / Rory the weeks back on / You can't have everything / Sally's revolution / Broadway bride / Just get that straight / Dream about tomorrow.

Beggars Banquet / Atlantic

Jan 93. (cd-ep) **FINGERS / WHOSE SIDE ARE YOU ON / WHAT WENT WRONG** -

Feb 93. (cd-ep) **LIGHTING FIRES / DARK SIDE OF TOWN / IF I SHOULD FALL BEHIND** -

Mar 93. (cd/c) *(BBQ CD/MC 127)* *<92387>* **FIREBOY** Jun94
– Lighting fires / Surround me / One million miles from here / The dark side of town / Things will change / The pawnbroker / Whose side are you on? / Fingers / Signs of life / The day my eyes Came back / Bathe (in the water) / When I close my eyes / Riddle in the rain.

Aug 94. (cd-ep) **DON'T YOU CRY / COMING UP FOR AIR / GIRL IN A BERET / PUT YOU DOWN / NO PEACE IN THE PALACE / THAT'S THAT** -

Nov 94. (d-cd/c) *(BBQ CD/MC 162)* **HORSEBREAKER STAR** -
– Simone & Perry / Ice in Heaven / What went wrong / Race day rag / Don't you cry for me no more / Put you down / Late afternoon in early August / Coming up for air / Ballad of Easy Rider / Open invitation / Open my eyes / From my lips / / Dropping you / Hot water / Keep my word / Do your own thing / That's that / If I was a girl / Head over heels / Girl in a beret / All her songs / No peace in the palace / I'll call you wild / Horsebreaker star. *(re-iss. d-cd Sep95 on 'Beggars Banquet-Lowdown'; BEGA 162CD)*

Jun 95. (cd-ep) *(BBQ 57CD)* **SIMONE & PERRY / DON'T YOU CRY FOR ME NO MORE / BALLAD OF EASY RIDER / WHAT WENT WRONG (original)** -

Jul 97. (cd) *(BBQCD 192)* **IN YOUR BRIGHT RAY** -
– In your bright ray / Cave in / One plus one / Sea breeze / Malibu '69 / Who said love was dead / Room for skin / All them pretty angels / Comet scar / Down here / Lamp by lamp / Do you see the lights / Parade of shadows.

GOD (see under ⇒ ICE)

Vic GODARD (& SUBWAY SECT)

Born: VIC KNAPPER, c.1959, Mortlake, London, England, although raised in nearby Barnes. Heavily inspired by the 1976 punk revolution and the SEX PISTOLS in particular, GODARD formed SUBWAY SECT along with schoolfriends, ROB SIMMONS, PAUL MYERS and PAUL PACKHAM, the band's short-lived original singer (who was later replaced by MARK LAFF). The lads made their live debut on the 20th of September that year, kicking off a punk festival at the 100 Club, a night that featured SIOUXSIE & THE BANSHEES, BUZZCOCKS, STINKY TOYS, VIBRATORS, CLASH and the 'PISTOLS. Their performance (free of the safety-pin chic favoured by their peers) prompted CLASH manager, Bernie Rhodes, to take them under his wing and release an early '78 single, 'NOBODY'S SCARED', for his own 'Braik' label. The track was a punk era classic although by this time, LAFF had been snatched up by GENERATION X and substituted with ROB WARD; Rhodes subsequently sacked both MYERS and SIMMONS, replacing them with three newcomers, STEVE ATKINSON, JOHNNY BRITTON and, fresh from school, COLIN SCOTT. This was the line-up to back VIC on SUBWAY SECT's more professional but sedate late 1978 follow-up, 'AMBITION', a one-off for 'Rough Trade'. A mooted album never appeared, VIC being groomed by his manager to try his hand at other vocal styles. In the Spring of 1980, having signed to an offshoot of 'M.C.A.', VIC GODARD & SUBWAY SECT re-emerged with a completely overhauled sound and style on the album, 'WHAT'S THE MATTER BOY?', leaving behind all traces of punk in the process. The record was nevertheless loved by the critics, although the follow-up, 'SONGS FOR SALE' (still co-crediting SUBWAY SECT), did not impress 'Island' who sold the rights to 'London' records for release in '82. VIC's Bristol-based backing band at the time (ROB MARCHE, DAVE COLLARD, CHRIS BOSTOCK and SEAN McLUSKY) soon pursued their own career as hitmakers, JoBOXERS, GODARD going into semi-retirement until the mid-80's. The former punk turned jazzy crooner was tempted back into the biz when Geoff Travis and Mike Always signed him to their newly formed 'Blanco Y Negro' imprint. However, the cost of numerous backing musicians led to them shelving a proposed album ('T.R.O.U.B.L.E.') and subsequently seeing VIC back on the dole and washing-up in a cafe to make ends meet. The aforementioned tapes were given another lease of life in Spring '86 when Travis' 'Rough Trade' label gave it a belated release; Always, meanwhile, had already issued a single, 'HOLIDAY HYMN', for his own 'El' label. Amid all the business wrangling etc, VIC retired from the music scene to become a postman in Kew (London), although he did return again in 1992 to pay tribute to the recently deceased 'JOHNNY THUNDERS' on a one-off single for 'Rough Trade Singles Club'. Perhaps inspired by some renewed interest from EDWYN COLLINS, GODARD, with help of both the former ORANGE JUICE frontman and dub producer, DENNIS BOVELL, recorded a 1993 comeback album, 'END OF THE SURREY PEOPLE', for the recently resurrected 'Postcard' label. • **Covered:** LANDSLIDE (Tony Clarke) / LOVE FOR SALE (Cole Porter) / etc.

Album rating: WHAT'S THE MATTER BOY? (*5) / SONGS FOR SALE (*6) / A RETROSPECTIVE compilation (*7) / Vic Godard: T.R.O.U.B.L.E. (*5) / END OF THE SURREY PEOPLE (*5)

SUBWAY SECT

VIC GODARD – vocals / **ROB SIMMONS** – guitar / **PAUL MYERS** – bass / **BOB WARD** – drums; repl. MARK LAFF (to GENERATION X) who repl. PAUL PACKHAM

Braik / not iss.

Mar 78. (7") *(BRS 01)* **NOBODY'S SCARED. / DON'T SPLIT IT** [ ] [-]

— **JOHNNY BRITTON** – guitar + **STEVE ATKINSON** – keyboards repl. SIMMONS / **COLIN SCOTT** (b.1962) – bass; repl. MYERS who later joined The PROFESSIONALS (former SEX PISTOLS)

Rough Trade / not iss.

Dec 78. (7") *(RT 007)* **AMBITION. / DIFFERENT STORY** [ ] [-]

VIC GODARD & SUBWAY SECT

VIC plus **BRITTON** /the returning **MYERS** + TERRY CHIMES – drums (ex-CLASH)

Oddball-MCA / not iss.

Apr 80. (7") *(MCA 585)* **SPLIT UP THE MONEY. / OUT OF TOUCH** [ ] [-]

Apr 80. (lp/c) *(MCF/+C 3070)* **WHAT'S THE MATTER BOY?** [ ] [-]
– Birth and death / Stand back / Watching the Devil / Enclave / Out of touch – View / Vertical integration / Split up the money / Stool pigeon / Double negative / Exit no return / Empty shell / Make me sad. *(re-iss. Jul82 lp/c; MCL/+C 1687) (<cd-iss. Apr96 on 'Mau Mau'; MAUCD 645>)*

— now backed by singers The BLACK ARABS

Rough Trade / not iss.

Jan 81. (7") *(RT 068)* **STOP THAT GIRL. / INSTRUMENTALLY SCARED / VERTICAL INTEGRATION** [ ] [-]

Club Left / not iss.

Nov 81. (7") *(CLUB 1)* **STAMP OF A VAMP. / HEY NOW (I'M IN LOVE)** [ ] [-]
(above was VIC GODARD solo)

VIC GODARD & THE SUBWAY SECT

— now with Bristol lads and future JO BOXERS; **ROB MARCHE** – guitar / **DAVE COLLARD** – keyboards / **CHRIS BOSTOCK** – bass / **SEAN McLUSKY** – drums

London / not iss.

May 82. (7") *(LON 005)* **HEY NOW (I'M IN LOVE). / JUST IN TIME** [ ] [ ]
(10"+=/12"+=) *(LON X/T 005)* – Mr. Bennett.

Jun 82. (lp/c) *(SH/KSAC 8549)* **SONGS FOR SALE** [ ] [ ]
– Hey now (I'm in love) / Crazy, crazy / Mr. Bennett / What's your name / Nola's salon / Be your age / Moving bed / Swing gently / Stamp of a vamp / Love for sale / Dilletante / Just in time / No style.

— VIC retired for a few years, although 'Rough Trade' were to have released single 'T.R.O.U.B.L.E.' mid-83 *RT 126)*

Rough Trade / not iss.

Feb 85. (lp) *(ROUGH 56)* **A RETROSPECTIVE (1977-81)** (compilation) [ ] [-]

VIC GODARD

with **SIMON BOOTH** + others from WORKING WEEK

El / not iss.

Jul 85. (7") *(EL 4)* **HOLIDAY HYMN. / NICE ON THE ICE** [ ] [-]
(12"+=) *(EL 4T)* – Stop that girl / Ice on the volcano / T.R.O.U.B.L.E.

Rough Trade / not iss.

Apr 86. (lp) *(ROUGH 86)* **T.R.O.U.B.L.E.** [ ] [-]
– Up on icing sugar mountain / T.R.O.U.B.L.E. / 20th century blues / Tidal wave / The Devil's in league with you / Caribb0blu / I'm gonna write a musical / Chainsmoking / (Stayin' outta) View / Stop that girl / Holiday hymn / Ice on a volcano / Miss Sadie / Wave. *(cd-iss. May98 as 'IN TROUBLE AGAIN' on 'Tugboat'; TUG 001CD)*

— retired for a long spell but returned on the same label

Sep 92. (7") *(45rev12)* **JOHNNY THUNDERS. / IMBALANCE** [ ] [-]

— now with **EDWYN COLLINS** – guitar (ex-ORANGE JUICE) / **CLAIRE KENNY** – bass (ex-AMAZULU) / **PAUL COOK** – drums (ex-SEX PISTOLS)

Postcard / not iss.

May 93. (7") *(DUBH 937)* **WON'T TURN BACK. / ('A'version)** [ ] [-]
(cd-s+=) *(DUBH 937CD)* – ('A'side) / The water was bad / Conscience be your guide / Same mistakes.

Jun 93. (lp/cd) *(DUBH 936/+CD)* **END OF THE SURREY PEOPLE** [ ] [-]
– Imbalance / Johnny Thunders / The water was bad / Malicious love / On the shore / Nullify my reputation (I'm gonna) / Won't turn back / Talent to follow / Same mistakes / The pain barrier / I can't stop you / The end of the Surrey people.

Garcia / not iss.

Sep 96. (7") *(POUM 002)* **NO LOVE NOW. / SHE'S MY BEST FRIEND** [ ] [-]

— Around this time, VIC was working with MARK PERRY (Alternative TV) in a band called The LONG DECLINE.

– compilations, etc. –

Apr 96. (7"ep/cd-ep) *Overground; (OVER 45/+CD)* **AMBITION / DIFFERENT STORY. / CHAIN SMOKING / AMBITION** [ ] [-]

GOD BULLIES

Formed: Kalamazoo, Michigan, USA . . . 1986 by vocalist MIKE HARD and three other angry young men, DAVID LIVINGSTONE, MIKE CORSO and ADAM BERG. Similar in some respects to The CRAMPS, The BUTTHOLE SURFERS and The STOOGES, the band gained a deal with US label, 'Amphetamine Reptile' (home of HALO OF FLIES, THROWN UPS and subsequently, HELMET), for whom they released a handful of releases from 1987's 'FEAR AND PAIN' single to 1991's double-7", 'JOIN SATAN'S ARMY'. Three years on, 'Alternative Tentacles' took up the reins for what was to become their swansong set, 'KILL THE KING' (1994).

Album rating: PLASTIC EYE MIRACLE (*5) / WAR ON EVERYBODY (*5) / KILL THE KING (*4)

MIKE HARD – vocals / **DAVID LIVINGSTONE** – guitar / **MIKE CORSO** – bass / **ADAM BERG** – drums

not iss. / Mad Queen

1988. (7") **ALL I WANT IS MY MAMMA. /** [-] [ ]

1988. (c) **PLASTIC EYE MIRACLE** (half studio/half live) [-] [ ]

Amphetam.Reptile / Amphetam.Reptile

1989. (7") *<Scale 10>* **FEAR AND PAIN. /** [-] [ ]

1989. (lp) **MAMAWOMBWOMB** [-] [ ]

— added **MARY KATE MURRAY + TABATHA PREDOVICH** – backing vocals

1990. (m-cd) *<ARR 181>* **DOG SHOW** [-] [ ]

— **TONY OLIVERI** – drums (ex-COWS) repl. BERG

1990. (d7") *(Scale 31>* **JOIN SATAN'S ARMY. /** [-] [ ]

Dec 91. (lp/cd) *(ARR 180/+CD)* **WAR ON EVERYBODY** [-] [ ]

— <also featured one track on Various EP, 'Ugly American Overkill'; Scale 34>

— split for a time in the early 90's

Sympathy F / Sympathy F

1990's. (7") *<(SFTRI 130)>* **HOW LOW. /** [ ] [ ]

Alternative Tentacles / Alternative Tentacles

Oct 94. (cd) *<(VIRUS 152CD)>* **KILL THE KING** [ ] [ ]
– Neighborhood kid / King of sling / How many times / Detain my brain / She's wild / Pretty on the inside / Space kid zoom / You have been warned / It's him / Artificial insemination by Aliens / Hate. *(re-iss. Nov97; VIRUSUK 152)*

Radical / Radical

Nov 95. (7") *(RDL 0087)* **MILLENIUM. / I FORGOT WHERE I LIVE** [ ] [ ]

— disbanded after above

GODFATHERS

Formed: London, England . . . 1983 as The SID PRESLEY EXPERIENCE by the COYNE brothers PETER and CHRIS, along with DEL BARTLE and KEVIN MOONEY. This basic post-punk aggregate released two singles, 'HUP TWO THREE FOUR' and a version of John Lennon's 'COLD TURKEY', before splintering early '85 into two factions that almost immediately fought over the group moniker. When the brothers lost out in the ensuing court battle to retain the group name, they chose The GODFATHERS instead, recruiting KRIS DOLLIMORE, MIKE GIBSON and GEORGE MAZUR and adopting a glowering, sharp-suited "Kray Twins" persona. After a clutch of fiery garage-punk/R&B singles on their own 'Corporate Image' imprint (namely 'LONELY MAN', 'THIS DAMN NATION', 'I WANT EVERYTHING' and 'LOVE IS DEAD'), they took the money and ran with 'Epic', the Brothers and Co finally issuing their first album proper in the shape of 'BIRTH, SCHOOL, WORK, DEATH' (early '88). Their second album for the label, 'MORE SONGS ABOUT LOVE AND HATE' (1989), cracked the UK Top 50 while, like its predecessor, the record made inroads into the US charts. With CHRIS BURROWS replacing DOLLIMORE, The GODFATHERS delivered a parting shot for 'Epic', in the shape of 'UNREAL WORLD' (1991), the label leaving the band to swim with the (indie) fishes after they'd failed to hit the sales target once again. Further personnel troubles dogged The GODFATHERS family when MAZUR and GIBSON went AWOL, leaving the inner core of the brothers to crack on with two 'Intercord' released sets, 'ORANGE' (1993) and 'AFTERLIFE' (1996). • **Songwriters:** COYNE brothers, except; SUN ARISE (Rolf Harris) / BLITZKRIEG BOP (Ramones) / HOW DOES IT FEEL TO FEEL (Creation).

Album rating: HIT BY HIT mini compilation (*6) / BIRTH, SCHOOL, WORK, DEATH (*6) / MORE SONGS ABOUT LOVE AND HATE (*5) / UNREAL WORLD (*5) / DOPE, ROCK'N'ROLL AND FU**ING IN THE STREETS collection (*5) / ORANGE (*4) / AFTERLIFE (*4) / BIRTH, SCHOOL, WORK, DEATH: THE BEST OF THE GODFATHERS compilation (*6)

SID PRESLEY EXPERIENCE

PETER COYNE – vocals / **DEL BARTLE** – guitar / **CHRIS COYNE** – bass / **KEVIN MOONEY** – drums

I.D. / not iss.

May 84. (7"/12") *(EYE/+T 4)* **HUP TWO THREE FOUR. / PUBLIC ENEMY NO.1** [ ] [-]

S.P.E. / not iss.

Dec 84. (7") *(SPE 41)* **COLD TURKEY. / FIREWATER / 'F' FOR FAKE** [ ] [-]

— split early '85. DEL and KEVIN formed The UNHOLY TRINITY (with bassist TIM ARROWSMITH), releasing a sole early '86 mini-set, 'RISE TO THE OCCASION' for 'Communique'.

The GODFATHERS

— were formed by the **COYNE** brothers **PETER + CHRIS** with also **MIKE GIBSON** (b. London) – guitar / **KRIS DOLLIMORE** (b.Isle Of Sheppey, Kent, England) – guitar / **GEORGE MAZUR** (b.Bradford, England) – drums

Corporate Image | not iss.

Oct 85. (7") *(GFTR 010)* **LONELY MAN. / I WANT YOU** [ ] [-]
(12"ep+=) **CAPO DI TUTTI EP** *(GFTR 010T)* – Sticks and stones.

Apr 86. (12") *(GRST 020)* **THIS DAMN NATION. / CAN'T LEAVE HER ALONE / JOHN BARRY** [ ] [-]

Sep 86. (7") *(GFTR 030)* **I WANT EVERYTHING. / SUN ARISE** [ ] [-]
(12"+=) *(GFTR 030T)* – I'm unsatisfied.

Nov 86. (m-lp) *(GFTRLP 010)* **HIT BY HIT** (compilation) [ ] [-]
– Lonely man / I want you / Sticks and stones / This damn nation / Can't leave her alone / John Barry / I want everything / Sun arise / I'm unsatisfied / Cold turkey. *(re-iss. Dec87 c/cd; GFTR C/CD 010) <US-iss.1987 on 'Link'; LINK 009>*

Feb 87. (7") *(GFTR 040)* **LOVE IS DEAD. / ANGELA** [ ] [-]
(12"+=) *(GFTR 040T)* – ('A'mix) / Gone to Texas.

Epic | Epic

Feb 88. (7"/7"box) *(GFT Z/B 1)* **BIRTH, SCHOOL, WORK, DEATH. / IF I ONLY HAD TIME** [ ] [-]
(12"+=/12"s+=) *(GFT ZT/Q 1)* – ('A'mix).

Feb 88. (lp/c/cd) *(460583-1/-4/-2) <40946>* **BIRTH, SCHOOL, WORK, DEATH** [80] [91]
– Birth, school, work, death / If I only had time / Tell me why / It's so hard / 'Cause I said so / Strangest boy / Obsession / S.T.B. / Just like you / Love is dead / When am I coming down.

Jul 88. (7"/7"pic-d) *(GFT/+P 2)* **'CAUSE I SAID SO. / WHEN AM I COMING DOWN** [ ] [-]
(12"+=/cd-s+=) *(GFTT/CDGFT 2)* – I can only give you everything / Cold turkey.

Nov 88. (7"/7"g-f/7"pic-d) *(GFT/+G/P 3)* **LOVE IS DEAD. / THESE DAYS ARE OVER (live)** [ ] [-]
(12"+=/cd-s+=) *(GFTT/CDGFT 3)* – ('A'original) / I'm satisfied (live).

Apr 89. (7"/7"box/7"pic-d) *(GFT/+B/P 4)* **SHE GIVES ME LOVE. / WALKING TALKING JOHNNY CASH BLUES** [ ] [-]
(12"+=/cd-s+=) *(GFTT/CDGFT 4)* – Just because you're not paranoid doesn't mean to say they're not out to get you!

May 89. (lp/c/cd) *(463394-1/-4/-2) <45023>* **MORE SONGS ABOUT LOVE AND HATE** [49] [ ]
– She gives me love / These days are over / How low is low? / Party girl / This is your life / I'm lost and then I'm found / I don't believe in you / Life has passed us by / Another you / Walking talking Johnny Cash blues / Halfway paralysed.

— **CHRIS BURROWS** – guitar, vocals; repl. DOLLIMORE

Feb 90. (7") *(GFT 5)* **I'M LOST AND THEN I'M FOUND. / STILL ALONE** [ ] [-]
(10") *(GFTQT 5)* – ('A'side) / Walking talking Johnny Cash blues / Blitzkreig bop / How low is low.
(12"/cd-s) *(GFT T/C 5)* – ('A'side) / Birth, school, work, death (extended) / She gives me love (Keith Le Blanc love mix) / She gives me love (mega dance authority mix).

Feb 91. (7"/c-s) **UNREAL WORLD. / SOMETHING GOOD ABOUT YOU** [ ] [-]
(12"+=/cd-s+=) – This is your life (live) / This damn nation (live).

Mar 91. (cd/c/lp) *(466952-2/-4/-1) <46026>* **UNREAL WORLD** [ ] [ ]
– Unreal world / Don't let me down / King of misery / Believe in yourself / I'll never forget what's his name / How does it feel to feel / Drag me down again / Something good about you / I love what's happening to me / This is war.

— MAZUR + GIBSON departed

Intercord | not iss.

Oct 93. (cd) *(986974)* **ORANGE** [ ] [-]

Feb 96. (cd) *(IRS 845255CD)* **AFTERLIFE** [ ] [-]

– compilations etc. –

Feb 89. (12"ep/cd-ep) *Night Tracks; (SFNT/+CD 019) / Dutch East India; <8011>* **THE EVENING SHOW SESSIONS** [ ] [ ] Oct91
– I want you / If I only had time / I want everything / I'm unsatisfied.

Jun 92. (cd/c/lp) *Corporate Image; (GFTR CD/MC/LP 020)* **DOPE, ROCK'N'ROLL AND FU**ING IN THE STREETS (live)** [ ] [-]
– Birth, school, work, death / She gives me love / Unreal world / I don't believe in you / Drag me down again / When am I coming down / Obsession / I love what's happening to me / If I only had time / Lonely man / Don't let me down / I want everything / 'Cause I said so / This damn nation / This is war / Cold turkey.

Apr 96. (cd) *Intercord; (IRS 988874CD)* **GOLDEN DELICIOUS** [ ] [-]

Jul 96. (cd) *Epic; (478423-2) <64789>* **BIRTH, SCHOOL, WORK, DEATH (THE BEST OF THE GODFATHERS)** [ ] [ ] Mar96

GOD IS MY CO-PILOT

Formed: New York City, New York, USA . . . 1990 by CRAIG FLANAGIN and SHARON TOPPER. Harking back to the late 70's when sonic noise terrorists such as POP GROUP, ESSENTIAL LOGIC and HALF JAPANESE were at the cutting edge, GIMC-P updated the form in typically experimental NY style. Lauded as the American equivalent of Riot Grrl campaigners HUGGY BEAR, FLANAGIN and TOPPER combined controversial, howling, gender-bending lyrics with a rhythmic, breakneck jazzcore assault that was initially showcased on debut album, 'SPEED YR TRIP' (1991). The following year's 'I AM NOT THIS BODY', confirmed their reputation as genre blurring funsters with an eye for the bizarre and an uncompromising social outlook. One of their biggest fans was John Peel, who invited the band onto his Radio One show for a handful of sessions between '93 and '95. Meanwhile, the group (who now included bassist FLY and twin-drummers, MICHAEL EVANS and DAN BROWN) went full steam ahead with their prolific release schedule, working with the likes of JOHN ZORN.

Album rating: SPEED YR TRIP (*6) / I AM NOT THIS BODY (*7)

SHARON TOPPER – vocals / **CRAIG FLANAGIN** – guitar, bass, etc / with **ALEX KLEIN** – bass / **SIOBHAN DUFFY** – drums, vox organ / + others at various times

not iss. | Making Of America

1991. (lp) **SPEED YR TRIP** [-] [ ]
– Little ghosts / Down down baby / They often look Fr. / In too deep / Angels in the air / Los mas sabrosa / No cross no crown / Anyone but you / Fat / C-etait une J. fille / Home / Woman enough / On lust / Catheter / Drave / Late last night / Comfort / Zonnebloem / Kingdom of the flesh / Hair in mouth / Poke / Complete control / Smirk / Got what / Brought up short / Scratch and sniff. *(cd-iss. Apr95 on 'Les Disques Du Soleil'; DSA 54237> (UK-iss.Nov96 on 'Runt'; RUNT 16)*

1992. (lp) *<4>* **I AM NOT THIS BODY** [-] [ ]
– List / Angels in the air / Heaven / Smooch / Thunder, perfect mind / Invisible rocket / Kissing frenzy / Grizzly gizzard / Fierce beast / 2 meats / Crushing a girl / Said and done / Out in the streets / Lonesome highway / Very very / This situation / Joan / God knows / The truth be told / Adrenalin jitters / Looken for a fat girl / Seashell / Liz Cohen caught looking / Theresa says / You up / Well / Animal rights / Southwestern jazz / The day I owned the sky / To yr scattered bodies go / You smell like sex / Tight and low / Anthem / That's how I like it. *<cd-iss. Apr95 on 'Les Disques Du Soleil'; DSA 54236> (UK-iss.Nov96 on 'Runt'; RUNT 15)*

May 93. (cd-ep) **MY SINISTER HIDDEN AGENDA EP** [ ] [ ]
– Straight not / etc

not iss. | Dark Beloved Cloud

1993. (7") *<008>* **WHEN THIS YOU SEE REMEMBER ME. /** [-] [ ]

1994. (7") *<017>* **SU VOT VOT ESTA SU VOZ. /** [-] [ ]

not iss. | Ajax

1994. (7") *<035>* **KITTYBAIT. /** [-] [ ]

— with now **FLY** – bass / **DAN BROWN + MICHAEL EVANS** – drums

Soul Static Sound | Making Of America

May 94. (7"ep) *(SOUL 3)* **SHARON QUITE FANCIES JO EP** [ ] [-]

Jun 94. (lp) *(SOUL 4) <11>* **HOW TO BE** [ ] [ ] Apr96

— following album incl. a plethora of session people

Knitting Factory | Knitting Factory

Nov 94. (cd) *<(KFWCD 148)>* **TIGHT LIKE FIST (live recording)** [ ] [ ] 1993
– Angels in the air / Handsome Molly / Eye contact / Get it / Katrinan Luala / Sun, wind / Heavy layer / Sound of wings / Crushing a girl / Lead w/ yr chin / Bicycle girls / Ot azoi – Igneous ejaculation / 2 meats beat as 1 / Miinan Laulu / Zonnebloem / Sleep not / Tourschr. – How I got over / Role model / Backstab / Lou explains it / Oyfn nil / Any # / Fierce beast / I'm not gonna lie / Smooch / Khad gad yo / Heaven / 4 steps / Pornography and rape / Make you fell / Home / Frauen U. nichtfrauen / Farm recording / Straight not / That's how I like it / Firecracker / Iko / Jailhouse / Can't stop now.

Runt | Runt

Jan 95. (7") *(RUNT 3)* **APPEAL TO REASON. /** [ ] [ ]

— below with **ELLIOT SHARP & ANTHONY COLEMAN**; most trad songs

Avant | Avant

Jan 95. (cd) *<(AVAN 032)>* **MIR SHLUFN NISHT** [ ] [ ] Dec94
– Vot vot ja niin niin / Hora / Tan Liz Cohane / Tuppasuita / Dayenu / Miyimalel / Double Dutch / Piramidn / B'nai! / Like – Park / We don't sleep / Raketa pisztoly / Miinan Laulu / Katrussya / Tantsukolena fin / Nya skor / Sissy dog / Khad gad yo / Churla / Palmcore / Hatikvah / Mia geht nach bodega / Oyfn nil / Tantsukolena yid.

— line-up:- **FLANAGIN, TOPPER, MICHAEL EVANS** – drums / **OTTO KENTROL** – bass / **ANDY DOGFACE** – guitar, viola, vocals / **JENNY WADE** – bass / **DAVID SIMONS** – drums / **ZOE TOBIER** – vocals / **FLY** – vocals

— **LAURA CROMWELL** – drums (appeared again) as did others

Les Disques Du Soleil | Les Disques Du Soleil

Jan 95. (cd) *<(DSA 54033)>* **SEX IS FOR MAKING BABIES** [ ] [ ]
– Tombstone / Runt hunt / Fly / In the forest / Tsifatelli / Interrogation / Sex is for making babies / What a goddess / High plains / Wetting the bed / Blue yodel #21 / (Fly) Tanja / Be nice to yr parents / Nechant / Work is love / Runt / Start / About how I hate boys / Then phat / Kantele / Imaginary friend / Sissy dog / Little red moon / Fat children.

Nov 95. (7"ep; split with GAG) *<(GUIDE 003)>* **GROW YOUR OWN COUNTRY EP** [ ] [ ]
(above issued on 'Guided Missile')

Dec 95. (cd) *<(DSA 54041)>* **PUSS 02** [ ] [ ]

not iss. | Outpunk

Apr 95. (cd,c,lp) *<8>* **STRAIGHT NOT** [-] [ ]

Miguel | Miguel

May 97. (cd) *<(MIGUEL 1)>* **CHILDREN CAN BE SO CRUEL** [ ] [ ]

Atavistic | Atavistic

Nov 98. (cd) *<(87)>* **GET BUSY** [ ] [ ]
– Menarche / Leave you alone / Chase scene / Far more attractive / Monkeys / Domestic partner / Kleines eisstuck / Lunch / Gras och granbarr / Shift and flicker / I can't dance / Hutulka / Nya skor / Abducted by aliens.

– compilations, etc. –

Nov 96. (cd) *Atavistic; <(ALP 82CD)>* **THE BEST OF GOD IS MY CO-PILOT** [ ] [ ]

Jan 97. (cd) *Strange Fruit; (SFRSCD 004)* **THE PEEL SESSIONS** [ ] [-]

GOD, MOTHER & COUNTRY (see under ⇒ RIP, RIG + PANIC)

GO HOLE (see under ⇒ GENE)

GOLDEN PALOMINOS

Formed: New York City, New York, USA . . . 1981 by drummer ANTON FIER, formerly of Cleveland, Ohio art-rockers, PERE UBU. FIER and his fellow ex-LOUNGE LIZARDS sidekick set about recruiting an array of musicians drawn largely from the NY experimental scene including BILL LASWELL, FRED FRITH JOHN ZORN, NICKY SKOPELITIS, DAVID MOSS and JAMAALADEEN TACUMA to name but a few. Locating a sympathetic stable in the shape of France's 'Celluloid', The GOLDEN PALOMINOS unleashed their eponymous debut album in 1983, a bravely experimental soundclash of avant-funk characterised by LINDSAY's crazed vocals. Heavily imported into Britain and the States, the album's cult success generated much anticipation for a follow-up. This arrived in the shape of 1985's 'VISIONS OF EXCESS', FIER looking beyond NY and bringing in a wildly disparate cast of the hip and not so hip including RICHARD THOMPSON, JACK BRUCE, JOHN LYDON, MICHAEL STIPE, CHRIS STAMEY and unknown female singer, SYD STRAW; most of these (and future) revolving-door guests contributed lyrics to songs written by FIER and guitarist JODY HARRIS. The project took a rootsier turn with 'BLAST OF SILENCE' (1986), new collaborators MATTHEW SWEET, PETER BLEGVAD, SNEAKY PETE KLEINOW and T-BONE BURNETT steering the 'PALOMINOS down the dusty paths of folk, blues and country. A core of FIER, LASWELL, SKOPELITIS, ROBERT KIDNEY (from NUMBERS BAND) and AMANDA KRAMER (from INFORMATION SOCIETY), meanwhile, formed the musical basis for 1989's '- A DEAD HORSE', KRAMER coming into her own on the THROWING MUSES-esque 'DARKLANDS'. The outfit continued to evolve into the 90's, FIER and LASWELL now utilising the talents of MICHAEL STIPE, RICHARD THOMPSON, BOB MOULD and CARLA BLEY on, astonishingly, their first major UK/US effort, 'DRUNK WITH PASSION' (1991). A few years later, the seasoned thoroughbreds were back on track once more with 'THIS IS HOW IT FEELS' (1993), KRAMER being eclipsed in her lead vocal role by co-writer/singer, LORI CARSON. Another new female voice, LYDIA KAVANAUGH, could be heard alongside stalwarts FIER, LASWELL, SKOPELITIS and master funksters, BOOTSY COLLINS and BERNIE WORRELL. The darkly ethereal 'PURE', appeared in 1994 (the following year's 'NO THOUGHT, NO BREATH, NO EYES, NO HEART' was a remixed version), while FIER pared things down dramatically with 1996's 'DEAD HORSE', choosing to work solely with poet, NICOLE BLACKMAN. • **Songwriters:** FIER aided by others too numerous to mention. Covered OMAHA (Moby Grape) / I'VE BEEN THE ONE + BRIDES OF JESUS (Little Feat) / DIAMOND (Peter Holsapple) / .

Album rating: THE GOLDEN PALOMINOS (*7) / VISIONS OF EXCESS (*7) / BLAST OF SILENCE (*6) / – A DEAD HORSE (*6) / DRUNK WITH PASSION (*7) / THIS IS HOW IT FEELS (*6) / PURE (*6) / DEAD INSIDE (*6) / THE BEST OF THE GOLDEN PALOMINOS 1983-1989 compilation (*7)

ANTON FIER (b.20 Jun'56, Cleveland, Ohio) – drums, programming (ex-PERE UBU, ex-FEELIES, ex-LOUNGE LIZARDS) / **ARTO LINDSAY** – vocals, guitar (ex-DNA, ex-LOUNGE LIZARDS) / **BILL LASWELL** – bass, piano (of MATERIAL) / **FRED FRITH** – guitar, violin / **DAVID MOSS** – percussion / **NICKY SKOPELITIS** – guitar / **JAMAALADEEN TACUMA** – bass / **JOHN ZORN** – saxophone / **M.E. MILLER** – vocals / **MICHAEL BEINHORN** – electronics / **PETER BLEGVAD** – vocals

Celluloid Celluloid

Jul 85. (lp) *(CEL 6662)* <5002> **THE GOLDEN PALOMINOS** [-] [ ] 1983
– Clean plate / Hot seat / Under the cap / Monday night / Cook out / I.D. / Two sided fist. *(cd-iss. Dec96 on 'Charly'; CPCD 8198) (cd re-iss. Jan98 on 'Movieplay Gold'; MPG 74049)*

— **ANTON, BILL, ARTO + NICKY** added **JODY HARRIS + RICHARD THOMPSON + HENRY KAISER + MIKE HAMPTON + CHRIS STAMEY** – guitar / **BERNIE WORRELL + CARLA BLEY** – organ / **SYD STRAW + MICHAEL STIPE + JOHN LYDON** – vocals

Apr 86. (lp) <*(CEL 6118)*> **VISIONS OF EXCESS** [-] [ ] French
– Boy (go) / Clustering train / Omaha / The animal speaks / Silver bullet / (Kind of) True / Buenos Aires / Only one party. *(cd-iss. Nov95 on 'Charly'; CPCD 8151) (cd re-iss. Jan98 on 'Movieplay Gold'; MPG 74050)*

Aug 87. (12") **BOY (GO). /** [-] [-] French

— **ROBERT KIDNEY** – vocals, guitar (of NUMBERS BAND) / **PETER BLEGVAD** – vocals / **T-BONE BURNETT** – vocals, co-producer / **DON DIXON** – vocals, co-producer / **ELLIOTT SHARP / SNEAKY PETE KLEINOW** – pedal steel guitar

Oct 87. (lp/c/cd) <*(CEL 6127/+C/CD)*> **BLAST OF SILENCE** [-] [ ] French
– I've been the one / Something becomes nothing / The push and the shove / (Something else is) Working harder / Angels / Diamond / Faithless heart / Work was new / Strong, simple silences / Brides of Jesus. *(cd re-iss. Mar98 on 'Movieplay Gold'; MPG 74051)*

— line-up:- **FIER, LASWELL, SKOPELITIS, KIDNEY / + AMANDA KRAMER** – vocals (ex-INFORMATION SOCIETY) / + featuring **BERNIE WORRELL / MICK TAYLOR** – guitar (ex-ROLLING STONES) / **JEFF BOVA + AIYB DIENG / CHUCK LEAVELL + LARRY SALTZMAN**

Aug 89. (lp/c/cd) <*(CEL 6138/+C/CD)*> **- A DEAD HORSE** [-] [ ] French
– Wild river / Shattered image / Angel of death / Lucky / Darklands / A letter back / Over. *(re-iss. cd Jun96 on 'Charly'+=; CPCD 8185)* – Simple silences / Brides of Jesus.

— **FIER, LASWELL, SKOPELITIS, KRAMER, BLEY, THOMPSON, KIDNEY** + MICHAEL STIPE – vocals / **BOB MOULD** – vocals, guitar (ex-HUSKER DU) / **AIYB DIENG**

Venture Nation – Charisma

Sep 91. (cd/c/lp) *(CD/TC+/VE 905)* <91745> **DRUNK WITH PASSION** [ ] [ ]
– Alive and living now / The haunting / When the kingdom cals / A sigh / Thunder cries / Hands of Heaven / Ding from the inside out / Begin to return.

— **FIER, LASWELL, SKOPELITIS, KRAMER, WORRELL** plus **BOOTSY COLLINS** – bass / **JEFF BOVA** – keyboards / **MATT STEIN** – programmer / **LORI CARSON + LYDIA KAVANAUGH** – vocals

Restless Restless

Nov 93. (cd-ep) *<72749>* **PRISON OF THE RHYTHM – THE REMIXES** [-] [ ]

Dec 93. (cd) <*(72735-2)*> **THIS IS HOW IT FEELS** [ ] [ ] Sep93
– Sleepwalk / Prison of the rhythm / I'm not sorry / This is how it feels / To a stranger / The wonder / Breakdown / These days / Rain holds / Twist the knife / Bird flying / A divine kiss.

— In Apr'94, ANTON FIER released a solo album, 'DREAMSPEED' for 'Avant'; *AVAN 009*

— **KNOX CHANDLER** – guitar repl.WORRELL, STEIN and BOVA

Oct 94. (cd) <*(72761-2)*> **PURE** [ ] [ ]
– Little suicides / Heaven / Anything / Wings / Pure / No skin / Gun / Break in the road / Touch you.

Dec 94. (12"ep) <*(72786)*> **NO SKIN – THE BANDALU REMIXES** [ ] [ ]

Mar 95. (cd) <*(72790-2)*> **NO THOUGHT, NO BREATH, NO EYES, NO HEART** (PURE remixes) [ ] [ ]
– Heaven (you have to be in Hell to see Heaven) / No skin (tempting fate) / Gun – Little suicides (brown stain walls, red jelly corners) / No skin (cold spells) / No skin (aural circumcision) / No skin (funky hornsey).

Apr 95. (cd-ep) *<72785>* **HEAVEN (mixes)** [-] [ ]

— now only **FIER** + NICOLE BLACKMAN – poet, etc / **KNOX CHANDLER** – guitars / **NICKY SKOPELITIS** – wah wah guitar

Oct 96. (cd) *<72907>* **DEAD INSIDE** [-] [ ]
– Victim / Belfast / Ride / Ambitions are / Drown / Holy / You are never ready / Metal eye / Thirst / Curses.

– compilations, etc. –

1991. (d-cd/d-c) *Oceana; <4105-2/-4>* **THUNDERING HERD: THE BEST OF THE GOLDEN PALOMINOS** [-] [ ]

Sep 92. (cd) *Mau Mau; (MAUCD 625) / Restless; <72651>* **A HISTORY (1982-1985)** [ ] [ ] Jul92
– Hot seat / Under the cap / Monday night / Cookout / I.D. / Two side fist / Boy (go) / Clustering train / Omaha / Animal speaks / Silver bullet / (Kind of) True / Buenos Aires / Only one party.

Sep 92. (cd) *Mau Mau; (MAUCD 626) / Restless; <72652>* **A HISTORY (1986-1989)** [ ] [ ] Jul92
– I've been the one / Something becomes nothing / The push and the shove / (Something else is) Working harder / Angels / Diamond / Faithless heart / Work was new / Strong, simple silences / Wild river / Shattered image / Angel of death / Lucky / Darklands / A letter black.

Oct 97. (cd) *Music Club; <(MCCD 316)>* **THE BEST OF THE GOLDEN PALOMINOS 1983-1989** [ ] [ ]

Oct 97. (cd) *Charly; (CDNEW 112)* **THE BEST OF THE GOLDEN PALOMINOS** [ ] [-]

GOLDEN SMOG

Formed: Minneapolis, Minnesota, USA . . . 1989 out of SKIDMARK T-SQUARE & Q-STOCK, by alternative country stars-to-be, DAN MURPHY (SOUL ASYLUM), GARY LOURIS (JAYHAWKS) and KRAIG JOHNSON (RUN WESTY RUN). Another SOUL ASYLUM frontman, DAVE PIRNER joined as an honorary member, in fact he became their drummer and back-up singer, although the drum parts on record were mainly taken up by CHRIS MARS (REPLACEMENTS). An EP of covers was delivered to mixed reviews as they all put the project on hold as their full-time commitments were come to fruition. When the supergroup returned to the fold for 1996's debut album, 'DOWN BY THE OLD MAINSTREAM', the outfit had added two further stars, MARC PERLMAN (another JAYHAWKS member) and JEFF TWEEDY (from WILCO). Americana was the subject matter for these songwriters of note, y'allternative was now the phrase on the media's lips and by 1998 (with the addition of JODY STEPHENS of BIG STAR), they had issued what was thought to be the years' best country-rock set, 'WEIRD TALES'. • **Covered:** COWBOY SONG (Thin Lizzy) / SHOOTING STAR (Bad Company) / SON (Michelangelo's) / EASY TO BE HARD (from 'Hair') / BACKSTREET GIRL (Don Nix) / SHE DON'T HAVE TO SEE YOU .

Album rating: DOWN BY THE OLD MAINSTREAM (*6) / WEIRD TALES (*8)

DAN MURPHY – vocals, guitar, keyboards (of SOUL ASYLUM) / **GARY LOURIS** – guitar, vocals (of JAYHAWKS) / **KRAIG JOHNSON** – vocals, guitar, piano (of RUN WESTY RUN) / added **DAVE PIRNER** – backing vocals (of SOUL ASYLUM) / **CHRIS MARS** – drums (of REPLACEMENTS)

not iss. Crackpot

Dec 92. (cd-ep) *<1219>* **ON GOLDEN SMOG** [-] [ ]
– Son / Easy to be hard / Backstreet girl / Shooting star / Cowboy song. *(UK-iss.Jan96 on 'Rykodisc'; RCD 30348)*

— **NOAH LEVY** – drums (of HONEYDOGS) repl. MARS

— added **MARC PERLMAN** – bass, guitar, vocals (of JAYHAWKS) / **JEFF TWEEDY** – vocals, guitar, harmonica, bass (of WILCO)

Rykodisc Rykodisc

Feb 96. (cd/c) <*(RCD/RAC 10325)*> **DOWN BY THE OLD MAINSTREAM** [ ] [ ]
– V / Ill-fated / Pecan pie / Yesterday I cried / Glad and sorry / Won't be coming home / He's a dick / Walk where he walked / Nowhere bound / The friend / She don't have to see you / Red headed step child / Williamton angel / Radio king.

— **JODY STEPHENS** – drums (of BIG STAR) repl. LEVY + PIRNER (back to SOUL ASYLUM)

Oct 98. (cd/c) <*(RAD/RAC 10446)*> **WEIRD TALES** [ ] [ ]
– To call my own / Looking forward to seeing you / Until you came along / Lost love / If I only had a car / Jane / Keys / I can't stop from talking / Reflections on me / Making waves / White shell road / Please tell my brother / Fear of falling / All the same to me / Jennifer save me.

GOMEZ

Formed: Southport, Yorkshire, England . . . 1997 originally as GOMEZ, KILL, KILL THE VORTEX by college lads BEN OTTERWELL, TOM GRAY, IAN BALL, PAUL BLACKBURN and OLLY PEACOCK. A home-recorded tape of the band found its way into the hands of record shop worker and former COMSAT ANGELS member, STEVE FELLOWS, who almost immediately became their manager. He in turn set up time in a Sheffield rehearsal studio in which he invited a plethora of A&R men to witness the unique talent of the band. After a fortnight, over thirty record labels were showing signs of interest, although FELLOWS and his protegees opted for Virgin offshoot, 'Hut'. Their early 70's to early 90's sound – like a hybrid of LOWELL GEORGE and BECK – was much in debt to the bluesy whisky-throated chords of lead singer, BEN, whose boyish, bespectacled look shocked an unsuspecting but appreciative audience on their debut single, '78 STONE WOBBLE'. It was their first UK Top 50 entry and was pursued a month later – in April '98 – by their classic debut album, 'BRING IT ON'. A critical and soon to be commercial success, its highlights were the tracks, 'GET MILES' (gruffly reminiscent of The BEATLES' 'Come Together'), 'WHIPPIN' PICCADILLY' and 'GET MYSELF ARRESTED', all of which helped it win the much lauded "Mercury" prize.

Album rating: BRING IT ON (*9)

BEN OTTERWELL – vocals / IAN BALL – guitar, vocals, harmonica (ex-SEV) / **TOM GRAY** – keyboards, vocals, guitar, multi / **PAUL BLACKBURN** – bass / **OLLY PEACOCK** – percussion

Hut | Virgin

Mar 98. (c-s) *(HUTC 95)* **78 STONE WOBBLE / WHAM BAM** [44] [-]
(12"+=/cd-s+=) *(HUT T/CD 95)* – Steve McCroski / Who's gonna go to the bar.

Apr 98. (cd-c/d-lp) *(CDHUT/HUTMC/HUTDLP 49) <45592>* **BRING IT ON** [11] [ ] May98
– Get miles / Whippin' Piccadilly / Make no sound / 78 stone wobble / Tijuana lady / Here comes the breeze / Love is better than a warm trombone / Get myself arrested / Free to run / Bubble gum years / Rie's wagon / The comeback.

Jun 98. (c-s) *(HUTC 97)* **GET MYSELF ARRESTED / THE COWBOY SONG** [45] [-]
(12"+=/cd-s+=) *(HUT T/CD 97)* – Flavours / Old school shirt.

Hut | E.M.I.

Aug 98. (c-s) *(HUTC 105) <95293>* **WHIPPIN' PICCADILLY / PUSSYFOOTIN'** [35] [ ] Nov98
(12"+=/cd-s+=) *(HUT T/CD 105)* – Pick up the pieces.

GOOBER PATROL

Formed: Norwich, England . . . 1989 by SIMON ROBERT SANDALL, his brother STUART SANDALL and TOM BLYTH. Taking their cue from the likes of SENSELESS THINGS and SNUFF and taking their moniker from the US slang term for hillbilly, the fresh-faced pop-punks made their debut in 1991 with the cheekily-titled 'TRUCK OFF'. By the release of 1992's 'DUTCH OVENS' (apparently a euphamism for breaking wind under the bed sheets!), the lads' irrepressible enthusiasm was being at least partially matched by musical expertise, their growing reputation leading to high-profile support slots with such up and coming US luminaries as GREEN DAY and NOFX. By this point, a fourth member, TIM SNELSON, had been added, the guitarist making his debut on the first of a batch of singles, 'BAD COMEDY'. Despite never achieving quite the same level of success as their US peers, GOOBER PATROL subsequently signed to FAT MIKE's 'Fat Wreck Chords' in the States ('Them's Good' in Britain), through whom they've since released two sets, 'VACATION' (1996) and 'UNBEARABLE LIGHTNESS OF BEING DRUNK' (1998).

Album rating: TRUCK OFF (*4) / DUTCH OVENS (*5) / VACATION (*5)

SIMON ROBERT SANDALL – vocals, guitar / **TOM BLYTH** – bass / **STUART SANDALL** – vocals, drums

Boss Tuneage | not iss.

1991. (lp) *(BOSTAGE 004)* **TRUCK OFF** [ ] [-]
– Timothy / Do it right / She knows / What's the point / I think it's time / Stop me / Hand in hand / Shadows and reflections / Playing with fire / 20 minute song / You can't repeat / Small gain / Wasn't it you. *(cd-iss. Aug98 on 'Them's Good'; GOOD 004CD)*

Oct 92. (lp/cd) *(BOSTAGE 009/+CD)* **DUTCH OVENS** [ ] [-]
(cd re-iss. Aug98 on 'Them's Good'; GOOD 001CD)

—— added **TIM SNELSON** – guitar

Lost & Found | not iss.

1993. (7") **BAD COMEDY. /** [-] [-] German

Them's Good | Fat Wreck Chords

Mar 96. (7") *(GOOD 003S)* **THE BIGGEST JOKE. / SMELL THE COFFEE** [ ] [-]

Apr 96. (cd) *(GOOD 002CD) <FAT 541>* **VACATION** [ ] [ ]
– Easy life / I'll do without / Empty / Crammin' / Egghead / The biggest joke / One more time / Happy tunes / Grabbers / 1000 ways / Duvet rising / Painless way / I'm not home / Piss off.
(re-iss. Aug98; same) (lp-iss.Oct96; as US)

Aug 98. (cd) *(GOOD 005CD)* **EXTENDED VACATION** [ ] [-]

Fat Wreck Chords | Fat Wreck Chords

Oct 98. (cd) *(<FAT 577>)* **UNBEARABLE LIGHTNESS OF BEING DRUNK** [ ] [ ]
– 1000th beer / Not that shrewd / Easy answers / Unbearable lightness of being drunk / Part-time SF ecologist / Stereophonic nutter / Don't you let nobody / High time / Watch us drown / Nothing can go wrong / Different window / I forget your name.

GOODBYE MR MACKENZIE

Formed: Bathgate, Scotland . . . 1984 by MARTIN METCALFE, JIMMY ANDERSON, RONA SCOBIE, SHIRLEY MANSON, FINLAY WILSON and DEREK KELLY. They recorded their first 45, 'DEATH OF A SALESMAN', via West Lothian College's 'Scruples' label before relocating to the thriving musical metropolis of Edinburgh. The band subsequently hooked up with Elliot Davis' (WET WET WET manager) 'Precious' label for the release of their debut single, 'THE RATTLER', in Autumn '86. A limited edition 12" follow-up, 'FACE TO FACE', was subsequently issued on the 'Mack' imprint, all proceeds going to the 'Rape Crisis' charity. With the addition of ex-EXPLOITED man and local legend, BIG JOHN DUNCAN, on guitar and a signing to 'Capitol' in 1988, the group looked set to follow in the footsteps of DEACON BLUE who'd broke big earlier that year. As intelligent and subtly creative as the latter outfit with a more alternative slant, GOODBYE MR MACKENZIE's sound hinged upon METCALFE's powerful BRUCE SPRINGSTEEN / NEIL DIAMOND-esque vocals and their knack for a rousing chorus. Continually tipped for the top, the band at last broke the Top 40 in early '89 with a re-recorded version of 'THE RATTLER', their much anticipated debut album, 'GOOD DEEDS AND DIRTY RAGS' making the Top 30 a few months later. Yet it wasn't to be, a flop set of live/rare tracks, 'FISH HEADS AND TAILS' (1989) and further clutch of minor hit singles no doubt convincing 'Capitol' to shelve a proposed follow-up album, 'HAMMER AND TONGS'. Help came in the form of M.C.A. subsidiary, 'Radioactive', who finally issued the record in Spring '91. By now, of course, much of the early buzz and momentum had been lost and the band drifted into obscurity. While various members went on to bigger and better things – DUNCAN as a roadie and sometime touring replacement with NIRVANA (these days he's a familiar face at Edinburgh's sterling Cafe Graffiti club) and MANSON with the massively successful GARBAGE – the remnants of the original line-up recorded albums such as 'FIVE' (1993) and 'JEZEBEL' (1995) to minimal interest. • **Songwriters:** All written by METCALFE-KELLY, except AMSTERDAM (Jaques Brel) / GREEN GREEN GRASS OF HOME (Engelbert Humperdinck) / HEROES (David Bowie) / CANDY SAYS (Velvet Underground) / FRIDAY'S CHILD (Lee Hazlewood) / THE WAY I WALK (J.Scott). • **Trivia:** METCALFE refused to pay his poll tax (community charge) early in 1990 due to the Scots being used as its guinea-pigs for the first year.

Album rating: GOOD DEEDS AND DIRTY RAGS (*7) / HAMMER AND TONGS (*6) / LIVE: ON THE DAY OF STORMS (*5) / FIVE (*5)

MARTIN METCALFE – vocals, guitar / **SHIRLEY MANSON** – vocals, keyboards / **JIMMY ANDERSON** – guitar / **RONA SCOBIE** – keyboards, vocals / **FINLAY WILSON** – bass / (DEREK) **KELLY** – drums

Scruples | not iss.

Nov 84. (7") *(YTS 1)* **DEATH OF A SALESMAN. / (other track by Lindy Bergman)** [ ] [-]

Precious | not iss.

Sep 86. (7") *(JEWEL 2)* **THE RATTLER. / CANDLESTICK PARK** [ ] [-]
(12"+=) *(JEWEL 2T)* – The end.

Clandestine | not iss.

Oct 87. (12"ltd) *(MACK 1)* **FACE TO FACE. / SECRETS. / GOOD DEEDS** [ ] [-]

—— (above proceeds went to Rape Crisis charity)

—— **BIG JOHN DUNCAN** – guitar (ex-EXPLOITED, ex-BLOOD UNCLES) repl. ANDERSON

Capitol | Capitol

Jul 88. (7") *(CL 501)* **GOODBYE MR. MACKENZIE. / GREEN TURN RED** [62] [-]
(ext.12"+=/ext.12"g-f+=)(ext.cd-s+=) *(12CL/+G 501)(CLCD 501)* – Knockin' on Joe.

Nov 88. (7"/7"g-f) *(CL/+G 513)* **OPEN YOUR ARMS. / SECRETS** [ ] [-]
(ext.12"+=/ext.12"pic-d+=) *(12CL/+P 513)* – Amsterdam.
(ext.12"g-f++=/ext.cd-s++=) *(12CLG/CLCD 513)* – Pleasure search.

Feb 89. (7"/7"g-f) *(CL/+G 52)* **THE RATTLER. / HERE COMES DEACON BRODIE** [37] [-]
(ext.12"+=) *(12CL 522)* – Calton Hill.
(12"w-poster++=/ext.cd-s++=) *(12CLG/CLCD 522)* – Drunken sailor.

Apr 89. (lp/c/cd) *(EST/TCEST/CDEST 2089) <92638>* **GOOD DEEDS AND DIRTY RAGS** [26] [ ]
– Open your arms / Wake it up / His master's voice / Goodwill city / Candlestick park / Goodbye Mr. Mackenzie / The rattler / Dust / You generous thing you / Good deeds. *(free-12"; GMM12 1) (c+=/cd+=)* – Amsterdam / Calton Hill / Secrets / Knockin' on Joe.

Jul 89. (7"/7"box/c-s) *(CL/CLX/TCCL 538)* **GOODWILL CITY. / I'M SICK OF YOU** [49] [ ]
(ext.12"+=) *(12CL 538)* – What's got into you.
(ext.12"g-f++=/cd-s++=) *(12CLG/CLCD 538)* – Insidious thing.

Oct 89. (lp/c/cd) *(CAPS/TCCAPS/CDCAPS 2001) <3357>* **FISH HEADS AND TAILS** (live & rare compilation) [ ] [ ]
– Amsterdam / Somewhere in China / Face to face / Knockin' on Joe / Sick of you / Green turn red / Pleasure search / Strangle your animal * / Mystery train / Here comes Deacon Brodie (live) *. *(cd+= *)*

Parlophone | Capitol

Apr 90. (7"/c-s) *(R/TCR 6247)* **LOVE CHILD. / HEROES** [52] [-]
(ext.12"+=) *(12R 6247)* – You generous thing you (live).
(dance.12"w-poster+=) *(12RX 6247)* – Goodwill city (Cava mix) / The rattler (live).
(cd-s) *(CDR 6247)* – ('A'side) / Goodwill city (live) / You generous thing you (live).

Jun 90. (7"/c-s) *(R/TCR 6257)* **BLACKER THAN BLACK. / GREEN GREEN GRASS OF HOME** [61] [-]
(ext.12"+=) *(12R 6257)* – Mad cow disease.
(12"pic-d++=/cd-s++=) *(12RPD/CDR 6257)* – His masters voice.

Radioactive M.C.A.

Feb 91. (7"/c-s) *(MCS/+C 1506)* **NOW WE ARE MARRIED. / FRIDAY'S CHILD** [ ] [-]
(ext.12"+=/ext.12"g-f+=/cd-s+=) *(MCST/+G/D 1506)* – Candlestick Park II/ Candy says.

Mar 91. (lp/c/cd) *(RAR/+C/D 10227)* *<10174>* **HAMMER AND TONGS** [61] [ ]
<US title 'GOODBYE MR MACKENZIE'>
– Blacker than black / Bold John Barleycorn / Diamonds / The burning / Now we are married / Sick baby / Down to the minimum / She's strong / Love child / Tongue-tied.

—— (album was scheduled for release 1990 but dropped by 'Capitol')

May 91. (cd-ep) *<54173>* **THE RATTLER / OPEN YOUR ARMS / DOWN TO THE MINIMUM / FRIDAY'S CHILD / GOODBYE MR MACKENZIE** [-] [ ]

Blokshok not iss.

Apr 93. (12"ep/cd-ep) *(BLOK 001 T/CD)* **GOODWILL CITY LIVE E.P. (live)** [ ] [-]
– Goodwill city / Mystery train / Open your arms / Working on the shoe-fly.

May 93. (cd/lp) *(BLOK CD/LP 001)* **LIVE: ON THE DAY OF STORMS (live)** [ ] [-]
– Goodwill city / Blacker than black / Face to face / Diamonds / Pleasure search / Sick baby / Goodbye Mr. Mackenzie / Dust / HMV / Tongue tied / The rattler / What's got into you / Working on the shoe-fly. *(re-iss. Apr96; same)*

Sep 93. (12"ep/cd-ep) *(BLOK 002 T/CD)* **HARD / NORMAL BOY. / BAD DAY / ZOO** [ ] [-]
(re-iss. Dec95)

Nov 93. (cd/lp) *(BLOK CD/LP 002)* **"FIVE"** [ ] [-]
– Hard / Bam bam / The grip / Jim's killer / Niagara / Touch the bullseye / The day of storms / Yelloueze / Bugdive / Normal boy / Hands of the receiver / Titanic. *(re-iss. Mar96; same)*

—— **METCALFE / WILSON / KELLY + DUNCAN** (vox on track 1)

Oct 94. (12"ep/cd-ep) *(BLOK 003 T/CD)* **THE WAY I WALK / SUPERMAN. / SICK BABY ('94) / YOU WILL** [ ] [-]

Jul 95. (m-cd) *(BLOKCD 004)* **JEZEBEL** (rare) [ ] [-]

—— now without SHIRLEY MANSON, who joined GARBAGE in 1995, after being heard in ANGELFISH (a GOODBYE MR MACKENZIE off-shoot, with her as frontperson and relegating MARTIN to guitarist). BIG JOHN had moonlighted with NIRVANA, as tour replacement for wayward KURT COBAIN.

– compilations, others, etc. –

Jul 98. (cd) *Blokshok; (BLOKCD 003)* **THE GLORY HOLE** [ ] [-]
– The ugly child / Smile trash it / She's got eggs / Troubling you / Space / Neurotic / Overboards / Concrete / Prince of Wales / Crew cut / House on fire / Neuromental.

ANGELFISH

—— **MANSON, METCALFE, WILSON + KELLY**

not iss. Wasteland

Jun 93. (c-ep/cd-ep) *<WSLD 9200-4/-2>* **SUFFOCATE ME / YOU CAN LOVE HER / KIMBERLEY / TRASH IT** [-] [ ]

not iss. Radioactive

Feb 94. (cd) *<RARD 10917>* **ANGELFISH** [-] [ ]
– Dogs in a cage / Suffocate me / You can love me / King of the world / Sleep with me / Heartbreak to hate / The sun won't shine / / Mummy can't drive / Tomorrow forever / The end.

GOOD MISSIONARIES (see under ⇒ ALTERNATIVE TV)

GOO GOO DOLLS

Formed: Buffalo, New York, USA . . . 1986 by ROBBY TAKAC, JOHNNY RZEZNICK and GEORGE TUTUSKA. Like a grunge-punk fusion of CHEAP TRICK, The LEMONHEADS and The DESCENDENTS, they debuted the following year with a low-rent eponymous debut album thankfully not given a release in Britain. A follow-up, 'JED' (1989), was also sprinkled with the odd cover version, a reading of Creedence Clearwater Revival's 'DOWN ON THE CORNER' presided over by guest crooner, LANCE DIAMOND. In the early 90's, 'Metal Blade' took over the reins, their powerful metal-punk winning new audiences after the release of their third set, 'HOLD ME UP' (1990). Three years on, the GOO GOO DOLLS returned with 'SUPERSTAR CARWASH', a transitional set preceding their break for the big time. GEORGE had now been replaced by MIKE MALININ, the sticksman coming in for the band's LOU GIORDANO-produced set, 'A BOY NAMED GOO' (1995), a US Top 30 success that featured Top 5 smash, 'NAME'. However, unlike many of their peers (GREEN DAY, OFFSPRING, etc), the 'DOLLS didn't really translate to the saturated British market despite having another two radio airplay hits in the States, both taken from 1998 album, 'DIZZY UP THE GIRL'. • **Covered:** I WANNA DESTROY YOU (Soft Boys) / DON'T FEAR THE REAPER (Blue Oyster Cult) / SUNSHINE OF YOUR LOVE (Cream) / I COULD NEVER TAKE THE PLACE OF YOUR MAN (Prince) / GIMME SHELTER (Rolling Stones) / I DON'T WANNA KNOW (Fleetwood Mac) / etc.

Album rating: GOO GOO DOLLS (*4) / JED (*4) / HOLD ME UP (*5) / SUPERSTAR CARWASH (*5) / A BOY NAMED GOO (*7) / DIZZY UP THE GIRL (*5)

JOHNNY RZEZNICK – vocals, guitar / **ROBBY TAKAC** – bass, vocals / **GEORGE TUTUSKA** – drums

Celluloid Mercenary

1987. (lp) *(2211)* *<97292-2>* **GOO GOO DOLLS** [-] [ ] French
– Torn apart / Messed up / Livin' in a hut / I'm addicted / Sunshine of your love / Hardsores / Hammering eggs (the metal song) / (Don't fear) The reaper / Beat me / Scream / Slaughterhouse / Different light / Come on / Don't beat my ass (with a baseball bat). *(re-iss. Nov95 on 'Metal Blade'; 14079-2)*

Roadracer Death-Enigma

Apr 89. (lp/cd) *(RO 9477-1/-2)* *<847859>* **JED** [ ] [ ]
– Out of sight / Up yours / No way out / 7th of last month / Love dolls / Sex maggot / Down on the corner / Had enough / Road to Salinas / Em Elbmuh / Misfortune / Artie / Gimme shelter / James Dean. *(cd re-iss. Feb94 on 'Metal Blade'; CDZORRO 70)*

Fun After All Metal Blade

Nov 90. (lp/cd) *(AFTER 8/+CD)* *<26259-1/-2>* **HOLD ME UP** [ ] [ ]
– Laughing / Just the way you are / So outta line / There you are / You know what I man / Out of the red / I could never take the place of your man / Hey / On your side / 22 seconds / Kevin's song / Know my name / Million miles away / Two days in February. *(cd re-iss. May96 on 'Metal Blade'; 3984 17018CD)*

Warners Warners

1993. (cd/c) *<9362 45206-2/-4>* **SUPERSTAR CARWASH** [-] [ ]
– Fallin' down / Lucky star / Cuz you're gone / Don't worry / Girl right next to me / Domino / We are the normal / String of lies / Another second time around / Stop the world / Already there / On the lie / Close your eyes / So far away.

—— **MIKE MALININ** – drums, vocals; repl. GEORGE

Apr 95. (cd/c) *<(9362 45750-2/-4)>* **A BOY NAMED GOO** [ ] [27]
– Long way down / Burnin' up / Naked / Flat top / Impersonality / Name / Only one / Somethin' bad / Ain't that unusual / So long / Eyes wide open / Disconnected / Slave girl.

May 95. (c-s) *(W 0293C)* **ONLY ONE / IMPERSONALITY** [ ] [ ]
(cd-s+=) *(W 0293CD)* – Hit or miss.

Sep 95. (c-s) *<17758>* **NAME / BURNIN' UP / HIT OR MISS** [-] [5]

Feb 96. (c-s) *(W 0333C)* **NAME / NOTHING CAN CHANGE YOU** [ ] [-]
(cd-s+=) *(W 0333CD)* – I wanna destroy you.

Jul 96. (c-s) *(W 0362C)* **LONG WAY DOWN / NAME (live)** [ ] [-]
(cd-s+=) *(W 0362CD)* – Don't change (live).

Jul 98. (c-s) *(W 0449C)* *<44525>* **IRIS / LAZY EYE** [50] [9] Sep98
(cd-s+=) *(W 0449CD)* – I don't want to know.

Sep 98. (cd/c) *<47058-2/-4>* **DIZZY UP THE GIRL** [-] [17]
– Dizzy / Slide / Broadway / January friend / Black balloon / Bullet proof / Amigone / All eyes on me / Full forever / Acoustic #3 / Iris / Extra pale / Hate this place.

Warners Imprint

Nov 98. (cd-s) *<1763>* **SLIDE** [-] [13]

Martin L. GORE (see under ⇒ DEPECHE MODE)

GORILLA BISCUITS (see under ⇒ CIV)

GORILLAS

Formed: Hammersmith, London, England . . . 1974 by JESSE HECTOR (formerly of mid-60's outfit, The CLIQUE) and his cohorts ALAN BUTLER and GARY ANDERSON. Around well before the punk explosion of '76, this dynamic R&B trio nevertheless became an integral part of the London scene, HECTOR's "You Beauty" mutton chops distinguishing them from the spiky-topped pack. Way back in '74, The HAMMERSMITH GORILLAS (as they were known then) debuted with a cover of the Kinks' 'YOU REALLY GOT ME' before signing to local label, 'Chiswick' (home of the COUNT BISHOPS and the 101'ERS). Wearing their influences proudly on their sleeves, The GORILLAS recalled the ghosts of everyone from ELVIS PRESLEY to JIMI HENDRIX (they subsequently covered 'FOXY LADY') with their hard-gigging escapades around the capital. In 1976, HECTOR and Co recorded two singles, 'SHE'S MY GAL' and 'GATECRASHER' for 'Chiswick', before moving on to the 'Raw' label (home of punk-rockers, The UNWANTED and The USERS) for a further couple of tracks, 'IT'S MY LIFE' and 'MESSAGE TO THE WORLD' (the latter the title track of their one and only album, released in '78).

Album rating: MESSAGE TO THE WORLD (*4)

JESSE HECTOR – vocals, guitar / **ALAN BUTLER** – bass / **GARY ANDERSON** – drums, percussion

Penny Farthing not iss.

Sep 74. (7"; as HAMMERSMITH GORILLAS) *(PEN 849)* **YOU REALLY GOT ME. / LEAVING 'OME** [ ] [-]
(re-iss. Aug77 on 'Raw'; RAW 2)

Chiswick not iss.

Jul 76. (7") *(S 4)* **SHE'S MY GAL. / WHY WAIT TILL TOMORROW** [ ] [-]

Jan 77. (7") *(S 8)* **GATECRASHER. / GORILLA GOT ME** [ ] [-]

Raw not iss.

Jan 78. (7") *(RAW 14)* **IT'S MY LIFE. / MY SON'S ALIVE** [ ] [-]

Nov 78. (7") *(RAW 26)* **MESSAGE TO THE WORLD. / OUTTA MY BRAIN** [ ] [-]

Dec 78. (lp) *(RWLP 103)* **MESSAGE TO THE WORLD** [ ] [-]
– Foxy lady / I'm a liar / I need her / Going fishing / New York groover / Outta my brain / Waitin' for you / No way in / Last train / Message to the world. *(cd-iss. Nov94 on 'Damaged Goods'; DAMGOOD 49)*

Chiswick not iss.

Aug 81. (7") *(CHIS 151)* **MOVE IT. / SONG FOR RITA** [ ] [-]

—— split in the early 80's, although a decade later HECTOR was still on the London live circuit

GORKY'S ZYGOTIC MYNCI

Formed: Camarthen, South Wales . . . early 1991 by EUROS CHILD, RICHARD JAMES and JOHN LAWRENCE. Naming themselves after the Russian writer MAXIM GORKY, they were signed to the Bangor-based 'Ankst' label by owner ALUN LLWYD and issued their 1992 debut 45,

'PATIO'. Two years later, their first album 'TATAY', found favour in the indie circuit, while they toured supporting The FALL (The GORKY's were banned in some Welsh clubs for combining the Welsh and English language!). A youthful Welsh-language psychedelic/folk/pop-rock outfit, they were largely influenced by the likes of The INCREDIBLE STRING BAND, early SOFT MACHINE, or the even medieval, GRYPHON. Two brilliant singles were released in 1995; 'MISS TRUDY' (from 'LLANFROG' EP) and the classic 'IF FINGERS WERE XYLOPHONES', while they progressed with their second album proper, 'BWYD TIME', in 1995 (another in 1994; 'PATIO' was demos, etc from '91-93). Early in '96, they inked a deal with the major 'Fontana' label, through A&R man Steve Greenberg. Their first single for the label, the excellent 'PATIO SONG', was their initial breakthrough into the UK Top 50. In April '97, this song and 15 others, were featured on on their best offering to date, the trippy 'BARAFUNDLE' which included the excellently folky 'SOMETIMES THE FATHER IS THE SON'. The following year, with cult glory seemingly at their feet, the GORKY'S released their fifth proper album, 'GORKY 5', a comparatively disappointing effort which, with mediocre reviews, only managed one week in the Top 75. • **Songwriters:** Mostly EUROS CHILDS, some by or with JOHN LAWRENCE and RICHARD JAMES, and a few by MEGAN. Covered; A DAY IN THE LIFE (Beatles) / WHY ARE WE SLEEPING? (Soft Machine) / O CAROLINE (Matching Mole).

Album rating: TATAY (*6) / PATIO (*5) / BWYD TIME (*6) / INTRODUCING . . . compilation US (*6) / BARAFUNDLE (*9) / GORKY 5 (*6)

EUROS CHILDS – vocals, keyboards, synthesizer / **RICHARD JAMES** – guitars, bass / **JOHN LAWRENCE** – bass, guitars, keyboards / **SION LANE** – keyboards / **STEFFAN** – violin

Mynci | not iss.

1991. (c) *(001)* **ALLUMETTE** [ ] [-]

—— **OSIAN EVANS** – drums; repl. SION + STEFFAN

G.Z.M. | not iss.

1992. (c) *(none)* **PEIRIANT PLESER** [ ] [-]

—— added **MEGAN CHILDS** – violin

Ankst | not iss.

1993. (10"lp;ltd) *(ANKST 40)* **PATIO** [ ] [-]
– Peanut dispenser / Lladd eich gwraig / Dafad yn sirad / Mr Groovy / Ti! Moses / Barbed wire / Miriam o Farbel / Oren, mefus a chadno / Gwallt rhegi Pegi / Sally Webster / Diamonds o Monte Carlo / Siwt nofio. *(re-iss. Jan95 & Apr97 cd+=/c+=; ANKST 055 cd/c)* – Blessed are the meek / Reverend Oscar Marzaroli / Oren, mefus a chadno / Dean ser / Siwmper heb grys / Llenni ar gloi / Anna apera / Siwf nofio / Hi ar gan.

Mar 94. (cd/c) *(ANKST 047 cd/c)* **TATAY** [ ] [-]
– Thema o cartref (Theme from home) / Beth sy'n digwydd i'r fuwch (What happens to the cow?) / Tatay / Y ffordd oren (Orange way) / Gwres prynhawn (Afternoon heat) / Amsermaemaiyndod (When May comes) – Cinema / O, Caroline / Naw.e.pimp (Nine for a pimp) / Kevin Ayers / When you hear the captain sing / O, Caroline II / Tatay (moog mix) / Anna apera:- a. Anna apera – b. Gegin nos (Night kitchen) – c. Silff ffenest (Window sill) – d. Backward dog. *(re-iss. Apr97; same)*

Jun 94. (7") *(ANKST 048)* **MERCHED YN GWALLT EI GILYDD. / BOCS ANGELICA / WHEN YOU LAUGH AT YOUR OWN GARDEN IN A BLAZER** [ ] [-]
(cd-s+=) *(ANKST 048cd)* – Mewn. *(re-iss. Apr97; same)*

Nov 94. (7") *(ANKST 053)* **THE GAME OF EYES. / PENTREF WRTH Y MOR** [ ] [-]
(cd-s+=) *(ANKST 053cd)* – Cwpwrdd sadwrn. *(re-iss. Apr97; same)*

—— **EUROS ROWLANDS** – percussion, drums; repl. EVANS

Mar 95. (10"ep/cd-ep) *(ANKST 056/+cd)* **LLANFWROG EP** [ ] [-]
– Miss Trudy / Eira / Methu aros tan haf / Why are we sleeping? *(re-iss. Apr97; same)*

Jun 95. (7"w-drawn) *(ANKST 058)* **GEWN NI GORFFEN. / 12 IMPRESSIONISTIC SOUNDSCAPES** [ ] [-]

Jul 95. (lp/c/cd) *(ANKST 059/+c/cd)* **BWYD TIME** [ ] [-]
– Bwyd time / Miss Trudy / Paid cheto ar Pam (Don't cheat on Pam) / Oraphis yndelphie / Eating salt is easy / Gewn ni gorffen (Let's finish) / Iechyd da (Good health) / Ymwelwyr a gwrachod (Visitors and witches) / The telescope and the bonfire / The man with salt hair / The game of eyes / Blood chant / Ffarm-wr. *(re-iss. Apr97; same)*

Nov 95. (7") *(ANKST 064)* **IF FINGERS WERE XYLOPHONES. / MOON BEATS YELLOW** [ ] [-]
(cd-s+=) *(ANKST 064cd)* – Pethau. *(re-iss. Apr97; same)*

Jul 96. (10"ep/cd-ep) *(ANKST 068/+cd)* **AMBLER GAMBLER EP** [ ] [-]
– Lucy's hamper / Heart of Kentucky / Sdim yr adar yn canu / 20. *(re-iss. Apr97; same)*

Fontana | Polygram

Aug 96. (cd) *<532818-2>* **INTRODUCING . . .** (compilation) [-] [ ]
– Merched ya neod gwalt eu gilydd / If fingers were xylophones / PenTree WRTH Y mor / Games of eyes / Kevin Ayers / Miss Trudy / Why are we sleeping? / Y ffordd oren / Meth aros tan haf / Era / Iechyd da / The moon beats yellow.

Oct 96. (7") *(GZMX 1)* **PATIO SONG. / NO ONE LOOKED AROUND** [41] [-]
(cd-s+=) *(GZMCD 1)* – Morwyr o hyd yn lladd eu hun ar y tir.

Mar 97. (7"/c-s/cd-s) *(GZM/+MC/CD 2)* **DIAMOND DEW. / QUEEN OF GEORGIA / TEARS IN DISGUISE** [42] [-]

Apr 97. (cd/c) *(534 769-2/-4)* *<536122>* **BARAFUNDLE** [46] [ ]
– Diamond dew / The barafundle bumbler / Starmoonsun / Patio song / Better rooms . . . / Heywood lane / Pen gwag glas / Bola bola / Cursed, coined and crucified / Sometimes the father is the son / Meirion Wylit / The wizard and the lizard / Miniature kingdoms / Dark night / Hwyl fawr i pawb / Wordless song.

Jun 97. (7"/c-s) *(GZM/+MC 3)* **YOUNG GIRLS & HAPPY ENDINGS. / DARK NIGHT** [49] [-]
(cd-s) *(GZMCD 3)* –

May 98. (7") *(GZM 4)* **SWEET JOHNNY. / UN HOGYN UN HOGAN DRIST** [60] [-]
(cd-s+=) *(GZMCD 4)* – Mifi Mihafan.

Aug 98. (7") *(GZM 5)* **LET'S GET TOGETHER (IN OUR MINDS) . / TONIGHT** [43] [-]
(cd-s) *(GZMCD 5)* – ('A'side) / Billy and the sugarloaf mountain / Hwiangerdd mair.

Aug 98. (cd/c/lp) *(558 822-2/-4/-1)* **GORKY 5** [67] [-]
– The tidal wave / Dyle fi / Let's get together (in our minds) / Tsunami / Not yet / Only the sea makes sense / Softly / Frozen smile / Sweet Johnny / Theme from Gorky 5 (Russian song) / Hush the warmth / Catrin.

Robert GORL (see under ⇒ D.A.F.)

GRAB GRAB THE HADDOCK (see under ⇒ MARINE GIRLS)

GRANDADDY

Formed: Modesto, California, USA . . . 1992 by ex-skater, JASON LYTE, who, with the help of HOWE GELB (of GIANT SAND), found a sympathetic ear at 'Big Cat' records. The line-up around this time also included JIM FAIRCHILD, TIM DRYDEN, KEVIN GARCIA and AARON BURTCH, although it took time aplenty to finally emerge with the mini-set, 'A PRETTY MESS BY THIS ONE BAND' (1995). 'UNDER THE WESTERN FREEWAY' followed in '98, another based on classic West Coast Americana, their NEIL YOUNG-esque sound marked them out as the Sunday drivers of the alt-country brigade.

Album rating: A PRETTY MESS BY THIS ONE BAND (*6) / UNDER THE WESTERN FREEWAY (*7)

JASON LYTE – vocals / **JIM FAIRCHILD** – guitar / **TIM DRYDEN** – keyboards / **KEVIN GARCIA** – bass / **AARON BURTCH** – drums

Big Cat | Will

1995. (m-cd) *<041>* **A PRETTY MESS BY THIS ONE BAND** [-] [ ]
– Away birdies with special sounds / Taster / Peeano / Kim, you bore me to death / Pre-merced / Gentle spike resort / Egg hit and Jack too.

Feb 98. (7") *(ABB 157S)* **EVERYTHING BEAUTIFUL IS FAR AWAY. /** [ ] [-]
(cd-s+=) *(ABB 157SCD)* –

Mar 98. (7"/cd-s) *(ABB 161S/+CD)* **LAUGHING STOCK. / G.P.C. / 12-INC – 599** [ ] [-]

Apr 98. (lp/cd) *(ABB 152/+CD)* *<33646>* **UNDER THE WESTERN FREEWAY** [ ] [ ] Oct97
– Nonphenomenal lineage / A.M. 180 / Collective dreamwish of upper class / Summer here kids / Laughing stock / Under the western freeway / Everything beautiful is far away / Poisoned at Hartsy Thai food / Go progress chrome / Why took your advice / Lawn and so on.

May 98. (7"/cd-s) *(ABB 162S/+CD)* **SUMMER HERE KIDS. /** [ ] [-]

Oct 98. (7") *(ABB 500350-7)* **AM 180. /** [ ] [-]

Dave GRANEY (see under ⇒ MOODISTS)

GRANT LEE BUFFALO

Formed: North Hollywood, California, USA . . . 1991 by GRANT LEE PHILLIPS (vocals, guitar), PAUL KIMBLE (bass, piano, vocals) and JOEY PETERS (drums, percussion) who had all played together in SHIVA BURLESQUE before splitting the group to concentrate on a new project, GRANT LEE BUFFALO, partly named after lead singer PHILLIPS. After BOB MOULD released 'FUZZY' as a one-off 7" on his own label, the band came to the attention of 'London'-offshoot, 'Slash', making their major label debut with an album, 'FUZZY' (1993). A compelling hybrid of country-rock, folk and feedback hum, the set was lauded by the press, PHILIPS' incisive lyrics cutting at the heart of America's broken dreams and drawing comparisons to NEIL YOUNG, The WATERBOYS and The DOORS. The album was also praised by MICHAEL STIPE of R.E.M. (spiritual forebears), who pronounced it his favourite release of the year. After a mini album, 'BUFFALONDON EP' (1993), featuring live versions of some of the debut's most sublime tracks ('JUPITER AND TEARDROP', 'THE SHINING HOUR'), the band released 'MIGHTY JOE MOON' (1994), a set that employed a richer sonic tapestry without losing the raw impact of the debut. At times, PHILIPS sounded like a more organic EDDDY VEDDER while on songs like 'IT'S THE LIFE', the effect was akin to a countryfied JAMES (decidedly more palatable in reality than on paper!) The breezy melancholy of 'HONEY DON'T THINK' was a highlight, as was 'ROCK OF AGES', rolling the final credits to the album's widescreen sweep. The band's third effort, 'COPPEROPOLIS' (1996), was even more ambitious, embellishing the sound with strings and mellotron amongst other instrumental exotica. The lyrics were more entrenched in threadbare Americana than ever, PHILIPS invoking the spirit of WOODY GUTHRIE in his sensitive portraits of his country's often tragic past. • **Covered:** BURNING LOVE (hit; Elvis Presley).

Album rating: FUZZY (*8) / MIGHTY JOE MOON (*7) / COPPEROPOLIS (*6) / JUBILEE (*5)

GRANT LEE PHILLIPS – vocals, guitars / **PAUL KIMBLE** – bass, piano, vocals, producer / **JOEY PETERS** – drums, percussion

Singles Only Label | not iss.

Dec 91. (7") *(227)* **FUZZY. / WE'RE COMING DOWN** [ ] [-]

Slash – London | Slash – Reprise

Jun 93. (cd/lp) *(828 389-2/-1)* *<45217>* **FUZZY** [74] [ ] Feb93
– The shining hour / Jupiter and teardrop / Fuzzy / Wish you well / The hook / Soft wolf tread / Stars n' stripes / Dixie drug store / America snoring / Grace / You just have to be crazy. *(cd re-iss. Sep97; same)*

Aug 93. (7") *(LAS 45)* **AMERICA SNORING. / WISH YOU WELL** [ ] [-]

(12"+=/cd-s+=) *(LAS H/CD 45)* – The hook / Burning love.

Sep 93. (7") *(LAS 46)* **FUZZY. / STARS & STRIPES** [ ] [-]
(12"+=/cd-s+=) *(LAS H/CD 46)* – Dixie drugstore (Ju Ju mix) / I will take him.

Nov 93. (12"ep/cd-ep) *(LAS H/CD 47)* **BUFFALONDON EP** [ ] [-]
– Jupiter and teardrop / Wish you well / Soft wolf tread / The shining hour.

Sep 94. (cd/c) *(828 541-2/-4)* <45714> **MIGHTY JOE MOON** [24] [ ]
– Lone star song / Mockingbirds / It's the life / Sing along / Mighty Joe Moon / Demon called Deception / Lady Godiva and me / Drag / Last days of Tecumseh / Happiness / Honey don't think / Side by side / Rock of ages.

Oct 94. (cd-ep) *(LASHCD 49)* **MOCKINGBIRDS / ORPHEUS / GOODNIGHT JOHN DEE** [ ] [-]
(12"ep+=) *(LASHX 49)* – Let go of my hand.
(cd-ep) *(LASPD 49)* – (first track) / Let go of my hand / We're coming down.

May 96. (12"ep/cd-ep) *(LAS H/CD 55)* **HOMESPUN / ARMCHAIR. / COMES TO BLOWS / CRASHING AT CORONA** [ ] [-]

Jun 96. (cd/c/lp) *(828 760-2/-4/-1)* <46250> **COPPEROPOLIS** [34] [ ]
– Homespun / The bridge / Arousing thunder / Even the oxen / Crackdown / Armchair / Bethlehem steel / All that I have / Two and two / Better for us / Hyperion and sunset / Comes to blows / Only way down.

— 3rd member **DAN ROTHCHILD** – bass; repl. KIMBLE

— additional **JON BRION** – keyboards / **RAMI JAFFE** – organ

— guests included ROBYN HITCHCOCK, MICHAEL STIPE & E (of The EELS)

Jun 98. (cd) *(556 048-2)* <46879> **JUBILEE** [ ] [ ]
– APB / Seconds / Change your tune / Testimony / Truly, truly / Superslomotion / Fine how'd ya do / Come to mama, she say / 8 mile road / Everybody needs a little sanctuary / My, my, my / Crooked dice / Jubilee / The shallow end.

GRAPES OF WRATH

Formed: Kelowna, British Columbia, Canada . . . 1983 by brothers TOM and CHRIS HOOPER, along with KEVIN KANE and VINCENT JONES. Obviously named after the John Steinbeck novel, this band were dubbed the Canadian R.E.M. due to their folksy, jangle-pop bent, although they weren't possessed of the same innovative spirit as their American cousins. Signing to 'Nettwerk' and uprooting to Vancouver, the quartet issued an eponymous debut EP as a Canadian-only release in '84. A few years passed before the release of their first full-length set, 'SEPTEMBER BOWL OF GREEN', which included the single 'MISUNDERSTANDING'. Characterised by ringing harmonies, 1987's 'TREEHOUSE' really began to see the R.E.M. comparisons kick in, while a move upstairs to 'Capitol' resulted in the acclaimed ANTON FIER-produced 'NOW AND AGAIN' (1989). Boasting a thicker production complete with strings and pedal-steel flourishes (courtesy of the legendary SNEAKY PETE KLEINOW), the record was arguably about the band's best chance to crack the US charts. 1991's 'THESE DAYS', meanwhile, fell some way short of its predecessor, JOHN LECKIE's production coming in for some flak. After almost ten years plugging away to little commercial reward, the band hadn't reached their Garden Of Eden and finally hitched up their wagon for good. • **Covered:** LET ME ROLL IT (Paul McCartney & Wings). • **Note:** Not to be confused with the 60's psychedelic outfit of the same name.

Album rating: SEPTEMBER BOWL OF GREEN (*5) / TREEHOUSE (*7) / NOW AND AGAIN (*8) / THESE DAYS (*5) / SEEMS LIKE FATE 1984-1992 compilation (*5) / Ginger: FAR OUT (*6) / SUDDENLY, I CAME TO MY SENSES (*5)

KEVIN KANE – vocals, guitar / **VINCENT JONES** – keyboards / **TOM HOOPER** – bass / **CHRIS HOOPER** – drums

Nettwerk Nettwerk

Jul 87. (12"ep) <(33NTWK 012)> **GRAPES OF WRATH** [ ] [ ] 1984

Nettwerk Capitol

1986. (7") **MISUNDERSTANDING. /** [-] [ ]

Jul 87. (lp)<lp,cd> *(NTL 30004)*<93337> **SEPTEMBER BOWL OF GREEN** [ ] [ ] Nov86
– Misunderstanding / Love comes around / Breaks my heart / A dream (about you) / Didn't you say something / And I know / Self abuse / Umbrella / Realistic birds / See her go / Lay out the trap / Down to the wire. <cd+=> – Laughing out loud / Breaks my heart.

1987. (lp/c/cd) <*CLT/C4T/C2 48018*> **TREEHOUSE** [-] [ ]
– O lucky man / Backward town / How long / Very special day / Try / At your soul / Peace of mind / Amused / So many times / Jewel in the hand / Completely lost / Run you down / Seems like fate.

Capitol Capitol

Feb 90. (cd/c/lp) *(CD/TC+/EST 2118)* **NOW AND AGAIN** [ ] [ ] Sep89
– All the things I wasn't / What was going through my head / Do you want to tell me? / The most / I'm gone / Blind / Stay / I can tell / Not the way it is / Hiding / The time is here / . . . But I guess we'll never know.

Mar 90. (7") *(CL 570)* **DO YOU WANT TO TELL ME. / BACKWARD TOWN (acoustic)** [ ] [ ]
(12"+=/cd-s+=) *(12/CD CL 570)* – I can tell.

Jul 91. (cd-ep) <*79169*> **YOU MAY BE RIGHT / DOWN SO CLOSE / LET ME ROLL IT / PEACE OF MIND** [-] [ ]

Feb 92. (cd/c) *(CD/TC EST 2168* **THESE DAYS** [ ] [ ] Aug91
– Away / You may be right / Consequences / I can't find my home / Days / I am here / No reason / Travelin' / A fishin' tale / Thru to you / Now / Miracle.

Jan 92. (cd-ep) <*15758*> **I AM HERE / ALL THE TIME / SEE EMILY PLAY / I AM HERE (version) / I AM HERE (version)** [-] [ ]

— KANE departed to go solo (in '96 they released, 'NEIGHBORHOOD WATCH') and the rest became GINGER

– compilations, etc. –

1994. (cd) *EMI Nettwerk;* **SEEMS LIKE FATE 1984-1992** [-] [ ]

GINGER

— **TOM + CHRIS HOOPER + VINCENT JONES**

Nettwerk Nettwerk

Dec 93. (cd-ep) <*6320*> **GINGER EP** [-] [-] Canada
– The earth revolves around you / Try to believe me / Dirge / Just like you / From now on.

Dec 94. (cd) <*30096*> **FAR OUT** [-] [ ]
– Far out / Solid ground / Feel like falling down / Saying sorry again / Keep looking back / On the road again / Ocean drain / The earth revolves around you / Mr. Attitude / Darkside of my mind / One who fell from grace on the news.

not iss. EMI Music

Nov 96. (cd) <*53959*> **SUDDENLY I CAME TO MY SENSES** [-] [ ]
– Evaporate / Here with me / Everything you're missing / What I need / Come to me / Everything's funny / Him with his foot in his mouth / Midnight man / Summertime / You're at it again / Love in my head / Sunday morning blues / All I wanted to say / Solid ground.

GRASSHOPPER & THE GOLDEN CRICKETS (see under ⇒ MERCURY REV)

GREAT DIVIDE (see under ⇒ BIBLE)

GREAT LEAP FORWARD (see under ⇒ BIG FLAME)

GREAT UNWASHED (see under ⇒ CLEAN)

GREEN DAY

Formed: Rodeo, nr. Berkeley, California, USA . . . early 90's out of The SWEET CHILDREN by BILLY JOE and MIKE. When TRE COOL replaced BILLY JOE's sister ANA on drums, they became GREEN DAY, this line-up releasing their debut lp, '39 / SMOOTH', which was recorded in under 24 hours. Their third album, 'DOOKIE' (their first for 'Reprise'), was a surprise US smash in 1994 due to its college/MTV favourite, 'BASKET CASE'. Retro punk-rock for young Americans (and now older Brits) who missed out on BUZZCOCKS, DICKIES, RAMONES (and even earlier 60's pop outfit, the MONKEES), GREEN DAY became a phenomenon in the States; like the SEX PISTOLS' revolution all over again, without the danger, unpredictability and raw excitement. Instead we got formulaic, annoyingly and yes, inanely catchy punk retreads that took you way back to '77. Still, the multi-millions who bought the record ensured that GREEN DAY were indeed radio friendly unit shifters. A follow-up set, 'INSOMNIAC' (1995), was another massive seller, although it had to compete with the hordes of equally faceless acts clogging up the charts with similar material. A fifth set, 'NIMROAD' (1997), made sure they were still in touch with their fanbase, the tried and tested formula again getting them into the Top 10. • **Songwriters:** Lyrics; BILLY JOE, group songs except TIRED OF WAITING FOR YOU (Kinks). • **Trivia:** DIRNT guested on The SCREAMING WEASEL album, 'How to Make Enemies And Irritate People'. BILLIE JOE was also a member of PINHEAD GUNPOWDER, who released an album, 'Jump Salty', plus a few EP's (also for 'Lookout').

Album rating: 39/SMOOTHED OUT SLAPPY HOUR compilation (*5) / KERPLUNK! (*5) / DOOKIE (*7) / INSOMNIAC (*6) / NIMROD (*6)

BILLY JOE ARMSTRONG (b.17 Feb'72, San Pablo, Calif.) – vocals, guitar / **MIKE DIRNT** (b. PRITCHARD, 4 May'72) – bass, vocals / **TRE COOL** (b. FRANK EDWIN WRIGHT III, 9 Dec'72, Germany) – drums repl. JOHN KIFTMEYER who had repl. AL SOBRANTE

not iss. Lookout

1989. (7"ep) <*LOOKOUT 17*> **1000 HOURS EP** [-] [ ]
– 1000 hours / Dry ice / Only of you / The one I want. *(UK-iss.Dec94; as above)*

1990. (lp) <*LOOKOUT 22*> **39 / SMOOTH** [-] [ ]
– At the library / Don't leave me / I was there / Disappearing boy / Green day / Going to Pasalacgua / 16 / Road to exceptance / Rest / The judge's daughter / Paper lanterns / Why do you want him? / 409 in your coffeemaker / Knowledge / 1000 hours / Dry ice / Only of you / The one I want / I want to be alone. *(re-iss. Nov91 lp/cd; LOOKOUT 22/+CD) (UK-iss.Sep94 as '1,039 / SMOOTHED OUT SLAPPY HOURS'; as above) (cd re-iss. Aug97 on 'Epitaph'; 6522-2)*

1991. (7"ep) <*LOOKOUT 35*> **SLAPPY EP** [-] [ ]
– Paper lanterns / Why do you want him? / 409 in your coffeemaker / Knowledge. *(UK-iss.Sep94; as above)*

Dec 91. (lp) <*LOOKOUT 46*> **KERPLUNK!** [-] [ ]
– 2000 light years away / One for the razorbacks / Welcome to Paradise / Christie Road / Private ale / Dominated love slave / One of my lies / 80 / Android / No one knows / Who wrote Holden Caulfield? / Words I might have ate. *(UK-iss.Sep94 on 'Lookout' lp/cd+=; LOOKOUT 46/+CD)* – Sweet children / Best thing in town / Strangeland / My generation. *(by SWEET CHILDREN and released US 1990 on 'Skene') (cd re-iss. Aug97 on 'Epitaph'; 6517-2)*

Reprise Reprise

Feb 94. (cd/c) <*(9362 45529-2/-4)*> **DOOKIE** [ ] [2]
– Burnout / Having a blast / Chump / Longview / Welcome to Paradise / Pulling teeth / Basket case / She / Sassafras roots / When I come around / Coming clean / Emenius sleepus / In the end / F.O.D. *(cd+=)* – (hidden track). *(re-dist.Jun94) (re-iss. Oct94 on green-lp soon hit UK No.13; 9362 45795-2/-4)*

Jun 94. (7") *(W 0247)* **LONGVIEW. / ON THE WAGON** [ ] [-]
(10"/cd-s) *(W 0247 T/CD)* – ('A'side) / Going to Pasalaqua / F.O.D. (live) / Christy Road (live).

Aug 94. (7"green/c-s) *(W 0257/+C)* **BASKET CASE. / TIRED OF WAITING FOR YOU** [55] [-]
(cd-s+=) *(W 0257CD)* – On the wagon / 409 in your coffeemaker.

Oct 94. (12"green/c-s/cd-s) *(W 0269 T/C/CDX)* **WELCOME TO PARADISE. / CHUMP (live) / EMENIUS SLEEPUS** [20] [-]

Jan 95. (7"green/c-s) *(W 0279/+C)* **BASKET CASE. / 2,000 LIGHT YEARS AWAY (live)** [7] [-] (cd-s+=) *(W 0279CD)* – Burnout (live) / Longview (live).

Mar 95. (7"/c-s) *(W 0278/+C)* **LONGVIEW. / WELCOME TO PARADISE (live)** [30] [ ]
(cd-s+=) *(W 0278CD)* – One of my lies (live).

May 95. (7"pic-d/c-s) *(W 0294/+C)* **WHEN I COME AROUND. / SHE (live)** [27] [-]
(cd-s+=) *(W 0294CD)* – Coming clean (live).

Sep 95. (7"red/c-s) *(W 0320/+C)* **GEEK STINK BREATH. / I WANNA BE ON T.V.** [16] [-]
(cd-s+=) *(W 0320CD)* – Don't wanna fall in love.

Oct 95. (cd/c/lp) *<(9362 46046-2/-4/-1)>* **INSOMNIAC** [8] [2]
– Armatage Shanks / Brat / Stuck with me / Geek stink breath / No pride / Bab's Uvula who? / 86 / Panic song / Stuart and the Ave. / Brain stew / Jaded / Westbound sign / Tight wad hill / Walking contradiction.

Dec 95. (7") *(W 0327X)* **STUCK WITH ME. / WHEN I COME AROUND (live)** [24] [-]
(c-s+=) *(W 0327C)* – Jaded (live).
(cd-s) *(W 0327CD)* – ('A'side) / Dominated love slave (live) / Chump (live).

Jun 96. (c-s) *(W 0339C)* **BRAIN STEW / JADED / GOOD RIDDANCE** [28] [-]
(cd-s+=) *(W 0339CD)* – Do da da.
(brain-shaped cd-s++=) *(W 0339CDX)* – Brain stew (radio).

Sep 97. (c-s) *(W 0424C) <43945>* **HITCHIN' A RIDE / SICK** [25] [ ] Jun98
(cd-s+=) *(W 0424CD)* – Espionage.

Oct 97. (cd/c) *<(9362 46794-2/-4)>* **NIMROD** [11] [10]
– Nice guys finish last / Hitchin' a ride / The grouch / Reduntant / Scattered / Worry rock / Desensitized / All the time / Platypus (I hate you) / Last ride in / Jinx / Haushinka / Walking alone / Suffocate / Uptight / Take back / King for a day / Good riddance / Prosthetic head.

Jan 98. (c-s) *(W 0430C) <43974>* **TIME OF YOUR LIFE (GOOD RIDDANCE) / DESENSITIZED** [11] [ ] Jun98
(cd-s+=) *(W 0430CD1)* – Rotting.
(cd-s) *(W 0430CD2)* – ('A'side) / Suffocate / You lied.

Apr 98. (7"/cd-s) *(W 0438/+CD1)* **REDUNDANT. / THE GROUCH (live) / PAPER LANTERN (live)** [27] [ ]
(cd-s) *(W 0438CD2)* – ('A'side) / Reject all American (live) / She (live).

Dave GREENFIELD & J. J. BURNEL

(see under ⇒ STRANGLERS)

GREEN ON RED

Formed: Tucson, Arizona, USA ... 1979 by DAN STUART, CHRIS CACAVAS, JACK WATERSON and VAN CRISTIAN. The latter was replaced by ALEX MacNICOL prior to the release of their eponymous mini-lp for STEVE WYNN's 'Down There' label. Their debut album, 'GRAVITY TALKS' (1984), drew comparisons with NEIL YOUNG's more rockyoutings, moving away from the ramshackle garage of their earlier releases. This influence was even more evident on their 1985 offering 'GAS FOOD LODGING', which featured the distinctive guitar style of the newly recruited CHUCK PROPHET. Signing to 'Mercury' the same year, they released the disappointing 'NO FREE LUNCH', an album that saw the band attempting a BYRDS-like country sound, and even included a WILLIE NELSON cover 'AIN'T IT FUNNY NOW'. After the similarly poor 'THE KILLER INSIDE ME' in 1987, the group disbanded although DAN and CHUCK re-formed, using session players to flesh out the sound. Always on the verge of a commercial breakthrough, they were dogged by label failures and by the time of 1989's 'HERE COME THE SNAKES', the band had signed to 'China' in the UK although the record, which showcased a bolshier, heavy guitar sound, was previously to have been issued in August '88 by the soon-to-be bust 'Red Rhino' records. Undaunted, the band played a blinding live set in London, documented on 'LIVE AT THE TOWN AND COUNTRY' (1989). The band issued another three albums (including AL KOOPER-produced 'SCAPEGOATS') to no commercial success and after the ironically titled 'TOO MUCH FUN' (1992), PROPHET and STUART went on to releaseswell-received solo albums. • **More covers:** KNOCKIN' ON HEAVEN'S DOOR (Bob Dylan) / SMOKESTACK LIGHTNIN' (Howlin' Wolf) / RAINY DAYS AND MONDAYS (Carpenters).

Album rating: GREEN ON RED mini (*6) / GRAVITY TALKS (*7) / GAS FOOD LODGING (*8) / NO FREE LUNCH mini (*4) / THE KILLER INSIDE ME (*5) / HERE COME THE SNAKES (*7) / LIVE AT THE TOWN AND COUNTRY (*4) / THIS TIME AROUND (*6) / SCAPEGOATS (*5) / ROCK'N'ROLL DISEASE – THE BEST OF GREEN ON RED compilation (*7) / TOO MUCH FUN (*4) / Danny & Dusty: THE LOST WEEKEND (*5) / Dan Stuart: RETRONEUVO (*5) / CANO'WORMS (*5)

DAN STUART – vocals, guitar / **CHRIS CACAVAS** – keyboards / **JACK WATERSON** – bass / **ALEX MacNICOL** – drums, repl. VAN CRISTIAN

not iss. / Private

1981. (12"ep) *<none>* **TWO BIBLES** [-] [ ]

not iss. / Down There

1982. (m-lp) *<71026>* **GREEN ON RED (UNTITLED)** [-] [ ]
– Death and angels / Hair and skin / Black night / Illustrated crawling / Aspirin / Lost world / Apartment 6. *(UK-iss.Jun85 on 'Zippo'; ZANE 002)*

Slash / Slash

Aug 84. (lp) *(SR 207) <23964-1>* **GRAVITY TALKS** [ ] [ ] 1983
– Gravity talks / Old chief / 5 easy pieces / Deliverance / Over my head / Snake bite / Blue parade / That's what you're here for / Brave generation / Abigail's ghost / Cheap wine / Narcolepsy. *(re-iss. Jan87 lp/c; SLM P/C 16)*

— added **CHUCK W. PROPHET** – steel guitar, vocals

Zippo / Enigma

May 85. (lp/c) *(ZONG/+CASS 005) <ST/4XT 73249>* **GAS FOOD LODGING** [ ] [ ] 1986
– That's what dreams / Black river / Hair of the dog / This I know / Fading away / Easy way out / Sixteen ways / The drifter / Sea of Cortez / We shall overcome. *(cd-iss. 1990 on 'Enigma'; D2-73249)*

— **KEITH MITCHELL** – percussion repl. ALEX

Mercury / Mercury

Oct 85. (m-lp/m-c) *(MERM/+C 78) <82646-1>* **NO FREE LUNCH** [99] [ ]
– Time ain't nothing / Honest man / Ballad of Guy Fawkes / No free lunch / Funny how time slips away / Jimmy boy / Keep on moving. *(c+=)* – Smokestack lightning.

Nov 85. (7") *(MER 202)* **TIME AIN'T NOTHING. / NO FREE LUNCH** [ ] [-]

Feb 87. (7") *(GOR 1)* **CLARKSVILLE. / NO DRINKIN'** [ ] [-]
(12"+=) *(GOR 1-12)* – Broken.

Mar 87. (lp/c)(cd) *(GOR LP/MC 1)(839122-2) <830912-2>* **THE KILLER INSIDE ME** [ ] [ ]
– Clarksville / Mighty gun / Jamie / Whispering wind / Ghost hand / Sorry Naomi / No man's land / Track you down (his master's voice) / Born to fight / We ain't feee / The killer inside me. *(cd+=)* – NO FREE LUNCH (m-lp)

Jun 87. (7") *(GOR 2)* **BORN TO FIGHT. / DON'T SHINE YOUR LIGHT ON ME** [ ] [-]
(ext.12"+=) *(GOR 2-12)* – While the widow weeps.

— Disbanded late 1987, DAN and CHUCK reformed and brought in new sessioners. WATERSON released an album 'WHOSE DOG' in 1988, while CHRIS CACAVAS & THE JUNKYARD LOVE released self-titled one in 1989.

China / Restless

Apr 89. (7") *(CHINA 16)* **KEITH CAN'T READ. / THAT'S THE WAY THE WORLD GOES ROUND / VAYA CON DIOS** [ ] [-]
(12") *(CHINX 16)* – (1st & 3rd tracks) / Tenderloin.

Apr 89. (lp/c/cd) *(839294-1/-4/-2) <72351-1>* **HERE COME THE SNAKES** [ ] [ ]
– Keith can't read / Rock and roll disease / Morning blue / Zombie for love / Broken radio / Change / Tenderloin / Way back home / We had it all / D.T. blues.

Aug 89. (ltd; 10"lp/c) *(841013-0/-4)* **LIVE AT THE TOWN & COUNTRY CLUB (live)** [ ] [-]
– 16 ways / Change / DT blues / Fading away / Morning blue / Are you sure Hank done it this way / Zombie for love / Hair of the dog. *(c+=)* – Rock and roll disease / We had it all.

— duo now with **RENE COMAN** – upright bass, bass / **MIKE FINNEGAN** – keyboards / **DAVID KEMPER** – drums, percussion / plus **BERNIE LEADON** – mandolin, acoustic guitar (4) / **PAT DONALDSON** – bass (4) / **SPOONER OLDHAM** – piano (3)

China / Catalina

Oct 89. (7") *(CHINA 21)* **THIS TIME AROUND. / FADING AWAY (live)** [ ] [-]
(12"+=/cd-s+=) *(CHINX/CHICD 21)* – 16 ways (live).

Nov 89. (lp/c/cd) *(841720-1/-4/-2) <841519-2>* **THIS TIME AROUND** [ ] [-]
– This time around / Cool million / Rev. Luther / Good patient woman / You couldn't get arrested / The quarter / Foot / Hold the line / Pills and booze / We're all waiting. *(free-7"w.a.)* – MORNING BLUE / ROCK AND ROLL DISEASE. / (interview) *(re-iss. Jul91 cd/c; WOL CD/MC 1019)*

Dec 89. (7") *(CHINA 22)* **YOU COULDN'T GET ARRESTED. / BROKEN RADIO** [ ] [-]
(ext.12"/ext.cd-s) *(CHINX/CHICD 22)* – Hair of the dog.

— DAN and CHUCK recruit **MICHAEL RHODES** – bass / **DAREN HESS** – drums

China / China

Mar 91. (7") **LITTLE THINGS IN LIFE. / CHERRY KIND** [ ] [-]
(12"+=/cd-s+=) – Sun goes down / Waiting for love.

Mar 91. (cd/c/lp) *<(WOL CD/MC/LP 1001)>* **SCAPEGOATS** [ ] [ ]
– A guy like me / Little things in life / Two lovers (waitin' to die) / Gold in the graveyard / Hector's out / Shed a tear (for the lonesome) / Blowfly / Sun goes down / Where the rooster crows / Baby loves her gun.

Jun 91. (7") **TWO LOVERS (WAITIN' TO DIE). / KEITH CAN'T READ** [ ] [-]

Sep 91. (cd/c/lp) *(WOL/+MC/CD 1021)* **THE BEST OF GREEN ON RED** (compilation) [ ] [-]
– Time ain't nothing / Born to fight / Hair of the dog / Keith can't read / Morning blue / This time around / Little things in life / You couldn't get arrested / That's what dreams / Zombie for love / Baby loves her gun.

— added **J.D. FOSTER**

Oct 92. (lp/c/cd) *<(WOL/+MC/CD 1029)>* **TOO MUCH FUN** [ ] [ ]
– She's all mine / Frozen in my headlights / Love is insane / Too much fun / The getaway / I owe you one / Man needs woman / Sweetest thing / Thing or two / Hands and knees / Wait and see / Rainy days and Mondays.

– compilations, others, etc. –

Sep 91. (cd/c) *Music Club; <(MC CD/TC 037)>* **THE LITTLE THINGS IN LIFE** [ ] [ ]

May 92. (cd) *Mau Mau; <(MAUCD 612)>* **GAS FOOD LODGING / GREEN ON RED** [ ] [ ] Jan96

Jun 94. (cd) *China; <(WOLCD 1047)>* **ROCK'N'ROLL DISEASE – THE BEST OF . . .** [ ] [ ] 1995

— DAN STUART also had appeared on album below.

DANNY & DUSTY

DUSTY being STEVE WYNN of DREAM SYNDICATE. Augmented by LONG RYDERS:- SYD GRIFFIN, TOM STEVENS + STEVE McCARTHY, plus DENNIS DUCK of DREAM SYNDICATE + CHRIS CACAVAS of GREEN ON RED

Zippo / A&M

Nov 85. (lp) *(ZONG 007) <5075>* **THE LOST WEEKEND** [ ] [ ]
– Down to the bone / The word is out / Song for the dreamers / Miracle mile / Baby, we all gotta go down / The king of the losers / Send me a postcard / Knockin' on Heaven's door. *<cd-iss. 1996 on 'Prima'; 6>*

— DAN was also guest on two of NAKED PREY albums. CHRIS guested on the GIANT SAND album 'VALLEY OF RAIN' in Mar'86. In Sep'90, CHUCK PROPHET issued solo album 'BROTHER ALDO' for 'Fire'. In 1993 for 'China', he issued 'BALINESE DANCER' foolowed by in '95; 'FEAST OF HEARTS'. Meanwhile CACAVAS on 'Normal' released 'PALE BLONDE HELL' (1994) & 'NEW IMPROVED PAIN' (1995).

DAN STUART

—— (on 1995 set) with **J.D. FOSTER, JON DEE GRAHAM, RANDY McREYNOLDS, JAMES VALENCIA, FERNANDO VALENCI, DAREN HESS + CRAIG SCHUMACHER**

Normal / Monkey Hill

Jul 94. (cd; by AL PERRY & DAN STUART) *(NORMAL 169CD)* **RETRONEUVO**
– Daddy's girl / Hermit of Jerome / I could run / Little slant 6 / Sick and tired / Better than I did / Mamcita / Eyes of a fool / Empty chair / Lone wolf.

Jul 95. (cd) *(NORMAL 189CD) <8131>* **CANO'WORMS**
– Panhandler / Home after dark / La pasionara / Who needs more / What a day / Expat blues / Waterfall / In Madrid / Filipina stripped / Can't get through / The greatest.

GREEN RIVER (see under ⇒ PEARL JAM)

GRENADINE (see under ⇒ UNREST)

Sid GRIFFIN (see under ⇒ LONG RYDERS)

GRIFTERS

Formed: Memphis, Tennessee, USA . . . 1990 out of A BAND CALLED BUD by DAVE SHOUSE, SCOTT TAYLOR and TRIPP LAMKINS, who were joined by STAN GALLIMORE after their radical name change. Debuting with the 'DISFIGUREHEAD' EP, these lo-fi noise terrorists differed from peers like ROYAL TRUX in that their sound was mired in the roots music of the American south. Following another breakneck blast of alt-rock distortion, 'SO HAPPY TOGETHER' (1992), The GRIFTERS took their feet off the accelerator for 1993's 'ONE SOCK MISSING'. Issued on their own 'Shangri-La' imprint, the record drew comparisons with a more extreme 'Stones circa 'Exile On . . .'. A further couple of low-key releases (including 'CRAPPIN' YOU NEGATIVE' and the mini-set 'EUREKA') preceded a prestigious signing to 'Sub Pop', taking the time to polish up their sound without losing the rough hewn charm on 1996's 'AIN'T MY LOOKOUT'. A follow-up set, 'FULL BLOWN POSSESSION' (1997), saw them once again put down'n'dirty rock'n'roll through the lo-fi shredder.

Album rating: SO HAPPY TOGETHER (*6) / ONE SOCK MISSING (*8) / CRAPPIN' YOU NEGATIVE (*7) / EUREKA mini (*5) / AIN'T MY LOOKOUT (*6) / FULL BLOWN POSSESSION (*6)

DAVE SHOUSE – guitar, vocals / **SCOTT TAYLOR** – guitar, vocals / **TRIPP LAMKINS** – bass / **STAN GALLIMORE** – drums

not iss. / Doink

1990. (10"ep) *<025>* **DISFIGUREHEAD EP**
– Disfigurehead / The kingdom of Jones.

Sonic Noise / Sonic Noise

Nov 92. (cd/lp) *<(SON 002-2/-1)>* **SO HAPPY TOGETHER**

Southern / Shangri-La

1993. (7"m) *<002>* **SODA POP. / DIVINE / SHE BLOWS BLASTS OF STATIC**

1993. (7") *<003>* **COROLLA HOIST. / THUMBNAIL SKETCH**

Jun 93. (cd/c/lp) *(18511-2/-4/-1) <004>* **ONE SOCK MISSING**

Mar 94. (7") *<006>* **BRONZE CAST. / CONFIDENTIAL**

May 94. (cd/lp) *(18519-2/-1) <008>* **CRAPPIN' YOU NEGATIVE**
– Rats / Maps of the sun / Dead already / Black fuel incinerator / Skin man palace / Arizona / Felt-tipped over / Holmes / Get outta that spaceship and fight like a man / Piddlebach / Bronze cast / Junkie blood / Here comes Larry / Cinnamon.

May 95. (m-cd) *<SON 013>* **EUREKA**
– Eureka I.V. / His Jesus song / Slow day for the cleaner / Whatever happened to Felix Cole / Founder's day parade / Banjo / X-ray hip.

not iss. / Derivative

1995. (7") *<018>* **STREAM. / COAT OF SILENCE**

Sub Pop / Sub Pop

Nov 94. (7") *<(SP 278)>* **QUEEN OF THE TABLE WATERS. /**

Jan 96. (7") *<(SP 339)>* **LAST MAN ALIVE. / PARTING SHOT**

Feb 96. (lp/cd) *<(SP/+CD 327)>* **AIN'T MY LOOKOUT**
– Covered with flies / Parting shot / Mysterious friends / Boho – Alt / Pretty notes / Day shift / The last man alive / My apology / Straight time / Return to cinder / Give yourself to me / Fixed in the sky / Radio city suicide.

Feb 96. (12"/cd-s) *(ALPHA 12/CD 001)* **AIN'T MY LOOKOUT. /**
(above issued on 'Alpha-Sub Pop')

Aug 97. (7") *<SP 382>* **WICKEDTHING. / ORGAN GRINDER**

Nov 97. (lp/cd) *<(SP/+CD 402)>* **FULL BLOWN POSSESSION** — Sep97
– Re-entry blues / Fireflies / Spaced out / Centuries / Sweetest thing / Happy / Wickedthing / Blood thirsty lovers / Hours / You be the stranger / Cigarette / Contact me now.

HOT MONKEY

—— **SCOTT TAYLOR** and Co.

not iss. / Shangri-la

Apr 94. (7") *<005>* **SHARK. / DEPENDS**

Jan 96. (m-cd) *<2>* **LION**
(above issued on 'Positive Force')

Sep 96. (cd) *<020>* **MORE THAN LAZY**
– Favors / That certain thing / 4 eyes / Steam / Wheel / Sometimes / Monty Carlo / Hide-n-seek / Wait up / Dandy lion / Other ideas / Strap / Sooner / I won't tell / Meat truck / Hours / Think I love you / Dinosaur angel / Sain.

GROOP DOGDRILL

Formed: Doncaster, England . . . early 1996 by tattooed "hard" lads, PETE SPIBY, DAMO FOWKES and HUG, who got together through ads put in American Army mag, 'Guns And Ammo'. Manic grinding, metallic punk like JON SPENCER BLUES EXPLOSION or THERAPY? on testosterone, GROOP DOGDRILL began their career in fine fettle with two independently issued 45's, 'GENTLEMEN'S SOIREE' and 'GRACELANDS'. The following year saw them sign to Beggars Banquet offshoot, 'Mantra', where they delivered a trio of greasy, Kerrang!-friendly singles prior to the release of their heavily touted debut set, 'HALF NELSON'.

Album rating: HALF NELSON (*8)

PETE SPIBY – vocals, guitar / **DAMO FOWKES** – bass / **HUG (KELLY)** – drums / 4th member **BOX** – lyrics, roadie

EXP Limited / not iss.

Aug 96. (7") *(GDD 7010)* **GENTLEMEN'S SOIREE. / SILVER BOOTS**

Nov 96. (7") *(EXP 7011)* **GRACELANDS. / SPOILER**
(cd-s) *(EXPCD 7011)* – Eyelash trauma.

Mantra / Imprint

Sep 97. (7") *(MNT 023)* **LOVELY SKIN. / ROCKABILLY WORKOUT**
(cd-s+=) *(MNT 023CD)* – Shrub.

Feb 98. (7") *(MNT 028)* **OILY RAG. / PACKMULE**
(cd-s+=) *(MNT 028CD)* – Feeding frenzy.

Apr 98. (7") *(MNT 033)* **JACKIE O. / SPORT OF KINGS**
(cd-s+=) *(MNT 033CD)* – New York sushi / Speedball.

Apr 98. (cd/c/lp) *(MNT CD/MC/LP 1010) <58844>* **HALF NELSON** — Aug98
– Lovely skin / Cocksuker blues / Gentleman's soiree / Lifestyle / Oily rag / Southbound tuxedo / Jackie O / Gracelands / Hessus / (That) Texaco feeling / Salt Peter / Personal / Silver boots.

Nov 98. (7"colrd) *(MNT 035)* **PERSONAL. / HOBOKEN THING / HEDLEY HADLEY (ODE TO LILLEY)**

GROTUS

Formed: San Francisco, California, USA . . . 1991 by LARS FOX, ADAM TANNER and JOHN CARSON. Taking grunge, Bay Area thrash and industrial experimentation as reference points, this innovative trio released their debut album, 'BROWN', in 1991. Subsequently signing to Jello Biafra's 'Alternative Tentacles' label, the group (bolstered by the addition of BRUCE BOYD, who replaced the drum machine with organic sticksmanship) released the vaguely Eastern-themed 'SLOW MOTION APOCALYPSE' (1993). While the artwork juxtaposed an assortment of Hindu deities with a backdrop of environmental desolation, the music was largely mid-paced jackhammer grunge-noise with occasional flourishes of tabla, sitar etc.; repeated listening to the likes of 'SHIVAYANAMA' was more likely to bring on catatonia than enlightenment. Later that year, the band released the first in a series of EP's, 'LUDDITE', following it up in summer '94 with a collaborative effort, 'THE OPIATE OF THE MASSES', recorded in partnership with world-beat specialists, TRANSGLOBAL UNDERGROUND. The attendant publicity, together with the band's growing undeground acclaim led to a deal with 'London' records, GROTUS making their major label debut with the 'HANDJOB' EP in early '96, while a third long player, 'MASS', surfaced the following month.

Album rating: BROWN (*6) / SLOW MOTION APOCALYPSE (*7) / MASS (*6)

LARS FOX – vocals, samples, percussion / **ADAM TANNER** – bass, guitar, synthesizer, samples / **JOHN CARSON** – bass, samples

not iss. / Spirit

1991. (cd) *<7>* **BROWN**
– Brown / Malthusela / City of the dead / Vegas power grid / Pharmaceutical / Edward Abbey / Daisy chain / Valhalla's Celtic Robbie / You fit the suit / Full metal Grotus / New York strip / Rust / Morning glory.

1992. (cd-ep) *<14>* **LUDDITE**
– Luddite / Marginal / Shelf life / What in the world. *(UK-iss.Aug93 on 'Alternative Tentacles' 12"ep/cd-ep; VIRIS 128/+CD)*

—— added **BRUCE BOYD** – drums

Alternative Tentacles / Alternative Tentacles

Apr 93. (cd) *<(VIRUS 118CD)>* **SLOW MOTION APOCALYPSE**
– Up rose the mountain / Good evening / The same old sauce / Hourglass / Shivayanama / Complications / Kali Yuga / Clean / Sleepwalking / Medicine / Slow motion apocalypse.

Jul 94. (12"ep/cd-ep; GROTUS & TRANSGLOBAL UNDERGROUND) *<(VIRUS 148/+CD)>* **THE OPIATE OF THE MASSES**

London / Polygram

Oct 95. (cd-s) *<850373>* **A BAD ITCH**

Feb 96. (cd-s) *<850521>* **HANDJOB EP**
– Hand to mouth / etc.

Mar 96. (cd/c/lp) *<(828604-2/-4/-1)>* **MASS**
– That's entertainment / A bad itch / White trash blues / Ebola Reston / Hand to mouth / T'ain't nobody's bizness if I do / Sick / Collect 'em all / Wild Bill / The bottom line / Back in the day.

GUADALCANAL DIARY

Formed: Marietta, Georgia, USA . . . 1981 by main songwriter MURRAY ATTAWAY and JEFF WALLS, along with RHETT CROWE and JOHN POE, naming themselves after a soldier's account of the WWII Guadalcanal operation. Trading in evocative countrified rock with a myriad of influences (although R.E.M. and the LONG RYDERS were the most prominent), GUADALCANAL DIARY issued the DON DIXON-produced debut single, 'WATUSI RODEO', in '83. A rootsy hoedown in the mould of DAVE EDMUNDS or NICK LOWE, the track featured on their inaugural album, 'WALKING IN THE SHADOW OF THE BIG MAN' (1984). Subsequently taken up by 'Elektra' on both sides of the Atlantic, the record was a fine example of 80's Americana with all the baggage that entails. Religion, war and the psychic landscape of the Yankee south were all familiar lyrical topics on 1986's follow-up, 'JAMBOREE', a patchwork of classic retro sounds stealthily rustled in a kinda cow-punk way from the likes of The BEATLES and The BYRDS. They finally managed to create something approaching greatness from the sum of their often derivative parts with the acclaimed '2x4' set in '87, a record that spent several weeks in the US Top 200. With a full commercial breakthrough seemingly just around the corner, GUADALCANAL DIARY struggled to live up to critical expectations with their slightly disappointing swansong, 'FLIP-FLOP' (1989), which also bubbled under the Top 100; ATTAWAY would find some work as a solo artist. Echoes of GUADALCANAL's musical ghost can be heard in the acoustic work of Seattle acts, the WALKABOUTS and NIRVANA; alternatively, try playing the chorus of 'SLEEPERS AWAKE' back to back with 'Penny Royal Tea'. • **Covered:** JOHNNY B GOODE (Chuck Berry).

Album rating: WALKING IN THE SHADOW OF THE BIG MAN (*7) / JAMBOREE (*6) / 2x4 (*8) / FLIP-FLOP (*6)

MURRAY ATTAWAY – vocals, electric guitar / **JEFF WALLS** – guitars / **RHETT CROWE** – bass / **JOHN POE** – drums

not iss. — Entertainment On Disc

1983. (7"ep) **WATUSI RODEO. / SLEEPERS AWAKE / JOHNNY B GOODE** -
(UK-iss.Aug85 on 'Elektra'; EKR 23)

Hybrid — D.B.

Feb 85. (lp) *(HYBLP 2) <13>* **WALKING IN THE SHADOW OF THE BIG MAN** Nov84
– Trail of tears / Fire from Heaven / Sleepers awake / Gilbert takes the wheel / Ghost on the road / Watusi rodeo / Why do the heathen rage? / Pillow talk / Walking in the shadow of the big man / Kumbaya. *(re-iss. Aug85 on 'Elektra' lp/c; 60429-2/-4)*

Elektra — Elektra

Jul 86. (lp/c) *(960 478-1/-4) <60478>* **JAMBOREE**
– Pray for rain / Cattle prod / Jamboree / Fear of God / Man hunt / Spirit train / Lonely street / Country club gun / Trouble / Michael Rockefeller / Please stop me / I see more / Dead eyes.

Sep 87. (lp/c) *(960 752-1/-4) <60752>* **2x4**
– Litany (life goes on) / Under the yoke / Get over it / Little birds / Things fall apart / Let the big wheel roll / Where angels fear to tread / Newborn / Winds of change / Say please / 3 a.m. / Lips of steel.

Feb 89. (lp/c/cd) *(960 848-1/-4/-2) <60848>* **FLIP-FLOP**
– Look up! / The likes of you / Whiskey talk / Everything but good luck / Fade out / Always Saturday / Happy home / Pretty is as pretty does / Ten laws / . . .Vista.

— they split soon after above; ATTAWAY going solo while POE joined LOVE TRACTOR

GUANA BATZ

Formed: Feltham, Middlesex, England . . . early '83 by MARK WHITE, PIP HANCOX, STUART OSBOURNE and DAVE TURNER. However, prior to the release of any material, co-founder WHITE was substituted by stand-up bass player, SAM SARDI. Psychobilly rockers in the vein of the METEORS, KING KURT and the STRAY CATS, the bequiffed GUANA BATZ signed to Chiswick off-shoot, 'Big Beat' and released a debut EP, 'YOU'RE SO FINE'. Next up was an appearance on compilation, 'Stompin' At The Klubfoot', an album that also premiered a host of similarly styled acts. Their inaugural long-player, 'HELD DOWN . . . AT LAST', finally saw the light of day in mid '85 and surprisingly nearly topped the indie charts. The record appeared on the 'I.D.' label, also home to an even better selling follow-up, 'LOAN SHARKS' (1986). The 'BATZ continued to sink their teeth into the heart of London's punkabilly scene over the latter half of the 80's, although bar a hardcore minority, the music scene had long since moved on by the turn of the decade. • **Covered:** I'M ON FIRE (Bruce Springsteen) / ENDLESS SLEEP (Joey Reynolds) / JOHNNY B. GOODE + NO PARTICULAR PLACE TO GO (Chuck Berry) / HIPPY HIPPY SHAKE (Swinging Blue Jeans) / YOU'RE MY BABY (Vacels) / SHAKE YOUR MONEYMAKER / TRAIN KEPT A-ROLLIN' / etc etc

Album rating: HELD DOWN . . .AT LAST (*6) / LOAN SHARKS (*7) / LIVE OVER LONDON (*5) / ROUGH EDGES (*4) / ELECTRA GLIDE IN BLUE (*4) / GET AROUND (*3)

PIP HANCOX – vocals / **STUART OSBOURNE** – guitar / **SAM SARDI** – double bass; repl. MARK WHITE / **DAVE 'DIDDLE' TURNER** – drums

Big Beat — not iss.

Nov 83. (12"ep) *(SW 89)* **YOU'RE SO FINE / ROCKIN' IN MY COFFIN. / JUNGLE RUMBLE / GUANA ROCK** -

Apr 84. (7") *(NS 96)* **THE CAVE. / WEREWOLF BLUES** -

I.D. — not iss.

Jul 85. (lp) *(NOSE 4)* **HELD DOWN . . .AT LAST** -
– Down on the line / Got no money / Can't take the pressure / Nightwatch / Lady Bacon / King Rat / You're my baby / Nightmare fantasy / Please give me something / Bust out. *(cd-iss. Nov97 on 'Anagram'; CDMPSYCHO 18)*

Feb 86. (12"ep) *(EYET 6)* **SEETHROUGH. / BATMAN THEME (live) / B SIDE BLUES** -

Jul 86. (7") *(EYE 9)* **I'M ON FIRE. /** -
(12"+=) *(EYET 9)* –

Oct 86. (lp/c) *(NOSE/KOSE 10)* **LOAN SHARKS** -
– Pile driver boogie / My way / Slippin' in / Tiny minds / Radio Sweetheart / Life's a beach / Loan shark / Shake your moneymaker / I'm weird / Hippy hippy shake / Live for the day / No particular place to go / I'm on fire.

Dec 86. (7") *(EYE 12)* **LOAN SHARKS. / RADIO SWEETHEART** -

May 87. (7") *(EYE 13)* **ROCK THIS TOWN. / JUST LOVE ME** -

Jun 87. (lp) *(NOSE 14)* **LIVE OVER LONDON (live)** -
– Can't take the pressure / Rockin' in the graveyard / My way / Live for the day / Rocky road / Seethrough / Loan shark / B side blues / Just love me / Baby blue eyes / I'm on fire / Dynamite / Rock this town / Endless sleep / King Rat / Shake your moneymaker – Tear it up / The overture. *(cd-iss. Jun93 on 'Dojo'; DOJOCD 133)*

— **GINGER** – drums (ex-METEORS) repl. TURNER

Apr 88. (lp/c/cd) *(NOSE/KOSE/CDOSE 20)* **ROUGH EDGES** -
– Streetwise / Open your mouth / One night / Good news / Rocking on Creek Road / Fight back / Spy catcher / Love generator / Bring my Cadillac back / Rocking with Ollie Vee / Two shadows / You can run.

— **JOHNNY BOWLER** – drums (ex-GET SMART) repl. GINGER

World Service

Mar 90. (12"one-sided) *(SERT 001)* **ELECTRA GLIDE IN BLUE** -

Mar 90. (lp/cd) *(SERV/+CD 009)* **ELECTRA GLIDE IN BLUE**
– Electra glide in blue / Green eyes / Texas eyes / No matter how / Wonderous place / Katherine / Stylin' / Spector love / Self made prison / Who needs it / Lover man / Take a rocket.

— **MARK PENNINGTON** – bass (ex-CARAVANS) repl. SARDI

— continued to tour, but mainly in Europe where they were more popular

Jappin' & Rockin' — not iss.

Mar 94. (cd/lp) *(JR CD/LP 008)* **GET AROUND** -
– Every night and every day / Breakdown / Tell her / Native beat / Lady of the night / Heart of stone / Shake it up / She's neat / Soul disbeliever / Chill out blues / Don't take this to heart / Such a night / Hot stuff / Sunsets / You're my baby.

– compilations, etc. –

Oct 88. (lp/cd) *Wrongco; (WRONG/+CD 001)* **THE BEST OF THE BATZ** -
– King Rat / Nightmare fantasy / I'm on fire / You're my baby / Dynamite / Radio sweetheart / Streetwise / lease give me something / Seethrough / Baby blue eyes / Rock this town / Loan shark / Spy catcher / Bring my Cadillac back.

Jun 89. (cd) *I.D.; (CDOSE 4-10)* **LOAN SHARKS / HELD DOWN . . . AT LAST** -
(re-iss. Apr93 on 'Loma'; LOMACD 13)

Dec 91. (cd) *Streetlink; (STRCD 020)* **GUANA BATZ 1985-1990** -
(<re-iss. Mar93/Oct94 on 'Dojo'; DOJOCD 120>)

Oct 92. (cd) *Street Link; (STRCD 033)* **THE KLUB FOOT CONCERTS (live)** -

May 93. (cd) *Loma; (LOMACD 14)* **ELECTRIC GLIDE IN BLUE / ROUGH EDGES** -

Sep 95. (cd) *Anagram; (CDPSYCHE 07)* **UNDER COVER** -

GUIDED BY VOICES

Formed: Dayton, Ohio, USA . . . mid-80's by ROBERT POLLARD, his brother JIM and TOBIN SPROUT. Making their debut in 1986 with the 'FOREVER SINCE BREAKFAST' EP, GUIDED BY VOICES became something of a cult phenomenon via a series of independently released, limited edition albums. From 1987's 'DEVIL BETWEEN MY TOES' onwards, the band garnered a reputation for inaccessible lo-fi musings issued under such characteristically long-winded titles as 'SELF INFLICTED AERIAL NOSTALGIA' (1989) and 'SAME PLACE THE FLY GOT SMASHED' (1990). A subsequent deal with leading US indie label, 'Matador', led to a full British release for 1993's 'VAMPIRE ON TITUS', the band's increasing critical plaudits reaching a peak with the following year's 'BEE THOUSAND'. By this point the line-up had expanded to include MITCH MITCHELL and KEVIN FENNELL, GBV's angular, surreal sketches sharing – in spirit at least – the same astral plane as MERCURY REV while drawing comparisons with fellow lo-fi pioneers such as PAVEMENT. Following on from live set, 'CRYING YOUR KNIFE AWAY' (1994), GUIDED BY VOICES kept up their unflaggingly prolific recording schedule with 'ALIEN LANES' (1995). Featuring a marathon 28 tracks on a single CD, the album veered from the CHRIS BELL/BEATLES-esque '(I WANNA BE A) DUMBCHARGER' to the almost TEENAGE FANCLUB-style harmonies of 'CIGARETTE TRICKS' and the soaraway pop brilliance of 'MOTOR AWAY'. The latter was an obvious choice for a single release while the sublime 'MY VALUABLE HUNTING KNIFE' was hailed as one of the finest songs POLLARD had yet penned. 1996's 'UNDER THE BUSHES UNDER THE STARS' moved in an increasingly accessible direction, the same year also seeing solo sets from both ROBERT POLLARD ('NOT IN MY AIRFORCE') and TOBIN SPROUT ('CARNIVAL BOY' and ~'SUNFISH HOLY BREAKFAST'). Any rumours of an imminent split were dispelled with 1997's 'MAG EARWHIG!' long-player; their album tally now in double figures, GUIDED BY VOICES remain one of America's more enigmatic indie institutions. • **Songwriters:** R. POLLARD and some with SPROUT.

Album rating: DEVIL BETWEEN MY TOES (*5) / SANDBOX (*5) / SELF INFLICTED AERIAL NOSTALGIA (*5) / SAME PLACE THE FLY GOT SMASHED (*5) / PROPELLER (*6) / I AM THE SCIENTIST (*5) / VAMPIRE ON TITUS (*6) / BEE THOUSAND (*7) / CRYING YOUR KNIFE AWAY (*6) / ALIEN LANES (*7) / UNDER THE BUSHES, UNDER THE STARS (*6) / SUNFISH HOLY BREAKFAST (*6) / MAG EARWHIG! (*7) / BOX compilation (*7) / Robert Pollard: NOT IN MY AIRPORT (*6) / WAVED OUT (*6) / Tobin Sprout: CARNIVAL BOY (*6) / MOONFLOWER PLASTIC (WELCOME TO MY WIGWAM) (*6)

ROBERT POLLARD – vocals, guitar / **TOBIN SPROUT** – guitar, bass / **JIM POLLARD** – drums

not iss. I Wanna

1986. (12"ep) **FOREVER SINCE BREAKFAST EP**

not iss. Schwa

1987. (lp) **DEVIL BETWEEN MY TOES**

not iss. Halo

1988. (lp) **SANDBOX**

1989. (lp) **SELF INFLICTED AERIAL NOSTALGIA**

not iss. Rocket

1990. (lp) *<No.9>* **SAME PLACE THE FLY GOT SMASHED**

not iss. Rockathon

1992. (cd) **PROPELLER**
– Over the Neptune – Mesh gear fox / Weedking / Particular damaged / Quality of amor / Metal mothers / Lethargy / Unleashed! the large hearted boy / Red gas circle / Exit flagger / 14 cheerleader coldfront / Back to Saturn X radio report / Ergo space pig / Circus world / Some drilling implied / On the tundra. *<cd-iss. Nov96 on 'Scat'; 49>*

not iss. Scat

1992. (7"ep) *(SCT 028)* **THE GRAND HOUR**
– I'll get over it / Shocker in Gloomtown / Alien lanes / Off the floor / Break even / Bee thousand. *(UK-iss.Oct94; same)*

1992. (cd) *(SCT 038-CD)* **I AM THE SCIENTIST**
– I am a scientist / The curse of the black ass buffalo / Do the earth / Planet's own brand. *(UK-iss.Jan95; same)*

City Slang Scat

1993. (cd/lp) *<31>* **VAMPIRE ON TITUS**
– Wished I was a giant / No.2 in the model home series / Expecting brainchild / Superior sector janitor X / Donkey school / Dusted / Marchers in orange / Sot / World of fun / Jar of cardinals / Unstable journey / E-5 / Cool off kid kilowatt / Gleemer (the deeds of fertile Jim) / Wondering boy poet / What about it? / Perhaps now the vultures / Non-absorbing. *(re-iss. Oct94 w/ PROPELLER on 'Matador' cd/lp; OLE 083-2/-1)*

Nov 93. (7") *(EFA 049397)* **STATIC AIRPLANE JIVE EP**

Domino Luna

Feb 94. (7"ep/cd-ep) *(RUG 11/+CD) <010>* **CLOWN PRINCE OF THE MENTHOL TRAIL EP**
– Matter eater land / Broadcaster house / Hunter complex / Pink gun / Scalping the guru / Grandfather Westing house / Johnny appleased.

not iss. Lo-Fi

Jun 94. (m-cd) **CRYING YOUR KNIFE AWAY: LIVE AT STACHE'S, COLUMBUS (live)**

Matador Scat

Jul 94. (cd/lp) *(OLE 084-2/-1) <SCT 35>* **BEE THOUSAND** Jun94
– Hardcore UFO's / Buzzards and dreadful crows / Tractor rape chain / Golden heart mountain top queen directory / Hot freaks / Smothered in hugs / Yours to keep / Echos Myron / Awful bliss / Mincer Ray / Big fan of pigeon / Queen of cans and jars / Her psychology day / Kicker of elves / Esther's day / Demons are real / I am a scientist / Peep-hole / You're not an airplane.

Matador Matador

Apr 95. (cd/lp) *<(OLE 123-2/-1)>* **ALIEN LANES** Mar95
– A salty salute / Evil speakers / Watch me jumpstart / They're not witches / As we go up, we go down / (I wanna be a) Dumbcharger / Game of pricks / The ugly vision / A good flying bird / Cigarette tricks / Pimple zoo / Big chief Chinese restaurant / Closer you are / Auditorium / Motor away / Hit / My valuable hunting knife / Gold hick / King and Caroline / Stripped white jets / Ex-supermodel / Blimps go 90 / Strawdogs / Chicken blows / Little whirl / My son cool / Always crush me / Alright.

Jun 95. (7") *(OLE 148-7)* **MOTOR AWAY. / COLOR OF MY BLADE**

—— added (or before) **MITCH MITCHELL** – guitar / **KEVIN FENNELL** – drums / **DON TOOHEY** – bass (latter repl. by **JIM GREER + GREG DEMOS + PETE JAMISON**)

Nov 95. (7"ep) *(OLE 168-7)* **TIGERBOMB EP**
– My valuable hunting knife / Game of pricks / Mice feel nice (in my room) / Not good for the mechanism / Kiss only the important ones / Dodgy invisible rays.

Feb 96. (7"ep/cd-ep) *<(OLE 184-7/-2)>* **THE OFFICIAL IRONMEN RALLY SONG / DEAF EARS. / WHY DID YOU LAND / JUNE SALUTES YOU!**

Mar 96. (cd/d-lp) *<(OLE 161-2/-1)>* **UNDER THE BUSHES, UNDER THE STARS**
– Man called Aerodynamics / Rhine jive click / Cut-out witch / Burning flag birthday suit / The official ironmen rally song / To remake the young flyer / No sky / Bright paper werewolves / Lord of Overstock / Your name is wild / Ghosts of a diferent dream / Acorns & orioles / Look at them / The perfect life / Underwater explosions / Atom eyes / Don't stop now / Office of hearts / Big boring wedding / It's like soul man / Drag days / Sheetkickers / Redmen and their wives / Take to the sky. *(cd w/bonus cd)* – My valuable hunting knife / Game of pricks / Mice feel nice (in my room) / Not good for the mechanism / Kis only the important ones / Dodging invisible rays / Delayed reaction brats / He's the uncle / The key losers.

Jun 96. (7"pic-d) *(OLE 218-7)* **CUT-OUT WITCH. /**

Nov 96. (7"ep) *(OLE 208-7)* **PLANTATIONS OF PALE PINK. /**
– System crash / Cat food on the earwig / Who vs. Porky pig / Life in finer clothing / Worryin' song / Subtle gear shifting.

Nov 96. (cd/lp) *<(OLE 185-2/-1)>* **SUNFISH HOLY BREAKFAST**
– Jabberstroker / Stabbing a star / Canteen plums / Beekeeper seeks truth / Cocksoldiers and their postwar stubble / Contest featuring human beings / If we wait / Trendspotter acrobat / Winter crows / Heavy metal country.

Mar 97. (7") *(OLE 10)* **/ (other by Cobra Verde)**
(above a split single on 'Wabana')

May 97. (7"ep/cd-ep) *(OLE 217-7/-2)* **BULLDOG SKIN / SINGING RAZORBLADE. / NOW TO WAR / MANNEQUINS COMPLAINT**

May 97. (cd/lp) *<(OLE 241-2/-1)>* **MAG EARWHIG!**
– Can't hear the revolution / Sad if I lost it / I am a tree / Old grunt / Bullskin skin / Are you faster / I am produced / Knock 'em flying / Not behind the fighter jet / Choking Tara / Hollow cheek / Portable men's society / Little lines / Learning to hunt / Finest joke is upon us / Mag earwhig / Now to war / Jane of the waking universe / Colossus crawls west / Mute in the bee-hive.

Aug 97. (7"ep) *(OLE 264-7)* **I AM A TREE**
– I am a tree / (I'll name you) The flame that cries / The ascended master's grogshop. (cd-ep+=) *(OLE 264-2)* – Do they teach you the chase?

– compilations, etc. –

Feb 95. (5xcd-box/5xlp-box) *Scat; <(SCT 040-2/-1)>* **BOX**

Sep 97. (7")(cd-s) *Siltbreeze; <(SB 028)>(EAR 002CD)* **GET OUT OF MY STATIONS. /** 1994

Nov 97. (d-lp) *Surefire; (LUNA 1)* **JELLYFISH REFLECTOR (live)**

—— they also released a number of live lp's (very limited)

ROBERT POLLARD

Sep 96. (cd/lp) *<(OLE 215-2/-1)>* **NOT IN MY AIRFORCE**
– Maggie turns to flies / Quicksilver / Girl named Captain / Get under it / Release the sunbird / John strange school / Parakeet troopers / One clear minute / Chance to buy an island / I've owned you for centuries / Ash gray proclamation / Flat beauty / King of Arthur avenue / Roofer's union fight song / Psychic pilot clocks out / Prom is coming / Party / Did it play? / Double standards Inc. / Punk rock gods / Meet my team / Good luck sailor.

Jun 98. (cd/lp) *<(OLE 316-2/-1)>* **WAVED OUT**
– Make use / Vibrations in the woods / Just say the word / Subspace biographies / Caught waves again / Waved out / Whiskey ships / Wrinkled ghost / Artificial light / People are leaving / Steeple of knives / Rumbling joker / Showbiz opera walrus / Pick seeds from my skull / Second step next language.

TOBIN SPROUT

Sep 96. (cd/lp) *<(OLE 216-2/-1)>* **CARNIVAL BOY**
– Natural alarm / Cooler jocks / E's navy blue / Bone yard / Carnival boy / Martin's mounted head / Gas daddy gas / To my beloved Martha / White flyer / I didn't know / Gallant men / It's like soul man / Hermit stew / Last man well known to kingpin.

Aug 97. (cd/lp) *<(OLE 244-2/-1)>* **MOONFLOWER PLASTIC (WELCOME TO MY WIGWAM)**
– Get out of my throat / Moonflower plastic (you're here) / Paper cut / Beast of souls / Little odd / Angels hang their socks on the moon / All used up / Since I . . . / Back chorus / Curious things / Exit planes / Little bit of dread / Hit junky dives / Water on the boater's back.

Recordhead Recordhead

Dec 97. (7"ep) *<(LUNA 04)>* **POPSTRAM EP**

Line not iss.

Mar 98. (cd) *(LUNA 08)* **TOBIN SPROUT**

GUMBALL (see under ⇒ B.A.L.L.)

GUN CLUB

Formed: Los Angeles, California, USA . . . 1980 as CREEPING RITUAL by ex-'Splash' magazine editor, JEFFREY LEE PIERCE and KID CONGO POWERS; they subsequently changed their name at the suggestion of CIRCLE JERKS' KEITH MORRIS. 1981 saw the independent release of their red-raw CHRIS D (Flesheaters)-produced debut album, 'FIRE OF LOVE', 'Beggars Banquet' picking it up for UK release, while CHRIS STEIN (of BLONDIE) was impressed enough to sign the band to his 'Animal' label in '82. Trading in a low-slung fusion of punk and primal rockabilly/blues, the band were favourably compared with contemporaries The CRAMPS, PIERCE, like his counterpart LUX INTERIOR, equal parts damned preacher and demented sinner if not quite managing the same level of leering lasciviousness. Appropriately enough then, the band reinterpreted blues legend, Robert Johnson's 'PREACHIN' THE BLUES' (as well as Tommy Johnson's 'COOL DRINK OF WATER') alongside unhinged originals in the vein of 'SHE'S LIKE HEROIN TO ME', 'SEX BEAT' and the vicious 'JACK ON FIRE'. Although he had co-written the warped 'FOR THE LOVE OF IVY', guitarist POWERS had bailed out prior to the recording of the debut, WARD DOTSON recruited in his place. Despite being previewed by the dark, brooding malevolence of the 'WALKING WITH THE BEAST' single, follow-up set, 'MIAMI' (1982), didn't meet with such an enthusiastic critical reception and PIERCE struggled to keep the creative fires burning. The singer's battle with alcoholism was also a factor and although The GUN CLUB had established themselves as one of America's leading alternative acts, the first phase of the band's career stumbled to a halt following the more sophisticated 'THE LAS VEGAS STORY' (1984). PIERCE cut only one solo album, 'WILDWEED' (1985) before The GUN CLUB unexpectedly reformed in 1987 with KID CONGO back in the fold (he'd also returned briefly in the early 80's) alongside new members NICK SANDERSON and ROMI MORI. Setting themselves up in the UK, the group signed to indie label, 'Red Rhino', procuring the production services of COCTEAU TWIN, ROBIN GUTHRIE, for the resulting album, 'MOTHER JUNO' (1987). More experimental and considered than their previous output, the record saw The GUN CLUB briefly regain their popularity. PIERCE & co. switched to 'Fire' for the belated release of 'PASTORAL HIDE AND SEEK' (1990), while '91's 'DIVINITY' was a half live/half studio affair. It was also, finally, the band's epitaph, as KID CONGO went walkabout and PIERCE cut a further solo set, 'RAMBLIN' JEFFREY LEE & CYPRESS GROVE WITH WILLIE LOVE' (1992) before his health deteriorated inexorably. • **Songwriters:** PIERCE except; RUN THROUGH THE JUNGLE (Creedence Clearwater Revival) / etc.

Album rating: FIRE OF LOVE (*7) / MIAMI (*6) / THE BIRTH, THE DEATH, THE GHOST live collection (*4) / THE LAS VEGAS STORY (*5) / MOTHER JUNO (*7) / PASTORAL HIDE AND SEEK (*7) / DIVINITY (*6) / LUCKY JIM (*5) / Jeffrey Lee Pierce: WILDWEED (*6) / RAMBLIN' JEFFREY LEE . . . (*5)

JEFFREY LEE PIERCE (b.27 Jun'58, El Monte, Calif.) – vocals, guitar / **WARD DOTSON** – lead guitar repl. KID CONGO POWERS who joined The CRAMPS / **ROB RITTER** – bass / **TERRY GRAHAM** – drums (ex-BAGS)

Beggars Banquet / Ruby

May 82. (lp/c) *(BEGA/BEGC 37)* <*JRR 102*> **FIRE OF LOVE** Sep81
– Sex beat / Preachin' the blues / Jack on fire / She is like heroin to me / For the love of Ivy / Fire spirit / Ghost on the highway / Jack on fire / Black train / Promise me / Cool drink of water / Goodbye Johnny. *(re-iss. Jan86 on 'New Rose' blue-lp/cd; ROSE 8/+CD) (cd re-iss. May94 on 'New Rose'; 42216-2)*

Jul 82. (7") *(BEG 80)* **SEX BEAT. / GHOST ON THE HIGHWAY**

Chrysalis-Animal / Chrysalis-Animal

Aug 82. (7") *(CHCAT 2635)* **WALKING WITH THE BEAST. / FIRE OF LOVE**

Sep 82. (lp) <*(CHR 1398)*> **MIAMI**
– Carry home / Like calling up thunder / Brother and sister / Run through the jungle / A devil in the woods / Texas serenade / Watermelon man / Bad Indian / John Hardy / Fire of love / Sleeping in Blood city / Mother of Earth. *(cd-iss. 1990; X213065)*

— **KID CONGO POWERS** (b.BRIAN TRISTIAN) – guitar returned to repl. RITTER + DOTSON (latter formed PONTIAC BROTHERS)

— **PIERCE** recruited new members **JIM DUCKWORTH** – lead guitar (ex-TAV FALCO'S PANTHER BURNS) repl. KID CONGO who later formed FUR BIBLE / **DEE POP** – drum (ex-BUSH TETRAS) repl. TERRY GRAHAM

Apr 83. (7") *(GUN 1)* **DEATH PARTY. / HOUSE OF HIGHLAND AVENUE / THE LIE**
(12"+=) *(GUN12 1)* – Light of the world / Come back Jim.

— added **PATRICIA MORRISON** – bass

Jun 84. (lp) <*(CHR 1477)*> **THE LAS VEGAS STORY**
– The Las Vegas story / Walking with the beast / Eternally is here / The stranger in our town / My dreams / The creator was a master plan / My man's gone now / Bad America / Moonlight hotel / Give up the sun. *(cd-iss. 1990; X 213064)*

— Split late 1984. PATRICIA joined FUR BIBLE (released a one-off 12"EP in 1985 for 'New Rose', 'PLUNDER THE TOMBS') and later joined English goth outfit, The SISTERS OF MERCY

JEFFREY LEE PIERCE

— went solo with **MURRAY MITCHELL** – guitar / **JOHN McKENZIE** – bass / **ANDY ANDERSON** – drums

Statik / not iss.

Apr 85. (lp/c) *(STAT LP/C 25)* **WILDWEED** -
– Love and desperation / Sex killer / Cleopatra dreams on / From temptation to you / Sensitivity / Hey Juana / Love Circus / Wildweed / From temptation to you / The midnight promise. *(cd-iss. Jun89 +=; CDST 25)* – The Fertility Goddess / Portrait of an artist in Hell / Love & Desperation (long) / Chris and Maggie meet Blind Willie McTell at . . . *(cd re-iss. Jan94 on 'Solid'; 527501220)*

— **PIERCE** brought in **HIROMI** – guitar / **DEAN DENNIS** – bass / **NICK SANDERSON** – drums (both ex-CLOCKDVA)

Aug 85. (7") *(TAK 36)* **LOVE AND DESPERATION. / THE FERTILITY GODDESS** -
(12"+=) *(TAK 36-12)* – Portrait of an artist in Hell.

Nov 85. (12"ep) *(STAB 5)* **FLAMINGO (part 1 & 2). / GET AWAY / FIRE / NO MORE FIRE / LOVE AND DESPERATION** -

GUN CLUB

— were reformed by **PIERCE, KID CONGO** and **SANDERSON plus ROMI MORI** – bass

Red Rhino / Solid

Oct 87. (lp/c/cd) *(RED LP/C/CD 084)* **MOTHER JUNO**
– Breaking hands / Araby / Hearts / My cousin Kim / Port of souls / Bill Bailey / Thunderhead / Lupita screams / Yellow eyes. *(cd re-iss. Nov92 on 'Solid'; 527500420)*

Mar 88. (12"m) *(REDT 089)* **BREAKING HANDS. / CRABDANCE / NOBODY'S CITY** -

— split again, KID CONGO went solo, but last line-up soon reformed

Fire / Solid

Sep 90. (12"ep/cd-ep) *(BLAZE 47 T/CD)* **THE GREAT DIVIDE. / CRABDANCE / ST. JOHN'S DIVINE (part 2)** -
(re-iss. Oct91; BLAZE 44047)

Oct 90. (cd/c/lp) *(FIRE CD/MC/LP 28)* **PASTORAL HIDE AND SEEK**
– Humanesque / The straits of love and hate / Emily's changed / I hear your heart singing / St.John's divine / The great divide / Another country's young / Flowing / Temptation and I. *(cd+=)* – Eskimo blue day. *(cd re-iss. Feb92 on 'New Rose'; NEW 162) (cd re-iss. Jun93 on 'Solid'; 52790020)*

New Rose / Solid

Oct 91. (cd/d-lp) *(ROSE 262CD)* **DIVINITY** (some live) - French
– Sorrow knows / Richard Speck / Keys to the kingdom / Black hole / Yellow eyes (live) / Hearts (live) / Fire of love (live). *(cd+=)* – St. John's divine. *(cd re-iss. Jun93 on 'Solid'; 527900920)*

Triple X / Triple X

May 93. (cd/lp) <*(527001020)*> **LUCKY JIM**
– Lucky Jim / A house is not a home / Kamata / Hollywood city / Idiot waltz / Up above the world / Day turn the night / Blue moonspoons / Anger blues. *(cd+=)* – Desire.

– compilations etc. –

Feb 84. (lp/c) *A.B.C.; (ABCLP/KAS 1)* **THE BIRTH, THE DEATH, THE GHOST (live 1983)** -
– Bo Diddley's a gunslinger / Railroad Bill / Seven miles with the Devil / Preachin' the blues / Goodbye Johnny / Black train / Walking with the beast / Bad mood / Not that much / Going down the red river / Willie Brown / Field Holler / Sex beat. *(cd-iss. Apr89; ABCD 1)*

Oct 84. (lp) *Lolita;* **SEX BEAT '81 (live)** -

Jul 85. (lp) *Dojo; (JOJOLP 8)* **TWO SIDES OF THE BEAST** -
– Walking with the beast / Like calling up thunder / Mother of Earth / Run through the jungle / Eternally is here / The Las Vegas story / Death party / Seven miles with the Devil (live) / Bo Diddley's a gunslinger (live) / Preaching the blues (live) / Goodbye Johnny (live) / Going down the red river (live) / Sex beat (live). *(re-iss. Apr86; same)*

Nov 85. (lp) *Eva; (OFFENCE 9002)* **LOVE SUPREME (live '82)** - - French

Dec 85. (lp) *Roadrunner; (MD 7979)* **DANCE KALINDA BOOM (live In Pandora's Box)** -
– Eternally is here / Bad America / Sytranger in town / Gila monster, New Mexico / Preaching the blues / Sleeping in Blood City / Goodbye Johnny / Give up the sun. *(cd-iss. Jun93 on 'Solid'; 527500120)*

May 89. (cd-ep) *New Rose; (NEAT 1CD)* **SEX BEAT / FOR THE LOVE OF IVY / BLACK TRAIN** - -

Aug 92. (cd) *Triple X; (511003-2)* **IN EXILE**
– Breaking hands / Thunderhead / Lupita screams / Yellow eyes / Hearts / Port of souls / Pastoral hide 'n' seek / Straights of love and hate / Emily's changed / I hear your heart singing / St. John's divine (remix) / Another country's young / Flowing / Temptation and I /Richard Speck / Keys to the kingdom / Black hole / Sorrow knows.

Jun 93. (cd) *Solid; (527500220)* **AHMED'S WILD DREAM (live)**
– (The creator has a) Master plan / Walking with the beast / I hear your heart singin' / Another country's young / Sex beat / Lupita screams / Go tell the mountain / Preachin' the blues / Stranger in my heart / Goodbye Johnny / Port of souls / Black hole / Little wing / Yellow eyes.

May 94. (cd) *New Rose; (89001-2)* **DEATH PARTY** -

May 98. (d-cd) *Sympathy For The Record Industry; (SFTRI 478)* **EARLY WARNING**

JEFFREY LEE PIERCE

Solid / Solid

May 92. (cd) *(527901220)* **RAMBLIN' JEFFREY LEE & CYPRESS GROVE WITH WILLIE LOVE**
– Goin' down / Pony blues / Future blues / Long long gone / Bad luck and trouble / Alabama blues / Good times / Stranger in my heart / Go tell the mountain / Moanin' in the moonlight / Hardtime / Killin' floor blues

— On 31st March '96, PIERCE died of a blood clot to the brain

GUTTERBALL (see under ⇒ DREAM SYNDICATE)

GYMSLIPS

Formed: East London, England . . . 1982 by the all-girl trio of PAULA RICHARDS, KAREN YARNELL and SUZANNE SCOTT. Lending a glam sheen to the austerity of the post-punk era, The GYMSLIPS debuted with a cover of Suzi Quatro's '48 CRASH', issued on 'Abstract' later that year. A follow-up, 'BIG SISTER', appeared in early '83, after which the girls took on KATHY BARNES as a full-time member (she'd already augmented the band at live gigs), the one and only album, ROCKIN' WITH THE RENEES' (1983), surfacing a few months later. Personnel upheavals led to sporadic releases, PAULA and SUZANNE recruiting LISA HINDLEY and SUE VICKERS for a final workout in '85, 'EVIL EYE'. RICHARDS subsequently joined The DELTONES until she and KAREN were back in the early 90's with short-lived new band, The RENEES.

Album rating: ROCKIN' WITH THE RENEES (*5)

PAULA RICHARDS (b. 1 Aug'63, Kent, England) – vocals, guitar / **SUZANNE SCOTT** – bass, vocals / **KAREN YARNELL** (b. 2 Apr'61) – drums, vocals

Abstract / not iss.

Oct 82. (7") *(ABS 011)* **48 CRASH. / MISS NUN SWEETA** -

Jan 83. (7") *(ABS 014)* **BIG SISTER. / YO-YO / PIE 'N MASH** -

— added **KATHY BARNES** – keyboards (was already 4th live member)

May 83. (lp) *(ABT 006)* **ROCKIN' WITH THE RENEES** -
– Drink problem / Barbara Cartland / Face lifts / Thinking of you / Angels / Robot man / Dear Marje / Wandering stars / Yo-yo / Some girls / Complications / Big sister / 48 crash.

Jul 83. (7") *(ABS 016)* **ROBOT MAN. / MULTI COLOURED SUGAR** -

— **LISA HINDLEY** – drums; repl. KAREN who joined SERIOUS DRINKING

— **SUE VICKERS** – keyboards; repl. KATHY

May 85. (7") *(ABS 033)* **EVIL EYE. / WONDERLAND** -
(12"+=) *(ABS 033-12)* – Don't lead me on.

— split in 1986 when PAULA joined The DELTONES then POTATO 5

RENEES

— **PAULA + KAREN** reunited, enlisting also **JACQUI CALLIS** – vocals (ex-DELTONES) / **KATRINA SLACK** (b.14 Jul'62) – bass / **PAUL SEACROFT** – lead guitar (ex-POTATO 5)

unknown / not iss.

1991. (7") **HE CALLED ME A FAT PIG (AND WALKED OUT ON ME). /** -

Square / not iss.

1991. (cd) **HAVE YOU GOT IT!** -

— split after above

GYRES

Formed: Blantyre, Glasgow, Scotland . . . 1995 by brothers ANDY and PAUL McLINDEN, together with PETER LYONS, MARK McGILL and PAT FLAHERTY. Blessed with opportunities that many (more deserving) young Scottish bands would jump at, The GYRES were lucky enough to be docu-filmed during their gestation period. They were also jammy enough to land an arena support slot to BOWIE, promoting their first three singles, 'BREAK', 'POP COP' and 'ARE YOU READY', in style. Released on the 'Sugar' label, the latter two tracks hit the Top 75, although a long lay-off meant these OASIS clones failed to break through with the 'FIRST' (1997) album.

Album rating: FIRST (*4)

ANDY McLINDEN – vocals / **PAUL McLINDEN** – guitar, vocals / **PETER LYONS** – guitar, vocals / **MARK McGILL** – bass / **PAT FLAHERTY** – drums

		Sugar	not iss.
Jan 96.	(7") *(SUGA 7V)* **BREAK. /**		-
Apr 96.	(7"/c-s) *(SUGA 9 V/T)* **POP COP. /**	71	-
	(cd-s+=) *(SUGA 9CD)* –		
Jun 96.	(7"/c-s) *(SUGA 11/+T)* **ARE YOU READY. / A MILLION MILES**	71	-
	(cd-s+=) *(SUGA 11CD)* – Top of the tree.		
Jul 97.	(7") *(SUGA 17V)* **SLY. / CONTACT DAY**		-
	(7") *(SUGA 17VX)* – ('A'side) / Sleepless nights.		
	(cd-s++=) *(SUGA 17CD)* – (all 3 tracks).		
Jul 97.	(cd/lp) *(SUGA 16 CD/LP)* **FIRST**		-
	– Sly / Hi-fi driving / Break / A million miles / Hooligan / Are you ready? / Falling down / On a roll / I'm alright / Pop cop / Downtime.		

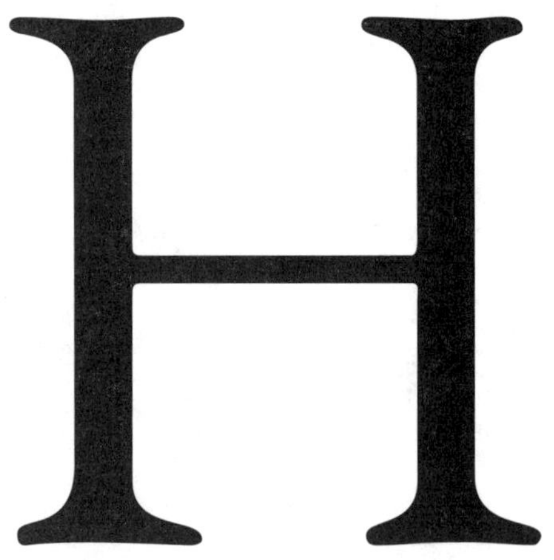

HAGAR THE WOMB

Formed: London, England . . . 1983 by the largely pseudonymous sextet of MISS K. PENFOLD (aka JULIE), THE HON. RUTHLESS SAVAGE, EL JANETTI RAVIOLI, HASTA PAUL CENTIPEDE, COM. MITCH JAIL BATE (aka VEG) and MR. CHRIS ENGELBERT FUNKADINK. Early the following year, the 'orribly titled HAGAR THE WOMB made their debut on the heavy/protest label, 'Mortarhate' (home of CONFLICT) with the 'WORD OF THE WOMB' EP. Moving on to the more appropriate indie imprint, 'Abstract', the band came into their own with early '85 EP, 'FUNNERY IN A NUNNERY', a record characterised by an unusual hybrid of The BANSHEES behind DELTA 5 or the SLITS with chunky guitars chopping up "Essex-girl" chorus hooklines. Although this proved to be their final vinyl, four members, JULIE, VEG, PAUL and CHRIS resurfaced under a new, equally distasteful moniker, WE ARE GOING TO EAT YOU. Following the independently released debut single, 'I WISH I KNEW', they secured a longer-term deal with 'Big Cat' and released a follow-up, 'HEART IN HAND'. A subsequent appearance on BBC2's indie video show, 'Snub', led to serious major label A&R interest, although contractual hassles resulted in delays that effectively negated the buzz already created. While they did sign to 'TVT' in America, the group remained with 'Big Cat' for the UK release of debut album, 'EVERYWHEN', at the turn of the decade. The group then underwent a second metamorphosis as two members later re-emerged as the short-lived MELT, recording only one 1991 EP, 'NEVERLAND'.

Album rating: We Are Going To Eat You: EVERYWHEN (*4)

MISS K. PENFOLD (b. JULIE SORRELL) – vocals / **THE HON. RUTHLESS SAVAGE** – vocals / **EL JANETTI RAVIOLI** – guitar / **HASTA PAUL CENTIPEDE** (b. PAUL HARDING) – guitar / **COM. MITCH JAIL BATE** (b. PAUL VENABLES; aka VEG) – bass / **MR. CHRIS ENGELBERT FUNKADINK** (b. CHRIS KNOWLES) – drums

Mortarhate — not iss.

Jan 84. (12"ep) *(MORT 2)* **WORD OF THE WOMB** — [ ] [-]

Abstract — not iss.

Feb 85. (12"ep) *(12ABS 29)* **FUNNERY IN A NUNNERY** — [ ] [-]
– A song of deep hate / One bright spark / Come into the soul / Armchair observer / Once proud now dead.

WE ARE GOING TO EAT YOU

— aka **CHRIS, VEG, PAUL + JULIE**

All The Madmen — not iss.

Jul 87. (12"ep) *(MADT 16)* **I WISH I KNEW / LET'S FLY. / FINE DAY / LET'S FLY (greedy mix)** — [ ] [-]

Big Cat — TVT

Nov 88. (7") *(ABB 07)* **HEART IN HAND. / JUST ANOTHER ONE (WHO GOT IT WRONG?)** — [ ] [-]
(12"+=) *(ABB 07T)* – What have the flowers got to do with it?

Oct 89. (12"ep) *(ABB 12T)* **RIDE UPON THE TIDE. /** — [ ] [-]

Jan 90. (lp/c)(cd) *(ABB 14/+C)(ABBCD 14)* **EVERYWHEN** — [ ] [ ]
– If I could / Heart in hand / This conspiracy / Each life a mystery / Glory / Ride upon the tide / Eye to eye / On a day like this / Just another one / Here always / If you believe / Her dreamworld.

MELT

— were formed by two of the group

Apr 91. (12"ep) *(ABB 025T)* **NEVERLAND EP** — [ ] [-]

— checking if below releases are actualy theirs

Kudos — not iss.

Sep 95. (12") *(7FKF 12V)* **FEEL. /** — [ ] [-]

Midi Circus — not iss.

Apr 96. (12") *(PROJECT 15)* **CALLING. /** — [ ] [-]

Nina HAGEN

Born: KATHERINA HAGEN, 11 Mar'55, East Berlin, Germany. Raised in the Eastern Bloc by her mother and dissident poet/songwriter stepfather, Walter Biermann, HAGEN excelled in her musical studies while moonlighting in dance groups such as AUTOMOBIL and FRITZENS DAMPFERBAND. In 1976, she followed her stepfather into exile in West Germany where she found it easy to secure a record deal with 'C.B.S.'. Inspired by her subsequent experience of the burgeoning London punk scene (where she met the SLITS), NINA formed her own posse of German musicians and proceeded to record an eponymous debut album, 'THE NINA HAGEN BAND' (1978). Despite the record's sizeable success on the continent, HAGEN chose to temporarily neglect her budding musical career and instead moved to the Netherlands where she struck up a friendship with HERMAN BROOD and LENE LOVICH, both of whom appeared with her in the late 70's cult movie, 'Cha Cha'. The LOVICH connection ultimately proved fairly profitable as HAGEN recycled her UK smash, 'LUCKY NUMBER' (having already tackled The Tubes' 'WHITE PUNKS ON DOPE' – aka 'TV GLOTZER' – on her debut) for German then American fans. A contract filling second album, 'UNBEHAGEN' (1980), was all the rage in her German homeland, while Austrians also developed a taste for her after allegedly witnessing the singer's simulated masturbation on TV. Having relocated to Los Angeles, she released her esoteric third set, 'NUNSEXMONKROCK' (1982), a US Top 200 record inspired by an apparent sighting of a UFO; HAGEN's newfound mysticism coincided with her decision to "sing" in English, the result being a banshee howl compared by many to a more extreme YOKO ONO. For her next project, the 1984 GIORGIO MORODER/KEITH FORSEY-produced set, 'FEARLESS', HAGEN moved into electro-dance territory, even roping in the fledgling RED HOT CHILI PEPPERS on the track, 'WHAT IT IS'. HAGEN subsequently fused her newfound dance leanings with metal-punk, although the choice of cover material on 'IN EKSTASY' (1985), suggested NINA was running out of ideas. She reunited with her old friend, LENE LOVICH on a one-off single in '87, 'DON'T KILL THE ANIMALS', while the same year saw her controversially marry one of her teenage fans! It would be 1989 before the release of another HAGEN long-player, the virtually ignored eponymous 'Mercury' set being followed a few years later by 'STREET' (1991). Her final album to date, 'REVOLUTION BALLROOM' (1995), failed to renew any interest in her flagging career, HAGEN's heyday long gone. • **Covered:** MY WAY (Paul Anka) / SPIRIT IN THE SKY (Norman Greenbaum) / MOVE OVER (Janis Joplin) / VIVA LAS VEGAS (hit; Elvis) / AVE MARIA + THE LORD'S PRAYER (trad.) / etc.

Album rating: THE NINA HAGEN BAND (*5) / UNBEHAGEN (*4) / NUNSEXMONKROCK (*4) / FEARLESS (*5) / IN EKSTASY (*3) / NINA HAGEN (*3) / STREET (*3) / REVOLUTION BALLROOM (*4) / 14 FRIENDLY ABDUCTIONS: BEST OF compilation (*5)

NINA HAGEN BAND

NINA HAGEN – vocals / with **BERNHARD POTSCHKA** – guitar (ex-LOK KREUZBERG) / **MANFRED PRAEKER** – bass (ex-LOK KREUZBERG) / **HERWIG MITTEREGGER** – drums / **REINHOLD HEIL** – keyboards

C.B.S. — Columbia

Dec 78. (lp) *(CBS 83136)* **THE NINA HAGEN BAND** — [ ] [ ]
– TV glotzer / Rangehn / Unbeschreiblich weiblich / Auf'm bahnhof / Naturtrane / Superboy / Heiss / Fisch im wasser / Auf'm Friedhof / Der spinner Pank. *(cd-iss. 1988; CD 83136)*

Aug 79. (7") *(CBS 7804)* **TV GLOTZER (WHITE PUNKS ON DOPE). / NATURTRANE** — [ ] [ ]

Feb 80. (7") *(CBS 8304)* **AFRICAN REGGAE. / WAU WAU** — [ ] [ ]

Apr 80. (lp) *(CBS 84159)* **UNBEHAGEN** — [ ] [ ]
– African reggae / Alptraum / Wir leben immer noch / Wenn oich ein junge war / Hermann heiss er / Auf'n rummel / Wau wau / Fall in love mit mir / No way.

NINA HAGEN

— now with **ALLAN SCHWARTZBERG** – drums / **KARL RUCKER** – bass / **CHRIS SPEDDING** – guitar / **PAUL SCHAFFER + PAUL ROSTLER** – piano + synthesizer / **AXEL GOTHE** – clarinet, wind

Jul 82. (lp) *(CBS 85774)* <38008> **NUNSEXMONKROCK** — [ ] [ ]
– Antiworld / Smack Jack / Taitschi – Tarot / Dread love / Future is now / Born in Xixax / Iki maska / Dr. Art / Cosma shiva / U.F.O.

— her main band:- **KARL RUCKER** – bass, keyboards / **STEVE SCHIFF** – guitar, keyboards / **RICHIE ZITO** – guitar

Jan 84. (lp) *(CBS 25667)* <39214> **ANGSTIOS** <US-title 'FEARLESS'> — [ ] [ ]
– New York New York / What it is / Flying saucers / Zarah / Springtime in Paris / I love Paul / My sensation / T.V. snooze / The change.

Feb 84. (7") *(A 4216)* **ZARAH. / (version)** — [ ] [ ]

— **PETER KRAUSE + ALEX LAROQUE** – drums; repl. SCHIFF + ZITO

— she used a plethora of musicians from now on

May 85. (7"/12") *(A/TX 6278)* **UNIVERSAL RADIO. / PRIMA NINA IN EKSTASY** — [ ] [ ]

May 85. (lp) *(CBS 26421)* **IN EKSTASY** — [ ] [ ]
– Universal radio / Gods of Aquarius / Russian reggae / My way / 1983 Ekstasy Drive / Prima Nina in Ecstasy / Spirit in the sky / Atomic flash deluxe / The Lord's prayer / Gott im Himmel.

Arista — Arista

Jan 87. (7"/12"; NINA HAGEN & LENE LOVICH) *(RIS/+T 3)* **DON'T KILL THE ANIMALS. /** — [ ] [ ]

Mercury Mercury

Sep 89. (lp/c/cd) *(838505-1/-4/-2)* **NINA HAGEN**
– Move over / Super freak family / Love heart attack / Hold me / Viva Las Vegas / Live on Mars / Dope sucks / Only seventeen / Where's the party / Michail, Michail (Gorbachev rap) / Ave Maria. *(cd re-iss. Feb96 on 'Activ'; ACTIVCD 6)*

Aug 91. (cd/c/lp) *(848716-2/-4/-1)* **STREET**
– Blumen fur die damen / Divine, love, sex and romance / Ruler of my heart / Nine 4 president / Keep it live / Berlin / In my world / Gretchen / Erfurt and Gera / All 4 Frankie. *(cd re-iss. Feb96 on 'Activ'; ACTIVCD 4)*

Activ not iss.

Jun 95. (cd/c/lp) *(ACTIV CD/MC/LP 3)* **REVOLUTION BALLROOM**
– So bad / Revolution ballroom / Right on time / Pollution pirates / King of hearts / L'amore / Pillow talk / Berlin / I'm going to live the life / Gypsy love / Dmhadahandi.

Sep 95. (c-s/12"/cd-s) *(C/12/CD TV 4)* **SO BAD (Utah Saints mixes)**

– compilations, etc. –

1987. (lp) *Polygram; (460454)* **LOVE**

Oct 93. (cd) *Sony Europe; (471675-2)* **THE GOLD COLLECTION**

Feb 96. (cd) *Legacy;* **14 FRIENDLY ABDUCTIONS: BEST OF**

Paul HAIG / RHYTHM OF LIFE

(see under ⇒ JOSEF K)

HAIR & SKIN TRADING CO.

Formed: London, England . . . 1991 by LOOP members, NEIL McKAY and JOHN WILLS, originally as a side project. Recruiting NIGEL WEBB, they went full-time upon the demise of LOOP and signed a deal with 'Situation 2'. Setting to work with producer ROLI MOSIMANN (ex-SWANS), they delivered their debut set, 'JO IN NINE G HELL' (1992), an out of control CAN meets FAUST affair carrying on in the darkly experimental tradition of their former outfit. The following year, the trio moved upstairs to 'Beggars Banquet', although the resulting album, 'OVER VALENCE' (1993), was met with slightly less enthusiasm. Retreating to lick their wounds after being dropped by the label, HAIR & SKIN TRADING CO. returned after an extended musical manicure with their third and final album, 'PSYCHEDELIC MUSIQUE' (1995).

Album rating: JO IN NINE G HELL (*5) / OVER VALENCE (*5) / PSYCHEDELIC MUSIQUE (*5)

NEIL McKAY – bass (ex-LOOP) / **JOHN WILLS** – drums (ex-LOOP, ex-SERVANTS) / **NIGEL WEBB** – guitar

Situation 2 Beggars Banquet

Apr 92. (12"ep/cd-ep) **GROUND ZERO EP**

Apr 92. (cd) *(SITU 40CD)* *<66136>* **JO IN NINE G HELL** Dec92
– Elevenate / Flat truck / Torque / Monkies / Kak / Where's gala / Ground zero / $1000 pledge / The final nail / Pipeline.

Beggars Banquet Atlantic

Jul 93. (10"ep/cd-ep) *(BBQ 16 T/CD)* *<95983>* **GO ROUND / DEEPS. / A MINE / SYMBOLS** Oct93

Sep 93. (cd) *(BBQCD 141)* *<92324>* **OVER VALENCE**
– On again, off again / Go round / K-funk / Loa / F.D.M. / Machine gun / Take control / Carrier wave / Levers / Lock-up / Take control II / Sub surface / Static.

Oct 93. (12"ep/cd-ep) *(BBQ 23 T/CD)* **LOA**
– Bath song / Snowballs.

Freek Freek

May 95. (cd/lp) *(<FRR 11 CD/LP>)* **PSYCHEDELIC MUSIQUE (LAVA SURF KUNST)** (outtakes from '92-'93)

—— had already disbanded

HALF JAPANESE

Formed: Uniontown, Maryland, USA . . . 1977 by San Franciscan-born brothers JAD and DAVID FAIR; a few years previously, together with friend, DAVID STANSKY, the pair had practised daily in the basement of their parents' Michigan home. A debut EP, 'CALLING ALL GIRLS . . . ' was released that year, its deliberate amateurism and wilful experimentation heralding a long and chequered career for the FAIR siblings. After they issued a further EP in 1979, 'NO DIRECT LINE FROM MY BRAIN TO MY HEART', the pair decided to recruit two other brothers, RUCKY and JOHN DREYFUSS, their inaugural appearance coming in the shape of 1980's UK-only single, 'THE ZOMBIES OF MORA-TAU'. By 1981, they had amassed enough material to fill a triple album, 'HALF GENTLEMEN, NOT BEASTS', a schizoid trip through the brothers' warped muse featuring numerous crazed cover versions (see below) alongside defiantly DIY creations which set the tone for homemade US underground music throughout the 80's. From then on they assembled various musicians to augment them on each album project, JAD simultaneously juggling a prolific solo career with HALF JAPANESE albums such as 'LOUD' (1981), the KRAMER-produced 'MUSIC TO STRIP BY' (1987), 'CHARMED LIFE' (1988) and 'THE BAND THAT WOULD BE KING' (1989); DAVID would now be just part-time in '88. JAD subsequently worked with the likes of DON FLEMING (of VELVET MONKEYS, etc), JOHN ZORN and FRED FRITH (ex-HENRY COW), to mention but a few. At the turn of the decade, JAD collaborated with fellow maverick, DANIEL JOHNSTON on their demon-exorcising 1989 album and went on to work with Scottish spiritual cousins, The PASTELS. In 1993, a feature-length film, 'HALF JAPANESE: THE BAND THAT WOULD BE KING' was being screened in art-house cinemas, while the band came perilously close to fame as fans, NIRVANA, asked them to support them on tour. • **Songwriters:** JAD FAIR except; 10th AVENUE FREEZE OUT (Bruce Springsteen) / TANGLED UP IN BLUE (Bob Dylan) / RAVE ON (Buddy Holly) / AIN'T TOO PROUD TO BEG (Temptations) / I CAN'T STAND IT ANYMORE (Velvet Underground) / THE SPY (Doors) / BLUE MONDAY (Fats Domino) / GLORIA (Them) / HIDDEN CHARMS (Willie Dixon) / LA BAMBA (Richie Valens) / TOMORROW NEVER KNOWS (Beatles) / SHANTY TOWN (Desmond Dekker) / GOING HOME (. . . Lee) / EVERY HOUR (Little Richard) / ALL OF ME (Marks-Simons) / EAR (. . . Brookings) / MEMPHIS TENNESSEE + CHARMED LIFE (Chuck Berry) / I'LL CHANGE MY STYLE (Jerry Reed) / CHERRY PIE (. . . Josea) / FUTURISTIC LOVERS (Laureate-Mitchell) / SILVER AND KATHERINE (trad) / CASPER (c/o cartoon; Carmichael) / etc. • **Trivia:** In 1991, they were produced by MO TUCKER (former VELVET UNDERGROUND drummer).

Album rating: HALF GENTLEMEN, NOT BEASTS compilation (*7) / LOUD (*5) / OUR SOLAR SYSTEM (*4) / SING NO EVIL (*4) / MUSIC TO STRIP BY (*6) / CHARMED LIFE (*7) / THE BAND THAT WOULD BE KING (*7) / WE ARE THEY WHO ACHE WITH AMOROUS LOVE (*6) / FIRE IN THE SKY (*6) / HOT (*6) / GREATEST HITS compilation (*8) / BONE HEAD (*6) / Jad Fair: EVERYBODY KNEW. BUT ME (*6) / MONARCHS (*4) / BEST WISHES (*5) / GREAT EXPECTATIONS (*6) / ROLL OUT THE BARREL (*4) / JAD FAIR AND DANIEL JOHNSTON (*7) / I LIKE IT WHEN YOU SMILE (*6) / HONEY BEE (*5)

JAD FAIR – vocals, guitar, drums / **DAVID FAIR** – guitar, vocals, drums

not iss. Watts

1977. (7"ep) *<7094-18>* **CALLING ALL GIRLS (50,000,000,000,000,000,000,000,000,000 WATTS) EP**

1979. (7") **NO DIRECT LINE FROM MY BRAIN TO MY HEART. / (I DON'T WANT TO HAVE) MONO (NO MORE) / NO**

—— added **RUCKY DREYFUSS** – drums / **JOHN DREYFUSS** – saxophone

Armageddon not iss.

Jun 80. (7"ep) *(AEP 003)* **THE ZOMBIES OF MORA-TAU**
– Frankenstein must die / Dead men talk / The thing with the atomic brain / Angela / It walks at night / The zombies of Mora-Tau / The invisible ray.

May 81. (7"/12") *(AS 009)* **SPY. / I KNOW HOW IT FEELS . . .BAD / MY KNOWLEDGE WAS WRONG**

Oct 81. (t-lp-box) *(ABOX 1)* **1/2 GENTLEMEN, NOT BEASTS** (compilation 77-79)
– No direct line from my brain to my heart / 10th Ave. freezeout / Ta Shari ta ta / My girlfriend lives like a beatnik / Her parents came home / Shhh shhh shhh / Girls like that / Rrrrrr / No more Beatlemania / Tangled up in blue / Patti Smith / School of love / Jodi Foster / Shy around girls / Grrr rrrrr / Bogue millionaires / Cool millionaires / Tn tn tn tn ki / I can't stand it anymore / I love Oriental girls / Dream date / Du du du du du du / Ain't too proud to beg / Ann Arbor Mi / I'm going to the zoo / Shi Yi Yi / Rave on / I ta na si na mi eee / Till victory / Rip my shirt to shreds / I don't want to have mono no more / She cracked / Bbbbbb-bbbbbb-bbbbbb / Funky Broadway medley / I'm sorry / TT-T-T-T-T-T-T / The worst I'd ever do / Live.

—— added **MARK JICKLING** – guitar / **LANA ZABKO** – saxophone

May 82. (lp) *(ARM 7)* **LOUD**
– My concentration, oh no / 2 hearts = 1 / If my father answers, don't say nothing / Scientific devices / Gift / Dumb animals / Popular / I know how it feels . . .bad / Perfume / New brides of Frankenstein / Forget you / Loud, louder, loudest / Spy / No danger / Love lasts forever / Nurse / Only dancing / Bad to your best friend / Baby wants music / High school tonight.

not iss. Compendium

1983. (12"ep) **HORRIBLE**
– Think with a hook / Rosemary's baby / Vampire. *(UK-iss.Jul86 on 'Press'; P 2005)*

not iss. Iridescence

Dec 84. (lp) *<IRID K-6>* **OUR SOLAR SYSTEM**

Dec 85. (lp) *<IRID K-10>* **SING NO EVIL**

not iss. K

1986. (c; shared with VELVET MONKEYS) **BIG BIG SUN**

not iss. 50 Skidillion Watts

1987. (lp) *<HJ 2>* **MUSIC TO STRIP BY**
– Stripping for cash / Thick and thin / Diary / Big mistake / Hot dog and hot damn / Price was right / Blue Monday / U.S. teens are spoiled bums / Point – Counterpoint / Sex at your parents house / The lst straw / Gator bait / La bamba / Colleen / Ouija board summoning Satan / You must obey me / Salt and pepper / Ancient life / Silver and Katherine / Money to burn / Hidden charms / How / My sordid past / Silver and Katherine / Dusk to dawn / Everybody knows / Go go go go go / Scratch / Colleen / Salt and pepper / 'T' for Texas / Terminator / Shiek of Araby. *(cd-iss. Jul93 on 'Paperhouse'; PAPCD 017) <cd-iss. 1994; 80002>*

Shadowline ShimmyDisc

Feb 88. (7") *(SR 0188)* **SILVER AND KATHERINE. /**

No Man's Land 50 Skidillion Watts

Nov 88. (lp) *(NML 8815)* *<HJ 5>* **CHARMED LIFE**
– Said and done / Penny in the fountain / Evidence / Vietnam / Roman candles / Love at first sight / Snake line / Bright lights, big city / Face rake / Later in a magazine / Red dress / Charmed life / Day and night / 1,000,000,000 kisses / Terminator / I'll change my style / Charmed life / Trouble in the water / Miracles / Happen every day / Fortunate / Poetic license / Day and night / 1,000,000,000 kisses / Madonna nude / I'll change my style / George Steele / Real cool time / How many moe years / King Kong Bundy / Something new in the ring / Terminator. *(cd-iss. Jul93 on 'Paperhouse'; PAPCD 016) <cd-iss. 1994; 80005>*

Apr 89. (lp/c/cd) *<HALF 8-1/-4/-2>* **THE BAND WHO WOULD BE KING**
– Open your eyes – Close your eyes / Daytona beach / Lucky star / Some things last a long time / My most embarrassing moment / Buried treasure / Open book / Little records / Deadly alien spawn / Postcard from faraway / Ventriloquism made easy / Something in the wind / Bingo's not his name / Put some sugar on it / What more can I do. *(re-iss. cd Jul93 on 'Paperhouse'+=; PAPCD 018)* – Brand new moon / Another world / Every word is true / I live for love / Werewolf / Ride ride ride /

Sugar cane / I wish I may / Ashes on the ground / Curse of the doll people / Horse shoes / Bluebirds / Frankenstein meets Billy The KId / My bucket's got a hole in it / Africans built the pyramids / Better than before / Daytona / Back home / Mule skinner blues / Sugar cane / Jump up / Postcard from far away / Big wheels / Ordeal / Jump down / Cowboys / Man without a head. *<cd-iss. 1994; 80008>*

not iss. T.E.C.

Jan 91. (cd/d-lp) *<TEC 90602>* **WE ARE THEY WHO ACHE WITH AMOROUS LOVE**
– Every hour / Elevator boy / Gloria / Ear / Titanic / Our eyes / Spin / Up and down / Run / All of me / Hand without a body / Going home / Three rings / How did you know? Then we walk / Secret / Best / The house I live in / Shanty town / Everything is right?

Seminal Twang not iss.

Jun 91. (7") *(2)* **EVERYBODY KNOWS. /**
Apr 92. (7") **EYE OF THE HURRICANE. /**

Rockville Safe House

Jun 93. (cd) *<2113>* **FIRE IN THE SKY**
– UFO expert / Tears stupid tears / This could be the night / Possum head / Frosty head / Turn your life around / I love a mystery / 12 houses / Hangar 18 / Magic kingdom / It's no wonder / Fire in the sky / Good luck / Gates of glory / Everyone knows / I heard her call my name / Eye of the hurricane.
Jun 93. (7") *(HJ 4)* **US TEENS ARE SPOILED BUMS. /**

not iss. TEC Tones

May 94. (cd) *<94602>* **BOO! LIVE IN EUROPE 1992 (live)**
– Open your eyes / Big mistake / One million kisses / Fire to burn / Mule in the corn / If he says he did / King Kong / Postcard / I'll change my style / Cherry pie / Rrrrrsssssstttttt / Sex at your parent's house / Secret / Said and done / Charmed life / Casper / Around around / Rocking chair / Turn your life around / Firecracker / Silver and Katherine / Frankenstein must fie! / By and by / Fire in the sky.

— with **MICK HOBBS** – bass, guitar / **JOHN SLUGGETT** – guitar / **JASON WILLETT** – bass, guitar

Fire Safe House

Jun 95. (cd) *(FIRECD 47) <2125>* **HOT** Aug95
– Drum straight / True believers / Well / Dark night / Part of my plan / Vampire / Lucky ones / Vast continent / Guess again / Black fruit / Sleep talk / Smile / Lucky town.
Mar 96. (m-cd) *<2132>* **TBD**

— retained only **SLUGGETT** + enlisted other co-writers **TIM FOLJAHN** – guitar / **GILLES V. RIEDER** – percussion, drums, etc

Alternative Tentacles Alternative Tentacles

Mar 97. (cd/lp) *<(VIRUS 197 CD/LP)>* **BONE HEAD**
– Monkey hand / A night like this / Sometimes / Zombie eye / Song of joy / Oww / Do it / He walks among us / Diamonds and / Kiss me like a frog / Rhumba / Intergalactic aliens / Celebration / C'mon baby / Somehow I knew / Now I know / Brand new sky / Should I? / Song of joy / Futuristic lovers / Movin' on up.

– compilations, etc. –

Nov 96. (d-cd) *Safe House; <(SH 2118-2)>* **GREATEST HITS** Mar95
– Firecracker / Daytona beach / Said and done / Dance when I say dance / Postcard from far away / Worst I'd ever do / Horseshoes / Open/close your eyes / This could be the night / Put some sugar on it / Caling all girls / Bamba / Love at first sight / Rub every muscle / Silver and Katherine / My sordid past / Ride, ride, ride / Day and night / Last straw / Nicole / Miracles happen every day / U.S. teens / School of love / T for Texas / Colleen / Red dress / Charmed life / Rosemary's baby / I know how it feels . . . bad / Roman candles / Dream date / Moving on up / No more Beatlemania / How did you know? / Penny in the fountain / King Kong / Secret / B./C. millionaires / Amazing clock / Thick and thin / 1,000,000 kisses / Big mistake / Little records / No direct line / The house I live in / UFO expert / Identical twins / Double trouble / Evidence / Stripping for cash / On the one hand / Snake line / Too much adrenalin / Trouble in the water / Ball and chain / Her parents came home / Deadly alien spawn / Ancient life / Poetic license / Uncertain feelings / Something new / Fire to burn / Acupuncture / Salt and pepper / Guitar solo / A little bit more / Mono / Better than before / Everything is right?
Nov 97. (cd) *Emperor Jones; <(EJ 12CD)>* **HEAVEN SENT**

JAD FAIR

not iss. Press

1982. (lp) **EVERYBODY KNEW . . . BUT ME**

not iss. Iridescence

1984. (lp) **MONARCHS**
(cd-iss. Jul97 on 'Dr.Jim'; DRJIM 20)
1987. (lp) **BEST WISHES**

Bad Alchemy not iss.

1988. (d-lp) *(BAAL 22)* **GREAT EXPECTATIONS** German
– Snake on my head / Everyone knew but me / Outlaw blues / Space sound / Want / Roses for Karen / Rocket ship / Moon / Tiger / Robot / Love research / Baseball / Lion / All my love / Hogwild / Like a bird / Shakespear / Parade / Angela / The tracks of my tears / Frankenstein must die / Weee / All / Amy / You / Frankenstein monster / Checkers / It saw me / Jambalaya / Horses / Dog / Whale / I got you / Deadmen walk / Fish / Zombies of Mora-Tau / Another silent night / This / New Orleans / Vampire / Amy you went away / Owl / Radio / Romeo and Juliet / Girl-trouble / Shoestrings / Mule / I want to be loved / Thing with the atomic brain / Lonely weekends / Again / Invisible ray / Duck / I'm gonna go out / XXOO / Went / Hotdog / I'm gonna come back to you / Eifel Tower / Cherry pie / Linda Lou / Bear / Will you go out with me? / Hillbillies / It walks at night / Monster is land / Elephant / Things with eyes / Pajamas / Wild West / Me and the boys / Fish can talk / I heard his footsteps beat against the attic floor / I knew my time had come / Don't you want to live forever? / Face your lord and master / There is no escape / The time has come / Nosferatu is among us.

— next with also **SONIC YOUTH, JOHN ZORN, DAVID LICHT**, etc

Black Lion ShimmyDisc

Jan 89. (lp; by JAD FAIR & KRAMER) *(BLP 60904) <SD 8912>* **ROLL OUT THE BARREL**

50 Skidillion Watts 50 Skidillion Watts

Apr 89. (lp/c/cd; by JAD FAIR AND DANIEL JOHNSTON) *<(JAD 9-1/-4/-2)>* **JAD FAIR AND DANIEL JOHNSTON**
– It's spooky / Summertime / I met Roky Erickson / Happy talk / McDonalds on the brain / I did acid with Caroline / If I'd only known / Tongues wag in this town / Tomorrow never knows / Oh honey / A vow of love / When love calls / Frankenstein conquers the world / Hands of love / Kicking the dog / What I've seen / Something's got a hold on me / Villain / Chords of fame / Ostrich / Casper the friendly ghost / First day at work / Nothing left / Memphis, Tennessee / Come back / Tears stupid tears / The making of the album / Get yourself together / What the world needs now / Sweet loafed. *(cd-iss. Jul93 as 'IT'S SPOOKY' on 'Paperhouse'; PAPCD 019)*

not iss. Shimmy Disc

1990. (cd; by JAD FAIR & KRAMER) **THE SOUND OF MUSIC**
– Beverly / Candace / Elenor / Faceless man / Our cause to worry / Here comes Roxanne / Zorro's black whip / Sleeping beauty / Pretty angel eyes / Something to sing about / Annie Oakley / The sound of music.

— now with **TERRY ADAMS** – harmonica, percussion, keyboards / plus guests **DON FLEMING + MICK HOBBS + STEVE SHELLEY + J MASCIS**etc

not iss. Psycho

Mar 92. (cd/lp) *<9260-2>* **I LIKE IT WHEN YOU SMILE**
– A little bit more / Only one left / Sunny side of the street / Something inside of me / Surprise party / Secret life / Dot / Roadrunner / If he says he did / You'll never know / Big as the sun / Crown / Take a chance / I like candy / Mule in the corn / Big top / I had a dream last night / Angel / Eyes of the world / Brand new moon / Texas / Better than before.

JAD FAIR & THE PASTELS

— yes the same Scottish band

Paperhouse TEC Tones

Feb 92. (12"ep/cd-ep) *(PAPER 013 T/CD)* **THIS COULD BE THE NIGHT. /**
Jun 92. (12"ep/cd-ep) *(PAPER 018 T/CD)* **HE CHOSE HIS COLOURS WELL. /**
Jan 94. (cd; by JAD FAIR & NAO) *(PAPCD 015)* **HALF ROBOT**
– Population is only 2 / Walk right in / Art? ha! / Hope-Bogart / ETC's / Happy together / Smile pretender / Our love has come / Neat beings / I like it / Gone with window / Pu-14 is is 4 of GB 10 / Brigham's coffee shop / Distorted moon / Kukaimanimani / Navel cake / Intuition / Broom of love / Zui zui zukkorobash / Amy's smile / Coffee me / Water / I don't know / April / Egg'n'ham / Haircuts / Do hachamecha / Nihon no Otoko / 999 years loan / Fresh meat / Pepper and salt / Forever / Hana o meshimasho / Junkful junk / Made in Paradise / The band / Do you like America? / Debt for debt / Beast wishes / Charlie Chaplin / As seen on T.V. / Oh! my buddha / $1.99, $2.99, $3.99 / Time / Protecting / Simon, not Simon / Nynyusa / Bride with cowboy boots / Candy / Pornographies in the safe / Happy birthday / Can't buy my money / Typewriter / Curious crowd's faces / My nane is Jad Fair / Morale booster / Bob Hope / Industrial refuse / Freaks / Miserable shit / Yes, I'm not tired / Too much car / Tattoo of hello Kitty / Cold summer / Vegetarian puts leather / Kiss tribe / Sleep / Newborn babies / Tokolo de Kowela Nani / Cato and Dogu / 40 monsters / Watch T.V. 'til you die / Taking a bath / Rocky mountain oyster / Blue suede shoes / Homosexual teacher.

JAD FAIR

Derivative not iss.

Oct 95. (7"; as JAD FAIR & PHONO COMB) *(DVH 020)* **IN A HAUNTED HOUSE. /**

— now with **KIM M. RANCOURT** – sax, vocals, etc / + others

not iss. Avant

Apr 97. (cd; as JAD FAIR & THE SDAPJA-O'RAMA) *<52>* **WE ARE THE RAGE**
– Meet me by the prison wall / I comb my hair with my hand / The book of love / Love in stores / Jamboree / I love honey / I saw Chris Economaki / Caterpillar / We are the rage / Shnella / Call me / Electric / I knew I know (just one look) / Convert / Lots of room for love / Party / Olives / Evelyn day / Don't change a thing / Summer – Winter / Rice a roni / Be it again / And I love her.

Dr. Jim not iss.

Jul 97. (cd; by JAD FAIR & JASON WILLET) *(DRJIM 19)* **HONEY BEE**
(re-iss. Apr98 on 'Lissys'; LISS 26)

Kill Rock Stars Kill Rock Stars

May 98. (cd; by JAD & DAVID FAIR) *<(KRS 292)>* **26 MONSTER SONGS FOR CHILDREN**

Matador Matador

Oct 98. (cd; by JAD FAIR & YO LA TENGO) *<(OLE 309)>* **STRANGE BUT TRUE**
– Helpful monkeys wallpapers entire / Texas man abducted by aliens for / National sports association hires / Dedicated thespian has teeth pulled / Three-year-old genius graduates high / Embarrassed teen accidentally / uses / Principal punishes students with bad / Retired grocer constructs tiny mount / X-ray reveals doctor left wristwatch / Clumsy grandmother serves delicious / Retired woman starts new career in / Circus strongman runs for PTA / High school shop class constructs / Clumsy grandmother serves delicious / Ohio town saved from killer bees by hungry vampire bats / Nevada man invents piano with 21 / Clever chemist makes chewing gum from / Minnesota man claims monkey bowled / Ingenius scientist invents car of / Car gears stick in reverse, daring / Shocking fashion statement terrorizes / Feisty millionaire fills potholes.

– compilations, etc. –

Jun 96. (cd) *Shake; <226>* **MONSTERS, LULLABIES & OCCASIONAL FLYING SAUCERS**

HALF MAN HALF BISCUIT

Formed: Birkenhead, England . . . 1984 by lyricist, NIGEL BLACKWELL and his brother SIMON, who enlisted NEIL CROSSLEY, DAVID LLOYD and PAUL WRIGHT (SIMON and the latter having previously played together with the WILDING brothers, ROY and MICHAEL, in late 70's act, ATTEMPTED MOUSTACHE; one single, 'SUPERMAN' / 'NO WAY OUT', appeared on

'Skeleton'). Late in '85, HALF MAN HALF BISCUIT stormed the bastions of good taste with debut album, 'BACK IN THE D.H.S.S', a record that re-introduced caustic wit and twisted humour back into the overly serious mid-80's rock/pop world; The BONZOS had shown the way in the 60's, The ALBERTOS carried the flame for the 70's, and now The 'BISCUITS were having a laugh at the expense of Britain's less glamourous TV celebs. Stalwart people's DJ, John Peel, took to them immediately, wearing out his stylus night after night on such eccentric post-punk (near-plagiarised) ditties as 'I HATE NERYS HUGHES – FROM THE HEART', 'FUCKIN' 'ELL, IT'S FRED TITMUS' and '99% OF GARGOYLES LOOK LIKE BOB TODD', while the tongue-in-cheek 'TIME FLIES BY (WHEN YOU'RE THE DRIVER OF A TRAIN)' took the Michael out of our long lost TV childhood. The following year, the album topped the indie charts for an extended period and even scraped into the national Top 60. Their indie imprint, 'Probe Plus', surely should have scored their first UK chart hit when the HMHB team unleashed their pastiche of a Kim Carnes number ('Bette Davies Eyes') in the shape of 'DICKIE DAVIES EYES', the accompanying thigh-slapping video parodying the Flake TV commercial with the long-haired beauty bearing a frightening resemblance to the moustachioed sports presenter in question! In fact, the band's love of sport, or at least football (they supprted Tranmere Rovers!), was a recurring theme in their work, obsessively expressed in the Subbuteo tribute, 'ALL I WANT FOR CHRISTMAS IS A DULKA PRAGUE AWAY KIT'. Having amassed more acclaim than they could have dreamed of in their brief year long recording career, HMHB decided to abandon the game before any major crowd trouble. It wouldn't be until 1990 that the band re-emerged onto the musical pitch of that year's Reading Festival, their first single in four years being 'LET'S NOT'. The following Spring, the band enlisted the help of Northern sex symbol, MARGI CLARKE, to spice up their version of the Walker Brothers' 'NO REGRETS'. Virtually six years in the making, their follow-up album (barring exploitation sets), 'McINTYRE, TREADMORE AND DAVITT' (1991), inevitably failed to live up to the genius of its predecessor, although it did contain one throwback to their scathing past in 'OUTBREAK OF VITAS GERULAITIS'. Without exerting themselves too much, the Scouse chancers continued to document the duller side of British life with perverse enthusiasm over such albums as 'THIS LEADEN PALL' (1993), 'SOME CALL IT GODCORE' (1995), 'VOYAGE TO THE BOTTOM OF THE ROAD' (1997) and 'FOUR LADS WHO SHOOK THE WIRRAL' (1998). • **Trivia for the uninitiated:** FRED TITMUS (former England cricketer) / BOB TODD (comic on Benny Hill show) / LEN GANLEY (snooker referee) / NERYS HUGHES (actress & children's TV presenter) / DEAN FRIEDMAN + ALBERT HAMMOND (US singers) / TED MOULT (TV presenter) / VITAS GERALAITIS (US tennis player).

Album rating: BACK IN THE D.H.S.S. (*8) / ACD (*8)

NIGEL BLACKWELL – vocals, guitar / **NEIL CROSSLEY** – bass, vocals / **SIMON BLACKWELL** – lead guitar (ex-ATTEMPTED MOUSTACHE) / **DAVID LLOYD** – keyboards / **PAUL WRIGHT** – drums (ex-ATTEMPTED MOUSTACHE)

Probe Plus / not iss.

Nov 85. (lp) *(PROBE 4)* **BACK IN THE D.H.S.S.** [59] [-]
– God gave us life / "Fuckin' 'ell, it's Fred Titmus" / Seal-clubbing / 99% of gargoyles look like Bob Todd / Time flies by (when you're the driver of a train) / I hate Nerys Hughes – from the heart / The Len Ganley stance / Venus in flares / I love you because (you look like Jim Reeves) / Reflections in a flat. *(re-iss. Apr94 & Oct97 cd/c +=; PROBE 4 CD/C)* – TRUMPTON RIOTS

Mar 86. (7") *(TRUM 17)* **TRUMPTON RIOTS. / ALL I WANT FOR CHRISTMAS IS A DULKA PRAGUE AWAY KIT** [ ] [-]
(12"+=) *(TRUMP 1)* – Architecture morality / Ted and Alice / 1966 and all that / Albert Hammond bootleg.

Sep 86. (7") *(PP 21)* **DICKIE DAVIES EYES. / LEFT MY HEART (IN PAPWORTH GENERAL)** [ ] [-]
(12"+=) *(PP 21T)* – ('A'&'B'remixes) / The bastard son of Dean Friedman.

Feb 87. (lp/c) *(PROBE 8/+C)* **BACK IN THE D.H.S.S. AGAIN** (sessions & 12" singles) [ ] [-]
– The best things in life / D'ye ken Ted Moult? / Reasons to be miserable (part 10) / Rod Hull is alive – why? / Dickie Davies eyes / The bastard son of Dean Friedman / I was a teenage armchair Honved fan / Arthur's farm / Carry on cremating / Albert Hammond bootleg / Reflections in a flat / Sealclubbing / Architecture and morality Ted and Alice / Fuckin' hell it's Fred Titmus / Time flys by (when you're the driver of a train) / All I want for Christmas is a Dulka Prague away kit / The Trumpton riots. *(cd re-iss. Apr94 & Oct97; same)*

Feb 89. (cd) *(PROBE 8CD)* **ACD** (same as above plus live tracks and rare singles) [ ] [-]

—— split late '86, but re-formed in 1990

Oct 90. (7") **LET'S NOT. / OUR TUNE** [ ] [-]
(12"+=/cd-s+=) – Ordinary to Enschede.

Apr 91. (7"/c-s) **NO REGRETS. / 1966 AND ALL THAT** [ ] [-]
(12"+–/cd-s+–) – ('A'-long version).
(above 'A' with MARGI CLARKE)

Oct 91. (lp/c/cd) *(PROBE 030/+C/CD)* **McINTYRE, TREADMORE AND DAVITT** [ ] [-]
– Outbreak of Vitas Geralaitis / Prag Veg at the Melkweg / Christian rock concert / Let's not / Yipps (my baby got the) / Medley verity save / A lilac happy Queen / Our tune / Girlfriend's finished with him / Everything's A.O.R. *(re-iss. Apr94 & Oct97; same)*

Oct 93. (lp/c/cd) *(PROBE 036/+C/CD)* **THIS LEADEN PALL** [ ] [ ]
– M-6 ster / 4ad3dcd / Running order / Squabble fest / Whiteness thy name is Meltonian / This leadon pall / Turned up clocked on laid off / Improv workshop mimeshow gobshite / 13 Eurogoths floating in the dead sea / Whit week malarkey / Doreen / Quality janitor / Floreat inertia / Malayan jelutong / Numanoid hang glide / Footprints.

May 95. (lp/c/cd) *(PROBE 041/+C/CD)* **SOME CALL IT GODCORE** [ ] [ ]
– Sensitive outsider / Fretwork homework / Faithlift / Song for Europe / Even men with steel hearts / £24.99 from Argos / Sponsoring the moshpits / Fear my wraith / Styx gig / Friday night / I Trog / Tour jacket (with detachable sleeves).

Aug 96. (7") *(PP 30)* **ENO COLLABORATION. / HAIR LIKE BRIAN MAY BLUES** [ ] [-]
(cd-s+=) *(PP 30CD)* – C.A.M.R.A. man / Get Kramer.

Jun 97. (lp/cd) *(PROBE 45/+CD)* **VOYAGE TO THE BOTTOM OF THE ROAD** [ ] [-]
– Shropshire lad / Bad review / Eno collaboration / Dead men don't need season tickets / Deep house victims minibus appeal / C.A.M.R.A. man / P.R.S. yearbook (quick the drawbridge) / Tonight Matthew I'm going to be with Jesus / Song of encouragement for the Orme ascent / Monmore hares running / Itma / He who would alium take / See that my bike's kept clean / Paintball coming home.

Jun 98. (lp/cd) *(PROBE 46/+CD)* **FOUR LADS WHO SHOOK THE WIRRAL** [ ] [-]

– compilations etc. –

Nov 88. (12"ep/cd-ep) *Strange Fruit; (SFPS/+CD 057) / Dutch East India; <8331>* **THE PEEL SESSIONS (10.11.85)** [ ] [ ]
– D'ye ken Ted Moult / Arthur's farm / All I want for Christmas is a Dulka Prague away kit / Trumpton riots / Old Tiger.

Toni HALLIDAY (see under ⇒ CURVE)

HALO OF FLIES

Formed: Minneapolis, Minnesota, USA . . . 1985 by TOM HAZELMYER, who had previously been frontman for Seattle outfit, the U-MEN, after earlier enlisting for the US Marines. The brains behind the 'Amphetamine Reptile' label, TOM recruited a rhythm section of TIM 'MAC' McLAUGHLIN and JOHN ANGLIM, releasing 'RUBBER ROOM' as a debut single and the second release for that label. The latter track was issued as a strictly limited edition, as were subsequent 7"er's, 'SNAPPING BACK ROSCOE BOTTLES EP', 'CIRCLING THE PILE', 'RICHIE'S DOG', 'NO TIME' and 'LEDERHOSEN' (a collaboration with KILLDOZER's BILL HOBSON under the pseudonym, POGO THE CLOWN). Combining crazed rockabilly-based attitude with head-on crashing noise, HAZELMYER and Co continued to slash'n'burn their way through the alternative jungle, cutting a couple of EP's for 'Twin/Tone' ('GARBAGE ROCK' and 'HEADBURN'). Collected together as 'GARBAGEBURN', the records were licensed to 'What Goes On' for European release in 1988. A further two singles (including one in '91 shared with MUDHONEY) and a couple of compilation sets rounded up the band's career as HAZELMYER devoted more time to his ever growing 'Amphetamine Reptile'.

Album rating: GARBAGEBURN mini (*6) / SINGLES GOING NOWHERE compilation (*6) / MUSIC FOR INSECT MINDS compilation (*6)

TOM HAZELMYER – vocals, guitar / **JOHN ANGLIM** – drums / **TIM 'MAC' McLAUGHLIN** – bass

What Goes On / Amphetam. Reptile

1986. (7") <Scale 2> **RUBBER ROOM. / THOUGHTS IN A BOOTH** [-] [ ]

1986. (7") <Scale 3> **SNAPPING BLACK ROSCOE BOTTLES EP** [-] [ ]
– Can't touch her / D.D.T. / Fin 13.

1986. (7") <Scale 4> **CIRCLING THE PILE EP** [-] [ ]
– Sinner sings / Pipebomb / M.D. 20-20.

1987. (7") <Scale 6> **RICHIE'S DOG. / HOW DOES IT FEEL TO FEEL** [-] [ ]

1987. (c) <Scale 11> **FOUR FROM THE BOTTOM** [-] [ ]

1988. (7") <Scale 13> **NO TIME. / YOU GET NOTHING** [-] [ ]

1988. (7"; as POGO THE CLOWN) <Scale 15> **LEDERHOSEN. /** [-] [ ]
(above was TOM's collaboration with KILLDOZER's BILL HOBSON)

1988. (m-lp) *(GOES ON 24)* **GARBAGEBURN** (a compilation of two 'Twin/Tone' EP's, 'GARBAGE ROCK' <TTR 87132> & 'HEADBURN') [ ] [-]
– Garbage rock / D.D.T. beat 69 / One barrel spent / I'm clean // Headburn / Easy or hard / Father paranoia / Drunk (in Detroit).

1990. (7") <Scale 19> **DEATH OF A FLY. / CLOWNS** [-] [ ]

not iss. / Forced Exposure

1990. (12"ep) <FE 019> **WINGED EP** [-] [ ]

not iss. / Silt Breeze

1991. (12"ep) **LIVE EP (live)** [-] [ ]

—— HAZELMYER split the trio in 1991

– compilations, etc. –

1990. (lp) *Amphetamine Reptile; <001>* **SINGLES GOING NOWHERE** [-] [ ]

1991. (7",7"maroon; shared with MUDHONEY) *<Scale 35/36>* **BIG MOD HATE TRIP EP** [-] [ ]
– Wasted time / Tired & cold / etc.

1991. (cd) *Amphetamine Reptile; <002>* **MUSIC FOR INSECT MINDS** [ ] [ ]

HANATARASH (see under ⇒ BOREDOMS)

The HANDSOME FAMILY

Formed: Chicago, Illinois, USA . . . 1993 by songwriter BRETT SPARKS, his wife and co-conspirator RENNIE SPARKS plus third bespectacled member, drummer MIKE WERNER. The husband and wife team were the Gomez and Morticia of alt-country (or even a distorted, updated version of TIMBUK 3!) to the GEORGE JONES and TAMMY WYNETTE of classic Nashville, although BRETT and RENNIE's sound was, well . . . er . . . miles apart. Born of acute personal difficulties, The HANDSOME FAMILY's music set against a background of strife; BRETT suffered a mental breakdown attempting to write his own bible!, while RENNIE was the "school freak" who immersed herself in literature (Greek classic, 'The Iliad', is apparently her favourite). From the onset, the trio toured extensively promoting their early releases, 'ODESSA' (1995), 'MILK AND SCISSORS' (1996) and 'INVISIBLE HANDS' (1997), dark country tales and lifesize plastic animals unsettling audiences in both America and Europe. Initially aided by co-producer DAVE TRUMFIO, the band of renegade "true country" folk were augmented on the aforesaid releases by studio helpers, et all. Recorded on collaborator JEFF TWEEDY's (WILCO/UNCLE TUPELO) mobile studio, 1998's pioneering (in every sense of the word!) 'THROUGH THE TREES' kicked-off with the delightfully disturbing 'WEIGHTLESS AGAIN'. These peerless lyrics describe their 'Dead Man' emotions; "This is why people O.D. on pills, And jump . . . from the Golden Gate Bridge, Anything to feel weightless again". Cloaked in the gothic NEIL YOUNG/BILLY BRAGG-esque vocals of BRETT, The HANDSOME FAMILY's mournful tales of tragic 19th century Wild West folklore conjure up cinematic images of barren canyons and Red Indian ghosts dancing on General Custer's grave.

Album rating: ODESSA (*5) / MILK AND SCISSORS (*5) / INVISIBLE HANDS (*5) / THROUGH THE TREES (*7)

BRETT SPARKS – vocals, guitar, keyboards / **RENNIE SPARKS** – bass, vocals / **MIKE WERNER** – drums / with additional musicians DAVE TRUMFIO – acoustic guitar, keyboards, co-producer / MICHAEL HAGLER – guitar / STEVE THOMAS – pedal steel

not iss. Carrot Top

Jan 95. (cd) <5> **ODESSA** [-] [ ]
– Here's hopin' / Arlene / Pony / One way up / Water into wine / Giant ant / Everything that rises must converge / Gorilla / The last / Claire said / Moving furniture around / Big bad wolf / She awoke with a jerk / Happy harvest. *(German-iss.Jan96 on 'Scout'; RTD 306-1004-2)*

— the trio's guests included MICHAEL, DAVE, HARRY TRUMFIO, DARRELL SPARKS and MARK STRUZYNSKI

Feb 96. (cd) *<11>* **MILK AND SCISSORS** [-] [ ]
– Lake Geneva / Winnebago skeletons / Drunk by noon / The house carpenter / The Dutch boy / The king who wouldn't smile / Emily Shore 1819-1839 / 3-legged dog / #1 country song / Amelia Earhart vs. the dancing bear / Tin foil / Puddin' fingers. *(German-iss.Sep96 on 'Scout'; RTD 306-1011-2)*

Sep 97. (m-cd) *<RTD 306-1012-2>* **INVISIBLE HANDS** [-] [-] German

— now without WERNER, the husband and wife duo added guests DAVE, JEFF TWEEDY, JESSICA BILLEY, DAVE SMITH and DAVE WINER

Loose Carrot Top

Apr 98. (cd) *(VJCD 105)* *<20>* **THROUGH THE TREES** [ ] [ ] Jan98
– Weightless again / My sister's tiny hands / Stalled / Where the birch trees lean / Cathedrals / Down in the ground / The giant of Illinois / Down in the valley of hollow logs / I fell / The woman downstairs / Last night I went out walking / Bury me here / My ghost.

HAPPY FLOWERS

Formed: Charlottesville, USA . . . 1986 by Mr. ANUS (alias CHARLIE KRAMER) and Mr. HORRIBLY CHARRED INFANT (alias JOHN BEERS), who had previously met in the hardcore group The LANDLORDS (also run by bassman EDDIE JETLAG and TRISTAN PUCKETT on drums). ANUS had also been part of other early 80's outfit, The CHARLIE KRAMER BAND, while Mr. HCI featured in two bands, LOWEST COMMON DENOMINATOR and PSYCHODELIC TRASHCAN. The LANDLORDS issued one EP, 'OUR FAVORITE SONGS!' and an album, 'HEY! IT'S A TEENAGE HOUSE PARTY!', before a few members splintered into BIGFOOT (without Mr. ANUS and Mr. HCI). After a few EP's on 'Catch Trout' in the mid-80's, The HAPPY FLOWERS signed to 'Homestead' in 1987, releasing debut album, 'MY SKIN COVERS MY BODY', a basic attempt to resurrect the embryonic of SONIC YOUTH and DIY noise/punk and screaching non-tunes. A handful of 45's (the second 'BB GUN' their classiest) and albums ('I CRUSH BOZO', 'OOF' and 'LASTERDAY I WAS BEEN BAD') appeared in the late 80's/early 90's, before they unhappily went to ground. • **Songwriters:** except BRING ON THE DANCING HORSES (Echo & The Bunnymen) / PENNY LANE (Beatles) / MRS. LENNON (Yoko Ono) / REAGANOMICS (DRI) / THIRTEEN (Big Star) / POX ON YOU (Simeon-Taylor) / LOVE HURTS (Everly Brothers).

Album rating: FLOWERS ON 45: THE HOMESTEAD SINGLES (*5)

MR. ANUS (b. CHARLIE KRAMER) – guitar / **MR. HORRIBLY CHARRED INFANT** (b. JOHN BEERS) – drums

not iss. Catch Trout

1985. (12"ep) **SONGS FOR CHILDREN** [-] [ ]
1986. (12"ep) **NOW WE ARE SIX** [-] [ ]
1987. (lp) **MAKING THE BUNNY PAY** (compilation) [-] [ ]

Homestead Homestead

1987. (lp) *<HMS 085-1>* **MY SKIN COVERS MY BODY** [ ] [ ]
Jun 88. (7"m) *<HMS 105>* **THEY CLEANED MY CUT OUT WITH A WIRE BRUSH. / JUST WAIT TILL I'M BIGGER THAN YOU / MY MOTHER S A FISH** [ ] [ ]
Jul 88. (lp/c) *<HMS 106/+C>* **I CRUSH BOZO** [ ] [ ]
Apr 89. (7"m) *<HMS 135>* **BB GUN. / CHARLIE GOT A HAIRCUT / I ATE SOMETHING OUT OF THE MEDICINE CABINET** [ ] [ ]
May 89. (lp/c/cd) *<HMS 136-1/-4/-2>* **OOF (live)** [ ] [ ]
– Stop touching my food / Unhappy meal / Pickin' scabs / There's soft spot on the baby's . . . / Finger in my crackerjacks / Ain't got nothin' / I said I wanna watch cartoons / My arm won't wake up / My evil twin / I'm gonna have an accident / Let's eat the baby (like my gerbils . . .) / BB gun / Let me out / I don't wanna go to school / Mrs. Lennon / Charlie said the F-word again.

Dec 89. (cd-ep) *<HMS 137-2>* **TOO MANY BUNNIES** [ ] [ ]
1990. (7"m) *<HMS 159>* **CALL ME PUDGE. / CALL ME PUDGE (live) / GERMAN FOLK SONG (live)** [ ] [ ]
1990. (cd/lp) *(HMS 160-2/-1)* **LASTERDAY I WAS BEEN BAD** [ ] [ ]
– We rock / Leave me alone / I don't want to shave / Rock bottom / Not a happy birthday / Embryo / Simon / Call me Pudge / I shouldn't have eaten that stuff / Mr. Fuck / Thirteen / If this gun were real (I could shoot you) / Pull off its head / Pox on you.
1991. (7"ep) *<HMS 161-7>* **THE PEEL SESSIONS** [ ] [ ]
– My head's on fire / Mom and dad like the baby more than me / Ruckwerts essen jetzt / I dropped my ice cream cone / These peas are so green.
1991. (cd) *<HMS 161-2>* **FLOWERS ON 45: THE HOMESTEAD SINGLES** (compilation) [ ] [ ]
– (the singles/tracks above) / Bring on the dancing horses / Penny Lane / Reaganomics / Love hurts / I wanna BB gun (and some glass eyes) / I'm first on the swing / The big picture / Hitting / The butcher (by The CHARLIE-CRAMER BAND) / Loser city (by LOWEST COMMON DENOMINATOR) / Fish (I like . . .) / Joe hates work (by PSYCHODELIC TRASHCAN) / Home in the jungle (by BIGFOOT) / Avsnit Frya / Fleekor / Tak so meeka (by The LANDLORDS) / Mrs. Butcher / Empty rhetoric / Press the bar / The strange house / Critical toast.

— split after playing final show on 18 August, 1990 at Firenze Tavern, Philadelphia. However, they did play a reunion gig on 20 July 1991 at Fallout Shelter, Raleigh, North Carolina.

HAPPY MONDAYS

Formed: Salford, Manchester, England . . . 1984 by brothers SHAUN and PAUL RYDER. In 1985, with the help of A&R man and producer Mike Pickering, they signed a contract with Tony Wilson's 'Factory' records, issuing a debut 12", 'FORTY-FIVE'. With the addition of MARK BERRY aka BEZ on 'percussion', the band released the 'FREAKY DANCIN' single, as good a description as any for BEZ's onstage contortions. A JOHN CALE-produced debut album followed in 1987, the acclaimed mutant indie funk of 'SQUIRREL AND G-MAN . . . ' winning the band many converts in the music press and the beginnings of a cult following. The early live shoes have been elevated to almost mythical status, SHAUN & Co. allegedly giving away drugs on the door to their own fans in true scally style. Despite sounding like it'd been recorded in a shed, the Martin Hannett-produced 'BUMMED' (1988) was a classic, a freewheeling groovy noise, punctuated intermittently by RYDER's stoned Mancunian slur. 'MAD CYRIL', 'LAZYITIS' and 'WROTE FOR LUCK' were all brilliant singles, the latter given a dance remix treatment by VINCE CLARKE (Erasure). 'Factory' supremo WILSON decided to take this a step further and set the band to work with the DJ/production team of PAUL OAKENFOLD and STEVE OSBORNE. The result was the pivotal 'MADCHESTER RAVE ON EP', a druggy mash-up of dance, indie, pop and funk that acted as a catylyst for the "Baggy" scene alongside The STONE ROSES' 'FOOL'S GOLD' single (spookily released exactly the same month), inspiring a whole string of bands in Manchester and beyond, some good, some not so good (just don't mention The FARM). Early the following year, The 'MONDAYS hit the Top 5 with their anthemic remake of JOHN KONGOS' 'He's Gonna Step On You Again', retitled 'STEP ON' and injected with typically laissez faire funk. 'KINKY AFRO' also made the Top 5, preceding the band's biggest success of their career, the 'PILLS 'N' THRILLS AND BELLYACHES' (1990) album. This time around there was a cleaner production and a melodic accessibilty coating the trademark melange of dirty 'STONES'-style guitar, raggedy-assed funk and cheesy disco. In addition to the singles, the album's highlights included a tribute to 60's folk-popster DONOVAN, a leering piece of porn-funk, 'BOB'S YER UNCLE' and the classic 'GOD'S COP' (featuring the timeless RYDER line "God laid his E's all on me"). While much of the band's music sounded continuously on the point of collapse and live, The HAPPY MONDAYS often seemed as if they'd arrived onstage purely by accident, RYDER was no space cadet, his inimitable lyrical couplets sussed, sharp and dryly witty. Almost inevitably though, the backlash began in earnest with an NME interview painting RYDER and BEZ as dim witted homophobes. Whatever RYDER actually said, it's likely that his tongue was planted firmly in cheek, and besides, to expect The HAPPY MONDAYS to stand up as right-on, PC role models for student NME readers displays a naivety that begs belief. Retreating to the Bahamas with Talking Heads' CHRIS FRANTZ and TINA WEYMOUTH at the production helm, the band struggled through sessions for the ' . . .YES PLEASE!' album, amid tales of general strife, severe drug abuse and obligatory debauchery. The album, an expensive disaster (critically and commercially) that reputedly bankrupted 'Factory', eventually emerged in late '92. Generally ignored and panned by the press, the album nevertheless contained some stellar 'MONDAYS moments, not least the low-key brilliance of 'STINKIN' THINKIN' and the darkly hypnotic 'ANGEL', both tracks using female backing vocals to impressive effect. After a wash out of a tour, The HAPPY MONDAYS drifted apart, a messy end for a band that were capable of true musical genius against all the odds. The loose limbed spirit of The 'MONDAYS lives on, though, in BLACK GRAPE, the band RYDER formed along with rapper KERMIT, while BEZ is up to all sorts, including a TV spot dedicated to science and writing an autobiography, no really man! "sorted". • **Songwriters:** Group compositions except; DESMOND (Ob-la-di Ob-la-da; Beatles) / LAZYITIS (Ticket To Ride; Beatles) / TOKOLOSHE MAN (John Kongos) / KINKY AFRO (parts of 'Lady Marmalade'; LaBelle).

Album rating: SQUIRREL AND G-MAN TWENTY FOUR HOUR PARTY . . . (*8) /

BUMMED (*8) / PILLS N' THRILLS AND BELLYACHES (*9) / YES PLEASE (*6)

SHAUN RYDER (b.23 Aug'62) – vocals / **PAUL RYDER** (b.24 Apr'64) – bass / **MARK DAY** (b.29 Dec'61) – guitar / **PAUL DAVIS** (b. 7 Mar'66) – keyboards / **GARY 'GAZ' WHELAN** (b.12 Feb'66) – drums

Factory | Rough Trade

Sep 85. (12"ep) *(FAC 129)* **FORTY-FIVE EP** [ ] [-]
– Delightful / This feeling / Oasis.

—— added **BEZ** (b. MARK BERRY, 18 Apr'64) – percussion, dancer

Jun 86. (7") *(FAC 142)* **FREAKY DANCIN'. / THE EGG** [ ] [-]
(ext.12"+=) *(FAC 142)* – ('A'live).

Mar 87. (12") *(FAC 176)* **TART TART. / LITTLE MATCHSTICK OWEN'S RAP** [ ] [-]

Apr 87. (lp) *(FACT 170)* **SQUIRREL & G-MAN TWENTY-FOUR HOUR PARTY PEOPLE PLASTIC FACE CARNT SMILE (WHITE OUT)** [ ] [-]
– Kuff dam / Tart tart / 'Enery / Russell / Olive oil / Weekends / Little matchstick Owen / Oasis / Desmond * / Cob 20. *(re-iss. Nov88; same)(track * repl. by)* – Twenty four hour party people. *(cd-iss. Mar90 +=; FACD 170)* – Little matchstick Owen's rap.

Oct 87. (12") *(FAC 192)* **TWENTY FOUR HOUR PARTY PEOPLE. / YAHOO / WAH WAH (THINK TANK)** [ ] [-]

Nov 88. (7") *(FAC 212-7)* **WROTE FOR LUCK. / BOOM** [ ] [-]
(12"+=/cd-s+=) *(FAC/+D 212)* – ('A'dance mix) / ('A'club mix).

Nov 88. (lp/cd)(d/dat) *(FACT/FACD 220)(FACT 220 C/D)* **BUMMED** [ ] [-]
– Country song / Moving in with / Mad Cyril / Fat lady wrestlers / Performance / Brain dead / Wrote for luck / Bring a friend / Do it better / Lazyitis. *(hit UK 59 UK Jan90)*

May 89. (12"/7"/c-s; as HAPPY MONDAYS & KARL DENVER) *(FAC 222/+7/C)* **LAZYITIS – ONE ARMED BOXER. / MAD CYRIL – HELLO GIRLS** [85] [-]
(re-iss. May90; same); hit No.46)

Sep 89. (12"/7") *(FAC 232/+7)* **WFL (Vince Clarke mix). / WFL – THINK ABOUT THE FUTURE (the Paul Oakenfold mix)** [68] [-]
(cd-s+=) *(FACD 232)* – Lazyitis – one armed boxer.

Nov 89. (7"clear/12"clear) **MAD CYRIL – HELLO GIRLS. / DO IT BETTER** [-] [ ]

Nov 89. (12"ep/cd-ep)(7"ep/c-ep) *(FAC/+D 242)(FAC 242-7/-C)* **MADCHESTER RAVE ON EP** [19] [-]
– Hallelujah / Holy ghost / Clap your hands / Rave on.
(7") *(FAC 242R-7)* **Hallelujah (the MacColl mix). / Hallelujah (in out mix).**
(c-s)(12"/cd-s) *(FAC 242RC)(FAC/+D 242R)* – ('A'club mix) / Rave on (club mix).

—— added guest **ROWETA** – backing vocals to repl. other guest KIRSTY MacCOLL

Factory | Elektra

Mar 90. (12"/7") *(FAC 272/+7)* *<64899>* **STEP ON (stuff it in mix). / ('A'-One louder mix)** [5] [57] Feb91
(c-s+=)(cd-s+=) *(FAC 272C)(FACD 272)* – ('A'-Twistin' my melons mix).

Oct 90. (12"/7"/c-s) *(FAC 302/+7/C)* **KINKY AFRO. / KINKY AFRO (live)** [5] [ ]
(cd-s+=) *(FACD 302)* – ('A'radio edit).

Nov 90. (cd/lp)(c) *(FACD/FACT 320)(FAC 320C)* *<60986>* **PILLS 'N THRILLS AND BELLYACHES** [4] [89]
– Kinky Afro / God's cop / Donovan / Grandbag's funeral / Loose fit / Dennis & Lois / Bob's your uncle / Step on / Holiday / Harmony.

Feb 91. (12"/7"/c-s) *(FAC 312/+7/C)* **LOOSE FIT. / BOB'S YOUR UNCLE** [17] [ ]
(cd-s+=) *(FACD 312)* – Kinky Afro (Euro mix).

Sep 91. (cd/d-lp)(c) *(FACD/FACT 322)(FAC 322C)* **LIVE** (live BABY BIG HEAD Bootleg album) [21] [-]
– Hallelujah / Donovan / Kinky Afro / Clap your hands / Loose fit / Holiday / Rave on / E / Tokoloshe man / Dennis and Lois / God's cop / Step on / W.F.L. *(d-lp+=)(c+=)* – Bob's your uncle.

Nov 91. (12"/7"/c-s) *(FAC 332/+7/C)* **JUDGE FUDGE. / TOKOLOSHE MAN** [24] [ ]
(cd-s+=) *(FACD 332)* – ('A'version).

Sep 92. (7"/c-s) *(FAC 362 7/C)* **STINKIN' THINKIN'. / ('A'-Boys Own mix)** [31] [ ]
(12"+=/cd-s+=) *(FAC/+D 362)* – ('A'-Terry Farley mix) / Baby bighead.

Oct 92. (cd/lp)(c) *(FACD/FACT 420)(FAC 420C)* **. . . YES PLEASE!** [14] [ ]
– Stinkin' thinkin' / Monkey in the family / Sunshine & love / Dustman / Angel / Cut 'em loose Bruce / Theme from Netto / Love child / Total Ringo / Cowboy Dave.

Nov 92. (7"/c-s) *(FAC 372 7/C)* **SUNSHINE & LOVE. / STAYING ALIVE (mix) / TWENTY FOUR HOUR PARTY PEOPLE (remix)** [62] [ ]
(12"+=/cd-s+=) *(FAC/+D 372)* – ('A'dance mix).

—— They disbanded early '93, with SHAUN and other two briefly forming The MONDAYS, which evolved into BLACK GRAPE.

– compilations, etc. –

May 90. (12"ep/c-ep/cd-ep) *Strange Fruit; (SFPS/+C/CD 077)* **THE PEEL SESSION** [ ] [-]
– Tart tart / Mad Cyril / Do it better. *(cd-ep re-iss. Feb92; same)*

Nov 91. (cd-ep) *Strange Fruit;* **THE PEEL SESSION (1986)** [ ] [-]
– Freaky dancin' / Kuff dam / Olive Oil / Cob 20.

Sep 93. (cd) *Elektra;* **DOUBLE EASY: THE US SINGLES** [-] [ ]

Oct 95. (cd/c) *London; (520036-2/-4)* **LOADS** [41] [ ]
– Step on / W.F.L. / Kinky Afro / Hallelujah – MacColl mix / Mad Cyril / Lazyitis / Tokoloshe man / Loose fit / Bob's yer uncle / Judge fudge / Stinkin' thinkin' / Sunshine & love / Angel / Tart tart / Kuff dam / Twenty four hour party people. *(some cd's w/ free cd+=)* **LOADS MORE** – Lazyitis – one armed boxer mix / W.F.L. (Perfecto mix) / Bob's yer uncle (Perfecto mix) / Loose fit (Perfecto mix) / Hallelujah (Deadstock mix) / Freaky dancing / Delightful.

Pearl HARBOR & THE EXPLOSIONS

Formed: San Francisco, California, USA . . . late '78 by PEARL E. GATES. Of American-Filipino parentage, she was once a dancer/backing singer with The TUBES' live troupe before hooking up with fellow member, JANE DORNACKER, to form the musically similar LEILA & THE SNAKES. Subsequently acquiring the group's rhythm section, JOHN and HILARY STENCH, while also finding guitarist, PETER BILT, GATES initiated PEARL HARBOR & THE EXPLOSIONS. Their independently released debut single, 'DRIVIN', set the underground New Wave scene alight, leading to 'Warners' harnessing their potential and releasing an eponymous debut album late in '79. Its failure to reach the US Top 100 resulted in her band bailing out for more mainstream waters (although they did later work with CHROME), while PEARL based herself in London for the recording of a MICKEY GALLAGHER-produced solo set, 'DON'T FOLLOW ME, I'M LOST TOO' (1981). A few years laters, it emerged that the singer tied the knot with The CLASH's PAUL SIMONON, although this didn't help her musical fortunes as a final album for 'Island', 'PEARLS GALORE!' (1985), bombed!

Album rating: PEARL HARBOR & THE EXPLOSIONS (*5) / Pearl Harbor: DON'T FOLLOW ME, I'M LOST TOO (*4) / PEARLS GALORE! (*5) / HERE COMES TROUBLE (*3)

PEARL E. GATES (b. 1958, Germany) – vocals, percussion / **PETER BILT** – guitar, vocals / **HILARY STENCH** – bass, vocals / **JOHN STENCH** – drums, percussion

not iss. | 415 Records

1979. (7") *<S 0003>* **DRIVIN'. / RELEASE IT** [-] [ ]

Warners | Warners

Dec 79. (7") *<WBS 49143>* **YOU GOT IT (RELEASE IT). / BUSY LITTLE B SIDE** [-] [ ]

Jan 80. (lp) *(K 56769)* *<BSK 3404>* **PEARL HARBOR & THE EXPLOSIONS** [ ] [ ]
– Drivin' / You got it / Don't come back / Keep going / Shut up and dance / The big one / So much for love / Get a grip on yourself / Up and over.

Feb 80. (7") *<WBS 49207>* **DRIVIN'. / THE BIG ONE** [-] [ ]

Apr 80. (7") *(K 17554)* **UP AND OVER. / BUSY LITTLE B SIDE** [ ] [-]

—— now without the STENCH brothers who joined VITAL PARTS (JORMA KAUKONEN). They later became part of CHROME (DAMON EDGE, HELIOS CREED)

PEARL HARBOR

—— now apparently backed by producer, **MICKEY GALLAGHER / OTIS WATKINS** – keyboards (ex-SHAKIN' STEVENS) / **NIGEL DIXON**

Jan 81. (7") *(K 17740)* **FUJIYAMA MAMA. / NERVES** [ ] [-]

Jan 81. (lp) *(K 56885)* *<BSK 3515>* **DON'T FOLLOW ME, I'M LOST TOO** [ ] [ ]
– Alone in the dark / Fujiyama mama / Everybody's boring but my baby / You're in trouble again / Do your homework / Cowboys & Indians / Losing to you / Filipino baby / Let's go upstairs / Rough kids / Out with the girls / Heaven is gonna be empty / At the dentist.

Apr 81. (7") *(K 17781)* **COWBOYS & INDIANS. / YOU'VE GOT ME ALL WRONG** [ ] [-]

not iss. | Test Press

Jan 82. (7") *<TPB 6>* **VOODOO VOODOO. / YOU DON'T FOOL ME** [-] [ ]

Island | Island

Jul 84. (7"/10") *(IS/10IS 191)* **HULA LOVE. / PLEASE COME HOME** [ ] [ ]

Feb 85. (lp) *(ILPS 9824)* **PEARLS GALORE!** [ ] [ ]

—— PEARL E retired from the music biz

– compilations, etc. –

1996. (cd) *Backtrip;* **HERE COMES TROUBLE** [-] [ ]

HARD-ONS

Formed: Sydney, Australia . . . 1982 out of The PLEBS and The DEAD RATS, by PETER BLACK, RAY AHN and KEISH DE SILVA, all ex-patriots from Yugoslavia, Korea and Sri Lanka. A fun lovin', if not exactly PC, this bunch of Aussie ne'er do wells initially traded exclusively in the 7" single market, releasing such sniggeringly titled "classics" as 'SURFIN' ON MY FACE' and 'SUCK 'N' SWALLOW' (both from 1985). More toilet humour followed with a debut album, the enticingly named 'SMELL MY FINGER' (no relation to the GEORGE CLINTON album!), their primary school punk RAMONES meets The DEAD KENNEDYS rehashes predictably finding a loyal, largely male audience. The MACC LADS of three-chord hardcore carried on inflicting their "hilarious" compositions on a largely uninterested metal scene throughout the 80's with the likes of 'HOT FOR YOUR LOVE, BABY' (aka 'THE WORST OF THE HARD-ONS) (1987), 'DICKCHEESE' (1988), 'LOVE IS A BATTLEFIELD OF WOUNDED HEARTS' (1989), 'YUMMY!' (1991) and 'TOO FAR GONE' (1993). Apart from a split album with The STUPIDS, their most high profile outing was probably the collaboration with HENRY ROLLINS, a 1991 cover of AC/DC's 'LET THERE BE ROCK'.

Album rating: SMELL MY FINGER (*4) / HOT FOR YOUR LOVE, BABY (*4) / DICKCHEESE (*4) / LOVE IS A BATTLEFIELD OF WOUNDED HEARTS (*5) / YUMMY! (*6) / TOO FAR GONE (*4)

KEISH DE SILVA – vocals, drums / **PETER BLACK** – guitar / **RAY AHN** – bass

Vi-Nil — Big Time

1985. (7"ep) **SURFIN' ON MY FACE EP** [-] [-] Austra
1985. (7") **SUCK 'N' SWALLOW. /** [-] [-] Austra
1986. (7") **GIRL IN A SWEATER. /** [-] [-] Austra
1986. (lp) *<6040>* **SMELL MY FINGER** <US title 'THE HARD-ONS'> [-] [ ] Austra
– Buddies / Squat house / Then I kissed her / Lolipop / I farted / Dancing girls / Wog food / Think about you everyday / I heard her call my name. *(UK-iss.Sep87 on 'Waterfront'; DAMP 37)*

Vinyl Solution — Taang!

Feb 88. (lp) *(SOL 8)* **HOT FOR YOUR LOVE, BABY** (other title 'THE WORST OF THE HARD-ONS') [ ] [ ]
– All set to go / Long song for Cindy / Coffs harbour blues / School days / It's cold outside / Then I kissed her (Arabic version) / By my side / I'll come again / Fifteen / Keish's new song / From my window / Rock'n'roll all nite.
Apr 88. (lp) *(SOL 10) <26>* **DICKCHEESE** [ ] [ ]
– Made to love you / What am I supposed to do? / Oozing for pleasure / Everytime I do a fart / Get away / Pretty face / There was a time / Mickey juice / Figaro / F**k society / Yuppies sick / Something about you / All washed up / Ache to touch you / Why don't you shut up / Nerds / Got a baby / Stairway to punchbowl.
Oct 89. (lp/cd) *(SOL 19/+CD) <35>* **LOVE IS A BATTLEFIELD OF WOUNDED HEARTS** [ ] [ ]
– Don't wanna see you cry / Rejects / Chitty chitty bang bang / Been has before / You're a tease / Who do you wanna fool / Get wet / Rich scrag / Do it with you / Missing you missing me / Throw it in / Kill your mum / Made to love you / What am I 'spose to do / Everytime I do a fart / Get away / Pretty face.

—— in 1989, split an album with The STUPIDS; 'NO CHEESE' on 'Waterfront'

Jan 91. (7") **WHERE DID SHE COME FROM? /** [ ] [-]
Feb 91. (lp/c/cd) *(SOL 26/+C/CD)* **YUMMY!** [ ] [ ]
– Where did she come from? / Raining / Dull / Cool hand Luke / Something I don't want to do / Sit beside you, Jaye's song / On and on / Ain't gonna let you go / Me or you / Spew / Fade away / Little Miss Evil / Wait around / Feast on flash / Stairway to Heaven.
Jul 91. (12"/cd-s/<7"> HENRY ROLLINS & The HARD-ONS) *(VS 30/+CD) <CZ 035>* **LET THERE BE ROCK. / CARRY ME DOWN** [ ] [ ]
Sep 91. (12"ep/cd-ep) **DULL EP** [ ] [-]

Survival — Skene

Sep 93. (lp/cd) *(SUR 538/+CD) <29>* **TOO FAR GONE** [ ] [ ]
– Crazy crazy eyes / Notice me / If it makes you happy / Carphone / Test / I do I do I do / Lost / Blade / No one can stop you / Cat scan / If she only knew / It's up to me / Stressed out / Sleepy.

—— above was their last release, although they shared a single with The CELIBATE RIFLES, 'WHERE THE THINGS ARE' on 'Waterfront'

HARMONY ROCKETS (see under ⇒ MERCURY REV)

Charlie HARPER (see under ⇒ UK SUBS)

Jerry HARRISON (see under ⇒ TALKING HEADS)

Deborah / Debbie HARRY (see under ⇒ BLONDIE)

HARRY CREWS (see under ⇒ LUNCH, Lydia)

Grant HART (see under ⇒ HUSKER DU)

PJ HARVEY

Born: POLLY JEAN HARVEY, 9 Oct'69, Corscombe, nr.Yeovil, England. Born to music-loving hippie parents, HARVEY was acquainted with music and musicians from an early age. Her first songwriting experience was with rootsy outfit The POLEKATS, HARVEY later joining Somerset-based group AUTOMATIC DLAMINI, who had been around for some five years. Numbered in their ranks were ROBERT ELLIS on drums, JOHN PARISH (ex-THIEVES LIKE US) on guitar and vocals (both ex-HEADLESS HORSEMEN; alongside bassist DAVE DALLIMORE). With bassist JAMIE ANDERSON, they finally released a well-received debut EP, 'THE CRAZY SUPPER', in June '86 on the 'D For Drum' label (DLAM 1). PARISH also went into production work for The CHESTERFIELDS and BRILLIANT CORNERS. Early members of AUTOMATIC DLAMINI included ex-CLEANERS FROM VENUS keyboard man and future rock critic GILES SMITH, and IAN OLLIVER. 1987 was their busiest year, releasing a single, 'I DON'T KNOW YOU BUT . . .' / 'I'VE NEVER BEEN THAT COLOUR ANYWHERE BEFORE' (DLAM 2) / 7"+12" 'ME AND MY CONSCIENCE' for 'Idea' (IDEA+T 009), and album, 'THE D IS FOR DRUM' (on 'Idea' IDEALP 001). ELLIS departed soon after and POLLY finally convinced PARISH to let her play guitar, sax and contribute backing vocals. Unfortunately, recordings (i.e. 12" 'WATER', an album, 'HERE CATCH SHOUTED HIS FATHER') didn't quite reach the retail stage. In August 1992, the group released 'FROM A DIVA TO A DIVER' (BOT/+CD 04), after which PARISH took time out to produce WALL OF VOODOO and play with ENSENADA JOYRIDE, whose 'Hey Lady' POLLY has always wanted to cover. She then turned up on GRAPE's single 'BABY IN A PLASTIC BAG' and two tracks by The FAMILY CAT; 'COLOUR ME GREY' and 'RIVER OF DIAMONDS'. With ELLIS and OLLIVER, she had already formed PJ HARVEY in 1991, and they signed for 'Too Pure'. With POLLY on vocals, their first release, 'DRESS', immediately caught the attention of JOHN PEEL and achieved the dubious honour of a Melody Maker single of the week. A driving, primal howl of a record, it introduced HARVEY's lyrical preoccupation with the darker corners of female sexuality, a theme continued with 'SHEELA-NA-GIG' (without OLLIVER who was subsequently replaced by STEPHEN VAUGHAN) in early '92. The single hit the UK Top 75 and and there was enough of a buzz around the band for the debut album, 'DRY', to reach the fringes of the Top 10. HARVEY's impact had been immediate, her raw, defiantly individual interpretation of feminism sparking much debate in the music press, especially after an NME cover shot in which she appeared topless, back to the camera. Signing to 'Island', PJ HARVEY began work on the Steve Albini (ex-BIG BLACK)-produced follow-up, 'RID OF ME', which went Top 3 upon its release in the Spring of '93. As one might expect from the man who gave us 'Songs About Fucking', Albini's production didn't exactly make for an easy listen, HARVEY turning in her most ferocious performance to date. With the likes of 'LEGS', 'MAN SIZE' and 'RUB TILL IT BLEEDS', the singer continued to explore the contradictory and unsavoury aspects of sexuality/relationships with unparallelled feminine fury. Following the departure of ROB ELLIS, HARVEY assembled a backing band that includued JOHN PARRISH (guitar, ex-AUTOMATIC DLAMINI), NICK BAGNALL (keyboards/bass), JOE GORE (guitar) and ERIC FELDMAN (keyboards) and JEAN-MARC BUTTY (drums). In 1995, with FLOOD and BAD SEED, MICK HARVEY on production duties, she/they unleashed HARVEY's finest work to date, 'TO BRING YOU MY LOVE', which also hit the US Top 40 and was nominated for a UK "Mercury" award. A more balanced affair, HARVEY's dark rage chose to simmer below the surface this time around, creating the feeling of creeping unease that runs through much of NICK CAVE's work (her new acquaintance!?). In 1996, she gave JOHN PARISH a full credit on their dual album 'DANCE HALL AT LOUSE POINT', which sold relatively poorly. • **Songwriters:** POLLY, and covers; HIGHWAY 61 (Bob Dylan) / DADDY (Willie Dixon) / BALLAD OF THE SOLDIER'S WIFE (Kurt Weill).

Album rating: DRY (*9) / RID OF ME (*8) / TO BRING YOU MY LOVE (*9) / DANCE HALL AT LOUSE POINT with John Parish (*5) / IS THIS DESIRE (*6)

POLLY HARVEY – vocals, guitar, cello, violin, organ / **IAN OLLIVER** – bass / **ROBERT ELLIS** (b.13 Feb'62, Bristol, England) – drums, vocals

Too Pure — Indigo

Oct 91. (12"ep) *(PURE 5)* **DRESS. / WATER (demo) / DRY (demo)** [ ] [-]
(cd-iss. Mar92; PURECD 5)

—— **STEPHEN VAUGHAN** (b.22 Jun'62, Wolverhampton, England) – bass repl. OLLIVER who returned to brief reformation of AUTOMATIC DLAMINI

Feb 92. (7"ltd.) *(PURE S8)* **SHEELA-NA-GIG. / JOE (demo)** [69] [-]
(12"+=/cd-s+=) *(PURE 8/+CD)* – Hair (demo).
Mar 92. (lp/cd/s-lp) *(PURE 10/+CD/D) <ING 5001>* **DRY** [11] [ ] Jun92
– Oh my lover / O Stella / Dress / Victory / Happy and bleeding / Sheela-na-gig / Hair / Joe / Plants and rags / Fountain water. *(s-lp w/ free 'Demonstration' lp; PURED 10)*

Island — Island

Apr 93. (7"/c-s) *(IS/CIS 538)* **50FT QUEENIE. / REELING / MAN-SIZE (demo)** [27] [-]
(12"+=/cd-s+=) *(12IS/CID 538)* – Hook (demo).
Apr 93. (cd/c/lp) *(CID/ICT/ILPS 8002) <514696>* **RID OF ME** [3] [ ] May93
– Rid of me / Missed / Legs / Rub 'til it bleeds / Hook / Man-size sextet / Highway '61 revisited / 50ft Queenie / Yuri-G / Man-size / Dry / Me-Jane / Snake / Ecstasy.

Jul 93. (12"ep/cd-ep) *(12IS/CID 569)* **MAN-SIZE. / WANG DANG DOODLE / DADDY** [42] [-]

— drummer ELLIS departed after above.

Oct 93. (cd/c/lp) *(IMCD/ICT/ILPM 2079) <518450>* **4-TRACK DEMOS** (demos) [19] [ ] Nov93
– Rid of me / Legs / Reeling / Snake / Hook / 50ft Queenie / Driving / Ecstasy / Hardly wait / Rub 'til it bleeds / Easy / M-bike / Yuri-G / Goodnight.

— POLLY now with **JOHN PARISH** – drums, guitar / **JOE GORE** (b. San Francisco) – guitar (ex-TOM WAITS) / **NICK BAGNALL** – keyboards, bass / **ERIC FELDMAN** (b. San Francisco) – keyboards (ex-CAPTAIN BEEFEART) / **JEAN-MARC BUTTY** (b. France) – drums

Feb 95. (7"ep/12"ep/cd-ep) *(IS/12IS/CID 607)* **DOWN BY THE WATER. / LYING IN THE SUN / SOMEBODY'S DOWN, SOMEBODY'S NAME** [38] [-]

Feb 95. (cd/c/lp) *(CID/ICT/ILPS 8035) <524085>* **TO BRING YOU MY LOVE** [12] [40]
– To bring you my love / Meet ze monsta / Working for the man / C'mon Billy / Teclo / Long snake moan / Down by the water / I think I'm a mother / Send his love to me / The dancer. *(re-iss. d-cd Dec95 w/ extra B-sides; CIDZ 8035)*

Jul 95. (12"/cd-s) *(12IS/CID 614)* **C'MON BILLY. / DARLING BE THERE / MANIAC** [29] [-]
(cd-s+=) *(CIDX 614)* – One time too many.

Oct 95. (7"pic-d) *(IS 610)* **SEND HIS LOVE TO ME. / LONG TIME COMING (session)** [34] [-]
(cd-s+=) *(CID 610)* – Harder.
(cd-s) *(CIDX 610)* – ('A'side) / Hook (live) / Water (live).

— Enjoyed more chart success on duet with NICK CAVE; 'Henry Lee' single released early '96.

JOHN PARISH & POLLY JEAN HARVEY

— with **JEREMY HOGG** – guitar / **ERIC DREW FELDMAN** – bass, keyboards (ex-CAPTAIN BEEFHEART) / **ROB ELLIS** – drums

Island Island

Sep 96. (cd/c/lp) *(CID/ICT/ILPS 8051) <524278>* **DANCE HALL AT LOUSE POINT** [46] [ ]
– Girl / Rope bridge crossing / City of no sun / That was my veil / Urn with dead flowers in a drained pool / Civil war correspondent / Taut / Un cercle autour du soleil / Heela / Is that all there is / Dance hall at Louse Point / Lost fun zone.

Nov 96. (7") *(IS 648)* **THAT WAS MY VEIL. / LOSING GROUND** [75] [-]
(12"+=/cd-s+=) *(12IS/CID 648)* – Who will love me now? / Civil war correspondent (Global Communications mix).

— ELLIS joined 'Too Pure' outfit, LAIKA

PJ HARVEY

— In 1998, she featured with TRICKY on his 'Broken Homes' single.

Island Polygram

Sep 98. (7") *(IS 718) <572408>* **A PERFECT DAY ELISE. / SWEETER THAN ANYTHING / INSTRUMENTAL #3** [25] [ ] Oct98
(cd-s) *(CID 718)* – (first & third tracks) / The Northwood.
(cd-s) *(CIDX 718)* – (first two tracks) / The bay.

Sep 98. (cd/c/lp) *(CID/ICT/ILPS 8076) <524563>* **IS THIS DESIRE?** [17] [54]
– Angelene / Sky lit up / Wind / My beautiful Leah / A perfect day Elise / Catherine / Electric light / Garden / Joy / River / No girl so sweet / Is this desire?

HARVEY DANGER

Formed: Seattle, Washington, USA ... 1991 by local students SEAN NELSON, JEFF J. LINN, AARON HUFFMAN and EVAN SULT. The lads played grunge covers at local parties until 1996 when producer John Goodmanson was drafted in to flesh out their alt-rock sound. A debut album, 'WHERE HAVE ALL THE MERRYMAKERS GONE?', was originally issued on New York's indie imprint 'Arena Rock' in 1997 before the quartet were picked up by 'Slash' the following year. Summer '98 saw HARVEY DANGER make their UK debut with the Top 60 'FLAGPOLE SITTA' single, a bouncy but lyrically barbed geek-rock effort with a melodic singalong factor in the vein of the dB's and the REPLACEMENTS. The album had already been re-issued a month earlier in the States where its slow-burning chart progress eventually saw it broach the Top 70.

Album rating: WHERE HAVE ALL THE MERRYMAKERS GONE? (*6)

SEAN NELSON – vocals / **JEFF J. LIN** – guitar / **AARON HUFFMAN** – bass / **EVAN SULT** – drums

Slash Slash

Jul 98. (7"/c-s) *(LASH/LASCS 64) <570261>* **FLAGPOLE SITTA. / WRECKING BALL** [57] [ ] Sep98
(cd-s+=) *(LASCD 64)* – The ballad of the tragic hero (pity and fear).

Aug 98. (cd) *(314-556 000-2) <55600>* **WHERE HAVE ALL THE MERRYMAKERS GONE?** [ ] [70] Jun98
– Carlotta Valdez / Flagpole sitta / Woolly muffler / Private helicopter / Problems and bigger ones / Jack the lion / Old hat / Terminal annex / Wrecking ball / Radio silence. *(originally iss.May97 on 'Arena Rock'; AR 006)*

Juliana HATFIELD

Born: 27 Jul'67, Wiscasset, Maine, USA. After fronting a high school covers band, HATFIELD met her future musical collaborators, JOHN STROHM and FREDA LOVE BONER, while studying at Boston's Berklee College of Music. The trio subsequently formed The BLAKE BABIES, releasing a debut mini-set, 'NICELY, NICELY' (1987), on the independent 'Chewbud' label (licensed to BILLY BRAGG's 'Utility' imprint in the UK). Not straying too far from the established Boston sound, the group's indie strumming brought comparisons with early R.E.M. and THROWING MUSES, although HATFIELD's distinctive girly vocals marked them out from the pack. The LEMONHEADS connection was there from the start, STROHM having previously played alongside EVAN DANDO and Co.; DANDO became a BLAKE BABY temporarily for a second mini-set, 'SLOW LEARNER' (1989), before returing to The LEMONHEADS as a drummer. Signing with 'Mammoth', The BLAKE BABIES subsequently released a full length set, 'EARWIG' (1990), an expanded version of their earlier release, while a follow-up, 'SUNBURN' (1992), upped the grunge factor and increased their already burgeoning college fanbase. After a further mini-set, the acclaimed 'ROSY JACK WORLD' (1992), the band surprised the music press by announcing a split; HATFIELD sang and played on The LEMONHEADS' breakthrough set, 'It's A Shame About Ray' (1992) album, before cutting her own solo album, 'HEY BABE', the same year. Despite the record's merits, the press were more concerned with the nitty gritty of her much publicised relationship with DANDO and the revelation that she was still a virgin at 25. Undeterred, the singer formed The JULIANA HATFIELD THREE (along with DEAN FISHER and TODD PHILIPS), signed to 'East West' and released a second solo set, 'BECOME WHAT YOU ARE' (1993), developing her hard-edged GO-GO's sound against lyrics which were as disarmingly angst-ridden as ever. A third set, 'ONLY EVERYTHING' (1995), packed more of a punch although its downbeat tone was obviously symptomatic of HATFIELD's continuing struggles; mirroring the personal strife of former beau, DANDO, HATFIELD suffered a nervous breakdown later that year. After an album ('GOD'S FOOT') was shelved by 'Mammoth', she severed ties with the label and returned in '97 with a six-song mini-set, 'PLEASE DO NOT DISTURB', a stopgap until her first full-set for three years, 'BED' (1998). • **BLAKE BABIES covered:** TEMPTATION (Grass Roots) / SEVERED LIPS (Dinosaur Jr).

Album rating: Blake Babies: NICELY, NICELY mini (*6) / EARWIG (*7) / SUNBURN (*7) / ROSY JACK WORLD (*5) / INNOCENCE AND EXPERIENCE compilation (*8) / Juliana Hatfield: HEY BABE (*8) / BECOME WHAT YOU ARE (*7) / ONLY EVERYTHING (*6) / BED (*5)

BLAKE BABIES

JULIANA HATFIELD – vocals, guitar / **JOHN STROHM** (b.23 Mar'67, Bloomington, Indiana) – guitar (of-LEMONHEADS) / **FREDA LOVE BONER** (b. 3 ep'67, Nashville, Tennessee) – drums

Utility Chewbud

Dec 87. (m-lp) *<CBTW-001>* **NICELY, NICELY** [-] [ ]
– Wipe it up / Her / Tom & Bob / A sweet burger lp / Bye / Let them eat chewy granola bars / Julius fast body / Better'n'you / Swill and the cocaine sluts. *(UK-iss.Oct94 on 'Mammoth' cd/c; MR 0086-2/-4)*

— added **EVAN DANDO** – bass, vocals (of-LEMONHEADS)

Jul 89. (m-lp/cd) *(UTIL/UTICD 6)* **SLOW LEARNER** [ ] [-]
– Lament / Grateful / Your way or the highway / Take your head off my shoulder / Rain / From here to Burma / Putta my head. *(re-iss. Mar93 as 'BLAKE BABIES' cd/lp; same)*

— now without DANDO who returned to The LEMONHEADS as drummer!

Mammoth Mammoth

Mar 90. (cd/lp) *<(MR 0016-2/-1)>* **EARWIG** [ ] [ ] 1989
– Cesspool / Dead and gone / Grateful you / You don't give up / Your way on the highway / Rain / Lament / Alright / Loose / Take your head off my shoulder / From here to Burma / Don't suck my breath / Outta my head / Steamy Gregg / Not just a wish. *(cd-iss. Oct92; same)*

Mar 92. (cd/lp) *<(MR 0022-2/-1)>* **SUNBURN** [ ] [ ] 1990
– I'm not your mother / Out there / Star / Look away / Sanctify / Girl in a box / Train / I'll take anything / Watch me now I'm calling / Gimme some mirth / Kiss and make up / A million years.

Nov 92. (m-cd/m-lp) *<(MR 0025-2/-1)>* **ROSY JACK WORLD** [ ] [ ] Jun91
– Rosy Jack world / Temptation eyes / Downtime / Take me / Nirvana.

— HATFIELD joined The LEMONHEADS on mid-92 album 'IT'S A SHAME ABOUT RAY', before forming The JULIANA HATFIELD three. STROHM and BONER had already formed ANTENNA, who released for same label 'SWAY' album mid-92 and eponymous album Mar93.

– compilations, etc. –

Oct 93. (cd) *Mammoth; <(MR 0058-2)>* **INNOCENCE AND EXPERIENCE** [ ] [ ]
– Wipe it up / Rain / Boiled potato / Lament / Cesspool / You don't give up / Star / Sanctify / Out there / Girl in a box / I'm not your mother / Temptation eyes / Downtime / Over and over.

JULIANA HATFIELD

— with **EVAN DANDO + JOHN WESLEY HARDING** (b. WESLEY HARDING STACE, 22 Oct'65, Hastings, England) – guitar, vocals

Mammoth Mammoth

Jul 92. (12"ep/cd-ep) *<MR 0041-1/-2>* **FOREVER BABY / NIRVANA / EVERYBODY LOVES ME BUT YOU. / RAISANS / TAMARA** [-] [ ]

Aug 92. (cd/c/lp) *<(MR 0035-2/-4/-1)>* **HEY BABE** [ ] [ ] Mar92
– Everybody loves me but you / Lost and saved / I see you / The lights / Nirvana / Forever baby / Ugly / No outlet / Quit / Get off your knees / No answer.

Nov 92. (12"ep/cd-ep) *<(MR 0045-1/-2)>* **I SEE YOU / UGLY RIDER. / HERE COMES THE PAIN / FEED ME** [ ] [ ]

JULIANA HATFIELD three

— **JULIANA HATFIELD** – vocals, guitar / **DEAN FISHER** – bass / **TODD PHILIPS** – drums (ex-BULLET LaVOLTA)

— guests **PETER HOLSAPPLE** – keyboards (ex-dB's) / **DENNY FONGHEISER** – percussion ('Mammoth' now taken over by the majors)

East West / Atco

Aug 93. (cd/lp) <(4509 93529-2/-1)> **BECOME WHAT YOU ARE** 44 □
– Supermodel / My sister / This is the sound / For the birds / Mabel / A dame with a rod / Addicted / Feelin' Massachusetts / Spin the bottle / President Garfield / Little pieces / I got no idols.

Sep 93. (7"/c-s) *(YZ 767/+C)* **MY SISTER. / PUT IT AWAY** 71 □
(10"+=/cd-s+=) *(YZ 767 T/CD)* – A dame with a rod (demo) / Ruthless.

Nov 93. (7"ep/c-ep/10"ep/cd-ep) *(YZ 791/+C/EP/CD)* **FOR THE BIRDS / HELLO, MY NAME IS BABY. / I GOT NO IDOLS)piano version) / BATWING** □ □

Aug 94. (c-s) *(YZ 819C)* **SPIN THE BOTTLE / MY DARLING** □ -
(10"+=/cd-s+=) *(YZ 819 TE/CD)* – My sister (acoustic) / Nirvana.

Nov 94. (c-s) <64207> **SPIN THE BOTTLE / (track by Ethan Hawke)** - 97
(above issued US on 'RCA', and from the film 'Reality Bites')

Mar 95. (c-s) *(YZ 916C)* **UNIVERSAL HEART-BEAT / GIRL IN OLD BLUE VOLVO DISOWNS SELF** 65 -
(10"+=/cd-s+=) *(YZ 916 TE/CD)* – Where would I be without you / Yardsailing.

Mar 95. (c-s) <98179> **UNIVERSAL HEART-BEAT / WHERE WOULD I BE WITHOUT YOU** - 84

Mar 95. (cd/c) <(4509 99886-2/-4)> **ONLY EVERYTHING** 59 □
– What a life / Fleur de lys / Universal heart-beat / Dumb fun / Live on tomorrow / Dying proof / Bottles and flowers / Outsider / Ok Ok / Congratulations / Hang down from Heaven / My darling / Simplicity is beautiful / You blues.

— In August '95, JULIANA suffered a nervous breakdown and took a break from the music business until '97

— now with **MIKE LEAHY** – guitar / **TODD PHILIPS** – drums

not iss. / Bar/None

Oct 97. (m-cd) <100> **PLEASE DO NOT DISTURB** - □
– Sellout / Trying not to think about it / As if your life depended on it / Give me some of that / Get off / Edge of nowhere.

not iss. / Zoe

Aug 98. (cd.c) <431001> **BED** - □
– Down on me / I want to want you / Swan song / Sneaking around / Backseat / Live it up / You are the camera / Running out / Bad day / Let's blow it all.

HAYDEN

Born: HAYDEN DESSER, 1971, Toronto, Ontario, Canada. This enigmatic and wilfully obscure singer/songwriter caused something of a stir on the alt-country underground with his debut set, 'EVERYTHING I LONG FOR', drawing comparisons to the likes of WILL OLDHAM, BECK and HOWIE GELB. Initially released on tiny Canadian label, 'Hardwood/Sonic Unyon', the record was a hauntingly downbeat trawl through torn and frayed acoustic Americana with occasional bouts of grizzled grunge, all set, of course, to a lyrical world view of gritted-teeth realism/miserabilism. Vocally, the man occasionally sounded like he'd been gargling with razorblades yet it was difficult to ignore the high, lonesome spectre of NEIL YOUNG throughout the record, especially bearing in mind the Toronto connection. Although HAYDEN subsequently signed a worldwide deal with MCA offshoot label, 'Outpost', (possibly) the most mysterious man in the alt-country canon released follow-up set, 'MOVING CAREFUL', on the 'Sonic Unyon' imprint later the same year.

Album rating: EVERYTHING I LONG FOR (*7)

HAYDEN – vocals, guitar, piano / with **JOAO CARVALHO** (some) drums

M.C.A. / Outpost-MCA

May 96. (cd/c) <(OPD/OPC 30000)> **EVERYTHING I LONG FOR** □ □
– Bad as they seem / In September / We don't mind / Tragedy / Stem / Skates / I'm to blame / Assignment in space with Rip Foster / Driveway / Hardly / You were loved / When this is over / My parent's house / Lounging.

— (orig.iss.1995 in Canada on 'Hardwood-Sonic Unyon')

Sonic Unyon / Sonic Unyon

Dec 96. (cd) <(SUNCD 032)> **MOVING CAREFUL** □ □ May97
– Pots and pans / Stride / Middle of July / Old fashioned way / Half of me / Choking / You are all I have.

— with a plethora of session people

Outpost / Outpost-MCA

May 98. (cd) <30006> **THE CLOSER I GET** □ □
– The closer I get / Stride / Hazards of sitting beneath palm trees / Bullet / Waiting for a chance to see her / Two doors / Between us to hold / Better off inside / Instrumental with mellotron / Memphis / Nights like these / You are all I have / I'll tell him tonight.

Charles HAYWARD (see under ⇒ THIS HEAT)

HAZELDINE

Formed: Albuquerque, New Mexico . . . mid 90's by the songwriting team of TONYA LAMM and SHAWN BARTON alongside JEFFREY RICHARDS, ANNE TKACH and DAVE SINCLAIR. If sensual, feminine country-rock seems a contradiction in terms, HAZELDINE aren't too concerned right now; a knack for penning goosebump melodies combined with a refreshingly risque attitude to lyric writing has seen this combo avoid both the airbrushed sterility of Nashville central and the beery laddishness of some alt-country. Initially signed to Germany's alt-country stalwart, 'Glitterhouse', the group debuted with '97's 'HOW BEES FLY', an album that featured two covers, Eric Trip's 'ALLERGIC TO LOVE' and Grant Lee Buffalo's 'FUZZY'. Having built up a sizeable fanbase on the continent, the band subsequently secured a major deal with 'Polydor'. 1998 saw the release of a covers set, 'ORPHANS' and a track, 'TARMAC' (from their debut), included on the sterling 'Uncut' magazine compilation, 'Sounds Of The New West' (a perfect beginner's guide to the genre). With a new four-track EP in the shops for Christmas, 'SUMMER WINE' (LEE/NANCY cover), there's absolutely no excuse for confusing HAZELDINE with HAZEL DEAN, even with the imminent catastrophe of an 80's revival! • **The covers:** APRIL 8th (Jeff Mangum) / HEART OF DARKNESS (Sparklehorse) / CUCKOO COCOON (Genesis) / HERE WE GO (East River Pipe) / LUCKY (Radiohead) / WHISKEY IN THE JAR (hit; Thin Lizzy) / SONG FOR YOU (Gram Parsons), etc.

Album rating: HOW BEES FLY (*8) / ORPHANS (*5)

TONYA LAMM – vocals, acoustic guitar / **SHAWN BARTON** – vocals, acoustic guitar / **JEFFREY RICHARDS** – guitar / **ANNE TKACH** – bass / **DAVE SINCLAIR** – drums

Glitterhouse / not iss.

Jul 97. (cd) *(GRCD 416)* **HOW BEES FLY** □ -
– Apothecary / Tarmac / My Magdalene / Yer shoes / Allergic to love / Rosemary cries / Fuzzy / Daddy / Bastard son of Medora / Postcard.

Polydor / E Squared

Oct 98. (cd) <51063> **ORPHANS** - □
– Moning camp blues / Wild and blue / April 8th / Cuckoo cocoon / Here we go / Lucky / It's only love / Heart of darkness / Whiskey in the jar / Song for you.

Dec 98. (cd-ep) **SUMMER WINE** □ -

Jowe HEAD (see under ⇒ SWELL MAPS)

Michael HEAD (see under ⇒ PALE FOUNTAINS)

Thee HEADCOATS (see under ⇒ CHILDISH, Wild Billy)

HEADS (see under ⇒ TALKING HEADS)

HEARTBREAKERS (see under ⇒ THUNDERS, Johnny)

HEART THROBS

Formed: Reading, England . . . 1986 by ROSE CARLOTTI and fellow residential college student, STEPHEN WARD. The pair were subsequently joined by ROSE's sister, RACHAEL DeFREITAS and MARK SIDE, releasing the 'TOY' single as their debut for 'In-Tape' a year later. Moving on to 'Rough Trade', The HEART THROBS released a further two 45's, promoting the car crash-themed 'BANG' on a support jaunt to the JESUS & MARY CHAIN. Naming their own label, 'Profumo', after the infamous 60's political sex scandal, the seductive quartet self-financed another two singles, 'HERE I HIDE' and 'BLOOD FROM A STONE'; ROSE was controversially snapped CHRISTINE KEELER-like for promo shots! At the turn of the decade, however, ROSE and RACHEL were to suffer tragedy when their brother, PETE DeFRIETAS (of ECHO & THE BUNNYMEN), died in a road accident. Happier times were ahead though, as the group signed a fresh record deal with 'One Little Indian' ('Elektra' in the States), their long awaited GIL NORTON-produced debut album, 'CLEOPATRA'S GRIP', finally arriving in 1990. By this time, guitarist ALAN BARCLAY had been added, although a further period of upheaval saw the band being dropped by both 'Elektra' and their successors 'A&M'. Former PARACHUTE MEN bassist, COLEEN BROWNE, was drafted in to replace RACHEL, making her first appearance on the largely disappointing follow-up set, 'JUBILEE TWIST' (1992). Their third and final long-player, 'VERTICAL SMILE' (1993), was a marked improvement, its title apparently a genital reminder of The HEART THROBS' naughty and unique appeal. • **Covered:** PUMPING MY HEART (Patti Smith).

Album rating: CLEOPATRA GRIP (*6) / JUBILEE TWIST (*5) / VERTICAL SMILE (*6)

ROSE CARLOTTI (b. ROSEMARIE DeFREITAS, 16 Dec'63, Barbados) – vocals, guitar / **RACHAEL DeFREITAS** (b.25 May'66, Reading) – bass / **STEPHEN WARD** (b.19 Apr'63, Chelmsford, England) – guitar, vocals / **MARK SIDE** (b.24 Jun'69, Reading) – drums

In-Tape / not iss.

Jul 87. (7") *(IT 043)* **TOY. / MAKE MY DAY** □ -
(12"+=) *(ITT 043)* – I, the jury.

Rough Trade / not iss.

Oct 87. (12"ep) *(RTT 211)* **BANG. / SICK AT HEART / NAKED BANG** □ -

Jun 88. (7"/12"blue) *(RT/+T 221)* **TOO MANY SHADOWS. / ?** □ -

Profumo / not iss.

Oct 88. (7"/12") *(PROS/+T 1)* **HERE I HIDE. / PALE FACE** □ -

Feb 89. (7") *(PROS 2)* **BLOOD FROM A STONE. / BECAUSE IT'S BEAUTIFUL** □ -
(12"+=) *(PROST 2)* – Smothered.

— added **ALAN BARCLAY** (b. 4 Apr'68, Singapore) – guitar

One Little Indian / Elektra

Feb 90. (7") *(33 TP)* **I WONDER WHY. / ?** □ -
(12"+=/cd-s+=) *(12TP/TPCD 33)* –

May 90. (7") *(39 TP)* **DREAMTIME. / SHUTDOWN** □ -

(12"+=/cd-s+=) *(12/CD 39TP)* –
Jul 90. (lp/c/cd) *(TPLP 23/+C/CD) <60961>* **CLEOPATRA'S GRIP**
– Tossed away / Dreamtime / Big commotion / In vain / Slip and slide / Here I hide / Calavera / I wonder why / Trance / Blood from a stone / Kiss me when I'm starving / White laughter.
Oct 91. (12"ep/cd-ep) *(50 TP12/TP7CD)* **TOTAL ABANDON / PUMPING MY HEART. / + 2** | -
Mar 92. (7"ep/12"ep/cd-ep) *(60 TP7/TP12/TP7CD)* **SPONGY THING EP** | -
– So far / Hooligan / Laughing & falling / Kiss me when I'm starving (Mastodon mix).
— above with guests; NOKO – bass / STEVE MONTI – drums
— **COLEEN BROWNE** (b.25 Aug'66, Kelowna, Canada) – bass (ex-PARACHUTE MEN) repl. RACHE

One Little Indian | A&M

May 92. (7"ep/cd-ep) *(70 TP7/+CD)* **SHE'S IN A TRANCE / DREAMTIME (Martin Hannett remix). / IN VAIN (acoustic) / GIRL BECAME THE STAIRS (acoustic) / KISS ME WHEN I'M STARVING (acoustic)** | -
(12"+=) *(70 TP12SP)* – ('A'-Mark Saunders remix).
(12"+=/cd-s+=) *(70 TP12/TP7CD)* – ('A'-Martin Hannett remix) / ('A'-Mutations mix).
Jun 92. (lp/c/cd) *(TPLP 33/+C/CD) <75021 5399-1/-4/-2>* **JUBILEE TWIST**
– Tiny feet / Winter came too soon / Hooligan / Outside / The girl became the stairs / So far / Bright green day / Too late / Tuna / Gone.
Apr 93. (12"ep/cd-ep) *(80 TP12/TP7CD)* **WORSER / AVALANCHE. / WE CONNECT / VISIONARY SONG** | -
Jun 93. (lp/c/2xcd) *(TPLP 43/+C/CD)* **VERTICAL SMILE** | -
– Perry said / Stunned / Love is stretching / Incense of you / Avalanche / Brood bitch / Apple pie / Tranquilised, naked and shy / Go / Solemn child / Worser.
— split after above, BROWNE subsequently joined The PALE SAINTS

Reverend Horton HEAT

Born: JIM HEATH, Corpus Christi, Dallas, Texas. Initially conceived as a one-off gospel send-up, the hick REVEREND scoured the proverbial music biz congregation for a rhythm section of JIMBO WALLACE and TAZ BENTLEY. A hard-drinking, pot-smoking, card-gambling, women-chasing, bar-brawling kinda guy, The REVEREND's high-octane, CRAMPS-esque punkabilly sermons presented him as the 'Sub Pop' generation's answer to 50's wildman, JERRY LEE LEWIS. The preacher man's vinyl Christening, 'SMOKE 'EM IF YOU GOT 'EM', certainly kicked up an unholy racket upon its release late in '91, whipping his boys into a beer-soaked rock'n'roll frenzy. The musical equivalent of tearing down Route 66 in a stolen Cadillac convertable high on Jack Daniels and Holy Water, 1993's 'THE FULL CUSTOM GOSPEL SOUNDS' even outstripped most of his heathen peers in the alternative/grunge sphere; the trio (with SCOTT CHURILLA replacing TAZ) were to support SOUNDGARDEN in '94. Subsequently making a pact with the Dev.. sorry, 'Interscope', The REV's next ten commandments (well er, thirteen actually!) came in the shape of the AL JOURGENSEN-produced 'LIQUOR IN THE FRONT' (1994), although the title was surely open to interpretation. Finally getting through to the non-believers and sinners among the American public, the REV hit the US Top 200 with his 1996 set, 'IT'S MARTINI TIME' (containing a cover of Bill Haley's 'ROCK THE JOINT'), a record that critically fell on its knees and suggested that the drink-saddled HEAT was in need of a bit of musical "heeeeaaling" himself. Likewise, 1998's 'SPACE HEATER', indicated that the REVEREND's reliable but increasingly predictable brand of metallic rockabilly was closer to anachronism than evangelism – praise the Lord!

Album rating: SMOKE 'EM IF YOU GOT 'EM (*7) / THE FULL CUSTOM GOSPEL SOUNDS (*8) / LIQUOR IN THE FRONT (*6) / IT'S MARTINI TIME (*4) / SPACE HEATER (*5)

REVEREND HORTON HEAT (b. JIM HEATH) – vocals, guitar / **JIMBO WALLACE** – stand-up bass / **TAZ BENTLEY** – drums

Sub Pop | Sub Pop

Dec 90. (7",7"blue) *(<SP 96>)* **PSYCHOBILLY FREAKOUT. / BABY YOU-KNOW-WHO**
Nov 91. (10"lp,c,cd) *<(SP 25-177)>* **SMOKE 'EM IF YOU GOT 'EM**
– Bullet / I'm mad / Bad reputation / Put it to me straight / Marijuana / Baby, you-know-who / Eat steak / Love whip. *(cd+=/c+=)* – It's a dark day / Big dwarf rodeo / Psychobilly freakout / D for Dangerous.
Apr 93. (lp/cd) *(SP/+CD 248) <SP 202/+B>* **THE FULL CUSTOM GOSPEL SOUNDS**
– Wiggle stick / 400 bucks / The Devil's chasing me / Livin' on the edge (of Houston) / You can't get away from me / Beer / Big little baby / Lonesome train whistle / Bales of cocaine / Loaded gun / Nurture my pig! / Gin and tonic blues. *(cd re-iss. Sep98; same as US)*
May 94. (7") *<(SP 125-308)>* **CALIENTE. / (other side by SUPERSUCKERS)**
— **SCOTT CHURILLA** – drums; repl. TAZ

Interscope | Interscope

Jul 94. (cd/c) *<(6544 92364-2/-4)>* **LIQUOR IN THE FRONT**
– Big sky / Baddest of the bad / One time for me / Five-o Ford / In your wildest dreams / The entertainer / Rockin' dog / Jezebel / I can't surf / Liquor, beer and wine / I could get used to it / Cruisin' for a bruisin' / Yeah right. *(cd re-iss. Jul96; IND 92364)*
— added guests **TIM ALEXANDER** – keyboards + **DAN PHILLIPS** – steel guitar
Dec 96. (cd/c) *<(INTD 90065-2/-4)>* **IT'S MARTINI TIME** | Jul96
– Big red rocket of love / Slow / It's martini time / Generation why / Slingshot / Time to pray / Crooked cigarette / Rock the joint / Cowboy love / Now, right now / Spell on me / Or is it just me / Forbidden jungle / That's showbiz.
Sep 98. (cd) *<(INTD 90168)>* **SPACE HEATER**
– The price of San Jacinto / Lie detector / Hello Mrs. Darkness / Jimbo song / Revolution under foot / Starlight lounge / Goin' manic / Mi amor / For never more / Prophet stomp / Native tongue of love / Couch surfin' / Cinco de Mayo / Texas rock-a-billy rebel / Baby I'm drunk / Space heater.
Sep 98. (cd-s) *<(IND 97357)>* **LIE DETECTOR /**

HEATMISER (see under ⇒ SMITH, Elliott)

HEAVENLY (see under ⇒ TALULAH GOSH)

HEAVY STEREO

Formed: London-based, England . . . 1993 by songwriter GEM ARCHER, alongside PETE DOWNING, NEZ (aka NEIL) and NICK JONES. Although they spent two years at 'Food' records under a different moniker, their release sheet remained blank until they became HEAVY STEREO. Having moved from the home of BLUR to the stable of OASIS ('Creation'), they hit the Top 50 in mid '95 with the debut single, 'SLEEP FREAK'. Despite their name, the band were revealed to be glam-rock devotees influenced by BOLAN or even the SWEET. The following year saw further minor hits, 'SMILER', 'CHINESE BURN' and 'MOUSE IN A HOLE', the latter's relative failure putting paid to any commercial hopes for their debut album, 'DEJA VOODOO' (1996). Further strife befell the band at that year's Phoenix Festival (July '96), when NICK was bitten in the arm (not too seriously) by a one-legged crusty. A month later, NEZ was also attacked by an unknown assailant, suffering a broken nose, broken ribs and concussion.

Album rating: DEJA VOODOO (*6)

GEM (ARCHER) – vocals (ex-CONTENDERS, ex-WHIRLPOOL) / **PETE DOWNING** – guitar / **NEZ** (aka NEIL) – bass / **NICK JONES** – drums

Creation | unknown

Jul 95. (7"red/c-s) *(CRE/+CS 203)* **SLEEP FREAK. / MAGIC SPONGE** | 46 | -
(cd-s+=) *(CRESCD 203)* – Pleasure dip.
Oct 95. (7"purple/c-s) *(CRE/+CS 213)* **SMILER. / CARTOON MOON** | 46 | -
(cd-s+=) *(C-CRE 213)* – Wonder fools.
Feb 96. (7"/c-s) *(CRE/+CS 218)* **CHINESE BURN. / WORM BRAIN** | 45 | -
(cd-s+=) *(CRESCD 218)* – Big apple pie.
Aug 96. (7"/c-s) *(CRE/+CS 230)* **MOUSE IN A HOLE. / NO SMALL PRINT** | 53
(cd-s+=) *(CRESCD 230)* – Freedom bug.
(cd-s) *(CRESCD 230X)* – ('A'live) / Smiler (live) / Cartoon moon (live) / Chinese burn (live).
Oct 96. (cd/lp) *(CRE CD/LP 85)(C-CRE 185)* **DEJA VOODOO**
— disbanded after above

HEFNER

Formed: East London, England . . . late '96 by the Hugh Hefner (Playboy mogul)-monikered trio of songwriter DARREN HAYMAN, ANTHONY HARDING and JOHN MORRISON. Similar in approach to BUILT TO SPILL, they worked on perfecting their fragile meanderings over three very rare independent singles. Early the following year, they found a home at 'Too Pure', the resulting 'HEFNER SOUL' EP immediately converting new fans. After two more instalments of heartbreaking, SOFT BOYS-esque lyricism, the indie press were beginning to take note, hooking onto the excellent debut set, 'BREAKING GOD'S HEART', its jazzy, fragile alternative-soul a critical success.

Album rating: BREAKING GOD'S HEART (*8)

DARREN HAYMAN – vocals, guitar / **JOHN MORRISON** – bass / **ANTHONY HARDING** – drums

Boogie Wonderland | not iss.

Apr 97. (12") *(BWL 020)* **A BETTER FRIEND. /** | -
Aug 97. (12") *(INERT 4)* **CAR CHASE. /** | -
(above issued on 'Inertia')
Feb 98. (12") *(BWL 023)* **LEE REMICK. /** | -

Too Pure | Too Pure

Mar 98. (10"ep) *(PURE 64X)* **THE HEFNER SOUL EP** | -
– Flowers / Hymn for the coffee / Brood mare / Girl from the coast / Christian girls.
May 98. (7") *(PURE 80S)* **PULL YOURSELF TOGETHER. / CHRIST** | -
(cd-s+=) *(PURE 80CDS)* – Smoking girlfriend / Wicker girl.
Jul 98. (cd/lp) *(<PURE 83 CD/LP>)* **BREAKING GOD'S HEART** | Nov98
– The sweetness lies within / The sad witch / A hymn for the postal service / Love will destroy us in the end / The librarian / God is on my side / Another better friend / Love inside the stud farm / Tactile / Eloping. *(re-dist.Nov98; same)*
Jul 98. (7") *(PURE 84S)* **LOVE WILL DESTROY US IN THE END. / DESTROYED COWBOY FALLS** | -
(cd-s+=) *(PURE 84CDS)* – Blind girl with a halo / Goethe's letter to Vic Chestnut.
Aug 98. (12") *(INERT 8)* **AN EVENING WITH HEFNER (pt.1-3). / ACTIONSLACKS** | -
(above on 'Inertia' records)
Oct 98. (7") *(PURE 87S)* **THE SWEETNESS LIES WITHIN. / HELLO KITTEN** | -
(cd-s+=) *(PURE 87CDS)* – Normal Molly / Hymn for Berlin.

HELEN LOVE

Formed: Swansea, Wales . . . 1992 by the all-female trio of HELENE (yes, Helene) LOVE and her companions, SHEENA and ROXY. Having met up at design college, they began to rehearse in HELENE's mum's kitchen; this cosy family affair continued as SHEENA's brother dispatched a demo of their cutie indie-pop to 'Damaged Goods'. The track in question, 'FORMULA ONE RACING GIRLS' was released on the label in summer '93, while a second 7"-only single 'SHEENA'S IN LOVE WITH JOEY RAMONEY', was a tribute to their US punk hero. The RAMONES frontman always seemed to crop up in future 45's (of which there was no shortag~e!), compiled on the albums, 'RADIO HITS' (1994) and 'RADIO HITS VOL.2' (1997). Although they never played a gig until 1995, the girls are staunch advocates of the 7 inch single and general indie traditionalism, subsequently signing to 'Che' in '97 where they finally broached the British Top 75 a year later with the hopefully titled 'LONG LIVE THE UK MUSIC SCENE'. • **Trivia:** ASH covered their song, 'PUNKBOY'.

Album rating: SUMMER POP PUNK POP mini (*5) / RADIO HITS compilation (*5) / RADIO HITS VOL.2 compilation (*5)

HELENE LOVE – vocals, guitar / **SHEENA** – guitar, keyboards / **ROXY** – bass, drum machine

		Damaged Goods	Damaged Goods
Jul 93.	(7") *(DAMGOOD 18)* **FORMULA ONE RACING GIRLS. /**		-
Oct 93.	(7") *(DAMGOOD 27)* **SHEENA'S IN LOVE WITH JOEY RAMONEY. /**		-
Dec 93.	(7"split with WAT TYLER) *(DAMGOOD 33)* **XMAS SINGLE**		-
Jun 94.	(7") *(DAMGOOD 38)* **PUNK BOY. /**		-
Jul 94.	(10"m-lp) *(DAMGOOD 42)* **SUMMER POP PUNK POP** *(re-iss. Oct94 & Sep98; same)*		-
Oct 94.	(cd) *(DAMGOOD 51CD)* **RADIO HITS** (compilation) *(lp-iss.Mar97; DAMGOOD 51) (re-iss. Sep97 & Sep98 lp/cd; same)*		-
Apr 95.	(7") *(DAMGOOD 61)* **BUBBLEGUM. /**		-
Dec 95.	(7") *(DAMGOOD 80)* **AHEAD OF THE RACE. /** (cd-s+=) *(DAMGOOD 80CD)* –		-
Jan 96.	(7") *(<DAMGOOD 89>)* **BEAT HIM UP. /** (cd-s+=) *(<DAMGOOD 89CD>)* –		
Jun 96.	(7") *(<DAMGOOD 95>)* **WE LOVE YOU. /** (cd-s+=) *(<DAMGOOD 95CD>)* –		
Mar 97.	(lp/cd) *(DAMGOOD 117/+CD)* **RADIO HITS VOL.2** (compilation) *(re-iss. Sep97 & Sep98; same)* *(also note; all previous singles were re-iss. Sep98)*		-

		Che	not iss.
Sep 97.	(7") *(Che 72)* **DOES YOUR HEART GO BOOM. /** (cd-s+=) *(Che 72cd)* –		-
Aug 98.	(7") *(Che 82)* **LONG LIVE THE UK MUSIC SCENE. /** (cd-s+=) *(Che 82cd)* –	65	-

HELIUM

Formed: Boston, Massachusetts, USA . . . late '92 out of CHUPA (a band that featured JULIANNA HATFIELD's brother, JASON) by SHAUN KING DEVLIN, BRIAN DUNTON and former AUTOCLAVE member, MARY TIMONY. The trio debuted in '93 with the self-financed single, 'THE AMERICAN JEAN' (a track that subsequently appeared on V/A compilation, 'End Of The Trail, Vol.II'), closely followed by another import-only 7", 'HOLE IN THE GROUND'. Signing to 'Matador' after an A&R scramble, TIMONY furthered her hardline feminist agenda on 1994's mini-set, 'PIRATE, PRUDE'. Drawing comparisons to MADDER ROSE, the record was characterised by the singer's sinister, childlike vocals against a churning, turgid musical backing. A full-length set, 'THE DIRT OF LUCK', followed in '95, although by the time of the record's release, DUNTON had made way for ASH BOWIE (moonlighting from POLVO). TIMONY's vocal capabilities were further strengthened on 1997's 'MAGIC CITY', although the overall impression was as uncompromising as ever.

Album rating: PIRATE, PRUDE mini (*5) / THE DIRT OF LUCK (*7) / MAGIC CITY (*6)

MARY TIMONY – vocals, guitar / **BRIAN DUNTON** – bass / **SHAUN KING DEVLIN** – drums (ex-DUMPTRUCK)

		not iss.	Warped
May 93.	(7") **THE AMERICAN JEAN. /**	-	

		not iss.	Pop Narcotic
Jul 93.	(7") **HOLE IN THE GROUND. /**	-	

		Matador	Matador
May 94.	(m-cd/m-lp) *<(OLE 078-2/-1)>* **PIRATE, PRUDE** – Baby vampire made me / Wanna be a vampire too, baby / XXX / OOO / I'll get you, I mean it / Love $$$.		Apr94
Apr 95.	(cd/lp) *<(OLE 124-2/-1)>* **THE DIRT OF LUCK** – Pat's trick / Trixie's star / Silver angel / Baby's going underground / Medusa / Comet / Skeleton / Superball / Heaven / Oh the wind and rain / Honeycomb / Latin song.		
Sep 95.	(7") *<(OLE 144-7)>* **SUPERBALL. / WHAT INSTITUTION** (cd-s+=) *<(OLE 144-2)>* – Lucky charm / Elephant / Do you think you'll die.		

— **ASH BOWIE** – bass (of POLVO) repl. DUNTON

Apr 97.	(cd-ep) *<OLE 225>* **NO GUITARS EP** – Silver strings / Dragon #2 / King of electric guitars / Sunday / 13 bees / Riddle of the chamberlin.	-	
Sep 97.	(cd/lp) *<(OLE 195-2/-1)>* **MAGIC CITY** – Vibrations / Leon's space song / Oceans of wine / Ageing astronauts / Medieval people / . . . the fire / Lullaby of the moths / Revolution of hearts pt.1 & 2 / Ancient cryme / Cosmic rays / Devil's tear / Clementine / Blue rain soda / Walk away.		

Richard HELL

Born: RICHARD MYERS, 2 Oct'49, Lexington, Kentucky, USA. Raised in Wilmington, Delaware, he later moved to New York in his late teens, where he wrote poetry and experimented with drugs. Along with his sidekick, TOM MILLER and BILLY FICCA, he formed The NEON BOYS in 1971. By '73, they'd metamorphasized into TELEVISION, MYERS adopting his RICHARD HELL moniker (while MILLER became TOM VERLAINE) and helping to initiate the city's new wave/punk scene. As legend has it, a sharp eyed MALCOLM McLAREN was rather taken by HELL's dragged-through-a-hedge-backwards attire and mop of spiked hair, initially attempting to secure his services for his new baby, The SEX PISTOLS; when this failed, well, at least could go back to England with a few ideas . . . HELL subsequently split with VERLAINE and co., briefly joining JOHNNY THUNDERS in The HEARTBREAKERS, where he co-penned (along with a RAMONE!) the seminal 'CHINESE ROCKS'; like THUNDERS, HELL was well acquainted with the pleasures of heroin, which no doubt accounted for his haphazard career. HELL subsequently formed his own outfit, RICHARD HELL & THE VOIDOIDS along with future LOU REED guitarist ROBERT QUINE, IVAN JULIAN and MARC BELL. They hastily recorded an independently released debut EP before signing to 'Sire'; with the resulting 'BLANK GENERATION' (1977) album, HELL had finally succeeded in capturing his brutally nihilistic poetical/musical vision, if only fleetingly. With his drug problems reaching critical levels, HELL's only release over the next five years was 'THE KID WITH THE REPLACEABLE HEAD', a 1978 NICK LOWE-produced single. A belated follow-up album, 'DESTINY STREET' (1982), eventually appeared in Spring '82, although the momentum had long since disippated. HELL was absent from the music scene for the next ten years (although he did star in the film, 'Smithereens' as well as scoring a cameo role as MADONNA's boyfriend in 'Desperately Seeking Susan'), finally re-emerging with art-noise veterans, THURSTON MOORE and DON FLEMING for a solo EP, before adding STEVE SHELLEY and recording an album under the DIM STARS moniker. • **Songwriters:** HELL penned all, co-writing 'LOVE COMES IN SPURTS' with VERLAINE. DIM STARS covered RIP OFF (Marc Bolan) / NATCHEZ BURNING (Johnny Burnette). • **Trivia:** He also wrote a column for East Village Eye in the 80's. His biography 'Artifact: Notebooks from Hell' was issued by Hanuman in 1990.

Album rating: BLANK GENERATION (*7)

RICHARD HELL & THE VOID-OIDS

RICHARD HELL – vocals, bass / **ROBERT QUINE** (b.30 Dec'42, Akron, Ohio) – guitar, vocals / **IVAN JULIAN** (b.26 Jun'55, Washington, D.C.) – guitar, vocals / **MARC BELL** (b.15 Jul'56, New York City) – drums (ex-WAYNE COUNTY & THE ELECTRIC CHAIRS)

		Stiff	Ork
Nov 76.	(7"ep) *(BUY 7) <81976>* **(I COULD LIVE WITH YOU IN) ANOTHER WORLD. / YOU GOTTA LOSE / (I BELONG TO THE) BLANK GENERATION** *(re-iss. Jun94 on 'Overground' 7"ep/cd-ep; OVER 36/+CD)*		

		Sire	Sire
Sep 77.	(7") *(6078 608) <SRE 1003>* **BLANK GENERATION. / LOVE COMES IN SPURTS** (12") *(6078 608)* – ('A'side) / Liars beware / Who says.		
Sep 77.	(lp) *(SR 6037) <6037>* **BLANK GENERATION** – Love comes in spurts / Liars beware / New pleasure / Betrayal takes two / Down at the rock and roll club / Who says / Blank generation / Walking on the water / The plan / Another world. *(cd-iss. Jun90; 7599 26137-2)*		

— **FRED MAURO** – drums repl. BELL who joined RAMONES

— added **JERRY ANTONIUS** – keyboards, vocals

		Radar	not iss.
Nov 78.	(7") *(ADA 30)* **THE KID WITH THE REPLACEABLE HEAD. / I'M YOUR MAN**		-

— **HELL** and **JULIAN** recruited **FRED MAHER** – drums repl. MAURO / **NAUX** (b.29 Jul'51, San Jose, Calif.) – guitar repl. QUINE to LYDIA LUNCH

		I.D.	Red Star
May 82.	(lp) *(NOSE 2)* **DESTINY STREET** – The kid with the replaceable head / You gotta move / Going going gone / Lowest common dominator / Downtown at dawn / Time / I can only give you everything / Ignore that door / Staring in her eyes / Destiny street. *(cd-iss. Sep93 & Mar95 on 'Danceteria';)*		

— Split 1982, RICHARD HELL starred in the film 'Smithereens'. MAHER joined SCRITTI POLITTI. In 1986, he made brief cameo in the film 'Desperately Seeking Susan' as Madonna's boyfriend.

RICHARD HELL

— (solo) **with THURSTON MOORE + DON FLEMING** – guitar (of GUMBALL)

		Overground	not iss.
Feb 92.	(7"ep/cd-ep) *(OVER 24/+CD)* **3 NEW SONGS EP** – The night is coming on / Baby Huey (Baby do you wanna dance?) / Frank Sinatra.		-

		Codex	Tim Kerr
Apr 95.	(cd-ep/10"ep) *(CODE 3/+X) <TK 9410 080 CD>* **GO NOW** (spoken word)		Oct96

– compilations etc. –

Feb 80. (7"ep; The NEON BOYS) *Shake; <SHK 101>* **DON'T DIE / TIME. / LOVE COMES IN SPURTS ('73) / THAT'S ALL I KNOW (RIGHT NOW)** [-] [ ]
(UK-iss.Feb90 as 'TIME EP' on 'Overground' 7"purple; OVER 11)

Dec 84. (c) *R.O.I.R.;* **R.I.P. (live)** [-] [ ]
(UK cd-iss. Jun90 on 'Danceteria'; DANCD 040)

Apr 90. (c) *R.O.I.R.;* **FUNHUNT** [ ] [ ]
(cd-iss. Jul92;)

Apr 91. (12"clear/cd-ep; A-side as The NEON BOYS) *Overground; (OVER 19/+CD)* **THAT'S ALL I KNOW (RIGHT NOW) / LOVE COMES IN SPURTS / HIGH HEELED WHEELS. / DON'T DIE / TIME** [ ] [-]

DIM STARS

RICHARD HELL + DON FLEMING with **THURSTON MOORE + STEVE SHELLEY** (both of SONIC YOUTH)

Paperhouse Caroline

Apr 92. (12"ep/cd-ep) *(PAPER 015 T/CD) <CAROL 1468>* **THE PLUG / DIM STAR THEME. / CHRISTIAN RAP ATTACK / YOU GOTTA LOSE** [ ] [ ]

Jun 92. (cd/lp) *(PAP CD/LP 014) <CAROL 1724>* **DIM STARS** [ ] [ ]
– She wants to die / All my witches come true / Memo to Marty / Monkey / Natchez burning / Stop breakin' down / Baby Huey (do you wanna dance?) / The night is coming on / Downtown at dawn / Try this / Stray cat generation / Rip off.

HELMET

Formed: New York City, New York, USA . . . 1989 by Oregon raised, jazz-trained guitarist, PAGE HAMILTON, who had briefly played with BAND OF SUSANS. He completed his line-up around 1990, when PETER MENGEDE, HENRY BOGDAN and JOHN STAINER were added. After a one-off release for 'Amphetamine Reptile', they were signed to 'East West', who released their debut album, 'STRAP IT ON' late in 1990. Unconventional non-image anti-fuss hardcore metal, channelling HENRY ROLLINS-like aggression with avant-garde rhythmic structures, HELMET drew influences from BLACK SABBATH to BLACK FLAG. The band's reputation was such that former BIG BLACK mainman STEVE ALBINI, deigned to produce their major label debut, 'MEANTIME', a Top 75 breakthrough in America despite its punishing musical content. MENGEDE departed the following year, his replacement being ROB ECHEVERRIA, who subsequently played on the track, 'JUST ANOTHER VICTIM' (a collaboration with HOUSE OF PAIN recorded for the 'Judgment Night' soundtrack). TODD RAY was at the controls for their third set, 'BETTY', a transatlantic Top 50 success which included a BUTCH VIG-produced number, 'MILQUETOAST' (also used on 'The Crow' film soundtrack). Three years in the making, 'AFTERTASTE' proved to be their most realised and accessible recording to date, if somewhat overlooked.

Album rating: STRAP IT ON (*6) / MEANTIME (*7) / BETTY (*5) / AFTERTASTE (*8)

PAGE HAMILTON (b.18 May'60, Portland, Oregon) – vocals, guitar (ex-BAND OF SUSANS) / **PETER MENGEDE** – guitar / **HENRY BOGDAN** (b. 4 Feb'61, Riverside, Calif.) – bass / **JOHN STANIER** (b. 2 Aug'68, Baltimore, Maryland; lived a time in Australia?) – drums

Amphetam. Reptile / Amphetam. Reptile

1989. (7") *<SCALE 22>* **BORN ANNOYING. / RUMBLE** [-] [ ]
1991. (7") *<SCALE 34>* **TAKEN. /** [-] [ ]
1991. (7") *<SCALE 41>* **. / YOUR HEAD** [-] [ ]
Nov 91. (cd/c/m-lp) *<SCALE 202>* **STRAP IT ON** [-] [ ]
– Repetition / Rude / Bad mood / Sinatra / FBLA / Blacktop / Distracted / Make room / Murder. *(UK-iss.Jul93 on 'East West' cd/c; 7567 92235-2/-4) (re-iss. cd Jul96 on 'Interscope'; IND 92235)*

—— early '92, 'Sub Pop' issued d7" 'OVEN' alongside various artists

1992. (7") *<SCALE 47>* **. / NO NICKY NO** [-] [ ]

East West / Interscope

Jun 92. (cd/c/lp) *<(7567 92162-2/-4/-1)>* **MEANTIME** [ ] [68]
– In the meantime / Iron head / Give it / Unsung / Turned out / He feels bad / Better / You borrowed / FBLA II / Role model. *(cd re-iss. Jul96; IND 92162)*

Nov 92. (7"/c-s) *(A 8484/+C)* **UNSUNG. / FBLA (live)** [ ] [ ]
(cd-s+=) *(A 8484CD)* – FBLA II (live).
(12") *(A 8484T)* – ('A'side) / Better (live) / Bad mood (live) / Distracted (live).

—— **ROB ECHEVERRIA** (b.15 Dec'67) – guitar repl. MENGEDE who joined HANDSOME

not iss. / Sony

Aug 93. (12") *<77037>* **JUST ANOTHER VICTIM** [-] [ ]

Interscope / Interscope

Jun 94. (7"/c-s/12") *(A 8291/+C/T)* **BISCUITS FOR SMUT. / MILQUETOAST** [ ] [ ]
(cd-s+=) *(A 8291CD)* – Flushings.

Jun 94. (cd/c) *<(7567 92404-2/-4)>* **BETTY** [38] [45]
– Wilma's rainbow / I know / Biscuits for smut / Milquetoast / Tie / Rollo / Street crab / Clean / Vaccination / Beautiful love / Speechless / The silver Hawaiian / Overrated / Sam Hell. *(cd re-iss. Jul96; IND 92404)*

Nov 94. (m-cd) *<(6544 92492-2)>* **WILMA'S RAINBOW EP** [ ] [ ]
– Wilma's rainbow / Sam Hell / Sinatra (live) / FBLA 11 (live) / TIC (live) / Just another victim (live) / In the meantime (live).

—— In 1996, ECHEVERRIA joined BIOHAZARD and was repl. by **CHRIS TRAYNOR** – guitar

Apr 97. (cd) *<(IND 90073)>* **AFTERTASTE** [ ] [47] Mar97
– Pure / Renovation / Exactly what you wanted / Like I care / Driving nowhere / Birth defect / Broadcast emotion / It's easy to get bored / Diet aftertaste / Harmless / (High) Visibility / Insatiable / Crisis king.

– compilations, etc. –

1993. (7") *Amphetamine Reptile; <SCALE 55>* **PRIMITIVE. / BORN ANNOYING (1993)** [-] [ ]

Apr 95. (lp/cd)(c) *Amphetamine Reptile; (ARR/+CD 60-003)(ARR 13C) <16>* **BORN ANNOYING** [ ] [ ]
– Born annoying (1989) / Rumble / Shirley MacLaine / Geisha to go / Taken / Your head / Oven / No Nicky no / Primitive / Born annoying (1993).

Brian HENNEMAN (see under ⇒ BOTTLE ROCKETS)

Kristin HERSH (see under ⇒ THROWING MUSES)

HE SAID (see under ⇒ WIRE)

Boo HEWERDINE (see under ⇒ BIBLE)

HEX (see under ⇒ CHURCH)

HIGH

Formed: Manchester, England . . . late 80's by ex-member of The STONE ROSES, ANDY COUZENS. Recruiting a line-up of JOHN MATTHEWS, SIMON DAVY and CHRIS GOODWIN, COUZENS attempted to secure his band a place in the lucrative 'Madchester' scene which his former bandmates had unwittingly helped form and from which they'd assumed near legendary status. Signed to 'London' in the rush to find the "next big thing' from Manchester, The HIGH achieved minor chart success at the dawn of the 90's with their first three singles. Trading in a melodic yet predictable retro, quasi psychedelic "baggy" sound encompassing the likes of The LA's, The BYRDS and of course The STONE ROSES, COUZENS & Co. finally cracked the Top 30 in early '91 with a revamped version of their debut single, 'BOX SET GO'. Yet by this point the press were sharpening the knives for one of the most vicious backlashes of the 90's and as the debut album, 'SOMEWHERE SOON' (1990) languished in relative obscurity, The HIGH's inextricable link with the scene was to be their downfall. The band at least had a sense of humour, titling their second album, 'HYPE' (1992) even as it almost instantaneously hit the bargain bins along with excess copies of The FARM's debut.

Album rating: SOMEWHERE SOON (*6) / HYPE (*4)

JOHN MATTHEWS (b.23 Sep'67, Torquay, Devon, England) – vocals / **ANDY COUZENS** (b.15 Jul'65) – guitar (ex-STONE ROSES, ex-BUZZCOCKS FOC) / **SIMON DAVY** (b.24 Jan'67) – bass / **CHRIS GOODWIN** (b.10 Aug'65) – drums (ex-BUZZCOCKS FOC, ex-INSPIRAL CARPETS)

London / not iss.

Jun 90. (7"/c-s) *(LON/+CS 261)* **BOX SET GO. / P.W.A.** [ ] [-]
(12"+=/cd-s+=) *(LON X/CD 261)* – P.W.A. (instrumental).

Aug 90. (7"/c-s) *(LON/+CS 272)* **UP AND DOWN. / MAKE IT HAPPEN** [53] [-]
(12"+=/cd-s+=) *(LON X/CD 272)* – ('A'-Bombay mix).

Oct 90. (7"/c-s) *(LON/+CS 280)* **TAKE YOUR TIME. / ('A'-Bombay mix-live)** [56] [-]
(12"+=/cd-s+=) *(LON X/CD 280)* – ('A'extended).
(12"+=) *(LONXX 280)* – Box set go / A minor turn.

Oct 90. (cd/c/lp) *(828 224-2/-4/-1)* **SOMEWHERE SOON** [59] [-]
– Box set go / Take your time / This is my world / Rather be Marsane / So I can see / A minor turn / Dreams of Dinesh / Up and down / P.W.A. / Somewhere soon.

Jan 91. (7"/7"g-f) *(LON/+G 286)* **BOX SET GO. / P.W.A.** [28] [-]
(12"/cd-s) *(LON X/CD 286)* – ('A'side) / ('A'original) / Up & down / This is my world.

Mar 91. (7"/c-s) *(LON/+CS 297)* **MORE . . . / 4.30 / MAKE IT HAPPEN** [67] [-]
(12"+=/cd-s+=) *(LON X/CD 297)* – Blue tourist.
(10"+=) *(LONT 297)* – More madness.

Aug 92. (7") **BETTER LEFT UNTOLD. / HICKORY SMOKE** [ ] [-]
(12"+=/cd-s+=) – Joustabout.

Sep 92. (cd/c/lp) *(828 354-2/-4/-1)* **HYPE** [ ] [-]
– Better left untold / The healer / Sweet liberty / This is your life / Let nothing come between us / Goodbye girl / Keep on coming / Slowly happens here / Can I be / Lost and found.

Feb 93. (12"ep/cd-ep) **SWEET LIBERTY. / THIS IS YOUR LIFE / BETTER LEFT UNTOLD** [ ] [-]

—— split after the hype had faded

HIGH FIVE

Formed: Liverpool, England . . . 1982 by ASA HAYES, MARK BRABEN, PHIL JONES and his brother ROB JONES (the latter from WAH!). A politically motivated indie-pop act, they toured supporting AZTEC CAMERA and The STYLE COUNCIL before unsuccessfully auditioning for 'E.M.I.' and subsequently securing a deal with 'Probe Plus' (later home to HALF MAN HALF BISCUIT). The HIGH FIVE's debut single, 'COLD STEEL GANG', was released towards the end of '83 and re-issued early in '86 to promote their first album, 'DOWN IN THE NO GO'. By this time, TIM O'SHEA had replaced MARK, although no other releases were forthcoming.

Album rating: DOWN IN THE NO GO (*4)

ASA HAYES – vocals, acoustic guitar / **MARK BRABEN** – guitar / **PHIL JONES** – bass / **ROB JONES** – drums (ex-WAH!)

Probe Plus / not iss.

Nov 83. (7") *(PP 8)* **COLD STEEL GANG. / ARE YOU HAPPY** [ ] [-]

Big Village / not iss.

Oct 84. (7") *(BIGV 1)* **WORKING FOR THE MAN. / WALK BACK THEME** [ ] [-]

— **TIM O'SHEA** – guitar (ex-SEND NO FLOWERS) repl. MARK

No-Go / not iss.

Mar 86. (7") *(GO 1)* **COLD STEEL GANG. / CONFESSIONS** [ ] [-]
(12"+=) *(12GO 1)* – Turn this car around / On the banks.

Apr 86. (lp) *(lp/c) (GOLP/TC-GOLP 1)* **DOWN IN THE NO-GO** [ ] [-]
– Cold steel gang / If they come in the morning / etc

— split not long after above

HIGH LLAMAS

Formed: London, England . . . 1991 by Irish-born, ex-MICRODISNEY co-leader, SEAN O'HAGAN. Following his split with former songwriting partner and future FATIMA MANSIONS man, CATHAL COUGHLAN, O'HAGAN spent the bulk of the ensuing three years crafting his first solo work, 'HIGH LLAMAS' (1990). Released on retro specialist, 'Demon', the record was the toast of classic West Coast pop connoiseurs, critics already mentioning O'HAGAN's work in the same breath as BRIAN WILSON (a constant reference point for reviewers over the course of HIGH LLAMAS/O'HAGAN's career). Confusingly enough, by the release of 1992's mini-set, 'APRICOTS', he'd decided to promote his backing musicians (JOHN FELL, MARK PRINGLE and old MICRODISNEY man, TOM FENNER) to full band status, naming the project the HIGH LLAMAS. An eagerly anticipated full-length follow-up, the very BEACH BOYS-esque 'GIDEON GAYE', finally appeared in 1994 (the Europe-only 'SANTA BARBARA' album was also released in '94 although it was subsequently re-issued in the UK after O'HAGAN signed to 'V2' in the late '90's), its luxuriant, hypnotic blend of orchestration and harmonies suggesting that O'HAGAN's part-time work with STEREOLAB had been at least as much of an influence as his penchant for vintage transatlantic sounds. Another superlative-heavy critical reception led to a Stateside deal with 'Epic', while O'HAGAN set up his own 'Alpaca Park' label to re-issue the album in the UK the following year. 1996's 'HAWAII' set was even more ambitious, a kitsch, pseudo-psychedelic mesh of O'HAGAN's favourite things very much in the BEACH BOYS' late 60's/early 70's mould. After the band had finally secured a British major label deal with Richard Branson's new 'V2' label, a further HIGH LLAMAS album, 'COLD AND BOUNCY', appeared in 1998.

Album rating: HIGH LLAMAS (*6) / APRICOTS mini (*5) / SANTA BARBARA (*5) / GIDEON GAYE (*6) / HAWAII (*6) / COLD AND BOUNCY (*6)

SEAN O'HAGAN – vocals, guitar, keyboards (ex-MICRODISNEY) / with **JOHN FELL** – bass / **TOM FENNER** – drums (ex-MICRODISNEY) / **MARK PRINGLE** – piano, bass

Demon / not iss.

Sep 90. (lp/c/cd; by SEAN O'HAGAN) *(FIEND/+C/CD 90)* **HIGH LLAMAS** [ ] [-]
– Perry Como / Edge of the sun / Pretty boy / Hoping you would change your mind / C'mon let's go / Paint & pets / Doggy / Half face cut / Trees / Have you heard the latest news. *(cd re-iss. Jul98 on 'Diabolo'; DIAB 866)*

— SEAN joined STEREOLAB on a part-time basis while continuing with his own band **JOHN BENNETT + ROB ALLUM** + others

Plastic / not iss.

Jan 92. (m-cd/m-lp) *(PLAS CD/LP 003)* **APRICOTS** [ ] [-]
– Travel / Banking on karma / Birdies sing / Period music / Black balloon / Apricots. *(cd re-iss. Dec95; same)*

Feb 92. (7") **TRAVEL. / APRICOTS** [ ] [-]

Vogue-Mute / V2

1994. (cd) **SANTA BARBARA** [-] [-] Europe
– Put yourself down / Birdies sing / Banking on karma / Market traders / Travel / Taximan's daughter / Period music / Holland / Apricots. *(UK-iss.Jan98 on 'V2'; VVR 100108-2) <US-iss.Jan98 on 'V2'; 27011>*

Target / Epic

Apr 94. (cd) *(TGT 012CD)* **GIDEON GAYE** [ ] [-]
– Giddy strings / Dutchman / Giddy and gay / Easy rod / Checking in, checking out / Goat strings / Up in the hills / The goat looks on / Taog skool no / Little collie / Track goes by / Let's have another look / Goat. *(re-iss. Feb95; same) (re-iss. Jul95 on 'Alpaca Park' cd/c/lp; CD/MC/LP WOOL 1)*

Alpaca Park / Alpaca Park

Jun 95. (c-s) *(WOOLM 1)* **CHECKING IN CHECKING OUT /** [ ] [ ]
(12"+=/cd-s+=) *(WOOL/+D 1)* –

Mar 96. (cd/c/lp) *(CD/MC/LP WOOL 2) <27004>* **HAWAII** [ ] [ ]
– Cuckoo casino / Sparkle up / Literature is fluff / Nomads / Snapshot pioneer / Ill-fitting suits / Recent orienteering / The hot revivalist / Phoney racehorse / Dressing up the old Dakota / D.C.8 / Doo-wop property / Theatreland / A friendly pioneer / Cuckoo's out / Peppy / There's nobody home / The hokey curator / Campers in control / Double drift / Island people / Incidentally N.E.O. / Tides / Nomad strings / Pilgrims / Rustic vespa / Folly time / Hawaiian smile / Untitled. *(cd re-iss. Jan98 on 'V2'; VVR 100109-2) (d-cd re-iss. Apr98 +=; 27004-2)* – NOMADS

Jun 96. (12"ep/cd-ep) *(WOOL T/D 2)* **NOMADS EP** [ ] [ ]
– Might as well be Dumbo / Cropduster / Mini-management / Chimes of a city clock / Literature is fluff / 3 frame offset.

V2 / V2

Jan 98. (cd/d-lp) *(VVR 100073-2/-1) <27007>* **COLD AND BOUNCY** [ ] [ ]
– Twisto teck / Sun beats down / Hiball Nova Scotia / Tilting windmills / Glide time / Bouncy glimmer / Three point scrabble / Homespin rerun / Painters paint / Evergreen vampo / Showstop hip hop / Over the river / End on tick tock / Didball / Jazzed carpenter / Lobby bears.

Mar 98. (7") *(VVR 500146-7)* **SUN BEATS DOWN. /** [ ] [ ]
(cd-s+=) *(VVR 500146-3)* –

Oct 98. (cd) *<27034>* **LOLLO ROSSO** [-] [ ]
– Showstop hic hup / Homespin rerun / Homerun ubershow / Mini-management / Space raid remix / Reflections in a plastic glass / Milting tindmills.

HIGSONS

Formed: Norwich, England . . . 1980 by university students CHARLIE 'SWITCH' HIGSON, TEZ EDWARDS, STUART McGEACHIN, SIMON CHARTERTON and COLIN WILLIAMS (DAVE CUMMINGS was also an early member but left before any recordings). Trading in a wiry strand of eccentric indie/funk characterised by EDWARDS' bleating sax and CHARLIE's often surreal lyrics, The HIGSONS made their debut in summer '81 with 'I DON'T WANT TO LIVE WITH MONKEYS'. Released on the tiny 'Romans In Britain' label and backed with the similarly bizarre 'INSECT LOVE', the single was championed by Radio One DJ and alternative guru, John Peel. A further clutch of singles appeared over the early to mid 80's including a couple for the legendary '2-Tone' label ('TEAR THE WHOLE THING DOWN' and 'RUN ME DOWN'), while a cover of Andy Williams' recently resurrected 'MUSIC TO WATCH GIRLS BY' possibly proves that The HIGSONS were ahead of their time. This was followed by the band's one and only album, 'CURSE OF THE HIGSONS' (1984), their final effort save for a final single, 'TAKE IT', on 'EMI'-offshoot, 'R4'. Following the band's split in March '86, TERRY EDWARDS became part of YEAH JAZZ, having already released the 1983 single, 'ROGER WILSON SAID' under the NEW YORK NEW YORK moniker (later suffixing the word EXPERIENCE and becoming a 4-piece; one single, 'I WANNA BE LIKE YOU', surfaced in late '85). He subsequently worked with the 8-TRACK CARTRIDGE FAMILY before teaming up with MARK BEDDERS (of MADNESS) to form the BUTTERFIELD 8. This bunch released one 1988 album, 'BLOW' for 'Go! Discs', preceded by the obligatory single, a version of Herbie Hancock's 'WATERMELON MAN'. EDWARDS later issued two fun tribute EP's to The FALL and The JESUS & MARY CHAIN. Meanwhile, SIMON formed BRAZILIAN NIGHTMARE with PETE SAUNDERS and JEM MOORE (both ex-SERIOUS DRINKING, former ex-DEXY'S). CUMMINGS joined LLOYD COLE & THE COMMOTIONS before doing the same for DEL AMITRI. Mainman and all round genius, CHARLIE HIGSON, meanwhile, took up writing, penning comedy material for Harry Enfield and Vic Reeves as well as completing a series of novels. He was also one of the team (including Paul Whitehouse) behind BBC 2's now legendary 'The Fast Show' and can currently be witnessed (1998) presenting a film guide on Channel 4 alongside actress, Kathy Burke. • **Covered:** THEM CHANGES (Buddy Miles).

Album rating: CURSE OF THE HIGSONS (*6) / THE ATTACK OF THE CANNIBAL ZOMBIE BUSINESSMEN compilation (*6)

CHARLIE 'SWITCH' HIGSON – vocals / **TERRY 'TEZ' EDWARDS** (b. Hornchurch, Essex, England) – guitar, saxophone, trumpet / **STUART McGEACHIN** – guitar / **COLIN WILLIAMS** – bass / **SIMON CHARTERTON** – drums

Romans In Britain / not iss.

Jul 81. (7") *(HIG 2)* **I DON'T WANT TO LIVE WITH MONKEYS. / INSECT LOVE** [ ] [-]

Waap / not iss.

Dec 81. (12"/7") *(12+/WAAP 1)* **GOT TO LET THIS HEAT OUT. / IT GOES WAAP** [ ] [-]

Mar 82. (7") *(WAAP 2)* **CONSPIRACY. / TOUCHDOWN** [ ] [-]

2-Tone – Chrysalis / not iss.

Oct 82. (7") *(CHSTT 21)* **TEAR THE WHOLE THING DOWN. / YLANG, YLANG** [ ] [-]

Feb 83. (7") *(CHSTT 24)* **RUN ME DOWN. / PUT THE PUNK BACK INTO FUNK** [ ] [-]
(ext.12"+=) *(CHSTT12 24)* – ('A'instrumental) / ('B'part 2).

Waap / not iss.

Oct 83. (7") *(WAAP 4)* **PUSH OUT THE BOAT. / ROUND AND ROUND** [ ] [-]

Dec 83. (7") *(WAAP 5)* **THE LOST AND THE LONELY. / Virgin Prunes: JIGSAW MENTALLAMA** [ ] [-]
(above was originally given away with Vinyl mag in Dec81)

Upright / not iss.

Sep 84. (7") *(UP 9)* **MUSIC TO WATCH GIRLS BY. / LYING ON THE TELEPHONE** [ ] [-]
('A'-BOYS version;12"+=) *(12UP 9)* – Clanking my bucket (live) / I don't want to live with monkeys (live).

Sep 84. (lp) *(UPLP 6)* **THE CURSE OF THE HIGSONS** [ ] [-]
(re-iss. Mar87; same) (cd-iss. Apr92 on 'Mixture'; SORT 2CD)

— **DAVE CUMMINGS** – guitar; returned to repl. STUART

R4 – EMI / not iss.

Jun 85. (7") *(FOR 2)* **TAKE IT. / I WALK THE LAND (live)** [ ] [-]
(12"+=) *(12FOR 2)* – ('A'instrumental).

– compilations, etc. –

Oct 87. (lp) *Waap; (WAAPLP 1)* **THE ATTACK OF THE CANNIBAL ZOMBIE BUSINESSMEN** (all the singles & more) [ ] [-]
(cd-iss. Apr92 on 'Mixture'; SORT 3CD)

HINDU LOVE GODS (see under ⇒ R.E.M.)

HIS NAME IS ALIVE

Formed: Livonia, Michigan, USA . . . 1987 by WARREN DEFERER (also of group, ELVIS HITLER) alongside schoolfriends, ANGELA CAROZZO and KARIN OLIVER. Over the course of the next few years they issued a series of self-financed recordings, the last of which, 'EUTECTIC', was a commission for Detroit's Harbinger Dance Company. Subsequently snapped up by arty UK indie label, '4 a.d.', HIS NAME IS ALIVE made their British debut with the avant-garde, pseudo-gothic experimentalism of the 'LIVONIA' (1990) album. Sounding something like the COCTEAU TWINS fused with ENO, the record found DEFERER feeding his guitar flurries and folky strumming through an echo chamber, the resulting sonic debris melting into OLIVER's graceful harmonies. Follow-up set, 'HOME IS IN YOUR HEAD' (1991), continued in a similarly dark vein, focusing, as ever, on the more disturbing aspects of human nature, while 'THE DIRT EATERS' EP featured a surprising coice of cover material in Rainbow's 'MAN ON THE SILVER MOUNTAIN' alongside the HNIA classic, 'WE HOLD THE LAND IN GREAT ESTEEM'. 1993's more upbeat 'MOUTH BY MOUTH', meanwhile, divided the songs between HNIA and sister act, confusingly enough also titled the DIRT EATERS; the result was a complementary collection of raucous DE guitar workouts alongside the glacial ambience and haunting harmonies of the HNIA material. The product of a songwriting partnership between DEFERER nd new collaborators, SMITH and IAN MASTERS (ex-PALE SAINTS), 1996's 'STARS ON E.S.P.' was HIS NAME IS ALIVE at their most accessible, turning in a collection of largely acoustic, BEACH BOYS influenced folk-pop. Two years later, DEFERER changed direction once more on the rockier 'FORT LAKE', the likes of 'WISH I HAD A WISHING RING' sounding like a scuzzier SKUNK ANANSIE!

Album rating: LIVONIA (*8) / HOME IS IN YOUR HEAD (*7) / MOUTH BY MOUTH (*7) / KING OF SWEET out-takes (*5) / SOUND OF MEXICO cassette (*4) / STARS ON E.S.P. (*8) / FORT LAKE (*6)

WARREN DEFERER (b.1969) – guitar, bass, vocals, samples / **KARIN OLIVER** – vocals, guitar / **ANGELA CAROZZO** – vocals

not iss. | own label

1987. (c-ep) **RIOTOUSNESS AND POSTROPHE** [-] [ ]
1987. (lp) **HIS NAME IS ALIVE** [-] [ ]
1988. (c) **I HAD SEX WITH GOD** [-] [ ]
1988. (lp) **EUTECTIC** [-] [ ]

4 a.d. | Rykodisc

Jun 90. (lp/cd)(c) *(CAD 0008/+CD)(CADC 0008)* <10244> **LIVONIA** [ ] [ ]
– As we could ever / E-Nicolle / If July / Some and I / E-Nicolle / Caroline's supposed demon / Fossil / Reincarnation / You and I have seizures / How ghosts affect seizures / How ghosts affect relationships / Darkest dreams. *(cd re-iss. Jul98; GAD 0008CD)*

— CAROZZO departed and was repl. by **DENISE JAMES** – vocals / **MELISSA ELLIOTT** – guitar / **JYMN AUGE** – guitar / **DAMIAN LANG** – drums

Sep 91. (lp/cd)(c) *(CAD 1013/+CD)(CADC 1013)* <20243> **HOME IS IN YOUR HEAD** [ ] [ ] Jul92
– This week / Eyes were / Charmer / Hope (song of schizophrenia) / Feathers (song of schizophrenia) / Well (song of schizophrenia) / Something / Ice / Are we still married? / Put your finger in your eye / Home / Why people disappear / Eyes are / Birds / Chances are we are mad / Mescalina / Sitting / Very bad / Beautiful / Tempe / Spirit / Fish eye / Dreams. *(cd re-iss. Jul98; GAD 1013CD)*

Apr 92. (12"ep/cd-ep) *(BAD 2005/+CD)* **THE DIRT EATERS EP** [ ] [ ]
– Man on the silver mountain / Are we still married? / Is this the way the tigers? / We hold the land in great esteem.

4 a.d. | 4ad-Warners

Apr 93. (lp/cd)(c) *(CAD 3006/+CD)(CADC 3006)* <45214> **MOUTH BY MOUTH** [ ] [ ]
– Baby fish mouth / Lip / Cornfield / In every Ford / Lord, make me a channel of your peace / Drink, dress and ink / Where knock is open wide / Can't go wrong without you / Jack rabbits / Sort of / Sick / Blue moon / Ear / Lemon ocean / The torso / The dirt eaters. *(cd re-iss. Jul98; GAD 3006CD)*

— **DEFERER with SMITH + IAN MASTERS**

May 96. (7") *(AD 6007)* **UNIVERSAL FREQUENCIES. / SUMMER OF ESP** [ ] [-]
(cd-s+=) *(BAD 6007CD)* –

Jun 96. (lp/cd) *(CAD 6010/+CD)* <46207> **STARS ON E.S.P.** [ ] [ ] Jul96
– Dub love letter / This world is not my home / Bad luck girl / What are you wearing tomorrow / The bees / What else is new list / Wall of speed / Universal frequencies / The sand that holds the lakes in place / I can't live in this world anymore / Answer to rainbow at midnight / Famous goodbye king / Across the street / Movie. *(cd re-iss. Jul98 +=; GAD 6010CD)* – NICE DAY EP

Apr 97. (7"ep; with LITTLE PRINCESS) *(MOTOR 016)* **PET FARM EP** [ ] [-]
(above on 'Motorway' & below on 'Friendly Science')

Aug 97. (7") *(FS 02)* **SOUND SYSTEM WANTS IT SWEET. /** [ ] [-]

Nov 97. (cd-ep) <46838> **NICE DAY** [ ] [ ]
– Nice day / Baby you feel me up / Hot / Crashed up on the corner / Whale, you ease my mind / Drive around the clock.

Jun 98. (cd) *(CAD 8009CD)* <97673> **FT. LAKE** [ ] [ ] Aug98
– Don't glue the world / Everything takes forever / Waitress / No hiding place down her / Can't always be loved / Wish I had a wishing ring / Red haired girl / A spirit needs a spirit too / Up your legs forever / How it got to be / Always turn me on / Rock'n'roll girl from rock'n'roll / Last American blues.

Aug 98. (7"m) *(AD 8015)* **CAN'T ALWAYS BE LOVED. / CAN'T WAIT FOREVER / WISH I HAD A WISHING RING (first one 04:09)** [ ] [ ]
(cd-s) *(BAD 8015CD)* – ('A'side) / Wish I had a wishing ring (uncut 17:14).

– compilations, etc. –

1993. (cd) *Perdition Plastics;* **KING OF SWEET** (out-takes, etc) [-] [ ]
1995. (c) *Time Stereo;* **SOUND OF MEXICO** [-] [ ]

Robyn HITCHCOCK

Born: 3 Mar'53, East Grinstead, London, England. Aged 21, he set out for CAMBRIDGE to locate the home of his idol, SYD BARRETT but ended up busking instead. 1976 found him forming a string of bands including The WORST FEARS, The BEETLES, MAUREEN & THE MEATPACKERS and, finally by the end of the year, DENNIS AND THE EXPERTS, who were the embryonic SOFT BOYS; alongside ROBYN were ALAN DAVIES, ANDY METCALFE and MORRIS WINDSOR. In March '77, they were offered a deal with indie label, 'Raw', who soon issued their debut release, 'GIVE IT TO THE SOFT BOYS EP'. The record included three trash-punk songs, notably 'WADING THROUGH A VENTILATOR'. KIMBERLEY REW replaced DAVIES before the band embarked on a UK tour supporting ELVIS COSTELLO and The DAMNED. This, in turn, led to a contract with 'Radar', although after only one 45 and many disagreements, they parted company. Taking matters into their own hands, the SOFT BOYS set up their own label, 'Two Crabs', and issued a debut album, 'A CAN OF BEES' (1979). The record was a resounding failure although it has since been the subject of many re-issues in different versions. In 1980 – by which time MATTHEW SELIGMAN had replaced METCALFE – they eventually established themselves, critically at least, with the much loved follow-up, 'UNDERWATER MOONLIGHT'. HITCHCOCK and Co. had finally managed to translate their quirky post-punk psychedelia to vinyl, pointing the way towards the direction of the frontman's erratic solo career. By the following year The SOFT BOYS had split, playing their final shows to more appreciative US audiences. HITCHCOCK subsequently completed a solo album, 'BLACK SNAKE DIAMOND ROLE' (1981), featuring the cult classics, 'BRENDA'S IRON SLEDGE' and the single, 'THE MAN WHO INVENTED HIMSELF'. Clearly the man had lost none of his BARRETT-esque lyrical daftness in the interim, his tongue-in-cheek, surreal humour occasionally even outstripping CAPTAIN BEEFHEART. After the disastrous STEVE HILLAGE-produced 'GROOVY DECAY' (1982), however, ROBYN decided enough was enough. Until 1984, that is, when he returned with an affecting acoustic album, 'I OFTEN DREAM OF TRAINS', the record seeing him reinstate the SOFT BOYS rhythm section (MORRIS WINDSOR and ANDY METCALFE) under the guise of ROBYN HITCHCOCK & THE EGYPTIANS. In 1985, their first product, 'FEGMANIA!', hit the shops, songs like 'THE MAN WITH THE LIGHTBULB HEAD' and 'EGYPTIAN CREAM', ressurecting the man's public profile. After a few more albums in the mid-80's, he and his band were signed to 'A&M', the resulting album, 'GLOBE OF FROGS' (1988), worthy of anything he'd previously recorded. It brought recommendations from R.E.M., who were longtime fans of HITCHCOCK. His band became firm faves on the US college circuit, especially when indie idols, MICHAEL STIPE and PETER BUCK guested on the two mediocre either-side-of-the-decade albums, 'QUEEN ELVIS' and 'PERSPEX ISLAND'. In 1993, he returned to the eccectric brilliance of old with the highly regarded, John Leckie-produced 'RESPECT', a creative renaissance of sorts which even inspired him to re-unite The SOFT BOYS early in 1994 for some Bosnia benefit concerts. A further couple of solo sets appeared in the mid-90's, 'YOU AND OBLIVION' (1995) and 'MOSS ELIXIR' (1996), the latter with a quintessentially HITCHCOCK, engagingly fantastical life-after-death yarn printed on the inner sleeve.

Album rating: A CAN OF BEES (*7) / UNDERWATER MOONLIGHT (*8) / INVISIBLE HITS compilation (*7) / THE SOFT BOYS 1976-81 compilation (*8) / Robyn Hitchcock: BLACK SNAKE DIAMOND ROLE (*6) / GROOVY DECAY (*4) / I OFTEN DREAM OF TRAINS (*7) / FEGMANIA! (*8) / GOTTA LET THIS HEN OUT (*8) / ELEMENT OF LIGHT (*7) / INVISIBLE HITCHCOCK collection (*5) / GLOBE OF FROGS (*7) / QUEEN ELVIS (*7) / EYE (*7) / PERSPEX ISLAND (*4) / RESPECT (*5) / YOU & OBLIVION (*4) / MOSS ELIXIR (*6) / GREATEST HITS compilation (*8)

SOFT BOYS

ROBYN HITCHCOCK – vocals, guitar, bass / **ALAN DAVIS** – guitar / **ANDY METCALFE** – bass / **MORRIS WINDSOR** (aka OTIS FAGG) – drums

Raw | not iss.

Jul 77. (7"ep) *(RAW 5)* **GIVE IT TO THE SOFT BOYS** [ ] [-]
– Wading through a ventilator / The face of death / Hear my brane. *(re-iss. Oct79; RAW 37)*

— **KIMBERLEY REW** – guitar, harmonica, vocals repl. DAVIS

Radar | not iss.

May 78. (7") *(ADA 8)* **(I WANT TO BE AN) ANGELPOISE LAMP. / FAT MAN'S SON** [ ] [-]

Two Crabs | not iss.

Feb 79. (lp) *(CLAW 1001)* **A CAN OF BEES** [ ] [-]
– Give it to the soft boys / The pigworker / Human music / Leppo and the jooves / The rat's prayer / Do the chisel / Sandra's having her brain out / The return of the sacred crab / Cold turkey / Skool dinner blues / Wading through a ventilator. *(re-iss. Feb80 on 'Aura'; AUL 709) (re-iss. Jun84 on 'Two Crabs'; same) (cd-iss. Feb95 on 'Rhino'+=; RCD 20231)* – Leppo and the jooves / Sandra's having her brain out / Skool dinner blues / Fatman's son / (I want to be an) Angelpoise lamp / Ugly Nora. *(<cd re-iss. May96 on 'Rykodisc'; RCD 20231>)*

— In Oct'79, 'Raw' quickly withdrew release of 45 'WHERE ARE THE PRAWNS'; *RAW 41)*

— **MATTHEW SELIGMAN** – bass, keyboards (ex-SW9) repl. ANDY to FISH TURNED HUMAN

Armageddon | Armageddon

Jun 80. (7"ep) *(AEP 002)* **NEAR THE SOFT BOYS** [ ] [-]
– Kingdom of love / Vegetable man / Strange.

Jul 80. (lp) *(ARM 1)* **UNDERWATER MOONLIGHT** [ ] [-]
– I wanna destroy you / Kingdom of love / Positive vibrations / I got the job / Insanely

jealous / Tonight / You'll have to go sideways / Old pervert / The queen of eyes / Underwater moonlight. *(cd-iss. Feb95 on 'Rhino'+=;)* – Vegetable man / Strange / Only the stones remain / Where are the prawns / Dreams / Black snake diamond role / There's nobody like you / Song No.4. *(<cd re-iss. May96 on 'Rykodisc'; RCD 20232>)*

Aug 80. (7") *(AS 005)* **I WANNA DESTROY YOU. / (I'M AN) OLD PERVERT (DISCO)**

Oct 81. (7") *(AS 029)* **ONLY THE STONES REMAIN. / THE ASKING TREE**

Mar 82. (lp) *(BYE 1)* **TWO HALVES FOR THE PRICE OF ONE** (half live) Oct81
– Only the stones remain / Where are the prawns / The bells of Rhymney / There's nobody like you / Innocent box / Black snake diamond role / Underwater moonlight / Astronomy domine / Outlaw blues / Mystery train. *<US-title; ONLY THE STONES REMAIN>*

— Disbanded in 1982, SELIGMAN who joined The THOMPSON TWINS

– compilations, others, etc –

1982. (7"w/mag) *Bucketful Of Brains; (BOB 1)* **LOVE POISONING. / WHEN I WAS A KID**

Nov 83. (7") *Midnight Music; (DING 4)* **HE'S A REPTILE. / SONG NO.4**

Nov 83. (7") *Midnight Music; (CHIME 0002)* **INVISIBLE HITS**
– Wey-wey-hep-uh-hole * / Have a heart Betty (I'm not fireproof) * / The asking tree / Muriel's hoof / The rout of the clones / Let me put it next to you / When I was a kid * / Rock & roll toilet * / Love poisoning * / Empty girl / Blues in the dark / He's a reptile. *(cd-iss. Feb95 on 'Rhino" +=;)* – (alt.takes of *). *(cd re-iss. May96 on 'Rykodisc'; RCD 20233)*

Aug 85. (lp/pic-lp) *De Laurean; (SOFT 1/+P)* **WADING THROUGH A VENTILATOR**

1987. (7"flexi; w-mag) *Bucketful Of Brains; (BOB 17)* **DECK OF CARDS. / Robyn Hitchcock & Peter Buck: FLESH NO.1**

Dec 87. (lp) *Midnight Music; (MOIST 4)* **LIVE AT THE PORTLAND ARMS (live)**

1989. (7"yellow,7"white; ltd) *Overground; (OVER 4)* **THE FACE OF DEATH. / THE YODELLING HOOVER**

Sep 93. (d-cd) *Rykodisc; (RCD 10234-35)* **1976-81**
– (mostly all of their material).

ROBYN HITCHCOCK

was already solo, using session people, including most ex-SOFT BOYS

Armageddon not iss.

Apr 81. (7") *(AS 008)* **THE MAN WHO INVENTED HIMSELF. / DANCING ON GOD'S THUMB**
(free 7"flexi w-above) (4SPURT 1) IT'S A MYSTIC TRIP. / GROOVING ON AN INNER PLANE

May 81. (lp) *(ARM 4)* **BLACK SNAKE DIAMOND ROLE**
– The man who invented himself / Brenda's iron sledge / Do policemen sing? / The lizard / Meat / Acid bird / I watch the cars / Out of the picture / City of shame / Love. *(re-iss. May86 on 'Aftermath'; AFT 1) (cd-iss. 1988; AFTCD 1) (cd re-iss. Feb95 on 'Rhino-Sequel'+=; RSACD 819)* – Dancing on God's thumb / Happy the golden prince / I watch the cars / It was the night / Grooving on an inner plane.

— now w / **SARA LEE** – bass / **ANTHONY THISTLETWAITE** – sax / **ROD JOHNSON** – drums repl. SELIGMAN to THOMAS DOLBY (and REW who re-joined The WAVES, who added Czech KATRINA; now KATRINA & THE WAVES)

Albion not iss.

Mar 82. (7") *(ION 103)* **AMERICA. / IT WAS THE NIGHT / HOW DO YOU WORK THIS THING?**

Mar 82. (lp) *(ALB 110)* **GROOVY DECAY**
– Night ride to Trinidad / Fifty-two stations / Young people scream / The rain / America / The cars she used to drive / Grooving on an inner plane / St. Petersburg / When I was a kid / Midnight fish. *(some with free various 'Albion' artists; RH track '52 STATIONS') (re-iss. Dec85 on 'Midnight Music'; CHIME 00.15) (cd-iss. Nov89 & Oct94 on 'Line'; ALCD 9.000008) (cd-iss. Feb95 as 'GRAVY DECO (THE COMPLETE GROOVY DECAY / DECOY SESSIONS)' on 'Rhino-Sequel'+=; RSACD 820)* – (extra mixes)

Midnight Music Slash

Nov 82. (7"m) *(DING 2)* **EATEN BY HER OWN DINNER. / LISTENING TO THE HIGSONS / DR. STICKY**
(12"ep; Oct86) *(DONG 2)* – ('A'side) / Grooving on an inner plane / Messages of the dark / The abandoned brain / Happy the golden prince.

— now w / **WINDSOR + METCALFE / + ROGER JACKSON** – keyboards

Aug 84. (lp) *(CHIME 00.05S)* **I OFTEN DREAM OF TRAINS**
– Nocturne / Uncorrected personality traits / Sounds great when you're dead / Flavour of night / This could be the day / Trams of old London / Furry green atom bowl / Heart full of leaves / Autumn is your last chance / I often dream of trains. *(cd-iss. Oct86; CHIME 00.05CD) (cd re-iss. Feb95 on 'Rhino-Sequel'+=; RSACD 821)* – Ye sleeping knights of Jesus / Sometimes I wish I was a pretty girl / Cathedral / Mellow together / Winter love / The bones in the ground / My favourite buildings / I used to say I love you.

Nov 84. (12"m) *(DONG 8)* **THE BELLS OF RHYMNEY / FALLING LEAVES. / WINTER LOVE / THE BONES IN THE GROUND**

ROBIN HITCHCOCK & THE EGYPTIANS

— same as solo line-up

Mar 85. (lp) *(CHIME 00.08) <25316>* **FEGMANIA!**
– Egyptian cream / Another bubble / I'm only you / My wife and my dead wife / Goodnight I say / The man with the lightbulb head / Insect mother / Strawberry mind / Glass / The fly / Heaven. *(cd-iss. 1986 +=; CHIME 00.08CD)* – The bells of rhymney / Dwarfbeat / Some body. *(re-iss. Mar95 on 'Rhino-Sequel'+=; RSACD 822)* – Egyptian cream (demo) / Heaven (live) / Insect mother (demo) / Egyptian cream (live) / The pit of souls: I) The plateau – II) The descent – III) The spinal dance – IV) Flight of the iron lung.

May 85. (12"m) *(DONG 12)* **HEAVEN. / DWARFBEAT / SOME BODY**

Midnight Relativity

Oct 85. (lp/c) *(CHIME 00.15 S/C)* **GOTTA LET THIS HEN OUT (live)**
– Sometimes I wish I was a pretty girl / Kingdom of love / Acid bird / The cars she used to drive / My wife and my dead wife / Brenda's iron sledge / The fly * / Only the stones remain * / Egyptian cream * / Leppo & the Jooves / America / Heaven / Listening to The Higsons / Face of death. *(cd-iss. Oct86 += *; CHIME 00.15CD) (re-iss. cd Mar95 on 'Rhino-Sequel'; RSACD 823)*

Feb 86. (12"ep) *(DONG 17)* **BRENDA'S IRON SLEDGE (live). / ONLY THE STONES REMAIN (live) / THE PIT OF SOULS (part I-IV)**

Mar 86. (pic-lp)(c) *(BM 80)(BMC 80-4) <EMC 8074>* **EXPLODING IN SILENCE**

Glass Fish Combat

Jun 86. (lp) *(MOIST 2)* **INVISIBLE HITCHCOCK** (compilation)
– All I wanna do is fall in love / Give me a spanner, Ralph / A skull, a suitcase, and a long red bottle of wine / It's a mystic trip / My favourite buildings / Falling leaves / Eaten by her own dinner / Pits of souls / Trash / Mr. Deadly / Star of hairs / Messages of dark / Vegetable friend / I got a message for you / Abandoned brain / Point it at gran / Let there be more darkness / Blues in A. *(re-iss. cd Mar95 on 'Rhino-Sequel'+=; RSACD 825)* – Listening to the higsons / Dr. Sticky.

Sep 86. (lp/cd) *(MOIST 3/+CD) <885618130>* **ELEMENT OF LIGHT**
– If you were a priest / Winchester / Somewhere apart / Ted, Woody and Junior / The president / Raymond Chandler evening / Bass / Airscape / Never stop bleeding / Lady Waters & the hooded one / The black crow knows / The crawling / The leopard / Tell me about your drugs. *(re-iss. cd Mar95 on 'Rhino-Sequel'+=; RSACD 824)* – The can opener / Raymond Chandler evening (demo) / President (demo) / If you were a priest (demo) / Airscape (live) / The leopard (demo).

Jan 87. (7") *(OOZE 1)* **IF YOU WERE A PRIEST. / THE CRAWLING**
(12"+=) *(OOZE 1T)* – Tell me about your drugs / The can opener.

A&M A&M

Feb 88. (lp/c/cd) *<(AMA/AMC/CDA 5182)>* **GLOBE OF FROGS**
– Trapped flesh Mandela / Vibrating / Balloon man / Luminous rose / Sleeping with your devil mask on / Unsettled / Flesh number one / Chinese bones / A globe of frogs / Beatle Dennis / The shapes between us / Turn to animals.

Apr 88. (7") **GLOBE OF FROGS. / BALLOON MAN**

— still with **METCALFE + WINDSOR** + guest **PETER BUCK** – guitar (of R.E.M.)

Mar 89. (lp/c/cd) *<395241-1/-4/-2>* **QUEEN ELVIS**
– Madonna of the wasps / The Devils coachman / Wax doll / Knife / Swirling / One long pair of eyes / Veins of the Queen / Freeze / Autumn sea / Superman. *(cd+=)* – Veins of the Queen (royal mix) / Freeze (shatter mix).

Jul 89. (7") **MADONNA OF THE WASPS. / RULING CLASS**
(12"+=/cd-s+=) – Veins of the queen (royal mix) / Freeze (shatter mix).

ROBIN HITCHCOCK

Glass Fish Twin/Tone

Nov 90. (lp/cd) *(MOIST 8/CD) <89175>* **EYE**
– Cynthia mask / Certainly clickot / Queen Elvis / Flesh cartoons / Chinese water python / Executioner / Linctus House / Sweet ghosts of light / College of ice / Transparent lover / Beautiful girl / Raining twilight coast / Clean Steve / Agony of pleasure / Glass hotel / Satellite / Aquarium / Queen Elvis II. *(UK cd-iss. Mar95 on 'Rhino-Sequel'+=; RSACD 826)* – Raining twilight coast (demo) / Agony of pleasure (demo) / Queen Elvis III (demo).

Go! Discs A&M

Oct 91. (cd/c) *(828 292-2/-4) <75021 5368-2>* **PERSPEX ISLAND** Aug91
– Oceanside / So you think you're in love / Birds in perspex / Ultra unbelievable love / Vegetations and dines / Lysander / Child of the universe / She doesn't exist / Ride / If you go away / Earthly Paradise.

Jan 92. (7") *(GOD 65)* **SO YOU THINK YOU'RE IN LOVE. / WATCH YOUR INTELLIGENCE**
(12"+=/cd-s+=) *(GOD X/CD 65)* – Dark green energy.
(above featured STIPE + BUCK of R.E.M.)

Jun 93. (cd/c; with ARCHIE ROACH) *(RHE CD/MC 1) <540064>* **RESPECT** Feb93
– The yip song / The arms of love / The moon inside / Railway shoes / When I was dead / The wreck of Arthur Lee / Driving aloud (radio storm) / erpnt at the gates of wisdom / Then you're dust / Wafflehead.

Rhino-Sequel Rhino-Sequel

Mar 95. (cd) *(<RSACD 827>)* **YOU & OBLIVION**
– You've got / Don't you / Birdshead / She reached for a light / Victorian squid / Captain Dry / Mr. Rock I / August hair / Take your knife out of my back / Surgery / The dust / Polly on the shore / Aether / Fiend before the shrine / Nothing / Into it / Stranded in the future / Keeping still / September clones / Ghost ship / You & me / If I could look.

Feb 95. (cd-ep) *(CDSEQ 2)* **MY WIFE AND MY DEAD WIFE / I SOMETHING YOU / ZIPPER IN MY SPINE / MAN WITH A WOMAN'S SHADOW**

— now with **DENI BONET** – violin / **NITSHUKS BONGA** – sax / **TIM KEEGAN** – guitar / **JAKE KYLE** – bass / **PATCH HANNAN** – drums / **MORRIS WINDSOR** – vocals, percussion / etc

Warners Warners

Aug 96. (cd/c) *(<9362 46302-2/-4>)* **MOSS ELIXIR**
– Sinister but she was happy / The Devil's radio / Heliotrope / Alright, yeah / Filthy bird / The speed of things / Beautiful queen / Man with a woman's shadow / I am not me / De Chirico Street / You and oblivion / This is how it feels.

– his compilations, etc. –

May 83. (12"ep) *Albion; (12ION 1036)* **NIGHT RIDE TO TRINIDAD (long version). / KINGDOM OF LOVE / MIDNIGHT FISH**

1984. (7"flexi; w-mag) *Bucketful Of Brains; (BOB 8)* **HAPPY THE GOLDEN PRINCE**

Jun 94. (cd) *Strange Roots; (ROOTCD 001)* **KERSHAW SESSIONS**

Mar 95. (cd) *Rhino-Sequel;* **RARE & UNRELEASED**

Sep 96. (cd) *A&M;* **GREATEST HITS**

Oct 97. (cd) *Warners; <46846>* **STOREFRONT HITCHCOCK: MUSIC FROM DEMME PICTURE (live)**
– 1974 / Let's go thundering / I'm only you / Glass hotel / I something you / Yip! song / Freeze / Alright, yeah / Where do you go when you die? / The wind cries Mary / No, I don't remember Guildford / Beautiful queen.

HOLE

Formed: Los Angeles, California, USA . . . late 1989 by COURTNEY LOVE and 6 foot 4 inch guitarist and Capitol records employee, ERIC ERLANDSON. LOVE, who had previously worked as an exotic dancer and an actress, and played alongside JENIFER FINCH (L7) and KAT BJELLAND (Babes In Toyland) in a band called SUGAR BABY DOLL, was also involved in an early incarnation of FAITH NO MORE. Taking the name HOLE from a line in Euripides' Medea, they placed an ad in a local paper, 'Flipside', finding a bassist and drummer, namely JILL EMERY and CAROLINE RUE. In the Spring of 1990, HOLE released the 'RAT BASTARD' EP, subsequently relocating to the burgeoning Seattle area. Early the following year, 'Sub Pop' issued the 'DICKNAIL' EP, the band duly signing to 'Caroline' records for their debut album, 'PRETTY ON THE INSIDE'. Produced by KIM GORDON and DON FLEMING, it hit the lower regions of the US charts, the record being voted album of the year by New York's Village Voice magazine. A harrowing primal howl of a record, LOVE's demons were confronted mercilessly on such psyche-trawling dirges as 'TEENAGE WHORE' and 'GARBAGE MAN'. Around the same time, LOVE's relationship with NIRVANA's KURT COBAIN, was the talk of the alternative rock world, the singer subsequently marrying him in February '92, giving birth to his daughter, Frances Bean, later that summer. The following year, with newcomers PATTY SCHEMEL (drums) and KRISTEN PFAFF (bass), the group secured a deal with the David Geffen Company ('D.G.C.'), much to the dismay of MADONNA who wanted HOLE for her newly formed 'Maverick' label. In Spring 1994, LOVE finally celebrated a UK Top 20 album, 'LIVE THROUGH THIS', although its success was overshadowed by the shocking suicide of KURT on the 8th of April. She subsequently held a memorial two days later, hailing everyone there to call him an asshole. More press coverage followed later that summer, when their new bassist KRISTIN PFAFF was found dead in her bath on the 16th June (it was believed to be another tragic drug related death). Despite the press circus surrounding LOVE, the band played a rather disappointing Reading Festival stint in August that year, her at times lethargic vox letting some of the more diserning fans down (EVAN DANDO of The LEMONHEADS was rumoured to be her new boyfriend, although a number of lucky people – including DANDO – were privy to her womanly charms – both of them – when she "flashed" at the side of the stage). With a new bassist, MELISSA AUF DER MAUR, the group released two UK hits, 'DOLL PARTS' and 'VIOLET', LOVE certainly back on top form with her incendiary Top Of The Pops performances (LYDIA LUNCH eat your heart out!?). Back in the news again, she was fined for assaulting BIKINI KILL's KATHLEEN HANNA, LOVE and SCHEMEL conversely taking three security guards to court following an alleged assault incident while signing autographs stagefront at a GREEN DAY concert in Lakefront Arena (yet more column inches were devoted to the controversial singer in August '96, when LOVE was acquitted of a stage assault nine months previous on two teenage fans in Florida). More recently, LOVE has played down her wild child character, exchanging the Seattle grunge mantle for a more respectable Hollywood career. This was largely down to her acclaimed roles in the movies, 'Feeling Minnesota' and more so with the controversial, 'The People Vs. Larry Flint'. On the recording front, only a lone version of FLEETWOOD MAC's 'GOLD DUST WOMAN' has surfaced (this was included on the film soundtrack from 'The Crow II: City Of Angels'). In 1998, LOVE was once again writing new material with her (very patient) band, material tentatively scheduled for the summer. • **Covers:** STAR BELLY sampled DREAMS (Fleetwood Mac) + INTO THE BLACK (Neil Young) / DO IT CLEAN (Echo & The Bunnymen) / CREDIT IN THE STRAIGHT WORLD (Young Marble Giants) / HUNGRY LIKE THE WOLF (Duran Duran) / SEASON OF THE WITCH (Donovan) / HE HIT ME (IT FELT LIKE A KISS) (Goffin-King). 'I THINK THAT I WOULD DIE' was co-written w / KAT BJELLAND (Babes In Toyland). • **Note:** Not to be confused with band who released in the late 80's; OTHER TONGUES, OTHER FLESH (lp) and DYSKINSIA (12") both on 'Eyes Media'.

Album rating: PRETTY ON THE INSIDE (*7) / LIVE THROUGH THIS (*9) / MY BODY, THE HAND GRENADE collection (*6) / CELEBRITY SKIN (*7)

COURTNEY LOVE (b. MICHELLE HARRISON, 9 Jul'65, San Francisco, Calif.) – vocals, guitars / **ERIC ERLANDSON** (b. 9 Jan'63) – guitars / **JILL EMERY** – bass, vocals / **CAROLINE RUE** – drums

		not iss.	Sympathy F
Jul 90.	(7"white-ep) <*SFTRI 53*> **RETARD GIRL. / PHONEBILL SONG / JOHNNIES IN THE BATHROOM**	-	
	(UK-iss.cd-ep Sep97 +=; SFTRI 53CD) – Turpentine.		
		not iss.	Sub Pop
Apr 91.	(7"colrd-various) *(SP 93)* **DICKNAIL. / BURNBLACK**	-	
		City Slang	Caroline
Aug 91.	(7"colrd-various) *(EFA 04070-45)* **TEENAGE WHORE. / DROWN SODA**		
	(12"+=/cd-s+=) *(EFA 04070-02/-03)* – Burnblack.		
Oct 91.	(cd/c/lp-some red) *(EFA 0407-2/-C/-1)* <*SLANG 012*> **PRETTY ON THE INSIDE**	59	Jul91
	– Teenage whore / Babydoll / Garbage man / Sassy / Goodsister – bad sister / Mrs. Jones / Berry / Loaded / Star belly / Pretty on the inside / Clouds. *(re-iss. Sep95; same)*		

— **LESLEY** – bass repl. JILL / **PATTY SCHEMEL** (b.24 Apr'67, Seattle Washington) – drums repl. CAROLINE

		City Slang	D.G.C.
Apr 93.	(7") *(EFA 04916-45)* **BEAUTIFUL SON. / OLD AGE**	54	-
	(12"+=/cd-s+=) *(EFA 04916-02/-03)* – 20 years in the Dakota.		

— **KRISTEN PFAFF** – bass, piano, vocals repl. LESLEY

Mar 94.	(7"some pink) *(EFA 04936-7)* **MISS WORLD. / ROCK STAR (alternate mix)**	64	
	(cd-s+=) *(EFA 04936-2)* – Do it clean (live).		
Apr 94.	(cd/c/lp;some white) *(EFA 04935-2/-4/-1)* <*24631*> **LIVE THROUGH THIS**	13	52
	– Violet / Miss World / Plump / Asking for it / Jennifer's body / Doll parts / Credit in the straight world / Softer, softest / She walks on me / I think that I would die / Gutless / Rock star. *(re-iss. cd/lp Mar95 on 'Geffen'; GED/GEF 24631)*		

— KRISTEN was found dead in her bath 16th June 1994. COURTNEY, ERIC + PATTI continued and later recruited **MELISSA AUF DER MAUR** (b.17 Mar'72, Montreal, Canada) – bass. As HOLEZ (HOLE + PAT SMEAR of GERMS) they released tribute GERMS cover 'CIRCLE 1' on 'Dutch East India' Mar95.

		Geffen	D.G.C.
Nov 94.	(c-s) <*19379*> **DOLL PARTS / PLUMP (live)**	-	58
Apr 95.	(7") *(GFS 91)* **DOLL PARTS. / THE VOID**	16	-
	(cd-s+=) *(GFSTD 91)* – Hungry like the wolf (live).		
	(cd-s) *(GFSXD 91)* – ('A'side) / Plump (live) / I think that I would die (live) / Credit in the straight world (live).		
Jul 95.	(7") *(GFS 94)* **VIOLET. / OLD AGE**	17	
	(7"colrd) *(GFSP 94)* – ('A'side) / He hit me (it felt like a kiss).		
	(cd-s++=) *(GFSCD 94)* – Who's porno you burn (black).		
Nov 96.	(etched-d7") *(573164-7)* **GOLD DUST WOMAN. / (NY LOOSE: Spit)**		
	(above 45 was a limited edition on 'Polydor' UK, 'Hollywood' US)		
Sep 98.	(7"/c-s) *(GFS/+C 22345)* <*radio play*> **CELEBRITY SKIN. / BEST SUNDAY DRESS**	19	85
	(cd-s+=) *(GFSTD 22345)* – Dying.		
Sep 98.	(cd/c/lp) <*(GED/GEC/GEF 25164)*> **CELEBRITY SKIN**	11	9
	– Celebrity skin / Awful / Hit so hard / Malibu / Reasons to be beautiful / Dying / Use once & destroy / Northern star / Boys on the radio / Heaven tonight / Playing your song / Petals.		
Dec 98.	(7"/c-s) *(GFS/+C 22369)* **MALIBU. /**		
	(cd-s+=) *(GFSTD 22369)* –		

– compilations, etc. –

Oct 95. (m-cd) *Caroline; <1470>* **ASK FOR IT** (radio session) [-] [ ]
Sep 97. (cd/c/lp) *City Slang; <(EFA 04995-2/-4/-1)>* **MY BODY, THE HAND GRENADE** [ ] [ ] Oct97
– Turpentine / Phonebill song / Retard girl / Burn black / Dicknail / Beautiful son / 20 years in Dakota / Miss World / Old age / Softer softest / He hit me (it felt like a kiss) / Season of the witch / Drown soda / Asking for it.

HOLLY & THE ITALIANS

Formed: Los Angeles, California, USA ... 1978 by HOLLY BETH VINCENT, who recruited her Italians in the shape of MARK HENRY and STEVE YOUNG. Inspired by London's punk explosion, HOLLY relocated her troops to the UK capital and set about securing a record deal. Discovered by future GLR DJ, Charlie Gillett, and signed to his 'Oval' imprint, the trio released 'TELL THAT GIRL TO SHUT UP' (later covered by TRANSVISION VAMP) as their debut single in early 1980. After a series of low-key pub gigs, the band scored support slots to BLONDIE and The CLASH, raising their profile and landing them a deal with 'Virgin'. Two singles, 'MILES AWAY' and 'YOUTH COUP', introduced the band to an appreciative post-punk, new-wave crowd although a debut album, 'THE RIGHT TO BE ITALIAN' (1981) was perhaps too one-dimensional and stuck in a New York groove for many UK fans. Following a further single, 'JUST FOR TONIGHT', the band fell apart and HOLLY subsequently recorded with her mate, JOEY RAMONE, on a cover of Sonny & Cher's 'I GOT YOU BABE'. Confusingly enough, the singer went on to release a solo album, 'HOLLY & THE ITALIANS' (1982) as HOLLY BETH VINCENT, although the record's more thoughtful textures distanced it from her earlier work, HOLLY'S retro influences showing through on a cover of Buffalo Springfield's 'FOR WHAT IT'S WORTH'. After a brief spell in The WAITRESSES, she later hooked up with WATERBOY, ANTHONY THISTLETHWAITE, on his side project, The WILD THINGS. More recently, HOLLY re-surfaced as a collaborator with CONCRETE BLONDE frontwoman, JOHNETTE NAPOLITANO, on 1995's 'VOWEL MOVEMENT'.

Album rating: THE RIGHT TO BE ITALIAN (*5) / Holly Beth Vincent: HOLLY & THE ITALIANS (*5)

HOLLY BETH VINCENT (b. Chicago, Illinois, USA) – vocals, guitar, synthesizer / **MARK HENRY** (b. SIDGWICK) – bass (ex-BOYFRIENDS, ex-TOYAH) / **STEVE YOUNG** – drums

Oval / not iss.

Jan 80. (7") *(OVAL 1016)* **TELL THAT GIRL TO SHUT UP. / CHAPEL OF LOVE** [ ] [-]
(re-iss. Jul82; HOLLY 16)

— added **PAUL SCHAFFER** – keyboards / **MIKE OSBORN** – drums

Virgin / Virgin

May 80. (7") *(VS 341)* **MILES AWAY. / IT'S ONLY ME** [ ] [-]
Feb 81. (7") *(VS 391)* **YOUTH COUP. / POSTER BOY** [ ] [-]
May 81. (7") *(VS 411)* **I WANNA GO HOME. / FANZINE** [ ] [-]
May 81. (lp) *(V 2186) <37359>* **THE RIGHT TO BE ITALIAN** [ ] [ ]
– I wanna go home / Baby gets it all / Youth coup / Just young / Miles away / Tell that girl to shut up / Just for tonight / Do you say love / Means to a den / Rock against romance.
Jun 81. (7") *(VS 429)* **JUST FOR TONIGHT. / BABY GETS IT ALL** [ ] [ ]

— split in the summer '81 (next A-side a duet with JOEY RAMONE)

Jan 82. (7"; HOLLY & JOEY) *(VS 478)* **I GOT YOU BABE. / ONE MORE DANCE** [ ] [-]

HOLLY BETH VINCENT

— went solo augmented by **BOBBY VALENTINO** – violins, mandolin (ex-FABULOUS POODLES) / **BOBBY COLLINS** – bass / **KEVIN WILKINSON** – drums (ex-THOSE NAUGHTY LUMPS)

Aug 82. (7") *(VS 539)* **HONALU. / REVENGE** [ ] [-]
Sep 82. (lp/c) *(V/TCV 2234) <38287>* **HOLLY & THE ITALIANS** [ ] [ ]
– Honalu / For what it's worth / Only boy / Revenge / Samurai and courtesan / Cool love / Uptown / We danced / Unoriginal sin / Just like me.
Oct 82. (7"/12") *(VS 517-12)* **FOR WHAT IT'S WORTH. / DANGEROUSLY** [ ] [-]

— she joined The WAITRESSES for a brief stint and subsequently became part of ANTHONY THISTLETWAITE's moonlight combo, The WILD THINGS. In the mid-90's, HOLLY collaborated with JOHNETTE NAPOLITANO (CONCRETE BLONDE) project, VOWEL MOVEMENT, who released one eponymous album in '95.

HOLLYWOOD BRATS

Formed: London, England ... 1973 by Canadian frontman ANDREW MATHESON, Norwegian keyboard man CASINO STEEL, along with EUNON BRADY, WAYNE MANOR and LOUIS SPARKS. Despite their failure to secure a UK deal, the 'BRATS did actually record an album, 'GROWN UP WRONG', for a Scandinavian label although it was subsequently withdrawn. Definitely ahead of their time, the band were belatedly acknowledged as progenitors of underground sleaze/glam-punk upon the release of the album (now re-titled simply, 'HOLLYWOOD BRATS') by 'Cherry Red' at the turn of the decade. By this point, however, they had been defunct for nearly five years, STEEL having had minor success with power-pop punks, The BOYS.

Album rating: HOLLYWOOD BRATS (*6)

ANDREW MATHESON – vocals / **CASINO STEEL** – keyboards / **EUNON BRADY** – guitar / **WAYNE MANOR** – bass / **LOUIS SPARKS** – drums

— split in 1975 with an impending album, 'GROWN UP WRONG', withdrawn from release in Scandinavia and America; the 1973 recordings surfaced below. MATHESON and BRADY went into sessions with WRECKLESS ERIC's LAST ORDERS, while STEEL found a little fame with The BOYS.

– posthumous, etc. –

Cherry Red / not iss.

May 79. (7") *(CHERRY 6)* **THEN HE KISSED ME. / SICK ON YOU** [ ] [-]
Feb 80. (lp) *(ARED 6)* **HOLLYWOOD BRATS** [ ] [-]
– Chez maximes / Another schoolday / Nightmare / Empty bottles / Courtesan / Then he kissed me / Tumble with me / Zurich 17 / Southern belles / Drowning sorrows / Sick on you. *(cd-iss. Dec93; CDMRED 106)*

Chris HOLMES

Born: 1971, Chicago, Illinois, USA. A musical jack-of-all-trades, CHRIS HOLMES (obviously NOT the blonde-maned, spandex-wearing one-time guitarist with schlock-rockers, WASP!) was apparently inspired by PRINCE's virtuosity, collecting and mastering an eclectic array of instruments while attending the University Of Chicago. The bespectacled intellectual also hosted his own Uni radio programme on aliens and conspiracy theory, his sci-fi obsession influencing his first musical outfit, SABLON GLITZ (named after a Dr. Who character!). Although formed in 1992 as a synth-based solo project inspired by space-rockers, HAWKWIND, no material would be commercially released until HOLMES secured a deal with 'Atlantic' in the mid-90's. Side by side with this, he was also operating a second space-themed enterprise, ASHTAR COMMAND, although as yet no official releases have materialised. The multi-faceted American had also been writing a wealth of 60's influenced psychedelic pop songs, the cream of which were released in summer 1996 as the 'DAN LOVES PATTI' album. Recorded with a full band (SARA DOMINIS, BARBARA GRETSCH, JIM NEWBERRY, MICHAEL KIRTS, HILARY RACHEL PORISS and DARCY VAUGHN) and issued under the YUM-YUM moniker, the record drew much praise for its orchestral sweeps, oblique complexity and strange melancholy vocals; in Britain, the record was released early in 1997 under his own name, UK audiences unlikely to get confused with the aforementioned ageing headbanger.

Album rating: DAN LOVES PATTI (*6)

CHRIS HOLMES – vocals, guitar, multi / with **SARA DOMINIS** – vocals / **BARBARA GRETSCH** – vocals / **JIM NEWBERRY** – organ / **HILARY RACHEL PORISS** – violin / **DARCY VAUGHN** – viola / **MICHAEL KIRTS** – percussion, drums, vocals

Atlantic / Tag-Atlantic

Nov 96. (c-s/cd-s) *(A 5652 C/CD)* **APIARY / RAINBOW CONNECTION** [ ] [ ]
Feb 97. (cd; as YUM-YUM; in US-only) *<(7567 92710-2)>* **DAN LOVES PATTI** [ ] [ ] May96
– I'm not telling / Apiary / Dan loves Patti / Doot-doot / Train of thought / Sister / Cross my heart / Ring / Jealous of the stars / Uneasy / Words will fail / Lament.
Apr 97. (c-s/cd-s) *(A 5617 C/CD)* **DOOT DOOT /** [ ] [ ]

SABLON GLITZ

CHRIS HOLMES – vocals, synthesizers

Organico / Trixie

1995. (12") *(ORG 016) <8>* **UFONIC** [ ] [ ]
(UK-iss.Feb98; same)

HOLY JOY (see under ⇒ BAND OF HOLY JOY)

HONEYCRACK

Formed: London, England ... August '94 by WILDHEARTS outcasts, CJ and WILLIE DOWLING, along with MARK McRAE. As unadorned and unpretentious as The WILDHEARTS themselves, HONEYCRACK signed to 'Epic' records, scoring the following year with their first UK Top 50 hit, 'SITTING AT HOME'. Multi-racial Brit-rock similar to TERRORVISION and METALLICA fused with the harmony of The BEACH BOYS, the group enjoyed a further two chart encounters, before releasing their GIL NORTON-produced debut set, 'PROZAIC' (1996). This Top 40 album gave 'Epic' another stab at the charts with the re-issued 'SITTING AT HOME', the band subsequently moving to another label later that year. • **Covered:** HEY BULLDOG (Beatles).

Album rating: PROZAIC (*7)

CJ (CHRIS JAGDHAR) – vocals, guitar (ex-WILDHEARTS, ex-TATTOOED LOVE BOYS) / **WILLIE DOWLING** – bass / **MARK McRAE** – guitar / **PETE CLARKE** – bass / **HUGO DEGENHARDT** – drums

Epic / not iss.

Nov 95. (7"/c-s) *(662538-7/-4)* **SITTING AT HOME / IF I HAD A LIFE** [42] [-]
(cd-s+=) *(662538-2)* – 5 minutes / Hey bulldog.
Feb 96. (7"yellow) *(662864-7)* **GO AWAY. / GUN** [41] [-]
(cd-s+=) *(662864-2)* – Where do you come from?
(cd-s) *(662864-5)* – ('A'side) / Sitting at home (live) / Powerless (live).

May 96. (7"blue) *(663147-7)* **KING OF MISERY. / GO AWAY (live)** 32 -
(cd-s+=) *(663147-2)* – Paperman (live) / Hey bulldog (live).
(cd-s) *(663147-5)* – ('A'side) / Mr. Ultra sheen / All gone wrong / Still dead (. . .and then there were three).
May 96. (cd/c/lp/white-lp) *(484230-2/-4/-1/-0)* **PROZAIC** 34 -
– King of misery / No – please don't / Go away / Powerless / The genius is loose / Good good feeling / If I had a life / I hate myself and everybody else / Animals / Samantha Pope / Paperman / Sitting at home / Parasite.
Jul 96. (c-s) *(663503-4)* **SITTING AT HOME / ('A'-Renegade Soundwave remix)** 32 -
(cd-s+=) *(663503-2)* – Animals (Martin Steib remix).
(cd-s) *(663503-5)* – ('A'side) / Good, good feeling (live) / No – please don't / Samantha Pope (live).
E'G not iss.
Nov 96. (cd-s) *(EGO 52-A)* **ANYWAY / MORE THAN I WAS / ANYWAY (demo)** 67 -
(cd-s) *(EGO 52-B)* – ('A'side) / You're not worth it / ('A'-Papa Brittle mix).
— split early in 1997

JELLYS

— were formed by **CJ** who recruited
Proud not iss.
Mar 98. (cd-ep) *(PROUDCD 1)* **JELLY BELLY EP** -
Mission Impossible not iss.
Apr 98. (cd-ep) *(MIRCDS 1)* **HEADS FIRST . . . LEGS LAST EP** -
Aug 98. (cd-ep) *(MIRCDS 2)* **FEELS LIKE SUNSHINE /** -

HOODOO GURUS

Formed: Sydney, Australia . . . 1981 as LE HOODOO GURUS by singer/songwriter, DAVE FAULKNER, JAMES BAKER, ROD RADALJ and KIMBEL RENDALL. Following the release of debut single, 'LEILANI', CLYDE BRAMLEY and BRAD SHEPPARD replaced the latter pair and after a few minor homeland hits they inked a Stateside deal with 'A&M'. Already popular in American underground circles, 1984's debut album, 'STONEAGE ROMEOS' presented The HOODOO GURUS as garage-punk/pop connoiseurs touching all bases from the crypt-kicking CRAMPS-esque shockabilly of 'DIG IT UP' to the harmonica-stomping groove of '(LET'S ALL) TURN ON'. Like The CRAMPS, the band were also self confessed American trash culture junkies, dedicating the album to US sitcom luminaries, ARNOLD 'The Pig' ZIFFEL and LARRY STORCH (Who?!). Despite the subsequent departure of founding member, BAKER (replaced by MARK KINGSMILL), the band bounced back with 'MARS NEEDS GUITARS!' (1985), a more professional sounding effort (released on 'Chrysalis' in the UK and 'Elektra' in the States) which saw the band become a hit on US college radio. Although the sloppy charm of old might've been missing, their newfound accessibility saw the 'BITTERSWEET' single making the Top 20 back home in Australia. After tours of Europe and America, the band began work on 'BLOW YOUR COOL!' (1987), FAULKNER further refining his songwriting skills on an album that was even more mainstream-friendly with help from fellow 60's revivalists The BANGLES on singles, 'WHAT'S MY SCENE' and 'GOOD TIMES'. Although the turn of the decade saw the 'GURUS release two of their strongest eforts in 'MAGNUM CUM LOUDER' (1989) and the raucous 'KINKY' (1991), the long awaited commercial breakthrough consistently failed to materialise and by 1994's 'CRANK' (featuring guest ex-BANGLE, VICKI PETERSON) FAULKNER and co. were beginning to sound tired. • **Trivia:** In the early 90's, GROSSMAN (with MIDNIGHT OIL's ROB HIRST) had his own project, The GHOSTWRITERS. They released two albums, 'GHOSTWRITERS' (1991) for 'Virgin' and 'SECOND SKIN' (1996) for 'Mercury'.

Album rating: STONEAGE ROMEOS (*8) / MARS NEEDS GUITARS! (*7) / BLOW YOUR COOL (*7) / MAGNUM CUM LOUDER (*6) / KINKY (*5) / CRANK (*4) / BLUE CAVE (*5) / ELECTRIC SOUP: THE SINGLES COLLECTION compilation (*8) / GORILLA BISCUIT: THE B SIDES AND RARITIES compilation (*5)

DAVE FAULKNER (b. 2 Oct'54, Perth, Australia) – vocals, guitar (ex-VICTIMS, ex-SCIENTISTS) / **ROD RADALJ** – guitar (ex-SCIENTISTS) / **KIMBLE RENDALL** – guitar / **JAMES BAKER** – drums (ex-SCIENTISTS)
not iss. Phantom
1983. (7") **LEILANI. /** -
— **BRAD SHEPHERD** (b. 1 Feb'61) – lead guitar (ex-SUPER K) repl. ROD
— **CLYDE BRAMLEY** – bass; repl. KIMBLE
1983. (7") **TOJO. /** -
Demon A&M
Dec 84. (lp) *(FIEND 32) <7502 15012-1>* **STONEAGE ROMEOS** 1986
– (Let's all) Turn on / I want you back / Arthur / Death ship / Dig it up / My girl / Zanzibar / Leilani / Tojo / In the echo chamber / I was a kamikaze pilot.
Jan 85. (7") *(D 1028)* **I WANT YOU BACK. /**
Jun 85. (7") *(D 1033)* **MY GIRL. / LEILANI**
— **MARK KINGSMILL** (b. 4 Dec'56) – drums; repl. BAKER
Chrysalis Elektra
Oct 85. (7") *(CHS 2926)* **BITTERSWEET. / BRING THE HOODOO DOWN**
(12"+=) *(CHS12 2926)* – Turkey dinner.
Oct 85. (lp/c) *(CHR/ZCHR 1520) <60485-1>* **MARS NEEDS GUITARS!**
– Bittersweet / Poison pen / In the wild / Death defying / Like wow – Wipeout / Hayride to Hell / Show some emotion / The other side of Paradise / Mars needs guitars! / She. *(cd-iss. Jul86; CCD 1520)*
Apr 87. (7") *(CHS 3123)* **WHAT'S MY SCENE. / HEART OF DARKNESS**
(12"+=) *(CHS12 3123)* – Where nowhere is.
May 87. (lp/c) *(CHR/ZCHR 1601) <60728-1>* **BLOW YOUR COOL!**
– Out that door / What's my scene / Good times / I was the one / Hell for leather / Where nowhere is / Middle of the road / Come on / My caravan / On my street / Party machine.
Jul 87. (7") *(CHS 3151)* **GOOD TIMES. / ON MY STREET**
(12"+=) *(CHS12 3151)* – Like wow – Wipeout.
— **RICK GROSSMAN** (b. 2 Nov'55) – bass (ex-DIVINYLS) repl. BRAMLEY
R.C.A. R.C.A.
Aug 89. (7") *(PB 49347)* **COME ANYTIME. / CAJUN COUNTRY**
(12"+=/cd-s+=) *(PT/PD 49350)* – Hallucination.
Aug 89. (lp/c/cd) *(PL/PK/PD 90362) <9781>* **MUGNUM CUM LOUDER** Jun89
– Come anytime / Another world / Axegrinder / Shadow me / Glamourpuss / Hallucination / All the way / Baby can dance parts 2-4) / I don't know anything / Where's that hit? / Death in the afternoon.
Apr 91. (cd/c/lp) *(PD/PK/PT 90558) <3009 R13>* **KINKY**
– Head in the sand / A place in the sun / Castles in the air / Something's coming / Miss Freelove '69 / 1000 miles away / Desiree / I don't mind / Brainscan / Too much fun / Dressed in black.
Jun 91. (7"/c-s) *(PB/PK 44577)* **1000 MILES AWAY. / THINK YOU KNOW**
(12"+=/12"pic-d+=)(cd-s+=) *(PT/+P 44636)(PD 49196)* – Stomp the tumba rumba.
1991. (cd-s) *<2805-2>* **MISS FREELOVE '69 / STOMP THE TUMBARUMBA / BRAINSCAN** -
L.D. Zoo
Aug 94. (14169> **RIGHT TIME /** -
Sep 94. (cd/c) *(LD 9453 CD/MC) <31094>* **CRANK**
– The right time / Crosed wires / Quo Vadis / Nobody / From a circle / Fading slow / Gospel train / Less than a feeling / You open my eyes / Hypocrite blues / I see you / Judgement day / Mountain.
Mushroom Volcano-Zoo
Oct 96. (cd) *(TVD 93455) <31123>* **BLUE CAVE** Aug96
– Big deal / Down on me / Mine / Waking up tired / Please yourself / If only . . . Mind the spider / Why? / All i know / Get high! / Always something / Son-of-a-gun / The night must fall.

– compilations, etc. –

1992. (cd) *R.C.A.; <74321 10741-2>* **ELECTRIC SOUP: THE SINGLES COLLECTION** -
– What's my scene / Bittersweet / Come anytime / My girl / 1000 miles away / Axegrinder / Generation gap / Death defying / A place in the sun / Tojo / In the middle of the land / Good times / Castles in the air / Leilani / Poison pen / Another world / Like wow – Wipeout / Miss Freelove '69
1993. (cd) *R.C.A.; <107422>* **GORILLA BISCUIT: THE B SIDES AND RARITIES** -
Apr 98. (d-cd) *Mushroom; (33066)* **ELECTRIC CHAIR**

Peter HOPE (see under ⇒ BOX)

HOPPER

Formed: London, England . . . 1992 by RACHEL MORRIS, PAUL SHEPHERD, CHRIS BOWERS and MATT ALEXANDER, who met at the capital's 'Brain Club'. Signed to 'Damaged Goods', the band bounced onto the scene with a single, 'HUNTER', followed in summer '94 with the equally promising 10" mini-set, 'BABY OIL APPLICATOR'. MORRIS's feisty attitude turned the head of 'Factory (Too)' boss, Tony Wilson, who signed the quartet up for a series of singles and a debut album, 'ENGLISH AND FRENCH' (1996). While the 'WASTED' single kicked and snarled like a chained rottweiler, producer BERNARD BUTLER (ex-SUEDE) overlayed the band's sweet'n'sour guitar attack with lofty string touches and lent the album (their one and only) a more accessible sheen.

Album rating: ENGLISH AND FRENCH (*5)

RACHEL MORRIS – vocals / **PAUL SHEPHERD** – guitar / **CHRIS BOWERS** – bass / **MATT ALEXANDER** – drums
Damaged Goods not iss.
Nov 93. (7") **HUNTER. /** -
Jul 94. (10"m-lp) *(DAMGOOD 39)* **BABY OIL APPLICATOR** -
Factory Too not iss.
Jul 95. (7") *(FAC 2.05)* **WASTED. /** -
(cd-s+=) *(FACD 2.05)* –
Nov 95. (7") *(FAC 2.12)* **OH MY HEARTLESS. /** -
(cd-s+=) *(FACCD 2.12)* –
(re-iss. Apr97; same)
May 96. (7") *(FAC 2.22)* **BAD KID. /** -
(cd-s+=) *(FAC 2.22CD)* –
Jul 96. (7") *(FAC 2.32)* **RIDICULOUS DAY. /** -
(cd-s+=) *(FAC 2.32)* –
Jul 96. (cd/c/lp) *(FAC D/MC/T 2.10)* **ENGLISH AND FRENCH** -
– Bad kid / Placebo / Nice set up / Oh my heartless / 'Cause I rock / Someone phoned / Germolene / Ridiculous day / Four goodbyes / Interference / Homesick / English and French / Wasted / Joytown.

HORMONES

Formed: London, England . . . 1996 by Dublin-born MARC CARROLL, who had led Irish band, PUPPY LOVE BOMB. The latter outfit were part of the 'Rough Trade' stable for a brief period in 1994, releasing the singles, 'NOT LISTENING' and 'BOBBY MILK EP, before splitting the following year.

Moving to the English capital, a mutual friend introduced the guitar-weilding frontman to his new band-to-be, JIMI BOLIN, JEZ HOUSDON and PAT WALTERS. The HORMONES made their debut on 'Trade 2' with the single, 'ARE YOU WITH US', a unique fusion of NIRVANA, the BEACH BOYS and a hint of Irish folk! Signed to Richard Branson's ever-expanding punk-pop-metal label, 'V2', the group embarked upon a prolific singles release schedule culminating with the debut album, 'WHERE OLD GHOSTS MEET', in the summer of '98.

Album rating: WHERE OLD GHOSTS MEET (*6)

MARC CARROLL – vocals, guitar / **JIMI BOLIN** – guitar / **JEZ HOUSDON** – bass / **PAT WALTERS** – drums

Trade 2 not iss.

Sep 96. (7") *(TRDSC 001)* **ARE YOU WITH US. / THE DEVIL GOES TO MOSCOW (GOOD TO KNOW YOU)** [ ] [-]
(cd-s+=) *(TRDSCCD 001)* –

V2 Imprint

Jul 97. (7") *(VVR 500041-7)* **THIS IS THE SOUND. / LOVE THE GIRL** [ ] [-]
(cd-s+=) *(VVR 500041-3)* – Bitched, balloxed and bewildered / G'night, g'luck (I'm going home).

Mar 98. (7"ep/cd-ep) *(VVR 500125-7/-3)* **STAY AHEAD / GOOD TO KNOW YOU. / PATTERNS / TIRED OLD SOULS** [ ] [-]

May 98. (7"ep/cd-ep) *(VVR 500158-7/-3)* **DON'T LET THEM GET YOU DOWN / BE WHAT YOU ARE. / BALLAD OF A DRIFTER (LET'S GO HOME) / OH LORD, SOMETIMES I COULD DIE** [ ] [-]

Jul 98. (7"ep/cd-ep) *(VVR 500189-7/-3)* **MR. WILSON /** [ ] [-]

Aug 98. (cd/lp) *(VVR 100165-2/-1)* *<112031>* **WHERE OLD GHOSTS MEET** [ ] [ ]

HOTALACIO (see under ⇒ FLUX OF PINK INDIANS)

HOT MONKEY (see under ⇒ GRIFTERS)

HOUSEMARTINS

Formed: Hull, England ... late 1983 by PAUL HEATON and STAN CULLIMORE, CHRIS LANG and TED KEY soon completing the line-up. After local gigs, many of them for political causes (i.e. the miners & CND), they signed to Andy McDonald's new 'Go! Discs' label. With HUGH WHITAKER replacing LANG, they released their debut single, 'FLAG DAY', a record that left you in no doubt where the band's political loyalties lay. Although the single failed to chart, with the follow-up, 'SHEEP' (prior to which, NORMAN COOK replaced TED KEY) faring little better, The HOUSEMARTINS imprinted themselves on mid-80's consciousness with 'HAPPY HOUR'. An outrageously catchy single, this was Brit-pop before Brit-pop was even invented; shiny, happy melodies, chiming guitars and nifty footwork, as always with an underlying right-on message. The record reached No.3 in the UK charts, the debut album, 'LONDON 0 HULL 4' (1986) attaining the same position later that summer. An endearing collection of witty, finely crafted songs which, above all, had a big heart and a deep soul, something not exactly at a premium in those dark 80's days with the twin spectres of Thatcher and Stock, Aitken & Waterman never far away. That Christmas, the band became a household name when they scaled the charts with a lovely a cappella cover of ISLEY JASPER ISLEY's 'CARAVAN OF LOVE'. The following Spring, WHITAKER was replaced by DAVE HEMMINGWAY, the band releasing their follow-up album later that year, 'THE PEOPLE WHO GRINNED THEMSELVES TO DEATH'. Even more politically pointed than the debut, the record nevertheless delivered its barbs in unerringly melodic packages, its highlight being the gorgeous gospel-pop of penultimate single, 'BUILD'. Yet the band had almost reached the end of their woefully short lifespan, HEATON and CULLIMORE agreeing from the start that it shouldn't exceed three years. Bowing out with a cover of Burt Bacharach's 'THERE'S ALWAYS SOMETHING THERE TO REMIND ME', The HOUSEMARTINS officially split in early '88. While HEATON went on to even greater success with The BEAUTIFUL SOUTH, the pseudo-Christian, Socialist sentiments he propounded in his earlier career seem a little hollow in light of his alleged penchant for soccer hooliganism. Working Class to the bone, eh mate? WHITAKER's subsequent conduct was little better, the man being sentenced to six years in prison in 1993 for assault and arson offences. NORMAN COOK, on the other hand, became a major player on the dance scene under various aliases, including BEATS INTERNATIONAL, PIZZAMAN and more recently the storming FATBOY SLIM. • **Songwriters:** Penned by HEATON-CULLIMORE except covers; HE AIN'T HEAVY, HE'S MY BROTHER (Hollies) / CARAVAN OF LOVE (Isley Jasper Isley). • **Trivia:** LONDON 0 HULL 4, stemmed from group's promotional hometown pride. They often described themselves as Hull's 4th best group. Who were better? RED GUITARS, EVERYTHING BUT THE GIRL and GARGOYLES?

Album rating: LONDON 0 HULL 4 (*8) / THE PEOPLE WHO GRINNED THEMSELVES TO DEATH (*7) / NOW THAT'S WHAT I CALL QUITE GOOD compilation (*8)

PAUL HEATON (b. 9 May'62, Bromborough, England) – vocals / **STAN CULLIMORE** (b.IAN, 6 Apr'62) – guitar, vocals / **TED KEY** – bass / **HUGH WHITAKER** – drums; repl. CHRIS LANG

Go! Discs Elektra

Oct 85. (7") *(GOD 7)* **FLAG DAY. / STAND AT EASE** [ ] [-]
(12"+=) *(GODX 7)* – Coal train to Hatfield Main.

— **NORMAN COOK** (b. QUENTIN COOK, 31 Jul'63, Brighton, England) – bass repl. TED KEY who formed GARGOYLES

Mar 86. (7"/7"pic-d) *(GOD/+P 9)* **SHEEP. / DROP DOWN DEAD** [54] [-]
(d7"+=) *(GOD 9/+7)* – Flag day / Stand at ease.
(12"+=) *(GODX 9)* – I'll be your shelter / Anxious / People get ready.

May 86. (7"/7"sha-pic-d) *(GOD/+P 11)* *<69515>* **HAPPY HOUR. / THE MIGHTY SHIP** [3] [ ] Sep86
(12"+=) *(GODX 11)* – Sitting on a fence / He ain't heavy.

Jun 86. (lp/c)(cd) *(A/Z GOLP 7)(CCD 1537)* *<60501>* **LONDON 0 HULL 4** [3] [ ] Feb87
– Happy hour / Get up off our knees / Flag day / Anxious / Reverends revenge / Sitting on a fence / Sheep / Over there / Think for a minute / We're not deep / Lean on me / Freedom. *(c+=)* – I'll be your shelter. *(cd++=)* – People get ready / The mighty ship / He ain't heavy. *(re-iss. Oct92 cd/c; same)*

Sep 86. (7"/7"sha-pic-d) *(GOD/+P 13)* **THINK FOR A MINUTE. / WHO NEEDS THE LIMELIGHT** [18] [ ]
(12"+=) *(GODX 13)* – I smell winter / Joy joy joy / Rap around the clock.

Nov 86. (7"/7"sha-pic-d) *(GOD/+P 16)* **CARAVAN OF LOVE. / WHEN I FIRST MET JESUS** [1] [-]
(12"+=) *(GODX 16)* – We shall not be moved / So much in love / Heaven help us all.
(7"box-set+=) *(GODB 16)* **THE HOUSEMARTINS CHRISTMAS BOX SET** – (all 4 singles +=; *GOD 9)* – I'll be your shelter. – hit No.84

Feb 87. (7") *<69491>* **FLAG DAY. / THE MIGHTY SHIP** [-] [ ]

— **DAVE HEMMINGWAY** (b.20 Sep'60) – drums; repl. WHITAKER who joined GARGOYLES full-time

May 87. (7") *(GOD 18)* **FIVE GET OVER EXCITED. / REBEL WITHOUT THE AIRPLAY** [11] [-]
(c-s+=/12"+=) *(XGOD/GODX 18)* – So glad / Hopelessly devoted to them.

Aug 87. (7") *(GOD 19)* **ME AND THE FARMER. / I BIT MY LIP** [15] [-]
(c-s+=/12"+=) *(XGOD/GODX 19)* – He will find you out / Step outside.

Sep 87. (lp/c) *(A/Z GOLP 9)* *<60761>* **THE PEOPLE WHO GRINNED THEMSELVES TO DEATH** [9] [ ] Jan88
– The people who grinned themselves to death / I can't put my finger on it / The light is always green / The world's on fire / Pirate aggro / We're not coming back / Me and the farmer / Five get over excited / Johannesburg / Bow down / You better be doubtful / Build. *(re-iss. Oct92 cd/c; same)*

Nov 87. (7") *(GOD 21)* **BUILD. / PARIS IN FLARES** [15] [-]
(c-s+=)(10"+=/12"+=/cd-s+=) *(ZGOD 21)(GOD X/T/CD 21)* – Forwards and backwards / The light is always green (cheaper version).

Apr 88. (7") *(GOD 22)* **THERE IS ALWAYS SOMETHING THERE TO REMIND ME. / GET UP OFF YOUR KNEES (live)** [35] [-]
(12"+=/cd-s+=) *(GOD X/CD 22)* – Five get over excited (live) / Johannesburg (live).

Apr 88. (d-lp/d-c/cd) *(AGOLP/ZGOLP/AGOCD 11)* **NOW THAT'S WHAT I CALL QUITE GOOD** (compilation) [8] [-]
– I smell winter / Bow down / Think for a minute / There is always something there to remind me / The mighty ship / Sheep / I'll be your shelter / Five get over excited / Everybody's the same / Build / Step outside / Flag day / Happy hour / You've got a friend / He ain't heavy / Freedom / The people who grinned themselves to death / Caravan of love / The light is always green / We're not deep / Me and the farmer / Lean on me.

— They had already decided to split up late '87. NORMAN COOK developed several solo projects including the unashamedly commercial BEATS INTERNATIONAL. HEATON and HEMINGWAY formed The BEAUTIFUL SOUTH.

HOUSE OF LOVE

Formed: Camberwell, London, England ... 1986 by vocalist GUY CHADWICK (ex-KINGDOMS), guitarist TERRY BICKERS (ex-COLENSO PARADE), guitarist ANDREA HEUKAMP, bassist CHRIS GROOTHIZEN and drummer PETE EVANS. Their demo tape soon caught the attention of Creation's ALAN McGEE who signed the act and released their debut single, the sublime and enigmatic 'SHINE ON'. The song was well-received although it didn't make the charts until 1990 when it went Top 20 in its remixed form. John Peel, in particular, was a great fan of the record and played it out over the course of the year. The follow-up, 'REAL ANIMAL' was rather underwhelming in comparison although a sample single for the band's PAT COLLIER (Vibrators)-produced debut album, 'CHRISTINE', picked up where 'SHINE ON' left off, all glistening guitar and darkly mysterious vocals. Sick of touring, HEUKAMP had departed the previous year, leaving the band to record the eponymous debut as a four piece. 'THE HOUSE OF LOVE' (1988) succeeded in living up to the band's early promise, a hypnotic VELVET UNDERGROUND/BYRDS/ONLY ONES hybrid that went down with The STONE ROSES' debut as one of the key releases of the decade. Touted as the future of British guitar music by the press, the band released a final single on 'Creation', 'DESTROY THE HEART', before being snapped up by the 'Polygram'-affiliated 'Fontana' label. A prolonged period of delays and problems ensued as the record company released the 'NEVER' single against the band's wishes in 1989 and the recording of the follow-up album went seriously awry. Another single, 'I DON'T KNOW WHY I LOVE YOU', lingered outside the Top 40 and the year ended with BICKERS departing on less than amicable terms to form his own act, LEVITATION. With SIMON WALKER replacing BICKERS, 'FONTANA' eventually emerged early in 1990 to a varied critical reception although it made the Top 10 and produced another minor Top 40 hit in 'BEATLES AND THE STONES'. A further round of touring followed and later that year ANDREA HEUKAMP returned to the fold. It was to be another year before any new material surfaced, 'THE GIRL WITH THE LONELIEST EYES' eventually being released in October '91. It was a classic CHADWICK composition and despite garnering critical favour again languished in the lower reaches of the charts. During the recording of the band's third album, 'BABE RAINBOW' (1992), WALKER departed, various personnel guesting on the album including WARNE LIVESAY (guitar, keyboards), CAROLE KENYON (vocals) and PANDIT DESH (tablas). Despite CHADWICK's pained deliberation in the studio the album failed to receive resounding critical acclaim and following a similarly underwhelming attempt to revive the band's earlier sound, 'AUDIENCE WITH THE MIND' (1993), CHADWICK called it a day. He eventually resurfaced in 1997, talking to the press about the drink and drug abuse, in-fighting and poor decisions that had marked the downfall of his band, shouldering the lion's share of the blame. Having inked a new deal with 'Setanta', he issued the mellow 'THIS STRENGTH' single in November, lifted from his soon-to-be released comeback album, 'LAZY, SOFT AND SLOW' (scheduled early '98). • **Covered:** I CAN'T STAND IT (Velvet Underground) / PINK FROST (Chills) / IT'S ALL TOO MUCH (Beatles) / STRANGE BREW (Cream) / ROCK YOUR BABY (George McCrae).

Album rating: THE HOUSE OF LOVE (*8) / FONTANA (*7) / BABE RAINBOW (*6) / SPY IN THE HOUSE OF LOVE collection (*5) / AUDIENCE WITH THE MIND (*6) / Guy Chadwick: LAZY SOFT AND SLOW (*6)

GUY CHADWICK (b.21 Mar'56, Hanover, Germany) – vocals, guitar (ex-KINGDOMS) / **TERRY BICKERS** (b. 6 Sep'65) – guitar (ex-COLENSO PARADE) / **ANDREA HEUKAMP** (b.1965, Germany) – guitar, vocals / **CHRIS GROOTHUIZEN** (b. 8 Jul'65, Otahuhu, New Zealand) – bass / **PETE EVANS** (b.22 Oct'57, Swansea, Wales) – drums

Creation | Creation

May 87. (12"m) *(CRE 043T)* **SHINE ON. / LOVE / FLOW** [ ] [-]
Sep 87. (12"m) *(CRE 044T)* **REAL ANIMAL. / PLASTIC / NOTHING TO ME** [ ] [-]

— Now a quartet when ANDREA returned to Germany

Apr 88. (7") *(CRE 053)* **CHRISTINE. / LONELINESS IS A GUN** [ ] [-]
(12"+=) *(CRE 053T)* – The hill.
May 88. (lp/cd) *(CRELP 034/+CD) <88561 8245>* **THE HOUSE OF LOVE** [ ] [ ]
– Christine / Hope / Road / Sulphur / Man to child / Salome / Love in a car / Happy / Fisherman's tale / Touch me. *(lp w/ free 7") (CREFRE 01)* – CHRISTINE (demo). / SHINE ON (demo) *(re-iss. Aug94 cd/c;)*
Aug 88. (7") *(CRE 057)* **DESTROY THE HEART. / BLIND** [ ] [-]
(12"+=) *(CRE 057T)* – Mr Jo.

Fontana | Polygram

Apr 89. (7") *(HOL 1)* **NEVER. / SOFT AS FIRE** [41] [-]
(12"+=/cd-s+=) *(HOL 1-12/CD1)* – Safe.
Nov 89. (7") *(HOL 2)* **I DON'T KNOW WHY I LOVE YOU. / SECRETS** [41] [-]
(c-s+=)(12"+=) *(HOLMC 2)(HOL 2-12)* – I can't stand it.
(cd-s++=) *(HOLCD 2)* – Clothes.
(remix.12"+=) *(HOLR 2-12)* – Clothes / The spy.
(7"g-f) *(HOLG 2)* – ('A'side) / Love II / Clothes.

— **SIMON WALKER** – guitar (of DAVE HOWARD SINGERS) repl. BICKERS

Jan 90. (7"/7"g-f) *(HOL/+G 3)* **SHINE ON (remix). / ALLERGY** [20] [-]
(c-s+=)(12"+=) *(HOLMC 3)(HOL 3-12)* – Scratched inside.
(cd-s++=) *(HOLCD 3-2)* – Love III.
(12"+=) *(HOL 3-22)* – Rosalyn.
(cd-s++=) *(HOLCD 3)* – Rough.
Feb 90. (cd/c/lp) *(842 293-2/-4/-1)* **FONTANA** [8] [-]
– Hannah / Shine on / Beatles and the Stones / Shake and crawl / Hedonist / I don't know why I love you / Never / Somebody's got to love you / In a room / Blind / 32nd floor / Se dest. *(re-iss. Mar94; same)*
Mar 90. (7") *(HOL 4)* **BEATLES AND THE STONES. / LOVE IV** [36] [-]
(12"+=) *(HOL 4-22)* – Phone.
(12"+=) *(HOL 4-12)* – Cut the fool down / Glorify me.
(cd-s+=) *(HOLCD 4-22)* – Marble.
(cd-s+=) *(HOLCD 4)* – Phone (extended) / Soft as fire.
(7"pic-d) *(HOLP 4)* – ('A'side) / Love IV / Love V.
Nov 90. (cd/c/lp) *(846 978-2/-4/-1)* **SPY IN THE HOUSE OF LOVE** (rare material, etc.) [49] [-]
– Safe / Marble / D song '89 / Scratched inside / Phone (full version) / Cut the fool down / Ray / Love II / Baby teen / Love III / Soft as fire / Love IV / No fire / Love V. *(re-iss. cd Aug94; same)*

— (Sep90) added returning **ANDREA HEUKAMP** – guitar, vocals

Oct 91. (7"/c-s) *(HOL/+MC 5)* **THE GIRL WITH THE LONELIEST EYES. / PURPLE KILLER ROSE** [58] [-]
(12"+=)(cd-s+=) *(HOL 5-12)(HOLCD 5)* – Tea in the sun / Pink frost.
Apr 92. (7") *(HOL 6)* **FEEL / IT'S ALL TOO MUCH** [45] [-]
(10"+=) *(HOL 6-10)* – Let's talk about you / Strange brew.
(cd-s++=) *(HOLCD 6)* – Real animal.

— During recording of following album, SIMON left. He was succeeded by **SIMON MAWBEY** (b.24 Dec'60, Leicester, England) – guitar + album guests **ANDREA HEUKAMP** – guitar, vox / **WARNE LIVESEY** – guitar, keyboards, etc. / **CAROL KENYON** – vocals / **PANDIT DENESH** – tablas

Jun 92. (7") *(HOL 7)* **YOU DON'T UNDERSTAND. / SWEET ANATOMY** [46] [-]
(10"+=)(cd-s+=) *(HOL 7-10)(HOLCD 7)* – Kiss the mountain / Third generation liquid song.
(cd-s+=) *(HOLCD 7-2)* – Destroy the heart / Blind / Mr Jo.
Jul 92. (cd/c/lp) *(512549-2/-4/-1)* **BABE RAINBOW** [34] [-]
– You don't understand / Crush me / Crue / High in your face / Fade away / Feel / The girl with the loneliest eyes / Burn down the world / Philly Phile / Yer eyes. *(re-iss. cd Aug94; same)*
Nov 92. (7") *(HOL 8)* **CRUSH ME. / LOVE ME** [67] [-]
(10"+=) *(HOL 8-10)* – Last edition of love / Skin 2 phase 2.
(cd-s) *(HOLCD 8)* – ('A'side) / Christine / Ladies is a gun / The hitch.
Jun 93. (cd/c/lp) *(514880-2/-4/-1) <3145>* **AUDIENCE WITH THE MIND** [38] [ ]
– Sweet anatomy / Audience with the mind / Haloes / Erosion / Call me / Shining on / Portrait in Atlanta / Corridors / Hollow / All night long / Into the tunnel / You've got to feel. *(re-iss. Aug94 cd/c; same)*

— CHADWICK was left with group name after the rest departed. He went solo in 1997.

– compilations, etc. –

Aug 95. (d-cd) *Fontana; (528602-2)* **HOUSE OF LOVE (FONTANA) / SPY IN THE HOUSE OF LOVE** [ ] [-]

GUY CHADWICK

Setanta | Setanta

Nov 97. (cd-ep) *(SETCD 052)* **THIS STRENGTH / WASTED IN SONG / FAR AWAY** [ ] [-]
Feb 98. (cd) *(<SETCD 053>)* **LAZY SOFT AND SLOW** [ ] [ ] May98
– Soft and slow / You've really got a hold of me / One of these days / In her heart / Song for Gala / Mirrored in her mind / Wasted in song / Fall in love with me / This strength / Crystal love song / Close your eyes.
Apr 98. (7") *(SET 048)* **YOU'VE REALLY GOT A HOLD OF ME. / QUESTIONAIRE** [ ] [-]
(cd-s+=) *(SETCD 048)* – Laughter and honey / Slaughterhouse friend.

Dave HOWARD

Born: Toronto, Canada. Relocating to Camberwell, London, he formed the DAVE HOWARD SINGERS (with PAUL MYERS, MARTIN HEATH and PAT AHERN). Taking the organ-grinding of 60's garage punk (? & THE MYSTERIANS, etc) and injecting it with the amphetamine drive of punk, HOWARD created the primitive pulse of 'BEAT BOX BABY', the lead track on his late 1985 DAVE FORMULA (MAGAZINE)-produced debut EP, 'WHO IS HE?'. Although the latter track sounded not too far removed from MARC RILEY & THE CREEPERS, the rest of the EP veered schizophrenically from the FRANKIE GOES TO HOLLYWOOD-esque industrial-pop of 'ROAD WARRIOR' to the slick GLENN GREGORY/HEAVEN 17 pastiche of 'STUFF ME IN YOUR BLENDER' and on to the BILLY MacKENZIE/ASSOCIATES crooner, 'WHEN WILL IT END'. The following Spring, HOWARD and Co titled their second EP after American actor, Karl Malden (famous for his lead role in TV cop show, 'The Streets Of San Francisco'), while the acting connection continued with a cover of David Essex's 'ROCK ON' later that year. 1987's 'IT DOESN'T CUT LIKE A KNIFE' meanwhile, refuted BRYAN ADAMS' earlier claims, the excellent uptempo 'YON YONSON' subsequently namechecking TV sex therapist, Dr. Ruth. DAVE continued his low-key solo exploits for the next couple of years, he never quite got around to release a full-length album.

Album rating: never released any

DAVE HOWARD – vocals, organ, beatbox / **PAUL MYERS** – guitar (ex-SUBWAY SECT) / **MARTIN HEATH** – bass (ex-ANGELTRAX, of POISON GIRLS) / **PAT AHERN** – drums

Hallelujah | not iss.

Dec 85. (12"ep; by DAVE HOWARD SINGERS) *(HALQT 1)* **WHO IS HE?** [ ] [-]
– Beat box baby / Road warrior / Stuff me in your blender / When will it end.

— **NICK SMASH** – drums; repl. AHERN

May 86. (12"ep; by DAVE HOWARD SINGERS) *(HALT 2)* **GOODNIGHT KARL MALDEN** [ ] [-]
– Pleasure of pain / Shakin' all over / How was I to know.
Oct 86. (7") *(FAA 106)* **ROCK ON. /** [ ] [-]
(12"+=) *(12FAA 106)* –
(above issued on 'Fun After All')
Jan 87. (12") *(HALT 3)* **IT DOESN"T CUT LIKE A KNIFE. /** [ ] [-]
Jun 87. (12") *(HALT 4)* **YON YONSON MEETS DR. RUTH (SEX SAMPLE SEQUEL). /** [ ] [-]

— joined by **SIMON WALKER** – guitar

Oct 88. (7"/12") *(HALT 5)* **CHANCES. /** [ ] [-]

Pinpoint | not iss.

Feb 89. (7") *(572 911-31)* **WHAT DO YOU SAY TO AN ANGEL. / SABATA 88** [ ] [-]
(12"+=/cd-s+=) *(572 911-36/+CZ)* –

Ghetto | not iss.

Oct 90. (7") **ALL MY RELATIVES LOOK THE SAME. / SO WHAT** [ ] [-]
(12"+=/cd-s+=) –

— retired from music business after above

H.P. ZINKER

Formed: Innsbruck, Austria . . . 1988, although founding members, HANS PLATZGUMMER and FRANK PUEMMEL took flight to New York in July '89 where they subsequently based themselves permanently after completing national service. After playing the still-going-strong CBGB's club, the duo came to the attention of NY producer Wharton Tiers, who produced a debut album, ' . . .AND THEN THERE WAS LIGHT'. In the event, the record didn't gain an official release until summer '91, by which time the pair had replaced their drum machine with real live jazz-loving drummer, DAVID WASIK. They also had a second album, 'BEYOND IT ALL' (1990) and EP, 'SUNSHINE' (1991), under their belts, both released on Brit indie label, 'Roughneck'. The latter boasted a cameo appearance by chief LEMONHEAD, EVEN DANDO (on the track, 'TO ONE IN PARADISE') whom the band met when playing DANDO's hometown of BOSTON. That said, there was little similarity between the two bands, HP ZINKER trading in a noised-up hybrid of BEEFHEART, the HEARTBREAKERS and the 'CHILI PEPPERS, PLATZGUMMER openly citing his love for, and the influence of, heads down heavy metal on his guitar playing and writing style. Possibly a little too dense and schizophrenic for the average indie fan, the Euro trio called it a day after a further two albums, 'HOVERING' (1991) and 'PERSEVERANCE' (1992).

Album rating: BEYOND IT ALL (*6) / . . . AND THEN THERE WAS LIGHT (*6) / HOVERING (*5) / PERSEVERANCE (*5) / STAYING LOOSE compilation (*6)

HANS PLATZGUMMER – vocals, guitar / **FRANK PUEMMEL** – bass / + a drum machine in '89 (repl. by drummer **DAVID WASIK**)

Roughneck Roughneck

Oct 90. (cd/lp) *(NECK CD/LP 003)* **BEYOND IT ALL**
– Me and my misery / Schwindling / Spmetimes I just don't feel like talking / I don't know what's going on / Die todesdrodge / The offense / Sunbeam First Ave.

May 91. (10"ep/cd-ep) **SUNSHINE EP**
– To one in Paradise / etc.

Jul 91. (m-cd/m-lp) *(NECK CD/LP 004)* **. . . AND THEN THERE WAS LIGHT** (rec.1989)
– Dancing days / My days seem to be long / Sip of death / Hurdles on my way / Sunshine / Down in the basement.

Oct 91. (cd/c) *(NECK CD/MC 006)* **HOVERING**
– Das testament: The shelling / The attack / Wounded / Epilog / Our precious love / Fish are burning / Abandoned feelings / The floating mind / Flug nach Alpha Centauri.

Jun 92. (10"ep/cd-ep) *(HYPE 16 T/CD)* **MYSTERIOUS GIRL**

Sep 92. (cd/lp) *(NECK CD/LP 010)* **PERSEVERANCE**
– Invitation / Warzone city / Reason / Trapped / Mysterious girl / Soulmate / A million sparks are riding my mind / Twister / Desperate moves / Mirror / Now that you're gone.

Nov 93. (cd) *(NECKCD 14)* **STAYING LOOSE** (compilation)
– Reason / Billion dollar babies / Trapped / Our precious love / Soulmate / Hurdles on my way / Fish are burning / Die todesdrodge / To one in Paradise / The know-it-all / Mysterious girl / Flug nach Alpha Centauri / Sunshine / Mirror / My days seem to be long / Warzone city / Trampled to death / Sunbeam First Ave.

— had already disbanded the previous year, HP now runs 'Matador'.

H.R. (see under ⇒ BAD BRAINS)

H2O

Formed: New York, USA . . . 1993 initially as SICK OF IT ALL's stage party piece when roadie, TOBY MORSE, picked up a mic and augmented their encores (during a tour he had sang on the hard-rock pastiche, 'MY LOVE IS REAL'). H2O were really born late in '94, when TOBY and ex-SOIA drummer, MAX CAPSHAW, played their first NY gig (he subsequently drafted in new sticksman, TODD FRIEND plus TOBY – his older brother – and RUSTY PISTACHIO). The angst-ridden spirit of the mid to late 80's hardcore scene was resurrected once again with the release of their eponymous debut album in '96. Adding ex-SHELTER bassist, ADAM BLAKE to the fold, H2O released a second set (their first for 'Epitaph'), 'THICKER THAN WATER', the following year. Their love of hardcore punk shined through, although the band always interspersed their tracks with melody.

Album rating: H2O (*6) / THICKER THAN WATER (*6)

TOBY MORSE – vocals / **TODD MORSE** – guitar (ex-OUTCROWD) / **RUSTY PISTACHIO** – guitar / **ERIC RICE** – bass / **TODD FRIEND** – drums (ex-OUTCROWD) repl. MAX CAPSHAW

Blackout Blackout

Jun 96. (cd) <*(BLK 030E-CD)*> **H2O**
– 5 yr. plan / Scene report / Spirit of '84 / I know why / Gen-eric / Surrounded / Here today, gone tomorrow / Family tree / Hi-low / My curse / My love is real. *(lp-iss.Sep96; BLK 030E-LP)*

— **ADAM BLAKE** – bass (ex-SHELTER) repl. RICE

Epitaph Epitaph

Nov 97. (cd/c/lp) <*(6505-2/-4/-1)*> **THICKER THAN WATER**
– Universal language / Everready / Talk too much / I see it in us / Sacred heart / Innocent kids / Scarred / Go / This time / Friend / Plus / The phone song / Responsible / Wake up / Thicker than water.

Jun 98. (cd-ep) <*(1004-2)*> **EVERREADY / FRIEND / UNIVERSAL LANGUAGE / HERE TODAY, GONE TOMORROW**

HUGGY BEAR

Formed: Brighton, England . . . 1992 as a girl/boy group of neo-feminists. With a line-up comprising of JO JOHNSON, NIKI ELLIOT, KAREN, CHRIS and JOHN, HUGGY BEAR spearheaded the UK 'Riot Grrrl' movement aimed at tackling misogynism and breaking down the illusory barriers between the sexes. Although their intentions might have been honourable, much of the message and the music was buried under an avalanche of (partly self-created) media hype and controversy. Signed to 'Wiiija' (home of CORNERSHOP, SILVERFISH, etc), HUGGY BEAR released a couple of 7" EP's in the latter half of '92, namely 'RUBBING THEE IMPOSSIBLE TO BURST' and 'KISS CURL FOR THE KID'S LIB. GUERILLAS', the former opening with the inflammatory 'KATHOLIC KUNT'. The following year, they found themselves in the news again after objecting to a feature on Channel 4's 'The Word' (they had actually performed their new single, 'HER JAZZ', on the show that night), the band embroiled in an alleged bust-up with security. A shared lp, 'OUR TROUBLED YOUTH / YEAH YEAH YEAH' – with fellow femme agitators, BIKINI KILL – surfaced later that year, an anarchic fusion of The POISON GIRLS and The DOLLY MIXTURES. Meanwhile, JO and NIKI found time to collaborate with members of another likeminded outfit, CEE CEE BEAUMONT; naming themselves BLOOD SAUSAGE, the group issued an EP (an NME Single Of The Week) and a 10" LP, 'HAPPY LITTLE BULLSHIT BOY' (1993). A busy year all round, HUGGY BEAR dodged the press backlash and defiantly delivered another 7"-only EP and a 10"mini-set, TAKING THE ROUGH WITH THE SMOOCH', both featuring the RSPCA-worrying 'SHAVED PUSSY POETRY'. With the 'Riot Grrrl' movement soon to be overtaken by the diluted corporate equivalent of Girl Power (yeah yeah yeah, right~), HUGGY BEAR became extinct after 1994's 'WEAPONRY LISTENS TO LOVE'.

Album rating: OUR TROUBLED YOUTH shared (*6) / TAKING THE ROUGH WITH THE SMOOCH (*6) / WEAPONRY LISTENS TO LOVE (*5) / Blood Sausage: HAPPY LITTLE BULLSHIT BOY (*6)

JO JOHNSON – vocals, bass / **NIKI ELLIOT** – vocals / **CHRIS** – vocals / **JOHN** – guitar / **KAREN** – drums

Wiiija Kill Rock Stars

Sep 92. (7"ep) **RUBBING THEE IMPOSSIBLE TO BURST** –
– Katholic kunt / Jupiter supercone / Snail messenger loss / Single bullets.

Dec 92. (7"ep) **KISS CURL FOR THE KID'S LIB. GUERILLAS** –
– Sizzle meet / Carn't kiss / Derwin / Concrete life.

Feb 93. (7"ep) *(TROUBLE 001)* **HER JAZZ. / WORDCORE // PRAYER / PRO NO FROM NOW** –
(above & below each jointly issued on 'Catcall-Wiiija')

Mar 93. (lp; with BIKINI KILL) *(PUSS 001)* **OUR TROUBLED YOUTH / YEAH YEAH YEAH** –
– Jupiter re-entry / My song No.1 / T-shirt tucked in / Blow dry / Nu song / Into the mission / Hopscortch / Aqua girl star / February 14. // (+ 7 tracks by BIKINI KILL).

Aug 93. (7"ep) *(WIJ 023V)* **DON'T DIE** –
– Dissthentic penetration / Teen tightens / No sleep till . . . / Shaved pussy poetry / Pansy twist.

Sep 93. (10"lp/cd) *(BOMB 015/+CD)* <*KRS 214*> **TAKING THE ROUGH WITH THE SMOOCH**
– Dissthentic penetration / Sizzle meat / Shaved pussy poetry / Pansy twist / Concrete life / Pro no from now / Prayer / Her jazz / Teen tightens / Derwin / No sleep / Carn't kiss.

Nov 94. (cd/lp) *(WIJ 037 CD/V)* <*KRS 236*> **WEAPONRY LISTENS TO LOVE** Dec94
– Immature adolescence / F*** your heart / Face down / Warning rails / On the wolves tip / Erotic bleeding / Sixteen and suicide / Obesity and speed / Insecure offenders / Why am I a lawbreaker / Local arrogance.

not iss. Fellaheen

Nov 96. (m-cd) <*11*> **MAIN SQUEEZE** –

BLOOD SAUSAGE

JO JOHNSON – bass, drums / **NIKI ELLIOT** – drums, vocals / plus **DALE SHAW** – vocals, guitar / **OWEN THOMAS** – guitar, percussion (also of CEE CEE BEAUMONT) / **A.J.W. BOURTON** – guitar, bass, flute, keyboards (also of CEE CEE BEAUMONT)

Wiiija K

Feb 93. (7"ep) *(WIJ 020V)* **TOUCHING YOU IN WAYS THAT DON'T FEEL COMFORTABLE / WHAT LAW AM I BREAKING NOW? / FUCK YOU AND YOUR UNDERGROUND / KNOCK OUT DROPS / THE GIRL WHO KISSED HIS FACE LIKE A CLOCK** –

Jul 93. (10"lp) *(WIJ 024V)* **HAPPY LITTLE BULLSHIT BOY** –

1993. (7") **DENNIS LAVANT. /** –

HULA

Formed: Sheffield, England . . . 1981 as the city's umpteenth industrial unit by MARK ALBROW, RON WRIGHT, ALAN FISH and ALAN WATT. Signing to Leeds-based 'Red Rhino', HULA delivered their debut EP, 'BLACK POP WORKOUT', an exercise in hard electro-funk that drew comparisons with 23 SKIDOO and CABARET VOLTAIRE. Having enlisted the services of CHAKK's MARK BRYDON (to replace WATT), the quartet unleashed their inaugural long-player, 'CUT FROM INSIDE' (1983), although personnel upheavals resulted in the subsequent departures of both BRYDON (briefly substituted by CHRIS BRANE) and FISH. Their respective replacements were JOHN AVERY and NORT, the more stable line-up cutting their finest three minutes in the shape of '(NO ONE LEAVES THE) FEVER CAR' and a slightly improved second set, 'MURMUR' (1984). Like many bands of their ilk, HULA livened up their stage show with the use of graphics and videos, their often enigmatic approach leaving them open to allegations of pretentiousness. From the release of the single, 'GET THE HABIT' onwards, the quartet experimented with jazzed-up dance rhythms and lost some of their underground kudos. Although they were now working from their home-built Sheffield studio, mid-80's albums, '1,000 HOURS' (1986) and 'SHADOWLAND' (1986), were made up largely of live material. Following the collapse of their label, 'Red Rhino', however, 1987's studio set, 'VOICE' proved to be their swansong (not counting compilation, 'THRESHOLD').

Album rating: CUT FROM INSIDE (*6) / MURMUR (*7) / 1,000 HOURS (*4) / SHADOWLAND (*4) / VOIVE (*5) / THRESHOLD compilation (*6) / THE BEST OF HULA compilation (*6)

RON WRIGHT – vocals, guitar, clarinet, tapes / **MARK ALBROW** – keyboards, tapes / **ALAN FISH** – drums, percussion / **ALAN WATT** – bass

Red Rhino not iss.

Sep 82. (12"ep) *(REDT 18)* **BLACK POP WORKOUT** –
– Feeding the animal / Ignoring the famine / Sacred serials.

— **MARK BRYDON** – bass, percussion (of CHAKK) repl. WATT

Nov 83. (lp) *(REDLP 35)* **CUT FROM INSIDE** –

— **NORT** – drums, percussion; repl. FISH who joined CABARET VOLTAIRE

— **JOHN AVERY** – bass; repl. CHRIS BRANE, who repl. MARK BRYDON

Sep 84. (12"ep) *(REDT 47)* **(NO ONE LEAVES THE) FEVER CAR / BATS LOST. / BLOOD RUSH / HARD STRIPES / IN THE SHUTOUT** –

Dec 84. (lp) *(REDLP 53)* **MURMUR** -
– Invisible / Tear-up / Jump the gun / etc

Jun 85. (12") *(REDT 56)* **GET THE HABIT. / BAD BLOOD** -

Dec 85. (12") *(REDT 62)* **WALKS ON THE STALKS OF SHATTERED GLASS. / (version)** -

Mar 86. (lp) *(REDLP 63)* **1,000 HOURS** (half live at the Milky Way, Amsterdam) -
– At the heart / Big heat / etc.

Apr 86. (12") *(REDT 64)* **FREEZE OUT (club version). / FREEZE OUT (radio version)** -

—— added guest **ADAM BARNES**

Oct 86. (lp) *(REDLP 71)* **SHADOWLAND (live in Sheffield)** -

Nov 86. (12"ep) *(REDT 72)* **BLACK WALL BLUE. / STOCKY / 2 A.M.** -

—— added guests **ALAN FISH, JUSTIN BENNETT + DARRELL D'SILVA**

Mar 87. (12") *(REDT 74)* **POISON. /** -

May 87. (lp/c) *(RED LP/C 75)* **VOICE** -
– Give me money / See you tomorrow / Cut me loose / Bush mark 2 / Cold stare / Clear water / Torn silk / Seven sleepers / Poison.

Jul 87. (12"ep) *(REDT 80)* **CUT ME LOOSE / CUT ME UP. / BURN IT OUT / INVISIBLE (live) / WALK ON STALKS OF SHATTERED GLASS (live)** -

—— split when their label folded. NORT guested on an album with IAN ELLIOTT, while the others also kept busy in session work

– compilations, etc. –

Nov 87. (lp/cd) *Red Rhino; (RED LP/CD 83)* **THRESHOLD** -

Dec 87. (c) *Red Rhino; (REDC 85)* **CUT FROM INSIDE / MURMUR** -

Jun 94. (cd) *Anagram; (CDMGRAM 81)* **THE BEST OF HULA** -
– (No one leaves the) Fever car / Get the habit / Freeze out (club mix) / Ghost rattle / Black wall blue / Big heat / Mother courage / Walk on stalks of shattered glass / Tear up / Hard stripes / Poison (club mix) / Seven sleepers / Junshi.

HUM

Formed: Champaign, Illinois, USA . . . 1989 by JEFF DIMPSEY, TIM LASH, BRYAN ST. PERE and MATT TALBOTT. Enterprising and self-reliant, HUM built up a grassroots following through heavy touring while initiating their own label, '12 Inch Records', for the release of debut album, 'ELECTRA 2000' (1993). A few years later, a follow-up set, 'YOU'D PREFER AN ASTRONAUT' was bubbling under the US Top 100; released on 'R.C.A.' ('Dedicated' in the US), the record set layers of mid-paced, muscular guitar against TALBOTT's complex, cryptic lyrics to compelling effect. In early '98, HUM were back with a third long-player, 'DOWNWARD IS HEAVENWARD', carrying on in much the same vein.

Album rating: ELECTRA 2000 (*5) / YOU'D PREFER AN ASTRONAUT (*6) / DOWNWARD IS HEAVENWARD (*5)

MATT TALBOTT (b.27 Jun'67, Geneseo, Illinois) – vocals, guitar / **TIM LASH** (b.16 Jun'74) – guitar / **JEFF DIMPSEY** (b.23 May'67) – bass / **BRYAN ST. PERE** (b. 2 Apr'66, Evergreen Park, Illinois) – drums

not iss. 12-Inch Records

1993. (cd) **ELECTRA 2000** -
– Iron clad Lou / Pinch and roll / Shovel / Pewter / Scraper / Fire head / Sun dress / Double dip / Winder. *(hidden track+=)* – Diffuse. *(UK-iss.Sep97 on 'Martians Go Home'; MGH 001)*

Dedicated R.C.A.

Feb 96. (7"green) *(HUM 001)* **STARS. / STARS (version)** -
(cd-s) *(HUM 001CD)* – ('A'side) / Boy with stick / Baby, baby.

Mar 96. (cd/lp) *(DED CD/LP 023)* **YOU'D PREFER AN ASTRONAUT** Apr95
– Little dipper / The pod / Stars / Suicide machine / The very old man / Why I like the robins / I'd like your hair long / I hate it too / Songs of farewell and departure. *(originally issued in the UK Oct95 as lp on '12 Inch Inch Records'; TIN 012)*

May 96. (7") *(HUM 002)* **THE POD. / MS LAZARUS**
(cd-s+=) *(HUM 002CD)* – Firehead.

Jan 98. (cd) *<67446>* **DOWNWARD IS HEAVENWARD** -
– Isle of the cheetah / Comin' home / If you are to bloom / Ms. Lazarus / Afternoon with the Axolotis / Green to me / Dreamboat / The inuit promise / Apollo / The scientists.

HUMAN LEAGUE

Formed: Sheffield, England . . . Autumn 1977 by computer operators MARTYN WARE and IAN CRAIG-MARSH. As The FUTURE, with vocalist ADI NEWTON, they recruited former hospital porter PHIL OAKEY, who soon replaced ADI (later to CLOCKDVA). Now as HUMAN LEAGUE, the trio recorded demo, which was accepted by Edinburgh-based indie 'Fast', run by Bob Last. Their debut 45 'BEING BOILED', became NME single of the week in mid-78. They added ADRIAN WRIGHT on visuals and synths, and after a dire instrumental EP 'THE DIGNITY OF LABOUR', they signed to 'Virgin' in Apr'79. Their first 45 for the label, 'I DON'T DEPEND ON YOU', was credited to The MEN, but their credibility was restored later that year when 'EMPIRE STATE HUMAN', nearly gave them a hit. This was duly followed by a debut album, 'REPRODUCTION', which failed to build on their early promise. In Spring 1980, they went into UK Top 60 with double-7" EP, 'HOLIDAY '80', and Top 20 with album, 'TRAVELOGUE'. In October '80, OAKEY and WRIGHT brought in teenage girls JOANNE and SUZANNE to replace WARE and CRAIG-MARSH who left to form HEAVEN 17. Twelve months later, with new additions IAN BURDEN and JO CALLIS, they were at No.1 with both the 'DARE' album, and 'DON'T YOU WANT ME' single, which also peaked at the top in the States. By now, the experimental industrial leanings of their early work had given way to a chart dominating new romantic/pop synth sound which made 'DARE' one of the definitive albums of the era. They were also repsonsible, or at least OAKEY was, for perhaps the worst 80's haircut of them all (yes, even worse than the mullet), the accident-with-a-pair-of-garden-shears number that featured one side long and erm . . . one side short! Barnet's aside, the hits were consistent ('KEEP FEELING FASCINATION', 'MIRROR MAN', 'THE LEBANON'), if not exactly prolific and, like many similar 80's acts, by the time they got around to releasing a follow-up set, the fuss had died down. Nevertheless, 'HYSTERIA' (1984) made the UK Top 3, while OAKEY teamed up with disco veteran, GIORGIO MORODER, for the soppy but brilliant 'TOGETHER IN ELECTRIC DREAMS', another massive Top 5 hit in Autumn '84 (the pair subsequently recorded a full length album together, 'CHROME'). Produced by the soul/R&B team of Jimmy Jam and Terry lewis, 'CRASH' (1986) didn't do the band any favours, although it did spawn the melancholy 'HUMAN', a surprise US No.1 and their biggest hit single since the early 80's heyday. Though a 1988 greatest hits album kept the band's profile high, poor sales of 'ROMANTIC' (1990) saw the end of their tenure with 'Virgin', and it looked like permanent relegation was imminent. A new deal with 'East West' and a 1994 Top 10 album, 'OCTOPUS', suggested otherwise, things coming full circle when a remixed version of 'DON'T YOU WANT ME' made the Top 20 in late '95. • **Songwriters:** WARE and CRAIG-MARSH before their departure, and OAKEY and WRIGHT on all since early 80's. The 90's, featured OAKEY composing alongside new member NEIL SUTTON. Covered:- YOU'VE LOST THAT LOVIN' FEELIN' (Righteous Brothers) / ROCK'N'ROLL (Gary Glitter) / NIGHTCLUBBIN' (Iggy Pop) / ONLY AFTER DARK (Mick Ronson).

Album rating: REPRODUCTION (*5) / TRAVELOGUE (*5) / DARE (*8) / LOVE AND DANCING (*4) / HYSTERIA (*5) / CRASH (*5) / GREATEST HITS compilation (*8) / ROMANTIC? (*4) / OCTOPUS (*6) / Phil Oakey & Giorgio Moroder: CHROME (*4)

PHIL OAKEY (b. 2 Oct'55) – vocals / **IAN CRAIG-MARSH** (b.19 Nov'56) – synthesizers / **MARTYN WARE** (b.19 May'56) – synthesizers

Fast not iss.

Jun 78. (7") *(FAST 4)* **BEING BOILED. / CIRCUS OF DEATH** -
(re-iss. Jan82 reached No.6 UK; same)

—— added **ADRIAN WRIGHT** (b.30 Dec'56) – synthesizers, visuals

Apr 79. (12"ep) *(FAST 10)* **THE DIGNITY OF LABOUR** -
– (part 1 / part 2 / part 3 / part 4) *(contains free spoken word flexi; VF 1)*

Virgin A&M

Jul 79. (7"/12"; as The MEN) *(VS 269/+12)* **I DON'T DEPEND ON YOU. / CRUEL (instrumental)**

Sep 79. (7") *(VS 294)* **EMPIRE STATE HUMAN. / INTRODUCING** -

Oct 79. (lp/c) *(V/TCV 2133)* **REPRODUCTION** -
– Almost medieval / Circus of death / The path of least resistance / Blind youth / The word before last / Empire state human / Morale / You've lost that lovin' feelin' / Austerity / Girl one / Zero as a limit. *(re-pro.Aug81, hit UK No.49) (re-iss. Jun88 lp/c; OVED/+C 114) (cd-iss. Dec88; CDV 2133)*

Apr 80. (d7"ep) *(SV 105)* **HOLIDAY '80** 56 -
– Rock'n'roll / Being boiled / Nightclubbing / Dancevision. *(re-iss. Nov81 as 12"ep+=)* – Marianne. *(hit UK No.46)*

May 80. (lp/c) *(T/TCV 2160)* **TRAVELOGUE** 16 -
– The black hit of space / Only after dark / Life kills / Dreams of leaving / Toyota city / Crow and a baby / The touchables / Gordon's Gin / Being boiled / WXJL tonight. *(re-iss. Jun88 lp/c; OVED/+C 115)*

Jun 80. (7") *(VS 351)* **ONLY AFTER DARK. / TOYOTA CITY** 62 -
(free 7" w/) – EMPIRE STATE HUMAN. / INTRODUCING

—— **JO CATHERALL** (b.18 Sep'62) & **SUSANNE SULLEY** (b.22 Mar'63) – b.vocals repl. WARE and MARSH who formed HEAVEN 17. also added **IAN BURDEN** (b.24 Dec'57) – bass, synthesizers

Feb 81. (7") *(VS 395)* **BOYS AND GIRLS. / TOM BAKER** 48 -

Apr 81. (7"/ext.12"; as HUMAN LEAGUE RED) *(VS 416/+12)* **THE SOUND OF THE CROWD. / ('A'instrumental)** 12 -

—— added **JO CALLIS** (b. 2 May'55, Glasgow, Scotland) – guitar (ex-REZILLOS, ex-BOOTS FOR DANCING, ex-SHAKE)

Jul 81. (7"; as HUMAN LEAGUE RED) *(VS 435)* **LOVE ACTION (I BELIEVE IN LOVE). / HARD TIMES** 3 Apr82
(12"+=) *(VS 435-12)* – ('A'&'B'instrumental).
(cd-ep.iss.Jun88; – the four 12"tracks)

Oct 81. (7"; as HUMAN LEAGUE BLUE) *(VS 453)* **OPEN YOUR HEART. / NON-STOP** 6 -
(12"+=) *(VS 453-12)* – ('A'instrumental) / ('B'instrumental).

Oct 81. (lp/pic-lp/c) *(T/TP/TCV 2192)* *<4892>* **DARE** 1 3 Feb82
– Things that dreams are made of / Open your heart / The sound of the crowd / Darkness / Do or die / Get Carter / I am the law / Seconds / Love action (I believe in love) / Don't you want me. *(cd-iss. 1983; OVED 177) (re-iss. Sep90 lp/c; OVED/+C 333)*

Nov 81. (7"; as HUMAN LEAGUE 100) *(VS 466)* *<2397>* **DON'T YOU WANT ME. / SECONDS** 1 1 Feb82
(2"+=) *(VS 466-12)* – ('A'extended).

Jul 82. (lp/c; as LEAGUE UNLIMITED ORCHESTRA) *(OVED/OVEC 6)* *<3209>* **LOVE AND DANCING** 6 Sep92
– (instrumental versions of "DARE" except;) / Get Carter / Darkness. *(cd-iss. Jan86; CDOVED 6)*

Aug 82. (7") **THINGS THAT DREAMS ARE MADE OF. / ('A' instrumental)** -

Oct 82. (7"; as LEAGUE UNLIMITED ORCHESTRA) **DON'T YOU WANT ME. / (part 2)** -

Nov 82. (7"/7"pic-d) *(VS/+Y 522)* **MIRROR MAN. / (YOU REMIND ME OF) GOLD** 2 -
(ext.12"+=) *(VS 522-12)* – Gold (instrumental).

Apr 83. (7"; as HUMAN LEAGUE RED) *(VS 569)* *<2547>* **(KEEP FEELING) FASCINATION. / TOTAL PANIC** 2 8 May83
(ext.12"+=) *(VS 569-12)* – ('A'improvisation).
Jul 83. (m-lp) *<12501>* **FASCINATION** (import, recent hits) - 22
Sep 83. (7") *<2587>* **MIRROR MAN. / NON-STOP** - 30
Apr 84. (7") *(VS 672)* *<2641>* **THE LEBANON. / THIRTEEN** 11 64 Jul84
(ext.12"+=) *(VS 672-12)* – ('A'instrumental).
May 84. (lp/c/cd) *(T/TCV/CDV 2315)* *<4923>* **HYSTERIA** 3 62
– I'm coming back / I love you too much / Rock me again and again and again and again and again / Louise / The Lebanon / Betrayed / The sign / So hurt / Life on your own / Don't you know I want you. *(re-iss. Feb88 lp/c; OVED/+C 177)*
Jun 84. (7") *(VS 688)* **LIFE ON YOUR OWN. / THE WORLD TONIGHT** 16 -
(12"+=) *(VS 688-12)* – ('A'extended).
Aug 84. (7") **DON'T YOU KNOW I WANT TO. / THIRTEEN** -
Oct 84. (7"/7"pic-d)(12") *(VS/+Y 723)(VS 723-12)* **LOUISE. / THE SIGN** 13 -
Oct 84. (7") **LOUISE. / THE WORLD TONIGHT** -

—— Trimmed down to main trio of **PHIL, SUSANNE, JOANNE** plus **ADRIAN / JIM RUSSELL** – synthesizer repl. BURDEN and CALLIS

Aug 86. (7") *(VS 880)* *<2861>* **HUMAN. / ('A'instrumental)** 8 1
(ext.12"+=) *(VS 880-12)* – ('A'acappella).
Sep 86. (lp/c/cd) *(V/TCV/CDV 2391)* *<5129>* **CRASH** 7 24
– Money / Swang / Human / Jam / Are you ever coming back? / I need your loving / Party / Love on the run / The real thing / Love is all that matters
Nov 86. (7") *(VS 900)* **I NEED YOUR LOVING. / ('A'instrumental)** 72 -
(ext.12"+=) *(VS 900-12)* – ('A'dub).
Nov 86. (7") *<2893>* **I NEED YOUR LOVING. / ARE YOU EVER COMING BACK** - 44
Jan 87. (7") **LOVE IS ALL THAT MATTERS. / ('A'instrumental)** -
Apr 87. (7") **ARE YOU EVER COMING BACK. / JAM** -
Oct 88. (7") *(VS 1025)* **LOVE IS ALL THAT MATTERS. / I LOVE YOU TOO MUCH** 41
('B'dub.12"+='B'dub.cd-s+=) *(VS T/CD 1025)* – ('A'extended).
Nov 88. (lp/c/cd/pic-cd) *(HL TV/MC/CD/CDP 1)* **GREATEST HITS** (compilation) 3
– Mirror man / (Keep feeling) Fascination / The sound of the crowd / The Lebanon / Human / Together in electric dreams (PHIL OAKEY & GIORGIO MORODER) / Don't you want me? / Being boiled (re-boiled) / Love action (I believe in love) / Louise / Open your heart / Love is all that matters / Life on your own. *(re-iss. Nov95 cd/c;)*

—— The basic trio, added **RUSSELL BENNETT** – guitar / **NEIL SUTTON** – keyboards

Aug 90. (7"/c-s) *(VS/+C 1262)* *<1520>* **HEART LIKE A WHEEL. / REBOUND** 29 32 Sep90
(12"+=) *(VST 1262)* – ('A'extended).
(cd-s++=) *(VSCDT 1262)* – ('A'remix).
(cd-s++=) *(VSCDX 1262)* – A doorway (dub mix).
Sep 90. (cd/c/lp) *(V/TCV/CDV 2624)* **ROMANTIC?** 24
– Kiss the future / A doorway / Heart like a wheel / Men are dreamers / Mister Moon and Mister Sun / Soundtrack to a generation / Rebound / The stars are going out / Let's get together again / Get it right this time.
Nov 90. (7"/c-s) *(VS/+C 1303)* **SOUNDTRACK TO A GENERATION. / ('A'instrumental)**
(12"+=) *(VST 1303)* – ('A'-Orbit mix).
(cd-s++=) *(VSCDT 1303)* – ('A'-Pan Belguin mix).
(cd-s) *(VSCDX 1303)* – ('A'-Pan Belguin dub) / ('A'-808 instrumental mix) / ('A'-Dave Dodd's mix) / ('A'-acapella).

East West East West

Dec 94. (c-s) *(YZ 882C)* *<64443>* **TELL ME WHEN. / ('A'mix 1)** 6 31 Mar95
(cd-s+=) *(YZ 882CD1)* – Kimi ni mune kyun / The bus to Crookes.
(12"/cd-s) *(YZ 882 T/CD2)* – ('A'side) / ('A'-Overworld mix) / ('A'-Red Jerry mix) / ('A'-Strictly blind dub mix).
Jan 95. (cd/c/lp) *(4509 98750-2/-4/-1)* **OCTOPUS** 6
– Tell me when / These are the days / One man in my heart / Words / Filling up with Heaven / House full of nothing / John Cleese; is he funny? / Never again / Cruel young lover.
Mar 95. (c-s/cd-s) *(YZ 904 C/CD1)* **ONE MAN IN MY HEART / THESE ARE THE DAYS (Ba ba mix)** 13
(cd-s+=) *(YZ 904CD2)* – These are the days (sonic radiation) / ('A'version).
(12") *(YZ 904T)* – ('B'side) / ('B'-Symphone Ba Ba mix) / ('B'instrumental) / ('A'-T.O.E.C. unplugged).
Jun 95. (c-s/cd-s) *(YZ 944 C/CD1)* **FILLING UP WITH HEAVEN / JOHN CLEESE, IS HE FUNNY?** 36
(cd-s) *(YZ 944CD2)* – ('A'side) / ('A'-Hardfloor mix) / ('A'-Neil McLellen mix).
Jan 96. (c-s) *(EW 020C)* **STAY WITH ME TONIGHT / ('A'mix)** 40
(cd-s) *(EW 020CD)* – ('A'mixes).

– compilations, etc. –

Oct 90. (3xcd-box) *Virgin; (TPAK 3)* **DARE / HYSTERIA / CRASH** -
Oct 95. (c-s) *Virgin; (VSC 1557)* **DON'T YOU WANT ME (remix) / ('A'-Snap remix) / (2-'A'-Red Jerry mix)** 16
(12") *(VST 1557)* – ('A'-Snap remix extended) / ('A'-Red Jerry remix extended).
(cd-s) *(VSCDT 1557)* – (all 6-'A'versions).

PHIL OAKEY & GIORGIO MORODER

– synthesizers

Virgin A&M

Sep 84. (7"/7"pic-d/ext.12") *(VS/+Y 713/+12)* **TOGETHER IN ELECTRIC DREAMS. / ('A'instrumental)** 3
Jun 85. (7") *(VS 772)* **GOODBYE BAD TIMES. / ('A'instrumental)** 44
Jul 85. (lp/c/cd) *(V/TCV/CDV 2351)* **CHROME** 52
– Goodbye bad times / Together in electric dreams / Valerie / Why must the show go on / Be me lover now / Shake it up / Brand new lover / In transit / Now. *(re-iss. Oct87; OVED 187)*
Aug 85. (7"/12") *(VS 800/+12)* **BE MY LOVER NOW. / ('A' instrumental)**
Nov 88. (7") *Old Gold; (OG 9825)* **TOGETHER IN ELECTRIC DREAMS. / GOODBYE BAD TIMES** -

HUNGRY I (see under ⇒ EYELESS IN GAZA)

HUNTERS + COLLECTORS

Formed: Melbourne, Australia . . . 1981 by MARK SEYMOUR, MARTIN LUBRAN, GEOFF CROSBIE, JOHN ARCHER, GREG PERANO, DOUG FALCONER, MICHAEL WATERS and live soundman, ROBERT MILES. After a couple of Australian-only released EP's, the ensemble speared their first major deal with 'Virgin' ('A&M' in the States) and unleashed an eponymous debut set early in '83. Featuring such marathon brooding gems as 'TALKING TO A STRANGER' and 'RUN RUN RUN' alongside 'SCREAM WHO' and 'TOW TRUCK', the record sounded like TOM BAILEY (of THOMPSON TWINS) fronting a more intense TALKING HEADS or GANG OF FOUR without forgetting their homeland's ethnic heritage. However, a rushed follow-up, 'FIREMAN'S CURSE' (1983), was something of a let-down which resulted in a move to 'Epic' records, who, in turn, released a third album, 'JAWS OF LIFE' (1984), a year later. A period of musical transition while the band were out of contract, resulted in the group issuing their own very rare white label set, 'WAY TO GO OUT' (1985). Subsequently signing to 'I.R.S.' the following year, H+C released a comeback album of sorts in 'HUMAN FRAILTY' (1986), revealing the more romantic side of the macho Aussie posse with a collection of radio-friendly pop rockers. Despite failing to shake off the cult listening tag, the group attracted an increasingly varied audience through constant touring, releasing 'FATE' (1988) as the creative pinnacle of this period. With CROSBIE, LUBRAN, PERANO and MILES out of the proverbial picture on 1990's 'GHOST NATION', a new band comprising BARRY PALMER, JACK HOWARD and JEREMY SMITH failing to find a focus. Going on musical safari, so to speak, over the next couple of years, HUNTERS & COLLECTORS eventually returned on 'Mushroom' records with two further albums, 'CUT' (1993) and 'DEMON FLOWER' (1994), although by this point, their mainstream sound wasn't so much dated as antique.

Album rating: HUNTERS + COLLECTORS (*7) / FIREMAN'S CURSE (*5) / JAWS OF LIFE (*6) / WAY TO GO OUT (*5) / HUMAN FRAILTY (*7) / FATE (*7) / GHOST NATION (*4) / COLLECTED WORKS compilation (*7) / CUT (*6) / DEMON FLOWER (*5)

MARK SEYMOUR – vocals, guitar / **MARTIN LUBRAN** – guitar / **GEOFF CROSBIE** – keyboards / **JOHN ARCHER** – bass / **DOUG FALCONER** – drums / **GREG PERANO** – percussion / **ROBERT MILES** – live sound / **MICHAEL WATERS** – trombone

WhiteLabel not iss.

1982. (12"ep) *(X 14002)* **PAYLOAD** - - Austra
– Towtruck / Droptank / Mouthtrap / Lumps of lead.

Virgin A&M

Feb 83. (7"/12") *(VS 566/+-12)* **TALKING TO A STRANGER. / ALLIGATOR ENGINE** -
Apr 83. (lp) *(V 2260)* *<4973>* **HUNTERS + COLLECTORS** -
– Tow truck / Drop tank / Mouthtrap / Lumps of lead / Talking to a stranger / Scream who / Run run run. *(re-iss. Aug88 lp/c; OVED/+C 92)*
Aug 83. (7") *(VS 616)* **JUDAS SHEEP. / MR. NIGHT** -
(12"+=) *(VS 616-12)* – Eggheart.
Oct 83. (lp) *(V 2279)* **THE FIREMAN'S CURSE** -
– Sway / Judas sheep / Eggheart / Drinking bomb / Curse / Fish roar / Blind snake sundae / Mr. Right.

Epic Slash

Aug 84. (7") *(A 4648)* **CARRY ME. / UNBELIEVER** -
(12"+=) *(TA 4648)* – Follow me no more.
Sep 84. (lp/c) *(EPC/40 26310)* **JAWS OF LIFE**
– 42 wheels / Holding down a "D" / The way to go out / I couldn't give it to you / It's early days yet / I believe / Betty's worry or the slab / Hayley's doorstep / Red lane / Little Chalkie.

White label not iss.

1985. (lp) **WAY TO GO OUT (live)** - - Austra

I.R.S. I.R.S.

Aug 86. (lp/c) *(IRS/+C 5801)* **HUMAN FRAILTY** -
– Say goodbye / Throw your arms around me / Dog / Everything's on fire / Relief / Living daylight / Inside a fireball / January rain / The finger / 99th home positions / Is there anybody in there / Stuck on you / This morning. *<US cd-iss. 1987 +=; IRSD 42024>* – LIVING DAYLIGHT
1987. (m-lp) *<IRS 36017>* **LIVING DAYLIGHT** -
– Inside a fireball / Living daylight / January rain / Slab / Carry me.
Aug 88. (7"/12") *(IRM/+T 171)* **DO YOU SEE WHAT I SEE. /** -
Sep 88. (lp/c)(cd) *(MIRF/+C 1037)(DMIRF 1037)* *<IRSCD 42110>* **FATE**
– Back on the breadline / Wishing well / You can have it all / Do you see what I see / Around the flame / Faraway man / Under the sun / What are you waiting for / So long ago / Real world / Something to believe in / Breakneck road / What's a few men.
Nov 88. (7") *(IRM 177)* **BACK ON THE BREADLINE. / ('A'version)** -
(12"+=/cd-s+=) *(IRMT/DIRM 177)* – Under the sun.

—— **BARRY PALMER** – guitar / **JACK HOWARD** – keyboards, trumpet / **JEREMY SMITH** – french horn, guitar, keyboards repl. PERANO, CROSBIE, LUBRAN + MILES

Elektra Atlantic

Apr 90. (cd)(lp/c) *(<7567 82096-2>)(WX 348/+C)* **GHOST NATION**
– When the river runs dry / Blind eye / Love all over again / Crime passion / You stole my thunder / Ghost nation / The way you live / Gut feeling / Lazy summer day / Running water.
May 90. (7"/c-s) *(A 7914/+MC)* **WHEN THE RIVER RUNS DRY. / TWO ROADS** -
(12"+=/cd-s+=) *(A 7914 T/CD)* – Price of freedom.

Mushroom Shake

1993. (cd) *(TVD 93364)* **CUT** [-] [ ]
(UK-iss.Feb96; same)

Apr 94. (cd-s) *(D 11579)* **HOLY GRAIL /** [ ] [-]

May 94. (cd/c) *(TVD/TVC 93401) <220>* **DEMON FLOWER** [ ] [ ] Jul95
– Easy / Panic in the shade / Back in the hole / The one & only you / Mr Bigmouth / Courtship of America / Drop in the ocean / Newborn / Tender / Desert where her heart is / Betrayer / Ladykiller / Holy grail.

1995. (cd) *(TVD 98017)* **LIVING IN LARGE ROOMS AND LOUNGES (live)** [-] [-] Austra
– Slab / Say goodbye / True tears of joy / Throw your arms around me / Easy / Courtship of America / Betrayer / Back in the hole / Ladykiller / Most unoriginal sin / Holy grail / When the river runs dry / Easy / Stuck on you / Say goodbye / Chalkie / Blind eye / Everything's on fire / 42 wheels / Head above water / Mr. Bigmouth / Where do you go? / One and only you / Do you see what I see?

unknown not iss.

1998. (cd) **JUGGERKNAUT** [-] [-] Austra

—— disbanded in '98

– compilations, etc. –

May 91. (cd/c) *I.R.S.; (X2/X4 13053)* **COLLECTED WORKS** [ ] [ ] Aug90

Nov 98. (cd-s) *Mushroom; (794)* **TALKING TO A STRANGER** [ ] [-]

Nov 98. (cd) *Mushroom; (TVD 33176)* **UNDER ONE ROOF (live)** [ ] [-]

HURRAH!

Formed: Newcastle, England ... early 80's briefly as the GREEN-EYED CHILDREN by main songwriters PAUL HANDYSIDE and TAFFY HUGHES, the pair enlisting ANTHONY PRICE and MARK SIM (the latter was soon to be replaced by DAMIEN MAHONEY). Opting for the punchier moniker, HURRAH!, the quartet were one of the first signings to local independent, 'Kitchenware' (others being PREFAB SPROUT, MARTIN STEPHENSON & THE DAINTEES and The KANE GANG), releasing their debut single, 'THE SUN SHINES HERE', in '82. It would be at least a year before HURRAH! followed it up with a second 7", 'HIP HIP' gaining some support in the music press and giving them an indie chart hit. DAVID PORTERHOUSE filled the shoes of the departing PRICE, while yet another two singles, 'WHO'D HAVE THOUGHT' and 'GLORIA', endeared them to fans of melodic mainstream jangle-pop but occasionally strayed too far into HAIRCUT 100 territory for comfort. Thankfully, HURRAH! celebrated their move (as part and parcel of Kitchenware's deal) to major label land ('Arista') with a shift towards a more rock-based sound on two singles, 'SWEET SANITY' and 'LOVE COULD KILL', and an accompanying UK Top 75 album, 'TELL GOD I'M HERE'. Appropriately enough, the lads secured a support slot with U2 (then going through their Messianic stage!) at the Wembley leg of their 'Joshua Tree' tour. Nevertheless, the party poppers remained under wraps as HURRAH! failed to make a breakthrough with 1989's 'THE BEAUTIFUL', ADRIAN EVANS substituting recent recruit STEVE PRICE for a final single and a posthumous live set entitled 'THE SOUND OF PHILADELPHIA' (1993).

Album rating: BOXED compilation (*6) / TELL GOD I'M HERE (*5) / THE BEAUTIFUL (*4) / THE SOUND OF PHILADELPHIA (*5)

PAUL HANDYSIDE (b.28 Sep'60, Newcastle-Upon-Tyne, England) – vocals, guitar / **TAFFY HUGHES** (b. DAVID, 16 Mar'61, Southmoor, Northumberland, England) – guitar, vocals / **ANTHONY PRICE** – bass / **DAMIEN MAHONEY** – drums; repl. MARK SIM

Kitchenware not iss.

Jun 82. (7") *(SK 2)* **THE SUN SHINES HERE. / I'LL BE YOUR SURPRISE** [ ] [-]

Sep 83. (7") *(SK 6)* **HIP HIP. / FLOWERS** [ ] [-]

—— **DAVE PORTERHOUSE** (b.17 Aug'61, Gateshead, England) – bass; repl. PRICE

Oct 84. (7") *(SK 14)* **WHO'D HAVE THOUGHT. / WHO'D HAVE THOUGHT (SLIGHT RETURN)** [ ] [-]
(12"+=) *(SKX 14)* – Celtic (who wants to live by love alone).

May 85. (7") *(SK 18)* **GLORIA. / FUNNY DAY** [ ] [-]
(12"+=) *(SKX 18)* – Tame / This boy.

Nov 85. (lp) *(SKINT 1)* **BOXED** (compilation) [ ] [-]

—— trimmed to a trio for a while when MAHONEY joined the police force

—— added **STEVE PRICE** – drums; replaced him

Kitchenware Arista

Oct 86. (7") *(SK 28)* **SWEET SANITY. / HEART AND HAND** [ ] [ ]
(12"+=) *(SKX 28)* – Don't need food.

Jan 87. (7") *(SK 29)* **IF LOVE COULD KILL. / TELL ME ABOUT YOUR PROBLEMS** [ ] [-]
(12"+=) *(SKX 29)* – Girl of my dreams.
(d7"++=) *(SKD 29)* – Gloria.

Feb 87. (lp/c/cd) *(208/408/258 201)* **TELL GOD I'M HERE** [71] [ ]
– I would if I could / Better times / Sweet sanity / Celtic (who wants to live by love alone) / A walk in the park / How many rivers? / If love could kill / Miss the kiss / How high the moon / Mr. Sorrowful. *(also cd; KWCD 6)*

May 87. (7") *(SK 31)* **HOW MANY RIVERS? / THREE WISHES** [ ] [-]
(12"+=) *(SKX 31)* – If it rains.

Nov 88. (7") *(111 911)* **SWEET SANITY. / HEART AND HAND** [ ] [-]
(12"+=/cd-s+=) *(611/661 911)* – Gloria / How many rivers?

Apr 89. (7") *(SK 42 – 111 770)* **BIG SKY. / SATURDAY'S TRAIN** [ ] [-]
(12"+=/3"cd-s+=) *(SK X/CD 42 – 611/661 770)* – The secret life.
(10"pic-d+=) *(SKPD 42 – 612 207)* – A walk in the park.

Apr 89. (lp/c/cd) *(SK LP/C/CD 10)* **THE BEAUTIFUL** [ ] [ ]
– Big sky / Troubled brow / Wisdom waits / Diana Diana / Velveteen / Let it be her / Call for me / Sad but true / Girls of Janla / She said. *(cd+=)* – The secret life.

—— **ADRIAN EVANS** (b. 6 Mar'63, County Durham, England) – drums; repl. STEVE PRICE

unknown not iss.

Apr 91. (7") **THAT'S DREAM'S OVER NOW. /** [ ] [-]

—— split up as their final single above might suggest, leaving behind . . .

Creation Rev-Ola not iss.

Aug 93. (cd) *(CREV 014CD)* **THE SOUND OF PHILADELPHIA (live)** [ ] [-]
– (live intro tape) / The sun shines here / I'll be your surprise / Don't need food / Saturday's train / Lonely room / Hip hip / Around and around (when in Rome) / If it rains / The point of perfection / Who'd have thought / Celtic (who wants to live by love alone) / Big sky / This boy / Gloria / Funny day / A walk in the park / Suffer and see / Sweet sanity / How many rivers? / Miss this kiss / If love could kill / I would if I could.

HURRICANE #1

Formed: Oxford, England ... 1996, by former RIDE guitarist/songwriter, ANDY BELL. Having procured his new recruits from a variety of disparate sources (i.e. WILL PEPPER from THEE HYPNOTICS, ALEX LOWE – via a newspaper ad placed by Creation boss ALAN McGEE – a former boxer from Glasgow and GAZ from the crowd at a BELL solo gig), the band changed their name to HURRICANE #1 to avoid confusion with another similarily named act. In the Spring of '97, Creation records released 'STEP INTO MY WORLD', which stormed into the Top 30. They gained further exposure via an appearance at The Brighton Essential Music Festival before hitting the charts again with follow-up, 'JUST ANOTHER ILLUSION'. Their third 45, 'CHAIN REACTION', also made the UK Top 30 and preceded their fairly cliched self-titled album, which although nearly hitting the Top 10, failed to carve out a distinctive sound to set it apart from the legions of sub Brit-pop no-hopers. To end a fairly successful year, the live favourite, 'STEP INTO MY WORLD' was given the remix treatment resulting in their highest chart position so far, 19. • **Trivia:** BELL married Creation solo artist IDHA in the mid 90's.

Album rating: HURRICANE #1 (*5)

ALEX LOWE (b. Tayside, Scotland) – vocals / **ANDY BELL** – lead guitar, keyboards, vocals (ex-RIDE) / **WILL PEPPER** – bass (ex-THEE HYPNOTICS) / **GARETH FARMER** – drums, percussion

Creation Alex-Warners

Apr 97. (7"/c-s) *(CRE/+C 253) <6097>* **STEP INTO MY WORLD. /** [29] [ ] May98
(cd-s+=) *(CRESCD 253)* –

Jun 97. (7") *(CRE 264) <6042>* **JUST ANOTHER ILLUSION. /** [35] [ ] Feb98
(cd-s+=) *(CRESCD 264)* –
(cd-s) *(CRESCD 264X)* –

Aug 97. (7") *(CRE 271)* **CHAIN REACTION. / KEEP WALKING** [30] [-]
(cd-s+=) *(CRESCD 271)* – Why don't you do it?
(cd-s) *(CRESCD 271X)* – ('A'mixes).

Sep 97. (cd/c/lp) *(CRECD/CCRE/CRELP 206) <46763>* **HURRICANE #1** [11] [ ] Oct97
– Just another illusion / Faces in a dream / Step into my world / Mother Superior / Let go of the dream / Chain reaction / Lucky man / Strange meeting / Monday afternoon / Stand in line.

Oct 97. (7") *(CRE 276)* **STEP INTO MY WORLD (Perfecto edit). / ('A'mix)** [19] [-]
(cd-s) *(CRESCD 276)* – ('A'-Paul Oakenfold edit) / If you think it's easy / Never mind the rain.
(cd-s) *(CRESCD 276X)* – ('A'-Perfecto mix) / ('A'-Kahuna mix) / ('A'-Andy Bell remix) / ('A'-Get it together mix).

Feb 98. (7") *(CRE 285)* **ONLY THE STRONGEST WILL SURVIVE. /** [19] [-]
(cd-s+=) *(CRESCD 285)* –
(cd-s) *(CRESCD 285X)* –

Creation Imprint

Oct 98. (7") *(CRE 303) <111580>* **RISING SIGN. /** [47] [ ] Nov98
(cd-s) *(CRESCD 303)* –
(cd-s) *(CRESCD 303X)* –

HUSKER DU

Formed: St. Paul, Minnesota, USA ... 1978 by MOULD, HART and NORTON. In 1980-82, they issued a few 45's and a live lp 'LAND SPEED RECORD', on their own label, 'New Alliance'. The record typified the band's early uncompromising hardcore which was often tediously workmanlike in its adherence to the steadfast confines of the genre. 'EVERYTHING FALLS APART' (1983) was also unflinching in its intensity and it was all the more surprising when the band showed glimmers of noise-pop greatness on their 1983 debut for 'SST', 'METAL CIRCUS'. They consolidated this by cross fertilising the previously polarised worlds of psychedelia and hardcore punk on an electrifying cover of The BYRDS' 'EIGHT MILES HIGH' (1984). The follow-up double set, 'ZEN ARCADE' (1984) was a further giant step for hardcore kind. A concept album no less, the twin songwriting attack of MOULD and HART was becoming sharper and even the sprawling, unfocused feel of the whole affair wasn't enough to blunt the edges of songs like 'WHATEVER' and 'TURN ON THE NEWS'. The songwriting on 'NEW DAY RISING' (1985) was even more trenchant, the band's adrenaline fuelled pop-core hybrid developing at breakneck speed. 'FLIP YOUR WIG' (1985), the band's last indie release, marked a stepping stone to their major label debut for 'Warners', 'CANDY APPLE GREY' (1986). While HART perfected HUSKER DU's melodic dischord on tracks like 'DEAD SET ON DESTRUCTION', MOULD showcased darkly introspective, acoustic elegies 'TOO FAR DOWN' and 'HARDLY GETTING OVER IT'. The more musically-challenged among HUSKER DU's following were none too taken with this new fangled unplugged business although the album was released to unanimous critical acclaim. The band's swansong, 'WAREHOUSE: SONGS AND STORIES' (1987) was the culmination of a decade's experimentation and possessed an unprecedented depth, clarity and consistence. By the time of its release, though, tension in the band was reaching breaking point and HUSKER DU was disbanded in 1987. While GRANT HART and BOB MOULD went on to solo careers, as well as respectively forming NOVA MOB and SUGAR, they were always better together and the magic of HUSKER DU is inestimable in its influence on a generation of alternative guitar bands. • **Songwriters:** MOULD-HART compositions except; SUNSHINE SUPERMAN (Donovan) / TICKET TO RIDE + SHE'S A WOMAN + HELTER SKELTER (Beatles) / EIGHT MILES HIGH (Byrds). NOVA MOB covered I JUST WANT TO MAKE LOVE TO YOU (Willie Dixon) / SHEENA IS A PUNK ROCKER (Ramones). Solo GRANT HART covered SIGNED D.C. (Love). • **Trivia:** HUSKER DU means DO YOU REMEMBER in Swedish.

Album rating: EVERYTHING FALLS APART (*5) / ZEN ARCADE (*9) / NEW DAY RISING (*9) / FLIP YOUR WIG (*9) / CANDY APPLE GREY (*7) / WAREHOUSE: SONGS & STORIES (*9) / THE LIVING END live compilation (*6) / Grant Hart: INTOLERANCE (*6) / Nova Mob: THE DAYS DAYS OF POMPEII (*6) / NOVA MOB (*6) / ECCE HOMO (*5)

BOB MOULD (b.12 Oct'60, Malone, N.Y.) – vocals, guitar, keyboards, percussion / **GRANT HART** (b. GRANTZBERG VERNON HART, 18 Mar'61) – drums, keyboards, percussion, vocals / **GREG NORTON** (b.13 Mar'59, Rock Island, Illinois) – bass

not iss. — Reflex

1980. (7") *<38285>* **STATUES. / AMUSEMENT (live)** [-] [ ]

Alternative Tentacles — New Alliance

1982. (lp) *(VIRUS 25) <NAR 007>* **LAND SPEED RECORD (live)** [-] [ ]
– All tensed up / Don't try to call / I'm not interested / Big sky / Guns at my school / Push the button / Gilligan's Island / MTC / Don't have a life / Bricklayer / Tired of doing things / You're naive / Strange week / Do the bee / Ultracore / Let's go die / Data control. *(re-iss. Nov88 on 'S.S.T.'; SST 195) (re-iss. cd/c/lp Oct95)*

1982. (7"m) *<NAR 010>* **IN A FREE LAND. / WHAT DO I WANT? / M.I.C.** [-] [ ]

not iss. — Reflex

Jul 83. (lp) *<D>* **EVERYTHING FALLS APART** [-] [ ]
– From the gut / Blah, blah, blah / Punch drunk / Bricklayer / Afraid of being wrong / Sunshine Superman / Signals from above / Everything falls apart / Wheels / Obnoxious / Gravity. *(cd-iss. May93 on 'WEA'+=; 8122 71163-2)* – In a free land / What do I want / M.I.C. / Statues / Let's go die / Amusement (live) / Do you remember?

S.S.T. — S.S.T.

Dec 83. (m-lp) *<(SST 020)>* **METAL CIRCUS** [ ] [ ]
– Real world / Deadly skies / It's not funny anymore / Diane / First of the last calls / Lifeline / Out on a limb.

Apr 84. (7"colrd) *(SST 025)* **EIGHT MILES HIGH. / MASOCHISM WORLD** [ ] [ ]
(cd-s iss.Dec88; SST 025CD)

Sep 84. (d-lp) *<(SST 027)>* **ZEN ARCADE** [ ] [ ]
– Something I learned today / Broken home, broken heart / Never talking to you again / Chartered trips / Dreams reoccurring / Indecision time / Hare Krishna / Beyond the threshold / Pride / I'll never forget you / The biggest lie / What's going on / Masochism world / Standing by the sea / Somewhere / One step at a time / Pink turns to blue / Newest industry / Monday will never be the same / Whatever / The tooth fairy and the princess / Turn on the news / Reoccurring dreams. *(cd-iss. Oct87; SST 027CD) (re-iss. cd/c/d-lp Oct95 & Jun97; same)*

Feb 85. (lp) *<(SST 031)>* **NEW DAY RISING** [ ] [ ]
– New day rising / Girl who lives on Heaven Hill / I apologize / Folklore / If I told you / Celebrated summer / Perfect example / Terms of psychic warfare / 59 times the pain / Powerline / Books about UFO's / I don't know what you're talking about / How to skin a cat / Watcha drinkin' / Plans I make. *(cd-iss. Oct87; SST 031CD) (re-iss. cd/c/lp Oct95; same)*

Aug 85. (7") *<(SST 051)>* **MAKE NO SENSE AT ALL. / LOVE IS ALL AROUND (MARY'S THEME)** [ ] [ ]

Oct 85. (lp) *<(SST 055)>* **FLIP YOUR WIG** [ ] [ ]
– Flip your wig / Every everything / Makes no sense at all / Hate paper doll / Green eyes / Divide and conquer / Games / Find me / The baby song / Flexible flyer / Private plane / Keep hanging on / The wit and the wisdom / Don't know yet. *(cd-iss. Oct87; SST 055CD) (re-iss. cd/c/lp Oct95; same)*

Warners — Warners

Feb 86. (7") *(W 8746)* **DON'T WANT TO KNOW IF YOU ARE LONELY. / ALL WORK NO PLAY** [ ] [ ]
(12"+=) *(W 8746T)* – Helter skelter (live).

Mar 86. (lp/c) *(WX 40/+C) <25385>* **CANDY APPLE GREY** [ ] [ ]
– Crystal / Don't want to know if you are lonely / I don't know for sure / Sorry somehow / Too far down / Hardly getting over it / Dead set on destruction / Eiffel Tower high / No promises have I made / All this I've done for you. *(cd-iss. Nov92; 7599 25385-2)*

Sep 86. (7") *(W 8612)* **SORRY SOMEHOW. / ALL THIS I'VE DONE FOR YOU** [ ] [ ]
(d7+=/12"+=) *(W 8612 F/T)* – Flexible flyer / Celebrated summer.

Jan 87. (7") *(W 8456)* **COULD YOU BE THE ONE. / EVERYTIME** [ ] [ ]
(12"+=) *(W 8456T)* – Charity, chastity, prudence, hope.

Jan 87. (d-lp/d-c) *(925544-1/-4) <25544>* **WAREHOUSE: SONGS & STORIES** [72] [ ]
– These important years / Charity, chastity, prudence and hope / Standing in the rain / Back from somewhere / Ice cold ice / You're a soldier / Could you be the one? / Too much spice / Friend, you've got to fall / Visionary / She floated away / Bed of nails / Tell you why tomorrow / It's not peculiar / Actual condition / No reservations / Turn it around / She's a woman (and now he is a man) / Up in the air / You can live at home. *(cd-iss. Oct92; 7599 25544-2)*

Jun 87. (7") *(W 8276)* **ICE COLD ICE. / GOTTA LETTA** [ ] [ ]
(12"+=) *(W 8276T)* – Medley.

—— Disbanded in 1987 after manager, DAVID SAVOY Jr., committed suicide. GRANT HART went solo in '89, as did BOB MOULD. In 1992 the latter formed SUGAR.

– compilations, etc. –

May 94. (cd/c) *Warners; <(9362 45582-2/-4)>* **THE LIVING END (live)** [ ] [ ]
– New day rising / Heaven Hill / Standing in the rain / Back from somewhere / Ice cold ice / Everytime / Friend you're gonna fall / She floated away / From the gut / Target / It's not funny anymore / Hardly getting over it / Terms of psychic warfare / Powertime / Books about UFO's / Divide and conquer / Keep hangin' on / Celebrated summer / Now that you know me / Ain't no water in the well / What's goin' on / Data control / In a free land / Sheena is a punk rocker.

GRANT HART

S.S.T. — S.S.T.

Oct 89. (7"ep/cd-ep) *(SST 219/+CD)* **2541. / COME HOME / LET'S GO** [ ] [-]

Nov 89. (lp/cd) *<(SST 215/+CD)>* **INTOLERANCE** [ ] [ ]
– All of my senses / Now that you know me / The main / Roller risk / Fanfare in D major (come, come) / You're the victim / 2541 / Anything / She can see the angels coming / Reprise.

May 90. (12"ep/cd-ep) *(SST 262/+CD)* **ALL OF MY SENSES. / THE MAIN (edit) / SIGNED D.C.** [ ] [ ]

NOVA MOB

(GRANT HART) & his group:- **TOM MERKL** – bass / **MICHAEL CRECO** – drums

Rough Trade — Rough Trade

Feb 91. (cd/c/lp) *<(R 2081261-2/-4/-1)>* **THE LAST DAYS OF POMPEII** [ ] [ ]
– Introduction / Woton / Getaway (gateway) in time / Admiral of the sea (79 a.d. version) / Wernher Von Braun / Space jazz / Where you grave land (next time you fall off of yo) / Over my head / Admiral of the sea / Persuaded / Lavender and grey / Medley:- The last days of Pompeii / Benediction.

Feb 91. (12"ep/cd-ep) *(RTT/RCD 267)* **ADMIRAL OF THE SEA (first avenue mix) / ('A' milk off mix) / THE LAST DAYS OF POMPEII (mix) / GETAWAY IN TIME (instrumental) / I JUST WANT TO MAKE LOVE TO YOU (live)** [ ] [ ]

—— **MARK RELISH** – drums repl. CRECO

Southern — Big Store

Jul 92. (cd-ep) *<EFA 04669CD>* **SHOOT YOUR WAY TO FREEDOM / BALLAD NO.19 / OH! TO BEHOLD / CHILDREN IN THE STREET** [ ] [ ]

—— **HART** with **CHRIS HENSLER** – guitar / **TOM MERKL** – bass / **STEVE SUTHERLAND** – drums

World Service — Restless

May 94. (cd/lp) *(1571744-2/-1) <72762>* **NOVA MOB** [ ] [ ]
– Shoot your way to freedom / Puzzles / Buddy / See and feel and know / Little Miss Information / I won't be there anymore / Please don't ask / The sins of their sons / Beyond a reasonable doubt / I was afraid – Coda.

Sep 94. (cd-ep) **OLD EMPIRE / PLEASE DON'T ASK / LITTLE MISS INFORMATION / BEYOND A REASONABLE DOUBT** [ ] [-]

Dec 95. (cd; GRANT HART) *<(RTD 1573096-2)>* **ECCE HOMO** (live) [ ] [ ]
– Ballad No.19 / 2541 / Evergreen / Memorial drive / Come come / Pink turns to blue / She floated away / The girl who lives on Heaven hill / Admiral of the sea / Back somewhere / Last days of Pompeii / Old Empire / Never talking to you again / Please don't ask / The main.

ICE

Formed: South London, England ... late 1993 by former GOD members, KEVIN MARTIN, DAVE COCHRANE and J. JOBBAGY, plus ex-GODFLESH mainman, JUSTIN BROADRICK. The blasphemously-monikered GOD released several jazzy METALLICA meets BUTTHOLE SURFERS-esque albums, including 'SWEET LIFE' (1988) and 'POSSESSION' (1992), before the dub-wise KEVIN and the aforementioned JUSTIN initiated two projects, TECHNO ANIMAL and ICE. The former duo delivered a landscape CABS/THROBS-type set, 'GHOSTS' (1991), the most challenging track being 'THE DREAM FORGER'. In 1993, ICE thawed-out their take on Mogadon-rock, brutal guitars and dub-hop landscapes filling their debut album, 'UNDER THE SKIN'. The quartet subsequently featured on two Virgin compilation sets, 'Isolationism' and 'Macro-Dub Infection', mixing a couple of techno/ambient pieces with sensory precision. Meanwhile, TECHNO ANIMAL raged its ambient head once more; the double-cd set, 'RE-ENTRY' (1995), was masterful in all its blips, noises and an additional bonus, the superb playing of the veteran trumpet-blower, JON HASSELL. ICE's long-awaited follow-up, 'BAD BLOOD', was finally let loose early in '98. A return to more conventional hardcore, it nevertheless blitzkreig'd the eardrums with appropriately off-kilter vocals by BLIXA BARGELD (of EINSTURZENDE NEUBAUTEN).

Album rating: UNDER THE SKIN (*7) / BAD BLOOD (*6) / Techno Animal: RE-ENTRY (*8)

GOD

KEVIN MARTIN – saxophone, synthesizer, voice / **SHAUN** – guitar / **DAVE COCHRANE** – bass / plus others including producer JOHN ZORN, with HENRY COW, SLAB! and TERMINAL CHEESECAKE members

Konkurrel / not iss.

May 88. (lp) *(K 031-110)* **SWEET LIFE** -
– See smoke, smell fire / The finger / Settling down / Lust / Wimps / Teste marce / Stomping ground / Sack B / So be it / The asset of punishment.

1989. (lp) *(K 031-120)* **THE SHAME TREE** -

Shakin Street / not iss.

May 89. (7") *(YEAHHUP 002)* **FOR LOVERS ONLY. /** -

Situation 2 / not iss.

Mar 90. (12"ep) *(SIT 65T)* **BREACH BIRTH EP** -

— **KEVIN MARTIN, JUSTIN BROADRICK, TIM HODGKINSON, STEVE BLAKE, JOHN EDWARDS, DAVE COCHRANE, GARY JEFF, LOU CICCOTELLI + SCOTT KIEHL**

Venture / Venture

Jan 92. (cd-s/pic-cd-s) **LOCO /**

Mar 92. (cd/c) <*(CD/TC VE 910)*> **POSSESSION** Nov93
– Pretty / Fucked / Return to Hell / Soul fire / Hate meditation / Lord, I'm on my way / Love / Black Jesus.

Sentrax / not iss.

1993. (cd) *(SET 5CD)* **CONSUMED** -

P.D.C.D. / not iss.

Jan 94. (cd) *(PPP 106CD)* **GOD LIVE AT ST. MARY'S CHURCH (live)** -

Big Cat / Big Cat

May 94. (cd) <*(ABB 62CD)*> **THE ANATOMY OF ADDICTION** Oct94
– On all fours / Body horror / Tunnel / Lazarus / Voodoo head blows / Bloodstream / White pimp cut up / Driving the demons out / Gold teeth / Detox.

Jun 95. (cd-ep) <*(ABB 79XCD)*> **APPEAL TO HUMAN GREED** (remixes) Oct95
– Gold teeth (Charles Atlas mix) / Bloodstream (the evening redness in the west mix) / On all fours (biomechanical mix) / Tunnel (electro-convulsive mix) / Bloodstream (Peckinpah mix).

TECHNO ANIMAL

KEVIN MARTIN – instruments / **JUSTIN BROADRICK** – guitars

Pathological / Revolver

Jul 91. (lp/cd) *(PATH 008/+CD)* **GHOSTS** 1994
– Burn / Walk then crawl / Freak fucker / Tough cop – soft cop / The dream forger / etc

— added **JON HASSELL** – trumpet (ex-jazz groups)

Virgin Ambient / Caroline

May 95. (d-cd) *(AMBT 8)* **RE-ENTRY** Jun95
– DREAM MACHINERY:- Flight of the Hermaphrodite / The mighty atom smasher / Masterdon Americanus / City heathen dub / Narco agent vs the medicine man / Demodex invasion // HEAVY LIDS:- Evil spirits – Angel dust / Catatonia / Needle park / Red Sea / Cape Canaveral / Resuscitator.

— In Oct'95, JUSTIN BROADRICK & ANDY HAWKINS released a cd, 'SUBSONIC 3' on 'Sub Rosa'; (SR 90)

not iss. / EFA

May 98. (cd) **TECHNO ANIMAL VS. REALITY** -
– Demonoid / Version – Porter Ricks / Declaration / Version – Ui / Baka / Version – Spectre / Bionic beatbox / Version – Tortoise / Atomic buddha / Version – Alex Empire.

Sep 98. (cd) **RADIO HADES** -
– The myth – Illogical / Intercranial toxicity / Return of the venom / Interplanetary war chant / The disciples of dark / Dread time warp / Fistfunk / Be headed / Needle / Bass concussion / Ill sommer / Phantom tribe / Excavator.

ICE

KEVIN MARTIN / ALEX BUESS (of 16/17) / **JOHN JABBAGY** – drums (ex-TERMINAL CHEESECAKE) / **JUSTIN BROADRICK** – guitar (ex-GODFLESH)

Pathological / not iss.

Jul 93. (cd) *(PATH 11CD)* **UNDER THE SKIN** -
– Juggernaut kiss / Survival of the fattest / Out of focus / .357 Magnum is a monster / Skyscraper / The flood / Stick insect / Implosion / The swimmer.

— note: KEVIN + JUSTIN augmented ALEX in his Swiss trio's debut, 'Gyatso'

— **LOU CICCOTELLI** – drums (ex-GOD) repl. JABBAGY + BUESS

Morpheus / Reprise

May 98. (cd) *(MORPH 001CD)* **BAD BLOOD** Oct98
– X-1 / The snakepit / Trapped in three dimensions / Dusted / A new breed of rat / Devils / When two worlds collide.

Nov 98. (12"ep) *(MORPH 001EP)* **HEADWRECK EP** -
– Headwreck / Trapped in 3-D (El Producto mix) / Year of the snake / Dusted (Dick Smothers mix).

ICICLE WORKS (see under ⇒ McNABB, Ian)

IDHA

Born: IDHA OVELIUS, 22 May'72, Sodertalje, Sweden. Having been a fully paid up Goth living in London at the turn of the decade (80's/90's), the stunning redhead's fortunes took a turn for the better after chancing upon her future boyfriend/husband, ANDY BELL, at a RIDE concert. Inspired to take up the guitar herself, IDHA subsequently found herself on the roster of 'Creation' (home to RIDE), co-writing some of her debut album, 'MELODY INN' (1994) with BELL. Also boasting ex-(SMALL) FACES keyboard man, IAN McLAGAN, the record was a rootsy, countrified affair featuring an array of choice cover versions (i.e. Gram Parsons' 'HICKORY WIND' and 'SAFE AT HOME' side by side with Tim Hardin's 'RED BALLOON'). Later that year, another high profile guest artist, EVAN DANDO, was to feature on the EP, 'A WOMAN IN A MAN'S WORLD', while BELL again shared the songwriting duties on slightly improved follow-up set, 'TROUBLEMAKER' (1997). • **Covered:** COMING DOWN (Byrd-Moskowitz)

Album rating: MELODY INN (*6) / TROUBLEMAKER (*7)

IDHA – vocals, guitar / with **IAN McLAGAN** – Hammond organ, piano / **CREEDENCE J. WRIGHT** – Hammond organ

Creation / Tristar

Jan 94. (cd/c/lp) *(CRECD/C-CRE/CRELP 160)* <*66191*> **MELODY INN**
– High over Hollywood / Red balloon / From me to you / More love / Another door / Stockholm / All my loving / Hickory wind / Get undressed / Safe at home / Music carries on.

Apr 94. (12"ep)(cd-ep) *(CRE 161T)(CRESCD 161)* **GET UNDRESSED / DO RIGHT BY ME. / SHE / COMING DOWN** -

Oct 94. (7") *(CRE 166)* **A WOMAN IN A MAN'S WORLD. /** -
(cd-s+=) *(CRESCD 166)* –

— now with **ANDY BELL** – guitar (ex-RIDE, of HURRICANE #1) / **TONY BARBER + ALAN WHITE**

May 97. (7") *(CRE 265)* **SORRY SORRY. /** -
(cd-s+=) *(CRESCD 265)* –

Jul 97. (7") *(CRE 268)* **GOING DOWN SOUTH. / SWEET 16** -
(cd-s+=) *(CRESCD 268)* –

Aug 97. (cd/lp) *(CRE CD/LP 184)* **TROUBLEMAKER** -

IDLEWILD

Formed: Edinburgh, Scotland ... late '95 by RODDY WOOMBLE, ROD JONES and COLIN NEWTON, each having a penchant for noise veterans, SONIC YOUTH and FUGAZI. Having met at a party, the erstwhile students whittled away their revision time with ramshackle rehearsals, eventually channelling their frustrations into a debut single, 'QUEEN OF THE TROUBLED TEENS'. Famously financed by a student loan (and issued on their own 'Human Condition' imprint), the track was championed by Radio 1 DJ Steve Lamacq, duly rescuing the band from eternal toilet gig hell and setting in motion the mechanics of A&R overload. A follow-up single, 'CHANDELIER', appeared on 'Fierce Panda' while an acclaimed mini-album on 'Deceptive', 'CAPTAIN', kickstarted '98 and became their final fully fledged indie release prior to a deal with 'Food'. Somewhere along the way the band also picked up bassist BOB FAIRFOULL and began to coax some melancholic tunefulness from the blizzard of sound and fury that characterises their youthful approach. 'A FILM FOR THE FUTURE' announced their major label arrival in fittingly convulsive style, the first of many minor hits which have cemented the band's reputation as one of Scotland's most talked about and possibly most dedicated sonic abusers. Their highly anticipated first album proper, 'HOPE IS IMPORTANT' (late '98), made the UK Top 60 and the band's steady rise proves that noisy guitars never go out of fashion; Idle? Nah. Wild? Definitely.

Album rating: HOPE IS IMPORTANT (*7)

RODDY WOOMBLE (b.1976) – vocals / **ROD JONES** (b.1976) – guitar / **PAUL** – bass / **COLIN NEWTON** (b.1977) – drums

		Human Condition	not iss.
Mar 97.	(7") *(HC 0017)* **QUEEN OF THE TROUBLED TEENS. /** *(re-iss. Jan98; same)*		-
—	**BOB FAIRFOULL** (b.1976) – bass; repl. PAUL		
		Fierce Panda	not iss.
Dec 97.	(ltd-7") *(NING 42)* **CHANDELIER. / I WANT TO BE A WRITER**		-
		Deceptive	not iss.
Jan 98.	(m-cd) *(BLUFF 058CD)* **CAPTAIN**		-
Feb 98.	(7") *(BLUFF 057)* **SATAN POLAROID. / HOUSE ALONE**		-
		Food	unknown
Apr 98.	(7") *(FOOD 111)* **A FILM FOR THE FUTURE. / MINCE SHOWERCAP (part I)**	53	-
	(cd-s+=) *(CDFOOD 111)* – What am I going to do?		
Jul 98.	(7") *(FOOD 113)* **EVERYONE SAYS YOU'RE SO FRAGILE. / MINCE SHOWERCAP (part II)**	47	-
	(cd-s+=) *(CDFOOD 113)* – Theory of achievement.		
Oct 98.	(7") *(FOOD 114)* **I'M A MESSAGE. / MINCE SHOWERCAP (part III)**	41	-
	(cd-s+=) *(CDFOOD 114)* – This is worse.		
	(cd-s) *(CDFOODS 114)* – ('A'side) / Satan polaroid (session) / You've lost your way (session).		
Oct 98.	(cd/c/lp) *(497132-2/-4/-1)* **HOPE IS IMPORTANT**	53	
	– You've lost your way / A film for the future / Paint nothing / When I argue I see shapes / 4 people do good / I'm happy to be here tonight / Everyone says you're so fragile / I'm a message / You don't have the heart / Close the door / Safe and sound / Low light.		

James IHA (see under ⇒ SMASHING PUMPKINS)

I, LUDICROUS

Formed: Finsbury, South London, England . . . early 1985 by the duo of WILL HUNG and JOHN PROCTER, the pair having met at work four years previously. Influenced by Mancunian punk poets such as JOHN COOPER CLARKE and er, well, MARK E. SMITH (of The FALL), WILL and JOHN procured a basic instrumental set-up of a Casio keyboard and a cheap guitar, securing an album deal with JOE FOSTER's 'Kaleidoscope' records on the strength of a few gigs. The band's first release however, came via a free fanzine ('Blah Blah Blah') flexi-disc in the Spring of '87, the track in question, 'PREPOSTEROUS TALES IN THE LIFE OF KEN MacKENZIE', showcasing their quirky, DIY narrative style and later turning up on John Peel's Festive 50. After being invited by the DJ to record a Radio One session, I, LUDICROUS finally delivered their debut lp, 'IT'S LIKE EVERYTHING ELSE' (1987), critics divided over its merits. After a further single for the label, 'QUITE EXTRAORDINARY', they were forced to move on to the smaller indie imprint, 'Rodney, Rodney!', where they welcomed in the new decade with two albums in 1990, 'A WARNING TO THE CURIOUS' and 'LIGHT AND BITTER' (an official release of 'PREPOSTEROUS TALES' was also on the cards). A few years later, they re-emerged with a surprise NME Single Of The Week in the shape of 'WE STAND AROUND', lifted from the accompanying self-financed album, 'IDIOTS SAVANTS' (1992). A further one-off 7" in 1994, 'HATS OFF TO ELDORADO', was their final instalment of off-the-cuff humour, the pair parting ways that year.

Album rating: IT'S LIKE EVERYTHING ELSE (*6) / A WARNING TO THE CURIOUS (*5) / LIGHT AND BITTER (*5) / IDIOTS SAVANTS (*5)

WILL HUNG (b. DAVID RIPPINGALE, 4 Nov'56) – vocals / **JOHN PROCTER** (b. 9 May'57) – keyboards, guitar

		Kaleidoscope	not iss.
Sep 87.	(lp) *(KSLP 004)* **IT'S LIKE EVERYTHING ELSE**		-
Apr 88.	(7") *(KS 707)* **QUITE EXTRAORDINARY. / AT THE END OF THE DAY**		-
	(12"+=) *(KS 107)* – Kick down the stumps / Mistakes.		
		Rodney, Rodney!	not iss.
Jan 90.	(lp/c) *(RODNEY 2/+C)* **A WARNING TO THE CURIOUS**		-
	(above was scheduled for release in 1988 as 'I, LUDICROUS'; *KSLP 008)*		
Apr 90.	(12"ep) *(RODNEY 3)* **PREPOSTEROUS TALES IN THE LIFE OF KEN MacKENZIE. / THREE ENGLISH FOOTBALL GROUNDS / SPOCK'S BRAIN**		-
Nov 90.	(lp/cd) *(RODNEY 6/+CD)* **LIGHT AND BITTER**		-

		Old King Lud	not iss.
Aug 92.	(cd) *(LUD 001)* **IDIOTS SAVANTS**		-
Sep 92.	(7"ep) *(LUD 002)* **WE STAND AROUND. /**		-
Jul 93.	(7"ep) *(LUD 003)* **HATS OFF TO ELDORADO / HACKY'S WINE BAR. / MAN'S MAN / OUR MATES**		-
—	looked to have split after above		

IMPERIAL DRAG (see under ⇒ JELLYFISH)

I'M SO HOLLOW

Formed: Sheffield, England . . . 1979 by ROD LEIGH and singer, JANE WILSON, alongside JOSEF SAWICKI and DAYTON MARSDEN. The quartet made their initial appearances on a handful of V/A releases including the EP, 'The First 15 Minutes' (on 'Neutron') and 'The Hicks From The Sticks' album (for 'Rockburgh'). The following year, I'M SO HOLLOW issued their debut 45, 'DREAMS TO FILL THE VACUUM', a post-punk favourite very much in the mould of ENO (c.1974) and MAGAZINE. The band's characteristic strained vocals and fuzz guitars were showcased on their one and only CABARET VOLTAIRE-produced album, 'EMOTION, SOUND, MOTION' (1981).

Album rating: EMOTION, SOUND, MOTION (*6)

JANE WILSON – vocals, synthesizer / **ROD LEIGH** – guitar, vocals / **DAYTON MARSDEN** – bass / **JOSEF SAWICKI** – hipercussion

		Hollogram	not iss.
Jan 81.	(7"clear) *(ISH 002)* **DREAMS TO FILL THE VACUUM. / DISTRACTION**		-
		Illuminated	not iss.
Oct 81.	(lp) *(JAMS 5)* **EMOTION/SOUND/MOTION**		-
	– Entrance / Which way? / Unbroken line / Touch / Collisions / Excitement = chance / The triangular hour / Emotion, sound, motion / Nosferatu / Distraction.		
—	disappeared the following year		

INBREDS

Formed: Kingston, Ontario, Canada . . . early '92 by songwriter, MIKE O'NEILL and DAVE ULRICH. Launching their own 'P.F.' label the same year with a Canadian-only demo cassette, 'DARN FOUL DOG', The INBREDS initiated a steady release schedule that saw them issuing a 7" EP, 'LET'S GET TOGETHER', a CD-EP, 'EGROG' and their first full album, 'HILARIO' (1993) over the course of a year. A subsequent round of touring brought the band's distorted, minimalist Lo-Fi sound to a bigger audience, ensuring a higher profile for follow-up album, 'KOMBINATOR' (1994). A prestigious support slot to BUFFALO TOM helped them secure a licensing deal with soon-to-be 'Atlantic' subsidiary, 'Tag', who re-issued the aforementioned second set in early '96.

Album rating: HILARIO (*6) / KOMBINATOR (*6)

MIKE O'NEILL – vocals, bass / **DAVE ULRICH** – drums

		not iss.	P.F.
1992.	(c) *(PF 001)* **DARN FOUL DOG**	-	Canada
1992.	(7"ep) **LET'S GET TOGETHER EP**	-	Canada
Jan 93.	(cd-ep) **EGROG EP**	-	Canada
Jun 93.	(cd) **HILARIO**	-	Canada
		not iss.	Summershine
1995.	(7") <020> **YELVERTON HILL. / CATHY'S CLOWN**	-	
		Seed-Tag	Seed-Tag
Oct 95.	(7"ep/cd-ep) *(TAG 001/+CD)* **YOU WILL KNOW / MATTERHORN. / HE NEVER / TELL THE TRUTH / SHE'S ACTING**		
Jan 96.	(cd/lp) *<92606-2/-1>* **KOMBINATOR**		
	– Kimbinator / Round 12 / You will know / Any sense of time / Turn my head / Dale says / She's acting / Scratch / Link / Dangerous / Don't try so hard / Cruise control / Last flight / Amelia Earhart. *(orig.rel.Aug94 in Canada)*		
Jan 96.	(cd-s) *(95650-2)* **ANY SENSE OF TIME / DERAILLEUR / OLIVER / CARNIVAL**		

INCA BABIES

Formed: Manchester, England . . . 1982 by BILL BONNEY, HARRY STAFFORD and vocalist/drummer PETE. A whirling, hard-hitting thrash-punk outfit in the grinding mould of LIVING IN TEXAS or a punkabilly BIRTHDAY PARTY, they formed their own 'Black Lagoon' label and proceeded to release a string of well-received (in indie circles at least) 45's beginning with 1983's 'THE INTERIOR'. Two full albums, 'RUMBLE' and 'THIS TRAIN', also surfaced in the mid 80's, although the INCA BABIES would be best remembered for the presence of CLINT BOON (later of The INSPIRAL CARPETS), who played on their final effort, 'EVIL HOUR' (1988).

Album rating: RUMBLE (*5) / THIS TRAIN (*5) / OPIUM DEN mini (*4) / EVIL HOUR (*5)

PETE – vocals, drums / **HARRY STAFFORD** – guitar / **BILL BONNEY** – bass

		Black Lagoon	not iss.
Nov 83.	(7") *(INC 001)* **THE INTERIOR. / SENSE OF LOSS**		-

Mar 84. (7") *(INC 002)* **GRUNT CADILLAC. / NO SACRED SOUND** ☐ -
May 84. (12"ep) *(INC 003)* **BIG JUGULAR** ☐ -
Aug 84. (7") *(INC 004)* **THE JUDGE. / BUS BREAKER** ☐ -
(12"+=) *(INC 004T)* –

— added **MIKE LOUIS** – vocals, harmonica (PETE no vocals)

Feb 85. (lp) *(INCLP 005)* **RUMBLE** ☐ -
– She mercenary / The interior / Blind man (the chiller) / The diseased stranger's waltz / Leucotomy meat boss / Big jugular / 16 tons of fink / Cactus mouth informer / Greaseball mechanic.
Oct 85. (12"ep) *(INC 007)* **SURFIN' IN LOCUSTLAND** ☐ -
Mar 86. (7") *(INC 009)* **SPLATTER BALLISTICS COP. / BURY THE SWAGGER** ☐ -
(12"+=) *(INC 009T)* – ('A'version).
May 86. (lp) *(INCLP 010)* **THIS TRAIN** ☐ -
– Plenty more mutants / Correction stack / Hole in the gulley / Candy mountain / Splatter ballistics cop / The depths / Backyard bones / Daniella / Call me enemy.
Jun 87. (m-lp) *(INCMLP 012)* **OPIUM DEN** ☐ -
– Opium den / Thirst / Devil in my room / Ramblin' man / Big Cyprus / A grim thought / Dresden.
Oct 87. (7") *(CON! 00027)* **BUSTER'S ON FIRE. /** - - German
(above issued for 'Constrictor')

— **HARRY + BILL** recruited newcomers **TONY CLARKE** – drums / **CLINT BOON** – keyboards / **DIRK BULLOWS + SIMON HINSON**

May 88. (lp) *(INCLP 013)* **EVIL HOUR** ☐ -
– Evil hour / Long uphill trek / Partisan's river / A madman's demise / Bad hombre / Artillery switchback / Two rails to nowhere / Volts / Burning town / Young blood. *(re-iss. Oct88 on 'Vinyl Drip'; SUK 002) (cd-iss. Jan89 on 'Communion'; COMM 6CD)*

— split after above, CLINT joined The INSPIRAL CARPETS

INDIANS IN MOSCOW

Formed: Hull, England . . . 1981 by ADELE NOZEDAR, a shaven-headed, seemingly schitzoid punk-angel/she-devil, akin to the third cousin thrice removed of ALTERED IMAGES lass, CLARE GROGAN. Early the following year, this post-punk act were initially heard on a V/A double-lp collection, 'Your Secret's Safe With Us', although the public were still blissfully unaware of ADELE's brutal image. Given exposure on Channel 4's pop/rock programme, 'The Tube', their debut single, 'NAUGHTY MIRANDA' (in which she took on the role of the wicked MIRANDA), hit the top of the indie charts at the turn of '83/'84. By the time of their follow-up, 'I WISH I HAD', a posse was sent out for the rest of the INDIANS IN MOSCOW (STUART WALTON, RICH HORNBY + PETE RICHES) who had gone AWOL for a while. Early in 1985, ADELE's body was witnessed painted purple on the sleeve of the group's Nigel Gray-produced eponymous album, their last release before she formed another 4-piece, The FEVER TREE.

Album rating: INDIANS IN MOSCOW (*5)

ADELE NOZEDAR – vocals / **STUART WALTON** – keyboards / **PETE RICHES** – keyboards / **RICH HORNBY** – drums

Kennick not iss.

Nov 83. (7"/12") *(KNK 1002/+T)* **NAUGHTY MIRANDA. / MIRANDA** ☐ -

— not sure if her band stayed on at this point after a disagreement

Mar 84. (7"/12") *(KNK 1003/+T)* **I WISH I HAD. / SLICE** ☐ -
Jun 84. (7"/12") *(KNK 1004/+T)* **JACK PELTER AND HIS SEX-CHANGE CHICKEN. / SALT** ☐ -
Sep 84. (7") *(KNK 1005)* **BIG WHEEL. / DESIRE** ☐ -
(12"+=) *(KNK 1005T)* – Price of love / Indians in Moscow.
Feb 85. (lp/c) *(KLNK/KCNK 1)* **INDIANS IN MOSCOW** ☐ -
– Big wheel / Meeting place / Witches & heroes / Howard's at lunch / Puppet dance / Square dance in the republic / Love song / I wish I had / Singing to French / Naughty Miranda / Jack Pelter and his sex-change chicken.

— ADELE decided to form a new band, The FEVER TREE, although only one single, 'THE PIXIE SHOP' / 'HIS HANDS GIVE HIM AWAY' came out late '85

IN EMBRACE

Formed: London, England . . . 1981 by Coventry lads CAMERON LINDO and GARY KNIGHT. Possibly a precursor to mid-80's TALK TALK, IN EMBRACE made their vinyl debut in '82 with a 5-track EP on 'Glass' records, 'INITIAL CARESS'. Adding ex-SINATRAS drummer, JOBY PALMER and temp vocalist CLAIRE JOHNSON, the duo really got things underway with an inaugural long-player, 'PASSION FRUIT PASTELS' (1983), an appropriately-titled collection of post-New Wave romantic, awkwardly funky piano'n'drums that could have easily passed for a softer EYELESS IN GAZA. Later in the year, LINDO was replaced by RICHARD FORMBY, the follow-up, 'TOO' (1983) also illustrating their ability to combine stark, melancholic piano with the EDWYN COLLINS-esque vocal chords of KNIGHT. He, in turn, enlisted yet another partner, CLIVE DOVE, their subsequent singles appearing on 'Cherry Red'. However, a last ditch long-playing effort for 'Glass' (recorded with who else but EYELESS IN GAZA's PETE BECKER), 'SONGS ABOUT SNOGGIN' (1987) only served to underline that the band's time had come and gone.

Album rating: PASSION FRUIT PASTELS (*5) / TOO (*5) / SONGS ABOUT SNOGGIN' (*4) / WANDERLUST 82-84 mini compilation (*5)

GARY KNIGHT – vocals, keyboards, guitar / **CAMERON LINDO** – bass

Glass not iss.

May 82. (12"ep) *(GLASS 019)* **INITIAL CARESS EP** ☐ -
– Breathless with passion explicit / For lovers / Clutching / The air inbetween / Precious.

— added **JOBY PALMER** – drums, percussion (ex-SINATRAS)

— added **CLAIRE JOHNSON** – vocals

Feb 83. (7") *(GLASS 024)* **SUN BRINGS SMILES. / PLAY IN LIGHT** ☐ -
Mar 83. (lp) *(GLALP 001)* **PASSION FRUIT PASTELS** ☐ -
– Tears turn fresh / Half-awake (mountains) / We fail each other / Our star drawn through planes / The ball rolling / Sun brings smiles / At east / (Sigh!) / Tickling the ivanes / To friends (an open letter) / Caroline beginning.

— **RICHARD FORMBY** – guitar, keyboards (ex-RELIGIOUS OVERDOSE) repl. CAMERON LINDO

Sep 83. (7") *(GLASS 030)* **LIVING DAYLIGHTS. / BLUE BEACH / MAKE** ☐ -
Oct 83. (lp) *(GLALP 004)* **TOO** ☐ -
– Embrace the base on Sunday / Love among the crumbs / Trying too hard / Under the skin / Emotional punchbags / With a satin finish / Uniform & unicorn / If we choose / Stretch / Pine needles / Kiss a cold shoulder.

— added **STEPHAN REES** – bass

Mar 84. (7") *(GLASS 034)* **YOU'RE HEAVEN SCENT (PLAYS HELL WITH ME). / FLUID** ☐ -
(12") *(GLASS12 034)* – ('A'side) / The newer living daylights / The longer living daylights / Liquid / Trying too hard.

— sole original **KNIGHT** added **CLIVE DOVE** – keyboards, guitar

Cherry Red not iss.

Feb 85. (7") *(CHERRY 84)* **SHOUTING IN CAFES. / CHOCOLATES FOR BREAKFAST** ☐ -
Oct 85. (7") *(CHERRY 90)* **THIS BRILLIANT EVENING. / THE DARKEST HORSE** ☐ -
(12"+=) *(12CHERRY 90)* – ('A'instrumental).

— added **AMANDA LYDON** – vocals / **PETER BECKER** – keyboards, bass, drum machine (of EYELESS IN GAZA)

Glass not iss.

Dec 86. (7") *(GLASS 051)* **A ROOM UPSTAIRS. / ('A'version)** ☐ -
(12") *(12GLASS 051)* – ('A'side) / My worst behavoir / Red blue eyes.
May 87. (lp) *(GLALP 022)* **SONGS ABOUT SNOGGIN'** ☐ -
– Mirror mirror / Perfect stranger / What's got into me / You can laugh / Bedtime / A room upstairs / Shipwrecks / Somebodys / Stay here / Wallpaper, bathroom, perfume & God / Lovelorn.
Jul 87. (7"ep) *(GLAEP 106)* **WHAT'S GOT INTO ME** ☐ -

— disbanded after above

– compilations, etc. –

May 86. (m-lp) *Glass;* **WANDERLUST 82-84** ☐ -

INFA RIOT

Formed: England . . . 1981 by LEE WILSON, BARRY D'AMERY, FLOYD WILSON and MARK REYNOLDS. Another bunch of "oi" hopefuls to emerge on the 'Secret' label, INFA RIOT debuted with a couple of simplistic three minute singles, 'KIDS OF THE 80'S' and 'THE WINNER', before knocking off a surprise Top 50 placing for their 1982 album, 'STILL OUT OF ORDER'. However, with all the (un)healthy competition around in such a crowded scene, the band evolved into The INFAS and inflicted one more album, 'SOUND AND FURY' (1984) upon the post-punk populace.

Album rating: STILL OUT OF ORDER (*4) / Infas: SOUND AND FURY (*2)

LEE WILSON – vocals / **BARRY D'AMERY** – guitar, vocals / **FLOYD WILSON** – bass, vocals / **MARK REYNOLDS** – drums, vocals

Secret not iss.

Oct 81. (7") *(SHH 117)* **KIDS OF THE 80'S. / STILL OUT OF ORDER** ☐ -
Apr 82. (7") *(SHH 133)* **THE WINNER. / SCHOOL'S OUT** ☐ -
Jul 82. (lp/c) *(SEC/TSEC 7)* **STILL OUT OF ORDER** 42 -
– Emergency / You ain't seen nothing yet / Five minute fashion / Each dawn I die / The drug squad / Still out of order / Catch 22 / Power / Boot boys / The winner / Friday oh Friday / Catalogue kids / In for a riot.

— changed their moniker to . . .

INFAS

Pancake not iss.

Feb 84. (lp/c) *(PAN LP/CA 501)* **SOUND AND FURY** ☐ -
– Rock all ye faithful / These dangerous days / Sound and fury / Punch the air with glory / There's gotta be a better way / Birds and bees / A spirit wild / Manthing / Don't want to be (the in-crowd) / Pushers on the rampage / Triffic spiff ya o.k. / Captain England.
Mar 84. (7") *(PAN 101)* **SOUND AND FURY. / TRIFFIC SPIFF YA O.K.** ☐ -

— they split after above

INSPIRAL CARPETS

Formed: Manchester, England . . . 1980 initially as The FURS, by schoolboy GRAHAM LAMBERT. He was joined in the mid-80's by STEPHEN HOLT, TONY WELSH and CHRIS GOODWIN. In 1986, as The INSPIRAL CARPETS, they replaced GOODWIN and WELSH with CRAIG GILL, DAVE SWIFT and CLINT BOON. Early in '87, they recorded a version of 'GARAGE' for a 7" flexi-disc given free with 'Debris' magazine. After gigs supporting the WEDDING PRESENT, JAMES, STONES ROSES and The SHAMEN, they issued their official debut, the 'PLANE CRASH EP' in mid-'88 for indie, 'Playtime' records. Early in 1989, they set up their own 'Cow' label, after their distributers, 'Red Rhino', went bust. At the same time, HOLT and SWIFT left to form The RAINKINGS, and were replaced by HINGLEY and WALSH. After a late 1988 recording, 'TRAIN SURFING EP', was issued, they recorded the 808 STATE-produced 'JOE' single/EP. A year later, they had their first UK Top 50 entry with 'MOVE', which led to Daniel Miller of 'Mute' records taking on both band and label. In April 1990, they broke into UK Top 20 with the poignant single, 'THIS IS HOW IT FEELS', pushing their debut album, 'LIFE', to No. 3. A heavy, organ-orientated psychedelic-pop group, their music lay somewhere between The DOORS and The FALL. The INSPIRAL CARPETS continued with a run of hit singles that included, 'SHE COMES IN THE FALL', 'CARAVAN' and 'DRAGGING ME DOWN', the latter two featured on the Top 5 album, 'THE BEAST INSIDE' (1991). The following year, with a further clutch of hit singles under their belt, they scraped into the Top 20 with 'REVENGE OF THE GOLDFISH', a weaker effort. A year of reflection in 1993 preceded a return to form with a MARK E. SMITH (The Fall) collaboration 45, 'I WANT YOU' (now featured on a certain TV ad). This helped the album, 'DEVIL HOPPING', reach the Top 10 but when their next single, 'UNIFORM', failed to even dent the Top 50, they were unceremoniously dropped by their label, 'Mute'. The band split soon after, leaving behind the customary cash-in compilation. • **Songwriters:** Group penned except; 96 TEARS (? & The Mysterians) / GIMME SHELTER (Rolling Stones) / TAINTED LOVE (Soft Cell) / PARANOID (Black Sabbath). • **Trivia:** To promote debut album, they employed the services of the Milk Marketing Board who ran a TV ad on their bottles. Early 1990, they penned 'THE 8.15 FROM MANCHESTER' (theme) from children's Saturday morning TV show.

Album rating: LIFE (*8) / THE BEAST INSIDE (*7) / REVENGE OF THE GOLDFISH (*6) / DEVIL HOPPING (*5) / THE SINGLES compilation (*8)

GRAHAM LAMBERT (b.10 Jul'64, Oldham, England) – guitar / **STEPHEN HOLT** – vocals / **DAVE SWIFT** – bass repl. TONY WELSH / **CRAIG GILL** (b. 5 Dec'71) – drums repl. CHRIS GOODWIN who joined ASIA FIELDS (later BUZZCOCKS F.O.C. and The HIGH) / added **CLINT BOON** (b.28 Jun'59, Oldham) – organ, vocals (ex-INCA BABIES)

Playtime / not iss.

Jul 88. (7"ltd.) *(AMUSE 2)* **KEEP THE CIRCLE AROUND. / THEME FROM COW** [ ] [-]
(12"ep+=) **PLANE CRASH EP** *(AMUSE 2T)* – Seeds of doubt / Garage full of flowers / 96 tears.

Cow / not iss.

Mar 89. (12"ep) *(MOO 2)* **TRAIN SURFING** [ ] [-]
– Butterfly / Causeway / You can't take the truth / Greek wedding song.

— **TOM HINGLEY** (b. 9 Jul'65, Oxford, England) – vocals (ex-TOO MUCH TEXAS) repl. HOLT who formed RAINKINGS **MARTIN WALSH** (b. 3 Jul'68) – bass (ex-NEXT STEP) repl. SWIFT who formed RAINKINGS

May 89. (12"ep) *(MOO 3)* **JOE. / COMMERCIAL MIX / DIRECTING TRAFFIK / COMMERCIAL RAIN** [ ] [-]
May 89. (c;ltd) *(DUNG 4)* **DEMO CASSETTE** (rec.Dec'87) [ ] [-]
– Keep the circle around / Seeds of doubt / Joe / Causeway / 26 / Inside my head / Sun don't shine / Theme from Cow / 96 tears / Butterfly / Garage full of flowers.
Aug 89. (7") *(DUNG 5)* **FIND OUT WHY. / SO FAR** [ ] [-]
(12"+=/cd-s+=) *(DUNG 5 T/CD)* – Plane crash (live).
Oct 89. (7"/s7") *(DUNG 6/+X)* **MOVE. / OUT OF TIME** [49] [-]
(12"+=/cd-s+=) *(DUNG 6 T/CD)* – Move in.

Cow-Mute / Elektra

Mar 90. (7") *(DUNG 7)* <66581> **THIS IS HOW IT FEELS. / TUNE FOR A FAMILY** [14] [ ]
(12"+=/cd-s+=) *(DUNG 7 T/CD)* – ('A'extended) / Seeds of doubt.
(c-s+=) *(DUNG 7MC)* – ('A'extended) / Whiskey.
(12") *(DUNG 7R)* – ('A'-Robbery mix) / ('B'drum mix).
Apr 90. (lp/c/cd) *(DUNG 8/+C/CD)* <60987> **LIFE** [2] [ ] Oct90
– Real thing / Song for a family / This is how it feels / Directing traffik / Besides me / Many happy returns / Memories of you / She comes in the fall / Monkey on my back / Sun don't shine / Inside my head / Move * / Sackville. *(cd+= *) <US++=>* – Commercial rain / Weakness / Biggest mountain / I'll keep it in mind.
Jun 90. (7") *(DUNG 10)* **SHE COMES IN THE FALL. / SACKVILLE** [27] [-]
(12"+=/cd-s+=) *(DUNG 10 T/CD)* – Continental reign (version).
(12"+=) *(DUNG 10R)* – ('A'acappella version).
Nov 90. (7"ep/12"ep) *(DUNG 11/+T)* **ISLAND HEAD** [21] [ ]
– Biggest mountain / I'll keep it in mind / Weakness / Gold to . . .
(cd-ep+=) *(DUNG 11CD)* – Mountain sequence.
Mar 91. (7") *(DUNG 13)* <66543> **CARAVAN. / SKIDOO** [30] [ ] Apr91
(7"/12") *(DUNG 13 R/T)* – ('A'side) / ('B'-Possession mix).
(cd-s) *(DUNG 13CD)* – ('A'-What noise rethink mix) / ('B'side).
Apr 91. (lp/c/cd) *(DUNG 14/+C/CD)* <61089> **THE BEAST INSIDE** [5] [ ] May91
– Caravan / Please be cruel / Born yesterday / Sleep well tonight / Grip / Beast inside / Niagara / Mermaid / Further away / Dreams are all we have.
Jun 91. (7"/c-s) *(DUNG/+C 15)* **PLEASE BE CRUEL. / THE WIND IS CALLING YOUR NAME** [50] [-]
(12"+=/cd-s+=) *(DUNG 15 T/CD)* – St.Kilda (version).
Feb 92. (7") *(DUNG 16)* **DRAGGING ME DOWN. / I KNOW I'M LOSING YOU** [12] [-]
(12"+=/cd-s+=) *(DUNG 16 T/CD)* – (2 other 'A'mixes).
May 92. (7") *(DUNG 17)* **TWO WORLDS COLLIDE. / BOOMERANG** [32] [-]
(12"+=/cd-s+=) *(DUNG 17 T/CD)* – ('A'-Mike Pickering remix).
Sep 92. (7") *(DUNG 18)* **GENERATIONS. / ('A'remix)** [28] [-]
(c-s) *(DUNG 18C)* – Lost in space again.
(12"/cd-s) *(DUNG 18 T/CD)* – ('A'side) / She comes in the fall (live) / Move (live) / Directing traffik (live).
(cd-s) *(DUNG 18CDR)* – ('A'side) / Joe (live) / Commercial rain (live) / Butterfly (live).
Oct 92. (lp/c/cd) *(DUNG 19/+C/CD)* <61397> **REVENGE OF THE GOLDFISH** [17] [ ]
– Generations / Saviour / Bitches brew / Smoking her clothes / Fire / Here comes the flood / Dragging me down / A little disappeared / Two worlds collide / Mystery / Rain song / Irresistable force.
Nov 92. (c-ep/12"ep) *(DUNG 20 C/T)* **BITCHES BREW / TAINTED LOVE. / BITCHES BREW (Fortran 5 remix) / IRRESISTABLE FORCE (Fortran 5 mix)** [36] [-]
(cd-ep+=) *(DUNG 20CD)* – Mermaid (live) / Born yesterday (live) / Sleep well tonight (live).
(cd-ep+=) *(DUNG 20CDR)* – Dragging me down (live) / Smoking her clothes (live) / Fire (live).

— parted company with 'Cow' co-founder/manager Anthony Boggiano.

May 93. (7"/c-s) *(DUNG 22/+C)* **HOW IT SHOULD BE. / IT'S ONLY A PAPER MOON** [49] [-]
(12"+=/cd-s+=) *(DUNG 22 T/CD)* – I'm alive.
Jan 94. (7"/c-s) *(DUNG 23/+C)* **SATURN 5. / PARTY IN THE SKY** [20] [-]
(cd-s+=/12"+=) *(DUNG 23 T/CD)* – ('A'mixes).
(cd-s) *(DUNG 23CDR)* – ('A'side) / Well of seven heads / Two cows / Going down.
Feb 94. (7"/c-s; by INSPIRAL CARPETS featuring MARK E. SMITH) *(DUNG 24/+C)* **I WANT YOU. / I WANT YOU (version)** [18] [-]
(cd-s+=) *(DUNG 24CD)* – We can do everything / Inside of you.
(cd-s) *(DUNG 24CDR)* – ('A'side) / Dragging me down / Party in the sky / Plutoman.
Mar 94. (lp/c/cd) *(DUNG 25/+C/CD)* <61632> **DEVIL HOPPING** [10] [ ]
– I want you / Party in the sky / Plutoman / Uniform / Lovegrove / Just Wednesday / Saturn 5 / All of this and more / The way the light falls / Half way there / Cobra / I don't want to go blind. *(w / free ltd-cd of 'BBC SESSIONS' or free ltd.red-10"lp)*
Apr 94. (7"/c-s/cd-s) *(DUNG 26/+C/CD)* **UNIFORM. / PARANOID** [51] [-]
(cd-s) *(DUNG 26 CDR)* – ('A'side) / Paranoid (Collapsed Lung mix).
Aug 95. (7"m) *(DUNG 27L)* **JOE (acoustic). / SEEDS OF DOUBT / WHISKEY** [37] [-]
(7"m) *(DUNG 27R)* – Joe (live) / Sackville (live) / Saviour (live).
(cd-s) *(DUNG 25CD)* – ('A'side) / I want you / I'll keep it in mind / Tainted love.
Sep 95. (cd/c/d-lp) *(CD/C+/MOOTEL 3)* <9010> **THE SINGLES** (compilation) [17] [ ]
– Joe / Find out why / Move / This is how it feels / (extended) / She comes in the fall / Commercial reign / Sackville / Biggest mountain / Weakness / Caravan / Please be cruel / Dragging me down / Two worlds collide / Generations / Bitches brew / How it should be / Saturn 5 / I want you / Uniform.

— Had already been dropped from the 'Mute' roster late in 1994.

– compilations, etc. –

Jul 89. (12"ep/cd-ep) *Strange Fruit; (SFPS/+CD 072) / Dutch East India; <8305>* **THE PEEL SESSIONS** [ ] [ ]
– Out of time / Directing traffic / Keep the circle around / Gimme shelter.
Aug 92. (cd/10"lp) *Strange Fruit;* **PEEL SESSIONS** [ ] [-]

— also released import 7"colrd/12"colrd/pic-cd-s 'GIMME SHELTER'.

CLINT BOON EXPERIENCE

Rabid Badger / not iss.

Nov 98. (7") *(NANG 006)* **WHITE NO SUGAR. / NOT ENOUGH PEOPLE, TOO MUCH GREY** [ ] [-]
(cd-s+=) *(NANG 006CD)* – Philip Glass, Astronaut.

INTASTELLA (see under ⇒ LAUGH)

IN THE NURSERY

Formed: Sheffield, England . . . 1982 by two sets of twins, NIGEL and KLIVE HUMBERSTONE alongside ANT and DOLORES BENNETT. Specialising in military marching drum effects mixed with COCTEAU TWINS/DEAD CAN DANCE-esque vocals and guitars mellowed down by romantic cello (bow on bass), this lot issued a string of low-key releases beginning with '83's mini-set, 'WHEN CHERISHED DREAMS COME TRUE'. Unfortunately, the group ran into a few problems with their follow-up 7", 'WITNESS TO A SCREAM', the artwork printed wrongly and John Peel uncharacteristically fading the record out due to its poor quality. 'New European Records' (home of DEATH IN JUNE) took them on for a one-off 12", 'SONORITY', this, and subsequent releases taking on a more orchestrated feel. During the second half of the 80's, IN THE NURSERY brushed aside charges of Fascist sympathies and concentrated on a prolific release schedule for the 'Sweatbox' imprint. By the time of 1990's 'Third Mind' ('Wax Trax' US) album, 'L'ESPRIT', ITN had fused their industrial sound with MORRICONE-type atmospherics, while 1992's 'DUALITY', saw them sampling the voice of actor, Richard Burton. With music press recognition seemingly as far off as ever, the band continued to deliver an album a year before founding their own 'ITN Corporation' label in the mid 90's.

Album rating: TWINS (*4) / KODA (*4) / COUNTERPOINT compilation (*5)

NIGEL HUMBERSTONE – bow on bass, vocals, etc / **KLIVE HUMBERSTONE** – drum machine, vocals, etc / **ANT BENNETT** – guitar / **DOLORES BENNETT** – vocals

Paragon / not iss.

Jul 83. (m-lp) *(VIRTUE 2)* **WHEN CHERISHED DREAMS COME TRUE** [ ] [-]
Mar 84. (7") *(VIRTUE 5)* **WITNESS TO A SCREAM. / 1984** [ ] [-]

New Europ. Records / not iss.

Mar 85. (12"ep) *(BADVC 55)* **SONORITY – A STRENGTH** [ ] [-]
– Deus / Ex machina / Lost prayer / And your eyes.

Sweatbox efa

Nov 85. (12"ep) *(SOX 008)* **TEMPER. / BREACH BIRTH / JOAQUIN / ARM ME AUDACITY** [ ] [-]

— ANT + DOLORES were repl. by **GUS FERGUSON** – cello / **ELAINE McLEOD** – vocals

Sep 86. (lp) *(SAX 014)* **TWINS** [ ] [-]
– Timbre / Twins / Workcorps / Profile 63 / Huntdown / Outsider / Judgement of music / Joaquin / Intertwine. *(cd-iss. 1988; SAX 014CD) (cd re-iss. Jun95 on 'ITN Corporation'; CORP 009CD)*

May 87. (12"ep) *(SOX 019)* **TRINITY: ELEGY. / TRINITY: ELEGY (reprise) / BLIND ME** [ ] [-]

Jul 87. (lp/c) *(SAX/+C 021)* **THE STORY HORSE** [ ] [-]
(cd-iss. Feb88 +=; SAX 021CD) – Trinity: elegy / Trinity: elegy (reprise) / Blind me.

Nov 87. (12") *(SOX 027)* **COMPULSION. / LIBERTAIRE** [ ] [-]

Nov 88. (lp/cd) *(SAX 034/+CD)* **KODA** [ ] [-]
– Rites / Maiden / Te deum / Triumph / Burnished days / Ascent / Scherzo / Guarded rites / Suspire / Kotow / The seventeenth parallel. *(cd+=)* – Compulsion / Libertaire. *(cd re-iss. Jun95 on 'ITN Corporation'; CORP 008CD)*

Third Mind Wax Trax

Feb 90. (cd/lp) *(TMCD/TMLP 48)* <*WAX 7120*> **L'ESPRIT** [ ] [ ]
– To the faithful / At first sight / Seudient / Azure wings / Soeurette / Inamorata / Retaliation / Scenes of childhood / The pearl / L'esprit / Reverie / Alluvion / Across the ruins / To the faithful (reprise). *(cd re-iss. Jun95 on 'ITN Corporation'; CORP 010CD)*

Jul 90. (12") **SESUDIENT. /** [ ] [-]

— featured the vox of **DOLORES (MARGUERITTE)**

Sep 91. (cd) *(TM 9271-2)* **SENSE** [ ] [-]
– Blue religion / A rebours / Boy behind the curtain / Temporis / Syntonic / Sense / Epigraph / Memoirs / Angelchrome / Sinistroi / Sense datum / Contre – coeur. *(cd re-iss. Jan98 on 'ITN Corporation'; CORP 018CD)*

Jun 92. (cd) *(TM 9163-2)* **DUALITY** [ ] [ ]
– Belle epoque / Always / Red harvest / Duality / Corruption: (I) thorns – (II) Pulse – (III) Valediction / Universe / The engraver / Mecciano.

Nov 93. (cd) *(TM 9038-2)* **AN AMBUSH OF GHOSTS (soundtrack)** [ ] [ ]
– After great pain / Sedation / Lipstick / Disorientated / Atchaize / White robe / Cop shed / Running scene / Christian returns / Christian decides / Silk robe / Sedation 2 / Cop house / Funeral (part 1) / Funeral (part 2) / Dear Grover / Casus Belli / Syntonic / The hidden fortress / Hallucinations.

May 94. (12"/cd-s) *(TM 2369-6/-3)* **HALLUCINATIONS** [ ] [-]

Oct 94. (cd) *(TM 8976-2)* **ANATOMY OF A POET** [ ] [ ] Feb98
– Bombed / Anatomy of a poet / In perpetuum / Motive / Hallucinations? (dream world mix) / Blue lovers / Paper desert / Byzantium / The seventh sea / The golden journey / Touched with fire / Hallucinations – The tower III / November trees / Hallucinations? – A sense of reality.

ITN Corporation EFA

Jun 95. (cd) *(CORP 011CD)* **SCATTER** [ ] [-]
– Libertaire / Belle epoque / Mystere / Huntdown / Pearl / Tempest / Twins / Epitaph / To the faithful / Painter / Seraphic / 17th parallel / Sixth sense / Workcorps / Haunted dancehall / Miracle of the rose II.

May 96. (cd) *(CORP 014CD)* <*70114*> **DECO** [ ] [ ] Jun96
– Deco / Precedent / Syracuse / Mallarme / Woman / Cedione / Caprice / Mandra / Bassilica / Harmonica / Moreau.

Nov 96. (cd) *(CORP 015CD)* **IN THE CABINET OF DR. CAGLIARI** [ ] [-]

Oct 97. (cd) *(CORP 017CD)* <*70117*> **ASPHALT** [ ] [ ] Jan98
– Asphalt / Sobriety / Bergen's / Precious / Metropole / Entrapment / Seduction / Sobriety II / Underworld / De-Luxe / Opulence / Reflux / Necessity / Crime passionel / Judgement walk.

Apr 98. (cd) *(CORP 019CD)* <*70119*> **LINGUA** [ ] [ ] Jul98
– Poema / Mute harmony / A ask for grace / Profundus / Living tongue / Shonen no hi / Biello dumlo / Salient / El secreto.

– compilations, etc. –

Nov 88. (lp/cd) *Normal; (NORMAL 74/+CD)* **PRELUDE** [ ] [-]
(cd re-iss. Jun95 on 'ITN Corporation'; CORP 007CD)

May 89. (lp/cd) *Sweatbox; (SAX 042/+CD)* **COUNTERPOINT** (compilation) [-] [ ]
– Breach birth / Compulsion / Workcorps / Twins / Iskra / Arm me audacity / Sentiment / Blind me / Libertaire / Elegy / Joaquin / Butyrki / Breach birth (inception mix).

Apr 97. (cd) *EFA;* **COMPOSITE – THE BRASILIAN ISSUE** [-] [ ]
– Libertaire / Belle epoque (scatter mix) / The pearl / Harmonia / A rebours / To the faithful / Te deum / Retaliation / Judgement of Paris / Miracle of the rose II / Triumph / Burnished days / Sedudient / Elegy / Always (strive to be) / Anatomy of a poet (instrumental).

INTO A CIRCLE

Formed: Yorkshire, England . . . mid '85 from the ashes of SOUTHERN DEATH CULT offshoot band, GETTING THE FEAR (other two members being BUZZ and AKY) by BARRY JEPSON and BEE. The latter RCA-signed pop-goth outfit only managed to unveil one solitary flop single, 'LAST SALUTE', before BUZZ and AKY took off to form JOY. Meanwhile, BARRY and BEE (aka EDDIE TEMPLE MORRIS), drafted in BILLY MORRISON and PASQUELLE, almost immediately releasing the 12"EP, 'RISE' (as IN TWO A CIRCLE). Moving from their own 'Arcadia' imprint to the more experienced and credible 'Abstract' label, INTO A CIRCLE delivered a follow-up EP, 'INSIDE OUT'. 1987 looked promising for the duo when their producer, Larry Steinbeck, booked former STRAWBERRY SWITCHBLADE chanteuse, ROSE McDOWELL, to take on the vocal duties for single, 'FOREVER'. She subsequently became an integral part of the group and appeared on their debut album, 'ASSASSINS' (1988), although this was the last we heard of the act.

Album rating: ASSASSINS (*4)

BARRY JEPSON – bass (ex-SOUTHERN DEATH CULT, ex-GETTING THE FEAR) / **BEE** (b. EDDIE TEMPLE MORRIS) – instruments (ex-GETTING THE FEAR, ex-DANSE SOCIETY) / **BILLY MORRISON** – guitar / **PASQUALE I SERNIA** – drums (ex-UNDER TWO FLAGS)

Arcadia not iss.

Jan 86. (12"ep; as IN TWO A CIRCLE) *(ARC 001)* **RISE. / AND IN FLAMES / GABRIEL** [ ] [-]

Abstract not iss.

Nov 86. (12"ep) *(12ABS 42)* **INSIDE OUT** [ ] [-]
– Reward / Flow / Field of sleep.

— now with **ROSE McDOWELL** – vocals (ex-STRAWBERRY SWITCHBLADE)

Jul 87. (7"/12") *(ABS/12ABS 44)* **FOREVER. / O SIREN** [ ] [-]

Mar 88. (7"/12") *(ABS/12ABD 50)* **EVERGREEN. /** [ ] [-]

Jun 88. (lp) *(ABT 018)* **ASSASSINS** [ ] [-]

— split the circle after above

INTO PARADISE

Formed: Churchtown, nr. Dublin, Ireland . . . 1986 as BACKWARDS INTO PARADISE by DAVE LONG, JAMES EADIE, RACHAEL TIGHE and RONAN CLARKE. Slightly shortening their moniker, INTO PARADISE shipped themselves over to South London after initially being ignored by the Irish music press. They signed a deal with Celtic-friendly imprint, 'Setanta', who released their debut EP in 1989, 'BLUE LIGHT'. Their inaugural long-player, 'UNDER THE WATER' (1990), won many enthusiastic reviews, its uncompromising and uncommercial doom-laden alt-rock drawing a line through The COMSAT ANGELS, The SOUND (it was produced by ADRIAN BORLAND) and fellow Emerald-Isle upstarts, MICRODISNEY. Their major label follow-up, 'CHURCHTOWN', (1991), for 'Ensign', was given the thumbs down and the band moved back to familiar territory with 'Setanta'. While the label's A HOUSE and FRANK & WALTERS found a cult audience among the British indie fraternity, INTO PARADISE's more miserablist rock failed to strike a chord on third and fourth albums, 'DOWN ALL THE DAYS' (1992) and 'FOR NO ONE' (1993).

Album rating: UNDER THE WATER (*8) / CHURCHTOWN (*6) / DOWN ALL THE DAYS (*5) / FOR NO ONE (*4)

DAVE LONG – vocals, guitar / **JAMES EADIE** – lead guitar, keyboards / **RACHAEL TIGHE** – bass / **RONAN CLARKE** – drums

Setanta Chrysalis

Jun 89. (7"ep) *(SET 002)* **BLUE LIGHT EP** [ ] [-]

Feb 90. (cd/lp) *(SET CD/LP 1)* **UNDER THE WATER** <US title 'INTO PARADISE> [ ] [ ]
– Bring me closer / Here with you / Red light / The pleasure is you / The circus came to town / Bring me closer (version) / The world won't stop / Hearts and flowers / Blue moon express / Say goodnight / Beautiful day / Going home.

May 90. (12"ep) *(12SET 004)* **CHANGE EP** [ ] [ ]
– Under the water / Change / Heaven / Bring me closer.

Ensign Chrysalis

Jan 91. (7") **BURNS MY SKIN. /** [ ] [ ]
(12"+=/cd-s+=) –

Mar 91. (cd)(c/lp) *(CCD 1836)(Z+/CHEN 18)* **CHURCHTOWN** [ ] [ ] Aug91
– Rain comes down / Burns my skin / Yesterday's men / I'm still waiting / Winter / Bring me up / All down from here / Angel / Dreaming / Dive / Tears in your eyes / Gently falls.

May 91. (7"/c-s) **ANGEL. /** [ ] [-]
(12"+=/cd-s+=) –

Setanta not iss.

Aug 92. (lp/c/cd) *(SET LPM/MCM/CDM 007)* **DOWN ALL THE DAYS** [ ] [-]

Sep 92. (7") **TOMORROW. / ANGELUS** [ ] [-]
(cd-s+=) –

Dec 92. (7") **WHY DON'T YOU. /** [ ] [-]
(cd-s+=) –

Apr 93. (m-cd/m-lp) *(SET CDM/LPM 008)* **FOR NO ONE** [ ] [-]

— output dried up after above

I START COUNTING

Formed: London, England . . . early 1984 by SIMON LEONARD – formerly of 1979 act, FILE UNDER POP, who issued one single, 'HEATHROW' for 'Rough Trade'; (RT 011) – and DAVID BAKER, a one-time teen-mag pin up and a survivor of the Istanbul ferry disaster. I START COUNTING began their mathematical/robotic musical sojourn when producer, Daniel Miller (of 'Mute') – on the lookout for a new DEPECHE MODE – spotted their electro-pop potential. Basically a singles act, they also released two albums, 'MY TRANSLUCENT HANDS' (1986) and 'FUSED' (1989), during their commercially unfruitful mid to late 80's career. Like many of their peers, ISC made liberal use of pioneering sampling technology, even incorporating a snatch of Dee D Jackson's 1978 hit, 'Automatic Lover' on their 1988 'LOSE HIM' single.

Album rating: MY TRANSLUCENT HANDS (*3) / FUSED (*4)

DAVID BAKER – vocals, keyboards / **SIMON LEONARD** – keyboards (ex-FILE UNDER POP)

Mute not iss.

Jun 84. (7"/12") *(7/12 MUTE 34)* **LETTERS TO A FRIEND. / ADAM'S DREAM** [ ] [-]

Apr 85. (7"/12") *(7/12 MUTE 35)* **STILL SMILING. / THERE IS ALWAYS THE UNEXPECTED** [ ] [-]

Aug 86. (7"/12") *(7/12 MUTE 49)* **CATCH THAT LOOK. / COOLER THAN CALCUTTA** [ ] [-]

Oct 86. (7") *(7MUTE 54)* **MY TRANSLUCENT HANDS. /** [ ] [-]
Nov 86. (cd/lp) *(CD+/STUMM 30)* **MY TRANSLUCENT HANDS** [ ] [-]
– Introduction / My translucent hands / Catch that look / You and I / Lose him / Keep the sun away / Cranley gardens / Which way is home / Letters to a friend / Still smiling / Small consolation / There is always the unexpected.
Jan 88. (7") *(7MUTE 69)* **LOSE HIM. / SEE HOW IT CUTS** [ ] [-]
(12"+=) *(12MUTE 69)* – Tie me tight.
(12") *(L12MUTE 69)* – ('A'-Pascal Gabriel remix) / ('B'-extended club dub dance remix version by Paul Kendall & ISC).
Sep 88. (7") *(12") (12MUTE 81)* **RA RA RAWHIDE. /** [ ] [-]
Apr 89. (7") *(7MUTE 95)* **MILLION HEADED MONSTER. /** [ ] [-]
(12"+=/cd-s+=) *(12/CD MUTE 95)* –
Jun 89. (cd/lp) *(CD+/STUMM 50)* **FUSED** [ ] [ ]
– Money / Million headed monster / House / Modern sunbathing / Ra Ra Rawhide / Lose him / Grassnake / Only after dark / Empty room / Car theme from "The Blessing" / Birmingham / Listen / Ad man's dream.

— it was only a matter of time before they split

IT'S IMMATERIAL

Formed: Liverpool, England . . . 1980 by JOHN CAMPBELL, HENRY PRIESTMAN, MARTIN DEMPSEY and PAUL BARLOW. All but BARLOW were ex-members of art-popsters, The YACHTS, and there was certainly something of the latter outfit's quirkiness in IT'S IMMATERIAL unassuming strum and droll humour. The band's erratic output remains strewn across a variety of indie labels, the wryly titled 'YOUNG MAN (SEEKS INTERESTING JOB)' the first in a series of singles which found a comfortable niche but hardly troubled the mainstream charts. Pared down to a duo of CAMPBELL and WHITEHEAD following PRIESTMAN and BARLOW's mid-80's departure (the latter two both decamped to fellow scousers, The MIGHTY WAH!), IT'S IMMATERIAL enjoyed some belated Top 20 chart success with the low-key brilliance of 'DRIVING AWAY FROM HOME (JIM'S TUNE)'. Yet despite a re-released 'ED'S FUNKY DINER' scraping into the Top 75 and a fine (if long awaited), similarly placed debut album, 'LIFE'S HARD AND THEN YOU DIE' (1986), the group's eccentric musings seemed doomed to cult appeal. Although PRIESTMAN was still working with the band on a casual, part-time basis, he subsequently became a full-time member of The CHRISTIANS in the late 80's. CAMPBELL and WHITEHEAD meanwhile, returned in 1990 with a follow-up album, 'SONG', only their second in a decade. Sadly, afficionados of thinking man's pop have since had to look elsewhere for understated thrills, the duo finally throwing in the towel in the early 90's.

Album rating: LIFE'S HARD AND THEN YOU DIE (*6)

JOHN 'JJ' CAMPBELL – vocals, bass (ex-YACHTS) / **HENRY PRIESTMAN** – keyboards (ex-YACHTS, of WAH!) / **MARTIN DEMPSEY** – guitar (ex-YACHTS, ex-PINK MILITARY) / **PAUL BARLOW** – drums

Hit Machine — not iss.

Jul 80. (7") *(HIT 001)* **YOUNG MAN (SEEKS INTERESTING JOB). / DOOSHA (A SUCCESS STORY)** [ ] [-]

Inevitable — not iss.

Jul 81. (7") *(INEV 9)* **A GIGANTIC RAFT (IN THE PHILLIPINES). / NO PLACE FOR A PROMTER** [ ] [-]
(re-iss. Oct82 on 'Wonderful World Of'; WW 4)

I.H.M. — not iss.

Nov 81. (7") *(IHM 002)* **IMMITATE THE WORM. / THE WORM TURNS** [ ] [-]

— **JARVIS WHITEHEAD** (b.Newcastle, England) – guitar; repl. DEMPSEY who joined MEL-O-TONES

Eternal — not iss.

Oct 83. (7") *(JF 2)* **WHITE MAN'S HUT. / THE WORM TURNS** [ ] [-]
(12"+=) *(JF 2T)* – Solid piles of food.
Feb 84. (7"/12") *(JF 4/+T)* **A GIGANTIC RAFT (IN THE PHILLIPINES). / THE MERMAID** [ ] [-]

— trimmed to a duo of **CAMPBELL + WHITEHEAD** when PRIESTMAN + BARLOW joined The MIGHTY WAH!

Ark — not iss.

Mar 85. (12"ep) *(DOVE 3)* **FISH WALTZ EP** [ ] [-]
– Fish waltz / Several brothers / The better idea / Lullaby.

— the duo added backing musicians **HENRY PRIESTMAN, The CHRISTIANS, RODDY LORIMER, STEVE WICKHAM, BRENDA KENNY, GILLIAN MILLER, MERRAN LAGINESTRA** + 70 year-old **TARRANT BAILEY JNR** – banjo (on 'Rope')

Siren — A&M

Oct 85. (7") *(SIREN 8)* **ED'S FUNKY DINER. / PUSH OUT THE BOAT** [ ] [-]
(12"+=) *(SIREN 8-12)* – Washing the air / We'll turn things upside down.
Mar 86. (7") *(SIREN 15)* **DRIVING AWAY FROM HOME (JIM'S TUNE). / TRAINS, BOATS, PLANES** [18] [-]
(12"+=) *(SIREN 15-12)* – ('A'-Wicked Weather For Walking mix) / A crooked tune.
Jul 86. (7") *(SIREN 24)* **ED'S FUNKY DINER (FRIDAY NIGHT, SATURDAY MORNING). / ONLY THE LONELY** [65] [-]
(12"+=) *(SIREN 24-12)* – Driving away from home (I mean after all it's only Dead Man's Curve).
(d7"++=) *(SIREN 24)* – We'll turn things upside down.
Sep 86. (lp/c/cd) *(SRNLP/SRNMC/CDSRN 4)* <5169> **LIFE'S HARD AND THEN YOU DIE** [62] [ ]
– Driving away from home (Jim's tune) / The sweet life / Lullaby / Happy talk / Festival time / Hang on sleepy town / Rope / Ed's funky diner / The better idea / Space. *(re-iss. Apr90 on 'Virgin' lp/c; OVED/+C 289)*
Oct 86. (7") *(SIREN 34)* **HE CALLED FROM THE KITCHEN . . . SPACE. / HEREBY HANGS A TALE** [ ] [-]
(12"+=) *(SIREN 34-12)* – Space (version).
Feb 87. (7") *(SIREN 38)* **ROPE. / VERY** [ ] [-]
(12"+=) *(SIREN 38-12)* – Festival time.

— part-timer PRIESTMAN joined The CHRISTIANS

Jun 90. (cd/c/lp) *(SRN CD/MC/LP 27)* **SONG** [ ] [-]
– New Brighton / Endless holiday / An ordinary life / Heaven knows / In the neighbourhood / Missing / Homecoming / Summer winds / Life on the hill / Your voice.
Aug 90. (7") **HEAVEN KNOWS. /** [ ] [-]
(12"+=/cd-s+=) – Driving away from home (I mean after all it's only 'Dead Man's Curve').

— the duo split soon after above

– compilations, etc. –

Nov 88. (3"cd-ep) *Virgin; (CDT 26)* **DRIVING AWAY FROM HOME (JIM'S TUNE) / ED'S FUNKY DINER / DRIVING AWAY FROM HOME (I MEAN AFTER ALL IT'S ONLY 'DEAD MAN'S CURVE'** [ ] [-]

David J (see under ⇒ BAUHAUS)

JACK

Formed: Cardiff, Wales ... 1994 by ANTHONY REYNOLDS and MATTHEW SCOTT, who subsequently enlisted others RICHARD ADDERLEY, GEORGE WRIGHT, COLIN WILLIAMS and PATRICK PULZER. After a move to London, the sextet signed a deal with maverick indie label, 'Too Pure', scoring a Melody Maker Single Of The Week towards the end of '95 with their debut 7", 'KID STARDUST' (a tribute to cult writer, Charles Bukowski). Enhancing their lush sound with the addition of cellist, AUDREY MORSE, the band created a minor stir with early '96's 'WINTERCOMESSUMMER', a track centering on girlfriend/boyfriend violence. A third single, 'WHITE JAZZ', previewed the band's inaugural long-player, 'PIONEER SOUNDTRACKS' (1996); it was hardly a coincidence that the record was overseen by Peter Walsh, a one-time producer for SCOTT WALKER, a JACK icon alongside moodmeisters such as NICK CAVE and JACQUES BREL. Following a one-off collaboration with fellow BREL afficionado, MOMUS, frontman REYNOLDS reunited with his JACK cohorts for a second set, 'THE JAZZ AGE' (1998).

Album rating: PIONEER SOUNDTRACKS (*6) / THE JAZZ AGE (*7)

ANTHONY REYNOLDS – vocals, guitar, keyboards / **MATTHEW SCOTT** – guitar / **RICHARD 'DICKO' ADDERLEY** – guitar / **GEORGE WRIGHT** – keyboards / **COLIN WILLIAMS** – bass / **PATRICK PULZER** – drums, percussion

Too Pure — American

Nov 95. (ltd.7") *(PURE 049)* **KID STARDUST. /** — [ ] [-]

— added 7th member **AUDREY MORSE** – cello

Jan 96. (7") *(PURE 052)* **WINTERCOMESSUMMER. / HEY JOSEPHINE** — [ ] [-]
(cd-s+=) *(PURECD 052)* – I was drunk in the underworld.

Apr 96. (7") *(PURE 053)* **WHITE JAZZ. / BALLAD OF MISERY AND HEAVEN** — [ ] [-]
(cd-s+=) *(PURECD 053)* – Ballad for a beautiful blonde eye.

Jun 96. (lp/cd) *(PURE/+CD 055)* *<43073>* **PIONEER SOUNDTRACKS** — [ ] [ ]
– Of lights, . . . / Wintercomessummer / White jazz / Biography of a first son / Filthy names / I didn't mean it, Marie / F.U. / Dress you in mourning / Hope is a liar.

Aug 96. (7") *(PURE 059)* **BIOGRAPHY OF A FIRST SON. / FOR LUNA** — [ ] [-]
(cd-s+=) *(PURECD 059)* – Seventh day / Kid Stardust.

Jan 98. (7") *(ER 176)* **CINEMATIC. /** — [ ] [-]
(above issued on 'Elefant')

Jun 98. (7") *(PURE 079S)* **3 O'CLOCK IN THE MORNING. / LOLITA ELLE** — [ ] [-]
(cd-s+=) *(PURE 079CDS)* – Ballad of swing and solar.

Aug 98. (lp/cd) *(PURE 072/+CD)* **THE JAZZ AGE** — [ ] [-]
– 3 o'clock in the morning / Pablo / My world vs. your world / Saturday's plan / Nico's children / Lolita Elle / Cinematic / Steamin' / Love and death in the afternoon / Half cut wholly yours.

Oct 98. (7"ep) *(PURE 081)* **STEAMIN'. / FALL IN LOVE WITH ME AGAIN / LAST MOMENTS IN THE MIND OF DANNY SAMMY JNR** — [ ] [-]
(cd-s) *(PURE 081CDS)* – ('A'side) / Yuka's life / You will forget me.

JACK FROST (see under ⇒ CHURCH)

JACK OFFICERS (see under ⇒ BUTTHOLE SURFERS)

JACOB'S MOUSE

Formed: Bury St.Edmunds, Suffolk, England ... 1991 by identical twins, HUGO and JEBB BOOTHBY alongside singing drummer SAM MARSH. Formed when the lads had barely reached puberty, the band had rather murky heavy metal beginnings, churning out STATUS QUO numbers until a chance TV sighting of Scots noisemongers The DOG FACED HERMANS turned their musical world around. Older and wiser, the trio made their vinyl debut in 1990 with the 'Dot' EP, issued on their own indie label, 'Liverish' and the proud winner of a Single Of The Week award from Sounds. A string of high profile support slots ensued including prestigious dates with NIRVANA, the band most widely mentioned when tackling any objective description of the JACOB'S MOUSE sound. While many noted the similarity with NIRVANA's 'Nevermind', the Bury St.Edmunds camp pointed out that debut album, 'NO FISH SHOP PARKING' (1992) – released on the band's own 'Blithering Idiot' label – had actually been recorded before the NIRVANA landmark had been released. Still, in terms of attitude and melodic, CARTER USM-style blitzkreig spirit, there was a definite musical kinship, indie label 'Wiiija' finally signing them after intially turning the band down. Another EP, 'TON UP', surfaced later that year, as did a follow-up album, 'I'M SCARED' (1992), the lyrical intensity matching the sonic barrage note by searing note. Two more EP's, 'GOOD', and 'GROUP OF SEVEN', appeared in 1993 and while the predicted indie domination never quite materialised, the following year's 'RUBBER ROOM' album was testament to their talents.

Album rating: NO FISH SHOP PARKING (*6) / I'M SCARED (*6) / WRYLY SMILING compilation (*6) / RUBBER ROOM (*5)

HUGO BOOTHY – guitar / **JEBB BOOTHY** – bass / **SAM MARSH** – vocals, drums

Liverish — not iss.

Jan 91. (12"ep) *(LIVES 001)* **THE DOT** — [ ] [-]
– Sign / Enterprise / Hey dip sugar / Ho-hum / Microfish. *(re-iss. Oct94; same)*

Blithering Idiot — not iss.

Feb 92. (lp/cd) *(BLIT 001/+CD)* **NO FISH SHOP PARKING** — [ ] [-]
– Tumbleswan / Twist / She is dead / A place to go / Carfish / Caphony / Justice / The vase. *(cd re-iss. Sep94; same)*

Wiiija — not iss.

Sep 92. (12"ep/cd-ep) *(WIJ V/CD)* **TON-UP** — [ ] [-]
– Oblong / This room / Motorspare / Fridge.

Apr 93. (cd/lp) *(WIJ 021 CD/V)* **I'M SCARED** — [ ] [-]
– Kettle / Deep canvas lake / This room / Zig zag / Solo / Coalmine dig / Thin sound / Ash tray / Body shop / Box hole / Colum. *(re-iss. Sep93 on green-lp)*

Oct 93. (7"ep/cd-ep) *(WIJ 26 V/CD)* **GOOD. / DUSTY / LIP AND CHEEK** — [ ] [-]

Nov 93. (7"ep/cd-ep) *(WIJ V/CD)* **GROUP OF SEVEN. / PALACE / SAG BAG** — [ ] [-]

Apr 94. (7"ep/cd-ep) *(WIJ 32 V/CD)* **FANDANGO WIDEWHEELS. / B12 MARMITE / 3 POUND APATHY / KEEN APPLE** — [ ] [-]

Sep 94. (cd/lp) *(JCOB 001 CD/V)* **WRYLY SMILING** (compilation) — [ ] [-]
– Good / Dusty / Lip and cheek / Group of seven / Palace / Sag bag / Fandango widewheels / B12 marmites / 3 pound apathy / Keen apple.

Feb 95. (7"one-sided) *(LTD 001)* **HAWAIIAN VICE** — [ ] [-]

Feb 95. (cd/lp) *(WIJ 040 CD/V)* **RUBBER ROOM** — [ ] [-]
– Kuff prang / Hawaiian vice / Public oven / James John Robert / Foam face / Snivelling / Hostile / Rubber room / Club scare / Domstic / Poltergeist / Blither.

— haven't returned as a group for some time now

JAGS

Formed: Scarborough, England . . . 1977 by songwriters NICK WATKINSON and JOHN ADLER, who subsequently recruited a rhythm section of STEVE PRUDENCE and ALEX BAIRD. Signed to 'Island', The JAGS released one of the power-punk/pop scene's finest three minutes in 'BACK OF MY HAND (I'VE GOT YOUR NUMBER)'. Complete with lip-curling, faux-American accents, a melody to die for and a rapid fire chorus that injected the track into the collective consciousness, the record gatecrashed the Top 20 in summer '79 (Top 100 in the States the following Spring!). Yet the JAGS were to become one of the era's many one-hit wonders, follow-up single, 'WOMAN'S WORLD' falling woefully short of requirements and only managing a Top 75 position. Debut album, 'EVENING STANDARD' (1980) also failed to live up to the high standards they'd already set themselves and following the release of the ALEX SADKIN-produced second set, 'NO TIES TO THE PRESENT' (1981), they sank without trace.

Album rating: EVENING STANDARD (*5) / NO TIES TO THE PRESENT (*4)

NICK WATKINSON – vocals, guitar / **JOHN ADLER** – guitar / **STEVE PRUDENCE** – bass / **ALEX BAIRD** – drums

Island — Island

Aug 79. (7"/12") *(WIP/12XWIP 6501)* *<49202>* **BACK OF MY HAND. / DOUBLE VISION – BWM** — [17] [84] May80

Jan 80. (7") *(WIP 6531)* **WOMAN'S WORLD. / DUMB BLONDE** — [75] [ ]

Jan 80. (lp) *(ILPS 9603)* **EVENING STANDARD** — [ ] [ ]
– Desert island discs / Woman's world / She's so considerate / Little boy lost / Single vision – BWM / Evening standard / Party games / Tune into Heaven / Last picture show / The tourist.

Apr 80. (7") *(WIP 6587)* **PARTY GAMES. / SHE'S SO CONSIDERATE** — [ ] [ ]

Jan 81. (7") *(WIP 6666)* **I NEVER WAS A BEACH BOY. / TUNE INTO HEAVEN** [ ] [ ]
Feb 81. (lp) *(ILPS 9655)* **NO TIE LIKE A PRESENT** [ ] [-]
– Here comes my baby / I never was a beach boy / Another town, another place / The train and the plane / Silver birds / The sound of G-O-O-D-B-Y-E / Small change / Mind reader / Little Lloyd Wright / Fearing a tornado.
Apr 81. (7") *(WIP 6683)* **SOUND OF G-O-O-D-B-Y-E. / THE HURT** [ ] [ ]
—— disbanded after above

JALE

Formed: Halifax, Nova Scotia, Canada . . . Spring '92 by the all-girl line-up of JENNIFER PIERCE, ALYSON MacLEOD, LAURA STEIN and EVE HARTLING, taking their moniker from the first letter of each member's christian name. Having all attended the same art school, the bespectacled librarian-like ladies decided to try their hand at alternative pop-rock, borrowing instruments from classmates and intially playing PIXIES/BREEDERS covers at parties. Making quick progress, they soon began writing their own material (as a group effort) and issued their debut 7", 'AUNT BETTY', in 1993. This led to the inclusion of a track on the 'Sub Pop' sampler, 'Never Mind The Molluscs', the JALE birds subsequently signing a bonafide deal with the label (having turned down 'Island') and releasing a further couple of singles prior to a debut album, 'DREAMCAKE' (1994). Intelligent, fresh and exciting, the record combined the sweet-lipped harmonies of classic pop with the kick of ELASTICA and dark undercurrent of THROWING MUSES, the highlights of which could be witnessed live on that summer's trial-by-fire L7 tour and Reading Festival appearance. Barring a US-only EP, the group kept a low profile until 1996's well-received follow-up set, 'SO WOUND', by which time MacLEOD been replaced by a guy(!), MIKE BELITSKY. The subsequent departure of HARTLING the following year looked to have put away the band for good.

Album rating: DREAMCAKE (*6) / SO WOUND (*7)

JENNIFER PIERCE – vocals, guitar / **EVE HARTLING** – vocals, guitar / **LAURA STEIN** – vocals, bass / **ALYSON MacLEOD** – drums, vocals

not iss. Cinnamon Toast

1993. (7"ep) *<015>* **GOLD LEATHER WITH HEEL DETAIL** [-] [ ]
– Aunt Betty / etc.

Sub Pop Sub Pop

Jun 94. (7") *(SP 134-331) <SP 235>* **3 DAYS. / PROMISE** [ ] [ ]
(cd-s+=) *(SPCD 134-331)* –
Aug 94. (cd/lp) *<(SP 256A/127-317)>* **DREAMCAKE** [ ] [ ] Jul94
– Not happy / Nebulous / 3 days / To be your friend / Again / River / I'm sorry / Mend / Unseen guest / Love letter / Emma / Promise.
1995. (cd-ep) *<018>* **CLOSED EP** [-] [ ]
—— <above issued on 'Murderchords'>
—— **MIKE BELITSKY** – drums; repl. ALYSON who joined HARDSHIP POST
May 96. (7") *<(SP 346)>* **HEY HEY. /** [ ] [ ]
(cd-s+=) *<(SPCD 346)>* –
Jun 96. (lp/cd) *<(SP/+CD 350)>* **SO WOUND** [ ] [ ]
– Ali / Hey hey / Sign of life / All ready / Tumble / Blue / Mosquito / Storm / Drag / Back on track / Over you / Despite / Superstar.

Derivative Derivative

Nov 96. (7") *<(DUH 008)>* **EMMA. /** [ ] [ ]
—— HARTLING departed in 1997 and it seemed the band would split

JAM

Formed: Woking, Surrey, England . . . late '73 by PAUL WELLER, BRUCE FOXTON, RICK BUCKLER and 4th member STEVE BROOKS – guitar. This quartet first gigged mid-74, progressing to the likes of London's Marquee, 101 Club & Red Cow in late '76, by which time BROOKS had departed. Peddling amphetamine charged retro R&B, the band rode in on the first wave of punk's brave new musical world. Incendiary live performances had generated a loyal following and considerable record company interest, the band signing with 'Polydor' early the following year via A&R man Chris Parry. In Spring '77, their debut, 'IN THE CITY', cracked the UK Top 40, an album of the same name following a month later. Image wise, the band were kitted out in unashamed allegiance to the mod masterplan of yore; sharp suits, parkas, scooters etc., another factor that set the band apart from the anti-fashion of punk. Something WELLER did share with his glue-sniffing peers was anger; yep, before WELLER the 'red-wedge' soul smoothie and WELLER the patron of 'Dad Rock' came WELLER the angry young man, so angry in fact, that he professed to voting conservative. Politics aside, 'IN THE CITY' was a cut above the average three chord punk thrash, bristling with adolescent fury yet possessed of an irresistible melodic verve. 'THIS IS THE MODERN WORLD' (1977) was a hastily recorded follow-up, and it showed. Only the pounding title track (the single backed with a cover of Arthur Conley's ~'SWEET SOUL MUSIC') really hit the target, the rest of the album pointlessly recycling WHO riffs ad nauseum. With 'ALL MOD CONS' (1978), however, The JAM were onto something big, WELLER's cutting social reportage and songwriting genius translating into such gems as 'DOWN IN THE TUBE-STATION AT MIDNIGHT', a cover of The Kinks' 'DAVID WATTS' indicating the heights he was aiming for. Come 'SETTING SONS' (1979), and with the bile-spewing 'ETON RIFLES', in particular, WELLER came pretty damn close to updating RAY DAVIES' class-conscious agenda for a harsh new age. The single gave the band their first Top 5 success and the album achieved a similar feat upon its release a month later. In February of the following year, the band went straight in at No.1 with 'GOING UNDERGROUND', a snarling critique of the establishment. The band followed this up with 'START!', a virtual remake (well, intro definitely) of George Harrison/Beatles' 'TAXMAN', quite why there's never been a court case over the matter remains a mystery. Still, the single marked a move into more ambitious musical territory, WELLER penning his most accomplished tune to date in the lilting, understated ennui of 'THAT'S ENTERTAINMENT'. The album, 'SOUND AFFECTS' (1980), confirmed the shift away from powerchord aggression with the use of horns and more obviously black music-derived rhythms. By this point, THE JAM were one of, if not the, biggest band in Britain although, despite repeated attempts, the American market was apparently impossible for the band to crack. Then again, it's not hard to see that their defiantly British sound just didn't translate in the States, in much the same way as, more recently, BLUR's idiosyncratic Englishness has precluded US recognition. Back home though, the band were No.1 again in early 1982 with the heavily Motown-influenced 'TOWN CALLED MALICE', 'THE GIFT' album being released the following month. It was to be the band's swansong as WELLER, at the peak of the band's fame later that summer, announced he was to break the group up to explore his soul fixation with The STYLE COUNCIL. After a final kiss-off with 'THE BITTEREST PILL' and the brilliant 'BEAT SURRENDER', the band were no more. While WELLER went on to a undergo many musical rebirths, there was no such joy for FOXTON, who later joined aging punks STIFF LITTLE FINGERS. BUCKLER, meanwhile, forsook the evils of the music business for furniture restoration. Thankfully, with no reunion so far, and the possibility of one rather slim, the legend of The JAM remains intact. • **Songwriters:** WELLER penned except; BACK IN MY ARMS AGAIN (Holland-Dozier-Holland) / DAVID WATTS (Kinks) / MOVE ON UP (Curtis Mayfield). • **Trivia:** In Oct'81, WELLER started own record company 'Respond', and signed acts The QUESTIONS and TRACIE.

Album rating: IN THE CITY (*6) / THIS IS THE MODERN WORLD (*5) / ALL MOD CONS (*8) / SETTING SONS (*8) / SOUND EFFECTS (*8) / THE GIFT (*6) / DIG THE NEW BREED live collection (*6) / SNAP! compilation (*10) / GREATEST HITS compilation (*8) / DIRECTION REACTION CREATION boxed compilation (*9) / THE VERY BEST OF THE JAM compilation (*8)

PAUL WELLER (b. JOHN WELLER, 25 May'58) – vocals, guitar / **BRUCE FOXTON** (b. 1 Sep'55) – bass, vocals / **RICK BUCKLER** (b. PAUL RICHARD BUCKLER, 6 Dec'55) – drums

Polydor Polydor

Apr 77. (7") *(2058 866)* **IN THE CITY. / TAKIN' MY LOVE** [40] [ ]
(re-iss. Apr80) – hit No.40 *(re-iss. Jan83)* – hit No.47
May 77. (lp) *(2383 447) <6110>* **IN THE CITY** [20] [ ]
– Art school I've changed my address / Slow down / I got by in time / Away from the numbers / Batman / In the city / Sounds from the street / Non stop dancing / Time for truth / Takin' my love / Bricks and mortar. *(re-iss. Aug83 lp/c; SPE LP/MC 27) (re-iss. Jul90 cd/c/lp; 817124-2/-4/-1) (cd re-iss. Jul97; 537417-2)*
Jul 77. (7") *(2058 903)* **ALL AROUND THE WORLD. / CARNABY STREET** [13] [-]
(re-iss. Apr80) – hit No.43 *(re-iss. Jan83)* – hit No.38
Oct 77. (7"m) *(2058 945)* **THE MODERN WORLD. / SWEET SOUL MUSIC (live) / BACK IN MY ARMS AGAIN (live) / BRICKS AND MORTAR (live)** [36] [-]
(re-iss. Apr80) – hit No.52 *(re-iss. Jan83)* – hit No.51
Nov 77. (lp) *(2383 475) <6129>* **THIS IS THE MODERN WORLD** [22] [ ]
– The modern world / London traffic / Standards / Life from the window / The combine / Don't tell them you're sane / In the street today / London girl / I need you / Here comes the weekend / Tonight at noon / In the midnight hour. *(re-iss. Aug83 lp/c; SPE LP/MC 66) (re-iss. Jul90 cd/c/lp; 823281-2/-4/-1) (cd re-iss. Jul97; 537418-2)*
Feb 78. (7") *<14462>* **I NEED YOU. / IN THE CITY** [-] [ ]
Mar 78. (7"m) *(2058 995)* **NEWS OF THE WORLD. / AUNTIES AND UNCLES / INNOCENT MAN** [27] [-]
(re-iss. Apr80) – hit No.53 *(re-iss. Jan83)* – hit No.39
Aug 78. (7") *(2059 054)* **DAVID WATTS. / 'A' BOMB IN WARDOUR STREET** [25] [-]
(re-iss. Apr80) – hit No.54 *(re-iss. Jan83)* – hit No.50
Oct 78. (7"m) *(POSP 8)* **DOWN IN THE TUBE STATION AT MIDNIGHT. / SO BAD ABOUT US / THE NIGHT** [15] [-]
(re-iss. Apr80) (re-iss. Jan83) – hit No.30
Nov 78. (lp/c) *(POLD/+C 5008) <6218>* **ALL MOD CONS** [6] [ ]
– All mod cons / To be someone (didn't we have a nice time) / Mr. Clean / David Watts / English rose / In the crowd / Billy Hunt / It's too bad / Fly 3.18 / The place I love / 'A' bomb in Wardour Street / Down in the tube station at midnight. *(cd-iss. 1989; 823282-2) (cd re-iss. Jul97; 537419-2)*
Mar 79. (7") *(POSP 34) <14553>* **STRANGE TOWN. / THE BUTTERFLY COLLECTOR** [15] [ ]
(re-iss. Apr80) – hit No.44 *(re-iss. Jan83)* – hit No.42
Jun 79. (7") *<14566>* **DOWN IN THE TUBE STATION AT MIDNIGHT. / MR. CLEAN** [-] [ ]
Aug 79. (7") *(POSP 69)* **WHEN YOU'RE YOUNG. / SMITHERS-JONES** [17] [-]
(re-iss. Jan83) – hit No.53
Oct 79. (7") *(POSP 83)* **THE ETON RIFLES. / SEE-SAW** [3] [-]
(re-iss. Jan83) – hit No.54
Nov 79. (lp/c) *(POLD/+C 5028) <6249>* **SETTING SONS** [4] [ ]
– Girl on the phone / Thick as thieves / Private hell / Little boy soldiers / Waste land / Burning sky / Smithers-Jones / Saturday's kids / The Eton rifles / Heat wave. *(cd-iss. May88; 831314-2) (cd re-iss. Jul97; 537420-2)*
Dec 79. (7") *<2051>* **THE ETON RIFLES. / SMITHERS-JONES** [-] [ ]
Feb 80. (7") *(POSP 113)* **GOING UNDERGROUND. / DREAMS OF CHILDREN** [1] [-]
(d7"+=) *(POSPJ 113 – 2616 024)* – The modern world (live) / Away from the numbers (live) / Down in the tube station at midnight (live). *(re-iss. Jan83)* – hit No.21

Apr 80. (7") *<2074>* **SATURDAY'S KIDS. / (LOVE IS LIKE A) HEATWAVE** [-] [ ]

Aug 80. (7") *(2059 266)* **START! / LIZA RADLEY** [1] [-]
(re-iss. Jan83) – hit No.60

Sep 80. (7") *<2155>* **START! / WHEN YOU'RE YOUNG** [-] [ ]

Nov 80. (lp/c) *(POLD/+C 5035) <6315>* **SOUND AFFECTS** [2] [72]
– Pretty green / Monday / But I'm different now / Set the house ablaze / Start! / That's entertainment / Dreamtime / Man in the cornershop / Music for the last couple / Boy about town / Scrape away. *(re-iss. Apr90 cd/c/lp; 823284-2/-4/-1) (cd re-iss. Jul97; 537421-2)*

Jan 81. (7") *(0030 364)* **THAT'S ENTERTAINMENT. / DOWN IN THE TUBE STATION AT MIDNIGHT (live)** [21] [-]
(above 45, was actually imported into Britain by German 'Metrognome') *(re-iss. Jan83 on 'Polydor'; 2059 482)* – hit No.60

May 81. (7") *(POSP 257)* **FUNERAL PYRE. / DISGUISES** [4] [ ]
(re-iss. Jan83)

Oct 81. (7") *(POSP 350)* **ABSOLUTE BEGINNERS. / TALES FROM THE RIVERBANK** [4] [ ]
(re iss. Jan83)

Dec 81. (m-lp) *<503>* **THE JAM** [-] [ ]
– Absolute beginners / Funeral pyre / Liza Radley / Tales from the riverbank / Disguises.

Feb 82. (7"/12") *(POSP/+X 400)* **TOWN CALLED MALICE. / PRECIOUS** [1] [ ]
(re-iss. Jan83) – hit No.73

Mar 82. (lp/c) *(POLD/+C 5055) <6349>* **THE GIFT** [1] [82]
– Happy together / Ghosts / Precious / Just who is the 5 o'clock hero? / Trans-global express / Running on the spot / Circus / The planner's dream goes wrong / Carnation / Town called Malice / The gift. *(re-iss. Apr90 cd/c/lp; 823285-2/-4/-1) (cd re-iss. Jul97; 537422-2)*

Jun 82. (7") *(2059 504)* **JUST WHO IS THE 5 O'CLOCK HERO?. / THE GREAT DEPRESSION** [6] [ ]
(12"+=) *(2141 558)* – War.

Sep 82. (7") *(POSP 505)* **THE BITTEREST PILL (I EVER HAD TO SWALLOW). / PITY POOR ALFIE / FEVER – PITY POOR ALFIE** [2] [ ]

<US-iss.Nov82 as 12"m-lp> – Great depression.

Nov 82. (7") *(POSP 540)* **BEAT SURRENDER. / SHOPPING** [1] [ ] Mar83
(d7"+=)<m-lp> *(POSPJ 540 – JAM 1) <810751>* – Move on up / War / Stoned out of my mind.

Dec 82. (lp/c) *(POLD/+C 5075) <6365>* **DIG THE NEW BREED (live 77-82)** [2] [ ]
– In the city / All mod cons / To be someone / It's too bad / Start! / Big bird / Set the house ablaze / Ghosts / Standards / In the crowd / Going underground / Dreams of children / That's entertainment / Private hell. *(re-iss. Jun87 lp/c; SPE LP/MC 107) (re-iss. Jun90 cd/c/lp; 810041-2/-4/-1) (cd re-iss. Sep95)*

—— They split late '82. WELLER formed The STYLE COUNCIL, before making it huge as a solo star. FOXTON, meanwhile, went solo, delivering a solitary solo album, 'TOUCH SENSITIVE' (May 1984) for 'Arista'; the Top 75 breaker contained his only Top 30 hit, 'FREAK', released a year earlier. BUCKLER formed TIME UK who had one minor hit, 'THE CABARET' (Sep'83), before he and FOXTON teamed up with TIME UK singer, JIMMY EDWARDS, to become mid-late 80's outfit, SHARP.

– compilations, etc. –

on 'Polydor' unless mentioned otherwise

Sep 80. (d-lp) *(2683 074)* **IN THE CITY / THIS IS THE MODERN WORLD** [ ] [-]
(re-iss. Jan91 cd/c; 847730-2/-4)

Jan 83. (d-c) *(TWOMC 1)* **SOUND AFFECTS / THE GIFT** [ ] [-]

Feb 83. (d-c) *(1574 098)* **ALL MOD CONS / SETTING SONS** [ ] [-]

Oct 83. (d-lp/d-c) *(SNAP/+C 1)* **SNAP!** [2] [-]
– In the city / Away from the numbers / All around the world / The modern world / News of the world / Billy Hunt / English Rose / Mr. Clean / David Watts / 'A' bomb in Wardour Street / Down in the tube station at midnight / Strange town / The butterfly collector / When you're young / Smithers-Jones / Thick as thieves / The Eton rifles / Going underground / Dreams of children / That's entertainment / Start! / Man in the cornershop / Funeral pyre / Absolute beginners / Tales from the riverbank / Town called Malice / Precious / The bitterest pill (I ever had to swallow) / Beat surrender. *(d-lp.with free 7"ep)* **LIVE AT WEMBLEY (live)** – The great depression / But I'm different now / Move on up / Get yourself together. *(cd-iss. Sep84 as 'COMPACT SNAP'; 821712-2)* – omits 8 tracks. *(re-iss. Jun90 cd/c/lp; 815537-2/-4/-1)*

Mar 90. (7") *Old Gold; (OG 9894)* **TOWN CALLED MALICE. / ABSOLUTE BEGINNERS** [ ] [-]

Mar 90. (7") *Old Gold; (OG 9895)* **BEAT SURRENDER. / THE BITTEREST PILL (I EVER HAD TO SWALLOW)** [ ] [-]

Mar 90. (7") *Old Gold; (OG 9896)* **THE ETON RIFLES. / DOWN IN THE TUBE STATION AT MIDNIGHT** [ ] [-]

Mar 90. (7") *Old Gold; (OG 9897)* **GOING UNDERGROUND. / START!** [ ] [-]

Sep 90. (12"ep/cd-ep) *Strange Fruit; (SFPS/+CD 080)* **THE PEEL SESSIONS** (26.4.77) [ ] [-]
– In the city / Art school / I've changed my address / The modern world. *(cd-ep re-iss. Sep96; same)*

Jun 91. (7"/c-s) *(PO/+CS 155)* **THAT'S ENTERTAINMENT. / DOWN IN THE TUBE-STATION AT MIDNIGHT (live)** [57] [-]
(12"+=/cd-s+=) *(PZ/+CD 155)* – Town called Malice (live).

Jul 91. (cd/c/lp) *(849554-2/-4/-1)* **GREATEST HITS** [2] [-]

Mar 92. (7"/c-s) *(PO/+CS 199)* **THE DREAMS OF CHILDREN. / AWAY FROM THE NUMBERS (live)** [ ] [-]
(12"+=/cd-s+=) *(PZ/+CD 199)* – This is the modern world (live).

Apr 92. (cd/c/lp) *(513177-2/-4/-1)* **EXTRAS: A COLLECTION OF RARITIES** [ ] [-]

Oct 92. (cd/c) *Pickwick; (PWK S/MC 4129P)* **WASTELAND** [ ] [-]

Oct 93. (cd/c/d-lp) *(519667-2/-4/-1)* **LIVE JAM (live)** [28] [ ]
– The modern world / Billy Hunt / Thick as thieves / Burning sky / Mr. Clean / Smithers-Jones / Little boy soldiers / The Eton Rifles / Away from the numbers / Down in the tube station at midnight / Strange town / When you're young / 'A' Bomb In Wardour Street / Pretty green / Boy about town / Man in the cornershop / David Watts / Funeral pyre / Move on up / Carnation / The butterfly collector / Precious / Town called Malice / Heatwave.

Jul 96. (d-cd/d-c/d-lp) *(531493-2/-4/-1)* **THE JAM COLLECTION** [58] [-]

May 97. (5xcd-box) *(537143-2)* **DIRECTION REACTION CREATION** [8] [-]

Sep 97. (7"/c-s) *(571598-7/-4)* **THE BITTEREST PILL (I EVER HAD TO SWALLOW). / THE BUTTERFLY COLLECTOR** [30] [-]
(cd-s+=) *(571598-2)* – That's entertainment / ('A'version).

Oct 97. (cd/c) *(537423-2/-4)* **THE VERY BEST OF THE JAM** [9] [-]

JAMES

Formed: Manchester, England . . . 1982 by JIM GLENNIE, TIM BOOTH, LARRY GOTT and GAVAN WHELAN. In 1983 they signed to Tony Wilson's 'Factory' label, issuing a debut 3-track, the 'JIMONE EP'. Their folksy idiosyncracy and wilful weirdness was beloved of the music press almost from the off and their cult standing increased considerably after their 2nd classic 45, 'HYMN FROM A VILLAGE', topped the indie chart early in '85. They were soon snapped up by Seymour Stein's 'Sire', legendary underground mover and shaker Lenny Kaye producing the debut album, 'STUTTER'. BOOTH's overtly accented vocals were the primary focus of the band's often erratic and unorthodox, cerebral, improvisation-driven indie rock/folk and this bizarre combination made the band a compelling live act. However, financial difficulties led to the band moving label to WEA subsidiary 'Blanco Y Negro', where they released 'STRIP MINE' (1988). In 1990, after a change of personnel and a spell on 'Rough Trade', JAMES had their first Top 40 hit on 'Fontana' with 'HOW WAS IT FOR YOU?'. It was soon followed by a Top 20 album, 'GOLD MOTHER', that when re-promoted early 1991 with No.2 hit, the outrageously anthemic and subsequently tediously annoying 'SIT DOWN', also hit No.2. Suddenly the band were riding on the frayed, flared coat-tails of the baggy scene alongside fellow Manchester bands like The HAPPY MONDAYS and The STONE ROSES. Their obstinately obscure sound of old had now been bolstered by chant-along choruses of almost terrace proportions and the ubiquitous JAMES t-shirt was de rigeur for fresher students up and down the country. The band were now playing to stadium-sized audiences and they made their follow-up, 'SEVEN' (1992), to match, all big production and bombast that went down like a lead balloon with critics. With 'LAID' (1993), the band roped in BRIAN ENO, and went for a more opaque, stripped-down sound that recalled their experimental, earlier work. Lyrically, the album was as complex and as vivid as ever while the gorgeous 'SOMETIMES' gave the band their first Top 20 hit since early '92. The ENO sessions also provided the material for the 'WAH WAH' (1994) album, a collection of ambient improvisations with the aging electronic wizard. Of late, TIM BOOTH teamed up with ANGELO BADALAMENTI (he of 'Twin Peaks' fame') and ex-SUEDE guitarist, BERNARD BUTLER to release one-off set, 'BOOTH AND THE BAD ANGEL' (1996). Last year (1997), JAMES were again in the UK Top 10, the single 'SHE'S A STAR' and its parent album, 'WHIPLASH', both achieving the feat. • **Songwriters:** TIM BOOTH penned, except SUNDAY MORNING (Velvet Underground).

Album rating: STUTTER (*6) / STRIP MINE (*6) / ONE MAN CLAPPING (*6) / GOLD MOTHER (*8) / SEVEN (*8) / LAID (*7) / WAH WAH (*6) / WHIPLASH (*6) / Booth & The Bad Angel: BOOTH & THE BAD ANGEL (*5)

TIM BOOTH (b. TIMOTHY, 4 Feb'60) – vocals / **LARRY GOTT** (b. JAMES GOTT) – guitar / **JIM GLENNIE** (b.10 Oct'63) – bass / **GAVAN WHELAN** – drums

Factory / not iss.

Sep 83. (7") *(FAC 78)* **JIMONE** [ ] [-]
– What's the world / Fire so close / Folklore.

Feb 85. (7") *(FAC 119)* **JAMES II** [ ] [-]
– Hymn from a village / If things were perfect.

Jun 85. (12"ep) *(FAC 138)* **VILLAGE FIRE** [ ] [-]
– What's the world / Fire so close / Folklore / Hymn from a village / If things were perfect.

Sire / Warners

Feb 86. (7") *(JIM 3)* **CHAIN MAIL. / HUP STRINGS** [ ] [-]
(12"+=) *(JIM 3T)* **SIT DOWN EP** – Uprising.

Jul 86. (7") *(JIM 4)* **SO MANY WAYS. / WITHDRAWN** [ ] [-]
(12"+=) *(JIM 4T)* – Just hipper.

Jul 86. (lp/c) *(JIM LP/C 1)* **STUTTER** [68] [-]
– Skullduggery / Scarecrow / So many ways / Just hip / Johnny Yen / Summer song / Really hard / Billy's shirts / Why so close / Withdrawn / Black hole. *(cd-iss. Nov91; 7599 25437-2)*

Blanco Y Negro / Sire

Sep 87. (7") *(NEG 26)* **YAHO. / MOSQUITO** [ ] [-]
(12"+=) *(NEG 26T)* – Left out of her will / New nature.

Mar 88. (7") *(NEG 31)* **WHAT FOR. / ISLAND SWING** [ ] [-]
(c-s+=/12"+=) *(NEG 31 C/T)* – Not there.

Sep 88. (lp/c)(cd) *(JIM LP/C 2)(925657-2)* **STRIP MINE** [90] [ ]
– What for / Charlie Dance / Fairground / Are you ready / Yaho / Medieval / Not there / Riders / Vulture / Strip mining / Refrain. *(re-iss. Jul91; same) (cd re-iss. Feb95; 925657-2)*

Rough Trade / not iss.

Mar 89. (lp/c/cd) *(ONEMAN 001/+C/CD)* **ONE MAN CLAPPING (live in Bath)** [ ] [-]
– Chain mail / Sandman (hup strings) / Whoops / Riders / Why so close / Leaking / Johnny Yen / Scarecrow / Are you ready / Really hard / Burned / Stutter. *(cd+=)* – Yaho.

—— **DAVE BAIGNTON-POWER** – drums repl. WHELAN / added **SAUL DAVIS** – violin, percussion, guitar / **MARK HUNTER** – keyboards

Jun 89. (7") *(RT 225)* **SIT DOWN. / SKY IS FALLING** [ ] [-]
(12"+=/3"cd-s+=) *(RTT 225/+CD)* – Goin' away / Sound investment.

—— added **ANDY DIAGRAM** – trumpet (ex-PALE FOUNTAINS, ex-DIAGRAM BROS)

Nov 89. (7") *(RT 245)* **COME HOME. / PROMISED LAND** [ ] [-]
(12"+=/cd-s+=) *(RTT 245/+CD)* – ('A'extended) / Slow right down (demo).

Fontana / Mercury

May 90. (7") *(JIM 5)* **HOW WAS IT FOR YOU? / WHOOPS (live)** [32] [-]
(12") *(JIM 5-12)* – ('A'side) / Hymn from a village (live) / Lazy.
(cd-s) *(JIMCD 5)* – ('A'side) / Hymn from a village (live) / Undertaker.
(12") *(JIMM 5-12)* – ('A'side) / ('A'different mix) / Lazy / Undertaker.

Jun 90. (cd/c/lp) *(<846189-2/-4/-1>)* **GOLD MOTHER** [16] [ ] Aug90
– Come home / Government walls / God only knows / You can tell how much suffering (on a face that's always smiling) / How was it for you? / Crescendo / Hang on / Walking the ghost / Gold mother / Top of the world. *(re-iss. Apr91 cd/c/lp; 848595-2/-4/-1); hit No.2) (cd+=)* – Sit down / Lose control.

Jul 90. (7"/c-s) *(JIM/+C 6)* **COME HOME (Flood mix). / DREAMING UP TOMORROW** [32] [-]
(12") *(JIM 6-12)* – ('A'extended) / Stutter (live) / Fire away.
(cd-s) *(JIMCD 6)* – ('A'side) / ('A'extended) / Gold mother (remix) / Fire away.
(12") *(JIMM 6-12)* – ('A'live) / Gold mother (Warp remix) / ('A'-Andy Weatherall Boys own remix).

Nov 90. (7"/c-s) *(JIM/+C 7)* **LOSE CONTROL. / SUNDAY MORNING** [38] [-]
(ext.12"+=/ext.cd-s+=) *(JIM 7-12/CD7)* – Out to get you.

Mar 91. (7"/c-s) *(JIM/+C 8)* **SIT DOWN. / ('A'live)** [2] [ ]
(12"+=/cd-s+=) *(JIM 8-12/CD8)* – Tonight.

Nov 91. (7"/c-s) *(JIM/+C 9)* **SOUND. / ALL MY SONS** [9] [ ]
(12"+=/cd-s+=) *(JIM 9-12/CD9)* – ('A'extended) / Come home (Youth mix).

Jan 92. (7"/c-s) *(JIM/+C 10)* **BORN OF FRUSTRATION. / BE MY PRAYER** [13] [ ]
(12"+=/cd-s+=) *(JIM 10-12/CD10)* – Sound (mix).

Feb 92. (cd/c/lp) *(<510932-2/-4/-1>)* **SEVEN** [2] [ ] Mar92
– Born of frustration / Ring the bells / Sound / Bring a gun / Mother / Don't wait that long / Live a life of love / Heavens / Protect me / Seven. *(cd+=/c+=)* – Next lover. *(re-iss. Aug98; same)*

Mar 92. (7"/c-s) *(JIM/+C 11)* **RING THE BELLS. / FIGHT** [37] [ ]
(12"+=/cd-s+=) *(JIM 11-12/CD11)* – The skunk weed skank / Come home (live dub version).
(12"++=) *(11)* – Once a friend.

Jul 92. (7"ep/c-ep/cd-ep) *(JIM/+C/CD 12)* **SEVEN (remix) / GOALIES BALL. / WILLIAM BURROUGHS / STILL ALIVE** 46 -

Sep 93. (7"/c-s) *(JIM/+C 13)* **SOMETIMES. / AMERICA** 18
(12"+=/cd-s+=) *(JIM 13-12/CD13)* – Building a charge.

Sep 93. (cd/c/lp) *(<514943-2/-4/-1>)* **LAID** 3 72 Oct93
– Out to get you / Sometimes (Lester Piggott) / Dream thrum / One of the three / Say something / Five-o / P.S. / Everybody knows / Knuckle too far / Low, low / Laid / Lullaby / Skindiving. *(re-iss. Aug98; same)*

Nov 93. (7"/c-s) *(JIM/+C 14) <858217>* **LAID. / WAH WAH KITS** 25 61 Jan94
(cd-s+=) *(JIMCD 14)* – The lake / Seconds away.
(cd-s) *(14)* – ('A'live) / Five-O / Say something / Sometimes.

Mar 94. (c-s) *(JIMMC 15)* **JAM J / SAY SOMETHING** 24
(12"+=)(cd-s+=) *(JIMX 15)(JMCD 15)* – Assassin / ('B'-version).
(cd-s) *(JIMCD 15)* – JAM J – James vs The Sabres Of Paradise (i) Arena dub (ii) Amphetamine pulsate / JAM J – James vs The Sabres Of Paradise (i) Sabresonic tremelo dub (ii) Spaghetti steamhammer.

Sep 94. (cd/c/d-lp;ltd) *(<314 526 408-2/-4/-1>)* **WAH WAH** (w / BRIAN ENO) 11 Oct94
– Hammer strings / Pressure's on / Jam J / Frequency dip / Lay the law down / Burn the cat / Maria / Low clouds (1) / Building a fire / Gospel oak / DVV / Say say something / Rhythmic dreams / Dead man / Rain whistling / Low clouds (2) / Bottom of the well / Honest Joe / Arabic agony / Tomorrow / Laughter / Sayonara.

— **ADRIAN OXAAL** – repl. DIAGRAM

Feb 97. (cd-s) *(JIMED 16)* **SHE'S A STAR / STUTTER (live) / JOHNNY YEN (live)** 9 -
(cd-s) *(JIMDD 16)* – ('A'side) / Chunney chops / Fishknives / Van Gogh's dog.
(cd-s) *(JIMCD 16)* – ('A'-Dave Angel mix) / ('A'-Biosphere mix) / Come home (Weatherall mix).

Mar 97. (cd/c/lp) *(<534354-2/-4/-1>)* **WHIPLASH** 9
– Tomorrow / Lost a friend / Waltzing along / She's a star / Greenpeace / Go to the bank / Play dead / Avalanche / Homeboy / Watering hole / Blue pastures.

Apr 97. (cd-ep) *(JIMCD 17)* **TOMORROW / GONE TOO FAR / HONEST PLEASURE / ALL ONE TO ME** 12 -
(cd-s) *(JIMDD 17)* – ('A'side) / Lost a friend (session) / Come home (session) / Greenpeace (session).
(cd-s) *(JIMED 17)* – ('A'mixes; Fila Brazilia / Archive / Dirty Beatnik).

Jun 97. (cd-s) *(JIMCD 18)* **WALTZING ALONG /** 23 -
(cd-s) *(JIMED 18)* – ('A'side) / (live) / (live).
(cd-s) *(JIMDD 18)* – ('A'remixes by; Midfield General & Flytronix).

Mar 98. (cd-ep) *(JIMCD 19)* **DESTINY CALLING / GOALIE'S BALL / ASSASSIN / THE LAKE** 17 -
(cd-ep) *(JIMDD 19)* – ('A'side) / Jam J (live) / Honest Joe (live) / Sound (live).
(cd-s) *(JIMED 19)* – ('A'side) / She's a star (CD-Rom video).

Mar 98. (cd/c) *(<536898-2/-4>)* **THE BEST OF** (compilation) 1
– Come home / Sit down / She's a star / Laid / Waltzing along / Say something / Tomorrow / Born of frustration / Destiny calling / Out to get you / Runaground / Lose control / How was it for you? / Seven / Sound / Ring the bells / Sometimes / Hymn from a village.
(also d-cd-iss. ; 558173-2)

May 98. (cd-ep) *(JIMCD 20)* **RUNAGROUND / CRESCENDO / HANG ON / BE MY POWER** 29 -
(cd-ep) *(JIMDD 20)* – ('A'side) / Say something / Laid / Lose control.
(cd-ep) *(JIMED 20)* – ('A'side) / Egoiste / Lost a friend.

Nov 98. (c-s/cd-s) *(JIM MC/CD 21)* **SIT DOWN (1998 remix) /** 7 -
(cd-s) *(JIMDD 21)* –

BOOTH AND THE BAD ANGEL

— **TIM BOOTH / ANGELO BADALAMENTI / + BERNARD BUTLER** (ex-Suede)

Fontana Mercury

Jun 96. (c-s) *(BBMC 1)* **I BELIEVE (edit) / I BELIEVE (long version)** 25 -
(cd-s+=) *(BBCD 1)* – When you smiled.
(cd-s+=) *(BBDD 1)* – Melting away.

Jul 96. (cd/c) *(<526 852-2/-4>)* **BOOTH AND THE BAD ANGEL** 35
– I believe / Dance of the bad angels / Hit parade / Fall in love with me / Old ways / Life gets better / Heart / Rising / Butterfly's dream / Stranger / Hands in the rain.

— (below lifted from the film 'Martha Meet Franky, Daniel & Laurence'.

Jun 98. (c-s) *(MERMC 503)* **FALL IN LOVE WITH ME (live) / I BELIEVE (live)** 57 -
(cd-s+=) *(MERCD 503)* – Hit parade (live).
(cd-s) *(MERDD 503)* – ('A'side) / Butterfly's dream (live) ('A'live).

JAMIE WEDNESDAY (see under ⇒ CARTER THE UNSTOPPABLE SEX MACHINE)

JANE (& BARTON) (see under ⇒ MARINE GIRLS)

JANE'S ADDICTION

Formed: Los Angeles, California, USA . . . 1984 by Miami-raised PERRY FARRELL. The band's debut effort was a self-financed eponymous live album on 'Triple XXX', the record's naked intensity going some way towards capturing FARRELL's skewed musical vision. More successful was the band's debut for 'Warner Brothers', 'NOTHING'S SHOCKING' (1988), a wilfully perverse and eclectic blend of thrash, folk and funk that, musically and lyrically, made L.A.'s cock-rock brigade look like school boys. FARRELL's creepy shrill was something of an acquired taste, although it complemented the abrasive, mantra-like music perfectly, from the juddering 'PIGS IN ZEN' to the bleakly beautiful 'JANE SAYS'. The record courted controversy almost immediately, with its cover art depicting naked siamese twins strapped to an electric chair. Live, the band were just as confrontational, FARRELL stalking the stage like some transexual high priest. 'RITUAL DE LO HABITUAL' (1990) was JANE'S' masterstroke, combining the compelling musical dynamics of the debut with more rhythm and melody. The result was a UK Top 40 hit for 'BEEN CAUGHT STEALING', a funky paeon to the delights of shoplifting. Inevitably, JANE'S ADDICTION incurred, yet again, the wrath of America's moral guardian's and the record was banned from several US retail chains. The band replied by re-releasing it in a plain white sleeve with only the First Ammendment printed on it. The following year, FARRELL organised the first Lollapalooza tour, a travelling festival of indie, rap and alternative acts. It was while headlining this jaunt that the band reached its messy conclusion, FARRELL eventually coming to blows with guitarist NAVARRO and splitting soon after. While NAVARRO subsequently joined the RED HOT CHILI PEPPERS, FARRELL formed PORNO FOR PYROS with PERKINS and a cast of likeminded musicians. The 1993 eponymous debut was like a more aggressive, less mysterious JANE'S ADDICTION, reaching the Top 5. Following personal problems and a drug bust, the band eventually released a follow-up three years later, 'GOOD GOD'S URGE', a more heavy-lidded, narcotic-centric affair which even featured NAVARRO on one track, 'FREEWAY'. JANE'S ADDICTION have since reformed (with the 'CHILI's FLEA on bass), initially for some live work in 1997, although a handful of new tracks surfaced on the odds'n'sods collection, 'KETTLE WHISTLE'. • **Songwriters:** Group penned, except SYMPATHY FOR THE DEVIL (Rolling Stones).

Album rating: JANE'S ADDICTION (*7) / NOTHING'S SHOCKING (*8) / RITUAL DE LO HABITUAL (*9) / KETTLE WHISTLE part compilation (*6) / Porno For Pyros: PORNO FOR PYROS (*6) / GOOD GOD'S URGE (*8)

PENNY FARRELL (b. PERRY BERNSTEIN, 29 Mar'59, Queens, N.Y.) – vocals / **DAVE NAVARRO** (b. 6 Jun'67, Santa Monica, Calif.) – guitar / **ERIC AVERY** (b.25 Apr'65) – bass / **STEPHEN PERKINS** (b.13 Sep'67) – drums

not iss. Triple X

Aug 87. (lp) *<XXX 51004>* **JANE'S ADDICTION (live)** -
– Trip away / Whores / Pigs in Zen / 1% / I would for you / My time / Jane says / Rock'n'roll / Sympathy / Chip away. *<re-iss. Dec88 lp/c/cd; TX 510041 LP/MC/CD> (UK-iss.Dec90 on 'WEA' cd/c/lp; 7599 26599-2/-4/-1)*

Warners Warners

Sep 88. (lp/c)(cd) *(WX 216/+C)(925727-2) <25727>* **NOTHING'S SHOCKING**
– Up the beach / Ocean size / Had a dad / Ted, just admit it . . . / Standing in the shower . . . thinking / Summertime rolls / Mountain song / Idiots rule / Jane says / Thank you boys. *(cd+=)* – Pigs in Zen.

Mar 89. (7") *<27520>* **MOUNTAIN SONG. / STANDING IN THE SHOWER . . . THINKING** -

May 89. (7") *(W 7520)* **MOUNTAIN SONG. / JANE SAYS** -
(12"ep+=) **THE SHOCKING EP** *(W 7520T)* – Had a dad (live).

— added guest **MORGAN** (a female) – violin

Aug 90. (cd)(lp/c) *(7599 25993-2)(WX 306/+C) <25993>* **RITUAL DE LO HABITUAL** 37 19
– Stop / No one's leaving / Ain't no right / Obvious / Been caught stealing / Three days / Then she did . . . / Of course / Classic girl.

Aug 90. (7"/c-s) *(W 9584/+C)* **THREE DAYS. / (part 2)**
(12"/cd-s) *(W 9584 T/CD)* – ('A'side) / I would for you (demo) / Jane says (demo).

Mar 91. (7"/c-s) *(W 0011/+C) <19574>* **BEEN CAUGHT STEALING. / HAD A DAD (demo)** 34
(12"+=/12"box+=/cd-s+=) *(W 0011 T/TB/CD)* – ('A'remix) / L.A. medley:- L.A. woman / Nausea / Lexicon devil.

May 91. (7"/c-s) *(W 0031/+C)* **CLASSIC GIRL. / NO ONE'S LEAVING** 60
(12"pic-d+=/cd-s+=) *(W 0031 TP/CD)* – Ain't no right.

— Had already disbanded when FARRELL looked liked heading into film acting. NAVARRO had briefly filled in for IZZY STRADLIN in GUNS N' ROSES, before joining RED HOT CHILI PEPPERS.

PORNO FOR PYROS

— **FARRELL + PERKINS** with **PETER DISTEFANO** (b.10 Jul'65) – guitar, samples, vocals / **MARTYN LE NOBLE** (b.14 Apr'69, Vlaardingen, Netherlands) – bass (ex-THELONIUS MONSTER) / and guest **DJ SKATEMASTER TATE** – keyboards, samples

Warners Warners

Apr 93. (cd/c/lp) *<(9362 45228-2/-4/-1)>* **PORNO FOR PYROS** 13 3
– Sadness / Porno for pyros / Meija / Cursed female – cursed male / Pets / Badshit / Packin' / • 25 / Black girlfriend / Blood rag / Orgasm.

Jun 93. (7"/c-s) *(W 0177/+C) <18480>* **PETS. / TONIGHT (from 'West Side Story')** 53 67
(12"pic-d+=/cd-s+=) *(W 0177 T/CD)* – Cursed female – cursed male (medley).

— **MIKE WATT** – bass (ex-fIREHOSE, ex-MINUTEMEN, ex-CICCONE YOUTH) repl. MARTYN (on most)

— added **THOMAS JOHNSON** – samples, engineer and co-producer

May 96. (cd/c/lp) *<(9362 46126-2/-4/-1)>* **GOOD GOD'S URGE** 40 20
– Porpoise head / 100 ways / Tahitian moon / Kimberly Austin / Thick of it all / Good God's:// Urge! / Wishing well / Dogs rule the night / Freeway / Bali eyes.

JANE'S ADDICTION

— reformed **PERRY FARRELL / DAVE NAVARRO / STEPHEN PERKINS + FLEA**

Dec 97. (cd/c) *<(9362 46752-2/-4)>* **KETTLE WHISTLE** (4 new + live, demos & out-takes) 21 Nov97
– Kettle whistle / Ocean size / Maceo / Hadadad / So what / Jane says / Mountain song / Slow divers / Three days / Ain't no right / Up the beach / Stop / Been caught stealing / Whores / City.

JANITORS

Formed: Sunderland & Newcastle, England . . . late 1984 by DENTOVER, CRAIG HOPE, SIMON HARRIES and TIM. Signing to John Grayland's (YEAH YEAH NOH) imprint, 'In-Tape', they released a couple of singles in the mid-80's, 'CHICKEN STEW' and 'GOOD TO BE KING', both a mixture of MEMBRANES meeting CAPTAIN BEEFHEART. In the summer of '86, The JANITORS worked with producer, JON LANGFORD (MEKONS/THREE JOHNS) on their debut 12", 'THUNDERHEAD', their last for the label before moving to 'Abstract'. A year later and side by side with a new single, 'FAMILY FANTASTIC', CRAIG and DENTOVER teamed up as BIG ZAP with MARY GOLIGHTLY (of GAYE BYKERS ON ACID), SARAH CORINA (BOMB PARTY) and DJ/producer, STEVE McINTOSH on a version of The Temptations' 'PSYCHEDELIC SHACK' (B-side, 'ZAP ATTACK'). The JANITORS returned to their own playground in 1988 with a single, 'MOONSHINE', taken from their first album proper, 'DEAFHEAD' (produced by Pat Collier), although their return was short-lived.

Album rating: DEAFHEAD (*5)

DENTOVER (b. DENTON) – vocals / **CRAIG HOPE** – guitar, keyboards / **SIMON HARRIES** – bass / **TIM** – drums

In-Tape | not iss.

Jul 85. (7") *(IT 017)* **CHICKEN STEW. / THE DEVIL'S GONE TO WHITLEY BAY** [ ] [-]
May 86. (7") *(IT 031)* **GOOD TO BE KING. / WALL STAR** [ ] [-]
Aug 86. (m-lp) *(IT 028)* **THUNDERHEAD** [ ] [-]
– Thunderhead Johnny / Wall star / Long neck bottles / Mexican kitchen.

—— **PETE** – bass; repl. SIMON

Abstract | not iss.

Jun 87. (7") *(ABS 045)* **FAMILY FANTASTIC. /** [ ] [-]
(12"+=) *(12ABS 045)* –
Mar 88. (7") *(ABS 047)* **MOONSHINE. / ONLY ONE** [ ] [-]
(12"+=) *(12ABS 047)* –
Jun 88. (lp) *(ABT 019)* **DEAFHEAD** [ ] [-]
– Moonshine / Spin / Only one / Halfway to a happening / Get a load (get a job) / Happy / What can I say / The country song / Proud Mary / Time goes on / Going to be.
Dec 88. (7") *(ABS 054)* **HALFWAY TO A HAPPENING. / DEAD SET ON DESTRUCTION / HUBBA HUBBA (SHE'S A WEIRD ANIMAL)** [ ] [-]

—— disbanded after above

Bill JANOVITZ (see under ⇒ BUFFALO TOM)

JANUS STARK

Formed: Grantham, England . . . 1983 as young punk act, The ENGLISH DOGS by ex-DESTRUCTORS frontman/guitarist GIZZ BUTT, Muslim bassist SHOP and drummer PINCH. After a number of releases in the mid-80's (most notably the 1986 album, 'ALL THE WORLD'S A RAGE'), the group were another to move from oi/punk to metal, although their mid-90's material went unnoticed. By good fortune, GIZZ (who had taught music therapy to handicapped children) then found employment playing guitar for The PRODIGY on stage. When the three duly came back together in 1994, they added new vocalist SHAUN ATKINS and became metal/punk outfit, DOWN RIVER NATION. The following year, they toured supporting BLAGGERS ITA while trying to find a label for their 'SUBWORLD DISCIPLES' demo. However, ATKINS was to subsequently depart and the trio opted for another change of moniker, this time to JANUS STARK (taken from a 70's comic character). Their direction too, had shifted to a more accessible, spiritual! punk/metal/pop (DESCENDENTS/ALL and FOO FIGHTERS were quoted), although it was with 'Earache' records that they found a home. JANUS STARK's debut, 'GREAT ADVENTURE CIGAR' (1998) received some fine reviews in the all new metal/punk Kerrang!, their constant dedication finally bearing fruits; GREEN DAY eat your heart out! • **Covered:** ENGLISH DOGS covered CRANKED UP REALLY HIGH (Slaughter & The Dogs).

Album rating: GREAT ADVENTURE CIGAR (*7) / English Dogs: ALL THE WORLD'S A RAGE (*6)

ENGLISH DOGS

GIZZ BUTT – vocals, guitar / **SHOP** – bass / **PINCH** – drums

Clay | not iss.

Oct 83. (12"ep) *(PLATE 6)* **MAD PUNX & ENGLISH DOGS** [ ] [-]
Jun 84. (lp) *(CLAYLP 10)* **INVASION OF THE PORKY MEN** [ ] [-]
– The fall of Max / World War 2 / Your country / Blind men / Mercenary / Never die / Astrophs waiting / Newsflash / Ghost of the past / Carol / Spoils of war / Cranked up really high / Invasion of the Porky men / Cavemen brain.

Rot | not iss.

Nov 84. (12"ep) *(ASS 17)* **TO THE END OF THE EARTH** [ ] [-]
1985. (lp) *(ASS 20)* **FORWARD INTO BATTLE** [ ] [-]

Under One Flag | not iss.

Nov 86. (lp) *(FLAG 4)* **WHERE LEGEND BEGAN** [ ] [-]
– Trauma / The eye of Shamahn / Enter the domain / Premonition / Calm before the storm / Flashback / A tomb of traveller's past / Middle earth / Epilogue. *(cd-iss. Jun97 on 'Powerage'; PRAGE 003CD)*
Dec 86. (12"ep) *(12FLAG 101)* **METALMORPHOSIS EP** [ ] [-]
– Nightmare of reality / Absolution / Let the killing begin.

—— split for a while until their reformation in the mid 90's

Impact | Century Media

Jun 94. (cd/lp) *(IR-C-021 CD/LP)* **BOW TO NONE** [ ] [ ] Oct94
– Nipper tripper / Amsterdam / Face pollution / Criminal justice / Fun door enlightening / Psycho killer / Bastard / Barnaby Hoofer / The fall of Max / Surgical cocoon / Left me for dead / The hanging wanker / D.N.A. / Balloon. *(lp-iss.Aug94; IR-C-023) (re-iss. Mar97; same)*

Impact | S.P.V.

Dec 95. (cd) *(IMR 22CD)* **ALL THE WORLD'S A RAGE** [ ] [ ] Aug98
– Shoot your own head off / I've got a gun (body guard) / Last one standing / This is not a war / Delete it / Out in the cold / Wrecking spree / Die waiting / Under a privare attack / Fortress Europe / A cog in their machine / Poor air quality / Be what you are / Grass / Reduction lane / Body on the line / Disarm. *(re-iss. Jun96 on 'S.P.V.'; 084.5363-2) (re-iss. Jun97 on 'Impact'; IR-C-053)*

Retch | not iss.

Jun 97. (cd-s) *(RRCD 006)* **WHAT A WONDERFUL FEELING, TO BE FUCKED BY EVERYONE. / WASTED LIFE** [ ] [-]

JANUS STARK

—— same line-up

Earache | not iss.

Dec 97. (ltd-7") **DYNAMO. / FLAG OF DISCONTENT** [ ] [-]
Mar 98. (7") *(7MOSH 206)* **FLOYD – WHAT ARE YOU ON?. / HYPERMANIA (demo)** [ ] [-]
(cd-s) *(MOSH 206CD)* – ('A'side) / Black box / No way / Barriers.
May 98. (cd) *(MOSH 186CD)* **GREAT ADVENTURE CIGAR** [ ] [-]
– Enemy lines / Panic attack / Every little things counts / Floyd, what are you on? / Dynamo / White man speak with fork tongue / Clique / New slant on nothing / 200 duty frees / Barriers.

JAPAN

Formed: Catford / Lewisham, London, England . . . mid-70's by DAVID SYLVIAN, his brother STEVE JANSEN, MICK KARN and RICHARD BARBIERI. In 1977, they added a second guitarist, ROB DEAN, subsequently signing to 'Ariola-Hansa' after winning a talent competition run by the label. They released a debut album, 'ADOLESCENT SEX', in the Spring of '78, followed six months later by 'OBSCURE ALTERNATIVES'. Basically pop music at the more accessible end of the avant-garde spectrum, JAPAN's proto-New Romantic image contrasted with SYLVIAN's (FERRY-esque) monotone croon. The following year, JAPAN scored a major hit in (of all places) Japan, with the GIORGIO MORODER-produced single, 'LIFE IN TOKYO'; a year on they finally gained a UK chart placing with 'QUIET LIFE'. By the turn of the decade, they'd secured a deal with 'Virgin', releasing the John Porter-produced Top 50 album, 'GENTLEMEN TAKE POLAROIDS'. The next year, after three minor hits in Britain, they went overground with a top selling classic album, 'TIN DRUM'. The record subsequently spawned the spectral 'GHOSTS' single in early '82, which hit the UK Top 5 after their former label had initiated a string of re-issues with 'EUROPEAN SON'; these exploitation releases graced the charts over the course of the next eighteen months while JAPAN officially folded. All band members went on to other projects, DAVID SYLVIAN enjoying most success. After a 1982 collaboration with RYUICHI SAKAMOTO ('BAMBOO HOUSES' and 'FORBIDDEN COLOURS' from the movie, 'Merry Xmas Mr. Lawrence'), the immaculately fringed frontman released his debut solo album, 'BRILLIANT TREES' (1984). The Top 5 album utilised the talents of world trumpeter, JON HASSELL, while JAPAN cohorts JANSEN and BARBIERI also helped to sculpt its sophisticated ambience. On future albums such as 'GONE TO EARTH' (1986), 'SECRETS OF THE BEEHIVE' (1987), 'PLIGHT AND PREMONITION' (1988) and 'FLUX AND MUTATION' (1989) – the latter two were collaborations with HOLGER CZUKAY (ex-CAN) – he worked with left-field luminaries like BILL NELSON and ROBERT FRIPP. In 1991, JAPAN re-formed as RAIN TREE CROW, although it became clear this set-up was only temporary, as all members (especially SYLVIAN), continued to pursue solo careers. SYLVIAN briefly returned to the charts in 1993 with the ROBERT FRIPP collaboration, 'THE FIRST DAY', a more accessible yet still inventive set. Although MICK KARN began a solo career at the same time as SYLVIAN (the bassist's work reminiscent of ENO or BILL NELSON), he went on to work as a sculptor; his track, 'TRIBAL DAWN' (from the album, 'TITLES' – 1982), was used on Channel 4's arty TV programme, 'Altered States'. • **Songwriters:** SYLVIAN lyrics / group compositions except; DON'T RAIN ON MY PARADE (Rogers-Hammerstein) / AIN'T THAT PECULIAR (Marvin Gaye) / I SECOND THAT EMOTION (Smokey Robinson) / ALL TOMORROW'S PARTIES (Velvet Underground).

Album rating: ADOLESCENT SEX (*6) / OBSCURE ALTERNATIVES (*6) / QUIET LIFE (*6) / GENTLEMEN TAKE POLAROIDS (*7) / TIN DRUM (*9) / ASSEMBLAGE compilation (*7) / OIL ON CANVAS live (*6) / EXORCISING GHOSTS compilation (*9) / Rain Tree Crow: RAIN TREE CROW (*4) / David Sylvian: BRILLIANT TREES (*8) / GONE TO EARTH (*6) / SECRETS OF THE BEEHIVE (*7) / PLIGHT AND PREMONITION with Holger Czukay (*7) / FLUX AND MUTABILITY with Holger Czukay (*6) / THE FIRST DAY with Robert Fripp (*6) / Mick Karn: TITLES (*7) / DREAMS OF REASON PRODUCE (*6) / BESTIAL CLUSTER (*5) / POLLYTOWN (*5) / THE TOOTH MOTHER (*5) / Jansen & Barbieri: CATCH THE FALL (*5) / STORIES ACROSS THE BORDER (*5) / BEGINNING TO MELT with Karn (*5) / SEED with Karn (*5) / STONE TO FLESH (*5) / OTHER WORLDS IN A SMALL ROOM (*4)

DAVID SYLVIAN (b. DAVID BATT, 23 Feb'58) – vocals, guitar, keyboards / **RICHARD BARBIERI** (b.30 Nov'57) – keyboards, synthesizers / **ROB DEAN** – guitar, mandolin / **MICK KARN** (b. ANTHONY MICHAELIDES, 24 Jul'58) – bass, saxophone / **STEVE JANSEN** (b. STEVE BATT, 1 Dec'59) – drums, percussion

Ariola Hansa / Ariola

Mar 78. (7") *(AHA 510)* **DON'T RAIN ON MY PARADE. / STATELINE** [ ] [-]
Apr 78. (lp) *(AHAL 8004)* **ADOLESCENT SEX** [ ] [ ]
– Transmission / The unconventional / State line / Wish you were black / Performance / Lovers on Main Street / Don't rain on my parade / Suburban love / Adolescent sex / Communist China / Television. *(re-iss. Sep82; same) (re-iss. Sep84 on 'Fame' lp/c; FA41 3108-1/-4) (cd-iss. 1989 on 'Hansa Germany'; VDP 1153)*
Aug 78. (7") *(AHA 525)* **THE UNCONVENTIONAL. / ADOLESCENT SEX** [ ] [-]
Nov 78. (lp) *(AHAL 8007)* **OBSCURE ALTERNATIVES** [ ] [ ]
– Automatic gun / Rhodesia / Love is infectious / Sometimes I feel so low / Obscure alternatives / Deviation / Suburban Berlin / The tenant. *(re-iss. Sep82; same) (re-iss. Apr84 on 'Fame' lp/c; FA41 3098-1/-4) (cd-iss. 1989 on 'Hansa Germany'; CDP 1154)*
Nov 78. (7",7"blue) *(AHA 529)* <7727> **SOMETIMES I FEEL SO LOW. / LOVE IS INFECTIOUS** [ ] [ ]
May 79. (7"red/ext.12"red) *(AHA/+D 540)* **LIFE IN TOKYO. / LIFE IN TOKYO (part 2)** [ ] [-]
Jul 79. (12") <7756> **LIFE IN TOKYO. / LOVE IS INFECTIOUS** [-] [ ]
Jan 80. (lp) *(AHAL 8011)* **QUIET LIFE** [53] [ ]
– Quiet life / Fall in love with me / Despair / In-vogue / Halloween / All tomorrow's parties / Alien / The other side of life. *(re-iss. Sep82 on 'Fame' lp/c; FA/TCFA 3037) (cd-iss. 1989 on 'Hansa Germany'; VDP 1155)*
Feb 80. (7",7"maroon) *(AHA 559)* **I SECOND THAT EMOTION. / QUIET LIFE** [ ] [-]

Virgin / Virgin

Oct 80. (7") *(VS 379)* **GENTLEMEN TAKE POLAROIDS. / THE EXPERIENCE OF SWIMMING** [60] [ ]
(d7"+=) *(VS 379)* – The width of a room / Burning bridges.
Oct 80. (lp/c) *(V/TCV 2180)* **GENTLEMEN TAKE POLAROIDS** [45] [ ]
– Gentlemen take polaroids / Swing / Some kind of fool / My new career / Methods of dance / Ain't that peculiar / Night porter / Taking islands in Africa. *(re-iss. Aug88 lp/c; OVED/+C 138) (cd-iss. Jun88; CDV 2180)*

—— Trimmed to quartet when ROB DEAN left, to later form ILLUSTRATED MAN

Apr 81. (7"/12") *(VS 409/+12)* **THE ART OF PARTIES. / LIFE WITHOUT BUILDINGS** [48] [-]
Oct 81. (7") *(VS 436)* **VISIONS OF CHINA. / TAKING ISLANDS IN AFRICA** [32] [-]
(12"+=) *(VS 436-12)* – Swing. *(re-iss. Dec84; same)*
Nov 81. (lp/c) *(V/TCV 2209)* **TIN DRUM** [12] [ ]
– The art of parties / Talking drum / Ghosts / Canton / Still life in mobile homes / Visions of China / Sons of pioneers / Cantonese boy. *(re-iss. Apr86 lp/c; OVED/+C 158) (cd-iss. Jun88; CDV 2209)*
Jan 82. (7"/7"pic-d/12") *(VS/+Y 472)(VS 472-12)* **GHOSTS. / THE ART OF PARTIES (version)** [5] [ ]
Feb 82. (7") **VISIONS OF CHINA. / CANTON** [-] [ ]
May 82. (d7") *(VS 502)* **CANTONESE BOY. / BURNING BRIDGES // GENTLEMEN TAKE POLAROIDS / THE EXPERIENCE OF SWIMMING** [24] [ ]

—— They had earlier in the year quietly branched out into new projects. DAVID SYLVIAN went solo after a brief collaboration with RYUICHI SAKAMOTO. MICK KARN went solo, had one-off single with MIDGE URE, then went into sessions before forming DALI'S CAR with PETE MURPHY in '84. BARBERI and JANSEN produced Swedes LUSTAN LAKEJER. The pair formed their own duo (The DOLPHIN BROTHERS) before joining DAVID SYLVIAN again.

– compilations, exploitation releases etc. –

—— on 'Hansa-Ariola' unless otherwise mentioned

Apr 81. (7"/12") *(HANSA/+12 4)* **LIFE IN TOKYO. / EUROPEAN SON** [ ] [-]
Aug 81. (7"/12") *(HANSA/+12 6)* **QUIET LIFE. / A FOREIGN PLACE / FALL IN LOVE WITH ME** [19] [-]
Sep 81. (lp)(c) *(HANLP 1)(ZCHAN 003)* **ASSEMBLAGE** [26] [-]
– Adolescent sex / State line / Communist China / Rhodesia / Suburban Berlin / Life in Tokyo / European son / All tomorrow's parties / Quiet life / I second that emotion. *(c+=)* – (12"extended versions). *(re-iss. Sep85 on 'Fame' lp/c; FA41 3136-1/-4)*
Jan 82. (7"/12") *(HANSA/+12 10)* **EUROPEAN SON. / ALIEN** [31] [-]
Jun 82. (7"/12") *(HANSA/+12 12)* **I SECOND THAT EMOTION. / HALLOWEEN** [9] [-]
Sep 82. (7"/12") *(HANSA/+12 17)* **LIFE IN TOKYO. / THEME** [28] [-]

—— now on 'Virgin' unless mentioned otherwise

Nov 82. (7") *(VS 554)* **NIGHT PORTER. / AIN'T THAT PECULIAR** [29] [-]
(12"+=) *(VS 554-12)* – Methods of dance.
Feb 83. (7"/12") *Hansa; (HANSA/+12 18)* **ALL TOMORROW'S PARTIES. / IN VOGUE** [38] [-]
May 83. (7") *(VS 581)* **CANTON (live). / VISIONS OF CHINA (live)** [42] [-]
Jun 83. (d-lp/c) *(VD/TCVD 2513)* **OIL ON CANVAS (live)** [5] [ ]
– Oil on canvas / Sons of pioneers / Gentlemen take polaroids / Swing / Cantonese boy / Visions of china / Ghosts / Voices raised in welcome, hands held in prayer / Night porter / Still life in mobile homes / Methods of dance / Quiet life / The art of parties / Canton / Temple of dawn. *(cd iss. Apr85; CDVD 2513)*
Aug 83. (d-c) *(XTWO 24)* **ADOLESCENT SEX / OBSCURE ALTERNATIVES** [ ] [-]
Nov 84. (d-lp/c/cd) *(VGD/+C/CD 3510)* **EXORCISING GHOSTS** [45] [ ]
– Methods of dance / Swing / Gentlemen take polaroids / Quiet life / A foreign place * / Night porter / My new career / The other side of life / Visions of China / Sons of pioneers * / Talking drum / The art of parties / Taking islands in Africa / Voices raised in welcome, hands held in prayer / Life without buildings / Ghosts. *(cd-omits *)*
Jun 88. (3"cd-ep) *(CDT 11)* **GHOSTS / THE ART OF PARTIES / VISIONS OF CHINA** [ ] [ ]
Nov 88. (3"cd-ep) *(CDT 32)* **GENTLEMEN TAKE POLAROIDS / CANTONESE BOY / METHODS OF DANCE** [ ] [ ]
Sep 87. (7") *Old Gold; (OG 9666)* **I SECOND THAT EMOTION. / ALL TOMORROW'S PARTIES** [ ] [-]
(12"+=) *(OG 4020)* – Life in Tokyo.
Nov 87. (7") *Old Gold; (OG 4031)* **QUIET LIFE. / LIFE IN TOKYO** [ ] [-]
Nov 88. (7") *Old Gold; (OG 9817)* **GHOSTS. / CANTONESE BOY** [ ] [-]
Dec 89. (c/cd) *R.C.A.; (410/260 360)* **A SOUVENIR FROM JAPAN** [ ] [-]
Nov 90. (3xcd-box) *(TPAK 6)* **COLLECTOR'S EDITION** [ ] [ ]
– (GENTLEMEN TAKE POLAROIDS / TIN DRUM / OIL ON CANVAS)
Nov 92. (cd-ep) *Old Gold; (OG 6187)* **I SECOND THAT EMOTION / QUIET LIFE / LIFE IN TOKYO** [ ] [-]
Oct 91. (cd/c) *Receiver; (RR CD/MC 150)* **THE OTHER SIDE OF JAPAN** [ ] [-]
Aug 96. (cd) *B.M.G.; (74321 39338-2)* **IN VOGUE** [ ] [ ]

DAVID SYLVIAN

—— - vocals, instruments (ex-JAPAN) / **RYUICHI SAKAMOTO** – synthesizers (ex-YELLOW MAGIC ORCHESTRA)

Virgin / Virgin

Jul 82. (7"/ext.12"; by SYLVIAN / SAKAMOTO) *(VS 510)* **BAMBOO HOUSES. / BAMBOO MUSIC** [30] [ ]

—— (below from the the film soundtrack 'Merry Christmas Mr.Lawrence')

Jun 83. (7"; by DAVID SYLVIAN & RYUICHI SAKAMOTO) *(VS 601)* **FORBIDDEN COLOURS. / THE SEED AND THE SOWER (by RYUICHI SAKAMOTO)** [16] [ ]
(12"+=) *(VS 601-12)* – Last regrets.
(3"/5"cd-ep of SYLVIAN tracks was iss.Aug88; CDT 18)

—— now solo – vocals, keyboards, guitar, percussion, with **RICHARD BARBIERI** and **STEVE JANSEN** (ex-JAPAN) / **RYUICHI SAKAMOTO** – synthesizers / **HOLGER CZUKAY** – tapes / **DANNY THOMPSON** – upright bass / **KENNY WHEELER** – horns

May 84. (7"/7"pic-d)(12") *(VS/+Y 633)(VS 633-12)* **RED GUITAR. / FORBIDDEN COLOURS (version)** [17] [ ]
Jun 84. (lp/c/cd) *(V/TCV/CDV 2290)* **BRILLIANT TREES** [4] [ ]
– Pulling punches / The ink in the well / Nostalgia / Red guitar / Weathered wall / Backwaters / Brilliant trees. *(re-iss. Apr90 lp/c; OVED/+C 239)*
Aug 84. (7"/12") *(VS 700/+12)* **THE INK IN THE WELL (remix). / WEATHERED WALL (instrumental)** [36] [ ]
Oct 84. (7"/ext.12") *(VS 717/+12)* **PULLING PUNCHES. / BACKWATERS (remix)** [56] [ ]

—— now with **JOHN HASSELL** and **ROBERT FRIPP** – guitar / **HOLGER CZUKAY** – tapes / **KENNY WHEELER** – horns

Nov 85. (12"ep) *(VS 835-12)* **WORDS WITH THE SHAMEN** [72] [ ]
– Part 1:- Ancient evening / Part 2:- Incantation / Part 3:- Awakening.
Dec 85. (c) *(SLY 1)* **ALCHEMY (AN INDEX OF POSSIBILITIES)** [ ] [-]
– WORDS WITH THE SHAMEN / Preparations for a journey / Steel cathedrals.

—— now with **ROBERT FRIPP** and **BILL NELSON** – guitar / **PHIL PALMER** – accoustic guitar / **MEL COLLINS** – soprano sax. / **KENNY WHEELER** – flugel horn

Jul 86. (7"/7"sha-pic-d) *(VS/+Y 815)* **TAKING THE VEIL. / ANSWERED PRAYERS** [53] [ ]
(remix-12"+=) *(VS 815-12)* – Bird of prey vanishes into a bright blue sky.
Aug 86. (d-lp)(c)(cd) *(VDL/TCVDL/CDVDL 1)* **GONE TO EARTH** [24] [ ]
– Taking the veil / Laughter and forgetting / Before the bullfight / Gone to earth / Wave / River man / Silver moon / The healing place / Answered prayers * / Where the railroad meets the sea / The wooden cross * / Silver moon over sleeping steeples * / Campfire: Coyote country * / A bird of prey vanishes into a blue cloudless sky * / Sunlight seen through the towering trees * / Upon this Earth. *(cd-omits tracks *)*
Sep 86. (7"/s7") *(VS/+P 895)* **SILVER MOON. / GONE TO EARTH** [ ] [ ]
(12"+=) *(VS 895-12)* – Silver moon over sleeping steeples.

—— DAVID was also credited on VIRGINIA ASTLEY's Feb87 'Some Small Hope'.

—— now with **SAKAMOTO, PALMER, JANSEN** plus **DANNY CUMMINGS** – percussion / **DAVID TORN** – guitar / **DANNY THOMPSON** – d. bass / **MARK ISHAM** – trumpet

Oct 87. (lp)(c)(cd) *(V/TCV/CDV 2471)* **SECRETS OF THE BEEHIVE** [37] [ ]
– September / The boy with the gun / Maria / Orpheus / The Devil's own / When poets dreamed of angels / Mother and child / Let the happiness in / Waterfront.
Oct 87. (7") *(VS 1001)* **LET THE HAPPINESS IN. / BLUE OF MOON** [66] [ ]
(12"+=) *(VS 1001-12)* – Buoy (remix).
Apr 88. (7") *(VS 1043)* **ORPHEUS. / THE DEVIL'S OWN** [ ] [ ]
(12"+=) *(VS 1043-12)* – Mother and child.

—— His touring band **JANSEN, BARBIERI, TORN, ISHAM** plus **IAN MAIDMAN** – bass, percussion / **ROBBY ALEDO** – guitar

DAVID SYLVIAN & HOLGER CZUKAY

with **JAKI LIEBEZEIT** – drums (ex-CAN)

Venture-Virgin / Venture

Mar 88. (lp/c/cd) *(VE/TCVE/CDVE 11)* **PLIGHT AND PREMONITION** [71] [ ]
– Plight (the spiralling of winter ghosts) / Premonition (giant empty iron vessel).

—— with **LIEBEZEIT, MICHAEL KAROLI** – guitar / **MARKUS STOCKHAUSEN** – flugel horn / **MICHI** – vocals

Sep 89. (lp/c/cd) *(VE/TCVE/CDVE 43)* **FLUX AND MUTABILITY** [ ] [ ]
– Flux (a big, bright, colourful world) / Mutability ("a new beginning is in the offing").

DAVID SYLVIAN

Virgin / Virgin

Nov 89. (7") *(VS 1221)* **POP SONG. / A BRIEF CONVERSATION ENDING IN DIVORCE** [ ] [ ]
(12"+=/cd-s+=) *(VST/VSCDX 1221)* – ('A'remix).
(cd-s+=) *(VSCD 1221)* – Stigmas of childhood.
Nov 89. (5-cd-box) *(DXCD 1)* **WEATHERBOX** [ ] [ ]
– (BRILLIANT TREES / GONE TO EARTH / GONE TO EARTH (instrumental) / SECRETS OF THE BEEHIVE / ALCHEMY – AN INDEX OF POSSIBILITIES)
Nov 91. (cd) *(DSRM 1)* **EMBRE GLANCE (THE PERMANENCE OF MEMORY)** [ ] [-]
– The beekeeper's apprentice / Epiphany.

—— JAPAN had reformed quartet in 1990, but as . . .

RAIN TREE CROW

Virgin Virgin

Mar 91. (7"/c-s) *(VS/+C 1340)* **BLACK WATER. / RAIN TREE CROW / I DRINK TO FORGET** [62]
(12") *(VST 1340)* – (1st + 3rd track) / Red Earth (as summertime ends).
(cd-s) *(VSCD 1340)* – (all above 4).

Apr 91. (cd/c/lp) *(CD/TC+/V 2659)* **RAIN TREE CROW** [24]
– Big wheels in Shanty town / Every colour you are / Rain tree crow / Red Earth (as summertime ends) / Rocket full of charge / Boat's for burning / New Moon Red Deer wallow / Black water / A reassuringly dull Sunday / Blackcrow hats shoe shine city.

SLYVIAN – SAKAMOTO

— next with **INGRID CHAVEZ**

Virgin America Virgin Am.

Jun 92. (7"/c-s) *(VUS/+C 57)* **HEARTBEAT (TAINAI KAIKI II) RETURNING TO THE WOMB. / NUAGES** [58]
(cd-s+=) *(VUSCD 57)* – The lost emperor.
(cd-s) *(VUSCDG 57)* – ('A'side) / Forbidden colours / Heartbeat.

DAVID SYLVIAN & ROBERT FRIPP

with **FRIPP** – guitar (of-KING CRIMSON & solo artist) / **TREY GUNN** – synthesizers, vocals, co-writer plus band **DAVID BOTTRILL** – synthesizers / **JERRY MAROTTA** – drums, percussion / **MARC ANDERSON** – percussion / **INGRID CHAVEZ** – backing vocals

Virgin Virgin

Jul 93. (cd/c/lp) *(CD/TC+/V 2712)* **THE FIRST DAY** [21]
– God's monkey / Jean the birdman / Firepower / Brightness falls / 20th century dreaming (a shaman's song) / Darshan (the road to Graceland).

Aug 93. (c-ep/cd-ep) *(VSC/DG 1462)* **JEAN THE BIRDMAN / EARTHBOUND – STARBLIND / ENDGAME** [68]
(cd-ep) *(VSCDT 1462)* – ('A'side) / Tallow moon / Dark water / Gone to Earth.

Dec 93. (cd/c/lp) *(SYL CD/MC/LP 1)* **DARSHAN** (mixes) [-]
– Darshan (the road to Graceland) (remixed by The GRID & others).

Sep 94. (cd) *(DAMAGE 1)* **DAMAGE (live)**
– Damage / God's monkey / Brightness falls / Every colour you are / Firepower / Gone to Earth / 20th century dreaming (a shaman's song) / Wave / Riverman / Darshan (the road to Graceland) / Blinding light of Heaven / The first day.

— In 1996, SYLVIAN was credited on soundtrack of 'Marco Polo' film alongside NICOLA ALESINI & PIER LUIGI ANDREONI. It was released on 'Materiali Sonori'; *MASOCD 90069)*

MICK KARN

– vocals, bass, keyboards, synthesizers (ex-JAPAN) with session

Virgin Virgin

Jun 82. (7"/12") *(VS 508/+12)* **SENSITIVE. / THE SOUND OF WAVES**

Nov 82. (lp/c) *(V/TCV 2249)* **TITLES** [74]
– Tribal dawn / Lost affections in a room / Passion in moisture / Weather the windmill / Saviour, are you with me / Trust me / Sensitive / Piper blue. *(re-iss. Aug88 lp/c; OVED/+C 91)*

— In Jun83, he teamed up with ULTRAVOX's MIDGE URE, on the single AFTER A FASHION which reached UK No.39. In 1984 KARN formed **DALI'S CAR** with PETE MURPHY (ex-BAUHAUS) and PAUL VINCENT LAWFORD.

— MICK KARN returned to solo '86

Jan 87. (lp/c/cd) *(V/TCV/CDV 2389)* **DREAMS OF REASON PRODUCE MONSTERS** [89]
– First impression / Language of ritual / Buoy / Land / The three fates / When love walks in / Dreams of reason / Answer.

Jan 87. (7"; by MICK KARN featuring DAVID SYLVIAN) *(VS 910)* **BUOY. / DREAMS OF REASON** [63]
(12"+=) *(VST 910)* – Language of ritual.

C.M.P. not iss.

Oct 93. (cd) *(CMPCD 1002)* **BESTIAL CLUSTER** [-]
– Bestial cluster / Back in the beginning / Beard in the letterbox / The drowning dream / The sad velvet breath of Summer & Winter / Saday, Maday / Liver and lungs / Bones of mud.

May 94. (cd; by DAVID TORN, MICK KARN + TERRY BOZZIO) *(CMPCD 1006)* **POLLYTOWN**

— with **RICHARD BARBIERI** – keyboards / **STEVE JANSEN** – drums / **DAVID TORN** – guitar / **DAVID LIEBMAN** – soprano sax

May 95. (cd) *(CMPCD 1008)* **THE TOOTH MOTHER** [-]
– Thundergirl mutation / Plaster the magic tongue / Lodge of skins / Gossip's cup / Feat funk / The tooth mother / Little less hope / There was not anything but nothing.

JANSEN / BARBIERI

JANSEN – vocals, etc / **BARBIERI** – keyboards, etc

Pan-East not iss.

Oct 86. (lp/c/cd) *(NEW LP/MC/CD 105)* **WORLD IN A SMALL ROOM** [-]

— (at same time JANSEN w/ YUKIHURO TAKAHASHI released 7"; STAY CLOSE. / BETSU-NI on 'Rime'; *RIM 1)*

— The JAPAN duo now

The DOLPHIN BROTHERS

— with **DAVID RHODES** – guitar / **DANNY THOMPSON** – ac. bass / **MATTHEW SELIGMAN + ROBERT BELL** – bass / **PHIL PALMER** – acoustic guitar / **MARTIN DITCHAM** – percussion

Virgin Virgin

Jun 87. (7") *(VS 969)* **SHINING. / MY WINTER** [-]
(12"+=) *(VS 969-12)* – ('A'-Am-ex mix).

Jul 87. (lp/c/cd) *(V/TCV/CDV 2434)* **CATCH THE FALL**
– Catch the fall / Shining / Second sight / Love that you need / Real life, real answers / Host to the holy / My winter / Pushing the river. *(cd re-iss. Mar91; same)*

Aug 87. (7"/12") *(VS 997/+12)* **SECOND SIGHT. / HOST TO THE HOLY** [-]

STEVE JANSEN & RICHARD BARBIERI

Venture Virgin

Sep 91. (cd) *(CDVE 908)* **STORIES ACROSS BORDERS**
– Long tales, tall shadows / When things dream / Luman / The insomniac's bed / The night gives birth / Celebration 1988 remix (saw) / Nocturnal sightseeing / One more zombie.

Medium not iss.

Mar 94. (cd; by STEVE JANSEN, RICHARD BARBIERI & MICK KARN) *(MPCD 1)* **BEGINNING TO MELT** [-]
– Beginning to melt / The wilderness / March of the innocents / Human agie / Shipwrecks / Ego dance / The orange asylum. *(re-iss. Oct96; same)*

Oct 94. (cd; by STEVE JANSEN, RICHARD BARBIERI & MICK KARN) *(MPCD 2)* **SEED** [-]
– Beginning to melt / In the black of desire / The insect tribe / Prey.

Oct 95. (cd) *(MPCD 3)* **STONE TO FLESH** [-]
– Mother London / Sleepers awake / Ringing the bell backwards: Siren – Drift / Swim there / Closer than "I" / Everything ends in darkness. *(re-iss. Oct96 & Apr97; same)*

Oct 96. (cd) *(MPCD 4)* **OTHER WORLDS IN A SMALL ROOM** [-]
– Remains of a fragile illusion / Light years / Disturbed sense of distance / Breaking the silence / Blue lines / Way the lights falls / Distant fire.

JARBOE (see under ⇒ JARBOE)

JASMINE MINKS

Formed: Aberdeen, Scotland . . . 1983 by young lads ADAM SHEPHERD, TOM SANDERSON, JIM BALE and MARTIN ALVEY, as a 60's nostalga outfit into BYRDS-esque jangle-pop psychedelia and influenced by the geographical proximity of Glasgow's 'Postcard' scene. Signing to Alan McGee's 'Creation' label, The JASMINE MINKS released a couple of decent 45's and an lp, '1,2,3,4,5,6,7, ALL GOOD PREACHERS GO TO HEAVEN' (1984), before the band moved down south to London; DAVE MUSKER was subsequently drafted in for one single, 'COLD HEART'. By the release of the 'ANOTHER AGE' album in '88, The 'MINKS had sharpened up their melodies, hooklines and overall approach, as heard on the likes of 'CUT ME DEEP', also one of the standout tracks on 'Creation' V/A sampler, 'Doing It For The Kids'.

Album rating: SUNSET compilation (*5)

ADAM SHEPHERD – guitar, vocals / **TOM SANDERSON** – vocals, guitar / **JIM BALE** – bass / **MARTIN ALVEY** – drums

Creation not iss.

Mar 84. (7") *(CRE 004)* **THINK! / WORK FOR NOTHING** [-]

Aug 84. (7") *(CRE 008)* **WHERE THE TRAFFIC GOES. / MR. MAGIC** [-]

Dec 84. (m-lp) *(CRELP 003)* **1,2,3,4,5,6,7, ALL GOOD PREACHERS GO TO HEAVEN** [-]

Jul 85. (7") *(CRE 018)* **WHAT'S HAPPENING. / BLACK AND BLUE** [-]

— added guest **DAVE MUSKER** – organ (ex-TV PERSONALITIES)

Apr 86.(7") *(CRE 025)* **COLD HEART. / WORLD'S NO PLACE** [-]
(12"+=) *(CRE 025T)* – Forces network (AFM version) / You got me wrong.

— MUSKER left to form SLAUGHTER JOE

Jun 86. (lp) *(CRELP 007)* **JASMINE MINKS** [-]
(cd-iss. Oct90; CRECD 007)

Oct 86. (lp) *(CRELP 013)* **SUNSET** (compilation) [-]
– Think / Work for nothing / Where the traffic goes / Ghost of a young man / Sunset / What's happening / Black and blue / Cold heart / World's no place / Forces network / Mr. Magic.

— **ED DE FLAM** – guitar; repl. ADAM

Nov 87. (7"ep) *(PACE 1)* **PURE EP (live)** [-]
(above issued on 'Esurient Communications')

Jan 88. (lp) *(CRELP 025)* **ANOTHER AGE** [-]
– Veronica / Still waiting / Summer! where? / Follow me away / Cut me deep / Living out your dreams / Don't wait too long / Nothing can stop me / Soul station / Time for you / Another age / Sad.

Feb 89. (lp/cd) *(CRELP 044/+CD)* **SCRATCH THE SURFACE** [-]
– Lost and living / Little things / I've lost her / Marcella misery / Can you hear me? / Take / Reaching out / Too young (my home town) / Shiny and black / Scratch the surface / Playing for keeps.

— folded after above

– compilations, etc. –

Oct 91. (cd/lp) *Creation; (CRE CD/LP 112)* **SOUL STATION** [-]
– Cold heart / Forces network / Veronica / Somers town / Think! / Where the traffic goes / The 30 second set up / Ghost of a young man / Still waiting / Cut me deep / The ballad of Johnny Eye / Soul station.

JAWBOX

Formed: Washington DC, USA . . . 1988 by J. ROBBINS, BILL BARDOT, KIM COLETTA and ZACHARY BAROCAS. Older than, and untypical of (both lyrically and musically) many 'Dischord' bands, a label for whom they signed during the early 90's and for whom KIM had previously worked, JAWBOX nevertheless won respect from both their peers and the press. After releasing two albums, 'GRIPPE' (1991) and 'NOVELTY' (1992) for IAN MacKAYE's fiercely independent operation, JAWBOX were tempted by the greater opportunities available as a new addition to Atlantic's new sideline, 'Tag' (although they remained independent in the UK via 'City Slang'). Early in '94, the quartet made their major label debut with the acclaimed 'FOR YOUR OWN SPECIAL SWEETHEART', previewed by the laid-back post-grunge reflections of the 'SAVORY' single. Yet by the release of 1996's eponymous fourth set, the buzz had died down and JAWBOX had become yet another casualty of the US major label Grunge goldrush. • **Covered:** SOUND ON SOUND (Big Boys) / CORNFLAKE GIRL (Tori Amos).

Album rating: GRIPPE (*5) / NOVELTY (*5) / FOR YOUR OWN SPECIAL SWEETHEART (*7) / JAWBOX (*5)

J. ROBBINS – vocals, guitar, Hammond organ / **(W.C.3db) BILL BARDOT** – guitar, vocals, sax, Hammond organ / **KIM COLETTA** – bass, vocals / **ZACHARY BAROCAS** – drums

Dischord Dischord

May 91. (cd/c/lp) <(DIS 52 CD/C/V)> **GRIPPE**
– Freezeburn / Impossible figure / Tools and chrome / Paint out the light / Consolation prize / Grip / Ballast / Something must break / Green-line delayed / Bullet park / Manatee bound. *(re-iss. Jun94; same)*

May 92. (cd/c/lp) <(DIS 69 CD/C/V)> **NOVELTY**
– Cutoff / Tracking / Dreamless / Channel 3 / Spiral fix / Linkwork / Chump / Static / Spit – Bite / Send down / Tongues / Ones and zeros.
(re-iss. Jun94; same)

Feb 93. (7") <(DIS 77V)> **MOTORIST. / JACKPOT PILS!**

Touch & Go Touch & Go

Feb 93. (7"; shared with TAR) <(TG 113)> **STATIC X2**

City Slang Tag-Atlantic

Feb 94. (7") *(EFA 04931-7)* **SAVORY. / SOUND ON SOUND**
(cd-d+=) *(EFA 04931-2)* – Lil' shaver / 68.

Mar 94. (cd/lp) *(EFA 04932-2/-1)* **FOR YOUR OWN SPECIAL SWEETHEART**
– FF=66 / Savory / Breathe / Motorist / LS/MFT / Cooling card / Green glass / Cruel swing / Jackpot lus! / Chicago piano / Reel / U-trau / Whitney walks.

Jun 96. (cd/lp) *(EFA 04981-2/-1)* **JAWBOX**
– Mirrorful / Livid / Iodine / His only trade / Chinese fork tie / Won't come off / Excandescent / Spoiler / Desert sea / Empire of one / Mule / Stall / Nickel nickel millionaire / Capillary life / Absenter. *(cd hidden track+=)* – Cornflake girl.

– compilations, etc. –

Dec 95. (10"lp/cd; shared with LEATHERFACE) *Your Choice Live; (YCLS 23/+CD)* **YOUR CHOICE LIVE**

JAYHAWKS

Formed: Minneapolis, Minnesota, USA . . . 1985 by MARK OLSON and GARY LOURIS, who formed the core of the band through an ever changing series of line-ups. After two American-only albums of rough-hewn country rock, 'THE JAYHAWKS' (1986) and 'BLUE EARTH' (1989), the band were taken under the wing of producer GEORGE DRAKOULIAS. In a well-thumbed tale, they were signed to Rick Rubin's 'Def American' label after roots maestro DRAKOULIAS allegedly phoned 'Twintone' mainman DAVE AYERS and heard a JAYHAWKS tape playing in the background. He was immediately spellbound, as were the country rock faithful among the record buying public when they heard the band's debut for 'Def American', the seminal 'HOLLYWOOD TOWN HALL' (1992). While many fans were under the impression this was the band's first album, the pristine harmonies of OLSON and LOURIS suggested otherwise. Like a fine malt whiskey, The JAYHAWKS's songwriting and harmonising had been maturing over almost a decade and the result was something to savour. There wasn't a duff track in sight, and with veteran piano player NICKY HOPKINS on board, this was an essential purchase. Following its release, the band embarked on a heavy round of touring, sparking, along with peers like UNCLE TUPELO, a mini country-rock revival. Expectations were high for the follow-up, 'TOMORROW THE GREEN GRASS' (1995), the band bypassing the dilemma of matching 'HOLLYWOOD's perfection by going for a more eclectic approach. The crystal clear harmonising was still intact, the single 'BLUE' perhaps the JAYHAWKS' finest moment, as affecting a piece of resigned melancholy as ever graced a slab of vinyl. After a further tour, OLSON left and, after a long period of uncertainty and personal crisis, The JAYHAWKS re-emerged, albeit in a radically altered form. 'THE SOUND OF LIES' (1997) was a decidedly low-key affair and despite receiving a 'Masterpiece' award from retro music mag Mojo, the record has largely gone unnoticed. Something of a departure musically and lyrically, the album was downbeat and edgy, not as immediate as the older material but well worth persevering with; the likes of 'TROUBLE' and 'DYING ON THE VINE' the sound of a band exorcising their demons, coming through bruised but wiser. • **Songwriters:** OLSON-LOURIS except; REASON TO BELIEVE (Tim Hardin). In 1996 LOURIS co-wrote with other members after OLSON left. • **Trivia:** OLSON and LOURIS can also be heard on sessions for MARIA McKEE, COUNTING CROWS and former stablemates SOUL ASYLUM. The latter's DAN MURPHY and DAVE PIRNER (latter part-time) were in the offshoot band, GOLDEN SMOG, which featured LOURIS and PERLMAN.

Album rating: THE JAYHAWKS (*6) / BLUE EARTH (*6) / HOLLYWOOD TOWN HALL (*8) / TOMORROW THE GREEN GRASS (*7) / THE SOUND OF LIES (*6)

MARK OLSON – vocals, guitar, harmonica / **GARY LOURIS** – vocals, electric guitar / **KAREN GROTBERG** – keyboards / **MARC PERLMAN** – bass repl. KEN CALLAHAN

not iss. Bunkhouse

1986. (lp) **THE JAYHAWKS** [-]

not iss. Twin/Tone

1989. (lp/cd) <TTR 89151-1/-2> **THE BLUE EARTH** [-]
– Two angels / She's not alone anymore / Will I be married / Dead end angel / Commonplace streets / Ain't no end / Five cups of coffee / The Baltimore sun / Red firecracker / Sioux City / I'm still dreaming now I'm yours / Martin's song. *(UK-iss.cd Jul95; same) (cd re-iss. Sep98 on 'R.C.A.'; 74321 60575-28)*

— session **NICKY HOPKINS** – keyboards (ex-JEFF BECK GROUP, etc)

Def American Def American

Sep 92. (cd/c/lp) *(512 986-2/-4/-1)* <26829> **HOLLYWOOD TOWN HALL**
– Waiting for the sun / Crowded in the wings / Clouds / Two angels / Take me with you / Sister cry / Settled down like rain / Witghita / Nevada, California / Martin's song. *(re-iss. cd Apr95 on 'American-RCA'; 74321 23994-2)*

Aug 93. (7"/c-s) *(DEFA/MC 28)* **SETTLED DOWN LIKE RAIN. / SISTER CRY**
(cd-s+=) *(DEFCD 28)* – Live medley: Settled down like rain – Martin's song.

Nov 93. (7"/c-s) *(DEFA/MC 25)* **WAITING FOR THE SUN. / MARTIN'S SONG**
(cd-s+=) *(DEFCD 25)* – Up above my head / Keith & Quentin.
(cd-s+=) *(DEFCDX 25)* – Reason to believe / Sister cry / Medley: Martin's song – Settled down like rain.
(cd-s) *(DEFCDXX 25)* – ('A'side) / Up above my head.

American-RCA American-RCA

— now on drums **DON HEFFINGTON** (studio) / **TIM O'REAGAN** (tour)

Feb 95. (cd/c) *(74321 23680-2/-4)* <43006> **TOMORROW THE GREEN GRASS** [41] [92]
– Blue / I'd run away / Miss Williams' guitar / Two hearts / Real light / Over my shoulder / Bad time / See him on the streets / Nothing left to borrow / Ann Jane / Pray for me / Red's song / Ten little kids.

Feb 95. (7"/c-s) *(74321 25797-7/-4)* **BLUE. / TOMORROW THE GREEN GRASS** [-]
(cd-s+=) *(74321 25797-2)* – Darling today.

Jul 95. (7"/c-s) *(74321 29163-7/-4)* **BAD TIME. / LAST CIGARETTE** [70] [-]
(cd-s+=) *(74321 29163-2)* – Get the load out / Sing me back home.

— now without OLSON / line-up **LOURIS, PERLMAN, GROTBERG + O'REAGAN** plus **KRAIG JOHNSON + JESSY GREENE**

Apr 97. (cd/c) <(74321 46406-2/-4)> **SOUND OF LIES** [61]
– The man who loved life / Think about it / Trouble / It's up to you / Stick in the mud / Big star / Poor little fish / Sixteen down / Haywire / Dying on the vine / Bottomless cup / Sound of lies / I hear you cry.

Jun 97. (c-s) *(74321 48755-4)* **BIG STAR / SLEEPYHEAD** [-]
(cd-s+=) *(74321 48677-2)* – Dying on the vine / I'd run away.

JAZZATEERS

Formed: Glasgow, Scotland . . . 1981 by MATTHEW WILCOX, IAN BURGOYNE, KEITH BAND and KENNY McDONALD. Being the last act to sign for the soon-to-be defunct indie label, 'Postcard' (home of ORANGE JUICE, AZTEC CAMERA and JOSEF K), they found themselves in the unenviable position of having their debut single shelved. However, a year later the JAZZATEERS were on the books of 'Rough Trade', releasing their eponymous set and an accompanying single, 'SHOW ME THE DOOR', in the summer of '83. The album received some decent reviews with regards to the LOU REED/GORDON GANO-esque approach of lead singer, WILCOX. Unfortunately, the frontman's services were no longer required when the band metamorphosised into minor hitmakers, BOURGIE BOURGIE, their new vocalist being the crooning great, PAUL QUINN. The JAZZATEERS story was not yet over though, as WILCOX and BAND reformed the group in '85, recruiting MICK SLAVEN and COLIN AULD to record a self-financed one-off single, 'PRESSING ON'. Over a decade later – after WILCOX and BAND had spent the late 80's/early 90's in The WILD ANGELS – The JAZZATEERS returned for a comeback set, 'I SHOT THE PRESIDENT' (1997).

Album rating: JAZZATEERS (*6) / I SHOT THE PRESIDENT (*5)

MATTHEW WILCOX – vocals / **IAN BURGOYNE** – guitar / **KEITH BAND** – bass / **KENNY McDONALD** – drums

Postcard not iss.

Jan 82. (7"; w-drawn) *(81-14)* **SINGLE. /** [-]

Rough Trade not iss.

Jul 83. (7") *(RT 138)* **SHOW ME THE DOOR. / SIXTEEN REASONS** [-]

Jul 83. (lp) *(ROUGH 46)* **JAZZATEERS** [-]
– Sixteen reasons / Nothing at all / First blood / Heartbeat / Baby that's a no no / Show me the door / etc

— all but WILCOX took off to form BOURGIE BOURGIE (⇒) with PAUL QUINN

— **WILCOX + BAND** re-formed The JAZZATEERS with **MICK SLAVEN** – guitar / **COLIN AULD** – drums

Stampede not iss.

Jun 85. (12") *(STAMP 1)* **PRESSING ON. / SPIRAL** [-]

— after their demise, SLAVEN joined DEL AMITRI while AULD joined FRUITS OF PASSION

WILD ANGELS

— were formed by **WILCOX + BAND** plus **STEPHEN LIRONI** – keyboards (ex-ALTERED IMAGES, ex-FLESH) / **DOUGLAS McINTYRE** – guitar (ex-BATHERS, ex-WHITE SAVAGES, ex-FLESH)

Supreme not iss.

Jul 87. (12") *(EDITION 87.13)* **SHE'S BLACK AND WHITE. /** [-]

Valentine not iss.

Jul 88. (cd) *(VALD 8060)* **ROCKIN' ON THE RAILROAD** [-]
– Rockin' on the railroad / Don't leave me now / Miss Froggie / Weekend / Boogie woogie country boy / It'll be me / Old black Joe / Lights out / Blue Monday /

Moonshine boogie / Ballad of a teenage queen / There's a fight going on / Little G.T.O. / Break up / Lucille / The sledgehammer strikes back.

JAZZATEERS

— **WILCOX** and

Marina | not iss.

May 97. (cd) *(MA 30)* **I SHOT THE PRESIDENT** -

JAZZ BUTCHER

Formed: Oxford, England . . . 1982 as an outlet for the off-beat but acute musical observations of PAT FISH (real name PATRICK HUNTRODS), the multi-instrumentalist/singer-songwriter having played in various outfits (including WOW FEDERATION) during his time as a student in Oxford. Securing a deal with the 'Glass' label, FISH rounded up former colleague MAX EIDER – who'd remain a pivotal part of the JAZZ BUTCHER operation for the next five years – and proceeded to record a debut album, 'BATH OF BACON'. More successful was 1984's 'SCANDAL IN BOHEMIA' (which saw the addition of ex-BAUHAUS man, DAVID J.), the record drawing cult underground acclaim with its droll cabaret-pop humour and eclectic array of musical styles (JONATHAN RICHMAN, LOU REED, FAD GADGET and MONOCHROME SET come to mind). Another fine offering surfaced the following year in the shape of mini-set, 'SEX AND TRAVEL', FISH taking a more relaxed but even more sardonic approach on the priceless 'HOLIDAY' and coming on like a Home Counties NICK CAVE on 'WALK WITH THE DEVIL'. Yet enthusiasm from the music press and public alike remained muted and FISH concentrated on building up a fanbase in Europe and America, this mid-80's period of instability seeing the departure of both DAVID J. and EIDER. After a final, poorly received album, 'DISTRESSED GENTLEFOLK' (1986; released under the moniker of JAZZ BUTCHER CONSPIRACY) for 'Glass', FISH re-emerged via a new deal with 'Creation' in 1988. The resulting album, 'FISHCOTHEQUE', saw him working with new guitarist KIZZY O'CALLAGHAN, a revised line-up subsequently forming around the pair and comprising ALEX GREEN, LAURENCE O'KEEFE and PAUL MULREANY. Under Alan McGee's benevolent wing, FISH & Co. were free to experiment to their heart's content, turning out a further series of highly individual albums including 'CULT OF THE BASEMENT' (1990) and 'CONDITION BLUE' (1991). Despite continuing success in the US alternative market, The JAZZ BUTCHER finally tired of domestic indifference and shut up shop following the release of 1995's 'ILLUMINATE'. • **Covered:** SPEEDY GONZALES (Pat Boone) / KNOCKIN' ON HEAVEN'S DOOR (Bob Dylan) / etc.

Album rating: IN BATH OF BACON (*7) / A SCANDAL IN BOHEMIA (*6) / SEX AND TRAVEL mini (*5) / DISTRESSED GENTLEFOLK (*6) / FISHCOTHEQUE (*6) / BIG PLANET SCAREY PLANET (*5) / CULT OF THE BASEMENT (*6) / BLACK EG (*5) / CONDITION BLUE (*5) / WESTERN FAMILY (5) / EDWARD'S CUPBOARD compilation (*6) / WAITING FOR THE LOVE BUS (*5) / ILLUMINATE (*5) / DRAING THE GLASS (*5)

PAT FISH (b. PATRICK HUNTRODS) – vocals / **MAX EIDER** – lead guitar / **FELIX RAY** – bass / **MR. O.P. JONES** – drums / guests incl. **ROLO + ALICE** (future WOODENTOPS)

Glass | Big Time

Aug 83. (lp) *(GLALP 002)* **IN BATH OF BACON** -
– Gloop jiving / Jazz Butcher theme / Party time / Bigfoot motel / Sex engine thing / Chinatown / Zombie love / Grey flanellette / La mer / Poisoned by food / Love kittens / Bath of Bacon / Girls who keep goldfish. *(re-iss. Feb85; same) (cd-iss. Aug88; GLACD 002)*

Sep 83. (7") *(GLASS 027)* **SOUTHERN MARK SMITH. / JAZZ BUTCHER MEETS COUNT DRACULA** -

Mar 84. (7") *(GLASS 033)* **MARNIE. / CAROLINE WHEELER'S BIRTHDAY PRESENT (bedroom version)** -
(12") *(GLASS 12-033)* – ('A'extended) / Zombie love / Girls who keep goldfish / Sweet Jane / Cowgirl fever.

Jul 84. (7") *(GLASS 040)* **ROADRUNNER. / RAIN** -
(ext.12"+=) *(GLASS 12-040)* – Drink.

— guests incl. **DAVID J + KEVIN HASKINS** (ex-BAUHAUS)

Nov 84. (lp) *(GLALP 009)* **A SCANDAL IN BOHEMIA** -
– Southern Mark Smith (big return) / Real men / Soul happy hour / I need meat / Just like Betty Page / Marnie / Caroline Wheeler's birthday present / Mind like a playgroup / Girlfriend / My desert. *(cd-iss. Sep88; GLACD 009)*

Feb 85. (7") *(GLASS 041)* **REAL MEN. / THE JAZZ BUTCHER VS THE PRIME MINISTER** -
(12"+=) *(GLASS 12-041)* – Southern Mark Smith (original).

Mar 85. (lp) *(GLEX 101)* **THE GIFT OF MUSIC** (compilation) -
– Southern Mark Smith / Roadrunner / Real men / Jazz Butcher meets Count Dracula / Zombie love / Goldfish / Sweet Jane / Jazz Butcher vs the prime minister / Party time / Lost in France / Drink. *(cd-iss. Jun88; GLEXCD 101)*

Jun 85. (m-lp) **SEX AND TRAVEL** -
– Big Saturday / Holiday / Red pets / Only a rumour / President Reagan's birthday present / What's the matter, boy? / Walk with the Devil / Down the drain.

Aug 85. (7") *(GLASS 043)* **HUMAN JUNGLE. / DEATH DENTIST** -
(ext.12"+=) *(GLASS 12-043)* – The Devil is my friend.

Feb 86. (7") *(GLASS 046)* **HARD. / GROOVIN' IN THE BUS LANE** -
(ext.12"+=) *(GLASS 12-046)* – Vienna song / Thing.

Jun 86. (7"ep; as JAZZ BUTCHER VS MAX EIDER) *(GLAEP 104)* **THE CONSPIRACY EP** -
– Conspiracy / A joy forever / Peter Lorre / Big old wind.

Jun 86. (lp) *<6007>* **BLOODY NONSENSE** (compilation of recent singles, etc) -

— **FISH + KIZZY O'CALLAGHAN** – guitar / **LAURENCE O'KEEFE** – bass / **PAUL MULREANY** – drums / **ALEX GREEN** – saxophone

Sep 86. (7"; as JAZZ BUTCHER CONSPIRACY) *(GLASS 049)* **ANGELS. / REBECCA WANTS HER BIKE BACK** -
(12"+=) *(GLASS 12-049)* – Mersey.

Oct 86. (lp/c) *(GLA LP/MC 020) <6021>* **DISTRESSED GENTLEFOLK**
– Falling in love / Big bad thing / Still in the kitchen / (Too much) Falling in love / Czechoslovakian love song / The new world / South America / Who loves you now? / Domestic animal / Buffalo shame / Nothing special / Angels. *(cd-iss. 1990's; GLACD 20)*

— MAX EIDER went solo and released 1987 album 'THE BEST KISSER IN THE WORLD' for 'Big Time'.

Apr 87. (lp) *(GLASS 023)* **BIG QUESTIONS (THE GIFT OF MUSIC VOL.2)** (compilation) -
– The human jungle / Hard / Death dentist / South America / Groovin' in the bus lane / Mersey / Conspiracy / Thing / Peter Lorre / Vienna song / Olof Palme / Rebecca wants her bike back / City of night / The hairbrush & the tank / Big old wind / Forever. *(w/ free 7"ep)* **BIG QUESTIONS EP** – Speedy Gonzalez / Knockin' on Heaven's door / May I? / Over you. *(cd-iss. Aug88; GLACD 023)*

— added guests **GREENWOOD GOULDING** – bass / **DAVE MORGAN** – drums / **ERAL SULLEYMAN** – bass / **BLAIR MacDONALD** – drums

Creation | Combat

Feb 88. (lp/cd) *(CRELP 027/+CD) <8223>* **FISHCOTHEQUE**
– Next move sideways / Out of touch / Get it wrong / Living in a village / Swell / Looking for lot 49 / The best way / Chickentown / Susie / Keeping the curtains closed. *(re-iss. lp May94; same)*

Sep 88. (7") *(CRE 059)* **SPOOKY. / BLAME** -
(12"+=) *(CRE 059T)* – The best way.

Creation | Genius

Jul 89. (lp/c/cd) *(CRELP/+C/CD 49) <GENI 008/+C/CD>* **BIG PLANET SCARY PLANET**
– New invention / Line of death / Hysteria / The word I was looking for / Bicycle kid / Burglar of love / Nightmare being / Do the bubonic plague / Bad dream lover / The good ones.

Oct 89. (12") *(CRE 069T)* **NEW INVENTION. /** -

Creation | Rough Trade

May 90. (7") *(CRE 077)* **GIRL GO. /** -
(12"+=/cd-s+=) *(CRE 077 T/CD)* –

Jun 90. (lp/c/cd) *(CRELP/+C/CD 62) <ROUGHUS 83>* **CULT OF THE BASEMENT**
– The basement / She's on drugs / Pineaple Tuesday / The onion field / Daycare nation / My zeppelin / Mr. Odd / After the great Euphrates / Panic in room 109 / Girl go / Turtle bait / Sister death.

Feb 91. (cd/lp)(c) *(CRE CD/LP 078)(C-CRE 078)* **EDWARD'S CUPBOARD** (compilation) -
– Mr. Odd / The best way (Edgar Wallace mix) / Spooky / Pineapple Tuesday / Keeping the curtains closed / She's on drugs / Line of death / Girl go / Susie / The good ones.

— **PAT FISH** now with **ALEX LEE + RICHARD FORMBY** – guitar / **ALEX GREEN** – saxophones / **JOE ALLEN** – bass / **PETER PAUL MULREANY** – drums

Jul 91. (cd/lp; by BLACK EG) *(CRE CD/LP 086)* **BLACK EG** -
– Just Vincent / British gas makes it alright / The good, the bad and the ugly / Get a job / My radio / The Mi-Lai hotel / African disease / Drugs / Monster man / Jesus right now / The twilight zone / So easy (no New York).

Creation | Skyclad

Aug 91. (cd/c/lp) *(CRECD/C-CRE/CRELP 110) <5080>* **CONDITION BLUE** Jan92
– Girls says yes / Our friends the filth / Harlan / Still and all / Monkeyface / She's a yo-yo / Honey / Shirley MacLaine / Racheland.

Feb 93. (cd) *(CRECD 148)* **WESTERN FAMILY (live)** -
– Southern Mark Smith / Shirley MacLaine / Sister death / Still and all / Pineapple Tuesday / Angels / Beautiful snow-white hair / She's on drugs / Girl go / She's a yo-yo / Racheland / Everybody's talkin' / Tugboat captain / Over the rainbow.

the JAZZ BUTCHER CONSPIRACY

— **PAT FISH** with **RICHARD FORMBY** – guitars, prog/tapes / **DOOJ** – bass, vocals / **NICK BURSON** – drums / **PETER CROUCH** – guitars, keyboards / **PASCAL LEGRAS + MARK BOWN** – whatever?

Creation | TriStar

Aug 93. (cd) *(CRECD 156) <57563>* **WAITING FOR THE LOVE BUS** Mar94
– Rosemary Davis world of sound / Bakersfield / Kids in the mall – Kaliningrad / Whaddya? / Sweet water / Ghosts / Baltic / Killed out / Ben / Penguins / President Chang / Angel station / Rosemary Davis world of sound (reprise).

Mar 95. (cd-s) *(CRESCD 167)* **SIXTEEN YEARS /** -

Apr 95. (cd/lp) *(CRE CD/LP 182)* **ILLUMINATE** -

- compilations, etc. -

Dec 85. (lp) *Rebel; (RE 0010)* **THE JAZZ BUTCHER AND THE SIKKORSKIS FROM HELL – HAMBURG – A LIVE ALBUM** -
– Bath of Bacon / Soul happy hour / Death dentist / Walk with the Devil / Rain / Roadrunner / The Jazz Butcher meets Count Dracula / Bigfoot motel / Only a rumour / Real men / Girlfriend / Sweet Jane.

Aug 96. (cd) *Nectar; (NTMCD 529)* **DRAINING THE GLASS (THE JAZZ BUTCHER CONSPIRACY 1982-1986)** -

Jun 98. (cd) *Reactive; (REMCD 527)* **THE BEST OF DRAINING THE GLASS 1982-1986** -

JELLYFISH

Formed: Pleasanton, San Francisco, California, USA . . . 1990 out of BEATNIK BEACH by ANDY STURMER and JASON FALKNER, alongside brothers CHRIS and ROGER MANNING. Updating power-pop in day-glo retro style, JELLYFISH were a shrewd investment by 'Charisma', which in turn, employed the services of veteran disco producer, Albhy Galuten, more famous for his work on the 'Saturday Night Fever' soundtrack. The kitschy 4-piece became the toast of muso types and pop fans alike with their classic debut 45, 'THE KING IS HALF UNDRESSED', a surprise UK Top 40 hit. The track was a fairly representative taster for their 1990 debut album, 'BELLYBUTTON', critics marvelling over the band's clever combination of BEACH BOYS/10CC/QUEEN harmonies and BEATLES-style intricacies. After a further handful of minor hits, including US breakthrough, 'BABY'S COMING BACK', JELLYFISH were stung by the departure of two founding members, CHRIS and JASON (the latter was to become a well respected solo artist in his own right). Replacing them with ERIC DOVER and TIM SMITH, the band resurfaced in Spring 1993 with possibly their finest three minutes, 'GHOST AT NUMBER ONE', another UK Top 50 hit and lifted from the accompanying near Top 20 second set, 'SPILT MILK'. Amid a rising tide of rumours, JELLYFISH were finally left high and dry as ROGER MANNING undertook two separate projects, the tongue-in-cheek covers album, 'The MOOG COOKBOOK' (1996) and cult glam-pop/rock outfit, IMPERIAL DRAG, with frontman, ERIC DOVER. The latter band released an eponymous album for 'Columbia' in '96 which featured a minor UK hit, 'BOY OR A GIRL'; MANNING is currently earning a crust as a member of UMAJETS. • **Songwriters:** STURMER, or most with MANNING, except covers; NO MATTER WHAT (Badfinger) / LET 'EM IN + JET (Paul McCartney & Wings).

Album rating: BELLYBUTTON (*8) / SPILT MILK (*6) / Moog Cookbook: MOOG COOKBOOK (*5) / Imperial Drag: IMPERIAL DRAG (*5)

ANDY STURMER – vocals, drums, keyboards / **JASON FALKNER** (b.1968) – guitar (ex-THREE O'CLOCK) / **CHRIS MANNING** – bass / **ROGER MANNING** – keyboards, vocals

Charisma – Virgin | Charisma

Jan 91. (7"/c-s) *(CUS S/C 1)* **THE KING IS HALF UNDRESSED. / CALLING SARAH** [39] [ ]
(12"+=/cd-s+=) *(CUS X/DG 1)* – The man I used to be.

Feb 91. (c-s) *<98837>* **BABY'S COMING BACK / THE KING IS HALF UNDRESSED** [-] [62]

Mar 91. (cd/c/lp) *(CDCUS/CUSMC/CUSLP 3) <91400>* **BELLYBUTTON** [ ] [ ] Nov90
– The man I used to be / That is why / The king is half undressed / I wanna stay home / She still loves him / All I want is everything / Now she knows is wrong / Bedspring kiss / Baby's coming back / Calling Sarah. *(free 12"w/ lp + on c+=/cd+=)* – No matter what / Medley live:- Let 'em in – That is why / The king is half undressed (live) / Jet (live) / Now she knows she's wrong (live). *(re-iss. Feb92 cd/c; CDCUX/CUSMX 3)*

Apr 91. (7"/c-s) *(CUS S/C 2))* **BABY'S COMING BACK. / ALL I WANT IS EVERYTHING (live)** [51] [-]
(12"+=/cd-s+=) *(CUS X/DG 2)* – No matter what (live).

Jul 91. (7"ep) *(CUSS 3)* **THE SCARY-GO-ROUND EP** [49] [ ]
– Now she knows she's wrong / Bedspring kiss / She still loves him (live) / Baby's coming back (live).
(12"ep) *(CUSX 3)* – (1st-2 tracks) / The man I used to be (live) / Calling Sarah (live).
(cd-ep) *(CUSDG 3)* – (1st-2 tracks) / Let 'em in – That is why (live) / The king is half undressed (live).

Oct 91. (7"/c-s) *(CUS S/C 4)* **I WANNA STAY HOME. / JET (live)** [59] [ ]
(10"+=/cd-s+=) *(CUS T/DG 4)* – Now she knows she's wrong (live).

— now a duo of **ANDY** + **ROGER** after the departure of CHRIS + JASON (the latter joined The GRAYS for one album, 'Bo Sham Bo', before going solo with the much improved 'Elektra' set, 'JASON FALKNER PRESENTS ANOTHER UNKNOWN', in 1996)

— added **ERIC DOVER** – guitar / + **TIM SMITH** – bass, vocals / and guest guitarists **LYLE WORKMAN + JON BRION** / additional bass – **T-BONE**

Apr 93. (7"/c-s) *(CUS S/C 10)* **THE GHOST AT NUMBER ONE. / ALL IS FORGIVEN** [43] [ ]
(cd-s+=) *(CUSDG 10)* – Worthless heart / Ignorance is bliss.
(cd-s) *(CUSCD 10)* – ('A'side) / Watchin' the rain / Family tree.

May 93. (cd/c/lp) *(CDCUS/CUSMC/CUSLP 20) <86459>* **SPILT MILK** [21] [ ]
– Hush / Joining a fan club / Sabrina, paste & Plato / New mistake / The glutton of sympathy / The ghost at mumber one / Bye, bye, bye / All is forgiven / Russian hill / He's my best friend / Too much, too little, too late / Brighter day.

Jul 93. (7"/c-s) *(CUS S/C 11)* **NEW MISTAKE. / HE'S MY BEST FRIEND** [55] [ ]
(cd-s+=) *(CUCDG 11)* – All is forgiven / Russian Hill (demos).
(cd-s) *(CUSCD 11)* – ('A'side) / Sabrina, Paste & Patto (demo) / The man I used to be (demo) / Bedspring kiss (demo).

— split-up after above

ROGER MANNING

S.S.T. | S.S.T.

Dec 88. (lp/c/cd) *<(SST 203 LP/CA/CD)>* **ROGER MANNING** [ ] [ ]
– The #14 blues / The pearly blues / The lefty rhetoric blues / The hitch-hikers' blues / The west valley blues / strange little blues / The airport blues / The #16 blues / The #17 blues / Blues for the chosen few / The 1010 blues / The Sicilian train blues. *(re-iss. Aug93 on 'Shimmy Disc' cd/c/lp; SHIMMY 067 CD/MC/LP)*

MOOG COOKBOOK

ROGER MANNING + BRIAN KEHEW – both keyboards, synths

Restless | Restless

Jun 96. (cd) *<(72914-2)>* **THE MOOG COOKBOOK** [ ] [ ]
– Black hole sun / Buddy Holly / Basket case / Come out and play / Free fallin' / Are you gonna go my way / Smells like teen spirit / Even flow / The one I love / Rockin' in the free world.

IMPERIAL DRAG

— formed 1994 by **ROGER JOSEPH MANNING JR.** – keyboards, vocals / **ERIC DOVER** – vocals, guitar (ex-SLASH'S SNAKEPIT) / **JOSEPH KARNES** – bass, vocals / **ERIC SKODIS** – drums, vocals

Columbia | Work-Sony

Aug 96. (cd/c) *(484178-2/-4) <67378>* **IMPERIAL DRAG** [ ] [ ]
– Zodiac sign / Boy or a girl / Crosseyed / The man in the moon / "Breakfast" by tiger (kiss it all goodbye) / Playboy after dark / Illuminate / Spyder / Overnight sensation / The salvation army band / Dandelion / Stare into the sun / Scaredy cats and egomaniacs.

Sep 96. (cd-ep) *(663299-2)* **BOY OR A GIRL / HEY HONEY PLEASE / MOTHER NATURE / SHE CRIES ALL NIGHT** [54] [-]

— MANNING subsequently joined Atlanta semi-supergroup, UMAJETS, with TIM SMITH, ROB ALDRIDGE, releasing 'DEMOLOTION', early '98

JELLYFISH KISS

Formed: Huddersfield, England . . . 1988 by DAVID LALJEE and NICK. The pair subsequently issued a debut album, 'GASOLINE JUNKIE', the following year before relocating to Leeds and becoming a trio with the addition of bassist/vocalist, JOHN GALVIN. Signing a one-off deal with 'Demon', JELLYFISH KISS cut a follow-up album, 'PLANK', in 1990, although their psychedelic hardcore sound was more suited to the environs of New York where they recorded 'ANIMAL RIGHTS' with 'Shimmy Disc' boss, KRAMER later that year. However, things went badly awry when on tour (26th November, 1991) to support their 4th album, 'STRANGE WEATHER', they were attacked and stung for over £5,000 worth of equipment. • **Covered:** I'M STICKING WITH YOU (Velvet Underground).

Album rating: GASOLINE JUNKIE (*4) / PLANK (*5) / ANIMAL RIGHTS (*4) / STRANGE WEATHER (*4)

NICK – vocals / **DAVID LALJEE** – guitar

Longpig | not iss.

Jul 89. (lp) *(LPIG 001)* **GASOLINE JUNKIE** [ ] [-]

— added **JOHN GALVIN** – bass, vocals

Demon | not iss.

Jun 90. (lp/cd) *(FIEND/+CD 190)* **PLANK** [ ] [-]
– Crazy bong / Melo / A.C. 801 A / Burn / La ronde (Viennese waltz) / Soul apart / Pre-mortem / Astro Z / Off the floor! *(cd+=)* – (6 alt. versions).

Shimmy Disc | Shimmy Disc

Dec 90. (lp)(cd) *(<SHIMMY 038>)(<SDE 9028>)* **ANIMAL RIGHTS** [ ] [ ]

Oct 91. (cd) *(<SHIMMY 047CD>)* **STRANGE WEATHER** [ ] [ ]

Longpig | not iss.

May 92. (7"ep) **BIG DRIVING EP** [ ] [-]

— split after above

JELLYS (see under ⇒ HONEYCRACK)

JENNIFERS (see under ⇒ SUPERGRASS)

JESSAMINE

Formed: Galion, Ohio, USA . . . 1992 by REX RITTER, DAWN SMITHSON, ANDY BROWN and MICHAEL FAETH. Moving wholesale to the more sympathetic climes of Seattle, the quartet released a one-off single, 'YOUR HEAD IS SO SMALL IT'S LIKE A . . .' for 'Sub Pop' in '94 before signing to 'Kranky' (home of LABRADFORD). The first phase of the band's interstellar drone-pop experimentation came in the shape of 1995's 'JESSAMINE', harking back to the heady days of SPACEMEN 3's tripped-out sound manipulation. Appropriately enough, the latter band's co-pilot, SONIC BOOM (i.e. SPECTRUM), would subsequently work with JESSAMINE on a collaborative EP, 'A POX ON YOU'. Their second long-player, 'THE LONG ARM OF COINCIDENCE' (1996), followed in much the same heavy-lidded vein, seeing a UK release – along with the debut – in Spring '97. A singles compilation, 'ANOTHER FICTIONALIZED HISTORY', surfaced later in the year, prior to a third and final album, 'DON'T STAY TOO LONG' (1998).

Album rating: JESSAMINE (*7) / THE LONG ARM OF COINCIDENCE (*6) / DON'T STAY TOO LONG (*5) / ANOTHER FICTIONALIZED HISTORY compilation (*7)

REX RITTER – vocals, guitar / **DAWN SMITHSON** – vocals, bass / **ANDY BROWN** – keyboards / **MICHAEL FAETH** – drums

not iss. | Sub Pop

1994. (7") **YOUR HEAD IS SO SMALL IT'S LIKE A . . . /** [-] [ ]

Kranky | Kranky

May 95. (lp/cd) *<(KRANK 003/+CD)>* **JESSAMINE** [ ] [ ]
– Another fictionalized history / Secret / Royal jelly eye cream / Ordinary sleep / Inevitably / Cellophane / / You have ugly talents, Martha / One trick pony / Don't you know that yet? / Lisboa. *(re-iss. Mar97; same)*

May 96. (cd-s; shared JESSAMINE & SPECTRUM) *(ORBIT 003CD)* **A POX ON YOU** [ ] [-]
(above issued on 'Space Age') (below issued on 'Darla')

Nov 96. (7") *(DRL 014)* **split with the Transparent Thing** [ ] [-]

Mar 97. (lp/cd) *<(KRANK 012/+CD)>* **THE LONG ARM OF COINCIDENCE** [ ] [ ] Sep96
– Say what you can / Or what you mean, . . . / Periwinkle / Step down / You may have forgotten / Polish countryside / Schisandra / The long arm of coincidence makes my radio / All the same.

Sep 98. (lp/cd) *<(KRANK 030/+CD)>* **DON'T STAY TOO LONG**
– Elsewards / It was already Thursday / Pilot-free ignition / Continuous / Corrupted endeavor / Burgundy / Hand held.

– compilations, etc. –

Sep 97. (cd) *Histrionic; <(HIST 1CD)>* **ANOTHER FICTIONALIZED HISTORY**
– Cheree / Reflections / (I'm not afraid of) Electricity / Your head is so small it's like a . . . / Soon the world of fashion will take . . . / Oscillations / It shouldn't take so long for a man . . . / Air from another world / The moon is made of cheese / From hereto and now otherwise / Live at off the record. *(d-lp-iss.Jan98; HIST 1LP)*

JESSE GARON & THE DESPERADOES

Formed: Edinburgh, Scotland . . . 1986 by FRAN SCHOPPLER, ANGUS McPAKE and two ROTE KAPELLE members, ANDREW TOLLY and MARGARITA VASQUEZ-PONTE (in fact this drummer/vocalist also moonlighted for a third "Burgh" act, The FIZZBOMBS, alongside the aforementioned ANGUS). ROTE KAPELLE – who also included CHRIS HENMAN, IAN DUNN, MALCOLM KERGAN and JONATHAN WIND – evolved a few years earlier, releasing their debut EP, 'THE BIG SMELL DINOSAUR', towards the end of '85. Signing with MARC RILEY's 'In-Tape' label, they issued a handful of other indie-pop releases, notably the JON LANGFORD-produced 'FIRE ESCAPE' single in the Spring of '88. Meanwhile, the 'Nardonik' stable (run by part-timer, EDDY) was home for JESSE GARON & THE DESPERADOES (confusingly enough, there wasn't actually a JESSE GARON in the band!), a country-tinged, fun-loving bunch of indie-rockers who made their first break for the border late in '86 with the DOUGLAS HART-produced 45, 'SPLASHING DOWN'. They also delivered a string of 45's before finally getting around to their full-set proper (a compilation, 'A CABINET FULL OF CURIOSITIES', had already hit the shops in '88) at the turn of the decade with 'NIXON'. Released discreetly on TOLLY's own 'Avalanche' records, the lp was followed by what was to be their last offering, 'HOLD ME NOW', a mini-set that featured covers of Bachman Turner Overdrive's 'YOU AIN'T SEEN NOTHIN' YET' and Lulu's 'LOVE LOVES TO LOVE LOVE'.

Album rating: A CABINET OF CURIOSITIES compilation (*6) / NIXON (*5)

FRAN SCHOPPLER – vocals / **ANDREW TOLLY** – vocals, guitar / **ANGUS McPAKE** – bass / **MARGARITA VASQUEZ-PONTE** – drums / **KEVIN + STUART** – guitars

Nardonik / not iss.

Oct 86. (7") *(NRK 001)* **SPLASHING DOWN. / PRESENCE DEAR** [ ] [-]
Mar 87. (7") *(NRK 002)* **THE RAIN FELL DOWN. / I'M UP HERE** [ ] [-]

— **BRUCE HOPKINS + JOHN ROBB** – guitars; repl. KEVIN + STUART

May 87. (12"ep) *(NRK 005T)* **THE BILLY WHIZZ EP** [ ] [-]

— **MICHAEL KERR** – lead guitar (of MEAT WHIPLASH) repl. BRUCE + JOHN

Wild Rumpus / not iss.

1987. (7"flexi) *(SHEP 001)* **HANK WILLIAMS IS DEAD. / Fizzbombs: YOU WORRY ME** [ ] [-]

Velocity / not iss.

Jan 88. (7") *(SPEED 001)* **THE ADAM FAITH EXPERIENCE. /** [ ] [-]
(12"+=) *(SPEEDT 001)* –
Jun 88. (7") *(SPEED 002)* **YOU'LL NEVER BE THAT YOUNG AGAIN. / AND IF THE SKY SHOULD FALL** [ ] [-]
Jan 89. (lp) *(SPEEDLP 111)* **A CABINET FULL OF CURIOSITIES** (compilation) [ ] [-]
(re-iss. Aug90 on 'Avalanche'; ONLYLP 004)

— now without KERR who joined the DARLING BUDS on tour

Avalanche / not iss.

Jan 90. (7"one-sided) *(AGAP 002)* **GRAND HOTEL** [ ] [-]
Mar 90. (cd/lp) **NIXON** [ ] [-]
Oct 90. (m-lp) *(AGAP 001)* **HOLD ME NOW EP** [ ] [-]
– You ain't seen nothin' yet / + 5

— disbanded towards the end of 1990

ROTE KAPELLE

ANDREW TOLLY – vocals / **MARGARITA VASQUEZ-PONTE** – vocals / **CHRIS HENMAN** – guitar / **IAN DINN** – keyboards (also of The STAIRCASE) / **MALCOLM KERGAN** – bass / **JONATHAN WIND** – drums

Big Smell Dinosaur / not iss.

Dec 85. (7"ep) *(SMELL 1)* **THE BIG SMELL DINOSAUR** [ ] [-]
– King Mob / Evolution / Fergus! the sheep! / A gas fire.

In-Tape / not iss.

Oct 86. (7") *(IT 037)* **THESE ANIMALS ARE DANGEROUS. / SUNDAY** [ ] [-]
Aug 87. (12"ep) *(IT 044)* **IT MOVES BUT DOES IT SWING?** (John Peel Sessions) [ ] [-]
– Marathon man / Jellystone park / Acid face baby / Sunday / You don't know.
Apr 88. (7") *(IT 051)* **FIRE ESCAPE. /** [ ] [-]
Jun 88. (12"ep) *(IT 054)* **SAN FRANCISCO AGAIN** [ ] [-]

— they disbanded later in the year, MARGARITA having joined another indie outfit, the re-formed SHOP ASSISTANTS

FIZZBOMBS

MARGARITA + ANGUS with **ANN DONALD** – drums (ex-SHOP ASSISTANTS)

Nardonik / not iss.

Apr 87. (7") *(NRK 3)* **SIGN ON THE LINE. / THE WORD THAT** [ ] [-]

Calculus / not iss.

Mar 88. (7"ep/12"ep) *(KIT 002/+T)* **THE SURFIN' WINTER EP** [ ] [-]

— short-lived due to other commitments (see above)

JESUS & MARY CHAIN

Formed: East Kilbride, Scotland . . . 1983, by brothers WILLIAM and JIM REID, who took their name from a line in a Bing Crosby film. After local Glasgow gigs, they moved to Fulham in London, having signed for Alan McGhee's independent 'Creation' label in May'84. Their debut SLAUGHTER JOE-produced 45, 'UPSIDE DOWN', soon topped the indie charts, leading to WEA subsidiary label, 'Blanco Y Negro', snapping them up in early 1985. They hit the UK Top 50 with their next single, 'NEVER UNDERSTAND', and they were soon antagonising new audiences, crashing gear after 20 minutes on set. Riots ensued at nearly every major gig, and more controversy arrived when the next 45's B-side 'JESUS SUCKS', was boycotted by the pressing plant. With a new B-side, the single 'YOU TRIP ME UP', hit only No.55, but was soon followed by another Top 50 hit in October, 'JUST LIKE HONEY'. A month later they unleashed their debut album, 'PSYCHOCANDY', and although this just failed to breach the UK Top 30, it was regarded by many (NME critics especially) as the album of the year. Early in '86, BOBBY GILLESPIE left to concentrate on his PRIMAL SCREAM project and soon after, JAMC hit the Top 20 with the softer single, 'SOME CANDY TALKING'. In 1987 with new drummer JOHN MOORE, the single 'APRIL SKIES' and album 'DARKLANDS' both went Top 10. Later that year, they remixed The SUGARCUBES' classic 'Birthday' single.'BARBED WIRE KISSES' (1988) was a hotch-potch of B-sides and unreleased material, essential if only for the anarchic trashing of The Beach Boys' 'SURFIN' U.S.A.'. By the release of the 'AUTOMATIC' album in 1989, the Reid brothers had become the core of the band, enlisting additional musicians as needed. The record sounded strangely muted and uninspired although the 'ROLLERCOASTER' EP and subsequent tour (alongside MY BLOODY VALENTINE and a pre-'PARKLIFE' BLUR) were an improvement. True to controversial style, the band returned to the singles chart in 1992 with the radio un-friendly, post-industrial mantra, 'REVERENCE'. Perhaps the last great piece of venom-spewing noise the 'MARY CHAIN produced, the follow-up album, 'HONEY'S DEAD', was tame in comparison. No surprise then, that it recieved mixed reviews although there were a few low key highlights, notably the melodic bubblegum grunge of 'FAR GONE AND OUT'. After 1993's 'SOUND OF SPEED' EP, the band hooked up with MAZZY STAR'S Hope Sandoval for 'STONED AND DETHRONED', a mellow set of feedback free strumming. While still echoing the brooding portent of the THE VELVETS, the style of the record was more 'PALE BLUE EYES' than 'SISTER RAY'. Predictably, the band were seen as having 'sold out' by Indie-Rock dullards and a 1995 single, 'I HATE ROCK'N'ROLL', didn't even scrape the Top 50. • **Songwriters:** All written by JIM and WILLIAM except; VEGETABLE MAN (Syd Barrett) / SURFIN' USA (Beach Boys) / WHO DO YOU LOVE (Bo Diddley) / MY GIRL (Temptations) / MUSHROOM (Can) / GUITAR MAN (Jerry Lee Hubbard) / TOWER OF SONG (Leonard Cohen) / LITTLE RED ROOSTER (Willie Dixon) / (I CAN'T GET NO) SATISFACTION (Rolling Stones) / REVERBERATION (13th Floor Elevators) / GHOST OF A SMILE (Pogues) / ALPHABET CITY (Prince) / NEW KIND OF KICK (Cramps). • **Trivia:** Their 1986 single 'SOME CANDY TALKING' was banned by Radio 1 DJ Mike Smith, due to its drug references. The following year in the States, they were banned from a chart show due to their blasphemous name. Although yet not overwhelming, their success in the US, have made albums reach between 100 & 200. On 1994's 'STONED AND DETHRONED', they were joined by William's girlfriend HOPE SANDOVAL (of MAZZY STAR).

Album rating: PSYCHOCANDY (*10) / DARKLANDS (*8) / BARBED WIRE KISSES collection (*7) / AUTOMATIC (*7) / HONEY'S DEAD (*8) / THE SOUND OF SPEED compilation (*7) / STONED AND DETHRONED collection (*6) / I HATE ROCK N ROLL (*5) / MUNKI (*5)

JIM REID (b.29 Dec'61) – vox, guitar / **WILLIAM REID** (b.28 Oct'58) – guitar, vox / **MURRAY DALGLISH** – drums (bass tom & snare) / **DOUGLAS HART** – bass

Creation / not iss.

Nov 84. (7") *(CRE 012)* **UPSIDE DOWN. / VEGETABLE MAN** [ ] [-]
(12"+=) *(CRE 012T)* – ('A' demo).

— **BOBBY GILLESPIE** – drums (ex-WAKE, of PRIMAL SCREAM) repl. DALGLISH who formed BABY'S GOT A GUN

Blanco Y Negro / Reprise

Feb 85. (7") *(NEG 8)* **NEVER UNDERSTAND. / SUCK** [47] [-]
(12"+=) *(NEGT 8)* – Ambition.
Jun 85. (7") *(NEG 13)* **YOU TRIP ME UP. / JUST OUT OF REACH** [55] [-]
(12"+=) *(NEGT 13)* – Boyfriend's dead.
Oct 85. (7") *(NEG 017)* **JUST LIKE HONEY. / HEAD** [45] [-]
(12"+=) *(NEGT 17)* – Just like honey (demo) / Cracked.
(d7"+=) *(NEGF 17)* – ('A'demo) / Inside me.
Nov 85. (lp/c) *(BYN/+C 11) <25383>* **PSYCHOCANDY** [31] [ ]
– Just like honey / The living end / Taste the floor / Hardest walk / Cut dead / In a hole / Taste of Cindy / Never understand / It's so hard / Inside me / Sowing seeds / My little underground / You trip me up / Something's wrong. *(cd-iss. Aug86 & Jan97 +=; K 242 000-2)* – Some candy talking.

— **JOHN LODER** – drums (on stage when BOBBY was unavailable)

Jul 86. (7") *(NEG 19)* **SOME CANDY TALKING. / PSYCHO CANDY / HIT** [13] [-]
(12"+=) *(NEGT 19)* – Taste of Cindy.
(d7"+=) *(NEGF 19)(SAM 291)* – Cut dead (acoustic) / You trip me up (acoustic) / Some candy talking (acoustic) / Psycho candy (acoustic).

— now basic trio of **JIM, WILLIAM** and **DOUGLAS** brought in **JOHN MOORE** (b.23 Dec'64, England) – drums repl. GILLESPIE (who was busy with PRIMAL SCREAM) / **JAMES PINKER** – drums (ex-DEAD CAN DANCE) repl. MOORE now on guitar

Apr 87. (7") *(NEG 24)* **APRIL SKIES. / KILL SURF CITY** [8] [-]
(12"+=) *(NEGT 24)* – Who do you love.
(d7"+=) *(NEGF 24)* – Mushroom / Bo Diddley is Jesus.

Aug 87. (7") *(NEG 25)* **HAPPY WHEN IT RAINS. / EVERYTHING IS ALRIGHT WHEN YOU'RE DOWN** [25] [-]
(ext.12"+=) *(NEGT 25)* – Happy place / F-Hole.
(ext.10"+=) *(NEGTE 25)* – ('A'demo) / Shake.

— trimmed to basic duo of REID brothers.

Sep 87. (lp/c)(cd) *(BYN/+C 25)(K 242 180-2) <25656>* **DARKLANDS** [5] [ ]
– Darklands / Deep one perfect morning / Happy when it rains / Down on me / Nine million rainy days / April skies / Fall / Cherry came too / On the wall / About you. *(cd re-iss. Nov94; K 242 180-2)*

Oct 87. (7"/7"g-f) *(NEG/+F 29)* **DARKLANDS. / RIDER / ON THE WALL (demo)** [33] [-]
(12"+=/12"g-f+=) *(NEGTF 29)* – Surfin' U.S.A.
(10"+=/cd-s+=) *(NEG TE/CD 29)* – Here it comes again.

— **DAVE EVANS** – rhythm guitar repl. MOORE who formed EXPRESSWAY

Mar 88. (7") *(NEG 32)* **SIDEWALKING. / TASTE OF CINDY (live)** [30] [-]
(12"+=) *(NEGT 32)* – ('A'extended) / April skies (live).
(cd-s++=) *(NEGCD 32)* – Chilled to the bone.

Apr 88. (lp/c)(cd) *(BYN/+C 29)(K 242 331-2) <25729>* **BARBED WIRE KISSES** (part compilation) [9] [ ]
– Kill Surf City / Head / Rider / Hit / Don't ever change / Just out of reach / Happy place / Psychocandy / Sidewalking / Who do you love / Surfin' USA / Everything's alright when you're down / Upside down / Taste of Cindy / Swing / On the wall. *(c+=/cd+=)* – Cracked / Here it comes again / Mushroom / Bo Diddley is Jesus. *(cd re-iss. Jan97; same)*

— In Nov'88, DOUGLAS HART moonlighted in The ACID ANGELS, who released 7"promo 'SPEED SPEED ECSTASY' on 'Product Inc.'; *FUEL 1)*

Nov 88. (7") *<27754>* **KILL SURF CITY. / SURFIN' USA (summer mix)** [-] [ ]

— Basically REID brothers, HART and EVANS. (added **RICHARD THOMAS** – drums) / **BEN LURIE** – rhythm guitar repl. EVANS

Sep 89. (7") *(NEG 41)* **BLUES FROM A GUN. / SHIMMER** [32] [-]
(10"+=) *(NEG 41TE)* – Break me down / Penetration.
(12"+=/c-s+=) *(NEG 41 T/C)* – Penetration / Subway.
(3"cd-s+=) *(NEG 41CD)* – Penetration / My girl.

Oct 89. (lp/c)(cd) *(BYN/+C 20)(K 246 221-2) <26015>* **AUTOMATIC** [11] [ ]
– Here comes Alice / Coast to coast / Blues from a gun / Between planets / UV ray / Her way of praying / Head on / Take it / Halfway to crazy / Gimme hell. *(cd re-iss. Jan97; same)*

Nov 89. (7") *(NEG 42)* **HEAD ON. / IN THE BLACK** [57] [-]
(12"+=) *(NEG 42T)* – Terminal beach.
(3"cd-s++=) *(NEG 42CD)* – Drop (acoustic re-mix).
(7") *(NEG 42XB)* – ('A'side). / DEVIANT SLICE
(7") *(NEG 42Y)* – ('A'side). / I'M GLAD I NEVER
(7") *(NEG 42Z)* – ('A'side). / TERMINAL BEACH

Mar 90. (7") *<19891>* **HEAD ON. / PENETRATION** [-] [ ]

Aug 90. (7") *(NEG 45)* **ROLLERCOASTER. / SILVER BLADE** [46] [-]
(12"+=) *(NEG 45T)* – Tower of song.
(7"ep++=/cd-ep++=) *(NEG 45 D/CD)* – Low-life.

— Trimmed again, when THOMAS joined RENEGADE SOUNDWAVE on U.S.tour. HART became video director. The **REID** brothers and **BEN** recruited **MATTHEW PARKIN** – bass + **BARRY BLACKER** – drums (ex-STARLINGS)

Blanco Y Negro / American

Feb 92. (7") *(NEG 55)* **REVERENCE. / HEAT** [10] [-]
(12"+=/cd-s+=) *(NEG 55 T/CD)* – ('A'radio remix) / Guitar man.

Mar 92. (cd/c/lp) *(9031 76554-2/-4/-1) <26830>* **HONEY'S DEAD** [14] [ ]
– Reverence / Teenage lust / Far gone and out / Almost gold / Sugar Ray / Tumbledown / Catchfire / Good for my soul / Rollercoaster / I can't get enough / Sundown / Frequency. *(cd re-iss. Jan97; same)*

Apr 92. (7") *(NEG 56)* **FAR GONE AND OUT. / WHY'D DO YOU WANT ME** [23] [-]
(12"+=/cd-s+=) *(NEG 56 T/CD)* – Sometimes you just can't get enough.

Jun 92. (7") *(NEG 57)* **ALMOST GOLD. / TEENAGE LUST (acoustic)** [41] [-]
(12"+=) *(NEG 57T)* – Honey's dead.
(gold-cd-s+=) *(NEG 57CD)* – Reverberation (doubt) / Don't come down.

Jun 93. (7"ep/c-ep/10"ep/cd-ep) *(NEG 66/+C/TE/CD)* **SOUND OF SPEED EP** [30] [-]
– Snakedriver / Something I can't have / White record release blues / Little red rooster.

Jul 93. (cd/c/lp) *(4509 93105-2/-4/-1)* **THE SOUND OF SPEED** (part comp '88-'93) [15] [-]
– Snakedriver / Reverence (radio mix) / Heat / Teenage lust (acoustic version) / Why'd you want me / Don't come down / Guitar man / Something I can't have / Sometimes / White record release blues / Shimmer / Penetration / My girl / Tower of song / Little red rooster / Break me down / Lowlife / Deviant slice / Reverberation / Sidewalking (extended version). *(cd re-iss. Jan97; same)*

— next album feat. guest vox HOPE SANDOVAL (Mazzy Star) + SHANE MacGOWAN / **STEVE MONTI** – drums repl. BLACKER

Jul 94. (7"/c-s) *(NEG 70/+C)* **SOMETIMES ALWAYS. / PERFECT CRIME** [22] [-]
(10"+=/cd-s+=) *(NEG 70 TE/CD)* – Little stars / Drop.

Aug 94. (cd/c/lp) *(4509 93104-2/-4/-1) <45573>* **STONED AND DETRONED** [13] [98]
– Dirty water / Bullet lovers / Sometimes always / Come on / Between us / Hole / Never saw it coming / She / Wish I could / Save me / Till it shines / God help me / Girlfriend / Everybody I know / You've been a friend / These days / Feeling lucky. *(cd re-iss. Jan97; same)*

Oct 94. (c-s) *<18078>* **SOMETIMES ALWAYS / DROP** [-] [96]

Oct 94. (7"/c-s) *(NEG 73/+C)* **COME ON. / I'M IN WITH THE OUT-CROWD** [52] [-]
(cd-s+=) *(NEG 73CD)* – New York City / Taking it away.
(cd-s) *(NEG 73CD)* – ('A'side) / Ghost of a smile / Alphabet city / New kind of kick.

Jun 95. (c-ep/12"ep/cd-ep) *(NEG 81 C/TEX/CD)* **I HATE ROCK N ROLL / BLEED ME. / 33 1-3 / LOST STAR** [61] [-]

Sep 95. (cd,c) *<43043>* **HATE ROCK N ROLL** (compilation of B-sides & rarities) [-] [ ]
– I hate rock'n'roll / Snakedriver / Something I can't have / Bleed me / Thirty three and a third / Lost star / Penetration / New York City / Taking it away / I'm in with the out crowd / Little stars / Teenage lust / Perfect crime.

— **JIM, WILLIAM + BEN** were joined by **NICK SANDERSON** – drums / **TERRY EDWARDS** – horns / + guests vocalists **HOPE SANDOVAL + SISTER VANILLA**

Creation / Sub Pop

Apr 98. (7") *(CRE 292)* **CRACKING UP. /** [35] [-]
(cd-s+=) *(CRESCD 292)* –

May 98. (7"/c-s) *(CRE/+CS 296)* **I LOVE ROCK N ROLL. / EASYLIFE, EASYLOVE** [38] [-]
(cd-s+=) *(CRESCD 296)* – 40,000k / Nineteen 666.

Jun 98. (cd/c/d-lp) *(CRECD/CCRE/CRELP 232) <SP 426>* **MUNKI** [47] [ ]
– I love rock n roll / Birthday / Stardust remedy / Fizzy / Moe Tucker / Perfume / Virtually unreal / Degenerate / Cracking up / Commercial / Supertramp / Never understood / I can't find the time for times / Man on the moon / Black / Dream lover / I hate rock n roll.

– compilations, etc. –

Sep 91. (m-lp/m-c/m-cd) *Strange Fruit; (SFP MA/MC/CD 210)* **THE PEEL SESSIONS (1985-86)** [ ] [-]
– Inside me / The living end / Just like honey / all / Hapy place / In the rain.

Jun 94. (cd+book) *Audioglobe;* **LIVE (live)** [ ] [-]

JESUS LIZARD

Formed: Austin, Texas, USA ... late 80's by DAVID YOW and DAVID SIMS, who had just folded SCRATCH ACID. This band, who also had in their ranks, BRETT BRADFORD, REY WASHAM and brief frontman STEVE ANDERSON, released a clutch of demented hardcore punk releases including the eponymous 'SCRATCH ACID' (1984), 'JUST KEEP EATING' (1986) and 'BERSERKER' (1986) before WASHAM joined STEVE ALBINI in RAPEMAN. YOW and SIMS subsequently recruited Chicago-born DUANE DENISON and MAC McNEILLY to complete the JESUS LIZARD formation, embarking on extensive US and UK tours. Roping in the ubiquitous ALBINI to produce their debut release, 'PURE' (a 1989 mini-set), YOW delivered a ferocious fusion of howling punk metallic blues that called to mind prime(evil) BIRTHDAY PARTY, IGGY POP and The BUTTHOLE SURFERS. Live, the JESUS LIZARD experience was a psychotic, apocalyptic cabaret with the bare-chested YOW a deranged focal point. He was renowned for launching himself into the audience mid set, at times disappearing from view, other times crowd-surfing while remarkably still managing to sing! In the early 90's, the group released a series of uncompromising, lyrically disturbing albums for 'Touch & Go', the last of these 'LIAR' (1992) omitted possibly their most gross track/single to date, a cover of The Dicks' 'WHEELCHAIR EPIDEMIC'. YOW and Co. enjoyed an unexpected taste of success (UK Top 20) the following year when they shared a split 45 with NIRVANA, JESUS LIZARD contributing the lovely 'PUSS'. The group released an unofficial live affair before leaving their label with a final effort, 'DOWN', an album that witnessed them at their grimy, bass-heavy best. Surprisingly signing a lucrative deal with 'Capitol' records (having earlier rejected 'Atlantic'), they signalled that their twisted musical vision remained resolutely uncommercial with the 1996 'SHOT' album. • **Covered:** SUNDAY YOU NEED LOVE (Remmler – Cralle).

Album rating: Scratch Acid: SCRATCH ACID (*6) / JUST KEEP EATING (*6) / BERSERKER (*6) / Jesus Lizard: PURE mini (*5) / HEAD (*6) / GOAT (*7) / LIAR (*7) / SHOW (*5) / DOWN (*6) / SHOT (*7) / BLUE (*7) / Denison – Kimball Trio: WALLS IN THE CITY (*6) / SOUL MACHINE (*5) / NEUTRONS (*5)

SCRATCH ACID

DAVID YOW – vocals, bass / **BRETT BRADFORD** – guitar, vocals / **DAVID WILLIAM SIMS** bass, guitar / **REY WASHAM** – drums, piano (ex-BIG BOYS)

Fundamental / RabidCat

Apr 86. (lp) *(HOLY 1)* **SCRATCH ACID** [ ] [ ]
– Cannibal / Greatest gift / Monsters / Owners lament / She said / Mess / El spectro / Lay screaming.

Jul 86. (m-lp) *(SAVE 012)* **JUST KEEP EATING** [ ] [ ]
– Crazy Dan / Eyeball / Big bone lick / Unlike a beast / Damned for all time / Ain't that love / Holes / Albino slug / Spit a kiss / Amicus / Cheese plug.

Mar 87. (lp) *(HOLY 2)* **BERSERKER** [ ] [ ]
– Mary had a little drug problem / For crying out loud / Moron's moron / Skin drips / Thing is bliss / Flying houses.

— In 1988, YOW joined RAPEMAN alongside STEVE ALBINI (BIG BLACK). WESHAM joined TAD.

– compilations, etc. –

Oct 91. (lp/cd) *Touch & Go; <(TG LP/CD 76)>* **THE GREATEST GIFT** [ ] [ ]

JESUS LIZARD

— **DAVID YOW** – vocals / **DUANE DENISON** – guitar / **DAVID WILLIAM SIMS** – bass / **MAC McNEILLY** – drums

Touch & Go | Touch & Go

Feb 89. (m-lp) *<TGLP 30>* **PURE** [-]
– Blockbuster / Bloody Mary / Rabid pigs / Starlet / Happy bunny goes fluff fluff along. *(UK-iss.Jul93; same)*

Feb 90. (7") *<TG 53>* **CHROME. /**

May 90. (lp) *<TGLP 54>* **HEAD**
– One evening / S.D.B.J. / My own urine / If you had lips / 7 vs 8 / Pastoral / Waxeater / Good thing / Tight 'n shiny / Killer McHann. *(cd-iss. Jul93+=; TGCD 54)* – PURE

Nov 90. (7") *<TG 66>* **MOUTH BREATHER. / SUNDAY YOU NEED LOVE**

Feb 91. (lp/cd) *<TG 68/+CD>* **GOAT**
– Then comes Dudley / Mouthbreaker / Nub / Monkey trick / Karpis / South mouth / Lady shoes / Rodeo in Joliet / Seasick. *(re-iss. Apr94; same)*

— In Apr'91, YOW featured for super techno-punks PIGFACE on their 'GUB' album

May 92. (7") *<TG 87>* **WHEELCHAIR EPIDEMIC. / DANCING NAKED LADIES**

Oct 92. (lp/c/cd/pic-lp) *<TG 100/+C/CD/P>* **LIAR**
– Boilermaker / Gladiator / The art of self-defence / Slave ship / Puss / Whirl / Rope / Perk / Zachariah / Dancing naked ladies.

Feb 93. (7"/cd-s) *<TG 83/+CD>* **PUSS. / (b-side by NIRVANA)** [12]

Jun 93. (cd/lp) **SHOW (live)** [-]
(imported into UK Jul94 on 'Collision Arts-Giant')

Sep 93. (12"ep/cd-ep) *<TG 121/+CD>* **LASH** [-]
– Glamorous / Deaf as a bat / Ladyshoes (live) / Killer McHaan (live) / Bloody Mary (live) / Monkey trick (live).

Nov 93. (12"/cd-s) *<TG 128/+CD>* **FLY ON THE WALL. / WHITE HOLE**

Aug 94. (lp/c/cd) *<TG 131/+C/CD>* **DOWN (live)** [64]
– Fly on the wall / Mistletoe / Countless backs of sad losers / Queen for a day / The associate / Destroy before reading / Low rider / 50 cents / American BB / Horse / Din / Elegy / The best parts.

Capitol | Capitol

May 96. (cd/c/lp) *<CD/TC+/EST 2284>* **SHOT**
– Thumper / Blue shot / Thumbscrews / Good riddance / Mailman / Skull of a German / Trephination / More beautiful than Barbie / Too bad about the fire / Churl / Now then / Inamorata / Pervertedly slow.

— **JIM KIMBALL** – drums (ex-MULE, ex-LAUGHING HYENAS) repl. MAC

Feb 98. (ltd-10"/cd-s) *(TWA 10/+CD)* **THE JESUS LIZARD**
– Cold water / Inflicted by hounds / Eyesore / Valentine / Needles for teeth.
(above issued on 'Jet Set'; as was below on lp; *TWA 12LP)*

Mar 98. (cd-s) *(882656-2)* **THUMPER EP**

Apr 98. (cd) *(859266-2)* **BLUE** [-]
– I can learn / Horse doctor man / Eucalyptus / A tale of two women / Cold water / And then the rain / Postcoital glow / Until it stopped to die / Soft damage / Happy snakes / Needles for teeth / Terremoto.

DENISON / KIMBALL TRIO

— aka **DUANE + JAMES** on a soundtrack for a film starring YOW

Skin Graft | Skin Graft

Oct 94. (lp/cd) *<GR 16/+CD>* **WALLS IN THE CITY**
– Prelude / Cold light of day / Walk away / Reunion / Harry's theme / One if by land . . . / Romantic interlude / Separate checks / Blue corridor / Postlude / . . . Two if by sea.

May 95. (m-cd) *<GR 22CD>* **SOUL MACHINE**

Quarter Stick | Quarter Stick

Aug 97. (cd/lp) *<QS 48 CD/LP>* **"NEUTRONS"**
– Downriver / Landshark pt.2 / Monte's casino / Heavy water / Traveling salesman / Neutrons / Issa / Lullaby.

J.F.A.

Formed: Phoenix, Arizona, USA . . . 1983 by BRIAN, DON, MICHAEL C and BAM BAM. Originally an out-and-out punk outfit, they slipped into skateboard-punk and surf-punk with two rare, fun-packed albums, 'VALLEY OF THE YAKES' (1986) and 'J.F.A.' (1988), both for 'Fundamental' records. What did happen to them and what did their moniker mean? (one can only guess?).

Album rating: VALLEY OF THE YAKES (*6)

BRIAN – vocals / **DON** – guitar / **MICHAEL C** – bass / **BAM BAM** – drums

Fundamental | Fundamental

Jul 87. (lp) *<SAVE 023>* **VALLEY OF THE YAKES** 1986
– Kick you / The great equaliser / Preppie / Little big man / Johnny D / Walk don't run / Skateboard / We know you suck / Too late / Sadistic release / Axed at Howard's / One-ten / Guess what?

Feb 88. (lp) *<SAVE 044>* **J.F.A.**
– Deltitnu / Tent peg / Aba / It's not right / The day Walt Disney died / Standin' on the verge / I love broads / Ramp song / Pipetruck / Zimbobway / Untitled / I still could not forget you.

— split in the late 80's

JILTED JOHN

Born: GRAHAM FELLOWS, Manchester, England. Having been an actor from the mid 70's, GRAHAM turned his attention to er . . . "singing" after being slightly influenced by the New Wave/Punk scene. His eponymous debut single, 'JILTED JOHN', was unleashed in the summer of '78 by local independent label, Rabid'. Its woeful tales of two-timing teen-angst were backed up by a pogo-punk beat, the record's potential leading to major 'EMI International' taking up its cause. Helped by daytime radioplay and an appearance on the prestigious (at the time!) Top Of The Pops TV show, the record shot up to No.4 in the charts and gave him not fifteen, but three minutes of fame. Subsequent follow-ups, including a MARTIN HANNETT-produced pseudo-concept long-player, 'TRUE LOVE STORIES' (1978) and two 45's by his winning rival/alter-ego, GORDON THE MORON, failed to shake off the one hit wonder/novelty tag and GRAHAM returned to acting; amongst other things, he went on to work in TV soap, 'Coronation Street'. After virtually disappearing throughout the 80's, the following decade saw GRAHAM resurface as Northern entertainer, JOHN SHUTTLEWORTH. Introduced through Jonathan Ross' Channel 4 TV show, the "old man" SHUTTLEWORTH character embarrassingly sang while programming his Bontempi organ, gaining cult status in the process. He went on to star in his own TV series, '500 Bus Stops' and did a mock Eurovision entry in 1997, singing the gloriously catchy 'Pigeons In Flight' (would have been a winner for me anyway!?).

Album rating: TRUE LOVE STORIES (*5)

JILTED JOHN – vocals / with session people

Rabid | not iss.

Jul 78. (7") *(TOSH 105)* **JILTED JOHN. / GOING STEADY** [-]

Sep 78. (7"; as GORDON THE MORON) *(TOSH 107)* **DE DO DOUGH DON'T BE DOUGH. /** [-]

Dec 78. (7"; as GORDON THE MORON) *(TOSH 111)* **FIT FOR NOTHING. / SOLD ON YOU** [-]

EMI Internat. | not iss.

Aug 78. (7") *(INT 567)* **JILTED JOHN. / GOING STEADY** [4]

Nov 78. (lp) *(INS 3024)* **TRUE LOVE STORIES**
– Baz's party / I know I'll never / I was a pre-pubescent / Fancy mice / Jilted John / The birthday kiss / The paperboy song / True love / In the bus shelter / Karen's letter / Shirley / Goodbye Karen.

Jan 79. (7") *(INT 577)* **TRUE LOVE. / I WAS A PRE-PUBESCENT** [-]

Apr 79. (7") *(INT 587)* **BIRTHDAY KISS./ BAZ'S PARTY** [-]

— made one last effort, 'SOME BOYS', under the moniker, GOING RED (with fellow nutters, FAMILY FODDER), before retiring from the business. He subsequently re-appeared in the early 90's as tongue-in-cheek comedian/singer, JOHN SHUTTLEWORTH.

Richard JOBSON (see under ⇒ SKIDS)

JOCASTA

Formed: London, England . . . Autumn '94 by the much-travelled TIM ARNOLD, together with former school friend, JACK REYNOLDS, ANDY LEWIS and ADRIAN MEEHAN. Taking their mythological moniker from the Greek legend of Oedipus, the lads lubricated their musical partnership with infamous drinking sessions around their favourite Soho haunts. Initially forming their own label ('V4'), they released their debut single, 'GO', in Spring '96, resulting in much hype from the London-based music press. Following a further single, 'CHANGE ME', JOCASTA were the subject of a surprise signing to 'Epic', the label subsequently re-issuing both tracks as a build up to their debut album, 'NO COINCIDENCE' (1997). Basically an unstartling US-influenced Brit-pop band with strings attached (well, they did employ a 22-piece orchestra!), JOCASTA were never destined to achieve the historical fame of their namesake.

Album rating: NO COINCIDENCE (*5)

TIM ARNOLD – vocals / **JACK REYNOLDS** – guitar / **ANDY LEWIS** – bass / **ADRIAN MEEHAN** – drums

V4 | not iss.

Mar 96. (7") *(V4V 001)* **GO. /** [-]
(cd-s+=) *(V4V 001CD)* –

May 96. (7") *(V4V 002)* **CHANGE ME. /**
(cd-s+=) *(V4V 002CD)* –

Epic | not iss.

Nov 96. (7"red/c-s) *(663767-7/-4)* **SOMETHING TO SAY. / SWINGS AND ROUNDABOUTS** [-]
(cd-s+=) *(663767-2)* – Mesmerizing Milla / Don't know when to stop.

Feb 97. (7"blue) *(664141-7)* **GO. / STOP TO THINK** [50] [-]
(cd-s+=) *(664141-2)* – Clean ash / The land of do as you please.
(cd-s) *(664141-5)* – ('A'side) / Something to say (session) / Change me (session).

Apr 97. (7"purple) *(664390-7)* **CHANGE ME. /** [60] [-]
(cd-s) *(664390-2)* – ('A'side) / Relativity / Best of both worlds / The apple and the strawberry.
(cd-s) *(664390-5)* – ('A'side) / Portion of my heart / Only no one / The skin we're in.

Jun 97. (cd/c) *(487861-2/-4)* **NO COINCIDENCE** [-]
– Laughing / Go / Life in a day / Change me / Actress / Leave the light on / Something to say / Single as hell / Perfect / Face you / Crackbaby / Inside out.

JODY & THE CREAMS (see under ⇒ DEEP FREEZE MICE)

JOHNBOY

Formed: Austin, Texas, USA . . . 1991 by BARRY STONE, TONY BICE and JASON MEADE. Not a band destined for the alt-rock mainstream, JOHNBOY were picked up by local label, 'Trance Syndicate' (also home of CRUNT amongst others), who issued their debut album, 'PISTOLSWING' (1993). A nihilistic blast of mutant R&R, the record caught the ear of both BOB MOULD (who offered them a support slot) and STEVE ALBINI, the latter working on their 1994 follow-up, 'CLAIM DEDICATION'.

Album rating: PISTOLSWING (*6) / CLAIM DEDICATION (*5)

BARRY STONE – guitar, vocals / **TONY BICE** – bass, vocals / **JASON MEADE** – drums

Trance Syndicate / Trance Syndicate

Jun 93. (lp/cd) *<TR 16/+CD>* **PISTOLSWING**
– Admiration / Sourmouth / Sunday two / Pistolswing / Hold / Freestanding / New Jersey roadbase / Yellow / I.

Sep 94. (lp/cd) *<TR 27/+CD>* **CLAIM DEDICATION** — Aug94
– Shortstack / Quick to drain / Driving reservoirs up noses / 10 W 40 / Chair / Genius / Pivotal / Lorac / Flung circles.

— disbanded after above

JOHNNY & THE SELF-ABUSERS (see under ⇒ SIMPLE MINDS)

Matt JOHNSON (see under ⇒ THE THE)

Mike JOHNSON (see under ⇒ DINOSAUR JR)

Daniel JOHNSTON

Born: West Virginia, USA. A tortured, troubled but incredibly gifted and prolific legend of the US underground, DANIEL JOHNSTON has spent a lifetime balancing the unpredictable demands of mental illness with a recording career. Presumably self taught, JOHNSTON issued a series of early cassette-only releases on his own 'Stress' label, beginning with 1980's self-explanatory 'SONGS OF PAIN'. Hardly musical genius, the appeal lay in the heart-rending emotional nakedness of JOHNSTON's amateur guitar strumming, keyboard plonking and singing, his lyrics focusing on the day to day difficulties, heartaches and small victories of JOHNSTON's world. Having based himself in Austin, Texas, he finally broke from obscurity after MTV filmed him as part of a profile on the city's thriving alternative music scene. While his name soon became more famous than his music, 'Homestead' redressed the balance in the late 80's by reissuing 1983's 'YIP JUMP MUSIC', an acclaimed set featuring heartfelt tributes to The BEATLES and cartoon legend, Caspar The Friendly Ghost against a backdrop of skeletal organ. The late 80's also found DANIEL collaborating with fellow maverick, JAD FAIR, on an eponyous album for the latter's '50 Skidillion Watts' label. By this point, JOHNSTON had already survived two periods of hospitalisation yet his work rate showed no sign of slowing. A move to KRAMER's 'Shimmy Disc' in the early 90's resulted in the appropriately titled '1990' and 'ARTISTIC VICE' (1992). Around the same time, DANIEL performed an acappella version of his classic 'SPEEDING MOTORCYCLE' (later covered by Scots shamblers, The PASTELS) down a transatlantic phoneline to John Peel, one of the more memorable moments from the veteran DJ's Radio One show over the past decade. Against all the odds, the irrepresible troubadour subsequently signed a major label deal with 'Atlantic', releasing the well received 'FUN' in 1994. With production assistance from BUTTHOLE SURFER, PAUL LEARY, the record displayed a marked leap in confidence with a strong set of songs which brought widespread critical plaudits.

Album rating: YIP JUMP MUSIC (*6) / HI, HOW ARE YOU (*6) / 1990 (*6) / ARTISTIC VICE (*6) / FUN (*7)

DANIEL JOHNSTON – vocals, guitar, keyboards

not iss. / Stress

1980. (c) **SONGS OF PAIN** — -
1982. (c) **DON'T BE SCARED** — -
1982. (c) **THE WHAT OF WHOM** — -
1983. (c) **MORE SONGS OF PAIN** — -
1983. (c) **THE LOST RECORDINGS VOLUME 1** (compilation) — -
1983. (c) **THE LOST RECORDINGS VOLUME 2** (compilation) — -
1984. (c) **RETIRED BOXER** — -
1985. (c) **RESPECT** — -

Furthur / Homestead

1983. (lp) **YIP / JUMP MUSIC** — -
– Chord organ blues / The Beatles / Sorry entertainer / Speeding motorcycle / Caspar the friendly ghost / Don't let the sun down on your grievances / Danny don't rapp / Sweet heart / King Kong / The creature – 3rd chair / I live for love / Almost got hit by a truck / Worried shoes / Dead lover's twisted heart / Rocket ship / God / Love defined / Museum of love / Rarely / I remember painfully. *(UK-iss.Nov94 on 'Homestead' lp/c/cd; HMS 142-1/-4/-2)*

1985. (c) **CONTINUED STORY** — -

Oct 88. (lp) *(FU 4) <HMS 117/+C>* **HI, HOW ARE YOU**

— In 1989, he collaborated with JAD FAIR (ex-HALF JAPANESE) on the album, 'JAD FAIR & DANIEL JOHNSTON', released on '50 Skadillion Watts'.

not iss. / Stress

1990. (c) **LIVE AT SXSW (live)** — -

Shimmy Disc / Shimmy Disc

Nov 90. (lp) *(SDE 9015LP) <SHIMMY 028>* **1990**
– Devil town / Spirit world rising / Held the hand / Lord give me hope / Some things last a long time / Tears stupid tears / Don't play cards with Satan / True love will find you in the end / Got to get you into my life / Careless soul / Funeral home / Softly and tenderly. *(cd-iss. Apr98; SHIMMY 028)*

Mar 92. (lp) *<(SDE 9237)>* **ARTISTIC VICE**
– My life iis starting over / Honey I sure miss you / I feel so high / A ghostly story / Tell me now / Easy listening / I know Casar / The startling facts / Hoping / It's got to be good / Happy soul / The dream is over / Love of my life / I killed the monster / Laurie / Fate will get done.

Seed / Atlantic

Sep 94. (7") *(SEED 010)* **HAPPY TIME. /**

Sep 94. (cd,c) *<82659>* **FUN** — -
– Love wheel / Life in vain / Crazy love / Catie / Happy time / Mind contorted / Jelly beans / Foxy girl / Sad sac + Tarzan / Psycho nightmare / Silly love / Circus man / Love will see you through / Lousy weekend / Delusion + confusion / When I met you / My little girl / Rock'n'roll – EGA.

— will return in 1999 with a new album for 'Tim/Kerr', 'REJECTED'

Freedy JOHNSTON

Born & Raised: 1961 . . . on a farm in rural Kinsley, Kansas. JOHNSTON began writing songs at university, moving to the more sympathetic climes of New York in the mid 80's. Securing a deal with indie label, 'Bar/None' ('Demon' in the UK), JOHNSTON released his debut album in 1990. Although acclaimed by critics for its pithy, keenly observed lyrics and downbeat authenticity, the singer/songwriter found a more appreciative audience in Europe than the States. Famously financed by the sale of the family farm, follow-up set, 'CAN YOU FLY' (1992) suggested that JOHNSTON's self belief was anything but misguided. Released on 'Rough Trade' in Britain, the record's wide-eyed, broken-down charm marked JOHNSTON out as one of America's most promising young singer/songwriters, even if his rootsy authenticity didn't sit well with the prevailing grunge craze. A stopgap EP, 'UNLUCKY' (featuring a wholly appropriate cover of Jimmy Webb's 'WICHITA LINEMAN'), followed in '93 prior to JOHNSTON moving on up to major label status and releasing third set, 'THIS PERFECT WORLD', on 'Elektra'. Produced by Butch Vig, the record was a deeply satisfying and emotive series of character sketches from the fringes of American culture, encapsulating the idea of the songwriter as spokesperson for the downcast and dispossessed. Although the critics raved once more, FREEDY's genius surprisingly seemed to bypass the bulk of the record buying public. A shame, as 1997's 'NEVER HOME' was another masterful collection of short story style creations brought to life by the emotive empathy and unique musical vision of their author.

Album rating: THE TROUBLE TREE (*6) / CAN YOU FLY (*6) / THIS PERFECT WORLD (*8) / NEVER HOME (*7)

FREEDY JOHNSTON – vocals / with various personnel

Demon / Bar/None

Nov 90. (cd) *(FIENDCD 208) <18>* **THE TROUBLE TREE**
– Innocent / Down on the moon No.1 / No violins / That's what you get / Fun ride / Gina / Nature boy / Bad girl / After my shocks / Tucumcari / Down on the moon No.2 / Little red-haired girl.

Rough Trade / Bar/None

Apr 92. (cd/c/lp) *(R 287-2/-4/-1) <24>* **CAN YOU FLY**
– Trying to tell you I don't know / In the new sunshine / Tearing down this place / Remember me / Wheels / Lucky one / Can you fly / Responsible / Mortician's daughter / Sincere / Down in love / California thing / We will shine. *(re-iss. Sep93 on 'Elektra' cd/c; 7559 61587-2/-4)*

Aug 93. (cd-ep) *<AHAON 024>* **UNLUCKY EP** — -
– The lucky one / Death of stars / For a lost key / Caroline / Wichita lineman / The lucky one (demo).

Elektra / Elektra

Jul 94. (cd/c) *<(7559 61655-2/-4)>* **THIS PERFECT WORLD** — Jun94
– Bad reputation / Evie's tears / Can't sink this town / This perfect world / Cold again / Two lovers stop / Across the avenue / Gone like the water / Delores / Evie's garden / Dissapointed man / I can hear the laughs.

Nov 94. (cd-s) **BAD REPUTATION** — -

Mar 97. (cd) *<(7559 61920-2)>* **NEVER HOME** — Feb97
– On the way out / I'm not hypnotised / Western sky / One more thing to break / He wasn't murdered / You get me lost / Hotel seventeen / Gone to see the fire / Seventies girl / If it's true / Something's out there.

JOLT (see under ⇒ SENSELESS THINGS)

JONATHAN FIRE*EATER

Formed: New York, USA . . . mid 90's having all attended a private school in Washington DC. STEW, PAUL, WALT, TOM and MATT eventually secured a semi-permanent residency at NY's The Continental club. In 1995, their debut album was made available at gigs, creating a buzz which led to a single on the 'P.C.P.' label. Stardom beckoned after David Geffen's 'Dreamworks' secured their signature, the mini-cd, 'TREMBLE UNDER BOOM LIGHTS', finally surfacing late in 1996. This was issued in Britain having signed to 'Deceptive' (home of ELASTICA) and kicked up a storm with its comparisons to The BIRTHDAY PARTY and The CRAMPS (the latter, at one time having numbered their new-found buddy KID CONGO).

Album rating: TREMBLE UNDER BOOM LIGHTS (*8) / WOLF SONGS FOR LAMBS (*6)

STEW LUPTON (b.1975) – vocals / **PAUL MAROON** – guitar / **WALT MARTIN** – organ / **TOM FRANK** – bass / **MATT BARRICK** – drums

P.C.P. P.C.P.

Sep 95. (7"/cd-s) *<(PCP 028-7/-2)>* **THE PUBLIC HANGING OF A MOVIE STAR. / THE CAKEWALK / WHEN PRIME WAS A HIT** Jun95

Deceptive Medicine

Oct 96. (7") *(BLUFF 037)* **GIVE ME DAUGHTERS. / SEARCH FOR CHERRY RED** -

Jan 97. (m-cd) *(BLUFF 038CD) <79603>* **TREMBLE UNDER BOOM LIGHTS**
– The search for cherry red / Make it precious / Give me daughters / Beautician / Winston Plum: undertaker / When Prince was a kid. *(lp-iss.Oct97 on 'Crippled Dick'; EFA 04396-1)*

Deceptive Dreamworks

Aug 97. (7") *(BLUFF 048)* **WHEN THE CURTAIN CALLS FOR YOU. / A NIGHT IN THE NURSERY** -
(cd-s+=) *(BLUFF 048CD)* – Don't forget me.

Sep 97. (cd/lp) *(BLUFF 049 CD/LP) <50024>* **WOLF SONGS FOR LAMBS** Oct97
– When the curtain calls for you / Shape of things that never come / This is my room / There is no love like that / Bi-polar summer / I've changed hotels / Everybody plays the mime / These little monkeys / Station coffee / Night in the nursery / In-patient talent show.

Feb 98. (7") *(BLUFF 059)* **THESE LITTLE MONKEYS. / TOMORROW'S NEWS TONIGHT** -
(cd-s+=) *(BLUFF 059CD)* – The city that never sleeps.

—— disbanded that August

JOOLZ

Born: Bradford, England. A socially aware and extreme feminist punk poetess, the tattooed and sultry JOOLZ recited her work on stage, pricking the conscience of laddish men looking for a night on the town. Finding an outlet for her work via 'Abstract' records (through her live-in boyfriend, SLADE THE LEVELLER of NEW MODEL ARMY), she released a couple of EP's and a mini-album, 'NEVER NEVER LAND' (1985), a set that included the poignant 'JACKANORY'. When NEW MODEL ARMY made it big time by signing to 'E.M.I.', she was also invited to step up to the majors, although this unsteady partnership only produced a handful of 45's and a much delayed first album proper, 'HEX' (1987); the record was to have been issued a year earlier as 'MUSKET, FIFE AND DRUM'.

Album rating: RECORDED 1983-85 compilation (*5)

JOOLZ – words / with **JAH WOBBLE** – dub effects

Abstract not iss.

Oct 83. (12"ep) *(12ABS 018)* **DENISE / THE LATEST CRAZE. / WAR OF ATTRITION / PROTECTION** -

—— added guest **OLLIE MARLAND** – saxophone

Jul 84. (12"ep) *(12ABS 025)* **THE KISS. / THE KISS (dub) / PAVED WITH GOLD** -

Jun 85. (m-lp) *(ABT 011)* **NEVER NEVER LAND** -
– Jackanory / Violation / etc

—— now with **SLADE THE LEVELLER** – backing

E.M.I. not iss.

Nov 85. (7") *(JLZ 1)* **LOVE IS (SWEET ROMANCE). / MUSKET, FIFE AND DRUM** -
(12"+=) *(12JLZ 1)* – Fury.

Aug 86. (7") *(EMI 5582)* **MAD, BAD AND DANGEROUS TO KNOW. / LEGEND** -
(12"+=) *(12EMI 5582)* – Babies.

Oct 87. (7") *(JLZ 3)* **PROTECTION. / A DAY IN THE LIFE** -
(12"+=) *(12JLZ 3)* –

Columbia not iss.

Oct 87. (lp/c)(cd) *(SCX/TC-SCX 6711)(CDP 748537-2)* **HEX** -
– Protection / The cat / Facade / Love is (sweet romance) / The stand / Storm / Mummy's boy / Ambition / House of dreams / Requiem. *(cd+=)* – Musket, fife and drum / Legend / Mad, bad and dangerous to know. *(re-iss. Apr90 on 'Anagram' cd+=/lp; CD+/GRAM 44)*

Intercord not iss.

Feb 92. (lp) *(IRS 951946)* **WEIRD SISTER** -
– The game / TRacy / The ballad of Steve & Joe / The boy next door but one / Bad blood / Fuel to the flame / Vendetta / The wait / Pandora / May / Miami / Treasure in the heart / Pamela.

—— she again retired from solo studio work

– compilations, etc. –

Jun 93. (cd) *Get Back; (GBR 004CD)* **RECORDED 1983-85** -

JOSEF K

Formed: Edinburgh, Scotland . . . 1979 by PAUL HAIG, MALCOLM ROSS, DAVID WEDDELL and RONNIE TORRANCE. Named after the main character from one of Franz Kafka's darkly paranoid novels and influenced by New York "No Wave" bands like TALKING HEADS, HAIG & Co. debuted in late '79 with the self-financed 'ROMANCE'. Subsequently signed to Alan Horne's ultra-hip Glasgow-based 'Postcard' label, the band were heralded as "The Sound Of Young Scotland" alongside labelmates ORANGE JUICE and AZTEC CAMERA. A string of singles, including 'RADIO DRILL TIME' and the low-end lurch of 'SORRY FOR LAUGHING', brought fawning press acclaim with one critic moved to describe their awkward, indie-noir sound as a "cross between CAPTAIN BEEFHEART and CHIC". Problems arose, however, with a proposed debut album, 'SORRY FOR LAUGHING', the band unhappy with the production and scrapping it at the last minute; some copies did filter through, mint editions now change hands for over £100. Recorded in Belgium, 'THE ONLY FUN IN TOWN' eventually surfaced as their debut long player in summer '81. Yet no sooner was the record out than HAIG, sticking rigidly by one of punk's guiding principles, decided that they'd reached an artistic peak and had to split. After a final single, 'THE MISSIONARY', JOSEF K disbanded in early '82, TORRANCE and WEDDELL forming HAPPY FAMILY while ROSS joined ORANGE JUICE and later AZTEC CAMERA. HAIG, meanwhile, embarked on a solo career via Belgian label, 'Crepuscule', following an ill-advised, vaguely SIMPLE MINDS-ish synth-pop/rock direction with 1983's 'RHYTHM OF LIFE' album. The singer continued releasing albums throughout the 80's, never drawing more than minor cult acclaim and modest sales; while HAIG's influence was apparent in the more commercially successful material of LLOYD COLE, for instance, the man himself had to make do with recognition on the continent. • **Covered:** APPLEBUSH (Alice Cooper).

Album rating: THE ONLY FUN IN TOWN (*6) / YOUNG AND STUPID compilation (*8) / Paul Haig: RHYTHM OF LIFE (*7)

PAUL HAIG (b.1960) – vocals, guitar / **MALCOLM ROSS** (b.31 Jul'60) – guitar, keyboards / **DAVID WENDELL** – bass; repl. GARY McCORMACK who later joined The EXPLOITED / **RONNIE TORRANCE** – drums

Absolute not iss.

Dec 79. (7") *(ABS 1)* **ROMANCE. / CHANCE MEETING** -

Postcard not iss.

Aug 80. (7") *(80-3)* **RADIO DRILL TIME. / CRAZY TO EXIST (live)** -

Dec 80. (7") *(80-5)* **IT'S KINDA FUNNY. / FINAL REQUEST** -

Feb 81. (7") *(81-4)* **SORRY FOR LAUGHING. / REVELATION** -

May 81. (7") *(81-5)* **CHANCE MEETING. / PICTURES (OF CINDY)** -

Jun 81. (lp) *(81-7)* **THE ONLY FUN IN TOWN** -
– Fun 'n' frenzy / Revelation / Crazy to exist / It's kinda funny / The angle / Forever drone / Heart of song / 16 years / Citizens / Sorry for laughing. *(cd-iss. Sep90 on 'Les Tempes Modernes'; LTMCD 2305)* – (with lost album 'SORRY FOR LAUGHING')

Operation Twilight not iss.

Feb 82. (7") *(7TWI 053)* **MISSIONARY. / ONE ANGLE / SECOND ANGLE** -

—— split early '82 when MALCOLM joined ORANGE JUICE (later AZTEC CAMERA). TORRANCE joined BOOTS FOR DANCING and subsequently teamed up with DAVID to form The HAPPY FAMILY. In 1992, MALCOLM reunited with DAVID forming the MAGIC CLAN in the process.

– compilations, etc. –

Mar 87. (12") *Supreme; (87-7)* **HEAVEN SENT / RADIO DRILL TIME (demo). / HEADS WATCH / FUN 'N' FRENZY** -

Jun 87. (lp) *Supreme; (87-6)* **YOUNG AND STUPID** -
– Heart of song / Endless soul / Citizens / Variation of scene / It's kinda funny / Sorry for laughing / Chance meeting / Heaven sent / Drone / Sense of guilt / Revelation / Romance. *(re-iss. Mar89 as 'ENDLESS SOUL'; same) (cd-iss. Sep90 on 'Les Tempes Modernes'; LTMCD 2307)*

RHYTHM OF LIFE

—— **PAUL HAIG** – vocals, etc. / + various people

Rational – Rhythm not iss.

Jan 82. (7") *(RATE 6 – RHYTHM 1)* **SOON. / SUMMERTIME** -

Apr 82. (7") *(RATE 7 – RHYTHM 2)* **UNCLE SAM. / PORTRAIT OF THE HEART** -

1982. (c) **DRAMA** - - gigs

PAUL HAIG

—— (solo) – vocals, guitar with various session people

Operation Twilight not iss.

May 82. (7") *(OPT 03)* **RUNNING AWAY. / TIME** -

Crepescule not iss.

Sep 82. (7") *(OPT 001)* **CHANCE. / JUSTICE** -

Dec 82. (12") *(TWI 106)* **BLUE FOR YOU. / ('A'version)** -

Crepescule-Island not iss.

May 83. (7"/ext-12") *(IS/12IS 111)* **HEAVEN SENT. / RUNNING AWAY, BACK HOME** 74 -

Jul 83. (7"/ext-12") *(IS/12IS 124)* **NEVER GIVE UP (PARTY, PARTY). / HEARTACHE** -

Oct 83. (lp/c) *(ILPS/ICT 9742)* **RHYTHM OF LIFE** 82 -
– Heaven sent / Never give up (party, party) / Adoration / In the world / Stolen love / Don't rush in / Blue for you / Justice / Work together.

Oct 83. (7") *(IS 138)* **JUSTICE. / ON THIS NIGHT OF DECISION** -
(12"+=) *(12IS 138)* – Justice '82.

Sep 84. (7") *(IS 198)* **THE ONLY TRUTH. / GHOST RIDER** -
(12"+=) *(ISX 198)* – ('A'-US remix).

—— with **ALAN RANKINE** – lead guitar / **MIKE McCANN** – bass / **JAMES LOCK** – drums

Operation Twilight not iss.

Sep 85. (7") *(OPA 2)* **HEAVEN HELP ME NOW. / WORLD RAW** -
(12"+=) *(12OPA 2)* – ('A'version) / Chance.
(re-iss. Aug88; TWI 624)

Nov 85. (lp) *(OPA 3)* **THE WARP OF PURE FUN** -
– Silent motion / Heaven help me now / Love eternal / This dying flame / Sense of fun / Scare me / Big blue world / The only truth / One lifetime away / Love & war. *(re-iss. Feb87 on 'Crepescule' lp/cd; TWI 669/+CD)*

Feb 86. (7"/12") *(OPA/12OPA 6)* **LOVE ETERNAL. / ('A'version)** [ ] [-]
(re-iss. Sep88; TWI 660)

Crepescule not iss.

Jan 88. (lp) *(TWI 829)* **EUROPEAN SUN: ARCHIVE COLLECTION 1982-1987** [ ] [-]
– Running away / Chance / JUstice / Swinging for you / Shining hour / Fear and dancing / Psycho San Jose / Ghost rider / Totchomatic / The executioner / Painless song.

Mar 88. (12"ep) *(TWI 832)* **TORCHOMATIC. / BEAT PROGRAMME / CHASE MANHATTAN / WHITE HOTEL / SONG FOR** [ ] [-]

—— with **ALAN RANKINE** – keyboards, guitar, co-producer / **JOHN TURNER** – piano

Circa not iss.

Mar 89. (lp/c/cd) *(CIR CA/C/CD 7)* **CHAIN** [ ] [-]
– Something good / True blue / Communication / Swinging for you / True of her life / Faithless / Times can change / Tune the vision / Sooner or later / Chained.

Jun 89. (7") *(YR 25)* **SOMETHING GOOD. / OVER YOU** [ ] [-]
(12"+=/12"g-f+=/3"cd-s+=) *(YR T/TX/CD 25)* – ('A'version) / Free to go.

Sep 90. (7") **I BELIEVE IN YOU. / FLIGHT X** [ ] [-]
(12"+=/cd-s+=) – ?

Feb 91. (12") **FLIGHT X. / ('A'-DJ mix)** [ ] [-]

Les Tempes Modernes not iss.

Jan 92. (cd/c/lp) **CINEMATIQUE – THEMES FOR UNKNOWN FILMS, VOLUME ONE** [-] [-] Belgian

Crepescule not iss.

May 93. (cd-ep) *(TWI 9892)* **SURRENDER / HEAVEN HELP YOU NOW ('93 remix) / COINCIDENCE VS FATE** [ ] [-]

Nov 93. (cd) *(TWI 9622)* **COINCIDENCE VS FATE** [ ] [-]
– I believe in you / Flight X / Born innocence / My kind / Si senorita / Right on line / Out of mind / Surrender / Stop and stare / The originator / 1959.

—— seems to have retired from the recording studio

– compilations, etc. –

Jun 84. (7"/12") *Operation Twilight; (TWI 230/231)* **BIG BLUE WORLD. / ('A'version)** [ ] [-]

Jun 84. (7"ep) *Operation Twilight; (7TWI 240)* **HEAVEN SENT EP** (5 remixes) [ ] [-]
– Heaven sent / Blue for you / Party party / Justice / Stolen love.

Apr 85. (12"ep) *Crepescule;* **SWING '82** [ ] [-]
– All of you / Love me tender / + 2.

JOY DIVISION

Formed: Salford, Manchester, England . . . mid'77 initially as The STIFF KITTENS by IAN CURTIS, BERNARD ALBRECHT, PETER HOOK and STEPHEN MORRIS. By the time they were ready to take the stage for the first time, the group were going under the WARSAW moniker, finally settling on JOY DIVISION later that year. A term used by the Nazis for Jewish prostitutes, the band had taken the name from the book, 'House Of Dolls'; unsurprisingly, they ran into a little media trouble, the press subsequently speculating about their supposedly fascistic tendencies and unfairly branding them little Adolfs. Particularly controversial was the track, 'AT A LATER DATE', included on the 'Virgin' various artists punk sampler, 'Short Circuit: Live At The Electric Circus'. A vinyl debut proper came with the limited EP, 'AN IDEAL FOR LIVING', although it was through manager Rob Gretton and a subsequent deal with the emerging 'Factory' records that JOY DIVISION's career really got off the ground. Their first recordings for the label were a couple of tracks, 'GLASS' and 'DIGITAL', featured on a 'Factory' sampler (In mid-'79, a further two tracks, 'AUTO-SUGGESTION' and 'FROM SAFETY TO WHERE', surfaced on the 'Fast' records compilation EP, 'Earcom 2'), while their legendary Martin Hannett-produced debut album, 'UNKNOWN PLEASURES' was finally released later that summer. Groundbreaking in its bass-heavy, skeletal sound and evocation of urban alienation, isolation and despair, the record ensured CURTIS's position as a latter day messiah of existential angst; while his lyrics trawled the underbelly of the human psyche with disturbing clarity, his sub-JIM MORRISON ruminations were a blueprint for every pasty-faced goth pretender of the next decade. Tony Wilson's faith in the band was such that he contributed his life savings of over £8,000 towards the album's cost, t~he 'Factory' supremo's investment rewarded as the record topped the indie charts and JOY DIVISION became the foremost post-punk cult act. Yet even as the hypnotic rhythms of sublime new single, 'TRANSMISSION', hinted at an equally compelling new direction, CURTIS's robotic contortions and trance-like stage presence were giving way to epileptic fits as the singer struggled to cope with the increasing demands of live work. Tragically, on the 18th May, 1980, depressed with the break-up of his marriage and his worsening illness, CURTIS hanged himself. Ironically, JOY DIVISION scored their first chart hit a month later with the seminal 'LOVE WILL TEAR US APART'; the loss of such a fiercely individual talent was underlined as the track suggested a singer (and indeed, band) at the very apex of their creative potential. CURTIS had actually recorded a full album's worth of material before his death, released that summer as 'CLOSER'; even more lyrically unsettling, the record's bleak vision nevertheless pre-empted rock's dancefloor embrace on the synth-laced likes of 'ISOLATION', as well as forming the basis for NEW ORDER's experiments in cross-genre innovation. The latter act were formed later that year from JOY DIVISION's ashes, while further CURTIS-era material was posthumously released in late '81 as 'STILL'. The band remain one of the most revered and certainly one of the most influential outfits to emerge from the punk 'revolution', the best of NEW ORDER's work an indication as to what musical heights JOY DIVISION might have scaled had CURTIS prolonged the battle with his personal demons.

Album rating: UNKNOWN PLEASURES (*10) / CLOSER (*10) / STILL part compilation/live (*8) / SUBSTANCE compilation (*9) / PERMANENT: JOY DIVISION 1995 remixes (*6)

IAN CURTIS (b.15 Jul'56, Macclesfield, England) – vocals / **BERNARD ALBRECHT** (b. BERNARD DICKEN, 4 Jan'56) – guitar, vocals / **PETER HOOK** (b.13 Feb'56, Salford, Manchester) – bass / **STEPHEN MORRIS** (b.28 Oct'57, Macclesfield) – drums

Enigma not iss.

Jun 78. (7"ep) *(PSS 139)* **AN IDEAL FOR LIVING** [ ] [-]
– An ideal for living / Warsaw / Leaders of men / No love lost / Failures. *(re-iss. Jul78 on 'Anonymous' 12"ep; ANON 1)*

Factory not iss.

Aug 79. (lp) *(FACT 10)* **UNKNOWN PLEASURES** [ ] [-]
– Disorder / Day of the lords / Candidate / Insight / New dawn fades / She's lost control / Shadowplay / Wilderness / Interzone / I remember nothing. *(re-dist.Jul80, hit No.71)* (re-iss. Jul82; *same) (c-iss.Nov84; FACT 10C) (cd-iss. Apr86; FACD 10) (re-iss. Jul93 on 'Centredate-London' cd/c; 520016-2) <US-iss.1989 on 'Qwest' lp/c/cd; 1-/4-/2-25840>*

Oct 79. (7") *(FAC 13)* **TRANSMISSION. / NOVELTY** [ ] [-]
(re-iss. Oct80 as 12"; FAC 13-12)

Mar 80. (7") *(SS 33-002)* **ATMOSPHERE. / DEAD SOULS** [-] [-] France
(above single released on 'Sordide Sentimentale' & now worth lots)

Jun 80. (7") *(FAC 23)* **LOVE WILL TEAR US APART. / THESE DAYS** [13] [-]
(re-iss. Oct80 as 12"+=; FAC 23-12) – ('A'version). *(re-iss. Oct83; same); hit UK No.19)*

Jul 80. (lp) *(FACT 25)* **CLOSER** [6] [-]
– Heart and soul / 24 hours / The eternal / Decades / Atrocity exhibition / Isolation / Passover / Colony / Means to an end. *(c-iss.Jul82; FACT 25C) (cd-iss. Apr86; FACD 25) (re-iss. Jul93 on 'Centredate-London' cd/c; 520015-2) <US-iss.1989 on 'Qwest' lp/c/cd; 1-/4/-2-25841>*

—— After another fit of depression, IAN CURTIS hanged himself 18th May 1980. The others became NEW ORDER

– compilations, others, etc. –

Sep 80. (12") *Factory Benelux; (FACTUS 2)* **ATMOSPHERE. / SHE'S LOST CONTROL** [ ] [-]

Apr 81. (free 7"flexi) *Factory; (FAC 28)* **KOMAKINO. / INCUBATION** [-] [-]

May 81. (7"ep/12"ep; as WARSAW) *Enigma; (PSS 138)* **THE IDEAL BEGINNING** [ ] [-]
– Inside the line / Gutz / At a later date.

Oct 81. (d-lp) *Factory; (FACT 40)* **STILL (live & rare)** [5] [-]
– Exercise one / Ice age / The sound of music / Glass / The only mistake / Walked in line / The kill / Something must break / Dead souls / Sister Ray / Ceremony / Shadowplay / Means to an end / Passover / New dawn fades / Transmission / Disorder / Isolation / Decades / Digital. *(c-iss.Dec86; FACT 40C) (cd-iss. Mar90; FACD 40) (re-iss. Jul93 on 'Centredate-London' cd/c; 520014-2/-4) <US-iss.1989 on 'Qwest' lp/c/cd; 26495>*

Nov 86. (12"ep) *Strange Fruit; (SFPS 013)* **THE PEEL SESSIONS (31.1.79)** [ ] [-]
– Exercise one / Insight / She's lost control / Transmission. *(re-iss. Jul88 cd-ep; SFPSCD 013)*

Sep 87. (12"ep) *Strange Fruit; (SFPS 033)* **THE PEEL SESSIONS 2 (26.11.79)** [ ] [-]
– Love will tear us apart / 24 hours / Colony / The sound of music. *(re-iss. Jul88 cd-ep; SFPSCD 033)*

1987. (7"ep+book) *Stampa; (SCONIC 001)* **YOU'RE NO GOOD FOR ME / KOMAKINO / INCUBATION / INCUBATION (version)** [-] [-] Italy

Jun 88. (7") *Factory; (FAC 213-7)* **ATMOSPHERE. / THE ONLY MISTAKE** [34] [-]
(12"+=) *(FAC 213)* – The sound of music.
(cd-s) *(FACD 213)* – ('A'side) / Love will tear us apart / Transmission.

Jul 88. (lp/c/dat)(cd) *Factory; (FACT 250/+C/D)(FACD 250) / Qwest; <1-/4-/2-25747>* **SUBSTANCE** (The best of..) [7] [ ]
– She's lost control / Dead souls / Atmosphere / Love will tear us apart / Warsaw / Leaders of men / Digital / Transmission / Auto-suggestion. *(cd+=)* – (7 extra tracks). *(re-iss. Jul93 on 'Centredate-London' cd/c; 520 014-2/-4)*

Sep 90. (cd/c) *Strange Fruit; (SFR CD/MC 111)* **COMPLETE PEEL SESSIONS** [ ] [-]

Jun 95. (c-s) *London; (YOJC 1)* **LOVE WILL TEAR US APART (radio version) / ('A'-original version)** [19] [ ]
(12"+=/cd-s+=) *(YOJ T/CD 1)* – These days / Transmission.

Jun 95. (cd/c/d-lp) *London; (828 624-2/-4/-1) / Warners; <45979>* **PERMANENT: JOY DIVISION 1995** (remixes) [16] [ ] Aug95
– Love will tear us apart / Transmission / She's lost control / Shadow play / Day of the lords / Isolation / Passover / Heart and soul / 24 hours / These days / Novelty / Dead souls / The only mistake / Something must break / Atmosphere / Love will tear us apart (Permanent mix).

Jan 98. (4xcd-box) *London; (<828 968-2>)* **HEART AND SOUL** (all material) [70] [ ]

Feb 98. (cd+book) *Sonic Book; (SB 10)* **ALL THE LYRICS** [ ] [-]

JOYRIDER

Formed: Portadown, N.Ireland . . . 1992 by PHIL WOOLSEY, CLIFF MITCHELL, SIMON HADDOCK and BUCK HAMILL. Signed to Dublin-based indie label, 'Blunt', they released a few singles in 1994 produced by ANDY CAIRNS (Therapy?). Akin to a cross between THERAPY? and TERRORVISION, their bouncy hard-rock endeared them to A&M off-shoot 'Paradox' later that year. They released a string of EP's over the course of the next year, before finally unleashing a debut album, 'BE SPECIAL' in the Spring of '96. The record boasted a few hits, the biggest (and most annoying) being the near UK Top 20 cover of Jane Wiedlin's (ex-GO-GO's) 'RUSH HOUR'. Unfortunately the group had more than rush hour traffic to deal with when their tour van (complete with instruments) was blown up in London by the bomb disposal squad. Moving upstairs to 'A&M', they released a second set, 'SKID SOLO' (1997).

Album rating: BE SPECIAL (*6) / SKID SOLO (*6)

PHIL WOOLSEY – vocals, guitar / **CLIFF 'Mitch' MITCHEL** – guitar / **SIMON HADDOCK** – bass / **BUCK HAMILL** – drums

Blunt / not iss.

Apr 94. (7"pink-ep) *(BLUNT 003)* **JOYRIDER EP** [ ] [-]
– Dweeb king / Happy / In a car.

Aug 94. (7"ep) *(BLUNT 004)* **GETTING THAT JOKE. / GONE / ON A MISSION** [ ] [-]

Paradox / not iss.

Feb 95. (7"colrd-ep/cd-ep) *(PDOX/+D 001)* **SEVEN SISTERS EP** [ ] [-]
– Something new / Fear / They all hate me.

Mar 95. (7"colrd-ep) *(PDOX 002)* **IT MOVED. / GONE / E.T.U.** [ ] [-]
(cd-ep+=) *(PDOXD 002)* – Dweeb king.

May 95. (7"colrd-ep/cd-ep) *(PDOX/+D 004)* **SELF INFLICTION / WANTING IT. / THAT TIRED / KINDA LOSING IT** [ ] [-]

Nov 95. (7"ep/cd-ep) *(PDOX/+D 006)* **FABULAE / IN A CAR. / SPECIAL ONE / STICKS AND STONES** [ ] [-]

Feb 96. (7"ep/cd-ep) *(PDOX/+D 008)* **VEGETABLE ANIMAL MINERAL / ALL WE HAVE TO FEAR IS EACH OTHER. / WE'LL JUST DO IT / T&DA IN WHITE SOCKS** [ ] [-]

Mar 96. (cd/c/lp) *(PDOX CD/MC/LP 003)* **BE SPECIAL** [ ] [-]
– Fabulae / Strikes sparks everywhere / That tired / Said she to me / Bible blackbelt / I cursed you / Nobody home / Another skunk song / Vegetable animal mineral / I don't give in / Are you sure you're alright / Imagine dead language / Rush hour / All gone away. *(re-iss. Aug96; PDOX CD/MC 005)*

— (Jan'96) **CARL ALTY** – drums repl. BUC

May 96. (7") *(PDOX 011)* **ANOTHER SKUNK SONG. / LOST IN TIME** [ ] [-]
(cd-s+=) *(PDOXD 011)* – Lost in time / 50 blanks / More about yerself.

Jul 96. (7"ep/cd-ep) *(PDOX/+D 012)* **RUSH HOUR / WHAT YOU GET. / ANOTHER SKUNK SONG (acoustic) / BIBLE BLACK BELT (acoustic)** [22] [-]
(cd-ep) *(PDOXDX 012)* – ('A'side) / Fabulae (live) / Said she to me (live) / Animal vegetable mineral (live).

Sep 96. (7") *(PDOX 013)* **ALL GONE AWAY. /** [54] [-]
(cd-s+=) *(PDOXD 013)* –
(cd-s) *(PDOXDX 013)* –

A&M / A&M

May 97. (cd/c) *(540740-2/-4)* **SKID SOLO** [ ] [ ]
– Skid solo / Chop logic / What do you think of me / Learn the ropes / Whole reason / Confession / Mongoose / Tonight is stolen / Day in the sun / Growing pains / Hub of the north / Wise is nice / The devil you know / Hit for fun.

JUNE BRIDES

Formed: Coventry, England . . . 1983 out of INTERNATIONAL RESCUE by PHIL WILSON and SIMON BEESLEY, the pair recruiting FRANK SWEENEY, ADE CARTER and BRIAN ALEXIS before any recordings. Influenced initially by JOSEF K, the sextet's sound was also distinguished by the trumpet playing of JON HUNTER. Having signed a deal with Rough Trade offshoot, 'Pink', The JUNE BRIDES released a couple of effervescent indie-pop singles, the second of which, 'EVERY CONVERSATION' stood out. However, a full year passed (during which time CHRIS NINEHAM replaced BRIAN) before the band followed up with their debut 12", a mini-set comprising the aforementioned song and an unusual cover of The Radiators From Space's 'ENEMIES'. Further personnel changes blighted the band's career as PHIL WILSON was left to go it alone following a final couple of 45's. Signing to Alan McGee's 'Creation', WILSON pursued a short-lived solo career and later resurrected The JUNE BRIDES for a brief period in the mid 90's.

Album rating: THERE ARE EIGHT MILLION STORIES mini (*5) / FOR BETTER OR WORSE 1983-1986 compilation (*6)

PHIL WILSON – vocals, guitar / **SIMON BEESLEY** (b. Shrewsbury, England) – guitar, vocals / **FRANK SWEENEY** (b. Lewisham, England) – organ, viola, etc / **JON HUNTER** – trumpet / **ADE CARTER** – bass / **BRIAN ALEXIS** – drums

Pink / not iss.

Jun 84. (7") *(PINKY 1)* **IN THE RAIN. / SUNDAY TO SATURDAY** [ ] [-]

Sep 84. (7") *(PINKY 2)* **EVERY CONVERSATION. / DISNEYLAND** [ ] [-]
(12"ep of above two 45's iss.Apr86; PINKY 9)

— **CHRIS NINEHAM** – drums; repl. BRIAN

— FRANK left to join The RINGING (who also comprised of his brother NICK, plus JENNY BENWELL, DIRK HIGGINS and CHRIS BLAWAT), releasing one single early '85, 'CAPRICE' / 'DOCTOR' for 'Pinky' *(PINKY 3)*. FRANK subsequently formed YEAH JAZZ.

Sep 85. (m-lp) *(PINKY 5)* **THERE ARE EIGHT MILLION BRIDES** [ ] [-]
– Every conversation / Enemies / Sick tired and drunk / Sunday to Saturday / Have you heard / Instrumental.

— **MARTIN PINK** – drums (of BATFISH BOYS) repl. CHRIS

In-Tape / not iss.

Nov 85. (7") *(IT 024)* **NO PLACE LIKE HOME. / WE BELONG** [ ] [-]
(12"+=) *(ITT 024)* – On the rocks / Josef's gone.

May 86. (7"m/12"m) *(IT/+T 030)* **THIS TOWN. / COLD / JUST THE SAME** [ ] [-]

— they split after above with most going into session work

– compilations, etc. –

Apr 87. (12"ep) *Strange Fruit; (SFPS 023)* **PEEL SESSIONS** (22/10/85) [ ] [-]
– This town / Waiting for a change / We belong / One day.

Jan 95. (cd) *Overground; (OVER 40CD)* **FOR BETTER OR WORSE (1983-1986)** [ ] [-]

PHIL WILSON

— went solo

Creation / not iss.

Feb 87. (7") *(CRE 036)* **WAITING FOR A CHANGE. / EVEN NOW** [ ] [-]
(12"+=) *(CRE 036T)* – A cowboy's lament.
(d7"+=) *(CRE 036D)* – Down in the valley / Love in vain.

Jun 87. (7") *(CRE 046)* **TEN MILES. / JINGLE** [ ] [-]
(12"+=) *(CRE 046T)* – Jackson.

Caff / not iss.

1989. (ltd-7") *(CAFF 3)* **BETTER DAYS. / YOU WON'T SPEAK** [ ] [-]

— PHIL retired from the indie limelight until a brief JUNE BRIDES reformation in the mid 90's

JUSTIFIED ANCIENTS OF MU MU (see under ⇒ KLF)

KALIMA (see under ⇒ A CERTAIN RATIO)

KANTE

Formed: Hamburg, Germany . . . mid 90's by a quintet which numbered SEBASTIAN VOGEL. Sharing some members with the equally obscure band, BLUMFELD (two albums, 'ISCH MASCHINE' for 'Cargo' 2915-2 in October '94 & 'LETAT AT MOI' for 'Big Cat' ABB 73/+CD in February '95), they played conventional instruments with an electronic feel, merging political lyrics with CAN, TORTOISE and STEREOLAB-esque soundscapes. It was no surprise when their first release was a cover of Gang Of Four's, 'AT HOME HE FEELS LIKE A TOURIST', almost a year passing before the appearance of a bonafide debut album, 'ZWEISCHEN DEN ORTEN' (1998).

Album rating: ZWEISCHEN DEN ORTEN (*6)

PETER THIESSEN – vocals, guitar / **FELIX MULLER** – guitar / **MICHAEL BUGMANN** – keyboards / **ANDREAS KRANE** – bass / **SEBASTIAN VOGEL** – drums

Kitty-Yo | Kitty Hawk

Nov 97. (7") *(KITTY 013)* **AT HOME HE FEELS LIKE A TOURIST. /** [ ] [-]
Oct 98. (cd/lp) *(<EFA 55207-2/-1>)* **ZWEISCHEN DEN ORTEN** [ ] [ ] Jul99
– Tourisme / Paradizer / California / Technique du sport / Anatomie / Highway / Gospel.

Mick KARN (see under ⇒ JAPAN)

Edward KA-SPEL (see under ⇒ LEGENDARY PINK DOTS)

KENICKIE

Formed: Tyne & Wear, Sunderland, England . . . August '94 by songwriters JOHNNY XAVERRE and MARIE DU SANTIAGO, along with LAUREN LE LAVERNE (JOHNNY's younger sister) and EMMY-KATE MONTROSE. After releasing two indie 7"er's, the second being, 'COME OUT 2NITE', in early '96 on the influential 'Fierce Panda' label. Their fusion of radical punk-pop and femme-power endeared them to 'Creation', KENICKIE subsequently turning their noses up at the offer in favour of a more lucrative deal with 'Emidisc'. This shrewd move paid off with a Top 50 hit, 'PUNKA', re-issued a year later when it fared a little better. In fact, 1997 saw KENICKIE become regular chart fixtures with no less that two Top 30 hits, 'IN YOUR CAR' and 'NIGHTLIFE', plus a Top 10 album, 'AT THE CLUB'. • **Covers:** SAVE YOUR KISSES FOR ME (Brotherhood Of Man).

Album rating: AT THE CLUB (*6)

LAUREN LE LAVERNE – vocals, guitar, keyboards, etc / **MARIE DU SANTIAGO** – lead guitar, vocals, keyboards / **EMMY-KATE MONTROSE** – bass, vocals, keyboards, trumpet / **X** (b. JOHNNY XAVERRE) – drums, keyboards, percussion

Slampt Underground | not iss.

Jun 95. (7"ep) *(SLAMPT 31)* **CATSUIT CITY EP** [ ] [-]

Fierce Panda | not iss.

Feb 96. (7"ep) *(NING 16)* **THE SKILLEX EP** [ ] [-]
– They come out 2nite / How I was made / etc.

Emidisc | Warners

Sep 96. (c-s/7") *(TC+/DISC 001)* **PUNKA. / COWBOY SONG** [43] [-]
(cd-s+=) *(CDDISC 001)* – Drag race / Walrus.
Nov 96. (c-s/7") *(TC+/DISC 002)* **MILLIONAIRE SWEEPER. /** [60] [-]
(cd-s) *(CDDISC 002)* – ('A'side) / Perfect plan / Kamikaze Annelids / Girl's best friend.
Jan 97. (7") *(DISC 005)* **IN YOUR CAR. / CAN I TAKE U 2 TO THE CINEMA?** [24] [ ]
(cd-s+=) *(CDDISCX 005)* – I'm an agent.
(cd-s) *(CDDISC 005)* – ('A'side) / Private Buchowski / Killing fantasy.
Apr 97. (7") *(DISC 006)* **NIGHTLIFE. / "J-P"** [27] [ ]
(cd-s+=) *(CDDISCX 006)* – Eat the angel.
(cd-s) *(CDDISC 006)* – ('A'side) / Kenix / Skateboard song.
May 97. (cd/c) *(7243-8-56147-2/-4)* *<46552>* **AT THE CLUB** [9] [ ]
– In your car / People we want / Spies / How I was made / Brother John / Millionaire sweeper / Robot song / Classy / Punka / Nightlife / P.V.C. / Come out 2nite / I never complain / Acetone.
Jun 97. (7"pic-d) *(DICS 007)* **PUNKA. / LIGHT OUT IN A PROVINCIAL TOWN** [38] [-]
(7") *(DISC 007)* – ('A'side) / Waste you.
(cd-s) *(CDDISC 007)* – (3 tracks above).
(cd-s) *(CDDISCS 007)* – ('A'side) / Brighter shade of blue / We can dream.

E.M.I. | Imprint

May 98. (c-s) *(TCEM 513)* **I WOULD FIX YOU. / ROUGH BOYS & MODERN GIRLS / I WOULD FIX YOU (Mint Royale mix)** [36] [-]
(cd-s) *(CDEM 513)* – (first 2 tracks) / ('A'-DJ Downfall mix).
(cd-s) *(CDEMS 513)* – (first & third tracks) / Packed in.
Aug 98. (7") *(EM 520)* **STAY IN THE SUN. / HOORAY FOR EVERYTHING** [43] [-]
(c-s+=) *(TCEM 520)* – Save your kisses for me.
(cd-s+=) *(CDEM 520)* – ('A'-Fridge remix).
(cd-s) *(CDEMS 520)* – ('A'side) / ('A'-Maxwell Implosion Influenza mix) / Save your kisses for me.
Aug 98. (cd/c) *(495851-2/-4)* *<113438>* **GET IN** [32] [ ]
– Stay in the sun / Lunch at Lassiters / I would fix you / 60's bitch / Run me over / And that's why / Magnatron / Weeknights / Psychic defence / 5 a.m. / 411 (la la la) / Something's got to give. *(cd+=)* – Disco Xmas on the dole.

KEPONE

Formed: Richmond, Virginia, USA . . . early 90's by the imposingly bearded MICHAEL BISHOP, along with TIM HARRISS and SETH HARRIS, taking the group name from a dangerous chemical manufactured by a local firm (previously detailed by musical mentor JELLO BIAFRA on The DEAD KENNEDYS' 'Kepone Factory'). Signed to noted US indie label, 'Quarter Stick', the band premiered their blend of idiosyncratic yet powerful mutant punk-blues on the debut album, 'UGLY DANCE' (1994). Like a downhome JESUS LIZARD, they flavoured their music and especially their lyrics with a Deep South small-town weirdness. Now without SETH – who was replaced by EDWARD JEFFERSON TRASK – KEPONE issued a second set, 'SKIN' (1995), which was followed by 1997's acclaimed eponymous album.

Album rating: UGLY DANCE (*6) / SKIN (*6) / KEPONE (*7)

MICHAEL BISHOP – vocals, bass / **TIM HARRISS** – guitar, vocals / **SETH HARRIS** – drums

Tenderizer | Tenderizer

Jun 93. (7") *(TZR 002)* **HENRY. /** [ ] [-]

not iss. | Alternative Tentacles

Dec 93. (7") *<VIRUS 144>* **295. / PHOBIC** [-] [ ]

Quarter Stick | Quarter Stick

Aug 94. (lp/cd) *<(QS 27/+CD)>* **UGLY DANCE** [ ] [ ]
– Loud / Dickie boys / Leadbreath / Brainflower / Some pig / Henry / Shit talk / Fly bop / Wrong / Eenie meenie / Sick river / Silly Sally / Ugly dance.

—— **EDWARD JEFFERSON TRASK** – drums; repl. SETH

Sep 95. (lp/cd) *<(QS 33/+CD)>* **SKIN** [ ] [ ] Aug95
– Knifethrower / Velveteen / Blue-devil / Stay down / Ed's sad party / Idiot ball drop / Superfucker / Prisoners / Left Eskimo / Thin solution.
Sep 96. (7") *(QS 45)* **THE GHOST. / DANGERMANE** [ ] [-]
Apr 97. (cd) *<(QS 46CD)>* **KEPONE** [ ] [ ] Mar97
– Bring it down / Joe / Pointless / Ghost / Liner hymn / Thaw/ Clicking jam / Leave your bones / I am an alien / Slow build / Jimmy Spit / Scrub / Virginia creeper / Dead pop ideal.

Tara KEY (see under ⇒ ANTIETAM)

Steve KILBEY (see under ⇒ CHURCH)

KILBURN & THE HIGH ROADS (see under ⇒ DURY, Ian)

David KILGOUR (see under ⇒ CLEAN)

KILLDOZER

Formed: Madison, Wisconsin, USA . . . 1986 by brothers BILL and DAN HOBSON alongside MICHAEL GERALD. Politically aware punks with an acute sense of humour/observation and a penchant for gritty country, KILLDOZER made their debut in 1984 with the wonderfully titled mini-set, 'INTELLECTUALS ARE THE SHOESHINE BOYS OF THE RULING ELITE'. Subsequently picked up by Chicago's 'Touch & Go' label, the band ran off a series of BUTCH VIG-produced records – 'SNAKEBOY' (1986), 'BURL' (1987) and 'LITTLE BABY BUNTIN' (1988) – exploring the backwoods mentality of rural America from differing narrative perspectives. Occasionally unsettling and often highly amusing, the band's lyrical caricatures were put on hold for 1989's 'FOR LADIES ONLY', wherein the boys KILLDOZER-ed their way through a selection of prime 70's FM rock classics. Following the release of '12 POINT BUCK' later that year, the band entered a period of instability as BILL departed due to family commitments. After periods of sporadic touring, KILLDOZER finally re-emerged – complete with new guitarist, PAUL ZAGORES – in 1994 with 'UNCOMPROMISING WAR ON ART UNDER THE DICTATORSHIP OF THE PROLETARIAT'. While the latter set revisited the political sentiments of the band's debut, 1995's STEVE ALBINI-produced 'GOD HEARS PLEAS OF THE INNOCENT' and 1997's 'THE LAST WALTZ' saw the band bow out with some of the most skull-crushing music of their career. • **Covered:** FUNK #49 (James Gang) / CINNAMON GIRL (Neil Young) / RUN THROUGH THE JUNGLE (John Fogerty) / AMERICAN PIE (Don McLean) / GOOD LOVIN GONE BAD (Bad Company) / TAKE THE MONEY AND RUN (Steve Miller Band) / HUSH (Joe South) / EVERY CHRISTIAN HEARTED MAN WILL (Bee Gees) / CONQUISTADOR (Procol Harum) / AQUARIUS – LET THE SUNSHINE IN (Fifth Dimension) / POUR MAN (Lee Hazlewood) / WHEN THE LEVEE BREAKS + NO QUARTER + HOT DOG (Led Zeppelin) / etc.

Album rating: INTELLECTUALS ARE THE SHOESHINE BOYS OF THE RULING ELITE (*5) / SNAKEBOY (*5) / BURL mini (*5) / LITTLE BABY BUNTIN' (*6) / FOR LADIES ONLY (*7) / 12 POINT BUCK (*7) / UNCOMPROMISING WAR ON ART UNDER THE DICTATORSHIP OF THE PROLETARIAT (*6) / GOD HEARS PLEAS OF THE INNOCENT (*7) / THE LAST WALTZ (*5)

MICHAEL GERALD – vocals, bass / **DAN HOBSON** – guitar / **BILL HOBSON** – drums

not iss. | Bone Air

1984. (m-lp) **INTELLECTUALS ARE THE SHOESHINE BOYS OF THE RULING ELITE** [-] [ ]
– Man of meat! / Pile driver! / Parade! / Farmer Johnson! / Ed Gein! / A man's gotta be a man . . .! / Dead folks! / Run through the jungle! *(re-iss. Oct89 on 'Touch & Go' lp/cd+=; T&G LP/CD 47)* – SNAKEBOY

Touch & Go | Touch & Go

Aug 86. (lp) *(T&GLP 6)* **SNAKEBOY** [ ] [ ] 1985
– King of sex / Going to the beach / River / L.Y.L.L.Y.D.E. / Don't cry / Cinnamon girl / Gone to Heaven / Revelations / Burning house.

1987. (m-lp) *(T&GLP 17)* **BURL** [ ] [ ] 1986
– Hamburger martyr / Cranberries / Slackjaw / Hot n' tot / One for the people / I'm not Lisa.

Mar 88. (lp) *(T&GLP 26)* **LITTLE BABY BUNTIN'** [ ] [ ] 1987
– Little Baby Buntin' / Cotton bolls / The puppy / Hi there / Ballad of my old man / The rub / 3/4 inch drill bit / I am I said / Cyst / Never gave me a kiss / The noble art of self defence.

Apr 89. (lp-ltd.) *(T&GLP 39)* **FOR LADIES ONLY** [ ] [ ]
– Hush / Good lovin' gone bad / Burnin' love / You've never been this far before / One tin soldier / Take the money and run / American pie / Funk #49 . *(re-iss. Sep90 lp/c/cd/pic-lp/pic-cd; T&GLP 39/+C/CD/PD/CP)*

Sep 89. (12"ep) *<T&G 44>* **YOW EP** [-] [ ]

Nov 89. (lp/cd) *(T&G LP/CD 48)* **TWELVE POINT BUCK** [ ] [ ] 1988
– Twelve point buck / New pants and shirt / Space 1999 / Lupus / Richard / Man versus nature / Gates of Heaven / Pigfoot and bear / Seven thunders / Free love in Amsterdam / Ted Key beef. *(cd+=)* – LITTLE BABY BUNTIN'

— **PAUL ZAGORAS** – guitar; repl. GERALD who took accountancy exams until he returned in '93

Mar 94. (lp/c/cd) *<(TG 82/+C/CD)>* **UNCOMPROMISING WAR ON ART UNDER THE DICTATORSHIP OF THE PROLETARIAT** [ ] [ ]
– Final market / Knuckles the dog (who helps people) / Turkey shoot / Grandma Smith said a curious thing / Hot 'n' nasty / Peach pie / Enemy of the people / Earl Scheib / Das kapital / The pig was cool / Working hard, or hardly working?

Sep 94. (12") *<TG 122>* **THE PIG WAS COOL. /** [-] [ ]

Feb 95. (lp/cd) *<(TG 139/+CD)>* **GOD HEARS PLEAS OF THE INNOCENT** [ ] [ ]
– A mother has a hard road / Porky's dead / Pour man / The buzzard / Paul doesn't understand jazz / Daddy's boy / The Nobbies (a sea chanty) / Big song of Hell / Cannonball run II '95 / I have seen grown men cry / Spork.

May 96. (7"ep/cd-ep; with ALICE DONUT) *<(TG 146/+CD)>* **MICHAEL GERALD'S PARTY MACHINE EP** [ ] [ ] Apr96
– Every Christian lion hearted man will / Conquistador / Medley: Aquarius – Let the sunshine in.

Man's Ruin | Man's Ruin

Sep 96. (12"ep) *<(MR 007)>* **WHEN THE LEVEE BREAKS. / NO QUARTER / HOT DOG** [ ] [ ]

Aug 97. (7") *(ISM 27V)* **GO BIG RED. /** [ ] [-]
(above issued on 'Ismist')

Sep 97. (cd) *<(MR 065CD)>* **THE LAST WALTZ** [ ] [ ]
– Porky's dad / The nobbies / Man of meat / I've seen grown men cry / A mother's road / Space: 1999 / Richard / A Xmas song / Knuckles the dog / Cannonball run III '97 / Mama's boy / Way down in old Alabam' / Songs for grand folks.

KILLING JOKE

Formed: Notting Hill, London, England . . . 1979 by JAZ COLEMAN and PAUL FERGUSON, who subsequently added GEORDIE (K. WALKER) and YOUTH (MARTIN GLOVER). After borrowing money to finance a debut EP (contained three tracks including 'TURN TO RED'), the band were the subject of some interest to DJ John Peel who championed their alternative rock sound. This immediately led to KILLING JOKE signing a deal with 'Island', who virtually re-issued the aforementioned single/EP in abbreviated 7" form (A-side, 'NERVOUS SYSTEM'), adding a fourth track on the 12". While supporting the likes of JOY DIVISION and The RUTS, they released a follow-up double A-sided single, 'WARDANCE' / 'PSYCHE', resurrecting their own 'Malicious Damage' label in the process. The left-field 'E.G.' operation were quick to spot the group's potential, taking on both KILLING JOKE and their label. The first results of this partnership came in the form of 'REQUIEM', the single taken from their pioneering eponymous UK Top 40 album. Replacing the anger of punk with apocalyptic doom mongering, KILLING JOKE were akin to a sonically disturbing, industrialised BLACK SABBATH. Now regarded as a catalystic classic in metal circles, the album also inspired many US hardcore acts, as well as such big guns as METALLICA, MINISTRY, SOUNDGARDEN and NIRVANA. By the release of follow-up set, 'WHAT'S THIS FOR' (1981), KILLING JOKE had taken their occult punk-like chants/anthems to extreme new dimensions. Nevertheless, they retained a strange accessiblity which saw the single, 'FOLLOW THE LEADERS' attaining a minor UK chart placing and incredibly, a hit on the American dancefloors! A third set, 'REVELATIONS' (1982), eased up a little on the intensity factor, although it peaked at No.12 having already spawned another hit single, 'EMPIRE SONG'. Convinced of imminent world destruction, the occult-fixated COLEMAN remained in Iceland after a tour, YOUTH initially returning home but later following his lead to the frozen north. He subsequently flew back to England, teaming up with FERGUSON and newfound friend, PAUL RAVEN to form BRILLIANT. However, both FERGUSON and RAVEN soon departed from YOUTH's group, taking off for Iceland in search of the missing COLEMAN. Eventually locating their frontman, all three returned to UK shores and re-entered the studio (GEORDIE also in tow) with a view to recording new KILLING JOKE material. The resulting album, 'FIRE DANCES' (1983), only managed to scrape into the Top 30, its lack of bite and experimentation possibly a hangover from their northern treks. The following year, KILLING JOKE released only two 45's, although one of them, 'EIGHTIES' (a minor hit), was showcased in all it's eccentric glory on Channel 4's new pop show, 'The Tube'. Having overcome the mental obstacle of 1984 (and all of its apocalyptic implications), COLEMAN and Co. unleashed their most focused work to date in 'NIGHT TIME' (a near Top 10 album), the 'LOVE LIKE BLOOD' single preceding the set and breaking into the Top 20 in early '85. The latter half of the eighties weren't so kind, both critically and commercially, the albums, 'BRIGHTER THAN A THOUSAND SUNS' (1986) and 'OUTSIDE THE GATE' (1988), taking a more self-indulgent keyboard-orientated approach. Following major personnel upheavals, KILLING JOKE decided to take a brief sabbatical, COLEMAN finding time to release a collaborative album with ANNE DUDLEY (ex-ART OF NOISE), 'SONGS FROM THE VICTORIOUS CITY' (1990). The same year, COLEMAN, GEORDIE, RAVEN and newcomer MARTIN ATKINS, returned with the acclaimed 'EXTREMITIES, DIRT AND VARIOUS REPRESSED EMOTIONS' album. Having spent most of the early 90's globetrotting in various exotic locations, KILLING JOKE (now COLEMAN, GEORDIE and the returning YOUTH), were back with a vengeance on 1994's 'PANDEMONIUM'. Their biggest selling album to date, the record and the 'PANDEMONIUM' single from it, both making the Top 30 (the previous 'MILLENIUM' made Top 40), while also seeing an American release on the 'Zoo' label. Another, increasingly metallic/industrial set, 'DEMOCRACY' followed in 1996, although COLEMAN now spends the bulk of his time in New Zealand, where he is composer in residence for the country's Symphony Orchestra.

Album rating: KILLING JOKE (*9) / WHAT'S THIS FOR . . .! (*7) / REVELATIONS (*5) / HA! KILLING JOKE LIVE (*5) / FIRE DANCES (*7) / NIGHT TIME (*7) / BRIGHTER THAN A THOUSAND SUNS (*6) / OUTSIDE THE GATE (*6) / EXTREMITIES, DIRT AND VARIOUS REPRESSED EMOTIONS (*7) / LAUGH? I NEARLY BOUGHT ONE! compilation (*8) / PANDEMONIUM (*8) / DEMOCRACY (*6)

JAZ COLEMAN (b. JEREMY, 26 Feb'60, Cheltenham, England; raised Egypt) – vocals, keyboards / **GEORDIE** (b. K.WALKER, 18 Dec'58, Newcastle-upon-Tyne, England) – guitar, synthesizers / **YOUTH** (b. MARTIN GLOVER, 27 Dec'60, Africa) – bass, vocals (ex-RAGE) / **PAUL FERGUSON** (b.31 Mar'58, High Wycombe, England) – drums

Malicious Damage | not iss.

Oct 79. (10"ep) *(MD 410)* **ARE YOU RECEIVING ME. / TURN TO RED / NERVOUS SYSTEM** [ ] [-]

Island | not iss.

Nov 79. (7") *(WIP 6550)* **NERVOUS SYSTEM. / TURN TO RED** [ ] [-]
(12"+=) *(12WIP 6550)* – Almost red / Are you receiving me.

Malicious Damage | not iss.

Mar 80. (7") *(MD 540)* **WARDANCE. / PSYCHE** [ ] [-]

E.G. – Malicious Damage | Editions

Sep 80. (7") *(EGMD 1.00)* **REQUIEM. / CHANGE** [ ] [-]
(12"+=) *(EGMX 1.00)* – Requiem 434 / Change (version).

Oct 80. (lp/c) *(EGMD/+C 545)* **KILLING JOKE** [39] [-]
– Requiem / Wardance / Tomorrow's world / Bloodsport / The wait / Complications / S.O. 36 / Primitive. *(re-iss. Jan87 lp/c/cd; EG LP/MC/CD 57) <US cd-iss. 1987 on 'Caroline'; 1538>*

May 81. (7") *(EGMDS 1.01)* **FOLLOW THE LEADERS. / TENSION** [55] [-]
(10"+=) *(EGMDX 1.010)* – Follow the leaders – dub.

Jun 81. (lp/c) *(EGMD/+C 550) <111>* **WHAT'S THIS FOR . . .!** [42] [ ]
– The fall of Because / Tension / Unspeakable / Butcher / Follow the leaders / Madness / Who told you how? / Exit. *(re-iss. Jan87 lp/c/cd; EG LP/MC/CD 58) <US cd-iss. 1987 on 'Caroline'; 1539>*

E.G. | Caroline

Mar 82. (7") *(EGO 4)* **EMPIRE SONG. / BRILLIANT** [43] [-]

— **GUY PRATT** – bass; repl. YOUTH who formed BRILLIANT

Apr 82. (lp/c) *(EGMD/+C 3)* **REVELATIONS** [12] [-]
– The hum / Empire song / We have joy / Chop chop / The Pandys are coming / Chapter III / Have a nice day / Land of milk and honey / Good samaritan / Dregs. *(re-iss. Jan87 lp/c/cd; EG LP/MC/CD 59) <US cd-iss. 1987 on 'Caroline'; 1540>*

Jun 82. (7") *(EGO 7)* **CHOP CHOP. / GOOD SAMARITAN** [ ] [-]

Oct 82. (7") *(EGO 10)* **BIRDS OF A FEATHER. / FLOCK THE B-SIDE** [64] [-]
(12"+=) *(EGOX 10)* – Sun goes down.

Nov 82. (10"m-lp/m-c) *(EGMD T/C 4)* **HA – KILLING JOKE LIVE (live)** [66] [-]
– Psyche / Sun goes down / The Pandys are coming / Take take take / Unspeakable / Wardance.

— **PAUL RAVEN** – bass (ex-NEON HEARTS) repl. PRATT who joined ICEHOUSE

Jun 83. (7") *(EGO 11)* **LET'S ALL GO (TO THE FIRE DANCES). / DOMINATOR (version)** 51 -
(12"+=) *(EGOX 11)* – The fall of Because (live).

Jul 83. (lp/c) *(EGMD/+C 5)* **FIRE DANCES** 29 -
– The gathering / Fun and games / Rejuvenation / Frenzy / Harlequin / Feast of blaze / Song and dance / Dominator / Let's all go (to the fire dances) / Lust almighty. *(re-iss. Jan87 lp/c/cd; EG LP/MC/CD 60) <US cd-iss. 1987 on 'Caroline'; 1541>*

Oct 83. (7") *(EGOD 14)* **ME OR YOU?. / WILFUL DAYS** 57 -
(with free 7") *(KILL 1-2)* – ('A'side) / Feast of blaze.
(d12"++=) *(EGOXD 14)* – Let's all go (to the fire dances) / The fall of Because (live) / Dominator (version).

Mar 84. (7") *(EGO 16)* **EIGHTIES. / EIGHTIES (Coming mix)** 60 -
(12"+=) *(EGOX 16)* – ('A'-Serious dance mix).

Jun 84. (7") *(EGO 17)* **A NEW DAY. / DANCE DAY** 56 -
(12"+=) *(EGOX 17)* – ('A'dub).

Jan 85. (7") *(EGO 20)* **LOVE LIKE BLOOD. / BLUE FEATHER** 16 -
(12"+=) *(EGOY 20)* – ('A'-Gestalt mix).
(12"++=) *(EGOX 20)* – ('A'instrumental).

Feb 85. (lp/c) *(EGMD/+C 6) <1531>* **NIGHT TIME** 11
– Night time / Darkness before dawn / Love like blood / Kings and queens / Tabazan / Multitudes / Europe / Eighties. *(re-iss. Jan87 lp/c/cd; EG LP/MC/CD 61)*

Mar 85. (7") *(EGO 21)* **KINGS AND QUEENS. / THE MADDING CROWD** 58 -
(12"+=) *(EGOX 21)* – ('A'-Right Royal mix).
(12"+=) *(EGOY 21)* – ('A'-Knave mix).

Aug 86. (7") *(EGO 27)* **ADORATIONS. / EXILE** 42 -
(d7"+=) *(EGOD 27)* – Ecstacy / ('A'instrumental).

E.G. Virgin

Oct 86. (7") *(EGO 30)* **SANITY. / GOODBYE TO THE VILLAGE** 70 -
(free c-s with-7") *(above tracks)* – Wardance (remix).
(12"+=) *(EGOX 30)* – Victory.

Nov 86. (lp/c/cd) *(EG LP/MC/CD 66) <90568-1/-4/-2>* **BRIGHTER THAN A THOUSAND SUNS** 54
– Adorations / Sanity / Chessboards / Twilight of the mortal / Love of the masses / A southern sky / Wintergardens / Rubicon. *(c+=/cd+=)* – Goodbye to the village / Victory.

E.G. Caroline

Apr 88. (7") *(EGO 40)* **AMERICA. / JIHAD (Beyrouth edit)** -
(12"+=) *(EGOX 40)* – ('A'extended).
(cd-s++=) *(EGOCD 40)* – Change (original 1980 mix).

Jun 88. (lp/c/cd) *(EG LP/MC/CD 73) <1378>* **OUTSIDE THE GATE** 92
– America / My love of this land / Stay one jump ahead / Unto the ends of the Earth / The calling / Obsession / Tiahuanaco / Outside the gate. *(cd+=)* – America (extended) / Stay one jump ahead (extended).

Jul 88. (7") *(EGO 43)* **MY LOVE OF THIS LAND. / DARKNESS BEFORE DAWN** -
(12"+=) *(EGOX 43)* – Follow the leaders (dub) / Psyche.
(10"+=) *(EGOT 43)* – Follow the leaders (dub) / Sun goes down.

— **JAZ + GEORDIE** brought in new members **MARTIN ATKINS** (b. 3 Aug'59, Coventry, England) – drums (ex-PUBLIC IMAGE LTD.) repl. FERGUSON / **TAFF** – bass repl. ANDY ROURKE (ex-SMITHS) who had repl. RAVEN. Early 1990, **JAZ COLEMAN** teamed up with ANNE DUDLEY (see; ART OF NOISE)

— **KILLING JOKE** reformed (**COLEMAN, GEORDIE, ATKINS + RAVEN**)

Noise Int. R.C.A.

Nov 90. (cd/c/lp) *(AGR 054-2/-4/-1) <4828-2/-4>* **EXTREMITIES, DIRT AND VARIOUS REPRESSED EMOTIONS**
– Money is not our god / Age of greed / Beautiful dead / Extremities / Inside the termite mound / Intravenus / Solitude / North of the border / Slipstream / Kalijuga struggle.

Jan 91. (12"/cd-s) *(AG 054-6/-3)* **MONEY IS NOT OUR GOD. / NORTH OF THE BORDER** -

Invisible Invisible

Jul 93. (d-lp) *(<INV 004>)* **THE COURTHOLD TALKS**
– (spoken word with JAZ, GEORDIE & JAFF SCANTLEBURY on percussion)

— **YOUTH** returned to repl. RAVEN

— **GEOFF DUGMORE** – drums (ex-ART OF NOISE) repl. ATKINS (to PIGFACE, etc)

Butterfly Volcano-Zoo

Mar 94. (10"ep/cd-ep) *(BFL T/D 11)* **EXORCISM. / ('A'live) / ('A'-German mix) / WHITEOUT (Ugly mix) / ANOTHER CULT GOES DOWN (mix) / ('A'-Bictonic revenge mix)** -

Apr 94. (7"clear/c-s) *(BFL/+C 12)* **MILLENIUM. / ('A'-Cybersank remix)** 34 -
(12"+=/cd-s+=) *(BFL T/D 12)* – ('A'-Drum Club remix) / ('A'Juno Reactor remix).

Jul 94. (12"/c-s/cd-s) *(BFL T/C/D 17) <14178>* **PANDEMONIUM. / ('A'mix)** 28 Oct94
(cd-s) *(BFLD 17)* – ('A'side) / Requiem (Kris Weston & Greg Hunter remix).

Jul 94. (cd/c/d-lp) *(BFL CD/MC/LP 9) <31085>* **PANDEMONIUM** 16 Aug94
– Pandemonium / Exorcism / Millenium / Communion / Black Moon / Labyrinth / Jana / Whiteout / Pleasures of the flesh / Mathematics of chaos.

— re-united originals **JAZ COLEMAN / GEORDIE + YOUTH**

Jan 95. (cd-ep) *(BFLDA 21)* **JANA (Youth remix) / JANA (Dragonfly mix) / LOVE LIKE BLOOD (live) / WHITEOUT** 54 -
(12"ep/cd-ep+=) *(BFL T/DB 21)* – Jana (live) / Wardance (live) / Exorcism (live) / Kings and queens (live).

Mar 96. (cd-s) *(BFLDA 33) <34262>* **DEMOCRACY / DEMOCRACY (Rooster mix by Carcass) / MASS** 39
(cd-s) *(BFLDB 33)* – ('A'-United Nations mix) / ('A'-Russian tundra mix) / ('A'-Hallucinogen mix).

Apr 96. (cd/c) *(BFL CD/MC 17) <31127>* **DEMOCRACY** 71
– Savage freedom / Democracy / Prozac people / Lanterns / Aeon / Pilgrimage / Intellect / Medicine wheel / Absent friends / Another bloody election.

– compilations, etc. –

on 'Virgin' unless mentioned otherwise

Sep 92. (12"/c-s) *(VST/VSC 1432)* **CHANGE. / REQUIEM** -
(cd-s) *(VSCDT 1432)* – ('A'spiral tribe mix). / ('B'trash Greg Hunter mix).
(cd-s) *(VSCDX 1432)* – ('A'-Youth mix). / ('B'-Youth mix).

Oct 92. (cd/c) *(CDV/TCV 2693) / Caroline; <1596>* **LAUGH? I NEARLY BOUGHT ONE!**
– Turn to red / Psyche / Requiem / Wardance / Follow the leaders / Unspeakable / Butcher / Exit / The hum / Empire song / Chop-chop / The Sun goes down / Eighties / Darkness before dawn / Love like blood / Wintergardens / Age of greed.

May 95. (cd) *(CDOVD 440) / Caroline; (1884>* **WILFUL DAYS** (remixes)

Oct 95. (cd) *Windsong; (WINCD 068)* **BBC LIVE IN CONCERT (live)** -

Apr 98. (12") *Dragonfly; <48>* **LOVE LIKE BLOOD. / INTELLECT** -

Aug 98. (cd) *Imprint; <114151>* **WAR DANCE** (remix album) -

KILLJOYS

Formed: Stoke, England . . . 1977 by main writer, KEVIN ROLAND (aka ROWLAND, i.e. future lead singer for DEXY'S MIDNIGHT RUNNERS), alongside HEATHER TONGE, MARK PHILLIPS, GEM STONE (later bass player of GIRLSCHOOL) and JOE 45 (apparently, only half the man of puppet, JOE 90!). The KILLJOYS managed only one blasting raw punk anthem, 'JOHNNY WON'T GET TO HEAVEN' (a prophetic tale for JOHNNY ROTTEN!), before all but KEVIN disappeared from punk's underground limelight. However, an "oi" crew formed another KILLJOYS (not this lot!) for a one-off single, 'THIS IS NOT LOVE', late in 1982.

Album rating: NAIVE mini compilation (*4)

KEVIN ROLAND – vocals / **GEM (STONE)** – bass / **HEATHER TONGE** – vocals / **MARK PHILLIPS** – guitar / **JOE 45** – drums

Raw not iss.

Nov 77. (7") *(RAW 3)* **JOHNNY WON'T GET TO HEAVEN. / NAIVE** -

— they split for a long period while KEVIN advanced his DEXY's career

— GEM joined RUBELLA BALLET and later GIRLSCHOOL

– compilations, etc. –

May 92. (m-lp) *Damaged Goods; (FNARRLP 10)* **NAIVE** -

— Note: another KILLJOYS (not this one!) issued an album for 'Mushroom'.

James KING

Born: Glasgow, Scotland. KING first came to the attention of the public when his "hardman" persona, JIMMY LOSER, played guitar for punk combo, the REV VOLTING BACKSTABBERS. This group subsequently evolved into FUN 4 (alongside REV THOMAS, COLIN McNEIL and STEVEN DALY), finally issuing their debut EP, 'SINGING IN THE SHADOWS', at the turn of the decade. In 1981, with DALY now an ORANGE JUICE recruit, KING was signed to 'Virgin', although only two singles made it to release stage. Rumours were rife (at the time) that KING had once allegedly pulled a knife on a young EDWYN COLLINS, normal practice for an up and coming bovver boy you could say; KING's guitarist, JAMES MASON (no, not the actor!), also allegedly spent some time in jail. Now competing with the likes of LLOYD COLE & THE COMMOTIONS, JAMES KING & THE LONE WOLVES embarked on their own mid-80's mission to make the charts. Unfortunately, after only a couple of singles, 'TEXAS LULLABY' and 'THE ANGELS KNOW', KING split the group up.

Album rating: never released any

JAMES KING – guitar / **REV THOMAS** – vocals / **COLIN NEIL** – bass / **STEVEN DALY** – drums

N.M.C. not iss.

Jan 80. (7"ep; as FUN 4) *(NMC 010)* **SINGING IN THE SHADOWS EP** -
– Singing in the shadows / Elevator crash / By products.

— **KING** – (now on vocals & guitar) + **NEIL** recruited **JAMES MASON** – guitar / **FRASER SCOTT** – drums

Virgin not iss.

Feb 81. (7") *(VS 405)* **BACK FROM THE DEAD. / MY REWARD / AS TEARS GO BY** -

Oct 81. (7"; as JAMES KING & THE LONE WOLVES) *(VS 454)* **I TRIED. / SO ALONE** -

— **MICK + JAKE** repl. JAMES MASON (to jail) + FRASER SCOTT

Thrush not iss.

Nov 83. (12"ep; as JAMES KING & THE LONE WOLVES) *(THRUSH 2)* **TEXAS LULLABY EP** -
– Texas lullaby / Sacred heart / Chance I can't deny / Until the dawn / Lost.

Swamplands not iss.

Jan 85. (7"; as JAMES KING & THE LONE WOLVES) *(SWP 3)* **THE ANGELS KNOW. / DON'T CARE IF YOU LIVE OR DIE** -
(12"+=) *(SWX 3)* – Ready to fall.

Expansion not iss.

Jun 87. (7") *(EXPAND 8)* **EASY LOVE. / HEARTBREAK, SORROW AND PAIN** -

Apr 88. (12") *(EXPAND 12)* **STORYTELLER (dance mix). / STORYTELER (version)** -

— retired from his solo career after above (a different JAMES KING released stuff on 'Rounder' in the mid-90's)

KING BISCUIT TIME (see under ⇒ BETA BAND)

KING BLANK (see under ⇒ LOWERY, Ian)

KINGMAKER

Formed: Hull, England . . . late 1990 by ex-TOMBSTONE GRAFFITI members, LOZ HARDY (the main songwriter) and MILES HOWELL. Subsequently recruiting JOHN ANDREW, the band made their vinyl debut with the 'CELEBRATED WORKING MAN' EP, released on their own 'Sacred Heart' label. Impressive enough to get the band signed to 'Chrysalis'-offshoot, 'Scorch', the record was followed by a 7", 'WHEN LUCY'S DOWN' and another EP, 'TWO HEADED, YELLOW BELLIED HOLE DIGGER', prior to a debut album, 'EAT YOURSELF WHOLE' (1991). While the band initially found favour with the press, KINGMAKER subsequently became an easy target for critical hatchet-jobs on the premise that they represented all that was ordinary about indie-pop. Not that the band suffered too much as a result, their natural constituency of WONDER STUFF/CARTER USM-type fans not likely to pay too much attention to journalistic snobbery. Early '92 saw KINGMAKER bag their first Top 40 hit while the debut's title track made the Top 20 six months later, follow-up album, 'SLEEPWALKING' (1993) finding HARDY's lyrical invective as succinct and razor sharp as it had ever been. A further two minor hits followed in 'QUEEN JANE' and 'SATURDAY'S NOT WHAT IT USED TO BE' but KINGMAKER's star eventually faded with the onset of Brit-pop in the mid-90's. While Spring '95's 'YOU AND I WILL NEVER SEE THINGS EYE TO EYE' scraped a Top 40 placing, the accompanying album, 'IN THE BEST POSSIBLE TASTE', sank like a stone and KINGMAKER finally called it a day later that year. • **Covered:** LADY MADONNA (Beatles).

Album rating: EAT YOURSELF WHOLE (*7) / SLEEPWALKING (*6)

LOZ HARDY (b.LAWRENCE, 14 Sep'70) – vocals, guitar / **MILES HOWELL** (b.23 Jan'71, Rugby, England) – bass (ex-RAIN) / **JOHN ANDREW** (b.27 May'63, Hull, England) – drums

Sacred Heart — not iss.

Jan 91. (12"ep) *(NONE 1)* **THE CELEBRATED WORKING MAN / LITTLE MISS KINGMAKER. / FREEWHEELIN' / POCKETS OF ST.MALACHI** [ ] [-]
(re-iss. Feb92; same)

Scorch – Chrysalis — Chrysalis

Apr 91. (c-s/7") *(TC+/SCORCH 1)* **WHEN LUCY'S DOWN. / WHERE YOU STAND** [ ] [-]
(12"+=/cd-s+=) *(12/CD SCORCH 1)* – High as a kite / Join the human race.

Aug 91. (12"ep/cd-ep) *(12/CD SCORCH 2)* **TWO HEADED, YELLOW BELLIED HOLE DIGGER. / THIS TIME THIS TOWN THIS SEA. / WONDERFUL GARDEN / POCKETS OF ST. MALACHI (live)** [ ] [-]

Sep 91. (cd/c/lp) *(<CCD/ZCHR/CHR 1878>)* **EAT YOURSELF WHOLE** [69] [ ]
– Revelation / Really scrape the sky / Two headed, yellow bellied hole digger / Hard times / Loveless-defamed / When Lucy's down / Wave / Lady Shakespeare's bomb / Everything in life / High as a kite. *(re-dist.Feb92)* – hit No.29

Jan 92. (7"ep) *(SCORCH 3)* **IDIOTS AT THE WHEEL EP** [30] [-]
– Really scrape the sky / Every teenage suicide / Strip away.
(12"ep+=/cd-ep+=) *(12/CD SCORCH 3)* – Revelation (Bombay mix).

Mar 92. (12"ep/cd-ep; w-drawn) *(12/CD SCORCH 4)* **KILLJOY WAS HERE EP** [-] [-]
– Eat yourself whole / Highway's gate / Pyjama girl.

May 92. (c-s/7") *(TC+/SCORCH 5)* **EAT YOURSELF WHOLE. / PYJAMA GIRL** [15] [-]
(12"+=/cd-s+=) *(12/CD SCORCH 5)* – Highway's gate.

Oct 92. (12"ep/cd-ep/7"ep) *(12/CD+/SCORCH 6)* **ARMCHAIR ANARCHIST / EVERYTHING'S CHANGED (SINCE YOU'VE BEEN TO LONDON). / KISSING UNDER ANAESTHETIC** [47] [-]

Apr 93. (c-ep/7"ep) *(TC+/SCORCH 8)* **10 YEARS ASLEEP. / BROADMOOR HOTEL / DON'T COME OVER / I'M IN LOVE** [15] [-]
(cd-ep) *(CDSCORCH 8)* – ('A'side) / Genuine liar / Lady Madonna / When Lucy's down (live).
(cd-ep) *(CDSCORCHS 8)* – ('A'side) / Shiver / High as a kite (live) / Hard times (live).

May 93. (cd/c/lp) *(<CD/TC+/CHR 6014>)* **SLEEPWALKING** [15] [ ]
– Playground reality / Armchair anarchist / Queen Jane / Sad to see you go / Help yourself / Tomorrow's world / 10 years asleep / Honesty kills / Sequinned thug / Sleepwalking in the five o'clock shadow / Stay free / Pyromaniacs anonymous.

Jun 93. (7"/7"s) *(SCORCH/+P 9)* **QUEEN JANE. / SICK AND ANGRY CHILDREN** [29] [-]
(12"+=) *(12SCORCH 9)* – Flesh phobia / Sequinned thug ('92 version).
(cd-s) *(CDSCORS 9)* – ('A'side) / Your place / Electric Sue.
(cd-s) *(CDSCORCH 9)* – ('A'side) / No way out / Sequinned thug ('92 version).

Oct 93. (cd-ep) *(CDSCORCH 10)* **SATURDAY'S NOT WHAT IT USED TO BE / ARMCHAIR ANARCHIST (live) / HIGHWAY'S GATE (live) / FREEWHEELIN' (live)** [63] [-]
(10") *(10SCORCH 10)* – (1st track) / Eat yourself whole (live) / Everything's changed (since you've . . .) (live) / Every teenage suicide (live).

Nov 93. (m-cd/m-c/m-lp) *(CD/TC+/CHR 6055)* **TO HELL WITH HUMDRUM** (part compilation) [ ] [-]
– Saturday's not what it used to be / Never too high to fall / Lies before kisses / Loose lips sink ships / Ten years asleep / Honesty kills / Sleepwalking (in the five o'clock shadow) / Queen Jane.

Apr 95. (c-s) *(TCSCORCH 11)* **YOU AND I WILL NEVER SEE THINGS EYE TO EYE / BITCH OF A SON / YOU OF ALL PEOPLE** [33] [-]
(cd-s) *(CDSCORCH 11)* – ('A'side) / When Lucy's down / Queen Jane / Saturday's not what it used to be.
(cd-s) *(CDSCORCHS 11)* – ('A'side) / Friends in low places / S*T*A*R / Warm heart, cold feet.

Apr 95. (cd/c/lp) *(<CD/TC+/CHR 6098>)* **IN THE BEST POSSIBLE TASTE** [ ] [ ]
– In the best possible taste (part 2) / You and I will never see things eye to eye / Hey, birdman / Frustrated gangster / Story of my life / Sometimes I think she takes me along just for the ride / One false move / Side by side / A fool like you / End of the line / In the best possible taste (part 1).

May 95. (7"pink) *(SCORCHS 12)* **IN THE BEST POSSIBLE TASTE (part 2). / AMATEUR'S LULLABY / IF YOU WERE MINE** [41] [-]
(cd-s) *(CDSCORCH 12)* – ('A'side) / Two headed yellow bellied hole digger / Sad to see you go / Never too high to fall.
(cd-s) *(CDSCORCHS 12)* – ('A'side) / Backroom boys / Another bad dose of home truths / Dissatisfaction guarenteed.

— split October 1995

– compilations, etc. –

Sep 98. (cd) *EMI Gold; (CDCHRM 104)* **BLOODSHOT & FANCY FREE (THE BEST OF & THE REST OF KINGMAKER)** [ ] [-]
– 10 years asleep / Armchair anarchist / Really scrape the sky / You and I will never see things eye to eye / Hard times / Two headed yellow bellied hole digger / Freewheeling / Everything's changed (since you've been to London) / Queen Jane / When Lucy's down / In the best possible taste / High as a kite / Frustrated gangster / In the best possible taste / Honesty kills / Don't come over.

KING MISSILE

Formed: New York, USA . . . 1987 by wordsmith/poet/singer, JOHN S. HALL. A mainstay of NY's Lower East Side "anti-folk" scene, HALL began putting his crazed poetical mutterings to music with the addition of guitarist DOGBOWL and his girlfriend, REBECCA KORBETT (on the drumstool). Also roping in the services of harmonica player, ALEX DeLASZLO, HALL secured a deal with 'Shimmy Disc' and recorded a KRAMER-produced debut album, 'FLUTING ON THE HUMP' (1987). This was released under the moniker, KING MISSILE – DOG FLY RELIGION, as was the following year's set, 'THEY', a more musically adventurous opus that saw STEPHEN DANZIGER replace KORBETT. Further personnel shuffles (DAVD RICK replaced DOGBOWL while CHRIS XEFOS was added on bass) were effected prior to the release of 'MYSTICAL SHIT' (1989), a record that benefitted from the beefed-up alt-rock backing and featured the college-rock minor-classic, 'JESUS WAS WAY COOL'. Subsequently securing a deal with 'Atlantic', KING MISSILE aimed straight at the heart of the alternative market with major label debut, 'THE WAY TO SALVATION' (1992), another entertaining selection of surreal vignettes including 'THE BOY WHO ATE LASAGNE AND COULD JUMP OVER A CHURCH' and a tribute to that great land of heather 'n' haggis, 'SCOTLAND'. 1993's 'HAPPY HOUR', meanwhile, featured such toilet humour fantasies as 'THE VULVAVOID' and 'DETACHABLE PENIS', the latter scaling the college charts to bring KING MISSILE their closest brush with fame. A Daniel Ray-produced follow-up failed to build on this success and HALL subsequently put the band on hold before re-emerging on 'Shimmy Disc' as KING MISSILE III with the string-enhanced 'FAILURE'.

Album rating: FLUTING ON THE HUMP (*6) / MYSTICAL SHIT (*6) / REAL MEN (by JOHN S. HALL with KRAMER; *6) / THE WAY TO SALVATION (*6) / HAPPY HOUR (*6) / KING MISSILE (*6)

JOHN S. HALL – vocals / **DOGBOWL** – guitars / **ALEX DeLASZLO** – harmonica / **REBECCA KORBETT** – percussion

Shadowline — Shimmy Disc

Dec 87. (lp; as KING MISSILE – DOG FLY RELIGION) *(SR 6987) <SHIMMY 003>* **FLUTING ON THE HUMP** [ ] [ ]
– Love you more / Fourthly / Lou / At Dave's / Muffy / Take stuff from work / Sensitive artist / Wuss / Heavy holy man / Fluting on the hump / Dick / That old dog.

— **STEVE DANZIGER** – percussion; repl. REBECCA

Shimmy Disc — Shimmy Disc

Nov 88. (lp; as KING MISSILE – DOG FLY RELIGION) *(SHIMMY 015) <SDE 9023>* **THEY** [ ] [ ]
– Now / I'm open / Mr. Johnson / She had nothing / He needed / The love song / Margaret's eyes / The bunny song / The blood song / Stonehenge / They / When she closed her eyes / Hemopheliac of love / The box / Fish / Leather clown / WW3 is a giant ice cream cone / Farm / As I walked thru queens / Hey Jesus / If only / Double fucked by 2 black studs.

— In '89, the departing DOGBOWL issued his solo debut, 'Tit! An Opera'. Two years later, he made another, 'Cyclops Nuclear Submarine Captain'.

— added **DAVE RICK** – guitar (ex-BONGWATER) / **CHRIS XEFOS** – multi (of WHEN PEOPLE WERE SHORTER)

Feb 90. (lp) *<SDE 9016LP>* **MYSTICAL SHIT** [ ] [ ]
– Mystical shit / Rock'n'roll will never die / No point / Gary and Melissa / Frightened and freezing / How to remember your dreams / The fish that played the ponies / Jesus was way cool / Open / The sandbox / The neither world / She didn't want / Cheesecake truck / Equivalencies.

Atlantic — Atlantic

Aug 91. (12") *<85974>* **MY HEART IS A FLOWER. /** [-] [ ]

Mar 92. (cd/c/lp) *<(7567 82208-2/-4/-1)>* **THE WAY TO SALVATION** [ ] [ ]
– The way to salvation / Life / The boy who ate lasagna & could jump over a church / The story of Willy / Dinosaurs / I wish / The Indians / It's / My heart is a flower / Pickaxe / Sex with you / art two / Betrayal takes two / Listen to me / Come closer / Scotland / To walk among the pigs.

Feb 93. (cd/c) *<(7567 82589-2/-4)>* **HAPPY HOUR**
– Sink / Martin Scorcese / (Why are we) Trapped? / It's Saturday / The vulvavoid / Metanoia / Detachable penis / Take me home / Ed / Anywhere / The evil children / Glass / And / King Murdoch / I'm sorry / Happy hour.

Jun 94. (cd) *<(7567 82589-2)>* **KING MISSILE**
– Love is / Let's have sex / Pigs will fly / Tongue / The dishwasher / Bloodletting / Socks / King David's dirge / What if / These people / Open up / Wind up toys / Delores / Lies / The commercial / Psalm / Happy note.

— split but reformed as KING MISSILE III:- **HALL / + SASHA FORTE** – vocals, guitar, violin, viola, bass, bells / **BRADFORD REED** – vocals, multi / **JANE SCARPANTONI** – cello, synthesizer / **CHARLES CURTIS** – vocals, guitar, cello

Shimmy Disc | Shimmy Disc

Sep 98. (cd-s) **GAY – NOT GAY! /**

Oct 98. (cd) *<(SHM 5090)>* **FAILURE** — Sep98
– Failure / The boy made out of bone China / A good hard look / Up my ass / The little sandwich that got a guilt complex because he was the sole survivor of a horrible bus crash / Despair / Monks / Gay – Not gay / Happiness / Mr. Pomerantz / Juniper dog / Tour diary: Louisville / The adventures of Planky / I dare to hope.

KING OF THE SLUMS

Formed: Salford, Manchester, England ... mid 80's by writer/poet, CHARLEY KEIGHER along with electric violinist, SARAH CURTIS. The duo made their vinyl debut around Xmas '86 with the independently released 'SPIDER PSYCHIATRY', subsequently spending the following year locating a solid rhythm section and finally settling on JON CHANDLER and STUART OWEN (the latter replacing a succession of drummers after their early 1988 second EP, 'ENGLAND'S FINEST HOPES'). All the aforementioned tracks along with early 89's single and EP package, 'BOMBS AWAY ON HARPURHEY' and 'VICIOUS BRITISH BOYFRIEND', were collected together on that year's debut long-player, 'BARBAROUS ENGLISH FAYRE'. Avant-garde but danceable, the focal point of this unorthodox alternative act was KEIGHER's scathing lyrical diatribes against the British establishment and its inherent racism, class divide and nationalistic bent. Having already taken on a new bass and drum team of ADAM and CHARLIE, KEIGHER and CURTIS added guitarist GARY SPARKES and yet another bassist, JAMES CASHAN prior to the release of a debut album proper, 'DANDELIONS' (1989). Undergoing yet more personnel upheaval as PETE MASON replaced SPARKES, the band would move from 'Midnight Music' to 'Cherry Red' for what would turn out to be their swansong offering, 'BLOWZY WEIRDOS' (1991).

Album rating: BARBAROUS ENGLISH FAYRE (*6) / DANDELIONS (*6) / BLOWZY WEIRDOS (*5)

CHARLIE KEIGHER – vocals / **SARAH CURTIS** – electric violin

S.L.R. | not iss.

Dec 86. (7"m) *(SLR 001)* **SPIDER PSYCHIATRY. / THE LODGE / LOSING GROUND** — -

— added **JON CHANDLER** – bass / drummers in the 80's; **TREVOR RISING, ROSS CAIN + GED O'BRIEN**

Play Hard | not iss.

Feb 88. (12"ep) *(DEC 88)* **ENGLAND'S FINEST HOPES** — -
– The Pennine splitter / England's leading light / Venerate me utterly / Bedevilment's favourite son.

— **STUART OWEN** – drums (now more permanent)

Jan 89. (7") *(DEC 13)* **BOMBS AWAY ON HARPURHEY. / BIG GIRL'S BLOUSE** — -

Feb 89. (12"ep) *(DEC 14)* **VICIOUS BRITISH BOYFRIEND** — -
– Fanciable headcase / Leery bleeder / Hardcore pornography star / Bombs away on Harpurhey.

— new rhythm for '89 **ADAM + CHARLIE**

Jun 89. (lp) *(DEC 22)* **BARBAROUS ENGLISH FAYRE** — -
– Simpering blonde bombshell / Bombs away on Harpurhey / England's leading light / Mere slip of a lad / The Pennine splitter / Up to the fells / Full speed ahead / Venerate me utterly / Bedevilment's favourite son / Leery bleeder / Fanciable headcase / Hardcore pornography star. *(re-iss. Jan91 on 'Midnight Music' lp/cd; CHIME 109/+CD)*

— **JAMES CASHAN** – bass; repl. CHANDLER

— added **GARY SPARKES** – guitar

Midnight Music | not iss.

Oct 89. (7") *(DING)* **ONCE A PERFECT. / ?** — -
(12"+=) *(DONG)* –

Nov 89. (lp/c/cd) *(CHIME 104/+C/CD)* **DANDELIONS** — -

— **PETE MASON** – guitar; repl. SPARKES

Jul 90. (7"one-side) *(DING 63)* **IT'S DEAD SMART** — -
(12+=) *(DONG 63)* –

Sep 90. (7") *(DING)* **BEAR WIV ME. / ?** — -
(12"+=) *(DONG)* –

Cherry Red | not iss.

May 91. (cd/lp) *(CD+/BRED 93)* **BLOWZY WEIRDOS** — -
– Gone all weirdo / Smile so big / Casin' the joint / Hot pot shebeen / Keeping it all sweet / Clubland gangs / Joy / Rimo / Hard arse / Mood on / Blowzy luv of life. *(cd+=)* – Casin' the joint (rollin') / Gone all weirdo (reaper mix) / Joy (skunkweed) / Smiles (big smiles mix).

— split later in 1991

KING PRAWN

Formed: East London, England . . . 1995 by AL-FARABI RUMJEN, ARYAN DEVIL, BABAR LUCK and SLUGBOYE. Their debut album, 'FIRST OFFENCE', was produced by SKUNK ANANSIE's ACE, apparently for free. A manic burst of speedball hardcore with a list of diverse influences as long as your arm (er, DEAD KENNEDYS to RAGE AGAINST THE MACHINE), the KING PRAWN sound was developed over a series of 7" singles culminating with a second long-player, 'FRIED IN LONDON' (1998). Known to dislike each other . . . immensly! • **Covered:** BIG A LITTLE A (Crass).

Album rating: FIRST OFFENCE (*5) / FRIED IN LONDON (*5)

AL-FARABI RUMJEN – vocals / **ARYAN DEVIL** – guitar / **BABAR LUCK** – bass / **NICK 'SLUG' SWINDONBOYE** – drums

Word Of Warning | Word Of Warning

Nov 95. (7") *(WOW 45)* **POISON ON THE AIR. /** — -
(cd-s+=) *(WOWCD 45)* –

Jun 96. (cd) *(WOWCD 46)* **FIRST OFFENCE** — -

Jun 97. (7") *(WOW 52)* **DEPTHS OF MY SOUL. / FELLED** — -

Nov 97. (7") *(WOW 53)* **NOT YOUR PUNK. / BIG A LITTLE A** — -
(cd-s+=) *(WOW 53CD)* – Ruthless.

Apr 98. (cd) *(<WOWCD 54>)* **FRIED IN LONDON** — Jul98
– Sound of we / Not your punk / Felled / Increase the pressure / Role model / Racist copper / Survive / Depths of my soul / Clocked / Rewards and prizes / Last request.

KINKY MACHINE (see under ⇒ RIALTO)

Richard H. KIRK (see under ⇒ CABARET VOLTAIRE)

KITCHENS OF DISTINCTION

Formed: Tooting Broadway, London, England . . . 1986 by the multicultural trio of PATRICK FITZGERALD, JULIAN SWALES and DANIEL GOODWIN. Named after a "fitted kitchen" ad slogan, this bunch achieved almost instantaneous acclaim when their self-financed debut single, 'LAST GASP DEATH SHUFFLE', was awarded an NME Single Of The Week award. Acclaimed for their innovative amalgam of indie guitar strumming, pre-shoegazing effects and dub-style dynamics, The KITCHENS continued to impress with a further two singles, 'THE PRIZE' and 'THE THIRD TIME WE OPENED THE CAPSULE' and a debut album, 'LOVE IS HELL' (1989) via a deal with Derek Birkett's (ex-FLUX OF PINK INDIANS) 'One Little Indian' label. Much was made of FITZGERALD's openly homosexual lyrical stance, hardly a common topic of discussion in indie/alternative circles, at least not since the heyday of TOM ROBINSON. Whether this affected the band's popularity is a moot point but there was no question that column inches weren't being matched by record sales despite another fine release in the 'ELEPHANTINE' EP. The trio's cult ascendancy slowed considerably with follow-up album, 'STRANGE FREE WORLD' (1991), a minor chart placing as near to mainstream success as The KITCHENS would ever come. Moreover, by the release of 1992's 'THE DEATH OF COOL', the band's dark appeal had become slightly diluted with an overblown, almost U2-esque "big rock" sound. Wider recognition was looking as unlikely as ever, 'One Little Indian' bailing out after 'COWBOYS AND ALIENS' (1994). Scaling down their ambitions, the band subsequently clipped their moniker to KITCHENS OD and signed to hip indie label, 'Fierce Panda', for a one-off single, 'FEEL MY GENIE'.

Album rating: LOVE IS HELL (*7) / STRANGE FREE WORLD (*8) / THE DEATH OF COOL (*7) / COWBOYS AND ALIENS (*6)

PATRICK FITZGERALD (b. 7 Apr'64, Basel, Switzerland) – vocals / **JULIAN SWALES** (b.23 Mar'64, Gwent, Wales) – guitar / **DANIEL GOODWYN** (b.22 Jul'64, Salamanca, Spain) – drums (ex-AR KANE)

Goldrush | not iss.

Oct 87. (7") *(GRR 3)* **ESCAPE. / THE LAST GASP DEATH SHUFFLE** — -

One Little Indian | A&M

Oct 88. (12"ep) *(12 TP12)* **THE PRIZE. / CONCEDE / INNOCENT** — -

May 89. (12"ep) *(19 TP12)* **THE THIRD TIME WE OPENED THE CAPSULE / 4 MEN. / INTO THE SEA / THE PRIZE (demo)** — -

May 89. (lp/c/cd) *(TP LP/C/CD 9) <540098-2>* **LOVE IS HELL**
– In a cave / Time to groan / Shiver / Prize / The 3rd time we opened the capsule / Her last day in bed / Courage, mother / Mainly mornings / Hammer.

Oct 89. (12"ep/cd-ep) *(29 TP 12/7CD)* **ELEPHANTINE / MARGARET'S INJECTION. / THE 1000st FAULT / ANVIL DUB** — -

Apr 90. (12"ep/cd-ep) *(43 TP 12/7CD)* **QUICK AS RAINBOWS. / MAINLY MORNINGS (live) / IN A CAVE (live) / SHIVER** — -

Feb 91. (12"ep/cd-ep) *(49 TP 12/7CD)* **DRIVE THIS FAST / THESE DRINKERS. / ELEPHANTLY / THREE TO BEAM UP** — -

Mar 91. (cd/c/lp) *(TP CD/C/LP 19) <5340>* **STRANGE FREE WORLD** 45
– Railwayed / Quick as rainbows / Hypnogogie / He holds her, he needs her / Polaroids / Gorgeous love / Aspray / Drive that fast / Within the days of passion / Under the sky, inside the sea.

May 92. (12"ep) *(59 TP12)* **BREATHING FEAR / GOODBYE VOYAGER. / SMILING / WHEN IN HEAVEN** — -
(12"/cd-s) *(59 TP 12/CD)* – (first two tracks) / Skin (instrumental) / Air shifting (instrumental).

Aug 92. (lp/c/cd) *(TPLP 39/+C/CD) <5402>* **THE DEATH OF COOL** 72
– What happens now? / 4 men / On Tooting Broadway station / Breathing fear / Gone world gone / When in Heaven / Mad as snow / Smiling / Blue pedal / Can't trust the waves.

Sep 92. (12"ep/cd-ep) *(69 TP 12/7CD)* **WHEN IN HEAVEN / GLITTERY DUST. / DON'T COME BACK / SPACEDOLPHINS** □ -

Sep 94. (c-s/12"/cd-s) *(111 TP 7C/12/7CD)* **NOW IT'S TIME TO SAY GOODBYE. / JESUS NEVADA / WHITE HORSES / WHAT WE REALLY WANTED TO DO** □ -

Sep 94. (lp/c/cd) *(TPLP 53/+C/CD)* <540227> **COWBOYS AND ALIENS** □ □
– Sand on fire / Get over yourself / Thought he had everything / Cowboys and aliens / Come on now / Remember me? / One of these sometimes is now / Here comes the swans / Now it's time to say goodbye / Pierced / Prince of Mars.

Fierce Panda — not iss.

May 96. (7"/cd-s; as KITCHENS O.D.) *(NING 19/+CD)* **FEEL MY GENIE. /** □ -

— subsequently split

KLEENEX

Formed: Geneva, Switzerland . . . 1978 by RAMONA CARLER, MARLENE MARDER, KLAUDI SCHIFF and LISLOT HA. One of the first bands to sign with 'Rough Trade', this highly regarded Euro punk outfit released only two singles, 'AIN'T YOU' and 'HEIDI'S HEAD' before the threat of legal action from the tissue giant of the same name convinced them to adopt the LILIPUT moniker. With the addition of sax, the band's jerky, stop-start chants assumed a new depth and a vaguely X-RAY SPEX/SLITS-like sound, especially on the moody 'DIE MATROSSEN' (the B-side of debut single, 'SPLIT'). A second single, 'EISERGWIND', preceded an eponymous debut set in 1983, yet by the time of the album's release the band had already ceased to exist. A further album, 'SOME SONGS', surfaced as a German-only release later the same year, MARDER subsequently formed DANGER MICE before going on to work in record retail.

Album rating: LILIPUT (compilation (*7)

REGULA SING (b. RAMONA CARLIER) – vocals / **MARLENE MARDER** – guitar / **KLAUDI SCHIFF** – bass, vocals / **LISLOT HA** – drums

Rough Trade — not iss.

Nov 78. (7") *(RT 009)* **AIN'T YOU. / HEIDI'S HEAD** □ -

— **CRIGELE FREUND** – vocals repl. REGULA who joined MO-DETTES

May 79. (7") *(RT 014)* **YOU. / U** □ -

LILIPUT

— added **ANGIE BARRACK** – saxophone

Rough Trade — not iss.

Jun 80. (7") *(RT 047)* **SPLIT. / DIE MATROSEN** □ -

Feb 81. (7") *(RT 062)* **ELSIGER WIND. / WHEN THE CAT'S AWAY, THE MICE WILL PLAY** □ -

— **ASTRID SPIRIT** – vocals, violin, bass, percussion repl. CRIGELE and LISLOT

1982. (lp) *(ROUGH 43)* **LILIPUT** □ -
– Do you mind my dream / In a mess / Birdy / Feel like snakes, twisting / Through the fog / Tschik-Mo / Outburst / Umamm / Might is right / Like it or lump it / Ichor / Tong-tong. *(re-iss. Aug84)*

Jul 83. (7") *(RTD 01)* **YOU DID IT. / THE JAZZ** - - German

— added guest drummer **BEAT SCHLATTER**

Dec 83. (lp) *(RTD 15)* **SOME SONGS** - - German
– Ring-a-ding-dong / A silver key can open an iron lock, somewhere / Yours is mine / Blue is all in rush / Terrified / Etoile / On streets without names / Boat-song / His head all red.

— disbanded after above. MARDER went onto form DANGER MICE who released two singles, 'I HAVE GOT YOU' & 'BROKEN NEW HEART'. She returned to Zurich to run a record shop, while SCHIFF became one of her countries best known modern painters.

– compilations, etc. –

1993. (cd) *Off Course;* **LILIPUT** □ -
– (contains the KLEENEX material)

KLF

Formed: KOPYRIGHT LIBERATION FRONT. Based; London, England . . . 1986 by BILL DRUMMOND and JIM CAUTY. Raised in Clydebank, Scotland, DRUMMOND was already a seasoned music industry veteran when he teamed up with CAUTY, having helped to form the pivotal 'Zoo' label in the late 70's, initially home to such Merseyside legends as TEARDROP EXPLODES and ECHO & THE BUNNYMEN. DRUMMOND also worked as an A&R bod for 'WEA', signing up the band BRILLIANT with whom CAUTY played guitar. Eventually, the pair ditched their existing music industry responsibilities with the intention of subverting the notion of the 'pop star' and began working on their first project, JUSTIFIED ANCIENTS OF MU MU. Under that improbably titled moniker, the pair released their first album, '1987 – WHAT THE FUCK IS GOING ON' (1987), a question one might well have asked oneself in those dark, RICK ASTLEY-dominated days. The JAMS answer was to desecrate the works of such revered musical greats as The BEATLES, LED ZEPPELIN and ABBA, the latter taking great offence to this and demanding that the band destroy the offending copies . . . all 500 of them. The JAMS went on to bigger and better things with their dancefloor-friendly Dr. Who/GARY GLITTER pastiche, 'DOCTORIN' THE TARDIS' (released under The TIMELORDS moniker) at the height of the first house explosion in 1988. The record went to No.1, prompting the group to make their ninth official release a mock-guide book to the music industry, detailing how to make No.1 with the minimum of effort. Next was the pair's most famous incarnation as the KLF, DRUMMOND and CAUTY experimenting with house and ambient music to create a string of tracks that were massive club hits as well as Top 5 singles, at the turn of the decade. 'WHAT TIME IS LOVE?', 'LAST TRAIN TO TRANSCENTRAL' and '3 A.M. ETERNAL' were all collected on 'THE WHITE ROOM' (1991) album, the latter single even reaching the US Top 5 in 1990. The album went to No.3 in Britain, becoming a consistent seller until the band deleted it the following year. A fertile period for the KLF, the outfit also released the highly regarded ambient album, 'CHILL OUT' (1990), while CAUTY played a major part in the formation of The ORB. Taking the opportunity to resurrect the JAMMS, the duo released 'IT'S GRIM UP NORTH', a hilarious run through of dismal English towns, as well as roping in TAMMY WYNETTE for an improbable duet on 'JUSTIFIED AND ANCIENT (STAND BY THE JAMMS)'. While the single was a massive cross-Atlantic hit, the lines were becoming blurred as to who was taking the piss out of who. But the KLF had yet to play their trump card, and after a suitably overwrought version of 'WHAT TIME IS LOVE' went Top 5, they decided enough was enough and set out to sabotage the success they'd created. Invited to play at the annual Brit awards ceremony in 1992, the KLF proceeded to obliterate 'WHAT TIME IS LOVE' with the help of hardcore punk/thrash merchants 'EXTREME NOISE TERROR'. The numerous rumours about the duo mutilating a dead sheep on stage never materialised although they created enough of a furore to keep the press speculating for weeks. A couple of months later the duo announced that the KLF was officially no more, the back catalogue promptly deleted. CAUTY and DRUMMOND subsequently turned their guerilla tactics on the art world, and under the guise of the mysterious K Foundation, awarded Rachel Whitehead a £40,000 prize for the worst art piece of the year. The Foundation's shortlist for the prize was identical to that of the shortlist for the Turner prize, an annual award for the best piece of non-mainstream art which Whiteread had also scooped. The K Foundation further bemused a sceptical art world when they exhibited £1,000,000 in banknotes, profits from their hit making which they nailed to a board for a private viewing. CAUTY and DRUMMOND then made the most radical statement of their career and one of the most radical "art" statements in history when they literally torched the money in a farmhouse on a remote Scottish island, even filming the event for posterity. Roundly condemned as a highly irresponsible waste of cash that could have been donated to charity etc, etc, the questions that the duo raised were predictably ignored. More recently, CAUTY was allegedly cautioned by police after scaring cows with high freqency electronic sound waves (!), while the duo contributed a suitably bizarre track to the 1995 'HELP' Warchild charity album. The K Foundation also released a single, 'F**K THE MILLENIUM', in late '97, asking people to phone in and cast their 'vote' on the matter.

Album rating: SHAG TIMES (*6) / THE WHITE ROOM (*8)

JUSTIFIED ANCIENTS OF MU MU

(aka J.A.M.M.s) **KING BOY D** (aka BILL DRUMMOND) (b.29 Apr'53, Butterworth, South Africa) – synths (ex-BIG IN JAPAN, ex-LORI & THE CHAMELEONS) / **ROCKMAN ROCK** (aka JIM CAUTY) (b.1954) – guitar (ex-BRILLIANT, etc.)

KLF Comm. — not iss.

May 87. (one-sided-12") *(JAMS 23)* **ALL YOU NEED IS LOVE** □ -
(12"+=) *(JAMS 23T)* – Ivum naya / Rap, rhyme and scratch yourself.
(7") *(JAMS 23s)* – ('A'-Me Ru Con mix) / ('A'-Ibo version).

Jun 87. (lp; w-drawn) *(JAMS LP1)* **1987 (WHAT THE FUCK IS GOING ON?)** - -

Sep 87. (one-sided-12") *(JAMS 24T)* **WHITNEY JOINS THE JAMS (120 bpm)** - - Scots

Nov 87. (12") *(JAMS 25T)* **1987 – THE 45 EDITS** □ -
– (excerpts from the unissued lp)

Dec 87. (12") *(JAMS 27)* **DOWN TOWN (A-side mix). / DOWN TOWN (B-side mix)** □ -
(above also available as 2 one-sided-12"; same)
(7"/ext.12") *(JAMS 27 s/T)* – Down town (118 bpm) / Down town.

Dec 87. (12"; as DISCO 2000) *(D 2000)* **I GOTTA CD. / I LOVE DISCO 2000** □ -

Feb 88. (lp) *(JAMS LP2)* **WHO KILLED THE JAMS?** □ -
– The candy store / The candy man / Disaster fund collection / King boy's dream / The porpoise song / The Prestwich prophet's grin / Burn the bastards. *(w/ free KLF 1987 COMPLETIST LIST discography; KLF 001)*

Mar 88. (export-12"ep) *(JAMS 26T)* **BURN THE BEAT EP** - -
– Burn the bastards / Burn the beat (I) / Prestwich prophet's grin (dance mix 90 bpm) / The porpoise song (dance mix 114 bpm).

Mar 88. (one-sided-12"grey) *(JAMS 28T)* **IT'S GRIM UP NORTH** □ -

K.L.F.

— just a justified change of name

KLF Comm. — TVT

Mar 88. (7") *(KLF 002)* **BURN THE BEAT (II). / THE PORPOISE SONG** □ -
(12") *(KLF 002T)* – ('A'side) / Burn the bastards.

Apr 88. (12"; as DISCO 2000) *(D 2002)* **ONE LOVE NATION. / ('A'edit) / ('A'instrumental)** □ -

May 88. (7"/7"sha-pic-d; as TIMELORDS) *(KLF 003 s/P)* <4025> **DOCTORIN' THE TARDIS. / ('A'-minimal version)** 1 66 Nov88
(12"+=) *(KLF 003T)* – ('A'club version).
(video-cd-s++=) *(KLFCD 003)* – ('A'-video mix).
(12"+=) *(KLF 003R)* – ('A'-with Gary Glitter).

Jan 89. (7"; as DISCO 2000) *(D 2003)* **UPTIGHT (EVERYTHING'S ALRIGHT (Banana 2000 mix). / MR. HOTTY LOVES YOU (edit)** ☐ –
(12") *(D 2003)* – ('A'-discorama mix) / ('B'side).

—— JIM CAUTY released eponymous album under **SPACE** banner mid-1990 on 'Space-Rough Trade'; *LP/CD 1.*

Jun 89. (12") *(KLF 004T)* **WHAT TIME IS LOVE? (trance). / ('A'mix 2)** ☐ –
(12") *(KLF 004R)* – ('A'-primal remix) / ('A'-Techno slam) / ('A'-Trance mix).

Sep 89. (12") *(KLF 005T)* **3 A.M. ETERNAL. / ('A'-Break for love mix) / ('A'-Pure trance mix)** ☐ –
(remix.12") *(KLF 005R)* – ('A'original) / ('A'-Blue Danube Orbital mix) / ('A'-Moody Boy mix).

Oct 89. (lp/cd) *(JAMS LP/CD 4)* **THE WHAT TIME IS LOVE STORY** ☐ –
– What time is love? (original) / Relax your body / What time is love? (Italian) / Heartbeat / No limit (dance mix) / What time is love? (live at the Land of Oz).

Dec 89. (12"; not issued) *(KLF 008R)* **LAST TRAIN FROM TRANCENTRAL** – –

Mar 90. (cd/lp) *(JAMS CD/LP 5)* **CHILL OUT** ☐ –

Jul 90. (7"/ext.12") *(KLF 010 s/PT)* **KYLIE SAID TO JASON. / KYLIE SAID TRANCE** ☐ –
(cd-s+=) *(KLF 010CD)* – Madrugaral eternal.

—— added **MAXINE HARVEY** – vocals

KLF | Arista

Aug 90. (7"/12"/c-s) *(KLF 004/+X/C)* **WHAT TIME IS LOVE (live at Trancentral). / ('A'-Techno gate mix)** 5 ☐
(12") *(KLF 004P)* – ('A'side) / ('A'-Wandafull mix).
(cd-s) *(KLF 004CD)* – ('A'radio) / ('A'side) / ('A'-Trance).
(remix.12") *(KLF 004Y)* – ('A'-Moody Boys vs. the KLF) / ('A'-Echo & The Bunnymen mix) / ('A'-Virtual reality mix).

Jan 91. (7"/12"/c-s) *(KLF 005 R/X/C)* *<2230>* **3 A.M. ETERNAL (live at SSL). / ETERNAL (GUNS OF MU MU)** 1 5 Jun91
(12"+=/cd-s+=) *(KLF 005 Y/CD)* – ('A'-Break for love mix).

Mar 91. (cd/c/lp) *(JAMS CD/MC/LP 6)* *<8657>* **THE WHITE ROOM** 3 39 Jun91
– What time is love? / Make it rain / 3 a.m. eternal (live at the S.S.L.) / Church of the KLF / Last train to Transcentral / Build a fire / The white room / No more tears / Justified and ancient.

Apr 91. (7"/12"/c-s) *(KLF 008/+X/C)* **LAST TRAIN TO TRANSCENTRAL. / THE IRON HORSE** 2 ☐
(12"+=) *(KLF 008T)* – Live from the Lost Continent.
(cd-s++=) *(KLF 008CD)* – ('A'-Pure trance version '89).

Oct 91. (c-s,cd-s) *<2365>* **WHAT TIME IS LOVE? / BUILD A FIRE** – 57

Nov 91. (7"/12"/c-s; as JUSTIFIED ANCIENTS OF MU MU) *(JAMS 028/+T/C)* **IT'S GRIM UP NORTH. / (part 2)** 10 ☐
(cd-s+=) *(JAMS 028CD)* – Jerusalem on the Moors.

Nov 91. (7"/c-s; as The KLF featuring THE FIRST LADY OF COUNTRY: TAMMY WYNETTE) *(KLF 099/+C)* *<12401>* **JUSTIFIED AND ANCIENT (STAND BY THE JAMS). / ('A'original version)** 2 11 Jan92
(12"+=/cd-s+=) *(KLF 099 T/CD)* – Let them eat ice-cream / Make mine a 99 / All bound for Mu Mu land (with MAXINE).

Jan 92. (7"/c-s) **P.O. 3 A.M. ETERNAL / ('A'-Guns of MuMu mix)** ☐ –
(12"+=/cd-s+=) – ('A'diff.versions).

Feb 92. (7"/c-s) *(KLFUSA 004/+C)* *<12366>* **AMERICA: WHAT TIME IS LOVE. / AMERICA NO MORE** 4 ☐
(12"+=/cd-s+=) *(KLFUSA 004 T/CD)* – (other 'A'mixes).

—— both now used KLF as art movement, causing controversy with their large inner city billboards nearly gaining Turner prize. Late in 1993, they collaborated on EXTREME NOISE TERROR version of '3 A.M. ETERNAL'.

– compilations, etc. –

Jan 89. KLF; (d-lp/cd; as JUSTIFIED ANCIENTS OF MU MU) *(DLP/DCD 3)* **SHAG TIMES** ☐ –
– All you need is love / Don't take five (take what you want) / Whitney joins the JAMS / Downtown / Candyman / Burn the bastards / Doctorin' the tardis / 114 BPM / 90 BPM / 118 BPM / 125 BPM / 120 BPM / 118 BPM / 120 BPM (all releases, from all aliases)

BILL DRUMMOND

Creation | not iss.

Nov 86. (lp) *(CRELP 014)* **THE MANAGER** ☐ –
– True to the trail / Ballad for a sex god / Julian Cope is dead / I want that girl / Going back / Queen of the south / I believe in rock'n'roll / Married man / I'm the king of joy / Son of a preacher man / Such a parcel of rogues in a nation. *(re-iss. Sep90 lp/c/cd; CRE LP/C/CD 14)*

Mar 87. (12") *(CRE 039T)* **KING OF JOY. / THE MANAGER** ☐ –

KMFDM

Formed: Germany . . . 1984 by the trio of EN-ESCH, SASCHA KONIETZKO and NAINZ WATTS. KMFDM (which apparently stands for KEIN MEHRHEIT FUR DIE MITLEID – No Majority For Compassion) were one of the pioneers of the mid-80's hardbeat/industrial revolution that swept Europe and threw up acts like FRONT 242, YOUNG GODS and NITZER EBB. Following an eponymous German-only debut album and its follow-up, 'WHAT DO YOU KNOW, DEUTSCHLAND?', the group became part of the burgeoning 'Wax Trax!' stable, the tastemakers of the US industrial scene and home to MINISTRY, REVOLTING COCKS, etc. The late 80's also saw the appearance of two further sets, 'DON'T BLOW YOUR TOP' (1988) and 'UAIOE' (1989), the band's growing cult popularity based on their uncompromising steamhammer beats 'n distorted guitar/vocals formula. Varying their brutal musical strategy only slightly, the Germans maintained their prolific release schedule throughout the first half of the 90's, the nihilistic minimalism of the music extending to the album titles:- 'NAIVE' (1990), 'MONEY' (1992), 'SUCKS' (1993), 'ANGST' (1993) and 'NIHIL' (1995). Subsequently signing to 'TVT' (home of industrial chart slayers, NINE INCH NAILS), KMFDM continued to take no prisoners with 1996's 'XTORT'.

Album rating: KMFDM (*5) / NAIVE (*7) / MONEY (*6) / ANGST (*6) / NIHIL (*4) / XTORT (*5) / SYMBOLS (*5)

SASCHA KONIETZKO + EN-ESCH + NAINZ WATTS

Zensor | not iss.

1986. (lp) *(ZR 2016)* **KMFDM (KEIN MEHRHEIT FUR DIE MITLEID)** – – German
– Zip / Deutsche schuld / Sieg-Sieg / Positive / Conillon / What do you know / Me I funk.

Skysaw | Wax Trax!

Feb 88. (lp/cd) *(SAW/CDSAW 004)* **WHAT DO YOU KNOW, DEUTSCHLAND?** ☐ –
– Kickin' ass / Me I funk / What do you know? / Zip / Conillon / Itchy bitchy / Deutsche schuld / Sieg sieg / Positiv / Lufthans / Itchy bitchy (dance version) / The unrestrained use of excessive force.

Nov 88. (lp/cd) *(SAW/CDSAW 006)* *<WAX 052>* **DON'T BLOW YOUR TOP** ☐ ☐
– Don't blow your top / No meat no man / Oh look / What a race / King Kong / No news / Oh look.

Dec 88. (12") *(SAW 008)* *<WAX 049>* **DON'T BLOW YOUR TOP. /** ☐ ☐

Strikeback | Wax Trax!

May 89. (lp/cd) *(SBR 032/+CD)* *<WAX 7083>* **UAIOE** ☐ ☐
– Murder / UAIOE / Loving can be an art / More & faster 243 / Rip the system / Thrash up / En Esch / Ganja rock / Thumb thumb / Rot the system / More & faster / Naff off.

1989. (12") *<WAX 9077>* **MORE & FASTER** – ☐
(above produced by FM EINHEIT / mixed by ADRIAN SHERWOOD)

Nov 89. (12"/cd-s) *(SBR 034 T/CD)* *<WAX 9108>* **VIRUS. / MURDER / M&F 244 (MORE AND FASTER remix)** ☐ ☐
(re-iss. Oct94; same)

Wax Trax! | Wax Trax!

Sep 90. (cd/lp) *(WAX CD/LP 148)* *<WAXCD 7148>* **NAIVE** ☐ ☐
– Welcome / Naive / Die now – Live later / Piggy bank / Achtung! / Friede (remix) / Liebeslied / Go to hell / Virus (dub) / Disgust (live) / Godlike.

Transglobal | Wax Trax!

Feb 92. (cd/c/lp) *(GLOBAL 2 CD/C/LP)* *<WAXCD 7177>* **MONEY** ☐ ☐
– Money / Vogue / Help us – save us – take us away / Bargeld / Spiritual house / Sex on the flag (Jezebeelzebuttfunk mix) / I will pray / We must awaken / Under Satan (dub) / Vogue (2000) / Money (Deutschmark mix).

May 92. (12"/cd-s) *(TRAN 07 T/CD)* *<9172>* **MONEY. / ('A'mix) / BARGELD** ☐ ☐ Jul91

—— line-up now **KONIETZKO, ESCH, WATTS + GUNTER SCHULZ** – bass, guitar, piano / **MARK DURANTE** – guitar, slide guitar

Roadrunner | T.V.T.

May 93. (cd-ep) *<TVT 8703>* **SUCKS (mixes) / MORE 'N' FASTER** – ☐

Jul 94. (cd,c) *(RR 8987-2)* *<TVT 7202>* **ANGST** ☐ ☐ Oct93
– Light / A drug against war / Blood evil / Lust / Glory / Move on / No peace / A hole in the wall / Sucks / The problem.

Intercord | Wax Trax!

Feb 96. (cd) *(IRS 993603CD)* *<7199>* **NIHIL** ☐ ☐ Apr95
– Ultra / Juke joint Jezebel / Flesh / Beast / Terror / Search and destroy / Disobedience / Revolution / Brute / Trust.

T.V.T. | T.V.T.

Mar 95. (12") *<TVT 8730>* **YEAR OF THE PIG (mixes)** – ☐

Oct 95. (12",cd-s) *<TVT 8733>* **BRUTE (mixes)** – ☐

—— **KONIETZKO + SCHULZ + EN ESCH** with **DURANTE, CHRIS CONNELLY, FM EINHEIT + NICOLE BLACKMAN**

Apr 96. (cd-s) *<TVT 8719>* **GLORY (mixes)** – ☐

Jun 96. (cd,c) *<TVT 7242>* **XTORT** – 92
– Power / Apathy / Rules / Craze / Dogma / Inane / Blame / Son of a gun / Ikons / Wrath.

Aug 96. (12") *<TVT 8740>* **POWER (mixes)** – ☐

Nov 96. (12"/cd-s) *<(TVT 8746-0/-2)>* **RULES. / SON OF AS GUN / INANE** ☐ ☐

Dragnet-Sony | T.V.T.

Oct 97. (cd/lp) *(488971-2/-1)* *<TVT 7245-2>* **SYMBOLS** ☐ ☐ Sep97
– Meglomaniac / Stray bullet / Leid und elend / Mercy / Torture / Spit sperm / Anarchy / Down and out / Unfit / Waste.

Jan 98. (m-cd) *<TVT 8753>* **MDFMK** – ☐
– Megalomaniac / Anarchy / Megalomaniac / Unfit / Anarchy / Megalomaniac.

Nov 98. (cd,c) *<8741>* **RETRO** (compilation) – ☐
– POwer / Juke-joint Jezebel / Brute / Drug against war / Light / Money / Vogue / Godlike – Doglike / Virus – Pestilence / Liebeslied-Liebeslied / More and faster / Rip the system / What do you know, Deutschland? / Don't blow your top.

—— note: there were a number of other US promos on 'Wax Trax-TVT'

Chris KNOX (see under ⇒ TALL TWARFS)

Peter KOPPES (see under ⇒ CHURCH)

KRAMER (see under ⇒ BONGWATER)

KREIDLER

Formed: Dusseldorf, Germany . . . 1994 by STEFAN SCHNEIDER (also of TO ROCOCO ROT), THOMAS KLEIN and ANDREAS REIHSE, who subsequently recruited DJ, DETLEF WEINRICH. Taking their moniker from an old clapped-out motorbike, KREIDLER conceived their own blend of Krautrock, fusing TORTOISE-esque musings with organic pop. A debut album, 'WEEKENDER' (1996), found its own groovy niche among the avant-garde indie anorak brigade. Now similar to MOUSE ON MARS, although a tad more conformist, the 'COLDNESS' single (remixed by Mute boss, DANIEL MILLER), was taken from their second set, 'APPEARANCE AND THE PARK' (1998).

Album rating: WEEKENDER (*7) / APPEARANCE AND THE PARK (*7)

STEFAN SCHNEIDER – bass / **ANDREAS REIHSE** – keyboards / **THOMAS KLEIN** – drums / **DETLEF WEINRICH** – turntables, etc

Kiff/SM Mute

Nov 96. (lp/cd) *(KIFF 004/+CD)* **WEEKENDER** -
– Traffic way / Shaun / Spat / La capital / Sand colour classic / Lio / Polaroid / Desto / Reflections / Hillwood / Telefon / La fille en beige / If / Schodringers katze. *(re-iss. Jun97 on 'Play It Again Sam' cd/lp; PIAS 556500-20/-10)*

Jun 97. (12"ep) *(EFA 07323-2/-1)* **RESPORT EP** -
(re-iss. & remixed Nov97; STU 04)
(above on 'Stewardess' and could have been earlier in Germany)

Jul 97. (12"ep) *(KIFF 006)* **FECHTERIN. / SHIVER / OBJEKT METAL** -

Apr 98. (12"ep) *(KIFF 010)* **AU PAIR (mixes). / GAIN / AUTOMATIC TUNNEL** -
(cd-ep) *(KIFF 010CD)* – (first 2 tracks) / Now the necessity.

May 98. (cd/lp) *(KIFF 011 CD/LP)* <9088> **APPEARANCE AND THE PARK** Mar99
– Tuesday / Il songo di una cosa / Plus / She woke up and the world had changed / Necessity now / Good morning city / Sneak preview / Au pair / After the preview / Coldness / Venetian blind / Cube. *(cd+=)* – Coldness (Sunroof mix).

Sep 98. (12") *(KIFF 013)* **COLDNESS (mixes:- Sunroof mix / Shantel mix / April & Clyne velocity mix / In cold dub)** -
(cd-s+=) *(KIFF 013CD)* – ('A'-Sunroof instrumental).

Die KREUZEN

Formed: Milwaukee, Wisconson, USA . . . early 80's by DAN KUBINSKI, BRIAN EGENESS, KEITH BRAMMER and ERIC TUNISON. Beginning life as a frantic metallic punk outfit, DIE KREUZEN thrashed their way onto the scene in 1982 with the 'COWS AND BEER' EP, reworking the tracks a couple of years later for their seminal eponymous debut on US indie label, 'Touch & Go'. Subsequent albums such as 'OCTOBER FILE' (1986) and 'CENTURY DAYS' (1988) saw the group attempt to assimilate a greater diversity of styles and influences into their uncompromising yet increasingly accessible sound. BRAMMER departed prior to the release of the Butch Vig-produced 'CEMENT' (1991) set, a record which saw the group explore the grunge sound which they had helped to develop.

Album rating: CENTURY DAYS (*5)

DAN KUBINSKI – vocals / **BRIAN EGENESS** – guitar / **KEITH BRAMMER** – bass / **ERIC TUNISON** – drums

not iss. Version Sound

1982. (7") **COWS AND BEER. / PINK FLAG** -

Touch & Go Touch & Go

1984. (lp) <*(TGLP 4)*> **DIE KREUZEN**
– Rumors / This hope / In school / I'm tired / On the street / Enemies / Get 'em fighting / No time / All white / Pain / Sick people / Hate me / Live wire / Not anymore / Mannequin / Fuck ups / Think for me / Dirt and decay / Don't say please / No name. *<US cd-iss. Aug94; TGCD 4>*

1986. (lp) <*(TGLP 7)*> **OCTOBER FILE**
– Man in the trees / Uncontrolled passion / It's been so long / Imagine a light / Cool breeze / Counting cracks / Red to green / Among the ruins / Hear and feel / Hide and seek / Conditioned / There's a place / Open lines / Melt. *<US cd-iss. 1992 +=; TG 07CD>* – DIE KREUZEN

Aug 88. (lp/cd) <*(TGLP 30/+CD)*> **CENTURY DAYS**
– Earthquakes / Lean into it / Different ways / So many times / These days / Elizabeth / Stomp / Slow / The bone / Bitch magnet / Number three / Dream sky / Halloween.

Jul 90. (12"ep) <*(TGEP 40)*> **GONE AWAY** (part live compilation)
– Cows and beer / Gone away / Seasons of wither / Pink flag / Land of treason / Stomp / Cool breeze / Man in the trees / Bitch magnet / Number three / Different ways / In school / Think for me / Hate me / Pain / Don't say please / Enemies / On the street / All white / Fighting.

1991. (12") <*TG 62*> **PINK FLAG. /** -

—— BRAMMER joined WRECK

Oct 91. (12") <*TG 79*> **BIG BAD DAYS. /** -

Nov 91. (lp/cd) <*(TG LP/CD 80)*> **CEMENT**
– Wish / Shine / Big bad days / Holes / Downtime / Blue song / Best goodbye / Heaven / Deep space / Shake loose / Over and the edge / Black song.

—— split after above

Die KRUPPS

Formed: Dusseldorf, Germany . . . 1980 by JURGEN ENGLER (formerly of punk outfit, MALE) and ROLF DORPER. Initially a hard-edged new-beat/industrial act in the vein of FRONT 242, NITZER EBB etc., DIE KRUPPS firmly established themselves in the vanguard of the German independent scene through domestic releases like 'VOLLE KRAFT VORAUS' (1982) and 'ENTERING THE ARENA' (1985). With their churning teutonic rhythms and the growling vox of ENGLER, the group were something of a precursor for bands like MINISTRY, NINE INCH NAILS and FEAR FACTORY. Though the group split during the latter half of the 80's, ENGLER, DORPER and CHRIS LIETZ reformed DIE KRUPPS at the turn of the decade. Inspired by the pioneering work of METALLICA, ENGLER was moved to introduce grinding guitar parts to thrilling effect on '1' (1992), going the whole hog later that year with a METALLICA tribute set, 'METAL FOR THE MASSES PART II – A TRIBUTE TO METALLICA' (reportedly loved by LARS ULRICH). For their next set, 'THE FINAL OPTION' (1993), DIE KRUPPS even recruited a real drummer, DARREN MINTER, and a guitarist, ex-HEATHEN man, LEE ALTUS, although it was with 'III: ODYSSEY OF THE MIND' (1995) that the group finally allowed heavy guitars free reign in the mix. The album marked their debut for metal label, 'Music For Nations', DIE KRUPPS continuing in an overtly rock vein for 1997's 'PARADISE NOW'.

Album rating: I (*7) / III: ODYSSEY OF THE MIND (*6) / PARADISE NOW (*6)

JURGEN ENGLER – vocals, guitar, electronics / **ROLF DORPER** – synthesizer, vocals / **BERNARD MALAKA** – bass, vocals / **FRANK KOLLGES** – drums, vocals / **EVA GOSSLING** – sax

Zick Zack not iss.

1981. (lp) *(ZZ 30)* **STAHWERKSYNFONIE** ('STEELWORKS SYMPHONY') - - German

—— **TINA SCHNECKENBURGER** – electronic drums; repl. FRANK + EVA

1981. (12") **WAHRE ARBEIT, WAHRER LOHN** - - German

WEA not iss.

Jun 82. (7") *(K 191390)* **GOLDFINGER. / ZUEI HERZEN** -

Jul 82. (lp) *(K 58463)* **VOLLE KRAFT VORAUS** -
– Volle kraft voraus / Goldfinger / Fur einen Augenblink / Tod und Teufel / Das ende der traume / Neue helden / Wahre arbeit, wahrer lohn / . . . Denn du lebst nur einmal / Zwei herzen, ein rhythmus / Laerm macht spass.

—— **CHRIS LIETZ** – drum programming + **WALTER JAGER** – bass; repl. DORPER who went solo and joined PROPAGANDA

Quiet not iss.

Jun 84. (12") *(PST 03)* **GOLDFINGER. / ZUEI HERZEN**

Statik Virgin

Jul 85. (lp) *(STAB 2)* <*207260*> **ENTERING THE ARENA**
– Risk / The rise and fall / Communication breakdown / Risky soul version / Gladiators / Your voice.

—— split after above, although **JURGEN, CHRIS + ROLF** did reform in the late 80's.

Mute Geffen

May 89. (7") *(MUTE 101)* <*21291*> **MACHINERIES OF JOY. /** -
(12"+=/cd-s+=) *(12/CD MUTE 101)* – ('A'mixes).

Grey Area Mute

Aug 91. (d-lp/cd) *(KRUPPS 1/+CD)* <*61128-4/-2*> **METALL MASCHINEN MUSIK 91-81 PAST FORWARD**
– Maniac / The machineries of joy.

Rough Trade Hollywood

Aug 92. (cd/lp) *(RTD 1951266-2/-1)* **I** -

Dec 92. (m-cd/m-lp) *(1951240-2/-1)* <*61515-2/-1*> **A TRIBUTE TO METALLICA** Sep93
– Enter sandman / Nothing else matters / Blackened / Battery / For whom the bell tolls.

—— added **LEE ALTUS** – guitar (ex-HEATHEN) + **DARREN MINTER** – drums

Equator Rough Trade

Oct 93. (12"/cd-s) *(AXIS T/CD 002)* **FATHERLAND / FATHERLAND (mixes) / METAL MACHINE MUSIC** -

Oct 93. (cd/c/lp) *(ATLAS CD/MC/LP 004)* <*1587*> **II: THE FINAL OPTION**

Feb 94. (12") *(AXIST 003)* <*1662*> **TO THE HILT. / THE DAWNING OF DOOM (live)**
(cd-s) *(AXISCD 003)* – ('A'mixes) / Bloodsuckers (live).

Jul 94. (12"/cd-s) *(AXIS T/CD 008)* <*19516933*> **CROSSFIRE (mixes)** -

Sep 94. (d-cd/d-lp) *(ATLAS CDD/LPD 006)* <*1995*> **THE FINAL REMIXES**
– To the hilt / Paradise of sin / Language of reality / Fatherland / Worst case scenario / Shellshocked / Crossfire / Bloodsuckers / Iron man / Inside out / New temptation / Dawning of doom / Ministry of fear / Hi tech low life / Metal machine music / Rings of steel.

—— (remixes by:- ANDREW ELDRITCH, JIM MARTIN, GUNSHOT, JULIAN BEESTON)

Nov 94. (12"/cd-s) *(AXIS T/CDD 010)* <*9579*> **BLOODSUCKERS (mixes; Biohazard / original / Julian Beeston / live)** Aug95
(cd-s) *(AXISCDS 010)* – Dawning of doom (live) / High tech low life (Julian Beeston remix) / Metal machine music (Cassandra Complex remix) / Rings of steel (Pro-pain remix).

—— **GEORGE LEWIS** – drums + **RUDIGER ESCH** – bass; repl. MINTER

Music For Nations Cleopatra

Jul 95. (cd) *(CDMFN 187)* <*9668*> **III: ODYSSEY OF THE MIND**
– The last flood / Scent / Metamorphasis / Isolation / The final option / Alive / Odyssey / LCD / Eggshell / Jekyll or Hyde.

Oct 95. (cd-ep) <*9578*> **FATHERLAND (the Sisters Of Mercy & original mixes) / GERMANIC (live) / CROSSFIRE (original & Gunshot remixes) / IRON MAN (original & N-factor remixes) / SHELLSHOCKED (Einsturzende Neubauten remix)** -

May 96. (cd-ep) <*9730*> **ISOLATION / ISOLATION (Luc Van Acker mix) / SCENT (club) / ISOLATION (Clawfinger mix) / THE LAST FLOOD (live) / THE FINAL OPTION (S.P.Q.R. mix)** -

Apr 97. (cd) *(CDMFN 218)* **PARADISE NOW** -
– Moving beyond / Gods of void / Paradise now / Black beauty / Reconstruction / Behind taste of taboo / Rise up / Fire / Full circle / Vortex / 30 seconds / Society treaty.

– compilations, etc. –

Sep 93. (3xcd-box) *Rough Trade; (RTD 1951542-2)* **DIE KRUPPS BOX** -

Nov 95. (cd) *Rough Trade; (RTD 19532003)* **SCENT** -

Oct 96. (cd) *Cleopatra; (CLP 9812)* **METAMORPHOSIS 1981-1992** -

Jul 97. (cd) *Captain Trip; (CTCD 057)* **FOUNDATION** -

K'S CHOICE

Formed: Brussels, Belgium . . . 1993 by the brother and sister team of GERT and SARAH BETTENS, alongside JAN VAN SICHEM JR, ERIC GROSSMAN and BART VAN DER ZEEUW. Emotional charged post-grunge alt-rockers fronted by English-speaking KURT COBAIN wannabe, SARAH, K'S CHOICE were as capable as any of their US counterparts. A major label deal with Epic's offshoot, '550', reflected as much, resulting in 1994's promising debut album, 'THE GREAT SUBCONSCIOUS CLUB'. However, the band's choicest compositions were to be found on 'PARADISE IN ME' (1996), an impressive follow-up that found a more appreciative audience in America and mainline Europe and featured the acoustic tongue-in-cheek live favourite, 'SOMETHING'S WRONG'. Although they remained virtually unknown in Britain, K'S CHOICE satisfied their loyal following with the release of a third set, 'COCOON CRASH' (1998).

Album rating: THE GREAT SUBCONSCIOUS CLUB (*5) / PARADISE IN ME (*7) / COCOON CRASH (*5)

GERT BETTENS – guitar, keyboards, vocals / **SARAH BETTENS** – vocals, guitar / **JAN VAN SICHEM JR** – guitar / **ERIC GROSSMAN** – bass / **BART VAN DER ZEEUW** – drums, percussion

550-Epic 550-Epic

Sep 94. (cd/c) **THE GREAT SUBCONSCIOUS CLUB** [-] [ ]
– Me happy / Breakfast / I smoke alot / Walk away / Elegia / My heart / I wanna meet the man / What the hell is love / I will return to you / The ballad of Lea & Paul / Winter / Laughing as I pray.

Mar 96. (cd/c) *(481305-2/-4)* **PARADISE IN ME** [ ] [ ] Aug96
– Not an addict / A sound that only you can hear / White kite fauna / Mr. Freeze / Song for Cathrine / To this day / Iron flower / Wait / Paradise in me / My record company / Only dreaming / Dad / Old woman / Something's wrong.

Apr 96. (c-ep/cd-ep) *(669283-4/-2)* **NOT AN ADDICT / SOMETHING'S WRONG / LITTLE MAN / BASICALLY THE SAME** [ ] [ ]

Jun 98. (cd/c) **COCOON CRASH** [-] [ ]
– Believe / In your room / Everything for free / Now is mine / Butterflies instead / If you're not scared / 20,000 seconds / Too many happy faces / Cocoon crash / Hide / Freestyle / Quiet little place / God in my bed / Winners.

Ed KUEPPER (see under ⇒ LAUGHING CLOWNS)

KUKL (see under ⇒ BJORK)

KULA SHAKER

Formed: Highgate, London, England . . .mid 90's out of mods The KAYS by CRISPIAN MILLS. They played down the fact his mother was the famous English actress HAYLEY MILLS (daughter of SIR JOHN MILLS). In the late 80's, CRISPIAN and ALONZA BEVIN set up a school group, The LOVELY LADS, later becoming The OBJECTS. In 1995, after jointly winning the 'In The City' new band competition and a Glastonbury appearance, KULA SHAKER signed to 'Columbia', through A&R man Ronnie Gurr. They debuted that Xmas with the limited edition single, 'TATTVA'. Their first single proper, 'GRATEFUL WHEN YOU'RE DEAD', was a tribute of sorts to the late, great JERRY GARCIA and earned them their first Top 40 hit. Their follow-up, a re-vamped version 'TATTVA', fared even better, making the Top 5. 'HEY DUDE', the next single, kept up the momentum, reaching No.2 following a blinding 'T In The Park' appearance in Scotland (they returned there in 1997 as headliners). CRISPIAN MILLS' songwriting was heavily influenced by a combination of classic 60's psychedelia and grandoise 70's rock, much in evidence on their debut album 'K' (1996). Relying on similar Eastern influences as 'TATTVA', 'GOVINDA' was another slice of elaborate, but cliched psychedelia, while 'HUSH' (1997) was workman-like in its similarity to the DEEP PURPLE version of the JOE SOUTH original.

Album rating: K (*7)

CRISPIAN MILLS – vocals, guitars / **ALONZA BEVIN** – bass, piano, tabla, vocals / **JAY DARLINGTON** – keyboards / **PAUL WINTERHART** – drums

Columbia Columbia

Dec 95. (ltd;7"/cd-s) *(KULA 71/CD1)* **TATTVA (Lucky 13 mix)/ HOLLOW MAN (part II)** [ ] [-]

Apr 96. (c-s) *(KULAMC 2)* **GRATEFUL WHEN YOU'RE DEAD – JERRY WAS THERE. / ANOTHER LIFE** [35] [-]
(cd-s+=) *(KULACD 2)* – Under the hammer.

Jun 96. (7") *(KULA 3)* **TATTVA. / TATTVA ON ST. GEORGE'S DAY / DANCE IN YOUR SHADOW** [4] [-]
(cd-s) *(KULACD 3)* – (first & third tracks) / Moonshine / Tattva (lucky 13).
(cd-s) *(KULACD 3K)* – (second & third tracks) / Red balloon (Vishnu's eyes).

Aug 96. (7"/c-s) *(KULA/+MC 4)* **HEY DUDE. / TROUBLED MIND** [2] [-]
(cd-s+=) *(KULACD 4)* – Grateful when you're dead (Mark Radcliffe session) / Into the deep (Mark Radcliffe session).
(cd-s) *(KULACD 4K)* – ('A'side) / Tattva / Drop in the sea / Crispian reading from the Mahabharata.

Sep 96. (cd/c/lp) *(SHAKER CD/MC/LP 1)* <67822> **K** [1] [ ] Oct96
– Hey dude / Knight on the town / Temple of the everlasting light / Govinda / Smart dogs / Magic theatre / Into the deep / Sleeping jiva / Tattva / Grateful when you're dead – Jerry was there / 303 / Start all over / Hollow man (parts 1 & 2). *(also ltd-cd; SHAKER CD1K)*

Nov 96. (c-s) *(KULAMC 5)* **GOVINDA / GOKULA** [7] [-]
(cd-s+=) *(KULACD 5)* – Hey dude (live) / Alonza Bevan's The Leek.
('A'-Hari & St.George mix-cd-s+=) *(KULACD 5K)* – ('A'-Monkey Mafia Pigsy's vision) / ('A'-Monkey Mafia Ten to ten version).
(7"mail-order+=) *(KULA 75)* – Temple of everlasting light.

Feb 97. (c-s) *(KULAMC 6)* **HUSH / RAAGY ONE (WAITING FOR TOMORROW)** [2] [-]
(cd-s+=) *(KULACD 6)* – Knight on the town (live) / Smart dogs (live).
(cd-s+=) *(KULACD 6K)* – Under the hammer (hold on to the magical key) / Govinda (live).

— (all above cd-singles were re-iss. Jul98; *KULA 71-76CD)*

Jul 97. (cd-ep) <68514> **SUMMER SUN EP** [-] [ ]
– Govinda / Gokula / Dance in your shadow / Raagy one (waiting for tomorrow) / Moonshine / Troubled mind.

Apr 98. (c-s) *(KULA 21MC)* **SOUND OF DRUMS / HURRY ON SUNDOWN (HARI OM SUNDOWN)** [3] [-]
(cd-s+=) *(KULA 21CD)* – Reflections of love / Fairyland (featuring DON PECKER).
(cd-s+=) *(KULA 21CDX)* – The one that got away / Smile.

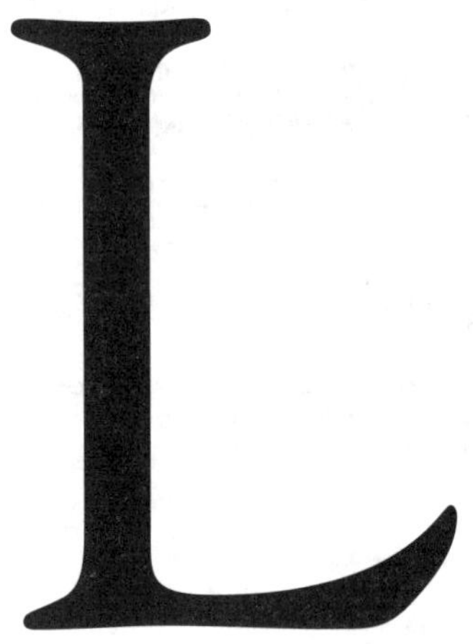

LABRADFORD

Formed: Richmond, Virginia, USA ... 1991, by MARK NELSON and CARTER BROWN. They set-up CARTER's Moog synthesizer in MARK's house and eventually acquired gigs supporting low-grade Virginia punk bands. In 1992, Chicago-based label 'Kranky' took up an option to sign them, subsequently releasing 'PRAZISION' in 1994. Drummerless Krautrock revivalists likened to CLUSTER, SPACEMEN 3 and MAIN, LABRADFORD specialised in creating space-rock dreamscapes and ambient drones of uneasy-listening while resurrecting the nearly forgotten Moog. After the album's cult success, they retreated back home, although the pair were lured back to sign for the UK arm of New Zealand-based, 'Flying Nun'. The label subsequently released a follow-up set, 'A STABLE REFERENCE' (1995), the music press hailing it as one of the year's most essential releases. In November '96, 'Blast First' issued their eponymous third effort to similar acclaim, their increasingly minimalist tendencies moving them to even cut the song titles of 1997's 'MI MEDIA NARANJA' down to single letters.

Album rating: PRAZISION (*7) / A STABLE REFERENCE (*8) / LABRADFORD (*8) / MI MEDIA NARANJA (*7)

CARTER BROWN – synthesizers / **MARK NELSON** – vocals, guitars, tapes / (ROBERT DONNE was only part-time until later)

Flying Nun / Kranky

1994. (cd,d-lp) *<1>* **PRAZISION**
– Listening in depth / Accelerating on a smoother road / Splash down / Disremembering / Experience the gated oscillator / Soft return / Sliding grass / C of people / New listening / Gratitude / Skyward with motion / Everlast. *(UK-iss.Feb96 & Sep98 lp/cd; FN/+CD 342)*

1994. (cd-s) *<2>* **EVERLAST /**

—— added **ROBERT DONNE** – bass (ex-BREADWINNER)

Jun 95. (lp/cd) *(FN/+CD 329) <6>* **A STABLE REFERENCE**
– Mas / El Lago / Streamlining / Banco / Eero / Balanced on its own flame / Star City, Russia / Comfort / SEDR 77.

Duophonic / not iss.

Feb 96. (10") *(DS 4512)* **SCENIC RECOVERY. / UNDERWOOD 5IVE**

Blast First / Kranky

Nov 96. (lp/cd) *(BFFP 136/+CD) <13>* **LABRADFORD**
– Phantom channel crossing / Midrange / Pico / The cipher / Lake speed / Scenic recovery / Battered. *(cd re-iss. Sep98 on 'Flying Nun'; FNCD 329)*

—— (below release on 'Trance Syndicate')

Jun 97. (12"; as LABRADFORD & STARS OF THE LID) *<(TR 60)>* **KAHANEK INCIDENT VOL.3** — Aug97

Oct 97. (lp/cd) *(BFFP 144/+CD) <23>* **MI MEDIA NARANJA**
– S / P / WR / CM / G / V / P.

LAIBACH

Formed: Trbovlje, Slovenia, the former Yugoslavia ... 1980 by TOMAZ HOSTNIK, MILAN FREZ, DEJAN KNEZ and ERVIN MARKOSEK. A musical, nay cultural one-off, LAIBACH took their moniker from the old German name for Slovenia's capital, Ljubljana, a statement of intent that set out their direct opposition to the communist-controlled state of Yugoslavia. One part of a wider art collective, NSK (Neue Slowenische Kunst or New Slovenian Art), LAIBACH worked in tandem with the movement's painting and theatre divisions in a fashion designed to both parody and speak out against the individual subjugation of the communist industrial machine. The early 80's proved tumultuous as the band attempted to develop their crude electro minimalism amid compulsory military service and the suicide of mainman HOSTNIK (his place was taken by IVAN NOVAK). They also experienced open hostility from the Yugoslav authorities, a deal with the state record company severed at the last minute. Following a series of releases through European labels, the band's growing UK profile and numerous art appearances eventually led to a long-term deal with 'Mute'. The result was 'OPUS DEI' (1987), LAIBACH moving away from the avant-garde experimentalism of their earlier releases towards a thunderous, po-faced (and let's face it, often hilarious) industrial-rock sound. Full marks for turning Opus' Euro cheese classic, 'LIFE IS LIFE' into a Balkan funeral march under the title of 'LEBEN HEIST LEBEN', the thrusting broadsword reworking of Queen's 'ONE VISION' aka 'GEBURT EINER NATION', meanwhile, raising disturbing questions about where exactly the band's political sympathies lie; accusations of fascist undercurrents were inevitable, only serving to furher shroud the band in myth. Two of rock's holiest cows, The BEATLES and The ROLLING STONES, were next in line for the LAIBACH treatment as the group proceeded to stomp their musical jackboot over the whole 'LET IT BE' (1988) album and 'STONES' classic, 'SYMPATHY FOR THE DEVIL' (1990). While 1990 also saw the release of their acclaimed 'MACBETH' soundtrack (for a production by German theatre company, 'Deutsches Scauspielhaus'), LAIBACH's political context was irrevocably altered with the beginnings of the Balkans confict as Slovenia declared its independence. The new decade has seen the band tackle techno in suitably Wagnerian style with 'KAPITAL' (1992), KRAFTWERK covers set, 'TRANS-SLOVENIA EXPRESS' (1994) and 'NATO' (even more covers), while 1996's 'SARAJEVO – OCCUPIED EUROPE NATO TOUR 1994-1995' documented the band's live excursions against the backdrop of turmoil and war which continues to afflict the region.

Album rating: THROUGH OCCUPIED EUROPE (*4) / LAIBACH (*5) / NOVA AKRPOLA (*5) / OPUS DEI (*6) / LET IT BE (*6) / MACBETH (*6) / KAPITAL (*6) / JESUS CHRIST SUPERSTARS (*6)

IVAN NOVAK – vocals; repl. TOMAZ HOSTNIK who committed suicide in '81 / **MILAN FREZ + DEJAN KNEZ + ERVIN MARKOSEK**

Staal / not iss.

Dec 83. (c) **THROUGH THE OCCUPIED NETHERLANDS** — Dutch
– De Kapal-den Haag (soundboard rec. 30.11.83) / NL Centrum-Amsterdam (live rec. 1.12.83).

Laylah / not iss.

Mar 84. (12") *(LAY 002)* **BOJI. / SILA / BRAT MOJ**

East-West Trading Co. / not iss.

May 84. (12") *(12EW 3)* **PANORAMA. / DECREE**

Walter Ulbright / not iss.

1985. (d-lp) **REKAPITULACIJA** (compilation 1980-84) — German
– Jaruzelelski / Tod fur Tod / Macht / In mitten von Kampfen / Bruder mein / Du, der du herausforderst / Wir schmieden die Zukunft.

S.K.U.C. / not iss.

May 85. (lp) **LAIBACH** — Yugo
– Cari Amici / Sila / Sredi Bojev / Drzava / Dekret / Mi Kujemo bodocnost / Brat moj / Panorama. *(cd-iss. Aug95 on 'Nika'; EFA 13132-2)*

Cherry Red / Wax Trax!

Dec 85. (12") *(12CHERRY 91)* **DIE LIEBE. / DIE LIEBE IST GROSSTE KRAFT, DIE ALLES SCHAFFT**

Jan 86. (m-lp/m-cd) *(B/CDM RED 67) <WX/+CS/CD 7080>* **NOVA AKROPOLA**
– Vier personen / Nova Akropola / Krvav Gruda – Ploona Zemlja / Vojna poena / Ti, zi izzivas / Die liebe / Drzava / Vade retro / Panorama. *(w/ free-lp)* – NEW KONSTERVATIW HAMBURG 1985 (live) – Vier personen / Nova Akropola / Vade retro Satanas / Die liebe / Du der du herausforderst / Der staat. *(re-iss. cd Apr93; same) <US cd re-iss. 1994 on 'Cleopatra'; 9483>*

Side Effects / not iss.

Jul 86. (lp) *(SER 08)* **THE OCCUPIED EUROPE TOUR 1985 (live)**
– Vade retro / Perspektive / Panorama / Die liebe / Dsava / Vier personen / Slovenska Akropola / Vojna poema / Nova Akropola / Ti, zi izzivas. *<US cd-iss. 1991 on 'Mute'; 61071-2>*

Mute / Wax Trax!

Mar 87. (12") *(12 MUTE 60)* **GEBURT EINER NATION (ONE VISION). / LEBEN HEIBT LEBEN (LIFE IS LIFE)**

Mar 87. (cd/lp) *(CD+/STUMM 44) <WAXCD 030>* **OPUS DEI**
– Leben heibt leben / Geburt einer nation / Leben-Tod / F.I.A.T. / Opus dei / Trans-national / How the west was won / The great seal. *(cd+=)* – Herz-Felde / Jagerspiel / Koza (skin) / Krst (baptism).

Jul 87. (7") *(MUTE 62)* **LIFE IS LIFE. / GERMANIA**
(12"+=) *(12MUTE 62)* – Life (Opus).

Mute / Mute

Sep 88. (7") *(MUTE 80) <71404>* **SYMPATHY FOR THE DEVIL (WHO KILLED THE KENNEDYS). / SYMPATHY FOR THE DEVIL (SOUL TO WASTE)**
(12"ep+=/cd-ep+=) *(MUTE 80 T/CD)* – ('A'numerous versions). *(re-iss. Feb90 cd/c/lp) (CD/MC/LP MUTE 80)*

Oct 88. (cd/c/lp) *(CD/C+/STUMM 58) <75404>* **LET IT BE**
– Let it be / Get back / Two of us / Dig a pony / I me mine / Across the universe / Dig it / I've got a feeling / The long and winding road / One after 909 / For you blue / Maggie Mae (auf der Luneburger Heide & was gleicht wohl auf Erden). *(d-c+=)* – OPUS DEI

Dec 88. (7") *(MUTE 91)* **ACROSS THE UNIVERSE. / MAGGIE MAE**
(12"+=/cd-s+=) *(12/CD MUTE 91)* – Get back. *(re-iss. Dec89)*

Mute / Restless

Jan 90. (cd/c/lp) *(CD/C+/STUMM 70) <71458>* **MACBETH**
– Preludium / Agnus dei (Acropolis) / Wutach schlucht / Die zeit / Ohne geld / U.S.A. / 10.05.1941 / Expectans expectavos / Coincidentia oppositorium / Wolf / Agnus dei (Exil und Tod).

Mute / Elektra

Apr 92. (12"/cd-s) **WIRTSCHAFT IST TOT (THE ECONOMY IS DEAD). /**

Apr 92. (cd/c/lp) *(CD/C+/STUMM 82) <61282>* **KAPITAL (live)**
– Decade null / Everlasting in union / Ilumination / Le privilege des morts / Codex Durex / Hymn to the black Sun / Young Europa / The hunter's funeral procession / White law / Wirtschaft ist tot / Torso / Entartete welt / Kinderreich (English version) / Sponsored by Mars / Regime of confidence / State of gravity.

Sep 94. (12"/cd-s) *(12/CD MUTE 117)* **FINAL COUNTDOWN. / ('A'mixes)**

Oct 94. (cd/c/lp) *(CD/C+/STUMM 121) <61714>* **NATO**
– NATO / War / Final countdown / In the army now / Dogs of war / Alle gegen alle / Anational reservation / 2 3 2 5 / Mars on River Drina.
Apr 95. (12"/cd-s) *(12/CD MUTE 170)* **IN THE ARMY NOW. / WAR** -
Oct 96. (cd-ep) *(CDMUTE 197)* **JESUS CHRIST SUPERSTAR / GOD IS GOD (optical vocal mix) / GOD IS GOD (coptic rain mix) / GOD IS GOD (diabolical mix) / JESUS CHRIST SUPERSTAR (random logic mix)** -
Oct 96. (cd/lp) *(CD+/STUMM 136) <69027>* **JESUS CHRIST SUPERSTARS**
– God is God / Jesus Christ superstar / Kingdom of God / Abuse and confession / Declaration of freedom / Message from the black star / The cross / To the new light / Deus ex machina.

Robot Robot

Jul 97. (cd) *(<efacd 20447-2>)* **ALSO SPRACH JOHANN PAUL II**
– Also Sprach Johann Paul II / Transcendental storm / Human redemption / Hell's march epilepsye / Prolaiare proelis domini / Resurrection of the kinderreich / Divine order / Zoroaster 2000 (reces).

– compilations, etc. –

1985. (c) *Staal;* **EIN SCHAUSPIELER** - - Yugo
Mar 87. (lp) *S.K.U.C.;* **SLOVENSKA AKROPOLA** - - Yugo
(UK cd-iss. Aug95 on 'Nika'; EFA 20025-2)
Nov 87. (d-lp/cd) *Sub Rosa; (SUB 33006 7/9)* **A BAPTISM** -
(re-iss. cd Nov88 & Oct94; SR 0019CD)
Feb 89. (cd-ep) *Wax;* **PANORAMA / DECREE / DIE LIEBE / DIE LIEBE IST GROSSTE KRAFT, DIE ALLES SCHAFFT** -
Jun 93. (cd) *Grey Area-Mute; (NSK 1CD)* **LJUBLJANA, ZAGREB, BEOGRAD** -
Jul 95. (cd) *Roir USA; (RUSCD 8211)* **LAIBACH**
Aug 96. (cd) *Grey Area-Mute; (NSK 2CD)* **OCCUPIED EUROPE NATO TOUR 1994-95 (live)** -
Jun 97. (cd) *Grey Area-Mute; (NSK 3CD)* **MB DECEMBER 21st, 1984** -

LAIKA

Formed: London, England ... early '94 by ex-MOONSHAKE pair, MARGARET FIEDLER and JOHN FRENETT, along with that band's former producer, GUY FIXSEN. Completing the line-up with LOU CICCOTELLI and 5th member LOUISE ELLIOTT, LAIKA took their name from the first dog in space and set about creating otherworldly sounds in line with their label, Too Pure's eclectic music policy. Keen to expound on the inter-related nature of life, philosophy graduate, FIEDLER, explained that LAIKA's driving force was an attempt to break down the illusive musical barriers between indie, dance technology and the avant-garde. The first results came in the shape of 1994's debut album, 'SILVER APPLES OF THE MOON', a multi-layered, CAN meets TRICKY (FIEDLER's ghostly vocal reminiscent of the latter's sidekick, NICOLETTE) affair bringing 70's Krautrock/pop up to date. A month or two after its completion, former PJ HARVEY drummer, ROB ELLIS came into the fold and, by the release of their follow-up set, 'SOUNDS OF THE SATELLITES' (1997), FRENETT had made way for percussion man, ALONZO MENDOZA. Another experimental fusion of pop electronics and haunting avant-jazz, a definite highlight was 'SHUT OFF / CURL UP', a subversive alternative cousin to MADONNA's 'Justify My Love' (!). • **Note:** not the same as LAIKA & THE COSMONAUTS on 'Upstart' records

Album rating: SILVER APPLES OF THE MOON (*7) / SOUNDS OF THE SATELLITES (*7)

MARGARET FIEDLER – vocals, samples, etc (ex-MOONSHAKE) / **GUY FIXSEN** – guitar, bass, etc / **LOU CICCOTELLI** – drums, percussion / **JOHN FRENETT** – bass (ex-MOONSHAKE) / plus **LOUISE ELLIOTT** – flute, sax

Too Pure Warners

Oct 94. (cd) *(purecd 042) <43010>* **SILVER APPLES OF THE MOON** Feb95
– Sugar daddy / Marimba song / Let me sleep / Itchy & Scratchy / Coming down glass / If you miss / 44 robbers / Red river / Honey in heat / Thomas / Spider happy hour.

— added **ROB ELLIS** – drums, piano, percussion (ex-PJ HARVEY) — **ALONZO MENDOZA** – vibraphone; repl. FRENETT

Jan 97. (2x12") *(pure/+cd 067)* **BREATHER. / LOOKING FOR THE JACKALOPE / ('A'&'B'mixes)** -
Feb 97. (d-lp/cd) *(pure/+cd 062) <31002>* **SOUNDS OF THE SATELLITES**
– Prairie dog / Breather / Out of sight and snowblind / Almost sleeping / Starry night / Bedbugs / Martinis on the Moon / Poor gal / Blood + bones (moody mix) / Shut off – Curl up / Spooky Rhodes / Dirty feet + giggles.
Sep 97. (12"ep/cd-ep) *(pure 071 rt/cds)* **ALMOST SLEEPING / PRAIRIE DOG (Maxwell House mix). / SHUT OFF – CURL UP (Cabbage Boy mix) / BREATHER (Luke Vibert mix)** -

Steve LAKE (see under ⇒ ZOUNDS)

L/A/L

Formed: Seattle, Washington, USA ... 1993 by SAM JAYNE, a one-time member of LYNC and collaborator of BECK. Issued under the unabbreviated moniker of LOVE AS LAUGHTER, 'THE GREKS BRING GIFTS' album was a SAM JAYNE solo project in all but name. One-man touring soon took its toll however and in early 1998, L/A/L became a 4-piece band, JAYNE enlisting friends, DAVE SCHNEIDER, JESSICA ESPELETA and his girlfriend LESLIE. This line-up completed a second set, '*1 USA', a rockier affair that broke from the lo-fi roots.

Album rating: THE GREKS BRING GIFTS (*5) / *1 USA (*6)

SAM JAYNE – vocals, guitar, etc (ex-LYNC, ex-BECK) / with **DIANA ARENS + STEVE 'THE WIZARD' DORE**

K K

Feb 96. (cd; as LOVE AS LAUGHTER) *<(KLP 51CD)>* **THE GREKS BRING GIFTS** Dec95
– It's only Lena / TTFL / You gotta bug / Keep your shade / Uninvented trumpets / Next time you fall apart / The youth are plastic / Singing sores make perfect swords / A tune and a comfortable ride / Let's talk radar / I am seldom reared / High noon / Eeyore crush it / Half-assed / Kung Fu exercise fountain / If I ever need someone like you.

— added **JESSICA ESPELETA** – guitar / **DAVE SCHNEIDER** – drums / **LESLIE** – bass

Feb 98. (cd) *<(KLP 76CD)>* ***1 USA** Jan98
– Old gold / #1 U.S.A. / I'm a bee / Slow river fever / Vacation / Tonight / Puger sound sanitation / PhoBias.

LAMBCHOP

Formed: Nashville, Tennessee, USA ... 1993 by KURT WAGNER, the 90's country-lounge answer to 60's icons, CAT STEVENS and TIM HARDIN. His hesitant but heavy-lidded vocal monotone sat perfectly against the lethargic drowsiness of the country-jazz played by his large backing ensemble. Although they could hardly be termed rock, LAMBCHOP emerged from the flourishing alternative roots scene with an album on 'Merge' ('City Slang' UK) 'I HOPE YOU'RE SITTING DOWN' (1995). A post-modern cousin of CHET ATKINS (although at times at least twice removed!), the record revealed WAGNER's love of vintage string-laden production and his penchant for beer-soaked, meandering tales of ordinary madness. Early the following year, KURT and LAMBCHOP delivered another collection of near comatose country vignettes, 'HOW I QUIT SMOKING', this time around wrapped up in a classic 70's Nashville production sheen courtesy of arranger, John Mock. One of the record's highlights, 'THE MAN WHO LOVED BEER', was issued as the first LAMBCHOP single and has since been adopted as author, Martin C. Strong's theme tune. Joking aside, 1996 also saw the release of a third set, the critically acclaimed live/festival (1995) recorded 'HANK', relaxzzzed audiences no doubt giving WAGNER and Co. the first ever horizontal standing ovation. A third studio album, meanwhile, sauntered onto the scene in 1997, the LAMBCHOP man surely being just a tad ironic in naming it 'THRILLER', although opening cuts, 'MY FACE YOUR ASS' and 'YOUR SUCKING FUNNY DAY', raised the pulse a little. Prolific as ever, WAGNER and his entourage returned in 1998 with possibly his/their best album to date, 'WHAT ANOTHER MAN SPILLS', featuring croonsome classic, 'THE SATURDAY OPTION', alongside a few covers by F.M. CORNOG (i.e. EAST RIVER PIPE) and one by Curtis Mayfield, 'GIVE ME YOUR LOVE'.

Album rating: I HOPE YOU'RE SITTING DOWN (*6) / HOW I QUIT SMOKING (*7) / HANK (*7) / THRILLER (*6) / WHAT ANOTHER MAN SPILLS (*7)

KURT WAGNER – vocals / with various members including **JOHN DELWORTH, DEANNA VARAGONA, PAUL NIEHAUS, ALLEN LOWREY, JONATHAN MARX, C. SCOTT CHASE, MARC TROUVILLION, PAUL BIRCH, MARK NEVERS, DENNIS CRONIN, ALEX McMANUS, MIKE DOSTER, MIKE GRIFFITH, VIC CHESNUTT + TONY CROW**

City Slang Merge

Mar 95. (cd/d-lp) *(efa 04953-2/-1) <MRG 70>* **I HOPE YOU'RE SITTING DOWN** Sep94
– Begin / Betweemus / Soaky in the pooper / Because you are the very aire he . . . / Under the same moon / I will drive slowly / Oh, what a disappointment / Hellmouth / Bon soir, bon soir / Hickey / Breathe deep / So I hear you're moving / Let's go howling / What he was wearing / Cowboy on the moon / Pack-up song.
Jan 96. (cd/d-lp) *(efa 04969-2/-1) <MRG 97>* **HOW I QUIT SMOKING**
– For which we are truly thankful / The man who loved beer / Militant / We never argue / Life's little tragedy / Suzieju / All smiles and mariachi / Scary caroler / Smuckers / Militant / Garf / Your life as a sequel / Theone / Again.
Apr 96. (7"m)(cd-s) *(efa 04974-45)(efa 04977-03)* **THE MAN WHO LOVED BEER. / ALUMNI LAWN / BURLY & JOHNSON** -
Jul 96. (m-cd/m-lp) *(efa 04979-2/-1) <MRG 108>* **HANK (live)**
– I'm a stranger here / Blame it on the brunettes / The tin chime / Randi / Doak's need / Poor bastard / I sucked my boss's dick.
Jul 97. (7") *<(MRG 124)>* **CIGARETIQUETTE. /**
(above & below 45's released on 'Merge' only)
Sep 97. (7") *<(MRG 126)>* **WHITEY. /**
Sep 97. (cd/lp) *(efa 04998-2/-1) <MRG 130>* **THRILLER**
– My face your ass / Your sucking funny day / Hey where's your girl / Crawl away / Gloria Leonard / Thriller / The old fat robin / Superstar in France.
Nov 97. (cd-ep) *(efa 0870-03)* **YOUR SUCKING FUNNY DAY / PETRIFIED FLORIST / THEME FROM THE NEIL MILLER SHOW** -
Sep 98. (cd/lp) *(efa 08711-2/-1) <MRG 146>* **WHAT ANOTHER MAN SPILLS**
– Interrupted / The Saturday option / Shucks / Give me your love (love song) / Life #2 / Scamper / It's not alright / N.O. / I've been lonely for so long / Magnificent obsession / King of nothing never / The theme from the Neil Miller show.

Mark LANEGAN (see under ⇒ SCREAMING TREES)

Jon LANGFORD (see under ⇒ MEKONS)

Gerard LANGLEY & Ian KEAREY (see under ⇒ BLUE AEROPLANES)

LARD (see under ⇒ DEAD KENNEDYS)

LA'S

Formed: Liverpool, England . . . 1986 by LEE MAVERS (guitar/vocals), JOHN POWER (bass), PAUL HEMMINGS (guitar) and JOHN TIMSON (drums). The band signed to 'Go! Discs' in 1987, releasing the charming retro pop of debut single, 'WAY OUT'. The record was well recieved but failed to chart and replacing TIMSON with CHRIS SHARROCK, the band followed up the single with the seminal BYRDS-like pop genius of 'THERE SHE GOES', all soaring melodies and youthful vigour. Incredibly, the single failed to chart, although it later reached the Top 20 when it was re-released in 1990 at the same time as the eponymous debut. Over the two year period it took to record the album, MAVERS' brother Neil replaced SHARROCK on the drum stool while JAMES JOYCE was recruited for the departing POWER (who went on to form the highly successful CAST). CAMMY, another guitarist, was also added. Part of the problem was the notoriously perfectionist MAVERS who obsessed over every tiny detail of the recording process in his search for an 'authentic' sound. 'Go! Discs' became increasingly worried about the escalating cost of the project and decided to go ahead and release the album against MAVERS' wishes. He retaliated by critiscising the company in press interviews and dismissed the debut as a collection of demos. In reality, the album was a seamless collection of post-baggy guitar pop, drawing comparisons with the STONE ROSES and garnering almost universal acclaim. After a tour of America and Japan in 1991, the band went to ground and little has been heard from them since, save a brief, disastrous appearance supporting PAUL WELLER in 1994. While rumours continue to abound, the band remain one of the greatest modern day musical enigmas. • **Songwriters:** LEE MAVERS penned. • **Trivia:** Steve Lilywhite produced them in 1990.

Album rating: THE LA'S (*8)

LEE MAVERS (b. 2 Aug'62) – vocals, guitar / **JOHN BYRNE** – guitar / **JOHN POWER** (b.14 Sep'67) – bass / **PAUL HEMMINGS** – guitar / **JOHN TIMSON** – drums

		Go! Discs	London
Oct 87.	(7") *(GOLAS 1)* **WAY OUT. / ENDLESS**		
	(12"+=) *(GOLAS 1-12)* – Knock me down.		
	(12"++=) *(GOLAR 1-12)* – Liberty ship (demo) / Freedom song (demo).		

—— **CHRIS SHARROCK** – drums (ex-ICICLE WORKS) repl. TIMSON

Nov 88.	(7") *(GOLAS 2)* **THERE SHE GOES. / COME IN, COME OUT**	59	
	(12"+=)(cd-s+=) *(GOLAS 2-12)(LASCD 2)* – Who knows / Man I'm only human.		
	(7"ep+=) *(LASEP 2)* – Who knows / Way out (new version).		
May 89.	(7";w-drawn) *(GOLAS 3)* **TIMELESS MELODY. / CLEAN PROPHET**	-	-
	(10"+=; w-drawn) *(LASEP 3)* – All by myself / There she goes.		
	(cd-s+=; w-drawn) *(LASCD 3)* – All by myself / Ride yer camel.		

—— **NEIL MAVERS** (b. 8 Jul'71) – drums repl. SHARROCK / **JAMES JOYCE** (b.23 Sep'70) – bass repl. POWER who formed CAST / added **CAMMY** (b.PETER JAMES CAMELL, 30 Jun'67) – guitar (ex-MARSHMALLOW)

Sep 90.	(7"/c-s) *(GOLAS/LASMC 4)* **TIMELESS MELODY. / CLEAN PROPHET**	57	
	(12"purple+=)(cd-s+=) *(GOLAS 4-12)(LASCD 4)* – Knock me down / Over.		
Oct 90.	(cd/c/lp) *(<828 202-2/-4/-1>)* **THE LA'S**	30	
	– Son of a gun / I can't sleep / Timeless melody / Liberty ship / There she goes / Doledrum / Feelin' / Way out / I.O.U. / Freedom song / Failure / Looking glass.		
Oct 90.	(7"/c-s) *(GOLAS/LASMC 5)* **THERE SHE GOES (new version). / FREEDOM SONG**	13	-
	(12"+=)(cd-s+=) *(GOLAS 5-12)(LASCD 5)* – All by myself.		
Feb 91.	(7"/c-s) *(GOLAS/LASMC 6)* **FEELIN'. / DOLEDRUM**	43	
	(12"+=)(cd-s+=)(7"ep+=) *(GOLAS 6-12)(LASCD 6)(GOLAB 6)* – I.O.U. (alt.version) / Liberty ship.		
Jun 91.	(c-s) *<869 370-4>* **THERE SHE GOES / ALL BY MYSELF**	-	49

—— had already disbanded just prior to above. In Apr'97 a various artists EP (taken from the movie, 'Fever Pitch', featured 'THERE SHE GOES' (issued on 'Blanco Yo Negro'; *NEG 104 C/T/CD)*

LAUGH

Formed: Manchester, England . . . 1985 by MARTIN WRIGHT, MARTIN MITTLER and SPENCER BIRTWHISTLE. Together with guitarist, IAN BENDELOW, the fun-loving indie-pop bunch (later namechecked by TIM BURGESS of The CHARLATANS) issued five singles before the release of a debut album in 1988, 'SENSATION No.1' (one of these 45's, 'PAUL McCARTNEY', was obviously named after their pop idol). In the early 90's, the lads found vocalist, STELLA GRAY, and metamorphosised into indie-dance outfit, INTASTELLA. The new-look group subsequently secured a deal with 'M.C.A.' and had a few minor UK hits in 1991, although STELLA and Co. were dogged by bad luck as she broke her arm in a motorcycle accident. Subsequently dropped by their label, INTASTELLA returned in '93 on a new imprint, 'Planet 3', SHAUN RYDER working with them on a comeback EP, 'DRIFTER'. Despite the record's hype and controversy, the band failed to make any significant breakthrough, although they did breach the UK Top 60 a few years later with 'IN THE NIGHT' (taken from their second set, 'WHAT YOU GONNA DO').

Album rating: SENSATION No.1 (*6) / Intastella: INTASTELLA AND THE FAMILY OF PEOPLE (*5) / WHAT YOU GONNA DO (*4)

MARTIN WRIGHT – vocals, guitar, keyboards / **IAN BENDELOW** – guitar / **MARTIN MITTLER** – bass / **SPENCER BIRTWHISTLE** – drums

		Debris	not iss.
Dec 85.	(7"flexi w/mag) *(DEB 01)* **TAKE YOUR TIME YEAH! / (TWANG: What's the rub)**	-	-
		Remorse	not iss.
Nov 86.	(12"m) *(LOST 3)* **TAKE YOUR TIME YEAH!. / NEVER HAD IT SO BAD / I'M STILL THINKING**		-
Aug 87.	(7") *(LOSS 5)* **PAUL McCARTNEY. / COME ON**		-
Apr 88.	(7"/12") *(LOS S/T 7)* **TIME TO LOSE IT. / TIME TO ABUSE IT GUESS WHAT**		-
		Sub Aqua	not iss.
Oct 88.	(lp) *(AQUALP 001)* **SENSATION No.1**		-
Nov 88.	(7"ep/12"ep) *(AQUA 3/+12)* **SENSATION No.1 EP**		-

INTASTELLA

STELLA GRAY – vocals (+ dancer **LITTLE ANTHONY**) repl. IAN

		M.C.A.	M.C.A.
Apr 91.	(7") *(MCS 1520)* **DREAM SOME PARADISE. / SOME DREAMS**	69	
	(12"+=/cd-s+=) – Paradise / It will end when it's over.		
Aug 91.	(7"/12") *(MCS/+T 1559)* **PEOPLE. / BENDY**	74	
	(cd-s) *(MCSCD 1559)* – ('A'side) / Bendy – in the disco / Thor is Bendy.		
Nov 91.	(cd/c/lp) **INTASTELLA AND THE FAMILY OF PEOPLE**		
	– Overdrive / Bendy / People / Are you happy / Mr. Everything / France / Century / Soulsalito / Arrival.		
Nov 91.	(7"/12") *(MCS/ 1585)* **CENTURY. / STRAWBERRY JAM**	70	
	(12"/cd-s) – ('A'side) / Intastella meets Adamski / Bendy – in the disco.		
		Planet 3-China	unknown
Oct 93.	(12"ep/cd-ep) *(GXY TR/CD 2001)* **DRIFTER EP**		-
	– Can you fly like we mean it? / (other mix).		
Feb 94.	(c-s) *(GXY 2002MC)* **POINT HOPE /**		-
	(12"+=/cd-s+=) *(GXY 2002 T/CD)* –		
	(12") *(GXY 2002TR)* – ('A'remixes).		
Aug 95.	(c-s) *(GXY 2005MC)* **IN THE NIGHT /**	60	-
	(cd-s+=) *(GXY 2005CD)* –		
	(12"+=) *(GXY 2005T)* –		
Oct 95.	(cd/c) *(SATURN CD/MC 1)* **WHAT YOU GONNA DO**		-
Feb 96.	(c-s) *(GXY 2009MC)* **GRANDMASTER / ('A'mix)**		-
	(12"+=/cd-s+=) *(GXY 2009 T/CD)* – ('A'mixes).		
Jul 96.	(c-s) *(GXY 2011MC)* **PAST / ('A'mix)**		-
	(12"+=/cd-s+=) *(GXY 2011 T/CD)* – ('A'mixes).		
Apr 97.	(c-s) *(GXY 2015MC)* **SKYSCRAPER KOOLAID. / ('A'mix)**		-
	(12"+=/cd-s+=) *(GXY 2015 T/CD)* – ('A'mixes).		
Sep 97.	(7") *(GXY 2017)* **SOON WE'LL FLY. / ('A'mix)**		-
	(cd-s) *(GXY 2017CD1)* – ('A'mixes).		
	(cd-s) *(GXY 2017CD2)* – ('A'mixes).		

LAUGHING APPLE (see under ⇒ BIFF BANG POW!)

LAUGHING CLOWNS

Formed: Sydney, Australia . . . late 70's by former SAINTS guitarist/singer, EDMUND KUEPPER. Following his departure from the band in early '79, KUEPPER returned to his beloved Australia and, along with cousins DAN and BEN WALLACE-CRABBE, ROBERT FARRELL and JEFFREY WEGENER, formed The LAUGHING CLOWNS. Signed to Aussie label, 'Prince Melon', the group debuted in late 1980 with an EP, 'SOMETIMES . . . THE FIRE DANCE', following it up with a second four-tracker, '3', early in '81. Avant-garde but surprisingly listenable, The LAUGHING CLOWNS sound was certainly a departure from the sweaty R&B of The SAINTS, employing often dense collages of screeching sax and trumpet (courtesy of new recruits PETER DOYLE and LOUISE ELLIOT), awkward rhythms, off-kilter time signatures and occasional bursts of eastern-tinged jazz improvisation. KUEPPER and Co. even made a foray into vaguely Afro-Cuban/mariachi territory with the melancholy brilliance of 'KNIFE IN MY HEAD', one of the standout tracks on the band's debut album, 'MR UDDICH SCHMUDDICH GOES TO TOWN' (1982). LAUGHING CLOWNS material finally saw a British release via an eponymous compilation on indie label, 'Red Flame', by which point the WALLACE-CRABBE brothers had departed. Despite the pockets of critical acclaim afforded a further two albums, 'LAW OF NATURE' (1984) and 'GHOSTS OF AN IDEAL WIFE' (1985) – the latter's title track featuring some nifty banjo playing from KUEPPER – The LAUGHING CLOWNS split in the mid-80's and KUEPPER set about carving a niche as solo artist. Generally more accessible than The LAUGHING CLOWNS, KUEPPER's solo career got underway with 1985's 'ELECTRICAL STORM' album, the atmospheric, widescreen guitar assault of the title track a long held favourite of KUEPPER obsessives. Playing most of the instruments himself with additional help from a revolving cast of musicians (of whom drummer MARK DAWSON has been the most prominent), KUEPPER kept fans and critics alike rapt by a succession of dazzling albums (almost one a year), displaying a chameleon-like ability to flit between different musical styles. While KUEPPER's striking originality makes any comparisons only a vague pointer, he has at various times sounded vaguely akin to THE THE, The SMITHS (especially on 'BLACK TICKET DAY', originally recorded for 1988's 'HAPPY AS HELL' EP), TEARDROP EXPLODES, JAMES and even R.E.M.. Critics have continually marvelled at KUEPPER's guitar technique (he can also blow a mean harmonica!), while his distinctive vocal is akin to a bastard cross between LLOYD COLE and MARK E SMITH! The archetypal

cult hero, this enigmatic Aussie has gathered rave reviews without sales to match over the course of the last decade, albums such as 'ROOMS OF THE MAGNIFICENT' (1986), 'EVERYBODY'S GOT TO' (1988), 'TODAY WONDER' (1990), 'HONEY STEEL'S GOLD' (1991), 'BLACK TICKET DAY' (1992) and 'SERENE MACHINE' (1993) often featuring in the upper reaches of annual writers polls and even netting him a couple of awards back in Australia. Still going strong in the 90's, 'CHARACTER ASSASSINATION' (1994) and 'A KING IN THE KINDNESS ROOM' (1995) have shown little sign of KUEPPER mellowing, while his simultaneous career with The 'AINTS (so named as a reaction to the still-lumbering-on SAINTS) has produced a series of blistering guitar workouts via 'S.L.S.Q.' (1991), 'ASCENSION' (1991), 'AUTOCANNIBALISM' (1992) and 'AFTERLIFE' (1993), all available – as with KUEPPER's solo output – on Aussie indie label, 'Hot'.
• **Songwriters:** KUEPPER except IF I WERE A CARPENTER (Tim Hardin) / WHITE HOUSES (Eric Burdon & The Animals) / ETERNALLY YOURS .

Album rating: MR UDDICH SCHMUDDICH GOES TO TOWN (*6) / LAUGHTER AROUND THE TABLE (*6) / LAW OF NATURE (*5) / GHOSTS OF AN IDEAL WIFE (*5) / HISTORY OF ROCK'N'ROLL VOLUME ONE compilation (*7) / Ed Kuepper: ELECTRICAL STORM (*7) / ROOMS OF THE MAGNIFICENT (*6) / EVERYBODY'S GOT TO (*6) / TODAY WONDER (*7) / HONEY STEEL'S GOLD (*6) / BLACK TICKET DAY (*6) / SERENE MACHINE (*7) / THE BUTTERFLY NET compilation (*7) / CHARACTER ASSASSINATION (*6) / THE KING IN THE KINDNESS ROOM (*6) / SINGS HIS GREATEST HITS FOR YOU compilation (*6) / FRONTIERLAND (*5) / STARSTRUCK (*5) / THE WHEELIE BIN AFFAIR (*5) / WITH A KNAPSACK ON MY BACK (*6) / CLOUD SURFING (*5) / LIVE (*5) / 'Aints: ASCENSION (*5) / AUTOCANNIBALISM (*5) / S.L.S.Q. (*6) / AFTERLIFE (*5)

EDMUND KUEPPER (b. Germany, 1955) – vocals, guitar (ex-SAINTS) / **DAN WALLACE-CRABBE** – piano / **BEN WALLACE-CRABBE** – bass / **ROBERT FARRELL** – saxophone / **JEFFREY WEGENER** – drums

Missing Link — not iss.

May 80. (m-lp) *(MLB 001)* **THE LAUGHING CLOWNS** [-] [-] Austra
– Clown town / Holy Joe / I want to scream / etc.

Prince Melon — not iss.

Oct 80. (12"ep) *(pm 01)* **SOMETIMES . . . THE FIRE DANCE** [-] [-] Austra
– Sometimes (I just can't live with anyone) / The fire might fall / Crying dance.

—— added **PETER DOYLE** – trumpet

Jan 81. (12"ep) *(pm 05)* **3** [-] [-] Austra
– I don't know what I want / Mr Ridiculous / Ghost beat / Collapse board.

Jul 81. (7") *(pm 2000)* **REIGN OF TERROR. / THRONE OF BLOOD** [-] [-] Austra

—— **LOUISE ELLIOT** – saxophone; repl. BOB + DAN

—— **LESLIE MILLAR** – bass; repl. BEN

Mar 82. (lp) *(pm 5000)* **MR UDDICH SCHMUDDICH GOES TO TOWN** [-] [-] Austra
– Knife in the head / Song of joy / Come one, come all / etc.

Aug 82. (7") *(pm 020)* **MAD FLIES, MAD FLIES. / MR UDDICH** [ ] [-]

Red Flame — not iss.

Aug 82. (lp) *(rf 14)* **LAUGHING CLOWNS** (compilation) [ ] [-]
– The fire might fall / Crying dance / I don't know what I want / Knife in the head / Mr Ridiculous / Sometimes . . . / Ghost beat / Song of joy / Come one, come all / Collapse board.

May 83. (12"ep) *(rf 12-23)* **EVERYTHING THAT FLIES (IS NOT A BIRD). / THE YEAR OF THE BLOATED GOAT / KNIFE IN THE HEAD** [ ] [-]
(above was also rel.in Australia; last track being repl. by 'NOTHING THAT HARMS ' & 'EVERY DOG HAS ITS DAY')

Rough Trade — not iss.

Aug 83. (lp) *(RTD 14)* **LAUGHTER AROUND THE TABLE** [-] [-] German
– Everything that flies (is not a bird) / Nothing that harms / Every dog has its day / Laughter around the table / Theme from Mad Flies, Mad Flies / Sometimes . . . / Crying dance / The fire might fall / When what you see.

—— **KUEPPER + WEGENER** recruited new members; **PETER MILTON-WALSH** – bass (ex-APARTMENTS) (repl. MILLAR who went solo making one eponymouse set in 1986 for 'Directional'; another lp, 'THE KEY – CONSUMOSOCIETY') / guest **CHRIS ABRAHAMS** – piano (of BENDERS)

—— (below 'Hot' releases were issued months earlier in Australia)

Hot — not iss.

Oct 84. (7") *(HOT)* **JUST BECAUSE I LIKE. /** [-] [-] Austra

Dec 84. (lp) *(HOT 1004)* **LAW OF NATURE** [ ] [-] Jun84
– Written in exile / Law of nature / Possessions / Eternally yours / The year is more important / Just because I like / etc. *(cd-iss. Nov92; HOT 1004CD)*

Jan 85. (12"/7") *(HOT 12+/001)* **ETERNALLY YOURS. /** [ ] [-] Apr84

Aug 85. (lp) *(HOT 1013)* **GHOSTS OF AN IDEAL WIFE** [ ] [-] Feb85
– Crystal clear / Diabolical creature / No words of honour / Winter's way / Ghosts of an ideal wife / The only one that knows / New bully in town / It gets so sentimental / The flypaper. *(cd-iss. Nov93; HOT 1013CD)*

—— had already disbanded late in '84. MILTON-WALSH rejoined The APARTMENTS, while WEGENER guested for NICK CAVE & THE BAD SEEDS

– compilations, etc. –

Sep 86. (lp) *Hot; (HOT 1010)* **HISTORY OF ROCK'N'ROLL VOLUME 1** [ ] [-] Oct84
(cd-iss. Mar93; HOT 1010CD)

Aug 95. (cd) *Hot; (HOT 1055CD)* **GOLDEN DAYS . . . WHEN GIANTS WALKED THE EARTH** [ ] [-]
– Eternally yours / Theme from Mad Flies, Mad Flies / Winter's way / Mr Uddich Smuddich / Holy Joe / I don't know what I want / Possessions / Eulogy / The flypaper / Every dog has its day.

ED KUEPPER

—— with **PAUL SMITH** – bass / **MARK DAWSON** – drums / **CHRIS ABRAHAMS** – keyboards / + guest LOUIS TILLET – viola (on debut)

—— (below material released months earlier on 'True Tone' Australia)

Hot — not iss.

May 86. (lp) *(HOT 1020)* **ELECTRICAL STORM** [ ] [-] Sep85
– Master of two servants / When the sweet turns sour / etc *(re-iss. Nov91; same) (cd-iss. Jan93; HOT 1020CD)*

Oct 86. (7") **ALSO SPRACH THE KING OF EURO-DISCO. /** [-] [-] Austra

Jan 87. (7") **I AM YOUR PRINCE. /** [-] [-] Austra

Feb 87. (lp) *(HOT 1027)* **ROOMS OF THE MAGNIFICENT** [ ] [-] Nov86
– Rooms of the magnificent / Also Sprach the king of Euro-disco / Sea air / The sixteen days / Without your mirror / No point in working / I am your prince / Spent five years / Show pony / Nothing you can do. *(cd-iss. Feb93; HOT 1027CD)*

—— **JIM BOWMAN** – keyboards; repl. ABRAHAMS

Apr 87. (7") **NOT A SOUL AROUND. /** [-] [-] Austra

Sep 87. (12"ep) **NOTHING CHANGES IN MY HOUSE. / AT TIMES SO EMOTIONAL** [-] [-] Austra

Apr 88. (7") **(WHEN THERE'S) THIS PARTY. /** [-] [-] Austra

Jun 88. (7") **TOO MANY CLUES. /** [-] [-] Austra

Sep 88. (12") **BURNED MY FINGERS. /** [-] [-] Austra

1988. (12"ep) **HAPPY AS HELL EP** [-] [-] Austra
– Everything's fine / Sometimes / Ghost of an ideal wife / New bully in the town.

Capitol — Capitol

Jun 89. (cd/c/lp) *(CD/TC+/EST 2099)* <790513-2/-4/-1> **EVERYBODY'S GOT TO** [ ] [ ] Apr88
– Everybody's got to / Too many clues / (When there's) This party / Standing in the cold, in the rain / Lonely paradise / Burned my fingers / Not a soul around / Nothing changes in my house / Spartan spirituals / No skin off your nose. *(cd re-iss. Jun94 on 'Hot'; HOT 1044CD)*

Rattlesnake — not iss.

Nov 90. (lp/cd) *(RAT 506/+CD)* **TODAY WONDER** [ ] [-] Jun90
– Horse under water / Always the woman pays / Everything I've got belongs to you / What you don't know / I'd rather be the Devil / There's nothing natural / Medley: Pretty Mary – Eternally yours – If I were a carpenter. *(cd re-iss. Sep93 on 'Hot'; HOT 1032CD)*

Hot — Restless

Nov 91. (cd) *(HOT 1036CD)* <72950> **HONEY STEEL'S GOLD** [ ] [ ] Jun95
– King of vice / Everything I've got belongs to you / Friday's blue / Honey steel's gold / The way I made you feel / Not too soon / Closer (but disguised) / Summerfield / Cheer – Libertines of Oxley. *(re-iss. Nov93; same) (c-iss.Jun94; HOT 1036MC)*

Apr 92. (cd-ep) **THE WAY I MADE YOU FEEL** [ ] [-]

Jun 92. (cd-ep) **REAL WILD LIFE. / BLACK TICKEY DAY** [ ] [-]

Sep 92. (lp/cd) *(HOT 1040/+CD)* **BLACK TICKET DAY** [ ] [-]
– It's lunacy / Blind girl stripper / Real wild life / All my ideas run to crime / Black ticket day / Helps me understand / There's nothing natural / Walked thin wires. *(c-iss.Jun94; HOT 140MC)*

May 93. (cd) *(HOT 1042CD)* **SERENE MACHINE** [ ] [-]
– When she's down / Sleepy head (serene machine) / Who's been talkin' / It's happening before / I wish you were here / Maria Peripatetica / Sounds like mysterious wind / Reasons / This hideous place / (You) Don't know what to steal / You can't please everybody (Sweete reprise) / Married to my lazy life. *(c-iss.Jun94; HOT 1042MC)*

Jul 93. (cd) *(HOT 1045CD)* **THE BUTTERFLY NET** (compilation) [ ] [-]
– Not a soul around / At times, so emotional / Nothing changes in my house / Sometimes / Everything's fine / Also Sprach the king of Euro-disco / Ghost of an ideal wife / New bully in the town / Sea air / Electrical storm / What you don't know / Black ticket day / The way I made you feel / Real wild life / Always the woman pays / It's lunacy / Honey steel's gold / Everything I've got belongs to you. *(c-iss.Jun94; HOT 1045MC)*

Sep 94. (d-lp/c/cd) *(HOT 1049/+MC/CD)* <72953> **CHARACTER ASSASSINATION** [ ] [ ]
– By the way / Little fiddle (and the ghost of Christmas past) / The cockfighter / My best interests at heart / Take it by the hand / La di doh / I'm with you / Ill wind / So close to certainty / A good soundtrack / Ring of fire / If I had a ticket.

Jul 95. (cd) *(HOT 1052CD)* **THE KING IN THE KINDNESS ROOM** [ ] [-]
– Confessions of a window cleaner / Pissed off / Highway to Hell / Messin' (part 2) / They call me Mr Sexy / Sundown / Space pirate / Diving board.

Mar 96. (cd) *(HOT 1057CD)* **SINGS HIS GREATEST HITS FOR YOU** (compilation) [ ] [-]
– The way I made you feel / Pissed off / The real wild life / If I had a ticket / Sleepy head / This hideous place / La di doh / It's lunacy / Highway to Hell / I'm with you / Black ticket day / Everything I've got belongs to you / Confessions in Paradise / I wish you were here / Dark sad eyes.

Oct 96. (cd) *(HOT 1058CD)* <89343> **FRONTIERLAND** [ ] [ ] Jan97
– All of these things / Fireman Joe / Weepin' willow / How would you plead / MDDP Limited / Pushin' fear / Roughneck blues / Someone told me / Poor Howard.

May 97. (cd-ep) *(HIT 014)* **WEEPIN' WILLOW / ALL OF THESE THINGS / CHLORINE VENDOR / FRIEND OR LENDER** [ ] [-]

Jul 97. (cd-ep) *(HOT 13)* **ALL OF THESE THINGS EP** [ ] [-]
– All of these things / Hardhats and handbags / No.3 runaway / All of these things #2.
(cd-ep) *(HOT 13X)* – ('A'side) / Perry rests his case / Shushin' fear / More of those things.

Hot — Hot

Jul 97. (cd) *(HOT 1064CD)* <1/2> **STARSTRUCK** <US-titles 'I WAS A MAIL ORDER BRIDEGROOM' & 'EXOTIC MAIL ORDER MOODS'> [ ] [ ]
– Lion to your lamb / Hardhats and handbags / No.3 runaway / Rape of Cornelius / Love and happiness / Eightball / Spook / Annie 1 / Spook strain / Spring Is sprung / Rachel owns the creek / Favourite angel / Wenleslas' daughter / Too many things / Angel's lament / Messin' with the tall / Diving board / Love me splendour / Christmas cake / Tom's theme / Green hat / Paul and Laurie have a party / Supermarket – Heaven / Evetbody's got to / Pleading ignorance / International playboys vs. the third reich.

Jul 98. (cd) *(HOT 1065CD)* **THE WHEELIE BIN AFFAIR** [ ] [-]
– Highway to Hell / Edmund the confessor / Steam train / No wonder – Built for comfort / It's still nowhere / Car headlights / Chlorine vendor / Indian reservation / Cyprus Grove blues / Wasn't I pissed off today sayeth Bing Bing the techno king / Milk cow blues / Someone's responsible / Lament for a lousy lover / Eternally yours / Romance in Karaoke hell.

Jul 98. (cd) *(HOT 1066CD)* **WITH A KNAPSACK ON MY BACK (live)** [ ] [-]
– Sleepy head / Sam Hall / Highway to Hell / All of these things / Little fiddle / Weepin' willow / I'm with you / Messin' / La di doh / Eternally yours / Crowd rain chant / Poor Howard / When I first came to this land / I'd rather be the Devil / Sea air / Blind girl stripper.

Jul 98. (cd) *(HOT 1069CD)* **CLOUDSURFIN'** -
– Gun runnin' / Three stigmata of James Ulmer / Last of the knucklemen / Delegation for the masses / Don't say you don't say / My dog killed ma gurski's cook / Thickness of two planks / Bikie groupie.

Jul 98. (cd) *(HOT 1070CD)* **LIVE (live)** -
– Intro / Electrical storm / Honey's steel gold / Confessions of a window cleaner / Liddle fiddle / La di doh / My best interests at heart / Weeping willow blues / When I first came to this land / Black ticket day / Poor little fool.

- compilations, etc. -

Sep 93. (cd/c) *Castle; (<CCS CD/MC 384>)* **THE LEGENDARY BULLY** Oct94

The AINTS!

— **ED KUEPPER** – vocals, guitar / **KENT STEEDMAN** – bass / **TIM REEVES** – drums

UFO not iss.

Nov 91. (lp/cd) *(UF 0005/+CD)* **ASCENSION** -
– It's still nowhere / What's it like out there? / A good soundtrack / Like an oil spill / Both worlds / Ascension. *(cd re-iss. Nov93 Aug95 & & May97 on 'Hot'; HOT 1035CD)*

Hot Restless

Jun 92. (cd) *(HOT 1037CD)* **AUTOCANNIBALISM** -
– You can't please everybody / Other side of the creek / Linda and Abilene / Ill wind / Red aces / The 'Aints go pop-camping. *(re-iss. Aug95 & May97; same)*

Apr 93. (cd) *(AINTONECD)* **S.L.S.Q. - VERY LIVE! (live SAINTS reworkings 1991)** -
– Intro / This perfect day / Erotic neurotic / Runaway / Know your product / River deep, mountain high / Audience rain chant / Messin' with the kid / Nights in Venice. *(re-iss. Aug95; same)*

Aug 93. (cd) *(HIT 004CD)* **CHEAP EROTICA** -

Dec 93. (cd) **AFTERLIFE** - - Austra

Jul 95. (lp/cd) *(HOT 1053/+CD)* **THE MOST PRIMITIVE BAND IN THE WORLD (live from the Twilight Zone, Brisbane 1974)** -
– Wild about you / Do the robot / One way street / Knock on wood / Erotic neurotic / River deep, mountain high / Lies / Misunderstood / Messin' with the kid / Stranded.

Aug 95. (cd) *(HOT 1054CD) <72957>* **SHELFLIFE UNLIMITED!! HOTTER THAN THE BLAZING PISTOLS!!!**
– Like an oil spill / Ill wind / River deep, mountain high / It's still nowhere / Erotic neurotic / The Aints go pop-camping / What's it like out there? / Linda and Abilene.

LEAD INTO GOLD (see under ⇒ MINISTRY)

Paul LEARY (see under ⇒ BUTTHOLE SURFERS)

LEATHER NUN

Formed: Goreburg, Sweden ... 1979 by JONAS ALMQUIST, a DJ and fanzine editor with a penchant for the Godfather of Punk, IGGY POP. Coming into contact with GENESIS P. ORRIDGE (a member of THROBBING GRISTLE at the time) at a London gig, JONAS handed him a demo of the track, 'DEATH THREATS'. ORRIDGE subsequently released it (as part of the 'SLOW DEATH' EP) on his own 'Industrial' imprint after JONAS had returned from Sweden with a studio ready band drawn from punk group, the STRAIT JACKET (BENGT ARONSSON, FREDDIE WADLING and GERT CLAESSON). The following year, the re-hashed demo also found its way onto a live cassette, 'AT THE SCALA CINEMA', which circulated at gigs around the same time. The gigs in question fuelled controversy after the band used background hardcore gay-pornography to provoke attention, although the focus was obviously peroxide blonde, ALMQUIST, an exotic post-punk clone of IGGY POP and LOU REED (circa '69) complete with cool wraparound shades. FREDDIE departed just after the recording of the long-awaited 'PRIME MOVER' single in 1983, while a revamped version of 'SLOW DEATH' appeared on the similarly titled mini-set in '84, the record featuring guest slots by GENESIS P. and MONTE CAZAZZA. Adding NILS WOHLRABE and replacing recent member, HAKEN with ANDERS OLSSON, the LEATHER NUN finally came up with some fresh songs for the 'Wire' label in mid-85, the result being the appropriately titled 'ALIVE'. The band took a slightly more commercial turn the following year when they "un-covered" the ABBA pop classic, 'GIMME GIMME GIMME (A MAN AFTER MIDNIGHT)'. Such unsavoury albums as 'LUST GAMES' (1986) and 'STEEL CONSTRUCTION' (1987) found their way to the shops before Miles Copeland's 'I.R.S.' imprint took them on in early '88. Although they failed to convert many mainstream indie fans, their dark gospel was enthusiastically received by their cult following on two further albums, 'INTERNATIONAL HEROES' (1990) and 'NUN PERMANENT' (1991), the latter produced by MICK RONSON.

Album rating: SLOW DEATH mini (*5) / ALIVE (*6) / LUST GAMES (*5) / STEEL CONSTRUCTION (*5) / FORCE OF HABIT compilation (*7) / INTERNATIONAL HEROES (*5) / NUN PERMANENT (*5)

JONAS ALMQVIST – vocals / **BENGT ARONSSON** – guitar / **FREDDIE WADLING** – bass / **GERT CLAESSON** – drums

Industrial not iss.

Dec 79. (7"ep) *(IR 0006)* **SLOW DEATH EP** -
– No rule / Death threats / Slow death / Ensam I natt.

1980. (c) *(IRC 27)* **THE LEATHER NUN AT THE SCALA CINEMA (live)** -

Subterranean not iss.

Jan 84. (7") *(SUB 40)* **PRIME MOVER. / F.F.A.** -

— **HAKEN** – bass repl. FREDDIE

Criminal D not iss.

May 84. (m-lp) *(CRI 12113)* **SLOW DEATH** -
(re-iss. Aug86 on 'Wire'; WRMLP 100)

— added **NILS WOHLRABE** – guitar

Wire not iss.

Jul 85. (12") *(WRMS 005)* **506. / FLY, ANGELS, FLY / I'M ALIVE** -

— **ANDERS OLSSON** – bass repl. HAKEN

Dec 85. (lp) *(WRLP 002)* **ALIVE** -
– Prime mover / Fly, angels, fly / Son of a good family / I'm alive / Busted knee caps / F.F.A. / On the road / Here comes life / For the love of your eyes / Lollipop.

Feb 86. (7") *(WRS 007)* **ON THE ROAD. / DESOLATION AVENUE** -
(12"+=) *(WRMS 007)* – Son of a good family.

May 86. (7") *(WRS 009)* **GIMME GIMME GIMME (A MAN AFTER MIDNIGHT). / LOLLIPOP** -
(12"+=) *(WRMS 009)* – ('A'-Chopper mix).
(12") *(WRXS 009)* – ('A'+'B'versions) / ('A'-Chopper version).

Oct 86. (7") *(WRS 010)* **PINK HOUSE. / SPEED OF LIFE** -
(12"+=) *(WRMS 010)* – Lucky strike.

Oct 86. (lp) *(WRMLP 200)* **LUST GAMES** -

May 87. (7") *(WRS 014)* **I CAN SMELL YOUR THOUGHTS (remix). / FALLING APART** -
(12"+=) *(WRMS 014)* – 506 (re-visited).

Aug 87. (7") *(WRS 016)* **COOL SHOES. / I WISH** -
(12"+=) *(WRMS 016)* – Special agent.

Aug 87. (lp/c) *(WR LP/TC 005)* **STEEL CONSTRUCTION** -
– Dance, dance, dance / Someone special like you / Lost and found / Ride to live / Just a hustler / Cool shoes / Summer's so short / Trail of pain / Godzilla is back / Let me be. *(cd+=)* – I wish / Special agent.

Oct 87. (7") *(WRS 020)* **LOST AND FOUND. / SOMEONE SPECIAL LIKE YOU** -
(12") *(WRMS 020)* – ('A'side) / Dance, dance, dance / Ride like a Cheyenne.

Jan 88. (cd) *(WRCD 008)* **FORCE OF HABIT** (compilation) -
– I can smell your thoughts / Jesus came driving along / Pink house / For the love of your eyes / No rule / 506 / Desolation avenue / Gimme gimme gimme (a man after midnight) / Prime mover / Death threats / Have sex with me / F.F.A. / Lollipop / Fly, angels, fly / On the road. *(lp-iss.May88; WRLP 008)*

Oct 88. (12") *(WRMS 021)* **DEMOLITION LOVE. /** -

I.R.S. I.R.S.

Nov 90. (cd/lp) *(WIRE CD/LP 011)* **INTERNATIONAL HEROES**
– Ride into your town / How does it feel / A thousand nights / Whama-lama-bam-bam-boy / Waiting for your train / Reach out / Velvet sky / Hooked to your lips / Toxic darlings / She said / Red guitars.

— basic trio **ALMQVIST, ARONSSON, CLAESSON** + on session **FREDRIK ADLERS** – keyboards / **ULF WIDLUND** – bass / **MATS GRUNDSTROM** – guitar / etc.

1991. (cd/lp) *(WIRE CD/LP 012)* **NUN PERMANENT**
– Take me home / At your doorstep / Girls / These eyes cannot lie / She's so bad / Big city / Desperation drive / She's had a past / Even a fool can learn to love / The sun still shines. *(cd+=)* – I ain't turning back.

— disbanded in the early 90's

- compilations, etc. -

Nov 88. (12"ep) *Nighttracks; (SFNT 014)* **THE EVENING SHOW SESSIONS** (13.7.86) -
– Lust for love / Pure heart / Desolation avenue / Prime mover.

Thomas LEER

Born: THOMAS WISHART, c.1960, Port Glasgow, Scotland. As a young teenager at school, the young THOMAS played and sang in a variety of local experimental pop groups, although with the advent of punk rock he moved down south to London, forming the group, PRESSURE, in the process. By late 1978, again returning to his love of electro-pop and CAN, LEER self-financed his debut single, 'PRIVATE PLANE', a machine-friendly minor classic. The following year, together with ROBERT RENTAL (former musical associate of The NORMAL), he issued a collaboration set, 'THE BRIDGE', although only one track, 'ATTACK DECAY', stood out. In the summer of '81, THOMAS resurfaced as a solo artist with the EP, '4 MOVEMENTS', his first of three promising releases for the stalwart indie imprint, 'Cherry Red'. The last of these, 'ALL ABOUT YOU' (a single and his most commercial so far), paved the way for 'Arista' to snap him up (partly reviving his 'Oblique' set-up), although their idea to release his debut's B-side, 'INTERNATIONAL', was certainly questionable. However, the mid-80's was definitely his most creative period, the long-awaited debut album proper, 'THE SCALE OF TEN', finally delivered towards the end of '85. Two years later, LEER abandoned his ineffectual solo career to help initiate the 'Z.T.T.' duo, ACT, with former PROPAGANDA chanteuse, CLAUDIA BRUCKEN. This partnership began reasonably well with a minor hit single, 'SNOBBERY AND DECAY', although their short-lived professional affair was over after their one and only long-player, 'LAUGHTER, TEARS AND RAGE' (1988), was panned by the press. • **ACT covered:** WHITE RABBIT (Jefferson Airplane) / HEAVEN KNOWS I'M MISERABLE NOW (Smiths).

Album rating: THE SCALE OF TEN (*5) / CONTRADICTIONS – THE CHERRY RED COLLECTION compilation (*7) / Act: LAUGHTER, TEARS & RAGE (*4)

THOMAS LEER – vocals, keyboards, synthesizer

Oblique not iss.

Nov 78. (7") *(ER 101)* **PRIVATE PLANE. / INTERNATIONAL** -

Industrial not iss.

1979. (lp; by THOMAS LEER & ROBERT RENTAL) *(IR 0007)* **THE BRIDGE** -
– Attack decay / Monochrome days / Day breaks, night heals / Connotations / Fade away / Interferon / 6 a.m. / The hard way & the easy way out / Perpetual. *(cd-iss. Jun92 on 'Grey Area'; BRIDGE 1CD)*

Cherry Red — not iss.

Jul 81. (12"ep) *(12CHERRY 28)* **4 MOVEMENTS** [ ] [-]
– Don't / Letter from America / Light as a drum / West End.

Jan 82. (2x12"m-lp) *(ERED 26)* **CONTRADICTIONS** [ ] [-]
– Hear what I say / Mr. Nobody / Contradictions / Looks that kill / Soul gypsy / Choices / Gulf stream.

Nov 82. (7"/12") *(CHERRY/12CHERRY 52)* **ALL ABOUT YOU. / SAVING GRACE** [ ] [-]

Arista — Arista

Jul 84. (7"/12") *(LEER/+12 1)* **INTERNATIONAL. / EASY WAY** [ ] [-]

Feb 85. (7"/12") *(LEER/+12 2)* **HEARTBEAT. / CONTROL YOURSELF** [ ] [-]

May 85. (7") *(LEER 3)* **NO.1. / CHASING THE DRAGON** [ ] [-]
(12"+=) *(LEER 3T)* – Trust me.

Nov 85. (lp/c) *(207/407 208)* **THE SCALE OF TEN** [ ] [ ]

ACT

— **THOMAS LEER + CLAUDIA BRUCKEN** – vocals (ex-PROPAGANDA)

Z.T.T. — Island

May 87. (7") *(ZTAS 28)* **SNOBBERY AND DECAY. / POISON** [60] [ ]
('A'-That's Entertainment mix-12"+=) *(12ZTAS 28)* – I'd be surprisingly good for you.
(12") *(12ZACT 28)* – ('A'-Naked Civil remix) / Strong poison / ('A'- . . .Theme from).
(cd-s) *(CID 28)* – ('A'extended) / I'd be surprisingly good for you / Poison / ('A'- . . .Theme from).
(c-s) *(CTIS 28)* – Snobbery and Decay Cabaret Cassette.

Aug 87. (7") *(IMM 1)* **ABSOLUTELY IMMUNE. / BLOODRUSH** [ ] [-]
(12"+=) *(TIMM 1)* – White rabbit.
(12"+=) *(VIMM 1)* – States of logic.

Feb 88. (7") *(IMM 2)* **I CAN'T ESCAPE FROM YOU. / DEAR LIFE** [ ] [-]
(12"+=/cd-s+=) *(T/CD IMM 2)* – ('A'-Love And Hate) / Heaven knows I'm miserable now.

Jun 88. (7"; w-drawn) *(BET 1)* **CHANCE. / WINNER '88** [-] [-]
(12"+=/cd-s+=) *(BET T/CD 1)* – Chance (we give you another chance).

Jul 88. (lp/c/cd) *(ZQ CD/MC/LP 1)* **LAUGHTER, TEARS & RAGE** [ ] [ ]
– Absolutely immune / Chance / Laughter / I can't escape from you / Poison / Under the nights of Germany / Gestures / A friendly warning / Certified / Where love lies bleeding / Snobbery and decay. *(c+=)* – Bloodrush / Poison. *(cd++=)* – Heaven knows I'm miserable now / The 3rd planet.

— when CLAUDIA went solo the duo split and LEER retired

– (THOMAS LEER) compilation –

Jan 94. (cd) *Cherry Red; (CDBRED 105)* **CONTRADICTIONS – THE CHERRY RED COLLECTION** [ ] [-]
– Private plane / International / Kings of sham / Dry land / Don't / Letter from America / Tight as a drum / West end / CONTRADICTIONS (tracks) / All about you / Love and flowers / Togetherness and unity.

LEFTFIELD

Formed: London, England . . . 1990 by ex-teacher of English NEIL BARNES and PAUL DALEY, formerly of Balearic housers A MAN CALLED ADAM. Barnes had previously released the 'Mississippi Burning'-sampling 'NOT FORGOTTEN' on dance indie Outer Rhythm and when the single became an underground club hit, contractual problems ensued. Undeterred, the duo kept a high profile with remix work (including David Bowie and Inner City) before setting up the Hard Hands label and cutting two singles in 1992, 'RELEASE THE PRESSURE' and 'SONG OF LIFE', the latter a slow building progressive house epic which further enhanced their dancefloor reputation and nudged into the lower regions of the pop charts. But the song that really branded LEFTFIELD into the musical consciousness of the nation was the pounding crossover hit, 'OPEN UP'. A collaboration with P.I.L.'s JOHN LYDON, his blood curdling wail of 'BURN HOLLYWOOD BURN' was scarier than Michael Bolton's mullet cut and was enough to have the video banned from ITV's Chart Show. Spookily enough, the song was released at the same time as a spate of Californian fires . . . The single was a corking tune into the bargain and climbed to No.13 in the charts. The debut album, 'LEFTISM' was greeted with critical plaudits galore upon its release in 1995, reaching No.3 in the U.K. and even being nominated for The Mercury Music Prize . An exhilirating cross-fertilisation of musical stylings, the album took pumping techno trance as its base ingredient, interspersing this with everything from cerebral sonic tapestries ('MELT') to dark, foreboding drum 'n' bass ('STORM 3000'). It contained all the aforementioned singles (save the earlier 'NOT FORGOTTEN') as well as a vocal-led collaboration with goth goddess Toni Halliday. LEFTFIELD enjoyed further chart success with tracks and remixes from the album and contributed material to both the 'Shallow Grave' and 'Trainspotting' film soundtracks. A nationwide tour and a series of legendary festival appearances in 1996 cemented their position as one of the key players in the new techno vanguard alongside Underworld, Prodigy et al. • **Songwriters:** BARNES / DALEY / guests and some samples. • **Trivia:** Their label 'Hard Hands' run by manager LISA HORRAN, also included acts VINYL BLAIR, DELTA LADY, DEE PATTEN and SCOTT HARRIS.

Album rating: BACKLOG compilation (*6) / LEFTISM (*9)

NEIL BARNES – DJ, percussion, synthesizers / **PAUL DALEY** – samples (ex-A MAN CALLED ADAM)

Outer Rhythm — not iss.

Mar 90. (12") *(FOOT 3)* **NOT FORGOTTEN. / PATELL'S ON THE CASE / ('A'version)** [ ] [-]

Feb 91. (12") *(FOOT 9)* **NOT FORGOTTEN (Hard Hands mix). / MORE THAN I KNOW** [ ] [-]
(12") *(FOOT 9R)* – ('A'&'B'remixes).

Hard Hands — Medicine

Aug 92. (12"ltd.; featuring EARL SIXTEEN) *(HAND 001T)* **RELEASE THE PRESSURE (3 track vocal)** [ ] [-]
(12"ltd.) *(HAND 001R)* – Release the dubs (instrumental mixes).

Nov 92. (12"ltd.) *(HAND 002T)* **SONG OF LIFE. / FANFARE OF LIFE / DUB OF LIFE** [59] [ ]
(12") *(HAND 002R)* – ('A'-3 Underworld mixes).
(cd-s) *(HAND 002CD)* – ('A'side) / Fanfare of life / Release the dub.

Dec 92. (cd) *(OUTERCD 1)* **BACKLOG** (compilation of above material on 'Outer Rhythm') [ ] [-]

— Below single with JOHN LYDON (of PUBLIC IMAGE LTD) on vocals

Nov 93. (7"/c-s; as LEFTFIELD / LYDON) *(HAND 9/+MC) <42232>* **OPEN UP (radio edit). / ('A'instrumental)** [13] [ ] Feb94
(12"+=)(cd-s+=) *(HAND 9 T/CD)* – ('A'vocal 12"mix) / ('A'-Dervish overdrive mix) / ('A'-Andrew Weatherall mix) / ('A'-Dust Brothers mix).
(12") *(HAND 9R)* – ('A'remixes).

Hard Hands — Sony-Columbia

Jan 95. (cd/c/d-lp) *(HAND CD/MC/LP 2/+D) <67231-2/-4/-1>* **LEFTISM** [3] [ ]
– Release the pressure / Afro-left / Melt / Song of life / Original / Black flute / Space shanty / Inspection (check one) / Storm 3000 / Open up / 21st century poem. *(iss.Apr95, 3x12"+=) (HANDLP 2T)* – Half past dub. *(cd w/ bonus disc)* – Afro-left (Afro-ride) / Release the pressure (release one) / Original (live dub) / Filter fish / Afro-left (Afro-Central) / Release the pressure (release four).

— Below single as featured TONI HALLIDAY (ex-CURVE) on vocals

Mar 95. (c-ep/cd-ep; as LEFTFIELD & HALLIDAY) *(HAND 18 MC/CD)* **ORIGINAL / ('A'-live mix) / ('A'jam mix) / FILTER FISH** [18] [-]
(12"ep) *(HAND 18T)* – ('A'-Drift version) – repl. ('A'live)

Jul 95. (12"ep/c-ep/cd-ep; LEFTFIELD featuring DJUM DJUM) *(HAND 23 T/MC/CD) <78045>* **AFRO-LEFT EP** [22] [ ]
– Afro left / Afro ride / Afro sol / Afro central.

Jan 96. (c-s) *(HAND 29MC)* **RELEASE THE PRESSURE (remix 96 vocal): RELEASE ONE / RELEASE TWO** [13] [ ]
(12"+=) *(HAND 29T)* – Release four.
(cd-s++=) *(HAND 29CD)* – Release three.

LEGENDARY PINK DOTS

Formed: London, England . . . late 1980 by EDWARD KA-SPEL and PHILIP KNIGHT (aka THE SILVERMAN). This outfit released their debut album, 'BRIGHTER NOW' (1982), for the Birmingham-based indie label, 'In-Phaze', although they subsequently moved to the Netherlands a few years later after the disappointing reception afforded 'THE TOWER' album. Signing to Belgium's 'Play It Again Sam', they issued the first of several albums, 'FACES IN THE FIRE' (1984). Experimental and exploratory, this electro-psychedelic outfit were akin to FAUST or CAN meeting STEVE HILLAGE or SYD BARRETT, a less than commercial approach which left them as perennial alternative fringe players. Nevertheless, KA-SPEL moonlighted as a solo artist around the same time, releasing the first of many albums, 'LAUGH CHINA DOLL'. He also collaborated with SKINNY PUPPY on the TEARGARDEN project for the 1987 album, TIRED EYES SLOWLY BURNING'. Various LPD personnel came and went and, in the 90's they came up with their best efforts to date, 'THE MARIA DIMENSION' (1991) and 'SHADOW WEAVER' (1992). The latter was promoted by a US tour, KA-SPEL and Co. having previously been refused work permits due to the "lack of artistic merit" rule!

Album rating: BRIGHTER NOW (*5) / THE TOWER (*7) / STONE CIRCLES (*7) / THE MARIA DIMENSION (*8) / SHADOW WEAVER (*7) / 9 LIVES TO WONDER (*7)

EDWARD KA-SPEL (as D'ARCHANGEL) – vocals, instruments / **PHILIP KNIGHT** (as THE SILVERMAN) – keyboards, tapes, samples

In-Phaze — not iss.

Jan 82. (lp) *(IPNER 1)* **BRIGHTER NOW** [ ] [-]
– Red castles / Louder after six / The wedding / Apocalypse then / Legacy / City ghosts / Hanging gardens / Soma bath / Premonition four. *(re-iss. Jun86 on 'Terminal Kaleidoscope'; TK 001)*

— added **ROLAND CALLOWAY** (as PRUUMPTJE JUSTE) – bass / **STRET MAJEST** – guitars / **APRIL ILIFFE** – vocals, keyboards

Aug 83. (lp) *(PHA 2)* **CURSE** [ ] [-]
– Love puppets / Wallpurges night / Lisa's party / Arzhklahh Olgevezh / Pruumptje kurss / Waving at the aeroplanes / Hiding / Doll's house / The palace of love / Stoned obituary. *(re-iss. Dec86 on 'Terminal Kaleidoscope'; TK 002) (cd-iss. Aug88; TK 002CD)*

— added **PAT PAGANINI** (aka WRIGHT) – violin, keyboards, vocals

May 84. (lp) *(PHA 3)* **THE TOWER** [ ] [-]
– Black zone / Break day / Tower one / Vigil-anti / A lust for powder / Poppy day / Tower two / Astrid / Rope and glory / Tower three / Tower four / Tower five. *(cd-iss. Aug88 with 'BRIGHTER NOW' on 'Terminal Kaleidoscope'; TK 003CD)*

Ding Dong — not iss.

Jan 85. (lp) *(DDD 3333)* **THE LOVERS** [-] [-] Dutch
– MMMmmmmmmmmmm / Geisha mermaid / The heretic / Jungle / The lovers (part 1) / Silverture / Flowers for the silverman / The lovers (part 2). *(cd-iss. 1990 on 'Play It Again Sam'+=; CDBIAS 156)* – Curious guy / Premonition 16.

Play It Again Sam — S.P.V.

Jun 84. (lp) *(BIAS 01)* **FACES IN THE FIRE** [ ] [-]
– Blasto / Love in a plain brown envelope / Sleeso / Neon gladiators / Kitto / Eight minutes to live. *(cd-iss. Aug88; CDBIAS 001)*

— added **GRAHAM WHITEHEAD** –

Sep 85. (d-lp) *(BIAS 12)* **ASYLUM** [ ] [-]

– Echo police / Gorgon Zola's baby / Fifteen flies in the marmalade / Femme mirage / The hill / Demonism / Prisoner / So gallantly screaming / I am the way, the truth, the light / Agape / Golden dawn / The last straw / A message from our sponsor / Go ask Alice / This could be the end. *(cd-iss. Mar88; CDBIAS 012)*

— added **HANS MEYER** – saxophone, flute, electronics / **BOB PISTOOR** – guitar, bass (to KA-SPEL, THE SILVERMAN)

Aug 86. (12") *(BIAS 030)* **CURIOUS GUY. / PREMONITION 16** [ ] [-]
Nov 86. (lp) *(BIAS 041)* **ISLAND OF JEWELS** [ ] [-]
– Tower six / The red and the black / The dairy / Emblem parade / Jewel on an island / Rattlesnake arena / The shock of contact / Jewel in the crown / Our lady in chambers / Our lady in Kharki / Our lady in darkness / The guardians of Eden. *(cd-iss. 1988; CDBIAS 041)*
Oct 87. (12"ep) *(BIAS 074)* **UNDER GLASS. / THE LIGHT IN MY LITTLE GIRL'S EYES / THE PLASMA TWINS** [ ] [-]
Nov 87. (cd/lp) *(CD+/BIAS 080)* **ANY DAY NOW** [ ] [ ]
– Casting the runes / A strychnine kiss / Laguna beach / The gallery / Neon mariners / True love / The peculiar funfair / Waiting for the cloud / Cloud zero / Under glass / The light in my little girl's eyes / The plasma twins.
Nov 88. (lp) *(BIAS 101)* **STONE CIRCLES** (compilation) [ ] [-]
– Love puppets / Black zone / Golden dawn / Curious day / The hanging gardens / Fifteen flies / Our lady in darkness / Apocalypse / Gladiators (version). *(cd-iss. Apr89; CDBIAS 101)*
Jul 89. (cd/c/lp) *(CD/C+/BIAS 103)* **THE GOLDEN AGE** (compilation) [ ] [-]
Oct 89. (12"ep/cd-ep) *(BIAS 109/+CD)* **BLACK-LIST. / METHODS / OUR LADY OF CERVETORI** [ ] [-]
Feb 90. (12"ep/cd-ep) *(BIAS)* **PRINCESS COLDHEART / THE PLEASURE PALACE. / THE COLLECTOR / C.V.A.** [ ] [-]
Mar 90. (cd/c/lp) *(CD/C+/BIAS 149)* **THE CRUSHED VELVET APOCALYPSE** [ ] [ ]
– I love you in your tragic beauty / Green gang / Hellsville / Hellowe'en / The safe way / Just a lifetime / he death of Jack The Ripper / New tomorrow. *(cd+=)* – Princess Coldheart / The pleasure palace / The collector / C.V.A.

— **KA-SPEL, KNIGHT + PISTOOR** added **NIELS VAN HOORNBLOWER** – wind, bass

Mar 91. (cd/lp) *(CD+/BIAS 184)* **THE MARIA DIMENSION** [ ] [ ]
– Disturbance / Pennies for Heaven / The third secret / The grain kings / The ocean cried "blue murder" / Belladonna / A space between / Evolution. *(cd w/free cd-ep+=)* – I DREAM OF GEANNIE / LITTLE OYSTER / SHE GAVE ME AN APPLE / STIRRED BUT NOT SHAKEN / WHERE NO MAN *(cd+=)* – Cheraderama / Lilith / Fourth secret / Expresso noir / Home / Crushed velvet.
Sep 92. (cd) *(BIAS 225CD)* **SHADOW WEAVER** [ ] [ ]
– Zero zero / Guilty man / Ghosts of unborn children / City of needles / Stitching time / Twilight hour / Key to heaven / Laughing guest / Prague Spring / Leper colony.

— **RYAN MOORE** – bass (of TEARGARDEN) repl. PISTOOR

— added **MARTYN DE KLEER** – guitar

Mar 93. (cd) *(BIAS 236CD)* **MALACHAI** (Shadow Weaver pt.2) [ ] [ ]
– Joey the canary / Kingdom of the flies / Encore une fois / Wildlife estate / Pavane / Window of the world / On the boards / We bring the day / Paris 4 a.m.

— with drummer **CEVIN KEY** (of SKINNY PUPPY)

Mar 94. (cd) *(BIAS 280CD)* **NINE LIVES TO WONDER** [ ] [ ]
– Madame Guillotine / On another shore / Softly softly / Crumbs on the carpet / Hotel Z / Oasis Malade / A crack in melancholy time / Siren / The angel trail / Nine shades to a circle / A terra firma welcome.

Terminal Kaleidoscope — not iss.

1994. (ltd-cd) **FOUR DAYS** [ ] [-]

Mirrodot — not iss.

1995. (d-cd) **CHEMICAL PLAYSCHOOL 10** [ ] [-]
– Scarlet wish / Inside / Colour wheel / Disaster area / Nouveaux modes exotiques / Glasshouse / The man with the cut-glass heart / Little Romeo / Kleine Juliet / Saucers #1 / Premonition 19 / Wonderdome.

Soleilmoon — Staalplaat

Sep 95. (cd) *(28)* *<STCD 099)>* **FROM HERE YOU'LL WATCH THE WORLD GO BY** [ ] [ ]
– Clockwise / Citadel / Friend / A velvet resurrection / Kollusim / 1001 commandments / Remember me this way / This one-eyed man is king / Straight on 'til morning / Damien / This hollowed ground.

Soleilmoon — Soleilmoon

Jan 96. (cd-ep) *(SOL 31CD)* **REMEMBER ME THIS WAY EP** [ ] [-]
Sep 96. (cd) *(SOL 43CD)* **IT'S RAINING IN HEAVEN** [ ] [-]
Jan 98. (cd-ep) *(SOL 56CD)* **STERRE** [ ] [-]
– Sterre / Spike psychomix / Elefant's graveyard / Sterre.
Dec 98. (12"ep/cd-ep) *(SOL 74/+CD)* **PRE MILLENNIAL SINGLE EP** [ ] [-]
– Hellsville '98 / Needles / Andromeda suite '98 / Abracadabra zzzz.
Dec 98. (lp/cd) *(<SOL 75/+CD>)* **NEMESIS ONLINE** [ ] [ ]
– Dissonance / Jasz / As long as it's purple and green / Under your wheels / Sunset for a swan / Is it something I said? / Zoo / Fate's faithful punchline / Cheating the shadow / Abracadabra / Slaapliedje.

– compilations, etc –

on 'Play It Again Sam' unless mentioned otherwise

Jul 83. (cd) *Third Man Tapes; (TMT 08)* **BASILISK** [ ] [-]
Nov 88. (lp) *Materiali Sonori; (MASO 70009)* **GREETING 9** [-] [-] Italy
1989. (3xlp-box/d-cd) *(BIAS 834/+CD)* **THE LEGENDARY PINK BOX** [ ] [-]
1996. (cd) *Terminal Kaleidoscope;* **PRAYER FOR ARCADIA** [ ] [-]
Aug 96. (cd) *(BIAS 325CD)* **CANTA MIENTRAS PUEDAS** ('90-'95) [ ] [-]
– Belladonna / I love you in your tragic beauty / Green gang / Princess coldheart / Disturbance / The grain kings / Prague spring / A triple moon salute / Joey the canary / Siren / The angel trail / A velvet resurrection (version) / Friend (version).
May 97. (cd) *R.O.I.R.; (RUSCD 8231)* **UNDER TRIPLE MOONS** (very early material) [ ] [-]
– As if / Splash / Submerged / Amphitheatre / Digital / Dying for the emperor / Oceans of emotion / Small anthem / Intruder / Premonition 2 / Frosty / One for the pearl moon / Whore of Babylon / War of silence / Garlands / Lust for powder / Punishment / Down from the country / Premonition 1.

EDWARD KA-SPEL

with **PATRICK Q. WRIGHT** – violin, keyboards, vocals / **PATRICK WRIGHT** – guitars, keyboards

In-Phaze — not iss.

Jun 84. (12") *(HAZ 6)* **DANCE, CHINA DOLL. /** [ ] [-]
Sep 84. (lp) *(PHA 6)* **LAUGH CHINA DOLL - NOTHING ELSE** [ ] [-]
– Lilith's daughter / Eye contact / Lady sunshine / Find the lady / Requiem / Suicide pact / Paradise then / Irrational anthem / Lisa's funeral / The glass moved by itself / Atomic roses. *(cd-iss. Jan90 on 'Licensed'; LD 894) (cd re-iss. Sep95 on 'Staalplaat'; STCD 090)*

— now with **LADY SUNSHINE** (EDWARD's wife ELKE KA-SPEL) – vocals / **HERO WOUTERS** – keyboards / **NEEL HOLST** – saxophone / **MATTHIEU KEIZER** – percussion

Scarface — not iss.

Aug 85. (lp) *(FACE 13)* **EYES! CHINA DOLL** [ ] [-]
– Mirror soul / Avengelist / God in a cupboard / Blowing bubbles (part 2) / Six cats on a dead man's chest / "Joey" – the video / The char char / Intermezzo / Hotel Blanc.

— with **STAPLETON + SUNSHINE + WRIGHT**(latter as PAGANINI)

Torso — not iss.

Mar 86. (lp) *(TORSO 33-013)* **CHYEKK CHINA DOLL** [-] [-] Dutch
– Lines / The infinity waltz / Prelude for a splash / The price of salvation / Chyekk 1 / Lisa's christening / Chyekk 2 / Beautiful, naked / Klazh, Tristurr / Lisa's resurrection / The power, the power / The glory, the glory. *(cd-iss. Nov88; TORSO CD013) (d-cd incl. AAAZHYD CHINA DOLL* – Forbidden zone / Colour me vexed, Desiree / AA-Zhyd China doll / Flesh parade / Qa'spell / The unfortunate demise of the fabulous fool / Nuts in May / Traitor's gate / Blowing bubbles (pt.3) / Fool / Witchfinder suite pt.1-6.

Play It Again Sam — not iss.

1989. (lp) **PERHAPS WE'LL ONLY SEE A THIN BLUE LINE** [ ] [-]

Third Mind — not iss.

Oct 91. (cd) *(TM 92671)* **TANITH AND THE LION TREE** [ ] [-]
– O' from the great sea / Tanith and the lion tree / Interference / Four out of ten / Loop 1 / Loop 2 / Bakersman / Prithee / Prisoners of war / Three times daily / Hotel X / Epilogue / Phoney war / Old man trouble. *<(re-iss. Jan98 on 'Soleilmoon'; SOL 85CD>)*

Soleilmoon — not iss.

Oct 95. (cd) *(SOL 29CD)* **DOWN IN THE CITY OF HEARTBREAK & NEEDLES** [ ] [-]

Staalplaat — not iss.

Feb 96. (cd) *(1009)* **KHATACLIMICI CHINA DOLL** [ ] [-]
Jan 98. (cd) *(60)* **LYVV CHINA DOLL** (rec.1994) [ ] [-]
– Char char / Wenn alte gotter sterben / Tower 8 / Bleak house / Corridors of deceit / Dada / Infirmary waltz / (untitled) / Lying oin state / Sneezing choirs / March of the anorexic locusts / Beautiful, plastic / Pretty ribbons / Vla / Culumnyeiz / God bless the cavalry (pt.1) / God bless the cavalry (pt.2) / Zyrrup / Horn section / Intent / Bleeding finale.

Terminal Kaleidoscope — not iss.

1996. (cd) **THE SCRIPTURES OF ILLUMINA** [ ] [-]

Soleilmoon — not iss.

Dec 98. (cd) *(SOL 60CD)* **DOWN IN THE CITY OF HEARTBREAK & NEEDLES, VOL.2** [ ] [-]
– Even now / Lady sunshine / Find the lady / Inferno / Illusion / The man who never was / Paradise then / Atomic roses / Crack in melancholy time / Fool with spanners / Number nine number nine number nine . . .

— Also, RYAN MOORE as TWILIGHT CIRCUS released 2 cd's 'IN DUB' (1995) & 'OTHER WORLDS OF DUB' both for 'M Records – Terminal Kaleidoscope'. Other members of LPD collaborated with CHRISTOPH & ANDREAS HEEMANN became MIMIR. Issued 'MIMIR' (1991) & 'MIMYRIAD' (1993) on 'Streamline' See SKINNY PUPPY for TEARGARDEN releases. SILVERMAN (aka KNIGHT) issued the album, 'DREAM CELL' in 1996 for Terminal Kaleidoscope'.

LEMONHEADS

Formed: Boston, Massachusetts, USA . . . 1983 by EVAN DANDO. Raised by middle-class parents (they were divorced when he was 12), the singer was originally the band's drummer and in March '86 he was joined by one-time school-friend, jazz-bassist JESSE PORETZ. With BEN DEILY completing the line-up, this early incarnation of The LEMONHEADS released their debut EP, the amateurish indie squall of 'LAUGHING ALL THE WAY TO THE CLEANERS' on the recently formed Boston label, 'Taang!'. The band stayed with the label for their first three releases, belting out spirited melodic punk (drawing comparisons with DINOSAUR JR, HUSKER DU, REPLACEMENTS etc,) on 'HATE YOUR FRIENDS' (1987), 'CREATOR' (1988) and 'LICK' (1989), the latter the pick of the bunch with a beguiling cover of Suzanne Vega's 'LUKA'. 'Atlantic' records were sufficiently confident in the band's pop-grunge abilities to offer them a deal, the initial fruits of which, the well received 'LOVEY' (1990), saw DANDO take more of a leading role following the departure of DEILY. From this point on he steered the band in an increasingly mellow, country-flavoured direction (an area he'd already explored on his 1990 solo EP, 'FAVOURITE SPANISH DISHES') with a brilliant cover of Mike Nesmith's 'DIFFERENT DRUM', while 'LOVEY' featured a fairly faithful rendition of his hero Gram Parson's 'BRASS BUTTONS'. Yet the ever unpredictable DANDO split the band up after the major label debut, eventually reforming with the help of girlfriend JULIANA HATFIELD and DAVE RYAN, the latter having played on 'LOVEY'. A spell in Australia seemed to have further mellowed the singer and the resultant album, 'IT'S A SHAME ABOUT RAY', was the most accessible LEMONHEADS release to date, heavy on harmonies and melody. Despite a favourable critical reception, the album lingered in the lower reaches of the album chart and it was only when 'Atlantic' issued the band's power pop cover of Simon & Garfunkel's 'MRS. ROBINSON', that The LEMONHEADS became a household name. Re-released to include the track, 'IT'S A SHAME ABOUT RAY' enjoyed a commercial comeback, eventually making it into the UK Top 40. Suddenly DANDO's long-haired, slacker-extraordinaire visage was staring out from every magazine cover from NME to The FACE, although this sudden thrust into the limelight seemed to drive DANDO further into drug abuse, a follow-up album, 'COME ON FEEL THE LEMONHEADS', eventually surfacing in late 1993. The record was another mellow beauty, powering into the UK Top 5 on the back of a successful Love Positions' cover, 'INTO YOUR ARMS', and even featuring contributions from legendary pedal steel player, SNEAKY PETE KLEINOW. Predictably, the Yanks just didn't get it, preferring the bluster of PEARL JAM instead. Lack of success in his home country sent DANDO spiralling further into drug use, although he had apparently cleaned up by the end of the year, undertaking a solo acoustic tour of the US. However, after a much criticised appearance at the 1995 Glastonbury festival, DANDO went to ground, spending much of his time in Australia strung out on heroin and LSD. A shorn, torn and frayed DANDO eventually surfaced in 1997 with 'CAR BUTTON CLOTH', the first LEMONHEADS album in four years, finding DANDO in reflective and world weary mood, the melancholy side of his songwriting more pronounced than ever. • **Songwriters:** DANDO, although DELLY or MADDOX were contributors early on. Covered; I AM A RABBIT (Proud Scum) / HEY JOE + AMAZING GRACE (trad.) / MOD LANG (Big Star) / STRANGE (Patsy Cline) / YOUR HOME IS WHERE YOU ARE HAPPY (C. MANSON / PLASTER CASTER (Kiss) / SKULLS (Misfits) / GONNA GET ALONG WITHOUT YA NOW (Hoagy Carmichael) / STEP BY STEP (New Kids On The Block) / FRANK MILLS (from 'Hair' musical) / KITCHEN (Hummingbirds) / MISS OTIS REGRETS (Cole Porter) / FADE TO BLACK (Metallica) / LIVE FOREVER (Oasis) / KEEP ON LOVING YOU (Reo Speedwagon) / TENDERFOOT (Tom Morgan / Adam Young) / GALVESTON (Jimmy Webb) / PIN YR HEART (Jacobites). Between 1994-1996, he co-wrote 'PURPLE PARALLELOGRAM' with Noel Gallagher (Oasis) + 'IF I COULD TALK I'D TELL YOU' with Eugene Kelly (Eugenius). • **Trivia:** DANDO and JOHN STROHM appeared on BLAKE BABIES lp, 'Slow Learners'.

Album rating: IT'S A SHAME ABOUT RAY (*8) / COME ON FEEL THE LEMONHEADS (*9) / LICK (*7) / CAR BUTTON CLOTH (*8)

EVAN DANDO (b. 4 Mar'67) – vocals, guitar + some drums / **JESSE PERETZ** – bass / **BEN DEILY** – guitar, + some drums

not iss. ArmoryArms

Jul 86. (7"ep) *<1-2-Huh-Bag 1>* **LAUGHING ALL THE WAY TO THE CLEANERS** [-] [ ]
– Glad I don't know / I like to / I am a rabbit / So I fucked up.

— added **DOUG TRACHTON** – drums

World Service Taang!

May 88. (lp)<US-lp some colrd> *(SERVM 001) <T 15>* **HATE YOUR FRIENDS** [ ] [ ] Jun87
– I don't wanna / 394 / Nothing time / Second change / Sneakyville / Amazing Grace / Belt / Hate your friends / Don't tell yourself it's ok / Uhhh / Fed up / Rat velvet. *(US-cd 1989; same +=)* – Glad I don't know / I like to / I am a rabbit / So I fucked up / Ever / Sad girl / Buried alive / Gotta stop. *(re-iss. cd Mar93 with the extra tracks)*

— **EVAN,** on bass, also joined BLAKE BABIES in 1988, alongside girlfriend JULIANA HATFIELD. **JOHN STROHM** – drums (ex-BLAKE BABIES) repl. DOUG.

Sep 88. (lp)(c) *(SERV 001) <T 23>* **CREATOR** [ ] [ ]
– Burying ground / Sunday / Clang bang clang / Out / Your home is where you're happy / Falling / Die right now / Two weeks in another town / Plaster caster / Come to my window / Take her down / Postcard / Live without. *(US-cd 1989; same +=)* – Luka (live) / Interview / Mallo cup. *(re-iss. Sep92 on 'Taang!', with 6 extra live tracks included) (re-iss. cd Mar93 with all re-issued tracks + 2 acoustic)*

— **COREY LOOG BRENNAN**– guitar (ex-BULLET LAVOLTA) repl. JOHN STROHM

Apr 89. (7"colrd) *<T 31>* **LUKA. / STRANGE / MAD** [ ] [-]
(scheduled UK Nov89 unissued 12"/cd-s; SEVS 010/+CD)
(UK-iss. 7"/12"/cd-s Apr93)

May 89. (lp/cd) *(SERV/+CD 007) <T 32>* **LICK** [ ] [ ]
– Mallo cup / Glad I don't know / 7 powers / A circle of one / Cazzo di ferro / Anyway / Luka / Come back D.A. / I am a rabbit / Sad girl / Ever. *(US-cd+=)* – Strange / Mad. *(re-iss. cd Mar93)*

— **MARK "BUDOLA"** – drums, toured until he checked out mid '89. (COREY also left to concentrate on his PhD.

Roughneck not iss.

Jun 90. (7") *(HYPE 3)* **DIFFERENT DRUM. / PAINT** [ ] [-]
(12"+=)(cd-s+=) *(12 HYPE 3)(HYPE 3CD)* – Ride with me. *(re-iss. Feb93 12"ep/cd-ep; HYPE 3 T/CD)*

Atlantic Atlantic

Jun 90. (cd ep) *<786088-2>* **FAVORITE SPANISH DISHES EP** [-] [ ]
– Different drum / Paint / Ride with me / Skulls / Step by step.

— **DAVID RYAN** (b.20 Oct'64, Fort Wayne, Indiana) – drums repl. DEILY

Oct 91. (cd/c/lp) *<(7567 82137-2/-4/-2)>* **LOVEY** [ ] [ ] Aug90
– Ballarat / Half the time / Year of the cat / Ride with me / Li'l seed / Stove / Come downstairs / Left for dead / Brass buttons / (The) Door. *(re-iss. cd/c/lp Nov93)*

— In Sep'90, **DANDO** recruited **BEN DAUGHTY** – drums (ex-SQUIRREL BAIT) repl. RYAN / **BYRON HOAGLAND** – bass (ex-FANCY PANTS) repl. PERETZ.

Sep 91. (7") *(A 7709)* **GONNA GET ALONG WITHOUT YA NOW. / HALF THE TIME** [ ] [-]
(12"ep+=) *(TA 7709)* – PATIENCE AND PRUDENCE EP: Stove (remix) / Step by step.

— **DANDO, RYAN + JULIANA HATFIELD** (b. 2 Jul'67, Wiscasset) – bass, vocals (ex-BLAKE BABIES)

Jul 92. (cd/c/lp) *<(7567 82137-2/-4/-1)>* **IT'S A SHAME ABOUT RAY** [69] [68]
– Rockin' stroll / Confetti / Rudderless / My drug buddy / The turnpike down / Bit part / Alison's starting to happen / Hannah and Gaby / Kitchen / Ceiling fan in my spoon / Frank Mills. *(album hit UK No.33 Jan'93) (re-iss. Feb95)*

Oct 92. (7"/c-s) *(A 7423/+C)* **IT'S A SHAME ABOUT RAY. / SHAKEY GROUND** [70] [-]
(10"+=/cd-s+=) *(A 7423 TE/CD)* – Dawn can't decide / The turnpike down.

Nov 92. (7"/c-s) *(A 7401/+C)* **MRS. ROBINSON. / BEING AROUND** [19] [-]
(10"+=/cd-s+=) *(A 7401 TE/CD)* – Divan / Into your arms.

— 1993 line-up: **DANDO, RYAN, NIC DALTON** (b.14 Jun'64, Australia) although she did provide b.vox for 1993 releases. – bass HATFIELD formed own trio)

Jan 93. (7"/c-s) *(A 7430/+C)* **CONFETTI (remix). / MY DRUG BUDDY** [44] [-]
(10"+=/cd-s+=) *(A 7430 TE/CD)* – Ride with me (live) / Confetti (acoustic).

Mar 93. (c-s) *(A 5764C)* **IT'S A SHAME ABOUT RAY / ALISON'S STARTING TO HAPPEN** [31] [-]
(cd-s+=) *(A 5764CD)* – Different drum (Evan acoustic) / Stove (Evan acoustic).
(10"+=) *(A 5764TE)* – Different drum (acoustic) / Rockin' stroll (live).
(cd-s) *(A 5764CDX)* – ('A'live) / Confetti / Mallo cup / Rudderless (all 4 live).

Oct 93. (7"/c-s) *(A 7302/+C) <87294>* **INTO YOUR ARMS. / MISS OTIS REGRETS** [14] [67]
(10"+=/cd-s+=) *(A 7302 TE/CD)* – Little black egg / Learning the game.

Oct 93. (cd/c/lp) *<(7567 82537-2/-4/-1)>* **COME ON FEEL THE LEMONHEADS** [5] [56]
– The great big no / Into your arms / It's about time / Down about it / Paid to smile / Big gay heart / Style / Rest assured / Dawn can't decide / I'll do it anyway / Rick James style / Being around / Favourite T / You can take it with you / The jello fund. *(lp+=)* – Miss Otis regrets.

Nov 93. (7"/c-s) *(A 7296/+C)* **IT'S ABOUT TIME. / RICK JAMES ACOUSTIC STYLE** [57] [-]
(10"+=/cd-s+=) *(A 7296 TE/CD)* – Big gay heart (demo) / Down about it (acoustic). (above 'A'side was written about JULIANA. I'LL DO IT ANYWAY for BELINDA CARLISLE)

May 94. (c-ep/10"ep/cd-ep) *(A 7259 C/TE/CD)* **BIG GAY HEART / DEEP BOTTOM COVE. / HE'S ON THE BEACH / FAVORITE T (session)** [55] [-]

— Offending lyrics to above 'A'side, were changed; with Stroke & Brick.

— DALTON departed Sep '94

— **PATRICK MURPHY** – drums (ex-DINOSAUR JR) repl.RYAN

— other members with DANDO; **BILL GIBSON** – bass, guitar / **DINA WAXMAN** – bass / **KENNY LYON** – guitar / **RICH GILBERT** – pedal steel / **BRYCE GOGGIN** – vocals, keyboards / etc.

Sep 96. (c-s) *(A 5495C)* **IF I COULD TALK I'D TELL YOU /** [39] [-]
(cd-s) *(A 5495CD)* – ('A'side) / How will I know (acoustic & electric version) / I don't want to go home / Seagulls aren't free.
(cd-s) *(A 5495CDX)* – ('A'side) / It's all true (acoustic – no drums) / Sexual bryceulidge.

Oct 96. (cd/c) *<(7567 92726-2/-4)>* **CAR BUTTON CLOTH** [28] [ ]
– It's all true / If I could talk I'd tell you / Break me / Hospital / The outdoor type / Losing your mind / Something's missing / Knoxville girl / 6ix / C'mon daddy / One more time / Tenderfoot / Secular rockulidge.

Nov 96. (c-s) *(A 5635C)* **IT'S ALL TRUE / LIVE FOREVER** [61] [-]
(10"+=/cd-s+=) *(A 5635 TE/CD)* – Fade to black / Keep on loving you.

Mar 97. (c-s) *(A 5620C)* **THE OUTDOOR TYPE (remix) / PIN YR HEART** [ ] [-]
(cd-s+=) *(A 5620CD)* – Losing your mind (live acoustic).

Aug 97. (7") *(AT 0012)* **BALANCING ACTS. / GALVESTON** [ ] [-]

– compilations, etc. –

1990. (cd) *Taang!; <T 15/T23>* **CREATE YOUR FRIENDS** [-] [ ]
– (HATE YOUR FRIENDS / CREATOR / LAUGHING E.P.)

Aug 98. (cd/c) *Atlantic; <(7567 80851-2/-4)>* **THE BEST OF THE LEMONHEADS** [ ] [ ]
– Confetti / Into the arms / Mrs. Robinson / Rudderless / It's a shame about Ray / The great big no / Ride with me (acoustic) / My drug buddy / Big gay heart / It's about time / The outdoor type / It's all true / If I could talk I'd tell you / Hospital / Rudy with a flashlight / Into your arms (acoustic) / Down about it (acoustic) / Being around / Rick James acoustic style.

LEMON INTERRUPT (see under ⇒ UNDERWORLD)

LET'S ACTIVE

Formed: Winston-Salem, North Carolina, USA ... 1981 by multi-instrumentalist, MITCH EASTER, who'd set up a studio in the late 70's after playing alongside moonlighting members of the dB's in a group called The SNEAKERS. His first solo outing was heard on UK V/A compilation, 'Shake To Date' a record which featured other US artists. In 1983, his new group, LET'S ACTIVE (which included long-time girlfriend, FAYE HUNTER), debuted with mini-lp, 'AFOOT', released around the same time as he chanced upon the up and coming, R.E.M., who he subsequently produced and toured alongside; he also worked with PYLON and The dB's. LET'S ACTIVE were really up and running with 1984's DON DIXON-produced set, 'CYPRESS', a 60's fixated jingle-jangle rock/pop (likened to the KINKS, the MONKEES or the BEATLES) affair given the thumb down by music press. In 1986, they finally made a critical impact with album, 'BIG PLANS FOR EVERYBODY', although it would be three years before they were back again with 'EVERY DOG HAS HIS DAY' (1989). Although this proved to be their final album, EASTER's production pedigree ensured he was never short of work.

Album rating: AFOOT mini (*6) / CYPRESS (*4) / BIG PLANS FOR EVERYBODY (*6) / EVERY DOG HAS HIS DAY (*5)

MITCH EASTER (b.15 Nov'54) – vocals, guitar / **FAYE HUNTER** (b.13 Sep'53) – bass, vocals / **SARA ROMWEBER** (b.13 Feb'64, Indiana) – drums

I.R.S. I.R.S.

Nov 83. (m-lp) <4497-70505> **AFOOT** -
– Every word means no / Make up with me / Edge of the world / Room with a view / In between / Leader of men.

Sep 84. (lp/c) *(IRSA 7047)* <70648> **CYPRESS**
– Easy does / Waters part / Lowdown / Gravel truck / Crows on a phone line / Ring true / Blue line / Flags for everything / Prey / Co-star / Grey scale.

—— **ERIC MARSHALL** (b.1962) – drums + **ANGIE CARLSON** (b.13 Sep'60, Minnesota) – backing vocals, guitar, keyboards

Jun 86. (7") *(IRM 116)* **IN LITTLE WAYS. / TWO YOU'S**
(12"+=) *(IRMT 116)* –

Jul 86. (lp/c) *(MIRF/+C 1011)* **BIG PLANS FOR EVERYBODY**
– In little ways / Talking to myself / Writing on the book of last pages / Last chance town / Won't go wrong / Badger / Fell / Still dark out / Whispered news / Reflecting pool / Route 67.

Apr 89. (lp/c) *(EIRSA/+C 1001)* **EVERY DOG HAS HIS DAY**
– Every dog has his day / Horizon / Sweepstakes winner / Orpheus in Hades lounge / Mr. Fool / Ten layers down / Too bad / Night train / Forty years / Bad machinery / I feel funny / Terminate.

—— EASTER went back to production. He returned to tour with VELVET CRUSH.

LETTERS TO CLEO

Formed: Boston, Massachusetts, USA . . . 1993 by frontwoman, KAY HANLEY (b. New England), along with SCOTT RIEBLING, GREG McKENNA, MICHAEL EISENSTEIN and STACY JONES. Enthusiastic, young and fresh-faced (well, KAY anyway!), these US wannabe Brit-poppers made their debut in 1994 via Stateside imprint, 'CherryDisc' with the 'AURORA GORY ALICE' album. After one of the record's tracks, 'HERE AND NOW', hit the US Top 60 the following Spring (after being aired on US TV series, 'Melrose Place'), 'Warners/Giant' re-promoted the debut set, which bubbled under the US Top 100. The hastily put together follow-up set, 'WHOLESALE MEATS AND FISH', arrived in August that year, failing to do the band any favours in the power-pop market place despite spawning another minor hit, 'AWAKE'. A new drummer, TOM POLCE, was posted in 1996 after JONES had been despatched to VERUCA SALT, the band's newly bolstered sound showcased on 'GO!' (1997). • **Covered:** SECRET AGEN (Lee Hazlewood) / DREAMS (Fleetwood Mac) / YOU DIRTY RAT (. . . Chesterman).

Album rating: AURORA GORY ALICE (*5) / WHOLESALE MEATS AND FISH (*4) / GO! (*5)

KAY HANLEY – vocals / **MICHAEL EISENSTEIN** – guitar / **GREG McKENNA** – guitar / **SCOTT RIEBLING** – bass / **STACY JONES** – drums

not iss. CherryDisc

1994. (cd) <24598> **AURORA GORY ALICE** -
– Big star / I see / Rim shak / Wasted / Get on with it / Here and now / From under the dust / Mellie's comin' over / Come around / Step back. *<re-prom.Mar95 by 'Giant'; same> (UK-iss.Apr95 on 'China' cd/c; WOL CD/MC 1057)*

China Warners

Mar 95. (7"/c-s) *(WOK/+MC 2049)* <17913> **HERE AND NOW. / BIG STAR** 56
(cd-s+=) *(WOKCD 2049)* –

Jan 96. (7") *(WOK 2069)* <17823> **AWAKE. / ACID JED** 88 Aug95
(cd-s+=) *(WOKCD 2069)* –

Jan 96. (cd) *(WOLCD 1068)* <24613> **WHOLESALE MEATS AND FISH** Aug95
– Demon rock / Fast way / Jennifer / Awake / Laudanum / Acid Jed / Pizza cutter / St. Peter / Little Rosa / Do what you want, yeah / He's got an answer / I could sleep (the wuss song).

—— **TOM POLCE** – drums; repl. JONES who joined VERUCA SALT

Warners Warners

Oct 97. (cd/c) <24688-2/-4> **GO!** -
– I got time / Because of you / Anchor / Find you dead / Veda very shining / Co-pilot / Go! / Sparklegirl / Alouette & me / I'm a fool / Disappear.

not iss. WickedDisc

Nov 98. (cd) <1010> **SISTER** -
– I see / Sister / Pete beat / He's stayin' / Clear blue water / Never tell / Boy / Green eggs / You dirty rat / Secret agent / Dreams.

LEVELLERS

Formed: Brighton, England . . . early '88 by MARK CHADWICK, JEREMY CUNNINGHAM, CHARLIE HEATHER, JON SEVINK and ALAN MILES. Taking their name from the English political radicals of the 17th Century, The LEVELLERS were one of the most successful and consistent bands to emerge from the free festival/crusty scene, building up a loyal grassroots fanbase with their raggle-taggle blend of folk and punk. After Phil Nelson took over as manager the following year, he released a couple of raw EP's on his own 'Hag' imprint, before the band signed to European label, 'Musidisc', and began work on a debut album with WATERBOYS producer, Phil Tennant. While 'WEAPON CALLED THE WORD' helped introduce their rootsy assault to a larger audience, the band subsequently broke from their contract and signed to 'China', while MILES was replaced by songwriter/guitarist, SIMON FRIEND. Another hectic UK tour followed and by Autumn '91, The LEVELLER's popularity was such that the 'LEVELLING THE LAND' album made the Top 20 with only the support of minor hit single, 'ONE WAY'. With a more accessible anthemic rock/folk approach, the album took the band's defiantly pro-earth, pro-equality philosophy overground and into the mainstream, 'BATTLE OF THE BEANFIELD' commemorating the famous festival stand-off between hippies and police. In Spring '92, The LEVELLERS scored their biggest hit to date with the 'FIFTEEN YEARS' EP, almost making the Top 10, while they chose to end the year with a series of 'Freakshows' combining the likes of fellow agit-poppers, CHUMBABWAMBA with such established crusty pastimes as juggling and fire-eating. The following year's eponymous album missed the No.1 spot by a whisker, spawning a trio of Top 20 singles in 'BELARUSE', 'THIS GARDEN' and the lovely 'JULIE'; although The LEVELLERS were now rather unlikely but fully fledged pop stars, they also became embroiled in a war of words with the music press and fellow musicians. Not that this affected their popularity one iota, the band finally topping the UK charts with 'ZEITGEIST' (1995) as they found themselves surfing the new wave of enthusiasm for British music in general. Certainly one of the UK's more conscientious bands, The LEVELLERS are sadly part of a dying breed who still believe that music and politics are a feasible combination. • **Songwriters:** Group compositions except; THE DEVIL WENT DOWN TO GEORGIA (Charlie Daniels Band) / TWO HOURS (McDermott) / GERM FREE ADOLESCENCE (X-Ray Spex) / PRICE OF LOVE (Everly Brothers) / HANG ON TO YOUR EGO (Frank Black). • **Trivia:** The FENCE released one single in May '87 on 'Flag'; FROZEN WATER / EXIT.

Album rating: LEVELLING THE LAND (*8) / WEAPON CALLED THE WORD (*7) / LEVELLERS (*6)

MARK CHADWICK – vocals, guitar, banjo (ex-FENCE) / **JEREMY CUNNINGHAM** – bass, bazouki / **CHARLIE HEATHER** – drums / **JON SEVINK** – violin (ex-FENCE) / **ALAN MILES** – vocals, guitar, mandolin, harmonica

Hag not iss.

May 89. (12"ep) *(HAG 005)* **CARRY ME** -
– Carry me / What's in the way / The lasy days of winter / England my home /

Oct 89. (12"ep) *(HAG 006)* **OUTSIDE INSIDE. / HARD FIGHT / I HAVE NO ANSWERS / BARREL OF A GUN** -

Musidisc not iss.

Apr 90. (7") *(105 577)* **WORLD FREAK SHOW. / BARREL OF A GUN (acoustic)** -
(12"+=) *(108 936)* – What you know.

Apr 90. (cd/c/lp) *(10557-2/-4/-1)* **WEAPON CALLED THE WORD** -
– World freak show / Carry me / Outside-inside / Together all the way / Barrel of a gun / Three friends / I have no answers / No change / Blind faith / The ballad of Robbie Jones / England my home / What you know.

Oct 90. (7") *(106897)* **TOGETHER ALL THE WAY. / THREE FRIENDS (re-mix) (Arfa mix short version)** -
(12"+=) *(106896)* – Cardboard box city / Social insecurity.

—— **SIMON FRIEND** – guitars, vocals repl. ALAN.

China Elektra

Sep 91. (7"/c-s) *(WOK/+MC 2008)* **ONE WAY. / HARD FIGHT (acoustic) / THE LAST DAYS OF WINTER** 51 -
(12"+=/cd-s+=) *(WOK T/CD 2008)* – ('A'-Factory mix) / The Devil went down to Georgia.

Oct 91. (lp/c/cd) *(WOL/+MC/CD 1022)* <61325-1/-4/-2> **LEVELLING THE LAND** 14 May92
– One way / The game / The boatman / The liberty song / Far from home / Sell out / Another man's cause / The road / The riverflow / Battle of the beanfield. *(re-iss. Jun92 hit No.22)*

Nov 91. (7"/c-s) *(WOK/+MC 2010)* **FAR FROM HOME. / WORLD FREAK SHOW (live)** 71 -
(12"+=/cd-s+=) *(WOK T/CD 2010)* – Outside inside (live) / The boatman (live) / Three friends (live).

May 92. (c-ep/10"pic-d-ep/12"ep/cd-ep) *(WOK MC/X/T/CD 2020)* **15 YEARS / DANCE BEFORE THE STORM. / RIVERFLOW (live) / PLASTIC JEEZUS** 11 -

Jun 93. (c-s) *(WOKMC 2034)* **BELARUSE / SUBVERT (live at Trancentral) / BELARUSE RETURN** 12 -
(12"+=/cd-s+=) *(WOK T/CD 2034)* – Is this art?

Sep 93. (lp/c/cd) *(WOL/+MC/CD 1034)* <61532> **LEVELLERS** 2
– Warning / 100 years of solitude / The likes of you and I / Is this art? / Dirty Davey / This garden / Broken circles / Julie / The player / Belaruse.

Oct 93. (7"pic-d/c-s) *(WOK P/MC 2039)* **THIS GARDEN. / LIFE (acoustic)** 12 -
(12"+=/cd-s+=) *(WOK T/CD 2039)* – ('A'-Marcus Dravs remix) / ('A'-Banco De Gaia remix).

May 94. (7"clear-ep/c-ep/10"pic-d-ep/cd-ep) *(WOK/+MC//CD 2042)* **THE JULIE EP** 17 -
– Julie (new version) / English civil war / Warning (live) / 100 years of solitude / The lowlands of Holland.

Jul 95. (7"pic-d) *(WOKP 2059)* **HOPE ST. / LEAVE THIS TOWN** 12 -
(7"pic-d) *(WOKPX 2059)* – ('A'side) / Miles away.
(cd-s++=/c-s++=) *(WOK CD/MC 2059)* – Busking on Hope Street.

Aug 95. (lp/c/cd) *(WOL/+MC/CD 1064)* <61887> **ZEITGEIST** 1
– Hope St. / The fear / Exodus / Maid of the river / Saturday to Sunday / 4.am / Forgotten ground / Fantasy / P.C. Keen / Just the one / Haven't made it / Leave this town / Men-an-tol.

Oct 95. (7"/c-s/cd-s) *(WOK/+MC/CD 2067)* **FANTASY. / SARA'S BEACH / SEARCHLIGHTS (extended)** 16 -

—— (below featured JOE STRUMMER (ex-CLASH) on piano)

Dec 95. (7"ep/c-ep/cd-ep) *(WOK/+MC/CD 2076)* **JUST THE ONE / A PROMISE. / YOUR 'OUSE / DRINKING FOR ENGLAND** 12 -

Jul 96. (7"ep/c-ep/cd-ep) *(WOK/+MC/CD 2082)* **EXODUS – LIVE (live)** 24 -
– Exodus / Another man's cause / Leave this town / P.C. Keen.

Aug 96. (cd/c) *(WOL CDX/MC 1074)* **HEADLIGHTS, WHITE LINES, BLACK TAR RIVERS – BEST LIVE (live)** 13 -
– Sell out / Hope St. / 15 years / Exodus / Carry me / The boatman / 3 friends / Men-an-tol / The road / One way / England my home / England my home / Battle of the beanfield / Liberty / The riverflow.

Aug 97. (c-s/cd-s) *(WOK MC/CD 2088)* **BEAUTIFUL DAY / BAR ROOM JURY / ALL YOUR DREAMS** 13 -

(cd-s) *(WOKCDX 2088)* – ('A'side) / Germ free adolescence / Price of love / Hang on to your ego.

Aug 97. (lp/c/cd) *(WOL/+MC/CD 1084)* **MOUTH TO MOUTH** 5 -
– Dog train / Beautiful day / Celebrate / Rain and snow / Far away / C.C.T.V. / Chemically free / Elation / Captains' courageous / Survivors / Sail away / Too real.

Oct 97. (c-ep/cd-ep) *(WOK MC/CD 2089)* **CELEBRATE / RAIN & SNOW (The White Mountain Yarn mix) / SEA OF PAIN / SURVIVORS** 28 -
(cd-s) *(WOKCDX 2089)* – ('A'side) / Men-an-tol (live acoustic) / 4 + 20 / Ring of fire.

Dec 97. (12"/c-s) *(WOK/+MC 2090)* **DOG TRAIN. /** 24 -
(cd-s+=) *(WOKCD 2090)* –

Mar 98. (12"/c-s) *(WOK/+MC 2091)* **TOO REAL. /** 46 -
(cd-s+=) *(WOKCD 2091)* –

Oct 98. (7"/c-s) *(WOK/+M 2096)* **BOZOS. / DON'T YOU GRIEVE** 44 -
(cd-s) *(WOKCD 2096)* – Plastic factory.
(cd-s) *(WOKCDR 2096)* – ('A'side) / New York mining disaster 1941 / Supercharger (heavy mental mix).

Oct 98. (cd/c) *(052173-2/-4)* **ONE WAY OF LIFE (THE BEST OF . . .)** (compilation) 15 -
– One way / What a beautiful day / Fifteen years / Shadow on the sun / Hope street / Belaruse / Celebrate / Too real (12"mix) / Bozos / This garden / Carry me / Fantasy / Julie / Dog train / Far from home / Just the one. *(ltd.d-cd+=)* – Far from home / Just the one / PC Keen / Sell out / Hope Street / 15 years / Men-an-to.

Nov 98. (7"/c-s) *(WOK/+MC 2102)* **ONE WAY '98. /** -
(cd-s+=) *(WOKCD 2102)* –
(cd-s) *(WOKCDX 2102)* –

– compilations, etc. –

Jan 92. (7") *Musidisc; (105 557)* **WORLD FREAK SHOW (remix). / WHAT YOU KNOW** -
(12"+=/cd-s+=) *(10893 6/2)* – Barrel of a gun / What you know.

Mar 93. (lp/c/cd) *China; (WOL 1035/+MC/CD)* **SEE NOTHING, HEAR NOTHING, DO SOMETHING** (early material) -

Jackie LEVEN (see under ⇒ DOLL BY DOLL)

LEVITATION

Formed: London, England . . . 1989 by main songwriter, TERRY BICKERS, who had just split less than amicably with GUY CHADWICK and his HOUSE OF LOVE. Hooking up with DAVE FRANCOLLINI (ex-SOMETHING PRETTY BEAUTIFUL), they invited seasoned indie campaigners, CHRISTIAN 'Bic' HAYES, BOB WHITE and JOE ALLEN to join. Signed to 'Ultimate' records, they lived up to the hype with the release of their debut EP, 'COPPELIA', in 1991, an intense affair highlighting BICKERS' swirls of sensuround sound and guitar effects. Later that year, LEVITATION proved it wasn't a fluke with a second EP, 'AFTER EVER BE', the two collected together as 'THE COTERIE ALBUM' (early 1992). Prior to its release, the quintet became the first outfit to issue a 7" ('SQUIRREL') for the 'Rough Trade Singles Club' series, which led to them signing a full album deal with the label ('Capitol' in the States). LAURENCE O'KEEFE had by now taken the place of JOE ALLEN, making his debut on the incendiary UK Top 50 album, 'NEED FOR NOT' (1992), produced by TIM SMITH (of The Cardiacs) and featuring former MAGAZINE guitarist, JOHN McGEOGH, in a guest capacity. LEVITATION must have been literally floating on air after signing a major record deal with 'Chrysalis', however, after only one poorly received single, 'EVEN WHEN YOUR EYES ARE OPEN', BICKERS took off to pursue his own wayward muse (he subsequently contributed to the debut album by OEDIPUSSY). The remaining members (HAYES, FRANCOLLINI and O'KEEFE) struggled on with new frontman, STEVE LUDWIN, although the chemistry of their prime line-up was missing on the Australian-only set, 'MEANWHILE GARDENS' (1994). After spells with HEATHER NOVA, the aforementioned trio re-emerged to critical acclaim in the late 90's as DARK STAR, HAYES, O'KEEFE and FRANCOLINI forming the band during a live SONIC YOUTH experience. Maintaining their love of noisy psychedelia, DARK STAR surfaced late in '98 with the groundbreaking 'GRACEADELICA' EP.

Album rating: THE COTERIE ALBUM compilation (*6) / NEED FOR NOT (*7) / MEANWHILE GARDENS (*4)

TERRY BICKERS – vocals, guitar (ex-HOUSE OF LOVE, ex-COLENSO PARADE) / **CHRISTIAN 'Bic' HAYES** – guitar (ex-CARDIACS) / **BOB WHITE** – keyboards, vocals / **JOE ALLEN** – bass / **DAVE FRANCOLLINI** – drums (ex-SOMETHING PRETTY BEAUTIFUL)

Ultimate Capitol

Feb 91. (7") *(TOPP 003)* **NADINE. / SMILE** -
(12"+=/cd-ep+=) **COPPELIA EP** *(TOPP 003 T/CD)* – Paid in kind / Rosemary Jones.

Aug 91. (7"ep/12"ep/cd-ep) *(TOPP 005/+T/CD)* **AFTER EVER BE EP** -
– Firefly / Attached / Bedlam.

Jan 92. (cd/lp) *(TOPP CD/LP 001)* <C2/C4 97959> **THE COTERIE ALBUM** (compilation)
(re-iss. Jul94; same)

Rough Trade Sing. Club not iss.

1991. (7") *(45REV 1)* **SQUIRREL. / IT'S TIME** -

— **LAURENCE O'KEEFE** – bass (ex-JAZZ BUTCHER) repl. JOE

Rough Trade Capitol

Feb 92. (cd-ep) *(R 285-3)* **WORLD AROUND / JAY / USHER** -

May 92. (cd/c/lp) *(R 286-2/-4/-1)* <C2/C4 98501> **NEED FOR NOT** 45
– Against nature / World around / Hangnail / Resist / Arcs of light and dew / Pieces of Mary / Smile / Embedded / Coterie.

Chrysalis Chrysalis

Apr 93. (12"ep/cd-ep) *(12/CD CHS 3972)* **EVEN WHEN YOUR EYES ARE OPEN. / EVERGREEN / MANTRA**

— Later in 1993, BICKERS announced his departure, although an album 'MEANWHILE GARDENS' was recorded for the Australian label 'Festival' (D-31018). He was replaced by **STEVE LUDWIN** – vocals. Meanwhile, BICKERS formed The CRADLE in 1995, while a few years later, HAYES, FRANCOLINI and O'KEEFE formed DARK STAR after spells in HEATHER NOVA, production work and DEAD CAN DANCE respectively. An entirelt different LEVITATION issued a CD in '97 entitled, 'Nous Ka Woule'.

DARK STAR

— **HAYES + O'KEEFE + FRANCOLINI**

E.M.I. unknown

Oct 98. (10"ep/cd-ep) *(10EM/CDEM 523)* **GRACEADELICA EP** -
– Graceadelica / The crow song / New model worker / Solitude song.

LEYTON BUZZARDS

Formed: Leyton, East London, England . . . late '77 by GEOFFREY DEANE (aka NICK NAYME) and DAVID JAYMES (DAVE DEPRAVE), who almost immediately recruited VERNON AUSTIN (CHIP MONK) and KEVIN STEPTOE (GRAY MARE). Leaving behind their pub rock beginnings, The LEYTON BUZZARDS got in on the punk/New Wave act and signed a one-off deal with the indie imprint, 'Small Wonder', releasing their debut, '19 AND MAD', the following year. Subsequently scooping first prize in a high profile Battle Of The Bands competition (jointly run by BBC Radio One and The Sun), the group were rewarded with a major label deal courtesy of 'Chrysalis'. Early in '79, they swooped into the lower regions of the UK charts with the easier-going 'SATURDAY NIGHT (BENEATH THE PLASTIC PALM TREES)', their claim to fame being a Top Of The Pops appearance. However, their follow-up single, 'I'M HANGING AROUND', failed to take them any higher up the proverbial pecking order, even an abbreviation of their moniker to The BUZZARDS not helping to stave off the encircling critical vultures. A debut album, 'JELLIED EELS TO RECORD DEALS' (1979), was savaged by the critics, leaving the band with only a bucketful of the former as their contract flew out the window, so to speak. Once bitten, twice shy(te), should have been the guiding motto of DEANE and JAYMES as they returned to terrorise the pop charts with the frankly embarrassing MODERN ROMANCE ("The Best Years Of Our Lives", "Ay Ay Ay Ay . . ." right!).

Album rating: Buzzards: JELLIED EELS TO RECORD DEALS (*4)

GEOFF DEANE (b.10 Dec'54) – vocals / **VERNON AUSTIN** – guitar / **DAVID JAYMES** (b.28 Dec'54, Woodford, Essex, England) – bass / **KEVIN STEPTOE** – drums

Small Wonder not iss.

Jul 78. (7") *(SMALL 7)* **19 AND MAD. / VILLAIN / YOUTHANASIA** -

Chrysalis not iss.

Feb 79. (7") *(CHS 2288)* **SATURDAY NIGHT (BENEATH THE PLASTIC PALM TREES). / THROUGH WITH YOU** 53 -

May 79. (7") *(CHS 2328)* **I'M HANGING AROUND. / I DON'T WANT TO GO TO ART SCHOOL / NO DRY ICE OR FLYING PIGS** -

BUZZARDS

Aug 79. (7") *(CHS 2360)* **WE MAKE A NOISE. / DISCO ROMEO** -

Oct 79. (lp) *(CHR 1213)* **JELLIED EELS TO RECORD DEALS** -
– Sharp young men / Saturday night (beneath the plastic palm trees) / I don't want to go to art school / British justice / The greatest story ever told / Land of the free / I'm hanging around / Can't get used to losing you / Sweet dreams little one / Mixed marriages / We make a noise / 19 and mad / People on the street / Disco Romeo / Through with you / No dry ice or flying pigs / Baby if you love me say yes if you don't say no.

WEA not iss.

Jul 80. (7"; as LEYTON BUZZARDS) *(K 18284)* **CAN'T GET USED TO LOSING YOU. / WEIRD FRENZ** -

— DEANE and JAYMES evolved the group into salsa popsters, MODERN ROMANCE, enjoying a string of hits in the first half of the 80's.

LIBERTY CAGE (see under ⇒ MEN THEY COULDN'T HANG)

LIBIDO

Formed: Bergen, Norway . . . 1995 by EVEN JOHANSEN, CATO EIKELAND and JORGEN LANDHAUGH. Described by some sections of the press as Brit-pop for Scandinavians, these lusty young English-speaking lads were signed to 'Fire' on the strength of a demo cassette. After making their vinyl debut in June '97 with the 'BLOW' single, the trio played the Phoenix festival the following month, showcasing their feisty melodic indie-pop to the sunburnt hordes. Musically lying somewhere between OASIS and The LA'S, LIBIDO attracted further media coverage with the 'SUPERSONIC DAYDREAM' single, even hitting the UK Top 60 early in '98 with 'OVERTHROWN'. The accompanying album, 'KILLING SOME DEAD TIME' (1998), didn't perform so well, the Bergen boys not exactly firing on all cylinders. • **Note:** Not to be confused with the dance act of the same name who had releases on 'Hooj Choons' and 'Top Banana'.

Album rating: KILLING SOME DEAD TIME (*6)

EVEN JOHANSEN – vocals, guitar / **CATO EIKELAND** – bass / **JORGEN LANDHAUGH** – drums (ex-SUNFLOWER)

Fire / Velvel

Jun 97. (7") *(BLAZE 113)* **BLOW. /**
(cd-s+=) *(BLAZE 113CD)* –

Sep 97. (7") *(BLAZE 116)* **SUPERSONIC DAYDREAM. /**
(cd-s+=) *(BLAZE 116CD)* –

Jan 98. (7") *(BLAZE 119)* **OVERTHROWN. / LYING THROUGH HER TEETH** [53]
(cd-s+=) *(BLAZE 119CD)* – Man inside my head.
(cd-s) *(BLAZE 119CDX)* – ('A'side) / Choking / Time of the month.

Feb 98. (cd/c) *(FIRE CD/MC 62)* *<79743>* **KILLING SOME DEAD TIME** Mar98
– Overthrown / Supersonic daydream / Strange news / Crash out / In my shadow / Blow / Remarkably abnormal (good intentions) / Revolving / Molest me / Comfort / God's guest list / Magic mushroom night.

Mar 98. (7") *(BLAZE 121)* **REVOLVING. /**
(cd-s+=) *(BLAZE 121CD)* –
(cd-s) *(BLAZE 121CDX)* –

LIGHT A BIG FIRE

Formed: Dublin, Ireland . . . 1983 by PETE DENCH, OWEN CONROY and Belfast-born TOM McLAUGHLIN (other two, PAT DISKIN and HUGHIE GALLAGHER were also present). Playing mainly SPRINGSTEEN-esque guitar-rock in local clubs, they finally lit the proverbial fuse after supporting ZZ TOP at the RDS stadium 1985. Having found an outlet for their work on UK indie label, 'Statik', LIGHT A BIG FIRE won 1986's 'Hot Press' magazine award for best Irish band (U2 were having a wee break!). Described by some critics at this point as a fusion of The GO-BETWEENS and a manic RIGHTEOUS BROTHERS, the quintet signed to 'Siren' records, finally releasing their debut album proper, the Craig Leon-produced 'SURVEILLANCE' (1987). However, just when things looked bright, the band decided to put a dampener on things by splitting.

Album rating: SURVEILLANCE (*5)

PETE DENCH – vocals / **TOM McLAUGHLIN** – vocals, guitar / **OWEN CONROY** – vocals, guitar / **PAT DISKIN** – bass / **HUGHIE GALLAGHER** – drums

Hotwire / not iss.

1985. (7") **C.I.A. /** [-] [-] Irish

1985. (7") *(HWS 856)* **I SEE PEOPLE. / MOONS** [-] [-]

Statik / not iss.

Nov 85. (m-lp) *(STAB 4)* **GUNPOWDERS** [-]
– Tommy's got a good job / The boom boom room / etc

— **PETE HOLIDAI** – guitar, keyboards (ex-RADIATORS FROM SPACE) repl. PAT

Siren / unknown

Aug 86. (7") *(SIREN 25)* **CHARLENE. / THE SHAPE I'M IN** [-]
(12"+=) *(SIREN 25-12)* – Hunger.

Nov 86. (7"/12") *(SIREN 28/+12)* **MR. TWILIGHT. / LOVERS** [-]

Mar 87. (7") *(SRN 45)* **I SEE PEOPLE. / JONNY ON ALL FOURS (live)** [-]
(12"+=) *(SRN 45-12)* – Mr. Twilight (live).

Apr 87. (lp/c) *(SIREN LP/C 6)* **SURVEILLANCE**
– I see people / C.I.A. / Hunger / Mr. Twilight (live in London) / Women / You can love a woman / Shop on the prarie / Charlene / Two jokes / Times we cried. *(re-iss. Nov90 lp/c; XID/CXID 29)*

— disbanded after above

LIGHTNING SEEDS

Formed: By IAN BROUDIE, 4 Aug'58, Liverpool, England. This seasoned scouser had previously been an integral part of BIG IN JAPAN (Autumn 77-78), before joining The SECRETS and then London-based band, ORIGINAL MIRRORS, in late '78. The latter outfit cut one eponymous album (c. early 1980) for 'Mercury', although BROUDIE left soon after to go into production work, chosen by ECHO & THE BUNNYMEN, The WAH!, The FALL and ICICLE WORKS, amongst the many to request his services. He subsequently helped form The CARE in 1983, with ex-WILD SWANS leader PAUL SIMPSON, although they disbanded after around a year and three singles; one of them, 'MY FLAMING SWORD', hit No.48 in the UK charts. After production work (mainly Merseyside bands), BROUDIE resurfaced in 1989, when he and a few session people formed The LIGHTNING SEEDS. The group signed to new indie label 'Ghetto', immediately scoring with surely one of the most fey, quintessentially indie-pop yet swoonsomely gorgeous singles ever, 'PURE'. This and its parent album, 'CLOUDCUCKOOLAND' (1990), surprised many by also making the US lists in '91 and BROUDIE garnered enough interest for 'Virgin' to sign him up for 1992's 'SENSE' album. Despite another batch of pristine, gilt-edged pop nuggets, the album hung around tentatively on the fringes of the album chart like a shy kid at the playground gates. Only 'THE LIFE OF RILEY' single managed to dent the Top 30. Perhaps as a response, 'JOLLIFICATION' (1994) was more blatantly commercial. The change was very subtle, but it was definitely there; in the way every track sounded like a muso rerun of 'PURE', in the way BROUDIE's little-boy-lost vocals now seemed to grate rather than soothe and in the way that the whole shebang continually teetered on the verge of self-parody. The resultant live shows, with their cack-handed rock approach, confirmed that BROUDIE was now writing for 20-something couples who had grown too old to go down the indie disco. The final nail in the coffin was the utterly nauseating England Euro '96 football theme, 'THREE LIONS', a track that sounded even more limp-wristed than NEW ORDER's World Cup effort two years previously. They think it's all over . . . it is now (we live in hope!?).
• **Songwriters:** BROUDIE obviously, except SOMETHING IN THE AIR (Thunderclap Newman) / HANG ON TO A DREAM (Tim Hardin) / LUCIFER SAM (Pink Floyd) / HERE TODAY (Beach Boys) / ANOTHER GIRL, ANOTHER PLANET (Only Ones) / WHOLE WIDE WORLD (Wreckless Eric) / OUTDOOR MINER (Wire) / YOU SHOWED ME (Byrds; minor hit Turtles). LUCKY YOU + FEELING LAZY + MY BEST DAY were co-written & sung w/ TERRY HALL + IAN McNABB + ALISON MOYET respectively. The track OPEN GOALS sampled; LOOK KA PY PY (Meters).
• **Trivia:** The track 'PERSUASION' featured IAN McCULLOCH (ex-ECHO & THE BUNNYMEN). He has also produced NORTHSIDE, PRIMITIVES and TERRY HALL.

Album rating: CLOUDCUCKOOLAND (*7) / PURE LIGHTNING SEEDS compilation (*8)

IAN BROUDIE – vocals, keyboards, guitar / with **PETER COYLE + PAUL SIMPSON** (ex-LOTUS EATERS + WILD SWANS)

Ghetto / M.C.A.

Jun 89. (7") *(GTG 004)* *<53816>* **PURE. / FOOLS** [16] [31] Apr90
(12"+=) *(GTGT 004)* – God help them.
(cd-s++=) *(GTG 004CD)* – All I want.

Aug 89. (lp/c/cd) *(GHETT/+C/CD 3)* *<MCA/+C/D 6404>* **CLOUDCUCKOOLAND** [50] [46]
– All I want / Bound in a nutshell / Pure / Sweet dreams / The nearly man / Joy / Love explosion / Don't let go / Control the flame / The price / Fools / Frenzy. *(c+=/cd+=)* – God help them. *(re-iss. cd May92; CDOVD 436)*

Oct 89. (7") *(GTG 6)* **JOY. / FRENZY**
(12"+=/cd-s+=) *(GTGT/CDGTG 6)* – Control The Flame.
(US cd-ep+=) – Hang on to a dream.

Apr 90. (7") *(GTG 9)* *<24054>* **ALL I WANT. / PERSUASION** Aug90
(12"+=/cd-s+=) *(GTGT/CDGTG 9)* – ('A'extended).

— BROUDIE made appearance on WILD SWANS non-UK album 'SPACE FLOWER'.

Virgin / M.C.A.

Mar 92. (7"/c-s) *(VS/VSC 1402)* *<54195>* **THE LIFE OF RILEY. / SOMETHING IN THE AIR** [28] [98]
(12"+=/cd-s+=) *(VST/VSCDG 1402)* – Marooned.
(US c-s) *<54195>* – ('A'side) / excerpts: Blowing bubbles – Sense – A cool place.

Apr 92. (cd/c/lp) *(CDV/TCV/V 2690)* *<MCA D/C 10388>* **SENSE** [53]
– Sense / The life of Riley / Blowing bubbles / A cool place / Where flowers fade / A small slice of heaven / Tingle tangle / Happy / Marooned / Thinking up, looking down.

May 92. (7"/c-s) *(VS/VSC 1414)* *<54431>* **SENSE. / FLAMING SWORD** [31] Jun92
(12"+=/cd-s+=) *(VST/VSCDT 1414)* – The life of Riley (remix) / Hang on to a dream.

May 92. (c-s) *<54425>* **SENSE / TINGLE TANGLE** [-]
(cd-s) *<54431>* – ('A'side) / The life of Riley / Flaming sword / Lucifer Sam.

— **BROUDIE** added **SIMON ROGERS** – instruments, co-producer / **CLIVE LAYTON** – Hammond organ / **MARINA VAN RODY** – vocals (Why Why Why). The live band **BROUDIE** – vocals, guitar / with **ALI KANE** – keyboards / **MARTYN CAMPBELL** – bass / **CHRIS SHARROCK** – drums

Epic / Trauma-Interscope

Aug 94. (7"/c-s) *(660 628-8/-4)* *<51002>* **LUCKY YOU. / ('A'lunar mix)** [43]
(12"/cd-s) *(660 628-6/-2)* – ('A'hard luck mix) / ('A'lucky devil mix) / ('A'lunar cabaret mix).

— Above was co-written w / **TERRY HALL**. They are now best known for contributing football theme to Match of the Day's 'Goal Of The Month'. ALISON MOYET wrote a track for the next album.

Sep 94. (cd/c/lp) *(477237-2/-4/-1)* *<71008>* **JOLLIFICATION** [12] Dec94
– Perfect / Lucky you / Open goals / Change / Why why why / Marvellous / Feeling lazy / My best day / Punch & Judy / Telling tales.

Jan 95. (7")(c-s) *(660 986-7/-4)* **CHANGE. / SAY YOU WILL** [13] [-]
(cd-s+=) *(660 986-5)* – Dust.
(cd-s) *(660 986-2)* – ('A'side) / The life of Riley (instrumental) / Lucky you (live).

Apr 95. (c-s) *(661 426-4)* **MARVELLOUS / LUCIFER SAM** [24] [-]
(cd-s+=) *(661 426-5)* – I met you.
(cd-s) *(661 426-2)* – ('A'side) / ('A'club mix) / ('A'dub mix) / All I want.

Jul 95. (c-s) *(662 179-4)* **PERFECT / HOWL** [18] [-]
(cd-s+=) *(662 179-2)* – ('A'acoustic) / Blowing bubbles (extended remix).
(cd-s) *(662 179-5)* – ('A'side) / Change (live) / Flaming sword (live).

Oct 95. (c-s) *(662 518-4)* **LUCKY YOU / LUCKY YOU (Lunar mix)** [15] [-]
(cd-s) *(662 518-2)* – ('A'side) / Life of Riley (live) / Pure (live) / Here today (live).
(cd-s) *(662 518-5)* – ('A'side) / Open your eyes / The likely lads.

Feb 96. (c-s) *(662 967-4)* **READY OR NOT / PUNCH AND JUDY (electric '96 version)** [20] [-]
(cd-s+=) *(662 967-5)* – Outdoor miner.
(cd-s) *(662 967-2)* – ('A'side) / Another girl, another planet / Whole wide world.

May 96. (7"/c-s; BADDIEL & SKINNER & The LIGHTNING SEEDS) *(663 273-7/-4)* **THREE LIONS (The Official Song Of The England Football Team) / ('A'-Karaoke version)** [1] [-]
(cd-s+=) *(663 273-2)* – ('A'-Jules Rimet extended version).
(the '98 World Cup version returned to No.1 in Jun'98)

Epic / Sony

Oct 96. (c-s) *(663863-4)* **WHAT IF . . . / HERE TODAY (live)** [14] [-]
(cd-s) *(663863-2)* – ('A'side) / Never / The crunch / ('A'-Leuroj's slo'n'easy mix).
(cd-s) *(663863-5)* – ('A'side) / Lightning Seeds mix'n'match / ('A'-Leuroj's easy disco dub mix).

Nov 96. (cd/c) *(486640-2/-4)* *<68054>* **DIZZY HEIGHTS** [11]
– Imaginary friends / You bet your life / Waiting for today to happen / What if . . . / Sugar coated iceberg / Touch and go / Like you do / Wishaway / Fingers and thumbs / You showed me / Ready or not / Fishes on the line.

Jan 97. (c-s) *(664043-4)* **SUGAR COATED ICEBERG / THIS POWER** 12
(cd-s+=) *(664043-2)* – S.F. sorrow is born / Porpoise song.
(cd-s) *(664043-5)* – ('A'side) / Why why why / Telling tales.

Apr 97. (cd-s) *(664328-2)* **YOU SHOWED ME (mixes by Attica Blues / The Wiseguys & DJ Pulse)** 8
(c-s+=) *(664328-4)* – (Todd Terry mix).
(cd-s) *(664328-5)* – (Todd Terry mixes).

Nov 97. (cd/c) *(<489034-2/-4>)* **LIKE YOU DO . . . THE BEST OF** (compilation) 5
– What you say / Life of Riley / Lucky you / You showed me / Change / Waiting for today to happen ('97 mix) / Pure / Sugar coated iceberg / Ready or not / All I want / Perfect / What if? / Sense / Marvellous / Three lions.

Epic — Alex

Nov 97. (c-s) *(665367-4)* **WHAT YOU SAY / BE MY BABY** 41 Apr98
(cd-s+=) *(665367-2)* *<6090>* – Weirdaway / Blue.
(cd-s) *(665367-5)* *<6050>* – ('A'-Psyche Beach trip pts.1-3) / ('A'mixes by Ballistic Brothers & Wiseguys).

– compilations, etc. –

on 'Virgin' unless otherwise mentioned

May 96. (cd/c/lp) *(CDV/TCV/V 2805)* **PURE LIGHTNING SEEDS** 27 -

May 96. (c-s) *(VSC 1586)* **LIFE OF RILEY / SOMETHING IN THE AIR** -
(cd-s+=) *(VSCDT 1586)* – Marooned.
(cd-s) *(VSCDX 1586)* – ('A'side) / Control the flame / ('A'remix).

LIGOTAGE

Formed: Bristol, England . . . July '83 by petite punkette, BEKI BONDAGE (formerly of VICE SQUAD) and her seasoned punk crew of LINC (ex-CHELSEA), STEVE ROBERTS (ex-UK SUBS) and er, HOMO SEX (ex-MY EYES MY EYES). A surprise signing to 'E.M.I.', LIGOTAGE lasted only one single, 'CRIME AND PASSION', before moving on to 'Picasso' for a live album, 'FORGIVE AND FORGET' (1984). Opening with a ridiculous rendition of Holzt's 'MARS THE BRINGER OF WAR', the band went on to murder Nancy Sinatra's 'THESE BOOTS ARE MADE FOR WALKING' and Jimi Hendrix's 'PURPLE HAZE', many longtime, er BONDAGE fans not forgiving or forgetting in a hurry. The gorgeous BEKI subsequently released three forgettable solo singles before tying up her career for good.

Album rating: FORGIVE AND FORGET (*3)

BEKI BONDAGE (b. REBECCA LOUISE BOND, 3 Jun'63) – vocals / **HOMO SEX** – guitar (ex-MY EYES MY EYES) / **LINC** – bass (ex-CHELSEA) / **STEVE ROBERTS** – drums (ex-UK SUBS, ex-CYANIDE)

E.M.I. — not iss.

Jan 84. (7") *(EMI 5446)* **CRIME AND PASSION. / VANITY** -
(12"+=) *(12EMI 5446)* – Execution.

Picasso — not iss.

Dec 84. (lp) *(PIKM 005)* **FORGIVE AND FORGET (live)** -
– Mars the bringer of war / The corporation / Crime and passion / The fun goes on / Forgive and forget / End of the century / Misfits / Coming for you / Vanity / Curate / These boots are made for walking / Purple haze.

BEKI BONDAGE

— solo with an unknown backing band

Communique — not iss.

Nov 85. (7"m) *(COMM 2)* **DON'T TURN AWAY. / DOLPHINS / HARD TO GET** -
(12"+=) *(COMM12-2)* – The wheel of fortune.

Mar 86. (c-s/7"; as BEKI) *(C+/LITTLE 5)* **OUT OF THE DARKNESS. /** -
(12"+=/12"pic-d+=) *(12LITTLE/+P 5)* –

Ranch Red — not iss.

Oct 87. (7"; as BEKI BONDAGE & THE BOMBSHELLS) **ONCE AIN'T ENOUGH. / LOVE OF MONEY** -

— BEKI retired from the music business

LILAC TIME (see under ⇒ DUFFY, Stephen)

LILIPUT (see under ⇒ KLEENEX)

LILYS

Formed: Boston, Massachusetts, USA . . . early 90's by KURT HEASLEY, who now lives in Hartford, Connecticut. He/they recorded their first album, 'IN THE PRESENCE OF NOTHING' in 1992, a noisily rough affair in the mould of MY BLOODY VALENTINE. A few singles for 'Slumberland' and 'Summershine' were delivered prior to the 1994 twelve-inch, 'A BRIEF HISTORY OF AMAZING LETDOWNS'. It featured the lead track, 'GINGER', the guitar intro soon to be used on the CK1 (Calvin Klein) commercial. A second, more accomplished set, 'ECCSAME THE PHOTON BAND' came out at the end of '94 and was picked up by UK 'Che' records, who licensed its release in Britain, having found KURT in Denver playing bass for APPLES IN STEREO. In 1996, after extensive touring around the States and Europe, they issued their third album, 'BETTER CAN'T MAKE YOUR LIFE BETTER', which highlighted a retro "new wave" approach, especially on the classy MONKEES-esque pop tune, 'A NANNY IN MANHATTAN'. In fact a year later, at the end of '97, the song was discovered by fan, Roman Coppola (son of director, Francis Ford Coppola), who used a new remixed version on a Levi commercial. This gave the song a fresh lease of life, helping it to soar high in the UK charts early the following year (the highest position so far for 'Che', although this was through Seymour Stein at Warners).

Album rating: IN THE PRESENCE OF NOTHING (*5) / ECCSAME THE PHOTON BAND (*7) / BETTER CAN'T MAKE YOUR LIFE BETTER (*6)

KURT HEASLEY (b.1971) – vocals, guitars, etc / with various musicians incl. **TONY EMMENDOLIO + DAVE JONES** (members of VELOCITY GIRL, SUDDENLY, TAMMY! and The ROPERS)

not iss. — Slumberland

1991. (7") **FEBRUARY 14. /** -

1992. (cd/lp) *<20>* **IN THE PRESENCE OF NOTHING** -
– There's no such thing as black orchids / Elizabeth colour wheel / Collider / Tone bender / Preiscope / It does nothing for me / Snowblinder / The way snowflakes fall / Claire hates me.

— In 1993, they released two US-only 45's for 'Slumberland' and 'Summershine'.

SpinArt — SpinArt

Mar 94. (m-lp) *<SPART 11>* **A BRIEF HISTORY OF AMAZING LETDOWNS** -
– Ginger / etc.

— **KURT** recruited **MIKE DEMING** – organ, bass, etc / **DAVE FRANK** – drums / **RICH COSTEY** – synthesizer, producer

Jan 95. (cd/lp) *<(SPART 43-2/-1)>* **ECCSAME THE PHOTON BAND** Dec94
– High writer at home / Day of the monkey / FBI and their Toronto knowing / Hermit crab / Overlit canyon (the obscured wingtip . . .) / Hubble kodiak / Radiotricity / Your guest and host.

— current line-up; **KURT HEASLEY + TORBEN PASTORE** – guitar / **TIMOTHY WEIDMAN** – keyboards / **THOM MONAHAN** – bass / **AARON FIRE SPERSKE** – drums

Che — Primary-Sire

Apr 96. (7") *(che 51)* **RETURNS EVERY MORNING. /** -

Sep 96. (cd/lp) *(che 52 cd/lp)* *<61956>* **BETTER CAN'T MAKE YOUR LIFE BETTER**
– Cambridge California / Nanny in Manhattan / Shovel into spade kit / Elevator is temporary / Can't make your life better / Who is moving / Tennis system (and its stars) / Daz en el Hogar / Bring up the stamp / Sammael sea / Returns every morning.

Nov 96. (7") *(che 65)* **A NANNY IN MANHATTAN. / MORE THAN IT IS DESERVED** -

Dec 96. (7"ep) *(SP 356)* **WHICH STUDIES THE PAST? EP** -
(above released on 'Sub Pop')

Apr 97. (cd-ep) *<63956>* **SERVICES (FOR THE SOON TO BE DEPARTED) EP** -
– Hark, an open channel / Energy channel / Icy water, water everywhere / First half second / Pookah / Gravity free atmosphere of Msa.

Feb 98. (7"/c-s) *(che 77/+c)* **A NANNY IN MANHATTAN. / THE FIRST HALF SECOND** 16
(cd-s+=) *(che 77cd)* – Hark, the open energy channel is icy water, water everywhere / Gravity free atmosphere of MSA.

Arto LINDSAY (see under ⇒ DNA)

LINUS

Formed: Tufnell Park, London, England . . . 1989 by American sisters, TAMMY and JENNIFER DENITTO, plus ANDY ROBERTS and a drummer named PETER. The siblings initially attracted attention via their own 'Riot Grrrl'-style fanzine, 'Plague Your Eyes', although LINUS traded in a more inventive brand of experimental pop-punk witnessed on their self-financed eponymous EP in '93. Having turned down the likes of 'E.M.I.', the 4-piece signed to 'El-e-mental' instead, releasing their well-received debut album, 'YOUGLI', the following year. One of the tracks, 'SUPER GOLGOTHA CRUCIFIXION SCENE' was issued as a single and was actually playlisted on night time Radio One. Although a couple of EP's were released in '95, they retired from the limelight for around three years, returning with the 'DON'T FORGET' EP, in '98.

Album rating: YOUGLI (*6)

TAMMY DENITTO – vocals / **JENNIFER DENITTO** – bass, guitar, vocals / **ANDY ROBERTS** – guitar / **PETER** – drums

Bone — not iss.

Jul 93. (7"ep) *(BUD 001)* **LINUS EP** -
– Driven thing / Dripped shit / Jack T. chick / Light blues.

El'e'mental — not iss.

Apr 94. (7") *(ELM 18S)* **SUPER GOLGOTHA CRUCIFIXION SCENE. / LA LA** -
(cd-s+=) *(ELM 18CD)* – Take my hand Lord Jesus, I'm coming home / Arlo baby.

Apr 94. (lp/cd) *(ELM 19/+CD)* **YOUGLI** -
– Riding with Rick and Darryl / Choose your own adventure / Rumor volat / Peeping Tam / Zap gun / Queen be / Sizafitz / Adolesce / Super Golgotha crucifixion scene / You're corroded / The bearded tomato / Fume / Maybe tonight / Slight / Lullah bye bye / Yougli.

— **STEVE HUGHES** – drums; repl. PETER

1995. (cd-ep) **SUPERCOOL** -

1995. (cd-ep) **BETTER GENES** -

Mole In The Ground — not iss.

Aug 98. (12"ep) *(MIGI 12)* **DON'T FORGET EP** -

LITTLE VILLAGE (see under ⇒ LOWE, Nick)

LIVE

Formed: York, Pennsylvania, USA ... early 90's by EDWARD KOWALCZYK, CHAD TAYLOR, PATRICK DAHLHEIMER and CHAD GRACEY. Coming up with a moniker that both displayed a complete lack of imagination and confused prospective fans, they nevertheless released a competent neo-grunge debut, 'MENTAL JEWELRY' (1991). Produced by JERRY HARRISON (ex-TALKING HEADS), the record (on MCA subsidiary, 'Radioactive') found a large US audience with its rather derivative hybrid of PEARL JAM and R.E.M. Three years in the making, 'THROWING COPPER' eventually scaled the US charts, largely due to a clutch of harder-edged tracks/singles such as, 'SELLING THE DRAMA' and the MTV fave, 'I ALONE'. These semi-classics also cracked the British charts, setting the scene for a show-stealing (LIVE!) slot at the 1995 Glastonbury Fest. A third album, 'SECRET SAMADHI' (1997), repeated the winning formula, although the more discerning fans considered the album a slight let down. • **Covered:** LOVE MY WAY (Psychedelic Furs) / SUPERNATURAL (Vic Chesnutt).

Album rating: MENTAL JEWELRY (*6) / THROWING COPPER (*7) / SECRET SAMADHI (*6)

EDWARD KOWALCZYK – vocals, guitar / **CHAD TAYLOR** – guitar, vocals / **PATRICK DAHLHEIMER** – bass / **CHAD GRACEY** – drums, vocals

		Radioactive	Radioactive
Jan 92.	(7") *<54387>* **PAIN LIES ON THE RIVERSIDE. / HEAVEN WORE A SHIRT**	-	
Apr 92.	(lp/c/cd) *<(RAR/+C/D 10346)>* **MENTAL JEWELRY** – Pain lies on the riverside / Operation spirit (the tyranny of tradition) / The beauty of Gray / Brothers unaware / Tired of me / Mirror song / Waterboy / Take my anthem / You are the world / Good pain / Mother Earth is a vicious crowd / 10,000 years (peace is now).		73 Jan92
Apr 92.	(cd-ep) *<54442>* **OPERATION SPIRIT (THE TYRANNY OF TRADITION) (live) / THE BEAUTY OF GRAY (live) / GOOD PAIN / LIES ON THE RIVERSIDE (live)**	-	
Jun 92.	(7") *(RAX 1)* **OPERATION SPIRIT. / HEAVEN WORE A SKIRT**		-
	(12"+=/cd-s+=) *(RAX T/TD 1)* – Negation / Good pain.		
May 94.	(c-s) *<54816>* **SELLING THE DRAMA / LIGHTNING CRASHES**	-	43
Sep 94.	(c-s/cd-s) *(RAX C/TD 11)* **SELLING THE DRAMA. / ('A'acoustic) / WHITE DISCUSSION**		-
Oct 94.	(cd/c) *<(RAD/RAC 10997)>* **THROWING COPPER** – The dam at Otter Creek / Selling the drama / I alone / Iris / Lightning crashes / Top / All over you / Shit towne / T.B.D. / Stage / Waitress / Pillar of Davidson / White discussion. *(cd hidden track +=)* – Horse.	37	1 May94
Feb 95.	(7"clear/c-s) *(RAX/+C 13)* **I ALONE. / PAIN LIES ON THE RIVERSIDE**	48	-
	(cd-s+=) *(RAXTD 13)* – ('A'mix).		
Jun 95.	(c-s/cd-s) *(RAX C/TD 17)* **SELLING THE DRAMA / THE DAN AT OTTER CREEK**	30	-
	(cd-s+=) *(RAXXD 17)* – ('A'acoustic).		
Sep 95.	(c-s) *(RAXC 20)* **ALL OVER YOU / SHIT TOWNE**	48	-
	(cd-s+=) *(RAXTD 20)* – ('A'live at Glastonbury).		
	(cd-s) *(RAXXD 20)* – ('A'side) / Waitress (live) / Iris (live at Glastonbury).		
Jan 96.	(c-s/cd-s) *(RAX C/TD 23)* **LIGHTNING CRASHES / THE BEAUTY OF GRAY (bootleg) / TBD (acoustic) ,**	33	-
	(cd-s) *(RAXXD 23)* – ('A'side) / ('A'-live at Glastonbury) / White discussion (live at Glastonbury).		
Mar 97.	(7"silver) *(RAX 28)* **LAKINI'S JUICE. / SUPERNATURAL (remix)**	29	-
	(cd-s+=) *(RAXXD 28)* – White discussion (remix).		
	(cd-s) *(RAD 49023)* – ('A'side) / Pain lies on the riverside (remix) / Selling the drama (acoustic).		
Mar 97.	(cd/c/d-lp) *<(RAD/RAC/RAR2 11590)>* **SECRET SAMADHI** – Rattlesnake / Lakini's juice / Graze / Century / Ghost / Unsheathed / Insomnia and the hole in the universe / Turn my head / Heropsychodreamer / Freaks / Merica / Gas Hed goes west.	31	1
Jun 97.	(7") *(RAX 29)* **FREAKS. / LOVE MY WAY (live)**	60	
	(cd-s+=) *(RAXTD 29)* – Freaks (Labor, Labor, Labor remix).		
	(cd-s) *(RAXD 29)* – ('A'side) / Lakini's juice (live) / Freaks (live).		

Richard LLOYD (see under ⇒ TELEVISION)

Robert LLOYD (see under ⇒ NIGHTINGALES)

LODGER

Formed: London, England ... 1997 by the indie supergroup line-up of DANNY GOFFEY (of SUPERGRASS) and his collaborative songwriting girlfriend, PEARL LOWE (ex-POWDER), who enlisted two former members of DELICATESSEN, NEIL CARLILL and WILL FOSTER. An unusual set-up due to the fact that DANNY was moonlighting with the permission from his aforementioned group and record label, although no publicity was allowed. Stranger still was the fact that PEARL and NEIL took on a barbed vocal tete-a-tete, a NANCY SINATRA and LEE HAZLEWOOD for the 90's you could say! This was much in evidence on their excellent debut single, 'I'M LEAVING', its dual counterplay helping it to scrape into the Top 40. A follow-up, 'ALWAYS ROUND HERE', was much of the same although not faring as well in the commercial world of pop.

Album rating: WALK IN THE PARK (*4)

PEARL LOWE – vocals (ex-POWDER) / **NEIL CARLILL** (b. 1966) – vocals (ex-DELICATESSEN) / **WILL FOSTER** (b. 1973) – bass (ex-DELICATESSEN) / **DANNY GOFFEY** (b. 1975) – drums (of SUPERGRASS)

		Island	Imprint
Apr 98.	(c-s/7") *(C+/IS 693)* **I'M LEAVING. / CIAO**	40	
	(cd-s+=) *(CID 693)* – Jacko's baby.		
Jun 98.	(7") *(IS 704)* **ALWAYS ROUND HERE. / SEE ME ROUND**		
	(cd-s+=) *(CID 704)* – Many mistakes.		
	(cd-s) *(CIDX 704)* – ('A'side) / Safe (instrumental) / Not in a million tears.		
Aug 98.	(7") *(IS 713)* **SMALL CHANGE. / DRUNK**		
	(cd-s+=) *(CID 713)* – Eric.		
	(cd-s) *(CIDX 713)* – ('A'side) / Compass point / Toby said kick me.		
Sep 98.	(cd) *<120494>* **WALK IN THE PARK**		Nov98

LO-FIDELITY ALLSTARS

Formed: London, England ... mid 90's by THE WREKKED TRAIN (aka DAVE), SHERIFF JOHN STONE (aka MATT), THE ALBINO PRIEST (aka PHIL), THE SLAMMER (aka JOHNNY), A ONE MAN CROWD CALLED GENTILEE (aka ANDY) and THE MANY TENTACLES (aka MARTIN); DAVE and MATT were brought up in Sussex, while JOHNNY and engineer MARTIN hail from Leeds. Having met while working in Tower Records, PHIL and MATT found that they had similar tastes, i.e. FUNKADELIC, BOOTSY COLLINS and late, great writer, CHARLES BUKOWSKI. Signed to trendy Big Beat label, 'Skint', they debuted in 1997 with the 'KOOL ROC BASS' EP, the music press heralding them as leaders of the new skool skunk-rock brigade that would also include The REGULAR FRIES. As well as creating a bastard 90's fusion of HAPPY MONDAYS, FLOWERED UP and trippy electro, these bands also shared a greasy haired, dishevelled druggy image. Later the same year, they scored their first Top 50 entry with 'DISCO MACHINE GUN', followed by an even bigger success (Top 30) with 'VISION INCISION', both lifted from their excellent sampletastic Top 20 debut set, 'HOW TO OPERATE WITH A BLOWN MIND' (1998); the record also featured a cover/collaboration of Pigeonhed's 'BATTLEFLAG', which became another hit single later in the year.

Album rating: HOW TO OPERATE WITH A BLOWN MIND (*8)

THE WREKKED TRAIN (aka DAVE) – vocals / **THE ALBINO PRIEST** (aka PHIL) – decks, samples / **A ONE MAN CROWD CALLED GENTILEE** (aka ANDY) – bass / **THE SLAMMER** (aka JOHNNY) – drums / **SHERIFF JOHN STONE** (aka MATT) – keyboards / plus **THE MANY TENTACLES** (aka MARTIN) – engineering, keyboards

		Skint	Sony
Jun 97.	(12"ep/cd-ep) *(skint 24/+cd)* **KOOL ROC BASS EP** *(re-iss. Jun98; same)*		-
Sep 97.	(12"ep/cd-ep) *(skint 30/+cd)* **DISCO MACHINE GUN** *(withdrawn after 3 days due to a sample of The BREEDERS 'Cannonball')*	50	-
Apr 98.	(12"ep/cd-ep) *(skint 33/+cd)* **VISION INCISION**	30	-
	(12"ep) *(skint 33x)* – ('A'remixes).		
Apr 98.	(cd/c/d-lp) *(brassic 8 cd/mc/lp) <69654>* **HOW TO OPERATE WITH A BLOWN MIND** – Warming up the brain farm / Kool roc bass / Kasparov's revenge / Blisters on my brain / How to operate with a blown mind / I used to fall in love / Battleflag (feat. Pigeonhed) / Lazer sheep dip funk / Will I get out of jail / Vision incision / Nightime story.	15	May98
Nov 98.	(12"/cd-s; featuring PIGEONHED) *(SKINT 38/+CD) <41551>* **BATTLEFLAG / PONY PRESSURE / BONUS BEATS**	36	
	(cd-s) *(SKINT 38XCD)* – ('A'edit) / ('A'-Space Raiders mix) / ('A'live).		

LOFT (see under ⇒ WEATHER PROPHETS)

LOFTUS (see under ⇒ RED RED MEAT)

Lora LOGIC

Born: SUSAN WHITBY, c.1961, London, England. Alongside POLY STYRENE, she came to prominence in 1977 as the saxophonist with punk group, X-RAY SPEX. LORA departed however, immediately after the release of their debut 45, 'Oh Bondage Up Yours'; the classic punk track was originally a highlight on the infamous 'Live At The Roxy' V/A album. The following year, LORA re-emerged with a new outfit, ESSENTIAL LOGIC, a frenetic avant-New Wave project who debuted with the single, 'AEROSOL BURNS'. After signing a one-off deal with 'Virgin' in 1979 for a follow-up single, 'WAKE UP', they secured a longer-term contract with 'Rough Trade'. By this time, ESSENTIAL LOGIC were comprised of LORA, PHILIP LEGG, MARK TURNER, WARBLING DAVID WRIGHT and RICH TEA, this line-up featuring on a debut album, 'BEAT RHYTHM NEWS' (1979). During this period, LORA guested for the likes of the SWELL MAPS, RED CRAYOLA, the STRANGLERS and the RAINCOATS, prior to initiating her own short-lived solo career. However, after only one solitary lp in 1982, 'PEDIGREE CHARM', LORA chose the same spiritual path as her former X-RAY SPEX bandmate, giving up the music business to join the Hare Krishna movement.

Album rating: Essential Logic: BEAT RHYTHM NEWS (*6) / PEDIGREE CHARM (*6)

ESSENTIAL LOGIC

LORA LOGIC – vocals, saxophone (ex-X-RAY SPEX) / **STUART ACTION** – guitar / **TIM WRIGHT** – bass / **RICH TEA** – drums

Cells | not iss.

Jun 78. (7") *(CELLS ONE)* **AEROSOL BURNS. / WORLD FRICTION** [ ] [-]

— STUART + TIM were repl. **PHILIP LEGG** – guitar / **WILLIAM BENNETT** – guitar / **MARK TURNER** – bass / **WARBLING DAVID WRIGHT** – tenor sax

Virgin | not iss.

May 79. (12"ep) *(VS 261-12)* **ESSENTIAL LOGIC EP** [ ] [-]
– Wake up / Eagle bird / Quality crayon wax O.K. / Bod's message.

— now without BENNETT

Rough Trade | not iss.

Oct 79. (7") *(RT 029)* **POPCORN BOY. / FLORA FORCE** [ ] [-]
Oct 79. (lp) *(ROUGH 5)* **BEAT RHYTHM NEWS** [ ] [-]
– Quality crayon wax o.k. / The order form / Shabby Abbott / World friction / Wake up / Albert / Alkaline loaf in the area / Collecting dust / Popcorn boy.
Nov 80. (7") *(RT 050)* **EUGENE. / TAME THE NEIGHBOURS** [ ] [-]
Jan 81. (7") *(RT 053)* **MUSIC IS A BETTER NOISE. / MOONTOWN** [ ] [-]
Jun 81. (7") *(RT 074)* **FANFARE IN THE GARDEN. / THE CAPTAIN** [ ] [-]

— split soon after above, some members joined RIP, RIG & PANIC

LORA LOGIC

— with **PHIL LEGG + BEN ANNESLEY** – bass / **RICH TEA + CHARLES HAYWARD** (ex-THIS HEAT) – drums

Rough Trade | not iss.

Oct 81. (7") *(RT 087)* **WONDERFUL OFFER. / STEREO** [ ] [-]
Feb 82. (lp) *(ROUGH 28)* **PEDIGREE CHARM** [ ] [-]
– Brute fury / Horrible party / Stop halt / Wonderful offer / Martian man / Hiss and shake / Pedigree charm / Rat alley / Crystal gazing.

— split when she converted to Hare Krishna. LEGG joined The GIST.

LONDON

Formed: er, London, England . . . early 1977 by RIFF REGAN, DAVE WIGHT, STEVE VOICE and JON MOSS. Signed straight out of obscurity to major label, 'M.C.A.', LONDON made their vinyl debut during the summer of '77 with the hopefully titled 'EVERYONE'S A WINNER', a chart duffer that didn't bode well for future releases. The lightweight punks persevered with a further two forgettable singles, both tracks available on their one and only full-length set, 'ANIMAL GAMES', released early the following year. Although frontman, RIFF REGAN went solo, the band's only claim to fame lies in the fact that JON MOSS subsequently drummed for CULTURE CLUB (after a brief spell with The DAMNED and the more obscure EDGE).

Album rating: ANIMAL GAMES (*3)

RIFF REGAN – vocals / **DAVE WIGHT** – guitar / **STEVE VOICE** – bass / **JON MOSS** – drums

M.C.A. | not iss.

Jun 77. (7") *(MCA 305)* **EVERYONE'S A WINNER. / HANDCUFFED** [ ] [-]
Sep 77. (7"ep/12"ep) *(MCA 319/+T)* **SUMMER OF LOVE EP** [ ] [-]
– Summer of love / Friday on my mind / No time / Siouxsie Sue.
Nov 77. (7") *(MCA 336)* **ANIMAL GAMES. / US KIDS COLD** [ ] [-]
Jan 78. (lp) *(MCF 2823)* **ANIMAL GAMES** [ ] [-]
– No time / Reaction / Everyone's a winner / Summer of love / Us kids cold / Young / Good looking girls / Animal games / Out on the skids / Speed speed / Swinging London. *(cd-iss. Nov97 as 'PUNK ROCK COLLECTION' on 'Captain Oi' +=; AHOYCD 077)* – Everyone's a winner / Handcuffed / Friday on my mind / Siouxsie Sue.

— they split in 1978, MOSS going off to join The DAMNED before helping to form the EDGE (he subsequently became part of CULTURE CLUB).

RIFF REGAN

Apr 78. (7") *(MCA 363)* **ALL THE NICE BOYS & GIRLS. / STRANGERS** [ ] [-]
Feb 79. (7") *(MCA 406)* **JAPANESE GIRLS. / TERROR BABY** [ ] [-]
Jan 80. (7") *(MCA 548)* **YOU CALL ME LUCKY. / JACOBY ISLAND** [ ] [-]
Mar 80. (7") *(MCA 573)* **THE ONLY ONE. / THE LUCKY DUB** [ ] [-]

Epic | not iss.

Apr 81. (7") *(EPCA 1124)* **HARD HEARTS DON'T CRY. / MISS MIDWEST FARMER'S DAUGHTER** [ ] [-]

LONGPIGS

Formed: Sheffield, England . . . 1993 by mainman, CRISPIN HUNT, RICHARD HAWLEY, SIMON STAFFORD and DEE BOYLE. The band's career got off to a less than encouraging start when a car crash left CRISPIN in a coma, their problems compounded when a deal with the UK arm of 'Elektra' went awry; they were effectively prevented from recording and playing live for two years, that is, until lawyer, John Stratham, bailed them out. With an album's worth of previously recorded, GIL NORTON-produced material in limbo, LONGPIGS eventually secured a new contract with 'Mother', re-recording their debut and soon breaking into the UK Top 75 with their second single, 'SHE SAID'. Finally released in the Spring of '96, 'THE SUN IS OFTEN OUT' spawned a handful of classy hit singles ('FAR', 'ON & ON', a re-issued 'SHE SAID' – Top 20 and 'LOST MYSELF') calling to mind the heady swagger of SUEDE, AUTEURS and occasionally the dark majesty of RADIOHEAD.

Album rating: THE SUN IS OFTEN OUT (*7)

CRISPIN HUNT – vocals, guitar / **RICHARD HAWLEY** – guitar, vocals / **SIMON STAFFORD** – bass, piano / **DEE BOYLE** – drums, vocals (ex-CHAKK)

Mother | Polygram

Mar 95. (7") *(MUM 63)* **HAPPY AGAIN. / SALLY DANCES** [ ] [-]
Jul 95. (7"/c-s) *(MUM/+C 66)* **SHE SAID. / TAKE IT ALL** [67] [-]
(cd-s+=) *(MUMCD 66)* – Devoted / Juicy.
Oct 95. (7"red/c-s) *(MUM/+C 68)* **JESUS CHRIST. / SWEETNESS** [61] [-]
(cd-s+=) *(MUMCD 68)* – Vagina song / Whiteness.
Feb 96. (7"/c-s) *(MUM/+C 71)* **FAR. / BLAH BLAH BLAH** [37] [-]
(cd-s+=) *(MUMCD 71)* – Amateur dramatics / Far (Sheffield version).
Apr 96. (7"ep/c-ep/cd-ep) *(MUM/+C/CD 74)* *<569238>* **ON & ON / YOUR FACE. / DOZEN WICKED WORDS / SLEEP** [16] [ ] Jan97
May 96. (cd/c/lp) *(MUM CD/MC/LP 9602)* *<531542>* **THE SUN IS OFTEN OUT** [26] [ ]
– Lost myself / She said / Far / On and on / Happy again / All hype / Sally dances / Jesus Christ / Dozen wicked words / Elvis / Over our bodies.
Jun 96. (7") *(MUM 77)* **SHE SAID. / FLARE IS METEOR** [16] [-]
(c-s+=/cd-s+=) *(MUM C/CD 77)* – Soap opera credo / Tendresse.
(cd-s) *(MUMXD 77)* – ('A'side) / I lost myself / Far / On and on.
Sep 96. (7"/c-s) *(MUM/+C 82)* **LOST MYSELF. / FLOSS** [22] [-]
(cd-s+=) *(MUMCD 82)* – Wonder drug / When you're alone.
Mar 97. (7"/c-s) *(MUM/+C 90)* **SWIM. /** [ ] [-]
(cd-s+=) *(MUMCD 90)* –

LONG RYDERS

Formed: Paisley, Los Angeles, California, USA . . . March '82, out of The UNCLAIMED by SID GRIFFIN, BARRY SKANK, MATT ROBERTS and STEVE WYNN. The latter soon formed his own band, The DREAM SYNDICATE and was superseded by STEPHEN McCARTHY. This revised line-up made an EP for 'Moxie', which included the tracks, 'Time to Time' and 'Deposition Central'. As The LONG RYDERS (named so after the Walter Hill film, 'The Long Riders), they issued a debut album, '10-5-60' (a mini-set), on their own 'Jem' label, a distinctive hybrid of jagged garage rock, psychedelia and country. While the band were lumped in with their mates under the catch-all term, "Paisley Underground", The LONG RYDERS always wore their country influences more proudly. 'NATIVE SONS' (1984), their debut for 'Zippo', marked the fruition of that experimentation, a finely hewn tapestry of alternative country which featured GENE CLARK on the keening 'IVORY TOWER'. Heralded by the critics, the band signed to 'Island' in 1985 and recorded a further two albums, 'STATE OF OUR UNION' (1985) and 'TWO FISTED TALES' (1987). More overtly country and lyrically politically pointed than their previous efforts, the latter proved to be the band's swansong and they split the following year. SID GRIFFIN subsequently relocated to London where he concentrated on his band The COAL PORTERS. The man has also helped to keep the 'Cosmic American Music' flame burning by penning a GRAM PARSONS biog and he continues to write for various music mags. • **Songwriters:** GRIFFIN-McCARTHY compositions, except YOU'RE GONNA MISS ME (13th Floor Elevators) / I SHALL BE RELEASED + MASTERS OF WAR (Bob Dylan) / DIRTY OLD TOWN (Ewan MacColl) / PRISONERS OF ROCK'N'ROLL (Neil Young) / ANARCHY IN THE UK (Sex Pistols) / PUBLIC IMAGE (P.I.L. w/ STEVE MACK of THAT PETROL EMOTION on vox). • **Trivia:** Will Birch produced them in 1985. SID, STEPHEN + TOM featured on 'Zippo' lp THE LOST WEEKEND by DANNY & DUSTY. They also guested on DREAM SYNDICATE album 'Medicine Show'.

Album rating: 10-5-60 (*6) / NATIVE SONS (*8) / STATE OF OUR UNION (*6)

SID GRIFFIN (b.18 Sep'55, Louisville, Kentucky) – vocals, guitar / **STEPHEN McCARTHY** (b.12 Feb'58, Richmond, Virginia) – steel guitar, vocals, repl. STEVE WYNN (to DREAM SYNDICATE) / **DES BREWER** – bass repl. BARRY SKANK / **MATT ROBERTS** – drums

not iss. | P.V.C.

1983. (m-lp) *<PVC 5906>* **10-5-60** [-] [ ]
– Join my gang / I don't care what's right, I don't care what's wrong / 105-60 / And she rides / Born to believe in you. *(UK-iss.1985 on 'P.V.C.'; PVC 50) (re-iss. Nov85 on 'Zippo'+=; ZANE 004)* – The trip. *(cd-iss. Aug87 on 'Zippo'; CMCAD 31038)*

— **TOM STEVENS** (b.17 Sep'56, Elkhart, Indiana) – drums repl. DON McCALL who had repl. DES BREWER

— **GREG SOWDERS** (b.17 Mar'60, La Jolla, Calif.) – drums, repl. ROBERTS

Zippo | Frontier

Nov 84. (lp) *(ZONG 004)* *<4606-1>* **NATIVE SONS** [ ] [ ] 1983
– Final wild sun / Still by / Ivory tower / Run Dusty run / (Sweet) Metal revenge / Fair game / Tell it to the judge on Sunday / Too close to the light / Wreck of the 809 / Never get to meet the man / I had a dream. *(cd-iss. Jan88; ZONGCD 003)* – (w/ last m-lp tracks). *(cd re-iss. Jun96 on 'Diablo'; DIAB 821)*
Apr 85. (7") *(ZIPPO 45-2)* **I HAD A DREAM. / TOO CLOSE TO THE LIGHT (Buckskin mix)** [ ] [ ]

Island | Island

Sep 85. (7") *(IS 237)* **LOOKING FOR LEWIS & CLARK. / CHILD BRIDE** [59] [ ]
(d7"+=/10"+=) *(ISD/10IS 237)* – Southside of the story / If I were a bramble and you were a rose.
Oct 85. (lp/c) *(ILPS/ICT 9802)* *<422842863-1>* **STATE OF OUR UNION** [66] [ ]
– Looking for Lewis & Clark / Lights of downtown / WDIA / Mason-Dixon line / Here comes that train again / Years long ago / Good times tomorrow, hard times today / Two kinds of love / You just can't ride the boxcars anymore / Capturing the flag / State of my union. *(cd-iss. Mar95 on 'Prima'+=; SID 003)* – If I were a bramble and you were a rose / Southside of the story / Child bride / Christmas in New Zealand.
Jun 87. (lp/c/cd) *(ILPS/ICT/CID 9869)* *<422842864-1>* **TWO FISTED TALES** [ ] [ ]
– Gunslinger man / I want you bad / A stitch in time / The light gets in the way /

Prairie fire / Baby's in toyland / Long short story / Man of misery / Harriet Tubman's gonna carry me home / For the rest of my life / Spectacular fall. *(cd re-iss. cd Mar96 on 'Prima'+=; SID 005)* – Ring bells / Time keeps travelling / State of our union (live) / Baby we've all got to go down (live).

Jun 87. (7") *(IS 330)* **I WANT YOU BAD. / RING BELLS**
(12"+=) *(12IS 330)* – State of our union.

— They split New Year '88. In Spring '90, GRIFFIN formed country-rock band The COAL PORTERS, who released first album 'REBELS WITHOUT APPLAUSE' in 1992. McCARTHY later appeared in GUTTERBALL with STEVE WYNN. GRIFFIN released a solo album in 1997.

– compilations, others, etc. –

Jan 91. (cd) *Overground; (OVER 16CD)* **METALLIC B.O.** (covers) -
– You're gonna miss me / Route 66 / Brand new headache / Prisoners of rock'n'roll / Dirty old town / Billy Jean / Circle round the sun / Six days on the road / Anarchy in the U.K. / Masters of war / Sandwich man / Blues theme / P.I.L. theme / I shall be released. *(re-iss. Dec94; same)*

May 94. (cd) *Windsong; (WINCD 058)* **BBC RADIO 1 LIVE IN CONCERT (live)** -

COAL PORTERS

GRIFFIN w / **ST.JOHN + McGARVEY**

Rubber Rubber

Aug 92. (cd) *<(RUB 17)>* **REBELS WITHOUT APPLAUSE**
– Roll Columbia roll / I tell her all the time / The light that shines within / Rhythm and blues angel / Stealin' horses / Sittin' in an isle of palms (live). *(UK+=)* – Stuck on an island / John F. Kennedy blues (live) / March of the tap-dancing rats.

Prima Prima

Sep 94. (cd) *<(SID 002)>* **THE LAND OF HOPE AND CROSBY**
– Imperial beach / Death like a valentine / She loved me / What am I doing? (in this thing called love) / How did we get this far? / You can see them there / Windy city / Playing dumb £1 / Everybody's fault but mine / What about tomorrow / All the colours of the world / The pipsqueaks theme.

Sep 95. (cd) *<(SID 004)>* **LOS LONDON**
– Me, here at the door / Crackin' at the seams / Chasing rainbows / A woman to love / Apple tree / It happened to me / Santa Mira / After it's broken / A Jacobite at heart / Someone's gonna love you too / Help me / Ain't no way I'll be your cowboy.

SID GRIFFIN

May 97. (cd) *<(SID 007)>* **LITTLE VICTORIES**
– When I'm out walking with you / Jimmy Reed / Good times tomorrow, hard times today / Rate of exchange / I wish I was a mountain / Distant trains / Sailors and soldiers / Man who invented the blues / Monk's moods / Flak jacket / Alma mater / Jerusalem road.

LOOP

Formed: Croydon, London, England . . . 1986 by ROBRT HAMPSON, who replaced the old rhythm section for JOHN WILLS and NEIL MacKAY. They issued their own releases on 'Head' records, their debut album seeing the light of day in November 1987. A remshackle affair, it nevertheless sowed the seeds for 1989's 'FADE OUT'. Released on the small indie label, 'Cheree', the album showcased the band's queasily churning, endlessly repetitive riffs enveloping HAMPSON's broooding vocals. The sound and atmosphere conjured up nothing less than a hallcinogenic fever and indeed, the band's alleged stated intention was to sonically reproduce an acid trip gone wrong. While their indie compadres were getting 'sorted' during the supposed second summer of love, Loop concerned themselves with darkness and despair and it was obvious they never really fitted with the mood of the times. Their swansong, 'A GILDED ETERNITY', was a distillation of their sound, a hypnotic trip to the scarier side of the human psyche. In early 1991 they finally split with McKAY and WILLS going off to form the rockier HAIR AND SKIN TRADING COMPANY. HAMPSON and newcomer SCOTT DAWSON formed the tripped-out MAIN, releasing 'HYDRA' in November, the first of a series of long E.P.'s and mini-albums that were more sculptured trance-ambient than the SPACEMEN 3/MC5 hybrid of LOOP. Throughout the last half of 1995, their unique 'HERTZ' series demonstrated their continuing break from the rock world. • **Songwriters:** All penned by HAMPSON and group, except MOTHER SKY (Can) / CINNAMON GIRL (Neil Young).

Album rating: ETERNAL – THE SINGLES compilation (*7) / A GILDED ETERNITY (*7) / Main:- FIRMAMENT (*6) / MOTION POOL (*7) / LIGATURE (*6) / FIRMAMENT II (*7) / FIRMAMENT III & IV (*5)

ROB 'Josh' HAMPSON – vocals, guitar / **JAMES** – guitar / **GLEN** – bass repl. PHILIP KING (ex-SERVANTS) / **JOHN WILLS** – drums (ex-SERVANTS)

Head Mute

Jan 87. (12"m) *(HEAD 5)* **16 DREAMS. / HEAD ON / BURNING WORLD** -

Jun 87. (7"pic-d) *(HEAD 7L)* **SPINNING. / SPINNING (part 2)** -
(12") *(HEAD 7)* – ('A'side) / Deep hit / I'll take you there.

Nov 87. (lp) *(HEADLP 1) <61154>* **HEAVEN'S END**
– Soundhead / Straight to your heart / Forever / Heaven's end / Too real to feel / Fix to fall / Head on / Carry me / Rocket U.S.A. / Spinning / Brittle head girl. *(cd-iss. Mar88; HEADCD 1) (re-iss. Jul91 & Mar94 on 'Reactor' cd/c/lp ; REACTOR CD/C/LP 001)*

— **NEIL MacKAY** – bass repl. GLEN / **SCOTT DOWSON** – guitar repl. JAMES

Chapter 22 not iss.

Apr 88. (7") *(LCHAP 27)* **COLLISION. / CRAWLING HEART** -
(12"+=) *(12CHAP 27)* – Thief of fire / Thief.

Cheree Rough Trade

1988. (7"flexi) *(CHEREE 1)* **SOUNDHEAD (live). / (other by The TELESCOPES)** -

— trimmed to trio when NEIL departed

Dec 88. (12"m) *(12CHAP 32)* **BLACK SUN. / CIRCLE GRAVE / MOTHER SKY** -

Jan 89. (2x12"lp/lp/c/cd) *(CHAP LLP/LP/C/CD 34) <ROUGHUS 52/+C/CD>* **FADE OUT** 51
– Black sun / This is where you end / Fever knife / Torched / Fade out / Pulse / Vision strain / Got to get it over / Collision / Crawling heart / Thief of fire / Thief (motherfucker) / Mother sky. *(cd re-iss. Nov92 on 'Reactor'+=; REACTORCD 004)* – Where you end.

Situation 2 Beggars Banquet

Nov 89. (7") *(SIT 64)* **ARC-LITE (SONAR). / ARC-LITE (RADIATED)** -
(12"+=/cd-s+=) *(SIT 64 T/CD)* – Sunburst.

Jan 90. (cd)(c/2x12"m-lp) *(SITU 27CD)(SIT C/U 27) <2061>* **A GILDED ETERNITY** 39
– Vapour / Afterglow / The nail will burn / Blood / Breathe into me / From centre to wave / Be here now. *(free-7"w/above)* – SHOT WITH A DIAMOND. / THE NAIL WILL BURN (BURN OUT) *(cd++=)* – Arc-lite (sonar). *(cd re-iss. Sep95 on 'Beggars Banquet'; BBL 27CD)*

— Disbanded early in 1991; WILLS founded HAIR & SKIN TRADING CO (with McKAY)

– compilations, others, etc. –

Aug 88. (lp)<cd/c> *Head; (HEADLP 2) / Mute; <61155-2/-4>* **THE WORLD IN YOUR EYES**
– 16 dreams / Head on / Burning world / Rocket U.S.A. / Spinning / Deep hit / I'll take you there / Brittle head girl / Burning prisma / Spinning (spun out). *(re-iss. Jul91 & Mar94 on 'Reactor' cd/c/lp; REACTOR CD/C/LP 002)*

Nov 89. (lp) *Chapter 22; (CHAPLP 44)* **ETERNAL – THE SINGLES 1988** (all Chapter 22 singles) -

May 91. (cd/c/2x12"m-lp) *Reactor; (REACTOR CD/C/LP 003)* **WOLF FLOW** (The John Peel sessions 1987-91) -
– Soundhead / Straight to your heart / Rocket U.S.A. / Pulse / This is where you end / Collision / From centre to wave / Afterglow / Sunburst. *(re-iss. Mar94 on 'Reactor'; same)*

Mar 94. (cd/lp) *Reactor; (REACTOR CD/LP 5)* **DUAL** -

MAIN

were founded by **HAMPSON + DOWSON**

Situation 2 not iss.

Nov 91. (12"ep) *(SIT 83T)* **HYDRA** -
– Flametracer / Time over (dub) / Suspension.

May 92. (12"ep) *(SIT 89T)* **CALM** -
– There is only light / Remain / Feed the collapse / Sever.
(cd-ep+=) *(SITL 89CD)* – Thirst.

— HAMPSON joined GODFLESH, when MAIN split temporarily.

Beggars Banquet Beggars Banquet

Jul 93. (12"ep/cd-ep) *(BBQM 18 T/CD)* **DRY STONE FEED** -
– Cypher / Above axis / Blown / Pulled from the water / Dry stone feed.

Aug 93. (cd-ep) *(BBQ 19CD)* **FIRMANENT (cloudscape). / CYPHER (pentode) / HEAT REALM (shortwave) / SUSPENSION (hyaline) / CODE RAYS** -
(re-iss. Oct94; 12"ep/cd-ep as 'LIGATURE'; BBQM 43 T/CD)

Apr 94. (cd/3x12"m-lp) *(BBQ CD/LP 148) <92382>* **MOTION POOL**
– VII / Rail / Crater star / Core / Spectra decay / Rotary eclipse / Reformation / Heat realm / VIII / Liquid reflection.

Nov 94. (cd) *(BBQCD 168) <92512>* **FIRMAMENT II** – (part IX, X)

Jun 95. (cd-ep) *(HERTZ 1)* **CORONA** – (part I & II) -

Aug 95. (cd-ep) *(HERTZ 2)* **TERMINUS** – (part I, II & III) -

Sep 95. (cd-ep) *(HERTZ 3)* **MASER** – (part I, II, III & IV) -

Oct 95. (cd-ep) *(HERTZ 4)* **HALOFORM** – (part I, II, III) -

Nov 95. (cd-ep) *(HERTZ 5)* **KAON** (part I, II, III, IV & V) -

Dec 95. (cd-ep) *(HERTZ 6)* **NEPER** – (part I, II & III) -

Jan 96. (cd/d-lp) *(HERTZ 16 CD/LP) <84016>* **HZ** May96
– (the 'HERTZ' singles) *(re-iss. Jan98; same)*

Nov 96. (cd) *(BBQCD 179)* **FIRMAMENT III** -

Aug 97. (cd) *(BBQCD 196)* **DELIQUESCENCE (live)** -
– Particle suspension / Phase space / Outer Corona / Carrier wave / Cavitation / Valency.

May 98. (cd) *(BBQCD 202)* **FIRMAMENT IV** -

Sep 98. (cd) *<80202>* **FIRMAMENT III & IV** -
– XI / XII / XIII / XIV / XV / XVI / XVII / XVIII / XIX / XX / XXI / XXII / XXIII / XXIV / XXV / XXVI.

Mary Lou LORD

Born: 1967, Salem, Massachusetts, USA. Despite briefly attending Boston's Berklee Music College, LORD payed her dues the hard way as a street busker after relocating to London. Upon her return to Boston, she was spotted by the 'Kill Rock Stars' label, releasing a debut single, 'ABOUT A BOY', in 1994. There was much speculation that the lyrics referred to KURT COBAIN, a one-time close friend of MARY's; the singer subsequently became the focus of COURTNEY LOVE's ire as the HOLE frontwoman openly criticised LORD in the press. Preferring to concentrate on her music, the songstress delivered an eponymous mini-set in early '95, its knowing lyrics and bittersweet indie-folk instigating a major label A&R scramble. Eventually opting for 'Sony' subsidiary, 'Work', LORD was augmented by an impressive cast of alternative luminaries (including ELLIOT SMITH, MONEY MARK, JULIANA HATFIELD and the BEVIS FROND's NICK SALOMAN) on her belated debut full length album, 'GOT NO SHADOW' (1998). Branching out from her trademark acoustic strum, she pumped up the volume with a newly electrified sound that bore the polished hallmarks of a major label recording budget, LORD covering tracks by the BEVIS FROND (the alias of the aforementioned NICK SALOMAN), ELIZABETH COTTON and FREEDY JOHNSTON.

Album rating: MARY LOU LORD (*6) / GOT NO SHADOW (*6)

MARY LOU LORD – vocals, guitar

Kill Rock Stars | Kill Rock Stars

Jan 95. (m-cd/m-lp) <(KRS 238 CD/EP)> **MARY LOU LORD**
– The lights are changing / Helsinki / That kind of girl / He'd be a diamond / The bridge / I'm talking to you / His indie world / Speeding motorcycle.

Jan 97. (12"ep/cd-ep) <KRS 264/+CD> **MARTIAN SAINTS!** [-]
– Martian saints! / Salem '76 / I figured you out / Sunspot stopwatch / Cinderella backstreet.

— next – like above – with a plethora of session people incl. NICK SALOMAN, ELLIOTT SMITH, ROGER McGUINN, MONEY MARK, JOSH FREESE, etc

Work-Sony | Work-Sony

Jan 98. (cd) <(OK 67574)> **GOT NO SHADOW**
– His latest flame / Western union desperate / The lights are changing / Seven sisters / Throng of Blowtown / Lucky one / She had you / Some jingle jangle morning / Shake sugaree / Two boats / Supergun / Down along the sea / Subway.

LORDS OF THE NEW CHURCH (see under ⇒ DEAD BOYS)

LORI & THE CHAMELEONS

Formed: Liverpool, England . . . 1979 by art college student, LORI LARTY alongside DAVE BALFE and BILL DRUMMOND. Basically a studio outfit for 'Zoo' (label) keeper and ECHO & THE BUNNYMEN manager, DRUMMOND, LORI and Co only managed to scrape out four tracks in their short musical lifetime. Spread over three singles starting with the minor hit, 'TOUCH', LORI's sensuous voice should have been reason enough to secure a wider audience. An OMD-influenced/JAMES BOND movie sampling second single, 'THE LONELY SPY' (released on 'Korova' in 1980), was followed by a double header of both the aforementioned indie favourites, although this proved to be their final outing.

Album rating: didn't release any

LORI LARTY – vocals / **DAVE BALFE** – keyboards (of TEARDROP EXPLODES) / **BILL DRUMMOND** – guitar, vocals (ex-BIG IN JAPAN) / with **TIM WHITAKER** – drums (ex-DEAF SCHOOL, ex-PINK MILITARY)

Zoo | not iss.

Oct 79. (7") (CAGE 006) **TOUCH. / LOVE ON THE GANGES** [-]
(re-iss. Nov79 on 'Sire' SIR 4025) – (hit No.70)

Korova | not iss.

Apr 80. (7") (KOW 5) **THE LONELY SPY. / PERU** [-]

— **GARY DWYER + RAY MARTINEZ** – drums; repl. TIM

Oct 81. (7") (KOW 20) **TOUCH. / THE LONELY SPY** [-]
(12"+=) (KOW 20T) – Love on the ganges.

— split after above, DRUMMOND went solo and created JUSTIFIED ANCIENTS OF MU MU and KLF. BALFE was already part of DALEK I LOVE YOU. He later formed the label, 'Food'.

LOTION

Formed: New York, USA . . . 1991 by TONY ZAJKOWSKI, BILL FERGUSON, JIM FERGUSON and ROB YOUNGBERG. Veterans of the alternative scene (TONY, BILL and ROB had been playing in bands since meeting up at Syracuse Uni in the 80's), the LOTION lads started out as Madchester devotees before realising that New York's social/cultural climate just wasn't right for beany hats and floppy middle partings. Instead, they looked to homegrown legends like R.E.M. and HUSKER DU for inspiration, releasing a debut single, 'HEAD', on KRAMER's 'Kokopop' label in early '93. Entering the studio later that summer with ULTRA VIVID SCENE mainman, KURT RALSKE, at the production helm, they began work on their acclaimed debut set, 'FULL ISAAC'. The record eventually emerged in Spring '94 on the 'SpinArt' label to almost universally positive reviews, subsequently notching up an album of the year award in the 'Village Voice' and generally reducing music journalists to gibbering wrecks. While the band cited the obscure MIRACLE LEGION and the not so obscure LEO SAYER (!) as influences, there was no denying the freshness of their post-grunge musical pot-pourri that effortlessly moved between stinging noise assault and goosebump melancholy. British fans wondering what all the fuss was about were saved from stumping up import prices after 'Big Cat' signed LOTION for the UK, Creation head honcho, Alan McGee having allegedly passed them up. The band were also praised for their contribution to 'Chairman Of The Board' (1994), a Frank Sinatra tribute album wherein LOTION convincingly crooned their way through 'FLY ME TO THE MOON'. Released on 'Warners' in the States, 'NOBODY'S COOL' (1995) was an impressive follow-up set that again met with encouraging reviews and boasted sleeve notes by cult writer, Thomas Pynchon. Later the same year, they released the 'AGNEW FUNERAL' EP before taking a lengthy sabbatical, eventually returning in 1998 with 'THE TELEPHONE ALBUM' (1998).

Album rating: FULL ISAAC (*7) / NOBODY'S COOL (*6) / THE TELEPHONE ALBUM (*6)

TONY ZAJKOWSKI – vocals, guitar / **JIM FERGUSON** – guitar / **BILL FERGUSON** – bass / **ROB YOUNGBERG** – drums

Kokopop | Kokopop

Dec 92. (cd-s) <KOKO 6CD> **HEAD. / SHE IS WEIRD CITY / PEACHTREE** [-]

Dec 93. (7"ep/cd-ep) <(KOKO 14/+CD)> **TEAR EP**
– Tear / Chrome PKG / 22+ / Really drunk.

Big Cat | SpinArt

Mar 94. (lp/cd) (ABB 60/+CD) <SPART 27> **FULL ISAAC**
– Tear / Dr. Link / Paas / Boost / Long / Pajamas / Around / Head / Dock Ellis / She is weird city / Love theme from Santo Gold.

Aug 94. (12"ep/cd-ep) (ABB 66 T/SCD) **AROUND EP** [-]

Big Cat | Warners

Jun 95. (lp/cd) (ABB 89/+CD) <24643> **NOBODY'S COOL**
– Dear sir / New Timmy / Sad part / Rock chick / Blind for now / Enormous room / Sandra / Juggernaut / Namedropper / Dalmacia 007 / Precious Tiny / Switch.

SpinArt | SpinArt

Oct 95. (12"ep/cd-ep) <SPART 45/+CD> **AGNEW FUNERAL EP** [-]
– Marijuana Vietnam / Walk away Renee / Switch / Famous redheads / Treat me.

Mar 98. (lp/cd) <(SPART 58/+CD)> **THE TELEPHONE ALBUM**
– Rich cop / Poor cop / Feedback queen / I love me / No.99 / Mr. Mosquito / Glorified / Mr. President / My name is Prince / Drop dead / West of here / Blackjack / 5th fret – Diatant cousin.

LOTUS EATERS (see under ⇒ WILD SWANS)

LOUD FAMILY (see under ⇒ GAME THEORY)

LOUDSPEAKER

Formed: New York, USA . . . 1986 out of 'Alternative Tentacles' combo, The CRUCIFUCKS (singer – DOC CORBIN DART), a controversially named hardcore/punk act with subsequent LOUDSPEAKER hailers, MATT BORRUSO and CHRISTOPHER DOUGLAS. Enlisting former PUSSY GALORE member, KURT WOLF and ex-RHYTHM & NOISE merchant, CHARLES HANSON, the band delivered a one-off 1987 debut single for UK's 'One LIttle Indian', 'PSYCHOTIC MACHINE'. Resurfacing in the early 90's with singles on 'Sympathy For The Record Industry' and 'Lung', LOUDSPEAKER also delivered their long-awaited debut album, entitled 'SUPERNATURAL' (1992). However, the group went AWOL yet again, only to return with the 1996 follow-up, 'RE-VERTEBRATE'.

Album rating: SUPERNATURAL (*4) / RE-VERTEBRATE (*4) / Crucifucks: CRUCIFUCKS (*4) / WISCONSIN (*6)

CRUCIFUCKS

DOC CORBIN DART – vocals / **JAKE** – guitar / **MATT BORRUSO** – bass / **CHRIS DOUGLAS** – drums

Alternative Tentacles | Alternative Tentacles

Dec 84. (lp) <(VIRUS 38)> **THE CRUCIFUCKS**
– Democracy spawns bad taste / Go bankrupt and die / You give me the creeps / Marching for trash / Legal genocide / I am the establishment / Cops for fertilizer / Hinkley had a vision / By the door / Oh where, oh where? / I was / Similar items / Official terrorism / No one can make me play along with this / Down on my kness.

— **CHRIS DOUGLAS** – drums; repl. SHELLEY who joined SONIC YOUTH

Dec 85. (lp) <(VIRUS 53)> **WISCONSIN**
– Annual report – Intro / Mountain song / Washington / Resurrection / Earth by invitation only / Laws against laughing / Pig in a blanket / When the top comes off / Concession stand / Wisconsin / Artificial competition / Holiday parade / Savior.

Feb 92. (cd) <(VIRUS 111)> **OUR WILL BE DONE** (compilation of above albums)

— DART released a solo set, 'PATRICIA', in 1990

LOUDSPEAKER

— **MATT + CHRISTOPHER** plus **KURT WOLF** – guitar (ex-PUSSY GALORE) / **CHARLES HANSON** – bass (ex-RHYTHM & NOISE)

One Little Indian | unknown

Apr 87. (12") (12TP 5) **PSYCHOTIC MACHINE. / LIVING WITH THE DEAD**

EFA | Patois

Feb 92. (cd) (EFA 16821CD) <004> **SUPERNATURAL**

— had US singles issued on 'Lung' & 'Sympathy For The Record Industry'

1990's. (7") <SFTRI 105> **PRAY. /** [-]
1990's. (7") <SFTRI 218> **KNOCKOUT. /** [-]
(UK-iss.Jul98; same)

not iss. | Sympathy F

Apr 95. (12"ep) <SFTRI 285> **RUBBERNECKERS VS. TAI** [-]

Another Planet | Another Planet

Jul 96. (cd) <(AP 6020-2)> **RE-VERTEBRATE**
– California son / Vaporize / Scientific / (Don't) Kill the messenger / Rerun / Supermantra / Lit / April fool / X-ray / Twin / Bassman 10.

CRUCIFUCKS

— re-formed with DART + BREHER

Alternative Tentacles | Alternative Tentacles

Sep 96. (m-cd/m-lp) <VIRUS 186> **L.D. EYE** [-]
– The L.D. eye theme / Lights over Baghdad / The story of Thomas McElwee / Suicide / Officer Powell / Artificial girl / Jeanetta Jones.

LOVE CORPORATION (see under ⇒ BALL, Edward)

LOVE DELEGATION (see under ⇒ FLESHTONES)

LOVER SPEAKS (see under ⇒ FLYS)

LOVE SPIT LOVE (see under ⇒ PSYCHEDELIC FURS)

LOVE TRACTOR

Formed: Athens, Georgia, USA ... 1980 by MIKE RICHMOND, ALFREDO VILLAR and KIT SCHWARTZ, all three seasoned players in their own respective groups, The METHOD ACTORS, The FANS and The SIDE EFFECTS. ARMISTEAD WELLFORD and MARK CLINE, were subsequently added although VILLAR had departed following the release of their eponymous 1982 debut album. Routinely compared to labelmates, PYLON, this initially instrumental band made their mark '83's 'AROUND THE BEND', MIKE RICHMOND taking on some vocal chores. The 'TRACTOR crew continued to plough their unorthodox furrow of hip-shaking alternative pop throughout the 80's with albums such as 'TILL THE COWS COME HOME' (1984), 'WHEEL OF PLEASURE' (1984) and 'THIS AIN'T NO OUTER SPACE SHIP' (1987), the latter featuring a cover of the Gap Band's 'PARTY TIME'. By this point the beat farmers of Athens had signed to 'Big Time', although only one further set, 'THEMES FROM VENUS' (1989) would surface; WELLFORD went on to sow his musical oats with GUTTERBALL alongside one-time DREAM SYNDICATE mainman, STEVE WYNN and BOB RUPE. • **Covered:** NEON LIGHTS (Kraftwerk).

Album rating: LOVE TRACTOR (*5) / AROUND THE BEND (*6) / TILL THE COWS COME HOME (*5) / WHEEL OF PLEASURE (*6) / THIS AIN'T NO OUTER SPACE SHIP (*6) / THEMES FROM VENUS (*7)

MIKE RICHMOND – guitar (bassist of METHOD ACTORS) / **ALFREDO VILLAR** – keyboards (bassist of FANS) / **KIT SCHWARTZ** – drums (guitarist of SIDE EFFECTS) / **ARMISTEAD WELLFORD** – guitar / **MARK CLINE** – bass / + guest **ANDREW CARTER** – guitars, drums

DB DB

1982. (lp) *<DB 60>* **LOVE TRACTOR** [-] [ ]
– Buy me a million dollars / Sixty degrees below / Motorcade / Festival / Cowboy songs / Hairy beat / Tropical / Wheel of pleasure.

— RICHMOND (some vocals) (WELLFORD + CLINE swopped instruments)

1983. (lp) *<DB 67>* **AROUND THE BEND** [-] [ ]
– Highland sweetheart / Cutting corners / Spin your partner / Pretty / Fat birds / Paint (your face and stand in the mirror) / Slum dungeon / J.E.B. Pharoahs / Timberland. *<cd-iss. 1997 on 'Ichiban'; 4548>*

1984. (lp,cd) *<DB 71>* **TILL THE COWS COME HOME** [-] [ ]
– Chilly damn Willy / Seventeen days / Fun to be happy / Neon lights / March / Cutting corners / Greedy dog / Seventeen days. *<cd+=>* – LOVE TRACTOR *<cd re-iss. 1997 on 'Ichiban'; 4547>*

Nov 84. (lp) *<(DB 74)>* **WHEEL OF PLEASURE** [ ] [ ]
– Neon lights / March / Jeb Pharaoh's / Fun to be happy / Highland sweetheart / Spin your partner / Wheel of pleasure / Chilly damn Willy / Slum dungeon / Seventeen days / Paint / Timberland.

Big Time Big Time

Jun 87. (lp/c) *(ZL/ZK 71273) <6015-1/-4>* **THIS AIN'T NO OUTER SPACE SHIP** [ ] [ ]
– Cartoon kiddies / Small town / Chili part two / Night club scene / Outside with ma / Rudolf Nureyev / Beatle boots / Amusement park / Party train / We all loved each other so much.

Oct 87. (7") *(ZB 41421)* **PARTY TRAIN. / RUDOLF NUREYEV** [ ] [ ]
(12"+=) *(ZT 41422)* – Got to give it up.

not iss. DB

1989. (lp,c,cd) *<DB 92>* **THEMES FROM VENUS** [-] [ ]
– I broke my saw / Themes from Venus / Crash / Satan / Crystal world / Venice / Hey mess / Nova express / Fantasy / Here comes the cops / Crash / Satan.

— disbanded and WELLFORD subsequently joined GUTTERBALL (with STEVE WYNN, ex-DREAM SYNDICATE and BOB RUPE, ex-HOUSE OF FREAKS)

Lene LOVICH

Born: LILI MARLENE PREMILOVICH, 30 Mar'49, Detroit, Michigan, USA, the daughter of a Yugoslavian father and English mother. In the early 60's, LENE and her mother took up residence in London, although she ran away from home a few years later. The budding singer/songwriter subsequently received a place at London's Central School of Art where she studied sculpture and met future husband and writing partner, LES CHAPPELL. Together they formed a band, The DIVERSIONS, signing to 'Polydor' in the mid-70's. Their one and only album was rejected however, although a solo LENE did release an embarrassing Xmas novelty (1976) single, 'I SAW MOMMY KISSING SANTA CLAUS'. Influenced by the onset of Punk Rock/New Wave and having also put her distinctive shriek to good use in the horror-film industry, LENE moved to the forefront of the musical revolution via a deal with 'Stiff'. Although the label's magic touch didn't work first time around with the flop cover of Tommy James & The Shondells' 'I THINK WE'RE ALONE NOW', her breakthrough came early in '79 with UK Top 3 smash, 'LUCKY NUMBER'. An infectious, quirky pop tune, its robotic simplicity focused around LOVICH's banshee-on-speed vocal style while a Top Of The Pops appearance found her cast as a more extravagant, intense punk cousin to KATE BUSH. Over the course of the following year, LENE and her shaven-headed sidekick, LES, completed two moderately successful albums, 'STATELESS' (1979) and 'FLEX' (1980), both of which contained further hits including the Top 20 third single, 'SAY WHEN'. However, the limited appeal of this singer/sax-player was all too obvious as subsequent releases – including third set, 'NO MAN'S LAND' (1982) – failed miserably both critically and commercially. As well as scoring bit parts in the movies, 'Cha Cha' and 'Mati Hari', LENE also hooked up with German punkstress, NINA HAGEN, for a one-off pro-Animal Rights single, 'DON'T KILL THE ANIMALS'. The latter track represented her only musical excursion during a 7-year itch, finally broken when she made a belated comeback album, 'MARCH', in '89.

Album rating: THE VERY BEST OF LENE LOVICH compilation (*6)

LENE LOVICH – vocals, saxophone; with session people

Polydor not iss.

Nov 76. (7") *(2058 812)* **I SAW MOMMY KISSING SANTA CLAUS. / CHRISTMAS SONG (MERRY CHRISTMAS TO YOU) / HAPPY CHRISTMAS** [ ] [-]

Stiff Stiff

Aug 78. (7") *(BUY 32)* **I THINK WE'RE ALONE NOW. / LUCKY NUMBER** [ ] [-]

Feb 79. (7"/12") *(BUY/12BUY 42)* **LUCKY NUMBER. / HOME** [3] [ ]

Mar 79. (lp,pic-lp,red-lp) *(SEEZ 7) <36102>* **STATELESS** [35] [ ]
– Home / Sleeping beauty / Lucky number / Too tender (to touch) / Say when / Writing on the wall / Telepathy / Momentary breakdown / I think we're alone now / One in a million / Tonight. *(cd-iss. May94 on 'Disky'; STIFFCD 20) (cd re-iss. Oct94 on 'Line'; LICD 901066)*

Apr 79. (7") *(BUY 46)* **SAY WHEN. / ONE LONELY HEART** [19] [ ]
(12"+=) *(12BUY 46)* – ('A'version).

Sep 79. (7") *(BUY 53)* **BIRD SONG. / TRIXI** [39] [ ]
(12"+=) *(12BUY 53)* – Too tender to touch.

Jan 80. (7") *(BUY 63)* **ANGELS. / THE FLY** [ ] [ ]
(12"+=) *(12BUY 63)* – The fall.

Jan 80. (lp) *(SEEZ 19) <36308>* **FLEX** [19] [94]
– Bird song / What will I do without you / Angels / The night / You can't kill me / Egg head / Wonderful one / Monkey talk / Joan / The freeze. *(cd-iss. May94 on 'Disky'; STIFFCD 21) (cd re-iss. Oct94 on 'Line'; LICD 901071)*

Mar 80. (d7") *(BUY 69)* **WHAT WILL I DO WITHOUT YOU. / JOAN // MONKEY TALK (live) / THE NIGHT (live). / TOO TENDER (live) / YOU CAN'T KILL ME (live)** [58] [ ]

Feb 81. (7"/12") *(BUY/+IT 97)* **NEW TOY. / CATS AWAY** [53] [ ]
(c-s+=) *(ZBUY 97)* – ('A'extended).

Oct 82. (lp/c) *(SEEZ/ZSEEZ 44) <38399>* **NO-MAN'S-LAND** [ ] [ ]
– It's you, only you (mein schmerz) / Blue hotel / Rocky road / Sister video / Faces / Special star / Maria / Savages / Walking low. *(cd-iss. May94 on 'Disky'; STIFFCD 22)*

Nov 82. (7"/7"pic-d) *(BUY/+P 164)* **IT'S YOU, ONLY YOU (MEIN SCHMERZ). / BLUE** [68] [ ]

— She retired for a while until a recording with German solo star, NINA HAGEN, appeared in 1986. The one-off single, 'DON'T KILL THE ANIMALS', was released in 7"/12" on 'Arista'; *RIS/+T 3)*

not iss. Pathfinder

1989. (cd/c) *<PAT 8909>* **MARCH** [-] [ ]
– Life / Wonderland / Nightshift / Hold on to love / Rage / Natural beauty / Make believe / Shadow walk / Vertigo / Sharman. *(Uk-iss.Oct95 on 'Evidence'; ECD 28001-2)*

– compilations, etc. –

Sep 90. (cd) *Great Expectations; (PIPCD 007)* **THE STIFF YEARS VOL.1** [ ] [-]

Sep 90. (cd) *Great Expectations; (PIPCD 008)* **THE STIFF YEARS VOL.2** [ ] [-]
(above 2 re-iss. cd Feb94 on 'Disky'; HRCD 8035)

May 97. (cd) *Disky; (DC 87858-2)* **THE VERY BEST OF LENE LOVICH** [ ] [-]
– Lucky number / Tonight / Say when / Be stiff / What will I do without you / Angels / Too tender (to touch) / New toy / Momentary breakdown / It's you, only you (mein schmerz) / Once in a million / Home / Bird song / Writing on the wall / Telepathy / I think we're alone now / Special star / Big bird / Sleeping beauty.

LOW

Formed: Duluth, Minnesota, USA ... 1993 by Mormons ALAN SPARHAWK, his wife MIMI PARKER and third member, ZAK SALLY. Their early efforts, 'I COULD LIVE IN HOPE' (1994) and 'LONG DIVISION' (1995), were more or less ignored, although critics pricked up their ears for the low-key lo-fi/ambient classic, 'THE CURTAIN HITS THE CAST' (1996). LOW subsequently completed a few UK gigs to promote it later that summer and later cut a single for the legendary 'Sub Pop', 'VENUS'. Of late, the trio have delivered a further two sets, namely 'SONGS FOR A DEAD PILOT' (1997) and 'ONE MORE REASON TO FORGET' (1998). • **Songwriters:** Group except SUNSHINE (Mitchell – Davis) / JACK SMITH (Supreme Dicks) / Transmission (Joy Division).

Album rating: I COULD LIVE IN HOPE (*7) / LONG DIVISION (*8) / THE CURTAIN HITS THE CAST (*7)

ALAN SPARHAWK – vocals, guitar / **ZAK SALLY** (r.n. NICHOLS) – bass / **MIMI PARKER** – drums

Quigley Quigley

Aug 94. (cd) *<(QUIGD 5)>* **I COULD LIVE IN HOPE** [ ] [ ]
– Words / Fear / Cut / Slide / Lazy / Lullaby / Sea / Down / Drag / Rope / Sunshine.

Vernon Yard Vernon Yard

1995. (cd) *<YARDCD 014>* **LONG DIVISION** [-] [ ]
– Violence / Below and above / Shame / Throw out the line / Swingin' / See-through / Turn / Caroline / Alone / Streetlight / Stay / Take. *(UK-iss.Feb97; same)*

Hi-Rise not iss.

Feb 96. (cd-ep) *(FLATSCD 24)* **TRANSMISSION EP** [ ] [-]
– Transmission / Bright / Cardine / Hands / Jack Smith / Untitled.

— NICHOLS repl. by **MICHELETI**

May 96. (cd-ep) *(YARD 022CD)* **FINALLY**
– Anon / Tomorrow one / Prisoner / Turning over.

Aug 96. (d-lp/cd) *(YARD/+CD 018)* **THE CURTAIN HITS THE CAST**
– Anon / The plan / Over the ocean / Mom says / Coat tails / Standby / Laugh / Lust / Stars gone out / Same / Do you know how to waltz / Dark. *(d-lp+=)* – Prisoner / Tomorrow one.

Nov 96. (7"/cd-s) <*(YARD 024/+CD)*> **OVER THE OCEAN. / CIOLENCE / BE THERE**

Sub Pop — Sub Pop

Sep 97. (7") <*(SP 392)*> **VENUS. / BOYFRIEND**

Wurlitzer Jukebox — not iss.

Oct 97. (7") *(WJ 44)* **IF YOU WERE BORN TODAY (A SONG FOR LITTLE BABY JESUS). / BLUE CHRISTMAS**

Kranky — Kranky

Oct 97. (m-lp/m-cd) <*(KRANK 021/+CD)*> **SONGS FOR A DEAD PILOT**
– Will the night / Condescend / Born by the wires / Be there / Landlord / Hey Chicago.

Tugboat — unknown

May 98. (7") *(TUG 001)* **JOAN OF ARC. / LONG LONG LONG**

Bluesanct Musak — not iss.

Jul 98. (cd-ep) *(INR 1040CD)* **ONE MORE REASON TO FORGET** — –

– compilations, etc. –

Jul 98. (cd) *Vernon Yard;* <*27*> **OWL** (LOW remixes) –
– Down / Annon (spore) / Over the ocean / Laugh / Anon (pollen) / Do you know how to waltz / Over the ocean / Words.
(above includes remixes by other artists)

Nick LOWE

Born: 24 Mar'49, Woodchurch, Suffolk, England. In 1963, LOWE formed his first semi-serious musical enterprise, SOUND 4 PLUS 1, with schoolfriend, BRINSLEY SCHWARZ. This subsequently evolved into KIPPINGTON LODGE, a pseudo-psychedelic outfit which released a series of flop singles before re-launching in 1969 under the BRINSLEY SCHWARZ banner. Despite a disastrous beginning (see separate entry), the band became one of the leading lights of the 70's pub-rock scene and released a clutch of fine, rootsy albums before their eventual demise in 1975. As well as handling bass and vocal duties, LOWE had penned the bulk of the band's material, finally embarking on a solo career the following year. Although his first releases were a couple of pseudonymous, tongue-in-cheek singles (TARTAN HORDE – 'Bay City Rollers We Love You' / 'Rollers Theme' and DISCO BROTHERS – 'Let's Go To The Disco' / 'Everybody Dance'), LOWE was also making a name for himself as a producer (GRAHAM PARKER & THE RUMOUR, DR. FEELGOOD etc.) and in 1976 had a hand in setting up Jake Rivera's seminal 'Stiff' label. His debut single, 'SO IT GOES', was also ~Stiff's very first release, LOWE helping to shape both the operation's identity and the careers of its artists i.e. The DAMNED, IAN DURY, ELVIS COSTELLO amongst others. LOWE joined the latter in late '77 at Rivera's new venture, 'Radar', where he recorded the UK Top 10 single, 'I LOVE THE SOUND OF BREAKING GLASS', and Top 30 album, 'THE JESUS OF COOL' (1978). Released in America under the title, 'PURE POP FOR NOW PEOPLE', the album saw LOWE's writing take a distinctly more sardonic turn although his lyrical barbs were rarely as razor sharp as those of labelmate COSTELLO. He nevertheless proved himself to be witty, articulate and intelligent as well as a consummate musical chameleon capable of traversing rock'n'roll boundaries while injecting his songs with a rootsy authenticity. 1979's 'LABOUR OF LUST' spawned a second major hit single in 'CRUEL TO BE KIND', the song also making the American Top 20. From the summer of '77 onwards, LOWE had also been a member of DAVE EDMUND's band, ROCKPILE (EDMUNDS and other band members played on LOWE's solo material), the outfit graduating from live work to releasing an album, 'Seconds Of Pleasure', in 1980. Although the record was a minor success, the group folded shortly after and LOWE divided his time between production (working with The PRETENDERS, PAUL CARRACK, FABULOUS THUNDERBIRDS and JOHN HIATT amongst others) and solo work. The turn of the decade also saw him marrying CARLENE CARTER (daughter of JOHNNY CASH), a successful country singer in her own right who numbered among LOWE's production clients. Recorded with new backing band, The CHAPS (subsequently NOISE TO GO), 'NICK THE KNIFE' (1980) was his first album for 'Columbia' and his last to enjoy any kind of chart success. The 80's were a difficult period for LOWE; increasingly countrified sets such as 'THE ABOMINABLE SHOWMAN' (1983) and 'NICK LOWE & HIS COWBOY OUTFIT' (1984) were enjoyable enough if never threatening to break him into the mainstream. Towards the end of the decade, he sunk into depression and considered retiring from the music business before making a convincing return to form with 1990's 'PARTY OF ONE', an infectious, invigorating album which saw him reunited with EDMUNDS and featured the likes of JIM KELTNER and RY COODER. The latter two hooked up with LOWE and JOHN HIATT in a kind of critics' supergroup, LITTLE VILLAGE (the same formation that played on HIATT's 1987 album, 'Bring The Family'), releasing an eponymous, one-off album in 1992. A fairly average affair, the album nevertheless saw LOWE back in the UK Top 30 for the first time in more than a decade. Yet this success failed to have a knock-on effect in terms of his solo career, 'THE IMPOSSIBLE BIRD' (1994) failing to cross over to a wider audience despite widespread critical acclaim. It's typical of LOWE's career, the man remaining something of an unsung, backroom hero when at the very least, he deserves some kind of recognition for his contributions to popular music over a career spanning more than thirty years. • **Songwriters:** Self-penned except; PEACE, LOVE & UNDERSTANDING (Brinsley Schwarz) / HALFWAY TO PARADISE (Billy Fury) / ENDLESS SLEEP (Joey Reynolds) / I KNEW THE BRIDE (Dave Edmunds) / etc.

Album rating: BASHER: THE BEST OF NICK LOWE compilation (*7)

NICK LOWE (solo) – vocals, bass, guitar (ex-BRINSLEY SCHWARZ) He was also a member of DAVE EDMUNDS' ROCKPILE group between Jul77-Feb81. His solo band included **EDMUNDS** – guitar and other ROCKPILE members **BILLY BREMNER** – guitar and **TERRY WILLIAMS** – drums (ex-MAN, etc.) used mainly on 2 albums below.

Stiff — not iss.

Aug 76. (7") *(BUY 1)* **SO IT GOES. / HEART OF THE CITY** — –

May 77. (7"ep) *(LAST 1)* **BOWI** — –
– Born a woman / Shake that rat / Marie Provost / Endless sleep.

Oct 77. (7") *(BUY 21)* **HALFWAY TO PARADISE. / I DON'T WANT THE NIGHT TO END** — –

Radar — Columbia

Feb 78. (7") *(ADA 1)* **I LOVE THE SOUND OF BREAKING GLASS. / THEY CALLED IT ROCK** — 7 —

Feb 78. (lp/c) *(RAD/RAC 1)* <*35329*> **THE JESUS OF COOL** <US-title 'PURE POP FOR NOW PEOPLE'> — 22
– Music for money / I love the sound of breaking glass / Little Hitler / Shake & pop / Tonight / So it goes / No reason / 36 inches high / Marie Provost / Nutted by reality / Heart of the city. *(re-iss. Oct88 on 'Demon' lp/c/cd; FIEND/+CASS/CD 131)*

May 78. (7") *(ADA 12)* **LITTLE HITLER. / CRUEL TO BE KIND** — –

Jul 78. (7") <*10734*> **HEART OF THE CITY. / SO IT GOES** — –

Sep 78. (7") <*10844*> **I LOVE THE SOUND OF BREAKING GLASS. / ENDLESS SLEEP** — –

Nov 78. (7") *(ADA 26)* **AMERICAN SQUIRM. / Nick Lowe & His Sound: (WHAT'S SO FUNNY 'BOUT) PEACE, LOVE AND UNDERSTANDING** — –

May 79. (7") *(ADA 34)* **CRACKING UP. / BASING STREET** — 34 — –

Jun 79. (lp/c) *(RAD/RAC 21)* <*36087*> **LABOUR OF LUST** — 43 — 31
– Cruel to be kind / Cracking up / Big kick, plain scrap / Born fighter / You make me / Skin deep / Switchboard Susan / Grey ribbon / Without love / Dose of you / Love so fine. *<US cd-iss. Jun88; CK 36087> (cd-iss. Apr90 on 'Demon'; FIENDCD 182)*

Aug 79. (7") *(ADA 43)* <*11018*> **CRUEL TO BE KIND. / ENDLESS GREY RIBBON** — 12 — 12 Jul79

Dec 79. (7") <*11131*> **SWITCHBOARD SUSAN. / BASING STREET** — –

— After he split from ROCKPILE in Feb'81, LOWE formed his own band, **NICK LOWE & THE CHAPS**

— (They became NOISE TO GO early '82) **MARTIN BELMONT** – guitar / **PAUL CARRACK** – keyboards / **BOBBY IRWIN** – drums

F-Beat — Columbia

Feb 82. (7") *(XX 20)* **BURNING. / ZULU KISS** — –

Feb 82. (lp/c) *(XX LP/MC 14)* <*37932*> **NICK THE KNIFE** — 99 — 50
– Burning / Heart / Stick it where the sun don't shine / Queen of Sheba / My heart hurts / Couldn't love you (any more than I do) / Let me kiss ya / Too many teardrops / Ba doom / Raining raining / One's too many / Zulu kiss. *(cd-iss. Apr90 on 'Demon'; FIENDCD 183)*

Apr 82. (7") *(XX 23)* **MY HEART HURTS. / PET YOU AND HOLD YOU** — –
(d7"+=) *(XX 23F – SAM 147)* – Cracking up / (What's so funny 'bout) Peace, love and understanding.

Apr 82. (7") <*02813*> **MY HEART HURTS. / STICK IT WHERE THE SUN DON'T SHINE** — –

— added **JAMES ELLER** – bass

Apr 83. (7") *(XX 31)* **RAGIN' EYES. / TANGUE-RAE** — –
(12"+=) *(XX 31T)* – Cool reaction.

Jun 83. (lp/c) *(XX LP/MC 18)* **THE ABOMINABLE SHOWMAN**
– We want action / Ragin' eyes / Cool reaction / Time wounds all heels / Man of a fool / Tanque-Rae / Wish you were here / Chicken and feathers / Paid the price / Mess around with love / Saint beneath the paint / How do you talk to an angel. *(cd-iss. Apr90 on 'Demon'; FIENDCD 184)*

Jun 83. (7") <*03837*> **HOW DO YOU TALK TO AN ANGEL / I WISH YOU WERE HERE** — –

NICK LOWE AND HIS COWBOY OUTFIT

— with **PAUL CARRACK, etc**

F-Beat/ RCA — Columbia

May 84. (7") *(XX 340)* **HALF A BOY AND HALF A MAN. / AWESOME** — 53 — –
(12"+=) *(XX 34T)* – Cruel to be kind.

May 84. (lp/c) *(ZL/ZK 79338)* <*39371*> **NICK LOWE & HIS COWBOY OUTFIT**
– Half a boy and half a man / You'll never get me up / (in one of those) / Maureen / God's gift to women / The Gee and the Rick and the three card trick / (Hey big mouth) Stand up and say that / Awesome / Breakaway / Love like a glove / Live fast, love hard, die young / L.A.F.S.

Aug 84. (7") *(XX 36)* **L.A.F.S. / (HEY BIG MOUTH) STAND UP AND SAY THAT** — –
(12"+=) *(XX 36T)* – Baby it's you.

Jul 85. (7") *(ZB 40303)* **I KNEW THE BRIDE (WHEN SHE USE TO ROCK AND ROLL). / DARLIN' ANGEL EYES** — –
(12"+=) *(ZT 40303)* – Seven nights to rock.

Aug 85. (lp/c) *(ZL/ZK 70765)* <*39958*> **THE ROSE OF ENGLAND**
– Darlin' angel eyes / She don't love nobody / 7 nights to rock / Long walk back / The rose of England / Lucky dog * / I knew the bride (when she use to rock and roll) / Indoor fireworks / (Hope to God) I'm right / I can be the one you love / Everyone * / Bobo ska diddle daddle. *(re-iss. Dec88 on 'Demon' lp/c/cd; FIEND/+CASS/CD 73)* – (omits tracks *)

Nov 85. (7") <*05570*> **I KNEW THE BRIDE (WHEN SHE USE TO ROCK AND ROLL). / LONG WALK BACK** — – — 77

NICK LOWE

Demon / Columbia

Jan 88. (7") **CRYING IN MY SLEEP. / LOVER'S JAMBOREE** [-] [ ]
Feb 88. (lp/c/cd) *(FIEND/+CASS/CD 99)* **PINKER AND PROUDER THAN PREVIOUS** [ ] [ ]
– (You're my) Wildest dream / Crying in my sleep / Big hair / Love gets strange / I got the love / Black Lincoln Continental / Cry it out / Lover's jambouree / Geisha girl / Wishing well / Big big love.

— now with **DAVE EDMUNDS, PAUL CARRACK, JIM KELTNER /** plus **BILL KIRCHEN** – electric guitar / **AUSTIN DE LONE** – piano, guitar / **RY COODER** – steel guitar

Warners / Reprise

Apr 90. (7") *(W 9821)* **ALL MEN ARE LIARS. / GAI-GIN MAN** [ ] [-]
(12"+=/cd-s+=) *(W 9821 T/CD)* – I love the sound of breaking glass / Cruel to be kind.
Apr 90. (cd)(lp/c) *(<7599 26132-2>)(WX 337/+C)* **PARTY OF ONE** [ ] [ ]
– You got the look I like / (I want to build a) Jumbo ark / Gai-gin man / Who was that man? / What's shakin' on the hill / Shting-shtang / All men are liars / Rocky road / Refrigerator white / I don't know why you keep me on / Honeygun. *(cd re-iss. Nov95 on 'Demon'; FIENDCD 767)* – (extra tracks)

LITTLE VILLAGE

were another amalgamation of near superstars; **NICK LOWE** – vocals, bass / **RY COODER** – vocals, guitar / **JOHN HIATT** – vocals, guitar / **JIM KELTNER** – drums, percussion, guitar, composer

Reprise / Reprise

Feb 92. (cd)(lp/c) *(<7599 26713-2>)(WX 462/+C)* **LITTLE VILLAGE** [23] [66]
– Solar sex panel / The action / Inside job / Big love / Take another look / Do you want my job / Don't go away mad / Fool who knows / She runs hot / Don't think about her when you're trying to drive / Don't bug me when I'm working.
Mar 92. (7"/c-s) **SOLAR SEX PANEL. / DO WITH ME WHAT YOU WANT TO DO** [ ] [ ]
(12"+=/cd-s+=) – Haunted house.
May 92. (7"/c-s) **DON'T GO AWAY MAD. / BIG LOVE** [ ] [ ]
(12"+=/cd-s+=) – Do with me what you want to do.

NICK LOWE

Demon / not iss.

Nov 94. (cd-s) *(NICKA 315)* **TRUE LOVE TRAVELS ON A GRAVEL ROAD. /** [ ] [-]
Nov 94. (cd) *(FIENDCD 757)* **THE IMPOSSIBLE BIRD** [ ] [-]
– Soulful wind / The beast in me / True love travels on a gravel road / Trail of tears / Shelly my love / Where's my everything / 12-step program / Lover don't go / Drive-thru man / Withered on the vine / I live on a battlefield / 14 days / I'll be there.
Jan 98. (cd) *(FIENDCD 939)* **DIG MY MOOD** [ ] [ ]
– Faithless lover / Lonesome reverie / You inspire me / What lack of love has done / Time I took a holiday / Failed Christian / The man that I've become / Freezing / High on a hilltop / Lead me not / I must be getting over you / Cold grey light of dawn.
Jun 98. (cd-ep) *(VEXCD 17)* **YOU INSPIRE ME /** [ ] [-]

– compilations etc. –

on 'Demon' unless mentioned otherwise

Sep 84. (lp/c) *(FIEND/+CASS 20)* **16 ALL-TIME LOWES** [ ] [-]
– Born fighter / Marie Provost / American squirm / Skin deep / When I write the book / Little Hitler / Cruel to be kind / Heart of the city / Switchboard Susan / (I love the sound of) Breaking glass / Big kick plain scrap / Cracking up / Without love / Nutted by reality / So it goes / They called it rock. *(cd-iss. 1986 as '20 ALL-TIME LOWES'; FIENDCD 20)* – (4 extra tracks). *(cd re-iss. Oct93 on 'Diablo'; DIAB 801)*
Mar 86. (lp/c/cd) *(FIEND/+CASS/CD 59)* **NICK'S NACK** [ ] [-]
Aug 89. (d-lp/c/cd) *(FIEND/+CASS/CD 142)* **BASHER: THE BEST OF NICK LOWE** [ ] [-]
Jun 91. (cd) *(FIENDCD 203)* **THE WILDERNESS YEARS** [ ] [-]
– (rare material 1974-1977)
Jan 94. (4xcd-box) *(NICK 1)* **BOXED SET** [ ] [-]
– (JESUS OF COOL / ROSE OF ENGLAND / NICK LOWE AND HIS COWBOY OUTFIT / PINKER AND PROUDER THAN PREVIOUS)

Ian LOWERY

Born: London, England. Initially the singer with 'Small Wonder' outfit, The WALL (on two singles), LOWERY subsequently formed his own outfit, SKI PATROL, alongside NICK CLIFT, PETER BALMER and BRUCE ARCHIBALD. The latter was replaced after their debut 45, 'EVERYTHING IS TEMPORARY', by drummer ALAN COLE, a man who would join LOWERY's next outfit, The FOLK DEVILS. Formed in 1983, they released a few platters on their own 'Ganges' imprint, the first of which, 'HANK TURNS BLUE', was a thrashy rock'n'roll number not unlike the early DOORS. Quarrelling and personnel changes dogged this outfit and by late 1987, LOWERY was fronting yet another group, KING BLANK. Signing to 'Situation 2', LOWERY finally issued his/their first album proper (not including compilations), 'THE REAL DIRT', in 1988. Confusingly, the man returned the following year with the IAN LOWERY GROUP, releasing the 'KING BLANK TO . . .' album; the record proved to be his swansong effort as nothing's been heard of him since.

Album rating: King Blank: THE REAL DIRT (*5) / Ian Lowery Group: KING BLANK TO . . . (*5)

SKI PATROL

IAN LOWERY – vocals (ex-WALL) / **NICK CLIFT** – guitar / **PETER BALMER** – bass, vocals / **BRUCE ARCHIBALD** – drums

Clever Metal / not iss.

Apr 80. (7") *(VIN 1)* **EVERYTHING IS TEMPORARY. / SILENT SCREAMS** [ ] [-]

— **ALAN COLE** – drums; repl. BRUCE

Malicious Damage / not iss.

Nov 80. (7") *(MD 2)* **AGENT ORANGE. / DRIVING** [ ] [-]
Jul 81. (7") *(MD 3)* **FAITH IN TRANSITION. / CUT** [ ] [-]

— disbanded in mid-81 when IAN formed the short-lived, F FOR FAKE

— re-formed with **NICK CLIFT** taking over all instruments (LOWERY still in there; BALMER joined FAD GADGET, COLE to FOLK DEVILS)

— new recruits:- **TRINA WILSON + TRACY HALL** – vocals / **MATTHEW FOX** – saxophone

Clever Metal / not iss.

Sep 82. (7") *(VIN 2)* **BRIGHT SHINY THINGS. / ELECTRIC BELLS GIRLS** [ ] [-]

FOLK DEVILS

IAN LOWERY – vocals, acoustic guitar, piano / **ALAN COLE** – drums / **KRIS JOZAJTIS** – guitar, vocals / **WHITELY** – bass

Ganges / not iss.

Mar 84. (7") *(RAY 1)* **HANK TURNS BLUE. / CHEWING THE FLESH** [ ] [-]
Aug 84. (7") *(RAY 2)* **BEAUTIFUL MONSTER. / NICE PEOPLE** [ ] [-]
(12") *(RAY 2T)* – ('A'side) / Brian Jones.

Karbon / not iss.

Jul 85. (12"ep) *(KAR 601T)* **FIRE & CHROME** [ ] [-]
– Evil eye / Where the buffalo roam / Wait / English disease.
Oct 85. (7";w-drawn) **IT DRAGS ON. /** [-] [-]

— now a 5-piece, newcomers being **JOHN HAMILTON** – bass / **ROB JONES** – drums (ex-WAH!, ex-HIGH FIVE)

Situation 2 / Beggars Banquet

Jun 87. (12"m) *(SIT 47T)* **THE BEST PROTECTION. / YOUR MISTAKE / THE THIRD STROKE** [ ] [-]
Oct 87. (lp/c) *(SIT UP/CP 19)* **GOODNIGHT IRONY** (compilation) [ ] [-]

KING BLANK

— **LOWERY + JOZAJTIS** plus **NIGEL PULSFORD** – guitar, keyboards / **HUGH GARRETY** – bass / **KEVIN ROONEY** – drums

May 88. (7") *(SIT 51)* **MOUTH OFF. / DRUNK ON TEARS** [ ] [-]
(12"+=) *(SIT 51T)* – Bagman.
Jul 88. (12"m) *(SIT 53T)* **BLIND BOX. / THOUGHT I WAS WELL / FILL ME UP** [ ] [-]
Jul 88. (lp/c)(cd) *(SITU/SITC 21)(SITU 21CD)* **THE REAL DIRT** [ ] [-]
– Howl upside down / Blind box / The real dirt / Big pink bang / Guilty as hell / Map of pain / Shot full of holes / Killer in the rain / Uptight / Bulletproof (cross symbol). *(re-iss. 1989 on 'Situation 2-Lowdown' lp/cd; SITL 21/+CD)*
Oct 88. (7") *(SIT 55)* **UPTIGHT. / HOWL UPSIDE DOWN** [ ] [-]
(12"+=) *(SIT 55Z)* – Slack jaw man.

IAN LOWERY GROUP

— nearly the same as above

Jul 89. (7") *(SIT 57)* **BEED. / SAILOR ON HORSE** [ ] [-]
(12"+=) *(SIT 59T)* – 13th floor.
Aug 89. (lp/c/cd) *(SITU 24/+C/CD) <9992-1/-4/-2>* **KING BLANK TO . . .** [ ] [-]
– Need / I said skin / A kind of loathing / Sick little minds / Wild times / You're gonna pay / Beach fire / Never trust me / Driver's arrived / The party / One last blast. *(cd+=)* – Jack dust. *(re-iss. Nov91 on 'Situation 2-Lowdown' lp/c)(cd; SITL/+C 24)(SITL 24CD)*

— LOWERY looks to have retired in the 90's

LOWLIFE

Formed: Grangemouth, Scotland . . . 1985 from the ashes of former rockabilly outfit, The DEAD NEIGHBOURS (who released two albums, 'HARMONY' and 'STRANGE DAYS, STRANGE WAYS'), by CRAIG LORENSTON and GRANT McDOWELL. The pair recruited disillusioned ex-COCTEAU TWIN bassist, WILL HEGGIE and guitarist, STUART EVEREST, subsequently setting about forming their own 'Nightshift' label. LOWLIFE debuted early in '86 with the mini-set, 'RAIN', following it up with first album proper, 'PERMANENT SLEEP' (1986). However, it was 1987's 'DIMENUENDO' which best captured their deep, atmospheric, vaguely gothic alt-rock sound, subsequent albums failing to progress and leaving the band sounding increasingly dated. This was particularly evident on 1991's 'SAN ANTORIUM', recorded without the talents of EVEREST and McDOWELL. After going to ground for almost four years, LORENSTON, HEGGIE and Co resurfaced with a much-improved new album, 'GUSH' (1995), the sound lent an added edge by the presence of new secondary vocalist, JENNIFER BACHEN.

Album rating: PERMANENT SLEEP (*4) / DIMINUENDO (*6) / FROM A SCREAM TO A WHISPER compilation (*5) / GODHEAD (*4) / SAN ANTORIUM (*4) / GUSH (*6)

CRAIG LORENTSON – vocals (ex-DEAD NEIGHBOURS) / **STUART EVEREST** – guitar, keyboards / **WILL HEGGIE** – bass, keyboards, sampling (ex-COCTEAU TWINS) / **GRANT McDOWELL** – drums (ex-DEAD NEIGHBOURS)

Nightshift not iss.

Jan 86. (12"ep) *(LOLIF 1)* **RAIN** [ ] [-]
– Sometime something / Gallery of shame / Reflections of 1 (for Kelly) / Sense of fondness / Hail ye / Again and again.

Oct 86. (lp/cd) *(LOLIF 2/+CD)* **PERMANENT SLEEP** [ ] [-]
– Cowards way / As it happens / Mother tongue / Wild swan / Permanent sleep / A year past July / The betting and gaming act 1964 / Do we party?.

Jan 87. (12"ep) *(LOLIF 3T)* **VAIN DELIGHTS** [ ] [-]
– Vain delights / Hollow gut / Permanent sleep (steel mix) / From side to side.

Mar 87. (lp/cd) *(LOLIF 4/+CD)* **DIMINUENDO** [ ] [-]
– Off pale yellow / Given to dreaming / A sullen sky / Big uncle ugliness / From side to side / Ragged rise to Tumbledown / Wonders will never cease / Tongue tied and twisted / Licked ones wounds.

Nov 87. (7"/12") *(LOLIF 5-7/5T)* **ETERNITY ROAD. / OFF PALE YELLOW** [ ] [-]

Jan 88. (12"ep) *(LOLIF 6T)* **SWIRL, IT SWINGS EP** [ ] [-]
– Swing / Colours blue / Ramified / Eternity road.

Feb 89. (lp/cd) *(LOLIF 7/+CD)* **FROM A SCREAM TO A WHISPER** (a retrospective 85-88) [ ] [-]
– Ramified / Sometime something / Cowards way / Big uncle ugliness / Wild swan / Hollow gut / Again and again / A sullen sky / Eternity road / Swing / From side to side.

Jul 90. (lp/cd) *(LOLIF 8/+CD)* **GODHEAD** [ ] [-]
– In thankful hands / Where I lay, I'll lie / Marjory's dream / I don't talk to me / Drowning leaves / Bittersweet / River of woe / I the cheated / Mising the kick / Forever filthy / Never ending shroud.

— **HUGH DOUGIE** – guitar / **CALUM MacLEAN** – programming, guitars, bass; repl. EVEREST + McDOWELL

Sep 91. (lp/cd) *(LOLIF 9/+CD)* **SAN ANTORIUM** [ ] [-]
– Jaw / Inside in / My mothers fatherly father / Big fat funky whale / Good as it gets / Suddenly violently random / June Wilson / Give up giving up / Bathe / As old as new.

— without CALUM but added; **JASON TAYLOR** – guitar, bass, keyboards, sampling / **JENNIFER BACHEN** – backing vocals

Nov 95. (cd) *(LOLIF 10CD)* **GUSH** [ ] [-]
– Bleach / Kiss me kick / Former comrade / Truth in needles / Tocopherol / Loaded. primal / And pulled / Wicked papa / Tantalus / Petricide / Swell.

L7

Formed: Los Angeles, California, USA ... 1986 by DONITA SPARKS (guitar/vocals) and SUZI GARDNER (guitar/vocals). Recruiting seasoned L.A. punk veteran JENNIFER FINCH on bass and drummer ANNE ANDERSON, the band signed for the small 'Epitaph' label. The feisty punk-metal noise of their 1988 eponymous debut attracted the attention of the now-famous 'Sub Pop' label the following year, DEE PLAKAS replacing ANDERSON and 'SMELL THE MAGIC' (1990) fuelling the band's growing cult reputation. 1990 also saw the girls touring with a relatively unknown NIRVANA, L7's infamous onstage antics almost causing as much of a stir as the headliners. The band were soon snapped up by 'Slash', hitting the UK Top 20 in 1992 with the pop-grunge of the 'PRETEND WE'RE DEAD' single. This was closely followed by the 'BRICKS ARE HEAVY' album, a hard hitting collision of girl power grunge and ultra hard line, often humerous, post-feminist lyrics. The band caused further uproar later that year when DONITA exposed her womanly charms on 'The Word', having already blessed that year's Reading Festival audience with a used tampon. Irreverant yet committed, L7 also formed 'Rock For Choice', a pro-abortion pressure group which won unprecedented support in the male-dominated environs of the music business. 'HUNGRY FOR STINK' (1994) was equally blistering, the frenetic 'FUEL MY FIRE' later covered by The PRODIGY on their landmark 'THE FAT OF THE LAND' album. • **Songwriters:** Group or SPARKS penned except THREE DAYS (Willie Nelson).

Album rating: L7 (*6) / BRICKS ARE HEAVY (*8) / HUNGRY FOR STINK (*6) / THE BEAUTY PROCESS: TRIPLE PLATINUM (*6)

DONITA SPARKS (b. 8 Apr'63, Chicago, Illinois) – vocals, guitar / **SUZI GARDNER** (b. 1 Aug'60, Altus, Oklahoma) – guitar, vocals / **JENNIFER FINCH** (b. 5 Aug'66) – bass, vocals / **ANNE ANDERSON** (b.Chicago) – drums repl.by **ROY KOUTSKY**

not iss. Epitaph

Dec 88. (lp/c/cd) *<E 86401-1/-4/-2>* **L7** [-] [ ]
– Bite the wax tadpole / Cat-o'-nine-tails / Metal stampede / Let's rock tonight / Uncle Bob / Snake handler / Runnin' from the law / Cool out / It's not you / I drink / Ms. 45. *(UK-iss.Jun92; same)*

— **(DEMETRA) DEE PLAKAS** (b. 9 Nov'60, Chicago) – drums repl. ROY

Glitterhouse Sub Pop

Jan 90. (7",7"green) *<SP 58>* **SHOVE. / PACKIN' A ROD** [-] [ ]
(UK-iss.Jan91 on 'Sub Pop'; EFA 08105)

Nov 90. (12"ep,12"purple-ep) *<(SP 79)>* **SMELL THE MAGIC** [ ] [ ] Aug90
– Shove / Til the wheels fall off / Fast'n'frightening / (Right on) Thru / Deathwish / Broomstick. *(cd-ep Oct95+= ; SPCD 79)* – Packin' a rod / Just like me / American society.

Slash Slash

Mar 92. (7"red/c-s) *(LASH/LACS 34)* **PRETEND WE'RE DEAD. / SHIT LIST** [21] [ ]
(12"+=/cd-s+=) *(LASHX/LASCD 34)* – Lopsided head / Mr. Integrity.

Apr 92. (cd/c/lp) *(828 307-2/-4/-1) <26784>* **BRICKS ARE HEAVY** [24] [ ]
– Wargasm / Scrap / Pretend we're dead / Diet pill / Everglade / Slide / One more thing / Mr. Integrity / Monster / Shit list / This ain't pleasure.

May 92. (7"green) *(LASH 36)* **EVERGLADE. / FREAK MAGNET** [27] [ ]
(12"+=/cd-s+=) *(LASHXP/LASHCD 36)* – Scrap.

Sep 92. (7"/c-s) *(LASH/LACS 38)* **MONSTER. / USED TO LOVE HIM** [33] [ ]
(12"+=/cd-s+=) *(LASHX/LASCD 38)* – Diet pill.

Nov 92. (7"/c-s) *(LASH/LACS 42)* **PRETEND WE'RE DEAD. / FAST 'N' FRIGHTENING (live)** [50] [-]
(cd-s+=) *(LASCD 42)* – (Right on) Thru / Shove / Shit list / Diet pill.

— L7 appeared as CAMEL LIPS group in the film 'Serial Mom'.

Jun 94. (7"colrd/12"colrd) *(LASH/LASCS 48)* **ANDRES. / BOMB** [34] [ ]
(cd-s+=) *(LASCD 48)* – (KRXT radio interview).

Jul 94. (cd/c/lp) *<(828 531-2/-4/-1)>* **HUNGRY FOR STINK** [26] [ ]
– Andres / Baggage / Can I run / The bomb / Questioning my sanity / Riding with a movie star / Stuck here again / Fuel my fire / Freak magnet / She has eyes / Shirley / Talk box.

— After recording 1996 album, FINCH left to form LYME. She was repl. by **GRETA BRINKMAN** who appeared on next album, before **GAIL GREENWOOD** (ex-BELLY) took over

Feb 97. (cd/c) *(828 868-2/-4)* **THE BEAUTY PROCESS: TRIPLE PLATINUM** [ ] [ ]
– Beauty process / Drama / Off the wagon / I need / Moonshine / Bitter wine / Masses are asses / Bad things / Must have more / Non existant Patricia / Me, myself and I / Lorenza, Giada, Alessandra / Guera.

LUDUS

Formed: Manchester, England ... 1978 by vocalist LINDER (aka LINDA MULVEY), along with ARTHUR CADMAN, WILLIE TROTTER and PHIL 'TOBY' TOLMAN. Managed by Richard Boon, they subsequently signed to the 'New Hormones' imprint (former DIY home of The BUZZCOCKS; LINDER was also then girlfriend of their original frontman, HOWARD DEVOTO) and debuted early 1980 with the EP, 'THE VISIT'; prior to this however, co-writer IAN DEVINE replaced ARTHUR CADMON. TROTTER was also to leave during a period in which LINDER might have secured a better mainstream following, although their indie-jazz experimentation (likened to RED CRAYOLA or ESSENTIAL LOGIC) failed to secure more than a cult audience. Several years later, DEVINE was to form a duet with another Welsh-born indie luminary, ALISON STATTON (ex-YOUNG MARBLE GIANTS), the pair recording two albums at the turn of the decade, 'THE PRINCE OF WALES' (1989) and 'CARDIFFIANS' (1991).

Album rating: PICKPOCKET (*6) / THE SEDUCTION (*5)

LINDER (b. LINDA MULVEY, 1954, Liverpool, England) – vocals / **IAN DEVINE** (b. IAN PINCOMBE, Cardiff, Wales) – guitar, vocals repl. ARTHUR CADMAN (b. PETER SADLER) / **WILLIE TROTTER** (b. 1959) – bass / **TOBY** (b. PHIL TOLMAN) – drums (ex-ED BANGER & THE NOSEBLEEDS, also of DURUTTI COLUMN)

New Hormones not iss.

Feb 80. (12"ep) *(ORG 4)* **THE VISIT (4 COMPOSITIONS)** [ ] [-]
– Lullaby cheat / Unveil / Sightseeing / I can't swim, I have nightmares.

Aug 80. (7") *(ORG 8)* **MY CHERRY IS IN SHERRY. / ANATOMY IS NOT DESTINY** [ ] [-]

May 81. (c) *(CAT 1)* **PICKPOCKET** [ ] [-]
– Mutilate / Box / Mouthpiece / Patient / The fool / Hugo Blanco.

— **DIDS** – drums, synthesizers repl. TROTTER

Jul 81. (7") *(ORG 12)* **MOTHER'S HOUR. / PATIENT** [ ] [-]

Dec 81. (2x12"ep) *(ORG 16)* **THE SEDUCTION** [ ] [-]
– Seduction (unveiled) / A woman's travelogue / My cherry is in Sherry / See the keyhole / Her story.

Sep 82. (m-lp) *(ORG 20)* **DANGER CAME SMILING** [ ] [-]

1983. (c) **LINDER SINGS BARDOT** [ ] [-]

Interior not iss.

Jan 88. lp) *(IM 013)* **NUE AU SOLEIL COMPLETEMENT** [ ] [-]
(above was to have been issued in 1985 as 'LET ME GO WHERE THE PICTURES GO' for 'Les Disques Du Crepescule')

DEVINE & STATTON

IAN DEVINE + ALISON STATTON – vocals (ex-WEEKEND, ex-YOUNG MARBLE GIANTS)

LesDisques not iss.

Jan 89. (7") *(TWI 878)* **UNDER THE WEATHER. /** [ ] [-]

Mar 89. (lp/cd) *(TWI 873-1/-2)* **THE PRINCE OF WALES** [ ] [-]

Jun 89. (7") *(TWI 895)* **DON'T IT MAKE MY BROWN EYES BLUE. /** [ ] [-]

Nov 89. (12") *(TWI 891-12)* **BIZARRE LOVE TRIANGLE** [ ] [-]

Jun 90. (7") *(TWI 908)* **HIDEAWAY. /** [ ] [-]

— below with guest ROBERT FRIPP – guitar (of KING CRIMSON)

Jan 91. (lp) **CARDIFFIANS** [ ] [-]

LUNA (see under ⇒ GALAXIE 500)

LUNACHICKS

Formed: Brooklyn, New York, USA ... 1988 by BECKY, SQUID SID, GINA and SINDI. Reportedly recommended to the influential indie label, 'Blast First' by NY noisemongers, SONIC YOUTH, LUNACHICKS were a garish explosion of colour and scuzzy punk/grunge, North Eastern cousins to the likes of BABES IN TOYLAND and L7. The sassy grunge girls weren't afraid of controversy, taking the name of their debut album, 'BABYSITTERS ON ACID' (1990) from a real-life incident (when a drug-crazed babysitter phoned her employers to tell them their child would be ready and cooked for them arriving back. She was obviously arrested! Sick), the crazed fem-rockers bashing out a racket that would probably scare most black-hearted Norwegian metallers. Their live show was equally raucous, the intergalactic noise terrorists subsequently releasing a slightly improved follow-up set in 1993, 'BINGE PURGE'. Switching labels to 'Go Kart' and replacing BECKY with CHIP, the band staggered on with a further two releases, 'JERK OF ALL TRADES' (1995) and 'PRETTY UGLY' (1997).

Album rating: BABYSITTERS ON ACID (*5) / BINGE AND PURGE (*6) / JERK OF ALL TRADES (*6) / PRETTY UGLY (*6) / DROP DEAD LIVE (*5)

THEO – vocals / **SINDI** – guitar / **GINA** – guitar / **SQUID SID** – bass / **BECKY** – drums

Blast First | Plan 9 – Caroline

Apr 89. (d7"ep/cd-ep) *(BFFP 44/+CD)* **SUGAR LUV. / GET OFF THE ROAD // MAKIN' IT (WITH OTHER SPECIES). / JAN BRADY** ☐ -

Nov 89. (lp/c/cd) *(BFFP 52/+C/CD)* <2105> **BABYSITTERS ON ACID** <US-title 'LUNACHICKS'> ☐ ☐
– Jan Brady / Glad I'm not yew / Babysitters on acid / Makin' it (with other species) / Mabel rock / Theme song / Born 2B mild / Pin eye woman 665 / Cookie core / Octopussy / Sugar luv / Complication. *(re-iss. Oct90; same)*

Apr 90. (7"ep) *(BFFP 55)* **COMPLICATION EP** ☐ -
– Cookie monster / etc.

Zuma | Safe House

Aug 92. (12"ep/cd-ep) <2105> **APATHETIC EP** - ☐

Mar 93. (lp/cd) *(ELUNA 1/+CD)* <SH 2107-1/-2> **BINGE AND PURGE** ☐ Sep92
– Apathetic / Plugg / P.S. Hell / Binge and purge / Mom / Superstrong / This is serious / Whole lotta B.S. / 2 bad 4 U / 11 / Rip U / C.I.L.L. *(re-iss. Mar96 on 'SPV'; SPV 0844543-2)*

Go Kart | Go Kart

Oct 95. (cd/lp) <(GK 013/+CD)> **JERK OF ALL TRADES** ☐ May95
– Drop dead / Fingerful / F.D.S. / Light as a feather / Edgar / Dogyard / Butt plugg / Bitterness Barbie / Deal with it / Brickface and Stucco / Jerk off all trades / Spoilt / Ring and run / Fallopian rhapsody / Insomnia / Why me. *(UK-iss.May97; same)*

Feb 97. (cd) <(GK 024CD)> **PRETTY UGLY** ☐ ☐
– Yeah / Thrown it away / The day Squibs gerbil died / Dear Dotti / Mr. Lady / Spork / What's left / Gone kissin' / Don't want you / Baby / #%@!* / Wing Chun / MMM donuts / Missed it.

Aug 98. (cd) <GK 42CD> **DROP DEAD LIVE (live)** - ☐
– Yeah / FDS / The day Squid's gerbil died / Gong kissin / Fingerful / Thrown it away / Don't want you / Jerk of all trades / Wing Chun / Bitterness Barbie / Drop dead / Donuts / Passenger / Buttplug / Crash / Dear Dotti / #%@!* / Spoilt.

Lydia LUNCH

Born: LYDIA KOCH, 2 Jun'59, Rochester, New York, USA. She became part of New York's 'No Wave' scene in 1976-78 when her punk band, TEENAGE JESUS & THE JERKS exploded onto the scene with their discordant, tortured classic, 'ORPHANS'. Towards the end of the decade, the stunning (in more ways than one!) punk banshee disbanded the 'JERKS, forming the short-lived BEIRUT SLUMP. After a solitary US-only single, 'TRY ME', LYDIA embarked on a solo career with the more vocally subdued debut album, 'QUEEN OF SIAM' (1980), a schizoid record that found LUNCH entertaining a gamut of styles including avant-swing-jazz in the shape of the TOM WAITS-esque 'LADY SCARFACE' (!). Ever the experimentalist, LYDIA tried out R&B and funk in her next project, 8-EYED SPY, although this too was just as brief as only a single and a mini eponymous set appeared in '81. The following year, LYDIA unleashed her second solo album, '13:13', an intense, heavy-duty precursor to the girl-grunge likes of HOLE and BABES IN TOYLAND, it featured three of her most effective numbers, 'AFRAID OF YOUR COMPANY', 'THIS SIDE OF NOWHERE' and 'STARES TO . . .'. Subsequent collaborations with The BIRTHDAY PARTY, ROWLAND S. HOWARD, EINSTURZENDE NEUBAUTEN, DIE HAUT and Danish band, SORT SOL, took her overseas to Berlin, although she returned in her own right in 1984 with 'IN LIMBO' (released on CABARET VOLTAIRE's indie imprint, 'DoubleVision'). The following year, LYDIA founded her own 'Widowspeak' label, issuing her 'UNCENSORED' cassette which unearthed her girlhood traumas in the shape of 'DADDY DEAREST'. This mid-80's period also found the provocative punk queen featuring in a series of NY~ "artistic" films, including 'Fingered', in which she gets to grips, so to speak, with long-time beau, JIM THIRLWELL (of FOETUS). Musically, LUNCH kept up her profile via a collaborative effort with mates SONIC YOUTH, 'DEATH VALLEY '69', a spiralling maelstrom of disturbing guitar-noise (inspired by the MANSON killings) over which she stamped her uncompromising authority. In between further solo work, LYDIA spent time in the studio with MICHAEL GIRA (Swans) and JIM FOETUS (as STINKFIST), while also lending her talents to the all-female project, HARRY CREWS, alongside KIM GORDON (of SONIC YOUTH) in late 80's splinter group HARRY CREWS. In the 90's, LUNCH continued to swim against the musical mainstream, her solo albums interspersed with further collaborative work featuring the likes of former X singer, EXENE CERVENKA. • **Songwriters:** LYDIA, except SPOOKY (Association) / DON'T FEAR THE REAPER (Blue Oyster Cult) / WHY DON'T WE DO IT IN THE ROAD (Beatles) / IN MY TIME OF DYING (trad/ Led Zeppelin).

Album rating: QUEEN OF SIAM (*6) / 8-EYED SPY mini (*5) / 13:13 (*7) / IN LIMBO (*5) / THE UNCENSORED (*5) / THE DROWNING OF LUCY HAMILTON mini (*5) / HYSTERIE compilation (*7) / HONEYMOON IN RED (*6) / ORAL FIXATION (*5) / NAKED IN GARDEN HILLS with Harry Crews (*6) / CONSPIRACY OF WOMEN (*6) / SHOTGUN WEDDING with Rowland S. Howard (*5) / RUDE HIEROGLYPHICS with Exene Cervenka (*5) / CRIMES AGAINST NATURE compilation (*7)

TEENAGE JESUS & THE JERKS

LYDIA LUNCH – vocals, guitar / **GORDON STEVENSON** – bass; repl. JIM SCLAVUNOS who repl. JAMES CHANCE / **BRADLY FIELD** – drums; repl. RECK who joined FRICTION

not iss. | Migraine

Apr 78. (7") <CC-333> **ORPHANS. / LESS OF ME** - ☐

Mar 79. (7") <CC-334> **BABY DOLL. / FREUD IN FLOP / RACE MIXING** - ☐

Aug 79. (12"ep,12"pink-ep) <CC-336> **PINK** - ☐
– Freud in flop / Race mixing / Baby doll / Burning rubber / Red alert / Orphans / Less of me.

not iss. | Ze

Nov 79. (12"ep) <12011> **PRE-TEENAGE JESUS** - ☐
– The closet / Less of me / My eyes.

disbanded when she formed . . .

BEIRUT SLUMP

— **LYDIA LUNCH** – vocals, guitar / **ROBERT QUINE** – guitar / **PAT IRWIN** – sax / **GEORGE SCOTT** – bass

not iss. | Migraine

Apr 79. (7") <CC-335> **TRY ME. / STAIRCASE** - ☐

LYDIA LUNCH

— went solo added piano & was backed by **ROBERT QUINE** – guitar / **PAT IRWIN** – guitar, keyboards / **JACK RUBY** – bass / **DOUGLAS BROWNE** – drums

Celluloid | Ze

Nov 80. (lp) *(CEL 2-6561)* <33006> **QUEEN OF SIAM** ☐ ☐
– Mechanical flattery / Gloomy Sunday / Tied and twisted / Spooky / Los banditos / Atomic bongos / Lady Scarface / A cruise to the Moon / Carnival fat man / Knives in the drain / Blood of tin. *(cd-iss. Jul91 on 'UFO'; WSP 001) (re-iss. cd Aug95 on 'Triple X')*

8 EYED SPY

— were formed by **LUNCH / IRWIN + SCOTT** plus **JIM SCLAVUNOS** – sax / **MICHAEL PAUMGARDEN** – drums

Fetish | not iss.

Oct 81. (m-lp) *(FR 2003)* **8 EYED SPY** ☐ -
– Lazy in love / etc.

Feb 82. (7") *(FE 19)* **DIDDY WAH DIDDY. / DEAD YOU ME B SIDE** ☐ -

— Had already disbanded, after SCOTT died late in 1981.

LYDIA LUNCH

— went solo, but she first half shared an album with The BIRTHDAY PARTY, then a single with their guitarist ROWLAND S. HOWARD

4 a.d. | not iss.

Feb 82. (lp) *(JAD 202)* **THE AGONY & THE ECSTASY** (other side 'Drunk On The Pope's Blood' by BIRTHDAY PARTY) ☐ ☐
– Afraid of your company / (2).

Sep 82. (12") *(BAD 210)* **SOME VELVET MORNING. ("ROWLAND S.HOWARD & LYDIA LUNCH") / I FELL IN LOVE WITH A GHOST** ☐ ☐

— now w / **DIX DENNEY** – guitar / **GREG WILLIAMS** – bass / **CLIFF MARTINEZ** – drums

Situation2 | Ruby

Jun 82. (lp) *(SITU 6)* <JRR 806> **13:13** ☐ ☐
– Stares to . . . / 3*3 / This side of nowhere / Snakepit breakdown / Dance of the dead children / Suicide ocean / Lock your door / Afraid of your company. *(cd-iss. Oct89 + Oct94 on 'Line'; LICD 9.00096)*

— Between 1982 + Aug83, she guested on 2 German 12"ep's on labels 'Ripoff' & 'Zensor' respectively. These were; **EINSTURZENDE NEUBAUTEN** – 'DURSTIGES TIER' the B-side of 'THIRSTY ANIMAL' + **DIE HAUT** – 'DER KARIBISCHE WESTERN'.

— Next with musicians **PAT PLACE** – guitar / **THURSTON MOORE** – bass + RICHARD EDSON – drums (of SONIC YOUTH) / **KRISTIAN HOFFMAN** – piano / **JIM SCLAVUNOS** – sax

DoubleVision | not iss.

Sep 84. (m-lp; some red) *(DVR 5)* **IN LIMBO** ☐ ☐
– I wish . . . I wish / Friday afternoon / 1000 lies / Some boys / Still burning / What did you do. *(re-iss. 1986 on 'Widowspeak'; WSP 6)*

— Early in 1985, she was again credited on a 12", this time **SONIC YOUTH's** 'DEATH VALLEY '69, which was released on 'Blast First' UK 'Iredescence' US.

Widowspeak | Widowspeak

Mar 85. (c) *(WSP 1)* **THE UNCENSORED** - ☐
– Dear whores / Shotgun / Black Romeo / Daddy dearest. *(cd-see ORAL . . .)*

Jun 85. (lp) *(WSP 2)* **THE DROWNING OF LUCY HAMILTON** ☐ -
– Emerald pale has disappeared / The drowning / How men die in their sleep / Lucy's lost her head again / 3:20 Thursday morning / A quiet night of murder in . . .

Oct 85. (10"ep) *(WSP 3)* **HEART OF DARKNESS (with NO TREND)** ☐ -

Mar 87. (d-lp) *(WSP 8)* **HYSTERIE** (compilation of all material 1976-1986) ☐ -
(cd-iss. 1989; WSP 008CD)

Mar 88. (12"m) *(WSP 013T)* **THE CRUMB. (with THURSTON MOORE) / DONE DUN / DEAD RIVER** ☐ -

— next featured backing from **BIRTHDAY PARTY** + recorded 1983-84

Apr 88. (lp) *(WSP 12)* **HONEYMOON IN RED** ☐ -
– Done dun / Still burning / Fields of fire / Dead in the head / Some velvet morning / Come fall / So your heart / Dead river / Three kings. *(cd-iss. May90; WSP 12CD)*

Nov 88. (m-lp) *(WSP 14)* **STINKFIST (with CLINT RUIN)** ☐ -
– Stinkfist / Meltdown oratorio (part 1,2,3) / Son of Stink.

Sep 89. (lp) *(WSP 16)* **ORAL FIXATION** (spoken word live in Detroit) ☐ -
– Dear whores / Shotgun / Black Romeo / Daddy dearest / Oral fixation.

HARRY CREWS

LYDIA LUNCH – vocals, guitar / **KIM GORDON** – bass (of SONIC YOUTH) **/ SADIE MAE** – drums

Big Cat | not iss.

Apr 90. (lp/cd) *(ABB 21/+CD)* **NAKED IN GARDEN HILLS (live in Vienna; late 1988)** ☐ ☐
– About the author / Distopia / Gospel singer / (She's in a) Bad mood / Bring me

down / S.O.S. / Man hates a man / You're it / Knockout artist / Way out / Car / Orphans.

LYDIA LUNCH

Big Cat / not iss.

Oct 91. (12"ep)(cd-ep) *(ABB 26T)(ABBSCD 26)* **(with CLINT RUIN): DON'T FEAR THE REAPER / CLINCH. / SERPENTINE / WHY DON'T WE DO IT IN THE ROAD** [ ] [-]

Pathological / not iss.

May 91. (cd) *(PATH 6CD)* **C.O.W. (CONSPIRACY OF WOMEN)** [ ] [-]
– The right to revolt / The conspiracy of women.

UFO / not iss.

Oct 91. (cd)(lp) *(UFO-WSP 2CD)(WSP 002)* **SHOTGUN WEDDING** (with ROWLAND S. HOWARD) [ ] [-]
– Burning skulls / In my time of dying / Solar hex / Endless fall / What is memory / Pigeon town / Cisco sunset / Incubator / Black juju. *<(re-iss. cd Aug95 on 'Triple X'+=; 51111)>* – Gospel singer. *(d-cd Sep94 w /'TRANCE MUTATION' cd on 'Trident')*

Clawfist / not iss.

Feb 93. (7") *(X-PIG 19)* **UNEARTHLY DELIGHTS. / BUSTED** [ ] [ ]

Rykodisc / Rykodisc

Nov 95. (cd; LYDIA LUNCH & EXENE CERVENKA) *<(RCD 10326)>* **RUDE HIEROGLYPHICS** [ ] [ ]
– Rude hieroglyphics.

– compilations, etc. –

on 'Widowspeak' unless mentioned otherwise

May 81. (c) *R.O.I.R.; <A 101>* **LIVE (8 EYED SPY)** [-] [ ]
(UK-iss.1992 on 'Danceteria' cd/lp; DAN CD/LP 087)

Feb 90. (cd) *(WSP 19CD)* **DROWNING IN LIMBO** [ ] [ ]
– (THE DROWNING OF LUCY HAMILTON / IN LIMBO) *<US cd-iss. 1995 on 'Atavistic'; 52>*

May 90. (cd) *(WSP 20CD)* **STINKFIST / THE CRUMB** [ ] [-]

Jul 90. (cd) *(WSP 23CD)* **THE UNCENSORED / ORAL FIXATION** [ ] [-]

Jul 93. (3xcd-box) *Triple X; <51157-2>* **CRIMES AGAINST NATURE** [-] [ ]
– Crimes against nature / The beast / Unearthly delights / Cruel story of youth / Daddy dearest / Terminal distraction / Shock corridor / Oral fixation / The right to revolt / Conspiracy of women. *(re-iss. Aug95; same)*

LURKERS

Formed: Uxbridge, London, England ... late 1976 by HOWARD WALL, ARTURO BASSICK, PETE STRIDE and MANIC ESSO. The first act to be signed to fledgling DIY independent, 'Beggars Banquet', The LURKERS' debut single, 'SHADOW' / 'LOVE STORY', was initially handed out free at gigs in the summer of '77. The flipside, rather than the lead track, stood out for its relentless, uncompromising barrage of 100 mph raw punk rock, taking its lead from the RAMONES but replacing the bubblegum factor with an aggressive edge more akin to MOTORHEAD. ARTURO was soon to be replaced by KYM BRADSHAW in time for their next single, 'FREAK SHOW', another brutally simplistic two and a half minutes which came packaged in artwork courtesy of SAVAGE PENCIL (an illustrator for Sounds and the frontman of fellow punk conspirators, The ART ATTACKS). Another personnel change ensued when brief member, KYM, was substituted for the more experienced NIGEL MOORE, the revised line-up hitting the Top 50 with the more chorus-friendly 'AIN'T GOT A CLUE'. A taster from their Top 60 debut set, 'FULHAM FALLOUT' (1978), its moderate success consolidated by their second Top 50 entry, 'I DON'T NEED TO TELL HER'. 1979 started off promisingly enough when the single, 'JUST THIRTEEN', dented the charts, although the accompanying album, 'GOD'S LONELY MEN', failed to generate much interest either critically or commercially. After two further 45's only just managed to scrape into the charts, The LURKERS began a long slide into oblivion after losing their frontman. Although replacement, MARK FINCHAM took up the reins from 1982's 'THIS DIRTY TOWN', the band joined the bulging ranks of the redundant punk has-beens and continued to churn out albums of limited appeal throughout the 80's and even the 90's. • **Songwriters:** WALL lyrics / STRIDE music. In 1982 STRIDE and EAGLE were the main writers with BASSICK returning in '88 replacing EAGLE. Covered; LITTLE OL' WINE DRINKER ME (Dean Martin) / etc? • **Trivia:** Their early sleeve artwork was created by Sounds journalist and ART ATTACKS frontman SAVAGE PENCIL.

Album rating: FULHAM FALLOUT (*6) / GOD'S LONELY MEN (*5) / LAST WILL AND TESTAMENT – GREATEST HITS compilation (*7) / THIS DIRTY TOWN (*4)

HOWARD WALL – vocals / **PETE STRIDE** guitar / **ARTURO BASSICK** (b. ARTHUR BILLINGSLEY) – bass / **MANIC ESSO** (b. PETE HAYNES) – drums

Beggars Banquet / not iss.

Jul 77. (7") *(BEG 1)* **SHADOW. / LOVE STORY** [ ] [-]
(re-iss. Aug78 red, blue or white; same)

— **KYM BRADSHAW** – bass; repl. ARTURO

Oct 77. (7") *(BEG 2)* **FREAK SHOW. / MASS MEDIA BELIEVER** [ ] [-]

— **NIGEL MOORE** – bass repl. KYM

May 78. (7") *(BEG 6)* **AIN'T GOT A CLUE. / OOH OOH I LOVE YOU** [45] [-]
(with free gold 7"flexi) *(BEG 6 1/2)* **CHAOS BROTHERS FULHAM FALLOUT FIRTY FREE!')**

Jun 78. (lp) *(BEGA 2)* **FULHAM FALLOUT** [57] [-]
– Ain't got a clue / I don't need to tell her / Total war / Hey you / Shadow / Then I kicked her / Go go go / Jenny / Time of year / Self destruct / It's quiet here / Gerald / I'm on heat / Be my prisoner. *(cd-iss. Nov97 on 'Captain Oi'+=; AHOYCD 073)* – Shadow / Love story / Freak show / Mass media believer / Ohh ohh I love you / Pills / We are the Chaos brothers / Be my prisoner / Total war / Then I kissed her / I love the dark / Freak show.

Jul 78. (7") *(BEG 9)* **I DON'T NEED TO TELL HER. / PILLS** [49] [-]

Jan 79. (7") *(BEG 14)* **JUST THIRTEEN. / COUNTDOWN** [66] [-]

Apr 79. (lp/c) *(BEGA/BEGC 8)* **GOD'S LONELY MEN** [ ] [-]
– She knows / God's lonely men / Out in the dark / Cyandide / Whatever happened to Mary / Take me back to Babylon / Room 309 / I'll be with you / Non contender / Seven o'clock someday / Sleep on diamonds / Bad times. *(cd-iss. Nov97 on 'Captain Oi'+=; AHOYCD 074)* – Just thirteen / Countdown / Suzie is a floozie / Cyanide / New guitar in town / Little old wine drinker / Cold old night / Pick me up / Mary's coming home / New guitar in town / Little old wine drinker.

May 79. (7") *(BEG 19)* **OUT IN THE DARK. / CYANIDE** [72] [-]
(d7"+=) *(BEG 19)* – Suzie is a floozie / Cyanide (pub version).

Nov 79. (7") *(BEG 28)* **NEW GUITAR IN TOWN. / PICK ME UP / LITTLE OL' WINE DRINKER ME** [72] [-]

— STRIDE teamed up with BOYS member JOHN PLAIN (see below).

— Split for a while. STRIDE, HAYNES and MOORE brought in new members **MARK FINCHAM** – vocals repl. WALL

Clay / not iss.

Jun 82. (7") *(CLAY 12)* **THIS DIRTY TOWN (I CAN'T FIND WAY OUT). / WOLF AT THE DOOR** [ ] [-]

Jul 82. (lp) *(CLAY 104)* **THIS DIRTY TOWN** [ ] [-]
– This dirty town / Drag you out / Frankenstein again / Heroin it's all over / One man's meat / Wolf at the door / Shut out the light / Let's dance now / Midnight hour / By the hat. *(re-iss. Dec89; same)* *<(cd-iss. Apr93; CLAYCD 104)>*

Nov 82. (7"/7"pic-d) *(CLAY 17/+P)* **DRAG YOU OUT. / HEROIN (IT'S ALL OVER)** [ ] [-]

Feb 83. (7") *(CLAY 21)* **FRANKENSTEIN AGAIN. / ONE MAN'S MEAT . . .** [ ] [-]

Mar 84. (12"ep) *(PLATE 7)* **FINAL VINYL** [ ] [-]
– Let's dance now (no time to be strangers) / Midnight hour / By the heart / Frankenstein again.

May 84. (7") *(CLAY 32)* **LET'S DANCE NOW. / MIDNIGHT HOUR** [ ] [-]

— split '84. Re-formed late '88, **STRIDE & BASSICK** plus **ESSO + MOORE**

Weser / not iss.

Feb 89. (lp) *(efa 2433)* **WILD TIMES AGAIN** [ ] [-]
(cd-iss. Nov94; WL 024332CD)

Link / not iss.

Jun 89. (m-lp) *(LINKLP 087)* **KING OF THE MOUNTAIN** [ ] [-]
– Brou blue / Never had a beech head / Unfinished business / Going monkee again / King of the mountain (part 1) / Lucky John / King of the mountain (pt.2).

Nov 89. (lp) **LIVE AND LOUD (live early '89)** [ ] [-]
– Ain't got a clue / I don't need to tell her / Unfinished business / Pills / Barbara blue / Rubber room / Just thirteen / Uptown or downtown / Going Monkee again (hey hey hey) / Shadow / New guitar in town / Miss World / I'm on heat / Freak show / Take me back to Babylon / Then I kissed her / Drag you out / Cyanide / Jenny.

Released Emotions / not iss.

Oct 90. (cd)(lp) *()* **POWERJIVE** [ ] [-]
– Powerjive / Lipstick and shampoo / Solitaire / Waiting for you / Things will never be the same / The world of Jenny Brown / Walk like a superstar (talk like a zombie) / Go go girl / Strange desire (burn, burn, burn) / Raven's wings / I close my eyes / Lullaby

Jun 92. (cd/lp) **LIVE IN BERLIN (live)** [ ] [-]

— **DAN TOZER** – drums joined STRIDE, PLAIN + BASSICK

Weser / Weser

Nov 94. (cd) *(<WL 02460CD>)* **NON-STOP NITROPOP** [ ] [ ] Jul96
– Don't need a reason / Melt away / Can't stand my room / Hand in the fire / She's another man / Unknown / The show goes on / Frozen out / Jungle creature / Storm in my mind / Rags to riches / Feel it coming / In a dark room.

– compilations, etc. –

on 'Beggars Banquet' unless mentioned otherwise

1979. (d7"ep) *(BACK 1)* **SHADOW / LOVE STORY. / FREAK SHOW / MASS MEDIA BELIEVER** [ ] [-]

1979. (d7"ep) *(BACK 3)* **I DON'T NEED YO TELL HER. / PILLS / JUST THIRTEEN / COUNTDOWN** [ ] [-]

Nov 80. (lp) *(BOPA 2)* **LAST WILL AND TESTAMENT – GREATEST HITS** [ ] [-]
– I'm on heat / Cyanide / Shadow / Little ol' wine drinker me / Out in the dark / Freak show / Jenny / Self destruct / Ain't got a clue / Take me back to Babylon / Total war / Love story / Then I kicked her / Just thirteen / New guitar in town / She knows. *(re-iss. Jul88 on 'Beggars Banquet-Lowdown' lp/c)(cd; BBL/+C 2)(BBL 2CD)*

Dec 92. (cd) *Dojo; (DOJOCD 74)* **TOTALLY LURKERED** [ ] [-]

Nov 95. (cd) *Anagram; (CDPUNK 69)* **POWERJIVE / KING OF THE MOUNTAIN** [ ] [-]

May 97. (cd) *Anagram; (CDPUNK 94)* **THE BEGGARS BANQUET PUNK SINGLES** [ ] [-]

Dec 97. (cd) *Receiver; (<RRCD 243>)* **TAKE ME BACK TO BABYLON** [ ] [ ]

PETE STRIDE and JOHN PLAIN

(PLAIN was from The BOYS) + **TONY BATEMAN** – bass / **JACK BLACK** – drums

Beggars Banquet / not iss.

Jan 80. (lp) *(BEGA 17)* **NEW GUITAR IN TOWN** [ ] [-]
– Laugh at me / School girls / Cold cold night / He'll have to go / Just like a clown / Half the time / New guitar in town / Cure for love / Restless kind / You better move on / Pick me up.

May 80. (7") *(BEG 41)* **LAUGH AT ME. / JIMMY BROWN** [ ] [-]

LUSCIOUS JACKSON

Formed: New York City, New York, USA ... 1991 by JILL CUNNIFF and GABRIELLE GLASER (both main songwriters), plus KATE SCHELLENBACH (an early BEASTIE "BOY"). In fact, LJ signed to the latter band's Capitol subsidiary, 'Grand Royal', releasing the acclaimed debut set, 'IN SEARCH OF MANNY', in 1992. The last word in alternative indie hip-hop, the record fused ungainly rock/pop with NY street suss to impressive effect. 1994 saw the release of their first full-length set, 'NATURAL INGREDIENTS', although critics were not so enamoured this time around. They returned three years later with a new member, VIVIAN TRIMBLE and 'FEVER IN FEVER OUT', their most consistent, mature release to date. Produced by the esteemed DANIEL LANOIS (aided by TONY MANGURIAN), the record was big on ambient atmospherics and shifted its fare share of units on both sides of the Atlantic, spawning their first hit single, 'NAKED EYE'.

Album rating: IN SEARCH OF MANNY (*8) / NATURAL INGREDIENTS (*5) / FEVER IN FEVER OUT (*7)

JILL CUNNIFF – vocals, bass, guitar / **GABRIELLE GLASER** – vocals, guitar / **KATE SCHELLENBACH** – drums (ex-BEASTIE BOYS)

Big Cat / Grand Royal – Capitol

May 93. (m-lp/m-cd) *(ABB 46X/+CD)* <GR 001 – 27582> **IN SEARCH OF MANNY** Nov92
– Let yourself get down / Life of leisure / Daughters of the kaos / Keep on rockin' it / She be wantin' it more / Bam-bam / Satellite. *(cd re-iss. Aug95; same) (re-iss. Apr97 on 'Grand Royal' lp/cd; same as US)*

Capitol / Grand Royal – Capitol

Jun 94. (12"/cd-s) *<GR 007 – 58220>* **CITYSONG. /** –
Aug 94. (cd/c/lp) *(CD/TC+/EST 2234)* *<GR 009 – 28356>* **NATURAL INGREDIENTS**
– Citysong / Deep shag / Angel / Strongman / Energy sucker / Here / Find your mind / Pele Merengue / Rock freak / Rollin' / Surprise / LP retreat.
Mar 95. (c-s) *(TCCL 739)* *<GR 011>* **DEEP SHAG / CITY SONG** 69 Jan95
(12"+=/cd-s+=) *(12/CD CL 739)* – Daddy.
Oct 95. (c-s)<12"/cd-s> *(TCCL 758)* *<GR 017 – 58372>* **HERE / BAM BAM (live)** 59 Jun95
(cd-s) *(CDCL 758)* – ('A'side) / Queen of bliss.
(cd-s) *(CDCLS 758)* – ('A'mixes) / Surprise (live).

—— added **VIVIAN TRIMBLE** – keyboards, vocals

Mar 97. (12"/cd-s) *(12/CD CL 786)* *<GR 036> 58619>* **NAKED EYE. / ('A'mixes)** 25 36 Oct96
(cd-s) *(CDCLS 786)* – ('A'side) / Banana's box / Foster's lover.
Apr 97. (cd/lp) *(CD+/EST 2290)* *<GR 038 – 35534>* **FEVER IN FEVER OUT** 53 72 Oct96
– Naked eye / Don't look back / Door / Mood swing / Under your skin / Electric / Take a ride / Water your garden / Soothe yourself / Why do I lie? / One thing / Parade / Faith / Stardust.
Jul 97. (12") *<1122>* **UNDER YOUR SKIN. /** –

LUSH

Formed: Camberwell, London, England . . . October '88 by girls MIKI BERENYI (half-Japanese / half-Hungarian) and EMMA ANDERSON, plus lads STEVE RIPPON and CHRIS ACLAND. After supports slots to DARLING BUDS, etc, they signed to top independent label '4.a.d.' in 1989 (MERIEL BARHAM was also a member before she joined The PALE SAINTS). A 1989 debut EP, 'SCAR', introduced the band's delicate wash of sound, all hazy guitar effects and celestial harmonies; immediately hailed by the press as one of the front runners in the 'shoegazing' scene, the band even attracted the attentions of ROBIN GUTHRIE (of 'shoegazing' forebears, COCTEAU TWINS) who produced a follow-up, the 'MAD LOVE' EP. Along with MY BLOODY VALENTINE, RIDE etc., LUSH were now the toast of the UK indie scene, while also enjoying minor success in Europe and America. A further EP, 'BLACK SPRING', followed in Autumn '91 prior to the departure of RIPPON. With former NME employee, PHIL KING (ex-FELT, SERVANTS etc.) drafted in as a replacement, the band eventually completed work on a debut album, 'SPOOKY'. Issued to a mixed critical reaction in early '92, the record reached the UK Top 10 despite complaints about the suffocating GUTHRIE production. Nevertheless, the scene which had spawned LUSH was dying on its feet (still staring at its shoes, presumably) with the influx of American grunge and the group took time out to reconsider their approach. The resultant follow-up, 'SPLIT' (1994), was well received by fans but failed to break the band out of the indie margins. Finally, with the advent of Brit-pop, LUSH re-emerged with a more straightforward, spiky pop sound, the fey vocal affectations of old giving way to unashamed cockney wide-girl attitude on the 'LADYKILLERS' single while 'SINGLE GIRL' was as breezy as anything they'd ever recorded. An album, 'LOVELIFE', made the Top 10 later that summer and although older fans might've mourned the haunting textures of old, the simple approach suited them down to the ground. Yet this mini-revival in the band's fortunes was tragically marred later that year when the 30-year old CHRIS ACLAND took his own life. • **Songwriters:** MIKI and EMMA, except HEY HEY HELEN (Abba) / FALLIN' IN LOVE (Dennis Wilson) / OUTDOOR MINER (Wire) / LOVE AT FIRST SIGHT (Young Marble Giants) / I WANNA BE YOUR GIRLFRIEND (Rubinoos). • **Trivia:** In 1990, they all posed topless for an NME cover shot, although they were given the body paint treatment.

Album rating: SPOOKY (*8) / GALA (*7) / SPLIT (*6) / LOVELIFE (*8)

MIKI BERENYI (b.18 Mar'67) – vocals, guitar / **EMMA ANDERSON** (b.10 Jun'67) – guitar, vocals / **STEVE RIPPON** – bass / **CHRIS ACLAND** (b. 7 Sep'66, Lancaster, England) – drums

4 a.d. / Nesak

Oct 89. (m-lp/m-c/m-cd) *(JAD/+C 911/+CD)* *<911>* **SCAR**
– Baby talk / Thoughtforms / Scarlet / Bitter / Second sight / Etheriel.
Feb 90. (12"ep/c-ep/cd-ep) *(BAD/+C 0003/+CD)* **MAD LOVE EP** 55 –
– De luxe / Leaves me cold / Downer / Thoughtforms.

4 a.d. / 4 a.d.-Reprise

Oct 90. (7"/c-s) *(AD/+C 0013)* **SWEETNESS AND LIGHT. / BREEZE** 47 –
(12"+=/cd-s+=) *(BAD 0013/+CD)* – Sunbathing.
Dec 90. (lp/c/cd) *(CAD/+C 0017/+CD)* *<26463>* **GALA**
– Sweetness and light / Sunbathing / Breeze / De luxe / Leaves me cold / Downer / Baby talk / Thoughtforms / Scarlet / Bitter / Second light / Etheriel / Hey hey Helen / Scarlet (alt.take).
Sep 91. (7"/c-s) *(AD/+C 1016)* *<40231>* **NOTHING NATURAL. / GOD'S GIFT** 43
(12"ep+=/cd-ep+=) *(BAD 1016/+CD)* – 'BLACK SPRING EP' – Fallin' in love / Monochrome.
Dec 91. (12"ep/c-ep)(cd-ep) *(BAD/+D/C 2001)(BAD 2001CD)* **FOR LOVE / STARLUST. / OUTDOOR MINER / ASTRONAUT** 35 –

—— Although on above + below recording RIPPON had left Oct'91.

Jan 92. (lp/d-10"lp/c)(cd)(s-cd) *(CAD/+D/C 2002)(CAD/+D 2002CD)* *<26798>* **[SPOOKY]** 7
– Stray / Nothing natural / Tiny smiles / Covert / Ocean / For love / Superblast! / Untogether / Fantasy / Take / Laura / Monochrome.

—— RIPPON was replaced by **PHIL KING** (b.29 Apr'60) – bass (ex-SEE SEE RIDER, ex-APPLE BOUTIQUE, ex-FELT)

4 a.d. / Warners

May 94. (7") *(AD 4008)* **HYPOCRITE. / LOVE AT FIRST SIGHT** 52 –
(12"+=/cd-s+=) *(BAD 4008/+CD)* – Cat's chorus / Undertow.
May 94. (7") *(AD 4010)* **DESIRE LINES. / WHITE WOOD** 60 –
(12"+=)(cd-s+=) *(BAD 4010/+CD)* – Girl's world / Lovelife (suga bullit remix).
Jun 94. (lp/c/cd) *(CAD/+C 4011/+CD)* *<45578>* **SPLIT** 19
– Light from a dead star / Kiss chase / Blackout / Hypocrite / Lovelife / Desire lines / The invisible man / Undertow / Never-never / Lit up / Stardust / When I die.
Jan 96. (7"clear) *(AD 6001)* **SINGLE GIRL. / SWEETIE** 21 –
(cd-s) *(BAD 6001CD)* – ('A'side) / Tinkerbell / Outside world / Cul de sac.
(cd-s) *(BADD 6001CD)* – ('A'side) / Pudding / Demystification / Shut up.
Feb 96. (7"green) *(AD 6002)* **LADYKILLERS. / I WANNA BE YOUR GIRLFRIEND** 22 –
(cd-s) *(BAD 6002CD)* – ('A'side) / Matador / Ex / Dear me.
(cd-s) *(BADD 6002CD)* – ('A'side) / Heavenly / Carmen / Plums and oranges.
Mar 96. (clear-lp/c/cd) *(CAD/+C 6004/+CD)* *<46170>* **LOVELIFE** 8
– Ladykillers / Heavenly nobodies / 500 / I've been here before / Papasan / Single girl / Ciao! / Tralala / Last night / Runaway / The childcatcher / Olympia.

—— JARVIS COCKER (Pulp) featured vox with MIKI on the track 'Ciao!'.

Jul 96. (7"red) *(AD 6009)* **500 (SHAKE BABY SHAKE). / I HAVE THE MOON** 21 –
(cd-s+=) *(BAD 6009CD)* – Piledriver / Olympia (acoustic).
(cd-s) *(BADD 6009CD)* – ('A'side) / I'd like to walk around your mind / Kiss chase (acoustic) / Last night (hexadecimal dub mix).

—— Sadly on the 17th of October '96, 30 year-old ACLAND committed suicide after returning from the States and splitting with his girlfriend. LUSH virtually gave up with the group after that. A dance group of the same name issued a single, 'GOLD', late '97 (nothing to do with the real LUSH). In 1998, EMMA teamed up with vocalist, LISA ONEIIL, to form SING-SING, debuting that year with a single, 'FEELS LIKE SUMMER'. It was released on the indie label, 'Bella Union' (with help of COCTEAU TWINS' ROBIN GUTHRIE and SIMON RAYMONDE), when EMMA couldn't find a new one after severing her association with '4 a.d.'.

– compilations, etc. –

May 98. (cd) *4 a.d.; <1102>* **TOPOLINO** –
– 500 (shake babyt shake) / I have the moon / Ex / I wanna be your girlfriendc / Matador / Outside world / I'd like to walk around in your mind / Carmen / Shut up / Cul de sac / Demystification.

LUXURIA (see under ⇒ MAGAZINE)

John LYDON (see under ⇒ PUBLIC IMAGE LTD)

LYRES

Formed: Boston, Massachusetts, USA . . . 1979 by (MONOMAN) JEFF CONNOLLY (ex-DMZ), RICK CORACCIO and PAUL MURPHY. Initially a surfadelic/garage trio in the mould of early LOVE, the MISUNDERSTOOD and the TROGGS, The LYRES surfaced in September that year with a debut 7", 'HOW DO YOU KNOW'. Two years on, CONNOLLY and Co were back with an eponymous 12" EP, although it would be some time before The LYRES were plucking garage fans' musical heartstrings again. Eventually picked up by the French-based 'New Rose' label, the retro-fixated Farfisa freaks re-emerged with the blistering 'ON FYRE' (1984), a record that burned up reverberating semi-recycled KINKS riffs (borrowing a couple of RAY DAVIES in the process), crazed vocals and general sonic mayhem on such stand-out tracks as 'HELP YOU ANN' and 'I'M TELLING YOU GIRL'. 1986 saw The LYRES mellowing out (in relative terms) with 'LYRES, LYRES', although their fire'n'brimstone approach to garage-punk remained undimmed. After a change of label to 'Fundamental' (US home of EUGENE CHADBOURNE, etc) for third set, 'A PROMISE IS A PROMISE' (1988), the band finally imploded, although a resurgence of interest saw CONNOLLY re-form his troops for a last ditch effort on 'Taang!', 'NOBODY BUT ME' (1993). Of late, younger audiences have been catching up on what they've missed via a 'Matador' re-issue programme while another label, 'Sundazed', have re-activated 'HELP YOU ANN'.

Album rating: ON FYRE (*7) / LYRES, LYRES (*5) / A PROMISE IS A PROMISE (*5) / NOBODY TOLD ME (*5) / SOME LYRES compilation (*6)

(MONOMAN) JEFF CONNOLLY – vocals, organ (ex-DMZ) / **RICK CORACCIO** – guitar / **PAUL MURPHY** – drums

not iss. / Sounds Intriguing

Sep 79. (7") *<SI45 002>* **HOW DO YOU KNOW. / DON'T GIVE IT UP NOW** -

not iss. / Ace Of Hearts

1981. (12"ep) *<AHS 1005>* **LYRES EP** -
– Buried alive / In motion / High on yourself / What a girl can't do. *(UK-iss.Aug86 on 'Fan Club'; FC 016)*

New Rose / not iss.

Jul 84. (lp) *(ROSE 35)* **ON FYRE** -
– Don't give it up now / Help you Ann / I confess / I'm telling you girl / Love me till the sun shines / I really want you right now / Tired of waiting / Dolly / Soapy / The way I feel about you / Not like the other one / Never met a girl like you / How could I have done all these things / Swing swift / Trying to please you / Busy body / Someone who'll treat you right now / She pays the rent / You've been wrong / I'll try anyway. *(cd-iss. Sep84; ROSE 35CD) (cd re-iss. Jun98 on 'Matador';)*

Dec 85. (12"ep) *(NEW 60)* **SOMEONE WHO'LL TREAT YOU RIGHT / SHE PAYS THE RENT. / YOU'VE BEEN WRONG / I'LL TRY ANYWAY** -

Nov 86. (lp/cd) *(ROSE 103/+CD)* **LYRES, LYRES** -
– Not looking back / She pays the rent / You'll never do it baby / I love her still, I always will / No reason to complain / Only think / Stacey / How do you know / You won't be sad anymore / If you want my love / Busy men / Teach me to forget you / Stormy. *(cd re-iss. Jun98 on 'Matador'; OLE 304-2)*

Dec 87. (12") *(NEW 97)* **HOW DO YOU KNOW** -

Feb 88. (12") *(NEW 116)* **TOUCH** -

Fundamental / Fundamental

Jun 88. (12") *(PRAY 008)* **HERE'S A HEART (ON FYRE)** -

Jul 88. (lp/cd) *(SAVE 059/+CD)* **A PROMISE IS A PROMISE**
– A promise is a promise / Here's a heart (on fyre) / Every man for himself / Feel good / I'll try you anyway / Worried about nothing / Touch / Running through the night / She's got eyes that tell lies / Jagged time lapse / Knock my socks off / Sick and tired / Trying just to please / Witch. *(also on 'New Rose'; ROSE 153/+CD)*

—— split around the late 80's, although they reformed for below

Taang! / Taang!

Jan 93. (lp/cd) *<(TAANG 58/+CD)>* **NOBODY BUT ME**

– compilations, etc. –

Jan 86. (lp) *New Rose; (LYRES 001)* **THE BOX SET** -

Aug 94. (lp/cd) *Taang!; <(TAANG 82/+CD)>* **SOME LYRES**

Apr 97. (cd) *Crypt; (EFA 11578)* **THE EARLY YEARS**

Sep 98. (7") *Sundazed; (LSD 6)* **HELP YOU ANN. / (other track by The Chesterfield Kings)** -

Shane MacGOWAN & THE POPES

Formed: King's Cross, London, England . . . early 1994 by ex-NIPPLE ERECTORS (1978), ex-NIPS (1978-'81) and ex-POGUES (1983-1991) frontman/legend, SHANE MacGOWAN (b.25 Dec'57, Kent, England), along with PAUL McGUINESS, BERNIE FRANCE, DANNY POPE and TOM McMANAMON. Following his messy departure from The POGUES in the early 90's, the Irish KEITH RICHARDS (though even RICHARDS' mythical debauchery would struggle to match MacGOWAN's self-destructiveness in terms of sheer dogged determination) threatened to form his own outfit, The POPES; sceptics who doubted the man could even form an opinion were at least partly silenced by MacGOWAN's late '92 duet with fellow maverick, NICK CAVE, on a brilliantly skewed cover of Louis Armstrong's 'WONDERFUL WORLD'. Two years on and much press rumination later, The POPES' debut single, 'THE CHURCH OF THE HOLY SPOOK', finally put an end to the speculation and announced that MacGOWAN's muse was as darkly fertile as ever. Released on 'Z.T.T.', the song's uptempo thrash recalled the unholy spirit of The POGUES' classic 'SICK BED OF CUCHULAINN', scraping into the UK Top 75. Follow-up single, 'THAT WOMAN'S GOT ME DRINKING' (excuses, excuses), made the Top 40, while Hollywood hearthrob, JOHNNY DEPP, played guitar on their debut Top Of The Pops appearance. The accompanying album, 'THE SNAKE', was the best album The POGUES never recorded in the last decade, finding MacGOWAN back at his cursing, doomed romantic best. Alongside the obligatory traditional songs ('THE RISING OF THE MOON' and 'NANCY WHISKEY'), the record featured an amusingly appropriate cover of Gerry Rafferty's 'HER FATHER DIDN'T LIKE ME ANYWAY', while 'HAUNTED' was a collaboration with SINEAD O'CONNOR which made the Top 30 when released as a single in Spring '95. CLANNAD's MAIRE BRENNAN also hooked up with MacGOWAN for 'YOU'RE THE ONE', underlining the depth of respect afforded the wayward genius, even among his more conventional peers. The live appearances which followed the record's release mightn't have matched the ferocious abandon of The POGUES in full flow but came damn near it, while MacGOWAN followed in SID VICIOUS' footsteps (the man's love of the SEX PISTOLS was recently revealed to the nation via a barely coherent admission on Jo Whiley's Channel 4 TV show) by recording a version of 'MY WAY' in gloriously two-fingered style. 1997 saw the release of a disappointing follow-up set, 'THE CROCK OF GOLD', a record that was at times easier on the ear but hardly threatened to set the pulse racing. • **Songwriters:** MacGOWAN except CRACKLIN' ROSIE (Neil Diamond) / THE RISING OF THE MOON + NANCY WHISKEY (trad). • **Trivia:** Their/his debut album also featured guest appearances from ex-POGUES; SPIDER and FINER, plus DUBLINERS musician/friend BARNEY McKENNA. 'VICTORIA' was written about his writer girlfriend at the time, VICTORIA CLARKE. MacGOWAN is still a reader & fan of writer JAMES JOYCE and Spanish poet LORCA.

Album rating: THE SNAKE (*8) / THE CROCK OF GOLD (*5)

SHANE McGOWAN – vocals (ex-POGUES, ex-NIPS) / **PAUL McGUINNESS** – guitar / **BERNIE FRANCE** – bass / **DANNY POPE** – drums / **TOM NcMANAMON** – banjo

Z.T.T. — Warners

Sep 94. (7"/c-s/cd-s) *(ZANG 57/+C/CD)* **THE CHURCH OF THE HOLY SPOOK. / RAKE AT THE GATES OF HELL** [74] [-]
(cd-s+=) *(ZANG 57CDX)* – King of the bop / Nancy Whiskey.

Oct 94. (c-s) *(ZANG 56C)* **THAT WOMAN'S GOT ME DRINKING / HER FATHER DIDN'T LIKE ME ANYWAY** [34] [-]
(12"+=/cd-s+=) *(ZANG 56 T/CD)* – Roddy McCorley / Minstrel boy.

Oct 94. (cd/c/lp) *(4509 98104-2/-4/-1)* *<45821>* **THE SNAKE** [37] [ ] Jan95
– The church of the holy spook / That woman's got me drinking / The song with no name / Aisling / I'll be your handbag / Her father didn't like me anyway / A Mexican funeral in Paris / The snake with the eyes of Garnet / Donegal express / Victoria / The rising of the moon / Bring down the lamp. *(re-iss. Jun95 cd/c; 0630 10402-2/-4)* – Haunted (with SINEAD O'CONNOR) / You're the one (with MAIRE BRENNAN) / Cracklin' Rosie / Bring down the lamp.

Dec 94. (c-s) *(ZANG 60C)* **THE SONG WITH NO NAME / NANCY WHISKEY** [ ] [-]
(12"+=/cd-s+=) *(ZANG 60 T/CD)* – Cracklin' Rosie.

Apr 95. (c-s; SHANE MacGOWAN & SINEAD O'CONNOR) *(ZANG 65C)* **HAUNTED. / THE SONG WITH NO NAME** [30] [-]
(cd-s+=) *(ZANG 65CD)* – Bring down the lamp / Cracklin' Rosie.

Jun 95. (c-s; SHANE MacGOWAN & MAIRE BRENNAN) *(ZANG 68C)* **YOU'RE THE ONE / AISLING** [ ] [-]
(cd-s) *(ZANG 68CD)* – Victoria.

Apr 96. (c-s; SHANE MacGOWAN) *(ZANG 79C)* **MY WAY / SONG WITH NO NAME** [29] [-]
(cd-s+=) *(ZANG 79CD)* – Aisling / My way (your way).

— **LUCKY DOWLING** – bass; repl. BERNIE

— added **KIERAN KIELY** – accordions, whistles, vocals + **JOHN MYERS** – fiddle, whistle, guitar

Oct 97. (cd-s) *(MACG 001CD)* **LONESOME HIGHWAY /** [ ] [-]

Oct 97. (cd/c) *(MACG 002 CD/C)* **THE CROCK OF GOLD** [59] [-]
– Paddy rolling stone / Rock'n'roll Paddy / Paddy public enemy No.1 / Back in County Hell / Lonesome highway / Come to the bower / Ceilidh cowboy / More pricks than kicks / Truck drivin' man / Joey's in America / B&I ferry / Mother mo chroi / Spanish lady / St. John of gods / Skipping rhymes / Maclennan / Wanderin' star.

Mar 98. (cd-s) *(MACG 003CD)* **ROCK'N'ROLL PADDY /** [ ] [-]

Billy MacKENZIE (see under ⇒ ASSOCIATES)

MADDER ROSE

Formed: Greenwich Village, New York, USA . . . 1991 by MARY LORSON and BILLY COTE, together with MATT VERTA-RAY and JOHNNY KICK. With the release of an eponymous debut EP on 'Rockville' in Spring '93, the VELVET UNDERGROUND comparisons flew thick and fast while the UK music press hailed them as the next big thing. Picked up by 'Atlantic' subsidiary, 'Seed', the group released their debut album, 'BRING IT DOWN', in summer '93. Again, the influences of NY forebears such as VU and TELEVISION were obvious although the guitar noise was contrasted with an emerging rootsiness and LORSON's high register harmonies were reminiscent of SUZANNE VEGA. By the release of follow-up set, 'PANIC ON' (1994), LORSON had developed even further as a songwriter, stamping her presence over much of the material and acting as a catylyst in effecting a more melodic, haunting sound. The album also took MADDER ROSE to the outer fringes of the UK Top 50 while the title track and the hypnotic 'CAR SONG' made the Top 75. With VERTA-RAY having departed around the time of the album's release, a replacement bassist, CHRIS GIAMMALVO, was recruited in time for the attendant touring commitments. Strangely, MADDER ROSE were conspicuous by their absence, until that is 1997's comeback set, 'TRAGIC MAGIC'. • **Covered:** I WANNA SLEEP IN YOUR ARMS (Jonathan Richman) / RULER OF MY HEART (. . . Neville).

Album rating: BRING IT DOWN (*7) / PANIC ON (*8) / TRAGIC MAGIC (*6)

MARY LORSON – vocals, guitar, keyboards / **BILLY COTE** – guitars, bass, vibes / **MATT VERTA-RAY** – bass, rhythm guitar, slide guitar, organ, violin, vibes / **JOHNNY KICK** – drums, keyboards, vocals, vibes

Rockville — Seed

Mar 93. (7"ep/12"ep/cd-ep) *(ROCK 6100-7/-1/-2)* *<14238-2>* **MADDER ROSE** [ ] [ ]
– Swim / Z / I wanna sleep in your arms / Amnesia / Baby gets high / Take it away. *(cd-ep re-iss. Apr97; same)*

Seed — Seed

May 93. (7"ep/cd-ep) *(SEED 003/+CD)* **BEAUTIFUL JOHN / BABY GETS HIGH. / LIGHTS GO DOWN / TAKE IT AWAY** [ ] [ ]

Jun 93. (cd/c/lp) *<(14229-2/-4/-1)>* **BRING IT DOWN** [ ] [ ]
– Beautiful John / While away / Bring it down / 20 foot red / Swim / Lay down low / Altar boy / Lights go down / (Living a) Daydream / Sugarsweet / Razor pilot / Waiting for engines / Pocket fulla medicine.

Oct 93. (7") *(SEED 006)* **SWIM (remix). / LIKED YOU MORE (WHEN YOU WERE HIGH)** [ ] [ ]
(12"+=) *(SEED12 006)* – Z.
(cd-s++=) *(SEECD 006)* – Amnesia.

Atlantic — Atlantic

Mar 94. (7") *(A 8301)* **PANIC ON. / ONE ARMED BANDIT** [65] [ ]
(10"+=/cd-s+=) *(A 8301 TE/CD)* – Mad dog.

Mar 94. (cd/c/lp) *<(7567 82581-2/-4/-1)>* **PANIC ON** [52] [ ]
– Sleep, forever / Car song / Panic on / What Holly sees / Almost lost my mind / Drop a bomb / Ultra anxiety (teenage style) / Happy new year / Day in, day out / Margaret / Foolish ways / Black eye town / When you smile / Mad dog.

Jul 94. (7"/c-s) *(A 7256/+C)* **CAR SONG. / JENNY TAKE A RIDE** [68] [-]
(10"+=/cd-s+=) *(A 7256 TE/CD)* – The widow song / Holiday.

— (Feb'94) **CHRIS GIAMMALVO** – bass; repl. MATT who joined SPEEDBALL BABY

Apr 95. (7") *(SEED 014)* **THE LOVE YOU SAVE. / DIANE** [ ] [-]
(cd-s+=) *(SEEDCD 014)* – No avail / Ruler of my heart.
(above issued on 'Seed')

Aug 97. (7") *(A 5438)* **MY STAR. / LILI MARLENE** [ ] [-]
(c-s) *(A 5438C)* – ('A'side) / Peter and Victor.
(cd-s++=) *(A 5438CD)* – See her every night.

Jun 97. (cd/c) *<83009>* **TRAGIC MAGIC** [-] [ ]
– My star / Real feel / Float to the top / Hung up in you / Delight's pool / (She's a) Satellite / Peter and Victor / Best friend / Scenes from "Starbright" / Midnight on the dot / Don Greene / Not perfect.

MAGAZINE

Formed: Manchester, England . . . Spring 1977 by former BUZZCOCKS frontman, HOWARD DEVOTO and guitarist JOHN McGEOGH, who recruited the rhythm section of BARRY ADAMSON and MARTIN JACKSON along with keyboard player, BOB DICKINSON. After six months of rehearsals, they played their debut gig on the final night of legendary Manchester punk club, The Electric Circus, subsequently signing to 'Virgin' on the strength of a demo. A classic debut single, 'SHOT BY BOTH SIDES' established MAGAZINE's post-punk credentials, its stark, uncompromising approach and lyrical despair paving the way for countless gaggles of miserable young men in trenchcoats. Although DICKINSON had left prior to recording the single, the band had recruited a replacement, DAVE FORMULA, in time for the debut album, 'REAL LIFE' (1978). Its icy keyboard textures and spiky sonic artistry announced the arrival of a unique talent although DEVOTO's hyper-intelligent wayward genius was nothing new for fans who'd admired the punk maverick since his BUZZCOCKS days. With major radio support from John Peel and a growing cult fanbase, the album made the UK Top 30, while JACKSON was replaced with JOHN DOYLE following the obligatory tour. A follow-up set, 'SECONDHAND DAYLIGHT' (1979), was even more liberal in its use of keyboards although MAGAZINE's leftfield approach could hardly be accused of straying into New Romantic territory (some of MAGAZINE did dip a toe into these waters when they guested for VISAGE). Although a further three singles (including the unsettling 'A SONG FROM UNDER THE FLOORBOARDS' and an unlikely cover of Sly Stone's 'THANK YOU') failed to chart, a third album, 'THE CORRECT USE OF SOAP' (1980), became their most successful to date. DEVOTO wasn't happy with the direction the band were headed, however, and the defection of McGEOGH to SIOUXSIE & THE BANSHEES led to a slow decline and a patchy final effort in 'MAGIC, MURDER AND THE WEATHER' (1981). By the time of the album's release, DEVOTO had already announced his departure, effectively ending MAGAZINE's limited shelf life. The singer went on to release a solo set, 'JERKY VERSIONS OF THE DREAM' before forming LUXURIA with NOKO. He subsequently quit the music business; BARRY ADAMSON has enjoyed greater recognition, initially with NICK CAVE & The BAD SEEDS and latterly with his acclaimed solo career. • **Songwriters:** DEVOTO penned all except; I LOVE YOU BIG DUMMY (Captain Beefheart). LUXURIA covered JEZEBEL (Marty Wilde).

Album rating: REAL LIFE (*9) / THE CORRECT USE OF SOAP (*8) / MAGIC, MURDER AND THE WEATHER (*6) / RAYS AND HAIL compilation (*8)

HOWARD DEVOTO – vocals (ex-BUZZCOCKS) / **JOHN McGEOGH** – guitar / **BARRY ADAMSON** – bass / **MARTIN JACKSON** – drums / **BOB DICKINSON** – keyboards

— (BOB left before debut recording)

Virgin | Int

Jan 78. (7") *(VS 200)* **SHOT BY BOTH SIDES. / MY MIND AIN'T SO OPEN** 41 | -

Apr 78. (7") *(VS 207)* **TOUCH AND GO. / GOLDFINGER** | -

— added **DAVE FORMULA** – keyboards

Jun 78. (lp/c) *(V/TCV 2100)* **REAL LIFE** 29 |
– Definitive gaze / My tulpa / Shot by both sides / Recoil / Burst / Motorcade / The great beautician in the sky / The light pours out of me / Parade. *(re-iss. Mar84; OVED 62) (cd-iss. Oct88; CDV 2100)*

— **JOHN DOYLE** – drums repl. JACKSON (to CHAMELEONS, then SWING OUT SISTER)

Nov 78. (7") *(VS 237)* **GIVE ME EVERYTHING. / I LOVE YOU, YOU BIG DUMMY** | -

Feb 79. (7") *(VS 251)* **RHYTHM OF CRUELTY. / T.V. BABY** | -

Mar 79. (lp/c) *(V/TCV 2121)* **SECONDHAND DAYLIGHT** 38 |
– Feed the enemy / Rhythm of cruelty / Cut-out shapes / Talk to the body / I wanted your heart / The thin air / Back to nature / Believe that I understand / Permafrost. *(re-iss. 1987 lp/c; OVED/+C 84) (cd-iss. Oct88; CDV 2121)*

Feb 80. (7") *(VS 321)* **A SONG FROM UNDER THE FLOORBOARDS. / TWENTY YEARS AGO** | -

Mar 80. (7") *(VS 328)* **THANK YOU (FALETTINME BE MICE ELF AGIN). / THE BOOK** | -

Apr 80. (7") *(VS 334)* **UPSIDE DOWN. / THE LIGHT POURS OUT OF ME (live)** | -

May 80. (lp/c) *(V/TCV 2156)* *<13144>* **THE CORRECT USE OF SOAP** 28 |
– Because you're frightened / Model worker / I'm a party / You never knew me / Philadelphia / I want to burn again / Thank you (falettinme be mice elf agin) / Sweetheart contract / Stuck / A song from under the floorboards. *(re-iss. 1988 lp/c; OVED/+C 116) (cd-iss. Oct88; CDV 2156)*

Jul 80. (d7/12"ep) *(VS 368/+12)* **SWEETHEART CONTRACT. / FEED THE ENEMY (live) // TWENTY YEARS AGO. / SHOT BY BOTH SIDES (live)** 54 | -

— **ROBIN SIMON** – guitar (ex-ULTRAVOX) repl. McGEOGH who joined SIOUXSIE . . . (above now alongside **DEVOTO, ADAMSON, FORMULA** and **DOYLE**)

Virgin | I.R.S.

Nov 80. (lp/c) *(V/TCV 2184)* *<70015>* **PLAY (live at Melbourne Festival Hall)** 69 |
– Give me everything / A song from under the floorboards / Permafrost / The light pours out of me / Model worker / Parade / Thank you (falettinme be mice elf agin) / Because you're frightened / Twenty years ago / Definitive gaze. *(re-iss. 1988 lp/c; OVED/+C 117) (cd-iss. Oct88; CDV 2184)*

— **BEN MANDELSON** – guitar (ex-AMAZORBLADES) repl. ROBIN.

May 81. (7") *(VS 412)* **ABOUT THE WEATHER. / IN THE DARK** | -
(12"+=) *(VS 412-12)* – The operative.

Jun 81. (lp/c) *(V/TCV 2200)* *<70020>* **MAGIC, MURDER AND THE WEATHER** 39 |
– About the weather / So lucky / The honeymoon killers / Vigilante / Come alive / The great man's secrets / This poison / Naked eye / Suburban Rhonda / The garden. *(re-iss. 1988 lp/c; OVED/+C 141) (cd-iss. Oct88; CDV 2200)*

— They split mid '81. DEVOTO went solo with help from FORMULA (see below). BEN MANDELSON joined The MEKONS, JOHN DOYLE later joined ARMOURY SHOW. BARRY ADAMSON joined PETE SHELLEY then later NICK CAVE & THE BAD SEEDS. FORMULA had also joined the group DESIGN FOR LIVING.

– compilations, etc. –

on 'Virgin' unless mentioned otherwise

May 82. (lp/c) *(VM/+C 1)* **AFTER THE FACT** (best of) | -

May 83. (12"ep) *(VS 592-12)* **SHOT BY BOTH SIDES** | -
– Shot by both sides / Goldfinger / Give me everything / A song from under the floorboards.

May 87. (cd) *(COMCD 5)* **RAYS AND HAIL 1978-81** (best of) | -
– Shot by both sides / Definitive gaze / Motorcade / The light pours out of me / Feed the enemy / Rhythm of cruelty / Back to nature / Permafrost / Because you're frightened / You never knew me / A song from under the floorboards / I want to burn again / About the weather / Parade. *(re-iss. Jul93; CDVM 9020)*

Jul 90. (cd) *(CDOVD 312)* **SCREE** (rarities 76-81) | -

Aug 93. (cd) *Windsong; (WINCD 040)* **BBC RADIO 1 LIVE IN CONCERT** | -

HOWARD DEVOTO

— went solo, with **DAVE FORMULA** – keyboards / **PAT AHORN** – drums / **ALAN ST. CLAIR** – guitar / **NEIL PYZER** – keyboards,synth / **MARTIN HEATH** – bass

Virgin | I.R.S.

Jun 83. (7"/12") *(VS 598/+12)* **RAINY SEASON. / RAIN FOREST** | -

Aug 83. (lp/c) *(V/TCV 2272)* *<SP 70036>* **JERKY VERSIONS OF THE DREAM** 57 |
– Cold imagination / Topless / Rainy season / I admire you / Way out of shape / Some will pay (for what others pay to avoid) / Waiting for a train / Out of shape with me / Taking over Heaven / Seeing is believing. *(re-iss. Aug88; OVED 129) (cd-iss. Apr90; CDV 2272)*

Aug 83. (7"/12") *(VS 642/+12)* **COLD IMAGINATION. / OUT OF SHAPE WITH ME** | -

— PYZER and ST.CLAIR joined SPEAR OF DESTINY. HEATH and AHORN joined DAVE HOWARD SINGERS, DEVOTO guested for B.SZAJNER a French electronic wizard. He then took 4 years off before his new venture . . .

LUXURIA

DEVOTO with **NOKO** (b.Liverpool) – guitar, co-composer

Beggars Banquet | Beggars Banquet

Jan 88. (7") *(BEG 204)* **REDNECK. / SHE'S YOUR LOVER NOW (pt.1)** | -
(12"+=) *(BEG 204T)* – She's your lover now (pt.2).

Feb 88. (lp/c)(cd) *(BEGA/BEGC 90)(BEGA 90CD)* *<6990>* **THE UNANSWERABLE LUST** |
– Redneck / Flesh / Public highway / Pound / Lady 21 / Celebrity / Rubbish / Mile / Luxuria.

May 88. (7") *(BEG 211)* **PUBLIC HIGHWAY (Short cut) / SICKLY THUG AND I** | -
(12"+=) *(BEG 211T)* – Luxuria (The wilderness mix).

Mar 90. (7"ep/12"ep/cd-ep) *(BEG 233/+T/CD)* **THE BEAST BOX IS DREAMING / BEAST BOX / USELESS LOVE** | -

Apr 90. (cd)(c/lp) *(BEGA 106CD)(BEGC/BEGA 106)* *<2233-2/-4/-1>* **BEAST BOX** |
– The beast box is dreaming / Stupid blood / Against the past / Our curious leader / We keep on getting there / Ticket / Animal in the mirror / Dirty beating heart / Smoking mirror / I've been expecting you / Karezza / Beast box / Jezebel.

May 90. (7") **JEZEBEL. / SMOKING MIRROR (instrumental)** | -
(12"+=) – Sickly thug and I.
(cd-s++=) – Luxuria (live).

— after their split, NOKO went to ground for a while, re-emerging later in the 90's with hard techno act, APOLLO 440

MAGIC HOUR (see under ⇒ GALAXIE 500)

MAGNAPOP

Formed: Atlanta/Athens, Georgia, USA . . . 1988 by LINDA HOPPER and RUTHIE MORRIS, plus SHANNON MULVANEY and DAVID McNAIR who had recently departed from the group OH-OK (the latter act numbered MATTHEW SWEET and LINDA STIPE – sister of MICHAEL STIPE – in their ranks!). With the production skills and industry experience of R.E.M. figurehead, MICHAEL STIPE, on their side, the band won a fanatical following in the Benelux countries with their debut single, 'SUGARLANDS' (a Top 20 hit in the Netherlands). Another early supporter was ex-HUSKER DU man, BOB MOULD, who produced their ensuing eponymous 1992 debut album. The two man/two woman combination proved a winning formula with HOPPER's insinuating, accusatory vocals sparking off a grunge-pop chemistry and occasionally bringing to mind prime THROWING MUSES. Their failure to secure an American major deal meant that European alternative label, 'Play It Again Sam', remained their home for a further two albums, 'HOT BOXING' (1994) and 'RUBBING DOESN'T HELP' (1996). Yet the band couldn't seem to translate their continental success into substantial British or American sales despite continuing critical support. • **Songwriters:** HOPPER-MORRIS penned except; SONG NUMBER ONE (Fugazi).

Album rating: MAGNAPOP (*7) / HOT BOXING (*6) / RUBBING DOESN'T HELP (*5)

LINDA HOPPER – vocals / **RUTHIE MORRIS** – guitar / **SHANNON MULVANEY** – bass / **DAVE McNAIR** – drums

Play It Again Sam | Play It Again Sam

Jun 92. (12"ep/cd-ep) **SUGARLAND. / MERRY** [ ] [-]

Jul 92. (lp/c/cd) *<BIAS 220/+MC/CD>* **MAGNAPOP** [ ] [ ] Oct92
– Garden / Guess / Ear / 13 / Spill it / Chemical / Favourite writer / Complicated / Merry.

Aug 93. (12"ep/cd-ep) *(BIAS 243/+CD)* **KISS MY MOUTH EP** [ ] [-]
– Texas / Lay it down / Precious / Nowhere.

Jan 94. (12"ep/12"white-ep/cd-ep) *(BIAS 257/+X/CD)* **SLOWLY, SLOWLY / SONG NUMBER ONE. / HERE IT COMES / PUFF** [ ] [-]

Feb 94. (lp/c/cd) *(BIAS 251/+MC/CD)* *<53909>* **HOT BOXING** [ ] [ ] Jul94
– Slowly, slowly, Texas / Lay it down / Here it comes / Piece of cake / Free mud / Leo / The crush / Ride / In the way / Idiot song / Get it right / Emergency / Skinburns.

May 94. (12"ep/cd-ep) *(BIAS 267 X/CD)* **LAY IT DOWN. / SLOWLY, SLOWLY (demo) / THE CRUSH (demo) / PIECE OF CAKE (demo)** [ ] [-]

— McNAIR was repl. by temp **JOSH FREESE** – drums

Feb 96. (7"ep/cd-ep) *(BIAS 287 7/CD)* **FIRE ALL OF YOUR GUNS AT ONCE** [ ] [-]
– Come on inside / Voice without a sound / Down on me / Hold you down.

Apr 96. (7") *(BIAS 297-7)* **OPEN THE DOOR. / RE-HAB** [ ] [-]
(cd-s+=) *(BIAS 297CD)* – True love.

May 96. (cd/red-lp) *(BIAS 321 CD/LP)* *<53992>* **RUBBING DOESN'T HELP** [ ] [ ]
– This family / I don't care / Open the door / Come on inside / Down on me / An apology / My best friend / Juicy fruit / Firebrand / Cherry bomb / Radio waves / Snake / Dead letter.

MAGNETIC FIELDS

Formed: 1990 . . . by STEPHIN MERRITT, who based his underground one-man outfit in Boston, Massachusetts. A prolific singer/songwriter (writes more than 100 songs a year!), the experimental minimalist with a penchant for pop – ABBA and BRIAN WILSON were obvious influences! – released a plethora of albums during the first half of the 90's. The first of these, 'DISTANT PLASTIC TREES' (1990/91), found him working with a cast of collaborators (CLAUDIA GONSON and SAM DAVOL) that would remain fairly constant over the next few years. Their kitschy yet lovelorn and desolate second set, 'THE WAYWARD BUS', was easily their best, although it was their last with singer, SUSAN AMWAY. Taking over vocal duties, STEPHIN was revealed to be a kind of lugubrious, lo-fi LEONARD COHEN on electro-pop pills. His/their next two long-players, 'HOLIDAY' (1994) and 'THE CHARM OF THE HIGHWAY STRIP' (1994/5), further developed the nomadic spirit possessing STEPHIN's muse. His first of many side projects, The 6ths, utilized the eclectic vocal talents of such underground indie figureheads as LOU BARLOW, MITCH EASTER and BARBARA MANNING, to name but a few on the 1995 album, 'WASPS NESTS' (one of the last albums on Tony Wilson's now defunct UK imprint, 'Factory'). Reprising the MAGNETIC FIELDS moniker, STEPHIN delivered their final instalment of wayward synth-pop, 'GET LOST' (1996), the openly gay schizophrenic retiring from the limelight before re-inventing himself as the FUTURE BIBLE HEROES alongside ever faithful sidekick, CLAUDIA. Remaining with 'Setanta' records, the pair added a third member, CHRIS EWEN, for the 'MEMORIES OF LOVE' album in the first half of '98.

Album rating: DISTANT PLASTIC TREES (*6) / THE WAYWARD BUS (*8) / HOLIDAY (*7) / THE CHARM OF THE HIGHWAY (*6) / GET LOST (*6) / 6ths: WASPS' NESTS (*7)

STEPHEN MERRITT – keyboards, guitar / **CLAUDIA GONSON** – percussion / **SAM DAVOL** – cello, flute / **SUSAN AMWAY** – vocals

Red Flame | not iss.

Feb 91. (cd) *(RFCD 3)* **DISTANT PLASTIC TREES** [ ] [-]
– Railroad boy / Smoke signals / You love to fail / Kings / Babies falling / Living in an abandoned firehouse with / Tar-heel boy / Falling in love with the wolfboy / Josephine / 100,000 fireflies.

not iss. | Fell Good All Over

Jan 92. (cd) **THE WAYWARD BUS** [-] [ ]
– When you were my baby / The saddest story ever told / Lovers from the moon / Candy / Tokyo a go-go / Summer lies / Old orchard beach / Jeremy / Dancing in your eyes / Suddenly there is a tidal wave.

— now without SUSAN (STEPHIN took over vocals)

1994. (cd) *<26>* **HOLIDAY** [-] [ ]
– BBC radiophonic workshop / Desert island / Strange powers / Torn green velvet eyes / Flowers she sent and the flowers she . . . / Swinging London / In my secret place / Sad little moon / The trouble I've been looking for / Sugar world / All you ever do is walk away / In my car / Take ecstasy with me.

— next with guest vocalists, **LOU BARLOW, MITCH EASTER, BARBARA MANNING, ANNA DOMINO, GEORGIA HUBLEY, ROBERT SCOTT, CHRIS KNOX, JANET UNDERHILL, MAC McCAUGHAN, AMELIA FLETCHER + AYAKO ALASHIBA**

Factory Too | Polygram

Jul 95. (cd/c; as The 6ths) *(FAC D/MC 206)* *<828592>* **WASPS' NESTS** [ ] [ ] Mar95
– San Diego zoo / Ageing spinsters / All dressed up in dreams / Winter in July / Pillow fight / Dream hat / Movies in my head / In the city in the rain / Looking for love (in the hall of mirrors) / Heaven in a black leather jacket / Here in my heart / Puerto Rico way / You can't break a broken heart / When I'm out of town.

Setanta | Merge

Aug 95. (cd/lp) *(SET CD/LP 021)* *<MRG 55>* **THE CHARM OF THE HIGHWAY STRIP** [ ] [ ] Dec94
– Lonely highway / Long Vermont roads / Born on a train / I have the Moon / Two characters in search of a country song / Crowd of drifters / Fear of trains / When the open road is closing in / Sunset city / Dustbowl.

Dec 95. (7") *<MRG 73>* **ALL THE UMBRELLAS IN LONDON. / RATS IN THE GARBAGE OF THE WESTERN WORLD** [-] [ ]

Mar 96. (cd) *(SETCD 023)* *<MRG 91>* **GET LOST** [ ] [ ]
– Famous / The desperate things you made me do / Smoke and mirrors / With whom to dance? / You and me and the moon / Don't look away / Save a secret for the moon / Why I cry / Love is lighter than air / When you're old and lonely / Village in the morning / All the umbrellas in London / Dreaming moon. *(also other cd; SETCD 023L)*

not iss. | Feel Good All Over

Apr 96. (cd-ep) *<7007>* **THE HOUSE OF TOMORROW** [-] [ ]
– Young and insane / Technical (you're so) / Alien being / Love goes home to Paris in the Spring / Either you don't love me or I don't. *(UK-iss.Mar97 as 'THE MAGNETIC FIELDS' on 'Data'; DAT 008)*

Merge | Merge

Aug 98. (7") *<(MRG 143)>* **I DON'T BELIEVE YOU. /** [ ] [ ]

– compilations, etc. –

Jan 95. (cd) *Merge; <MRG 75>* **THE WAYWARD BUS / DISTANT PLASTIC TREES** [-] [ ]

FUTURE BIBLE HEROES

— **STEPHIN + CLAUDIA GONSON** recruited **CHRISTOPHER EWEN** (ex-FIGURES ON A BEACH)

Setanta | Slow River

Mar 98. (7") *(SET 059)* **LONELY DAYS. / HOPELESS** [ ] [-]
(cd-s) *(SETCD 059)* – ('A'side) / Love is blue / How to get laid in Japanese / Berlin on $10 a day.

Apr 98. (cd) *(SETCD 056)* *<24>* **MEMORIES OF LOVE** [ ] [ ] May97
– Lonely days / She-devils of the deep / Hopeless / Death opened a boutique / You pretend to be the moon / Blonde adonis / But you're so beautiful / You, you never knew / Real summer / Memories of love / You steal the scene.

MAGOO

Formed: King's Lynn, Norfolk, England . . .. 1991 by ANDREW RAYNER, ADAM BLACKBOURN, OWEN TURNER and DAVID BAMFORD. Finally signing to the appropriately titled 'Noisebox' label, these Lo-Fi pop alchemists began making a name for themselves with the first of three EP's, 'MUDSHARK', in Spring '95. A year on MAGOO had a further two under their belt, 'ROBOT CARNIVAL' and the seven track 7", 'EYE SPY'. Taking their cue from transatlantic experimentalists like GUIDED BY VOICES, MAGOO thrived on the sonic possibilities inherent in combining distortion, noise and melody. As such they were an obvious choice for up and coming Scottish indie institution, 'Chemikal Underground', already home to MOGWAI, ARAB STRAP and The DELGADOS. By the time they'd signed up in early '97, the group had been reduced to a trio following the departure of ADAM, two part-time members, CHRIS THORPE-TRACEY and CHRIS WYATT helping out on their debut album, 'THE SOATERAMIC SOUNDS OF MAGOO' (1997). The following year, they took on the task (along with MOGWAI) of covering a classic BLACK SABBATH track – MAGOO's choice being the highly unlikely 'BLACK SABBATH' – on the split CD single, ' . . .. DO THE ROCK BOOGALOO'. Returning to the headspinning creative spark of their own material, the Norfolk lads released a second album proper, 'VOTE THE PACIFIST TICKET TODAY' (1998), six months on from a 'Noisebox' singles compilation, 'CLOSE CONTINENTAL D.N.A.'.

Album rating: THE SOATERAMIC SOUNDS OF MAGOO (*7) / VOTE THE PACIFIST TICKET TODAY (*7) / CLOSE CONTINENTAL D.N.A. compilation (*6)

ANDREW RAYNER – vocals, guitar, bass, piano / **ADAM BLACKBOURN** – guitar, bass / **OWEN TURNER** – guitar, effects / **DAVID BAMFORD** – drums

Noisebox | not iss.

May 95. (7"ep) *(nbx 013)* **MUDSHARK EP** [ ] [-]
– Pop your mouth / Tom, Lou and me / Elsie's skinny arms.

Sep 95. (7"ep) *(nbx 016)* **ROBOT CARNIVAL / SAMPA CALMIDA (LAND OF JOY). / CANDLE BUDDHA / ROCKET TO SPECTOR CITY** [ ] [-]

— the track, 'PEANUT BOY', appeared on a various artists EP, 'Now That's What I Call Noisebox' (nbx 018)

Apr 96. (7"yellow-ep) *(nbx 020)* **EYE SPY / MOTEL MINING / SOATERAMA. / POLKA PARTY NO.2 / SILVER SCREEN / WORD IS OUT / DIVING BELL** [ ] [-]

— the track, 'GOLDWYN', appeared on a 'Fierce Panda' collection, 'Songs About Picniking' (ning 018)

— ADAM left the band

— the track, 'STRUCK A CHORD', appeared on a various artists cd, 'C96'

— ADAM was replaced by two part members **CHRIS THORPE-TRACEY** – guitar, bass, organ / **CHRIS WYATT** – drums, effects

Chemikal Underground | Beggars Banquet

Mar 97. (7"ep/cd-ep) *(Chem 011/+cd)* *<85006>* **A TO Z AND BACK AGAIN. / THE BIG COMEBACK STARTS HERE / SOME DARK ACTION / BAXTER PREMINGER / IT'S GOOD FOR YOU** [ ] [ ] Jun97

Apr 97. (lp/cd) *(Chem 012/+cd)* *<85008>* **THE SOATERAMIC SOUNDS OF MAGOO** [ ] [ ] Sep97
– The starter's gun / A to Z and back again / Your only friend / Telling you lies / Red lines (are fine) / The guilt club / The advantage of noise / Have you heard? / The social event of the year / Soaterama / The queen of the 8-bus singers / It's not going

to stop / Hello . . . / Playing cards with the stars / British cars / This red earth / Say goodnight. *(cd+=/+free-7"ep)* – Lonely legionaire / Careering dice (a loose dear Santa) / Melodra / Bebe alights / Dutch dynamico / Train of thought.

Jun 97. (7"ep/cd-ep) *(Chem 016/+cd)* **RED LINES (ARE FINE). /** [ ] [-]

Dec 97. (ltd-7") *(ER 157)* **TREMOR, TREMOR, TREMOR. /** [ ] [-]
(above 45 released on 'Elefant') (below on 'Fierce Panda')

Mar 98. (cd-s;split) *(NING 47CD)* **. . ... DO THE ROCK BOOGALOO** [ ] [-]
– Black sabbath / Sweat Leaf (by MOGWAI).

Jun 98. (7"ep/cd-ep) *(Chem 025/+cd)* **HOLY SMOKE. / PINK DUST / MEETING OF THE MINDS** [ ] [-]

Sep 98. (7"ep/cd-ep) *(Chem 028/+cd)* **SWISS BORDER ESCAPE. / SWITCHED AROUND / I FORGOT ALL THE THINGS I EVER KNEW** [ ] [-]

Nov 98. (cd/lp) *(Chem 030 cd/lp)* **VOTE THE PACIFIST TICKET TODAY** [ ] [-]
– Vote the pacifist ticket today / Pink dust / Swiss border escape / Get on it superhero / Acid goldbar / The casino effect / Billion dollar brain / Holy smoke / Keep it pure / My vote is you / Cable tuned and sabre toothed / The spectre closes in / Implicate the targets / Airmen afraid.

– compilations, etc. –

Apr 98. (cd) *Noisebox; (nbx 036)* **CLOSE CONTINENTAL D.N.A. {NOISEBOX 94-96}** [ ] [-]

MAIN (see under ⇒ LOOP)

MAKE-UP

Formed: Washington DC, USA . . . Spring '88 initially as NATION OF ULYSSES. This sharp-suited politi-core terrorist outfit consisted of JAMES CANTY, TIM GREEN, STEVE KRONER, STEVE GAMBOA plus the "sassy" frontman, IAN SVENONIUS. Until their demise in the Autumn of '92, NOU issued two IAN MacKAYE-produced albums, '13-POINT PROGRAM TO DESTROY AMERICA' (1991) and 'PLAYS PRETTY FOR BABY' (1992). CANTY, SVENONIUS and GAMBOA formed the short-lived CUPID CAR CLUB with former FRUMPIES bassist, MICHELLE MAE, although the name was thankfully shelved for the more basic MAKE-UP. Like JON SPENCER BLUES EXPLOSION and ROCKET FROM THE CRYPT rolled into one, their legendary "greaseball" stage shows were recorded for posterity in the guise of their debut release, 'DESTINATION: LOVE – LIVE AT COLD RICE' (1996). 'Dischord' (home of MacKAYE's FUGAZI) delivered one more set, 'AFTER DARK' (1997), before they released 'SOUND VERITE' (1997), for 'K' records (NOU guitarist, TIM GREEN, had worked for the label since the split). • **Covered:** BLACK WIRE (MC5).

Album rating: DESTINATION: LOVE – LIVE AT COLD RICE (*6) / AFTER DARK (*6) / SOUND VERITE (*5) / Nation Of Ulysses: 13-POINT PROGRAM TO DESTROY AMERICA (*5) / PLAYS PRETTY FOR BABY (*6)

NATION OF ULYSSES

IAN SVENONIUS – vocals, trumpet / **TIM GREEN** – guitar / **STEVE KRONER** – guitar / **STEVE GAMBOA** – bass / **JAMES CANTY** – drums

Dischord Dischord

Sep 91. (cd/c/lp) *<DIS 57 CD/C/V>* **13-POINT PROGRAM TO DESTROY AMERICA** [ ] [ ]
– Spectra sonic sound / Look out! soul is back / Today I met the girl I'm going to marry / Ulythium / A kid who tells on another kid is a dead kid / Cool senior high school (fight song) / Diptheria / Aspirin kid / Hot chocolate city / P. Power / You're my Miss Washington, D.C. / Target: U.S.A. / Love is a bull market / The sound of young America / Channel One Ulysses / Atom bomb.

Oct 92. (cd/c/lp) *<DIS 71 CD/C/V>* **PLAYS PRETTY FOR BABY** [ ] [ ]
– N-sub Ulysses / A comment on ritual / The hickey underworld / Perpetual motion / Machine / N.O.U. future-vision / Hypothesis / 50,000 watts of goodwill / Maniac dragstrip / Last train to cool / Shakedown / Mockingbird, yeah! / Depression III / S.S. Explorer / The kingdom of Heaven must be taken by storm.

— disbanded when supposedly one of them (possibly KRONER begat a baby

MAKE-UP

IAN SVENONIUS – vocals / **STEVE GAMBOA** – drums / **MICHELLE MAE** – bass, vocals (ex-FRUMPIES) / **JAMES CANTY** – drums, organ

Dischord Dischord

Apr 96. (cd/lp) *<DIS 99 CD/V>* **DESTINATION: LOVE – LIVE AT COLD RICE (live)** [ ] [ ]
– Intro "Hold it" / Here comes the judge / You + I vs. the world / They live by night / Bring the birds down / Don't mind the mind / Evidence is everywhere / We can't be contained / Introductions / Don't step on the children / How pretty can U get / R U a believer (part 2) / International airport / We gotta get offa this rock / So . . . chocolatey – Destination: love / Outro "Hold it".

Oct 96. (7") *<TBI 38>* **SUBSTANCE ABUSE. /** [ ] [ ]
(above issued on 'Time Bomb')

Feb 97. (cd/lp) *<DIS 105 CD/V>* **AFTER DARK** [ ] [ ]
– Spoken intro / Prelude to comedown – Can I hear U say . . ..?? / Blue is beautiful / At the tone . . . (the time will be) / We can't be contacted / Gospel 2000 / Vs. culture / We're having a baby / Make up is: lies / R U a believer / The final comedown / Don't mind the mind / Here comes the judge.

Mar 97. (lp/cd) *<KLP 64/+CD>* **SOUND VERITE** [ ] [ ]
– If they come in the morning / Make up is: lies / At the tone, the time will be / Tell it like it will be / What's the rumpus? / Gospel 2000 / Hot coals / Gold record (part 1) / Gold record (part 2) / Have U got the new look.
(above & below on 'K' records)

Oct 97. (7") *(IPU 85)* **FREE ARTHUR LEE. /** [ ] [ ]

Jan 98. (7") *(ACMU 1)* **WADE IN THE WATER. /** [ ] [ ]
(above on 'All City' & below on 'Woo Me')

Mar 98. (7") *(WOOME 001)* **UNTOUCHABLE SOUND. /** [ ] [ ]

Mar 98. (cd/lp) *<DIS 113 CD/V>* **IN MASS MIND** [ ] [ ]
– Black wire / Live in the rhythm-hive / Joy of sound / Watch it with that thing / Drop the needle / Earth worm / Do you like gospel music? / Come up to the microphone / Centre of the earth / (I've heard about) Saturday nite / Earth worm / Time machine / Caught up in the rapture / Black wire.

Jun 98. (7"; split with LUNG) *(POMP 16)* **split** [ ] [ ]
(above on 'Vesuvius' records)

Stephen MALLINDER (see under ⇒ CABARET VOLTAIRE)

MANIC STREET PREACHERS

Formed: Blackwood, Gwent, South Wales . . . 1988 by JAMES DEAN BRADFIELD (vocals, guitar) and cousin SEAN MOORE (drums). With the addition of former school friends NICKY WIRE (bass) and RICHEY EDWARDS (rhythm guitar), the line-up was complete and the band set about recording their self-financed debut single, 'SUICIDE ALLEY'. The group began to attract attention with the release of the 'NEW ART RIOT' EP (1990), derivative but impassioned neo-punk which drew interest more for the band's defiant slurs on a range of targets (fellow musicians were shown no mercy) than its musical content. While the band looked the part (low rent glamour chic) and namechecked all the right people (RIMBAUD, The CLASH, etc.), their philosophy of kill your idols and then burn out, smacked of contrivance to say the least. When journalist STEVE LAMACQ said as much in an interview with EDWARDS in 1991, the guitarist proceeded to carve '4 REAL' into his arm with a razor, upping the ante in the band's already precarious relationship with the music press and causing furious debate between doubters and obsessive fans. The group proceeded to release a couple of raging singles on 'Heavenly', 'MOTOWN JUNK' and the stinging 'YOU LOVE US' (aimed at the press), before signing to 'Columbia' in 1991. After a couple of minor hits, 'STAY BEAUTIFUL' and 'LOVE'S SWEET EXILE', the MANICS cracked the Top 20 with a re-released 'YOU LOVE US', their much anticipated debut album, 'GENERATION TERRORISTS' following in February 1992. A sprawling double set, it kicked convincingly against the pricks, lashing out at such deserving targets as high street banks ('NAT WEST-BARCLAYS-MIDLAND-LLOYDS') and our beloved monarch ('REPEAT'). The band also proved they had a way with melody and songwriting in the soaring melancholy of 'MOTORCYCLE EMPTINESS'. Despite their original well intentioned claims to break up after the debut, the band rather predictably toured the album and began work on a new colection, 'GOLD AGAINST THE SOUL' (1993). Lacking the vicious kick of the debut, the record nevertheless contained some fine moments in the likes of 'LA TRISTESSE DURERA (SCREAM TO A SIGH)' and 'LIFE BECOMING A LANDSLIDE', reaching No.8 in the album charts. The MANIC STREET PREACHERS continued to court controversy with NICKY WIRE making his infamous comments about about MICHAEL STIPE at the 1993 Reading Festival. The following year RICHEY EDWARDS' depression, self-mutilation and anorexia reaced a head, the guitarist eventually admitted to a clinic for several weeks. His trauma was detailed in the harrowing '4st 7lb' from their third album, 'The HOLY BIBLE' (1994), a dark night of the soul which centred on such grim topics as Nazi genocide. Then, on 1st February '95, with EDWARDS apparently recovered, he went AWOL from his London hotel. A fortnight later, his abandoned car was found at the Severn Bridge, and rumours of suicide abounded. Even after a protracted police search, there was no trace of the guitarist and at the time of writing , he is still missing. Numerous sightings have since been reported, most notably in Goa, India although the Police have continued to draw a blank. The remaining members eventually decided to carry on, contributing a poignant 'RAIN DROPS KEEP FALLING ON MY HEAD' to the 1995 Warchild charity album, 'HELP', and releasing their fourth album, 'EVERYTHING MUST GO' (1996). The group's most accomplished work to date, the record was preceeded by their biggest hit single (No.2), the bitter 'A DESIGN FOR LIFE'. Embellished with soaring strings and lavish arrangements, the band scored with a succession of brilliant songs including 'AUSTRALIA' and the title track, compositions that were almost transcendant in their emotive power, the memory of EDWARDS never far away. It seemed that at last the MANIC STREET PREACHERS had lived up to their early boasts and in early 1997 their talent was recognised when 'EVERYTHING MUST GO' won the coveted Mercury Music Award. • **Covered:** IT'S SO EASY (Guns n' Roses) / UNDER MY WHEELS (Alice Cooper) / SUICIDE IS PAINLESS (Theme from 'Mash') / CHARLES WINDSOR (McCarthy) / THE DROWNERS (Suede) / STAY WITH ME (Faces) / WROTE FOR LUCK (Happy Mondays) / RAINDROPS KEEP FALLING ON MY HEAD (Bacharach-David) / VELOCITY GIRL (Primal Scream) / TAKE THE SKINHEADS BOWLING (Camper Van Beethoven) / I CAN'T TAKE MY EYES OFF YOU (hit; Andy Williams).

Album rating: GENERATION TERRORISTS (*8) / GOLD AGAINST THE SOUL (*9) / THE HOLY BIBLE (*9) / EVERYTHING MUST GO (*9)

JAMES DEAN BRADFIELD (b.21 Feb'69, Newport) – vocals, guitar / **RICHEY JAMES EDWARDS** (b.27 Dec'69) – rhythm guitar / **NICKY WIRE** (b. JONES, 20 Jan'69, Tredegar) – bass / **SEAN MOORE** (b.30 Jul'70, Pontypool) – drums

S.B.S. not iss.

Aug 89. (7") *(SBS 002)* **SUICIDE ALLEY. / TENNESSEE (I FEEL SO LOW)** [ ] [-]

EAT THE RICH
A DESIGN FOR LIFE
DESTROY WORK
4 REAL

Damaged Goods / not iss.

Jun 90. (12"ep) *(YUBB 4)* **NEW ART RIOT** [ ] [-]
– New art riot / Stip it down / Last exit on yesterday / Teenage 20-20. *(re-iss. Dec91, Jul93 + Sep96, 12"pink-ep/cd-ep; YUBB 4 P/CD)*

Heavenly / not iss.

Jan 91. (12"ep/cd-ep) *(HVN8 12/CD)* **MOTOWN JUNK. / SORROW 16 / WE HER MAJESTY'S PRISONERS** [92] [-]

May 91. (7") *(HVN 10)* **YOU LOVE US. / SPECTATORS OF SUICIDE** [62] [-]
(12"+=/cd-s+=) *(HVN 10 12/CD)* – Starlover / Strip it down (live).

Caff / not iss.

Jul 91. (7") *(CAFF 15)* **FEMININE IS BEAUTIFUL: NEW ART RIOT. / REPEAT AFTER ME** [ ] [-]

Columbia / Columbia

Jul 91. (7") *(657337-7)* **STAY BEAUTIFUL. / R.P. McMURPHY** [40] [ ]
(12"+=/12"w-poster/cd-s+=) *(657337-6/-8/-2)* – Soul contamination.
(US-cd-ep+=) – Motown junk / Sorrow 16 / Star lover.
(cd-ep re-iss. Sep97 on 'Epic' hit No.52; MANIC 1CD)

Nov 91. (7") *(657582-7)* **LOVE'S SWEET EXILE. / REPEAT** [26] [-]
(12"+=/cd-s+=) *(657582-6/-2)* – Democracy coma.
(12"ltd.++=) *(657582-8)* – Stay beautiful (live).
(cd-ep re-iss. Sep97 on 'Epic' hit No.55; MANIC 2CD)

Jan 92. (7"/c-s) *(657724-7/-4)* **YOU LOVE US. / A VISION OF DEAD DESIRE** [16] [-]
(12"+=) *(657724-6)* – It's so easy (live).
(cd-s++=) *(657724-2)* – We her majesty's prisoners.
(cd-ep re-iss. Sep97 on 'Epic' hit No.49; MANIC 3CD)

Feb 92. (pic-cd/cd/d-c/d-lp/pic-d-lp) *(471060-0/-2/-4/-1/-9)* *<52474>* **GENERATION TERRORISTS** [13] [ ]
– Slash 'n' burn / Nat West-Barclays-Midland-Lloyds / Born to end / Motorcycle emptiness / You love us / Love's sweet exile / Little baby nothing / Repeat (stars and stripes) / Tennessee / Another invented disease / Stay beautiful / So dead / Repeat (UK) / Spectators of suicide / Damn dog / Crucifix kiss / Methadone pretty / Condemned to rock'n'roll.

Mar 92. (7"/c-s) *(657873-7/-4)* **SLASH 'N' BURN. / AIN'T GOING DOWN** [20] [-]
(12"+=) *(657873-6)* – Motown junk.
(cd-s++=/gold-cd-s++=) *(657873-2/-0)* – ('A'version).
(cd-ep re-iss. Sep97 on 'Epic' hit No.54; MANIC 4CD)

Jun 92. (7"/c-s) *(658083-7/-4)* **MOTORCYCLE EMPTINESS. / BORED OUT OF MY MIND** [17] [-]
(12"pic-d+=) *(658083-8)* – Under my wheels.
(cd-s++=/s-cd-s++=) *(658083-2/-9)* – Crucifix kiss (live).
(cd-ep re-iss. Sep97 on 'Epic' hit No.41; MANIC 5CD)

Sep 92. (7"/cd-s) *(658382-7/-2)* **THEME FROM M.A.S.H. (SUICIDE IS PAINLESS). / ('b'side by 'Fatima Mansions' – Everything I Do (I Do It For You)** [7] [-]

Nov 92. (7") *(658796-7)* **LITTLE BABY NOTHING. / SUICIDE ALLEY** [29] [-]
(12"+=/cd-s+=) *(658796-6/-2)* – Yankee drawl / Never want again.
(cd-ep re-iss. Sep97 on 'Epic' hit No.50; MANIC 6CD)

Jun 93. (c-s) *(659337-4)* **FROM DESPAIR TO WHERE. / HIBERNATION** [25] [-]
(12"+=) *(659337-6)* – Spectators of suicide (Heavenly version).
(cd-s+=) *(659337-2)* – Star lover (Heavenly version).

Jun 93. (cd/c/lp/pic-lp) *(474064-2/-4/-1/-9)* *<57386>* **GOLD AGAINST THE SOUL** [8] [ ]
– Sleepflower / From despair to where / La tristesse durera (scream to a sigh) / Yourself / Life becoming a landslide / Drug drug druggy / Roses in the hospital / Nostalgic pushead / Symphony of tourette / Gold against the soul.

Jul 93. (7"/c-s) *(659477-7/-4)* **LA TRISTESSE DURERA (SCREAM TO A SIGH). / PATRICK BATEMAN** [22] [-]
(12"+=) *(659477-6)* – Repeat (live) / Tennessee.
(cd-s+=) *(659477-2)* – What's my name (live) / Slash'n'burn (live).

Sep 93. (7"/c-s) *(659727-7/-4)* **ROSES IN THE HOSPITAL. / US AGAINST YOU / DONKEY** [15] [-]
(cd-s+=) *(659727-2)* – Wrote for luck.
(12") *(659727-6)* – ('A'side) / (5-'A' mixes).

Epic / Epic

Feb 94. (c-s) *(660070-4)* **LIFE BECOMING A LANDSLIDE / COMFORT COMES** [36] [-]
(12"+=) *(660070-6)* – Are mothers saints.
(cd-s++=) *(660070-2)* – Charles Windsor.

Jun 94. (7"/c-s) *(660447-7/-4)* **FASTER. / P.C.P.** [16] [-]
(10"+=) *(660447-0)* – Sculpture of man.
(cd-s++=) *(660447-2)* – New art riot (in E-minor).

Aug 94. (10"/c-s) *(660686-0/-4)* **REVOL. / TOO COLD HERE** [22] [-]
(cd-s+=) *(660686-2)* – You love us (original Heavenly version) / Love's sweet exile (live).
(cd-s) *(660686-5)* – ('A'side) / (3 live at Glastonbury tracks).

— RICHEY booked himself into a health clinic, after wasting himself down to 5 stone.

Aug 94. (cd/c/pic-lp) *(477421-2/-4/-0)* *<66967>* **THE HOLY BIBLE** [6] [ ]
– Yes / Ifwhiteamericatoldthetruthforonedayit'sworldwouldfallapart / Of walking abortion / She is suffering / Archives of pain / Revol / 4st 7lb / Mausoleum / Faster / This is yesterday / Die in the summertime / The intense humming of evil / P.C.P.

Oct 94. (10"/c-s) *(660895-0/-4)* **SHE IS SUFFERING. / LOVE TORN US UNDER (acoustic)** [25] [-]
(cd-s+=) *(660895-2)* – The drowners / Stay with me (both live w/ BERNARD BUTLER).
(cd-s) *(660895-5)* – ('A'side) / La tristesse durera (scream to a sigh) / Faster (Dust Brothers remixes).

— RICHEY was now fully recuperated . . . but on 1st Feb '95, he went AWOL again after walking out of London's Embassy Hotel at 7 that morning. Two weeks later, his car was found abandoned and after police frog search the Severn, it was believed he might be dead. By the end of 1995, with RICHEY still missing, the group carried on as a trio.

— Meanwhile, BRADFIELD produced the debut of NORTHERN UPROAR.

Apr 96. (c-s) *(663070-4)* **A DESIGN FOR LIFE / BRIGHT EYES (live)** [2] [-]
(cd-s) *(663070-2)* – ('A'side) / Mr Carbohydrate / Dead passive / Dead trees and traffic islands.
(cd-s) *(663070-5)* – ('A'side) / ('A'-Howard Grey remix) / ('A'-Apollo 440 remix) / Faster (Chemical Brothers remix).

May 96. (cd/c/lp) *(483930-2/-4/-1)* *<67709>* **EVERYTHING MUST GO** [2] [ ]
– Elvis impersonator: Blackpoool pier / A design for life / Kevin Carter / Enola – alone / Everything must go / Small black flowers that grow in the sky / The girl who wanted to be God / Removables / Australia / Interiors (song for Willem De Kooning) / Further away / No surface at all.

Jul 96. (c-s) *(663468-4)* **EVERYTHING MUST GO / RAINDROPS KEEP FALLING ON MY HEAD (live)** [5] [-]
(cd-s) *(663468-2)* – ('A'side) / Hanging on / Black garden / No-one knows what it's like to be me.
(cd-s) *(663468-5)* – ('A'side) / ('A'-Stealth Sonic Orchestra remix) / ('A'-Chemical Brothers remix).

Sep 96. (c-s) *(663775-4)* **KEVIN CARTER / EVERYTHING MUST GO (acoustic)** [9] [-]
(cd-s) *(663775-2)* – ('A'side) / Horses under starlight / Sepia / First republic.
(cd-s) *(663775-5)* – Kevin Carter busts loose (Jon Carter remix) / ('A'-Stealth Sonic Orchestra mixes).

Dec 96. (c-s) *(664044-4)* **AUSTRALIA / A DESIGN FOR LIFE (live)** [7] [-]
(cd-s) *(664044-2)* – ('A'side) / Velocity girl / Take the skinheads bowling / I can't take my eyes off you (acoustic).
(cd-s) *(664044-5)* – ('A'side) / ('A'-Lionrock remix) / Motorcycle emptiness (Stealth Sonic Orchestra version).

Epic / Imprint

Aug 98. (c-s) *(666345-4)* **IF YOU TOLERATE THIS YOUR CHILDREN WILL BE NEXT / KEVIN CARTER (live)** [1] [-]
(cd-s) *(666345-2)* – ('A'side) / Prologue to history / Montana Autumn '78.
(cd-s) *(666345-5)* – ('A'side) / ('A'-Massive Attack remix) / ('A'-The Class Reunion Of The Sunset Marquis mix; aka David Holmes).

Sep 98. (cd/c/lp) *(491703-2/-4/-1)* *<111820>* **THIS IS MY TRUTH TELL ME YOURS** [1] [ ]
– The everlasting / If you tolerate this your children will be next / You stole the sun from my heart / Ready for drowning / Tsunami / My little empire / I'm not working / You're tender and you're tired / Born a girl / Be natural / Black dog on my shoulder / Nobody loved you / S.Y.M.M.

Nov 98. (c-s) *(666686-4)* **THE EVERLASTING / SMALL BLACK FLOWERS THAT GROW IN THE SUN (live at Nunex)** [11] [ ]
(cd-s) *(666686-2)* – ('A'side) / Blackholes for the young / Valley boy.
(cd-s) *(666686-5)* – ('A'extended) / ('A'-Deadly Avenger's Psalm 315) / ('A'-Stealth Sonic Orchestra mix).

Barbara MANNING

Born: San Diego, California, USA. Beginning her career with local folk-rock act, 28TH DAY (who also comprised COLE MARQUIS and MIKE CLOWARD), MANNING recorded a solitary eponymous mini-set in 1985 before embarking on a solo career. Subsequently basing herself in San Francisco, the singer/songwriter/guitarist cut two albums worth of her own material, 'LATELY I KEEP SCISSORS' (1989) and 'ONE PERFECT GREEN PLANET' (1991). The former found MANNING backed by the WORLD OF POOH (featuring ex-CAT HEADS member, MELANIE CLARIN and KIM OSTERWALD) while the latter saw her working with the TABLESPOONS, an act that numbered MICHELLE CERNUTO and LINCOLN ALLEN alongside two future members (the aforementioned MELANIE and KIM), of her soon-to-be-formed outfit, S.F. SEALS. Still based in the Bay Area, the experimental, retro-pop influenced trio signed to hip US indie label, 'Matador', debuting late in 1993 with a homage to three of their World Series heroes in the shape of the 'BASEBALL TRILOGY' EP. The band (with additional personnel including MARGARET MURRAY and BENTLEY PUSSER) went on to record two full sets, 'NOWHERE' (1994) and 'TRUTH WALKS IN SLEEPY SHADOWS' (1995), while MANNING herself found time to fit in another solo album, ' . . . SINGS WITH THE ORIGINAL ARTISTS' (1995), a collaborative effort with English post-punk stalwarts, The MEKONS. A few years later, the indie-roots maverick returned with a surprisingly strong set of songs in '1212' (1997).

Album rating: LATELY I KEEP SCISSORS (*6) / ONE PERFECT GREEN PLANET compilation (*6) / . . . SINGS WITH THE ORIGINAL ARTISTS (*5) / 1212 (*7) / 28th Day: 28th DAY mini (*5) / S.F. Seals: NOWHERE (*6) / TRUTH WALKS IN SLEEPY SHADOWS (*6)

28th DAY

BARBARA MANNING – vocals, guitar / **COLE MARQUIS** – guitar / **MIKE CLOWARD** – drums

not iss. / Enigma

1985. (m-lp/m-c) *<72047-1/-4>* **28th DAY** [-] [ ]
(cd-iss. 1990's on 'Skyclad'; 128>

— MANNING and CLOWARD split up, with the latter and MARQUIS forming SUN BIRDS. MARQUIS subsequently joined The DOWNSIDERS and later the SNOWMEN.

BARBARA MANNING

- vocals, guitar, cello, bass / with **BRANDON KEARNEY** – clarinet / also her band **WORLD OF POOH**

Heyday / Heyday

May 89. (lp) *<(HEY 002)>* **LATELY I KEEP SCISSORS** [ ] [ ] Nov88

— now with her group the **TABLESPOONS** including **KIM OSTERWALD + MELANIE CLARIN + MICHELLE CERNUTO + LINCOLN ALLEN**

Sep 91. (cd/c/lp) *<(HEY 018 CD/CS/LP)>* **ONE PERFECT GREEN PLANET** (compilation) [ ] [ ]

– Straw man / Smoking her wings / Don't rewind / Sympathy wreath / Green / Lock yer room (uptight) / Someone wants you dead / Sympathy wreath (reprise) / Scissors / Breathe lies / Somewhere soon / Talk all night / Make it go away / Never park / Every pretty girl / Mark E. Smith and Brix / Something you've got (isn't good) / Prophecy written. *(cd re-iss. Mar94 on 'Normal'; NORMAL 138CD)*

— In 1993, BARBARA augmented STUART MOXHAM & THE ORIGINAL ARTISTS (aka The MEKONS) on an album, 'SIGNAL PATH'.

S.F. SEALS

— **BARBARA MANNING** with **MELANIE CLARIN** – drums, accordion, vocals / **KIM OSTERWALD** – cello / also with 4th member **MARGARET MURRAY** – bass (ex-U.S. SAUCER) / toured with **CHRIS MILNER** – bass (of MOLECULES) / **JAY PAGE** – drums

Matador / Matador

1993. (7") **NOWHERICA. / BEING CHEATED** [ ] [-]

Dec 93. (7"ep/cd-ep) *<OLE 064-7/-2>* **BASEBALL TRILOGY** [ ] [ ]
– Joltin' Joe DiMaggio / The ballad of Denny McLain / Dock Ellis.

— added 5th member **BRENTLY PUSSER** – guitar (of 3-DAY STUBBLE)

May 94. (7") *<OLE 088-7>* **STILL? / DON'T UNDERESTIMATE ME** [ ] [ ]

Jun 94. (cd/lp) *<OLE 089-2/-1>* **NOWHERE** [ ] [ ]
– Back again / Don't underestimate me / 8's / Janine's dream / Still / Day 12 / Winter song / Baby blue / Demons on the corner / Missing.

Sep 95. (cd/lp) *<OLE 162-2/-1>* **TRUTH WALKS IN SLEEPY SHADOWS** [ ] [ ]
– S.F. Sorrow / Ladies of the sea / Ipecac / Locked out / Bold letters / Flashback Caruso / Pulp / Soul of Patrick Lee / Kid's pirate ship / How did you know / Stellar lullabye.

Nov 95. (7") *<OLE 176-7>* **IPECAC. / HOW DID YOU KNOW** [ ] [ ]

BARBARA MANNING

— with The MEKONS, etc

not iss. / Feel Good All Over

1995. (cd) <7001> **BARBARA MANNING SINGS WITH THE ORIGINAL ARTISTS** [-] [ ]
– My first gun / Gold brick / When I dream / Here comes love / Daddy bully / Untitled #2 / Optimism is it's own reward / Martian man / Big eye / Cry me a river / You were the one.

— with **JIM O'ROURKE, JOHN CONVERTINO, JOEY BURNS, CRAIG SCHUMACHER**

Matador / Matador

Jun 97. (cd/d-lp) *<OLE 221-2/-1>* **1212** [ ] [ ]
– Arsonist story: Fireman – Evil plays piano – Evil craves attention – Trapped and drowning / End of the rainbow / Blood of feeling / Rickity tikity tin / Stain on the sun / Isn't lovely lovely? / That kid / First line (seven the row) / Marcus Leid / Stammtisch.

Roger MANNING (see under ⇒ JELLYFISH)

MANSUN

Formed: Chester, England . . . 1995 originally as MANSON, by songwriter PAUL DRAPER, DOMINIC CHAD, STOVE, THE HIB and MARK STENT. After one single under this moniker ('TAKE IT EASY CHICKEN'), they caused a minor rumpus with the legal team of notorious killer CHARLES MANSON. The band claimed their name was taken from a VERVE b-side, 'A MAN CALLED SUN', deliberately slightly altering it to avoid court action. With name change now complete, they issued their follow-up, 'SKIN UP PIN UP'. A month later with the help of A&R man, Keith Wozencroft, they were part of Parlophone's enviable roster. Their blend of melodic, alternative rock, was described as a 90's indie update of TEARS FOR FEARS. Two UK Top 40 hits appeared as the EP's, 'ONE' & 'TWO' in 1996, paving the way for further successes, 'STRIPPER VICAR' and 'WIDE OPEN SPACE'. The year 1997, began on a high note with a Top 10 hit, the charmingly titled 'SHE MAKES MY NOSE BLEED' and a No.1 album, 'ATTACK OF THE GREY LANTERN'. Ambitious in its stylistic diversity, it contained additional Top 20 hits, 'TAXLO$$' and 'CLOSED FOR BUSINESS'. In the summer of '98, MANSUN were back in the hit parade with two EP's, 'LEGACY' (their eighth in the series) and 'NINE' (leading in with 'BEING A GIRL'), both taken from their pseudo-concept follow-up album, 'SIX', which, spookily enough, reached the same number in the charts. • **Covers:** RAILINGS (Howard Devoto). Everyone Must Win was co-written with the ex-MAGAZINE frontman.

Album rating: ATTACK OF THE GREY LANTERN (*8) / SIX (*7)

PAUL DRAPER – vocals, guitars, piano, synthesizer / **DOMINIC CHAD** – lead guitar, piano, vocals, synthesizer / **STOVE KING** – bass / **THE HIB** – drums / **MARK 'SPIKE' STENT** – beatbox

Regal / not iss.

Sep 95. (7"; as MANSON) *(REG 2)* **TAKE IT EASY CHICKEN. / ('A'version)** [ ] [-]
(above also issued on own 'Sci Fi Hi Fi' label; MANSON 1)

Nov 95. (7"white) *(REG 3)* **SKIN UP PIN UP. / FLOURELLA** [ ] [-]
(cd-s+=) *(REG 3CD)* – Take it easy chicken.

— early '96, MARK suddenly departed

Parlophone / Sony

Mar 96. (cd-ep/c-ep/7"ep) *(CDRS/TCR/R 6430)* **MANSUN – ONE** [37] [-]
– Egg shaped Fred / Ski jump nose / Lemonade secret drinker / Thief.

Jun 96. (cd-ep/c-ep/7"ep) *(CD/TC+/R 6437)* **MANSUN – TWO** [32] [-]
– Take it easy chicken / Drastic sturgeon / The greatest pain / Moronica.

— lost another member when THE HIB quit

— **ANDIE RATHBONE** – drums; repl. temp. JULIAN (ex-KINKY MACHINE)

Sep 96. (7"clear) *(R 6447)* **STRIPPER VICAR. / NO ONE KNOWS US** [19] [-]
(cd-ep+=) *(CDR 6447)* **THREE EP** – An open letter to the lyrical trainspotter / Things keep falling off buildings.
(cd-ep) *(CDRS 6447)* **THREE EP** – ('A'side) / The edge / Duchess.

Nov 96. (7"white) *(R 6453)* **WIDE OPEN SPACE. / REBEL WITHOUT A QUILT** [15] [-]
(cd-s+=) *(CDR 6453)* **FOUR EP** – Vision impaired / Skin up pin up.
(cd-s) *(CDRS 6453)* **FOUR EP** – ('A'side) / The gods of not very much / Moronica (acoustic) / Lemonade secret drinker (acoustic).

Feb 97. (7"red) *(R 6458)* **SHE MAKES MY NOSE BLEED. / THE HOLY BLOOD AND THE HOLY GRAIL** [9] [-]
(cd-s+=) *(CDRS 6458)* **FIVE EP** – Live open space / Drastic sturgeon (live).
(cd-s) *(CDR 6458)* **FIVE EP** – ('A'side) / The most to gain / Flourella / ('A'acoustic).

Feb 97. (cd/c/d-lp) *(CD/TC+PCS 3787)* *<67935>* **ATTACK OF THE GREY LANTERN** [1] [ ]
– The Chad who loved me / Mansun's only love song / Taxloss / You, who do you hate? / Wide open space / Stripper vicar / Disgusting / She makes my nose bleed / Naked twister / Egg shaped Fred / Dark Mavis.

May 97. (cd-ep) *(CDR 6465)* **SIX EP** [15] [-]
– Taxloss / Grey lantern / Taxloss (Lisa Marie Experience remix).
(cd-ep) *(CDRS 6465)* – ('A'side) / The impending collapse od it all / Ski jump nose (live) / Wide open space (acoustic).
(12"ep) *(12R 6465)* – ('A'mixes:- John '00' Fleming remix / album version / Slam remix / Gaudi remix).

Oct 97. (7"clear) *(R 6482)* **CLOSED FOR BUSINESS. / EGG SHAPED FRED (acoustic)** [10] [-]
(cd-s) *(CDR 6482)* **SEVEN EP** – ('A'side) / K.I.Double.S.I.N.G. / Everyone must win / The world's still open.
(cd-s) *(CDRS 6482)* **SEVEN EP** – ('A'side) / Dark Mavis (acoustic) / Stripper vicar (live) / Taxloss (video for PC or Mac).

Jun 98. (c-ep) *(TCR 6497)* *<57396>* **LEGACY EP (EIGHT EP)** [7] [ ] Aug98
– Legacy / Wide open space (the Perfecto remix) / The acoustic collapse of it all / Ski jump nose (acoustic).
(cd-ep) *(CDR 6497)* – ('A'side) / Wide open space (the Perfecto remix) / GSOH / Face in the crowd.
(cd-ep) *(CDRS 6497)* – ('A'side) / Can't afford to die / Spasm of identity / Check under the bed.

Aug 98. (c-ep) *(TCR 6503)* **NINE EP** [13] [-]
– Being a girl (part 1) / Wide open space (Trouse Enthusiasts mix) / Mansun's only acoustic song.
(cd-ep) *(CDR 6503)* – ('A'side) / Railings / Been here before.
(cd-ep) *(CDRS 6503)* – ('A'side) / Hideout / Wide open space (Trouser Enthusiasts mix).

Sep 98. (cd/c/d-lp) *(96723-2/-4/-1)* *<69748>* **SIX** [6] [ ] Apr99
– (Part one):- Six / Negative / Shotgun / Inverse Midas / Anti-everything / Fall out / Serotonin / Cancer / (interlude) / Witness to a murder (part two) / (Part two):- Television / Special – Blown it (delete as appropriate) / Legacy / Being a girl.

Oct 98. (7") *(R 6508)* **NEGATIVE. / MANSUN'S ONLY LIVE SONG** [27] [-]
(cd-s) *(CDR 6508)* – ('A'side) / I deserve what I get / Take it easy chicken (live).
(cd-s) *(CDRS 6508)* – ('A'side) / When the wind blows / King of beauty.

MANTARAY

Formed: Braintree, Essex, England . . . 1993 by the trio of frontmouth, CHRIS LATTER, bassist DAVE STANDEN and drummer SIMON. Despite vociferously denying any association with the New Wave Of New Wave scene, MANTARAY made their debut on 'Fierce Panda's celebrated 'Shagging In The Streets' EP back to back with THESE ANIMAL MEN and S*M*A*S*H. Soon making a name for themselves in the press with their rent-a-quote opinions, The JAM-loving neo-Mod throwbacks subsequently signed to the 'Dead Dead Good' label, debuting in late '94 with a couple of singles, 'INSOMNIAC'S DREAM' and ADORATION'. Dismissing mainstream party politics, the power Brit-pop trio instead took a more individualistic lyrical stance which nevertheless failed to mask the average quality of the songwriting on debut album, 'SOME POP' (1994). Only two further singles surfaced in as many years before MANTARAY signed a major record deal with 'Fontana', only to let down both fans and critics alike with comeback single, 'KNOW WHERE TO FIND YOU' and follow-up album, 'THE REDS AND THE BLUES' (1997). • **Note:** A different MANTARAY released the 'Numinous Island' CD for 'Silent' in October '95 (SR 9592CD).

Album rating: SOME POP (*5) / THE REDS AND THE BLUES (*4)

CHRIS LATTER – vocals, guitar / **DAVE STANDEN** – bass / **SIMON** – drums

Dead Dead Good / not iss.

Sep 94. (7") *(GOOD 25)* **INSOMNIAC'S DREAM. / HARD SELF CENTRE** [ ] [-]
(cd-s+=) *(GOOD 25CD)* –

Oct 94. (7") *(GOOD 26)* **ADORATION. /** [ ] [-]
(cd-s+=) *(GOOD 26CD)* –

Nov 94. (cd/c) *(GOOD CD/MC 3)* **SOME POP** [ ] [-]

Feb 95. (7") *(GOOD 30)* **HIDE & SEEK. /** [ ] [-]
(cd-s+=) *(GOOD 30CD)* –

Apr 96. (7") *(GOOD 36)* **I DON'T MAKE PROMISES. /** [ ] [-]
(cd-s+=) *(GOOD 36CD)* –

Fontana / not iss.

Feb 97. (7") *(MAN 1)* **KNOW WHERE TO FIND YOU. / TIME WITH THE ANGELS** [ ] [-]
(cd-s+=) *(MANCD 1)* – Unstuck.

May 97. (7") *(MAN 2)* **PATIENT MAN. / TRUST TO FATE** [ ] [-]
(cd-s+=) *(MANCD 2)* – Full circle.
(cd-s) *(MANDD 2)* – ('A'side) / I know you too well / Pollen.

May 97. (cd/c) *(534205-2/-4)* **THE REDS AND THE BLUES** [ ] [-]
– Know where to find you / I don't make promises / Always tomorrow / Look after myself / Just a ride / Something special / Everybody looks the same / Rise

above it all / Blackburn / Behind the clouds / Patient man / Don't believe in me.

MARCH VIOLETS

Formed: Leeds, England . . . late 1981 by SIMON DENBIGH and LOZ ELLIOT. Featuring a line-up completed by guitarist HUGH and secondary vocalist, ROSIE GARLAND, this fledgling goth outfit emerged from the same scene that spawned The SISTERS OF MERCY, releasing the cheesy 'RELIGIOUS AS HELL' as their debut single on the latter outfit's 'Merciful Release' imprint in summer '82. Like the SISTERS, they also powered their rhythm section with a tinny drum machine for that quintessential 80's sound. After a further single, 'GROOVING ON GREEN', the band signed to the 'Rebirth' label, subsequently bringing in TOM ASHTON as a replacement for HUGH. This served to bolster the sound and by the release of early '84's classy 'SNAKE DANCE', the band had progressed to a kind of CULT-esque groove with GARLAND providing far more effective backing vocals. Later that year, the 'NATURAL HISTORY' compilation collected together the cream of the band's work to date although the departure of founding member DENBIGH (to form The BATFISH BOYS) reduced The MARCH VIOLETS to a trio of newcomer CLEO MURRAY, ELLIOT and ASHTON. Fresh material finally surfaced in the shape of Spring '85's 'DEEP' single and its 1986 follow-up, 'TURN TO THE SKY', although unlike their more famous contemporaries, the MARCH VIOLETS failed to effect a major critical and commercial coup.

Album rating: NATURAL HISTORY compilation (*6)

SIMON DENBIGH – vocals / **LOZ ELLIOTT** – bass / **HUGH** – guitar / **ROSIE GARLAND** – vocals

Merciful Release / not iss.

Aug 82. (7"ep) *(MR 013)* **RELIGIOUS AS HELL / FODDER. / CHILDREN ON STUN / BON BON BABIES** -

Nov 82. (7") *(MR 017)* **GROOVING IN GREEN. / STREAM** -

Rebirth / Relativity

May 83. (7") *(RB 18)* **CROW BABY. / ONE TWO I LOVE YOU** -
(12"=Mar85+=) *(RB 18-12)* – Long pig / Crow bait.

— **TOM ASHTON** – guitar; repl. HUGH

Jan 84. (7") *(RB 21)* **SNAKE DANCE. / SLOW DRIP LIZARD** -
(12"+=) *(RB 21-12)* – It's hot / ('A'extended).

May 84. (7") *(RB 23)* **RESPECTABLE. / MICROWAVES** -

Jul 84. (7") *(VRB 24)* **WALK IN THE SUN. / LIGHTS GO OUT** -
(12"+=) *(VRB 24-12)* – Essence.

Oct 84. (lp) *(VRB 25)* **NATURAL HISTORY** (compilation) -

— now without ROSIE + SIMON D (the latter formed the BATFISH BOYS)

— Autumn '84, both were repl. by **CLEO** – vocals

— late '84 – briefly added **TRAVIS** – drums to repl. drum machine

— now a trio of **CLEO + TOM + LOZ**

Apr 85. (7") *(VRB 26)* **DEEP. / ELDORADO** -
(12"+=) *(VRB 26-12)* – Electric shades.

1985. (lp) **ELECTRIC SHADES** -

Feb 86. (7") *(VRB 27)* **TURN TO THE SKY. / NEVER LOOK** -
(12"+=) *(VRBX 27)* – Deep (deeper mix).

— split after their latest failure

- compilations, etc. -

Sep 93. (cd) *Jungle; (FREUDCD 42) / Cleopatra; <1030>* **THE BOTANIC VERSES** Feb94
– Snake dance (extended) / Walk into the sun / Slow drip lizard / The lights go out / Essence / Crow baby / 1 2 I love you / Grooving in green / It's hot / Long pig / Steam / Fodder / Radiant boys / Bob bon babies / Religious as hell / Children on stun / Crow bait / Snake dance.

MARINE GIRLS

Formed: Hatfield, Hertfordshire, England . . . 1980 by TRACEY THORN, alongside sisters ALICE and JANE FOX. This quirky but charming post-New Wave trio issued their first official release in 1981, the cassette-only '(BEACH PARTY – Catch The Cod)'. Subsequently re-issued on vinyl by TV PERSONALITY, DAN TREACY's 'Whaam!' imprint, the album showcased the girls' YOUNG MARBLE GIANTS-esque, cheap but effective pop minimalism with TRACEY THORN's sultry vocal rapidly blossoming among the mainly ALICE FOX-led 2-minutes tales of lovelorn angst. THORN, however, was to take the lead vocals on their debut single, 'ON MY MIND', its child-like simplicity no doubt persuading 'Cherry Red' to net their signatures. Having re-released the single and given THORN a solo shot ('A Distant Shore' mini-set), the MARINE GIRLS finally began making waves with the more widely distributed follow-up lp, 'LAZY WAYS', early in '83. However, by this time, TRACEY had met her beau, BEN WATT, at Hull University, the pair releasing their first joint recording, Cole Porter's 'NIGHT AND DAY' as EVERYTHING BUT THE GIRL in summer '83. Inevitably, THORN found it increasingly difficult to juggle two/three careers and opted to part ways with the FOX sisters later that year. JANE, too, was attempting to balance group and solo commitments, having already released the summer single, 'IT'S A FINE DAY', a starkly atmospheric, acappella gem which was radically overhauled by OPUS III for a massive disco hit nine years later. JANE subsequently found her "Ben Watt" in rhythm man, BARTON, the partnership extended to a mini-set, 'JANE AND BARTON' (1983). The following year, the dreamy singer was re-united with ALICE in another maritimed-themed outfit, GRAB GRAB THE HADDOCK, although they only surfaced for a couple of 45's.

Album rating: BEACH PARTY (*6) / LAZY WAYS (*6) / Jane And Barton: JANE AND BARTON mini (*4)

ALICE FOX (b.1966) – vocals / **TRACEY THORN** (b.26 Sep'62) – guitar, vocals / **JANE FOX** (b.1963) – bass

In-Phaze / not iss.

1980. (ltd-c; various) *(Tapes 001)* **A DAY BY THE SEA** -

1981. (c) *(Tapes 002)* **(BEACH PARTY – Catch The Cod)** -
– In love / Fridays / Tonight / Times we used to spend / Honey / Flying over Russia / Tuti lo sanno / Dishonesty / Promises / Silent red / He got the girl / All dressed up / Holiday song / Day-night dream / 20,000 leagues / Marine girls. *(lp-iss.Dec81 on 'Whaam!-InPhaze'; COD 1) (re-iss. lp Apr87 on 'Cherry Red'; BRED 75)*

Mar 82. (7") *(COD 2)* **ON MY MIND. / THE LURE OF THE ROCKPOOLS** -
(re-iss. May82 on 'Cherry Red'; CHERRY 40)

Cherry Red / not iss.

Jan 83. (7") *(CHERRY 54)* **DON'T COME BACK. / YOU MUST BE MAD** -

Mar 83. (lp) *(BRED 44)* **LAZY WAYS** -
– A place in the sun / Leave me with the boy / Falling again / Love to know / A different light / Sunshine blue / Second sight / Don't come back / That fink, jazz-me-blues boy / Fever / Shell island / Lazy ways / Such a thing / You must be mad. *(cd/c iss.Aug88 w/ BEACH PARTY; CD/C MRED 44)*

— TRACEY had already gone solo and formed EVERYTHING BUT THE GIRL with BEN WATT

JANE

— augmented by **BARTON** on rhythm

May 83. (7") *(CHERRY 65)* **IT'S A FINE DAY. / OF ALL / LEAVES WERE FALLING** -
(cd-s iss.Jul93; CDCHERRY 65)

Sep 83. (7"; by JANE & BARTON) *(CHERRY 69)* **I WANT TO BE WITH YOU. / ('A'version)** -

Sep 83. (m-lp; by JANE & BARTON) *(MRED 53)* **JANE & BARTON** -
– There is a man / It's a fine day / You are over there (part 1) / I want to be with you / You are over there (part 2) / Ha bloody ha.

GRAB GRAB THE HADDOCK

— **ALICE + JANE** plus **LESTER NOEL** – guitar + **STEVEN GOLLOWAY** – drums

Sep 84. (12") *(12CHERRY 83)* **I'M USED NOW. / NOTHING TO SAY** -

Apr 85. (7"ep/12"ep) *(CHERRY/12CHERRY 86)* **THE LAST FOND GOODBYE / ONE BUT SMILING. / FOR ALL WE KNOW / THAT BIG WORD BUT** -

— the sisters & co. retired from the music biz

MARION

Formed: Macclesfield, Manchester, England . . . 1992 by JAIME HARDING, TONY GRANTHAM and PHIL CUNNINGHAM, who had been together in numerous teenage bands since the mid-80's. Beefing up the sound with the rhythm section of JULIAN PHILLIPS and MURAD MOUSSA, MARION issued a one-off 1994 debut, 'VIOLENT MEN', for 'Rough Trade'. This led to 'London' records taking over the reins, the group going from strength to strength throughout '95 and the STEPHEN STREET/AL CLAY – produced album, 'THIS WORLD AND BODY' scraping into the UK Top 10. Trawling the same sub-SMITHS territory as the likes of GENE, HARDING and Co. enjoyed a brief period of singles success culminating in the UK Top 20 re-issue of 'SLEEP' zzz . . . However, JAIME's heroin and cocaine habit took its toll, the band's lengthy hiatus resulted in the difficult second album syndrome, in that of 'THE PROGRAM' (1998), selling poorly.

Album rating: THIS WORLD AND BODY (*6)

JAIME HARDING (b.1975) – vocals, harmonica / **TONY GRANTHAM** – guitar, piano / **PHIL CUNNINGHAM** – guitar / **JULIAN PHILLIPS** – bass / **MURAD MOUSSA** – drums, percussion

Rough Trade / not iss.

May 94. (7") *(RT 319-7)* **VIOLENT MEN. / TOYS FOR BOYS** -
(cd-s+=) *(RT 319-3)* – Today and tonight.

London / Polygram

Feb 95. (7") *(LON 360)* **SLEEP./ FATHER'S DAY** 53 -
(12"+=/cd-s+=) *(LON X/CD 360)* – Moving fast.

Apr 95. (7"/c-s) *(LON 366)* **TOYS FOR BOYS. / DOWN THE MIDDLE WITH YOU** 57 -
(cd-s+=) *(LONCD 366)* – Changed for the same.

— **NICK GILBERT** – bass repl.PHILLIPS who joined ELECTRAFIXION

Oct 95. (7"yellow/c-s) *(LON 371)* **LET'S ALL GO TOGETHER. / LATE GATE SHOW** 37 -
(cd-s+=) *(LONCD 371)* – The only way (live).

Jan 96. (7"/c-s) *(LON/+CS 377)* **TIME. / CHANCE** 29 -
(cd-s+=) *(LONCD 377)* – Let's all go together.

Jan 96. (cd/c/lp) *(<828695-2/-4/-1>)* **THIS WORLD AND BODY** 10
– Fallen through / Sleep / Let's all go together / Wait / The only way / I stopped dancing / All for love / Toys for boys / Time / Vanessa / Your body lies / My children. *(lp w/ free 7")*– VIOLENT MEN

Mar 96. (7"/c-s) *(LON/+CS 381)* **SLEEP (remix). / VIOLENT MEN** 17 -
(cd-ep) *(LONCD 381)* – ('A'acoustic) / Wait (acoustic) / Time (acoustic).

Feb 98. (7") *(LON 403)* **MIYAKO HIDEAWAY. /** [45] [-]
(cd-s+=) *(LOCDP 403)* –
(cd-s) *(LONCD 403)* –
Apr 98. (7") *(LON 409)* **SPARKLE. / PRESENT** [ ] [-]
(cd-s+=) *(LONCD 409)* – Journey to the centre / Miyako hideaway.
(cd-s) *(LONDP 409)* – ('A'side) / Psycho killer / Our place.
Aug 98. (cd/c) *(828994-2/-4)* **THE PROGRAM** [ ] [-]

MARS

Formed: New York, USA . . . 1977 by DON BURG, SUMNER CRANE, NANCY ARLEN and MARK CUNNINGHAM. The following year, the quartet made it onto vinyl with a four track contribution ('PUERTO RICAN GHOST', 'HELEN FORDSADALE', 'TUNNEL' and 'HAIRWAVES') to the BRIAN ENO-produced V/A set, 'No New York' alongside fellow No Wavers, TEENAGE JESUS & THE JERKS, The CONTORTIONS and DNA. 1978 also saw the band record a debut single in their own right, '3E', released on the 'Ze' label (then home of SUICIDE) as well as an eponymous EP. By the time of the latter's belated release in 1980, MARS had already entered the black hole of music business oblivion, the various space cadets engaging in their own solar missions; BURG and CUNNINGHAM resurfaced in the band, DON KING, alongside DUNCAN LINDSAY. The latter and his brother, ARTO, together with three MARS originals (NANCY wasn't involved) and DNA's IKUE MORI released a critically savaged reworking of the famous opera, 'Don Giovanni', released in 1981 as 'JOHN GAVANTI'.

Album rating: 78 compilation (*6) / JOHN GAVANTI (*2)

DON BURG – vocals, guitar / **SUMNER CRANE** – vocals, guitar / **MARK CUNNINGHAM** – vocals, bass / **NANCY ARLEN** – drums

not iss. / Ze
1978. (12") *<ZE12 010>* **3E. / 11,000 VOLTS** [-] [ ]
not iss. / Lust-Unlust
Jun 80. (12"ep) *<JMB 232>* **MARS** (rec.1978) [-] [ ]
– N.N. end / Scorn / Outside Africa / Monopoly / The immediate stages of the erotic.

— had already split; BURG and CUNNINGHAM forming DON KING with DUNCAN LINDSAY (brother of ARTO). All three (and ARTO) with CRANE and IKUE MORI (of DNA) re-worked DON GIOVANNI below

not iss. / Hyrax
Jan 81. (lp) *<HY 101>* **JOHN GAVANTI** [-] [ ]

– compilation, etc. –

Dec 86. (lp) *Widowspeak; <(WSP 10)>* **78** [ ] [ ]
– 3-E / 11,000 volts / Tunnel / Helen Forsdale / Puero Rican ghost / Immediate stages of the erotic / Monopoly / Cats / Cairo / Hairwaves / Outside Africa. *(cd-iss. 1996 on 'Atavistic'; 48)*
Apr 90. (lp) *Danceteria; <(DANLP 360)>* **VENUS FLY TRAP** [ ] [ ]
Mar 94. (cd) *Semantic; (CDSA 54025)* **MARS LIVE (live)** [ ] [ ]

Chris MARS (see under ⇒ REPLACEMENTS)

MARTHA & THE MUFFINS

Formed: Toronto, Canada . . . late '77 by ex-CADS organist, MARTHA JOHNSON (one single, 'DO THE CRABWALK'), alongside CARL FINKLE, MARK GANE, TIM GANE and ANDY HAAS; MARTHA LADLY was soon added. A Canadian-only debut single, 'INSECT LOVE', appeared in 1978, the track introduced to the British market a year later via a deal with Virgin subsidiary, 'Dindisc'. Its follow-up, the infectious 'ECHO BEACH', struck a chord in the collective post-New Wave consciousness and heralded a new era of futuristic 80's style pop, the MARK GANE-penned classic climbing into the UK Top 10. Unfortunately, their accompanying album, 'METRO MUSIC' (1980), received mixed reviews and was unable to sustain its Top 40 chart run as a further single, 'SAIGON', failed miserably. Seemingly not concerned with saturating the market for want of another hit, MARTHA & THE MUFFINS tried to shake off the one-hit wonder tag with another two flop singles and an equally unsuccessful second album, 'TRANCE AND DANCE', all in the same year. By the time they returned to the studio, only one MARTHA remained as LADLY first opted for a one-off solo career then went on to join The ASSOCIATES. FINKLE had also bailed out, the remaining members bringing in then unknown producer, DANIEL LANOIS, in a dual capacity on their third set, 'THIS IS THE ICE AGE' (1981). With LANOIS' sister, JOCELYN, now in tow, the group moved in an increasingly Euro-pop direction, the result being a German-only release for their 1983 set, 'DANSEPARC'. The following year, MARK GANE and MARTHA JOHNSON sweetened their moniker by slimming it down to M + M, the revamp initially paying off with a transatlantic Top 75 dancefloor hit, 'BLACK STATIONS – WHITE STATIONS'. However, the failure of two albums, 'MYSTERY WALK' (1984) and 'THE WORLD IS A BALL' (1985), led to the outfit taking several years out during which they dabbled in soundtrack work.

Album rating: FARAWAY IN TIME compilation (*5)

MARTHA JOHNSON – vocals, keyboards / **MARK GANE** – guitar / **ANDY HAAS** – saxophone / **CARL FINKLE** – bass / **TIM GANE** – drums / **MARTHA LADLY** – keyboards, trombone, vocals

not iss. / M+M
Jun 78. (7") *<MM 001>* **INSECT LOVE. / SUBURBAN DREAM** [-] [-] Canada

Dindisc / Virgin
Oct 79. (7") *(DIN 4)* **INSECT LOVE. / CHEESIES AND GUM** [ ] [-]
Feb 80. (7") *(DIN 9)* **ECHO BEACH. / TEDDY THE DINK** [10] [ ]
Mar 80. (lp) *(DID 1) <13145>* **METRO MUSIC** [34] [ ] Aug80
– Echo beach / Paint by number heart / Saigon / Indecision / Terminal twilight / Hide and seek / Monotone / Sinking land / Revenge (against the world) / Cheesie and gum. *(re-iss. Mar84 lp/c; OVED/+C 54)*
Apr 80. (7") *(DIN 17)* **SAIGON. / COPACABANA** [ ] [ ]
Jun 80. (7"green) *(DIN 19)* **ABOUT INSOMNIA. / 1 4 6** [ ] [-]
Aug 80. (7") *(DIN 21)* **SUBURBAN DREAM. / GIRL FAT** [ ] [-]
Sep 80. (lp/c) *(DID/+C 5)* **TRANCE AND DANCE** [ ] [-]
– Luna park / Suburban dream / Was ezo / Teddy the dink / Symptomatic love / Primal weekend / Halfway through the week / Am I on / Motorbikin' / About insomnia / Be blase / Trance and dance. *(re-iss. Aug88; OVED 78)*
Nov 80. (7") *(DIN 27)* **WAS EZO. / TRANCE AND DANCE** [ ] [-]

— now without FINKLE + LADLY (the latter joined the ASSOCIATES after one solo single in May'81, 'FINLANDIA' / 'TASMANIA'; *DIN 32)*

— added **DANIEL LANOIS** – producer, etc

Aug 81. (7") *(DIN 34)* **WOMEN AROUND THE WORLD AT WORK. / TWENTY-TWO IN CINCINNATI** [ ] [-]
Sep 81. (lp) *(DID 10)* **THIS IS THE ICE AGE** [ ] [-]
– Swimming / Women around the world at work / Casualties of glass / Body without filters / Jets seem slower in London skies / This is the ice age / One day in Paris / You sold the cottage / Three hundred years / Chemistry. *(re-iss. 1988; OVED 79)*

— (Mar'82) **JOHNSON + MARK GANE** recruited **JOCELYN LANOIS** – bass, vocals / **NICK KENT** – drums, percussion (also many guests)

R.C.A. / R.C.A.
May 83. (7"/12") *(RCA/+T 331)* **DANSEPARC (EVERY DAY IT'S TOMORROW). / WHATEVER HAPPENED TO RADIO VALVE ROAD?** [ ] [ ]
May 83. (lp) *(PL 14664) <4664>* **DANSEPARC** [-] [ ] German
– Obedience / World without borders / Walking into walls / Danseparc / Sins of children / Several styles of blonde girls dancing / Boys in the bushes / What people do for fun / Whatever happened to radio valve road?

M + M

— was adopted by the duo (**MARK + MARTHA**) plus a plethora of session people incl. **DANIEL LANOIS** / **TINKER BARFIELD + DAVID PILTCH** – bass / **YOGI HORTON + FRED MAHER** – drums / etc

R.C.A. / Current
Jul 84. (7"/12") *(RCA/+T 426) <13824>* **BLACK STATIONS – WHITE STATIONS. / XOA OHO** [46] [63] Jun84
Aug 84. (lp/c) *(PL/PK 70246) <3>* **MYSTERY WALK** [ ] [ ] Jul84
– Black stations – white stations / Cooling the medium / Come out and dance / I start to stop / Big trees / In between sleep and reason / Garden in the sky / Nation of followers / Alibi room / Rhythm of life.
Sep 84. (7"/12") *(RCA/+T 452)* **COOLING THE MEDIUM. / COME OUT AND DANCE** [ ] [ ]
Nov 85. (lp) *(PL 70841)* **THE WORLD IS A BALL** [ ] [ ]
– The world is a ball / I watch, I wait / Watching the boys fall down / Only you / By the waters of Babylon / Song in my heart / Don't jump the gun / Stuck on the grid / Someone else's shoes / As a matter of fact.
Oct 86. (7"/12") *(PB/PT 40835)* **SONG IN MY HEART. / RIVERINE** [ ] [-]

— split up some time in the mid 80's

– compilations, etc. –

May 88. (cd) *Virgin; (COMCD 12)* **FARAWAY IN TIME** [ ] [-]
– Echo beach / Paint by number heart / Saigon / Indecision / Terminal twilight / Hide and seek / Monotone / Sinking land / Revenge (against the world) / Cheesies and gum / Insect love / About insomnia / Motorbikin' / Suburban dream / Was ezo / Women around the world at work / This is the ice age.
Nov 88. (7") *Old Gold; (OG 9824)* **ECHO BEACH. / WOMEN AROUND THE WORLD AT WORK** [ ] [-]

J. MASCIS (see under ⇒ DINOSAUR JR)

MASSIVE ATTACK

Formed: Bristol, England . . . 1988 by 3-D, MUSHROOM and DADDY G. Having founded their own label, 'Wild Bunch' (named after the loose Bristol collective of DJ's, producers and musicians of which MASSIVE ATTACK were an integral part) five years earlier, they were subsequently snapped up by Virgin subsidiary, 'Circa' in 1990 and with only their second single, 'UNFINISHED SYMPATHY' – released under the revised moniker of MASSIVE (to distance themselves for any affiliation with the UN Gulf War policy) – crashed into the Top 20. Featuring the velvet tones of SHARA NELSON and luxuriant string arrangements to die for, this hypnotically beautiful track is oft cited as one of the most perfectly singles ever crafted. While not boasting anything quite as tantalising, the classic debut album, 'BLUE LINES', hit the the Top 20 in Spring '91, a darkly sensual, spliff-heavy cocktail of sampladelic dub, hip-hop, funk and soul that can quite possibly lay claim to be the Big Daddy of that much-maligned genre, trip-hop. Alongside the aforementioned NELSON, the record featured guests vocalists, TRICKY (soon to carve out his own career in paranoid beats) and dub reggae veteran, HORACE ANDY. NELSON subsequently departed for a solo career and all was quiet from the MASSIVE' camp until the Autumn of '94, when they re-surfaced with the NELLEE HOOPER (Soul II Soul)-produced 'PROTECTION' album. An even darker, slinkier creature, it featured an array of guest vocalists, most effectively employing TRACY THORN on the aching 'BETTER THINGS' and the title track; TRICKY, meanwhile, sounded almost catatonic on the spellbinding voodoo bass-psyche of 'KARMACOMA' while the exotic tones of NICOLETTE graced a couple of tracks. More cohesive soundwise, the record was characterised by a haunting dub-reggae feel and while it was perhaps pushing it a bit to revamp a Doors track ('LIGHT MY FIRE'), the claustrophobic brilliance of 'SPYING GLASS' (featuring HORACE ANDY in peerless form) more than made up for it. London dub producer, The MAD PROFESSOR, later gave it a bowel quaking, full-on dub reworking early in '95, the results surfacing as the mind scrambling 'NO PROTECTION'. Stunningly original and defiantly self-sufficient, MASSIVE ATTACK continue to shrug off any labels hopeful journos may pin on them (and woe betide anyone who mentions tr*p h*p), and while their perfectionism means lengthy periods between new material, fans have learned to be patient. In the summer of '97, the trio returned with their darkest, scariest track to date, 'RISINGSON', a solitary taster for the following year's long-awaited UK chart-topper, 'MEZZANINE'. Yet again cleaning up across the critical board, MASSIVE ATTACK had created a work many regarded as the pinnacle of their career, an unflinchingly bleak, downbeat and introspective record mired in paranoia, despair and apocalyptic pre-millennium tension. Nevertheless, 3-D, MUSHROOM and DADDY-G explored more musical possibilities than most bands of their ilk put together, even hooking up with LIZ FRASER (of the COCTEAU TWINS) on the track, 'TEARDROPS', subsequently a Top 10 hit. • **Songwriters:** Group except; BE THANKFUL FOR WHAT YOU'VE GOT (William DeVaughn) / LIGHT MY FIRE (Doors) / MAN NEXT DOOR (John Holt) / EXCHANGE (Bob Hilliard & Mort Garson). Sampled JAMES BROWN, PIECES OF A DREAM, YOUNG HOLT TRIO. • **Trivia:** Remixed PETER GABRIEL, LES NEGRESSES VERTES.

Album rating: BLUE LINES (*9) / PROTECTION (*9) / NO PROTECTION (*8; MASSIVE ATTACK V MAD PROFESSOR) / MEZZANINE (*9)

3-D (b. DEL NAJA) – vocals / **MUSHROOM** (b. A.VOWLES) – keyboards / **DADDY-G** (b. MARSHALL) – keyboards

Warners Warners

Jul 88. (12") *(MASS 001)* **ANY LOVE. / ('A'mix)** [ ] [ ]

— w / **SHARA NELSON** – vocals / **NELLEE HOOPER** – programmer / arranger

Wild Bunch-Circa Virgin

Nov 90. (7"/c-s) *(WBR S/C 1)* **DAYDREAMING. / ('A'instrumental)** [ ] [-]
(12"+=/cd-s+=) *(WBR T/X 1)* – Any love (2).
(12") *(WBR TX 1)* – ('A'-luv it mix) / ('A'-Brixton bass mix) / ('A'-luv it dub).

Feb 91. (7"/c-s; as MASSIVE) *(WBR S/C 2)* **UNFINISHED SYMPATHY. / ('A'-Nellee Hooper mix)** [13] [-]
(12"/cd-s) *(WBR T/X 2)* – ('A'side) / ('A'-Paul Oakenfold mix) / ('A'-P.O. instrumental) / ('A'instrumental).

— Below also featured **HORACE ANDY** – vox

Apr 91. (cd/c/2x12"lp) *(WBR CD/MC/LP 1)* <91685> **BLUE LINES** [13] [ ] Aug91
– Safe from harm / One love / Blue lines / Be thankful for what you've got / Five man army / Unfinished sympathy / Daydreaming / Lately / Hymn of the big wheel. *(re-iss. Sep96; same); hit UK 21)*

May 91. (7"/c-s) *(WBR S/C 3)* <96332> **SAFE FROM HARM. / ('A'version)** [25] [ ]
(cd-s+=) *(WBRX 3)* – ('A'-Perfecto mix).
(12") *(WBRT 3)* – ('A'-Perfecto mix) / ('A'dub mix) / ('A'instrumental).

Feb 92. (7"ep/c-ep/12"ep/cd-ep) *(WBR S/C/T/X 4)* **MASSIVE ATTACK** [27] [-]
– Hymn of the big wheel / Home of the whale / Be thankful / Any love.

— now w / **TRACY THORN** (Everything But The Girl) / **NICOLETTE / TRICKY + HORACE ANDY** – vocals. **CRAIG ARMSTRONG** – piano / **CHESTER KAMEN** – guitar / **ROB MERRIL** – drums

Sep 94. (cd/c/lp) *(WBR CD/MC/LP 2)* <39883> **PROTECTION** [4] [ ]
– Protection / Karmacoma / Three / Weather storm / Spying glass / Better things / Eurochild / Sly / Heat miser / Light my fire (live).

Oct 94. (c-s/cd-s) *(WBR C/X 5)* <38465> **SLY / ('A'mix by UNDERDOG) / ('A'-Mad Professor mix) / ('A'-Tim Simenon mix)** [24] [ ] Nov94
(12"s+=/cd-s+=) *(WBR T/DX 5)* – (extra-'A'mix).

Jan 95. (cd-s; by MASSIVE ATTACK with TRACY THORN) *(WBRDX 6)* <38471> **PROTECTION / ('A'-J.Sw!ft mix) / THREE (Don T's house mix)** [14] [ ] Feb95
(c-s/cd-s) *(WBR C/X 6)* – (1st 2 tracks) / ('A'-Radiation for the nation mix) / ('A'-Eno mix).
(12"+=) *(WBRT 6)* – ('A'-Mad Professor mix).

Feb 95. (cd/c/lp; as MASSIVE ATTACK VS MAD PROFESSOR) *(WBR CD/MC/LP 3)* **NO PROTECTION** [10] [-]
– Radiation ruling the nation (Protection) / Bumper ball dub (Karmacoma) / Trinity dub (Three) / Cool monsoon (Weather storm) / Eternal feedback (Sly) / Moving dub (Better things) / I spy (Spying glass) / Backward sucking (Heat miser).

Mar 95. (12"ep) *(WBRT 7)* **KARMACOMA. / ('A'-Napoli trip mix) / ('A'-Unkle mix) / BLACKSMITH – DAYDREAMING** [28] [ ] Jul95
(cd-ep+=) *(WBRX 7)* – ('A'-Portishead experience mix) / ('A'-Bumper ball mix).
(c-ep++=/cd-ep++=) *(WBR C/DX 7)* – ('A'-Portishead mix).

— next album/releases saw the addition of vocalists **HORACE ANDY, ELIZABETH FRASER, SARA JAY, ROBERT DEL NAJA + GRANT MARSHALL** / guitars – **ANGELO BRUSCHINI** / bass – **JOHN HARRIS, BOB LOCKE + WINSTON** / drums – **ANDY GANGADEEN**

Jul 97. (12"/cd-s) *(WBR T/X 8)* **RISINGSON. / SUPERPREDATORS** [11] [ ]

Apr 98. (cd/c/lp) *(WBR CD/MC/LP 4)* <45599> **MEZZANINE** [1] [60] May98
– Angel / Risingson / Teardrop / Inertia creeps / Exchange / Dissolved girl / Man next door / Black milk / Mezzanine / Group four / (Exchange).

— (below single featured LIZ FRAZER on vocals)

Apr 98. (c-s) *(WBRC 9)* **TEARDROP / EURO ZERO HERO** [10] [ ]
(12"+=/cd-s+=) *(WBR T/X 9)* – ('A'mixes).

Jul 98. (c-s) *(WBRC 10)* **ANGEL / GROUP 4** [30] [ ]
(12"+=/cd-s+=) *(WBR T/X 10)* – ('A'mixes by Blur & the Mad Professor).

Oct 98. (d12"ep/cd-ep) *(WBR TD/DDX 11)* **INERTIA CREEPS (mixes:- Manic Street Preachers mix / State of Bengal mix / Alpha mix / Back she comes – Inertia mixed by Mad Professor / Reflection)** [-] [-] -non

Eric MATTHEWS

Born: 12 Jan'69, Gresham, Portland, Oregon, USA. A one time student of the San Francisco Conservatory classical music college, MATTHEWS' first love was trumpet although his penchant for classic orchestral pop and his decision to take up the guitar eventually led him to the thriving alternative music scene in Boston, Massachusetts. There, he hooked up with SEBADOH's LOU BARLOW and BOB FAY, with whom he cut an obscure EP in 1993 under the name of BELT BUCKLE. Subsequently finding a musical foil in Australian ex-MOLES leader, RICHARD DAVIES, MATTHEWS found an outlet for his lush arranging/instrumental talent as one-half of the acclaimed duo, The CARDINAL. Although they only lasted one album – an eponymous 1994 effort – the publicity generated helped MATTHEWS secure a solo deal with Seattle label, 'Sub Pop'. Hardly a typical signing for the former bastion of grunge, MATTHEWS surpassed all expectations with his 1995 solo debut, 'IT'S HEAVY IN HERE', a darkly luxuriant sequence of equisitely arranged and executed orchestral pop. Showcasing a breathy, wistful vocal style that frequently brought comparisons with NICK DRAKE, MATTHEWS showed himself to be a master pop craftsman, layering trumpets, chiming guitars and melancholy string flourishes in a manner reminiscent of past masters like BRIAN WILSON, VAN DYKE PARKS and the largely unsung ROBERT KIRBY (NICK DRAKE's string arranger on his first two albums). Despite boasting a more extensive array of guest musicians, follow-up set, 'THE LATENESS OF THE HOUR' (1997) lost little of the debut's focus or sense of continuity, consolidating MATTHEWS' position as grand master of modern baroque pop for the thinking indie fan. • **Covered:** A CERTAIN KIND (Soft Machine).

Album rating: IT'S HEAVY IN HERE (*8) / THE LATENESS OF THE HOUR (*7)

ERIC MATTHEWS – on usual instruments & vocals (also conducts orchestra & produces) musicians mostly **JASON FALKNER** – guitars, bass / **STEVE HANFORD** – drums

Sub Pop Sub Pop

Nov 95. (lp/c/cd) <(SP/+MC/CD 312)> **IT'S HEAVY IN HERE** [ ] [ ]
– Fanfare / Forging plastic pain / Soul nation select them / Faith to clay / Angels for crime / Fried out broken girl / Lust takes time / Hop and tickle / Three-cornered moon / Distant mother reality / Flight and lion / Poison will pass me / Sincere sensation / Fanfare (reprise).

Feb 96. (7") <(SP 319)> **FANFARE. / LIDS, NAILS, SCREWS** [ ] [ ]
(cd-s+=) <(SPCD 319)> – A certain kind / Distant mother reality (S H mix).

— now with **JASON FALKNER** – guitar, bass, piano, drums / **WES MATTHEWS** – guitar, bass, piano / **GREGG WILLIAMS** – drums, percussion / **TONY LASH** – drums, percussion, piano / **SPOOKEY RUBEN** – bass / plus others **DON SCHWARTZ** – bass / **ANDREW SHAW** – sax / **STEVEN HANFORD** – drums / **STEVEN MATTHEWS** – acoustic guitar

Nov 97. (lp/cd) <(SP 404/+CD)> **THE LATENESS OF THE HOUR** [ ] [ ]
– Ideas that died that day / My morning parade / Pair of cherry / To clear the air / Yes, everyone / Everything so real / Becomes dark blue / The pleasant kind / Gilded cages / dopeyness / Since the wheel free / Festival fun / No gnashing teeth.

MAXIMUM JOY (see under ⇒ GLAXO BABIES)

MAZZY STAR

Formed: Santa Monica, Los Angeles, California, USA . . . by Paisley Underground veteran, DAVID ROBACK and the young HOPE SANDOVAL. She had met him around six years previous after a friend, KENDRA SMITH (erstwhile member of RAINY DAY alongside ROBACK), had introduced the pair. SANDOVAL initially joined ROBACK's band, OPAL, a short-lived affair which came to a premature end after a tour in '87. The couple were reunited at the beginning of '89 as MAZZY STAR, a darkly languid, soft-VELVETS style project which fused haunting folk/country and dreamy psychedelia to mesmerising effect. The resulting album, 'SHE HANGS BRIGHTLY' (1990), surprised many in the rock world, although it was their 1993 set, 'SO TONIGHT THAT I MIGHT SEE' which cracked the US Top 50. An even more soporific set of stoned acoustic rock, the album even spawned a near Top 40 hit with the gorgeously melancholy 'FADE INTO YOU'. Fans had to wait another three long years before their next fix, 'AMONG MY SWAN' delighting the faithful if not exactly taking any risks. • **Covers:** BLUE FLOWER (Slapp Happy) / I'M GONNA BAKE MY BISCUIT (McCoy) / I'M SAILIN' (Lawler) / FIVE STRING SERENADE (. . . Lee) / GIVE YOU MY LOVIN'. RAINY DAY covered I'LL KEEP IT WITH MINE (Bob Dylan) / SLOOP JOHN B. (Beach Boys) / I'LL BE YOUR MIRROR (Velvet Underground). • **Trivia:** HOPE SANDOVAL guested on The JESUS & MARY CHAIN's 1994 single, 'SOMETIMES ALWAYS'.

Album rating: SO TONIGHT THAT I MIGHT SEE (*8) / SHE HANGS BRIGHTLY (*8) / AMONG MY SWAN (*6) / Rainy Day: RAINY DAY (*6) / Opal: HAPPY NIGHTMARE BABY (*7) / EARLY RECORDINGS compilation (*6)

RAINY DAY

DAVID ROBACK – guitar, vocals, piano, bass (ex-RAIN PARADE) / **WILL GLENN** – violin, cello (of RAIN PARADE) / **MICHAEL QUERICO** – vocals, bass, guitar (of THREE O'CLOCK) / **MATT PIUCCI** – guitar (of RAIN PARADE) / **KENDRA SMITH** – bass, vocals + **KARL PRECODA** – guitar + **DENNIS DUCK** – drums (3 of DREAM SYNDICATE) / **ETHAN JAMES** – keyboards / + **SUSANNA HOFFS + VICKI PETERSON** – backing vocals (of BANGLES)

Rough Trade Llama

Apr 84. (lp) *(ROUGH 70) <E-1024>* **RAINY DAY** [ ] [ ]
– I'll keep it with mine / John Riley / Flying on the ground is wrong / Sloop John B. / Holocaust / On the way home / I'll be your mirror / Rainy day, dream away.

Jun 84. (7") *(RT 140)* **I'LL KEEP IT WITH MINE. / HOLOCAUST** [ ] [-]

OPAL

DAVID ROBACK / + KENDRA SMITH – bass

One Big Guitar not iss.

1986. (12"ep) *(OBG 002T)* **NORTHERN LINE. / EMPTY BOTTLES / SOUL GIVER** [ ] [-]

— split but left compilation below . . .

not iss. S.S.T.

Sep 87. (lp/c/cd) *<SST/+C/CD 103>* **HAPPY NIGHTMARE BABY** [-] [ ]
– Rocket machine / Magick power / Revelation / Falling star / She's a diamond / Supernova / Siamese trap / Happy nightmare baby / Soul giver.

— when KENDRA left ROBACK, he introduced friend **HOPE SANDOVAL** – vocals, guitar (ex-GOING HOME); disbanded sometime in '88

Rough Trade not iss.

Nov 89. (cd/c/lp) *(CD/C+/ROUGH 128)* **EARLY RECORDINGS** [ ] [-]
– Empty box blues / She's a diamond / My only friend / Empty bottles / Grains of sand / Brigit on Sunday / Northern line / Strange delight / Fell from the sun / Harriet Brown / Lullabye / All souls. *(cd+=)* – Hear the wind blow.

MAZZY STAR

— **ROBACK + HOPE SANDOVAL** – vocals (ex-GOING HOME)

Rough Trade Capitol

Apr 90. (cd/c/lp) *(CD/TC+/R 158) <C2/C4 96508>* **SHE HANGS BRIGHTLY** [ ] [ ] Feb91
– Halah / Blue flower / Ride it on / She hangs brightly / I'm sailin' / Give you my lovin' / Be my angel / Taste of blood / Ghost highway / Free / Before I sleep. *(re-iss. May93 + Sep94 on 'Capitol' cd/c; CD/TC EST 2196)*

Capitol Capitol

Oct 93. (cd/c/lp) *(CD/TC+/EST 2206) <98253>* **SO TONIGHT THAT I MIGHT SEE** [68] [36]
– Fade into you / Bells ring / Mary of silence / Five string serenade / Blue light / She's my baby / Unreflected / Wasted / Into dust / So tonight that I might see. *(re-iss. Jun94; same)*

Aug 94. (c-s) *<58286>* **FADE INTO YOU / HALAH** [-] [44]
(cd-s) *<58121>* – ('A'side) / I'm gonna take my biscuit / Under my car / Bells ring.

Aug 94. (cd-s) *(CDCL 720)* **FADE INTO YOU / BLUE FLOWER / I'M GONNA BAKE MY BISCUIT** [48] [-]
(10") *(10CL 720)* – ('A'side) / Five string serenade / Under my car / Bells ring (acoustic).

— The track 'TELL ME NOW' featured in the film 'Batman Forever' and the was on B-side of U2's 'Hold Me, Kiss Me, Kill Me!'.

Oct 96. (7"/cd-s) *(CL/CDCLS 781)* **FLOWERS IN DECEMBER. / TELL YOUR HONEY / HAIR AND SKIN** [40] [-]
(cd-s) *(CDCL 781)* – ('A'side) / Ride it on (live) / Had a thought.

Nov 96. (cd/c) *(CD/TC+/EST 2288) <27224>* **AMONG MY SWAN** [57] [68] Oct96
– Disappear / Flowers in December / Rhymes of an hour / Cry cry / Take everything / Still cold / All your sisters / I've been let down / Roseblood / Happy / Umbilical / Look on down from the bridge.

David McALMONT

Born: 1967, Croydon, London, England. After being raised in Norfolk until the age of eleven, McALMONT spent the remainder of his unhappy adolescence in Guyana, eventually moving back to London due to the country's lack of tolerance for homosexuality. Flamboyant and blessed with a celestial voice, McALMONT's chief influences were DANNY LA RUE, AL GREEN, MARVIN GAYE and DAVID BOWIE, the singer eventually setting out on his musical career and teaming up with SAUL FREEMAN to form the short-lived THIEVES in the early 90's. Although their avant-soul was lauded by the music press, the duo never actually released an album, the material they were working on when they split later surfacing as DAVID's early '95 solo album on 'Hut', simply titled 'McALMONT'. Later that year, the singer hooked up with ex-SUEDE guitar maestro, BERNARD BUTLER. Musically, at least, it was a match made in heaven, the classic single 'YES' floating into the Top 10 upon waves of soaring strings, heart-stopping melody and sublime vocals. A follow-up, 'YOU DO', repeated the magic, making the Top 20 a few months later, although the shaky alliance was soon on the rocks following accusatory press comments by McALMONT against his colleague. Although these remarks were later retracted, it seemed it was too late to save the partnership and the pair duly went their separate ways, leaving behind an album, 'THE SOUND OF McALMONT & BUTLER' (1995) which collected the two singles along with B-sides and studio outtakes. While fans can only guess at what they might have produced together, McALMONT and BUTLER are both currently working on solo projects, the latter signed to 'Creation' and apparently developing into a latter day NEIL YOUNG. • **Covered:** YOU'LL LOSE A GOOD THING (Ozen-Meaux).

Album rating: THE SOUND OF . . . McALMONT & BUTLER (*7)

THIEVES

DAVID McALMONT – vocals / **SAUL FREEMAN** – guitar / + 2 earlier members

Nursery not iss.

Nov 92. (12"/cd-s) *(12NYS/NYSCD 011)* **THROUGH THE DOOR. / PLACED ASIDE / THE SAME** [ ] [-]

Hut Caroline

Sep 93. (7"/c-s) **UNWORTHY. / THE NIGHT** [ ] [-]
(12"+=/cd-s+=) – They hide / ('A'version).

Mar 94. (c-s) **EITHER /** [ ] [-]
(cd-s+=) –

May 94. (cd; w-drawn see below) *(CDHUT 12)* **THIEVES** [ ] [-]

McALMONT

DAVID McALMONT – vocals (with BERNARD BUTLER, etc.)

Hut Caroline

Sep 94. (cd/c/lp) *(CDHUT/HUTMC/HUTLPX 12)* **McALMONT** [ ] [-]
– Either / Not wiser / Unworthy / Misunderstood / Is it raining? / Conversation / He loves you / Worn away / It's always this way / My grey boy / They hide. *(cd had ltd.bonus cd) (re-iss. Jan 95; same)*

Dec 94. (7") *(HUT 42)* **EITHER. / YOU MADE ME** [ ] [-]
(12"+=/cd-s+=) *(HUT T/DG 42)* – As if I'd known (live) / ('A'mix).

— On the 19th June '95, he made available for one day a cdep 'SATURDAY (GAY PRIDE EP) *(PRIDE 1)*. The tracks were:- Saturday / Fort James / My grey boy.

McALMONT & BUTLER

DAVID McALMONT – vocals / **BERNARD BUTLER** – guitar, instruments / **ANN STEPHENSON + GINI BALL + JOHNNY TAYLOR + JOTE OSAHN** – violins / **CLAIRE ORSLER + JOSS POOK** – violas

Hut Gyroscope

May 95. (c-s) *(HUTC 53)* **YES / DON'T CALL IT SOUL** [8] [-]
(cd-s+=) *(HUTDG 53)* – How about you?.
(cd-s) *(HUTDX 53)* – ('A'side) / What's the excuse this time? / Disappointment.

Oct 95. (c-s) *(HUTC 57)* **YOU DO / ALTHOUGH** [17] [-]
(cd-s+=) *(HUTDG 57)* – The debitor.
(cd-s) *(HUTDX 57)* – ('A'side) / Tonight / You'll lose a good thing.

Nov 95. (cd/c/lp) *(CD/TC+/HUT 32) <6633>* **THE SOUND OF . . . McALMONT & BUTLER** [33] [ ] Jan96
– Yes (full version) / What's the excuse this time? / The right thing / Although / Don't call it soul / Disappointment – (interval) / The debitor / How about you? / Tonight / You'll lose a good thing / You do (full version).

DAVID McALMONT

Jul 97. (c-s) *(HUTC 87)* **LOOK AT YOURSELF / I'M IN LOVE AGAIN** [40] [-]
(cd-s+=) *(HUTCD 87)* – Alfie.
(cd-s) *(HUTDX 87)* – ('A'side) / Misty blue / The unforgiven.

— In Nov'97, McALMONT featured on DAVID ARNOLD's version of the Bond theme song 'DIAMONDS ARE FOREVER', which hit UK No.39.

McCARTHY

Formed: Barking Abbey, Essex, England . . . 1984 by school mates MALCOLM EDEN, TIM GANE, JOHN WILLIAMSON and GARY BAKER; all attended the same school as BILLY BRAGG. Following a self-financed, limited edition debut single, 'IN PURGATORY', the band signed to the Rough Trade offshoot 'Pink' and released the acclaimed 'RED SLEEPING BEAUTY'; all guitar crescendos and rolling, tumbling drums, the track was a lullaby for socialism amid the rampant Thatcherism of the mid-80's. One of a string of overtly left-wing bands of the era – prior to the final nail in the coffin of the 1987 Conservative victory – McCARTHY came to greater prominence via the inclusion of the very SMITHS-esque 'CELESTIAL CITY' on the NME's C86 compilation tape. The following year saw the release of a debut album, 'I'M A WALLET' (1987), two further politically barbed sets, 'THE ENRAGED WILL INHERIT THE EARTH' and 'BANKING, VIOLENCE AND THE INNER CITY LIFE TODAY' emerging at the turn of the decade as the band hopped from label to label. With wider recognition seemingly as far off as ever and the political climate as stagnant as ever, McCARTHY finally split in 1990, GANE going on to cult hero status with avant-popsters, STEREOLAB. As well as being the latter outfit's home from home, GANE's 'Duophonic' label also handled EDEN's solo venture, 'HERZFELD'.

Album rating: I AM A WALLET (*8) / THE ENRAGED WILL INHERIT THE EARTH (*7) / BANKING, VIOLENCE AND THE INNER LIFE TODAY (*7) / THAT'S ALL VERY WELL BUT compilation (*8)

MALCOLM EDEN (b. 1 Sep'63, Ilford, Essex, England) – vocals, guitar / **TIM GANE** (b.12 Jul'64) – guitar / **JOHN WILLIAMSON** (b.28 Dec'63, Ilford) – bass / **GARY BAKER** (b. 8 Sep'63) – drums

Wall Of Salmon not iss.

Feb 86. (7"m) *(MAC 001)* **IN PURGATORY. / THE COMRADE ERA / SOMETHING WRONG SOMEWHERE** [ ] [-]

Pink not iss.

Oct 86. (7") *(PINKY 12)* **RED SLEEPING BEAUTY. / FROM THE DAMNED** [ ] [-]
(12"+=) *(PINKY 12T)* – The comrade era / For the fat lady.

Mar 87. (7") *(PINKY 17)* **FRANS HALS. / THE FALL (remix)** [ ] [-]
(12"+=) *(PINKY 17T)* – Kill kill kill kill / ('A'version).

September / not iss.

Oct 87. (7") *(SEPT 1)* **THE WELL OF LONELINESS. / ANTIAMERICANCRETIN / UNFORTUNATELY** [ ] [-]
(12"+=) *(SEPT 1T)* – Bad dreams / Someone worse off.
Oct 87. (lp) *(SEPT 2)* **I AM A WALLET** [ ] [-]
– The well of loneliness / An M.P. speaks / The international narcotics traffic / The funeral / The procession of popular capitalism / Antinature / The vision of Peregrine Worsthome / God made the virus / The wicked palace revolution / Monetaries / Charles Windsor. *(re-iss. Jan89 on 'Midnight Music' lp/c/cd+=; CHIME 0045 S/CC/CD)* – Unfortunately / Bad dreams / Someone worse off / Antiamericancretin.
Feb 88. (12"ep) *(SEPT 4T)* **THIS NELSON ROCKERFELLER / THE FALL. / THE FUNERAL / THE ENEMY IS AT HOME (FOR THE FAT LADY) / THE WAY OF THE WORLD** [ ] [-]
Apr 88. (12"ep) *(SEPT 5T)* **SHOULD THE BIBLE BE BANNED? /** [ ] [-]

Midnight Music / not iss.

Feb 89. (7"m/12"m) *(DING/DONG 045)* **KEEP AN OPEN EYE OR ELSE. / TWO CRIMINALS POINT OF VIEW / THE NEW LEFT REVIEW #1** [ ] [-]
Mar 89. (lp/c/cd) *(CHIME 047 S/CC/CD)* **THE ENRAGED WILL INHERIT THE EARTH** [ ] [-]
– Boy meets girl, so what / Governing takes brains / An address to the better off / Hands off or die / What our boys are fighting for / Two criminal points of view / The new left review / Keep an open mind or else / We are all born creeps / I'm not a patriot but / The home secretary briefs the forces of law and order / Throw him out he's breaking my heart.
May 89. (12"ep/cd-ep) *(DONG 48/+CD)* **McCARTHY AT WAR** [ ] [-]
– Boy meets girl, so what / (+3).
Apr 90. (cd/c/lp) **BANKING, VIOLENCE AND THE INNER LIFE TODAY** [ ] [-]
Apr 90. (7"/12") *(DONG 061/+T)* **GET A KNIFE BETWEEN YOUR TEETH EP** [ ] [-]
—— Disbanded after above and TIM quickly formed his complete diversion STEREOLAB. EDEN formed HERZFELD while studying literature. BAKER was last heard working as a radiographer.

– compilations, etc. –

May 88. (lp) *Danceteria; (TUE 871)* **A LA GUILLOTINE** [ ] [-]
Jul 91. (cd/c/d-lp) *Midnight Music;* **THAT'S ALL VERY WELL BUT** [ ] [-]
(cd re-iss. May96 on 'Cherry Red'; CDMRED 125)
1991. (cd/lp) *Midnight Music;* **WE'LL GET YOU SOON YOU CREEPS** [ ] [-]

David McCOMB & Adam PETERS (see under ⇒ TRIFFIDS)

Ian McCULLOCH (see under ⇒ ECHO & THE BUNNYMEN)

G.W. McLENNAN (see under ⇒ GO-BETWEENS)

Ian McNABB

Born: ROBERT IAN McNABB, 3 Nov'60, Liverpool, England. After a spell with CITY LIGHTS, then SUNSET BOULEVARD, he formed The ICICLE WORKS in 1979 with CHRIS LAYHE and CHRIS SHARROCK. A cassingle appeared on 'Probe' in 1981, followed a year later by their vinyl debut 'NIRVANA', the single surfacing on manager Tony Barwood's 'Troll Kitchen' label. After their classy 45, 'BIRDS FLY' won over numerous indie legions, they moved upstairs in 1983 to 'Beggars Banquet' and immediately made an impact in the Top 20 with 'LOVE IS A WONDERFUL COLOUR'. A re-issue of 'BIRDS FLY (WHISPER TO A SCREAM)', didn't fare as well, although it surprisingly broke them into the US Top 40. Their eponymous debut album also cracked the American market having already went Top 30 in the UK. Still sounding SCOTT WALKER-ish at this early stage, McNABB (complete with attached microphone gadget) was a compelling frontman for this college circuit power-rock trio. Follow-up set, 'THE SMALL PRICE OF A BICYCLE' (1985), featured a number of good reasons ('SEVEN HORSES' and 'ALL THE DAUGHTERS' for starters) why they deserved promotion from Rock's second division, while 'IF YOU WANT TO DEFEAT YOUR ENEMY SING HIS SONG' (1987) finally gave them a UK Top 30 album. The following year, 'BLIND' also scraped into the Top 40, although this was their final effort for the label having signed to 'Epic'. Major label status did them no favours, the disappointing 'PERMANENT DAMAGE' seeing a slide in their popularity and leading to them being dropped. McNABB was virtually left in the cold, that is until 'Way Cool' released his debut solo single, 'GREAT DREAMS OF HEAVEN' in 1991. This was closely followed by another independently released 45, McNABB's deserved break coming the following year when ANDREW LAUDER signed him to his 'This Way Up' label. Early in 1993, McNABB was back in the album charts, 'TRUTH & BEAUTY' nearly making the UK Top 50. He subsequently realised one of his longheld musical dreams when he secured the services of the legendary CRAZY HORSE, initially for live work before going into the studio to record a whole album together. The resulting 'HEAD LIKE A ROCK' (1994), was short-listed for a Mercury Music Award, his critical rehabilitation now complete. In 1996, McNABB released his third solo set, 'MERSEYBEAST', his second consecutive Top 30 achievement and a worthy addition to his increasingly impressive back catalogue. • **Songwriters:** Mostly McNABB compositions for ICICLE WORKS except; SEA SONG (Robert Wyatt) / NATURE'S WAY (Spirit) / COLD TURKEY (John Lennon) / INTO THE MYSTIC (Van Morrison) / YOU AIN'T SEEN NOTHIN' YET (Bachman-Turner Overdrive) / SHOULD I STAY OR SHOULD I GO (Clash) / ROCK'N'ROLL (Led Zeppelin) / PRIVATE REVOLUTION (World Party) / ROADHOUSE BLUES (Doors) / TRIAD – CHESTNUT MARE (Byrds) / MR SOUL + FOR WHAT IT'S WORTH (Buffalo Springfield). McNABB covered UNKNOWN LEGEND + THE NEEDLE AND THE DAMAGE DONE (Neil Young) / CAROLINE NO (Brian Wilson). • **Trivia:** In Aug'85, an ICICLE WORKS off-shoot MELTING POT, were supposed to have had a single 'IT MAKES NO DIFFERENCE' issued.

Album rating: THE BEST OF THE ICICLE WORKS compilation (*8) / TRUTH & BEAUTY (*6) / HEAD LIKE A ROCK (*8) / MERSEYBEAST (*6)

ICICLE WORKS

IAN McNABB – vocals, guitar, keyboards / **CHRIS LAYHE** – bass, keyboards, vocals / **CHRIS SHARROCK** – drums, percussion

Probe / not iss.

Mar 81. (c-ep) *(private)* **ASCENDING** [ ] [-]

Troll Kitchen / not iss.

Oct 82. (7"m) *(WORKS 001)* **NIRVANA. / LOVE HUNT / SIROCCO** [ ] [-]

Situation2 / not iss.

Jun 83. (7") *(SIT 22)* **BIRDS FLY (WHISPER TO A SCREAM). / REVERIE GIRL** [ ] [-]
(12"+=) *(SIT 22T)* – Gunboys.

Beggars Banquet / Arista

Oct 83. (7"/7"pic-d) *(BEG 99/+P)* **LOVE IS A WONDERFUL COLOUR. / WATERLINE** [15] [ ]
(ext.12"+=/ext.12"pic-d+=) *(BEG 99 T/TP)* – In the dance the Shamen led.
(d7"++=) *(BEG 99 + ICE 1)* – The Devil on horseback.
Mar 84. (7") *(BEG 108)* **BIRDS FLY (WHISPER TO A SCREAM). / IN THE CAULDRON OF LOVE** [53] [-]
(12"+=) *(BEG 108T)* – Ragweed campaign / Scarecrow.
(12"+=) *(BEG 108TD)* – ('A'-Frantic mix).
Mar 84. (lp/c) *(BEGA/BEGC 50) <8202>* **THE ICICLE WORKS** [24] [40]
– Chop the tree / Love is a wonderful colour / Reaping the rich harvest / As the dragonfly flies / Lover's day / In the cauldron of love / Out of season / A factory in the desert / Birds fly (whisper to a scream) / Nirvana. *(cd-iss. Jul86; BEGA 50CD) (re-iss. Jul88 lp/c/cd; BBL/+C 50/+CD)*
Mar 84. (7") *<9155>* **BIRDS FLY (WHISPER TO A SCREAM). / IN THE DANCE THE SHAMEN LED** [-] [37]
Sep 84. (7") *(BEG 119)* **HOLLOW HORSE. / THE ATHEIST** [ ] [-]
(12"+=) *(BEG 119T)* – Nirvana (live).
(12"+=) *(BEG 119TR)* – ('A'remix).
May 85. (7") *(BEG 133)* **ALL THE DAUGHTERS (OF HER FATHER'S HOUSE). / A POCKETFUL OF NOTHING** [ ] [-]
(12"+=) *(BEG 133T)* – Mr. Soul.
Jul 85. (7") *(BEG 142)* **SEVEN HORSES. / SLINGSHOT** [ ] [-]
(d7"+=) *(BEG 142D)* – Beggars legacy / Goin' back.
(12") *(BEG 142T)* – ('A'-American) / ('B'side) / Beggars legacy.
Sep 85. (lp/c) *(BEGA/BEGC 61)* **THE SMALL PRICE OF A BICYCLE** [55] [-]
– Hollow horse / Perambulator / Seven horses / Rapids / Windfall / Assumed sundown / Saint's sojourn / All the daughter's (of her father's horse) / Book of reason / Conscience of kings. *(re-iss. Jan89 lp/c/cd; BBL/+C 61/+CD)*
Oct 85. (7") *(BEG 151)* **WHEN IT ALL COMES DOWN. / (LET'S GO) DOWN TO THE RIVER** [ ] [-]
('A'unabridged-12"+=) *(BEG 151T)* – Cold turkey.
Feb 86. (m-lp/c) *(BEGA/BEGC 71)* **SEVEN SINGLES DEEP** (compilation) [52] [-]
– Hollow horse / Love is a wonderful colour / Birds fly (whisper to a scream) / All the daughters (of her father's house) / When it all comes down / Seven horses / Rapids. *(c+=)* – I never saw my hometown 'til I went around the world / (Let's go) Down to the river / Slingshot / The atheist / Into the mystic / A pocketful of nothing / Goin' back. *(re-iss. Sep88 lp/c/cd; BBL/+C 71/+CD) (cd+=)* – Perambulator / Lover's day / Out of season / Saints sojourn / Nirvana / Conscience of kings.

Beggars Banquet / Beggars Banquet

Jun 86. (7") *(BEG 160)* **UNDERSTANDING JANE. / I NEVER SAW MY HOMETOWN 'TIL I WENT AROUND THE WORLD** [52] [-]
(12"+=) *(BEG 160T)* – Into the mystic.
(d7"+=) *(BEG 160 + ICE 3)* – Hollow horse (live) / You ain't seen nothin' yet (live).
(c-s+=) *(BEG 160C)* – Seven horses (live) / Perambulator (live) / Rapids (live).
Sep 86. (7") *(BEG 172)* **WHO DO YOU WANT FOR YOUR LOVE. / UNDERSTANDING JANE (live)** [54] [-]
(w/ free c-s+=) *(BEG 172F)* – John Geoffrey Muir shopkeeper / Impossibly three lovers.
(12"+=) *(BEG 172T)* – Should I stay or should I go (live) / Roadhouse blues (live).
Dec 86. Situation2; (12"ep) *(SIT 45T)* **UP HERE IN THE NORTH OF ENGLAND. / SEA SONG (Ian McNabb) / NATURE'S WAY / IT MAKES NO DIFFERENCE / WAYLAID (Chis Layhe)** [ ] [-]
Jan 87. (7") *(BEG 181)* **EVANGELINE. / EVERYBODY LOVES TO PLAY THE FOOL** [53] [-]
(12"+=) *(BEG 181T)* – Waiting in the wings / ('A'demo).
(c-s+=) *(BEG 181C)* – It makes no difference / Nature's way / Sea song.
Mar 87. (lp/c)(cd) *(BEGA/BEGC 78)(BEGA 78CD) <6447>* **IF YOU WANT TO DEFEAT YOUR ENEMY SING HIS SONG** [28] [ ]
– Hope springs eternal / Travelling chest / Sweet Thursday / Up here in the north of England / Who do you want for your love / When you were mine / Evangeline / Truck driver's lament / Understanding Jane / Walking with a mountain. *(c+=)* – Everybody loves to play the fool / Don't let it rain on my parade. *(cd++=)* – I never saw my hometown 'til went around the world / Into the mystic. *(re-iss. Feb90 lp/c/cd; BBL/+C 78/+CD)*
Nov 87. (7"/s7") *(BEG 203/+S)* **HIGH TIME. / BROKEN HEARTED FOOL** [ ] [-]
(12"+=) *(BEG 203T)* – Travelling chest (live) / Private revolution (live).

Feb 88. (7") *(BEG 208)* **THE KISS OFF. / SURE THING** -
(12"ep/c-ep+=/cd-ep+=) *(BEG 1W/+C/CD)* – THE NUMB EP – High time (acoustic) / Whipping boy.

Apr 88. (7") *(BEG 220)* **LITTLE GIRL LOST. / TIN CAN** 59 -
(12"+=/pic-cd-s+=) *(BEG 215 T/CD)* – Hot profit gospel / One time.

May 88. (lp)(c)(cd) *(IWA/IWC 2)(IWA 2CD) <8424>* **BLIND** 40
– (intro) Shit creek / Little girl lost / Starry blue-eyed wonder / One true love / Blind / Two two three / What do you want me to do? / Stood before Saint Peter / The kiss off / Here comes trouble / Walk a while with me.

Jun 88. (7") *(BEG 220)* **HERE COMES TROUBLE. / STARRY BLUE-EYED WONDER**
(12"+=)(12"box) *(BEG 220T)(IW 3)* – Rock'n'roll (live) / For what it's worth (medley live).

— **ZAK STARKEY** (b.13 Sep'65, London, England, son of RINGO) – drums repl. LAYHE SHARROCK who joined WILD SWANS + The LA'S / added **DAVE GREEN** – keyboards / **ROY CORKHILL** – bass (both ex-BLACK)

— (1989) **IAN and ROY** brought in **DAVE BALDWIN** – keyboards / **MARK REVELL** – guitar, vocals / **PAUL BURGESS** – drums

Epic Work-Epic

Mar 90. (7") *(WORKS 100)* **MOTORCYCLE RIDER. / TURN ANY CORNER** 73
(12"+=/12"etched+=) *(WORKS T/E 100)* – People change.
(cd-s++=) *(WORKS C100)* – Victoria's ghost.
(12") *(WORKS Q100)* – ('A'side) / Let's get loaded / Red lightning.

May 90. (cd/c/lp) *(466 800-2/-4/-1)* **PERMANENT DAMAGE** -
– I still want you / Motorcycle rider / Melanie still hurts / Hope street rag / I think I'm gonna be OK / Baby don't burn / What she did to my mind / One good eye / Permanent damage / Woman on my mind / Looks like rain / Dumb angel.

May 90. (7") *(WORKS 101)* **MELANIE STILL HURTS. / WHEN THE CRYING'S DONE** -
(12"+=) *(WORKS T101)* – Mickey's blue.
(7"ep++=/cd-ep++=) *(WORKS Q/C 101)* – I dreamt I was a beautiful woman.

Jul 90. (7"/c-s) *(WORKS/+M 102)* **I STILL WANT YOU. / I WANT THAT GIRL** -
(12"+=) *(WORKST 102)* – It's gonna rain forever.
(10"++=/cd-ep++=) *(WORKS Q/C 102)* – Sweet disposition.

— McNABB joined the WILD SWANS briefly before going solo.

– compilations, etc. –

Nov 88. (12"ep) *Nighttracks; (SFNT 015)* **THE EVENING SHOW SESSIONS** (14.11.82) -
– Birds fly (whisper to a scream) / Lover's day / Love hunt / As the dragonfly flies.

Jan 90. (7") *Old Gold; (OG 9918)* **LOVE IS A WONDERFUL COLOUR. / BIRDS FLY (WHISPER TO A SCREAM)** -

Aug 92. (cd)(c) *Beggars Banquet; (BEGA 124CD)(BEGC 124)* **THE BEST OF THE ICICLE WORKS** 60 -
– Hollow horse (long version) / Love is a wonderful colour / Birds fly (whisper to a scream) / Understanding Jane ('92 version) / Shit creek / High time (acoustic) / Who do you want for your love? / Evangeline / Little girl lost / When it all comes down ('92 version) / Starry blue eyed wonder / Out of season / The kiss off / Up here in the North of England / Firepower / Blind. *(ltd. w/ free cd 'BEST KEPT SECRET'; BEGA 124CD2) (re-iss. cd Sep95; BBL 124CD)*

Aug 92. (7") *Beggars Banquet; (BEG 262)* **UNDERSTANDING JANE '92. / LITTLE GIRL LOST** -
(12"+=) *(BEG 262T)* – When it all comes down '92 / Firepower.
(cd-s+=) *(BEG 262CD)* – Solid ground / Like weather.

Mar 94. (cd) *Windsong; (<WINCD 053>)* **BBC RADIO 1 LIVE IN CONCERT (live)**

Jul 97. (cd) *Dutch East India; <8004>* **THE PEEL SESSIONS** -

IAN McNABB

Way Cool not iss.

Jun 91. (12"ep/cd-ep) *(WAYCOOL 14 T/CD)* **GREAT DREAMS OF HEAVEN / THAT'S WHY I BELIEVE. / MAKE LOVE TO YOU / POWER OF SONG** -

Fat Cat not iss.

Oct 91. (12"ep/cd-ep) *(FC 001/+CD)* **THESE ARE THE DAYS. / TRAMS IN AMSTERDAM / GREAT DREAMS OF HEAVEN (acoustic)** -

This Way Up not iss.

Jan 93. (7") *(WAY 211)* **IF LOVE WAS LIKE GUITARS. / TRAMS IN AMSTERDAM** 67 -
(cd-s+=) *(WAY 233)* – Great dreams of Heaven.

Jan 93. (cd/c/d-lp) *(514 378-2/-4/-1)* **TRUTH AND BEAUTY** 51 -
– (I go) My own way / These are the days / Great dreams of Heaven / Truth and beauty / I'm game / If love was like guitars / Story of my life / That's why I believe / Trip with me / Make love to you / Presence of the one. *(re-iss. cd/c Apr95; same)*

Mar 93. (7"/c-s) *(WAY 811/844)* **GREAT DREAMS OF HEAVEN. / UNKNOWN LEGEND** -
(12"+=/cd-s+=) *(WAY 822/833)* – I'm game / Caroline no.

Jun 93. (7") *(WAY 1211)* **I'M GAME. / A PIRATE LOOKS AT FORTY** -
(cd-s) *(WAY 1233)* – ('A'side) / What's it all about / ('A'version).

Sep 93. (7"/c-s/cd-s) *(WAY 1611/1644/1655)* **(I GO) MY OWN WAY / PLAY THE HAND THEY DEAL YOU** -
(10"+=/cd-s+=) *(WAY 1688/1633)* – If my daddy could see me now / For you, angel.

— with **RALPH MOLINA + BILLY TALBOT** (of NEIL YOUNG's CRAZY HORSE) + **MIKE 'TONE' HAMILTON** (of SMITHEREENS)

Jun 94. (7"/c-s) *(WAY 3111/3144)* **YOU MUST BE PREPARED TO DREAM. / THAT'S WHY THE DARKNESS EXISTS** 54 -
(12"/cd-s) *(WAY 3122/3133)* – ('A'side) / Sometimes I think about you / Woo yer.
(cd-s) *(WAY 3199)* – ('A'side) / ('A'radio) / Love is a wonderful colour / When it all comes down (both acoustic).

Jul 94. (cd/c) *(522 298-2/-4)* **HEAD LIKE A ROCK** 29 -
– Fire inside my soul / You must be prepared to dream / Child inside a father / Still got the fever / Potency / Go into the light / As a life goes by / Sad strange solitary Catholic mystic / This time is forever / May you always.

Aug 94. (c-s) *(WAY 3644)* **GO INTO THE LIGHT / TIME YOU WERE IN LOVE** -
(cd-s+=) *(WAY 3633)* – For you, angel.
(12") *(WAY 3622)* – ('A'side) / ('A'-Celestial dub mix) / For you, angel.
(cd-s) *(WAY 3699)* – ('A'side) / I stood before St.Peter / Rock / ('A'-Celestial dub mix).

Apr 96. (7"/c-s) *(WAY 5011/5044)* **DON'T PUT YOUR SPELL ON ME. / DON'T PATRONISE ME** -
(cd-s+=) *(WAY 5033)* – What she did to my mind.

May 96. (cd/c/d-lp) *(524 215-2/-4/-1)* **MERSEYBEAST** 30 -
– Merseybeast / Affirmation / Beautiful old mystery / Love's young dream / Camaraderie / Don't put your spell on me / Heydays / Little bit of magic / You stone my soul / Too close to the sun / They settled for less than they wanted / I'm a genius / Available light / Merseybeast (reprise). *(some cd's w/ free cd 'NORTH WEST COAST'; 524 240-2)*

Jun 96. (7") *(WAY 5211)* **MERSEYBEAST. / UP HERE IN THE NORTH OF ENGLAND (demo Jan 86)** 74 -
(cd-s+=) *(WAY 5233)* – Permanent damage (demo Sept 88) / Merseybeast (demo March 95).
(cd-s) *(WAY 5266)* – ('A'side) / Pretty boys with big guitars / The slider / Snaked.

MEAT BEAT MANIFESTO

Formed: Swindon, England ... 1985 as PERENNIAL DIVIDE by main writer, JACK DANGERS and JONNY STEPHENS. A radical politico industrial dance outfit with similarities to CABARET VOLTAIRE, they issued a few EP's and one album, 'PURGE' (1986) before STEPHENS became institutionalised. Meanwhile, DANGERS formed his own group, MEAT BEAT MANIFESTO, recruiting BIRDHNA JONES and GREG RITCH. A series of 12" singles were collected together as 'STORM THE STUDIO' (1989), DANGERS pioneering an aural equivalent of WILLIAM BURROUGHS' "cut-up" method by splicing sampled breakbeats, slogans and dub basslines. At the dawn of the 90's, MEAT BEAT MANIFESTO switched labels from 'Sweatbox' to 'Play It Again Sam', recalling STEPHENS in the process. The seminal 'RADIO BABYLON' (which sampled BONEY M's 'Rivers Of Babylon', incidentally JACK's most hated song!) has since been cited as a guiding influence on The PRODIGY (LIAM was a big fan!), NINE INCH NAILS and The CHEMICAL BROTHERS to name but a few, the track subsequently used as the base material for another defining piece of electronic music, FUTURE SOUND OF LONDON's 'Papua New Guinea'. In the same year, 1990, DANGERS and Co, unveiled their first studio album proper, '99%', although inevitably it proved difficult to maintain the impact of their best work over the course of the whole album. Previewed by the blisteringly intense 'EDGE OF NO CONTROL' single (and featuring their only Top 60 entry to date, 'MINDSTREAM'), 1992's 'SATYRICON' was their last long-player for some time as DANGERS moved to the more sympathetic climes of San Francisco, signing to TRENT REZNOR's 'Nothing' imprint in 1994. A much in-demand remixer (for such luminaries as DAVID BOWIE, The SHAMEN and DAVID BYRNE), DANGERS finally completed his MBM comeback set in '96, 'SUBLIMINAL SANDWICH', a wildly diverse double-set containing a cover of World Domination Enterprises' 'ASBESTOS LEAD ASBESTOS'.
• **Trivia:** Around the mid-90's, DANGERS was responsible for the reformation of HERBIE HANCOCK's backing group, The HEADHUNTERS; HERBIE also joined MEAT BEAT on stage!

Album rating: STORM THE STUDIO (*7) / 99% (*6) / ARMED AUDIO WARFARE (*6) / VERSION GALORE remixes (*6) / SATYRICON (*7) / SUBLIMINAL SANDWICH (*6) / ORIGINAL FIRE (*6) / ACTUAL SOUNDS & VOICES (*6) / Perennial Divide: PURGE (*5)

PERENNIAL DIVIDE

JACK DANGERS (b. CORRIGAN) – keyboards / **JONNY STEPHENS** – keyboards / **JOHNNY WARD** – / **FREEGARD + SEARLY**

Sweatbox not iss.

Jul 86. (12"ep) *(SOX 018)* **BURN DOWN EP** -
– Burn down / The permanent way / New foundation of mankind.

Aug 86. (lp) *(SAX 016)* **PURGE** -
– Blow / Parricide / Word of the Lord / Captain Swing / Rescue / The fall / Trip / Tuna hell / Burning dogs / End of the line. *(re-iss. May87 w/ free 12") – BURN DOWN EP*

May 87. (12"ep) *(SOX 020)* **BEE HEAD EP** -
– Bee head / Word spread / Gentle as a fawn is warm / Clamp.

Oct 88. (12"/cd-s) *(SOX 036/+CD)* **LEATHER NECKS** -

MEAT BEAT MANIFESTO

JACK DANGERS – keyboards / **BIRDHNA JONES** – keyboards / **GREG RETCH** – DJ

Sweatbox Wax Trax

Dec 87. (12"ep) *(SOX 023)* **SUCK HARD (I GOT THE FEAR). / KICK THAT MAN / KNEEL AND BUZZ** -
(12") *(SOX 023R)* – I got the fear Titanium mix) / I got the fear (without fuck).

Feb 88. (lp) *(SAX 029)* **SUCK HARD** -

Jun 88. (7") *(OX 032)* **STRAP DOWN. / GIVE YOUR BODY IT'S FREEDOM** -
(12"/cd-s) *(SOX 023 R/CD)* – ('A'-The sound defence policy remix) / Wall to wall.

Sep 88. (one-sided-12"; by "SPACE CHILDREN" aka JACK DANGERS) *(SOX 038)* **LET'S GO DISCO** -

Oct 88. (12"/cd-s) *(SOX 039/+CD)* **GOD O.D. / MARS NEEDS WOMEN** -

Jan 89. (d-lp/cd) *(SDX 040/+CD)* **STORM THE STUDIO** -
– God O.D. (parts 1-4) / Re-animator (parts 1-4) / Strap down (parts 1-4) / I got the fear (parts 1-4).

— **JONNY STEPHENS** re-joined set-up with **DANGERS** + **CRAIG MORRISON** + **MARCUS ADAMS**

Play It Again Sam / Elektra

Jan 90. (12") *(BIAS 142)* **DOGSTAR MAN. / STILL FALLING** [ ] [-]
(cd-s+=) *(BIAS 142CD)* – Dog star / D.V.A.

May 90. (12"/cd-s) *(12+/BIAS 004/+CD)* **HELTER SKELTER. / RADIO BABYLON** [ ] [-]

May 90. (lp/cd) *(BIAS 180/+CD) <61026-1/-2>* **99%** [ ] [ ]
– Now / Psyche out / All the things you are / Hello teenage America / 10 x faster than the speed of love / 99% / Dogstar man – Helter skelter / Think fast / Hallicination generation / Deviate. *(re-iss. cd Sep93)*

Aug 90. (lp/c/cd) *(LD 9048/+MC/CD) <WAX 7106>* **ARMED AUDIO WARFARE** [ ] [-]
– Genocide / Repulsion / Mister President / Reanimator / I got the fear / Kneel and buzz / Fear (version) / Give your body it's freedom. *(cd+=)* – Mars needs women / Cutman.
(above issued on 'Licensed' records / 'Wax Trax~' in the US)

Sep 90. (12") *(BIAS 182)* **PSYCHE OUT (version 1). / PSYCHE OUT (version 2)** [ ] [-]
(cd-s+=) *(BIAS 182CD)* – Psyche dub.
(12") *(BIAS 182R)* – ('A'-Andy Weatherall sex skank stripdown remix) / Radio Babylon (original mix).

Feb 91. (lp/c/cd) *(BIAS 192/+C/CD)* **VERSION GALORE** [ ] [-]
– Radio Babylon (Space Children intro remix) / Radio Babylon (version galore) / Psyche out (sex skank stripdown) / Psyche out (version) / Psyche out (dub) / Radio Babylon. *(cd+=)* – Psyche out (sex skank mix).

Aug 92. (12"ep) *(BIAS 222)* **EDGE OF NO CONTROL. / ORBITAL CONTROL (version 3) / THE CIRCULAR COSMIC SPOT** [ ] [-]
(12"ep) *(BIAS 222R)* – ('A'-Take control Orbital reply) / ('A'-Satyriconsolidated – Consolidated reply) / DJ interruptus.
(cd-ep) *(BIAS 222CD)* – (as above except last track repl. by 'Circular . . .').

Sep 92. (lp/c/cd) *(BIAS 202/+C/CD) <61395>* **SATYRICON** [ ] [ ]
– Potsounds / Mindstream / Drop / Original control (version 1) / Circles / The sphere / Euthanasia / Edge of no control (part 1 & 2) / Untold stories / Placebo. *(free 12") (BIAS 202X) (cd+=/c+=)* – ORIGINAL CONTROL (version 2) / BRAINWASHED THIS WAY – ZOMBIE THAT SHIRT. / YOUR MIND BELONGS TO THE STATE / TRACK 15 / SON OF SAM

— In Nov'92 some MBM members became SUPEREAL and released 'ELIXIR' on 'Guerilla' records.

Play It Again Sam / Interscope

Feb 93. (12"/12"remix) *(BIAS 232/+R)* **MINDSTREAM. / PARADISE FOUND** [55] [ ]
(cd-s/cd-s remix) *(BIAS 232CD/+R)* – ('A'side) / ('A'mixes) / Original control (electro the robot).

— trio of DANGERS + 2

Mar 96. (12"/cd-s) *(BIAS 292/+CD)* **TRANSMISSION (mixes) / MAD BOMBER / THE WOODS** [ ] [ ]

Apr 96. (12"/cd-s) *(BIAS 252/+CD)* **ASBESTOS LEAD ASBESTOS (mixes) / UNTITLED** [ ] [ ]
(above was scheduled for an earlier release thus its low cat.no.)

May 96. (d-cd) *(BIAS 302CD) <90069>* **SUBLIMINAL SANDWICH** [ ] [ ]
– Sound innovation / Nuclear bomb / Long periods of time / 1979 / Future worlds / What's your name? / She's unreal / Asbestos lead asbestos / Mass producing hate / Radio mellotron / Assisinator / Phone calls from the dead / Lucid dream / No purpose no design / Cancer / Transmission / We done / Set your receivers / Mad bomber – The woods / Utterer / United nations / Stereophrenik / Teargas / lexus / Electric people / Tweekland / Simulacra. *(also ltd; cd/lp; BIAS 302 CDX/LPX)*

Nov 96. (12"/cd-s) *(BIAS 322/+CD)* **IT'S THE MUSIC / I CONTROL (AUDIO COLLAGE 2) / ASBESTOS LEAD ASBESTOS** [ ] [ ]

Jun 97. (cd) *(<INTD 90127>)* **ORIGINAL FIRE** [ ] [ ]
– Helter skelter '97 / It's the music / I am electro / I am organic / Radio Babylon / I got the fear (part 5) / Asbestos lead asbestos / It's the music / Radio Babylon / Radio Babylon (version).

Jun 98. (12"/cd-s) *(BIAS 342/+CD)* **ACID AGAIN. /** [ ] [ ]

Sep 98. (d-lp/cd) *(BIAS 345/+CD)* **ACTUAL SOUNDS + VOICES** [ ] [ ]
– Everything's under control / Prime audio soup / Book of shadows / Oblivion – Humans / Let's have fun / Tweek / Acid again / Let go / Where are you? – Enuff / Hall to the bopp / 3 floors above you / Funny feeling / The thumb / Wavy line / Wildlife.

Nov 98. (12"ep) *(BIAS 352)* **PRIME AUDIO SOUP. / ('A'-Herbaliser mix) / ('A'-Boards Of Canada mix).**
(cd-ep+=) *(BIAS 352CD)* – ('A'-Biomuse mix).

– compilations, etc. –

Nov 93. (c-ep) *Strange Fruit; (SFPSCD 088)* **THE PEEL SESSIONS** [ ] [-]
– Fire number 9 / Soul driver / Drop / Radio Babylon.

MEAT PUPPETS

Formed: Tempe, Phoenix, Arizona, USA . . . 1980 by brothers CURT and CRIS KIRKWOOD. They were soon snapped up by rising US indie label 'SST' in 1981, after a debut on their own label. Their first recording for the company, 'MEAT PUPPETS 1' (1982), was a demanding blast of howling noise and twisted country that barely hinted at the compelling sound they'd invent with the follow-up 'MEAT PUPPETS II' (1983). A hybrid of mystical GRATEFUL DEAD-like psychedelia that short-fused hardcore punk rock and the country-boy slur of CRIS, the record was the blueprint for most of their subsequent output. 'UP ON THE SUN' (1985) was slightly more polished and saw the band garner snowballing critical acclaim. By the release of 'MIRAGE' (1987), the band had fully realised their desert-rock vision with a collection of weather beaten, psychedelic country classics; tracks like 'BEAUTY' and 'CONFUSION FOG' rank among the MEAT PUPPET's best. Yet the record failed to sell and the band returned to a rawer, ZZ TOP-influenced sound on 'HUEVOS'. This album, together with the more mainstream 'MONSTERS' (1989) and continuing critical praise led to a deal with 'London'. Their major label debut, 'FORBIDDEN PLACES' (1991) was accomplished but lacked the high-noon intensity of their earlier work. After a step-up from KURT COBAIN (see below), the raw 'NO JOKE' (1995) album at last saw The MEAT PUPPETS reaping some financial rewards, sales of the album going on to break the half million mark. • **Songwriters:** Most by CURT, some with CRIS or DERRICK. Covered TUMBLIN' TUMBLEWEEDS (Bob Nolan) / EL PASO CITY (Marty Robbins) / GOODNIGHT IRENE (Leadbelly). • **Trivia:** On 18 Nov'93, CURT & CRIS guested with NIRVANA's on an unplugged MTV spot. The tracks they performed were 'PLATEAU', 'OH ME' & 'LAKE OF FIRE'.

Album rating: UP ON THE SUN (*8) / MONSTERS (*8) / TOO HIGH TO DIE (*7) / FORBIDDEN PLACES (*6) / MIRAGE (*9)

CURT KIRKWOOD (b.10 Jan'59, Amarillo, Texas) – guitar, vocals / **CRIS KIRKWOOD** (b.22 Oct'60, Amarillo) – vocals, bass, rhythm guitar / **DERRICK BOSTROM** (b.23 Jun'60, Phoenix) – drums

not iss. / World Inv.

Sep 81. (7"ep) **IN A CAR / BIG HOUSE. / DOLFIN FIELD / OUT IN THE GARDINER / FOREIGN LAWNS** [-] [ ]
(cd-ep iss.Nov88 on 'S.S.T.'; SST 044CD)

S.S.T. / S.S.T.

Jan 82. (m-lp) *<SST 009>* **MEAT PUPPETS I** [-] [ ]
– Reward / Love offering / Blue green god / Walking boss / Melons rising / Saturday morning / Our friends / Tumblin' tumbleweeds / Milo, Sorghum and maize / Meat puppets / Playing dead / Litterbox / Electromud / The goldmine. *(re-iss. May93 lp/c/cd; SST 009/+C/CD)*

Apr 84. (lp) *<SST 019>* **MEAT PUPPETS II** [ ] [ ] 1983
– Split myself in two / Magic toy missing / Lost plateau / Aurora Borealis / We are here / Climbing / New gods / Oh, me / Lake on fire / I'm a mindless idiot / The whistling song. *(re-iss. May93 lp/c/cd; SST 019/+C/CD)*

Apr 85. (lp) *<SST 039>* **UP ON THE SUN** [ ] [ ]
– Up on the Sun / Maiden's milk / Away / Animal kingdom / Hot pink / Swimming ground / Bucket head / Too real / Enchanted pork fist / Seal whales / Two rivers / Creator. *(cd-iss. Sep87; SST 039CD) (re-iss. May93 cd/c; SST 039 CD/C)*

Aug 86. (m-lp) *<SST 049>* **OUT MY WAY** [ ] [ ]
– She's hot / Out my way / Other kinds of love / Not swimming ground / Mountain line / Good golly Miss Molly. *(cd-iss. Sep87; SST 049CD) (re-iss. May93 cd/c; SST 049 CD/C)*

Apr 87. (lp/cd) *<SST 100/+CD>* **MIRAGE** [ ] [ ]
– Mirage / Quit it / Confusion fog / The wind and the rain / Mighty zero / Get on down / Leaves / I am a machine / Beauty / A hundred miles / Love your children forever / Liquified: Mighty zero – I am a machine – Liquified – Rubberneckin'. *(re-iss. May93 cd/c; SST 100 CD/C)*

Oct 87. (lp/cd) *<SST 150/+CD>* **HEUVOS** [ ] [ ]
– Paradise / Look at the rain / Bad love / Sexy music / Crazy / Fruit / Automatic mojo / Dry rain / I can't be counted on at all. *(re-iss. May93 cd/c; SST 150 CD/C)*

Oct 87. (12") *<PSST 150>* **I CAN'T BE COUNTED ON AT ALL. / PARADISE** [ ] [ ]

Oct 89. (lp/cd) *<SST 253/+CD>* **MONSTERS** [ ] [ ]
– Attacked by monsters / Light / Meltdown / In love / The void / Touchdown king / Party till the world obeys / Flight of the fire weasel / Strings on your heart / Like being alive.

Nov 90. (d-lp/cd) *<SST 265/+CD>* **NO STRINGS ATTACHED** (compilation) [ ] [ ]
– Big house / In a car / Tumblin' tumbleweeds / Reward / The whistling song / New gods / Lost / Lake of fire / Split myself in two / Up on the Sun / Swimming ground / Maiden's milk / Bucket head / Out my way / Confusion fog / I am a machine / Quit it / Beauty / Look at the rain / I can't be counted on at all / Automatic mojo / Meltdown / Like being alive / Attacked by monsters.

London / London

Nov 91. (cd/c/lp) *<828254-2/-4/-1>* **FORBIDDEN PLACES** [ ] [ ]
– Sam / Nail it down / This day / Open wide / Another Moon / That's how it goes / Whirlpool / Popskull / No longer gone / Forbidden places / Six gallon pie.

Mar 94. (cd/c/lp) *<828484-2/-4/-1>* **TOO HIGH TO DIE** [ ] [62]
– Violet eyes / Never to be found / We don't exist / Severed goddess head / Flaming heart / Shine / Backwater / Roof with a hole / Station / Things / Why / Evil love / Comin' down / Lake of fire.

Jul 94. (cd-ep) *<857553>* **BACKWATER / OPEN WIDE / ANIMAL / UP ON THE SUN / WHITE SPORT COAT** [-] [47]

Dec 94. (10"ep) *<1109>* **RAW MEAT EP** [-] [ ]
– We don't exist / Up on the sun / El Paso city / White sport coat / Goodnight Irene.

Oct 95. (cd/c) *<828665-2/-4>* **NO JOKE!** [ ] [ ]
– Scum / Nothing / Head / Taste of the sun / Vampires / Predator / Poison arrow / Eyeball / For free / Cobbler / Inflamable / Sweet ammonia / Chemical garden.

MEAT WHIPLASH (see under ⇒ MOTORCYCLE BOY)

MEDALARK 11 (see under ⇒ BODINES)

MEDICINE

Formed: Los Angeles, California, USA . . . Spring 1991 by BETH THOMPSON, BRAD LANER, JIM PUTNAM, JIM GOODALL and ED RUSCHA (son of pop artist of the same name). All seasoned campaigners on the local music scene (GOODALL having previously played with a latter day line-up of the 'BURRITOS), MEDICINE secured initial airplay on Rodney Bingenheimer's West Coast radio show. A year later, the 5-piece debuted for UK label, 'Creation' ('American Recordings' in the States), on their self-titled EP, which opened with the track, 'ARUCA'. Attempting to combine the classic sounds of West Coast Americana with Krautrock and MBV-style guitar atmospherics, MEDICINE dispensed a pretty gloomy prescription with their inagural album, 'SHOT FORTH SELF LIVING', in '92. The following year, the darkly addictive quintet mixed up the medicine, so to speak, on remix set, 'THE BURIED LIFE', although it would be another two years before the appearance of their second album proper, 'HER HIGHNESS' (1995). After their subsequent split, only PUTTNAM found a degree of success in both MAIDS OF GRAVITY and the RADAR BROTHERS.

Album rating: SHOT FORTH SELF LIVING (*7) / THE BURIED LIFE (*5) / HER HIGHNESS (*5)

BETH THOMPSON (b.12 Jun'67, St. Louis, Missouri) – vocals (ex-FOUR WAY CROSS) / **BRAD LANER** (b. 6 Nov'66) – vocals, guitar (ex-SAVAGE REPUBLIC, ex-STEAMING COILS) / **JIM PUTTNAM** (b.30 Sep'67, Hollywood, Calif.) – guitar (ex-SDF, ex-BUS ENGINES, ex-MAGIC BEARD) / **ED RUSCHA** (b.14 Dec'68, Inglewood, Calif.) – bass (ex-SDF, ex-MAGIC BEARD, ex-PITA HAWKS, ex-MAIDS OF GRAVITY, ex-DUMB SPEEDWAY CHILDREN) / **JIM GOODALL** (b. 9 May'52, Burbank, Calif.) – drums (ex-FLYING BURRITO BROTHERS, ex-CANADIAN SWEETHEART, ex-ROGER McGUINN)

Creation / Def American

Aug 92. (12"ep)(cd-ep) *(CRE 135T)(CRESCD 135)* **MEDICINE EP**
– Aruca / Onion flower / The powder / World hello.

Oct 92. (lp/cd) *(CRE LP/CD 142) <45067>* **SHOT FORTH SELF LIVING**
– One more / Aruca / Defective / A short happy life / 5ive / Sweet explosion / Queen of tension / Miss Drugstore / The Christmas song.

Feb 93. (12"ep)(cd-ep) *(CRE 141T)(CRESCD 141)* **5IVE E.P.** [-]
– 5ive / Title baby II / Lime 6 / Wrought.

American / Warners

Nov 93. (cd/lp) *(ARB CD/LP 5) <45443>* **THE BURIED LIFE**
– The pink / Babydoll / Slut / She knows everything / Something goes wrong / Never click / Fried awake / Beneath the sands / Emmeline / I hear / Live it down / The earth is soft and white.

Jan 94. (12"/cd-s) *(ARB 3 T/CD)* **NEVER CLICK. / WHILE / TIL I DIE**

Jun 94. (12"ep/cd-ep) *(ARB 6 T/CD) <45609>* **TIME BABY 3** <US-title 'SOUNDS OF MEDICINE'>
– Time baby 3 / Little Miss Drugstore / She knows everything / Little slut / Zelzah / Lime 6.

Oct 95. (cd) *(74321 28757-2) <43016>* **HER HIGHNESS**
– All good things / Wash me out / Candy Candy / Feel nothing at all / A fractured smile / Farther dub / Further down / Aarhus / Seen the light alone / Heads.

—— the band went off on their own projects, PUTTNAM to MAIDS OF GRAVITY and RADAR BROTHERS

not iss. / Next Century

Jun 98. (12") *<12-013>* **I'M SICK. / BLEACH** [-]

MEDIUM MEDIUM (see under ⇒ C-CAT TRANCE)

MEGA CITY FOUR

Formed: Farnborough, England . . . early 1987 by CHRIS JONES and ex-CAPRICORN members, GERRY BRYANT and brothers WIZ and DANNY BROWN. Taking their name from '2000 A.D.' comic hero/lawman, Judge Dredd's home city, MC4 never quite achieved the wild abandon or political influence of near-namesakes MC5 but nevertheless attempted to put the worlds to rights with their patented brand of late 80's melodic punk so beloved of the crusty scene. Along with hard-gigging peers like The SENSELESS THINGS, MC4 regularly traipsed the length and breadth of the country living out the back of a transit van. These were the experiences which informed their debut album, 'TRANZOPHOBIA' (1989), released on indie label 'Decoy' following a couple of acclaimed singles, 'DISTANT RELATIVES' and 'LESS THAN SENSELESS'. The album itself scaped into the UK Top 75 and topped the indie chart, the 'MEGA's regular features in the weekly music press pre-Madchester. As the admittedly more colourful 'baggy' scene came to dominate the media, the more worthy strains of thrash-pop weren't such hip currency and MC4's cause wasn't helped by a lacklustre production on follow-up set, 'WHO CARES WINS' (1990). Nevertheless, it was enough to get them signed up by happening label, 'Big Life', through whom they released the minor hit EP, 'WORDS THAT SAY' and their first Top 40 single, 'STOP'. The accompanying album, 'SEBASTOPOL RD' (1992) confirmed a newfound musical and lyrical maturity which combined intelligent comment with contagiously hook-laden buzz-pop. Yet it seemed the band had missed out yet again with the record frustratingly stalling just outside the Top 40. Unsurprisingly perhaps, WIZ's songwriting took a gradually more downbeat turn and 1993's 'MAGIC BULLETS' album generated even less interest. Subsequently parting company with 'Big Life', the band spent a couple of years in label limbo before signing to 'Fire' in 1995 and releasing a couple of singles,'SKIDDING' and 'SUPERSTAR'. The following year saw the release of a comeback album (of sorts), 'SOULSCRAPER', although this did little to re-establish the band. • **Covered:** DON'T WAN'T TO KNOW IF YOU ARE LONELY (Husker Du) / A HARD DAY'S NIGHT (Beatles).

Album rating: TRANZOPHOBIA (*8) / SEBASTAPOL RD (*7) / WHO CARES WINS (*7).

DARREN 'WIZ' BROWN – vocals, guitar / **DANNY BROWN** – guitar / **GERRY BRYANT** – bass / **CHRIS JONES** – drums (ex-EXIT EAST) repl. MARTIN

Primitive / not iss.

Mar 88. (7"ltd.) *(PRIME 009)* **MILES APART. / RUNNING IN DARKNESS** [-]
(re-iss. Jul88 on 'Mega City'; MEGA 1)

Decoy / not iss.

Nov 88. (7") *(DYS 1)* **DISTANT RELATIVES. / CLEAR BLUE SKY** [-]

Feb 89. (7") *(DYS 2)* **LESS THAN SENSELESS. / DANCING DAYS ARE OVER** [-]

May 89. (lp/cd) *(DYL 3/+CD)* **TRANZOPHOBIA** [67] [-]
– Start / Pride and prejudice / Severe attack of the truth / Paper tiger / January / Twenty one again / On another planet / Things I never said / New years day / Occupation / Alternative arrangements / Promise / What you've got / Stupid way to die.

Oct 89. (7") *(DYS 5)* **AWKWARD KID. / CRADLE** [-]

Mar 90. (7"ep/12"ep) *(DYS 10/+T)* **FINISH / SEVERANCE. / THANX / SQUARE THROUGH A CIRCLE** [-]

Sep 90. (lp/c/cd) *(DYL 20/+C/CD)* **WHO CARES WINS** [-]
– Who cares? / Static interference / Rose coloured / Grudge / Me not you / Messenger / Violet / Rail / Mistook / Open / Revolution / No such place as home / Storms to come / Balance.

Apr 91. (lp/c/cd) *(DYL 24/+C/CD)* **TERRIBLY SORRY BOB** (compilation) [-]

Big Life / Caroline

Sep 91. (7"ep/7"green-ep/12"ep/cd-ep) *(MEGA/+R/T/D 3)* **WORDS THAT SAY / UNTOUCHABLE. / LIPSCAY / MANSION** [66] [-]
(re-iss. Aug93 12"ep/cd-ep; same)

Jan 92. (7"red-ep/12"ep/cd-ep) *(MEGA R/T/D 3)* **STOP / DESERT SONG. / BACK TO ZERO / OVERLAP** [36] [-]
(ltd.live-7"ep) *(MEGA R3)* – Stop / Revolution / Who cares / Finish / Props.
(re-iss. Aug93 7"ep/12"ep/cd-ep; same)

Feb 92. (cd/c/lp) *(MEG CD/MC/LP 1) <2800>* **SEBASTOPOL RD** [41]
– Ticket collector / Scared of cats / Callous / Peripheral / Anne Bancroft / Prague / Clown / Props / What's up? / Vague / Stop / Wasting my breath. *(re-iss. Sep93; same)*

May 92. (7"ep/12"ep/cd-ep) *(MEGA/+T/D 4)* **SHIVERING SAND. / EVERYBODY LOVES YOU / DISTURBED** [35] [-]
(ltd.live-7"ep) *(MEGAL 4)* – Shivering sand / Words that say / Callous / Don't want to know if you are lonely. *(re-iss. Aug93 7"ep/12"ep/cd-ep; same)*

Nov 92. (cd/c/lp) *(MEG CD/C/LD 2)* **INSPIRINGLY TITLED (THE LIVE ALBUM) (live)** [-]
– Who cares / Finish / Thanx / Shivering sand / Props / Messenger / Stop / Revolution / Words that say / Callous / Lipscar / Peripheral / Clown / Open / What've you've got / Don't want to know if you are lonely. *(re-iss. Sep93)*

Apr 93. (7"ep/c-ep/10"ep/cd-ep) *(MEGA/+C/T/D 5)* **IRON SKY. / ON THE EDGE / SOMETIMES** [48] [-]

May 93. (cd/c/lp) *(MEG CD/MC/LP 003)* **MAGIC BULLETS** [57] [-]
– Perfect circle / Drown / Rain man / Toys / Iron sky / So / Enemy skies / Wallflower / President / Shadow / Underdog / Greener / Speck.

Jul 93. (7"/c-s) *(MEGA/+C 6)* **WALLFLOWER. / INAMORATA** [69] [-]
(12"+=/cd-s+=) *(MEGA T/D 6)* – Wilderness.

Fire / not iss.

Sep 95. (7") *(BLAZE 93)* **SKIDDING. / STAY DEAD** [-]
(cd-s+=) *(BLAZE 93CD)* – Lazergaze.

Nov 95. (7") *(BLAZE 97)* **SUPERSTAR. / CHRYSANTH** [-]
(cd-s+=) *(BLAZE 97CD)* –

Jan 96. (7") *(BLAZE 102)* **ANDROID DREAMS** [-]
(cd-s+=) *(BLAZE 102CD)* –

Mar 96. (cd/c/lp) *(FIRE CD/MC/LP 54)* **SOULSCRAPER** [-]

– compilations, others, etc. –

Nov 93. (cd) *Strange Fruit; (SFRCD 124) / Dutch East India; <8415>* **THE PEEL SESSIONS** Mar94

MEKONS

Formed: Leeds, England . . . 1977 by art students TOM GREENHALGH and JON LANGFORD. The pair signed to Edinburgh's 'Fast' records, soon surfacing on vinyl in early '78 with the two-chord wonder, 'NEVER BEEN IN A RIOT', reputedly a reply to the macho overtones of the CLASH's 'White Riot'. This three song ultra-DIY assault was played to death by late night DJ, John Peel, a fervent supporter through thick and thin over the ensuing two decades. To end the year, The MEKONS delivered the classic lovesick punk anthem, 'WHERE WERE YOU', a track which perhaps encapsulated the genre's yellow-haired heyday more vividly than many of their peers (i.e. the BUZZCOCKS and WIRE). Limited by the extent of their musical talent and subject to the pressures of a major label deal ('Virgin'), LANGFORD and GREENHALGH enlisted the help of ANDY CARRIGAN, MARK WHITE, KEVIN LYCETT and ROS ALLEN, the latter borrowed from fellow Leeds cohorts, DELTA 5. At the turn of the decade, The MEKONS finally delivered their debut album, 'THE QUALITY OF MERCY IS NOT STRNEN' (1980), an overly ambitious collection which marked a premature departure from their early ramshackle charm in favour of GANG OF FOUR-style politico experimentation. They were subsequently dropped by their record label the following year amid poor sales, a string of low-key independent releases via various labels, namely 'Red Rhino' and the more political 'C.N.T.'. The core trio of GREENHALGH, LANGFORD and LYCETT (although the latter was soon to leave) recruited various musicians (SALLY TIMMS and SUSIE HONEYMAN being the more stable) over the years, their style of music constantly evolving in line with the personnel comings and goings; LANGFORD moonlighted with the THREE JOHNS. Although maintaining their uncompromising punk ideals and politics (especially with regards to the plight of the miners), 1985's 'FEAR AND WHISKEY' saw The MEKONS baptised by country/roots/folk fire. 'THE MEKONS HONKY TONKIN' (1987) and 'SO GOOD IT HURTS' (1988), continued in a rootsy, if more eclectic vein, the latter encompassing elements of various world music folk styles. Moving from their own 'Sin' records to UK's 'Blast First' ('A&M' in America), the band were once more critically reborn with the blisteringly defiant 'MEKONS ROCK'N'ROLL' (1989), proving they weren't yet ready to sink into worthy middle age. In the early 90's, they (GREENHALGH, LANGFORD, TIMMS and HONEYMAN) continued to release the odd album, although geographical problems (half the band had taken flight to the States!) precluded an overly prolific release schedule. Having signed to 'Quarter Stick' in 1993, they issued a number of albums including the 1996 collaborative set,

'PUSSY, KING OF THE PIRATES', featuring narration by American writer, KATHY ACKER. Of late, the ever-industrious LANGFORD has completed his first solo set, 'SKULL ORCHARD' (1998), a disappointing album which seemed to be retreading the heady radical politics of the mid 80's. • **Covered:** MAKES NO DIFFERENCE (Robbie Robertson) / HAVING A PARTY (Kevin Coyne) / etc. • **Trivia:** Named themselves after the green-headed alien in the 50's US comic-strip 'Dan Dare'.

Album rating: THE QUALITY OF MERCY IS NOT STRNEN (*6) / UNTITLED (*4) / THE MEKONS STORY compilation (*7) / FEAR AND WHISKEY (*6) / THE EDGE OF THE WORLD (*6) / THE MEKONS HONKY TONKIN' (*5) / SO GOOD IT HURTS (*5) / MEKONS ROCK'N'ROLL (*6) / THE CURSE OF THE MEKONS (*6) / I LOVE MEKONS (*5) / RETREAT FROM MEMPHIS (*5) / PUSSY, KING OF THE PIRATES with Kathy Acker (*6) / Jon Langford: SKULL ORCHARD (*5)

TOM GREENHALGH (b. 4 Nov'56, Stockholm, Sweden) – vocals, guitar / **JON LANGFORD** (b.11 Oct'57, Newport, Wales) – drums, vocals

Fast Prod. not iss.

Feb 78. (7"m) *(FAST 1)* **NEVER BEEN IN A RIOT. / 32 WEEKS / HEART AND SOUL** -

Dec 78. (7") *(FAST 7)* **WHERE WERE YOU? / I'LL HAVE TO DANCE THEN (ON MY OWN)** -

— added **ANDY CARRIGAN** – vocals / **MARK WHITE** – lyrics / **KEVIN LYCETT** – guitar / **ROSS ALLEN** – bass (of DELTA 5)

Virgin not iss.

Sep 79. (7") *(VS 300)* **WORK ALL WEEK. / UNKNOWN WRECKS** -

Feb 80. (lp) *(V 2143)* **THE QUALITY OF MERCY IS NOT STRNEN** -
– Like spoons no more / Join us in the countryside / Rosanne / Trevira trousers / After 6 / What are we going to do tonight? / What / / Watch the film / Beetroot / I saw you dance / Lonely and wet / Dan Dare. *(cd-iss. Apr90 +=; VCD 2143)* – Teeth / Guardian / Kill / Stay cool / Work all week / Unknown wrecks. *<US cd-iss. 1990 on 'Caroline'; 1621>*

Mar 80. (d7") *(VS 101)* **TEETH. / GUARDIAN // KILL. / STAY COOL** -

Red Rhino not iss.

Dec 80. (lp) *(RR 001)* **UNTITLED** (aka 'DEVILS RATS AND PIGGIES A SPECIAL MESSAGE FROM GODZILLA') -
– Snow / St. Patrick's day / D.P. Miller / Institution / I'm so happy / Chopper squad / Business tango / Trimden Grange explosion / Karen / Corporal Chalkie / John Barry / Another one / Killer Ken / Another set of teeth. *(re-iss. Jun85; same)* <*US cd-iss. 1997 on '1/4 Stick'; QS 66*>

Sep 81. (7") *(RED 7)* **SNOW. / ANOTHER ONE TIME** -

C.N.T. not iss.

Oct 81. (12"m) *(CNT 1)* **THIS SPORTING LIFE. / FRUSTRATION / (mystery live track; NEVER BEEN IN A RIOT)** -

Nov 82. (7"ltd.) *(CNT 008)* **THIS SPORTING LIFE. / FIGHT THE CUTS** -

Nov 82. (lp) *(CNT 009)* **THE MEKONS STORY – IT FALLETH LIKE GENTLE RAIN FROM HEAVEN** (compilation) -
– The letter's in the post / Not a bitterman (born to be mild) / Dance and drink the Mekons / Bomb train / Trouble down south / Car-men / Eden / Frustrations / Fight the cuts / Byron / This sporting life / Rosanne / Garden fence of sound / Miriam always / The walking song / Building / I'm so happy / I bought you these / He beat up his boyfriend / 1st guitarist. <*US cd-iss. 1993 on 'Feel Good All Over'*>

— **GREENHALGH, LANGFORD + LYCETT** recruited new members **BEN MANDELSON** – guitar (ex-MAGAZINE) / **DICK TAYLOR** – guitar (ex-PRETTY THINGS) / **ROB WAREY** – bass (all these 3 left after 1985 recordings)

Sep 83. (12"ep) *(CNT 014)* **THE ENGLISH DANCING MASTER** -
– The last dance / No confess / No country dance / Parsons farewell.

— **LU KNEE** (aka LU EDMUNDS) – bass, guitar (ex-DAMNED, ex-EDGE) repl. LYCETT / added **SALLY TIMMS** – vocals (ex-guest & solo artist) / **SUSIE HONEYMAN** – violin / **STEVE GOULDING** – drums (ex-RUMOUR)

Sin not iss.

Jul 85. (lp) *(SIN 001)* **FEAR AND WHISKEY** -
– Chivalry / Trouble down south / Hard to be human again / Darkness and doubt / Psycho cupid (danceband on the edge of town) / Flitcraft / Country / Abernant 1984-1985 / The last dance / Lost highway. *(cd-iss. Mar89 as 'ORIGINAL SIN' on 'R.T.D.'+=; RTDCD 105)* *<US cd-iss. Mar89 as 'ORIGINAL SIN' on 'Twin/Tone'+=; 89164>* – (A dancing master such as) Mr Confess / Beaten and broken / Chop that child in half / Hey! Susan / Garage d'or / Slightly south of the border / Coal hole / $1000 wedding / Rescue mission.

Feb 86. (12"ep) *(SIN 002R)* **CRIME AND PUNISHMENT** (Peel session) -
– Beaten and broken / Chop that child in half / Hey! Susan / Deep end.

Jun 86. (lp) *(SIN 003)* **THE EDGE OF THE WORLD** -
– Hello cruel world / Bastard / Oblivion / King Arthur / Ugly band / Shanty / Garage d'or / Big zombie / Sweet dreams / Dream dream dream / Slightly south of the border / Alone and forsaken / The letter. *(<cd-iss. 1996 on '1/4 Stick'; 42)>*

Jun 86. (7") *(SIN 004)* **HELLO CRUEL WORLD. / ALONE AND FORSAKEN** -

Oct 86. (10"ep) *(SIN 005)* **SLIGHTLY SOUTH OF THE BORDER / $1,000 WEDDING. / COOL HOLE / RESCUE MISSION** -

— trimmed slightly when LU (already a brief PUBLIC IMAGE LTD member) joined SHRIEKBACK

— over the next few years, they (**GREENHALGH, LANGFORD, TIMMS, HONEYMAN + GOULDING**) used others:- **RICO BELL** – accordion / **BRENDAN CROKER** – guitar / **JOHN GILL** – mellotron / **SARAH CORINA** – bass / etc.

Sin Twin/Tone

Mar 87. (lp/c) *(SIN/+C 006)* *<TTR 87113/+C>* **THE MEKONS HONKY TONKIN'**
– I can't find my money / Hole in the ground / Sleepless nights / Keep hoppin' / Charlie cake park / If they hang you / Prince of darkness / Kidnaped / Sympathy for The Mekons / Spit / The Trimdon Grange explosion / Please don't let me love you / Gin palace. *(c+=)* – Sin city / Derion.

Aug 87. (12"m) *(SIN 007T)* **HOLE IN THE GROUND. / SIN CITY / PRINCE OF DARKNESS** -

Mar 88. (lp/c/cd) *(SIN/+C/CD 008)* *<TTR 88114/+C/CD>* **SO GOOD IT HURTS**
– I'm not here (1967) / Ghosts of American astronauts / Road to Florida / Johnny miner / Dora / Poxy lips / (Sometimes I feel like) Fletcher Christian / Fantastic voyage / Robin Hood / Heart of stone / Maverick / Vengeance. *(cd+=)* – Revenge.

Apr 88. (7") *(SIN 009)* **GHOSTS OF AMERICAN ASTRONAUTS. / ROBIN HOOD** -
(12") *(SIN 009T)* – ('A'side) / 1967 (revisited) / Revenge.

Blast First A&M

Aug 89. (10"ep/cd-ep) *(BFFP 53/+CD)* **DREAM AND LIE OF THE MEKONS** -
– Amnesia / Heaven and back / Club Mekon / Blow your tuneless trumpet.

Sep 89. (lp/c/cd) *(BFFP 40/+C/CD)* *<75021 5277-1/-4/-2>* **MEKONS ROCK'N'ROLL**
– Memphis, Egypt / Club Mekon / Only darkness has the power / Ring o'roses / Learning to live on your own / Cocaine Lil / Empire of the senseless / Someone / Amnesia / I am crazy / Heaven and back / Blow your own tuneless trumpet / Echo / When darkness falls.

Oct 90. (m-lp/c/cd) *(BFFP 62/+C/CD)* **F.U.N.'90** -
– Makes no difference / Having a party / Sheffield park / One horse town / Hashis in Marseilles / One horse dub.

Feb 91. (7") **MAKES NO DIFFERENCE. / HAVING A PARTY** -

Jun 91. (lp/c/cd) *(BFFP 80/+C/CD)* **THE CURSE OF THE MEKONS** -
– The curse / Blue arse / Wild and blue / Authority / Secrets / Nocturne / Socerer / Brutal / Funeral / Lyric / Waltz / 100% song.

— now 2 boy/ 2 girl (**GREENHALGH, LANGFORD, TIMMS + HONEYMAN**) with others on call at various times

not iss. Loud-WEA

Dec 92. (12"ep) *<89014>* **WICKED MIDNITE / ALL I WANT. / THE CURSE (live) / WALTZ (live) / AMNESIA (live)** -

1/4 Stick 1/4 Stick

Oct 93. (lp/c/cd) *(<QS 19/+C/CD>)* **I LOVE MEKONS**
– Millionaire / Wicked midnite / I don't know / Dear sausage / All I want / Special / St. Valentine's day / I love apple / Love letter / Honeymoon in Hell / Too personal / Point of no return.

Nov 93. (cd-s) *(<QS 823CD>)* **MILLIONAIRE EP**
– Millionaire / He beat up his boyfriend / All I want (live) / Blow your tuneless trumpet (live) / Fletcher Christian, (sometime I feel like) (live).

May 94. (cd/lp) *(<QS 26 CD/LP>)* **RETREAT FROM MEMPHIS**
– Eve future / Lucky devil / Insignificance (conversation with . . .) / His bad dream / Our bad dream / The flame that killed John Wayne / Ice rink in Berlin / Spinning round in flames / Machine / Hostile mascot / Chemical wedding / Spirals of paranoia / Missing you all / Submerged / Soldier / Never work.

May 95. (7") *(<QS 31>)* **UNTITLED 1. / UNTITLED 1 (continued) / UNTITLED 2**

Jan 96. (cd/lp; as MEKONS & KATHY ACKER) *(<QS 36 CD/LP>)* **PUSSY, KING OF THE PIRATES**
– Ange's song as she crawled through London / Song of the dogs / Ostracism's song to pussycat / Antigone speaks about herself / My song at night / Into the strange / Captured by pirates / A prayer for all sailors / My name is O / I want to tell you about myself / We're just outside London / Antigone, you see her / Now let me tell you / Since Ange and me are innocent.

May 98. (cd) *(<QS 53>)* **ME**
– Enter the lists / Down / Narrative / Tourettes / Flip flop / Gin & it / Back to back / Come and have a go if you think you're hard enough / Men united / Mirror / Far sub dominant / Whiskey sex shack / Thunder / Belly to belly.

– compilations, etc. –

Jan 88. (c)<cd> *R.O.I.R.; (A 154) / Combat; <5026>* **MEKONS N.Y.. (live)**
– (Chicago introduction) Big zombie / Trouble down south / Slightly south of the border / The story of nothing / Flitcraft at the Iron Horse / Prince of darkness / Abernant 84-87 / I can't find my money / The shape I'm in / Hard to be human / Beaten and broken / Not long ago / Shanty / Revenge / Sophie / Chivalry.

1988. (12") *Materiali Sonori; (MASO 70008)* **GREETINGS EIGHT** - - Italy

Mar 94. (cd) *Anagram; (CDMGRAM 76)* **THE MEKONS** -

JON LANGFORD

with **ALAN DOUGHTY** – bass, vocals / **MARC DURANTE** – guitars / **STEVE GOULDING** – drums

Sugar Free Sugar Free

Jul 98. (cd) *(<sf 006>)* **SKULL ORCHARD** Feb98
– Tubby brothers / Penny arcades / Butter song / Sentimental marching song / Youghal / Trapdoor / Inside the whale / I am the law / Pill sailor / The last count / My own worst enemy / I'm stopping this train / Deep sea diver / Tom Jones levitation.

MEL-O-TONES (see under ⇒ WALKING SEEDS)

MELT (see under ⇒ HAGAR THE WOMB)

MELVINS

Formed: Aberdeen, Washington, USA . . . early '85 by BUZZ OSBOURNE, who found LORI BECK and other floating members. Debuting early in 1987 with the patchy 'GLUEY PORCH TREATMENTS', they improved enough in the early 90's to sign for major label 'Atlantic'. In the interim period, this endearingly amateurish outfit (revered by KURT COBAIN, he had been their roadie!) graced a handful of largely ignored albums with their noisy BLACK SABBATH/SWANS fusions. Future MUDHONEY man, MATT LUKIN, appeared on their 1989 set, 'OZMA', before he was replaced by JOE PRESTON. In 1992, the three members simultaneously issued three solo EP's, much in the same way as KISS did in the late 70's. Still a long-time fan, KURT COBAIN worked with them on 1993's 'HOUDINI' set, although his continued patronage didn't do much for their record sales. A couple of uninspiring albums have surfaced during the past few years, the last of which, 'HONKY' was released on the 'Amphetamine Reptile' label. • **Songwriters:** OSBOURNE except; WAY OF THE WORLD + SACRIFICE (Flipper) / BALLAD OF DWIGHT FRY (Alice Cooper).

Album rating: GLUEY PORCH TREATMENTS (*5) / OZMA (*5) / BULLHEAD (*6) / LYSOL (*7) / HOUDINI (*5) / PRICK (*5) / STONER WITCH (*5) / STAG (*5) / HONKY (*4)

BUZZ OSBOURNE (aka KING BUZZO) – vocals, guitar / **LORI BECK** – bass / **DALE CROVER** – drums

Volume Alchemy

Feb 87. (lp) *(VM 103) <24>* **GLUEY PORCH TREATMENTS**

Tupelo Boner

Feb 90. (lp/cd) *(TUPLP 7) <BR 16/+CD>* **OZMA** 1989
– Vile / Oven / At a glance / Let God be your gardener / Creepy smell / Kool legged / Green honey / Agonizer / Raise a paw / Love thing / Ever since my accident / Revulsion – We reach / Dead dressed / Cranky Messiah / Claude / My small percent shows most / Candy-O / Eye flys / Echo head – Don't piece me / Heater moves and eyes / Steve Instant Newman / Influence of atmosphere / Exact paperbacks / Happy grey or black / Leeech / Glow god / Big as a mountain / Heaviness of the load / Flex with you / Bitten into sympathy / Gluey porch treatments / Clipping roses / As was it / Over from under the excrement. *<cd+=>* – GLUEY PORCH TREATMENTS

— **MATT LUKIN** – bass; repl. LORI

— **JOE PRESTON** – bass repl. LUKIN who joined MUDHONEY

Tupelo Boner

Feb 91. (cd/lp) *(TUP CD/LP 26) <BR 25CD>* **BULLHEAD**
– Boris / Anaconda / Ligature / It's shoved / Zodiac / If I had an exorcism / Your blessened / Cow.

Sep 91. (10"ep/cd-ep) *(TUP EP/CD 31) <BR 28CD>* **EGG NOG**
– Wispy / Antitoxidote / Hog leg / Charmicarmicat.

Aug 92. (12"ep/cd-ep) *(TUP 39 1/-2) <BR 32/+CD>* **KING BUZZO**
– Isabella / Porg / Annum / Skeeter.

— BUZZO augmented by **DALE NIXON** – guitars, etc (on above)

Aug 92. (12"ep/cd-ep) *(TUP 40 1/-2) <BR 33/+CD>* **DALE CROVER**

Aug 92. (12"ep/cd-ep) *(TUP 41 1/-2) <BR 34/+CD>* **JOE PRESTON**
– The eagle has landed / Bricklebrit / Hands first flower.

Nov 92. (cd/c/lp) *(TUP 42 2/4/1) <BR 35CD>* **LYSOL**

not iss. Amphetam. Reptile

Dec 92. (7") **NIGHT GOAT. / ADOLESCENT WET DREAM** -

East West Atlantic

Sep 93. (cd/c) *<(7567 82532-2/-4)>* **HOUDINI**
– Hooch / Set me straight / Sky pup / Joan of Arc / Pearl bomb / Spread eagle Beagle / Night goat / Lizzy / Going blind / Honey bucket / Hag me / Teet / Copache.

— **MARK DEUTROM** – bass; repl. JOE PRESTON

Nov 94. (cd/c/lp) *<(7567 82704-2/-4/-1)>* **STONER WITCH** Oct94
– Skweetis / Queen / Sweet Willy Rollbar / Revolve / Goose freight train / Roadbull / At the stake / Magic pig detective / Shevil / June bug / Lividity.

Mammoth Mammoth

Jul 96. (cd/c/lp) *<(7567-82878-2/-4/-1)>* **STAG**
– The bit / Hide / Bar-X-the rocking M / Yacob's lab / The bloat / Tipping the lion / Black bock / Goggles / Soup / Buck Owens / Sterilized / Lacrimosa / Skin horse / Captain Pungent / Berthas / Cottonmouth.

Amphetam. Reptile Amphetam. Reptile

May 97. (cd) *<(AR 64)>* **HONKY**
– They all must be slaughtered / Mombius Hibachi / Lovely butterfly / Pitfalls in serving warrants / Air breather in the arms of Morphius / Laughing with Lucifer ar Satans's sideshow / How / Harry Lauders walking stick tree / Grin / In the freaktose the bugs are dying.

Jun 98. (cd-ep) **MELVINS ALIVE AT CLUB F*CKER** -

– compilations, others, etc. –

1990's. (7") *Sympathy For The Record Industry; <(SFTRI 81)>* **WITH YO HEART NOT YO HANDS. / FOUR LETTER WOMAN / ANAL SATAN**

1991. (cd/c) *C/Z; <CZ 002/+A>* **MELVINS (live in 1996)** -
– Easy as it was / Now a Limo / Grinding process / #2 pencil / At a crawl / Disinvite / Snake appeal / Show off your red hands / Over the underground / Crayfish.

Jan 92. (cd) *Your Choice; <(YCR 012/+CD)>* **MELVINS** (early material) Mar94

Nov 92. (5"clear-ep) *Scooby Doo; (SAH 13)* **LOVE CANAL. / CANAL** -

Aug 94. (lp/cd) *Amphetamine Reptile; <(ARR/+CD 58-333)>* **PRICK**
– How about / Rickets / Pick it n' flick it / Montreal / Chief ten beers / Underground / Chalk people / Punch the lion / Pure digital silence / Larry / Roll another one.

Aug 97. (cd) *<AR 63CD>* **1996, VOL.1-12** -
– Lexicon devil / Pigtro / In the rain / Spread eagle / Leech / Queen / Way of the world / Theme / It's shoved / Forgotten principles / GGIIBBYY / Theresa screams / Poison / Double troubled / Specimen / All at once / Jacksonville / Dallas / Bloat / Fast forward / Nasty dogs and funky kings / HDYF / How – Walking stick tree / Brutal truth – Zodiac.

MEMBERS

Formed: Camberley, Surrey, England . . . 1977 by NICKY TESCO and French-born JEAN-MARIE CARROLL along with GARY BAKER and ADRIAN LILLYWHITE. Following the subsequent replacement of BAKER with NIGEL BENNETT and the addition of CHRIS PAYNE the band made their first foray into DIY punk with the raw 'FEAR ON THE STREETS' single. Released on the tiny (self-financed) 'X.S.' label, the track alerted the recently formed 'Stiff' who signed them to a one-single deal. The result was 'SOLITARY CONFINEMENT', a paean to the delights of living in the bedsit-land of London's lovely Earls Court. Amateurish but addictive, it landed them a major label deal with 'Virgin', Richard Branson's operation releasing punk classic, 'THE SOUND OF THE SUBURBS', in 1979. A singalong mob anthem for semi-detached youth up and down the country, the track was the finest example of The MEMBERS' knack for three-chord chaos baited on the sharpest of hooklines; the band were memorably described as the intelligent bloke's SHAM 69. The fact that both a TV series (charting the history of the genre) and a best selling compilation album – both part of the ever enduring nostalgia for punk's heyday – were named in the track's honour is testament to its importance. Yet like many of their peers, the band made the tragic mistake of recording a cod-reggae follow-up; it may have been amusing but 'OFFSHORE BANKING BUSINESS' fell flat. A Steve Lillywhite (brother of ADRIAN)-produced debut album, 'AT THE CHELSEA NIGHTCLUB' (1979), met with some positive critical noises but the lack of a worthy successor to 'SOUND . . .' eventually sounded the death knell on The MEMBERS' career. A second 'Virgin' album, 'THE CHOICE IS YOURS' (1980), met with little enthusiasm and signalled the end of their contract. The independently released 'GOING WEST' (1983) was a last-ditch effort, TESCO already having long since abandoned ship.

Album rating: AT THE CHELSEA NIGHTCLUB (*5) / THE CHOICE IS YOURS (*4) / GOING WEST (*4)

NICKY TESCO – vocals / **GARY BAKER** – lead guitar / **J.C. MAINMAN** (b. JEAN-MARIE CARROLL) – guitar, vocals / **CHRIS BAYNE** – bass, vocals / **ADRIAN LILLYWHITE** – drums

X.S. not iss.

Jul 77. (7"; w-drawn) *(XS 1)* **FEAR ON THE STREETS. /** -

One Off-Stiff not iss.

May 78. (7") *(OFF 3)* **SOLITARY CONFINMENT. / RAT UP A DRAINPIPE** -

— **NIGEL BENNETT** – lead guitar; repl. BAKER

Virgin not iss.

Jan 79. (7"clear) *(VS 242)* **THE SOUND OF THE SUBURBS. / HANDLING THE BIG JETS** 12 -

Mar 79. (7"/12") *(VS 248/+12)* **OFFSHORE BANKING BUSINESS. / SOLITARY CONFINEMENT** 31 -

Apr 79. (lp) *(V 2120)* **AT THE CHELSEA NIGHTCLUB** 46 -
– Love in a lift / Electricity / Don't push / Offshore banking business / Soho a go-go / Frustrated bagshot / The sound of the suburbs / Solitary confinment / Sally / Stand up and spit / Phone-in show / Chelsea nightclub. *(re-iss. Mar84; OVED 44)*

Sep 79. (7") *(VS 292)* **KILLING TIME. / G.L.C.** -

Mar 80. (7") *(VS 333)* **ROMANCE. / THE BALLAD OF JOHN MARTIN** -

Apr 80. (lp) *(V 2153)* **THE CHOICE IS YOURS** -
– Brian was / Killing time / Clean men / Romance / Flying again / Solitary confinement / Chelsea nightclub / Gang war / Police car.

May 80. (d7") *(VS 352)* **FLYING AGAIN. / DISCO OUI OUI // LOVE IN A LIFT. / RAT UP A DRAINPIPE** -

— now a quartet when TESCO went solo (J.C. & C.B. took over vocals)

Albion not iss.

May 81. (7") *(ION 1012)* **WORKING GIRL. / HOLIDAY IN TANGANIKA** -
(12"+=) *(12ION 1012)* – Everybody's a holiday.

Island Arista

Apr 82. (7") *(WIP 6773)* **RADIO. / IF YOU CAN'T STAND UP** -

Jan 83. (7") **BOYS LIKE US. / AT THE ARCADE** -

Albion not iss.

Jul 83. (7") *(ION 1050)* **WORKING GIRL (re-recorded). / THE FAMILY** -
(12"+=) *(12ION 1050)* – The arcade.

Aug 83. (lp) *(ALB 115)* **GOING WEST** -
– Working girl / The family / You and me against the world / Chairman of the board / Boys like us / Going west / Radio / Fire (in my heart) / The model / We, the people.

Aug 83. (7"/12") *(ION/12ION 153)* **GOING WEST. / MEMBERSHIP** -

— split 1983

– compilations, others, etc. –

on 'Virgin' unless mentioned otherwise

Apr 83. (7"/12") *(VS 584/+12)* **THE SOUND OF THE SUBURBS. / OFFSHORE BANKING BUSINESS** -

Feb 91. (cd) *(CDOVD 310)* **THE CHOIVE IS YOURS / AT THE CHELSEA NIGHTCLUB** -

Mar 95. (cd) *(CDOVD 455)* **THE SOUND OF THE SUBURBS . . .THE FINEST MOMENTS** -
– Handling the big jets / Sally / G.L.C. / Offshore banking business / Pennies in the pound / Soho a go-go / Muzak machine / Rat up a drainpipe / Sound of the suburbs / Phone-in show / Brian was / Killing time / Clean men / Romance / Flying again / Solitary confinement / Chelsea nightclub / Gang war / Police car.

MEMBRANES

Formed: Preston, Lancashire . . . 1977 by JOHN ROBB alongside MARK TILTON, MARTIN CRITCHLEY and MARTIN KELLY. Their first recording, 'ICE AGE', was for Various Artists compilation EP, 'BLACKPOOL ROX', released on 'Vinyl Drip'. With CRITCHLEY subsequently replaced by COOFY SID, The MEMBRANES gained instant notoriety in 1980 via their flexi-disc 45, 'FLEXIBLE MEMBRANE' and a debut single proper, 'MUSCLES'. Raved over by both the music press and John Peel, the track's cult success secured the band a deal with 'Rondolet' records through whom they released a follow-up track, 'PIN STRIPE HYPE', complete with extra guitarist STEVE FARMBRY. His tenure was brief, however, the group reverting to a three piece and signing to 'Criminal Damage' for 1984's 'PULP BEATING AND ALL THAT'. Featuring the infamous blast of cacophonous noise that was 'SPIKE MILLIGAN'S TAPE RECORDER', the record fully displayed ROBB's ability for subhuman wailing together with the band's talent for generating bass-crunching sonic chaos; a challenging listen to say the least, The MEMBRANES augmented their unholy racket with bleating sax on 1985's 'GIFT OF LIFE', their first and only effort for 'Creation'. Constant personnel changes blighted the band's career and as ROBB increasingly concentrated on a career in music journalism, The MEMBRANES gradually fell by the wayside. The STEVE ALBINI (of spiritual heirs, BIG BLACK)-produced 'KISS ASS GODHEAD' (1988) surfaced on US label, 'Homestead', while 1989's 'TO SLAY THE ROCK PIG' was to be The MEMBRANES' parting shot as ROBB became enmeshed in the emerging dance culture with SENSURROUND. One of the UK's more respected music scribes, ROBB went on to pen an acclaimed biography of The STONE ROSES as well as fronting rock'n'roll renegades, GOLD BLADE. • **Songwriters:** PENAL LANDSCAPE GARDENER (Dead Kennedys) / ICE CREAM FOR CROW (Captain Beefheart) / ANGIE (Rolling Stones) / VOODOO CHILE (Jimi Hendrix) / BIG DECISION (That Petrol Emotion).

Album rating: THE GIFT OF LIFE (*5) / GIANT (*4) / SONGS OF LOVE AND FURY (*5) / KISS ASS . . . GODHEAD! (*4) / TO SLAY THE ROCK PIG (*4) / PULP BEATING AND ALL THAT compilation (*6)

JOHN ROBB (b. 4 May'61, Preston, England) – vocals, bass, dustbin lids / **MARK TILTON** – guitar, vocals / **T.P. KELLY** – guitar, keyboards / **COOFY SID (COULTHART)** – drums; repl. vocalist MARTIN CRITCHLEY

Vinyl Drip · not iss.

Dec 80. (7"flexi) *(VD 005)* **FLEXIBLE MEMBRANE** –
– Fashionable junkies / Almost China.

Jan 82. (7") *(VD 007)* **MUSCLES. / ALL ROADS LEAD TO NORWAY** –

Rondelet · not iss.

May 82. (7"ep/12"ep) *(ROUND/12ROUND 19)* **MUSCLES / ALL ROADS LEAD TO NORWAY. / GREAT MISTAKE / ENTERTAINING FRIENDS** –

— **STEVE FARMBRY** – guitar; repl. KELLY

Nov 82. (7"ep/12"ep) *(ROUND/12ROUND 28)* **PIN STRIPE HYPE** –
– High St. Yanks / Funny old world / The hitch / Man from Moscow.

— now a trio when STEVE departed

Criminal Damage · not iss.

Dec 83. (m-lp) *(CRIMLP 105)* **CRACK HOUSE** –
– (re-iss. Jun85; same)

Jun 84. (7") *(CRI 115)* **SPIKE MILLIGAN'S TAPE RECORDER. / KENNEDY '63** –
(re-iss. Sep86 with PHILIP BOA on 'Constrictor'; CON 9)

Jan 85. (12"ep) *(CRI 12-125)* **DEATH TO TRAD ROCK** –
– Shine on Pumpkin Moon / The kite-man / Big nose and the howling wind / Myths and legends.

— **STAN BATCOW** – bass, vocals, guitar; repl. TILTON who was still co-producer and part-time member until he joined The CREEPERS (MARC RILEY)

Creation · not iss.

Aug 85. (lp) *(CRELP 006)* **THE GIFT OF LIFE** –
– Shot by my own gun / I am fisheye / Dreadful saint engine / Green and ghostly land / More skin and bone / Mr. Charisma brain / Barbest snake fish thing / Chewing the fat / Typical male penis / Fire face / Gift of life.

In-Tape · not iss.

Mar 86. (7") *(IT 029)* **EVERYTHING'S BRILLIANT. / CLEANSED AGAIN** –
(12"+=) *(ITT 029)* – ('A'mix) / New blood for young skulls / King Cotton Whiplash.

Constrictor · not iss.

Jun 86. (lp) *(CON 00004)* **GIANT** – – German
– Sexy? big tongue! / Everything's brilliant / Mr. Charisma brain / King cotton whiplash / Gift of life (parts 1 & 2) / Shot by my own gun / Everyone's going, triple bad acid yeah! / New blood for young skulls / Chwing the fat.

— **WALLAS TERROR** – bass, vocals; repl. STAN

— brought in guests **TIM HYLAND** – sax / **NICK BROWN** – violin, guitar / **TED CHIPPINGTON** – vocals (Solo artist) / **KEITH CURTIS** – guitar, bass / **NOEL KILBRIDE** – guitar

Oct 86. (lp) *(IT 038) (CON 00010)* **SONGS OF LOVE AND FURY** –
– Big fun tonight / Kennedy '63 / Postdetergent / Vacuum cleaner man / The day my universe changed / Bang! / Snaffleflatch / The murder of Sister George / Spaceships / 1986 / Thank heavens for the iron horse / Sleazeball / Phoney T.V. repair man / The Elvis I knew was no junkie / Everyone's going triple bad acid, yeah! / Jaw cracker fuzz.

— **NICK + KEITH** were now added full-time

— Early in '87, the group were credited on 'Past Caring' with PIG BROS.

1987. (7"orange) *(CON 00024)* **GROOVY F---ERS. / TIME WARP 1991 (mix) / GREAT MISTAKE** – – German

Glass · Homestead

Aug 87. (7") *(GLASS 052)* **TIME WARP 1991. / TOO FAST TO LIVE, TOO FAST TO DIE** –
(12"+=) *(GLASS12 052)* – ('A'mix) / Groovy / Dragon fly.

Apr 88. (lp) *(GLALP 028) (CON 00034) <HMS 108>* **KISS ASS . . . GODHEAD!**
– Long live the hooligan! / Viva! Spanish turncoat / Tatty seaside town / Electric storm / (The world acclaims) . . . Eternal protein man / Let's take the death trip / Flyspray / Your puppy / Bulbous love child / Corn dolly fear / Punk out, baby / Bacon factory / Cheap male aggression / John Robb's 91st nightmare.

— **PAUL MORLEY** – bass, vocals (ex-SLUM TURKEYS) repl. WALLAS

Vinyl Drip · not iss.

Jul 89. (12"ep) *(SUK 8)* **EURO PIG VS. AUTO FLESH** –
– Auto flesh / Tatty seaside town II / Voodoo smile / Hey Bryn Maer.

Nov 89. (lp/cd) *(SUK 9/+CD) <CON 00041>* **TO SLAY THE ROCK PIG** –
– Auto flesh / Space hopper ignites / Caretaker mentality / Life, death and the scary bits inbetween / Tuff veggie aggro / More than a kiss (the freak remains high) / 24 hour drinking at northern prices / Vile antics of supa yob! / Missive from couch potato command / England expects every man to do his booty (Starfucker No.2) / Growling people.

Clawfist · not iss.

1991. (7") *(XPIG 6)* **BIG DECISION (SLIGHT RETURN). / (B-side by THAT PETROL EMOTION)** –

— Disbanded when ROBB formed SENSURROUND

– compilations, etc. –

Apr 86. (lp) *Criminal Damage; (CRIMLP 130)* **PULP BEATING AND ALL THAT** –

Jun 87. (lp) *Vinyl Drip; (DRIPLP 1)* **THE VIRGIN MARY VERSUS PETER SELLERS – BACK CATALOGUE** –

Jul 93. (cd) *A-Bomb / Constrictor; (13) / (CCON 001CD)* **WRONG PLACE AT THE WRONG TIME** –

Jun 97. (cd) *Anagram; (CDMGRAM 112)* **THE BEST OF THE MEMBRANES** –
– Ice age / Fashionable junkies / Muscles / High St. Yanks / Man from Moscow / Kafka's dad / Spike Milligan's tape recorder / Myths and legends / Shine on pumpkin moon / I am fish eye / Mr. Charisma brain / Everything's brilliant / Kennedy '63 / Spaceships / Everyone's going triple bad acid yeah / Time warp 1991 / Love your puppy / Electric storm / Tatty seaside town / Voodoo chile.

SENSURROUND

JOHN ROBB – bass, etc / **TRACEY CARMEN** – vocals / **GREG WILSON** – DJ (ex-manager of RUTHLESS RAP ASSASSINS) / **PATRICK + ADAM**

Ice Rink · not iss.

Jun 92. (12") *(DAV 02-12)* **BLIND FAITH. / ('A'mix)** –

Apr 93. (12"/cd-s) *(DAV 05 12/CD)* **WHEN I GET TO HEAVEN. / ('A'mixes) / DEEP INSIDE YOUR LOVE (Hulme mix)** –

ME ME ME (see under ⇒ ELASTICA)

MENSWEAR

Formed: Camden, London, England . . . 1994 by JOHNNY DEAN, CHRIS GENTRY and STUART BLACK, who subsequently completed the line-up with SIMON WHITE and TODD PARMENTER (the latter being replaced by MATT EVERITT in 1994). The following year, they scored their first of three major UK hits with the WIRE-sounding, 'DAYDREAMER'. Other influences of BLUR and the MONKEES were apparent on the other two 'STARDUST' and 'SLEEPING IN', both taken from the Top 10 album, 'NUISANCE' (1995). However, two further chart appearances with 'BEING BRAVE' and 'WE LOVE YOU' (both in '96) were the last with EVERITT, who has since been replaced by former roadie, TUD. • **Trivia:** CHRIS GENTRY is (still?) the boyfriend of DONNA from ELASTICA.

Album rating: NUISANCE (*7)

JOHNNY DEAN (b.12 Dec'71) – vocals / **SIMON WHITE** – guitar, vocals / **CHRIS GENTRY** (b.23 Feb'77) – guitars / **STUART BLACK** – bass, acoustic guitar / **MATT EVERITT** – drums, percussion; repl. TOOD PARMENTER

Laurel-London · London

Apr 95. (7"/cd-s) *(LAU/+CD 4)* **I'LL MANAGE SOMEHOW. / SECONDHAND** 49 –

Jun 95. (7"/c-s) *(LAU/+MC 5)* **DAYDREAMER. / GENTLEMAN JIM** 14 –
(cd-s+=) *(LAUCD 5)* – Around you again.

Sep 95. (7"/c-s) *(LAU/+MC 6)* **STARDUST. / DAYDREAMER (dub dreamer)** 16 –
(cd-s+=) *(LAUCD 6)* – Back in the bar / Satellite.

Oct 95. (cd/c/lp) *(<828 676-2/-4/-1>)* **NUISANCE** 11
– 125 West 3rd Street / I'll manage somehow / Sleeping in / Little Miss Pinpoint eyes / Daydreamer / Hollywood girl / Being brave / Around you again / The one / Stardust / Piece of me / Stardust (reprise).

Nov 95. (7"/c-s) *(LAU/+MC 7)* **SLEEPING IN. / SUNDAY DRIVER** 24 –
(cd-s+=) *(LAUCD 7)* – Now is the hour / 26 years.

Mar 96. (7") *(LAU 8)* **BEING BRAVE. / PUBLIC IMAGE** 10 –
(cd-s+=) *(LAUCD 8)* – Sunlight on the moon / This will be our year.
(cd-s) *(LAUDP 8)* – ('A'side) / I'll manage somehow (live) / Daydreamer (live) / Stardust (live).

Aug 96. (c-s) *(LAUMC 11)* **WE LOVE YOU / CRASH** 22
(cd-s+=) *(LAUCD 11)* – Phat kid music (demo) / Hanging in the blue sky (demo).
(cd-s) *(LAUDP 11)* – ('A'side) / The one (live) / Sleeping in (live) / Little Miss Pinpoint eyes (live).

— **TUD** – drums (ex-roadie) repl. EVERITT, who joined the MONTROSE AVENUE

MEN THEY COULDN'T HANG

Formed: London, England . . . 1983 by former buskers, (PHIL) SWILL, his brother JOHN, PAUL SIMMONDS, STEPHAN CUSH and SHANNE HASLER, who got together for an impromptu performance at the Alternative Country Festival in London. Though they never intended to become a professional outfit, their performance was so well received that promoters were queuing up to offer them gigs and ELVIS COSTELLO was so impressed he signed them to his 'Imp' label. Though they were initially lumped in with the "cowpunk" scene (and compared to The POGUES, HASLER having been a member of The NIPPLE ERECTORS with SHANE MacGOWAN), the MTCH's hard-edged folk-rock/thrash was always more politically motivated, tracing the linage of historical protest and choosing a cover of Scottish folkie, Eric Bogle's anti-war anthem, 'THE GREEN FIELDS OF FRANCE', as a debut single in late '84. One of their biggest fans was the evergreen John Peel, whose audience rated the song at No.3 in his Radio 1 Festive 50. A follow-up, 'IRONMASTERS', was even more frenetic and just as cutting, while the debut album, 'NIGHT OF A 1,000 CANDLES' (1985) brought widespread acclaim. A final, NICK LOWE-produced single for 'Imp' later that year, 'GREENBACK DOLLAR', preceded a major label deal with

'M.C.A.'. The resulting album, 'HOW GREEN IS MY VALLEY' (1986), was a disappointment in comparison, the band's material not translating well to big budget production values. Though it made the Top 75, the album failed to achieve the crossover success that their new label were obviously hoping for and the band duly found themselves dropped. Picking up where they left off with 'Magnet', the band eventually released the much improved 'WAITING FOR BONAPARTE' (1988), missing the UK Top 40 by a whisker. After being subjected to record company pressure for a name change, the band again parted company with their label. Subsequently finding a more sympathetic home at 'Silvertone', the band released the superior 'SILVERTOWN' (1989), a record which found SIMMONDS at his most lyrically scathing and provided them with the only Top 40 entry of their career. Finally, shortly after the release of 1990 set, 'THE DOMINO CLUB', the band called it a day, the concert set, 'ALIVE, ALIVE-O' (1991) a document of their final night at London's Town and Country Club and testament to the onstage intensity of these musical vagabonds. Surprisingly, The MEN THEY COULDN'T HANG came back to haunt the scene in late '96 with an EP on 'Demon'. This was followed by a full-length album, 'NEVER BORN TO FOLLOW' (1996) and mini-set, 'SIX PACK' (1997), although their profile remains low. • **Covered:** DONALD WHERE'S YOUR TROOSERS? (hit; Andy Stewart) / RAWHIDE (Link Wray) / MAN IN THE CORNER SHOP (Paul Weller) / GOODBYE T'JANE (Slade) / HARVEST MOON (Neil Young) / NEVER BORN TO FOLLOW (Goffin-King) / etc. • **Trivia:** GREENBACK DOLLAR was produced by NICK LOWE.

Album rating: FIVE GLORIOUS YEARS compilation (*7) / NIGHT OF 1,000 CANDLES (*8) / HOW GREEN IS MY VALLEY (*6)

PHIL 'SWILL' ODGERS – vocals, accoustic guitar, tin whistle, melodia / **PAUL SIMMONDS** – guitar, vocals, mandolin, keyboards / **STEFAN CUSH** (b.Wales) – guitar, vocals / **SHANNE HASLER** – bass (ex-NIPPLE ERECTORS, ex-NIPS) / **JON ODGERS** – drums, percussion

Imp-Demon / not iss.

Oct 84. (7") *(IMP 003)* **THE GREEN FIELDS OF FRANCE. / ('A'version)** [ ] [-]
(12"+=) *(IMP 003T)* – Hush little baby.

Jun 85. (7") *(IMP 005)* **IRONMASTERS. / DONALD WHERE'S YOUR TROOSERS?** [ ] [-]
(12"+=) *(IMP 005T)* – Rawhide.

Demon / not iss.

Jul 85. (lp/c) *(FIEND/+CASS 50)* **NIGHT OF A 1,000 CANDLES** [91] [-]
– The day after / Jack Dandy / A night to remember / Johnny comes home / The green fields of France (no man's land) / Ironmasters / Hush little baby / Walkin' talkin' / Kingdom come / Scarlet ribbons. *(cd-iss. 1988; FIENDCD 50) <US cd-iss. 1997 on 'Diablo'; 839>*

Nov 85. (7") *(D 1040)* **GREENBACK DOLLAR. / A NIGHT TO REMEMBER** [ ] [-]
(12"+=) *(D 1040T)* – The bells.

M.C.A. / M.C.A.

Jun 86. (7") *(SELL 1)* **GOLD RUSH. / GHOSTS OF CABLE STREET** [ ] [-]
(12"+=) *(SELLT 1)* – Walkin' talkin'.

Oct 86. (7") *(SELL 2)* **SHIRT OF BLUE. / JOHNNY COME HOME** [ ] [-]
(12"+=) *(SELLT 2)* – Whiskey in me giro / Scarlet ribbons.

Oct 86. (lp/c) *(MCF/+C 3337)* **HOW GREEN IS MY VALLEY** [68] [ ]
– Gold strike / Gold rush / Ghosts of Cable Street / Dancing on the pier / The bells / Wishing well / Going back to Coventry / Shirt of blue / Rabid underdog / Tiny soldiers / The parade / Parted from you. *(cd-iss. Jan90; DMCF 1898) (re-iss. Nov92 cd/c; MCL D/C 19075)*

Mar 87. (7"/12") *(SELL/+T 3)* **GHOSTS OF CABLE STREET. / DREAM MACHINE** [ ] [-]
(c-s+=) *(SELLC 3)* – Liverpool lullaby.

— **RICKY McGUIRE** – bass; repl. SHANNE

Magnet / Warners

Oct 87. (7"/7"pic-d) *(SELL/+P 5)* **ISLAND IN THE RAIN. / COUNTRY SONG** [ ] [-]
(7"ep+=/12"ep+=) *(SELL E/T 5)* – Silver dagger / Restless highway.

Mar 88. (7") *(SELL 6)* **THE COLOURS. / RORY'S GRAVE** [61] [-]
(12"+=) *(SELLT 6)* – Big iron.
(cd-s++=) *(CDSELL 6)* – ('A'-full remix).

Apr 88. (lp/c/cd) *(MAGL/MAGC/DMAG 5075)* **WAITING FOR BONAPARTE** [41] [-]
– The crest / Smugglers / Dover lights / Bounty hunter / Island in the rain / The colours / Midnight train / Father's wrong / Life of a small fry / Mary's present. *(cd+=)* – The crest (12"version). *(c+=)* – Silver dagger / Restless highway / Country song. *(re-iss. May88 lp/c)(cd; WX 183/+C)(242380-2)*

WEA / not iss.

Jun 88. (7"/12") *(YZ 193/+T)* **THE CREST. / TIME AT THE BAR** [ ] [-]
(cd-s+=) *(YZ 193CD)* – Goodbye t'Jane / Ironmasters.

— added p/t **NICKY MUIR** – keyboards, accordion

Silvertone / not iss.

Feb 89. (7") *(ORE 4)* **RAIN, STEAM AND SPEED. / SHIRT OF BLUE** [ ] [-]
(12"+=) *(ORET 4)* – Scarlet ribbons.
(cd-s++=) *(ORECD 4)* – Iron masters.

Apr 89. (lp/c/cd) *(ORE LP/MC/CD 503)* **SILVERTOWN** [39] [-]
– Rosettes / A place in the sun / Home fires / Diamonds, gold & fur / Company town / Lobotomy gets 'em home / Blackfriar's bridge / Rain, steam and speed / Down all the days / Hellfire and damnation / Homefires / El vaquero. *(cd+=)* – A map of Morocco / Rain, steam and speed (12"mix).

May 89. (7") *(ORE 7)* **A PLACE IN THE SUN. / A MAP OF MOROCCO** [ ] [-]
(12"+=) *(ORET 7)* – Scarlet ribbons.
(cd-s++=) *(ORECD 7)* – The day after (live).

Dec 89. (7") *(ORE 14)* **A MAP OF MOROCCO. / ROSETTES / THE DAY THE CLOCK WENT BACK** [ ] [-]
(12"+=/12"s+=) *(ORE T/X 14)* – Rosettes (live).
(cd-s++=) *(ORECD 14)* – The iron men of rap (with ATTILA THE STOCKBROKER).

Jul 90. (7") *(ORE 19)* **GREAT EXPECTATIONS. / MARGARET PIE** [ ] [-]
(cd-s+=) *(ORECD 19)* – Green fields of France.
(12"+=) *(ORET 19)* – (excerpts from forthcoming album below).

Aug 90. (cd/c/lp) *(ORE CD/MC/LP 512)* **THE DOMINO CLUB** [53] [-]
– The lion and the unicorn / Great expectations / The family man / Handy man / Kingdom of the blind / Grave rosting in gig harbour / Industrial town / You're the one / Australia / Dog eyes, owl meat, man-chops / Billy Morgan / On the razzle.

Oct 90. (10"/cd-s) **THE LION AND THE UNICORN. / KINGDOM OF THE BLIND** [ ] [-]

— Disbanded February '91 after some farewell gigs (& periodical one-offs)

Fun After All / not iss.

May 91. (cd/c/lp) *(CD/T+/AFTER 10)* **ALIVE, ALIVE-O (live)** [ ] [-]
– The crest / Billy Morgan / You're the one / Home fires / Going back to Coventry / The colours / Ironmasters / Lobotomy, gets 'em home / Man in the corner shop / Australia / Night to remember / Scarlet ribbons.

LIBERTY CAGE

— **SIMMONDS + ODGERS / + DAVE KENT** – whistle, harmonica, trumpet, vocals / **NEIL SIMMONDS** – double bass, sax, bass, guitar

Line / not iss.

Sep 94. (cd) *(LICD 9.01293)* **SLEEP OF THE JUST** [ ] [-]
– Everything's different now / Fires below / Throwing stones at the sea / On her majesty's service / Swimming against the tide / One for the road / Judgement day / You make my mind stand still / Mercy of the guards / Cat and mouse affair / Murder in cell #9 / C.D.C.

Kronk / not iss.

Sep 95. (cd-ep) **I'LL KEEP IT WITH MONE / THE RIVERS RUN DRY / SLIP AWAY GENTLY / HEAVEN'S PRISONERS** [ ] [-]
(above a DYLAN song) **PAUL HOWARD** – guitar, c-vocals (ex-TENDER TRAP) repl. KENT, although they subsequently split after

MEN THEY COULDN'T HANG

— re-formed in 1996, **KENNY HARRIS** – drums, percussion; repl. JON

Demon / Demon

Oct 96. (cd-ep) *(D 2000)* **THE EYE / HARVEST MOON / PERRY BORDER / PIECES OF PARADISE** [ ] [-]

Nov 96. (cd) *(<FIENDCD 788>)* **NEVER BORN TO FOLLOW** [ ] [ ]
– The eye / Glittering prize / Never born to follow / I survived / Contenders / Our day / Gangland / House of cards / Denis Law & Ali MacGraw / To have and to hold / The spell is broken / Jennifer Grey.

— **ANDY SELWAY** – drums, percussion; repl. HARRIS

Jul 97. (m-cd) *(<VEXCD 15>)* **SIX PACK** [ ] [ ]
– Nightbird / The wonder of it all / Moving on / Refugee / Come forward / Henry Krinkle: Alone inna ugly town.

– compilations, others, etc. –

Aug 88. (12"ep) *Strange Fruit; (SFNT 012)* **THE EVENING SHOW SESSIONS (15.6.86)** [ ] [-]
– Dancing on the pier / Ghosts of Cable Street / Going back to Coventry / Tiny tin soldiers.

Apr 90. (cd/c/lp; w-drawn) *Silvertone; (ORE CD/MC/LP 509)* **FIVE GLORIOUS YEARS** [ ] [-]

1992. (7"ep/12"ep/cd-ep) **GREAT EXPECTATIONS (BIG DREAMS) / THE COLOURS (live). / GHOSTS OF CABLE STREET (live) / KINGDOM OF THE BLIND** [ ] [-]

Apr 98. (cd) *Demon; (<FIENDCD 940>)* **MAJESTIC GRILL: THE BEST OF THE MEN THEY COULDN'T HANG** [ ] [ ]
– Ironmasters / Ghosts of Cable Street / Shirt of blue / Scarlet ribbons / The crest / Colours / Islands in the rain / Rosettes / Dogs' eyes, owl meat and man chop / Map of Morocco / Denis Law and Ali Maggraw / Australia / Eye / Our day / Nightbird / Green fields of France (no man's land).

MEN WITHOUT HATS

Formed: Montreal, Canada . . . 1980 by brothers IVAN and JEREMIE ARROBAS. North America's premier electro-pop purveyors if only because of a dearth of any peers, these mad hatters issued two US-only 12"ers for the Stateside branch of 'Stiff', 'FOLK OF THE 80's' and 'NATIONALE 7'. However, these were the only two recordings to feature the brothers together, JEREMIE leaving his more talented sibling to recruit a full band (including brothers STEFAN and COLIN DOROSCHUK alongside ALLAN McCARTHY) and sign to 'Backstreet' ('Statik' in the UK). Initially the act struggled, two singles and an album failing to sell any significant quota while even the 'SAFETY DANCE' single made little impact the first time round. A quirky but irresistably infectious, post-PETER GABRIEL new wave pop classic, the latter track finally entered the US charts in the summer of '83. Promoted by an innovative video (with IVAN as the colourful court jester!) and featuring fashionable pre-1984/anti-nuclear sentiments, the single rocketed into the American Top 3 before making the Top 20 in both Britain and Europe. The aforementioned debut album, 'RHYTHM OF YOUTH' (1982/3), made Stateside inroads after being re-promoted, although this was their only long-playing success. Unfortunately, 'SAFETY DANCE', became the proverbial albatross around their necks with further singles and albums – 'FOLK OF THE 80's PART III' (1984) and 'POP GOES THE WORLD (1987) – selling only moderately; the fact that "WEIRD AL" YANKOVIC graced them with a parody certainly didn't help their cause.

Album rating: RHYTHM OF YOUTH (*5) / FOLK OF THE 80'S PART III (*4) / POP GOES THE WORLD (*4)

IVAN ARROBAS – vocals, synths / **JEREMIE ARROBAS** – drums, synths not iss. Stiff

1981. (12"ep) <TEES12 01> **FOLK OF THE 80'S** [-] [ ]
– Modern(e) dancing / Utter space / Antartica / Security (everybody feels better with it).

—— <above originally issued for 'Trend' in Canada; HATS 001>

1981. (12") <TEES12 08> **NATIONALE 7. / FREEWAYS** [-] [ ]

—— **IVAN** (now without JEREMIE) recruited **STEFAN DOROSCHUK** – guitar, violin + **ALLAN McCARTHY** – electronics, piano, percussion / plus **COLIN DOROSCHUK** – guitar / **ANNE DUSSAULT** – vocals / **DANIEL VERMETTE** – guitar / **MARTIN CARTIER** + **MICHEL JEROME** – percussion

Statik Backstreet

Mar 82. (7") *(STAT 13)* **ANTARTICA. / MODERN DANCING** [ ] [ ]
Aug 82. (7") *(STAT 20)* **I GOT THE MESSAGE. / UTTER SPACE** [ ] [ ]
Oct 82. (lp/c) *(STAT LP/C 10)* <39002> **RHYTHM OF YOUTH** [ ] [13] Jul83
– Ban the game / Living in China / The great ones remember / I got the message / Cocoricci (le tango des voleurs) / Safety dance / Ideas for walls / Things in my life / I like / The great ones remember – reprise. *(cd-iss. Oct85; CDST 10)*
Mar 83. (7") *(TAK 1)* **SAFETY DANCE. / SECURITY** [ ] [ ]
(12"+=) *(TAK 1-12)* – I got the message.
(re-iss. Sep83; same) – hit No.6
Jun 83. (7") <52232> **SAFETY DANCE. / LIVING IN CHINA** [-] [3]
Oct 83. (7") <52293> **I LIKE. / THINGS IN MY LIFE** [-] [84]
Jan 84. (7") *(TAK 3)* **LIVING IN CHINA. / COCORICCI (LE TANGO DES VOLEURS)** [ ] [ ]
(12"+=) *(TAK 3-12)* – Modern dancing.

—— now a 4-piece of **IVAN, ALLAN, STEFAN + COLIN** with guest ANNE

Jun 84. (7"/12") *(TAK 15/+12)* **WHERE DO THE BOYS GO? / EUROTHEME** [ ] [ ]
Sep 84. (lp/c) *(STAT LP/C 18)* <5487> **FOLK OF THE 80'S (PART III)** [ ] [ ]
– No dancing / Unsatisfaction / Where do the boys go? / Mother's opinion / Eurotheme / Messiahs die young / I know their name / Folk of the 80's / I sing last – Not for tears. *(cd-iss. Oct85; CDST 18)*

—— **IVAN** recruited an entire new line-up **JOHNNY** – guitar / **JENNY** – bass / **J. BONHOMME** – drums

Mercury Mercury

Oct 87. (7") *(MER 257)* <888859> **POP GOES THE WORLD. / THE END (OF THE WORLD)** [ ] [20]
(12"+=/cd-s+=) *(MER X/CD 257)* – ('A'-dance mix).
Nov 87. (lp) <832730> **POP GOES THE WORLD** [-] [73]
– Intro / Pop goes the world / On Tuesday / Bright side of the sun / O sole mio / Lose my way / The real world / Moonbeam / In the name of angels / La valese d'Euge'nie / Jenny wore black / Intro – Walk on water / The end (of the world).

Polydor Polydor

1989. (lp/cd) *(842000-1/-2)* **IN THE 21ST CENTURY** [-] [-] German
– In the 21st century / Hey men / You and me / Everybody's selling something / Here come the 90's / All we do / I'm in love / Louise and I / Underneath the rainbow / 21st century safety dance.

—— above was their final release

Natalie MERCHANT

Born: 26 Oct'63, Jamestown, New York, USA. Focal point with the 10,000 MANIACS since 1981, she embarked on a solo career in 1993. Spending over a year in the studio, she returned in fine style with her debut album, 'TIGERLILY' (1995), an emotive and eclectic collection of songs that stayed high in the American charts for some time. Three singles were lifted from it, 'CARNIVAL', 'WONDER' and 'JEALOUSY', all stirring up enough support for Top 30 placings; the latter's B-side featured a cover of The Rolling Stones' 'SYMPATHY FOR THE DEVIL'.

Album rating: TIGERLILY (*6)

NATALIE MERCHANT – vocals / with **JENNIFER TURNER** – guitars, vocals / **BARRY MAGUIRE** – bass, guitar / **PETER YANOWITZ** – drums, percussion

Elektra Elektra

Jun 95. (cd/c) <(7559 61745-2/-4)> **TIGERLILY** [39] [13]
– San Andreas fault / Wonder / Beloved wife / River / Carnival / I may know the word / The letter / Cowboy romance / Jealousy / Where I go / Seven years.
Jul 95. (c-s) *(EKR 203C)* <64413> **CARNIVAL / I MAY KNOW THE WORD** [ ] [10]
(cd-s+=) *(EKR 203CD)* – ('A'edit).
Nov 95. (c-s) <64376> **WONDER / BABY I LOVE YOU** [-] [20]
Apr 96. (c-s/cd-s) *(EKR 217 C/CD1)* **WONDER / TAKE A LOOK (live) / THE WORK SONG (live)** [ ] [-]
(cd-s) *(EKR 217CD2)* – ('A'side) / Sympathy for the Devil (live) / All I want (live medley).
May 96. (c-s) <64301> **JEALOUSY / SYMPATHY FOR THE DEVIL (live)** [-] [23]
Jun 98. (cd/c) <(7559 62196-2/-4)> **OPHELIA** [52] [8] May98
– Ophelia / Life is sweet / Kind & generous / Frozen Charlotte / My skin / Break your heart / King of May / Thick as thieves / Effigy / The living / When they ring the golden bells / Ophelia (reprise).
Nov 98. (cd-s) *(E 3831CD)* **KIND & GENEROUS / FROZEN CHARLOTTE / WANDER** [ ] [ ]

MERCURY REV

Formed: Buffalo, New York, USA ... 1988 by JONATHAN DONAHUE, DAVID BAKER, GRASSHOPPER (aka SEAN MACKIOWIAK), DAVE FRIDMANN, JIMY CHAMBERS and SUZANNE THORPE, who claimed they had all met while attending a psychiatric hospital. Admittedly, their sound, which came about by playing their own soundtrack to nature TV programmes! ('VERY SLEEPY RIVERS' indeed) was certainly deliciously deranged enough for this explanation of their secret history. Just over two years of rehearsals passed (DONAHUE, co-producer FRIDMANN and GRASSHOPPER were part-time members of FLAMING LIPS and utilised some spare studio time), before they finally surfaced with the mini-lp, 'YERSELF IS STEAM' (1991). Perhaps the most immaculate marriage of searing noise and crystalline pop ever committed to vinyl, this freaky guitar-angst rock classic mixed up psychedelia, noise, film dialogue and exhilirating experimentation in a way only previously matched by The FLAMING LIPS; other indie influences were also apparent (i.e. BIRTHDAY PARTY, STUMP, VERY THINGS and MY BLOODY VALENTINE). The inspired opening salvo of 'CHASING A BEE', 'SYRINGE MOUTH' and 'CONEY ISLAND CYCLONE', alone was enough to give the album a resounding thumbs-up by the British press and record buying public alike. Later that year, the 'CAR WASH HAIR' EP/track (recorded with DEAN WAREHAM of GALAXIE 500), further convinced commentators of MERCURY REV's volatile genius although squabbling and widely publicised, wildly unpredictable live shows led to break-up rumours. These were subsequently quashed when the band were snapped up by 'Beggars Banquet', a follow-up album, 'BOCES' (1993), carrying on in the established schizophrenic mould but too often straying into wanton self-indulgence at the expense of conventional tunes. However, it did satisfy some punters by becoming their first record to hit the UK Top 50. The following year, the band's infamous in-fighting reach a head as the proverbial time-honoured musical differences led to the wayward BAKER pursuing a noisier career of his own as SHADY. Although a solitary MERCURY REV single, 'EVERLASTING ARM', appeared in summer '94 (featuring ALAN VEGA of SUICIDE), it would be another long year before the release of 'SEE YOU ON THE OTHER SIDE' (1995), although by this time the first chapter of MERCURY REV's maverick career had already drawn to a close. While critics marvelled over the album's more accessible but wonderfully eclectic pop-jazz experiments, DONAHUE and GRASSHOPPER were in the process of completing a debut album, 'PARALYZED MIND OF THE ARCANGEL VOID' (1995) for their revamped side-project, HARMONY ROCKETS. A few years later, the pair resurrected the MERCURY REV moniker with a complete new cast (namely ADAM SNYDER, JUSTIN RUSSO, JASON RUSSO and JEFF MERCEL), although the subsequent return of THORPE, FRIDMANN and CHAMBERS (SNYDER was retained) resulted in a more fully-fledged reformation. V.I.P. HARMONY ROCKETS guests, LEVON HELM and GARTH HUDSON of The BAND, were also brought on board for the album no one thought was possible, 'DESERTER'S SONGS' (1998). Issued on Richard Branson's new imprint, 'V2' ('Epic' in the States), the record was widely hailed as THE album of the year as MERCURY REV enjoyed one of the critical rebirths of the decade. Older and wiser, the band (or THE BAND, take your pick!) had possibly stumbled upon what GRAM PARSONS really meant when he dreamt of his "cosmic American music", a wistful (in a far-out sort of way) melange of quixotic pop, spacey orchestration and lullaby romanticism quite possibly unlike anything you've ever heard. If long-time fans were hoping to hear the anarchic spark of old they were in for a drastic shock, tracks such as 'TONITE IT SHOWS', 'OPUS 40', 'DELTA SUN BOTTLENECK BLUES' and 'ENDLESSLY', meandering to a more mature muse, the latter even incorporating their own heavy-lidded interpretation of traditional carol, 'Silent Night'. A couple of months previous to the album's release, GRASSHOPPER & His GOLDEN CRICKETS (including flautist, SUZANNE THORPE) had taken their own, more off-beat journey into the psychedelic musical galaxy with the album, 'THE ORBIT OF ETERNAL GRACE'. • **Covered:** IF YOU WANT ME TO STAY (Sly Stone) / SHHH – PEACEFUL (Miles Davis) / The HARMONY ROCKETS covered I'VE GOT A GOLDEN TICKET (from 'Charlie & The Chocolate Factory') / L'APOCALYPSE DES ANIMAUX (Vangelis) / etc..

Album rating: YERSELF IS STEAM (*8) / BOCES (*6) / SEE YOU ON THE OTHER SIDE (*8) / DESERTER'S SONGS (*9) / Harmony Rockets: PARALYZED MIND OF THE ARCANGEL VOID (*6) / Grasshopper & The Golden Crickets: THE ORBIT OF ETERNAL GRACE (*7)

DAVID BAKER – vocals / **JONATHAN DONAHUE** – vocals, guitar (ex-FLAMING LIPS) / **SEAN 'Grasshopper' MACKIOWIAK** – guitar / **DAVID FRIDMANN** – bass / **JIMY CHAMBERS** – drums / **SUZANNE THORPE** – woodwind

Mint Films Mint Films

Feb 91. (cd/c/blue-lp) <(MINT CD/C/LP 4)> **YERSELF IS STEAM** [ ] [ ]
– (Rocket): Chasing a bee / Syringe mouth / Coney Island cyclone / Blue and black / Sweet oddysee of a cancer cell t' th' center of yer heart / (Harmony): Frittering / Continuous trucks and thunder under a mother's smile / Very sleepy rivers. *(re-iss. Nov92 on 'Beggars Banquet' as d-cd+=/d-c+=/d-lp+=; BBQ CD/MC/LP 125)* **LEGO MY EGO** – If you want me to stay / Shhh – Peaceful – Very sleepy rivers / Frittering / Coney Island cyclone / Car wash hair / Syringe mouth / Blood on the moon / Chasing a girl (inside a car). / etc Space patrol / Uh . . . it's out there / I better let my pants back on / My mom is coming over. *<US cd re-iss. Nov92 on 'Columbia'; 53030>*
Nov 91. (12"ep/cd-ep) <(MINT 5 T/CD)> **CAR WASH HAIR (The Bee's Chasing me) full pull / CHASING A BEE (demo) / CONEY ISLAND CYCLONE (demo)** [ ] [ ]

Rough Trade not iss.

Apr 92. (7") *(45REV 6)* **IF YOU WANT ME TO STAY. / THE LEFT-HANDED RAYGUN OF PAUL SHARITS (RETIREMENT JUST LIKE THAT)** [ ] [-]

Beggars Banquet Columbia

Nov 92. (12"/cd-s) *(BBQ 1/+CD)* <74717> **CHASING A BEE. / CONEY ISLAND CYCLONE** [ ] [ ]
Mar 93. (10"/cd-s) *(BBQ 5 T/CD)* <74907> **THE HUM IS COMING FROM HER. / SO THERE (with ROBERT CREELY)** [ ] [ ] Apr93

May 93. (7") *(BBQ 14)* **SOMETHING FOR JOEY. / THREE SPIDER'S EGGS (live)** [ ] [-]
(12"+=) *(BBQ 14/+T)* – Suzanne peels out.
(cd-s++=) *(BBQ 14CD)* – Noise. *(re-iss. Jul93)*

Jun 93. (cd/c/lp) *(BBQ CD/MC/LP 140) <53217>* **BOCES** [43] [ ]
– Meth of a rockette's kick / Trickle down / Bronx cheer / Boys peel out / Downs are feminine balloons / Something for Joey / Snorry mouth / Hi-speed boats / Continuous drunks and blunders / Girlfren.

Jul 93. (cd-ep) *<CSK 5532>* **SOMETHING FOR JOEY / SO THERE / BOYS PEEL OUT / VERY SLEEPY RIVERS / (Ron Jeremy interview)** [-] [ ]

Feb 94. (cd-ep) *<77112>* **BRONX CHEER / THERE'S SPIDER EGGS IN BUBBLA YHUM / SUZANNE PEELS OUT** [-] [ ]

— now without BAKER, who became SHADY and released solo album, 'WORLD', which included members of SWERVEDRIVER and The BOO RADLEYS

Jun 94. (12"white/cd-s) *(BBQ 37 T/CD)* **EVERLASTING ARM. / DEAD MAN** [ ] [ ]

May 95. (cd/c/lp)(pic-lp) *(BBQ CD/MC/LP 176)(BBQ 176P) <64362>* **SEE YOU ON THE OTHER SIDE** [ ] [ ] Sep95
– Empire state (Sun house in excelsis) / Young man's stride / Sudden ray of hope / Everlasting arm / Racing the tide / Close encounters of the third grade / A kiss from an old flame (a trip to the Moon) / Peaceful night.

— split late '94, as DONAHUE and GRASSHOPPER were already moonlighting as the HARMONY ROCKETS. The former and MERCURY REV collaborated on The CHEMICAL BROTHERS 'Dig Your Own Hole' track, 'Private Psychedelic Reel'.

HARMONY ROCKETS

— **DONAHUE + GRASSHOPPER** plus **LEVON HELMS + GARTH HUDSON** (The BAND) (they also guested on MERCURY REV's comeback album) / **ZOOT ROLLO HORN** (ex-CAPTAIN BEEFHEART)

Rockville Rockville

Jun 93. (7") *(ROCK 6113-7)* **SKELETON MAN. /** [ ] [ ]

Big Cat Big Cat

Oct 95. (lp/cd) *<(ABB 90/+CD)>* **PARALYZED MIND OF THE ARCHANGEL VOID** [ ] [ ] Sep98
– Paralyzed mind of the archangel void.

Big Cat No.6

Oct 97. (cd-s) *(ABB 151SCD) <45>* **GOLDEN TICKET EP** [ ] [ ] Nov98
– I've got a golden ticket / L'apocalypse des animaux / Tale scendeva l'etternale adore / +1

MERCURY REV

— **JONATHAN + GRASSHOPPER** reformed the band in the summer of '97 with **ADAM SNYDER** – keyboards / **JUSTIN RUSSO** – keyboards / **JASON RUSSO** – bass / **JEFF MERCEL** – drums

— by 1998, **SNYDER** was the only person that **JONATHAN + GRASSHOPPER** retained, bringing back **DAVE FRIDMANN, SUZANNE THORPE + JIMY CHAMBERS**

V2 Epic

Oct 98. (cd/lp) *(VVR 100277-2/-1) <27027>* **DESERTER'S SONGS** [56] [ ] Sep98
– Holes / Tonite it shows / Endlessly / I collect coins / Opus 40 / Hudson line / The happy end (the drunk room) / Goddess on a hiway / The funny bird / Pick up if you're there / Delta sun bottleneck stomp. *(also on special cd; VVR 100379-2)*

Nov 98. (7") *(VVR 500332-7)* **GODDESS ON A HIWAY. /** [51] [-]
(cd-s+=) *(VVR 5000332-3)* –

GRASSHOPPER AND THE GOLDEN CRICKETS

with **SUZANNE THORPE** – flute, co-producer (of MERCURY REV) + others

Beggars Banquet Beggars Banquet

Jul 98. (7") *(BBQ 325)* **SILVER BALLOONS. / SOLAR POWERED HORNET BEYOND THE SHADOWS OF OVERLOOK MOUNTAIN** [ ] [-]
(cd-s+=) *(BBQ 325CD)* – ('A'mix).

Aug 98. (cd/lp) *(BBQ CD/LP 201) <80201>* **THE ORBIT OF ETERNAL GRACE** [ ] [ ]
– Silver balloons / The ballad of the one-eyed angelfish / O-ring (baby talk) / Nickel in a lemon / The orbit of eternal grace / September's fool / Univac bug track / Smpte for the Devil / N.Y. avenue playground / Sketches of Saturn (love in space) / Midnight express / N.Y. avenue playground (reprise).

METAL URBAIN

Formed: Paris, France . . . 1977 as possibly the first Gallic punk-rock act. The band also took the honour of being the first act to release a record on British independent, 'Rough Trade', the track in question being early '78's 'PARIS MAQUIS'. However, CLAUDE PANIK, ERIC DEBRIS, HERMAN SCHWARTZ and NANCY LUGER (a male!) had already issued a French-only debut 7", 'PANIK', two months previously. Pitting growling, politically motivated lyrics against a background/foreground blast of cheap fuzz noise-guitar and a bizarre syncopated drumbeat, METAL URBAIN were musically distinct from most of their UK cousins. Over the course of next year or so, the Frenchmen released two more singles, 'HYSTERIE CONNECTIVE' and 'SWEET MARILYN', the latter the first to appear under the moniker of the METAL BOYS. DEBRIS also fronted another 'Rough Trade' act, DR. MIX & THE REMIX, releasing a cover of The Stooges' 'NO FUN'. Towards the end of the decade, DEBRIS and Co tackled another cover, 'I CAN'T CONTROL MYSELF', once a hit for the Troggs. The two acts continued to release material simultaneously although both had disappeared in the space of a year.

Album rating: L'AGE D'OR compilation (*6)

CLAUDE PANIK – vocals / **ERIC DEBRIS** – synthesizer, electric drums / **HERMAN SCHWARTZ** – guitar / male **NANCY LUGER** – guitar

Cobra not iss.

Oct 77. (7") *(COB 7004)* **PANIK. / LADY COCA COLA** [-] [-] French

Rough Trade not iss.

Jan 78. (7") *(RT 001)* **PARIS MAQUIS. / CLE DE CONTACT** [ ] [-]

Radar not iss.

Sep 78. (7") *(ADA 20)* **HYSTERIE CONNECTIVE. / PAS POUBELLE** [ ] [-]

— now without DEBRIS who joined METAL BOYS and DR. MIX & THE REMIX

— METAL URBAIN issued two further albums, 'LES HOMMES MORT SONT DANGEREUX' (1980 – Byzz; BLPS 8101) and 'DEAD MEN' (1981 – Byzz; BLPS 8107). The former had a free 7" below on 'Celluloid'

Sep 80. (7") *(CEL 16216)* **HYSTERIE CONNECTIVE (mix 2). / ATLANTIS** [-] [-] French

DR. MIX & THE REMIX

— **ERIC DEBRIS** – vocals / **PAT VINCENT** – guitar / **MARK TURNER** – bass, synthesizers / **JEAN-PIERRE** – bass, synthesizers / **NICK TURNER** – drums / **LUCY** – saxophone

Rough Trade not iss.

Jun 79. (7"; as METAL BOYS) *(RT 016)* **SWEET MARILYN. / FUGUE FOR A DARKENED ISLAND** [ ] [-]

Jun 79. (7") *(RT 017)* **NO FUN. / NO FUN (Dr.Mix alone version)** [ ] [-]

Dec 79. (7") *(RT 032)* **I CAN'T CONTROL MYSELF. / ('A'version)** [ ] [-]

Dec 79. (m-lp) *(ROUGH 6)* **WALL OF NOISE** [ ] [-]
– Out of the question / Grey lagoons / No fun / Six dreams / I can't control myself / Supermen / Sister Ray.

Celluloid not iss.

Oct 80. (12"ep) *(CEL 6585)* **PSYCHEDELIC DESERT EP** [ ] [-]

Dec 80. (lp; as METAL BOYS) *(CEL 2.6560)* **TOKIO AIRPORT** (John Peel session) [ ] [-]

Oct 81. (lp) *(CEL 6589)* **DR. MIX & THE REMIX** [ ] [-]

— disappeared after above

– (METAL URBAIN) compilations

1989. (lp/cd) *Fan Club; (FC 011/+CD)* **L'AGE D'OR** [ ] [-]
– Hysterie connective / Ghetto / Cle de contact / Lady Coca Cola / Panik / Futurama / Paris maquis / Pop poubelle / 50-50 / Anarchie au palace / E 202 / Numero / Colt 45 / Lady Coke / No fun / Metal urbain / Atlantis / Creve salope / Snuff movie / Ultra violence / Tango sudiste.

METEORS

Formed: London, England . . . 1980 as RAW DEAL by alleged self-confessed Satanist, P. PAUL FENECH, alongside NIGEL LEWIS and MARK ROBERTSON. All veterans of the rockabilly/R'n'R scene (specifically the bands The SOUTHERN BOYS and ROCK THERAPY) despite their youthfulness, the trio made their vinyl debut via an appearance on 'Alligator' records' various artists compilation, 'Home Grown Rockabilly'. Subsequently adopting the METEORS moniker, the band released a debut EP, 'METEOR MADNESS', combining a rockabilly rebel stance with gothic punk in much the same fashion as the more outlandish CRAMPS, substituting the latter outfit's fetishism for a more Oi!-like gang mentality. This ethos was neatly summed up with 'WRECKIN' CREW' (1986), the title of the band's second album and a phrase associated with the band for the rest of their career. In the meantime, they'd released a debut set, 'IN HEAVEN' (1981) on their own 'Lost Souls' imprint, LEWIS later striking out to form his own outfit, The TALL BOYS. New members MICK WHITE, RUSSELL JONES and STEVE MEADHAM were in place for the galloping, lip-curling minor hit rendition of John Leyton's 'JOHNNY REMEMBER ME', one of the highlights on the aforementioned 'WRECKIN' CREW'. Issued on the 'I.D.' label, the record was confirmation of The METEORS' psychobilly credentials; by this point, the band's gigs had already become notorious for raucous activities as be-quiffed boot boys became as regular an 80's subcultural feature as punks and skinheads. More personnel changes ensued as WHITE also departed to form his own outfit, GUANA BATZ, a temporary replacement found in RICK ROSS before IAN CUBITT was brought in for the recording of the 'STAMPEDE' (1984) album. In keeping with their spirit as a live act, a couple of unoffical live sets appeared in 1986/87 before the band signed to 'Anagram' for the release of 'SEWERTIME BLUES' (1987). This lovingly titled METEORS artefact featured a cover of Jan & Dean's 'SURF CITY', adding to their extensive back catalogue of trademark interpretations which already included the likes of Creedence Clearwater Revival's 'BAD MOON RISING'. Albums such as 'DON'T TOUCH THE BANG BANG FRUIT' (1987), 'ONLY THE METEORS ARE PURE PSYCHOBILLY' (1988) and 'MUTANT MONKEY AND THE SURFERS FROM ZORCH' (1988) continued to please the faithful if not exactly offering up anything to tempt the casual listener save the usual cover material, The Ramones' 'SOMEBODY PUT SOMETHING IN MY DRINK' given the honours this time around. While they may have had a more fanatical following (obsessed fan, Mark Silman, turned into a mad psycho killer!) than The CRAMPS for example, The METEORS never enjoyed the same level of support from the press and while the latter act are still going fairly strong more than twenty years on, The METEORS seemed to have burned out at the dawn of the 90's. • **Covered:** GET OFF MY CLOUD (Rolling Stones) / GET ME TO THE WORLD ON TIME (Electric Prunes) / WIPEOUT (Surfaris) / WILD THING (Troggs) / GO BUDDY GO (Stranglers) / THESE BOOTS ARE MADE FOR WALKING (hit; Nancy Sinatra) / RAWHIDE (Link Wray) / PLEASE DON'T TOUCH (Johnny Kidd) / etc. • **Note:** Not to be confused with Dutch band of the early 80's (out of ALQUIN) who were on 'E.M.I.'.

Album rating: ONLY THE METEORS ARE PURE PSYCHOBILLY compilation (*7)

P. PAUL FENECH – vocals, guitar / **NIGEL LEWIS** – bass, vocals / **MARK ROBERTSON** – drums

Ace / not iss.

Jul 81. (7"ep) *(SW 65)* **METEOR MADNESS** [ ] [-]
– Voodoo rhythm / Maniac rockers from Hell / My daddy's a vampire / You can't keep a good man down.

Jul 81. (m-lp) *(MAD 1)* **THE METEORS MEET SCREAMING LORD SUTCH** [ ] [-]
– (4 above) + tracks by SCREAMING LORD SUTCH (yes! that one!).

Chiswick / not iss.

Nov 81. (7") *(CHIS 147)* **RADIOACTIVE KID. / GRAVEYARD STOMP** [ ] [-]

Upright / not iss.

Dec 81. (7"; as CLAPHAM SOUTH ESCALATORS) *(UPYOUR 1)* **GET ME TO THE WORLD ON TIME. / LEAVE ME ALONE / CARDBOARD CUT OUTS** [ ] [-]

Lost Souls / not iss.

Dec 81. (lp) *(LOSTLP 3001)* **IN HEAVEN** [ ] [-]
– In Heaven / Shout so loud / Earwigs in my brain / In the cards / Attack of the Zorch men / The crazed / Get off my cloud / Love you to death / Teenagers from outer space / Maniac / Into the darkness / Death dance / Psycho for your love / The room / Rockabilly psychosis. *(<cd-iss. Feb97 on 'Edsel'; ED 509>)*

Jan 82. (7") *(LOST 101)* **THE CRAZED. / ATTACK OF THE ZORCH MEN** [ ] [-]

— **FENECH** brought in **MARK WHITE** – bass to repl. LEWIS who joined The TALL BOYS

— **RUSSELL JONES** – drums repl. WOODY who repl. ROBERTSON

WXYZ / not iss.

Aug 82. (7") *(ABCD 5)* **MUTANT ROCK. / THE HILLS HAVE EYES** [ ] [-]

— **STEVE 'Ginger' MEADHAM** – drums repl. JONES

I.D. / not iss.

Dec 82. (7"/7"pic-d) *(EYE 1/+P)* **JOHNNY REMEMBER ME. / FEAR OF THE DARK / WRECKIN' CREW** [66] [-]

Jan 83. (lp) *(NOSE 1)* **WRECKIN' CREW** [ ] [-]
– Insane / I ain't ready / Johnny remember me / I don't worry about it / Axe attack / Zombie noise / Rattlesnakin' daddy / When a stranger calls / Phantom of the opera / Blue sunshine / Wreckin' crew / Sick things / Wild thing / I'm not mad / Get off my cloud. *(cd-iss. Dec91 on 'Streetlink';) (<re-iss. cd Apr93 on 'Dojo'; DOJOCD 121>)*

— **RICK ROSS** – bass, vocals repl. WHITE who formed GUANA BATZ

Wreckin' / not iss.

Nov 83. (lp) *(WRECK 1)* **THE METEORS LIVE (live)** [ ] [-]
– Wipe out / Maniac rockers from Hell / Lonesome train / I ain't ready / Ain't gonna bring me down / Sick things / Crazy love / When a stranger calls / Rawhide / I don't worry about it / Voodoo rhythm / You crack me up / Mutant rock / Graveyard stomp / Wreckin' crew / These boots were made for walking / Long blonde hair.

— **IAN 'Spider' CUBITT** – bass repl. ROSS who went to America

Mad Pig / not iss.

Oct 84. (lp) *(CHOP 1)* **STAMPEDE** [ ] [-]
– Night of the werewolf / Ain't gonna bring me down / Electro / Stampede / I'm just a dog / In too deep / Cecil drives a combined harvester / Michael Myers / Out of the dark / Only a fury in my heart / Do the demolition / You're out of time. *(cd-iss. Jul89; CDCHOP 1)*

Oct 84. (7") *(PORK 1)* **I'M JUST A DOG. / YOU CRACK ME UP** [ ] [-]
(12"+=) *(PORK 1T)* – Ain't gonna bring me down.
(12") *(PORR 1)* – ('A'-Wild hog mix down) / Hoover rock / Electro rock.

May 85. (7") *(PORK 2)* **FIRE, FIRE. / LITTLE RED RIDING HOOD** [ ] [-]
(12"+=) *(PORK 2T)* – Stampede (King Ray bat scalator in the dark mix).

— **NEVILLE HUNT** – bass repl. CUBITT

Oct 85. (7") *(PORK 3)* **BAD MOON RISING. / RHYTHM OF THE BELL** [ ] [-]
(12"+=) *(PORK 3T)* – Hogs and cuties (What? another cover mix).

Nov 85. (lp) *(CHOP 2)* **MONKEY'S BREATH** [ ] [-]
– Ex man boogie / Power of steel / Hoover rock / Kick boy / Eat the baby / Maybe tomorrow / Hogs and cuties / Alligator man / Rhythm of the bell / Sweet love on my mind / Meat is meat / Take a ride / Just the three of us / Joba's snake.

Anagram / not iss.

Aug 86. (7") *(ANA 31)* **SURF CITY. / THE EDGE** [ ] [-]
('A'-Has Beens From Outer Space mix-12"+=) *(12ANA 31)* – Johnny's here.

Dec 86. (lp/c) *(GRAM/CGRAM 27)* **SEWERTIME BLUES** [ ] [-]
– Ain't takin a chance / So sad / Here's Johnny / Mind over matter / Acid and psyam / Sewertime blues / Return of Ethel Merman / Deep dark jungle / Never get away / I bury the living / Vibrate / Surf city. *(cd-iss. Jul89 +=; CDGRAM 27)* – DON'T TOUCH THE BANG BANG FRUIT *(cd re-iss. Apr95 as above on 'Anagram'; CDMPSYCHO 03)*

— **TOBY 'Jug' GRIFFIN + AUSTIN H. JONES** – bass repl. NEVILLE

Jun 87. (7") *(ANA 35)* **GO BUDDY GO. / WILDKAT WAYS** [ ] [-]
('A'-Wonkey Donkey mix-12"+=) *(12ANA 35)* – You crack me up.

— **LE BROWN** – bass (ex-PHAROAHS) repl. above temp. bassists

Sep 87. (lp/c) *(GRAM/CGRAM 30)* **DON'T TOUCH THE BANG BANG FRUIT** [ ] [-]
– Go buddy go / Midnight people / Low livin' daddy / Your worst nightmare / Wildkat ways / Repo man / You crack me up / Shakey shakey / Psycho kat / Let's go / Revenge of El Trio Los Bastardos / Don't touch the bang bang fruit.

Oct 87. (7") *(ANA 39)* **DON'T TOUCH THE BANG BANG FRUIT. / DATELESS NITES** [ ] [-]
(12"+=) *(12ANA 39)* – Corpse grinders.

Feb 88. (12") *(12ANA 41)* **SOMEBODY PUT SOMETHING IN MY DRINK** [ ] [-]

Feb 88. (lp/c/cd) *(GRAM/CGRAM/CDGRAM 33)* **ONLY THE METEORS ARE PURE PSYCHOBILLY** (compilation) [ ] [-]
– Voodoo rhythm / Graveyard stomp / Wreckin' crew / Sick things / Blue sunshine / Mutant rock / The hills have eyes / Fire, fire / Power of steel / Eat the baby / Rhythm of the bell / Surf city / Go buddy go / Somebody put something in my drink.

Oct 88. (7") *(ANA 43)* **RAWHIDE. / SURFIN' ON THE PLANET ZORCH** [ ] [-]
(12"+=) *(12ANA 43)* – Little Red Riding Hood.

Nov 88. (lp/cd) *(GRAM/CDGRAM 37)* **MUTANT MONKEY AND THE SURFERS FROM ZORCH** [ ] [-]
– Swamp thing / Electro II (the revenge) / Side walk psycho / I'm invisible man / She's my baby again / Surfin' on the Planet Zorch / Spine bender / Dance crazy baby / Rawhide / Oxygen dog / Yellow zone / Meet me in the morgue / Little Red Riding Hood.

— **MARK HOWE** – drums repl. MEADHAM

Sep 89. (lp/c/cd) *(GRAM/CGRAM/CDGRAM 43)* **UNDEAD, UNFRIENDLY AND UNSTOPPABLE** [ ] [-]
– Razorback / Disneyland / My kind of rockin' / Lonesome train / Johnny God / I go to bed with the undead / Out of the attic / Brains as well / Charlie, Johnny, Redhead and me / Lies in wait / Surf mad pig / Please don't touch. *(re-iss. cd Apr85; CDMPSYCHE 02)*

Dec 89. (12"m) *(12ANA 51)* **PLEASE DON'T TOUCH. / DISNEYLAND / MY KINDA ROCKIN'** [ ] [-]

May 90. (lp/c/cd) *(GRAM/CGRAM/CDGRAM 45)* **LIVES OF THE SICK AND SHAMELESS (live)** [ ] [-]
– Ex-men boogie / Wipe out / Rattle snake daddy / Mutant rock / Maniac / Blue sunshine / Mind over matter / These boots are made for walking / Little Red Riding Hood / The hills have eyes / Wild thing / I go to bed with the undead / Voodoo rhythm / I ain't ready / Wreckin' crew. *(cd+=)* – Lonesome train / Rock bop / Ain't gonna bring me down / Graveyard stomp.

— disbanded after above

– compilations, etc. –

Feb 85. (lp) *Dojo; (DOJOLP 2)* **THE CURSE OF THE MUTANTS** [ ] [-]
– Mutant rock / Insane / Scream of the mutants / When a stranger calls / Fear of the dark / The hills have eyes / Wild thing / Get off my cloud / Wreckin' crew / Zombie noise / Johnny remember me / Phantom of the opera / Blue sunshine / I don't worry about it / Axe attack / Rattlesnakin' daddy.

Sep 85. (pic-lp) *Dojo; (DOJOLP 4P)* **LIVE** [ ] [-]
(re-iss. Jan86; DOJOLP 4) (cd-iss. 1988; DOJOCD 4)

Apr 86. (lp) *Dojo; (DOJOLP 22)* **HORRIBLE MUSIC FOR HORRIBLE PEOPLE: LIVE VOL.2 (live)** [ ] [-]

Jun 86. (lp/cd) *Big Beat; (WIKA/CDWIK 47)* **TEENAGERS FROM OUTER SPACE** [ ] [-]
– Voodoo rhythm / Maniac rockers from Hell / My daddy is a vampire / You can't keep a good man down / Graveyard stomp / Radioactive kid / Leave me alone / Dog eat robot / Walter Mitty blues / Just the three of us / Blue sunshine insight / Attack of the Zorch men / Jupiter stroll. *(cd+=)* – Another half hour till sunrise / Island of the lost souls / The Napoleon solo / Get me to the world on time.

Aug 86. (12"ep) *Archive 4; (TOF 106)* **WRECKIN' CREW / JOHNNY REMEMBER ME. / I DON'T WORRY BOUT IT / WILD THING** [ ] [-]

Sep 86. (7"green-ep/12"green or blue) *I.D.; (EYE/+T 10)* **MUTANT ROCK** [ ] [-]
– Wreckin' crew / Scream of the mutants / The hills have eyes / Mutant rock.

Jul 87. (d-lp) *Anagram; (DCHOP 1)* **MONKEY'S BREATH / STAMPEDE** [ ] [-]
(cd-iss. Oct95; CDMPSYCHE 09)

Nov 87. (pic-lp) *Dojo; (DOJOLP 56P)* **NIGHT OF THE WEREWOLF** [ ] [-]

Dec 87. (lp) *Link; (LINK LP06)* **LIVE AND LOUD** [ ] [-]

Sep 93. (cd) *Anagram; (CDGRAM 66)* **THE BEST OF THE METEORS** [ ] [-]

Feb 95. (cd) *Dojo; <213>* **LIVE, LEARY & FUCKIN' LOUD!** [ ] [ ]

Apr 95. (cd) *Receiver; (<RRCD 217>)* **WELCOME TO THE WRECKIN' PIT** [ ] [ ] May96

Sep 95. (cd) *Nectar; (NTMCD 508)* **GRAVEYARD STOMP (BEST OF THE METEORS)** [ ] [-]

1995. (cd) *Cleopatra; <CLEO 9647>* **CORPSE GRINDER** [-] [ ]

Oct 96. (cd) *Receiver; (<RRCD 230>)* **INTERNATIONAL WRECKERS 2: THE LOST TAPES OF ZORCH** [ ] [ ] Nov96

MIAOW (see under ⇒ CARROLL, Cath)

MICE (see under ⇒ ALL ABOUT EVE)

MICRODISNEY (see under ⇒ COUGHLAN, Cathal)

MIDGET

Formed: Stamford, Lincolnshire, England . . . 1995 by the youthful trio of RICHARD GOMBAULT, ANDY HAWKINS and LEE MAJOR (no, not the six million dollar man!). Taking up the punky-pop sound normally peddled by ASH, GREEN DAY and SUPERGRASS, the lads inked a deal with 'Radarscope' in '96. Early the following year, MIDGET delivered a sort of tribute debut, 'KYLIE AND JASON' (MINOGUE and DONOVAN), the first in a series of eight singles released over the course of the next two years. Their first album proper, 'JUKEBOX' (had already issued mini-cd, 'ALCO-POP!') hit the shops in the summer of '98 and showed they had promise if nothing else. • **Covered:** DAYDREAM BELIEVER (Monkees) / SENSES WORKING OVERTIME (Xtc). • **Note:** 'THE TOGGLE SWITCH' cd on 'Au Go Go' ANDA 203 Mar97 was not theirs.

Album rating: JUKEBOX (*6)

RICHARD GOMBAULT – vocals, guitar / **ANDY HAWKINS** – bass / **LEE MAJOR** – drums

Radarscope / Sire

Jan 97. (7") *(TINY 1)* **KYLIE AND JASON. / PATHETICALLY DEVOTED TO YOU** [ ] [-]

Mar 97. (7") *(TINY 2)* **CAMOUFLAGE. / FIRST THING IN THE MORNING** [ ] [-]
(cd-s+=) *(TINYCDS 2)* – So damn creepy.
May 97. (7"blue) *(TINY 3)* **WELCOME HOME JELLYBEAN. / DOROTHY** [ ] [-]
(cd-s+=) *(TINYCDS 3)* – Wendyhouse.
(cd-s) *(TINYCDS 3X)* – ('A'side) / Solitudinational / Family man / How?
Aug 97. (7") *(TINY 4)* **OPTIMISM. / STILL** [ ] [-]
(cd-s+=) *(TINYCDS 4)* – Bleached Queenie.
(cd-s) *(TINYCDS 4X)* – ('A'side) / You're back again / Meeting the parents / The way things turn out.
Nov 97. (cd-ep) *(TINYCDS 5)* **ALCO-POP! EP** [ ] [-]
Jan 98. (7") *(TINY 6)* **ALL FALL DOWN. / DESIGNER FRIEND** [57] [-]
(cd-s) *(TINYCDS 6)* – ('A'side) / Daydream believer / Heavier than a really heavy thing.
(cd-s) *(TINYCDS 6X)* – ('A'side) / Tigger had a good idea / The victim.
Mar 98. (7") *(TINY 7)* **INVISIBLE BALLOON. / OPTIMISM (acoustic)** [ ] [-]
(cd-s) *(TINYCDS 7)* – ('A'side) / Three little words / All fall down (demo).
(cd-s) *(TINYCDS 7X)* – ('A'side) / Prince Valium / Kevin's girl.
Jun 98. (7") *(TINY 8)* **THE DAY OF YOUR LIFE. / INVISIBLE BALLOON (demo)** [ ] [-]
(cd-s) *(TINYCDS 8)* – ('A'side) / Senses working overtime / Kylie and Jason (live) / ('A'album version).
(cd-s) *(TINYCDS 8X)* – ('A'side) / The good, the bad and the beautiful / Parting shot (live) / ('A'album version).
Jun 98. (cd/c) *(TINY CD/MC 9)* *<31024>* **JUKEBOX** [ ] [ ] Jul98
– Invisible balloon / Ben wants to be a secret agent / The day of your life / Magic lamp / You cope / The one who should save me / All fall down / On the run / Canada / A guy like me / Optimism / The way things turn out.

not iss. Imprint

Aug 98. (cd) *<111979>* **B-SIDE TRACKS** (compilation) [-] [ ]

MIDWAY STILL

Formed: Bexleyheath, South London, England . . . early 90's as The MELON PITS by PAUL THOMPSON, DECLAN KELLY and JOHN KANOPKA. Vaguely crusty indie-rockers following in the wake of CARTER USM, MEGA CITY 4 etc., MIDWAY STILL enjoyed a brief period of media enthusiasm as the music press cast around blindly trying to locate a new scene following the demise of both the baggy and shoegazing movements. The band were also given vocal support via John Peel, the DJ airing the band's impressive 'Roughneck' debut single, 'I WON'T TRY'. Characterised by THOMPSON's gravel-throated growl atop a roughly hewn yet melodic guitar sound, MIDWAY STILL's US-influenced appeal (HUSKER DU and NEIL YOUNG) saw their DON FLEMING-produced debut album, 'DIAL SQUARE' (1992) notch up respectable sales in the independent market and win over the cynicism of hardened hacks. Fickle as ever, the press soon forgot about them as the full force of the Seattle grunge wave hit Britain, leaving MIDWAY STILL, and their follow-up effort, 'LIFE'S TOO LONG' (1993), washed up on the shores of indifference. • **Covered:** YOU MADE ME REALISE (My Bloody Valentine).

Album rating: DIAL SQUARE (*6) / LIFE'S TOO LONG (*4)

PAUL THOMPSON – vocals, guitar / **JOHN KANOPKA** – bass / **DECLAN KELLY** – drums

Roughneck not iss.

Aug 91. (7") *(HYPE)* **I WON'T TRY. /** [ ] [-]
(12"+=/cd-s+=) *(HYPE T/CD)* – Apple / Daynight.
Oct 91. (7") *(HYPE 013)* **WISH. / YOU MADE ME REALISE** [ ] [-]
(12|+=/cd-s+=) *(HYPE 013 T/CD)* –
Mar 92. (7") *(HYPE 015)* **BETTER THAN BEFORE. /** [ ] [-]
(12"+=/cd-s+=) *(HYPE 015 T/CD)* –
Apr 92. (cd/c/lp) *(NECK CD/MC/LP 8)* **DIAL SQUARE** [ ] [-]
– Found / Better than before / Me in you / Gun / Making time / Killing time / Come down / Make a start / What you said / Wish / Brand new / Sweat / Heaven.
Feb 93. (10"ep/cd-ep) *(HYPE 019 T/CD)* **SLUGABED EP** [ ] [-]
– Just get stuck / Abnegate / Three five nine / Still get by.
May 93. (7") *(HYPE 023)* **COUNTING DAYS. / MOD SONG NO.2** [ ] [-]
(cd-s+=) *(HYPE 023CD)* – Fragments.
Jun 93. (cd/lp) *(NECK CD/LP 12)* **LIFE'S SO STRONG** [ ] [-]
– Jamie and Gigi / Lies / Straight line / Out pf view / Sell these ears / Counting days / Kemper / Disappear / Cyclops / Summercide / Strange how / Goodbye.

—— split after disaster of above

Thee MIGHTY CAESARS (see under ⇒ CHILDISH, Wild Billy)

MIGHTY LEMON DROPS

Formed: Dudley, Midlands, England . . . 1984 by PAUL MARSH, DAVID NEWTON, TONY LINEHAN and KEITH ROWLEY. All veterans of the local music scene, various band members had played alongside each other in ACTIVE RESTRAINT, this outfit releasing a one-off single, 'TERROR IN MY HOME', the previous year. Encouraged by the band's pedigree and no doubt hoping to cash in on the much hyped C-86 movement, 'Chrysalis' signed them following a one-off single, 'HAPPY HEAD' issued on the independent 'Dreamworld' label. A Stephen Street-produced debut album of the same name surfaced later in '86, developing the tinny guitar clatter of their first single. Despite their Midlands origins, the band's sound and image bore a heavy debt to Liverpool legends ECHO & THE BUNNYMEN, with MARSH's gloomy vocals in particular bearing comparison to IAN McCULLOCH. Despite generally favourable reviews, subsequent albums such as 'WORLD WITHOUT END' (1988) and 'LAUGHTER' (1989) proved too one dimensional for wider pop consumption, alternating between introspective laments and jingle/jangle indie fare. Popularity on America's college scene led to a brief dalliance with 'Sire' for 1991's 'SOUND . . . GOODBYE TO YOUR STANDARDS' album, their parting shot save for a posthumous live effort recorded in the States. • **Covered:** SPLASH #1 (13th Floor Elevators) / PAINT IT BLACK + WE LOVE YOU (Rolling Stones).

Album rating: HAPPY HEAD (*6) / WORLD WITHOUT END (*5) / LAUGHTER (*5) / SOUND . . . GOODBYE TO YOUR STANDARDS (*5)

ACTIVE RESTRAINT

PAUL MARSH – vocals / **DAVID NEWTON** – guitar / **TONY LINEHAM** – bass / **MARTIE GILKS** – drums

Sticky not iss.

Nov 83. (7") *(PEEL OFF 3)* **TERROR IN MY HOME. / TURNS OUT ROSES** [ ] [-]

MIGHTY LEMON DROPS

Dreamworld not iss.

Nov 85. (12"ep) *(DREAM 005)* **LIKE AN ANGEL. / SOMETHING HAPPENS / SYMPATHISE WITH US** [ ] [-]
Apr 86. (7") *(DREAM 006)* **LIKE AN ANGEL. / NOW SHE'S GONE** [ ] [-]

—— **KEITH ROWLEY** – drums; repl. MARTIE who joined The WONDER STUFF

Blue Guitar Sire

Aug 86. (7") *(AZUR 1)* **THE OTHER SIDE OF YOU. / UPTIGHT** [51] [-]
(12"+=) *(AZURX 1)* – Pass you by.
Sep 86. (lp/c) *(AZLP/ZAZLP 1)* *<25532>* **HAPPY HEAD** [58] [ ]
– The other side of you / My biggest thrill / Behind your back / All the way / Hypnotised / Like an angel / Pass you by / Take me up / On my mind / Something happens / Turn me around. *<US+=>* – Out of hand / Going under / Count me out / Splash #1 (now I'm home) / Rollercoaster / My biggest thrill / Hypnotised / The other side of you.
Oct 86. (7") *(AZUR 3)* **MY BIGGEST THRILL. / OPEN MIND** [ ] [-]
(12"+=) *(AZURX 3)* – Take my heart.
Apr 87. (7"/12") *(AZUR/+X 4)* *<25595>* **OUT OF HAND. / GOING UNDER** [66] [-]
Jan 88. (7") *(AZUR 6)* **INSIDE OUT. / SHINE** [74] [-]
(12"+=) *(AZURX 6)* – Head on the block. *<US; b-side>*
Feb 88. (lp/c/cd) *(AZLP/ZAZLP/CDAZ 4)* *<25701>* **WORLD WITHOUT END** [34] [ ]
– Inside out / One by one / In everything you do / Hear me call / No bounds / Fall down (like the rain) / Crystal clear / Hollow inside / Closer to you / Breaking down.
Apr 88. (7") *(AZUR 9)* **FALL DOWN (LIKE THE RAIN). / PAINT IT BLACK** [ ] [-]
(c-s+=) *(ZAZURX 9)* – Laughter.
(12"++=/cd-s++=) *(AZUR X/CD 9)* – Happy head / Hollow inside (live).

—— **MARCUS WILLIAMS** – bass; repl. LINEHAM

Aug 89. (7"/7"s/c-s) *(AZUR/+B/MC 12)* **INTO THE HEART OF LOVE. / RUMBLE TRAIN** [ ] [-]
(12"+=/cd-s+=) *(AZUR X/CD 12)* – Sometimes good guys don't wear white / ('A'extended).

Chrysalis Sire

Sep 89. (lp/c/cd) *(CHR/ZCHR/CCD 1733)* *<26017>* **LAUGHTER** [ ] [ ]
– At midnight / Into the heart of love / Where do you go from Heaven / The heartbreak thing / One in a million / Written in fiction / The real world / All that I can do / Second time around / Beautiful shame. *<US-only+=>* – Rumbletrain?
Oct 89. (7") **BEAUTIFUL SHAME. / AT MIDNIGHT (live club mix)** [ ] [-]
(12"+=/cd-s+=) – Like an angel.

—— added **. . . DAVIES** –

Sire Sire

Apr 91. (7"/c-s) **TOO HIGH. / YOU DON'T ASK** [ ] [ ]
(12") – ('A'side) / Discontent / We love you.
(cd-s) – (all 4 tracks).
May 91. (cd/c/lp) *(<7599 26512-2/-4/-1>)* **SOUND . . . GOODBYE TO YOUR STANDARDS** [ ] [ ]
– Too high / Unkind / My shadow girl / Barry's poem / Always / Big surprise / Cold, cold heart / Annabelle / You don't appreciate anything / Colorful-loving-me / Ready, steady, no!.
Jun 91. (7"/c-s) **UNKIND. / ANOTHER GIRL, ANOTHER PLANET** [ ] [ ]
(12"+=/cd-s+=) – ('A'version) / Colour-loving-me (original demo).
Feb 92. (cd/c) *<2-/4-26993>* **RICOCHET** [-] [ ]
– Nothing / Into the sun / Sense / From the sky / (She's so) Out of touch / Falling deep / Reach out / Between the lines / More / Blues inside / Hallowed ground.

—— disbanded after above

– compilations, etc. –

Jul 87. (12"ep) *Night Tracks; (SFNT 004)* **THE EVENING SHOW SESSIONS** [ ] [-]
– The other side of you / Now she's gone / Waiting for the rain / When I dream.
1993. (cd) *Overground;* **ALL THE WAY – LIVE IN CINCINNATI** [-] [ ]
Feb 97. (cd) *Chrysalis; (CDCHRM 103)* **ROLLERCOASTER (THE BEST OF THE MIGHTY LEMON DROPS 1986-1989)** [ ] [ ]
– Happy head / Into the heart of love / My biggest thrill / Inside out / The other side of you / Out of hand / Like an angel / Fall down (like the rain) / Splash #1 (now I'm home) / Beautiful shame / Rollercoaster / In every thing you do / Uptight / Shine / Where do you go from Heaven / Count me out / Something happens / Sympathise with us / Now she's gone.

MIGHTY MIGHTY

Formed: Birmingham, England . . . mid 80's by HUGH HARKIN, MICK GEOGHEGAN, brother PETER GEOGHEGAN, RUSSELL BURTON and DAVID HENNESSY. Having formed their own 'Girlie' label, MIGHTY MIGHTY released their debut single, 'EVERYBODY KNOWS THE MONKEY', around the same time as they contributed a track to the fresh-faced NME newcomers V/A compilation, C-86. Harkin' er, back to the golden era of 'Postcard' Scot-pop, HUGH and Co subsequently jangled their way onto the 'Chapter 22' label after a second self-financed release, 'IS THERE ANYBODY OUT THERE?'. Over the ensuing year and a half, the lads issued a string of largely uninspired singles, culminating in their debut album and swansong effort, 'SHARKS' (1988).

Album rating: SHARKS (*4)

HUGH HARKIN – vocals / **MICK GEOGHEGAN** – guitar / **PETER GEOGHEGAN** – organ / **RUSSELL BURTON** – bass, vocals / **DAVID HENNESSEY** – drums

Girlie | not iss.

Mar 86. (7") *(GAY 001)* **EVERYBODY KNOWS THE MONKEY. / YOU'RE ON MY MIND** [ ] [-]
Jul 86. (12"ep) *(XGAY 2)* **IS THERE ANYBODY OUT THERE? / SETTLE DOWN. / LET'S CALL IT LOVE / MAN OR BOY** [ ] [-]

Chapter 22 | not iss.

Nov 86. (7") *(CHAP 10)* **THROWAWAY. / CEILING TO THE FLOOR** [ ] [-]
(12"+=) *(12CHAP 10)* – Lionheart.
Mar 87. (7") *(CHAP 12)* **BUILT LIKE A CAR. / I DON'T NEED YOU ANYMORE** [ ] [-]
(12"+=) *(12CHAP 12)* – Twilight / Love so strong.
Oct 87. (7") *(CHAP 19)* **ONE WAY. / LAW** [ ] [-]
(12"+=) *(12CHAP 19)* – I never imagined / Night after night.
Jan 88. (7") *(CHAP 21)* **BORN IN A MAISONETTE. / POSITIVELY SESAME STREET** [ ] [-]
(12"+=) *(12CHAP 21)* – Precious moments / Loose end.
Feb 88. (lp) *(CHAPLP 24)* **SHARKS** [ ] [-]

— disbanded after above

MIGHTY WAH! (see under ⇒ WAH!)

Thee MILKSHAKES (see under ⇒ CHILDISH, Wild Billy)

Roger MILLER (see under ⇒ MISSION OF BURMA)

MILLTOWN BROTHERS

Formed: Colne, Lancashire, England . . . early '88 by brothers MATT and SIMON NELSON (who had originally called themselves The WORD ASSOCIATION), the group completed by BARNEY JAMES, JAMES FRASER and NIAN BRINDLE. After a few releases – including the original of 'WHICH WAY SHOULD I JUMP' – on their own 'Big Round' imprint, the MILLTOWN BROTHERS were signed to 'A&M' by A&R man, Sean O'Sullivan in 1990. Basically an acoustic/keyboard outfit influenced by R.E.M. and The GO-BETWEENS, the band initially flopped with 'APPLE GREEN' before breaking through early the following year with a revamped version of the easy-rocking 'WHICH WAY . . .' single. The accompanying album, 'SLINKY' (1991), showed definite promise, although with subsequent singles hovering around the Top 50 mark, their second division status was confirmed. Amid protracted difficulties over the musical direction of new material, follow-up set, 'VALVE' (1993), was delayed. As a preview to the album's release, the 'BROTHERS scored their last (minor) hit with a cover of Bob Dylan's 'IT'S ALL OVER NOW BABY BLUE', the cd-EP actually featured three other DYLAN classics, namely 'POSITIVELY 4th STREET', 'HURRICANE' and 'I SHALL BE RELEASED'.

Album rating: SLINKY (*6) / VALVE (*4)

MATTHEW NELSON – vocals / **SIMON NELSON** – guitar (ex-BLUE BERLIN) / **BARNEY JAMES** – keyboards / **JAMES FRASER** – bass / **NIAN BRINDLE** – drums

Big Round | not iss.

Feb 89. (7") *(BIGR 101)* **COMING FROM THE MILL 1989: ROSES. / WE'VE GOT TIME** [ ] [-]
(12"+=/cd-s+=) *(BIGR 101 T/CD)* – Something on my mind / We've got time (version).
Oct 89. (7") **WHICH WAY SHOULD I JUMP. / SILVERTOWN** [ ] [-]
(12"+=) – Why should I.

Orea Milltown | not iss.

Apr 90. (7"/12") *(MTOWN 001/+T)* **SEEMS TO ME. / NATURAL** [ ] [-]

A&M | A&M

Oct 90. (7"/c-s) **APPLE GREEN. / WHEN IT COMES** [ ] [-]
(12"+=/cd-s+=) – My favourite place.
Jan 91. (7"/c-s) *(AM/+C 711)* **WHICH WAY SHOULD I JUMP. / DIPLOMAT** [38] [-]
(12"+=/cd-s+=) *(AM X/CD 711)* – Knives and forks / Drop out.
(10"+=) *(AMT 711)* – Natural / Silvertown.
Mar 91. (cd/c/lp) *(395346-2/-4/-1)* <5346> **SLINKY** [27] [ ]
– Apple green / Here I stand / Sally Ann / Which way should I jump? / Real / Nationality / Never come down again / Something cheap / Seems to me / Sandman.
Apr 91. (7") *(AM 758)* **HERE I STAND. / DON'T BREATHE IN** [41] [-]
(cd-s+=) *(AMCD 758)* – Jack Lemon.
(12"++=) *(AMX 758)* – Something on my mind.
Jun 91. (7") *(AM 787)* **APPLE GREEN. / SALLY ANNE (demo)** [43] [-]
(12"+=/cd-s+=) *(AM X/CD 787)* – Nationality (demo) / Never come down again (demo).
May 93. (7") *(580269-7)* **TURN OFF. / WORLD WIDE** [55] [-]
(12"+=) *(580269-6)* – Got this feeling.
(cd-s) *(580269-2)* – ('A'side) / Caroline / Rosemary Page / Alice.
Jul 93. (7") *(580333-7)* **IT'S ALL OVER NOW BABY BLUE. / SWEET NOTHING** [48] [-]
(cd-s) *(580333-2)* – ('A'side) / Roses / Which way should I jump (original) / Seems to me.
(10"/cd-s) *(580333-0/-2)* – ('A'side) / Positively 4th Street / Hurricane / I shall be released.
Aug 93. (cd/c/lp) *(540132-2/-4/-1)* **VALVE** [ ] [-]
– When it comes / Turn off / Killing all the good men, Jimmy / Pictures (round my room) / Turn me over / Trees / Sleepwalking / Falling straight down / Crawl with me / Someday / It's all over now baby blue / Cool breeze. *(cd re-iss. May95; same)*
Sep 93. (7"/c-s) **SLEEPWALKING. / FE-FI-FO-FUM** [ ] [-]
(cd-s+=) – You don't know me no more / Long time.
(cd-s) – ('A'side) / Everybody knows / Can't find the time / Freedom song.

— disbanded after above

MINISTRY

Formed: Chicago, Illinois, USA . . . 1981 by ex-SPECIAL EFFECT member AL JOURGENSEN. The latter bunch included FRANKIE NARDIELLO (who'd replaced TOM HOFFMAN), MARTY SORENSON and HARRY RUSHAKOFF, this synth-pop aggregation releasing a couple of 7" singles and a soundtrack album at the turn of the decade. Continuing in this vein, JOURGENSEN co-formed the 'Wax Trax' label and issued a debut MINISTRY 12" in 1982, 'COLD LIFE'. A further string of limp electro singles and a debut album, 'WITH SYMPATHY' (1983; European title 'WORK FOR LOVE') followed, before JOURGENSEN adopted a decidedly harder electronic sound on 'TWITCH' (1986). Around the same time, the MINISTRY mainman initiated a number of offshoot projects, the most high profile being The REVOLTING COCKS, who included in the ranks RICHARD 23, LUC VAN ACKER (the former later replaced by CHRIS CONELLY of FINI TRIBE). JOURGENSEN was said to have described this bunch as "Disco For Psychopaths", the 12", 'NO DEVOTION' and the long-player, 'BIG SEXY LAND' were aural proof. Another single, 'YOU OFTEN FORGET' (1987) was equally controversial, having already annoyed the PMRC (Parental Music Resource Center) with their overtly blasphemous debut. A live album, 'GODDAMNED SON OF A BITCH' was The REVOLTING COCKS next release in 1988, drummer BILL RIEFLIN now a steady part of both JOURGENSEN's groups. Meanwhile, MINISTRY had recruited bassist PAUL BARKER (and brother ROLAND BARKER), the outfit consolidated their harsher industrial approach with the vicious 1989 set, 'LAND OF RAPE AND HONEY'. To end the decade, MINISTRY unleashed yet another uncompromisingly bleak set of industrial grinding, 'THE MIND IS A TERRIBLE THING TO TASTE', while four months later, The REVOLTING COCKS offered some light relief with a decidedly unsympathetic version of Olivia Newton John's '(LET'S GET) PHYSICAL'. This was lifted from parent album, 'BEERS, STEERS AND QUEERS', the title track a brilliant must-hear send-up of backwoods American perversion. The REVOLTING COCKS gained even more notoriety when a proposed tour (which was to include onstage strippers and livestock) was the subject of an outraged House Of Commons discussion. Having briefly collaborated with JELLO BIAFRA (ex-DEAD KENNEDYS) on a project entitled LARD, JOURGENSEN released a one-off single under the 1000 HOMO DJ's banner, the main track being a cover of Black Sabbath's 'SUPERNAUT'. With the addition of guitarist MIKE SCACCIA and the unhinged guest vocals of GIBBY HAYNES (Butthole Surfers), MINISTRY recorded arguably their finest moment to date, 'JESUS BUILT MY HOTROD'. This was closely followed by MINISTRY's breakthrough Top 40 (on both sides of the Atlantic!) album, 'PSALM 69: THE WAY TO SUCCEED AND THE WAY TO SUCK EGGS', a highly regarded set which saw the group veering towards searing sonic metal. A Top 50 single, 'N.W.O.' followed a successful near headlining slot on the Lollapalooza' 1992 tour, PAUL BARKER also moonlighting in yet another MINISTRY offshoot, LEAD INTO GOLD (releasing the 'AGE OF REASON' a follow-up to 1990's mini-cd 'CHICKS & SPEED'). A year later, The REVOLTING COCKS returned with their inimitably twisted brand of black humour, a version of Rod Stewart's 'DO YA THINK I'M SEXY' one of the highlights of their 1993 album, 'LINGER FICKEN' GOOD'. The two main MINISTRY men, AL JOURGENSEN and PAUL BARKER, replaced the departing RIEFLIN with RAY WASHAM and moved the operation to Texas (JOURGENSEN set up a country label). Late in 1995, after AL escaped a drugs bust, MINISTRY ventured even further into metal territory with the 'FILTH PIG' opus, a collection that contained a murderous version of Bob Dylan's 'LAY LADY LAY'.

Album rating: LAND OF RAPE AND HONEY (*7) / PSALM 69: HOW TO SUCCEED AND HOW TO SUCK EGGS (*8) / FILTH PIG (*6) / Revolting Cocks: BEERS, STEERS & QUEERS (*7)

SPECIAL EFFECT

AL JOURGENSEN (b. 9 Oct'58, Havana, Cuba) – guitar / **FRANKIE NARDIELLO** – vocals; repl. TOM HOFFMAN / **MARTY SORENSON** – bass / **HARRY RUSHAKOFF** – drums not iss. / Special Effect

1979. (7"ep) <2955> **MOOD MUSIC EP** [-] [ ]
– I know a girl / Vertigo feeling / Innocense / Dress me dolls.

1980. (lp; soundtrack) <008028> **TOO MUCH SOFT LIVING** [-] [ ]

— also flexidisc from 'Praxis' magazine; HEADACHE. / NUCLEAR GLOOM

not iss. / Thermidor

Oct 81. (7") <T 5> **EMPTY HANDED. / THE HEAT** [-] [ ]

MINISTRY

AL JOURGENSEN – guitar, keyboards, synthesizers, vocals / **LAMONT WELTON** – bass / **STEVO** – drums

Situation 2 / Wax Trax

Mar 82. (12"m) *(SIT 17T)* <110072X> **COLD LIFE. / I'M FALLING / COLD LIFE (dub) / PRIMENTAL** [ ] [ ]

— AL used musicians on next lp; **SHAY JONES** – vocals / **WALTER TURBETT** – guitar / **JOHN DAVIS** – keyboards / **ROBERT ROBERTS** – keyboards / **STEPHEN GEORGE** – drums / **MARTIN SORENSEN** – bass

Arista / Arista

Feb 83. (7"/12") *(ARIST/+12 510)* **WORK FOR LOVE. / FOR LOVE (instrumental)** [ ] [-]

Apr 83. (7"/12") *<9021>* **REVENGE (YOU DID IT AGAIN). / SHE'S GOT A CAUSE** [-] [ ]

Jun 83. (7") *(ARIST 533)* <9068> **I WANTED TO TELL HER. / A WALK IN THE PARK** [ ] [ ]
(12"+=) *(ARIST12 533)* <9102> – ('A'-Tongue Tied mix).

Sep 83. (lp/c) *(205/405 306)* <6608> **WORK FOR LOVE** <US title 'WITH SYMPATHY'> [ ] [96] Jun83
– Work for love / Do the Etawa / I wanted to tell her / Say you're sorry / Here we go / Effigy / Revenge / She's got a cause / Should have known better. *(cd-iss. 1989 as 'WITH SYMPATHY'+=; ARCD 8016) (cd-iss. Mar93 +=; 255 306)* – What He Say.

Nov 83. (7") *(ARIST 549)* **REVENGE (YOU DID IT AGAIN). / EFFIGY** [ ] [-]
(12"+=) *(ARIST12 549)* – Work for love.

— now basically AL solo

Wax Trax / Wax Trax

Oct 85. (12") *(WAXUK 009)* **NATURE OF LOVE. / ('A'-Cruelty mix)** [ ] [-]

Sire / Sire

Apr 86. (lp/c) *(925309-1/-4)* <25309> **TWITCH** [ ] [ ]
– Just like you / We believe / All day remix / The angel / Over the shoulder / My possession / Where you at now? / Crash and burn / Twitch (version II). *(cd+=)* – Over the shoulder (mix) / Isle Of Man.

— added partner **PAUL BARKER** (b. 8 Feb'50, Palo Alto, Calif.) – bass, programming (ex-FRONT 242) + **WILLIAM RIEFLIN** (b.30 Sep'60, Seattle, Washington) – drums / **ROLAND BARKER** (b.30 Jun'57, Mountainview, Calif.) – keyboards

Jan 89. (lp/c/cd) *(925799-1/-4/-2)* <25799> **THE LAND OF RAPE AND HONEY** [ ] [ ] Nov88
– Stigmata / The missing / Deity / Golden dawn / Destruction / The land of rape and honey / You know what you are / Flashback / Abortive. *(cd+=)* – Hizbollah / I prefer. *(cd re-iss. Dec92; 7599 25799-2)*

Feb 90. (cd/c/lp) *<(7599 26004-2/-4/-1)>* **THE MIND IS A TERRIBLE THING TO TASTE** [ ] [ ] Dec89
– Thieves / Burning inside / Never believe / Cannibal song / Breathe / So what / Test / Faith collapsing / Dream song. *(cd re-iss. Dec92)*

Sep 90. (cd/lp) *<7599 26266-2/-1>* **IN CASE YOU DIDN'T FEEL LIKE SHOWING UP (live)** [-] [ ]
– The missing / deity / So what / Burning inside / Seed / Stigmata. *(UK cd-iss. Dec92 on 'WEA'; same)*

— next with guest **GIBBY HAYNES** (of BUTTHOLE SURFERS)

— added **MIKE SCACCIA** (b.14 Jun'65, Babylon, N.Y.) – guitar

Apr 92. (7") *(W 0096)* **JESUS BUILT MY HOTROD. / TV SONG** [ ] [ ]
(12"+=/cd-s+=) *(W 0096 T/C)* – ('A'-Red line-white line version).

Jul 92. (cd/c/10"lp) *<(7599 26727-2/-4/-1)>* **PSALM 69: HOW TO SUCCEED AND HOW TO SUCK EGGS** [33] [27]
– N.W.O. / Just one fix / TV II / hero / Jesus built my hot rod / Scarecrow / Psalm 69 / Corrosion / Grace.

Jul 92. (10") *(W 0125)* **N.W.O. / F***ED (non lp version)** [49] [ ]
(cd-s+=) *(W 0125CD)* – ('A'extended dance mix).

— **JOURGENSEN + PAUL BARKER + SCACCIA** recruited **RAY WASHAM** – drums (of JESUS LIZARD) / **DUANE BUFORD** – keyboards / **LOUIS SVITEK** – guitar (ex-MINDFUNK)

W.E.A. / Warners

Dec 95. (c-s) *(W 0328C)* **THE FALL / RELOAD** [53] [ ]
(cd-s+=) *(W 0328CD)* – TV III.

Jan 96. (cd/c/lp) *<(9362 45838-2/-4/-1)>* **FILTHPIG** [43] [19]
– Reload / Filth pig / Crumbs / Useless / Lava / Dead guy / The face / Brick windows / Gane show / Lay lady lay / Reload (edit).

Feb 96. (c-s) *(W 0338C)* **LAY LADY LAY / LAY LADY LAY (album version)** [ ] [ ]
(cd-s+=) *(W 0338CD)* – Paisley / Scarecrow (live).

– compilation, others, etc. –

1985. (lp) *Hot Trax; (WAXC 35)* **12" INCH SINGLES 1981-1984** [-] [ ]

REVOLTING COCKS

AL's studio outfit, with FRONT 242 members; LUC and RICHARD 23. The latter was soon replaced CHRIS CONNELLY of FINI TRIBE.

Wax Trax / Wax Trax

Feb 86. (12"m) *(WAXUK 011)* **NO DEVOTION. / ATTACK SHIPS / ON FIRE** [ ] [ ]

Nov 86. (lp)(cd) *(WAXUK 017)(WAX 017CD)* **BIG SEXY LAND** [ ] [ ]
– 38 / We shall cleanse the world / Attack ships on fire / Big sexy land / Union carbide (West Virginia version) / T.V. mind / No devotion / Union carbide (Bhopal version). *(re-iss. Mar92 on 'Devotion' cd/c/lp; CD/T+/DVN 6)*

Feb 87. (12") *(WAXUK 022)* **YOU OFTEN FORGET. / ('A'version)** [ ] [ ]

AL now with **BARKER, VAN ACKER, RIEFLIN + CONNELLY** – vocals

Jun 88. (d-lp/cd) *(WAX UK/CD 037)* **LIVE! – YOU GODDAMNED SON OF A BITCH** (live + 2 studio) [ ] [ ]
– You Goddamned son of a bitch / Cattle grind / We shall cleanse the world / 38 / In the neck / You often forget / TV mind / Union carbide / Attack ships on fire / No devotion. *(re-iss. May92 on 'Devotion' cd/c/lp; CD/T+/DVN 8)*

Mar 89. (12") *<(WAX 042)>* **STAINLESS STEEL PROVIDERS. / AT THE TOP** [ ] [ ]

— **AL + PHIL** were also part of JELLO BIAFRA's (Dead Kennedys) group LARD.

May 90. (cd/c/lp) *(WAX 063 CD/MC/LP)* **BEERS, STEERS + QUEERS** [ ] [ ]
– Beers, steers + queers / (Let's get) Physical / In the neck / Get down / Stainless steel providers / Can't sit still / Something wonderful / Razor's edge. *(cd+=)* – (Let's talk) Physical. *(re-iss. Feb92 on 'Devotion' cd/c/lp; CD/T+/DVN 4)*

May 90. (cd-s) *(WAX 086CD)* **(LET'S GET) PHYSICAL. / (LET'S TALK) PHYSICAL** [ ] [ ]

— now without RIEFLIN (on below only TRENT REZNOR of NINE INCH NAILS)

Apr 91. (12"ep/cd-ep; 1000 HOMO DJ'S) *<WAX 032>* **SUPERNAUT / HEY ASSHOLE / APATHY / BETTER WAYS** [ ] [ ] 1987

Devotion / Devotion

Sep 93. (12"ep/cd-ep) *(12/CD DVN 111)* **DA YA THINK I'M SEXY? / SERGIO GUITAR / WRONG (sexy mix)** [61] [ ]

Sep 93. (cd/c/d-lp) *(CD/T+/DVN 22)* **LINGER FICKEN' GOOD . . . AND OTHER BARNYARD ODDITIES** [39] [ ]
– Gila copter / Creep / Mr.Lucky / Crackin' up / Sergio / Da ya think I'm sexy? / The rockabye / Butcher flower's woman / Dirt / Linger ficken' good.

Jun 94. (12"/cd-s) *(12/CD DVN 112)* **CRACKIN' UP. / ('A'-Amylnitrate mix) / GUACOPTER (version 2)** [ ] [-]

PTP

AL, PAUL + WILL (SCORPIO + ALIEN DOG STAR + FRENCHIE L'AMOUR)

Wax Trax / Wax Trax

1989. (12) *(WAX 9073)* **RUBBER GLOVE SEDUCTION. / MY FAVOURITE THINGS** [ ] [ ]

ACID HORSE

GALLOPIN' SCORPIO SADDLEBUTT + TENNESSEE KING BIFF + HAROLD SANDOZ + ALIEN DOG STAR

1989. (12") *(WAX 9081)* **NO NAME NO SLOGAN. / ('A'-produced by CABARET VOLTAIRE)** [ ] [ ]

LEAD INTO GOLD

PAUL BARKER with **AL JOURGENSEN + WILD BILL RIEFLIN**

not iss. / SPV

1990. (m-cd) *<SPV 91942>* **CHICKS & SPEED** [-] [ ]
– Faster than light / The stripper / Beauty / Idiot / Blackened heart / Hatred.

— added **STUART BANG ZECHMAN** – guitar

Wax Trax / Wax Trax

Aug 90. (lp/cd) *<(WAX 116/+CD)>* **AGE OF REASON** [ ] [ ]
– Age of reason / Unreason / Snake oil / A giant on Earth / Faster than light / Lunatic – Genius / Sweet thirteen / Fell from Heaven. *(re-iss. Mar92 on 'Devotion' cd/c/lp; CD/T+/DVN 7)*

MINK DeVILLE

Formed: San Francisco, California, USA . . . 1974 by WILLY DeVILLE (he had lived in London for the past few years), the singer relocating his new outfit – who included RUBEN SIGUENZA, THOMAS 'MANFRED' ALLEN and LOUIS X. ERLANGER – to his native New York where they became favourites on the New York new wave underground scene. Snapped up by 'Capitol' on the strength of a few tracks on the celebrated V/A collection, 'Live At CBGB'S', the group broke through with their 1977 debut 45, 'SPANISH STROLL'. A surprise UK chart hit in light of its characteristic Hispanic singing crossed between LOU REED and the more soulful R&B American singers, the track was one of the few highlights from their patchy eponymous debut set. Produced by Jack Nitzsche, the album failed to generate anticipated interest, although it was notable for the inclusion of Patti & The Emblems cover, 'MIXED UP, SHOOK UP GIRL'. Follow-up set, 'RETURN TO MAGENTA' (1978), fared little better, DeVILLE turning his interpretive skills this time around to a cover of Moon Martin's 'ROLENE'. Ever the ladies man, WILLY relocated his musical endevours to Paris for the recording of third album, 'LE CHAT BLEU' (1980), he and ERLANGER joined by a clutch of seasoned former session men enlisted to make the most of the part-DOC POMUS penned songs. With each subsequent release, MINK DeVILLE (or just basically WILLY solo) became an increasingly mainstream/AOR operation, culminating in a collaborative effort with MARK KNOPFLER, 'Storybook Love', in 1988.

Album rating: SAVOIR FAYRE compilation (*5)

WILLY DeVILLE (b. WILLIAM BORAY, 27 Aug'53, New York City) – vocals, guitar, mouth harp / **RUBEN SIGUENZA** – bass / **THOMAS 'MANFRED' ALLEN** – drums / **LOUIS X. ERLANGER** – guitar, vocals / **BOBBY LEONARDS** – keyboards

Capitol / Capitol

Jun 77. (7") **SPANISH STROLL. / MIXED UP, SHOOK UP** [-] [ ]

Jun 77. (7"/12") *(CL/12CLX 103)* **SPANISH STROLL. / GUNSLINGER** [20] [-]

Jun 77. (lp/c) *<(EST/TC-EST 11631)>* **MINK DeVILLE** [ ] [ ]
– Venus of Avenue D / Little girl / One way street / Mixed up, shook up girl / Gunslinger / Can't do without it / Cadillac walk / Spanish stroll / She's so tough / Party girls. *(re-iss. Feb87 on 'Razor'; as 'CABRETTA'; RAZ 24) (cd-iss. Mar93 as 'SPANISH STROLL' on 'Raven'; RVCD 32)*

Sep 77. (7") *(CL 15942)* **LITTLE GIRL. / SHE'S SO TOUGH** [ ] [-]
Nov 77. (7") *(CL 15952)* **CADILLAC WALK. / CAN'T DO WITHOUT IT** [ ] [-]
Dec 77. (7") **CADILLAC GIRL. / LITTLE GIRL** [-] [-]
May 78. (7") *(CL 15989)* **JUST YOUR FRIEND. / ONE WAY STREET** [ ] [-]
Jun 78. (7") **GUARDIAN ANGEL. / EASY SLIDER** [-] [-]
Jul 78. (lp/c) *<(EST/TC-EST 11780)>* **RETURN TO MAGENTA** [ ] [ ] Jun78
– Guardian angel / Soul twist / "A" train lady / Rolene / Desperate days / Just your friends / Steady drivin' man / Easy slider / I broke that promise / Confidence to kill. *(cd-iss. May93 on 'Wotre Music'; WM 339003)*
Aug 78. (7") *(CL 16005)* **SOUL TWIST. / ROLENE** [ ] [-]

— **WILLY** retained **ERLANGER** and brought in new men **RICK BORGIA** – guitar / **KENNY MARGOLIS** – keyboards / **JERRY SCHEFF** – bass / **RON TUTT** – drums

Apr 80. (7") *(CL 16134)* **THIS MUST BE THE NIGHT. / MIXED UP, SHOOK UP GIRL** [ ] [-]
(12"+=) *(CLX 16134)* – Lipstick traces.
Apr 80. (lp/c) *(EST/TC-EST 25390) <11955>* **LE CHAT BLEU** [ ] [ ] Sep80
– This must be the night / Savoir faire / That world outside / Slow drain / You just keep holding on / Lipstick traces / Bad boy / Mazurka / Just to walk that little girl home / Heaven stood still. *(cd-iss. May93 on 'Wotre Music'; WM 339002)*
Jun 80. (7") **LIPSTICK TRACES. / JUST TO WALK THAT LITTLE GIRL HOME** [-] [ ]

— disbanded in Spring 1980

C.B.S. Columbia

Sep 80. (7"; by WILLY DeVILLE) *(CBS 8526)* **HEAT OF THE MOMENT. / PULLIN' MY STRING** [ ] [ ]

— MINK DEVILLE re-grouped in 1981. **WILLY, RICK + KENNY** recruited **JOEY VASTA** – bass / **TOMMY PRICE** – drums

Atlantic Atlantic

Oct 81. (7") *(K 11688)* **YOU BETTER MOVE ON. / SHE WAS MINE** [ ] [ ]
Oct 81. (lp/c) *(K/K4 50833) <19311>* **COUP DE GRACE** [ ] [ ]
– Just give me one good reason / Help me to make it / Maybe tomorrow / Teardrops must fall / You better move on / Love & emotion / So in love are we / Love me like you did before / She was made in Heaven / End of the line.
Jan 82. (7") *(K 11703)* **MAYBE TOMORROW. / SO IN LOVE ARE WE** [ ] [-]
Dec 83. (lp/c) *(780115-1/-4)* **WHERE THE ANGELS FEAR TO TREAD** [ ] [ ]
– Each word's a beat of my heart / River of tears / Demasiado / corazon (Too much heart) / Lilly's daddy's Cadillac / Around the corner / Pick up the pieces / Love's got a hold on me / Keep your monkey away from my door / Are you lonely tonight / The moonlight let me down.
Apr 84. (7") *(A 9750) <89750>* **EACH WORD'S A BEAT OF MY HEART. / RIVER OF TEARS** [ ] [89] Jan84
(12"+=) *(AT 9750)* – Harlem nocturne / Maybe tomorrow.
Apr 84. (7") **PICK UP THE PIECES. /** [-] [ ]

— now with complete new personnel of session people

Jun 85. (7") *(POSP 745)* **IN THE HEART OF THE CITY. / PRIDE AND JOY** [ ] [-]
(12"+=) *(POSPX 745)* – Italian shoes (New York mix).
Jun 85. (lp/c/cd) *(825776-1/-4/-2)* **SPORTIN' LIFE** [ ] [ ]
– In the heart of the city / I must be dreaming / Italian shoes / Slip away / When you walk my way / A woman's touch / Easy street / Little by little / There's no living (without your loving) / Something beautiful is dying.
Oct 85. (7") *(POSP 773)* **I MUST BE DREAMING. / IN THE HEART OF THE CITY** [ ] [ ]
(12"+=) *(POSPX 773)* – ('A'mix).

— split late '85

WILLY DE VILLE

— continued a solo career

Polydor A&M

Nov 87. (7") **ASSASSIN OF LOVE. / I CALL YOUR NAME** [-] [ ]
Nov 87. (7") *(POSP 887)* **MIRACLE. / I CALL YOUR NAME** [ ] [-]
(12"+=) *(POSPX 887)* – Stand by me.
(c-s+=/cd-s+=) *(PO C/CD 887)* – Could you would you.
Jan 88. (lp/c)(cd) *(POLH/+C 39)(833669-2)* **MIRACLE** [ ] [ ]
– (Due to) Gun control / Could you would you / Heart & soul / Assassin of love / Spanish Jack / Miracle / Angel eyes / Nightfalls / Southern politician / Storybook love. *(cd-iss. Dec94 on 'Raven'; RVCD 41)*
Feb 88. (7") *(POSP 904)* **ASSASSIN OF LOVE. / SPANISH JACK** [ ] [-]
(12"+=) *(POSPX 904)* – ('A'extended remix) / Spanish stroll (live).
(cd-s++=) *(POCD 904)* Desperate ways (live).

— WILLY was credited with MARK KNOPFLER (Dire Straits) on 'Storybook Love', (circa Mar88).

Skyranch Skyranch

Mar 92. (cd) *<(SR 652304)>* **VICTORY MIXTURE** [ ] [ ]
– Hello my lover / It do me good / Key to my heart / Beating like a tom-tom / Every dog has its day / Big blue diamonds / Teasin' you / Ruler of my heart / Who shot the la-la / Junker's blues. *(re-iss. Mar95; same)*

F.N.A.C. not iss.

Apr 94. (cd) *(592254)* **WILLY DeVILLE LIVE (live)** [ ] [ ]

not iss. Forward-Rhino

May 94. (cd-s) **HEY! JOE /** [-] [ ]
May 94. (cd) *<71686>* **BACKSTREETS OF DESIRE** [-] [ ]
– Empty heart / All in the name of love / Lonely hunter / Even while I sleep / Voodoo charm / Come to poppa / Chemical warfare / Hey! Joe / I call your name / I can only give you everything / Jump city / Bamboo road / All in the name of love (reprise).

East West WEA

Nov 95. (c-s) *(EW 019C)* **STILL / WHEN YOU'RE AWAY FROM ME** [ ] [ ]
(cd-s+=) *(EW 019CD)* – Still (I love you still).
Jan 96. (cd/c) *<(0630 12456-2/-4)>* **LOUP GAROU** [ ] [ ]

– (MINK DeVILLE) compilations, etc. –

Nov 81. (lp/c) *Capitol; (EST/TC-EST 26716)* **SAVOIR FAIRE** [ ] [ ]
– This must be the night / "A" train lady / Spanish stroll / Cadillac walk / Soul twist / Just your friends / Mixed up, shook up girl / Gunslinger / One way street / Mazurka / I broke that promise / Just to walk that little girl home.
Jul 84. (7") *EMI Gold; (G45 27)* **SPANISH STROLL. / CADILLAC WALK** [ ] [-]
Nov 95. (3xcd-box) *E.M.I.; (CDOMB 013)* **CABRETTA / RETURN TO MAGENTA / LE CHAT BLEU** [ ] [ ]
Jan 96. (cd; by WILLY DeVILLE) *Wotre Music; (122151)* **BIG EASY FANTASY** [ ] [ ]
Oct 96. (cd) *Raven; (RVCD 59)* **CABRETTA / RETURN TO MAGENTA** [ ] [-]
Sep 97. (cd) *E.M.I.; (CTMCD 333)* **THE CENTENARY COLLECTION (THE BEST OF MINK DeVILLE)** [ ] [-]

MINNY POPS

Formed: Amsterdam, Netherlands ... September '78 by songwriter and er, "singer", WALLY VAN MIDDENDORP and his synthesized accomplice WIM DEKKER. A year on, the gruesome twosome released their debut single, 'KOJAK', following it up with a Dutch-only long-player, 'DRASTIC MEASURES, DRASTIC MOVEMENT' (1979). Fleshing out the minimalist sound with the addition of guitarist, GERARD WALHOF and bassist LION VAN ZOEREN, they delivered another heavy dose of mogadon electronica in the shape of the EP, 'LIVE 33'. One of its tracks, 'DOLPHIN SPURT', was seemingly interesting enough for 'Factory' boss, Tony Wilson to give it a full UK release. Thanks Tony! Further personnel shuffles were effected as P. MULDER substituted GERARD and LION, while the group were shunted onto Factory's continental branch 'Benelux' for a further two singles and album, 'SPARKS IN A DARK ROOM' (1982). Designed to make your party go with a bang (if you were playing Russian roulette with all barrels loaded, that is), this was possibly the most depressing material ever to be released by 'Factory' (and they've had some beauties, haven't they); imagine IAN CURTIS at 16 rpm inside a medieval monastery or alternatively an android on prozac and you're probably still nowhere near the full suicidal impact of the well named WALLY VAN MIDDENDORP's vocal drone.

Album rating: DRASTIC MEASURES, DRASTIC MOVEMENT (*4) / SPARKS IN A DARK ROOM (*3)

WALLY VAN MIDDENDORP – vocals / **WIM DEKKER** – synthesizer

Plurex not iss.

Mar 79. (7"ep) *(005)* **KOJAK. / FOOTSTEPS / NERVOUS** [ ] [-]
Sep 79. (lp) *(009)* **DRASTIC MEASURES, DRASTIC MOVEMENT** [-] [-] Dutch
– Springtime 1 / Minny pops / Hologram / Total confusion / Dolphins spurt / Motor city / Springtime 2 / Monica / Flash goes the eyes / M.D. mania / R.U. 21 / Mono / New muzak. *(re-iss. Dec81; same)* (with free 7") – KOGEL. / STRALERS

— added **GERARD WALHOF** – guitar / **LION VAN ZOEREN** – bass

Jun 80. (7"ep) *(0016)* **MINNY POPS – LIVE 33** [-] [-] Dutch
– Mental / Night out / Dolphin spurt.

Factory not iss.

Oct 80. (7") *(FAC 31)* **DOLPHIN SPURT. / GODDESS** [ ] [-]

— **P. MULDER** – instruments; repl. GERARD + LION

Factory Benelux not iss.

Nov 81. (7"ep) *(FACBN 11)* **TIME. / TRANCE / NIGHT VISIT** [ ] [-]
Nov 81. (7") *(FACBN 13)* **EIN KUS. / (other side by the band, MENTAL)** [-] [-] Dutch
Jul 82. (lp) *(FBN 15)* **SPARKS IN A DARK ROOM** [ ] [-]
– Black eye / Dream / Night visit / A feeling / Crack / Tracking / Vital / Blue roses / Mountains.

Les Tempes not iss.

Jun 84. (7") *(CSBT 4-5)* **EIN KUS. / SON** [ ] [-]

— had already split prior to above release

MINOR THREAT (see under ⇒ FUGAZI)

MINUTEMEN

Formed: San Pedro, California, USA ... 1979 originally as The REACTIONARIES, by D. BOON and MIKE WATT (third member GEORGE HURLEY replaced FRANK TONCHE). The band featured on Various Artists US lp's on indie labels 'Radio Tokyo', 'New Alliance' and 'Posh Boy', before signing for 'S.S.T.' (home base of BLACK FLAG and MEAT PUPPETS). For five years they committed many songs (mostly hardcore/jazz! around a minute long!) to EP and LP before having to disband late in 1985 after the untimely death of BOON. From 'PARANOID TIME' to '3-WAY TIE (FOR LAST)', MINUTEMEN showcased their politically leftfield attacks on the establishment including RONNIE REAGAN and JOE McCARTHY. In 1986 the remaining two, MIKE WATT and GEORGE HURLEY re-formed as fIREHOSE alongside guitarist ED CRAWFORD. This trio debuted with an album, 'RAGIN' FULL ON' (1987), their sound slightly mellowing. After an acclaimed 1989 third album 'fROMOHIO', they shifted to 'Columbia', where they scored minor hit albums in the early 90's. • **Covered:** HEY LAWDY MAMA (Steppenwolf) / HAVE YOU EVER SEEN THE RAIN + GREEN RIVER (Creedence Clearwater Revival) / DOCTOR WU (Steely Dan) / THE RED AND THE BLACK (Blue Oyster Cult). fIREHOSE covered WALKING THE COW (Daniel Johnston) / SLACK MOTHERFUCKER (Superchunk). DOS covered PACIFIC COAST HIGHWAY (Sonic Youth) + DON'T EXPLAIN (Billie Holiday).

Album rating: PARANOID TIME (*5) / THE PUNCH LINE mini (*4) / WHAT MAKES A MAN START FIRES? (*7) / DOUBLE NICKELS ON THE DIME (*8) / 3-WAY TIE (FOR LAST) (*6) / PROJECT: MERSH mini n(*6) / BALLOT RESULTS (*7) / firehose: RAGIN', fULL-ON (*6) / fROMOHIO (*8) / FLYING THE FLANNEL (*6) /

Mike Watt: BALL-HOG OR TUGBOAT? (*7) / CONTEMPLATING THE ENGINE ROOM (*7) / Dos: DOS (*6)

D. BOON (b. DENNES DALE BOON, 1 Apr'58) – vocals, guitar / **MIKE WATT** (b.20 Dec'57, Portsmouth, Virginia) – bass (also of DOS) / **GEORGE HURLEY** (b. 4 Sep'58, Brockton, Massachusetts) – drums; repl. FRANK TONCHE

S.S.T. S.S.T.

Dec 80. (7"ep) *<SST 002>* **PARANOID TIME** [-] [ ]
– Untitled song for Latin America / Political song for Michael Jackson to sing / Validation / The maze / Definitions / Fascist / Joe McCarthy's ghost. *(UK-iss.Mar83, cd-ep iss.Nov88; same)*

Sep 81. (7"ep) *<NAR 004>* **JOY / BLACK SHEEP. / MORE JOY** [-] [ ]
<above issued on 'New Alliance'>

Nov 81. (m-lp) *<SST 004>* **THE PUNCH LINE** [-] [ ]
– Search / Tension / Games / Boiling / Disguises / Struggle / Monuments / Ruins / Issued / The punch line / Song for El Salvador / History lesson / Fanatics / No parade / Straight jacket / Gravity / Warfare / Static. *<(cd/c-iss.May93; SST CD/C 004)>*

Feb 83. (lp) *<SST 014>* **WHAT MAKES A MAN START FIRES?** [-] [ ]
– Bob Dylan wrote propaganda songs / One chapter in the book / Fake contest / Beacon sighted through fog / Mutiny in Jonestown / East wind – Faith / Pure joy / '99 / The anchor / Sell or be sold / Only minority / Split red / Colors / Plight / Tin roof / Life as rehearsal / This road / Polarity. *(UK-iss.Aug91 & May93 cd/c; SST 014 CD/C)*

Nov 83. (m-lp) *<SST 016>* **BUZZ OR HOWL UNDER THE INFLUENCE OF HEAT** [-] [ ]
– Self-referenced / Cut / Dream told by Moto / Dreams are free, motherfucker! / Tow jam / I felt like a gringo / Product / Little man with a gun in his hand. *(UK-iss.May93 cd/c; SST 016 CD/C)*

Oct 84. (d-lp) *<(SST 028)>* **DOUBLE NICKELS ON THE DIME** [ ] [ ]
– D.'s car jam – Anxious Mo-Fo / Theatre is the life of you / Vietnam / Cohesion / It's expected I'm gone / Number 1 hit song / Two heads at the end / Do you want new wave or do you want . . . / Don't look now / Shit from an old notebook / Nature without man / One reporter's opinion / Political song for Michael Jackson to sing / Maybe partying will help / Toadies / Retreat / Big foist / God bows to math / Corona / Glory of man / Take 5, D. / My heart and the real world / History lesson, pt.2 / You need the glory / Roar of the masses could be farts / West Germany. *<(cd-iss. Oct87 +=; SST 028CD)>* – THE POLITICS OF TIME lp

Jun 85. (12"ep) *<(SST 034)>* **PROJECT: MERSH** [ ] [ ]
– Cheerleaders / King of the hill / Hey lawdy mama / Take our test / Tour-spiel / More spiel.

— tragedy struck on the 23rd December '85 when D.BOON was killed in a car crash

Jan 86. (lp) *<(SST 058)>* **3 WAY TIE (FOR LAST)** [ ] [ ]
– The price of Paradise / Lost / The big stick / Political nightmare / Courage / Have you ever seen the rain? / The red and the black / Spoken word piece / No one / Stories / What is it? / Ack ack ack / Just another soldier / Situations at hand / Hittin' the bong / Bermuda. *(cd-iss. Aug87; SST 058CD)*

— Broke-up early 1986. WATT guested for CICCONE YOUTH (aka SONIC YOUTH).

– compilations, etc. –

1984. (lp/cd) *New Alliance;* **THE POLITICS OF TIME** (early REACTIONARIES material) [-] [ ]
– The politics of time / Themselves / Please don't be gentle with me / Nothing indeed / No exchange / There ain't shit on TV tonight / This ain't no picnic / Spillage / Untitled song for Latin America / Jesus and tequila / June 16th / Storm in my house / Martin's story / Dr. Wu / World according to nouns / Love dance / Three car jam. *<cd-iss. May93 on 'S.S.T.'; >*

Apr 85. (7"ep) *Reflex; (REFLEX L)* **TOUR SPIEL (live)** [ ] [ ]

Dec 86. (d-lp/cd) *S.S.T.; <(SST 068)>* **BALLOT RESULTS** [ ] [ ]
– Little man with a black gun in his hand / Political song for Michael Jackson to sing / I felt like a gringo / Jesus and tequila / Courage / King of the hill / Bermuda / No one / Mr.Robot's holy orders / Ack ack ack / History lesson (part two) / This ain't no picnic / The cheerleaders / Time / Cut / Split red / Shit you hear at parties / Hell (second take) / Tour-spiel / Take our test / The punch line / Search / Bob Dylan wrote propaganda songs / Badges / Tension / If Reagan played disco / No! no! no! to draft and war – Joe McCarthy ghost. *(re-iss. May93)*

1987. (lp/cd) *S.S.T.; <SST 138/+CD>* **POST-MERSH, VOL.I** [-] [ ]
– THE PUNCH LINE ep / WHAT MAKES A MAN START FIRES lp *(re-iss. May93)*

1987. (lp/cd) *S.S.T.; <SST 139/+CD>* **POST-MERSH, VOL.II** [-] [ ]
– BUZZ OR HOWL UNDER THE INFLUENCE OF HEAT lp / PROJECT: MERSH ep *(re-iss. May93)*

Sep 87. (7"ep) *New Alliance;* **JOY / BLACK SHEEP. / MORE JOY** [ ] [ ]
(re-iss. Feb90 on 'S.S.T.' 10"colrd; SST 214)

May 89. (cd) *S.S.T.; <(SST 165)>* **POST-MERSH, VOL.III** [ ] [ ]

fIREHOSE

MIKE WATT – bass (also of **CRIMONY**, with **PAUL ROESSLER** – keyboards) / **GEORGE HURLEY** – drums / **ED CRAWFORD** (b.26 Jan'62, Steubenville, Ohio) – vocals, guitar (of COLUMBUS)

S.S.T. S.S.T.

Apr 87. (lp/c/cd) *<(SST 079/+C/CD)>* **RAGIN' FULL-ON** [ ] [ ]
– Caroma / Mutiny / Perfect pairs / Chemical wires / Choose and memory / Relating dudes to jazz? / Another theory shot to shit on your . . . / Under the influence of the Meat Puppets / Locked in / Brave captain. *(re-iss. Mar93; same)*

Mar 88. (lp/c/cd) *<(SST 115/+C/CD)>* **IF'N** [ ] [ ]
– Sometimes / Hear me / Honey, please / Backroads / From one cums one / Making the freeway / Anger / For the singer of R.E.M. / Operation solitaire / Windmilling / Me & you, remembering / In memory of Elizabeth Cotton / Soon / Thunder child. *(re-iss. Mar93; same)*

Jun 88. (12"ep) *<(SST 131)>* **SOMETIMES. / RHYMIN' SPILIN' / SHE PAINTS PICTURES** [ ] [ ]
(re-iss. Aug93 cd-ep+=; SST 131CD) – For the singer of R.E.M.

Mar 89. (lp/c/cd) *<(SST 235/+C/CD)>* **FROMOHIO** [ ] [ ]
– In my mind / Whisperin' while hollerin' / Mas cojones / What gets heard / Fiddle of the eighties / Time with you / If 'n / Understanding / The softest hammer / Vastapol / Let the drummer have some / Liberty for our friend / Some things / Not that shit George.

not iss. New Alliance

1989. (lp,c,cd; as BOOTSTRAPPERS) *<46>* **BOOTSTRAPPERS** [-] [ ]
– Memory is a muscle / Spider baby / New boots / Taxita / Flicker / Third rail / Media dub / D-I-A-L-C-A-S-H / X – Delta / Their faces are green and their hands / Presidential apology / Mud / Indeed / Empty-vee / Long beach dub – Feen / Maneuvres.
(above:- WATT + HURLEY with ELLIOTT SHARP)

Columbia Columbia

Oct 91. (cd/c/lp) *(468422-2/-4/-1)* **FLYIN' THE FLANNEL** [ ] [ ]
– Down with the bass / Up Finnegan's ladder / Can't believe / Walking the cow / Flyin' the flannel / Epoxy for example / O'er the town of Pedro / Too long / The first class / Anti-misogyny manoever / Toolin' song for Dave Alvin / Tienan man dream again / Lost colors / Towin' the line / Losers, boozers and heroes.

Feb 92. (m-cd) *<74152>* **THE LIVE TOTEM POLE EP** [-] [ ]
– The red and the black / Sophisticated bitch / Revolution part 2 / Slack motherfucker / What gets heard / Mannequin / Making the freeway safe for the freeway.
<re-iss. Feb95 as 'THE RED AND THE BLACK'; same>

Mar 93. (cd/c/lp) *(472967-2/-4/-1)* **MR. MACHINERY OPERATOR** [ ] [ ]
– Formal introduction / Blaze / Herded into pools / Witness / Number seven / Powerful hankerin' / Rocket sled-fuel tank / Quicksand / Disciples of the 3-way / More famous quotes / Sincerely / Hell-hole / 4.29.92 / The cliffs thrown down.

1994. (cd-ep) *<5122>* **BIG BOTTOM POW-WOW** [-] [ ]

— disbanded on the 12th of February 1994 after playing a small unadvertised gig. MIKE WATT joined PORNO FOR PYROS after a solo album.

MIKE WATT

Columbia Columbia

Mar 95. (cd/c) *(478375-2/-4) <67086>* **MIKE WATT: BALL-HOG OR TUGBOAT?** [ ] [ ]
– Big train / Against the 70's / Drove up from Pedro / Piss-bottle man / Chinese firedrill / Song for Madonna to sing / Tuff gnarl / Sexual military dynamics / Max and Wells / E-ticket ride / Forever – one reporter's opinion / Song for Igor / Tell 'em boy! / Sidemouse advice / Heartbeat / Maggot brain / Coincidence is either hit or miss.

— now with **NELS CLINE** – guitar / **STEPHEN HODGES** – drums

Oct 97. (cd,c) *<68161>* **CONTEMPLATING THE ENGINE ROOM** [-] [ ]
– In the engine room / Red bluff / The bluejackets' manual / Pedro bound! / The boilerman / Black gang coffee / Topsiders / No one says old man (to the old man) / Fireman Hurley / Liberty calls! / In the bunk room / Navy wife / Crossing the equator / Breaking the choke hold / Wrapping around the screw / Shore duty.

DOS

MIKE WATT + his wife **KIRA ROESSLER** – bass (ex-BLACK FLAG)

not iss. New Alliance

1986. (lp) *<NAR 032>* **DOS** [-] [ ]
– The fisherman & his wife / Forever / Funk one / Number four / Number one / Number three / Number two / The rabbit and the porcupine / Slow little turtle / Snapshot / Taking away the fire. *(UK cd-iss. May93; NAR 032CD)*

1989. (12"ep) *<NAR 044>* **NUMERO DOS** [-] [ ]
– Don't explain / Heartbeat / PCH / I worry, my son / Silence / Number six.

Aug 91. (cd) *<NAR 061>* **UNO CON DOS** (compilation of above 2) [-] [ ]
(UK-iss.May93; NAR 061CD)

not iss. Kill Rock Stars

Jun 96. (cd) *<KRS 256>* **JUSTAMENTE TRES** [-] [ ]
– Down in the dumps / Dream of San Pedro / Image that / Intense song for Madonna / 'Til the blood ran / Sidemouse advice / Excerpts from a captain's log / To each his dulcinea / Powerful hankerin' / Little doll / Willow weep for me / Even the pain has changed / Formal introduction / Angel face is the Devil's daughter / Number seven / Do you want new wave or do you want the truth? / Number five.

MIRACLE LEGION

Formed: Connecticut, USA . . . 1984 by MARK MULCAHY, RAY NEAL, JEFF WIEDERSCHALL and JOEL. Yet another American act to emerge in the seismic wake of R.E.M., MIRACLE LEGION first marched onto the scene the following year with a mini-set, 'THE BACKYARD'. Subsequently picked up by 'Rough Trade', the band finally released a full length album, 'SURPRISE, SURPRISE, SURPRISE', in summer '87, their rickenbacker-ringing alterna-pop finding an audience among post-Paisley Underground fans. By this point, STEVEN WEST had replaced JOEL on bass although the band was subsequently reduced to a core of MULCAHY and NEAL for 1989's stripped down, rootsy acoustic effort, 'ME AND MR. RAY'. While they did recruit another rhythm section (in the shape of DAVE McCAFFREY and SCOTT BOUTLER) and even had IAN McLAGAN (ex-SMALL FACES) guesting for them, MULCAHY and NEAL disbanded MIRACLE LEGION after the country influenced 1992 album, 'DRENCHED'. MULCAHY took up a low-key solo career before he hooked up with NEAL once more to deliver a comeback set, 'PORTRAIT OF A DAMAGED FAMILY' (1997).

Album rating: THE BACKYARD mini (*5) / SURPRISE SURPRISE SURPRISE (*5) / ME AND MR. RAY (*5) / DRENCHED (*6) / PORTRAIT OF A DAMAGED FAMILY (*4)

MARK MULCAHY – vocals (ex-DUMPTRUCK) / **RAY NEAL** – guitar / **JOEL** – bass / **JEFF WIEDERSCHALL** – drums

Making Waves Incas

Nov 85. (m-lp) *(SPIN 302)* **THE BACKYARD** [ ] [ ] May85
– Butterflies / Steven are you there? / The backyard / Closer to the wall / Just say hello / The heart is attached.

Feb 86. (7") *(SURF 112)* **THE BACKYARD. / UNTIL SHE TALKS** [ ] [ ]

— **STEVEN WEST** – bass; repl. JOEL

Rough Trade Rough Trade

Jul 87. (lp/c) *(ROUGH/+C 112)* **SURPRISE, SURPRISE, SURPRISE**
– Storyteller / Truly / Little man / Mr. Mingo / Crooked path / Paradise / Everyone in Heaven / Country boy / Wonderment / All for the best. *<US-iss.May88 as 'GLAD'; ROUGHUS 34>*

Jan 89. (lp/c/cd) *(ROUGH/+C/CD 136) <ROUGHUS 57>* **ME AND MR. RAY**
– The ladies from town / And then / Old & new / Sailors and animals / If she could cry / Pull the wagon / You're the one Lee / Even better / Cold shoulder balcony / Gigantic transatlantic trunk call.

Feb 89. (7") *(RT 226)* **YOU'RE THE ONE LEE. /**
(12"+=) *(RTT 226)* –

— (briefly before their split in 1991) **MARK + RAY** enlisted **DAVE McCAFFREY** – bass / **SCOTT BOUTLER** – drums

not iss. Morgan Creek

1992. (cd/c) *<2959-20006-2/-4>* **DRENCHED** -
– Sooner / Sea hag / Snacks and candy / So good / Everything is rosy / With a wish / Little blue light / Out to play / Velvetine / Waiting room / Maybelline.

1992. (7") **OUT TO PLAY. /** -

not iss. Mezzotint

Feb 97. (cd) **PORTRAIT OF A DAMAGED FAMILY** -
– You're my blessing / Screamin' / Homer / Say I had a lovely time / La muerte di gardenier / Accidentally on purpose / Please / 6 months / Madison park / I wish I was Danny Kaye / K.K.M. / 30.06 (you better watch out) / Good for her / Gone to bed at 21.

MIRANDA SEX GARDEN

Formed: London, England . . . early 90's by 19 year-olds, KATHARINE BLAKE and KELLY McCUSKER, both classically trained musicians (at Harrow's Purcell Music School) with piercing falsetto voices. Together with violinist JOCELYN WEST, the pair spent the early part of their career busking around the capital, performing madrigals ("16th-17th century part song for unaccompanied voices" according to the dictionary) to impressed passers by. BARRY ADAMSON was sufficiently bewitched to secure the girls an appearance on his 'Delusion' soundtrack, the group – completed by keyboard player BEN GOLOMSTOCK and percussionist TREVOR SHARPE – subsequently joining ADAMSON as part of the diverse 'Mute' roster. Complete with gothic typeface and arty photography, the haunting 'GUSH FORTH MY TEARS' served as the debut MIRANDA SEX GARDEN single in 1991 as the trio went on to support BLUR. An avant-ambience mix courtesy of ORB man, THRASH, provided an interesting juxtaposition between austerity and modernity, the press reacting with a mixture of bemusement and surprise amid charges of pretentiousness as debut album, 'MADRA' (1991) hit the shops. Mini-set, 'IRIS', followed in 1992 while a further two full length albums, 'SUSPIRIA' (1993) and 'FAIRYTALES OF SLAVERY' (1994) – remaining member KATHARINE now with DONNA McKEVITT, BEN GOLOMSTOCK and TREVOR SHARPE – put paid to any ideas of classical prudishness as BLAKE explored sado-masochism and allegedly performed semi-naked at fetish clubs. • **Songwriters:** Group except; GUSH FORTH MY TEARS (William Holborne) / SEE AMARYLLIS SHAMED (Michael West) / FULL FATHOM FIVE (Robert Johnson) / MY FUNNY VALENTINE (Hart-Rogers) / IN HEAVEN (Ivers-Lynch) / HAVANA LIED (Brecht-Weill).

Album rating: MADRA (*6)

KATHARINE BLAKE – vocals, percussion, violin, keyboards / **JOCELYN WEST** – vocals, some instruments / **KELLY McCUSKER** – vocals, strings, keyboards, etc

Mute Mute-Elektra

Jun 91. (7") *(MUTE 123) <66497>* **GUSH FORTH MY TEARS. / SEE AMARYLLIS SHAMED**
(12"+=) *(12MUTE 123)* – ('A'-Danny Rampling mix) / ('A'-Thrash & Paul Kendal mix).
(cd-s+=) *(CDMUTE 123)* – ('A'-A Cappella mix) / ('A'-remix).

Jul 91. (cd/c/d-lp) *(CD/C+/STUMM 91) <61126>* **MADRA**
– Seek sweet content / While joyful springtime lasteth / Go wailing accents / Gush forth my tears / Fly not so fast / The nightingale / Lady those eyes / Through my carriage be but careless / All creatures now are merry minded / Full fathom five / See Amaryllis shamed // It was a lover and his lass / Those sweet delightful lillies / Ah, look upon these eyes / If it be love / Away, thou shalt not love me / How merrily we live / Sweet Kate / This love is but a wanton fit / Sure there is no god of love / See my own sweet jewel / When first I saw thee / The silver swan / Sweet honey-sucking bees.

May 92. (cd/c/m-lp) *(CD/C+/STUMM 97) <61277>* **IRIS**
– Lovely Joan / Falling / Fear / Blue light / Iris.

— **KATHARINE + DONNA** brought in **BEN GOLOMSTOCK** – keyboards / **DONNA McKEVITT** – violin / **TREVOR SHARPE** – percussion / etc

Jan 93. (12"ep/cd-ep) *(12/CD MUTE 139)* **PLAY. / INFERNO (version II) / MY FUNNY VALENTINE** -

Feb 93. (cd/c/lp) *(CD/C+/STUMM 112) <61460>* **SUSPIRIA**
– Ardera sempre / Open eyes / Sunshine / Distance / Play / In Heaven / Bring down the sky / Feed / Inferno / Willie Biddle and his amazing maggot / My funny valentine.

Mar 93. (12"ep/cd-ep) *(12/CD MUTE 154)* **SUNSHINE / WILLIE BIDDLE. / FEAR (live) / MUFF DIVING SIZE QUEEN** -

— **KATHARINE, BEN, TREVOR** with newcomer **HEBZIBAH SESSA** – strings, keyboards

Apr 94. (12"ep/cd-ep) *(12/CD MUTE 163)* **PEEP SHOW. / THE WOODEN BOAT / FREEZING** -

May 94. (cd/c/lp) *(CD/C+/STUMM 129) <61666>* **FAIRYTALES OF SLAVERY**
– Cut / Fly / Peep show / Wooden boat / Havana lied / Cover my face / Transit / Freezing / Serial angels / The wheel / Intermission / Monk song / Fairytale about slavery.

— disbanded after above

MISFITS

Formed: Lodi, New Jersey, USA . . . 1977 by GLENN DANZIG and JERRY ONLY. B-movie punks dominated by the brooding presence and sneering croon of DANZIG, the group (BOBBY STEELE and JOEY IMAGE completing the line-up) gigged at the usual N.Y. haunts such as CBGB's before releasing their debut single, 'COOL COUGH', on the self-financed 'Plan 9' label. This was closely followed by such endearingly amateurish slices of low-rent melodic splatter-punk as 'HORROR BUSINESS' and 'NIGHT OF THE LIVING DEAD EP', as well as a special 'HALLOWEEN' single released in, you guessed it, October (1980). Around the same time, GLENN and Co. supported The DAMNED on a European tour, during which DANZIG wound up in jail after fisticuffs with their roadies. By this point, STEELE had been replaced with JERRY's broher DOYLE, this line-up playing on the belated debut album, 'WALK AMONG US' (1982; one of their only releases issued in the UK). Taking DANZIG's horror/sci-fi obsession to its comic-book conclusion, tracks like 'ASTRO ZOMBIES' and 'I TURNED INTO A MARTIAN' would've done ROKY ERICKSON proud. The painful 'LIVE/EVIL' (1983) featured a guest spot from HENRY ROLLINS on 'We Are 138', while the final album, 'EARTH A.D. / WOLFSBLOOD' (1984) saw the group opting for a decidedly more brutal sonic assault. Although their career spanned only six short years during which time they struggled to achieve even the most passing interest, The MISFITS have since come to be regarded as eminent cult heroes, GUNS N' ROSES, METALLICA and more recently MARILYN MANSON admitting their fondness for the band. A Various Artists tribute compilation, 'VIOLENT WORLD', was released early in 1997 featuring PRONG, NOFX, THERAPY?, while the original band, well at least JERRY and DOYLE, along with new members DR. CHUD and MICHAEL GRAVES, reformed for an album on 'Geffen', 'AMERICAN PSYCHO' (1997) thankfully without the more heavy frontman DANZIG.

Album rating: WALK AMONG US (*8) / AMERICAN PSYCHO (*6) / STATIC AGE (*6)

GLENN DANZIG (b.23 Jun'55, Lodi, New Jersey) – vocals / **BOBBY STEELE** – guitar / **JERRY ONLY** – bass / **JOEY IMAGE** – drums

not iss. Plan 9

1977. (7") *<PL 1001>* **COUGH COOL. / SHE BLANK** -

1977. (7") *<PL 1009>* **BULLET EP** -
– Horror business / Teenagers from Mars / Children in heat.

1979. (7"ep) *<PL 1011>* **NIGHT OF THE LIVING DEAD EP** -
– Night of the living dead / Where eagles dare / Rat fink.

— **DOYLE ONLY** – guitar; repl. STEELE who joined The UNDEAD

— **(ARTHUR) GOOGY** (aka EERIE VON) repl. JOEY

Apr 81. (7"ep) *<PL 1013>* **THREE HITS FROM HELL EP** -
– London dungeon / Horror hotel / Ghoul's night out.

— (below release licensed to 'Cherry Red' in the UK)

Jul 81. (m-lp) *(PLP 9)* **BEWARE EP** -

Oct 81. (7") *<PL 1017>* **HALLOWEEN. / HALLOWEEN II** -

not iss. Ruby-WEA

1982. (lp) *<925756-1>* **WALK AMONG US**
– 20 eyes / I turned into a Martian / All Hell breaks loose / Vampira / Nike a go-go / Hate breeders / Mommy, can I go out & kill tonight / Night of the living dead / Skulls / Violent world / Devils whorehouse / Astro zombies / Brain eaters. *(re-iss. +cd Sep88 on 'Ruby-WEA')*

not iss. Aggressive Rock

1983. (lp) *<AG 023>* **EVIL – LIVE (live)** -
– 20 eyes / Night of the living dead / Astro zombies / Horror business / London dungeon / All Hell breaks loose / We are 138. *(re-iss. Sep87 on 'Plan 9'; PL 908) (UK-iss.Mar97 on 'Plan 9' lp/cd; PL9/+CD 08)*

— **ROBO** – drums; repl. GOOGY

Feb 84. (lp) *<AG 024>* **EARTH A.D. / WOLF'S BLOOD** -
– Earth a.d. / Queen wasp / Devilrock / Death comes ripping / Green Hell / Wolf's blood / Demonomania / Bloodfeast / Hellhound / Die die my darling / We bite. *(cd-iss. Jul91; AGO 572) (cd re-iss. Jan97 on 'Plan 9' lp/cd+=; PL9 02)* – DIE DIE MY DARLING ep

— had already split the previous year. DANZIG released a solo single and formed SAMHAIN with EERIE VON. JERRY and DOYLE formed KRYST THE CONQUEROR, releasing five track EP augmented by future SKID ROW frontman DAVID SABO.

— The MISFITS reformed in 1996 with **JERRY ONLY** – bass / **DOYLE** – guitar / **MICHAEL GRAVES** – vocals / DR. CHUD – drums

Geffen Geffen

May 97. (cd) *<(GED 24939)>* **AMERICAN PSYCHO**
– Abominable Dr. Phibes / American psycho / Speak of the Devil / Walk among us / The hunger / From Hell they came / Dig up your bones / Blacklight / Resurrection / This island Earth / Crimson ghost / The day of the dead / The haunting / Mars attacks / Hate the living, love the dead / The shining / Don't open til doomsday.

– compilations, etc. –

1986. (lp/cd) *Plan 9; <PL9/+CD 06>* **LEGACY OF BRUTALITY** -
– Angelfuck / Who killed Marilyn? / Where eagles dare / She / Halloween / American nightmare / Static age / T.V. casualty / Hybrid moments / Spinal remains / Come back / Some kinda hate / Theme for a jackal. *(UK-iss.Jul97; same)*

Jul 86. (lp) *Revolver; (REVLP 74)* **BEST OF THE MISFITS** -

Nov 87. (12"ep) *Plan 9; <PL9-03>* **DIE DIE MY DARLING** -

May 88. (cd) *Plan 9; <PL9CD 1>* **THE MISFITS COLLECTION** -
(UK-iss.Jul97 cd/lp; same)

Oct 95. (cd/lp) *Caroline; (CAROL 7515-2/-1)* **THE MISFITS COLLECTION VOL.2**

Feb 97. (4xcd-box) *Caroline; (CDCAR 7529-2)* **THE MISFITS BOX SET**

Jul 97. (cd/lp) *Caroline; (CAROL 7520-2/-1)* **STATIC AGE** [ ] [ ]
– (debut album GLENN DANZIG, JERRY ONLY, FRANCHE COME, MR. JIM) – 14 tracks +; 'She', 'Spinal Remains' and 'In The Doorway')

MISSION

Formed: Leeds, England ... late 1985 by ex-SISTERS OF MERCY members WAYNE HUSSEY and CRAIG ADAMS. After falling out with the aforementioned band's singer ANDREW ELDRITCH, the pair recruited SIMON HINKLER (ex-ARTERY) and MICK BROWN (ex-RED LORRY YELLOW LORRY), forming a new band originally under The SISTERHOOD moniker. Calculated to annoy their former colleague, ELDRITCH retaliated by releasing a single under a similar name, HUSSEY and Co. subsequently switching to The MISSION. In Spring '86, the band signed to indie label, 'Chapter 22', releasing the enjoyably amateurish goth theatrics of the 'SERPENT'S KISS' single a couple of months later. Another single, 'GARDEN OF DELIGHT', appeared that summer before the band were snapped up by 'Mercury'. The debut album, 'GOD'S OWN MEDICINE', appeared towards the end of the year, almost making the UK Top 10. Given a bit of a rough ride by critics for its often overbearing goth pompousness, the record was nevertheless a fairly accomplished set of adult rock, a bit like what U2 might have sounded like had they been born in Leeds and developed a penchant for wearing pointy shoes and smearing their faces with flour. The grandiose 'WASTELAND' made No.11 when it was released as a single early the following year, staking The MISSION's claim as the new Goth messiahs and no doubt making ELDRITCH sick to his stomach. But much as they liked to be serious fellows on record, they liked to party hard behind the scenes, CRAIG ADAMS coming a cropper on a particularly gruelling US tour and briefly leaving the band. His temporary replacement was PETE TURNER who filled in for the remainder of the tour and also played at The MISSION's triumphant Reading Festival headlining appearance later that summer. With ADAMS back in the fold, the band began work on a new album with LED ZEPPELIN bassist JOHN PAUL JONES on production chores. The less than impressive result was 'CHILDREN' (1988), a No.2 hit despite its critical lashing. Preceeded by the delicate 'BUTTERFLY ON A WHEEL', the 'CARVED IN SAND' album was eventually released to expectant fans in early 1990. More elegantly refined than their normal heavy handed approach, the set remains their most listenable effort, if not their most successful. The band resumed heavy touring following the album's release, HINKLER subsequently storming out on the American jaunt. His replacement for the remainder of the tour was another ex-RED LORRY YELLOW LORRY man, DAVID WOLFENDEN, the band eventually recruiting guitarist ETCH (PAUL ETCHELLS, ex-GHOST DANCE) as a semi-permanent fixture later that year. Following the ambitious 'MASQUE' (1992) set (which featured the violin playing of FAIRPORT CONVENTION's RIC SAUNDERS), MARK THWAITE (ex-SPEAR OF DESTINY) and RIK CARTER (ex-PENDRAGON) were brought in after the departure of ADAMS. Two further albums appeared on the band's own label, 'Equator', following the end of their tenure with 'Mercury', none making any substantial commercial headway. • **Songwriters:** HUSSEY penned, except LIKE A HURRICANE (Neil Young) / DANCING BAREFOOT (Patti Smith) / SHELTER FROM THE STORM (Bob Dylan) / OVER THE HILLS AND FAR AWAY (Led Zeppelin) / LOVE (John Lennon) / ATOMIC (Blondie). • **Trivia:** In 1991, HUSSEY was ushered off James Whale's late night TV show for being drunk and abusive to its ever-polite presenter!!

Album rating: SUM AND SUBSTANCE compilation (*8)

WAYNE HUSSEY (b.26 May'59, Bristol, England) – vocals, guitar (ex-SISTERS OF MERCY, ex-DEAD OR ALIVE, ex-HAMBI & THE DANCE, ex-WALKIE TALKIES) / **CRAIG ADAMS** – bass (ex-SISTERS OF MERCY, ex-EXPELAIRES) / **SIMON HINKLER** – guitar (ex-ARTERY) / **MICK BROWN** – drums (ex-RED LORRY YELLOW LORRY)

Chapter 22 / not iss.

May 86. (7") *(CHAP 6-7)* **SERPENT'S KISS. / WAKE (R.S.V.)** [70] [-]
(12"+=) *(CHAP 6)* – Naked and savage.

Jul 86. (7") *(CHAP 7)* **GARDEN OF DELIGHT. / LIKE A HURICANE** [50] [-]
(12"+=) *(12CHAP 7)* – Over the hills and far away / The crystal ocean.
(12"+=) *(L12CHAP 7)* – Dancing barefoot / The crystal ocean.

Mercury / Mercury

Oct 86. (7") *(MYSG 1)* **STAY WITH ME. / BLOOD BROTHER** [30] [ ]
(12"+=) *(MYSGX 1)* – Islands in a stream.

Nov 86. (lp/c)(cd) *(MERH/+C 102)(<830603-2>)* **GODS OWN MEDICINE** [14] [ ]
– Wasteland / Bridges burning / Garden of delight (hereafter) / Stay with me / Blood brother * / Let sleeping dogs lie / Sacrilege / Dance on glass / And the dance goes on / Severina / Love me to death / Island in a stream *. *(c+=/cd+= *)*

Jan 87. (7") *(MYTH 2)* **WASTELAND. / SHELTER FROM THE STORM** [11] [ ]
(12"+=) *(MYTHX 2-1)* – Dancing barefoot (live).
('A'-Anniversary mix.12"+=) *(MYTHX 2-2)* – 1969 (live) / Wake (live).
(d7") *(MYTHB 2)* – 1969 (live) / Serpent's kiss (live).

Mar 87. (7"/7"s) *(MYTH/+P 3)* **SEVERINA. / TOMORROW NEVER KNOWS** [25] [ ]
(12"+=) *(MYTHL 3)* – Wishing well.

— **PETE TURNER** – bass; took over on tour while ADAMS recovered from illness

— **CRAIG ADAMS** was soon back after a 4 month lay-off.

Jan 88. (7") *(MYTH 4)* **TOWER OF STRENGTH. / FABIENNE** [12] [ ]
(ext.12"+=) *(MYTHX 4)* – Dream on / Breathe (instrumental).
(ext.cd-s+=) *(MTHCD 4)* – Dream on / Breathe (vocal).

Mar 88. (lp/c)(cd) *(MISH/+C 2)(<834263-2>)* **CHILDREN** [2] [ ]
– Beyond the pale / A wing and a prayer / Fabienne * / Heaven on Earth / Tower of strength / Kingdom come / Breathe / Child's play / Shamera kye / Black mountain mist / Dream on * / Heat / Hymn (for America). *(c+=/cd+= *)*

Jul 88. (7") *(MYTH 6)* **BEYOND THE PALE. / TADEUSZ (1912-1988)** [32] [ ]
('A'-Armageddon mix.12"+=) *(MYTHX 6)* – Love me to death / For ever more.
('A'-Armageddon mix.cd-s+=) *(MTHCD 6-2)* – Tower of strength (Bombay edit).

Nov 88. (7") *(MYTH 7)* **KINGDOM COME. / CHILD'S PLAY (live)** [ ] [ ]
(12"+=) *(MYTHX 7)* – The crystal ocean.
(cd-s++=) *(MTHCD 7)* – Garden of delight (live).

— (all formats on above single withdrawn)

Jan 90. (7"/c-s) *(MYTH/MTHMC 8)* **BUTTERFLY ON A WHEEL. / THE GRIP OF DISEASE** [12] [ ]
(12"+=/cd-s+=/box-cd-s+=)(10"+=) *(MYTHX/MTHCD/MYCDB 8)(MYTH 8-10)* – ('A'-Magni-octopus) / Kingdom come (forever and again).

Feb 90. (cd/c/lp) *(<842251-2/-4/-1>)* **CARVED IN SAND** [7] [ ]
– Amelia / Into the blue / Butterfly on a wheel / Sea of love / Deliverance / Grapes of wrath / Belief / Paradise (will shine like the Moon) / Hungry as the hunter / Lovely.

Mar 90. (7"/c-s) *(MYTH/MTHMC 9)* **DELIVERANCE. / MR. PLEASANT** [27] [ ]
(12"+=/cd-s+=/pic-cd-s+=)(10"+=) *(MYTHX/MTHCD/MYCDB 9)(MYTH 9-10)* – Heaven sends us.

May 90. (7"/c-s) *(MYTH/MTHMC 10)* **INTO THE BLUE. / BIRD OF PARADISE** [32] [ ]
(12"+=/cd-s+=) *(MYTHX/MTHCD 10)* – Divided we fall.

— **DAVID WOLFENDEN** – guitar (ex-RED LORRY YELLOW LORRY) repl. HINKLER.

— (Oct'90) added **ETCH** – guitar (ex-GHOST DANCE)

Oct 90. (cd/c/lp) *(846937-2/-4/-1)* **GRAINS OF SAND** (out-takes) [28] [ ]
– Hands across the ocean / The grip of disease / Divided we fall / Mercenary / Mr.Pleasant / Kingdom come (forever and again) / Heaven sends you / Sweet smile of a mystery / Love / Bird of passage. *(c+=/cd+=)* – Tower of strength (Casbah mix) / Butterfly on a wheel (Troubadour mix).

Nov 90. (7"/c-s) *(MYTH/MTHMC 11)* **HANDS ACROSS THE OCEAN. / AMELIA / LOVE** [28] [-]
(12"+=) *(MYTHX 11)* – Amelia (live) / Tower of strength (mix) / Mercenary.
(cd-s+=) *(MTHCD 11)* – Amelia (live) / Stay with me / Mercenary.

Vertigo / Mercury

Apr 92. (7"/c-s) *(MYTH/MTHMC 12)* **NEVER AGAIN. / BEAUTIFUL CHAOS** [34] [-]
(12"+=/cd-s+=) *(MYTHX/MTHCD 12)* – ('A'-F1 mix) / ('A'-Zero G mix.

Jun 92. (cd/c/lp) *<(512121-2/-4/-1)>* **MASQUE** [23] [ ]
– Never again / Shades of green (part II) / Even you may shine / Trail of scarlet / Spider and the fly / She conjures me wings / Sticks and stones / Like a child again / Who will love me tomorrow? / You make me breathe / From one Jesus to another / Until there's another sunrise. *(re-is.cd/c Aug94; same)*

Jun 92. (7"/c-s) *(MYTH/MTHMC 13)* **LIKE A CHILD AGAIN (remix). / ALL TANGLED UP IN YOU** [30] [-]
(12"+=/cd-s+=) *(MYTHX/MTHCD 13)* – ('A'-Mark Saunders remix) / Hush a bye baby (child again) (Joe Gibbs remix).

Oct 92. (7"/c-s) *(MYTH/MTHMC 14)* **SHADES OF GREEN. / YOU MAKE ME BREATHE** [49] [-]
(cd-s) *(MTHCD 14)* – ('A'side) / Sticks and stones / Trail of scarlet / Spider and the fly.
(etched-12"+=) *(MYTHX 14)* – ('A'mix).

— (Nov'92) **MARK THWAITE** – guitar (ex-SPEAR OF DESTINY) repl. HINKLER + ADAMS. Note:- **RIC SAUNDERS** – violin (of FAIRPORT CONVENTION) on last lp

Jan 94. (7") *(MYTH 15)* **TOWER OF STRENGTH (Youth remix). / WASTELAND** [33] [-]
(12"+=) *(MYTHX 15)* – Serpent's kiss.
(cd-s) *(MYTCD 15)* – ('A'mixes) / ('A'-East India Cairo mix) / Deliverance.

Feb 94. (cd/c/d-lp) *<(518447-2/-4/-1)>* **SUM AND SUBSTANCE** (compilation) [49] [ ]
– Never again / Hands across the ocean / Shades of green / Like a child again / Into the blue / Deliverance / Tower of strength / Butterfly on a wheel / Kingdom come / Beyond the pale / Severina / Stay with me / Wasteland / Garden of delight / Like a hurricane / Serpent's kiss / Sour puss / Afterglow.

Mar 94. (7") *(MYTH 16)* **AFTERGLOW. / SOUR-PUSS** [53] [-]
(cd-s+=) *(MYTCD 16)* – Cold as ice / Valentine.

Equator / not iss.

Oct 94. (7"ep/cd-ep) *(HOOK S/CD 001)* **MISSION 1 EP** [ ] [-]
– Raising Cain / Sway / Neverland.

Jan 95. (7"ep/cd-ep) *(HOOK S/CD 002)* **MISSION 2 EP** [73] [-]
– Swoon / Where / Wasting away.
(cd-ep+=) *(HOOKCDR 002)* – ('A'-Resurrection mix).

Feb 95. (cd/c/lp) *(SMEE CD/MC/LP 001)* **NEVERLAND** [58] [-]
– Raising Cain / Sway / Lose myself / Swoon / Afterglow (reprise) / Stars don't shine without you / Celebration / Cry like a baby / Heaven knows / Swim with the dolphins / Neverland / Daddy's going to Heaven now.

Jun 96. (cd/c/lp) *(SMEE CD/MC/LP 002)* **BLUE** [73] [-]

– compilations, others, etc. –

Jun 87. (lp/c) *Mercury; (MISH/+C 1) <832527-1/-4>* **THE FIRST CHAPTER** [35] [ ] May88
(cd-iss. May88; 832527-2)

Jul 94. (cd/lp) *Nighttracks; (CDNT/LPNT 005)* **SALAD DAZE** [ ] [-]

Aug 95. (d-cd) *Mercury; (528805-2)* **CHILDREN / CARVED IN SAND** [ ] [-]

MISSION OF BURMA

Formed: Boston, Massachusetts, USA ... 1979 from the ashes of The MOVING PARTS by the classically trained ROGER MILLER and CLINT CONLEY. They subsequently completed the line-up with a further two members, backing tape man MARTIN SWOPE and PETE PRESCOTT, the pair supplying the rhythm behind their classic 1980 debut 45, 'ACADEMY FLIGHT SONG' (later covered by R.E.M.). At this stage of the career, MISSION OF BURMA were known for their uncomfortable wall-of-noise punk sound, likened to WIRE, HUSKER DU or MC5. A mini-set, 'SIGNALS,

CALLS AND MARCHES' (1981), featured the seminal 'THAT'S WHEN I REACH FOR MY REVOLVER', a favourite among the US hardcore fraternity and later, much later, revived by ambient punkmeister, MOBY. Unfortunately, after an astounding debut album proper, 'VS.' (1982), the short-lived outfit had no choice but to retire due to MILLER's worsening tinnitus (a hearing disorder). Nevertheless, the frontman coped with his ailment as best he could throughout a prolific solo career (at times as NO MAN IS ROGER MILLER) which he pursued simultaneously with another band project, BIRDSONGS OF THE MESOZOIC. • **Covered:** HEART OF DARKNESS (Pere Ubu) / 1970 (Stooges).

Album rating: MISSION OF BURMA compilation cd (*9)

ROGER MILLER (b.24 Feb'52, Ann Arbor, Michigan) – guitar, vox / **CLINT CONLEY** (b.16 May,55, Indianapolis, Indiana) – bass, vox / **PETE PRESCOTT** (b.26 Oct'57, Nantucket Island, Mass.) – drums (ex-MOLLS) / **MARTIN SWOPE** (b. 1 Jun'55, Ann Arbor) – tapes

not iss. / Ace Of Hearts

Jun 80. (7") *<AHS 104>* **ACADEMY FLIGHT SONG. / MAX ERNST** [-] [ ]

1981. (m-lp) *<AHS 10006>* **SIGNALS, CALLS, AND MARCHES** [-] [ ]
– That's when I reach for my revolver / Outlaw / Fame and fortune / This is not a photograph / Red / All world cowboy romance.

1982. (lp) *<AHS 210>* **VS.** [-] [ ]
– Secrets / Train / Trem two / New nails / Dead pool / Learn how / Mica / Weatherbox / The ballad of Johnny Burma / Einstein's day / Fun world / That's how I escaped my certain fate / Ok – No way / Laugh the world away / Progress. *<cd-iss. 1997 on 'Rykodisc'; 10340>*

—— split to MILLER's tinnitus, although he did release quieter solo stuff and form BIRDSONGS OF THE MESOZOIC, with SWOPE. PRESCOTT had formed and continued to tour with VOLCANO SUNS (an SST label band who in 1989 released d-lp,cd 'THING OF BEAUTY'; *SST 257*). CONLEY later produced for YO LA TENGO.

– compilations, etc. –

Nov 85. (lp) *New Rose; (ROSE 76)* **THE HORRIBLE TRUTH ABOUT BURMA (live)** [ ] [-]
– That's when I reach for my revolver / Tremelo / Dumbells / Peking Spring / 1970 / Learn how / New disco / Dirt / Red / Heart of darkness / Them two / Blackboard / He is, she is / Go fun burn man. *<cd-iss. 1997 on 'Rykodisc'; 10341>*

1987. (m-lp) *Taang!; (TAANG 20)* **MISSION OF BURMA EP** [-] [ ]
(UK cd-iss. Jun92; TAANG 20CD)

1988. (cd) *Rykodisc; <RCD 40072>* **MISSION OF BURMA** [-] [ ]
– Academy fight song / That's when I reach for my revolver / Outlaw / Fame and fortune / This is not a photograph / Red / All world cowboy romance / Forget / Laugh the world away / Ok no way / Secrets / Train / Trem two / New nails / Dead pool / Learn how / Mica / Weatherbox / The ballad of Johnny Burma / Einstein's day / Fun world / That's how I escaped my certain fate / Go fun burn man / 1970. *(re-iss. Jun92 & Mar94 cd/c; RCD4/RACS 0072)*

Mar 89. (lp) *Taang!; <(TAANG 24)>* **FORGET** [ ] [ ] 1987
– Execution / Progress / Playland / House flaming / Eyes of men / Manic incarnation / Anti aircraft warning / Active in the yard / Hunt again / Smoldering fuselage / Head over head / Forget. *(re-iss. Jan93 lp/cd; TAANG 024/+CD)*

Sep 90. (cd) *Emergo; (EM 94081) / Relix; <983608>* **LET THERE BE BURMA** [ ] [ ]
– Execution / Progress / Playland / House flaming / Eyes of men / Manic incarnation / Anti-aircraft warning / Active in the yard / Hunt again / Smoldering fuselage / Head over head / Forget / This is not a photograph / Peking spring / Dumbells / Dirt / Sing-a-long / He is – she is / Black board / Go fun burn man / Nu disco / Foreign country / Einstein's day.

BIRDSONGS OF THE MESOZOIC

ROGER MILLER – keyboards, percussion, vocals / **MARTIN SWOPE** – tapes, guitar, cymbals / **RICK SCOTT** – organ / **ERIK LINDGREN** – synthesizers (of SPACE NEGROS, ex-FAMILY FUN) / guest **PETE PRESCOTT** – percussion

not iss. / Ace Of Hearts

1983. (m-lp) *<AHS 1008>* **BIRDSONGS OF THE MESOZOIC EP** [-] [ ]
– Sound valentine / Transformation of Oz / Drift / The orange ocean / Triassic Jurassic, Cretaceous.

not iss. / Rykodisc

1986. (cd) *<RCD 20073>* **SONIC GEOLOGY** [-] [ ]
– Shiny golden snakes / Ptoccata / Waterwheel / Pulse piece / The rite of spring / The orange ocean / The tyger / Scenes from a . . . / The beat of the Mesozoic (part 1) / International tours / Drift / Final motif / Theme from Rocky and Bullwinkle / The fundamental / Sound valentine / The common sparrow / Lost in the B-zone / Triassic, Jurassic, Cretaceous. *(UK-iss.Apr92; same)*

not iss. / C.U.N.

1989. (cd) *<RUNE 19>* **FAULTLINE** [-] [ ]
– The true wheelbase / They walk among us / Coco Boudakian / I don't need no crystal ball / Chariots of fire / Magic fingers / Faultline / On the street where you live / Maybe I will / There is no one / Slo-boy / Pterobold / Just say yes.

ROGER MILLER

Fundamental / Fundamental

1988. (lp) *<SAVE 054>* **THE BIG INDUSTRY** [ ] [ ]
– Portrait of a mechanical dog / Boil away / Hammers / Upon this boat in the sea / The age of reason / Groping hands / Manic depression / The big industry / We don't know why.

NO MAN

—— aka **MILLER + ANDREW DECKARD** – percussion, drums

S.S.T. / S.S.T.

Jul 89. (lp/c/cd) *<(SST/+C/CD 243)>* **WIN! INSTANTLY!** [ ] [ ]
– Run water, run water / No man's landing / Calling the animals / Scratch / This is not a photograph / The promised land / The quarry / Renegades / Volumptuous airplane.

1990. (7") *<(SST 912)>* **DIAMONDBACK. /** [-] [ ]

Sep 90. (lp/c/cd) *<(SST/+C/CD 267)>* **WHAMON EXPRESS** [ ] [ ]
– Oppression / Zelia / The man who sold the world / Red ants 1v / S.O.B. / Not enough / Diamondback / (I live on) Heaven Street / Save me / Goodbye paper / Floated – Overflow / Broke a string.

—— added **RUSS SMITH** – guitar / **KEN WINOKUR** – percussion

Dec 91. (lp/c/cd; as NO MAN IS ROGER MILLER) *<(SST/+C/CD 281)>* **HOW THE WEST WAS WON** [ ] [ ]
– Cartoon, cartoon (where's the exit?) / Boomerang / How the west was won / Reach for the sun / Here we go / Set-up / Wounded world / Grabbed star / It's just a day / No warning / Call on me / (Astronomy engine).

—— An entirely different NO MAN; the UK one featuring STEVEN WILSON of PORCUPINE TREE released stuff from 1989 onwards (mostly for 'One Little Indian' label).

ROGER MILLER

New Alliance / New Alliance

Apr 91. (lp/c/cd) *<(NAR/+C/CD 051)>* **XYLYL & A WOMAN IN HALF** [ ] [ ]
– Lampbase / Wheelstop / Childrum / Palmsandr / House rock compost / V-2 / Pecan box lope.

Apr 94. (cd) *<(NAR 097CD)>* **OH, GUITARS ETC** [ ] [ ]
– We grind open (in) / Meltdown man / Chinatown samba / Firetruck / Cosmic battle / You son of a bitch / War bolts / Fun world reductions / Space is the place / Forest / Kalgastak.

S.S.T. / S.S.T.

Oct 94. (cd/c; as ROGER MILLER'S EXQUISITE CORPSE) *<(SST 307 CD/C)>* **UNFOLD** [ ] [ ]
– Entry / Dance in the poet's eye / Djinn / Mentabolism / Looney tunes / Mooche / Nothing what / Game #2 / Gargoyle / Owl / Machete hacker's boogie-woogie / Game #3 / Cheese and the worms / Prelude to the demolition of the teal / Dream interpretation No.1 / Exit (Bach).

Sep 95. (cd/c) *<(SST 318 CD/CA)>* **ELEMENTAL GUITAR** [ ] [ ] Aug95
– Misunderstanding the time / Lost eyes / Repair / Dream interpretation No.7 / Warp zombie / Broken head / Off-On / Dream interpretation No.8 / Talamin Yarka / Are you experienced?

Jul 96. (cd) *<SST 331>* **BENEVOLENT DISRUPTIVE RAY** [-] [ ]

Aug 97. (cd) *<SST 349>* **THE BINARY SYSTEM LIVE AT THE IDEA ROOM** [-] [ ]
– The fish, he laughs at his own commands / Peerd rail se / Plate glass w/ Tornado / Moon dance (Ra) / Machete Hacker's boogie-woogie / Abruption / What's up, Ched Voogis? / Djinn / Binary mechanics (Oct.4, 10:37 pm) / Turbo wheel (Oct.4, 10:58pm) / Tibet (Oct.5, 10:31pm) / Last oak king (Oct.4, 11:06pm).

MOB (see under ⇒ BLYTH POWER)

MOBY

Born: RICHARD MELVILLE HALL, 11 Sep'65, New York City, New York, USA. After being raised by his middle-class mother in Darien, Connecticut, he joined hardcore outfit The VATICAN COMMANDOES, which led to him having a brief stint in the similar, FLIPPER. He didn't record anything with the band and moved back to New York to become a DJ, making hardcore techno/dance records under the guise of BRAINSTORM and UHF3, etc. He subsequently became a mixer for The PET SHOP BOYS, ERASURE and MICHAEL JACKSON, before and during his return into solo work in the early 90's. His UK debut, 'GO', hit the Top 10 in October '91, having just breached the charts 3 months earlier. Sampling the 'Twin Peaks' theme, the song was a compelling piece of techno-pop that remains a dancefloor favourite. Little was subsequently heard of him barring a few US imports, although this led to UK semi-indie, 'Mute', taking him on board in mid'93. First up was his near Top 20 single, 'I FEEL IT', beginning a series of hits, albeit sporadic. Early in 1995, his album 'EVERYTHING IS WRONG' had critics lavishing praise on the man for his combination of acid-dance and ambience. In 1996, his 'ANIMAL RIGHTS' follow-up added a new dimension; heavy industrial punk-metal which gave him a new found 'Kerrang' audience. • **Songwriters:** Himself, and a few with singer, MIMI GOESE:- 'Into The Blue' + 'When It's Cold I'd Like To Die'. Other singers on 1995 album; ROZZ MOREHEAD / MYIM ROSE / NICOLE ZARAY / KOOKIE BANTON / SAUNDRA WILLIAMS. Samples BADALAMENTI's 'Twin Peaks' on 'GO'. Covered NEW DAWN FADES (Joy Division) / THAT'S WHEN I REACH FOR MY REVOLVER (Mission Of Burma). • **Trivia:** RICHARD is a Christian vegan. In 1992, he remixed JAM & SPOON's club smash 'Stella', which had sampled his 'GO'. He also provided vox for RECOIL's 1992 album , 'Bloodline'. MOBY remixed The B-52's, ESKIMOS AND EGYPT, LFO, FORTRAN 5, ORBITAL, ENO, PET SHOP BOYS + The OTHER TWO.

Album rating: THE STORY SO FAR (*6) / EVERYTHING IS WRONG (*9) / ANIMAL RIGHTS (*8)

MOBY – vocals, keyboards, etc.

Outer Rhythm / Instinct

Jul 91. (12") *(FOOT 15) <237>* **GO (analog mix). / ('A'-Night time mix) / ('A'-Soundtrack mix)** [46] [ ] Jan92
(12") *(FOOT 15R)* – ('A'side) / ('A'-video aux w/ LYNCH & BADALAMENTI) / ('A'-Rain forest mix).
(cd-s) *(FOOT 15CD)* – ('A'side) / ('A'-Low spirit mix) / ('A'-Woodtick mix). *(re-iss. Oct91, hit No.10; same)*

1992. (12"/cd-s) *<240>* **DROP A BEAT (mixes)** [-] [ ]

1992. (m-cd/m-c) *<241>* **MOBY** [-] [ ]
– Drop a beat / Everything / Yeah / Electricity / Next is the E / Mercy. *<cd re-iss.*

1995 on 'Elektra'+=; 61838> – Go / Help me to believe / Have you seen my baby / Ah ah / Slight return / Stream.

1992. (12"/cd-s) *<247>* **NEXT IS THE E (mixes)** [–] [ ]

Jan 93. (cd) *<253>* **AMBIENT** [–] [ ]
– My beautiful blue sky / Heaven / Tongues / J Breas / Myopia / House of blue leaves / Bad days / Piano & string / Sound / Dog / 80 / Lean on me. *(UK-iss.Oct93 on 'Equator Arctic' cd/c/lp; ATLAS CD/MC/LP 002)*

Equator / Instinct

Jun 93. (c-s) *(AXISMC 001)* **I FEEL IT. / THOUSAND** [38] [ ]
(12"/cd-s) *(AXIS T/CD 001)* – (3-'A'mixes).
(12") *(AXISM 001)* – ('A'remixes).

Aug 93. (cd/c/lp) *(ATLAS CD/MC/LP 001)* **THE STORY SO FAR** [ ] [–]
– Ah ah / I feel it / Everything / Help me to believe / Go (woodtick mix) / Yeah / Drop a beat (the new version) / Thousand / Slight return / Go (sublimal mix unedited version) / Stream. *(cd+=)* – Mercy.

Mute / Elektra

Sep 93. (c-s) *(CMUTE 158) <61568>* **MOVE (YOU MAKE ME FEEL SO GOOD). / ('A'-disco threat mix)** [21] [ ]
(12"/cd-s) *(12/CD MUTE 158)* – ('A'side) / ('A'-Subversion) / ('A'-xtra mix) / ('A'-MK-Blades mix).
(cd-s) *(LCDMUTE 158)* – ('A'side) / All that I need is to be loved / Unloved symphony / Rainfalls and the sky shudders.
(12") *(L12MUTE 158)* – (last track repl. by)- Morning dove.

May 94. (c-s) *(CMUTE 161)* **HYMN – THIS IS MY DREAM (extended) / ALL THAT I NEED IS TO BE LOVED (H.O.S. mix)** [31] [ ]
(cd-s+=) *(CDMUTE 161)* – ('A'-European edit) / ('A'-Laurent Garnier mix).
(12") *(12MUTE 161)* – ('A'extended) / ('A'-Laurent Garnier mix) / ('A'-Upriver mix)/ ('A'-Dirty hypo mix).
(cd-s) *(LCDMUTE 161)* – Hymn (alternate quiet version 33 mins).

Oct 94. (c-s) *(CMUTE 173) <66180>* **FEELING SO REAL. / NEW DAWN FADES** [30] [ ]
(cd-s+=) *(CDMUTE 173)* – ('A'-Unashamed ecstatic piano mix) / ('A'-Old skool mix).
(cd-s) *(LCDMUTE 173)* – ('A'-Westbam remix) / ('A'-Ray Keith remix) / ('A'dub mix) / Everytime you touch me (remix parts).
(12") *(12MUTE 173)* – ('A'side) / (4-versions from cd's above).

Feb 95. (c-s/7"dinked) *(C+/MUTE 176/+D) <66154>* **EVERYTIME YOU TOUCH ME / THE BLUE LIGHT OF THE UNDERWATER SUN** [28] [ ]
(cd-s+=) *(CDMUTE 176)* – ('A'-Beatmasters mix) / ('A'-competition winner; Jude Sebastian mix) / ('A'Freestyle mix).
(cd-s++=) *(LCDMUTE 176)* – ('A'-Uplifting mix).
(12") *(12MUTE 176)* – ('A'-Sound Factory mix) / ('A'-SF dub) / ('A'-Follow me mix) / ('A'-Tribal mix).

Mar 95. (cd/c/d-lp) *(CD/C+/Stumm 130) <61701>* **EVERYTHING IS WRONG** [21] [ ]
– Hymn / Feeling so real / All that I need is to be loved / Let's go free / Everytime you touch me / Bring back my happiness / What love? / First cool hive / Into the blue / Anthem / Everything is wrong / God moving over the face of the waters / When it's cold I'd like to die. *(cd/c w/free cd/c) (XLCD/XLC+/Stumm 130)* – Underwater (parts 1-5).

Jun 95. (c-s) *(CMUTE 179)* **INTO THE BLUE / ('A'-Shining mix)** [34] [ ]
(cd-s+=) *(LCDMUTE 179)* – ('A'-Summer night mix) / ('A'-Beastmasters mix).
(12"/cd-s) *(12/CD MUTE 179)* – ('A'-Beastmasters mix) / ('A'-Jnr Vasquez mix) / ('A'-Phil Kelsey mix) / ('A'-Jon Spencer Blues mix).

Jan 96. (cd/c) *(XLStumm 130)* **EVERYTHING IS WRONG – MIXED AND REMIXED** [25] [ ]

— The track 'GOD MOVING OVER THE FACE OF THE WATERS' was used for the Rover 400 TV commercial. Toyota had earlier sampled his 'GO'.

Aug 96. (12") *(12MUTE 184)* **THAT'S WHEN I REACH FOR MY REVOLVER. / ('A'-Rollo & Si Star Bliss mix)** [50] [ ]
(cd-s) *(CDMUTE 184)* – ('A'side) / Lovesick / Displaced / Sway.
(cd-s) *(LCDMUTE 184)* – ('A'side) / Every one of my problems / God moving over the face of the waters (dark mix).

Oct 96. (cd/c/d-lp) *(CD/C+/Stumm 150) <62031>* **ANIMAL RIGHTS** [38] [ ]
– Now I let it go / Come on baby / Someone to love / Heavy flow / You / My love will never die / Soft / Say it's all mine / That's when I reach for my revolver / Face it / Living / Love song for my mom. *(cd w/ free cd)* **LITTLE IDIOT** *(LCDStumm 150)* – Degenerate / Dead city / Walnut / Old / A season in Hell / Love song for my mom / The blue terror of lawns / Dead sun / Reject.

Nov 96. (12"ep) *(12MUTE 200)* **COME ON BABY / LOVE HOLE / WHIP IT / GO / ALL THAT I NEED TO BE IS LOVED / HYMN** [ ] [ ]
(cd-ep) *(CDMUTE 200)* – ('A'-Eskimos And Egypt mix) / ('A'-Crystal method mix) / ('A'-Eskimos And Egypt extended).

Jul 97. (7") *<SP 377>* **THAT'S WHEN I REACH FOR MY REVOLVER. /** [–] [ ]
<above issued on 'Sub Pop'>

Nov 97. (c-s/12"/cd-s) *(C/12/CD MUTE 210) <040>* **JAMES BOND THEME: TOMORROW NEVER DIES** [8] [ ]
– (mixes:- extended dance / Grooverider's Jeep remix / Da Bomb remix / CJ Bolland remix / Dub Pistols remix / CJ Bolland – Dubble-oh Heaven remix).
(12") *(XL12MUTE 210)* – ('A'mixes; re-version / Grooverider / Danny Tenaglia dub).

Nov 97. (cd/c/lp) *(CD/C+/Stumm 168) <62094>* **I LIKE TO SCORE** [ ] [ ]
– Novio / James Bond theme / Go / Ah ah / I like to score / Oil / New dawn fades / God moving over the face of the waters / First cool hive / Nash / Love theme / Grace.

Aug 98. (cd-s) *(CDMUTE 218) <2186>* **HONEY / HONEY (Mario Caldato Jnr. mix) / MICRONESIA / MEMORY GOSPEL** [33] [ ]
(cd-s) *(LCDMUTE 218)* – ('A'-Rollo & Sister Bliss blunt edit) / ('A'-Moby's 118 mix) / ('A'-Westbam & Hardy mix) / ('A'-Aphrodite & Micky Finn mix).
(12") *(12MUTE 218)* – ('A'-Rollo & Sister Bliss mix) / ('A'-Sharam Jey's sweet honey mix) / ('A'-Moby's low side mix).

– compilations, specials, etc

Nov 93. (12") *Mute; (12NEMY 2)* **ALL THAT I NEED IS TO BE LOVED. / (3 other 'A'mixes)** [ ] [–]

Sep 94. (c-s) *Mute; (CNOCAR 1)* **GO (woodtick mix). / ('A'-Low spirit mix)** [ ] [–]
(12"+=) *(12NOCAR 1)* – ('A'-Voodoo chile mix).
(12"+=) *(12LNOCAR 1)* – ('A'-Appathoski mix) / ('A'-Amphemetix mix).
(cd-s+=) *(CDNOCAR 1)* – ('A'-Delirium mix).

Mar 95. (10"ltd.) *Soapbar; (SBR 15)* **FEELING SO REAL (mixes)** [ ] [–]

MOCK TURTLES

Formed: Manchester, England ... 1985 by former JUDGE HAPPINESS frontman, MARTIN COOGAN. The aforementioned outfit won a local Battle Of The Bands competition before releasing what proved to be a one-off single, 'HEY JUDGE'. COOGAN subsequently recruited STEVE GREEN, STEVE COWEN and KRZYSZTOF KORAB and adopted the name MOCK TURTLES, signing to Alan Duffy's indie label 'Imaginary' in the process. Summer '87's 'POMONA' (after the release of which they added MARTIN GLYN MURRAY) was the first of several 12"ep's for the label, many of them dented the higher regions of the indie charts. By the turn of the decade, ANDREW STEPHENSON and JOANNE GENT had replaced GREEN and KORAB, their psychedelic retro leanings now becoming more attuned to the prevailing indie dance movement. The long-awaited debut album, 'TURTLE SOUP' (1990), consolidated their jangly 60's influences – The BYRDS and the original TURTLES – and their love of BE-BOP DELUXE/BILL NELSON (the latter featuring on a 1989 B-side, 'TAKE YOUR TIME') with a newfound baggy groove. Although this wasn't an immediate recipe for success, the subsequent re-release of 'CAN YOU DIG IT?' by new label 'Siren', led to a UK Top 20 hit single and a minor resurgence in sales of the album; the essential compilation of their early work, '87-90', also benefitted from the fresh interest. Their most famous four minutes and latterly an albatross round their their necks, 'CAN YOU DIG IT?' was also – alongside other 1991 singles – the main attraction on their second album proper, the Top 40 entry, 'TWO SIDES'. However, the glare of the limelight proved too bright for The MOCK TURTLES and they ended up crawling back into their proverbial shells. While MURRAY found work as an actor (bit part in TV soap, Families'), COOGAN and his old muckers KORAB and GREEN formed mid 90's outfit, UGLI. • **Songwriters:** COOGAN wrote all, except covers; PALE BLUE EYES (Velvet Underground) / BIG-EYED BEANS FROM VENUS (Captain Beefheart) / BIG SKY (Kinks) / WHY (Byrds) / ARE YOU EXPERIENCED? (Jimi Hendrix) / NO GOOD TRYING (Syd Barrett) / THE WILLOW SONG (from film 'The Wicker Man').

Album rating: TURTLE SOUP (*7) / 87-90 compilation (*8) / TWO SIDES (*6)

MARTIN COOGAN – vocals, guitar / + unknown others

Mynah / not iss.

1985. (7"; as JUDGE HAPPINESS) *(SCS 8501)* **HEY JUDGE. / PIG IN PINK** [ ] [–]

— **MARTIN** was joined by **KRZYSZTOF KORAB** – keyboards / **STEVE GREEN** – bass / **STEVE COWAN** – drums

Imaginary / Relativity

Jun 87. (12"ep) *(MIRAGE 003)* **POMONA** [ ] [–]
– John O'War / Bathing in blue / Mary's garden / Watching the waning moon.

— added **MARTIN GLYN MURRAY** – guitar

May 89. (12"m) *(MIRAGE 003)* **WICKER MAN / THE WILLOW SONG. / ANOTHER JESUS WALKS ON WATER / FIONNUALA** [ ] [–]

— **ANDREW STEPHENSON** – bass, viola, violin repl. GREEN

Nov 89. (12"m) *(MIRAGE 015)* **AND THEN SHE SMILES. / CALM BEFORE THE STORM / SHANGRI-LA** [ ] [–]

— **JOANNE GENT** – keyboards repl. KORAB

Apr 90. (12"/cd-s) *(MIRAGE 017/+CD)* **LAY ME DOWN. / CAN U DIG IT?** [ ] [–]

May 90. (cd/c/lp) *(ILLCD/ILLCASS/ILLUSION 012) <1058>* **TURTLE SOUP** [ ] [ ]
– Kathy come home / Head run wild / Lay me down / Another Jesus walks on water / Oh Helen how? / How does it feel? / And then she smiles / The willow song / Mary's garden / Can you dig it? / Wicker man. *(re-dist.May91; hit No.54)*

Oct 90. (7") **MAGIC BOOMERANG. / TAKE YOUR TIME** [ ] [–]
(12"+=/cd-s+=) – ('A'version).

Mar 91. (cd/c/lp) *(ILLCD/ILLCASS/ILLUSION 019)* **87-90** (rare singles + demo for the label) [ ] [–]

Siren / unknown

Mar 91. (7"/c-s) *(SRN/ 136)* **CAN U DIG IT. / LOSE YOURSELF** [18] [ ]
(12"+=/cd-s+=) *(SRN/ 136)* – Lay me down (live) / ('A'-Yeah version).

Jun 91. (7"/c-s) *(SRN/ 139)* **AND THEN SHE SMILES. / ANOTHER JESUS WALKS ON WATER (live)** [44] [ ]
(12"+=/cd-s+=) *(SRN/ 139)* – How does it feel (live).

Jul 91. (cd/c/lp) *(CDSRN/SRNMC/SRNLP 31)* **TWO SIDES** [33] [ ]
– Strings and flowers / And then she smiles / Shine on me / Baby and the stars / Words of wisdom / Pearls for my girl / Brush of a butterfly's wing / Can u dig it? / You move me / Deep down / Why must I share this air with foolish men?

Sep 91. (7"/c-s) **STRINGS AND FLOWERS. / SHE TOLD ME** [ ] [ ]
(12"+=) – ('A'-Steve Proctor mix).
(cd-s++=) – Deep down (remix).

— MURRAY departed to become an actor (he played a bit part in the TV soap, 'Families'). COOGAN, KORAB and GREEN re-formed in the mid-90's as UGLI, although as yet, no records.

MODELS

Formed: London, England . . . 1977 by CLIFF HARRIS, MICK ALLEN, MARCO PIRRONI and TERRY LEE MIALL, the short-lived punk-rock group a launching pad for ADAM & THE ANTS members (the latter two actually) and subsequently The WOLFGANG PRESS, through the line of REMA REMA and MASS member, MICK ALLEN. Although they only ever released one single, 'FREEZE', for 'Step Forward' (home of CHELSEA and The CORTINAS), the track was raw and hard-hitting enough to ensure The MODELS a minor footnote in punk history. Worth tracking down for its 'PISTOLS-style attitude and radical political stance, the single still sounds as fresh today as it ever did, only serving to underline the lack of any discernible charisma or drive in the current crop of Kerrang's pseudo heavy/punk brigade.

Album rating: never released any

CLIFF HARRIS – vocals, guitar / **MARCO PIRRONI** (b.27 Apr'59) – guitar (ex-INFANTS, ex-SIOUXSIE & THE BANSHEES) / **MICK ALLEN** – bass / **TERRY LEE MIALL** (b. 8 Nov'58) – drums

Step Forward | not iss.

Aug 77. (7") *(SF 003)* **FREEZE. / MAN OF THE YEAR** [ ] [-]

— just prior to their split, **MARK ROBERTSON** – drums; repl. MIALL + HARRIS (both formed MUSIC CLUB); the former later joined ADAM & THE ANTS. MARCO + MICK formed REMA REMA, the latter evolving the group into the WOLFGANG PRESS. ROBERTSON later joined The TALL BOYS.

MODELS

Formed: Melbourne, Australia . . .late 70's by songwriter SEAN KELLY, MARK FERRIE, JANIS 'JOHNNY CRASH' FRIEDENFIELDS and ANDREW DUFFIELD (the latter having replaced short-lived member ASH WEDNESDAY). One of the leading lights of the Antipodean post-New Wave scene, The MODELS' first vinyl release was a split 7" effort with BOYS NEXT DOOR (who evolved into The BIRTHDAY PARTY) entitled 'EARLY MORNING BRAIN'. Like its follow-up, 'OWE YOU NOTHING', the record was mainly given away free at gigs as the band built up their fanbase. Having already signed to 'Mushroom' (in 1980), through whom they issued their long-winded debut LP, 'ALPHABETACHARLIEDELTAECHOFOXTROT', The MODELS secured a worldwide deal with 'A&M', ensuring a 1981 UK release for the latter. A second album, 'LOCAL AND/OR GENERAL' (1982) was the last to feature FERRIE, his replacement arriving in the shape of former solo artist, JAMES FREUD, who was soon sharing songwriting duties with KELLY. An Australian-only set, 'THE PLEASURE OF YOUR COMPANY' (1983) was next to appear, already hinting at the more commercial direction to come; that year, the band even supported BOWIE on his Down Under tour dates. A protracted period of instability ensued as founding members FRIEDENFIELDS and DUFFIELD departed, three new recruits ROGER MASON, BARTON PRICE and JAMES VALENTINE filling the gap as the band ploughed a more mainstream furrow. The mid-80's saw The MODELS signing to 'Geffen' (outside Australia), strutting their stuff in the US Top 40 with the 'OUT OF MIND OUT OF SIGHT' single, the title track of their accompanying Top 100 album. However, they couldn't sustain their high profile outside of their homeland and finally stepped off the musical catwalk following the release of 1987's 'MEDIA'. • **Note:** The MODELS of 1997 who issued 'Jaana Hai Bollywood' were in fact an Asian 3-piece girl trio.

Album rating: ALPHABRAVOCHARLIEDELTAECHOFOXTROT (*6) / LOCAL AND/OR GENERAL (*6) / PLEASURE OF YOUR COMPANY (*5) / OUT OF MIND OUT OF SIGHT (*5) / MEDIA (*5)

SEAN KELLY – vocals, guitar (ex-TEENAGE RADIO STAR) / **ANDREW DUFFIELD** – keyboards; repl. ASH WEDNESDAY / **MARK FERRIE** – bass, vocals / **JANIS 'Johnny Crash' FRIEDENFIELDS** – percussion

Crystal Ball – Missing Link | not iss.

Nov 79. (7"freebie) *(CBR 1)* **EARLY MORNING BRAIN (IS NOT THE SAME AS SOBRIETY). / (B-side by BOYS NEXT DOOR)** [-] [-] Austra

— signed to 'Mushroom' in Australia, where debut gets released 1980

Aug 80. (7"freebie) *(MA 7356)* **OWE YOU NOTHING. / PROGRESSIVE OFFICE POOLS** [-] [-] Austra

A&M | A&M

May 81. (lp) *(AMLH 68529)* **ALPHABRAVOCHARLIEDELTAECHOFOXTROTGOLF** [ ] [-]
– Strategic air command / Two people per sq. km. / Pull the pin / Twice removed / Pate pedestrian / Kissing round corners / All stop / Uncontrollable boy (I'm just an) / Young rodents / Hands stand (war record) / Happy birthday.

Aug 81. (m-lp) *(L 20001)* **CUT LUNCH** [-] [-] Austra

Jan 82. (7") *(AMS 8204)* **LOCAL AND/OR GENERAL. / BANTAM HAD** [ ] [ ]

Feb 82. (lp) *(AMLH 68536)* **LOCAL AND/OR GENERAL** [ ] [ ]

Mar 82. (7") *(AMS 8212)* **UNHAPPY. / RATE OF CHANGE** [ ] [ ]

— **JAMES FREUD** – bass, vocals (ex-Solo Artist / 1 album for 'Carrere' in 1982 'BREAKING THE SILENCE') repl. FERRIE

1983. (lp) **THE PLEASURE OF YOUR COMPANY** [-] [-] Austra

— (1983) **ROGER MASON** – keyboards; repl. DUFFIELD

— **BARTON PRICE** – drums (ex-DRAGON) repl. JANIS

— added **JAMES VALENTINE** – saxophone

— Still signed to 'Mushroom' in Australia.

Geffen | Geffen

Mar 86. (7") *(GEF 1)* <28762> **OUT OF MIND OUT OF SIGHT. / DOWN IN THE GARDEN** [ ] [37] Apr86
(12"+=) *(GEF 1T)* – Seeing is believing.

Mar 86. (lp/c) *(924100-2/-4)* <24100> **OUT OF MIND OUT OF SIGHT** [ ] [84] Apr86
– Out of mind out of sight / Big on love / Ringing like a bell / Stormy tonight / These blues / Cold fever / Sooner in Heaven / Seeing is believing / Barbados / King of kings.

1986. (7") **BARBADOS. /** [-] [ ]
(12"+=) –

Mushroom | not iss.

1986. (7") **KING OF KINGS. /** [-] [-] Austra

1987. (7") **EVOLUTION. /** [-] [-] Austra

1987. (lp) **MEDIA** [-] [-] Austra

1987. (7") **LET'S KISS. /** [-] [-] Austra

1987. (7") **HOLD ON. /** [-] [-] Austra

— Disbanded and FREUD worked on new solo work, while PRICE joined WA WA NEE, who released an eponymous album early 1988 for 'Columbia'. KELLY co-formed ABSENT FRIENDS with GARRY BEERS of INXS. They released one album 'HERE'S LOOKING UP YOUR ADDRESS' in 1990.

MODERN ENGLISH

Formed: Colchester, Essex, England . . . 1979 by ROBBIE GREY, GARY McDOWELL, MICHAEL CONROY and RICHARD BROWN. Signed to '4 a.d.' after a debut single on the tiny 'Limp' label, the band were initially inspired by the post-punk morbidity of JOY DIVISION, as heard on their early singles and debut album, 'MESH AND LACE' (1981). However, it was a strikingly different MODERN ENGLISH which emerged in Spring '82 with follow-up set, 'AFTER THE SNOW', a far more accessible, keyboard heavy effort bringing to mind SIMPLE MINDS, PETER GABRIEL, DAVID DOWIE and perhaps even a more credible DURAN DURAN! With po-faced English pop all the rage in America at the time, MODERN ENGLISH actually made No.70 in the billboard chart, achieving a similar feat with the uncharacteristically jangly 'I MELT WITH YOU'. Relocating to New York, the band worked on third set, 'RICOCHET DAYS' (1984), another fine album which again made the US Top 100 and featured some subtle french horn touches amid an overall more mature sound. 'Sire', who had been handling the band's Stateside releases, took over completely from '4 a.d.' with 1986's disappointing 'STOP START'. Following the subsequent split, GREY later reappeared briefly with '4 a.d.' "supergroup", THIS MORTAL COIL, before re-forming MODERN ENGLISH for a one-off album, 'PILLOW LIPS' (1990) on US label, 'T.V.T.'.

Album rating: MESH AND LACE (*5) / AFTER THE SNOW (*5) / RICOCHET DAYS (*4) / STOP START (*4) / PILLOW LIPS (*4)

ROBBIE GREY – vocals, guitar / **GARY McDOWELL** – guitar / **STEPHEN WALKER** – keyboards / **MICK CONROY** – bass / **RICHARD BROWN** – drums

Limp | not iss.

Sep 79. (7") *(LMP 2)* **DROWNING MAN. / SILENT WORLD** [ ] [-]

4 a.d. | Sire

Apr 80. (7") *(AD 6)* **SWANS ON GLASS. / INCIDENT** [ ] [-]

Oct 80. (7") *(AD 15)* **GATHERING DUST. / TRANQUILITY OF A SUMMER MOMENT** [ ] [-]

Apr 81. (lp) *(CAD 105)* **MESH & LACE** [ ] [-]
– Gathering dust / 16 days / Just a thought / Move in light / Grief / The token man / A viable commercial / Black houses / Dance of devotion (a love song) / Smiles and laughter / Mesh and lace . *(cd-iss. Nov92 +=; CAD 105CD)* – Tranquility of a summer moment / Home / Swans on glass / Incident.

Aug 81. (7") *(AD 110)* **SMILES AND LAUGHTER. / MESH AND LACE** [ ] [-]

Apr 82. (lp/c) *(CAD/+C 206)* <23821> **AFTER THE SNOW** [ ] [70] Feb83
– Someone's calling / Life in the gladhouse / Face of wood / Dawn chorus / I melt with you / After the snow / Carry me down / Tables turning. *(cd-iss. Nov92 +=; CAD 206CD)* – Someone's calling (version) / Life in the gladhouse (version) / I melt with you (mix) / The prize / The choicest view.

Jun 82. (7") *(AD 208)* **LIFE IN THE GLADHOUSE (remix). / THE CHOICEST VIEW** [ ] [-]
(12"+=) *(BAD 208)* – Fragments of fear / Legion.

Oct 82. (7") *(AD 212)* <29339> **I MELT WITH YOU. / THE PRIZE** [ ] [78] Mar83

Sep 83. (7"/12") *(AD/BAD 309)* **SOMEONE'S CALLING. / LIFE IN THE GLADHOUSE** [ ] [-]

Jan 84. (7") *(AD 401)* **CHAPTER 12. / RINGING IN THE CHANGES** [ ] [-]
(12"+=) *(BAD 401)* – Reflection.

Feb 84. (lp/c) *(CAD/+C 402)* <25066> **RICOCHET DAYS** [ ] [93]
– Rainbow's end / Machines / Spinning me round / Ricochet days / Hands across the sea / Blue waves / Heart / Chapter 12 . *(cd-iss. Nov92 +=; CAD 402CD)* – Chapter 12 (extended) / Ringing in the change / Reflection / Breaking away.

Mar 84. (7") <29339> **HANDS ACROSS THE SEA. /** [-] [91]

Sire | Sire

Aug 86. (lp/c) *(925343-1/-4)* <25343> **STOP START** [ ] [ ] Mar86
– The border / Ink and paper / Night train / I don't know the answer / Love breaks down / Breaking away / The greatest show / Love forever / Start stop – Stop start .

— future MARCH VIOLETS member **AARON DAVIDSON** – guitar, keyboards ; repl. McDOWELL + WALKER before they broke up in 1986. ROBBIE GREY joined THIS MORTAL COIL on some of their output.

— **GREY, DAVIDSON + CONROY** reformed in 1990 after moving to the States.

not iss. | T.V.T.

Jun 90. (cd/c) <TVT 2810-2/-4> **PILLOW LIPS** [-] [ ]
– I melt with you / Life's rich tapestry / Beauty / You're too much / Beautiful people / Care about you / Let's all dream / Coming up for air / Take me away / Pillow lips.

Jun 90. (c-s/cd-s) <TVT 2812-4/-2> **I MELT WITH YOU / BEAUTIFUL PEOPLE** [-] [76]

— split in 1991. GREY formed ENGINE.

– compilations, etc. –

Jun 83. (12"ep) *4 a.d.; (BAD 306)* **THE SINGLES** [ ] [-]
– Gathering dust / Mesh and lace / Smiles and laughter / Swans on glass / Home.

MODERN EON

Formed: Liverpool, England . . . 1979 out of the LUGLO SLUGS by ALIX PLAIN and DANNY HAMPSON, who enlisted BOB WAKELIN, JOEY McKECHNIE and GED ALLEN (the latter was replaced by TIM LEVER). Thankfully abandoning earlier names such as TANK TIME, ONE-TWO and J&J MODERN EON, these Merseyside hopefuls were one of the many post-punk acts to emerge as part of the burgeoning Liverpool music scene. Appropriately enough, MODERN EON kicked off the new decade with a self-financed debut EP, 'PIECES', a very rhythmically militaristic, JOY DIVISION-esque affair, at least musically; vocally, the high-pitched but throaty PLAIN came across as an FM rock combination of JON ANDERSON and DON HENLEY! A follow-up single, 'EUTHENTICS' appeared towards the end of 1980 prior to the replacement of PASSAGE-bound McKECHNIE with CLIFF HEWITT and a subsequent signing to 'Dindisc'. Following the release of a revamped version of the aforementioned track, MODERN EON delivered their debut long-player, 'FICTION TALES' (1981), collecting together most of their vinyl repertoire to date and featuring forthcoming singles, 'CHILD'S PLAY' and 'MECHANIC'. Although this marked the end of the road for the band, LEVER went on to join DEAD OR ALIVE while various members resurfaced with BONE a decade on.

Album rating: FICTION TALES (*6)

ALIX PLAIN – vocals, guitar, piano / **TIM LEVER** – guitar, saxophone; repl. GED ALLEN / **BOB WAKELIN** – keyboards, synthesizer, vocals / **DANNY HAMPSON** – bass / **JOEY McKECKNIE** – drums, percussion

Modern Eon / not iss.

Jan 80. (7"ep) *(EON 001)* **PIECES** [ ] [-]
– Second still / Special patrol / Choreography / The look a smack.

Inevitable / not iss.

Nov 80. (7") *(INEV 3)* **EUTHENTICS. / WAITING FOR THE CAVALRY** [ ] [-]

— **CLIFF HEWITT** – drums, timpani; repl. JOEY who joined The PASSAGE

Dindisc / not iss.

Feb 81. (7") *(DIN 30)* **EUTHENTICS (new version). / CARDINAL SINS** [ ] [-]

May 81. (lp) *(DID 11)* **FICTION TALES** [ ] [-]
– Second still / The grass still grows / Playwrite / Watching the dancers / Real hymn / Waiting for the cavalry / High noon / Child's play / Choreography / Euthentics / In a strange way / Mechanic.

Jun 81. (7") *(DIN 31)* **CHILD'S PLAY. / VISIONARY** [ ] [-]

Aug 81. (7") *(DIN 35)* **MECHANIC. / SPLASH** [ ] [-]

— disbanded late 1981 and LEVER joined DEAD OR ALIVE. Two members formed BONE in 1990 and released ep 'AN ARM AND A LEG' for 'Belly Up'.

MODERN LOVERS (see under ⇒ RICHMAN, Jonathan)

MO-DETTES

Formed: London, England . . . 1979 by American-born ex-SLITS member, KATE KORUS along with Swiss frontwoman RAMONA CARLIER, JANE CROCKFORD and JUNE MILES-KINGSTON. Trading in a spiky new wave sound despite their moniker and the (then) current mod revival, this all-female outfit debuted the same year with the self-financed 'WHITE MICE' single. CARLIER's Euro-centric pronunciation and "hiccuping" vocal style was reminiscent of LENE LOVICH while the backing harmonies and handclaps added a retro touch to proceedings. A debut album, 'THE STORY SO FAR', followed in 1980 but failed to generate the anticipated interest and preceded a period of upheaval with both CARLIER and KORUS departing for pastures new in 1981. Despite the recruitment of respective replacements, SUE SLACK and MELISSA RITTER, the band came to a halt the following year amid yet more internal strife. MILES-KINGSTON went on to gain most recognition, initially as a member of FUN BOY THREE's backing band before going on to join The COMMUNARDS. She also released a one-off single for 'Go! Discs', while KORUS subsequently recorded a collaborative effort with BELLE STAR, JENNIE McKEOWN.

Album rating: THE STORY SO FAR (*6)

RAMONA CARLIER – vocals (ex-KLEENEX) (as REGULA SING) / **KATE KORRIS** – guitar (ex-SLITS) / **JANE CROCKFORD** – bass / **JUNE MILES-KINGSTON** – drums

Mode – Rough Trade / not iss.

Dec 79. (7") *(MODE 1)* **WHITE MICE. / MASOCHISTIC OPPOSITE** [ ] [-]

Deram / not iss.

Jun 80. (7") *(DET-R-1)* **PAINT IT BLACK. / BITTA TRUTH** [42] [-]
(free ltd 7"flexi) *(MODE 1-2)* – TWIST AND SHOUT.

Oct 80. (lp) *(SML 1120)* **THE STORY SO FAR** [ ] [-]
– White mouse disco / Fandango / Satisfy / Foolish girl / He's no rebel / Paint it black / The Kray twins / Bedtime stories / Norman / Dark park creeping / Masochistic opposite / Mi lord / The sparrow.

Oct 80. (7") *(DET 2)* **DARK PARK CREEPING. / TWO CAN PLAY** [ ] [-]

Jun 81. (7") *(DET 3)* **TONIGHT. / WALTZ IN BLUE MINOR** [ ] [-]

Human / not iss.

Jul 81. (7") *(HUM 10)* **WHITE MICE. / THE KRAY TWINS (live)** [ ] [-]

— **SUE SLACK** – vocals; repl. RAMONA

— **MELISSA RITTER** – guitar; repl. KATE who teamed up with JENNY (BELLE STARS)

— They split late 1982. JANE married someone from MADNESS. JUNE MILES-KINGSTON went solo after a spell with FUN BOY THREE.

MOGWAI

Formed: Glasgow, Scotland . . . 1995 by DOMINIC AITCHISON, STUART LESLIE BRAITHWAITE and MARTIN BULLOCH. In the Spring of '96, the band debuted with 'TUNER' / 'LOWER', a precursor to the band's double whammy NME Singles Of The Week, 'SUMMER' and 'NEW PATHS TO HELICON'. Early in 1997, they signed to the suffocatingly hip Glasgow-based 'Chemikal Underground' (home of BIS and friends, ARAB STRAP), the first outing being 'THE 4 SATIN EP'. A fine collection of their early singles was released a month later in June, although another label was responsible. That summer, the new 5-piece MOGWAI (complete with JOHN CUMMINGS and former TEENAGE FANCLUB member, BRENDON O'HARE) alternately bludgeoned/charmed the NME tent at Scotland's premier festival 'T In The Park' with their striking hybrid of SONIC YOUTH, METALLICA and pre-'Blue Monday' NEW ORDER! The feverishly anticipated "proper" debut album, 'MOGWAI YOUNG TEAM' was released late '97 to rave reviews, also scraping into the Top 75. Stunningly dynamic, the record shifted seamlessly from tranquil, bleakly beautiful soundscapes to brain scrambling white noise and sledgehammer riffing. Prime examples were 'LIKE HEROD', 'WITH PORTFOLIO' and 'MOGWAI FEAR SATAN', while 'TRACY' was a near 10-minute collage of drifting, childlike charm segueing into a taped phone conversation. Another track, 'R U STILL IN 2 IT', featured the mumbling vocal talents of ARAB STRAP's AIDAN MOFFAT. Prior to the album's release, O'HARE was summarily dismissed, apparently for yapping his way through an ARAB STRAP gig (tsk, tsk!). • **Covered:** HONEY (Spacemen 3).

Album rating: MOGWAI YOUNG TEAM (*9) / KICKING A DEAD PIG: MOGWAI SONGS REMIXED (*7) / TEN RAPID compilation (*8)

pLasmatroN (b. STUART BRAITHWAITE) – guitar, vocals / **DEMONIC** (b. DOMINIC AITCHISON) – bass / **bionic** (b. MARTIN BULLOCH) – drums

Rock Action / not iss.

Feb 96. (ltd-7") *(RAR 001)* **TUNER. / LOWER** [ ] [-]

Che / not iss.

May 96. (ltd-7"green) *(che 61)* **ANGELS VERSUS ALIENS. / (other side by DWEEB)** [ ] [-]

Love Train / not iss.

Sep 96. (ltd-7"; "CAMDEN CRAWL II") *(PUBE 011)* **A PLACE FOR PARKS. / (other artists)** [ ] [-]

Oct 96. (ltd-7"; "TEN DAY WEEKEND") *(PUBE 012)* **I AM NOT BATMAN. / (other artists)** [ ] [-]

Nov 96. (ltd-7") *(PUBE 014)* **SUMMER. / ITHICA 27 o 9** [ ] [-]

Wurlitzer Jukebox / not iss.

Jan 97. (ltd-7") *(WJ 22)* **NEW PATHS TO HELICON** [ ] [-]
– Helicon 1 / Helicon 2.

— added **Cpt. Meat** (aka JOHN CUMMINGS) – guitar

F&J/13th Note / not iss.

Mar 97. (ltd-7"; "CLUB BEATROOT part four") *(SHAG 13.05)* **STEREO DEE (live). / (other side by Ph FAMILY)** [ ] [-]

Chemikal Underground / Jetset

May 97. (12"ep/cd-ep) *(chem 015/+cd)* <TWA 14CD> **4 SATIN EP** [ ] [ ]
– Superheroes of BMX / Now you're taken / Stereo Dee. <US++> – Guardians of space.

— added **+the relic+** (aka BRENDAN O'HARE – piano (of-MACROCOSMICA, ex-TEENAGE FANCLUB, ex-TELSTAR PONIES)

Oct 97. (cd/d-lp) *(chem 018 cd/lp)* <7> **MOGWAI YOUNG TEAM** [75] [ ]
– Yes! I am a long way from home / Like Herod / Radar maker / Tracy / Summer (Priority version) / With portfolio / R u still in 2 it / A cheery wave from stranded youngsters / Mogwai fear Satan.

— now without O'HARE, who was sacked (see above)

Mar 98. (7"split w/MAGOO) *(NING 47CD)* **. . .. DO THE ROCK BOOGALOO** [60] [-]
– Black Sabbath (by MAGOO) / Sweet leaf.
(above obviously covers of two well-known BLACK SABBATH classics)
(above issued on 'Fierce Panda', below 2 for 'eye q' / US 'Jetset')

Apr 98. (cd-ep) *(eyeuk 032cd)* **FEAR SATAN remixes** [57] [-]
– Mogwai remix / U-ziq remix / Surgeon remix / My Bloody Valentine remix.

May 98. (cd/d-lp) *(eyeuk cd/lp)* <TWA 13 CD/LP> **KICKING A DEAD PIG: MOGWAI SONGS REMIXED** [ ] [ ] Jun98
– Like Herod (Hood remix) / Helicon 2 (Max Tundra remix) / Summer (Klute's weird winter remix) / Gwai on 45 (Arab Strap remix) / A cheery wave from stranded youngsters (Third Eye Foundation tet offensive remix) / Like Herod (Alec Empire's face the future remix) / Mogwai fear Satan (Surgeon remix) / R U still in to it? (DJ Q remix) / Tracy (Kid Loco's playing with the young team remix) / Mogwai fear Satan (Mogwai remix).

Jun 98. (12"ep/cd-ep) *(chem 026/+cd)* <111230> **NO EDUCATION = NO FUTURE (FUCK THE CURFEW) e.p.** [68] [ ]
– Xmas steps / Rollerball / Small children in the background.

– compilations, etc. –

Aug 98. (cd) *Rock Action; (rock act 05cd) / Jetset;* <TWA 05LP> **TEN RAPID (collected recordings 1996-1997)** [ ] [ ] Aug97
– Summer / Helicon 2 / Angels versus aliens / I am not Batman / Tuner / Ithica 27 o 9 / A place for parks / Helicon 1 / End.

MOISTBOYZ (see under ⇒ WEEN)

MOJAVE 3 (see under ⇒ SLOWDIVE)

MOLES (see under ⇒ DAVIES, Richard)

MOLLY HALF HEAD

Formed: Manchester, England . . . 1992 out of mysterious beginnings by PHIL MURPHY and ANDY PICKERING who subsequently recruited PAUL BARDSLEY and NEIL DALY. Despite an A&R stampede at that year's 'In The City' music biz conference, the quartet ended up signing with local indie label, 'Playtime', through whom they issued a debut single, 'TASTE OF YOU'. Complaining to the music press that the dole were still on their backs, the band put their money where their mouth was and discounted the single for UB40 card holders. Musically, the band traded in inventive but unpretentious alternative pop with a leftfield streak compared to fellow Manc mavericks, MAGAZINE (whose track, 'THE LIGHT POURS OUT OF ME', they later covered), while lyrically, BARDSLEY was located somewhere between the impenetrability of MARK E. SMITH and the colourful laddishness of SHAUN RYDER. A further two singles, 'JUST' and 'BARNY', previewed a debut album, 'SULK' (1993), although the media hype had obviously failed to impress the average indie fan and the anticipated breakthrough never really materialised. Nevertheless, the band were given a second chance by 'Columbia', re-emerging in 1995 (by which time DALY had been replaced with GRAHAM ATKINSON) with an OASIS-friendly comeback single, 'BREAKING THE ICE'. Unfortunately, it failed to cut any ice in the charts although MOLLY HALF HEAD did manage to scrape into the Top 75 with subsequent single, 'SHINE'. The accompanying album, meanwhile, 'DUNCE' (1995), failed miserably and MOLLY HALF HEAD were soon out on their ear.

Album rating: SULK (*6) / DUNCE (*6)

PAUL BARDSLEY – vocals / **PHIL MURPHY** – guitar / **NEIL DALY** – bass / **ANDY PICKERING** – drums

Playtime Columbia

Mar 93. (7"one-sided) *(AMUSE 015L)* **TASTE OF YOU** [ ] [-]
(10"+=/cd-s+=) *(AMUSE 015 T/CD)* – Treehouse steps / Vivid Whitsun.

May 93. (7") *(AMUSE 018)* **JUST. / TOE TO SAND** [ ] [-]
(10"+=/cd-s+=) *(AMUSE 018 T/CD)* – The light pours out of me.

Sep 93. (7") *(AMUSE 019L)* **BARNY. / SUCKING BLANKETS** [ ] [-]
(10"+=/cd-s+=) *(AMUSE 019 T/CD)* – Aeroplane mother / ('A'-Bernard Chevron mix).

Nov 93. (cd/c/lp) *(AMUSE 020 CD/MC/LP)* *<64296>* **SULK** [ ] [ ] Feb94
– Vivid whitsun / Barny / Promote / Just / Arty breakfast / Bone idle / Spectacle clear / Taste of you / Hopscotch / Inkwell / Writing time / Ginger Pat's avenue / Toe to sand.

— **GRAHAM ATKINSON** – bass; repl. NEIL

Columbia Columbia

Feb 95. (c-s) *(661216-4)* **BREAKING THE ICE. / BLISTERED** [ ] [-]
(10"+=) *(661216-0)* – Airwaves.
(cd-s++=) *(661216-2)* – Ginger Pat's avenue.
(cd-s) *(661216-5)* –

May 95. (7"clear) *(662073-7)* **SHINE. / PUMP IT UP** [73] [-]
(cd-s+=) *(662073-5)* – Stay as you are / 1 DY.
(cd-s) *(662073-2)* – ('A'side) / Exactly / P.G. / Are 'friends' electric.

Jul 95. (cd/c/lp) *(<478314-2/-4/-1>)* **DUNCE** [ ] [ ]

MOMUS

Born: NICHOLAS CURRIE, 1960, Paisley, Scotland. A kind of Scottish MORRISSEY with a wordy, occasionally pretentious penchant for painstakingly examining controversial subject material, especially with regards to sexual morality, CURRIE (ironically the cousin of JUSTIN CURRIE, mainman with coffee table chart-schmoozers DEL AMITRI) has courted more criticism than success (at least in Britain) over the course of his lengthy career. Initially the frontman of Scots alternative popsters The HAPPY FAMILY (who also numbered ex-JOSEF K members DAVE WENDELL and RONNIE TORRANCE), CURRIE split the group up after what he saw as "indifference" by their label, '4 a.d.', leaving behind a solitary album, 'THE MAN ON YOUR STREET' (1982). Relocating to Sloane Square in London and adopting the MOMUS moniker (a name taken from the god who was dismissed from Heaven and who inspired the modern day poet, Peter Porter), CURRIE's debut release came in the shape of the 'BEAST WITH NO BACKS' EP, issued by the 'El' label and quickly followed by an excellent but quickly forgotten debut album, 'CIRCUS MAXIMUS' (1986). An enthusiastic fan of French legends like JACQUES BREL and SERGE GAINSBOURG – obvious influences – CURRIE relied on mood, atmopsphere and lyrical expression to capture the listener's attention, setting about lyrically ridiculing everything in sight, at times transfiguring himself into the past. His episodes of infidelity and injustice were romantically delivered in a vocal vein reminiscent to a cross between the fragility of NICK DRAKE and the effete camp of NEIL TENENT. Finding a welcoming home at 'Creation', MOMUS released 'THE POISON BOYFRIEND' album in 1987 but it was the following year's 'TENDER PERVERT' which really caused a stir. A compelling set of narratives centering on such cheery everyday topics as incest, paedophilia and bestiality, the album won him a cult following but predictably came in for flak from the usual quarters, as did 1991's 'HIPPOPOTAMOMUS', the NME famously awarding it a big round zero out of ten. In his defence, MOMUS argued that he was simply performing one the basic functions of pop since its inception i.e. to help angst-ridden teenagers come to terms with their sexual identity. The album, which was dedicated to French pensmith SERGE GAINSBOURG, was initially removed from the record shops, due to its cover of the TV ad for the 'Michelin Man'! Whatever, the man continued to shock and delight throughout the 90's with albums such as 'THE ULTRACONFORMIST' (1992) – a mock-live affair which featured the sleazy BRECHT-WEILL-esque gems, 'THE MOTHER-IN-LAW' and 'THE LADIES UNDERSTAND' – and 'THE PHILOSOPHY OF MOMUS' (1995). No doubt having given up on winning over the sexually repressed British public long ago, MOMUS could content himself with the fact that he was big in Japan. He was even commisioned to pen a song for a Japanese cosmetics commercial; the result was the quasi-psychedelic BEATLES via BOOKER T. strangeness of 'GOOD MORNING WORLD', a Top 5 hit in the land of saki and one of the more interesting moments on the '20 VODKA JELLIES' (1996) album. The latter set also featured a number of songs apparently written during CURRIE's grunge phase, an interesting diversion – at least musically – from the usual wistful, intellectual forays into cabaret style alternative pop. Love him or loathe him, MOMUS should at least be given credit for having the courage to write about the stuff most people would rather sweep under the carpet. • **Covers:** ORGASM ADDICT (Buzzcocks). Trivia: MANFRED MANN'S EARTH BAND covered his 'COMPLETE HISTORY OF SEXUAL JEALOUSY' in the early 90's! He also composes for Japanese singers KAHIMI KARIE and NORIKO SEKIGUCHI, THE POISON GIRLFRIEND.

Album rating: CIRCUS MAXIMUS (*6) / THE POISON BOYFRIEND (*6) / THE TENDER PERVERT (*7) / DON'T STOP THE NIGHT (*4) / MONSTERS OF LOVE compilation (*7) / HIPPOPOTAMOMUS (*5) / THE ULTRACONFORMIST (*7) / VOYAGER (*6) / TIMELORD (*6) / PHILIOSOPHY OF MOMUS (*6) / SLENDER SHERBET (*6) / 20 VODKA JELLIES (*5) / PING PONG (*6) / Happy Family: THE MAN ON YOUR STREET (*5)

HAPPY FAMILY

NICHOLAS CURRIE – vocals, guitar / **DAVE WENDELL** – bass, vocals (ex-JOSEF K)

4 a.d. not iss.

Mar 82. (7"ep) *(AD 204)* **PURITANS. / INNERMOST THOUGHTS / THE MISTAKE** [ ] [-]

— added **RONNIE TORRANCE** – drums (ex-JOSEF K, ex-BOOTS FOR DANCING) / **NEIL MARTIN** – synthesizer / **PAUL MASON** –

Nov 82. (lp) *(CAD 214)* **THE MAN ON YOUR STREET** [ ] [-]
– The salesman / Letter from Hall / The luckiest citizen / Revenge / The courier / The man on your street / A night underground / Two of a kind / March in Turin. *(cd-iss. Nov92 +=; CAD 214CD)* – Puritans / Innermost thoughts / The mistake.

— split in 1983, leaving behind last recordings below . . .

Les Tempes not iss.

Oct 84. (c) **THE BUSINESS OF LIVING** [ ] [-]

MOMUS

NICHOLAS CURRIE – vocals, guitar / with **NEIL MARTIN** / + on album only **JANE DAVIES** – vocals

El not iss.

Jul 85. (12"ep) **THE BEAST WITH 3 BACKS** [ ] [-]
– The ballad of the barrel organist / Third party fire and theft / Hotel Marquis de Sade.

Jan 86. (lp) *(ACME 2)* **CIRCUS MAXIMUS** [ ] [-]
– Lucky like St. Sebastian / The lesson of Sodom (according to Lot) / John the Baptist Jones / King Solomon's song and mine / Little Lord Obedience / The day the circus came to town / The rape of Lucretia / Paper wraps rock / Rules of the game of quoits. *(cd-iss. Jul89 & Jun97 +=; ACME 2CD)* – Nicky / Don't leave / See a friend in tears.

Jun 86. (12"m) *(GP 09T)* **NICKY. / DON'T LEAVE / SEE A FRIEND IN TEARS** [ ] [-]

— with **DEAN KLERAT** – keyboards / **FEIN O'LOCHLAINN** – bass / **TERRY NEILSON** – drums / **ARUN G. SHENDURNIKAR** – percussion

Creation not iss.

Mar 87. (12"ep) *(CRE 037T)* **MURDERERS, THE HOPE OF WOMEN. / ELEVEN EXECUTIONERS / WHAT WILL DEATH BE LIKE?** [ ] [-]

Jul 87. (lp) *(CRELP 021)* **THE POISON BOYFRIEND** [ ] [-]
– The gatecrasher / Violets / Islington John / Three wars / Flame into being / Situation comedy blues / Sex for the disabled / Closer to you. *(cd-iss. Apr88 +=; CRELP 021CD)* – Murderers, the hope of women / Eleven executioners / What will death be like?

Jul 88. (lp/cd) *(CRELP 036/+CD)* **THE TENDER PERVERT** [ ] [-]
– The angels are voyeurs / Love on ice / I was a Maoist intellectual / The homosexual / Bishonen / A complete history of sexual jealousy (parts 17-24) / Ice king / In the sanatorium / The charm of innocence / The angels are voyeurs (reprise). *(w/ free 7")*

Jan 89. (7") *(CRE 063L)* **HAIRSTYLE OF THE DEVIL. /** [ ] [-]
(12"+=) *(CRE 063LT)* –

Oct 89. (7") **LIFESTYLES OF THE RICH AND FAMOUS. /** [ ] [-]
(12"+=/3"cd-s+=) –

Nov 89. (cd)(c/lp) *(CRECD 59)(C+/CRE 59)* **DON'T STOP THE NIGHT** [ ] [-]
– Trust me, I'm a doctor / Right hand heart / Lord of the dance / Lifestyles of the rich and famous / How do you find my sister? / The hairstyle of the Devil * / Don't stop the night / Amongst women only / The guitar lesson / The cabriolet / Shaftesbury Avenue. *(cd+= *)*

Mar 90. (cd)(c/lp) *(CRECD 59)(C+/CRE 59)* **MONSTERS OF LOVE: SINGLES 85-89** (readings of my early years) [ ] [-]
– Morality is vanity / Ballad of the barrel organist / Third party, fire and theft / Hotel Marquis de Sade / Murderers, the hope of women / What will death be like? / Eleven executioners / Gilda / The hairstyle of the Devil / Monsters of love.

Jul 91. (cd)(c/lp) *(CRECD 97)(C+CRE 97)* **HIPPOPOTAMOMUS** -
– Hippopotamomus / I ate a girl right up / Michelin man / A dull documentary / Marquis of sadness / Bluestocking / Ventriloquists & dolls / The painter & his model / A monkey for Sallie / Pornography / Song in contravention.

May 92. (lp/cd) *(MONDE 3/+CD)* **THE ULTRACONFORMIST** (live whilst out of fashion) -
– Sinister themes / Last of the window cleaners / The ladies understand / Cape and stick gang / The ultraconformist / The mother-in-law / La Catrina / The cheques in the post / Spy on the moon / Forests. *(cd re-iss. Jun97; same)*

— above issued on 'Richmond-Cherry Red'.

Jun 92. (cd)(lp/c) *(CRECD 113)(C+/CRE 113)* **VOYAGER** -
– Cibachrome blue / Virtual reality / Vocation / Conquistador / Spacewalk / Summer holiday 1999 / Afterglow / Trans Siberian express / Voyager / Momutation 3.

Sep 92. (12")(cd-s) *(CRE 134T)(CRESCD 134)* **SPACEWALK (Deja vu remix). / CONQUISTADIOR (Lovecut db remix) / MOMUTATION 3** -

Nov 93. (cd/lp) *(CRE CD/LP 151)* **TIMELORD** -
– Platinum / Enlightenment / You've changed / Landrover / Rhetoric / Suicide pact / Christmas on Earth / Breathless.

Cherry Red / Cherry Red

Apr 95. (cd-s) *(CDCHERRY 137)* **THE SADENESS OF THINGS /** -

Jun 95. (cd) *(CDBRED 119)* **PHILOSOPHY OF MOMUS** -
– Toothbrushead / The madness of Lee Scratch Perry / It's important to be trendy / Quark and charm, the robot twins / Girlish boy / Yokohama Chinatown / Withinity / K's diary / Virtual Valerie / Red pyjamas / The cabinet of Kuniyoshi Kaneko / Slide projector, lie detector / Microworlds / Complicated / I had a girl / The philosophy of Momus / The loneliness of lift music / Paranoid acoustic seduction machine / The sadeness of things.

Nov 95. (cd) *(CDBRED 123)* **SLENDER SHERBET – CLASSIC SONGS REVISITED** (readings of my early years) -
– The complete history of sexual jealousy / The guitar lesson / Closer to you / The homosexual / Charm of innocence / Lucky like St. Sebastian / I was a Maoist intellectual / Lifestyles of the rich and famous / Angels are voyeurs / Hotel Marquis de Sade / The gatecrasher / Hairstyle of the Devil / Bi shonen / Angels (reprise).

Sep 96. (cd) *(<CDMRED 133>)* **20 VODKA JELLIES** (an assortment of curiosities and rarities) Jan97
– I am a kitten / Vogue Bambini / The poisoners / Nikon 2 / Giapponese a Roma / Paolo / The end of history / London 1888 / Streetlamp soliloquy / An inflatable doll / Saved / Someone / Howard Hughes / Three beasts / Good morning world / Germania / The girl with no body / Radiant night / Orgasm addict / Nobody.

Satyricon / Bungalow-Setanta

Nov 97. (cd) *(SATYR 001)* <031> **PING PONG**
– Ping pong with Hong Kong King Kong / His majesty the baby / My pervert doppleganger / I want you, but I don't need you / Professor Shaftenberg / Shoesize of the angel / Age of information / Sensation of orgasm / Anthem of Shibuya / Lolitapop dollhouse / Tamagotchi press officer / Space Jews / My kindly friend the censor / Animal that desires / How to get – and stay – famous / 2 p.m.

MONACO (see under ⇒ NEW ORDER)

MONOCHROME SET

Formed: London, England . . . early 1978 by BID and LESTER SQUARE, who had comprised one half of punk outfit The B-SIDES. While the other half formed ADAM & THE ANTS, BID and SQUARE recruited a rhythm section in JEREMY HARRINGTON and J.D. HANEY, signing to 'Rough Trade' and releasing a string of quirky but compelling singles, 'HE'S FRANK (SLIGHT RETURN)', 'EINE SYMPHONIE DES GRAUENS' and subtropical signature tune, 'THE MONOCHROME SET (I PRESUME)', SETting the tone for an eclectic and generally low-key career. Characterised by the lugubrious, sardonic vocals of BID – the alternative JAKE THACKARY! – The MONOCHROME SET's offbeat guitar-based musings won them a cult following and a modicum of critical acclaim but precious little in the way of commercial rewards. Hardly surprising then, that they were shunted around from label to label, the band moving on to 'Dindisc' for 1980's debut album, 'STRANGE BOUTIQUE'. As well as marking the arrival of ANDY WARREN (another ex-B-SIDE who had initially played with ADAM & THE ANTS), the album stands as the band's one and only flirtation with the charts, skirting the UK Top 60. A further two singles followed in '405 LINES' and 'APOCALYPSO', previewing another full length album, 'LOVE ZOMBIES' (1980) in the space of only six months. Yet the band were dogged by personnel changes, LEXINGTON CRANE replacing HANEY for 'ELIGIBLE BACHELORS' (1982). The first fruits of a new deal with 'Cherry Red', the record featured such memorable MONOCHROME SET moments as ironic Latin America commentary, 'JET SET JUNTA' and the wry 'MATING GAME', the latter set to a hilarious 'Young Ones'-era CLIFF RICHARD style tune. Despite indie chart success and an obvious influence on upcoming bands like The SMITHS, BID & co. couldn't quite manage a significant breakthrough, the line-up changes continuing apace as CARRIE BOOTH joined on keyboards and (ex-SOFT BOYS) MORRIS WINDSOR took up the vacant drum seat. The latter pair were subsequently replaced by FOZ and NICK WESOLOWSKI as the band moved to 'Blanco Y Negro' and came close to wider recognition with their most accessible singles – 'JACOB'S LADDER', 'WALLFLOWER' – and album, 'THE LOST WEEKEND' (1985) to date. It wasn't to be though and disillusioned, the band split soon after with BID subsequently becoming involved in the short-lived RAJ QUARTET. Come 1989, BID, SQUARE and WARREN regrouped to give it another go, recruiting new member, ORSON PRESENCE, and releasing an album, 'DANTE'S CASINO' on 'Vinyl Japan'. The revamped MONOCHROME SET subsequently renewed their acquaintance with 'Cherry Red' in the early 90's, delivering material at their usual prolific pace to a generally disinterested music scene.

Album rating: STRANGE BOUTIQUE (*5) / LOVE ZOMBIES (*4) / ELIGIBLE BACHELORS (*6) / VOLUME, BRILLIANCE, CONTRAST compilation (*7) / THE LOST WEEKEND (*5) / DANTE'S CASINO (*5) / JACK (*5) / CHARADE (*5) / MISERIE (*5) / TRINITY ROAD (*5)

BID (b. J.BIVOUAC, Calcutta, India) – vocals, guitar / **LESTER SQUARE** – lead guitar, vocals (ex-ADAM & THE ANTS, ex-B-SIDES) / **JEREMY HARRINGTON** – bass, percussion (ex-GLORIA MUNDI and MEAN STREET) repl. SIMON CROFT who had replaced CHARLIE / **J.D. HANEY** – drums (ex-ART ATTACKS) / plus 5th member **TONY POTTS** – visuals

Rough Trade / I.R.S.

Dec 78. (7") *(RT 005)* <IR 9002> **ALPHAVILLE. / HE'S FRANK** Oct79

Apr 79. (7") *(RT 019)* **EINE SYMPHONIE DES GRAUENS. / LESTER LEAPS IN** -

Sep 79. (7") *(RT 028)* **THE MONOCHROME SET (I PRESSUME). / MR. BIZARRO** -

Disques Bleu / not iss.

Dec 79. (7") *(BL 1)* **HE'S FRANK (SLIGHT RETURN). / SILICON CARNE / FALLOUT (all live)** -

— **ANDY WARREN** – bass (ex-ADAM & THE ANTS, ex-B SIDES) repl. JEREMY

Dindisc / not iss.

Apr 80. (7") *(DIN 18)* **STRANGE BOUTIQUE. / SURFING S.W.12** -

Apr 80. (lp) *(DID 4)* **STRANGE BOUTIQUE** 62 -
– The Monochrome Set (I pressume) / Expresso / The Puerto Rican fence climber / Martians go home / Love goes down the drain / Ici les enfants / The ecetera stroll / Goodbye Joe / Strange boutique / The lighter side of dating / Tomorrow will be too long. *(re-iss. Mar84 on 'Virgin'; OVED 55)*

Jun 80. (7") *(DIN 23)* **405 LINES. / GOODBYE JOE** -

Oct 80. (7") *(DIN 26)* **APOCALYPSO. / FIASCO BONGO** -

Oct 80. (lp) *(DID 8)* **LOVE ZOMBIES** -
– Apocalypso / Adesta fiedes / Love zombies / 405 lines / Kama Sutra / B.I.D. spells Bid / R.S.V.P. / The man with the black moustache / In love, cancer? / The weird, wild and wonderful world of Tony Potts. *(re-iss. Mar84 on 'Virgin'; OVED 56)*

Pre / not iss.

Jul 81. (7") *(PRE 018)* **TEN DON'TS FOR HONEYMOONERS. / STRAITS OF MALACCA** -

— **LEXINGTON CRANE** – drums; repl. HANEY

Cherry Red / not iss.

Jul 82. (7") *(CHERRY 42)* **THE MATING GAME. / J.D.H.A.N.E.Y.** -

Aug 82. (lp) *(BRED 34)* **ELIGIBLE BACHELORS** -
– The jet-set junta / The mating game / Cloud 10 / The ruling class / The great barrier reef / I'll cry instead / Fun for all the family / The Devil rides out / On the 13th day / March of the eligible bachelors. *(cd-iss. May91; CDBRED 34)*

— **CARRIE BOOTH** – keyboards (ex-THOMPSON TWINS) repl. LESTER who went solo

— **MORRIS WINDSOR** – drums (ex-SOFT BOYS) repl. LEXINGTON

Oct 82. (7") *(CHERRY 51)* **CAST A LONG SHADOW. / THE BRIDGE** -

May 83. (7"m) *(CHERRY 60)* **THE JET-SET JUNTA. / LOVE GOES DOWN THE DRAIN / NOISE** -

May 83. (lp) *(MRED 47)* **VOLUME! BRILLIANCE! CONTRAST!** (compilation) -
– Eine symphonie des grauens / The jet-set junta / Love zombies / Silicon Carne / The ruling class / Viva death row / The man with the black moustache / He's Frank (slight return) / Fun for all the family / Lester leaps in / Ici les enfants / Fat fun / Alphaville / Avanti. *(cd-iss. May91 & Jul93; CDBRED 47)*

— **BID + WARREN** recruited **NICK WESOLOWSKI** – drums; who repl. WINDSOR

— **FOZ** (b. JAMES FOSTER) – guitar; repl. CARRIE (to The SING MARKET)

Blanco Y Negro / not iss.

Jan 85. (7") *(NEG 4)* **JACOB'S LADDER. / ANDIANO** -
(12"+=) *(NEG 4T)* – La boom boom / Sailor beware / Starry nowhere.

May 85. (7"/12") *(NEG 12/+T)* **WALLFLOWER. / BIG BEN BONGO** -

Jun 85. (lp/c) *(BYN/+C 5)* **THE LOST WEEKEND** -
– Wallflower / Sugar plum / Take Foz / Starry nowhere / Jacob's ladder / Cargo / Don't touch / Letter from Viola / The twitch / Cowboy country / La boom boom.

— disbanded after above album

BID

El / not iss.

Jun 86. (7") *(GPO 10)* **REACH FOR YOUR GUN. / SWEET CHARIOTS** -
(12"+=) *(GPO 10T)* – Love.

RAJ QUARTET

were formed by **BID**

El / not iss.

Mar 87. (12"ep) *(GPO 26T)* **WHOOPS: WHAT A PALAVER / INVOCATION OF TOTH. / RAZBOYNIKA / THE MANEATER OF SURREY GREEN** -
Split, and BID went onto join KING OF LUXEMBOURG in '86-87

MONOCHROME SET

re-formed 4-piece late 1989 with **BID, LESTER, WARREN** plus **ORSON PRESENCE** – guitar, keyboards

Vinyl Japan / not iss.

Sep 90. (lp/cd) *(ASK 4/+CD)* **DANTE'S CASINO** -

Honeymoon / not iss.

Nov 91. (12"/cd-s) **KILLING DAVE. / HOUSE OF GOD (live) / SWEET DEATH** -

Nov 91. (cd/c/lp) *(MONO CD/MC/LP 1)* **JACK** -
– Big wheel / Jack / Blood act / Sweet death / Cerebella / Killing Dave / Jane / Black are the flowers / Yo Mo fo / Ground zero. *(re-iss. Nov93; same)*

Cherry Red / not iss.

Mar 93. (cd/lp) *(CD+/BRED 102)* **CHARADE**
– Prelude / Forever young / Clover / Snowgirl / White garden / Her pain / Little noises / Crystal chamber / Girl / Oh Angie / Talking about you / No time for girls / Christine / Tilt.

Mar 93. (cd-ep) *(CDCHERRY 126)* **FOREVER YOUNG / HURTING YOU / LITTLE NOISES** [ ] [-]

May 94. (cd) *(CDBRE 114)* **MISERIE** [ ] [-]
– Milk and honey / Pauper / Dr. Robinson / Achilees / Leather jacket / Bed / Handsome / The ethereal one / UFO / Intergrate me / Twang 'em high.

Sep 95. (cd-ep) *(CDCHERRY 138)* **I LOVE LAMBETH / KISSY KISSY / ALL OVER / CLOSING TIME** [ ] [ ]

Sep 95. (cd) *(CDBRED 122)* **TRINITY ROAD** [ ] [-]
– Flamen dialis / All over / I love Lambeth / Kissy kissy / The mousetrap / Snake-fingers / Hula honey / Albert Bridge / Two fists / The wurst is yet to come / The golden apples of the sun / Hobb's end / Bar Madiera / Bliss / The April dance affair.

– compilations, etc. –

Jun 86. (lp) *El; (ACME 1)* **FIN! (live)** [ ] [-]
– He's Frank / Martians go home / Straits of Malacca / Sugar plum / B-I-D spells BID / Alphaville / Heaven can wait / Goodbye Joe / The strange boutique / Jacob's ladder / Wallflower / Apocalypso / Mr. Bizarro / I'll cry instead / Expresso / 405 lines / Ein symphonie des grauens / The Monochrome Set.

Jun 87. (cd) *Virgin; (COMCD 9)* **COLOUR TRANSMISSION** [ ] [-]
– The Monochrome Set (I pressume) / The lighter side of dating / Expresso / The Puerto Rican fence climbler / Tomorrow will too long / Martians go home / Love goes down the drain / Ici les enfants / The etcetera stroll / Goodbye Joe / The strange boutique / Love zombies / Adeste fideles / 405 lines / B-I-D spells BID / R.S.V.P> / Apocalypso / Karma sutre / The man with the black moustache / The weird, wild and wonderful world of Tony Potts / In love cancer?

Aug 88. (lp/cd) *El; (ACME 17/+CD)* **WESTMINSTER AFFAIR – BANDE ORIGINALE DU FILM** [ ] [-]
– The jet-set junta / Cast a long shadow / The ruling class / Lester leaps in / The mating game / On the 13th day / March of the eligible bachelors / Devil rides out / Fun for all the family / Andiamo / Cowboy country / J.D.H.A.N.E.Y. / Noise / Eine symphonie des grauens / Avanti. *(cd+=)* – Viva death row / Jacob's ladder / Ici les enfants. *(cd re-iss. Nov93; same)*

Apr 92. (lp/cd) *Richmond; (MONDE 2/+CD)* **WHAT A WHOPPER!** [ ] [-]

Oct 92. (cd) *Richmond; (MONDE 8CD)* **THE GOOD LIFE** [ ] [-]

May 93. (cd) *Code 90; (<NINETY 4>)* **LIVE (live)** [ ] [ ] Nov95

Mar 95. (cd) *Virgin; (CDOVD 458) / Caroline; <1252>* **TOMORROW WILL BE TOO LONG – THE BEST OF THE MONOCHROME SET** [ ] [ ] Apr95

Mar 95. (cd) *Cherry Red; (CDMRED 118)* **BLACK & WHITE MINSTRELS – 1975-1979** [ ] [-]

May 96. (cd) *Cherry Red; (CDBRED 128)* **HISTORY: 1978-1996** [ ] [-]

Sep 97. (d-cd) *Snapper; (SMDCD 134) / Recall; <134>* **CHAPS** [ ] [ ]

MOODISTS

Formed: Melbourne, Australia . . . 1980 by DAVE GRANEY, formerly of the short-lived SPUTNIKS, who released one single, 'OUR BOYS' / 'SECOND GLANCE', in late '79. Joined by STEVE MILLER (no, not that one), MICK TURNER, CHRIS WALSH and CLARE MOORE, GRANEY instigated The MOODISTS, a longer term garage/psyche outfit that enjoyed much cult acclaim in their native Australia. After a couple of homegrown 45's, they secured a UK deal with the small independent, 'Red Flame', subsequently issuing a string of releases including two mini-sets, 'ENGINE SHUDDER' (1983) and 'DOUBLE LIFE' (1985) either side of a full-length album, 'THIRSTY'S CALLING' (1984). The mid-80's also saw the band (who were now without TURNER) release a one-off single, 'JUSTICE AND MONEY TOO', for Alan McGee's yet-to-be-massive 'Creation' label. Ex-ORANGE JUICE bassist, DAVID McCLYMONT, was soon to be drafted in for the departing WALSH, although two further singles rounded off their seven year career. GRANEY was to enjoy greater commercial success with his own outfit, DAVE GRANEY & THE CORAL SNAKES (who included another former ORANGE JUICE member, MALCOLM ROSS), his songwriting prowess and balladeering style seeing him elevated to the critical heights scaled by fellow countrymen, DAVE McCOMB, NICK CAVE and GRANT McLENNAN. Signed to UK 'Fire', GRANEY and Co delivered three albums between '89 and '92, namely 'WORLD FULL OF DAUGHTERS', 'MY LIFE ON THE PLAINS' and 'I WAS THE HUNTER . . . AND I WAS THE PREY'. In 1993, he surpassed expectations with the much praised 'NIGHT OF THE WOLVERINE'; the album was given a belated UK release three years later by the astute 'This Way Up' label, who were due to issue its follow-up, 'THE SOFT 'N' SEXY' (1996). • **Trivia:** CLARE MOORE is the younger sister of LINDY MORRISON (of The Go-Betweens).

Album rating: ENGINE SHUDDER mini (*5) / THIRSTY'S CALLING (*6) / DOUBLE LIFE mini (*4) / Dave Graney: WORLD FULL OF DAUGHTERS (*6) / MY LIFE ON THE PLAINS (*6) / I WAS THE HUNTER . . . AND I WAS THE PREY (*6) / NIGHT OF THE WOLVERINE (*8) / THE SOFT 'N' SEXY (*6)

DAVE GRANEY – vocals / **STEVE MILLER** – guitar / **MICK TURNER** – guitar / **CHRIS WALSH** – bass / **CLARE MOORE** – drums

Au Go Go / not iss.

Sep 81. (7") *(ANDA 15)* **WHERE THE TREES WALK DOWN HILL. / I SHOULD HAVE BEEN THERE** [-] [-] Austra

Apr 82. (7") *(ANDA 18)* **GONE DEAD. / CHAD'S NEW CAR** [-] [-] Austra

Red Flame / not iss.

Mar 83. (7") *(RF 721)* **THE DISCIPLES KNOW. / SHE CRACKLES** [ ] [-]

Jun 83. (m-lp) *(RFM 21)* **ENGINE SHUDDER** [ ] [-]
– Kept spectre / The road is holy / Junkyard / etc.

Apr 84. (lp) *(RFA 39)* **THIRSTY'S CALLING** [ ] [-]
– That's Frankie's negative / Bad cabin / Some kinda Jones / Do the door, friend / Runaway / Machine machine / Pure gold flesh / You could be his killer / Swingy George / Thirsty's calling / Boss shitkicker.

May 84. (7") *(RFB 39)* **RUNAWAY. / CHEVROLET ROSE** [ ] [-]
(12"+=) *(RFB 39-12)* – Busy splinters.

Sep 84. (7"/10") *(RFB/10RFB 41)* **ENOUGH LEGS TO LIVE ON. / CAN'T LOSE HER** [ ] [-]

— now without TURNER

Sep 85. (m-lp) *(RFM 44)* **DOUBLE LIFE** [ ] [-]
– Double life / Enough legs to live on / Chevrolet rise / That's how you'll cry / Can't lose her / Six dead birds.

Creation / not iss.

Dec 85. (12"ep) *(CRE 023T)* **JUSTICE AND MONEY TOO. / YOU'VE GOT YOUR STORY / TAKE US ALL HOME** [ ] [-]

— **DAVID McCLYMONT** – bass (ex-ORANGE JUICE) repl. CHRIS

Tim / not iss.

Oct 86. (12"ep) *(12MOT 1)* **TAKE THE RED CARPET OUT OF TOWN. / JACK OF DIAMONDS / EVERYBODY DON'T TELL HER** [ ] [-]

May 87. (7") *(MOT 5)* **HEY LITTLE GARY. / SOMEONE'S GOT TO GIVE** [ ] [-]
(12"+=) *(12MOT 5)* – Somebody to love / It takes a thief.

DAVE GRANEY

— first credited with The CORAL SNAKES AT HIS STONE BEACH

— included in group **MALCOLM ROSS** – guitar (ex-ORANGE JUICE)

Fire / Fire

Oct 88. (12"ep) *(BLAZE 32T)* **LISTEN TO HER LOVERS SING / THE GREATEST SHOW IN TOWN. / A DEAL MADE FOR SOMEBODY ELSE / WORLD FULL OF DAUGHTERS** [ ] [-]

1989. (lp/cd) **WORLD FULL OF DAUGHTERS** [ ] [-]

Mar 90. (m-cd/m-lp) *(<FIRE CD/LP 20>)* **MY LIFE ON THE PLAINS** [ ] [ ] Jul91
– Brass buttons / In a misty morning / Dolphins.

Nov 90. (cd-ep) **CODINE (live EP** [ ] [-]

Feb 92. (cd; by DAVE GRANEY with The CORAL SNAKES) *(FIRE 33029)* **I WAS THE HUNTER . . . AND I WAS THE PREY** [ ] [-]
– $1,000,000 in a red velvet suit / You could be mine / I got myself a beautiful nightmare / Same place another time / A love that blinds a love / Somebody tryin' to hold you now / I was the hunter and I was the prey / I caught my head in a crack of time / We were going faster / Everybody does what they want to / Belong to you / Everything flies away / Codine / Jack of diamonds.

This Way Up / not iss.

Apr 96. (7"ep) *(WAY 48-33)* **YOU'RE JUST TOO HIP, BABY. / THAT'S THE WAY IT'S GONNA BE / 3220 BLUES** [ ] [-]

May 96. (cd/c) *(532 129-2/-4)* **NIGHT OF THE WOLVERINE** (rec.1993) [ ] [-]

Sep 96. (cd) *(528 416-2)* **THE SOFT 'N' SEXY** [ ] [-]

MOOD SIX

Formed: Margate, England . . . 1981 by SIMON SMITH, songwriter TONY CONWAY, ANDY GODFREY, PAUL SHUREY, GUY MORLEY and PHIL WARD. Although most members were from Mod backgrounds, The MOOD SIX chose retro psychedelia as the inspiration for their new style, making their vinyl debut in 1982 on WEA's V/A compilation, 'A Splash Of Colour'. The two featured MOOD SIX tracks ('JUST LIKE A DREAM' and 'PLASTIC FLOWERS') were certainly highlights, resulting in an interview on BBC-TV's 'Nationwide' news programme. They subsequently secured a deal with 'E.M.I.' and debuted with the single, 'HANGING AROUND' (soon to be covered by US pop star, TONI BASIL), a sales flop that did little to further their relationship with the label. Finally dropped after the withdrawal of their follow-up, 'SHE'S TOO FAR (OUT)', the group took a lengthy sabbatical while SMITH went off to join The TIMES. By the time of his return, CHRIS O'CONNOR had been chosen to replace PAUL and GUY, a long-awaited debut album, 'THE DIFFERENCE IS . . .', finally hitting the racks in early '85. The following year, The MOOD SIX found a new home at 'Cherry Red', through whom they released a second album, 'A MATTER OF!' (1986), the last recording to feature O'CONNOR who was substituted with SIMON TAYLOR. Following the collapse of Cherry Red, it would be several years before loyal fans were furnished with a third and final set, 'AND THIS IS IT' (1993), by which point WARD had made way for GERRY O'SULLIVAN.

Album rating: THE DIFFERENCE IS . . . (*6) / A MATTER OF! (*7) / AND THIS IS IT (*5)

PHIL WARD – vocals / **TONY CONWAY** (b.28 Feb'58, Newbury, England) – guitar / **PAUL SHUREY** – (ex-V.I.P.'s) / **GUY MORLEY** – (ex-V.I.P.'s) / **ANDY GODFREY** (b.28 Dec'57, Ilford, Essex, England) – bass (ex-SECURITY RISK) / **SIMON SMITH** (b. 3 Dec'58, Merton Park, London) – drums (ex-MERTON PARKAS)

E.M.I. / not iss.

May 82. (7") *(EMI 5300)* **HANGING AROUND. / MOOD MUSIC** [ ] [-]

Sep 82. (7"w/drawn) *(EMI 5336)* **SHE'S TOO FAR (OUT). / VENUS** [-] [-]

— **CHRIS O'CONNOR** – keyboards repl. PAUL SHUREY + GUY MORLEY

Psycho / not iss.

Feb 85. (lp) *(PSYCHO 33)* **THE DIFFERENCE IS . . .** [ ] [-]
– She's too far (out) / Party time / It's your life / Victim / Hanging around / Plastic flowers / Brief encounter / Stay this way / The rain falls on Mary / The difference is . . .

Apr 85. (7") *(PSYCHO 2001)* **PLASTIC FLOWERS. / IT'S YOUR LIFE** [ ] [-]
(12"+=) *(PSYCHO 4001)* **PLASTIC FLOWERS EP** – Is it right? / I wanna destroy you / Starting points.

Cherry Red — not iss.

Aug 86. (12") *(12CHERRY 94)* **WHAT HAVE YOU EVER DONE. /** [ ] [-]
Sep 86. (lp/c) *(BRED/CBRED 71)* **A MATTER OF!** [ ] [-]
– The contemporary scene / The voice of reason / Eternal / Back to the day / The life that Jack built / A matter of! / What have you ever done? / Love of money / Far away / When the time came / The perfect life / Game show.

— **SIMON TAYLOR** (b.28 Dec'60, Redhill, Surrey) – keyboards repl. O'CONNOR

May 87. (7") *(CHERRY 97)* **I SAW THE LIGHT. / FLOWERS AND BOXES** [ ] [-]
(12"+=) *(12CHERRY 97)* – Light music / Theme from 'The Chase'.

— not much happened after 'Cherry Red' went bust. Re-formed in 1993.

— **GERRY O'SULLIVAN** (b.25 Mar'63, Paddington, London) – vocals repl. WARD

Lost Recording Co. — not iss.

1993. (cd) **AND THIS IS IT** [ ] [-]

— SIMON SMITH would subsequently join SMALLTOWN PARADE

MOOG COOKBOOK (see under ⇒ JELLYFISH)

MOONFLOWERS

Formed: Bristol, England ... 1987 by THE REVEREND SONIK RAY alongside SMOKIN' SAM, JESSIE JAMES VERNON, ELECTRIC PUSSY, DOUGAL MacSHAGGER and ELMO. After a debut EP, 'WE DIG YOUR EARTH', in summer '89 and a cover of Sly Stone's 'GET HIGHER' on 'Heavenly' the following year, RAY formed his own label, 'Pop God'. He quickly signed local lads, The FAMILY who released their own mini-lp while The MOONFLOWERS themselves were afforded free publicity and ensuing hype after appearing in court for not paying the dreaded Poll Tax. A fews months later – to promote their limited 7"single, 'WARSHAG' – the latter day hippies were again a talking point after appearing naked (hand over parts) in the NME. Despite their dedication to the free festival circuit and community benefit work, their prolific release schedule continued apace and a long awaited debut album, 'HASH SMITS', appeared towards the tail end of '91. Influenced by a freaky hybrid of US West Coast psychedelic pop, GONG weirdness, GEORGE CLINTON's colourful funk experimentation, dub reggae and even ZODIAC MINDWARP, MOONFLOWERS were clearly out on a musical limb. As for playing the music business game, the band were content to communicate with the media by hand-written letter and defiantly refused to be lumped in with any music press-created scene. A couple of 1992 covers EP's showed the band weren't lacking a sense of humour while a follow-up album, 'FROM WHALES TO JUPITER BEYOND THE STARS OF RAINBOWHEMIA' (1993) preached a new, unceasingly optimistic hippy gospel for the crusty generation. 1995's 'SHAKE IT TOGETHER' EP, meanwhile, was something of a minor classic, a possible precursor to the stoned genius of The BETA BAND. The lead track was taken from the longest titled album in history 'WE WOULD FLY AWAY ...' (see discography), The MOONFLOWERS last epistle before their mid-90's demise. • **Covered:** NORWEGIAN WOOD (Beatles) / ARMAGEDDON TIME (Clash) / TIGHTEN UP (Archie Bell & The Drells) / I JUST CAN'T BE DISCOMAN TODAY (Damned). • **Trivia:** All their mothers sang backing vocals on their last 1991 EP.

Album rating: HASH SMITS (*6) / FROM WHALES TO JUPITER BEYOND THE STARS OF RAINBOWHEMIA (*6) / WE WOULD FLY AWAY... (*6)

THE REVEREND SONIK RAY (b. SEAN O'NEIL) – vocals, guitar / **SMOKIN' SAM** (b. SAM BURNS) – keyboards, saxophone, vocals / **JESSIE JAMES VERNON** – guitar / **ELECTRIC PUSSY** (b. YODDOM POPE) – drums / **DOUGAL MacSHAGGER** (b. PAUL WATERWORTH) – bass / **ELMO** – DJ

Electric Stars — not iss.

Jul 89. (7"ep/12"ep) *(EST/+T 1)* **WE DIG YOUR EARTH EP** [ ] [-]
– Rock'n'roll / My baby don't love me anymore / All or nothing / Johnny.

— **PRAISE THE ELECTRIC MOONCHILLUM** (b. TOBY PASCOE) – percussion, vocals; repl. ELMO

Heavenly — not iss.

Oct 90. (12") *(HVN 5-12)* **GET HIGHER. / ('A'-rather large in the Bristol area mix) / ('A'-dub mix by Mark Lusardi)** [ ] [-]

Pop God — not iss.

Jan 91. (12"etched) *(PGTT 003)* **WARSHAG** [ ] [-]
May 91. (7"etched) *(PGTT 7)* **FIRE** [ ] [-]
(12"+=) *(PGTT 7)* – Bring me down gently / I want to chill your.
Oct 91. (12"ep) *(PGTT 010)* **THE GROOVEPOWER BIG FAST DUB EP** [ ] [-]
– Big / Fast / Dub.
Dec 91. (cd/lp) *(PG CD/LP 012)* **HASH SMITS** [ ] [-]
May 92. (12"ep/cd-ep) *(PG TT/CD PGTT 15)* **TIGHTEN UP ON THE HOUSEWORK BROTHERS AND SISTERS EP** [ ] [-]
– Tighten up / Housework / Brothers and sisters.
Nov 92. (12"ep/cd-ep) *(PGTT 023)* **THE COVERS EP** [ ] [-]
– I've just got to be discoman today / Armageddon time / Tighten up / Norwegian wood.

— **GINA GRIFFIN** – violin, viola, vocals; repl. POPE

Jun 93. (cd/c/lp) *(PG CD/MC/LP 025)* **FROM WHALES TO JUPITER BEYOND THE STARS OF RAINBOWHEMIA** [ ] [-]
– There we will find the sun / Conitations / Summer long / Goldmine / UG / Come by ours, love / Smile and the face of evil and dance / Planet Dodo / Serpents of the deep / Share your good love / Jupiter / Dream lovers.
May 95. (12"ep/cd-ep) *(PG TT/CD 032)* **SHAKE IT TOGETHER / SOUL HEAVY. / DUB IT TOGETHER / I WOULD LIKE TO SEE EGYPT ONE OF THESE DAYS** [ ] [-]
May 95. (cd/d-lp) *(PG CD/LP 034)* **WE WOULD FLY AWAY (WE COULD FLY AWAY NEVER LOOK BACK AND LEAVE THE WORLD TO SPIN SILENTLY IN A SUICIDE PACT AND ALL THE COLOURS AND SOUNDS THAT PASS THROUGH US IN SPACE FALL DOWN TO THE EARTH AND PUT A SMILE ON IT'S FACE)** [ ] [-]
– Future alien / What is going to happen? / The Nopar king / World leaves the world / Shake it together / The revolution / Path of the free / Whitebird / Sun and Moon / The winkstress / I have a friend / Too much love / Colours and sounds / Keepers of the fire / The world's most famous unknown people.

— disbanded later in '95

MOONSHAKE (see under ⇒ WOLFHOUNDS)

Thurston MOORE (see under ⇒ SONIC YOUTH)

MOOSE

Formed: London, England ... Spring 1990 by RUSSELL YATES, KEVIN 'MOOSE' McKILLOP and DAMIEN WARBURTON (LINCOLN FONG was to become a member mid '91 after short-lived recruit MICK CONROY decamped to STEREOLAB). One of the prime movers in the shoegazing scene of the early 90's, MOOSE stood out from the glacial-guitar pack by dint of their country/folk stylings; the initial three debut EP's ('THE JACK', 'COOL BREEZE' and 'REPRISE') suggested hints of what was to come although it was 1992's impressive 'XYZ' album – released on 'Virgin' subsidiary, 'Hut' – which had critics reaching for the thesaurus. Produced (partly naked, according to the sleeve!) by US veteran, MITCH EASTER (and augmented by DOLORES from The CRANBERRIES and ROXANNE of Th' FAITH HEALERS), the album combined the obligatory guitarscapes with a rootsy twang and subtle strings. Granted, RUSSELL's rather fey vocal style – pitched somewhere between MORRISSEY and DAMON ALBARN – wasn't exactly an ideal bed partner for the country hoedown of 'SOON IS NEVER ENOUGH' yet it worked just fine on mellower numbers like 'DON'T BRING ME DOWN' and the canter through Fred Neil's 'EVERYBODY'S TALKIN''. Unfortunately for MOOSE, the scene they'd played a large part in forming was already on its last legs by this time and inevitably they ended up taking the same one-way ticket to obscurity as CHAPTERHOUSE, SLOWDIVE, LUSH etc. (although the latter outfit did enjoy a subsequent reincarnation). Recorded for Euro label, 'Play It Again Sam', 1993's 'HONEY BEE' album saw MOOSE move even further away from their indie beginnings yet despite positive press from some loyal critics, both the record and MOOSE themselves sank without trace. • **Trivia:** The PIXIES' KIM DEAL produced their debut single. RUSSELL was also part of STEREOLAB live act in Spring 1991, while McKILLOP does the same for SEE SEE RIDER.

Album rating: XYZ (*8) / HONEY BEE (*6)

RUSSELL YATES – vocals, guitar / **KEVIN McKILLOP** – guitar / **DAMIEN WARBURTON** – drums

Hut — Virgin

Mar 91. (12"ep/cd-ep) *(HUT T/CD 3)* **THE JACK E.P.** [ ] [-]
– Jack / Ballad of Adam and Eve / Boy / I'll take tomorrow.
Jun 91. (7") *(HUT 5)* **SUZANNE. / BUTTERFLY COLLECTOR** [ ] [-]
(12"ep+=/cd-ep+=) **COOL BREEZE** *(HUT T/CD 5)* – Untitled love song / Speak to me.

— **LINCOLN FONG** – bass; repl. MICK CONROY who joined STEREOLAB then formed TREETOP

Nov 91. (7"ep/12"ep/cd-ep) *(HUT/+T/CD 8)* **REPRISE EP** [ ] [-]
– Last night I fell again / This river will never run dry / Do you remember? / Reprise.
Jan 92. (m-cd) *(HUTCD 11)* <96266> **SONNY AND SAM** (1991 ep's) [ ] [ ]

— **RICHARD THOMAS** – drums (ex-JESUS & MARY CHAIN, ex-DIF JUZ) repl. DAMIEN

Aug 92. (7") *(HUT 020)* **LITTLE BIRD (ARE YOU HAPPY IN YOUR CAGE)? / THERE I GO AGAIN** [ ] [-]
(12"+=) *(HUT 020T)* – Theme from 'Ace Conroy'.
(cd-s++=) *(HUT 020CD)* – ZYX.
Sep 92. (cd/c/lp) *(HUT CD/MC/LP 55)* **XYZ** [ ] [-]
– Soon is never soon enough / I'll see you in my dreams / High flying bird / Screaming / Friends / XYZ / Slip & slide / Little bird / Don't bring me down / Polly / The whistling song / Everybody's talking / Sometimes loving is the hardest thing. (cd+=/c+=/free-7"w-lp) – This river is nearly dry (live).

Cool Badge — not iss.

Feb 93. (12"ep/cd-ep) *(CB 001 T/CD)* **LIQUID MAKE-UP EP** [ ] [-]
– I wanted to see you to see if I wanted you / There's a place / Ramon.

— added **ROXANNE STEPHEN, JOE DILWORTH, RUSSELL FONG + STEVEN YOUNG**

Play It Again Sam — not iss.

Sep 93. (12"ep/cd-ep) *(BIAS/+CD 254)* **UPTOWN INVISIBLE / CALL IT WHAT YOU WANT, ANYTHING. / NEVERGREEN / TOWER OF CRUMBS** [ ] [-]
Oct 93. (cd/lp) *(BIAS 260 CD/LP)* **HONEY BEE** [ ] [-]
– Uptown invisible / Meringue / Mondo cane / You don't listen / Joe Courtesy / Asleep at the wheel / I wanted to see you to see if I wanted you / Around the warm bed / Stop laughing / Dress you the same / Hold on. (lp w /free lp)
Mar 94. (12"ep/cd-ep) *(BIAS 264/+CD)* **BANG BANG EP** [ ] [-]
– I wanted to see you to see if I wanted you / Welcome to the mind of Mr. Breeders / Following in my own footsteps / Sexy M.O.R. (take your clothes off).
Feb 96. (cd) *(BIAS 320CD)* **LIVE A LITTLE, LOVE A LOT** [ ] [-]
– Play God / The man who hanged himself / First balloon to Nice / Rubdown / Poor man / Eve in a dream / Old man Time / Love on the dole / So much love so little time / Last of the good old days / Regulo 7.

Johnny MOPED

Born: PAUL HALFORD, Croydon, London, England. PAUL/JOHNNY initially started out in the early 70's playing under various guises: BLACK WITCH CLIMAX BLUES BAND, The GENETIC BREAKDOWN, The ARROGANT SUPERSTARS and JOHNNY MOPED'S ASSAULT AND BUGGERY. The latter numbered RAY BURNS (aka CAPTAIN SENSIBLE) among their rank, The CAPTAIN asking MOPED to support his band The DAMNED after they became more famous. The JOHNNY MOPED outfit also featured more permanent members, the BERK brothers (aka DAVE and FRED), although SENSIBLE's brother PHIL and astonishingly, CHRISSIE HYNDE (later of The PRETENDERS), also passed through briefly. Early in 1977, SLIMEY TOAD became the band's resident guitarist, playing on a the original (very rough!) version of 'HARD LOVIN' MAN' from the infamous V/A live album, 'Live At The Roxy'. Moronic punk'n'roll fusing future 'Chiswick' labelmates, MOTORHEAD with the manic humour of JOHN OTWAY, the latter track a pogo-floor favourite at many a punk disco. The aforementioned London independent were either brave or stupid enough to give the man a break, releasing his/their debut single, 'NO ONE', in the summer of '77. Romantically inclined, or at least in his own mind, MOPED delivered his somewhat mellower follow-up, 'DARLING, LET'S HAVE ANOTHER BABY', a taster from his retrospectively feted debut long-player, 'CYCLEDELIC' (1978). The collection featured his inimitable interpretation of Chuck Berry's R&R classic, 'LITTLE QUEENIE', a laugh a minute for those with a sense of humour, sacrilege for anyone over forty (at the time!). However, HALFORD dismounted his JOHNNY MOPED and subsequently quit the music scene altogether; that is, until 1991, when the outfit played live again and released a comeback album, 'THE SEARCH FOR XERXES' (the name referring to a mysterious early member).

Album rating: CYCLEDELIC (*8) / THE SEARCH FOR XERXES (*5)

JOHNNY MOPED – vocals, organ / **SMILEY TOAD** – guitar, piano / **FRED BERK** – bass, piano, guitar / **DAVE BERK** – drums, percussion / **CAPTAIN SENSIBLE + PHIL BURNS** also contributed

Chiswick | not iss.

Aug 77. (7") *(NS 15)* **NO ONE. / INCENDIARY DEVICE** [ ] [-]

Jan 78. (7") *(NS 27)* **DARLING, LET'S HAVE ANOTHER BABY. / SOMETHING ELSE / IT REALLY DIGS** [ ] [-]

Apr 78. (lp) *(WIK 8)* **CYCLEDELIC** [ ] [-]
– Mystery track / V.D. boiler / Panic button / Little Queenie / Maniac / Darling, let's have another baby / Groovy Ruby / 3D time / Wee wee / Make trouble / Wild breed / Hell razor / Incendiary device. *(some w/ free 7")* – BASICALLY, THE ORIGINAL JOHNNY MOPED TAPE

Jun 78. (7") *(NS 41)* **LITTLE QUEENIE. / HARD LOVIN' MAN** [ ] [-]

—— split after above and DAVE joined The DAMNED to replace RAT SCABIES on tour. SLIMEY TOAD as SLIME issued a single in 1978; 'CONTROVERSIAL'.

—— **CAPTAIN SENSIBLE, KIRSTY MacCOLL** and revived group featured on return album.

Deltic | not iss.

May 91. (cd/lp) **THE SEARCH FOR XERXES** [ ] [-]

– compilations, etc. –

Sep 95. (cd) *Chiswick; (CDWIKD 144)* **BASICALLY (THE BEST OF JOHNNY MOPED)** (all & live) [ ] [-]

MORCHEEBA

Formed: London, England . . . mid 90's by the GODFREY brothers, PAUL and ROSS, who subsequently recruited female singer, SKYE EDWARDS. Launched into musical orbit at roughly the same time as fellow trip-hoppers PORTISHEAD, TRICKY et al., MORCHEEBA offered up a London-centric take on what was still essentially a Bristol-based phenomenon. With a bit of Southern-fried slide guitar thrown in for good measure, MORCHEEBA's paranoid beat collages were even compared to LYNYRD SKYNYRD at one point! Before you start dusting down your old copy of 'Freebird', however, be rest assured that this bunch deal in a musical hybrid throughly 90's in make-up. Blessed with the satin-silk vocals of SKYE, the debut 'IndoChina' album, 'WHO CAN YOU TRUST?' (1996) enjoyed lavish praise among even the most bpm-hardened journos. Liable to lull the listener into a soporific sense of insecurity with its deceptively laid back grooves, MORCHEEBA's edgy trip-hop sound reflected the urban unease of its native environment. Yet this bunch retain a certain warmth and accessibility missing in their contemporaries, an obvious fondness for folk, blues and vintage hammond grooves occasionally melting the glacial veneer of icy coolness. Autumn '96 saw the band's first Top 40 success with a re-released 'TRIGGER HIPPIE', a series of festival appearances and a growing fanbase seeing follow-up album, 'BIG CALM' make the UK Top 20. Another consumate collection of sculptured soundscapes infused with a healthy helping of pastoral strumming, the album garnered universal praise and was high on the year-end lists of many critics and music fans alike.

Album rating: WHO CAN YOU TRUST? (*7) / BIG CALM (*8)

SKYE EDWARDS – vocals / **PAUL GODFREY** – programming, scratching, live drums, lyrics / **ROSS GODFREY** – guitars, sitar, keyboards, synthesizer, bass / plus **PETE NORRIS** – synthesizer programming

China | not iss.

Feb 96. (c-s) *(WOKMC 2081)* **TRIGGER HIPPIE /** [ ] [-]
(12"+=/cd-s+=) *(WOK T/CD 2081)* –

Indochina | Discovery

Apr 96. (12"/cd-s) *(INDO 44 T/CD)* **NEVER AN EASY WAY (mixes)** [ ] [-]

Apr 96. (cd/c/lp) *(ZEN 009 CD/MC/LP)* <77050> **WHO CAN YOU TRUST?** [ ] [ ] Sep96
– Moog Island / Trigger hippie / Post houmous / Tape loop / Never an easy way / Howling / Small town / Enjoy the wait / Col / Who can you trust? / Almost done / End theme. *(re-dist.Apr97 hit No.70) (cd re-iss. Nov97 / US=Dec98 on 'Sire'+= 'BEATS AND B-SIDES'; ZEN 009CDX)<31049>* – Killer hippie / On the Rhodes again / Tape loop / Dungeness / Baby sitar / Ray payola / Shoulder holster / Post houmous.

Jul 96. (c-s/cd-s) *(INDO 45 MC/CD)* **TAPE LOOP (mixes)** [42] [-]

Oct 96. (c-s/cd-s) *(INDO 52 MC/CD)* **TRIGGER HIPPIE / TRIGGER HIPPIE (mix) / THE SEA** [40] [-]
(cd-s) *(INDO 52CDR)* – ('A'remixes).

Indochina | China-Sire

Feb 97. (c-s) *(INDO 54MC)* <35001> **THE MUSIC THAT WE HEAR (MOOG ISLAND) / (Arthur Baker mix)** [47] [ ] Dec97
(cd-s+=) *(INDO 54CD)* – ('A'-Omni Trio mix).
(cd-s) *(IDO 54CDR)* – ('A'remixes).

Sep 97. (c-s/cd-s) *(IDO 64 MC/CD)* **SHOULDER HOLSTER / ('A'-Diabolical Brothers mix) / ('A'instrumental) / Payola (Curly Wurly mix)** [53] [ ]
(cd-s) *(IDO 64CDX)* – ('A'side) / ('A'-DJ Swamp mix) / ('A'-Rolling Boulder mix) / ('A'-Nation Of Teflon Souls mix) / ('A'-Low Pressure mix).

Feb 98. (cd-s) *(IDO 66CD)* **THE SEA /** [ ] [-]

Mar 98. (cd/c/lp) *(ZEN 017 CD/MC/LP)* <31020> **BIG CALM** [18] [ ]
– The sea / Shoulder holster / Part of the process / Blindfold / Let me see / Bullet proof / Over and over / Friction / Diggin' a watery grave / Fear and love / Big calm.

Mar 98. (ltd;12"ep/pic-cd-ep) *(IDO 70 T/CD)* **BLINDFOLD / THE SEA / THREE ORANGE WHIPS** [56] [ ]

Indochina | WEA

Jun 98. (c-s) *(IDO 76C)* <42387> **LET ME SEE / LET ME SEE (Magnus Fiennes mix) / DON'T LET IT GET YOU DOWN** [46] [ ] Nov98
(cd-s+=) *(IDO 76CD)* – ('A'-Talvin Singh mix).
(cd-s) *(IDO 76CDX)* – (first & third track) / ('A'mix by Reflections Eternal, Circa 1963 & QD 111) / Trigger hippie (live CD-Rom).

China | Indochina

Aug 98. (c-s) *(WOKMC 2097)* **PART OF THE PROCESS / THE DYSLEXIC PORN STAR WHO FUNKED IN HER SPACE** [38] [ ]
(12"+=/cd-s+=) *(WOK T/CD 2097)* – ('A'-The Americruiser Morfeedback mix).

Dec 98. (c-s) *(WOKMC 2102)* <2101> **SUMMERTIME /** [ ] [ ]
(cd-s+=) *(WOKCD 2102)* –

MORPHINE

Formed: Boston, Massachusetts, USA . . . 1990 out of TREAT HER RIGHT by MARK SANDMAN and DANA COLLEY, who subsequently added drummer JEROME DUPREE. Certainly not your average Boston indie band, MORPHINE employed a musical set-up that defied standard rock convention; while SANDMAN offered up subtle, often treated vocals and a pioneering two-string bass played like a bottleneck guitar, COLLEY contributed breathless baritone/tenor sax over DUPREE's spare, jazzy backbeat. The trio quickly made their mark with an independently released US-only debut album, 'GOOD' (1992), the record drawing across the board praise from America's alternative media network and resulting in a long term deal with 'Rykodisc'. The label subsequently gave it a new lease of life as well as releasing the set in Britain where MORPHINE were also fast rising cult stars. Although new drummer BILLY CONWAY was soon to replace DUPREE, the musical chemistry was even stronger than ever on 1993's follow-up, 'CURE FOR PAIN', another inspired set of avant blues/jazz. Two years on, MORPHINE had the critics intoxicated yet again with, 'YES' (1995) a more spontaneous album that swung between low-key introspection and upfront affirmation. One of the few alt-rock acts to be honoured with a 'DreamWorks' contract (US-only), SANDMAN and Co finally eased their way into chart territory (Top 75) via their fourth album, 'LIKE SWIMMING' (1997).

Album rating: GOOD (*7) / CURE FOR PAIN (*6) / YES (*8) / LIKE SWIMMING (*8) / B-SIDES AND OTHERWISE compilation (*7)

MARK SANDMAN – vocals, 2-string bass (ex-TREAT HER RIGHT) / **DANA COLLEY** – saxophones / **JEROME DUPREE** – drums

not iss. | Accurate-Distortion

Jan 92. (cd) **GOOD** [-] [ ]
– Good / Saddest song / Have a lucky day / You speak my language / You look like rain / Do not go quietly unto your grave / Lisa / Only one / Test tube baby / Shoot'm down / Other side / I know you (pts.1 & 2). *<(cd re-iss. Sep92=US/Jul93=UK & Apr97 on 'Rykodisc'; RCD 10263)>*

Rykodisc | Rykodisc

—— **BILLY CONWAY** – drums (ex-TREAT HER RIGHT) repl. JEROME

Jan 94. (cd/c) *<(RCD/RACS 10262)>* **CURE FOR PAIN** [ ] [ ] Sep93
– Dawna / Buena / I'm free now / All wrong / Candy / Head with wings / In spite of me / Thursday / Cure for pain / Mary, won't you call my name / Let's take a trip together / Sheila / Miles Davis' funeral. *<(cd re-iss. Apr97; same)>*

Jan 94. (cd-s) *<RCD 51033>* **CURE FOR PAIN /** [-] [ ]

Mar 94. (cd-ep) *<(RCD 51035)>* **BUENA / SHAME / MORPHINE PROFILE – INTERVIEW** [ ] [ ]

Mar 94. (7") *<(RA7 1036)>* **THURSDAY. / MARY WON'T YOU CALL MY NAME?** [ ] [ ]
(cd-s+=) *<(RCD5 1036)>* – You look like rain.

Mar 95. (7") *<(RA7 1046)>* **SUPERSEX. / I KNOW YOU** [ ] [ ]
(cd-s+=) *<(RCD5 1046)>* – All wrong.

Apr 95. (cd/c/lp) *<(RCD/RAC/RALP 10320)>* **YES** [ ] [ ]
– Honey white / Scratch / Radar / Whisper / Yes / All your way / Supersex / I had my chance / Jury / Sharks / Free love / Gone for good. *<(cd re-iss. Apr97; same)>*

Jun 95. (7"clear) <*(RA7 1047)*> **HONEY WHITE. / BIRTHDAY CAKE** ☐ ☐
(cd-s+=) <*(RCD5 1047)*> – Lucky day / Sunday afternoon weightlessness.

Rykodisc DreamWorks

Mar 97. (cd/c) *(RCD/RAC 10362)* <*50009*> **LIKE SWIMMING** ☐ 67
– Lilah / Potion / I know you (part 3) / Early to bed / Wishing well / Like swimming / Murder for my money / French lines with pepper / Empty box / Eleven o'clock / Hanging on a curtain / Swing it low.

May 97. (cd-s) *(RCD5 1057)* **MURDER FOR MY MONEY / KEROUAC** ☐ ☐

– compilations, etc. –

Sep 97. (cd) *Rykodisc;* <*(RCD 10387)*> **B SIDES AND OTHERWISE** ☐ ☐
– Have a lucky day (live) / All wrong (live) / I know you (live) / Bo's veranda / Mile high / Shame / Down love's tributaries / Kerouac / Pulled over the car / Sunday afternoon weightlessness / Virgin bride / Mail / My brain.

MORRISSEY

Born: STEPHEN PATRICK MORRISSEY, 22 May'59, Manchester, England. After his bust up with SMITHS guitarist JOHNNY MARR in August '87, MORRISSEY, one of rock music's most intellectually incisive wordsmiths, hastily embarked upon a relatively successful solo career. Remaining with 'E.M.I.', his debut effort, 'VIVA HATE', was subsequently released on the re-activated 'H.M.V.' imprint in Spring '88. With the music co-written by his new producer, STEPHEN STREET, and a backing band that numbered VINI REILLY (guitar, keyboards; ex-DURUTTI COLUMN) and ANDREW PARESI (drums), the album was a strong start, reaching No.2 in the UK charts on the back of the catchy 'SUEDEHEAD' single (incredibly, the singer's first ever Top 5 hit single). Another stand-out track was the lavish melancholy of 'EVERYDAY IS LIKE SUNDAY', arguably his best solo track to date and a song which gave him another Top 10 hit later that summer. Though the album received a relatively warm critical reception, it was, as ever, not without controversy. 'BENGALI IN PLATFORMS' was an ambiguous address to immigrants which he later unsuccessfully attempted to play down while 'MARGARET ON THE GUILLOTINE' was self explanatory, no doubt meeting with a little more empathy. Recruiting a new band composed of NEIL TAYLOR (guitar) and ex-SMITHS', CRAIG GANNON, ANDY ROURKE and MIKE JOYCE, MORRISSEY returned the following year with another couple of fine singles, the playfully coy 'LAST OF THE INTERNATIONAL PLAYBOYS' and 'INTERESTING DRUG', both records going Top 10. The line-up didn't last, however, and he brought in a completely new cast for his next single 'OUIJA BOARD, OUIJA BOARD', a song that suffered scathing reviews in the music press and barely made the Top 20. The following year, a projected album was scrapped although its title, 'BONA DRAG', was retained for an impressive career resume that appeared in late 1990. The collection also contained some new material, notably the grim 'NOVEMBER SPAWNED A MONSTER' and the contentious narrative, 'PICCADILLY PALARE', both released as singles. With a fresh backing group that included ex-MADNESS bassist BEDDERS and MORRISSEY's new writing partner, MARK E. NEVIN (ex-FAIRGROUND ATTRACTION), the singer cut the 'KILL UNCLE' opus. Released in 1991 to mixed reviews, the album failed to deliver on the promise of the earlier singles, although MORRISSEY subsequently recruited a rockabilly backing band: ALAIN WHYTE (guitar), GARY DAY (bass), BOZ BOORER (guitar, ex-POLECATS) and SPENCER COBRIN (drums), touring the album around the world, his first live appearances since the prime of The SMITHS. The tour was largely a success and, enlivened and inspired, MORRISSEY cut the 'YOUR ARSENAL' (1992) set. Produced by MICK RONSON and co-penned with WHYTE, the album took the watered down glam-rock of 'KILL UNCLE' and kickstarted it with some raw rockabilly, resulting in MORRISSEY's highest chart placing for years (No.4). Though the record failed to spawn any major hits, it contained such thoughtful material as 'I KNOW IT'S GONNA HAPPEN SOMEDAY' and 'YOU'RE THE ONE FOR ME, FATTY', the former subsequently covered by DAVID BOWIE, another of MORRISSEY's idols. The same year, MORRISSEY hit the headlines with his scathing criticism of Johnny Rogan, author of the SMITHS biography, 'Morrissey & Marr: The Severed Alliance'. It wasn't the last time the 'Oscar Wilde of Rock' would be in the news, MORRISSEY subsequently losing a well publicised court battle with MIKE JOYCE over unpaid SMITHS royalties. More controversy surrounded the singer following his disastrous appearance at the 1993 'Madstock' concert in London's Finsbury Park. Supporting headliners MADNESS, MORRISSEY was given an extremely hostile reception after coming out draped in a Union Jack, further fuelling debate over the perceived ambiguity of his motivations. Following all this strife, 'VAUXHALL AND I' (1994) resurrected MORRISSEY's career, a sympathetic production by STEVE LILLYWHITE setting the scene for his most considered and consistent album to date. The record was also MORRISSEY's first No.1, a critically acclaimed opus that was marked by more emotionally-charged lyrics, laying off the trademark caustic barbs. Moving to 'R.C.A.', MORRISSEY released 'SOUTHPAW GRAMMER' almost a year later, a bizarre album that focussed on the singer's apparent boxing fixation. Unsurprisingly, the record met with bewilderment from critics, though it consolidated his position as one of rocks few genuine mavericks. In 1997, MORRISSEY once again shifted stables, this time to 'Island' who got their chance to showcase the bard on some new work, 'MALADJUSTED'. • **Covered:** THAT'S ENTERTAINMENT (Jam) / SKIN STORM (Bradford). • **Trivia:** In the late 80's, MORRISSEY made a cameo appearance in Channel 4's 'Brookside' off-shoot, 'South'.

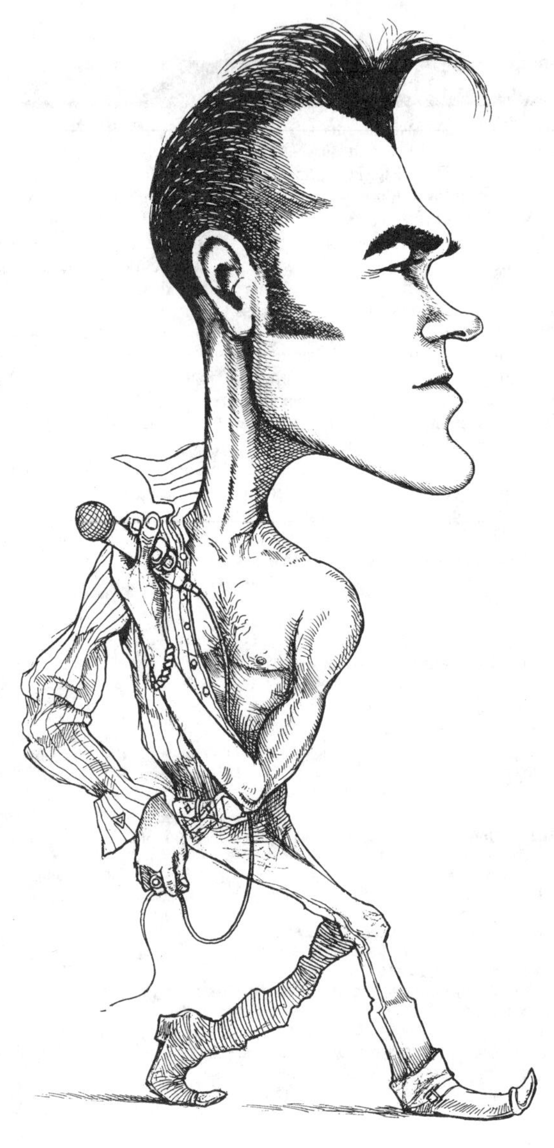

Album rating: VIVA HATE (*9) / KILL UNCLE (*8) / YOUR ARSENAL (*8) / VAUXHALL AND I (*9) / SOUTHPAW GRAMMAR (*6)

MORRISSEY – vocals (ex-SMITHS) with **STEPHEN STREET** – guitar, bass, producer, co-writer / **ANDREW PARESI** – drums / **VINI REILLY** – guitar, keyboards (of DURUTTI COLUMN)

H.M.V. Sire

Feb 88. (7") *(POP 1618)* **SUEDEHEAD. / I KNOW VERY WELL HOW I GOT MY NAME** 5 ☐
(12"+=) *(12POP 1618)* – Hairdresser on fire.
(c-s++=/cd-s++=) *(TC/CD POP 1618)* – Oh well, I'll never learn.

Mar 88. (cd/c/lp) *(CD/TC+/CDS 3787)* <*25699*> **VIVA HATE** 2 48
– Alsatian cousin / Little man, what now? / Everyday is like Sunday / Bengali in platforms / Angel, angel, down we go together / Late night, Maudlin Street / Suedehead / Break up the family / The ordinary boys / I don't mind if you forget me / Dial-a-cliche / Margaret on the guillotine. *(re-iss. Mar94 on 'Parlophone' cd/c; same) (cd re-iss. Mar97 on 'E.M.I.'+=; CDCNTAV 2)* – Let the right one slip in / Pashernate love / At amber / Disappointed (live) / Girl least likely to / I'd love to / Michael's bones / I've changed my plea to guilty.

Jun 88. (7") *(POP 1619)* **EVERYDAY IS LIKE SUNDAY. / DISAPPOINTED** 9 ☐
(12"+=) *(12POP 1619)* – Sister I'm a poet.
(c-s++=/cd-s++=) *(TC/CD+/POP 1619)* – Will never marry.

— **MORRISSEY** only retained **STREET.** He brought in **NEIL TAYLOR** – guitar and re-united with (ex-SMITHS):- **CRAIG GANNON, ANDY ROURKE + MIKE JOYCE**

Feb 89. (7") *(POP 1620)* **THE LAST OF THE FAMOUS INTERNATIONAL PLAYBOYS. / LUCKY LIPS** 6 ☐
(12"+=/cd-s+=) *(12/CD POP 1620)* – Michael's bones.

Apr 89. (7"/etched-12") *(POP/12POPS 1621)* **INTERESTING DRUG. / SUCH A LITTLE THING MAKES SUCH A BIG DIFFERENCE** 9 ☐
(c-s+=/12"+=/cd-s+=) *(TC/12/CD POP 1621)* – Sweet and tender hooligan (live).

— He brought in complete new line-up:- **KEVIN ARMSTRONG** – guitar / **MATTHEW SELIGMAN** – bass / **STEVE HOPKINS** – drums and returning **ANDREW PARESI** – keyboards

Nov 89. (7") *(POP 1622)* **OUIJA BOARD, OUIJA BOARD. / YES, I AM BLIND** 18 ☐
(c-s+=/12"+=/cd-s+=) *(TC/12/CD POP 1622)* – East west.

— **ANDY ROURKE** returned to repl. SELIGMAN + HOPKINS / added guest **MARY MARGARET O'HARA** – vocals (up & coming solo artist)

Apr 90. (c-s/7") *(TC+/POP 1623)* **NOVEMBER SPAWNED A MONSTER. / HE KNOWS I'D LOVE TO SEE HIM** 12
(12"+=/cd-s+=) *(12/CD POP 1623)* – The girl least likely to.

Oct 90. (c-s/7") *(TC+/POP 1624)* **PICCADILLY PALARE. / GET OFF THE STAGE** 18
(12"+=/cd-s+=) *(12/CD POP 1624)* – At amber.

Oct 90. (cd/c/lp) *(CD/TC+/CSD 3788) <26221>* **BONA DRAG** 9 59
– Piccadilly palare / Interesting drug / November spawned a monster / Will never marry / Such a little thing makes such a big difference / The last of the famous international playboys / Ouija board, ouija board / Hairdresser on fire / Everyday is like Sunday / He knows I'd love to see him / Yes, I am blind / Lucky lisp / Suedehead / Disappointed. *(re-iss. Mar94 on 'Parlophone' cd/c; same)*

— He now retained **ANDREW PARESI.** Newcomers were **BEDDERS** – bass (ex-MADNESS) / **MARK E.NEVIN** – guitars, co-composer (ex-FAIRGROUND ATTRACTION) plus **STEVE HEART + SEAMUS BEAGHAN** – keyboards / **NAWAZISH ALI KHAN** – violin

Feb 91. (c-s/7") *(TC+/POP 1625)* **OUR FRANK. / JOURNALISTS WHO LIE** 26
(12"+=/cd-s+=) *(12/CD POP 1625)* – Tony the pony.

Feb 91. (cd/c/lp) *(CD/TC+/CSD 3789) <26514>* **KILL UNCLE** 8 52 Mar91
– Our Frank / Asian rut / Sing your life / Mute witness / King Leer / Found found found / Driving your girlfriend home / The harsh truth of the camera eye / (I'm) The end of the family line / There's a place in Hell for me and my friends.

— His tour band Spring '91; **ALAIN WHYTE** – guitar / **GARY DAY** – bass / **BOZ BOORER** – guitar (ex-POLECATS) / **SPENCER COBRIN** – drums

Apr 91. (c-s/7") *(TC+/POP 1626)* **SING YOUR LIFE. / THAT'S ENTERTAINMENT** 33
(12"+=/cd-s+=) *(12/CD POP 1626)* – The loop.

Jul 91. (c-s/7") *(TC+/POP 1627)* **PREGNANT FOR THE LAST TIME. / SKIN STORM** 25
(12"+=/cd-s+=) *(12/CD POP 1627)* – Cosmic dancer (live) / Disappointed (live).

Oct 91. (c-s/7") *(TC+/POP 1628)* **MY LOVE LIFE. / I'VE CHANGED MY PLEA TO GUILTY** 29
(12"+=/cd-s+=) *(12/CD POP 1628)* – There's a place in Hell for me and my friends.

late 91. (cd-ep) **MORRISSEY AT KROQ (live)** –
– There's a place in Hell for my friends / My love life / Sing your life.

May 92. (c-s/7") *(TC+/POP 1629)* **WE HATE IT WHEN OUR FRIENDS BECOME SUCCESSFUL. / SUEDEHEAD** 17
(12"+=) *(12POP 1629)* – Pregnant for the last time.
(cd-s+=) *(CDPOP 1629)* – I've changed my plea to guilty.

Jul 92. (c-s/7") *(TC+/POP 1630)* **YOU'RE THE ONE FOR ME, FATTY. / PASHERNATE LOVE** 19
(12"+=/cd-s+=) *(12/CD POP 1630)* – There speaks a true friend.

Jul 92. (cd/c/lp) *(CD/TC+/CSD 3790) <26994>* **YOUR ARSENAL** 4 21
– You're gonna need someone on your side / Glamorous glue / We'll let you know / The National Front disco / Certain people I know / We hate it when our friends become successful / You're the one for me, Fatty / Seasick, yet still docked / I know it's gonna happen someday / Tomorrow.

Dec 92. (c-s/7") *(TC+/POP 1631)* **CERTAIN PEOPLE I KNOW. / JACK THE RIPPER** 35
(12"+=/cd-s+=) *(12/CD POP 1631)* – You've had her.

Parlophone E.M.I.

May 93. (cd/c/lp) *(CD/TC+/CSD 3791) <89061>* **BEETHOVEN WAS DEAF (live)** 13
– You're the one for me, Fatty / Certain people I know / National Front disco / November spawned a monster / Seasick, yet still docked / The loop / Sister I'm a poet / Jack the ripper / Such a little thing makes such a big difference / I know it's gonna happen someday / We'll let you know / Suedehead / He knows I'd love to see him / You're gonna need someone on your side / Glamorous glue / We hate it when our friends become successful. *(re-iss. Sep94 on 'Parlophone' cd/c; same)*

— **BOZ BOORER + ALAIN WHYTE** – guitars / **JONNY BRIDGEWOOD** – bass / **WOODIE TAYLOR** – drums

Parlophone Sire

Mar 94. (c-s/7") *(TCR/R 6372) <18207>* **THE MORE YOU IGNORE ME, THE CLOSER I GET. / USED TO BE A SWEET BOY** 8 46
(12"+=/cd-s+=) *(12R/CDR 6372)* – I'd love to.

Mar 94. (cd/c/lp) *(CD/TC+/PCSD 148) <45451>* **VAUXHALL AND I** 1 18
– Now my heart is full / Spring-heeled Jim / Billy Budd / Hold on to your friends / The more you ignore me, the closer I get / Why don't you find out for yourself / I am hated for loving / Lifeguard sleeping, girl drowning / Used to be a sweet boy / The lazy sunbathers / Speedway.

Jun 94. (c-s/7") *(TCR/R 6383)* **HOLD ON TO YOUR FRIENDS. / MOONRIVER** 47
(12"/cd-s) *(12R/CDR 6383)* – (extended versions).

Aug 94. (c-s/7"; by MORRISSEY and SIOUXSIE) *(TCR/R 6365)* **INTERLUDE. / ('A'extended)** 25
(12"+=/cd-s+=) *(12R/CDR 6365)* – ('A'mix).

Jan 95. (c-s/7") *(TC+/R 6400)* **BOXERS. / HAVE-A-GO MERCHANT** 23
(12"+=/cd-s+=) *(12/CD R 6400)* – Whatever happens, I love you.

Feb 95. (cd/c/lp) *(CD/TC+/PCSD 163) <45879>* **WORLD OF MORRISSEY** (part compilation) 15
– Whatever happens, I love you / Billy Budd / Jack the ripper (live) / Have-a-go merchant / The loop / Sister I'm a poet (live) / You're the one for me, Fatty (live) / Boxers / Moon river (extended) / My love life / Certain people I know / The last of the famous international playboys / We'll let you know / Spring-heeled Jim.

— **SPENCER JAMES COBRIN** – drums repl. WOODIE

RCA Victor RCA Victor

Aug 95. (7"/c-s) *(74321 29980-7/-4)* **DAGENHAM DAVE. / NOBODY LOVES US** 26
(cd-s+=) *(74321 29980-2)* – You must please remember.

Aug 95. (cd/c/lp) *(74321 29953-2/-4/-1) <45939>* **SOUTHPAW GRAMMAR** 4 66
– The teachers are afraid of the pupils / Reader meet author / The boy racer / The operation / Dagenham Dave / Do your best and don't worry / Best friend on the payroll / Southpaw.

Nov 95. (7") *(74321 33294-7)* **THE BOY RACER. / LONDON (live)** 36
(cd-s) *(74321 33295-2)* – Billy Budd (live).
(cd-s) *(74321 33294-2)* – ('A'side) / Spring heeled Jim (live) / Why don't you find out for yourself (live).

Parlophone Capitol

Dec 95. (c-s/7") *(TC+/R 6243)* **SUNNY. / BLACK-EYED SUSAN** 42
(cd-s+=) *(CDR 6243)* – A swallow on my neck.

Island Polygram

Jul 97. (c-s/7") *(C+/IS 667)* **ALMA MATTERS. / I CAN HAVE BOTH** 16
(12"+=/cd-s+=) *(12IS/CID 667)* – Heir apparent.

Aug 97. (cd/c/lp) *(CID/ICT/ILPS 8059) <536036>* **MALADJUSTED** 8 61
– Maladjusted / Alma matters / Ambitious outsiders / Trouble loves me / Papa Jack / Ammunition / Wide to receive / Roy's keen / He cried / Satan rejected my soul.

Oct 97. (c-s/7") *(C+/IS 671)* **ROY'S KEEN. / LOST** 42
(12"+=/cd-s+=) *(12IS/CID 671)* – The edges are no longer parallel.

Dec 97. (c-s/7") *(C+/IS 686)* **SATAN REJECTED MY SOUL. / NOW I AM I WAS** 39
(cd-s+=/12"+=) *(CID/12IS 686)* – This is not your country.

– compilations, etc. –

Sep 97. (cd/c/lp) *E.M.I.; (<CD/TC+/EMC 3771>)* **SUEDEHEAD (THE BEST OF MORRISSEY)** 26
– Suedehead / Interesting drug / Boxers / Last of the famous international playboys / Sunny / Tomorrow / Interlude / Everyday is like Sunday / Hold on to your friends / My love life / Our Frank / Piccadilly palare / Ouija board, ouija board / You're the one for me, fatty / We hate it when our friends become successful / Pregnant for the last time / November spawned a monster / The more you ignore me, the closer I get / That's entertainment. *(special edition; CDEMCX 3771)*

Elton MOTELLO

Born: ALAN WARD, London, England. A one-time member of BASTARD (which included noneother than soon-to-be DAMNED guitarist, BRIAN JAMES), WARD changed his stage name to ELTON MOTELLO and released a one-off Belgian-only single, 'JET BOY JET GIRL', at the tail end of '77. While MOTELLO's version sank without trace, PLASTIC BERTRAND would subsequently take the track into the UK Top 10 early the following year as 'Ca Plane Pour Moi'. Roping in a cast of backing musicians who included ex-PINK FAIRIES and PRETTY THINGS drummer, TWINK, ELTON continued to record in Belgium, putting together the album 'VICTIM OF TIME' (1979). With a fresh bunch of sidemen, the singer worked on a follow-up set, 'POP ART', released this time around in North America and Britain. In the event, it proved to be MOTELLO's final effort despite never having had a proper UK release to his name.

Album rating: VICTIM OF TIME (*5) / POP ART (*5)

ELTON MOTELLO – vocals (ex-BASTARDS) / with session people

Pinball not iss.

Dec 77. (7") *(6.12186)* **JET BOY JET GIRL. / POGO POGO** – – Belgian
(UK-iss.Feb78 on 'Lightning'; LIG 508)

— now with **PETER GOFF** – guitar / **WILLIE CHANGE** – bass / **NOBBY GOFF** – drums / + guests **JET STAXX** – guitar / **TONY BOAST** – guitar / **TWINK** – drums (ex-PINK FAIRIES, ex-PRETTY THINGS)

Mar 79. (lp) *(623650)* **VICTIM OF TIME** – – Belgian
– Victim of time / I am the marshall / Jet boy jet girl / He's a rebel / He's crying / Pipe line / Get the guy / Tuttie fruttie Teen pimp / Sha la la la lee / Artificial incemination / Pogo pogo / Apocalipstic.

— with **MIKE BUTCHER** – guitar / **ANDREW GOLDBERG** – keyboards / **J.P. MARTINS** – bass, guitar / **WALTER METER** – drums

Edge Passport

Jan 80. (lp) *(HOB 1) <PB 9846>* **POP ART** Jan81
– Pop art / In the heart of the city / Queen / Pocket calculator / When all the boys are English / Out of limit / Night sister / Falling like a domino / Can't explain / Pay the radio / Out cast / 20th century fox.

Oct 80. (7") *(EDGE 4)* **20th CENTURY FOX. / FALLING LIKE A DOMINO** –

Nov 80. (7") *<PS 7920>* **POP ART. / 20th CENTURY** –

— ELTON/ALAN retired from the music business

MOTHER LOVE BONE (see under ⇒ PEARL JAM)

MOTOR BOYS MOTOR (see under ⇒ SCREAMING BLUE MESSIAHS)

MOTORCYCLE BOY

Formed: East Kilbride, Scotland ... early 1985 as MEAT WHIPLASH (named after a FIRE ENGINES b-side!) by PAUL McDERMOTT, MICHAEL KERR (also part-time with JESSE GARON & THE DESPERADOS), EDDY CONNOLLY and STEPHEN McLEAN. They signed to Alan McGee's 'Creation' independent, supporting The JESUS & MARY CHAIN while the REID brothers produced their one and only single, 'DON'T SLIP UP'. All but STEPHEN resurfaced as MOTORCYCLE BOY (after the hero in cult film, 'Rumblefish') a few years later and, with the recruitment of female, ALEX TAYLOR (ex-SHOP ASSISTANTS) on vocals and SCOTTIE on aggressive guitar, they became a big signing for 'Rough Trade'. However, the band moved on up to 'Chrysalis', having only issued one single, 'BIG ROCK CANDY MOUNTAIN', in 1987. For a few years little was heard from ALEX's wonderful vocals until 1989 brought forth two singles, 'TRYING TO BE KIND' and 'YOU AND ME AGAINST THE WORLD', both taken from their one and only album, 'SCARLET'.

Album rating: SCARLET (*5)

MEAT WHIPLASH

PAUL McDERMOTT – vocals, percussion / **MICHAEL KERR** – guitar / **EDDY CONNOLLY** – bass / **STEPHEN McLEAN** – drums

Creation | not iss.

Sep 85. (7") *(CRE 020)* **DON'T SLIP UP. / HERE IT COMES** | | –

MOTORCYCLE BOY

— added **ALEX TAYLOR** – vocals (ex-SHOP ASSISTANTS)

— **SCOTTIE** (b. DAVID SCOTT) – guitar; repl. STEPHEN

Rough Trade | not iss.

Sep 87. (7") *(RT 210)* **BIG ROCK CANDY MOUNTAIN. /** | | –
(12"+=) *(RTT 210)* –

Chrysalis | not iss.

Jun 89. (7") *(CHS 3310)* **TRYING TO BE KIND. / THE WORLD FALLS INTO PLACE** | | –
(12"+=) *(CHS12 3310)* – ('A'version) / Will you love me tomorrow.

Sep 89. (7") *(CHS 3398)* **YOU AND ME AGAINST THE WORLD. / UNDER THE BRIDGE** | | –
(12"+=) *(CHS12 3398)* – Some girls.

Sep 89. (lp/c/cd) *(CHR/ZCHR/CCD 1689)* **SCARLET** | | –

Nymphaea Pink | not iss.

Apr 90. (12") *(NPST 001)* **THE ROAD GOES ON FOREVER. /** | | –

— split for the rest of the 90's, TAYLOR became a "real" shop assistant

MOTORS

Formed: London, England . . . early 1977 by NICK GARVEY and RICKY WERNHAM, out of the ashes of The SNAKES. The pair united with BRAM TCHAIKOVSKY and GARVEY's ex-DUCKS DELUXE songwriting sidekick, ANDY McMASTERS (DUCKS DELUXE had released two albums in the mid-70's, 'Ducks Deluxe' and 'Taxi To The Terminal Zone') to kickstart The MOTORS. Following a debut gig at The Marquee that March, the band were signed to Richard Branson's 'Virgin' label, releasing their first 45 in September, 'DANCING THE NIGHT AWAY'. Although a UK Top 50 hit, it would be another year before this New Wave pub-rock combo went into top gear with the keyboard-heavy chartbusting smash, 'AIRPORT'. During this breakthrough period, The MOTORS also cruised into the album charts with both 'MOTORS 1' (1977) and 'APPROVED BY THE MOTORS' (1978), the latter featuring the aforementioned 'AIRPORT' and another major hit 'FORGET ABOUT YOU' (which was a tad reminiscent of the Grandstand TV sports theme at the time!). With the band now basically catering for the pop market, BRAM and RICKY bailed out and were superceded by two Welsh music scene veterans, MARTIN ACE and TERRY WILLIAMS (both ex-MAN!). It was this line-up which would wheel out The MOTORS' final album, 'TENEMENT STEPS' (1980), after which the band were finally consigned to the proverbial scrapyard with GARVEY going solo (one album, 'BLUE SKIES' in '82) and WILLIAMS taking up the drum-stool in the massively successful DIRE STRAITS. • **Trivia:** In 1976, The SNAKES released one single, 'LIGHTS OUT' / 'TEENAGE HEAD', on 'Dynamite' records.

Album rating: MOTORS 1 (*5) / APPROVED BY THE MOTORS (*5) / TENEMENT STEPS (*4) / MOTORS' GREATEST HIT compilation (*5)

NICK GARVEY (b.26 Apr'51, Stoke-On Trent, England) – vocals, guitar / **BRAM TCHAIKOVSKY** (b. PETER BRAMALL) – guitar, vocals / **ANDY McMASTERS** (b.27 Jul'47, Glasgow, Scotland) – bass, vocals / **RICKY WERNHAM** – drums (ex-SNAKES, ex-BAZOOKA JOE)

Virgin | Virgin

Sep 77. (7"/12") *(VS 186/+12)* **DANCING THE NIGHT AWAY. / WHISKEY AND WINE** | 42 |

Sep 77. (lp/c) *(V/TCV 2089) <34924>* **MOTORS 1** | 46 |
– Dancing the night away / Emergency / Whiskey and wine / Bring in the morning light / Freeze / Cold love / Phoney Heaven / Summertime (is calling). *(cd-iss. Oct90; CDV 2089)*

Dec 77. (7") *(VS 194)* **BE WHAT YOU WANNA BE. / YOU BEAT THE HELL OUTTA ME** | | –

Jan 78. (7") **PHONEY HEAVEN. / COLD LOVE** | – |

Apr 78. (7") *(VS 206)* **SENSATION. / THE DAY I FOUND A FIVER** | |

Apr 78. (red-lp/c) *(V/TCV 2101) <35348>* **APPROVED BY THE MOTORS** | 60 |
– Airport / Forget about you / Do you mind / Breathless / Mama rock'n'roller / Today / Soul redeemer / Sensation / Dreaming your life away / You beat the hell outta me. *(re-iss. 1988; OVED 202) (cd-iss. Oct90; CDV 2101)*

Jun 78. (7"/12"blue) *(VS 219/+12)* **AIRPORT. / COLD LOVE (live)** | 4 | –

Jul 78. (7") **AIRPORT. / MAMA ROCK 'N' ROLLER** | – |

Aug 78. (7") *(VS 222)* **FORGET ABOUT YOU. / PICTURAMA** | 13 | –
(12"red+=) *(VS 222-12)* – The middle bit / Soul surrender.

Sep 78. (7") **FORGET ABOUT YOU. / BREATHLESS** | – |

Nov 78. (7") *(VS 236)* **TODAY. / HERE COMES THE HUSTLER** | |

— (Aug'78) **MARTIN ACE** – bass (ex-MAN, etc.) repl. BRAM who formed BATTLEAXE / **TERRY WILLIAMS** – drums (ex-MAN, etc.) repl. RICKY

Feb 80. (10"red-green-blue-yellow) *(VS 263) <67007>* **LOVE AND LONELINESS. / TIME FOR MAKE-UP** | 58 | 78

Mar 80. (lp/c) *(V/TCV 2151) <VA 13139>* **TENEMENT STEPS** | |
– Love and loneliness / Metropolis / Modern man / That's what John said / Tenement steps / Slum people / Here comes the hustler / Nightmare zero.

May 80. (7") *(VS 349)* **THAT'S WHAT JOHN SAID. / CRAZY ALICE** | | –

Sep 80. (7") *(VS 363)* **METROPOLIS. / LOVE ROUND THE CORNER** | | –

— broke-up after above 45. WILLIAMS joined DIRE STRAITS. GARVEY went solo.

– compilations, others, etc. –

Jul 81. (lp/c) *Virgin; (V/TCV 2204)* **MOTORS' GREATEST HIT** | | –
– Dancing the night away / Sensation / Airport / Metropolis / Crazy Alice / Love and loneliness / Forget about you / Emergency / Tenement steps / Today. *(cd-iss. Dec94; CDVM 9032)*

Nov 88. (7") *Old Gold; (OG 9830)* **AIRPORT. / FORGET ABOUT YOU** | | –

NICK GARVEY

— solo, with **GORDON HAAN** – instruments, co-composer / guest **ANGELA TOPPING**

Virgin | not iss.

Jul 82. (7") *(VS 504)* **TAKE A LOOK OVER MY SHOULDER. / THE LION AND ME** | | –

Sep 82. (lp/c) *(V/TCV 2231)* **BLUE SKIES** | |
– So slow / Think / Take a look over my shoulder / Now is the time / Emotional ammunition / Looking at you / Skin / Play the game / Humming / Sometimes / Don't you know.

Bob MOULD (see under ⇒ HUSKER DU)

MOVING TARGETS

Formed: Ipswich, Massachusetts, USA . . . early 80's as the brainchild of KEN CHAMBERS. MOVING TARGETS first made it onto vinyl by contributing a handful of tracks to local V/A album sampler, 'Bands That Would Be God', although it would be some time before the band would record in their own right. Eventually securing a deal with fledgling US indie, 'Taang!', CHAMBERS and Co showcased their blistering punk wares on 1986's 'BURNING IN WATER, DROWNING IN FLAMES'. Despite a postive reception, KEN would pursue a number of side projects, BULLET LAVOLTA being the most high profile. CHAMBERS later reassembled MOVING TARGETS with a new line-up that included guitarist, PAT LEONARD, the band slightly off the mark with a belated follow-up set, 'BRAVE NOISE' (1989). The 'TARGETS mainman began a new decade with yet another line-up that boasted the former rhythm section of JONES VERY, JEFF GODDARD and JAMIE VAN BRAMER, along with guitarist BEN SEGAL (prior to the next recording, 'FALL', another backing team were used). Although CHAMBERS continued to record into the 90's, he gradually phased out the MOVING TARGETS name, releasing 'NO REACTION' (1994) in a solo capacity.

Album rating: BURNING IN WATER, DROWNING IN FLAMES (*7) / BRAVE NOISE (*6) / FALL (*5) / TAKE THIS RIDE (*5) / Ken Chambers: NO REACTION (*4)

KEN CHAMBERS – vocals, lead guitar / **unknown**

What Goes On | Taang!

May 88. (lp) *(GOES ON 14) <TAANG 11>* **BURNING IN WATER, DROWNING IN FLAMES** | | 1986
– The other side / Faith / Let me know why / Shape of somethings / Less than gravity / Almost certain – Drone / Urban dub / Always calling / Underground / MTV / Funtime / This world / Squares and circles. *(re-iss. Nov92 on 'Taang!'; TAANG 11LP)*

— CHAMBERS went into other projects, DRED FOOLE & THE DIN, The GROINOIDS and BULLET LAVOLTA (albums, 'THE GUN DIDN'T KNOW I WAS LOADED' (1992) and 'THE GIFT' (1993)

— **PAT LEONARD** – bass; returned to repl. CHUCK FREEMAN

1989. (lp/cd) *<TAANG 30/+CD>* **BRAVE NOISE** | – |
– Falling / Brave noise / Nothing changes / Things are going by / Car crash / Separate hearts / Instrumental No.3 / In the way / 2500 club / Into the forest / June 7th / Through the door / Lights. *(UK-iss.Mar93; same as US)*

— **CHAMBERS** recruited **JEFF GODDARD** – bass / **JAMIE VAN BRAMER** – drums (both ex-JONES VERY) **BEN SEGAL** – guitar

— now **CHAMBERS, LEONARD + PAT BRADY** – drums / **CHUCK FREEMAN** – bass

Roadrunner | Taang!

May 91. (cd/lp) *(TG 9304-2/-1) <TAANG 54>* **FALL** | |
– Taang intro / Only fun in life / Fumble / Answer / Can you blame me / Travel music / Away from me / No soul / Blind / Once upon a time / Overrated / Awesome sky / Fake it.

— now with **PAT** + new drummer **J. ARCARI**

Plastic Head | Plastic Head

May 93. (7"; by KEN CHAMBERS) *(PHD 001)* **TAKE THIS RIDE. /** | |

Taang! | Taang!

Jun 93. (lp/cd/cd) *<(TAANG 73/+MC/CD)>* **TAKE THIS RIDE** | |
– Last of the angels / Story / A thousand times / Unwind / The right way / Take this ride / Alright / Reason to believe / Take that away / Answer II / Erase / Drown it out.

Jun 93. (cd-ep) **LAST OF THE ANGELS EP** | – |
– Last of the angels / Babble / No quarter / Answer II.

Aug 94. (7"; by KEN CHAMBERS) *<(TAANG 83)>* **ABOVE YOU. / TEMPTATION** | |
(cd-s+=) *<(TAANG 83CD)>* – Jesus Christ superstar / Wiped out / Above you (demo).

— with **JEFF GODDARD** – bass / **GLENN FOSTER BROWN** – keyboards

Nov 94. (cd; by KEN CHAMBERS) *<(T 84CD)>* **NO REACTION** | |
– Smile / No reaction / In between / Above you / Temptation / Too hard to wait / Here and gone / Operation / No sin / Play the blues / Wintergreen.

Stuart MOXHAM & THE ORIGINAL ARTISTS (see under ⇒ YOUNG MARBLE GIANTS)

MUDHONEY

Formed: Seattle, Washington, USA . . . 1988 by MARK ARM (vocals, guitar), STEVE TURNER (guitar), MATT LUKIN (bass) and DAN PETERS (drums). A band boasting impeccable credentials, ARM and TURNER had both graduated from the seminal GREEN RIVER (and The THROWN UPS), while LUKIN had previously been a member of Seattle noisemongers, The MELVINS. With as much a claim to the 'Godfathers of Grunge' crown as labelmates NIRVANA, MUDHONEY released the definitive 'Sub Pop' single in 1988 with 'TOUCH ME I'M SICK'. Arguably one of the few tracks to ever match the primal howl of The STOOGES, the single was a revelation, a cathartically dumb three chord bludgeon with ARM shrieking over the top like a man who was, erm, very sick indeed. A mini-album followed shortly after, the wonderfully titled 'SUPERFUZZ BIGMUFF' (rather disappointingly named after STEVE TURNER's favourite effects pedals, apparently). Visceral, dirty, fuzz-drenched rock'n'roll, this was one of the seminal records of the 80's and the blueprint for "grunge", a term that would later become bastardised to represent a glut of snooze-worthy, sub-metal toss. There was also a deep, underlying sense of unease and melancholy to these songs (especially 'NO ONE HAS' and 'NEED') that gave MUDHONEY an edge over most of their contemporaries, a subsequent cover of SONIC YOUTH'S 'HALLOWEEN' (released as a split single with SONIC YOUTH covering 'TOUCH ME..') sounding positively evil. Given all this, then, the debut album proper, 'MUDHONEY', was regarded as something of a disappointment when it was finally released in late '89. Nevertheless, 'THIS GIFT' and 'HERE COMES SICKNESS' were worth the price of admission alone. By summer '91, MUDHONEY had modified their sound somewhat, releasing the 'LET IT SLIDE' EP as a taster for the forthcoming 'EVERY GOOD BOY DESERVES FUDGE' album (a UK Top 40 hit). The intensity of the EP harked back to 'SUPERFUZZ..', this time with more of a retro garage-punk feel on the blistering 'PAPERBACK LIFE' and 'OUNCE OF DECEPTION'. The album continued in this direction, adding funky (in the loosest sense of the term) hammond organ and harmonica to the mutant guitar buzz. Hell, they even came close to a pop song with 'GOOD ENOUGH'. Following a financial dispute with 'Sub Pop', MUDHONEY followed NIRVANA into the big league, signing with 'Reprise' and releasing the lacklustre 'PIECE OF CAKE' (1992). Having sold their souls to the corporate 'devil', it seemed MUDHONEY had had the life sucked out of them, the rough edges smoothed into a major production gloss. The mini-album, 'FIVE DOLLAR BOB'S MOCK COOTER STEW' (1993) was an improvement but it took Seattle legend, Jack Endino to summon forth the raw spontaneity of old on 'MY BROTHER THE COW' (1995), a return to form of sorts, notably on 'INTO YOUR SCHTIK' and 'GENERATION SPOKESMODEL'. MUDHONEY subsequently took a few years hiatus in which ARM went on tour with his side-project, BLOODLOSS, while TURNER continued with his label, 'Super-Electro' (MUDHONEY were allowed dual output for the imprint) and PETERS guested for solo MIKE JOHNSON (DINOSAUR JR). In the Autumn of '98, the quartet were back once again, although the album, TOMORROW HIT TODAY', disappointed most of their hardcore fanbase. • **Covers:** HATE THE POLICE (Dicks) / EVOLUTION (Spacemen 3) / OVER THE TOP (Motorhead) / PUMP IT UP (Elvis Costello) / TONIGHT I THINK I'M GONNA GO DOWNTOWN (Jimmie Dale Gilmore) / BUCKSKIN STALLION BLUES (Townes Van Zandt). MARK ARM solo:- MASTERS OF WAR (Bob Dylan).

Album rating: SUPERFUZZ BIGMUFF mini (*9) / MUDHONEY (*6) / BOILED BEEF & ROTTING TEETH (*6) / EVERY GOOD BOY DESERVES FUDGE (*7) / PIECE OF CAKE (*5) / MY BROTHER THE COW (*5)

MARK ARM (b.21 Feb'62, California) – vocals, guitar (ex-GREEN RIVER, ex-THROWN UPS) / **STEVE TURNER** (b.28 Mar'65, Houston, Texas) – guitar (ex-GREEN RIVER, ex-THROWN UPS) / **MATT LUKIN** (b.16 Aug'64, Aberdeen, Washington) – bass (ex-MELVINS) / **DAN PETERS** (b.18 Aug'67) – drums

Glitterhouse | Sub Pop

Aug 88. (7",7"brown) *<SP 18>* **TOUCH ME I'M SICK. / SWEET YOUNG THING AIN'T SWEET NO MORE** [-] [ ]

Oct 88. (12"ep) *(GR 0034)* *<SP 21>* **SUPERFUZZ BIGMUFF** [ ] [ ]
– No one has / If I think / In 'n' out of grace / Need / Chain that door / Mudride.

Jan 89. (7",7"clear) *<SP 26>* **('A'side by 'Sonic Youth'). / TOUCH ME I'M SICK** [-] [ ]

Jun 89. (7",7"white) *(GR 060)* *<SP 33>* **YOU GOT IT (KEEP IT OUTTA MY FACE). / BURN IT CLEAN / NEED (demo)** [ ] [ ]
(re-iss. May93; same)

Oct 89. (7",7"purple,12") *(GR 0070)* *<SP 44AA>* **THIS GIFT. / BABY HELP ME FORGET / REVOLUTION** [ ] [ ]
(re-iss. May93; same)

Oct 89 (lp/c/cd) *(GR 0069)* *<SP 44/+A/B>* **MUDHONEY** [ ] [ ]
– This gift / Flat out f***ed / Get into yours / You got it / Magnolia caboose babyshit / Come to mind / Here comes sickness / Running loaded / The further I go / By her own hand / When tomorrow hits / Dead love.

Jun 90. (7",7"pink) *(GR 0102)* *<SP 63>* **YOU'RE GONE. / THORN / YOU MAKE ME DIE** [60] [ ]
(re-iss. May93; same)

Sub Pop | Sub Pop

Jul 91. (7",12"grey) *(SP 15154)* *<SP 95>* **LET IT SLIDE. / OUNCE OF DECEPTION / CHECKOUT TIME** [60] [ ]
(cd-s+=) *(SP 95B)* – Paperback life / The money will roll right in.

Aug 91. (lp/c/cd) *<(SP 160/+A/B)>* **EVERY GOOD BOY DESERVES FUDGE** [34] [ ]
– Generation genocide / Let it slide / Good enough / Something so clear / Thorn / Into the drink / Broken hands / Who you drivin' now / Move out / Shoot the Moon / Fuzzgun '91 / Poking around / Don't fade IV / Check out time.

—— MARK + STEVE took up time in MONKEYWRENCH, and DAN joined SCREAMING TREES, after below album.

Warners | Reprise

Oct 92. (7"/c-s) *(W 0137/+C)* **SUCK YOU DRY. / DECEPTION PASS** [65] [-]
(12"+=/cd-s+=) *(W 0137 T/CD)* – Underride / Over the top.

Oct 92. (cd/c) *<(4509 90073-2/-4)>* **PIECE OF CAKE** [39] [ ]
– No end in sight / Make it now / Suck you dry / Blinding sun / Thirteenth floor opening / Youth body expression explosion / I'm spun / Take me there / Living wreck / Let me let you down / Ritzville / Acetone.

Jan 93. (cd-s) *<40741>* **BLIDING SUN /** [-] [ ]

Oct 93. (m-cd/m-c/m-lp) *<(9362 45439-2/-4)>* **FIVE DOLLAR BOB'S MOCK COOTER STEW** [ ] [ ]
– In the blood / No song III / Between you & me kid / Six two one / Make it now again / Deception pass / Underide.

—— In Mar'94, MUDHONEY released a collab with JIMMIE DALE GILMOUR; 7"yellow/cd-ep 'BUCKSKIN STALLION BLUES' for 'Sub Pop' *(SP 124/305/+CD)* Also a single, 'PUMP IT UP, was released by 'Fox' in April '94

Reprise | Reprise

Mar 95. (cd/c/lp) *<(9362 45840-2/-4/-1)>* **MY BROTHER THE COW** [70] [ ]
– Judgement, rage, retribution and thyme / Generation spokesmodel / What moves the heart? / Today, is a good day / Into yer schtik / In my finest suit / F.D.K. (Fearless Doctor KIllers) / Orange ball-pen hammer / Crankcase blues / Execution style / Dissolve / 1995.

Apr 95. (7") **INTO YOUR SCHTIK. / YOU GIVE ME THE CREEPS** [ ] [ ]
(above single on 'Super Electro')

May 95. (7"colrd/c-s) *(W 0292/+C)* **GENERATION SPOKESMODEL. / NOT GOING DOWN THAT ROAD AGAIN** [ ] [ ]
(cd-s+=) *(W 0292CD)* – What moves the heart live) / Judgement, rage, retribution and thyme (live).

Amphetam. Reptile | Amphetam. Reptile

Aug 95. (7") **GOAT CHEESE. /** [ ] [ ]
(above on 'Amphetamine Reptile' and below on 'Super Electro')

May 98. (ltd-7") *(SE 716)* **NIGHT OF THE HUNTED. / BRAND NEW FACE** [ ] [ ]

Sep 98. (cd) *<(9362 47054-2)>* **TOMORROW HIT TODAY** [ ] [ ]
– A thousand forms of mind / I have to laugh / Oblivion / Try to be kind / Poisoned water / Real low vibe / This is the life / Night of the hunted / Move with the wind / Ghost / I will fight no more forever / Beneath the valley of the underdog.

– compilations, etc. –

Nov 89. (cd-ep) *Tupelo; (TUPCD 009) / Sub Pop; <SP 62>* **BOILED BEEF AND ROTTING TEETH** [ ] [ ]

THE FREEWHEELIN' MARK ARM

Sub Pop | Sub Pop

Feb 91. (7",7"red,7"green) *<(SP 87)>* **MASTERS OF WAR. / MY LIFE WITH RICKETS** [ ] [ ] Dec90

THROWN UPS

STEVE TURNER + MARK ARM + two others

not iss. | Amphetam. Reptile

1987. (7") *<Scale 5>* **FLECH. /** [-] [ ]
1987. (7") *<Scale 7>* **SMILING PANTIES. /** [-] [ ]
1987. (7") *<Scale 9>* **EAT MY DUMP. /** [-] [ ]
1990. (3x7"box) *<Scale 26>* **MELANCHOLY GIRLHOLE** (3 singles boxed) [-] [ ]

Jan 97. (cd) *<AR 55>* **SEVEN YEARS GOLDEN** (compilation) [-] [ ]
– Your band sucks / She's fat / Eat my dump / Flubber mate / Bucking retards / Dude pump / The person in my bowel (is sad) / Fleshy web pit / Elephant crack / My cock is the coin / Hairy crater man / Sparse tits / Smiling panties / Be correct / Melancholy girlhole / Stock boy, superhero / Flech / Lard Butt / Sloppy pud love / Hot lunch / Ladies love me / Scabby like my love / My love is simple / R ladies R bitches / Patty has a problem / Slick lip / Thorp, Thorp.

MONKEYWRENCH

—— **MARK + STEVE** plus **TOM PRICE, TIM KERR + MARTIN BLAND**

Sub Pop | Sub Pop

1992. (cd) *<(SP 129CD)>* **CLEAN AS A BROKE-DICK DOG** [ ] [ ]

MUFFS (see under ⇒ PANDORAS)

MUMPS

Formed: New York City, New York, USA . . . 1977 by LANCE LOUD, alongside songwriter KRISTIAN HOFFMAN, TOBY DUPREY, KEVIN KIELEY and PAUL RUTNER. The toast of the NY punk/New Wave elite, The MUMPS were more infamous for their unhinged stage show than their studio output, although they did manage to release two one-off singles in 1977/78. The first of these, 'CROCODILE TEARS', was jointly issued by Greg Shaw's 'Bomp' label and 'Exhibit', while 'ROCK & ROLL THIS, ROCK & ROLL THAT', appeared on 'Perfect'. A precursor to the likes of The B-52's or REDD KROSS, The MUMPS' infectious update of 70's kitsch was more fully showcased on 1994's 'Eggbert' outtakes/rare/demos compilation, 'FATAL CHARM'.

Album rating: FATAL CHARM compilation (*7)

LANCE LOUD – vocals / **KRISTIAN HOFFMAN** – keyboards (vocalist with the SWINGING MADISONS, ex-JAMES CHANCE) / **TOBY DUPREY** – guitar / **KEVIN KIELEY** – bass / **PAUL RUTNER** – drums

not iss. Bomp-Exhibit

1977. (7") *<BES 1>* **CROCODILE TEARS. / I LIKE TO BE CLEAN** -

not iss. Perfect

1978. (7") *<PR 1>* **ROCK & ROLL THIS, ROCK & ROLL THAT. / MUSCLEBOYS / THAT FATAL CHARM** -

— split in the late 70's after KIELEY + RUTNER departed

– compilations, etc. –

Dec 97. (cd) *Eggbert; <(ER 80011CD)>* **FATAL CHARM** 1994
– I like to be clean / Crocodile tears / Crocodile tears / Rock and roll this, rock and roll that / Muscleboys / Fatal charm / Brain massage / Scream and scream again / Just look, don't touch / Did you get the girl? / Anyone but you / Not again / Awkward age / Before the accident / Forget me not / Teach me / S.O.S. / We ended up / Dutch boy / Stupid / Dance tunes for underdogs / Photogenia / Gimme gimme / Crocodile tears.

MUNDY

Born: EDMUND ENRIGHT, 1976, Birr, Offaly, Ireland (er. . . on a Monday!). Having spent his formative years in a rural backwater of Southern Ireland away from the constant flux of youth culture, ENRIGHT's primary source of inspiration came largely from the 60's vinyl stocked by his local record shop. This was no doubt partly accountable for the initial flurry of acclaim over the freshness of his sound when he emerged as fledgling singer/songwriter, MUNDY, in 1996. Signed to 'Epic' after an A&R chequebook race, MUNDY became routinely mentioned in the same breath as VAN MORRISON, NEIL YOUNG and MIKE SCOTT (of WATERBOYS fame), although it was the latter to which debut single, 'TO YOU I BESTOW' was closest to in spirit. All bold Celtic poetry and lilting romance, the track edged into the UK Top 60 on the initial wave of hype, its B-side featuring a grooved-up cover of Donovan's 'SEASON OF THE WITCH'. Follow-up, 'LIFE'S A CINCH', was also a minor chart hit although the fortunes of the much touted YOUTH-produced debut album, 'JELLY LEGS' (1996), seemed to buckle under the weight of critical and commercial expectation despite showing definite promise.

Album rating: JELLY LEGS (*6)

MUNDY – vocals, guitar / with **STEPHEN FARRELL** – guitars / **SHANE FITZSIMMONS** – bass / **CION O'CALLAGHAN** – drums

Epic Sony

Jul 96. (7"/c-s) *(MUNDY 1 7/MC)* **TO YOU I BESTOW. / SEASON OF THE WITCH** 60 -
(cd-s+=) *(MUNDY 1CD)* – ('A'live).

Sep 96. (7"/c-s) *(MUNDY 2)* **LIFE'S A CINCH. / PUFFY EYES** 75 -
(cd-s+=) *(MUNDY 2CD)* – ('A'mix).

Oct 96. (cd/c) *(MUNDY 3 CD/MC) <67894>* **JELLY LEGS** Feb97
– Reunion / Pardon me / Life's a cinch / Song for my darlin' / Gin and tonic sky / Blown away / To you I bestow / Stone / Springtown / Sisters / Arrow of gold / Private paradise / Mundy in wonderland.

Feb 97. (7"/c-s) *(MUNDY 4 7/MC)* **PARDON ME. / REUNION (live)** -
(cd-s+=) *(MUNDY 4CD)* – To you I bestow (live).

MURDER INC. (see under ⇒ CONNELLY, Chris)

Peter MURPHY (see under ⇒ BAUHAUS)

Pauline MURRAY & INVISIBLE GIRLS (see under ⇒ PENETRATION)

MUSIC FOR PLEASURE

Formed: Leeds, England . . . 1980 by MARK COPSON, DAVE WHITAKER and MARTIN KING, the trio adding ex-GIRLS AT OUR BEST drummer, CHRIS OLDROYD, following the release of their debut 45, 'THE HUMAN FACTOR'. Very much part of the uptempo-electro-pop-with-droning-vocals brigade, MFP delivered a similarly themed follow-up single, 'FUEL TO THE FIRE', before signing a major label deal with 'Polydor'. In 1982, with KING having made way for IVAN ROBERTS, the synth crew issued an inaugural long-player, 'INTO THE RAIN', a more reflective effort mapping out similar territory to OMD and early SIMPLE MINDS. Moving back to the more sympathetic climes of the indie sector, MUSIC FOR PLEASURE began recording for the tiny 'Whirlpool' imprint, releasing a few singles and a mini-album, 'BLACKLANDS' (1986), before calling it a day. Two of their members, WHITAKER and OLDROYD, took up more high profile posts with DANSE SOCIETY and RED LORRY YELLOW LORRY respectively.

Album rating: INTO THE RAIN (*6) / BLACKLANDS mini (*4)

MARK COPSON – vocals / **DAVE WHITAKER** – keyboards, synthesizer / **MARTIN KING** – bass / **. . . PEACE** – guitar / **. . . LEWIS** – drums

Rage-DJM not iss.

Nov 80. (7") *(RAGE 1)* **THE HUMAN FACTOR. / MURDER AT THE MISSION** -

— **CHRIS OLDROYD** – drums (ex-GIRLS AT OUR BEST) repl. LEWIS + PEACE

Feb 81. (7") *(RAGE 2)* **FUEL TO THE FIRE. / DEBRIS** -

— **IVAN ROBERTS** – bass; repl. KING

Polydor not iss.

Jul 82. (7") *(POSP 464)* **SWITCHBACK. / I RECALL** -

Aug 82. (lp/c) *(POLS/+C 1070)* **INTO THE RAIN** -
– Light / Switchback / Nostalgia / Time / New day / Lost detail / Winterscene / Aim to life / Warehouse / Underworld.

Oct 82. (7") *(POSP 533)* **LIGHT. / MALEFICE** -
(12") *(POSPX 533)* – ('A'side) / Nostalgia.

Jan 83. (7") *(POSP 553)* **TIME. / SLIDE** -
(12") *(POSPX 553)* – ('A'side) / Switchback.

May 83. (7") *(POSP 594)* **DARK CRASH. / URBAN POISON** -
(12"+=) *(POSPX 594)* – Blacklands.

Whirlpool not iss.

Jan 84. (7") *(WH 1)* **DISCONNECTION. / WHIPLASH CARESS** -

May 84. (12"ep) *(WH 4)* **CHROME HIT CORROSION** -
– Pleasure ride / Grey parade / Walking / The rise.

Jan 86. (m-lp) *(WHLP 6)* **BLACKLANDS** -
– Remember the sun / Disconnection (part 1) / Look around you / Blue / Whiplash caress / Grey parade / Disconnection (part 2) / Drive.

— had already disbanded before above. WHITAKER joined DANSE SOCIETY while OLDROYD was snapped up by RED LORRY YELLOW LORRY

MUTTON BIRDS

Formed: Auckland, New Zealand . . . 1989 by DON McGLASHAN, a singer-songwriter with Scottish ancestory and former member of various obscure Kiwi outfits including The ERIC GLANDY MEMORIAL BIG BAND. With a line-up initially completed by fellow musical veterans, RUSS BURGE and DAVID LONG, prior to the addition of ALAN GREGG, they debuted with the NZ-only 'HEATER' EP in 1994 (the lead track a highlight from that year's eponymous debut set), revealing them to be darker, more experimental, cinematic cousins of countrymen, CROWDED HOUSE (especially on the haunting 'HE TURNED AROUND'). A further domestic single, 'ANCHOR ME' – lifted from the acclaimed, best selling 'SALTY' album – netted a major songwriting award and amid the ensuing acclaim, The MUTTON BIRDS secured a contract with Virgin subsidiary, 'Dindisc' and a more permanent vacation. Their first long-player for the label, 'NATURE' was compiled from the deep, earthy early recordings on the first two albums, while the aforementioned 'ANCHOR ME' was re-issued as a UK single. 1996 saw the band release a broodingly impressive cover of Blue Oyster Cult's 'DON'T FEAR THE REAPER' (as the B-side to NZ-only single, 'SHE'S BEEN TALKING'); originally recorded for a film by Kiwi director, Peter Jackson, the track became a minor hit in Australia (where the band were signed to 'E.M.I.') and was subsequently tacked on to Aussie and Canadian versions of third album, 'ENVY OF ANGELS' (1997). Recorded at Rockfield studios in Wales, the latter set gave the band their first UK chart placing, scraping into the Top 75. • **Covered:** IT HAPPENED ONE NIGHT (Jody Harris).

Album rating: THE MUTTON BIRDS (*6) / SALTY (*6) / NATURE compilation (*6) / ENVY OF ANGELS (*7) / TOO HARD BASKET compilation (*6)

DON McGLASHAN – vocals, guitar / **RUSS BURGE** – drums / **ALAN GREGG** – bass / **DAVID LONG** – guitar

E.M.I. not iss.

1994. (12"ep) **THE HEATER EP** - - New Z.
– The heater / It happened one night / He turned around / The ballad of Kelvin.

1994. (cd) **THE MUTTON BIRDS** - - New Z.

1994. (7") **ANCHOR ME. / THE HEATER (Careful With . . . version)** - - New Z.

1994. (7") **NGAIRE. / THE QUEEN'S ENGLISH (Annus Horribilis mix)** - - New Z.

1995. (cd) **SALTY** - - New Z.

Dindisc Virgin

Aug 95. (c-s) *(DINSC 148)* **DOMINION ROAD / YOU WILL RETURN** -
(cd-s+=) *(DINSD 148)* – Wellington / Ngaire.

Sep 95. (cd) *(CDVIR 39)* **NATURE** (compilation of first two NZ albums) -
– Nature / Dominion road / Anchor me / The heater / Giant friend / Your window / White valient / In my room / A thing well made / The Queen's English / There's a limit / Too close to the sun.

Feb 96. (c-s) *(DINSC 149)* **ANCHOR ME / ESTHER / DON'T FIGHT IT MARSHA, IT'S BIGGER THAN BOTH OF US** -
(cd-s) *(DINSD 149)* – ('A'side) / When the wind comes round.

1996. (7") **SHE'S BEEN TALKING. / DON'T FEAR THE REAPER** - - New Z.

Feb 97. (c-s) *(DINSC 157)* **COME AROUND / WHEN THE WIND COMES ROUND** -
(cd-s+=) *(DINSD 157)* – Along the boundary / Face in the paper.
(cd-s) *(DINSDX 157)* – ('A'side) / Dominion road / Anchor me.

Jun 97. (cd/c) *(CD/MC VIR 55) <842584-2>* **ENVY OF ANGELS** 64
– Straight to your head / She's been talking / Trouble with you / April / Like this rain / Another morning / Ten feet tall / Come around / Crooked mile / While you sleep / Inside my skin / Envy of angels.

Jun 97. (c-s) *(DINSC 160)* **SHE'S BEEN TALKING / WHITE VALIANT** -
(cd-s+=) *(DINSD 160)* – Inbetween man.
(cd-s) *(DINSDX 160)* – ('A'side) / He turned around / The heater.

– compilations, etc. –

Dec 98. (cd) *Gravy Train; (GRAVY cd2)* **"TOO HARD BASKET" – B SIDES AND BASTARDS** -
– It happened one night / He turned around / The ballad of Kelvin / Three minutes / So long / The heater (careful with . . . version) / The Queen's English (annus horribilis mix) / Cinema of unease – credit music / Don't fear the reaper / Ash Wednesday / Ranchslider / Answerphone / Face in the paper / Inbetween man / Along the boundary.

MX-80 SOUND

Formed: Bloomington, Indiana, USA . . . 1975 by BRUCE ANDERSON, DAVE SOPHIEA and JEFF ARMOUR. Relocating to San Francisco, they were joined by RICH STIM and DAVE MAHONEY, releasing a few low-key singles for a local independent imprint. Signed to a UK deal with 'Island', they issued their debut album, 'HARD ATTACK' in 1977, an experimental New Wave affair that, being American, lay closer in spirit to BEEFHEART or ZAPPA. They resurfaced a further twice in the early 80's on The RESIDENTS, 'Ralph' records with 'OUT OF THE TUNNEL' (1980) and 'CROWD CONTROL' (1981), although little was heard of them since; ANDERSON and SOPHIEA were said to be behind The GIZZARDS, HALF-LIFE and O-TYPE on their 'Quadroped' label. Save for MAHONEY (who was replaced by MARC WEINSTEIN), the original members re-formed MX-80 SOUND in the early 90's and recorded one final album, 'DAS LOVE BOAT'.

Album rating: HARD ATTACK (*7) / OUT OF THE TUNNEL (*6) / CROWD CONTROL (*6) / DAS LOVE BOAT (*4)

RICH STIM – vocals, guitar, keyboards, sax / **BRUCE ANDERSON** – guitar / **DAVE SOPHIEA** – bass / **DAVE MAHONEY** – drums / **JEFF ARMOUR** – drums

not iss. | 6r6q

1976. (7"ep) **BIG HITS – HARD POP FROM THE HOSSIERS** [-] [ ]
– Train to loveland / You turn me on / SCP / Till death do us part / Myonga von Bontee / Boy trouble girl trouble / Tidal wave. *<re-iss. 1977 on 'Gulcher'; GULCH 003>*

Island | not iss.

Oct 77. (lp) *(ILPS 9520)* **HARD ATTACK** [ ] [-]
– Man on the move / Kid stuff / Fascination / Summer 77 / P.C.B.'s / Crushed ice / Tidal wave / Checkmate / Facts – facts / You're not alone / Civilised – Demeyes / Afterbirth – Aftermath. *(UK cd-iss. Apr97 on Atavistic'+=; ALP 30CD)* – BIG HITS EP

— **KEVIN TEARE** – drums repl. ARMOUR (although he left in 1979)

not iss. | Ralph

Mar 80. (7") *<MX 8001S>* **SOMEDAY YOU'LL BE KING. / WHITE KNIGHT** [-] [ ]
Mar 80. (lp) *<MX 8002L>* **OUT OF THE TUNNEL** [-] [ ]
– It's not my fault / Follow that car / Fender bender / I walk among them / Someday you'll be king / Frankie I'm sorry / Gary and Priscilla / Man in a box / Metro-teens.
Dec 80. (7") *<MX 8055-2>* **O TYPE (part 1). / O TYPE (part 2)** [-] [ ]
Mar 81. (lp) *<8102>* **CROWD CONTROL** [-] [ ]
– Face of the Earth / Crowd control / Why are we here / Obsessive devotion / More than good / Night rider / City of fools / Theme from Sisters / Cover to cover / Pharoah's sneakers / Promise of love.

— split after above. STIM entered law school and ANDERSON joined The HENRY KAISER BAND. MX-80 SOUND re-formed, although drummer MAHONEY was replaced by **MARC WEINSTEIN**

not iss. | A&R Enter.

Oct 90. (lp) **DAS LOVE BOAT** [-] [ ]
(UK-iss.Apr97 on 'Atavistic'; ALP 56CD)

– compilations, etc. –

Apr 97. (cd) *Atavistic; (ALP 32CD)* **OUT OF CONTROL** [ ] [ ]
Apr 97. (cd) *Atavistic; (ALP 67CD)* **I'VE SEEN ENOUGH** [ ] [ ]

MY BLOODY VALENTINE

Formed: Dublin, Ireland . . . 1984 by KEVIN SHIELDS and COLM O'CIOSOIG. Later the same year, the pair travelled to Germany where they hooked up with DAVE CONWAY and TINA to record a mini-lp, 'THIS IS YOUR BLOODY VALENTINE', for the small 'Tycoon' records. This was issued the following year although only 50 copies seem to have emerged (now very rare!). They subsequently moved to London, DEBBIE GOODGE replacing TINA for the recording of the 'GEEK!' EP on 'Fever'. After more 45's for 'Kaleidoscope' then 'Lazy' (home of The PRIMITIVES), the band really began to move away from their early twanging, IGGY POP-style sound following a move to 'Creation' in 1988 (masterminded by SLAUGHTER JOE FOSTER, ex-TV PERSONALITIES). With co-"vocalist", BILINDA BUTCHER now also on board, SHIELDS and Co. finally made the breakthrough in 1990 when the 'GLIDER' EP nearly went Top 40 in the UK, hot on the heels of the acclaimed 'ISN'T ANYTHING' (1988) album. The full extent of their pioneering guitar manipulation – responsible for a whole scene of "shoegazing" musical admirers, stand up RIDE, MOOSE, LUSH etc., etc. – was revealed as MBV released their most challenging and inventive track to date in 'TO HERE KNOWS WHEN' (from the Top 30 'TREMOLO' EP). Creating a whole new concept and language of sound, the song either enveloped the listener in blissful noise or just seemed out of bloody tune, there was no middle ground. 'LOVELESS' (1991), MBV's long awaited and much heralded follow-up, was a revelation. Its hypnotic, undulating noisescapes sounded not-of-this-earth and 'Creation' were saddled with an astronomical studio bill to match, almost going bankrupt as a result. They subsequently signed to 'Island' records, and eight (!!!) years on, fans are still awaiting some new product. Although MY BLOODY VALENTINE have arguably been the most influential indie band of the last decade and few doubt their potential to return with a masterpiece, their reclusive silence makes the late Stanley Kubrick appear prolific. Nevertheless, SHIELDS has surfaced occasionally as a remixer, notably for the single release of PRIMAL SCREAM's 'Stuka' and many more. • **Songwriters:** SHIELDS writes most of material, with words after 1987 by BILINDA. Covered MAP REF 41 (Wire). • **Trivia:** A track, 'SUGAR', was given away free with 'The Catalogue' magazine of February '89.

Album rating: THIS IS YOUR BLOODY VALENTINE (*5) / ISN'T ANYTHING (*8) / ECSTASY AND WINE compilation (*7) / LOVELESS (*9)

KEVIN SHIELDS (b.21 May'63, Queens, New York) – guitar, vocals, occasional bass / **DAVE CONWAY** – vocals / **COLM CUSACK** (b. COLM MICHAEL O'CIOSOIG, 31 Oct'64) – drums / **TINA** – keyboards

Tycoon | not iss.

1985. (m-lp) *(ST 7501)* **THIS IS YOUR BLOODY VALENTINE** [-] [-] German
– Forever and again / Homelovin' guy / Don't cramp my style / Tiger in my tank / The love gang / Inferno / The last supper.

— **DEBBIE GOOGE** (b.24 Oct'62, Somerset, England) – bass repl. TINA

Fever | not iss.

Apr 86. (12"ep) *(FEV 5)* **GEEK!** [ ] [-]
– No place to go / Moonlight / Love machine / The sandman never sleeps.
Jun 86. (7") *(FEV 5X)* **NO PLACE TO GO. / MOONLIGHT** [ ] [-]

Kaleidoscope Sound | not iss.

Oct 86. (12"ep) *(KS 101)* **THE NEW RECORD BY MY BLOODY VALENTINE** [ ] [-]
– Lovelee sweet darlene / By the danger in your eyes / On another rainy Sunday / We're so beautiful.

Lazy | not iss.

Feb 87. (7") *(LAZY 04)* **SUNNY SUNDAE SMILE. / PAINT A RAINBOW** [ ] [-]
(12"+=) *(LAZY 04T)* – Kiss the eclipse / Sylvie's head.

— **BILINDA BUTCHER** (b.16 Sep'61, London, England) – vocals, guitar repl. CONWAY

Nov 87. (m-lp) *(LAZY 08)* **ECSTASY** [ ] [-]
– (Please) Lose yourself in me / The things I miss / I don't need you / Clair / (You're) Safe in your sleep / She loves you no less / Strawberry wine / Lovelee sweet darlene.
Nov 87. (12"m) *(LAZY 07)* **STRAWBERRY WINE. / NEVER SAY GOODBYE / CAN I TOUCH YOU** [ ] [-]

Creation | Relativity

Jul 88. (7") *(CRE 055)* **YOU MADE ME REALISE. / SLOW** [ ] [-]
(12"+=) *(CRE 055T)* – Thorn / Cigarette in your bed / Drive it all over me. *(re-iss. Mar90 as cd-ep; CRECD 55)*
Oct 88. (7") *(CRE 061)* **FEED ME WITH YOUR KISSES. / EMPTINESS INSIDE** [ ] [-]
(12"+=) *(CRE 061T)* – I believe / I need no trust. *(re-iss. Mar90 as cd-ep; CRECD 61)*
Nov 88. (lp/cd)(c) *(CRELP 040/+CD)(C-CRELP 040) <1006>* **ISN'T ANYTHING** [ ] [ ]
– Soft as snow (but warm inside) / Lose my breath / Cupid come / (When you wake) You're still in a dream / No more sorry / All I need / Feed me with your kiss / Sue is fine / Several girls galore / You never should / Nothing much to lose / I can see it (but I can't feel it). *(free 7"w/ lp)* – INSTRUMENTAL. / INSTRUMENTAL *<US cd re-iss. 1993 on 'Warners'; 45231>*

Creation | Sire

Apr 90. (7"ep/12"ep)(cd-ep) *(CRE 73/+T)(CRESCD 73) <26313>* **GLIDER** [41] [ ]
– Soon / Glider / Don't ask why / Off your face.
Feb 91. (7"ep/12"ep)(cd-ep) *(CRE 085/+T)(CRESCD 085) <40024>* **TREMOLO** [29] [ ] Apr91
– To here knows when / Swallow / Honey power / Moon song.
Nov 91. (cd/lp)(c) *(CRE CD/LP 060)(C-CRELP 060) <26759>* **LOVELESS** [24] [ ]
– Only shallow / Loomer / Touched / To here knows when / When you sleep / I only said / Come in alone / Sometimes / Blown a wish / What you want / Soon.

— During there long hiatus, KEVIN SHIELDS contributed (1996) to an album 'Beyond The Pale' by EXPERIMENTAL AUDIO RESEARCH. It also featured SONIC BOOM (ex-SPACEMEN 3), KEVIN MARTIN (of GOD) & EDDIE PREVOST (of AMM). Meanwhile, DEBBIE GOOGE teamed up with KATHERINE GIFFORD and MAX CORRADI to form SNOWPONY. Late in 1996, they issued their debut single, 'COME HERE AND SIT ON YOUR DADDY', for 'Rough Trade Singles Club' (45REV 41). The following year, their new label, 'See No Evil', released their follow-up, 'CHOCOLATE' / 'EASY WAY DOWN' (EVIL 002/+CD).

– compilations, others, etc. –

Feb 89. (lp/cd) *Lazy; (LAZY 12/+CD)* **ECSTASY AND WINE** [ ] [-]
– Strawberry wine / Never say goodbye / Can I touch you / She loves you no less / The things I miss / I don't need you / Safe in your sleep / Clair / You've got nothing / Lose yourself in me.

MY LIFE STORY

Formed: London, England . . . 1990 by JAKE SHILLINGFORD and arranger AARON CAHILL. The son of artist/musician parents and cousin of noted producer, Warne Livesey, SHILLINGFORD decided on a course of pop stardom at an early age, forming his first band at high school. Subsequently relocating to London, he secured work as an artist and DJ at Camden's Dingwall's club before hooking up with CAHILL and setting about realising his musical vision of glamorous, orchestral pop set to gritty lyrics. After a couple of years spent writing and performing low profile gigs around the capital, JAKE and Co. finally secured a deal with indie label, 'Mother Tongue'. The winner of a Single Of The Week award in both the NME amd Melody Maker, the debut 'MY LIFE STORY' EP introduced SHILLINGFORD's trademark cockney-style vocals and featured fans' favourite, 'YOU DON'T SPARKLE (IN MY EYES)', released as a single in its own right the following year. The subject of comparisons with everyone from 80's stars, ABC and The BLOW MONKEYS to 90's fops, DIVINE COMEDY and PULP, MY LIFE STORY were hailed as the perfect antidote to grunge scruffiness with the release of their highly praised debut album, 'MORNINGTON CRESCENT', in 1995. Seemingly unable to turn the acclaim into sales, JAKE was on the verge of throwing in the towel when 'Parlophone' came to the rescue, signing the band up and releasing what turned out to be their first Top 40 hit, '12 REASONS WHY I LOVE HER'. A third-time-lucky 'SPARKLE' followed into the Top 40 while JAKE's credentials as a self-styled Prince Of Suave were confirmed with 'THE KING OF KISSINGDOM'. All featured on follow-up album, 'THE GOLDEN MILE' (1997), as did future single, 'STRUMPET', the sad story of a fading groupie. Possibly too contrived to be everyone's cup of tea, MY LIFE STORY nevertheless make for an entertaining listen, especially in the live arena where their grandiose stage show incorporates the full-on orchestral experience.

Album rating: MORNINGTON CRESCENT (*6) / THE GOLDEN MILE (*5)

JAKE SHILLINGFORD (b.15 May'66, Southend, England) – vocals / **AARON CAHILL** – instruments, arrangements / **OLLIE KRAUS** – cello, keyboards / **LUCY WILKINS** – viloin / **BECKI DOE** – violin / **ROXANNA SHIRLEY** – trumpet / **RUTH THOMAS** – trumpet / **MARK BRADLEY** – trumpet / **BEN SPENCER** – saxophone

		Mother Tongue	not iss.
Oct 93.	(12"ep/c-ep/cd-e) *(MOTHER 2 T/MC/CD)* **GIRL A, GIRL B, BOY C / YOU DON'T SPARKLE (IN MY EYES). / STAR COLLIDING / YOU DON'T SPARKLE (BIG SCREEN SOUNDTRACK)**		-
Feb 94.	(7") *(MOTHER 3S)* **FUNNY HA HA. / THE LADY IS A TRAMP**		-
	(12"+=/cd-s+=) *(MOTHER 3 T/CD)* – These words are haunting / Funny peculiar.		
Apr 94.	(7") *(MOTHER 4S)* **YOU DON'T SPARKLE (IN MY EYES). / FIRST PERSON SINGULAR**		-
	(12"+=/cd-s+=) *(MOTHER 4 T/CD)* – Stood amongst friends / You don't sparkle (quintet).		
Jan 95.	(cd/lp) *(MOTHER CD/LP 1)* **MORNINGTON CRESCENT**		-
Jun 95.	(cd-ep) *(MOTHER 5CD)* **MORNINGTON CRESCENT COMPANION EP**		-

—— added **DANNY TURNER** – piano, harpsicord / **PAUL SIEPEL** – bass (ex-DIRECTION) / **SIMON WRAY** – drums, timpani

		Parlophone	Alex
Aug 96.	(c-s/7") *(TC+/R 6442)* **12 REASONS WHY I LOVE HER. / LOVER'S RECIPE**	32	-
	(cd-s) *(CDR 6442)* – ('A'side) / Lady Somerset / Silent screaming / Heaven suitcase.		
Oct 96.	(7"clear) *(R 6450)* **SPARKLE. / EMERALD GREEN**	34	-
	(cd-s+=) *(CDRS 6450)* – Megaphone theology / ('A'-concert hall).		
	(cd-s) *(CDR 6450)* – ('A'side) / Garden fence affair / 17 reasons why I lover her / ('A'-Jazz club).		
Feb 97.	(7") *(R 6457)* <6052> **THE KING OF KISSINGDOM. / A BOY CALLED DAYDREAM**	35	Apr98
	(cd-s+=) *(CDR 6457)* – Sir Richard Steele.		
	(cd-s) *(CDRS 6457)* – ('A'side) / Stuck up your own era / I love you like gala.		
Mar 97.	(cd/c/lp) *(CD/TC+/PCS 7386)* **THE GOLDEN MILE**	36	
	– 12 reasons why I love her / Suited and booted / Marriage blister / Strumpet / Claret / Mr. Boyd / King of Kissingdom / I dive (unanswered questions and questionable answers) / You can't unheat the apple / Sparkle / April 1st / November 5th / Duchess.		
May 97.	(7"yellow) *(R 6464)* **STRUMPET. / WELCOME TO MY ARCHIPELAGO**	27	-
	(cd-s+=) *(CDR 6464)* – The return of emerald green / Wallpaper.		
	(cd-s) *(CDRS 6464)* – ('A'side) / Waiting to explode / I faced the music / March 9th.		
Aug 97.	(7") *(R 6476)* **DUCHESS. / SILENTLY SCREAMING**	39	-
	(cd-s+=) *(CDRS 6476)* – Suited and booted / Mr. Boyd.		
	(cd-s) *(CDR 6476)* – ('A'side) / Birthday suit / Emerald green strikes back / Love scene.		
Nov 97.	(7") *(R 6485)* **YOU CAN'T UNEAT THE APPLE. / CHERRIES**		-
	(cd-s+=) *(CDRS 6485)* – Emerald green blah blah blah / History of the world on ice.		
	(cd-s) *(CDR 6485)* – ('A'side) / Florence's theme / My sweet little death / Emerald green vs. Dr.Who.		

NADA SURF

Formed: Los Angeles, California, USA . . . mid 90's out of BECAUSE BECAUSE BECAUSE by MATTHEW CAWS and DANIEL LORCA, who invited IRA ELLIOT to replace the original drummer. A veteran of the local indie scene and former music journo (with 'Guitar World'), CAWS took on the role of both frontman and songwriter, his tales of adolescent angst set to a SONIC YOUTH meets post-NIRVANA grunge sound. Almost immediately finding an audience among disaffected American youth, NADA SURF hit a raw nerve with the single, 'POPULAR', opening track on their moderately successful 'Elektra' debut album, 'HIGH/LOW' (1996). The aforementioned signature tune would become something of an albatross around their necks as a 1998 follow-up set, 'THE PROXIMITY EFFECT', suffered from minimal press interest.

Album rating: HIGH/LOW (*5) / THE PROXIMITY EFFECT (*4)

MATTHEW CAWS – vocals, guitar / **DANIEL LORCA** – bass / **IRA ELLIOT** – drums (ex-FUZZTONES)

not iss. / No.6

Mar 96. (cd-ep) <38> **KARMIC EP** [-] [ ]
– Telescope / Sea knows when / Everybody lies / Tree house / Nothing.

Elektra / Elektra

Oct 96. (cd/c) <(7559 61913-2/-4)> **HIGH/LOW** [ ] [63] Jul96
– Popular / Plan / Sleep / Psychic caramel / Stalemate / Hollywood / Zen brain / Icebox / Treehouse / Deeper well.

Feb 97. (c-s) *(EKR 231C)* **POPULAR / PRESSURE FREE** [ ] [ ]
(cd-s+=) *(EKR 231CD)* – Oh no.

Jul 98. (7") *(DER 352)* **DEEPER WELL. /** [ ] [ ]
(above issued on 'Deep Elm')

Sep 98. (cd/c) <(7559 61913-2/-4)> **THE PROXIMITY EFFECT** [ ] [ ]
– Hyperspace / Amateur / Why are you so mean to me? / Mother's day / Troublemaker / 80 windows / Bacardi / Bad best friend / Dispossession / Voices / Firecracker / Slow down / Robot.

NAKED PREY

Formed: Tucson, Arizona, USA . . . 1981 by ex-SERFERS and KRELS frontman, VAN CHRISTIAN, alongside DAVID K. SEGER, RICHARD BADEN and SAM BLAKE. Part of the early-mid 80's roots/retro US rock revival that also included DREAM SYNDICATE, GREEN ON RED and GIANT SAND, NAKED PREY were first given a break by the scene's pivotal but tiny 'Down There' label. The eponymous DAN STUART (GREEN ON RED)-produced mini-set (in '84) showed a lot of promise, enough for 'Frontier' records ('Zippo' in the UK) to take them on for a debut album proper, 'UNDER THE BLUE MARLIN', a few years later. Galloping desert-rock fusing NEIL YOUNG & CRAZY HORSE-esque dirgy guitar solos with sun-parched, whiskey-throated vocals, the record was a far more metallic – in a LYNYRD SKYNYRD kind of way – affair than the material offered by their aforementioned peers. Having already covered the Stooges 'DIRT' on the latter set, NAKED PREY swooped on the Rolling Stones' 'SILVER TRAIN' and Jim Webb's 'WICHITA LINEMAN', for the otherwise disappointing mini-set, '40 MILES FROM NOWHERE' (1987). Having never quite made the breakthrough they had threatened early on, NAKED PREY were fed to the critical vultures with their final live set, 'KILL THE MESSENGER', in 1989. However, CHRISTIAN and Co did recover enough to return to the studio for one more long-player, 'AND THEN I SHOT EVERYONE' (1995).

Album rating: NAKED PREY mini (*6) / UNDER THE BLUE MARLIN (*7) / 40 MILES FROM NOWHERE mini (*4) / KILL THE MESSENGER (*4) / AND THEN I SHOT EVERYONE (*5)

VAN CHRISTIAN – vocals, guitar / **DAVID K. SEGER** – guitar, vocals / **RICHARD BADEN** – bass, vocals / **SAM BLAKE** – drums

not iss. / Down There

1984. (m-lp) <71126> **NAKED PREY** [-] [ ]

— **TOM LARKINS** – drums; repl. BLAKE

Zippo / Frontier

1986. (lp/c) *(ZONG/+CASS 011)* <FLP/FCX 1016> **UNDER THE BLUE MARLIN** [ ] [ ]
– The ride / A stranger (never says goodbye) / Dirt / Train whistle / How I felt that day / Come on down / Rawhead / Voodoo godhead / Fly away / What price for freedom.

Jan 88. (m-lp) *(ZANE 006)* **40 MILES FROM NOWHERE** [ ] [ ]
– 40 miles from nowhere / Find my way / Silver train / The carnival / Wichita lineman / Too far gone.

Fundamental / Fundamental

Jul 89. (lp/cd) <(SAVE 073/+CD)> **KILL THE MESSENGER (live in Tucson)** [ ] [ ]
– One even stand / Doctor Brown / Plastic Jesus / I saw the light / Blind man / Yardman / Blue tick hound / Life on Mars / Road crash / Night crew.

— **VAN C + LARKINS** brought in session band for below

not iss. / Epiphany

Oct 95. (cd) <1005> **AND THEN I SHOT EVERYONE** [-] [ ]
– Grande market / Fortune teller / Now I know / Love me to death / Lucky lager / Space / It's on me / That's how much I love you / Mop it up / Bitter end / Dillionious skunk.

NAKED RAYGUN

Formed: based- Chicago, Illinois, USA . . . 1981 by JEFF PEZZATI, his brother MARCO PEZZATI (who was almost immediately replaced by CAMILO GONZALEZ) and future BIG BLACK member, SANTIAGO DURANGO (who in turn was substituted by JOHN HAGGERTY) with subsequent addition of drummer JIM COLAO. Having garnered an early live reputation for raw (the lads played with their boots on – and nothing else!) hardcore, their first vinyl outing came in the shape of four tracks, 'BOMB SHELTER', 'LIBIDO', 'PARANOIA' and 'WHEN THE SCREAMING STOPS', featured on an Autumn 1981 V/A compilation, 'Busted At Oz' (alongside the EFFIGIES and STRIKE UNDER). With ERIC SPICER newly installed on the drumstool, NAKED RAYGUN fired out a debut EP, 'BASEMENT SCREAMS' before signing to 'Homestead' (stamping ground of DINOSAUR JR and SONIC YOUTH) for whom they released debut album, 'THROB THROB' (1984). Following the replacement of GONZALEZ with PIERRE KEZDY, the band established themselves as one of the Windy City's premier guitar assault units (alongside STEVE ALBINI's noisemongers, BIG BLACK) with 1985's sophomore album, 'ALL RISE'. After parting company with 'Homestead', NAKED RAYGUN initiated their own short-lived imprint, 'Sandpounder' – only a one-off 45, 'VANILLA BLUE', would materialise – before signing to 'Caroline' for 1988's 'JETTISON' (released in the UK as 'UNDERSTAND?'). One further personnel change (BILL STEPHENS for HAGGERTY) was effected prior to the band's disappointing swansong set, 'RAYGUN . . . NAKED RAYGUN', in 1990.

Album rating: THROB THROB (*5) / ALL RISE (*7) / UNDERSTAND? (*5) / RAYGUN . . . NAKED RAYGUN (*4)

JEFF PEZZATI – vocals, guitar / **JOHN HAGGERTY** – guitar; repl. SANTIAGO DURANGO / **CAMILO GONZALEZ** – bass; repl. MARCO PEZZATI / **ERIC SPICER** – drums; repl. JIM COLAO

not iss. / Ruthless

1983. (7"ep) <RRNR 03> **BASEMENT SCREAMS** [-] [ ]

Homestead / Homestead

Mar 85. (lp) <(HMS 008)> **THROB THROB** [ ] [ ] Nov84
– Rat patrol / Surf combat / Gear / Metastasis / Leeches / Roller queen / On / I don't know / Libido / Only in America / No sex / Stupid / Managua. *(cd-iss. Jul88 & Mar98; HMS 008CD)*

— **PIERRE KEZDY** – bass; repl. GONZALEZ

May 86. (lp) <(HMS 045)> **ALL RISE** [ ] [ ] Nov85
– Home of the brave / Dog at large / Knock me down / Mr. Gridlock / The strip / I remember / Those who move / The envelope / Backlash Jack / Peacemaker / New dreams. *(cd-iss. Jul88; HMS 045CD)*

not iss. / Sandpounder

1987. (7") <SR 001> **VANILLA BLUE. /** [-] [ ]
(UK-iss.Oct97; same)

Caroline / Caroline

Feb 89. (lp/c) *(CAR LP/C/CD 6)* <CAROL 1348/+C/CD> **UNDERSTAND?** <US-title 'JETTISON'> [ ] [ ] May88
– Treason / Hips swingin' / Understand? / Entrapment / Bughouse / Wonder beer / Never follow / Too much of you / Vagabond dog / O.K. wait / The sniper song / Which side you're on.

— **BILL STEPHENS** – guitar; repl. HAGGERTY who joined PIGBOY

1990. (cd/c/lp) <CAROL 1642-2/-4/-1> **RAYGUN . . . NAKED RAYGUN** [-] [ ]
– Home / Fever island / The grind / Jazz gone bad / Prepare to die / The promise / Holding you / Strange days / In my head / Camarilla / Terminal.

— disbanded after above

– compilations, etc. –

Jan 98. (cd) *Dyslexic;* <(DYS 21)> **LAST OF THE DEMOHICANS** [ ] [ ]

NAMES

Formed: Brussels, Belgium . . . late 70's out of Benelux outfit The PASSENGERS by a deliberately anonymous team of musicians. After touring under the banner of N.I.M. (aka NAMES IN MUTATION), the group finally got underway with the release of a French-only EP, 'SPECTATORS OF LIFE'. Picked up by Manchester's 'Factory' records, the English-speaking/singing Belgians made their UK debut early in '81 with the single, 'NIGHTSHIFT'. Farmed out to 'Factory Benelux', the NAMES released a further track, 'POSTCARDS', prior to cutting a full-length album, 'SWIMMING' (1982) for homegrown imprint, 'Les Disques Du Crepescule'. Vaguely reminiscent of early CURE and JOHN FOXX-era ULTRAVOX!, the record was swathed in mogadon-paced but atmospheric synth flourishes while the occasional discordant piano plonked away in the background. Accessible for 'Factory' but too obscure for many indie fans, the NAMES were struck off the register for good after a final single, 'THE ASTRONAUT', in 1983.

Album rating: SWIMMING (*5)

unknown

		Celluloid	not iss.
May 80.	(12"ep) *(CEL-2 6554)* **SPECTATORS OF LIFE** – Spectators of life / White life / The drive.	[-]	[-] French
		Factory	**not iss.**
Jan 81.	(7") *(FAC 29)* **NIGHTSHIFT. / I WISH I COULD SPEAK YOUR LANGUAGE**	[ ]	[-]
		Factory Benelux	**not iss.**
Oct 81.	(7"/12") *(FACBN 9/+12)* **POSTCARDS. / CALCUTTA**	[ ]	[-]
		Crepescule	**not iss.**
Apr 82.	(lp) *(TWI 065)* **SWIMMING** – (This is) Harmony / Shanghai gesture / Leave her to Heaven / Light / Discovery / Floating world / The fire / Life by the sea.	[ ]	[-]
		Operation Twilight	**not iss.**
Oct 83.	(12") **THE ASTRONAUT. /**	[-]	[-] Belgian
—	disbanded around this time		

NATION OF ULYSSES (see under ⇒ MAKE-UP)

NATIVE HIPSTERS

Formed: London, England . . . late 70's by WILLIAM WILDING and South African-born BLATT (aka NANETTE GREENBLATT). Setting up their own 'Heater Volume' imprint while recruiting ROBERT CUBITT and TOM FAWCETT, The WILDINGS – as they were then known – released a solitary album, 'WHY DID I BUY THOSE PYJAMAS', at the turn of the decade. After issuing a one-off 45 as The PATTERNS, the group changed their moniker once again, this time releasing an EP, 'THERE GOES CONCORDE AGAIN', as (AND THE) NATIVE HIPSTERS. Enthusiastically playlisted by noneother than John Peel, the track's whimsical novelty factor saw it cruise into the upper reaches of the indie charts. With CUBITT subsequently out of the picture, the band's line-up was bolstered by three extra members, MICK LOUGHRAN, LUCINDA VAN DER SMAN and YUM YUM MOSELEY (the latter two both sax players). A further couple of singles, 'TENDERLY HURT ME' and 'LARRY'S COMING BACK', never caught the public imagination in quite the same way although their maverick musical hotch-potch attracted an underground following.

Album rating: BLATT ON THE LANDSCAPE compilation cassette (*6)

WILLIAM WILDING (b.18 May'53, Romford, Essex, England) – vocals, bass / **BLATT** (b. NANETTE GREENBLATT, 9 Mar'52, Cape Town, South Africa) – vocals / **ROBERT CUBITT** – guitar, tapes, sax / **TOM FAWCETT** – guitar, synthesizer, trombone

		Heater Volume	not iss.
Dec 79.	(lp; as The WILDINGS) *(HVR 001)* **WHY DID I BUY THOSE PYJAMAS**	[ ]	[-]
Aug 80.	(7"; as The PATTERNS) *(HVR 002)* **THE BISHOP'S IN THE FRIDGE (part 2). / NO VIOLENT PACING**	[ ]	[-]
Oct 80.	(7"ep; as AND THE NATIVE HIPSTERS) *(HVR 003)* **THERE GOES CONCORDE AGAIN . . . / STANDS STILL THE BUILDING / I WANNA BE AROUND (PAUL)**	[ ]	[-]
—	**LUCIANA VAN DER SMAN + YUM YUM MOSELEY** – sax + **MICK LOUGHRAN** – guitar; repl. CUBITT		
		Illuminated – Glass	**not iss.**
Feb 82.	(12"ep) *(MAP 1)* **TENDERLY HURT ME EP** – Tenderly hurt me / Stuck / Poor prince / Hang ten.	[ ]	[-]
		Plattekop	**not iss.**
Jul 83.	(7") *(KOP 1)* **LARRY'S COMING BACK. /**	[ ]	[-]
—	**WILDING + BLATT** recruited a host of backers, namely **LESTER SQUARE** – guitar (ex-MONOCHROME SET) / **SIMON DAVIDSON** – piano / **ANNIE WHITEHEAD** – trombone / **CHRIS CORNETTO** – cornet		
		own	**not iss.**
1988.	(c) **BLATT ON THE LANDSCAPE**	[ ]	[-]

NAVIGATOR

Formed: Norwich, England . . . 1994 by NICK MELIA, JENNY ROBOTTOM and SAM RICHARDS, while attending the city's university. The very antithesis of raucous indie guitar-pop, this experimental trio forged their delicate sound while testing the waters around the student circuit. Signed to the local 'Noisebox' label (home of MAGOO), they released a debut EP, 'KILLTAKER', in summer '96, its sedative appeal reminiscent of LABRADFORD or even "a Sunday morning MOGWAI", as one journalist commented. 'A LITTLE ASTRONOMY' followed later that year, another audibly obscured slice of mogadon-paced melancholia that whetted appetites for early '97's classically-influenced marathon, 'WHEN THE WIRES FALL'. NAVIGATOR mapped out further directions in minimalist stereo that summer with an eponymous EP, while a debut album, 'NOSTALGIE', finally arrived on new label, 'Swarf Finger' a full year later.

Album rating: NOSTALGIE (*6)

NICK MELIA – guitar, vocals / **JENNY ROBOTTOM** – bass, vocals / **SAM RICHARDS** – drums

		Noisebox	not iss.
Jun 96.	(7"ep/cd-ep) *(NBX 022/+CD)* **KILLTAKER EP**	[ ]	[-]
Oct 96.	(7"blue) *(NBX 026)* **A LITTLE ASTRONOMY. /**	[ ]	[-]
Feb 97.	(7") *(NBX 027)* **WHEN THE WIRES FALL. /**	[ ]	[-]
Jun 97.	(7"ep/cd-ep) *(NBX 028/+CD)* **NAVIGATOR EP** – Assay / Diving bell / On all you hold sacred / II.	[ ]	[-]
		Swarf Finger	**not iss.**
Jul 98.	(lp/cd) *(SF 032/+CD)* **NOSTALGIE**	[ ]	[ ]

NEARLY GOD (see under ⇒ TRICKY)

NECROS

Formed: Maumee, Ohio, USA . . . summer '79 by BARRY HENSSLER, BRIAN POLLACK, COREY RUSK and TODD SWALLA. One of the first acts to sign for 'Touch & Go', the NECROS unleashed their debut EP, 'SEX DRIVE', in early '81, experimenting with hardcore punk. Youthful, brash and 'orrible, this outfit was not to be confused with Washington DC's similarly named hardcore troopers who released an eponymous set for 'Dischord' the same year. The Ohio NECROS returned in '83 with a new guitarist, ANDY WENDLER (to replace POLLACK), the man taking up his post for their debut long-player, 'CONQUEST FOR DEATH'. Another sabbatical ensued before the NECROS came back to life with an album on 'Restless', 'TANGLED UP' (1987), a more straight-down-the-line metallic affair that featured the track, 'BIG CHIEF', a title that departing frontman HENSSLER would later use as the moniker for his new band.

Album rating: CONQUEST FOR DEATH (*6) / TANGLED UP (*6) / LIVE OR ELSE (*4)

BARRY HENSSLER – vocals / **BRIAN POLLACK** – guitar / **COREY RUSK** – bass / **TODD SWALLA** – drums

		not iss.	Touch & Go
Feb 81.	(7"ep) **SEX DRIVE / POLICE BRUTALITY. / BETTER NEVER THAN LATE / CASTE SYSTEM**	[-]	[ ]
Oct 81.	(7"ep) *<No.4 1/2>* **THE NECROS EP** – I.Q. 32 / Youth camp / Peer pressure / Race riot / Wargame / I hate my school / Past comes back to haunt me / Reject / Public high school. (above was probably the NECROS from Washington DC on 'Dischord')	[-]	[ ]
—	**ANDY WENDLER** – guitar; repl. POLLACK		
1983.	(lp) **CONQUEST FOR DEATH** – Search for fame / Tarnished words / No one / Satisfy / Bad dream / Police brutality / Andy's shit for brunch / Conquest for death / Count me out / Change / Crying form / Face forward / Friend to all.	[-]	[ ]
		Enigma	**Restless**
Jun 87.	(lp) *(2203-1) <971295>* **TANGLED UP** – Gun / Blizzard of glass / Big chief / Open wound / Tangled up / Power of fear / Black water / Noise / 500 years a pack of kools / Nile song / A house full of drunks.	[ ]	[ ]
—	HENSSLER bailed out and subsequently formed BIG CHIEF		
		not iss.	**Enigma**
1989.	(lp) *<72220>* **LIVE OR ELSE**	[-]	[ ]
—	disbanded after above		

NECTARINE No.9 (see under ⇒ FIRE ENGINES)

NED'S ATOMIC DUSTBIN

Formed: Stourbridge, West Midlands, England . . . late '87 by JOHN PENNEY, RAT, ALEX GRIFFIN, MAT CHESLIN, and DAN WARTON. The 'Sound of Stourbridge' along with neo-crustie contemporaries like THE WONDER STUFF and the more rhythmically inclined POP WILL EAT ITSELF, NED'S took their name from a character on BBC TV's infamous 'Goon Show'. The group didn't quite reach the same giddy heights, though, admittedly they gave it their best shot. With the dubious advantage of two bass players, the group developed an engagingly spiky indie-pop sound prone to bursts of manic guitar thrashing and the odd sample. After the underground success of the 'INGREDIENTS', 'KILL YOUR TELEVISION' and 'UNTIL YOU FIND OUT' EP's, the band were picked up by 'Sony' who jointly released all their forthcoming product on 'Furtive'. The NED'S major label debut, 'HAPPY', soared into the Top 20, while the album, 'GOD FODDER', made the Top 5. The group then embarked on a punishing touring schedule including an appearance at that bastion of indie-dom, The Reading Festival (where the ubiquitous NED's T-shirt was almost as de rigeur as the NIRVANA Dante's Inferno job). Further Top 20 singles followed with 'TRUST' and 'NOT SLEEPING AROUND', while that difficult second album, 'ARE YOU NORMAL' (1992) again made the UK Top 20. Yet while other Brit hopefuls like EMF and JESUS JONES were sparking proclamations of another full scale American invasion (where are they now?, a nation probably doesn't ask), NED'S couldn't seem to break the lucrative US market despite heavy touring. Maybe their sound was just too 'British' and anyhow, with the success of the aforementioned NIRVANA, the yanks were back on top of their game, the dream of a British invasion fading faster than sales of The FARM's 'SPARTACUS' album. In the three years prior to the release of 'BRAINBLOODVOLUME' (1995), the musical landscape of the UK had undergone a sea change in attitude, attitude, of course, being the operative word. The likes of NED'S were just no longer fashionable, despite the album being their most rounded and consistent to date. Inevitably, the band split the following year, another act, dare I say it, consigned to the dustbin of history. Who knows, maybe the lads will re-emerge in a BENTLEY RHYTHM ACE fashion, NED'S ATOMIC BREAKBEAT, anyone?

Album rating: GOD FODDER (*8) / ARE YOU NORMAL (*7) / BRAINBLOODVOLUME (*6)

JONN PENNEY (b.17 Sep'68) – vocals / **RAT** (b.GARETH PRING, 8 Nov'70) – guitar / **ALEX GRIFFIN** (b.29 Aug'71) – bass / **MAT CHESLIN** (b.28 Nov'70) – bass / **DAN WARTON** (b.28 Jul'72) – drums

Chapter 22 / not iss.

Mar 90. (12"ep) *(12CHAP 047)* **THE INGREDIENTS** [ ] [-]
– Aim / Plug me in / Grey cell green / Terminally groovy.

Jul 90. (cd-ep/12"ep/7"ep) *(CD/12+/CHAP 048)* **KILL YOUR TELEVISION** [53] [-]
– Kill your television / That's nice / Sentence / Kill your remix.

Oct 90. (7") *(CHAP 52)* **UNTIL YOU FIND OUT. / FLEXIBLE HEAD** [51] [-]
(12"+=/cd-s+=) *(12/CD CHAP 52)* – Bite.

Furtive – Columbia / Columbia

Feb 91. (7"/c-s) *(656680-7/-4)* **HAPPY. / TWENTY THREE HOUR TOOTHACHE** [16] [-]
(12"+=/cd-s+=) *(656680-6/-2)* – Aim (at the Civic – live) / 45 second blunder.

Apr 91. (cd/c/lp) *(468112-2/-4/-1)* *<47929>* **GOD FODDER** [4] [91]
– Kill your television / Less than useful / Selfish / Grey cell green / Cut up throwing things / Capital letters / Happy / Your complex / Nothing like until you find out / You / What gives my son. *(re-iss. cd May95; same)*

Sep 91. (7") *(657462-7)* **TRUST. / FACELESS** [21] [-]
(12"+=/cd-s+=) *(657462-6/-2)* – Titch.

Feb 92. (c-s) *<74141>* **GREY CELL GREEN / TRUST** [-] [ ]
(cd-s+=) *<73991>* – Titch / Faceless / Until you find out.

Apr 92. (cd-ep) *<74202>* **KILL YOUR TELEVISION. / TERMINALLY GROOVIE / SENTENCE / KILL YOUR REMIX** [-] [ ]

Oct 92. (7") *(658386-7)* **NOT SLEEPING AROUND. / CUT UP** [19] [ ]
(12"+=/cd-s+=) *(658386-6/-2)* – Scrawl.
(US c-s+=) *<74718>* – N.S.A. (NAD VS. NOX).

Oct 92. (cd/c/lp) *(472633-2/-4/-1)* *<53154>* **ARE YOU NORMAL?** [13] [ ]
– Suave and suffocated / Walking through syrup / Legoland / Swallowing air / Who goes first / Tantrum / Not sleeping around / You don't want to do that / Leg end in his own boots / Two and two made five / Fracture / Spring / Intact.

Nov 92. (7") *(658816-7)* **INTACT. / PROSTRATE** [36] [-]
(10"+=) *(658816-0)* – NAD & NDX = Intact.
(12"+=/cd-s+=) *(658816-6/-2)* – Swiss legoland (live).

Furtive / Chaos

Mar 95. (c-s) *(661356-4)* **ALL I ASK OF MYSELF IS THAT I HOLD TOGETHER / CAPSIZE** [33] [-]
(12"+=) *(661356-6)* – ('A'-Just together mix) / ('A'-No answer mix).
(cd-s++=) *(661356-2)* – ('A'-In control mix).
(cd-s+=) *(661356-5)* – Take me to the cleaners / Premonition (need to know mix).

Jul 95. (7") *(662056-7)* **STUCK. / A TEMPTED FATE** [64] [-]
(cd-s+=) *(662056-2)* – . . .To be right (acoustic) / ('A'acoustic).
(12") *(662056-6)* – ('A'side) / Premonition (as I thought mix) / Premonition (dirty caller mix).

Jul 95. (cd/c/lp) *(478330-2/-4/-1)* *<67040>* **BRAINBLOODVOLUME** [ ] [ ]
– All I ask of myself is that I hold together / Floote / Premonition / Talk me down / Borehole / Your only joke / Stuck / . . .To be right / I want it over / Traffic / Song eleven could take forever.

— disbanded October 1995

– compilations, etc. –

Jan 91. (lp/cd) *R.T.D. Euro; (1401183-1/-2)* **BITE** (imported) [72] [-]

Nov 94. (cd) *Sony S2; (477984-2)* **5.22** (B-sides, etc) [ ] [-]

NEGATIVLAND

Formed: Berkeley, California, USA . . . 1979 by MARK HOSLER, DAVID WILLS and RICHARD LYONS (PETER DAYTON was part-time member). Taking their name from a track by Kraut-rockers, NEU~!, these suburban experimentalists initially began mixing 'n' matching disparate material in the early 80's, both with vinyl LP's, 'NEGATIVLAND' (1980), 'POINTS' (1981), 'A BIG 10-8 PLACE' (1983) and their own radio show, 'OVER THE EDGE, VOL.1: JAM CON '84' (1985). 1987's debut for 'S.S.T.', 'ESCAPE FROM NOISE' kicked up a storm of controversy as the band fooled the media into believing the track, 'CHRISTIANITY IS STUPID', had inspired a brutal inter-family murder. Outrage aside, the record's media-manipulating sonic terrorism was created with the help of such anti-establishment luminaries as The RESIDENTS, JELLO BIAFRA, FRED FRITH, JERRY GARCIA, HENRY KAISER and er, DEVO's MARK MOTHERSBAUGH. Come the turn of the decade, NEGATIVLAND turned their satirical sights on America's redundant MOR history with a full album's worth of chestnut send-ups, 'HELTER STUPID' (1989). The latter's title was perhaps a reference to U2 whom they ripped to shreds with the EP, 'THE LETTER U AND THE NO.2', sending up their pomp-rock classic, 'I Still Haven't Found What I'm Looking For'. Needless to say, BONO and Co weren't amused, dispatching their legal team to tackle the copyright breach; U2 subsequently dropped the case although the incident didn't discourage the NEGATIVLAND posse from further risky shenanigans.

Album rating: NEGATIVLAND (*5) / POINTS (*5) / A BIG 10-8 PLACE (*5) / OVER THE EDGE, VOL.1: JAM CON '84 (*5) / ESCAPE FROM NOISE (*6) / HELTER STUPID (*6) / FREE (*4) / DISPEPSI (*5) /

MARK HOSLER – keyboards, bass, guitar, tapes, etc / **DAVID WILLS** – synthesizer, keyboards, vocals, etc / **RICHARD LYONS** – clarinet, keyboards, etc / 4th member **PETER DAYTON** – bass, guitar

not iss. / Seeland-Optional

1980. (lp) *<OPTLP 001>* **NEGATIVLAND** [-] [ ]
<US re-iss. 1991 on 'SST'; 272>

1981. (lp) *<OPTLP 002>* **POINTS** [-] [ ]
– Harry to the ferry / The answer is . . . / Scolding box / That darn keet / Dear Mary / Clutch cargo '81 / Babac d'babc . . . / Nice place to live / Bee fly / No hands / Potty air.

1983. (lp) *<OPTLP 003>* **A BIG 10-8 PLACE** [-] [ ]
– Theme from a big place / A big 10-8 place (pt.1) / Clowns and ballerinas / Introduction / Four fingers / 180-G, a big 10-8 place (pt.2).

1985. (cd) *<OPTCD 004>* **OVER THE EDGE, VOL.1: JAM CON '84 (radio compiled)** [-] [ ]
– Introduction – JamJamJam – A little history – Jam this guy: An interview with W6DR – Jamming the "S / Crosley Bendix reviews JamArt and cultural jamming / The worst programming ever – Mind jamming – A report by Rex Everything / C. Eliot Friday's presidential campaign shortwave broadcast (live from Howland Island) / Two or three people listening – You motherfucking son of a sack of piece of shit – Attempts to jam / Introduction to the show – Parade of condiments – Walking and driving and hiking to the picnic / Stockholders' meeting (with Crosley Bendix) – Insects in your pop bottle – An abrupt ending / Body English. *<(c-iss.Mar89 on 'S.S.T.'; SSTC 233)>*

— DAYTON repl. by **DON JOYCE** – tapes, synthesizer / **CHRIS GRIGG** – drums, synthesizer, computers

Recommended / S.S.T.

Dec 87. (lp) *(REC 017)* *<SST 133>* **ESCAPE FROM NOISE** [ ] [ ]
– Announcement / Quiet please / Michael Jackson / Escape from noise / The Playboy channel / Stress in marriage / Nesbitt's lime soda song / Over the hiccups / Sycamore / Car bomb / Methods of torture / Yellow black and rectangular / Backstage pass / Christianity is stupid / Time zones / You don't even live here / The way of it / Endscape. *(cd-iss. Jun93; RECDEC 17)*

S.S.T. / S.S.T.

Nov 89. (c) *<(SST 901)>* **OVER THE EDGE, VOL.2 – PASTOR DICK: MURIEL'S PURSE FOUND** (radio compiled) [ ] [ ]
– Thrilling choice – Dayle Embree / Ask Pastor Dick – Muriel's purse found / Hell car / The men's continental breakfast / Christianity and the cults – Joseph / I love my B.I.B.L.E. – More bible / Whisper a prayer / Drunk at last – A date with ham – etc / Forty-three fuck you's – Sign off. *(cd-iss. May93; SST 901)*

Nov 89. (c) *<(SSTC 902)>* **OVER THE EDGE, VOL.3: THE WEATHERMAN** (radio compiled) [ ] [ ]
– One of them / Clorox cowboy. *<US cd-iss. Aug98 on 'Seeland'; SEE 19>*

Recommended / S.S.T.

Apr 90. (lp/c/cd) *(REC 029)* *<SST 252/+C/CD>* **HELTER STUPID** [ ] [ ] Nov89
– Prologue / Helter stupid / The perfect cut (Canned music) / The perfect cut (Rooty poops) / The perfect cut (Good as gold) / The perfect cut (Piece of meat) / The perfect cut (White rabbit – Dog named Gidget) / The perfect cut (11 minutes) / The perfect cut (48 hours). *(re-iss. May93 lp/c/cd; SST 252/+C/CD) (cd-iss. Jul93 as 'HELTER STUPID: THE PERFECT CUT'; RECDEC 29)*

1990. (m-lp) *(REC 051)* **THE LETTER U AND THE NO.2 EP** [ ] [-]
(cd-iss. Jul93; RECDEC 51)

1990. (c-ep) *<SSTC 904>* **DICK VAUGHN** [-] [ ]

1991. (12") *<SST 272>* **---------** [-] [ ]

Feb 92. (12"ep/c-ep/cd-ep) *<SST/+C/CD 291>* **GUNS EP** [-] [ ]
(re-iss. May93; same)

Seeland / Seeland

Mar 93. (cd) *<SEE 8CD>* **U2** [-] [ ]

Jun 93. (cd) *<(SEE 9CD)>* **FREE** [ ] [ ]
– Freedom's waiting / Cityman / The gun and the bible / Truck stop drip drop / The bottom line / Crumpled farm / Happy the harmonica / Pip digs Pep / We are driven / View to the sun / I am God / Our national anthem.

Oct 93. (cd) *<SEE 10>* **OVER THE EDGE, VOL.5: CROSLEY BENDIX RADIO REVIEWS** (radio compiled) [-] [ ]

Mar 94. (cd) *(SEE 11>* **OVER THE EDGE, VOL.6: THE WILLSAPHONE STUPID SHOW** (radio compiled) [-] [ ]

1994. (d-cd) *<SEE 12>* **OVER THE EDGE, VOL.7: TIME ZONES EXCHANGE PROJECT** (radio compiled) [-] [ ]
– Executive window – Memo to Friday – Memo from the future – Dickie Diamond and the media shifter / The piddle diddle report 1: Sandamanians – Transinfiltration – Nothing is too wonderful to be true / The piddle diddle report 2: Human values – Where is Friday? – Call from Howland Island and the priest / The piddle diddle report 3: Stike it rich – This fabled island – Cary Grant tapes a ghost / The piddle diddle report 4: After the rain – Let's take a few calls – Photos of Mrs. Gorbachev – Com / The piddle diddle report 5: Sergio Caracus – Frankenstein meets cyclops – What was on the island? / The piddle diddle report 6: A future confronting the past which is our future – Last call from Howl / A unique cultural simulcast / Cubulax guidelines / Dickie Diamond grabs the gusto / Russian nationa / Americo-Soviet free market osmosis – Mertz – Intercontinental phone mess / Russian factoids – Natural woman – Tiolet paper ads and smiles / Hey you-buy this! – Innovation – Shilling for attention / Mertz – A force of nature – Hard and soft thinking – The good life – Cars / One bar of soap – Rubles – Mertz – It's as if we never left home – Negativ thoughts – Nuts-oh-nuts! / Passage to the 4th dimension – Memo to Howland – Calling Radio Moscow / A presidential campaign shortwave broadcast by C. Eliot Friday / The piddle report 7: What's to come – The quantum edge – Fiber optics – Experimental sharpner / A place in time to put time in it's place – Do you have a job? – Das vedanya – Mertz – Credits – So.

Feb 95. (cd) *<SEE 13>* **FAIR USE THE STORY OF THE LETTER U AND THE NUMERAL 2** [-] [ ]

Jul 95. (cd) *<SEE 14>* **OVER THE EDGE, VOL.1 1/2: STARTING LINE** (radio compiled) [-] [ ]
– The drive line: World's most beloved & exalted status symbol – Metallic root beer –

Lada – etc / Stir the stumps: Answer man – Hitler's staff car – Chappaquiddick – Transient peaks – Carnuba wax – etc / Receptacle programming – Fear of freeways mix – Defend the fuel – Total asshole – etc / Auto trivia: Cool cars – Cheaper cheese – Limousines of Pope Paul VII – etc / Chevy innovation and JamJamJam / It fell from Port Costa – Rototiller mix – Bottlebrush bushes – etc / Phone-in singalong – Song list – What the world needs now / Tammy / Drug free / Transient peaks – etc / This disco's out of sight – A lot about mucus – Sammy the whammy – A prayer to O.T.E. – Life's unanamous / Pure full stereo rototiller and so long.

Nov 95. (cd) *<SEE 14>* **OVER THE EDGE, VOL.8: SEX DIRT** (radio compiled)

Jul 97. (cd) *<SEE 17>* **DISPEPSI**
– A smile you can't hide / Drink it up / Why is this commercial? / Happy hero / A most successful formula / The greatest taste around / Hyper real / All she called about / I believe it's L / Humanitarian effort / Voice in my head / Aluminium or glass: the memo / Bite back.

May 98. (m-cd) *<SEE 18>* **HAPPY HEROES**
– Mertz #1 / Jolly green giant / Mertz #2 / Chicken diction / Black hole tube / O.J. and his personal trainer kill Ron and Nicole / Happy hero: the remedia megamix / Mertz end.

– compilations, etc. –

Jan 94. (d-cd) *ReR; (CD 1806)* **NEGATIV CONCERT LAND**

1994. (lp) *Knitting Factory; <128>* **LIVE AT THE KNITTING FACTORY (live)**

Jun 97. (7") *Eerie Materials; <(EM 01)>* **TRUTH IN ADVERTISING. /**

Aug 97. (cd) *S.S.T.; <355>* **LIVE ON TOUR (live)**
– Christianity is stupid / Murder and music / Escape from noise / Time / Fourfingers / Record industry / Christianity is stupid (part 2).

NEPHILIM (see under ⇒ FIELDS OF THE NEPHILIM)

NERVES

Formed: San Francisco, California, USA . . . 1976 by JACK LEE, PETER CASE and PAUL COLLINS, although it would be in L.A. that they would establish their Stateside power-pop base. Towards the end of the year, The band self-financed the release of their debut EP, a record that contained the original LEE-penned version of 'HANGIN' ON THE TELEPHONE'. By the time it became a massive hit for BLONDIE in 1978, The NERVES had broken down as COLLINS formed The BREAKAWAYS and CASE formed the more fruitful PLIMSOULS. LEE, meanwhile, put together a solo set which featured another future BLONDIE track, 'WILL ANYTHING HAPPEN?'. In the late 70's, COLLINS was reunited with CASE when the former founded The BEAT (the trio also included HARLAN HOLLANDER), although the latter was already occupied with own group. Under the wing of veteran manager, Bill Graham, The BEAT (no relation to the UK 2-Tone act of the same name who were forced to prefix the moniker with ENGLISH for American releases) inked a deal with 'Columbia'. COLLINS and his new cohorts (i.e. LARRY WHITMAN, STEVEN HUFF and MICHAEL RUIZ) released a couple of strident, college-friendly pop singles before delivering their eponymous debut set (issued as 'PAUL COLLINS' BEAT' for the UK market) in the Spring of 1980. After a poor performance on the sales front, The BEAT downshifted slightly to 'Passport' records, emerging with what proved to be their final releases, 'THE KIDS ARE THE SAME' (1982) album and 'TO BEAT OR NOT TO BEAT' (1983) EP.

Album rating: THE NERVES compilation (*6)

JACK LEE – vocals, guitar / **PETER CASE** (b. 5 Apr'54, Buffalo, New York, USA) – bass, vocals / **PAUL COLLINS** (b. New York) – drums

not iss. Nerves

Dec 76. (7"ep) *<N45-01>* **THE NERVES EP**
– Hangin' on the telephone / When you find out / Give me some time / Working too hard. *(rel.1985 on French 'Fence' as lp + =;) –* (6 demos).

—— disbanded early in '78 when COLLINS formed The BREAKAWAYS, CASE formed The PLIMSOULS and JACK LEE went solo in 1981, 'JACK LEE'S GREATEST HITS VOL.1' lp was released by 'Maiden America'.

BEAT

PAUL COLLINS – vocals, drums / **PETER CASE** – bass, vocals / **HARLAN HOLLANDER** – guitar

—— actually named PAUL COLLINS' BEAT (In the UK only), after CASE formed The PLIMSOULS and HOLLANDER departed

—— **COLLINS** – (now) vocals, guitar / **LARRY WHITMAN** – guitar, vocals / **STEVEN HUFF** – bass, vocals / **MICHAEL RUIZ** – drums

C.B.S. Columbia

Jan 80. (7") *<1-11161>* **WALKING OUT ON LOVE. / LET ME INTO YOUR LIFE**

Feb 80. (7") *(CBS 8135)* **DON'T WAIT UP FOR ME. / WALK OUT ON LOVE**

Apr 80. (7") *<1-11211>* **DON'T WAIT UP FOR ME. / WORKING TOO HARD**

May 80. (7") *(CBS 8575)* **ROCK'N'ROLL BEAT. / LOOK BUT DON'T TOUCH**

May 80. (lp) *(CBS 83895) <36195>* **PAUL COLLINS' BEAT** Nov79
– Rock'n'roll girl / I don't fit in / Different kind of girl / Don't wait up for me / You won't be happy / Walking out on love / Work a day world / USA / Let me into your life / Working too hard / You and I / Look but don't touch.

not iss. Passport

Mar 82. (lp) *<ARC 36794>* **THE KIDS ARE THE SAME**
– That's what life is all about / Dreaming / On the highway / Will you listen / Crying won't help / The kids are the same / Trapped / It's just a matter of time / Met her yesterday / I will say no / Down. *<cd-iss. 1995 on 'Wagon Wheel'; 3>*

—— **JIMMY RIPP** – guitar; repl. WHITMAN

—— **JAY DEE DAUGHERTY** – drums (ex-PATTI SMITH) repl. RUIZ

1983. (12"ep) *<5002>* **TO BEAT OR NOT TO BEAT**

—— split after above failed to sell

NEUROTICS (see under ⇒ NEWTOWN NEUROTICS)

NEUTRAL MILK HOTEL

Formed: Ruston, Louisiana, USA . . . 1989 by singer-songwriter, JEFF MANGUM, along with WILLIAM CULLEN HART and BILL DOSS, although the latter two soon bailed out to form OLIVIA TREMOR CONTROL. Confusingly enough, however, this would be after NMH evolved out of Athens, Georgia outfits, CRANBERRY LIFE CYCLE and SYNTHETIC FLYING MACHINE, leaving MANGUM to flit once more, this time to Denver, Colorado. After a period helping out his Ruston-born buddy, ROBERT SCHNEIDER, in his outfit APPLES (IN STEREO), MANGUM finally got NEUTRAL MILK HOTEL underway, releasing a series of obscure singles and demos before signing to 'Merge' and releasing the single, 'EVERYTHING IS', following it up with a debut album, 'ON AVERY ISLAND' (1996). Apparently recorded on SCHNEIDER's bedroom four track and released in the UK on 'Fire', the record bore inevitable comparison with OLIVIA TREMOR CONTROL's 'Dusk At Cubist Castle', if only for its fantastical concept strangeness. Not as overtly psychedelic as the latter album but rampantly experimental, 'ON AVERY ISLAND' was a collision of seemingly spontaneous, barely formed musical ideas, samples and sound effects, underlaid by a frazzled pop genius and executed with delirious abandon. MANGUM continue to indulge his passion for conceptual weirdness with 1998's 'IN THE AEROPLANE OVER THE SEA', released this time around on 'Blue Rose'

Album rating: ON AVERY ISLAND (*7) / IN THE AEROPLANE OVER THE SEA (*6)

JEFF MANGUM – vocals, multi / with **ROBERT SCHNEIDER** – xylophone, etc / **HILARIE SIDNEY** – multi / **AARON REEDY** – multi / **RICK BENJAMIN** – trombone

Fire Merge

Jul 95. (7") *(BLAZE 79)* **EVERYTHING IS. /**
(cd-s+=) *(BLAZE 79CD)* –

Sep 96. (cd) *(FIRECD 53) <MRG 53>* **ON AVERY ISLAND** Mar96
– Song against sex / You've passed / Someone is waiting / Baby for Pree / Marching theme / Where you'll find me now / Avery Island – Leave me alone / Three peaches / Naomi / April 8th / Pree-sisters swallowing a donkey's . . .

Blue Rose Merge

Jun 98. (cd) *(BRRC 1019-2) <MRG 136>* **IN THE AEROPLANE OVER THE SEA** Feb98
– King of carrot flowers (part 1) / The king of carrot flowers (parts 2 & 3) / In the aeroplane over the sea / Two-headed boy / The fool / Holland, 1945 / Communist daughter / Oh comely / Ghost / 10 / Two-headed boy (part 2).

NEW BOMB TURKS

Formed: Columbus, Ohio, USA . . . 1990 by Ohio University students ERIC DAVIDSON, JIM WEBER, MATT REBER, BILL BRANDT. Akin to a fusion of IGGY POP, DEAD BOYS and The DWARVES, their brand of melody-fuelled punk was initially heard on US-only singles before they signed to 'Crypt' and issued a highly praised (in underground circles at least) debut album, '!!DESTROY-OH-BOY!!' (1993). A follow-up, 'INFORMATION HIGHWAY REVISITED' (1994), appeared a couple of years later to equally effusive praise and despite a resurgence in interest for nu-punk in the wake of grunge, the band's profile and sales remained low. 1995 saw the release of a collaboration with The ENTOMBED, misanthropically titled 'I HATE PEOPLE', as well as a double set, 'PISSIN' OUT THE POISON', which collected the group's early singles; including a plethora of covers: SUMMER ROMANCE (Rolling Stones) / I WANNA SLEEP (Modern Lovers) / BAD GIRL (New York Dolls) / CHRISTMAS (Phil Spector, etc) / YOUNGBLOOD (Wild Billy Childish) / etc. Subsequently signing with the seminal 'Epitaph' label, the group released 'SCARED STRAIGHT' in 1996 and needless to say turned a tad heavier.

Album rating: !!DESTROY-OH-BOY!! (*5) / INFORMATION HIGHWAY REVISITED (*7) / PISSIN' OUT THE POISON compilation (*6) / SCARED STRAIGHT (*7) / AT ROPE'S END (*6)

ERIC DAVIDSON – vocals / **JIM WEBER** – guitar / **MATT REBER** – bass / **BILL RANDT** – drums

not iss. Munster

1990's. (7") **DRAGSTRIP RIOT. / CRYIN' INTO THE BEER OF A DRUNK MAN**

not iss. Bag Of Hammers

1990's. (7") **SHARPEN-UP TIME. / LAISSEZ FAIR STATE**

not iss. Sympathy F

Jan 93. (cd-s) *<SFTRI 228>* **TRYING TO GET BY. / LAST LOST FIGHT**

Crypt Crypt

Apr 93. (lp/cd) *(EFA 11560/+D) <32>* **!!DESTROY-OH-BOY!!**
– Born Toulouse-Lautrec / Tail crush / Up for a downside / Tattooed apathethic boys / Dragstrip riot / We give a rat's ass / Runnin' on go / Lone gone sister / Mr. Suit / Let's dress up the naked truth / Hapless attempt / I want my baby . . . dead? / Sucker

punch / I'm weak / Tryin' to get by / Cryin' into the beer of a drunk man.
Oct 93. (7") *(DAM 26)* **BOTTLE ISLAND. /**
(above issued on 'Damaged Goods') (below on 'Helter Skelter')
Feb 94. (7") *(EFA 402977)* **DOGS ON 45. / (other track by DEVIL DOGS)**
—— (below on 'Sympathy For The . . .')
Oct 94. (7") <*(SFTRI 319)*> **(GOTTA, GOTTA) SINKING FEELING. /**
Oct 94. (lp/cd) *(EFA 11585-1/-2)* <49> **INFORMATION HIGHWAY REVISITED**
– It slips in / Bullish on / If I only could / Brother Orson Welles / T.A.S. / Fingernail chomp / Dented 'n' spent / Girl can't help it / (Gotta gotta) Sinking feeling / Grandpa atomic / Never will / Apocalyptic dipstick / Lyin' on our backs / I got you bitter end / Straight-on chaser.
—— (In Jun'95, they shared a single with The ENTOMBED, 'I HATE PEOPLE')
Oct 95. (d-lp/cd) *(EFA 11598-1/-2)* <58> **PISSIN' OUT THE POISON**
(compilation of all early 45's)
– Tail crush / Out of my mind / Cryin' in the beer of a drunk man / Just head / Let's dress up to the naked truth / Do the pop / Sucker punch / Spinnin' clock / Summer romance / The girl can't help it / Got no proof / Polyester thinking cap / Last lost fight / We need more / Sharpen-up time / Laissez faire state / Croonin' into the beer of a drunk man / Pist / Deathbedside manner / I wanna sleep / Youngblood / Taller order / Bad girl / Ejection / Christmas (baby please come home) / Anal swipe.
Fat Wreck Chords / Fat Wreck Chords
Jul 96. (7") <*(FAT 542-7)*> **STICK IT OUT. / STILL NEVER WILL / JOB**
Epitaph / Epitaph
Aug 96. (cd/c/lp) <*(86479-2/-4/-1)*> **SCARED STRAIGHT**
– Hammerless nail / Bachelor's high / Professional gangster / Cultural elite sign-up sheet / Jukebox lean / Jeers of a clown / Look alive jive / Staring down the gift horse / Shoot the offshoot / Drop what you're doin' / Telephone numbrrr / Wrest your hands.
Jun 97. (7") *(WAL 015)* **PROFESSIONAL AGAINSTER. /**
(above single on 'Wallabies' & below on 'Munster')
Jul 97. (7") *(DLM 179)* **DRAGSTRIP RIOT. /** -
Mar 98. (7") *(SFTRI 553)* **SNAP DECISION. / JAGUAR RIDE**
(above on 'Sympathy For The Record Industry')
Mar 98. (cd/c/lp) *(6515-2/-4/-1)* **AT ROPE'S END**
– Scapegoat soup / Snap decisions / Ally smile / So long silver lining / Veronica Lake / Defiled / Bolan's crash / Raw law / Minimum wages of sin / At rope's end / Common cold shoulder / Aspirin aspirations / Streamline yr skull.
Mar 98. (7"ep/cd-ep) *(1001-7/-2)* **VERONICA LAKE EP**
– Veronica Lake / Snap decision / Double Marlon (rough mix) / Don't Kimosabe me (demo).
Nov 98. (7"ep/cd-ep) *(1011-7/-2)* **RAW LAW / SO LONG SILVER LINING / HAMMERLESS NAIL / TAIL CRUSH**

Martin NEWELL (see under ⇒ CLEANERS FROM VENUS)

NEW FAST AUTOMATIC DAFFODILS

Formed: Manchester, England . . . 1988 out of punk group PARIAH, with an initial line-up of guitarist DOLAN HEWISON, bassist JUSTIN CRAWFORD and drummer PERRY SAUNDERS, vocalist ANDY SPEARPOINT and precussionist ICARUS WILSON-KNIGHT joining later. In 1989, just as the 'Madchester' scene was crystallising, the group unleashed their indie 45, 'LIONS', reminiscent of the alternative funk-rock of the early 80's (i.e. PIGBAG, ACR, FIRE ENGINES or 23 SKIDOO) and heralded as the best debut for years. By late 1990, a fresh move to a new label ('Play It Again Sam') gave them a brief entry into the UK chart with a debut album, 'PIGEONHOLE', showcasing the band's diverse, often breakneck style and SPEARPOINT's intelligent, highly articulate lyrics. Produced by Craig Leon (FALL, RAMONES), 'BODY EXIT MIND' was a decidedly darker affair featuring the defiant likes of 'WHAT KIND OF HELL IS THIS' and 'HOW MUCH LONGER SHALL WE TOLERATE MASS CULTURE'. Following the reord's release the band's moniker was subject to a slight abbreviation to NEW FADS, SPEARPOINT and Co. following a more rhythmic direction on their well-received 1995 release, 'LOVE IT ALL'. Produced by JEREMY ALLOM (MASSIVE ATTACK), the record further illustrated the band's willingness to experiment with diverse musical styles and ideas. • **Songwriters:** Group penned except; I'M SET FREE (Velvet Underground). • **Trivia:** Around mid'91, 20,000 copies of 'Getting Better' were stolen by Basque separatists of Spain.

Album rating: PIGEONHOLE (*7) / BODY EXIT MIND (*8)

ANDY SPEARPOINT – vocals / **DOLAN HEWISON** (b.Newcastle) – guitar / **JUSTIN CRAWFORD** – bass / **PERRY SAUNDERS** – drums / **ICARUS WILSON-KNIGHT** – percussion
Playtime / not iss.
Jun 89. (12"ep) *(AMUSE 4T)* **LIONS / FATE DON'T FAIL ME NOW. / YOUR DREAMS, MY NIGHTMARES** -
Oct 89. (12"ep/cd-ep) *(AMUSE 6 T/CD)* **MUSIC IS SHIT** -
– Beam me up / Men without qualities / Music is shit (parts 1, 2 & 3) / Lions.
Mar 90. (7"one-sided) *(AMUSE 7)* **BIG** -
(12"+=/cd-s+=) *(AMUSE 7 T/CD)* – ('A'instrumental) / Baka / ('A'-Baka mix).
Play It Again Sam / Elektra
Sep 90. (7") *(BIAS 162-7)* **FISHES EYES. / FISHES EYES (UNDERWATER)** -
(ext;12"+=/cd-s+=) *(BIAS 162/+CD)* – White.
Nov 90. (lp/c/cd) *(BIAS 185/+MC/CD)* <61102> **PIGEONHOLE** 49 Jan91
– Get better / Fishes eyes / Working for him / Part 4 / Big / You were lying when you said you loved me / Amplifier / Reprise / Partial. *(free-7") (BIAS 185X)* – I'M SET FREE. / PENGUINS *(cd re-iss. Sep93; same)*
Apr 91. (7") *(BIAS 193-7)* **GET BETTER. / PIGEONHOLE** -
(ext.12"+=) *(BIAS 193)* – I found myself in another room.
(ext.cd-s++=) *(BIAS 193CD)* – ('A'extended).
Nov 91. (7") *(BIAS 199-7)* **ALL OVER MY FACE. / WHY THE HARD MEN FAIL** -
(12"/cd-s) *(BIAS 199/+CD)* – ('A'-split decision mix) / ('A'-off the road mix) / ('B'side).
Jan 92. (cd-s) <66510> **BIG /** -
Aug 92. (7") *(BIAS 219-7)* **IT'S NOT WHAT YOU KNOW. / BEAUTIFUL** -
(12"+=/cd-s+=) *(BIAS 219/+CD)* – Head on / Beatlemania.
Sep 92. (7") *(BIAS 229-7)* **STOCKHOLM (radio mix). / CANNES** -
(12"+=/cd-s+=) *(BIAS 229/+CD)* – ('A'extended).
(10") *(BIAS 229-LTD)* – ('A'demo) / Hexagon spray / It's not what you know (demo).
Oct 92. (lp/c/cd) *(BIAS 205/+MC/CD)* <61398> **BODY EXIT MIND** 57 Mar93
– Bong / It's not what you know / Stockholm / I take you to sleep / Bruises / Kyphos / Beatlemania / What kind of Hell is this? / American money / Missing parts of famous people / Patchwork lies / Music. *(cd+ = cd-ep)* – How much longer shall we tolerate mass culture? / Teenage combo / Exit body, exit mind.
Jan 93. (cd-ep) <61438> **BONG** -
– Bong / It's not what you know / Head on / Beautiful / Cannes.

NEW FADS

—— change of name but same line-up
Sep 94. (12"m) *(BIAS 249)* **LIFE IS AN ACCIDENT. / EVERY ONCE IN A WHILE (Fuzzy Logic remix) / MAD POP** -
(cd-s) *(BIAS 249CD1)* – (1st 2 tracks) / Aches and pains.
(cd-s) *(BIAS 249CD2)* – (1st & 3rd tracks) / PSV (VPL remix).
Nov 94. (10") *(BIAS 269)* **THESE FOOLISH THINGS. / EVERY ONCE IN A WHILE** -
(cd-s+=) *(BIAS 269CD)* – Bassdrum (H.Nicholson mix) / Lions (live).
Jan 95. (cd/c/lp) *(BIAS 285 CD/MC/LP)* **LOVE IT ALL** -
– These foolish things / Life is an accident / Left right / Every once in a while / Why waste your love / What I feel / Saxophone / Monday it is / P.S.V. / Kill my instincts / Souvenir.
—— disbanded after above

– compilations, others, etc. –

Jul 91. (m-lp/m-cd) *Strange Fruit; (SFPMA/+CD 209) / Dutch East India; <8410>* **THE PEEL SESSIONS** (19.12.89 – 11.11.90) Feb92
– Purple haze / Man without qualities II / Jaggerbog / Big II (instrumental) / Get better / Part 4 / Man without qualities I.

Colin NEWMAN (see under ⇒ WIRE)

NEW MODEL ARMY

Formed: Bradford, England . . . 1980 by SLADE THE LEVELLER (aka JUSTIN SULLIVAN) alongside STUART MORROW and ROBB HEATON, taking their name from Oliver Cromwell's forces in the 11th century English civil war. Following a one-off release, 'BITTERSWEET', on the small 'Quiet' label, the band moved on to the larger independent operation, 'Abstract'. By the release of a debut mini-set, 'VENGEANCE' (1984), the group had attracted a notoriously partisan, clog-footed following, their uncompromising anti-Thatcherite stance and crusty-punk musical assault endearing them to those actively dropping out of the prevailing 80's ethos. Songs such as 'NO MAN'S LAND', 'SPIRIT OF THE FALKLANDS' and the raging title track laid out their political agenda in bruising style, NEW MODEL ARMY's growing popularity subsequently leading to a deal with 'E.M.I.'. The irony of signing with a multi-national corporation wasn't wasted on the band's more scathing critics, although the fact that their music was now more widely available than ever before was no doubt justification enough for such a move; a major label debut single, 'NO REST' / 'HEROIN' (the latter's subject matter resulting in an IBA ban), made the UK Top 30, while a full-length follow-up album, 'NO REST FOR THE WICKED' (1985), almost made the Top 20. In light of this chart success, a ban from performing in America – reputedly on the grounds of poor artistic quality – looked all the more untenable. With JASON 'MOOSE' HARRIS replacing MORROW, the band continued to kick against the pricks throughout the latter half of the 80's on such grimly defiant albums as 'THE GHOST OF CAIN' and 'THUNDER AND CONSOLATION' (1989). In line with the new age travelling movement's increasing concern with environmental matters and the rise of band's like The LEVELLER's, NEW MODEL ARMY gradually moved away from jackboot punk towards a more traditional folky approach, the tellingly titled 'THE LOVE OF HOPELESS CAUSES' (1993) marking the first fruits of a new deal with 'Epic'. Never strangers to controversy, their was a minor storm over the attendant 'HERE COMES THE WAR' single, its enclosed instructions on how to construct a nuclear device typical of NEW MODEL ARMY's militantly subversive approach. • **Songwriters:** All written by SULLIVAN / HEATON. • **Trivia:** SULLIVAN and HEATON played back-up to the former's girlfriend poet JOOLZ on many stage shows.

Album rating: HISTORY THE SINGLES (*7) / VENGEANCE (*8)

SLADE THE LEVELLER (b. JUSTIN SULLIVAN, 1956) – vocals, guitar / **STUART MORROW** – bass / **ROBB HEATON** (b.1962) -drums

Quiet not iss.

May 83. (7"m) *(QS 002)* **BITTERSWEET. / BETCHA / TENSION** [ ] [-]
(w/free flexi-7") – FASHION / CAUSE.

Abstract not iss.

Nov 83. (7") *(ABS 0020)* **GREAT EXPECTATIONS. / WAITING** [ ] [-]
(re-iss. Feb90 – 7"blue; ABS 090)

Apr 84. (m-lp) *(ABT 006)* **VENGEANCE** [73] [-]
– Christian militia / Notice me / Smalltown England / A liberal education / Vengeance / Sex (the black angel) / Running / Spirit of the Falklands. *(c-iss.Nov85; ABTC 006) (cd-iss. Jun87 +=; ABT 006CD)* – Great expectations / Waiting / The price / 1984 / No man's land. *(blue-lp iss.Nov87 with 6xlp-box-set of 'Abstract' label records: 'SIX DISQUES BLEU')*

Oct 84. (7") *(ABS 0028)* **THE PRICE. / 1984** [ ] [-]
(12"+=) *(12ABS 0028)* – No man's land / Notice me / Great expectations.

E.M.I. Capitol

Apr 85. (c-s/7") *(TC+/NMA 1)* **NO REST. / HEROIN** [28] [-]
(d12"+=) *(12NMA 1 – PSLP 387) – Vengeance (live) / The price (live) / No greater love (live).*

May 85. (lp/c) *(EJ 240335-1/-4) <12432>* **NO REST FOR THE WICKED** [22] [ ]
– Frightened / Ambition / Grandmother's footsteps / Better than them / My country / No greater love / No rest / Young, gifted & skint / Drag it down / Shot 18 / The attack. *(re-iss. May88 on 'Fame' lp/c; FA/TC-FA 3198) (cd-iss. Jul89; CDFA 3198)*

Jun 85. (d7") *(NMA 2)* **BETTER THAN THEM. / NO SENSE // ADRENELIN. / TRUST** [49] [-]
(7"ep)(12"ep) *(NMAD – NMA 22)(12NMA 2)* – THE ACOUSTIC EP

— **JASON 'MOOSE' HARRIS** repl. MORROW

Nov 85. (7") *(NMA 3)* **BRAVE NEW WORLD. / R.I.P.** [57] [-]
(12"+=) *(12NMA 3)* – Brave new world 2.
(d12"+=) *(12NMA 3 – PSLP 395)* – Young, gifted & skint (live) / Sex (the black angel) (live)

Sep 86. (lp/c) *(EMC/TC-EMC 3516)* **THE GHOST OF CAIN** [45] [ ]
– The hunt / Lights go out / 51st state / All of this / Poison street / Western dream / Love songs / Heroes / Ballad / Master race. *(cd-iss. Jul89; CDP 746695-2) (re-iss. Jul90 on 'Fame' cd/c/lp; CD/TC+/FA 3237)*

Oct 86. (7") *(NMA 4)* **51st STATE. / TEN COMMANDMENTS** [71] [-]
(d12"+=) *(NMA 4 – PSLP 348)* – A liberal education (live) / No rest (live) / No man's land (live).

Feb 87. (7",7"red) *(NMA 5)* **POISON STREET. / COURAGE** [64] [-]
(12"+=) *(12NMA 5)* – ('A'extended version).
(d12"+=) *(12NMA 5 – PSLP 1002)* – All of this (live) / My country (live).

Jun 87. (7"ep/12"ep) *(NMA/12NMA 6)* **WHITE COATS / THE CHARGE. / CHINESE WHISPERS / MY COUNTRY** [50] [-]

Dec 88. (m-lp/m-c) *<CLP/C4P 46928>* **SEVEN SONGS** [-] [ ]
– My country (live) / Waiting / 51st state / The hunt (live) / White coats / The charge / Chinese whispers.

Jan 89. (7"/7"g-f) *(NMA/+G 7)* **STUPID QUESTIONS. / NOTHING TOUCHES** [31] [-]
(12") *(12NMA 7)* – ('A'extended) / Betcha (live).
(cd-s++=) *(CDNMA 7)* – 51st state.

Feb 89. (cd/c/lp) *(CD/TC+/EMC 3552)* **THUNDER AND CONSOLATION** [20] [ ]
– I love the world / Stupid questions / 225 / Inheritence / Green and grey / Ballad of Bodmin Pill / Family / Family life / Vagabonds / Archway towers. *(re-iss. Aug91 on 'Fame', cd+=/c/lp; CD/TC+/FA 3257)*– The charge / Chinese whispers / Nothing changes / White coats.

Feb 89. (7"/7"g-f/7"pic-d) *(NMA/+G/P 8)* **VAGABONDS. / DEAD EYE** [37] [-]
(12"+=) *(12NMA 8)* – ('A'extended) / White coats (live).
(cd-s++=) *(CDNMA 8)* – Lights go out (extended).

Jun 89. (7"/7"pic-d) *(NMA/+P 9)* **GREEN AND GREY. / THE CHARGE (live)** [37] [-]
(12") *(12NMA 9)* – ('A'side) / Family life (live) / 125 mph (live).
(cd-s+=) *(CDNMA 9)* – Green and grey (live).

— **NELSON** – bass (ex-HIDING PLACE) repl. JASON

Aug 90. (7") *(NMA 10)* **GET ME OUT. / PRISON** [34] [-]
(10"+=) *(10NMA 10)* – ('A'extended) / Waiting (live).
(12"+=) *(12NMA 10)* – ('A'extended) / White coats (live).
(cd-s+=) *(CDNMA 10)* – White coats (live) / Waiting (live).

Sep 90. (cd/c/lp) *(CD/TC+/EMC 3581)* **IMPURITY** [23] [ ]
– Get me out / Space / Innocense / Purity / Whirlwind / Lust for power / Bury the hatchet / 11 years / Lurkstop / Before I get old / Vanity. *(cd+=)* – Marrakesh. *(re-iss. Oct92 & Jul98 on 'Fame' cd/c; CD/TC FA 3273)*

Oct 90. (c-s/7") *(TC+/NMA 11)* **PURITY (IS A LIE). / CURSE** [61] [-]
(12"+=/cd-s+=) *(12/CD NMA 12)* – ('A'extended) / Vengeance (live).

May 91. (c-s/7") *(TC+/NMA 13)* **SPACE (live). / FAMILY LIFE** [39] [-]
(12") *(12NMA 13)* – ('A'side) / No rest (live) / Stupid questions (live).
(cd-s) *(CDNMA 13)* – ('A'side) / 225 (live) / Ambition (live).
(10") *(10NMA 13)* – ('A'side) / Bury the hatchet (live) / Stupid questions (live).

Jun 91. (cd/c/lp) *(CD/TC+/EMC 3595)* **RAW MELODY MEN (live)** [43] [-]
– Whirlwind / The charge / Space / Purity / White coats / Vagabonds / Get me out / Lib. fol / Better than them / Innocense / Love songs / Innhstaap / Archway towers / Smalltown England / Green & grey / The world. *(re-iss. Jun93 on 'Fame' cd/c; CD/TC FA 3296)*

Apr 92. (cd/c/lp) *(CD/TC+/EMC 3622)* **HISTORY THE SINGLES 1985-91** (compilation) [ ] [ ]
– No rest / Better than them / Brave new world / 51st state / Poison street / White coats / Stupid questions / Vagabonds / Green and grey / Get me out / Purity / Space (live). *(incl.free 12")*– Far Better Thing / Higher Wall / Adrenalin (version) Luurstaap (acoustic). *(cd+=/c+=)* – (2 extra tracks *)

— Jun'92, JUSTIN was nearly killed when he was electrocuted on stage.

Epic Epic

Jan 93. (7") *(658 935-7)* **HERE COMES THE WAR. / MODERN TIMES** [25] [-]
(12"+=/cd-s+=) *(658 935-6/-2)* – Ghost of your father.

Mar 93. (cd/c/lp) *(473 356-2/-4/-1)* **THE LOVE OF HOPELESS CAUSES** [22] [ ]
– Here comes the war / Fate / Living in the rose / White light / Believe it / Understand U / My people / These words / Afternoon song / Bad old world.

Jul 93. (12"ep/cd-ep) *(659 244-6/-2)* **THE BALLADS EP** [51] [-]
– Living in a rose / Drummy B / Marry the sea / Sleepwalking.

— split around 1994, although they arrived back four years later. Line-up: **SULLIVAN, HEATON, NELSON** plus **DAVE BLOMBERG** – guitar, keyboards, vocals / **DEAN WHITE** – keyboards, clarinet / plus a string & brass section

Eagle unknown

Apr 98. (cd/c) *(EAG CD/MC 021)* **STRANGE BROTHERHOOD** [72] [-]
– Wonderful way to go / Whites of their eyes / Aimless desire / Over the wire / Queen of my heart / Gigabyte wars / Killing / No pain / Headlights / Big blue / Long goodbye / Lullaby.

Apr 98. (c-s) *(EAGCS 021)* **WONDERFUL WAY TO GO / REFUGEE** [ ] [-]
(cd-s+=) *(EAGXA 021)* – South west / ('A'-radio edit).
(cd-s) *(EAGXS 021)* – ('A'side) / F?NY / BD7 / Ballad of Bodmin Pill.

– compilations, others, etc. –

on 'Abstract' unless mentioned otherwise

Apr 88. (m-lp/cd) *(ABT 017/+CD)* **RADIO SESSIONS (1983-1984 rare)** [ ] [-]

Dec 93. (cd) *Windsong; (WINCD 051)* **BBC RADIO 1 LIVE IN CONCERT (live)** [ ] [-]

Sep 94. (cd) *E.M.I.; (CDEMC 3688)* **B SIDES AND ABANDONED TRACKS** [ ] [-]

Oct 94. (12"ep/cd-ep) **VENGEANCE 1994. / ('A'-Zion Train mix) / ('A'-The Headman mix) / ('A'-Pressure Of Speech mix)** [ ] [-]

Jun 95. (d-cd) *(NMA 001CD)* **VENGEANCE / RADIO SESSIONS** [ ] [-]

NEW ORDER

Formed: Manchester, England ... mid-'80, from the fragments of JOY DIVISION following the death of frontman IAN CURTIS on the 18th of May 1980. The remaining JOY DIVISION members, vocalist/guitarist BERNARD ALBRECHT (now SUMNER), bassist PETER HOOK and drummer STEPHEN MORRIS remained with 'Factory' records, subsequently adopting the NEW ORDER moniker at the suggestion of manager Rob Gretton. With SUMNER taking over vocal duties, the group gigged around Manchester, eventually releasing a debut single, 'CEREMONY' in 1981. This broke the Top 40, as did the Martin Hannett-produced follow-up, 'PROCESSION' / 'EVERYTHING'S GONE GREEN' although in reality, these releases weren't much of a departure from the rumbling, melodic bass sound of old, critics unimpressed with SUMNER's weak vocals. With their debut album, 'MOVEMENT' (1981), however, NEW ORDER were beginning to crystallise their own unique sound, new recruit GILLIAN GILBERT embellishing the music with cutting keyboard swathes. A subtle dance feel was also edging it's way in and with the release of 'TEMPTATION' the following year, NEW ORDER had begun experimenting openly with sequencing technology. The single married the raw cut 'n' thrust of alternative rock to danceable rhythms, echoing hip-hop's similar experimentation with European electronica (see AFRIKA BAMBAATAA's seminal KRAFTWERK-sampling 'Planet Rock') and creating sonic waves that are still rippling through the eclectic musical free-for-all of the 90's. Fittingly then, NEW ORDER's tour de force, 'BLUE MONDAY' was produced by cult US hip-hop producer, Arthur Baker. The best selling 12 inch single in the history of rock, the record was dominated by compelling, almost militaristic dancefloor beats behind SUMNER's moodily introspective, melancholy vocal musings and HOOK's insidious bass melody. A true crossover single, the record appealed to indie fans, B-boys and club posers alike, cementing NEW ORDER's reputation as one of the UK's most street-cred acts. The accompanying album (an inferior demo version of 'BLUE MONDAY', '5-8-6' was included at the expense of the original single), 'POWER, CORRUPTION AND LIES' (1983) made the Top 5, confirming NEW ORDER's commitment to electronic experimentation via a hypnotic, slightly hazy set. A further Arthur Baker-produced 12 inch single followed, 'CONFUSION', the New Yorker also collaborating on the 1984 follow-up, 'THIEVES LIKE US'. But it wasn't until the acclaimed 'LOW LIFE' the following year that NEW ORDER successfully integrated the various strands which made up their imimitable sound. Previewed by the affecting 'PERFECT KISS' single and arguably the most consistently listenable NEW ORDER long player, the record convincingly welded driving, bass-heavy rock onto dance rhythms as well as featuring some interesting stylistic diversions. 'BROTHERHOOD' (1986) was a harder-edged affair, enjoyable enough and boasting the brilliant 'BIZARRE LOVE TRIANGLE', although hardly breaking new ground. 'TRUE FAITH' was another landmark NEW ORDER single; co-written and produced by STEPHEN HAGUE (who'd worked wonders on the PET SHOP BOYS' early material), the single was a hauntingly infectious piece of dance-pop, possibly the most commercial material NEW ORDER had ever released. Following the release of the best selling compilation, 'SUBSTANCE (1980-1987)' later that summer, the band went to ground, finally resurfacing in 1989 with 'TECHNIQUE' and quashing rumours of an imminent split. Heavily influenced by the house explosion of the late 80's and partly recorded on the Balearic Island of Ibiza, the album fully indulged the band's dancier leanings with a verve and passion that's missing from much of their later work. Deservedly, the album rode into the No.1 spot on the back of the club zeitgeist, a scene NEW ORDER had a major hand in creating. The single, 'FINE TIME', almost made the Top 10, an uncharacteristically humerous ditty featuring parodic mock-medallion man, BARRY WHITE-esque vocal rumblings. The following year, NEW ORDER were back at No.1 with their World Cup theme tune, 'WORLD IN MOTION'. Nationalist prejudice aside, this song seemed to set the trend for the nauseous, 'Enger-land' limp-wristed crap that the LIGHTNING SEEDS would update six years later for the European championships. Maybe NEW ORDER felt the same way, as the various members soon drifted away to their respective side projects; HOOK to the muscular REVENGE (subsequently stiffing with the 'ONE TRUE PASSION' album), GILBERT and MORRIS to The OTHER TWO ('93's 'THE OTHER TWO AND YOU' album getting lost in the ether when 'Factory' went belly-up) and SUMNER hooking up with JOHNNY MARR (ex-SMITHS) and occasionally NEIL TENNANT (PET SHOP BOYS) to form ELECTRONIC. By far the most successful NEW ORDER-offshoot, the group scored three Top 20 hit singles, including the pop wistfulness of 'GETTING AWAY WITH IT'. They also narrowly missed No.1 with their 1991 eponymous album, their akin to a breezier NEW ORDER, fusing house and indie-pop with wry, intelligent lyrics. With 'Factory' going bust following HAPPY MONDAYS' bank-breaking 'SUNSHINE AND LOVE' debacle, a belated NEW ORDER follow-up, 'REPUBLIC' (1993), was subsequently released on 'London' records. A strangely muted collection, the record nevertheless spawned a succession of Top 30 singles including the aptly named Top 5 hit, 'REGRET'. Rumours of tensions within the group persisted and after a final appearance at the 1993 Reading Festival, the various members soon went off to do their own thing once more. ELECTRONIC charted with another set, 'RAISE THE PRESSURE' in 1996 and HOOK came up with the highly-NEW ORDER-esque MONACO project the following year. • **Songwriters:** All group compositions except; TURN THE HEATER ON (Keith Hudson). • **Trivia:** In 1987, they contributed some tracks to the movie, 'Salvation'.

Album rating: MOVEMENT (*8) / POWER, CORRUPTION AND LIES (*9) / LOW-LIFE (*8) / BROTHERHOOD (*8) / TECHNIQUE (*9) / SUBSTANCE 1980-1987 compilation (*10) / THE BEST OF NEW ORDER compilation (*9) / Electronic: ELECTRONIC (*8) / Monaco: MUSIC FOR PLEASURE (*6)

BERNARD SUMNER (b.BERNARD DICKEN, 4 Jan'56) – vocals, guitar / **PETER HOOK** (b.13 Feb'56) – bass / **STEPHEN MORRIS** (b.28 Oct'57, Macclesfield, England) – drums

Factory Streetwise

Mar 81. (7"/ext.12") *(FAC 33/+T)* **CEREMONY. / IN A LONELY PLACE** [34] [-]
(re-iss. Jul81 re-recorded; FAC 33-12)

— added **GILLIAN GILBERT** (b.27 Jan'61) – keyboards, synth.

Sep 81. (7") *(FAC 53)* **PROCESSION. / EVERYTHING'S GONE GREEN** [38] [-]

Nov 81. (lp) *(FACT 50)* **MOVEMENT** [30] [-]
– Dreams never end / Truth / Senses / Chosen time / I.C.B. / The him / Doubts even here / Denial. *(re-iss. Nov86 c)(cd; FACT 50C)(FACD 50) (re-iss. Jul93 on 'Centredate' cd/c;)*

Dec 81. Factory Benelux; (12"m) *(FBN 8)* **EVERYTHING'S GONE GREEN (extended). / MESH / CRIES AND WHISPERS** [-] [-] Belg.
(re-iss. cd-ep Jul90; FBN 8CD)

May 82. (7"/ext.12") *(FAC 63/+T)* **TEMPTATION. / HURT** [29] [-]

Nov 82. Factory Benelux; (m-lp) *(FACTUS 8)* **NEW ORDER 1981-82** (compilation) [-] [-] Belg.

Mar 83. (12") *(FAC 73)* **BLUE MONDAY. / THE BEACH** [9] [ ]

May 83. (lp)(c) *(FACT 75)(FACTUS 12C)* <25308> **POWER, CORRUPTION AND LIES** [4] [ ]
– Your silent face / Ultraviolence / Ecstasy / Leave me alone / Age of consent / We all stand / The village / 5-8-6. *(re-iss. Nov86 c)(cd; FACT 75C)(FAC 75CD)* – Blue Monday / The beach. *(re-iss. Jul93 on 'Centredate' cd/c;)*

Aug 83. (12"ep) *(FAC 93)* **CONFUSION. / CONFUSED BEATS / CONFUSION (instrumental & Rough mixes)** [12] [ ]

Apr 84. (12") *(FAC 103)* **THIEVES LIKE US. / LONESOME TONIGHT** [18] [ ]

May 84. Factory Benelux; (12") *(FBN 22)* **MURDER. / THIEVES LIKE US (instrumental)** [-] [-] Belg.

Factory Qwest

May 85. (7") *(FAC 123)* **THE PERFECT KISS. / THE KISS OF DEATH** [46] [-]
(12"+=) *(FAC 123-12)* – Perfect pit.

Jun 85. (7") **THE PERFECT KISS. / PERFECT PIT** [-] [ ]

May 85. (lp/c)(cd) *(FACT 100/+C)(FACD 100)* <25289> **LOW-LIFE** [7] [94]
– Sooner than you think / Sub-culture / Face up / Love vigilantes / Elegia / The perfect kiss / This time of the night / Sunrise. *(c+=)* – The perfect kiss / The kiss of death / Perfect pit. *(re-iss. Jul93 on 'Centredate' cd/c;)*

Nov 85. (7"/ext.12") *(FAC 133/+T)* **SUB-CULTURE. / DUB-CULTURE** [63] [-]

Mar 86. (7") *(FAC 143)* **SHELLSHOCK. / THIEVES LIKE US (instrumental)** [20] [-]
(12") *(FAC 143T)* – ('A'extended) / Shellshock (dub).

Sep 86. (ext.12"/7") *(FAC 153/+7)* **STATE OF THE NATION. / SHAME OF THE NATION** [30] [-]

Oct 86. (lp/c/s-lp)(cd) *(FACT 150/+C/SP)(FACD 150)* <25511> **BROTHERHOOD** [9] [ ]
– Paradise / Weirdo / As it was when it was / Broken promise / Way of life / Bizarre love triangle / All day long / Angel dust / Every little counts. *(cd+=)* – State of the nation. *(re-iss. Jul93 on 'Centredate' cd/c;)*

Nov 86. (ext.12"/7") *(FAC 163/+7)* **BIZARRE LOVE TRIANGLE. / BIZARRE DUB TRIANGLE** [56] [-]

Mar 87. (7") **BIZARRE LOVE TRIANGLE. / EVERY LITTLE COUNTS** [-] [ ]

Jul 87. (ext-12"/7") *(FAC 183/+7)* <28271> **TRUE FAITH. / 1963** [4] [32] Oct87
(remix-12"+=) *(FAC 183R)* – True dub.

Aug 87. (d-lp/d-c)(d-cd) *(FACT 200/+C)(FACD 200)* <25621> **SUBSTANCE (1980-1987)** (compilation) [3] [36]
– Ceremony / Everthing's gone green / Temptation / Blue Monday / Confusion / Thieves like us / Perfect kiss / Subculture / Shellshock / State of the nation / Bizarre love triangle / True faith. *(d-c+=)* – Procession / Mesh / Hurt / In a lonely place / The beach / Confused / Murder / Lonesome tonight / Kiss of death / Shame of the nation / 1963. *(cd++=)* – Cries and whispers / Dub culture / Shellcock / Bizarre dub triangle. *(re-iss. Jul93 on 'Centredate' cd/c;); hit UK No.32) (d-cd re-iss. Jun98; 520008-2)*

Dec 87. (ext.12"/7") *(FAC 193/+7)* **TOUCHED BY THE HAND OF GOD. / TOUCHED BY THE HAND OF DUB** [20] [-]
(cd-s) *(FACD 193)* – ('A'extended) / Confusion (dub '87) / Temptation (original).

Mar 88. (7") **TOUCHED BY THE HAND OF GOD. / BLUE MONDAY 1988** [-] [ ]

Dec 88. (7") *(FAC 223-7)* **FINE TIME. / DON'T DO IT** [11] [ ]
(12"+=) *(FAC 223)* – Fine line.
(cd-s+=) *(FACCD 223)* – ('A'-Silk mix) / ('A'-Messed around mix).

Jan 89. (cd)(lp/c/dat) *(FACD 275)(FACT 275/+C/D)* <25845> **TECHNIQUE** [1] [32]
– Fine time / All the way / Love less / Round & round / Guilty partner / Run / Mr. Disco / Vanishing point / Dream attack. *(re-iss. Jul93 on 'Centredate' cd/c;)*

Mar 89. (ext.12"/7") *(FAC 263/+7)* <27524> **ROUND & ROUND. / BEST AND MARSH** [21] [64]
(ext.& club-12"+=) *(FAC 263R)* – ('A'-Detroit mix).
(cd-s+=) *(FACD 263)* – Vanishing point (instrumental 'Making Out' mix) / ('A'-12"mix).
(3"cd-s) *(FACD 263R)* – ('A'-Detroit) / ('A'-12") / ('A'-club).

Sep 89. (7") *(FAC 273-7)* **RUN 2. / MTO** [49] [-]
(12"+=) *(FAC 273)* – ('A'extended) / ('B'-Minus mix).

May 90. (12"/7"/c-s; as ENGLAND / NEW ORDER) *(FAC 293/+7/C)* **WORLD IN MOTION . . .. / THE B SIDE** [1] [-]
(cd-s+=) *(FACD 293)* – No alla violenzia / ('A'-Subbuteo mix).
(12") *(FAC 293R)* – ('A'-Subbuteo mix) / ('A'-Subbuteo dub) / No alla violenzia mix / ('A'-Carabinieri mix).

— Around the late 80's/early 90's, all members splintered to do own projects

Centredate Qwest

Apr 93. (7"/c-s) *(NUO/+C 1)* <18586> **REGRET. / ('A'mix)** [4] [28]
(cd-s+=) *(NUOCD 1)* – ('A'-Fire Island mix) / ('A'-Junior's dub mix).
(12") *(NUOX 1)* – ('A'-Fire Island mix) / ('A'-Junior's dub mix) / (2-'A' Sabres mixes)

May 93. (cd/c/lp) *(828413-2/-4/-1)* <45250> **REPUBLIC** [1] [11]
– Regret / World / Ruined in a day / Spooky / Everyone everywhere / Young offender / Liar / Chemical / Times change / Special / Avalanche.

Jun 93. (7"/c-s) *(NUO/+C 2)* **RUINED IN A DAY. / VICIOUS CIRCLE (mix)** [22] [-]
(cd-s+=) *(NUOCD 2)* – ('A'mixes).
(cd-s) *(NUOCDX 2)* – ('A'mixes).
(12") *(NUOX 2)* – ('A'side) / World (the price of dub mix).

Aug 93. (c-s) *(NUOC 3)* <18432> **WORLD (THE PRICE OF LOVE) / ('A'mixes)** [13] [-]
(12"+=/cd-s+=) *(NUOX/NUOCD 3)* – ('A'-Perfecto + sexy club mixes).
(cd-s) *(NUOCDX 3)* – ('A'-Brothers in rhythm mix) / ('A'dubstramental mix) / ('A'-World in action mix) / ('A'-Pharmacy dub).

Sep 93. (c-s,cd-s) <18432> **WORLD (THE PRICE OF LOVE) / RUINED IN A DAY** [-] [92]

Dec 93. (c-s/12"/cd-s) *(NUO MC/X/CD 4)* **SPOOKY. / (3 'A' mixes-magimix-minimix-moulimix)** [22] [ ]
(cd-s) *(NUCDP 4)* – ('A'-Out of order mix) / ('A'-Stadium mix) / ('A'-In Heaven mix) / ('A'-Boo-dub mix) / ('A'-Stadium instrumental).

Nov 94. (7"/c-s) *(NUO/+MC 5)* **TRUE FAITH '94. / ('A'-Perfecto mix)** [9] [ ]
(12"+=) *(NUOX 5)* – ('A'-sexy disco dub mix) / ('A'-TWA Gim Up North mix).
(cd-s++=) *(NUOCD 5)* – ('A'radio mix).

Nov 94. (cd/c/d-lp) *(828 580-2/-4/-1)* <45794> **? (THE BEST OF)** (compilation) [4] [78]
– True faith '94 / Bizarre love triangle '94 / 1963 / Regret / Fine time / The perfect kiss / Shellshock / Thieves like us / Vanishing point / Run (2) / Round and round '94 / World (price of love) / Ruined in a day / Touched by the hand of God / Blue Monday '88 / World in motion.

Jan 95. (c-s) *(NUOMC 6)* **NINETEEN63 (Arthur Baker remix) / ('A'-'94 album version) / ('A'-Lionrock full throttle mix) / ('A'-Joe T Venelli remix)** [21] [ ]
(12") *(NUOX 6)* – ('A'-Lionrock & Joe T mixes / True faith (Eschreamer mix)/ ('A'-Eschreamer dub).
(cd-s) *(NUOCD 6)* – ('A'-Arthur Baker remix) / Let's go/ Spooky (Nightstripper mix)/ True faith '87 (Shep Pettibone mix).

Jul 95. (c-s) *(NUOMC 7)* **BLUE MONDAY '95 / ('A'-original)** [17] [-]
(12"+=/cd-s+=) *(NUO X/CD 7)* – ('A'-Hardfloor mix) / ('A'-Jam & Spoon mix).

Jul 95. (cd-ep) <20546> **BIZARRE LOVE TRIANGLE (2 mixes) / STATE OF THE NATION (2 mixes)** [-] [98]

Aug 95. (cd/c) *(828 661-2/-4)* **THE REST OF NEW ORDER** (remixes, etc) [5] [ ]

– compilations, etc. –

Sep 86. (12"ep) *Strange Fruit; (SFPS 001)* **PEEL SESSIONS** (1.6.82.) [54] [-]
– Turn the heater on / We all stand / 586 / Too late. *(re-iss. Jul87 c-ep; SFPSC 001) (re-iss. Mar88 cd-ep; SFPSCD 001)*

Oct 87. (12"ep) *Strange Fruit; (SFPS 039)* **PEEL SESSIONS** (26.1.81.) [ ] [-]
– Truth / Senses / I.C.B. / Dreams never end. *(re-iss. May88 cd-ep; SFPSCD 039)*

Mar 88. (7"/12") *Factory; (FAC 73-7/R) / Qwest; <27979>* **BLUE MONDAY 1988. / BEACH BUGGY** [3] [68]
(cd-s+=) *(FACD 73)* – ('A'original).

Sep 90. (m-cd/m-c/m-lp) *Strange Fruit; (SFR CD/C/LP 110)* **PEEL SESSIONS** (2 ep's combined) [ ] [-]

Feb 92. (cd/c/lp) *Windsong; (WIN CD/MC/LP 011)* **BBC RADIO 1 LIVE IN CONCERT (live June '87)** [33] [-]
– Touched by the hand of God / Temptation / True faith / Your silent face / Every second counts / Bizarre love triangle / Perfect kiss / Age of consent / Sister Ray.

Sep 97. (12") *Touch; (502780314769)* **TOUCH TONE 7.1** [ ] [-]

— In Mar'89, issued two 5"cd-videos of TRUE FAITH + BLUE MONDAY '88.

ELECTRONIC

BERNARD SUMNER – vocals, guitar / **JOHNNY MARR** – guitar (ex-SMITHS) + both programmers. also with **NEIL TENNANT** – vocals (of PET SHOP BOYS)

Factory Warners

Dec 89. (7"/c-s) *(FAC 257-7/-C)* <19880> **GETTING AWAY WITH IT. / LUCKY BAG** [12] [38]
(12"+=/cd-s+=) *(FAC 257)* – ('A'extended).
(12"+=) *(FAC 257)* – ('A'extra mixes).

— added further guests **CHRIS LOWE, DONALD JOHNSON, DAVID PALMER, DENISE JOHNSON, HELEN POWELL + ANDREW ROBINSON** (on same track)

Apr 91. (7"/c-s) *(FAC 287-7/-C)* **GET THE MESSAGE. / FREE WILL** [8] [ ]
(cd-s+=) *(FACD 287)* – ('A'-DNA groove mix).
(12"+=) *(FAC-12 287)* – ('A' 2 other mixes).

May 91. (cd)(lp/c) *(FACD 290)(FACT 290/+C) <26387>* **ELECTRONIC** 2
– Idiot country / Reality / Tighten up / The patience of a saint / Gangster / Soviet / Get the message / Try all you want / Some distant memory / Feel every beat. *(re-iss. Feb94 on 'Parlophone' cd/c; CD/TC PRG 1012)*
Sep 91. (7"/c-s) *(FAC 328-7/-C)* **FEEL EVERY BEAT. / LEAN TO THE INSIDE** 39
(12"+=) *(FAC-12 328)* – ('A'dub version).
(cd-s+=) *(FACD 328)* – Second to none / ('A' DNA mix)

— next with NEIL TENNANT again

Parlophone Warners

Jun 92. (c-s/7") *(TC+/R 6311)* **DISAPPOINTED. / IDIOT COUNTRY TWO** 6
(12"+=/cd-s+=) *(12R/CDR 6311)* – ('A'-808 State mix) / ('B'-Ultimatum mix).
Jun 96. (c-s/7") *(TC+/R 6436)* **FORBIDDEN CITY. / IMITATION OF LIFE** 14
(cd-s+=) *(CDR 6436)* – A new religion.
Jul 96. (cd/c) *(CD/TC+/PCS 7382) <45955>* **RAISE THE PRESSURE** 8
– Forbidden city / For you / Dark angel / One day / Until the end of time / Second nature / If you've got love / Out of my league / Interlude / Freefall / Visit me / How long / Time can tell.
Sep 96. (c-s) *(TCR 6445)* **FOR YOU / ALL THAT I NEED** 16
(cd-s+=) *(CDR 6445)* – I feel alright.
(cd-s) *(CDRS 6445)* – ('A'side) / Free will (12"mix) / Disappointed / Get the message (DNA mix).
Feb 97. (c-s) *(TCR 6455)* **SECOND NATURE / TURNING POINT** 35
(cd-s+=) *(CDRS 6455)* – Feel every beat (12"remix).
(cd-s) *(CDR 6455)* – ('A'side) / ('A'-Plastik mix) / ('A'-Trance Atlantic dub) / ('A'-Sweet remix).

REVENGE

PETER HOOK – bass / with **DAVE HICKS** – words, vocals / **C. JONES**

Factory Capitol

Nov 89. (7") *(FAC 247-7)* **REASONS. / JESUS I LOVE YOU**
(12"+=) *(FAC 247)* – Love you 2.
(cd-s+=) *(FACD 247)* – ('B'version) / Bleach boy.
May 90. (7"/c-s) *(FAC 267-7/-C)* **PINEAPPLE FACE. / 14K**
(12"+=) *(FAC 267)* – ('A'-Revenge version).
(cd-s+=) *(FACD 267)* – ('A'-Last Lunge version).
Jun 90. (cd)(lp/c) *(FACD 230)(FAC 230/+C) <94053>* **ONE TRUE PASSION**
– Pineapple face / Big bang / Lose the chrome / Slave / Bleachman / Surf Nazi / Fag hag / It's quiet.
Sep 90. (7") **(I'M NOT YOUR) SLAVE. / AMSTERDAM**
(12"+=)(cd-s+=) – ('A' II version) / Slave.

— DAVE HICKS departed Apr'91, replaced by **POTTSY**

Dec 91. (12"ep/cd-ep) *<98479>* **GUN WORLD PORN** Feb92
– Deadbeat (remix) / Cloud nine / State of shock / Little pig.

MONACO

PETER HOOK – bass (now departed from NEW ORDER) / **DAVID POTTS** – guitar, vocals

Polydor A&M

Mar 97. (7"/c-s) *(573 190-7/-4)* **WHAT DO YOU WANT FROM ME? / BICYCLE THIEF** 11 –
(cd-s+=) *(573 191-2)* – Ultra.
May 97. (c-s) *(571 054-4)* **SWEET LIPS / SHATTERED** 18 –
(cd-s+=) *(571 055-2)* – ('A'-Tony De Vit mix) / ('A'-arley & Heller mix).
(cd-s) *(571 057-1/-2)* – ('A'side) / ('A'-Farley & Heller mix) / ('A'-Joey Negro mix).
Jun 97. (cd/c/lp) *(<537 242-2/-4/-1>)* **MUSIC FOR PLEASURE** 11
– What do you want from me? / Shine / Sweet lips / Buzz gum / Blue / Junk / Billy Bones / Happy Jack / Tender / Sedona.
Sep 97. (7"/c-s) *(571 418-7/-4)* **SHINE. /**
(cd-s+=) *(571 418-2)* –

The OTHER TWO

STEPHEN + GILLIAN

Parlophone Warners

Oct 91. (7"/c-s) *(FAC 329-7/-C)* **TASTY FISH (Pascal mix). / ('A'mix)** 41 –
(12"+=/cd-s+=) *(FAC/+D 329)* – ('A'-Almond slice mix).

London London

Oct 93. (7"/c-s) *(TWO/+CD 1)* **SELFISH. / SELFISH (that pop mix)** 46
(12"+=/cd-s+=) *(TWO X/CD 1)* – ('A'-East Village vocal mix) / ('A'-Waterfront mix).
Nov 93. (cd/c/lp) *(<520028-2/-4/-1>)* **THE OTHER TWO AND YOU**
– Tasty fish / The greatest thing / Selfish / Movin' on / Ninth configuration / Feel this love / Spirit level / Night voice / Innocence. *(cd+=)* – Love it.

NEW RACE (see under ⇒ RADIO BIRDMAN)

NEWTOWN NEUROTICS

Formed: Harlow, Essex, England . . . mid 1978 by STEVE DREWETT, COLIN DREDD and TIGGY BARBER. Instigating their own 'No Wonder' label, these agit power-poppers struggled to make an impact at the turn of the decade with their first two 45's, 'HYPOCRITE' and 'WHEN THE OIL RUNS OUT'. With SIMON LOMOND having replaced TIGGY, the newlook trio returned with a harder hitting political agenda on 1982's 'KICK OUT THE TORIES!'. The campaign continued with a second single for 'C.N.T.' (then home to SISTERS OF MERCY), 'LICENSING HOURS', before the latter imprint went bust. A cover of the Ramones' 'BLITZKRIEG BOP', marked their debut for 'Razor' records, heralding a full-length album, 'BEGGARS CAN BE CHOOSERS' (1983); left-wing/social sentiments mixed with short-circuit guitars on a set that veered towards the overt politicism of The REDSKINS and NEW MODEL ARMY. The RAMONES influence resurfaced on 1984's solitary single, 'SUZI IS A HEARTBREAKER', while a subsequent name change to The NEUROTICS saw the band heading in a more lyrically militant but musically adept direction with the string-enhanced 'REPERCUSSIONS' (1985) set. They continued in a similar vein with two further albums, 'KICKSTARTING A BACKFIRING NATION' (1986) and 'IS YOUR WASHROOM BREEDING BOLSHEVIKS?' (1988), before calling it a day in the late 80's as political pop lost its way.

Album rating: BEGGARS CAN BE CHOOSERS (*5) / Neurotics: REPERCUSSIONS (*5) / KICKSTARTING A BACKFIRING NATION (*5) / IS YOUR WASHROOM BREEDING BOLSHEVIKS? (*4) / 45 REVOLUTIONS PER MINUTE compilation (*5)

STEVE DREWETT – vocals, guitar / **COLIN DREDD** – bass, vocals / **TIGGY BARBER** – drums

No Wonder not iss.

Nov 79. (7") *(CUS 363)* **HYPOCRITE. / YOU SAID NO** –
Nov 80. (7") *(NOW 4)* **WHEN THE OIL RUNS OUT. / OH NO** –

— **SIMON LOMOND** – drums; repl. TIGGY

C.N.T. not iss.

Jun 82. (7") *(CNT 005)* **KICK OUT THE TORIES! / MINDLESS VIOLENCE!** –
Dec 82. (7") *(CNT 010)* **LICENSING HOURS. / NO SANCTUARY** –

Razor not iss.

Aug 83. (7"m) *(RZS 107)* **BLITZKRIEG BOP. / HYPOCRITE (new version) / I REMEMBER YOU** –
Sep 83. (lp) *(RAZ 6)* **BEGGARS CAN BE CHOOSERS** –
– Newtown people / Does anybody know where the march is / Life in their hands / My death / Living with unemployment / Wake up / The mess / Get up and fight / No respect / Agony. *(cd-iss. Jan95 on 'Dojo'; DOLECD 111)*

No Wonder not iss.

Oct 84. (7"/12") *(NOW/+T 6)* **SUZI IS A HEARTBREAKER. / FOOLS** –

NEUROTICS

— same line-up, **STEVE, COLIN + SIMON**

Jungle not iss.

Jul 85. (lp) *(FREUD 07)* **REPERCUSSIONS** –
– Screaming / Sects / Creatures from another world / This fragile life / etc
Jul 86. (7") *(JUNG 29)* **LIVING WITH UNEMPLOYMENT. / AIRSTRIP 1** –
(12"+=) *(JUNG 29T)* – My death / Oh no / Mindless violence / Porky the poet / Peter Campbell.
Sep 86. (lp/c) *(FREUD/+C 10)* **KICKSTARTING A BACKFIRING NATION** –
(c+=) – REPERCUSSIONS
Mar 88. (12"ep) *(JUNG 39T)* **NEVER THOUGHT / SCREAMING (live) / STAND BY ME. / MIND OF VALERIE / SECTS / MY DEATH** –
Jul 88. (lp) *(FREUD 19)* **IS YOUR WASHROOM BREEDING BOLSHEVIKS?** –

— disbanded later in 1988, DREWETT later formed The UNSTOPPABLE FORCE

– compilations, etc. –

Nov 90. (cd) *Jungle; (FREUDCD 31)* **45 REVOLUTIONS PER MINUTE – THE SINGLES 1979-1984** –
Oct 92. (cd/lp) *Terz;* **HIS MASTER'S VOICE** –
Mar 97. (cd) *Anagram; (CDPUNK 91)* **PUNK SINGLES COLLECTION** –
– Hypocrite / You said no / When the oil runs out / Oh no / Kick out the Tories! / Mindless violence / Licensing hours / No sanctuary / Blitzkrieg bop / Hypocrite (new version) / I remember you / Suzi is a heartbreaker / Fools / Living with unemployment / Airstrip 1 / My death / Never thought / Screaming / Stand by me / Mind of Valerie / Sect / My death.

NIGHTINGALES

Formed: Birmingham, England . . . 1978 out of punk band, The PREFECTS, by mainman ROBERT LLOYD along with brother ANDY LLOYD, PAUL APPERLEY and JOW CROW. After one single, 'GOING THROUGH THE MOTIONS', they added EAMONN DUFFY. Now going under The NIGHTINGALES moniker, a follow-up single, 'IDIOT STRENGTH', appeared in Spring '81 (their second for 'Rough Trade'), benefitting from the continuing support of DJ John Peel – who had already recorded a PREFECTS session – and paving the way for a deal with the independent 'Cherry Red' label. By the recording of the band's first album, 'PIGS ON PURPOSE' (1982), CROW had been replaced by JOHN NESTOR. While the record displayed LLOYD's barbed lyrical wit on such slyly humourous ditties as 'USE YOUR LOAF', commentators criticised the lacklustre production. A move to Red Flame's 'Ink' provided a more vibrant showcase for the NIGHTINGALES' grating, angular approach with follow-up set, 'HYSTERICS' (1983) while the addition of new member, multi-instrumentalist PETE BYRCHMORE lent a new, more accessible dimension to the band's sound. Recorded with NICK BEALES in place of NESTOR, third set, 'JUST THE JOB' (1984), appeared on the new 'Vindaloo' imprint, LLOYD subsequently developing a roster that included the likes of WE'VE GOT A FUZZBOX . . . AND WE'RE GONNA USE IT and comedian TED CHIPPINGTON. The violin-enhanced (courtesy of MARIA COLLINS) 'IN THE GOOD OLD COUNTRY WAY' (1986) proved to be the NIGHTINGALES' swansong as the band's head honcho devoted his time to his label and a subsequent solo career (with his NEW FOUR SEASONS!). As vociferous in his support of the band as ever, John Peel added to his tally of NIGHTINGALES sessions by writing sleevenotes for the 1991 compilation, 'WHAT A SCREAM'. • **Note:** A different PREFECTS released two singles YOUNG WORLD + LOVE IS ALL AROUND in 1981 + 1982.

Album rating: PIGS ON PURPOSE (*5) / HYSTERICS (*4) / JUST THE JOB (*5) / IN THE GOOD OLD COUNTRY WAY (*5) / WHAT A SCREAM compilation (*6) / Robert Lloyd & The New Four Seasons: ME AND MY MOUTH (*6)

ROBERT LLOYD – vocals / **ANDY LLOYD** – guitar / **JOE 'Motivator' CROW** – bass / **PAUL APPERLEY** – drums

Rough Trade / not iss.

Jun 80. (7"; as PREFECTS) *(RT 040)* **GOING THROUGH THE MOTIONS. / THINGS IN GENERAL** ☐ -

— added **EAMONN DUFFY** – guitar, bass

Apr 81. (7") *(RT 075)* **IDIOT STRENGTH. / SECONDS** ☐ -

Cherry Red / not iss.

Feb 82. (7"ep) *(CHERRY 34)* **USE YOUR LOAF EP** ☐ -
– Use your loaf / Inside out / Under the lash.

Apr 82. (7") *(CHERRY 38)* **PARAFFIN BRAIN. / ELVIS – THE LAST TEN DAYS** ☐ -

Jul 82. (12"ep) *(12CHERRY 44)* **4 PIECE SESSION** (John Peel sessions) ☐ -
– Which hi-fi? / My brilliant career / Give 'em time / The son of God's mate.

Nov 82. (lp) *(BRED 39)* **PIGS ON PURPOSE** ☐ -
– Blood for dirt / Start from scratch / One mistake / Well done underdog / The crunch / The hedonists sigh / It lives again / Make good / Don't blink / Joking apart / Yeah it's o.k. / Use your loaf / Blisters.

— **JOHN NESTOR** – bass; had already repl. CROW who went solo

Feb 83. (7") *(CHERRY 56)* **URBAN OSPREYS. / CAKEHOLE** ☐ -

— **PETE BYRCHMORE** – guitar; repl. DUFFY

Ink / not iss.

Nov 83. (7") *(INK 71)* **CRAFTY FAG. / HOW TO AGE** ☐ -

Nov 83. (lp) *(INK 1)* **HYSTERICS** ☐ -

— **NICK BEALES** – bass, guitar; repl. NESTOR

Vindaloo / not iss.

May 84. (12"ep) *(YUS 1)* **THE CRUNCH EP** ☐ -
– The crunch / All talk / Look satisfied / Not man enough.

Sep 84. (lp) *(VILP 1)* **JUST THE JOB** ☐ -

— **ROBERT, ANDY, PETE + PAUL** recruited **HOWARD JENNER** – bass to repl. BEALES who formed The PIG BROS

Feb 85. (7") *(UGH 9)* **IT'S A CRACKER. / HERE WE GO NOW** ☐ -

Sep 85. (12"ep) *(YUS 4)* **WHAT A CARRY ON / CARRY ON CARRYING ON. / COMFORT AND JOY / FIRST MY JOB** ☐ -
(free-7"flexi w.a.) – HOW TO AGE. / HEROIN

— **MARIA COLLINS** – violin; repl. ANDY who formed LITTLE RED SCHOOL HOUSE / **RON COLLINS** – drums; repl. PAUL

Mar 86. (lp) *(YUS 7)* **IN THE GOOD OLD COUNTRY WAY** ☐ -
– Leave it out / Coincidence / The headache collector / How to age / No can do / etc.

— In Jul'86, they featured on their labels' VINDALOO SUMMER SPECIAL 7", which featured WE'VE GOT A FUZZBOX AND WE'RE GONNA USE IT and TED CHIPPINGTON. This hit UK No.56 with tracks ROCKIN' WITH RITA (HEAD TO TOE) / LET'S SURF

— Disbanded later in '86. MARIA and PETE formed The CAPITOLS, MARIA also being part of RUMBLEFISH, who issued a trio of 45's, 'TUG BOAT LINE', 'MEDICINE' and 'DON'T LEAVE ME', before splitting summer '88

– compilations, etc. –

Apr 87. (12"ep; as PREFECTS) *Strange Fruit; (SFPS 025)* **THE PEEL SESSIONS** (8.1.79) ☐ -
– Faults / Motions / Barbarella's / Total luck.

Jul 88. (12"ep) *Strange Fruit; (SFPS 052)* **THE PEEL SESSIONS** ☐ -
– Start from scratch / Butter bricks / Torn / 12 years.

Jun 91. (cd) *Mau Mau; (MAUCD 607)* **WHAT A SCREAM (1980-1986)** ☐ -
– Bristol road leads to Dachau / Hark my love / Nowhere to run (alternative mix) / Blisters / Idiot strength / Seconds / Return journey / The crunch / The hedonists sigh / My brilliant career / Use your loaf / Which hi-fi? / Parrafin brain / Only my Opinion / Urban ospreys / This / Surplus and scarcity / Crafty fag / It's a cracker / Here we go now / Heroin / What a carry on / Faithful lump / At the end of the day.

ROBERT LLOYD & The NEW FOUR SEASONS

— ROBERT had early in 1986 released with VI SUBVERSA (of POISON GIRLS) the single 'KEEP LYING, I LOVE IT' for 'Vindaloo'.

In-Tape / not iss.

Jul 88. (7") *(IT 056)* **SOMETHING NICE. / ALL THE TIME IN THE WORLD** ☐ -
(12"+=) *(ITT 056)* – Of course you can't.

Oct 88. (7") *(IT 059)* **NOTHING MATTERS. / MAMA NATURE'S SKIN** ☐ -
(12"+=) *(ITT 059)* – The race is on / Something nice.

Virgin / not iss.

Mar 90. (7") *(VS 1196)* **FUNERAL STOMP. / STRAYED** ☐ -
(12"+=) *(VST 1196)* – The last laugh.
(cd-s++=) *(VSCD 1196)* – All the time in the world.

May 90. (7"/c-s) *(VS/+TC 1256)* **NOTHING MATTERS. / MAMA NATURE'S SKIN** ☐ -
(12"+=) *(VST 1256)* – The race is on.
(cd-s++=) *(VSCD 1256)* – Something nice.

Jun 90. (cd/c/lp) *(CD/TC+/V 2623)* **ME AND MY MOUTH** ☐ -
– Cheap as sin / Nothing matters / Something nice / Top floor to let / Not forever / Sweet Georgia Black / Funeral stomp / Of course you can't / Man oh man / Hey Roberta / Better to have / The part of the anchor.

— In 1992, ROBERT re-surfaced in TERMINAL HOEDOWN.

NINE INCH NAILS

Formed: San Francisco, California, USA . . . 1989 by classically trained pianist, TRENT REZNOR. He turned his attention to the darker textures of 'PRETTY HATE MACHINE' in the late 80's following a stint working in a recording studio. A solo effort – the album was written and played wholly by REZNOR – its despair and bitter self-pity were set against walls of churning synths and industrial rhythms, the compelling 'HEAD LIKE A HOLE' subsequently becoming a minor hit thanks to heavy MTV rotation. Around the same time, REZNOR recruited a band and struck out on that year's Lollapolooza trek, previewing a harder hitting, guitar influenced sound. Although the debut album was equal parts DEPECHE MODE/MINISTRY, REZNOR's follow-up, the mini-album, 'BROKEN' (1992), followed the metal/industrial fusion of the live shows. REZNOR seemed more tormented than ever on the likes of 'HELP ME I AM IN HELL', an explicitly masochistic video for the 'HAPPINESS IN SLAVERY' single courting not inconsiderable controversy. A punishing album of remixes, 'FIXED' followed a couple of months later, featuring such good-time party favourites as 'FIST FUCK' and 'SCREAMING SLAVE'. Clearly, REZNOR was rather discontented with his lot, his scary reputation heightened when it was revealed that he'd rented the L.A. pad where Charles Manson and Family had murdered Sharon Tate and her friends back in 1969. While REZNOR was allegedly unaware of this spook factor when he rented the property, it nevertheless gave 'THE DOWNWARD SPIRAL' (1994) a grim new resonance (the album was recorded in said abode). The consummation of everything REZNOR had been working towards, the record was a masterful alternative metal/industrial landmark, exploring the depths of human despair and depravity in its multifarious forms. REZNOR's tormented musings obviously struck a chord with the American populace, the album making No.2 in the US charts while NIN were given a rapturous reception at that year's Woodstock anniversary festival. Another album of remixes, 'FURTHER DOWN THE SPIRAL', appeared the following year, while REZNOR set up his own 'Nothing' label, nurturing such famous talent as the equally scary MARILYN MANSON. • **Songwriters:** 'The Terminator' REZNOR penned except PHYSICAL YOU'RE SO (Adam Ant). • **Trivia:** REZNOR appeared in the 1987 film 'LIGHT OF DAY'.

Album rating: PRETTY HATE MACHINE (*7) / BROKEN (*7) / THE DOWNWARD SPIRAL (*8)

TRENT REZNOR (b.17 May'65, Mercer, Pennsylvania, USA) – vocals, guitar, keyboards, bass, drums, programming / **JAMES WOOLEY** – keyboards / **RICHARD** – guitar / **CHRIS VRENNA** – drums

Island / Nothing-TVT

Nov 90. (12"ep/cd-ep) *(12IS/CID 482)* **DOWN IN IT (skin). / TERRIBLE LIE (mix) / DOWN IN IT (shred – demo)** ☐ ☐

Sep 91. (7"/10") *(IS/10ISP 484)* **HEAD LIKE A HOLE. / ('A'-Copper mix)** 45 ☐
(12"+=/cd-s+=) *(12IS/CID 484)* – ('A'-Opal mix).

Sep 91. (cd/c/lp) *(CID/ICT/ILPS 9973) <2610>* **PRETTY HATE MACHINE** 67 75 Nov90
– Head like a hole / Terrible lie / Down in it / Sanctified / Something I can never have / Kinda I want to / Sin / That's what I get / The only time / Ringfinger.

Nov 91. (c-s/7") *(C+/IS 508)* **SIN. / GET DOWN MAKE LOVE** 35 ☐
(10"+=/cd-s+=) *(10IS/CID 508)* – Sin (dub).

Sep 92. (m-cd/m-c/m-lp) *(IMCD/ICM/ILPM 8004) <92246>* **BROKEN** 18 7
– Pinion / Wish / Last / Help me I am in Hell / Happiness is slavery / Gave up. *(free 7"+/cd+=)* – Physical (you're so) / Suck.

Nov 92. (m-cd/m-c/m-lp) *(IMCD/ICM/ILPM 8005)* **FIXED** (remixes) ☐ -
– Gave up / Wish / Happiness is slavery / Throw this away / Fist fuck / Screaming slave.

— Below was controversally recorded at the house of the Charles Manson murders (some produced by /with FLOOD). Guests on 1 track each were **ADRIAN BELEW + DANNY LOHNER** – guitar / **CHRIS VRENNA + STEPHEN PERKINS + ANDY KUBISZEWSKI +** – drums (live:- **VRENNA, LOHNER, WOOLLEY + ROBIN FINCK**)

Mar 94. (cd/c/d-lp) *(CID/ICT/ILPSD 8012) <92346>* **THE DOWNWARD SPIRAL** 9 2
– Mr. Self destruct / Piggy / Heresy / March of the pigs / Closer / Ruiner / The becoming / I do not want this / Big man with a gun / A warm place / Eraser / Reptile / The downward spiral / Hurt.

Mar 94. (cd-ep) *<95938>* **MARCH OF THE PIGS / REPTILLIAN / ALL THE PIGS, ALL LINED UP / A VIOLET FLUID / UNDERNEATH THE SKIN** - 59

Mar 94. (etched-7") *(IS 592)* **MARCH OF THE PIGS. / A VIOLENT FLUID** 45 -
(9"+=) *(9IS 592)* – All the pigs, all lined up / Underneath the skin.
(cd-s) *(CID 592)* – ('A'side) / Underneath the skin / Reptillian.
(cd-s+=) *(CIDX 592)* – All the pigs, all lined up / Big man with a gun.

Jun 94. (12"ep/cd-ep) *(12IS/CID 596)* **CLOSER / CLOSER TO GOD / MARCH OF THE FUCKHEADS / HERESY (BLIND) / MEMORABILIA** 25 -
(12"ep/cd-ep) *(12ISX/CIDX 596)* – ('A'side) – (deviation) – (further away) / ('A'original) / ('A'-Precursor) / ('A'-Internal).

Jun 94. (c-s) *<98263>* **CLOSER / MARCH OF THE PIGS (live)** - 41

Jun 95. (cd/c) *(IMCD/IMA 8041) <95811>* **FURTHER DOWN THE SPIRAL** (remixes) ☐ 23
– Piggy (nothing can stop me) / The art of destruction (part one) / Self destruction (part three) / Heresy (version) / The downward spiral (the bottom) / Hurt / At the heart of it all / Ruiner (version) / Eraser (denial: realization) / Self destruction: final.

Sep 97. (cd-ep) *(IND 95542)* **THE PERFECT DRUG (mixes; original / Meat Beat Manifesto / Plug / Nine Inch Nails / Spacetime Continuum / The Orb)** 43 46
(above from the movie 'Lost Highway')

999

Formed: London, England . . . 1977 as 48 HOURS by former KILBURN & THE HIGH ROADS man, NICK CASH along with GUY DAYS, PABLO LABRITAIN and JON WATSON. Building on CASH's pub-rock CV, the band amassed a healthy live following in the capital and snagged a deal with 'United Artists' on the strength of a self-financed debut single, 'I'M ALIVE'. A headlong rush of anti 9-5 rebellion complete with a bruising power-pop punk guitar attack and rent-a-yob pitched-in vocals, the track was quickly followed with 'NASTY NASTY' and 'EMERGENCY' while an eponymous debut album confirmed their position in punk's vanguard. Things began to go awry, however, with follow-up set, 'SEPARATES' (1978), an album which embraced a more straightahead but colourful rock sound and thus appealed more to the US market. Subsequently taking off for a prolonged bout of transatlantic touring, the band were criticised for losing direction and neglecting British fans who had to make do with a live set, 'BIGGEST PRIZE IN SPORT' (1980). The latter represented the first fruits of a new deal with 'Polydor' while a long awaited studio set, 'CONCRETE' (1981), failed to cement their fading profile at home. The same year, 999 almost broke into the Top 50 with their version of John D. Loudermilk's 'INDIAN RESERVATION'. 1983's '13TH FLOOR MADNESS' saw many fans give up the ghost and the band looked all but washed up; as it was, they redeemed themselves with a more accomplished final effort, 'FACE TO FACE' (1985). Almost a decade later, they answered the call of duty once more, touring the punk nostalgia circuit and releasing an album's worth of new material, 'YOU, US, IT' (1993). Still pounding the beat, 999 rarely instigate a real emergency these days but still command a fair sized audience, issuing their sixth proper album, 'TAKEOVER', in '98.

Album rating: 999 (*5) / SEPARATES (*5) / THE BIGGEST PRIZE IN SPORT (*5) / CONCRETE (*5) / THIRTEENTH FLOOR MADNESS (*4) / FACE TO FACE (*5) / YOU, US, IT (*3) / THE SINGLES ALBUM compilation (*6)

NICK CASH (b. KEITH LUCAS, 6 May'50, Gosport, England) – vocals, guitar / **GUY DAYS** – guitar, vocals / **JON WATSON** – bass / **PABLO LABRITAIN** – drums

LaBritain / not iss.

Jul 77. (7") *(LAB 999)* **I'M ALIVE. / QUITE DISAPPOINTING** [ ] [-]
(re-iss. 1979 on 'United Artists'; UP 36519)

U.A. / S.P.V.

Oct 77. (7",7"green) *(UAG 36299)* **NASTY NASTY. / NO PITY** [ ] [-]

Mar 78. (lp) *(UAG 30199)* **999** [53] [-]
– Crazy / Hit me / Emergency / No pity / Pick it up / I'm alive / Your number is my number / Direct action briefing / Me and my desire / Chicane destination / Titanic (my over) reaction / Nobody knows. *(re-iss. Jun87 on 'Fan Club'; FC 026) (cd-iss. 1990 +=; FC 026CD)* – (3 extra). *(cd re-iss. Sep93 on 'Dojo'; DOJOCD 145)*

Apr 78. (7") *(UP 36376)* **ME AND MY DESIRE. / CRAZY** [ ] [-]

Jun 78. (7") *(UP 36399)* **EMERGENCY. / MY STREET STINKS** [ ] [-]

Aug 78. (7") *(UP 36435)* **FEELING ALRIGHT WITH THE CREW. / TITANIC (MY OVER) REACTION** [ ] [-]

Sep 78. (lp) *(UAG 30209)* **SEPARATES** [ ] [-]
– Let's face it / Homocide / Feeling alright with the crew / Tulse Hill night / Real man / Out of reach / High energy plan / Wolf / Crime (part 1 & 2) / Subterfuge / Brightest view. *(re-iss. Jun87 on 'Fan Club'; FC 027) (cd-iss. 1990 +=; FC 027CD)* – (4 extra). *(cd re-iss. Sep93 on 'Dojo'; DOJOCD 150)*

Oct 78. (7",7"green) *(UP 36467)* **HOMOCIDE. / SOLDIER** [40] [-]

LaBritain / not iss.

Dec 78. (12"freebie) *(12FREE 10)* **WAITING. / ACTION** [-] [-] mail-o

Radar / not iss.

Sep 79. (7") *(ADA 46)* **FOUND OUT TOO LATE. / LIE LIE LIE** [69] [-]

—— **ED CASE** – drums; repl. LABRITAIN

Polydor / not iss.

Jan 80. (7") *(POSP 99)* **TROUBLE. / MAKE A FOOL OF YOU** [ ] [-]

Jan 80. (lp) *(POLS 1013)* **THE BIGGEST PRIZE IN SPORT** [ ] [-]
– Boys in the gang / Inside out / Trouble / So long / Fun thing / The biggest prize in sport / Hollywood / Stranger / Stop stop / English wipeout / Shake / Boiler. *(cd-iss. Nov95 on 'Anagram'; CDPUNK 67)*

Apr 80. (7") **HOLLYWOOD. / BOILER** [-] [ ]

—— **PABLO LABRITAIN** – drums; returned to repl. CASE

Albion / Polydor

Apr 81. (7"m) *(ION 1011)* **OBSESSED. / CHANGE / LIE LIE LIE (live)** [71] [-]

Apr 81. (lp) *(ITS 999)* **CONCRETE** [ ] [-]
– So greedy / Li'l red riding hood / Break it up / Taboo / Mercy mercy / Fortune teller / Obsessed / Silent anger / That's the way it goes / Bongos on the Nile / Don't you know I need you / Public enemy No.1. *(re-iss. Oct87 on 'Link'; NALLP 400017) (cd-iss. May91; ALCD 9.00017)*

May 81. (7") **OBSESSED. / FORTUNE TELLER** [-] [ ]

Jun 81. (7"m) *(ION 1017)* **LI'L RED RIDING HOOD. / WAITING FOR YOUR NUMBER TO BE CALLED / I AIN'T GONNA TELL YA (live)** [59] [-]

Nov 81. (7",7"clear) *(ION 1023)* **INDIAN RESERVATION. / SO GREEDY (remix) / TABOO (remix)** [51] [-]

Jun 82. (7"red-or-yellow) *(ION 1033)* **WILD SUN. / SCANDAL IN THE CITY / BONGOS ON THE NILE** [ ] [-]
(12"red-or-yellow+=) *(12ION 1033)* – Don't you know I need you.

Oct 83. (7") *(ION 155)* **13th FLOOR MADNESS. / NIGHTSHIFT** [ ] [-]
(12"+=) *(12ION 155)* – Arabesque.

Nov 83. (lp/c) *(AS/CAS 8502)* **13th FLOOR MADNESS** [ ] [-]
– Use your imagination / Lookin' like you do / Book of love / It's what you've got / Don't want you back / 13th floor madness / Good to see you / Arabesque / Custer's last stand / Hang it all / Night shift. *(c+=)* – (4 extra). *(cd-iss. May91; ALCD 9.00073)*

—— **DANNY PALMER** – bass repl. WATSON on tour

LaBritain / not iss.

Mar 85. (lp) *(LABLP 1000)* **FACE TO FACE** [ ] [-]
– Hallelujah / Black sunshine / 20 years / Walk in the meadow / Dancing on me / Spiritual independence / Vicious circle / Lucy dead / I can't face it / Maybe someday / This is just a lie / Dancing in the wrong shoes. *(cd-iss. Jun93 on 'Obsession'; OBSESSCD 003)*

A.B.C. / Rough Trade

May 87. (lp/c/cd) *(ABC LP/K/D 11)* **LUST POWER AND MONEY (live)** [ ] [ ]
– Inside out / Hit me / Don't you know I need you / White trash / Feelin' alright with the crew / Obsessed / On the line / Let's face it / Emergency / English wipe out / Nasty nasty / Homocide / Lust power and money / My street stinks / Titanic reaction / I'm alive. *(cd-iss. Jun93 on 'Dojo'+=; DOJOCD 129)* – (2 extra). *(cd re-iss. Oct92 as 'GREATEST HITS LIVE' on 'Streetlink'; STRCD 026)*

—— split but re-formed in 1993

Anagram / not iss.

Nov 93. (cd) *(CDGRAM 71)* **YOU, US, IT** [ ] [-]
– Black flowers for the bride / There is no glory in Mary's story / Signed dangerous from Hollywood / Bye bye bones / Everybody needs it / It's over now / Bye bye England / All of the days / Big fast car / Absolution / Deep in the shadow / Run for your life / Don't tell me / Crazy crazy crazy / White light.

—— **ARTURO** – bass (ex-LURKERS) repl. DANNY

Get Back / not iss.

Mar 98. (cd) *(GBR 010CD)* **TAKEOVER** [ ] [-]

– compilations, etc. –

Jun 80. (lp/c) *United Artists; (SOS 999)* **THE SINGLES ALBUM** [ ] [-]
– Nasty nasty / No pity / Me and my desire / Crazy / Emergency / My street stinks / Feelin' alright with the crew / Titantic (my over) reaction / You can't buy me / Homocide / Soldier / I'm alive / Quite disappointing / Waiting / Action.

Mar 84. (lp/c) *Albion; (ALB/CALB 118)* **IDENTITY PARADE** [ ] [-]
(c+=) – (4 extra).

Nov 86. (lp) *Dojo; (DOJOLP 31)* **IN CASE OF EMERGENCY** [ ] [-]

Nov 89. (lp/c) *Link; (LINK LP 107)* **LIVE AND LOUD (live)** [ ] [-]
(cd-iss. Jan91; LINKCD 107)

May 92. (cd) *E.M.I.; (CDGO 2032)* **THE EARLY STUFF (THE UNITED ARTISTS YEARS)** [ ] [-]

Dec 92. (lp) *Link; (LINKLP 125)* **THE CELLBLOCK TAPES** [ ] [-]

Dec 94. (d-cd; shared with SLAUGHTER & THE DOGS) *Step 1; (STEPCD 045)* **THE CELLBLOCK TAPES / The Slaughterhouse Tapes** [ ] [-]

Dec 95. (d-cd; shared with SHAM 69) *Step 1; (STEPCD053)* **LOVE AND LOUD / Live And Loud** [ ] [-]

Jun 96. (cd) *Anagram; (CDPUNK 78)* **THE ALBION PUNK YEARS (THE INDEPENDENT PUNK SINGLES COLLECTION)** [ ] [-]

Apr 97. (cd) *Anagram; (CDPUNK 93)* **LIVE AT THE NASHVILLE 1979 (live)** [ ] [-]

Aug 97. (cd) *Receiver; (RRCD 245)* **EMERGENCY** [ ] [-]
– Don't know I love you / Crazy / Feeling alright with the crew / Emergency / Pick it up / Indian reservation / Quite disappointing / My street stinks / Rael raen / Subterfuge / Hollywood / Inside out / The biggest prize in sport / Chicane destination / Obsessed / Hit me / Nasty nasty / Tulse Hill nights / Mercy mercy / English wipeout / Fun thing / Titanic reaction / Boys in the gang / Lil' red riding hood / Me and my desire / Homocide / Let's face it / I'm alive / Found out too late.

NIPPLE ERECTORS / NIPS (see under ⇒ POGUES)

NIRVANA

Formed: Aberdeen, Washington, USA . . . 1987 by singer/songwriter/guitarist KURT COBAIN and bassist KRIST NOVOSELIC. Recruiting drummer CHAD CHANNING, they soon became a talking point and pivotal band in nearby Seattle where the likes of SOUNDARDEN and MUDHONEY were major players in the emerging grunge scene. Whereas those bands dealt in raw garage punk/metal, NIRVANA immediately stood out from the pack by dint of the subtle pop melodies which COBAIN craftily incorporated into his songs. They also fast gained a reputation for their ferocious live shows which drew comparisons with early WHO, if only for their sheer nihilistic energy, invariably ending in trashed equipment. Signing, of course, with the hub of the Seattle scene, 'Sub Pop', NIRVANA released their debut single, 'LOVE BUZZ' in October 1988, the album, 'BLEACH', following a year later. One of the seminal 'Sub Pop' releases alongside, MUDHONEY's 'SUPERFUZZ BIGMUFF' and TAD's 'GOD'S BALLS', this was a darkly brooding, often savagely angry collection, driven by bass and fuzz and interspersed with pockets of melody. The likes of 'SCHOOL' and the throbbing 'NEGATIVE CREEP' saw COBAIN lapse into his trademark howl, an enraged, blood curdling shriek, almost primal in its intensity. Conversely, 'ABOUT A GIRL' was an achingly melodic semi-acoustic shuffle, as steeped in hurt as the rest of the album but more resigned than angry. New guitarist JASON EVERMAN had contributed to the record's sonic bludgeon as well as paying for recording costs, although he soon parted ways (he went on to play with the much hyped MINDFUNK) with COBAIN and NOVOSELIC over the ever reliable, 'musical differences'. 'BLEACH' was heartily received by the indie/metal press, NIRVANA embarking on a heavy round of touring, first in the States, then Europe. Following the departure of CHANNING, MUDHONEY's DAN PETERS joined briefly and was involved with the 'SLIVER' single, a brilliant chunk of pop-noise which further enhanced NIRVANA's underground kudos and raised expectations for a follow-up album to fever pitch. 'NEVERMIND' (1991) let down no-one, except possibly the anally-retentive sad-kids who accused the band of selling out to a major label ('Geffen'). Released immediately after a blinding set at England's Reading festival (where NIRVANA, who probably drew the most frenetic crowd reaction of the day,

had to make do with a paltry afternoon slot; the following year they'd be headlining), and with appetites whetted via import copies of 'SMELLS LIKE TEEN SPIRIT', the record was met with an ecstatic press reaction. While the album brought the grunge phenomenon into the mainstream, NIRVANA had already moved on to a blistering power pop/punk sound, best evidenced in the sardonic fury of the aforementioned 'SMELLS . . .'. Here was an anthem for the blank generation, for all the people who'd given up before even starting; COBAIN had condensed the collective frustration/despair/apathy into an incendiary slice of pop genius not witnessed since The SEX PISTOLS' heyday. 'COME AS YOU ARE' was another piece of semi-acoustic bruised beauty while 'TERRITORIAL PISSINGS' was as extreme as the record went, a rabid blast of hardcore punk introduced with a sarcastic send-up pilfered from The YOUNGBLOOD's 60's love 'n' peace classic, 'GET TOGETHER'. Most of the other tracks lay somewhere in between, COBAIN never letting up the intensity level for a minute, whether on the deceptively breezy 'IN BLOOM' or the stinging 'BREED'. For a three piece (the drum seat had now been filled by DAVE GROHL, ex-SCREAM), the group made one hell of a racket, but it was a racket which was never less than 100% focused, the GROHL/NOVOSELIC rhythmic powerhouse underpinning every track with diamond-edged precision. It's fair to say that 'NEVERMIND' literally changed the face of music, American indie bands coming to dominate the scene until the arrival of OASIS in the mid-90's. COBAIN was heralded as the spokesman of a generation, although it was a role he was both unwilling and unable to cope with. As the inevitable, punishing round of touring ensued, the singer's health began to suffer once more; never the healthiest of people, COBAIN suffered from a chronic stomach complaint as well as narcolepsy, a condition which causes the sufferer to sleep for excessive periods of time. What's more, he was concerned that the irony of his lyrics was missed on his growing legions of fans (which now included the macho 'jocks' whom COBAIN so despised) who now doted on his every word. Amid all this confusion, COBAIN was married to HOLE's COURTNEY LOVE on the 24th February '92, the couple almost losing custody of their newborn child, Frances, later that summer following revelations of drug abuse. The end of the year saw the release of a compilation of rare material, 'INCESTICIDE', including two storming VASELINES' (obscure but brilliant Scottish punk-popsters) covers, 'MOLLY'S LIPS' and 'SON OF A GUN'. Rumours of COBAIN's heroin abuse were rife, however, and the singer overdosed twice the following year. 'IN UTERO' (1993) reflected the turmoil, an uncompromising wall of noise (courtesy of STEVE ALBINI) characterising most of the album. The melodies were still there, you just had to dig deeper in the sludge to find them. Despite 'Geffen's misgivings, the record was a transatlantic No.1, its success engendering another round of live work. After a final American show in January, the group set off for Europe, taking a break at the beginning of March. COBAIN remained in Rome, where, on the 4th March, LOVE found him unconscious in their hotel room, the result of an attempted tranquilizer overdose. Although COBAIN eventually recovered, the tour was abandoned and the couple returned to their Seattle home. Though it didn't come as a complete surprise, the music world was stunned nonetheless when, on the 8th April, news broke that COBAIN had finally killed himself, blowing his own head off with a shotgun. The most widely mourned rock'n'roll death since JOHN LENNON, COBAIN's suicide even sparked off a series of 'copycat' incidents in America by obsessive fans. Posthumously released later that year, the acoustic 'UNPLUGGED IN NEW YORK' (1994) live set was heavy going, a tragic poignancy underpinning the spare beauty of tracks like 'DUMB' and 'PENNYROYAL TEA' (from 'IN UTERO') while the heart-rendingly resigned 'ALL APOLOGIES' sounds like COBAIN's final goodbye to a world that he could no longer bear to be a part of. Eventually picking up the pieces, GROHL formed The FOO FIGHTERS, turning his hand to guitar playing/songwriting and recruiting ex-GERM, PAT SMEAR. After time spent campaigning for his native, war torn Yugoslavia, NOVOSELIC returned with his own band, SWEET 75, a collaboration with diminutive Venezuelan lesbian folk-singer, YVA LAS VEGAS. They finally released one unstartling eponymous set in 1997, which just might be their only outing. • **Songwriters:** COBAIN wrote late 80's work. In the 90's, the group were credited with COBAIN lyrics. Covers; LOVE BUZZ (Shocking Blue) / HERE SHE COMES NOW (Velvet Underground) / DO YOU LOVE ME? (Kiss) / TURNAROUND (Devo) / JESUS WANTS ME FOR A SUNBEAM (Vaselines) / D7 (Wipers) / THE MAN WHO SOLD THE WORLD (David Bowie) / WHERE DID YOU SLEEP LAST NIGHT (Leadbelly).

Album rating: BLEACH (*8) / NEVERMIND (*10) / INCESTICIDE (*7) / IN UTERO (*9) / UNPLUGGED IN NEW YORK (*9) / FROM THE MUDDY BANKS OF THE WISHKAH (*8) / Sweet 75: SWEET 75 (*4)

KURT COBAIN (b.20 Feb'67, Hoquaim, Washington) – vocals, guitar / **CHRIS NOVOSELIC** (b.16 May'65) – bass / **CHAD CHANNING** (b.31 Jan'67, Santa Rosa, Calif.) – drums

	Tupelo	Sub Pop
Oct 88. (7") <*SP 23*> **LOVE BUZZ. / BIG CHEESE**	-	

—— Early '89, added **JASON EVERMAN** – guitar Also guest drummer on 2 tracks **DALE CROVER**

Aug 89. (lp,white or green-lp/cd) *(TUP LP/CD 6)* <*SP 34*> **BLEACH**		Jun89

– Blew / Floyd the barber / About a girl / School / Paper cuts / Negative creep /

Scoff / Swap meet / Mr.Moustache / Sifting / Big cheese. *(cd+=)* – Love buzz / Downer. *<US re-iss. Dec91 hit 89> (re-iss. Feb92 on 'Geffen'; GEFD 24433) (hit UK No.33) (c+=)* – Big cheese. *(re-iss. Oct95 on 'Geffen' cd/c; GFLD/GFLC 19291)*

Dec 89. (12"ep/cd-ep) *(TUP EP8/CD8)* **BLEW / LOVE BUZZ. / BEEN A SON / STAIN** [ ] [-]

—— **DAN PETERS** – drums (of MUDHONEY) repl. CHANNING (Apr90)

Jan 91. (7",7"green) *(TUP 25)* **SLIVER. / DIVE** [ ] [ ] Sep 90
(12"+=) *(TUP EP25)* – About a girl (live). *(US-iss.7"blue; SP 72)*
(cd-s++=) *(TUP CD25)* – Spank thru (live).

Feb 91. (7",7"green) *<SP 97>* **MOLLY'S LIPS. / ('Candy' by FLUID)** [-] [ ]

not iss. Communion

Mar 91. (7"colrd) *<Communion 25>* **HERE SHE COMES NOW. / ('Venus In Furs' by MELVINS)** [-] [ ]

—— (Apr91 trio) **DAVE GROHL** (b.14 Jan'69, Warren, Ohio) – drums, vocals (ex-SCREAM) repl. PETERS and EVERMAN, who joined MIND FUNK.

Geffen Geffen

Sep 91. (lp/c/cd) *<(DGC/+C/D 24425)>* **NEVERMIND** [7] [1]
– Smells like teen spirit / In bloom / Come as you are / Breed / Lithium / Polly / Territorial pissings / Drain you / Lounge act / Stay away / On a plain / Something in the way. *(cd+=)* – Endless nameless.

Oct 91. (c-s/cd-s) *<19050>* **SMELLS LIKE TEEN SPIRIT / EVEN IN HIS YOUTH** [-] [6]

Nov 91. (7"/c-s) *(DGC/+C 5)* **SMELLS LIKE TEEN SPIRIT. / DRAIN YOU** [7] [-]
(12"pic-d+=) *(DGCTP 5)* – Aneurysm.
(cd-s++=) *(DGCCD 5)* – Even in his youth.
(12") *(DGCT 5)* – ('A'side) / Even in his youth / Aneurysm.

Mar 92. (c-s/cd-s) *<19120>* **COME AS YOU ARE. / DRAIN YOU (live)** [-] [32]

Mar 92. (7"/c-s) *(DGC/+C 7)* **COME AS YOU ARE. / ENDLESS NAMELESS** [9] [-]
(12"+=/12"pic-d+=) *(DGCT/+P 7)* – School (live).
(cd-s++=) *(DGCTD 7)* – Drain you (live).

Jul 92. (7"/c-s) *(DGCS/+C 9)* **LITHIUM. / CURMUDGEON** [11] [-]
(12"pic-d+=) *(DGCTP 9)* – Been a son (live).
(cd-s++=) *(DGCSD 9)* – D7 (Peel session).

Jul 92. (c-s,cd-s) *<19134>* **LITHIUM / BEEN A SON (live)** [-] [64]

Nov 92. (7"/c-s) *(GFS/+C 34)* **IN BLOOM. / POLLY** [28] [-]
(12"pic-d+=/cd-s+=) *(GFST P/D 34)* – Sliver (live).

Dec 92. (cd/c/lp) *<(GED/GEC/GEF 24504)>* **INCESTICIDE** (rare material) [14] [39]
– Dive / Sliver / Stain / Been a son / Turnaround / Molly's lips / Son of a gun / (New wave) Polly / Beeswax / Downer / Mexican seafood / Hairspray queen / Aero zeppelin / Big long now / Aneurysm.

—— In Feb'93, NIRVANA's 'OH, THE GUILT' appeared on double'A'side with JESUS LIZARD's 'Puss'. Issued on 'Touch & Go' 7"blue/cd-s; *(TG 83/+CD)*. It had UK No.12, and crashed out of the Top 60 the following week!.

—— GOODBYE MR MACKENZIE's BIG JOHN played guitar for them in mid'93.

—— In Aug'93, KURT COBAIN and WILLIAM S.BURROUGHS narrated 'The Priest, They Call Him By' on 10"lp/cd 'Tim Kerr'; *(92 10/CD 044)*

Aug 93. (7"/c-s) *(GFS/+C 54)* **HEART-SHAPED BOX. / MARIGOLD** [5] [-]
(12"+=/cd-s+=) *(GFST/+D 54)* – Milk it.

Sep 93. (cd/c/lp)<clear-lp> *<(GED/GEC/GEF 24536)><DGC 24607>* **IN UTERO** [1] [1]
– Serve the servants / Scentless apprentice / Heart-shaped box / Rape me / Frances Farmer will have her revenge on Seattle / Dumb / Very ape / Milk it / Penny royal tea / Radio friendly unit shifter / Tourette's / All apologies. *(cd+=)* – Gallons of rubbing alcohol flow through the strip.

Dec 93. (7"/c-s) *(GFS/+C 66)* **ALL APOLOGIES. / RAPE ME** [32] [-]
(12"+=/cd-s+=) *(GFST/+D 66)* – MV.

—— On the 4th March '94, KURT overdosed while on holiday in Italy and went into a coma. A month later, on the 8th April he committed suicide, by shooting himself through the mouth. He was only 27, and this was certainly the biggest rock star death since JOHN LENNON. For more details see HOLE and the COURTNEY LOVE story.

—— below album featured **LORI GOLDSTON** – cello + **MEAT PUPPETS' Curt & Cris Kirkwood** on 3rd, 4th & 5th last songs.

Nov 94. (cd/c/white-lp) *<(GED/GEC/GEF 24727)>* **UNPLUGGED IN NEW YORK** (live acoustic) [1] [1]
– About a girl / Come as you are / Jesus doesn't want me for a sunbeam / Dumb / The man who sold the world / Pennyroyal tea / Polly / On a plain / Something in the way / Plateau / Oh me / Lake of fire / All apologies / Where did you sleep last night.

—— GROHL (now vox, guitar) formed The FOO FIGHTERS with ex-GERMS guitarist PAT SMEAR. Meanwhile NOVOSELIC formed the trio SWEET 75.

– compilations, etc. –

on 'Geffen' unless mentioned otherwise

Jul 95. (d-cd) *<(GES 00001)>* **BLEACH / INCESTICIDE** [ ] [ ]

Nov 95. (6xcd-s-box) *<(GED 24901)>* **6 CD SINGLE BOXED SET** [ ] [ ]

Oct 96. (cd/c/lp) *<(GED/GEC/GEF 25105)>* **FROM THE MUDDY BANKS OF THE WISHKAH (live)** [4] [1]
– Intro / School / Drain you / Aneurysm / Smells like teen spirit / Been a son / Lithium / Sliver / Spank thru / Scentless apprentice / Heart-shaped box / Milk it / Negative creep / Polly / Breed / Tourette's / Blew.

SWEET 75

KRIST NOVOSELIC – guitar (ex-NIRVANA) / **YVA LAS VEGAS** – vocals, bass / **ADAM WADE** – drums

Geffen Geffen

Aug 97. (cd/c) *<(GED/GEC 25140)>* **SWEET 75** [ ] [ ]
– Fetch / Lay me down / Bite my hand / Red dress / La vida / Six years / Take another stab / Poor Kitty / Ode to Dolly / Dogs / Cantos de Pilon / Nothing / Japan trees / Oral health.

NITZER EBB

Formed: Chelmsford, Essex, England . . . 1983 by schoolfriends DOUGLAS McCARTHY and BON HARRIS, who were soon joined by DAVID GOODAY. Inspired by industrial pioneers like SUICIDE and DAF, the trio released a series of independent singles ('ISN'T IT FUNNY HOW THE BODY WORKS?', 'WARSAW GHETTO', 'LET YOUR BODY LEARN' and 'MURDEROUS') before being snapped up by premier electronic experimentation outlet, 'Mute' ('Geffen' in the States). A long awaited, FLOOD-produced debut album, 'THAT TOTAL AGE' (including a revamped version of 'LET YOUR BODY LEARN'), surfaced in 1987 and saw NITZER EBB join the new vanguard of synth abusers alongside the likes of MINISTRY, FRONT 242, KMFDM etc. As the 80's progressed into the 90's, the band's jackboot approach became increasingly dancefloor friendly as the impact of the house/techno explosion slowly filtered through to the industrial scene. Certainly, 1991's 'EBBHEAD' was their highest profile album release to date, drawing generally favourable comments from the press and spawning a near Top 50 hit with 'GODHEAD'. Yet a gap of four years before 1995's 'BIG HIT' led to a loss of momentum, the harder end of the industrial spectrum hogging the limelight with massive selling albums by the likes of MINISTRY and especially NINE INCH NAILS. • **Trivia:** Pronounced NIGHT-ZER EBB.

Album rating: THAT TOTAL AGE (*6) / BELIEF (*6) / SHOWTIME (*5) / EBBHEAD (*7) / BIG HIT (*4)

DOUGLAS McCARTHY (b. 1 Sep'66) – vocals / **BON HARRIS** (b. 12 Aug'65) – percussion, vocals / **DAVID GOODAY** – electronics

Power Of Voice not iss.

Jan 85. (12"ep) *(NEB 1)* **ISN'T IT FUNNY HOW THE BODY WORKS? / THE WAY YOU LIVE / CRANE / COLD WAR** [ ] [-]

Oct 85. (12") *(NEB 2)* **WARSAW GHETTO. / SO BRIGHT, SO STRONG** [ ] [-]
(Feb86; d12") *(NEB/NEBX 2)* – ('A'rap & dub mix) / ('B'radio mix). *(tracks issued 1988 as 'SO BRIGHT, SO STRONG' on EURO 'Up Front'; NITZ 8009)*

Apr 86. (12") *(NEB 3)* **LET YOUR BODY LEARN. / ('A'instrumental) / GET CLEAN** [ ] [-]

Nov 86. (12"/7") *(12+/NEB 4)* **MURDEROUS. / FITNESS TO PURPOSE** [ ] [-]

Mute Geffen

May 87. (12") *(12MUTE 58)* **LET YOUR BODY LEARN. / ('A'instrumental) / GET CLEAN** [ ] [-]

May 87. (cd/c/lp) *(CD/C+/STUMM 45) <24155>* **THAT TOTAL AGE** [ ] [ ] Nov87
– Fitness to purpose / Violent playground / Murderous / Smear body / Join in the chant / Alarm / Let your body learn / Let beauty loose / Into the large air. *(cd+=)* – Join in the chant (metal mix) / Fitness to purpose (mix 2) / Murderous (instrumental).

Aug 87. (12") *(12MUTE 64)* **JOIN IN THE CHANT (bass mix). / CONTROL I'M HERE (dance mix)** [ ] [-]

—— **JULIAN BEESTON** – drums, percussion repl. GOODAY

Oct 88. (12"/cd-s) *(12/CD MUTE 71) <21111>* **CONTROL I'M HERE. / ('A'mix)** [ ] [ ] Jul91
(12") *(L12MUTE 71)* – Control I'm here (strategic dance floor initiative mix) / k.i.a. / Join in the chant (burn mix).

Jan 89. (cd/c/lp) *(CD/C+/STUMM 61) <24213>* **BELIEF** [ ] [ ]
– Hearts and minds / Nitzer Ebb for fun / Control I'm here / Captivate / TWA / Blood money / Shame / Drive / Without belief / k.i.a. / Control I'm here (SDI mix) / Without belief (instrumental).

Jan 89. (12"ep/cd-ep) *(12/CD MUTE 78) <21193>* **HEARTS AND MINDS (subsonic mix). / NITZER EBB FOR FUN (lp version) / TIME SLIPS BY (PK mix)** [ ] [ ] Jul91
(12") *(L12MUTE 78)* –

Oct 89. (7") *(MUTE 96)* **SHAME. / CAPTIVATE** [ ] [-]
(12"+=/cd-s+=) *(12/CD MUTE 96)* – Backlash.
(12"ep) *(L12MUTE 96)* – Re-design shame / Shame / Captivate (William Orbit mixes).

Feb 90. (12"/cd-s) *(12/CD MUTE 106) <21465>* **LIGHTNING MAN. / WHO WE ARE** [ ] [ ] Mar90
(12") *(L12MUTE 106)* – ('A'-Renegade Soundwave mix) / ('A'-The Industry Vs. The Ebb mix).

Feb 90. (cd/c/lp) *(CD/C+/STUMM 72) <24284>* **SHOWTIME** [ ] [ ]
– Getting closer / All over / Rope / Nobody knows / My heart / Hold on / One man's burden / Lightning man / Fun to be had.

Jun 90. (12"/cd-s) *(12/CD MUTE 115) <21606>* **GETTING CLOSER. / ('A'-George Clinton remix)** [ ] [ ]
(12"ep) *(L12MUTE 115)* – Fun To Be Had (long mix) / Getting Closer (kitten mix)/ Taken From me (servant mix).

Jun 91. (12"ep/cd-ep) *(12/CD MUTE 122) <21658>* **AS IS. / FAMILY MAN** [ ] [ ]
(12") *(LMUTE 122)* – ('A'+'B'mixes).

Aug 91. (10"ep/cd-ep) *(10/CD MUTE 133)* **I GIVE TO YOU (elemental). / I GIVE TO YOU (pestilence) / STRAY CAT BLUES (adventurous)** [ ] [-]

Nov 91. (cd/c/lp) *(CD/C+/STUMM 88) <24456>* **EBBHEAD** [ ] [ ] Sep91
– Reasons / Lakeside drive / I give to you / Sugar sweet / DJVD / Time / Ascend / Godhead / Trigger happy. *(cd+=)* – Family man (extended).

Dec 91. (12"ep/cd-ep) *(12/CD MUTE 135) <21705>* **GODHEAD EP** [56] [ ]
– Godhead (remix) / Let your body learn – Murderous (live) / Control (I'm here) (live).
(12"ep/cd-ep) *(LMUTE 135)* – ('A'live) / Getting closer (live) / Join in the chant (live).

Apr 92. (10"ep/cd-ep) *(1-10/CD MUTE 145)* **ASCEND** [52] [-]
(10") *(2-10 MUTE 145)* –

—— added **JASON PAYNE** – instruments; to repl. JULIAN

Feb 95. (12"/cd-s) *(12/CD MUTE 155)* **KICK IT. / ('A'mixes)** [75] [ ] Mar96
(cd-s+=) *(LCDMUTE 155)* – Skin tight.
(cd-s) *(XLCDMUTE 155)* – ('A'mixes).

Mar 95. (cd/cd/c/lp) *(LCD/CD/S+/STUMM 118)* <24718> **BIG HIT**
– Cherry blossom / Hear me say / Kick it / I thought / Floodwater / Border talk / In decline / Living out of a bag / Boy / Our own world.

Apr 95. (12"/cd-s) *(12/CD MUTE 164)* **I THOUGHT. / FRIEND / BEATS ME**
(cd-s) *(LCDMUTE 164)* – ('A'mixes) / Cherry blossom.

Mojo NIXON

Born: NEILL KIRBY McMILLAN Jr., 2 Aug'57, Chapel Hill, North Carolina, USA. Allegedly a former Virginia state cycling champion, McMILLAN adopted the MOJO NIXON moniker after hooking up with SKID ROPER in 1984, duly putting his full pedal power into offending as much of America's conservative population as possible (and no doubt some liberals to boot). With ROPER on washboard, mandolin etc., and NIXON on primitive guitar/effected hillbilly hectoring vocals, the duo wreaked aural havoc in amateurish cowpunk style on their eponymous, independently released debut album. The likes of 'JESUS AT McDONALD'S' gained airplay on college radio, while 'STUFFIN' MARTHA'S MUFFIN' (an erm, touching ode to MTV VJ, Martha Quinn) – from follow-up set, 'FRENZY' (1986) – became a minor college chart hit. Ironically, Mr NIXON subsequently became something of an MTV celebrity, recording promo shorts for the channel, who returned the favour by actually screening material (including the demented KING homage, 'ELVIS IS EVERYWHERE') from 'BO-DAY-SHUS!!!' (1987), the duo's debut for 'Enigma'. 1989's 'ROOT HOG OR DIE', meanwhile, featured the inimitible 'DEBBIE GIBSON IS PREGNANT WITH MY TWO-HEADED LOVE CHILD', the straw which broke the hog's back, at least as far as MTV were concerned. NIXON vowed to carry on his debauched crusade alone, splitting with ROPER and recording a solo set for 'Enigma', 'OTIS' (1991). Despite the inclusion of such considered material as 'DON HENLEY MUST DIE', the album went down the pan as the label went belly up, NIXON becoming embroiled in legal disputes over the next four years. In the meantime, he recorded the festive (or not so festive) 'HORNY HOLIDAYS!' album under the TOAD LIQUORS moniker and worked with arch subversive JELLO BIAFRA on the 'PRAIRIE HOME INVASION' set, released on the 'Alternative Tentacles' label. It wasn't until 1995 that NIXON released a solo follow-up proper, 'WHEREABOUTS UNKNOWN', proving that, if not lost completely, his muse was still as wayward as ever and likely to stick a particularly sharp pitchfork into America's bloated ass at the first opportunity (just listen to his version of the Smiths' 'GIRLFRIEND IN A COMA').

Album rating: UNLIMITED EVERYTHING (*6) / HORNY HOLIDAYS (*5)

MOJO NIXON & SKID ROPER

MOJO NIXON – vocals, guitar / **SKID ROPER** (b. RICHARD BANKE, 19 Oct'54, National City, Calif.) – washboard, harmonica, mandolin, percussion / with various country session people

not iss. R.B.I.

1985. (lp) <72056> **MOJO NIXON & SKID ROPER** [-]
– Jesus at McDonald's / Mushroom maniac / Moanin' with your mama / Promised land tonight / Guns to my head / I'm in love with your girlfriend / Rockin' religion / Big payback / Comin' down / Mama possums / King of the couch / Art fag shuffle / Black yo' eye.

Enigma Enigma

1986. (lp,cd) <971127> **FRENZY** [-]
– The amazing Bigfoot diet / Stuffin' Martha's muffin / I hate banks / Feeling existential / Be my lover / Where the hell is my money / Gonna put my face on a nuclear bomb / Ain't got no boss / I'm living with a three-foot anti-Christ / Gonna eat them words / Twilight's last gleaming / 23 mile ride / In-a-gadda-da-vida / The ballad of Wendell Scott / Get out of my way / Rutabagas / Burn down the walls.

Oct 87. (lp) <(73272-1)> **BO-DAY-SHUS!!!** Sep87
– Elvis is everywhere / We gotta have more soul / Ain't gonna piss in no jar / The polka polka / I'm gonna dig up Howlin' Wolf / The story of one chord / Gin guzzlin' frenzy / B.B.Q. U.S.A. / Positively bodies parking lot / Wash no dishes no more / Lincoln logs / Wide open / Don't want no foo-foo haircut on my head.

Apr 89. (lp/c/cd) *(ENVLP/TCENV/CDENV 520)* <73335> **ROOT HOG OR DIE**
– Debbie Gibson is pregnant with my two-headed love child / This land is your land / Chicken drop / I'm a wreck / Circus mystery / (619) 239 – K.I.N.G. / Pirate radio / Louisiana liplock / Legalize it / She's vibrator dependent.

Jun 90. (cd/c/lp) *(CDENV/TCENV/ENVLP 1005)* **UNLIMITED EVERYTHING**
– The amazing Bigfoot diet / Debbie Gibson is pregnant with my two- headed love child / Jesus at McDonald's / Amsterdam dogshit blues / Stuffin' Martha's muffin / Burn down the malls / Elvis is everywhere / Louisiana liplock / (619) 239 – K.I.N.G. / Burn your money! / Rockin' religion / I gotta connect.

— ROPER went solo, releasing several albums starting with 1989's 'Trails Plowed Under'.

MOJO NIXON

— now with **BILL DAVIS** – guitar (of DASH RIP ROCK) / **JOHN DOE** – bass (of X) / **ERIC AMBEL** – guitar (of DEL-LORDS)

not iss. I.R.S.

Sep 90. (cd/c) <X2/X4 13095> **OTIS** [-]
– Don Henley must die / Destroy all lawyers / Rabies baby / Perry Mason of love / Gonna be a new world / Ain't high falutin' / I wanna race Bigfoot trucks / Put a sex mo-sheen in the White House / Shane's dentist / Star spangled mojo / You can dress 'em up / Took out the trash and never came back.

not iss. Triple X

Dec 92. (cd; MOJO NIXON & THE TOAD LIQUORS) <51117> **HORNY HOLIDAYS!** (festive; not!) [-]
– Happy birthday / Trim yo' tree / Good King Wenceslas / Mr. Grinch / Head crushing yuletide sing-a-long / It's Christmas time / Jungle bells / Boogie woogie Santa Claus / Santa Claus go straight to the ghetto / Run Rudolph run / We three kings / Everyday will be like a holiday / Sleigh ride / Little man song / Go tell it on a mountain / 'Twas the night before Christmas. *(UK-iss.May94 on 'New Rose'; 422427)*

Jun 93. (7"; as MOJO NIXON & THE WORLD FAMOUS BLUE JEANS) **UFO'S. /**

— NIXON subsequently teamed up with The PLEASURE BARONS who included DAVE ALVIN (ex-BLASTERS)

— In 1994, NIXON collaborated with (ex-DEAD KENNEDYS) frontman JELLO BIAFRA on an album, 'PRAIRIE HOME INVASION'.

Last Call Ripe & Ready

May 95. (cd) *(42205-2)* <3825> **WHEREABOUTS UNKNOWN**
– Gotta be free / Not as much as football / Mr. Correct (don't tell me what to do) / Buck up and stop your whinin' / My free will just ain't willin' / Girlfriend in a coma / Pleasurelegionce / Don't ask me why I drink / My TV is watchin' me / Take a look in my eyes / Tie my pecker to my leg / You can't kill me / If I can dream.

Danbert NOBACON (see under ⇒ CHUMBAWAMBA)

NOFX

Formed: Hollywood, California, USA . . . 1984 by 'FAT' MIKE RAKHABIT, ERIC MELVIN, IZZY DREW LYNN and GROGGY NODBEGGAR. Punk-metal/hardcore stalwarts, NOFX's albums (the band have never released a single on principal and hardly do any interviews) are noted primarily for their black humour and cutting wit, their music akin to a more adventurous fusion of BLACK FLAG and BAD RELIGION. The latter band's label, 'Epitaph', recognised NOFX's distinctive talents and the label's mainman GUREWITZ signed them for a debut album, 'LIBERATION ANIMATION' (1988). A further couple of albums followed over the ensuing two years, 'S & M AIRLINES' (1989) and 'RIBBED' (1990), the latter set, in particular, seeing the group gaining more widespread recognition for their wicked way with a humerous lyric and a skull-crushing sonic assault. NOFX (AL HEFE and ERIK SANDON replaced IZZY and GROGGY respectively) continued a fairly prolific recording schedule throughout the 90's (MIKE formed his own 'Fat Wreck Chords' label), and following the success of bands like GREEN DAY, finally made the US and UK charts (Top 75) with 1996's 'HEAVY PETTING ZOO'. True to the band's confrontational style, the artwork depicted a sheep shearer, eh . . . shearing very close to the bone . . . so to speak. In the same year at a New York gig, they dressed up in bizarre female clothing copying the style of tourmates, The LUNACHICKS.

Album rating: RIBBED (*5) / WHITE TRASH, TWO HEEBS AND A BEAN (*5) / PUNK IN DRUBLIC (*7) / HEAVY PETTING ZOO (*5)

'FAT' MIKE RAKHABIT – vocals, bass / **ERIC MELVIN** – guitar / **IZZY DREW LYNN** – guitar / **GROGGY NODBEGGAR** – drums

not iss. own label

1988. (lp) **LIBERATION ANIMATION** [-]
– Shut up already / Freedumb / Here comes the neighbourhood / A 200 club / Sloppy English / You put your chocolate in my peanut butter / Mr. Jones / Vegetarian mumbo jumbo / Beer bong song / Piece / I live in a cake / No problems / On the rag / Truck stop blues. *(UK-iss.Jan92 on 'Epitaph' cd/lp; E 86417-2/-1)*

Epitaph Epitaph

1989. (lp/cd) <E 86405-1/-2> **S & M AIRLINES** [-]
– Day to daze / Five feet under / Professional crastination / Mean people suck / Vailla sex / S&M airlines / Drug free America / Life O'Riley / You drink you drive you spill / Screamin for change / Jaundiced eye / Go your own way. *(UK-iss.Nov92 cd/c/lp; same)*

Mar 91. (cd/lp) <86410-1/-2> **RIBBED** [-]
– Green corn / Moron brothers / Showerdays / Food, sex and ewe / Just the flu / El lay / Cheese – Where's my slice? / Together on the sand / Nowhere / Brain constipation / Gonoherpasyphilaids / I don't want you around / Malachi crunch. *(UK-iss.Nov92 cd/c/lp; 6410-2/-4/-1)*

— **EL HEFE** – guitar, trumpet, vocals / **ERIK GHINT** (b. SANDON) – drums; repl. IZZY DREW + GROGGY NODBEGGAR

Jun 92. (m-cd/m-lp) <(FAT 503-2/-1)> **THE LONGEST LINE**
– The death of John Smith / The longest line / Stranded / Remnants / Kill all the white man.
(above issued on 'Fat Wreck Chords')

Jun 93. (cd/lp) <(E 86418-2/-1)> **WHITE TRASH, TWO HEEBS AND A BEAN** Nov92
– Soul doubt / Stickin' in my eye / Bob / You're bleeding / Straight edge / Liza and Louise / Bag / Please play this song on the radio / Warm / I wanna be your baby / Johnny Appleseed / She's gone / Buggley eyes.

Jul 94. (cd/c/lp) <(E 86435-2/-4/-1)> **PUNK IN DRUBLIK**
– Linoleum / Leave it alone / Dig / Cause / Don't call me white / My heart is yearning / Perfect government / Brews / Quass / Dying degree / Fleas / Lori Meyers / Jeff wears birkenstocks? /

Sep 95. (10"/cd-s) *(WOOS 6 TOT/CDS)* **LEAVE IT ALONE. /**
(above issued on 'Out Of Step')

Jan 96. (cd/c) <(E 86457-2/-4)> **HEAVY PETTING ZOO** 60 63
– Hobophobic / Philthy Phil Philanthropist / Freedom lika shopping cart / Bleeding heart disease / Hot dog in a hallway / Release the hostages / Liza / What's the matter with kids today? / Love story / Black and white / Whatever Didi wants / August 8th / Drop the world.

Nov 97. (cd/c/lp) <(6518-2/-4/-1)> **SO LONG – AND THANKS FOR ALL THE SHOES (live)** 79
– 180 degrees / I'm telling him / Dad's bad news / Falling in love / Kill rock stars / Punk rock elite / Murder the government / Stuck in the k-hole again / Desperation's

gone / All outta angst / Champs Elysees / Quart in session / Mono syllabic girl / Eat the meek.

– compilations, etc. –

Jun 94. (7"ep) *Fat Wreck Chords; (FAT 514-7)* **DON'T CALL ME WHITE EP**
Oct 94. (cd) *Mystic; (MYSTICCD 180)* **MAXIMUM ROCK'N'ROLL** -
Jul 95. (12") *Fat Wreck Chords; (FAT 5261)* **WE AIN'T SHIT. /**
Sep 95. (cd/c/lp) *Fat Wreck Chords; (FAT 528-2/-4/-1)* **WE HEARD THEY SUCK LIVE (live)**
Nov 97. (7") *Fat Wreck Chords; (FAT 561)* **ALL OF ME. / DESPERATIONS GONE**

NO-MAN (see under ⇒ PORCUPINE TREE)

NO MAN IS ROGER MILLER (see under ⇒ MISSION OF BURMA)

NOMEANSNO

Formed: Victoria, British Columbia, Canada ... 1983 by the WRIGHT brothers ROB and JOHN (their name a reference to a woman's right to refuse sexual advances). Deliberately anti-image and fiercly independent from the beginning, NOMEANSNO delivered their debut set, 'MAMA', in 1983 on their own label, 'Wrong'. With darkly causic social commentary and fragmented, avant-garde fuzzcore their forte, this trio (having recently added ANDREW KERR) certainly weren't in the game of rock stardom. They found a soul mate in JELLO BIAFRA, who subsequently signed/licensed them to the ever bulging roster of 'Alternative Tentacles' in 1984. Several albums followed through the 80's, namely 'SEX MAD' (1987), 'SMALL PARTS ISOLATED AND DESTROYED' (1988), 'WRONG' (1989) and '0+2=1' (1991). A year previously, they were one of the many acts to collaborate with BIAFRA, recording an album, 'THE SKY IS FALLING AND I WANT MY MOMMY' together. More recently, the trio have issued two further, equally barbed sets, 'WHY DO THEY CALL ME MR. HAPPY?' (1993) (Mr. HAPPY being ROB's solo alter-ego) and 'THE WORLDHOOD OF THE WORLD (AS SUCH)' (1995).

Album rating: SEX MAD (*5) / SMALL PARTS ISOLATED AND DESTROYED (*6) / WHY DO THEY CALL ME MR. HAPPY? (*6) / WRONG (*5) / 0+2=1 (*6) / THE WORLDHOOD OF THE WORLD (AS SUCH) (*6)

ANDREW KERR – guitar (joined after debut) / **ROB WRIGHT** – bass / **JOHN WRIGHT** – drums

not iss. Wrong

1983. (lp) <*WRONG 001*> **MAMA** -
– Living is free / My roommate is turning into a monster / Red devil / Mama's little boy / We are the chopped / No sex / Rich guns / No rest for the wicked / Living in Detente. *(UK-iss.Nov92 on 'Wrong' cd/c; WRONG 001 CD/C)*
1985. (12"ep) <*WRONG* > **YOU KILL ME** -
– Body bag / Stop it / Some bodies / Manic depression / Paradise (with BILLY & SARAH GAINES). <*re-iss. 1990 on 'Alternative Tentacles'; VIRUS 86*>

Alternative Tentacles Alternative Tentacles

Jan 87. (lp) <*(VIRUS 56)*> **SEX MAD**
– Sex mad / Dad / Obsessed / No fkucign / Hunt the she beast / Dead Bob / Long days / Metrognome / Revenge / Self pity. <*cd-iss. Jun91 +=; VIRUS 56CD*> – YOU KILL ME
Feb 88. (7") <*VIRUS 60*> **DAD. / REVENGE** -
May 88. (12"ep) <*(VIRUS 62)*> **THE DAY EVERYTHING BECAME NOTHING**
– The day everything became nothing / Dead souls / Forget your life / Beauty and the beast.
May 88. (lp/c/cd) <*(VIRUS 63/+MC/CD)*> **SMALL PARTS ISOLATED AND DESTROYED**
– Brother rat / What Slayde says / Dark ages / Junk / And that's sad / Small parts isolated and destroyed / Victory / Teresa give me that knife / Real love / Lonely. *(cd-iss. as 'THE DAY EVERYTHING BECAME ISOLATED AND DESTROYED', which included last ep)*
Nov 89. (lp/c/cd) <*(VIRUS 77/+MC/CD)*> **WRONG**
– It's catching up / The tower / Brainless wonder / Tired of waiting / Stocktaking / The end of all things / Big Dick / Two lips, two lungs, and one tongue / Rags and bones / Oh no! Bruno! / All lies. *(cd+=)* – Life in Hell / I am wrong.
Apr 90. (12"/cd-s) <*(VIRUS 81/+CD)*> **THE POWER OF POSITIVE THINKING. / MANIC DEPRESSION**

— early 1991, collaborated with JELLO BIAFRA (Dead Kennedys) on album 'THE SKY IS FALLING AND I WANT MY MOMMY'

Oct 91. (lp/c/cd) <*(VIRUS 98/+MC/CD)*> **0 + 2 = 1**
– Now will you be good? / The fall / 0 + 2 = 1 / The valley of the blind / Mary / Everyday I start to ooze / When putting it all in order ain't enough / The night nothing became everything / I think you know / Ghosts / Joyful reunion.

— now without KERR who formed HISSANOL with their engineer, SCOTT HENDERSON

Jun 93. (lp/c/cd) <*(VIRUS 123/+MC/CD)*> **WHY DO THEY CALL ME MR. HAPPY?**
– The land of the living / The river / Machine / Madness and death / Happy bridge / Kill everyone now / I need you (with TONYA WYNNE). *(c+=/cd+=)* – Slowly melting / Lullaby / Cats, sex and Nazis.

— added guitarist/keyboardist (**TOMMY**) and uncredited drummer

Nov 95. (cd/lp) <*(VIRUS 171 CD/LP)*> **THE WORLDHOOD OF THE WORLD (AS SUCH)** Oct95
– Joy / Humans / Angel or devil / He learned how to bleed / I've got a gun / My politics / Lost / Predators / Wiggley worm / Tuck it away / Victim's choice / State of grace / The jungle.
Dec 97. (12"ep/cd-ep) <*(VIRUS 207/+CD)*> **WOULD WE BE ALIVE? / YOU ARE NOT THE ONE. / RISE / BIG DICK (alternate version)**

– compilations, others, etc. –

1990's. (7") *Wrong; (WRONG 2)* **BETRAYAL. /**
1990's. (7") *Plastic Head; (ALLIEDN 010)* **OH CANADUH. /**
Jun 91. (d-lp/c/cd) *Konkurrel; (K 031-130) / Alternative Tentacles;* <*VIRUS 97/+MC/CD*> **LIVE + CUDDLY (live in Europe)**
Oct 94. (cd) *Wrong; (WRONG 13)* **ONE DOWN, TWO TO GO (NO MEANS NO PRESENTS: MR WRIGHT & MR WRONG)**

Stina NORDENSTAM

Born: 1969, Stockholm, Sweden. Inspired by jazz and classical from an early age (mainly JOHN COLTRANE and ERIK SATIE), STINA began writing her own material during adolescence, having survived the harrowing break-up of her parent's marriage. After leaving school, the elfin-like musical prodigy (she had mastered piano, violin and guitar!) cut her teeth in jazz outfit, The FLIPPERMEN. NORDENSTAM (now aged 21) signed to 'Telegram' and soon cut her debut album, 'MEMORIES OF A COLOUR', an acclaimed record of melancholy, monochromatic beauty which was deservedly picked up by Warners global offshoot, 'East West', in '92. A self-confessed depressive compared to movie director and fellow gloom-meister, Ingmar Bergman, NORDENSTAM was given the honour of playing for the Swedish parliament and royal family despite her maverick reputation. In 1994, she left behind the JONI MITCHELL and TORI AMOS comparisons by digging even deeper into her troubled psyche, unearthing a series of tragic tales frosted by her icy, deceivingly childlike vocals and coloured by the jazz textures of veteran, JON HASSELL. The following year, another veteran of the ambient/pop music world, VANGELIS, invited her to sing on his single, 'Ask The Mountains', although the collaboration didn't work out commercially. STINA's third album, 'DYNAMITE' (1996), saw the diminutive Swede take a mood swing of sorts away from her morbidly established mould towards a more forthright sound.

Album rating: MEMORIES OF A COLOUR (*7) / AND SHE CLOSED HER EYES (*7) / DYNAMITE (*6)

STINA NORDENSTAM – vocals, guitar, piano, violin / with session people

East West East West

Sep 92. (cd/c) *(<4509 90767-2/-4>)* **MEMORIES OF A COLOUR**
– Memories of a colour / The return of Alan Bean / Another story girl / His song / He watches her from behind / I'll be cryin' for you / Alone at night / Soon after Christmas / A walk in the park.
Mar 93. (7"/c-s) *(YZ 711/+C)* **ANOTHER STORY GIRL. / A WALK IN THE PARK**
(cd-s+=) *(YZ 711CD)* –
Mar 94. (7"/c-s) *(YZ 807/+C)* **LITTLE STAR. / FIRST DAY IN SPRING**
(cd-s+=) *(YZ 807CD)* – He watches her from behind.
Apr 94. (cd/c) *(<4509 93898-2/-4>)* **AND SHE CLOSED HER EYES**
– Little star / When Debbie's back from Texas / Viewed from the spire / Crime / Murder in Mairyland Park / So this is goodbye / Something nice / And she closed her eyes / Fireworks / Proposal / Hopefully yours / I see you again.
Sep 94. (c-s) *(YZ 853C)* **SOMETHING NICE / WHEN DEBBIE'S BACK FROM TEXAS**
(cd-s+=) *(YZ 853CD)* – Soon after Christmas.

— another 'East West' artist, VANGELIS, invited STINA to sing on their early '96 collaboration single, 'Ask The Mountains'.

Jul 96. (c-ep/10"ep/cd-ep) *(EW 055 C/TE/CD)* **THE PHOTOGRAPHER'S WIFE E.P.** -
– I could still (be an actor) / Now when I see you / The things you said.
Oct 96. (cd/c) *(<0630 15605-2/-4>)* **DYNAMITE**
– Under your command / Dynamite / Almost a smile / Mary Bell / The man with the gun / This time John / C.O.D. / Down Desire Avenue / Now that you're leaving.
Mar 97. (10"/c-s/cd-s) *(EW 091 TE/C/CD)* **DYNAMITE. / GREETINGS FROM THE OLD WORLD**
Jun 97. (c-s/cd-s) *(EW 106 C/CD)* **LITTLE STAR / THE MAN WITH THE GUN**

NORMAL

Formed: London, England ... 1977/78 as the brainchild of futuristic electronic entrepreneur-to-be, DANIEL MILLER. He created and self-financed The NORMAL's one and only single (the first on his 'Mute' imprint), the classic double-header, 'T.V.O.D.' & 'WARM LEATHERETTE'. Almost immediately, both sides were compared to KRAFTWERK / THROBBING GRISTLE on punk pills, the latter track being subsequently covered in impressively monotonic fashion by GRACE JONES. However, with MILLER's indie label now in full swing, he abandoned The NORMAL (after his/their last live appearance was on the 6th March 1979 with ROBERT RENTAL), choosing instead to sign his first act, FAD GADGET; he would soon snap up DEUTSCH AMERIKANISCHE FREUNDSCHAFT, SILICON TEENS and DEPECHE MODE. The rise of such prestigious loyal acts like the aforementioned DEPECHE MODE, YAZOO and later ERASURE and NICK CAVE, ensured MILLER and his 'Mute' crew would be shopping at Harrod's (so-to-speak) for years to come.

Album rating: never released any

DANIEL MILLER – electronics, vox

Mute / not iss.

Feb 78. (7") *(MUTE 001)* **T.V.O.D. / WARM LEATHERETTE** ☐ -
(re-iss. Jun95 on cd-s; 771400-2)

— The NORMAL with ROBERT RENTAL issued a live one-sided lp, 'LIVE – AT WEST RUNTON PAVILLION' on 'Rough Trade' *(ROUGH 17)<ROUGHUS 2>*

NORTHERN UPROAR

Formed: Manchester, England . . . 1994 by schoolfriends LEON MEYA, PK (aka PAUL KELLY), JEFF FLETCHER and KEITH CHADWICK. Not exactly one of Heavenly's deftest signings, this bunch were snapped up by the label on the strength of an 'In The City' industry showcase. Produced by JAMES DEAN BRADFIELD (of The MANICS) and released amid a veritable tidal wave of hype, 'ROLLERCOASTER' was a promising enough debut single in late '95. While the record stalled just outside the Top 40, the band had no such problems with follow-up, 'FROM A WINDOW', crashing into the Top 20 and drawing the tired and inevitable "next OASIS" comparisons. While they might've espoused the same boorish philosophy as their Manc compatriots, they had neither the looks/attitude of LIAM nor the common-man songwriting talent of NOEL; one thing they did share was the ability to somehow splice soundalike fragments of rock'n'pop history into an easily consumed whole i.e. the echoes of MARVIN GAYE/TAMMI TERRELL classic, 'It Takes Two' and The STONE ROSES' 'She Bangs The Drum' on 'IN MY WORLD'. 1996's eponymous debut album confirmed matters, an enjoyable trad-rock romp along the obligatory SMALL FACES/WHO/CLASH/JAM lineage but hardly strong enough to justify the lads' well publicised boasting. Critics were divided on their merits although the music buying public voted with their feet and ensured that despite another respectable offering in 1997's 'TOMORROW, TODAY AND YESTERDAY', NORTHERN UPROAR fizzled out with merely a whimper along with Brit-pop itself. • **Songwriters:** Most by MEYA (or with KELLY) except MY MIND'S EYE (Small Faces) / I AM THE COSMOS (Chris Bell). • **Trivia:** LEON MEYA was called up for national service to the Spanish army although he only lived there during the first five years of his life!

Album rating: NORTHERN UPROAR (*6) / TOMORROW, TODAY AND YESTERDAY (*5)

LEON MEYA – vocals, bass / **PK (PAUL KELLY)** – guitar / **JEFF FLETCHER**– guitar, vocals / **KEITH CHADWICK**– drums, piano

Heavenly / Alex

Oct 95. (7"/c-s) *(HVN 047/+CS)* **ROLLERCOASTER. / SMOOTH GEEZER** 41 -
(cd-s+=) *(HVN 047CD)* – Rough boy / Waiting on (acoustic).

Jan 96. (7"/c-s) *(HVN 051/+CS)* **FROM A WINDOW. / THIS MORNING** 17 -
(cd-s+=) *(HVN 051CD)* – My mind's eye / Credibility.

Apr 96. (7"ep/c-ep/cd-ep) *(HVN 052/+CS/CD)* **LIVIN' IT UP / STONEFALL. / GOODBYE / IN MY WORLD** 24 -

May 96. (cd/c/lp) *(HVN CD/MC/LP 12)* **NORTHERN UPROAR** 22 -
– From a window / Rough boy / Town / Kicks / Breakthrough / Memories / Waiting on / Livin' it up / Head under water / Moods / Rollercoaster / Living in the red.

Jun 96. (7"/c-s) *(HVN 054/+CS) <6053>* **TOWN. / KICKS (acoustic)** 48 ☐ Apr98
(cd-s+=) *(HVN 054CD)* – Memories / I am the cosmos.

May 97. (c-s) *(HVN 73CS)* **ANY WAY YOU LOOK / BREAKING THE ICE** 36 -
(10"+=/cd-s+=) *(HVN 70-10/CD)* – I remember.

Aug 97. (7"/c-s/cd-s) *(HVN 73 7/CS/CD)* **A GIRL I ONCE KNEW /** 63 -

Aug 97. (cd/c/lp) *(HVN CD/MC/LP 19)* **TOMORROW, TODAY AND YESTERDAY** ☐ -
– Any way you look / A girl I once knew / Down to me / What's it gonna be? / Blind / Goodbye / One of those things / Blown away / So much / More than this / Another day / I'm coming undone.

Nov 97. (7"/c-s) *(HVN 77/+CS)* **GOODBYE. /** ☐ -
(cd-s+=) *(HVN 77CD)* –

NORTHSIDE

Formed: Manchester, England . . . 1989 by DERMO (WARREN DERMODY), CLIFF OGIER and the WALSH brothers, TIMMY and PAUL. One of the many second division stragglers to follow in the 'Madchester' wake of The HAPPY MONDAYS and The STONE ROSES, the band were picked up by local indie institution, 'Factory', through whom they released a debut single, 'SHALL WE TAKE A TRIP'. The title alone was enough to fuel accusations of bandwagoneering and neither follow up single, 'RISING STAR', nor the aptly named debut album, 'CHICKEN RHYTHMS' (1991) cut much ice with the critics. They didn't do much sales wise either, the group sinking back into deepest, darkest Manchester along with the scene that spawned them as the press turned its attention to the more intelligent sounds of London shoegazing. • **Songwriters:** Group compositions, although they did Peter Gabriel's 'SOLISBURY HILL' on stage.

Album rating: CHICKEN RHYTHMS (*6)

WARREN 'Dermo' DERMODY – vocals / **TIMMY WALSH** – guitar / **CLIFF OGIER** – bass / **PAUL 'Walt' WALSH** – drums

Factory / Geffen

May 90. (7"/ext.12") *(FAC/12FAC 268)* **SHALL WE TAKE A TRIP. / MOODY PLACES** 50 -

Oct 90. (7") *(FAC 298-7)* **MY RISING STAR. / ('A'instrumental)** 32 -
(12"+=) *(12FAC 298)* – ('A'extended).
(cd-s+=) *(FACD 298)* – Shall we take a trip / Moody places.

May 91. (7") *(FAC 308-7)* **TAKE 5. / WHO'S TO BLAME (instrumental)** 40 ☐
(12")(cd-s+=) *(12FAC 308)(FACD 308)* – ('A'version).

Jun 91. (cd)(lp/c) *(FACTD 310)(FACT 310/+C) <24412>* **CHICKEN RHYTHMS** 19 ☐
– Take 5 / Weight of air / Funky Munky / A change is on it's way / Yeah man / Tour de world / Wishful thinking / Shall we take a trip / Who's to blame / Practice makes perfect.

— disbanded later in the year. Another NORTHSIDE were around in the mid-90's and were mainly club/dance orientated

NOSEBLEEDS

Formed: Manchester, England . . . 1977 by ED BANGER, VINI REILLY, PETE CROOKS and TOBY. Although this raw punk outfit only managed to bring out one single, the brilliant 'AIN'T BIN TO NO MUSIC SCHOOL' (complete with orchestra intro, chunky guitars and griping chorus line!), each member went on to better things: ED to fellow 'Rabid' combo, SLAUGHTER & THE DOGS and VINI (with later PETE and TOBY) to the more subdued DURUTTI COLUMN. Billed at times as ED BANGER & THE NOSEBLEEDS, it was no surprise when the loud frontman went solo leaving the rest to audition the likes of STEPHEN MORRISSEY (yes, that one!); future CULT guitarist, BILLY DUFFY, also made an appearance before their final demise.

Album rating: never released any

ED BANGER – vocals / **VINI REILLY** – guitar / **PETE CROOKS** – bass / **TOBY** – drums

Rabid / not iss.

Sep 77. (7") *(TOSH 102)* **AIN'T BIN TO NO MUSIC SCHOOL. / FASCIST PIGS** ☐ -

— ED joined SLAUGHTER & THE DOGS after a solo single, VINI joined V2 (prior to any releases) and later recalled PETE and TOBY to his DURUTTI COLUMN, the latter also becoming part of The BLUE ORCHIDS.

ED BANGER

Jul 78. (7") *(TOSH 106)* **KINNEL TOMMY. / BABY WAS A BABY** ☐ -
(re-iss. Aug78 on 'EMI International'; INT 570)

Spiv / not iss.

Nov 81. (7") *(DIV 1)* **I'VE JUST HAD ME CAR NICKED. / P.C. PLOD / SPONGE** ☐ -

Cloud Nine / not iss.

Jan 83. (7") *(CNS 01)* **POOR PEOPLE. / VICARS IN THE PARK** ☐ -

— ED retired from solo work

NOTHING BUT HAPPINESS (see under ⇒ ULTRA VIVID SCENE)

NOTSENSIBLES

Formed: Burnley, Lancashire, England . . . 1978 by frontman HAGGIS, and his motley crew of SAGE, KEV, ROG and GARY. "Celebrating" the election of a new Conservative government, these northern lads made their memorable debut with a frantic, fun-packed JILTED JOHN-esque ode to the Iron Lady, '(I'M IN LOVE WITH) MARGARET THATCHER'. Tongue-in-cheek shoutalong punk at its vintage best, the track was a turn of the decade favourite and even laid into Sun pundit, Gary Bushell on the B-side. A possible precursor to the TOY DOLLS, they never quite managed to send-up any target as entertainingly as their debut, although they made a fair attempt with their one and only LP, 'INSTANT CLASSIC' (1980)

Album rating: INSTANT CLASSIC (*4)

HAGGIS – vocals / **SAGE** – guitar / **ROG SENSIBLE** – keyboards, bass / **GARY BROWN** – bass / **KEV HEMMINGWAY** – drums

Redball / not iss.

Nov 79. (7"m) *(RR 02)* **(I'M IN LOVE WITH) MARGARET THATCHER. / LITTLE BOXES / GARY BUSHELL'S BAND OF THE WEEK** ☐ -
(re-iss. Jan80 on 'Snotty Snail'; NELCOL 1)

Bent / not iss.

Feb 80. (7"m) *(SMALL BENT 5)* **DEATH TO DISCO. / CORONATION STREET HUSTLE / LYING ON THE SOFA** ☐ -

Snotty Snail / not iss.

Mar 80. (lp) *(SSLP 1)* **INSTANT CLASSIC** ☐ -
– Instant classic / Girl with scruffy hair / Freedom / King Arthur / Death to disco / Ploppy / I am a clone / Little boxes / Sick of being normal / (Love is like) Banging my head against a brick wall / Because I'm mine / Wrong love / Blackpool rock / Daddy won't let me love you song / Don't wanna work anymore.

1980. (7"m) *(NELCOL 3)* **I THOUGHT YOU WERE DEAD. / I MAKE A BALLS OF EVERYTHING I DO / TEENAGE REVOLUTION** ☐ -

Sep 81. (7") *(NELCOL 6)* **I AM THE BISHOP. / THE TELEPHONE RINGS AGAIN** ☐ -

— sensibly split up after above

– compilations, etc. –

Sep 94. (cd) *Anagram; (CDPUNK 38)* **INSTANT PUNK CLASSICS** (all material) ☐ -

NOTWIST

Formed: Weilheim, Germany . . . 1987 by the ACHER brothers, MARKUS and MICHA. A few years later, the pair found drummer MECKI MESSERSCHMID and completed their US hardcore influenced debut set, 'LIVE'. To obtain cash, the siblings played traditional drums and trumpets respectively at Dixieland jazz parties and weddings. Breaking from the hardcore and metal mould (early DINOSAUR JR, etc) on a number of albums, they marked a career change into alternative ambient-jazz on 1997's, '12' (which featured a cover of Robert Palmer's 'JOHNNY AND MARY'). Shortly afterwards they added the sampling delights of MARTIN GRETSCHMANN, who stuck around for a similar 'Duophonic' (home of STEREOLAB) release, 'SHRINK'. Meanwhile, the brothers moonlighted in the brassy, avant-jazz outfit, THE TIED AND TICKLED TRIO.

Album rating: 12 (*7) / SHRINK (*6)

MARKUS ACHER – guitar / **MICHA ACHER** – bass / **MECKI MESSERSCHMID** – drums

Subway / not iss.
Aug 94. (cd) *(3550003-2)* **NOTWIST** [ ] [-]

Big Store / not iss.
Aug 94. (cd) *(BST 035)* **NOOK** [ ] [-]

Your Choice / Your Choice
Aug 94. (cd) *<(YCLS 021)>* **LIVE (live)** [ ] [ ]

Diversity / unknown
Nov 95. (7") *(WACCY 014)* **NOTWIST. /** [ ] [-]

Zero Hour / Zero Hour
Jan 97. (7") *(ZERS 10014)* **TORTURE DAY. /** [ ] [ ]

Community / Zero Hour
Jun 97. (cd/d-lp) *(COM 1003216-2/-1) <2180>* **12** [ ] [ ]
– Torture day / My phrasebook / Puzzle / M / Noah / My faults / String / Instr / 12 / String / Incredible change of our alien / Johnny and Mary / Torture day "loup" / Noah.

—— added **MARTIN GRETSCHMANN** – samples, etc (of CONSOLE; one album – PAN OR AMA)

Jul 97. (12"ep) *(COM 00923) <3181>* **DAY 7 EP** [ ] [ ] Oct98

Duophonic / Zero Hour
Sep 98. (cd/lp) *(DS45CD/DS33 023) <3180>* **SHRINK** [ ] [ ]
– Day 7 / Chemicals / Another planet / Moron / Electric bear / No encores / N.L. / Shrink / Your signs / 0-4.

Oct 98. (12") *<3182>* **CHEMICALS (mixes)** [-] [ ]

Heather NOVA

Born: 1968 . . . Bermuda. HEATHER was raised on a sailboat around the Caribbean, an idyllic upbringing which allowed her plenty of time to sit around and learn the guitar. Moving to dry land at the age of 19, she studied film at art college in Providence, Rhode Island, subsequently finding a more permanent base in London after a spell in New York. After working on music for her own films, NOVA found a kindred spirit in former KILLING JOKE/BRILLIANT bassman turned cult producer, YOUTH, who took the budding singer/songwriter under the wing of his own 'Butterfly' records. The resulting album, 'GLOWSTARS' (1993), recorded at her own London home studio, received mixed but generally encouraging reviews and NOVA's growing reputation secured support slots to SUGAR/BOB MOULD, etc. A live mini-set, 'BLOW' (1993), filled in time between her next studio album, the acclaimed UK Top 75, YOUTH-produced 'OYSTER' (1994). Fusing together the pop-folk influences of her childhood with the more worldly-wise standpoint of a maturing wordsmith, HEATHER had created a thought-provoking collection of songs, not least the thorny document of domestic abuse, 'ISLAND'. After touring the world on the much vaunted NEIL YOUNG / PEARL JAM "Mirrorball" trek, she took time out to collect her thoughts before emerging on Richard Branson's new 'V2' imprint with 1998's Top 60 album, 'SIREN'.

Album rating: GLOWSTARS (*6) / BLOW (*6) / OYSTER (*8) / SIREN (*6)

HEATHER NOVA – vocals, guitar; with a few people on session

Butterfly / Big Cat
Apr 93. (cd-ep) *(BSL 3)* **SPIRIT IN YOU / GLOWSTARS / EAR TO THE GROUND / SHAKING THE DOLL** [ ] [-]

May 93. (cd/c/lp) *(BFL CD/MC/LP 002)* **GLOWSTARS** [ ] [-]
– Bare / My fidelity / Spirit in you / Shell / Glowstars / Ear to the ground / Second skin / Mother tongue / All the way / Frontier / Shaking the doll / Talking to strangers. *(re-iss. Aug95 cd/c; same)*

Oct 93. (cd/c) *(BFLCD 008) <ABB 57 CD/C>* **BLOW (live)** [ ] [ ]
– Light years / Sugar / Maybe an angel / Blessed / Mother tongue / Talking to strangers / Shaking the doll. *(cd re-iss. Aug95 +=; BFLCD 8)* – Frontier / Doubled up. *(cd re-iss. Sep98 on 'Big Cat'; same as US)*

Feb 95. (c-s) *(BFLC 19)* **WALK THIS WORLD / HOME** [69] [ ]
(cd-s+=) *(BFLD 19)* – Blind.
(12"++=) *(BFT 19)* – ('A'acoustic).

Butterfly / Work-Columbia
Oct 94. (cd/c) *(BFL CD/MC 12) <67113>* **OYSTER** [72] [ ]
– Walk this world / Heal / Island / Throwing fire at the sun / Maybe an angel / Truth and bone / Blue black / Walking higher / Light years / Verona / Doubled up.

Sep 95. (c-s) *(BFLC 27)* **MAYBE AN ANGEL / THROWING FIRE AT THE SUN** [ ] [-]
(cd-s+=) *(BFLDA 27)* – Talking to strangers / ('A'-Undertow mix).
(cd-s) *(BFLDB 27)* – ('A'side) / Verona / Heal / My fidelity.

Jan 96. (cd-ep) *<67046>* **LIVE FROM THE MILKY WAY (live)** [-] [ ]
– Maybe an angel / Throwing fire at the sun / Talking to strangers / Sugar / Walking higher / Verona.

Apr 96. (c-s) *(BFLC 34)* **TRUTH AND BONE /** [ ] [ ]
(cd-s+=) *(BFLD 34)* –

V2 / Sony
May 98. (cd-s) *(VVR 5001188-3)* **LONDON RAIN (NOTHING HEALS ME LIKE YOU DO) / SHIP SONG / LONDON RAIN (acoustic)** [ ] [ ]
(cd-s) *(VVR 5001188-8)* – ('A'side) / Grow young / Water from wine.

Jun 98. (cd) *(VVR 100187-2) <67953>* **SIREN** [55] [ ]
– London rain (nothing heals me like you do) / Blood of me / Heart and shoulder / What a feeling / Valley of sound / I'm the girl / Winterblue / I'm alive / Widescreen / Paper cup / Avalanche / Make you mine / Ruby red / Not only human.

– compilations, etc. –

Feb 97. (cd-ep) *Big Cat; (ABB 132SCD)* **THE FIRST RECORDING** [ ] [ ]

NOVA MOB (see under ⇒ HUSKER DU)

NOVOCAINE

Formed: Newport, Wales . . . 1994 by STEVE EVANS, RUSSELL EDWARDS, RICHARD JACKSON and BERT LEWIS. They made their vinyl debut that year with 'MODERN MAN', raw, gut-wrenching punk-grunge with turps-gargling vocals provided by EVANS. A follow-up, 'TENSION', appeared on the 'Townhill' label a year later, leading to a contract with the more experienced indie imprint, 'Fire'. NOVOCAINE injected even more energy into 1997 albums, 'FRUSTRATION No.10' and 'NERVOUS DISPOSITION'; although the band were saddled with the usual NIRVANA or RADIOHEAD comparisons, they were hotly tipped for greater things in '98/'99.

Album rating: FRUSTRATION No.10 (*7) / NERVOUS DISPOSITION (*7)

STEVE EVANS – vocals / **RICHARD JACKSON** – guitar / **RUSSELL EDWARDS** – bass / **BERT LEWIS** – drums

Liberty Place / not iss.
Jun 94. (7") *(LP 004)* **MODERN MAN. / BRAIN** [ ] [-]

Townhill / not iss.
Jul 95. (7") *(TIDY 002)* **TENSION. / DADDY'S MONEY** [ ] [-]

Fire / not iss.
Nov 96. (7") *(BLAZE 107)* **CELLOPHANE WRAPPED NEW HEAD. / 'E'** [ ] [-]

Jan 97. (m-cd) *(FIREMCD 61)* **FRUSTRATION NO.10** [ ] [ ]

May 97. (7") *(BLAZE 114)* **MOTHER – FATHER. / IN MY HEAD** [ ] [ ]
(cd-s+=) *(BLAZE 114CD)* – My big business.

Jul 97. (7") *(BLAZE 117)* **STONEFACE. / FLAMES** [ ] [-]
(cd-s+=) *(BLAZE 117CD)* – Bury the hate.

Aug 97. (cd) *(FIRECD 67)* **NERVOUS DISPOSITION** [ ] [ ]
– Walls / Mother – Father / Awake / Bittersoul / Stoneface / Frustration No.10 / Pondlife / Million miles / Sorry (scum like me) / Boring git / Waiting / Analyse / Horses / She knows nothing.

Dec 97. (7") *(BLAZE 118)* **POND LIFE. / BEDROOM ADDICT (alternative version)** [ ] [ ]
(cd-s+=) *(BLAZE 118CD)* – Astronaut / Modern man (radio version).

Feb 98. (7") *(BLAZE 120)* **MILLION MILES. / YOU KNOW ME BETTER THAN THAT** [ ] [ ]
(cd-s+=) *(BLAZE 120CD)* – Control / Asylum.

NUBILES

Formed: Oxford, England . . . 1994 by TARA MILTON, PENNY SCHUELLER, GEORGIO CURCETTI and DAN GODDARD. Propelled by the anti-hero revolutionary vision of mainman TARA MILTON, The NUBILES launched their first sonic attack on the mainstream with the incendiary 'LAYABOUT'. Veering between indie-pop melody and blitzkreig guitar noise, the single was vaguely reminscent of RADIOHEAD, at least in spirit. The lovesick 'WITHOUT WAKING' followed a similar formula, building up to a raging climax of frustration and bitterness while B-side, 'A SAP'S GUIDE TO ROCK'N'ROLL' wasn't exactly short on sarcasm; you could tell MILTON had been through the music biz mill at least once before (with also-ran power mods, 5:30). Despite initial press acclaim, a further clutch of singles – 'TATJANA', 'I WANT TO BE YOUR KUNTE KINTE' and a revamped 'LAYABOUT' – and a debut album, 'MINDBLENDER' (1998) were afforded only minimal interest.

Album rating: MINDBLENDER (*5)

TARA MILTON – vocals, bass (ex-FIVE THIRTY) / **PENNY SCHUELLER** – guitar, keyboards / **GEORGIO CURCETTI** – guitar / **DAN GODDARD** – drums

Lime Street / not iss.
Feb 95. (7") *(LS 01)* **LAYABOUT. / MOTHER & FATHER** [ ] [-]

May 95. (7") *(LS 02)* **WITHOUT WAKING. / A SAP'S GUIDE TO ROCK'N'ROLL** [ ] [-]
(cd-s+=) *(LS 02CD)* – Toodle pip.

Oct 95. (7") *(LS 03)* **TATJANA (ALL OVER ME). / BIG CHILD** [ ] [-]
(cd-s+=) *(LS 03CD)* – Chasing 10 (acoustic).

Jun 96. (12") *(LS 04)* **I WANT TO BE YOUR KUNTA KINTE. /** [ ] [-]
(cd-s+=) *(LS 04CD)* –

Mar 98. (cd-s) *(LS 08)* **LAYABOUT (Mindblender remix)** [ ] [-]

May 98. (cd) *(LSCD 01)* **MINDBLENDER** [ ] [-]

Gary NUMAN

Born: GARY WEBB, 8 Mar'58, Hammersmith, London, England. Inspired by 70's glam icons such as BOLAN and BOWIE as well as synthmeisters like KRAFTWERK, NUMAN formed punk outfit, MEAN STREET in 1977,

subsequently appearing on the Various Artists compilation, 'Live At The Vortex'. To end the year, he set up TUBEWAY ARMY, basically his solo project although he was accompanied on live work by PAUL GARDINER and his uncle, GERALD LIDYARD. The debut vinyl outing, 'THAT'S TOO BAD', was issued by indie punk label, 'Beggars Banquet' in early '78. An eponymous debut album passed virtually unnoticed, although things changed dramatically in June '79, when they/he had a first No.1 with the monotonic synth-noir of 'ARE FRIENDS ELECTRIC', spurred on by a compelling appearance on UK's 'Top Of The Pops'. Its parent album, 'REPLICAS', also shot to the top the same month. A busy year for NUMAN, in addition to collaborating with ROBERT PALMER, of all people (he was initially part of offshoot outfit, DRAMATIS), he found time to record a second No.1 album, 'THE PLEASURE PRINCIPLE'. This collection was previewed with the hypnotic, sweeping electronica of the 'CARS' single, by far his most well known track and one that enjoyed a rejuvination only last year (1996) after it was used in a British TV advert. NUMAN scored yet another No.1 album with 'TELEKON' (1980) the following year, his futuristic synth-based pop/rock gracing the upper reaches of the singles chart in the form of 'WE ARE GLASS' and 'I DIE: YOU DIE'. By this point, however, NUMAN was well on his way to becoming perhaps one of most visible targets of critical derision in the whole of the music industry, his neo-futurist posturing, dalek vocals, pretentious lyrics and worst of all, his vocal support of Margaret Thatcher raising the not inconsiderable ire of the music press. Nevertheless, NUMAN had a fiercely loyal grassroots following of clone-like fans (second only to NUMAN himself as figures of fun among rock circles) who ensured most of his subsequent output made the Top 50 at least. Despite the presence of such luminaries as MICK KARN (JAPAN), ROGER TAYLOR (QUEEN) and erm, NASH THE SLASH (solo artist from Canada, apparently), 'DANCE' (1981) was a decidedly ungroovy set of steely electronica and his last to achieve mainstream success. NUMAN released two further, increasingly pompous albums, 'I, ASSASSIN' (1982) and 'WARRIORS' (1983) before forming his own label, 'Numa', in 1984 to issue his own product along with material by his brother JOHN's outfit, HOHOKAM. 80's albums like 'THE FURY' (1985), 'STRANGE CHARM' (1986), 'METAL RHYTHM' (1988) and 'AUTOMATIC' (1989) continued to appeal mainly to hardcore fans although 'OUTLAND' (1991) managed to nudge into the Top 40. However, since the awful 'MACHINE AND SOUL' (1992), NUMAN has fallen further into cult status, his releases failing to even break the Top 100. • **Songwriters:** Wrote own material, with inspiration from psi-fi writers (i.e. WILLIAM S. BURROUGHS). Covered 1999 + U GOT THE LOOK (Prince). • **Trivia:** In the early 80's, he took up flying planes and bought his own aircrafts (mainly warplanes).

Album rating: THE GARY NUMAN COLLECTION (*7) / THE PLEASURE PRINCIPLE (*6) / REPLICAS (*7; TUBEWAY ARMY)

TUBEWAY ARMY

GARY NUMAN – vocals, guitar, synthesizer, keyboards (ex-MEAN STREET) / **PAUL 'Scarlett' GARDINER** – bass / **GERALD 'Rael' LIDYARD** – drums

		Beggars Banquet	Atco
Feb 78.	(7") *(BEG 5)* **THAT'S TOO BAD. / OH! DIDN'T I SAY**		-
—	**BARRY BENN** – drums repl. BOB SIMMONDS who had repl. LIDYARD / added **SEAN BURKE** – guitar		
Jul 78.	(7"m) *(BEG 8)* **BOMBERS. / O.D. RECEIVER. / BLUE EYES**		-
Aug 78.	(lp,blue-lp) *(BEGA 4)* **TUBEWAY ARMY** – Listen to the sirens / My shadow in vain / The life machine / Friends / Something's in the house / Every day I die / Steal and you / My love is a liquid / Are you real / The dream police / Jo the waiter / Zero bass. *(re-iss. Aug79 lp/c; BEGA/BEGC 4); hit No.14) (re-iss. May83 on 'Fame' lp/c; FA/TC-FA 3060) (re-iss. Jul88 lp/c; BBL/+C 4)*		-
—	**JESS LIDYARD** – drums returned to replace BARRY and SEAN		
Mar 79.	(7") *(BEG 17)* **DOWN IN THE PARK. / DO YOU NEED THE SERVICE?** (12"+=) *(BEG 17T)* – I nearly married a human 2.		-
May 79.	(7"/7"pic-d) <US-7"/c-s> *(BEG 18/+P)* **ARE 'FRIENDS' ELECTRIC?. / WE ARE SO FRAGILE?**	1	
Jun 79.	(lp/c) <credited as GARY NUMAN & TUBEWAY ARMY> *(BEGA/BEGC 7) <117>* **REPLICAS** – Me I disconnect from you / Are 'friends' electric? / The machman / Praying to the aliens / Down in the park / You are in my vision / Replicas / It must have been years / When the machines rock / I nearly married a human. *(re-iss. +cd.Sep88) (re-iss. cd/c Apr95 on 'Music Club')*	1	

GARY NUMAN

Date	Release	UK	US
—	solo retaining **PAUL GARDINER** – bass / **CEDRIC SHARPLEY** – drums / **CHRIS PAYNE** – synth, viola / **BILLY CURRIE** – keyboards		
Aug 79.	(7") *(BEG 23)* **CARS. / ASYLUM**	1	-
Sep 79.	(lp/c) *(BEGA/BEGC 10) <38120>* **THE PLEASURE PRINCIPLE** – Airplane / Metal / Complex / Films / M.E. / Tracks / Observer / Conversation / Cars / Engineers. *(re-iss. Sep88 lp/c; BBL/+C 10)*	1	16 Jan80
Nov 79.	(7") *(BEG 29)* **COMPLEX. / BOMBERS (live)** (12"+=) *(BEG 29T)* – Me I disconnect from you (live).	6	
Jan 80.	(7") *<7211>* **CARS. / METAL**	-	9
—	**DENNIS HAINES** – keyboards repl. CURRIE who returned to ULTRAVOX and VISAGE; added **RUSSELL BELL** – guitar (on tour) .		
May 80.	(7") *(BEG 35)* **WE ARE GLASS. / TROIS GYMNPEDIES (1st MOVEMENT)**	5	
Aug 80.	(7") *(BEG 46)* **I DIE: YOU DIE. / DOWN IN THE PARK (piano version)**	6	-
Sep 80.	(lp/c) *(BEGA/BEGC 19) <32103>* **TELEKON** – This wreckage / The aircrash bureau / Telekon / Remind me to smile / Sleep by windows / I'm an agent / I dream of wires / Remember I was a vapour / Please push no more / The joy circuit. *(free-7"w/ lp)* – REMEMBER I WAS A VAPOUR. / ON BROADWAY *(re-iss. Jul88 lp/c; BBL/+C 19)*	1	64
Sep 80.	(7") **I DIE: YOU DIE. / SLEEP BY WINDOWS**	-	
Dec 80.	(7") **REMIND ME TO SMILE. /**	-	
Dec 80.	(7") *(BEG 50)* **THIS WRECKAGE. / PHOTOGRAPH**	20	
Apr 81.	(d-lp/c) *(BOX/C 1)* **LIVING ORNAMENTS 1979-1980 (live)**	2	-
Apr 81.	(lp) *(BEGA 24)* **LIVING ORNAMENTS 1979 (live)** – Airplane / Cars / We are so fragile? / Films / Something's in the house / My shadow in vain / Conversation / The dream police / Metal.	47	-
Apr 81.	(lp) *(BEGA 25)* **LIVING ORNAMENTS 1980 (live)** – This wreckage / I die: you die / M.E. / Everyday I die / Down in the park / Remind me to smile / The joy circuit / Tracks / Are 'friends' electric? / We are glass.	39	-
—	GARY now recruited famous stars to replace BELL, SHARPLEY, HAINES and PAYNE. They became DRAMATIS. Jul'81 he guested on PAUL GARDINER single 'STORMTROOPER IN DRAG' *(BEG 61/+T)*, which hit UK No.49. Next with stars **MICK KARN** – bass (of JAPAN) / **ROGER TAYLOR** – drums (of QUEEN) + **NASH THE SLASH** – violin (Canadian solo artist)		
Aug 81.	(7") *(BEG 62)* **SHE'S GOT CLAWS. / I SING RAIN** (12"+=) *(BEG 62T)* – Exhibition.	6	
Sep 81.	(lp/c) *(BEGA/BEGC 28) <38143>* **DANCE** – Slowcar to China / Night talk / A subway called you / Cry the clock said / She's got claws / Crash / Boys like me / Stories / My brother's time / You are you are / Moral. *(re-iss. Jan89 lp/c; BBL/+C 28)*	3	
Nov 81.	(7"; by GARY NUMAN and DRAMATIS) *(BEG 68)* **LOVE NEEDS NO DISGUISE. / TAKE ME HOME** (12"+=) *(BEG 68T)* – Face to face.	33	
—	GARY NUMAN now used session people.		
Feb 82.	(7") *(BEG 70)* **MUSIC FOR CHAMELEONS. / NOISE NOISE** (ext.12"+=) *(BEG 70T)* – Bridge? what bridge.	19	
Jun 82.	(7") *(BEG 77)* **WE TAKE MYSTERY (TO BED). / THE IMAGE IS** (ext.12"+=) *(BEG 77T)* – ('A'early version).	9	
Aug 82.	(7") *(BEG 81)* **WHITE BOYS AND HEROES. / WAR GAMES** (ext.12"+=) *(BEG 81T)* – Glitter and ash.	20	
Sep 82.	(lp/c) *(BEGA/BEGC 40) <900141>* **I, ASSASSIN** – White boys and heroes / War songs / A dream of Siam / Music for chameleons / This is my house / I, assassin / The 1930's rust / We take mystery (to bed). *(re-iss. Jan89 lp/c; BBL/+C 40)*	8	
Aug 83.	(7"/7"sha-pic-d) *(BEG 95/+P)* **WARRIORS. / MY CAR SLIDES (1)** (ext.12"+=) *(BEG 95T)* – My car slides (2).	20	
Sep 83.	(lp/c) *(BEGA/BEGC 47)* **WARRIORS** – Warriors / I am render / The iceman comes / This prison moon / My centurion / Sister surprise / The tick tock man / Love is like clock law / The rhythm of the evening. *(re-iss. Jan89 lp/c; BBL/+C 47)*	12	-
Oct 83.	(7") *(BEG 101)* **SISTER SUPRISE. / POETRY AND POWER** (ext.12"+=) *(BEG 101T)* – Letters.	32	
		Numa	Warners
Oct 84.	(7"/7"sha-pic-d) *(NU/+P 4)* **BERSERKER. / EMPTY BED, EMPTY HEART** (12"+=) *(NUM 4)* – ('A'extended).	32	

Nov 84. (lp/c) *(NUMA/+C 1001)* **BERSERKER** 45 [ ]
– Berserker / This is new love / The secret / My dying machine / Cold warning / Pump it up / The God film / A child with the ghost / The hunter. *(c+=)* – (6 extra tracks). *(cd-iss. Dec95; NUMACD 1001)*

Dec 84. (7") *(NU 6)* **MY DYING MACHINE. / HERE I AM** 66 [ ]
(ext.12"+=) *(NUM 6)* – She cries.

— next 45 with BILL SHARPE of SHAKATAK; and on 'Polydor' album 'Famous People'.

Feb 85. (7"/7"pic-d; by SHARPE & NUMAN) *(POSP/+P 722)* **CHANGE YOUR MIND. / REMIX, REMAKE, REMODEL** 17 [ ]
(ext.12"pic-d+=) *(POSPX 722)* – Fools in a world of fire.

Apr 85. (d-lp/c) *(NUMA D/C 1002)* **WHITE NOISE (live)** 29 [-]
– (intro) / Berserker / Metal / Me, I disconnect from you / Remind me to smile / Sister surprise / Music for chameleons / The iceman comes / Cold warning / Down in the park / This prison moon / I die; you die / My dying machine / Cars / We take mystery (to bed) / We are glass / This is new love / My shadow in vain / Are 'friends' electric?. *(d-cd-iss. May93; NUMACD 1002)*

May 85. (7"ep/12"ep,12"blue-ep,12"white-ep) *(NU/+M 7)* **THE LIVE EP (live)** 27 [ ]
– Are 'friends' electric? / Berserker / Cars / We are glass.

Jul 85. (7"/7"pic-d) *(NU/+P 9)* **YOUR FASCINATION. / WE NEED IT** 46 [ ]
(ext.12"+=/ext.12"pic-d+=) *(NUM/+P 9)* – Anthem.

Sep 85. (7") *(NU 11)* **CALL OUT THE DOGS. / THIS SHIP COMES APART** 49 [ ]
(ext.12"+=) *(NUM 11)* – No shelter.

Sep 85. (lp/pic-lp/c) *(NUMA/+P/K 1003)* **THE FURY** 24 [ ]
– Call out the dogs / This disease / Your fascination / Miracles / The pleasure skin / Creatures / Tricks / God only knows / Creatures / I still remember. *(c+)* – (all tracks extended). *(cd-iss. 1986; CDNUMA 1003) (re-iss. cd Nov96; NUMACDX 1003)*

Nov 85. (7",7"red,7"white/ext-12",ext-12"red,ext-12"white) *(NU/+M 13)* **MIRACLES. / THE FEAR** 49 [ ]

Apr 86. (7"/7"pic-d/ext-12"/ext-12"pic-d) *(NU/+P/M/MP 16)* **THIS IS LOVE. / SURVIVAL** 28 [ ]
(all w/ free 7"flexi)
(d12"+=) *(NUMX 16)* – Call out the dogs (extended) / No shelter / This ship comes apart.

Jun 86. (7"/7"sha-pic-d/ext-12"/picture-12"pic-d/club-10") *(NU/+P/M/MP/DJ 17)* **I CAN'T STOP. / FACES** 27 [ ]
(all w/ free 7"flexi)

Sep 86. (7"/7"pic-d/ext-12"/ext-12"pic-d; as SHARPE & NUMAN) *(NU/+P/M/MP 19)* **NEW THING FROM LONDON TOWN. / TIME TO DIE** 52 [ ]

Oct 86. (lp/c)(cd) *(NUMA/+C 1005)(CDNUMA 1005)* **STRANGE CHARM** 59 [ ]
– My breathing / Unknown and hostile / The sleep room / New thing from London Town / I can't stop / Strange charm / The need / This is love. *(re-iss. cd Nov96; NUMACDX 1005)*

Nov 86. (7"/7"pic-d/ext-12"/ext-12"pic-d) *(NU/+P/M/MP 21)* **I STILL REMEMBER. / PUPPETS** 74 [-]

— Early in 1987, he teamed up with RADIO HEART (see further below)

Polydor Warners

Jan 88. (7",7"white,7"blue,7"clear/7"pic-d/ext-12"/ext-12"pic-d; as SHARPE & NUMAN) *(POSP/+P/X/PX 894)* **NO MORE LIES. / VOICES** 34 [ ]
(cd-s+=) *(POCD 894)* – ('A'extended) / Change your mind.

I.R.S. I.R.S.

Sep 88. (7"/7"w-poster) *(ILS/+P 1003)* **NEW ANGER. / I DON'T BELIEVE** 46 [ ]
(12"+=/12"g-f+=) *(ILST/ILSG 1003)* – Children.
(cd-s+=) *(ILSCD 1003)* – Creatures (live) / I can't stop (live).

Oct 88. (lp/c/cd) *(ILP/+C/CD 035)* *<IRS/+D 82005>* **METAL RHYTHM** 48 [ ]
– Respect / Don't call my name / New anger / America / Hunger / Voix / Young heart / Cold metal rhythm / This is emotion. *(pic-lp iss.Mar89; ILPX 035)*

Nov 88. (7"/7"pic-d) *(ILS/+PD 1004)* **AMERICA (remix). / RESPECT (live)** 49 [ ]
(12"+=) *(ILST 1004)* – New anger (live).
(cd-s++=) *(ILSCD 1004)* – Call out the dogs (live).

— again with **ROGER ODELL** – drums / **TESSA MILES + LINDA TAYLOR** – backing vocals

SHARPE & NUMAN

Polydor M.C.A.

May 89. (7"/7"pic-d) *(PO/+PD 43)* **I'M ON AUTOMATIC. / LOVE LIKE A GHOST** 44 [ ]
(ext.12"+=/ext.12"pic-d+=) *(PZ/+PD 43)* – Voices ('89 remix).
(7"w-poster) *(POPB 43)* – ('A'side) / No more lies (new version).
(cd-s+=) *(POCD 43)* – (all 4 above).

Jun 89. (lp/c/cd) *(839520-1/-4/-2)* **AUTOMATIC** 59 [ ]
– Change your mind / Turn off the world / No more lies / Breathe in emotion / Some new game / I'm on automatic / Rip it up / Welcome to love / Voices / Nightlife. *(cd+=)* – No more lies (12"version) / I'm on automatic (12"version).

GARY NUMAN

— solo with **RUSSELL BELL** – guitar / **CHRIS PAYNE** – keyboards, violin / **ADE ORANGE** – keyboards / **CEDRIC SHARPLY** – drums / **JOHN WEBB** – saxophone / **ANDY COUGHLAN** – bass / **VAL CHALMERS + EMMA CHALMER** – backing vocals

I.R.S. I.R.S.

Oct 89. (lp/cd) *(EIRSA/+CD 1019)* **THE SKIN MECHANIC (live Sep88)** 55 [ ]
– Survival / Respect / Call out the dogs / Cars / Hunger / Down in the park / New anger / Creatures / Are 'friends' electric / Young heart / We are glass / I die: you die.

Mar 91. (7",7"red/c-s) *(NUMAN 1/+C)* **HEART. / SHAME** 43 [ ]
(12") – ('A'side) / Icehouse.
(cd-s) – ('A'side) / Tread careful.
(12") – ('A'side) / Are 'friends' electric?.

Mar 91. (lp/c/cd) *(EIRSA/+MC/CD 1039)* **OUTLAND** 39 [ ]
– Confession / My world storm / Interval 1 / From Russia infected / Interval 2 / They whisper you / Dark Sunday / Heart / Devotion / Outland / Interval 3 / 1999 / Dream killer.

Numa Numa

Sep 91. (7"/c-s) *(NUD/NUC 22)* **EMOTION. / IN A GLASSHOUSE** [ ] [ ]
(12"+=) *(NUM 22)* – Hanoi.
(cd-s++=) *(NUCD 22)* – ('A'-different mix).

Mar 92. (7"/c-s) *(NU/+C 23)* **THE SKIN GAME. / DARK MOUNTAIN** 68 [ ]
(12"+=/cd-s+=) *(NUM/NUCD 23)* – U got the look / ('A'-digi mix).

Jul 92. (7") *(NU 24)* **MACHINE + SOUL. / ('A'-promo mix)** 72 [-]
(cd-s+=) *(NUCD1 24)* – Cry baby / Wonder eye.
(cd-s+=) *(NUCD2 24)* – 1999 / The hauntings.
(12"+=) *(NUM1 24)* – Your fascination (live) / Outland (live) / Respect (live).
(12") *(NUM2 24)* – ('A'side) / Soul protection (live) / Confession (live) / From Russia infected (live).

Jul 92. (lp/c/cd) *(NUMA/+C/CD 1009)* **MACHINE + SOUL** 42 [ ]
– Machine + soul / Generator / The skin game / Poison / I wonder / Emotion / Cry / U got the look / Love isolation. *(ext.cd re-iss. Sep93)*

— Apr 94; He guested for GENERATOR on their version of 'ARE FRIENDS' ELECTRIC'.

— NUMAN & DADAGANG; Apr 94 12"/cd-s LIKE A REFUGEE (I WON'T CRY) on 'Record Label', re-iss. Aug 94 as GARY NUMAN & FRIENDS

Aug 94. (12"ep/cd-ep) *(NU M/CD 25)* **DREAM CORROSION** [ ] [-]

Aug 94. (t-lp/d-c/d-cd) *(NUMA/+C/CD 1010)* **DREAM CORROSION (live)** [ ] [-]
– Mission / Machine and soul / Outland / Me, I disconnect from you / We are so fragile / Respect / Shame / Films / Dream killer / Down in the park / My world storm / Machman / Generator / Noise, noise / Cars / Voix / You are in my vision / It must have been years / That's too bad / Remind me to smile / I'm an agent / Are 'friends' electric / My breathing / I don't believe / Bombers / Jo the waiter / We are glass.

Oct 94. (12"ep/cd-ep) *(NU M/CD 26)* **A QUESTION OF FAITH** [ ] [ ]

Mar 95. (cd/c/lp) *(NUMA/+C/CD 1011)* **SACRIFICE** [ ] [ ]

Mar 95. (12"/12"pic-d/cd-s/pic-cd-s) *(NU/+MP/CD/CDP 27)* **ABSOLUTION. / MAGIC (trick mix) / MAGIC (extended)** [ ] [-]

Jun 95. (12"ep/cd-ep) *(NUM/+CD 28)* **DARK LIGHT LIVE E.P. (live)** [ ] [-]
– Bleed / Everyday I die / The dream police / Listen to the sirens.

Jul 95. (d-cd/d-c) *(NUMA CD/C 1012)* **DARK LIGHT (live)** [ ] [ ]
– Pray / A question of faith / I dream of wires / Noise noise / Listen to the sirens / Everyday I die / Desire / Friens / Scar / Magic / Praying to the aliens / Replicas I / Mean street / Stormtrooper in drag / Dead liner / Bleed / The dream police / I die, you die / The hunter / Remind me to smile / Are friends "electric"? / Do you need the service? / Love and napalm / Jo the waiter / I'm an agent.

Nov 95. (d-c/d-cd; with MICHAEL R. SMITH) *(NUMA C/CD 1013)* **HUMAN** [ ] [-]
– Navigators / Bombay / We fold space / Cry in the dark / Manic / Empire / Little lost soul / Visitor / Magician / Undercover / Halloween / Embryo / Elm Street / Harmonos / Big alten / Blind faith / New life / Fairy tales / Disease / Tidal wave / Alone and afraid / Sahara / Cold / Do you wonder / Betrayal / Suspicion / Unborn / Lethal injection / Frantic / Mother / Black heart / Thunder road / Law and order / Needles / Climax / Inferno.

When! not iss.

Feb 96. (cd) *(WHENCD 006)* **TECHNO ARMY** [ ] [-]

Eagle not iss.

Oct 97. (cd/c) *(EAG CD/MC 008)* **EXILE** 48 [-]
– Dominion day / Prophecy / Dead heaven / Dark / Innocence bleeding / The angel wars / Absolution / An alien cure / Exile.

Apr 98. (c-s) *(EAGCS 008)* **DOMINION DAY / ANGEL WARS (extended)** [ ] [-]
(cd-s) *(EAGXS 008)* – ('A'side) / Voix (20th anniversary) / Dead heaven (extended) / Cars (live).
(cd-s) *(EAGXA 008)* – ('A'side) / Metal (20th anniversary) / Down in the park (20th anniversary) / Dominion day (live).

– compilations, etc. –

on 'Beggars Banquet' unless otherwise mentioned / * = TUBEWAY ARMY

Aug 79. (d7"*) *(BACK 2)* **THAT'S TOO BAD. / OH! I DIDN'T SAY// BOMBERS. / O.D. RECEIVER / BLUE EYES** [ ] [-]

Apr 81. (c-s*) *WEA; (SPC 4)* **ARE 'FRIENDS' ELECTRIC? / WE ARE SO FRAGILE? / DOWN IN THE PARK** [ ] [-]

Nov 82. (lp/c) *TV-Virgin; (TVA/TVC 7)* **NEW MAN NUMAN – THE BEST OF GARY NUMAN** 45 [-]

Apr 83. (12"ep,12"yellow-ep*) *(BEG 92E)* **TUBEWAY ARMY '78 VOL.1** [ ] [-]
– That's too bad (alternate mix) / Oh! didn't I say / Bombers / O.D. receiver / Blue eyes / Do you need the service.

Sep 84. (lp/pic-lp*) *(BEGA 55/+P)* **THE PLAN** 29 [-]
(re-iss. Jul88 lp/c; BBL/+C 55)

Dec 84. (12"ep,12"red-ep*) *(BEG 123E)* **TUBEWAY ARMY '78-'79 VOL.2** [ ] [-]
– Fade out / 1930 / The crazies / Only a downstate / We have a technical.

Dec 84. (12"ep,12"blue-ep*) *(BEG 124E)* **TUBEWAY ARMY '78-'79 VOL.3** [ ] [-]
– The Monday troup / Crime of assikon / The life machine / A game called Echo / Random / Oceans.

Aug 87. (12"ep/c-ep;*) *Strange Fruit; (SFPS/+C 032)* **THE PEEL SESSIONS** [ ] [-]
– Me I disconnect from you / Down in the park / I nearly married a human.

Aug 87. (7"/7"pic-d) *(BEG 199/+P)* **CARS (E-REG MODEL). / ARE FRIENDS ELECTRIC?** 16 [ ]
(c-s+=/ext-12"+=) *(BEG 199 C/T)* – We are glass / I die: you die.
(ext-12"+=) *(BEG 199TR)* – ('A'-Motorway mix).

Sep 87. (d-lp/d-cd) *(BEGA 88/+CD)(BEGC 88)* **EXHIBITION** 43 [-]
– Me, I disconnect from you / That's too bad / My love is a liquid / Music for chameleons / We are glass / Bombers / Sister Surprise / Are 'friends' electric / I dream of wires / Complex / Noise noise / Warriors / Everyday I die / Cars / We take mystery to bed / I'm an agent / My centurion / Metal / You are in my vision / I die: you die / She's got claws / This wreckage / My shadow in vain / Down in the park / The iceman comes. *(d-cd+=)* – (11 tracks)

Dec 87. (cd) *(BEGA 4CD)* **REPLICAS / THE PLAN** -
(re-iss. d-cd Dec93; BEGA 152CD)
Dec 87. (cd) *(BEGA 7CD)* **TUBEWAY ARMY / DANCE** -
(re-iss. d-cd Dec93; BEGA 151CD)
Dec 87. (cd) *(BEGA 10CD)* **THE PLEASURE PRINCIPLE / WARRIORS** -
(re-iss. d-cd Dec93; BEGA 153CD)
Dec 87. (cd) *(BEGA 19CD)* **TELEKON / I, ASSASSIN**
(re-iss. d-cd Dec93; BEGA 154CD)
(above series of cd's, omitted some tracks on each)
Oct 89. (d-lp/cd) *Castle; (CCS LP/CD 229)* **THE GARY NUMAN COLLECTION** -
Dec 89. (m-lp/cd) *Strange Fruit; (SFPMA/+CD 202)* **DOUBLE PEEL SESSIONS** -
1990. (pic-cd-ep) **THE SELECTION** -
– Cars ('E' reg.model) / Down in the park / I die: you die / Are 'friends' electric? / We are glass / Music for chameleons.
1990. (7") *Old Gold; (OG 9917)* **ARE FRIENDS ELECTRIC?. / I DID YOU** -
1990. (7") *Old Gold; (OG 9919)* **CARS. / WE ARE GLASS** -
Mar 92. (lp/c/cd) *Numa; (NUMA/+C/CD 1008)* **ISOLATE** -
Oct 92. (d-cd) *Numa; (NUMACD 1007)* **GHOST** -
Oct 92. (cd/lp) *Receiver; (RR CD/LP 170)* **THE OTHER SIDE OF GARY NUMAN** -
Dec 92. (cd) *Connoisseur; (CSAPCD 113)* **DOCUMENT SERIES PRESENTS . . .** -
Aug 93. (7"/c-s) *(BEG 264/+C)* **CARS. / ('A'mix)** 53
(12"sha-pic-d+=/cd-s+=) *(BEG 264 L/CD)* – Cars ('93 sprint mix) / Cars (Top Gear mix).
Sep 93. (d-cd)(c) *(BEGA 150CD)(BEGC 150)* **THE BEST OF GARY NUMAN 1978-1983** 70 -
Jul 94. (cd) *Receiver; (RRCD 186)* **HERE I AM** -
Mar 95. (cd/c) *Polygram TV; (531 149-2/-4)* **GREATEST HITS** -
Mar 96. (7"/c-s/cd-s) *Premier; (PRM/+MC/CD 1)* **CARS (premier mix) / ARE FRIENDS ELECTRIC (live) / DOWN IN THE PARK (live)** 17
Mar 96. (cd/c) *Premier;* **THE PREMIER HITS** (compilation) 21 -
Jul 96. (3xcd) *Receiver; (RRXCD 505)* **THE STORY SO FAR** -
Sep 96. (cd/c) *Emporio; (EMPR CD/MC 666)* **THE BEST OF GARY NUMAN** -
Oct 97. (12") *Random; (RANDOM 2.1)* **METAL (remixes). / DANS LE PARC** -
Nov 97. (12"green) *Random; (RANDOM 2.2)* **I DIE YOU DIE (Greenhaus mix) / CARS (Mike Dearborn mix) / CARS (Dave Clarke mix)** -
Jan 98. (12"blue) *Random; (RANDOM 2.3)* **WARRIORS (Dave Angel mix). / ARE 'FRIENDS' ELECTRIC (Liberator DJ's mix) / REMEMBER I WAS VAPOUR (Steve Stoll mix)** -
Feb 98. (12") *Random; (RANDOM 2.4)* **WE ARE GLASS (Claude Young mix) / FILMS (Alex Hazzard remix) / THE ICEMAN COMES (Peter Lazonby mix)** -
— GARY has also contributed to other DRAMATIS recordings.

NUMBER ONE CUP

Formed: Chicago, Illinois, USA . . . 1993 by SETH COHEN, MICHAEL LENZI and PAT O'CONNELL. Apparently conceived as a combination of GASTR DEL SOL, UNREST and STEREOLAB, NUMBER ONE CUP was the brainchild of bespectacled intellectual, SETH COHEN, who was contacted by MICHAEL LENZI and PAT O'CONNELL after the pair read about his intentions in a local newspaper article. Signed to 'Flydaddy', the band released their debut album, 'POSSUM TROT PLAN', in Spring '96, to encouraging reviews. With an attention-span challenging twenty tracks, the appeal of the album lay in quieter moments such as 'STRANGE & SILENT STAIRCASE' and 'PATCH KIT', chessy electric piano and COHEN's wonderfully off-the-cuff lyrics drawing the listener in. Among the noisier stuff, the synth enhanced, soarway ba-ba-ba melodica of subsequent single, 'DIVEBOMB', was the cream of the crop, preceding the 'KIM CHEE IS CABBAGE' EP later that year. 1997 was equally prolific with a handful of singles (including a split affair with RED RED MEAT) and a follow-up album, 'WRECKED BY LIONS' (1997).

Album rating: POSSUM TROT PLAN (*6) / WRECKED BY LIONS (*4)

SETH COHEN – vocals, guitar / **MICHAEL LENZI** – guitar / **PATRICK O'CONNELL** – drums / with also JOHN PRZYBOROWSKI + MIKE KIRTS + DAVE TRUMFIO (the producer) + MIKE HAGLER + JENNI SNYDER

Flydaddy Flydaddy
Nov 95. (cd) *<(FLY 012)>* **POSSUM TROT PLAN**
– Birth of a gasser / Just let go / Autumn lever / No particular style / 'Til Tuesday / Aspirin burns / Outboard motors / Why did you piss yourself? / Strange & silent staircase / Static / Divebomb / Pocket / Seminar for backward pupils / Let me know / Patch kit / Apple cider / Lustrous poppies / Ohio arts / She plays the numbers / & Nico.
Blue Rose Flydaddy
Feb 96. (7"/c-s) *(BRRC 1003-7/-4)* **DIVEBOMB. /** -
(cd-s+=) *(BRRC 1003-2)* –
Jul 96. (7"/c-s) *(BRRC 1005-7/-4)* **JUST LET GO. /** -
(cd-s+=) *(BRRC 1005-2)* –
Nov 96. (cd-ep) *<FLY 021-2>* **KIM CHEE IS CABBAGE EP** -
– Malcolm's X-ray picnic / Not quite reading / Caught sliding / The house is falling down / Stereo / High diver / As men will.
Mar 97. (7") *(FLY 019-7)* **split with band, RED RED MEAT** -
Blue Rose Flydaddy
Mar 97. (7") *(BRRC 1014-7)* **MONKEY SONG. / MALCOLM'S X-RAY PICNIC** -
(cd-s+=) *(BRRC 1014-3)* –
May 97. (7") *(BRRC 1007-7)* **EASE BACK DOWN. /** -
(cd-s+=) *(BRRC 1007-2)* –
Jun 97. (cd/lp) *(BRRC 1013-2/-1) <FLY 018>* **WRECKED BY LIONS** Mar97
– Ease back down / Backlit / Chisel / Paris / Bright orange fireball sun / Black choppers cry / Astronaut / Waiting on the lions / Maybe there's a thread / Tree song / Concordia / Malcolm's x-ray picnic / Flickers and flames / So inclined / Three miles from talent.
Oct 97. (7") *(BRRC 1009-5)* **MONEY PIT VOL.1. /** -

NUNS

Formed: San Francisco, California, USA . . . 1977 by RITCHIE DETRICK, ALEJANDRO ESCOVEDO, JENNIFER MIRO, PAT RYAN and JEFF RAPHAEL. One of many bands said to have pioneered the US hardcore/punk scene (which paved the way for fellow Californians The DEAD KENNEDYS and The GERMS), The NUNS made their vinyl debut late in 1978 with the blistering single, 'SAVAGE'. The following few years saw the lads release a couple of 45's for the 'Rosco' imprint, before signing to the influential 'Posh Boy' (home of BLACK FLAG, etc). However, immediately prior to this they disbanded for a while, only to re-form again early 1980 with slightly new personnel on their eponymous debut album. A few more line-up changes ensued, leading to another break-up soon after, although a new look NUNS completed a comeback pop-orientated album, 'RUMANIA', in the mid 80's. In the interim, ESCOVEDO had helped form RANK & FILE with former DILS members.

Album rating: NUNS (*7) / RUMANIA (*5)

RITCHIE DETRICK – vocals / **ALEJANDRO ESCOVEDO** – guitar / **JENNIFER MIRO** – keyboards / **PAT RYAN** – bass / **JEFF RAPHAEL** – drums

not iss. 415
Nov 78. (7"m) *<S 0001>* **SAVAGE. / DECADENT JEW / SUICIDE CHILD** -
not iss. Rosco
1979. (7") **THE BEAT. / MEDIA CONTROL** -
1980. (7") *<4166>* **WW III. / COCK IN MY POCKET** -
— split after recording of above. **KEVIN FOLEY** – drums; repl. RAPHAEL / **JOEY TERRANOVA** – bass; repl. PAT
not iss. Posh Boy
Nov 80. (lp) *<PBS 105>* **THE NUNS** -
Butt Watteau
Jan 82. (7") *(FUN 2) <002>* **WILD. / SUICIDE CHILD** Nov81
Mar 82. (lp) *(ALSO 001)* **1ST** (UK-issue of US debut) -
— ESCOVEDO helped form RANK AND FILE in 1981. The NUNS re-formed later
— **MIKE VARNEY** – bass; repl. JOEY TERRANOVA
— **JEFF OLENER** – vocals repl. DETTRICK
Hive P.V.C.
1986. (lp) **RUMANIA** -
May 87. (7") *(HIVE 8)* **THE SUN IS GONNA GET TO ME. /**
— no more heard of them after above.

– compilations, etc. –

Feb 94. (cd) *Musical Tragedies; (EFA 122012)* **4 DAYS IN A MOTEL ROOM**

NURSE WITH WOUND

Formed: London, England . . . 1979 by STEPHEN STAPLETON, a graphic designer who resided in Ireland. Although he wrote and performed most of the material himself, he occasionally employed members of spiritual cousins, CURRENT 93, who shared releases with NWW. That year, STAPLETON and the 'United Dairies' imprint debuted with 'CHANCE MEETING ON A DISSECTING TABLE OF A SEWING MACHINE AND AN UMBRELLA', the first limited-edition album in a mindbogglingly prolific career that took in the whole of the 80's and most of the 90's. A tireless noise/sample experimentalist, STAPLETON utilised any sound he could get his hands on, the more humdrum or the more exotic the better. Unsurprisingly, his audience was restricted to restricted to those with an enquiring and patient mind, not to mention a healthy bank balance; many of NWW's early albums now fetch between £50 and £100 at record fairs. • **Trivia:** STAPLETON produced The LEGENDARY PINK DOTS among others.

Album rating: CHANCE MEETING . . . (*4) / + most others depending on your point of view averaging around the same

STEPHEN STAPLETON – instruments

United Dairies not iss.
1979. (lp) *(UD 01)* **CHANCE MEETING ON A DISSECTING TABLE OF A SEWING MACHINE AND AN UMBRELLA** -
1980. (lp) *(UD 03)* **TO THE QUIET MEN FROM A TINY GIRL** -
1980. (lp) *(UD 04)* **MERZBILD SCHWET** -
1981. (lp) *(UD 08)* **INSECT AND INDIVIDUALS SILENCED** -
– Alvin's funeral / Absent old queen underfoot / Mutiles De Guerre.
Feb 84. (lp) *(YMR 03)* **OSTRANENIE 1913** -
(above issued on 'Third Mind')
Jul 85. (lp) *(UD 012)* **HOMOTOPY TO MARIE** -
May 86. (lp) *(UD 019)* **AUTOMATING VOL.1** -
Jul 86. (lp) *(UD 020)* **A MISSING SENSE** (shared with ORGANUM) -
Nov 86. (lp) *(TORSO 33-016)* **SPIRAL INSANA** -
(above released on 'Torso')

— In 1987, they shared a single 'CRANK' with TERMITE QUEEN's 'Wisecrack' for 'Crystal-Wisewound' label; *WW 01)*

Nov 87. (lp) *(UD 025)* **DRUNK WITH THE OLD MAN OF THE MOUNTAINS** [ ] [-]

Jun 88. (m-lp) *(UD 027)* **ALAS THE MADONNA DOES NOT FUNCTION** [ ] [-]
– Cut glass poison /

— In 1988, shared 12" 'FAITH'S FAVOURITES' with CURRENT 93 on 'Yankhi' label; *YANKHI 002)*

Jun 89. (lp) *(UD 030)* **AUTOMATING II** [ ] [-]

Sep 89. (12"ep/cd-ep) *(UD 031/+CD)* **SORESUCKER. / JOURNEY THROUGH CHEESE** [ ] [-]

Dec 89. (lp/cd) *(UD 032/+CD)* **A SUCKED ORANGE** [ ] [-]
– Paradise lost / Internal torment II / Autopsy / Stillborn / Deviated instinct / The resurrection encore / Doom / A means to an end / Confessor / Uncontrolled / Talion / Laws of retaliation / Electro hippies / Freddy's revenge (live) / Toranga / Dealers in death.

— In 1990, shared another single 'BURIAL OF THE STONED SARDINE' with CURRENT 93 for 'Harbinger' label; *001)*

Jan 91. (lp) *(UD 038)* **CREAKINESS** (with SPASM) [ ] [-]

Apr 91. (lp/cd) *(UD 09/+CD)* **THE 150 MURDEROUS PASSIONS** [ ] [-]

1992. (cd) **THUNDER PERFECT MIND** [ ] [-]

Clawfist — not iss.

1992. (7") *(Clawfist 12)* **STEEL DREAM MARCH OF THE METAL MEN. / THE DADDA'S INTOXICATION** [ ] [-]

1993. (10"ep) *(Clawfist 20)* **CRUMB DUCK** (shared with STEREOLAB) [ ] [-]

World Serpent — not iss.

1993. (7") *(WS 7004)* **ALIEN. /** [ ] [-]

– other releases, etc. –

Laylah — not iss.

Dec 84. (12") *(LAY 007)* **BRAINED BY FALLING MASONARY. / SHORT DIP IN THE GLORY HOLE** [ ] [-]

Sep 85. (lp) *(LAY 015)* **SYLVIE & BABS HIGH-THIGH COMPANION** [ ] [-]
(cd-iss. 1989; LAY 015CD)

Nov 89. (cd) *(LAY 030CD)* **GYLLENSKOLD** [ ] [-]
(lp-iss.Mar90; LAY 030)

Idle Hole — not iss.

1988. (3xlp-box) *(MIRROR ONE)* **SOLILOQUY FOR LILITH** [ ] [-]

1988. (lp) *(MIRROR 1C)* **SOLILOQUY FOR LILITH PTS 5/6** [ ] [-]

1989. (lp) *(MIRROR TWO)* **PRESENTS THE SISTERS OF PATAPHYSICS** [ ] [-]

1989. (12") *(MIRROR 003)* **COOLOORTA MOON. / GREAT EMPTY SPACE** [ ] [-]

Shock — not iss.

1990. (7") *(SX 004)* **SINISTER SENILE: HUMAN HUMAN HUMAN. / PSYCHEDELIC UNDERGROUND** [ ] [-]

Torso — Torso

. (lp) *(TORSO 33016)* **SPIRAL INSANA** [ ] [ ]

NUT

Born: 1972, Northumbria, England. This unusually named (after an Egyptian Goddess, apparently) singer/songwriter left home at the age of 14, initially living with her boyfriend in Newcastle before relocating to London and trying her hand at acting. Subsequently hooking up with writing partner, PETER EVANS, NUT began creating music in her late teens, primarily on an acoustic basis and influenced – in spirit if not in execution – by the timeless sounds of BILLIE HOLIDAY, ELLA FITZGERALD etc. Signed to 'Epic', she released her debut single, 'BRAINS', in Spring '96, hitting the Top 75 and drawing comparisons with the likes of PJ HARVEY and SINEAD O'CONNOR. Follow-up single, 'CRAZY', notched her up almost ten chart places, a compelling blend of vaguely unsettling lyrics, inventive acoustic pop and cute, elfin vocals. Both tracks featured on debut set, 'FANTANICITY' (1996), a surprising chart failure despite a further single, 'SCREAM', narrowly missing the Top 40.

Album rating: FANTANICITY (*6)

NUT – vocals / with **PETE EVANS** – co-writer, producer, drums / **JONNY BRIDGEWOOD** – bass (of MORRISSEY)

Epic — Epic

May 96. (c-s) *(nutmc 2)* **BRAINS /** [64] [ ]
(cd-s+=) *(nutcd 2)* –

Sep 96. (c-s) *(nutmc 5)* **CRAZY / JUNK** [56] [ ]
(cd-s+=) *(nutcd 5)* –

Sep 96. (cd/c) *(nut cd/mc 3)* **FANTANICITY** [ ] [ ]
– Brains / Scream / Sticky / Giant / Junk / Fantanicity / Pleased / Crazy / Bitter / Burn / Bluegenes.

Dec 96. (7"/c-s) *(nut vi/mc 6)* **SCREAM. / AMAZING** [43] [-]
(cd-s) *(nutcd 6)* – ('A'side) / Get lost / Brains (live) / ('A'live).

Judy NYLON (see under ⇒ SNATCH)

NY LOOSE

Formed: Manhattan, New York, USA … 1993 as LOOSE by vocalist/guitarist, BRIJETTE WEST and drummer JOHN MELVILLE. With another band already operating under that name, the pair were forced to prefix their moniker with NY prior to the release of a self-financed debut single, 'BITCH'. A potted history of streetwise punk/New Wave from the Big Apple's skool of kool, the track kicked the stagnant Grunge-fixated US indie squarely in the bollocks. BRIJETTE's tough-talking patter and feminist invective also had the critics chattering, some even daring to compare her with COURTNEY LOVE. Bolstering the line-up with two battle-scarred veterans of the NY scene, GARY SUNSHINE (formerly of the blistering but criminally overlooked CIRCUS OF POWER) and DANNY NORDAHL (ex-STIV BATORS), BRIJETTE and Co delivered two further 45's, 'GREEN LITTLE SEMAPHORE' and 'SPIT', the latter a one-off for Chris Parry's offshoot label, 'Non-Fiction'. After a period of label-less instability, the hard-bitten quartet found a home at 'Hollywood' (well, the company, that is) and finally got round to freeing up a debut long-player, 'YEAR OF THE RAT', in '96.

Album rating: YEAR OF THE RAT (*6)

BRIJETTE WEST – vocals, guitar / **JOHN MELVILLE** – drums

not iss. — Loose

1994. (7") **BITCH. /** [-] [ ]

— added **GARY SUNSHINE** – guitar (ex-CIRCUS OF POWER) / **DANNY NORDAHL** – bass (ex-STIV BATORS)

not iss. — Holy Plastic

1994. (7") **GREEN LITTLE SEMAPHORE. /** [-] [ ]

Non-Fiction — unknown

Apr 95. (7") *(YES 12)* **SPIT. / PRETTY SUICIDE** [ ] [-]

Flipside — Flipside

Sep 95. (m-cd) *<(FLIP 70)>* **LOOSEN UP** [ ] [-]

Polydor — Hollywood

Sep 96. (cd) *(162049-2)* **YEAR OF THE RAT** [ ] [ ]

Phil OAKEY & Giorgio MORODER (see under ⇒ HUMAN LEAGUE)

(see under ⇒ HUMAN LEAGUE)

OASIS

Formed: Manchester, England . . . summer 1992, by frontman LIAM GALLAGHER, rhythm guitarist PAUL 'BONEHEAD' ARTHURS, bassist PAUL McGUIGAN and drummer TONY McCARROLL. Initially called RAIN, they were soon joined by LIAM's older brother NOEL who had worked as a roadie for The INSPIRAL CARPETS. He was also a budding songwriter/guitarist with a concrete self-belief and after a year of rehearsals and occasional local gigs, they were signed by Creation's ALAN McGEE, after the eagle-eared Scotsman clocked them at a Glasgow gig in mid-1993. With a groundswell of interest not witnessed since the heady early days of The STONE ROSES, OASIS secured a near UK Top 30 placing with 'SUPERSONIC', a sneering, leering anthem with lyrics that SHAUN RYDER would've been proud to call his own. Later that summer the band released the follow-up, 'SHAKER MAKER', a rather tame effort in comparison which appeared to be modelled on the NEW SEEKERS' chestnut, 'I'd Like To Teach The World To Sing'. Nevertheless, what the single lacked in originality, it made up for in controversy and the stage was set for OASIS' first Top 10 hit, the classic 'LIVE FOREVER'. A life-affirming rush celebrating the strength of the human spirit, the song was lauded as single of the year, closely followed by the epochal debut album, 'DEFINITELY MAYBE' (1994). There were no maybes about it, this album defined an era in the same way that The SEX PISTOLS (an obvious influence) focused the frustrations of a generation with 'Never Mind The Bollocks', it's just a pity that the dubious 'Britpop' era spawned an interminable glut of production line indie chancers. The record opens on the same wave of freefall exhiliration as say, 'Exile On Main Street', (The ROLLING STONES were another oft cited influence), 'ROCK'N'ROLL STAR' alive with a palpable sense of what it actually means to want fame that badly. The feeling that this was "for real, man", never lets up until the last track fades, a visceral, exhaustive listen and one of the most consistent debut albums ever released. Another highlight from the album, the T.REX-esque nihilism of 'CIGARETTES AND ALCOHOL' was the next single, peaking at No.7 in late '94. Basically, OASIS were like all your favourite bands rolled into one, a kind of potted history of rock, NOEL having a unique talent for constructing classic songs that seemed somehow familiar yet annoyingly difficult to pin down. On top of this, LIAM was a natural, his piercing stare and cooly motionless stage presence coupled with his inimitably lethargic sneer a vital component of OASIS' rock'n'roll juggernaut. That Christmas the band narrowly missed No.1 with the string-laden, overtly BEATLES-esque 'WHATEVER', a poppier effort that hinted at the band's future direction. By this point, OASIS were a headline act, the scramble for tickets that accompanied any announcement of a gig becoming all too familiar over the next few years. As would the brothers' press profile, their loudmouth self-aggrandising and embaressingly public fisticuffs becoming a regular feature of OASIS' increasingly cartoonish image. The first casualty of the well documented in-fighting was McCARROLL, his place in the drum seat subsequently filled by ALAN WHITE. The boasting was backed up by consistently strong material, however, and in the Spring of '95, OASIS deservedly scored their first No.1 with the soaring, yearning 'SOME MIGHT SAY'. The band's single releases had always been good value for money, the B-sides usually better than most indie bands' half-arsed lead tracks. This release was no exception, containing the affecting 'TALK TONIGHT' (NOEL on vocals) and the brilliant melodic noise of 'ACQUIESCE', arguably one of the group's finest tracks. Thus the stage was set for the media-created battle with the recently revitalised BLUR, both bands releasing a single simultaneously that August. In the event, despite the verbal jousting, BLUR took the top spot with 'Country House', OASIS forced to bite their tongue and, erm, 'ROLL WITH IT' at No.2. The Mancs had the last laugh, however, when their follow-up album '(WHAT'S THE STORY) MORNING GLORY' (1995) proceeded to sell multi-millions, catapulting OASIS into the musical stratosphere alongside U2 etc., something unheard of for a group who started out as, basically, another guitar band from Manchester. While the album lacked the serrated edge and amphetamine rush of the debut, the songwriting was once again faultless, tracks like 'WONDERWALL' (almost a Christmas No.1), 'DON'T LOOK BACK IN ANGER', and 'CHAMPAGNE SUPERNOVA' reflecting a newfound maturity and a more coffee-table friendly pop-rock sound. The rapid ascent of the GALLAGHERS continued the following year, with awards galore and a significant dent into the US market. The latter wasn't achieved without some cost to the band, however, as LIAM and NOEL had their most serious and most widely reported fracas to date, LIAM flying home midway through a US tour amid rumours that the band had split. It was merely a case of another day, another fight however, and the band went on to break British concert attendance records with two sell-out shows at Knebworth in August ('96). All that said then, OASIS' most recent material, the 'STAND BY ME' (1997) album, was underwhelming to say the least. The posturing and epic feel of '(WHAT'S THE STORY) . . .' were still there but the record sounded like a parody of OASIS, if that's not a contradiction in terms. While the album broke records with its first day sales figures, it has hardly achieved the same momentum as its predecessor and if NOEL doesn't come up with material a tad more inspiring next time then its doubtful if OASIS can fully realise their long-held aim to be "best band in the world". • **Songwriters:** NOEL, except I AM THE WALRUS (Beatles) / CUM ON FEEL THE NOIZE (Slade) / STREET FIGHTING MAN (Rolling Stones) / FEELIN' LONELY by Noel (Small Faces). • **Trivia:** NOEL wrote 'SLIDE AWAY' on a Les Gibson guitar, which he bought from friend JOHNNY MARR (ex-Smiths) and which was once the property of PETE TOWNSHEND (The Who). After a long on-off relationship, LIAM married PATSY KENSIT (singer/actress and former estranged wife of Simple Minds voxman, JIM KERR) in 1997.

Album rating: DEFINITELY MAYBE (*10) / (WHAT'S THE STORY) MORNING GLORY? (*10) / BE HERE NOW (*7) / THE MASTERPLAN compilation (*7)

LIAM GALLAGHER (b.21 Sep'72) – vocals / **NOEL GALLAGHER** (b.29 May'67) – guitar / **PAUL 'BONEHEAD' ARTHURS** (b.23 Jun'65) – guitar / **PAUL McGUIGAN** (b.19 May'71) – guitar / **TONY McCARROLL** – drums

		Creation	Epic
Apr 94.	(7") *(CRE 176) <55332>* **SUPERSONIC. / TAKE ME AWAY**	31	Jul94
	(12"+=) *(CRE 176T)* – I will believe (live). (cd-s++=) *(CRECD 176)* – Columbia (demo). *(re-iss. Nov96 c-s repl.7" as so below; same); hit No.47)*		
Jun 94.	(7"/c-s) *(CRE/+CS 182)* **SHAKERMAKER. / D'YER WANNA BE A SPACEMAN?**	11	-
	(12"+=) *(CRE 182T)* – Alive (demo). (cd-s++=) *(CRECD 182)* – Bring it on down (live). *(re-iss. Nov96; same); hit No.48)*		
Aug 94.	(7"/c-s) *(CRE/+CD 185)* **LIVE FOREVER. / UP IN THE SKY (acoustic)**	10	-
	(12"+=) *(CRE 185T)* – Cloudburst. (cd-s++=) *(CRECD 185)* – Supersonic (live). *(re-iss. Nov96; same); hit No.42)*		
Aug 94.	(cd/c/d-lp) *(CRE CD/MC/LP 169) <66431>* **DEFINITELY MAYBE**	1	58 Jan95
	– Rock'n'roll star / Shakermaker / Live forever / Up in the sky / Columbia / Supersonic / Bring it down / Cigarettes and alcohol / Digsy's dinner / Slide away / Married with children. *(d-lp+=)* – Sad song. *(re-iss. Nov96 as ' . . .SINGLES BOX – SILVER' cd/5xcd-s-box; CREDM 001/002); hit No.23)*		
Oct 94.	(7"/c-s) *(CRE/+CS 190)* **CIGARETTES AND ALCOHOL. / I AM THE WALRUS (live)**	7	-
	(12"+=) *(CRE 190T)* – Fade away. (cd-s++=) *(CRECD 190)* – Listen up. *(re-iss. Nov96; same); hit No.38)*		
Dec 94.	(7"/c-s) *(CRE/+CS 195)* **WHATEVER. / (IT'S GOOD) TO BE FREE**	3	-
	(12"+=) *(CRE 195T)* – Slide away. (cd-s++=) *(CRECD 195)* – Half the world away. *(re-iss. Nov96; same); hit No.34)*		

— After a punch-up McCARROLL left and was replaced by drummer **ALAN WHITE** (b.26 May'72, London) (ex-IDHA) and brother of STEVE WHITE (long-time sticksman with PAUL WELLER)

Apr 95.	(7"/c-s) *(CRE/+CS 204)* **SOME MIGHT SAY. / TALK TONIGHT**	1	-
	(12"+=) *(CRE 204T)* – Acquiesce. (cd-s++=) *(CRECD 204)* – Headshrinker. *(re-iss. Nov96; same); hit No.40)*		

— Their first 5 singles re-entered UK Top 60 in Jun'95. The next single lost the battle with rivals BLUR to the No.1 spot. It was a year of running verbal battles between them, although LIAM's arrogance and NOEL's songwriting abilities on next album, finally won over the public.

Aug 95.	(7"/c-s) *(CRE/+CS 212)* **ROLL WITH IT. / IT'S BETTER, PEOPLE**	2	-
	(12"+=) *(CRE 212T)* – Rockin' chair. (cd-s+=) *(CRECD 212)* – Live forever (live). *(re-iss. Nov96; same)hit No.55)*		
Oct 95.	(cd/c/d-lp) *(CRE CD/MC/LP 189) <67351>* **(WHAT'S THE STORY) MORNING GLORY?**	1	4
	– Hello / Roll with it / Wonderwall / Don't look back in anger / Hey now! / Some might say / Cast no shadow / She's electric / Morning glory / Champagne supernova. *(d-lp+=)* – Bonehead's bank holiday. *(re-iss. Nov96 as ' . . .SINGLES BOX – GOLD' cd/5xcd-s-box; CREMG 001/002); hit No.24)*		
Oct 95.	(7"/c-s) *(CRE/+CS 215)* **WONDERWALL / ROUND ARE WAY**	2	-
	(12"+=) *(CRE 215T)* – The swamp song. (cd-s+=) *(CRECD 215)* – The masterplan. *(re-iss. Nov96; same); hit No.36)*		
Jan 96.	(c-s,cd-s) *<78216>* **WONDERWALL / ROUND ARE WAY / TALK TONIGHT**	-	8

DUBLIN
12 m
MANCHESTER

— NOEL also part of one-off supergroup The SMOKIN' MOJO FILTERS alongside PAUL WELLER and PAUL McCARTNEY. They had Top 20 hit with 'COME TOGETHER'.

Feb 96. (7"/c-s) *(CRE/+CS 221) <78356>* **DON'T LOOK BACK IN ANGER. / STEP OUT** 1 -
(12"+=) *(CRE 221T)* – Underneath the sky.
(cd-s++=) *(CRECD 221)* – Cum on feel the noize.
(re-iss. Nov96; same); hit No.53)

Jul 96. (c-s,cd-s) *<78356>* **DON'T LOOK BACK IN ANGER / CUM ON FEEL THE NOIZE** - 55

— NOEL met up with great pensmith and fan! BURT BACHARACH who wanted to do a collaboration. He also refused to accept his Ivor Novello award for best songwriter of the year, after he was told it would be shared with rivals BLUR. In Aug'96, NOEL objected to The SMURFS releasing 'WONDERWALL' on their album. LIAM was posted missing on US tour (actually the tabloids caught him buying a new house). NOEL and the lads had to play to packed out stadiums on own. LIAM joined them after around a week, but walked out again after a bust-up with NOEL. Speculation over the next months, will be about an impending split. Meanwhile, NOEL featured on CHEMICAL BROTHERS No.1 UK smash 'Setting Sun'.

Jul 97. (7"/c-s) *(CRE/+CS 256)* **D'YOU KNOW WHAT I MEAN? / STAY YOUNG** 1 -
(12"+=) *(CRE 256T)* – Angel child (demo).
(cd-s++=) *(CRESCD 256)* – Heroes.

Aug 97. (cd/c/lp) *(CRECD/CCRE/CRELP 219) <68530>* **BE HERE NOW** 1 2
– D'you know what I mean? / My big mouth / Magic pie / Stand by me / I hope I think I know / Girl in the dirty shirt / Fade in-out / Don't go away / Be here now / All around the world / It's gettin' better (man) / All around the world (reprise).

Sep 97. (7"/c-s) *(CRE/+CS 278)* **STAND BY ME. / (I GOT) THE FEVER** 2 -
(12"+=) *(CRE 278T)* – My sister lover.
(cd-s++=) *(CRESCD 278)* – Going nowhere.

Jan 98. (7"/c-s) *(CRE/+CS 282)* **ALL AROUND THE WORLD. / THE FAME** 1 -
(12"+=) *(CRE 282T)* – Flashbox.
(cd-s++=) *(CRESCD 282)* – Street fighting man.

Nov 98. (cd/d-lp)(c) *(CRE CD/LP 241)(C-CRE 241) <69647>* **THE MASTERPLAN** (compilation) 2 51
– Acquiesce / Underneath the sky / Talk tonight / Going nowhere / Fade away / The swamp song / I am the walrus / Listen up / Rockin' chair / Half the world away / (It's good) To be free / Stay young / Headshrinker / The masterplan.

OBLIVIANS

Formed: Memphis, Tennessee, USA ... summer '93 by JACK, GREG and ERIC 'OBLIVIAN' (real surnames in no particular order, YARBER, CARTWRIGHT and FRIEDL). Instrumentally interchangable, the average OBLIVIANS live set was characterised by much guitar and drum swapping as the trio belted out the filthiest blues/garage groove this side of one-time fellow 'Crypt'-kicker, JON SPENCER. The latter label was home to The OBLIVIANS' debut album, 'SOUL FOOD', a record that boasted warped interpretations of tracks by Lightnin' Hopkins, Dave Clark Five(!) and German one-hit wonders, Trio(!). Weird if not wonderful, the er . . . trio were wont to invent their own inter-band subdivisions, e.g. GREG OBLIVIAN & THE TIP TOPS, the pseudonymous moniker of 1998's 'HEAD SHOP'. Previous to this, the OBLIVIAN "brothers" had issued two further albums, 'POPULAR FAVOURITES' (1996) and 'PLAY 9 SONGS WITH MR. QUINTRON' (1997). • **Songwriters:** JACK's 'SO LOW' album in late '98 featured a handful of covers including the New York Dolls' 'TRASH', Memphis Minnie's 'LET ME BE YOUR CHAUFFER' and Otis Rush's 'ALL YOUR LOVIN''.

Album rating: SOUL FOOD (*5) / POPULAR FAVOURITES (*5) / PLAY 9 SONGS WITH MR. QUINTRON mini (*4) / HEAD SHOP solo (*4) / SO LOW solo (*5)

GREG 'OBLIVIAN' – guitar, drums, vocals / **ERIC 'OBLIVIAN'** – guitar, drums, vocals / **JACK 'OBLIVIAN'** (YARBER) – guitar, drums, vocals

Crypt Crypt

Jan 95. (7") *(EFA 11582-7)* **SUNDAY YOU NEED LOVE. /** -

Feb 95. (cd/lp) *(EFA 11589-2/-1) <55>* **SOUL FOOD** May95
– Viet Nam war blues / And then I fucked her / Big black hole / Jim Cole / Mad lover / Sunday you need love / Never change / No reason to live / I'm not a sicko, there's a plate in . . . / Cannonball / Nigger rich / Bum a ride / Anyway you want it / Static party / Ja ja ja.

Jan 96. (7") *(DR 001)* **GO PILL-POPPER. /** -
(above issued on 'Drug Racer')

Jul 96. (cd/lp) *(EFA 12876-2/-1) <65>* **POPULAR FAVOURITES** Oct96
– Christina / Trouble / Leather / Guitar shop asshole / Hey mama, look at sis / Part of your plan / Do the milkshake / The strong come on / She's a hole / Bad man / He's your man / Drill / You better behave / Pinstripe Willie / You fucked me up, you put me down / Emergency.

Aug 96. (d7") *(SFTRI 412)* **KISS YOUR ASS**
(above issued on 'Sympathy For The Record Industry') *(re-iss. Jul98; same)*

Jun 97. (m-lp/m-cd) *(EFA/+CD 12892) <82>* **PLAY 9 SONGS WITH MR. QUINTRON**
– Feel all right / Live the life / I may be gone / I don't wanna live alone / The final stretch / What's the matter now? / Ride that train / If mother knew / Mary Lou.

Sympathy F Sympathy F

Mar 98. (lp/cd; by GREG OBLIVIAN & The TIP TOPS) *<(SFTRI 513/+CD)>* **HEAD SHOP** Jan98

— next solo with **SCOTT BOMAR** – bass / **STUART SIKES** – drums

Nov 98. (cd; by JACK OBLIVIAN) *<(SFTRI 535)>* **SO LOW**
– Intro – Midnight hour queen / Shake it off / Trash / So low / Downtown / Let me be your chauffer / Mama don't get off / You made me crazy / Human being / All your lovin' / All the way down.

OCEAN COLOUR SCENE

Formed: Moseley, Birmingham, England . . .mid-'89 out of The FANATICS, by SIMON FOWLER, DAMON MINCHELLA and OSCAR HARRISON, who released a one-off '45 for the 'Chapter 22' label before recruiting BOYS' guitarist STEVE CRADOCK. In the summer of 1990, OCS found manager JOHN MOSTYN, who signed them to his new '!Phffft' stable. A debut track, 'SWAY', helped secure a joint venture with 'Phonogram' for a follow-up, 'YESTERDAY TODAY'. The latter track breeched the Top 50 in March '91, and, just when it seemed as if a breakthrough was imminent, '!Phffft' was sold during the recording of their JIMMY MILLER-produced debut album. Now on 'Fontana', the momentum was lost as they re-recorded the whole project, a 1992 re-issue of 'SWAY' and the follow-up, 'GIVING IT ALL AWAY' sinking without trace. In April, the aforementioned eponymous album finally surfaced, although it brought criticism for its over-cooked production. After another 45, 'DO YOURSELF A FAVOUR' bombed, the group subsequently found themselves without a recording contract and up to their necks in debt. Aided by lawyer, Michael Thomas, they were successful in persuading Fontana's DAVE BATES to waive the million £'s they were still owing. OCS returned with a support slot to their newfound mate, PAUL WELLER, CRADOCK and FOWLER guested on his Autumn '93 classic 'Wildwood' album; CRADOCK subsequently became an integral part of WELLER's band over the course of the next year. Meanwhile in the summer of '94, OCEAN COLOUR SCENE supported OASIS and completed a 'Fontana' tour of the States supporting HOUSE OF LOVE and The CATHERINE WHEEL. A year later, all group members played for WELLER at some point, with CRADOCK and MINCHELLA guesting on his No.1 album, 'Stanley Road'. 1995 also saw the band recording their long-awaited follow-up album, having earlier signed to 'M.C.A.'. Early in '96 (with WELLER on organ), they scored their first of many Top 20 hits with 'THE RIVERBOAT SONG' (later chosen for Chris Evans' TFI Friday Show theme song). Dropping the indie-dance trappings of old, OCS adopted a heavier, funkier, white-soul/mod sound and a retro image to boot, dominating the charts in the wake of WELLER's massively successful return to a rootsier sound. 'YOU'VE GOT IT BAD' fared even better, followed by a BRENDAN LYNCH-produced album, 'MOSELEY SHOALS' (name of their own studio), which hit the UK Top 3. The record inevitably featured WELLER on a few other tracks and the man augmented the group on their 'Later With Jools Holland' spot. Two further Top 10 smashes, 'THE DAY WE CAUGHT THE TRAIN' (their classiest so far) and 'THE CIRCLE' were culled from the album, an odds'n'sods collection, 'B-SIDES, SEASIDES & FREERIDES' keeping their profile high prior to the release of new material. A couple of Top 5 hits, 'HUNDRED MILE HIGH CITY' and 'TRAVELLERS TUNE', preceded an Autumn '97 album, 'MARCHIN' ALREADY', a lesser work which nevertheless reached the top of the UK charts. An easy target for the critics, only time will tell whether OCS's retro-lite and almost wholly teenage audience can stay the course. • **Songwriters:** FOWLER lyrics / group music; except DO YOURSELF A FAVOUR (Stevie Wonder & Syreeta) / DAY TRIPPER (Beatles).

Album rating: OCEAN COLOUR SCENE (*6) / MOSELEY SHOALS (*8) / MARCHIN' ALREADY (*6)

FANATICS

SIMON FOWLER – vocals, acoustic guitar, harmonica / **DAMON MINCHELLA** – bass / **PAUL WILKES** – guitar / **OSCAR HARRISON** – drums, piano, vocals (ex- ECHO BASE) who repl. CAROLINE BULLOCK

Chapter 22 not iss.

Mar 89. (12"ep) *(12CHAP 38)* **SUBURBAN LOVE SONGS** -
– Suburban love songs / 1.2.3.4. / My brother Sarah / Tight rope.

OCEAN COLOUR SCENE

STEVE CRADOCK – guitars, piano, vocals (ex-BOYS; late 80's mods) repl. WILKES

!Phffft not iss.

Sep 90. (7") *(FIT 001)* **SWAY. / TALK ON** -
(ext-12"+=/ext-cd-s+=) (FITX/FITCD 001) – One of these days.

Mar 91. (7") *(FIT 002)* **YESTERDAY TODAY. / ANOTHER GIRL'S NAME / FLY ME** 49
(12"+=/cd-s+=) *(FITX/FITCD 002)* – No one says.

Fontana not iss.

Feb 92. (7") *(OCSS 1)* **SWAY. / MY BROTHER SARAH** -
(12"+=/cd-s+=) *(OCS 112/CD1)* – Mona Lisa eyes / Bellechoux.

Apr 92. (7") *(OCSS 2)* **GIVING IT ALL AWAY. / THIRD SHADE OF GREEN** -
(12"+=/cd-s+=) *(OCS 212/CD2)* – Flowers / Don't play.

Apr 92. (cd/c/lp) *(<512269-2/-4/-1>)* **OCEAN COLOUR SCENE** Sep92
– Talk on / How about you / Giving it all away / Justine / Do yourself a favour / Third shade of green / Sway / Penny pinching rainy Heaven days / One of these days / Is she coming home / Blue deaf ocean / Reprise. *(re-iss. Sep96, hit UK 54)*

May 92. (7") *(OCSS 3)* **DO YOURSELF A FAVOUR. / THE SEVENTH FLOOR** -
(12"+=/cd-s+=) *(OCS 312/CD3)* – Patsy in green / Suspended motion.

M.C.A. M.C.A.

Feb 96. (7"/c-s) *(MCS/+C 40021)* **THE RIVERBOAT SONG. / SO SAD** 15 -
(cd-s+=) *(MCSTD 40021)* – Charlie Brown says.

Apr 96. (c-s) *(MCSTD 40036) <55217>* **YOU'VE GOT IT BAD / I WANNA STAY ALIVE WITH YOU** 7 Jul96
(cd-s+=) (MCSTD 40036) – Robin Hood / Huckleberry Grove.
(cd-s) (MCSXD 40036) – ('A'demo) / Here in my heart / Men of such opinion / Beautiful losers.

Apr 96. (cd/c/d-lp) *(<MCD/MCC/MCA 60008>)* **MOSELEY SHOALS** [2] [ ]
– The riverboat song / The day we caught the train / The circle / Lining your pockets / Fleeting mind / Forty past midnight / One for the road / It's my shadow / Policeman and pirates / Downstream / You've got it bad / Get away.

Jun 96. (c-s) *(MCSC 40046)* **THE DAY WE CAUGHT THE TRAIN / THE CLOCK STRUCK 15 HOURS AGO** [4] [-]
(cd-s+=) *(MCSTD 40046)* – I need a love song / Chicken bones and stones.
(cd-s) *(MCSXD 40046)* – ('A'acoustic) / Travellers tune / Justine.

Sep 96. (c-s) *(MCSC 40077)* **THE CIRCLE /** [6] [-]
(cd-s) *(MCSTD 40077)* –
(cd-s) *(MCSXD 40077)* –

Mar 97. (cd/c/d-lp) *(<MCD/MCC/MCA 60034>)* **B SIDES • SEASIDES & FREERIDES** (compilation) [4] [ ]
– Huckleberry grove / The day we caught the train (acoustic) / Mrs Jones / Top of the world / Here in my heart / I wanna stay alive with you / Robin Hood / Chelsea walk / Outside of a circle / The clock struck 15 hours ago / Alibis / Chicken bones and stones / Cool cool water / Charlie Brown says / Day tripper / Beautiful losers.

Jun 97. (7"/c-s) *(MCS/+C 40133)* **HUNDRED MILE HIGH CITY. /** [4] [-]
(cd-s+=) *(MCSTD 40133)* –

Aug 97. (7"/c-s) *(MCS/+C 40144)* *<Alex 6055>* **TRAVELLERS TUNE /** [5] [ ] Apr98
(cd-s) *(MCSTD 40144)* –

Sep 97. (cd/c/d-lp) *(<MCD/MCC/MCA 60048>)* **MARCHIN' ALREADY** [1] [ ]
– Hundred mile high city / Better day / Travellers tune / Big star / Debris road / Besides yourself / Get blown away / Tele he's not talking / Foxy's folk faced / All up / Spark and Cindy / Half a dream away / It's a beautiful thing. *(<also enhanced-cd; MCD 60053>)*

Nov 97. (7"/c-s) *(MCS/+C 40151)* **BETTER DAY. / THE BEST BET ON CHINASKI** [9] [-]
(cd-s+=) *(MCSTD 40151)* – On and on.

Feb 98. (7"/c-s) *(MCS/+C 40157)* **IT'S A BEAUTIFUL THING. / MARINERS WAY** [12] [ ]
(cd-s+=) *(MCSTD 40157)* – Going nowhere for a while / Expensive chair.
(above featured singer, P.P. ARNOLD)

Hazel O'CONNOR

Born: 16 May'55, Coventry, England. After initially working as a nude model, HAZEL travelled to Beirut where she became an exotic dancer, subsequently teaching English in Japan in the late 70's. In 1979, after a bit part in the movie, 'Girls Come First', she returned to London, performing local solo gigs and signing to 'Albion' records. After a few flop singles for the label, she landed the role of a futuristic punk rock star in the 1980 film, 'BREAKING GLASS'. The movie was a great success at the Cannes Film Festival, critics raving over O'CONNOR's acting and firebrand vocal style. The accompanying 'A&M' soundtrack hit the UK Top 5, spawning a number of hit single cuts, namely 'EIGHTH DAY' and 'WILL YOU?'. Still signed to 'Albion' as a solo artist, her late 1980 follow-up, 'SONS AND LOVERS', sold poorly and failed to consolidate her recent movie related inroads into the music business. Nevertheless, the blonde bombshell did manage one last Top 10 hit with 'D-DAYS', a track previewing the Top 40 album, 'COVER PLUS' (1981). Later releases such as 1984's dismal 'SMILE', failed to make the grade and O'CONNOR increasing concentrated on her acting career; her television work included plays, 'Girlfriends', 'Jangles' and 'Fighting Back'. • **Covered:** HANGING AROUND (Stranglers) / SUFFRAGETTE CITY (David Bowie) / BRING IT ON HOME TO ME (Sam Cooke) / DANNY BOY (trad) / WHITE ROOM (Cream) / etc. • **Trivia:** Her biography, appropriately titled 'Uncovered Plus' was published in 1982.

Album rating: BREAKING GLASS (*5) / SONS AND LOVERS (*4) / COVER PLUS (*4) / SMILE (*4)

HAZEL O'CONNOR – vocals, keyboards / with **BOB CARTER** – guitar, keyboards / **WESLEY McGOOGHAN** – saxophone / **RICK FORD** – bass / **ANDY DUNCAN** – drums

Albion / not iss.

Oct 79. (7") *(DEL 2)* **EE-I-ADIO. / TIME IS FREE** [ ] [-]

Apr 80. (lp; w-drawn) *(DAI 002)* **GLASS HOUSES** [-] [-]

A&M / A&M

Jun 80. (7") *(AMS 7530)* **WRITING ON THE WALL. / BIG BROTHER** [ ] [-]

Jul 80. (lp/c) *(AMLH/CAM 64820)* *<4820>* **BREAKING GLASS (Original Motion Picture Soundtrack)** [5] [ ]
– Writing on the wall / Monsters in disguise / Come into the air / Big brother / Who needs it / Will you / Eighth day / Top of the wheel / Calls the tune / Blackman / Give me an inch / If only. *(re-iss. Mar91 cd/c; CD/C MID 124)*

Aug 80. (7") *(AMS 7553)* **EIGHTH DAY. / MONSTERS IN DISGUISE** [5] [-]

Oct 80. (7") *(AMS 7569)* **GIVE ME AN INCH. / IF ONLY** [41] [ ]

Nov 80. (7") **WILL YOU? / BIG BROTHER** [-] [ ]

Jan 81. (7") **EIGHTH DAY. / BIG BROTHER** [-] [ ]
later singles from the soundtrack

May 81. (7") *(AMS 8131)* **WILL YOU?. / SONS AND LOVERS** [8] [-]

Jan 82. (7"m) *(AMS 8203)* **CALLS THE TUNE. / EIGHTH DAY / GIVE ME AN INCH** [60] [-]

— Her band **MEGAHYPE** included her brother **NEIL O' CONNOR** – guitar (ex-FLYS) + **WESLEY** plus **ANDY QUNTA** – keyboards / **ED CASE** – drums / **STEVE KINCH** – bass

— Meanwhile, she was still contracted to . . .

Albion / not iss.

Oct 80. (lp) *(LB 104)* **SONS AND LOVERS** [ ] [ ]
– D-days / Waiting / Who will care / Zoo / Gigolo / Do what you do / Glass houses / Sons and lovers / Ain't it funny / Time / Danny boy / Bye bye. *(re-iss. Nov87 on 'Link' lp/cd; ALLP4/ALCD9 00030)*

Nov 80. (7") *(ION 1006)* **TIME. / AIN'T IT FUNNY** [ ] [-]
(12"+=) *(12ION 1006)* – Suffragette city.

Mar 81. (7") *(ION 1009)* **D-DAYS. / TIME IS FREE** [10] [ ]
(12"+=/free c-s w-7"+=) *(12/C ION 1009)* – Zoo.

Jul 81. (7"/12") *(ION/12ION 1018)* **(COVER PLUS) WE'RE ALL GROWN UP. / WHITE ROOM** [41] [-]

Aug 81. (lp/c) *(ALB/CALB 108)* **COVER PLUS** [32] [ ]
– We're all grown up / Hanging around / Ee-i-adio / Not for you / Hold on / So you're born / Dawn chorus / Animal farm (we will be happy?) / Runaway / Do what you gotta do / Men of good fortune / That's life. *(re-iss. Nov87 on 'Link' lp/cd; ALLP4/ALCD9 00010) (re-iss. cd Sep95 on 'Music De-Luxe'; MSCD 23)*

Sep 81. (7"m) *(ION 1022)* **HANGING AROUND. / HOLD ON / NOT FOR YOU (German version)** [45] [ ]

Apr 82. (7") *(ION 1032)* **THAT'S LIFE. / WAITING** [ ] [-]

B.B.C. / not iss.

1982. (7") *(RESL 109)* **ENNAL'S POINT. / DAWN LIGHT** [ ] [-]

— she now used various session people

R.C.A. / R.C.A.

Jan 84. (7"/7"pic-d) *(RCA/ACAP 387)* **DON'T TOUCH ME. / BRING IT ON HOME TO ME** [ ] [ ]
(12"+=) *(RCAT 387)* – ('A'extended).

Jul 84. (7"/12") *(RCA/+T 422)* **JUST GOOD FRIENDS. / FIRE AWAY** [ ] [ ]

Sep 84. (lp/c) *(PL/PK 70268)* **SMILE** [ ] [ ]
– Just good friends / Don't touch me / I'm sorry / Cuts too deep / Tell me a story / The man I love / I don't know / Bring it home to me / Mystified / Spancill hill.

Sep 84. (7") *(RCA 442)* **CUTS TOO DEEP. / I'M SORRY** [ ] [-]
(12"+=) *(RCAT 422)* – Fire away.

Greenpeace / not iss.

Jun 85. (7"/12"; HAZEL O'CONNOR & CHRIS THOMPSON) *(FND 1/12)* **PUSH AND SHOVE. / SAVE** [ ] [-]

Red Bus / not iss.

Mar 86. (7") *(RBUS 2209)* **TODAY COULD BE SO GOOD. / WE TRIED** [ ] [-]

B.B.C. / not iss.

Jul 86. (7"/12"; HAZEL O'CONNOR with the ARTS FREEDOM SINGERS) *(RESL/12RESL 182)* **FIGHTING BACK. / REACH** [ ] [-]

First Night / not iss.

Oct 87. (7"; HAZEL O'CONNOR with DAVID EASTER) *(SCORE 13)* **AND I DREAM. / WAKE ME OH WAKE ME** [ ] [-]

— she retired from music scene continuing with acting career, this was mainly in a leading role for TV play, 'Girlfriends' (she had earlier featured in other TV plays, 'Jangles' & 'Fighting Back').

- compilations, etc. -

Sep 85. (7") *Old Gold; (OG 9544)* **WILL YOU? / EIGHTH DAY** [ ] [-]
(re-iss. Jun88; same)

Apr 88. (cd-ep) *A&M; (AMCD 902)* **COMPACT HITS** [ ] [-]
– Eighth day / Calls the tune / Give me an inch / Will you?

Feb 94. (cd) *Line; (ALCD 901291)* **SEE THE WRITING ON THE WALL** [ ] [-]

Jul 94. (cd/c) *Success;* **GREATEST HITS** [ ] [-]

Feb 97. (cd) *Start; (SRH 804)* **LIVE IN BERLIN (live)** [ ] [-]

Gene OCTOBER (see under ⇒ CHELSEA)

OEDIPUSSY (see under ⇒ PERFECT DISASTER)

OFFSPRING

Formed: Orange County, California, USA . . . 1984 out of MANIC SUBSIDAL and CLOWNS OF DEATH, by main songwriter DEXTER HOLLAND and GREG KRIESEL. With the addition of JAMES LILJA and KEVIN 'NOODLES' WASSERMAN they adopted THE OFFSPRING moniker, releasing a debut 45, 'I'LL BE WAITING' on the self-financed 'Black' label. With RON WELTY subsequently replacing LILJA, the band began working on demo material, eventually going into the studio with Thom Wilson. The results eventually surfaced in the form of the eponymous 'OFFSPRING' (1989), issued on the 'Nitro' label. An ambitious and experimental fusion of exotic hardcore, its schizoid ramblings not endearing the band to many outside the scene. The next few years were tough for the band as they struggled to find a steady record deal, even tougher for NOODLES who was stabbed at a benefit concert. They eventually found a sympathetic ear in the form of BRAD GUREWITZ (ex-BAD RELIGION) and his burgeoning 'Epitaph' operation, releasing a much improved follow-up album, 'IGNITION' in 1992. However, it wasn't until 1994 and their follow-up, 'SMASH', that OFFSPRING pogo'd into the US charts. Hard on the heels of GREEN DAY's phenomenal worldwide success, the 4-piece found a very successful niche in the larger than life, lads-together ska-core punk rock complete with dayglo choruses and brutally addictive hooklines. The album went on to sell over a million copies in the States and finally gained deserved recognition in Britain, especially after the 'SELF ESTEEM' track became a Top 40 smash early '95! Over the course of the ensuing two years, OFFSPRING almost became part of 'Columbia's roster, although in the end a follow-up, 'INXAY ON THE HOMBRE' appeared on 'Epitaph' in 1997. Building on the winning formula of its predecessor, the album scored another transatlantic Top 20. The dreadlocked DEXTER subsequently teamed up with JELLO BIAFRA (ex-DEAD KENNEDYS) to play some charity gigs under the banner of F.S.U. in aid of the homeless, human rights, etc. • **Covers:** HEY JOE (hit; Jimi Hendrix) / SMASH IT UP (Damned) / KILLBOY POWERHEAD (Didjits).

Album rating: THE OFFSPRING (*4) / IGNITION (*6) / SMASH (*7) / IXNAY ON THE HOMBRE (*6)

DEXTER HOLLAND (b. BRYAN HOLLAND, 1966) – vocals, guitar / **NOODLES** (b. KEVIN WASSERMAN, 4 Feb'63, L.A.) – guitar / **GREG KRIESEL** (b.20 Jan'65, Glendale, Calif.) – bass / **JAMES LILJA** – drums

not iss. / Black

1986. (7") **I'LL BE WAITING. /** [-] [ ]

— **RON WELTY** (b. 1 Feb'71) – drums (ex-FQX) repl. LILJA

not iss. — Nitro

1989. (lp) *<86460-1>* **THE OFFSPRING** [–] [ ]
– Jennifer lost the war / Elders / Out on patrol / Crossroads / Demons / Beheaded / Tehran / A thousand days / Black ball / I'll be waiting / Kill the president. *(UK-iss.Nov95 on 'Epitaph' cd/c; E 86460-2/-4)*

not iss. — Plastic Head

1991. (7") *<NEM 38>* **BAGHDAD. /** [–] [ ]

Epitaph — Epitaph

Oct 92. (cd/c/lp) *<(E 86424-2/-4/-1)>* **IGNITION** [ ] [ ]
– Session / We are one / Kick him when he's down / Take it like a man / Get it right / Dirty magic / Hypodermic / Burn it up / No hero / L.A.P.D. / Nothing from something / Forever and a day.

Sep 94. (cd/c/lp) *<(E 86432-2/-4/-1)>* **SMASH** [21] [4] Apr94
– Time to relax / Nitro (youth energy) / Bad habit / Gotta get away / Genocide / Something to believe in / Come out and play / Self esteem / It'll be a long time / Killboy powerhead / What happened to you / So alone / Not the one / Smash.

Sep 94. (12"/cd-s) *(EPUK/+CD 001)* **COME OUT AND PLAY. / SESSION / ('A'acoustic)** [ ] [–]

Oct 94. (7") *<IGN 3H)> <65572>* **COME OUT AND PLAY. / COME OUT AND PLAY** [ ] [ ]
(above on 'Ignition'/<'Phantom'> (below ltd. on 'Flying')

Dec 94. (10"ep) *(GOD 008)* **COME OUT AND PLAY EP** [ ] [–]

Feb 95. (c-s/12"/cd-s) *(MC/12/CD HOLE 001)* **SELF ESTEEM. / JENNIFER LOST THE WAR / BURN IT UP** [37] [–]

Aug 95. (7"/c-s/cd-s) *(WOOS 2/+CS/CDS)* **GOTTA GET AWAY. / SMASH** [43] [–]
(above single on 'Out Of Step' UK)

— In the Spring of '96, they were fighting Epitaph and boss BRETT GUREWITZ for the right to sign with another label 'Columbia' in the US-only.

Jan 97. (7"m/cd-s) *(6495-7/-2)* **ALL I WANT. / WAY DOWN THE LINE** [31] [–]
(cd-s+=) *(6491-2)* – Smash it up.

Feb 97. (cd/lp) *(6487-2/-1)* *<67810>* **IXNAY ON THE HOMBRE** [17] [9]

Apr 97. (7"/cd-s) *(6504-7/-2)* **GONE AWAY. / D.U.I.** [42] [–]
(cd-s+=) *(6498-2)* – Cool to hate / Hey Joe.

Columbia — Columbia

Nov 98. (cd/c) *(491656-2/-4)* *<69661>* **AMERICANA** [75] [6]
– Welcome / Have you ever / Staring at the sun / Pretty fly (for a white guy) / Kids aren't alright / Feelings / She's got issues / Walla walla / End of the line / No brakes / Why don't you get a job / Americana / Pay the man.

Nov 98. (cd-s) *<41579>* **PRETTY FLY (FOR A WHITE GUY)** [–] [59]

OI POLLOI

Formed: Edinburgh, Scotland . . . early 80's by DEEK ALLAN and Co. Although their moniker might have suggested an association with the "oi" movement, this band had more in common with the likes of CRASS and CONFLICT. After building up a loyal fanbase in the capital, these politically correct anarcho-punks finally made it onto vinyl in early '86, sharing the 'UNLIMITED GENOCIDE' lp with AOA. In fact, OI POLLOI also shared their following two sets, 'MAD AS FUCK (DON'T YOU THINK?)' and 'SKINS 'N' PUNKS II', with TOXIC EPHEX and BETRAYED respectively. Lending their weight to the anti-censorship movement, OI POLLOI contributed one track, 'NO FILTHY NUCLEAR POWER', to the JELLO (BIAFRA) AID compilation album, 'Censorship Sucks', the proceeds from which went towards the cost of the DEAD KENNEDYS frontman's impending court case (cover art by the illustrious Harry Horse!). In 1987, moving in an increasingly punk-metal hybrid direction, the band delivered their first exclusive set, 'UNITE AND WIN', a subsequent two year hiatus broken with the impassioned protest of 'IN DEFENCE OF OUR EARTH' (1990). Having earlier signed to 'Words Of Warning' (home of fellow anti-Nazis, BLAGGERS ITA), they went on to issue a compilation, 'OUTRAGED BY THE ATOMIC MENACE' (1991) and the following year's 'OMNICIDE' EP. Despite being largely ignored by the indie press, OI POLLOI battled on with the self-explanatory 'TOTAL ANARCHOI' (1992), although little was heard of them until 1997's 'FIGHT BACK'.

Album rating: UNLIMITED GENOCIDE (*4) / MAD AS FUCK (DON'T YOU THINK?) (*4) / SKINS' N' PUNKS II (*4) / UNITE AND WIN (*5) / IN DEFENCE OF OUR EARTH (*5) / OUTRAGE BY ATOMIC MENACE compilation (*5) / TOTAL ANARCHOI (*5) / FIGHT BACK (*5)

DEEK ALLAN – vocals / (+)

Children Of The Revolution — not iss.

Jan 86. (lp; shared with AOA) *(GURT 12)* **UNLIMITED GENOCIDE** [ ] [–]

Endangered Musik — not iss.

May 86. (7") *(EDR 5)* **RESIST THE ATOMIC MENACE. /** [ ] [–]

Words Of Warning — not iss.

Aug 86. (7"ep; Various Artists) *(WOW 1)* **YOU ARE NOT ALONE EP** [ ] [–]

Green Vomit — not iss.

Oct 86. (lp; shared with TOXIC EPHEX) *(PUKE 15)* **MAD AS FUCK (DON'T YOU THINK?)** [ ] [–]

Oi! — not iss.

Jan 87. (lp; shared with BETRAYED) *(OIR 008)* **SKINS 'N' PUNKS II** [ ] [–]

Oct 87. (lp) *(OIR 011)* **UNITE AND WIN** [ ] [–]

Words Of Warning — not iss.

Jul 90. (lp) *(WOWLP 10)* **IN DEFENCE OF OUR EARTH** [ ] [–]

Jan 91. (lp) *(WOWLP 13)* **OUTRAGED BY THE ATOMIC MENACE** (compilation) [ ] [–]

Jan 92. (7"ep) *(WOW 17)* **OMNICIDE EP** [ ] [–]

Released Emotions — not iss.

Apr 92. (cd) *(REM 017)* **TOTAL ANARCHOI (live)** [ ] [–]
(re-iss. Nov97 on 'Step 1' cd/lp; STEP CD/LP 073)

— disbanded during the early 90's, although they re-formed later

Campary — not iss.

Mar 97. (lp) *(CAMPARY 024)* **FIGHT BACK** [ ] [–]

OINGO BOINGO

Formed: Los Angeles, California, USA . . . 1979 out of performance art/comedy collective, the MYSTIC KNIGHTS OF OINGO BOINGO, by frontman/songwriter, DANNY ELFMAN, who completed the line-up with STEVE BARTEK, KERRY HATCH and drummer DAVID EAGLE (a brass section of LEON SCHNEIDERMAN, SAM PHIPPS and DALE TURNER augmented the New Wave synth sound). Possibly America's answer to XTC, OINGO BOINGO mined a similar vein of surreal humour/downright quirkiness as Ohio-based spiritual cousins, DEVO, on their eponymous debut EP in 1980. After signing to 'A&M' and acquiring the services of fresh drummer, JOHNNY 'VATOS' HERNANDEZ, the increasingly electro-pop styled combo found some degree of success with their first full-set, 'ONLY A LAD' (1981). Subsequent albums, 'NOTHING TO FEAR' (1982) and the ROBERT MARGOULEFF (formerly of late 60's electronic experimentalists, TONTO'S EXPANDING HEADBAND)-produced 'GOOD FOR YOUR SOUL' (1983), also made appearances in the US Top 200, although ELFMAN and his spaced-out crew (HATCH having made way for JOHN AVILA) only really cracked the charts with the 1985 title track to teen movie, 'WEIRD SCIENCE'. By this point, the band had signed a long term deal with 'M.C.A.', going on to further left-field pop successes throughout the mid to late 80's. ELFMAN, however, was to garner greater acclaim for his TV/film soundtrack work, writing scores for such Hollywood blockbusters as 'Beetlejuice', 'Batman' and 'Dick Tracy'. More importantly, ELFMAN was the man behind the backing music for ~'The Simpsons', all this activity putting BOINGO (as his outfit were now called) on ice until 1994 when they returned with a Top 75 eponymous album on 'Giant'.

Album rating: ONLY A LAD (*4) / NOTHING TO FEAR (*4) / GOOD FOR YOUR SOUL (*5) / DEAD MAN'S PARTY (*6) / BOI-NGO (*4) / BOINGO ALIVE: CELEBRATION OF A DECADE 1979-1988 (*4) / DARK AT THE END OF THE TUNNEL (*4) / SKELETONS IN THE CLOSET: THE BEST OF OINGO BOINGO compilation (*5) / BOINGO (*3) / FAREWELL: LIVE . . . (*4) / Danny Elfman: also released solo material mainly soundtracks except '84's 'SO-LO'.

DANNY ELFMAN – vocals / **STEVE BARTEK** – lead guitar / **KERRY HATCH** – bass / **RICHARD GIBBS** – keyboards / **DAVID EAGLE** – drums / **LEON SCHNEIDERMAN** – saxophone / **SAM PHIPPS** – saxophone / **DALE TURNER** – trumpet

I.R.S. — I.R.S.

Aug 80. (10"ep) *<SP 70400>* **OINGO BOINGO EP** [–] [ ]
– Only a lad / Violent love / Ain't this the life / I'm so bad.

Jun 81. (7") *(PFP 1002)* **ONLY A LAD. / AIN'T THIS THE LIFE** [ ] [ ]

— **JOHNNY 'VATOS' HERNANDEZ** – drums; repl. EAGLE

A&M — A&M

Aug 81. (lp) *(AMLH 64863)* *<4863>* **ONLY A LAD** [ ] [ ]
– Little girls / Perfect system / On the outside / Capitalism / You really got me / Only a lad / What you see / Controller / Imposter / Nasty habits.

Aug 82. (7") *(AMS 8244)* **PRIVATE LIFE. / WILD SEX** [ ] [ ]

Sep 82. (lp) *(AMLH 64903)* *<4930>* **NOTHING TO FEAR** [ ] [ ] Aug82
– Nothing to fear / Grey matter / Reptiles and Samurai / Insects / Whole day of / Islands / Running on a treadmill / Private life / Wild sex / Why'd we come.

Sep 83. (lp) *(AMLH 64959)* *<4959>* **GOOD FOR YOUR SOUL** [ ] [ ]
– Who do you want to be / Little guns / Nothing bad ever happens / Fill the void / Good for your soul / Cry of the Vatos / No spill blood / Wake up (it's 1984) / Pictures of you / Dead or alive / Sweat.

— **JOHN AVILA** – bass; repl. HATCH

M.C.A. — M.C.A.

Aug 85. (7") *<52633>* **WEIRD SCIENCE. / (other track by Ira & The Geeks)** [–] [45]
(above songs from the film of the same name)

Nov 85. (lp/c/cd) *<(MCA/+C/D 5665)>* **DEAD MAN'S PARTY** [ ] [98]
– Just another day / Dead man's party / Heard somebody cry / No one loves forever / Stay / Fool's paradise / Help me / Same man as I was before / Weird science.

Jan 86. (7") *<52726>* **JUST ANOTHER DAY. / DEAD MAN'S PARTY** [–] [85]

— **MIKE BACICH** – keyboards; repl. R.GIBBS

Mar 87. (lp/c/cd) *<(MCA/+C/D 5811)>* **BOI-NGO** [ ] [77]
– Home again / Where do all my friends go / Elevator man / New generation / We close our eyes / Not my slave / My life / Outrageous / Pain.

Oct 88. (d lp/d-cd) *<MCA/+D 8030>* **BOINGO ALIVE – CELEBRATION OF A DECADE 1979-1988 (live July '88)** [–] [90]
– Dead man's party / Dead or alive / No spill blood / Stay / Cinderella undercover / Home again / Help me / Just another day / Only makes me laugh / My life / Nothing to fear (but fear itself) / Not my slave / We close our eyes / Elevator man / Return of the dead man / Winning side / Wild sex (in the working class) / Grey matter / Private life / Gratitude / No one lives for ever / Mama / Capitalism / Who do you want to be / Sweat / Violent love / On the outside / Only a lad / Goodbye-goodbye / Country sweat / Return of the dead man 2.

— **CARL GRAVES** – keyboards, vocals; repl. BACICH

Mar 90. (cd/c/lp) *<MCA 6363>* **DARK AT THE END OF THE TUNNEL** [ ] [72]
– When the lights go out / Skin / Out of control / Glory be / Long breakdown / Flesh 'n' blood / Run away (the escape song) / Dream somehow / Is this / Try to believe. *(cd+=/c+=)* – Right to know.

— around this time ELFMAN concentrated writing scores for movies, namely 'Beetlejuice', 'Batman', 'Dick Tracy' and of course 'The Simpsons' TV series

Giant Giant

Oct 94. (cd/c; as BOINGO) *(74321 18971-2/-4)* <24555> **BOINGO** [ ] [71] May94
– Insanity / Hey! / Mary / Can't see (useless) / Pedestrian wolves / Lost like this / Spider / War again / I am the walrus / Tender lumplings / Change / Helpless.

not iss. A&M

Apr 96. (d-cd/d-lp) *<540504>* **FAREWELL – LIVE FROM THE UNIVERSAL AMPHITHEATRE, HALLOWEEN 1995 (live)** [-] [ ]
– Insanity / Little girls / Cinderella undercover / Controller / Burn me up / Insects / No one lives forever / Hey! / Reptiles and Samurai / Water / I am the walrus / Piggies / We close our eyes / Mary / Can't see (useless) / Helpless / I'm so bad / Change / Stay / Who do you want to be / On the outside / Wild sex (in the working class) / Dead man's party / Nasty habits / Clowns of death / Ain't this the life / A whole day off / Grey matter / No spill blood / Only a lad.

– compilations, etc. –

Feb 89. (lp,cd) *A&M; <5217>* **SKELETONS IN THE CLOSET: THE BEST OF OINGO BOINGO** [ ] [-]

Will OLDHAM (see under ⇒ PALACE BROTHERS)

O-LEVEL (see under ⇒ BALL, Ed)

OLIVIA TREMOR CONTROL

Formed: Athens, Georgia, USA . . . 1992 out of CRANBERRY LIFE CYCLE and SYNTHETIC FLYING MACHINE by WILLIAM CULLEN HART and BILL DOSS. A true lo-fi enigma, OTC emerged from the 'Elephant 6' musical collective, a kind of Wild Bunch for the US underground which also boasted NEUTRAL MILK HOTEL and APPLES (IN STEREO). OTC mainmen/singer-songwriters, HART and DOSS began playing together at school, developing their musical partnership at university. Together with childood friend, JEFF MANGUM, the pair formed CRANBERRY LIFE CYCLE after relocating to Athens, Georgia. Following the subsequent replacement of MANGUM with JOHN FERNANDES, the band changed name to SYNTHETIC FLYING MACHINE before finally adopting the OTC moniker just prior to the addition of PETE ERCHICK and ERIC HARRIS. Initiating their own 'Drug Racer' label, the band made their debut in 1995 with the 'CALIFORNIA DEMISE' EP. A concept affair influenced by 60's psychedelia, the record was the first part in an ongoing saga conceived by DOSS and HART as a pseudo film script. Follow-up EP, 'GIANT DAY' served as a link into the weird and wonderful complexities of OLIVIA TREMOR CONTROL's debut double set, 'DUSK AT CUBIST CASTLE' (1997). Released on 'Flydaddy' and previewed by two singles, 'OPERA HOUSE' and 'JUMPING FENCES', the record found DOSS and HART employing classic psychedelic techniques and fusing everything from space-rock to BYRDS-ian pop with cutting edge lo-fi noise. While many critics noted the influence of late 60's BEATLES and guiding spirit of BRIAN WILSON, a more contemporary comparison might've been SEAN O'HAGAN and his HIGH LLAMAS (had they grown up listening to PAVEMEMT!)

Album rating: DUSK AT CUBIST CASTLE (*7) / EXPLANATION VOL.2 (*5) / OLIVIA TREMOR CONTROL VS BLACK SWAN NETWORK (*6)

WILLIAM CULLEN HART – vocals, multi / **BILL DOSS** – vocals, multi / + others unknown

not iss. Drug Racer

1995. (7"ep) *<DR 1>* **CALIFORNIA DEMISE EP** [-] [ ]
1996. (7"ep) *<DR 2>* **THE GIANT DAY EP** [-] [ ]
(UK-iss.Jun97; same as US)

Blue Rose Flydaddy

Oct 96. (7") *(BRRC 1011-7)* **OPERA HOUSE. / BLACK SWAN RADAR** [ ] [ ]
(cd-s+=) *(BRRC 1011-2A)* –
(cd-s+=) *(BRRC 1011-2B)* –
May 97. (12"/cd-s) *(BRRC 1015-6/-3)* **JUMPING FENCES. /** [ ] [ ]
Jun 97. (d-cd/d-lp) *(BRRC 1008-2/-1)* *<FLY 17>* **DUSK AT CUBIST CASTLE** [ ] [ ] Aug96
– Opera house / Frosted ambassador / Jumping fences / Define a transparent dream / No growing (exegesis) / Holiday surprise / Courtyard / Memories of Jacqueline 1906 / Tropical bells / Can you come down with us? / Marking time / Tracks 12-21: Green typewriters / Spring succeeds / Theme for a very delicious grand piano / I can smell the leaves / Dusk at Cubist castle / Gravity car / N.Y.C.-25. *(d-cd+=)* – EXPLANATION II

Flydaddy Flydaddy

Nov 97. (cd) *<(FLY 017X)>* **EXPLANATION II (INSTRUMENTAL THEMES AND SEQUENCES)** [ ] [ ]
Jun 98. (m-cd; by OLIVIA TREMOR CONTROL VS BLACK SWAN NETWORK) *<FLY 030)>* **COLLABORATION (A.K.A. THE TOUR EP)** [ ] [ ]

OMD (see under ⇒ ORCHESTRAL MANOEUVRES IN THE DARK)

OMEGA TRIBE

Formed: North London, England . . . 1982 by ex-FATAL MICROBES guitarist, PETE FENDER, who had previously issued a solo EP, 'FOUR FORMULAS', for 'Xntrix'. Alongside him were a young team of oi/punks, namely HUGH, RADLY and PETER (aka PETEROLEUM YORKIE) and this line-up toured supporting The NIGHTINGALES and TOXIC SHOCK. The 'TRIBE debuted a year later on the 'Crass' label with the EP, 'ANGRY SONGS', following it up with a mini-set, 'NO LOVE LOST' (1983). YORKIE was subsequently replaced by SUNNY and saxophonist, JANE, although only a solitary single and a cassette were forthcoming before they became extinct.

Album rating: NO LOVE LOST mini (*3)

HUGH TWITM'N – vocals, guitar / **PETE LOUDM'N** (b. PETE FENDER) – guitar, vocals (ex-FATAL MICROBES) / **RADLY HARDM'N** (b. DARYL) – bass, vocals / **PETEROLEUM YORKIE BIGM'N** – drums, vocals

Crass not iss.

May 83. (7"ep) *(221984-10)* **ANGRY SONGS** [ ] [-]

Corpus Christi not iss.

Dec 83. (m-lp) *(ITS 5)* **NO LOVE LOST** [ ] [-]
– Duty calls / Profit / Aftermath / Freedom, peace and unity / What the hell / Mother of cultivation / My tears / Nature wonder / Pictures / Man made / My tears – reprise (no more wars).

—— **SUNNY** – drums; repl. YORKIE / added **JANE** – sax, flute

Sep 84. (7"/12") *(ITS/+T 12)* **IT'S A HARD LIFE. / YOUNG JOHN** [ ] [-]

96 Tapes not iss.

Mar 85. (c) *(96-11)* **LIVE AT THE CLARENDON** [ ] [-]

—— disbanded in 1985

101'ERS

Formed: Brixton, London, England . . . summer '74 by JOE STRUMMER, CLIVE TIMPERLEY, DAN KELLEHER and RICHARD DUDANSKI, their first gig being on the 7th of September, 1974, at the local Telegraph venue. However, eighteen months later the quartet had broken-up, only a posthumous issue – in June '76 – of their modern R&B gem, 'KEYS TO YOUR HEART', hitting the small record shops. All four group members went on to greater things, frontman, STRUMMER, becoming a punk icon when he joined The CLASH (KELLEHER subsequently formed MARTIAN SCHOOLGIRLS, while TIMPERLEY joined The PASSIONS and DUDANSKI initially played with PUBLIC IMAGE LTD and The RAINCOATS).

Album rating: ELGIN AVENUE BREAKDOWN posthumous (*4)

JOE STRUMMER (b. JOHN MELLOR, 21 Aug'52, Ankara, Turkey) – vocals, guitar / **CLIVE TIMPERLEY** – guitar, vocals (ex-DERELICTS) / **DAN KELLEHER** – bass, vocals / **RICHARD DUDANSKI** – drums

Chiswick not iss.

Jun 76. (7") *(NS 3)* **KEYS TO YOUR HEART. / 5 STAR ROCK'N'ROLL PETROL** [ ] [-]

—— had already split (see biog for details).

– postumous collections, etc. –

Feb 81. (7") *Chiswick; (NS 63)* **SWEET REVENGE. / RABIES (FROM THE DOGS OF LOVE)** [ ] [-]
Sep 81. (lp) *Andalucia; (AND 101)* **ELGIN AVENUE BREAKDOWN** [ ] [-]
(live recordings & rare items)

ONLY ONES

Formed: South London, England . . . 1976 by singer/guitarist PETER PERRETT out of the recently defunct ENGLAND'S GLORY (which also comprised HARRY KAKOULLI – bass and JON NEWEY – drums). They were initially managed by HARRY's sister, ZENA, who also provided some backing vocals alongside fourth member, MICHAEL KEMP – keyboards. When HARRY quit to join SQUEEZE in 1974, PERRETT found seasoned musicians, JOHN PERRY, MIKE KELLIE and ALAN MAIR, subsequently adopting The ONLY ONES tag. Their vinyl debut, 'LOVERS OF TODAY', was released in Summer '77 on Zena & Peter's own 'Vengeance' label, selling sufficiently to attract the attentions of major label, 'C.B.S.'. April '78 saw the release of their exhilarating 'ANOTHER GIRL, ANOTHER PLANET', a legendary track that remains to this day in the "One That Got Away" bracket. An eponymous debut album followed a few months later, its low-rent, faded glamour tales of life's seedier side drawled out by the charismatic PERRETT against an authentic but professional new wave backdrop. The record's humble Top 60 position was a poor reflection of its quality bearing in mind the number of two-bit amateurs clogging up the charts at the time. With bountiful critical acclaim on their side, The ONLY ONES ploughed on, releasing a second instalment of PERRETT's doomed romanticism in 1979's 'EVEN SERPENTS SHINE'. Another impressive self-produced effort, the album's success was hindered by the snowballing tensions, both internally within the group itself and with their record company. Perhaps as a result, a third set, 'BABY'S GOT A GUN' (1980) sounded flaccid and tired in comparison, although it did provide PERRETT and Co. with a belated Top 40 placing. Sales weren't sufficient to please CBS, however, and, minus a deal, the group called it a day. While PERRY formed DECLINE AND FALL, PERRETT faded into drug-fuzzed obscurity, only re-emerging more than a decade later as PETER PERRETT IN THE ONE. An album, 'WOKE UP STICKY' (1996), appeared on 'Demon' in summer '96 to encouraging reviews, although whether he can last the course this time around remains to be seen. • **Songwriters:** PERRETT compositions except; FOOLS (Johnny Duncan) / MY WAY OF GIVING (Small Faces) / SILENT NIGHT (trad.carol) / I'M NOT LIKE EVERYBODY ELSE (Kinks). • **Trivia:** PERRETT is known to have made recordings with SQUEEZE man, GLENN TILBROOK, in the mid-70's.

Album rating: THE ONLY ONES (*8) / THE IMMORTAL STORY compilation (*8)

PETER PERRETT – vocals, guitar (ex-ENGLAND'S GLORY) / **JOHN PERRY** – lead guitar, keyboards (ex-RATBITES FROM HELL) / **MIKE KELLIE** (b.24 Mar'47, Birmingham, England) – drums (ex-SPOOKY TOOTH, ex-FRAMPTON'S CAMEL) / **ALAN MAIR** – bass (ex-BEATSTALKERS)

Vengeance not iss.

Jun 77. (7",12") *(VEN 001)* **LOVERS OF TODAY. / PETER AND THE PETS** [ ] [-]

C.B.S. Epic

Apr 78. (7") *(S-CBS 6228)* **ANOTHER GIRL, ANOTHER PLANET. / SPECIAL VIEW** [ ] [ ]

May 78. (lp/c) *(CBS/40 82830)* **THE ONLY ONES** [56] [-]
– The whole of the law / Another girl, another planet / Breaking down / City of fun / The beast / Creature of doom / It's the truth / Language problem / No peace for the wicked / Immortal story. *(re-iss. 1984; CBS 32077) (re-iss. cd Sep94 on 'Columbia'; 477379-2)*

Aug 78. (12") *(S-CBS12 6576)* **ANOTHER GIRL, ANOTHER PLANET. / AS MY WIFE SAYS** [ ] [-]

Feb 79. (7") *(S-CBS 7086)* **YOU'VE GOT TO PAY. / THIS AIN'T ALL (IT'S MADE OUT TO BE)** [ ] [ ]

Mar 79. (lp/c) *(CBS/40 83451)* **EVEN SERPENTS SHINE** [42] [-]
– From here to eternity / Flaming touch / You've got to pay / No solution / In betweens / Out there in the night / Curtains for you / Programme / Someone who cares / Miles from nowhere / Instrumental. *(re-iss. 1985; same) (cd-iss. Feb95 on 'Columbia'; 478503-2)*

Apr 79. (7") *(S-CBS 7285)* **OUT THERE IN THE NIGHT. / LOVERS OF TODAY** [ ] [-]
(12"blue+=) *(SCBS12-7285)* – Peter and the pets.

Jun 79. (lp) *<36199>* **SPECIAL VIEW** (compilation 77-79) [-] [ ]
– Another girl, another planet / Lovers of today / Peter and the pets / The beast / City of fun / The whole of the law / Out there in the night / Someome who cares / You've got to pay / Flaming torch / Curtains for you / From here to eternity.

Nov 79. (7") *(S-CBS 7963)* **TROUBLE IN THE WORLD. / YOUR CHOSEN LIFE** [ ] [-]

Apr 80. (lp/c) *(CBS/40 84089) <36584>* **BABY'S GOT A GUN** [37] [ ]
– The happy pilgrim / Why don't you kill yourself / Me and my shadow / Deadly nightshade / Strange mouth / The big sleep / Oh Lucinda (love becomes a habit) / Reunion / Trouble in the world / Castle built on sand / Fools / My way out of here. *(re-iss. 1985; same) (cd-iss. Mar96 on 'Columbia'; 483662-2)*

May 80. (7"; ONLY ONES with PAULINE MURRAY) *(S-CBS 8535)* **FOOLS. / CASTLE BUILT ON SAND** [ ] [-]

— Disbanded March '81, PERRY formed DECLINE AND FALL but soon disappeared. In Autumn 91, PERRETT augmented the HEARTTHROBS live in Canada.

– compilations, others, etc. –

Jan 83. (7") *Vengeance; (VEN 002)* **BABY'S GOT A GUN. / Peter Perrett: SILENT NIGHT** [ ] [-]
(re-press.Aug85; same)

— (next lp featured on session **GLENN TILBROOK + GORDON EDWARDS** to repl. KELLIE + MAIR.

Jun 84. (m-lp) *Closer; (CL 012)* **REMAINS** (out-takes from last album) [-] [-] France
(cd-iss. Dec88; CLCD 012) (UK-iss.Sep93 on 'Anagram'; CDMGRAM 67)

Oct 86. (lp) *Dojo; (DOJOLP 43)* **ALONE IN THE NIGHT** [ ] [-]
(cd-iss. Oct91; DOJOCD 43)

May 87. (lp; by ENGLAND'S GLORY) *5 Hours Back; (TOCK 004)* **ENGLAND'S GLORY – THE LEGENDARY LOST RECORDINGS** [ ] [-]
– Devotion / The wide waterway / City of fun / First time I saw you / Broken arrows / Bright lights / It's been a long time / The guest / Peter and the pets / Showdown / Predictably blonde / Weekend / Trouble in the world. *(this was originally privately released in 1973 for 'Vengeance'; VEN 105) (cd-iss. Apr94 on 'Anagram'; CDMGRAM 73)*

Aug 89. (lp/cd) *Mau Mau; (MAU/+CD 603)* **THE ONLY ONES LIVE (live)** [ ] [-]
(cd has extra tracks)

Dec 89. (lp/c/cd) *Strange Fruit; (SFR/+MC/CD 102) / Dutch East India; <8109>* **DOUBLE PEEL SESSIONS** [ ] [ ]
(re-iss. Jul94; same)

Jan 92. (7") *Columbia; (657750-7)* **ANOTHER GIRL, ANOTHER PLANET. / ('B' by 'Psychedelic Furs')** [57] [-]
(12"+=/12"red+=/cd-s+=) *(657750-6/-2)* – Lovers of today.

May 92. (cd/c/d-lp) *Columbia; (471267-2/-4/-1)* **THE IMMORTAL STORY** [ ] [-]
– Lovers of today / Peter and the pets / The whole of the law / Another girl, another planet / Special view (aka Telescopic love) / The beast / It's the truth / No peace for the wicked / The immortal story / From here to eternity / In betweens / No solution / Curtains for you / Someone who cares / Miles from nowhere / Instrumental / Your chosen life / Baby's got a gun / Why don't you kill yourself / Oh Lucinda (love becomes a habit) / Big sleep.

Nov 93. (lp/cd) *Jungle; (FREUD/+CD 045)* **THE BIG SLEEP** [ ] [-]

Dec 95. (cd) *Windsong; (WINCD 080)* **IN CONCERT** [ ] [-]

PETER PERRETT

Dwarf not iss.

Nov 94. (12"ep/cd-ep; as PETER PERRETT IN THE ONE) **CULTURED PALATE** [ ] [-]
– Baby don't talk / etc.

Demon Demon

Apr 96. (7"one-sided) *(VEX 14)* **WOKE UP STICKY** [ ] [-]
(cd-s+=) *(VEXCD 14)* – Transfixed / Wildlife / Dead love syndrome.

Jun 96. (lp/c/cd) *(<FIEND/+CASS/CD 773>)* **WOKE UP STICKY** [ ] [ ]
– Deep freeze / Woke up sticky / Nothing worth doing / Falling / The shame of being you / I'm not like everybody else / Sirens / Law of the jungle / Land of the free / Shivers / My sweet angel.

OPAL (see under ⇒ MAZZY STAR)

OPERATION IVY (see under ⇒ RANCID)

'O'RANG (see under ⇒ TALK TALK)

ORANGE JUICE (see under ⇒ COLLINS, Edwyn)

ORB

Formed: South London, England ... 1989 by remix supremo and ex-KILLING JOKE roadie Dr. ALEX PATERSON. Working as an A&R bod for ambient label EG (home to he likes of BRIAN ENO), PATTERSON began recording similar ambient sounds in his spare time. He hooked up with the KLF's JIMMY CAUTY in 1988 and recorded an EP, 'KISS', using samples from NEW YORK's Kiss FM. The duo traded under the ORB moniker (which PATTERSON had taken from the WOODY ALLEN sci-fi film 'Sleepers') and released the record the following year on the 'WAU!Mr Modo' label, a joint venture between PATTERSON and ex-KILLING JOKE bassist YOUTH. Around this time the multi-talented PATTERSON was doing a spot of DJ'ing in the chill-out room of PAUL OAKENFOLD's Land of Oz club, where, in a well documented incident, he met STEVE HILLAGE (ex-GONG). The two struck up an immediate friendship (HILLAGE no doubt impressed by the fact that PATTERSON had been spinning one of his old tracks at the time) and a series of mutual collaborations ensued. Meanwhile, the ORB carved out a place in the cobwebbed corners of music history by making what was arguably the first ever ambient dance track, entitled, pause for breath, 'A HUGE EVER GROWING PULSATING BRAIN THAT RULES FROM THE CENTRE OF THE ULTRAWORLD'. The psychedelic/progressive rock influence was glaringly obvious, not only in the overblown title but in the slowly shifting rhythms and tripped-out dub effects. The ORB's heavy use of samples continued, this time running into trouble with MINNIE RIPPERTON's 'LOVING YOU'. Come 1990, the band found themselves in the enviable position of being in-demand remixers and amid their growing reputation released another single, the celestial 'LITTLE FLUFFY CLOUDS'. This time penned by PATTERSON/YOUTH, the single saw the ORB run into sample trauma again, with RICKIE LEE JONES reportedly none too happy that her, frankly, out-of-it sounding tones were used on the single. During the sessions for the single, PATTERSON met a young engineer, THRASH, who would go on to become a fully fledged ORB member in late '91 as a replacement for the recently departed CAUTY. The much anticipated debut album, 'ADVENTURES BEYOND THE ULTRAWORLD', released in April '91 on Big Life, was a sprawling double set of blissed-out almost-beats and shimmering ambience. It was also a catalyst for the burgeoning ambient scene that would spawn the likes of MIXMASTER MORRIS and the APHEX TWIN, the music spilling out of chill-out rooms across the country into fully paid-up ambient club nights. In June '92, the ORB stormed into the top 10 with the 'BLUE ROOM' single. At a record breaking 39 minutes long, it wasn't exactly radio-friendly although the band 'performed' it on Top Of The Pops, sitting nonchalantly playing chess and the act's cult popularity saw the subsequent album, 'UFORB', go straight in at No.1. Following a dispute with YOUTH, PATTERSON signed with Island, fighting a protracted battle for the ORB name which he eventually won. His first release for the label was a live album, imaginatively titled 'LIVE '93', and culled from the legendary ORB stage show at various locations around the globe. A collaboration with German techno exponent THOMAS FEHLMAN resulted in the harder sounding 'POMMEFRITZ' album which included such wonderfully titled tracks as 'MORE GILLS, LESS FISHCAKES'. Another two albums, 'ORBUS TERRARUM' (1995) and 'ORBLIVION' (1997) ploughed similarly obscure furrows and divided critical opinion, although both hit top 20. Along with the likes of PRIMAL SCREAM, the ORB helped define an era, bringing overt pychedelia back into the pop charts and updating the genre for the 90's. • **Songwriters:** Most by WESTON and PATERSON. • **Trivia:** The ORB have remixed many including 'Mute' label stars; DEPECHE MODE / ERASURE & WIRE. In 1992, they caused upset in the Asian community by using their religious chants.

Album rating: UF ORB (*9) / ADVENTURES BEYOND THE ULTRAWORLD (*9) / POMME FRITZ (*6) / ORBLIVION (*7)

ALEX PATERSON – synth, keyboards / with **JIM CAUTY**

Wau! Mr Modo not iss.

May 89. (ltd.12"ep; as ROCKMAN ROCK & LX DEE) *(MWS 010T)* **KISS EP** [ ] [-]
– Kiss your love / Suck my kiss mix / The roof is on fire / Ambiorix mix.

Oct 89. (12"ep) *(MWS 017T)* **A HUGE EVER GROWING PULSATING BRAIN THAT RULES FROM THE CENTRE OF THE ULTRAWORLD: LOVIN' YOU (Orbital mix). / ('A'bucket and spade mix) / WHY IS 6 SCARED OF 7?** [ ] [-]

Big Life Mercury

Jun 90. (12"ep) *(BLR 270T)* **(above with new vocals)** [ ] [-]
(cd-ep) *(BLR 270CD)* – (above) / Loving you (ambient house).

Jul 90. (12"ep/cd-ep) *(BLR 27 T/CD)* **(above remixed) / ('A'-9 a.m. radio mix) / ('A'-Aubrey mix I)** [ ] [-]

Nov 90. (7") *(BLR 33)* **LITTLE FLUFFY CLOUDS. / ('A'-Ambient mix Mk.1)** [ ] [-]
(dance mix-12"ep+=/cd-ep+=) *(BLR 33 T/CD)* – Into the fourth dimension (Essenes beyond control).

(12"ep) *(BLR 33R)* – ('A'side) / ('A'-drum & vox version) / Into the fourth dimension.

— In Nov90, they collaborated on STEVE HILLAGE's SYSTEM 7 release 'Sunburst'.

— CAUTY was replaced by **STEVE HILLAGE** – guitar (ex-Solo artist, ex-GONG) / **MIQUETTE GIRAUDY** (ex-GONG) / **ANDY FALCONER**

Apr 91. (d-cd/d-c/d-lp) *(BLR CD/MC/LP 5)* *<511034>* **ADVENTURES BEYOND THE ULTRAWORLD** 29 Nov91
– Little fluffy clouds / Earth (Gaia) / Supernova at the end of the universe / Back side of the Moon / Spanish castles in space / Perpetual dawn / Into the fourth dimension / Outlands / Star 6 & 7 8 9 / A huge ever growing pulsating brain that rules from the centre of the Ultraworld.

Jun 91. (7"/c-s) *(BLR 46/+C)* **PERPETUAL DAWN (SOLAR YOUTH). / STAR 6&789 (phase II)** 61 -
(cd-ep+=) *(BLR 46CD)* – Perpetual dawn: Solar flare.
(12"ep+=) *(BLRT 46)* – (above version) / ('B'side) / ('A'-Ultrabass 1 mix).
(12"ep) *(BLR 46R)* – ORB IN DUB: Towers of dub (ambient mix) / Perpetual dawn (ultrabass II). *(re-iss. Jan94; same)* – (hit No.18)

— In Nov91, SYSTEM 7 issued another release on '10-Virgin'; 'Miracle'.

Dec 91 (cd/c/lp) *(BLR CD/MC/LP 14) / Caroline; <CAROL 1717>* **THE AUBREY MIXES: THE ULTRAWORLD EXCURSIONS** (deleted after 1 day) 44
– Little fluffy clouds / (Pal Joey mix) / Black side of the moon (Steve Hillage remix) / Spanish castles in Spain (Youth remix) / Outlands (Ready made remix) / A huge ever growing pulsating brain (Jim Cauty & Dr. Alex Patterson remix).

— **PATERSON** now with **THRASH (KRISTIAN WESTON)** – guitars, synthesizers, samplers, percussion, plus guests **YOUTH, STUART McMILLAN, GUY PRATT, JAH WOBBLE, STEVE HILLAGE, MIQUETTE GIRAUDY, THOMAS FEHLMANN, GREG HUNTER, ORDE MEIKLE, TOM GREEN, MARNEY PAX.**

Jun 92. (12"ep) *(BLRT 75)* **THE BLUE ROOM (part 1). / (part 2)** 8 -
(cd-ep) *(BLRDA 75)* – The blue room (40 minute version).
(cd-ep) *(BLRDB 75)* – The blue room (radio 7) / The blue room (excerpt 605) / Towers of dub (Mad Professor mix).

Jul 92. (d-cd/d-c/t-lp) *(BLR CD/MC/LP 18)* *<513749>* **UF ORB** 1
– O.O.B.E. / U.F. Orb / Blue room / Towers of dub / Close encounters / Majestic / Sticky end. *(free live lp at some shops 'Soundtrack To The Film: ADVENTURES BEYOND THE ULTRAWORLD: PATTERNS & TEXTURES') (re-iss. Apr96 on 'Island; (cd)(c) IMCD 219)(ICM 8033)*

Oct 92. (c-s) **ASSASSIN (the oasis of rhythm mix)** 12
(12"ep+=/cd-ep+=) *(BLR T/DA 81)* – U.F. ORB (Bandulu remix).
(cd-ep) *(BLRDB 81)* – ('A'-radio 7 mix) / ('A'-another live version) / ('A'-Chocolate hills of Bohol mix).

Nov 93. (c-ep/12"ep/cd-ep) *(BLR C/T/D 98)* **LITTLE FLUFFY CLOUDS. / ('A'mixes)** 10 -

Island Island

Nov 93. (d-cd/d-c/q-lp) *(CIDD/ICTT/ILPSQ 8022) <535004>* **LIVE 93 (live)** 23
– Plateau / The valley / Oobe / Little fluffy clouds / Star 6, 7, 8 & 9 / Towers of dub / Spanish castles in space / The blue room / Perpetual dawn / Assassin / Outlands / A huge ever pulsating brain that rules from the centre of the ultraworld. *(d-cd-iss. Mar97; IMCD 245)*

Jun 94. (cd/c/lp) *(ORB CD/MC/LP 1) <535007>* **POMMEFRITZ** 6
– Pommefritz / More gills less fishcakes / We're paste to be grill you / Banger'n'chips / Allers ist schoen / His immortal logness.

— now w /out KRIS WESTON, who was repl. (after 1995 recording by) **ANDY HUGHES**

Mar 95. (cd/cd/c/d-lp) *(CID/CIDX/ICT/ILPSD 8037) <524099>* **ORBUS TERRARUM** 20 Apr95
– Valley / Plateau / Oxbow lakes / Montagne d'or (der gute berg) / White river junction / Occidental / Slug dub.

May 95. (c-s) *(CIS 609)* **OXBOW LAKES / ('A'-Everglades mix)** 38 -
(12"+=) *(12IS/CID 609)* – ('A'-Sabres No.1 mix).
(12") *(12ISX 609)* – ('A'-Carl Craig psychic pals family wealth plan mix) / ('A'-Evensong string arrangement mix).
(cd-s) *(CIDX 609)* – (all 5 mixes above).

— In Jul'96, the label 'Deviant' released various artists compilation of their mixes 'AUNTIE AUBREY'S EXCURSIONS BEYOND THE CALL OF DUTY'.

— line-up **LX PATERSON / ANDY HUGHES / THOMAS FEHLMANN**

Jan 97. (12"/cd-s) *(12IS/CID 652) <854907>* **TOXYGENE. / DELTA Mk.II** 4
(cd-s) *(CIDX 652)* – ('A'side) / Rose tinted.

Feb 97. (cd/c/d-lp) *(CID/ICT/ILPSD 8055) <524347>* **ORBLIVION** 19
– Delta mk II / Ubiquity / Asylum / Bedouin / Molten love / Pi / S.A.L.T. / Toxygene / Log of deadwood / Secrets / Passing of time / 72.

May 97. (12"/cd-s) *(12IS/CID 657)* **ASYLUM. / ('A'-Blood Sugar's mix 1) / ('A'-Andrea Parker's Bezirkskrankenhaus mix)** 20
(cd-s) *(CIDX 657)* –

Oct 98. (cd/d-lp) *(CID/ILPSD 8078)* **U.F.OFF – THE BEST OF** (compilation) 38
– A huge ever growing pulsating brain rule from the centre of the world / Little fluffy clouds / Perpetual dawn / Blue room / Assassin / Pomme Fritz / Toxygene / Outlands / DJ Asylum / Mickey Mars / Towers of dub (part 1) / Oxbow lakes. *(d-cd+=; CIDD 8078)* – (other mixes).

Nov 98. (d12"ep) *(12ISD 729)* **LITTLE FLUFFY CLOUDS (mixes:- Danny Tenaglia's downtempo groove / Danny Tenaglia's detour mix / Adam Freeland Tsunami one mix / Cumulo nimbus mix / One True Parker mix)** - - -non

– compilations, others, etc. –

Nov 91. (cd/c/lp) *Strange Fruit; (SFR CD/MC/LP 118)* **THE PEEL SESSIONS** -
– A huge ever growing brain that rules from the centre of the ultraworld. *(re-iss. Apr96; same)*

APOLLO XI

DR. ALEX PATERSON + guest **BEN WATKINS** (of SUNSONIC)

Wau! Mr Modo not iss.

Feb 91. (12"/cd-s) *(APOLLO 11/+CD)* **PEACE (IN THE MIDDLE EAST) / ('A'-Sea Of Tranquility mix). / ('A'radio) / ('A'-Is This Really The Orb mix?)** -

F.F.W.D.

aka **ROBERT FRIPP** – guitar / **THOMAS FEHLMANN** – electronics / **KRIS WESTON** – electronics / **DR. ALEX PATERSON**

Intermodo not iss.

Aug 94. (cd/c/d-lp) *(INTA 001 CD/TC/LP)* **F.F.W.D.** 48 -
– Hidden / Lucky saddle / Drone / Hempire / Collosus / What time is clock / Can of bliss / Elauses / Meteor storm / Buckwheat and grits / Klangtest / Suess wie eine nuss.

ORBITAL

Formed: Seven Oaks, London, England . . . late 80's by brothers PHIL and PAUL HARTNOLL. United by a shared love of electro and punk, they were inspired by the outdoor party scene of '89 and named themselves after the infamous circular motorway which ravers used in delirious pursuit of their next E'd-up shindig. A home produced 4-track demo, 'CHIME', brought the band almost instant fame and remains one of their best loved songs. Originally released on the small 'Oh-Zone' label, the track was given a full release in March 1990 on 'London' offshoot 'Ffrr', it's subtly euphoric charms elevating 'CHIME' into the top 20 and the brothers onto a memorable 'Top Of The Pops' appearance where they sported defiant 'No Poll Tax' t-shirts. Although dance culture has since become increasingly politiscized as a result of heavy handed legislation, it was unusual at the time for a techno act to be so passionately anti-establishment, an ethos the HARTNOLL brothers had carried over from their punk days and which would become a recurring theme throughout their career. Meanwhile, ORBITAL followed their debut with a trio of largely instrumental, synth-driven singles, the highlight being the pounding white noise of the BUTTHOLE SURFERS-sampling 'SATAN'. The track reached No.31 upon its release in August '91 although a subsequent live version stormed into the top 5 earlier this year. Their untitled debut album, released in September of the same year, showcased cerebral electronic soundscapes which nevertheless retained a melancholy, organic warmth while their live shows moved feet and minds en masse. Alongside events like the Shamen's Synergy, which attempted to mix the spectacle of rock 'n' roll with the communal energy of house, ORBITAL were pivotal in pioneering dance music in the live evironment. Rather than reproducing the songs live on stage, they improvised, restructuring tracks which had been pre-set into sequencers. This spontaneity was enhanced by an innovative light show utilising state of the art technology, a heady combination that saw ORBITAL headline the Glastonbury festival two years running during the mid-90's. They were no less effective in the studio and their second untitled album was a finely tuned extension of the debut, encompassing such exotica as a sample from an Australian pedestrian crossing (!) With their third long player, 1994's cynically titled 'SNIVILISATION', the music took on an uneasy paranoia, seething with a bitter undercurrent that railed against the state of humanity in general, as well as issues closer to home such as the much hated Criminal Justice Bill. The record also introuced elements of drum 'n' bass, a dalliance that continued with their 'IN SIDES' album. Preceded by the near-half hour strangeness of 'THE BOX' single, the record marked the pinnacle of ORBITAL's sonic explorations, a luminous trip to the final frontiers of electronica. In spite of their experimentalism, a loyal following ensures that the duo are never short of chart success, the 'IN SIDES' album reaching No.5, while 1997 saw ORBITAL go top 3 in the singles chart twice (first with the aforementioned live version of 'SATAN' and then with their celebrated remake of 'THE SAINT'). • **Songwriters:** The duo, except cover of THE SAINT (E. Astley) and noted samples; O EUCHARI (performed by Emily Van Evera). • **Trivia:** Vox on tracks 'SAD BUT TRUE' & 'ARE WE HERE?' by ALISON GOLDFRAPP.

Album rating: UNTITLED (ORBITAL 1) (*7) / UNTITLED (ORBITAL II) (*7) / SNIVILIZATION (*8) / IN SIDES (*9)

PHIL HARTNOLL – keyboards / **PAUL HARTNOLL** – keyboards

Oh-Zone not iss.

Jan 90. (12"ep) *(ZONE 001)* **CHIME. / DEEPER (full version)** -

Ffrr-London Ffrr-London

Mar 90. (7"/c-s) *(F/+CS 135)* **CHIME. / DEEPER** -
(cd-ep+=) *(FCD 135)* – ('A'version).
(12"ep) *(FX 135)* – ('A'-JZM remix) / ('A'-Bacardi mix).

Jul 90. (7"ep) *(F 145)* **OMEN. / 2 DEEP / OPEN MIND** -
(cd-ep) *(FCD 145)* – (1st & 3rd track) / ('A'edit)
(12"ep) *(FX 145)* – Omen: The chariot / The tower / Wheel of fortune / The fool.
(12"ep) *(FXR 145)* – ('A'remixes).

Jan 91. (7") *(F 149)* **SATAN. / BELFAST** 31 -
(12"ep+=/cd-ep+=) *(FX/FCD 149)* – L.C.1. *(cd-ep re-iss. Aug95 on 'Internal'; LIECD 25)*
(12"ep) *(FXR 149)* – ('A'-rhyme & reason mix) / L.C.2 (outer limits mix) / Chime.

Aug 91. (12") *(FX)* **MIDNIGHT. / CHOICE** -
(12"ep) *(FX)* – Midnight (Sasha mix) / Choice (Orbital & Eye & I mix).
(cd-ep+=) *(FCD)* – Analogue test Feb'90. *(re-iss. Aug95 on 'Internal'; LIECD 26)*

Sep 91. (cd/c/lp) *(828248-2/-4/-1) <351001>* **UNTITLED (ORBITAL 1)** 71
– The moebius / Speed freak / Oolaa / Desert storm / Fahrenheit 303 / Steel cube

idolatry / High rise / Chime (live) / Midnight (live) / Belfast / Macrohead. *(cd w-out last track, repl. by)* – I think it's disgusting. *(c+=)* – Untitled. *(re-iss. Apr96 & Apr97 on 'Internal' cd/c; TRU CD/MC 9)*

Feb 92. (12"ep) *(FX 181)* **MUTATIONS (I): OOLAA (Joey Beltram remix) / OOLAA (Meat Beat Manifesto mix) / CHIME (Joey Beltram). / SPEED FREAK (Moby mix)** [24] [-]
(12"ep) *(FX 181)* – MUTATIONS (II): Chime (Ray Keith mix) / Chime (Crime remix) / Steel cube idolatory / Farenheit 303.
(cd-ep) *(FCD 181)* – Oolaa (Joey Beltram mix) / Chime (Ray Keith mix) / Speed freak / Fahrenheit 303.

Internal / Ffrr-London

Sep 92. (12"ep/cd-ep) *(LIARX/LIECD 1)* **RADICCIO EP** [37] [-]
– Halycon / The naked and the dead.
(cd-ep) *(LIECd 2)* – The naked and the dead / Sunday.
(cd-ep re-iss. Aug95; LIECD 27)

Apr 93. (12"ep/c-ep) *(LIARX/LIEMC 7)* **LUSH 3-1. / LUSH 3-2 / LUSH 3-3 (Underworld mix)** [ ] [-]
(12"ep) *(LIAXR 7)* – LUSH 3-4 (Psychick Warriors Ov Gaia) / LUSH 3-5 (CJ Bollard).
(cd-ep) *(LIECD 7)* – (all 5 tracks).

Jun 93. (cd/c/lp) *(TRU CD/MC/LP 2)* *<351026>* **UNTITLED (ORBITAL II)** [28] [ ]
– Time becomes / Planet of the shapes / Lush 3-1 / Lush 3-2 / Impact (the Earth is burning) / Remind / Walk now . . . / Monday / Halycon + on + on / Input out. *(re-iss. Aug95; same)*

Mar 94. (cd-ep/12"ep) *(LIECD/LIARX 12)* **THE JOHN PEEL SESSIONS EP** [ ] [-]
– Lush (Euro-tunnel disaster '94) / Walk about / Semi detached / Attached.
(cd-ep) **DIVERSIONS EP** *(LIEDC 12)* – Impact USA / Lush 3 (Euro-Tunnel disaster '94) / Walkabout / Lush 3-5 (CJ Bolland) / Lush 3-4 (Warrior drift) / Lush 3-4 (Underworld).

Aug 94. (cd/c/d-lp) *(TRU CD/MC/LP 5)* *<124027>* **SNIVILIZATION** [4] [ ]
– Forever / I wish I had duck feet / Sad but true / Crash and carry / Science friction / Philosophy by numbers / Kein trink wasser / Quality seconds / Are we here? / Attached. *(re-iss. Aug95 & Apr97; same)*

Sep 94. (12"ep/c-ep) *(LIARX/LIEMC 15)* **ARE WE HERE? EP** [33] [-]
– Are we here?: Who are they? – Do they here? – They did it (mix).
(cd-ep+=/s-cd-ep+=) *(LIE CD/DC 15)* – Are we here?: What was that? – Criminal Justice bill? – Industry standard?.

— In May'95, they issued 'Belfast'/'Wasted (vocal mix)' on special cd-s which hit UK No.53. THERAPY? was on flip side with 'Innocent X'.

Aug 95. (d7"ep/12"ep/cd-ep/s-cd-ep) *(LIE/LIARX/LIECD/LIEDP 23)* **UNTITLED EP** [ ] [-]
– Times fly (slow) / Sad but new / Times fly (fast) / The tranquilizer.
(above was not eligible for UK chart position due to it's length)

Apr 96. (12"/cd-s) *(LIARX/LIECD 30)* **THE BOX. / THE BOX** [11] [-]
(cd-s+=) *(LICDP 30)* – (2 extra mixes).

Apr 96. (cd/cd/c/3x12"lp) *(TRU DC/CD/MC/LP 10)* *<124087>* **IN SIDES** [5] [ ]
– The girl with the sun in her head / P.E.T.R.O.L. / The box / Dwr budr / Adnan's / Out there somewhere? *(cd re-iss. Apr97 on 'Dutch East India'; 124129CD)*

Jan 97. (cd-s) *(LIECD 37)* *<850990>* **SATAN (live at New York) / OUT THERE SOMEWHERE (live at New York)** [3] [ ] Sep97
(cd-s) *(LICDP 37)* – ('A'-live at Chelmsford) / Lush 3 (live at Boston) / The girl with the sun in her head (live at Boston).
(cd-s) *(LICDD 37)* – ('A'-Industry standard edit) / Chime (live at Chelmsford) / Impact (live at Chelmsford).

— (due to length of above it also hit No.48 in the UK album charts)

Apr 97. (c-s/12"/cd-s) *(FCS/FX/FCD 296)* **THE SAINT / THE SINNER** [3] [ ]
(cd-s+=) *(FCDP 296)* – Belfast (live) / Petrol (live).
(above issued on 'Ffrr'-London')

Aug 97. (cd/c/lp) *(828939-2/-4)* **EVENT HORIZON (soundtrack)** [ ] [ ]

ORCHESTRAL MANOEUVRES IN THE DARK

Formed: West Kirby, Liverpool, England . . . Autumn 1978, initially as The ID, by ANDREW McCLUSKEY and PAUL HUMPHREYS. After a one-off indie single, the coldly pulsing 'ELECTRICITY', for 'Factory', they signed to 'Virgin' subsidiary label, 'Dindisc'. Early in 1980, the group hit the UK Top 75 with 'RED FRAME – WHITE LIGHT', paving the way for an eponymous Top 30 parent album. Later that summer, they scored further chart successes with 'MESSAGES' and 'ENOLA GAY' (the name of the plane which dropped the Hiroshima bomb), the latter an infectiously melancholy swirl of electronica which belied its horrific subject matter. The song was also the highlight of the 'ORGANISATION' (1980) album, wherein the drum machines of previous recordings had been replaced with a live drummer, MALCOLM HOLMES. Heavily influenced by KRAFTWERK, OMD's cerebral electro-pop became progressively warmer and more commercial as the decade wore on. Beginning with the soporific lilt of 'SOUVENIR', McCLUSKEY and HUMPHREYS embarked upon the most successful period of their career, releasing a string of Top 5 hits and well-received albums, namely 'ARCHITECTURE & MORALITY' (1981), 'DAZZLE SHIPS' (1983), 'JUNK CULTURE' (1984) and 'CRUSH' (1985). O.M.D. were a constant feature in the singles chart through the early to mid 80's, like a more pretentious, less claustrophobic cousin to DEPECHE MODE, their biggest hit of the era being the breezy 'LOCOMOTION' (mercifully, not a cover of the LITTLE EVA number!), complete with horn stabs courtesy of the WEIR BROTHERS (NEIL & GRAHAM) who later joined the group as a permanent fixture. With the 'CRUSH' album, OMD enjoyed a brief flurry of Stateside success via the twee romanticism of the 'SO IN LOVE' and 'SECRET' singles, although by the release of the patchy 'PACIFIC AGE' (1986) the following year, the writing partnership of McCLUSKEY and HUMPHREYS was beginnning to falter. The latter eventually departed in 1989 to form The LISTENING POOL, while McCLUSKEY carried on with OMD as a solo project, resurfacing in early '91 with the annoying 'SAILING ON THE SEVEN SEAS', a Top 3 hit. The subsequent album, 'SUGAR TAX' (1991) also made the Top 3 although the revamped OMD was clearly an entirely different beast, airbrushed pop lacking the mystery and romance of the early material. A further album, 'LIBERATOR', carried on in a similar vein. • **Songwriters:** All material written by McCLUSKEY & HUMPHREYS, until the latters exit. Covered; I'M WAITING FOR THE MAN (Velvet Underground) / NEON LIGHTS (Kraftwerk). • **Trivia:** An ID track 'JULIA'S SONG', appeared on an 'Open Eye' indie compilation album, 'Street To Street' in 1978.

Album rating: THE BEST OF O.M.D. compilation (*8)

ANDREW McCLUSKEY (b.24 Jun'59, Wirral, England) – vocals, bass, synthesizers (ex-DALEK I) / **PAUL HUMPHRIES** (b.27 Feb'60, London, England) – keyboards, synths. (ex-The ID) with backing from computer 'Winston'.

Factory / not iss.

May 79. (7") *(FAC 6)* **ELECTRICITY. / ALMOST** [ ] [-]

Dindisc / not iss.

Sep 79. (7") *(DIN 2)* **ELECTRICITY (re-recorded). / ALMOST** [ ] [-]

Feb 80. (7"/12") *(DIN 6/+12)* **RED FRAME – WHITE LIGHT. / I BETRAY MY FRIENDS** [67] [-]

— guests **DAVID FAIRBURN** – guitar / **MALCOLM HOLMES** – drums / **MARTIN COOPER** – sax

Feb 80. (2x12"lp/c) *(DID/+C 2)* **ORCHESTRAL MANOEUVRES IN THE DARK** [27] [-]
– Bunker soldiers / Almost / Mystereality / Electricity / The Messerschmit twins / Messages / Julia's song / Red frame – white light / Dancing / Pretending to see the future. *(re-iss. Aug84 on 'Virgin' lp/c; OVED/+C 96) (cd-iss. Jul87; DIDCD 2)*

May 80. (7") *(DIN 15)* **MESSAGES. / TAKING SIDES AGAIN** [13] [-]
(ext-10") *(DIN 15-10)* – Waiting for the man.

— added **DAVID HUGHES** – keyboards (ex-DALEK I LOVE YOU, ex-SECRETS) and now f/t member **MALCOLM HOLMES** – drums (ex-CLIVE LANGER & THE BOXES, ex-ID)

Sep 80. (7"/ext.12") *(DIN 22/+12)* **ENOLA GAY. / ANNEX** [8] [-]

Oct 80. (lp/c) *(DID/+C 6)* **ORGANISATION** [6] [-]
– Enola Gay / 2nd thought / VCL XI / Motion and heart / Statues / The misunderstanding / The more I see you / Promise / Stanlow. *(free 7"ep)* – INTRODUCING RADIOS / PROGRESS. / DISTANCE FADES BETWEEN US / WHEN I WAS SIX *(re-iss. Aug88 on 'Virgin' lp/c; OVED/+C 147) (cd-iss. Jul87; DIDCD 6)*

— **MALCOLM COOPER** – saxophone, keyboards (ex-DALEK I LOVE YOU) repl. HUGHES

Dindisc / Epic

Aug 81. (7"/ext.10") *(DIN 24/+10)* **SOUVENIR. / MOTION AND HEART (Amazon version) / SACRED HEART** [3] [-]

Oct 81. (7"/ext.12") *(DIN 36/+12)* **JOAN OF ARC. / THE ROMANCE OF THE TELESCOPE (unfinished version)** [5] [ ]

Nov 81. (lp/c) *(DID/+C 12)* *<37721>* **ARCHITECTURE & MORALITY** [3] [ ]
– New stone age / She's leaving / Souvenir / Sealand / Joan Of Arc / Joan Of Arc (Maid of Orleans) / Architecture and morality / Georgia / The beginning and the end. *(cd-iss. 1988 on 'Virgin' lp/c; OVED/+C 276) (re-iss. Apr90; DIDCD 12) (cd re-iss. Jan95; CDIDX 12)*

Jan 82. (7") *(DIN 40)* **MAID OF ORLEANS (THE WALTZ JOAN OF ARC). / NAVIGATION** [4] [ ]
(12"+=) *(DIN 40-12)* – Of all the things we've made.
(3"cd-s iss.Jun88; CDT 27)

Jan 82. (7") **SOUVENIR. / NEW STONE AGE** [-] [ ]

Virgin / Epic-Virgin

Feb 83. (7"/7"pic-d)(12") *(VS/+Y 527)<VS 527-12)* **GENETIC ENGINEERING. / 4-NEU** [20] [-]

Mar 83. (lp/c) *(V/TCV 2261)* *<38543>* **DAZZLE SHIPS** [5] [ ]
– Radio Prague / Genetic engineering / ABC auto-industry / Telegraph / This is Helena / International / Dazzle ships / The romance of the telescope / Silent running / Radio waves / Time zones / Of all the things we've made. *(cd-iss. 1985; CDV 2261) (re-iss. 1987 lp/c; OVED/+C 106) (cd re-iss. Apr97 on 'Virgin-VIP'; CDVIP 170)*

Apr 83. (7"/7"pic-d)(12") *(VS/+Y 580)(VS 580-12)* **TELEGRAPH. / 66 AND FADING** [42] [-]

May 83. (7") **TELEGRAPH. / THIS IS HELENA** [-] [ ]

Virgin / A&M

Apr 84. (7"/7"sha-pic-d) *(VS/+Y 660)* **LOCOMOTION. / HER BODY IN MY SOUL** [5] [ ] Nov84
(ext.12") *(VS 660-12)* – The avenue. *(3"cd-s-iss.Jun88; CDT 12)*

May 84. (lp/c) *(V/TCV 2310)* *<5027>* **JUNK CULTURE** [9] [ ] Nov84
– Junk culture / Tesla girls / Locomotion / Apollo / Never turn away / Love and violence / Hard day / All wrapped up / White trash / Talking loud and clear. *(cd-iss. 1986; CDV 2310) (re-iss. Mar90 lp/c; OVED/+C 215) (cd re-iss. Aug98 on 'Virgin-VIP'; CDVIP 215)*

Jun 84. (7"/7"pic-d)(12") *(VS/+Y 685)(VS 685-12)* **TALKING LOUD AND CLEAR. / JULIA'S SONG** [11] [-]

Aug 84. (7") *(VS 705)* **TESLA GIRLS. / TELEGRAPH (live)** [21] [-]
(12"+=)(c-s+=) *(VS 705-12)(TVS 705)* – Garden city.

Oct 84. (7"/7"pic-d) *(VS/+Y 727)* **NEVER TURN AWAY. / WRAP-UP** [70] [-]
(ext.12") *(VS 727-12)* – Waiting for the man (live).

May 85. (7") *(VS 766)* *<2746>* **SO IN LOVE. / CONCRETE HANDS** [27] [26] Aug85
(ext;12")(ext.12"pic-d) *(VS 766-13)(VSY 766-14)* – Maria Gallante.
(d7"++=) *(VS 766)* – White trash (live).

Jun 85. (lp)(c) *(V/TCV 2349)* *<5077>* **CRUSH** [13] [38] Jul85
– So in love / Secret / Bloc bloc bloc / Women III / Crush / 88 seconds in Greensboro / The native daughters of the west / La femme accident / Hold you / The lights are going out. *(cd-iss. Jan86; CDV 2349) (cd re-iss. Oct96 on 'Virgin-VIP'; CDVIP 155)*

Jul 85. (7") *(VS 796)* **SECRET. / DRIFT** [34] [-]
(ext-d12"+=) *(VS 796-12)* – Red frame – white light / I betray my friends.

Oct 85. (7"/7"sha-pic-d) *(VS/+S 811)* **LA FEMME ACCIDENT. / FIREGUN** [42] [ ]
(ext.d12"+=) *(VSD 811-12)* – Locomotion (live) / Enola Gay (live).
Nov 85. (7") *<2794>* **SECRET. / FIREGUN** [-] [63]
Feb 86. (7") *<2811>* **IF YOU LEAVE. / LA FEMME ACCIDENT** [-] [4]
Apr 86. (7") *(VS 843)* **IF YOU LEAVE. / 88 SECONDS IN GREENSBORO** [48] [-]
(12") *(VS 843-12)* – ('A'extended) / Locomotion (live).

—— added The **WEIR BROTHERS** (NEIL & GRAHAM) (had guested on earlier songs)

Aug 86. (7"/7"pic-d) *(VS/+Y 888) <2872>* **(FOREVER) LIVE AND DIE. / THIS TOWN** [11] [19]
(12"+=) *(VS 888-13)* – ('A'extended).
Sep 86. (cd/c/lp) *(CD/TC+/V 2398) <5144>* **THE PACIFIC AGE** [15] [47] Oct86
– Stay (the black rose and the universal wheel) / (Forever) Live and die / The Pacific age / The dead girls / Shame / Southern / Flame of hope / Goddess of love / We love you / Watch us fall.
Nov 86. (7") *(VS 911)* **WE LOVE YOU. / WE LOVE YOU (dub)** [54] [ ]
(12"+=) *(VS 911-12)* – ('A'extended).
(d7"+=) *(VSD 911)* – If you leave / 88 seconds on Greensboro.
(free c-s w7"+=) *(VSC 911)* – Souvenir / Electricity / Enola Gay / Joan of Arc.
Apr 87. (7") *(VS 938)* **SHAME (re-recorded). / GODDESS OF LOVE** [52] [ ]
(12"+=) *(VS 938-12)* – ('B're-recorded version).
(cd-s+=) *(MIKE 938-12)* – (Forever) Live and die / Messages.
Jan 88. (7") *(VSG 987) <3002>* **DREAMING. / SATELLITE** [50] [16] Feb88
(ext.12"pic-d) *(VS 987-12)* – Gravity never failed.
(cd-s++=/3"cd-s++=) *(VDCD/+X 987)* – Dreaming.
(re-dist.Jun88, hit Uk No.60)
(10") *(VS 987-10)* – ('A'side) / ('A'William Orbit mix) / Messages / Secret.
Feb 88. (pic-cd/cd/c/lp) *(CDP/CD/TC+/OMD 1) <5186>* **IN THE DARK – THE BEST OF O.M.D.** (compilation) [2] [46]
– Electricity / Messages / Enola Gay / Souvenir / Joan of Arc / Maid of Orleans (Joan Of Arc waltz) / Talking loud and clear / Tesla girls / Locomotion / So in love / Secret / If you leave / (Forever) Live and die / Dreaming. *(cd+=)* – Telegraph / We love you (12"version) / La femme accident (12"version) / Genetic engineering. *(re-iss. Sep94; same)*

OMD

—— **ANDY McCLUSKEY** now sole survivor after others left 1989. HUMPHREYS formed The LISTENING POOL in the early 90's. / added **STUART BOYLE** – guitar / **NIGEL IPINSON** – keyboards / **PHIL COXON** – keyboards / **ABE JUCKS** – drums

Virgin Virgin

Mar 91. (7"/c-s) *(VS/+C 1310)* **SAILING ON THE SEVEN SEAS. / BURNING** [3] [ ]
(12") *(VS 1310-12)* – ('A'extended) / Floating on the seven seas.
(cd-s) *(VSCDX 1310)* – ('A'extended) / Dancing on the seven seas / Big town.
(cd-s) *(VSCD 1310)* – ('A'side) / Floating on the seven seas / Dancing on the seaven seas (Larrabee mix) / Sugartax.
May 91. (cd/c/lp) *(CD/TC+/V 2648) <91715>* **SUGAR TAX** [3] [ ]
– Sailing on the seven seas / Pandora's box / Then you turn away / Speed of light / Was it something I said / Big town / Call my name / Apollo XI / Walking on air / Walk tall / Neon lights / All that glitters.
Jun 91. (7"/c-s) *(VS/+C 1331)* **PANDORA'S BOX. / ALL SHE WANTS IS EVERYTHING** [7] [ ]
(cd-s+=) *(VSCD 1331)* – ('A'-Constant pressure mix) / ('A'-Diesel fingers mix).
(12") *(VS 1331-12)* – (2-'A'mixes).
(cd-s) *(VSCDX 1331)* – (3-'A'mixes).
Sep 91. (7"/c-s) *(VS/+C 1368)* **THEN YOU TURN AWAY. / SUGAR TAX** [50] [ ]
(cd-s+=) *(VSCD 1368)* – Area / ('A'-Inforce repeat mix).
(cd-s) *(VSCDG 1368)* – ('A'side) / ('A'-Repeat mix) / Sailing on the seven seas / Vox humana.
Nov 91. (7"/c-s) *(VS/+C 1380)* **CALL MY NAME. / WALK TALL** [50] [ ]
(12") *(VS 1380-12)* – ('A'side) / Brides of Frankenstein.
(cd-s++=) *(VSCD 1380)* – ('A'side) / ('A'version) / Brides . . . (dub).
May 93. (7"/c-s) *(VS/+C 1444)* **STAND ABOVE ME. / CAN I BELIEVE YOU** [21] [ ]
(cd-s+=) *(VSCDG 1444)* – ('A'-Transcendental mix) / ('A'-Hynofunk mix).
(12") *(VS 1444-12)* – ('A'side) / ('A'-Transcendental mix) / ('A'-10 minute version).
Jun 93. (cd/c/lp) *(CD/TC+/V 2715) <88225>* **LIBERATOR** [14] [ ]
– Stand above me / Everyday / King of stone / Dollar girl / Dream of me (based on Love's theme) / Sunday morning / Agnus Dei / Love and hate you / Heaven is / Best years of our lives / Christine / Only tears. *(cd re-iss. Aug98 on 'VIP-Virgin'; CDVIP 217)*
Jul 93. (7"/c-s) *(VS/+C 1461)* **DREAM OF ME (BASED ON LOVE'S THEME). / ('A'mix)** [24] [ ]
(cd-s+=) *(VSCDT 1461)* – Strange sensations / The place you fear the most.
(cd-s) *(VSCDX 1461)* – ('A'side) / Enola Gay / Dreaming / Call my name.
Sep 93. (7"/c-s) *(VS/+C 1471)* **EVERYDAY. / ELECTRICITY (live)** [59] [ ]
(cd-s+=) *(VSCDT 1471)* – Walk tall (live) / Locomotion (live).

—— **STUART KERSHAW** – drums; repl. JUCKS

Aug 96. (c-s/cd-s) *(VSC/+DT 1599)* **WALKING ON THE MILKY WAY / MATTHEW STREET / NEW DARK AGE** [17] [-]
(cd-s) *(VSCDG 1599)* – ('A'side) / Joan of Arc (live) / Maid of Orleans (live) / Walking on air (live).
Sep 96. (cd/c) *(CDV/TCV 2807)* **UNIVERSAL** [24] [-]
– Universal / Walking on the Milky Way / The Moon & the Sun / The Black Sea / Very close to far away / The gospel of St Jude / That was then / Too late / The boy from the chemist is here to see you / If you're still in love with me / New head / Victory waltz.
Oct 96. (c-s) *(VSC 1606)* **UNIVERSAL / HEAVEN IS** [55] [-]
(cd-s+=) *(VSCDT 1606)* – Messages (live).
(cd-s) *(VSCDG 1606)* – ('A'side) / King of stone (live) / Talking loud & clear (live) / ('A'-abum version).
Sep 98. (cd-s) *(VSCDT 1694)* **THE OMD REMIXES: ENOLA GAY (OMD vs SASH!) / ELECTRICITY (Micronauts mix) / SOUVENIR (Moby mix)** [35] [-]
(12") *(VST 1694)* – (first mix) / Souvenir (hard house) / Souvenir (7am version).
(12") *(VSTX 1694)* – (first two mixes) / Apollo XI (Northern electric soul remix).
Sep 98. (cd/c) *(CDV/TCV 2859) <46520>* **THE OMD SINGLES** (compilation) [16] [ ] Nov98
– Electricity / Messages / Enola Gay / Souvenir / Joan of Arc / Maid of Orleans / Tesla girls / Locomotion / Talking loud and clear / So in love / If you leave / (Forever) Live and die / Dreaming / Sailing the seven seas / Pandora's box / Call my name / Dream of me (based on love's theme).

– compilations, etc. –

May 84. (lp) *Epic;* **ORCHESTRAL MANOEUVRES IN THE DARK** [-] [ ]
– (compilation of first 2 albums)
Feb 89. (12") *Old Gold; (OG 4099)* **ENOLA GAY. / ELECTRICITY** [ ] [-]
Mar 89. (12") *Old Gold; (OG 4109)* **SOUVENIR (extended). / TALKING LOUD AND CLEAR (extended)** [ ] [-]
Feb 89. (12") *Virgin; (SP12 285)* **BRIDES OF FRANKENSTEIN (OMD megaremixes: LOCOMOTION / SO IN LOVE / SECRET / IF YOU LEAVE / WE LOVE YOU)** [-] [ ]
Nov 90. (3xpic-cd-box) *Virgin; (TPAK 7)* **CD BOXED SET** [ ] [-]
– (first 3 albums)

ORCHIDS

Formed: Govan, Glasgow, Scotland . . . by main songwriter, JAMES HACKETT, alongside MATTHEW DRUMMOND, CHRIS QUINN, JAMES MOODY and JOHN. A surprise signing to 'Sarah' records late in 1987, they released their first official debut, 'I'VE GOT A HABIT', early the following year having previously recorded a flexi-disc track for indie fanzine 'Sha La La'. A popsicle bedsit-land band with a sound similar to The BATHERS or The WEATHER PROPHETS, they released a series of singles, most of them appearing on their IAN CARMICHAEL (ONE DOVE)-produced debut set, 'UNHOLY SOUL' (1991). The ORCHIDS continued to flower over subsequent albums, namely 'EPICUREAN: A SOUNDTRACK' (1992) and 'STRIVING FOR THE LAZY PERFECTION' (1994). • **Note:** Obviously not the same group, who issued eponymous lp in 1980 for 'M.C.A.', and there is no connection between them and 1963 band on 'Decca'.

Album rating: UNHOLY SOUL (*5) / EPICUREAN: A SOUNDTRACK (*5) / STRIVING FOR THE LAZY PERFECTION (*5)

JAMES HACKETT – vocals / **MATTHEW DRUMMOND** – guitar / **JOHN** – guitar / **JAMES MOODY** – bass / **CHRIS QUINN** – drums

Sha La La not iss.

Jun 87. (7"flexi) *(Sha La La Ba Ba Ba 5)* **FROM THIS DAY. / Sea Urchins:- Summertime** [ ] [-]

Sarah not iss.

Feb 88. (7") *(SARAH 002)* **I'VE GOT A HABIT. / GIVE ME SOME PEPPERMINT FREEDOM / APOLOGIES** [ ] [-]
Nov 88. (7"ep) *(SARAH)* **UNDERNEATH THE SINK, UNDERNEATH THE WINDOW / WALTER. / TINY WORDS / DEFY THE LAW** [ ] [-]
Aug 89. (10"m-lp) *(SARAH 401)* **LYCEUM (live)** [ ] [-]
Sep 89. (7") *(SARAH 023)* **WHAT WILL WE DO NEXT. / ?** [ ] [-]
Feb 90. (12") *(SARAH 029)* **SOMETHING FOR THE LONGING. / FAREWELL, DEAR BONNIE / ON A SUNDAY** [ ] [-]
(below single on 'Caff')

—— DRUMMOND + MOODY were also part of The WAKE in the early 90's

Sep 90. (7"ltd) *(CAFF 11)* **AN ILL WIND THAT BLOWS. / ALL THOSE THINGS** [ ] [-]
Feb 91. (12"ep) *(SARAH 042)* **PENETRATION** [ ] [-]
May 91. (lp/cd) *(SARAH 605/+CD)* **UNHOLY SOUL** [ ] [-]
– Me and the black & white dream / Women priests and addicts / Bringing you the love / Frank De Salvo / Long drawn Sunday night / Peaches / Dirty clothing / Moon lullaby / Coloured stone / The sadness of sex (part 1) / Waiting for the storm / You know I'm fine.
Sep 92. (7") *(SARAH 066)* **THAUMATURGY. / I WAS JUST DREAMING** [ ] [-]
(cd-s+=) *(SARAH 066CD)* – Between sleeping and waking.
Sep 92. (lp/cd) *(SARAH 611/+CD)* **EPICUREAN: A SOUNDTRACK** [ ] [-]
– Peaches / A place called home / Tiny words / Moon lullaby / Walter / It's only obvious / Long drawn Sunday night / Blue light / Yawn / Sigh / Something for the longing / The York song / Bemused, confused and bedraggled / Caveman / Underneath the window, underneath the sink / Pelican blonde / Women priests and addicts / Carole-Anne / Tropical fishbowl / The sadness of sex (part 1).
Jan 94. (lp/cd) *(SARAH 617/+CD)* **STRIVING FOR THE LAZY PERFECTION** [ ] [-]
– Obsession No.1 / Striving for the lazy perfection / The searching / Welcome to my curious heart / Avignon / A living Ken and Barbie / Beautiful liar / A kind of Eden / Prayers to St. Jude / Lovechild / Give a little honey / I've got to wake up / The perfect reprise.

—— went to ground after above

ORIGINAL MIRRORS

Formed: Liverpool, England . . . early '79 by veterans of the new wave scene, songwriters STEVE ALLEN (ex-DEAF SCHOOL) and IAN BROUDIE (ex-BIG IN JAPAN), who enlisted the help of London-based musicians, PHIL SPALDING, JONATHAN PERKINS and PETE KIRCHNER. Signing to 'Mercury' records, they debuted with the single, 'COULD THIS BE HEAVEN', previewing their 1980 eponymous debut album. A combination of uptempo, keyboard-tinkling New Wave pop and hookline choruses, the record plumbed the depths with an awful cover of Diana Ross & The Supremes' 'REFLECTIONS' (pun intended?). SPALDING was then substituted with

JIMMY HUGHES prior to the release of their second collection, 'HEART, TWANGO & RAW BEAT' (1981), thankfully their last effort. However, IAN BROUDIE did go on to greater things, most notably, The LIGHTNING SEEDS, while KIRCHNER was given a call-up by none other than ageing blues rockers STATUS QUO!

Album rating: HEARTBEAT – THE BEST OF THE ORIGINAL MIRRORS compilation (*4)

STEVE ALLEN – vocals, piano, guitar (ex-DEAF SCHOOL) / **IAN BROUDIE** (b. 4 Aug'58) – guitar, keyboards, vocals (ex-BIG IN JAPAN, ex-SECRETS) / **JONATHAN PERKINS** – keyboards, guitar (ex-XTC, ex-STADIUM DOGS) / **PHIL SPALDING** – bass (ex-BERNIE TORME) / **PETE KIRCHNER** – drums

Mercury | Arista

Nov 79. (7") *(6007 245)* **COULD THIS BE HEAVEN. / NIGHT OF THE ANGELS** -

Feb 80. (7") *(MER 5)* **BOYS CRY. / CHAINS OF LOVE** -

Feb 80. (lp) *(9102 039) <4264>* **ORIGINAL MIRRORS**
– Sharp words / Reflections / The boys, the boys / Flying / Chains of love / Could this be Heaven / Boys cry / Night of the angels / Panic in the night / Feel like a train.

—— **JIMMY HUGHES** – bass; repl. SPALDING

Apr 81. (7") *(MER 65)* **DANCING WITH THE REBELS. / SURE YEAH** -
(12"+=) *(MERX 65)* – On Broadway.

May 81. (lp) *(6359 046)* **HEART, TWANGO & RAW BEAT** -
– Heart, twango and raw beat / Dancing with the rebels / Teen beat / When you're young / Things to come / Darling . . . in London / Don't cry baby / Please don't wear red / Swing together / Time has come.

Jun 81. (7") *(DREAM 1)* **20,000 DREAMERS. / TIME HAS COME** -
(12"+=) *(DREAM 12)* – Dancing with the rebels.

—— after they split BROUDIE became a producer and formed The CARE (with WILD SWANS members) before he was the man behind The LIGHTNING SEEDS. KIRCHNER got a surprise call-up from STATUS QUO in later years.

- compilations, etc. -

Jun 96. (cd) *Mercury; (532594-2)* **HEARTBEAT – THE BEST OF THE ORIGINAL MIRRORS** (combination of both albums) -

ORLANDO

Formed: London, England . . . 1994 by keyboard player/composer, DICKON EDWARDS and his singing accomplice, TIM CHIPPING, a former funeral director. Conceived as an attempt to parody the archetypal girlie indie band, ORLANDO additionally consisted of SIMON KEHOE and STEPHEN JEFFRIS in its initial incarnation. As the sound gradually became heavier than EDWARDS had envisaged, he split the group before later reuniting with TIM and recording the 'REPRODUCTION IS POLLUTION' single for 'Sarah' under the moniker, SHELLEY, in Spring '95. Sinking without trace, the record's failure spurred on the duo to resurrect ORLANDO, bringing in backing musicians, NEIL TURNER and MIKE AUSTIN. In September '96, 'Blanco Y Negro' delivered their debut single proper, 'JUST FOR A SECOND', a mutton-dressed-as-lamb synth-pop effort that was shamelessly hyped as ORLANDO were placed firmly in the vanguard of the hopelessly contrived, Melody Maker-created 'Romo' scene. An embarrassing attempt to revive the early 80's 'New Romantic' movement, the kids stayed at home in their droves and the accompanying 'Club Skinny' package tour fell flat. Hardly even built up before they were knocked down, ORLANDO were left licking their wounds among the wreckage of 'Romo' as debut album, 'PASSIVE SOUL' (1997), was virtually ignored.

Album rating: PASSIVE SOUL (*6)

DICKON EDWARDS (b. Bildeston, Suffolk, England) – keyboards, vocals / **SIMON KEHOE** – vocals, keyboards (left before debut) / added **TIM CHIPPING** (b. TIMOTHY MARK) – vocals / **STEPHEN JEFFRIS** – guitar (left before debut)

Sarah | not iss.

Apr 95. (7"/cd-s; as SHELLEY) *(SARAH 098/+CD)* **REPRODUCTION IS POLLUTION. / PREJUDICE / HERO** -

—— revived ORLANDO with **DICKON + TIM** plus augmentation from **NEIL TURNER + MIKE AUSTIN**

Blanco Y Negro | not iss.

Sep 96. (c-s) *(NEG 91C)* **JUST FOR A SECOND / SOMETHING TO WRITE HOME ABOUT** -
(12"+=/cd-s+=) *(NEG 91/+CD)* – ('A'mixes).

Nov 96. (7"ep/c-ep/cd-ep) *(NEG 98/+C/CD)* **THE MAGIC EP** -
– Don't kill my rage / Fatal / Up against it / Contained.

Apr 97. (7"/c-s) *(NEG 101/+C)* **NATURE'S HATED. / SOMEDAY SOON** -
(cd-s+=) *(NEG 101CD)* – ('A'mixes).

Sep 97. (cd) *(0630 19718-2)* **PASSIVE SOUL** -
– Introduction / Furthest point away / Just for a second / Nature's hated / On dry land / Contained / Afraid again / Happily unhappy / Don't sleep alone / Save yourself / Three letters / Here (so find me).

Beth ORTON

Born: Dec'70, Norwich, England. A one-time Buddhist nun, she was discovered in 1991/2 by WILLIAM ORBIT who saw her performing in a play. Her collaborative work with ORBIT was subsequently heard by The CHEMICAL BROTHERS and RED SNAPPER, the former act employing her downbeat but poignant vocals on the 1995 'Exit Planet Dust' album track, 'Alive Alone'. The following year, she found herself on the books of 'Heavenly' records, delivering her debut album, 'TRAILER PARK' soon after. An affecting blend of fragile folk and subtle lo-fi trip-hop rhythms, it won praise from such diverse camps as Folk Roots magazine and Mixmag (it was even nominated for the 1997 Mercury Music Prize). The same year (1997), BETH's four singles scored successively higher chart placings, the re-released 'SHE CRIES YOUR NAME', revealing the melancholy depths of her NICK DRAKE/SANDY DENNY-esque muse. ORTON ended the year on a high note, collaborating with her long-time hero, TERRY CALLIER on the Top 40 EP 'BEST BIT'. • **Songwriters:** Most with rhythm FRIEND and BARNES, except SHE CRIES YOUR NAME; she co-wrote with WILLIAM ORBIT. Covered IT'S NOT THE SPOTLIGHT (Bobby Bland; c.) / I WISH I NEVER SAW THE SUNSHINE (Spector – Greenwich – Barry) / DOLPHINS (Fred Neil).

Album rating: TRAILER PARK (*8)

BETH ORTON – vocals; with **TED BARNES** – guitar (of JUNCTIONS) / **ALI FRIEND** – double bass (of RED SNAPPER) / **WILL BLANCHARD** – drums (of SANDALS) / guest **DAVID BOULTER** – harmonium / + string section

Heavenly | Dedicated

Jul 96. (7"one-sided) *(HVN 056)* **I WISH I NEVER SAW THE SUNSHINE** -

Sep 96. (10"ep/cd-ep) *(HVN 60 10/CD)* **SHE CRIES YOUR NAME / TANGENT. / SAFETY / IT'S NOT THE SPOTLIGHT** -

Oct 96. (cd/c/lp) *(HVNLP 17 CD/MC/LP) <44007>* **TRAILER PARK** 68
– She cries your name / Tangent / Don't need a reason / Live as you dream / Sugar boy / Touch me with your love / Whenever / How far / Someone's daughter / I wish I never saw the sunshine / Galaxy of emptiness.

Jan 97. (10"ep/cd-ep) *(HVN 64 10/CD)* **TOUCH ME WITH YOUR LOVE. / PEDESTAL / GALAXY OF EMPTINESS** 60 -

Mar 97. (c-ep/10"ep/cd-ep) *(HVN 65 CS/10/CD)* **SOMEONE'S DAUGHTER. / I WISH I NEVER SAW THE SUNSHINE / IT'S THIS I AM I FIND** 49 -

Jun 97. (c-s) *(HVN 68CS)* **SHE CRIES YOUR NAME (1997 version) / IT'S NOT THE SPOTLIGHT** 40 -
(10"+=/cd-s+=) *(HVN 68-10/CD)* – Bullet / Best bit.

Heavenly | Heavenly

Dec 97. (c-ep; BETH ORTON featuring TERRY CALLIER) *(<HVN 72CS>)* **BEST BIT EP** 36
– Best bit / Skimming stone / Dolphins.
(12"ep+=/cd-ep+=) *(<HVN 72 12/CD>)* – Lean on me.

OTHER TWO (see under ⇒ NEW ORDER)

OUR DAUGHTER'S WEDDING

Formed: New York, USA . . . 1980 by KEITH SILVA, LAYNE RICO and SCOTT SIMON. Following in the geek electroid wake of DEVO and GARY NUMAN, this NY trio delivered a couple of singles for the 'Design' label, the second of which, 'LAWNCHAIRS', was issued by 'EMI America' in the UK where they had now settled. The latter track became a surprise Top 50 hit in Britain, although an EP, 'THE DIGITAL COWBOY', failed to build on their modest success. By the 1982 release of their debut album, 'MOVING WINDOWS', their earlier hit (which wasn't even included on the set) had long since been forgotten. Following the failure of their one and only long-player, the various members of OUR DAUGHTER'S WEDDING left the party and eloped back to New York.

Album rating: MOVING WINDOWS (*4)

KEITH SILVA – vocals, keyboards / **LAYNE RICO** – synthesizer / **SCOTT SIMON** – synthesizer, saxophone

EMI America | Design

Aug 80. (7") *<ODW 521>* **NIGHT LIFE. / RAINCOATS & SILVERWARE** -

Jul 81. (7"/12") *(EA/12EA 124) <ODW 913LR>* **LAWNCHAIRS. / AIRLINE** 49 Nov80

Oct 81. (7"ep/12"ep) *(EA/12EA 129)* **THE DIGITAL COWBOY EP** -
– Target for life / Hotel room / Dance floor / No one's watching.

Aug 82. (7"/12") *(EA/12EA 144)* **AUTO MUSIC. / TRACK ME DOWN** -

Oct 82. (lp) *(AML 3025)* **MOVING WINDOWS** -
– Auto music / She was someone / Elevate her / Track me down / Daddy's slave / Longtitude 60 / Love machine / Always be true / Moving windows / Paris / Buildings.

—— disbanded after the failure of above

OUR LADY PEACE

Formed: Toronto, Canada . . . 1994 by RAINE MAIDA (a former criminology student), Bradford-born MIKE TURNER, DUNCAN COUTTS and jazz-trained JEREMY TAGGART. Almost immediately signing to 'Epic' records, they released their debut album 'NAVEED' in '95, a disc that went on to achieve record-breaking triple platinum sales in their native Canada. Unfortunately, DUNCAN didn't appear on the album as he spent a year at university, his temporary substitute being, CHRIS EACRETT Issued early '96 in the UK, the record's dreamy emotional guitar-rock was akin to a more cerebral LIVE, ALICE IN CHAINS or even U2. • **Songwriters:** TURNER, MAIDA (+ lyrics), EACRETT and producer ARNOLD LANNI.

Album rating: NAVEED (*8) / CLUMSY (*6)

RAINE MAIDA (b.1972) – vocals / **MIKE TURNER** (b.1965) – guitars / **CHRIS EACRETT** (b.1971) – bass; repl. DUNCAN COUTTS / **JEREMY TAGGART** (b.1977) – drums

Epic Relativity

Jan 96. (cd-s) **STARSEED /** [-] [ ]

Feb 96. (cd/c) *(478383-2/-4)* *<88561-1507-2/-4>* **NAVEED** [ ] [ ] Mar95
– The birdman / Supersatellite / Starseed / Hope / Naveed / Dirty walls / Denied / Is it safe? / Julia / Under Zenith / Neon crossing.

— **DUNCAN COUTTS** – bass; returned in '96 to repl. CHRIS

Epic Epic

Sep 97. (cd/c) *(487408-2/-4)* *<67940>* **CLUMSY** [ ] [76]
– Superman's dead / Automatic flowers / Carnival / Big dumb rocket / 4 a.m. / Shaking / Clumsy / Hello Oskar / Let you down / Story of 100 aisles / Car crash.

Jun 98. (7") *(664331-7)* **SUPERMAN'S DEAD. / STARSEED** [ ] [ ]
(cd-s+=) *(664331-2)* – Let you down.

OUTCASTS

Formed: Belfast, N.Ireland . . . 1977 by the COWAN brothers, MARTIN (the main songwriter), COLIN and GREG, the trio invited GETTY to join a little later. Early the following year, the quartet issued their debut 7", 'FRUSTRATION', before signing to up and coming local imprint, 'Good Vibrations' (who'd just had a hit with The UNDERTONES' 'Teenage Kicks'). Towards the end of '78, The OUTCASTS delivered their take on the classic punk-pop anthem with 'JUST ANOTHER TEENAGE REBEL', glammin' it up for unsavoury murder "ballad", 'THE COPS ARE COMIN', which subsequently featured on a V/A EP, 'Battle Of The Bands'. Their final single for the label, 'SELF CONSCIOUS OVER YOU', was also the title track of the accompanying debut album, released at the turn of the decade as punk's initial spark was dying out. Rejecting the majors and adamantly refusing to budge from the independent sector, The OUTCASTS delivered a further handful of 45's (including two on their own imprint), although tragedy struck when COLIN was killed in a car crash in '82. While the band struggled on with new drummer, RAYMOND FALLS, they failed to recapture the bite of their early work.

Album rating: BLOOD AND THUNDER (*5) / SEVEN DEADLY SINS (*5)

GREG COWAN (b.1961) – vocals, bass / **MARTIN COWAN** (b.1955) – guitar, vocals / **GETTY** (b. COLIN GETGOOD, 1960) – lead guitar / **COLIN COWAN** (b.1957) – drums

It not iss.

Mar 78. (7"m) *(IT 4)* **FRUSTRATION. / DON'T WANT TO BE NO ADULT / YOU'RE A DISEASE** [ ] [-]

Good Vibrations not iss.

Nov 78. (7") *(GOT 3)* **JUST ANOTHER TEENAGE REBEL. / LOVE IS FOR SOPS** [ ] [-]

Feb 79. (d7"; with Various Artists) *(GOT 7)* **THE COPS ARE COMIN' (from 'Battle Of The Bands')** [ ] [-]

Nov 79. (7") *(GOT 17)* **SELF CONSCIOUS OVER YOU. / LOVE YOU FOR NEVER** [ ] [-]

Dec 79. (lp) *(BIG 1)* **SELF CONSCIOUS OVER YOU** [ ] [-]
– Self conscious over you / Clinical love / One day / Love is for sops / Love you for never / The princess grew up a frog / Cyborg / School teacher / Spiteful Sue / The cops are comin'. *(cd-iss. Feb94 on 'Dojo'+=; DOJOCD 182)* – Just another teenage rebel.

G.B.H. not iss.

Aug 81. (7") *(GBH 001)* **MAGNUM FORCE. / GANGLAND WARFARE** [ ] [-]

Outcasts Only not iss.

Nov 81. (7") *(OO 001)* **PROGRAMME LOVE. / BEATING AND SCREAMING (pt.1 & 2) / MANIA** [ ] [-]

Jun 82. (7") *(OO 200)* **ANGEL FACE. / GANGLAND WARFARE** [ ] [-]

— **RAYMOND FALLS** – drums; repl. COLIN (on some of below album) when he died in a car crash in '82

Abstract not iss.

Jan 83. (lp) *(ABT 004)* **BLOOD AND THUNDER** [ ] [-]
– Winter / Machine gun / Sex and glory / Gangland warfare / Programme love / Frustration / Magnum force / Beating and screaming (parts 1 & 2) / Mania. *(cd-iss. 1984 on 'New Rose'; ROSE 16CD)*

Jun 83. (7") *(ABS 017)* **NOWHERE LEFT TO RUN. / THE RUNNING'S OVER TIME TO PRAY** [ ] [-]
(12"+=) *(12ABS 017)* – ('A'instrumental) / Ruby.

New Rose not iss.

Aug 84. (7") *(NEW 38)* **SEVEN DEADLY SINS. / SWAMP FEVER** [ ] [-]

Aug 84. (lp) *(NEW 40)* **SEVEN DEADLY SINS** [ ] [-]

Jul 85. (12"m) *(NEW 52)* **1969 (extended). / PSYCHOTIC SHAKEDOWN / BLUE MURDER** [ ] [-]

— disbanded after above

– compilations, etc. –

Sep 95. (cd) *Anagram; (CDPUNK 62)* **PUNK SINGLES COLLECTION** [ ] [-]

OUT OF MY HAIR

Formed: London, England . . . mid 90's by COMFORT (aka SIMON EUGENE). Clearly a man who likes to control his own destiny, COMFORT sent the original OUT OF MY HAIR line-up packing after they compained about his domineering ways. With the laid-back 'IN THE GROOVE' single already under his belt (OUT OF MY HAIR's debut single for 'R.C.A.'), the lone frontman played a series of solo gigs before reinstating original guitarist SEAN ELLIOT and recruiting a new rhythm section in JON GEORGE and KENNY RUMBLES. In an attempt to shake off the "hippie" tag which had dogged him since the debut, COMFORT came up with the harder-hitting 'HEART'S DESIRE' single, released in late '94. This was followed by the solitary 'MISTER JONES' in summer '95, before the soaraway dream-pop of 'SAFE BOY' previewed debut album, 'DROP THE ROOF', in 1996. Described at various times as glamorous, classic and authentic, the OUT OF MY HAIR sound is short on pretension and big on melody, rarely allowing the weight of COMFORT's obvious 60's influences to pen the band into a simple retro category.

Album rating: DROP THE ROOF (*6)

COMFORT (b. SIMON EUGENE, 1970) – vocals, guitar / **SEAN ELLIOT** – guitar / **JON GEORGE** – bass / **KENNY RUMBLES** – drums

R.C.A. not iss.

Jun 94. (7"/c-s) *(74321 2031-7/-4)* **IN THE GROOVE AGAIN. / RIVER OF GOLD** [ ] [-]
(cd-s+=) *(74321 2031-2)* – Strange company.

Nov 94. (7"/c-s) *(74321 23655-7/-4)* **HEART'S DESIRE. / HOW IS A MAN** [ ] [-]
(cd-s+=) *(74321 23655-2)* – Secret sleepers (f**k off 4 track) / That's all.

Jun 95. (7"/c-s) *(74321 26781-7/-4)* **MISTER JONES. / I'D RATHER BE** [73] [-]
(cd-s+=) *(74321 26781-2)* – Comfort in my life.

Aug 95. (7"/c-s) *(74321 30361-7/-4)* **IN THE GROOVE AGAIN. /** [ ] [-]
(cd-s+=) *(74321 30361-2)* –

Mar 96. (7"/c-s) *(74321 32932-7/-4)* **SAFE BOY. / YOU SEE ME** [ ] [-]
(cd-s+=) *(74321 32932-2)* –

Apr 96. (cd/c/lp) *(74321 34837-2/-4/-1)* **DROP THE ROOF** [ ] [-]
– In the groove again / Safe boy / Wide together / Drop the roof / I'd rather be / Why it doesn't snow / Mary / Gracie's social please me's / Thieves in the fanclub / That's all / Mister Jones / Wendy / Judas flip. *(re-iss. Jun97; same)*

OUTSIDERS (see under ⇒ SOUND)

OZRIC TENTACLES

Formed: London, England . . . after meeting at Stonehenge in 1982. Brothers ED and ROLY WYNNE, together with the others, decamped to Trowbridge, Somerset, in the early 90's, having issued their second album proper (a double), 'ERPLAND', on manager JOHN BENNETT's own 'Dovetail' label. Their unashamedly retro style was developed over six low key cassette-only releases throughout the 80's and countless festival appearances. The aforementioned double album, 'ERPLAND', released in 1990, distilled the essence of their sprawling open-ended jams into an epic of ethnic-inflected trip-rock. Coming on like a younger, hipper Hawkwind, the band fitted neatly into the crusty/rave crossover scene, galvanising space cadets the length and breadth of the country. Taking the OZRIC's occasional ambient techno dabbling to its ultimate conclusion, PEPLER and HINTON formed EAT STATIC along with new recruit STEVE EVERITT. They peddled beat-friendly trance-athons that eschewed high minded techno purism for lyrics that centred on aliens, UFO's etc. After the success of the 'ABDUCTION' (1993) and 'IMPLANT' (1994) albums, PEPLAR and HINTON left OZRIC TENTACLES to make their new act a full time concern, releasing a string of well-recieved EP's. Meanwhile, the OZRIC's brushed aside a sneering music press and stormed into the top 20 with the 'JURASSIC SHIFT' album in 1993. Their grassroots following of crusties and students accounting largely for this sudden leap into the spotlight, the follow-up album, 'ABORESCENCE' (1994) also gained a respectable chart placing. After riding out a near fatal bankruptcy following a copyright run-in with Kellog's (the band had designed the 6-CD retrospective of their earlier work in the guise of a cereal packet) and a financially draining American tour, the band bounced back with the psychotropic explorations of the 'BECOME THE OTHER' (1995) album. • **Songwriters:** Group / or ED and JOIE. • **Trivia:** JOIE bet their record company that aliens!!! would land on Earth by the year 2000.

Album rating: STRANGEITUDE (*7) / JURASSIC SHIFT (*7) / ARBORESCENCE (*7)

ED WYNNE – guitar, synthesizers / **ROLY WYNNE** – bass / **JOIE 'OZROONICULATOR' HINTON** – synthesizers / **NICK 'TIG' VAN GELDER** – drums / **GAVIN GRIFFITHS** – guitar / added in 1983; **TOM BROOKES** – synthesizers / **PAUL HANKIN** – percussion

— In 1984, GRIFFITHS left to form ULLINATORS, and a year later BROOKES also left. HINTON sidelined with group ULLINATORS and OROONIES. Released cassette-only albums which I think were untitled.

— **MERV PEPLER** – drums, percussion repl. VAN GELDER

Demi-Monde not iss.

Feb 89. (lp) *(DMLP 1017)* **PUNGENT EFFULGENT** [ ] [-]
– Dissolution (the clouds disperse) / 0-1 / Phalarn dawn / The domes of G'bal / Shaping the pelm / Ayurvedic / Kick muck / Agog in the ether / Wreltch. *(re-iss. Mar91 on 'Dovetail' cd/c/lp; DOVE CD/MC/LP 2)*

Dovetail Dovetail

Nov 90. (cd)(d-lp) *(DOVE CD/MC/LP 1)* **ERPLAND** [ ] [-]
– Eternal wheel / Toltec spring / Tidal convergence / Sunscape / Mysticum Arabicola / Crackerblocks / The throbbe / Erpland / Valley of a thousand thoughts / Snakepit / Iscence / A gift of wings. *<US cd-iss. 1994 on 'Alex'; 4399>*

Jul 91. (12"/cd-s) *(DOVE EST/CD 3)* **SPLOOSH!. / LIVE THROBBE** [ ] [-]

Aug 91. (cd/c/lp) *(DOVE CD/MC/LP 3)* **STRANGEITUDE** [70] [-]
– White rhino tea / Sploosh / Saucers / Strangeitude / Bizzare bazaar / Space between your ears. *(cd+=)* – Live Throbbe. *<US cd-iss. 1993 on 'I.R.S.'; 13215>*

— **STEVE EVERETT** – synthesizers repl. BROOKES

— added **MARCUS CARCUS** – percussion / **JOHN EGAN** – flute

Jan 92. (d-cd) *(<DOVECD 4>)* **AFTERWISH** (compilation 1984-1991) [ ] [ ]
– Guzzard / Chinatype / The sacred turf / Og-ha-be / Thyroid / Omnidibectional Bhadba / Afterwish / Velmwend / Travelling the great circle / Secret names / Soda

water / Fetch me the pongmaster / Zall! / Abul Hagag / It's a hup ho world / The dusty pouch / Thrashing breath texture / Floating seeds / Invisible carpet / The code for Chickendon / Kola b'pep / Mae Hong song / Symetricum / Jabular / Sliding and gliding.

Apr 92. (cd/c/d-lp) *(DOVE CD/MC/LP 5)* **LIVE UNDERSLUNKY (live)** [ ] [-]
– Dot thots / Og-ha-be / Erpland / White rhino tea / Bizzare bazaar / Sunscrape / Erpsongs / Snake pit / Kick muck / 0-1 / Ayurvedic.

— **ZIA GEELANI** – bass repl. ROLY (late'92)

— (5-piece **ED, JOIE, JON, MERV + ZIA**)

Dovetail I.R.S.

Apr 93. (cd/c/lp) *(DOVE CD/MC/LP 6)* <X2/X4 13236> **JURASSIC SHIFT** [11] [ ] Jul93
– Sun hair / Stretchy / Feng Shui / Jurassic shift / Pteranodon / Train oasis / Vita voom.

Jul 94. (cd/c/lp) *(DOVE CD/MC/LP 7)* <29486> **ARBORESCENCE** [18] [ ]
– Astro Cortez / Yog-bar-og / Arborescence / Al-salooq / Dance of the Loomi / Myriapod / There's a planet here / Shima Koto.

— JOIE + MERV were now EAT STATIC full-time. They had splintered as said outfit since summer '92.

— line-up:- **ED WYNNE, JOHN EGAN, ZIA** + new members **SEAWEED** – keyboards / **RAD** – drums, percussion

Oct 95. (cd/c) *(DOVE CD/MC 8)* **BECOME THE OTHER** [ ] [-]
– Og-ha-be / Shards of ice / Sniffing dog / Music to gargle at / Ethereal cereal / Atmosphear / Ulluvar gate / Tentacles of Erpmiad / Trees of eternity / Mescalito / Odhanshan / Become the other / Gnuthlia / Sorry style / The Aun shuffle.

Snapper Snapper

Oct 97. (cd/c/lp) *(<SNA CD/MC/LP 502>)* **CURIOUS CORN** [ ] [ ] Dec97
– Spyroid / Oolite grove / Afroclonk / Curious corn / Oddentity / Papyrus / Meander.

– compilations, etc. –

on 'Dovetail' unless mentioned otherwise

Nov 93. (6xcd-box) *(DOVEBOX 1)* **VITAMIN ENHANCED** [ ] [-]
– (the 6 cd's below)

Feb 94. (cd) *(OTCD 1)* **ERPSONGS** [ ] [-]

Feb 94. (cd) *(OTCD 2)* **TANTRIC OBSTACLES** [ ] [-]

Feb 94. (cd) *(OTCD 3)* **LIVE ETHEREAL CEREAL** [ ] [-]

Feb 94. (cd) *(OTCD 4)* **THERE IS NOTHING** [ ] [-]

Feb 94. (cd) *(OTCD 5)* **SLIDING GLIDING WORDS** [ ] [-]

Feb 94. (cd) *(OTCD 6)* **THE BITS BETWEEN THE BITS** [ ] [-]

— were originally as cassettes between 1985 & 1989

EAT STATIC

JOIE + MERV + STEVE

C.J.P. not iss.

1991. (12"; as COSMIC JOURNEY PROJECT) *(CJP 1)* **BASS PROBE** [ ] [-]

White label not iss.

1992. (12") *(HAB 01)* **HABBI BEEP. / MONKEY MAN** [ ] [-]

Alien not iss.

1992. (12"ep) *(AR 01)* **EAT STATIC EP** [ ] [-]
– Inaana / Medicine wheel.

1992. (c) *(AR 01C)* **PREPARE YOUR SPIRIT** [ ] [-]
– Hallucinate / Fudge / Wormlips / Instinct / Eat-Static / Destroy / Raga / Almost human / Om machine / Cyper-funk / The watcher / Higher-state / Woman is life / Medicine wheel / Fourt dimension.

Nov 92. (12"ep/cd-ep) *(AR/+CD 02)* **ALMOST HUMAN / FOURTH DIMENSION. / PUPAE (THE LOCUST SONG) / MOTHER PLANET** [ ] [-]

Planet Dog Mammoth

May 93. (cd/c/d-lp) *(BARK CD/MC/LP 1)* **ABDUCTION** [62] [-]
– Prana / Gulf breeze / Kalika / Splitting world / Kinetic flow / Forgotten rites / Abduction / Intruder / Xenomorph / Inner peace. *<US cd-iss. Sep95 on 'Mammoth'; MR 118>*

Nov 93. (12"ep/cd-ep) *(BARK 2 T/CDS)* **LOST IN TIME. / GULF BREEZE (Zetan mix) / THE BRAIN** [ ] [-]

Mar 94. (12"ep/cd-ep) *(BARK 002/+CD)* **GULF BREEZE (remix). / ('A'-Ashoshashoz mix) / ('A'-Qat mix)** [ ] [-]

Jun 94. (cd/c/d-lp) *(BARK CD/MC/LP 005)* <MR 112> **IMPLANT** [13] [ ]
– Survivors / Abnormal interference / Implant / Dzhopa dream / Panspermia / Area 51 / Cydonia / Uforic undulance.

Jul 94. (etched-12") *(BARK 003T)* **SURVIVORS** [ ] [-]

Mar 95. (c-ep/12"ep/d12"ep/cd-ep) *(BARK 009 MCS/T/TS/CDS)* <MR 117> **EPSYLON EP** [ ] [ ]
– Epsylon / Dionysiac / Peeow! / Undulattice.

Dec 95. (12") <MR 116> **DIONYSIAC (mixes)** [-] [ ]

Feb 96. (cd-ep) *(BARK 016CDS)* **BONY INCUS EP** [ ] [-]
– (mixes:- original / man with no name / shape head / mucor).

Feb 97. (12"ep/cd-ep) *(BARK 024 T/CDS)* **HYBRID. / (The Infinity Project remix) / (PFM remix)** [41] [-]
(cd-ep) *(BARK 024CDX)* – ('A'-Eat Static & OTT remix) / ('A'-Yum Yum remix) / ('A'-Dave Angel remix).

Sep 97. (12"/cd-s) *(BARK 030 T/CDS)* **INTERCEPTOR** [44] [-]
(12"/cd-s) *(BARK 030 TX/CDX)* – ('A'remixes).

Oct 97. (cd/c/lp) *(BARK CD/MC/LP 029)* <MR 146> **SCIENCE OF THE GODS** [60] [ ]
– Science of the gods / Interceptor / Kryll / Spawn / Dissection / Pseudopod / Body stealers / Contact / Hangar.

Jun 98. MW (12"/cd-s) *(BARK 033 T/CD)* **CONTACT (mixes; radio / original / De Niro)** [67] [-]
(12"/cd-s) *(BARK 033 TX/CDX)* – ('A'side) / ('A'-Jon The Dentist mix) / ('A'live version).

Aug 98. (cd) *(BARKCD 034)* **B-WORLD** [ ] [-]

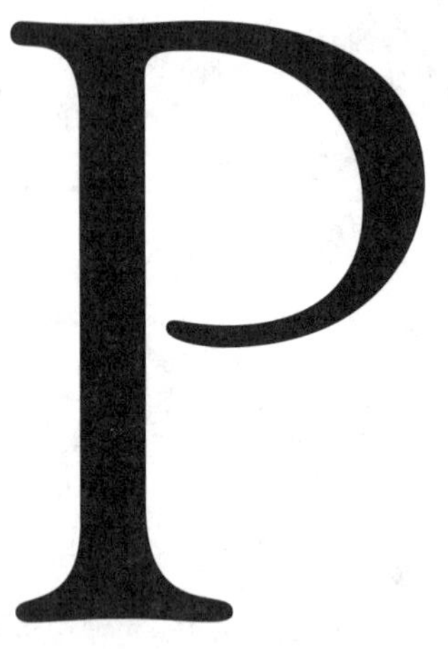

P (see under ⇒ BUTTHOLE SURFERS)

PAGANS

Formed: Cleveland, Ohio, USA . . . 1977 by MIKE HUDSON and TOMMY GUNN METOFF along with TIM ALLEE and BRIAN MORGAN. Hailing from the same American city that spawned PERE UBU, DEAD BOYS, etc, The PAGANS certainly kicked up an ungodly racket while their brutally defiant lyrics took no prisoners, thriving on alienation and offence. Despite being overlooked during punk's first wave, the greasoid garage crew were subsequently namechecked by a host of latter day hardcore/punk bands. Only four (independently-released) singles appeared during their short career span, the first three on 'Drome': 'THE STREET WHERE NOBODY LIVES', 'NOT NOW, NO WAY' and 'DEAD END AMERICA'. A final 7", 'SIX AND CHANGE', surfaced on 'Neck' records at the turn of the decade, rounding up their short sharp legacy. They re-formed for the odd gig or two throughout the 80's, sparking interest in a handful of retrospective releases for Mark Trehus' 'Treehouse' imprint. • **Covered:** HEART OF STONE (Rolling Stones) / CAN'T EXPLAIN (Who) / SEVENTH SON WIPED OUT (Willie Dixon) / BOY I CAN DANCE GOOD (. . . Carlton) / LITTLE BLACK EGG (. . . Conlon).

Album rating: BURIED ALIVE compilation (*7) / THE GODLIKE POWER OF THE PAGANS compilation (*7) / EVERYBODY HATES YOU compilation (*7)

MIKE HUDSON – vocals / **TOMMY GUNN METOFF** – guitar (ex-CHRONIC) / **TIM ALLEE** – bass / **BRIAN MORGAN** – drums

		not iss.	Drome
1978.	(7") *<DR 1>* **THE STREET WHERE NOBODY LIVES. / WHAT'S THIS SHIT CALLED LOVE?**	-	
1978.	(7") *<DR 5>* **NOT NOW, NO WAY. / I JUVENILE**	-	
1978.	(7") *<DR 7>* **DEAD END AMERICA. / LITTLE BLACK EGG**	-	
		not iss.	Neck
1979.	(7") *<1143>* **SIX AND CHANGE. / SIX AND CHANGE**	-	

—— disbanded Sep'79, METOFF went on to work with DAVE DELUCA, MORGAN with The FRENCHMEN

– compilations, etc. –

1986.	(lp) *Treehouse;* **BURIED ALIVE**	-	
Sep 87.	(lp) *Treehouse; <(TR 004)>* **THE GODLIKE POWER OF THE PAGANS**		
May 89.	(lp)(cd) *Resonance; (R33 8921)(08908-2)* **THE STREET WHERE NOBODY LIVES (live)**		-
May 95.	(cd) *Crypt; <36>* **EVERYBODY HATES YOU** – What's this shit called love / Dead end America / Eyes of Satan / The street where nobody lives / Boy I can dance good / Give up / Real world / Six and change / Haven't got the time / Little black egg / Yeah yeah / Heart of stone / Not now no way / I juvenile / Can't explain / Nowhere to run / Give till it hurts / Slow street / Cry 815 / Angela / Seventh son wiped out / Multiple personalities / When I die / Cleveland confidential (real world) / Dead end America / Wall of shame / She's a cadaver (and I gotta have her) / I stand alone / I don't understand / Her name was Jane.	-	
Apr 98.	(cd) *Sonic Swirl; (SWIRL 024)* **LIVE ROAD KILL 1978-1979 (live)**		-

PAIN TEENS

Formed: Houston, Texas, USA . . . 1988 by SCOTT AYERS, his girlfriend BLISS BLOOD, along with KIRK CARR and FRANK GARYMARTIN. Fixated on twisted sexuality and and the more unsavoury impulses of the human psyche, The PAIN TEENS were a natural choice for KING COFFEY's 'Trance Syndicate' imprint, having previously debuted in '89 with the 'CASE HISTORIES' set. First up for the label was 1990's 'BORN IN BLOOD', a sample-hungry collection of fractured but accessible noise experimentation that set the tone for the bulk of their 90's output. Memorably described as the Marquis de Sade put to music, The PAIN TEENS uneasy listening experience continued with 'STIMULATION FESTIVAL' (1992), 'DESTROY ME LOVER' (1993) and 'BEAST OF DREAMS' (1995), the latter recorded after the band had been reduced to a duo of BLISS and SCOTT; by this point their partnership was purely musical. Having already given up live work, the pair retired for an extended sabbatical.

Album rating: CASE HISTORIES (*6) / BORN IN BLOOD (*6) / STIMULATION FESTIVAL (*6) / DESTROY ME, LOVER (*7) / BEAST OF DREAMS (*6)

BLISS BLOOD – vocals, percussion / **SCOTT AYERS** – guitar, samples, drums / **KIRK CARR** – bass / **FRANK GARYMARTIN** – drums

		not iss.	Anomie
1988.	(12"ep) **PAIN TEENS** – Inside me / Unameable / Brown Jenkin / Knife / Shoemaker / Amidst the rubble / World of destruction / Valley of the sun / Symptoms / Where madness dwells / Continuing nightmare / Count Magnus / Tapes / Innsmouth / Freezing wind / The somnambulist. *<cd-iss. Apr98 on 'Charnel'; 32>*	-	
1989.	(lp) *<3>* **CASE HISTORIES**	-	
		Trance Syndicate	Trance Syndicate
Nov 90.	(lp/c/cd) *<(TR 03/+CS/CD)>* **BORN IN BLOOD** – The basement / Pleasures of the flesh / Shotguns / Bad in my head / The way love used to be / Secret is sickness / Lady of flame / Desu evol yaw / She shook me / Christo / My desire / Noh jam.		
Jun 92.	(lp/cd) *<(TR 10/+CD)>* **STIMULATION FESTIVAL** – Shallow hole / The dead cannot / God told me / Poured out blood / Drowning / Living hell / Indiscreet jewels / Wild world / Daughter of chaos / Evil dirt / Bruised / Dog spirits / Hangman's rope / Apartment #213.		
Jul 93.	(lp/cd) *<(TR 17/+CD)>* **DESTROY ME, LOVER** – Cool your power / Prowling / Tar pit / Ru 486 / Dominant man / Sexual anorexia / Lisa knew / Body memory / Story of Isaac / Shock treatment.		

—— now pared down to the couple **BLISS + SCOTT**

Nov 95.	(lp/cd) *<(TR 41/+CD)>* **BEAST OF DREAMS** – Swimming / Manouche / Coral kiss / Accusing eyes / Swamp / Embers and ashes / Voluptus / Moonray / Frigid idol / Skids / Sweet sickness / Invitation.		Oct95

—— split up the following year

PALE FOUNTAINS

Formed: Liverpool, England . . . 1981 by MICK HEAD, his brother JOHN HEAD and CHRIS McCAFFREY, the three almost immediately recruiting THOMAS 'JOCK' WHELAN and ANDY DIAGRAM (the latter from DISLOCATION DANCE and The DIAGRAM BROS). Their debut single, '(THERE'S ALWAYS) SOMETHING ON MY MIND', set the scene for their melancholy, melodic, 60's-inspired alt-pop, like a cross between The BEATLES and LOVE. 'Virgin' were quick off the mark to sign them, their contract off to a promising start when follow-up single, 'THANK YOU', hit the Top 50 late in '82. However, sales of subsequent 45's and debut album, 'PACIFIC STREET' (1984), didn't quite meet expectations, its brassy tropical feel (with colourful image to match) a touch exotic for the average indie fan. A second album, the IAN BROUDIE-produced ' . . .FROM ACROSS THE KITCHEN TABLE', emerged early the following year, the pleasant but hardly inspiring 'JEAN'S NOT HAPPENING' summing up PALE FOUNTAINS appeal. With their chart potential having almost completely dried up, The PALE FOUNTAINS split as the brothers HEAD re-emerged as SHACK. Along with new boys, DAVE BUTCHER, JUSTIN SMITH and MICHAEL CURTIS, they were the first act to sign for the 'Ghetto Recording Company', the first fruits of their efforts being the 1988 set, 'ZILCH'. Displaying an even stronger BEATLES influence, the album was a sterling slab of subtle, intelligent indie-pop. However, it took all of two years for the band to return, the single 'I KNOW YOU WELL' calling to mind The BEATLES' 'Taxman' with its knotty stop-start rhythms. A solitary single, 'AL'S VACATION', arrived in Spring '91 and although an album was completed, a studio fire destroyed what was thought to be the only existing master tape. Fortunately, producer Chris Allison unearthed a DAT master, although he subsequently lost it again after leaving it in a hired car. Incredibly, the fabled tape later turned up in Germany (!), the belated album finally issued in '95 as 'WATERPISTOL' by 'Marina' records. MICHAEL HEAD was back in a solo capacity in 1998, members of SHACK backing him up on his inaugural release, 'THE MAGICAL WORLD OF THE STRANDS'.

Album rating: PACIFIC STREET (*6) / . . .FROM ACROSS THE KITCHEN TABLE (*4) / Shack: ZILCH (*7) / WATERPISTOL (*6) / Michael Head: THE MAGICAL WORLD OF THE STRANDS (*6)

MICK HEAD (b.28 Nov'61) – vocals, guitar / **JOHN HEAD** (b. 4 Oct'65) – lead guitar / **CHRIS McCAFFREY** – bass / **ANDY DIAGRAM** – trumpet (ex-DISLOCATION DANCE, ex-DIAGRAM BROS) / **THOMAS 'JOCK' WHELAN** – drums, percussion / + 6th member **M. BARRADAS** – oil drums, percussion

		Operation Twilight	not iss.
Jul 82.	(7") *(OPT 09)* **(THERE'S ALWAYS) SOMETHING ON MY MIND. / JUST A GIRL**		-
		Virgin	not iss.
Oct 82.	(7") *(VS 557)* **THANK YOU. / MEADOW OF LOVE**	48	-
May 83.	(7"/12") *(VS 568/+12)* **PALM OF MY HAND. / LOVE'S A BEAUTIFUL PLACE**		-
Jan 84.	(7"/12") *(VS 614/+12)* **UNLESS. / NATURAL**		-

Feb 84. (lp/c) *(V/TCV 2274)* **PACIFIC STREET** ☐ [-]
– Reach / Something on my mind / Unless / Southbound excursion / Natural / Faithful pillow (part 1) / (Don't let your love) Start a war / Beyond Friday's field / Abergele next time / Crazier / Faithful pillow (part 2). *(re-iss. Aug87 lp/c; OVED/+C 143) (cd-iss. Nov89; CDV 2274)*

Mar 84. (7"/12") *(VS 668/+12)* **(DON'T LET YOUR LOVE) START A WAR. / LOVE SITUATION** ☐ [-]

— now without BARRADAS

Jan 85. (7"/12") *(VS 735/+12)* **JEAN'S NOT HAPPENING. / BICYCLE THIEVES** ☐ [-]

Feb 85. (lp/c) *(V/TCV 2333)* **. . .FROM ACROSS THE KITCHEN TABLE** ☐ [-]
– Shelter / Stole the love / Jean's not happening / Bicycle thieves / Limit / 27 ways to get back home / Bruised arcade / These are the things / It's only hard / . . .From across the kitchen table / Hey / September sting. *(re-iss. Apr86 lp/c; OVED/+C 164) (cd-iss. Jul89; CDV 2333)*

Jun 85. (7") *(VS 750)* **. . .FROM ACROSS THE KITCHEN TABLE. / BICYCLE THIEVES** ☐ [-]
(12"+=) *(VS 750-12)* – Thank you.
(d7"++=) *(VS 750)* – Just a girl.

— disbanded when DIAGRAM returned to DISLOCATION DANCE (sadly, McCAFFREY was to die in August '89)

SHACK

— **MICK HEAD + JOHN HEAD** with **DAVE BUTCHER** – keyboards / **JUSTIN SMITH** – bass / **MICHAEL KURTIS** – drums

Ghetto | not iss.

Mar 88. (7") *(GTG 1)* **EMERGENCY. / LIBERATION** ☐ [-]
(12"+=) *(GTGT 1)* – Faith.
(cd-s+=) *(CDGTG 1)* – What's it like.

Mar 88. (lp/c/cd) *(GHETT/+C/D 1)* **ZILCH** ☐ [-]
– Emergency / Someone's knocking / John Kline / Realization / I need you / High rise, low life / Who killed Clayton Square? / Who'd believe it? / What's it like . . . / The believers.

Jun 88. (7") *(GTG 2)* **HIGH RISE LOW LIFE. / WHO KILLED CLAYTON SQUARE?** ☐ [-]
(12"+=/cd-s+=) *(GTGT/CDGTG 2)* – ('A'-Bert Hardy mix).

Jul 90. (7") *(GTG 11)* **I KNOW YOU WELL. / FEEL NO WAY** ☐ [-]
(ext.12") *(GTG 11T)* – ('A'-If you want it mix).
(cd-s++=) *(CDGTG 11)* – ('A'extended).

Apr 91. (7") **AL'S VACATION. /** ☐ [-]
(12"+=/cd-s+=) –

— an album was recorded but destroyed after a studio fire (see above).

Marina | not iss.

Nov 95. (cd) *(MA 16)* **WATERPISTOL** ☐ [-]
– Sgt. Major / Neighbours / Stranger / Dragonfly / Mood of the morning / Walter's song / Time machine / Mr. Appointment / Undecided / Hazy / Hey mama / London town. *(re-iss. Feb98; same)*

MICHAEL HEAD

— with other members of SHACK as backing

Megaphone | not iss.

Feb 98. (cd/lp) *(CD/LP MEGA 01)* **THE MAGICAL WORLD OF THE STRANDS** ☐ [-]
– Queen Matilda / Something like you / And luna / X hits the spot / The prize / Undecided (reprise) / Glynys and Jaqui / It's harvest time / Loaded man / Hocken's hey / Fontilan.

Apr 98. (7") *(7MEGA 02)* **SOMETHING LIKE YOU. /** ☐ [-]
(cd-s+=) *(CDMEGA 02)* –
(re-iss. Oct98; same)

PALE SAINTS

Formed: Leeds, England . . . 1987 by IAN MASTERS, GRAEME NAYSMITH and CHRIS COOPER with occasional help from ASHLEY HORNER. Clocked by indie stalwart, '4 a.d.' at their debut London gig, this proto-shoegazing outfit were signed up at the same time as more successful peers LUSH, the two bands sharing a fondness for combining intense, abstract guitar textures and distortion with pop melodies in the mould of The CHAMELEONS or The BOO RADLEYS. Following a debut EP, 'BARGING INTO THE PRESENCE OF GOD', the band scraped a Top 40 placing for their debut album, 'THE COMFORT OF MADNESS' (1990). Initial acclaim gave way to rather harsh and unecessary criticism in some quarters; while MASTERS' vocals could've done with a bit of a charisma boost, there was no denying the potential of their ideas and talent. With HORNER subsequently working full-time on his EDSEL AUCTIONEER project, female vocalist/guitarist MERIEL BARHAM added a new dimension to the band's sound and acted as a counterpoint to MASTERS. A second EP, 'HALF-LIFE', and a Top 75 cover of Nancy Sinatra's 'KINKY LOVE' preceded a follow-up album, 'IN RIBBONS' (1992). Highlights included the arpeggio atmospherics of 'HAIR SHOES' and the BARHAM-sung 'NEVERENDING NIGHT' yet by now all the shoegazing bands had been declared easy meat for a circling press and The PALE SAINTS were buried under the weight of the vicious backlash alongside SLOWDIVE, CHAPTERHOUSE etc. Even MASTERS had departed by the release of 'SLOW BUILDINGS' (1993), COLLEEN BROWNE sharing vocal duties with BARHAM, the latter having taken over songwriting duties. • **Songwriters:** Group penned except; REFLECTIONS FROM A WATERY WORLD (Slapp Happy) / FELL FROM THE SUN (Opal). • **Trivia:** PALE SAINTS issued a Japanese-only album in 1991 'MRS.DOLPHIN'. MERIEL guested on The BOO RADLEYS' 1993 album, 'Giant Steps'.

Album rating: THE COMFORT OF MADNESS (*8) / IN RIBBONS (*9)

IAN MASTERS (b.4 Jan'64, Potters Bar, Hertfordshire, England) – vocals, bass / **GRAEME NAYSMITH** (b. 9 Feb'67, Edinburgh, Scotland) – guitar / **CHRIS COOPER** (b.17 Nov'66, Portsmouth, England) – drums

4 a.d. | 4 a.d.-Warners

Sep 89. (12"ep/cd-ep) *(BAD 910/+CD)* **BARGING INTO THE PRESENCE OF GOD** ☐ [-]
– Sight of you / She rides the waves / Mother might.

— added **ASHLEY HORNER** – guitar

Feb 90. (lp/c/cd) *(CAD 0002/+C/CD) <7564>* **THE COMFORT OF MADNESS** [40] ☐
– True coming dream / Little hammer / You tear the world in two / The sea of sound / Way the world is / A deep sleep for Steven / Fell from the Sun / Time thief / Insubstantial / Language of flowers / Sight of you.

— **MERIEL BARHAM** (b.15 Oct'64, Germany) – guitar, vocals repl. HORNER who concentrated on own group EDSEL AUCTIONEER, whom he spent the last 2 years with

Oct 90. (12"ep/cd-ep) *(BAD 015/+CD)* **HALF-LIFE** ☐ [-]
– Half-life remembered / Baby maker / Two sick sisters / A revelation.

Jun 91. (7") *(AD 1009)* **KINKY LOVE. / HAIR SHOES** [72] [-]
(12"cp+–/cd-ep+=) **FLESH BALLOON EP** *(CAD 1009/+CD)* – Hunted / Porpoise.

Mar 92. (lp/c/cd) *(CAD 2004/+C/CD) <26913>* **IN RIBBONS** [61] ☐ Apr92
– Throwing back the apple / Ordeal / Thread of light / Shell / There is no day / Hunted / Hair shoes / Babymaker / Liquid / Neverending night / Featherframe / A thousand stars bust open. *(free 12"w/lp as "The TINWISTLE BRASS BAND") (RIB 1)* **A THOUSAND STARS BUST OPEN. / A REVELATION**

May 92. (12"ep/cd-ep) **THROWING BACK THE APPLE** ☐ [-]
– Throwing back the apple / Blue flower / Half-life remembered / Reflections from a watery world.

— **COLLEEN BROWNE** – bass, vocals (ex-PARACHUTE MEN) repl. MASTERS who formed The LOST SOUL BAND (album in May93; FRIDAY THE 13th / singles Jul93; OH YOUR EYES / Sep93; YOU CAN'T WIN 'EM / album Nov93; LAND OF DO AS YOU PLEASE / all on 'Silvertone')

Aug 94. (12"/cd-s) **FINE FRIEND. / SPECIAL PRESENT / MARIMBA / SURPRISE** ☐ [-]

Sep 94. (lp/c/cd) *(CAD 4014/+C/CD) <45625>* **SLOW BUILDINGS** ☐ ☐
– King Fade / Angel (will you be my) / One blue hill / Henry / Under your nose / Little gesture / Song of Solomon / Fine friend / Gesture of a fear / Always I / Suggestion.

— disbanded later in the year

PANDORAS

Formed: Los Angeles, California, USA . . . 1983 by PAULA PIERCE and her all-girl crew of BAMBI CONWAY, GWYNNE KELLY and CASEY. Using sex as a musical weapon, the bunch of likely lassies made their debut with an eponymous EP in '84. Over the course of the next five years, The PANDORAS released a clutch of spunky garage-pop albums, the last of which, 'NYMPHOMANIA' (1989), sacrificed their girly charm for a shambolic sub-metal noise. Later members KIM SHATTUCK and MELANIE VAMMEN re-emerged with The MUFFS, diving into a major deal with 'Elektra' and releasing an eponymous debut album in 1993. Appropriately enough, The MUFFS were compared to the tortured grunge of HOLE, especially with regards to their second set, 'BLONDER AND BLONDER' (1995).

Album rating: IT'S ABOUT TIME (*6) / STOP PRETENDING (*5) / LIVE NYMPHOMANIA (*1) / Muffs: THE MUFFS (*5) / BLONDER AND BLONDER (*6)

PAULA PIERCE – vocals, guitar / **GWYNNE KELLY** – organ, vocals / **BAMBI CONWAY** – bass, vocals / **CASEY** – drums

not iss. | Moxie

Apr 84. (12"ep) **THE PANDORAS** [-] ☐

Closer | Voxx

1984. (lp) *(CL 0017) <20002-1>* **IT'S ABOUT TIME** [-] ☐ French
– I want him / James / He's not far / I'm here I'm gone / That's your way out / High on a cloud / It's about time / The hook / I live my life / Want, need love / It just ain't true / Why / You lie / Going is away. *<re-iss. Aug88; same> (cd-iss. Jan94; VOXXCD 2021)*

not iss. | Rhino

May 86. (lp) *<RNLP 70857>* **STOP PRETENDING** [-] ☐

— **PAUL** recruited **RITA DALBERT** – rhythm guitar, vocals / **PAULA PIERCE** – rhythm guitar, vocals / **KIM SHATTUCK** – bass, vocals / **MELANIE VAMMEN** – keyboards, vocals

G.W.R. | Restless

Feb 89. (m-lp/m-c/m-cd) *(GWLP 38) <72292-1/-4/-2>* **ROCK HARD** ☐ ☐
– Run down love battery / Tryin' ain't good enough / Six times a day / He's coming / Craving / Close behind.

Jan 90. (cd) *<23362>* **NYMPHOMANIA (live)** [-] ☐
– Pacify me / Burned / Craving / Liar / Put the brakes on your heart / He's coming / Six times a day / Bad habit / Run down love battery.

— split up after above; **SUSAN HYATT** had been a later member and she subsequently joined PILLBOX

MUFFS

— formed by **KIM + MELANIE** with **RONNIE BARNETT** – bass / **CRISS CRASS** – drums

— released two 45's for 'Sub Pop' + 'Sympathy For The Record . . .'

Elektra | Elektra

Aug 93. (cd/c) *<(9362 45251-2/-4)>* **THE MUFFS** ☐ ☐
– Lucky guy / Saying goodbye / Everywhere I go / Better than me / From your girl / Not like me / Baby go round / North Pole / Big mouth / Every single thing / Don't waste another day / Stupid jerk / Another day / Eye to eye / I need you / All for nothing.

— now a trio when CRISS departed

— **ROY McDONALD** – drummer (ex-REDD KROSS) repl. VAMMEN who joined LEAVING TRAINS

Apr 95. (cd/c/lp) <(9362 45852-2/-4/-1)> **BLONDER AND BLONDER**
– Agony / Oh Nina / On and on / Sad tomorrow / What you've done / Red eyed troll / End it all / Laying on a bed of roses / I need a face / Won't come out to play / Funny face / Ethyl my love / I'm confused / Just a game.

Jul 95. (7"/c-s/cd-s) *(W 0298 X/C/CD)* **SAD TOMORROW. / GOODNIGHT NOW**

May 97. (cd/c) <46523> **HAPPY BIRTHDAY TO ME** [-]
– Crush me / That awful man / Honeymoon / All blue baby / My crazy afternoon / Is it all okey? / Pennywhore / Outer space / I'm a dick / Nothing / Where only I could go / Upside down / You and your parrot / Keep holding me / Best time around.

PANSY DIVISION

Formed: San Francisco, California, USA . . . 1991, when openly gay frontman, JON GINOLI, placed an ad in a newspaper looking for queer musicians into The Beatles, Buzzcocks and Ramones. He picked three like minded homosexuals, CHRIS FREEMAN, SALLY SCHLOSSTEIN and finally PATRICK GOODWIN, the self-professed "faggot quartet" getting around to releasing their debut album, 'UNDRESSED', in 1993. A couple more basic (s)punk rock sets appeared in the mid '90's before they slapped it on the table with a tongue-in-bum-cheek variation of an AC/DC number, 'FOR THOSE WHO SUCK COCK . . . WE SALUTE YOU'. The EP poked fun at two other covers of Judas Priest's 'BREAKING THE LAW' and Kiss's 'SWEET PAIN', while KIRK HAMMETT (don't tell anyone!) made a guest spot on 'HEADBANGER'.

Recommended: full protection (on the eardrums, that is!?)

JON GINOLI – vocals / **PATRICK GOODWIN** – guitar / **CHRIS FREEMAN** – bass / **SALLY SCHLOSSTEIN** – drums

Outpunk Outpunk

Jul 93. (7") <(OUT 006)> **BILL AND TED'S HOMO ADVENTURE. / BIG BOTTOM**

K not iss.

Oct 94. (7") *(IPU 52)* **JACKSON. / I REALLY WANTED YOU** [-]

Lookout Lookout

Oct 94. (cd) <(LOOKOUT 70CD)> **UNDRESSED** 1993
– Versatile / Fem in a black leather jacket / Bunnies / Boyfriend wanted / Story so far / Hippy dude / Curvature / Cocksucker club / Crabby day / Luck of the draw / Rock and roll queer bar / Surrender your clothing / Anthem.

Oct 94. (cd) <(LOOKOUT 87CD)> **DEFLOWERED**
– Reciprocate / Groovy underwear / Anonymous / Fluffy city / James bondage / Negative queen / Denny / Rachbottomoff / Beercan boy / Kissed / Song of remembrance for old queers / Deep water / Not enough of you to go around / New pleasures / Homosapien.

— rhythm section now **CHRIS BOWE + DAVID AYER**

Mar 95. (cd) *(DAMGOOD 60CD)* <LOOKOUT 110CD> **PILE UP** Feb95
– I can't sleep / Ring of joy / Fuck Buddy / Cowboys are frequently secretly fond . . . / Flower / Cry for shadow / Real men / Bill & Ted's homosexual adventure / Jack U off / Strip U down / Jackson / Big bottom / Touch my Joe camel / Biggest lie / Denny (naked) / Femme fatale / Trash / Homo Christmas / C.S.F. / Smells like queer spirit. (above issued on 'Damaged Goods' UK)

— now with drummer **DUSTIN DONALDSON**

Feb 96. (lp/cd) <(LOOKOUT 133/+CD)> **WISH I'D TAKEN PICTURES**
– Horny in the morning / Vanilla / I really wanted you / Dick of death / Expiration date / The summer you let your hair grow out / Wish I'd taken pictures / Pillow talk / This is your life / Don't be so sure / Kevin / Ache / Pee shy / Side walk sale.

Aug 96. (7"ep) *(LOOKOUT 147)* **FOR THOSE ABOUT TO SUCK COCK, WE SALUTE YOU EP** [-]
– For those about to suck cock, we salute you / Headbanger / Breaking the law / Sweet pain.

Apr 97. (7"ep) *(LOOKOUT 174)* **QUEER TO THE CORE EP**

Sep 98. (cd) <(LK 198CD)> **ABSURD POP SONG ROMANCE**
– – / February 17 / Sweet insecurity / It'll never be the same / Better off just friends / Too beautiful / – / Luv luv luv / – / Best revenge / Bad boyfriend / – / You're gonna need your friends / Tinted windows / – / Glenview / Used to turn me on / Obstacle course / Vicious beauty.

PANTHER BURNS (see under ⇒ FALCO, Tav)

PAPAS FRITAS

Formed: Somerville, Massachusetts, USA . . . 1993 by main songwriter TONY GODDESS, alongside girlfriend at-the-time, SHIVIKA ASTHANA and Houston-born KEITH GENDEL, who all met at Tufts University. Exploring paths once trod by The BEATLES, The BEACH BOYS and PHIL SPECTOR, they created a low-fi sonic sound which led to Chicago's 'Minty Fresh' label giving them a try-out. A couple of singles, namely 'PASSION PLAY' and 'WILD LIFE', previewed late 1995's critically acclaimed eponymous debut album, a record upon which the band's classic pop instincts came to the fore. A second set, 'HELIOSELF', surfaced a few years later, refining their sound and consolidating their wide ranging appeal.

Album rating: PAPAS FRITAS (*6) / HELIOSELF (*6)

TONY GODDESS – vocals, guitar, piano / **KEITH GENDEL** – bass, vocals / **SHIVIKA ASTHANA** – drums, vocals

not iss. Sunday Driver

1994. (7") **FRIDAY NIGHT. /** [-]

Minty Fresh Minty Fresh

May 95. (7") <(MF 10)> **PASSION PLAY. /**

Aug 95. (cd-ep) <(MF 13)> **PASSION PLAY EP** Apr96
– Passion play / Means / Howl / Radio days.

Nov 95. (cd-s) <(MFP 1)> **WILD LIFE / AFTER ALL**

Jan 96. (cd) <(MF 14)> **PAPAS FRITAS** Nov95
– Guys don't lie / Holiday / Wild life / Passion play / TV movies / My revolution / Kids don't mind / Smash this world / Lame to be / Possibilities / My own girlfriend / Explain / Afterall.

Apr 97. (cd) <(MF 22)> **HELIOSELF**
– Hey hey what you say / We've got all night / Say goodbye / Small rooms / Rolling in the sand / Live by the water / Words to sing / Sing about me / Just to see you / Captain of the city / Weight / Starting to be it.

Jun 97. (cd-ep) <(MF 21-3)> **HEY HEY YOU SAY / HOLIDAY / WORDS TO SING (demo) / WE'VE GOT ALL NIGHT (live)**

PARACHUTE MEN

Formed: Leeds, England . . .1985 by FIONA GREGG, STEPHEN H. GREGG, ANDREW HOWES and MARK BOYCE. Another better than average indie-guitar act to sign for 'Fire' (home of BLUE AEROPLANES, etc), The PARACHUTE MEN (and woman!) made their album debut in 1988 with 'THE INNOCENTS', an enjoyably sculpted slice of melodic alt-pop. However, all was not well in the ranks, the GREGG's trimmed to a duo until the arrival of newcomers MATTHEW PARKIN and PAUL WALKER. This line-up was responsible for the second and final set, 'EARTH, DOGS AND EGGSHELLS' (1990), although the PARACHUTE MEN will always be remembered for a classy John Peel-playlisted single, 'LEEDS STATION'.

Album rating: THE INNOCENTS (*6) / EARTH, DOGS AND EGGSHELLS (*6)

FIONA GREGG (b.26 Jul'63, Norwich, England) – vocals / **STEPHEN H. GREGG** (b.29 Nov'60, Bishop Auckland, England) – guitar / **ANDREW HOWES** – bass / **MARK BOYCE** – drums

Fire not iss.

May 88. (12"m) *(BLAZE 27T)* **SOMETIMES IN VAIN. / LEEDS STATION / HEADING THE WRONG WAY (J AT 41)** [-]

Aug 88. (lp/cd) *(FIRE LP/CD 14)* **THE INNOCENTS** [-]
– *(cd+=)* – Sometimes in vain / Leeds station / Heading the wrong way (J at 41). *(re-iss. Oct91 cd/lp; 33/11 014)*

— they became an acoustic duo until a little later in 1990

— **MATTHEW PARKIN** – bass; repl. HOWES

— **PAUL WALKER** (b. 7 Jul'66) – drums; repl. BOYCE

Oct 88. (7") *(BLAZE 30S)* **IF I COULD WEAR YOUR JACKET. / BURGESS MEREDITH** [-]
(12"+=) *(BLAZE 30T)* – That's too bad.

May 89. (7") *(BLAZE 33S)* **LEEDS STATION. / MAYBE IF I SAID** [-]
(12"+=/3"cd-s+=) *(BLAZE 33T)* – So mistaken.

Oct 89. (7") *(BLAZE 35S)* **BED AND BREAKFAST. / ?** [-]
(12"+=) *(BLAZE 35T)* –

Apr 90. (7") *(BLAZE 40S)* **EVERY OTHER THURSDAY. / ?** [-]
(12"+=) *(BLAZE 40T)* –

May 90. (cd/c/lp) *(FIRE CD/MC/LP 24)* **EARTH, DOGS AND EGGSHELLS** [-]
– Mad Sadie can't levitate / Mr. Gas / Never alone / Don't cry July / Miles away / Elizabeth / Earth, dogs and eggshells / Every other Thursday / . . .Yeah / Sleepless, sleepless, sleepless / Dream of kings / Fear of falling. *(re-iss. Oct91 cd/c/lp; 33/22/11 024)*

— **COLLEEN BROWNE** (b.25 Aug'66, Kelowna, Canada) – bass; repl. MATTHEW

— split after above

PARADISE MOTEL

Formed: Hobart, Tasmania . . . 1994 by main songwriter, CHARLES BICKFORD, plus MATTHEW AULICH, BJ AUSTIN, MATTHEW BAILEY and TIM O'SHANNESSY. To gain the attention a band needs to get on in the big wide world, they jumped ship to Melbourne, Australia, finding the beautifully bleak vocal talents of librarian turned professional singer, MERIDA SUSSEX. Like a fusion of the COCTEAU TWINS, MY BLOODY VALENTINE and the PIXIES, The PARADISE MOTEL recorded their debut album, 'LEFT OVER LIFE TO KILL' (1998), in a council squat CHARLES had been occupying at the time. Its subject matter was as uncomfortable and repressed as an emotionally sad life should be, although it seemed to possess a strange eerie tenderness not unlike that of other down under faves, DEAD CAN DANCE.

Album rating: LEFT OVER LIFE TO KILL (*6)

CHARLES BICKFORD – guitar, vocals / **MERIDA SUSSEX** – vocals / **MATTHEW AULICH** – guitar / **BJ AUSTIN** – Hammond organ / **MATTHEW BAILEY** – bass / **TIM O'SHANNESSY** – drums

Infectious not iss.

Feb 98. (7"ep/cd-ep) *(infect 46 s/cds)* **CALLING YOU / F HEART. / JACKSTAR / J STAR** [-]

Mar 98. (cd) *(infect 47cd)* **LEFT OVER LIFE TO KILL** [-]
– Calling you / Dead skin / Men who loved her / Watch illuminum / Skip bins / Desperate plan / Bad light / German girl / Ashes / Stones.

Apr 98. (7"ep/cd-ep) *(infect 53 s/cds)* **WATCH ILLUMINUM / THIN ARMS. / GLITTER / CIRCLES** [-]

Sep 98. (7") *(infect 68s)* **HOLLYWOOD LANDMINES. / FIND NINETEENS** [-]
(cd-s) *(infect 68cds)* – ('A'side) / Candeline Brazil / Foxholes.

PARIS ANGELS

Formed: Manchester/Liverpool, England ... 1989 by SCOTT CAREY, RIKKI TURNER, PAUL WAGSTAFF, SIMON WORRALL, who were subsequently joined by JAYNE GILL, MARK ADGE and computer wizard STEVEN TATJY BLAKE. Debuting with a self-financed cover of David Bowie's 'STAY', the band were picked up by independent label, 'Sheer Joy' and scooped an NME Single Of The Week award with follow-up track, 'PERFUME'. A further two tracks, 'SCOPE' and 'OH YES', garnered similar critical plaudits yet like so many bands of the era, PARIS ANGELS' marriage of indie guitars and dance dynamics was both a blessing and a curse, the "buzz" only lasting until the press decided the scene wasn't no longer trendy. A thing which largely coincided with the major labels getting in on the act, 'Virgin' picking up The PARIS ANGELS only to see their investment fail to meet expectations as a minor charting debut album, 'SUNDEW' (1991) fell victim to a combination of the baggy backlash and the band's own hype.

Album rating: SUNDEW (*5)

RIKKI TURNER – vocals, wind / **JAYNE GILL** – vocals, percussion / **PAUL WAGSTAFF** – guitar / **SCOTT CAREY** – bass, harmonica / **MARK ADGE** – rhythm guitar, percussion / **SIMON WORRALL** – drums / **STEVEN TATJY BLAKE** – programming, effects

own label | not iss.

Feb 90. (7") **STAY. /** [ ] [-]

Sheer Joy | not iss.

Jun 90. (7") *(SHEER 002)* **PERFUME. / MUFFIN 2** [ ] [-]
(12"+=) *(SHEER 002T)* – All on you (perfume).
(cd-s) *(SHEER 002CD)* –

Oct 90. (7") *(SHEER 004-7)* **SCOPE. /** [75] [-]
(12"/cd-s) *(SHEER 004 T/CD)* –

Apr 91. (7") *(SHEER)* **OH YES. /** [ ] [-]
(12"+=/cd-s+=) *(SHEER)* –

Virgin | not iss.

Jul 91. (7"/c-s) *(VS/+C 1360)* **PERFUME (loved up). / PURE** [55] [-]
(12") *(VS12 1360)* – ('A'-All do you mix) / ('B'-summer version).
(cd-s) *(VSCD 1360)* – ('A'version).

Aug 91. (cd/c/lp) *(CD/T+/V 2667)* **SUNDEW** [37] [-]
– Eternity / Fade / Smile / Slippery man / What goes on / Perfume (all on you) / Perfume (loved up) / Louise / Breathless / Chaos (stupid stupid) / Purest values / Oh yes.

Sep 91. (7"/c-s) *(VS/+C 1365)* **FADE. / FENCE** [70] [-]
(cd-s) *(VSCD 1365)* – ('A'-Tag mix) / ('A'-Polo mix).

—— split late 1991

John PARISH & POLLY JEAN HARVEY (see under ⇒ HARVEY, PJ)

Andy PARTRIDGE (see under ⇒ XTC)

PASSAGE

Formed: Manchester, England ... 1978 by multi-instrumentalist, DICK WITTS who recruited LORRAINE HILTON and ex-FALL bassist TONY FRIEL. WITTS' eccentricity was extended to both the musical and lyrical vision of his band, as heard on their first two EP's, 'NEW LOVE SONGS' and 'ABOUT TIME', in the late 70's. Their debut album, 'PINDROP', was issued late in 1980, although many were put off by WITTS' self-indulgent and often directionless musical experimentation and cryptic narratives. He was left in the dark following the departure of his bandmates, although their was light at the end of the tunnel when ANDREW WILSON, JOEY McKECHNIE and TERESA SHAW entered the fray. Another, slightly improved effort, 'FOR ALL AND NONE', hit the shops in summer '81, 'Cherry Red' subsequently signed The PASSAGE after they'd trimmed down to a duo of WITTS and WILSON. The third album, 'DEGENERATES', appeared a year later, its way-out, schizophrenic avant-indie occasionally reminiscent of a bizarre rock musical in which the campy WITTS played the lead role. One further set, 'ENFLAME' (1983), rounded off the 'Cherry Red' era and surprisingly the band signed to 'Arista'. Their major label tenure was short-lived however, only a solitary revamped version of 'SHARP TONGUE' being released before The PASSAGE finally reached a dead end. WITTS had already made his mark on television by presenting the music programme, The Oxford Road Show.

Album rating: PINDROP (*4) / FOR ALL AND NONE (*5) / DEGENERATES (*5) / ENFLAME (*5) / THROUGH THE PASSAGE compilation (*6)

DICK WITTS – vocals, drums, cello / **LORRAINE HILTON** – keyboards / **TONY FRIEL** – bass, guitar (ex-FALL)

Object | not iss.

Dec 78. (7"ep) *(OM 02)* **NEW LOVE SONGS** [ ] [-]
– Love song / Competition / Slit machine / New kind of love.

Oct 79. (7"ep) *(OM 08)* **ABOUT TIME** [ ] [-]
– Taking my time / Clock paradox / Sixteen hours / Time.

Nov 80. (lp) *(OBJ 11)* **PINDROP** [ ] [-]
– PIN: Fear / Troops out / Carnal / Watching you dance / Hunt / Anderton's hall / From the heart / DROP: Locust / 2711 / 16 hours / Carmen / A certain way to go / Prelude.

—— added **IZZY JOHNSON** –

Night & Day | not iss.

Feb 81. (7") *(AM:PM 24.00)* **DEVILS AND ANGELS. / WATCHING YOU DANCE** [ ] [-]

—— **JOEY McKECHNIE** – drums (ex-MODERN EON); repl. HILTON

—— **ANDREW WILSON** – guitar + **TERESA SHAW** – vocals; repl. FRIEL (to CONTACT)

May 81. (7") *(AM:PM 22.00)* **TROOPS OUT. / HIP REBELS** [ ] [-]

Jun 81. (lp) *(PM:AM 23.00)* **FOR ALL AND NONE** [ ] [-]
– Dark times / Lon Don / The shadows / Do the Bastinado / One to one / A good and useful life begun / A good and useful life revisited / Flag night / Shave your head / Tangled / Photo romance / The great refusal.

—— now a duo of **WITTS + WILSON**

Cherry Red | not iss.

Nov 81. (12") *(12CHERRY 30)* **TABOOS. / TABOO DUB** [ ] [-]

—— added **PAUL MAHONEY** – drums

May 82. (7") *(CHERRY 35)* **XOYO. / ANIMAL IN ME** [ ] [-]
(12"+=) *(12CHERRY 35)* – Born every minute.

Jun 82. (lp) *(BRED 29)* **DEGENERATES** [ ] [-]
– Revelation / Love is as / Flock / Time will tell / Ourselves / Xoyo / Go to seed / Armour / Empty words.

Oct 82. (7") *(CHERRY 50)* **WAVE. / ANGLELAND** [ ] [-]
(12"=) *(12CHERRY 50)* – Drugface.

—— **JOEY McKECHNIE** – drums; returned to repl. PAUL

Mar 83. (lp/c) *(BRED/CBRED 45)* **ENFLAME** [ ] [-]
– Sharp tongue / The half of it: Twats / Clear as crystal / Drugface / Man of war / Dogstar – ?th day / Horseplay / Sunburn / The half of it: Sissies / BRD USA GDR JFK.

Mar 83. (7") **SHARP TONGUE. / BRD USA GDR JFK** [ ] [-]

Nov 83. (lp) *(BRED 56)* **THROUGH THE PASSAGE** (compilation) [ ] [-]
– Xoyo / Sharp tongue / Devils and angels / Good and useful life / Taboos / Born every minute / Sixteen houses / Watching you dance / Love is as / Carnal / Wave.

Arista | not iss.

Apr 85. (7"/12") *(ARIST/+12 525)* **SHARP TONGUE. / ?** [ ] [-]

—— disbanded in 1983/4 (FRIEL was also part of CONTACT)

PASSENGERS (see under ⇒ U2)

PASSIONS

Formed: Ladbroke Grove, London, England ... summer '78 out of The RIVERS OF PASSION by Dublin-born singer, BARBARA GOGAN, the ex-DERELICTS girl recruiting MITCH BARKER, CLIVE TIMPERLEY, CLAIRE BIDWELL and RICHARD WILLIAMS. They debuted early the following year with 'NEEDLES & PINS' on the small 'Soho' label, subsequently signing to Polydor's 'Fiction' outlet (home to the CURE) after the departure of BARKER. A follow-up single, 'HUNTED', preceded their first album, 'MICHAEL AND MIRANDA' (1980), before CLAIRE upped and left. With DAVID AGAR filling her shoes, the band moved upstairs to 'Polydor', the initially disappointment of a flop single, 'THE SWIMMER', soon forgotten as they eased into the Top 30 with the moodily atmospheric 'I'M IN LOVE WITH A GERMAN FILMSTAR'. However, subsequent singles failed to have the same impact, their accompanying album, 'THIRTY THOUSAND FEET OVER CHINA' (1981), only managing to scrape into the Top 100. Introducing keyboards courtesy of JEFF SMITH and also enlisting KEVIN ARMSTRONG to replace TIMPERLEY, The PASSIONS made one final plea to the alt/indie scene with another ethereal guitar offering, 'SANCTUARY' (1982).

Album rating: MICHAEL AND MIRANDA (*5) / THIRTY THOUSAND FEET OVER CHINA (*6) / SANCTUARY (*4)

BARBARA GOGAN (b. Dublin, Ireland) – vocals, guitar / **MITCH BARKER** – vovals / **CLIVE TIMPERLEY** – guitar, vocals (ex-101'ERS) / **CLAIRE BIDWELL** – bass, vocals / **RICHARD WILLIAMS** – drums

Soho | not iss.

Jan 79. (7") *(SH 5)* **NEEDLES & PINS. / BODY & SOUL** [ ] [-]

—— now without BARKER

Fiction | not iss.

Nov 79. (7") *(FICS 8)* **HUNTED. / OH NO IT'S YOU** [ ] [-]

Apr 80. (lp) *(FIX 3)* **MICHAEL AND MIRANDA** [ ] [-]
– Pedal fury / Oh no it's you / Snow / Love song / Man on the tube / Miranda / Obsession / Suspicion / Palava / Absentee / Brick wall / Why me.

—— **DAVID AGAR** – bass; repl. BIDWELL who later joined The WALL

Polydor | not iss.

Oct 80. (7") *(POSP 184)* **THE SWIMMER. / WAR SONG** [ ] [-]

Jan 81. (7") *(POSP 222)* **I'M IN LOVE WITH A GERMAN FILMSTAR. / (DON'T TALK TO ME) I'M SHY** [25] [-]

Jun 81. (7") *(POSP 256)* **SKIN DEEP. / I RADIATE** [ ] [-]
(12"+=) *(POSPX 256)* – Small stones.

Sep 81. (7") *(POSP 325)* **THE SWIMMER. / SOME FUN** [ ] [-]

Sep 81. (lp/c) *(POLS/+C 1041)* **THIRTY THOUSAND FEET OVER CHINA** [92] [-]
– I'm in love with a German filmstar / Someone special / The swimmer / Strange affair / Small stones / Runaway / The square / Alice's song / Bachelor girls / Skin deep. *(re-iss. Sep91 on 'Great Expectations' cd/c/lp; PIP CD/MC/LP 028)*

—— **KEVIN ARMSTRONG** – guitar (ex-LOCAL HEROES SW9) + **JEFF SMITH** – keyboards (ex-LENE LOVICH) repl. TIMPERLEY

Jan 82. (7") *(POSP 384)* **AFRICA MINE. / I FEEL CHEAP** [ ] [-]
(with free 7"ep+=) *(CRUSH 1)* – The square / Why me / The snow / I'm in love with a German filmstar.

May 82. (7") *(POSP 435)* **JUMP FOR JOY. / THE STORY** [ ] [-]

Sep 82. (7") *(POSP 487)* **SANCTUARY. / TEMPTING FATE** [ ] [-]

Oct 82. (lp) *(POLS 1066)* **SANCTUARY** [ ] [-]
– Jump for joy / The letter / Into night / Small talk / White lies / Sanctuary / Love is essential / Your friend / Hold on, don't go / Cars driven fast.

—— split after **STEVE WRIGHT** had already repl. ARMSTRONG

– compilations, etc. –

Feb 85. (lp) *Polydor; (SPELP 85)* **PASSION PLAYS**
– I'm in love with a German filmstar / Runaway / The swimmer / Someone special / Bachelor girls / Skin deep / African mine / Jump for joy / The letter / Love is essential / Your friend / Sanctuary. *(cd-iss. Jul96; 529860-2)*

PASTELS

Formed: Glasgow, Scotland ... 1982 by STEPHEN McROBBIE, who subsequently changed his surname to PASTEL. After a few indie outings, the band eventually settled for Alan McGee's 'Creation' records in late 1983 with a relatively stable line-up of PASTEL, guitarist BRIAN SUPERSTAR, bassist MARTIN HAYWARD and drummer BERNICE An indie band in the truly classic sense of the term, The PASTELS' early mid-80's recordings such as 'SOMETHING GOING ON', 'MILLION TEARS' and 'I'M ALRIGHT WITH YOU' were endearingly amateurish jingle-jangle/VELVET UNDERGROUND swathes of melodic noise, the latter the band's final single for 'Creation' before they moved to the small 'Glass' label. Around this time, The PASTELS, along with fellow Scottish (then) 'shamblers' PRIMAL SCREAM and a host of others, were forever immortalised via the dubious honour of having a track included on the NME's semi-legendary C86 compilation. Perhaps inspired by this modest scrape with indie stardom (though the band remain defiantly unambitious), The PASTELS soon adopted a more coherent, harmonious sound as evidenced on their trio of 'Glass' singles and the debut album 'UP FOR A BIT WITH THE PASTELS' (1987), which included a few choice moments from their earlier days. The group label-hopped yet again for the follow-up, signing with 'Chapter 22' for 1989's 'SITTING PRETTY', arguably the band's most accomplished, if not exactly consistent work. With guest appearances by ubiquitous Glasgow scenesters like EUGENE KELLY (once of the seminal VASELINES and latterly CAPTAIN AMERICA) and TEENAGE FANCLUB's NORMAN BLAKE, the album featured some of sweetest, juiciest moments in The PASTELS' chequered career, including the fizzing 'NOTHING TO BE DONE'. The album also saw DAVID KEEGAN contributing guitar, the ex-SHOP ASSISTANT being a partner in STEPHEN's influential '53rd & 3rd' label (which signed Scots acts The SOUP DRAGONS and BMX BANDITS amongst others). At the turn of the decade, The PASTELS line-up was stabalised to a core of PASTEL, girlfriend AGGI WRIGHT and KATRINA MITCHELL, KEEGAN making occasional contributions. Signed to 'Paperhouse', the first release from the new-look PASTELS was a fine cover of American maverick DANIEL JOHNSTON's seminal 'SPEEDING MOTORCYCLE', the group subsequently teaming up with another respected US underground figure, JAD FAIR (HALF JAPANESE), on a collaborative album, JAD FAIR AND THE PASTELS' (1991). Working with GALAXIE 500 guru, DEAN WAREHAM (on the 1994 EP, 'OLYMPIC WORLD OF PASTELISM') further illustrated the band's cultish kudos while 'MOBILE SAFARI' (1995) was a wryly self-deprecating look at an indie band's lot. Highly influential, if never really groundbreaking, The PASTELS remain the Grandaddy's (and mammy's!) of the Glasgow music scene. • **Songwriters:** All written by STEPHEN and group except BOARDWALKIN' (. . . Larson)

Album rating: SUCK ON THE PASTELS (*8) / SITTIN' PRETTY (*7) / TRUCKLOAD OF TROUBLES: 1986-1993 compilation (*7)

STEPHEN PASTEL (b.STEPHEN McROBBIE) – vocals / **BRIAN SUPERSTAR** (b.BRIAN TAYLOR) – guitar / **MARTIN HAYWARD** – bass / **CHRIS GORDON** – drums

Whaam! / not iss.

Oct 82. (7") *(WHAAM 005)* **HEAVENS ABOVE! / TEA TIME TALES**

Creation Artefact / not iss.

Apr 83. (7"flexi) *(LYN 12903)* **I WONDER WHY (live) / (other track by LAUGHING APPLES)**
(above was initialy a freebie with CRE 001)

Rough Trade / not iss.

Oct 83. (7") *(RT 137)* **I WONDER WHY. / SUPPOSED TO UNDERSTAND**

Creation / not iss.

Mar 84. (7") *(CRE 005)* **SOMETHING GOING ON. / STAY WITH ME TILL MORNING**

Oct 84. (12"m) *(CRE 011T)* **A MILLION TEARS. / SUPRISE ME / BABY HONEY**

Nov 85. (12"m) *(CRE 023T)* **I'M ALRIGHT WITH YOU. / WHAT IT'S WORTH / COULDN'T CARE LESS**

Glass / Big Time

Jul 86. (7") *(GLASS 048)* **TRUCK TRAIN TRACTOR. / BREAKING LINES**
(12"+=) *(GLASS12 048)* – Truck train tractor (2).

— (in '87) they added **AGGI** – keyboards (ex-BUBA & THE SHOP ASSISTANTS) + **NORMAN BLAKE** – guitar (of The BOY HAIRDRESSERS)

Feb 87. (lp) *(GLALP 022) <6032>* **UP FOR A BIT WITH THE PASTELS**
– Ride / Up for a bit / Crawl babies / Address book / I'm alright with you / Hitchin' a ride / Get round town / Baby honey / Automatically yours / If I could tell you. *(cd-iss. Oct88; GLACD 021) (re-iss. Sep91 on 'Paperhouse')*

Feb 87. (7") *(GLASS 050)* **CRAWL BABIES. / EMPTY HOUSE**
(12"+=) *(GLASS12 050)* – The day I got certified.

Oct 87. (7") *(GLASS 053)* **COMING THROUGH. / SIT ON IT MOTHER**
(12"+=) *(GLASS12 053)* – Lonely planet boy / Not unloved.

— guest **EUGENE KELLY** (of VASELINES) who later formed CAPTAIN AMERICA then EUGENIUS

Chapter 22 / Homestead

Apr 89. (12"m) *(12CHAP 37)* **BABY YOU'RE JUST YOU. / HOLY MOLY. / UGLY TOWN**

Jun 89. (lp/c/cd) *(CHAP LP/MC/CD 43) <HMS 1441>* **SITTIN' PRETTY**
– Nothing to be done / Anne Boleyn / Sit on it mother / Holy moly / Ugly town / Zooom / Baby you're just you / Ditch the fool / Sittin' pretty / Swerve. *(also pic-lp; CHAPLP 43P) (lp re-iss. Feb95 on 'Homestead'; same as US)*

— now a trio **STEPHEN, AGGI + KATRINA MITCHELL** also with **FRANCES McDONALD** – drums (ex-BOY HAIRDRESSERS)

Paperhouse / Seed

Sep 91. (7") *(PAPER 008)* **SPEEDING MOTORCYCLE. / SPEEDWAY STAR**
(12"+=/cd-s+=) *(PAPER 008 T/CD)* – 4th band.

Nov 91. (7") *(PAPER 011)* **THRU YOUR HEART. / FIREBELL RINGING**
(12"+=/cd-s+=) *(PAPER 011 T/CD)* – My heart's my badge / Sign across me / Thru' your heart (home recording).

— In Feb + Jun 92, they teamed up with JAD FAIR (ex-HALF JAPANESE) on his singles; THIS COULD BE THE NIGHT + HE CHOSE HIS COLOURS WELL from his 1991 album 'JAD FAIR AND THE PASTELS'.

Nov 92. (cd/c/lp) *(PAP CD/MC/LP 008) <14239>* **TRUCKLOAD OF TROUBLES: 1986-1993** (compilation)
– Thank you for being you / Thru' your heart / Kitted out / Comin' through / Over my shoulder / Truck train tractor / Crawl babies / Nothing to be done / Different drum / Not unloved / Baby honey / Speeding motorcycle / Speedway star / What you said / Dark side of your world / Sometimes I think of you / Sign across me.

May 93. (7") *(PAPER 023)* **THANK YOU FOR BEING YOU. / KITTED OUT**
(cd-s+=) *(PAPER 023CD)* – Sometimes I think about you.

— now w/ guests: **GERARD LOVE** (Teenage Fanclub) / **DEAN WAREHAM** (Galaxie 500).

May 94. (7"ep/cd-ep) **OLYMPIC WORLD OF PASTELISM**
– Hot wheels / Three strip dynamite / Feedback Olympics.

— **STEPHEN, AGGI + KATRINA MITCHELL** plus various honorary PASTELS, including GERARD LOVE, NORMAN BLAKE, JONATHAN KILGOUR, DEAN WAREHAM, BILL WELLS, SARAH WARD, ISOBEL CAMPBELL, DAWN KELLY + GREGOR REID

Domino / Matador

Oct 94. (12"ep/cd-ep) *(RUG 28 T/CD) <114>* **YOGA / BOARDWALKIN'. / WINTER OLYMPIC GLORY / YOGA** — Apr95

Domino / Domino

Feb 95. (cd/c/lp) *(<WIG CD/MC/LP 17>)* **MOBILE SAFARI**
– Exploration team / Mandarin / Yoga / Mobile deli / Exotic arcade / Classic line-up / Flightpaths to each other / Basement scam / Strategic gear / Token collecting / Coolport / Worlds of possibility. (lp w/free 7") **SAFARI COMPANION** – 1 / 2 / 3 / 4.

Apr 95. (12"ep/cd-ep) *(RUG 36 T/CD)* **WORLDS OF POSSIBILITY / PHOTOGRAM. / EVER FAR / LOVE IT'S GETTING BETTER**

Domino / Up

Jul 97. (12"ep/cd-ep) *(RUG 55 T/CD) <UP 38>* **UNFAIR KIND OF FAME / FROZEN WAVE. / CYCLE (My Bloody Valentine remix) / FROZEN WAVE (Flacco remix)** — Sep97

Aug 97. (7") *(RUG 52)* **THE HIT HURTS. / WINDY HILL**
(cd-s+=) *(RUG 52CD)* – G12 nights.

Oct 97. (cd/lp) *(WIG CD/LP 34) <UP 41>* **ILLUMINATION**
– The hits hurt / Cycle / Thomson colour / Unfair kind of fame / Fragile gang / The viaduct / Remote climbs / Rough riders / On the way / Leaving this island / G12 nights / Attic plan / Mechanised.

– compilations, etc. –

Mar 85. (7"ep) *Villa 21; (VILLA 1)* **HEAVENS ABOVE! / TEA TIME TALES. / I WONDER WHY (live) / TEA TIME TALES (live)**

Dec 87. (d12") *Glass; (GLASS12 048)* **TRUCK TRAIN TRACTOR. / BREAKING LINES / TRUCK TRAIN TRACTOR 2 / / CRAWL BABIES. / EMPTY HOUSE / THE DAY I GOT CERTIFIED**

Jun 88. (lp/cd) *Creation; (CRE LP/CD 031)* **SUCK ON THE PASTELS**
– Baby honey / I wonder why / Something going on / Million tears / Surprise me / She always cries on Sunday / Baby honey / I'm alright with you / Couldn't care less / What's it worth. *(<cd-iss. Mar94 on 'Rockville'; 6048>)*
(above to be have been issued Mar'85 as 'SHE ALWAYS CRIES ON SUNDAY')

1990. (7"colrd-ep) *Overground; (OVER 06)* **HEAVENS ABOVE! / TEA TIME TALES. / SOMETHING GOING ON (demo) / UNTIL MORNING COMES (demo)**

PAVEMENT

Formed: Stockton, California, USA ... 1989 by frontman STEPHEN MALKMUS and longtime friend/guitarist, SCOTT KANNBERG. They were soon joined by drummer GARY YOUNG (although this was initially a loose arrangement), the band recording their early US-only EP's at YOUNG's home studio, the first of which, 1989's 'SLAY TRACKS', was released on the self-financed 'Treble Kicker' label. A further two EP's, 'DEMOLITION PLOT J-7' and 'SUMMER BABE', together with a mini-lp, 'PERFECT SOUND FOREVER', were subsequently issued on the US indie, 'Drag City' over the course of the ensuing two years. The lo-fi, shambling charm of the likes of 'SUMMER BABE' eventually secured the band a UK deal with 'Big Cat' records, PAVEMENT consistently hitting the charts in Britain throughout their career. The debut album, 'SLANTED AND ENCHANTED' was finally released amid much anticipation in early 1992, its covertly melodic, avant-indie drawing inevitable but favourable comparisons with The PIXIES, The VELVET UNDERGROUND and even KING CRIMSON! Masterfully combining chaotic dischord and shards of crystalline harmony, the record's most compelling moments lay in the lazy melancholia of 'TRIGGER CUT' or 'ZURICH IS STAINED'. MALKMUS' brilliantly cryptic lyrics and offhand phrasing together with the twisted beauty of their music saw the band consistently dubbed as an American FALL. No bad thing, and besides, the band were carving out their own niche on the live circuit, by now augmented with extra sticksman, BOB NASTANOVICH and bassist MARK IBOLD, wildman YOUNG's infamous onstage antics an added attraction. The debut reached the lower reaches of the UK chart while a compilation of the early EP's, 'WESTING (BY MUSKET & SEXTANT)' (1993) made the Top 30. Prior to the release of the follow-up proper, 'CROOKED RAIN CROOKED RAIN' (1994), the band parted company on less than amicable terms with YOUNG, his replacement being STEVE WEST. This folk-ish record marked the band's most enticingly melodic affair to date, the keening 'CUT YOUR HAIR' single almost making the Top 40, the record itself reaching No.15 and cementing PAVEMENT's position as the crown kings of lo-fi. Although PAVEMENT failed to breach the Billboard chart, they built up a loyal following on the US underground scene on the back of constant touring, the defiantly experimental and diverse 'WOWEE ZOWEE!' (1995) proving that the band were making no concessions to radio programmers. There were still perfect PAVEMENT moments of stark beauty, as on the single, 'FATHER TO A SISTER OF THOUGHT'. While the album may have put off those after the immediate pop fix of 'CROOKED . . .', PAVEMENT's next release, the meditative 'BRIGHTON THE CORNERS' (1997) took a different tack again. It was clear that MALKMUS' songwriting was fast maturing, his work taking on a new depth and resonance that eschewed the stylistic grab-bag of old for a more straightforwardly direct approach. Feted by the likes of BLUR, who had previously pooh-poohed the American scene, PAVEMENT remain one of music's most resolutely individual bands. • **Trivia:** MALKMUS produced early 90's album 'Eyes Wide Smile' for FAITH OVER REASON. BOB and STEVEN played on SILVER JEW's (David Berman) album 'Starlite Walter'.

Album rating: SLANTED AND ENCHANTED (*7) / WESTING (BY MUSKET & SEXTANT) compilation (*8) / CROOKED RAIN CROOKED RAIN (*7) / WOWEE ZOWEE (*8)

STEVEN MALKMUS (b. Santa Monica, California) – vocals, guitar / **SCOTT "SPIRAL STAIRS" KANNBERG** – guitar, vocals

not iss. — Treble Kicker

1989. (7"ep) <TK 001> **SLAY TRACKS 1933-1969** [–] [ ]
– You're killing me / Box elder / Maybe maybe / She believes / Price yeah!.

—— added **GARY YOUNG** (b.1953, Stockton) – drums

not iss. — Drag City

1990. (7"ep) <DC 2> **DEMOLITION PLOT J-7** [–] [ ]
– Forklift / Spizzle trunk / Recorder grot / Internal K-dart / Perfect depth / Recorder grot (rally).

—— (Aug90) added **BOB NASTANOVICH** – drums

1991. (10"m-lp) <DC 4> **PERFECT SOUND FOREVER** [–] [ ]
– Heckler spray / From now on / Angel carver blues – Mellow jazz docent / Drive by fader / Debris slide / Home / Krell vid-user.

—— (mid '91) added **MARK IBOLD** (b. New York) – bass

Jan 92. (7"ep) <DC 9> **SUMMER BABE (Winter version) / MERCY: THE LAUNDROMAT. / BAPTISS BLACKTICK / MY FIRST MINE / MY RADIO** [–] [ ]

Big Cat — Matador

Mar 92. (lp/c/cd) (ABB 034/+C/CD) <OLE 038-2> **SLANTED AND ENCHANTED** [72] [ ]
– Summer babe (winter version) / Trigger cut – Wounded – Kite at: 17 / No life singed her / In a mouth of a desert / Conduit for sale / Chesleys little wrists / Loretta's scars / Here / Two states / Perfume-V / Fame throwa / Jackals, false grails – The lonesome era / Our singer / Zurich is stained.

Jul 92. (7"/12"/cd-s) (ABB 35 S/T/CD) **TRIGGER CUT. / SUE ME JACK / SO STARK (YOU'RE A SKYSCRAPER)** [ ] [–]

Nov 92. (12"ep/12"pic-d-ep/cd-ep) (ABB 38 T/P/SCD) <OLE 044> **WATERY, DOMESTIC EP** [58] [ ]
– Texas never whispers / Frontwards / Feed 'em to the (Linden) lions / Shoot the singer (1 sick verse).

Mar 93. (lp/c/cd) (ABB 40/+C/CD) <Drag City; DC 14> **WESTING (BY MUSKET & SEXTANT)** (first 4 US singles material) [30] [ ]

—— **STEVE WEST** (b. Richmond, Virginia) – drums. repl. GARY YOUNG – solo (single; 'PLANET MAN' 94)

Jan 94. (7"/12"/cd-s) (ABB 55 S/T/CD) <OLE 082> **CUT YOUR HAIR. / CAMERA / STARE** [52] [ ]

Feb 94. (lp/c/cd) (ABB 56/+C/CD) <92343> **CROOKED RAIN CROOKED RAIN** [15] [ ]
– Silence kit / Elevate me later / Stop breathin / Cut your hair / Newark wilder / Unfair / Gold sound Z / 5-4 = unity / Range life / Heaven is a truck / Hit the plane down / Fillmore jive. (s-lp w/free 7") – HAUNT YOU DOWN. / JAM KIDS

Jul 94. (7") (ABB 70S) **GOLD SOUNDZ. / KNEELING BUS** [ ] [–]
(12"+=/cd-s+=) (ABB 70 T/SCD) – Strings of Nashville / The exit theory.

—— line-up= **STEPHEN MALKMUS / MARK IBOLD / ROBERT NASTANOVICH / STEVE WEST / SPIRAL STAIRS + FATAH RUARK**

Jan 95. (7") (ABB 77S) **RANGE LIFE. / COOLIN' BY SOUND** [ ] [ ]
(12"+=/cd-s+=) (ABB 77 T/SCD) – Raft.

Mar 95. (7"/12") (ABB 86 S/T) **RATTLED BY THE RUSH. / FALSE SKORPION / EASILY FOOLED** [ ] [–]
(cd-s+=) (ABB 86SCD) – Brink of the clouds.

Apr 95. (3-sided d-lp/c/cd) (ABB 84/+C/CD) <45898> **WOWEE ZOWEE!** [18] [ ]
– We dance / Rattled by the rush / Black out / Brinx job / Grounded / Serpentine pad / Motion suggests / Father to a sister of thought / Extradition / Best friends arm / Grave architecture / At & t / Flux = rad / Fight this generation / Kennel district / Pueblo / Half a canyon / Western homes.

Jun 95. (7"ep/12"ep/cd-ep) (ABB 91 S/T/SCD) **FATHER TO A SISTER OF THOUGHT. / KRIS KRAFT / MUSSLE ROCK (IS A HORSE IN TRANSITION)** [ ] [–]

Aug 95. (7") <3G-08> **DANCING WITH THE ELDERS. / (other artist)** [–] [ ]
<above released on 'Third Gear'>

Jan 96. (cd-ep) (ABB 110SCD) <OLE 188CD> **GIVE IT A DAY / GANGSTERS & PRANKSTERS / SAGANAW** [ ] [ ]
(7"ep+=) (ABB 110S) <OLE 188> – I love Perth.

—— now without FATAH

Domino — Capitol

Jan 97. (7") (RUG 51) **STEREO. / BIRDS IN THE MAJIC INDUSTRY** [48] [–]
(cd-s) (RUG 51CD) – ('A'side) / Westie can drum / Winner of the . . .

Feb 97. (cd/c/lp) (WIG CD/MC/LP 31) <55226> **BRIGHTEN THE CORNERS** [27] [70]
– Stereo / Shady lane / Transport is arranged / Date with IKEA / Old to begin / Type slowly / Embassy row / Blue Hawaiian / We are underused / Passat dream / Starlings of the slipstream / Infinite spark.

Apr 97. (7") (RUG 53) **SHADY LANE (KROSSFADER). / UNSEEN POWER OF THE PICKET FENCE** [40] [–]
(cd-s) (RUG 53CD) – ('A'side) / Slowly typed / Cherry area.
(cd-s) (RUG 53CDX) – ('A'side) / Wanna mess you around / No tan lines.

PAW

Formed: Lawrence, Kansas, USA . . . 1990 by the FITCH brothers; GRANT and PETER, plus CHARLES BRYAN and frontman MARK HENNESSY. Signed to 'A&M' on the strength of a Butch Vig-produced demo, PAW released the acclaimed 'DRAGLINE' in summer '93. Tracing their way back through the great American lineage of seminal hardcore/indie rock, PAW sculpted a visceral collection of contemporary yet classic, melody-conscious guitar abuse. Set to everyday tales of smalltwon love and life, the record's powerful, empathetic approach brought praise from the indie and metal press alike, PAW going on to tour with the likes of THERAPY and MONSTER MAGNET. A second set, 'DEATH TO TRAITORS', followed in 1995, although the group have yet to turn critical favour into major record sales.

Album rating: DRAGLINE (*8) / DEATH TO TRAITORS (*6)

MARK HENNESSY – vocals / **GRANT FITCH** – guitar / **CHARLES BRYAN** – bass / **PETER FITCH** – drums

A&M — A&M

May 93. (12"/cd-s) (580 293-1/-2) **JESSIE. / SLOW BURN / BRIDGE** [ ] [ ]

Jul 93. (7"/c-s) (580 344-7/-4) **COULDN'T KNOW. / BRIDGE** [ ] [ ]
(cd-s+=) (580 345-2) – Dragline.

Aug 93. (cd/c) <(540 065-2/-4)> **DRAGLINE** [ ] [ ]
– Gasoline / Sleeping bag / Jessie / The bridge / Couldn't know / Pansy / Lolita / Dragline / Veronica / One more bottle / Sugarcane / Hard pig.

Oct 93. (7"/c-s) (580 374-7/-4) **SLEEPING BAG. / IMAGINARY LOVER** [ ] [ ]
(10"+=/cd-s+=) (580 375-0/-2) – Suicide shift / Slow burn.

Mar 94. (7"/c-s) (580 560-7/-4) **JESSIE. / GASOLINE** [ ] [ ]
(cd-s+=) (580 561-2) – Slow burn / The bridge.
(12"red) (580 561-1) – ('A'side) / Pansy / Sleeping bag.

Aug 95. (cd/c) <(540 391-2/-4)> **DEATH TO TRAITORS** [ ] [ ]
– No such luck / Seasoned glove / Hope I die tonight / Swollen / Last one / Death to traitors / Built low / Glue mouth kid / Texas / Max the silent / Sweet Sally Brown / Badger / Peach / Sunflower.

—— not heard much from them since

PEARL JAM

Formed: Seattle, Washington, USA . . . 1991 by JEFF AMENT and STONE GOSSARD, who, together with MARK ARM, STEVE TURNER and ALEX VINCENT had previously played in pivotal Seattle band, GREEN RIVER (ARM and TURNER went on to form the noisier, and some still argue, superior MUDHONEY). Widely held to be the first ever "Grunge" act, GREEN RIVER's distortion-heavy mash-up of punk and metal is best sampled on the 'DRY AS A BONE' EP (1987), one of the first releases on the seminal 'Sub Pop' label. Following the band's demise, GOSSARD, AMENT and BRUCE FAIRWEATHER (who had replaced TURNER in GREEN RIVER) recruited vocalist ANDREW WOOD (ex-MALFUNKSHUN) and drummer GARY GILMOUR to form the short lived MOTHER LOVE BONE. After an EP and a cult debut album, 'APPLE' (1990), WOOD overdosed on heroin (March '90), effectively bringing the band to an untimely end. However, it was within these 70's influenced grooves that AMENT and GOSSARD laid the musical foundations for what would later become PEARL JAM. The group evolved from a tribute project for the dead WOOD put together by SOUNDGARDEN frontman, CHRIS CORNELL. Also featuring GOSSARD, AMENT, guitarist MIKE McCREADY, and SOUNDGARDEN sticksman MATT CAMERON, this loose aggregation released 'TEMPLE OF THE DOG' in 1991, a critically acclaimed opus that laid further groundwork for PEARL JAM's sound. With vocalist EDDIE VEDDER and drummer DAVE KRUSEN (subsequently superceded by DAVE ABBRUZZESE) replacing the SOUNDGARDEN boys, the outfit gradually evolved into PEARL JAM, the band still something of a cult act when their 'Epic' debut was released in America at the tail end of '91. 'TEN' eventually reached No.2 in the US chart and a hefty media buzz ensured a steady flow of UK imports, the record making the British Top 20 upon its Feb '92 release. With VEDDER penning the lyrics and GOSSARD and AMENT writing the music, 'TEN' was a powerfully assured debut, transforming the grunge monster into a sleekly melodic rock beast. VEDDER's soulful bellow was a key factor, the singer wringing emotion from every note of the anthemic 'ALIVE' and the affecting 'JEREMY'. Granted, comparisons to LED ZEPPELIN were a little unfair, but the band's lumbering sound seemed the antithesis of the cathartic rush with which NIRVANA had revolutionised a stale music scene and KURT COBAIN was spot on with his infamous critiscisms, despite cries of sour grapes. While their intentions may have been honourable, PEARL JAM ushered in a tidal wave of dull as dishwater, sub-metal masquerading as grunge, most of it, funnily enough, released on major labels. Nevertheless, the kids loved it, especially the American ones, and the band embarked on a punishing touring schedule, finding time to make a cameo appearance as Matt Dillon's band in 'Singles', the Cameron Crowe film based on the Seattle music scene. As well as standing in for JIM MORRISON when The DOORS were eventually inducted into the Rock 'n' Roll Hall Of Fame, VEDDER performed a heart stopping version of BOB DYLAN's 'Masters Of War' (playing mandolin) at the veteran's annniversary concert in 1993. The same year also saw the release of a PEARL JAM follow-up, 'VS', the band's fiercely loyal fanbase propelling the album straight in at No.1 in the US charts. A more ragingly visceral affair, 'GO' gave VEDDER something to get his teeth into while the more reflective 'DAUGHTER' proved how affecting the band (and particularly VEDDER) could be when they dropped the derivative hard rock assault. Along with their mate NEIL YOUNG, PEARL JAM seemingly have an abiding love of vinyl, releasing 'VITALOGY' (1994) initially on record only, something which didn't prevent the band scaling the US chart once again. While not exactly vital, as the title might suggest, the record saw PEARL JAM going back to basics and injecting their behemoth-rock with a bit of stripped down energy. The following year saw PEARL JAM backing NEIL YOUNG on the so-so 'MIRROR BALL' (1995) album, the fruition of their musical partnership that had begun some years previous. In 1995, each member (except ABBRUZZESE), took time to carry out other projects, although the following year they returned to full force with 'NO CODE', an album that showed a lighter, acoustic side. • **Songwriters:** VEDDER wrote lyrics / GOSSARD and AMENT the songs. GREEN RIVER covered AIN'T NOTHIN' TO DO (Dead Boys) / QUEEN BITCH (David Bowie). • **Trivia:** Backed actor MATT DILLON's band CITIZEN DICK in the 1992 film 'Singles'. VEDDER co-wrote and sang on 2 tracks; 'THE LONG ROAD' + 'THE FACE OF LOVE' on the 1996 movie 'Dead Man Walking'.

Album rating: TEN (*10) / VS (*8) / VITALOGY (*8) / NO CODE (*8) / Green River: REHAB DOLL (*7) / Mother Love Bone: MOTHER LOVE BONE (*8)

GREEN RIVER

MARK ARM (b.21 Feb'62, California) – vocals / **STEVE TURNER** (b.28 Mar'65, Houston, Texas) – guitar / **STONE GOSSARD** (b.20 Jul'66) – guitar / **JEFF AMENT** (b.10 Mar'63, Big Sandy, Montana) – bass / **ALEX VINCENT** – drums

not iss. Homestead

Sep 85. (12"ep) <*HMS 031*> **COME ON DOWN** [-] [ ]
– New god / Swallow my pride / Ride of your life / Corner of my eye / Tunnel of love. *(cd-ep-iss.May94; same)*

— **BRUCE FAIRWEATHER** – guitar repl. TURNER who later joined MUDHONEY

not iss. I.P.C.

Nov 86. (7"green) <*ICP 01*> **TOGETHER WE'LL NEVER. / AIN'T NOTHIN' TO DO** [-] [ ]

Glitterhouse Sup Pop

Jun 87. (12"ep) <*SP 11*> **DRY AS A BONE** [-] [ ]
– Unwind / Baby takes / This town / PCC / Ozzie. *(UK-iss.Mar91 on 'Tupelo'; TUPLP 17) (cd-iss. May94; same)*

Feb 89. (12"ep) *(GR 0031)* <*SP 15*> **REHAB DOLL** [ ] [ ] May88
– Searchin' / Ain't nothin' to do / Forever means / Rehab girl / Swallow my pride / Together we'll never / Smilin' and dyin' / Porkfist / Take a dive / One more stitch. (c-ep+=) <*SP 15A*> – Queen bitch. *(US re-iss. c+cd-lp Jul88 as 'DRY AS A BONE' / 'REHAB DOLL')*

— MARK ARM formed MUDHONEY

MOTHER LOVE BONE

formed by **AMENT, GOSSARD + FAIRWEATHER** plus **ANDREW WOOD** (b.1966) – vocals (ex-MALFUNKSHUN) / **GARY GILMOUR** – drums

Polydor Stardog

Mar 89. (m-lp) <*839011-2*> **SHINE** [-] [ ]
– Thru fade away / Midshaker meltdown / Halfass monkey boy / Medley:- Chloe dancer / Lady Godiva blues.

Jul 90. (cd/c/lp) <*(843191-2/-4/-1)*> **APPLE** [ ] [ ] Mar90
– This is Shangri-la / Stardog champion / Holy roller / Bone China / Come bite the apple / Stargazer / Heartshine / Captain hi-top / Man of golden words / Mr.Danny boy / Capricorn sister / Crown of thorns. *(above 2 re-iss. cd as 'STAR DOG CHAMPION' Sep92 on 'Polydor'; 514177-2 / <314512 884-2>) (hit US No.77)*

— ANDREW WOOD died on the 19th March '90 after a heroin overdose. AMENT and GOSSARD paid tribute to him by joining with SOUNDGARDEN ⇒ members in off-shoot outfit TEMPLE OF THE DOG. After this project was finished . . . PEARL JAM were formed

PEARL JAM

AMENT + GOSSARD with **EDDIE VEDDER** (b.23 Dec'66, Evanson, Illinois) – vocals / **MIKE McCREADY** (b. 5 Apr'65) – lead guitar / **DAVE ABBRUZZESE** (b.17 May'??) – drums repl. DAVE KRUZON

Epic Epic

Feb 92. (cd/c/lp/pic-lp) *(468884-2/-4/-1/-0)* <*47857*> **TEN** [18] [2] Dec91
– Once / Even flow / Alive / Why go / Black / Jeremy / Oceans / Porch / Garden / Deep / Release. *(re-dist.Dec92 yellow-cd+=/m-d; 468884-5/-3)* – Alive (live) / Wash / Dirty Frank.

Feb 92. (7"white/c-s) *(657572-7/-4)* **ALIVE. / WASH** [16] [ ]
(12"+=/pic-cd-s+=) *(657572-6/-5)* – Once.

Apr 92. (7"/c-s) *(657857-7/-4)* **EVEN FLOW (remix). / OCEANS** [27] [ ]
(12"white+=/cd-pic-s+=) *(657857-8/-2)* – Dirty Frank.

Sep 92. (7"white/c-s) *(658258-7/-4)* **JEREMY. / ALIVE (live)** [15] [ ]
(12"pic-d+=) *(658258-6)* – Footsteps (live).
(pic-cd-s+=) *(658258-4)* – Yellow Ledbetter.

Oct 93. (cd/c/lp) *(474549-2/-4/-1)* <*53136*> **VS** [2] [1]
– Go / Animal / Daughter / Glorified G / Dissident / W.M.A. / Blood / Rearviewmirror / Rats / Elderly woman behind the counter in a small town / Leash / Indifference.

Oct 93. (12"ep/cd-ep) *(659795-6/-2)* **GO. / ALONE / ELDERLY WOMAN BEHIND THE COUNTER IN A SMALL TOWN (acoustic)** [ ] [ ]
(free c-s+=) *(659795-4)* – Animal (live).

Dec 93. (7"red/c-s) *(660020-7/-4)* **DAUGHTER. / BLOOD (live)** [18] [ ]
(12"+=/cd-s+=) *(660020-6/-2)* – Yellow ledbetter (live).

May 94. (7"/c-s) *(660441-7/-4)* **DISSIDENT. / REARVIEWMIRROR (live)** [14] [ ]
(cd-s+=) *(660441-2)* – Release / Even flow (versions).
(cd-s) *(660441-5)* – ('A'side) / Deep / Even flow / Why go (versions).

— ABBRUZZESE departed and was repl. after below album by **JACK IRONS** (ex-RED HOT CHILI PEPPERS)

Nov 94. (7"/c-s/cd-s) *(661036-7/-4/-2)* <*77771*> **SPIN THE BLACK CIRCLE. / TREMOR CHRIST** [10] [58] [18]

Dec 94. (cd/c/d-lp) *(477861-2/-4/-1)* <*66900*> **VITALOGY** [6] [1]
– Last exit / Spin the black circle / Not for you / Tremor Christ / Nothingman / Whipping / Pry, to / Corduroy / Bugs / Satan's bed / Better man / Aye davanita / Immortality / Stupid mop.

— McCREADY now also moonlighted for MAD SEASON (see under ALICE IN CHAINS) due to lead singer being LAYNE STALEY. Meanwhile, STONE GOSSARD set up own record label 'Loosegroove' and signed MALFUNKSHUN, DEVILHEAD, WEAPON OF CHOICE, BRAD and PROSE AND CONCEPTS.

Feb 95. (7"colrd/c-s/cd-s) *(661203-7/-4/-2)* **NOT FOR YOU. / OUT OF MY MIND (live)** [34] [-]

Dec 95. (7"/cd-s) *(662716-7/-2)* <*78199*> **MERKINBALL** [25] [7]
– I got I.D. / Long road.
(above both recorded w/ NEIL YOUNG)

— Group had already featured on NEIL YOUNG's album 'MIRRORBALL'. GOSSARD featured on THERMIDOR's 1996 album 'Monkey On Rico'.

— mid-96; JEFF AMENT featured for minor supergroup THREE FISH.

Aug 96. (7"/c-s/cd-s) *(663539-7/-4/-2)* <*78389*> **WHO YOU ARE. / HABIT** [18] [31]

Sep 96. (cd/c/d-lp) *(484448-2/-4/-1)* <*67500*> **NO CODE** [3] [1]
– Sometimes / Habit / Who you are / In my tree / Smile / Hail hail / I'm open / Red mosquito / Lukin / Mankind / Black & red & yellow / Allnight.

Jan 98. (7"/c-s) *(665394-7/-4)* <*78797*> **GIVEN TO FLY. / PILATE** [12] [21]
(cd-s+=) *(665394-2)* – Leatherman.

Feb 98. (cd/c/lp) *(489365-2/-4/-1)* <*68164*> **YIELD** [7] [2]
– Brain of J / Faithful / No way / Given to fly / Wishlist / Pilate / Do the evolution / Untitled song / M.F.C. / Low light / In hiding / Push me pull me / All those yesterdays.

May 98. (7"/c-s) *(665790-7/-4)* <*78896*> **WISHLIST. / U** [30] [47]
(cd-s+=) *(665790-2)* – Brain of J (live).

Nov 98. (cd/c/d-lp) *(429859-2/-4/-1)* <*69752*> **LIVE ON TWO LEGS (live)** [68] [15]
– Corduroy / Given to fly / Hail hail / Daughter / Elderly woman behind the counter in a small town / Untitled / MFC / Go / Off he goes / Even flow / Red mosquito / Nothingman / Do the evolution / Better man / Black / F*ckin' up.

– others, etc. –

Jul 95. (cd-ep) *Epic;* <*77935*> **JEREMY / YELLOW LEDBETTER / FOOTSTEPS** [-] [79]

Jan 96. (cd-ep) *Epic;* <*77938*> **DAUGHTER / YELLOW LEDBETTER (live) / BLOOD (live)** [-] [97]

THREE FISH

JEFF AMENT – vocals, bass / **ROBBI ROBB** – vocals, guitar (of TRIBE AFTER TRIBE) / **RICHARD STUVERUD** – (of FASTBACKS)

Epic Epic

Jun 96. (cd/c/d-lp) *(484118-2/-4/-1)* **THREE FISH** [ ] [ ]
– Solitude / Song for a dead girl / Silence at the bottom / Intellgent fish / Zagreb / All messed up / Here in the darkness / Hall of intelligent fish / Strangers in my head / Lovely meander / Elusive ones / Build / Stupid fish / A secret place / Laced. *(d-lp+=)* – If miles were alive / Can I come along / Easy way.

Sep 96. (cd-s) **LACED /** [ ] [ ]

PENETRATION

Formed: Newcastle / Middlesborough, England . . . 1976 by PAULINE MURRAY and ROBERT BLAMIRE alongside GARY CHAPMAN and GARY SMALLMAN, all four hailing from the small mining village of Ferrybridge. Following a valuable support slot to GENERATION X at London's punk nerve centre, The Roxy, PENETRATION began to make a name for themselves in the capital and duly secured a deal with 'Virgin'. Late '77's debut single, 'DON'T DICTATE', revealed a decidedly more "rawk" proposition than many of the three-chord trainee anarchists on the scene, MURRAY drawing inevitable comparisons with both PATTI SMITH and SIOUXSIE SIOUX for her force of personality and the strength/style of her voice. Replacing CHAPLIN with NEALE FLOYD and adding keyboard player FRED PURSER, the band released a fine follow-up in 1978's 'FIRING SQUAD', the track, like its predecessor, generating only limited interest amid charges that the band were "going heavy". Certainly, the debut album, 'MOVING TARGETS' (1978) had a few nifty guitar solos but MURRAY's songs were firmly rooted in punk's guiding light of social awareness and integrity. Also featuring a sterling choice of cover material in the Buzzcocks' 'NOSTALGIA', the album met with a generally positive press reaction and narrowly missed the UK Top 20. Yet things went inexorably awry from here on in as the band struggled, both with live commitments and new material, 'Virgin' pressing them for a new album which arrived in the shape of 1979's 'COMING UP FOR AIR'. The response was less than enthusiastic and amid increasing frustration, the band split soon after its release. While PURSER confirmed the suspicions of the band's detractors and went on to play with NWOBHM (New Wave Of British Heavy Metal) band, TYGERS OF PAN TANG, MURRAY launched her solo career with 'PAULINE MURRAY & THE INVISIBLE GIRLS' (1980). Backed by BLAMIRE, STEVE HOPKINS, JOHN MAHER and MARTIN HANNETT, MURRAY had recorded a set of much poppier, more experimental/electronic material which cracked the Top 30. The project was short-lived, however, MURRAY only surfacing occasionally with the odd single over the coming decade before a releasing an album, 'STORM CLOUDS', in 1989. • **Songwriters:** MURRAY lyrics / group music. PAULINE solo: – CLOSE WATER (John Cale). • **Trivia:** In 1979, Pauline guested for THE ONLY ONES on their final album, 'Baby's Got A Gun', and duetted with their leader, PETER PERRETT, on a single/track, 'Fools'.

Album rating: MOVING TARGETS (*7) / COMING UP FOR AIR (*5) / DON'T DICTATE – THE BEST OF PENETRATION compilation (*8) / PAULINE MURRAY & THE INVISIBLE GIRLS (*7)

PAULINE MURRAY (b. 8 Mar'58, Durham, England) – vocals / **GARY CHAPLIN** – guitar / **ROBERT BLAMIRE** – bass / **GARY SMALLMAN** – drums

Virgin | not iss.

Nov 77. (7") *(VS 192)* **DON'T DICTATE. / MONEY TALKS** ☐ -

—— **NEALE FLOYD** – guitar repl. CHAPLIN. / added **FRED PURSER** – keyboards

May 78. (7") *(VS 213)* **FIRING SQUAD. / NEVER** ☐ -
Sep 78. (7") *(VS 226)* **LIFE'S A GAMBLE. / V.I.P.** ☐ -
Oct 78. (lp,luminous-lp/c) *(V/TCV 2109)* **MOVING TARGETS** 22 -
– Future daze / Life's a gamble / Lovers of outrage / Vision / Silent community / Stone heroes / Movement / Too many friends / Reunion / Nostalgia / Free money. *(re-iss. Mar84; OVED 40) (cd-iss. Dec89; CDV 2109)*
Apr 79. (7") *(VS 257)* **DANGER SIGNS. / STONE HEROES** ☐ -
(12"+=) *(VS 257-12)* – Vision (live).
Aug 79. (7") *(VS 268)* **COME INTO THE OPEN. / LIFELINE** ☐ -
Sep 79. (lp/c) *(V/TCV 2131)* **COMING UP FOR AIR** 36 -
– Shout about the noise / She is the slave / Last saving grace / Killed in the rush / Challenge / Come into the open / What's going on / The party's over / On reflection / Lifeline / New recruit. *(re-iss. 1988; OVED 203)*

—— (split late 1979) CHAPLIN later formed SOUL ON ICE. PURSER subsequently joined TYGERS OF PANG TANG.

– compilations, etc. –

Oct 79. (lp) *Cliffdayn; (PEN 1)* **RACE AGAINST TIME** (official bootleg) ☐ -
May 83. (12"ep) *Virgin; (VS 593-12)* **DON'T DICTATE / FREE MONEY. / LIFE'S A GAMBLE / DANGER SIGNS** ☐ -
Jan 92. (cd; shared with The RUTS) *Windsong; (WINCD 009)* **BBC RADIO 1 LIVE IN CONCERT (live)** ☐ -
Nov 93. (cd) *Burning Airlines; (PILOT 001)* **PENETRATION** ☐ -
– (live, demos, Peel sessions, solo PAULINE MURRAY, etc)
Mar 95. (cd) *Virgin; (CDOVD 450)* **DON'T DICTATE . . .THE BEST OF PENETRATION** ☐ -
– Come into the open / Lifeline / Firing squad / Never / Life's a gamble / V.I.P. / Danger signs / Stone heroes / Don't dictate / Free money / Shout above the noise / She is the slave / Party's over / Future daze.
Apr 97. (lp) *Get Back; (GET 13)* **THE EARLY YEARS** ☐ -

PAULINE MURRAY & THE INVISIBLE GIRLS

—— with **ROBERT BLAMIRE** – bass / **STEVE HOPKINS** – keyboards / **JOHN MAHER** – drums (ex-BUZZCOCKS) / **MARTIN HANNETT** – keyboards

Illusive | not iss.

Jul 80. (7"/10") *(IVE/+X 1)* **DREAM SEQUENCE 1. / DREAM SEQUENCE 2** 67 -
Sep 80. (lp) *(2934 277)* **PAULINE MURRAY & THE INVISIBLE GIRLS** 25 -
– Screaming in the darkness / Dream sequence 1 / European eyes / Shoot you down / Sympathy / Time slipping / Drummer boy / Thunder tunes / When will we learn / Mr. X / Judgement day. *(cd-iss. Jun93 on 'Trident'; PSTRCD 01) (cd re-iss. Mar97 on 'Burning Airlines'+=; PILOT 002)* – The visitor / Animal crazy / Searching for Heaven.
Oct 80. (7") *(IVE 2)* **MR. X. / TWO SHOTS** ☐ -
Apr 81. (7") *(IVE 3)* **SEARCHING FOR HEAVEN. / ANIMAL CRAZY** ☐ -
(10"+=) *(IVEX 3)* – The Visitor.

—— (split 1981)

PAULINE MURRAY

—— with **ROBERT BLAMIRE** – bass / **PAUL HARVEY** – guitar / **TIM JOHNSON** – drums

Polestar | not iss.

Oct 84. (7") *(PSTR 001)* **HOLOCAUST. / DON'T GIVE UP** ☐ -
(12"+=) *(PSTR 12-001)* – Aversion.
Oct 86. (7") *(PSTR 003)* **NEW AGE. / BODY MUSIC** ☐ -
(12"+=) *(PSTR 12-003)* – Archangel.

—— (from 1984-86 by PAULINE MURRAY & THE STORM, below with The SAINT)

Mar 87. (12"ep) *(PSTR 002)* **HONG KONG EP** ☐ -
– Close watch / All I want / Body music / Holocaust.

Cat&Mouse | not iss.

Apr 89. (12"m) *(ABBO 9T)* **THIS THING CALLED LOVE. / MR. MONEY / PRESSURE ZONE** ☐ -
Jul 89. (lp) *(ABB 10)* **STORM CLOUDS** ☐ -
– This thing called love / Holocaust / Soul power / No one like you / Another world / Don't give up / Pressure zone / Close watch / Everybody's talkin' / New age / Time. *(re-iss. Jun91 on 'Polestar'; 834445-1)*

PENNYWISE

Formed: Hermosa Beach, California, USA . . . 1988 by JIM, FLETCHER DRAGGE, JASON THIRSK and BYRON. Yet another band in the mould of OFFSPRING and GREEN DAY to sign to Brett Gurewitz's 'Epitaph' imprint, JIM and Co had obviously grown up listening to both the sounds of Bay Area thrash and classic US hardcore, as evidenced on their eponymous 1991 debut for the label; in 1989 the band had issued the very rare 'A WORD FROM THE WISE'. PENNYWISE finally came to prominence after the Americans finally discovered punk in the mid 90's, cracking the US Top 100 with 'ABOUT TIME' (1995). Tragically, a year after its completion, bass player, THIRSK, was to meet an untimely death, leaving the band very much down but not out. With new man RANDY on board, PENNYWISE scored an even bigger success with their fourth set, 'FULL CIRCLE' (1997); full circle right enough, as we in Britain had been listening to this stuff for the past two decades!

Album rating: PENNYWISE (*5) / UNKNOWN ROAD (*5) / ABOUT TIME (*5) / FULL CIRCLE (*5)

JIM – vocals / **FLETCHER DRAGGE** – guitar / **JASON THIRSK** (b.1967) – bass / **BYRON** – drums

not iss. | Thelogian

1989. (lp) *<3>* **A WORD FROM THE WISE** - ☐
– Final chapter / Covers / Depression / No way out / Gone / Wildcard / Maybes / Stand by me.

Epitaph | Epitaph

Oct 91. (cd/c/lp) *<(E 86412-2X/-4X/-1X)>* **PENNYWISE** ☐ ☐
– Wouldn't it be nice / Rules / Secret / Living for today / Come out fighting / Homeless / Open door / Pennywise / Who's to blame / Fun and games / Kodiak / Side one / No reason why / Bro hymn.
Aug 93. (cd/c/lp) *<(E 86429-2/-4/-1)>* **UNKNOWN ROAD** ☐ ☐
– Unknown road / Homesick / Time to burn / It's up to me / You can demand / Nothing / Vices / The city is burning / Dying to know / Tester / Try to conform / Give and get / Clear your mind.
May 95. (7"ep) *(T 002)* **WILD CARD EP** ☐ -
(above on 'Semaphore')
Jun 95. (cd/c/lp) *<(E 86437-2/-4/-1)>* **ABOUT TIME** ☐ 96
– Peaceful day / Waste of time / Perfect people / Every single day / Searching / Not far away / Freebase / It's what you do with it / Try / Same old story / I won't have it / Killing time.

—— (below on 'Out Of Step')

Sep 95. (7") *(WOOS 7S)* **SAME OLD STORY. /** ☐ ☐
(cd-s+=) *(WOOS 7CDS)* –

—— **RANDY** – bass; repl. JASON who died in 1996

Apr 97. (cd/c/lp) *<(86489-2/-4/-1)>* **FULL CIRCLE** ☐ 79
– Fight till you die / Date with destiny / Get a life / Society / Final day / Broken / Running out of time / You'll never make it / Every time / Nowhere fast / What if I / Go away / Did you really / Bro hymn tribute.

– others, etc. –

all issued on 'Thelogian'

Jun 95. (cd) *<(TF 003CD)>* **WILDCARD / A WORD FROM THE WISE** ☐ ☐ 1992
Jul 95. (7") *(RE 001)* **TOMORROW. / DON'T FEEL NOTHING** ☐ ☐
(re-iss. Apr97; TPW 02)
Apr 97. (7") *(TPW 01)* **A WORD FROM THE WISE. /** ☐ ☐

PENTHOUSE

Formed: Camden, London, England . . . mid 90's by CHARLIE FINKE, JON FREE, GRAEME FLYNN and TIM CEDAR. What the 'STONES might've sounded like had they been born twenty, thirty, or even fort~y (!) years later, PENTHOUSE traded in a similar scabby vein of dirty, distorted blues as JON SPENCER, if a bit more lascivious. After the release of two independent 45's, 'RIPPED 'N' HAPPY' and 'GAS PORTER BLUES', they signed to 'World Domination', releasing their debut album, 'GUTTER EROTICA', in 1997. From the devilish sleaze of the cover art to the explicit nature of the lyrics, especially opening track/single, 'VOYEUR'S BLUES', the record was the aural equivalent of Soho at its seediest.

Album rating: GUTTER EROTICA (*6)

CHARLIE FINKE – vocals, mouth harp / **JON FREE** – guitar / **GRAEME FLYNN** – bass / **TIM CEDAR** – drums

Kitty Kitty Corporation | not iss.

Nov 95. (7") *(CHOOSY 002)* **RIPPED 'N' HAPPY. / BABY PEELER** ☐ -
Apr 96. (7") *(CHOOSY 003)* **GAS PORTER BLUES. / STUNG TRUNKS** ☐ -

Syrup | not iss.

Jul 96. (ltd.7") *(SYRUP 001)* **LE STUNT. / Country Teasers: GETAWAY** ☐ -

World Domination | Beggars Banquet

Apr 97. (7") *(WDOM 33S)* **VOYEUR'S BLUES. / PLATE OF SLAGS** ☐ -
(cd-s+=) *(WDOM 33SCD)* – Le stunt / Tongue Kung Fu.
May 97. (lp/cd) *(WDOM 34/+CD) <80206>* **GUTTER EROTICA** ☐ ☐ Nov98
– Voyeur's blues / Gus' neck / La grotte d'amour / Road rash / The beauty in the beast / A deviant soiree / Harmonic surf spastic / Widow's chagrin / Mare Ingram's lament / The gin waltz / White coal / Lap dog shuffle / Face down. *(re-iss. Apr98; same)*
Nov 97. (cd-ep) *(CRH 00009)* **RECKS EP** ☐ -
(above single on 'Carcrashh')
Apr 98. (12"ep/cd-ep) *(PENT 001 T/CD)* **REMIX EP** ☐ -
– White coal / Voyeur's blues / Road rash / Lap dog shuffle.

PERENNIAL DIVIDE (see under ⇒ MEATBEAT MANIFESTO)

PERE UBU

Formed: Cleveland, Ohio, USA ... September '75 out of ROCKET FROM THE TOMBS, by DAVID THOMAS (aka CROCUS BEHEMOTH; his alter-ego) and PETER LAUGHNER. Along with CHARLIE WEINER (guitar), GLEN 'THUNDERHAND' HACH (guitar) and TOM 'FOOLERY' CLEMENTS (drums), they became residents at THOMAS's workplace, the Viking Saloon; he was apparently a bouncer! A revamped RFTT saw THOMAS and LAUGHNER being joined by CRAIG BELL (bass), GENE 'CHEETAH CHROME' O'CONNOR (guitar) and 'JOHNNY BLIZ' MADANSKY, and it was this line-up who recorded sessions for WMMS radio stations, later to surface as a posthumous 1990 cd, 'LIFE STINKS'. A few embryonic UBU tracks, 'FINAL SOLUTION' and '30 SECONDS OVER TOKYO', plus covers of 'SATISFACTION' (Rolling Stones) and 'SEARCH AND DESTROY' (Stooges), featured on these rare master tapes. Even 'SONIC REDUCER' was hijacked by The DEAD BOYS bound, CHEETAH and BLITZ, the pair being united with STIV BATORS, who replaced THOMAS before the ROCKETS split. Meanwhile, PERE UBU (THOMAS and LAUGHNER) recruited other musicians; TIM WRIGHT, ALLEN RAVENSTINE, TOM HERMAN plus SCOTT KRAUSS, and took their name from a play by French writer, Alfred Jarry. The large-framed THOMAS formed his own 'Hearthan' label, issuing a classic debut, '30 SECONDS OVER TOKYO', which led to gigs at (New York's) Max's Kansas City in early '76. Another gem, 'FINAL SOLUTION', was unleashed soon after, although LAUGHNER departed (at this stage the line-up numbered THOMAS, RAVENSTINE, HERMAN, KRAUSE and newcomer, TONY MAIMONE) prior to the release of their third and fourth rare 45's, 'STREET WAVES' and 'THE MODERN DANCE'. The latter subsequently became the name of their debut album which gained a release early in 1978 on the obscure US 'Blank' label (a few months later it surfaced in the UK on 'Mercury'). The sound was clearly a break from the "New Wave", echoing as it did a revival of the avant-garde (CAPTAIN BEEFHEART and ENO-era ROXY MUSIC). On the strength of this masterwork, they signed to the major 'Chrysalis' label and, six months later, wowed the music world with another abstract beauty, 'DUB HOUSING' (1978). After the disappointing 'NEW PICNIC TIME' (1979), however, they were unceremoniously dropped by their label, the band's wayward eccentricity floating right over the average pop picker's head. PERE UBU (who had replaced HERMAN with veteran, MAYO THOMPSON – formerly of RED CRAYOLA) subsequently found a home with UK indie, 'Rough Trade', although they split after two poorly-received studio sets, 'THE ART OF WALKING' (1980) and 'SONG OF THE BAILING MAN' (1982), the latter boasting the drumming talents of ANTON FIER. Over the course of the next five years, having released a debut album, 'THE SOUND OF THE SAND' early in '82, THOMAS embarked on an equally weird and anti-commercial solo career with albums, the live 'WINTER COMES HOME' (1983), 'VARIATIONS ON A THEME' (1983), 'MORE PLACES FOREVER; (1985), 'MONSTER WALKS THE WINTER LAKE' (1986) and 'BLAME THE MESSENGER' (1987). PERE UBU released a belated comeback album, 'THE TENEMENT YEARS', in 1988, a record which gathered together old UBU men, THOMAS, RAVENSTINE, MAIMONE and KRAUSE, while retaining CHRIS CUTLER and JIM JONES (previously part of THOMAS' solo band). For the 1989 set, 'CLOUDLAND', the group sought out former CAPTAIN BEEFHEART employee, ERIC DREW FELDMAN, who remained for a further two albums, 'WORLDS IN COLLISION' (1991) and 'STORY OF MY LIFE' (1993). Subsequently signing to 'Cooking Vinyl' (also now the rest home of BILLY BRAGG and The WEDDING PRESENT), PERE UBU cut one final effort, 'RAY GUN SUITCASE' (1995), before THOMAS once again opted for solo pastures with 'EREWHON' (1996). • **Songwriters:** All group compositions, except MIRROR MAN (Captain Beefheart) / DOWN BY THE RIVER (Neil Young). THOMAS collaborated with others on solo work and covered SLOOP JOHN B. (Beach Boys).

Album rating: TERMINAL TOWER: AN ARCHIVAL COLLECTION (*9) / THE MODERN DANCE (*9) / DUB HOUSING (*7) / NEW PICNIC TIME (*7) / CLOUDLAND (*6) / STORY OF MY LIFE (*6) / RAYGUN SUITCASE (*7) / David Thomas: THE SOUND OF THE SAND (*6) / VARIATIONS ON A THEME (*6)

DAVID THOMAS (b.14 Jun'53) – vocals / **PETER LAUGHNER** (b.1953) – guitar / **TIM WRIGHT** – bass, guitar / **TOM HERMAN** (b.19 Apr'49) – guitar, bass / **SCOTT KRAUSE** (b.19 Nov'50) – drums / **ALLEN RAVENSTINE** (b. 9 May'50) – synthesizer

not iss. / Hearthan

Dec 75. (7"ltd) *<HR 101>* **30 SECONDS OVER TOKYO. / HEART OF DARKNESS** – [ ]

— **DAVE TAYLOR** – synthesizer repl. RAVENSTINE

Mar 76. (7"ltd) *<HR 102>* **FINAL SOLUTION. / CLOUD 149** – [ ]

— **ALLEN RAVENSTINE** – synthesizer returned to repl. TAYLOR / **ALAN GREENBLATT** – guitar repl. LAUGHNER who formed FRICTION (he died of drug & alcohol abuse 22nd June '77)

— **TONY MAIMONE** (b.27 Sep'52) – bass, piano repl. WRIGHT who joined DNA. (GREENBLATT left also) (were now a quintet with **THOMAS, HERMAN, KRAUSE, MAIMONE + RAVENSTINE**)

Nov 76. (7"ltd) *<HR 103>* **STREET WAVES. / MY DARK AGES** – [ ]

Aug 77. (7"ltd) *<HR 104>* **THE MODERN DANCE. / HEAVEN** – [ ]

Mercury / Blank

Apr 78. (lp) *(9100 052) <001>* **THE MODERN DANCE** [ ] [ ] Jan78
– Non-alignment pact / The modern dance / Laughing / Street waves / Chinese radiation / Life stinks / Real world / Over my head / Sentimental journey / Humor me. *(re-iss. Jan81 on 'Rough Trade'; ROUGH 22) (re-iss. Feb88 on 'Fontana' lp/cd; SF LP/CD 3)*

Radar / not iss.

Apr 78. (12"ep) *(RDAR 1)* **DATAPANIK IN THE YEAR ZERO (remixes compilation)** [ ] –
– Heart of darkness / 30 seconds over Tokyo / Cloud 149 / Untitled / Heaven.

Chrysalis / Rough Trade

Nov 78. (lp) *(CHR 1207) <ROUGHUS 14>* **DUB HOUSING** [ ] [ ]
– Navy / On the surface / Dub housing / Cagliari's mirror / Thriller / I will wait / Drinking wine Spodyody / Ubu dance party / Blow daddy-o / Codex. *(cd-iss. Mar89 on 'Rough Trade'; ROUGHCD 6002)*

Sep 79. (lp) *(CHR 1248) <ROUGHUS 20>* **NEW PICNIC TIME** [ ] [ ]
– One less worry / Make hay / Goodbye / The voice of the sand / Jehovah's kingdom comes / Have shoes will walk / 49 guitars and 1 girl / A small dark cloud / Small was fast / All the dogs are barking. *(cd-iss. Mar89 on 'Rough Trade'; ROUGHCD 6003)*

Oct 79. (7"m) *(CHS 2372)* **THE FABULOUS SEQUEL (HAVE SHOES WILL WALK). / HUMOR ME (live). / THE BOOK IS ON THE TABLE** [ ] –

— **MAYO THOMPSON** (b.26 Feb'44) – guitar, vocals (ex-RED CRAYOLA) repl. HERMAN who went solo

Rough Trade / not iss.

Jun 80. (7") *(RT 049)* **FINAL SOLUTION. / MY DARK AGES** [ ] –

Sep 80. (lp) *(ROUGH 14)* **THE ART OF WALKING** [ ] –
– Go / Rhapsody in pink / Arabia * / Miles * / Misery goats / Loop / Rounder / Birdies / Lost in art / Horses / Crush this horn. *(re-iss. 1981; same)* – Arabian nights / Tribute to Miles; repl. *) *(cd-iss. Apr89 tracks as re-issue; ROUGHCD 14)*

Feb 81. (7") *(RT 066)* **NOT HAPPY. / LONESOME COWBOY DAVE** [ ] –

May 81. (lp) *(ROUGH 23)* **390° OF SIMULATED STEREO – UBU LIVE: VOLUME 1 (live 76-79)** [ ] –
– Can't believe it / Over my head / Sentimental journey / 30 seconds over Tokyo / Humor me / Real world / My dark ages / Street waves / Laughing / Non-alignment pact / Heart of darkness / The modern dance. *(cd-iss. Apr89; ROUGHCD 23)*

— added **ANTON FIER** (b.20 Jun'56) – drums, percussion (ex-FEELIES) / guest **EDDIE THORNTON** – trumpet

Jun 82. (lp) *(ROUGH 33)* **SONG OF THE BAILING MAN** [ ] –
– The long walk home / Use of a dog / Petrified / Stormy weather / West Side story / Thoughts that go by steam / Big Ed's used farms / A day such as this / The vulgar boatman bird / My hat / Horns are a dilemma. *(cd-iss. Apr89; ROUGHCD 33)*

— split mid 1982. MAYO returned to RED CRAYOLA (which also incl. most UBU's). KRAUSE + WRIGHT formed HOME & GARDEN, who released one album for 'Dead Man's Curve', 'HISTORY & GEOGRAPHY' (1986)

DAVID THOMAS & THE PEDESTRIANS

Rough Trade / Recommended

Dec 81. (12"ep; by DAVID THOMAS) *(TRADE 5-12)* **VOCAL PERFORMANCES** [ ] –

— included **THOMPSON, KRAUSE, FIER & RAVENSTINE** plus **CHRIS CUTLER** (b. 4 Jan'47) – drums / **JOHN GREAVES** – bass (both ex-HENRY COW) / **PHILIP MOXHAM** – multi (ex-YOUNG MARBLE GIANTS) / **RICHARD THOMPSON** – guitar

Jan 82. (lp) *(ROUGH 30)* **THE SOUND OF THE SAND AND OTHER SONGS OF THE PEDESTRIANS** [ ] [ ]
– The birds are good ideas / Yiki Tiki / The crickets in the flats / Sound of the sand / The new atom mine / Big dreams / Happy to see you / Crush this horn – part 2 / Confuse did / Sloop John B. / Man's best friend.

Oct 82. (7") **PETRIFIED. / ?** – [ ]

— w/ **CHRIS CUTLER & LINDSAY COOPER** – bassoon (ex-MIKE OLDFIELD)

Feb 83. (lp; DAVID THOMAS & HIS LEGS) *(DTLP)* **WINTER COMES HOME (live Munich, 1982)** [ ] –
– A day such as this / Winter comes home / West side story / Sunset / Stormy weather / Poetic license / Rhapsody in pink / Dinosaurs like me / Petrified / Bones in action / Contrasted views of the archaeopterix.

— added **RICHARD THOMPSON** etc. (CUTLER, COOPER)

Dec 83. (lp) *(ROUGH 60)* **VARIATIONS ON A THEME** [ ] –
– A day at the Botanical Gardens / Pedestrians walk / Bird town / The egg and I / Who is it / Song of hoe / Hurry back / The ram / Semaphore.

— **TONY MAIMONE** – bass repl. GREAVES who joined The FLYING LIZARDS

Rough Trade / Twin/Tone

May 85. (lp) *(ROUGH 80) <TTR 8551>* **MORE PLACES FOREVER** [ ] [ ]
– Through the magnifying glass / Enthusiastic / Big breezy day / About true friends / Whale head king / Song of the bailing man / The farmer's wife / New broom.

DAVID THOMAS & THE WOODEN BIRDS

(**DAVID** retained **MAIMONE** and **CUTLER**) brought in **RAVENSTINE** again. (**DAVID HILD** – accordion of LOS LOBOS guested)

Apr 86. (lp/cd) *(ROUGH 90) <TTR/+CD 8667>* **MONSTER WALKS THE WINTER LAKE** [ ] [ ]
– My theory of similtanious similtude – Red tin bus / What happened to me / Monster walks the winter lake / Bicycle / Coffee train / My town / Monster Magge king of the seas / Monster thinks about the good days / What happened to us.

— **JIM JONES** (b.12 Mar'50) – guitar was added

Mar 87. (lp) *(ROUGH 120) <TTR 87105>* **BLAME THE MESSENGER** [ ] [ ]
– The long rain / My town / King Knut / A fact about trains / When love is uneven / Storm breaks / Having time / Velikovsky / The two-step.

PERE UBU

(**THOMAS, RAVENSTINE, MAIMONE, CUTLER, JONES** and **KRAUSE**)

Fontana / Enigma

Mar 88. (lp/c)(cd) *(SF LP/MC 5)(834 537-2) <73343>* **THE TENEMENT YEAR** [ ] [ ]

THE MODERN DANCE

– Something's gotta give / George had a hat / Talk to me / Busman's honeymoon / Say goodbye / Universal vibration / Miss you / Dream the Moon / Rhythm kind / The hollow Earth / We have the technology.

Jul 88. (7") *(UBU 1)* **WE HAVE THE TECHNOLOGY. / THE B-SIDE** [ ] [-]
(12"+=/cd-s+=) *(UBU 1-12/CD1)* – The postman drove a caddy / ('A'-different mix).

— **ERIC DREW FELDMAN** (b.16 Apr'55) – drums (ex-CAPTAIN BEEFHEART) repl. RAVENSTINE + CUTLER

Fontana not iss.

Mar 89. (7") *(UBU 2)* **WAITING FOR MARY (WHAT ARE WE DOING HERE?). / WINE DARK SPARKS** [ ] [-]
(12"+=/cd-s+=) *(UBU 2-12/CD2)* – Flat.

May 89. (lp/c/cd) *(838 237-1/-4/-2)* **CLOUDLAND** [ ] [-]
– Breath / Bus called happiness / Race the sun / Waiting for Mary / Cry / Flat * / Ice cream truck / Lost nation road / Monday night / Pushin' / The wire * / The waltz. *(cd+= *)*

Jun 89. (7") *(UBU 3)* **LOVE LOVE LOVE. / FEDORA SATELLITE** [ ] [-]
(cd-s+=) *(UBUCD 3)* – Say goodbye.
(12") *(UBU 3-12)* – ('A'-cajun house mix) / ('A'132 bpm mix) / ('A'side).

Oct 89. (7") *(UBU 4)* **BREATH. / BANG THE DRUM** [ ] [-]
(12"+=) *(UBU 4-12)* – Over my head (live) / Universal initiation (live).
(cd-s+=) *(UBUCD 4)* – Humor me (live).

Mar 91. (7") *(UBU 5)* **I HEAR THEY SMOKE THE BARBEQUE. / INVISIBLE MAN** [ ] [-]
(12"+=/cd-s+=) *(UBU 5-12/CD5)* – Around the fire.

May 91. (cd/c/lp) *(848 564-2/-4/-1)* **WORLDS IN COLLISION** [ ] [-]
– Oh Catherine / I hear they smoke the barbeque / Turpentine / Goodnight Irene / Mirror man / Cry cry / World's in collision / Life of Riley / Over the Moon / Don't look back / Playback / Nobody knows / Winter in the Netherlands.

May 91. (7") *(UBU 6)* **OH CATHERINE. / LIKE A ROLLING STONE** [ ] [-]
(12"+=/cd-s+=) *(UBU 6-12/CD6)* – Down by the river.

Fontana Imago

Jan 93. (cd/c) *(514159-2/-4)* <21024> **STORY OF MY LIFE** [ ] [ ]
– Wasted / Come home / Louisiana train wreck / Fedora satellite II / Heartbreak garage / Postcard / Kathleen / Honey Moon / Sleep walk / The story of my life / Last will and testament.

— **THOMAS / KRAUSS / JONES / TEMPLE / YELLIN**

Cooking Vinyl Tim/Kerr

Aug 95. (cd) *(COOKCD 089)* <TK 100> **RAY GUN SUITCASE** [ ] [ ]
– Folly of youth / Electricity / Beach Boys / Turquoise fins / Vacuum in my head / Memphis / Three things / Horse / Don't worry / Ray gun suitcase / Surfer girl / Red sky / Montana / My friend is a stooge for the media priests / Down by the river II.

Oct 95. (cd-ep) *(FRYCD 043)* <TK 111-2> **FOLLY OF YOUTH / BALL 'N' CHAIN (jam) / DOWN BY THE RIVER II (demo) / MEMPHIS (demo)** [ ] [ ] Feb96

— **THOMAS** with **TOM HERMAN** + **JIM JONES** newcomer + **ROBERT WHEELER** – synthesizer / **MICHELE TEMPLE** – bass

Tim/Kerr Tim/Kerr

Mar 98. (cd) <(TK 155)> **PENNSYLVANIA** [ ] [ ]
– Woolie bullie / Highwaterville / Sad txt / Urban lifestyle / Drive / Indiangiver / Monday morning / Perfume / Silent spring / Mr. Wheeler / Muddy waters / Slow / Fly's eye / Duke's Saharan ambitions / Wheelhouse.

May 98. (cd-ep) <TK 830121> **BEACH BOYS / DOWN BY THE RIVER / LOUISIANA TRAIN WRECK / MONTANA** [-] [ ]

– compilations, others, etc. –

Nov 85. (lp/cd) *Rough Trade; (ROUGH 83) / Twin/Tone; <TTR/+CD 8561>* **TERMINAL TOWER: AN ARCHIVAL COLLECTION** [ ] [ ]
– (early 'Hearthan' sides + rare)

Mar 89. (cd) *Rough Trade; (ROUGHCD 93)* **ONE MAN DRIVES WHILE THE OTHER MAN SCREAMS – LIVE VOL.2: PERE UBU ON TOUR** [ ] [-]

Nov 95. (4x7"box) *Cooking Vinyl; (FRY 045) / Tim/Kerr; <TK 107>* **THE HEARTHAN SINGLES** [ ] [ ]

Nov 95. (d-cd) *Movieplay Gold; (MPG 74178)* **MODERN DANCE / TERMINAL TOWER** [ ] [-]

Sep 96. (5xcd-box) *Cooking Vinyl; (COOKCD 098) / Geffen; <24969>* **DATAPANIK IN THE YEAR ZERO** [ ] [ ]
– (first 5 albums + 1 free rarities album)

DAVID THOMAS

— with **ANDY DIAGRAM** – trumpet (ex-PALE FOUNTAINS) / **PAUL HAMANN** – upright bass / **JIM JONES** – backing vocals

Cooking Vinyl Tim/Kerr

Sep 96. (cd; DAVID THOMAS & TWO PALE BOYS) *(COOKCD 105)* *<TK 145>* **EREWHON** [ ] [ ]
– Obsession / Planet of fools / Nowheresville / Fire / Lantern / Morbid sky / Weird cornfields / Kathlen / Highway 61 revisited.

Jun 97. (5xcd-box) *(HR 110)* **MONSTER** (compilation of all his solo work) [ ] [-]

PERFECT DISASTER

Formed: London, England . . . early 80's as ORANGE DISASTER by PHIL PARFITT and the future rhythm section of FIELDS OF THE NEPHILIM, TONY PETTITT and NOD. This early incarnation only released one single, SOMETHING'S GOT TO GIVE', before changing their moniker to the ARCHITECTS OF DISASTER and issuing another one-off, 'CUCUMBER SANDWICH', in '82. Adopting the PERFECT DISASTER mantle, PHIL, along with ALISON PATES, JOHN SALTWELL and MALCOLM CATTO, crossed the English Channel to record their French-only eponymous debut (given a UK release on 'Glass' in 1987). They finally secured a domestic contract with 'Fire', the much-improved follow-up, 'ASYLUM ROAD', set free in early '88. By this time, they had undergone a sizeable personnel shift, JO WIGGS and DAN CROSS replacing SALTWELL and PATES respectively. Subterranean guitar rumblings and obsessively dark subject matter (PARFITT once worked as psychiatric nurse) were the order of the day, the band offering up another fix on 1989's 'UP' album. Yet more line-up upheavals occured when WIGGS left to join The BREEDERS, the returning SALTWELL taking up the slack on their fourth and final set, 'HEAVEN SCENT' (1990). PARFITT would subsequently work with SPIRITUALIZED man, JASON PIERCE, before returning in his own right with OEDIPUSSY; a solitary album, 'DIVAN', appeared in '95.

Album rating: THE PERFECT DISASTER (*4) / ASYLUM ROAD (*8) / UP (*6) / HEAVEN SCENT (*6)

PHIL PARFITT – vocals, guitar / **TONY PETTITT** – bass / **NOD** (b. ALEXANDER WRIGHT) – drums

Neuter not iss.

1982. (7"m; as ORANGE DISASTER) *(OD 1)* **SOMETHING'S GOT TO GIVE. / OUT OF THE ROOM / HIDING FROM FRANK** [ ] [-]

Neuter not iss.

Nov 82. (7"; as ARCHITECTS OF DISASTER) *(NEU 1)* **CUCUMBER SANDWICH. / FRIENDLY FIRE** [ ] [-]

— PETTITT and NOD formed the FIELDS OF NEPHILIM

— **PHIL PARFITT** recruited **ALISON PATES** – keyboards / **JOHN SALTWELL** – bass / **MALCOLM CATTO** – drums

Kampa not iss.

1985. (lp) **THE PERFECT DISASTER** [-] [-] France
(UK-iss.Sep87 on 'Glass'; GLALP 027)

Glass not iss.

Nov 87. (12"ep) *(GLAEP 107)* **HEY HEY HEY / THE NIGHT BELONGS TO CHARLIE. / THAT'S WHAT THE DOCTOR SAYS / ELUSIVE DREAMS** [ ] [-]

— **JOSEPHINE WIGGS** (b.26 Feb'65, Letchworth, England) – bass, cello, piano; repl. SALTWELL

— **DAN CROSS** – lead guitar, keyboards; repl. PATES

Fire Genius

May 88. (12") *(BLAZE 28T)* **TV (GIRL ON FIRE). / CRACK UP F SONG TV (version)** [ ] [-]

Aug 88. (lp) *(FIRELP 11)* *<5>* **ASYLUM ROAD** [ ] [ ]

Oct 88. (7") *(BLAZE 31S)* **TIME TO KILL. / GARAGE** [ ] [-]
(12"+=) *(BLAZE 31T)* – ('A'version).

— **PHIL 'Archie' OUTRAM** + **MARTIN LANGSHAW** – drums repl. CATTO

Jun 89. (lp/c/cd) *(FIRE LP/MC/CD 18)* **UP** [ ] [-]
– '55 / Shout / Up / It doesn't matter / Down (here I go) / Down (falling) / Down (down) / Hey now / Go away / B-52. *(cd+=)* – Garage / Time to kill.

Oct 89. (7"ep/12"ep) *(BLAZE 38 S/T)* **MOOD ELEVATORS** [ ] [-]

— **SALTWELL** returned to repl. WIGGS who joined The BREEDERS, then ULTRA VIVID SCENE

Sep 90. (12"ep) *(BLAZE 43T)* **RISE E.P.** [ ] [-]

Oct 90. (cd/lp) *(FIRE CD/LP 27)* **HEAVEN SCENT** [ ] [-]
– Rise / Father / Wires / Takin' over / Where will you go with me / Little sister (if ever days) / Shadows / Sooner or later / It's gonna come to you. *(cd+=)* – Lee / Mood elevators (original) / Bluebell live) / B-52 (live).

— disbanded soon after, PARFITT subsequently collaborating with JASON PIERCE (of SPIRITUALIZED) prior to initiating his own outfit, OEDIPUSSY

OEDIPUSSY

— **PARFITT** + others

Handsome not iss.

Apr 95. (cd/lp) *(HAN CD/LP 001)* **DIVAN** [ ] [-]

PERFUME

Formed: Leicester, England . . . late 1993 by MICK McCARTHY and TONY OWEN, who enlisted JOHNNY WADD. Having set up their own appropriately titled label, 'Aromasound', the whiffy wannabes made their debut with the single, 'YOGA', quite literally leaving a scented trail with a further two 45's, 'YOUNG' and 'LOVER'; the former actually smelled of perfume! Meanwhile, the lads built up their already swaggering confidence with a Jo Whiley session for Radio One and a tour supporting GENE with whom PERFUME bore at least a passing musical resemblance. After another indie hit, 'YESTERDAY FOLLOWS TODAY', they got their one solitary sniff at chartland (No.71) with early '96's 'HAVEN'T SEEN YOU'. A year on, the band had signed to 'Big Star', previewing their belated debut album, 'ONE' (1997) with a re-issue of 'LOVER'.

Album rating: ONE (*7) / YESTERDAY RISING compilation (*7)

MICK McCARTHY – vocals, guitar / **TONY OWEN** – bass / **JOHNNY WADD** – drums

Aromasound not iss.

Dec 93. (7") *(AROMA 001)* **YOGA. /** [ ] [-]

Apr 94. (7") *(AROMA 002)* **YOUNG. / ANOINTED** [ ] [-]

Jan 95. (7") *(AROMA 003)* **LOVER. / MORPHEUS** [ ] [-]
(cd-s+=) *(AROMA 003CDS)* – Lover (acoustic) / Yoga.

Jul 95. (7") *(AROMA 004)* **YESTERDAY FOLLOWS YOU. / RISING STAR** [ ] [-]
(cd-s+=) *(AROMA 004CDS)* – Aylestone lane / Walk into the wind.

Jan 96. (7"/c-s) *(AROMA 005/+MC)* **HAVEN'T SEEN YOU. / OPEN YOUR SHELL** [71] [-]
(cd-s+=) *(AROMA 005CDS)* – Walk like a god (live) / You've got something (live).

May 96. (7"/c-s) *(AROMA 006/+MC)* **CARVING YOUR NAME. / LOST IN YOU**
(cd-s+=) *(AROMA 006CDS)* – Climber / You kill me.

Big Star not iss.

Feb 97. (7"/c-s) *(STAR/+K7 103)* **LOVER. / MORPHEUS**
(cd-s+=) *(STARC 103)* – Lover (acoustic) / Yoga.

Mar 97. (cd/c) *(STAR C/K7 104)* **ONE**
– I'm alive / Lover / Watch me bleed / You and I / As I go blind / Carving your name / Your life is now / One / Haven't seen you / I'm no saint / Changes / Fallen / Things that I love / Wild honey.

Mar 97. (7"/c-s) *(STAR/+K7 106)* **YOU AND I. /**
(cd-s+=) *(STARC 106)* –

– compilations, etc. –

Feb 98. (cd) *Aromasound; (AROMALP 001CD)* **YESTERDAY RISING**
– Yesterday follows you / Rising star / Morpheus / Yoga / Lost in you / Climber / L.I.P.S. / Perfume / Anointed / Aylestone lane.

PERNICE BROTHERS

Formed: Boston, Massachusetts, USA . . . 1996 by er, the PERNICE BROTHERS, songwriter JOE (formerly of 'Sub Pop' outfit, SCUD MOUNTAIN BOYS, who made three albums in the mid 90's) and his elder sibling BOB, who doubled the line-up with PEYTON PINKERTON and THOM MONAHAN (formerly of the NEW RADIANT STORM KINGS and The LILYS respectively). America's country-rock equivalent to TEENAGE FANCLUB, JOE and Co issued a couple of low key 45's before delivering a set of orchestra-laden tunes in the shape of 1998's 'OVERCOME BY HAPPINESS'. This featured JOE's homage to his poet hero, CHARLES SIMIC, on the track, 'WHEREIN OBSCURITY'; lushness was back in musical city.

Album rating: OVERCOME BY HAPPINESS (*6)

JOE PERNICE – vocals, guitar (ex-SCUD MOUNTAIN BOYS) / **BOB PERNICE** – guitar, vocals / **PEYTON PINKERTON** – guitar / **THOM MONAHAN** – bass, vocals / + a 10-piece orchestra in the studio

Sub Pop Sub Pop

Sep 97. (7") <*(SP 381)*> **JIMMY COMA. / MONKEY SUIT** Jan97

not iss. Summershine

Dec 97. (7") <*SHINEUS 21*> **SQUARE WORLD. / IN PLAIN SIGHT**

Rykodisc Sub Pop

May 98. (cd) *(RCD 10447)* <*SPCD 427*> **OVERCOME BY HAPPINESS**
– Crestfallen / Overcome by happiness / Sick of you / Clear spot / Dimmest star / Monkey suit / Chicken wire / Wait to stop / All I know / Shoes and clothes / Wherein obscurity / Ferris wheel.

Mark PERRY (see under ⇒ ALTERNATIVE TV)

PETER & THE TEST-TUBE BABIES

Formed: Brighton, England . . . 1978 by PETER BYWATERS, DEREK GREENING, CHRIS MARCHANT and NICHOLAS LOIZIDES. Initially making an appearance with the track 'ELVIS IS DEAD' on 1978's 'Vaultage' compilation – released on local label, Attrix' – PETER and his cronies later surfaced as in-house jesters for the court of Oi!, releasing the self explanatory 'BANNED FROM THE PUBS' on the 'No Future' label in 1982. This was quickly followed by another synapse-shattering commentary, 'RUN LIKE HELL', detailing the trials of trying to chat up the "skirt" down the local disco. Subsequently setting up their own 'Trapper' label, the band released a further two slabs of yobbish three-chord aggro in 'ZOMBIE CREEPING FLESH' and 'THE JINX' prior to a full length debut album, 'THE MATING SOUNDS OF SOUTH AMERICAN FROGS' (1983). Just to make sure people got the message, 'PISSED AND PROUD' emerged as the second full length release of the year, while 'Hairy Pie' served as a vehicle for the cassette-only 'JOURNEY TO THE CENTRE OF JOHNNY CLARKE'S HEAD' (1984) and live set, 'ANOTHER NOISY, LOUD, BLARING PUNK ROCK LP' (1985). The mid-80's also saw the release of the 'ROTTING IN THE FARTSACK' EP, presumably how the boys occupied their time until 1990's assassination of STOCK, AITKEN & WATERMAN songs (artists; Kylie, Jason, Rick, Sinita, et all; yuk!) on the album, 'THE SHIT FACTORY – PLAY . . .'. An erm, pivotal influence on the feminist baiting likes of The MACC LADS, PETER & THE TEST TUBE BABIES could only have been a product of the 80's. • **Songwriters:** BYWATERS / GREENING except a few covers; LEADER OF THE GANG (Gary Glitter).

Album rating: THE BEST OF . . . compilation (*4)

PETER BYWATERS – vocals / **DEREK 'Greenback' GREENING** – guitar / **CHRIS 'Trapper' MARCHANT** – bass / **NICHOLAS 'Ogs' LOIZIDES** – drums

No Future not iss.

Jan 82. (7"m) *(OI 14)* **BANNED FROM THE PUB. / MOPED LADS / PEACEHAVEN WILD LADS**

Jul 82. (7") *(OI 15)* **RUN LIKE HELL. / UP YER BUM**

Trapper not iss.

Mar 83. (7"m/12"m) *(EARS/12EARS 1)* **ZOMBIE CREEPING FLESH. / NO INVITATION / SMASH AND GRAB**

Sep 83. (7"/12") *(EARS/12EARS 2)* **THE JINX. / TRAPPER AIN'T GOT A BIRD**

Nov 83. (lp) *(THIN 1)* **THE MATING SOUNDS OF SOUTH AMERICAN FROGS**
– September (part 1) / Guest list / One night stand / Let's burn / The jinx / Blown out again / Easter Bank Holiday / No invitation / Pissed punks (go for it) / Never made it / September (part 2). <*US cd-iss. 1997 on 'Dr.Strange'; 56*>

Mar 84. (12"ep) *(EARFIT 1)* **PRESSED FOR CASH / BLOWN OUT AGAIN (blender version). / (FITS: Peace and quiet but never dreamed it was going to be like this)**

Og & Dells not iss.

Sep 84. (c) *(OD 1)* **JOURNEY TO THE CENTRE OF JOHNNY CLARKE'S HEAD**
– The journey begins / Who the hell is jolly / What's up with Trapper records / Go for it (live) / Banned from the pubs (live) / From the heart / T.Q.G.G.B.J.'s (demo) / Go to the garage mate / The golden voice beckons you / Elvis is dead (live) / Wimpy's are shit (studio) / Reggae meets le punk movement / Tupperware party (demo) / Skin one up Ralph / Keep Britain untidy (demo) / Who the hell is jolly (part 2) / I lust for the disgusting things in life (demo) / All about love (rare demo) / Time to go home. *(cd-iss. Oct94 on 'Dojo'; DOJO 80CD) (cd re-iss. May95 on 'We Bite'; WB 3124-2)* <*US cd-iss. 1997 on 'Dr.Strange'; 57*>

Jungle not iss.

May 85. (12"white-ep) *(JUNG 21T)* **ROTTING IN THE FART-SACK**
(cd-ep-iss.May95 on 'We Bite'; WB 3127)

Hairy Pie not iss.

May 85. (lp) *(HP 1)* **ANOTHER NOISY, LOUD, BLARING PUNK ROCK LP**
(cd-iss. Oct94 on 'Dojo'; DOJO 67)

May 86. (7") *(TTB 1)* **KEYS TO THE CITY. / KEITH MOON**
(12"+=) *(TTB 12-1)* – Work hard.

Trapper not iss.

Oct 85. (lp) *(NO FEARS 1)* **3 X 45**

Dec 85. (7") *(EARS 3)* **WHIMPEEZ. / NEVER MADE IT**

Hairy Pie not iss.

Oct 86. (lp) *(HP 2)* **SOBERPHOBIA**
– Key to the city / Louise Wouldn't like it / Spirit of Keith Coleman / Allergic to life / All about love / He's on the whiskey (watch out) / Boozanza / Everytime I see her / Ghost in the bedsit / Every second counts. *(re-iss. Feb87 on 'Dojo'; DOJOLP 49) (cd-iss. May95 on 'We Bite'; 3128-2)*

A.B.T. not iss.

Nov 90. (cd/c/lp) **THE SHIT FACTORY (. . .PLAY STOCK, AITKEN AND WATERMAN)**
– I just can't wait / Toy boy / Nothings gonna stop us now / F.L.M. / I'd rather jack / When I fall in love / Love in the first degree / The harder I try / Hand on your heart / Venus / Especially for you / Never gonna give you up / Too many broken hearts / Who's leaving who.

Rebel not iss.

1991. (cd/c/lp) *(SPV 0843001-2/-4/-1)* **CRINGE**
– Cringe / Shit British tour / The gardener / Launch 'em now / Reality calling / The man who did nothing / Weekend warrior / V.D.U. head / Shit it all / There's a penis in my shoulder / Tuinal shuffle / Goodbye forever / Latent psychosis. *(re-iss. cd Mar96; same)*

We Bite Dr.Strange

Jan 96. (cd/lp) *(WB 1139-2/-1)* <*55*> **SUPERMODELS** Mar97

Pub City Royal Pub City Royal

Nov 98. (cd) *(<6>)* **ALIEN PUBDUCTION**
– Sour grapes / Early grave / 1.4.7.1 / I'm getting pissed for Christmas / Troublemakers / Talk show / Why bother? / Bloody Mary / Big disappointment / Long way from home / Meet you at the all night offy / Nutter / All in her head / Legless / Twenty years / Alien pubduction.

– compilations, etc. –

Dec 83. (lp/c) *No Future; (PUNK/CPUNK 3)* **PISSED AND PROUD**
– Moped lads / Banned from the pubs / Elvis is dead / Up yer bum / Smash and grab raid / Run like hell / Shit stirrer / Intensive care / Keep Britain untidy / Transvestite / Maniac / Disco / Leader of the gang (I am). *(cd-iss. Jul89 & Jun93; CDPUNK 3)* <*US cd-iss. Jun94 on 'Century Media'; 7768*>

Aug 88. (lp/cd) *Dojo; (DOJO LP/CD 57)* **THE BEST OF PETER & THE TEST-TUBE BABIES**

Jan 92. (cd) *;* **TOTALLY TEST TUBED**
(re-iss. May95 on 'We Bite'; WB 3126-2)

May 95. (cd) *We Bite; (WB 3127-2)* **TEN DEADLY SINS**

Oct 95. (cd) *Anagram; (CDPUNK 64)* **PUNK SINGLES COLLECTION**

Mar 97. (cd) *Dr.Strange; <58>* **TEST TUBE TRASH**

Mike PETERS (see under ⇒ ALARM)

Liz PHAIR

Born: 17 Apr'67, New Haven, Connecticut, USA. Chicago based, USA. After graduating in Art History, PHAIR concentrated full-time on her songwriting and, with the help of friend/COME guitarist, CHRIS BROKAW, eventually secured a contract with indie label, 'Matador' early in 1992. Hooking up with musicians BRAD WOOD, CASEY RICE and LEROY BACH, PHAIR translated her song sketches into a marathon double album, 'EXILE ON GUYVILLE', its title a typically PHAIR-esque play on the classic 'STONES album. An engagingly eclectic, often brazenly confessional affair, PHAIR had fashioned a folk-grunge mini-classic, fusing wry life-in-America / hard-hitting sexual lyrics with beautiful country harmonies in a similar vein to MAZZY STAR or THROWING MUSES. Critics loved it and in addition to the gushing reviews, PHAIR became the first woman since JONI MITCHELL (in 1974) to win the prestigious 'Village Voice' annual award. The sonic femme-thrust of 'SUPERNOVA' previewed follow-up, 'WHIP-SMART' (1994), a record that surprisingly received a less than enthusiastic response in comparison to its predecessor. While the album may have lacked a little of the debut's wayward charm, the songs were more focused and PHAIR's muse was as fertile, and occasionally as candid as ever (even if her much talked about stage-fright might've belied the bolshy, sexually liberated persona her music projected). While 1995 saw the release of a stop-gap odds'n'sods collection, 'JUVENILIA' (1995), it would be another three years before another studio set, 'WHITECHOCOLATESPACEEGG' (1998).

Album rating: EXILE IN GUYVILLE (*7) / WHIP-SMART (*8) / JUVENILIA compilation (*4) / WHITECHOCOLATESPACEEGG (*6)

LIZ PHAIR – vocals, guitar / **BRAD WOOD** – drums, percussion / **CASEY RICE** – guitar / **LEROY BACH** – bass

Minty Fresh / not iss.

Aug 93. (7") *(MF 4)* **CANARY. / CARNIVORE** [ ] [-]

Matador / Matador

Aug 93. (cd/c/lp) *<(OLE 051-2/-4/-1)>* **EXILE IN GUYVILLE** [ ] [ ] Jun93
– 6'1" / Help me Mary / Glory / Dance of the seven veils / Never said / Soap star Joe / Explain it to me / Canary / Mesmerizing / Fuck and run / Girls! girls! girls! / Divorce song / Shatter / Flower / Johnny Sunshine / Gunshy / Stratford-On-Guy / Strange loop.

Sep 94. (7") *(OLE 103-7) <98206>* **SUPERNOVA. / COMBO PLATTER** [ ] [78]

Atlantic / Atlantic

Sep 94. (cd/c/lp) *<(7567 92429-2/-4/-1)>* **WHIP-SMART** [ ] [27]
– Chopsticks / Supernova / Support system / X-ray man / Shane / Nashville / Go west / Cince de Mayo / Dogs of L.A. / Whip-smart / Jealousy / Crater lake / Alice Springs / May queen.

Oct 94. (7"/c-s) *(A 8224/+C)* **SUPERNOVA. / X-RAY MAN (remix)** [ ] [-]
(12"+=/cd-s+=) *(A 8224 T/CD)* – ('A'-clean version).

Matador / Capitol

Aug 98. (lp)<cd,c> *(MAT 191) <53554>*
WHITECHOCOLATESPACEEGG [ ] [35]
– Whitechocolatespaceegg / Big tall man / Perfect world / Johnny Feelgood / Polyester bride / Love is nothing / Baby got going / Uncle Alverez / Only son / Go on ahead / Headache / Ride / What makes you happy / Fantasize / Shitloads of money / Girls' room.

– compilations, etc. –

Aug 95. (d7"ep/cd-ep) *Matador; <(OLE 129-7/-2)>* **JUVENILIA** [ ] [ ]
– Jealousy / Turning Japanese / Animal girl / California / South Dakota / Batmobile / Dead shark / Easy.

Joel R.L. PHELPS (see under ⇒ SILKWORM)

PHISH

Formed: Burlington, Vermont, USA . . . 1983 by TREY ANASTASIO, JON FISHMAN and GORDON while they were students at the local university. Following the addition of PAGE McCONNELL, the band began touring in earnest, playing gigs across the States and in the process building up a grassroots fanbase and a reputation gained largely by word of mouth. Not since the heady days of the 70's have a band become so huge by dint of sheer hard graft and a resolutely "authentic" sound, proving that even in these days of 99p single giveaways, record company marketing muscle isn't everything. An archetypal 'Great American Band', PHISH have undoubtedly tapped into the same constituency of MOR-friendly, liberal/hippy Americans who once followed (and probably still do) the GRATEFUL DEAD and now dig HOOTIE & THE BLOWFISH. It is for exactly this reason that despite being honoured with the obligatory Ben & Jerry's ice cream flavour in the States, PHISH will probably only ever attract a minority audience in Britain. Still, BLIND MELON proved at least a one-hit wonder was possible and with their first two independently released albums, 'JUNTA' (1988) and 'LAWN BOY' (1990), PHISH explored elements of blues, jazz, funk and rock in a similarly improvisational spirit to The SPIN DOCTORS , BLUES TRAVELER etc. In fact, PHISH actually toured with these bands under the banner of HORDE (Horizon Of Rock Developing Everywhere)(!?), some sharp-witted Stateside critic memorably dubbing this lot the "Living Dead" in honour of their interminable jam sessions. Packing out venues in almost every State, it was only a matter of time before the band were picked up by a major, 'Elektra' winning out and releasing 1992's 'A PICTURE OF NECTAR' set. 'RIFT' (1993) was PHISH's first major chart entry, the band reigning in their more wayward musical tendencies and even securing radio play for a couple of tracks from 1994' 'HOIST' album. In the true spirit of JERRY GARCIA & co., 1995 saw PHISH releasing that most reviled of rock artefacts, a double live album. The mellow, ALLMANS-esque 'FREE' incredibly remains the band's only bonafide single release, one of the stand-out tracks from 1997's 'BILLY BREATHES' album, a US Top 10 and their most successful to date. Now something of an American institution, PHISH seem to have effortlessly navigated the shark-infested waters of the US music business without compromising their original vision, 'SLIP STITCH AND PASS' (1997) and 'THE STORY OF THE GHOST' (1998) finding them swimming as freely as ever.

Album rating: LAWN BOY (*6) / A PICTURE OF NECTAR (*6) / RIFT (*6) / HOIST (*6) / A LIVE ONE (*7) / STASH compilation (*7) / BILLY BREATHES (*8) / SLIP STITCH AND PASS (*7) / THE STORY OF THE GHOST (*7)

TREY ANASTASIO – vocals, guitar / **JON FISHMAN** – drums, vocals / **MIKE GORDON** – bass, vocals / **PAGE McCONNELL** – keyboards, vocals

not iss. / own label

1988. (lp) **JUNTA** [-] [ ]
– Fee / You enjoy myself / Esther / Golgi apparatus / Foam / Dinner and a movie / Divided sky / David Bowie / Fluffhead / Fluff's travels / Contact. *<US d-cd-iss. Dec97 on 'Elektra'+=; 61413-2>* – Union federal / Sanity / Icculus.

Absolute A-Go-Go / Absolute A-Go-Go

Sep 90. (lp/c/cd) *<(AGO 1992/+MC/CD)>* **LAWN BOY** [ ] [ ]
– Squirming coil / Reba / My sweet one / Split open and melt / Oh kee pa ceremony / Bathtub gin / Run like an antelope / Lawn boy / Bouncing around the room. *<cd re-iss. Jun97 on 'Elektra'; 7559 61273-2>*

Elektra / Elektra

May 92. (cd/c) *<(7559 61274-2/-4)>* **A PICTURE OF NECTAR** [ ] [ ]
– Llama / Eliza / Cavern / Poor heart / Stash / Manteca / Guelah papyrus / Magilla / Landlady / Glide / Tweezer / The mango song / Chalk dust torture / Faht / Catapult / Tweezer (reprise). *(cd re-iss. Jun97; same)*

Feb 93. (cd/c) *<7559 61433-2>* **RIFT** [-] [51]
– All things reconsidered / It's ice / Silent in the morning / Sparkle / Horn, Weigh / The wedge / Mound / My friend, my friend / Rift / Maze / Lengthwise / The horse / Fast enough for you. *(UK cd-iss Jun97; same)*

Mar 94. (cd/c) *<7559 61628-2/-4>* **(HOIST)** [-] [34]
– Julius / Down with disease / If I could / Riker's mailbox / Axill (part 2) / Lifeboy / Sample in a jar / Wolfman's brother / Scent of a mule / Dog faced boy / Demand. *(UK cd-iss. Jun97; same)*

Jul 95. (d-cd) *<7559 61772-2>* **A LIVE ONE (live)** [-] [18]
– Bouncing around the room / Harry Hood / Chalk dust torture / You enjoy myself / Tweezer / Wilson / Stash / Squirming coil / Slave to the traffic light / Simple / Montana / Gumbo.

Jul 96. (cd) *<(7559 61933-2)>* **STASH** (compilation) [ ] [ ]
– Stash / Scent of a mule / Maze / Bouncing around the moon / Gumbo / Sample in a jar / Split open and melt / Fast enough for you / Down with disease / You enjoy myself / If I could.

Feb 97. (cd/c) *<(7559 61971-2/-4)>* **BILLY BREATHES** [ ] [7] Oct96
– Free / Character zero / Waste / Taste / Cars trucks buses / Talk / Theme from the bottom / Train song / Bliss / Billy breathes / Swept away / Steep / Prince Caspian.

Mar 97. (c-s) *(A 4205C)* **FREE / STRANGE DESIGN** [ ] [ ]
(cd-s+=) *(A 4205CD)* – Theme from the bottom.

Oct 97. (cd/c) *<(7559 62121-2/-4)>* **SLIP STITCH AND PASS** [ ] [17]
– Cities / Wolfman's brother / Jesus just left Chicago / Weigh / Mike's song / Lawn boy / Weekapaug groove / Hello my baby / Taste.

Nov 98. (cd) *<(7559 62297-2)>* **THE STORY OF THE GHOST** [ ] [8]
– The ghost / Birds of a feather / Meat / Guyute / Fikus / Shafty / Limb by limb / Frankie says / Brian and Robert / Water in the sky / Roggae / Wading in the velvet sea / Moma dance / End of session.

PHOTOS

Formed: Evesham, Midlands, England . . . 1978 by former members of punk group, SATAN'S RATS, who comprised STEVE EAGLES, DAVE SPARROW and OLLY HARRISON; they released three singles namely, 'IN MY LOVE FOR YOU', 'YEAR OF THE RATS' and 'YOU MAKE ME SICK'. Having originally tried to prise JAYNE CASEY away from BIG IN JAPAN, they instead settled for WENDY WU, ex-manager of pub band CITY YOUTH. The latter was touted as Britain's dark-haired answer to DEBBIE HARRY, while the group's New-wave-ish pop-rock wasn't a million miles removed from BLONDIE. Probably on the strength of this, The PHOTOS signed to 'C.B.S.', although after only one flop single, 'I'M SO ATTRACTIVE', they moved along the corporate corridor to 'Epic'. During the following Spring of 1980, The PHOTOS developed some chart action as the single, 'IRENE', made the UK Top 60. That summer, surprisingly without a major hit to their name, WU and Co pulled off a chart coup when their eponymous debut album (complete with the purchase incentive of a free 'BLACKMAIL TAPES' lp) hit the UK Top 5. However, the exposure was to be short-lived as WENDY departed for a solo career, bailing out of a sinking ship as a series of singles had failed to chart. WU's own efforts also fell on deaf ears, while the band themselves (with new singer, CHE) took one last shot with the hopefully titled 1983 single, 'THERE'S ALWAYS WORK'. While WENDY teamed up with former VISAGE singer, STEVE STRANGE (in the pop duo, STRANGE CRUISE), EAGLES joined the more obscure BLURT and later co-founded early 90's act, BANG BANG MACHINE. • **Covered:** I SAW HER STANDING THERE (Beatles) / JE T'AIME (Serge Gainsbourg).

Album rating: THE PHOTOS (*5)

SATAN'S RATS

STEVE EAGLES (b. 1958) – guitar / **DAVE SPARROW** – bass / **OLLY HARRISON** – drums

D.J.M. / not iss.

Oct 77. (7") *(DJS 10819)* **IN MY LOVE FOR YOU. / FACADE** [ ] [-]
(re-iss. 1989 on 'Overground' 7"yellow/white; OVER 02)

Dec 77. (7") *(DJS 10821)* **YEAR OF THE RATS. / LOUISE** [ ] [-]
(re-iss. 1989 on 'Overground' 7"yellow/white; OVER 01)

Mar 78. (7") *(DJS 10840)* **YOU MAKE ME SICK. / LOUISE** [ ] [-]
(re-iss. 1991 on 'Overground' 7"clear; OVER 14)

The PHOTOS

— above recruited **WENDY WU** (b. WENDY CRUISE, 29 Nov'59, Winston Green)– vocals

C.B.S. / not iss.

Nov 79. (7") *(CBS 7984)* **I'M SO ATTRACTIVE. / GUITAR HERO** [ ] [ ]

Epic / Epic

Apr 80. (d7") *(EPC 8517)* **IRENE. / BARBARELLAS // SHY. / CRISSILLA** [56] [ ]

Jun 80. (lp) *(PHOTO 5) <NJE 36515>* **THE PHOTOS** [4] [ ]
– Do you have fun / Irene / Barbarellas / Now you tell me that we're through / Look at the band / Loss of contact / She's artistic / All I want / Maxine / Evelyn II / I just don't know what to do with myself. *(free-lp.w.a.)* **THE BLACKMAIL TAPES** – Last time / With honours / Sex object / Lady is a tramp / Do you wanna dance / Skateboard / Evelyn 1 / I saw her standing there.

Jul 80. (7";w-drawn) *(EPC 8785)* **FRIENDS. / JE T'AIME** [ ] [ ]

Sep 80. (7") *(EPC 8872)* **NOW YOU TELL ME THAT WE'RE THROUGH. / JE T'AIME** [ ] [ ]

Feb 81. (7") *(EPCA 1010)* **LIFE IN A DAY. / MORE THAN A FRIEND**
Mar 81. (lp) *(EPC 84849)* **CRYSTAL TIPS AND MIGHTY MICE** [ ] [-]
Jul 81. (7") *(EPC 1369)* **WE'LL WIN. / YOU WON'T GET TO ME**

— split late 1981 after WENDY was replaced by CHE

WENDY WU

Epic Epic

Mar 82. (7") *(EPCA 2128)* **FOR YOUR LOVE. / CHARLOTTE**
Sep 82. (7") *(EPCA 2676)* **RUN JILLY RUN. / NEANDERTHAL BOY**
Oct 83. (7"/12") *(A/TA 3834)* **LET ME GO. / LOVE TONIGHT**

The PHOTOS

— had also re-formed (as a trio) without WENDY who helped form STRANGE CRUISE.

— **ANGUS HINES** – drums; repl. HARRISON

Rialto not iss.

Apr 83. (7"/12") *(RIA/12RIA 16)* **THERE'S ALWAYS WORK. / WORK PHASE** [ ] [-]

— disbanded again for final time later in 1983. STEVE EAGLES joined BLURT before forming early 90's outfit, BANG BANG MACHINE

PHRANC

Born: SUSAN GOTTLIEB, 28 Aug'57, Santa Monica, California, USA. The words Jewish, folksinger and lesbian are those most commonly banded about when discussing this uncompromising performer, or indeed when she's describing herself. Changing her name to PHRANC in the mid-70's after dropping out of high school, the budding singer subsequently fell in with the notorious early 80's L.A. punk/hardcore scene, playing guitar with the likes of CASTRATION SQUAD and CATHOLIC DISCIPLINE. The latter of these (with also CLAUD BESSY – vocals, ROBERT LOPEZ – keyboards, RICKIE JAFFE – bass & CRAIG LEE – drums) had a few tracks on various artists albums, 'San Francisco Punks' and 'Decline Of The Western Civilization'. Eventually tiring of the scene's insularity and relentless negativity, she retraced her folk roots and in 1985 released a debut album, 'FOLKSINGER' for retro specialist, 'Rhino' records. A characteristically candid and honest exploration of politics, both sexual and otherwise, the record was heartily received by more radical critics and increased her small but loyal band of fans. PHRANC then signed to 'Island' at the end of the 80's and released a belated follow-up set, 'I ENJOY BEING A GIRL' (1989). The task of bringing PHRANC to a wider audience proved too great a challenge even for a label as eclectic as 'Island' and the singer parted company with them after 1991's 'POSITIVELY PHRANC'. A pity, as she demonstrated her wide ranging appeal by supporting MORRISSEY on his UK tour the same year. • **Covers:** THE LONESOME DEATH OF HATTIE CARROLL (Bob Dylan) / SURFER GIRL (Beach Boys) / etc.

Album rating: FOLKSINGER (*6) / I ENJOY BEING A GIRL (*6) / POSITIVELY PHRANC (*6)

PHRANC – vocals, acoustic guitar

Stiff Rhino

Nov 85. (7") *(BUY 233)* **AMAZON. / EL SALVADOR** [ ] [-]
(12"+=) *(BUYIT 233)* – Charlotte.
Jan 86. (lp) *(SEEZ 60)* <*RNDA 856*> **FOLKSINGER** [ ] [ ] Nov85
– Noguchi / Mary Hooley / Ballad of the dumb hairdresser / Caped crusader / One o' the girls / Female mudwrestling / The lonesome death of Hattie Carroll / Amazons / Liar liar / Handicapped / Carolyn / Lifeover.
Mar 86. (7") *(BUY 247)* **THE LONESOME DEATH OF HATTIE CARROLL. / EL SALVADOR** [ ] [-]

Island Island

Aug 89. (cd/c/lp) <*(CID/ICT/ILPS 9940)*> **I ENJOY BEING A GIRL**
– Folksinger / I enjoy being a girl / Double decker bed / Bloodbath / Individuality / Rodeo parakeet / Take off your swastika / Toy time / Martina / Myriam and Esther / The ballad of Lucy and Ted / Moonlight becomes you.
Jul 91. (cd/c/lp) <*(CID/ICT/ILPS 9981)*> **POSITIVELY PHRANC** [ ] [ ] Mar91
– I like you / I'm not romantic / '64 Ford / Hitchcock / Tipton / Dress code / Why? / Gertrude Stein / Surfer girl / Outta here.

Kill Rock Stars Kill Rock Stars

Aug 94. (7") *(KRS 230)* **BULLDAGGER SWAGGER. / HILARY'S EYEBROWS**

— Phrancly, it looks as if she's given it all up

Jeffrey Lee PIERCE (see under ⇒ GUN CLUB)

PIGBAG

Formed: based- Bristol, England . . . 1980 by JAMES JOHNSTONE and ex-POP GROUP man, SIMON UNDERWOOD alongside OLLIE MOORE, CHRIS LEIGH, CHIP CARPENTER and ROGER FREEMAN. Managed by Linda Neville, this experimental/instrumental combo formed their own label, 'Y Records' (named after The POP GROUP's semi-legendary debut) via 'Rough Trade', issuing their seminal 'PAPA'S GOT A BRAND NEW PIGBAG' single in Spring '81. Revelling in classic brass-led soul/funk yet retaining a residue of edgy paranoia from The POP GROUP, the single climbed to the UK Top 3 over the space of a year. By this point they'd already scored two minor hits with 'SUNNY DAY' and 'GETTING UP', the latter serving as the lead track on debut set, 'DR HECKLE AND MR JIVE' (1982). A dancefloor-friendly yet consistently intriguing listen, the record limbo-danced its way from the Latin party vibes of the aforementioned 'GETTING UP' to the rolling voodoo-bones percussion of 'DOZO DON' and the bass groove/jerky jazz workouts of 'BRIAN THE SNAIL' with snake-hipped ease. Despite the record's glowing praise and Top 20 success, the band found it difficult to follow-up their massive debut single and even with the addition of a female vocalist (ANDREA JAEGAR) to spice up the sound, follow-up set, 'LEND AN EAR' (1983), didn't even chart. By early '83, the band had already split with UNDERWOOD going on to play briefly with RIP, RIG & PANIC. This wasn't the end of the story, however, 'PAPA'S GOT A BRAND NEW PIGBAG' later re-released in 1987 to tie in with a retrospective compilation; of course it was a hit all over again, and again . . . in the early 90's when super-DJ PAUL OAKENFOLD and his PERFECTO ALLSTARS released a dance version.

Album rating: DR HECKLE & MR JIVE (*7) / LEND AN EAR (*4) / PIGBAG – LIVE (*4) / THE BEST OF PIGBAG compilation (*7)

JAMES JOHNSTONE – guitar, alto sax, steel drums / **OLLIE MOORE** – tenor sax, clarinet, sanza / **CHRIS LEIGH** – trumpet, percussion / **CHIP CARPENTER** – drums, percussion, tumbas / **SIMON UNDERWOOD** – bass, cello, violin (ex-POP GROUP) / **ROGER FREEMAN** – percussion, trombone, keyboards, piano

Y Records not iss.

May 81. (7") *(Y 10)* **PAPA'S GOT A BRAND NEW PIG BAG. / BACKSIDE** [ ] [-]
(12"+=) *(Y 10T)* – Another orangutango.
(above re-dist.Mar82, hit No.3)
Oct 81. (7") *(Y 12)* **SUNNY DAY. / ELEPHANTS WISH TO BECOME NIMBLE** [53] [-]
Jan 82. (7") *(Y 16)* **GETTING UP. / GIGGLING MUD** [61] [-]
(12"+=) *(Y 16T)* – Go cat.
Mar 82. (lp/c) *(Y/YK 17)* **DR HECKLE AND MR JIVE** [18] [-]
– Getting up / Bigbag / Dozo Don / Brian the snail / Wiggling / Brazil nuts / Orangutango / As it will be.

— **BRIAN** – drums / **+ OSCAR** – trombone repl. ROGER who joined DR. CALCULUS (signed to '10-Virgin', released a couple of singles and an album, 'DESIGNER BEATNIK' in '86)

Jul 82. (7"/12") *(Y/12Y 24)* **THE BIG BEAN. / SCUMDA** [40] [-]

— **ANGELA JAEGAR** (OLIVER) – vox (ex-RIP, RIG & PANIC, ex-DROWNING CRAZE)

Feb 83. (7"/12") *(Y/YT 101)* **HIT THE 'O' DECK. / SIX OF ONE** [ ] [-]
Feb 83. (lp/c) *(YLP/YK 501)* **LEND AN EAR** [ ] [-]
– Weak at the knees / Hit the 'O' deck / Ubud / One way ticket to Cubesville / Jump the line / Can't see for looking / No such thing as / Listen listen (liitle man).
Jun 83. (m-lp/m-c) *(YMP/YK 1001)* **PIGBAG LIVE (live)** [ ] [-]
– Shack of scraps / Smiling faces / Sunny day / Papa's got a brand new pigbag / Jump the line / Global terrain / End of Ubud / Can't see for looking.

— they had already disbanded early '83, SIMON joined RIP, RIG & PANIC

– compilations, others, etc. –

Nov 87. (cd) *Kaz; (KAZCD 3)* **THE BEST OF PIGBAG** [ ] [-]
– Papa's got a brand new Pigbag (extended) / Weak at the knees / Hit the 'O' deck / Getting up / Brazil nuts / Jump the line / Another orangutango (extended) / Sunny day (extended) / Big bean (extended) / Can't see for looking / Six of one / Big bag.
(re-iss cd+=) – Listen listen little man / Papa's got a brand new Pigbag.
Sep 94. (12") *Kaz; (KAZT 94)* **PAPA'S GOT A BRAND NEW PIGBAG (mixes)** [ ] [-]
(12") *(KAZX 94)* – ('A'mixes).

PIGFACE (see under ⇒ BRAIN, Brian)

PiL (see under ⇒ PUBLIC IMAGE LTD.)

PINK MILITARY

Formed: Liverpool, England . . . 1978 by former BIG IN JAPAN frontwoman, JAYNE CASEY. Recruiting JOHN HIGHWAY, WAYNE WADDEN, NICKY COOL and PAUL HORNBY, she initiated a career which, if not quite as high profile as her famous ex-bandmates (BILL DRUMMOND, IAN BROUDIE, HOLLY JOHNSON etc.), was held in equally high critical esteem. Released on independent local label, 'Eric's', a 1979 debut EP, 'BLOOD AND LIPSTICK', caused enough of a stir to catch the attention of 'Virgin', who subsequently handled distribution of debut album, 'DO ANIMALS BELIEVE IN GOD?' (1980). Featuring a replacement rhythm section of CHRIS JOYCE and MARTIN DEMPSEY along with pianist CHARLIE GRUFF, the record was an entrancing sequence of experimental new wave/pop boasting such enduring tracks as the needling 'BACK ON THE LONDON STAGE' and the haunting 'I CRY'. Unfortunately the album performed poorly sales wise and with the 'Virgin' deal dead in the water, CASEY took a completely different approach. Altering the name to PINK INDUSTRY, she subsequently hooked up with future FRANKIE GOES TO HOLLYWOOD member, AMBROSE REYNOLDS, for an acclaimed 1982 single, 'IS THIS THE END?' and an album, 'LOW TECHNOLOGY' (1983). Heavily electronic with snatches of samples, aberrant sax, bleeps, guitar abuse, hints of eastern promise and of course CASEY's powerful vocals, the record was a breathtakingly diverse lesson in how to apply modern technology without sounding like SPANDAU BALLET. A second set, 'WHO TOLD YOU YOU WERE NAKED' (1983), continued in a similar electro sound-collage vein later that year although it would be a further two years before the release of any new material. In the event, 1985's 'NEW BEGINNINGS' album was to be PINK INDUSTRY's death knell as CASEY decided to restructure and concentrate on a TV career. • **Trivia:** MORRISSEY's photo was on the cover of their single, 'WHAT WOULDN'T I GIVE'.

Album rating: DO ANIMALS BELIEVE IN GOD? (*8) / LOW TECHNOLOGY (*6) / WHO TOLD YOU – YOU WERE NAKED (*6) / NEW BEGINNINGS (*5)

JAYNE CASEY – vocals (ex-BIG IN JAPAN) / **JOHN HIGHWAY** – guitar / **NICKY COOL** – keyboards, synthesizers / **WAYNE WADDEN** – bass / **PAUL HORNBY** – drums

Last Trumpet | not iss.

Feb 79. (7") *(LT 001)* **BUDDHA WALKING / DISNEY SLEEPING (live; as "PINK MILITARY STANDS ALONE")** [ ] [-]
– Degenerated man / Sanjo Kantara / Dead lady of clowntown / Heaven / Hell.

— **STEVE TORCH** – bass repl. WADDEN

— **TIM WHITAKER** – drums (ex-DEAF SCHOOL) repl. PAUL

— **MARTIN DEMPSEY** – guitar (ex-YACHTS) repl. ROY who repl. HIGHWAY

Eric's | not iss.

Sep 79. (12"ep) *(ERIC'S 002)* **BLOOD AND LIPSTICK** [ ] [-]
– Spellbound / Blood and lipstick / I cry / Clowntown.

— **CHRIS JOYCE** – drums (of MOTHMEN) repl. TIM (later to)

— **CHARLIE GRUFF** – keyboards + **NEIL INNES** repl. TORCH

Jun 80. (lp) *(ERIC'S 004)* **DO ANIMALS BELIEVE IN GOD?** [ ] [-]
– Degenerated man / I cry / Did you see her / Wild west / Back on the London stage / After Hiroshima / Living in the jungle / Dreamtime / War games / Heaven – Hell / Do animals believe in God? *(re-iss. 1989 on 'Virgin'; OVED 231)*

Jul 80. (7") *(ERIC'S 005)* **DID YOU SEE HER. / EVERYDAY** [ ] [-]

— DEMPSEY joined IT'S IMMATERIAL and later MEL-O-TONES. CHRIS JOYCE joined DURUTTI COLUMN and later SIMPLY RED. NICKY formed FACTION.

PINK INDUSTRY

JAYNE CASEY – vocals / **AMBROSE REYNOLDS** – bass, keyboards (ex-BIG IN JAPAN, ex-HOLLYCAUST (w/ HOLLY JOHNSON), ex-NIGHTMARES IN WAX (pre-DEAD OR ALIVE), ex-WALKIE TALKIES) / **JAZIO JOOLOWSKI** –

Zulu | not iss.

Feb 82. (12"ep) *(ZULU 1)* **IS THIS THE END? / 47. / DON'T LET GO / FINAL CRY** [ ] [-]

Mar 83. (lp) *(ZULU 2)* **LOW TECHNOLOGY** [ ] [-]
– I wish / New aims / Don't let go / Creating hours / Enjoy the pain / Savage / Send them away / Remove the stain / Heavenly / Is this the end?.

Oct 83. (lp) *(ZULU 4)* **WHO TOLD YOU – YOU WERE NAKED** [ ] [-]
– Walk away / Not moving / Urban jazz / Fear of failure / Anyone's fashion / Situation / Two culture's / Extreme / The raft / This is the place / The only one / Time for change.

Jun 85. (7") *(ZULU 6)* **WHAT WOULDN'T I GIVE. / BOUND BY SILENCE** [ ] [-]

Jul 85. (lp) *(ZULU 7)* **NEW BEGINNINGS** [ ] [-]
– Stand alone / What wouldn't I give / Rain of pride / Bound by silence / The corpse / etc

Cathexis | not iss.

Nov 87. (12"ep) *(CRL 16)* **DON'T LET GO. / TICKET TO HEAVEN / EMPTY BEACH** [ ] [-]

May 88. (lp) *(CRL 18)* **PINK INDUSTRY** (compilation) [ ] [-]
– Enjoy the pain / Send them away / New aims / Is this the end? / Not moving / This is the place / Pain of pride / State of grace / Bound by silence / Cruel garden / What I wouldn't give / Don't let go / Ticket to Heaven / Empty beach.

— had already disbanded a year earlier

– other compilation –

Dec 95. (cd) *Audioglobe; (PINK 1CD)* **NEW NAKED TECHNOLOGY** [ ] [-]

PIXIES

Formed: Boston, Massachusetts, USA . . .1986 by L.A. born frontman and self-confessed UFO freak, BLACK FRANCIS (real name, deep breath . . . CHARLES MICHAEL KITRIDGE THOMPSON IV) along with guitarist JOEY SANTIAGO. Famously placing a newspaper ad requesting musicians with a penchant for PETER, PAUL AND MARY and HUSKER DU, the only taker was KIM DEAL who subsequently brought in drummer DAVID LOVERING. Originally trading under the moniker PIXIES IN PANOPLY, the band soon trimmed this down to the punchier PIXIES and began kicking up a storm on the Boston music scene with their spiky, angular noise-pop (that's two thirds noise, one third pop) and wilfully cryptic lyrics. Along with fellow Bostonians THROWING MUSES, the band were signed to '4 a.d.' by a suitably impressed Ivo Watts-Russell, the label releasing The PIXIES' debut 'COME ON PILGRIM' in late '87. Stunningly different, the record galvanised the early PIXIES sound, a bizarre hybrid of manic, strangulated vocals (often sung in Spanish), searing melodic noise and schizophrenic, neo-latin rhythms. The album drew an early core of believers but it wasn't until the release of 'SURFER ROSA' (1988) that the band were hailed as the saviours of indie rock. Taking the formula of the debut to its brain splintering conclusion, the likes of 'BONE MACHINE', the incendiary 'SOMETHING AGAINST YOU' and careering 'BROKEN FACE' were utterly compelling in their blistering intensity. The sheer unhinged abandon with which BLACK FRANCIS threw himself into these songs has to be heard to be believed. You begin to fear that the man really has lost it when he asks 'WHERE IS MY MIND' in his inimitable melancholy howl. DEAL was equally affecting on the gorgeous 'GIGANTIC', the track building from a metaphorical whisper to a scream. Truly essential, 'SURFER ROSA' remains one of the most pivotal alternative rock records of the last ten years. Following their first headline UK tour, the band hooked up with producer Gil Norton for the 'DOOLITTLE' (1989) album. Previewed by the haunting 'MONKEY GONE TO HEAVEN', the record showcased a cleaner, more pop-friendly sound, most notably on (then) upcoming single, 'HERE COMES YOUR MAN'. Swoonfully poptastic, this song was guaranteed to have even the most miserable SMITHS fan grinning ear to ear, putting the toss that passes for modern 'indie-pop' to eternal shame. The demented 'DEBASER' was another highlight, becoming a dependable fixture at indie discos for oh, aeons. As well as a mammoth world tour, DEAL found time for her side project, The BREEDERS. A collaboration with the delectable TANYA DONELLY (ex-THROWING MUSES), the pair released the acclaimed 'POD' album in 1990. Later that year came 'BOSSANOVA', another breathtaking collection that had the music press in rapture. Lyrically, BLACK was in his element, losing himself in science fiction fantasy while the band raged and charmed in equal measure. The album reached No.3 in the UK charts and The PIXIES could apparently do no wrong, consolidating their position as one of the biggest American acts in Europe. Yet the critics turned on them with the release of 'TROMPE LE MONDE' (1991), in keeping with the times a decidedly grungier affair. Accusations of "Heavy Metal" were way off the mark. In reality, the record was still chokka with stellar tunes, you just had to dig deeper to find them. 'PLANET OF SOUND', 'SPACE (I BELIEVE IN)' and 'MOTORWAY TO ROSWELL' were all quintessential PIXIES, FRANCIS as endearingly fascinated as ever with the mysteries of the universe. Sadly, the singer was soon to turn his obsession into a solo venture, The PIXIES gone almost as quickly as they had arrived, leaving behind a brief but rich sonic legacy. With FRANCIS changing his name to the rather dull FRANK BLACK, he went on to release a moderately successful eponymous solo debut in 1993 and a wryly titled follow-up, 'TEENAGER OF THE YEAR' (1994), DEAL going on to make a further album with The BREEDERS. Inevitably, none of these projects approached the deranged genius of The PIXIES. Rock will never see their like again. • **Songwriters:** BLACK FRANCIS penned except; WINTERLONG + I'VE BEEN WAITING FOR YOU (Neil Young) / EVIL HEARTED YOU (Yardbirds) / HEAD ON (Jesus & Mary Chain) / CECELIA ANN (Surftones) / BORN IN CHICAGO (Paul Butterfield's Blues Band) / I CAN'T FORGET (Leonard Cohen). FRANK BLACK solo:- JUST A LITTLE (Beau Brummels) / RE-MAKE, RE-MODEL (Roxy Music) / HANG ON TO YOUR EGO (Beach Boys).

Album rating: COME ON PILGRIM mini (*7) / SURFER ROSA (*10) / DOOLITTLE (*9) / BOSSANOVA (*8) / TROMPE LE MONDE (*7) / Frank Black: FRANK BLACK (*8) / TEENAGER OF THE YEAR (*8) / THE CULT OF RAY (*5)

BLACK FRANCIS (b. CHARLES MICHAEL KITRIDGE THOMPSON IV, 1965, Long Beach, Calif.) – vocals, guitar / **JOEY SANTIAGO** (b.10 Jun'65, Manila, Philippines) – lead guitar / **KIM DEAL** (Mrs.JOHN MURPHY) (b.10 Jun'61, Dayton, Ohio) – bass, vocals / **DAVE LOVERING** (b. 6 Dec'61) – drums

4.a.d. | Elektra

Oct 87. (m-lp) *(MAD 709) <61296>* **COME ON PILGRIM** [ ] [ ]
– Caribou / Vamos / Islade encounter / Ed is dead / The holiday song / Nimrod's son / I've been tried / Levitate me.

Mar 88. (lp/c)(cd) *(CAD/+C 803)(CAD 803CD) <61295>* **SURFER ROSA** [ ] [ ]
– Bone machine / Break my body / Something against you / Broken face / Gigantic / River Euphrates / Where is my mind? / Cactus / Tony's theme / Oh my golly! / Vamos / I'm amazed / Brick is red. *(cd+=)* – COME ON PILGRIM (m-lp)

Aug 88. (12"ep/cd-ep) *(BAD 805/+CD)* **GIGANTIC. / RIVER EUPHRATES. / VAMOS. / IN HEAVEN (LADY IN THE RADIATOR SONG)** [ ] [-]

Mar 89. (7") *(AD 904)* **MONKEY GONE TO HEAVEN. / MANTA RAY** [60] [ ]
(12"+=/cd-s+=) *(BAD 904/+CD)* – Weird at my school / Dancing the manta ray.

Apr 89. (lp/c)(cd) *(CAD/+C 905)(CAD 905CD) <60856>* **DOOLITTLE** [8] [98]
– Debaser / Tame / Wave of mutilation / I bleed / There goes my gun / Here comes your man / Dead / Monkey gone to Heaven / La la love you / Mr. Grieves / Crackity Jones / #13 baby / Silver / Hey / Gouge away.

Jun 89. (7") *(AD 909) <66694>* **HERE COMES YOUR MAN. / INTO THE WHITE** [54] [ ]
(12"+=/cd-s+=) *(BAD 909/+CD)* – Wave of mutilation (UK surf) / Bailey's walk.

— KIM DEAL was also part of amalgamation The BREEDERS

Jul 90. (7"/c-s) *(AD/+C 0009) <66616>* **VELOURIA. / I'VE BEEN WAITING FOR YOU** [28] [ ]
(12"+=/cd-s+=) *(BAD 0009/+CD)* – Make believe / The thing.

Aug 90. (cd)(lp/c) *(CAD 0010CD)(CAD/+C 0010) <60963>* **BOSSANOVA** [3] [70]
– Cecilia Ann / Rock music / Velouria / Allison / Is she weird / Ana / All over the world / Dig for fire / Down to the wall / The happening / Blown away / Hang wire / Stormy weather / Havalina.

Oct 90. (7"/c-s) *(AD/+C 0014) <66596>* **DIG FOR FIRE. / VELVETY (instrumental)** [62] [ ]
(12"+=/cd-s+=) *(BAD 0014/+CD)* – Winterlong / Santo.

May 91. (7") *(AD 1008)* **PLANET OF SOUND. / BUILD HIGH** [27] [ ]
(c-s+=)(12"+=/cd-s+=) *(BADC 1008)(BAD 1008/+CD)* – Evil hearted you / Theme from Narc.

Sep 91. (cd)(lp/c) *(CAD 1014CD)(CAD/+C 1014) <61118>* **TROMPE LE MONDE** [7] [92]
– Trompe de Monde / Planet of sound / Alec Eiffel / The sad punk / Head on / U-mass / Palace of the brine / Letter to Memphis / Bird dream Of the Olympus mons / Space (I believe in) / Subbacultcha / Distance equals rate times time / Lovely day / Motorway to Roswell / The Navajo know.

Nov 91. (12"ep) **ALEC EIFFEL / MOTORWAY TO ROSWELL. / PLANET OF SOUND (live) / TAME (live)** [ ] [-]

Feb 92. (12"ep) *<66444>* **ALEC EIFFEL / LETTER TO MEMPHIS (instrumental). / BUILD LIFE / EVIL HEARTED YOU** [-] [ ]

— Disbanded late in '92, with BLACK FRANCIS going solo as FRANK BLACK.

– compilations, etc. –

on '4 a.d.' / 'Elektra' unless otherwise mentioned

Sep 97. (7") *(AD 7010)* **DEBASER (demo). / £13 BABY** [23] [ ]
(cd-s) *(BAD 7010CD)* – ('A'studio) / Bone machine / Gigantic / Isla de Encanta.
(cd-s) *(BADD 7010CD)* – ('A'live) / Holiday song (live) / Cactus (live) / Nimrod's son (live).

Oct 97. (d-cd/d-c) *(DAD/+C 7011) / <62118>* **DEATH TO THE PIXIES** [28] [ ]
– Cecilia Ann / Planet of sound / Tame / Here comes your man / Debaser / Wave of mutilation / Dig for fire / Caribou / Holiday song / Nimrod's son / U mass / Bone machine / Gigantic / Where is my mind / Velouria / Gouge away / Monkey gone to Heaven / Debaser / Rock music / Broken face / Isla De Encanta / Hangfire / Dead / Into the white / Monkey gone to Heaven / Gouge away / Gouge away / Here comes your man / Alidon / Hey / Gigantic / Crackity Jones / Something against you / Tame / Wave of mutilation / Where is my mind / Ed is dead / Vamos / Tony's theme. *(de-luxe version hit No.20 q-lp/d-cd; DADD 7011/+CD)*

Jul 98. (cd) *(GAD 8013) <62185>* **PIXIES AT THE BBC (live)** [45] [ ]
– Wild honey pie / There goes my gun / Dead / Subbacultcha / Manta Ray / Is she weird? / Ana / Down to the well / Wave of mutilation / Letter to Memphis / Levitate me / Caribou / Monkey gone to Heaven / Hey / In Heaven (lady in the radiator song).

FRANK BLACK

— with **ERIC DREW FELDMAN** – bass, keyboards, synthetics (ex-CAPTAIN BEEFHEART) / **NICK VINCENT** – drums, percussion / + extra guitars **SANTIAGO, MORRIS TEPPER + DAVID SARDY**

4 a.d. | Elektra

Mar 93. (lp/cd)(c) *(CAD 3004/+CD)(CADC 3004) <61467>* **FRANK BLACK** [9] [ ]
– Los Angeles / I heard Ramona sing / Hang on to your ego / Fu Manchu / Places named after numbers / Czar / Old black dawning / Ten percenter / Brackish boy / Two spaces / Tossed (instrumental version) / Parry the wind high, low / Adda Lee / Every time I go around here / Don't ya rile 'em. *(cd re-iss. Jul98; GAD 3004CD)*

Apr 93. (7") *(AD 3005) <8782-2>* **HANG ON TO YOUR EGO. / THE BALLAD OF JOHNNY HORTON** [ ] [ ]
(cd-s+=) *(BAD 3005CD)* – Surf epic.

— same trio augmented by **SANTIAGO, TEPPER + LYLE WORKMAN** – guitar

May 94. (7") *(AD 4007)* **HEADACHE. / ('A'mix)** [53] [-]
(10"/cd-s) *(BADD 4007/+CD)* – ('A'side) / Men in black / At the end of the world / Oddball.
(cd-s) *(BAD 4007CD)* – ('A'side) / Hate me / This is where I belong / Amnesia.

May 94. (d-lp/cd)(c) *(DAD 4009/+CD)(DADC 4009) <61618>* **TEENAGER OF THE YEAR** [21] [ ]
– Whatever happened to Pong? / Thalassocracy / (I want to live on an) Abstract plain / Calistan / The vanishing spies / Speedy Marie / Headache / Sir Rockaby / Freedom rock / Two reelers / Fiddle riddle / Ole Mulholland / Fazer eyes / I could stay here forever / The hostess with the mostest / Superabound / Big red / Space is gonna do me good / White noise maker / Pure denizen of the citizens band / Bad, wicked world / Pie in the sky. *(re-iss. Jul98; GAD 4009CD)*

— FRANK BLACK had earlier in the year teamed up with ex-SEX PISTOL; GLEN MATLOCK to form tribute band FRANK BLACK & THE STAX PISTOLS

Noise Annoys | not iss.

Dec 95. (cd/d-lp) *(ANAN CD/V 7)* **THE BLACK SESSIONS (live in Paris)** [ ] [-]
(re-iss. Oct97; same)

— now w/ **LYLE WORKMAN** – lead guitar / **DAVID McCAFFREY** – bass / **SCOTT BOUTIER** – drums

Epic | Warners

Dec 95. (ltd-7") *(662 671-7)* **THE MARXIST. / BETTER THINGS** [ ] [-]

Jan 96. (7") *(662 786-7)* **MEN IN BLACK. / JUST A LITTLE** [37] [-]
(cd-s+=) *(662 786-2)* – Re-make, re-model.
(cd-s) *(662 786-5)* – ('A'side) / You never heard of me / Pray a little faster / Announcement.

Jan 96. (cd/c/lp) *(481 647-2/-4/-1) <43070>* **THE CULT OF RAY** [39] [ ]
– The Marxist / Men in black / Punk rock city / You ain't me / Jesus was right / I don't want to hurt you (every single time) / Mosh, don't pass the guy / Kicked in the taco / Creature crawling / Adventure and the resolution / Dance war / The cult of Ray / Last stand of Shazeb Andleeb.

Jul 96. (7") *(663 463-7)* **I DON'T WANT TO HURT YOU (EVERY SINGLE TIME). / YOU AIN'T ME (live)** [63] [-]
(cd-s+=) *(663 463-2)* – The Marxist / Better things.
(cd-s) *(663 463-5)* – ('A'live) / Men in black (live) / Village of the sun (live) / The last stand of Shazeb Andleeb (live).

FRANK BLACK AND THE CATHOLICS

Play It Again Sam | SpinArt

Apr 98. (7"ep/cd-ep) *(BIAS 347 7/CD)* **ALL MY GHOSTS / LIVING ON SOUL / HUMBOULDT COUNTY MASSACRE / CHANGING OF THE GUARDS** [ ] [-]

May 98. (cd/c/lp) *(BIAS 370 CD/MC/LP) <SPART 67>* **FRANK BLACK AND THE CATHOLICS** [61] [ ]
– All my ghosts / Back to Rome / Do you feel bad about it / Dog gone / I gotta move / I need peace / King and Queen of Siam / Six sixty six / Solid gold / Steak 'n' sabre / Suffering / Man who was too loud. *(ltd-cd+=; BIAS 370CDX)* – All my ghosts / Living on soul / Humboldt county massacre / Changing of the guards.

– his compilations, etc. –

Jul 95. (12"ep/cd-ep) *Strange Fruit; (SFPS/+CD 091)* **PEEL SESSION** [ ] [-]
– Handyman / The man who was too loud / The Jacques Tati / Sister Isabel.

Nov 97. (cd-ep; with TEENAGE FANCLUB) *Strange Fruit; (SFRSCD 042)* **THE JOHN PEEL SESSION** [ ] [-]

PIZZICATO FIVE

Formed: Tokyo, Japan ... 1979 by university students and part-time sound engineers, YASUHARA KONISHI and KEITARO TAKANAMI. After recruiting fellow Western music fan, RYO KAMAMIYA, they auditioned unsuccessfully for an English speaking vocalist. Eventually locating MAMIKO SASAKI, the quartet finally debuted in the mid-80's with the single, 'AUDREY HEPBURN COMPLEX', the first in a series of kitschy releases that plundered the cheesiest bits of 60's/70's US/UK pop history in search of the perfect post-modern collage. Amid a revolving door personnel situation, the founding duo remained intact throughout the 80's and into the 90's, their sizeable Japanese success promting US indie giant, 'Matador', to try them out on American alternative fans. However, after only one EP, 'FIVE BY FIVE', KONISHI was left to take up the reins alongside recent vocal addition, MAKI NOMIYA, after TAKANAMI finally bailed out. Suffocatingly hip and contrived or refreshingly funky according to taste, P5 were never really destined to capture the imagination of the average indie fan while their sampledelic pop deconstructions went over the head of chart audiences.

Album rating: NON-STANDARD YEARS '85-'86 compilation (*3) / COUPLES (*4) / BELISSIMA! (*5) / MADE IN USA compilation (*7) / THE SOUND OF MUSIC BY PIZZICATO FIVE (*6)

YASUHARA KONISHI + KEITARO TAKANAMI – electronics / **RYO KAMAMIYA** – electronics / **MAMIKO SASAKI** – vocals

Teichiku | not iss.

1985. (12"ep) **THE AUDREY HEPBURN COMPLEX EP** [-] [-] Japan
– 59th Street bridge song / Boy meets girl / September song / Audrey Hepburn complex.

1986. (12"ep) **PIZZICATO V IN ACTION EP** [-] [-] Japan
– From party to party / Action painting / Let's go away for awhile / What's new, Pizzicato?

1987. (cd) *(TECN 22333,223)* **NON-STANDARD YEARS** (compilation) [-] [-] Japan
(re-mixed Jun98; 15256)

CBS-Sony | not iss.

1987. (cd) *(32DH 637)* **COUPLES** [-] [-] Japan
– Magical connection / Summertime, summertime / They all laughed / Serial stories / Apartment / What now our love / Seven o'clock news / Odd couple and the others / My blue heaven / Party joke / Two sleepy people / Everytime we say goodbye.

— **TAJIMA TAKAO** – vocals; repl. SASAKI

1988. (cd) *(32DH 5126)* **BELISSIMA!** [-] [-] Japan
– Planets / Temptation talk / Holy triangle / World standard / Couples / Sunday impressions / Swim / Seventeen / This can't be love / Work of God.

— **MAKI NOMIYA** – vocals; repl. TAKAO who formed ORIGINAL LOVE

Matador | Matador

Aug 94. (m-cd/m-lp) *<(OLE 096-2/-1)>* **FIVE BY FIVE** [ ] [ ]
– Pizzacatomania / Twiggy, Twiggy / Baby love child / Me Japanese boy / This year's girl No.2.

Oct 94. (cd/c/lp) *<(OLE 099-2/-4/-1)>* **MADE IN USA** (compilation) [ ] [ ]
– I / Sweet soul revue / Magic carpet ride / Readymade FM / Baby love child / Twiggy, Twiggy / Twiggy vs James Bond / This year's girl / I wanna be like you / Go-go dancer / Catchy / Peace music.

Mar 95. (12"ep/cd-ep) *<(OLE 128-1/-2)>* **QUICKIE EP** [ ] [ ]
– Magic carpet ride (mixes) / Go-go dancer / I wanna be like you.

May 95. (12"ep/cd-ep) *<OLE 138-1/-2>* **QUICKIE TWO EP** [-] [ ]

Apr 96. (7") *<(OLE 167-7)>* **HAPPY SAD. / IF I WERE A GROUPIE** [ ] [ ]
(cd-s+=) *<(OLE 167-2)>* – CDJ.

Matador | Atlantic

Jun 96. (cd/d-lp) *(OLE 166-2/-2) <92622>* **THE SOUND OF MUSIC BY PIZZICATO FIVE** [ ] [ ] Oct95
– We love Pizzicato Five / Rock'n'roll / The night is still young / Happy sad / Groovy is my name / Sophisticated catchy / Strawberry sleighride / If I were a groupie / Sweet Thursday / CDJ / Fortune cookie. *(d-lp+=)* – Number five / Peace music / Airplane / Rock'n'roll.

Matador | Matador

Feb 97. (10"ep/cd-ep) *<(OLE 223-1/-2)>* **SISTER FREEDOM TAPES** [ ] [ ] Nov96
– Airplane '96 / Domino / Snowflakes / Chicken curry / Mini Cooper / Holger and Marcus / Cornflakes / To our children's children's children / Passing by

Mar 97. (10"ep/cd-ep) *<(OLE 224-1/-2)>* **COMBINAISON SPACIALE** [ ] [ ]
– Baby portable rock / Ice cream meltin' mellow / Contact / Good / Tokyo mon amour / Ice cream meltin' mellow.

Matador | Capitol

Sep 97. (cd/lp) *(OLE 198-2/-1) <59181>* **HAPPY END OF THE WORLD** [ ] [ ]
– The world is spinning at 45 rpm / The Earth goes round / Trailer music / It's a beautiful day / Love's prelude / Love's theme / My baby portable player sound / Mon amour Tokyo / Collision and improvisation / Porno 3003: Music for sofa – Galaxy / Arigato we love you / Ma vie, l'ete de vie / Happy ending.

Matador | Matador

Oct 97. (7") *(OLE 289-7)* **MON AMOUR TOKYO. / TRAILER MUSIC** [ ] [-]
(cd-s+=) *(OLE 289-2)* – Contact.
(cd-s+=) *(OLE 290-2)* – Happy birthday.

Oct 97. (12") *<(OLE 273-1)>* **THE WORLD IS SPINNING AT 45 RPM: P5 REMIXES VOL.1** [ ] [ ]

Oct 97. (12") *<(OLE 274-1)>* **THE WORLD IS SPINNING AT 45 RPM: P5 REMIXES VOL.2** [ ] [ ]

Nov 97. (12") *<(OLE 275-1)>* **THE WORLD IS SPINNING AT 45 RPM: P5 REMIXES VOL.3** [ ] [ ]

Nov 97. (12") *<(OLE 276-1)>* **THE WORLD IS SPINNING AT 45 RPM: P5 REMIXES VOL.4** [ ] [ ]

Dec 97. (12") *<(OLE 277-1)>* **THE WORLD IS SPINNING AT 45 RPM: P5 REMIXES VOL.5** [ ] [ ]

Dec 97. (12") *<(OLE 278-1)>* **THE WORLD IS SPINNING AT 45 RPM: P5 REMIXES VOL.6** [ ] [ ]

Jan 98. (12") *<(OLE 279-1)>* **THE WORLD IS SPINNING AT 45 RPM: P5 REMIXES VOL.7** [ ] [ ]

Jan 98. (12") <(OLE 280-1)> **THE WORLD IS SPINNING AT 45 RPM: P5 REMIXES VOL.8** [ ] [ ]

Apr 98. (12") *(GINA 03)* **IT'S A BEAUTIFUL DAY. / LOVE"S THEME / MON AMOUR TOKYO** [ ] [-]
(above issued on 'Gina')

Jun 98. (cd/d-lp) <(OLE 282-2/-1)> **HAPPY END OF YOU** (remixes) [ ] [ ] May98
– Love's theme (AUTOMATOR) / Trailer music (808 STATE) / Goes round (DADDY-O) / Porno 3003 (DJ DARA) / Porno 3000 (GUSGUS) / My baby portable player sound (SEAN O'HAGAN) / Happy ending (OVAL) / It's a beautiful day (JOHN OSWALD) / Love's theme (SAINT ETIENNE) / Trailer music (MOMUS) / Collision and improvisation (SHOOTER) / Contact (DIMITRI FROM PARIS) / The world is spinning at 45 rpm (DANIEL MILLER / GARETH JONES).

Aug 98. (cd/lp) <(OLE 333-2/-1)> **PLAYBOY AND PLAYGIRL** [ ] [ ]
– Depression / Rolls Royce / International Pizzicato 5 mansion / New song / Weekend / Magic twin candle tale / Concerto / Such a beautiful girl like you / Playboy playgirl / I hear a symphony / Drinking wine / Great invitations / Stars.

PLACEBO

Formed: South London, England . . . October '94 by the cosmopolitan pair of BRIAN MOLKO and STEFAN OLSDAL, who had attended the same school in Luxembourg. They met up again in a London tube having spent time in the States and Sweden respectively. Early the following year, they recruited Swedish drummer, ROBERT SCHULTZBERG, the trio subsequently becoming joint winners of the 'In The City' Battle Of The Bands competition. Late in '95, PLACEBO shared a one-off single, 'BRUISE PRISTINE', with the band, SOUP, on 'Fierce Panda' records. After only a handful of gigs, they signed for 'Deceptive' (home of ELASTICA), leading to tours with ASH, BUSH and WHALE. A solitary single later ('COME HOME'), MOLKO and Co., hit the proverbial jackpot via a deal with Virgin/Hut subsidiary, 'Elevator'. The openly bisexual, cross-dressing MOLKO, drew comparisons with 70's glam idols like BOLAN and BOWIE, the music, however, traded in the glitter for a darker listening experience. Taking the fast lane out of the post-grunge pile-up, they fused elements of avant-garde rock and cerebral metal, MOLKO's paint-stripping shrill drawing comparisons with Rush's GEDDY LEE and DAVID SURKAMP of the more obscure Pavlov's Dog. Their eponymous debut album was released in mid-'96 to a fawning music press, metal-mag Kerrang's strong support helping the record dent the UK Top 40. Hit singles 'TEENAGE ANGST' and the Top 5 'NANCY BOY', helped regenerate sales of a collection which many hailed as one of the years' best. In addition to the more incendiary tracks, the album also contained such hauntingly reflective songs as 'LADY OF THE FLOWERS' and 'HANG ON TO YOUR IQ'. • **Songwriters:** Group, except BIGMOUTH STRIKES AGAIN (Smiths) / 20TH CENTURY BOY (T.Rex).

Album rating: PLACEBO (*9) / WITHOUT YOU I'M NOTHING (*8)

BRIAN MOLKO (b.1972) – vocals, guitars, bass / **STEFAN OLSDAL** – bass, guitars, keyboards / **ROBERT SCHULTZBERG** – drums, percussion, didgeridoo

Fierce Panda / not iss.

Nov 95. (7") *(NING 13)* **BRUISE PRISTINE. / (Soup: 'Meltdown')** [ ] [-]

Deceptive / not iss.

Feb 96. (7") *(BLUFF 024)* **COME HOME. / DROWNING BY NUMBERS** [ ] [-]
(cd-s+=) *(BLUFF 024CD)* – Oxygen thief.

Elevator / Caroline

Jun 96. (7") *(FLOOR 001)* **36 DEGREES. / DARK GLOBE** [ ] [-]
(cd-s+=) *(FLOORCD 001)* – Hare Krishna.

Jun 96. (cd/c/lp) *(CD/MC/LP FLOOR 002)* <7575> **PLACEBO** [40] [ ] Jul96
– Come home / Teenage angst / Bionic / 36 degrees / Hang on to you IQ / Nancy boy / I know / Bruise pristine / Lady of the flowers / Swallow. *(re-dist.Jan97 hit UK No.5; same)*

Sep 96. (7"/cd-s) *(FLOOR/+CD 003)* **TEENAGE ANGST. / BEEN SMOKING TOO LONG / HUG BUBBLE** [30] [-]
(7"m) *(FLOORX 003)* – ('A'-V.P.R.O. radio session) / Flesh mechanic (demo) / HK farewell.

Jan 97. (7") *(FLOOR 004)* **NANCY BOY. / SLACKERBITCH** [4] [ ]
(cd-s+=) *(FLOORCD 004)* – Bigmouth strikes again / Hug bubble.
(cd-s) *(FLOORCDX 004)* – ('A'side) / Eyesight to the blind / Swallow (Brad Wood mix) / Miss Moneypenny.

May 97. (c-s/cd-s) *(FLOOR MC/CD 005)* **BRUISE PRISTINE / THEN THE CLOUDS WILL OPEN FOR ME / BRUISE PRISTINE (One Inch Punch remix)** [14] [-]
(cd-s) *(FLOORCDX 005)* – ('A'side) / Waiting for the sun of man / Serenity (Lionrock remix).

Elevator / Hut

Aug 98. (cd-ep) *(FLOORCD 6)* **PURE MORNING / MARS LANDING PARTY / LEELOO** [4] [-]
(cd-ep) *(FLOORCDX 6)* – ('A'-lp version) / Needledick / The innocence of sleep.

Sep 98. (c-s/cd-s) *(FLOOR C/CD 7)* <95363> **YOU DON'T CARE ABOUT US / 20TH CENTURY BOY / ION** [5] [ ]
(cd-s) *(FLOORDX 7)* – ('A'side) / ('A'-Les Rhythmes Digitales remix) / ('A'-Howie B remix).

Oct 98. (cd/c/lp) *(CDFLOOR/FLOORMC/FLOORLP 8)* <46531> **WITHOUT YOU I'M NOTHING** [7] [ ] Nov98
– Pure morning / Brick shithouse / You don't care about us / Ask for answers / Without you I'm nothing / Allergic (to thoughts of Mother Earth) / The crawl / Every you every me / My sweet prince / Summer's gone / Scared of girls / Burger queen.

PLANET WILSON (see under ⇒ RED GUITARS)

PLASMATICS

Formed: New York, USA . . . 1978 by porn magnate ROD SWENSON, the brains behind this outrageous, shock-hungry post-punk outfit. To front the band he recruited ex-stripper and porn-star WENDY O'WILLIAMS, backing her up with the colourful RITCHIE STOTTS, WES BEECH, STU DEUTSCH and CHOSEI FUNAHARA, the latter subsequently being replaced by JEAN BEAUVOIR. With a string of US-only indie 45's behind them, The PLASMATICS arrived in Britain under a storm of protest, especially from London's GLC who vehemently objected to their much publicised high-octane stage show (blowing up cars and chainsawing the odd instrument a speciality, while WENDY's topless, sometimes bottomless attire further provoked police heavy-handedness!). Appropriately signing to 'Stiff' records, the spiky-nippled O'WILLIAMS and her crew finally unleashed their debut set, 'NEW HOPE FOR THE WRETCHED' amid a sea of hype in 1980. Although lambasted by the critics it nevertheless hit the UK charts, as did the controversial 'BUTCHER BABY' single. WENDY and the band released two further forgettable albums the following year and it was quite surprising 'Capitol' records took up the option to sign them. Now without BEAUVOIR and DEUTSCH (who were replaced by JUNIOR ROMANELLI and T.C. TOLLIVER), they released the heavier 'COUP D'ETAT' (1982), a change in music and image which left them with few fans. This proved to be The PLASMATICS' epitaph, the bondage-loving WENDY going solo, taking her cue from wildman sidekick, LEMMY and releasing three albums in as many years. The last of these, 'MAGGOTS: THE RECORD', came in 1987, both its concept and cover art reaching a nadir in bad taste. She made her final stand for rock'n'roll excess with the aforementioned LEMMY on a version of Tammy Wynette's country standard, 'STAND BY YOUR MAN'. Spookily enough, both WENDY and TAMMY were to die on the same day (6th April '98), O'WILLIAMS taking her own life by shooting herself. • **Songwriters:** BEECH-BEAUVOIR penned most, until the latter's departure. Covered; DREAM LOVER (Bobby Darin) / JAILBAIT (Motorhead).

Album rating: NEW HOPE FOR THE WRETCHED (*5) / Wendy O'Williams: W.O.W. (*5)

WENDY O'WILLIAMS – vocals, saxophone, electric chain saw / **RITCHIE STOTTS** – lead guitar / **WES BEECH** – rhythm guitar / **JEAN BEAUVOIR** – bass; repl. CHOSEI FUNAHARA / **STU DEUTSCH** – drums

Vice Squad / P.V.C.

Nov 78. (7";7"red) <VS 101/102> **BUTCHER BABY. / FAST FOOD SERVICE / CONCRETE SHOES** [-] [ ]

Oct 79. (7"/7"lavender) <VS 103/104> **DREAM LOVER. / CORRUPTION / WANT YOU BABY** [-] [ ]

Dec 79. (12"ep/12"ep;yellow) <VS 105/106> **MEET THE PLASMATICS** [-] [ ]
– Sometimes I / Won't you? / Want you baby.

Stiff / Stiff

Jun 80. (7",7"multi-colrd) *(BUY 76)* **BUTCHER BABY. / TIGHT BLACK PANTS** [55] [-]

Jul 80. (12"ep) *(BUYIT 76)* **BUTCHER BABY (re-recorded). / LIVING DEAD (live) / SOMETIMES I (FEEL IT WHEN YOU'RE DOWN ON YOUR KNEES)** [ ] [-]

Sep 80. (7"multi-colrd) *(BUY 91)* **MONKEY SUIT. / SQUIRM (live)** [ ] [-]

Sep 80. (lp,multi-colrd-lp) *(SEEZ 24)* <USE 9> **NEW HOPE FOR THE WRETCHED** [55] [ ]
– Concrete shoes / Butcher baby / Squirm (live) / Corruption / Want you baby / Dream lover / Won't you / Sometimes I / Tight black pants / Monkey suit / Living dead / Test-tube babies. *(cd-iss. Dec92 on 'Dojo'; DOJOCD 79) (re-iss. cd Feb94 on 'Disky'; STIFFCD 16)*

— **JOEY REESE** – drums repl. DEUTSCH

Nov 81. (m-lp) <WOW 666> **METAL PRIESTESS** (The 2nd Album) [-] [ ]
– Lunacy / Doom song / Sex junkie / Black leather monster / 12 noon / Masterplan.

— **'JUNIOR' CHRIS ROMANELLI** – bass repl. BEAUVOIR who went solo, after joining LITTLE STEVEN & THE DISCIPLES OF SOUL

Jun 81. (lp) *(WOW 2)* **BEYOND THE VALLEY OF 1984** [ ] [ ]
– Incantation / Masterplan / Headbanger / Sumer nite / Nothing / Fast food service / Hit man / Living dead / Sex junkie / Plasma jam / Pig is a pig.

— **T.C. TOLLIVER** – drums, percussion repl. REESE

Capitol / Capitol

Nov 82. (lp/c) <(EST/TC-EST 12237)> **COUP D'ETAT** [ ] [ ]
– Put your love in me / Stop / Rock and roll / Counting fairs / No class / Just like on TV / Lightning breaks / Mistress of taboo / Path of glory. *(re-iss. 1986 on 'Revolver' lp/c; REV LP/MC 78) (cd-iss. Mar96 on 'Dojo'; DOJOCD 239)*

— split 1983

WENDY O'WILLIAMS

went solo, augmented by **ROMANELLI, BEECH + GENE SIMMONS** (of KISS, + their producer)

Music For Nations / not iss.

May 84. (7"/12") *(KUT/12KUT 111)* **IT'S MY LIFE. / PRIESTUS** [ ] [-]

Jul 84. (lp) *(MFN 24)* **W.O.W.** [100] [-]
– I love sex and rock and roll / It's my life / Priestess / Thief in the night / Opus in Cm7 / Ready to rock / Bump and grind / Legends never die / Ain't none of your business. <US-iss.1987 on 'Passport' lp/c/cd; PB/+C/CD 6034>

Zebra / not iss.

Feb 86. (lp) *(ZEB 7)* **KOMMANDER OF CHAOS** [ ] [-]
– Hoy hey (love to rock) / Pedal to the metal / Goin' wild / Ain't none of your business / Party / Jailbait / Bad girl / Fight for the right / F*** that booty.

— **O'WILLIAMS** re-formed The PLASMATICS with **RAY**

G.W.R. not iss.

Mar 87. (lp; as The PLASMATICS and WENDY O'WILLIAMS) *(GWLP 8)* **MAGGOTS: THE RECORD** [ ] [-]
– Overture / Introduction / You're a zombie / Full meal diner / The whites apartment / The day of the humans is gone / The central research laboratory / Valerie and Bruce on the phone / Destroyers / The whites apartment / Bruces bedroom / Brain dead / The whites apartment / Bruces bedroom / Propagators / The whites apartment / Fire escape / Finale.

— added **WES BEECH** – guitar / **KATRINA ASHTON** – guitar

Mar 88. (lp; as ULTRAFLY & THE HOMETOWN GIRLS) *<PAL 1258>* **DEEPEST AND BADDEST** [-] [ ]
– Rulers of rock / 10 million $ question / Super Jock / Early days / Know w'am sayin' / I.R.T. (out in space) / Lies intro & 41 / La la land / Laffin' & scratchin'.

– compilations, etc. –

1987. (lp/c/cd) *P.V.C.; <PVC/+C/CD 8929>* **BEYOND THE VALLEY OF 1984 / METAL PRIESTESS** [-] [ ]

PLASTIC BERTRAND

Born: ROGER JORRET, 1958, Belgium. A former musical child prodigy, ROGER went on to drum with New Wave ironists, HUBBLE BUBBLE, who issued a couple of singles and two French lp's for 'Barclay', 'HUBBLE BUBBLE' (1977) and 'FAKING' (1978). Subsequently plucked from Euro obscurity by 'Sire' records, the hyperactive BERTRAND thrilled UK audiences with his Top 10 teen-friendly pogo-punk classic, 'CA PLANE POUR MOI'. Bafflingly, his label declined to grant a UK release for a debut album of the same name, 'Vertigo' taking over his Brit business for a follow-up Top 40 version of The Small Faces' 'SHA LA LA LA LEE'. By the turn of the decade this colourful character had been sidelined to the more sympathetic markets of Belgium and French-speaking Canada. A more mature BERTRAND recently turned up as a guest on that naughtee leetle TV show, 'Eurotrash', talking about his failed bid for Eurovision glory!

Album rating: CA PLANE POUR MOI (*5)

PLASTIC BERTRAND – vocals / with session people incl. **ELTON MOTELLO**

Sire Sire

May 78. (7") *(6078 616) <1020>* **CA PLANE POUR MOI. / POGO POGO** [8] [ ] Apr78
(above was released in France 1977 on 'Vogue'; *140.316)*

— (below was released same time as 'AN 1' on 'Vogue'; *VO 15008)*

Jun 78. (lp) *<SRK 6061>* **CA PLANE POUR MOI** [-] [ ]
– Le petit toptillard / Bambino / Naif song / Ca plane pour moi / Sha la la la lee / Pognon pognon / Dance dance / 5-4-3-2-1 / Pogo pogo / Wha wha (je suis un chien, nous sommes des chiens, vous des chiens) / Solo naif song.

Vertigo not iss.

Jul 78. (7") *(6059 209)* **SHA LA LA LA LEE. / NAIF SONG** [39] [-]
Dec 78. (7") *(6059 215)* **C'EST LE ROCK'N'ROLL. / AFFECTION** [ ] [-]

Sire Sire

Mar 79. (7") *(SIR 4012)* **TOUT PETITE LA PLANETE. / JE FAIT UN PLAN / HIT 78** [ ] [-]

Vogue R.K.M.

1979. (7") *(VG 108)* **SENTIMENTALE MOI. / OUAIS, OUAIS, OUAIS, OUAIS** [-] [-] French
1979. (7") *<101.251)* **LE MONDE EST MERVEILLEUX. / J'TE FAIS UN PLAN** [-] [-] French
1979. (pink-lp) *(9250 8508)* **J'TE FAIS UN PLAN** [-] [ ] French
– J'te fais un plan / Affection / Telephone, telephone / Super cool / Hit 78 / C'est le rock'n'roll (walk like a man) / Cliche / Tout petit la planete.
1980. (7") *(101.394)* **SANS AMOUR. / PLASTIC BOY** [-] [-] French

not iss. Attic

1980. (7") *<ATF 506>* **TELEPHONE A TELEPHONE MON BIJOU. / STOP OU ENCORE** [-] [-] Canada
1980. (lp) *<LATF 5004>* **L'ALBUM** [-] [-] Canada
– Telephone a telephone mon bijou (mon rock'n'roll attrappe des cheveaux blancs) / Stop ou encore / Rock'n'roll je te hais / Je t'aime trop danger / Kangourou / Une fille moche / Express ca presse / Chacun son truc / Jeaune et insouciant.
1981. (lp) *<LATF 5006>* **GREATEST HITS** (compilation) [-] [-] Canada
– Telephone a telephone mon bijou / Sans amour / Super cool / Les monde est merveilleux / Tout petit la planete / Stop ou encore / Ouais, ouais, ouais, ouais / Intro / Je t'aime trop danger / Telephone a telephone / Ca plane pour moi / Hula hoop / Sentimentale moi / Au bout / Stop or go.
1982. (lp) *<LATF 5007>* **PLASTIQUEZ VON BAFFLES** [-] [-] Canada
– Jacques Cousteau / Coeur d'acier / Victime de l'amour / Si ma tete fait ding dong, . . . mon coeur est dingue donc / Le pantin / Shoe bi dou bi . . . baby / Baby doll / Boum dans le coeur / Kili watch / Chewing-gum / Paradis / Hula hoop.

— BERTRAND/ROGER retired from recording

PLASTICLAND

Formed: Milwaukee, Wisconsin, USA . . . 1980 by GLENN REHSE and JOHN FRANKOVIC, who had actually played together in a mid-60's garage band. They played some live psychedelic (PINK FLOYD / CREATION-like) shows, but by the early 70's they had "progressed" into rock outfit, WILLIE THE CONQUEROR. Influenced by Britain's new-found love of "Krautrock", they became AROUSING POLARIS, although it wasn't long before another quarrel split them apart. As PLASTICLAND (with extra members DAN MULLEN and BRIAN RITCHIE), they were once again re-united, taking their first fruitful sojourn into the studio with the 1981 single, 'MINK DRESS', after which, RITCHIE joined The VIOLENT FEMMES. With punk-rock now past its sell-by date, they fashioned themselves in 60's Carnaby Street wares although this image didn't go down too well back home in Milwaukee. In 1982 they made an appearance on "Battle Of The Garages", which led to a self-issued EP, 'VIBRASONGS FROM . . . POP! OP DROPS'. A debut album, 'COLOR APPRECIATION', was released for the French 'Lolita' label, its flowing dramas and sense of the absurd leading to a deal with 'Enigma' in 1985. Their first outing for the label, 'WONDER WONDERFUL WONDERLAND' (1985), was lush Lewis Carroll-style fantasy, although producer PAUL CUTLER (of DREAM SYNDICATE) might disagree. Their next groovy offering, 'SALON' (1987), showed a shift to a more "Psychedelic Shack"-style R&B/soul while the band refused to do a promotional tour, giving their label the "old age" excuse (they were now over 40!). Despite developing musically with some awe-inspiring, occasional gigs (complete with go-go dancers), they were dropped. This led to semi-retirement, the band only surfacing to play reunion gigs, also backing veteran, TWINK, on his live album. In 1994, their 1991 recorded comeback album, 'DAPPER SNAPPINGS', was finally released by the German 'Repulsion' label, a UK release still impending. More releases are in the pipeline, although FRANKOVIC is now a part-time solo artist, while other offshoots, The GOTHICS and FABULON TRIPTOMETER, are also underway. • **Songwriters:** REHSE-FRANKOVIC except covers ALEXANDER (Pretty Things) / etc.

Album rating: PLASTICLAND (*6) / WONDER WONDERFUL WONDERLAND (*7) / SALON (*6) / DAPPER SNAPPINGS (*6) / John Frankovic:- UNDER THE WATER LILY (*6)

GLENN REHSE – vocals, guitar, keyboards / **JOHN FRANKOVIC** – bass, vocals, percussion, bouzouki / **DAN MULLEN** – guitar, vocals / **BRIAN RITCHIE** – drums

Scadillac Scadillac

Jan 81. (7") *<SC-1001>* **MINK DRESS. / OFFICE SKILLS** [-] [ ]

— **ROB McCUEN** – drums; repl. RITCHIE who joined VIOLENT FEMMES

May 81. (12"ep) *<SC-1002>* **VIBRASONGS FROM . . . POP! OP DROPS** [-] [ ]
– Too many fingers / Standing in a room / The prince's playground / Pushy.
Mar 84. (7") *<(SC 05)>* **EUPHORIC TRAPDOOR SHOES. / RAT TAIL COMB** [ ] [ ]

Lolita not iss.

1984. (lp) **COLOR APPRECIATION** [-] [-] France
– Alexander / The garden in pain / Rat tail comb / etc. *<US-iss.1985 as 'PLASTICLAND'; > (UK-iss.Feb87 on 'Bam Caruso'; KIRI 034)*

Pink Dust-Enigma Pink Dust-Enigma

1985. (lp) *<70063-1>* **WONDER WONDERFUL WONDERLAND** [-] [ ]
– No shine for the shoes / Gloria Knight / Transparencies, friends / Fairytale hysteria / Don't let it all pass by / The gingerbread house / Flower scene / Processes of the silverness / Non-stop kitchen / Grassland of reeds and things / Gloria Knight (reprise) / Wonder wonderful wonderland.

— **VICTOR DEMICHI** – drums, repl. McCUEN

Jun 87. (lp) *<(ENIG 72179-1)>* **SALON** [ ] [ ]
– Go a go-go time / What am I to say / It's a dog life / Quick commentary on wax museums / Abcessed words to climb / House / Lie of great Sedan Pinocchio / We can't / Serene it's true / Reserving the right to change my mind / Window sills / Don't antagonize me.

Repulsion not iss.

1991. (12"ep) *(EFA 15651)* **LET'S PLAY POLLYANNA / RADIANT FUZZBOX WIG. / KALEIDOSCOPIC GLANCE / ENCHANTED FORESTRY** [ ] [-]
Feb 95. (cd) *(EFA 15660-2)* **DAPPER SNAPPINGS** [ ] [ ]

– compilations, etc. –

1995. (cd) ; **MINK DRESS AND OTHER CATS** [ ] [ ]

JOHN FRANKOVIC

Midnight Midnight

1994. (cd) **UNDER THE WATER LILY** [ ] [ ]

PLAY DEAD

Formed: Oxford, England . . . Autumn 1980 by ROB, PETE DEAN and WIFF, who were soon supporting the likes of UK DECAY the following summer. Their debut single, 'POISON TAKES A HOLD', was issued around the same time while its follow-up, 'TV EYE', saw the addition of guitarist, STEVE. In 1982, they recorded their first of many John Peel sessions and signed to goth/punk orientated label, 'Jungle', releasing 'PROPAGANDA' in the process. Subsequent tours supporting SEX GANG CHILDREN and KILLING JOKE – with whom they shared a spiritual similarity – paved the way for another string of anthemic singles including the pummelling 'PROPAGANDA'. They finally unleashed their debut album, 'FROM THE PROMISED LAND', in 1984, featuring live favourite 'WALK AWAY', which believe it or not, suggested a gothic BIG COUNTRY, if that's possible! Becoming one of the many acts on the books of the 'Clay' label, PLAY DEAD featured on a December '84 edition of 'The Tube', while going on to tour Scandinavia and other parts of Europe where they were more popular. However, by March '86 (and after another album, 'COMPANY OF JUSTICE'), PLAY DEAD had finally keeled over, metamorphasising into the short-lived BEASTMASTER GENERAL.

Album rating: FROM THE PROMISED LAND (*5) / INTO THE FIRE – LIVE mini (*4) / COMPANY OF JUSTICE (*4) / THE SINGLES 82-85 compilation (*5)

ROB – vocals / **PETE DEAN** – bass / **WIFF** – drums

Fresh not iss.

Jun 81. (7") *(FRESH 29)* **POISON TAKES A HOLD. / INTRODUCTION**

— added **STEVE** – guitar

Oct 81. (7") *(FRESH 38)* **T.V. EYE. / THE FINAL EPITAPH** [-]

Jungle not iss.

Nov 82. (7") *(JUNG 002)* **PROPAGANDA. / PROPAGANDA (mix)** [-]

Situation 2 not iss.

Sep 83. (7") *(SIT 28)* **SHINE. / PROMISE** [-]
(12"+=) *(SIT 28T)* – Gaze.

Clay not iss.

Apr 84. (7") *(CLAY 31)* **BREAK. / BLOODSTAINS** [-]
(12"+=) *(12CLAY 31)* – The pleasure.

May 84. (lp) *(CLAYLP 11)* **FROM THE PROMISED LAND** [-]
– Isabel / Torn on desire / Walk away / Pleasureland / Return to the east / Holy holy / No motive / Weeping blood.

Jul 84. (7"/12") *(CLAY/12CLAY 35)* **ISABEL. / SOLACE** [-]

Oct 84. (7"/12") *(CLAY/12CLAY 40)* **CONSPIRACY. / SILENT CONSPIRACY** [-]

Feb 85. (7") *(CLAY 42)* **SACROSANCT. / PALE FIRE** [-]
(12"+=) *(12CLAY 42)* – Holy holy / Sacrosanct.

May 85. (m-lp) *(CLAYLP 16M)* **INTO THE FIRE (live)** [-]
– Walk away / Shine / Return to the east / Break / Turn on desire / Sin of sins / The tenant / No motive.

Tanz not iss.

Sep 85. (12"'w-drawn) *(TANZ 1)* **THIS SIDE OF HEAVEN. / LAST DEGREE / THIS SIDE OF HEAVEN (serious mix)** [-]

Nov 85. (lp) *(TANZLP 1)* **COMPANY OF JUSTICE** [-]
(cd-iss. Sep93 on 'Jungle'; FREUDCD 41)

May 86. (12") *(TANZ 2)* **BURNING DOWN. / STILL IN CHAINS** [-]

— had already split in March when two members (not PETE) formed the BEASTMASTER GENERAL

– compilations, etc. –

Jul 84. (lp/c) *Jungle; (FREUD/+C 003)* **THE FIRST FLOWER** [-]
– Shine / Sin of sins / In silence / Gaze / Propaganda / The tenant / Time / Promise / Propaganda ('84 mix) / Don't leave without me. *(cd-iss. Sep92 +=; FREUDCD 003)* – Sin of sins ('84 mix) / Poison takes a hold / Introduction / T.V. eye / The final epitaph. *(cd re-iss. Jan94 on 'Cleopatra'; CLEO 7519CD)*

Sep 84. (12") *Jungle; (JUNG 17)* **PROPAGANDA (1984 mix). / SIN OF SINS (remix)** [-]

Feb 86. (12"ep) *Jungle; (JUNG 26T)* **IN THE BEGINNING – THE 1981 SINGLES** [-]

Jul 86. (m-lp) *Clay; (CLAYLP 20M)* **THE SINGLES '82-'85** [-]

Aug 86. (lp) *Dojo; (DOJOLP 34)* **CAUGHT FROM BEHIND – LIVE IN ENGLAND, FRANCE, GERMANY AND SWITZERLAND)** [-]
– Break / Last degree / Solace / Shine / Isabel / Sin of sins / Torn on desire / This side of Heaven / Sacrosanct / The tenant.

Mar 87. (lp) *Jungle; (FREUD 015)* **THE FINAL EPITAPH – LIVE (live)** [-]

Jun 92. (cd) *Clay; (CLAYCD 111)* **RESURRECTION** (w/ some remixes) [-]
– Break / Isabel / Walk away / Bloodstains / Solace / No motive / Pleasureland / Pale fire / Sacrosanct / Torn on desire / Holy holy / Return to the east / Conspiracy / Sin of sins (live) / Bloodstains pleasure / Solace / Holy holy.

PLIMSOULS

Formed: Los Angeles, California, USA . . . late '78 as The TONE DOGS by PETER CASE (a one-time member of The NERVES), DAVE PAHOA, LOU RAMIREZ and last but not least, EDDIE MUNOZ. Having taken their new moniker from the British slang for "gym shoes", The PLIMSOULS finally debuted at the turn of the decade with the independently released classic 'ZERO HOUR' EP. Inspired by the classic Brit bands of the 1960's American invasion (especially The BEATLES), CASE and Co specialised in rootsy power-pop that influenced a generation of Stateside bands. The quartet subsequently signed to Warner Brothers subsidiary, 'Planet', releasing an eponymous full-length album in 1981, a well-produced effort that won over many post-New Wave music lovers. After becoming part of David Geffen's recently established superlabel, the trademark PLIMSOULS sound was compromised on 1983's 'EVERYTHING AT ONCE', despite having already made their mark with the Hot 100 entry, 'A MILLION MILES AWAY'. Following the band's demise, CASE would concentrate on the rootsier side of his muse, recording sporadically throughout the latter half of the 80's with non-charting albums such as the eponymous 'PETER CASE' (1986) and 'THE MAN WITH THE BLUE POST MODERN FRAGMENTED NEO-TRADITIONALIST GUITAR' (1989).

Album rating: THE PLIMSOULS (*7) / EVERYWHERE AT ONCE (*7) / ONE NIGHT IN AMERICA compilation (*6) / Peter Case: PETER CASE (*6) / THE MAN WITH THE BLUE POST MODERN FRAGMENTED NEO-TRADITIONALIST GUITAR (*6) / SIX-PACK OF LOVE (*5) / SINGS LIKE HELL (*6) / TORN AGAIN (*7) / FULL SERVICE NO WAITING (*6)

PETER CASE (b. 5 Apr'54, Buffalo, New York, USA) – vocals, guitar (ex-NERVES) / **EDDIE MUNOZ** – guitar, vocals / **DAVE PAHOA** – bass, vocals / **LOU RAMIREZ** – drums, percussion

not iss. Beat

1980. (12"ep) *<BE 1001>* **ZERO HOUR EP** [-]
– Great big world / Zero hour / Hypnotized / How long will it take? / I can't turn you loose.

Planet – Warners Planet

Mar 81. (lp) *(PL 52277) <P 13>* **THE PLIMSOULS**
– Lost time / Now / In this town / Zero hour / Women / Hush, hush / I want what you got / Nickels and dimes / I want you back / Mini-skirt Minnie / Everyday things.

Apr 81. (7") *(K 12519)* **NOW. / WHEN YOU FIND IT**

Bomp Shaky City

May 82. (7")<12"> *(BOMP 2) <BMP12 134>* **A MILLION MILES AWAY. / I'LL GET LUCKY** Jan82

Geffen Geffen

Jul 83. (7") *<29600>* **A MILLION MILES AWAY. / PLAY THE BREAKS** [-] 82

Sep 83. (lp) *(GEF 25509) <4002>* **EVERYWHERE AT ONCE**
– Shaky city / Magic touch / Oldest story in the world / Lie, beg, borrow and steal / Play the breaks / How long will it take? / A million miles away / My life ain't easy / Inch by inch / I'll get lucky / Everywhere at once.

— disbanded the following year with CASE going solo

PETER CASE

Geffen Geffen

Jul 86. (lp/c) *<(924105-1/-4)>* **PETER CASE**
– Echo wars / Steel strings / Three days straight / More than curious / I shook his hand / Small town spree / Old blue car / Walk in the woods / Horse and crow / Ice water / Satellite beach / Brown eyes. *(re-iss. Feb 94 cd/c; GFL D/C 19189)*

Oct 86. (7"/12") *(GEF 14/+T)* **STEEL STRINGS. / SMALL TOWN SPREE**

Apr 89. (lp/c/cd) *<(K 924238-1/-4/-2)>* **THE MAN WITH THE BLUE POST MODERN FRAGMENTED NEO-TRADITIONALIST GUITAR**
– Charlie James / Travellin' light / Old part of town / Rise and shine / Hidden love / Put down the gun / Poor old town / Two angels / This town's a riot.

Mar 92. (cd/c) *<(GEF D/C 24466)>* **SIX-PACK OF LOVE**
– Vanishing act / Deja blues / Dream about you / When you don't come / Never comin' home / It's all mine / Why don't we give it a go? / Why? / Last time I looked / Wonderful 99 / I've been looking for you / Beyond the blues / It don't matter what people say.

Glitterhouse Vanguard

Dec 94. (cd) *(GRCD 351) <VND 79476>* **SINGS LIKE HELL** Apr94
– Brokedown engine / Rovin' gambler / So glad you're mine / Lakes of Ponchartrain / Walkin' bum / How 'bout you / Matchbox blues / Rose Conolly / Down in the alley / Waltz of the angels / Well runs dry / North coast blues / Down the line. *(re-iss. Apr97 on 'Vanguard'; same as US)*

Vanguard Vanguard

Apr 95. (cd) **TORN AGAIN** [-]

Mar 98. (cd) *<(VCD 79504)>* **FULL SERVICE NO WAITING**
– Spell of wheels / On the way downtown / Let me fall / Green blanket / Honey child / See through eyes / Until the next time / Crooked mile / Beautiful grind / Drunkard's harmony / Still playin'.

PLIMSOULS

— re-formed originals **PETER CASE, EDDIE MUNOZ + CLEM BURKE**

Musidisc Musidisc

Feb 98. (cd) *<(12125-2)>* **KOOL TRASH**
– Playing with Jack / Feeling strange / Down / Falling awake / Pile up / 12 o'clock midnight / Kool trash / Lost / Dangerous book / Not of this world.

– compilations, etc.

May 89. (lp/c/cd) *Fan Club; (FC 048/+C/CD)* **ONE NIGHT IN AMERICA (live 1981)** [-]
– Hush, hush / How long will it take? / I want what you got / In this town / Help yourself / I'll get lucky / Now / A million miles away / Time won't let me / One more heartache / Dizzy Miss Lizzy / Come on now. *(cd re-iss. May94 on 'New Rose'; 422266)*

PLUSH

Formed: Chigaco, Illinois, USA . . . 1994 by LIAM HAYES, a part-time keyboard-player with PALACE (aka WILL OLDHAM). The well-named PLUSH debuted early the following year with a fine 7" single, 'THREE-QUARTERS BLIND EYES', although it was the grandoise and symphonic flip-side, 'FOUND A LITTLE BABY', that created a mini-sensation. However, the introverted HAYES went into seclusion for a long period; stories were rife that he was spending time in a Californian commune. He was also rumoured to be working with an orchestra for his debut album, although this might have broken him financially. Late in 1997, he was back in action with a comeback single, 'NO EDUCATION', a balladesque, lo-fi number that was yet again acclaimed in some quarters. A tour in Australia with OLDHAM seemed to be going well, until he virtually disappeared once more. His debut album, 'MORE YOU BECOMES YOU' (a mini, compared to today's standards), finally reached the shops in the Autumn of '98, a hidden masterpiece that was actually recorded in 1995 (not the rumoured material mentioned above which was supposedly shelved).

Album rating: MORE YOU BECOMES YOU (*6)

LIAM HAYES (c.1960's) – vocals, piano, organ

Domino Drag City

Jan 95. (7") *(RUG 32) <DR 056>* **THREE-QUARTERS BLIND EYES. / FOUND A LITTLE BABY**

— went into retreat for a while (see above)

Nov 97. (7"/12") *(FLY 024/+T)* **NO EDUCATION. / SOARING AND BORING** [-]
(above issued on 'Flydaddy') *(re-iss. Aug98; same)*

Sep 98. (cd/lp) *(WIG CD/LP 50) <DC 070>* **MORE YOU BECOMES YOU**
– Virginia / More you becomes you / (I didn't know) I was asleep / The party I / The party II / Soaring and boring / (See it in the) Early morning / Instrumental / Save the people / The sailor.

POGUES

Formed: North London, England . . . late 1983 by Tipperary raised SHANE MacGOWAN, SPIDER STACEY and JEM FINER. MacGOWAN had earlier been part of punk outfit, The NIPPLE ERECTORS through 1978-1981; this motley crew released a solitary single, 'KING OF THE BOP' before shortening their name to The NIPS. A further few singles appeared and even an album, 'ONLY AT THE END OF THE BEGINNING', recommended for diehard POGUES fiends only. POGUE MAHONE (Gaelic for "kiss my arse") was subsequently formed by MacGOWAN and JAMES FEARNLEY (also a NIP), adding drinking buddies, ANDREW RANKEN, plus female singer/bassist CAIT O'RIORDAN. By Spring '84, they'd formed their own self-titled label, issuing a classic debut single, 'DARK STREETS OF LONDON'. Boasting all the Celtic melancholy, romance and gritted-teeth attitude which marked the best of the band's work, the track rather unfairly but predictably received an official BBC radio ban (apparently after the beeb managed to translate their name). A month later they secured a deal with 'Stiff', opting instead for The POGUES. Their Stan Brennan-produced debut album, 'RED ROSES FOR ME', broke into the UK Top 100 as they acquired growing support from live audiences the length and breadth of the country. Whether interpreting trad Irish folk songs or reeling off brilliant originals, the POGUES were apt to turn from high-spirited revelry ('STREAMS OF WHISKEY') to menacing threat ('BOYS FROM THE COUNTY HELL') in the time it took to neck a pint of guinness (in MacGOWAN's case, not very long at all). April '85 saw the release of perhaps their finest single (and first Top 20 hit), the misty-eyed, ELVIS COSTELLO-produced 'A PAIR OF BROWN EYES'. COSTELLO also oversaw the accompanying album, 'RUM, SODOMY & THE LASH' (1985), a debauched, bruisingly beautiful classic which elevated The POGUES to the position of modern day folk heroes. MacGOWAN's gift for conjuring up a feeling of time and place was never more vivid than on the likes of the aforementioned 'A PAIR..', the rousing 'SALLY MacLENNANE' and the cursing malice of 'THE SICK BED OF CUCHULAINN', while O'RIORDAN put in a spine-tingling performance as a Scottish laird on the traditional 'I'M A MAN YOU DON'T MEET EVERYDAY'. On the 16th of May '86, the latter married COSTELLO and when she subsequently left that November (after writing the Top 50 hit 'HAUNTED' for the Alex Cox film, 'Sid & Nancy'), a vital component of POGUES chemistry went with her. Around the same time, the group played 'The McMahon Gang' in Cox's movie 'Straight To Hell', meeting ex-CLASH singer JOE STRUMMER on the set: the veteran punk would subsequently deputise for the absent MacGOWAN on an early 1988 US tour. This period also saw them peak at No.3 in the album charts with 'IF I SHOULD FALL FROM GRACE WITH GOD', an album which spawned an unlikely No.2 Christmas 1987 hit in 'FAIRY TALE OF NEW YORK'. A drunken duet with KIRSTY MacCOLL, the track was certainly more subversive than the usual Yuletide fodder and for a brief period, The POGUES were bonafide pop stars, their rampant collaboration with The DUBLINERS on 'IRISH ROVER' earlier that year having already breached the Top 10. Live, the band were untouchable, MacGOWAN's errant, tin-tray wielding genius the stuff of legend, particularly for many who witnessed their storming Glasgow Barrowlands performances (needless to say, Rangers fans were mercifully thin on the ground at these celebratory Celtic shindigs). Inevitably, MacGOWAN's hard-drinking ways were beginning to affect his writing and 'PEACE AND LOVE' (1989) signalled a slow slide into mediocrity. 1990's 'HELL'S DITCH' carried on in much the same vein, although this was to be MacGOWAN's final album under The POGUES banner, his failing health incompatable with the demands of a successful major label band. While the gap-toothed frontman eventually got a solo career together, The POGUES bravely soldiered on with a surprisingly impressive hit single, 'TUESDAY MORNING', lifted from their 1993 UK Top 20 "comeback" album, 'WAITING FOR HERB'. Two years on, a nostalgically titled follow-up set, 'POGUE MAHONE', failed to rekindle their former glory, while MacGOWAN continued to dominate the limelight. • **Songwriters:** Group compositions, except; THE BAND PLAYED WALTZING MATILDA (Eric Bogle) / DIRTY OLD TOWN (Ewan MacColl) / WILD ROVER + MADRA RUM (trad.) / MAGGIE MAY (Rod Stewart) / HONKY TONK WOMAN (Rolling Stones) / WHISKEY IN THE JAR (Thin Lizzy) / MISS OTIS REGRETS (Cole Porter) / GOT A LOT O' LIVIN' TO DO (Elvis Presley) / HOW COME (Ronnie Lane) / WHEN THE SHIP COMES IN (Bob Dylan). FINER became main writer in the mid-90's with others contributed some material. • **Trivia:** In the early '90s, they supplied the soundtarack for TV play 'A Man You Don't Meet Every Day'. The song 'Fiesta' was subsequently used on Vauxhall-Tigra TV ad after the rights were sold from their 1988 album.

Album rating: RED ROSES FOR ME (*8) / RUM, SODOMY & THE LASH (*9) / IF I SHOULD FALL FROM GRACE WITH GOD (*8) / PEACE AND LOVE (*6) / HELL'S DITCH (*6) / WAITING FOR HERB (*6) / POGUE MAHONE (*5) / THE BEST OF THE POGUES compilation (*9) / THE BEST OF THE REST OF THE POGUES compilation (*7)

NIPPLE ERECTORS

SHANE MacGOWAN (b.25 Dec'57, Kent, England) – vocals, guitar / **ADRIAN THRILLS** – guitar (NME journalist) / **SHANE 'HASLER' BRADLEY** – bass / **ARCANE** – drums / + others

Soho | not iss.

Jun 78. (7") *(SH 1/2)* **KING OF THE BOP. / NERVOUS WRECK** [ ] [-]

NIPS

LARRY HINDRICKS – guitar repl. THRILLS

— **MARK HARRIS** – drums repl. ARCANE

Aug 79. (7") *(SH 4)* **ALL THE TIME IN THE WORLD. / PRIVATE EYES** [ ] [-]

— **GAVIN DOUGLAS** – drums repl. LARRY

— **JAMES FEARNLEY** (b.10 Oct'54, Manchester, England) – accordion (appeared on album)

Feb 80. (7") *(SH 9)* **GABRIELLE. / VENGEANCE** [ ] [-]
(re-iss. 1980 on 'Chiswick'; CHIS 119)

Oct 80. (lp) *(HOHO 1)* **ONLY AT THE END OF THE BEGINNING** [ ] [-]

Test Press | not iss.

Oct 81. (7") *(TP 5)* **HAPPY SONG. / NOBODY TO LOVE** [ ] [-]

— split in 1982. HASLER was soon to join MEN THEY COULDN'T HANG.

compilation

Nov 87. (m-lp) *Big Beat; (WIKM 66)* **BOPS, BABES, BOOZE & BOVVER** [ ] [-]
– King of the bop / Nervous wreck / So pissed off / Stavordale Rd. N5 / All the time in the world / Private eye / Gabrielle / Vengeance.

POGUES

MacGOWAN + FEARNLEY plus **SPIDER STACEY** (b.PETER, 14 Dec'58, Eastbourne, England) – tin whistle (ex-NIPS) / **JEM FINER** (b.JEREMY, 29 Jul'55, Stoke, England) – banjo, guitar / **CAIT O'RIORDAN** – bass, vocals / **ANDREW RANKEN** (b.13 Nov'53, London) – drums

Pogue Mahone | not iss.

May 84. (7"; as POGUE MAHONE) *(PM 1)* **DARK STREETS OF LONDON. / THE BAND PLAYED WALTZING MATHILDA** [ ] [-]
(re-iss. Jun84 as The POGUES on 'Stiff'; BUY 207)

Stiff | not iss.

Sep 84. (lp) *(SEEZ 55)* **RED ROSES FOR ME** [89] [-]
– Transmetropolitan / The battle of Brisbane / The auld triangle / Waxie's dargle / Boys from the county Hell / Sea shanty / Dark streets of London / Streams of whiskey / Poor daddy / Dingle regatta / Greenland whale fisheries / Down in the ground where the dead men go / Kitty. *(cd-iss. May87; CDSEEZ 55) (re-iss. Jan89 on 'WEA' lp/c; WX 240/+C)* (cd re-iss. Jan89; *244494-2)*

Oct 84. (7") *(BUY 212)* **BOYS FROM THE COUNTY HELL. / REPEALING OF THE LICENSING LAWS** [ ] [-]
(d7"+=) *(BUY 212 – 207)* – (see debut 45).

Mar 85. (7"/7"pic-d) *(BUY/DBUY 220)* **A PAIR OF BROWN EYES. / WHISKEY YOU'RE THE DEVIL** [72] [-]
(12"+=) *(BUYIT 22)* – Muirshin Durkin.

— added p/t **PHIL CHEVRON** (b. RYAN, 17 Jun'57, Dublin, Ireland) – guitar, producer (ex-RADIATORS FROM SPACE)

Jun 85. (7",7"green/7"sha-pic-d) *(BUY/PBUY 224)* **SALLY MacLENNANE. / WILD ROVER** [51] [-]
(12"+=) *(BUYIT 224)* – The leaving of Liverpool.
(c-s++=) *(BUYC 224)* – Wild cats of Kilkenny.

Aug 85. (lp/c/cd) *(SEEZ/CSEEZ/CDSEEZ 58)* **RUM, SODOMY & THE LASH** [13] [-]
– The sick bed of Cuchulainn / The old main drag / Wild cats of Kilkenny / I'm a man you don't meet every day / A pair of brown eyes / Sally MacLennane / Dirty old town / Jesse James / Navigator / Billy's bones / The gentleman soldier / And the band played waltzing Matilda. *(cd+=)* – A pistol for Paddy Garcia. *(re-iss. Jan89 on 'WEA' lp/c; WX 241/+C) (cd-iss. Jan89; 244495-2)*

Aug 85. (7"/7"pic-d) *(BUY/PBUY 229)* **DIRTY OLD TOWN. / A PISTOL FOR PADDY GARCIA** [62] [-]
(12"+=) *(BUYIT 229)* – The parting glass.

Feb 86. (7"ep/12"ep/c-ep/7"pic-ep) *(BUY/BUYIT/BUYC/PBUY 243)* **POGUETRY IN MOTION** [29] [-]
– A rainy night in Soho / The body of an American / London girl / Planxty Noel Hill.

Aug 86. (7") *(MCA 1084)* **HAUNTED. / JUNK THEME** [42] [-]
(12"+=) *(MCAT 1084)* – Hot dogs with everything.
(above single from the motion picture, 'Sid & Nancy' on 'MCA')

— **DARRYL HUNT** (b. 4 May'50, Bournemouth, England) – bass (ex-PRIDE O' THE CROSS) repl. CAIT

Mar 87. (7"; by The POGUES & THe DUBLINERS) *(BUY 258)* **THE IRISH ROVER. / THE RARE OLD MOUNTAIN DEW** [8] [-]
(12"+=) *(BUYIT 258)* – The Dubliners fancy.

— added **TERRY WOODS** (b. 4 Dec'47, Dublin) – banjo (now 8-piece)

Pogue Mahone-EMI | Island

Nov 87. (7"; The POGUES featuring KIRSTY MacCOLL) *(NY 7)* **FAIRYTALE OF NEW YORK. / BATTLE MARCH MEDLEY** [2] [ ]
(12"+=)(cd-s+=) *(NY 12)(CDNY 1)* – Shanne Bradley.

Jan 88. (cd/c/lp) *(CD/TC+/NYR 1) <90872>* **IF I SHOULD FALL FROM GRACE WITH GOD** [3] [88]
– If I should fall from grace with God / Turkish song of the damned / Bottle of smoke / Fairytale of New York (featuring KIRSTY MacCOLL) / Metropolis / Thousands are sailing / Fiesta / Medley:- The recruiting sergeant – The rocky road to Dublin – Galway races / Streets of Sorrow – Birmingham Six / Lullaby of London / Sit down by the fire / The broad majestic Shannon / Worms. *(cd+=)* – South Australia / The battle march medley. *(re-iss. Jan89 on 'WEA' lp/c; WX 243/+C) (cd-iss. Jan89; 244494-2)*

Feb 88. (7") *(FG 1)* **IF I SHOULD FALL FROM GRACE WITH GOD. / SALLY MacLENNANE (live)** [58] [ ]
(12"red-ep)(cd-ep+=) **ST. PATRICK'S NIGHT** *(SGG 1-12)(CDFG 1)* – A pair of brown eyes (live) / Dirty old town (live).

Jul 88. (7") *(FG 2)* **FIESTA. / SKETCHES OF SPAIN** [24] [-]
(12"+=)(cd-s+=) *(FG 2-12)(CDFG 2)* – South Australia.

WEA Island

Dec 88. (7") *(YZ 355)* **YEAH, YEAH, YEAH, YEAH, YEAH. / THE LIMERICK RAKE** 43 -
(12"+=/cd-s+=) *(YZ 355 T/CD)* – ('A'extended) / Honky tonk woman.

Jun 89. (7"/c-s) *(YZ 407/+C)* **MISTY MORNING, ALBERT BRIDGE. / COTTON FIELDS** 41 -
(12"+=) *(YZ 407T)* – Young ned of the hill.
(3"cd-s++=) *(YZ 407CD)* – Train of love.

Jul 89. (lp/c)(cd) *(WX 247/+C)(246086-2)* <91225> **PEACE AND LOVE** 5
– White City / Young ned of the hill / Misty morning, Albert Bridge / Cotton fields / Blue heaven / Down all the days / U.S.A. / Lorelei / Gartloney rats / Boat train / Tombstone / Night train to Lorca / London you're a lady / Gridlock.

Aug 89. (7"/c-s) *(YZ 409/+C)* **WHITE CITY. / EVERY MAN IS A KING** -
(12"+=) *(YZ 409TX)* – Maggie May (live).
(cd-s+=) *(YZ 409CD)* – The star of the County Down.

May 90. (7"/c-s; The POGUES & The DUBLINERS) *(YZ 500/+C)* **JACK'S HEROES. / WHISKEY IN THE JAR** 63 -
(12"+=/cd-s+=) *(YZ 500 T/CD)* – ('B'extended).

— (theme song used by Eire in World Cup)

Aug 90. (7") *(YZ 519)* **SUMMER IN SIAM. / BASTARD LANDLORD** 64 -
(12"+=/cd-s+=) *(YZ 519 T/CD)* – Hell's ditch (instrumental) / The Irish rover.

Sep 90. (cd)(lp/c) *(9031 72554-2)(WX 366/+C)* <422846> **HELL'S DITCH** 12
– The sunnyside of the street / Sayonara / The ghost of a smile / Hell's ditch / Lorca's novena / Summer in Siam / Rain street / Rainbow man / The wake of the Medusa / House of the gods / Five green onions and Jean / Maidria Rua / Six to go.

Apr 91. (cd-s) **SAYONARA / CURSE OF LOVE / INFINITY** -

Sep 91. (7") *(YZ 603)* **A RAINY NIGHT IN SOHO (remix). / SQUID OUT OF WATER** 67 -
(12"+=) *(YZ 603)* – Infinity.
(cd-s+=) *(YZ 603CD)* – POGUETRY IN MOTION (ep).

Sep 91. (cd)(lp/c) *(9031 75405-2)(WX 430/+C)* **THE BEST OF THE POGUES** (compilation) <US-title 'ESSENTIAL POGUES'> 11
– Fairytale of New York / Sally MacLennane / Dirty old town / The Irish rover / A pair of brown eyes / Streams of whiskey / A rainy night in Soho / Fiesta / Rain street / Misty morning, Albert Bridge / White City / Thousand are sailing / The broad majestic Shannon / The body of an American.

Dec 91. (7") *(YZ 628)* **FAIRYTALE OF NEW YORK. / FIESTA** 36 -
(12"+=/cd-s+=) *(YZ 628 T/CD)* – A pair of brown eyes / Sick bed of Cuchulainn / Maggie May.

— p/t JOE STRUMMER is deposed by member SPIDER who takes over vox.

May 92. (7"/c-s) *(YZ 673/+C)* **HONKY TONK WOMAN. / CURSE OF LOVE** 56 -
(12"+=) *(YZ 673T)* – Infinity.
(cd-s+=) *(YZ 673CD)* – The parting glass.

Jun 92. (cd)(lp/c) *(9031 77341-2)(WX 471/+C)* **THE BEST OF THE REST OF THE POGUES** (compilation out-takes)
– If I should fall from grace with God / The sick bed of Cuchulainn / The old main drag / Boys from the County Hell / Young Ned of the hill / Dark streets of London / The auld triangle / Repeal of the licensing laws / Yeah yeah yeah yeah yeah / London girl / Honky tonk women / Summer in Siam / Turkish song of the damned / Lullaby of London / The sunnyside of the street / Hell's ditch.

— (Sep'91) MacGOWAN left when his health deteriorated (JOE STRUMMER deputised for him on tour)

— added 8th member & producer **MICHAEL BROOK** – infinite guitar

WEA Chameleon

Aug 93. (7"/c-s) *(YZ 758/+C)* **TUESDAY MORNING. / FIRST DAY OF FOREVER** 18
(cd-s+=) *(YZ 758CD)* – Turkish song of the damned (live).
(cd-s) *(YZ 758CDX)* – ('A'side) / London calling / I fought the law (both live with JOE STRUMMER).

Sep 93. (cd/c/lp) *(4509 93463-2/-4/-1)* <61598> **WAITING FOR HERB** 20 Oct98
– Tuesday morning / Smell of petroleum / Haunting / Once upon a time / Sitting on top of the world / Drunken boat / Big city / Girl from the Wadi Hammamat / Modern world / Pachinko / My baby's gone / Small hours.

Jan 94. (7"/c-s) *(YZ 771/+C)* **ONCE UPON A TIME. / TRAIN KEPT ROLLING ON** 66 -
(12"+=/cd-s+=) *(YZ 771 T/CD)* – Tuesday morning / Paris St. Germain.

— FEARNEY and WOODS departed, apparently due to the brief Christmas comeback of SHANE MacGOWAN

— **SPIDER / JEM / DARRYL + RANKEN** added **JAMIE CLARKE** – banjo / **JAMES McNALLY** – accordion, uilleann pipes / **DAVID COULTER** – mandolin, tambourine

Sep 95. (7"colrd/c-s) *(WEA 011 X/C)* **HOW COME. / EYES OF AN ANGEL** -
(cd-s+=) *(WX 011CD)* – Tuesday morning (live) / Big city (live).

Oct 95. (cd/c/lp) *(0630 11210-2/-4/-1)* **POGUE MAHONE** -
– How come / Living in a world without her / When the ship comes in / Anniversary / Amadie / Love you 'till the end / Bright lights / Oretown / Pont Mirabeau / Tosspint / Four o'clock in the morning / Where that love's been gone / The sun and the moon.

— note:- The POGUES also appeared on the flip side to KIRSTY MacCOLL's Cole Porter tribute single, 'Miss Otis Regrets' on the track 'JUST ONE OF THOSE THINGS'.

POISON GIRLS

Formed: Brighton, England . . . 1977 by VI SUBVERSA, LANCE D'BOYLE and RICHARD FAMOUS. In her mid-40's by the time of the group's shared debut EP, 'FATAL MICROBES MEET THE POISON GIRLS' – the FATAL MICROBES being a punk band featuring VI's kids! – SUBVERSA was an unlikely but highly articulate and committed hippy-turned-punk frontwoman, guiding the band through more than a decade of anti-establishment, pro-feminist musical activity. The subsequent 'HEX' EP was released on CRASS' own label, while the 'GIRLS collaborated with the staunchly anarchist punks themselves on 1980's bludgeoning 'PERSONS UNKNOWN'. The POISON GIRLS also shared their beliefs and lifestyle, choosing to live in a London commune and spending their spare time campaigning against racism and fascism. A full length debut set, 'CHAPPAQUIDDICK BRIDGE' (1980) followed on the band's own 'Xentrix' label and by the release of 'WHERE'S THE PLEASURE' (1982), the group had begun to widen their musical scope and had moved on from their affiliation with CRASS. Following a brief dalliance with the 'Illuminated' label for 1983's 'SEVEN YEAR SCRATCH', the group reactivated 'Xentrix' with their swansong album, 'SONGS OF PRAISE' (1985), the material, at least lyrically, as uncompromising as ever. Although they kept on keeping on until the end of the 80's, The POISON GIRLS last vinyl release was 1986's EP, 'THE PRICE OF GRAIN AND THE PRICE OF BLOOD', railing against injustice to the last. While VI's occasionally cackling vocal style may be something of an acquired taste and the slightly GONG-hippy feel to some tracks may be off-putting, 1995's 4CD box set, 'STATEMENT', provides an interesting overview of the band's career.

Album rating: 7 YEAR SCRATCH compilation (*6)

VI SUBVERSA – vocals, guitar / **RICHARD FAMOUS** – guitar, vocals / **LANCE D'BOYLE** – drums / **PETE FENDER** – bass

Small Wonder not iss.

Mar 79. (12"ep) *(WEENY 3)* **FATAL MICROBES MEET THE POISON GIRLS** -
– Piano lessons / Closed shop / (2 by FATAL MICROBES).

— **BERNHARDT REBOURS** – bass repl. FENDER (of FATAL MICROBES)

Jul 79. (12"ep) *(WEENY 4)* **HEX** -
– Old tarts song / Crisis / Ideologically / Bremen song / Political love / Jump mama jump / Under the doctor / Reality attack. *(re-iss. Apr81 on 'Crass'; 421984-1)*

Crass not iss.

May 80. (7") *(421984-1)* **PERSONS UNKNOWN. / (other track by CRASS)** -

— added guests **GEM STONE** – vocals (ex-KILLJOYS) / **NIL** – violin

Oct 80. (lp) *(421984-2)* **CHAPPAQUIDICK BRIDGE** -
– Another hero / Hole in the wall / Underbitch / Alienation / Pretty Polly / Good time / Other / Daughter & sons.

Apr 81. (7"m) *(421984-8)* **ALL SYSTEMS GO. / PROMENADE IMMORTELLE / DIRTY WORK** -

Jun 81. (7"flexi-free) *(421984-10)* **PRETTY POLLY. / BULLY BOYS (live)** -

Xntrix not iss.

Oct 81. (lp) *(XN 2003)* **TOTAL EXPOSURE (live)** -
– Persons unknown / Old tart's song / State control / Tension / Bully boys / Another hero bites / Don't go home tonight / S.S. snoopers / Other / Daughters and sons / Alienation / Fucking mother / Dirty work.

— **CHRIS GRACE** + guest **PETE FENDER** – bass repl. REBOURS

Nov 82. (lp) *(XN 2006)* **WHERE'S THE PLEASURE** -
– Where's the pleasure / Lovers are they worth it / I've done it all before / Whisky voice / Menage abattoir / Take the toys / Soft touch / Take the toys – reprise / Velvet launderette / Rio disco stink / Cry no more / Mandy is having a baby / Fear of freedom.

— added **CYNTH ETHICS** – keyboards

Illuminated not iss.

Jul 83. (7") *(ILL 23)* **ONE GOOD REASON. / CINNAMON GARDEN** -

Oct 83. (7") *(ILL 25)* **ARE YOU HAPPY NOW?. / CREAM DREAM** -

— **MARTIN HEATH** – bass repl. CHRIS

Xntrix not iss.

Nov 84. (7") *(XN 2009)* **(I'M NOT A) REAL WOMAN. / TAKE THE TOYS FROM THE BOYS** -
(12"+=) *(12XN 2009)* – Perfect crime / Tension.

Jun 85. (lp) *(XN 2008)* **SONGS OF PRAISE** -

— **AGENT ORANGE** – drums repl. D'BOYLE

Upright not iss.

Nov 85. (12"ep) *(UPT 12)* **THE PRICE OF GRAIN AND THE PRICE OF BLOOD** -

— **MAX VOLUME** – bass repl. HEATH + ETHICS

— still until split in 1989 after Zagreb concert, but nothing new was released after '86. However, they did a one-off gig in June '95.

– compilations, etc. –

Mar 84. (d-lp) *Xntrix; (RM 101)* **7 YEAR SCRATCH** -

Mar 85. (12"ep) *Illuminated; (ILL 33-12)* **ARE YOU HAPPY NOW? (remix) / CREAM DREAM. / MENAGE ABATTOIR / WHISKY VOICE** -

May 95. (cd) *Cooking Vinyl; (<COOKCD 086>)* **REAL WOMAN** Feb97

May 95. (4xcd-box) *Cooking Vinyl; (<COOKCD 087>)* **STATEMENT – THE COMPLETE RECORDINGS**

Sep 98. (cd) *Recall; <137>* **POISONOUS**

POISON IDEA

Formed: Portland, Oregon, USA . . . late 1980 by JERRY A., PIG CHAMPION, CHRIS TENSE and DEAN JOHNSON. The latter pair were subsequently replaced by numerous rhythm men throughout a torrid decade which saw the remainder/bulk of the band (50 stone between them!) consistently fixated on alcohol and general debauchery. Their first release was an EP of 13 short songs entitled 'PICK YOUR KING', virtually a mini-set featuring an iconic sleeve depicting ELVIS on one side and JESUS on the other. The 1986 debut album, 'KINGS OF PUNK', showed little compromise

as they threw their weight behind a vicious set of foul-mouthed hardcore punk. The following year's 'WAR ALL THE TIME' was equally heavy going, while the hilariously titled 'RECORD COLLECTORS ARE PRETENTIOUS ARSEHOLES' (1989) suggested that POISON IDEA had little time for trainspotting. Still, they did drag out a surprisingly eclectic bag of covers on 1992's 'PAJAMA PARTY', including suitably harsh renditions of such soul classics as Jimmy Cliff's 'THE HARDER THEY COME' and Booker T & The MGs 'GREEN ONIONS'. By this point, the band had already signed to 'Vinyl Solution', disbanding after 'WE MUST BURN' (1993). After a brief (one album) stint with The GIFT in '94, POISON IDEA lumbered back into view in 1996, the resulting album, 'PIG'S LAST STAND' released for 'Sub Pop'.
• **Songwriters:** JERRY A. + PIG except covers album 'PAJAMA PARTY', which included; WE GOT THE BEAT (Go-Go's) / KICK OUT THE JAMS (MC5) / MOTORHEAD (Motorhead) / ENDLESS SLEEP (Joey Reynolds) / JAILHOUSE ROCK (Elvis Presley) / NEW ROSE (Damned) / etc. The GIFT covered SO THIS IS THE POPS (Tones On Tails).

Album rating: KINGS OF PUNK (*6) / RECORD COLLECTORS . . . (*7) / FEEL THE DARKNESS (*7)

JERRY A. – vocals / **PIG CHAMPION** (b. TOM ROBERTS) – guitar / **CHRIS TENSE** – bass / **DEAN JOHNSON** – drums

not iss. unknown

1985. (12"ep) **PICK YOUR KING E.P.** [-] [ ]
– Think twice / It's an action / This thing called progress / In my head ache / Underage / Self abuse / Cult band / Last one / Pure hate / Castration / Reggae (I hate) / Give it up / Think fast. <*US cd-iss. Oct91 on 'Taang!';* >

not iss. Pusmort

1986. (m-lp) *<6012-10>* **KINGS OF PUNK** [-] [ ]
– Lifestyles / Short fuse / God not God / Ugly American / Subtract / Cop an attitude / Death wish kids / Tormented imp / One by one / Out of the picture. *<(re-iss. Sep91 on 'Taang!' cd/lp; TG 9284-2/-1)>*

— **STEVE 'Three Slayer Hippy' SANFORD** – drums repl. JOHNSON

— added **VEGETABLE** – guitar (ex-MAYHEM)

— **MONDO** – bass (ex-MAYHEM) repl. TENSE (he had been replaced very briefly by TIM PAUL for only one song and one aborted gig; now in GUNTRUCK)

not iss. Alchemy

Nov 87. (lp/c) *<VM 106/+C>* **WAR ALL THE TIME** [-] [ ]
– Temple / Romantic self destruction / Push the button / Ritual chicken / Nothing is final / Motorhead / Hot time / Steel rule / Typical / Murderer / Marked for life. *(UK-iss.Oct93 on 'Vinyl Solution' cd/c/lp; SOL 40 CD/MC/LP)*

not iss. Bitzcore

1989. (m-lp) *<BC 1658>* **RECORD COLLECTORS ARE PRETENTIOUS ARSEHOLES** [-] [ ]
– A.A. / Legalize freedom / Cold comfort / Typical / Thorn in my side / Laughing boy / Rubber hisband / Right? / Rich get richer / Don't like it here / Die on your knees / Time to go. *(UK-iss.Sep91 on 'Taang!'; TG 9299-1) (cd-iss. Aug94 on 'Bitzcore'; 1568)*

not iss. InYourFace

Jul 89. (lp) *<FACE 6>* **POISON IDEA (aka 'GETTING THE FEAR')** [-] [ ]

— **MYRTLE TICKNER** – bass (ex-OILY BLOODMEN) repl. VEGETABLE

Sub Pop Sub Pop

Oct 90. (7",7"green) *(SP 86)* **WE GOT THE BEAT. / TAKEN BY SURPRISE** [ ] [ ]

Vinyl Solution Taang!

Oct 90. (lp/cd) *(SOL 025/+CD)* **FEEL THE DARKNESS** [ ] [ ]
– Plastic bomb / Deep slep / The badge / Just to get away / Gone for good / Death of an idiot blues / Taken by surprise / Alan's on fire / Welcome to Krell / Nation of finks / Backstab gospel / Painkiller / Feel the darkness. *(cd+=)* – Discontent. *(re-iss. Jan97 on 'Epitaph' cd/c/lp; 6463-2/-4/-1)*

Nov 90. (7") **FEEL THE DARKNESS. / ALAN'S ON FIRE** [ ] [ ]

— **KID COCKSMAN** – guitar (ex-GARGOYLE) repl. VEGETABLE

— **ALDINE STRYCHNINE** – guitar (ex-MAIMED FOR LIFE) repl. KID

Apr 91. (cd-ep) *(VS 32CD)* **OFFICIAL BOOTLEG EP** [ ] [ ]
– Plastic bomb / Punish me / etc.

— **MONDO** returned to add to the mayhem

Feb 92. (lp/cd) *(SOL 033/+CD) <T 63-2/-4/-1>* **BLANK, BLACKOUT, VACANT** [ ] [ ]
– Say good bye / Star of Baghdad / Icepicks at dawn / Smack attack / Forever and always / Punish me / Crippled angel / What happened to Sunday? / You're next / Drain / Brigandage / Amy's theme / Vietnamese baby. *(lp w/ free 7"live)*

Sep 92. (lp,pink-lp/c/cd) *(SOL 034/+MC/CD)* **PAJAMA PARTY** [ ] [ ]
– Kick out the jams / Vietnamese baby / We got the beat / Motorhead / Endless sleep / Laudy Miss Clawdy / Jailhouse rock / Flamethrower love / New rose / Doctor doctor / Up front / The harder they come / Green onions.

Apr 93. (cd-ep) *(VS 32CD)* **PUNISH ME EP** [ ] [-]

Apr 93. (lp/c/cd) *(SOL 037/+MC/CD)* **WE MUST BURN** [ ] [ ]
– In order to live / Hung like a saviour / Hard and cheap / Endless blockades for the pussyfooter / It's not the last / When I say stop / Foiled again / Jessie's arms / Slum lord / Stare at the sun / Religion and politics.

— disbanded when TENSE and JOHNSON formed APARTMENT 3G

GIFT

— **JERRY A.** with his wife **MAY MAY DEL CASTRO** – bass, vocals (ex-DESTROY ALL BLONDS) / **SAM HENRY** – drums (ex-WIPERS)

Tim/Kerr Tim/Kerr

Oct 94. (cd) *<(TK93CD 068)>* **MULTUM IN PARVA** [ ] [ ]
– Little deranged puppet (part 1) / Sinking ship / OK this is the pops / Don't need a reason / Restless spirit / Little deranged puppet (part 2) / Never too young / Social cleansing / A date with failure / Beyond the tears / Kelly K. / Jezebel / Little deranged puppet (part 3).

POISON IDEA

— reformed with **JERRY A. + CHAMPION**

Sub Pop Sub Pop

Apr 96. (cd) *<(SP 343)>* **PIG'S LAST STAND** [ ] [ ]
– Plastic bomb / Taken by surpise / Truth hurts / Death, agony and screams / Don't ask me why / A.A. / Crippled angle / Stare at the sun / Bela Lugosi is dead / Feel the darkness / Give it up / Blitzkreig bop / Hangover heart attack / Alan's on fire / Up front.

— In Feb'97, PIG CHAMPION was credited on an MDC single, 'I Don't Want To Hurt You Dude', issued on 'Honest Dons'; (DON 004).

– compilations, etc. –

Jan 92. (lp/cd) *Bitzcore; (BC 1667/+CD)* **DUTCH COURAGE** [ ] [ ]
(re-iss. Aug94; same)

1992. (cd; with JEFF DAHL) *Triple X; <51137>* **JEFF DAHL AND POISON IDEA** [-] [ ]

Aug 94. (cd) *Bitzcore; (BC 1684CD)* **THE EARLY YEARS** [ ] [ ]

POLAK (see under ⇒ ADORABLE)

POLARA

Formed: Minneapolis, Minnesota, USA . . . mid 80's out of 27 VARIOUS by ED ACKERSON. An enigmatic psychedelic guitar-pop proposition, the latter outfit released a series of obscure but noteworthy long-players over the course of the late 80's/early 90's. For his new combo, POLARA, ED recruited JENNIFER JURGENS, JASON ORRIS and PETER ANDERSON, exploring more experimental avenues that drew on the pioneering fusion of 60's influences and punk once initiated by fellow Minneapolis sons, HUSKER DU. Surfacing on local institution, 'TwinTone', ACKERSON and Co debuted early in '95 with an impressive eponymous album that caught the ear of leading major alternative bastion, 'Interscope'. While not as compellingly innovative as their earlier work, subsequent albums, 'C'EST LA VIE' (1997) and 'FORMLESS – FUNCTIONAL' (1998), were still worthy of attention.

Album rating: 27 Various: HI (*5) / YES, INDEEED (*5) / APPROXIMATELY (*6) / UP (*4) / FINE (*4) / Polara: POLARA (*7) / C'EST LA VIE (*6) / FORMLESS – FUNCTIONAL (*5)

the 27 VARIOUS

ED ACKERSON – vocals, guitar / **JED MAYER** – drums

not iss. Susstones

1987. (lp) **HI** [-] [ ]

— added two unknown members

1989. (lp) **YES, INDEED** [-] [ ]

— **MIKE REITER** – drums; repl. MAYER

— added **BART BAKKER** – bass

not iss. TwinTone

1990. (cd) *<TT 89200>* **APPROXIMATELY** [-] [ ]
– I feel damage (D) / You look a treat / Deposit / I can't wait till the end of my days / You reached me / Like the poison / Cold / Too long a day / Blue concourse / Things I wasn't surprised to see / Out of lungs.

Sep 91. (cd,c) *<89218>* **UP (live)** [-] [ ]
– Happening – Sometime / Lay it on, Elaine / Love somebody / Leave it / Never been told / Cavern eyes / Fare thee well / Whenever I'm gone / What to do? / Burned / Put me down / Doesn't matter to you.

Sep 92. (cd,c) *<89226>* **FINE** [-] [ ]
– Turn on and on / You've got it bad / Swoop factor: 9000 / Down the line / Shag / Song for mire / Out of mohair / C/O Anne / Make it through / Song for Juliana / Up / Contrast.

— ACKERSON joined the touring line-up of ANTENNA until . . .

POLARA

ED ACKERSON – vocals, guitar / **JENNIFER JURGENS** – guitar, organ, vocals / **JASON ORRIS** – bass, vocals / **PETER ANDERSON** – drums

Clean Up-Restless Clean Up-Restless

Feb 95. (cd) *<(CR 89276-2)>* **POLARA** [ ] [ ]
– Counting down / Allay / Source of light / Squelch / Listening now / Taupe / Avenue E / Anniversary 6 / One foot / a+b=y / State / Letter bomb.

not iss. Interscope

Nov 96. (cd-s) *<97011>* **PANTOMIME /** [-] [ ]

Apr 97. (cd/c) *90074>* **C'EST LA VIE** [-] [ ]
– Transformation / Sort it out / Light the fuse and run / Quebecois / So sue me / Make it easy / Incoming / Eleasticity / Idle hands / The other side / Pantomime / Shanghai bell / Untitled.

— now without ORRIS

Mar 98. (cd) *<90182>* **FORMLESS/FUNCTIONAL** [-] [ ]
– Whassup? / Brighter day / Trainwreck / Got the switch! / Halo / Peaking Charlie / I can believe / Semi-detatched / Verbing / Midtown greenway / Tread lightly / Corporate hegemony (smash the state!).

Robert POLLARD (see under ⇒ GUIDED BY VOICES)

POLVO

Formed: Chapel Hill, North Carolina, USA . . . early 90's by ASH BOWIE, DAVE BRYLAWSKI, STEVE POPSON and EDDIE WATKINS. Taking their cue from the complex, oblique noise experimentation once the domain of SONIC YOUTH and to a lesser extent, DINOSAUR JR and WIRE, POLVO often dismissed chorus/verse convention in favour of atonal guitar scree and sprawling stop-start song patterns. A deal with 'Merge' (licensed to 'Touch & Go' in the States) and a debut album, 'COR-CRANE SECRET' (1992), quickly established POLVO as one of the most challenging acts thrown up by the fertile Chapel Hill alternative scene. Working at a rate of almost an album a year, the quartet maintained an impressively prolific release schedule throughout the mid-90's while frontman ASH also found the time to moonlight for the band HELIUM.

Album rating: CRO-CRANE SECRET (*6) / TODAY'S ACTIVE LIFESTYLES (*5) / CELEBRATE THE NEW DARK AGE mini (*5) / THIS ECLIPSE mini (*5) / EXPLODED DRAWING (*5) / SHAPES (*5)

ASH BOWIE – guitar, vocals / **DAVE BRYLAWSKI** – guitar, vocals / **STEVE POPSON** – bass / **EDDIE WATKINS** – drums

not iss. unknown

1991. (cd-ep) **POLVO** -
– Can I ride / Leaf / Lull / Totemic / Tread on me / Teen dream / Snake fist fighter.

Touch & Go Merge

Jul 92. (lp/cd) *(TG 101/+CD)* <*MRG 22/+CD*> **COR-CRANE SECRET**
– Vibracobra / Kalgon / Bend or break / Can I ride / Sense of it / Ox scapula / Channel changer / In the hand, in the sieve / The curtain remembers / Well is deep / Duped.

May 93. (lp/cd) *(TG 114/+CD)* <*MRG 40/+CD*> **TODAY'S ACTIVE LIFESTYLES**
– Thermal treasure / Lazy comet / My kimono / Sure shot / Stinger (five wigs) / Tilebreaker / Shiska / Time isn't on my side / Action vs. vibe / Gemini cusp.

May 94. (m-cd/m-c) *(TG 133CD)* <*MRG 56 CD/C*> **CELEBRATE THE NEW DARK AGE**
– Fractured (like chandeliers) / City spirit / Tragic carpet ride / Solitary pet / Every holy shroud / Old Lystra / Virtual cold.

Nov 95. (m-cd) *(TG 156CD)* <*MRG 95*> **THIS ECLIPSE**
– Bat radar / Bombs that fall from your eyes / Titan up / Production values / Title track.

—— ASH BOWIE also moonlighted with HELIUM

Touch & Go Touch & Go

May 96. (lp/cd) <*(TG 162/+CD)*> **EXPLODED DRAWING**
– Fast canoe / Bridesmaid blues / Feather of forgiveness / Passive attack / Light of the moon / Crumbling down / Street knowledge / High-wire moves / Monolith / In this life / Secret's secret / Snowstorm in iowa / Purple bear / Taste of your mind / Missing receipts / When will I die / For the last time / In my dreams.

Sep 97. (cd/lp) <*(TG 179 CD/LP)*> **SHAPES**
– Enemy insects / Fighting kites / Rock post rock / Golden ladder / Downtown dedication / Pulchritude / Twenty white tents / Everything in flames / D.D. (S.R.) / El Rocio / Lantern.

—— split up in '98

POND

Formed: Portland, Oregon, USA . . . early 90's by Alaskan (Juneau, to be exact) lads CHRIS BRADY and CHARLIE CAMPBELL, who met one time molecular biologist DAVE GRIEBWASSER on a trip to Seattle. All veterans of various underachieving amateur outfits despite their youthfulness, the trio surfed the initial North-Western grunge wave with a melodic, retro-influenced debut single for 'T/K', 'YOUNG SPLENDOR'. POND were subsequently thrown in at the deep end when 'Sub Pop' netted them for a long term deal, the band swimming among the alternative scene's bigger fish with early 1993's eponymous debut album. Presumably immersing themselves in their beloved Star Trek, POND later resurfaced in the mid-90's with their second and final set, 'THE PRACTICE OF JOY BEFORE DEATH' (1995).

Album rating: POND (*7) / THE PRACTICE OF JOY BEFORE DEATH (*6)

CHRIS BRADY – bass, vocals / **CHARLIE CAMPBELL** – guitar, vocals / **DAVE GRIEBWASSER** – drums

not iss. Tim/Kerr

1991. (7") **YOUNG SPLENDOR. /** -

Sub Pop Sub Pop

Nov 92. (7") <*(SP 218)*> **WHEEL. /**
(12"+=/cd-s+=) *(SP/+CD 222)* –

Feb 93. (lp/cd) <*(SP/+CD 66-233)*> **POND**
– Young splendour / Perfect four / Gone / Agatha / Tree / Wheel / Spots / Foamy / Grinned / Filler.

Jul 94. (7") <*(SP 263)*> **MOTH. /**

Feb 95. (7") <*(SP 146-366)*> **SUNDIAL. / GLASS SPARKLES IN THEIR HAIR**

Mar 95. (lp/cd) *(SP/+CD 143-357)* <*SPCD 265*> **THE PRACTICE OF JOY BEFORE DEATH** Jan95
– Side road / Mubby's theme / Union / Magnifier / Patience / Ol' blue hair / Sundial / Glass sparkles in their hair / Van / Happy cow farm family / Carpenter ant / Artificial turf / Rock collection / Gagged and bound.

not iss. Sony

Apr 97. (cd,c) <*67630*> **ROCK COLLECTION** -
– Spokes / You're not an astronaut / Scoliosis / One day in the future / Twins / You're not a seed / Flawed / My dog is an astronaut though / Forget / Golden / Greyhound / Rebury me / Filterless / (untitled) / (untitled) / Ugly.

POOH STICKS

Formed: Swansea, Wales . . . 1987 by HUE WILLIAMS (the son of ex-MAN and DIRE STRAITS drummer, TERRY WILLIAMS) who recruited a largely (youthful) female line-up of TRUDI, ALISON, STEPHANIE and PAUL. Setting out to satirise the po-faced boys club that represented the indie scene of the time, The POOH STICKS cut 'ON TAPE' for tiny local label, 'Fierce'. A completely inappropriate boxed set of singles followed, the humour in the semi-legendary 'I KNOW SOMEONE WHO KNOWS SOMEONE WHO KNOWS ALAN McGEE QUITE WELL' as relevant today as it was then. Music wise, the general formula was a kitsch grab-bag of classic American pop/rock, from The RASPBERRIES to CHEAP TRICK; all fine and dandy but in reality, WILLIAMS' Anglophile indie-boy vocals – and often pretty flat vocals at that – weren't exactly complementary. Nevertheless, critics were generally enamoured with their bright-eyed charm, the band collecting their early material together for 1988's eponymous mini-set. This was followed by a couple of live albums, one for Scottish label, '53rd & 3rd' and one for US alternative bastion, 'Sympathy For The Record Industry'. A debut album proper, 'THE GREAT WHITE WONDER' was released on the latter label in 1991, The POOH STICKS' Stateside potential finally realised when they were signed to US-based 'BMG'-offshoot, 'Zoo'. Their major label debut, the hopefully (and no doubt ironically) titled 'MILLION SELLER' hit the shelves in 1993, the band's love of American teen-dream fantasy undimmed as they churned out another helping of three-chord guitar, cutesy harmonies and twee, occasionally humourous lyrics. That 'SUGAR BABY' was apparently inspired by a chance meeting with RANDY BACHMAN says it all really. Yet the record failed to really capture the record buying imagination – as did 1995's 'OPTIMISTIC FOOL' – The POOH STICKS remaining as curious a cult item as ever. • **Songwriters:** HUE penned except; DYING FOR IT (Vaselines).

HUE WILLIAMS (b. 4 Mar'68) – vocals / **PAUL WELLER** – guitar / **TRUDI** – keyboards, Moog synth / **ALISON** – bass / **STEPHANIE** – drums

Fierce Sympathy F

Feb 88. (7"etched) *(FRIGHT 011)* **ON TAPE** -

Aug 88. (7"etched) *(FRIGHT 021)* **1-2-3 RED LIGHT** -

Sep 88. (5x7"etched;box) *(FRIGHT 021)* **1-2-3 RED LIGHT /** *(FRIGHT 022)* **HEROES AND VILLAINS /** *(FRIGHT 023)* **HEARTBREAK /** *(FRIGHT 024)* **I KNOW SOMEONE WHO KNOWS SOMEONE WHO KNOWS ALAN McGEE QUITE WELL /** *(FRIGHT 025)* **INDIE POP AIN'T NOISE POLLUTION** -

Oct 88. (cd-ep) *(FRIGHT 026)* **ALAN McGEE CD** -
– (above tracks) / How to get to Hue Pooh-Stick / On tape / Please Hue, please.

Nov 88. (lp) *(FRIGHT 028)* **ON TAPE** -
– (above tracks).

Jan 89. (pink-m-lp) *(AGAMC 5)* **ORGASM (live)** -
(above originally album issued on '53rd & 3rd')

Feb 89. (m-lp;etched) *(FRIGHT)* **THE POOH STICKS** -

Mar 89. (7"one-sided) *(FRIGHT 034)* **DYING FOR IT** -

—— In the Spring of '89, they issued 7"flexi GO GO GIRL./ SIMON E from 'Cheree 3' fanzine. From their own Woosh fanzine 'HARD ON LOVE' was issued on yellow 7"flexi. In the Autumn, a one-sided 7" 'ENCORES EP' was issued by 'Anonymous'.

Nov 89. (lp; mail-order) *(FRIGHT 035)* **TRADEMARK OF QUALITY** -
(re-iss. Mar92 lp/cd; FRIGHT 048/+CD)

Apr 90. (lp) *(FRIGHT 037)* <*SFTRI 58*> **FORMULA ONE GENERATION**
– Intro / Radio ready / Teenage high / Time to time / Susan sleepwalking / All the good that's happening / Dare true kiss promise / Teenage high 2 / Tonight / Soft beds, hard battles / Dying for it.

Cheree Zoo

May 91. (7") *(CHEREE 17)* **WHO LOVES YOU. / GOOD TIMES** -

—— above featured vocals by AMELIA FLETCHER (of HEAVENLY)

Jun 91. (cd/c/lp) *(CHEREE 18 CD/MC/LP)* <*72445-11029-2/-4*> **THE GREAT WHITE WONDER** -
– Young people / Rhythm of love / Sweet baby James / Pandora's box / Desperado / Goodtimes / The wild one, forever / I'm in you / When Sunny gets blue.

Sep 91. (7") **YOUNG PEOPLE. /** -

Fierce-BMG not iss.

Oct 92. (7") *(FRIGHT 42)* **MILLION SELLER. /** -

Zoo-RCA not iss.

Oct 92. (7") *(WALES 1)* **THE WORLD IS TURNING ON. / GOODBYE DON'T MEAN I'M GONE** -
(12"/cd-s) *(WALES 1 T/CD)* – ('A'side) / Force fed by love / True love ('A'mix).

Feb 93. (cd/c/lp) *(7244 511043-2/-4/-1)* **MILLION SELLER** -
– Million seller / Let the good times roll / The world is turning on / Sugar baby / I saw the light / Susan sleepwalking / When the girl wants to be free / Baby wanna go round with me / Sugar mello / Rainbow rider / Goodbye don't mean I'm gone / Jelly on a plate / That was the greatest song.

Mar 93. (7"/c-s) **THE WORLD IS TURNING ON. / ROLL OVER EASY / WHEN THE GIRLS WANT TO BE FREE** -
(12"+=/cd-s+=) – Sugar baby (acoustic) / Let the good times roll (acoustic).

Seed Seed

Apr 95. (7") <*(SEED 013)*> **DIZGO GIRL. / COOL IN A CRISIS / WHEN THE NIGHT FALLS**
(cd-s+=) <*(SEEDCD 013)*> – She's the one.

May 95. (cd/lp) <*(92513-2/-1)*> **OPTIMISTIC FOOL**
– Opening night / Cool in a crisis / Starfishing / Optimistic fool / Who was it / Bad morning girl / Miss me / Working on a beautiful thing / Up on the roof / Prayer for my demo / All things must pass / Song cycle / First of a million songs.

– compilations, etc. –

Apr 91. (lp) *Overground; (OVER 018)* **PEEL SESSIONS 88/89** -

Mar 92. (lp/cd) *Fierce; (FRIGHT 047/+CD)* **MULTIPLE ORGASM** -

POP GROUP

Formed: Bristol, England . . . 1978 by MARK STEWART, JON WADDINGTON, DAVID WRIGHT, SEAN OLIVER and BRUCE SMITH. Inspired by punk's nihilistic energy and influenced by everyone from ROLAND KIRK to CAN and LEE PERRY, The POP GROUP harnessed their competing forces into a funky but defiant howl of rage at newly elected Prime Minister, Margaret Thatcher, with 1979's debut single, 'SHE IS BEYOND GOOD AND EVIL'. Issued on Jake Riviera's newly established 'Radar' label, the track was hailed as one of the most innovative releases of the post-punk era. With OLIVER and WRIGHT subsequently replaced by SIMON UNDERWOOD and GARETH SAGER – the latter introducing screeching free-jazz sax into the equation – The POP GROUP recorded a landmark debut album, 'Y' (1979). Produced by reggae veteran DENNIS BOVELL, the record presaged the primal intensity of The BIRTHDAY PARTY with spontaneous layers of visceral noise, militant lyrics and tortured vocals underpinned by CHIC-style basslines and dub dynamics. NICK CAVE, for one, was irrevocably changed after witnessing The POP GROUP in full flight, recently confessing (early 1999) on Channel 4 that the seminal 'WE ARE ALL PROSTITUTES' was among the most "violent, paranoid" music he'd ever heard. Essential ingredients for decent rock'n'roll of course, the band's first single for 'Rough Trade' offering it up in spades. A second album, 'FOR HOW MUCH LONGER DO WE TOLERATE MASS MURDER' (1980), was, if anything, even more intense but hardly helped widen the band's limited appeal. Something had to give and inevitably it all ended in tears, the band subsequently embroiled in legal wrangles with their label and signing off after a split single with The SLITS. STEWART went on to work with The ON-U SOUND posse, issuing records as MARK STEWART & THE MAFFIA (and later solo in his own right), while SAGER went on to form RIP, RIG + PANIC. UNDERWOOD achieved brief but enduring acclaim as founder of PIGBAG while WADDINGTON formed MAXIMUM JOY. OLIVER, sadly, was to die of heart failure in 1990, having recently co-written TERENCE TRENT D'ARBY's massive 'Wishing Well'. As cult as they come, The POP GROUP are widely acknowledged as laying the foundations for a fertile Bristol music scene which would subsequently spawn such revered artists as MASSIVE ATTACK, NENEH CHERRY, NELLEE HOOPER, PORTISHEAD, TRICKY etc. • **Songwriters:** STEWART lyricist / group compositions.

Album rating: Y (*7) / FOR HOW MUCH LONGER . . . (*8) / WE ARE TIME (*5) / Mark Stewart: LEARNING TO COPE WITH COWARDICE (*6) / AS THE VENEER OF DEMOCRACY BEGINS TO FADE (*6) / MARK STEWART (*5) / METATRON (*5) / CONTROL DATA (*5)

MARK STEWART – vocals / **JOHN WADDINGTON** – guitar / **DAVID WRIGHT** – saxophone / **SEAN OLIVER** – bass / **BRUCE SMITH** – drums, percussion

Radar | not iss.

Mar 79. (7"/12") *(ADA 29/1229)* **SHE IS BEYOND GOOD AND EVIL. / 3:38**

— **SIMON UNDERWOOD** – bass repl. OLIVER who joined ESSENTIAL LOGIC / **GARETH SAGER** – guitar, saxophone repl. WRIGHT who joined ESSENTIAL LOGIC

Apr 79. (lp) *(RAD 20)* **Y**
– Thief of fire / Snowgirl / Blood money / Savage sea / We are time / Words disobey me / Don't call me Pain / The boys from Brazil / Don't sell your dreams. *(re-iss. cd/lp; SCAN CD/LP 14)(+=)* – She is beyond good and evil.

— **DAN KATSIS** – bass (also of GLAXO BABIES) repl. SIMON who joined PIGBAG / added **TRISTAN HONSINGER** – cello

Rough Trade – Y | not iss.

Oct 79. (7") *(RT 023)* **WE ARE ALL PROSTITUTES. / OUR CHILDREN SHALL RISE UP AGAINST**

— **PAUL STUART** – drums; repl. SMITH who joined SLITS

Mar 80. (7") *(RT 039 – Y1)* **(In The Beginning – by SLITS). / WHERE THERE'S A WILL THERE'S A WAY**

Mar 80. (lp) *(ROUGH 9 – Y2)* **FOR HOW MUCH LONGER DO WE TOLERATE MASS MURDER?**
– Forces of oppression / Feed the hungry / One out of many / Blind faith / How much longer . . . / Justice / There are no spectators / Communicate / Rob a bank.

Dec 80. (lp) *(ROUGH 12 – Y5)* **WE ARE TIME (live)**
– Kiss the book / Amnesty report / Springer / Sense of purpose / We are time / Trap / Thief of fire / Genius or lunatic / Colour blind / Spanish inquisition. *(re-iss. Aug84; same)*

— split 1980, when GARETH formed RIP, RIG & PANIC with other ex-POP GROUP members, SEAN and BRUCE. WADDINGTON and CATSIS formed MAXIMUM JOY

MARK STEWART

Y Records | not iss.

May 82. (10"/7"; as MOUTH 2) *(10+/Y 20)* **WHO'S HOT. / CATCH A CAB**

— with **CHARLES 'ESKIMO' FOX** – drums / **EVAR** – bass / **NOAH** – keyboards

On-U-Sound | not iss.

Oct 82. (10"ep; as MARK STEWART & THE MAFFIA) *(ONUDP 5)* **JERUSALEM. / HIGH IDEALS AND CRAZY DREAMS / LIBERTY CITY**

— **FATFINGERS** – keyboards; repl. NOAH

Jun 83. (lp; as MARK STEWART & THE MAFFIA) *(ONULP 24)* **LEARNING TO COPE WITH COWARDICE**
– Learning to cope with cowardice / Liberty city / Blessed are those / Who struggle / None dare / Call it conspiracy / Don't you ever lay down / Your arms / The paranoia of power / To have the vision / Jerusalem.

— he again worked with **ADRIAN SHERWOOD** – producer / **KEITH LA BLANCA** – drums (ex-MALCOLM X) / **DOUG WIMBUSH** – bass / **SKIP McDONALD** – keyboards, guitar

Mute | Mute

May 85. (7") *(7MUTE 37)* **HYPNOTISED. / DREAMERS**
(12"+=) *(12MUTE 37)* – The veneer of democracy starts to fade.

Nov 85. (lp) *(<STUMM 24>)* **AS THE VENEER OF DEMOCRACY BEGINS TO FADE**
– Passcreation programme / Bastards / The resistance of the cell / As the veneer of democracy starts to fade / Hypnotised / Slave of love / The waiting room. *(cd-iss. Apr88 +=; CDSTUMM 24)* – Dreamers.

Sep 87. (7") *(MUTE 59)* **THIS IS STRANGER THAN LOVE. / ANGER IS HOLY**
(12"+=) *(12MUTE 59)* – Survival / ('A'dub).

Oct 87. (cd/lp) *(<CD+/STUMM 43>)* **MARK STEWART**
– Survival / Survivalist / Anger is holy / Hell is empty / Stranger / Forbidden colour – Forbidden dub / Fatal attraction / This is stranger than love.

Mar 90. (12"/cd-s) *(12/CD MUTE 92)* **HYSTERIA. /**

Apr 90. (cd/c/lp) *(<CD/C+/STUMM 62>)* **METATRON**
– Hysteria / Shame / Collision / Faith healer / These things happen / My possession / Possession dub / Mammon.

Mar 96. (12"/cd-s) *(12/CD MUTE 130)* **DREAM KITCHEN. /**

Apr 96. (cd/d-lp) *(CD+/STUMM 93) <69013>* **CONTROL DATA** Jun96
– Dream kitchen / Forbidden love / Red zone / Scorpio / Consumed / Data blast / Digital justice / Simulacra / Half / Blood money 2.

Aug 98. (cd-s/12") *(CD+/MUTE 213)* **CONSUMED (remix). /**

POPGUNS

Formed: Brighton, England . . . 1988 by lyricicst WENDY MORGAN, SIMON PICKLES, GREG DIXON and PAT WALKINGTON. Debut release, 'WHERE DO YOU GO' was recorded for flexidisc label, 'La Di Da', a split affair featuring the band, HOW MANY BEANS MAKE FIVE on the flip side. In April '89, indie label 'Way Cool' issued their debut proper, the 'LANDSLIDE' ep, the band subsequently jettisoning the drum machine in favour of sticksman, SHAUN CHARMAN (ex-Wedding Present). A second ep, 'WAITING FOR THE WINTER', followed later that year, its frantic yet melancholy title track the most promising shot from the POPGUNS' canon up to that point. Both EP's, together with 1990's 'SOMEONE YOU LOVE', were collected together on compilation set, 'EUGENIE' (1990), isued on the 'Midnight Music' label, while a bonafide debut album, 'SNOG' finally surfaced in 1991. Roundly acclaimed by the indie press, the album found MORGAN & Co.'s eager-beaver indie jangle finally coming of age, even if the 20-something angst remained. A further couple of EP's appeared later the same year although The POPGUNS went strangely silent for much of the early 90's, eventually staging a comeback in late '94 with an EP, 'STAR', for the '3rd Stone' label. A long awaited follow-up album, 'LOVE JUNKY', followed a few months later in early '95, although the press support wasn't offered a second time around. • **Covers:** HARLEY DAVIDSON (Serge Gainsbourg) / CAN I KICK IT? (A Tribe Called Quest) • **Songwriters:** Group. • **Trivia:** GENESIS P. ORRIDGE (late of PSYCHIC TV and THROBBING GRISTLE) guested on acclaimed debut 'SNOG'.

Album rating: EUGENIE (*6) / SNOG (*8)

WENDY MORGAN – vocals / **SIMON PICKLES** – guitar / **GREG DIXON** – guitar / **PAT WALKINGTON** – bass / drum machine

Way Cool | not iss.

Apr 89. (12"ep) *(MC 19T)* **LANDSLIDE. / DOWN ON YOUR KNEES / LEAVE IT ALONE**

— **SIMON CHARMAN** – drums (ex-WEDDING PRESENT) repl. drum machine

Midnight Music | not iss.

Nov 89. (12"ep) *(DONG 55)* **WAITING FOR THE WINTER. / EVERY DREAM / BECAUSE HE WANTED TO**

Apr 90. (12"ep) *(DONG 62)* **SOMEONE YOU LOVE. / THOSE OTHER THINGS / DON'T SMILE**

Aug 90. (cd/c/lp) *(CHIME 01.08)* **EUGENIE** (singles compilation)

Mar 91. (12"ep) *(DONG 68)* **STILL A WORLD AWAY**

Apr 91. (cd/c/lp) **SNOG**

Jul 91. (7"ep) **XXX EP**

Oct 91. (7"ep) **CRAZY**

3rd Stone | ZYX

Nov 94. (cd-ep) *(STONE 013CD)* **STAR / CRAZY / STAY ALIVE**

Feb 95. (cd/c) *(STONE 016 CD/MC) <20307>* **LOVE JUNKY** Oct95
– (I'll) Take you down / Get out / Star / Second time around / Someone to dream of / Under starlight / A miserable boy / How to face it / Here in Heaven / Over your head / So cold.

May 95. (cd-ep) *(STONE 019CD)* **GET OUT / WHAT ARE YOU WAITING FOR? / DAYBREAK**
(12"ep+=) *(STONE 019T)* – Can I kick it?

Tall Poppy | not iss.

Mar 96. (7") *(POPPY 002S)* **HARLEY DAVIDSON. /**

– compilations, etc. –

1996. (cd) *Tall Pop; (POP 001CD)* **A PLUS DE CENT**
– Harley Davidson / Star / Get out / Stay alive / So amazing / Crushed / What are you waiting for? / Daybreak / Can I kick it? / Crazy / Gesture.

POPINJAYS

Formed: Kentish Town, London, England . . . 1988 by WENDY ROBINSON and POLLY HANCOCK. Setting out to make sassy, sexy pop music as a reaction to the manufactured Stock, Aitken & Waterman fare of the day, the songwriting duo originally performed with the help of a drum machine, recruiting third member DANA BALDINGER prior to the inking of a contract with 'One Little Indian' (the deal sweetened by a supply of candy and biscuits!) and the release of debut single, 'DON'T GO BACK'. The latter was soon replaced by American-born ANNE ROGERS as they followed up with 'PLEASE LET ME GO' and feisty debut album, 'BANG UP TO DATE WITH THE POPINJAYS' (1990), the accompanying 'VOTE ELVIS' single going down well in the States and prompting an ill-fated American jaunt. With the subsequent addition of sticksman SEAMUS FEENEY, The POPINJAYS became a fully fledged, bonafide indie-pop band and proceeded to record the album they'd always been capable of in 'FLYING DOWN TO MONO VALLEY' (1992). Comparisons with VOICE OF THE BEEHIVE aside, the pop-brass cleverness and sing-song swooning of singles 'MONSTER MOUTH' and 'TOO JUNG' belied lyrics which ran deeper than their indie contemporaries, reflecting ROBINSON's belief in therapy and backing up her conviction that all pop lyrics are self analytical. This certainly seemed to be the case with 1994's 'TALES FROM THE URBAN PRAIRIE' set, a musical departure towards more rootsy territory inhabited by strumming introspection and beerglass melancholy. • **Covered:** I'M A BELIEVER (Monkees) / 59th STREET BRIDGE SONG (Simon & Garfunkel) / etc.

Album rating: BANG UP TO DATE . . . (*8)

WENDY ROBINSON (b. 6 Apr'64, Huddersfield, England) – vocals / **POLLY HANCOCK** (b.16 Jul'64, Berkshire, England) – vocals, guitar / **EMMA** – bass / drum machine

Big Cat | not iss.

Aug 88. (12"m) *(BBA 02)* **DON'T GO BACK. / SO CLOSE / MOVE TO PERISH** [ ] [–]

— **DANA BALDINGER** (b.26 Dec'63, California, USA) – bass repl. EMMA

One Little Indian | Epic

Mar 90. (12") *(40 TP12)* **PERFECT DREAM HOME. / PLEASE LET ME GO** [ ] [–]

— **ANNE ROGERS** (b.17 Oct'62, New York, USA) – bass repl. DANA

Apr 90. (cd/lp) *(TP CD/LP 28)* **BANG UP TO DATE WITH THE POPINJAYS** [ ] [–]
– Please let me go / Doctor fell / Rain / Hey! (back to the beginning) / Perfect dream home / I don't believe in anything / Thinking about the weather / Mr. Spacecase / Laughing at it all / Kissing cowboys.

— next with guest CATHAL COUGHLAN (of FATIMA MANSIONS)

Oct 90. (12"/cd-s) *(?? TP12) <73021>* **VOTE ELVIS** [ ] [ ] Mar91

Jan 91. (12") *(40 TP12)* **PLEASE LET ME GO. /** [ ] [–]

— added **SEAMUS FEENEY** (b.19 Nov'64, Middlesex, England) – drums repl. machine / **BEN KESTEVEN** – bass (ex-AIRHEAD) repl. ANNE

One Little Indian | Epic

May 92. (7") *(61 TP7)* **MONSTER MOUTH. / SOMETHING ABOUT YOU** [ ] [–]
(12"+=/cd-s+=) *(61 TP 12/7CD)* – Helicopter people (disco sex mix).

Jul 92. (7") *(71 TP7)* **TOO JUNG. / SUN** [ ] [ ]
(12"+=/cd-s+=) *(71 TP 12/7CD)* – Vote Elvis.

Aug 92. (lp/c/cd) *(TPLP 38/+C/CD) <52822>* **FLYING DOWN TO MONO VALLEY** [ ] [ ]
– Monster mouth / Too jung / The moon looks nice from here / Nothing / We love you / Sun / It doesn't matter / Snowblind / Getting better / See saw.

Nov 92. (7"/c-s) *(81 TP7/+C)* **I'M A BELIEVER. / 59th STREET BRIDGE SONG** [ ] [ ]
(12"+=/cd-s+=) *(81 TP 12/7CD)* –

One Little Indian | Sony

Jun 94. (lp/c/cd) *(TPLP 48/+C/CD) <64383>* **TALES FROM THE URBAN PRAIRIE** [ ] [ ]
– Queen of the parking lot / Feelin' / When I believed in you / Moonheart / Slowly I reach / Hurricane / Kentish town / Buffalo / Down / Drive the train.

POP RIVETS (see under ⇒ CHILDISH, Wild Billy)

POPSICLE

Formed: Stockholm, Sweden . . . early 90's by ANDREAS MATTSSON, FREDRIK NORBERG, KENNY VIKSTROM and PER-ARNE WIKANDER. Having already issued two albums (for 'M.N.W.') in Scandinavia, these UK indie-fixated Swedes finally gained a British release with 1993's award-winning 'LACQUER'. Despite ploughing the same furrow of upfront cutesy pop as countrymen, The WANNADIES and The CARDIGANS, POPSICLE never quite scaled the same chart-winning heights outside of their native Sweden. With ARVID LIND replacing VIKSTROM, the power-pop Vikings found a home with 'Warners' ('East West' UK) for 1995's 'ABSTINENCE' although they were back with homegrown imprint, 'Telegram', for subsequent releases.

Album rating: TEMPLATE (*5) / WHITSUN (*5) / LACQUER (*6) / ABSTINENCE (*5) / THE THIRD DIMENSION (*5) / POPSICLE (*5)

ANDREAS MATTSSON – vocals, guitar / **FREDRIK NORBERG** – vocals, guitar / **KENNY VIKSTROM** – bass / **PER-ARNE WIKANDER** – drums

Snap | not iss.

1991. (cd) **TEMPLATE** [–] [–] Swedish

1992. (cd) **WHITSUN** [–] [–] Swedish

Aug 93. (cd-ep) *(SNAPC 014)* **HEY PRINCESS / BLOW UP / NEVER KNOW** [ ] [–]

Sep 93. (cd) *(SNAP 011)* **LACQUER** [ ] [–]

Feb 94. (cd-ep) *(SNAPC 018)* **UNDULATE /** [ ] [–]

— **ARVID LIND** – bass; repl. VIKSTROM

East West | Warners

Feb 95. (7"/c-s/cd-s) *(YZ 900 X/C/CD)* **MAKE UP. / EVERYTHING'S THE ONLY THING** [ ] [ ]

Feb 95. (cd/c) *<4509 95679-2/-4>* **ABSTINENCE** [ ] [ ]
– Make up / Mayfly / Sunkissed / Could be / Step inside my mind / Soul lacquer drug / Join my stream / 9 / Diving bell / Spaniel / Prussian blue / Histrionics.

Jun 95. (c-s/cd-s) *(YZ 943 C/CD)* **HISTRIONICS / MAYFLY** [ ] [–]

Telegram | not iss.

1996. (cd) **THE THIRD DIMENSION** [–] [–] Swedish

1997. (cd) *(13287)* **POPSICLE** [–] [–] Swedish

POP WILL EAT ITSELF

Formed: Stourbridge, Midlands, England . . . early 1985 initially as WILD AND WANDERING by vocalist/guitarist CLINT MANSELL, guitarist/keyboardist ADAM MOLE, bassist RICHARD MARCH and drummer GRAHAM CRABB. After the wittily titled '2000 LIGHT ALES FROM HOME' EP, the band adopted the POP WILL EAT ITSELF moniker in early '86. Their debut release, 'POPPIES SAY GRRR . . . EP' was originally sold at a Dudley gig, although after this DIY effort was made more widely available, it subsequently became an NME single of the week and was playlisted on night time Radio One. Later that summer, the band signed to Craig Jennings' indie label, 'Chapter 22', Jennings becoming their manager after a few more singles (including a cover of SIGUE SIGUE SPUTNIK's brilliantly vacant 'LOVE MISSILE F1-11'). By the release of the impressive debut album, 'BOX FRENZY' (1987) these self-styled 'GREBO GURU's were in the process of progressing from their early guitar pop to a sample-driven hybrid of heavy punk (a la KILLING JOKE) and psyche-pop. While songs like 'BEAVER PATROL' were criticised for their schoolboy sexism, indie chart hits like the driven genius of 'THERE IS NO LOVE BETWEEN US ANYMORE' and the anthemic 'DEF CON ONE' proved they were major contenders. Fittingly then, they were duly signed up by 'R.C.A.' and scored further minor chart successes with 'CAN U DIG IT' and 'WISE UP! SUCKER', while a follow-up album, 'THIS IS THE DAY, THIS IS THE HOUR, THIS IS THIS' (1989) made the Top 30. By this point the band had long since abandoned a conventional drum kit for an electronic model and in the Spring of 1990, PWEI turned out their most dance-friendly track to date in 'TOUCHED BY THE HAND OF CICCIOLINA'. A collaboration with the infamous Italian porn star-turned MP (only in Italy!) of the same name, the record was released just in time for the World Cup, complete with crowd noises and chanting. That year's album, 'THE POP WILL EAT ITSELF CURE FOR SANITY', confirmed the trend with 'DANCE OF THE MAD BASTARDS' and 'X, Y AND ZEE'. Nevertheless, by the release of 'THE LOOKS OR THE LIFESTYLE' (1992), the band had reverted back to a living, breathing human drummer in the form of FUZZ. Although the record spawned their biggest hit to date, the Top 10 'GET THE GIRL! KILL THE BADDIES', PWEI were subsequently dropped by RCA after the live 'WEIRD'S BAR & GRILL' (1993), the band also largely dismissed by a music press that had new fish to fry. Down but not out, the grebo troopers signed a new deal with the indie label, 'Infectious', hooking up with 'FUN-DA-MENTAL' in 1994 for the anti-nazi effort, 'ICH BIN EIN AUSLANDER'. The record was a minor hit, although their fifth studio effort, the harder-edged 'DOS DEDOS MIS AMIGOS' became their highest charting album to date, almost reaching the Top 10 and proving that they could get along just fine without a major label. If any more proof was needed, the defiantly titled remix album, 'TWO FINGERS MY FRIENDS', showed that PWEI were nothing if not resilient. • **Songwriters:** Group compositions except; LIKE AN ANGEL (Mighty Lemon Drops) / ORGONE ACCUMULATOR (Hawkwind) / EVERYTHING THAT RISES (Eno) / ROCK-A-HULA BABY (Elvis Presley).

Album rating: BOX FRENZY (*8) / NOW FOR A FEAST compilation (*7) / THIS IS THE DAY (*7)

CLINT MANSELL (b. 7 Jan'63, Coventry, England) – vocals, guitar / **ADAM MOLE** (b. 8 Apr'62) – guitar, keyboards / **GRAHAM CRABB** (b.10 Oct'64, Sutton Coldfield, England) – drums / **RICHARD MARCH** (b. 4 Mar'65, York, England) – bass

Iguana | not iss.

Feb 86. (12"ep; as WILD & WANDERING) *(VYK 14)* **2000 LIGHT ALES FROM HOME** [ ] [–]
– Dust me down / Stand by me / Real cool time / Interlong / Apple tree (pt.1 & 2).

Desperate | not iss.

May 86. (7"ep) *(SRT 1)* **THE POPPIES SAY GRRRR . . . EP** [ ] [–]
– I'm sticking with you hoo / Sick little girl / Mesmerized / There's a psychopath in my soup / Candydiosis. *(re-iss. Jun86; DAN 1)*

Chapter 22 | Rough Trade

Oct 86. (7"ep) *(CHAP 9)* **POPPIECOCK** [ ] [–]
– The Black country chainsaw massacreee / Monogamy / Oh Grebo I think I love you / Titanic clown / B-B-B-Breakdown.
(12"ep+=) *(12CHAP 9)* – THE POPPIES SAY GRRRR . . . EP.

Jan 87. (12"/7") *(12+/CHAP 11)* **SWEET SWEET PIE. / DEVIL INSIDE / RUNAROUND** [ ] [–]

May 87. (7") *(CHAP 13)* **LOVE MISSILE F1-11. / ORGONE ACCUMULATOR** [ ] [ ]
(12"ep+=) **THE COVERS EP** *(12CHAP 13)* – Everything that rises / Like an angel.
(12"ep+=) *(L12CHAP 13)* – ('A'-Designer Grebo mix) / Everything that rises (new version).

Sep 87. (7"pink,7"clear/7") *(L+/CHAP 16)* **BEAVER PATROL. / BUBBLES** [ ] [-]
(12"+=) *(12CHAP 16)* – Oh Grebo I think I love you (new version).

Oct 87. (lp/c/cd) *(CHAP LP/MC/CD 18)* *<ROUGHUS 33/+C/CD>* **BOX FRENZY** [ ] [ ]
– Grebo guru / Beaver patrol / Let's get ugly / U.B.L.U.D. / Inside you / Evelyn / There is no love between us anymore / She's surreal / Intergalactic love mission / Love missile F1-11 / Hit the hi-tech groove / Razorblade kisses.

Jan 88. (7"pic-d/7") *(L+/CHAP 20)* **THERE IS NO LOVE BETWEEN US ANYMORE. / PICNIC IN THE SKY** [66] [-]
(12"+=) *(12CHAP 20)* – On the razor's edge / Kiss that girl.
(ext.12"+=) *(L12CHAP 20)* – ('A'extended high mix) / Hit the hi-tech groove (the M&K mix).
(12") *(CLUBCHAP 20)* – (above 2 tracks).

Jul 88. (7") *(PWEI 001)* **DEF CON ONE. / INSIDE YOU (live)** [63] [-]
(12"+=) *(PWEI 12-001)* – She's surreal (live) / Hit the hi-tech groove (live).
(12"+=) *(PWEIL 12-001)* – ('A'-Doomsday power mix) / She's surreal (live).

Dec 88. (lp/c/cd) *(CHAP LP/MC/CD 33)* **NOW FOR A FEAST** (compilation) [ ] [-]
– The Black country chainstore massacreee / Monogamy / Oh Grebo I think I love you / Titanic clown / B-B-B-Breakdown / Sweet sweet pie / Like an angel / I'm sniffin' with you hoo / Sick little girl / Mesmerized / There's a psychopath in my soup / Candydiosis / The devil inside / Orgone accumulator.

R.C.A. R.C.A.

Feb 89. (7"/7"orange,7"green/7"s) *(PB 42621/42619/42729)* **CAN U DIG IT. / POISON TO THE MIND** [38] [-]
(cd-s+=) *(PD 42620)* – Radio PWEI (acapella) / ('A'-12"version).
(12"++=) *(PT 42620)* – The fuses have been lit.

Apr 89. (7"/7"pic-d) *(PB PB 42761/42793)* **WISE UP! SUCKER. / ORGYONE STIMULATOR** [41] [-]
(c-s+=)(12"+=/cd-s+=) *(PK 42761)(PT/PD 42762)* – ('A'extended) / Can u dig it (riffs mix).
(10") *(PJ 42762)* – ('A'side) / ('A'extended) / ('A'version).

May 89. (lp/c/cd) *(PL/PK/PD 74106)* *<9742>* **THIS IS THE DAY, THIS IS THE HOUR, THIS IS THIS** [24] [ ]
– PWEI is a four letter word / Preaching to the peverted / Wise up! sucker / Sixteen different flavours of Hell / Inject me / Can u dig it? / The fuses have been lit / Poison to the mind / Def con one / Radio PWEI / Shortwave transmission on up to the minuteman / Satellite ecstatica / Now now James, we're busy / Wake up! time to die . . . *(cd+=)* – Wise up sucker (mix). *(re-iss. cd Nov93; 74321 15792-2)*

Aug 89. (7"ep)(7"g-f-ep)(7"sha-pic-ep)(c-ep)(12"ep)(cd-ep) *(PB 42883)(PB 43021)(PA 43022)(PK 43023)(PT 42884)(PD 42894)* **VERY METAL NOISE POLLUTION EP** [45] [-]
– Very metal noise pollution / P.W.E.I.-zation / 92° F / Def con one 1989 A.D.
(12") *(PT 43068)* – Def con 1989 AD including:- Twilight zone / Preaching to the perverted / P.W.E.I.-zation / 92° F.

May 90. (7"/c-s) *(PB/PK 43735)* **TOUCHED BY THE HAND OF CICCIOLINA. / THE INCREDI-BULL MIX** [28] [-]
(12"+=) *(PT 43736)* – ('A'-Extra time mix).
(cd-s) *(PD 43736)* – ('A'-Extra time mix) / ('A'-Diva Futura mix) / ('A'-Renegade Soundwave mix – Smoothneck).
(12") *(PT 43738)* – ('A'-Diva Futura mix) / ('A'-Renegade Soundwave mix – Smoothneck).

Oct 90. (7"/c-s) *(PB/PK 44023)* **DANCE OF THE MAD. / PREACHING TO THE PERVERTED** [32] [-]
(12"ep+=/cd-ep+=) **PWEI VS. THE MORAL MAJORITY EP** *(PT/PD 44023)* – ('A'other mix).

Oct 90. (cd/c/lp) *(PD/PK/PL 74828)* **CURE FOR SANITY** [33] [-]
– Incredible PWEI vs. The Moral Majority / Dance of the mad bastards / 88 seconds . . . and still counting / X Y & Zee / City Zen radio 1990-2000 FM / Dr. Nightmares medication time / Touched by the hand of Cicciolina / 1000 x no! / Psycho sexual / Axe of men / Another man's rhubarb / Medicine man speaks with forked tongue / Nightmare at 20,000 feet / Very metal noise pollution / 92 degrees (the 3rd degree) / Lived in splendour, died in chaos / The beat that refused to die. *(re-iss. May91 pic-lp; PL 75041) (re-iss. cd Nov93; 74321 15791-2)*

Jan 91. (7"/c-s) *(PB/PK 44243)* **X Y & ZEE. / AXE OF MEN** [15] [-]
(12"box+=) *(PT 44243)* – Psychosexual.
(12"+=/cd-s+=) *(PT/PD 44243)* – ('A'-Intergalactic mix) / ('A'-Sensory amp mix).

May 91. (7"/c-s) *(PB/PK 44555)* **92 DEGREES. / INCREDIBLE PWEI VS. DIRTY HARRY** [23] [-]
(10"+=/12"+=/cd-s+=) *(PX/PT/PD 44555)* – Another man's rhubarb.

May 92. (7"/c-s) *(PB/PK 45467)* **KARMADROME. / EAT ME DRINK ME LOVE ME** [17] [-]
(12"+=) *(PT 45467)* – Dread alert in the karmadrome / ('A'version).
(cd-s) *(PD 45467)* – ('A'side) / PWEI-zation (original metal noise pollution).
(12"pic-d+=) *(PTP 45467)* – PWEI-zation (original . . .) / Eat me drink me dub . . .

Aug 92. (7"/c-s) *(74321 11013-7/-4)* **BULLETPROOF! / ('A'-On-U-Sound mix)** [24] [-]
(12"pic-d+=/cd-s+=) *(74321 11013-6/-2)* – Good from far, far from good.
(12") *(74321 11013-8)* – ('A'-Mile high mix) / ('A'-No half measures mix).

Sep 92. (cd/c/lp) *(74321 10265-2/-4/-1)* **THE LOOKS OR THE LIFESTYLE** [15] [-]
– England's finest / Eat me, drink me, love me, kill me / Mother / Get the girl, kill the baddies! / I've always been a coward baby / Spoken drug song / Karmadrome / Urban futuristic (son of South Central) / Pretty pretty / I was a teenage grandad / Harry Dean Stanton / Bulletproof!. *(re-iss. cd Nov93; 74321 15790-2)*

— added 5th member **FUZZ TOWNSHEND** (b. JOHN TOWNSHEND, 31 Jul'64, Birmingham, England) – drums

Jan 93. (7"/c-s) *(74321 12880-7/-4)* **GET THE GIRL! KILL THE BADDIES!. / ('A'-Adrian Sherwood mix)** [9] [-]
(12"+=/cd-s+=) *(74321 12880-6/-2)* – ('A'-Black country & western mix) or ('A'boilerhouse mix).
(cd-s) *(74321 12880-5)* – ('A'side) / Urban futuristic (live) / Can u dig it? (live) / Wise up! sucker! (live).

Feb 93. (cd/c/lp) *(74321 13343-2/-4/-1)* **WEIRD'S BAR AND GRILL (live)** [44] [-]
– England's finest / Eat me drink me love me kill me / Get the girl, kill the baddies!! / Wise up! sucker / 88 seconds and counting / Karmadrome / Token drug song mother / Preaching to the perverted / Axe of men / Nightmare at 20,000 feet / Always been a coward / Can U dig it / Bullet proof / Urban futuristic / There is no love between us anymore / Def con one. *(cd+=/c+=)* – Harry Dean Stanton teenage grandad.

Oct 93. (cd/c/lp) *(74321 15317-2/-4/-1)* **16 DIFFERENT FLAVOURS OF HELL** (compilation) [73] [-]
– Def con one / Wise up! sucker / Can U dig it / Touched by the hand of Cicciolina (extra time mix) / Dance of the mad / X Y & Zee (sunshine mix) / 92 degrees (Boilerhouse The Birth mix) / Karmadrome / Bullet proof / Get the girl! kill the baddies! / Another man's rhubarb / Rockahula baby / Wise up sucker / Cicciolina (Renegade Soundwave mix). *(cd+=)* – Preaching to the perverted (remix) / Eat me drink me love me kill me / PWEI-zatin.

Infectious Nothing-Interscope

Oct 93. (c-s) *(INFECT 1MC)* *<95887>* **R.S.V.P. / FAMILUS HORRIBILUS** [27] [ ] Feb94
(cd-ep+=) *(INFECT 1CD)* – ('B'remixes) / ('B'live).
(12"ep+=/cd-ep+=) *(INFECT 1/+CDX)* – ('A'side) / ('B'-Higher later space mix agency vocal).

Feb 94. (7"/7"pic-d) *(INFECT 4 G/P)* **ICH BIN EIN AUSLANDER. / CP1 #2** [28] [-]
(12"+=/cd-s+=) *(INFECT 4/+CD)* – ('A'-Fun-Da-Mental instrumental) / ('A'-Fun-Da-Mental extra).
(12"+=) *(INFECT 4TX)* – ('A'-Drone ranger mix) / Intense.

Sep 94. (7"colrd) *(INFECT 9GG)* **EVERYTHING'S COOL. / LET IT FLOW** [23] [-]
(7"colrd) *(INFECT 9SO)* – ('A'side) / Wild west.
(cd-s) *(INFECT 9CD)* – ('A'side) / ('A'-Youth remix) / R.S.V.P. (Fluke mix).
(cd-s) *(INFECT 9CDX)* – ('A'side) / Ich bin ein Auslander (live) / Familus horribilus (live) / R.S.V.P. (live).

Sep 94. (cd/c) *(INFECT 10 CD/MC)* *<92393>* **DOS DEDOS MIS AMIGOS** [11] [ ]
– Ich bin ein Auslander / Kick to kill / Familus horribilus / Underbelly / Fatman / Home / Cape connection / Menofearthereaper / Everything's cool / R.S.V.P. / Babylon. *(also d-lp/d-c/d-cd; INFECT 10 LPX/MCX/CDX)*

Mar 95. (d-cd/d-c) *(INFECT 10 CDR/MCR)* *<22>* **TWO FINGERS MY FRIENDS!** (remixes) [25] [ ]
– Ich bin ein Auslander (Fun-Da-Mental) / Kick to kill (Jim Foetus seersucker mix) / Familus horribilus (mega web 2) / Underbelly (Renegade Soundwave blackout mix) / Fatman (Hoodlum Priest Fatboy mix) / Home (Orb sweet sin and salvation mix) / Cape Connection (Transglobal Underground Cossack in UFO encounter mix) / Menofearthereaper (concrete no fee, no fear mix) / Everything's cool (safe as milk mix) / R.S.V.P. (made in Japan, live at the Budokan double live Gonzo F mix) / Babylon (Loop Guru Babylon a dub fire mix) // Ich bin ein Auslander (Die Krupps mix) / Familus horribilus (Hia Nyg vocal mix) / Cape Connection (golden claw versus clock and dagger mix) / Intense / C.P.I. #2 / Cape Connection (TGV aliens, bodacious aliens mix) / Everything's cool (Dragonfly mix) / RSVP (Fluke lunch mix) / Cape Connection (Secret Knowledge transfered up mix) / Underbelly (The Drum Club bugsong mix).

— CRABB left to pursue own career. He formed The BUZZARD and other project, The Golden Claw Music.

– compilations, etc. –

Jun 96. (cd) *Camden; (74321 39339-2)* **WISE UP SUCKERS** [ ] [-]

PORCUPINE TREE

Formed: London, England . . . 1989 by STEVEN WILSON, a self-taught guitarist and pianist. He had originally surfaced in the duo, ALTAMONT (in 1983, aged 15), issuing the cassette, 'PRAYER FOR THE SOUL' (half solo, half with SI VOCKINGS on keyboards). Released on 'Acid Tapes', it featured lyrics by the label's owner, ALAN DUFFY, who later founded 'Imaginary' records. WILSON was also sidelining with the heavier KARMA, an outfit that released a few private tapes, 'THE JOKE'S ON YOU' (1983) and 'THE LAST MAN TO LAUGH' (1985), before splitting in 1986; several tracks from these were to take on a new lease of life with PORCUPINE TREE, an ambient retro-progressive/psychedelic outfit akin to PINK FLOYD fused with HAWKWIND and rave! STEVEN then compiled a progressive rock collection, 'Exposure', which featured several new bands alongside his own new project, NO MAN IS AN ISLAND EXCEPT THE ISLE OF MAN (with the track, 'From A Toyshop Window'). He shortened the moniker slightly to NO MAN for another compilation, 'Double Exposure', adding ex-PLENTY frontman, TIM BOWNESS, on the song, 'FAITH'S LAST DOUBT'. NO MAN continued for two years and issued a few items for 'Plastic Head', including a couple of tracks for the label's 'Expose It' V/A album. WILSON's next venture, PORCUPINE TREE (also with ALAN DUFFY), continued in much the same vein, releasing the cassette-only 'TARQUIN'S SEAWEED FARM' (which featured a PRINCE cover, 'THE CROSS'). Two more cassettes surfaced in the early 90's, namely 'LOVE, DEATH AND MUSSOLINI' and 'THE NOSTALGIA FACTORY', whose tracks appeared on the excellent debut album proper, 'ON THE SUNDAY OF LIFE', in 1992. A single, 'VOYAGE 34' (a 30 minute track!), was issued soon after while STEVEN continued with NO MAN, the one-man unit expanding into a band featuring members of JAPAN (i.e. STEVE JANSEN, RICHARD BARBIERI and MICK KARN). STEVEN returned the favour in 1994 when he featured on two of their post-JAPAN albums, 'Seed' and 'Stone To Flesh' (the latter without KARN). In 1996, PORCUPINE TREE were back on form with 'SIGNIFY', while WILSON's NO MAN project had signed to '3rd Stone', releasing the more commercial 'WILD OPERA'. • **NO MAN covers:**- COLOURS (Donovan).

Album rating: ON THE SUNDAY OF LIFE (*8) / UP THE DOWNSTAIR (*6) / THE SKY MOVES SIDEWAYS (*6) / SIGNIFY (*7) / COMA DIVINE (*6) / No Man: LOVEBLOWS AND LOVECRIES (*6) / WILD OPERA (*6) / DRY CLEANING RAY (*5)

ALTAMONT

STEVEN WILSON + ALAN DUFFY

Acid Tapes / not iss.

1983. (c) *(TAB 004)* **PRAYER FOR THE SOUL** — -
1985. (c) *(TAB 010)* **EVERYDAY HEROES** (compilation) — -

— also with KARMA who also released private cassettes (see above).

NO-MAN

STEVEN WILSON – guitar, keyboards / **TIM BOWNESS** – vocals / **BEN COLEMAN** – violin

Plastic Head / not iss.

Jun 89. (12"ep; as NO MAN IS AN ISLAND) *(PLASS 012)* **THE GIRL FROM MISSOURI / FOREST ALMOST BURNING. / NIGHT SKY SWEET EARTH / THE BALLET BEAST** — -

Hidden Art / not iss.

Jul 90. (7") *(HA 4)* **COLOURS. / COLOURS (remodelled)** — -

Probe Plus / not iss.

Nov 90. (12"ep) *(PP 27T)* **COLOURS. / DRINK JUDAS / COLOURS (remodelled)** — -

One Little Indian / not iss.

Jul 91. (12"ep/cd-ep) *(57TP 12/7CD)* **DAYS IN THE TREES EP** — -
– Days in the trees (Mahler / Ives / Bartok / Reich versions).

Apr 92. (m-lp/m-cd) *(TPLP 47 M/CD)* **LOVESIGHS – AN ENTERTAINMENT** — -
– Heartcheat pop / Days in the trees (Mahler) / rink Judas / Heartcheat motel / Kiss me stupid / Colours / Iris Murdoch cut me up / Days in the trees (Reich).

— added JAPAN (RAIN TREE CROW) members **STEVE JANSEN** – drums / **RICHARD BARBIERI** – keyboards / **MICK KARN** – bass

Sep 92. (12"ep/cd-ep) *(63TP 12/7CD)* **OCEAN SONG. / BACK TO THE BURNING SHED / SWIRL** — -

Jan 93. (cd-ep mail-order) *(73TP 7CD)* **SWEETHEART RAW / BLEED / SAY BABY SAY GOODBYE** - -

Mar 93. (12"ep/cd-ep) *(83TP 12/7CD)* **ONLY BABY (Move For Me) / ONLY BABY (Breathe For Me) / ONLY BABY (Be For Me) / LONG DAY FALL** — -

May 93. (d-lp/c/cd) *(TPLP 57/+C/CD)* **LOVEBLOWS AND LOVECRIES – A CONFESSION** — -
– Loveblow / Only baby / Housekeeping / Sweetheart raw / Lovecry / Tulip / Break Heaven / Beautiful and cruel / Painting Paradise / Heaven's break. *(ltd.cd w/ free cd) (TPLP 57CDL)*- **LOVESIGHS**

Jun 93. (12"/cd-s) *(93TP 12/7CD)* **PAINTING PARADISE. / HEAVEN TASTE** — -

— JAPAN members dislodged by ROBERT FRIPP (King Crimson) – guitar

Jun 94. (d-lp/c/cd) *(TPLP 67/+C/CD)* **FLOWERMOUTH** — -
– Angel gets caught in the beauty trap / You grow more beautiful / Animal ghost / Soft shoulders / Shell of a fighter / Teardrop falls / Watching over me / Simple / Things change.

— now without COLEMAN

Hidden Art / HiddenArt

Oct 95. (cd) *(HI-ART 1)* **HEAVEN TASTE** — -
(re-iss. Oct96; same)

Oct 95. (cd) *(HI-ART 2)* **FLOWERMIX** — Jan96
– Angeldust / Faith in you / All I see / Natural neck / Heal the madness / You grow more beautiful / Sample / Why the noise? / Born simple. *(re-iss. Oct96; same)*

— now without COLEMAN

3rd Stone / not iss.

May 96. (cd-ep) *(STONE 026CD)* **HOUSEWIVES HOOKED ON HEROIN / HIT THE CEILING / HOUSEWIVES HOOKED ON METHADONE (Scanner mix) / URBAN DISCO / WHERE I'M CALLING FROM** — -

Aug 96. (cd) *(STONE 027CD)* **WILD OPERA** — -
– Radiant city / Pretty genius / Infant phenomenon / Sinister jazz / Housewives hooked on heroin / Libertino libretto / Taste my dream / Dry cleaning Ray / Sheep loop / My rival Trevor / Time travel in Texas / My revenge on Seattle / Wild opera.

May 97. (7"ltd) *(STONE 034S)* **DRY CLEANING RAY. / TIME TRAVEL IN TEXAS / WATCHING OVER ME** — -

Jun 97. (cd) *(STONE 035CD)* **DRY CLEANING RAY** — -
– Dry cleaning Ray / Sweetside silver night / Jack the sax / Diet mothers / Urban disco / Punished for being born / Knightlinger / Evelyn (the song of slurs) / Sicknote.

Aug 98. (cd-ep) *(STONE 037CD)* **CAROLINA SKELETONS** — —
– Carolina skeletons / Something falls / Close your eyes / Carolina.

— TIM BOWNESS also moonlighted with DARKROOM, the project releasing 'DAYLIGHT' in 1998.

PORCUPINE TREE

STEVEN WILSON – guitar, keyboards, vocals

Delerium / C&S

1991. (ltd.c) *(DELC 0002)* **TARQUIN'S SEAWEED FARM** (originally very ltd.50 in 1989) - -

— LOVE, DEATH AND MUSSOLINI cassette released 1990 but only 10 copies.

1991. (ltd.c) *(DELC 0003)* **THE NOSTALGIA FACTORY** (originally very ltd.50 in 1990) - -

May 92. (cd/d-lp) *(DELEC CD/LP 008D)* **ON THE SUNDAY SIDE OF LIFE** — -
– Music for the head / Jupiter island / Third eye surfer / On the Sunday side of life . . . / The nostalgia factory / Space transmission / Message from a self-destructing turnip / Radioactive toy / Nine cats / Hymn / Footprints / Linton Samuel Dawson / And the swallows dance above the sun / Queen quotes Crowley / No luck with rabbits / Begonia seduction scene / This long silence / It will rain for a million years.

Nov 92. (12"ep/cd-ep) *(DELEC EP/CDEP 010)* **VOYAGE 34 PHASE 1. / PHASE 2** — -

— added **COLIN EDWIN** – bass / **CHRIS MAITLAND** – drums / **RICHARD BARBIERI** – keyboards

Jun 93. (cd/lp) *(DELEC CD/LP 020)* **UP THE DOWNSTAIR** — -
– What are you listening to / Synesthesia / Monuments burn into moments / Always never / Up the downstair / Not beautiful anymore / Siren / Small fish / Burning sky / Fadeaway.

Nov 93. (12"ep) *(DELEC EP 007)* **VOYAGE 34 REMIX: PHASE 3 (Astralasia Dreamstate). / PHASE 4 (A New Civilisation)** — -

— added **RICK EDWARDS** – percussion

Oct 94. (12"ep/cd-ep) *(DELEC EP/CDEP 032)* **STARS DIE. / MOONLOOP** — -

Oct 94. (cd-ep) *<CS 2024-2>* **STARS DIE / MOONLOOP / ALWAYS NEVER** - —

Jan 95. (cd,pic-cd/lp/blue-lp) *(DELEC CD/LP 028/+L)* **THE SKY MOVES SIDEWAYS** — -
– The sky moves sideways (part one) / Dislocated day / Moon touches your shoulder / Prepare yourself / The sky moves sideways (part two). *(cd+=)* – Moonloop.

Apr 96. (12"ep) *(DELEC EP 049)* **WAITING PHASE 1 / WAITING PHASE 2. / COLOURFLOW IN MIND / FUSE THE SUN** — -
(cd-ep) *(DELEC CDEP 049)* – (Phase 1 & 2) / The sound of no-one listening.

Sep 96. (cd/d-lp) *(DELEC CD/LP 045)* **SIGNIFY** — -
– Bornlivedie / Signify / Sleep of no dreaming / Pagan / Waiting phase one / Waiting phase two / Sever / Idiot prayer / Every home is wired / Intermediate Jesus / Light mass prayers / Darkmatter. *(d-lp+=)* – The sound of no-one listening.

Oct 97. (cd) *(DELECCD 067)* **COMA DIVINE** — -
– Bornlivedieintro / Signify / Waiting phase one & two / The sky moves sideways / Dislocated day / Sleep of no dreaming / Moonloop / Radioactive toy / Not beautiful anymore.

– compilations, others, etc –

Aug 94. (cd) *Magic Gnome; (MG 4299325)* **YELLOW HEDGEROW DREAMSCAPE** — -
– Mute / Landscape / Prayer / Daughters in excess / Delightful suicide / Split image / No reason to live, no reason to die / Wastecoat / Towel / Execution of the will of the Marquis De Sade / Track eleven / Radioactive toy / An empty box / The cross / Yellow hedgerow dreamscape / Music for the head.

Oct 94. (10"m-lp) *Lazy; (LE 3094)* **STAIRCASE INFINITIES** — -
(cd-iss. Oct95 on 'Blueprint'; BP 217CD)

PORNO FOR PYROS (see under ⇒ JANE'S ADDICTION)

PORTASTATIC (see under ⇒ SUPERCHUNK)

PORTISHEAD

Formed: Bristol, England . . . 1993 by duo GEOFF BARROW and BETH GIBBONS, who took their name from a local coastal town. After working as MASSIVE ATTACK's studio runner and writing one of the better songs on NENEH CHERRY's 'HOMEBREW' album, BARROWS recruited covers band stalwart GIBBONS and the band signed to 'Go! Discs' off-shoot 'Go! Beat'. Named after BARROW's faded seaside resort hometown of Portishead near Bristol, the group debuted with a short film, 'TO KILL A DEAD MAN'. A retro spy movie pastiche, the film (which starred PORTISHEAD in an acting capacity) and its accompanying soundtrack were indicative of the cinematic melodrama which would chracterise the band's groundbreaking debut. Released in August '94 amid much anticiption, and preceeded by the singles 'NUMB' and 'SOUR TIMES', 'DUMMY' was a wracked, claustrophobic melange of painfully slow hip hop rhythms, droning hammond, knife-edge guitar and rumbling bass. Spiced with a sprinkling of obscure samples and topped off by the sublime lament of GIBBONS' vocals, the sound PORTISHEAD had created was one of the most striking definitions of the phenomena that would come to be known as 'Trip Hop'. Along with MASSIVE ATTACK, TRICKY et al., the band insisted the label was a lazy attempt at pigeonholing but what really set PORTISHEAD apart was simply the otherness of their sound, a strange grace that made the unrelenting lyrical bleakness and despair bearable. Who knows, winning the Mercury Music Prize in 1995 may have cheered them up a bit, although a cover of 'SHINY HAPPY PEOPLE' looks unlikely. • **Songwriters:** BARROW-GIBBONS, but most with UTLEY. Sample; MORE MISSION IMPOSSIBLE (Lalo Schifrin) / SPIN IT JIG (Smokey Brooks) / ELEGANT PEOPLE (Weather Report) / MAGIC MOUNTAIN (War) / I'LL NEVER FALL IN LOVE AGAIN (Johnnie Ray; at slow speed!) / ISAAC MOODS (Isaac Hayes). • **Trivia:** Have remixed for the likes of DEPECHE MODE (In Your Room) / RIDE (I Don't Know Where It Comes From) / GRAVEDIGGAZ (Nowhere To Run).

Album rating: DUMMY (*10) / PORTISHEAD (*8) / PNYC (*6)

BETH GIBBONS – vocals / **GEOFF BARROW** (b.1971) – programming, synthesizer with **ADRIAN UTLEY** – guitar, bass / **CLIVE DEAMER** – drums / **DAVE McDONALD** – nose flute / **RICHARD NEWELL** – drum programme / **NEIL SOLMAN** – synthesizers, organ / **ANDY HAGUE** – trumpet

Go Beat / Polygram

Jun 94. (c-s) *(GODMC 114)* *<857561>* **NUMB / NUMBED IN MOSCOW** — —
(12"+=/cd-s+=) *(GOD X/CD 114)* – Revenge of the numbed / Numb: Earth under / Extra numb.
(cd-s++=) *(GOLCD 114)* – A tribute to Monk and Cantella.

Aug 94. (c-s) *(GODMC 116)* **SOUR TIMES / SOUR SOUR TIMES** 57 -
(12"+=) *(GODX 116)* – Lot more / Sheared times.
(cd-s++=) *(GODCD 116)* – Airbus reconstruction.
(cd-s) *(GOLCD 116)* – ('A'side) / It's a fire / Pedestal / Theme from 'To Kill A Dead Man'.
(re-iss. Apr95, hit UK No.13)

Aug 94. (cd/c/lp) *(<828552-2/-4/-1>)* **DUMMY** 2 79 Jan95

– Mysterons / Sour times / Strangers / It could be sweet / Wandering star / Numb / Roads / Pedestal / Biscuit / Glory box.

Oct 94. (c-s) *(GODMC 120)* **GLORY BOX / ('A'version)** [13] [ ]
(12"+=/cd-s+=) *(GOD X/CD 120)* – ('A'versions).

Jan 95. (cd-s) *<857816>* **SOUR TIMES (NOBODY LOVES ME) / AIRBUS RECONSTRUCTION** [-] [53]

— BARROW guested on EARTHLING's 1995 hit album 'Radar'.

Jun 97. (12"ltd) *(571277-1)* **COWBOYS** [ ] [-]

Sep 97. (7"/c-s) *(571597-7/-4) <871881>* **ALL MINE /** [8] [ ]
(12"+=/cd-s+=) *(571597-1/-2)* –

Oct 97. (cd/c) *(<539189-2/-4>)* **PORTISHEAD** [2] [21]
– Cowboys / All mine / Undenied / Half day closing / Over / Humming / Mourning air / Seven months / Only you / Elysium / Western eyes.

Nov 97. (12"/cd-s) *(571993-1/-2)* **OVER. / OVER (remix) / OVER (instrumental)** [25] [ ]
(cd-s) *(571995-2)* – ('A'side) / Half day closing / Humming (live).

Mar 98. (c-s) *(569474-4)* **ONLY YOU / ELYSIUM (Parlour Talk remix)** [35] [ ]
(12"+=) *(569475-1)* – ('A'instrumental).
(cd-s+=) *(569475-2)* – ('A'live).

Nov 98. (cd/c/d-lp) *(<559424-2/-4/-1>)* **PNYC (live)** [40] [ ]
– Humming / Cowboys / All mine / Mysterons / Only you / Half day crossing / Over / Glory box / Sour times / Roads / Strangers.

POSIES

Formed: Seattle, Washington, USA . . . 1987 by ex-SKY CRIES MARY members, JONATHON AUER and KEN STRINGFELLOW. Influenced by the twin strands of classic 60's/70's Brit/US pop and the alternative rock sounds of their hometown, these budding retro merchants first set up their stall in 1988 with the cassette-only release, 'FAILURE'. Carefully re-arranging their sound with the addition of rhythm section DAVE FOX and MIKE MUSBURGER, the band were an unlikely signing to 'Geffen' for 1990's John Leckie-produced 'DEAR 23'. Although it didn't fit into the emerging Grunge zeitgeist, the album was the toast of critics who liked their Power-Pop as lush, fresh and fragrant as a newly picked bouquet. Inevitably, the band were compelled to slide inexorably into grungier but still relatively composed musical territory with the long-awaited DON FLEMING-produced third album, 'FROSTING ON THE BEATER' (1993). Equally inevitably, The POSIES effeminate charm was partly buried although they did have a surprise minor UK hit with 'DEFINITE DOOR'. The latter's CD b-side featured a cover of Chris Bell's 'I AM THE COSMOS', both AUER and STRINGFELLOW having already followed in their idol's footsteps by joining a re-formed BIG STAR. In 1996, The POSIES confounded fans and critics alike by embracing Grunge wholesale on that year's disappointing 'AMAZING DISGRACE', the record featuring a tribute to another of their heroes, 'GRANT HART'.

Album rating: FAILURE (*5) / DEAR 23 (*7) / FROSTING ON THE BEATER (*5) / AMAZING DISGRACE (*4)

JONATHON AUER – vocals, guitar (ex-SKY CRIES MARY) / **KEN STRINGFELLOW** – vocals, guitar (ex-SKY CRIES MARY)

not iss. / 23

1988. (c) **FAILURE** [-] [ ]
– Blind eyes open / Longest line / Under easy / Like me too / I may hate you sometimes / Ironing Tuesdays / Paint me / Believe in something other / Compliment? / At least for now / Uncombined / What little remains. *(UK cd-iss. Feb95 on 'Pop Llama'; PLCD 2323)*

— added **DAVE FOX** – bass / **MIKE MUSBURGER** – drums

Geffen / Geffen

Nov 90. (cd/c/lp) *<(7599 24305-2/-4/-1)>* **DEAR 23** [ ] [ ]
– My big mouth / Golden blunders / Apology / Any other way / You avoid parties / Suddenly Mary / Help yourself / Mrs. Green / Everyone moves away / Flood of sunshine. *(re-iss. Aug93 cd/c; GFLD/GFLC 19223) (cd re-iss. Nov96; GED 24305)*

May 93. (cd/c/lp) *<(GED/GEC/GEF 24522)>* **FROSTING ON THE BEATER** [ ] [ ]
– Dream all day / Solar sister / Flavor of the month / Love letter boxes / Definite door / Burn & shine / Earlier than expected / 20 questions / When mute tongues can speak / Lights out / How she lied by living / Coming right along. *(cd re-iss. Oct95 & Feb98; GFLD 19298)*

Sep 93. (7"/c-s) *(GFS/+C 50)* **DREAM ALL DAY. / HOW SHE LIED BY LIVING** [ ] [ ]
(12"+=/cd-s+=) *(GFST/+D 50)* – Ever since I was alone / Open every window.

Oct 93. (7"mauve/c-s) *(GFS/+C 58)* **FLAVOR OF THE MONTH. / START A LIFE** [ ] [ ]
(cd-s+=) *(GFSTD 58)* – This one's taken.

Mar 94. (7") *(GFS 68)* **DEFINITE DOOR. / SONG OF THE BAKER** [67] [ ]
(cd-s+=) *(GFSTD 68)* – Ooh child / I am the cosmos.

— AUER and STRINGFELLOW became part of a re-formed BIG STAR before returning to The POSIES

Apr 96. (c-s) *(GFSC 22128)* **PLEASE RETURN IT /** [ ] [ ]
(cd-s+=) *(GFSTD 22128)* –

Apr 96. (cd/c) *<(GED/GEC 24910)>* **AMAZING DISGRACE** [ ] [ ]
– Daily mutation / Ontario / Throwaway / Please return it / Hate song / Precious moments / Fight it (if you want it) / Everybody is a fucking liar / World / Grant Hart / Broken record / Certainty / Song #1 / Will you ever ease your mind.

– compilations, others, etc. –

Oct 94. (7") *Elefant; (ER 121)* **THIS IS NOT A FISH** [ ] [ ]
(re-iss. Apr96; same)

Apr 98. (cd) *Pop Llama; (PLCD 3232)* **SUCCESS** [ ] [ ]

POSSUM DIXON

Formed: Los Angeles, California, USA . . . late 80's by ROBERT ZABRECKY who recruited members from likely candidates playing at his Jabber Jaw club. Concocting an awkward but original sound drawing influences from the likes of TALKING HEADS, XTC, WIRE and The STRANGLERS, ZABRECKY self-financed the release of three US-only 45's. Trading in a similarly quirky lyrical vein as acts like THEY MIGHT BE GIANTS, the POSSUM DIXON muse drew on a quintessentially American strand of fantasy and distorted reality to entertaining effect. The major-label backed 'Interscope' were quick to snap them up and 1994 saw the release of an eponymous debut album, the accompanying 'NERVES' single featuring a bleep frenzy rendition of The Yardbirds' 'FOR YOUR LOVE' on the B-side. A few years on, the POSSUM posse were back in town, still casting around for a musical identity with the follow-up set, 'STAR MAPS' (1996).

Album rating: POSSUM DIXON (*5) / STAR MAPS (*5) / NEW SHEETS (*5)

ROBERT ZABRECKY – vocals, bass / **ROBERT O'SULLIVAN** – electric piano / **CELSO CHAVEZ** – guitar / **RICHARD TREUEL** – drums

not iss. / unknown

— released 3 singles in the US

Interscope-Atlantic / Interscope-Atlantic

Mar 94. (7") *(A 8304)* **NERVES. / SHE DRIVES** [ ] [ ]
(12"+=/cd-s+=) *(A 8304 T/CD)* – For your love.

Apr 94. (cd/c) *<(6544 92291-2/-4)>* **POSSUM DIXON** [ ] [ ]
– Nerves / In buildings / Watch the girl destroy me / She drives / We're all happy / Invisible / Pharmaceutical itch / Executive slacks / Regina / John struck Lucy / Elevators. *(cd re-iss. Jul96; IND 92291)*

Jun 94. (7"/c-s) *(A 8297/+C)* **WATCH THE GIRL DESTROY ME. / EXECUTIVE SLACKS** [ ] [ ]
(12"+=/cd-s+=) *(A 8297 T/CD)* – Damn the rainbow.

Jul 96. (cd) *<(IND 92625)>* **STAR MAPS** [ ] [ ]
– Go west / In her disco / Radio comets / Party tonight / Emergency's about to end / General electric / Crashing your planet / Personals / Reds / Skid marks / Artificial sunlight / Apartment song. *(lp-iss.Jun96 on 'Revelation'; REV 2625)*

Aug 98. (cd/c/lp) *<90221-2/-4/-1>* **NEW SHEETS** [-] [ ]
– Songs from a box / Holding (Lenny's song) / Only in the summertime / Firecracker / New sheets / Always engines / Stop breaking me / Now what? / Plan B / Heavenly / Faultlines / What you mean / The end's beginning.

POSTER CHILDREN

Formed: Champaign-Urbana, Illinois, USA . . . 1987 by the VALENTIN brothers RICK and JIM, along with ROSE MARSHACK and HOWIE KANTOFF. These hyperactive punk-pop kids made an enterprising start to their career with a self-financed cassette-only release, 'TOREADOR SQUAT' (1988), their DIY skills extending to artwork, T-shirts, tour promotion, etc. Securing the services of STEVE ALBINI, The POSTER CHILDREN completed their first album for 'Limited Potential', in the shape of 'FLOWER POWER' (1990) which was subsequently licensed to 'Frontier'. Drawing comparisons with The PIXIES, BITCH MAGNET and SLINT, The POSTER CHILDREN found admirers across the US alt-rock spectrum (where they had signed to 'Sire-Reprise'); the buzz soon spread across the water where Creation's Alan McGee was quick to spot their more than limited potential. While they never quite reached pin-up status, The POSTER CHILDREN did enjoy underground critical acclaim with a further two albums, 'DAISYCHAIN REACTION' (1992) and 'TOOL OF THE MAN' (1992/93). Soon to be given a higher priority by their Stateside label ('Warner Bros.'), the band's mid-90's albums, 'JUNIOR CITIZEN' (1995) and 'RTFM' (1997) were aimed at the alternative crossover audience who'd taken GREEN DAY to the top.

Album rating: TOREADOR SQUAT (*6) / FLOWER POWER (*6) / DAISYCHAIN REACTION (*6) / TOOL OF THE MAN (*6) / JUNIOR CITIZEN (*6) / RTFM (*6)

RICK VALENTIN – vocals, guitar / **ROSE MARSHACK** – vocals, bass / **JIM VALENTIN** – bass / **HOWIE KANTOFF** – drums

not iss. / Limited Potential

1988. (c) **TOREADOR SQUAT** [-] [ ]

Frontier / Frontier

Feb 92. (cd/c) *<(34633-2/-4)>* **FLOWER POWER** [ ] [ ] Sep91
– Dangerous life / Wanna / Byron's song / Eye / Hollywood / Modern art / Evidence / She walks / 10,000 pieces / Question / Non-reggae song / Detective Tracy / Bump bump / Jeremy Straight / Rain on me.

Creation / Twin/Tone

Jul 92. (cd/lp) *(CRE CD/LP 131) <89205>* **DAISYCHAIN REACTION** [ ] [ ] Jul90
– Dee / Cancer / If you see Kay / L-O-V-E / Freedom rock / Space gun / Water / Want it / Carver's / Chain reaction / Frustration / Where we live.

Feb 93. (12"ep)(cd-ep) *(CRE 152T)(CRESCD 152)* **CLOCK STREET / EVERYTHING BURNS. / MATTER CRUSH / OUTSIDE IN** [ ] [-]

Creation / Sire-Reprise

Mar 93. (cd/lp) *(CRE CD/LP 155) <45178>* **TOOL OF THE MAN** [ ] [ ] Nov92
– Dynamite chair / Tommyhaus / In my way / Clock street / Redline / Shotguns & pickups / Blatant dis / Idiot show / Outside in / Three bullets.

WEA / Sire-Reprise

Mar 95. (cd/c) *<(9362 45737-2/-4)>* **JUNIOR CITIZEN** [ ] [ ]
– Get a life / Junior citizen / He's my star / Revolution year zero / The drug I need / New boyfriend / Wide awake / King for a day / Mustaine / Downwind / One of us.

Apr 95. (cd-ep) *<45772>* **JUST LIKE YOU EP** [-] [ ]
– Not like you / Sick of it all / Voight / What's inside the box / Uther / Just like you.

Apr 97. (cd/c) *<9362 46567-2/-4>* **RTFM** [-] [ ]
– Blackdog / Ofor 1 / Musicofamerica / Dreamsmall / Speedoflight / King of the hill / 21st century / Attack! / Sleep / Pearlygates / Afterglow / Happenseveryday.

PRAG VEC

Formed: London, England . . . 1978 by ex-DERELICTS members SUSAN GOGAN and JOHN STUDHOLME, plus DAVID BOYD and NICHOLAS CASH. Not one of the better female-fronted punk rock outfits, PRAG VEC delivered only two singles, 'CIGARETTES' and 'THE FOLLOWER' before New Wave fizzled out at the turn of the decade. While GOGAN's hard-nosed vocal chords were uncannily similar to those of PENETRATION's PAULINE MURRAY, the overall PRAG VEC effect was akin to a less entertaining hybrid of BLONDIE and the SLITS. In fact, the band were more famous for the inclusion of JIM THIRLWELL (soon-to-be FOETUS), who contributed synth-noise on their one and only LP, 'NO COWBOYS' (1981).

Album rating: NO-COWBOYS (*4)

SUSAN GOGAN – vocals / **JOHN STUDHOLME** – guitar / **DAVID BOYD** – bass / **NICHOLAS CASH** – drums

Spec | not iss.

Dec 78. (7"ep) *(SP 001)* **WOLF / CIGARETTES. / EXISTENTIAL / BITS** [ ] [-]

Jun 79. (7") *(SP 002)* **EXPERT. / THE FOLLOWER** [ ] [-]
(all tracks re-iss. Feb80 on French 'Celluloid'; LTD 1040)

—— they disbanded for around a year, returning in 1981 with additional musicians, **JIM THIRLWELL** – synthesizer, vocals / **SURESH SINGH** – vocals, marimba / + guest **ART MORAN** – alto sax

Oct 81. (lp) *(reSPECt 1)* **"NO-COWBOYS"** [ ] [-]
– Laugh / Nervous / Happy valley / By the sea / Uh oh erotic / Welcome home / You're the gun / Third person / Breaking point / Cigarettes.

—— split again after above; CASH joined FAD GADGET and THIRLWELL formed his own outfit, FOETUS

PRAM

Formed: Birmingham, England . . . 1990 by ROSIE CUCKSTON, who soon found kindred spirits, SAM OWEN, MATTHEW EATON and MAX SIMPSON. Taking their inspiration from cult femme punks, the RAINCOATS and the SLITS, PRAM wheeled out their self-financed debut mini-set, 'GASH', an impressive minimalist outing that caught the ever attentive ear of 'Too Pure'. Filling out their sound as drummer ANDY GARRETT replaced MAX, PRAM employed an array of toy instruments against CUCKSTON's haunting vocal style to create a sinister childlike atmosphere that served as a backdrop for the trials and traumas hinted at in their dark lyrics. The quartet also experimented with rhythm and repetition in a similar way to the likes of STEREOLAB, all the component parts coming scarily together on 1993's 'IRON LUNG' EP. Later that year, they finally unleashed their first full-length set, 'THE STARS ARE SO BIG, THE EARTH IS SO SMALL . . . STAY AS YOU ARE', an album that further explored the boundaries between spooky ambience and neo Kraut-rock. Come the mid-90's, PRAM were mapping out similar abstract, avant-jazz terrain to the likes of TORTOISE, raking in underground credit for albums, 'HELIUM' (1994) and especially 'SARGASSO SEA' (1995). However, a near three-year break between albums saw the band lose a bit of momentum on '98's comeback set, 'THE NORTH POLE RADIO STATION'.

Album rating: GASH (*4) / THE STARS ARE SO BIG . . . (*7) / HELIUM (*6) / SARGASSO SEA (*7) / THE NORTH POLE RADIO STATION (*5)

ROSIE CUCKSTON – vocals, theremin / **SAM OWEN** – bass / **MATT EATON** – multi / **MAX SIMPSON** – keyboards, sampler

unknown | not iss.

1992. (m-cd) **GASH** [ ] [-]
– Dead piano / Flesh / Inmate's clothes / I'm a war / Pram / Dirty children / Blue singer / The day the animals turned on the cars / Gooswalk / Sunset international / Bleed *<US-iss.Jun97 on 'World Domination'; 56>*

—— **ANDY GARRETT** – drums; repl. MAX

Too Pure | American

Feb 93. (12"ep/cd-ep) *(PURE 17/+CD)* **IRON LUNG EP** [ ] [-]
– Cumulus / Water toy / Blue singer / Iron lung (version).

Sep 93. (lp/cd) *(PURE/+CD 26)* **THE STARS ARE SO BIG, THE EARTH IS SO SMALL . . . STAY AS YOU ARE** [ ] [-]
– Loco / Radio freak in a storm / Loredo Venus / Milky / Dorothy / In dreams you too can fly / The ray / Cape St. Vincent.

May 94. (12"ep/cd-ep) *(PURE 35/+CD)* **MESHES EP** [ ] [ ]
– Life in the clouds / Chrysalis / The legacy band of Venus.
(ltd.12"ep) *(PURE 35LTD)* – Life in the clouds (remixes).

Jun 94. (lp/cd) *(PURE/+CD 41)* *<43012>* **HELIUM** [ ] [ ] Feb95
Gravity / Dancing on a star / Nightwatch / Things left on the pavement / Windy / My father the clown / Blue / Little angel, little monkey / Meshes in the afternoon / Shadows.

Sep 95. (lp/cd) *(PURE/+CD 46)* *<43021>* **SARGASSO SEA** [ ] [ ]
– Loose threads / Little scars / Earthling and protection / Cotton candy / Three wild Georges / Serpentine / Crystal tips / Crooked tiles / Eels / Sea swells and distant squalls.

Kooky Disc | not iss.

1996. (cd-ep) *(AE 004)* **MUSIC FOR YOUR MOVIES** [ ] [-]
– The last astronaut / Cinnabar.

Domino | not iss.

Mar 98. (cd/lp) *(WIG CD/LP 049)* **THE NORTH POLE RADIO STATION** [ ] [-]
– Omnichord / Cinnabar / El Topo / Bathysphere / Fallen snow / Clockwork lighthouse / Sleepy sweet / Cow ghosts / Doors of empty cupboards.

Aug 98. (12"ep/cd-ep) *(RUG 037 T/CD)* **SLEEPY SWEET / VERSION. / CINNABAR (PCM version) / CARNIVAL OF SOULS GOES TO RIO** [ ] [ ]

PRESIDENTS OF THE UNITED STATES OF AMERICA

Formed: Seattle, Washington, USA . . . late 1993 by long-time friends CHRIS BALLEW, JASON FINN and DAVE DEDERER. All veterans of the alternative rock scene in one way or another (BALLEW had even worked as part of BECK's backing band), this "wacky" outfit were akin to a head-on collision between The CARS and DEVO. Combining surreal animal-inspired lyrics and a youthfully enthusiastic, funky pop/punk approach, the band recorded their celebrated debut set. Initially released on the independent 'Pop Llama' label in 1994, the eponymous album was subsequently remixed and reissued the following year after 'Columbia' came out tops in the ensuing bidding war for their presidential signatures. Powered by the success of the 'LUMP' single, the album went on to sell well over a million copies in the States, eventually making the Top 10. The band also made a dent in the UK market, helped by the success of the bizarre 'PEACHES' single. A follow-up set, 'II', eventually appeared in 1996, although this time around they failed to capture the public's attention in quite the same fashion. • **Songwriters:** BALLEW and group except KICK OUT THE JAMS (MC5) / WE ARE NOT GOING TO MAKE IT (Ben Reiser) / VIDEO KILLED THE RADIO STAR (Buggles) / CA PLANE POUR MOI (Plastic Bertrand) / DEVIL IN A SLEEPING BAG (Willie Nelson) / CLEVELAND ROCKS (Ian Hunter). • **Trivia:** PEACHES video was directed by ROMAN COPPOLA, son of FRANCIS FORD COPPOLA.

Album rating: PRESIDENTS OF THE UNITED STATES OF AMERICA (*5) / II (*7) / PURE FROSTING (*3)

CHRIS BALLEW – vocals, two-string basitar (ex-SUPERGROUP) / **DAVE DEDERER** – three-string guitbass, vocals (ex- LOVE BATTERY) / **JASON FINN** – drums, vocals (ex-SKIN YARD, ex-HELIOS CREED)

—— released a single on 'Pop Llama' US Mar 95.

Columbia | Columbia

Oct 95. (cd/c) *(481039-2/-4)* *<67291>* **PRESIDENTS OF THE UNITED STATES OF AMERICA** [14] [6] Sep95
– Kitty / Feather pluckn / Lump / Stranger / Boll Weevil / Peaches / Dune buggy / We are not going to make it / Kick out the jams / Body / Back porch / Candy / Naked and famous. *(yellow-lp Apr96; 481039-0)* – (2 extra). *(re-iss. cd Jul96; 484334-2)* *(w/ free cd+=)* – Dune buggy / Kick / Peaches / Lump / Back porch (versions). *(lp re-iss. Jun98 on 'Munster'; MR 093)*
<above album was originally issued on 'Pop Llama' in the US>

Dec 95. (7"pic-d/c-s) *(662496-7/-4)* **LUMP. / WAKE UP** [15] [-]
(cd-s+=) *(662496-2)* – Carolyn's bootie / Candy's cigarette.

Feb 96. (c-s,cd-s) *<78254>* **PEACHES / CANDY CIGARETTE** [-] [29]

Mar 96. (7") **FUCK CALIFORNIA. / CAROLYN'S BOOTIE** [-] [ ]

—— above on US label 'C/Z'

Apr 96. (7"pic-d/c-s) *(663107-7/-4)* **PEACHES. / CONFUSION** [8] [-]
(cd-s) *(663107-2)* – ('A'side) / Feather pluckin (live) / Boll Weevil (live) / Dune buggy (live).

Jul 96. (7"pic-d/c-s) *(663489-7/-4)* **DUNE BUGGY. / PEACHES (live)** [15] [-]
(cd-s) *(663489-3)* – ('A'side) / Back porch (live) / Kick out the jams (live) / Video killed the radio star (live).

Oct 96. (7"pic-d) *(663881-7)* **MACH 5. / BODY (live)** [29] [-]
(c-s) *(663817-4)* – ('A'side) / Carolyn's bootie.
(cd-s) *(663817-2)* – ('A'side) / Tremelo blooz / Tiki lounge god.

Nov 96. (cd/c/lp) *(485092-2/-4/-1)* *<67577>* **II** [36] [31]
– Ladies and gentlemen part 1 / Lunatic to love / Volcano / Mach 5 / Twig / Bug city / Bath of fire / Tiki god / L.I.P. / Froggie / Toob amplifier / Supermodel / Puffy little shoes / Ladies and gentlemen part 2 / Basketball dream.

—— split leaving behind a few remnants below

Mar 98. (cd/c) *(489702-2/-4)* *<69201>* **PURE FROSTING** (part compilation) [ ] [ ]
– Love delicatessen / Video killed the radio star / Mobile home / Japan / Black porch / Man (deposable thumb) / Tiki lounge god / Teenage girl / Slip away / Tremolo blooz / Cleveland rocks / Lump.

Jul 98. (c-s/cd-s) *(W 0450 C/CD)* **VIDEO KILLED THE RADIO STAR / (other tracks by Ellen Dow & Sugarhill Gang / Culture Club** [52] [-]
(above issued on the 'Maverick/Warners' label)

—— BALLEW was now in a band called, The GIRAFFES

PRIMAL SCREAM

Formed: Glasgow, Scotland . . . mid'84 by JESUS & MARY CHAIN drummer BOBBY GILLESPIE. Signing to JAMC's label, 'Creation', in 1985, they cut two singles, GILLESPIE leaving The 'MARY CHAIN after the debut, 'ALL FALL DOWN' (1985). The first album, 'SONIC FLOWER GROOVE' (1987), was recorded by the current band line-up core of ANDREW INNES, ROBERT 'THROB' YOUNG and MARTIN DUFFY (save MANI, ex-STONE ROSES, who joined up in 1996) along with an ever-changing array of additional musicians. Released on 'Creation' boss ALAN McGEE's 'WEA' subsidiary label, 'Elevation', the album saw the band pretty much live up to their name, a primitive take on raw ROLLING STONES, STOOGES etc. with a bit of BYRDS jingle jangle thrown in. This sound served the band well through their second album, PRIMAL SCREAM (1989) until the release of 'LOADED' in early 1990. Back at 'CREATION' and enamoured with the Acid House explosion, the band had enlisted the esteemed ANDREW WEATHERALL to remix 'I'M LOSING MORE THAN I'LL EVER HAVE' from the second lp. More a revolution than a remix, WEATHERALL created the stoned funk shuffle of 'LOADED', in the process bringing indie and rave kids together on the same dancefloor for the first time. PRIMAL SCREAM were now set on pushing the parameters of rock, releasing a trio of singles that defined an era, 'COME TOGETHER' (1990) was 90's style hedonist gospel that converted even the most cynical of rock bores while 'HIGHER THAN THE SUN' (1991) was perhaps the 'SCREAM's stellar moment, a narcotic lullaby beamed from another galaxy. Combining all the aforementioned tracks with a trippy 13TH FLOOR ELEVATORS cover, a heavyweight dub workout and a clutch of STONES-like beauties, 'SCREAMADELICA' (1991) was flawless. Opening with the euphoric 'MOVIN' ON UP' (the best song the 'STONES never wrote), the album effortlessly proved that dance and rock were essentially carved out of the same soulful root source, a seam that's been mined by any artist that's ever mattered. A landmark album, 'SCREAMADELICA' was awarded the Mercury Music prize in 1992 and for sheer breadth of vision the record has yet to meet its match in the 90's. Inevitably, then, the GEORGE DRAKOULIAS-produced follow-up, 'GIVE OUT BUT DON'T GIVE UP' (1994) was a disappointment in comparison. Recorded in MEMPHIS, the record saw PRIMAL SCREAM trying far too hard to achieve a roughshod R&B grit. Where before they had made The STONES' sound their own, now they came across as mere plagiarists, and over-produced plagiarists at that. Granted, the likes of 'JAILBIRD' and 'ROCKS' were funkier than any of the insipid indie competition around at the time and GILLESPIE's epileptic handclap routine was always more endearing than the run-of-the-mill rock posturing. Rumours of severe drug abuse abounded at this point and few were shocked when, in January 1994, it emerged that DUFFY had survived a near fatal stabbing in America. For the next couple of years, the band kept a fairly low profile, only a contribution to the 'Trainspotting' soundtrack and an unofficial Scottish 'Euro '96' single confirmed the 'SREAM were still in existence. But while Scotland stumbled to defeat (again!!), PRIMAL SREAM cleaned up their act and recorded the wonderful 'VANISHING POINT' (1997). Apparently cut as an alternative soundtrack to cult 70's road movie 'Kowalski', this album was the true follow-up/comedown to the psychedelic high of 'SCREAMADELICA'. 'OUT OF THE VOID' was the band's darkest moment to date while the title track and 'STUKA' were fractured, paranoid psych-outs. Only the vintage screenshow of 'GET DUFFY' and the mellow 'STAR' offered any respite. Big on dub and low on derivation, the album was a spirited return to form for one of Scotland's most enduring and groundbreaking bands. • **Songwriters:** GILLESPIE, YOUNG and BEATTIE, until the latter's replacement by INNES. Covered CARRY ME HOME (Dennis Wilson) / UNDERSTANDING (Small Faces) / 96 TEARS (? & The Mysterians) / KNOW YOUR RIGHTS (Clash) / MOTORHEAD (Motorhead).

Album rating: SCREAMADELICA (*10) / PRIMAL SCREAM (*8) / GIVE OUT BUT DON'T GIVE UP (*7) / VANISHING POINT (*8) / ECHO DEK (*6)

BOBBY GILLESPIE (b.22 Jun'64) – vocals (ex-WAKE) (also drummer of JESUS & MARY CHAIN) / **JIM BEATTIE** – guitar / **ROBERT YOUNG** – bass / **TOM McGURK** – drums / **MARTIN ST.JOHN** – tambourine

Creation / not iss.

May 85. (7") *(CRE 017)* **ALL FALL DOWN. / IT HAPPENS** [ ] [-]

— added **PAUL HARTE** – rhythm guitar (GILLESPIE left JESUS & MARY)

Apr 86. (7") *(CRE 026)* **CRYSTAL CRESCENT. / VELOCITY GIRL** [ ] [-]
(12"+=) *(CRE 026T)* – Spirea X.

— **STUART MAY** – rhythm guitar (ex-SUBMARINES) repl. HARTE (Dec86) / **ANDREW INNES** – rhythm guitar (of REVOLVING PAINT DREAM) repl. MAY / Guest drummers **PHIL KING** (studio) + **DAVE MORGAN** (tour) repl. McGURK

Elevation / not iss.

Jun 87. (7") *(ACID 5)* **GENTLE TUESDAY. / BLACK STAR CARNIVAL** [ ] [-]
(12"+=) *(ACID 5T)* – I'm gonna make you mine.

Sep 87. (7") *(ACID 5)* **IMPERIAL. / STAR FRUIT SURF RIDER** [ ] [-]
(12"+=/s12"+=) *(ACID 5T/+W)* – So sad about us / Imperial (demo).

Oct 87. (lp/c)(cd) *(ELV 2/+C)(242-182-2)* **SONIC FLOWER GROOVE** [62] [ ]
– Gentle Tuesday / Treasure trip / May the sun shine bright for you / Sonic sister love / Silent spring / Imperial / Love you / Leaves / Aftermath / We go down slowly. *(re-iss. Jul91)*

— (Jun87) **GAVIN SKINNER** – drums repl. ST.JOHN

— (Feb88) Now a trio **GILLESPIE, YOUNG + INNES** augmented by **JIM NAVAJO** – guitar. (BEATTIE formed SPIREA X, and SKINNER also left)

— (Feb89) added **HENRY OLSEN** – bass (ex-NICO) / **PHILIP 'TOBY' TOMANOV** – drums (ex-NICO, ex-DURUTTI COLUMN, ex-BLUE ORCHIDS)

Creation / Mercenary

Jul 89. (7") *(CRE 067)* **IVY IVY IVY. / YOU'RE JUST TOO DARK TO CARE** [ ] [-]
(12"+=)(cd-s+=) *(CRE 067T)(CRESCD 067)* – I got you split wide open over me.

Sep 89. (lp/c/cd) *(CRE LP/C/CD 054) <2100>* **PRIMAL SCREAM** [ ] [ ]
– Ivy Ivy Ivy / You're just dead skin to me / She power / You're just too dark to care / I'm losing more than I'll ever have / Gimme gimme teenage head / Lone star girl / Kill the king / Sweet pretty thing / Jesus can't save me. *(free 7"ltd.)* – SPLIT WIDE OPEN (demo). / LONE STAR GIRL (demo)

— trimmed to a trio again (**GILLESPIE, YOUNG + INNES**)

Creation / Sire

Feb 90. (7") *(CRE 070)* **LOADED. / I'M LOSING MORE THAN I'LL EVER HAVE** [16] [-]
(ext.12"+=/'A'Terry Farley remix-12"+=)(ext.cd-s+=) *(CRE 070 T/X)(CRESCD 070)* – Ramblin' Rose (live).

Jul 90. (7"/c-s)(ext.12")(ext.cd-s) *(CRE/+CS 078)(CRE 078T(CRESCD 078) <26384>* **COME TOGETHER (Terry Farley mix). / COME TOGETHER (Andrew Weatherall mix)** [26] [ ] Aug90
(12") *(CRE 078X)* – ('A'-HypnotoneBrainMachine mix) / ('A'-BBG mix).

Jun 91. (7"/ext.12") *(CRE 096/+T)* **HIGHER THAN THE SUN. / ('A' American Spring mix)** [40] [-]
(cd-s+=) *(CRESCD 096)* – Higher than the Orb.

— guest spot on above from **JAH WOBBLE** – bass

Aug 91. (7"/ext.12")(c-s) *(CRE 110/+T)(CRECS 110)* **DON'T FIGHT IT, FEEL IT. / ('A'scat mix featuring Denise Johnson)** [41] [-]
(cd-s+=) *(CRESCD 110)* – ('A'extended version).

Sep 91. (cd/c/d-lp) *(CRE CD/C/LP 076) <26714>* **SCREAMADELICA** [8] [ ]
– Movin' on up / Slip inside this house / Don't fight it, feel it / Higher than the Sun / Inner flight / Come together / Loaded / Damaged / I'm comin' down / Higher than the Sun (a dub symphony in two parts) / Shine like stars.

Jan 92. (7"ep/c-ep) *(CRE/+CS 117) <40193>* **DIXIE-NARCO EP** [11] [ ]
– Movin' on up / Carry me home / Screamadelica.
(12"ep+=)(cd-ep+=) *(CRE 117T)(CRESCD 117)* – Stone my soul.

— In Jan'94, MARTIN DUFFY was stabbed in Memphis, although he recovered soon after.

— Line-up:- **GILLESPIE, YOUNG, INNES, DUFFY + DAVID HOOD + DENISE JOHNSON** + guest **GEORGE CLINTON** – vocals

Mar 94. (7"/c-s) *(CRE/+CS 129) <18189>* **ROCKS. / FUNKY JAM** [7] [ ] Apr94
(12")(cd-s) *(CRE 129T)(CRESCD 129)* – ('A'side) / Funky jam (hot ass mix) / Funky jam (club mix).

Apr 94. (cd/c/lp) *(CRE CD/C/LP 146) <45538>* **GIVE OUT, BUT DON'T GIVE UP** [2] [ ]
– Jailbird / Rocks / (I'm gonna) Cry myself blind / Funky jam / Big jet plane / Free / Call on me / Struttin' / Sad and blue / Give out but don't give up / I'll be there for you.

Jun 94. (7"/c-s) *(CRE/+CS 145)* **JAILBIRD. / ('A'-Dust Brothers mix)** [29] [-]
(12"+=) *(CRE 145T)* – ('A'-Toxic Trio stay free mix) / ('A'-Weathcrall dub chapter 3 mix).
(cd-s++=) *(CRESCD 145)* – ('A'-Sweeney 2 mix).

Nov 94. (7"/c-s) *(CRE/+CS 183)* **(I'M GONNA) CRY MYSELF BLIND (George Drakoulias mix). / ROCKS (live)** [51] [-]
(cd-s+=) *(CRESCD 183)* – I'm losing more than I'll ever have (live) / Struttin' (back in our minds) (Brendan Lynch remix).
(10") *(CRE 183X)* – ('A'side) / Struttin' (back in our minds) (Brendan Lynch remix) / Give out, but don't give up (Portishead remix) / Rockers dub (Kris Needs mix).

Jun 96. (c-s/cd-s; PRIMAL SCREAM, IRVINE WELSH AND ON-U SOUND PRESENT . . .) *(CRECS-CRESCD 194)* **THE BIG MAN AND THE SCREAM TEAM MEET THE BARMY ARMY UPTOWN (mixes:- full strength fortified dub / electric soup dub / a jake supreme)** [17] [-]

— In Oct'96, GILLESPIE, INNES, YOUNG & DUFFY were joined by **MANI MOUNFIELD** – bass (ex-STONE ROSES)

Creation / Creation

May 97. (c-s) *(<CRECS 245>)* **KOWALSKI / 96 TEARS** [8] [ ]
(cd-s+=) *(<CRESCD 245>)* – Know your rights / ('A'-Automator mix).

Jun 97. (c-s) *CRECS 263)* **STAR / JESUS** [16] [-]
(cd-s+=) *(CRESCD 263)* – Rebel dub / How does it feel to belong.
(12"+=) *(CRE 263T)* – ('A'mixes).

Jul 97. (cd/d-lp)(c) *(CRE CD/LP 178)(CCRE 178) <46559>* **VANISHING POINT** [2] [ ]
– Burning wheel / Get Duffy / Kowalski / Star / If they move, kill 'em / Out of the void / Stuka / Medication / Motorhead / Trainspotting / Long life.

Oct 97. (7") *(CRE 272)* **BURNING WHEEL. /** [17] [-]
(12")(cd-s) *(CRE 272T)(CRESCD 272)* – ('A'side) / ('A'-Chemical Brothers remix) / Hammond connection / Higher than the sun (original).

Oct 97. (cd/7"box) *(CRE CD/L7 224)* **ECHO DEK** (remixes) [43] [-]
– Living dub / Duffed up / Revolutionary / Ju-87 / First name unknown / Vanishing dub / Last train / Wise blood / Dub in vain.

Feb 98. (7") *(CRE 284)* **IF THEY MOVE, KILL 'EM. / BADLANDS** [ ] [-]
(12"+=)(cd-s+=) *(CRE 284T)(CRESCD 284)* – ('A'-My Bloody Valentine Arkestra mix) / ('A'-Darklands 12"disco mix).

— added on tour **JIM HUNT** – saxophone / **DUNCAN MACKAY** – trumpet / **DARREN MOONEY** – drums

– others, etc. –

Nov 97. (12") *Creation; (PSTLS 1)* **STUKA. / TWO LONE SWORDSMEN (mixes)** [ ] [-]

PRIMITIVES

Formed: Coventry, England . . . September '85 by PETE TWEEDIE, STEVE DULLAHAN and PAUL COURT, who had been part of EUROPEAN SUN with male singer KEIRON. Adopting the PRIMITIVES moniker, the band recruited striking Aussie blonde, TRACY TRACY as a frontwoman, setting up their own indie label, 'Lazy' with the help of manager WAYNE MORRIS. In '86/'87, the band's first three singles, 'THRU THE FLOWERS', REALLY STUPID', and 'STOP KILLING ME' were cult indie hits, quintessential 80's distortion-pop not unlike a fantasy collaboration between The RUNAWAYS and The JESUS AND MARY CHAIN. With a new 'R.C.A.' deal in the can (the company had taken over 'Lazy', which was now essentially a subsidiary), the comparisons with BLONDIE became more than just visual, the new wave, amphetamine melodica of 'CRASH' giving The PRIMITIVES immediate Top 5 success in early '88. Their debut album, 'LOVELY', cruised into the Top 10 the following month, the highly photogenic TRACY enjoying a concentrated fifteen minutes of fame as the style press fell over themselves to have her blonde barnet on their front covers. An infectious collection of neo-psychedelic power pop, the album nevertheless failed to deliver any further major hits. Problems were compounded by personnel changes; by the time the band came to record a follow-up, DULLAHAN and TWEEDIE had both departed to join the band HATE. Though replacements had been found in ANDY HOBSON (replaced in turn, by PAUL SAMPSON on the new album) and TIG WILLIAMS respectively, 'PURE' (1989) was regarded by many reviewers as distictly underwhelming, the album barely scraping into the Top 40. Worse, TRACY had gone ginger! The group bravely struggled on, releasing the 'GALORE' (1992) album, its commercial failure co-inciding with the wise decision to call it a day in Spring '92. • **Songwriters:** Penned by COURT, except I'LL BE YOUR MIRROR (Velvet Underground) / I WANNA BE YOUR DOG (Stooges; Iggy Pop) / AS TEARS GO BY (Rolling Stones) / (YOU'RE SO SQUARE) BABY I DON'T CARE (Elvis Presley). • **Trivia:** So far TRACY has still to reveal her surname, which is slightly irritating for a biographer.

Album rating: LOVELY (*7) / LAZY 86-88 compilation (*8)

TRACY TRACY (b. TRACY CATTELL, 18 Aug'67, Australia) – vocals repl. KIERON / **PAUL COURT** (b.27 Jul'65) – guitar, vocals / **STEVE DULLAHAN** (b.18 Dec'66) – bass / **PETE TWEEDIE** – drums

Lazy | not iss.

May 86. (12"ep) *(LAZY 01)* **THRU THE FLOWERS / ACROSS MY SHOULDER. / SHE DON'T NEED YOU / LAZY** [ ] [-]
Oct 86. (7") *(LAZY 02)* **REALLY STUPID. / WE FOUND A WAY TO THE SUN** [ ] [-]
(12"+=) *(LAZY 02T)* – Where the wind blows.
Feb 87. (7") *(LAZY 03)* **STOP KILLING ME. / BUZZ BUZZ BUZZ** [ ] [-]
(12"+=) *(LAZY 03T)* – Laughing up my sleeve.
May 87. (free gig-7") *(LAZY 05)* **OCEAN BLUE. / SHADOW** [-] [-]
Aug 87. (7") *(LAZY 06)* **THRU THE FLOWERS (new version). / EVERYTHING SHINING BRIGHT** [ ] [-]
(12"+=) *(LAZY 06T)* – Across my shoulder (original).
(7"ltd.+=) *(LAZY 06L)* – ('A'original).

— **TIG WILLIAMS** – drums repl. TWEEDIE who joined HATE

R.C.A. | R.C.A.

Feb 88. (7") *(PB 41761)* **CRASH. / I'LL STICK WITH YOU** [5] [ ] Apr88
(10"+=) *(PB 41761X)* – Crash (live in studio).
(12"+=) *(PT 41762)* – Crash (demo) / Things get in your way.
(7"ep+=) *(PB 41761E)* – Crash (again and again) / Crash (short).
Mar 88. (lp/c/cd) *(PL/PK/PD 71688)* <8443> **LOVELY** [6] [ ] Aug88
– Crash / Spacehead / Carry me home / Shadow / Thru the flowers / Dreamwalk baby / I'll stick with you / Nothing left / Stop killing me / Out of reach / Ocean blue / Run, baby, run / Anything to change / Buzz buzz buzz. *<later US copies +=> –* Way behind me.
Apr 88. (7") *(PB 42011)* **OUT OF REACH (remix). / REALLY STUPID (live)** [25] [-]
(12"+=) *(PT 42012)* – Crash (live) / ('A'lp version).
(cd-s+=) *(PD 42012)* – Ocean blue (lp version) / I wanna be your dog (live).
(7"ep+=) *(PB 42011E)* – Crash (live) / Dreamwalk baby (live).
Aug 88. (7"/7"red,7"green,7"yellow,7"blue) *(PB 42209/+E)* **WAY BEHIND ME. / ALL THE WAY DOWN** [36] [-]
(12"+=/c-s+=) *(PT 42210/+C)* – ('A'acoustic) / ('B'-beat mix).
Sep 88. (7") **WAY BEHIND ME. / THRU THE FLOWERS (lp version)** [-] [ ]

— Trimmed to a trio when DULLAHAN also departed to join HATE

Jul 89. (7"/7"g-f/7"box)(c-s) *(PB 42947/42993/43003)(PK 42948)* **SICK OF IT. / NOOSE** [24] [-]
(12"+=/cd-s+=) *(PT/PD 42948)* – I'll be your mirror.
(12"blue++=) *(PT 43134)* – As tears go by.

— added **ANDY HOBSON** – bass (ex-JUNK)

Sep 89. (7"/c-s) *(PB/PK 43173)* **SECRETS. / I ALMOST TOUCHED YOU** [49] [-]
(7"m+=) *(PB 43209)* – Dizzy heights.
(7"ep++=)(12"red-ep+=)(3"cd-ep++=) *(PB 43211)(PT 43212)(PD 43174)* – Secrets (demo).
(12"m+=) *(PT 43174)* – Secrets (demo).

— **PAUL SAMPSON** – bass repl. HOBSON (on lp)

Oct 89. (lp/c/cd) *(PL/PK/PD 74252)* <9934> **PURE** [33] [ ] Dec89
– Outside / Summer rain / Sick of it / Shine / Dizzy heights / All the way down / Secrets / Keep me in mind / Lonely streets / Can't bring me down / Way behind me / Never tell / Noose / I'll be your mirror. *(cd+=)* – All the way down (beat version) / I almost touched you. *<US cd+=)* – (4 tracks).
Jul 91. (7"/c-s) *(PB/PK 44481)* **YOU ARE THE WAY. / IN MY DREAM** [58] [-]
(12"+=/cd-s+=) *(PT/PD 44481)* – Sunpulse / Stop killing me.
Oct 91. (7") **EARTH THING. / EMPHASISE** [ ] [-]
(12"ep+=/cd-ep+=) **THE SPELLS EP** – Under my spell / Haunted.
(12"ep+=) **THE SPELLS EP** – All the way down (live) / Way behind me (live).
Mar 92. (7"/c-s) **LEAD ME ASTRAY. / OUTSIDE (live) / YOU ARE THE WAY (live)** [ ] [-]
(12") – ('A'side) / Slip away (live) / Earth thing (live) / Outside (live).
(12") – ('A'side) / See thru the dark (live) / Stop killing me (live).
(cd-s) – ('A'side) / Sick of it (live) / Give this world to me (live).
Apr 92. (cd/c/lp) **GALORE** [ ] [-]
– You are the way / Lead me astray / Earth thing / Give this world to you / Slip away / Cold enough to kill / Hello Jesus / Empathise / See thru the dark / Kiss mine / Smile / The little black egg.

— disbanded around Spring 1992.

– compilations, others, etc. –

Aug 89. (lp/c/cd) *Lazy; (LAZY/+C/CD 15)* **LAZY 86-88** (early material) [73] [-]
1995. (cd) *R.C.A.; <74321 2635>* **BOMBSHELL: THE HITS AND MORE** [-] [ ]
1996. (cd) *Camden; <39343>* **THE BEST OF THE PRIMITIVES** [-] [ ]

PRIMUS

Formed: Bay Area, San Francisco, USA . . . mid-80's by bassist/vocalist LES CLAYPOOL and guitarist TODD HUTH, initially as PRIMATE. Something of a cult phenomenon in their native city, the act's first release was a live affair, 'SUCK ON THIS' (1989), recorded at a local club and released on the band's own 'Prawnsong' label. By this point, JOE SATRIANI protege, LARRY LALONDE, had replaced HUTH who joined fellow Bay Area act, BLIND ILLUSION (CLAYPOOL had once been a member). PRIMUS were hardly purveyors of breakneck rifferama, however, CLAYPOOL's wayward muse fashioning instead a notoriously bizarre, bass-heavy fish stew of thrash, aquatic funk, avant-rock and surreal humour, CLAYPOOL's staccato-snorkle vocals colouring his marine-obsessed tales of fishermen and sturgeon. PRIMUS' first studio effort, 'FRIZZLE FRY' (1990), was released on the American independent label, 'Caroline' ('Virgin' in the UK), many of the songs from the debut reworked, including the brilliant 'JOHN THE FISHERMAN'. The band had also recruited a permanent drummer in TIM 'HERB' ALEXANDER, complementing CLAYPOOL's slippery, knottily intricate bass work. PRIMUS fitted in loosely with the burgeoning funk-metal scene of the day (supporting the likes of FAITH NO MORE, 24-7 SPYZ and LIVING COLOUR) and soon found themselves with a major label contract via 'Interscope', subsequently making their major label debut with the wonderfully titled 'SAILING THE SEAS OF CHEESE' (1991). The record's highlight was a reworked 'TOMMY THE CAT' (from the debut), complete with vocals courtesy of highly respected fellow weirdster, TOM WAITS. Touring with RUSH obviously hadn't damaged the band's street cred too much and the '93 follow-up, 'PORK SODA' made the US Top 10, proving that weird, in PRIMUS' case, was indeed wonderful. The same year, CLAYPOOL teamed up with old colleagues HUTH and JAY LANE to form a side project, SAUSAGE, releasing the album 'RIDDLES ARE ABOUND TONIGHT' (1993). A further (US) Top 10 PRIMUS album appeared in 1995, 'TALES FROM THE PUNCHBOWL', CLAYPOOL proving that he hadn't lost his technicolour, often flippant sense of humour with such lyrical vignettes as 'WYNONA'S BIG BROWN BEAVER'. Prior to the release of 'THE BROWN ALBUM' in '97, a rare line-up change occured with BRIAN MANTIA replacing ALEXANDER. The following year saw the release of a largely disappointing covers album, 'RHINOPLASTY', it looked like PRIMUS were sailing on cheese right enough. • **Covers:** MAKING PLANS FOR NIGEL + SCISSOR MAN (Xtc) / INTRUDER + THE FAMILY AND THE FISHING NET (Peter Gabriel) / HAVE A CIGAR (Pink Floyd) / TIPPY TOES (Meters) / SILLY PUTTY (Stanley Clarke) / AMOS MOSES (Jerry Reed) / BEHIND MY CAMEL (Police) / THE THING THAT SHOULD NOT BE (Metallica) / etc.

Album rating: SUCK ON THIS (*4) / FRIZZLE FRY (*7) / SAILING THE SEAS OF CHEESE (*7) / PORK SODA (*8) / TALES FROM THE PUNCH BOWL (*8) / THE BROWN ALBUM (*6) / RHINOPLASTY mini (*5)

LES CLAYPOOL (b.29 Sep'63, Richmond, Calif.) – vocals, bass (ex-BLIND ILLUSION) / **LARRY LaLONDE** (b.12 Sep'68, Richmond) – guitar (ex-POSSESSED) repl. TODD HUTH (b.13 Mar'63, San Leandro, Calif.) who joined BLIND ILLUSION / **JAY LANE** (b.15 Dec'64, San Francisco) – drums; repl. drum machine

not iss. | Prawn Song

Jan 90. (lp) *<CAROL 160-2>* **SUCK ON THIS (live)** [-] [ ]
– John the fisherman / Groundhog's day / The heckler / Pressman / Jelikit / Tommy the cat / Pudding time / Harold of the rocks / Frizzle fry. *(UK cd-iss. Mar92 on 'Atlantic'; 7567 91833-2) (re-iss. Jun97 on 'Caroline' lp/cd; CAR/+OLCD 1620)*

— **TIM 'HERB' ALEXANDER** (b.10 Apr'65, Cherry Point, New Connecticut) – drums repl. JAY who joined SAUSAGE

Virgin | Caroline

Jul 90. (cd/c/lp) *(CAR CD/C/LP 10) <CAROL 1619-2>* **FRIZZLE FRY** [ ] [ ] Feb90
– To defy the laws of tradition / Ground hog's day / Too many puppies / Mr.Know-it-all / Frizzle fry / John the fisherman / You can't kill Michael Malloy / The toys go winding down / Pudding time / Sathington Willoby / Spaghetti western / Harold of the rocks / To defy. *(cd re-iss. Jun97; CAROLCD 1619)*

Atlantic | Interscope

May 91. (cd/c/lp) *<(7567 91659-2/-4/-1)>* **SAILING THE SEAS OF CHEESE** [ ] [ ]
– Seas of cheese / Here come the bastards / Sgt. Baker / American life / Jerry was a race car driver / Eleven / Is it luck? / Grandad's lil ditty / Tommy the cat / Sathington waltz / Those damned blue collar tweekers / Fish on / Los bastardos. *(re-iss. Feb95; same)*
Jun 92. (cd-ep) *(A 6167CD)* **CHEESY EP 1** <US title 'MISCELLANEOUS DEBRIS'> [ ] [ ]
– Making plans for Nigel / Tommy the cat / Tippy toes / Have a cigar.
(cd-ep) **CHEESY 2** *(A 6167CDX)* – (1st 2 tracks) / Sinister exaggerator / Intruder.
May 93. (cd/c/lp) *<(7567 92257-2/-4/-1)>* **PORK SODA** [56] [7]
– Pork chop's little ditty / My name is mud / Welcome to this world / Bob / D.M.V. / The ol' Diamondback sturgeon (Fisherman's chronicles, part 3) / Nature boy / Wounded Knee / Pork soda / The pressman / Mr.Krinkle / The air is getting slippery / Hamburger train / Pork chop's little ditty / Hail Santa. *(cd re-iss. Jul96 on 'Interscope'; IND 92257)*
Jun 95. (cd/c) *<(IND/INC 92553)>* **TALES FROM THE PUNCHBOWL** [ ] [8]
– Professor Nutbutter's house of treats / Mrs. Blaileen / Wynona's big brown beaver / Southbound pachydern / Space farm / Year of the parrot / Hellbound 17 1/2 (theme from) / Glass sandwich / Del Davis tree farm / De Anza jig / On the tweak again / Over the electric grapevine / Captain Shiner. *(enhanced-cd re-iss. Jul96; IND 92665)*
Dec 95. (c-s) *(A 8129C)* **WYNONA'S BIG BROWN BEAVER /** [ ] [ ]
(cd-s) *(A 8129CD)* –
(above issued on 'Atlantic' in the UK)

— early '96, CLAYPOOL featured on ALEX LIFESON'S (Rush) VICTOR project

— (Sep'96) **BRIAN 'Brain' MANTIA** – drums (ex-GODFLESH) repl. TIM

Jul 97. (cd/d-lp) *<(IND/ISC 90126)>* **BROWN ALBUM** [ ] [21]
– The return of Sathington Willoughby / Fisticuffs / Golden boy / Over the falls / Shake hands with beef / Camelback cinema / Hats off / Puddin' Taine / Bob's party time lounge / Duchess and the proverbial mind spread / Restin' bones / Coddington / Kalamazoo / Chastasing of renegade / Arnie.
Aug 98. (m-cd) *<(IND 90214)>* **RHINOPLASTY** [ ] [ ]
– Scissor man / The family and the fishing net / Silly putty / Amos Moses / Behind my camel / Too many puppies / The thing that should not be / Tommy the cat / Bob's party time lounge.

SAUSAGE

LES CLAYPOOL – vocals, bass / **TODD HUTH** – guitar / **JAY LANE** – drums

East West East West

Apr 94. (cd/c) *<(6544 92361-2/-4)>* **RIDDLES ARE ABOUND TONIGHT**
– Temporary phase / Girls for single men / Caution should be used while driving a motor vehicle or operating machinery / Shattering song / Prelude to fear / Riddles are abound tonight / Here's to the man / Toyz 1988 / Recreating.

Peter PRINCIPLE (see under ⇒ TUXEDOMOON)

PRISONERS

Formed: Rochester / Medway, Kent, England . . . 1982 by GRAHAM DAY, ALLAN CROCKFORD, JAMIE TAYLOR and JOHNNY SYMONS. That year they created something of a stir when they released a self-financed debut album, 'A TASTE OF PINK!', TAYLOR's hammond organ proving the key element in an energetic sound which drew heavily on the more mod-influenced sounds of the 60's. They soon signed to Chiswick off-shoot, 'Big Beat', who unleashed the PHIL CHEVRON (future POGUES)-produced, tongue-twistingly titled but muted follow-up set, 'THE WISERMISERDEMELZA' (1983). The following year, an appearance on Channel 4's 'The Tube' afforded DAY and Co. valuable exposure and led to them contributing a track, 'REACHING MY HEAD', to their label's accompanying various artists EP, 'Four On Four: Trash On The Tube'. Subsequently striking out on their own once more, The PRISONERS released a second self-financed set, 'THE LAST FOURFATHERS', securing them an ill-fated deal with Stiff off-shoot, 'Countdown'. The resulting, TROY TATE-produced album, 'IN FROM THE COLD', was beset with problems and stretched the band's patience to breaking point. Following their 1986 demise, GRAHAM went on to join THEE MIGHTY CEASARS before forming The PRIME MOVERS (with CROCKFORD), while TAYLOR went on to greater recognition with his own JAMES TAYLOR QUARTET. Initially also comprising CROCKFORD alongside DAVID TAYLOR and SIMON 'WOLF' HOWARD, JTQ were inspired by the funky pop/theme tune interpretations of prime BOOKER T & THE MG'S, releasing a string of albums for their own 'Re-Elect The President' label. With London's rare groove/acid jazz scene beginning to move away from its inherent insularity and make an impact on the wider market, JTQ were snapped up by 'Polydor'-offshoot, 'Urban'. The group made their major label debut with 'THE THEME FROM STARSKY & HUTCH', a live favourite also featured on the accompanying album, 'WAIT A MINUTE'. Certainly, it was in a live environment that JTQ were (and still are!) best sampled, TAYLOR's mean Hammond licks guaranteed to set any dancefloor on fire. It could even be argued that TAYLOR pre-empted the current vogue for all things lounge/easy listening although his core audience of students and polo-necked groovers would undoubtedly refute any charges of cheesiness. While never actually charting, a cult following ensured that albums such as 'GET ORGANIZED' (1989) and 'DO YOUR OWN THING' (1990) were steady sellers; the uninitiated, however, are directed towards the recently released 'Music club' album, 'BLOW UP!', a fine collection featuring their legendary cover of Led Zeppelin's 'WHOLE LOTTA LOVE', eat your heart out GOLDBUG! • **Songwriters:** GRAHAM DAY. JAMES TAYLOR QUARTET covered many TV/film themes + GOLDFINGER (John Barry) / MRS. ROBINSON (Simon & Garfunkel) / ALFIE / etc, etc.

Album rating: A TASTE OF PINK! (*5) / THE WISERMISERDEMELZA (*7) / THE LAST FOURFATHERS (*5) / IN FROM THE COLD (*5) / James Taylor Quartet: BLOW UP! A JTQ COLLECTION compilation (*7)

GRAHAM DAY – vocals, guitar / **JAMES 'JAMIE' TAYLOR** – Hammond organ / **ALLAN CROCKFORD** – bass / **JOHNNY SYMONS** – drums

Own Up not iss.

1982. (lp) *(OWN UP U2)* **A TASTE OF PINK!** -
– Better in black / A taste of pink / Maybe I was wrong / Creepy crawlies / There can't be a place / Pretend / Coming home / Threw my heart away / Come to the / Mushroom / Till the morning light / Say your prayers / Don't call my name. *(cd-iss. Feb94; OWNUPU 002CD) (re-iss. Mar85 in pink vinyl)*

Big Beat not iss.

Nov 83. (7") *(NS 90)* **HURRICANE. / TOMORROW (SHE SAID)** -
Nov 83. (lp) *(WIK 19)* **THE WISERMISERDEMELZA** -
– Here come the misunderstood / A dream is gone / For now and forever / Unbeliever / Far away / Hurricane / Somewhere / Think of me / Love me lies / Tonight. *(cd-iss. May90 +=; CDWIKD 937)* – Tomorrow (she said) / Melanie / What I want / The last thing on your mind / Revenge of the Cybermen / Coming home / Reaching my head.

Ace-Chiswick not iss.

Aug 84. (7"ep) *(SW 98)* **ELECTRIC FIT** -
– Revenge of the Cybermen / Melanie / What I want / The last thing on your mind.

Own Up not iss.

Jul 85. (lp) *(OWN UP 3)* **THE LAST FOURFATHERS** -
– Nobody wants your love / Night of the Nazgul / Thinking of you (broken pieces) / I am the fisherman / Mrs. Fothergill / Take you for a ride / The drowning / F.O.P. / Whenever I'm gone / Who's sorry now / Explosion on Uranus / I drink the ocean. *(cd-iss. Feb94; OWNUPU 003CD)*

Empire not iss.

Jan 86. (lp) *(MIC 001)* **THE LAST NIGHT AT THE MIC CLUB (live)** (shared with The MILKSHAKES) -

Countdown not iss.

Mar 86. (7") *(VAIN 4)* **WHENEVER I'M GONE. / PROMISED LAND** -
(12"+=) *(12VAIN 4)* – Gravedigger.
May 86. (lp) *(DOWN 2)* **IN FROM THE COLD** -
– All you gotta do is say / Come closer / The more I teach you / Mourn my health / I know how to please you / Deceiving eye / In from the cold / Wish the rain / Be on your way / Find and seek / Ain't no telling / The lesser evil.

— split in 1986 when GRAHAM joined THEE MIGHTY CAESARS (an off-shoot of MILKSHAKES). He was soon to form The PRIME MOVERS.

– compilations, etc. –

1984. (lp) *Pink Dust;* **REVENGE OF THE PRISONERS** -
Apr 87. (lp) *Media Burn; (MB 17)* **THE MILKSHAKES VS. THE PRISONERS** -
Dec 88. (lp) *Hangman; (HANG 23UP)* **RARE AND UNISSUED** -

DAGGERMEN

— **TAYLOR** with ?

Empire not iss.

Feb 86. (7"ep) *(UPW 258J)* **INTRODUCING THE DAGGERMEN** -

Own Up not iss.

Nov 86. (lp) *(DAG 001)* **DAGGERS IN MY MIND** -

JAMES TAYLOR QUARTET

— **TAYLOR** – Hammond organ / **ALLAN CROCKFORD** – bass / **DAVID TAYLOR** – guitar / **SIMON 'WOLF' HOWARD** – drums

Re-Elect the President not iss.

Mar 87. (7") *(FORD 1)* **BLOW UP. / ONE MINT JULEP** -
Jul 87. (m-lp) *(REAGAN 2)* **MISSION: IMPOSSIBLE** -
– Blow up / One mint julep / Be my girl / Mission: impossible / Untitled No.1 / Goldfinger / The cat / Mrs. Robinson / Alfie / The stooge / Untitled NO.2 *<US cd-iss. 1996 on 'Hollywood'; 168040>*
Dec 87. (lp) *(KENNEDY 1)* **THE MONEY SPYDER** -
– The money spyder / One way street / Car chase / Spiral staircase / Mr. Cool's dream / Real mean time / Onion club / Stroll / Los cuevos Pablo / Midnight stomp / Buzy bee / In the park. *<us cd-iss. 1996 on 'Hollywood'; 168022>*
Jun 88. (cd) *(CARTER 1)* **THE FIRST 64 MINUTES** (compilation) -
– Blow up / One mint julep / Be my girl / Mission; impossible / Goldfinger / The cat / Mrs. Robinson / Alfie / The stooge / The money spyder / One way street / Car chase / The spiral staircase / Mr. Cool's dream / A real mean time / The onion club / The stroll / Los Cuevos Pueblo / etc.

— CROCKFORD joined PRIME MOVERS alongside GRAHAM DAY

Urban-Polydor Verve

Sep 88. (7"/12") *(URB/+X 24)* **THE THEME FROM 'STARSKY & HUTCH'. / ('A'version)** -
Oct 88. (lp/c/cd) *(837 340-1/-4/-2)* **WAIT A MINUTE** -
– Wait a minute / Lulu / Indian summer / Fat boy stomp / Eleven thru seven / Theme from 'Starsky & Hutch' / Jungle strut / Pocket change / Baion-ara / Out there / Kooks korner / The natural thing.
May 89. (7") *(URB 38)* **BREAKOUT. / DOWN BY THE RIVER** -
(12"+=/cd-s+=) *(URBX/URCD 38)* – Aquarius / Down by the river (version).
Jun 89. (lp/c/cd) *(<839 405-1/-4/-2>)* **GET ORGANIZED**
– Grooving home / Electric boogaloo / The stretch / It doesn't matter / Touchdown / Breakout / Brothers Batucada / Bluebird / Bossa pilante / Riding high.
Oct 90. (cd/c/lp) *(843 797-2/-4/-1)* **DO YOUR OWN THING** -
– Love the life / Killing time / The money / JTQ theme / Ted's asleep / Always there / Oscar / Samba for Bill & Ben / Valhalla / Fat / Peace song.

Acid Jazz Hollywood

Feb 95. (cd/lp) *(JAZID CD/LP 115) <168005>* **IN THE HAND OF THE INEVITABLE**
– Love will keep us together / Three Mile Island / Free your mind * / Haitian breakdown / A good thing / Let's go together / Segue No.1 / Steppin' into my life / Whole lotta love / The journey / Sounds of freedom / Keep on movin' * / In the hands of the inevitable. *(lp w/ free 12") (cd+= *)*
May 96. (cd) *(JAZIDCD 139) <168054>* **CREATION**
– Theme from Starsky and Hutch / Selectivity / Creation (fanfare for a 3rd . . .) / Staying active / Man of mystery / Theme from Dirty Harry / Summer fantasy / Don't let money be your god / Road rage / Check it out / The grass is not greener / Theme from a far away land / Austin's theme.
Jun 96. (cd/c/lp) *(JAZID CD/MC/LP 140)* **LIVING UNDERGROUND** -

JTI not iss.

May 98. (cd) *(JTI 002CD)* **LIVE AT THE MANCHESTER ACADEMY** -

– compilations, etc. –

Oct 95. (cd) *Nighttracks; (CDNT 010)* **RADIO 1 SESSIONS** -
Dec 97. (cd) *Strange Fruit; (SFRSCD 043)* **THE BBC SESSIONS** -
Mar 98. (cd) *Music Club; (MCCD 333)* **BLOW UP! A JTQ COLLECTION** -

PRISONSHAKE

Formed: Cleveland, Ohio, USA . . . 1987 by DOUG ENKLER and ROBERT GRIFFIN, the latter founding his own fanzine which eventually evolved into a bonafide indie record label, 'Scat'. A series of Stateside 7"ers and two albums ensued over the course of the early 90's, one of these albums, 'FAILED TO MENACE', finally surfacing on 'Matador' as their UK debut, their US debut 'THE ROARING THIRD', appeared later that year, although it seems PRISONSHAKE have gone on extended parole since then.

Album rating: THE ROARING THIRD (*6) / FAILED TO MENACE (*6)

DOUG ENKLER – vocals / **ROBERT GRIFFIN** – guitar / **CHRIS BURGESS** – bass / **SCOTT PICKERING** – drums, mandolin

not iss. Rubber

1991. (7") **THEN SHE PRAYED. /** -

not iss. Scat

1992. (7") *<001>* **DEANNA. / SHOOK LIKE ROSES** -
1992. (12"ep) *<021>* **DELLA STREET** -

– Molly / From down here / London – Stuck in St. Louis, 1985.

—— **BARRY BRANHAM** – bass + **TIM TOBIAS** – guitar; repl. rhythm

		Matador	Matador
Jul 94.	(cd) <*(OLE 085-2)*> **FAILED TO MENACE** – Last time I looked / Either way evil eye / A brilliant idea / Ever and ever / Some chick you fucked / Stumble / Asiento / Cigarette day / (Not without) Grace / Nothing has to hurt / Humor.	[ ]	[ ]
		Shake	**Scat**
Nov 94.	(7") <*SAL 206*> <*30*> **2 SISTERS. /**	[ ]	[ ]
Nov 94.	(lp/cd) *(SALD 209/+CD)* <*33*> **THE ROARING THIRD** – Kick up yer heels / Carthage burns! / Hurry / 2 sisters / Precious / Cigarette day / Quits / Always almost there / Asiento / Irene / Seemed a brilliant idea.	[ ]	[ ] Oct93
		not iss.	**Carcrashh**
Apr 96.	(7") <*007*> **JIMJIMMYJIMJIM. / IGNITION**	[-]	[ ]

PRODIGY

Formed: Braintree, Essex, England . . . early 90's by LIAM HOWLETT together with MC MAXIM REALITY, LEEROY THORNHILL and KEITH FLINT. With their roots in hip hop, this irrepressible quartet of techno terrorists spread their first waves of discontent through the harder end of the rave scene, releasing the 'WHAT EVIL LURKS' EP in March '91 on the (then) fledgling 'XL' label. One track, the rave call to arms of 'EVERYBODY IN THE PLACE' would rocket to No.2 the following Christmas, hot on the heels of the PRODIGY's seminal debut hit (No.3), 'CHARLY'. A masterstroke of genius, HOWLETT sampled a veteran Government TV ad warning children off playing with fire (a recurring lyrical obsession) and welded it to fuck-off, hoover synths and a juggernaut breakbeat. The mixed result: proof that ravers had a sense of humour/irony and a string of low-rent imitations sampling everything from 'Sesame Street' to 'Rhubarb and Custard'. Borrowing from ARTHUR BROWN's hoary old chestnut of the same name, 'FIRE' gave the PRODIGY their third Top 20 hit in a row, closely followed by 'THE PRODIGY EXPERIENCE' (1992). More assured and inventive than most of the weak cash-in album's to come out of the 12" dominated rave scene, the record proffered alternate versions of the hits and killer new tracks like the brilliant breakbeat-skank, 'OUT OF SPACE'. By this point the group were also making waves with their formidable live show, still largely gracing raves yet a far cry from your average P.A. featuring a scantily clad diva miming to a 15-minute set. By 1993, HOWLETT was extending his horizons; a much in demand remixer, he worked on material for such diverse acts as DREAM FREQUENCY and FRONT 242 as well as poring over new PRODIGY tracks. The first of these, the wailing 'ONE LOVE' was initially realeased as a white label, apparently to keep in touch with their underground roots. The record still charted of course, going Top 10 in late '93 after a full release. 'NO GOOD START THE DANCE' was the sound of a group in transition, a speeded-up female vocal alternating with a thundering techno assault. The single made the Top 5 in Spring '94, but it was hardly representative of what lay in store on 'MUSIC FOR THE JILTED GENERATION' later that summer. Opening with a sinister tap-tapping typewriter and spoken word intro, then slamming into a dark, twisting techno groove, it was clear HOWLETT was no longer "luvved up". The album was breathtaking in its sweep, mapping out the future of techno, PRODIGY style, incorporating heavy riffing (on the two fingered salute to the Criminal Justice Bill, 'THEIR LAW', a collaboration with POP WILL EAT ITSELF), 70's style funky flute (the evocative '3 KILOS') and even a trio of tracks, 'THE NARCOTIC SUITE', climaxing the album in blistering form. Obvious highlights were the utterly compelling 'VOODOO PEOPLE' (riffs AND funky flute!; arguably The PRODIGY's finest moment to boot) and the military stomp of 'POISON' (complete with techno-gothic video; a must-see). The album was a UK No.1, establishing the band as major contenders who had far outstripped the narrow confines of 'dance', as was evidenced at their shows over the ensuing two years. White-gloved ravers blew their whistles hopefully, waiting in vain for 'CHARLY' or 'NO GOOD START THE DANCE', while more recent converts contorted and thrashed wildly to the new material (when, that is, they weren't threatening to shove the raver's eardrum-rupturing whistles where the sun doesn't shine!). By late '95/early '96, The PRODIGY were also showcasing new material at live gigs, including an incendiary little ditty entitled 'FIRESTARTER'. Primarily KEITH's baby, the 'song' was released as a single in Spring '96, giving The PRODIGY their first No.1. FLINT had, by now, fashioned his once flowing locks into a formidable luminous green mohican and had also developed a stage act that made IGGY POP (circa The STOOGES) look like a librarian. The fine, upstanding British public were subsequently treated to the new improved KEITH via the brilliant video (claustrophobically shot in the London Underground) on Top Of The Pops, resulting in an avalanche of complaints. Of course, the kids loved it, even toddlers were heard to garble 'I'm a twisted firestarter' while dragging their hapless mums into Woolies to bag a copy. As for the song itself, FLINT took a starring role, spitting out his demented cockney threats over depth charge beats. The next single, 'BREATHE', was even better, an ominous JOY DIVISION-esque guitar riff segueing into the hardest funkiest breakbeats this side of The CHEMICAL BROTHERS. Arguably the single of the year, the track raised expectations for the forthcoming PRODIGY opus to fever pitch. Almost inevitably, then, 'THE FAT OF THE LAND' (1997) was something of a letdown. There was nothing to match the dark majesty of 'BREATHE' (included on the album along with 'FIRESTARTER'), but there were plenty of other tracks to 'melt some brains' as HOWLETT put it. The insistent techno-hop of 'DIESEL POWER' (with KOOL KEITH guesting) attested to the group's love of hardcore rap, while the BEASTIE BOYS-sampling 'FUNKY SHIT' and MC MAXIM-led 'MINDFIELDS' were high-octane PRODIGY crowd pleasers. Minus points, however, for the dull collaboration with CRISPIAN MILLS (KULA SHAKER), 'NARAYAN' and the pointless cover of L7's 'FUEL MY FIRE'. Far more compelling was the insidiously funky 'CLIMBATIZE'. But it was the album's opener which had the nation's moral guardians and pro-women groups in a tizzy; whatever the inspiration for 'SMACK MY BITCH UP', The PRODIGY were as defiant and unapologetic as ever. Politics aside, the album may not have fully met expectations but it still trampled on the competition. Live, The PRODIGY remain a revelation, an electric maelstrom of colour and sound (and grimacing!), with an abiltiy to mobilise a crowd unmatched in the musical spectrum. In saying that, if they rely on punk cliches without pushing the boundaries of dance music – which is what they do best – they risk becoming a caricature of themselves.
• **Songwriters:** HOWLETT except samples of BABY D ('Casanova') on 'BREAK & ENTER', and KELLY CHARLES on 'YOU'RE NO GOOD FOR ME'. 'FULL THROTTLE' is also reminiscent of JOAN ARMATRADING's 'Me Myself I'.

Album rating: EXPERIENCE (*8) / MUSIC FOR THE JILTED GENERATION (*10) / THE FAT OF THE LAND (*7)

KEITH FLINT (b.17 Sep'69) – vocals, dancer / **LIAM HOWLETT** (b.21 Aug'71) – keyboards / **MC MAXIM REALITY** (b.KEITH PALMER, 21 Mar'67) – rapper-vox, dancer / **LEEROY THORNHILL** (b.7 Oct'69) – dancer, vocals

		X.L.	Elektra
Mar 91.	(12"ep) *(XLT 17)* **WHAT EVIL LURKS / WE GONNA ROCK. / ANDROID / EVERYBODY IN THE PLACE**	[ ]	[-]
Aug 91.	(7"/c-s) *(XLS/XLC 21)* <*66411*> **CHARLY. / CHARLY (original mix)** (12"+=/cd-s+=) *(XLT/CDXLS 21)* – Pandemonium / Your love.	[3]	[ ]
Dec 91.	(7"/c-s) *(XLS/XLC 26)* **EVERYBODY IN THE PLACE. / G-FORCE (ENERGY FLOW)** (12"+=) *(XLT 26)* – Crazy man / Rip up the sound system. (cd-s++=) *(XLS 26CD)* – ('A'remix).	[2]	[-]
Sep 92.	(7"/c-s) *(XLS/XLC 30)* <*66370*> **FIRE. / JERICHO (original mix)** (12"+=/cd-s+=) *(XLT/XLS 30CD)* – Fire (sunrise version) / Jericho (genaside II remix).	[11]	[ ]
Oct 92.	(cd/c/lp) *(XLCD/XLMC/XLLP 110)* <*61365*> **EXPERIENCE** – Jericho / Music reach (1/2/3/4) / Wind it up / Your love (remix) / Hyperspeed (G-Force part 2) / Charly (trip into drum and bass version) / Out of space / Everybody in the place (155 and rising) / Weather experience / Fire (sunrise version) / Ruff in the jungle bizness / Death of the Prodigy dancers (live).	[12]	[ ]
Nov 92.	(7"/c-s) *(XLS/XLC 35)* <*66346*> **OUT OF SPACE (remix). / RUFF IN THE JUNGLE BIZNESS (uplifting vibes remix)** (12"+=)(cd-s+=) *(XLT/XLS 35CD)* – ('A'techno underworld remix) / Music reach (1,2,3,4) (live).	[5]	[ ] Dec92
Apr 93.	(7"/c-s) *(XLS/XLC 39)* <*66319*> **WIND IT UP (REWOUND). / WE ARE THE RUFFEST** (12"+=) *(XLT 39)* – Weather experience (remix). (cd-s++=) *(XLS 39CD)* – ('A'edit).	[7]	[ ]
Oct 93.	(c-ep/12"ep/cd-ep) *(XLC/XLT/XLS 47CD)* **ONE LOVE / RHYTHM OF LIFE (original mix). / FULL THROTTLE (original mix) / ONE LOVE (Jonny L remix)**	[8]	[-]
May 94.	(12"/c-s) *(XLT/XLC 51)* **NO GOOD (START THE DANCE) / NO GOOD (bad for you mix) / NO GOOD (CJ Bolland's museum mix)** (cd-s+=) *(XLS 51CD)* – No Good (original mix).	[4]	[-]

—— below album with **PHIL BENT** – flute / **LANCE RIDDLER** – guitar

		X.L.	Mute
Jul 94.	(cd/c/d-lp) *(XLCD/XLMC/XLLP 114)* <*55642*> **MUSIC FOR THE JILTED GENERATION** – Intro / Break & enter / Their law (featuring POP WILL EAT ITSELF) / Full throttle / Voodoo people / Speedway (theme from 'Fastlane') / The heat (the energy) / Poison / No good (start the dance) / One love (edit) – The narcotic suite / 3 kilos / Skylined / Claustrophobic sting.	[1]	[ ] Mar95
Sep 94.	(12"ep) *(XLT 54)* <*67007*> **VOODOO PEOPLE (original mix) / VOODOO PEOPLE (Dust Brothers remix). / VOODOO PEOPLE (Haiti Island mix) / GOA (THE HEAT, THE ENERGY PART 2)** (cd-ep) *(XLS 54CD)* – (3rd track repl.by) ('A'edit).	[13]	[ ]
Mar 95.	(c-s) *(XLC 58)* **POISON ('95) / ('A'-Rat Poison mix) / SCIENIDE** (12"+=/cd-s+=) *(XLT/XLS 58CD)* – ('A'-Environmental science dub mix).	[15]	[ ]
		X.L.	**Geffen**
Mar 96.	(c-s) *(XLC 70)* <*17387*> **FIRESTARTER / MOLOTIV BITCH** (12"+=/cd-s+=) *(XLT/XLS 70CD)* – ('A'-Empiron mix) / ('A'instrumental).	[1]	[30] Jan97

—— All singles re-issued Apr96 hitting UK Top 75.

Nov 96.	(c-ep/12"ep) *(XLC/XLT 80)* **BREATHE / THEIR LAW featuring PWEI (live at Phoenix fesival '96). / POISON (live at the Tourhout & Werchter festival '96)** (cd-ep+=) *(XLS 80CD)* – The trick.	[1]	[ ]
Jul 97.	(cd/c/lp) *(XL CD/MC/LP 121)* <*46606*> **THE FAT OF THE LAND** – Smack my bitch up / Breathe / Diesel power / Funky shit / Serial thrilla / Mindfields / Narayan / Firestarter / Climbatize / Fuel my fire.	[1]	[1]
Nov 97.	(12"/c-s) *(XLT/XLC 90)* <*43946*> **SMACK MY BITCH UP. / NO MAN ARMY** (cd-s+=) *(XLS 90CD)* – Minefields (heavy rock dub) / ('A'-DJ Hype remix).	[8]	[89]

PROFESSIONALS (see under ⇒ SEX PISTOLS)

PROLAPSE

Formed: Leicester, England . . . 1991 by Scotsman MICK DERRICK and LINDA STEELYARD, who soon expanded the unit to a sextet/septet with the addition of DAVE JEFFREYS, PAT MARSDEN, DONALD ROSS-SKINNER, MICK HARRISON and TIM PATTISON. Having met during a drinking binge, the band played some initial shows in Hanover (or is it hangover?!), Germany, before signing to 'Cherry Red' and debuting with a JOHN ROBB-produced EP, 'CRATE' early in '94. An album, 'POINTLESS WALKS TO DISMAL PLACES', followed later in the year, a THROBBING GRISTLE/NME C-86! industrial guitar-mangling hybrid. In 1997, after tours supporting PULP and STEREOLAB, PROLAPSE signed to Warner Brothers affiliated label, 'Radarscope', offering up their most accessible noisefest to date, 'ITALIAN FLAG'.

Album rating: ITALIAN FLAG (*6)

MICK DERRICK – vocals / **LINDA STEELYARD** – vocals / **DAVE JEFFREYS** – guitar / **PAT MARSDEN** – guitar / **DONALD ROSS-SKINNER** – keyboards / **MICK HARRISON** – bass / **TIM PATTISON** – drums

Cherry Red | not iss.

Jan 94. (7"ep) *(CHERRY 128)* **THE PROLAPSE 'CRATE' EP** [ ] [-]
– Psychotic now / etc.

Sep 94. (7") *(CHERRY 135)* **DOORSTEP RHYTHMIC BLOC. / PILE TENT** [ ] [-]
(cd-s+=) *(CDCHERRY 135)* – Muscovite parricide song / ('A'mix).

Oct 94. (cd) *(CDBRED 116)* **POINTLESS WALKS TO DISMAL PLACES** [ ] [-]
– Serpico (theme) / Headless in a beat motel / Surreal Madrid / Doorstep rhythmic bioc / Burgundy spine / Black death ambulance / Chili blown / Hungarian suicide song / Tina this is Matthew Stone.

Love Train | not iss.

Oct 95. (7") *(PUBE 06)* **TCR. / IRRITATING RADIATOR** [ ] [-]

Lissy's | Big Cat

Dec 95. (lp/cd) *(LISS 8/+CD)* *<1>* **BACK SATURDAY** [ ] [ ] Apr96
– Mein minefield, mine landmind / TCR / Framen Fr. Cesar / Every night I'm mentally crucified / Zen nun deb / Irritating radiator / Drown radio therapy / Flex / Strain contortion of bag.

1996. (7") *(LISS 17)* **FLEXED. / UNROADKILL** [ ] [-]

Radarscope | Radarscope

Apr 97. (7") *(SCAN 24)* **SNAPPY HORSE. / FEAR OF TEETH** [ ] [-]
(cd-s+=) *(SCANCD 24)* – Killing the bland.

Sep 97. (7") *(SCAN 26)* **AUTOCADE. /** [ ] [-]
(7") *(SCAN 26X)* –
(cd-s+=) *(SCANCD 26)* –

Oct 97. (cd/d-lp) *(<SCAN CD/LP 25>)* **ITALIAN FLAG** [ ] [ ]
– Slash / Deanshanger / Cacophony No.A / Killing the bland / I hate the clicking man / Autocade / Tunguska / Flat velocity curve / Return of shoes / Day at death seaside / Bruxelles / Visa for Violet and Van / Three wooden heads.

PROPAGANDA

Formed: Dusseldorf, Germany . . . 1983 by RALF DORPER alongside MICHAEL MERTENS, SUSANNE FREYTAG, ANDREAS THEIN and frontwoman CLAUDIA BRUCKEN. Signed to Paul Morley & Trevor Horn's 'ZTT' label and with added promotion from Channel 4's 'The Tube', their debut single 'DR. MABUSE', cracked the UK Top 30 in 1984. A rhythmic and heavily synthesized outfit initially influenced by KRAFTWERK and The HUMAN LEAGUE, PROPAGANDA were a consummate product of the era and follow-up single, 'DUEL', remains one of the finest and most evocative examples of 80's Europop. Dripping with the continental sensuality of BRUCKEN's voice and boasting a killer melody to boot, the track was a near-Top 20 hit and one of the many highlights of their one and only bonafide album, 'A SECRET WISH' (1985). Despite critical acclaim the album failed to take off on the quite the same scale as expected and a bitter battle between band and label ensued, prompting successive personnel shuffles on the subsequent tour as various members bailed out (DORPER had withdrawn before it had even begun). Inevitably the band split in late '86 amid the ongoing legal dispute, BRUCKEN marrying MORLEY and recording a one-off single with HEAVEN 17's GLENN GREGORY and forming ACT with THOMAS LEER. A modified PROPAGANDA re-emerged in 1990 with American frontwoman, BETSY MILLER, recording a sole, low-key album on 'Virgin', '1234'. • **Songwriters:** DORPER composed except covers; DISCIPLINE (Throbbing Gristle) / SORRY FOR LAUGHING (Josef K) / FEMME FATALE (Velvet Underground). • **Trivia:** The track DREAM WITHIN A DREAM contained a poem by Edgar Allan Poe.

Album rating: A SECRET WISH (*7) / 1234 (*5)

RALF DORPER

Operation Twilight | not iss.

Nov 82. (12"ep) *(OPT 018)* **RALF DORPER'S ERASERHEAD** [ ] [-]
– Dizziplin / Assault / Lorelia.

PROPAGANDA

RALF DORPER (b.11 Jan'60) – instruments / **MICHAEL MERTENS** (b.23 Oct'63) – keyboards, synth (ex-DUSSELDORF SYMPHONY) / **SUSANNE FREYTAG** – synthesizers, vocals / **CLAUDIA BRUCKEN** (b.12 Dec'63) – vocals (ex-TOPPOLINOS) / with **ANDREAS THEIN** – tapes

ZTT-Island | Island

Mar 84. (7") *(ZTAS 2)* **DR.MABUSE. / DR.MABUSE DER SPIELER (instrumental)** [27] [ ]
(12") *(12ZTAS 2)* – Das testaments des Mabuse / Femme fatale (the woman with the orchid) / The 9th life (of Dr.Mabuse).
(12") *(12ZTAS 2)* – Das testaments des Mabuse (the third side) / Femme fatale (the woman with the orchid) the fourth side.
(c-s) *(CTIS 101)* – Das testaments des Mabuse / The last word / Dr. Mabuse.

—— Now a quartet when ANDREAS departed

Apr 85. (7"sha-pic-d) *(ZTAS 8)* **DUEL. / JEWEL** [21] [ ]
(d7"+=) *(DUAL 1)* – Lied / The lesson.
(12") *(12ZTAS 8)* – Duel (bittersweet) / Jewel (cut rough).
(some copies with free 12") *(12ZTAS 2)* – Dr.Mabuse
(c-ep) *(CTIS 108)* – DO WELL:- The first cut / Duel / Jewel (cut rough) / Wonder / Bejewelled.

Jul 85. (lp/c)(cd) *(ZTTIQ/ZCIQ 3)(CID 126)* *<842496>* **A SECRET WISH** [16] [ ]
– Dream within a dream / The murder of love / Duel / P-machinery / Sorry for laughing / Dr. Mabuse (first life) / The chase / The last word / Strength to dream. *(cd+=)* – Frozen faces. *(re-iss. May94 on 'ZTT-Warners' cd/c; 450994749-2/-4)*

Aug 85. (7"clear/7") *(P+/ZTAS 12)* **P-MACHINERY. / FROZEN FACES** [50] [-]
('A'-Polish version 12"clear+=) *(12PZTAS 12)* – ('A'-Passive).
('A'-Beta version 12"+=) *(12ZZTAS 12)* – Complete machinery.
(d12"++=) *(12ZZTAST 12)* – (above two 12").
(c-ep) *(CTIS 12)* – COMPLETE MACHINERY:- Introduction / P-Machinery (connected) / P-Machinery (seperation) / Frozen faces.
(also issued in Dec85; ZTAS 21 / 12ZTAS 21 with free 12ZTAS 8)

Nov 85. (m-lp/m-c) *(ZTTIQ/CZAS 20)* **WISHFUL THINKING** (DISTURBED DANCE remixes) [82] [-]
– Abused / Machined / Laughed / Loving / Jewelled / Loved / Abuse / Thought. *(re-iss. May94 on 'ZTT-Warners' cd/c; 450994748-2/-4)*

—— split late 1986 when CLAUDIA married ZTT boss Paul Morley. She made one-off single with GLENN GREGORY (of HEAVEN 17) before forming ACT with soloist THOMAS LEER. **PROPAGANDA** re-formed in 1989 with **DORPER** bringing in **BETSY MILLER** – vocals / **DEREK FORBES** – bass (ex-SIMPLE MINDS)

Virgin | Charisma

Apr 90. (7"/c-s) *(VS/+C 1245)* **HEAVEN GIVE ME WORDS. / COUNT ZERO** [36] [-]
(12"+=/cd-s+=) *(VST/VSCDT 1245)* – ('A'-Money In Heaven version).
(cd-s+=) *(VSCDX 1245)* – ('A'-Doppelganger mix).

May 90. (cd/c/lp) *(CD/TC+/V 2625)* *<91375-2/-4/-1>* **1234** [46] [ ]
– Vicious circle / Heaven give me words / Your wildlife / Only one word / How much love / Vicious (reprise) / Ministry of fear / Wound in my heart / La carne, la morte e il diavolo. *(re-iss. Apr92 lp/c; OVED/+C 433)*

Aug 90. (7"/c-s) *(VS/+C 1271)* **ONLY ONE WORD. / LA CARTE, LA MORTE E IL DIAVOLO** [71] [-]
(12"+=/cd-s+=) *(VST/VSCDT 1271)* – ('A'extended).

—— split after above. In mid'96, BRUCKEN, featured on The BRAIN's 'Interpop' single, 'I'll Find A Way'. PROPAGANDA were back in '98

E.M.I. | E.M.I.

Jun 98. (cd) *(<87467>)* **PROPAGANDA** [ ] [ ]

– compilations, etc. –

Jul 95. (c-s/12"/cd-s) *Seven; (SEVE 04 C/T/CD)* **P-MACHINERY (mixes)** [ ] [-]

PSYCHEDELIC FURS

Formed: London, England . . . 1977 by RICHARD and TIM BUTLER, JOHN ASHTON, ROGER MORRIS and DUNCAN KILBURN, who eventually completed the line-up with drummer VINCE ELY. Gaining a bit of much needed credibilty via a Radio One John Peel session, the band signed to 'Epic-C.B.S.' in 1978 and released a debut single, 'WE LOVE YOU', late the following year. This was followed in early 1980 by a classic second single, 'SISTER EUROPE' and a Top 20 eponymous debut album. A vintage slice of post-punk miserabilism tracing the classic linage of VELVET UNDERGROUND, ROXY MUSIC, ~'BOWIE etc., the record's dischordant mesh of jagged melody, inwardly spiralling guitar and BUTLER's cracked monotone placed The PSYCHEDELIC FURS firmly at the forefront of the alternative rock scene. Subsequently relocating to New York, they worked on an even better follow-up, 'TALK TALK TALK' (1981), a record which might've made more concessions to pop/rock convention but made up for it with gloriously subversive songwriting; 'INTO YOU LIKE A TRAIN' was leeringly self explanatory, 'DUMB WAITERS' tripped out on a mangled STOOGES vibe while the lugubrious 'PRETTY IN PINK' provided the 'FURS with a near-Top 40 hit and remains their best known track. With ex-BIRTHDAY PARTY man, PHIL CALVERT, replacing ELY (who teamed up with ROBYN HITCHCOCK), the band hooked up with TODD RUNDGREN for the disappointing 'FOREVER NOW' (1982), a combination that looked intersting on paper but somehow failed to translate on vinyl. The record nevertheless made the UK Top 20, as did 1984's 'MIRROR MOVES', by which time line-up changes had seen KEITH FORSEY and MARS WILLIAMS replace CALVERT and founding members KILBURN and MORRIS. Despite flashes of darkly melodic inspiration, a suffocatingly slick production erased any traces of mystery or danger, further testing the patience of many longtime fans. A re-released 'PRETTY IN PINK' (issued to coincide with the film of the same name, inspired by the song itself) illustrated just how lifeless the newer material was, while the terminally dull 'MIDNIGHT TO MIDNIGHT' (1987) showed no signs of an imminent return to form. With ELY back on the drum stool, a further late 80's effort, 'BOOK OF DAYS' (1989), attempted a more credible approach to diminishing commercial returns and minimal critical reaction. Finally, after 1991's 'WORLD OUTSIDE', the band hung up their 'FURS for good, BUTLER going on to form LOVE SPIT LOVE with RICHARD FORTUS and FRANK FERRER, releasing a one-off eponymous album for 'Imago-R.C.A.' in 1994. • **Songwriters:** RICHARD BUTLER + FURS, except MACK THE KNIFE (Bobby Darin).

Album rating: THE PSYCHEDELIC FURS (*8) / TALK TALK TALK (*8) / FOREVER NOW (*7) / ALL OF THIS AND NOTHING compilation (*7)

RICHARD BUTLER (b. 5 Jun'56, Kingston-Upon-Thames, England) – vocals / **JOHN ASHTON** (b.30 Nov'57) – lead guitar / **ROGER MORRIS** – guitar / **TIM BUTLER** (b. 7 Dec'58) – bass / **DUNCAN KILBURN** – saxophone, keyboards / **VINCE ELY** – drums (ex-UNWANTED)

Epic | not iss.

Oct 79. (7") *(EPC 8005)* **WE LOVE YOU. / PULSE** [ ] [-]

C.B.S. | Columbia

Feb 80. (7") *(CBS 8179)* **SISTER EUROPE. / ****** [ ] [ ]
Mar 80. (lp/c) *(CBS/40 84084) <36791>* **THE PSYCHEDELIC FURS** [18] [ ]
– India / Sister Europe / Imitation of Christ / Fall / Pulse / We love you / Wedding song / Blacks / Radio / Flowers. *(re-iss. Mar83) (cd-iss. Apr89)*
Oct 80. (7") *(CBS 9059)* **MR. JONES. / SUSAN'S STRANGE** [ ] [ ]
Apr 81. (7") *(A 1166)* **DUMB WAITERS. / DASH** [59] [ ]
May 81. (lp/c) *(CBS/40 84892) <37339>* **TALK TALK TALK** [30] [89]
– Dumb waiters / Pretty in pink / I wanna sleep with you / No tears / Mr. Jones / Into you like a train / It goes on / So run down / All of this and nothing / She is mine. *(re-iss. Nov84 lp/c; CBS/40 32539) (cd-iss. Apr89; CD 32539) (cd re-iss. Mar96 on 'Columbia'; 483663-2)*
Jun 81. (7"/7"pic-d) *(A/WA 1327)* **PRETTY IN PINK. / MACK THE KNIFE** [43] [ ]
(12"+=) *(A13 1327)* – Soap commercial.

— **PHIL CALVERT** – drums (ex-BIRTHDAY PARTY) repl. ELY (to ROBYN HITCHCOCK)

Jul 82. (7") *(A 2549) <03197>* **LOVE MY WAY. / AEROPLANE (dance mix)** [42] [ ]
Sep 82. (lp/c) *(CBS/40 85909) <38261>* **FOREVER NOW** [20] [61]
– Love my way / President Gas / Sleep comes down / Forever now / Danger / You and I / Run and run / Merry-go-round / Goodbye / No easy street. *(c+=)* – Shadow. *(re-iss. Apr86 lp/c; CBS/40 85909)*
Oct 82. (7") *(A 2665) <03340>* **DANGER. / (I DON'T WANT TO BE YOUR) SHADOW** [ ] [ ]
(12"+=) *(TA 2665)* – Goodbye (mix).
Feb 83. (7") *<03340>* **LOVE MY WAY. / SHADOW** [-] [44]
May 83. (7") *<03930>* **PRESIDENT GAS. / RUN AND RUN** [-] [ ]

— **KEITH FORSEY** – drums repl. CALVERT who joined CRIME & THE CITY SOLUTION / **MARS WILLIAMS** – saxophone (ex-WAITRESSES) repl. KILBURN + MORRIS

Mar 84. (7"/12") *(A/TA 4300)* **HEAVEN. / HEARTBEAT (remix)** [29] [-]
May 84. (lp/c) *(CBS/40 25950) <39278>* **MIRROR MOVES** [15] [43]
– The ghost in you / Here come cowboys / Heaven / Heartbeat / My time / Like a stranger / Alice's house / Only a game / Highwire days. *(re-iss. Jan87 lp/c; 450356-1/-4) (cd-iss. May87; CD 25950) (re-iss. Jun94 on 'Columbia' cd/c; 450356-2/-4)*
May 84. (7"/7"pic-d) *(A/WA 4470) <04416>* **THE GHOST IN YOU. / CALYPSO DUB** [68] [59]
(12"+=) *(TA 4470)* – President Gas (live).
Jul 84. (7") *<04577>* **HERE COME COWBOYS. / ANOTHER EDGE** [-] [ ]
Sep 84. (7") *<04627>* **HEAVEN. / ALICE'S HOUSE** [-] [ ]
Oct 84. (7"/12") *(A/TA 4654)* **HEARTBEAT (Mendelssohn mix). / MY TIME** [ ] [-]
(d7"+=) *(DA 4654)* – Here comes cowboys / Heaven.

— **PAUL GARISTO** – drums repl. DORSEY. <below 45 on 'A&M' US>

Apr 86. (7") *<2826>* **PRETTY IN PINK. / (dub)** [-] [41]
Aug 86. (7"/7"pic-d) *(A/WA 7242)* **PRETTY IN PINK (film version). / LOVE MY WAY** [18] [-]
(12"+=) *(TA 7242)* – ('A'version).
(d7"+=) *(DA 7242)* – Heaven / Heartbeat.
Oct 86. (7") *(650183-7) <06420>* **HEARTBREAK BEAT. / NEW DREAM** [ ] [26] Mar87
(12"+=) *(650186-6)* – ('A'version).
(free c-s w/7"+=) *(650183-0)* – Sister Europe / Into you like a train / President Gas.
Jan 87. (7") *(FURS 3)* **ANGELS DON'T CRY. / NO RELEASE** [ ] [ ]
(free c-s w/7"+=) *(FURSD 3)* – We love you / Pretty in pink / Love my way.
Feb 87. (lp/c/cd) *(450256-1/-4/-2) <40466>* **MIDNIGHT TO MIDNIGHT** [12] [29]
– Heartbreak beat / Shock / Shadow in my heart / Angels don't cry / Midnight to midnight / One more word / Torture / All of the law / No release * / Petty in pink. *(cd+= *) (re-iss. Feb89 lp/c/cd; 463399-1/-4/-2)*
Apr 87. (7") *<07224>* **SHOCK. / PRESIDENT GAS (live)** [-] [ ]
Jun 87. (7") **ANGEL'S DON'T CRY. / MACK THE KNIFE** [-] [ ]

— **VINCE ELY** – drums returned to repl. GARISTO (to CURE) + WILLIAMS

Jul 88. (7") *(FURS 4) <07974>* **ALL THAT MONEY WANTS. / BIRDLAND** [75] [ ]
(12"+=) *(FURST 4)* – No easy street (live).
(d7"++=) *(FURSEP 4)* – Heaven (live).
(cd-s++=) *(CDFURS 4)* – No tears (live).
Aug 88. (lp/c/cd) *(461110-1/-4/-2) <44377>* **ALL OF THIS AND NOTHING** (compilation) [67] [ ]
– President Gas / All that money wants / Imitation of Christ / Sister Europe / Love my way / Highwire days / Dumb waiters / Pretty in pink / Ghost in you / Heaven / Heartbreak beat / All of this and nothing. *(cd+=)* – No easy street / She is mine. *(re-iss. Apr91 cd/c; 461110-2)*
Nov 88. (7") *<38-08499>* **HEAVEN. / INDIA** [-] [ ]
Nov 89. (lp/c/cd) *(465982-1/-4/-2) <45412>* **BOOK OF DAYS** [74] [ ]
– Entertain me / Book of days / Should God forget / Torch / Parade / Mother-son / House / Wedding / I don't mine.
Jan 90. (7"/7"pic-d) *(FURS/+P 5)* **HOUSE. / WATCHTOWER** [ ] [-]
(10") *(FURSQT 5)* – ('A'side) / ('A'-Flashback mix) / Badman / Totch (electric).
(cd-s+=) *(CDFURS 5)* – Badman / Torch (electric).

— **BUTLER, ASHTON + BUTLER** recruited **DON YALLITCH** – drums repl. ELY

East West | Epic

Jun 91. (7"/c-s) *(73855)* **UNTIL SHE COMES. / MAKE IT MINE** [ ] [-]
(12"+=/cd-s+=) *(73855)* – Sometimes / ('A'remix).
Jul 91. (c-s,cd-s) *<74055>* **UNTIL SHE COMES / SOMETIMES** [-] [ ]
Jul 91. (cd)(lp/c) *(9031 74669-2)(WX 422/+C) <74669>* **WORLD OUTSIDE** [68] [ ]
– Valentine / In my head / Until she comes / Don't be a girl / Sometimes / Tearing down / There's a world / Get a room / Better days / All about you. *(re-iss. cd Feb95; same)*
Sep 91. (7"/c-s) **DON'T BE A GIRL. / GET A ROOM (acoustic)** [ ] [ ]
(12"+=/cd-s+=) – (2 'A'versions).

— disbanded after above

– compilations, etc. –

on 'C.B.S.' unless mentioned otherwise

Nov 82. (c-ep) *(A 2909)* **GREATEST ORIGINAL HITS** [ ] [-]
– Sister Europe / Pretty in pink / Dumb waiters / Love my way. *(re-iss. Mar83.as 7"ep.)*
Sep 86. (c-ep) *(450130-4)* **THE 12" TAPE** [ ] [-]
– Pretty in pink / Love my way / Heaven / Heartbeat / Ghost in you.
Jan 92. (7") **PRETTY IN PINK. / (B-side by the Only Ones)** [ ] [-]
(cd-s+=) – (other track by Only Ones).
Oct 91. (cd) *Castle; (CCSCD 308)* **THE COLLECTION** [ ] [-]
May 95. (cd) *Columbia; (480363-2) <57889>* **B SIDES AND LOST GROOVES** [ ] [ ] Oct94
Feb 97. (cd) *Strange Fruit; (SFRSCD 003)* **RADIO ONE SESSIONS** [ ] [-]

LOVE SPIT LOVE

RICHARD BUTLER – vocals / **RICHARD FORTUS** – guitar / **TIM BUTLER** – bass / **FRANK FERRER** – drums

Imago-RCA | Imago-RCA

Oct 94. (cd/c) *(72787 21055-2/-4) <21030>* **LOVE SPIT LOVE** [ ] [ ]
– Seventeen / Superman / Half a life / Jigsaw / Change in the weather / Wake up / Am I wrong / Green / Please / Codeine / St. Mary's gate / More.
Oct 94. (c-s,cd-s) *<25073>* **AM I WRONG / CODEINE** [-] [83]

PSYCHED UP JANIS

Formed: Copenhagen, Denmark . . . late 1989 by Sonderborg-raised SUNE and JAKOB. They relocated to Brighton, England after being signed up by producer, Craig Leon, the man obviously impressed to see them carrying on after the ceiling caved in at a Copenhagen gig in 1994. By this time, the trio (who had added drummer, MARTIN) had already released their self-financed Scandinavian-only debut EP, 'I DIED IN MY TEENS', a trippy sonic-country affair with similarities to HOLE, although lyrically way out. They had also signed to Swedish label, 'Metrognome-Replay', which released their LEON-produced debut album, 'SWELL', its worldwide critical success prompting a UK deal in 1995 with Island off-shoot, 'This Way Up'. The band made their British debut with the 'VANITY' EP early the following year, previewing the re-release of both the single, 'I DIED IN MY TEENS' and album 'SWELL'.

Album rating: SWELL (*7)

SUNE – vocals, guitar / **JAKOB** – bass / **MARTIN** – drums

This Way Up | not iss.

Jan 96. (10"ep/cd-ep) *(WAY 4688/4633)* **VANITY EP** [ ] [-]
– Vanity / Modest us / Punk song (live) / Flabbergaster (live).
Mar 96. (7") *(WAY 4711)* **I DIED IN MY TEENS. / SHOOT THE BREEZE** [ ] [-]
(cd-s+=) *(WAY 4733)* – Dense high.
Mar 96. (cd/c/d-lp) *(532031-2/-4/-1)* **SWELL** [ ] [-]
– Vanity / I died in my teens / Shudder / Modest us / Subsonic why / Swirl like you / Chandelier / Dead green summer / Reddening star / New 5 / They / Fragments.

— (all above issued on Swedish 'Metrognome-Replay' a few years earlier)

PSYCHIC TV

Formed: London, England . . . 1982 from the ashes of THROBBING GRISTLE by NEIL MEGSON aka GENESIS P.ORRIDGE and PETER CHRISTOPHERSON. The latter soon departed to form COIL and P.ORRIDGE susbsequently steered PSYCHIC TV through its various incarnations over the course of the 80's and into the 90's. Drawing inspiration from situationist media manipulation, the cut-up technique of William Burroughs, the magick theories of Alistair Crowley and pagan/shamanistic ritual, P.ORRIDGE plotted a determinedly subversive path through what he perceived as a dysfunctional society controlled by "the managers" and organised religion. Throughout their weird and wonderful career PSYCHIC TV have been backed by the Temple Ov Psychick Youth (TOPY), a cult-style band of followers who take the P.ORRIDGE philosophy as gospel. Musically, PSYCHIC TV's early work – as heard on albums such as 'FORCE THE HAND OF CHANCE' (1982), 'DREAMS LESS SWEET' (1983) and 'THEMES' (1985) – carried on where THROBBING GRISTLE left off with an often barely listenable sonic barrage of scraping noise, jackboot rhythms and assorted disturbing samples ranging from guttural growls to the utterances of P.ORRIDGE favourites like Charles Manson and Crowley. The mid-80's proved a turning point, however, as PTV became more immersed in psychedelic culture and unveiled their own take on the movement which they dubbed 'Hyperdelic'. 1986 also saw PTV score an unlikely minor UK hit with their most accessible (and surprisingly affecting) recording to date, 'GODSTAR', a tribute to long time gone ROLLING STONES founder BRIAN JONES (another P.ORRIDGE obsession) which rather niftily cut-up the riff from 'Brown Sugar'. The 60's/rejuvenated psychedelia theme continued with the 'MAGICKAL MYSTERY D TOUR' EP, featuring a faithful, if rather droning cover of The Beach Boys' 'GOOD VIBRATIONS'. 1986 also saw the initiation of an ambitious project to release 23 different live albums from 23 different countries on the 23rd of each month (!), 23 apparently being a magickal number. P.ORRIDGE's interest in consciousness altering substances and their ability to transform society deepened with the advent of rave culture, a visit to Chicago inspiring a series of acid-house singles subsequently collected together as 1990's 'HIGH JACK: THE POLITICS OF ECSTASY'. Much like The SHAMAN, PSYCHIC TV espoused the transformational possibilities inherent in club culture and following PSYCHIC TV's exile to California, P.ORRIDGE found a natural home in the sunshine state's consciousness altering community and a natural collaborator in veteran acid guru TIMOTHY LEARY. The forced exile came in 1992 following a police raid on The Temple Ov Psychick Youth's Hackney base, officers confiscating videos, books and magazines after a clip from a P.ORRIDGE performance was screened as part of a TV documentary on child abuse; on holiday in Nepal at the time, P.ORRIDGE and his partner were warned they could face arrest and lose custody of their daughters should they return to the UK. Unsurprisingly they decamped to the more liberal climes of Cali. Intrigued readers are pointed towards the 1995 video, 'Beauty From Thee Beast', as an entertaining introduction to PTV, the songs interspersed with clips of P.ORRIDGE dispensing his eco-shaman-evolutionary philosophy.

Album rating: FORCE THE HAND OF CHANCE (*6) / DREAMS LESS SWEET (*5) / MOUTH OF THE NIGHT (*5) / THEMES II (*5) / BEAUTY FROM THEE BEAST compilation (*6)

GENESIS P.ORRIDGE (b. Feb'49) – vocals, keyboards, violin, bass, percussion (ex-THROBBING GRISTLE) / **PETER 'SLEAZY' CHRISTOPHERSON** – organ, synthesizer, vocals (ex-THROBBING GRISTLE) / **ALEX FERGUSSON** – guitar, vocals (ex-ALTERNATIVE TV) / with guests **KENNY WELLINGTON + CLAUDE DEPPA** – brass / **ANDREW POPPY** – strings / **MARC ALMOND** – vocals

Some Bizzare / not iss.

Dec 82. (lp) *(PSY 1)* **FORCE THE HAND OF CHANCE** [ ] [-]
– Just drifting / Terminus / Stolen kisses / Caresse / Guiltless / No go go / Ov power / Message from the temple. *(with free lp)* – THEMES:- The full pack / The mad organist / Catalan. *(<cd-iss. Jan97 on 'Cleopatra'; CLEO 9595-2>) (cd rom-iss.Nov97; SBZ 026CD)*
Dec 82. (7") *(PTV 1)* **JUST DRIFTING. / BREAKTHROUGH** [ ] [-]
(12") *(PTV 1T)* – ('A'side) / Just drifting (midnight).

— added **PAULA P.ORRIDGE** – drums, vibes / **GEOFF RUSHTON** – bass, vibes / + a cast of extra musicians & singers

C.B.S. / not iss.

Dec 83. (d-lp/c) *(CBS/40 25737)* **DREAMS LESS SWEET** [ ] [-]
– Hymn 23 / The orchids / Botanica / Glove / Iron / Always is always / White nights / Finale / Eleusis / Medmenham / Ancient lights / Proof on / Survival / Eden 1 / Eden 2 / Eden 3 / Clouds without water / Black moon / Silver and gold / In the nursery / Circle. *(cd-iss. Aug92 on 'Some Bizzare'; SBZCD 011) <US cd-iss. 1196 on 'Thirsty Ear'; 57021>*

— **BEE** – bass, vocals (ex-GETTING THE FEAR) repl. PETER who formed COIL / added **JORDI VALLIS** (JOHN GOSLING – ex-ZOS KIA, also a member at this time)

Sordid Sentimentale / not iss.

Jun 84. (7") *(SS33 000)* **ROMAN P. / TOPY: NEUROLOGY** [-] [-] French

Temple / Wax Trax

Aug 84. (12") *(TOPY 001)* **UNCLEAN. / MIRRORS** [ ] [-]
Dec 84. (ltd-lp) *(TOPY 002)* **NEW YORK SCUM HATERS** [ ] [-]
Dec 84. (pic-lp; deleted on next of release) *(TOPY 003)* **A PAGAN DAY – 25TH DECEMBER 1984** [ ] [-]
– Catalogue / W kiss / Opium / Cold steel / Los Angeles / Iceland / Translucent carriages / Paris / Baby's gone away / Alice / New sexuality / Farewell. *(black-lp re-iss. Mar87; TOPY 017) (cd-iss. Jul94 on 'Cleopatra'; CLEO 9469-2)*

— **MONTE CZAZZA** – guitar / **HILMAR ORN HILMARSSON** – keyboards / **MAX** – drums; repl. BEE + JORDI

Jul 85. (lp) *(TOPY 004)* **THEMES II** [ ] [-]
Sep 85. (lp) *(TOPY 008)* **THEMES 3** [ ] [-]
(re-iss. Feb87; TOPY 019)
Nov 85. (lp/c) *(TOPY/+C 010)* **MOUTH OF THE NIGHT** [ ] [-]
– Dawn / Ordeal of innocence / The wedding / Rebis / Separation and undressing / Discopravity / The immune zone / Climax. *(pic-lp; TOPIC 010) (cd-iss. Nov89; TOPY 034CD) (cd re-iss. Nov93 on 'Trident'; VAULT 23)*

— **PHILIP EBB** – keyboards / **MOUSE** – bass / **MATTHEW BEST** – drums; repl. recent three above

Mar 86. (7"; as PSYCHIC TV & The ANGELS OF LIGHT) *(TOPY 009)* **GODSTAR. / ('A'-BJ mix)** [67] [-]
(d7"+=) *(TOPYS 009)* – Discopravity (fish mix) / Yes it's the B side.
(12"/12"pic-d) *(TOPYH/TOPIC 009)* – ('A'-Hyperdelic mix) / ('A'-California mix).

— **GENESIS, PAULA + MATTHEW** recruited **SCOTT** – guitar / **DAVE TIBET** – bass (ex-23 SKIDOO); to repl. FERGUSSON

Sep 86. (7") *(TOPY 023)* **GOOD VIBRATIONS. / ROMAN P** [65] [-]
(12"ep+=) **MAGICKAL MYSTERY D-TOUR** *(TOPYD 023)* – Interzone / Hex-sex / Godstar (ugly mix) / Je t'aime.
(12"ep) *(TOPYT 023)* – ('A'&'B'mixes) / Interzone / Hex-sex.

— returned to anti-commercial antics by releasing a series of live albums issued on the 23rd of each month (interspersed with new recordings)

Nov 86. (lp) *(TOPY 014)* **LIVE IN PARIS** [ ] [-]
Dec 86. (lp) *(TOPY 015)* **LIVE IN TOKYO** [ ] [-]
Jan 87. (lp) *(TOPY 016)* **LIVE IN GLASGOW** [ ] [-]
Mar 87. (lp) *(TOPY 018)* **LIVE IN HEAVEN** [ ] [-]
– I hear vocals / The leg song / Paradise lost / Lies and spies / Revenge on God / Stolen lightning / Seat of broken glass / Redium.
Apr 87. (12") *(TOPY 022)* **MAGICK DEFENDS ITSELF. / PAPAL BREAKDANCE** [ ] [-]
Jun 87. (lp) *(TOPY 026)* **LIVE IN REYKJAVIK** [ ] [-]
Jul 87. (lp) *(TOPY 027)* **LIVE EN SUISSE** [ ] [-]
Aug 87. (lp) *(TOPY 028)* **LIVE IN TORONTO** [ ] [-]
Sep 87. (lp) *(TOPY 029)* **LIVE IN GOTTINGEN** [ ] [-]
Dec 87. (m-lp) *(TOPY 030)* **TEMPORARY TEMPLE** [ ] [-]
Feb 88. (pic-lp) *(TOPY 031)* **PSYCHIC TV** [ ] [-]
Mar 88. (pic-lp) *(TOPY 032)* **ALBUM 10** [ ] [-]
May 88. (lp) *(TOPY 036)* **LIVE AT MARDI GRAS** [ ] [-]
Jun 88. (blue-lp) *(TOPY 038)* **ALLEGORY AND SELF: (THEE STARLET FIRE)** [ ] [-]
(re-iss. Aug91 lp/cd; TOPY 038/+CD) (cd-iss. Sep94 on 'Cleopatra'; CLEO 9491-2)
Aug 88. (12"; PSYCHIC TV / JACK THE TAB) *(TOPY 037)* **TUNE IN (TURN ON TO THEE ACID TAB)** [ ] [-]
Oct 88. (12"; by GENESIS P. ORRIDGE) *(TOPY 040)* **JOY. / THEE POLITICS OV ECSTASY** [ ] [-]
Dec 88. (lp) *(TOPY 042)* **LIVE AT THEE CIRCUS** [ ] [-]
Apr 89. (lp) *(TOPY 045)* **LIVE AT THEE RITZ** [ ] [-]
May 89. (lp/c/cd) *(TOPY 46/+C/CD)* **KONDOLE / COPYCAT** [ ] [-]
(cd re-iss. Jan94 on 'Silent'; SR 933-2)
Aug 89. (lp) *(TOPY 047)* **LIVE AT THEE PYRAMID NYC 1988** [ ] [-]
Nov 89. (12") *(TOPY 048T)* **LOVE, WAR, RIOT. / EVE OF DESTRUCTION (vocoder mixes)** [ ] [-]

— TIBET had already joined DEATH IN JUNE (1989-90)

Feb 90. (12") *(TOPY 050)* **JE T'AIME (Mistress mix). / WICKED** [ ] [-]
Mar 90. (lp/c/cd) *(TOPY 049/+CC/CD) <WAX 7129>* **TOWARDS THEE INFINITE BEAT** [ ] [-]
– Infinite beat / Bliss / Drone zone / S.M.I.L.E. / I.C. water / Black rainbow / A short sharp taste OV / Mistress mix / Horror house / Jigsaw / Alien be-in / Stick insect / Money for E. *(cd re-iss. Sep94 on 'Visionary'; VICD 002)*
Jul 90. (12"ep)(cd-ep) *(TOPYT 051)(TOPY 051CD)* **BEYOND THEE INFINITE BEAT** (Ravemaster mixes) [ ] [-]
(cd re-iss. Dec94 on 'Visionary'; VICD 004)
Sep 90. (cd) *(TOPY 052CD)* **LIVE AT THEE BERLIN WALL VOLUME 1** [ ] [-]
Sep 90. (cd) *(TOPY 053CD)* **LIVE AT THEE BERLIN WALL VOLUME 2** [ ] [-]
Nov 90. (7"etched) *(TOPY 058)* **I.C. WATER. / ALIEN BE IN** [ ] [-]
(12"+=) *(TOPYT 058)* – ('A'versions).
Jan 91. (lp/cd) *(TOPY 020/+CD)* **LIVE IN BREGENZ** [ ] [-]
Apr 91. (cd) *(TOPY 054CD)* **THEE CITY OV TOKYO, THEE CITY OV NEW YORK, MIDNIGHT MUSIC** [ ] [-]
Nov 91. (cd) *(TOPY 055CD)* **CITY OV PARIS** [ ] [-]
Nov 91. (cd) *(TOPY 062CD)* **A REAL LIVE SWEDISH SHOW** [ ] [-]
Sep 93. (lp/cd) *(TOPY 068/+CD)* **PEAK HOUR** (compilation) [ ] [-]
Jan 94. (12") *(TOPY 070)* **RE-MIND. / TRIBAL** [ ] [-]
Jul 94. (12"/cd-s) *(TOPY 077/+CD)* **TRIBAL DRUM CLUB (four versions)** [ ] [-]

Visionary / not iss.

Sep 94. (cd) *(VICD 001)* **ULTRADRUG** [ ] [-]
– Scoring / Tempted / Swallow / Bloodstream / B-on-E / Constant high / Back to reality / Thee eagle has landed / S.U.C.K. or know / Tempter / Still B-on-E / Gone paranoid / Loose nuts.
Nov 94. (cd) *(VICD 003)* **A HOLLOW COST** [ ] [ ]
Apr 95. (cd) *(VICD 005)* **SIRENS** [ ] [ ]
– Stargods / Skreemer / Re-united (mixes 1,2,3 & 4) / Sirens.
Oct 95. (cd) *(VICD 006)* **BEAUTY FROM THEE BEAST (THEE BEAST OV GENESIS P.ORRIDGE & PSYCHIC TV)** (compilation) [ ] [ ]
– Roman P / Good vibrations / Hex sex / Godstar / Je t'aime / United '94 / Eve ov destruction / S.M.I.L.E. / I.C. water / Horror house / Back to reality / Godstar (hyperdelic mix) / Re-united (mix 4).

Etherworld / not iss.

Sep 97. (cd; by GENESIS P. ORRIDGE & THE WHITE STAINS) *(ETW 001)* **AT STOCKHOLM** [ ] [-]

– compilations, etc. –

Apr 87. (lp; shared with Z.EV) *Dossier; (ST 3001)* **BERLIN ATONAL (live)** [ ] [-]
– Nursery times / Skinhead moonstomp '84.
Aug 93. (cd) *Trident; (TIBCD 10)* **RARE AND ALIVE** [ ] [-]
Sep 93. (cd) *Dossier; (EFA 08441-2)* **TEMPORARY TEMPLE / ATONAL** [ ] [-]
Jan 94. (cd) *Semantic; (SSCDV 01)* **LISTEN TODAY** [ ] [-]
Feb 94. (cd) *Dossier; (EFA 08454-2)* **THEE TRANSMUTION OF MERCURY** [ ] [-]
Mar 94. (cd) *Cleopatra; (CLEO 6508-2)* **HEX SEX (THE SINGLES)** [ ] [-]
Jun 94. (cd) *Dossier; (EFA 06446-2)* **MEIN GOTTINGEN** [ ] [-]
Jan 95. (cd) *Dossier; (EFA 08459-2)* **ELECTRONIC NEWSPAPER** [ ] [-]
Mar 95. (cd) *Dossier; (EFA 08467-2)* **CATHEDRAL ENGINE** [ ] [-]
Apr 95. (cd) *Cleopatra; (CLEO 9518-2)* **GODSTAR (THE SINGLES PART II)** [ ] [-]
Jul 95. (cd) *Dossier; (EFA 08470-2)* **ELECTRONIC NEWSPAPER ISSUE 2** [ ] [-]
Nov 95. (cd) *Dossier; (EFA 08476-2)* **ELECTRONIC NEWSPAPER ISSUE 3** [ ] [-]
Apr 96. (cd) *Cleopatra; (CLEO 9665CD)* **TRIP RESET** [ ] [-]
Apr 96. (cd) *Cleopatra; (<CLEO 9711CD>)* **COLD BLUE TORCH** [ ] [-]
May 96. (cd) *Cold Spring; (CSR 10CD)* **THOSE WHO DO NOT** [ ] [-]
Jan 97. (cd) *Dossier; (DCD 9054)* **AL OR AL** [ ] [-]
Feb 98. (cd) *Cold Spring;* **THEMES 2 – A PRAYER FOR DEREK JARMAN** [ ] [-]

PSYCLONE RANGERS

Formed: Allentown, Pennsylvania, USA ... 1992 by JONATHAN VALANIA, who recruited SCOTT DANTZER, MICHAEL VALLONE and RACE BANNON. One of the first signings to DAVE ALLEN's (ex-

GANG OF FOUR) label, 'World Domination', the PSYCLONE RANGERS stormed on to the scene with 1994's 'FEEL NICE' set, featuring a reading of Jonathan Richman's 'I'M STRAIGHT'. As the name might suggest, the band's sound conjured up images of rural America's seedy underbelly, akin to a more updated, swamptrash CREEDENCE CLEARWATER REVIVAL (whose 'EFFIGY' they subsequently covered). A year later, the 'RANGERS posse were back in town for a follow-up Ian Caple-produced collection, 'THE DEVIL MAY CARE'. A third set, 'BEATIN' ON THE BAT POLE' (1996), confirmed their credentials as the 90's version of The GUN CLUB.

Album rating: FEEL NICE (*6) / THE DEVIL MAY CARE (*6) / BEATIN' ON THE BAT POLE (*6)

JONATHAN VALANIA – vocals / **SCOTT DANTZER** – guitar, vocals / **MICHAEL VALLONE** – bass / **RACE BANNON** – drums

World Domination | World Domination

May 94. (7"ep/cd-ep) *<(WDOM 001/2 S/+CD)>* **CHRISTIE INDECISION / I WANNA BE JACK KENNEDY. / BAD SEEDS / C.I.A.** [ ] [ ]

May 94. (lp/cd) *<(WDOM 005/+CD)>* **FEEL NICE** [ ] [ ]
– I wanna be Jack Kennedy / Spinnin' my head / Christie indecision / I feel nice / The hate noise / Stephen / Heaven / Riot girl / Bigger than a gun / Devil's down there / Perfect engine / You're not Edie Sedgewick.

Apr 95. (cd) *<(WDOM 015CD)>* **THE DEVIL MAY CARE** [ ] [ ]
– Deal / Ain't goin' down / Firenze / Tilt-a-whirl / Boyo / The awe song / Ehy the hell did I die? / I'm straight / Dejesus / Nazi mother / Dr. Softness / Mono town.

— **DAN McKINNEY** – organ + **P.R. BEHLER** – bass; repl. VALLONE

May 96. (7") *<(WDOM 25S)>* **LITTLE MAN WITH A GUN IN HIS HAND. /** [ ] [ ]

Jul 96. (cd/lp) *<(WDOM 036-2/-1)>* **BEATIN' ON THE BAT POLE** [ ] [ ]
– Fuel city! / (Can you feel the) Kingdom comin' / Little man with a gun in his hand / For the sake of Ivy / Meth carnival / Tim, are you home?

not iss. | Sympathy F

1990's. (7"ep) *<SFTRI 264>* **SWING, BABY, SWING EP** [-] [ ]

PUBLIC IMAGE LTD.

Formed: London, England . . . July '78 by ex-SEX PISTOLS frontman, JOHNNY ROTTEN, who reverted to his real name, JOHN LYDON. He recruited local friends, guitarist KEITH LEVENE (ex-CLASH), bassist JAH WOBBLE and Canadian drummmer JIM WALKER, re-signing to 'Virgin' in the process. 'PUBLIC IMAGE', both the debut single and the title track of the debut album was a raucous slice of post-PISTOLS sonic energy, the record coming wrapped in a mock-newspaper sleeve and reaching the UK Top 10 late in 1978. The album followed it into the Top 30 at the end of the year, hardly a departure from punk but a convincing statement of intent nevertheless; tracks such as 'RELIGION', 'ANNA LISA' and 'ATTACK' formed the basis for LYDON's subsequent experiments. Preceded by the bizarre 'DEATH DISCO' single, 'METAL BOX 1' (1979) was a strikingly differerent beast, its pristine packaging (three 12" 45's inside a metal film can, something much copied by record company marketing departments in the years to come) rather deceptively encasing a dark, often disturbing set of experimental, Eastern-influenced material. As far from punk as LYDON has ever ventured, the record utilised monotonic repitition, LEVENE's shards of splintered guitar dissecting the vague structures of WOBBLE's rubbery basslines while LYDON wailed and ranted like a damned soul. John Peel was a particular champion of the record, playlisting virtually all its disturbing but accessible tracks, 'CAREERING', 'POPTONES' and 'GRAVEYARD' highlighting what came to be regarded as one of the last classic "punk/alternative" albums of the 70's. Surely one of the most avant-garde releases to ever grace the Top 20, the album even hit the charts a second time (Top 50) when it was re-issued in double-album format as 'SECOND EDITION' two months later. Following a patchy live album, 'PARIS AU PRINTEMPS' (1980), WOBBLE departed on a sour note, leaving LYDON and LEVENE to mastermind 'FLOWERS OF ROMANCE' (1981). A comparatively weaker effort, the record nevertheless almost made the Top 10 and the more contrived moments were interspersed with a few gems, notably the Burundi-esque title track, a Top 30 hit single. LEVENE was also soon to leave in less than pleasant circumstances following the success of 'P.I.L.'s biggest hit single to date, the compelling 'THIS IS NOT A LOVE SONG'. LYDON subsequently completed the lacklustre 'THIS IS WHAT YOU WANT . . . THIS IS WHAT YOU GET' opus with the help of session musicians, disbanding the group around the time of the album's release in the summer of '84. By this point, LYDON had moved to Los Angeles and his career slowed up somewhat, although he subsequently reformed 'P.I.L.' in late '85. Using such respected (and glaringly un-punk) musos as STEVE VAI, RYUICHI SAKAMOTO, GINGER BAKER and RAVI SHANKAR, LYDON recorded the minimally titled 'ALBUM' (also released as 'CASSETTE' and 'COMPACT DISC', of course). The BILL LASWELL-produced effort remains his last consistent collection, the 'SINGLE', 'RISE', almost making the Top 10, a driving, resonating, infectiously commercial example of LYDON doing what he does best (although I could be wrong . . .). For the remainder of the 80's, LYDON was content to churn out formula 'JOHNNY ROTTEN'-to-order type material that often incorporated bland Americanised rock backing. This only served to further entrench him in the mire of self-parody. Albums like 'HAPPY?' (1987) and '9' (1989) achieved only minimal commercial success although LYDON was back in the Top 20 in 1990 with 'DON'T ASK ME', the punk veteran's comment on the topical subject of the environment. The single was cannily included by 'Virgin' on a best of set, the hopefully titled 'GREATEST HITS – SO FAR' (1990). Then again, LYDON proved he could still cut the mustard with his late '93 LEFTFIELD collaboration, 'OPEN UP'. When LYDON lets rip, as he does here (a blood curdling wail of 'Burn, Hollywood, burn'), he is still the most frightening man in rock, no contest. Just to prove it, he hooked up once more with the original SEX PISTOLS line-up for the aptly titled 'Filthy Lucre' tour, appearing on 'Top Of The Pops' and scaring young children all over again with his gravity-defying hairdo.

Album rating: PUBLIC IMAGE (*9) / METAL BOX 1 (*10) / FLOWERS OF ROMANCE (*6) / ALBUM (*7) / GREATEST HITS – SO FAR compilation (*9)

JOHN LYDON (b.31 Jan'56, Finsbury Park, London, England) – vocals (ex-SEX PISTOLS) / **KEITH LEVENE** (b. London, England) – guitar (ex-CLASH) / **JAH WOBBLE** (b. JOHN WORDLE) – bass / **JIM WALKER** (b. Canada) – drums (ex-FURIES) (most singles just credit "PiL")

Virgin | Warners

Oct 78. (7") *(VS 228)* **PUBLIC IMAGE. / THE COWBOY SONG** [9] [-]

Dec 78. (lp/c) *(V/TCV 2114) <3288>* **PUBLIC IMAGE** [22] [ ]
– Theme / Religion I / Religion II / Annalisa / Public image / Low life / Attack / Fodderstompf. *(re-iss. Apr86 lp/c; OVED/+C 160) (cd-iss. Jun88; CDV 2114)*

— **DAVE CROWE** – drums repl. WALKER who joined The PACK (with KIRK BRANDON) added **JEANNETTE LEE** – keyboards, synthesizer

Jun 79. (7") *(VS 274)* **DEATH DISCO. / NO BIRDS DO SING** [20] [-]
(12"+=) *(VS 274-12)* – Death disco megamix.

Sep 79. (7"/ext.12") *(VS 299/+12)* **MEMORIES. / ANOTHER** [60] [-]

Dec 79. (3x12"box)<lp> *(METAL 1) <3288>* **METAL BOX 1** <US-title 'SECOND EDITION'> [18] [ ] Jul80
– Albatross / Memories / Swan lake/ / Poptones / Careering / No birds / Graveyard / / The suit / Bad baby / Socialist – Chant – Radio 4. *(re-iss. Feb80 as 'SECOND EDITION' d-lp/c; VD/TCVD 2512); hit UK No.46) (cd-iss. Jun86; CDVD 2512) (original; cd-iss. Jun90; MTLLCD 1)*

— **RICHARD DUDANSKI** – drums (ex-101'ERS, ex-BASEMENT 5) repl. CROWE

— (he had joined during Apr-Sep'79) (below French titles of above songs)

Nov 80. (lp/c) *(V/TCV 2183)* **PARIS AU PRINTEMPS (live 'PARIS IN THE SPRING')** [61] [-]
– Theme / Psalmodie (Chant) / Precipitamment (Careering) / Sale bebe (Bad baby) / La vie ignoble (Low life) / Attaque (Attack) / Timbres de pop (Poptones). *(re-iss. Mar84 lp/c; OVED/+C 50)*

— (Jul80) Trimmed to a quartet when JAH WOBBLE went solo. / **MARTIN ATKINS** (b. 3 Aug'59, Coventry, England) (aka BRIAN BRAIN) – drums repl. DUDANSKI who joined RAINCOATS. (ATKINS was sacked Jul80, most of drums by LYDON and LEVENE)

Mar 81. (7") *(VS 397)* **FLOWERS OF ROMANCE. / HOME IS WHERE THE HEART IS** [24] [-]
(12"+=) *(VS 397-12)* – ('A'instrumental).

Apr 81. (lp/c) *(V/TCV 2189) <3536>* **FLOWERS OF ROMANCE** [11] [ ]
– Four enclosed walls / Track 8 / Phenagen / Flowers of romance / Under the house / Hymie's him / Banging the door / Go back / Francis massacre. *(re-iss. Mar84 lp/c; OVED/+C 51) (cd-iss. Apr90 & Mar94; CDV 2189)*

— **KEN LOCKIE** – keyboards (ex-COWBOYS INTERNATIONAL, ex-Solo) repl. LEE / added (May82) **MARTIN ATKINS** – drums / **PETE JONES** – bass

Aug 83. (7") *(VS 529)* **THIS IS NOT A LOVE SONG. / PUBLIC IMAGE** [5] [-]
(12"+=) *(VS 529-12)* – Blue water / ('A'remix).
(re-iss. Jun88 cd-ep; CDT 14)

— LYDON + ATKINS were joined by US session people from New Jersey; **JOSEPH GUIDA** – guitar / **TOM ZVONCHECK** – keyboards / **LOUIE BERNARDI** – bass

Virgin | Elektra

Sep 83. (2x12"/c) *(VGD/+C 3508)* **LIVE IN TOKYO (live)** [28] [-]
– Annalisa / Religion / Low life / Solitaire / Flowers of romance / This is not a love song / Death disco / Bad life / Banging the door / Under the house. *(cd-iss. 1986; VGDCD 3508)*

May 84. (7"/ext.12") *(VS 675/+12)* **BAD LIFE. / QUESTION MARK** [71] [-]

Jul 84. (lp/c) *(V/TCV 2309) <60365>* **THIS IS WHAT YOU WANT . . . THIS IS WHAT YOU GET** [56] [ ]
– Bad life / This is not a love song / Solitaire / Tie me to the length of that / The pardon / Where are you? / 1981 / The order of death. *(re-iss. 1986 lp/c; OVED/+C 176) (cd-iss. Apr90; CDV 2309)*

Aug 84. (lp; as KEITH LEVENE & PiL) *<XYZ 007>* **THE COMMERCIAL ZONE** [-] [ ]
– (as last album, with LEVENE's guitar parts more obvious)

— Disbanded mid'84, but reformed by LYDON late '85 with on session **STEVE VAI** – guitar (ex-ALCATRAZZ) / **RYUICHI SAKAMOTO** – keys (ex-YELLOW MAGIC ORCHESTRA) / **GINGER BAKER** (ex-CREAM, etc) / **TONY WILLIAMS** (ex-MILES DAVIES, etc) / **RAVI SHANKER** – violin

Jan 86. (7"/12") *(VS 841/+12)* **RISE. / ('A'instrumental)** [11] [-]

Feb 86. (cd/c/lp) *(CD/TC+/V 2366) <60438>* **ALBUM** [14] [ ]
– FFF / Rise / Fishing / Round / Bags / Home / Ease. *(re-iss. 1989 lp/c; OVED/+C 245)*

Apr 86. (7") *(VS 855)* **HOME. / ROUND** [75] [-]
(12"+=) *(VS 855-12)* – ('A'-lp version).
(d7"+=) *(VSD 855)* – Rise / ('A'instrumental).

— (Feb86) **LYDON** recruited **LU EDMUNDS** – guitar, keys (ex-DAMNED, ex-MEKONS) / **JOHN McGEOGH** – guitar (of ARMOURY SHOW, ex-SIOUXSIE & THE BANSHEES) / **ALAN DIAS** – bass / **BRUCE SMITH** – drums (ex-RIP, RIG & PANIC, ex-SLITS, ex-POP GROUP)

Virgin | Virgin

Aug 87. (7") *(VS 988)* **SEATTLE. / SELFISH RUBBISH** [47] [-]
(12"+=/c-s+=) *(VS/+C 988-12)* – The suit.

Sep 87. (cd/c/lp) *(CD/TC+/V 2455) <90642>* **HAPPY?** [40] [ ]
– Seattle / Rules and regulations / The body / Save me / Hard times / Open and revolving / Angry / Fat chance hotel. *(re-iss. Apr90 lp/c; OVED/+C 299)*

Oct 87. (7") *(VS 1010)* **THE BODY. / RELIGION (new version)** [100] [-]
(12"+=) *(VST 1010)* – Angry.
(12") *(VSR 1010)* – ('A'extended remix) / ('A'-U.S. remix) / Angry.

— trimmed to a quartet when EDMUNDS dispersed.

Apr 89. (7") *(VS 1181)* **DISAPPOINTED. / SAME OLD STORY** 38 -
(ext.12"+=/12"pic-d+=/3"cd-s+=) *(VS T/TY/CD 181)* – ('A'version).

Jun 89. (cd/c/lp) *(CD/TC+/V 2588) <91062>* **9** 36
– Happy / Disappointed / Warrior / U.S.L.S. 1 / Sand castles in the snow / Worry / Brave new world / Like that / Same old story / Armada.

Jul 89. (7"/7"g-f) *(VS 1195)* **WARRIOR. / U.S.L.S. 1** -
(ext.12"+=) *(VST 1195)* – ('A'instrumental).
(3"cd-s+=) *(VSCD 1195)* – ('A'extended).
(12") *(VSTX 1195)* – ('A'-Dave Dorrell remix) / ('A'instrumental).

Oct 90. (7"/c-s) *(VS/+C 1231)* **DON'T ASK ME. / RULES AND REGULATIONS** 22 -
(cd-s+=) *(VSCD 1231)* – Warrior (original).
(12") *(VST 1231)* – ('A'extended) / Warrior (remix).

Oct 90. (cd/c/lp) *(CD/TC+/V 2644)* **GREATEST HITS – SO FAR** (compilation) 20
– Public image / Death disco / Memories / Careering / Flowers of romance / This is not a love song / Rise / Home / The body / Rules and regulations / Disappointed / Warrior / Don't ask me / Seattle.

— **MIKE JOYCE** – drums (ex-SMITHS, ex-BUZZCOCKS) repl. BRUCE

Feb 92. (7") *(VS 1390)* **CRUEL. / LOVE HOPE** 49 -
(cd-s+=) *(VSCD 1390)* – Rise (live) / Home (live).
(10"+=) *(VST 1390)* – Happy (live).

Feb 92. (cd/c/lp) *(CD/TC+/V 2681) <86263>* **THAT WHAT IS NOT** 46
– Acid drops / Lucks up / Cruel / God / Covered / Love hope / Unfairground / Think tank / Emperor / Good things.

— In Nov'93, LYDON was credited on acclaimed dance hit & UK No.19 'Open Up' by LEFTFIELD / LYDON on 'Hard Hands' records.

— Stop press:- Early '96, JOHN LYDON (ROTTEN) re-grouped with The SEX PISTOLS for summer tours in Britain, Europe and America.

JOHN LYDON

Virgin America / Virgin America

Jun 97. (cd/c) *(CDVUS/VUSMC 130) <44209>* **PSYCHO'S PATH**
– Grave ride / Dog / Psychopath / Sun / Another way / Dis-ho / Take me / No and a yes / Stump / Armies / Open up.

Jul 97. (12"/cd-s) *(VUS T/CD 122)* **SUN. / GRAVE RIDE / PSYCHOPATH** 42 -

PULLMAN

Formed: Chicago, Illinois, USA ... by seasoned alternative/Lo-Fi campaigners, CHRIS BROKAW (of COME), CURTIS HARVEY (of REX), DOUG McCOMBS (of TORTOISE and ELEVENTH DREAM DAY) and BUNDY K BROWN (of TORTOISE and DIRECTIONS IN MUSIC). Taking influences from such acoustic "folk" artists as JOHN FAHEY, NICK DRAKE and RY COODER, the supergroup of sorts delivered a much talked about debut set, 'TURNSTYLES & JUNKPILES', in 1998. Entirely instrumental, the album's atmospheric, textured guitar highlights included 'GRAVENHURST', penned by another former TORTOISE cohort, DAVID PAJO (now of AERIAL-M).

Album rating: TURNSTYLES & JUNKPILES (*6)

CHRIS BROKAW – guitar / **CURTIS HARVEY** – guitar / **BUNDY K BROWN** – guitar, bass / **DOUG McCOMBS** – bass

Thrill Jockey / Thrill Jockey

Aug 98. (lp/cd) *<(THRILL 055/+CD)>* **TURNSTYLES & JUNKPILES**
– To hold down a shadow / Barefoot / In a box, under the bed / Sagamore bridge / Gravenhurst / Lyasnya / Two parts water / Beacon and Kent / Deer hill / So breaks yesterday / Fullerton / Sunday morning traffic / Tall grass / With hands.

PULP

Formed: Sheffield, England . . . 1981 originally as ARABACUS PULP by JARVIS COCKER while still at school. Following on in the tradition of geek heart-throbs like BUDDY HOLLY, JARVIS COCKER achieved the knicker-wetting adulation he'd always aspired to through sheer hard graft and the determination of the downtrodden. His long road to stardom began in the mid-80's with the release of the 'IT' mini-lp and a prestigious JOHN PEEL session. Further releases like the 'LITTLE GIRL AND OTHER PIECES' (1985) and 'DOGS ARE EVERYWHERE' (1986) EP's saw COCKER developing as a wry and sharply observant chronicler of working class drudgery and sexual frustration, his inimitable brand of camped-up showmanship unhampered by a spell in a wheel chair (his injuries allegedly sustained after falling from a window when trying to show off to a woman!). By the release of 'FREAKS' (1987), the core of the latter day PULP was in place, violinist/guitarist RUSSELL SENIOR and keyboardist CANDIDA DOYLE beginning to move away from the band's early LEONARD COHEN/FALL hybrid to a more arty MONOCHROME SET/ULTRAVOX (John Foxx era!) type vibe. Most of the band moved to London in the late 80's, with bassist STEVE MACKAY and drummer NICHOLAS BANKS stabilising the line-up. In this incarnation, the sleek, new-look PULP recorded the 'SEPARATIONS' (1991) album, a more ambitious affair which spawned the enduringly glitter-tastic 'MY LEGENDARY GIRLFRIEND' single. The track's success encouraged PULP to set up their own label, 'Gift', through which they released a string of early 90's EP's, becoming critical darlings with some sections of the music press alongside fellow pop sculptors like SAINT ETIENNE. It wasn't long before the enigmatic JARVIS and crew were on the roster of 'Island', releasing their breakthrough 'HIS 'N' HERS' album in 1994. Previewed by the driving, tongue-in-cheek query of the 'DO YOU REMEMBER THE FIRST TIME?' single (a short film was released to tie in with the track, featuring various biz figureheads candidly talking about their "first time"), the album expertly dissected the sexual undertow of working class Britain with a incisive accuracy, mordant humour and lashings of glam posturing. The album made the UK Top 10, becoming a consistent seller and setting COCKER up as a fashion icon (Bri-Nylon, national health specs etc.). The singer was to become a star on the same scale as BRETT ANDERSON (Suede) following the success of the landmark 'COMMON PEOPLE' single. A classic pop song that almost made No.2 on the back of the Britpop zeitgeist, the single was a brilliant portrayal of the British class divide set to an almost 80's style synth-led backdrop. After the headlining act dropped out, PULP stepped in to put in one of the most acclaimed performances of their career at the 1995 Glastonbury festival, releasing the 'DIFFERENT CLASS' album in October to round off the most successful year to date in the band's career. With the social commentary as cutting as ever (the controversial 'SORTED FOR E'S AND WHIZZ') and their gift for effortlessly poignant pop intact ('DISCO 2000'), PULP consolidated their position as Britain's leading exponents of home-grown pop genius. A more downbeat COCKER returned late in '97 with the Top 10 hit, 'HELP THE AGED' (all monies going to that particular charity), while Britain awaited with much anticipation the porn-inspired 'THIS IS HARDCORE' set in '98. • **Songwriters:** COCKER + SIMON HINKLER collaborated on debut. COCKER, SENIOR, C. DOYLE, MANSELL penned, until 90's when COCKER was main contributor. • **Trivia:** COCKER and MACKAY directed videos for TINDERSTICKS and The APHEX TWIN. • **Note:** Not to be confused with other band fronted by ANDY BEAN + PAUL BURNELL, who released in 1979; LOW FLYING AIRCRAFT single.

Album rating: IT (*4) / FREAKS (*4) / SEPARATIONS (*5) / PULPINTRO – THE GIFT RECORDINGS compilation (*7) / HIS 'N' HERS (*9) / DIFFERENT CLASS (*9) / THIS IS HARDCORE (*8) / MASTERS OF THE UNIVERSE compilation (*5)

JARVIS COCKER (b. Sep'62) – vocals, guitar, piano / **SIMON HINKLER** – keyboards, vocals repl. PETER DALTON / **PETER BOAM** – bass repl. JAMIE PINCHBECK who had repl. DAVID LOCKWOOD / **DAVID HINKLER** – keyboards, trombone / **GARY WILSON** – drums (of ARTERY) repl. WAYNE FURNISS who had repl. JIMMY SELLERS who had repl. MARK SWIFT

— plus guests **SASKIA COCKER** + **GILL TAYLOR** – b.vox / **TIMM ALLCARD** – keyboards

Red Rhino / not iss.

Apr 83. (m-lp) *(REDLP 29)* **IT** -
– My lighthouse / Wishful thinking / Joking aside / Boats and trains / Blue girls / Love love / In many ways. *(cd-iss. Mar94 on 'Cherry Red'; CDMRED 112 w/drawn)* *(cd+=)* – Looking for life / Everybody's problem / There was. *(re-iss. cd Dec94 on 'Fire'; REFIRE CD15)* *(cd+=)* – Looking for life. *<US cd-iss. 1997 on 'Velvel'; 79750>*

May 83. (7") *(RED 32)* **MY LIGHTHOUSE (remix). / LOOKING FOR LIFE** -

Sep 83. (7") *(RED 37)* **EVERYBODY'S PROBLEM. / THERE WAS** -

— **RUSSELL SENIOR** – guitar, violin, vocals repl. DAVID

— **CANDIDA DOYLE** – keyboards, vocals repl. SIMON who joined ARTERY then the MISSION)

— **MAGNUS DOYLE** – drums repl. GARY, SASKIA, GILL + TIMM

— **PETER MANSELL** – bass repl. BOAM

Fire / not iss.

Nov 85. (12"ep) *(FIRE 5)* **LITTLE GIRL AND OTHER PIECES** -
– Little girl (with blue eyes) / Simultaneous / Blue glow / The will to power. *(re-iss. Oct91)*

Jun 86. (12"ep) *(BLAZE 10)* **DOGS ARE EVERYWHERE / THE MARK OF THE DEVIL. / 97 LOVERS / ABORIGINE / GOODNIGHT** -
(re-iss. Oct91)

Jan 87. (7"/ext.12") *(BLAZE 17/+T)* **THEY SUFFOCATE AT NIGHT. / TUNNEL** -

Mar 87. (7"/12") *(BLAZE 21/+T)* **MASTER OF THE UNIVERSE (sanitised version). / MANON / SILENCE** -
(re-iss. Oct91)

May 87. (lp) *(FIRE LP5)* **FREAKS** -
– Fairground / I want you / Being followed home / Master of the universe / Life must be so wonderful / There's no emotion / Anorexic beauty / The never-ending story / Don't you know / They suffocate at night. *(cd-iss. Apr93; FIRE CD5)* *<US cd-iss. 1997 on 'Velvel'; 79752>*

— **STEPHEN MACKAY** – bass repl. STEPHEN HAVENLAND who had repl. PETER

— **NICHOLAS BANKS** – drums, percussion repl. MAGNUS

Sep 90. (12"ep) *(BLAZE 44T)* **MY LEGENDARY GIRLFRIEND. / IS THIS HOUSE? / THIS HOUSE IS CONDEMNED** -
(re-iss. Oct91)

Aug 91. (12"ep/cd-ep) *(BLAZE 51 T/CD)* **COUNTDOWN. / DEATH GOES TO THE DISCO / COUNTDOWN (edit)** -
(re-iss. Oct91)

Oct 91. (cd/c/lp) *(FIRE 33/22/11 026)* **SEPARATIONS** -
– Love is blind / Don't you want me anymore / She's dead / Separations / Down by the river / Countdown / My legendary girlfriend / Death II / This house is condemned. *(re-iss. Jun92; same)* *<US cd-iss. 1995 on 'Razor & Tie'; 2090-2>*

Gift / not iss.

May 92. (12"ep/cd-ep) *(GIF 1/+CD)* **O.U. (GONE GONE) / SPACE / O.U. (GONE GONE) (radio edit)** -

Oct 92. (12"ep/cd-ep) *(GIF 3/+CD)* **BABIES. / STYLOROC (NIGHTS OF SUBURBIA) / SHEFFIELD** – SEX CITY -

Feb 93. (7") *(7GIF 6)* **RAZZAMATAZZ. / INSIDE SUSAN (abridged; Stacks – 59 Lynhurst Grove)** -
(12"ep+/cd-ep+=) *(GIF 6/+CD)* – (B-side; A STORY IN 3 PARTS).

Island / Polygram

Oct 93. (cd/c)(lp) *(IMCD/IMCT 159)(ILPM 2076) <2076-518451>* **PULPINTRO – THE GIFT RECORDINGS** (compilation)

– Space / O.U. (gone gone) / Babies / Styloroc (nights of suburbia) / Razzamatazz / Sheffield – Sex city / Medley of stacks: Inside Susan (a story in 3 songs) Stacks – Inside Susan – 59 Lyndhurst Grove.

Nov 93. (7") *(IS 567)* **LIPGLOSS. / YOU'RE A NIGHTMARE** [50] [ ]
(12"+=)(cd-s+=) *(12IS/CID 567)* – Deep fried in Kelvin. *(re-iss. Aug96) (re-iss. Oct96 on 7"red)*

Mar 94. (7"/c-s) *(IS/CIS 574)* **DO YOU REMEMBER THE FIRST TIME?. / STREET LITES** [33] [ ]
(12"+=)(cd-s+=) *(12IS/CID 574)* - **The babysitter.** *(re-iss. Aug96, hit 73) (re-iss. Oct96 7"biege)*

Apr 94. (cd/c/lp) *(CID/ICT/ILPS 8025) <524006>* **HIS 'N' HERS** [9] [ ] Jun94
– Joyriders / Lipgloss / Acrylic afternoons / Have you seen her lately? / She's a lady / Happy endings / Do you remember the first time? / Pink glove / Someone like the Moon / David's last summer.(cd,c+=) – Babies (remix).

May 94. (7"ep/c-ep/12"ep/cd-ep) *(IS/CIS/12IS/CID 595)* **THE SISTERS EP** [19] [-]
– Babies / Your sister's clothes / Seconds / His'n'hers. *(re-iss. Aug96) (re-iss. Oct96 on white 7"ep)*

May 95. (c-s) *(CIS 613)* **COMMON PEOPLE. / UNDERWEAR** [2] [-]
(cd-s+=) *(CID 613)* – ('A'-Motiv8 mix) / ('A'-Vocoda mix). *(re-iss. Aug96) (re-iss. Oct96 7"yellow/12")*
(cd-s) *(CIDX 613)* – ('A'side) / Razzmatazz (acoustic) / Dogs are everywhere (acoustic) / Joyriders (acoustic).

— Below second side (double A) caused controversy with tabloids and parents, due to it's mis-use of drugs in JARVIS's lyrics. JARVIS was to become the hero to most and villain to the few early in 1996 at a certain awards ceremony (skinny J.C. vs. St.MICHAEL & the bouncers; who won – you decide).

Sep 95. (c-s) *(CIS 620)* **MIS-SHAPES / SORTED FOR E'S AND WIZZ** [2] [-]
(cd-s+=) *(CID 620)* – P.T.A. (Parent Teacher Association) / Common people (live at Glastonbury). *(re-iss. Oct96 7"blue/12")*
(cd-s+=) *(CIDX 620)* – Common people (Motiv8 mix). *(re-iss. Aug96)*

Oct 95. (cd/c/lp) *(CID/ICT/ILPS 8041) <524165>* **DIFFERENT CLASS** [1] [ ]
– Mis-shapes / Pencil skirt / Common people / I spy / Disco 2000 / Live bed show / Something changed / Sorted out for E's and wizz / F.E.E.L.I.N.G.C.A.L.L.E.D.L.O.V.E. / Underwear / Monday morning / Bar Italia.

Nov 95. (c-s) *(CIS 623)* **DISCO 2000 / ANSAPHONE** [7] [-]
(cd-s+=) *(CID 623)* – ('A'-Motiv8 Gimp dub & Discoid mixes). *(re-iss. Aug96) (re-iss. Oct96 7"orange/12")*
(cd-s+=) *(CIDX 623)* – Live bed show (extended).

Mar 96. (c-s) *(CIS 632)* **SOMETHING CHANGED / MILE END** [10] [-]
(cd-s+=) *(CID 632)* – F.E.E.L.I.N.G.C.A.L.L.E.D.L.O.V.E (The Moloko mix) / F.E.E.L.I.N.G.C.A.L.L.E.D.L.O.V.E. (live from Brixton Academy). *(re-iss. Aug96) (re-iss. Oct96 7"pink/12")*

— now without SENIOR, who wanted to pursue new projects

Nov 97. (c-s/7") *(C+/IS 679)* **HELP THE AGED. / LAUGHING BOY** [8] [-]
(cd-s+=) *(CID 679)* – Tomorrow never lies.

Mar 98. (c-s) *(CIS 695)* **THIS IS HARDCORE / LADIES MAN** [12] [-]
(cd-s+=) *(CID 695)* – Professional.
(cd-s) *(CIDX 695)* – ('A'mixes).

Mar 98. (cd/c/d-lp) *(ILPSD/ICT/CID 8066) <524492>* **THIS IS HARDCORE** [1] [ ]
– The fear / Dishes / Party hard / Help the aged / This is hardcore / TV movie / A little soul / I'm a man / Seductive Barry / Sylvia / Glory days / Day after the revolution.

Jun 98. (c-s) *(CIS 708)* **A LITTLE SOUL / COCAINE SOCIALISM** [22] [-]
(cd-s+=) *(CID 708)* – Like a friend.
(cd-s) *(CIDX 708)* – ('A'alternative mix) / ('A'-Lafayette Velvet revisited mix) / That boy's evil.

Sep 98. (c-s/cd-s) *(CIS/CID 719) <572418>* **PARTY HARD / WE ARE THE BOYZ / THE FEAR** [29] [ ]
(cd-s) *(CIDX 719)* – ('A'mixes by Stretch'n'Vern & All Seeing I).

– compilations, etc. –

Jun 94. (cd/c/lp) *Fire; (FIRE CD/MC/LP 36)* **MASTERS OF THE UNIVERSE – PULP ON FIRE 1985-86** [ ] [-]
– Little girl (with blue eyes) / Simultaneous / Blue glow / The will to power / Dogs are everywhere / The mark of the Devil / 97 lovers / Aborigine / Goodnight / They suffocate at night / Tunnel / Master of the universe (sanitised version) / Manon.

Mar 96. (d-cd/c/d-lp) *Nectar; (NTM CDD/C/LP 521)* **COUNTDOWN 1992-1983** [10] [-]
– Countdown / Death goes to the disco / My legendary girlfriend / Don't you want me anymore / She's dead / Down by the river / I want you / Being followed home / Master of the universe / Don't you know / They suffocate at night / Dogs are everywhere / Mark of the Devil / 97 lovers / Little girl (with blue eyes) / Blue glow / My lighthouse / Wishful thinking / Blue girls / Countdown (extended).

Jul 98. (cd) *Connoisseur; (VSOPCD 256)* **DEATH GOES TO THE DISCO** [ ] [-]

Sep 98. (cd) *E.M.I.; <79737>* **FRESHLY SQUEEZED (EARLY YEARS)** [-] [ ]

PUNISHMENT OF LUXURY

Formed: London, England . . . 1978 by NEVILLE LUXURY and his co-writer BRIAN BOND alongside RED HELMIT, JIMMY GIRO and LIQUID LES DENHAM. With their origins in radical theatre, this punk-era oddity was driven by an attempt to combine three-chord aggression with quirky prog-rock. Initially signed to the 'Small Wonder' label, the group released a debut single, 'PUPPET LIFE', in summer '78. A couple of John Peel sessions also added to their credibility, the band subsequently signing to 'United Artists' for whom they cut a further two singles, 'ENGINE OF EXCESS' and 'SECRETS', prior to their one and only album, 'LAUGHING ACADEMY' (1979). Retrospectively bestowed the honour of appearing in a 'Mojo' magazine poll of 100 all-time worst albums, the record's political sermonising and woefully self-indulgent guitar work was certainly not your average New Wave fare. A subsequent deal with 'Liberty' saw the release of the album's title track prior to a lengthy break. NEVILLE and JIMMY eventually resurfaced as PUNILUX (alongside new recruits STEVE SEKRIT and TIM MAGENTA) with a one-off single, 'HOLD ME (NEVER MOULD ME)' on 'Red Rhino' in 1983. The following year saw the outfit's swansong release, mini-set, '7', NEVILLE going on to release a solo album, 'FEELS LIKE DANCING WARTIME'.

Album rating: LAUGHING ACADEMY (*5)

BRIAN BOND – vocals, keyboards / **NEVILLE LUXURY** – guitars / **RED HELMIT** – guitar / **JIMMY GIRO** – bass / **LIQUID LES DENHAM** – drums

Small Wonder — not iss.

Jul 78. (7") *(SMALL 8)* **PUPPET LIFE. / THE DEMON** [ ] [-]

U.A. — not iss.

Apr 79. (7") *(UP 36507)* **ENGINE OF EXCESS. / JELLYFISH** [ ] [-]

Jul 79. (7") *(UP 36537)* **SECRETS. / BRAIN BOMB** [ ] [-]

Sep 79. (lp) *(UAG 30258)* **LAUGHING ACADEMY** [ ] [-]
– Puppet life / Funk me / The message / All white Jack / Obsession / Radar bug – Metropolis / British baboon / Babylon / Excess bleeding heart / Laughing academy. *(cd-iss. Sep93 on 'Dojo'+=; DOJOCD 147)* – Secrets / Brain bomb / Baby don't jump / Engine of excess / Jellyfish.

Liberty — not iss.

Feb 80. (7") *(BP 317)* **LAUGHING ACADEMY. / BABY DON'T JUMP** [ ] [-]

— (early in 1982) **NEVILLE + JIMMY** recruited new members **STEVE SEKRIT** – guitar + **TIM MAGENTA** – guitar

Red Rhino — not iss.

Mar 83. (7"; as PUNILUX) *(RED 33)* **HOLD ME (NEVER MOULD ME). / GOLDEN CORSETS** [ ] [-]

Sep 84. (m-lp; as PUNILUX) *(REDLP 34)* **7** [ ] [-]

— disbanded for the final time – NEVILLE LUXURY subsequently issued an album, 'FEELS LIKE DANCING WARTIME'; *REDLP 46)*

– compilations, etc. –

Aug 97. (lp/cd) *Overground; (OVER 66/+CD)* **REVOLUTION BY NUMBERS** [ ] [-]

PURE MORNING (see under ⇒ CLINIC)

PURESSENCE

Formed: Oldham, Lancashire, England . . . May '92 by JAMES MUDRICZKI, NEIL McDONALD, KEVIN MATTHEWS and TONY SZUMINSKI. Inspired by, or even idolising the STONE ROSES after their legendary 1990 Spike Island concert, PURESSENCE embarked on their own creative sojourn. In the summer of '92, their first of three singles over the course of the following year, the 'PETROL SKIN' EP, was issued by Northern imprint, '2 Damn Loud'. However, it wasn't until Island's Toby Chalmers took control, that the band's indie-rock direction started to take shape. In 1995, now signed to the aforementioned major, PURESSENCE found a larger fanbase with the much-improved 'I SUPPOSE' 45, having also supported MARION on tour. An eponymous debut set was in the shops by '96, although the track 'CASTING LAZY SHADOWS', should really have fared better when released as an accompanying single. However, the quartet finally made their long-awaited chart breakthrough when the track, 'THIS FEELING, burst into the UK Top 40 in 1998. Although the JOY DIVISION/MORRISSEY-laden, 'IT DOESN'T MATTER ANYMORE', just failed to do a similar feat, their second album, 'ONLY FOREVER', notched up sufficient sales. The high-pitched singer, JAMES, subsequently landed a bit part in the movie, 'Molly's Idle Ways', which starred SHAUN RYDER (of BLACK GRAPE), while the long-struggling PURESSENCE were happening big time in the Mediterranean sunspots of Greece and Israel.

Album rating: PURESSENCE (*6) / ONLY FOREVER (*6)

JAMES MUDRICZKI – vocals / **NEIL McDONALD** – guitar / **KEVIN MATTHEWS** – bass / **TONY SZUMINSKI** – drums

2 Damn Loud — not iss.

Jul 92. (12"ep) *(2DM 01)* **PETROL SKIN EP** [ ] [-]
– Telekenesis / Suck the knife / Polystyrene snow / Petrol skin.

Jan 93. (7") *(45rev 9)* **SIAMESE. / SCAPA FLOW** [ ] [-]
(above issued for the 'Rough Trade' singles club)

Apr 93. (12"/cd-s) *(2DM/+CD 02)* **OFFSHORE. / NONE HANDED / MIST** [ ] [-]

Island — not iss.

May 95. (12"/cd-s) *(12IS/CID 612)* **I SUPPOSE. / LET IT ALL GO / FREEFALL** [ ] [-]

Nov 95. (7") *(IS 619)* **FIRE. / YOU'RE ONLY TRYING TO TWIST MY ARM** [ ] [-]
(cd-s+=) *(CID 619)* – All star.

Apr 96. (7"/7"g-f) *(IS/+G 624)* **INDIA. / GUTTER GIRL** [ ] [-]
(cd-s+=) *(CID 624)* – Let down.

Apr 96. (cd/c/lp) *(CID/ICT/ILPS 8046)* **PURESSENCE** [ ] [-]
– Near distance / I suppose / Mr. Brown / Understanding / Fire / Traffic jam in memory lane / Casting lazy shadows / You're only trying to twist my arm / Every house on every street / India.

Jun 96. (7"/c-s) *(ISG/CIS 639)* **TRAFFIC JAM IN MEMORY LANE. / DIFFERENT SAND** [ ] [-]
(cd-s+=) *(CID 639)* – Sick of waiting.

Aug 96. (7"/c-s) *(IS/CIS 641)* **CASTING LAZY SHADOWS. / FIFTEEN YEARS** [ ] [-]
(cd-s+=) *(CID 641)* – Half the way you were.

May 98. (7") *(IS 688)* **THIS FEELING. / THINK OF THE TIMES** [33] [-]
(cd-s+=) *(CID 688)* – Walk on by.
(cd-s) *(CIDX 688)* – ('A'side) / Near distance (demo) / Northern framing company (demo) / London in the rain.
Jul 98. (7"/cd-s) *(IS 703)* **IT DOESN'T MATTER ANYMORE. / ANOTHER DAY ANOTHER NIGHT / TAKE A RIDE** [47] [-]
(cd-s) *(CIDX 703)* – ('A'side) / Drone / Deathtrap.
Aug 98. (cd/c/lp) *(CID/ICT/ILPS 8064)* **ONLY FOREVER** [36] [-]
Nov 98. (7") *(IS 722)* **ALL I WANT. / TURN THE LIGHTS (demo)** [39] [-]
(cd-s) *(CID 722)* – ('A'side) / Along the sure / This feeling.
(cd-s) *(CIDX 722)* – ('A'side) / Never be the same again / All I want (acoustic) / Casting lazy shadows (acoustic).

Jimmy PURSEY (see under ⇒ SHAM 69)

PUSHERMAN

Formed: London, England . . . 1994 out of baggy crusties, $KAW by Anglo-American six-piece of ANDY FRANK and YANK, who enlisted MARTIN HOYLAND, TONY ANTONIO, HARRY HARRISON and BO ELLERY. Taken under the wing of OASIS manager, Marcus Russell and signed to 'Ignition' ('Sony' in the States), PUSHERMAN were groomed for alternative crossover stardom with a series of support slots with the VERVE. Late in '95, the groovy punk/funk posse delivered their debut EP, 'FIRST TIME', followed over the course of the ensuing year by a further batch of singles culminating with a debut long-player, 'FLOORED' (1996).

Album rating: FLOORED (*6)

ANDY FRANK – vocals / **YANK** – vocals, harmonica / **MARTIN HOYLAND** – guitar / **TONY ANTONIO** – guitar / **HARRY HARRISON** – drums / **BO ELLERY** – bass

Ignition Sony

Nov 95. (12"ep/cd-ep) *(IGN TVE/CDE 1)* **FIRST TIME EP** [ ] [-]
Mar 96. (12"/cd-s) *(IGN TV/SCD 7)* **SHOW ME SLOWLY. / 95% / FIRST TIME (live)** [ ] [-]
May 96. (7") *(IGN 8)* **CHASE IT. / FAST CARS ARE DANGEROUS** [ ] [-]
(cd-s+=) *(IGNSCD 8)* – Lonely road.
Sep 96. (7") *(IGN 10)* **THE AIM INDEED. /** [ ] [-]
(cd-s+=) *(IGNSCD 10)* –
Sep 96. (cd/c/d-lp) *(IGN CD/MC/LP 1)* <67752> **FLOORED** [ ] [ ]
– Chase it / Sold / Aim indeed / So long ago / First time / Whole / Never coming back / Cos I lied / Show me slowly / Floored.
Jan 97. (7") *(IGN 11)* **SOLD. / NO LUCK** [ ] [-]
(cd-s+=) *(IGNSCD1 11)* – Clucking / Ducking.
(cd-s) *(IGNSCD2 11)* – ('A'side) / Whole (live) / Never coming back (live).

PUSSY GALORE

Formed: Washington DC, USA . . . 1985 by JON SPENCER and JULIE CAFRITZ, who first met at college in Providence, Rhode Island, the pair subsequently recruiting drummer JOHN HAMILL. The trio then invited photographer, CRISTINA MARTINEZ, to join up after she'd snapped them for the cover shot of their debut 7"ep, 'FEEL GOOD ABOUT YOUR BODY' (released on their own 'Shove' records). Featuring four tracks of primal hardcore, holocaustic industrial slime and scuzzy garage-punk, the band's nearest musical cousins were SONIC YOUTH, BIG BLACK and HUSKER DU, although PUSSY GALORE were in a noise terrorist league of their own. Adding NEIL HAGGERTY and replacing HAMMILL with former SONIC YOUTH man, BOB BERT, they took off to the more sympathetic New York, having slagged off local 'Dischord' label owner IAN McKAYE of MINOR THREAT (later FUGAZI). JON and CRISTINA set up home together, meeting up with the others to record their seriously deranged debut mini-set, 'GROOVY HATE FUCK' (1986), titles such as 'CUNT TEASE', 'TEENY PUSSY POWER' and 'YOU COOK LIKE A JEW', seeing the band court a sense of outrage that would characterise their whole career. In response to SONIC YOUTH's rumoured wholesale makeover of The BEATLES' 'White Album', SPENCER played up to the supposed rivalry by covering The ROLLING STONES' 'EXILE ON MAIN STREET' in its entirety, although only 550 cassettes were pressed. Release No.4 for the label (a joint effort with US label, 'Buy Our Records') came in the shape of 'PUSSY GALORE 5000' (1987), although by this point, CRISTINA, had opted to leave the band rather than further jeopardise her relationship with SPENCER, whom she later married. For their first full-length long-player, 'RIGHT NOW!' (1987), the band – who had now signed to 'Caroline' – were graced with the uncompromising production skills of former BIG BLACK leader, STEVE ALBINI, resulting in a marginally less shambolic, more focused slab of noise which saw the band begin to win over their critics. Later that year, NEIL was temporarily substituted with KURT WOLF, the latter's sole appearance being on the mini-set, 'SUGARSHIT SHARP' (1988). HAGGERTY returned to the pick up the pieces on follow-up proper, 'DIAL M FOR MOTHERFUCKER' (1989), although shortly prior to its release, JULIE added another nail to the band's coffin by finally taking her leave. SPENCER recalled HAGGERTY and BERT into the PUSSY GALORE fold for one last ditch attempt, coming in the shape of 'LA HISTORIA DE LA MUSICA ROCK' (1990), upon which the first twisted seeds of SPENCER's subsequent BLUES EXPLOSION were sown with swaggering covers of Elvis's 'CRAWFISH' and Willie Dixon's 'RED ROOSTER' (the latter disguised as 'ERIC CLAPTON MUST DIE'). The 90's saw HAGGERTY form ROYAL TRUX, while JULIE teamed up with SONIC YOUTH's KIM GORDON in FREE KITTEN; a musically re-united JON and CRISTINA also recorded a few albums under the BOSS HOG moniker. • **Songwriters:** JON and some with JULIE, except DAMAGED (Black Flag) / CRAWFISH (Elvis Presley) / YU GUNG (Einsturzende Neubauten) / LITTLE RED ROOSTER (Willie Dixon) / NO COUNT (Ty Wagner & The Scotchmen).

Album rating: EXILE ON MAIN STREET (*4) / RIGHT NOW! (*6) / DIAL M FOR MOTHERFUCKER (*6) / LA HISTORIA DE LA MUSICA ROCK (*5) / GROOVY HATE FUCK compilation UK (*6) / CORPSE LOVE: THE FIRST YEAR compilation (*6)

JON SPENCER – vocals, guitar / **JULIE 'Juicy' CAFRITZ** – guitar / **JOHN HAMMILL** – drums

not iss. Shove

Oct 85. (7"ep) <SHOV 1> **FEEL GOOD ABOUT YOUR BODY** [-] [ ]
– Die bitch / Car fantasy / Constant pain / HC rebellion.

— added **CRISTINA MARTINEZ** – guitar / **NEIL HAGGERTY** – guitar / **BOB BERT** – drums (ex-SONIC YOUTH); repl. HAMMILL who later joined ELEVATOR (he later appeared on supergroups' VELVET MONKEYS Oct90 album 'Rake'.

Jun 86. (m-lp) <SHOV 2> **GROOVY HATE FUCK (FEEL GOOD ABOUT YOUR BODY)** [-] [ ]
– Asshole / Cunt tease / Just wanna die / Kill yourself / Dead meat / Teeny pussy power / Spit'n'shit / You cook like a Jew / Get out / No count / Spin out. *(UK-iss.compilation Feb89 on 'Vinyl Drip'; SUK 001)*
Dec 86. (c;ltd) <SHOV 3> **EXILE ON MAIN STREET** [-] [ ]
(same tracks as ROLLING STONES d-lp from 1972)

— CRISTINA had departed in Autumn '86 and she later formed BOSS HOG

Jan 87. (m-lp) <SHOV 4> **PUSSY GALORE 5000** [-] [ ]
<also issued on US 'Buy Our Records'; BOR 12-010>

Product Inc. Caroline

Sep 87. (lp) *(33PROD 19)* <CAROL 1337> **RIGHT NOW!** [ ] [ ]
– Pig sweat / White noise / Uptight / Biker rock loser / Wretch / Rope legend / Fuck you, man / White people / New breed / Alright / Knock up / NYC 1999 / Punch out / Pussy stomp / Trash can oil drum / Fix it / Really suck / Rancid / Hell spawn. *(cd-iss. Feb88; PRODCD 19)*

— **KURT WOLF** – guitar; repl. NEIL

Oct 88. (m-lp/m-c) *(MPROD/+C 15)* **SUGAR SHIT SHARP** [ ] [ ]
– Yu gung / Adolescent wet dream / Brick / Handshake / Sweet little hi-fi / Renegade.

— **NEIL** returned to replace KURT who later joined LOUDSPEAKER

Apr 89. (lp/c/cd) *(INC LP/MC/CD 001)* <CAROL 1369-1/-4/-2> **DIAL M FOR MOTHERFUCKER** [ ] [ ]
– Understand my love / Kicked out / Undertaker / Dick Johnson / Eat me / Evil eye / Hang on / SM 57 / Solo = sex / D.W.D.A. / 1 hour later / Waxhead / A.D.W.D. 2. *(cd+=)* – Penetration of the centerfold / Handshake / Adolescent wet dream / Sweet little hi-fi / Brick / Renegade!. *(re-iss. Jun94; same)*

Sub Pop Sub Pop

Jun 89. (7") <SP 37> **DAMAGED. / (version by TAD)** [-] [ ]

not iss. Supernatural

1989. (7") **PENETRATION OF A CENTREFOLD / ?** [-] [ ]

— now a trio of **JON, NEIL + BOB,** when JULIE left later joining FREE KITTEN with KIM GORDON (SONIC YOUTH). She was also became part of VELVET MONKEYS.

Rough Trade Caroline

May 90. (lp/c/cd) *(ROUGH/+C/CD 149)* <CAROL 1618-1/-4/-2> **LA HISTORIA DE LA MUSICA ROCK** [ ] [ ]
– Dedication / Revolution summer / Will you still have me / Don't Jones me / (Do) The snake / Ship comin' in / Mono! man / Crawfish / Drop dead.

— disbanded finally just after above. JON formed JON SPENCER BLUES EXPLOSION while NEIL formed ROYAL TRUX (BOB joined ACTION SWINGERS). In 1990, an alter-ego of PUSSY GALORE going by the name of BOSS HOG, featured CRISTINA and 5 males. They released a few albums for 'Amphetamine Reptile', 'COLD HANDS' (1991) and 'GIRL POSITIVE' (Jun'93).

– compilations, etc. –

Apr 92. (cd/lp) *Hut; (HUT CD/LP 003) / Caroline; <CAROL 1706>* **CORPSE LOVE: THE FIRST YEAR** [ ] [ ] Feb92
– Die bitch / HC rebellion / Contact pain / Car fantasy / Fuck you, man / No count solo / Why would I say it to you / Groovy phone / Shit rain / Don't give a fuck about you / Soundcheck / D.M.P. / Teen pussy power / You look like a Jew / Cunt tease / Just wanna die / Dead meat / Kill yourself / Asshole / Spit 'n shit / Turd on the run / Ventilator blues / Just wanna see his face / Let it loose / Pretty fuck look / Spin out / Walk / Get out.

PYLON

Formed: Athens, Georgia, USA . . . 1980 by VANESSA BRISCOE, MICHAEL LACHOWSKI and RANDY BEWLEY, all having met at the University Of Georgia. Becoming a 4-piece with the addition of CURTIS CROWE, PYLON electrified both US and British audiences, promoting their early singles, 'COOL' and 'CRAZY', via a UK tour in 1982. Cool and Crazy was also an accurate description of their B-52's-esque sound, although their image was nothing out of the ordinary. After the release of debut album, 'GYRATE', late in '82, they took a sabbatical, returning four years later with their long-awaited follow-up, 'CHOMP' (1986). One of their biggest fans was MICHAEL STIPE (and his band R.E.M.), their aforementioned track, 'CRAZY', later covered by the Athens legends on their 'Dead Letter Office' collection. PYLON themselves, meanwhile, went to ground for another few years, the band coaxed back in '89 for a reformation and a tour supporting both R.E.M. and The B-52's. However, only a few releases on the low-key US 'Sky' label added to their existing legacy, namely the album, 'CHAIN' (1990) and the accompanying single, 'SUGARPOP'. • **Trivia:** JENNIFER BLAIR managed PYLON and can be contacted through JIM PARKER at Sky Records, 6400 Atlantic Blvd, Suite 220, Norcross, GA 30071, U.S.A.

Album rating: GYRATE (*6) / CHOMP (*7) / HITS compilation (*7) CHAIN (*5)

VANESSA BRISCOE – vocals / **RANDY BEWLEY** – guitar / **MICHAEL LACHOWSKI** – bass / **CURTIS CROWE** – drums

Armageddon D.B.

Feb 81. (10"ep) *(AEP 12-004)* **COOL. / DUB / DRIVING SCHOOL DANGER**

1981. (7") *<DB >* **CRAZY. / M TRAIN** -

Sep 83. (10"lp) *(ARM 5) <DB 54>* **GYRATE** Mar82
– Stop it / Precaution / Recent title / Volume / Gravity / Danger / Feast on my heart / Human body / Read a book / Working is no problem / Weather radio.

D.B. D.B.

Jul 86. (7") *(DB 61)* **GYRATE. / CRAZY**

Jul 86. (7") *(DB 62)* **BEEP. / ?**

Jul 86. (lp/c) *<(DB/+C 65)>* **CHOMP**
– K / Yo-yo / Beep / Italian movie theme / Crazy / M train / Buzz / No clocks / Reptiles / Spider / Gyrate / Attitude.

— disbanded 1986, although they re-formed in 1989

not iss. Sky

Oct 90. (lp/cd) *<SKY 2020/+CD>* **CHAIN** -
– Look alive / Catch / B-complex / Sugarpop / There it is / Springtime / This – That / Go / Crunch / Very right / Metal / Outside / Sloganistic. *(UK cd-iss. Aug94; same)*

Oct 90. (7") **SUGARPOP. /** -

— disbanded later in the 90's

– compilations, etc. –

1989. (cd) *D.B.; <DB 91>* **HITS** -
– Beep / Cool / Dub / Volume / Altitude / Gravity / Danger / Stop it / Feast on my heart / M-train / K / Driving school / Crazy / Yo-yo / Human body / Read a book / No clocks / Recent title / Working is no problem / Weather radio.

QUASI

Formed: Portland, Oregon, USA . . . mid 90's by former San Franciscans, SAM COOMES and JANET WEISS, both seasonal campaigners since 1989 for the likes of HEATMISER (ELLIOTT SMITH's old band) and SLEATER-KINNEY respectively. Trading in a unique hybrid of lo-fi drum'n'Hammond stylings, QUASI supported their old chum, ELLIOTT, in November to promote their second proper set, 'FEATURING "BIRDS"' (1998); previous albums being 'EARLY RECORDINGS' (1996) and 'R&B TRANSMOGRIFICATION' (1997).

Album rating: R&B TRANSMOGRIFICATION (*7) / FEATURING "BIRDS" (*7)

SAM COOMES – vocals, keyboards, guitar (ex-HEATMISER, ex-DONNER PARTY, ex-MOTORGOAT) / **JANET WEISS** – vocals, drums (of SLEATER-KINNEY)

not iss. | Key Op

Mar 96. (cd) *<23>* **EARLY RECORDINGS** [-] [ ]

Domino | Up

Mar 97. (cd) *<UP 40>* **R&B TRANSMOGRIFICATION** [-] [ ]
– Ghost dreaming / The ballad of mechanical man / In the first place / Bird's eye view / Two-faced / Ghost vs. vampire / R&B transmogrification / When I'm dead / Sugar / My coffin / Mama, papa, baby / Chocolate rabbit / Iron worm / Clouds.

Sep 98. (cd/lp) *(WIG CD/LP 055) <UP 54>* **FEATURING "BIRDS"** [ ] [ ] Apr98
– Our happiness is guarenteed / I never want to see you again / Poisoned well / Happy prole / Sea shanty / It's hard to turn me on / Nothing from nothing / Tomorrow you'll hide / California / You fucked yourself / Ape self prevails / Please do / I give up / Birds / Repetition / Only success can fail me now.

Kill Rock Stars | Kill Rock Stars

Oct 98. (7") *<(KRS 309)>* **QUASI. /** [ ] [ ]

QUEERS

Formed: North Hampton, USA . . . 1982 by the RAMONES obsessed teenagers, JOE QUEER, VAPID, B-FACE and DANNY PANIC. After the release of a 6-song EP that year they seemed to go into a 5-year hibernation, that is, until their debut album, 'LOVE SONGS' was issued in '88. They resurfaced again with a series of 'Lookout!' (once home of GREEN DAY) sets, including 'BEAT OFF' (1990), 'GROW UP' (1992), 'MOVE BACK HOME' (1995) and 'DON'T BACK DOWN' (1996). In 1998, still with a penchant for sounding like clones of the RAMONES, they moved to another label, 'Hopeless', which best describes their sixth album, 'PUNK ROCK CONFIDENTIAL'. Their blend of cartoon three-chord punk'n'roll will no doubt go down well with the new wave of poppy-punk that American acts were churning out, twenty-odd years too late! • **Covered:** THAT GIRL (Livermore) / GET OVER YOU (Undertones) / HAWAII + DON'T BACK DOWN + LITTLE HONDA (Brian Wilson/Beach Boys) / END IT ALL (Muffs) / SIDEWALK SURFIN' GIRL (Curb-Hatcher) / ANOTHER GIRL (Hernandez) / PRETTY FLAMINGO (Manfred Mann) / I ENJOY BEING A BOY (Banana Splits) + a complete tribute to the Ramones:- ROCKET TO RUSSIA.

Album rating: LOVE SONGS FOR THE RETARDED (*5) / BEAT OFF (*4) / GROW UP (*4) / MOVE BACK HOME (*6) / DON'T BACK DOWN (*4) / PUNK ROCK CONFIDENTIAL (*3)

JOE QUEER (b. KING) – vocals, guitar / **VAPID** – guitar, vocals / **B-FACE** (b. BARNARD) – bass, vocals / **DANNY PANIC** – drums

not iss. | unknown

1982. (7"ep) **6-SONG EP** [-] [ ]

Lookout | Lookout

1988. (lp) *<LOOKOUT 66>* **LOVE SONGS FOR THE RETARDED** [-] [ ]
– You're tripping / Ursula finally has tits / I hate everything / Teenage bonehead / Fuck this world / I can't stop farting / Feeling groovy / Debra Jean / Hi mom, it's me! / Noodlebrain / I can't stand you / Night of the livid queers / Granola head / I won't be / Monster zero / Daydreaming. *(UK-iss.Jul95 cd/c; LOOKOUT 66 CD/MC)*

1990. (lp) *<LOOKOUT 81>* **BEAT OFF** [-] [ ]
– Steak bomb / Drop the attitude fucker / You make me wanna puke / Teenage gluesniffer / Ben Weasel / Voodoo doll / Mirage / Grounded / Live this life / Half shitfaced / Too many twinkies / All screwed up. *(UK-iss.Jul95 cd/c; LOOKOUT 81 CD/MC)*

1990. (lp) *<LOOKOUT 90>* **GROW UP** [-] [ ]
– Squid omelet / Love love love / Boobarella / I met her at the rat / I'll be true to you / Burger king queen / Junk freak / Gay boy / Rambo rat / I don't wanna get involved / Goodbye California / Strip search. *(UK-iss.Jul95 cd/c/lp; LOOKOUT 90 CD/MC/LP)*

— **HUGH O'NEILL** – drums, bass; repl. VAPID + DANNY PANIC

Feb 95. (cd-ep) *<LOOKOUT 108>* **SURF GODDESS EP** [-] [ ]
– Mirage / Surf goddess / Get over you / +1

May 95. (cd/lp) *<(LOOKOUT 114 CD/LP)>* **MOVE BACK HOME** [ ] [ ]
– She's a cretin / Next stop rehab / High school psychopath II / If you only had a brain / I gotta girlfriend / Hawaii / From your body / Definitely / Everything's going my way / Cut it dude / I can't get invite to the prom / That girl / Peppermint girl.

Jan 96. (cd) *<LOOKOUT 130>* **A DAY LATE AND A DOLLAR SHORT** (compilation) [-] [ ]
– We'd have a riot doing heroin / Terminal rut / Fagtown / I want cunt / Trash this place / Love me / Kicked out the Webelos / Tuly is a wimp / At the mall / I spent the rent / I don't wanna work / I'm useless / This place sucks / Wimpy drives through Harlem / I like young girls / Nuni in New York / Nobody likes me / Nothing to do / Nowhere at all / Mac Arthurs park / Flesh for Tulu / Fuck you / Didn't want some / Meat wagon / Don't puke / Bonehead / Wimpy drives through Harlem / Nothing to do / Gay boy / Nobody likes me / Too many twinkies / Half shitfaced / I live this life / Live broadcast WFMJ 4/11/9?

Oct 96. (cd/lp) *<(LOOKOUT 140 CD/LP)>* **DON'T BACK DOWN** [ ] [ ] Aug96
– No tit / Punk rock girls / I'm ok, you're fucked / Number one / Don't back down / I only drink Bud / I always new / Born to do dishes / Janelle, Janelle / Brush your teeth / Sidewalk surfin' girl / Another girl / Love, love, love / I can't get over you.

Feb 97. (7"ep) *<(LOOKOUT 158)>* **BUBBLEGUM DREAMS EP** [ ] [ ]
– Punk rock girls / Never ever ever / Little Honda / End it all.

Hopeless | Hopeless

Jun 98. (cd-ep) *(HR 631CD)* **EVERYTHING'S OK / QUEERBAIT / GET A LIFE AND LIVE IT LOSER / I ENJOY BEING A BOY** [ ] [ ]

Oct 98. (cd/lp) *<(HR 636-2/-1)>* **PUNK ROCK CONFIDENTIAL** [ ] [ ]
– Tamara is a punk / Everything's OK / I didn't puke / Mrs. Brown, you've got an ugly daughter / The sun always shines around you / Rancid motherfuckers / Punk rock confidential / Today I fell in love / Pretty flamingo / Motherfucker / Like a parasite / Idiot savant / I enjoy being a boy / Don't mess it up / Sayonara sucker.

– compilations, etc. –

1994. (lp; shared with PINK LINCONS) *Just Add Water; <001>* **LIVE AT SOME PRICK'S HOUSE** [-] [ ]

Jan 98. (cd) *Clear View; <37>* **SUCK THIS LIVE (live)** [-] [ ]
– Squid omelet / We'd have a riot doing heroin / This place sucks / Tulu is a wimp / I want it now / Monster zero / Fuck up / Noodle brain / Granola gead / Hi mom . . . it's me!! / Teenage bonehead / Beer break / I spent the rent / Nothing to do / My old man's a fatso / Fuck you / Fuck the world / I hate everything / Ursula finally has tits / You're tripping.

Nov 98. (cd) *Clear View; <28>* **ROCKET TO RUSSIA** [-] [ ]

QUICKSPACE (SUPERSPORT) (see under ⇒ Th' FAITH HEALERS)

Paul QUINN

Born: 26 Dec'51, Glasgow, Scotland. He formed BOURGIE BOURGIE in 1983 with former JAZZATEERS members (IAN BURGOYNE, KEITH BAND and KENNY McDONALD) and scraped into the Top 50 early the following year with their much lawded 'M.C.A.' debut 45, 'BREAKING POINT'. A second, 'CARELESS' flopped and the band quickly disbanded, QUINN subsequently resurfacing on a collaboration single, 'PALE BLUE EYES' (a VELVET UNDERGROUND cover) with ORANGE JUICE mainman, EDWYN COLLINS. His first solo outing, 'AIN'T THAT ALWAYS THE WAY' was another for ALAN HORNE's (the man behind 'Postcard'; Glaswegian indie home of ORANGE JUICE, AZTEC CAMERA and JOSEF K) 'Swamplands' label, pursued by yet another top indie collaboration, this time 'ONE DAY' alongside ex-YAZOO and future ERASURE man VINCE CLARKE. For the rest of the 80's, QUINN's unique and extremely fluid voice took a back seat until the early 90's heralded his return with a sort of "Postcard" supergroup, 'PAUL QUINN AND THE INDEPENDENT GROUP. This included hip musicians featured were, JAMES KIRK (Orange Juice), BLAIR COWAN (Lloyd Cole & The Commotions), CAMPBELL OWENS (Aztec Camera), ROBERT HODGENS (Bluebells) and ALAN HORNE!, who had revived the 'Postcard' stable for this new act. In 1992, an album 'THE PHANTOMS AND THE ARCHETYPES' took rave reviews, QUINN's crooning voice never better on songs such as, 'HANGING ON', 'PUNK ROCK HOTEL' and the excellent title track. His retro film noir style (BILLY MacKENZIE or BILLY IDOL on mood pills) was again on song, when a follow-up, 'WILL I EVER BE INSIDE OF YOU' showed remarkable beauty, a re-working of 'STUPID THING' and a cover of 'MISTY BLUE' were top notch.

Album rating: THE PHANTOMS AND THE ARCHETYPES (*6) / WILL YOU EVER BE INSIDE OF ME (*6)

BOURGIE BOURGIE

PAUL QUINN – vocals / **IAN BURGOYNE** – guitar / **KEITH BAND** – bass (ex-JAZZATEERS) / **KENNY McDONALD** – drums

M.C.A. not iss.

Feb 84. (7") *(BOU 1)* **BREAKING POINT. / APRES SKI** 48 -
(12"+=) *(BOUT 1)* – ('A'extended).
Apr 84. (7") *(BOU 2)* **CARELESS. / CHANGE OF ATTITUDE** -
(12"+=) *(BOUT 2)* – ('A'extended).

PAUL QUINN

— first single a collaboration with the ex-ORANGE JUICE frontman

Swamplands not iss.

Aug 84. (7"; PAUL QUINN & EDWYN COLLINS) *(SWP 1)* **PALE BLUE EYES. / BURROW** -
Mar 85. (7") *(SWP 6)* **AIN'T THAT ALWAYS THE WAY. / PUNK ROCK HOTEL** -
(12"+=) *(SWX 6)* – Corrina Corrina.

— In Jun'85, QUINN collaborated with VINCE CLARKE (ex-YAZOO, ex-DEPECHE MODE, now ERASURE) on 7"/12", 'ONE DAY' (Mute; TAG/12TAG 1). (this was re-issued in Apr93; same cat.no.)

PAUL QUINN AND THE INDEPENDENT GROUP

PAUL QUINN with **JAMES KIRK** – guitar (ex-ORANGE JUICE) / **ALAN HORNE** – (creator of 'Postcard' label) / **CAMPBELL OWENS** – drums (of-AZTEC CAMERA) / **BLAIR COWAN** – bass (ex-LLOYD COLE & THE COMMOTIONS) / **ROBERT HODGENS** – rhythm guitar, vocals (ex-BLUEBELLS)

Postcard Thirsty Ear

Sep 92. (lp/c/cd) *(DUBH 921/+MC/CD)* **THE PHANTOMS AND THE ARCHETYPES** -
– The phantoms and the archetypes / Born on the wrong side of town / What can you do to me now / Punk rock hotel / Superstar / Call my name / The damage is done / Darling / I can't fight / Hanging on.
Jul 93. (7") *(DUBH 933)* **STUPID THING. / PASSING THOUGHT** -
(cd-s+=) *(DUBH 933)* – Superstar.

— HODGENS replaced by **MICK SLAVEN** – / **SLIP REID** – / **ANDY ALSTON** – / **JANE MARIE O'BRIEN** –

Oct 94. (lp/c/cd) *(DUBH 945/+MC/CD)* *<57024>* **WILL I EVER BE INSIDE OF YOU** 1996
– Will I ever be inside of you / You have been seen / Lover, that's all you over / Mooreefoc (misty blue) / A passing thought / Outre / Misty blue / Stupid thing / At the end of the night.
Jun 95. (cd-ep; PAUL QUINN, The NECTARINE NO.9 / JOCK SCOTT) *(DUBH 952CD)* **PREGNANT WITH POSSIBILITES EP** -
– Tiger tiger / Will I ever be inside of you / Just another f***ed-up little druggy on the scene / Grunge girl groan.

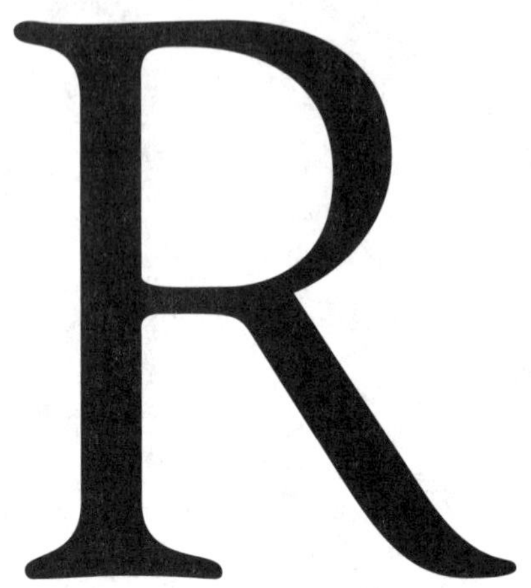

RADAR BROTHERS

Formed: San Fernando, California, USA . . . 1995 by former MAIDS OF GRAVITY and MEDICINE man, JIM PUTTNAM. Abandoning psychedelic noise for a life of reflective "sadcore", PUTTNAM recruited a rhythm section of SEONON WILLIAMS and STEVE GOODFRIEND, cobbling together ragged strands of COWBOY JUNKIES, NEIL YOUNG and early 70's era BEACH BOYS on their eponymous late '95 debut mini-set. Approximately a year later, the trio emerged with a full-length album on 'Restless', confusingly enough again entitled simply 'RADAR BROTHERS', the record cementing – especially among UK critics – PUTTNAM's reputation as a long lost musical cousin to the likes of SMOG's BILL CALLAHAN.

Album rating: RADAR BROTHERS (*7)

JIM PUTTNAM (b.30 Sep'67) – vocals, guitar (ex-MEDICINE) / **SEONON WILLIAMS** – bass / **STEVE GOODFRIEND** – drums

		not iss.	Fingerpaint
Nov 95.	(m-cd) *<4004>* **RADAR BROTHERS**	-	
		not iss.	Restless
Oct 96.	(cd) *<72927>* **RADAR BROTHERS** – Lose your face again / Capital gain / Wise mistake of you / Stay / Supermarket pharmacy / On the floor / We're over here / Distant mine / Underwater culprits / This drive / Take stuff / Goddess.	-	

RADIAL SPANGLE

Formed: Oklahoma City, Oklahoma, USA . . . 1991 by ALAN LAIRD, APRIL TIPPENS and RICHARD ENGLISH. Inspired by the redneck isolation of their dustbowl environment, LAIRD and Co befriended fellow musical mavericks, MERCURY REV, whose DAVID FRIDMANN and JONATHAN DONAHUE produced their debut album, 'ICE CREAM HEADACHE' (1993). There was one further connection between the bands in that both recorded first for the 'Mint Tea' label and later for 'Beggars Banquet', the 'BIRTHDAY' single being RADIAL SPANGLE's first effort for the latter imprint. A self-confessed archetypal middle class slacker, LAIRD admitted to being influenced by everything from The CARPENTERS to the MARQUIS DE SADE, the music an equally schizophrenic lunge between grating SONIC YOUTH-style noise and whimsical, SYD BARRETT-esque nursery pop. These tactics were employed to impressive effect on 1994's 'SYRUP MACRAME', after which the band dissolved; MERCURY REV also fell apart around the same time and while that group were reborn to great critical acclaim in the late 90's, RADIAL SPANGLE were left with only memories of their short-lived indie stardom.

Album rating: ICE CREAM HEADACHE (*6) / SYRUP MACRAME (*7)

ALAN LAIRD – vocals, guitar / **APRIL TIPPENS** – bass / **RICHARD ENGLISH** – drums

		Mint Tea	Mint Tea
May 93.	(cd/lp) *<MINT CD/LP 8>* **ICE CREAM HEADACHE** – Raze / Canopy and shoe / Dream problem / Drop / Snow / Birthday / Hand / Gutter chain / White paper basket / Copper.		
Jul 93.	(12"ep/cd-ep) *(MINT 7 T/CD)* **RAZE. / CURTAIN LEAF / SAPPHIRE**		-
		Beggars Banquet	Beggars Banquet
Nov 93.	(12"ep/cd-ep) *(BEG 24 T/CD)* **BIRTHDAY / TURPENTINE. / BIRTHDAY / SNOW**		-
	—— added **KENNEDY** – co-writer on 2 songs		
Aug 94.	(cd/lp) *(BBQ CD/LP 163) <92476>* **SYRUP MACRAME** – Marble / Special love / Caf, 'fine / Busy hole / Cross your legs / Knees / New dress / Dragonfly / Patio furniture / Sunflower graveyard.		

—— disbanded after above

RADIATORS FROM SPACE

Formed: Dublin, Ireland . . . 1976 initially as GRETA GARBAGE & THE TRASHCANS by STEVE RAPID and PETER HOLIDAI, the pair recruiting PHILIP CHEVRON, MARK MEGARAY and JAMES CRASH as they became The RADIATORS FROM SPACE. The first Irish band of the punk era to get a single out in the UK (having already signed to 'C.B.S.' in Eire), Spring '77's 'TELEVISION SCREEN' was a heady slice of R&B-influenced punk-pop. Having subsequently relocated to London (home of 'Chiswick' records), they issued a second single, 'ENEMIES' and an accompanying album, 'TV TUBE HEART', later that year. While rivals The BOOMTOWN RATS invaded their space, so to speak, the band trimmed down their moniker and their personnel after losing vocalist STEVE RAPID. The RADIATORS, as they were now known, returned in 1979 with a series of singles (including near hit, 'MILLION DOLLAR HERO'), all featuring on their belated and difficult second set, 'GHOSTOWN'. After another batch of 45's the wanna-be-stars finally burned out, HOLIDAI striking out to join LIGHT A BIG FIRE while CHEVRON issued a few solo singles. The RADIATORS were turned on again – but only briefly this time – releasing a one-off set for 'Warners' (Ireland), 'BUYING GOLD FROM HEAVEN' (1987), after which CHEVRON was invited to join The POGUES.

Album rating: THE RADIATORS FROM SPACE (*5) / GHOSTOWN (*5)

STEVE RAPID – vocals / **PHILIP CHEVRON** – guitar, vocals / **PETER HOLIDAI** – guitar, vocals / **MARK MEGARAY** – bass, vocals / **JAMES CRASH** – drums

		Chiswick	not iss.
Apr 77.	(7") *(NS 10)* **TELEVISION SCREEN. / LOVE DETECTIVE**		-
Oct 77.	(7") *(NS 19)* **ENEMIES. / PSYCHOTIC REACTION**		-
Oct 77.	(lp) *(WIK 4)* **TV TUBE HEART** – Television screen / Prison bars / Great expectations / Roxy girl / Press gang / Contact / Sunday world / Electric shares / Enemies / Ripped and torn / Not too late / Blitzin' at the Ritz / Party line.		-
Sep 78.	(7"w/drawn) *(NS 24)* **PRISON BARS. / (WHY CAN'T I BE A) TEENAGER IN LOVE**	-	-

RADIATORS

—— now without STEVE RAPID

Jan 79.	(7") *(NS 29)* **MILLION DOLLAR HERO (IN A FIVE AND TEN CENTS STORE). / BLITZIN' AT THE RITZ**		-
May 79.	(7"w/drawn) *(NS 45)* **WALKIN' HOME ALONE AGAIN. / TRY AND STOP ME / THE HUCKLEBUCK**	-	-
Jun 79.	(7") *(CHIS 113)* **LET'S TALK ABOUT THE WEATHER. / THE HUCKLEBUCK / TRY AND STOP ME**		-
Jun 79.	(lp) *(CWK 3003)* **GHOSTOWN** – Million dollar hero / Let's talk about the weather / Johnny jukebox / Confidential / They're looting in the town / Who are the strangers? / Ballad of Kitty Rickets / Song of the faithful departed / Walkin' home alone again / Dead the beast, dead the poison.		-
Aug 79.	(7") *(CHIS 115)* **KITTY RICKETS. / SONG OF THE FAITHFUL DEPARTED**		-
Jul 80.	(7") *(CHIS 126)* **STRANGER THAN FICTION. / PRISON BARS / WHO ARE THE STRANGERS?**		-
Sep 80.	(7") *(CHIS 133)* **THE DANCING YEARS. / (part 2 – instrumental)**		-
Dec 80.	(7") *(CHIS 144)* **SONG OF THE FAITHFUL DEPARTED. / THEY'RE LOOTING IN THE TOWN**	-	- Irish

—— split and HOLIDAI later joined LIGHT A BIG FIRE

PHILIP CHEVRON

		Mosa	not iss.
Nov 81.	(12"ep) *(MOEP 412)* **SONGS FROM BILL'S DANCE HALL**		-
		Imp-Demon	not iss.
Oct 83.	(7") *(IMP 002)* **THE CAPTAIN AND THE KINGS. / FAITHFUL DEPARTED**		-

RADIATORS

returned and signed to 'WEA' in Ireland.

		Hotwire	not iss.
Jun 87.	(lp) *(HWLP 8503)* **BUYING GOLD FROM HEAVEN**		-

—— PHIL CHEVRON went on to join The POGUES

– compilations, etc. –

Jul 79.	(7"ep) *Big Beat; (NS 57)* FOUR ON THE FLOOR – Enemies / Teenager in love / Television screen / Psychotic reaction.		-
Feb 89.	(7") *Ace-Chiswick; (NS 128)* **UNDER CLEARY'S CLOCK. / TAKE MY HEART AND RUN** (12"+=) *(NST 128)* – Strangers in fiction.		-
Oct 95.	(cd) *Chiswick; (CDWIKD 156)* **COCKLES & MUSSELS (THE BEST OF THE RADIATORS)** – Television screen / Love detective / Sunday world / Prison bars / Party line / Roxy girl / Enemies / Try and stop me / Million dollar hero (in a five and ten cents store) / Let's talk about the weather / Johnny Jukebox / Confidential / They're looting in the town / Who are the strangers / Kitty Ricketts / Ballad of the faithful departed / Walking home alone again / Dead the beast, dead the poison / Stranger than fiction / The dancing years / Under Cleary's clock / Plura bell / Television screen.		-
Jun 96.	(cd) *Chiswick; (CDWIKD 164)* **ALIVE ALIVE O! (live)**		-

RADICAL DANCE FACTION

Formed: Reading, England . . . 1987 from the remnants of Hungerford reggae collective, MILITARY SURPLUS by mainman CHRIS BOWSHER and Co. In the eyes of a largely hostile press, RDF were the archetypal crusty band, beloved of dog-on-string types who formed the bulk of their audience. To BOWSHER, his band were observers of the dispossessed, relaying their stories through a combination of roots, dub, punk and frantic beat poetry. Signed to the 'Earth Zone' label, the band debuted with the 'BORDERLAND CASES' album in 1989, following it up with 'WASTELAND' (1991), the latter set featuring a guest appearance by ROOTS RADICS man, STYLE SCOTT. Yet despite being continually on the verge of wider indie recognition, RDF never really managed the quantum leap of more commercial contemporaries like The LEVELLERS and BACK TO THE PLANET.

Album rating: BORDERLAND CASES (*5) / WASTELAND (*5) / RAGGAMUFFIN STATEMENT (*5)

CHRIS BOWSHER – vocals / + others (unknown)

Earth Zone / not iss.

Dec 89. (lp/cd) *(EZ 001/+CD)* **BORDERINE CASES** [ ] [-]
– Surplus people / Chinese poem / Borderline / Rogue trooper (live mix) / 4 Chuck Chant / Back in the same place / Riverwise / Hot on the wire / Sorepoint for a sickman / Firepower (MILITARY SURPLUS / RDF). *(re-iss. Jul94; same)*

Aug 91. (lp/c/cd; as RDF) *(EZ 003/+MC/CD)* **WASTELAND** [ ] [-]

Ax-s / not iss.

Jun 93. (12"ep/cd-ep) *(AXS93 12/CD 001)* **BEAST IN THE DOORWAY / DIRTY OLD TOWN. / BEAST IN THE DUB / MARTIN FORAN (demo)** [ ] [-]

Inna State / not iss.

Jun 95. (cd/c/lp) *(CD/MC/LP 4DS4A)* **RAGGAMUFFIN STATEMENT** [ ] [-]

RADIO BIRDMAN

Formed: Sydney, Australia . . . September 1974 by American medical students DENIZ TEK and PHILIP 'PIP' HOYLE, alongside ROB YOUNGER, WARWICK GILBERT, RON KEELY and CARL ROURKE. Being a part-time project, RADIO BIRDMAN weren't exactly the most prolific of New Wave acts, releasing only two domestic singles prior to their first UK visit early in '78. By this time, new guitarist CHRIS MUSUAK had replaced bassist CARL ROURKE and with their Australian singles selling well on import, 'Sire', signed them up for a debut album, 'RADIO APPEAR' (1978). Very much in the balls-out MC5/STOOGES mould, 'BIRDMAN couldn't quite break the already congested UK/US market and subsequently flew back to their homeland. After a further Australian-only album, 'LIVING EYES' (1981), YOUNGER, TEK and GILBERT hooked up with their long-time heroes, RON ASHETON (ex-STOOGES) and DENNIS THOMPSON (ex-MC5) to form The NEW RACE; the appropriately-title concert set, 'THE FIRST AND THE LAST', was the sole recorded output of this short-lived project. YOUNGER subsequently concentrated on a production career as well as playing in his own band, The NEW CHRISTS. A belated RADIO BIRDMAN reunion album, 'RITUALISM', saw the band briefly plucked from obscurity in 1997.

Album rating: RADIO APPEAR (*7) / LIVING EYES (*8) / RITUALISM (*4)

ROB YOUNGER – vocals / **DENIZ TEK** (b. Detroit, Michigan, USA) – guitar / **PIP HOYLE** (b. USA) – organ, guitar / **CHRIS MUSUAK** – guitar, piano; repl. CARL ROURKE / **WARWICK GILBERT** – bass / **RON KEELY** – drums

Trafalgar / not iss.

Oct 76. (7"ep) *(ME 109)* **BURN MY EYE EP** [-] [-] Austra
– Smith Wesson blues / Snake / 1-94 / Burned my eye.

Jun 77. (7") *(TRS 11)* **NEW RACE. / TV EYE** [-] [-] Austra

Sire / Sire

Mar 78. (7") *(6078 617)* **WHAT GIVES. / ANGLO GIRL DESIRE** [ ] [ ]

Apr 78. (lp) *(9103 332)* <SRK 6050> **RADIO APPEAR** [ ] [ ]
– What gives / Non stop girls / Do the pop / Man with the golden helmet / Descent into the maelstrom / New race / Aloha Steve & Danno / Anglo girl desire / Murder city nights / You're gonna miss me / Hand of law / Hit them again. *(cd-iss. +re-mast.Jan98 on 'Red Eye'; REDCD 49)*

Trafalgar / not iss.

May 78. (7") *(TRS 12)* **ALOHA STEVE AND DANNO. / ANGLO GIRL DESIRE** [-] [-] Austra

WEA / not iss.

Mar 81. (lp) *(600085)* **LIVING EYES** [-] [-] Austra
(cd-iss. +re-mast.Jan98 on 'Red Eye'; REDCD 53)

Apr 81. (7") *(100160)* **ALONE IN THE ENDZONE. / BREAKS MY HEART** [-] [-] Austra

— disbanded after above and YOUNGER became top-notch producer. In 1982, WARWICK and MUSUAK formed The HITMEN with ex-SAINTS drummer IVOR HAY and future HOODOO GURUS members (not to be confused with UK band of same name 1980-82).

NEW RACE

— **ROB YOUNGER** – vocals / **DENIZ TEK** – guitar / **WARWICK GILBERT** – bass / **RON ASHETON** – guitar (ex-STOOGES) / **DENNIS THOMPSON** – drums (ex-MC5)

Statik / not iss.

Jun 83. (lp) *(STATLP 16)* **THE FIRST AND THE LAST (live 1981)** [ ] [-]
– Crying sun / Haunted road / Sad T.V. / Breaks my heart / Looking at you / November 22, 1963 / Alone in the endzone / Love kills / Gotta keep movin' / Columbia. *(cd-iss. Oct97 on 'Total Energy'; NER 3013)*

— YOUNGER went on to form NEW CHRISTS, who made two turn of the decade albums for 'Citadel'; 'DISTEMPER' & 'DIVINE RITES'. On the latter, they (others being :- CHARLIE OWEN, JIM DICKSON + NICK FISHER) were joined by MUSUAK.

RADIO BIRDMAN

— re-formed the originals

Citadel / Crying Sun

Jun 97. (cd+book) *(CSREC 001)* **RITUALISM** [ ] [ ]

RADIOHEAD

Formed: Oxford, England . . . 1988 by frontman THOM YORKE, guitarist ED O'BRIEN and bassist COLIN GREENWOOD with drummer PHIL SELWAY completing the line-up. Dubbing themselves ON A FRIDAY, the band began gigging around Oxford, subsequently boasting a triple guitar attack following the addition of COLIN's brother, JONNY. Initially, the group also fleshed out their sound with a couple of saxaphone players (though it's now difficult to imagine what that must have sounded like). With the various members trooping off to complete their respective educations, the RADIOHEAD story really began in the summer of '91 when the band got back together and adopted the aforesaid moniker (after a TALKING HEADS song). Signed to the ever vigilant 'Parlophone', the band enjoyed some airplay with their first release, a Spring '92 EP with 'PROVE YOURSELF' as the lead track. Next up was the seminal 'CREEP', an incendiary anthem for anyone who'd ever felt rejected/alienated (and let's face it, that's most of the population), the song stiffing first time round but subsequently kickstarting RADIOHEAD's career. The track also used the group's trademark soft bit/quiet bit dynamics to stunning effect, a method which would come to form the basis for some of the band's best tracks. In the meantime, RADIOHEAD eventually scraped in to the lower regions of the Top 40 with the abrasive 'ANYONE CAN PLAY GUITAR', the debut album, 'PABLO HONEY' making the UK Top 30 around the same time in early '93. Though it had its moments, the album lacked consistency with YORKE seemingly searching for some kind of vocal identity. While the record found enthusiastic champions in some sections of the music press, by and large, RADIOHEAD were passed over. All that changed, however, when 'CREEP' exploded in the States, the record obviously striking a deep chord with the multitudes who weren't part of the 'American Dream'. Taking the first flight over there, RADIOHEAD capitalised on this surprise success, the band treated like homecoming heroes and selling out concerts night after night. In a bizarre reversal of the standard process, this US success laid the groundwork for the re-release of 'CREEP' in the UK, where it became a Top 10 hit, sales of the album also enjoying a healthy re-invigoration. With such a universal theme, it was no surprise that the track was also a massive hit all over the world, RADIOHEAD finding themselves in the strange position of being international pop stars yet at the same time, regarded merely as a competent indie band in their home country. 'THE BENDS' (1995) convincingly silenced the doubters once and for all, a groundbreaking album with a spectral musical vision which rarely failed to take the breath away. Opening with the searing, reverbating 'PLANET TELEX' the record proceeded to juxtaopse howling guitar menace against bleakly beautiful melodies, echoing synth and acoustic strumming, YORKE painting piercingly vivid images with his tortured musings on the nature of the human psyche. The fragile majesty of'FAKE PLASTIC TREES' was RADIOHEAD at their most sublime, YORKE's ability to hit those high notes pivotal to the resigned melancholy of his vocals. The churning claustrophobia of 'BLACK STAR' sounded like the final fling of a condemned man, positively revelling in its own pain and misery, while the funereal 'STREET SPIRIT' was a ghostly coda, its award-winning video perfectly evoking the track's haunting feeling of time standing still. Basically, the album wiped the floor with the competition, laying waste to the snot-nosed chaff of Brit-pop and confirming that there was indeed a thinking man's alternative to OASIS. R.E.M. felt the same way, inviting the band to support them on tour later that year, something of a dream come true for RADIOHEAD who had long been massive fans of STIPE & Co. The summer of '95 also saw the release of the 'HELP' album, a project involving the cream of the British music scene with proceeds from album sales donated to the War Child charity (which raised money for war torn Bosnia). RADIOHEAD contributed 'LUCKY', a song apparently written about the band's newfound position as one of the most highly regarded group's in the world. Stunning though the track is, it sounds more like a dirge than a celebration, the searing guitar line evoking a feeling of utter desolation and emptiness. Probably the best example of YORKE's self-acknowledged struggle to sound anything other than melancholy, the track was one of many highlights on 'OK COMPUTER' (1997), RADIOHEAD's feverishly anticipated follow-up to the poll-topping 'THE BENDS'. A densely complex, almost initally impenetrable album, 'OK..' was a demanding beast, previewed by the wildly ambitious 'PARANOID ANDROID', a kind of post-prog symphony in three parts. The oscillating guitar vibration of 'AIRBAG' kicked off proceedings in much the same fashion as 'PLANET TELEX', but then things started getting weird. 'SUBTERRANEAN HOMESICK ALIEN' was truly adrift in space, the guitars twinkling and shimmering like tiny constellations, while with 'EXIT MUSIC (FOR A FILM)' (written for closing sequence of the revamped 'Romeo And Juliet' movie), YORKE's vocal was so eerily intimate, it sounded as if he was in the same room, the song building to a majestic climax via unearthly choral parts and swooning synths. 'LET DOWN' was an almost BYRDS-esque follow-up to 'CREEP', its pealing guitar and infectious melody framing a similar theme and creating what was conceivably the nearest the record came to conventional rock. Much of the album was vaguely reminiscent of the more cerebral moments on U2's 'Unforgettable Fire', although YORKE has never come so close to sounding like BONO as on 'CLIMBING THE WALLS', for once managing to avoid the bruised resignation that normally colours his voice. With 'NO SURPRISES', RADIOHEAD cleverly contrasted an almost child-like musical lullaby with lyrics expressing a hopeless world weariness. Of their contemporaries, only SPIRITUALIZED and MOGWAI were making music this far out, RADIOHEAD once again almost sweeping the board at the end of year polls and bravely taking rock music into the future rather than fawning over a Union Jack-clad past.

Album rating: PABLO HONEY (*8) / THE BENDS (*9) / OK COMPUTER (*9)

THOM YORKE (b. 7 Oct'68) – vocals, guitar / **ED O'BRIEN** (b.15 Apr'68) – guitar, vocals / **JON GREENWOOD** (b. 5 Nov'71) – guitar / **COLIN GREENWOOD** (b.26 Jun'69) – bass / **PHIL SELWAY** (b.23 May'67) – drums

Parlophone / Capitol

May 92. (c-ep/12"ep/cd-ep) *(TCR/12R/CDR 6312)* **DRILL EP** [ ] [ ]
– Prove yourself / Stupid car / You / Thinking about you.

Sep 92. (c-ep/12"ep/cd-ep) *(TCR/12R/CDR 632?) <15978?* **CREEP / LURCEE. / INSIDE MY HEAD / MILLION $ QUESTION** [ ] [ ] Apr93

Feb 93. (c-ep/12"ep/cd-ep) *(TCR/12R/CDR 6333)* **ANYONE CAN PLAY GUITAR. / FAITHLESS, THE WONDER BOY / COKE BABIES** [32] [–]

Feb 93. (cd/c/lp) *(CD/TC+/PCS 7360) <81409>* **PABLO HONEY** [25] [32] Jun93
– You / Creep / How do you? / Stop whispering / Thinking about you / Anyone can play guitar / Ripcord / Vegetable / Prove yourself / I can't / Lurgee / Blow out.

May 93. (c-ep/12"ep/cd-ep) *(TCR/12R/CDR 6345)* **POP IS DEAD / BANANA CO. (acoustic). / CREEP (live) / RIPCORD (live)** [42] [–]

Jun 93. (c-s,cd-s) *<44932>* **CREEP / FAITHLESS, THE WONDER BOY** [–] [34]

Sep 93. (7"clear-ep/c-ep/cd-ep) *(RS/TCR/CDR 6359)* **CREEP / YES I AM. / BLOW OUT (remix) / INSIDE MY HEAD (live)** [7] [–]
(12"ep) *(12RG 6359)* – ('A'-acoustic KROQ) / You (live) / Vegetable (live) / Killer cars (live).

Oct 94. (c-ep/12"ep) *(TCR/12R 6984) <58274>* **MY IRON LUNG / THE TRICKSTER / LEWIS (mistreated) / PUNCHDRUNK LOVESICK SINGALONG** [24] [ ]
(cd-s) *(CDRS 6394)* – (1st & 4th track) / Lozenge of love.
(cd-s) *(CDR 6394)* – (1st & 2nd track) / Permanent daylight / You never wash up after yourself.

Mar 95. (c-s) *(TCR 6405) <58537>* **HIGH & DRY / PLANET TELEX** [17] [ ] Feb96
(cd-s+=) *(CDR 6405)* – Killer cars / Planet Telex (LFO JD mix).
(cd-s+=) *(CDRS 6405)* – Maquiladora / Planet Telex (hexadecimal mix).
(12") *(12R 6405)* – Planet Telex (hexadecimal mix) / Planet Telex (LFO JD mix) / Planet Telex (hexadecimal dub) / High & dry.

Mar 95. (cd/c/lp) *(CD/TC+/PCS 7372) <29626>* **THE BENDS** [6] [88]
– Planet Telex / The bends / High & dry / Fake plastic trees / Bones (nice dream) / Just / My iron lung / Bulletproof . . .I wish I was / Black star / Sulk / Street spirit (fade out).

May 95. (c-ep/cd-ep) *(TCR/CDRS 6411) <58424>* **FAKE PLASTIC TREES / INDIA RUBBER / HOW CAN YOU BE SURE?** [20] [ ] Jul95
(cd-s) *(CDR 6411)* – ('A'side) / ('A'acoustic) / Bulletproof..I wish I was (acoustic) / Street spirit (fade out) (acoustic).

Aug 95. (c-ep/12"ep) *(TCR/12R 6415)* **JUST / PLANET TELEX (Karma Sun Ra mix) / KILLER CARS (mogadon mix)** [19] [–]
(cd-s) *(CDR 6415)* – ('A'side) / Bones (live) / Planet Telex (live) / Anyone can play guitar (live).

Jan 96. (7"white) *(R 6419) <82523>* **STREET SPIRIT (FADE OUT). / BISHOP'S ROBES** [5] [ ]
(cd-s+=) *(CDRS 6419)* – Talk show host.
(cd-s) *(CDR 6419)* – ('A'side) / Banana co. / Molasses.

Feb 96. (c-s,cd-s) *<58537>* **HIGH AND DRY / FAKE PLASTIC TREES** [–] [78]

Jun 97. (7") *(NODATA 01)* **PARANOID ANDROID. / POLYETHYLENE (PARTS 1 & 2)** [3] [–]
(cd-s+=) *(CDNODATAS 01)* – Pearly.
(cd-s) *(CDNODATA 01)* – ('A'side) / A reminder / Melatonin.

Jun 97. (cd/c/d-lp) *(CD/TC+/NODATA 02) <55229>* **OK COMPUTER** [1] [21]
– Airbag / Paranoid android / Subterranean homesick alien / Exit music (for a film) / Karma police / Electioneering / Climbing up the walls / No surprises / Lucky / The tourist.

Aug 97. (cd-s) *(CDNODATA 03)* **KARMA POLICE / CLIMBING UP THE WALLS (Fila Brazillia & Zero 7 mixes)** [8] [ ]
(12"+=) *(12NODATA 03)* – Meeting in the aisle.
(cd-s) *(CDNODATAS 03)* – ('A'side) / Meeting in the aisle / Lull.

Jan 98. (12") *(12NODATA 04)* **NO SURPRISES. / PALO ALTO** [4] [ ]
(c-s+=/cd-s+=) *(TC/CD NODATA 04)* – How I made my millions.
(cd-s) *(CDNODATAS 04)* – ('A'side) / Airbag (live) / Lucky (live).

Apr 98. (m-cd) *(858701-2)* **AIRBAG / PEARLY (remix) / MEETING IN THE AISLE / A REMINDER / POLYTHENE (parts 1 & 2) / MELATONIN / PALO ALTO** [ ] [–]
(above wasn't legitimate to chart in Britain)

Apr 98. (m-cd) *<58071>* **AIRBAG / HOW AM I DRIVING (EP)** [–] [56]

RADIO STARS

Formed: London, England . . . early 1977 by former JOHN'S CHILDREN and JET frontman, ANDY ELLISON, alongside IAN McLEOD and MARTIN GORDON (also ex-JET). Almost immediately joined by NEO drummer, PAUL SIMON (no, not that one!), they signed a deal with 'Chiswick' records and wasted no time in getting debut single, 'DIRTY PICTURES', on the shelves (but not the top ones). Shifting to a different frequency from their past musical endeavours, The RADIO STARS presented a more refined blend of power-pop/new wave bandwagoneering. Finding a more permanent drummer in STEVE PARRY, the colourful quartet released an EP, 'STOP IT', prior to achieving short-lived chart glory with the Top 40, 'NERVOUS WRECK'. Towards the end of the year, the seasoned 'STARS delivered their first album, the sarcastically-titled 'SONGS FOR SWINGING LOVERS' (actually the name of a classic FRANK SINATRA lp). With new wave moving on to a more experimental channel, The RADIO STARS were left behind, the result being poor sales of their subsequent 45's and follow-up set, 'HOLIDAY ALBUM' (1978). Nevertheless, the band's off-kilter sense of humour shone through on the likes of '(I'VE GOT DEM OLD) SEX IN CHAINS BLUES (AGAIN MAMA)', alongside a cover of The Beatles' 'NORWEGIAN WOOD'. By this time, MARTIN had been replaced by JAMIE CROMPTON, although the latter was in turn succeeded by JOHN MACKIE and former SPARKS guitarist TREVOR WHITE. However, further personnel changes left the band effectively dead, although ELLISON briefly resurrected the name in 1982.

Album rating: SONGS FOR SWINGING LOVERS (*5) / HOLIDAY ALBUM (*4)

ANDY ELLISON – vocals, guitar (ex-JOHN'S CHILDREN, ex-JET) / **IAN McLEOD** – guitar (ex-JET) / **MARTIN GORDON** – bass (ex-JET) / **PAUL SIMON** – drums (also of NEO)

Chiswick / not iss.

Apr 77. (7") *(NS 9)* **DIRTY PICTURES. / SAIL AWAY** [ ] [–]

— (Jul'77) **STEVE PARRY** – drums; repl. PAUL who joined COWBOYS INTERNATIONAL

Aug 77. (7"ep) *(SW 17)* **STOP IT** [ ] [–]
– No Russians in Russia / Box 29 / Johnny Mekon / Sorry I'm tied up.

Oct 77. (7"/12") *(NS/+T 23)* **NERVOUS WRECK. / HORRIBLE BREATH** [39] [–]

Dec 77. (lp) *(WIK 5)* **SONGS FOR SWINGING LOVERS** [ ] [–]
– Good personality / Is it really necessary / Eric / The beast of Barnsley / Nervous wreck / Nothing happened today / Buy Chiswick records / Don't waste my time / Arthur is dead boring / Macaroni and mice / Nice girls / Talkin' 'bout you. *(free-7"w.a.)* – NO RUSSIANS IN RUSSIA. / DIRTY PICTURES

Apr 78. (7",6") *(NS 36)* **FROM A RABBIT. / TO A BEAST** [ ] [–]

— **JAMIE CROMPTON** – drums (ex-NEW HEARTS) repl. MARTIN to BLUE MEANIES

Sep 78. (7") *(CHIS 102)* **RADIO STARS. / ACCOUNTANCY BLUES** [ ] [–]

Sep 78. (lp) *(CWK 3001)* **THE RADIO STARS HOLIDAY ALBUM** [ ] [–]
– Radio stars / Boy meets girl / Baffin Island / (I've got dem old) Sex in chains blues (again mama) / Sitting in the rain / The real me / Rock and roll for the time being / Norwegian wood / Get on a plane / I'm down / No Russians in Russia / It's all over / Goodnight.

— (tour after lp) **JOHN MACKIE** – drums (ex-STUKAS) repl. CROMPTON / added **TREVOR WHITE** – guitar (ex-SPARKS)

Jan 79. (7") *(CHIS 109)* **THE REAL ME. / GOOD PERSONALITY** [ ] [–]

— (Feb'79) **STEVE PARRY** – drums; returned to repl. MACKIE + WHITE

— disbanded but re-formed in 1982 by **ELLISON,** etc

Moonlight / not iss.

May 82. (7") *(MNS 001)* **GOOD PERSONALITY. / TALKING 'BOUT YOU** [ ] [–]

May 82. (lp) *(MNA 001)* **TWO MINUTES MR. SMITH** [ ] [–]

Snap / not iss.

Sep 82. (7") **MY MOTHER SAID. / TWO MINUTES MR. SMITH** [ ] [–]

– compilations, etc. –

Oct 92. (cd) *Chiswick; (CDWIKD 107)* **SOMEWHERE THERE'S A PLACE FOR US** [ ] [–]

RADISH

Formed: Greenville, Texas, USA . . . 1993 by 12 year-old BEN KWELLER. After recruiting his schoolfriend JOHN KENT and BRYAN BLUR, a codgerly late 20-something in comparison, they were subsequently the subject of a frantic major bidding war. 'Mercury' came out on top and an album, 'RESTRAINING BOLT' was completed by 1997. Akin to a fusion of Brit-pack counterparts, ASH and SYMPOSIUM, the band were the pop-grunge alternative to HANSON, girlie haircuts intact. The group garnered further kudos, purportedly being adored by COURTNEY LOVE and MADONNA.

Album rating: RESTRAINING BOLT (*5)

BEN KWELLER (b.1982) – vocals, guitar / **BRYAN BLUR** (b.1968) – bass / **JOHN KENT** (b.1980) – drums

Mercury / Polygram

Oct 96. (cd-s) *<578680>* **DEAR AUNT ARCTICA** [–] [ ]

Aug 97. (7") *(MER 494)* **LITTLE PINK STARS. / MAKE IT UP (demo)** [32] [–]
(cd-s+=) *(MERCD 494)* – The you in me (live) / Dear Aunt Artica (live).

Sep 97. (cd/c/lp) *<(534 644-2/-4/-1)>* **RESTRAINING BOLT** [ ] [ ] Apr97
– Little pink stars / Simple sincerity / Falling and leaving / Dear Aunt Arctica / Sugar free / Today's bargain / You in me / Still in wait / Promise / Apparation of purity / My guitar / Bedtime.

Nov 97. (7") *(MER 498)* **SIMPLE SINCERITY. / LITTLE PINK STARS (live)** [50] [–]
(cd-s+=) *(MERCD 498)* – Dear Aunt Arctica (live) / Bedtime (live).
(cd-s) *(MERDD 498)* – ('A'side) / Take my seashell (demo) / Sugar tree (live) / P girl (live).

RAILWAY CHILDREN

Formed: Wigan, Lancashire, England . . . 1985 by teenagers GARY NEWBY (the band's songwriter), STEPHEN HULL, BRIAN BATEMAN and GUY KEEGAN. Signed to Manchester's 'Factory' label on the strength of a demo, the young hopefuls issued a couple of impressive singles (i.e. 'A GENTLE

SOUND' and 'BRIGHTER') prior to the release of a debut album, 'REUNION WILDERNESS' (1987). Having forged a highly marketable sound lying somehwere between ECHO & THE BUNNYMEN, The SMITHS and the indie soul-strumming of Scottish acts like AZTEC CAMERA and ORANGE JUICE, The RAILWAY CHILDREN were snapped up by 'Virgin', who subsequently moulded the band into an even more commercially palatable proposition. The new improved sound was unveiled on 1988's 'RECURRENCE' album, new improved sales proving more readily available abroad than in Britain. Two years on, 'NATIVE PLACE' (1990) was well timed to fit in with the burgeoning baggy culture and the band eventually broke into the UK Top 30 with a remixed version of 'EVERY BEAT OF THE HEART'. Yet like so many jangly guitar acts who benefitted from the indie-dance craze, The RAILWAY CHILDREN found only fleeting success, a further two singles, 'SOMETHING SO GOOD' and 'MUSIC STOP' running out of chart steam. Shunted into relative obscurity once more, the band finally decided to blow the whistle on their stop-start career once and for all in the early 90's.

Album rating: REUNION WILDERNESS (*7) / RECURRENCE (*4) / NATIVE PLACE (*5)

GARY NEWBY (b. 5 Jun'66, Australia) – vocals, guitar / **BRIAN BATEMAN** (b. 3 Aug'66) – guitar / **STEPHEN HULL** (b. 7 Jul'66) – bass / **GUY KEEGAN** (b.16 Jun'66) – drums

Factory Virgin

Sep 86. (7") *(FAC 162)* **A GENTLE SOUND. / CONTENT** -
Feb 87. (7") *(FAC 167)* **BRIGHTER. / HISTORY BURNS** -
(12"+=) *(FAC 167T)* – Careful.
Mar 87. (m-lp/m-c)(m-cd) *(FACT 185/+C)(FACD 185) <90636-1>* **REUNION WILDERNESS** Jul87
– Brighter / Another town / The first notebook / Big hands of freedom / Listen on / Railroad side / Careful. *(cd+=)* – A gentle sound / Content. *(cass-box-iss.Jan91; FACT 185C)*

Virgin Virgin

Mar 88. (7") *(VS 1070)* **IN THE MEANTIME. / MERCILESS** -
(12"+=) *(VST 1070)* – Swallowed / Second nature.
(cd-s+=) *(VSCD 1070)* – Second nature / Caught you.
May 88. (cd/c/lp) *(CD/TC+/V 2525) <90930>* **RECURRENCE** 96
– Somewhere south / Pleasure / Swallowed / Merciless / My word / In the meantime / Over and over / Monica's light / Chrysalis / No great objections. *(cd re-iss. Apr92; same)*
Jun 88. (7") *(VS 1084)* **SOMEWHERE SOUTH. / LISTEN ON** -
(12"+=) *(VST 1084)* – Darkness and colour.
(10"+=) *(VSA 1084)* – You can't follow the world / Waterfall.
Aug 88. (7") *(VS 1115)* **OVER AND OVER. / A GENTLE SOUND (demo)** -
(12"+=) *(VST 1115)* – Union city blue (live).
(cd-s++=) *(VSCD 1115)* – ('A'remix) / Big hands of freedom (live).
Mar 90. (7"/c-s) *(VS/+C 1237)* **EVERY BEAT OF THE HEART. / EVERYBODY** 68 -
(10"+=/12"+=/cd-s+=) *(VS A/T/CD 1237)* – Give it away / Strange altrader. *(re-iss. Jan91 – hit No.24)*
May 90. (7"/c-s) *(VS/+C 1255)* **MUSIC STOP. / TELL ME** 66 -
(d7"+=) *(VSX 1255)* – What she wants / It won't be long.
(12"+=) *(VST 1255)* – ('A'instrumental).
(cd-s+=) *(VSCD 1255)* – ('A'-Steve Proctor mix).
Jun 90. (cd/c/lp) *(CD/TC+/V 2627) <91385>* **NATIVE PLACE**
– Every beat of the heart / Music stop / You're young / Because / Cotton counting / It's Heaven / Something so good / Collide / Native place / Fall on / Harbour force / Blue sky. *(re-act.Mar91 – hit UK No.59)*
Oct 90. (7"/c-s) *(VS/+C 1289)* **SO RIGHT. / ('A'-Dakeyen mix)** 68 -
(12"+=) *(VST 1289)* – ('A'-strawberry mix).
(cd-s++=) *(VSCD 1289)* – Kinds of fuel.
Apr 91. (7"/c-s) *(VS/+C 1318)* **SOMETHING SO GOOD. / HOURS GO BY** 57 -
(12"+=) *(VST 1318)* – After the rain / Standing too still.
(cd-s+=) *(VSCD 1318)* – ('A'extended) / After the rain / Standing too still.
Jun 91. (7"/c-s) **MUSIC STOP. / WHAT SHE WANTS / TELL ME** -
(12") – ('A'side) / ('A'instrumental) / ('A'-Steve Proctor mix).
(cd-s) – ('A'side) / What she wants / ('A'-Steve Proctor mix) / ('A'extended).

—— split after above

– compilations, etc. –

Mar 93. (cd) *Nighttracks; (CDNT 2) / Dutch East India; <8122>* **RADIO 1 EVENING SHOW SESSIONS**
Feb 95. (cd) *Virgin; (<CDOVD 451>)* **LISTEN ON (THE BEST OF THE RAILWAY CHILDREN)**
– Every beat of the heart / Everybody / Give it away / Music stop / What she wants / Something so good / Hours go by / After the rain / You're young / Collide / Somewhere south / Listen on / Over and over (full remix) / A gentle sound (original demo) / Monica's light / So right (dakeyne full length remix) / In the mantime.

RAIN

Formed: Huyton, Liverpool, England . . . 1988 by songwriters NED CLARK and COLIN MURPHY, alongside MARTIN CAMPBELL and TONY McGUIGAN, having luckily received a 6-figure sum from a local trade union centre. Friends and sometime musical compadres of legendary scousers The LA's, RAIN were signed to 'Columbia' – along with fellow Liverpudlians The REAL PEOPLE – at the tail end of '89, prompting much excitement among the press as commentators predicted big things for their BYRDS-ian three-part harmony trad-pop. After an ensuing 18 month lull – during which initial sessions with NICK LOWE were abandoned – RAIN eventually surfaced with debut album, 'A TASTE OF RAIN' (1991), justifying the early hype with a star-crossed collection of anthemic, bass-heavy power rock/pop drawing comparisons with the likes of CREAM and R.E.M.. Critics weren't so enamoured with the record's cover art, however, a 70's heavy metal-style throwback shot of a moisture-soaked female torso framed off at the head and pubic area with the RAIN logo plastered over the breasts.

Album rating: A TASTE OF RAIN (*6)

NED CLARK – vocals, guitar / **COLIN MURPHY** – vocals, guitar / **MARTIN CAMPBELL** – bass, vocals / **TONY McGUIGAN** – drums

Columbia Columbia

Mar 91. (7"/c-s) **LEMONSTONE DESIRED. / OUTBACK BLUES** -
(cd-s+=) – Drive on (live).
(10"++=) – ('A'live).
Jun 91. (7") **A TASTE OF RAIN. / LAUGHING MAN** -
(12"+=/cd-s+=) – Tumble down.
Jul 91. (cd/c/lp) *(468442-2/-4/-1) <52437>* **A TASTE OF RAIN**
– All I want / Going / The beat goes on / Lemonstone desired / Hold on / Here they are / A taste of rain / She's on fire / Mother Earth / Inside out. *(cd+=/c+=)* – Outback blues. *(cd re-iss. Feb96 as 'LIVERPOOL – THE CALM BEFORE THE RAIN'; 483660-2)* – (shared with The REAL PEOPLE album).
Oct 91. (7") **LEMONSTONE DESIRED. / GOING** -
(12"+=/cd-s+=) – Outback blues.
(10"+=) – Drive on (live).

—— disbanded soon after above. Where are they now?

RAINCOATS

Formed: Ladbroke Grove, London, England . . . 1977 by ANA DA SILVA and GINA BIRCH (other early members included NICK TURNER, ROSS CRIGHTON, KATE KORUS (ex-SLITS), JEREMIE FRANK and SHIRLEY O'LOUGHLIN). Featuring a line-up subsequently completed by VICKY ASPINAL and future SLITS member, PALMOLIVE, this all-female outfit are held up as having redefined the musical possibilities for women in what was still – even with the supposed liberation of punk – a male dominated bastion. Signed to fledgling indie label, 'Rough Trade', the band debuted in 1979 with the groundbreaking guitar scree and distinctive drumroll chorus of the 'FAIRYTALE IN A SUPERMARKET' single, promptly notching up an NME Single Of The Week award. Later that year, they released their much acclaimed debut album, 'THE RAINCOATS', commentators falling over themselves to praise its emotionally stark noise collages. Somewhere in deepest Seattle, a young KURT COBAIN was similarly entranced, the future grunge architect at least partly responsible for resurrecting interest in the 90's. In the meantime, The RAINCOATS began writing material for a follow-up set, minus PALMOLIVE, who had departed for foreign shores in pursuit of spiritual enlightenment. The resulting album, 'ODYSHAPE' (1981) was more abstract than anything they'd recorded to date, eschewing conventional song structures for a near-improvisational approach and off-kilter time signatures. It was also largely recorded with the absence of a solid drum beat, deep, dubby bass and minimalist percussion the only instruments providing any kind of rhythmic anchor among the ethereal vocals, violin shards and angular guitar. The third and final RAINCOATS studio album, 'MOVING' (1984) was radically different again, far more accessible in a kind of knotty, avant-disco/funk stylee, lead track and single, 'ANIMAL RHAPSODY' carrying on where their cover of Sly Stone's 'RUNNING AWAY' left off and rendering the band virtually unrecognisable from their previous incarnation. ASPINALL's scraping violin was ever present of course, even if it did jar against the hotch-potch of competing musical strands. The disparate sound suggested a band coming apart at the seams, the girls subsequently going their separate ways for the remainder of the 80's. While the 90's has been characterised by reformation mania, few could've predicted The RAINCOATS reunion. As mentioned above, NIRVANA mainman, KURT COBAIN made sure their legacy lived on, instrumental as he was in the CD re-issue of their albums. The interest from COBAIN and many of his peers encouraged the girls to give it another go and in 1993, DA SILVA and BIRCH teamed up with violinist ANNE WOOD and SONIC YOUTH's STEVE SHELLEY to record an EP, 'EXTENDED PLAY' (1994) and an album, 'LOOKING IN THE SHADOWS' (1995). • **Songwriters:** BIRCH and ASPINALL, except LOLA (Kinks) / STILL WAITING (Prince). • **Trivia:** GINA was also part of RED CRAYOLA, and VICKY played violin for the NEW AGE STEPPERS.

Album rating: THE RAINCOATS (*7) / ODYSHAPE (*8) / MOVING (*8)

ANA DA SILVA (b.1949, Portugal) – vocals, guitar / **VICKY ASPINALL** – guitar, violin / **GINA BIRCH** (b.1956) – bass / **PALMOLIVE** (b.Spain) – drums (ex-SLITS)

Rough Trade Rough Trade

Apr 79. (7"m) *(RT 013)* **FAIRYTALE IN A SUPERMARKET. / IN LOVE / ADVENTURES CLOSE TO HOME** -
Nov 79. (lp) *(ROUGH 3)* **THE RAINCOATS** -
– Fairytale in a supermarket / No side to fall in / Adventures close to home / Off duty trip / Black and white / Lola / The void / Life on the line / You're a million / In love / No looking. *(cd-iss. Sep93; R 302-2) <US-iss.Sep93 on 'DGC'; 24622>*

—— **INGRID WEISS** (b.1961) – drums repl. PALMOLIVE who returned to Spain.

—— guests on next **ROBERT WYATT + CHARLES HAYWARD** (of THIS HEAT)

Jun 81. (lp/c) *(ROUGH 13/+C)* **ODYSHAPE**
– The Raincoats / Shouting out loud / Family treat / Only loved at night / Dancing in my head / And then it's o.k. / Baby song / Red shoes / Go away. *(cd-iss. Jan94; R 304-2) <US-iss.Jan94 on 'DGC'; 24623>*

—— **RICHARD DUDANSKI** – drums repl. INGRID

Jul 82. (7") *(RT 093)* **RUNNING AWAY. / NO-ONE'S LITTLE GIRL** -

—— basic trio **BIRCH, DA SILVA, ASPINALL + DUDANSKI** plus guests **PADDY O'CONNELL** – saxophone / **DEREK GODDARD** – percussion

Nov 83. (12"m) *(RT 153)* **ANIMAL RHAPSODY. / NO-ONE'S LITTLE GIRL / HONEY MAD WOMAN** [ ] [-]
Feb 84. (lp) *(ROUGH 66)* **MOVING** [ ] [-]
– Ooh ooh la la la / Dreaming in the past / Mouth of a story / Hoey mad woman / Rainstorm / The dance of the hopping mad / Balloon / I saw a hill / Overheard / The body / Avidoso / Animal rhapsody. *(cd-iss. Feb94; R 306-2) <US-iss.Feb94 on 'DGC'; 24624>*

— disbanded after above album

– compilations, etc. –

1983. (c) *R.O.I.R.; <A 120>* **THE KITCHEN TAPES (live)** [-] [ ]
(cd-iss. Feb 95 on 'ROIR Europe')

DOROTHY

were a duo formed by **GINA + VICKY**

BlueGuitar / not iss.

Jul 88. (7"/12") *(AZUR 8/+T)* **STILL WAITING. / THE FROG PRINCE** [ ] [-]
Jan 89. (7"/12"/cd-s) *(AZUR 11/+T/CD)* **LOVING FEELING. / SEXUAL OBSESSION** [ ] [-]

Cooltempo / not iss.

Jul 89. (7"/12") *(COOL 187/+T)* **REFLECTIONS. / ('A'version)** [ ] [-]

— They split after above dance flop.

RAINCOATS

— re-formed w / **BIRCH, DA SILVA, + ANNE WOOD** – violin / **STEVE SHELLEY** (b.23 Jun'62, Midland, Michigan) – drums (of SONIC YOUTH)

Blast First / Smells Like

Jun 94. (10"ep/cd-ep) *(BFFP 99/+CD) <12>* **EXTENDED PLAY** [ ] [ ] Apr95
– Don't be mean / We smile / No-one's little girl / Shouting out loud.

Rough Trade / Geffen

May 96. (7"ep/cd-ep) *(R 404-7/-3)* **DON'T BE MEAN** [ ] [-]
Jun 96. (cd/lp) *(R 403-2/-1) <24957>* **LOOKING IN THE SHADOWS** [ ] [ ] May96
– Only tonight / Don't be mean / Forgotten words / Pretty / Truth is hard / Babydog / You ask why / 57 ways to end it all / So damn early / You kill me / Love a loser / Looking in the shadows.

RAIN PARADE

Formed: Los Angeles, California, USA ... 1981 as The SIDEWALKS by Minneapolis college mates DAVID ROBACK and MATT PIUCCI. They also numbered DAVID's younger brother STEVEN and WILL GLENN, before they opted for a name change. Their vinyl debut came with the BYRDS-like 'WHAT'S SHE DONE TO YOUR MIND' in 1982 while they found a permanent drummer in EDDIE KALWA. DAVID moonlighted with another project, RAINY DAY, but a disappointing covers album was soon forgotten when 'EMERGENCY THIRD RAIL POWER TRIP' hit the shops. Purveyors of the burgeoning "Paisley Underground" scene, the set was throwback to the psychedelic sound of PINK FLOYD/KALEIDOSCOPE, while the guitar plucking was reminiscent of TELEVISION. The record gained a UK release on Demon's off-shoot 'Zippo' label, as did their 1984 mini-lp 'EXPLOSIONS IN THE GLASS PALACE'. The record was recorded without co-leader DAVID, however, who had left earlier in the year. 'Island' records gave them their break in '85 but surely damaged their growing reputation when they rush-released a live-set recorded in Japan, 'BEYOND THE SUNSET'. With MATT and STEVEN the sole remaining members, they recruited JOHN THOMAN and MARK MARCUM although the 1986 album, 'CRASHING DREAM', was appropriately titled, Island soon ditching them. They took a two-year hiatus before going back into the studio to finish off a double album. It never found its way to the shops, as PIUCCI joined a re-formed CRAZY HORSE, while the rest became VIVA SATURN. • **Songwriters:** All written by the ROBACK's and group, except AIN'T THAT NOTHIN' (Television).

Album rating: EMERGENCY THIRD RAIL POWER TRIP (*8) / EXPLOSIONS IN THE GLASS PALACE (*7) / CRASHING DREAM (*7)

DAVID ROBACK – vocals, guitar, percussion / **MATT PIUCCI** – guitar, vocals, sitar / **WILL GLENN** – keyboards / **STEVEN ROBACK** – bass, vocals / **EDDIE KALWA** – drums

not iss. / Llama

1982. (7") **WHAT'S SHE DONE TO YOUR MIND?. / ?** [-] [ ]

Zippo / Enigma

Aug 84. (lp) *(ZING 001) <ENIGMA 19>* **EMERGENCY THIRD RAIL POWER TRIP** [ ] [ ] 1983
– Talking in my sleep / This can't be today / I look around / 1 hr. half ago / Carolyn's song / What she's done to your mind / Look at Merri / Saturday's asylum / Kaleidoscope / Look both ways.

— trimmed to a quartet when DAVE left to form RAINY DAY (later OPAL). He is now part of duo MAZZY STAR

1984. (m-lp) *(ZANE 003) <71081>* **EXPLOSIONS IN THE GLASS PALACE** [ ] [ ]
– You are my friend / Prisoners / Blue / Broken horse / No easy way down.
Feb 85. (7") *(ZIPPO 45-1)* **YOU ARE MY FRIEND. / THIS CAN'T BE TODAY** [ ] [ ] 1984

— **MARK MARCUM** – drums repl. KALWA

— added **JOHN THOMAN** – guitar, vocals

Island / Restless

Jun 85. (lp/c) *(IMA/IMC 17) <72086>* **BEYOND THE SUNSET** (live in Tokyo 1984) [78] [ ]
– Night shade / Prisoners / This can't be today / Blue / Eyes closed / Ain't that nothin' / Don't feel bad / 1 hr. 1/2 ago / Blue / No easy way down / Cheap wine.

Island / Island

Oct 85. (lp/c) *(ILPS/ICT 9805) <90499-1/-4>* **CRASHING DREAM** [ ] [ ]
– Depending on you / My secret country / Don't feel bad / Mystic green / Sad eyes kill / Shoot down the railroad man / Fertile crescent / Invisible people / Gone west / Only business.

— Disbanded when PIUCCI formed GONE FISHIN', then joined CRAZY HORSE

– compilations, etc. –

Feb 92. (cd) *Mau Mau; (MAUCD 610)* **EMERGENCY THIRD RAIL POWER TRIP / EXPLOSIONS IN THE GLASS PALACE** [ ] [-]

VIVA SATURN

STEVEN ROBACK – guitar, piano, vocals / **JOHN THOMAN** – guitar / **MARK MARCUM**

World Service / Heyday

Jun 89. (lp) *(SERVS 003)* **VIVA SATURN** [ ] [ ]
– So glad / Brought it on yourself / Remember I'm dead / Old world / Wild town.

— **MATT PIUCCI** – guitar, vocals; repl. MARK

— added **ROSS INDEN** – bass / **CARLO NUCCIO** – drums

Normal / Heyday

May 94. (cd) *(NORMAL 139CD) <ADE 009CD>* **SOUNDMIND** [ ] [ ] 1992
– Still she waits / Love the sugar / Believe / Haven't felt like / Soundmind / Suicidal lamb / Raised / Better get your nerve Paradise / Mermaid / Waiting for the train.

Restless / Restless

Jul 95. (cd) *<(72909-2)>* **BRIGHTSIDE** [ ] [ ]
– Send a message / Black cloud / Brightside / Here comes April / Abondoned car string me out a line / Mourn the light / Distracted / Nothing helps / Heart of you / One for my baby.

RAIN TREE CROW (see under ⇒ JAPAN)

RAINY DAY (see under ⇒ MAZZY STAR)

RAMONES

Formed: Forest Hills, New York, USA ... August'74 as a trio by JOHNNY, JOEY and DEE DEE, who all took the working surname RAMONE (although they were brothers only in the loosest sense of the term). One of the prime movers (many would subsequently cite them as the first) in the emergent US punk scene, the band began a residency at the legendary NY club, CBGB's, TOMMY coming in on the drum stool in order to free JOEY up for suitably deranged vocal duties. In June '75, the band were dealt a slight setback when they failed an audition for RICK DERRINGER's 'Blue Sky' label in front of 20,000 fans at a JOHNNY WINTER concert, although later that year manager, Danny Fields, found up and coming new wave label, 'Sire' (run by Seymour Stein) considerably more receptive. Released around the same time as their pivotal (and highly influential) London Roundhouse gig, the band's eponymous summer '76 debut album presented a sound every bit as exhiliratingly juvenile and humerously warped as their leering, mop-topped scruffiness might suggest. Ripping out gloriously dumb, two-minute buzz-saw classics on such perennial punk subjects as solvent abuse ('I WANNA SNIFF SOME GLUE'), girls (most of the album) and erm, chainsaws ('CHAIN SAW'), The RAMONES had invented themselves as larger than life, cartoon yob no-wavers well ahead of their time, their attitude alone copped by countless two-bit punk bands (and a few great ones) the length and breadth of the British Isles. Barely pausing for breath (or whatever it was these guys inhaled), the new yoik brudders followed up with 'LEAVE HOME' (1977), another strychnine-fuelled session of primitive but tuneful terrace chant anthems, RAMONES style; from this point onwards, the words 'Gabba Gabba Hey' would be forever carved in the stone of the punk lexicon. The album even managed a minor dent in the UK charts, a full scale assault led later that year with the brilliantly throwaway 'SHEENA IS A PUNK ROCKER'. The climax of the early RAMONES blitzkreig came with 'ROCKET TO RUSSIA' (1977), the lads easing ever so slightly off the gas pedal and taking the credo of mangled, two minute surf-pop to its dayglo conclusion; the hilarious 'CRETIN HOP', 'ROCKAWAY BEACH' and 'TEENAGE LOBOTOMY' remain among the most definitive moments in the RAMONES' dog-eared catalogue. A rather disappointing Top 60 placing failed to do the record justice, although by this stage the band were beginning to make some inroads into the home market. Further evidence, if any was needed, that The RAMONES' chief writer was at the peak of his powers came with the blistering 'Chinese Rocks', a HEARTBREAKERS track co-penned by DEE DEE. With the departure of TOMMY (into production work) the following year, ex-VOID-OID MARC BELL was recruited in his place, rechristened, of course, MARKY RAMONE. Incredibly, the tried and tested formula (with a few notable exceptions, a guitar solo (!) on 'GO MENTAL' and a ballad, 'QUESTIONINGLY') continued to excite with 'ROAD TO RUIN' (1978), their first album to break into the UK Top 40 and the resting place of the legendary 'I WANNA BE SEDATED'. The riotous 'IT'S ALIVE' (1979) captured the RAMONES concert experience head-on, neatly wrapping up the first stage of the boys' career and providing a handy overview of their career to date. Every punk band coped with the scene's fragmentation in their own way, The RAMONES not so wisely choosing to indulge their love of classic 60's pop via the genre's guru, Phil Spector. The result were predictably confused, many longtime RAMONES headbangers balking at their UK Top 10 cover of The Ronettes' 'BABY I LOVE YOU'. Subsequent 80's efforts such as 'PLEASANT DREAMS' (1981)

and 'SUBTERRANEAN JUNGLE' (1983) lacked the ragged glory of their earlier work although with the replacement of MARKY with RICHIE (aka RICHARD REINHARDT) in 1984, 'TOO TOUGH TO DIE' (1985) found the band sharpening their attack and presenting a united front against the hardcore pretenders of the day. They couldn't keep it up though, and the limitations of their art really began to bite deep on the bedraggled 'ANIMAL BOY' (1986) and 'HALFWAY TO SANITY' (1987). DEE DEE bailed out after 'BRAIN DRAIN' (1989), replacement C.J. effecting something of a rejuvenation on 'MONDO BIZARRO' (1992). The following year's 'ACID EATERS' saw the band pay tribute to the 60's sounds which had actually inspired them, while in turn, many of the younger bands who had actually been inspired by The RAMONES would soon be calling the shots at America'a major labels. Yet despite this punk revival and the success of such acts as GREEN DAY and OFFSPRING, The RAMONES finally decided to call it a day in early 1996 following the release of the 'IL ADIOS AMOGOS!' set and the accompanying tour. • **Songwriters:** DEE DEE and group, except; DO YOU WANNA DANCE (Bobby Freeman) / SURFIN' BIRD (Trashmen) / BABY I LOVE YOU (Ronettes; Phil Spector) / NEEDLES AND PINS (Searchers) / STREET FIGHTIN' MAN (Rolling Stones) / TAKE IT AS IT COMES (Doors) / R.A.M.O.N.E.S. (Motorhead) / ANY WAY YOU WANT IT (Dave Clark) / SPIDER-MAN (Harris-Webster) / etc. In '77, DEE DEE co-wrote 'CHINESE ROCKS' for The HEARTBREAKERS. • **Trivia:** The RAMONES featured in the films 'Blank Generation' (1976) & 'Rock'n'roll High School' (Roger Corman 1979).

Album rating: RAMONES (*9) / LEAVE HOME (*8) / ROCKET TO RUSSIA (*8) / RAMONES MANIA compilation (*9)

JOEY RAMONE (b. JEFFREY HYMAN, 19 May'51) – vocals (was drummer) / **JOHNNY RAMONE** (b. JOHN CUMMINGS, 8 Oct'51, Long Island, N.Y.) – guitar, vocals / **DEE DEE RAMONE** (b. DOUGLAS COLVIN, 18 Sep'52, Fort Lee, Virginia) – bass, vocals / **TOMMY RAMONE** (b. TOM ERDELYI, 29 Jan'49, Budapest, Hungary) – drums

Sire Sire

Jul 76. (lp) *(9103 253)* *<7520>* **RAMONES** [ ] [ ] May76
– Blitzkrieg bop / Beat on the brat / Judy is a punk / I wanna be your boyfriend / Chain saw / Now I wanna sniff some glue / I don't wanna go down to the basement / Loudmouth / Havana affair / Listen to my heart / 53rd & 3rd / Let's dance / I don't wanna walk around with you / Today your love, tomorrow the world. *(re-iss. Sep78; SRK 6020)*

Jul 76. (7") *(6078 601)* *<725>* **BLITZKRIEG BOP. / HAVANA AFFAIR** [ ] [ ] May76

Oct 76. (7"m) *<734>* **I WANNA BE YOUR BOYFRIEND. / CALIFORNIA SUN (live) / I DON'T WANNA WALK AROUND WITH YOU (live)** [-] [ ]

Feb 77. (7"m) *(6078 603)* **I REMEMBER YOU. / CALIFORNIA SUN (live) / I DON'T WANNA WALK AROUND WITH YOU (live)** [ ] [-]

Mar 77. (lp) *(9103 254)* *<7528>* **LEAVE HOME** [45] [ ] Feb77
– Glad to see you go / Gimme gimme shock treatment / I remember you / Oh oh I love her so / Babysitter * / Suzy is a headbanger / Pinhead / Now I wanna be a good boy / Swallow my pride / What's your game / California sun / Commando / You're gonna kill that girl / You should never have opened that door / California sun. *(re-iss. Jun77 'Carbona Not Glue' replaced *; other re-iss's same) (re-iss. Sep78; SRK 6031) (re-iss. Nov87 on 'Mau Mau'; MAU 602)*

May 77. (7"m,12"m) *(6078 606)* *<746>* **SHEENA IS A PUNK ROCKER. / COMMANDO / I DON'T CARE** [22] [81]

Jul 77. (7"m) *(6078 607)* *<738>* **SWALLOW MY PRIDE. / PINHEAD / LET'S DANCE (live)** [36] [ ] Mar77

Nov 77. (7"m,12"m) *(6078 611)* **ROCKAWAY BEACH. / TEENAGE LOBOTOMY / BEAT ON THE BRAT** [ ] [-]

Nov 77. (7") *<1008>* **ROCKAWAY BEACH. / LOCKET LOVE** [-] [66]

Dec 77. (lp) *(9103 255)* *<6042>* **ROCKET TO RUSSIA** [60] [49] Nov77
– Cretin hop / Rockaway beach / Here today, gone tomorrow / Locket love / I don't care / Sheena is a punk rocker / We're a happy family / Teenage lobotomy / Do you wanna dance? / I wanna be well / I can't give you anything / Ramona / Surfin' bird / Why is it always this way. *(re-iss. Sep78; SRK 6042)*

Feb 78. (7") *<1017>* **DO YOU WANNA DANCE?. / BABYSITTER** [-] [86]

Mar 78. (7"m) *(6078 615)* **DO YOU WANNA DANCE? / IT'S A LONG WAY BACK TO GERMANY / CRETIN HOP** [ ] [-]

— **MARKY RAMONE** (b. MARC BELL, 15 Jul'56) – drums (ex-RICHARD HELL & THE VOID-OIDS, ex-DUST) repl. TOMMY who continued producing others.

Sep 78. (7",7"yellow,12"yellow,12"red) *(SRE 1031)* *<1025>* **DON'T COME CLOSE. / I DON'T WANT YOU** [38] [ ]

Oct 78. (yellow-lp) *<(SRK 6063)>* **ROAD TO RUIN** [32] [ ]
– I just want to have something to do / I wanted everything / Don't come close / I don't want you / Needles and pins / I'm against it / I wanna be sedated / Go mental / Questioningly / She's the one / Bad brain / It's a long way back.

Nov 78. (7") *<1045>* **NEEDLES AND PINS. / I WANTED EVERYTHING** [-] [ ]

Jan 79. (7") *(SIR 4009)* **SHE'S THE ONE. / I WANNA BE SEDATED** [ ] [-]

May 79. (d-lp/c) *(SRK/SRC 26074)* **IT'S ALIVE (live)** [27] [-]
– Rockaway beach / Teenage lobotomy / Blitzkrieg bop / I wanna be well / Glad to see you go / Gimme gimme shock treatment / You're gonna kill that girl / I don't care / Sheena is a punk rocker / Havana affair / Commando / Here today, gone tomorrow / Surfin' bird / Cretin hop / Listen to my heart / California sun / I don't wanna walk around with you / Pinhead / Do you wanna dance? / Chain saw / Today your love, tomorrow the world / Now I wanna be a good boy / Judy is a punk / Suzy is a headbanger / Let's dance / Oh oh I love her so / Now I wanna sniff some glue / We're a happy family. *(cd-iss. Nov93 on 'Warners'; 7599 26069-2) (cd re-iss. Jan96; 9362 46045-2)*
(above album features TOMMY on drums)

Sep 79. (7") *<1051>* **DO YOU WANNA DANCE? / ROCK'N'ROLL HIGH SCHOOL** [-] [ ]

Sep 79. (7") *(SIR 4021)* **ROCK'N'ROLL HIGH SCHOOL. / SHEENA IS A PUNK ROCKER (live) / ROCKAWAY BEACH (live)** [67] [-]

Jan 80. (lp/c) *<(SRK/SRC 6077)>* **END OF THE CENTURY** [14] [44]
– Do you remember rock'n'roll radio? / I'm affected / Danny says / Chinese rock / The return of Jackie and Judy / Let's go / Baby I love you / I can't make it on time / This ain't Havana / Rock'n'roll high school / All the way / High risk insurance. *(re-iss. cd Mar94; 7599 27429-2)*

Jan 80. (7") *(SIR 4031)* *<49182>* **BABY, I LOVE YOU. / HIGH RISK INSURANCE** [8] [ ]

Apr 80. (7") *<49261>* **DO YOU REMEMBER ROCK'N'ROLL RADIO?. / LET'S GO** [-] [ ]

Apr 80. (7") *(SIR 4037)* **DO YOU REMEMBER ROCK'N'ROLL RADIO?. / I WANT YOU AROUND** [54] [-]

Jul 81. (7") *(SIR 4051)* *<49812>* **WE WANT THE AIRWAVES. / ALL'S QUIET ON THE EASTERN FRONT** [ ] [ ]

Jul 81. (lp/c) *<(SRK/SRC 3571)>* **PLEASANT DREAMS** [ ] [58]
– We want the airwaves / All's quiet on the Eastern front / The KKK took my baby away / Don't go / You sound like you're sick / It's not my place / She's a sensation / 7-11 / You didn't mean anything to me / Come on now / This business is killing me / Sitting in my room. *(re-iss. cd Mar94; 7599 23571-2)*

Oct 81. (7") *(SIR 4052)* **SHE'S A SENSATION. / ALL'S QUIET ON THE EASTERN FRONT** [ ] [-]

May 83. (lp/c) *(WX/+C 3800)* *<23800>* **SUBTERRANEAN JUNGLE** [ ] [83]
– Little bit o' soul / I need your love / Outsider / What'd ya do / Highest trails above / Somebody like me / Psycho therapy / Time has come today / My-my kind of girl / In the park / Time bomb / Everytime I eat vegetables It makes me think of you. *(re-iss. cd Mar94; 7599 23800-2)*

Jun 83. (7") *(W 9606)* **TIME HAS COME TODAY. / PSYCHO THERAPY** [ ] [-]
(12"+=) *(W 9606T)* – Baby I love you / Don't come close.

— **RICHIE RAMONE** (b. RICHARD REINHARDT, aka BEAU) – drums (ex-VELVETEENS) repl. MARC

Beggars Banquet Sire

Nov 84. (7") *<29107>* **HOWLING AT THE MOON (SHA LA LA). / WART HOG** [-] [ ]

Jan 85. (lp/c) *(BEGA/BEGC 59)* *<25187>* **TOO TOUGH TO DIE** [63] [ ] Oct84
– Mama's boy / I'm not afraid of life / Too young to die / Durango 95 / Wart hog / Danger zone / Chasing the night / Howling at the Moon (sha-la-la) / Daytime dilemma (dangers of love) / Planet Earth 1988 / Human kind / Endless vacation / No go.

Jan 85. (7") *(BEG 128)* **HOWLING AT THE MOON (SHA-LA-LA). / CHASING THE NIGHT** [ ] [-]
(d7"+=)(12"pic-d+=) *(BEG 128D)(BEGTP 128)* – Smash you / Street fighting man.

Jun 85. (7") *(BEG 140)* **BONZO GOES TO BITBURG. / DAYTIME DILEMMA (DANGERS OF LOVE)** [ ] [-]
(12"+=) *(BEG 140T)* – Go home Annie.

Apr 86. (7") *(BEG 157)* **SOMETHING TO BELIEVE IN. / SOMEBODY PUT SOMETHING IN MY DRINK** [69] [-]
(12"+=) *(BEG 157T)* – (You) Can't say anything nice.

May 86. (lp/c) *(BEGA/BEGC 70)* *<25433>* **ANIMAL BOY** [38] [ ]
– Somebody put something in my drink / Animal boy / Love kills / Apeman hop / She belongs to me / Crummy stuff / My brain is hanging upside down (Bonzo goes to Bitburg) / She belongs to me / Mental hell / Eat that rat / Freak of nature / Hair of the dog / Something to believe in.

Jun 86. (7") *<28599>* **SOMETHING TO BELIEVE IN. / ANIMAL BOY** [-] [ ]

Jul 86. (7") *(BEG 167)* **CRUMMY STUFF. / SHE BELONGS TO ME** [ ] [-]
(12"+=,12"red+=) *(BEG 167 T)* – I don't want to live this life.

— **MARKY RAMONE** – drums returned to repl. CLEM BURKE (ex-BLONDIE) who had repl. RICKY (above now with originals JOEY, DEE DEE and JOHNNY)

Sep 87. (7") *(BEG 198)* **A REAL COOL TIME. / INDIAN GIVER** [ ] [-]
(12"+=) *(BEG 198T)* – Life goes on.

Sep 87. (lp/c) *(BEGA/BEGC 89)* *<25641>* **HALFWAY TO SANITY** [78] [ ]
– I wanna live / Bop 'til you drop / Garden of serenity / Weasel face / Go lil' Camaro go / I know better now / Death of me / I lost my mind / A real cool time / I'm not Jesus / Bye bye baby / Worm man. *(cd-iss. Dec87 +=; BEGA 89CD)* – Indian giver / Life goes on.

Nov 87. (7"/12") *(BEG 201/+T)* **I WANNA LIVE. / MERRY CHRISTMAS (I DON'T WANT TO FIGHT TONIGHT)** [ ] [ ]

Chrysalis Sire

Aug 89. (lp/c/cd) *(CHR/ZCHR/CCD 1725)* *<25905>* **BRAIN DRAIN** [75] [ ] Jun89
– I believe in miracles / Zero zero UFO / Don't bust my chops / Punishment fits the crime / All screwed up / Palisades Park / Pet sematary / Learn to listen / Can't get you outta my mind / Ignorance is bliss / Come back, baby / Merry Christmas (I don't want to fight tonight).

Sep 89. (7") *(CHS 3423)* **PET SEMATARY. / ALL SCREWED UP** [ ] [-]
(12"+=) *(CHS12 3423)* – Zero zero UFO.

Sep 89. (7") *<22911>* **PET SEMATARY. / SHEENA IS A PUNK ROCKER** [-] [ ]

— **C.J. RAMONE** (b. CHRISTOPHER JOSEPH WARD, 8 Oct'65, Long Island, N.Y.) – bass repl. DEE DEE who became rap artist DEE DEE KING

Oct 91. (cd/c/d-lp) *(CCD/ZCHR/CHR 1901)* **LIVE LOCO (live)** [ ] [ ]
– The good, the bad and the ugly / Django 95 / Teenage lobotomy / Psycho therapy / Blitzkrieg bop / Rock'n'roll radio / I believe in miracles / Gimme gimme shock treatment / Rock'n'roll high school / I wanna be sedated / The KKK took my baby away / I wanna live / Bonzo goes to Bitzburg / Too tough to die / Sheena is a punk rocker / Rockaway beach / Pet sematary / Don't bust my shape / Palisades park / Mama's boy / Animal boy / Wart hog / Surfin' bird / Cretin hop / I don't wanna walk around with you / Today your love, tomorrow the world / Pinhead / Somebody put something in my drink / Beat on the brat / Judy is a punk / Chinese rocks / Love kills / Ignorance is bliss.

Radioactive Radioactive

Sep 92. (cd/c/lp) *<(RAR D/C 10615)>* **MONDO BIZARRO** [ ] [ ]
– Censorshit / The job that ate my brain / Poison heart / Anxiety / Strength to endure / It's gonna be alright / Take it as it comes / Main man / Tomorrow she goes away / I won't let it happen again / Cabbies on crack / Heidi is a heartache / Touring.

Chrysalis Radioactive

Nov 92. (c-s/7"yellow) *(TC+/CHS 3917)* **POISON HEART. / CENSORSHIT (live)** [69] [-]
(12"+=) *(12CHS 3917)* – Chinese rocks (live) / Sheena is a punk rocker (live).
(cd-s+=) *(CDCHS 3917)* – Rock and roll radio (live).

Dec 93. (cd/c/lp) *(CD/TC+/CHR 6052)* *<10913>* **ACID EATERS** [ ] [ ]
– Journey to the center of the mind / Substitute / Out of time / The shape of things to come / Somebody to love / When I was young / 7 and 7 is / My back pages / Can't

seem to make you mine / Have you ever seen the rain / I can't control myself / Surf city.

— Album of covers; SUBSTITUTE (Who) / I CAN'T CONTROL MYSELF (Troggs) / SURF CITY (Jan & Dean) / OUT OF TIME (Rolling Stones) / THE SHAPE OF THINGS TO COME (Headboys) / etc.

Jun 95. (cd/c/lp) *(CD/TC+/CHR 6104) <11273>* **ADIOS AMIGOS!** [62] [ ]
– I don't want to grow up / I'm makin' monsters for my friends / It's not for me to know / The crusher / Life's a gas / Take the pain away / I love you / Cretin family / Have a nice day / Scattergun / Got a lot to say / She talks to rainbows / Born to die in Berlin.

— split after tour early the following year, although they had a brief reunion on the 6th August, 1996 at The Palace, Los Angeles

Eagle / Radioactive

Nov 97. (cd) *(EAGCD 010) <11555>* **WE'RE OUTTA HERE!** [ ] [ ]
– Durango 95 / Teenage lobotomy / Psycho therapy / Blitzkrieg bop / Do you remember rock and roll radio / I believe in miracles / Gimme gimme shock treatment / Rock'n'roll high school / I wanna be sedated / Spider-man / The K.K.K. took my baby away / I just want to have something to do / Commando / Sheena is a punk rocker / Rockaway beach / Pet sematary / The crusher / Love kills / Do you wanna dance / Someone put something in my drink / I don't want you / Wart hog / Cretin hop / R.A.M.O.N..S. / Today your love, tomorrow the world / Pinhead / 53rd & 3rd / Listen to your heart / We're a happy family / Chinese rock / Beat on the brat / Any way you want it.

– compilations, etc. –

Aug 80. (7") *R.S.O.; (RSO 70) / Sire; <2090 512>* **I WANNA BE SEDATED. / THE RETURN OF JACKIE AND JUDY** [ ] [ ]

— (above from Various Artists Film Soundtrack 'Rock'n'roll High School' also incl. 'Medley: Blitzkrieg bop – Teenage lobotomy – California sun – Pinhead – She's the one')

Nov 80. (7"ep) *Sire; (SREP 1)* **MELTDOWN WITH THE RAMONES** [ ] [ ]
– I just wanna have something to do / Questioningly / I wanna be your boyfriend / Here today, gone tomorrow.

Jun 88. (7") *Sire; <27663>* **I WANNA BE SEDATED. / (part 2)** [–] [ ]

Jun 88. (d-lp/c/cd) *Sire; (925709-1/-4/-2) <25709>* **RAMONES MANIA** [ ] [–]
– I wanna be sedated / Teenage lobotomy / Do you remember rock'n'roll radio? / Gimme gimme shock treatment / Beat on the brat / Sheena is a punk rocker / I wanna live / Pinhead / Blitzkrieg bop / Cretin hop / Rockaway beach / Commando / I wanna be your boyfriend / Mama's boy / Bop 'til you drop / We're a happy family / Bonzo goes to Bitburg / The outsider / Psycho therapy / Wart hog / Animal boy / Needles and pins / Howlin' at the Moon / Somebody put something in my drink / We want the airwaves / Chinese rocks / I just want to have something to do / The KKK took my baby away / Indian giver / Rock'n'roll high school.

Sep 90. (cd/c/d-lp) *Sire; (7599 2620-2/-4/-1)* **ALL THE STUFF (AND MORE)** (demos 1976-77, etc) [ ] [–]

Mar 93. (lp) *Selfless;* **THE SCREECHING WEASEL** [ ] [ ]

— JOEY also on "HOLLY & JOEY" 7" – 1982 'I Got You Babe' on 'Virgin'.

— In August '88, JOHNNY teamed up with DEBBIE HARRY for 7" – 'Go Lil Camara Go'.

DEE DEE RAMONE

writes with **REY**

World Dom. / World Dom.

Jun 94. (cd/lp) *(1571757-2/-1)* **I HATE FREAKS LIKE YOU** [ ] [ ]
– I'm making monsters for my friends / Don't look in my window / Chinese bitch / It's not for me to know / Runaway / All's quiet on the Eastern Front / I hate it / Life is like a little smart Alleck / I hate creeps like you / Trust me / Curse on me / I'm seeing strawberry's again / Lass mich in Fuhe / I'm making monsters for my friends.

Other People's Music / Other People's Music

Sep 97. (cd-ep) *(OPM 2118CD)* **ZONKED E.P.** [ ] [ ]

Blackout / Blackout

Oct 97. (7") *(BLK 5008E7)* **I AM SEEING UFO'S. / BAD HOROSCOPE** [ ] [–]

Nov 97. (cd) *(BLK 5008ECD)* **AIN'T IT FUN** [ ] [ ]
– I'm zonked los hombres / Fix yourself up / I am seeing UFO's / Get off the scene / Never never again / Bad horoscope / It's so bizarre / Get out of the room / Someone who doesn't fit in / Victim of society / My Chico / Disguises / Why is everyone always against Germany / Please kill me.

Lee RANALDO (see under ⇒ SONIC YOUTH)

RANCID

Formed: Albany, California, USA . . . 1987 as tattooed ska-punk act, OPERATION IVY, by TIM 'LINT' ARMSTRONG and MATT FREEMAN (alias MATT McCALL), who also numbered JESSE MICHAELS and DAVE MELLO in their ranks. This quartet would become a cult act of the late 80's, although they only managed to squeeze out one album, 'ENERGY', in 1989. ARMSTRONG and FREEMAN continued to work with various outfits, including MDC, a band that they often supported at the infamous Gilman Street Club in Berkeley. In 1990, the pair were joined by BRETT REED and thus RANCID were spawned. After the release of a self-financed EP, 'I'M NOT THE ONLY ONE' in '92, the trio inked a deal with BRETT GUREWITZ's 'Epitaph' records. They subsequently added second guitarist LARS FREDERIKSON, who was to swell the ranks following the release of their well-received eponymous debut in 1993. With the early 90's resurgence of punk and youthful peers such as OFFSPRING and GREEN DAY making commercial headway, RANCID were well placed to capitalise on their particular brand of gut-level hardcore. Following the release of a 1994 EP, 'RADIO RADIO RADIO' on FAT MIKE's (NOFX) independent 'Fat Wreck Chords' label, the band cracked the elusive US Top 100 with their second album, 'LET'S GO' (1994). The following year, RANCID scored with an even higher placed album, ' . . . AND OUT COME THE WOLVES', a Top 60 success. In 1998, like The CLASH over 20 years before them, RANCID adopted some roots reggae and ska into their umpteenth set, 'LIFE WON'T WAIT' (Jamaican, BUJU BANTON and MIGHTY MIGHTY BOSSTONES' mainman DICKY BARRETT guested). The results surprisingly worked as the album went Top 40 in America and Britain. • **Trivia:** ARMSTRONG also set up his own label, 'Hellcat', his best signings being DROPKICK MURPHYS, The PIETASTERS, GADJITS, HEPCAT and US BOMBS.

Album rating: RANCID (*6) / LET'S GO (*6) / . . .AND OUT COME THE WOLVES (*8) / LIFE WON'T WAIT (*7) / Operation Ivy: OPERATION IVY (*6)

OPERATION IVY

TIM ARMSTRONG – vocals, guitar / **MATT FREEMAN** (as MATT McCALL) – bass / **JESSE MICHAELS** – vocals / **DAVE MELLO** – drums

not iss. / Lookout

Jan 88. (7"ep) **HECTIC EP** [–] [ ]

Apr 91. (lp) *<LOOKOUT 10>* **OPERATION IVY** [–] [ ]
– Knowledge / Sound system / Jaded / Take warning / The crowd / Bombshell / Unity / Vulnerability / Bankshot / One of these days / Gonna find you / Bad town / Smiling / Caution / Freeze up / Artificial life / Room without a window / Big city / Missionary / Junkie's running dry / Here we go again / Hoboken / Yellin' in my ear / Sleep long / Healthy body / Officer / I got no. *(UK-iss.Oct94 lp/c/cd+=; LOOKOUT 10/+MC/CD)* – HECTIC EP

— they had already split in May '89, DAVE hoined SCHLONG while JESSE became a Buddhist monk! ARMSTRONG and FREEMAN worked with the DANCE HALL CRASHERS and DOWNFALL, while both joined MDC, FREEMAN more so; he featured on the group's 1990 set, 'Hey Cop, If I Had A face Like Yours'.

RANCID

— **ARMSTRONG + FREEMAN** added **BRETT REED** – drums (ex-SMOG)

not iss. / Lookout

1992. (7"ep) *<LOOK 059>* **I'M NOT THE ONLY ONE** [–] [ ]
(UK-iss.Dec95; same as US)

Epitaph / Epitaph

May 93. (cd/c/lp) *<(E 86428-2/-4/-1)>* **RANCID** [ ] [ ]

— added **LARS FREDERIKSON** – guitar (ex-UK SUBS)

Apr 94. (7"ep) *(FAT 509)* **RADIO, RADIO, RADIO EP** [ ] [ ]
(above single on 'Fat Wreck Chords') (below single on 'Lookout')

Dec 94. (7"ep) *(LOOKOUT 59)* **RANCID EP** [ ] [–]

Jan 95. (cd/c/d-10"lp) *<(E 86434-2/-4/-1)>* **LET'S GO** [ ] [97] Jun94
– Nihilism / Radio / Sidekick / Salvation / Tenderloin / Let's go / As one / Burn / Ballad of Jimmy & Johnny / Gunshot / I am the one / Gave it away / Ghetto box / Harry Bridges / Black and blue / St. Mary / Dope sick girl / International cover-up / Solidarity / Midnight / Motorcycle ride / Name / 7 years down.

Aug 95. (cd/c/lp) *<(E 86444-2/-4/-1)>* **. . .AND OUT COME THE WOLVES** [55] [45]
– Maxwell murder / 11th hour / Roots radicals / Time bomb / Olympia Wa. / Lock, step and gone / Junkie man / Listed M.I.A. / Ruby Soho / Daly city train / The way I feel / Avenues and alleyways / As wicked / You don't care nothin' / Wars end / Disorder and disarray / Old friend / She's automatic / Journey to the end of the East Bay.

Oct 95. (7"ep/cd-ep) *(WOOS 8 S/CDS)* **TIME BOMB** [56] [–]
(above issued on 'Out Of Step')

May 96. (7"ep/cd-ep) *(86464-7/-2)* **RUBY SOHO. / THAT'S ENTERTAINMENT / DISORDER AND DISARRAY** [ ] [–]

Jun 98. (d-cd/d-c/d-lp) *(6497-2/-4/-1) <86497>* **LIFE WON'T WAIT** [32] [35]
– Intro / Bloodclot / Black lung / Life won't wait / New dress / Warsaw / Hooligan / Crane fist / Leicester Square / Backslide / Who would've thought / Cas culture and violence / Wolf / 1998 / Lady Liberty / Wrongful suspicion / Turntable / Something in the world today / Corazon de oro / Coppers.

Aug 98. (7"ep/cd-ep) *(1005-7/-2)* **BLOODCLOT. / ENDRINA / STOP** [ ] [ ]

Dec 98. (7"ep/cd ep) *(1009-7/-2)* **HOOLIGANS / CASH, CULTURE AND VIOLENCE (bass drop mix) / THINGS TO COME (dance hall mix)** [ ] [ ]

Eric RANDOM

Born: Manchester, England. This one-man electronic/instrumental act first drew attention, however low-key, when his TILLER BOYS (a trio who included PETE SHELLEY of the BUZZCOCKS and FRANCIS COOKSON) released their one and only single, 'BIG NOISE FROM THE JUNGLE', in 1979. Remaining with the BUZZCOCKS' 'New Hormones' imprint (having collaborated again with SHELLEY on the FREE AGENTS lp in 1980), ERIC issued a further couple of 45's, 'THAT'S WHAT I LIKE ABOUT ME' EP and 'DOW CHEMICAL COMPANY'. During the recording of his debut solo album, 'EARTHBOUND GHOST NEED' (1982), he was also involved with two other projects, The JELL (their one and only track, 'I DARE SAY IT WILL HURT A LITTLE', featured on the 'Some Bizzare Album') and The PRESSURE COMPANY (a pseudonym for CABARET VOLTAIRE – an outfit he performed with), who issued one collaborative set, 'LIVE IN SHEFFIELD'. ERIC subsequently continued his solo career, releasing a couple of best forgotten albums that were augmented by his group, The BEDLAMITES.

Album rating: EARTHBOUND GHOST NEED (*4) / TIME SPLICE (*3) / ISHMAEL (*3)

ERIC RANDOM – vocals, keyboards, bass, guitar, saxophone / **PETE SHELLEY** – guitar, vocals / **FRANCIS COOKSON**

New Hormones / not iss.

1979. (7"m; by TILLER BOYS) *(ORG 3)* **BIG NOISE FROM THE JUNGLE. / SLAVES AND PYRAMIDS / WHAT ME WORRY?** [ ] [-]

— now with **LYNN 'SEED' WALTON** – keyboards, synthesizer / + other JELL member, **LISA LISA** – clarinet (not on solo material)

Sep 80. (12"ep) *(ORG 6)* **THAT'S WHAT I LIKE ABOUT ME** [ ] [-]
– Fade in / Dirty bongo / Call me / Fade out.

May 81. (7") *(ORG 11)* **DOW CHEMICAL COMPANY. / SKIN DEEP** [ ] [-]

Jul 81. (7") *(TWI 029)* **SUBLIMINAL. / 23 SKIDOO** [ ] [-]
(above issued for 'Les Disques Du Crepescule')

Jan 82. (lp) *(ORG 18)* **EARTHBOUND GHOST NEED** [ ] [-]

ERIC RANDOM & THE BEDLAMITES

DoubleVision / not iss.

Dec 84. (12") *(DVR 7)* **MAD AS MANKIND. / THE FLOOD** [ ] [-]

Feb 85. (lp) *(DVR 11)* **TIME SPLICE** [ ] [-]
– Himalaya sun / Destination / Hardcore / Father can't yell.

Fon / not iss.

Dec 86. (lp) *(BED 7)* **ISHMAEL** [ ] [-]

— ERIC retired from the studio . . .

RANK & FILE (see under ⇒ DILS)

RAPED (see under ⇒ CUDDLY TOYS)

RAPEMAN (see under ⇒ BIG BLACK)

RAZORCUTS

Formed: London, England . . . 1985 by songwriter GREGORY WEBSTER alongside TIM VASS. These 'Friends of the Earth' were part of the original C-86 anorak brigade and another pastel-hued outfit to sign for the 'Subway Organisation'. Their inaugural single, 'BIG PINK CAKE', was cut in Summer '86, prior to the arrival of Kiwi drummer, DAVID SWIFT. After a further 45, 'SORRY TO EMBARASS YOU', the SWIFT connection led to the band releasing a one-off single, 'I HEARD YOU THE FIRST TIME', for NZ imprint, 'Flying Nun'. Another label with hip indie credibility, 'Creation', was home to the band's debut album, 'STORYTELLER' (1988), a downbeat set of melancholy indie-pop suffering at times from WEBSTER's apathetic vocals. Despite bolstering their line-up with the addition of PETE MOMTCHILOFF, STRUAN ROBERTSON and RICHARD MASON (to replace SWIFT), the band failed to sharpen their sound on the follow-up set, 'THE WORLD KEEPS TURNING' (1989). The subsequent demise of The RAZORCUTS saw WEBSTER join The CAROUSEL while VASS formed his own outfit, RED CHAIR FADE AWAY; newcomer MOMTCHILOFF joined HEAVENLY. A posthumous RAZORCUTS ep appeared the following year, while a reunion between WEBSTER and VASS resulted in a one-off single for 'Sarah', released as the FOREVER PEOPLE.

Album rating: STORYTELLER (*6) / THE WORLD KEEPS TURNING (*6)

GREGORY WEBSTER – vocals, guitar / **TIM VASS** – bass / guest **ANGUS** – drums

Subway / not iss.

Jun 86. (7") *(SUBWAY 5)* **BIG PINK CAKE. / I'LL STILL BE THERE** [ ] [-]

— **DAVID SWIFT** (b. New Zealand) – drums; repl. ANGUS

Oct 86. (7") *(SUBWAY 8)* **SORRY TO EMBARASS YOU. / SUMMER IN YOUR HEART** [ ] [-]
(12"+=) *(SUBWAY 8T)* – Snowbirds don't fly / Mary Day.

Flying Nun / not iss.

Jun 87. (7") *(FNUK 9)* **I HEARD YOU THE FIRST TIME. / FIRST DAY** [ ] [-]
(12"+=) *(FNUK 9T)* – Eight times around the world / A is for alphabet.

Creation / not iss.

Feb 88. (lp) *(CRELP 026)* **STORYTELLER** [ ] [-]
– Storyteler / Try a little tenderness (live) / A contract with God / Sky high / Everyday eyes / Jade / Silhouette / Brighter now / I'll still be there / The last picture show.

— **STRUAN ROBERTSON** – drums; repl. SWIFT

— added **PETE MOMTCHILOFF** – guitar / **RICHARD MASON** – backing vocals / + producer **JOHN A. RIVERS** – hammond organ

Feb 89. (lp/cd) *(CRE LP/CD 045)* **THE WORLD KEEPS TURNING** [ ] [-]
– Goodnight England / Mile high towers / Change / I won't let you down / Waterfall / Flowers for Abigail / Across the meadow / Come my way / Snowbound / Steps to the sea / The world keeps turning. *(cd+=)* – STORYTELLER

— disbanded later in '89 when GREG joined The CAROUSEL, while the RAZORCUTS issued a further single. The same year, VASS's outfit, RED CHAIR FADE AWAY, released an eponymous lp for 'Cosmic English Music' *(CTA 103)*. PETER subsequently joined ex-TALULAH GOSH members in HEAVENLY.

Caff / not iss.

Sep 90. (ltd-7"ep) *(CAFF 10)* **SOMETIMES I WORRY ABOUT YOU / FOR ALWAYS. / SORRY TO EMBARRASS YOU / MUSIC FROM BIG PINK** [ ] [-]

— **WEBSTER + VASS** returned under another pseudonym

Sarah / not iss.

Feb 92. (7"; as FOREVER PEOPLE) *(SARAH 054)* **INVISIBLE. / SOMETIMES** [ ] [-]

— VASS subsequently re-formed RED CHAIR FADE AWAY, issuing two cd-albums for 'English Garden' in 1994 & 1997 respectively, 'MESMERIZED' *(ENG 1012CD)* and 'CURIOUSER AND CURIOUSER' *(ENG 1013CD)*

REAL KIDS

Formed: Boston, Massachusetts, USA . . . 1975 by songwriter, JOHN FELICE (also a sometime J.RICHMAN/MODERN LOVERS sidekick), who enlisted ALLEN 'ALPO' PAULINO, BILLY BORGIOLI and HOWARD FERGUSON. With the Punk/New Wave explosion providing a perfect platform for FELICE's brand of slap-dash high-octane rock'n'roll, the RAMONES-alike (definitely image wise at least) REAL KIDS were a regular draw at New York's CBGB's club. Bizarrely enough, the band became a leading light of the Paris punk scene after issuing their debut single, 'ALL KINDSA GIRLS', as a French-only release in '77. American and British fans had to wait for 1978's eponymous LP which featured the song as its opening track, the record subsequently achieving underground cult status for its combination of raw beer-drenched originals and spirited covers of material by BUDDY HOLLY and EDDIE COCHRAN. The band was put on hold however, as FELICE became part of the RAMONES' road crew, the man (along with a new cast of musicians) later releasing an EP as the TAXI BOYS, taking the moniker from an old REAL KIDS track. A near original line-up of the latter combo regrouped in '82, signing to French label 'New Rose' for a trio of albums, 'OUTTA PLACE' (1982), the live 'ALL KINDSA JERKS' (1983) and 'HIT YOU HARD' (1983). With the band again put on ice, JOHN FELICE & HIS LOWDOWNS returned in '88 with a collection of songs entitled 'NOTHING PRETTY'; The REAL KIDS were back on the block one last time in 1997 with their comeback set, 'GROWN UP WRONG'.

Album rating: THE REAL KIDS (*7) / OUTTA PEACE (*5) / ALL KINDSA JERKS (*4) / HIT YOU HARD (*4) / John Felice & The Lowdowns: NOTHING PRETTY (*5)

JOHN FELICE – vocals, guitar / **BILLY BORGIOLI** – guitar / **ALLEN 'ALPO' PAULINO** – bass / **HOWARD FERGUSON** – drums

Sponge / not iss.

1977. (7") *(SPSP 10)* **ALL KINDSA GIRLS. / COMMON AT NOON** [-] [-] French

Bronze / Red Star

Jun 78. (lp) *(BRON 509)* *<RS 2>* **THE REAL KIDS** [ ] [ ]
– All kindsa girls / Better be good / She's alright / Solid gold (thru and thru) / Just like darts / Do the boob / My baby's book / Reggae reggae / My ways / Taxi boys / Roberta / Rave on. *(re-iss. Jul85 on 'Fan Club'; FC 010)*

Jun 78. (7") *(BRO 54)* **ALL KINDSA GIRLS. / TAXI BOYS** [ ] [-]

— **SCOTT PARMENTAR** – guitar; repl. BORGIOLI

— **BILLY COLE** – bass; repl. PAULINO

— **BOBBY McNABB** – drums; repl. FERGUSON

not iss. / Bomp

Jul 81. (12"ep; as the TAXI BOYS) *<EC 4019>* **TAXI BOYS EP** [-] [ ]
– She / Bad to worse / Happens all the time / What she don't know / What's it to you / Everybody's girl.

— **ROBBY 'MOROCCO' MORIN** – drums; repl. McNABB

— **PAULINO + BORGIOLI** would return repl. SCOTT + BILLY

New Rose / Star-Rhythm

Jul 82. (lp) *(ROSE 14)* **OUTTA PLACE** [ ] [ ]

Dec 82. (7") *(NEW 17)* **SHE. /** [ ] [-]

Mar 83. (lp) *(ROSE 21)* **ALL KINDSA JERKS (live)** [ ] [-]

Jul 83. (lp) *(ROSE 24)* **HIT YOU HARD** [ ] [-]

— disbanded in 1984, but re-formed in the mid 90's

Norton / Norton

Jun 97. (cd) *<(CED 231)>* **GROWN UP WRONG** [ ] [ ]

Feb 98. (7") *<(45018)>* **HOT DOG. /** [ ] [ ]

– compilations, etc. –

1983. (lp) *Lolita;* **GIRLS! GIRLS! GIRLS!** [-] [-] French

JOHN FELICE & THE LOWDOWNS

New Rose / not iss.

Feb 88. (lp/cd) *(ROSE 141/+CD)* **NOTHING PRETTY** [ ] [-]
– Don't be telling me / Ain't we having fun / I'll never sing that song again / Not the one / Perfect love / Nowadaze kids / Nothing pretty / Dreams / Don't make me wait / Can't play it safe.

REAL PEOPLE

Formed: Bootle, Liverpool, England . . . 1989 by songwriting brothers TONY and CHRIS GRIFFITHS, who had cut their teeth as JO JO AND THE REAL PEOPLE. The pair were joined by SEAN SIMPSON and TONY ELSON, and, after many impressive local gigs, signed to 'CBS-Columbia'. However, a subsequent trip to India swallowed up most of their advance and it wasn't until early '91 that they issued their first single, 'OPEN UP YOUR MIND (LET ME IN)'. Hyped as leading the vanguard of the new Scally sound alongside RAIN and The LA'S, the band crept ever closer to the Top 40 with each single release. These tracks were all lifted from their eponymous debut album, a disappointingly average collection of pop-indie which lacked the headspinning charm of contemporaries The LA'S. After parting company with their major label paymasters, The REAL PEOPLE laid low for a while before returning on their own terms in 1995.

Album rating: THE REAL PEOPLE (*5)

TONY GRIFFITHS (b. 7 Apr'66) – vocals, bass / **CHRIS GRIFFITHS** (b.30 Mar'68) – guitar, vocals / **SEAN SIMPSON** (b. 9 Oct'69) – guitar / **TONY ELSON** (b. 2 Jan'66) – drums

Columbia Columbia

Feb 91. (7") *(656612-7)* **OPEN UP YOUR MIND (LET ME IN). /** 70
(12"+=/cd-s+=) *(656612-6/-2)* –

Apr 91. (7") *(656787-7)* **THE TRUTH. /** 73
(12"+=/cd-s+=) *(656787-6/-2)* –

May 91. (cd/c/lp) *(468084-2/-4/-1)* **THE REAL PEOPLE** 59

Jun 91. (7"ep/12"ep/cd-ep) *(656932-7/-6/-5)* **WINDOW PANE. / SEE THROUGH YOU / EVERYTHING MUST CHANGE** 60

Jan 92. (7") *(657698-7)* **THE TRUTH (remix). / WORDS (remix)** 41
(cd-s+=) *(657698-2)* – Easy (remix).
(12"ep/7"ep) *(657698-6/-)* – ('A'side) / Breathe / Ashamed / Easy.

May 92. (7"/c-s) *(658006-7/-4)* **BELIEVER. / IF I'M A FOOL** 38
(12"+=/cd-s+=) *(658006-6/-2)* – Sun shines down / Don't look now.

Jul 92. (7"/c-s) *(658195-7/-4)* **DREAM ON. /**
(12"+=/cd-s+=) *(658195-6/-2)* –

Oct 92. (7"/c-s) **TOO MUCH TOO YOUNG. /**
(12"+=/cd-s+=) –

— were casualties of the music biz in the New Year, although they were back around the mid-90's.

Egg not iss.

Apr 95. (cd-ep) *(1 EGG)* **REAL PEOPLE. /** -

Jun 95. (7"ep/cd-ep) *(2 EGG/+CD)* **BRING YOU DOWN** -

MGL Granite not iss.

Nov 95. (7"ep/cd-ep) *(MGGR 7/CD 9)* **EVERY VISION OF YOU / I DON'T MIND. / LIFE IS A BORE / LOST IN SPACE** -

Jun 96. (7"/c-s) *(MGGR/+MC 18)* **ROLLING STONE. /** -
(cd-s+=) *(MGGRCD 18)* –

– compilations, etc. –

Feb 96. (cd; shared with The RAIN) *Columbia; (483660-2)*
LIVERPOOL (/ THE CALM BEFORE THE STORM) -

RECORDS

Formed: Southend, England . . . early 1978 by ex-KURSAAL FLYERS, WILL BIRCH and JOHN WICKS, the pair creating a songwriting partnership in the process. The former was a veteran of the local music scene, having played drums in various bands beginning with mid-60's combo, The GEEZENSTACKS through to the aforementioned mid-70's pub-rock act. The RECORDS' line-up was completed by PHIL BROWN, HUW GOWER and IAN GIBBONS, the latter in place in time for their debut lp, 'SHADES IN BED' (1979); he subsequently became a full-time member thereafter. One track from the album, a revamped 'STARRY EYES' (the song had originally appeared in 1978 as RECORDS' independently released debut single prior to their deal with 'Virgin'), nudged into the Top 60 later that year, the band's one and only hit. Fine in small doses, their trademark power-pop was a mite too sickly to stomach over a whole album, the underwhelming 'CRASHES' (1980) being a point in case. Endless variations on the same squeaky clean harmonies and earnest, often cringeworthy lyrics (see 'MAN WITH A GIRLPROOF HEART' and 'WORRIERS') were the order of the day. By the time of the record's release, GOWER had decamped to play with former NEW YORK DOLL, DAVID JOHANSEN, his place filled initially by BILLY MARTIN and more permanently JUDE COLE. More line-up changes then ensued with the replacement of COLE and GIBBONS (who remained on a part-time basis) with CHRIS GENT and DAVE WHELAN prior to swansong album, 'MUSIC ON BOTH SIDES' (1982). Splitting after BIRCH embarked on a fruitful career in production, the band later reforming for a one-off album, 'A SUNNY AFTERNOON IN WATERLOO' (1988). • **Covers:** HAVE YOU SEEN HER MOTHER BABY . . . (Rolling Stonnes).

Album rating: SHADES IN BED (*5) / CRASHES (*4) / MUSIC ON BOTH SIDES (*4) / SMASHES, CRASHES & NEAR MISSES compilation (*5)

JOHN WICKS – vocals, rhythm guitar (ex-KURSAAL FLYERS) / **WILL BIRCH** (b.1950) – drums, vocals (ex-KURSAAL FLYERS) / **HUW GOWER** – lead guitar, vocals (ex-RATBITES FROM HELL) / **PHIL BROWN** – bass, vocals

N.B. not iss.

Nov 78. (7") *(NB 2)* **STARRY EYES. / PAINT HER FACE** -

Virgin Virgin

Mar 79. (7") *(VS 247)* **ROCK'N'ROLL LOVE LETTER. / WIVES AND MOTHERS OF TOMORROW** -
(12"+=) *(VS 247-12)* – Starry eyes.

— added as a guest at first, **IAN GIBBONS** – keyboards

May 79. (7") *(VS 250)* **TEENARAMA. / HELD UP HIGH**

Jun 79. (lp) *(V 2122)* <*VA 13130*> **SHADES IN BED** <US-title 'THE RECORDS'> 41 Aug79
– All messed up and ready to go / Teenarama / Girls that don't exist / Starry eyes / Up all night / Girl / Insomnia / Affection rejected / The phone / Another star. *(w/ free 7"ep)* **HIGH HEELS** – Abracadabra (have you seen her) / See my friends / 1984 / Have you seen her mother baby (standing in the shadows).

Aug 79. (7") <*VA 67000*> **STARRY EYES. / PAINT HER FACE** - 56

— **JUDE COLE** – guitar, vocals (ex-MOON MARTIN); repl. BILLY MARTIN, who repl. GOWER (latter to DAVID JOHANSEN group)

May 80. (7") *(VS 330)* **HEARTS IN HER EYES. / SO SORRY** -

Jun 80. (lp) *(V 2155)* <*VA 13140*> **CRASHES**
– Rumour sets the woods alight / Hearts in her eyes / I don't remember your name / Man with a girlproof heart / The same mistakes / Girl in golden disc / Spent a week with you last night / Hearts will be broken / Worriers / Guitars in the sky.

— **DAVE WHELAN** – guitar; repl. JUDE + IAN

— **CHRIS GENT** – vocals, saxophone; repl. GIBBONS (was p/t again)

Aug 81. (7") *(VS 442)* **IMMITATION JEWELLERY. / YOUR OWN SOUNDTRACK** -

Mar 82. (lp) *(V 2206)* **MUSIC ON BOTH SIDES** -
– Immitation jewellery / Heather and Hell / Selfish love / Clown around town / Not so much time / Keeping up with Joneses / Third hand information / Real life / King of kings / Cheap detective music / Everyday nightmare.

— split when BIRCH went into production work (re-formed late 80's for a one last recording session (**WICKS, BIRCH, GOWER + BROWN**)

Waterfront not iss.

Apr 88. (lp) *(WF 042)* **ON A SUNNY AFTERNOON IN WATERLOO** -
– Night driving / Lovin' in the back row / Level in the bottle / You changed the lock / In the eyes of a blindman / Third degree burns / 36-24-36 / Living out of a suitcase.

– compilations, etc. –

Oct 88. (cd) *Virgin; (COMCD 13)* **SMASHES, CRASHES AND NEAR MISSES** -
– Starry eyes / Girl in golden disc / Teenarama / Up all night / I don't remember your name / Girls that don't exist / Hearts will be broken / All messed up and ready to go / Hearts in her eyes / Girl / Spent a week with you last night / Held up high / Rumour set the woods alight / The same mistakes / Selfish love / Not so much the time / Affection rejected / Paint her face / Imitation jewellery / Rock and roll love letter. *(re-iss. Feb95; CDOVD 456)*

REDD KROSS

Formed: Hawthorne, California, USA . . . late 1978 by schoolboy brothers JEFF McDONALD (then 15) and STEVE (only 11), initially as The TOURISTS (not UK group with ANNIE and DAVE). Completing the line-up with GREG HETSON and RON REYES, they played their first gig in 1979 as RED CROSS, opening for BLACK FLAG. Spotted by DJ and entrepreneur, Rodney Bingenheimer, they subsequently recorded an EP for 'Posh Boy' which led to the "real" International Red Cross threatening to sue them if they didn't change the group name! REDD KROSS, as they were now known, lost GREG HETSON and RON REYES in the process, both moving on to similar hardcore acts, CIRCLE JERKS and BLACK FLAG respectively. Over the course of the early to mid 80's, personnel changed like the weather and output was sparse. However, a few albums had emerged during this lean period, namely 'BORN INNOCENT' (1982) and covers set, 'TEEN BABES FROM MONSANTO' (1984), REDD KROSS not exactly causing an emergency with their trashy psychedelic punk/glam, although their embryonic grunge sound was definitely ahead of its time. Just when recognition seemed to be forthcoming with 1987's 'NEUROTICA', luck ran out as their label, 'Big Time', came a cropper. The McDONALD brothers re-appeared in 1990 with their one-off covers side project, TATER TOTZ, before the pair resurfaced with a new REDD KROSS line-up and a major deal courtesy of 'Atlantic'. A comeback album, 'THIRD EYE', appeared in 1991, the band's subsequent UK output released through 'This Way Up' (home to TINDERSTICKS and IAN McNABB). Another new line-up (namely, EDDIE KURDZIEL, GERE FENNELLY and BRIAN REITZEL) was in place for 1993's 'PHASESHIFTER', which spawned three singles, 'SWITCHBLADE SISTER', 'LADY IN THE FRONT ROW' and 'VISIONARY', the latter scraping into the UK Top 75 early the following year. Later that summer, the band indulged their love of classic 70's pop with a kitschy cover of the Carpenters' 'YESTERDAY ONCE MORE', a shock UK Top 50 hit which featured SONIC YOUTH paying tribute to Karen & Richard on the B-side. A long hiatus ensued before REDD KROSS entered the fray once more in early '97 with another set of multi-coloured sonic-pop, 'SHOW WORLD', a collection that featured another minor hit single, 'GET OUT OF MYSELF'. • **Covered:** CITADEL (Rolling Stones) / HEAVEN ONLY KNOWS (Shangri-las) / DANCING QUEEN (Abba) / ANN (Stooges) / CEASE TO EXIST (Charles Manson) / etc. • **Trivia:** In 1990, REDD KROSS recorded a soundtrack for the Super-8 film, 'Desperate Teenage Lovedolls'.

Album rating: BORN INNOCENT (*4) / TEEN BABES FROM MONSANTO (*5) / NEUROTICA (*6) / THIRD EYE (*7) / PHASESHIFTER (*6) / SHOW WORLD (*7)

JEFF McDONALD (b.10 Aug'63, Los Angeles) – vocals / **GREG HETSON** – guitar / **STEVE McDONALD** (b.24 May'67) – bass, vocals / **RON REYES** – drums

not iss. Posh Boy

1981. (12"ep; as RED CROSS) <*PBS 1010*> **RED CROSS** -
– Cover band / Annette's got the hits / I hate my school / Clorox girls / S&M party / Standing in front of a poseur.

— now without HETSON (to CIRCLE JERKS) and REYES (to BLACK FLAG). They were repl. by a BANGLE!? (briefly) and various L.A. session people including **DEZ CADENA** (of BLACK FLAG)

not iss. Smoke 7

1982. (lp) <*smk7 103*> **BORN INNOCENT** -
– Linda Blair / White trash / Everyday there's someone new / Solid gold / Burn out / Charlie / Tatum O'Tot and the fried vegetables / St. Lita Ford blues / Self respect / Pseudo-intellectual / Kill someone you hate / Look on up at the bottom / Cellulite city / I'm alright / Cease to exist / Notes and chords mean nothing to me. *(UK-iss.Aug92 on 'Frontier' cd/lp; 4609-2L/1L)*

not iss. Enigma

1984. (lp) <*71110-1*> **TEEN BABES FROM MONSANTO** (covers) -

Big Time Big Time

Sep 87. (lp/c) <*(ZL/ZK 71427K)*> **NEUROTICA**
– Neurotica / Play my song / Frosted flake / Janus, Jeanie and George Harrison / Love is you / Peach Kelli Pop / McKenzie / Ballad of a love doll / What they say / Ghandii is dead (in the cartoon man) / Beautiful bye byes.

East West Atlantic

Apr 91. (cd/c/lp) <*(7567 82148-2/-4/-1)*> **THIRD EYE** Nov90
– The faith healer / Annie's gone / I don't know how to be your friend / Shonen Knife / Bubblegum factory / Where I am today / Zira (call out my name) / Love is not love / 1976 / Debbie & Kim / Elephant flares.

Apr 91. (7") **ANNIE'S GONE. /**
(12")(cd-s) –

Seminal Twang | not iss.

Jul 92. (7") **TRANCE. /** (cd-s+=) –

— **McDONALD's** plus **EDDIE KURDZIEL** (b.25 Sep'60, Philadelphia) – guitar / **GERE FENNELLY** (b. 5 Aug'60, San Mateo, Calif.) – keyboards / **BRIAN REITZEL** (b.24 Dec'65, Ukiah, Calif.) – drums

This Way Up | Polygram

Jun 93. (7") *(WAY 10-11)* **SWITCHBLADE SISTER. /** (cd-s) *(WAY 10-33)* –

Sep 93. (cd/c/lp) *<(518167-2/-4/-1)>* **PHASESHIFTER**
– Jimmy's fantasy / Lady in the front row / Monolith / Crazy world / Dumb angel / Huge wonder / Visionary / Pay for love / Ms. Lady Evans / Only a girl / Saragon / After school special.

Oct 93. (7"/10") *(WAY 20-11/88)* **LADY IN THE FRONT ROW. / I'LL MEET YOU HALFWAY**
(cd-s) *(WAY 20-33)* – ('A'side) / Standing in front of poseur / Oh my lover / Fancy.

Jan 94. (7") *(WAY 27-11)* **VISIONARY. /** [75] [-]
(12"+=/cd-s+=) *(WAY 27-/33)* –

— In Sep'94, they shared a single 'YESTERDAY ONCE MORE' with SONIC YOUTH's 'Superstar' (both CARPENTERS covers) hit UK No.45 for 'A&M'; *580792)*

Jan 97. (7"colrd) *(WAY 54-11)* **GET OUT OF MYSELF. / SOCALV8** [63] [-]
(cd-s+=) *(WAY 54-33)* – Teen competition (demo).
(cd-s) *(WAY 54-66)* – ('A'side) / Misery is mother / Jimmy's fantasy.

Feb 97. (cd/c/lp) *<(524 275-2/-4/-1)>* **SHOW WORLD**
– Pretty please me / Stoned / You lied again / Girl god / Mess around / One chord progression / Teen competition / Follow the leader / Vanity mirror / Secret life / Ugly town / Get out of myself / Kiss the goat.

Mar 97. (7") *(WAY 60-11)* **MESS AROUND. / WHAT CHA DOIN' TO THAT GIRL**
(cd-s) *(WAY 60-33)* – ('A'side) / Crazy world / Ugly town.
(cd-s) *(WAY 60-66)* – ('A'side) / Sick love / Popular cult.

Jun 97. (7") *(WAY 64-11)* **SECRET LIFE. / DANCING QUEEN**
(cd-s+=) *(WAY 64-33)* – Follow the leader.
(cd-s) *(WAY 64-66)* – ('A'side) / Its in the sky / You lied again.

TATER TOTZ

not iss. | Positive

1988. (lp) *<6010>* **ALIEN SLEESTACKS FROM BRAZIL** [-]

Jul 90. (cd/c/lp) **SGT. SHONEN'S EXPLODING PLASTIC EASTMAN BAND REQUESTS** [-]
(above was released on 'Gatanska-Giant')

1990. (cd) *<6027>* **MONO STEREO** [-]

Rockville | Rockville

Jul 93. (m-cd) *<(ROCK 6054-2)>* **TATER COMES ALIVE!**
– Tomorrow never knows / Rain / Sisters, o sisters / Don't worry Kyoko / Flowers / Sympathy for the Devil / Don't worry Kyoko.

RED GUITARS

Formed: Hull, England . . . 1982 by JEREMY KIDD and HALLAM LEWIS, alongside JOHN ROWLEY and MATT HIGGINS. Issued on their own 'Self-Drive' label in mid '83, the chugging irony of debut single, 'GOOD TECHNOLOGY' was followed by 'FACT!', an intelligent slice of alternative pop with an ominous guitar refrain and an anti-war message. The double re-issue of 'GOOD TECHNOLOGY' early in '84 appeared prior to the moody bass reverbations of 'STEELTOWN', the latter track underlining the band's political stance. Yet it was 'MARIMBA JIVE' which gave the band most success, climbing to the top of the indie charts and forming the centrepiece of debut album, 'SLOW TO FADE' (1984). KIDD left unexpectedly shortly after the record's release, taking his label with him. Recruiting ROBERT HOLMES as a replacement, The RED GUITARS moved swiftly onwards, signing to 'Virgin'-offshoot, 'One Way' and releasing a second long player, 'TALES OF THE EXPECTED' (1985). Despite further critical acclaim, the group ultimately went their separate ways with HALLAM forming PLANET WILSON and HOLMES releasing a solo set, 'AGE OF SWING' (1989) for 'Virgin'.

Album rating: SLOW TO FADE (*7) / TALES OF THE EXPECTED (*5)

JEREMY KIDD – vocals / **HALLAM LEWIS** – guitar, vocals / **JOHN ROWLEY** – guitar, keyboards / **LOU HOWARD** – bass / **MATT HIGGINS** – drums

Self-Drive | not iss.

Jul 83. (7") *(SD 006)* **GOOD TECHNOLOGY. / HEARTBEAT GO** [-]

Nov 83. (7") *(SD 007)* **FACT. / DIVE (live)** [-]

Jan 84. (12") *(SD 008)* **GOOD TECHNOLOGY. / FACT / PARIS FRANCE** [-]

Apr 84. (7"/12") *(SD 009/+T)* **GOOD TECHNOLOGY. / HEARTBEAT GO** [-]

Jun 84. (7"/12") *(SCAR 010/T)* **STEELTOWN. / WITHIN FOUR WALLS** [-]

Sep 84. (7"/12") *(SCAR 014/+T)* **MARIMBA JIVE. / HEARTBEAT GO** [-]

Nov 84. (lp) *(SCARLP 001)* **SLOW TO FADE** [-]
– Remote control / Dive / Astronomy / Cloak and dagger / Shaken not stirred / Crocodile tears / Sting in the tail / Marimba / Slow to fade. *(re-iss. Nov86 lp/c/cd; SCAR LP/C/CD 001)*– (with extra tracks).

— **ROBERT HOLMES** – vocals, guitar; repl. JEREMY KIDD who went solo

One-Way | not iss.

Apr 85. (7") *(OW 1)* **BE WITH ME. / ?** [-]
(12"+=) *(OW 1T)* –

— **LOU HOWARD** – bass; repl. BARLOW

Virgin | not iss.

Mar 86. (7") *(VS 832)* **NATIONAL AVENUE (SUNDAY AFTERNOON). / KING AND COUNTRY** [-]
(12"+=) *(VS 832-12)* – Things I want.

Mar 86. (lp/c) *(V/TCV 2373)* **TALES OF THE EXPECTED** [-]
– Be with me / Suspicion and fear / National Avenue (Sunday afternoon) / Love and understanding / Storyville / Marianne / Sweetwater ranch / House of love / Trains on time / Baby's got a gun. *(re-iss. Jun88 lp/c; OVED/+C 224) (cd-iss. 1988; CDV 2373)*

May 86. (7") *(VS 858)* **AMERICA AND ME. / MARIANNE** [-]
(12"+=) *(VS 858-12)* – ('A'version).

Sep 86. (7"/12") *(VS 899/+12)* **BLUE CARAVAN. / SUSPICION AND FEAR** [-]

— disbanded late 1986 and ROBERT HOLMES went solo releasing debut single, 'INTERNATIONAL SUNSHINE', in 1987. He subsequently issued one more, 'ANGEL IN THE HOUSE', from the parent set, 'AGE OF SWING' (1989)

– compilations, etc. –

Feb 93. (cd) *R.P.M.; (RPM 109)* **SEVEN TYPES OF AMBIGUITY** [-]
– Paris France / Fact / Dive / Marimba jive / Sting in the tale / Slow to fade / Steeltown / Heartbeat go! / Within four walls / Crocodile tears / Remote control / Shaken not stirred / Astronomy / Seven types of ambiguity / Jamaican homecoming / Be with me / Clean up / Age of swing / Train's on time / Good technology.

PLANET WILSON

— were formed by **HALLAM LEWIS + LOU HOWARD** plus **JONAH OXBURROW** – drums (ex-THAT NOBLE PORPOISE)

Virgin | not iss.

Mar 88. (7") *(VS 1053)* **WHITE LIES. / VISION ON** [-]
(12"+=) *(VST 1053)* – The big wheel.

Mar 88. (cd/c/lp) *(CD/TC+/V 2508)* **IN THE BEST OF ALL POSSIBLE WORLDS** [-]
– Flap the bird / The big wheel / Rolling balls / Distraction / Sinister Dexter / Seven days / Love by hand / Wish it was so / White lies. *(cd+=)* – Vision on / I remain outside.

Records Of Achievement | not iss.

Jan 89. (7") *(PLAN 2)* **TAKEN FOR A RIDE. / ?** [-]
(12"+=) *(12PLAN 2)* –

Mar 89. (lp/cd) *(PLAN 003/+CD)* **NOT DROWNING BUT WAVING** [-]
– Truth hurts / Taken for a ride / I remain outside / Golden touch / Honeymoon / Fly by night / How do I feel? / Mouth to mouth / Night swimming.

— HALLAM went on to run his own studio.

RED HOUSE PAINTERS

Formed: San Francisco, California, USA . . . 1989 by MARK KOZELEK (who had earlier sang in GOD FORBID) along with drummer ANTHONY KOUTSOS who he met in 1989, after moving from Ohio to Atlanta. Relocating once again, this time to San Francisco, the pair duly recruited guitarist GORDON MACK and bassist JERRY VESSEL. The outfit was basically KOZELEK's baby, however, and his writing and distictly melancholy musings dominated the group's work. Their debut album, 'DOWN COLOURFUL HILL', was virtually a bare demo which had arrived in the hands of '4 a.d.' supremo, Ivo Watts-Russell, via American Music Club miserabilist, MARK EITZEL. Spiritually akin to AMC, the debut showcased KOZELEK's moody pastel-rock introspections, downbeat but often hauntingly melodic. Though the press raved over it (comparisons were made with singer/songwriters like NEIL YOUNG and LOU REED), the album sold negligably. A further couple of RED HOUSE PAINTERS' releases followed in 1993, confusingly enough, both entitled 'RED HOUSE PAINTERS'. One was a spawling double set building on the wistfulness of the debut while the other was a mini-album featuring such endearing covers as Paul Simon's 'I AM A ROCK' and 'THE STAR SPANGLED BANNER'. It would be another two years before the group's next album, KOZELEK and Co. undertaking a rare UK tour, their first British dates since an early appearance at London's 'Borderline'. 'OCEAN BEACH' (1995) was a more robust set, KOZOLEK illustrating the breadth of his influences with a YES cover, 'LONG DISTANCE RUNAROUND', no doubt a crime punishable by public flogging in most indie bands' book. Though the critical plaudits continued to roll in, the album again failed to sell in any great quantity. With a move to 'Island' in 1996, surely a better home for the sparse melancholy of the bulk of KOZOLEK's material, the group released 'SONGS FOR THE BLUE GUITAR?'. • **Songwriters:** All by KOZELE K, except 'Dragonflies' by ROBYN RIEL-NAIL. Covers; STAR SPANGLED BANNER (US National Anthem) / SHOCK ME (Kiss). • **Trivia:** Their UK first gig (very rare) was at The Borderline in London in the Autumn of '92.

Album rating: RED HOUSE PAINTERS (*9; June '93 double album) / DOWN COLORFUL HILL (*8) / OCEAN BEACH (*7) / SONGS FOR A BLUE GUITAR (*8)

MARK KOZELEK – vocals / **GORDON MACK** – guitar / **JERRY VESSEL** – bass / **ANTHONY KOUTSOS** – drums

4 a.d. | 4ad-Warners

Sep 92. (cd)(lp/c) *(CAD 2014CD)(CAD/+C 2014) <45062>* **DOWN COLORFUL HILL**
– 24 / Medicine bottle / Down colourful hill / Japanese to English / Lord kill the pain / Michael.

May 93. (cd)(d-lp/c) *(DAD 3008CD)(DAD/+C 3008) <45256>* **RED HOUSE PAINTERS** [63]
– Grace cathedral park / Down through / Katy song / Mistress / Things mean a lot / Funhouse / Take me out / Rollercoaster / New Jersey / Dragonflies / Mistress (piano version) / Mother / Strawberry hill / Brown eyes.

Oct 93. (cd)(m-lp/c) *(CAD 3016CD)(CAD/+C 3016) <45441>* **RED HOUSE PAINTERS** 68
– Evil / Bubble / I am a rock / Helicopter / New Jersey / Uncle Joe / Blindfold / Star spangled banner.

Feb 94. (12"ep/cd-ep) *(BAD 4004/+CD)* **SHOCK ME / SHOCK ME (mix). / SUNDAYS AND HOLIDAYS / THREE-LEGGED CAT** -

Mar 95. (cd)(c)(2x10"lp) *(CAD 5005CD)(CADC 5005)(DAD 5005) <45859>* **OCEAN BEACH**
– Cabezon / Summer dress / San Geronimo / Shadows / Over my head / Red carpet / Brockwell Park / Moments / Drop. *(lp+=)* – Long distance runaround.

Island | Polygram

Jul 96. (cd/c) *(CID/ICT 8050) <531061>* **SONGS FOR A BLUE GUITAR**
– Have you forgotten / Song for a blue guitar / Make like paper / Priest alley song / Trailways / Feel the rain fall / Long distance runaround / All mixed up / Revelation Big Sur / Silly love songs / Another song for a blue guitar.

RED LETTER DAY

Formed: Portsmouth, England . . . 1983 by frontman ADE, IAN CAMPBELL, PETE WHITE and BRIAN LEE, the latter three soon posted missing and replaced over the course of the ensuing few years by guitarist DAVIE EGAN, bassist KEITH METCALFE and drummer DARYN PRICE respectively. This line-up debuted in early '86 with the single, 'WHEREVER YOU MAY RUN', the record's post-punk stylings catching the ear of Radio One DJ, John Peel, who invited the quartet on his show for a session. Subsequently signing to 'Quiet' records (former stable of NEW MODEL ARMY), they issued two further EP's, 'RELEASED EMOTIONS' and 'TAKE ME IN YOUR ARMS', the former also the name of the label they'd sign to for a shared LP (with The SECT), 'SOFT LIGHTS AND LOUD GUITARS' (1988). Never a prolific band, RED LETTER DAY were also dogged by further personnel changes (METCALFE and EGAN were despatched around '87/'88) although they did finally emerge with their own album proper, 'MORE SONGS ABOUT LOVE AND WAR' (1991). After taking another interminable sabbatical, RLD were back with a limited-edition one-off 7", 'INSOMNIA', in '97, while the following year saw the release of only their second album in a decade and a half, 'LETHAL'.

Album rating: SOFT LIGHTS AND LOUD GUITARS (*5) / MORE SONGS ABOUT LOVE AND WAR (*5)

ADE – vocals, guitar / **DAVIE EGAN** – guitar; repl. IAN CAMPBELL / **KEITH METCALFE** – bass; repl. PETE WHITE / **DARYN PRICE** – drums; repl. BRIAN LEE

Lost Generation | not iss.

Mar 86. (7") *(LG 003)* **WHEREVER YOU MAY RUN. / SUSIE'S BOMBED OUT TONITE** -

Quiet | not iss.

Sep 86. (12"ep) *(QST 15)* **RELEASED EMOTIONS EP** -
Jul 87. (7"ep) *(QS 018)* **TAKE ME IN YOUR ARMS. / MOVING ON / THE DAY I JOINED THE HUMAN RACE** -

— **STEVE** – bass (ex-ORIGINAL MIRRORS) repl. METCALFE

Released Emotions | not iss.

Jul 88. (lp; shared with The SECT) *(REM 001)* **SOFT LIGHTS AND LOUD GUITARS** -
– It's cold outside / American dream / The war starts at midnight / Fade away / Fall apart / Barely alive / Shades / The less i see the more I think of you / The whole world gets me down / Unclean.

— **RAY** – guitar; repl. EGAN

1991. (cd) **MORE SONGS ABOUT LOVE AND WAR** -

— disbanded but re-formed later

Mouthy | not iss.

Feb 97. (ltd-7") **INSOMNIA. /** -

Holier Than Thou | not iss.

Jul 98. (cd) *(HTT 032-2)* **LETHAL** -
– Choose noise / Alison / Insomnia / Lethal / Parallel suburbia / Diva / Clandestine / Wordstoomuch / Four / Insider / Drama queen / Thousand names for God.

RED LORRY YELLOW LORRY

Formed: Leeds, England . . . 1982 by CHRIS REED, MARTIN FAGEN, STEVE SMITH and MICK BROWN. With FAGEN and SMITH subsequently replaced by DANE WOLFENDEN (aka WOLFIE) and PAUL SOUTHERN, RED LORRY YELLOW LORRY emerged from the fertile Leeds goth scene via a deal with the local 'Red Rhino' label. Featuring their much loved signature tune, 'HOLLOW EYES', the debut mini-album, 'TALK ABOUT THE WEATHER', arrived in 1985 and received support from John Peel amongst others. Favouring the usual prophet-of-doom vocals over noisy, discordant guitars and an almost tribal rhythm, the band built up a following parallel to contemporaries like The SISTERS OF MERCY and FIELDS OF THE NEPHILIM without really achieving the same degree of cult status and fanatical following. Nevertheless, they carved out their own niche in the market, moving to 'Beggars Banquet' offshoot, 'Situation 2', for a third set, 'NOTHING'S WRONG' (1988). By the early 90's, the line-up had undergone so many changes that REED was the only founding member left, the band forging on with 1992's 'BLASTING OFF' album.

Album rating: THE SINGLES 1982-1987 compilation (*7)

CHRIS REED – vocals, guitar / **DANE WOLFENDEN** – guitar; repl. MARTIN EGAN / **PAUL SOUTHERN** – bass; repl. STEVE SMITH / **MICK BROWN** – drums

Red Rhino | not iss.

Sep 82. (7") *(RED 20)* **BEATING MY HEAD. / I'M STILL WAITING** -
Apr 83. (7") *(RED 28)* **TAKE IT ALL. / HAPPY** -
Oct 83. (7") *(RED 39)* **HE'S READ. / SET THE FIRE** -
Mar 84. (12"ep) *(RED 48)* **THIS TODAY / BEATING MY HEAD. / SEE THE FIRE / TAKE IT ALL/ HE'S READ** -
Jun 84. (7") *(RED 49)* **MONKEY'S ON JUICE. / PUSH** -
(12"+=) *(REDT 49)* – Silence.

— **LEON PHILLIPS** – bass; repl. PAUL

Oct 84. (7") *(RED 52)* **HOLLOW EYES. / FEEL A PIECE** -
(12"+=) *(REDT 52)* – Russia.
Jan 85. (lp) *(REDLP 50)* **TALK ABOUT THE WEATHER** -
– This today / Hollow eyes / Talk about the weather / Hand on heart / Happy / Strange dream / Feel a piece / Sometimes.
Apr 85. (7"/ext-12") *(RED/+T 55)* **CHANCE. / GENERATION** -

— **CHRIS OLDROYD** – drums (ex-MUSIC FOR PLEASURE, ex-GIRLS AT OUR BEST) repl. BROWN who joined The MISSION

Sep 85. (7") *(RED 60)* **SPINNING ROUND. / HOLD YOURSELF DOWN** -
(12"+=) *(REDT 60)* – ('A'version).
Feb 86. (lp/c/cd) *(RED LP/C/CD 65)* **PAINT YOUR WAGON** -
– Walking on your hands / Jipp / Last train / Head all fire / Mescal dance / Shout at the sky / Which side / Tear me up / Save my soul / Blitz. *(cd+=) (REDF 65)* – Hold yourself down / Generation. *(free-7"w/ lp)* – PAINT YOUR WAGON. / MORE JIPP (instrumental)
Jun 86. (7") *(RED 66)* **WALKING ON YOUR HANDS. / WHICH SIDE** -
(12"+=) *(REDT 66)* – More jipp (instrumental).
Oct 86. (7") *(RED 73)* **CUT DOWN. / RUNNING FEVER** -
(12"+=) *(REDT 73)* – Pushed me.
May 87. (7"; as The LORRIES) *(RED 76)* **CRAWLING MANTRA. / HANGMAN** -
(d7"+=/12"+=) *(RED D/T 76)* – All the same / Shout at the sky (live).

Situation 2 | Beggars Banquet

Nov 87. (7") *(SIT 49)* **OPEN UP. / ANOTHER SIDE** -
(12"+=) *(SIT 49T)* – You only get what you pay for.
Mar 88. (7") *(SIT 50)* **NOTHING WRONG. / DO YOU UNDERSTAND** -
(12"+=) *(SIT 50T)* – Calling.
May 88. (lp/cd)(c) *(SITU 20/+CD)(SITC 20) <8480>* **NOTHING WRONG**
– Nothing wrong / Big stick / Hands off me / She said / Time is right / Sayonara / World around / Hand-away / Never know / Only dreaming (wide awake) / Pushing on / Do you understand? / You only get what you pay for / Another side / Calling / Open up. *(re-iss. Jul91 lp/cd; SITL 20/+CD)*
Sep 88. (7") *(SIT 54)* **ONLY DREAMING (WIDE AWAKE). / THE RISE** -
(12"+=) *(SIT 54T)* –
Aug 89. (7") *(SIT 60)* **TEMPTATION. /** -
(12"+=) *(SIT 60T)* –
Sep 89. (lp/cd)(c) *(SITU 25/+CD)(SITU 25) <9937>* **BLOW**
– Happy to see me / Temptation / Shine a light / Too many colours / Heaven / Gift that shines / In a world / You are everything / West wakes up / It was wrong / Blow. *(cd+=)* – Heaven (acoustic version). *(re-iss. Jul91 lp/cd; SITL 25/+CD)*

— Disbanded after above album when new drummer CHIL broke his wrist. Reformed when **REED** brought in other new members **GARY WEIGHT** – lead guitar / **MARTIN SCOTT** – bass

Deathwish | Relapse

Sep 92. (cd/lp) *(DW 2355 6CD/5LP) <6109>* **BLASTING OFF** 1994
– This is energy / It's on fire / Don't think about it / Train of hope / Talking back / Down on ice / In my mind / Sea of tears / I can see stars / Driving me.

— split for the last time early in '93

– compilations, etc. –

Feb 88. (lp/c/cd) *Red Rhino; (RED LP/C/CD 86)* **SMASHED HITS** -
(cd-iss. May95 on 'Dojo'; DOJOCD 210)
Feb 94. (cd) *Cherry Red; (CDMRED 109)* **THE SINGLES 1982-87** -
– Beating my head / I'm still waiting / Take it all away / Happy / He's read / See the fire / Monkey's on juice / Push / Silence / Hollow eyes / Feel a piece / Chance / Generation / Spinning round / Hold yourself down / Regenerate / Walking on your hands / Which side / Jipp (instrumental mix) / Cut down / Burning fever / Pushed me / Crawling mantra / Hang man / All the same / Shout at the sky.
Jun 94. (cd) *Cherry Red; (CDMRED 115)* **TALK ABOUT THE WEATHER / PAINT YOUR WAGON** -
Jun 94. (cd) *Cleopatra; (cd) (<CLEO 9404>)* **GENERATION: THE BEST OF . . .**

RED RED MEAT

Formed: Chicago, Illinois, USA . . . 1992 by frontman/songwriter, TIM RUTILI (also a pop video maker for the likes of VERUCA SALT), GLENN GIRARD, TIM HURLEY and BRIAN DECK. Their eponymous 1993 debut didn't quite set the barbeque alight, although a deal with 'Sub Pop' won the band a wider audience. Brooding, laid-back and eerily melancholic, RED RED MEAT played at the opening New York party of controversial Spanish director Pedro Almodavar's film, 'Kika', although their Lo-fi psychedelic grunge-blues set wasn't quite appreciated by the arty dance crowd. A 1994 album, 'JIMMYWINE MAJESTIC', was highly regarded by many critics, a record they topped a year later with the semi-classic 'BUNNY GETS PAID'. Although a clutch of obscure singles and a fourth set, 'THERE'S A STAR ABOVE THE MANGER TONIGHT' (1997) appeared over the next two years, the band splintered when RUTILI and HURLEY (with newcomer BEN MASARALA) formed LOFTUS. Early in 1998, this short-lived project delivered their one and only album, 'LOFTUS', before the trio changed their name to CALIFONE, releasing a solitary eponymous set on the 'Flydaddy' label later that year. • **Covered:** CARPET OF HORSES (Polara) / SAD PETER PAN with Smashing Pumpkins (Vic Chesnutt).

Album rating: RED RED MEAT (*6) / JIMMYWINE MAJESTIC (*6) / BUNNY GETS PAID (*7) / THERE'S A STAR ABOVE THE MANGER TONIGHT (*6)

TIM RUTILI – vocals, guitar, keyboards, etc / **GLENN GIRARD** – guitar, etc / **TIM HURLEY** – bass, guitars, synthesizer / **BRIAN DECK** – synthesizer, drums, percussion

not iss. Red Red Meat

1993. (cd) <RRM 001> **RED RED MEAT** [-] [ ]
– Robo sleep / Snowball / Molly's on the rag / Flossy / Idaho durt / Cellophane / Grief giver / Rabbit eyed / Hot nickety monkey / Nice round numbers / X-diamond cutter blues / Stare box. *<(US/UK-iss.Oct94/Feb95 on 'Sub Pop'; 3)>*

Sub Pop Sub Pop

Sep 93. (7") *<(SP 232S)<* **FLANK. /** [ ] [ ]
Mar 94. (lp/cd)(c) *(SP/+CD 119-300)<(SP 243 A/B)>* **JIMMYWINE MAJESTIC** [ ] [ ]
– Flank / Stained and lit / Braindead / Smokey Mtn. cool dip / Moon calf tripe / Cillamange / Ball / Lather / Rusted water / Gorshin / Dowser / Comes / Roses.
Oct 94. (7"/10") *<(SP 272)>* **IDIOT SON. / GAUZE** [ ] [ ]
(10"+=) *<(SP 139/343)>* – Mouse-ish.

— added former guest **BEN MASSARELLA** – drums; to repl. GIRARD

Oct 95. (lp/cd) *<(SP 318/+B)>* **BUNNY GETS PAID** [ ] [ ]
– Carpet of horses / Chain chain chain / Rosewood, Wax, Voltz + Glitter / Buttered / Gauze / Idiot son / Variations on Nadia's theme / Oxtail / Sad cadillac / Taxidermy blues in reverse / There's always tomorrow.
Nov 96. (7") *(SP 376)* **THERE'S A STAR ABOUT THE MANGER TONIGHT. / WELCOME CHRISTMAS** [ ] [-]
Feb 97. (cd) *<(SPCD 387)>* **THERE'S A STAR ABOUT THE MANGER TONIGHT** [ ] [ ]
– Sulfur / There's a star above the manger tonight / Chinese balls / Second hand sea / All tied / Paul Pachal / Bury me / Airstream driver / Mecanix (from cold milk) / Quarter horses (B-slow) / Just like an egg on stilts.

Flydaddy Blue Rose

Mar 97. (7") *(FLY 019-7)* **split with group, NUMBER ONE CUP** [ ] [ ]

Generator not iss.

1997. (7") **LISTENING NOW. / Polara: Carpet Of Horses** [-] [ ]

LOFTUS

— were formed by **TIM RUTILI** + **TIM HURLEY** plus **BEN MASARALA**

Perishable not iss.

Jan 98. (cd) *(PERISH 03CD)* **LOFTUS** [ ] [-]

CALIFONE

— **RUTILI** plus **MASSARELLA** + **HURLEY**

Flydaddy Flydaddy

Sep 98. (cd) *<(FLY 031)>* **CALIFONE** [ ] [ ]
– On the steeple / Silvermine pictures / Pastry sharp / To hush a sick transmission / Dime fangs / Red food ole heat / Down Eisenhower sun up.

REDSKINS

Formed: York, England . . . 1981 as NO SWASTIKAS by NME journalist CHRIS DEAN (alias X MOORE) along with MARTIN HEWES and NICK KING. Delivering a steadfast anti-Thatcher, determinedly left-wing ideology – strongly based on the politics of the Socialist Workers Party – via a musical backdrop combining punk attitude and skinhead aggression with brassy northern soul, The REDSKINS made a brave attempt to unite youth culture under the red flag. Following a productive John Peel session, the band's independently released double A-side debut single, 'LEV BRONSTEIN' / 'PEASANT ARMY' hit the racks in summer '82, the campaign continuing the following year with another double header, 'LEAN ON ME' / 'UNIONIZE'. Championed by music journo, Gary Bushell, the band were subsequently signed to 'London' records, through whom they released the urgent call to arms of 'KEEP ON KEEPIN' ON' in 1984. With the shadow of the miners strike looming large over the mid-80's political landscape, The REDSKINS played a series of benefit gigs, pledging their solidarity and winning over new fans. The resulting interest saw them score a Top 40 hit with the highly charged 'BRING IT DOWN (THIS INSANE THING)', yet by the belated release of debut album, 'NEITHER WASHINGTON . . . NOR MOSCOW' in 1986, the miners were all but beaten and the unions were on the run from the Conservative Government. Despite its dancefloor-friendly celebration of socialist ideals and adrenaline-fuelled invective, the album received neither the critical praise nor the sales it deserved. Frozen out of the pro-Labour 'Red Wedge' movement (featuring the likes of BILLY BRAGG, PAUL WELLER, COMMUNARDS etc.) in the run-up to the 1987 election, The REDSKINS finally admitted defeat after a final single, 'IT CAN BE DONE'. Unfortunately it couldn't, even the efforts of 'Red Wedge' falling by the wayside as the Conservatives romped home again. • **Songwriters:** Group penned, except covers; 16 TONS (Tennessee Ernie Ford) / 99 AND A HALF WON'T DO (Dale Hawkins).

Album rating: NEITHER WASHINGTON . . . NOR MOSCOW (*8)

CHRIS DEAN – vocals, guitar, keyboards / **MARTIN HEWES** – bass, keyboards / **NICK KING** – drums

C.N.T. not iss.

Jul 82. (7") **LEV BRONSTEIN. / PEASANT ARMY** [ ] [-]
Jul 83. (7") **LEAN ON ME. / UNIONIZE!** [ ] [-]
(12") – ('A'&'B' different mixes)

Decca not iss.

Oct 84. (7") **KEEP ON KEEPIN' ON. / RED STRIKES THE BLUES** [43] [-]

— **STEVE WHITE** – drums (of STYLE COUNCIL) repl. KING

Jun 85. (7") **(BURN IT UP) BRING IT DOWN (THIS INSANE THING). / YOU WANT IT, THEY'VE GOT IT** [33] [-]
(12"+=) – ('A'remix).

— **PAUL HOOKHAM** – drums (ex-WOODENTOPS) repl. WHITE (re-to STYLE COUNCIL)

Nov 85. (7") **KICK OVER THE STATUES!. / YOUNG AND PROUD** [ ] [-]

— (above 45, was one-off issued on 'Abstract Dance')

Feb 86. (7") **THE POWER IS YOURS . . . / 99 1/2 (WON'T DO)** [59] [-]
(12"+=)(d7"+=) – Take 3 / Take your goods and bury them.

— Brass section were **RAY CARLESS** – sax / **KEVIN ROBINSON** – trumpet, flugelhorn / **TREVOR EDWARDS** – trombone, 1/4 bottle

Mar 86. (lp)(c) **NEITHER WASHINGTON . . . NOR MOSCOW . . .** [31] [-]
– The power is yours . . . / Kick over the statues! / Go get organized! / It can be done! / Keep on keepin' on! / (Burn it up) Bring it down! (this insane thing) / Hold on! / Turnin' loose (these furious flames) / Take no heroes! / Let's make it work! / Lean on me! / 'The return of the modern soul classic'.
May 86. (7") **IT CAN BE DONE!. / A PLATEFUL OF HEAVEN** [ ] [-]
(10"+=)(12"+=) – Let's make it work.

— Disbanded again, with HEWES returning to work as a despatch rider.

– compilations, others, etc. –

May 87. (12"ep) *Strange Fruit;* **THE PEEL SESSIONS** (9.10.82) [ ] [-]
– Unionize! / Red strikes the blues / Kick over the statues! / The peasant army.
Jun 94. (cd) *Dojo;* **LIVE (live)** [ ] [-]

RED SNAPPER

Formed: Hammersmith, London, England . . . 1993 by 30-somethings, RICHARD THAIR, ALI FRIEND, DAVID AYERS and ALLAN RIDING. Fusing elements of blues, jazz and dub, RED SNAPPER (now featuring late addition, BETH ORTON), complete with unconventional dance! instruments, double bass, etc, cut their musical teeth at the Black Sunshine club run by Ashley Beadle of the DISCO EVANGELISTS. Dance guru, ANDREW WEATHERALL, was their inspiration, while their sound was not too dissimilar to avant-funksters, A CERTAIN RATIO. A self-financed eponymous debut EP on THAIR's 'Flaw' imprint in 1994 was soon followed by two others, 'SWANK' and 'HOT FLUSH', all three collected together in 1995 as 'REELED AND SKINNED'. They soon elevated themselves to supporting the likes of MASSIVE ATTACK and BJORK after they signed with 'Warp'. RED SNAPPER's first album proper, 'PRINCE BLIMEY' (co-produced with TIM HOLMES), surfaced in '96, its fusion of stripped-down funk/jazz and dub were well-received by critics (it also scraped into the UK Top 60). A few years passed before RED SNAPPER returned to the fold in 1998 with 'MAKING BONES', another Top 60 entry featuring one-that-got-away, 'BOGEYMAN', track.

Album rating: REELED AND SKINNED compilation (*6) / PRINCE BLIMEY (*7) / MAKING BONES (*7)

RICHARD THAIR – drums / **ALI FRIEND** – double bass / **DAVID AYERS** – guitar / + **ALLAN RIDING** – saxophone, melodica / **BETH ORTON** – vocals (ex-SANDALS)

Flaw not iss.

May 94. (12"ep) *(FLAW 4)* **THE SNAPPER EP** [ ] [-]
– Snapper / Cortina / Lobster.
Nov 94. (12"ep) *(FLAW 7)* **SWANK EP** [ ] [-]
– In deep / One legged low frequency guy / Swank.
May 95. (12"ep) *(FLAW 9)* **HOT FLUSH EP** [ ] [-]
– Hot flush / Wesley don't surf / Hot flush (Sabres Of Paradise remix).

Warp Warp

Jun 95. (cd/c/d-lp) *(WARP CD/MC/LP 33)* **REELED AND SKINNED** [ ] [-]
– (compilation of above singles).

— now without RIDING + ORTON, repl. by **OLLIE MOORE** – violin

Feb 96. (12"ep) *(WAP 70)* **MOOKING. / ('A'mixes)** [ ] [-]
(12"/cd-s) *(WAP 70 R/CD)* – Son of Mook (Depth Charge remix) / Get some sleep tiger (Plaid remix).
Sep 96. (cd/c/lp) *(WARP CD/MC/LP 45)* **PRINCE BLIMEY** [60] [-]
– Crusoe takes a trip / Thomas the fib / Get some sleep tiger / Fatboy's dust / Moonbuggy / The paranoid / Space sickness / The last one / Digging doctor what what / Gridlock / Lo-beam.
Nov 96. (12"ep/cd-ep) *(WAP 84/+CD)* **LOOPASCOOPA EP** [ ] [-]
– The last one / Strike one / Thomas the fib / Crusoe takes a trip.

— basic trio of **RICHARD THAIR, ALI FRIEND + DAVID AYERS** added **BYRON WALLEN** – trumpet / and guests **MC DET + ALISON DAVID** – vocals / **JEZ FRIEND** – trombone

Jun 98. (12") *(WAP 104)* **BOGEYMAN. / ('A'-David Holmes mix) / ('A'-Two Lone Swordsmen 5 Day Wonder mix)** [ ] [-]
(cd-s+=) *(WAP 104CD)* – ('A'-Two Lone Swordsmen Blue Jam Cologne mix).
Sep 98. (12") *(WAP 108)* **THE SLEEPLESS. / ('A'-Shut Up & Dance mix) / SEEING RED (instrumental)** [ ] [-]
(cd-s) *(WAP 108CD)* – ('A'mixes; Shut Up & Dance / Shut Up & Dance instrumental).
Sep 98. (cd/lp) *(<WARP CD/LP 56>)* **MAKING BONES** [59] [ ]
– The sleepless / Crease / Image of you / Bogeyman / The tunnel / Like a moving truck / Spitalfields / Seeing red / Suckerpunch / 4 dead monks.
Nov 98. (12"/cd-s) *(WAP 111/+CD)* **IMAGE OF YOU (mixes; Rae & Christian / Saly City Orchestra / Shut Up & Dance)** [60] [-]
(cd-s) *(WAP 111CDR)* – ('A'mix) / Quicktemper.

REEGS (see under ⇒ CHAMELEONS)

REFLECTIONS (see under ⇒ ALTERNATIVE TV)

REFRESHMENTS

Formed: Tampe, Arizona, USA ... mid 90's by ROGER CLYNE, who recruited BRIAN BLUSH, BUDDY EDWARDS and P.H. NAFFAH. After a couple of releases on their own self-titled label, The REFRESHMENTS sparkled into commercial life with a major label deal courtesy of 'Polygram', the band scraping into the US Top 100 with their larger than life anti-depressant alt-rock set, 'FIZZY, FUZZY, BIG & BUZZY' (1996). A more earnest PAUL BRADY (BUTTHOLE SURFERS)-produced follow-up set, 'THE BOTTLE & FRESH HORSES' (1997), combined rootsy touches with beefy guitar-pop.

Album rating: WHEELIE (*6) / FIZZY, FUZZY, BIG & BUZZY (*6) / THE BOTTLE & FRESH HORSES (*6)

ROGER CLYNE – vocals, guitar / **BRIAN BLUSH** – guitar / **BUDDY EDWARDS** – bass / **P.H. NAFFAH** – drums

not iss. | Refreshments

1994. (cd-ep) **LO OUR MUCH PRAISED NOT YET ALTOGETHER SATISFACTORY LADY EP** [-] [ ]

1994. (cd) **WHEELIE** [-] [ ]

not iss. | Polygram

Feb 96. (cd,c) *<528999>* **FIZZY, FUZZY, BIG & BUZZY** [-] [97]
– Blue collar suicide / European swallow / Down together / Mekong / Don't wanna know / Girly / Banditos / Mexico / Interstate / Suckerpunch / Carefree / Nada.

Apr 96. (cd-s) **BANDITOS. /** [-] [ ]

Sep 97. (cd,c) *<536203>* **THE BOTTLE & FRESH HORSES** [-] [ ]
– Tributary Otis / Preacher's daughter / Wanted / Sin nombre / Heaven or the highway out of town / Buy American / Dolly / Good year / Fonder and blonder / Birds sing / Horses / Broken record / Una soda.

Riff REGAN (see under ⇒ LONDON)

REGULAR FRIES

Formed: North London, England ... 1997 by graphic designer WILL BEAVAN, film-maker PAUL MOODY and music journalist ANDY STARKE, who completed the line-up with DAVE BROTHWELL, RICH LITTLE, PAT O'SULLIVAN and STEPHEN GRIFFIN. Touted as one of the leading lights of the much hyped "skunk" rock movement, The REGULAR FRIES revisited the old stamping ground of early 90's baggy stars like HAPPY MONDAYS and FLOWERED UP, although live the septet came into their own with a blinding kaleidoscope of light and sound. On the recording front, they shared/split a 'Fierce Panda' single later that year with fellow indie hopefuls, CAMPAG VELOCET. 'Rabid Badger' (the label, that is!) almost immediately delivered their debut single proper, 'DUST IT, DON'T BUST IT', a classy 12"only effort that featured the inimitable lyrics, "Hey Vanessa! ciao Tessa!!". After gigging up and down the country, The 'FRIES prised themselves away from fast-food outlets long enough to ink a deal with independent dance label, 'J.B.O.', who delivered two promising EP's, 'FREE THE REGULAR FRIES' and 'FRIES ENTERTAINMENT', in the second half of '98.

Album rating: awaiting debut album

DAVE BROTHWELL – vocals / **RICH LITTLE** – vocals / **STEPHEN 'GRIFF' GRIFFIN** – guitars / **WILL BEAVAN** – keyboards / **PAT O'SULLIVAN** – bass / **PAUL MOODY** – Moog, vibes / **ANDY STARKE** – percussion

Fierce Panda | not iss.

Nov 97. (7"split) *(Ning 41)* **split with CAMPAG VELOCET** [ ] [-]

Rabid Badger | not iss.

Jan 98. (12"ep) *(Nang 02)* **DUST IT, DON'T BUST IT (full version) / SUPPOSED TO BE A GAS. / DUST IT, DON'T BUST IT (produced by Richard Fearless)** [ ] [-]

J.B.O. | not iss.

Sep 98. (cd-ep) *(JNR 500353-3)* **FREE THE REGULAR FRIES** [ ] [-]
– Hypnosis / The prayer / New moon / Christopher Colombus / Ray's garage.

Dec 98. (12"ep/cd-ep) *(JNR 500481-6/-3)* **FRIES ENTERTAINMENT EP** [-] [-]
– Cyanide / Mars hotel / Cyanide (beach detective mix) / Mars hotel (psychonauts mix).

Blaine L. REININGER (see under ⇒ TUXEDOMOON)

R.E.M.

Formed: Athens, Georgia, USA ... Spring 1980 by MICHAEL STIPE and PETER BUCK, who once meeting MIKE MILLS and BILL BERRY, played at a local party under the name TWISTED KITES. In 1981, through manager Jefferson Holt, they released their debut MITCH EASTER-produced 45, 'RADIO FREE EUROPE'. With its soaring melody and jangly guitar playing off STIPE's low-key vocals, the sound was unique and caught the ears of 'I.R.S.' label boss, MILES COPELAND. The latter duly signed them up and retained EASTER for the mini-lp 'CHRONIC TOWN' (1982). The five-song set was recieved with gushing enthusiasm and set the scene for R.E.M.'s first album proper, 'MURMUR' (1983). Co-produced by EASTER and DON DIXON, the album was a stunning debut which sharpened the hooks, honed the pealing guitar sound and generally engendered a compelling air of mystique. Much of this was down to STIPE's impenetrable lyrics and vague execution which enhanced rather than detracted from the melodic melancholy of songs like 'TALK ABOUT THE PASSION'. While this inventiveness wasn't quite consolidated with 'RECKONING' (1984), the album was slightly more accessible, leading to a Top 30 placing in the American charts. Boasting the ambling country poignancy of '(DON'T GO BACK TO) ROCKVILLE', what the record lacked in innovation it made up for in songwriting skill. Never content to tread water, the band recorded 'FABLES OF THE RECONSTRUCTION' (1985) in London with veteran folk producer JOE BOYD, an interesting pairing which made for a trippy, heavily atmospheric sound. Even the poppier 'DRIVER 8' wasn't free of the edginess which characterised the record. Dextrously combining sonic exploration and heart-melting melodies, 'LIFE'S RICH PAGEANT' (1986) was a bold step forward. Tracks like 'FALL ON ME', 'I BELIEVE' and 'CUYAHOGA' showed an assured poise which the band were undoubtedly developing through their ceaseless touring and snowballing critical acclaim. 'DOCUMENT' (1987) was even more focused, STIPE actually beginning to sound comprehensible. The sardonic, brooding 'THE ONE I LOVE' single gave R.E.M. their first US Top 10 hit, while the band's 'Warners' debut, 'GREEN' (1988), finally saw the band become a mainstream act, in terms of commercial success at least. The unashamed jaunty pop of 'STAND' (1989) gave the band their biggest hit to date while 'ORANGE CRUSH' (1989) echoed the muted moodiness of 'THE ONE I LOVE'. Elsewhere, gems like 'WORLD LEADER PRETEND' were artful examples of that rare ability to create subtle, intelligent songs that were still annoyingly hummable. After 'GREEN's release, R.E.M. undertook a mammoth world tour with the result that the next album, 'OUT OF TIME', didn't hit the shelves until 1991. For most people it was well worth the wait. Preceded by the starkly melancholy 'LOSING MY RELIGION' with its mournful mandolin refrain, 'OUT OF TIME' was a multi-million seller, hitting the top spot on both sides of the Atlantic. While 'SHINY HAPPY PEOPLE' was a mite sickly sweet after 10,000 listens, and 'RADIO' was an ill-advised foray into rap, acoustic flavoured diamonds like 'HALF A WORLD AWAY', 'COUNTRY FEEDBACK' and 'ME IN HONEY' rendered the album a classic. Equally successful but much harder going, 1992's 'AUTOMATIC FOR THE PEOPLE' was a moody masterpiece. Focusing on the more painful aspects of human existence, the album wasn't as immediate as its predecessor but the lucid beauty of tracks like 'NIGHTSWIMMING' and 'MAN ON THE MOON' soon slipped insidiously into your subconscious. Silencing rumours that MICHAEL STIPE was suffering from Aids, R.E.M. bounced back with the grungy 'MONSTER' (1994) album. Despite confident hits like 'WHAT'S THE FREQUENCY KENNETH' and 'CRUSH WITH EYELINER', R.E.M. were capable of more imaginative fare. The subsequent tour (the first since the late 80's) came to a premature halt when BILL BERRY suffered a brain haemhorrage. After a successful recovery, the band reconvened to record 1996's 'NEW ADVENTURES IN HI-FI' (sadly, the last with BERRY). Written mainly on the road, the album was a return to more familiar R.E.M. territory, rich in imagery and possessed of all the qualities that make R.E.M. one of rock's most respected bands. • **Songwriters:** Group compositions except 'B'side covers; THERE SHE GOES AGAIN + PALE BLUE EYES + FEMME FATALE (Velvet Underground) / TOYS IN THE ATTIC (Aerosmith) / KING OF THE ROAD (Roger Miller) / CRAZY (Pylon) / AFTER HOURS (Lou Reed) / LOVE IS ALL AROUND (Troggs) / FIRST WE TAKE MANHATTAN (Leonard Cohen) / LAST DATE (Floyd Cramer) / TIGHTEN UP (Booker T. & The MG's) / SEE NO EVIL (Television) / ACADEMY EIGHT SONG (Mission of Burma) / SUMMERTIME (Gershwin) / BABY BABY (Vibrators) / WHERE'S CAPTAIN KIRK? (Spizz) / PARADE OF WOODEN SOLDIERS (Tchaikovsky) / MOON RIVER (Henry Mancini) / THE ARMS OF YOU (Robyn Hitchcock) / THE LION SLEEPS TONIGHT (Tokens) / DARK GLOBE (Syd Barrett) / SPONGE (Vic Chesnutt). • **Trivia:** R.E.M. stands for Rapid Eye Movement.

Album rating: MURMUR (*9) / RECKONING (*9) / FABLES OF THE RECONSTRUCTION (*9) / LIFE'S RICH PAGEANT (*8) / DOCUMENT (*8) / DEAD LETTER OFFICE compilation (*7) / GREEN (*9) / THE BEST OF R.E.M. compilation (*9) / OUT OF TIME (*10) / AUTOMATIC FOR THE PEOPLE (*10) / MONSTER (*8) / NEW ADVENTURES IN HI-FI (*8) / UP (*7)

MICHAEL STIPE (b. JOHN MICHAEL STIPE, 4 Jan'60, Decatur, Atlanta) – vocals / **PETER BUCK** (b. 6 Dec'56, Oakland, Calif.) – guitar / **MIKE MILLS** (b.17 Dec'58, Orange County, Calif.) – bass, keyboards, vocals / **BILL BERRY** (b.31 Jul'58, Duluth, Minnesota) – drums, vocals

not iss. | Hib-Tone

Jul 81. (7") *(HT-0001)* **RADIO FREE EUROPE. / SITTING STILL** [-] [ ]

I.R.S. | I.R.S.

Aug 82. (m-lp) *<SP 70502>* **CHRONIC TOWN** [-] [ ]
– Wolves, lower / 1,000,000 / Gardening at night / Stumble / Carnival of sorts (box cars). *(re-iss. Feb85; IRS 70502)*

Aug 83. (7") *(PFP 1017) <9916>* **RADIO FREE EUROPE. / THERE SHE GOES AGAIN** [ ] [78] Jul83

Aug 83. (lp/c) *(SP/CS 70604) <70604>* **MURMUR** [ ] [36] May83
– Radio free Europe / Pilgrimage / Laughing / Talk about the passion / Moral kiosk / Perfect circle / Catapult / Sitting still / 9-9 / Shaking through / We walk / West of the fields. *(cd-iss. 1988; CDA 7014) (cd re-iss. Mar91 ++; CDMID 129)* – There she goes again / 9-9 (live) / Gardening at night (live) / Catapult (live).

Nov 83. (7") *(PFP 1026)* **TALK ABOUT THE PASSION. / SHAKING THROUGH** [ ] [-]
(12"+=) *(PFSX 1026)* – Carnival of sorts (box cars) / 1,000,000.

Mar 84. (7") *(IRS 105) <9927>* **S). CENTRAL RAIN (I'M SORRY). / KING OF THE ROAD** [ ] [85] Jun84
(12") *(PFSX 105)* – ('A'side) / Voice of Harold / Pale blue eyes.

Apr 84. (lp/c) *(IRS A/C 7045)* <70044> **RECKONING** [91] [27]
– Harborcoat / 7 Chinese Bros. / So. central rain (I'm sorry) / Pretty persuasion / Time after time (Annelise) / Second guessing / Letter never sent / Camera / (Don't go back to) Rockville / Little America. *(cd-iss. 1988 on 'A&M'; CDA 7045) (re-iss. Oct94 on 'A&M' cd/c;)*

Jun 84. (7") *(IRS 107)* **(DON'T GO BACK TO) ROCKVILLE. / WOLVES** [ ] [-]
(12"+=) *(IRSX 107)* – 9 minus 9 (live) / Gardening at night (live).

Jun 84. (7") *<IR 9931>* **(DON'T GO BACK TO) ROCKVILLE. / CATAPULT (live)** [-] [ ]

Jul 85. (7") *(IRM 102)* **CAN'T GET THERE FROM HERE. / BANDWAGON** [ ] [-]
(12"+=) *(IRT 102)* – Burning Hell.

Jul 85. (lp/c) *(MIR F/C 1003)* <5592> **FABLES OF THE RECONSTRUCTION – RECONSTRUCTION OF THE FABLES** [35] [28] Jun85
– Feeling gravitys pull / Maps and legends / Driver 8 / Life and how to live it / Old Man Kensey / Can't get there from here / Green grow the rushes / Kokoutek / Auctioneer (another engine) / Good advices / Wendell Gee. *(cd-iss. Apr87; DMIRF 1003) (re-iss. cd Jan90; DMIRL 1503)*

Oct 85. (7") <52678> **DRIVER 8. / CRAZY** [-] [ ]

Oct 85. (7") *(IRM 105)* **WENDELL GEE. / CRAZY** [ ] [-]
(d7"+=) *(IRMD 105)* – Ages of you / Burning down.
(12"+=) *(IRT 105)* – Driver 8.

Aug 86. (7") *(IRM 121)* <52883> **FALL ON ME. / ROTARY TEN** [ ] [94]
(12"+=) *(IRMT 121)* – Toys in the attic.

Aug 86. (lp/c) *(MIRG/+C 1014)* <5783> **LIFE'S RICH PAGEANT** [43] [21]
– Begin the begin / These days / Fall on me / Cuyahoga / Hyena / Underneath the bunker / The flowers of Guatemala / I believe / What if we give it away? / Just a touch / Swan swan H / Superman. *(cd-iss. Dec86; DMIRG 1014) (re-iss. cd Sep91; DMIRL 1507)*

Mar 87. (7") *(IRM 128)* **SUPERMAN. / WHITE TORNADO** [ ] [-]
(12"+=) *(IRMT 128)* – Femme fatale.

Aug 87. (7") *(IRM 145)* **IT'S THE END OF THE WORLD AS WE KNOW IT (AND I FEEL FINE). / THIS ONE GOES OUT (live)** [ ] [-]
(12"+=) *(IRMT 145)* – Maps and legends (live).

Sep 87. (7") <53171> **THE ONE I LOVE. / MAPS AND LEGENDS (Live)** [-] [9]

Oct 87. (lp/c/cd) *(MIRG/MIRGC/DMIRG 1025)* <42059> **DOCUMENT** [28] [10] Sep87
– Finest worksong / Welcome to the occupation / Exhuming McCarthy / Disturbance at Heron House / Strange / It's the end of the world as we know it (and I feel fine) / The one I love / Fireplace / Lightnin' Hopkins / King of birds / Oddfellows local 151. *(re-iss. cd Sep91; DMIRL 1508) (+=)* – Finest worksong (other mix) / Last date / The one I love (live) / Time after time etc. (live) / Disturbance at the Heron house (live) / Finest worksong (lengthy club mix).

Nov 87. (7") *(IRM 146)* **THE ONE I LOVE. / LAST DATE** [51] [-]
(12"+=/cd-s+=) *(IRMT/DIRM 146)* – Disturbance at the Heron House (live).

Jan 88. (7") *(IRM 161)* **FINEST WORKSONG. / TIME AFTER TIME, ETC.** [50] [-]
(12"+=) *(IRMT 161)* <23850> – ('A'-lengthy club mix).
(cd-s+=) *(DIRM 161)* – It's the end of the world and we know it (and I feel fine).

Jan 88. (7") <53220> **IT'S THE END OF THE WORLD AS WE KNOW IT (AND I FEEL FINE). / LAST DATE** [-] [69]

Warners Warners

Nov 88. (lp/c)(cd) *(WX 234/+C)*<(7599-25795-2)> **GREEN** [27] [12]
– Pop song '89 / Get up / You are the everything / Stand / World leader pretend / The wrong child / Orange crush / Turn you inside-out / Hairshirt / I remember California / Untitled song.

Jan 89. (7"/s7") *(W 7577/+X)* <27688> **STAND. / MEMPHIS TRAIN BLUES** [51] [6]
(12"+=/3"cd-s+=/3"s-cd-s+=) *(W 7577 T/CD/CDX)* – (The eleventh untitled song).

Mar 89. (7"/s7"/7"box/c-s) *(W 2960/+X/B/C)* **ORANGE CRUSH. / GHOST RIDERS** [28] [-]
(12"+=/3"cd-s+=) *(W 2960 T/CD)* – Dark globe.

Jun 89. (7") <27640> **POP SONG '89 / ('A'acoustic)** [-] [86]

Jul 89. (7"/s7") *(W 2833/+W)* **STAND. / POP SONG '89 (acoustic)** [48] [-]
(12"+=/3"cd-s+=/3"s-cd-s+=) *(W 2833 T/CD/CDX)* – Skin tight (live).

— (all above 7"singles were re-iss. in 4xbox Dec89)

Sep 89. (7") *(7-22791)* **GET UP. / FUNTIME** [-] [ ]

— R.E.M. toured early '91 as BINGO HAND JOB.

Feb 91. (7"/c-s) *(W 0015/+C)* <19392> **LOSING MY RELIGION. / ROTARY ELEVEN** [19] [4] Mar91
(12"+=/cd-s+=) *(W 0015 T/CD)* – After hours (live).
(cd-s) *(W 0015CDX)* – ('A'side) / Stand (live) / Turn you inside-out (live) / World leader pretend (live).

Mar 91. (cd/c/lp) <*(7599 26496-2/-4/-1)*> **OUT OF TIME** [1] [1]
– Radio song / Losing my religion / Low / Near wild Heaven / Endgame / Shiny happy people / Belong / Half a world away / Texarkana / Country feedback / Me in honey.

— (the album feat. PETER HOLSAPPLE – guitar (ex-DB'S) / KRS-1 – rapper) MICHAEL STIPE released album with KRS-1 'CIVILIZATION VS.TECHNOLOGY' Oct91.

May 91. (7"/c-s) *(W 0027/+C)* <19242> **SHINY HAPPY PEOPLE. / FORTY SECOND SONG** [6] [10] Jul91
(12"+=/cd-s+=) *(W 0027 T/CD)* – Losing my religion (live acoustic).
(cd-s) *(W 0027CDX)* – ('A'side) / I remember California (live) / Get up (live) / Pop song '89 (live).
(above 'A'side feat. KATE PIERSON of The B-52'S)

Aug 91. (7"/c-s) *(W 0055/+C)* **NEAR WILD HEAVEN. / POP SONG '89** [27] [-]
(12"+=) *(W 0055T)* – Half a world away (live).
(cd-s) *(W 0055CDX)* – ('A'side) / Tom's diner (live) / Low (live) / Endgame (live).

Nov 91. (7"/c-s) *(W 0072/+C)* **RADIO SONG. / LOVE IS ALL AROUND (live)** [28] [-]
(12"+=) *(W 0072T)* – Shiny happy people (music mix).
(cd-s) *(W 0072CDX)* – ('A'side) / You are my everything (live) / Orange crush (live) / Belong (live).

Oct 92. (7"/c-s) *(W 0136/+C)* **DRIVE. / WORLD LEADER PRETEND** [11] [-]
(cd-s+=) *(W 0136CD)* – First we take Manhattan /
(cd-s) *(W 0136CDX)* – ('A'side) / It's a free world, baby / Winged mammal theme / First we take Manhattan.

Oct 92. (c-s,cd-s) <18729> **DRIVE / WINGED MAMMAL THEME** [-] [28]

Oct 92. (cd)(lp/c) <*(9362 45055)*>*(WX 488/+C)* **AUTOMATIC FOR THE PEOPLE** [1] [2]
– Drive / Try not to breathe / The sidewinder sleeps tonight / Everybody hurts / New Orleans instrumental No.1 / Sweetness follows / Monty got a raw deal / Ignoreland / Star me kitten / Man on the Moon / Nightswimming / Find the river.

Nov 92. (7"/c-s) *(W 0143/+C)* **MAN ON THE MOON. / TURN YOU INSIDE-OUT** [18] [-]
(cd-s+=) *(W 0143CD)* – Arms of love.
(cd-s) *(W 0143CDX)* – ('A'side) / Fruity organ / New Orleans instrumental £2 / Arms of love.

Jan 93. (c-s,cd-s) <18642> **MAN ON THE MOON / NEW ORLEANS INSTRUMENTAL #2** [-] [30]

Feb 93. (7"/c-s) *(W 0152/+C)* **THE SIDEWINDER SLEEPS TONIGHT. / GET UP** [17] [-]
(cd-s) *(W 0152CD1)* – ('A'side) / The lion sleeps tonight (live) / Fretless.
(cd-s) *(W 0152CD2)* – ('A'side) / Organ song / Star me kitten (demo).

Apr 93. (7"/c-s) *(W 0169/+C)* **EVERYBODY HURTS. / POP SONG '89** [7] [-]
(cd-s) *(W 0169CD1)* – ('A'side) / Mandolin strum / New Orleans instrumental No.1 (long version).
(cd-s) *(W 0169CD2)* – ('A'side) / Dark globe / Chance (dub).

Jul 93. (7"/c-s) *(W 0184/+C)* **NIGHTSWIMMING. / LOSING MY RELIGION (live)** [27] [-]
(one-sided-12"pic-d/cd-s) *(W 0184 TP/CD)* – ('A'side) / World leader pretend (live) / Low (live) / Belong (live).

Aug 93. (c-s) <18638> **EVERYBODY HURTS / MANDOLIN STRUM** [-] [29]
(12"orange+=) <*9362 40989-04*> – Belong / Orange crush (live).
(12"white or blue)(cd-ep) <*9362 40992-08*> – ('A'side) / Star me kitten (demo) / Losing my religion (live) / Organ song.

Dec 93. (7"/c-s) *(W 0211/+C)* **FIND THE RIVER. / EVERYBODY HURTS (live)** [54] [-]
(cd-s+=) *(W 0211CD1)* – World leader pretend (live).
(cd-s+=) *(W 0211CD2)* – Orange crush (instrumental).

Sep 94. (7"/c-s) *(W 0265/+C)* <18050> **WHAT'S THE FREQUENCY, KENNETH? / ('A'instrumental)** [9] [21]
(cd-s) *(W 0265CD)* – ('A'side) / Monty got a raw deal (live) / Everybody hurts (live) / Man on the Moon (live).

Oct 94. (cd/c/lp) <*(9362 45740-2/-4/-1)*> **MONSTER** [1] [1]
– What's the frequency, Kenneth? / Crush with eyeliner / King of comedy / I don't sleep I dream / Star 69 / Strange currencies / Tongue / Bang and blame / I took your name / Let me in / Circus envy / You.

Nov 94. (7"/c-s) *(W 0275/+C)* <17994> **BANG AND BLAME / ('A'instrumental)** [15] [19]
(cd-s) *(W 0275CD)* – ('A'side) / Losing my religion (live) / Country feedback (live) / Begin the begin (live).

Jan 95. (7"/c-s) *(W 0281 X/C)* **CRUSH WITH EYELINER. / ('A'instrumental)** [23] [-]
(cd-s) *(W 0281CD)* – ('A'side) / Calendar bag / Fall on me (live) / Me in honey (live) / Finest worksong (live).

— On 1st March, 1995, BILL BERRY suffered a brain haemorrhage, after collapsing during a concert in Switzerland. Thankfully, he steadily recovered during the following few months.

Apr 95. (7"/c-s) *(W 0290 X/C)* <17900> **STRANGE CURRENCIES. / ('A'instrumental)** [9] [47]
(cd-s) *(W 0290CD)* – ('A'side) / Drive (live) / Funtime (live) / Radio free Europe (live).

Jul 95. (c-s) *(W 0308 X/C)* **TONGUE / ('A'instrumental)** [13] [-]
(cd-s) *(W 0308CD)* – ('A'side) / Bang and blame (live) / What's the frequency, Kenneth? (live) / I don't sleep, I dream (live).

Aug 96. (c-s) *(W 0369C)* <17529> **E-BOW THE LETTER / TRICYCLE** [4] [49]
(cd-s+=) *(W 0369CD)* – Wall of death / Departure.
(cd-s) *(W 0369CDX)* –

Sep 96. (cd/c/d-lp) <*(9362 46320-2/-4/-1)*> **NEW ADVENTURES IN HI-FI** [1] [2]
– How the west was won and where it got us / The wake-up bomb / New test leper / Undertow / E-bow the letter / Leave / Departure / Bittersweet me / Be mine / Binky the doormat / Zither / So fast, so numb / Low desert / Electrolite.

Oct 96. (c-s) *(W 0377C)* <17490> **BITTERSWEET ME / UNDERTOW (live)** [19] [46]
(cd-s+=) *(W 0377CDX)* – Wichita lineman (live) / New test leper (acoustic).
(cd-s) *(W 0377CD)* – ('A'side) /

Dec 96. (c-s) *(W 0383C)* <43810> **ELECTROLITE / THE WAKE-UP BOMB (live)** [29] [96]
(cd-s+=) *(W 0383CDX)* – King of comedy (808 State mix) / Binky the doormat (live).
(cd-s) *(W 0383CD)* – ('A'side) /

— now without BERRY whose place was taken up by guests

Oct 98. (c-s) *(W 0455C)* <17129> **DAYSLEEPER / EMPHYSEMA** [6] [57]
(cd-s+=) *(W 0455CD)* – Why not smile (Oxford American version).
(3"cd-s) *(W 0466CDX)* – Daysleeper / Sad professor (live in the studio).

Oct 98. (cd/c/lp) *(9362 47151-2/-4/-1)* <47112> **UP** [2] [3]
– Airportman / Lotus / Suspicion / Hope / At my most beautiful / The apologist / Sad professor / You're in the air / Walk unafraid / Why not smile / Daysleeper / Diminished / Parakeet / Falls to climb.

Dec 98. (c-s) *(W 466C)* **LOTUS / SURFING THE GANGES** [26] [ ]
(cd-s+=) *(W 466CD)* – Lotus (weird mix).
(3"cd-s) *(W 466CDX)* – Lotus / Suspicion (live in the studio).

– compilations, others, etc. –

— on 'I.R.S.' unless mentioned otherwise

May 87. (lp/c/cd) <*(SP/CS/CDA 70054)*> **DEAD LETTER OFFICE** (b-sides, rarities, etc.) [60] [52]

– Crazy / There she goes again / Burning down / Voice of Harold / Burning Hell / White tornado / Toys in the attic / Windout / Ages of you / Pale blue eyes / Rotary ten / Bandwagon / Femme fatale / Walters theme / King of the road. *(cd+=)* – CHRONIC TOWN *(re-iss. Oct94 on 'A&M' cd/c; CD/C MID 195)*

Oct 88. (lp/c/cd) *(MIRG/MIRGC/DMIRG 1038) <6262>* **EPONYMOUS** 69 44
– Radio free Europe / Gardening at night / Talk about the passion / So. central rain / (Don't go back to) Rockville / Can't get there from here / Driver 8 / Romance / Fall on me / The one I love / Finest worksong / It's the end of the world as we know it (and I feel fine).

Oct 88. (7") *(IRM 173)* **THE ONE I LOVE. / FALL ON ME** -
(12"+=/cd-s+=) *(IRMT/DIRM 173)* – So. central rain (I'm sorry).

May 90. (c) *A&M; (AMC 24109)* **MURMUR / RECKONING**

Sep 91. (cd/c/lp) *(DMIRH/MIRHC/MIRH 1)* **THE BEST OF R.E.M.** 7 -
– Carnival of sorts / Radio free Europe / Perfect circle / Talk about the passion / So. central rain / (Don't go back to) Rockville / Pretty persuasion / Green grow the rushes / Can't get there from here / Driver 8 / Fall on me / I believe / Cuyahoga / The one I love / Finest worksong / It's the end of the world as we know it (and I feel fine).

Sep 91. (7"/c-s) *(IRM/+C 178)* **THE ONE I LOVE. / CRAZY** 16
(cd-s) *(DIRMT 178)* – ('A'side) / This one goes out (live) / Maps and legends (live).
(cd-s) *(DIRMX 178)* – ('A'side) / Driver 8 (live) / Disturbance at the Heron House (live).

Dec 91. (7"/c-s) *(IRM/+C 180)* **IT'S THE END OF THE WORLD (AS WE KNOW IT). / RADIO FREE EUROPE** 39
(cd-s+=) *(DIRMT 180)* – Time after time, etc. (live).

— When MICHAEL STIPE went off guesting for groups incl. GOLDEN PALOMINOS; others splintered off into . . .

HINDU LOVE GODS

not iss. I.R.S.

Sep 85. (7") **NARRATOR. / GONNA HAVE A GOOD TIME TONIGHT** -

— with **WARREN ZEVON** – vocals They guested on his late '89 album; SENTIMENTAL HYGIENE.

Reprise Giant

Nov 90. (7") **RASPBERRY BERET. / WANG DANG DOODLE**
(12"+=/cd-s+=) – Mannish boy.

Nov 90. (cd/c/lp) *<7599 24406-2/-4/-1>* **HINDU LOVE GODS**
– Walkin' blues / Travelin' riverside blues / Raspberry beret / Crosscut saw / Junco pardner / Mannish boy / Wang dang doodle / Battleship chains / I'm a one woman man / Vigilante man.

— (all above HINDU songs were covers)

RENALDO & THE LOAF

Formed: Portsmouth, England . . . 1979 by BRIAN POOLE (aka RENALDO M.) and DAVE JANSSEN (aka TED THE LOAF). Originally a tribute to the RESIDENTS, RENALDO & THE LOAF combined avant-garde humour with ludicrous instrumentation that seemed to utilise everything including the kitchen sink. After handing a homemade demo tape in to the RESIDENTS' San Franciscan HQ, the pair were signed to the associated 'Ralph' records, officially debuting in '81 with the album, 'SONGS FOR SWINGING LARVAE' (they had already distributed a cassette-only release, ' . . . PLAY STRUVE AND SNEFF'). Follow-up set, 'ARABIC YODELLING' (1983), was another impenetrably experimental effort, the duo saving themselves a lot of uneccessary bother by employing readymade synth sounds. Around the same time, BRIAN and DAVE actually collaborated with their long-time heroes on a video project, the results hitting the independent shops as an LP, 'TITLE IN LIMBO' (1984). Later installing a home studio with the er . . . bread they'd earned, RENALDO and Co worked on material for Some Bizzare offshoot, 'Rotcod', releasing the albums, 'OLLEH OLLEH ROTCOD' (1985) and 'THE ELBOW IS TABOO' (1987) to a less than ecstatic response.

Album rating: SONGS FOR SWINGING LARVAE (*4) / ARABIC YODELLING (*6) / OLLEH OLLEH ROTCOD (*3) / THE ELBOW IS TABOO (*3)

BRIAN POOLE – guitar, percussion, piano, glockenspiel, bouzouki, vocals, harmonica, vocals / **DAVE JANSSEN** – clarinet, guitar, bouzouki, percussion

Do-It Ralph

Apr 81. (lp) *(RIDE 6) <RL 8108>* **SONGS FOR SWINGING LARVAE**
– Lime jelly grass / A medical man / Bali whine / Kimbolton gnome / Song / Frass / N 20 / B.P.M. / Spratt's medium / Honest Joe's Indian gets the goat on the way to the cowboy's conga / Ow! stew the red shoe / Bustle the burgoo / Is Guava a donut / A sob story / Hats off, gentlemen / Renaldo's trip to Venice / Ted's reverie.

— added guest **DAVE BAKER** – violin

May 83. (lp) *<RL 8308>* **ARABIC YODELLING** -
– Green candle / Night / Bearded cats / The blowflies dilemma / Dichotomy rag / A critical dance / Wilf in builth / Leery looks / Clean gender / Vitamin song / Lonely Rosa / J.P.W.B.C. / Like some Kous-Kous western / Nelda danced at daybreak / There's a cap on the lawn.

— late in '83, they collaborated with the RESIDENTS on an LP, 'TITLE IN LIMBO'

Rotcod not iss.

1985. (lp) *(RD 3)* **OLLEH OLLEH ROTCOD** -

Nov 86. (12") *(RD 4)* **HAMBU HODO. / HE LOVES US ALL** -

Sep 87. (lp) *(RD 5)* **THE ELBOW IS TABOO** -
– A street called Straight / Boule / Hambu hodo / Dance for sonambulists / Here's to the oblong boys / Bread song / A critical dance / Extracting the re-re. *(cd-iss. May98 on 'Some Bizzare'; SBZ 036CD)*

— above was their final release

RENEES (see under ⇒ GYMSLIPS)

RENEGADE SOUNDWAVE

Formed: West London, England . . . 1986 by ex-MASS members GARY ASQUITH and DANNY BRIOTETT, alongside CARL BONNIE. Largely unsung pioneers of bass-quaking, paranoid techno-dub, RENEGADE SOUNDWAVE began as a West London bedroom experiment, taking their influence from the militant punk/reggae stylings of The CLASH before graduating to the capital's mid-80's all-nighter warehouse scene. Released on dance label, 'Rhythm King' and dominated by ASQUITH's trademark cockney leer, debut single, 'KRAY TWINS', was a scary trip through London's underworld driven by a bowel-rupturing bassline. The twisted humour of follow-up, 'COCAINE SEX', ensured cult status while 'THE PHANTOM' reverberated around London's dancefloors as the trio moved on to the more sympathetically experimental confines of 'Mute' records. Debut album, 'SOUNDCLASH' (1990), confirmed RENEGADE SOUNDWAVE's electro outlaw credentials with an addictive fix of sample-frenzy innovation, bass-breaking beats and low-life commentary. While the novelty value of their one and only hit single, 'PROBABLY A ROBBERY', led to a lasting tag as "CHAS 'N' DAVE with a beatbox", the sonic attack of the towering 'IN DUB' album was further proof that this London posse were thinking long term. So long, in fact, that by the time they released a follow-up (the release date held back by legal hassles over sampling copyright), 'HOWYOUDOIN?' (1994), the buzz had long since died down amid the perpetual flux of the dance scene. Nevertheless, tracks like the SERGE GAINSBOURG-sampling 'RENEGADE SOUNDWAVE' illustrated just why this group were important in the first place and why they were still at the cutting edge, albeit reduced to a duo following the mysterious departure of BONNIE. Critical acclaim wasn't enough though, young pretenders like The PRODIGY and The CHEMICAL BROTHERS marauding through territory The RENEGADE's had once so fearlessly mapped out as their own. 1995's remix album, 'THE NEXT CHAPTER OF DUB', only served to underline that the lack of recognition afforded this pivotal act was indeed, probably a (daylight) robbery.

Album rating: SOUNDCLASH (*6) / IN DUB (*5) / HOWYOUDOIN' (*5) / THE NEXT CHAPTER OF DUB (*4) / RENEGADE SOUNDWAVE 1987-1995 compilation (*6)

GARY ASQUITH – vocals (ex-MASS, ex-REMA REMA) / **DANNY BRIOTTET** – electronics, percussion (ex-MASS) / **CARL BONNIE** – electronics

Rhythm King not iss.

May 87. (7") *(LEFT 8)* **KRAY TWINS. / RENEGADE THEME** -
(12"+=) *(LEFT 8T)* – (2-'A'versions).
(re-iss. Feb92 on 'Mute' 12"/cd-s; 12/CD MUTE 137)

Jan 88. (12") *(LEFT 20T)* **COCAINE SEX. / BONUS PORNO BEATS / ('A'versions)** -
(re-iss. Feb92 on 'Mute' 12"/cd-s; 12/CD MUTE 138)

Mute Mute-Elektra

Sep 88. (7") *(MUTE 82)* **BITING MY NAILS. / ('A'instrumental)** -
(12"+=/cd-s+=) *(12/CD MUTE 82)* – Kray twins / Cocaine sex.

Jul 89. (7") *(MUTE 88)* **THE PHANTOM (IT'S IN THERE). / OZONE BREAKDOWN** -
(12"+=) *(12MUTE 88)* – ('A'mix).

Sep 89. (7") *(MUTE 102)* **PROBABLY A ROBBERY. / OZONE BREAKDOWN (uprising '90 mix)** -
(12"+=/cd-s+=) *(12/CD MUTE 102)* – ('A'club mix) / ('B'original).
(re-iss. Jan90, also c-s/12"; C/L12 MUTE 102) – hit UK No.38

Oct 89. (7") *(MUTE 104)* **SPACE GLADIATOR. / THE PHANTOM** -
(12"+=/12"pic-d+=/cd-s+=) *(12/P12/CD MUTE 104)* – (2-'A'mixes).

Mar 90. (cd/c/lp) *(CD/C+/STUMM 63) <75422>* **SOUNDCLASH**
– Blue eyed boy / Lucky Luke / On TV / Probably a robbery / Traitor / Space gladiator / Murder music / Biting my nails / Pocket porn / Can't get used to losing you / Biting my nails (instrumental).

Jun 90. (12"/cd-s) *(12/CD MUTE 112)* **BITING MY NAILS (mixes)** -
(12") *(L12MUTE 112)* – ('A'remixes).

Oct 90. (cd/c/lp) *(CD/C+/STUMM 85) <61006>* **IN DUB**
– Thunder / Bocterio / Deadly / Transition / Pocket porn due / Women respond to bass / Holgertron / Recognise and respond / Transworld siren / Black eye boy.

Nov 90. (12"/cd-s) *(12/CD MUTE 124)* **THUNDER II. / MANPHIBIAN MARCH / MASH UP** -

— now with CARL who ventured on a solo career

May 92. (12"/cd-s) *(12/CD MUTE 147)* **WOMEN RESPOND TO BASS. / RSW MEGAMIX – LESSON 1** -

Jan 94. (12"/cd-s) *(12/CD MUTE 146)* **RENEGADE SOUNDWAVE (mixes)** 64 -

Apr 94. (cd/c/lp) *(CD/C+/STUMM 100) <61631>* **HOWYOUDOIN'?**
– Renegade soundwave / Bubbaluba / Positive I.D. / Funky dropout / Last freedom fighter / Howyoudoin? / Liquid up / Brixton / John Holmes / Blast 'em out.

Mar 95. (12"/cd-s) *(12/CD MUTE 165)* **BRIXTON (mixes)** -

May 95. (cd/c/lp) *(CD/C+/STUMM 90)* **NEXT CHAPTER OF DUB** (remixes)

Jun 95. (12"/cd-s) *(12/CD MUTE 182)* **POSTIVE I.D. /** -
(re-iss. Jul96; same)

Jul 96. (d-cd) *(CDSTUMM 152)* **RENEGADE SOUNDWAVE 1987-1995** (compilation)
– Kray twins / Cocaine sex / Biting my nails / Lucky Luke / Space gladiator (satellite of dub) / Murder music / Pocket porn / Can't get used to losing you / Probably a robbery / Women respond to bass / Renegade soundwave / How ya doin'? / Bubbaluba / Positive I.D. / Blast 'em out / Cocaine sex / The phantom / Ozone breakdown / Biting my nails (version) / Thunder II / Deadly / Transworld siren / Black eye boy / Renegade soundwave (version) / Last freedom fighter / Renegade priest / Positive mindscape / Blastik 1.

— the duo had already split the previous year

RENTALS (see under ⇒ WEEZER)

REPLACEMENTS

Formed: Minneapolis, Minnesota, USA ... 1980 originally as The IMPEDIMENTS by the STINSON brothers – TOMMY and BOB – along with CHRIS MARS and chief songwriter/frontman, PAUL WESTERBERG. Legendary purveyors of ramshackle three-chord punk rock, The REPLACEMENTS' early efforts were so lo-fi they were off the end of the scale. Signed to Minneapolis indie stalwart, 'Twin Tone', the band debuted with 'SORRY MA, FORGOT TO TAKE OUT THE TRASH' (1981), the record's raw-nerve attitude, cathartic melodies and twisted humour shining through the garden shed (and a particularly dilapidated one at that) production. The following year's 'STINK' stepped on the gas and upped the nihilism ('GIMME NOISE', 'FUCK SCHOOL') although 'HOOTENANNY' (1983) and 'LET IT BE' (1984) used the hormonal energy to more satisfying and constructive ends. The latter set, especially, saw WESTERBERG's breathtakingly intuitive way with a melody reach fruition; granted, the likes of 'GARY'S GOT A BONER' didn't suggest another ELVIS COSTELLO in the ascendant but the bruised beauty of 'SIXTEEN BLUE' put WESTERBERG head and shoulders above most of his contemporaries (with the honourable exception of, perhaps, HUSKER DU). The record's charms were powerful enough to attract the major label attentions of 'Sire' and in late '85, The REPLACEMENTS released the Tommy Erdelyi (formerly TOMMY RAMONE)-produced 'TIM'. Furnished with a bigger budget, the group tempered their ragged sound while retaining much of the threadbare authenticity, the hooks as razor sharp as ever. It was to be the last album to feature the departing BOB, the band's notoriously shambolic live appearances robbed of the man's more erm, eccentric tendencies (playing in a dress – radical for the time! – or indeed in the nude, was not uncommon). With ROBERT 'SLIM' DUNLAP brought in as a replacement (ha!), the band recorded what many fans and critics alike regard as their finest hour, 'PLEASED TO MEET ME' (1987). More musically adventurous in line with their growing eclecticism, the album also found WESTERBERG's songwriting prowess at its unprecedented best, 'SKYWAY' soaring heavenward while 'CAN'T HARDLY WAIT' was the killer pop song he'd been threatening to pen since the band's inception. Criminally, the rave reviews and positive momentum surrounding the album's release failed to translate into sales, The REPLACEMENTS sounding strangely muted on 1989's 'DON'T TELL A SOUL', despite the return of BOB STINSON. While the minor concessions to commerciality resulted in a Top 60 US chart entry, the band were on their last legs and 1990's 'ALL SHOOK DOWN' was a WESTERBERG solo effort in all but name. The split eventually came in 1992, TOMMY forming BASH & POP (who released an album, 'FRIDAY NIGHT IS KILLING ME' the following year), while WESTERBERG worked on his solo debut proper, '14 SONGS' (1993). Although the writing was faultless, the record lacked the unkempt charm of old, any chance of a full REPLACEMENTS reunion suffering a serious setback as BOB succumbed to a drugs overdose the following year. • **Songwriters:** Penned by WESTERBERG, except; I WILL DARE (Kiss) / ROUTE 66 (Nelson Riddle Orchestra) / 20TH CENTURY BOY (T-Rex) / HEY GOOD LOOKING (Bo Diddley) / CRUELLA DE VILLE (from '1001 Dalmations'). • **Trivia:** Were quoted after a tour as saying 'Better hours, 9 to 5; 9 at night to 5 in the morning, that is'. Their '87 single 'ALEX CHILTON', was dedicated to legendary BOX TOPS leader.

Album rating: BOINK!! (*8) / LET IT BE (*8) / TIM (*7) / PLEASED TO MEET ME (*8) / Paul Westerberg: 14 SONGS (*5) / EVENTUALLY (*6) / Chris Mars: HORSESHOES AND HAND GRENADES (*5) / 75% LESS FAT (*5) / TENTERHOOKS (*6) / ANONYMOUS BOTCH (*5)

PAUL WESTERBERG (b.31 Dec'60) – vocals, rhythm guitar / **BOB STINSON** (b.17 Dec'59) – lead guitar / **TOMMY STINSON** (b. 6 Oct'66, San Diego, Calif.) – bass / **CHRIS MARS** (b.26 Apr'61) – drums

not iss. | Twin Tone

1981. (lp) *<TTR 8123>* **SORRY MA, FORGOT TO TAKE OUT THE TRASH** [-] [ ]
– Takin' a ride / Careless / Customer / Hanging downtown / Kick your door down / Otto / I bought a headache / Rattlesnake / I hate music / Johnny's gonna die / Shiftless when idle / More cigarettes / Don't ask why / Something to do / I'm in trouble / Love you till Friday / Shut up / Raised in the city. *(UK-iss.Mar88 on 'What Goes On'; GOES ON 017) (cd-iss. Apr93 on 'Roadrunner'; RR 9089-2) (cd re-iss. Mar95; TTR 8123-2)*

1981. (7") *<TTR 8120>* **I'M IN TROUBLE. / IF ONLY YOU WERE LONELY** [-] [ ]

1982. m-(lp) *<TTR 8228>* **STINK** [-] [ ]
– Kids don't follow / Fuck school / Stuck in the middle / God damn job / White and lazy / Dope smokin' moron / Go / Gimme noise. *(UK-iss.Mar88 on 'What Goes On'; GOES ON 020) (cd-iss. Apr93 on 'Roadrunner'; RR 9090-2) (cd re-iss. Mar95; 8228-2)*

1983. (lp) *<TTR 8332>* **HOOTENANNY** [-] [ ]
– Hootenanny / Run it / Color me impressed / Will power / Take me down to the hospital / Mr. Whirly / Within your reach / Buck hill / Lovelines / You lose / Hayday / Treatment bound. *(UK-iss.Mar88 on 'What Goes On'; GOES ON 021) (cd-iss. Apr93 on 'Roadrunner'; RR 9091-2) (cd re-iss. Feb95; TTR 8332-2)*

1984. (12") *<TTR 8440>* **I WILL DARE. / 20TH CENTURY BOY / HEY GOOD LOOKING (live)** [-] [ ]

Zippo | Twin Tone

Oct 84. (lp) *(ZONG 002) <TTR 8441>* **LET IT BE** [ ] [ ]
– I will dare / We're comin' out / Tommy gets his tonsels out / Black diamond / Androgynous / Unsatisfied / Seen your video / Gary's got a boner / Sixteen blue / Answering machine. *(cd-iss. Apr93 on 'Roadrunner'; RR 9092-2) (cd-iss. Mar95)*

Sire | Sire

Nov 85. (lp/c) *(K 925330-1/-4) <25330>* **TIM** [ ] [ ]
– Hold my life / I'll buy / Kiss me on the bus / Dose of thunder / Waitress in the sky / Swingin' party / Bastards of young / Lay it down clown / Left of the dial / Litle mascara / Here comes a regular. *(cd-iss. Jul93; 7599 25330-2)*

Mar 86. (7") *(W 8727)* **SWINGIN' PARTY. / LEFT OF THE DIAL** [ ] [-]

May 86. (7") *(W 8679)* **KISS ME ON THE BUS. / LITTLE MASCARA** [ ] [-]

— **ROBERT 'SLIM' DUNLAP** (b.14 Aug'51, Plainview, Minnesota) – keyboards repl. BOB (he was to die on the 18th of February 1995 o.d.)

Apr 87. (lp/c/cd) *(K 925557-1/-4/-2) <25557>* **PLEASED TO MEET ME** [ ] [ ]
– I.O.U. / Alex Chilton / I don't know / Nightclub jitters / The ledge / Never mind / Valentine / Shooting dirty pool / Red red wine / Skyway / Can't hardly wait. *(cd re-iss. Jul93; 7599 25557-2)*

Jun 87. (7") *(W 8297)* **ALEX CHILTON. / ELECTION DAY** [ ] [-]
(12"+=) *(W 8297T)* – Nightclub jitters / Route 66.

Jul 87. (7") *<28151>* **CAN'T HARDLY WAIT. / COOL WATER** [-] [ ]

— **BOB STINSON** – guitar returned to repl. SLIM who went solo

Jan 89. (lp/c/cd) *(K 925721-1/-4/-2) <25721>* **DON'T TELL A SOUL** [ ] [57]
– Talent show / Back to back / We'll inherit the Earth / Achin' to be / They're blind / Anywhere's better than here / Asking me lies / I won't / Rock'n'roll ghost / Darlin' one. *(cd re-iss. Jul93; 7559 25831-2)*

Apr 89. (7") *<22992>* **I'LL BE YOU. / DATE TO CHURCH (with TOM WAITS)** [-] [51]
(below w/ guests **STEVE BERLIN / MICHAEL BLAIR / BELMONT TENCH / JOHN CALE /** etc.

Sep 90. (cd/c/lp) *<(7599 26298-2/-4/-1)>* **ALL SHOOK DOWN** [ ] [69]
– Merry go round / One wink at a time / Nobody / Bent out of shape / Sadly beautiful / Someone takes the wheel / When it began / All shook down / Attitude / Happy town / Torture / My little problem / The lost. *(cd re-iss. Jul93 & Feb95; same)*

— (Mar91) **STEVE FOLEY** – drums repl. MARS who went solo

— disbanded 1992, TOMMY formed BASH & POP, who released album 'FRIDAY NIGHT IS KILLING ME'.

– compilations, others, etc. –

Apr 86. (m-lp/m-c) *Glass; (MGA LP/MC 016)* **BOINK!!** [ ] [-]
– Color me impressed / White and lazy / Within your reach / If only you were lonely / Kids don't follow / Nowhere is my home / Take me down to the hospital / Go.

PAUL WESTERBERG

Sire | Warners

Jun 93. (cd/c) *<9362 45255-2/-4>* **14 SONGS** [ ] [44]
– Knockin' on mine / First glimmer / World class fad / Runaway wind / Dice behind your shades / Even here we are / Silver naked ladies / A few minutes of silence / Someone I once knew / Black eyed Susan / things / Something is me / Mannequin shop / Down love.

Jul 93. (7"/c-s) *(W 0183/+C)* **WORLD CLASS FAD. / SEEING HER** [ ] [ ]
(12"/cd-s) *(W 0183 T/CD)* – ('A'side) / Men without ties / Down love.

Oct 93. (7"/c-s) *(W 0209/+C)* **WORLD CLASS FAD. / CAN'T HARDLY WAIT (live)** [ ] [ ]
(cd-s+=) *(W 0209CD1)* – Left of the dial (live) / Another girl another planet (live).
(cd-s) *(W 0209CD2)* – ('A'side) / Waiting for somebody / Dyslexic heart / Answering machine (live).

Apr 96. (cd/c) *(9362 46251-2/-4) <46176>* **EVENTUALLY** [ ] [50]
– These are the days / Century / Love untold / Ain't got me / You've had it with you / Mamadaddydid / Hide n seekin' / Once around the weekend / Trumpet clip / Angels walk / Good day / Time flies tomorrow.

CHRIS MARS

plays multi-instruments + augmented by some guests

not iss. | Polygram

1992. (cd) *<513198>* **HORSESHOES AND HAND GRENADES** [-] [ ]
– Reverse status / Popular creeps / Outer limits / Before it began / Get out of my life / Monkey sees / Ego maniac / Midnight carnival / I, me, we, us, them / Don't you see it / Happy disconnections / Better days / City lights on Mars / Last drop.

not iss. | Smash

1993. (cd) *<8004>* **75% LESS FAT** [-] [ ]
– Stuck in rewind / No bands / Weasel / Public opinion / All figured out / Whining horse / Car camping / Skipping school / Bullshit detector / Candy liquor / Demolition / No more mud / Nightcap.

not iss. | Bar/None

1995. (cd) *<52A>* **TENTERHOOKS** [-] [ ]
– White Patty rap / Forkless tree / Mary / Lizard brain / Hate it / Brother song / Water biscuits / E.I.B. negative / Haunted town / Floater.

Sep 96. (cd) *<85A>* **ANONYMOUS BOTCH** [-] [ ]
– Conquering cow farmer / Sheep spine shimmy / Narrow / Down drag / Black days / Two dreams / It's a long life / Janet's new kidney / Weather / Where and why / Funeral hymn of the small critter / I'll be gone / Cadaver dogs / New day.

RESIDENTS

Formed: Shrieveport, Louisiana, USA . . .1966 by mysterious line-up. Soon relocating to San Mateo, California in the early 70's, they made a few untitled homemade recordings. They subsequently sent these to Hal Haverstadt of 'Warners' who promptly returned them, the address marked; 'for the attention of the residents'. Adopting the latter as their moniker, they later issued the two newly named tapes in the early 70's, 'RUSTY COAT HANGER FOR THE DOCTOR' and 'THE BALLAD OF STUFFED TRIGGER' respectively. In 1972, they shifted base to San Francisco, founding the independently distributed 'Ralph' records. Their "real" debut lp, 'MEET THE RESIDENTS' was issued in 1974, its title and cover art a tongue-in cheek take-off of The

BEATLES. They then released a series of very limited edition lp's, 'THIRD REICH AND ROLL' in 1976, a collection of mangled 50's and 60's covers, carrying on where FRANK ZAPPA left off (albeit in a much weirder fashion). Later in the year, The RESIDENTS and DEVO competed for the best re-constructed version of The STONES' 'SATISFACTION', however, the latter won out in the end. After more comical parodying of The BEATLES and others, they unleashed the 'ESKIMO' set in 1979. This seminal meisterwork was recorded over a lengthy period of time, weird in the extreme, it featured tribal rhythms behind sub-lingual voices (VIC REEVES in "club style" must have taken inspiration). In 1980, the 'COMMERCIAL ALBUM' was released, containing forty tracks of exactly one minute in length, it was another to explore the barren frontiers of possibilities in music. They continued throughout the 80's with even more obscurity than their earlier 70's work. They were infamous for their hilarious head disguises, which included giant eyeballs, etc.
• **Songwriters:** Group penned, except tribute/covers lp's of ELVIS PRESLEY, HANK WILLIAMS, GEORGE GERSHWIN and JAMES BROWN material.
Album rating: THE COMMERCIAL ALBUM (*7) / ESKIMO (*8)

The RESIDENTS (4) – instruments, vocals, noises / assisted by **SNAKEFINGER** (b. PHILIP LITHMAN) (ex-CHILLI WILLI & THE RED HOT PEPPERS)

not iss. Ralph

Dec 72. (d-7"ltd) *<RR 1272>* **SANTA DOG** -
– Aircraft damage (credited to ARR + OMEGA) / The COLLEGE WALKERS – Lightning /

Feb 74. (lp-ltd) *<RR 0274>* **MEET THE RESIDENTS** -
– Boots . . . Numb erone . . . Guylum Bardot . . . Breath and length . . . Consuelo's departure . . . Smelly tongues . . . Rest aria . . . Skratz . . . Spotted pinto bean . . . Infant tango . . . Seasoned greetings . . . N-er-gee (crisis blues). *(re-iss. re-mixed Aug77; RR 0677)* – (lost 7 minutes). *(re-iss. Dec88 on 'Torso' cd/lp; CD/40 416)*

— In Oct'75, they issued 500 copies US of lp 'BLORP ESETTE' for 'LAFMS'; *005>*

Feb 76. (lp-ltd) *<RR 1075>* **THE THIRD REICH AND ROLL** -
– Hitler was a vegetarian / Hey Jude / Swastikas on parade / The twist / Land of 1000 dances / Hanky panky. *<re-iss. 1978; same>*

Sep 76. (7"ltd) *<RR 0776>* **SATISFACTION. / LOSER = WEED** -
<re-iss. Aug78 as 7"yellow; RR 7803>

Jan 77. (7"ep-ltd) *<RR 0377>* **BABYFINGERS** -
<re-iss. 1979 on 'W.E.I.R.D.' 7"pink; 1>

Feb 77. (lp-ltd) *<RR 1276>* **FINGERPRINCE** -
– You yesyesyes / Home age conversation / Godsong / March de la winni / Bos sy / Boo who / Tourniquet of roses / You yesyesyes again / Six things to a cycle. *(re-iss. twice 1978; same) (cd-iss. Dec87 on 'Torso'; TORSOCD 047)*

Aug 77. (7") *<RR 0577>* **(THE BEATLES PLAY THE RESIDENTS AND THE RESIDENTS PLAY THE BEATLES)** -
– Beyond the valley of a day in the life /

Feb 78. (7"ep) *<RR 1177>* **DUCK STAB EP** -

Oct 78. (lp) *<RR 1174>* **NOT AVAILABLE** -
– Edweena / The making of a soul / Ships a going down / Never known questions epilogue. *(UK-iss.cd Sep94 on 'Indigo'; 7539-2)*

Nov 78. (lp) *<RR 0278>* **DUCK STAB / BUSTER AND GLEN** -
– Constantinople / Sinister exaggerator / The Booker tease / Blue rosebuds / Laughing song / Bach is dead / Elvis and his boss / Lizard lady / Semolina / Birthday boy / Weight-lifting Lulu / Krafty cheese / Hello skinny / The electrocutioner. *(cd-iss. Jul87 on 'Torso'; TORSOCD 406>*

Dec 78. (7") *<RR 7812>* **SANTA DOG 78. / SANTA DOG** -

Aug 79. (lp) *<SM 7908>* **SUBTERRANEAN MODERN** -

— more guests **CHRIS CUTLER** – percussion / **DON PRESTON** – synth

Sep 79. (lp,white-lp) *<ESK 7906>* **ESKIMO** -
– The walrus hunt / Birth / Arctic hysteria / The angry Angakok / A spirit steals a child / The festival of death. *(cd-iss. Jul87 on 'Torso'; TORSOCD 404) (cd re-iss. 1996 on 'Ralph Euro'; CD 016)*

Virgin Ralph

Sep 79. (lp; with SNAKEFINGER) *(VR 3) <DJ 7901>* **NIBBLES** <US title 'PLEASE DO NOT STEAL IT' – DJ compilation> Mar79
– Yesyesyesyes / Santa dog '78 / Gloria / Rest aria / Semolina / The spot / Never known questions / Constantinople / Laughing song / The mocking of a soul / Skratz / Good lovin' / Blue rosebuds / Six things to a cycle / The electrocutioner.

Pre Ralph

Oct 80. (lp) *(PREX 2) <6559>* **THE COMMERCIAL ALBUM**
– Easter woman / Perfect love / Picnic boy / End of home / Amber / Japanes watercolour / Red rider / My second wife / Suburban bathers / Floyd / Dimples and toes / The nameless souls / Die in terror / Love leaks out / Act of being polite / Medicine man / Tragic bells / Loss of innocence / The simple song / Ups and downs / Possessions / Give it someone else / Phantom / Less not more / My work is so behind / Birds in the trees / Handful of desire / Moisture / Love is . . . / Troubled man / La la loneliness / Nice old man / The talk of creatures / Fingertips / In between dreams / Margaret Freeman / The coming of the crow / When we were young.

Oct 80. (7"ep) *(PRE 009)* **THE COMMERCIAL SINGLE**
– Amber / Red rider / Picnic boy / When we were young / Phantom / Moisture.

1980. (12"ep) *<RZ 8006-D>* **DISKOMO** -
– Diskomo / Goosebump: Disasterplants – Farmers – Twinkle.

1981. (lp) *<8152>* **MARK OF THE MOLE** -
– Hole-worker at the mercies of nature / Voices of the air / The ultimate disaster / Won't you keep us working / First warning / Back to normality / The sky falls / Why are we crying / The tunnels are filling / It never stops / Migration / March to the sea / The observer / Hole-worker's new hymn / Hole-worker's vs Man and machine / Another land / Rumors / Arrival / Deployment / Saturation / The new machine / Idea / Construction / Failure / Reconstruction / Success / Final confrontation / Success / Final confrontation / Driving the moles away / Don't tread on me / The short war / Resolution. *(UK cd-iss. Sep94 on 'Indigo'; 7540-2)*

Ralph Recommended

May 82. (lp) *(RZ 8202)* **THE TUNES OF TWO CITIES** Mar82
– Serenade for Missy / Mousetrap / Smack your lips clap your teeth / A maze of jigsaws / God of darkness / Smokebams / Mourning the undead / Song of the wild / Happy home / The secret seed / The evil disposer.

Jul 83. (12"ep) *(RALPH 1) <RZ 8252>* **INTERMISSION**
– Lights out / Shorty's lament / Moles are coming / Would we be alive / New hymn. *(lp-iss.1989 on 'Torso'; TORSO 33-055)*

1983. (lp) *<RZ 8302>* **RESIDUE OF THE RESIDENTS** -
– The sleeper / Whoopy snorp / Kamakazi lady / Boy in love / Shut up! shut up! / Anvil forest / Diskomo / Jailhouse rock / Up & down / Walter Westinghouse / Saint Nix / Open up.

New Ralph New Ralph

Jan 84. (lp; with RENALDO & THE LOAF) *(RR 8351)* **TIME IN LIMBO**

Korova Recommended

Jul 84. (7") *(KOW 36)* **IT'S A MAN'S MAN'S MAN'S WORLD. / I'LL GO CRAZY**

Aug 84. (lp/c) *(KODE/CODE 9) <RZ 8402>* **GEORGE & JAMES** (some live)
– Rhapsody in blue / I got rhythm / Summertime / Live at the Apollo: I'll go crazy / Try me / Think / I don't mind / Lost someone / Please please please / Night train. *(c+=)* – (extra track). *(cd-iss. Sep94 on 'Indigo'; 2122-2)*

DoubleVision Ralph

Dec 84. (lp) *(DV 9) <RZ 8452>* **WHATEVER HAPPENED TO VILENESS FATS**
– Whatever happened to Vileness Fats / Atomic shopping carts / Adventures of a troubled heart / Search for the short man / The importance of evergreen / Broccoli and saxophone / Disguised as meat / Thoughts busily betraying / Lord, it's lonely / The knife fight. *(UK cd-iss. Sep94 on 'Indigo'; 7537-2)*

1985. (lp) *<RZ 8552>* **THE BIG BUBBLE – PART 4 OF THE MOLE TRILOGY** -
– Sorry / Hop a little / Go where ya wanna go / Gotta gotta get / Cry for the fire / Die stay-go / Vinegar / Fire fly / The big bubble / Fear for the future / Kula bocca says so. *(cd-iss. Sep94 on 'Indigo'; 7541-2)*

Sep 85. (red-lp) *(DVR 17)* **THE PAL TV LP** -

not iss. Rykodisc

Jan 86. (cd) *<RCD 20012>* **HEAVEN?** -
– The importance of evergreen / It's a man's man's man's world / H.E.L.L. no! / Japenese watercolours / I got rhythm / Ups and downs / Serenade for Missy / Eastern woman / Amber / The census taker / Happy home / Crashing / Redrider / Floyd / The moles are coming / Resolution / Mahogany wood / Simple song / Kula bocca says no / Love leaks out / New hymn / Whater happened to Vileness Fats / Twinkle / Festival of death (excerpt).

Jan 86. (cd) *<RCD 20013>* **HELL!** -
– The ultimate disaster (excerpt) / Lights out / Where is she? / The coming of the crow / Lizard lady / Die interior / Shut up! shut up! / Shorty's lament / Hello skinny / Kamikaze lady / Secret seed / Sonny / Smelly tongues / Monkey and Bunny / Farmers / Satisfaction / Sinister exaggerator / Loss of innocence / The sleeper / Final confrontation (excerpt).

Torso Torso

Oct 86. (d-lp) *(TORSO 33-018) <2614220>* **13TH ANNIVERSARY SHOW (live in Japan & Holland)**
– Jailhouse rock / Where is she? / Picnic in the jungle / I got rhythm / Passing in the bottle / Monkey and Bunny / This is a man's man's man's world / Walter Westinghouse / Easter woman guitar solo / Diskomo / Hello skinny / Constantinople / Hop a little / Cry for the fire / Kamikaze. *(cd-iss. Sep94 on 'Indigo'; 7534-2)*

Nov 86. (lp) *(TORSO33 022) <2614202>* **STARS & HANK FOREVER! – THE AMERICAN COMPOSER'S SERIES VOL.II (THE MUSIC OF HANK WILLIAMS AND JOHN PHILIP SOUSA)**
– Hank Williams:- Hey good lookin' / Six more miles (to the graveyard) / Kaw-liga / Ramblin' man / Jambalaya / John Philip Sousa:- Sousaside: a) Nobles of the mystic shrine, b) The stars & stripes forever, c) El capitan, d) The liberty bell, e) Semper fidelis, f) The Washington post. *(re-iss. Sep94 on 'Indigo'; 7530-1)*

Dec 86. (7"/12") *(TORSO 7/12 022)* **KAW-LIGA. / ?**
(re-iss. Mar89; cd-s; TORSOCD 322)

Jun 87. (7"/12") *(TORSO 7/12 032)* **HIT THE ROAD. / ?**

Aug 88. (d-lp/cd/dat) *(TORSO 33/CD/DAT 055) <2614226>* **GOD IN THREE PERSONS**
– Hard and tenderly / Devotion / The thing about them / Their early yearsx / Loss of a loved one / The touch / The service / Confused / Fine fat flies / Time / Silver sharp / Kiss of flesh / Pain and pleasure. *(re-iss. lp Sep94 on 'Indigo'; 7531-1)*

1989. (lp/cd) *<2614262>* **THE MOLE SHOW LIVE (live)** -
– Voices of the air / The secret seed / Narration / The ultimate disaster / God of darkness / Migration / Smack your lips clap your feet / Another land / The new machine / Call of the wild / Final confrontation / Satisfaction / Happy home. *(UK cd-iss. Sep94 on 'Indigo'; 7542-2)*

1989. (3"pic-cd-ep) *(TORSOCD 355)* **DOUBLE SHOT / LOSS OF LOVED ONE (extended) / KISS OF FLESH (instrumental)**

1989. (lp/cd) *<14263-26>* **THE KING AND EYE** -
– Blue suede shoes / Don't be cruel / Heartbreak hotel / All shook up / Return to sender / Teddy bear / Devil in disguise / Stuck on you / Big hunk o' love / A fool such as I / Little sister / His latest flame / Burning love / Viva Las Vegas / Love me tender / Hound dog. *(UK cd-iss. Sep94 on 'Indigo'; 7535-2)*

1989. (cd-ep) *(TORSOCD 421)* **DISKOMO / WHOOPY SNORP / SAINT NIX / DISKOMO LIVE** -

May 90. (7"ep)(12"ep)(cd-ep) **DON'T BE CRUEL. / DISKOMO / DISCO WILL NEVER DIE**

Indigo East Side Digital

1991. (cd,lp) *<80602>* **FREAKSHOW** -
– Everyone comes to the freak show / Harry the head / Herman the human mole / Wanda the worm woman / Jack the boneless boy / Benny the bouncing bum / Mickey the mumbling midget / Lillie / Nobody laughs when they leave. *(re-iss. Sep94 on 'Indigo' cd)(lp; 2125-2)(7532-1)*

— returned in 1998

Sep 98. (cd) *(8535-2) <81332>* **WORMWOOD: CURIOUS STORIES FROM THE BIBLE** Oct98
– In the beginning / Fire fall / They are the meat / Melncholy clumps / How to get a head / Cain and Abel / Mr. Misery / Tent peg in the temple / God's magic finger / Spilling the seed / Dinah and the unclean skin / Bathsheba bathes / Bridegroom of blood / Hanging by his hair / Seven ugly cows / Burn baby burn / Kill him / I hate Heaven / Judas slaves / Revelation.

– others, etc. –

Sep 94. (lp)(cd) *Torso; (TORSO 33-199)(7536-2)* **CUBE E**
Sep 94. (cd) *Indigo; (2124-2)* **POOR KAW LIGA'S PAIN**
Sep 94. (cd/lp) *Indigo; (7543-2/-6)* **POOR KAW LIGA (housey mix)**
Oct 94. (cd) *Cargo; (2129-2)* **THE RESIDENTS** -

– compilations, etc.

Oct 84. (lp/c) *Korova; (KODE/CODE 10)* **RALPH BEFORE '84 – VOLUME 1** ☐ [-]
– It's a man's man's man's world / Diskomo / Hello skinny / (I left my heart in) San Francisco / Happy home / Smack your lips / Yesyesyesyes / Jailhouse rock / Monkey and Bunny / Festival of death.

Jan 85. (lp) *Korova; (KODE 12)* **BEFORE RALPH VOLUME 2** ☐ [-]
– Eva's warning / Halloween / Evolution / What use / Mahogany wood / Same ole me / Tritone / Melvyn's repose / Yeti: what are you / Nelda danced at day break / Norrgarden nyvia.

Nov 92. (cd)(c)(lp) *Euro Ralph;* **PRESENT OUR FINEST FLOWERS** ☐ ☐
(re-iss. cd Sep94 on 'Indigo'; 2121-2)

May 97. (4xcd-box) *Cargo; (RESBOX 1)* **25th ANNIVERSARY BOX SET** ☐ [-]

Martin REV (see under ⇒ SUICIDE)

Graeme REVELL (see under ⇒ S.P.K.)

REVENGE (see under ⇒ NEW ORDER)

REVILLOS (see under ⇒ REZILLOS)

REVOLTING COCKS (see under ⇒ MINISTRY)

REVOLVER

Formed: Winchester, England . . . Autumn 1990 by songwriter MAT FLINT, alongside NICK DEWEY and HAMISH BROWN, who all met in London. Having played their first gig at the end of that year, they secured a deal with Virgin off-shoot label, 'Hut', issuing a debut single, 'HEAVEN SENT AN ANGEL', the following summer. Quintessential "shoegazers", REVOLVER had all the qualities of a typical early 90's band, i.e. neo-psychedelic effects-laden guitars, fey vocals and almost-hooklines. A further couple of singles, 'CRIMSIN' and 'VENICE', preceded their 1992 debut album, 'BABY'S ANGRY', its watered down, RIDE-esque fare bearing the full brunt of the music press backlash; a cover of Strawberry Switchblade's 'SINCE YESTERDAY' didn't help matters. 1993's follow-up set, 'COLD WATER FLAT', on the other hand, impressed even the most jaundiced of rock journos with its more robust approach. However, the trio weren't really a hit with the wider indie public and following the parting shot of single, 'I WEAR YOUR CHAIN', REVOLVER bit the bullet and called it a day.

Album rating: BABY'S ANGRY (*5) / COLD WATER FLAT (*7)

MAT FLINT – vocals, guitar, organ / **HAMISH BROWN** – bass / **NICK DEWEY** – drums

Hut Caroline

Aug 91. (12"ep/cd-ep) *(HUT T/CD 7)* **'45'** ☐ [-]
– Heaven sent an angel / Painting pictures / Molasses / Cherish.

Nov 91. (7") *(HUT 9)* **CRIMSIN. / DON'T EVER LEAVE** ☐ [-]
(12"+=/cd-s+=) *(HUT T/CD 9)* – Drowning inside / Further away.

Apr 92. (7"blue) **VENICE. /** ☐ [-]
(12"+=/cd-s+=) –

May 92. (cd/c/lp) *(HUT CD/MC/LP 15) <CAROL 1722CD>* **BABY'S ANGRY** ☐ ☐
– Venice / Painting pictures / Red all over / Heaven sent an angel / Drowning inside / Molasses / Cherish / Since yesterday / Don't ever leave.

Feb 93. (10"ep/12"ep/cd-ep) *(HUT EN/T/CD 26)* **CRADLE SNATCH / DON'T YOU WONDER WHY? / CRIMSIN / IF WE COULD SPEND SOME TIME** ☐ [-]

Apr 93. (cd/c/lp) *(CD/TC+/HUT 8) <CAROL 1734>* **COLD WATER FLAT** ☐ ☐
– Cool blue / Shakesdown / Cradle snatch / I wear your chain / Nothing without you / Bottled out / Coming back / Cold water flat / Makes no difference all the same / Wave.

Jul 93. (12"ep/cd-ep) *(HUT T/CD 34)* **I WEAR YOUR CHAIN /** ☐ [-]

— split after above

REVOLVING PAINT DREAM

Formed: Isle Of Dogs, London, England . . . 1983 by former LAUGHING APPLE conspirator, ANDREW INNES, a bit part guitarist with BIFF BANG POW!; both these outfits were ALAN McGEE projects, the 'Creation' boss launching RPD's debut single, 'FLOWERS ARE IN THE SKY' early '84. This retro-psychedelic gem was augmented by McGEE, plus the more steadier members, NICO-esque vocalist CHRISTINE WANLESS (whom ANDREW met at Queen Mary's College) and BIFF BANG POW!'s drummer, KEN POPPLE. However, this mysterious outfit (at the time) disappeared for over three years, INNES obviously a bit more concerned with performing with another group, er . . . PRIMAL SCREAM. RPD resurfaced in the summer of 1987 with the pop-come-psyche debut mini-album, 'OFF TO HEAVEN', a directionless collection of weird indie-rock tunes. LUKE HAYES was in the fold for their 1989 follow-up, 'MOTHER WATCH ME BURN', although this turned out to be INNES swansong.

Album rating: OFF TO HEAVEN (*5) / MOTHER WATCH ME BURN (*4)

ANDREW INNES – rhythm guitar, etc (ex-LAUGHING APPLE, of BIFF BANG POW!) / **CHRISTINE WANLESS** – vocals / **KEN POPPLE** – drums / **ALAN McGEE** – guitar, etc (also part-time)

Creation not iss.

Feb 84. (7") *(CRE 002)* **FLOWERS ARE IN THE SKY. / IN THE AFTERNOON** ☐ [-]

— INNES became part of PRIMAL SCREAM early in '87 while WANLESS took a job as a Creation press officer while both remained with RPD.

Jun 87. (m-lp) *(CRELP 018)* **OFF TO HEAVEN** ☐ [-]
– Flowers in the sky / Stop the world / 7 seconds.

— **LUKE HAYES** – ; repl. POPPLE

Jan 89. (lp) *(CRELP 039)* **MOTHER WATCH ME BURN** ☐ [-]
– The dune buggy attack battalion / Green sea blue / Fever mountain / (Burn this house) Down to the ground / Mother wash my tears away / Garbagebrain / Electra's crying loaded in the basement / Mandra Mandra / Untitled (love song) / 300 (coda) / Reprise: Mandro Mandro / Sun, sea, sand. *(cd-iss. Oct90 & May94 +=; CRECD 039)* – OFF TO HEAVEN

Feb 89. (7") *(CRE 062)* **SUN, SEA, SAND. / GREEN SEA BLUE** ☐ [-]

— INNES remained with his main job, PRIMAL SCREAM

REZILLOS

Formed: Edinburgh, Scotland . . . March '76 by EUGENE REYNOLDS and JO CALLIS (aka LUKE WARM), alongside art school colleagues MARK 'HI-FI' HARRIS, DR. D.K. SMYTHE, ANGEL PATERSON, GAYLE WARNING and imimitable frontwoman, FAY FIFE. Early in 1977, the band signed a one-off deal with Lawrie Love's 'Sensible' records and released the semi-legendary 'CAN'T STAND MY BABY'. Three-chord dumbness in the vein of The RAMONES with the added advantage of FIFE's Scots twang, the track was followed by '(MY BABY DOES) GOOD SCULPTURES' towards the end of the year. As well as being the first fruits of their deal with 'Sire', the record marked the debut of new man, WILLIAM MYSTERIOUS, recruited as a replacement for early departees, SMYTHE, HARRIS and WARNING. By the summer of '78, The REZILLOS were performing the tongue-in-cheek 'TOP OF THE POPS' on that self same programme as their multi-coloured freakshow crashed into the UK Top 20. A debut album, 'CAN'T STAND THE REZILLOS' also hit the Top 20 that summer, offering up for closer inspection the band's obsession with American beat/girl groups and general trash culture competing with British influences like DR. FEELGOOD. MYSTERIOUS didn't hang around long, replaced by SIMON TEMPLAR (yeah, right) as the 'DESTINATION VENUS' single carried on the sci-fi malarky but failed to crack the Top 40. Splitting before the year was out, The REZILLOS splintered in two, with CALLIS, TEMPLAR and PATERSON forming SHAKE – CALLIS would subsequently join the more successful HUMAN LEAGUE – while FIFE and REYNOLDS remained on much the same track with The REVILLOS. Featuring a line-up completed by ROCKY RHYTHM, a returning HARRIS and a trio of female backing singers, the new-look band immersed themselves even further in retro Americana with a string of singles, 'WHERE'S THE BOY FOR ME?', 'MOTORBIKE BEAT' and 'SCUBA SCUBA'. Despite encouraging press, neither these nor an album, 'REV UP' (1980) notched up sufficient sales as the group underwent constant personnel upheaval with MYSTERIOUS and new man KID KRUPA coming and going. Over the course of the next three years, the band hopped from label to label as thay continued to crank out inimitably titled material like '(SHE'S FALLEN IN LOVE WITH A) MONSTER MAN' and 'BONGO BRAIN'. Following a final couple of singles for 'E.M.I.', the band called it a day in 1985, FIFE moving into TV acting and subsequently appearing in the likes of 'Taggart' and 'The Bill'. Like spiritual descendents BIS, the band were big in Japan, choosing the Far East as their destination for a mid-90's reunion tour. • **Songwriters:** EUGENE and JO penned most, except; I WANNA BE YOUR MAN (Beatles) / I LIKE IT (Gerry & The Pacemakers) / GLAD ALL OVER (Dave Clark Five) / TWIST AND SHOUT (Isley Brothers) / BALLROOM BLITZ (Sweet) / TELL HIM (Exciters) / LAND OF A 1,000 DANCES (Cannibal & The Headhunters) / ON THE BEACH (Cliff Richard) / THUNDERBIRDS ARE GO (Barry Gray).

Album rating: CAN'T STAND THE REZILLOS (*7)

FAY FIFE (b. SHEILAGH HYNDE) – vocals / **EUGENE REYNOLDS** (b.ALAN FORBES) – vocals / **LUKE WARM** (b. JO CALLIS) – guitar, vocals (both ex-KNUTSFORD DOMINATORS) / **MARK 'HI-FI' HARRIS** – guitar / **Dr. D.K.SMYTHE** – bass / **ANGEL PATERSON** – drums / **GAYLE WARNING** – backing vocals

Sensible not iss.

Aug 77. (7") *(FAB 1)* **CAN'T STAND MY BABY. / I WANNA BE YOUR MAN** ☐ [-]
(re-iss. Aug79; SAB 1) – hit No.71

— **WILLIAM MYSTERIOUS** (b.DONALDSON) – bass finally repl. SMYTHE, HARRIS & WARNING

Sire Sire

Nov 77. (7") *(6078.612)* **(MY BABY DOES) GOOD SCULPTURES. / FLYING SAUCER ATTACK** ☐ [-]

May 78. (7";w-drawn) *(6198.215)* **COLD WARS. / WILLIAM MYSTERIOUS OVERTURE** [-] [-]

Jul 78. (7") *(SIR 4001)* **TOP OF THE POPS. / 20,000 REZILLOS UNDER THE SEA** [17] [-]
(c-s) *(SPC 3)* – ('A'side) / Destination Venus.

Jul 78. (lp/c) *(K/K4 56530) <SRK 6057>* **CAN'T STAND THE REZILLOS** [16] ☐
– Flying saucer attack / No / Someone's gonna get their heads kicked in tonight / Top Of The Pops / 2000 AD / It gets me / Can't stand my baby / Glad all over / My baby does good sculptures / I like it / Gettin' me down / Cold wars / Bad guy reaction. *(cd-iss. Jan96; 7599 26942-2)*

— **SIMON TEMPLAR** (b. BLOOMFIELD) – bass, vocals repl. WILLIAM

Nov 78. (7") *(SIR 4008)* **DESTINATION VENUS. / MYSTERY ACTION** [43] [-]

— disbanded late '78; JO, SIMON + ANGEL formed SHAKE, who released a couple of singles, 'CULTURE SHOCK' and 'INVASION OF THE GAMMA MEN', before releasing an EP for 'Pop Aural', 'WOAH YEAH!', in 1981. They subsequently became part of BOOTS FOR DANCING. The REZILLOS gave us a few more exploitation releases

Apr 79. (7"m) *(SIR 4014)* **COLD WARS. / FLYING SAUCER ATTACK (live) / TWIST AND SHOUT (live)** [ ] [-]

Apr 79. (lp/c) *(SRK/SRC 6069)* **MISSION ACCOMPLISHED . . . BUT THE BEAT GOES ON (live)** [30] [-]
– Top of the pops / Mystery action / Somebody's gonna get their head kicked in tonight / Thunderbirds are go / Cold wars / Teenbeat / Land of 10,000 dances / I need you / Gettin' me down / Culture shock / Ballroom blitz / Destination Venus / (My baby does) Good sculptures.

The REVILLOS

— (a slight change) brought together again **FAY & EUGENE** (also now on bass) / **HI-FI HARRIS** – guitar / **ROCKY RHYTHM** (b. NICKY FORBES) – drums (ex-PORK DUKES) / **JANE WHITE, JANE BROWN, TRICIA BRYCE** – backing vocals

Dindisc — not iss.

Sep 79. (7") *(DIN 1)* **WHERE'S THE BOY FOR ME?. / THE FIEND** [ ] [-]

— (Aug'79) added **KID KRUPA** – guitar (on tour) / **FELIX** – bass / **CHERIE & BABS REVETTE** – backing vocals repl. last backing trio

Jan 80. (7") *(DIN 5)* **MOTORBIKE BEAT. / NO SUCH LUCK** [45] [-]

— **WILLIAM MYSTERIOUS** – bass returned to repl. FELIX (to HEY ELASTICA)

Apr 80. (7") *(DINZ 16)* **SCUBA SCUBA. / BOY BOP** [ ] [-]

Sep 80. (lp) *(DIDX 3)* **REV UP** [ ] [-]
– Secret of the shadow / Rev up / Rock-a-boom / Voodoo / Bobby come back to me / Scuba scuba / Boy bop / Yeah yeah / Hungry for love / Jukebox sound / On the beach / Cool jerk / Hippy hippy sheik / Motorbike beat. *(re-iss. Mar84 on 'Virgin'; OVED 53)*

Sep 80. (7") *(DINZ 20)* **HUNGRY FOR LOVE. / VOODOO 2** [ ] [-]

— **KID KRUPA** (b. JON McLOUGHLIN) – guitar now totally repl. HARRIS / **DRAX** – b.vox repl. BABS / **VINCE SANTINI** – bass repl. MYSTERIOUS

Superville — not iss.

Sep 81. (7") *(SV 1001)* **(SHE'S FALLEN IN LOVE WITH A) MONSTER MAN. / MIND BENDING CUTIE DOLL** [ ] [-]

Jan 82. (lp;w-drawn) *(SV 4001)* **ATTACK** [-] [-]

Feb 82. (7"m) *(SV 2001)* **BONGO BRAIN. / HIP CITY / YOU WERE MEANT FOR ME** [ ] [-]

— **MAX ATOM** – guitar repl. KRUPA / **TERRI REVETTE** – b.vox repl. DRAX

Aura — not iss.

Nov 82. (7") *(AUS 135)* **TELL HIM. / GRAVEYARD GROOVE** [ ] [-]

— **FABIAN WONDERFUL** – guitar repl. ATOM

E.M.I. — not iss.

Oct 83. (7") *(RVL 1)* **BITTEN BY A LOVE BUG. / TRIGGER HAPPY JACK** [ ] [-]
(12"+=) *(12RVL 1)* – Cat call.

Mar 84. (7") *(RVL 2)* **MIDNIGHT. / Z-X-7** [ ] [-]
(12"+=) *(12RVL 2)* – ('A'extended).

— **BUDDY MOON** – bass; repl. SANTINI

— disbanded early 1985, FAY went into acting and later featured in 'Taggart' and 'The Bill'.

— REVILLOS re-formed with main originals (see above)

Vinyl Japan — not iss.

Dec 94. (12"ep/cd-ep) *(TASK/+CD 033)* **YEAH YEAH / CRUSH. / SCUBA SCUBA / SCUBA SCUBA (Japanese version)** [ ] [-]

May 95. (cd/lp) *(ASK CD/LP 046)* **LIVE AND ON FIRE IN JAPAN (live)** [ ] [-]
– Secret of the shadow / Bongo brain / Rockaboom / She's fallen in love with a monster man / Where's the boy for me? / Rev up! / Bitten by a lovebug / Mad from birth to death / Bobby come back to me / The fiend / Scuba scuba / My baby does good sculptures / Do the mutilation / Somebody's gonna get their head kicked in tonight / Yeah yeah.

Damaged Goods — not iss.

Sep 96. (7") *(DAMGOOD 93)* **JACK THE RIPPER. /** [ ] [-]

Sep 96. (cd) *(DAMGOOD 97CD)* **FROM THE FREEZER** [ ] [-]

– compilations, etc. –

Jul 95. (cd) *Mau Mau; (MAUCD 643)* **MOTORBIKE BEAT** [ ] [-]

Aug 95. (cd) *Receiver; (RRCD 204)* **ATTACK OF THE GIANT REVILLOS** [ ] [-]

Sep 98. (cd) *Vinyl Japan; (ASKCD 80)* **THE BBC RADIO SESSIONS** [ ] [-]

RHYTHM SISTERS

Formed: West Riding, Yorkshire, England . . . mid-80's, not surprisingly by two sisters, DEBI and MANDI LAEK. Attired in Doc Marten boots, these ladies of indie-pop played an unusual blend of quirky tunes as heard on their debut album, 'ROAD TO ROUNDHAY PIER' (1987). The RHYTHM SISTERS added a few guys to their project, former JAM man, BRUCE FOXTON and ex-UK SUBS drummer, STEVE STONES. Little was heard from the girls until 1990 when they worked with BILL NELSON, the great former BE-BOP DELUXE frontman signing the siblings to his 'Imaginary' imprint for what turned out to be their last outing, 'WILLERBY' (1991). The latter set was originally scheduled for release as 'INFOTAINMENT' a full year previously.

Album rating: ROAD TO ROUNDHAY PIER (*4) / WILLERBY (*4)

DEBI LAEK – vocals / **MANDI LAEK** – vocals / with session people

Red Rhino — not iss.

Nov 87. (lp/c/cd) *(RED LP/C/CD 87)* **ROAD TO ROUNDHAY PIER** [ ] [-]
– Gotham / Motor / Homework / Hooked / Elderberry avenue / American boys / Wild west party.

May 88. (7"/12") *(RED/+T 92)* **AMERICAN BOYS. /** [ ] [-]

— now augmented by other musicians (see above)

Imaginary — not iss.

Feb 91. (cd/c/lp) *(ILLCD/ILLCASS/ILLUSION 027)* **WILLERBY** [ ] [-]

— they disappeared back to the day jobs

RICH KIDS

Formed: London, England . . . Autumn 1977 by sacked SEX PISTOLS bass player, GLEN MATLOCK, who founded the band along with Scots-born MIDGE URE (a one-time chart-topping star with SLIK). Spoiled by press expectation, the RICH KIDS' wealth of talent (which also included STEVE NEW and RUSTY EGAN) promised much but delivered relatively little. Although MATLOCK and his fellow 'PISTOLS had been unceremoniously ousted from the 'E.M.I.' roster a year previously, the bass player was cynically welcomed back with open arms. A watered-down "Power-pop" version of what E.M.I. would probably have wanted the 'PISTOLS to sound like, the RICH KIDS' eponymous debut single confounded the label's expectations by stalling at No.24 in early 1978. Later that summer, The RICH KIDS dynasty went bankrupt, metaphorically speaking, as two further singles, 'MARCHING MEN' and 'GHOSTS OF PRINCES IN TOWERS', failed to chart. The accompanying MICK RONSON-produced album, 'GHOSTS OF PRINCES IN TOWERS', just missed the Top 50, the 'KIDS finally falling out with each other as the strained relationship between MATLOCK and URE came to a head. While the latter found fame and fortune with ULTRAVOX, a solo career and BAND AID, the former scraped a living on the fringes of the rock scene until 1996 when re-united with JOHNNY ROTTEN and Co for the self-explanatory 'Filthy Lucre' tour. At the same time, GLEN signed to 'Creation' for a one-off solo album, 'WHO'S HE THINK HE IS WHEN HE'S AT HOME'. • **Songwriters:** MATLOCK-URE penned most, except HERE COMES THE NICE (Small Faces).

Album rating: GHOSTS OF PRINCES IN TOWERS (*5)

MIDGE URE (b. JAMES URE, 10 Oct'53, Cambuslang, Scotland) – vocals, guitar (ex-SLIK, ex-PVC 2) / **STEVE NEW** – guitar (ex-SEX PISTOLS briefly '75) / **GLEN MATLOCK** (b. 21 Aug'56) – bass, vocals (ex-SEX PISTOLS) / **RUSTY EGAN** (b. 19 Sep'57) – drums

E.M.I. — not iss.

Jan 78. (7"red) *(EMI 2738)* **RICH KIDS. / EMPTY WORDS** [24] [-]

May 78. (7") *(EMI 2804)* **MARCHING MEN. / HERE COMES THE NICE** [ ] [-]

Aug 78. (7") *(EMI 2848)* **GHOSTS OF PRINCES IN TOWERS. / ONLY ARSENIC** [ ] [-]

Aug 78. (lp) *(EMI 3263)* **GHOSTS OF PRINCES IN TOWERS** [51] [-]
– Strange one / Hung on you / Ghosts of princes in towers / Cheap emotion / Marching men / Put you in the picture / Young girls / Bullet proff lover / Rich kids / Lovers and fools / Burning sounds. *(re-iss. Nov83 on 'Fame' lp/c; FA/TC-FA 4130771) (cd-iss. Sep93 on 'Dojo'; DOJOCD 154)*

— disbanded early 1979. MIDGE joined ULTRAVOX after a brief spell with THIN LIZZY!. He also was part of the initial guest list of VISAGE who had recruited RUSTY EGAN, who was later to join SKIDS. GLEN joined IGGY POP's band and later formed the SPECTRES in '81, followed by The LONDON COWBOYS. In the mid 90's, he was back with a re-united SEX PISTOLS (for live gigs) and released his first solo set, 'WHO'S HE THINK HE IS WHEN HE'S AT HOME?' for 'Creation. STEVE NEW formed UK act, PEARL HARBOUR.

Jonathan RICHMAN

Born: 16 May'51, Boston, Massachusetts, USA. After a period in the late 60's working as a contributor for local music papers, 'Vibrations' & 'Fusion', he formed his first real band, MODERN LOVERS, in 1971. With the help of producer KIM FOWLEY, they recorded a successful demo for 'Warners' in 1972, although the label subsequently shelved their JOHN CALE-produced debut album and soon dropped the group. RICHMAN & Co. finally split in late '74, only to re-form again six months later and record a debut single, 'ROADRUNNER', for 'United Artists'. They then moved to West Coast label 'Beserkley', who bought the unreleased Warners tapes and finally packaged the songs as an eponymous album in 1976. Featuring the classic MODERN LOVERS line-up of JERRY HARRISON, ERNIE BROOKS and DAVID ROBINSON, the album was one of the more genuine efforts to lay claim to the vastly oversubscribed 'first punk album' tag. Carrying on where his heroes The VELVET UNDERGROUND left off, RICHMAN fashioned an idiosyncratic update of late 60's garage-rock, his REED-y vocals carrying epistles of adolescent angst over a simplistic but effective musical backing. While UK Top 20 hit, 'ROADRUNNER', may have whetted fans appetites for more of the same, a belated follow-up album, 'JONATHAN RICHMAN & THE MODERN LOVERS' (1977) was a different beast altogether. While HARRISON and BROOKS were now tending greener new wave pastures with The TALKING HEADS and The CARS respectively, the revamped MODERN LOVERS line-up of ROBINSON, LEROY RADCLIFFE and GREG KERANEN were following RICHMAN's more whimsically eccentric path, cutting retro pop, acoustic-based tracks about aliens, insects and erm, abominable snowmen. A second album that year, 'ROCK'N'ROLL WITH THE MODERN LOVERS', confirmed RICHMAN's new strategy, hitting the

British Top 50 despite itself and spawning a second hit (Top 5) in the bizarre instrumental, 'EGYPTIAN REGGAE'. Critics were divided, some hailing the man as a wayward genius, some confounded at what they preceived as a waste of good talent. Whatever, after a late 70's lay-off, RICHMAN continued to plow his singular furrow throughout the following decade with an ever changing cast of musicians and different labels. Amid the grating childishness, the man was still capable of a wistful charm and the occasional sting of biting poignancy, fans and critics alike generally agreed that 'JONATHAN SINGS!' (1984) remains his finest release from this period. Towards the end of the decade, he recruited BRENDAN TOTTEN and JOHNNY AVILA for the leaner 'MODERN LOVERS '88' before abandoning the backup for good and going it alone. His 1989 eponymous solo debut was followed up with a misguided attempt at C&W, 'JONATHAN GOES COUNTRY' (1990), while a Spanish-language set, '!JONATHAN, TE VAS A EMOCIONAR!' (1994) surely tested the patience of even his most loyal fans. Much more promising were 1995's 'YOU MUST ASK THE HEART' and the following year's 'SURRENDER TO JONATHAN', the latter his first for a major label ('WEA') after years in the commercial wilderness. • **Songwriters:** RICHMAN compositions. • **Trivia:** JOHN CALE (ex-Velvet Underground), went on to record his brilliant 'PABLO PICASSO'.

Album rating: THE MODERN LOVERS (*7) / 23 GREAT RECORDINGS (*8)

The MODERN LOVERS

were formed by **RICHMAN** – vocals, guitar / with **JERRY HARRISON** – keyboards, vocals / **ERNIE BROOKS** – bass, vocals / **DAVID ROBINSON** – drums (left Nov73 to DMZ, after recording debut)

U.A. U.A.

Jun 75. (7") *(UP 36006)* **ROADRUNNER. / IT WILL STAND** [ ] [ ]

Beserkley Beserkley

Oct 76. (7") *<5701>* **ROADRUNNER. / Friday On My Mind (by Earthquake)** [-] [ ]

Oct 77. (lp/c) *(BSERK/BSERC 1) <BZ/+CA 0050>* **THE MODERN LOVERS** (1972 demos) [ ] [ ] Oct76
– Roadrunner / Astral plane / Old world / Pablo Picasso / I'm straight / She cracked / Hospital / Someone I care about / Girlfriend / Modern world. *(re-iss. Nov87; same> <re-iss. Nov89 on 'Rhino'; RNLP 70091> (cd-iss. Feb93 on 'Rev-Ola'+=; CREV 007CD)* – (3 extra tracks).

— HARRISON (also to TALKING HEADS) and BROOKS joined ELLIOTT MURPHY

JONATHAN RICHMAN & THE MODERN LOVERS

with also **LEROY RADCLIFFE** – guitar, vox / **GREG KERANEN** – bass, vox / **DAVID ROBINSON** – drums

Feb 77. (7") *<5743>* **NEW ENGLAND. / HERE COME THE MARTIAN MARTIANS** [-] [ ]

Jun 77. (7") *(BZZ 1)* **ROADRUNNER (once). / ROADRUNNER (twice)** [11] [-]
(re-iss. Jul82 on 'Old Gold'; OG 9113)

Oct 77. (lp/c) *(BSERK/BSERC 2) <BZ/+CA 0048>* **JONATHAN RICHMAN & THE MODERN LOVERS** [ ] [ ] Jul76
– Rockin' shopping center / Back in the U.S.A. / Important in your life / New England / Lonely financial zone / Hi dear / Abominable snowman in the market / Hey there little insect / Here comes the Martian Martians / Springtime / Amazing Grace. *<re-iss. Nov87; same> (cd-iss. Feb93 on 'Rev-Ola'; CREV 008CD)*

Aug 77. (lp/c) *(BSERK 9) <BZ/+CA 0053>* **ROCK'N'ROLL WITH THE MODERN LOVERS** [50] [ ]
– The sweeping wind (kwa ti feng) / Ice cream man / Rockin' rockin' leprechauns / Summer morning / Afternoon / Fly into the mystery / South American folk song / Roller coaster by the sea / Dodge veg-o-matic / Egyptian reggae / Coomyah / The wheels on the bus / Angels watching over you. *<re-iss. Nov87; same> (cd-iss. Feb93 on 'Rev-Ola'; CREV 009CD)*

Sep 77. (7") *(BZZ 2)* **EGYPTIAN REGGAE. / ROLLER COASTER BY THE SEA** [5] [ ]

— **D.SHARPE** – drums repl. ROBINSON / **ASA BREMNER** – bass repl. KERANEN

Dec 77. (lp/c) *(BSERK/BSERC 12) <BZ/+CA 055>* **THE MODERN LOVERS LIVE (live)** [ ] [ ]
– I'm a little airplane / Hey there little insect / Egyptian reggae / Ice cream man / I'm a little dinosaur / My little kookenhaken / South American folk song / New England / Morning of our lives. *<re-iss. Nov87; same> (cd-iss. Feb93 on 'Rev-Ola'; CREV 010CD) (cd re-iss. Apr97 on 'Wooded Hill'; HILLCD 15)*

Jan 78. (7"; as MODERN LOVERS) *(BZZ 7)* **MORNING OF OUR LIVES (live). / ROADRUNNER (thrice) (live)** [28] [ ]

Apr 78. (7"; as MODERN LOVERS) *(BZZ 14)* **NEW ENGLAND. / ASTRAL PLANE (live)** [ ] [-]

Jul 78. (7") *(BZZ 19)* **ABDUL & CLEOPATRA. / OH CAROL** [ ] [ ]

Dec 78. (7") *(BZZ 25)* **BUZZ BUZZ BUZZ. / HOSPITAL (live)** [ ] [ ]

Feb 79. (lp/c) *(BSERK/BSERC 17) <BZ/+CA 0060>* **BACK IN YOUR LIFE** [ ] [ ]
– Abdul and Cleopatra / (She's gonna) Respect me / Lover please / Affection / Buzz buzz buzz / Back in your life / Party in the woods tonight / My love is a flower (just beginning to bloom) / I'm nature's mosquito / Emaline / Lydia / I hear you calling me. *<re-iss. Nov86; same> (cd-iss. Feb93 on 'Rev-Ola'; CREV 011CD) (cd re-iss. Apr97 on 'Wooded Hill'; HILLCD 14)*

Mar 79. (7") *(BZZ 28)* **LYDIA. / IMPORTANT IN YOUR LIFE** [ ] [ ]

Jan 80. (lp) *(DSERK 19)* **JONATHAN RICHMAN SONGBOOK – THE BEST OF . . .** (compilation) [ ] [ ]

— JONATHAN retired in the late 70's, until 1982. Joining him were **KEN FORFIA** – keyboards / **BETH HARRINGTON** – guitar / **GREG KERANEN** – bass, vocals / **MICHAEL GUARDABASCIO** – drums, vocals / **ELLIE MARSHALL** – backing vocals

Rough Trade Sire

Aug 84. (lp/c) *(ROUGH/+C 52)* **JONATHAN SINGS!** [ ] [ ]
– That summer feeling / This kind of music / The neighbors / Somebody to hold me / These conga drums / Stop this car / Not yet three / Give Paris one more chance / You're the one for me / When I'm walking.

May 85. (7") *(RT 152)* **THAT SUMMER FEELING. / THIS KIND OF MUSIC** [ ] [ ]
(12"+=) *(RTT 152)* – The tag game.

— re-formed again with **JONATHAN, ELLIE, MICHAEL** and newcomer **ANDY PALEY** – toy piano

Jun 85. (lp/c) *(ROUGH/+C 72)* **ROCKIN' AND ROMANCE** [ ] [ ]
– The beach / My jeans / Bermuda / The U.F.O. man / Down in Bermuda / V. Van Gogh / Walter Johnson / I'm just beginning to live / The fenway / Chewing gum wrapper / The Baltimores / Up in the sky sometime / Now is better than before.

Aug 85. (7") *(RT 154)* **I'M JUST BEGINNING TO LIVE. / CIRCLE I** [ ] [ ]
(12"+=) *(RTT 154)* – Shirin & Fahrad.

Feb 86. (lp/c) *(ROUGH/+C 92)* **IT'S TIME FOR** [ ] [ ]
– It's you / Let's take a trip / This love of mine / Neon sign / Double chocolate malted / Just about seventeen / Corner store / The desert / Yo Jo Jo / When I dance / Shirin & Fahrad / Ancient and long ago.

— **JONATHAN** recruited complete new line-up **BRENDAN TOTTEN** – guitar / **JOHNNY AVILA** – drums

Demon Rounder

Feb 88. (lp/cd) *(FIEND/+CD 106) <ROUNDER/+CD 9014>* **MODERN LOVERS '88** [ ] [ ]
– Dancin' late at night / When Harpo played his harp / Gail loves me / New kind of neighborhood / African lady / I love hot nights / California desert party / Everything's gotta be right / Circle 1 / I have come out to play / The theme from 'Moulin Rouge'!.

JONATHAN RICHMAN

Special Delivery Rounder

Aug 89. (lp/c/cd) *<(SPD/+C/CD 1024)>* **JONATHAN RICHMAN** [ ] [ ]
– Malagueno de Jojo / Action packed / Everyday clothes / Fender Stratocaster / Blue Moon / Closer / I eat with Gusto / Damn!! you bet / Miracles will start to happen / Sleepwalk / Que reste t'll de nos amours / A mistake today for me / Cerca.

— now with **TOM BRUMLEY** – guitar

Aug 90. (lp/c/cd) *<(SPD/+C/CD 1037)>* **JONATHAN GOES COUNTRY** [ ] [ ]
– Since she started to ride / Reno / You're the one for me / Your good girl's gonna go bad / I must be king / You're crazy for takin' the blues / Rodeo wind / Corner store / The neighbours / Men walks among us / I can't stay mad at you / Satisfied mind.

Cheree Cheree

Nov 91. (cd) *(CHEREE 22)* **HAVING A PARTY (live US tour)** [ ] [ ]
– The girl stands up to me now / Cappuccino bar / my career as a homewrecker / She doesn't laugh at my jokes / When she kisses me / They're not tryin' on the dance floor / At night / When I say wife / 1963 / Monologue about bermuda / Our swingin' pad / Just for fun

Rounder Rounder

Dec 92. (cd/c) *<(ROU CD/C 9036)>* **I, JONATHAN** [ ] [ ]
– Parties in the U.S.A. / Tandem jump / You can't talk to the dude / Velvet underground / I was dancing in the lesbian bar / Rooming house on Venice beach / That summer feeling / Grunion run / A higher power / Twilight in Boston.

May 94. (cd) *<(ROUCD 9040)>* **!JONATHAN, TE VAS A EMOCIONAR!** [ ] [ ]
– Pantomima de el amor Brujo / Harpo en su Harpa / No te oye / No mas por fun / Papel de chicle / Los vecinos / Compadrito corazon / Melodia tradicional Ecuadoriana / Shirin y Farad / Reno / Cerca / El U.F.O. man / Ahora es Mejor / Sabor A.Mi / Una Fuerza alla.

May 95. (cd/c) *<(ROU CD/C 9047)>* **YOU MUST ASK THE HEART** [ ] [ ]
– To hide a little thought / The heart of Saturday night / Vampire girl / Just because I'm Irish / That's how I feel / Let her go into darkness / The rose / You must ask the heart / Nothing can change this love / Amorcito corazon / City vs. country / Walter Johnson / Nishi.

WEA WEA

Sep 96. (cd/c) *<(9362 46296-2/-4)>* **SURRENDER TO JONATHAN** [ ] [ ]
– Just look at me / That little sleeper car / Not just a plus list on the guest list anymore / My little girl's got a full time daddy now / Rock'n'roll drummer straight from the hospy-tel / atisfy / When she kisses me / Egyptian reggae / To hide a little thought / I was dancing in the lesbian bar / Surrender / Floatin' / French style.

– compilations, etc. –

Oct 81. (lp) *Bomp; <LBOM 1>* **THE ORIGINAL MODERN LOVERS** [-] [ ]
(UK-iss.Jun87 on 'Link';)

Jul 82. (7") *Old Gold; (OG 9112)* **EGYPTIAN REGGAE. / MORNING OF OUR LIVES (live)** [ ] [-]

1987. (cd) *Rhino; <RNCD 75889>* **THE BEST OF JONATHAN RICHMAN AND THE MODERN LOVERS** [-] [ ]

1988. (cd) *Rounder; (CDS1)* **JONATHAN RICHMAN & BARRENCE WHITFIELD** [-] [ ]

Feb 91. (cd/c/lp) *Essential; (ESS CD/MC/LP 128)* **23 GREAT RECORDINGS BY JONATHAN RICHMAN AND THE MODERN LOVERS** [ ] [-]
– Roadrunner / Dignified & old / Pablo Picasso / I'm straight / Astral plane / Girl friend / Government centre / New teller / It will stand / Morning of our lives / Abominable snowman in the market / Important in your life / My little kookenhaken / Dodge veg-o-matic / Lonely financial zone / Roller coaster by the sea / New England / Egyptian reggae / Ice cream man / Buzz buzz buzz / Abdul & Cleopatra / Roadrunner (twice). *(c+=)* – She cracked / Hospital. *(re-iss. cd Sep93 on 'Castle'; CSCD 397)*

1991. (lp) *Ubik; <BAKTUN 004>* **ORIGINAL MODERN LOVERS** [-] [ ]
(UK-iss.Feb97 on 'Bomp'; BLP 4021)

Apr 94. (cd) *Castle;* **THE COLLECTION** [ ] [-]

Apr 95. (cd; by MODERN LOVERS) *Rounder; (ROUCD 9042)* **PRECISE MODERN LOVERS ORDER** [ ] [-]
(originally issued in 1992 on French 'Fan Club'; 422439)

Jun 95. (cd) *Nectar; (NPMCD 506)* **A PLEA FOR TENDERNESS** [ ] [-]

RIDE

Formed: Oxford, England . . . 1988 by local art college students MARK GARDENER, ANDY BELL and LAURENCE COLBERT. They drafted in STEVE QUERALT and journalist/manager Dave Newton who subsequently secured them some London gigs. These led to a deal with 'Creation' records and they released their eponymous debut EP early in 1990, the record quickly selling out of its limited number and squeezing into the UK Top 75. The disc showcased the band's spiralling guitar-scapes and contained an early classic in the cathartic 'DRIVE BLIND'. It was hotly pursued by two further Top 40 EP's, 'PLAY' and 'FALL', the latter containing their best track to date (at that point) in 'TASTE'. Come October, with the "shoegazing" scene in full flow, they nearly secured a Top 10 place with their stunning debut album, 'NOWHERE'. 1991 was spent in the studio (excluding Reading Festival), and the fruits were heard early in '92 on their superb 8-minute single 'LEAVE THEM ALL BEHIND'. This slow burning psychedelic epic gave them their first Top 10 entry and was a prelude to their second, more BYRDS-esque album, 'GOING BLANK AGAIN'. The record went Top 5, despite being derided by certain music critics. Frictions began to appear and it was thought a two-year sabbatical would solve the problem. BELL took time off to help out his Swedish wife and stablemate IDHA (OVELIUS) on her debut album. In 1994, RIDE were back with 'CARNIVAL OF LIGHT', but again they received lukewarm reviews. Early the next year, GARDENER took off to the States, leaving them all behind (ouch!). Their swansong, 'TARANTULA' was annoyingly deleted after one week, as BELL and GARDENER considered separate solo ventures. • **Songwriters:** Lyrics MARK or ANDY / group compositions except covers EIGHT MILES HIGH (Byrds) / THE MODEL (Kraftwerk) / HOW DOES IT FEEL TO FEEL (Creation) / THAT MAN (Small Faces) / UNION CITY BLUE + ATOMIC (Blondie). • **Trivia:** In 1991, they headlined the Slough Music Festival in front of over 8,000 fans.

Album rating: NOWHERE (*8) / GOING BLANK AGAIN (*7) / CARNIVAL OF LIGHT (*6) / TARANTULA (*6)

MARK GARDENER – vocals, guitar / **ANDY BELL** – guitar, vocals / **STEPHAN QUERALT** – bass / **LAURENCE COLBERT** – drums

		Creation	Sire
Jan 90.	(12"ep)(cd-ep) *(CRE 072T)(CRESCD 072)* **RIDE** – Chelsea girl / Drive blind / Close my eyes / All I can see. *(re-iss. Oct90; same)*	71	-
Apr 90.	(12"ep)(cd-ep) *(CRE 075T)(CRESCD 075)* **PLAY** – Like a daydream / Silver / Furthest sense / Perfect time.	32	-
Jun 90.	(m-cd,m-c) *<26390>* **SMILE** (first two EP's) *(UK-iss.Nov92; CRECD 126)*	-	
Oct 90.	(12"ep)(cd-ep) *(CRE 087T)(CRESCD 087)* **FALL** – Dreams burn down / Taste / Here and now / Nowhere.	34	-
Oct 90.	(cd/lp)(c) *(CRE CD/LP 74)(CREC 74) <26462>* **NOWHERE** – Seagull / Kaleidoscope / Polar bear / Dreams burn down / In a different place / Decay / Paralysed / Vapour trail. *(cd+=)* – Taste / Here and now / Nowhere.	11	Dec90
Jan 91.	(cd-ep) *<40055>* **VAPOUR TRAIL**	-	
Mar 91.	(c-ep)(12"ep)(cd-ep) *(CRECS 100)(CRE 100T)(CRESCD 100)* **TODAY FOREVER** – Unfamiliar / Sennen / Beneath / Today.	14	-
Feb 92.	(c-ep)(12"ep)(cd-ep) *(CRECS 123)(CRE 123T)(CRESCD 123)* *<40332>* **LEAVE THEM ALL BEHIND. / CHROME WAVES / GRASSHOPPER**	9	
Mar 92.	(cd/2x12"lp)(c) (CRE CD/LP 124)(CCRE 124) <26836> **GOING BLANK AGAIN** – Leave them all behind / Twisterella / Not fazed / Chrome waves / Mouse trap / Time of her life / Cool your boots / Making Jusy smile / Time machine / OX4.	5	
Apr 92.	(c-ep)(12"ep)(cd-ep) *(CRECS 150)(CRE 150T)(CRESCD 150)* *<40448>* **TWISTERELLA / GOING BLANK AGAIN. / HOWARD HUGHES / STAMPEDE**	36	

—— In Oct'93, 'Fright' records issued 'UNION CITY BLUE' *(FRIGHT 060) (re-iss. Apr97; same)*

Apr 94.	(12"ep/12"clear-ep)(cd-ep) *(CRE 155T/+C)(CRESCD 155)* **BIRDMAN / ROLLING THUNDER 2. / LET'S GET LOST / DON'T LET IT DIE**	38	-
Jun 94.	(7"/c-s) *(CRE/+MC 184)* **HOW DOES IT FEEL TO FEEL? / CHELSEA GIRL** (12")(cd-s) *(CRES 184T)(CRESCD 184)* – ('A'side) / Walkabout / At the end of the universe.	58	-
Jun 94.	(pic-cd/d-lp)(c) *(CRE CD/LP 147)(C-CRE 147) <45610>* **CARNIVAL OF LIGHT** – Moonlight medicine / 1000 miles / From time to time / Natural grace / Only now / Birdman / Crown of creation / How does it feel to feel? / Endless road / Magical spring / Rolling thunder / I don't know where it comes from.	5	
Sep 94.	(c-s) *(CRECS 189)* **I DON'T KNOW WHERE IT COMES FROM. / TWISTERELLA** (12")(cd-s) *(CRE 189T)(CRESCD 189)* – ('A'side) / Drive blind / From time to time / How does it feel to feel (live w / The CREATION). (cd-s) *(CRESCD 189R)* – ('A'-Apollo 11 mix) / Moonlight medicine (ride on the wire mix by Portishead) / A journey to the end of the universe (version).	46	-

—— split officially early '96. MARK citing ANDY's near takeover of vocal duties.

Feb 96.	(12"ep/cd-ep) *(CRE 199T)(CRESCD 199)* **BLACK NITE CRASH**	67	-
Mar 96.	(cd/lp)(c) *(CRE CD/LP 180)(CCRE 180) <61893>* **TARANTULA** – Black nite crash / Sunshine – Nowhere to run / Dead man / Walk on water / Deep inside my pocket / Mary Anne / Castle on the hill / Gonna be alright / Dawn patrol / Ride the wind / Burnin' / Starlight motel.	21	

—— above was only available for 1 week only

—— On the 30th of June '96, MARK GARDENER released his limited solo cd-single 'MAGDALEN SKY / CAN'T LET IT DIE (demo)' for Oxford-based 'Shifty Disco' *(DISCO 9706)*. *(re-iss. Jun97; same)*

– compilations, etc. –

Oct 95.	(cd,c) *Elektra; <61884>* **LIVE LIGHT (live)** – Seagull / Magical Spring / From time to time / Chelsea girl / Birdman / Only now / Leave them all behind / Let's get lost.	-	

RIFF RAFF (see under ⇒ BRAGG ,Billy)

Marc RILEY & The CREEPERS

Formed: Manchester, England . . . late 1982, by MARC RILEY after he was dismissed from The FALL by life and soul of any party, MARK E SMITH. Backed by The CREEPERS (who included PAUL FLETCHER, PETE KEOGH and EDDIE FENN), RILEY formed his own indie imprint, 'In-Tape' with Jim Khambatta. The outfit's first release, 'FAVOURITE SISTER', arrived the following summer, an unusual collision of angular FALL-esque rhythms, stripped-down VELVETS atmosphere and grim Northern vocals. A second 45, 'JUMPER CLOWN', hit the indie shops in a matter of months, a repetitive neo-rockabilly marathon complete with beat-up Wurlitzer organ and droning barbed lyrics (I wonder who about?). The equally sarcastic, chunky punkabilly of 'CURE BY CHOICE', featured on their next release, early '84's 'CREEPING AT MAIDA VALE' EP. A filler mini-compilation, 'CULL', was followed by the 'POLLYSTIFFS' single, prior to the release of their debut album proper, 'GROSS OUT' (1984). Boasting the surreal noisefest, 'EARWIG O'DOWD', alongside the crude 'GROSS' and their finest organ-grinding three minutes, 'TEACHER TRAVEL', the album nevertheless failed to generate much interest outside the independent scene. They ended quite a prolific year with a disappointing fifth single, 'SHADOW FIGURE', marking time until their second collection of goodies, 'FANCY MEETING GOD' (1985). Although again not a classic album (MARK E was making much more progress), it did however contain a couple of wee gems in 'HARRY'S CHIN' (another reference to the mysterious Harry O'Dowd!) and 'BUNKER'. Another busy year was capped by a second 'MAIDA VALE' EP (which included a snipe at PAUL WELLER in the shape of 'BARD OF WOKING') and a live album, 'WARTS 'N' ALL', the latter featuring a version of Eno's 'BABY'S ON FIRE'. Subsequently abbreviating the group's moniker to The CREEPERS, RILEY found some new recruits, namely MARK TILTON and PHIL ROBERTS, the new line-up's first album-length outing being 'MISERABLE SINNERS' (1986). Signing to 'Red Rhino', RILEY and Co released their sawnsong set, 'ROCK'N'ROLL LICORICE FLAVOUR', in 1988, sadly not a patch on their awkward but pioneering early work (The INSPIRAL CARPETS certainly took note!). After a brief spell as The LOST SOUL CRUSADERS, The CREEPERS finally split and RILEY went on to co-host a Radio One show with MARK RADCLIFFE. In 1997, the pair were the main men behind the DJ supergroup, The SHIREHORSES, who scored with a Top 30 album, 'THE WORST ALBUM IN THE WORLD EVER . . . EVER!'.

Album rating: CULL mini-compilation (*6) / GROSS OUT (*6) / FANCY MEETING GOD (*6) / WARTS 'N' ALL (*4) / MISERABLE SINNERS (*4) / ROCK'N'ROLL LICORICE FLAVOUR (*4) / SLEEPER compilation (*7)

MARC RILEY – vocals, keyboards (ex-FALL) / **PAUL FLETCHER** – guitar (of TOOLS YOU CAN TRUST) / **PETE KEOGH** – bass (of KISS THE BLADE) / **EDDIE FENN** – drums (of KISS THE BLADE, ex-CRAWLING CHAOS)

		In-Tape	not iss.
Jul 83.	(7") *(IT 001)* **FAVOURITE SISTER. / CARRY MI CARD (DAFT HEAD)**		-
Oct 83.	(7") *(IT 002)* **JUMPER CLOWN. / VIOLIN**		-
Feb 84.	(7"ep) *(IT 004)* **CREEPING AT MAIDA VALE** – Cure by choice / Baby paints / Blow / +1		-
Apr 84.	(m-lp) *(IT 005)* **CULL** (compilation)		-
May 84.	(7") *(IT 006)* **POLLYSTIFFS. / RAILROAD**		-
Jun 84.	(lp) *(IT 007)* **GROSS OUT** – Teacher travel / Freaky sleeper / Make Joe / Gross / Less speed / Earwig O'Dowd / etc.		-
Sep 84.	(12"m) *(IT 009)* **SHADOW FIGURE. / HOLE 4 A SOUL / SHIRT SCENE**		-
Mar 85.	(lp) *(IT 015)* **FANCY MEETING GOD** – Breakneck 1 / Bunker / Cocktail / Harry's chin / Judas sheep / Poop scoop / We don't say / Breakneck 2 / Snipe / etc.		-
Oct 85.	(d7"/12"ep) *(IT/+T 025)* **4 A's FROM MAIDA VALE** – Goin' rate / Bard of Woking / Black dwarf / +1		-
Nov 85.	(10"lp) *(IT 026)* **WARTS'N'ALL – LIVE IN AMSTERDAM (live)** – Breakneck 1 / Black dwarf / Pollystiffs / Jumper clown / Goin' rate / Gross / Baby's on fire / Hole 4 a soul / Bard of Woking / Shirt scene / Snipe / Make Joe / Baby paints / Cure by choice.		-

CREEPERS

—— **RILEY** recruited **MARK TILTON** – guitar (ex-MEMBRANES); repl. PAUL / **PHIL ROBERTS** – bass (ex-SHRUBS); repl. PETE who remained with KISS THE BLADE (one single issued, 'YOUNG SOLDIER, late '86 and an album, STATIC WAIL' in Apr'89 on 'Soft Cushion'; *KISS 223123)*

May 86.	(7"/12") *(IT/+T 033)* **BABY'S ON FIRE. / ANOTHER SONG ABOUT MOTOR BIKES**		-
Nov 86.	(lp/c) *(IT 039/+C)* **MISERABLE SINNERS**		-
		Red Rhino	not iss.
Jun 87.	(7"/12") *(RED/+T 079)* **BRUTE. / ?**		-
Jan 88.	(lp/c/cd) *(RED LP/C/CD 082)* **ROCK'N'ROLL LIQUORICE FLAVOUR**		-

—— disbanded just after they became The LOST SOUL CRUSADERS. RILEY now works as the character, LARD.

- compilations, etc. -

Jul 89. (d-lp) *Bleed;* **SLEEPER: A RETROSPECTIVE** ☐ ☐

Penny RIMBAUD (see under ⇒ CRASS)

RIOT SQUAD

Formed: Mansfield, England . . . 1982, comprising WAYNE BUTLER, PAUL PALMER and two unknown members (not to be confused with another outfit around the same time who released 'Total Onslaught' – in fact, the RIOT SQUAD moniker was used by a reasonably successful mod combo in the mid-60's). Anyway, these hardcore skins with protest oi/punk leanings were a different kettle of fish altogether. Defiant and anarchic from the outset, RIOT SQUAD unleashed two anti-establishment 45's in 1982, namely 'FUCK THE TORIES' and 'RIOT IN THE CITY', before WAYNE and PAUL enlisted two new recruits, LEE BUTLER and CHEDD. This line-up completed three further similarly provocative singles for their own 'Rot' label, the musical blind alley of subsequent album, 'NO POTENTIAL THREAT' (1984), arresting their progress as the band split.

Album rating: THE COMPLETE PUNK COLLECTION compilation (*4)

– vocals / – guitar / **WAYNE BUTLER** – bass / **PAUL PALMER** – drums

Rondelet not iss.

Aug 82. (7"m) *(ROUND 23)* **FUCK THE TORIES. / WE ARE THE RIOT SQUAD / CIVIL DESTRUCTION** ☐ -

Sep 82. (7"m) *(ROUND 25)* **RIOT IN THE CITY. / WHY SHOULD WE / RELIGION DOESN'T MEAN A THING** ☐ -

— **LEE BUTLER** – vocals; repl.

— **CHEDD** (b. PAUL) – bass; repl. (WAYNE now lead guitar)

Rot not iss.

Jun 83. (7"ep) *(ASS 1)* **DON'T BE DENIED** ☐ -
– Lost cause / Suspicion / Unite and fight / Police power.

Sep 83. (7"ep) *(ASS 2)* **I'M OK FUCK YOU** ☐ -
– Society's fodder / In the future / Friday night hero.

Jan 84. (7") *(ASS 3)* **THERE AIN'T NO SOLUTION. / GOVERNMENT SCHEME** ☐ -

Mar 84. (lp) *(ASS 13)* **NO POTENTIAL THREAT** ☐ -
– No potential threat / Ten years time / Hate the law / Hidden in fear / Lost cause (demo) / Unite and fight (demo).

— disbanded later in '84

- compilations, etc. -

Jan 95. (cd) *Anagram; (CDPUNK 41)* **THE COMPLETE PUNK COLLECTION** ☐ -

RIP, RIG + PANIC

Formed: Bristol, England . . . late 1980 by former POP GROUP cohorts GARETH SAGER and BRUCE SMITH, the pair taking their moniker from an album by avant-jazz man, ROLAND KIRK. SMITH's 16 year-old girlfriend, NENEH CHERRY (step-daughter of the veteran jazz trumpeter, DON CHERRY), took up the invitation to join the growing ensemble, as did MARK SPRINGER and SEAN OLIVER. Shaking up a colourful cocktail of improvised freeform jazz, African tribal sounds and schizophrenic New Wave funk/reggae, RIP, RIG + PANIC weren't exactly an easy listening experience although their dense virtuosity and skewed musical logic occasionally threw up moments of genius. Signed to 'Virgin' on the strength of their live reputation and top musical pedigree, the collective debuted in 1981 with the 'GOD' album (actually a double mini-set!). The record introduced the group's penchant for cryptically long-winded song titles, gracing tracks that suggested a meeting of The SLITS and PIGBAG and sung with scat-ish soulful aplomb by the sultry-voiced NENEH. However, the latter would take temporary maternity leave, returning to Sweden to have a baby; her replacement was ANDREA OLIVER, who would actually remain a part of the expanding ensemble when NEHEH was fit enough to resume her vocal duties. Her step-father, DON, would augment the group on their second set, 'I AM COLD' (1982), an album that featured their most accessible and well-known track, 'YOU'RE MY KIND OF CLIMATE', aired to the nation via the very first episode of cult TV sitcom, 'The Young Ones'. A final set, 'ATTITUDE' (1983), took the experimental format as far as it could go although most members bar the solo bound SPRINGER, re-grouped in the short-lived FLOAT UP CP in 1984. This metamorposised into the even more short-lived GOD, MOTHER & COUNTRY, as SAGER went off to form HEAD. NENEH, meanwhile, would go on to carve out her own highly successful solo career.

Album rating: GOD (*5) / I AM COLD (*5) / ATTITUDE (*6)

NENEH CHERRY (b. NENEH MARIANN KARLSSON, 10 Mar'64, Stockholm, Sweden) – vocals (ex-NAILS) / **GARETH SAGER** – guitar (ex-POP GROUP) / **SEAN OLIVER** – bass (ex-ESSENTIAL LOGIC) / **MARK SPRINGER** – piano, keyboards / **BRUCE SMITH** – drums (ex-POP GROUP) / guest **SIMON UNDERWOOD** – bass

Virgin not iss.

Aug 81. (7") *(VS 445)* **GO GO GO (THIS IS IT). / THE ULTIMATE IN FUN (IS GOING TO A DISCO WITH MY BABY)** ☐ -
(12"+=) *(VS 445-12)* – Let me move on the Gord.

Sep 81. (2xm-lp) *(V 2213)* **GOD** ☐ -
– Constant drudgery is harmful to soul, spirit and health / Wilhelm show me the diagram (function of the orgasm) / Thru' nomad eyeballs / Change your life / Knee deep in shit / Totally naked (without lock or key) / Try box out of this box / Need (de school you) / Howl! caged bird / Those Eskimo women speak frankly / The blue blue third / Shadows only there because of the sun / Beware (our leaders love the smell of napalm) / Miss Pib / It don't mean a thing if it ain't got that brod. *(re-iss. Aug88; OVED 118)*

Nov 81. (7"/ext-12") *(VS 468/+12)* **BOB HOPE TAKES RISKS. / HEY MR.E! A GRAN GRIN WITH A SHAKE OF SMILE** ☐ -

— **ANDREA OLIVER** – vocals (temp.) repl. & was added to expanding line-up (NENEH returned to Sweden to have her baby – maternity leave – she was back in line-up for subsequent releases)

— **STEVE NOBLE** – drums (also came in) / guest **DON CHERRY** – trumpet / others on long/short-term **SARAH SARAHANDI** – viola / **DAVID DE FRIES** – tenor sax / **JEZ PARFITT** – baritone sax / **GILES LEAMAN** – percussion / **DEBBIE** – cello / **ALPH WATT** – trombone / **LOUIS MAHALO** – percussion

Jun 82. (7") *(VS 507)* **YOU'RE MY KIND OF CLIMATE. / SHE GETS SO HUNGRY AT NIGHT** ☐ -
(12"+=) *(VS 507-12)* – She eats her jewellery.

Jun 82. (lp) *(V 2228)* **I AM COLD** 67 -
– Storm the reality asylum / Warm: to the if in life / Liars shape up or ship out / Epi epi arp woosh! / Nurse increase the sedatives (the torment's no better) / Take a donkey to mystery / Tax sex / Hunger (the ocean roars it bites) / You're my kind of climate / Here gathers nameless energy (volcanos covered by snow) / Misa Luba Lone Wolf. *(free 12"ep)* – Another tampon up the arse of humanity / A dog's secret / Subversive wisdom / Fire eyes joyful silent tears. *(re-iss. Aug88; OVED 119)*

Aug 82. (7") *(VS 533)* **STORM THE REALITY ASLYLUM. / LEAVE YOUR SPITTLE IN THE POT** ☐ -
(12"+=) *(VS 533-12)* – It's always tit for tat you foolish brats.

— added **DAVID WRIGHT** – saxophone

Mar 83. (7"/ext-12") *(VS 577)* **BEAT THE BEAST. / IN 1619, A DUTCH VESSEL DOCKED IN THE U.S.A. WITH 20 HUMANS FOR SALE** ☐ -

Apr 83. (lp) *(V 2268)* **ATTITUDE** ☐ -
– Keep the sharks from your heart / Sunken love / Rip open, But oh so long thy wounds take to heal / Do the tightrope / Intimacy, just gently shimmer / How that spark sets me aglow / Alchemy in the cemetry / Beat the beast / The birth pangs of Spring / Eros, what brings colour up the stem / Push your tiny body as high as your desire can take you / Viva x dreams. *(re-iss. Aug87 lp/c; OVED/+C 63)*

May 83. (7"/ext-12") *(VS 582/+12)* **DO THE TIGHTROPE. / BLIP THIS JIG IT'S SHANANIC** ☐ -

— they split later in the year, MARK SPRINGER went solo and released (in Feb'85) a solo lp, 'PIANO', for 'Illuminated' *(JAMS 46)*

- compilations, etc. -

Oct 90. (cd) *Virgin; (CDOVD 329)* **KNEE DEEP IN HITS** ☐ -
– You're my kind of climate / Storm the reality asylum / Sunken love / Warm: to the if in life / Go go go (this is it) / Keep the sharks from your heart / Miss Pib / Thru' nomad eyeballs / Do the tightrope / Beat the beast / The ultimate in fun (is going to the disco with my baby) / Alchemy in the cemetry / Bob Hope takes risks / The blue blue third.

FLOAT UP CP

— **SAGER, CHERRY, SMITH, OLIVER + SARAHANDI**

Rough Trade not iss.

Jul 84. (7"/12") *(RT/+T 150)* **JOY'S ADDRESS. / DESERT HEART** ☐ -

Oct 85. (lp) *(ROUGH 77)* **KILL ME IN THE MORNING** ☐ -
– Chemically wet / Forever party / Secret desire / He loves me (no no no) / etc

— they had already disbanded, SAGER forming rock-orientated, HEAD

GOD, MOTHER & COUNTRY

— aka **BRUCE SMITH, NENEH CHERRY + DAVID WRIGHT**

Kaz not iss.

Aug 85. (7"/12") *(KAZ 60/+T)* **FOOT ON THE ROCK. / ('A'dub)** ☐ -

— SMITH + CHERRY split up their relationship, the former joining PUBLIC IMAGE LTD. (among others), while the latter joined the short-lived KABBALA before hooking up with a new boyfriend, CAMERON McVEY, and venturing on a fruitful solo career

Brian RITCHIE (see under ⇒ VIOLENT FEMMES)

Tom ROBINSON

Born: 1st June'50, Cambridge, England. Sent to reform school as a lad, the young ROBINSON met guitarist DANNY KUSTOW and subsequently formed DAVANQ in the early 70's. Duly relocating to London, ROBINSON put together cabaret-folk outfit, CAFE SOCIETY, releasing an eponymous solo album on RAY DAVIES' (KINKS) 'Konk' label in 1974. Relations between the band and DAVIES soon soured, the project falling by the wayside as ROBINSON formed his own outfit, The TOM ROBINSON BAND. With a stable line-up cementing around KUSTOW, MARK AMBLER and DOLPHIN TAYLOR, the group were signed up by 'E.M.I.', immediately hitching a ride on the emerging punk juggernaut with stompalong classic, '2-4-6-8 MOTORWAY'. The track's UK Top 5 success was followed with the live EP, 'RISING FREE', ROBINSON's radical political manifesto introduced with the celebratory 'SING IF YOU'RE GLAD TO BE GAY' and the defiant 'DON'T TAKE NO FOR AN ANSWER'. Adopted by the music press as something of a new wave cause celebre, TRB, along with the likes of The CLASH, espoused a more positive strand of protest than the bleak nihilism of many punk acts, their anti-racist, pro-individual freedom stance represented by the clenched fist logo on debut album, 'POWER IN THE DARKNESS' (1978). Brimming with anthemic rallying cries for the disaffected yet rarely lapsing into laboured preaching, the album confirmed ROBINSON's credentials as an articulate spokesman for the punk generation. And it wasn't just empty rhetoric, ROBINSON putting his politics where his mouth was and playing a host of benefit gigs (chiefly anti-racism and gay/lesbian rights events) both at home and in the States where he was something of a minor hero on the college circuit. Following the departure of AMBLER and TAYLOR, however, ROBINSON struggled through a TODD RUNDGREN-produced follow-up set, 'TRB 2' (1979). Preceded by the flop PETER GABRIEL collaboration, 'BULLY FOR YOU', the album's bland sloganeering was met with a frosty critical reception and relatively poor sales (despite a UK Top 20 placing); the TOM ROBINSON BAND fell apart, its mainman subsequently suffering a nervous breakdown. Upon his recovery, the singer formed a new outfit, SECTOR 27, initiating his own label, 'Panic' and releasing an eponymous album in 1980. A more experimental post-punk affair, the album was well received but failed to sell and again, ROBINSON changed his plans. Moving to Hamburg, Germany in early '82, he cut his first solo album proper, 'NORTH BY NORTHWEST', another strong effort which found him developing a more conventional singer/songwriter style. This paid dividends the following year when 'WAR BABY' made the UK Top 10, its laidback, swinging sophistication contrasting with the three-chord assault of old. An equally classy follow-up, 'LISTEN TO THE RADIO: ATMOSPHERICS', just nudged into the Top 40 later that year, another collaboration with PETER GABRIEL. Together with a further minor hit in Steely Dan's 'RIKKI DON'T LOSE THAT NUMBER', the singles were included on the fine 1984 set, 'HOPE AND GLORY', ROBINSON's most successful album since the late 70's. 'STILL LOVING YOU' (1986) saw the man's muse become increasingly mellow as he entered fatherhood (it emerged that he was actually bi-sexual, not homosexual) although the album failed to match even its predecessor's limited success. Throughout the remainder of the 80's and on into the 90's, ROBINSON regularly performed with original members of TRB as well as touring, writing and recording as a solo artist. Featuring such disparate guests as CHRIS REA and T.V. SMITH, 1994's 'LOVE OVER RAGE' album boasted ROBINSON's most confident set of songs in almost a decade, proving that he didn't have to rely on mere nostalgia to make a living. • **Songwriters:** Most written by ROBINSON, except covers; RIKKI DON'T LOSE THAT NUMBER (Steely Dan) / etc?

Album rating: POWER IN THE DARKNESS (*8) / HOPE AND GLORY (*6)

TOM ROBINSON BAND

TOM ROBINSON – vocals, bass (ex-CAFE SOCIETY, ex-DAVANQ) / **DANNY KUSTOW** – guitar (ex-DAVANQ) / **MARK AMBLER** – keyboards repl. ANTON MAUVE, BRET SINCLAIR & MARK GRIFFITHS / **DOLPHIN TAYLOR** – drums, vocals repl. NICK TREVISICK (ex-CAFE SOCIETY)

E.M.I. / Harvest

Oct 77. (7") *(EMI 2715) <4533>* **2-4-6-8 MOTORWAY. / I SHALL BE RELEASED** 5

Feb 78. (7"ep) *(EMI 2749)* **RISING FREE (live)** 18 -
– Don't take no for an answer / Right on sister / Sing if you're glad to be gay / Martin.

May 78. (7") *(EMI EMI 2787)* **UP AGAINST THE WALL. / I'M ALRIGHT JACK** 33 -

May 78. (lp/c) *(EMC/TC-EMC 3226) <11778>* **POWER IN THE DARKNESS** 4
– Up against the wall / Grey Cortina / Too good to be true / Ain't gonna take it / Long hot summer / Winter of 79 / Man you never saw / Better decide which side you're on / You gotta survive / Power in the darkness / 2-4-6-8 Motorway. *(re-iss. Aug83 lp/c; EMS/TC-EMS 106668-1/-4) (re-iss. Oct94 on 'Cooking Vinyl' cd/c; COOK C/CD 076) (cd re-iss. Aug96 on 'Razor & Tie'; RE 2018)*

Aug 78. (7") *(EMI 2847)* **TOO GOOD TO BE TRUE. / POWER IN THE DARKNESS** -

Sep 78. (7") *<4568>* **RIGHT ON SISTER. / GLAD TO BE GAY** -

— (mid'78) **IAN PARKER** – keyboards repl. NICK PLYTAS (ex-ROOGALATOR) who had repl. AMBLER (Apr'78).

— (Dec78) **PRESTON HEYMAN** – drums (ex-BRAND X) repl. DOLPHIN who joined STIFF LITTLE FINGERS.

Mar 79. (7") *(EMI 2916) <4726>* **BULLY FOR YOU. / OUR PEOPLE** 68

Mar 79. (lp/c) *(EMC/TC-EMC 3296) <11930>* **TRB TWO** 18
– All right all night / Why should I mind / Black angel / Let my people be / Blue murder / Bully for you / Crossing over the road / Sorry Mr. Harris / Law and order / Days of rage / Hold out. *(re-iss. Aug83 lp/c; EMS/TC-EMS 165215-1/-4) (re-iss. Oct94 on 'Cooking Vinyl' cd/c; COOK CD/C 077) (cd re-iss. Aug96 on 'Razor & Tie'; RE 2019)*

May 79. (7"; w-drawn) *(EMI 2946)* **ALRIGHT ALL NIGHT. / BLACK ANGEL** -

— **CHARLIE MORGAN** – drums repl. the returning TREVISICK who had repl. HEYMAN. The latter joined KATE BUSH. **GEOFF SHARKEY** – guitar repl. KUSTOW / added **GRAHAM COLLIER** – double bass / **GEOFF DALY** – saxophone

Aug 79. (7"; TOM ROBINSON & THE VOICE SQUAD) *(EMI 2967)* **NEVER GONNA FALL IN LOVE (AGAIN). / GETTING TIGHTER** -

— Disbanded late summer '79. **TOM ROBINSON** now vocals, guitar went solo with back-up from SECTOR 27. **STEVE BLANCHARD** – guitar / **DEREK QUINTON** – drums / **JO BURT** – bass (recorded one withdrawn lp, 'SECTOR 27', on 'Regal Zonophone')

SECTOR 27

— were now given full billing.

Panic / not iss.

Jul 80. (7") *(SEC 27)* **NOT READY. / CAN'T KEEP AWAY** -

Oct 80. (7") *(SEC 28)* **INVITATION, WHAT HAVE WE GOT TO LOSE? / DUNGANNON** -

Fontana / I.R.S.

Nov 80. (lp) *(6359 039) <70013>* **SECTOR 27**
– Invitation / Not ready / Mary Lynne / Looking at you / 523 / Total recall / Where can we go tonight / Take it or leave it / Bitterly disappointed / One fine day.

Panic / not iss.

Jan 81. (7") *(SEC 29)* **TOTAL RECALL. / STORNOWAY** -

May 81. (7") *(SEC 30)* **MARTIN'S GONE. / CHRISTOPHER CALLING** -

TOM ROBINSON

— went solo again. (SECTOR 27 as a trio branched out on own). **TOM** added **STEVE LAURIE** – drums / **RICHARD MAZDA** – guitar, producer / etc

Panic / Geffen

Jun 82. (lp) **NORTH BY NORTHWEST**
– Now Martin's gone / Atmospherics / Can't keep away (part 2) / Looking for a bonfire / Merrily up on high / Those days / In the cold / The night tide / Dungannon / Love comes. *(re-iss. 1986 on 'Castle' lp/c/cd; CLA LP/MC/CD 128)*

Jul 82. (7") *(NIC 1)* **NOW MARTIN'S GONE. / ATMOSPHERICS** -
(re-iss. Feb83 as 5-track-12"ep; NIC 1-12) – ATMOSPHERICS

Jun 83. (7") *(NIC 2)* **WAR BABY. / HELL YES** 6 Sep84
(12"+=) *(NIC 2-12)* – Martin's gone (original).

Nov 83. (7") *(NIC 3)* **LISTEN TO THE RADIO: ATMOSPHERICS. / DON'T DO ME ANY FAVOURS** 39
(12"+=) *(NIC 3-12)* – Out to lunch.

Castaway-RCA / Geffen

Jun 84. (7") *(TR 1)* **BACK IN THE OLD COUNTRY. / BEGGIN'**
(12"+=) *(TRT 1)* – ('A'live version).

Sep 84. (7"/12") *(TR/+T 2)* **RIKKI DON'T LOSE THAT NUMBER. / CABIN BOY (live)** 58 -

Sep 84. (lp/c) *(ZL/ZK 70483)* **HOPE AND GLORY** 21
– War baby / Atmospherics: Listen to the radio / Cabin boy / Blond and blue / Hope and glory / Murder at the end of the day / Prison / Rikki don't lose that number / Old friend / Looking for a bonfire.

May 85. (7"/12") *(ZB/ZT 400 19/20)* **PRISON. / MORE LIVES THAN ONE** -

— TOM brought back **BLANCHARD + BURT** plus **RED** – drums

Jul 86. (7") *(TR 3)* **(IT AIN'T NOTHIN' LIKE) THE REAL THING. / THE WEDDING** -
(12"+=) *(TRT 3)* – ('A'extended).

Sep 86. (lp/c/cd) *(ZL/ZK/ZD 71129)* **STILL LOVING YOU**
– Feels so good – Hurt so bad / (It ain't nothin' like) The real thing / Still loving you / Take me home again / You tattooed me / Drive all night / Living in a love town / Spain / This little romance / The wedding.

Sep 86. (7"/12") *(TR/+T 4)* **STILL LOVING YOU. / THE SATURDAY DISCO** -

Jan 87. (7"; TOM ROBINSON & KIKI DEE) *(TR 5)* **FEELS SO GOOD. / NORTHERN RAIN** -
(12"+=) *(TRT 5)* – You tattooed me / Change.

Jun 87. (7") *(ZB 41333)* **SPAIN. / DRIVE ALL NIGHT** -
(12"+=) *(ZT 41333)* – (It ain't nothin' like) The real thing.

Musidisc / not iss.

Oct 90. (cd/c/lp; TOM ROBINSON & JAKKO M. JAKSYSK) *(10666-2/-4/-1)* **WE NEVER HAD IT SO GOOD** -
– We never had it so good / Drinking through the desert / Blood brother / What have I ever done to you / The baby rages on / Tomboy / Kiss and roll over / Hard cases / Can't stop: Peter's theme / My own sweet way.

Nov 90. (7") **BLOOD BROTHER. / ('A'version)** -
(12"+=) – What have I ever done to you / Rigging.

Cooking Vinyl / Scarface

Sep 92. (lp/c/cd) *(COOK/+C/CD 052)* **LIVING IN A BOOM TIME** -
– Folk song (intro) / Living in a boom time / More lives than one / Yuppie scum / My own sweet way / Castle island / Digging it up / The Brits / War baby / Back in the old country. *(re-iss. Mar94 cd/c; same)*

Jan 93. (c-ep/cd-ep) *()* **WAR BABY. / BLOOD BROTHER / WE DIDN'T KNOW WHAT WAS GOING ON / WAR BABY** -

— now w / **ROBIN MILLAR** – rhythm guitar / **CHRIS REA** – slide guitar / **MARK AMBLER** – keyboards / **WINSTON BLISSETT** – bass / **MARTIN DITCHAM** – drums / **MARK RAMSDEN** – saxophone / **T.V.SMITH + ANDY MITCHELL** – backing vocals

May 94. (lp/c/cd) *(COOK/+C/CD 066) <53913>* **LOVE OVER RAGE**
– Roaring / Hard / Loved / Days / Driving / Green / DDR / Fifty / Silence / Chance.

Jun 94. (cd-ep) *(FRYCD 028)* **HARD / GREEN / LIVING IN A BOOM TIME / PORTOBELLO TERRACE** -

Jul 94. (cd-ep) *(FRYCD 029)* **LOVED / FIFTY / YUPPY SCUM / GLAD TO BE GAY '94** -

Sep 94. (cd-ep) *(FRYCD 031)* **DAYS (THAT CHANGED THE WORLD) / ROARING / THE BRITS COME ROLLING BACK** -

Jul 96. (cd-ep) *(FRYCD 050)* **CONNECTICUT / DISRESPECT / RUM THUNDERBIRD / CONNECTICUT (mix)** -

– compilations, etc. –

Dec 81. (lp) *E.M.I.; (EMS 1005)* **TOM ROBINSON BAND** -
(re-iss. May82 on 'Fame'; FA 3028)

Nov 82. (lp) *Panic; (ROBBO 2)* **CABARET '79 (live)** -

Oct 83. (7") *Old Gold; (OG 9379)* **2-4-6-8 MOTORWAY. / DON'T TAKE NO FOR AN ANSWER** -

Apr 87. (lp/c; TOM ROBINSON & THE CREW) *Dojo; (DOJO LP/CD 51)* **MIDNIGHT AT THE FRINGE (live)** -

Sep 87. (7") *E.M.I.; (EM 28)* **2-4-6-8 MOTORWAY (live). / ('A'original)** -
(12"+=) *(12EM 28)* – Sing if you're glad to be gay.

Sep 87. (cd/c/lp) *E.M.I.; (CD/TC+/EMC 3540)* **COLLECTION 77-87** [ ] [-]
Mar 89. (lp/cd) *Line; (MS LP4/CD9.00695)* **GLAD TO BE GAY CABARET** [ ] [-]
Jun 89. (cd) *Line; (LICD 9.005888)* **LAST TANGO** [ ] [-]
Oct 89. (d-lp/c/cd) *Connoisseur; (VSOP LP/MC/CD 138)* **BACK IN THE OLD COUNTRY** [ ] [-]
– Listen to the radio: Atmospherics / Too good to be true / Up against the wall / Northern rain / I shall be released / 2-4-6-8 motorway / Drive all night / Don't take no for an answer / Where can we go tonight / Back in the old country / Alright all night / War baby / Power in the darkness / Crossing over the road / Rikki don't lose that number / Looking for a bonfire / Hard cases / Still loving you / Not ready / Bully for you / Long hot summer. *(d-lp/c+=)* – Mary Lynne / Bitterly disappointed.
Jun 92. (d-cd) *Line; (LICD 921215)* **GLAD TO BE GAY / LAST TANGO** [ ] [-]
(re-iss. Aug95; same)
Aug 92. (cd) *Pop Almanac; (PACD 7005)* **WINTER OF '89** [ ] [-]
Jun 93. (cd/c) *Optima; (OPTM CD/C 012)* **TOM ROBINSON** [ ] [-]
Jul 94. (cd) *Music De-Luxe; (MSCD 6)* **MOTORWAY** [ ] [-]

R.O.C.

Formed: London, England . . . 1983 by PATRICK NICHOLSON and FRED BROWNING, the pair really getting underway musical after the addition of American singer KAREN SHERIDAN. Issued on the band's own 'Little Star' label, 'DEAD STEP' combined sampled answerphone messages with a lazy, hazy dub beat while follow-up, 'GOD WILLING', took spook-ambient to scary new frontiers. Early '94 got off to a rather "oo-er missus" start with the release of the darkly sensual/humerous 'WHITE STAINS', surely the best masturbation ode since The BUZZCOCKS' 'Orgasm Addict'. Following a further two singles, 'X-INE' and 'GIRL WITH A CROOKED EYE', R.O.C. (Reincarnation Of Christ) signed to Keith Cullen's 'Setanta' label and issued their breathily anticipated eponymous debut album in '96. Taking in a determinedly eclectic array of musical reference points and ranging from the aforementioned 'GOD . . .' to the positively upbeat, pseudo-bubblegum pop of subsequent single, 'HEY YOU CHICK', the album was characterised by SHERIDAN's insinuating vocals and barbed lyrics. Bizarre, compelling stuff, a sound that 'Virgin' decided they could bring to a wider audience. Following the addition of fourth member, GARETH HUW DAVIES, the group previewed their new album, 'VIRGIN' (1997) with '(DIS)COUNT US IN', a brace of dance mixes with something for everyone, even a Black Panthers sample.

Album rating: R.O.C. (*6) / VIRGIN (*6)

KAREN SHERIDAN (b. Denver, Colorado, USA) – vocals / **FRED BROWNING** – guitars / **PATRICK NICHOLSON** – samples, etc.

Little Star — not iss.

Feb 94. (12"ep/cd-ep) *(STAR 3/+CD)* **CAIRO / DEAD SEA. / WHITE STAINS / KIRSTI** [ ] [-]
Jul 94. (12"ep/cd-ep) *(STAR 4/+CD)* **X-INE (CHRIST FORSWORN) / COLE CHILL ON CALI. / EVERYTHING'S FINE NOW / DIRT ENTERS AT THE HEART** [ ] [-]
Sep 94. (12"ep/cd-ep) *(STAR 5/+CD)* **GIRL WITH A CROOKED EYE. /** [ ] [-]
—— added **GARETH HUW DAVIES** – bass

Setanta — Bar/None

Jan 96. (cd/c) *(SET CD/MC 22) <71>* **R.O.C.** [ ] [ ] May96
– "Desert wind" / Excised / God willing / Hey you chick / Balloon / Real time / Plastic Jesus / I want you I need you I miss you / Gold bug / La heredia / Thirteen summers / Dear Nicky / Sylvia's thighs / Ascension / Clouds / Old man.

Virgin — not iss.

Sep 96. (12"/cd-s) *(VST/VSCDT 1608)* **HEY YOU CHICK. / HEY YOU CHICK (remix) / SILVER LINING** [ ] [-]
Mar 97. (12"/cd-s) *(VST/VSCDT 1620)* **CHERYL. /** [ ] [-]
Aug 97. (12"/cd-s) *(VST/VSCDT 1644)* **(DIS)COUNT US IN (Nicky Holt remix) / ('A'edit). / ('A'-Atlas remix) / ('A'-ROC in France)** [ ] [-]
Sep 97. (cd/c) *(CDV/TCV 2829)* **VIRGIN** [ ] [-]
– Dada / (Dis)count us in / Mountain / Cheryl / Corner off / Dead pool / Ever since yesterday / 25 reasons to leave me / K.C. / Cold chill just lately / Said what I said / Ocean and England.

ROCKET FROM THE CRYPT

Formed: San Diego, California, USA . . . 1989 by half-Portuguese singer, SPEEDO (JOHN REIS), alongside PETEY X, ATOM, JC 2000 and ND. REIS left school and joined PITCHFORK, a hardcore band who rapidly evolved into DRIVE LIKE JEHU (other members of this outfit being RICK FROBERG, MIKE KENNEDY and MARK TROMBINO), the frontman continuing to moonlight for the latter outfit through his early career with the 'CRYPT. Kick-ass speedball R&R punks/greasers drawing on the earthiest of 50's tradition, ROCKET FROM THE CRYPT were as suave as Vegas-era ELVIS with the attitude and sound of their heroes, The MISFITS (who they initially supported). In a further bid to boost their street cred, RFTC also claimed to have opened for two of the most legendary figures in black music, JAMES BROWN and SUN RA. On the recording front, the lads issued a plethora of singles for various hip US underground labels (the tracks were later collected together for UK consumption as 'ALL SYSTEMS GO!'), along the way releasing a debut album, 'PAINT AS A FRAGRANCE' (1991) and picking up sax player, APOLLO NINE. They unearthed a second album, 'CIRCA: NOW!', a year later and although the ROCKET-fuelled formula varied little, there was an audible improvement in the musicianship. While their mid-90's release schedule was as prolific as ever, they finally settled on a long-term deal with 'Interscope' ('El-e-mental' in the UK) in 1995. Towards the end of that year, they finally made their critical breakthrough on the UK alt-rock scene with the 'SCREAM, DRACULA, SCREAM!' album. It also lent them a modicum of commercial success scraping into the UK Top 40 and spawning no less than three hit singles, the last of which, 'ON A ROPE', found them threatening the Top 10. In the best tradtion of the DEAD BOYS or the SAINTS, however, ROCKET FROM THE CRYPT were in their element on stage blasting out their visceral, three-chord mainline rock'n'roll, NME recognising their talent by bestowing upon them a Brat Award for Best Newcomer. In the summer of '98, the slicked-back six-piece resurfaced with their second major label album, 'RFTC', a slightly subdued, more pop/rock-orientated affair that only just scraped into the UK Top 75. • **Songwriters:** Group, except GOLD (MC5). • **Trivia:** SPEEDO recently married ND's sister.

Album rating: ALL SYSTEMS GO compilation (*7) / SCREAM, DRACULA, SCREAM! (*8) / RFTC (*6)

SPEEDO (b. JOHN REIS) – vocals, guitar / **ND** (aka ANDY) – guitar / **PETEY X** – bass, bass vocals / **ATOM** (aka ADAM) – drums / **JC 2000** (aka JAY) – trumpet, percussion, organ, vocals

not iss. — Pushead

1990. exist? (7"red) *<200772>* **CUT IT LOOSE. / GLAZED** [-] [ ]

Helter Skelter — not iss.

1991. (7"ep) *<HS 92712>* **YUM KIPPERED EP** [-] [-] Italian
– Bad Ninja / Goodbye / Kill the funk (there will be no funk in Outer Space). *(UK-iss.Apr95 c-s/cd-s; same)*

not iss. — Headhunter

Feb 91. (lp/c/cd) *<HED 003/+MC/CD>* **PAINT AS A FRAGRANCE** [-] [ ]
– French guy / Maybellene / Shy boy / Basturds / Velvet touch / Evil party / Stinker / Jiggy jig / Weak superhero / Thumbmaster. *(cd-iss. Mar93; same +UK)*
—— added **APOLLO NINE** (aka PAUL) – saxophone, vocals

not iss. — Sympathy F

Jun 92. (7"m) *<SFTRI 179>* **BOY CHUCKER. / JUMPER K. BALLS / LEFTY** [-] [ ]

not iss. — Sub Pop

Jun 92. (7"blue-ep) *<SP 154>* **NORMAL CARPET RIDE / WHERE ARE THE FUCKERS. / SLUMBER QUEEN / FLIP THE BIRD** [-] [ ]

not iss. — Drunken Fish

Jul 92. (one-sided-7"gold) *<DF 02>* **GOLD** [-] [ ]

not iss. — Standard

Oct 92. (7") *<SR 72>* **CHA CHA CHA. / (other track by DEADBOLT)** [-] [ ]

not iss. — Merge

Nov 92. (7") *<MRG 035>* **PIGEON EATER. / (THE) PASTE THAT YOU LOVE** [-] [ ]

not iss. — Pussheads

Dec 92. (d7") **PUSS MORT. / (other by SEPTIC DEATH)** [-] [ ]

Headhunter — Headhunter

Jan 93. (lp/c/cd) *<(HED 015/+MC/CD)>* **CIRCA: NOW!** [ ] [ ] Nov92
– Short lip fuser / Hippy dippy do / Ditch digger / Don't Darlene / Killy kill / Hairball alley / Sturdy wrists / March of dimes / Little arm / Dollar / Glazed.

not iss. — Drunken Fish

Apr 93. (7",7"clear) *<DF 05>* **PURE GENIUS. / LIFT AND LOVE** [-] [ ]

not iss. — Merge

Feb 94. (12") *<1994>* **BURNT MOUTH OFF LIAR. / UFO UFO UFO** [-] [ ]

Bacteria Sour — not iss.

May 94. (7") *(SOUR 2V/3V)* **BLOODY THIRSTY BUTCHERS. /** [ ] [ ]

not iss. — Sympathy F

1995. (10"ep) *<SFTRI 320>* **THE STATE OF THE ART IS ON FIRE** [-] [ ]
– Light me / A+ in arson class / Rid or ride / Human torch / Ratsize / Human spine / Trouble / Masculine intuition.

El-e-mental — Interscope

Oct 95. (m-lp) *(ELM 27LP) <92595>* **HOT CHARITY** [ ] [ ] Aug95
– Pushed / Guilt free / Poison eye / My arrow's aim / Feathered friends / Cloud over Branson / Lorna Doom / Shucks / Pity yr paws.
Dec 95. (cd/c)<lp> *(ELM 34 CD/MC) <92596-2/-4><Hed 54>* **SCREAM, DRACULA, SCREAM!** [40] [ ] Oct95
– Middle / Born in '69 / On a rope / Young livers / Drop out / Used / Ball lightning / Fat lip / Suit city / Heater hands / Misbeaten / Come see, come saw / Salt future / Burnt alive.

El-e-mental — Interscope

Jan 96. (7"/cd-s) *(ELM 32 S/CD)* **BORN IN '69. / CIAO PATSY** [68] [-]
Apr 96. (7"/c-s) *(ELM 33 S/MC)* **YOUNG LIVERS. / BURNING ARMY MEN** [67] [-]
(cd-s+=) *(ELM 33CD)* – Lumps.
Sep 96. (cd-ep) *(ELM 38CD1)* **ON A ROPE / ALONE / WHO NEEDS YOU / YOUNG LIVERS (Mark Radcliffe session)** [12] [-]
(cd-ep) *(ELM 38CD2)* – ('A'-White Room version) / Allergic reaction / Transcendent crankiness / Suit city (Mark Radcliffe session).
(cd-ep) *(ELM 38CD3)* – ('A'-Ghetto box mix) / You and I / Intro – Don't Darlene (Mark Radcliffe session) / Lorna Doom (Mark Radcliffe session).
Nov 96. (7"ep) *(SFTRI 373)* **PLAYS THE MUSIC MACHINE EP** [ ] [ ] Oct96
(above on 'Sympathy For The Record Industry' / 'Kill Rock Stars' US)
Jun 98. (10"pic-d-ep) *(ELM 47TPIC)* **WHEN IN ROME (DO THE JERK). / TARZAN / TIGER FEET TONITE** [ ] [-]
Jul 98. (cd/c/lp) *(ELM 50 CD/MC/LP) <90167>* **RFTC** [63] [ ] Jun98
– Eye on you (with HOLLY GOLIGHTLY) / Break it up / I know / Panic scam / Made for you / Lipstick / You gotta move / Your touch / Let's get busy / Dick on a dog / Back in the state / When in Rome / Run kid run. *(also ltd-cd; ELM 50CDQ)*
Aug 98. (10") *(ELM 48TEN)* **LIPSTICK. / HOT HEART** [64] [-]
(cd-s) *(ELM 48CDS1)* – ('A'side) / Heads are gonna roll / When in Rome.
(cd-s) *(ELM 48CD2)* – ('A'side) / Raped by ape / Stranglehold.
—— In Oct'98, the group were on a split 7" with JULIAN Y SUS HERMANOIS for 'Vinyl Communication' (VC 76)
Nov 98. (7") *(ELM 49S)* **BREAK IT UP. / TURKISH REVENGE** [ ] [-]
(cd-s+=) *(ELM 49CDS1)* – Crack attack.
(cd-s) *(ELM 49CDS2)* – ('A'side) / U.S. Army / Raped by ape.

– compilations, etc. –

Dec 93. (lp/cd) *Sympathy For The Record Industry; (SFTRI 558/+CD) / Hedhunter; <Hed 023>* **ALL SYSTEMS GO**
– Live the funk / Bad song Ninja / Goodbye / Boy chucker / Jumper K. balls / Lefty / Normal carpet ride / Where are the fuckers / Slumber queen / Flip the bird / Cha cha cha / Pressure's on / Pigeon eater / (The) Paste that you love / Pure genius / Lift and love / Press darlings / Filly fill again / Chantilly face. *(cd re-iss. Dec98; same)*

DRIVE LIKE JEHU

JOHN REIS – guitar / **RICK FROBERG** – vocals, guitar / **MIKE KENNEDY** – bass / **MARK TROMBINO** – drums

not iss. Merge

1992. (7") *<MRG 023>* **HAND OVER FIST. / BULLET TRAIN TO VEGAS** [-] [ ]

Headhunter Headhunter

Jan 93. (lp/cd) *<(HED/+CD 008)>* **DRIVE LIKE JEHU** [ ] [ ] Dec91
– Caress / Spikes to you / Step on chameleon / O pencil sharp / Atom Jack / If it kills you / Good luck in jail / Turn it off / Future home of Stucco monstrosity.

El-e-mental Cargo

May 94. (cd) *(ELM 22CD) <EFA 17690-2>* **YANK CRIME** [ ] [ ]
– Here come the Rome plows / Do you compute / Golden brown / Luau / Super unison / New intro / New math / Human interest / Sinews. *(lp-iss.Aug94 on 'Cargo'; HED 037)*

ROCKET FROM THE TOMBS (see under ⇒ PERE UBU)

ROCKINGBIRDS

Formed: Camden, London, England . . . 1990 by former squatters, ALAN TYLOR, ANDY HACKETT, PATRICK ARBUTHNOT, SHAUN REID, DAVE GOLDING and former WEATHER PROPHETS drummer, DAVE MORGAN. The ROCKINGBIRDS soon signed on the dotted line for Jeff Barrett's 'Heavenly', the label releasing their debut, 'A GOOD DAY FOR YOU IS A GOOD DAY FOR ME', the following year. Its B-side, the harmony-happy 'JONATHAN, JONATHAN' (a tribute to that RICHMAN bloke), was later used as a follow-up in its own right in 1992, previewing the eponymous, CLIVE LANGER-produced debut album. Shouldered with the nigh on impossible task of rehabilitating country for the younger generation, the album was an enjoyable enough saunter down the dusty paths once trod by GRAM PARSONS, GENE CLARK, etc. That year, they also took part in the Cambridge Folk Festival, even venturing out to the country heartland of Texas to promote themselves as part of their Stateside deal with 'Sony'. Sadly, the indie scene wasn't ready to don their cowboy shirts just yet and bar a one-off V/A charity single – upon which they had to perform a version of Right Said Fred's 'DEEPLY DIPPY' – they failed to chart, subsequent EP's, 'FURTHER DOWN THE LINE' and 'ROCKINGBIRDS 'R' US', selling poorly. With GOLDING now moving on, the Camden country-rockers returned in '95 on 'Cooking Vinyl' with a belated EDWYN COLLINS-produced follow-up set, 'WHATEVER HAPPENED TO THE ROCKINGBIRDS'. Exactly. • **Covered:** YOUR GOOD GIRL'S GONNA GO BAD (Tammy Wynette) / IN TALL BUILDINGS (John Hartford) / OLDER GUYS (Parsons – Hillman) / etc.

Album rating: THE ROCKINGBIRDS (*6)

ALAN TYLOR – vocals, guitar / **ANDY HACKETT** – guitar / **PATRICK ARBUTHNOT** – pedal steel guitar / **DAVE GOLDING** – bass / **SHAUN REID** – percussion, vocals / **DAVE MORGAN** – drums (ex-LOFT)

Heavenly Sony

Sep 91. (7") **A GOOD DAY FOR YOU IS A GOOD DAY FOR ME. / JONATHAN, JONATHAN** [ ] [-]
(12"+=/cd-s+=) – Only one flower.

— (In Nov'91, with LESLIE SILVERFISH on vox, they released a single for 'Clawfist'; 'YOUR GOOD GIRL'S GONNA GO BAD')

May 92. (7") **JONATHAN, JONATHAN. / TIME DRIVES THE TRUCK** [ ] [-]
(12"+=/cd-s+=) – Older guys.
Jul 92. (cd/c/lp) **THE ROCKINGBIRDS** [ ] [ ]
Aug 92. (7") **GRADUALLY LEARNING. / WHERE I BELONG** [ ] [-]
(12"+=) – Love has gone and made a mess of me.

— (In Nov'92, with other 'Heavenly' acts, they released their version of 'DEEPLY DIPPY' on 'FRED EP' *(HVN 19) (hit UK No.26)*

Feb 93. (cd-ep) *(HVN 027CD)* **FURTHER DOWN THE LINE. /** [ ] [ ]
Jul 93. (12"ep/cd-ep) *(HVN 031-12/-CD)* **ROCKINGBIRDS 'R' US: THE HEAVENLY EP** [ ] [-]
– Gladys . . . / I'm a little less lonely / It won't be long / Harden up your heart.
Oct 94. (7") *(HVN 043)* **BAND OF DREAMS. / EVERYBODY LIVES WITH US** [ ] [-]

— now without GOLDING

Cooking Vinyl not iss.

Apr 95. (lp/cd) *(COOK 084/+CD)* **WHATEVER HAPPENED TO THE ROCKINGBIRDS** [ ] [ ]
– Roll on forever / I like winter / Everybody lives with us / Band of dreams / We had it all / I woke up one morning / The high part / Bitter tear / Before we go to the end / Hell / Let me down slow.

— they disbanded after above

ROLLERSKATE SKINNY

Formed: Dublin, Ireland . . . early 90's by brothers KEN and GER GRIFFIN, together with JIMI SHIELDS (younger sibling of MY BLOODY VALENTINE's mainman, KEVIN SHIELDS) and STEVIE M. The lads subsequently set up home in Marble Arch/Wandsworth, London in 1992, making a name for themselves with the self-financed 'NOVICE' EP early the following year. Its 10-minute lead track, 'COMPLACENCY', was an ambitious beginning, suggesting they'd been listening to the awkward avant-noise of MERCURY REV or MY BLOODY VALENTINE. Beggars Banquet offshoot, 'Placebo' (also home of COME), were shrewd enough to pick them up, releasing a second 10" EP the following Spring, 'TROPHY'. Slightly less ferocious, the lead track, 'BOW-HITCH-HIKER', signalled a move towards a slightly more restrained PAVEMENT-style approach. This mapped out the sonic territory the band would explore throughout the subsequent debut album, 'SHOULDER VOICES' (1993) and EP, 'THRESHOLD'. The following year, ROLLERSKATE SKINNY actually supported spiritual cousins, PAVEMENT, on that summer's 'Lollapalooza' jaunt, the resulting upsurge in media coverage helping them find a home at 'Warners'. Complete with new drummer, CLIVE CARROLL (replacing JIMI), they finally unveiled their new material in the shape of early 1996's 'HORSE DRAWN WISHES'.

Album rating: SHOULDER VOICES (*6) / HORSE DRAWN WISHES (*6)

KEN GRIFFIN – vocals (also keyboards) / **GER GRIFFIN** – guitar / **JIMI SHIELDS** – guitar, drums (also vocals, keyboards) / **STEVIE M** – bass (also guitar, keyboards)

Showbiz not iss.

Sep 92. (10"ep) *(RSS 001)* **NOVICE** [ ] [-]
– Complacency / etc.

Placebo Beggars Banquet

Apr 93. (10"ep) *(PILL 5)* **TROPHY** [ ] [-]
– Bow-hitch-hiker / Violence to violence / Trophy.
Oct 93. (cd/lp) *(PILL CD/A 3) <92325-2/-4>* **SHOULDER VOICES** [ ] [ ] Feb94
– Miss leader / Violence to violence / Lunasa / Bring on stgmata / Bella / Ages / Bow hitch-hiker / Some give birth / Shallow thunder / Slave / So far down up to Heaven.
Feb 94. (10"ep/cd-ep) *(PILL 9/+CD)* **"THRESHOLD" – ACCEPT MORALITY . . . . . . (& FREEDOM IS YOUR BONE)** [ ] [-]
– Miss leader / Entropy / Goodbye balloon.

— **CLIVE CARROLL** – drums; repl. JIMI

WEA Warners

Feb 96. (cd/c) *(<9362 45943-2/-4>)* **HORSE DRAWN WISHES** [ ] [ ]
– Swing boat yawning / Cradle burns / One thousand couples / Swab the temples / Speed to my side / All morning break / Man under glass / Shimmer son like a star / Angela starling / Ribbon fat / Thirsty European / Bells jar away.
May 96. (c-s) *(W 0349C)* **SPEED TO MY SIDE / GOOD NIGHT DIAMOND** [ ] [ ]
(12"+=/cd-s+=) *(W 0349 T/CD)* – Trial of witness.

— disbanded after above

Henry ROLLINS

Born: HENRY GARFIELD, 13 Feb '61, Washington DC, USA. After cutting his teeth in the 'straight edge' (militantly clean living) hardcore punk scene of the late 70's, ROLLINS made his name with the seminal BLACK FLAG. Recruited in time for their 'DAMAGED' (1981) opus, ROLLINS added a manic intensity to the brilliant 'SIX PACK' as well as new numbers like 'LIFE OF PAIN' and the title track. So extreme was the record that MCA's top man, Al Bergamo, tried to block the record's release even though thousands of copies had already been pressed. ROLLINS honed his writing and performing talents over a further series of albums, eventually going solo after the release of 'LOOSE NUT' (1985). 'HOT ANIMAL MACHINE' (1987) was a crudely visceral debut, ROLLINS indicating that, if anything, his solo career was going to be even more uncompromising than his work with BLACK FLAG. Later the same year, the singer released the mini album, 'DRIVE BY SHOOTING' under the pseudonym, HENRIETTA COLLINS AND THE WIFE-BEATING CHILD HATERS, a taste of ROLLINS' particularly tart brand of black humour. By 1988, The ROLLINS BAND line-up had solidified around guitarist CHRIS HASKETT (who'd played on the earlier releases), bassist ANDREW WEISS and drummer SIMON CAIN, releasing the IAN MACKAYE (of hardcore gurus, FUGAZI)-produced 'LIFE TIME' (1988) album later that year. An incendiary opus, the record was The ROLLINS BAND blueprint, setting the agenda for future releases with a lyrical incisiveness and musical ferocity that would be hard to equal. Following a slot on the hugely successful 1991 Lollapalooza tour, The ROLLINS BAND moved from cult status to a major label deal with 'Imago/RCA', releasing 'THE END OF SILENCE' in early '92. Fiercely self-analytic, ROLLINS had always used the stage and the rock medium, to a certain extent, as a kind of therapy, dredging up his childhood demons and tackling them head on. With ' . . ..SILENCE', ROLLINS had penned his most introspective work to date, leaving no stone unturned. The fact that he'd had seen his best friend, Joe Cole, gunned down in cold blood had obviously deeply affected the singer and subsequently the material on the album. This intensely personal exorcism is what made ROLLINS' shows so damn compelling; for ROLLINS, this was far and beyond mere entertainment, for the most part at least, and this was no doubt a major contributing factor in the band's constant live work. As well as a punishing regime of physical exercise, ROLLINS found time to run his own publishing company, 2.13.61 (showcasing work of underground authors as well as ROLLINS' own material, including his acclaimed collection of short stories, 'Black Coffee Blues') and tour his darkly observant, often hilarious and ultimately inspiring spoken word sets. A choice selection of the latter were included on the double-set, 'BOXED LIFE' (1993). The ROLLINS BAND, meanwhile, returned in 1994 with 'WEIGHT', their most commercially successful set to date, and a record which finally made inroads into the UK market, almost making the Top 20. Musically, the album was more accessible than its predecessor, firmly establishing ROLLIN's & Co. as 'alternative rock' heavyweights. More recently, ROLLINS has expanded his jack-of-all-trades CV with another burst of acting (he'd made his onscreen debut alongside LYDIA LUNCH in 1991's 'Kiss Napoleon Goodbye'), appearing in 'The Chase' and 'Johnny Mnemonic' as well as scoring a cameo in the much heralded De Niro/Pacino face-off, 'Heat'. In mid '96, ROLLINS was the subject of a lawsuit (an 8-figure sum) by Imago for allegedly signing with 'Dreamworks' while under contract, the singer claiming he was let go by the major distributors of the label, 'B.M.G.'. Despite all this, the singer returned to the fray in 1997 with a new album, 'COME IN AND BURN', the record actually appearing on Dreamworks. With ROLLINS becoming something of an all-round celebrity, it remains to be seen whether he can retain the outsider intensity of old (though it wouldn't be an idea to argue with the man!). • **Covers:** GHOST RIDER (Suicide) / EX-LION TAMER (Wire) / DO IT (Pink Fairies) / LET THERE BE ROCK (Ac-Dc) / FRANKLIN'S TOWER (Grateful Dead).

Album rating: END OF SILENCE (*8) / WEIGHT (*6) / COME IN AND BURN (*6)

HENRY ROLLINS – vocals (ex-BLACK FLAG, ex-SOA) / with **CHRIS HASKETT** (b. Leeds, England) – guitar (ex-SURFIN' DAVE) / **BERNIE WANDEL** – bass / **MICK GREEN** – drums

Fundamental Texas Hotel

Jul 87. (lp) *(SAVE 024) <TXH 001>* **HOT ANIMAL MACHINE** ☐ ☐
– Black and white / Followed around / Lost and found / There's a man outside / Crazy lover / A man and a woman / Hot animal machine I / Ghost rider / Move right in / Hot animal machine 2 / No one. *(cd-iss. Oct88 +=; SAVE 024CD) – . (cd re-iss. Mar94 on 'Intercord'; 986976)*

— In Oct'87, he shared 'LIVE' lp with GORE, released on Dutch 'Eksakt' label; *EKSAKT 034*

Dec 87. (lp; solo) *<TXH 005>* **BIG UGLY MOUTH** (spoken word live early '87) [-] ☐
(UK cd-iss. Mar93 on '1/4 Stick'; QS 9CD)
(below saw him do a reverse MICHAEL JACKSON and black-up)

Jan 88. (12"ep; as HENRIETTA COLLINS and THE WIFEBEATING CHILDHATERS featuring HENRY ROLLINS) *(HOLY 5) <TXH 03>* **DRIVE BY SHOOTING** ☐ ☐ Aug87
– Drive by shooting (watch out for that pig) / Ex-lion tamer / Hey Henriezza / Can you speak this? / I have come to kill you / Men are pigs.

ROLLINS BAND

retained **HASKETT** and recruited **ANDREW WEISS** – bass / **SIMEON CAIN** – drums

Sep 88. (lp/cd) *(SAVE 065/+CD) <TXH >* **LIFE TIME** ☐ ☐
– Burned beyond recognition / What am I doing here / 1000 times blind / Lonely / Wreck-age / Gun in mouth blues / You look at you / If you're alive / Turned out. *(cd+=)* – What am I doing here? / Burned beyond recognition / Move right in / Hot animal machine 2. *(cd re-iss. Mar94 on 'Intercord'; 986977)*

World Service Texas Hotel

Jan 89. (lp) *(SERVM 004) <TXH 013CD>* **DO IT! (live/studio)** ☐ ☐ Apr89
– Do it / Move light in / Next time / Joe is everything, everything is Joe / Black and white / Lost and found / Followed around / Wreck age / Lonely / Hot animal machine £1 / You look at you / Gun in mouth blues / Turned out / Thousand times blind / No one. *(re-iss. cd Mar94 on 'Intercord'; 986978)*

Apr 89. (d-lp; solo) *<TXH 015>* **SWEATBOX** (spoken word live) [-] ☐
(UK d-cd-iss. Mar93 on '1/4 Stick'; QS 10CD)

Nov 89. (m-lp/cd) *(SERV 010 LP/CD) <TXH >* **HARD VOLUME** ☐ ☐
– Hard / What have I got / I feel like this / Planet Joe / Love song / Turned inside out / Down and away. *(cd+=)* – Joyriding with Frank. *(cd-iss. Mar94 on 'Intercord'; 986979)*

— In 1989, a Swiss cassette found its way into UK; 'READINGS: SWITZERLAND' on 'Action' *ACTIONK 001*

— In 1990, WARTIME was an extra-curricular activity headed by ROLLINS and ANDREW WEISS. An cd-ep surfaced 'FAST FOOD FOR THOUGHT' on 'Chrysalis'; *MPCD 1753*

1990. (lp; solo) *<TXH >* **LIVE AT McCABE'S (spoken word live)** [-] ☐
(UK cd-iss. Mar93 on '1/4 Stick'; QS 11CD)

not iss. Sub Pop

1990. (7",7"red,7"pink) *<SP 72>* **I KNOW YOU. / EARACHE MY EYE** [-] ☐

1/4 Stick 1/4 Stick

Nov 90. (lp/cd) *<(QS 02/+CD)>* **TURNED ON (live '89)** ☐ ☐
– Lonely / Do it / What have I got / Tearing / Out there / You didn't need / Hard / Followed around / Mask / Down & away / Turned inside out / The Dietmar song / Black & white / What do you do / Crazy lover.

— in July '91, HENRY ROLLINS & The HARD-ONS released their collaboration 'LET THERE BE ROCK' issued on 'Vinyl Solution' (VS 30/+CD)

Imago-RCA Imago-RCA

Feb 92. (12") *(PT 49113)* **LOW SELF OPINION. / LIE, LIE, LIE** ☐ ☐

Feb 92. (cd/c/d-lp) *(PD/PK/PL 90641) <21006>* **THE END OF SILENCE** ☐ ☐
– Low self opinion / The end of silence / Grip / Tearing / You didn't need / Almost real / Obscene / What do you do? / Blues jam / Another life / Just like you.

Aug 92. (7") *(72787 87250-18-7)* **TEARING. / EARACHE IN MY EYE (live)** [54] ☐
(12"+=/cd-s+=) *(72787 87250-18-1/-2)* – (There'll be no) Next time / Ghost rider.

Jan 93. (2xcd-box/2xc-box) *(72787 21009-2/-4)* **THE BOXED LIFE** (compilation of alter-ego workings) ☐ ☐

— In early '94, he acted in the film 'The Chase', and was about to be seen in 'Johnny Mnemonic'.

— **MELVIN GIBBS** – bass repl. HASKINS who left in 1993.

Apr 94. (cd/c/clear d-lp) *<(72787 21034-2/-4/-1)>* **WEIGHT** [22] [33]
– Disconnect / Fool / Icon / Civilized / Divine object of hatred / Liar / Step back / Wrong man / Volume 4 / Tired / Alien blueprint / Shine.

Aug 94. (7"/c-s) *(74321 213057-7/-4)* **LIAR. / DISCONNECT** [27] ☐
(cd-s+=) *(74321 213057-2)* – Right here too much / Nightsweat.

Dreamworks Dreamworks

Apr 97. (cd/c) *<(DRD/DRC 50011)>* **COME IN AND BURN** ☐ [89]
– Shame / Starve / All I want / The end of something / On my way to the cage / Thursday afternoon / During a city / Neon / Spilling over the side / Inhale exhale / Saying goodbye again / Rejection / Disappearing act.

Jul 97. (7") *(DRMS 22271)* **THE END OF SOMETHING. / ALSO RAN** ☐ [-]
(cd-s) *(DRMCD 22271)* – ('A'side) / ('A'-We Change remix) / Threshold.
(cd-s) *(DRMXD 22271)* – ('A'side) / ('A'-Grooverider remix) / Stray.

– compilations, etc. –

Mar 93. (d-cd) *1/4 Stick; (QS 12CD)* **HUMAN BUTT** (book readings) ☐ ☐ 1991

Mar 93. (cd-box) *1/4 Stick; (QS 13CD)* **DEEP THROAT** ☐ ☐
– (all 4 spoken word releases).

Nov 94. (d-cd) *Imago; <(74321 24238-2)>* **GET IN THE VAN** (book readings; life on the road with BLACK FLAG) ☐ ☐

Nov 94. (book) *Imago;* **HENRY: PORTRAIT OF A SINGER SINGER** (spoken word) ☐ ☐

1996. (cd) *Thirsty Ear; <2.13.61>* **EVERYTHING** [-] ☐

Apr 97. (m-cd) *Thirsty Ear; <21321>* **BLACK COFFEE BLUES** [-] ☐
– Black coffee blues / Invisible woman blues / Monster / Exhaustion blues / I know you.

ROME

Formed: Chicago, Illinois, USA . . . 1993 by the trio of RIK SHAW, LE DEUCE and ELLIOT DICK. Another experimental outfit to join the massed ranks of 'Thrill Jockey', ROME distinguished themselves from the post-rock pack by basing their futuristic sound around a "live in the studio" space/echo-chamber dub sound. This much was in evidence on their 1996 eponymous debut, the trio filtering disjointed ambient/synth textures through warped reverbating rhythms and disorientating effects. After an appearance on the 'In Memoriam' V/A compilation (on 'Mille Plateaux'), the group were reduced to a duo following the departure of sticksman, ELLIOT, SHAW and LE DEUCE only managing one further release to date, 1997's 12" EP, 'BEWARE BODY SNATCHERS'. • **Note:** Not to be confused with R&B singer, ROME (alias JEROME WOODS), who confusingly released his eponymous set for 'R.C.A.' in '97.

Album rating: ROME (*7)

RIK SHAW – bass / **LE DEUCE** – electronics / **ELLIOT DICK** – drums, percussion

Thrill Jockey Thrill Jockey

Jul 96. (cd) *<THRILL 29>* **ROME** [-] ☐
– Leaving perdition / Intermodal / Lunar white / She's a black belt / Rohm / Radiolucence / Deepest laws.

— now without ELLIOT

Jun 97. (12") *<(TJ12 02)>* **BEWARE BODY SNATCHERS EP** ☐ ☐

ROMEO VOID

Formed: Bay Area, San Francisco, California, USA . . . 1979 by lyricist/singer, DEBORA IYALL (a Cowlitz Indian), along with PETER WOODS, FRANK ZINCAVAGE, BENJAMIN BOSSI and JAY DERRAH (the latter was replaced a year later by JOHN STENCH). Driven by the smouldering but streetwise sensuality of IYALL, ROMEO VOID emerged in 1981 with a debut single, 'WHITE SWEATER', on the small '415' label. The record was characterised by IYALL's disaffected musings on the vagaries of romance while the bleating sax work of BOSSI brought comparisons to the likes of X-RAY SPEX; hypnotic and minimalist, ROMEO VOID's sound had critics spellbound. A RIC OCASEK-produced follow-up EP, 'NEVER SAY NEVER' meanwhile, boasted a glossier production edge and the more commercial bent of 'BENEFACTOR' found RV aiming straight for the alternative dancefloor although the inevitable BLONDIE comparisons missed the point. Yet despite the distribution muscle of 'CBS' (who'd taken over '415'), the record failed to spawn any hit singles and ironically, it took a return to the bite of their earlier sound on third set, 'INSTINCT' (1984), to provide a minor US Top 40 hit in the shape of 'A GIRL IN TROUBLE (IS A TEMPORARY THING)'. The album itself also scraped into the Top 75 yet depite this belated success, ROMEO VOID became null and er . . . void, after a final single, 'SAY NO', in early '85. IYALL went on to release a solitary solo album, 'STRANGE LANGUAGE' (1986) before concentrating on her literary aspirations. Although ROMEO VOID reunited in 1993, their activities were confined to live work.

Album rating: IT'S A CONDITION (*6) / BENEFACTOR (*6) / INSTINCTS (*6) / WARM, IN YOUR COAT compilation (*7)

DEBORA IYALL (b.1956) – vocals / **PETER WOODS** – guitar / **BENJAMIN BOSSI** – saxophone / **FRANK ZINCAVAGE** – bass / **JOHN STENCH** – drums (of PEARL HARBOR & THE EXPLOSIONS) repl. JAY DERRAH

not iss. 415

Feb 81. (7") **WHITE SWEATER. / APACHE** [-] ☐

Mar 81. (lp) *<A 0004>* **IT'S A CONDITION** [-] ☐
– Myself to myself / Nothing for me / Talk dirty (to me) / Love is an illness / White sweater / Charred remains / Confrontation / Drop your eyes / Fear to fear / I mean it.

— **LARRY CARTER** – drums, percussion; repl. STENCH
Nov 81. (7") **NOT SAFE. / SUCCESS STORY**
Feb 82. (12"ep) *<A 0007>* **NEVER SAY NEVER. / IN THE DARK / PRESENT TENSE / NOT SAFE**
C.B.S. Columbia
Sep 82. (7") *(A 2733)* **NEVER SAY NEVER. / FLASHFLOOD**
Nov 82. (lp) *(CBS 85929) <38182>* **BENEFACTOR** Aug82
– Never say never / Wrap it up / Flashflood / Undercover kept / Ventilation / Chinatown / Orange / Shake the hands of time / S.O.S.
— **AARON SMITH** – drums, percussion; repl. CARTER
Oct 84. (7") *(A 4756) <04534>* **A GIRL IN TROUBLE (IS A TEMPORARY THING). / GOING TO NEON** 35 Aug84
Oct 84. (lp) *(CBS 25969) <39155>* **INSTINCTS** 68 Aug84
– Out on my own / Just too easy / Billy's birthday / Going to Neon / Six days and one / A girl in trouble (is a temporary thing) / Your life is a lie / Instincts.
Jan 85. (7") *(A 5028)* **SAY NO. / SIX DAYS AND ONE**
(12"+=) *(TA 5028)* – Out on my own.
— split in 1985 when DEBORA IYALL went solo; she released one album, 'STRANGE LANGUAGE', in '86.

– compilations, etc. –

May 92. (cd/c) *Columbia-Legacy; <CK/CT 47964>* **WARM, IN YOUR COAT** -
– White sweater / I mean it / Charred remains / Talk dirty to me / Myself to myself / In the dark / Girl in trouble (is a temporary thing) / Out on my own / Just too easy / Wrap it up / Flashflood / Undercover kept / Chinatown / Never say never / One thousand shadows.

ROOM

Formed: Liverpool, England . . . early 80's by DAVE JACKSON, ROBYN ODLUM, BECKY STRINGER and CLIVE THOMAS. A series of singles (one on cassette!) on the tiny 'Box' label led to comparisons with local heroes ECHO & THE BUNNYMEN while JACKSON's vocals were, in retrospect, something of a cross between the rich expressiveness of OMD's ANDY McCLUSKEY and the lugubrious wallowing of MORRISSEY. Subsequently signing to noted indie, 'Red Flame', the band released a debut set, 'INDOOR FIREWORKS' (1982), containing at least three semi-classics, 'IN SICKNESS AND IN HEALTH', 'CANDLE' and 'BATED BREATH'. The mini-set, 'CLEAR', followed in '83 and featured the debut of three new recruits, 'ALAN WILLS (from The WILD SWANS), PAUL CAVANAGH and PETER BAKER, to replace the departed ROBYN and CLIVE; PHIL LUCKING was subsequently added for around half a year. A second album proper, 'IN EVIL HOUR' (1984) was partly produced by former TELEVISION mainman, TOM VERLAINE, many of the tracks taken from sessions recorded with Radio One DJ, Janice Long. Among the delights were the infectious 'NEW DREAMS FOR OLD' (with PHIL) and the sneering 'JACKPOT JACK', while the spiky guitar of 'THE FRIENDLY ENEMY' was straight from the JOHNNY MARR school of cool. Chart success remained tantalisingly out of sight, however, and ROOM called it a day. JACKSON went on to front the similarly obscure BENNY PROFANE although echoes of his deep throated monologue style can occasionally be discerned in the efforts of PULP mainman JARVIS COCKER.

Album rating: INDOOR FIREWORKS (*7) / CLEAR! (*6) / IN EVIL HOUR (*6)

DAVE JACKSON – vocals / **ROBYN ODLUM** – guitar / **BECKY STRINGER** – bass / **CLIVE THOMAS** – drums, percussion
Box not iss.
1980. (7") *(BOX 001)* **MOTION. / WAITING ROOM** -
1980. (c-s) *(BOX 002)* **BITTER REACTION** -
Jul 81. (7") *(BOX 003)* **IN SICKNESS AND HEALTH. / BATED BREATH** -
Red Flame not iss.
May 82. (7") *(RF7 03)* **THINGS HAVE LEARNT TO WALK THAT OUGHT TO CRAWL. / DREAMS OF FLYING** -
Jul 82. (lp) *(RF 3)* **INDOOR FIREWORKS** -
– No dream / Escalator / Rewind / Chatshows / This party stinks / Heat haze / Conversation / Things have learnt to walk that ought to crawl / Candle / Bated breath / In sickness and health .
Dec 82. (7") *(RF7 15)* **100 YEARS. / THE WHOLE WORLD SINGS** -
— **ALAN WILLS** – drums (ex-WILD SWANS) repl. CLIVE / **PAUL CAVANAGH** – guitar; repl. ROBYN / added **PETER BAKER** – keyboards
Nov 83. (m-lp) *(RFB 26)* **CLEAR!** -
– Ringing / Numb / The ride / Never / Sleep tight / On the beach.
— added **PHIL LUCKING** – trumpet, trombone
Jun 84. (7"/12") *(RFB 40/+12)* **NEW DREAMS FOR OLD. / ON THE BEAT** -
— Reverted to a quintet, when PHIL departed.
Oct 84. (lp/c) *(RFA/CRFA 42)* **IN EVIL HOUR** -
– A shirt of fire / Whirlpool / Naive / Crying red / The friendly enemy / New dreams for old / Calloused hands / Half forgotten thing / Jackpot Jack.
Mar 85. (12"ep) *(RF 12-42)* **JACKPOT JACK. / FRIENDLY ENEMY / SHIRT OF FIRE / CRYING RED / NAIVE (Janice Long sessions)** -
— Disbanded late 1985

– compilations, etc. –

Feb 86. (d-lp) *Red Flame; (RF 47)* **NEMESIS** -
– (CLEAR! / IN EVIL HOUR)
Nov 88. (12"ep) *Strange Fruit; (SFPS 062)* **THE PEEL SESSIONS** -
– The storm / Here comes the floor / But when do we start to live? / Jeremiah.

BENNY PROFANE

formed by **JACKSON + STRINGER** plus **JOE McKECHNIE** – guitar, drums (ex-MODERN EON) / **ROBIN SURTEES** – guitar / **FRANK SPARKS** – drums (ex-EX POST FACTO)
Sub Pop UK not iss.
May 86. (12") *(PURE 1)* **WHERE IS PIG?. / ?** -
Ediesta not iss.
Jul 87. (12") *(CALC 026)* **DEVIL LAUGHING. / ?** -
Apr 88. (12"ep) *(CALC 048)* **PARASITE / KAMIKAZE DRINKING. / HOLY COW / LITTLE GOD** -
Sep 88. (7") *(CALC 061)* **ROB A BANK. / ?** -
(12"+=) *(CALC 061T)* –
— **ROGER SINEK + DAVE BROWN** repl. SPARKS
Play Hard not iss.
May 89. (12") *(DEC 24)* **SKATEBOARD TO OBLIVION. / GHOST RIDERS SING RAWHIDE IN THE SKY** -
Jun 89. (lp) *(DEC 25)* **TRAPDOOR SWING** -
– Man on the sauce / Skateboard to oblivion / Pink snow / Quickdraw McGraw meets Deadeye Dick / A handful of nothing / Rob a bank / Tear the web / Wall to wall / Stitch that / Here comes the floor.
Imaginary not iss.
Feb 90. (7"one-sided) *(RED ONE)* **HEY WASTE OF SPACE** -
Feb 90. (lp) *(ILLUSION 7)* **DUMBLUCK CHARM** -
– Time bomb / Maureen / Devil laughing / Walkaway / Perfect girl / Everything / Hey waste of time / Beam me up / Imaginary / Ghoul friend / She. *(cd+=)* – TRAPDOOR SWING lp
— disbanded after above

ROSE OF AVALANCHE

Formed: Yorkshire, England . . . early 80's by PHILIP MORRIS and PAUL JAMES BERRY. Signed to 'L.I.L.' records, the band debuted in 1985 with the 'L.A. RAIN' single, following it up with the 'GODDESS' 12" and 'CASTLES IN THE SKY'. Akin to IGGY POP or even a more metallic, more accessible SISTERS OF MERCY, complete with deep-throat vocals and drumming by NICOL MACKAY (GLENN SCHULTZ on guitar and ALAN DAVIS on bass were also members at this point). They issued their debut album, 'ALWAYS THERE', the following year and with enthusiastic support from John Peel it looked as if the band were destined for more than just cult success. Following the 'FIRST AVALANCHE' (1986) album, they signed to the 'Fire' imprint, releasing a couple of singles, 'TOO MANY CASTLES IN THE SKY' and 'VELVETEEN', the latter lifted from another album that year, 'ALWAYS THERE'. After the lp, 'IN ROCK', a subsequent dispute with their label slowed down the momentum, leading to the band setting up their own label, 'Avalantic', through which they issued a string of progressively more mainstream albums beginning with 'NEVER ANOTHER SUNSET' (1989). The turn of the decade saw MORRIS and BERRY bringing in a new rhythm section of DARREN HOMER and ANDREW PARKER, this line-up completing two final sets, 'STRING 'A' BEADS' (1990) and 'I.C.E.' (1991).

Album rating: FIRST AVALANCHE (*5) / ALWAYS THERE (*6) / NEVER ANOTHER SUNSET (*5)

PHILIP MORRIS – vocals / **PAUL JAMES BERRY** – guitar / **GLENN SCHULTZ** – guitar / **ALAN DAVIS** – bass / **NICOL MACKAY** – drums
Leeds Independent Label Emergo
May 85. (7") *(LIL 1)* **L.A. RAIN. / RISE TO THE GROOVE** -
(12"+=) *(12LIL 1)* – Conceal me.
Jan 86. (12"m) *(12LIL 2)* **GODDESS / A THOUSAND LANDSCAPES. / GIMME SOME LOVIN'** -
— **MARK THOMPSON** – drums; repl. MACKAY
Mar 86. (lp) *(LILLP 003) <772286-1>* **FIRST AVALANCHE** -
– Stick in the works / Rise to the groove / A thousand landscapes / Conceal me / Assassin / Goddess / American girls / Gimme some lovin' / L.A. rain / Dizzy Miss Lizzy. *(re-iss. Aug89 on 'Fire'; REFIRELP 4) (re-iss. Oct91 cd/lp; FIRE 33/11 004)*
Fire Emergo
May 86. (7") *(BLAZE 9)* **TOO MANY CASTLES IN THE SKY. / ASSASSIN** -
(12"+=) *(BLAZE 9T)* – Dizzy Miss Lizzy.
Sep 86. (7") *(BLAZE 14)* **VELVETEEN. / WHO CARES** 1989
(12"+=) *(BLAZE 14T) <EM12 5482>* – Just like yesterday.
Sep 86. (lp) *(FIRE 7) <EM 9633>* **ALWAYS THERE** 1989
– Always there / Waiting for the sun / Majesty / Just like yesterday / Velveteen / Who cares / The mainline man / Always there . *(re-iss. Feb89 on 'Fire' lp/cd; FIRE LP/CD 7) (re-iss. Oct91 cd/lp; FIRE 33/11 007)*
Jan 87. (7") *(BLAZE 18)* **ALWAYS THERE. / WAITING FOR THE SUN** -
(12"+=) *(BLAZE 18T)* – Majesty.
('A'-Mainline mix-12"++=) *(BLAZE 18TR)* – The mainline man.
Apr 88. (lp) *(FIRELP 12) <772285-1>* **IN ROCK** -
– Dreamland / Not another day / Height of the clouds (part 1 & 2) / Darkorjan / Yesterday once more. *<US+=>* – ALWAYS THERE *(re-iss. Oct91 cd/lp; FIRE 33/11 012)*
Contempo not iss.
Nov 88. (lp/cd) *(CONTE/+CD 104)* **LIVE AT TOWN AND COUNTRY (live)** -
– Stick in the works / Just like yesterday / Mainline man / Velveteen / A thousand landscapes / Waiting for the sun / Always there / Dreamland / Too many castles in the sky / Gimme some lovin'.
Avalantic S.P.V.
Dec 88. (7") *(AVE 001)* **THE WORLD IS OURS. / ?** -
(12"+=) *(AVE 001T)* –

Feb 89. (7") *(AVE 002)* **NEVER ANOTHER SUNSET. / GIMME DANGER**
(12"+=) *(AVE 002T)* –

Apr 89. (lp/c/cd) *(AVE LP/C/CD 001)* *<84091-1>* **NEVER ANOTHER SUNSET**
– What's going down / Nowhere to run / You don't belong / The Devil's embrace / Never another sunset / Delusions / Don't fly too high / Her fatal charm / A romantic vision.

— **MORRIS + BERRY** recruited **DARREN HOMER** – bass / **ANDREW PARKER** – drums

Oct 90. (cd/lp) *(AVE CD/LP 002)* *<008-3096-1>* **STRING 'A' BEADS**
– Your lights on / All we want / Make it right / If you only knew – A certain truth / String 'A' beads / If it's right for you / Second sight / A different child / Be true to your love / Lights on.

Avantic Rebel

Nov 91. (cd/lp) *(AVE CD/LP 003)* *<084-3034-2>* **I.C.E.**
– Ride the storm / Two time baby / I love the ice / Destination nowhere / The garden / Lost the chance / Wall of pain / Everything's OK / Take all the money.

– compilations, etc. –

May 87. (d7"ep) *Fire; (BLAZE 19EP)* **ROSE OF AVALANCHE**
– (the mid-'86 ep's)

ROTE KAPELLE (see under ⇒ JESSE GARON & THE DESPERADOES)

ROYAL FAMILY AND THE POOR

Formed: Liverpool, England . . . early 80's by multi-instrumentalist, MIKE KEANE and seasoned campaigner AMBROSE REYNOLDS. Although relatively accessible, The ROYAL FAMILY & THE POOR (who also numbered JEFF TURNER, KAREN HALEWOOD, JOHN WALSH and KIF) were one of the more obscure 'Factory' acts, releasing a one-off EP, 'ART ON 45', before vanishing completely from the music scene. They finally returned in early '86 with a single, 'WE LOVE THE MOON', followed by a belated DONALD JOHNSON (A CERTAIN RATIO)-produced debut album, 'THE PROJECT'. This was an occasionally magikal if nowhere near magical record blighted by KEANE's directionless PINK MILITARY-esque sound and sub-PETE WYLIE vocals. Changing personnel, changing labels and changing style, KEANE and his musical family recorded 'IN THE SEA OF E' (1987) against the backdrop of the emerging, ecstasy-fuelled acid-house scene; danceable but always experimental, the album improved on the debut while failing to take the group to a higher level.

Album rating: THE PROJECT (*3) / IN THE SEA OF E (*4)

MIKE KEANE – vocals, guitar, bass, drum prog, synth, piano, percussion / **AMBROSE REYNOLDS** – bass, (ex-BIG IN JAPAN) / **JEFF TURNER** – sax, clarinet, guitar, violin / **KAREN HALEWOOD** – synthesizer, vocals / **JOHN WALSH** – bass, guitar / **KIF** – drums

Factory not iss.

Feb 82. (12"ep) *(FACT 43)* **ART ON 45. / DREAM / DOMINION**

— disappeared for around four years, until . . .

Jan 86. (7") *(FAC 139)* **WE LOVE THE MOON. / WHITE SATINS**

Apr 86. (lp) *(FACT 95)* **THE PROJECT**
– I love you (restricted in a moment) / Voices / Moonfish is here / Dark and light / Radio Egypt / Discipline / The dawn song / Ritaul 1 / Power of will / Motherland.

Recloose not iss.

1986. (lp) *(LOOSE 13)* **LIVE 1983-1985 (live)**
– Restrained in a moment / Dawn song / Visions / Transparent / Something someone / Destiny / Heartbeat.

— **MIKE** now with **SIMON CRAB** – tapes, synths, keyboards / **ANDY FRIZELL** – bass, flute / **MERLIN SHEPHERD** – sax, strings

Gaia not iss.

Jun 87. (lp) *(PHASE 003)* **IN THE SEA OF E**
– Living light / Mr. Crow / Song for freedom / Gaia / Journey / Honesty / Creatura / No more compromise / Wounded / When the cats away / Feast of the supersensualists.

Jan 88. (12") *(PHASE 004)* **RESTRAINED IN A MOMENT. / THE PROJECT**

— KEANE abandoned this project

ROYAL TRUX

Formed: Chicago, Illinois, USA . . . 1987 by Calvin Klein model and self-confessed junkie, JENNIFER HERRERA and PUSSY GALORE's NEIL HAGERTY, who had originally met in a New York sewer two years previously. Lo-fi avant-garde terrorists from the stable of BEEFHEART or ZAPPA that shifted more into The 'STONES (early 70's era), the difference being the sultry JANE BIRKEN style-vox of HERRERA. Following the junkie freeform chaos of earlier albums (by this point she had kicked her habit), the couple signed to 'Virgin'-offshoot, 'Hut' in 1994 and finally got it together for the most focused album of their career to date, the David Briggs-produced 'THANK YOU' (1995). Reportedly cleaned up and newly relocated to Virginia, HAGGERTY and HERRERA had created a work of hip swivelling, ground-in-the-dirt rock'n'roll drawing inevitable comparisons with the early 70's glory of The ROLLING STONES while recreating the spirit of such less readily remembered boogie merchants as BLACK OAK ARKANSAS and GRAND FUNK RAILROAD, the legendary 'TRUX musical bloody mindedness bubbling under the surface. An unlikely UK tour with TEENAGE FANCLUB helped raise their profile, yet perhaps not surprisingly, it seemed ROYAL TRUX weren't destined for mainstream indie success and following the release of 'SWEET SIXTEEN' (1997), the pair relocated to the more familiar surroundings of US indie label, 'Domino', issuing the 'ACCELERATOR' album in 1998.

Album rating: UNTITLED – ROYAL TRUX (*4) / TWIN INFINITIVES (*4) / CATS AND DOGS (*6) / THANK YOU (*6) / SWEET SIXTEEN (*5) / ACCELERATOR (*6)

JENNIFER HERRERA – vocals / **NEIL HAGERTY** – guitar, vocals (ex-PUSSY GALORE) / with guests

not iss. Royal

Jan 89. (lp) **UNTITLED**
– Air / Move / Hallucination / Sometimes / Lightning boxer / Blood flowers / Sun on the run. *<cd-iss. Jan92 & Dec96 as 'ROYAL TRUX' on 'Drag City'; DC 5>* *(UK-iss.Jun93 on 'Domino' cd/lp' WIG CD/LP 5)*

not iss. Drag City

1990. (d-lp) **TWIN INFINITIVES**
– Solid gold tooth / Ice cream / Jet pet / RTX – USA / Kool down wheels / Chances are the comets in our future / Yin Jum verses the vomit creature / Osiris / (Edge of the) Ape oven / Florida Avenue theme / Lick my boots / Glitterbust / Funky son / Ratcreeps / New York Avenue bridge. *(UK-iss.Jan94 on 'Domino'; WIGCD 8)*

— **KEN NASTA** – drums; repl. unknown

Domino Drag City

Jul 93. (cd/lp) *(WIG CD/LP 6)* *<DC 32CD>* **CATS AND DOGS** Jun93
– Teeth / The flag / Friends / The spectre / Skywood greenback mantra / Turn of the century / Up the sleeve / Hot and cold skulls / Tight pants / Let's get lost / Driving in that car (with the eagle on the hood).

Oct 93. (12"ep/cd-ep) *(RUG 8 T/CD)* **DOGS OF LOVE EP**

Oct 94. (7") *(RUG 27)* **MERCURY. / SHOCKWAVE RIDER**

— added **DAN BROWN** – bass / **CHRIS PYLE** – drums / **ROBBIE ARMSTRONG** – percussion / with guests RIAN MURPHY + DAVID BERMAN

Hut Virgin + Drag City

Feb 95. (7") *(HUT 50)* **MAP OF THE CITY. / NATIONAL MOTHER**

Feb 95. (cd)(c/lp) *(CDHUT 23)(HUT MC/LP 23)* *<40141><DG 66>* **THANK YOU**
– A night to remember / The sewers of Mars / Ray O Vac / Map of the city / Granny grunt / Lights on the levee / Fear strikes out / (Have you met) Horror James / You're gonna lose / Shadow of the wasp.

May 95. (10"/cd-s) *(HUT EN/CD 56)* **YOU'RE GONNA LOSE. / HIBISCUS (live) / HOT AND COLD (live)**

— now without 5th member

Apr 97. (cd) *(CDHUT 43)* *<42752>* **SWEET SIXTEEN** Feb97
– Don't try too hard / Morphic resident / Pickup / Cold joint / Golden rules / You'll be staying in romm 323 / Can't have it both ways / 10 days 12 nights / Microwave made / Sweet sixteen / I'm looking through you / Roswell seeds and stems / Pol Pot pie.

Domino Drag City

Apr 98. (7"m) *(RUG 065)* **I'M READY. / P.T. 20 / MR CRUMP DON'T LIKE IT**

Apr 98. (cd/lp) *(WIG CD/LP 045)* *<DC 145CD>* **ACCELERATOR**
– I'm ready / Yellow kid / Banana question / Another year / Juicy, juicy, juice / Liar / New bones / Follow the winner / Stevie.

Jun 98. (7") *(RUG 069)* **LIAR. / MONEY FOR NOTHING**
(cd-s+=) *(RUG 069CD)* – P.T. 20 / Mr. Crump don't like it.

Aug 98. (12"ep/cd-ep) *(RUG 076 T/CD)* *<DC 154>* **3 SONG EP**
– Deafer than blind / United States vs. one 1974 Cadillac El Dorado sedan / Run shaker life.

– compilations, etc. –

May 97. (7") *<(DC 42)>* **MERCURY. /**

Nov 97. (d-cd) *<DC 93>* **SINGLES LIVE UNRELEASED** (rarities, etc)
– Esso dame / Mercury / No fixed address / Red tiger / Lucy Peaupaux / June night afternoon / Steal your face / Back to school / Faca amolada / Luminous dolphin / Spike cyclone / Vile child / Law man / Shockwave rider / Chairman blow / Womban / Cut you loose / Baghdad buzz / Hero – Zero / Statik Jakl / Gett off / Teeth / Cleveland / Theme from M*A*S*H / Strawberry soda / Sunflavor / Love is . . . / Ratcreeps / Hair beach / Sometimes / Signed, confused / Aviator blues.

RUBELLA BALLET

Formed: London, England . . . mid '79 by ex-FATAL MICROBES guitarist, PETE FENDER. A second division punk supergroup of sorts, the band also numbered SID ATTION (ex-FLUX OF PINK INDIANS), GEM STONE (ex-KILLJOYS) and singer(!?), ZILLAH MINX (who had replaced a number of previous singers including ANNIE ANXIETY). After a handful of mainly single releases for 'Xntrix' and 'Jungle' records, the dayglo doom-punks released their first album proper for the newly-established 'Ubiquitous', 'AT LAST IT'S PLAYTIME' (1985). Chugging mid-paced stuff, many of the tracks were dominated by ZILLAH's steamroller-flat vox which were reminiscent of the heady "Roxy" days of a young SIOUXSIE SIOUX. By this point, FENDER and STONE had been replaced by STEVE and ZILLAH's sister RACHEL, the show finally coming to a close after the release of the album, 'IF' (1986).

Album rating: BALLET BAG (*5) / AT LAST IT'S PLAYTIME (*5) / IF (*4) / BIRTHDAY BOX compilation (*5) / GREATEST TRIPS compilation (*5)

ZILLAH MINX (b.31 Mar'61, Birkenhead, England) – vocals; repl. ANNIE ANXIETY who went solo (other early singers WOMBLE, COLIN AND IT) / **PETE FENDER** – guitar (of/ex-FATAL MICROBES) / **SID ATTION** (b.18 Apr'60, Sutton Coldfield, England) – drums (ex-FLUX OF PINK INDIANS) / **GEM STONE** – bass, vocals (ex-KILLJOYS, ex-FATAL MICROBES)

Xntrix / not iss.

Mar 82. (C-30 cass) *(XN 2004)* **BALLET BAG** [ ] [-]
(re-iss. Sep85; ZN 2004) (re-iss. 1986; same)

Sep 82. (7"ep) *(XN 2005)* **THE BALLET DANCE / SOMETHING TO GIVE. / UNEMPLOYED / KRAK TRAK** [ ] [-]

Jungle / not iss.

Jan 84. (12"ep) *(JUNG 12)* **42°F. / SLANT AND SLIDE / BLIND AMBITIONS** [ ] [-]

Ubiquitous / not iss.

Feb 85. (12") *(DAYGLO 1)* **MONEY TALKS. / DEATH TRAIN** [ ] [-]

—— **RACHEL MINX** (b.12 Nov'64, Birkenhead) – bass; repl. GEM

—— **STEVE** – guitar; repl. PETE who went solo

Jul 85. (lp) *(DAYGLO 2)* **AT LAST IT'S PLAYTIME** [ ] [-]
– Love life / Tangled web / T.V. scream / Trial thirteen / See saw / Twister / etc

Sep 86. (12") *(DAYGLO 3)* **ARCTIC FLOWERS. / FALSE FLOWERS** [ ] [-]

Oct 86. (lp) *(DAYGLO 4)* **IF** [ ] [-]
– Let us out / Plastic life / 'T' / Thugs / It'll never happen to me / Animal house / Rainbow love.

—— split on the 1st Jan'88

– compilations, etc. –

Mar 87. (lp) *Ubiquitous; (DAYGLO 5)* **THE COCKTAIL MIX** [ ] [-]
– (BALLET BAG tape + THE BALLET DANCE (EP)).

1988. (d-lp) *Ubiquitous; (DAYGLO 6)* **THE RUBELLA BALLET BIRTHDAY BOX** [ ] [-]

Feb 90. (cd/lp) *Brave – One Little Indian; (BND 2 CD/LP)* **AT THE END OF THE RAINBOW** [ ] [-]
– Money talks / False promise / Arctic flowers / Dreamer / Animal house / It'll never happen to me / Love potion / Rainbow love / 'T' (emotional blackmail).

Feb 90. (cd) *Brave – One Little Indian; (BND 3CD)* **GREATEST TRIPS** [ ] [-]
– The ballet dance / Something to give / Unemployed / Krak trak / 'T' (emotional blackmail) / Belfast / A dream of honey / Newz at 10 / Slant + slide / Krak trak (mk.2) / Blues (with DON BYAS) / Exit / Money talks (dub) / Love life / Tangled web / T.V. screen / Death train / See saw / Twister / Mecalito (acieed mix) / Cowboy hero (with KARA).

RUBICON (see under ⇒ FIELDS OF THE NEPHILIM)

RUBY (see under ⇒ SILVERFISH)

RUNAWAYS

Formed: Los Angeles, California, USA . . . mid-1974 by the notorious solo star turned record producer KIM FOWLEY (along with teen lyricist, KARI KROME), who set out to create a female RAMONES. After successfully applying to his music paper ad, JOAN JETT became the first to join, followed soon after by SANDY WEST and MICKI STEELE. With a few gigs under their belt, STEELE was replaced by CHERIE CURRIE, while the line-up was finalised with the addition of LITA FORD and JACKIE FOX. This was the formation that played a rooftop session on a Los Angeles apartment block in early 1976, an event that helped secure a record deal with 'Mercury'. While their eponymous debut was hitting the shops, the girls (average age 16) made their New York debut at CBGB's in September '76 supporting TELEVISION and TALKING HEADS. Dragging glam-metal by the pubic hair and injecting it with punk energy, tracks such as 'CHERRY BOMB' and 'HOLLYWOOD' saw The RUNAWAYS lumped in with the fermenting US New Wave scene. Early in '77, they released a second album, 'QUEENS OF NOISE', and like its predecessor it too failed to capitalize on the hype. Internal tensions were coming to a head around the time of the Japanese-only (The RUNAWAYS were huge in the Far East) live set, VICKI BLUE standing in for the worn out JACKIE FOX, while the blonde CURRIE finally split for a solo career (JOAN JETT taking over vocal duties). Adopting a harder-edged approach, the new line-up released yet another album, 'WAITIN' FOR THE NIGHT' (1978), the last to feature LITA FORD (another RUNAWAY to go onto a semi-successful solo career) and VICKI BLUE (who had attempted suicide). Although LAURIE McCALLISTER was brought in as a brief replacement, she didn't play on a posthumous covers set, 'AND NOW . . . THE RUNAWAYS', the band having already finally split. JOAN JETT was the third and most successful member to carve out a solo niche, however, FOWLEY subsequently resurrected the name (minus any original members!) for a less than impressive 1987 set, 'YOUNG AND FAST'. • **Trivia:** The JOAN JETT & THE RUNAWAYS album was entirely made up of covers; Slade's 'MAMA WEER ALL CRAZEE NOW' being one of them.

Album rating: THE RUNAWAYS (*6) / QUEENS OF NOISE (*6) / LIVE IN JAPAN (*6)

CHERIE CURRIE (b.1960) – vocals who repl. MICKI STEELE (was part-time vox, bass) / **LITA FORD** (b.23 Sep'59, London, England) – lead guitar, vocals / **JOAN JETT** (b.22 Sep'60, Philadelphia, Pennsylvania) – rhythm guitar, vocals / **JACKIE FOX** – bass / **SANDY WEST** (b.1960) – drums

Mercury / Mercury

Sep 76. (7") *(6167 392) <73819>* **CHERRY BOMB. / BLACKMAIL** [ ] [ ]

Nov 76. (lp) *(9100 029) <SRM1 1090>* **THE RUNAWAYS** [ ] [ ] Jun 76
– Cherry bomb / You drive me wild / Is it day or night? / Thunder / Rock and roll / Lovers / American nights / Blackmail / Secrets / Dead end justice.

Feb 77. (lp) *(9100 032) <SRM1 1126>* **QUEENS OF NOISE** [ ] [ ] Jan 77
– Queens of noise / Take it or leave it / Midnight music / Born to be bad / Neon angels on the road to ruin / Midnight music / I love playin' with fire / California Paradise / Hollywood heartbeat / Johnny Guitar.

Feb 77. (7") *<73890>* **HEARTBEAT. / NEON ANGELS ON THE ROAD TO RUIN** [-] [ ]

Feb 77. (7") *(6167 493)* **QUEENS OF NOISE. / BORN TO BE BAD** [ ] [-]

Oct 77. (lp) *(9100 046)* **LIVE IN JAPAN (live)** [ ] [-]
– Queens of noise / California Paradise / All right you guys / Wild thing / Gettin' hot / Rock and roll / You drive me wild / Neon angels on the road to ruin / I wanna be where the boys are / Cherry bomb / American nights / C'mon.

—— (Jul'77) **VICKI BLUE** – bass repl. FOX who suffers from nervous exhaustion. **JETT** took over lead vocals, when CURRIE left to go solo.

Oct 77. (7") *(6167 587)* **SCHOOL DAYS. / WASTED** [ ] [-]

Dec 77. (lp) *(9100 047) <SRM1 3075>* **WAITIN' FOR THE NIGHT** [ ] [ ]
– Little sister / Wasted / Gotta get out tonight / Wait for me / Fantasies / School days / Trash can murders / Don't go away / Waitin' for the night / You're too possessive.

—— **LAURIE McALLISTER** – bass repl. VICKI BLUE when she attempted suicide. Split late 1978, when LITA FORD went solo after the recording of final album below.

Cherry Red / not iss.

Jul 79. (lp,colrd-lp) *(ARED 3)* **AND NOW . . . THE RUNAWAYS** [ ] [-]
– Saturday night special / Eight days a week / Mama weer all crazee now / I'm a million / Right now / Takeover / My buddy and me / Little lost girls / Black leather. *<re-iss. US 1981 as 'LITTLE LOST GIRLS' on 'Rhino' lp><pic-lp; RNLP 70861><RNDF 250> <cd-iss. US 1987; R2 70861> (cd-iss. Jul93 on 'Anagram'; CDGRAM 63)*

Aug 79. (7") *(CHERRY 8)* **RIGHT NOW. / BLACK LEATHER** [ ] [-]

—— JOAN JETT went solo backed by her BLACKHEARTS

– compilations, others, etc. –

Feb 80. (lp) *Cherry Red; (BRED 9)* **FLAMING SCHOOLGIRLS** (live/studio) [ ] [-]

Sep 82. (lp/c) *Mercury; (MERB/+C 12)* **THE BEST OF THE RUNAWAYS** [ ] [ ]

1981. (12"ep) *Rhino; <RNEP 602>* **MAMA WEER ALL CRAZEE NOW** [-] [ ]

Apr 82. (pic-lp/lp; JOAN JETT & THE RUNAWAYS) *Cherry Red; (P+/LAKER 1)* **I LOVE PLAYING WITH FIRE** [ ] [-]

1992. (cd) *Mercury; <838 583-2>* **NEON ANGELS** [-] [ ]

Jun 94. (10"lp) *Marilyn; (FM 1004)* **BORN TO BE BAD** [-] [-] France

RUTS

Formed: London, England . . . 1978 by MALCOLM OWEN, PAUL FOX, SEGS and DAVE RUFFY. One of the most revered punk acts to emerge in the seismic wake of The SEX PISTOLS and The CLASH, The RUTS shared the latter outfit's love of reggae and dub as well as their Rock Against Racism politics. Released as a one-off by tiny reggae label, 'People Unite', the seething 'IN A RUT' served as the band's debut single in early '79, earning them a series of John Peel sessions and a major label contract courtesy of 'Virgin'. The tinderbox intensity of follow-up track, 'BABYLON'S BURNING' was enough to break The RUTS into the UK Top 10 later that summer while the equally anthemic 'SOMETHING THAT I SAID' scraped the Top 30 ahead of debut album, 'THE CRACK' (1979). Alternating scathing politico-punk with defiant dub excursions, the album cut to the fractured heart of late 70's youth culture with a precision lacking in some of their clumsier peers; third single, 'JAH WAR', recounted an anti-fascist riot to a hypnotic dub backing while 1980's classic 'STARING AT THE RUDE BOYS' displayed a spiritual solidarity with the emerging 2-tone movement. Sadly, it also proved to be the band's epitaph as OWEN succumbed to his heroin habit later that summer. While a compilation set of live and rare tracks, 'GRIN AND BEAR IT' (1980), served as a stop-gap release, the remainder of the band eventually resurfaced in early '81 as RUTS DC with FOX taking over lead vocals and GARY BARNACLE joining on sax. The subsequent two albums, 'ANIMAL NOW' (1981) and 'RHYTHM COLLISION' (1982) took a more commercial approach and met with little enthusiasm. Clearly struggling without OWEN's guiding influence, the band finally split in mid '83 with BARNACLE going on to work with VISAGE and RUFFY joining AZTEC CAMERA. • **Trivia:** In 1980, they were the backing band of KEVIN COYNE on his album, 'Sanity Stomp'.

Album rating: THE CRACK (*7) / SOMETHING THAT I SAID – THE BEST OF . . . compilation (*8)

MALCOLM OWEN – vocals / **PAUL FOX** – guitar, vocals / **SEGS** (b. JOHN JENNINGS) – bass / **DAVE RUFFY** – drums

PeopleUnite / not iss.

May 79. (7") *(SJP 795)* **IN A RUT. / H-EYES** [ ] [-]
(re-iss. Jun79; RUT 1)

Virgin / Virgin

Jun 79. (7"/12") *(VS 271/-12)* **BABYLON'S BURNING. / SOCIETY** [7] [-]

Aug 79. (7") *(VS 285)* **SOMETHING THAT I SAID. / GIVE YOUTH A CHANCE** [29] [-]

Sep 79. (lp/c) *(<V/TCV 2132>)* **THE CRACK** [16] [ ]
– Babylon's burning / Dope for guns / S.U.S. / Something that I said / You're just a . . . / It was cold / Savage circle / Jah war / Criminal mind / Backbiter / Out of order / Human punk. *(re-iss. Aug88; OVED 80) (cd-iss. Jul90; CDV 2132)(+=)* – Give youth a chance / I ain't so satisfied / The crack. *(re-iss. cd Mar94)*

Nov 79. (7") *(VS 298)* **JAH WAR. / I AIN'T SOFISTICATED** [ ] [-]

Apr 80. (7") *(VS 327)* **STARING AT THE RUDE BOYS. / LOVE IN VAIN** [22] [-]

—— On 14th July '80, MALCOLM OWEN died of a drug overdose. Postumous releases below.

Aug 80. (7") *(VS 370)* **WEST ONE (SHINE ON ME). / THE CRACK** [43] [-]

Oct 80. (lp/c) *(V/TCV 2188)* **GRIN AND BEAR IT** (new, live & rare) [28] [-]
– In a rut / Love in vain / S.U.S. / Babylon's burning / Society / West one (shine on me) / Staring at the rude boys / Demolition dancing / Secret soldier / H eyes. *(re-iss. Mar84; OVED 57)*

RUTS D.C.

remaining trio (with PAUL on lead vocals) / added **GARY BARNACLE** – saxophone, keyboards

Feb 81. (7") *(VS 396)* **DIFFERENT VIEW. / FORMULA BOYS** [ ] [-]
May 81. (lp/c) *(V/TCV 2193)* **ANIMAL NOW** [ ] [-]
– Mirror smashed / Dangerous minds / Slow down / Despondency / Different view / No time to kill / Fools / Walk or run / Parasites.

Bohemian **not iss.**

Jul 82. (7") *(BO 2)* **WHATEVER WE DO. / PUSH YOURSELF – MAKE IT WORK** [ ] [-]
Jul 82. (lp) *(BOLP 4)* **RHYTHM COLLISION** [ ] [-]
– Whatever we do / Militant / Push yourself (make it work) / Rhythm collision / Accusation / Pleasures of the dance / Weak heart (dub) / Love and fire.
Mar 83. (12"ep) *(12BO 3)* **WEAK HEART. / MILITANT / ACCUSATION** [ ] [-]

RUTS

May 83. (7"m) *(BO 4)* **STEPPING BONDAGE. / LOBOTOMY / RICH BITCH** [ ] [-]

— Folded mid'83. BARNACLE joined VISAGE, etc, and RUFFY joined AZTEC CAMERA.

– compilations, etc. –

Apr 83. (12"ep) *Virgin; (VS 583-12)* **BABYLON'S BURNING / SOMETHING THAT I SAID. / STARING AT THE RUDE BOYS / WEST ONE (SHINE ON ME)** [ ] [-]
Dec 86. (12"ep) *Strange Fruit; (SFPS 011)* **PEEL SESSIONS** (21.5.79) [ ] [-]
– S.U.S. / Society / You're just a . . . / It was cold / Something that I said. *(re-iss. Jun87 c-ep; SFPSC 011)*
Mar 87. (lp) *Dojo; (DOJOLP 52)* **LIVE! (live)** [ ] [-]
Aug 87. (c) *R.O.I.R.; <A 151>* **RHYTHM COLLISION DUB VOL.1** (with MAD PROFESSOR) [-] [ ]
(re-iss. Mar91 on French 'Danceteria' cd/lp; DANCD/DANLP 054)
1987. (cd) *Virgin; (COMCD 7)* **YOU'VE GOTTA GET OUT OF IT** [ ] [-]
Dec 87. (lp) *Link; (LINKLP 013)* **LIVE AND LOUD (live)** [ ] [-]
(cd-iss. Aug92 on 'Street Link'; LINKCD 013)
Nov 88. (7") *Old Gold; (OG 9829)* **BABYLON'S BURNING. / STARING AT THE RUDE BOYS** [ ] [-]
May 90. (cd/c/lp) *Strange Fruit; (SFR CD/MC/LP 109)* **PEEL SESSIONS – COMPLETE SESSIONS 1979-1981** [ ] [-]
Jan 92. (cd; shared with PENETRATION) *Windsong; (WINCD 009)* **BBC RADIO 1 LIVE IN CONCERT (live)** [ ] [-]
1992. (cd-ep; shared with SKIDS) *Virgin; (VSCDT)* **THE SKIDS VS THE RUTS EP** [ ] [-]
Mar 94. (cd) *Receiver; (RRCD 182)* **DEMOLITION DANCING** [ ] [-]
Mar 95. (cd) *Virgin; (CDOVD 454)* **SOMETHING THAT I SAID . . .THE BEST OF THE RUTS** [ ] [-]
– In a rut / Babylon's burning / Dope for guns / Sus / Something that I said / You're just a . . . / It was cold / Savage circle / Jah war / Criminal mind / Backbiter / Out of order / Human punk / Staring at the rude boys / Love in vain / West one (shine on me).
Mar 95. (cd; shared with The ADVERTS) *Step 1;* **LIVE AND LOUD (live)** [ ] [-]

SABALON GLITZ (see under ⇒ HOLMES, Chris)

SAD LOVERS AND GIANTS

Formed: Rickmansworth, England . . . 1980 by GARCE ALLARD, TRISTAN GAREL-FUNK, DAVID WOOD, CLIFF SILVER and NIGEL POLLARD. Subsequently basing themselves in Watford and releasing a couple of singles for the small indie imprint, 'Last Movement', SL&G made a brave attempt at combining trad folk influences and complex prog-rock elements with the jangly post-punk pop coming out of the US Paisley underground scene. Initiating their own 'Midnight Music' label, the quintet revealed their penchant for classically romantic lyrical wordplay with mini-set, 'EPIC GARDEN MUSIC' (1982). Their first album proper, 'FEEDING THE FLAME' (1983), found a more enthusiastic audience on the continent and while UK support came from the likes of Radio One DJ, John Peel, the band were on the verge of an imminent split. Following their demise, posthumous material surfaced in the shape of 'IN THE BREEZE' (outtakes and a Peel session) and 'TOTAL SOUND' (live on Dutch radio). ALLARD and POLLARD re-emerged early in 1987 with a new line-up (TONY McGUINNESS, JULIET SAINSBURY and IAN GIBSON) and a fresher, cleaner sound on comeback set, 'THE MIRROR TEST'. A series of 12" EP's ensued while the band set about recording a follow-up, although the collapse of their label eventually saw 'TREEHOUSE POETRY' secure a German-only release on 'Rough Trade' in 1991.

Album rating: EPIC GARDEN MUSIC mini (*4) / FEEDING THE FLAME (*5) / IN THE BREEZE (*5) / TOTAL SOUND (*5) / THE MIRROR TEST (*4) / LES ANNES VERTES (*4) / TREEHOUSE POETRY (*4)

GARCE ALLARD – vocals / **TRISTAN GAREL FUNK** – guitar / **DAVID WOOD** – keyboards / **CLIFF SILVER** – bass / **NIGEL POLLARD** – drums

Last Movement | not iss.

May 81. (7"ep) *(LM 003)* **CLE** [ ] [-]
– Imagination / Landslide / When I see you.

Oct 81. (7") *(LM 005)* **COLOURLESS DREAM. / THINGS WE NEVER DID** [ ] [-]

Midnight Music | not iss.

Sep 82. (m-lp) *(CHIME 0001)* **EPIC GARDEN MUSIC** [ ] [-]
– Echoplay / Clocktower lodge / Clint / Lope / Cloud 9 / Art / Alice / Far from the sea. *(cd-iss. Sep88; CHIME 0001CD)* – (with extra tracks)

Nov 82. (7") *(DING 1)* **LOST IN A MOMENT. / THE TIGHTROPE TOUCH** [ ] [-]

Oct 83. (7") *(DING 5)* **MAN OF STRAW. / COWBOYS** [ ] [-]
(12"+=) *(DONG 5)* – Close to the sea.

Nov 83. (lp) *(CHIME 0003)* **FEEDING THE FLAME** [ ] [-]
(cd-iss. Sep88; CHIME 0003CD) – (with extra tracks)

Nov 84. (lp) *(CHIME 0007M)* **IN THE BREEZE** [ ] [-]
– (rare demos, out-takes & John Peel sessions)

Oct 86. (m-lp) *(CHIME 0022)* **TOTAL SOUND** (live on Dutch radio in 1983) [ ] [-]

— Had already disbanded in 1984, although they re-formed in 1987.

— **GARCE + NIGEL** recruited **TONY McGUINNESS** – guitar / **JULIET SAINSBURY** – keyboards / **IAN GIBSON** – bass

Feb 87. (12"m) **SEVEN KINDS OF SIN. / THE OUTSIDER / OURS TO KILL** [ ] [-]

May 87. (lp) *(CHIME 0030)* **THE MIRROR TEST** [ ] [-]
– White Russians / Take seven / Seven kinds of sin / The green years / Cuckooland / Return to clocktower lodge / Wire lawn / House of clouds / Summer and smoke. *(cd-iss. Mar88 +=; CHIME 0030)* – Ours to kill / A map of the world / The outsider / Life under glass.

Jul 87. (12"m) *(DONG 34)* **WHITE RUSSIANS. / A MAP OF THE WORLD / LIFE UNDER GLASS** [ ] [-]

Mar 88. (12"ep) *(DONG 36)* **COWBOYS (remix) / LOST IN A MOMENT (remix). / THE BEST FILM HE EVER MADE / THINGS WE NEVER DID (live)** [ ] [-]

Nov 88. (lp) *(CHIME 40S)* **LES ANNES VERTES** (compilation) [ ] [-]

Apr 90. (12"ep) *(DONG 59)* **CLOCKS GO BACKWARDS** (re-rec) [ ] [-]

Rough Trade | not iss.

1991. (lp) *(351.0120.1)* **TREEHOUSE POETRY** [-] [-] German
– Toy planes in a southern sky / Lizard king / Still restless / Parachute of love / Christmas on Easter Island / Criminally sane / Jungle of lies / The sky is a glove.

— split after above

SAINT ETIENNE

Formed: North London, England . . . early 90's by music journo, BOB STANLEY and PETE WIGGS. Naming themselves after French football team, St. Etienne, after originally toying with the name, REARDON (the snooker player!), they signed to up-and-coming indie label 'Heavenly'. With MOIRA LAMBERT on vocals (borrowed from FAITH OVER REASON), the outfit's first vinyl foray was a sublime dub/indie-dance cover of Neil Young's 'ONLY LOVE CAN BREAK YOUR HEART'. Re-released after securing their first minor hit, 'NOTHING CAN STOP US', the track brought ST. ETIENNE to the attention of both the dance and indie scene. By this point however, a full-time vocalist (guest DONNA SAVAGE of the DEAD FAMOUS PEOPLE featured on their version of the Field Mice's 'KISS AND MAKE UP') had been recruited in the shape of SARAH CRACKNELL, whose sensuous, playful voice graced the bulk of 'FOXBASE ALPHA' (1991). A stunning debut album mixing and matching disco samples, trippy bass-lines and airy atmospherics into a pot-pourri of kitschy pop genius, the record was released to rave reviews and its relatively lowly chart position barely reflected its importance. With word now out, the group narrowly missed the UK Top 20 with their next single, 'JOIN OUR CLUB', although by early 1993 they found themselves bonafide pop stars when 'YOU'RE IN A BAD WAY' became their biggest hit to date. The accompanying album, 'SO TOUGH', cemented SAINT ETIENNE's position as top swoon-pop ironists, a masterfully sampledelic set featuring such classy compositions as 'HOBART PAVING', 'AVENUE' (also a Top 40 hit) and 'CALICO'. Following CRACKNELL's high profile collaboration with TIM BURGESS (Charlatans) for the Xmas hit, 'I WAS BORN ON CHRISTMAS DAY', the oufit completed their fourth set, 'TIGER BAY', a record which slightly disappointed their fan/fox base with its more experimental approach. Although the future of the group seemed in doubt with CRACKNELL working on solo material, a brilliant return to form with the 'HE'S ON THE PHONE' single boded well for the future. • **Songwriters:** STANLEY-WIGGS except a few with CRACKNELL plus outside covers WHO DO YOU THINK YOU ARE (Scott-Dyer) / MY CHRISTMAS PRAYER (Billy Fury) / WESTERN WIND (trad.) / STRANGER IN PARADISE (hit; Tony Bennett) / IS IT TRUE (Marc Bolan) / HOW I LEARNED TO LOVE THE BOMB (TV Personalities). • **Trivia:** Sang a version of RIGHT SAID FRED's 'I'M TOO SEXY' on a 1992 'Heavenly' compilation ep.

Album rating: FOXBASE ALPHA (*8) / SO TOUGH (*7) / TIGER BAY (*6).

BOB STANLEY (b.25 Dec'64, Horsham, Sussex) – keyboards / **PETE WIGGS** (b.15 May'66, Reigate, Surrey) – keyboards, synthesizers / **MOIRA LAMBERT** – vocals (of FAITH OVER REASON)

Heavenly | Warners

Jul 90. (7"/12") *(HVN 2/212)* **ONLY LOVE CAN BREAK YOUR HEART. / ('A'version)** [ ] [-]
(12") *(HVN 212R)* – ('A'-A mix of two halves mix by Andy Weatherall) / The Official Saint Etienne world cup theme.

— **DONNA SAVAGE** – vocals (of DEAD FAMOUS PEOPLE) repl. MOIRA

Sep 90. (7"/12") *(HVN 4/412)* **KISS AND MAKE UP. / SKY'S DEAD** [ ] [-]
(cd-s+=) *(HVN 412R)* – ('A'extended).
(12") *(HVN 4CD)* – ('A'mixes by Pete Helber incl. dub version).

— **SARAH CRACKNELL** – vocals repl. DONNA

May 91. (7"/12") *(HVN 9/912)* **NOTHING CAN STOP US. / SPEEDWELL** [54] [ ]
(cd-s+=) *(HVN 9CD)* – ('A'instrumental).
(12"++=) *(HVN 912R)* – ('B'-Flying mix) / ('B'-Project mix) / 3-D tiger.

— below A-side featured MOIRA LAMBERT / B-side featured Q-TEE

Aug 91. (7"/12"/c-s) *(HVN 12/+12/+CS)* **ONLY LOVE CAN BREAK YOUR HEART. / FILTHY** [39] [-]
(cd-s+=) *(HVN 12CD)* – ('A'-A mix of two halves).

Oct 91. (cd/c/lp) *(HVN CD/MC/LP 1) <26793>* **FOXBASE ALPHA** [34] [ ] Jan92
– This is Radio Etienne / Only love can break your heart / Wilson / Carnt sleep / Girl VII / Spring / She's the one / Stoned to say the least / Nothing can stop us / Etienne gonna die / London belongs to me / Like the swallow / Dilworth's theme.

Jan 92. (12"ep) *<0-40395>* **NOTHING CAN STOP US (mixes) / SPEEDWELL** [-] [ ]

Feb 92. (c-s) *<19078>* **ONLY LOVE CAN BREAK YOUR HEART / STONED TO SAY THE LEAST** [-] [97]
(12"+=) *<0-40196>* – ('A'mixes).

May 92. (7"/c-s) *(HVN 15/+CS)* **JOIN OUR CLUB. / PEOPLE GET REAL** [21] [-]
(12"+=/cd-s+=) *(HVN 15 12/CD)* – ('A'-Chemically friendly zoom mix) / Scene '93.

Sep 92. (c-ep/12"ep/cd-ep) *(HVN 23 CS/12/CD)* **AVENUE / SOME PLACE ELSE. / PAPER / JOHNNY IN THE ECHO CAFE** [40] [-]
(cd-s) *(HVN 23CDR)* – ('A'club mix) / ('A'-Marshall mix) / ('A'-Venusian mix) (all remixed by A.R. KANE or GORDON KING).

— added **IAN CATT** – guitar, programmer

Feb 93. (7"/c-s) *(HVN 25/+CS)* **YOU'RE IN A BAD WAY. / CALIFORNIA SNOW STORY** [12] [-]
(12"+=/cd-s+=) *(HVN 25 12/CD)* – Archway people / Duke Duvet.

Mar 93. (cd/c/lp) *(HVN CD/MC/LP 6) <45166>* **SO TOUGH** [7] [ ]
– Mario's cafe / Railway jam / Date with Spelman / Calico / Avenue / You're in

a bad way / Memo to Pricey / Hobart paving / Leafhound / Clock milk / Conchita Martinez / No rainbows for me / Here come clown feet / Junk the morgue / Chicken soup. *(re-iss. Jun93 with free ltd.cd 'YOU NEED A MESS OF HELP TO STAND ALONE' compilation; HVN CDX 6)* – Who do you think you are / Archway people / California snow storm / Kiss and make up / Duke duvet / Filthy / Join our club / Paper / Some place else / Speedwell.

May 93. (7"/c-s) *(HVN 29/+CS)* **HOBART PAVING. / WHO DO YOU THINK YOU ARE** 23 -
(12"+=/cd-s+=) *(HVN 29 12/CD)* – Your head my voice (voix revirement) / Who do you think you are (Quex-Rd) (Aphex Twin remixes).

Jun 93. (12"/cd-s) *<40910>* **WHO DO YOU THINK YOU ARE (mixes)** -

Dec 93. (7"/c-s) *(HVN 36/+CS)* **I WAS BORN ON CHRISTMAS DAY. / MY CHRISTMAS PRAYER** 37 -
(12"+=/cd-s+=) *(HVN 36 12/CD)* – Snowplough / Peterloo.
(above 'A' featured dual vocals with TIM BURGESS of The CHARLATANS)

Dec 93. (cd/c/lp) *(HVN CD/MC/LP 7)* **YOU NEED A MESS OF HELP TO STAND ALONE**
– (see last album)

Feb 94. (7"/c-s) *(HVN 37/+CS)* **PALE MOVIE. / HIGHGATE ROAD INCIDENT** 28 -
(12"/cd-s) *(HVN 37 12/CD)* – ('A'side) / ('A'-Stentorian dub) / ('A'-Secret Knowledge trouse assassin mix) / ('A'-Lemonentry mix).

Feb 94. (cd/c/lp) *(HVN CD/MC/LP 8) <45634>* **TIGER BAY** 8 Jun94
– Urban clearway / Former lover / Hug my soul / Like a motorway / On the shore / Marble lions / Pale movie / Cool kids of death / Western wind / Tankerville / Western wind / Boy scouts of America.

May 94. (7"/c-s) *(HVN 40/+CS)* **LIKE A MOTORWAY. / YOU KNOW I'LL MISS YOU WHEN YOU'RE GONE / SUSHI RIDER** 47 -
(12"/cd-s) *(HVN 40 12/CD)* – ('A'side) / ('A'-Chekhov warp mix) / ('A'-David Holmes mix) / (Skin up, you're already dead) (Dust Brothers mix).

Sep 94. (c-ep/cd-ep) *(HVN 42 CS/CD) <41591>* **HUG MY SOUL / I BUY AMERICAN RECORDS / HATE YOUR DRUG / LA POUPEE QUI FAIT NON (NO, NO, NO) (live)** 32
(12"ep) *(HVN 4012)* – ('A'side) / ('A'-Sure Is Pure) / ('A'-Motiv8) / ('A'-Secret Knowledge).
(cd-ep+=) *(HVN 42CDR)* – (above tracks) / ('A'-Juan "Kinky" Hernandez mix).

Feb 95. (fan club-cd) *(HVNCD 9)* **I LOVE TO PAINT** - -

Heavenly M.C.A.

Oct 95. (c-s) *(HVN 50CS) <55268>* **HE'S ON THE PHONE / ('A'-Motiv8 mix)** 11 Jan96
(cd-s+=) *(HVN 50CDR)* – Cool kids of death (Underworld mix) / How I learned to love the bomb.
(cd-s) *(HVN 50CD)* – ('A'side) / Groveley Road / Is it true / The process.

Nov 95. (cd/c/d-lp) *(HVN CD/MC/LP 10)* **TOO YOUNG TO DIE – THE SINGLES** (compilation) 17 -
– Only love can break your heart / Kiss and make up / Nothing can stop us / Join our club / People get real / Avenue / You're in a bad way / Who do you think you are / Hobart paving / I was born on Christmas day / Pale movie / Like a motorway / Hug my soul / He's on the phone. *(cd w/cd 'THE REMIX ALBUM'; HVN LP 10CDR)(+=)* – (9 remixes).

— next with French dance artist ETIENNE DAHO and on 'Dindisc'/'Alex'US.

Jan 96. (m-cd; as ST. ETIENNE DAHO) *(DINSD 150) <5567>* **RESERECTION** 50 Feb96

Oct 96. (d-cd/d-c/t-lp) *(HVNLP 16 CD/MC/LP)* **CASINO CLASSICS** 34 -
– remixes by Chemical Brothers / PFM / Underworld / Way out West / Andrew Weatherall / Lionrock / David Holmes / Monkey Mafia / Death In Vegas / Sure Is Pure / Billy Nasty / Gordon King / Secret Knowledge / The Aloof / Broadcast / Aphex Twin / Primax / Psychonauts / Balearico.

— SARAH had already tried out a solo career

SARAH CRACKNELL

Gut not iss.

Jul 96. (c-s/cd-s) *(CA/CD GUT 3)* **ANYMORE / OH BOY, THE FEELING WHEN YOU HELD MY HAND** 39 -
(cd-s+=) *(CXGUT 3)* – Fifth floor / Anymore (mix).

Apr 97. (c-s) *(CAGUT 7)* **GOLDIE / ('A'mix)** -
(cd-s+=) *(CDGUT 7)* – ('A'mixes).

May 97. (cd/c) *(GUT CD/MC 2)* **LIPSLIDE** -
– Ready or not / Desert baby / Coastal town / Home / Anymore / How far / Goldie / Taxi / Taking off for France / If you leave me / Penthouse girl, basement boy / Can't stop now.

SAINT ETIENNE

— **SARAH** returned to the fold in 1997

Creation not iss.

Jan 98. (c-s) *(CRECS 279)* **SYLVIE / AFRAID TO GO HOME** 12 -
(cd-s+=) *(CRESCD 279)* – Zipcode / Hill street connection.
(cd-s) *(CRESCD 279X)* – ('A'mixes).

Apr 98. (c-s) *(CRECS 290)* **THE BAD PHOTOGRAPHER / HIT THE . . .** 27 -
(cd-s+=) *(CRESCD 290)* – Swim swan swim / Madelaine.
(cd-s) *(CRESCD 290X)* – ('A'side) / 4.35 in the morning (Kid Loco remix) / Foto (Bronx Dogs mix) / Uri Geller bent my boyfriend (Add N To X mix).

May 98. (cd/lp) *(CRE CD/LP 225)* **GOOD HUMOR** 18 -
– Woodcabin / Sylvie / Split screen / Mr Donut / Goodnight Jack / Lose that girl / The bad photographer / Been so long / Postman / Erica America / Dutch TV. *(also ltd-cd; CRECD 225L)*

SAINTS

Formed: Brisbane, Australia . . . 1976 by ED KUEPPER and CHRIS BAILEY alongside KYM BRADSHAW and IVOR HAY. The quartet had barely begun an apprenticeship on the Sydney music scene when their debut effort, 'I'M STRANDED' (released on 'Fatal' in Australia), won a Single Of The Week award in punk-friendly music paper, 'Sounds'. Hi-octane rock'n'roll ignited by KUEPPER's scathing guitar playing and IGGY POP-style drawl, the domestically released track saw The SAINTS hailed as Australia's most vital contribution to the punk war effort and bagged them a major label deal with 'Harvest' into the bargain. Relocating to the UK, the band enjoyed widespread acclaim for their similarly titled debut album, released in the summer of '77 alongside their only Top 40 hit, 'THIS PERFECT DAY'. A subsequent EP, 'ONE TWO THREE FOUR', found them demolishing standards, 'LIPSTICK ON YOUR COLLAR' and 'RIVER DEEP MOUNTAIN HIGH', while 1978's 'KNOW YOUR PRODUCT' single and accompanying album, 'ETERNALLY YOURS', flirted with a brassier sound. Never a punk band in the conventional sense, The SAINTS refused to kow-tow to prevailing fashion and suffered the resulting damage to their credibilty. To make matters worse, KUEPPER left after the release of 1978's 'PREHISTORIC SOUNDS' with the remaining line-up having crumbled by the end of the year. While the former frontman went on to follow his own idiosyncratic path and enjoy cult acclaim with The LAUGHING CLOWNS and a subsequent solo career, CHRIS BAILEY later reformed The SAINTS at the turn of the decade with a line-up of CHRIS BARRINGTON, JANINE HALL, MARK BIRMINGHAM and IVOR HAY. Signed to French label, 'New Rose', the remodelled band released 'THE MONKEY PUZZLE' in 1981, the following year's 'CASABLANCA' and 1984's 'WHAT WE DID ON OUR HOLIDAYS' issued as BAILEY solo albums. Featuring former BIRTHDAY PARTY man, TRACY PEW, until his untimely death in 1986, The SAINTS continued to record sporadically throughout the 80's and on into the 90's with varying line-ups. • **Songwriters:** Penned by BAILEY and KUEPPER, until the latter's departure. Covered RIVER DEEP MOUNTAIN HIGH (Phil Spector) / LIPSTICK ON YOUR COLLAR (Connie Francis).

Album rating: I'M STRANDED (*6) / ETERNALLY YOURS (*6) / PREHISTORIC SOUNDS (*6) / THE MONKEY PUZZLE (*4) / A LITTLE MADNESS TO BE FREE (*5) / LIVE IN A MUD HUT (*5) / ALL FOOLS DAY (*6) / SONGS OF SALVATION compilation (*8)

CHRIS BAILEY – vocals / **ED KUEPPER** (b. EDMUND) – guitar / **KYM BRADSHAW** – bass / **IVOR HAY** – drums

Fatal Sire

Sep 76. (7") *(MA 7158) <1005>* **(I'M) STRANDED. / NO TIME** Jun77

Harvest Sire

May 77. (7") *(HAR 5123)* **EROTIC NEUROTIC. / ONE WAY STREET** -

May 77. (lp) *(SHSP 4065) <SRK 6039>* **(I'M) STRANDED**
– (I'm) Stranded / One way street / Wild about you / Messin' with the kid / Erotic neurotic / No time / Kissin' cousins / Story of love / Demolition girl / Nights in Venice. *(cd-iss. Nov97 on 'Triple X'; TX 51243CD)*

Jul 77. (7") *(HAR 5130)* **THIS PERFECT DAY. / LIES** 34
(12") *(12HAR 5130)* – ('A'side) / Do the robot.

— **ALGY WARD** – bass repl. BRADSHAW who joined The LURKERS

Sep 77. (7"ep) *(SHSM 2028)* **ONE TWO THREE FOUR** -
– Lipstick on your collar / One way street / Demolition girl / River deep mountain high.

Feb 78. (7") *(11673)* **KNOW YOUR PRODUCT. / RUN DOWN** -

Mar 78. (lp) *(SHSP 4078) <SRK 6055>* **ETERNALLY YOURS**
– Know your product / Lost and found / Memories are made of this / Private affair / A minor aversion / No, your product / This perfect day / Run down / Ostralia / New center of the universe / Untitled / Misunderstood. *(re-iss. Nov87 on 'Fan Club'; FC 035) (cd-iss. May94 on 'New Rose'; 422309) (cd re-iss. Nov97 on 'Triple X'; TX 51244CD)*

Aug 78. (7") *(11795)* **SECURITY. / ALL TIMES THROUGH PARADISE** -

Sep 78. (lp) *(SHSP 4094)* **PREHISTORIC SOUNDS** -
– Swing for the crime / All times through Paradise / Everyday's a holiday, every night's a party / Brisbane / Church of indifference / Crazy Googenheimer blues / Everything's fine / The prisoner / Security / This time / This heart of mine / The chameleon / Save me. *(re-iss. Nov87 on 'Fan Club'; FC 036) (cd-iss. May94 on 'New Rose'; 422312)*

— Disbanded late 1978. KUEPPER formed The LAUGHING CLOWNS and WARD joined The DAMNED. In 1980, **CHRIS BAILEY** re-formed The SAINTS recruiting **CHRIS BARRINGTON** – guitar / **JANINE HALL** – bass / **MARK BIRMINGHAM** – drums / guest **IVOR HAY** – keyboards

New Rose not iss.

Apr 80. (12"ep) *(NEW 1)* **PARALYTIC TONIGHT DUBLIN TOMORROW EP** -
– Simple love / Roses / On the waterfront / Call it mine.

Oct 80. (7") *(NEW 3)* **ALWAYS. / IN THE MIRROR** -

Jan 81. (lp) *(ROSE 1)* **THE MONKEY PUZZLE** -
– Miss wonderful / Always / Paradise / Let's pretend / Someday / Monkeys (let's go) / Mystery dream / Simple love / The ballad / Dizzy Miss Lizzy. *(free live 7"m w.a.)* – **(I'M) STRANDED. / SECURITY / THIS PERFECT DAY** *(cd-iss. 1980's+=; ROSE 1CD)* – (above 12"ep)

Flicknife not iss.

Feb 83. (7") *(FLS 215)* **FOLLOW THE LEADER. / ANIMAL** -

CHRIS BAILEY

New Rose not iss.

1983. (lp) *(ROSE 20)* **CASABLANCA** -

1984. (lp) *(ROSE 30)* **WHAT WE DID ON OUR HOLIDAYS** -
– In the midnight hour / Ghost ships / Cherokee dance / I'm drinking / Bring it on home to me / Careless love / I heard it through the grapevine / Amsterdam / All night long / Wak on / Another Saturday night / Home again / It's only time / Insurance on me / Junko partner / Look at me / Always the same / Why does it make me feel / Country boy. *(cd-iss. Aug90; ROSE 30CD)*

SAINTS

— **TRACY PEW** – bass (ex-BIRTHDAY PARTY) repl. JANINE HALL

New Rose | not iss.

Dec 84. (7") *(NEW 43)* **IMAGINATION. / PRISONER (live)** [ ] [-]
Dec 84. (lp) *(ROSE 38)* **A LITTLE MADNESS TO BE FREE** [ ] [-]
(cd-iss. 1985 +=; ROSE 38CD) – (extra live tracks)
Mar 85. (7") *(NEW 37)* **GHOST SHIP. / WRAPPED UP & BLUE** [ ] [-]
May 85. (lp) *(ROSE 55)* **LIVE IN A MUD HUT (live)** [ ] [-]
– Ghost ship / Imagination / Follow the leader / Know your product / etc.

— TRACY PEW died of cancer in November '86

— **BAILEY + HAY** with **RICHARD BURGMANN** – bass + **ARCHIE LaRIZZA** – drums

Polydor | TVT

Oct 86. (7") *(POSP 825)* **THE TEMPLE OF THE LORD. / CELTIC BALLAD** [ ] [-]
(12"+=) *(POSPX 825)* – How to avoid disaster.
Oct 86. (lp/c) *(POLD/+C 5203)* <*TVT 2111-1/-4/-2*> **ALL FOOLS DAY** [ ] [ ] 1987
– Just like fire would / First time / Hymn to Saint Jude / See you in Paradise / Love or imagination / Celtic ballad / Empty page / Big hits (on the underground) / How to avoid disaster / Blues on my mind / Temple of the Lord / All fools day.
Mar 87. (7") *(POSP 848)* **JUST LIKE FIRE WOULD. / EAST IS EAST** [ ] [-]
(12"+=) *(POSPX 848)* – Casablanca.

— split but BAILEY re-formed 1989 with **LaRIZZA / + IAIN SHEDDEN** – drums / **BARRINGTON 'BAZ' FRANCIS** – guitar / **JOE CHIOFALO** – keyboards

Mushroom | TVT

Jan 90. (7") *(MRI 01)* **GRAIN OF SAND. / MAD RACE** [ ] [-]
(12"+=) *(MRI 01T)* – Minus a ride.
Jan 90. (cd/c/lp) *(MRI CD/MC/LP 001)* <*TVT 2121-2/-4/-1*> **PRODIGAL SON** [ ] [ ] Nov89
– Grain of sand / Fire and brimstone / Friend of the people / Before Hollywood / Sold out / Ghost ships / Massacre / Tomorrow / Stay / Shipwreck / The music goes round my head.
1992. (cd) **PERMANENT REVOLUTION** [-] [ ]
– Grain of sand (Zydeco version) / One night with you / Wild and wicked world / Pick up the pieces / Running away / Revolution in my life / Friday the 13th / Love or imagination / Cartoon life / Idiot blues.
1992. (12"etched) **GRAIN OF SAND. / CARTOON** [-] [ ]

— disbanded after above but re-formed in the mid-90's

Blue Rose | Triple X

Oct 96. (cd) *(BLUCD 029)* <*TX 51245CD*> **HOWLING** [ ] [ ] Jan98
– Howling / Shadows / Something, somewhere, sometime / Something wicked / Only stone / Good Friday / Blown away / Last and laughing mile / You know I know / Only dreaming / Second coming / All for nothing.

Last Call | Amsterdamned

Apr 98. (cd) *(303777-2)* <*70019*> **EVERYBODY KNOWS THE MONKEY** [ ] [ ] Oct98
– What do you want / Easy money / Working overtime / Fall of an empire / Mustard / Vaguely Jesus / What are you waiting for / Everything turns sour / Playboy of the western world / Come back and visit / S+M+M's / Glorious wonder.

– compilations, etc. –

Aug 77. (7") *Power Exchange; (PX 242)* **(I'M) STRANDED. / (B-side by Chuck Stanley)** [ ] [-]
Mar 82. (lp) *New Rose; (ROSE 11)* **OUT IN THE JUNGLE** [ ] [-]
(cd-iss. 1988; ROSE 11CD) (re-iss. Oct90 on 'Flicknife'; SHARP 106)
Nov 86. (lp) *Razor; (RAZ 21)* **THE BEST OF THE SAINTS (77-78)** [ ] [-]
Dec 89. (lp) *Raven;* **SCARCE SAINTS** [-] [-] Austra
Jan 90. (lp/c/cd) *Fan Club; (FC 060/+C/CD)* **THE NEW ROSE YEARS (GREATEST HITS)** [ ] [-]
(cd+=) – (5 extra tracks)
Feb 91. (cd) *Raven; (<9>)* **SONGS OF SALVATION 1976-1988** [-] [ ] Austra
Jul 95. (lp/cd) *Hot; (HOT 1053/+CD)* **THE MOST PRIMITIVE BAND IN THE WORLD (live from The Twilight Zone, Brisbane 1974)** [ ] [-]
– Wild about you / Do the robot / One way street / Knock on wood / Erotic neurotic / River deep mountain high / Lies / Stranded / Messin' with the kid / Misunderstood.
Oct 96. (cd) *EMI Gold; (CDGO 2069)* **KNOW YOUR PRODUCT (THE BEST OF THE SAINTS)** [ ] [-]
– (I'm) Stranded / This perfect day / Lipstick on your collar / River deep mountain high / Demolition girl / One way street / Story of love / Kissin' cousins / No time / Wild about you / Messin' with the kid / Nights in Venice / Do the robot / Know your product / Run down / Lost and found / Memories are made of this / Private affaie / Minor aversion / No. your product / Swing for the crime / All times through paradise.

CHRIS BAILEY

East West | East West

Mar 91. (cd/lp) **DEMONS** [ ] [ ]
– Demons / Marquis of Queensberry / Return to zero / Bridges / Edgar Allan Poe / Running away from home / Fade away / Marie Antoinette / Rusting in the moonlight / That's the way it goes / Up all night.

Mushroom | not iss.

Mar 94. (cd) *(D 31145)* **54 DAYS AT SEA** [ ] [-]

SALAD

Formed: London, England ... 1992 by ex-MTV presenter and fashion model, MARIJNE VAN DER VLUGT, along with fellow ex-film student and boyfriend, PAUL KENNEDY, PETE BROWN and ROB WAKEMAN. Releasing the 'KENT' EP in summer '93 on their own 'Waldorf' label, the band aroused immediate interest from the indie press with their raw-edged alternative pop/rock sound, artfully convoluted lyrics adding extra cred. After a further 12" single, 'DIMINISHED CLOTHES', SALAD were picked up by 'Island's new indie offshoot label, 'Island Red', subsequently making inroads into the indie charts with classy singles, 'ON A LEASH' and 'YOUR MA' before 'DRINK THE ELIXIR' made the lower regions of the Top 75 and the SHANGRI-LAS influenced 'MOTORBIKE TO HEAVEN' narrowly missed the Top 40. All were included on their long awaited debut album, 'DRINK ME', released amid much anticipation the following month. Its patented combination of ALL ABOUT EVE, The PRIMITIVES and BLONDIE was unusual in that the songwriting was divided almost equally between KENNEDY, VLUGT and WAKEMAN, a democratic approach which made for interesting, if not always satisfying listening. Although the record made the Top 20, SALAD couldn't keep up the momentum and a further single, 'GRANITE STATUE', failed to make the all important leap into the Top 40. After a solitary single in late '96, the band eventually released a follow-up, 'ICE CREAM', in summer '97, although by this point the press had newer fish to fry and SALAD, rather unfairly, appeared to be off the menu. • **Cover:** IT'S FOR YOU (Lennon-McCartney; hit Cilla Black).

Album rating: DRINK ME (*8) / ICECREAM (*5) / SINGLES BAR compilation (*6)

MARIJNE VAN DER VLUGT – vocals, keyboards / **PAUL KENNEDY** – guitar, vocals / **PETE BROWN** – bass / **ROB WAKEMAN** – drums, samples

Waldorf | not iss.

Jun 93. (12"ep) **KENT EP** [ ] [-]
– Kent / The king of love / Heaven can wait / Mistress.
Oct 93. (12"/cd-s) **DIMINISHED CLOTHES. / CLEAR MY NAME / COME BACK TOMORROW** [ ] [-]

Island Red | not iss.

Apr 94. (7") *(IR 101)* **ON A LEASH. / WHAT DO YOU SAY ABOUT THAT?** [ ] [-]
(12"+=/cd-s+=) *(12IR/CIRD 101)* – Planet in the ocean / Problematique.
Jul 94. (7") *(IR 103)* **YOUR MA. / PLANK** [ ] [-]
(12"+=/cd-s+=) *(12IR/CIRD 103)* – Open.
Feb 95. (7"/c-s) *(IR/CIRS 104)* **DRINK THE ELIXIR. / KISS MY LOVE** [66] [-]
(12"+=/cd-s+=) *(12IR/CIRD 104)* – Julius / Diminished clothes (live).
Apr 95. (7"/c-s) *(IR/CIRS 106)* **MOTORBIKE TO HEAVEN. / DIARY HELL** [42] [-]
(cd-s+=) *(CIRD 106)* – I am December.
May 95. (cd/c/lp) *(CIRD/IRCT/IRLP 1002)* **DRINK ME** [16] [-]
– Motorbike to Heaven / Drink the elixir / Granite statue / Machine of menace / Overhear me / Shepherds' isle / Muscleman / Your ma / Warmth of the hearth / Gertrude Campbell / Nothing happens / No.1's cooking / A man with a box / Insomnia.
Aug 95. (7"/c-s) *(IR/CIRS 108)* **GRANITE STATUE. / IT'S FOR YOU** [50] [-]
(cd-s+=) *(CIRD 108)* – Ici les amigos.
(cd-s) *(CIRDX 108)* – ('A'side) / Rip goes love and lust / Roadsex.

Island | not iss.

Oct 96. (7") *(IS 646)* **I WANT YOU. / FLY IN A SHEET OF WINTER** [60] [-]
(cd-s) *(CID 646)* – ('A'side) / Decade of the brain / Ugly fashion town.
(cd-s) *(CIDX 646)* – ('A'side) / One in the bag / A size more woman than her.
May 97. (7") *(IS 654)* **CARDBOY KING. / MOTORBIKE TO HEAVEN (demo)** [65] [-]
(cd-s) *(CID 654)* – ('A'side) / Bridesmaids' gimmicks / Down at Monty's.
(cd-s) *(CIDX 654)* – ('A'side) / One imitation smile / Moon above my shoulder.
Jun 97. (cd/c/lp) *(CID/ICT/ILPS 8056)* **ICECREAM** [ ] [-]
– UV / Written by a man / Yeah yeah / Broken bird / Wanna be free / A size more woman than her / Cardboy king / Namedrops / Foreign cow / Terrible day / Wolves over Washington / The sky's our terminal.
Aug 97. (7") *(IS 660)* **YEAH YEAH. / PALM TREE ON THE MOON** [ ] [-]
(cd-s+=) *(CID 660)* – Sleepwalking.
(cd-s) *(CIDX 660)* – ('A'side) / Lovesong / Party.

– compilations, etc. –

Jun 95. (cd) *Island Red; (CIRM 1000)* <*23544*> **SINGLES BAR** [ ] [ ]

SALAKO

Formed: Hull, England ... 1995 by JAMES WAUDBY, DAVID LANGDALE, LUKE BARWELL and THOMAS SPENCER. Taking their moniker from a Native American rain god, they joined the hallowed ranks of 'Jeepster' alongside critical faves, BELLE & SEBASTIAN, making a small but perfectly formed mark on the indie scene with summer '98's debut set, '"rE-inVentiNg; Punc.tU!at?iOn>:'. Annoyingly smart-arsed title aside, the album proved SALAKO to be psychedelic folksters for the 21st century, melding found-sound elements of GORKY'S ZYGOTIC MYNCI, SUPER FURRY ANIMALS and THE BETA BAND into one surprisingly melodic, lighter-than-air jamboree. Pick of the bunch was the single, 'GROWING UP THE NIGHT' or possibly 'THE MOONLIGHT RADIATES A PURPLE GLOW IN HIS WORLD', released in its own right later that year.

Album rating: "rE-inVentiNg; Punc.tU!at?iOn>: (*8)

JAMES WAUDBY – vocals / **DAVID LANGDALE** – guitar / **LUKE BARWELL** – bass / **THOMAS SPENCER** – percussion

Jeepster | Imprint

Aug 98. (7") *(JPR7 006)* <*112024*> **GROWING UP IN THE NIGHT. / MY INTERNAL VISITOR** [ ] [ ] Nov98
(cd-s+=) *(JPRCDS 006)* – My booroo clow.
Aug 98. (cd/lp) *(JPR CD/LP 002)* <*112032*> **"rE-inVentiNg; Punc.tU!at?iOn>:** [ ] [ ]
– Each one unique / Words are not useful / Island life / Glass-bottom boat rides / For inspiration only / Colours merge and fly / Second age / Story of Bill / The moonlight radiates a purple glow in his world / In swoosh we trust / Sun and moon conspire / Go on then! enlighten me, why doncha? / Sunburst / Six part lullaby / Don't be afraid / When will be alone? / Porpoise sunlamp / In the morning / Growing up in the night / Could things be the same.
Nov 98. (7") *(JPR7 008)* **THE MOONLIGHT RADIATES A PURPLE GLOW IN HIS WORLD. / GO ON THEN! ENLIGHTEN ME~, WHY DONCHA?** [ ] [-]
(cd-s+=) *(JPRCDS 008)* – Easy to love you.

Walter SALAS-HUMARA (see under ⇒ SILOS)

Kim SALMON & THE SURREALISTICS (see under ⇒ SCIENTISTS)

SAMMY

Formed: New York, USA . . . 1993 by songwriters, LUKE WOOD and JESSE HARTMAN. Having worked in the NY offices of Geffen, WOOD was well placed to secure a US release (on STEVE SHELLEY's Geffen-backed subsidiary, 'Smells Like Records') for the pair's inaugural mini-set, 'KINGS OF THE INLAND EMPIRE' (1995), issued a year previously in Britain on 'Fire' records as simply 'DEBUT ALBUM'. Moving upstairs to 'Geffen' and taking on new drummer, ALEXIS FLEISIG (to replace original TONY MAXWELL, apparently who went by the zany nickname of CORN), WOOD and HARTMAN concocted a "real" debut album, 'TALES OF GREAT NECK GLORY', the angular grooves and incoherent but skybound pop refrains contained within once again seeing SAMMY charged as PAVEMENT clones.

Album rating: DEBUT ALBUM mini (*5) / TALES OF GREAT NECK GLORY (*5)

JESSE HARTMAN – vocals, guitar / **LUKE WOOD** – guitar, bass / with also **TONY 'CORN' MAXWELL** – drums

Fire | Smells Like

Jul 94. (m-cd/m-lp) *(FIRE CD/LP 40)* <13> **DEBUT ALBUM** <US-title 'KINGS OF THE INLAND EMPIRE'> [ ] [ ] Aug95
– Inland empire / Majik man / Teen hour / Cracked up. *(UK re-iss. Mar95 as 'KINGS OF THE INLAND EMPIRE' 7"ep/cd-ep; BLAZE 80/+CD)*

Sep 94. (7"ep/cd-ep) *(BLAZE 72/+CD)* **HI-FI KILLERS** [ ] [-]

Aug 95. (7") *(BLAZE 83)* **MAJIK MAN. /** [ ] [ ]
(cd-s+=) *(BLAZE 83CD)* –

— **ALEXIS FLEISIG** – drums; repl. MAXWELL

Fire | Geffen

May 96. (7") *(BLAZE 105)* **NEPTUNE AVENUE. / SLIM STYLE** [ ] [ ]
(cd-s+=) *(BLAZE 105CD)* – irr.

Jun 96. (cd/lp) *(FIRE CD/LP 58)* <24962> **TALES OF GREAT NECK GLORY** [ ] [ ]
– Possibly Peking / Encyclopedi-ite / Slim style / Neptune Ave. (ortho hi rise) / Buckle-up sunshine / Blue oyster bay / Chilling excerpts / Red lights flashing / Anything / Horse or ballet? / Kings pt. vs. steamboat.

Aug 96. (7") *(BLAZE 108)* **ENCYCLOPEDI-ITE. / PENCIL NECK** [ ] [ ]
(cd-s+=) *(BLAZE 108CD)* – Cafeteria hawker / Red lights flashing.

SAUSAGE (see under ⇒ PRIMUS)

SAVAGE REPUBLIC

Formed: Los Angeles, California, USA . . . early 80's initially as AFRICA CORPS, by UCLA students BRUCE LICHER and MARK ERSKINE. Enlisting the help of ETHAN PORT, ROBERT LOVELESS, PHIL DRUCKER and employing a startling array of industrial percussion that would make even TEST DEPT look like a school project, the duo created some of the most bleakly evocative avant-garde music of the US post-punk scene. Characterised by stark, tribal rhythms and gravel-voxed incantations, their debut album, 'TRAGIC FIGURES' (1982), favoured noise experimentalism over melody although by the time they re-emerged in 1985 (LOVELESS and DRUCKER had occupied the intervening years with side project, 17 PYGMIES), SAVAGE REPUBLIC were a relatively more accessible proposition. That year's 'CEREMONIAL' album (their second for LICHER's 'Independent Project' label) utilised off-kilter guitar as its focus, winding hypnotic riffs round exotic world music influenced melodies. Finding a more sympathetic audience in Europe, the group (which now included BRAD LANER) subsequently recorded a mini-set for 'Play It Again Sam', 'TRUDGE' (1986), before signing a long term deal with 'Fundamental'. Two further albums, 'JAMAHIRIYA' (1988) and 'CUSTOMS' (1989), surfaced before SAVAGE REPUBLIC faded from view. LICHER continued to operate his label from the relative seclusion of the Arizona desert, having already netted a Grammy for his packaging of the debut CAMPER VAN BEETHOVEN album. Musically, he returned to the fray as SCENIC along with JAMES BRENNER and BROCK WIRTZ, exploring more widescreen celluloid territory with 'INCIDENT AT CIMA' (1995) and 'ACQUATICA' (1996), tempering his past tendency to jarring repetition with a dust-bowl/soundtrack twang.

Album rating: TRAGIC FIGURES (*5) / TRUDGE mini (*6) / CEREMONIAL (*6) / LIVE TREK (*5) / JAMAHIIYA (*5) / CUSTOMS (*4) / LIVE IN EUROPE 1988 (*4) / Scenic: INCIDENT AT CIMA (*6) / ACQUATICA (*7)

BRUCE LICHER – guitar / **MARK ERSKINE** – drums, percussion / **ETHAN PORT** – guitars, bass, percussion / **ROBERT LOVELESS + PHIL DRUCKER** – rhythm, etc

Sordid Sentimental | Independent Project

Mar 84. (lp) *(SSLP 001)* <IP 004> **TRAGIC FIGURES** [ ] [ ] 1982
– When all else fails / Ivory Coast / Exodus / Machinery / Real men / Film noir / Attempted coup / Next to nothing / On the prowl / Zulu Zulu / Flesh that walks / Tragic figures. *(re-iss. Aug87 on 'Fundamental' lp/cd; SAVE 021/+CD)*

— took time off to recuperate in '83 after ROBERT LOVELESS and PHIL DRUCKER left to form the 17 PYGMIES

— added guest **LOUISE BAILIK** – vocals

Play It Again Sam | not iss.

Jan 86. (m-lp) *(BIAS 011)* **TRUDGE** [ ] [-]

Fundamental | Independent Project

Sep 87. (lp/cd) *(SAVE 022/+CD)* <IP 018> **CEREMONIAL** [ ] [ ] 1985

Nov 87. (d-lp) <*(SAVE 042-043)*> **LIVE TREK 86 (live)** [ ] [ ] 1986
(c-iss.Aug88; WEBOY 002C)

— added **BRAD LANER** – percussion

Fundamental | Fundamental

Aug 89. (lp/cd) <*(SAVE 061/+CD)*> **JAMAHIRIYA** [ ] [ ] 1988
– So it is written / Spice fields / Viva la rock'n'roll / Tabula rasa / Il papa sympatico / Pios den m pla yia ti lambri / Lethal musk / Lebanon 2000 / Moujahadeen / Jamahiriya.

Dec 89. (lp/cd) <*(SAVE 071/+CD)*> **CUSTOMS** [ ] [ ]
– Sucker punch / Sono Cairo / Mapia / The birds of pork / Rapeman's first EP / The world / Song for Adonis / Archetype.

Oct 90. (lp/cd) <*(SAVE 087/+CD)*> **LIVE IN EUROPE 1988 (live)** [ ] [ ]

— had already split; LANER formed MEDICINE, LICHER relocated to Sedona in Arizona and ran his label

– compilations, etc. –

1993. (cd) *Independent Project;* **RECORDINGS FROM LIVE PERFORMANCE, 1981-1983 (live)** [-] [ ]

SCENIC

— **BRUCE LICHER** – guitar, percussion, etc / **JAMES BRENNER** – bass, percussion, keyboards, etc (ex-SHIVA BURLESQUE) / **BROCK WRITZ** – drums, percussion / **ROBERT LOVELESS** – keyboards, flute, accordion, percussion, etc / **BRANDON CAPPS** – guitar, sitar

IP/World Domination | IP/World Domination

Jun 96. (cd-ep) <*(IP 054)*> **SAGE EP** [ ] [ ]
– Sage / Another way / Kelso run / East Mojave shuffle / Down black canyon road.

Nov 96. (cd) <*(IP 050CD)*> **INCIDENT AT CIMA** [ ] [ ] Nov95

Nov 97. (2x7"ep/cd-ep; split with LANTERNA) *(PAR/+CD 031)*<*IP 058*> **IN LIVE PERFORMANCE (live)** [ ] [ ]
(above issued with 'Parasol')

Apr 98. (cd) *(WD 0038-2)* <10844> **AQUATICA** [ ] [ ] Oct96
– Tones of Peloponnesus / Ionia / Parisia / Acquatica / All fish go to Heaven / Isle of Caldra / Deserted shores / Improvia / Angelica / Dronia / Ionic curve / Aca aludoma / Sidereal hands at the temple of . . . / Modula raga / Et tu, Dronius?

SCARCE (see under ⇒ ANASTASIA SCREAMED)

SCARFO

Formed: Andover, England . . . 1994 by former art college students, JAIME HINCE, AL SAUNDERS and NICK PRIOR. Relocating to a squat in Deptford, London, the trio gigged around the capitol and released a one-off single for 'Fierce Panda', 'SKINNY'. Snapped up by 'Deceptive' (home to ELASTICA and PLACEBO), the band fused JAM-esque power-chords with US noise influences on late '95's eponymous debut mini-set. While a further two singles raised their profile, things were subsequently put on hold when AL was hit square-on by a car when leaving a pub. This near-fatal accident (which left AL in hospital limbo for a number of months) only served to fan the flames of their fiercely passionate attitude to music, as witnessed on their belated full-length album, 'LUXURY PLANE CRASH' (1997). That year also saw a couple of minor hit singles, 'ALKALINE' and 'COSMONAUT No.7', although by the release of 'A YEAR FROM MONDAY', the 12-month delay had put paid to the momentum. • **Covered:** READ ABOUT SEYMOUR (Swell Maps).

Album rating: SCARFO mini (*6) / LUXURY PLANE CRASH (*7)

JAIME HINCE – vocals, guitar / **NICK PRIOR** – bass / **AL SAUNDERS** – drums

Fierce Panda | not iss.

May 95. (7") *(NING 08)* **SKINNY. /** [ ] [-]

Deceptive | Broken Rekids

Nov 95. (m-cd/m-lp) *(BLUFF 017 CD/LP)* <48> **SCARFO** [ ] [ ] Oct96
– Eyesore / Coin op / Skinny / Backwater / Car chase / Throw it all / Wailing words. <*US+=*> – Shuffling souls / Bingo England / Read about Seymour.

Dec 95. (7"etched) *(BLUFF 022)* **TUNNEL OF LOVE** [ ] [-]

Apr 96. (7"m) *(BLUFF 028)* **BINGO ENGLAND. / SHUFFLING SOULS / READ ABOUT SEYMOUR** [ ] [-]
(cd-s+=) *(BLUFF 028CD)* – Car chase (part 2).

May 97. (7") *(BLUFF 041)* **ELO. / FUJI** [ ] [-]
(cd-s+=) *(BLUFF 041CD)* – Porno.

Jul 97. (7") *(BLUFF 044)* **ALKALINE. / BRAZIL** [61] [-]
(7") *(BLUFF 044X)* – ('A'side) / El Topo / Montserrat.
(cd-s++=) *(BLUFF 044CD)* – (all 4 tracks).

Jul 97. (cd/lp) *(BLUFF 045 CD/LP)* **LUXURY PLANE CRASH** [ ] [-]
– Elo / Jet samshed flat / Safecracker / Don't let go / Japanese cameras / Jazz cigarette / Cosmonaut No.7 / Pajo gear / Chomsky airport / U-feline / Prison architect.

Oct 97. (7") *(BLUFF 053)* **COSMONAUT No.7. / ALCATRAZ** [67] [-]
(7"m) *(BLUFF 053X)* – ('A'side) / Assistant assassin / I want you.
(cd-s++=) *(BLUFF 053CD)* – (all 4 tracks above).

Sep 98. (7") *(BLUFF 064)* **A YEAR FROM MONDAY. / NOTHING DOING / SPECIAL COMMUNIQUES** [ ] [-]
(cd-s) *(BLUFF 064CD)* – ('A'side) / Off and on / Nothing doing.

SCARS

Formed: Edinburgh, Scotland . . . late '77 by ROBERT 'BOBBY' KING, PAUL RESEARCH, JOHN MACKIE and CALUMN MacKAY. This young post-punk outfit made their vinyl debut on the local 'Fast' label with the 'Adultery' single in Spring '79, 'Charisma' sufficiently impressed to sign the band to the 'Pre' offshoot. 'THEY CAME AND TOOK HER' marked the SCARS' major label debut in early 1980, while a much anticipated debut album, 'AUTHOR! AUTHOR!' arrived in Spring the following year. Ranging from the melodic new-wave guitar pop of 'ALL ABOUT YOU' to the CURE-style reverberations of 'JE T'AIME C'EST LA MORT', the record was an encouraging debut in what was a fine year for Scots artists with releases from contemporaries like JOSEF K, ORANGE JUICE etc. Unfortunately, like most of the new young Caledonian bands, the lifespan of SCARS proved surprisingly short and the band split with only one album to their name. Perhaps this was for the best as wearing tan jodphurs wrapped with garish climbing rope (!) was surely plunging New Romantic fashion to unnecessary depths.

Album rating: AUTHOR! AUTHOR! (*7)

ROBERT 'BOBBY' KING – vocals / **PAUL RESEARCH** – guitar / **JOHN MACKIE** – bass / **CALUMN MacKAY** – drums

Fast | not iss.

Mar 79. (7") *(FAST 8)* **HORRORSHOW. / ADULT-ERY** [ ] [-]

— **STEVE 'CHICK' McLAUGHLIN** – drums; repl. CALUMN

Pre | Stiff

Feb 80. (7") *(PRE 002)* **THEY CAME AND TOOK HER. / ROMANCE BY MAIL** [ ] [-]

May 80. (7") *(PRE 005)* **LOVE SONG. / PSYCHOMODO** [ ] [-]

Apr 81. (7") *(PRE 014)* **ALL ABOUT YOU. / AUTHOR! AUTHOR!** [ ] [-]

Apr 81. (lp) *(PREX 5)* **AUTHOR! AUTHOR!** [67] [-]
– Leave me in Autumn / Fear of the dark / Aquarama / David / Obsessions / Everywhere I go / The lady in the car with glasses on and a gun / Je t'aime c'est la mort / Your attention please / All about you.

Sep 81. (7") *(PRKS 5)* **AUTHOR! AUTHOR! / SHE'S ALIVE** [ ] [-]
(12"+=) *(PRKSX 5)* – Silver dream machine.

Oct 81. (12"ep) *<TEES12 04>* **AUTHOR! AUTHOR! / SHE'S ALIVE. / ALL ABOUT YOU / LEAVE ME IN AUTUMN** [-] [ ]

— split early 1982, KING subsequently went solo releasing one single, 'PAPER HEART', in 1982 *(PRE 23)*. He later formed LIP MACHINE, who released a handful of 45's for the 'Disposable Dance' imprint.

SCENIC (see under ⇒ SAVAGE REPUBLIC)

SCHEER

Formed: Magherafelt, County Derry, N.Ireland . . . early 90's by AUDREY GALLAGHER, NEIL CALDERWOOD, PADDY LEYDEN, PETER FLEMING and JOHN BATES. Following a self-financed debut single, 'I WISH YOU WERE DEAD', the band were picked up by U2's 'Mother' label as part of a development deal, resulting in the 'PSYCHOBABBLE' EP. Veteran indie label, '4 a.d.' were sufficiently impressed with the band's abrasive sound – memorably described as a cross between BJORK and the PIXIES – and hard gigging ways to offer them a fully fledged deal. The result was 1995's acclaimed 'SCHISM' EP, a record that saw SCHEER draw interest from both the indie and metal press, a testament to their crossover sound. Indeed, the long awaited debut album, 'INFLICTION' (1996) proved to be even heavier than their earlier material, carefully straddling the line between melody, noise and monster guitar licks.

Album rating: INFLICTION (*6)

AUDREY GALLAGHER – vocals / **NEAL CALDERWOOD** – guitar / **PADDY LEYDEN** – guitar / **PETER FLEMING** – bass / **JOHN BATES** – drums

Schism | not iss.

1995. (7") **I WISH YOU WERE DEAD. /** [-] [-] Irish

Son | not iss.

1995. (7"ep) **PSYCHOBABBLE EP** [-] [-] Irish

4 a.d. | Warners

Oct 95. (12"ep/cd-ep) *(BAD 5012/+CD)* **SCHISM EP** [ ] [-]
– Sometimes / You said / Baby size / Take you anywhere.

Feb 96. (7") *(AD 6003)* **SHEA. / YOU SAID (acoustic)** [ ] [-]
(cd-s) *(BAD 6003CD)* – ('A'side) / My world (live studio) / Demon (acoustic) / Nemesis (demo).

Apr 96. (7") *(AD 6005)* **WISH YOU WERE DEAD. / HANGING ON THE TELEPHONE** [ ] [-]
(cd-s+=) *(BAD 6005CD)* – Sad loved girl (acoustic) / Cannon (instrumental).

May 96. (cd)(lp/c) *(CAD 6006CD)(CAD/+C 6006) <46108>* **INFLICTION** [ ] [ ]
– Shea / Howling boy / Wish you were dead / In your hand / Demon / Babysize / Sad loved girl / Driven / Screaming / Goodbye. *(cd re-iss. Jul98;* **GAD 6006CD)**

Fred SCHNEIDER (see under ⇒ B-52's)

SCIENTISTS

Formed: Perth, Australia . . . 1978 by KIM SALMON, JAMES BAKER, BORIS SUJDOVIC and ROD RADALJ. During the recording of their debut 1979 single 'FRANTIC ROMANTIC', RADALJ departed as did SUJDOVIC a little later. The track found its way on to UK and US shores and was subsequently licensed to Greg Shaw's US 'Bomp' label. DENIS BYRNE then became a temp bass player until IAN SHARPLES and BEN JUNIPER (guitar) were recruited for 1980's 'LAST NIGHT' EP. The SCIENTISTS stripped down to a trio soon after as JUNIPER became another personnel casualty. However, the team finally disbanded after recording an eponymous album (aka 'the PINK album'). SALMON then moved to Sydney, forming LOUIE LOUIE with drummer BRETT RIXON, although this short-lived outfit soon metamorphasised into The SCIENTISTS (Mk.2), completing the line-up with TONY THEWIS and the returning SUJDOVIC. In 1982, this more settled version of the Aussie musical boffins delivered a new single, 'THIS IS MY HAPPY HOUR'. Initially not as experimental as their moniker might suggest, The SCIENTISTS moved from a retro sonic R&B sound (once the territory of 60's outfits The TROGGS and The STOOGES) to a more gothic, bass-heavy CRAMPS meets The BIRTHDAY PARTY style. This was evident on their 1983 follow-up mini-set, 'BLOOD RED RIVER', showing SALMON at his howling best. In 1985, they relocated to London, although they soon became disillusioned when RIXON quit. He again joined for 1987's 'THE HUMAN JUKEBOX', although the drummer would later die of a heroin overdose on the 24th of December '93. KIM SALMON, meanwhile, had formed his own solo project (backed by The SURREALISTICS) at the turn of the decade, having already initiated a simultaneous and ongoing moonlighting outfit, The BEASTS OF BOURBON. A plethora of releases (by both combos) ensued, including self-explanatory SALMON solo titles such as '94's 'SIN FACTORY' and 'HELL IS WHERE MY HEART LIVES'. • **Covered:** YOU ONLY LIVE TWICE (John Barry). BEASTS OF BOURBON covered GRAVEYARD TRAIN (John Fogerty).

Album rating: ABSOLUTE compilation (*7)

KIM SALMON – vocals, guitar / **ROD RADALJ** – guitar / **BORIS SUJDOVIC** – bass / **JAMES BAKER** – drums

not iss. | Bomp

Mar 79. (7") *<SMX 46960>* **FRANTIC ROMANTIC. / SHAKE (TOGETHER TONIGHT)** [-] [ ]

— **BEN JUNIPER** – guitar repl. RADALJ

— **IAN SHARPLES** – bass repl. DENIS BYRNE who repl. SUJDOVIC

not iss. | WhiteRider

Mar 80. (7"ep) *<WEEP 1>* **LAST NIGHT** [-] [ ]
– Last night / Bet your lyin' / It's for real / Pissed on another planet.

— now a trio without JUNIPER

Easter | not iss.

Aug 81. (lp) *<HAVE 1>* **THE SCIENTISTS** [-] [ ]
– Shadows of the night / Girl / I'm looking for you / She said she loves me / Sorry sorry sorry / That girl / High noon / Teenage dreamer / Another Sunday / Walk the plank / Larry / Making a scene / It'll never happen again.

— disbanded after recording of above. BAKER re-united with RADALJ in The HOODOO GURUS

— **SALMON** re-formed SCIENTISTS with **BRETT RIXON** – drums / **TONY THEWLIS** – guitar / **BORIS SUJDOVIC** – bass

Au Go Go | not iss.

1982. (7") *(ANDA 25)* **THIS IS THE HAPPY HOUR. / SWAMPLAND** [ ] [-] Austra

1983. (m-lp) *(ANDA 27)* **BLOOD RED RIVER** [ ] [-] Austra
– When fate deals it's mortal blow / The spin / Rev head / Burnout / Set it on fire / Blood red river.

Oct 83. (7") *(ANDA 31)* **WE HAD LOVE. / CLEAR SPOT** [ ] [-] Austra

Nov 84. (m-lp) *(ANDA 32)* **THIS HEART DOESN'T RUN ON BLOOD** [ ] [-] Aust.
– Nitro / Solid gold hell / I cried no tears / Crazy heart / This life of yours.

Jul 85. (m-lp) *(ANDA 37)* **ATOM BOMB BABY** [ ] [-] Aust.

Soundwork | not iss.

Aug 85. (12"ep) *(SW 12-007)* **DEMOLITION DERBY** [-] [-] Belg
– Demolition derby / Temple of love / Murderess in a purple dress / Backwards man.

Karbon | not iss.

Aug 85. (lp) *(KAR 101L)* **YOU GET WHAT YOU DESERVE** [ ] [-]
– Hell beach / It came out of the sky / etc

— **LEANNE CHOCK** – drums repl. PHILIP HERTZE (from USA) who repl. RIXON

Nov 85. (7") *(KAR 007)* **YOU ONLY LIVE TWICE. /** [ ] [-]

Oct 86. (lp) *(KAR 103L)* **WEIRD LOVE** (compilation) [ ] [-]
– Swampland / The wall / Fire escape / Raver / Clear spot / Happy hour / We had love / Temple of love / Murderess in a purple dress / Psycho cook supreme / Demolition derby. *(Australian title 'HEADING FOR A TRAUMA'; ANDA 39) (w/ free 7")* – THE OTHER PLACE. / SHE CRACKED

— now trio of **SALMON, THEWLIS +** new drummer **NICK COMBE** who repl. LEANNE + BORIS (latter formed DUBROVNIKS, with BAKER + RADALJ)

Aug 87. (lp) *(KAR 105L)* **THE HUMAN JUKEBOX** [ ] [-]
– The human jukebox / Shine / Distortion / Place called Bad / Hungry eyes / Brain dead / It must be nice.

— **BRETT RIXON** returned but the group soon split after tour. He was to die of a heroin overdose on 24th Dec'93.

– compilations, etc. –

May 94. (cd) *Red Eye; (REDCD 23)* **ABSOLUTE** [ ] [ ]

BEASTS OF BOURBON

TEX PERKINS – vocals, guitar / **KIM SALMON** – guitar, slide guitar / **SPENCER JONES** – guitar, vocals / **BORIS SUJDOVIC** – bass / **JAMES BAKER** – drums

Hybrid | not iss.

Apr 85. (lp) *(HYBLP 1)* **THE AXEMAN'S JAZZ** [ ] [-]
– Evil Ruby / Love & death / Graveyard train / Psycho / Drop out / Save me a place / Lonesome bones / The day Marty Robbins died / Ten wheels for Jesus. *(cd-iss. Mar94 on 'Red Eye'; REDCD 4)*

Red Eye | not iss.

Nov 88. (lp/cd) *(RED LP/CD 5)* **SOUR MASH** [-] [-] Austra
– Hard work drivin' man / Hard for you / Watch your step / Playground / Door to

your soul / These are the good old days / The hate inside / The big sleep / Pig / Driver man / Elvis impersonator blues / Today I started loving you again / Flathead (the fugitive) / This ol' shit / Sun gods. *(UK-iss.Mar94; same)*

Feb 89. (7") *(RED 017)* **HARD WORK DRIVIN' MAN. /** — -

Aug 90. (cd/lp) *(RED CD/LP 12)* **BLACK MILK** — -
– Black milk / Finger lickin' / Cool fire / Bad revisited / Hope you find your way to Heaven / Words from a woman to her man / I'm so happy I could cry / You let me down / Let's get funky / A fate much worse than life / El beasto / Blue stranger / I've let you down again / Blanc garcon / Execution day / Rest in peace. *(re-iss. Mar94; same)*

— **BRIAN HENRY HOOPER** – bass, guitar; repl. BORIS

— **TONY POLA** – drums; repl. BAKER

1991. (cd) *(REDCD 26)* **THE LOW ROAD** - - Austra
– Chase the dragon / The low road / Just right / There's a virus going round / Can't say no / Ride on / Straight, hard & long / Cocksucker blues / Something to lean on / Goodbye friends. *(Uk-iss.Mar94; same)*

1992. (m-cd) *(REDCD 20)* **JUST RIGHT** - - Austra
– Just right / Getcha money ready / There's no cure / Black milk / Let's get funky. *(Uk-iss.Mar94; same)*

Mar 94. (cd) *(REDCD 30)* **FROM THE BELLY OF THE BEASTS** — -

KIM SALMON & THE SURREALISTICS

SALMON with **BRIAN HOOPER** – bass, guitar, piano / **TONY POLA** – drums, percussion

Black Eye / not iss.

1989. (lp/cd) *(BLACK LP/CD 9)* **JUST BECAUSE YOU CAN'T SEE IT . . .** — -
– Melt (part 1) / Measure of love / Undying love / Sundown, sundown / Melt (part 2) / Weren't we bad / Sunday drive / Je t'aime / Your vicious omnipresence / You're gonna die / An articulation of the thoughts of one of society's bastards. *(cd+=)* – The surreal feel / Bad birth / Bellyful of slugs / Black velvet / Intense / Blue velvet / Torture / The surreal feel. *(re-iss. May94; same)*

Normal / not iss.

1991. (lp) *(305.062-1)* **ESSENCE** - - German
– I'm keeping you alive / The cockroach / Self absorbtion / The butterfly effect / A pox on you / Zero blank / Lightning scary / Essence of you / Looking at the picture / Down at the soul bank / Sea anemone / 26 good works. *(UK-iss.May94 on 'Red Eye'; REDCD 21)*

Red Eye / not iss.

Mar 94. (cd) *(REDCD 33)* **SIN FACTORY** — -

May 94. (cd) *(REDCD 34)* **HELL IS WHERE MY HEART LIVES** — -

Glitterhouse / In The Red

Nov 94. (cd; solo) *(GRCD 349)* **HEY BELIEVER** — -

Nov 95. (cd) *(GRCD 381)* **KIM SALMON & THE SURREALISTS** — -

Nov 96. (cd,lp) *<33>* **HIT ME WITH THE SURREAL FEEL** - —

not iss. / Imprint

Jul 98. (cd) *<111038>* **YA GOTTA LET ME DO MY OWN THING** - —

SCORPIO RISING

Formed: Birkenhead, Liverpool, England . . . 1989 by Manchester lads, MICKEY BANKS (frontman & lyricist), MARTIN ATHERTON, SPLOOTE, STEVE SOAR and COLIN OWENS. Taking their moniker from a 60's Kenneth Anger movie, the band set about combining the guitar assault of the Fraggle scene with the backbeat groove of the Baggy brigade. Unsurprisingly, the term 'Bagel' (another failed pigeon-hole attempt by the media) didn't really stick and in reality, the SCORPIO's were, if anything, more JAMES-ish. Initially produced by John A. Rivers, they toured supporting the NEDS, while releases came in the shape of two 1991 EP's for 'Chapter 22', 'STRANGEST TIMES' and 'THE WATERMELON'. A couple more singles, a mini-set, 'IF . . .' and a predictable press hype was enough to persuade 'Sire' that SCORPIO RISING were a commercialy viable proposition. However, the resulting 'PIG SYMPHONY' (1993) album failed to bring home the proverbial bacon, the SCORPIO's brief rise to fame cut short.

Album rating: IF . . . mini (*4) / PIG SYMPHONY (*5)

MICKEY BANKS – vocals / **MARTIN ATHERTON** – guitar / **SPLOOTE** – guitar / **STEVE SOAR** – bass / **COLIN OWENS** – drums

Chapter 22 / Sire

May 91. (12"ep) *(12CHAP 56)* **STRANGEST TIMES EP** — -
– Strangest times / Turn you on / Bliss.

Sep 91. (12"ep/cd-ep) *(12/CD CHAP 59)* **THE WATERMELON EP** — -

Jan 92. (cd/c/m-lp) *(CHAP CD/MC/MLP 62)* **IF . . .** — -

Jun 92. (m-cd/m-c) *<2-/4-45115>* **ZODIAC KILLERS** (compilation) - —

Jul 92. (12"ep/cd-ep) **SATURNALIA. / DISTURBANCE / PEACE FROG** — -
(10"ep+=) – Watermelon (Mark Goodier session).

Jan 93. (10"etched) *(10CHAP 71)* **SILVER SURFING / FOUNTAIN OF YOU** — -
(12"+=/cd-s+=) *(12CHAP/CHAPCD 71)* – Zero.

Sire / Sire

Jun 93. (cd/c) *(<9362 42570-2/-4)>* **PIG SYMPHONY** — —
– Talking backwards / Breathing underwater / Beautiful people / Watermelon / Oceanside / Silver surfing / Evelyn / Little pieces / Goofball / Sleeping sickness.

Aug 93. (7"/c-s) *(W 0197/+C)* **EVELYN. / IT'S OBVIOUS** — —
(cd-s+=) *(W 0197CD)* – Find your own way / Brutal deluxe.

— split after the commercial failure of above

Mike SCOTT (see under ⇒ WATERBOYS)

SCOTT 4

Formed: South Newington, London, England . . . 1996 by namesake, SCOTT BLIXEN, who, alongside JOHN MOODY and ED TILLEY (which makes 3 oddly enough!), blended a type of Stetson-rock; country, blues, hip-hop and lo-fi new wave. Inspired by The BYRDS' 'Sweetheart Of The Rodeo' and realising SPARKLEHORSE and BECK were selling loads of records, SCOTT 4 (named after a SCOTT WALKER album), delivered their 'Satellite' records debut, 'ELEKTRO AKOUSTIC AND VOLKMECHANIK', a 10" mini-album in 1997. Early the following year, the band received universal plaudits for their 'RECORDED IN STATE' album; country-rock was alive and kicking in London!

Album rating: RECORDED IN STATE (*7)

SCOTT BLIXEN – vocals / **JOHN MOODY** – guitar / **ED TILLEY** – drums

Satellite / Imprint

Jun 97. (10"m-lp; with free 7") *(STL 004)* **ELEKTRO AKOUSTIC UND VOLKMECHANIK** — -
– East winter / Work / Afternoons / You set the scene / Broken stones / I've been tamed / Lucky strike / On off. *(re-iss. Jul98 lp/cd; STL 004/+CD)*

Dec 97. (7"ep/cd-ep) *(STL 008/+CD)* **DEUTSCHE LP RECORDS / STRING 'A'. / WITH DRINKING / ROBERT HARRY** — -

Feb 98. (lp/cd) *(STL 009/+CD)* *<112765>* **RECORDED IN STATE** — — Aug98
– Start-up / Deutsche LP records / East winter / Aspirins / Your kingdom to dust / Plane / Cheese fourtracks / Miss Goddess nr.2 / Zilch / Choke bore / Philly's song.

V2 / unknown

Jun 98. (12"/cd-s) *(VVR 500181-6/-3)* **YOUR KINGDOM TO DUST. / YOU SET THE SCENE** — -
(above originally issued on 'Folk Archive' in 1997)

SCRATCH ACID (see under ⇒ JESUS LIZARD)

SCRAWL

Formed: Columbus, Ohio, USA . . . 1985 as SKULL by MARCY MAYS, SUE HARSHE and CAROLYN O'LEARY. Although the concept of an all-female rock band was hardly something new, this uncompromising trio were one of the first acts to bring seething feminist/emotional sentiments to the US indie underground. After a baptism by fire supporting the MEAT PUPPETS, the ladies cobbled together enough money to record a debut set, 'PLUS, ALSO, TOO' (1987), garnering praise from many established publications. The attendant rise in profile led to a transatlantic deal with 'Rough Trade', through whom they released a further two albums, 'HE'S DRUNK' (1989) and 'SMALLMOUTH' (1990), the former cut at PRINCE's recently built Paisley Park studio complex in Minneapolis. Although SCRAWL were already at loggerheads with their label over a proposed fourth album, the subsequent collapse of 'Rough Trade' meant that the scathing 'BLOODSUCKER' mini-album would eventually appear in 1991 on another indie imprint. In the meantime, the band were forced to bid for their own master tapes at a public auction, their back catalogue having been in limbo since Rough Trade's demise. While their all-girl exclusivity was gone following the substition of CAROLYN by DANA MARSHALL (a male!), the music on 1993's 'VELVET HAMMER' (the first album for 'Simple Machines') was as fiercely brooding as any they had recorded to date, reflecting the trials and tribulations of the past few years. SCRAWL's fortunes finally took a turn for the better as they signed to 'Elektra' in the mid-90's, releasing two further albums, 'TRAVEL ON, RIDER' (1996) and 'NATURE FILM' (1998); the latter was a consolidation of their career to date and featured revamped versions of a few old faves alongside a handful of fresh material and a cover of PiL's 'PUBLIC IMAGE'.

Album rating: PLUS, ALSO, TOO (*8) / HE'S DRUNK (*7) / SMALLMOUTH (*6) / BLOODSUCKER (*5) / VELVET HAMMER (*5) / TRAVEL ON, RIDER (*5) / NATURE FILM (*6)

MARCY MAYS – vocals, guitar / **SUE HARSHE** – bass / **CAROLYN O'LEARY** – drums

not iss. / No Other

May 87. (lp) **PLUS, ALSO, TOO** - —
– Gutterball / One word / I can't relax / Standing around / Loser / Sad / Slut / He's walkin' / Great American pastime / Afterthought. *<re-iss. Nov89 on 'Rough Trade'; ROUGHUS 64>*

Rough Trade / Rough Trade

Aug 89. (lp/c/cd) *(ROUGH/+C/CD 138)* *<ROUGHUS 51>* **HE'S DRUNK** — — Mar89
– 11 / Green beer / Ready / Breaker, breaker / For your sister / Believe / I feel your pain / Let it all hang out / Small day / Rocky top / Which one are you / Major, minor. *(cd+=)* – PLUS, ALSO, TOO

Apr 90. (lp/c/cd) *(ROUGH/+C/CD 150)* *<ROUGHUS 76>* **SMALLMOUTH** — —
– Begin / Charles / Enough / Rot / Out of mind / Absolute torture / Hymn / Tell you what / Time to come clean / I need you.

not iss. / Feel Good All Over

1991. (m-cd) *<17>* **BLOODSUCKER** - —
– VI ploriontos / Love's insecticide / Please have everything / Clock song / C.O.W. / High roller / Cold hearted snake. *(UK-iss.May93 on 'Simple Machines' cd/c/lp; same)*

— (May'92) **DANA MARSHALL** (male) – drums; repl. CAROLYN

Simple Machines / Simple Machines

Mar 93. (7") *(WHJAN)* **11.59 IT'S JANUARY. / Versus: TIN FOIL STAR** — —

Nov 93. (cd,c,lp) *<20>* **VELVET HAMMER** - —
– Your mother wants to know / Take a swing / Disappear without a trace / See / Face down / Tell me now, boy / Drunken fool / Prize / Blue green sea / Remember that day.

Apr 96. (7") <045> **CHAOS. / GOOD UNDER PRESSURE** [-] [ ]
not iss. Elektra
Aug 96. (cd,c) <61934> **TRAVEL ON, RIDER** [-] [ ]
– Good under pressure / Garden path / I'm not stuck / From deep inside her / Story Musgrave / Easy on her mind / Hunting me down / Come back then / Louis l'amour / He cleaned up / Story Musgrave / What did he give away?
May 98. (cd,c) <62186> **NATURE FILM** [-] [ ]
– Rot / You make it a crime / Charles / Don't we always get there? / Standing around / Public image / 11:59 it's January / Clock song / Everyone I saw tonight / Nature film / For your sister / 100 car pile-up / Guess I'll wait.

SCREAM

Formed: Washington, USA . . . 1982 by PETER STAHL, his brother FRANZ STAHL, SKEETER THOMPSON and KENT STAX. Signed to IAN McKAYE's (Minor Threat) label 'Dischord', they recorded three hardcore/punk albums, 'STILL SCREAMING' (1983), 'THIS SIDE UP' (1985) and 'BANGING THE DRUM' (1987). DAVE GROHL (later a member of NIRVANA and The FOO FIGHTERS) subsequently became their drummer in '88, sticking around for a couple of late 80's live albums and the studio set, 'NO MORE CENSORSHIP'. However, the group foundered at the turn of the decade, GROHL becoming a grunge figurehead alongside KURT COBAIN.

Album rating: STILL SCREAMING (*5)

PETER STAHL – vocals / **FRANZ STAHL** – guitar / **SKEETER THOMPSON** – bass / **KENT STAX** – drums

Dischord Dischord
1983. (lp) <DISCHORD 9> **STILL SCREAMING** [-] [ ]
(UK-iss.1988; same)
—— Also in 1984 they issued 'BOUNCING BABIES' compilation on 'Fountain Of Youth'.
1985. (lp) <DISCHORD 15> **THIS SIDE UP** [-] [ ]
(UK-iss.1988; same)
Nov 87. (lp/c) *(DISCHORD 25/+C)* **BANGING THE DRUM** [ ] [ ]
– Banging the drum / People, people / I.C.Y.U.O.D. / Nod to the east / Mineshaft burning / Rhythm beating / Feel like that / Walking by myself / When I rise / Sing it up kidz.
—— **DAVE GROHL** – drums; repl. KENT around this time
Konkurrel not iss.
Sep 88. (lp) *(K 001-113)* **LIVE IN EUROPE (AT VAN HALL, AMSTERDAM)** [ ] [-]
R.A.S. Torso
Dec 88. (lp/cd) *(RAS/RASCD 4001)* <2614248> **NO MORE CENSORSHIP** [ ] [ ]
– Hit me / No more censorship / Fucked without a kiss / No escape / Building dreams / Take it from the top / Something in my head / It's the time / Binge / Run to the sun / In the beginning.
YourChoice not iss.
1990. (lp) *(010)* **SCREAM – LIVE (live)** [ ] [-]
– C.W.W. Pt.II / I.C.Y.O.U.D. / The zoo closes / Hot smoke and sasafrass / Fight / American justice / Show and tell / Sunmaker / No escape / Take it from the top / Dancing madly backwards / Hit me.
—— disbanded in 1990 after GROHL joined NIRVANA and later FOO FIGHTERS. Another SCREAM were formed in the early 90's, but they were from L.A.
Jul 93. (lp/c) <(DIS 82 V/C)> **FUMBLE** [ ] [ ]
– Caffine dream / Sunmaker / Mardi Gras / Land torn down / Gods look down / Gas / Dying days / Poppa says / Rain. *(cd-iss. w/ 'BANGING THE DRUM'; DIS 82D)*

– compilations, etc. –

Jul 93. (cd) *Dischord;* <(DIS 81CD)> **STILL SCREAMING / THIS SIDE UP** [ ] [ ]
– Came without warning / Bedlam / Solidarity / Your wars – Killer / Piece of her time / Human behavior / Stand / Fight – American justice / New song / Laissez faire / Influenced / Hygiene / Cry wolf / Total mash / Who knows? who cares? / Amerarockers / U. suck A. – We're fed up / Ultra violence – Screamin' / Violent youth / Bet you never thought / Things to do today / This side up / Gluesniff / Still screaming / No money down / Show and tell me baby / Zoo closes at dark / I look when you talk / Iron curtain / Walking song dub.

SCREAMING BLUE MESSIAHS

Formed: London, England . . . 1983 from the remnants of MOTOR BOYS MOTOR (who released one single and self-titled album in '82) by American singer/songwriter BILL CARTER along with CHRIS THOMPSON and KENNY HARRIS. Picked up by indie label, 'Big Beat' (subsequently home to the CRAMPS), The SCREAMING BLUE MESSIAHS made their vinyl debut in 1984 with mini-set, 'GOOD AND GONE'. The attendant interest led to a major label deal with 'WEA' the following year, the company re-issuing the debut, releasing the acclaimed 'TWIN CADILLAC VALENTINE' 12" and promoting the band via a series of hard hitting TV performances. With both media and public expectation running high, 'GUNSHY' arrived fully formed in 1986 as one of the finest debut albums of that year. Fuelled by a turbo charged rhythm section (reminiscent of DR. FEELGOOD or The WHO), itchy/scratchy guitars and CARTER's hectoring vocals, highlights included the SMITHS-go-hillbilly stomp of 'PRESIDENT KENNEDY'S MILE' alongside the discordant shuffle of preceding single, 'TWIN CADILLAC..'. A previously recorded John Peel session served as a stop-gap prior to the unveiling of a follow-up album, 'BIKINI RED' (1987). Regarded by many as a let down, the record nevertheless blessed the 'MESSIAHS with their only sniff of chart action, the demented 'I WANNA BE A FLINTSTONE' scraping into the Top 30. Yet it would be another two years – during which time the band had moved to 'Atlantic' – before any further material surfaced, 'TOTALLY RELIGIOUS' (1989) falling flat commercially and generating interest only among the most faithful of 'MESSIAHS disciples. Finally giving up on making any new converts, the group split soon after the album's release, HARRIS and THOMAS going on to form LERUE.

Album rating: GOOD & GONE (*7) / GUNSHY (*6) / Motor Boys Motor: MOTOR BOYS MOTOR (*5)

MOTOR BOYS MOTOR

BILL CARTER (b.Redcar, Teeside, England) – guitar / **CHRIS THOMPSON** – bass, guitar / **TONY MOON** – vocals, harmonica / **JOHN KINGHAM** – drums, percussion

Silent not iss.
1981. (7") *(SSH 4)* **DRIVE FRIENDLY. / FAST 'N' BULBOUS / GROW FINS** [ ] [-]
Albion not iss.
Mar 82. (lp) *(ALB 111)* **MOTOR BOYS MOTOR** [ ] [-]
– Drive friendly / Hooves / Here come the Flintstones / Yes indeedy / Clean shirt and a shave / Sacred pie / Little boy and a fat man / One down, one down / Claw boy's claw / Freeze up the truth.

SCREAMING BLUE MESSIAHS

—— **CARTER** (now) vocals, guitar / **TONY** (now) bass / **CHRIS THOMPSON** – guitar (then bass) / **KENNY HARRIS** – drums; repl. JOHN

Big Beat not iss.
Jul 84. (m-lp) *(NED 7)* **GOOD & GONE** [ ] [-]
– Someone to talk to / I want up / You're gonna change / Tracking the dog / Good and gone / Happy home. *(re-iss. Apr85 on 'WEA' lp/c; WX 16/+C)*
—— now without TONY
W.E.A. Elektra
Oct 85. (7"m) *(YZ 73)* **TWIN CADILLAC VALENTINE. / GOOD AND GONE / GROWING FOR GOLD** [ ] [-]
(12"+=) *(YZ 50T)* – Happy home (live) / You're gonna change (live) / Someone to talk to (live).
Apr 86. (7") *(YZ 69)* **SMASH THE MARKET PLACE. / JUST FOR FUN** [ ] [-]
(12"+=) *(YZ 69T)* – The power glide.
May 86. (lp/c) *(WX 41/+C)* <60488> **GUNSHY** [90] [ ]
– Holiday head / Twin Cadillac valentine / Wild blue yonder / President Kennedy's mile / Let's go down to the woods and pray / Just for fun / Talking doll / Killer born man / Clear view.
Jun 86. (7") *(YZ 73)* **WILD BLUE YONDER. / KILLER BORN MAN** [ ] [-]
(12"+=) *(YZ 73T)* – I'm mad again.
Oct 87. (lp/c)(cd) *(WX 117/+C)(242212-2)* <60755> **BIKINI RED** [ ] [ ]
– Sweet water pools / Bikini red / Lie detector / 55-the law / Jesus Chrysler drives a Dodge / I wanna be a Flintstone / Waltz / Big brother muscle / I can speak American / All shook down.
Nov 87. (7") *(YZ 158)* **BIKINI RED. / ALL SHOOK DOWN** [ ] [-]
(12"+=) *(YZ 158T)* – 55-the law.
Jan 88. (7") *(YZ 166)* **I WANNA BE A FLINTSTONE. / JERRY'S ELECTRIC CHURCH** [28] [-]
(12"pic-d+=) *(YZ 166T)* – ('A'version).
Apr 88. (7") *(YZ 176)* **I CAN SPEAK AMERICAN. / GOOD AND GONE** [ ] [-]
(12"+=) *(YZ 176T)* – Twin Cadillac valentine.
Atlantic Atlantic
Oct 89. (lp/c/cd) *(<K9 60859-1/-4/-2>)* **TOTALLY RELIGIOUS** [ ] [ ]
– Four engines burning (over the USA) / Mega City one / Wall of shame / Nitro / Big big sky / Watusi's wedding / Here comes Lucky / Gunfight / Martian / All gassed up.
—— disbanded soon after above release; HARRIS and THOMAS formed LERUE

– compilations, others, etc. –

Jun 87. (12"ep) *Strange Fruit; (SFPS 003) / Dutch East India; <8315>*
THE PEEL SESSIONS (2.8.84) [ ] [ ]
– Tracking the dog / Someone to talk to / Good and gone / Let's go down to the woods and pray.
Nov 92. (cd) *Windsong; (WINCD 022)* **BBC RADIO 1 LIVE IN CONCERT (live)** [ ] [-]

SCREAMING TARGET (see under ⇒ DREADZONE)

SCREAMING TREES

Formed: Ellensburg, Washington, USA . . . 1985 by girthsome brothers VAN and GARY LEE CONNER along with frontman MARK LANEGAN and drummer MARK PICKEREL. Following early effort, 'CLAIRVOYANCE' (1986) for the tiny 'Velvetone' label, the group signed to respected US indie, 'S.S.T.', making their debut with the convincing 'EVEN IF AND ESPECIALLY WHEN' (1987). Fuelled by raging punk, The SCREAMING TREES were nevertheless characterised by the spectral hue of 60's psychedelia running through much of their music, LANEGAN's exotic, JIM MORRISON-esque vocals adding an air of brooding mystery on the likes of fans favourite, 'TRANSFIGURATION'. Another couple of stirring sets, 'INVISIBLE LANTERN' (1988) and 'BUZZ FACTORY' (1989), followed before the group released a one-off EP for 'Sub Pop'. With the emerging grunge phenomenon in nearby Seattle on the cusp of world domination, The SCREAMING TREES were obviously a promising prospect for major label A&R and it came as little surprise when they signed for 'Epic'. That same year, prior to their debut for the label, the various 'TREES occupied themselves with solo projects, GARY LEE forming PURPLE OUTSIDE and releasing 'MYSTERY LANE', while brother VAN issued the eponymous 'SOLOMON GRUNDY' set the same year, both appearing on 'New Alliance'. Best of the lot, however, was LANEGAN's windswept 'WINDING SHEET', an intense, largely acoustic collection featuring a cover of Leadbelly's 'WHERE DID YOU SLEEP LAST NIGHT' (as later covered in frightening style by KURT COBAIN). Co-produced by CHRIS CORNELL, the subsequent SCREAMING TREES effort, 'UNCLE ANAESTHASIA' (1991), saw the group moving towards a more overt 70's rock sound, while 'SWEET OBLIVION' (1992) saw PICKEREL replaced with BARRETT MARTIN on a more low-key set which stood at odds with the grunge tag unwillingly forced on the band. Augmented by such Seattle "luminaries" as TAD and DAN PETERS (MUDHONEY) along with DINOSAUR JR.'s J. MASCIS, LANEGAN cut an acclaimed solo follow-up, 'WHISKEY FOR THE HOLY GHOST' (1993), before beginning the long and arduous work on the material which would eventually come to make up 'DUST' (1996). Widely held up as the group's most affecting work to date, the George Drakoulias-produced album perfectly captured their threadbare grit and world-weary mysticism, the disparate elements of their sound finally fusing in harmony and exorcising the lingering spirit of grunge. • **Covered:** SLIDE MACHINE (13th Floor Elevators). • **Note:** Not to be confused with the English band on 'Native' records.

Album rating: OTHER WORLDS mini (*4) / EVEN IF AND ESPECIALLY WHEN (*7) / INVISIBLE LANTERN (*5) / BUZZ FACTORY mini (*5) / UNCLE ANAESTHESIA (*6) / SWEET OBLIVION (*7) / DUST (*9) / ANTHOLOGY – THE S.S.T. YEARS 1985-1989 compilation (*7) / Mark Lanegan: THE WINDING SHEET (*6) / WHISKEY FOR THE HOLY GHOST (*7) / SCRAPS AT MIDNIGHT (*5)

MARK LANEGAN (b.25 Nov'64) – vocals / **GARY LEE CONNER** (b.22 Aug'62, Fort Irwin, Calif.) – guitar, vocals / **VAN CONNER** (b.17 Mar'67, Apple Valley, Calif.) – bass, vocals / **MARK PICKEREL** – drums, percussion

not iss. Velvetone

1986. (m-lp) **CLAIRVOYANCE** -

S.S.T. S.S.T.

Feb 87. (m-lp/m-cd) *<SST/+C/CD 105>* **OTHER WORLDS** -
– Like I said / Pictures in my mind / Turning / Other worlds / Barriers / Now your mind is next to mine. *(UK-iss.May93; same as US)*

Sep 87. (lp/cd) *<(SST 132/+CD)>* **EVEN IF AND ESPECIALLY WHEN**
– Transfiguration / Straight out to any place / World painted / Don't look down / Girl behind the mask / Flying / Cold rain / Other days and different planets / The pathway / You know where it's at / Back together / In the forest. *(cd re-iss. May93; same)*

Sep 88. (lp/c/cd) *<(SST 188/+C/CD)>* **INVISIBLE LANTERN**
– Ivy / Walk through to the other side / Line & circles / Shadow song / Grey diamond desert / Smokerings / The second I awake / Invisible lantern / Even if / Direction of the sun / Night comes creeping / She knows.

Mar 89. (m-lp/m-cd) *<(SST 248/+CD)>* **BUZZ FACTORY**
– Where the twain shall meet / Windows / Black sun morning / Too far away / Subtle poison / Yard trip / Flower web / Wish bringer / Revelation revolution / The looking glass cracked / End of the universe.

Glitterhouse Sub Pop

Dec 89. (d7"w /1-white) *(GR 80) <SP 48B>* **CHANGE HAS COME. / DAYS / / FLASHES. / TIME SPEAKS HER GOLDEN TONGUE**
(re-iss. Dec90 cd-ep+=; GRCD 80) – I've seen you before. *(re-iss. May93; same)*

— LEE CONNER also formed PURPLE OUTSIDE in 1990, releasing 'MYSTERY LANE'. Brother VAN with SOLOMON GRUNDY issued eponymous same year also for 'New Alliance'.

Epic Epic

Oct 90. (12"ep) *<73539>* **UNCLE ANAESTHESIA / WHO LIES IN DARKNESS. / OCEAN OF CONFUSION / SOMETHING ABOUT TODAY (numb inversion version)** -

Jun 91. (cd/c/lp) *(467 307-2/-4/-1) <EK 46800>* **UNCLE ANAESTHESIA** Mar91
– Beyond this horizon / Bed of roses / Uncle anaesthesia / Story of her fate / Caught between / Lay your head down / Before we arise / Something about today / Alice said / Time for light / Disappearing / Ocean of confusion / Closer.

— **BARRETT MARTIN** (b.14 Apr'67, Olympia, Washington) – drums repl. PICKEREL who later joined TRULY

Oct 92. (cd/c/lp) *(471 724-2/-4/-1) <48996>* **SWEET OBLIVION**
– Shadow of the season / Nearly lost you / Dollar bill / More or less / Butterfly / For celebrations past / The secret kind / Winter song / Troubled times / No one knows / Julie Paradise.

Feb 93. (12"ep/pic-cd-ep) *(658 237-6/-2)* **NEARLY LOST YOU. / E.S.K. / SONG OF A BAKER / WINTER SONG (acoustic)** 50 -

Apr 93. (7"pic-d) *(659 179-7)* **DOLLAR BILL. / (THERE'LL BE) PEACE IN THE VALLEY FOR ME (acoustic)** 52 -
(12"colrd+=/cd-s+=) *(659 179-6/-2)* – Tomorrow's dream.

Jul 96. (cd/c/lp) *(483 980-2/-4/-1) <64178>* **DUST** 32
– Halo of ashes / All I know / Look at you / Dying days / Make my mind / Sworn and broken / Witness / Traveler / Dime western / Gospel plow.

Sep 96. (7") *(663 351-7)* **ALL I KNOW. / WASTED TIME**
(cd-s+=) *(663 351-2)* – Silver tongue.
(cd-s) *(663 351-5)* – ('A'side) / Dollar bill / Nearly lost you / Winter song (acoustic).

Nov 96. (7"white) *(663 870-7)* **SWORN AND BROKEN. / BUTTERFLY** -
(cd-s+=) *(663 870-2)* – Dollar bill (U.S. radio session) / Caught between – The secret kind (U.S. radio session).

— on a long holiday from each other, maybe for ever, VAN CONNER now moonlighting in VALIS with DAN PETERS of MUDHONEY, while BARRETT plays on tour with R.E.M. LANEGAN continued solo (see below)

– compilations, others, etc. –

Nov 91. (d-lp/d-cd) *<(SST 260/+CD)>* **ANTHOLOGY . . . THE S.S.T. YEARS 1985-1989**

MARK LANEGAN

— with on first **MICHAEL JOHNSON** – guitar / **JACK ENDINO** – bass, guitar / **KURT COBAIN** – guitar, vocals / **CHRIS NOVOSELIC** – bass / **MARK PICKEREL** – drums / **STEVE FISK** – keyboards

Glitterhouse Sub Pop

May 90. (red-lp/cd) *(GR 085/+CD) <SP 61>* **THE WINDING SHEET**
– Mockingbirds / Museum / Undertow / Ugly Sunday / Down in the dark / Wild flowers / Eyes of a child / The winding sheet / Woe / Ten feet tall / Where did you sleep last night? / Juarez / I love you little girl. *(c+cd+=)* – I love you little girl. *(re-iss. Apr94; same)*

Sep 90. (7") **DOWN IN THE DARK. /**

— next w / **J.MASCIS + MARK JOHNSON** (Dinosaur Jr.) / **TAD DOYLE** (Tad) / **DAN PETERS** (Mudhoney) / **KURT FEDORA** (Gobblehoof)

Sub Pop Sub Pop

Jan 94. (lp/cd) *<(SP/+CD 78249)>* **WHISKEY FOR THE HOLY GHOST**
– The river rise / Borracho / House a home / Kingdoms of rain / Carnival / Riding the nightingale / El Sol / Dead on you / Shooting gallery / Sunrise / Pendulum / Jesus touch / Beggar's blues.

May 94. (cd-ep) *<(SPCD 131-327)>* **HOUSE A HOME / SHOOTING GALLERY / UGLY SUNDAY / SUNRISE**

Beggars Banquet Sub Pop

Jul 98. (cd) *(BBQCD 204) <SP 419>* **SCRAPS AT MIDNIGHT**
– Hospital roll call / Hotel / Stay / Black bell ocean / Last one in the world / Wheels / Waiting on a train / Day and night / Praying ground / Because of this.

Sep 98. (7"colrd) *(BBQ 328)* **STAY. / SLIDE MACHINE**
(cd-s+=) *(BBQ 328CD)* – Death don't have no mercy.

SCRITTI POLITTI

Formed: London, England . . . late '77 by Leeds art student (and former Young Communist), 'GREEN' GARTSIDE, along with NIAL JINKS and TOM MORLEY. Politically motivated punks, their first release, 'SKANK BLOC BOLOGNA' (issued on their own 'St. Pancras' label) created enough interest for a John Peel session, the tracks subsequently released on 'Rough Trade' in 1979. By the release of the classic 'SWEETEST GIRL' single in summer '81, only MORLEY remained from the original line-up, GREEN now steering the band in an altogether more endearing new-wave art-pop/white reggae vein. The track (which featured the piano talents of ROBERT WYATT) was a minor chart hit, likewise the follow-up singles, 'FAITHLESS' and 'JERUSALEM'. All three were included on the much anticipated debut set, 'SONGS TO REMEMBER' (1982), GREEN's dreamy falsetto, musical eclecticism and unerring way with an insidious pop hook (not to mention clever-clever lyric) making him – by this juncture SCRITTI POLITTI were basically a studio vehicle for GREEN – a critical darling and one of 'Rough Trade's most unlikely success stories; the album almost made the UK Top 10, becoming the label's biggest selling release to date. Subsequently relocating to New York and moving up to 'Virgin', GREEN sought out such accomplished US musicians as MARCUS MILLER (former bassist for MILES DAVIS), who accompanied him on his first (UK) Top 10 hit, 'WOOD BEEZ (PLAY LIKE ARETHA FRANKLIN)' in 1984. A succession of different sessioners played on subsequent singles, 'ABSOLUTE', 'HYPNOTISE' and 'THE WORD GIRL', although FRED MAHER and DAVID GAMSON went on to augment GREEN on the follow-up album, 'CUPID AND PSYCHE '85' (1985). Again including all the singles, this slick set of Arif Mardin-produced dancefloor pop-soul also included 'PERFECT WAY', the track which broke SCRITTI POLITTI (albeit briefly) in the States and was later given the honour of a cover by aforementioned jazz legend, MILES DAVIS. The trumpeter also contributed to 'OH PATTI (DON'T FEEL SORRY FOR LOVERBOY)', GREEN's first single after three years of beavering away in the studio. The accompanying album, 'PROVISION' (1988), further refined the man's luxuriant pop vision with an altogether more straightforward approach, GAMSON again providing the lush synth textures. Despite the quality, further singles, 'FIRST BOY IN TOWN (LOVESICK)' and 'BOOM! THERE SHE WAS' lingered in the lower regions of the singles chart. After another interminable lay-off, GREEN returned in 1991 for a Top 20 collaborative cover of The Beatles' 'SHE'S A WOMAN' with ragga loveman, SHABBA RANKS, a further duet with SWEETIE IRIE (a version of Gladys Knight's hit, 'TAKE ME IN YOUR ARMS') not quite so successful. With no album forthcoming in the 90's so far, it does seem as if GREEN had finally abandoned SCRITTI POLITTI as a front for his musical activities although it's likely that this pop maverick will emerge at one point in one form or another. • **Trivia:** SCRITTI POLITTI is nearly Italian for political writing. MADNESS had a 1986 hit with 'THE SWEETEST GIRL'. That year also saw GREEN and GAMSON write the title track for AL JARREAU's album, 'L Is For Lover'.

Album rating: SONGS TO REMEMBER (*8) / CUPID & PSYCHE (*8).

GREEN (b.GREEN STROHMEYER-GARTSIDE, 22 Jun'56, Cardiff, Wales) – vox, guitar / **TOM MORLEY** – linn drum / **MATTHEW 'K'** – programme organiser / **NIAL JINKS** – bass

St.Pancras not iss.

Nov 78. (7") *(SCRIT 1)* **SKANC BLOG BOLOGNA. / IS AND OUGHT OF THE WESTERN WORLD** -

Rough Trade not iss.

Sep 79. (12"ep) *(RT 027T)* **4 A SIDES** -
– Doubt beat / Confidences / Bibbly O'tek / P.A.'s.

Nov 79. (7"ep) *(SCRIT 2 – RT 034)* **WORK IN PROGRESS** (PEEL SESSIONS) -
– Hegamony / Scritlocks door / Opec-Immac / Messthetics.

— added **MIKE MacEVOY** – synthesizers, vocoder / **MGOTSE** – d.bass / guest **ROBERT WYATT** – piano

Aug 81. (7"/12") *(RT 091/+T)* **THE SWEETEST GIRL. / LIONS AFTER SLUMBER** 64 -

— **JOE CANG** – bass repl. NIAL / **STEVE SIDWELL** – trumpet / **JAMIE TALBOT** – saxophone repl. MGOTSE

Apr 82. (7"/12") *(RT 107/+T)* **FAITHLESS. / FAITHLESS PART II (instrumental)** 56 -

Jul 82. (7"/7"pic-d) *(RT 111/+P)* **ASYLUMS IN JERUSALEM. / JAQUES DERRIDA** 43 -
(12"+=) *(RT 111T)* – ('A'extended).

Aug 82. (lp) *(ROUCH/+C 20)* **SONGS TO REMEMBER** 12 -
– Asylums in Jerusalem / A slow soul / Jacques Derrida / Lions after slumber / Faithless / Sex / Rock-a-boy blue / Gettin' havin' & holdin' / The sweetest girl. *(cd-iss. May87; ROUGH/+CD 20)*

— **GREEN** recruited US musicians **MARCUS MILLER** – bass (ex-MILES DAVIS) / **STEVE FERRONE** – drums (ex-BRIAN AUGER) / **PAUL JACKSON Jnr.** – guitar / (MORLEY went solo and released one 1985 single for 'Zarjazz', 'WHO BROKE THE LOVE?')

Virgin Warners

Mar 84. (7"/7"pic-d) *(VS 657/+P)* *<28811>* **WOOD BEEZ (PLAY LIKE ARETHA FRANKLIN). / ('A'dub)** 10 91 Jan86
(12"+=) *(VS 657T)* – ('A'extended).

— **GREEN** with **ROBBIE BUCHANAN + DAVID FRANK** – keys / **FRED MAHER** – drums

Jun 84. (7"/7"pic-d) *(VS 680/+P)* **ABSOLUTE. / ('A'version)** 17
(12"+=) *(VS 680T)* – ('A'extended).

— **GREEN** now with **DAVID GAMSON** – keyboards / **ALLAN MURPHY** – guitar

Nov 84. (7"/7"pic-d) *(VS 725/+P)* **HYPNOTISE. / ('A'version)** 68
(12"+=) *(VS 725T)* – ('A'extended).

— **NICK MOROCH** – guitar was added to above guests for album below.

May 85. (7"/7"sha-pic-d) *(VS 747/+P)* **THE WORD GIRL. / FLESH AND BLOOD** 6
(12"+=) *(VS 747-12)* – ('A'&'B'versions).

Jun 85. (lp/c/cd) *(V/TCV/CDV 2350)* *<25302>* **CUPID AND PSYCHE '85** 5 50
– The word girl / Small talk / Absolute / A liitle knowledge / Don't work that way / Perfect way / Lover to fall / Wood beez (pray like Aretha Franklin) / Hypnotize. *(cd+=)*– (other versions). *(re-iss. Apr90 lp/c; OVED/C 294)*

Aug 85. (7") *(VS 780)* *<28949>* **PERFECT WAY. / ('A'version)** 48 11
(12"+=) *(VS 780-12)* – ('A'extended).

— **GREEN** with numerous session people, + guest MILES DAVIS

Apr 88. (7") *(VS 1006)* **OH PATTI (DON'T FEEL SORRY FOR LOVERBOY). / ('A'instrumental)** 13
(12"+=/12"pic-d+=) *(VST/+P 1006)* – ('A'extended).
(cd-s+=) *(VSCD 1006)* – Best thing ever.
(c-s++=) *(VSTC 1006)* – ('A'-Drumless mix).

Jun 88. (lp/c/cd) *(V/TCV/CDV 2515)* *<25686>* **PROVISION** 8
– Boom! there she was / Overnite / First boy in this town / All that we are / Best thing ever / Oh Patti (don't feel sorry for loverboy) / Bam salute / Sugar and spice / Philosophy now. *(cd+=)* – Oh Patti (extended) / Boom! . . . (dub). *(re-iss. Aug91 cd/c;)*

Jul 88. (7") *(VS 1082)* **FIRST BOY IN TOWN (LOVESICK). / WORLD COME BACK TO LIFE** 63
(12"+=) *(VST 1082)* – ('A'instrumental).
(cd-s+=) *(VSCD 1082)* – ('A'extended remix).

Oct 88. (7") *(VS 1143)* *<27973>* **BOOM! THERE SHE WAS. / PHILOSOPHY NOW** 55 53 Jun88
(12"+=/3"cd-s+=) *(VS T/CD 1143)* – ('A'mix) / ('A'dub version).

Mar 91. (7"/c-s; SCRITTI POLITTI & SHABBA RANKS) *(VS/+C 1333)* **SHE'S A WOMAN. / LITTLE WAY (different)** 20
(12"+=) *(VST 1333)* – ('A'-Apollo 440 remix).
(cd-s+=) *(VSCD 1333)* – Wood beez (pray like Aretha Franklin).
(12") *(VSTX 1333)* – ('A'-William Orbit remix) / ('A'-Tutology business mix).

Jul 91. (7"/c-s) *(VS/+C 1346)* **TAKE ME IN YOUR ARMS. / ('A'instrumental) / ('A'mix)** 47
(12"+=/cd-s+=) *(VS T/CD 1346)* – She's a woman.

— above single credited SWEETIE IRIE on the sleeve. GREEN abandoned SCRITTI, although he still writes for and with others.

– compilations, others, etc. –

on 'Virgin' unless mentioned otherwise

Jun 88. (3"cd-ep) *(CDT 13)* **THE WORD GIRL / FLESH AND BLOOD / ('A'-Turntable mix)** -

Nov 88. (3"cd-ep) *(CDT 34)* **WOOD BEEZ (PRAY LIKE ARETHA FRANKLIN) / ('A'dub) / SMALL TALK** -

Apr 90. (3"cd-ep) *(VVCS 1)* **ABSOLUTE / (3 tracks by other artists)** -

SCUD MOUNTAIN BOYS

Formed: Northampton, Massachusetts, USA . . . 1991 originally as The SCUDS by JOE PERNICE, STEPHEN DESAULNIERS, BRUCE TULL and TOM SHEA. Eventually seeing the alt-country light after a few years banging out straight-down-the-line rock, the quartet recorded a debut cassette, 'PINE BOX', which was later given a limited CD release in the mid-90's on the miniscule 'Chunk' label. This was quickly followed up by 'DANCE THE NIGHT AWAY' (1995), their growing reputation enabling them to secure a deal with former grunge label, 'Sub Pop'. Graced with that peaceful, easy feeling, 1996's 'MASSACHUSETTS' was an unassuming but satisfying collection of acoustic, harmony-rich country-rock in the more traditional sense of the term. Despite glowing reviews and a wealth of material in the can, JOE would subsequently form The PERNICE BROTHERS, sibling BOB having already guested for the SCUD crew on the aforementioned swansong album.

• **Covered:** GYPSIES, TRAMPS AND THIEVES (hit; Cher) / PLEASE, MR. PLEASE (. . .Augustus) / WICHITA LINEMAN + WHERE'S THE PLAYGROUND SUSIE (Jim Webb) / HELEN (. . . Bonanno).

Album rating: PINE BOX (*6) / DANCE THE NIGHT AWAY (*6) / MASSACHUSETTS (*7)

JOE PERNICE – vocals, guitar / **STEPHEN DESAULNIERS** – bass, vocals / **BRUCE TULL** – lap steel guitar, vocals / **TOM SHEA** – drums, mandolin

not iss. Chunk

1995. (cd) **PINE BOX** -

1995. (cd) **DANCE THE NIGHT AWAY** -

Sub Pop Sub Pop

May 96. (7") **KNIEVEL. /** -

Jun 96. (lp/cd) *<(SP/+CD 342)>* **MASSACHUSETTS** Apr96
– In a ditch / Scratch ticket / Penthouse in the woods / Grudge **** / Big hole / Van drunk / Lift me up / Liquor store / Ride / Holy ghost / Cigarette sandwich / Massachusetts / Glass jaw / Kneivel.

— split when JOE formed The PERNICE BROTHERS

– compilations, etc. –

Apr 97. (d-cd) *Sub Pop; <SP 389>* **THE EARLY YEARS: PINE BOX & DANCE THE NIGHT AWAY** -
– Silo / Reservoir / Glacier bay / Peter Graves' anatomy / Freight of fire / Sweet Sally / Oklahoma! / Don't know how to tell her / Gypsies, tramps and thieves / There is no Hell (like the Hell on Earth) / Witchita lineman / Please, Mr. please / Down in writing / Closing time / Freight of fire / One hand / Letter to bread / Television / (She took his) Picture / Where's the playground Susie / Combine / Blood and bones / Silo / Sangre de Cristo / Kneeling / Fiery coffin / Helen.

SEA AND CAKE

Formed: Chicago, Illinois, USA . . . 1993 initially as a one-off part-time project by mainman, SAM PREKOP, along with ERIC CLARIDGE, the pair having frequently performed with the group, SHRIMP BOAT. Enlisting the help of guitarist ARCHER PREWITT and TORTOISE's head honcho, JOHN McINTIRE on drums, they recorded their excellent eponymous debut in '94. Another deliciously different 'Thrill Jockey' release (licensed to 'Rough Trade' in the UK), the album floated along on a current of subtle pop-lite noodling, propelled by shifting Afro-Caribbean influenced backbeats. Further albums, 'NASSAU' (1995), 'THE BIZ' (1995) and 'THE FAWN' (1997), seamlessly enveloped the diverse strands of laid back neo-jazz, exotic rhythmic excursions, burbling electronica and post-rock experimentalism that underpins many of the projects connected with McINTIRE, PREKOP and the rest of the Chicago indie mafia.

Album rating: THE SEA AND CAKE (*8) / NASSAU (*7) / THE BIZ (*8) / THE FAWN (*7)

SAM PREKOP – vocals, guitar / **ERIC CLARIDGE** – bass / **ARCHER PREWITT** – guitar (ex-COCKTAILS) / **JOHN McINTIRE** – drums (of TORTOISE)

Rough Trade Thrill Jockey

Feb 94. (cd/lp) *(R 310-2/-1)* *<THRILL CD/LP 016>* **THE SEA AND CAKE**
– Jacking the ball / Polio / Bring my car I feel to smash it / Flat lay the waters / Choice blanket / Culabra cut / Bombay / Showboat angel / So long to the captain / Lost in Autumn.

Lissy's Thrill Jockey

Jan 95. (7") *(LISS 1)* **GLAD YOU'RE RIGHT. /**

Moll Thrill Jockey

May 95. (cd/lp) *(EFA 12112-2/-1)* *<THRILL CD/LP 21>* **NASSAU** Jan95
– Nature boy / Parasol / A man who never sees a pretty girl that he doesn't love her a little / The world is against you / Lamont's lament / Soft and sleep / Cantina / Earth star / Alone, for the moment / I will hold the tea bag.

Oct 95. (cd/lp) *(EFA 12115-2/-1)* *<THRILL CD/LP 026>* **THE BIZ**
– The biz / Leeora / Kiss / Station in the valley / Darkest night / Sending / Escort / Assassin / Transaction / For minor sky.
(cd re-iss. Apr98 on 'Thrill Jockey'; TKCD 70951)

Thrill Jockey Thrill Jockey

Apr 97. (cd/lp) *<(THRILL CD/LP 39)>* **THE FAWN**
– Sporting life / Arguement / The fawn / Ravine / Rossignol / There you are / Civilise / Bird and flag / Black tree in the bee yard / Do now fairly well.

Sep 97. (12"ep/cd-ep) *<THRILL 48/+CD>* **TWO GENTLEMEN** -
– Cheech Wizard meets Baby Ultraman in . . . / Rinky-dink O.S. type rip / I took the opportunity to antique my . . . Early Chicago / Sewing machine.

– compilations, etc. –

Jun 98. (cd) *Thrill Jockey; <(TKCB 70952)>* **A BRIEF HISTORICAL . . .**

SEAFOOD

Formed: London, England . . . mid '96 by DAVID LINE and CHARLES MacLEOD, who recruited flatmates CAROLINE BANKS and KEVIN HENDRICK through an ad in the capital's premier exchange forum, 'Loot'. Twin-headed, youthful, shouty, pop noise merchants akin to a crossover of the PIXIES and SONIC YOUTH, SEAFOOD served up their first platter in the shape of early '98's 'SCORCHED COMFORT'. Having already been snapped up by cult indie launching pad, 'Fierce Panda', they delivered another fine 45 and a mini-cd, 'MESSENGER IN THE CAN' (1998). At Reading '98, with CHARLES suffering some sort of hand injury, they re-interpretated ALED

JONES' balls-clutching choirboy carol, 'WALKING IN THE AIR' (cockles and mussels, not so much alive alive-o!)

Album rating: MESSENGER IN THE CAN (*6)

DAVID LINE – vocals, guitar / **KEVIN HENDRICK** – vocals, bass / **CHARLES McLEOD** – guitar / **CAROLINE BANKS** – drums

		Fierce Panda	not iss.
Jan 98.	(7") *(NING 45)* **SCORCHED COMFORT. / DIG**		-
Mar 98.	(7") *(KOOKYDISC 005)* **PSYCHIC RAINY NIGHTS. /** (above issued on 'Kooky' records)		-
Jun 98.	(7") *(NING 54)* **PORCHLIGHT. /** (cd-s+=) *(NING 54CD)* –		-
Nov 98.	(m-cd) *(NONGCD 006)* **MESSENGER IN THE CAN** – Scorched comfort / Psychic rainy nights / Porchlight / Ukiah / Rot of the stars / Dope stars / We felt maroon / Dig.		-

SEAHORSES

Formed: based London, England . . . 1996 by ex-STONES ROSES guitarist JOHN SQUIRE, who allegedly 'discovered' frontman CHRIS HELME busking in his native Yorkshire. With STUART FLETCHER and ANDY WATTS completing the line-up, the band hooked up with producer Tony Visconti and quickly entered a studio in L.A. to begin work on their debut set, 'DO IT YOURSELF'. In stark contrast to the infamously drawn out sessions for the final 'ROSES album, all the tracks were laid down inside a month and the record was in the shops by Spring '97. Inevitably, the hype surrounding the whole thing tended to obscure the question of whether the record was actually any good or not; the bulk of critics (perhaps only too eager to get the boot in to SQUIRE, a previously unassailable indie guitar god) thought not, or at least panned the set for its inoffensive blandness. Certainly, there was nothing to match the quality of any track from the STONE ROSES sublime debut, although on its own terms, the record's vaguely enjoyable, bluesy indie-rock would've counted as a decent debut by a new band. Somewhat akin to a folk-ish cross between IAN BROWN and LIAM GALLAGHER (who, incidentally, co-penned 'LOVE ME AND LEAVE ME'), HELME's singing, as with SQUIRE's guitar flash, was as competent yet ultimately forgettable as any second division Brit-rock outfit. With the album lacking any real songwriting magic (bar say 'LOVE IS THE LAW' and 'BLINDED BY THE SUN'), some fans began to wonder just who put the mysterious X factor into the STONE ROSES (and talk is that IAN BROWN's forthcoming solo album might just have the self same critics who ridiculed the last STONE ROSES performance eating their ludicrously exaggerated words), although enough people thought differently to take the album to No.2 in the UK chart. With a string of successful singles and festival appearances also now under their belt, British sales of the debut are approaching the half million mark; SQUIRE may at last be achieving the success that has long seemed his due, ironically, with the most underwhelming material of his career.

Album rating: DO IT YOURSELF (*7)

JOHN SQUIRE – guitar / **CHRIS HELME** – vocals, acoustic guitar / **STUART FLETCHER** – bass / **ANDY WATTS** – drums, vocals

		Geffen	Geffen
May 97.	(7"/c-s/cd-s) *(GFS/+C/TD 22243)* **LOVE IS THE LAW. / DREAMER / SALE OF THE CENTURY**	3	-
May 97.	(cd/c/lp) *(<GED/GEC/GEF 25134>)* **DO IT YOURSELF** – I want you to know / Blinded by the sun / Suicide drive / The boy in the picture / Love is the law / Happiness is eggshaped / Love me and leave me / Round the universe / 1999 / Standing on your head / Hello.	2	
Jul 97.	(7"/c-s/cd-s) *(GFS/+C/TD 22266)* **BLINDED BY THE SUN. / KILL PUSSYCAT KILL / MOVING ON**	7	-
Sep 97.	(7"/c-s/cd-s) *(GFS/+C/TD 22282)* **LOVE ME AND LEAVE ME. / SHINE / FALLING IS EASY**	16	-
Dec 97.	(7"/c-s/cd-s) *(GFS/+C/TD 22297)* **YOU CAN TALK TO ME. / DON'T TRY / 3 WIDE**	15	-

SEAM

Formed: Chapel Hill, North Carolina, USA . . . 1986 as BITCH MAGNET by SOOYOUNG PARK and LEXI MITCHELL. This obscure but occasionally namedropped outfit released three albums at the turn of the decade before MAC McCAUGHAN (also of SUPERCHUNK) joined them to form SEAM. Signed to 'Homestead' ('City Slang' in Europe), the trio took a dynamic crescendo/release approach on debut album, 'HEADSPARKS' (1992), although most of the time the band crawled along at prozac pace alongside PARK's forlorn vocals. With MAC subsequently devoting all his time to the up and coming SUPERCHUNK, PARK and MITCHELL replaced him with BOB RISING while adding a second guitarist, CRAIG WHITE. Now residing in Chicago and signed to local imprint, 'Touch & Go', SEAM varied their heavy-lidded music policy little on 1993's 'THE PROBLEM WITH ME', although PARK was to recruit an entire new line-up of musicians (namely REG SHRADER, WILLIAM SHIN and CHRIS MANFRIN) for future releases. These came in the shape of 'ARE YOU DRIVING ME CRAZY?' (1995) and the long-awaited but directionless 'THE PACE IS GLACIAL' (1998), SEAM yet to mine any real crossover success.

Album rating: HEADSPARKS (*6) / THE PROBLEM WITH ME (*8) / ARE YOU DRIVING ME CRAZY? (*8) / THE PACE IS GLACIAL (*5)

BITCH MAGNET

SOOYOUNG PARK – vocals, guitar / **LEXI MITCHELL** – bass / – drums

		What Goes On	Communion
Apr 89.	(lp) *(GOESON 27)* <7> **STAR BOOTY**		Oct88
—	added **DAVID GRUBBS** – guitar (ex-SQUIRREL BAIT)		
Sep 89.	(lp) *(GOESON 35)* <12> **UMBER** – Motor / Navajo ace / Clay / Joan of Arc / Douglas leader / Goat-legged country god / Big pining / Joyless street / Punch and Judy / Americruiser / Carnation / Chord / Sea of pearls / Hatpins / Knucklehead / Circle K / Polio / Cantaloupe. *<US cd-iss. +=>* – STAR BOOTY		
		not iss.	Communion
1990.	(cd) *<21>* **BEN HUR** – Dragoon / Ducks and drakes / Mesentary / Lookin' at the Devil / Spite y malice / Crescent.	-	
—	split after above; PARK + MITCHELL formed SEAM, while GRUBBS formed SLINT		

SEAM

— **SOOYOUNG PARK** – vocals, guitar / **LEXI MITCHELL** – bass / **MAC McCAUGHAN** – drums (of SUPERCHUNK)

		City Slang	Homestead
Apr 92.	(lp/cd) *(EFA 04076/+CD)* *<HMS 177>* **HEADSPARKS** – Decatur / Grain / Sky city / Pins and needles / Feather / Atari / King rice / New year's / Shame / Granny 9x.		Mar92
		City Slang	Touch & Go
Mar 93.	(7") *(EFA 04912-45)* *<TG 112>* **KERNEL. / SWEET PEA** (12"+=/cd-s+=) *(EFA 04912-02/-03)* *<TG 112/+CD>* – Shame / Driving the dynamite truck.		
—	**BOB RISING** – drums; repl. McCAUGHAN (back to SUPERCHUNK)		
—	added **CRAIG WHITE** – guitar		
Sep 93.	(cd/c/lp) *(EFA 04923-26/-06/-08)* *<TG 118CD>* **THE PROBLEM WITH ME** – Rafael / Bunch / Road to Madrid / Stage 2000 / Sweet pea / Dust and turpentine / Something's burning / Wild cat / Autopilot.		
—	**SOOYOUNG** recruited new band **REG SHRADER** – guitar / **WILLIAM SHIN** – bass / **CHRIS MANFRIN** – drums		
Jun 95.	(7") *(che 32)* **HEY LATASHA. /** (above issued on 'Che')		-
Jul 95.	(cd/lp) *(EFA 04960-2/-1)* *<TG 144CD>* **ARE YOU DRIVING ME CRAZY?** – Berlitz / Hey Latasha / Port of Charleston / Rainy season / Two is enough / Haole redux / Tuff luck / Broken bones / Sometimes I forget / Petty thievery.		Jun95
		Touch & Go	Touch & Go
Sep 98.	(lp/cd) *<(TG 175/+CD)>* **THE PACE IS GLACIAL** – Little Chang, big city / Get higher / Wig / Intifada driving school / Kanawha / Nisei fight song / Prizefighters / In the sun / Inching towards Juarez / Pale marble movie / Aloha spirit.		

SEA URCHINS

Formed: West Bromwich, nr.Birmingham, England . . . 1986 by JAMES ROBERTS, SIMON WOODCOCK, MARK BEVIN, ROBERT COOKSEY, PATRICK ROBERTS and BRIDGET DUFFY. Another mid-80's indie band to kickstart their career via 7" flexi fanzine freebies (namely 'CLINGFILM' and 'SUMMERSHINE'), these jingle-jangle fops were a natural first signing for soon-to-be pastoral bastion 'Sarah'. The summer of '87 also saw the release of debut single proper, 'PRISTINE CHRISTINE', by which time BEVIN had been superseded by DARREN MARTIN. Releases proved sporadic with follow-up, 'SOLACE', taking around nine months to hit the shops, the subsequent departure of DUFFY and MARTIN resulting in an even longer lay-off before a third 45, 'A MORNING ODYSSEY', eventually surfaced in 1990. Musical differences led to a final split with 'Sarah', after which the SEA URCHINS signed to 'Cheree' for a one-off 7", 'PLEASE DON'T CRY'. JAMES, PATRICK and ROBERT would go to perform as The LOW SCENE (an old SEA URCHINS track) while a posthumous concert album (their debut!), 'LIVE IN LONDON' (1994), featured a cover of Donovan's 'SEASON OF THE WITCH'.

Album rating: LIVE IN LONDON posthumous (*5)

JAMES ROBERTS (b. 4 Mar'70) – vocals / **SIMON WOODCOCK** (b. 2 Dec'69) – guitar / **ROBERT COOKSEY** (b.14 Nov'69) – guitar / **MARK BEVIN** (b.21 Jan'70) – bass / **BRIDGET DUFFY** (b.28 Jun'70) – tambourine, vox organ (ex-VELVET UNDERWEAR drummer) / **PATRICK ROBERTS** – drums

		Kvatch	not iss.
May 87.	(7"flexi) *(KVATCH 001)* **CLINGFILM. / GROOVE FARM:- Baby Blue Marine**		-
		Sha La La	not iss.
Jun 87.	(7"flexi) *(Sha La La Ba Ba Ba 5)* **SUMMERSHINE. / ORCHIDS:- From This Day**		-
—	**DARREN MARTIN** (b.25 Mar'67) – bass; repl. BEVIN		
		Sarah	not iss.
Aug 87.	(7") *(SARAH 001)* **PRISTINE CHRISTINE. / SULLEN EYES / EVERGLADES**		-
Jun 88.	(7") *(SARAH 006)* **SOLACE. / PLEASE RAIN FALL**		-
—	now without DUFFY + MARTIN (WOODCOCK now bass + ROBERTS on guitar)		
Jul 90.	(7") **A MORNING ODYSSEY. /**		-

Fierce not iss.

1990. (7") *(FRIGHT 032)* **30.10.88 (live)**

Cheree not iss.

May 91. (7") *(CHEREE 15)* **PLEASE DON'T CRY. / TIME IS ALL I'VE SEEN**

— split after above, JAMES, PATRICK + ROBERT formed The LOW SCENE

– compilations, etc. –

Mar 94. (cd) *Fierce; (FRIGHT 061)* **LIVE IN LONDON (live)**
– Low scene / My ship is going down / A morning odyssey / Sullen eyes / I don't belong / Please don't cry / Season of the witch / Summershine / Open out / Rock and roll star / Slow scene / Solace / Jam / Hendrix / Pristine Christine.

SEBADOH

Formed: Boston, Massachusetts, USA . . . 1989 by LOU BARLOW, lo-fi overlord and former DINOSAUR JR member. After a less than amicable break from DINOSAUR mainman, J. MASCIS, BARLOW began writing and recording material with sticksman, ERIC GAFFNEY. Released on 'Homestead' over two albums, 'THE FREED MAN' (1989) and 'WEED FORESTIN' (1990), these acoustic sketches were (released in 1992 as a single CD package, 'FREED WEED') a taster for the fully fledged pop subversion of 'SEBADOH III' (1991). With the addition of bassist/guitarist, JASON LOWENSTEIN, the trio ventured into raucous electric territory, while keeping one foot in the acoustic camp, reconciling their love of lo-fi noise with barbed indie-folk. Though a US-only affair, the album was given a belated UK release in 1994; in the meantime, SEBADOH's output became more readily available following a deal with 'Sub Pop', the mini-set, 'ROCKIN' THE FOREST' (1992), boasting the semi-classic self-parody of 'GIMME INDIE ROCK', previously only available as an import 7". A second mini-album that year, 'SEBADOH VS HELMET', found BARLOW and Co. bravely tackling a Nick Drake cover (the timeless 'PINK MOON') with interesting results, while 'BUBBLE AND SCRAPE' (1992) was the band's most commercially successful release to date, making the UK Top 75. BARLOW continued to express his more lo-fi urges via side projects, releasing material as FOLK IMPLOSION with guitarist JOHN DAVIS and working on his own as LOU BARLOW AND HIS SENTRIDOH. Industriously (and confusingly for discographers!) prolific in the best indie tradition, BARLOW continued apace with his SEBADOH duties, releasing the acclaimed 'BAKESALE' in 1994. Though GAFFNEY had been replaced by BOB FAY, his playing still featured on an album which came as close to conventional alternative rock as anything BARLOW has yet recorded, the sound less self-consciously muted. It also marked their entry into the UK Top 40, just, while 1996's 'HARMACY' was even more accessible without compromising their indie/grunge ethos. BARLOW even had a hit single on his hands following the inclusion of FOLK IMPLOSION's 'NATURAL ONE' in Larry Clark's hotly debated 'Kids' movie, proving conclusively that lo-fi didn't necessarily entail lo-sales. • **Songwriters:** BARLOW and GAFFNEY (until latter repl. by FAY), some by LOWENSTEIN after 1992. Covered REJECT (Negros) / SICKLES AND HAMMERS (Minutemen) / WONDERFUL! WONDERFUL! (Edwards-Raleigh) / EVERYBODY'S BEEN BURNED (Byrds) / PINK MOON (Nick Drake) / RUN TO YOU (Bryan Adams) / BLONDE IN THE BLEACHERS (Joni Mitchell) / NAIMA (John Coltrane?). FOLK IMPLOSION covered SCHOOL (Nirvana) / WON'T BACK DOWN (Tom Petty) / I SMELL A RAT (Bags).

Album rating: BAKESALE (*8) / HARMACY (*6)

LOU BARLOW (b.17 Jul'66, Northampton, Massachusetts) – vocals, guitar (ex-DINOSAUR JR) / **ERIC GAFFNEY** – drums

Homestead Homestead

Dec 89. (lp/c) *<HMS 145-1/-4>* **THE FREED MAN**
– Temporary dream / New worship / Subtle holy gift / My own religion / Ride the darker wave / More simple / Jealous of Jesus / Mr. Genius eyes / Perfect power / Feeding evil / Sexual confusion / Three times a day / Gate to hell / Broken / Whiley peach / I can't see / Take my hand / Pound my skinny head / I believe in fate / Waited forever / Slightest suggestion / It's so hard to fall in love / Brand new love.

Nov 90. (lp/c) *<HMS 158-1/-4>* **WEED FORESTIN'**
– Healthy sick / Burning out / Little man / Punch in the nose / Loose 'n' screw / Jealous evil / Moldy bread / Solid brownies / The bridge was you / Bolder / Slit your wrists / True hardcore / Stop the wheel / Made real / Close enough / Level anything / Soul mate / Nest / Narrow stories / Ladybugs / Yellow submarine / Wall of doubt / Crumbs / Growin' up with you. *(UK cd-iss. Nov92 of above two as 'FREED WEED'; HMS 158-2)*

— added **JASON LOEWENSTEIN** – bass, guitar, drums, vocals

Jul 91. (7") *<HMS 165>* **GIMME INDIE ROCK. /**
(UK-iss.Apr97; same)

Sep 91. (cd/lp) *<HMS 168-2/-1>* **SEBADOH III**
– Freed pig / Sickles and hammers / Total peace / Violet execution / Scars, our eyes / Truly great thing / Kath / Perverted world / Wonderful! wonderful! / Limb by limb / Smoke a bowl / Black haired girl / Hoppin' up and down / Supernatural force / Rockstar / Downmind / Renaissance man / God told me / Holy picture / Hassle / No different / Spoiled / As the world does, the eyes of God. *(UK-iss.Jul94 & Jun98; same)*

not iss. Siltbreeze

Nov 91. (7") **OVEN IS MY FRIEND. /**

— In 1991, Sonic Life fanzine issued 'SPLIT WITH BIG STICK' for 'Blast First'.

not iss. Vertical

1992. (7") **ASSHOLE. /**

Domino Sub Pop

Aug 92. (m-cd/m-lp) *(WIG CD/LP 2)* **ROCKIN' THE FOREST**
– Gimme indie rock / Ride the darker wave / It's so hard to fall in love / Cry sis / Really insane II / Vampire / Junk bands / Mind-held.

— Sep 92; split an EP release w/ AZALIA SNAIL on 'Dark Beloved Cloud'; *DBC 001)*

Oct 92. (m-cd/m-lp) *(WIG CD/LP 3)* **SEBADOH VS HELMET**
– Notsur dnuora selcric / Brand new love / Mean distance / . . . Burned / New worship / Good things, proud man / P.Moon / Cecilia chime in Melee / Soulmate.

Nov 92. (cd) *<SP 176>* **SMASH YR HEAD ON PUNK ROCK**
(compilation of above 2)
– Crisis / Brand new love / Notsur dnuora selcric / Vampire / Good things / Cecelia chime in Melee / Everybody's been burned / Junk bonds / New worship / Pink moon / Mind meld. *(UK-iss.May98; same as US)*

Mar 93. (7") *(RUG 4)* **SOUL AND FIRE. / FANTASTIC DISASTER (amateur mix)**
(12"+=/cd-s+=) *(RUG 4 T/CD)* – Emma get wild / Reject.

Apr 93. (cd/c/lp) *(WIG CD/MC/LP 4)* *<SP 192>* **BUBBLE AND SCRAPE** 63
– Soul and fire / Two years two days / Telecosmic alchemy / Fantastic disaster / Happily divided / Sister / Cliche / Sacred attention / Elixir is Zog / Emma get wild / Sixteen / Homemade / Forced love / No way out / Bouquet for a siren / Think (let tomorrow be) / Flood.

Dec 93. (7") *(RUG 17)* **REBOUND. / CAREFUL**
(12"ep+=/cd-ep+=) **FOUR SONGS EP** *(RUG 17)* – Mar backlash / Not a friend / Foreground / Naima / 40203 / Mystery man / Drumstick jumble / Lime kiln.

— **BOB FAY** – drums; repl. GAFFNEY who went solo (although still on below album)

Jul 94. (7"ep/cd-ep) *(RUG 22/+CD)* **SKULL. / PUNCHING MYSELF IN THE FACE REPEATEDLY, PUBLICLY / SING SOMETHING – PLATE O'HATRED**

Aug 94. (cd/c/lp) *(WIG CD/MC/LP 11)* *<SP 260>* **BAKESALE** 40
– License to confuse / Careful / Magnet's coil / Not a friend / Not too amused / Dreams / Skull / Got it / S. soup / Give up / Rebound / Mystery man / Temptation tide / Drama mine / Together or alone. *(ltd. w / free 7")*

Jun 95. (7"/cd-s) *(RUG 38/+CD)* **NOT TOO AMUSED. / HANK WILLIAMS**

Jul 96. (7"ep/10"ep/cd-ep) *(RUG 47/+T/CD)* **BEAUTY OF THE RIDE / SIXTEEN. / RIDING / SLINTSTRUMENTAL** 74

Aug 96. (cd/c/d-lp) *(WIG CD/MC/LP 26)* *<SP 370>* **HARMACY** 38
– On fire / Prince – S / Ocean / Nothing like you / Crystal gypsy / Beauty of the ride / Mind reader / Sferzando! / Willing to wait / Hillbilly II / Zone doubt / Too pure / Worst thing / Love to fight / Perfect way / Can't give up / Open ended / Weed against speed / I smell a rat.

Oct 96. (7") *(RUG 50)* **OCEAN. /**
(cd-s+=) *(RUG 50CD)* –

Nov 98. (7") *(RUG 80)* **FLAME. / FLAME (4-track) / SWEET SURRENDER**
(cd-s) *(RUG 80CD1)* – (first 2 tracks) / Beautiful day in bed / Television.
(cd-s) *(RUG 80CD2)* – (first 2 tracks) / Crystal crossed / Saltwater gardens.

– compilations, others, etc. –

Feb 97. (cd) *Cortex; (CORX 016CD)* **MAGNET'S COIL**

LOU BARLOW AND HIS SENTRIDOH

— - vocals, guitar

not iss. Sub Pop

1993. (7"; as LOU BARLOW) **I AM NOT MOCKING YOU. /**

not iss. Smells Like

1992. (7") **LOSERCORE. / REALLY INSANE**

not iss. Little Bro.

1993. (7"ep) **THE MYSTERIOUS SENTRIDOH**

Smells Like Smells Like

Jun 94. (cd; LOU BARLOW'S ACOUSTIC SENTRIDOH) *<SLR 08>* **COLLECTION OF HOME RECORDINGS**
– Stronger / Chokechain / Only losers / Breakdown day / Rise below slowly / Dragdown memory / Not nice to be nice / Mellow, cool and painfully aware / Crackers and coffee / High school /

Oct 94. (cd; SENTRIDOH) *<(SM 11CD)>* **WINNING LOSERS**

Oct 94. (cd; LOU BARLOW & FRIENDS) *<(SM 12CD)>* **ANOTHER COLLECTION OF HOME RECORDINGS**
– Run to you / Puffin' / Queen of the shore / Blonde in the bleachers / What would it be like / Feel good / Symbiosis / Option / Alone to decide / Cranky / Machinery / Synthstrument.

— Also cd on 'Shrimper' cd+d-lp 'LOSING YEARS'.

City Slang City Slang

1995. (cd/d-lp) *<(EFA 04940-2/-1)>* **LOU BARLOW AND HIS SENTRIDOH**
– I am not mocking you / Survival / Helpless heartbreak / Dirty mind / Forever instant / Natural nature / Don't need / Endless tease / Paranoid revolution / Same old, say mold / Good in others / Spirit that kills / Weakness is the secret / Cold love / No one taught me / No matter what / Feel good / Symbiosis / Option / Alone to decide / Cranky / Machinery / Synthstrument.

the FOLK IMPLOSION

LOU BARLOW + JOHN DAVIS

Chocolate Drunken F.

1993. (c) **FOLK IMPLOSION**
(5 tracks were featured in Sep94 on cd+10"m-lp 'TAKE A LOOK INSIDE THE FOLK IMPLOSION' om 'Tupelo-Communion'UK / 'Shrimper'US)

imported Drunken F.

Aug 94. (7"ep) **WALK THRU THIS WORLD WITH THE FOLK IMPLOSION**
– My head really hurts / End of the first side / Won't back down / School.

Communion Communion

Sep 94. (m-cd/m-lp) *(COMM 32)* **TAKE A LOOK INSIDE . . . . . .**
– Blossom / Sputnik's down / Slap me / Chicken squawk / Spiderweb – Butterfly / Had to find out / Better than allrite / Why do they they hide / Winter's day / Boyfriend, girlfriend / Shake a little Heaven / Waltin' with yor ego / Take a look inside / Start again.

1996. (7") **PALM OF MY HAND. /**

Domino Domino

Mar 96. (7"; as DELUXX FOLK IMPLOSION) *(RUG 44)* **DADDY NEVER UNDERSTOOD. /**

London London

May 96. (12") *(LONX 382)* <0430> **NATURAL ONE. / ('A'-Unkle mix) / (Unkle instrumental)** 45 29 Nov95
(cd-s+=) *(LONCD 382)* – ('A'-Unkle No Skratch mix).
(above single taken from the movie, 'Kids)

— JOHN DAVIS for 'Communion' released cd/lp 'LEAVE HOME'. Alongside DENNIS CALLACI released cd/lp 'ROOM FOR SPACE' for 'Shrimper'.

Communion Communion

Feb 97. (7") <*(COMM 47)*> **POLE POSITION. / OPENING DAY**
(cd-s+=) <*(COMM 47CD)*> – Summer's over.
Apr 97. (7") <*(COMM 46)*> **INSINUATION. / KEEPING SCORE**
(cd-s+=) <*(COMM 46CD)*> – Trail burn.
Jun 97. (lp/cd) <*(COMM 45/+CD)*> **DARE TO BE SURPRISED**
– Pole position / Wide web / Insinuation / Barricade / That's the trick / Checking in / Cold night / Park dub / Burning paper / (Blank paper) / Ball and chain / Fall into NOvember / Dare to be surprised / River devotion.

SECOND LAYER (see under ⇒ SOUND)

SECTION 25

Formed: Blackpool, England . . . late '79 by songwriting brothers VINCENT and LARRY CASSIDY. Initially using a drum machine, the siblings soon bolstered the rhythm section with a real drummer and added guitarist PAUL WIGGIN. Signed to Manchester's 'Factory', the group made their debut in summer 1980 with the 'GIRLS DON'T COUNT' single, following it with a debut album, 'ALWAYS NOW', just over a year later. More suuccessful in Europe than Britain, SECTION 25's minimalist sound was drawn from a similar grey area to fellow 'Factory' acts, JOY DIVISION, NEW ORDER, ACR etc, as well as the likes of KRAFTERK and their ilk. Vocals, if there were any, echoed sinisterly as in 'ALWAYS NOW', from follow-up album, 'THE KEY OF DREAMS' (1982). Mid '83 saw a turning point, however, as the CASSIDY brothers recruited two female vocalists, ANGELA FLOWERS and JENNY ROSS (LARRY's wife), presenting a more accessible sound with the 'BACK TO THE WONDER' single and the subsequent album, 'FROM THE HIP' (1984). Yet the band seemed forever in the shadow of their more popular labelmates and after a further two 12"ers in 1986, 'LOVE AND HATE' and 'BAD NEWS WEEK', they finally called it day.

Album rating: ALWAYS NOW (*6) / THE KEY OF DREAMS (*5) / FROM THE HIP (*4)

VINCENT CASSIDY – electronics, drum machine / **LARRY CASSIDY** – vocals, guitar / **PHIL WIGGIN** – guitar / **JOHN BRIERLEY** – drums / **JOHN HURST** – sound engineer

Factory not iss.

Jul 80. (12") *(fac 18t)* **GIRLS DON'T COUNT. / KNEW NOISE / UP TO YOU** -
Jan 81. (7") *(fbn 3.006)* **CHARNEL GROUND. / HAUNTED** -
Jun 81. (7") *(fbn 5)* **JE VEUX TON AMOUR. / OYO ACHEL ADA** -
(above two were released on 'Factory Benelux')
Sep 81. (lp) *(fact 45)* **ALWAYS NOW** -
– Friendly fires / Dirty disco / Be brave / New horizon / Melt close / C.P. / Loose talk (costs lives) / Inside out / Hit / Babies in the Bardo. *(re-iss. Jan87; same) (cd-iss. Feb92 on 'Les Tempes Modernes'+=;)* – Girls don't count / After image / Red voice.

— **LEE SHALLCROSS** – drums; repl. PAUL who had repl. PHIL

Jul 82. (12") *(fac 66-12)* **THE BEAST / SAKURA. / SAKURA (matrix mix) / TRIDENT** -
Nov 82. (lp) *(fbn 14)* **THE KEY OF DREAMS** -
– There was a time / Wretch / Sutra / Always now / Visitation / Regions / The wheel / No abiding place / Once before. *(cd-iss. Feb92 on 'Les Tempes Modernes'+=;)* – Sutra.
Jun 83. (7") *(fac 68)* **BACK TO WONDER. / BEATING HEART** -

— added **JENNY ROSS** – vocals, keyboards / **ANGELA FLOWERS** – vocals, keyboards

May 84. (lp) *(fact 90)* **FROM THE HIP** -
– Beneath the blade / Inspiration / Looking from a hilltop / Desert / Program for light / The process / Reflection / Prepare to live. *(cd-iss. Feb92 on 'Les Tempes Modernes';)*
Jun 84. (7"/12") *(fac 108/+t)* **LOOKING FROM A HILLTOP./ ('A'version)** -
Sep 85. (12"m) *(fbn 45)* **CRAZY WISDOM. / THE GUITAR WALTZ / DIRTY DISC II** -

— **DAVID CRABTREE** – guitar + **STEWART HILTON** – drums; repl. ANGELA + LEE

Jul 86. (12") *(fac 160t)* **LOVE AND HATE. /** -
Dec 86. (12") *(fac 157t)* **BAD NEWS WEEK. / ('A'-Cough mix)** -

— disbanded in 1987

SEEFEEL

Formed: London, England . . . 1992 by college students JUSTIN FLETCHER and MARK CLIFFORD (the main songwriter), the lads soon finding DARREN 'Delores Throb' SEYMOUR, although they were still in search of a singer. Replying to SARAH PEACOCK's self-placed ad, CLIFFORD and Co had found themselves a frontwoman who assumed vocal duties on their 1993 debut, 'MORE LIKE SPACE EP'. Quite unlike anything else around at the time (although MY BLOODY VALENTINE was obviously a reference point) Radio One DJ, John Peel, found it hard to distinguish what speed to play the record at (33 or 45rpm!). Having signed for 'Too Pure' (the same label as PJ HARVEY, STEREOLAB and Th' FAITH HEALERS), they tried to break away from their inevitable pigeon-holed fate (their textured sound lay somewhere between chilled-out droning ambience and more guitar-led COCTEAU TWINS-style indie) via a collaboration with The APHEX TWIN, the 'PURE, IMPURE EP'. The 'TWIN's Sheffield based home, 'Warp', released their second, more sculpted album, 'SUCCOUR', in 1995. The following year, after CLIFFORD had issued a solo set (the others moonlighted as SIREN), SEEFEEL returned with an album on 'Rephlex' records, 'CH-VOX'.

Album rating: QUIQUE (*8) / SUCCOUR (*7) / CH-VOX (*6)

SARAH PEACOCK – vocals, guitars / **MARK CLIFFORD** – guitars / **DARREN SEYMOUR** – bass / **JUSTIN FLETCHER** – drums

Too Pure Astralwerks

Mar 93. (12"ep/cd-ep) *(PURE/+CD 20)* **MORE LIKE SPACE E.P.** -
– More like sace / Time to find me (come inside) / Come alive / Blue easy sleep.
Jun 93. (12"ep) *(PURE 23)* **PLAINSONG E.P.** -
– Plainsong / Moodwing / Minky starshine.
Jul 93. (12"ep; with APHEX TWIN) *(PURE 25)* **REMIXES E.P.** -
– Time to find me (AFX fast mix) / Time to find me (AFX slow mix) / Plainsong (sinebubble embossed dub).
(m-cd) **PURE, IMPURE** *(PURE/+CD 25)* – (the two 12"ep's above).
Oct 93. (cd/c/lp) *(PURE CD/MC/LP 28)* <6123> **QUIQUE**
– Climatic phase 3 / Polyfusion / Industrious / Imperial / Plainsong / Charlotte's mouth / Through you / Filter dub / Signals.

Warp not iss.

May 94. (12"ep/cd-ep) *(WAP 45/+CD)* **STARETHROUGH / ACR EYES. / SPANGLE / LUX 1** -
Jun 94. (12") <6124> **TIME TO FIND ME (remixes)** -
Jul 94. (cd) <6125> **POLYFUSIA** (compilation of MORE LIKE SPACE + PURE, IMPURE) -
Sep 94. (10"/cd-s) *(10+/WAP 53/+CD)* **FRACTURE. / TIED** -
Mar 95. (cd/c/d-lp) *(WARP CD/MC/LP 28)* **SUCCOUR** -
– Meol / Extract / When face was face / Fracture / Gatha / Ruby-ha / Rupt / Vex / Cut / Utreat.

— the outfit took time off for CLIFFORD to release a solo album, 'DISJEKTA', while the three others were moonlighting as SIREN

Rephlex not iss.

Nov 96. (cd/lp) *(CAT 038 CD/LP)* **CH-VOX** -

SEE SEE RIDER

Formed: based- East Kilbride, Scotland . . . late 1989 by LEWIS CHAMBERLAIN, alongside STEPHEN SANDS and female co-vocalist MAY ROCK MARSHALL. Naming themselves after a LEADBELLY song (widely covered by a variety of acts), they secured a support slot to both LLOYD COLE and The JESUS & MARY CHAIN, the latter's DOUGLAS HART augmenting the group on their inventive (shiny chrome indie-rock with darkly sexual lyrical undertones) debut recordings. SEE SEE RIDER snatched their break when BIRDLAND manager, Wayne Morris, signed them to his 'Lazy' imprint, recommending drummer PETE TWEEDIE (who had split from another band of his, The PRIMITIVES) in the process. Early in 1990, the band released their first 45/EP, 'SHE SINGS ALONE', although a series of very rock'n'roll, almost "Spinal Tap"-esque accidents put the brake on their momentum. The most serious of these occured when MAY came a cropper after travelling pillion on a motorbike, a case of No SEE SEE RIDER, at least as far as their fans were concerned, the subsequent delay holding up the release of a follow-up single, 'STOLEN HEART' (featuring The Rolling Stones' 'HAPPY' on the flip side), until Spring 1991. By this juncture, they had taken another passenger on board, namely ex-FELT man, PHIL KING. Although the band had signed to 'Elektra', their career skidded to a halt when TWEEDIE was involved in a bust-up on stage.

Album rating: never released any

LEWIS CHAMBERLAIN – vocals, bass / **MAY ROCK MARSHALL** – vocals, slide guitar / **STEPHEN SANDS** – guitar / **PETE TWEEDIE** – drums (ex-PRIMITIVES)

Lazy Elektra

Mar 90. (12"ep/cd-ep) *(LAZY 18 T/CD)* **SHE SINGS ALONE / SNOWFALL. / SLIP SO LOW / SEE SEE** -

— added **PHIL KING** – guitar (ex-SERVANTS, ex-FELT)

May 91. (7") *(LAZY 27)* **STOLEN HEART. / HAPPY** -
(12"+=/cd-s+=) *(LAZY 27 T/CD)* – Rosey singer.

— Aug'91, TWEEDIE departed after a bust-up on stage

— they disbanded when KING joined LUSH the following year

SENATE (see under ⇒ SPEAR OF DESTINY)

SENSELESS THINGS

Formed: Twickenham, London, England . . . late '86 by MARK KEDS and MORGAN NICHOLLS, who had played in a band together since their schooldays. By the release of their debut single (a 7" flexi given away free in early '88 with the fanzine, 'Shy Like You'), the line-up had solidified around BEN HARDING and CASS BROWNE, the fledgling pop punksters subsequently receiving the honour of a John Peel session. Their first release proper was the 'UP AND COMING' EP later that year, released on the self-financed 'Red' imprint. A debut mini-set, 'POSTCARD C.V.' (1989) followed on indie label, 'Way Cool', highlighting the band's continuing musical evolution. With the success of such crusty-esque fare as NED'S ATOMIC DUSTBIN and CARTER USM, along with the imminent explosion of grunge, 'Epic' deemed the SENSELESS THINGS a promising commercial possibility and, following a further couple of indie releases, the band made their major label debut in summer '91 with the 'EVERYBODY'S GONE' single. A minor Top 75 success, it was followed by the Top 50 mini-classic, 'GOT IT AT THE DELMAR', both singles featured on the album, 'THE FIRST OF TOO MANY' (1991). Displaying a quantum leap in songwriting and a newfound melodic verve, the record's promise was confirmed when the effervescent 'EASY TO SMILE' single finally took the SENSELESS THINGS into the UK Top 20 later that year. The following year's 'HOLD IT DOWN' repeated the success, although despite its admirable sentiments, the contentious 'HOMOPHOBIC ASSHOLE' single's radio-unfriendliness didn't do it any favours and it stiffed outside the Top 50. The accompanying album, 'EMPIRE OF THE SENSELESS' (1993) was another fine effort, but sank without trace after a brief appearance in the Top 40. Following 1995's 'TAKING CARE OF BUSINESS', KEDS joined The WILDHEARTS for two months before going AWOL, effectively ending The SENSELESS THINGS long running campaign. The singer eventually resurfaced in early '96 fronting The JOLT alongside BB METS and MARTIN SHAW, an EP, 'SEX AND CHEQUES' surfacing later that year. • **Songwriters:** KEDS penned most, except; SHOPLIFTING (Slits) / BREAK IT AWAY (Perfect Daze) / APACHE (Shadows) / ANSWERING MACHINE (Replacements). • **Trivia:** BEN HARDING was once a clerk for the BBC.

Album rating: THE FIRST OF TOO MANY (*7)

MARK KEDS – vocals, guitar / **BEN HARDING** – lead guitar / **MORGAN NICHOLLS** – bass, guitar / **CASS BROWNE** – drums

Yo Jo Jo | not iss.

Feb 88. (7"flexi) *(Yo Jo Jo 3)* **I'M MOVING / LOW TIME / (ALL YOU'VE GOT TO DO IS) STAY TOGETHER** | -
(above was given free with 'Shy Like You' fanzine)

Red | not iss.

Nov 88. (12"ep) *(RED 001T)* **UP AND COMING** | -
– Where the secret lies / I want to go back / I don't want to talk about it / You don't want me / When you let me down. *(re-iss. Feb91 12"ep+=/cd-ep+=; WC 006/+CD)* – Girlfriend / Standing in the rain.

Way Cool | not iss.

Mar 89. (7") *(WC 001)* **GIRLFRIEND. / STANDING IN THE RAIN** | -
Oct 89. (7") *(WC 003)* **TOO MUCH KISSING. / TREVOR** | -
Nov 89. (m-lp/cd) *(WC 004/+CD)* **POSTCARD C.V.** | -
– Trevor / Come together / Sneaking kisses / Laura Lamona / Shoplifting / Drunk & soppy / Back to nowhere / Teenage / Someone in you / Too much kissing / Girlfriend / Standing in the rain. *(cd+)* – UP AND COMING EP

Decoy | not iss.

May 90. (7") *(DYS 15)* **IS IT TOO LATE?. / LEO** | -
(12"+=/cd-s+=) *(DYS 15 T/CD)* – Andi in a karmann / Ponyboy.
May 90. (m-lp/m-cd) *(DYL 16/+CD)* **IS IT TOO LATE?** | - | - Euro
– Is it too late? / Leo / Andi in a karmann / Ponyboy / Celebrity / Tricia don't belong.
Jul 90. (12"ep/cd-ep) *(DYS 17 T/CD)* **CAN'T DO ANYTHING. / CAN'T EXPLAIN / TANGLED LINES** | -

Epic | Epic

Jun 91. (7"/c-s) *(656 980-7/-4)* **EVERYBODY'S GONE. / MYSTERY TRAIN** | 73 | -
(12"+=/cd-s+=) *(656 980-6/-2)* – I'm on black and white.
Sep 91. (7") *(657 449-7)* **GOT IT AT THE DELMAR. / FISHING AT TESCOS** | 50 | -
(c-s+=/12"+=/cd-s+=) *(657 449-4/-6/-2)* – Beat to Blondie / Can't remember.
Oct 91. (cd/c/lp/purple-lp) *(469 157-2/-4/-1) <48988>* **THE FIRST OF TOO MANY** | 66 | Mar92
– Everybody's gone / Best friend / Ex teenager / It's cool to hang out with your ex / 19 blues / Should I feel it / Lip radio / In love again / Got it at the Delmar / American dad / Radio Spiteful / Chicken / Wrong number / Different tongues / Fishing at Tescos. *(re-iss. Feb92 purple-lp; 469157-0)*
Dec 91. (7"pink/c-s) *(657 695-7/-4)* **EASY TO SMILE. / HAZEL** | 18 | -
(12"+=/cd-s+=) *(657 926-6/-2)* – Mollylove.
Mar 92. (7"orange/c-s) *(657 926-7/-4)* **HOLD IT DOWN. / CRUCIAL JUVENILIA** | 19 | -
(12"+=/pic-cd-s+=) *(657 926-6/-2)* – Splitting hairs.
Nov 92. (7"/c-s) *(658 833 7/-4)* **HOMOPHONIC ASSHOLE. / BODY BAG** | 52 | -
(12"+=) *(658 833-6)* – Just flirting.
(cd-s++=) *(658 833-2)* – ('A'radio edit).
Feb 93. (7") *(658 940-7)* **PRIMARY INSTINCT. / RUNAWAYS** | 41 | -
(12"colrd+=/cd-s+=) *(658 940-6/-2)* – Too much like I know you.
Mar 93. (cd/c/lp) *(473 525-2/-4/-1)* **EMPIRE OF THE SENSELESS** | 37 | -
– Homophobic asshole / Keepsake / Tempting Kate / Hold it down / Counting friends / Just one reason / Cruel moon / Primary instinct / Rise (song for Dean & Gene) / Ice skating at the Milky Way / Say what you will / Runaways. *(re-iss. Jun93 += cd/c/lp; 474 119-2/-4/-1)* – POSTCARD CV.
Jun 93. (7"/c-s) *(659 250-7/-4)* **TOO MUCH KISSING. / KEEPSAKE / SAY WHAT YOU WILL (demo)** | 69 | -
(cd-s) *(659 250 2)* (1st 2 tracks) / Cruel dub / ('A'original).
Oct 94. (7") *(660 957-7)* **CHRISTINE KEELER. / HIGH ENOUGH** | 56 | -
(12") *(660 957-6)* – ('A'side) / Jerk / The revivalist / Can't go back.
(cd-s) *(660 957-2)* – ('A'side) / Jerk / The revivalist / Driving on the right.
Jan 95. (7"colrd) *(661 116-7)* **SOMETHING TO MISS. / 16.18.21** | 57 | -
(12"+=/cd-s+=) *(661 116-6/-2)* – Never haunted / Answering machine.
Feb 95. (cd/c/lp) *(478 368-2/-4/-1)* **TAKING CARE OF BUSINESS** | -
– Christine Keeler / Something to miss / Page 3 valentine / Any which way / Marlene / Role models / Watching the pictures go / Scapegoats / 16.18.21 / Touch me on the heath / Wanted / Too late / Dead sun / The way to the drugstore.

— now without KEDS who joined WILDHEARTS for a few months before going AWOL, while HARDING joined 3 COLOURS RED. KEDS re-surfaced early in 1996 with The JOLT, while it took CASS a little longer to make his return with the more pop-friendly, DELAKOTA.

– compilations, etc. –

Feb 94. (cd) *Strange Fruit; (SFRCD 127)* **THE PEEL SESSIONS** | -

JOLT

KEDS – vocals, guitar / **BB METS** – vocals, bass / **MARTIN SHAW** – drums

Scared Of Girls | not iss.

Oct 96. (cd-ep) *(GIRL 001CD)* **SEX AND CHEQUES EP** | -
– Homebreaker / Call me if you wanna / Scared of girls / Sex and cheques.
Apr 97. (one-sided-7") *(GIRL 003)* **GOODBYE TO THE 80's** | -

Fluffy Bunny | not iss.

Apr 98. (7"ep/cd-ep) *(FLUFF 17/+CD)* **MADE MY DAY / RUDE BOY. / WAS IT WILD? (original) / MADE MY DAY (original).** | -

SENSER

Formed: Wimbledon, London, England . . . late 1990 initially as a trio by NICK MICHAELSON, KERSTIN HAIGH and JAMES BARRETT. With the line-up subsequently augmented by Saudi Arabian vocalist/rapper, HEITHAM AL-SAYED, DJ ANDY CLINTON, bassist/engineer HAGGIS and drummer JOHN MORGAN, SENSER developed into a formidably eclectic soundclash attracting such labelling attempts as "the British RAGE AGAINST THE MACHINE". They were certainly as fiercely indignant about political inertia and injustice, although they soundtracked their anger with a slightly more schizophrenic musical assault. Aligning themselves with the free festival/crusty scene, the group's first tour was supporting uber-hippies OZRIC TENTACLES in 1992, although the first SENSER single, 'EJECT' was more molten metal-hip hop than mushroom meandering. Released on 'Ultimate' in summer '93, the single enjoyed wildly enthusiastic reviews across the board, from the inkies to the metal and dance press. Likewise their two follow-up efforts, 'THE KEY' and 'SWITCH', the former scraping into the Top 50 while the latter featured a rivetting mash-up of Public Enemy's SLAYER-sampling classic, 'SHE WATCH CHANNEL ZERO'. It served as a brutal taster for the group's genre splicing debut album, 'STACKED UP' (1994), a groundbreaking collision of dub, rap, riffing, scratching and two-fingered defiance best evidenced in the frantic 'AGE OF PANIC', a subsequent single release later that summer. Despite continuing acclaim and riotous live appearances, however, the group splintered the following year with HEITHAM, MORGAN and HAGGIS forming LODESTAR alongside guitarist JULES HODGSON. Recruiting DJ AWE, SENSER carried on with its original core members, releasing a one-off single in summer '96, 'CHARMING DEMONS'. • **Songwriters:** Group except; SHE WATCH CHANNEL ZERO (Public Enemy). 'PEACE' was co-written w / TIM MORTON.

Album rating: STACKED UP (*8)

HEITHAM AL-SAYED (b.1970, Riyadh, Saudi Arabia) – vocals, piano, bongos / **KERSTIN HAIGH** (b.1969, Balham, London) – vocals, flute / **NICK MICHAELSON** (b.1969, London) – guitar / **JAMES BARRETT** (b. 1970, London) – bass / **ANDY CLINTON** (b. 1969, Buckinghamshire) – DJ / **HAGGIS** (b. 1966, Edinburgh, Scotland) – bass, soundman, engineer / **JOHN MORGAN** (b. London, 1970) – drums

Ultimate | A&M

Jun 93. (12"/cd-s) *(Topp 016 t/cd)* **EJECT / DON'T LOSE YOUR SOUL. / (other mixes)** | -
Sep 93. (7") *(Topp 019)* **THE KEY. / NO COMPLY** | 47 | -
(12"+=/cd-s+=) *(Topp 019 t/cd)* – ('A'-radio mix) / ('A'-Liquid lunch mix).
Mar 94. (7") *(Topp 022)* **SWITCH. / CHANNEL ZERO** | 39 | -
(12"+=/cd-s+=) *(Topp 022 t/cd)* – ('A'-Depth Charge mix) / Age of panic (Eat Static mix).
Apr 94. (cd/c/d-lp) *(Topp cd/mc/lp 008) <540347>* **STACKED UP** | 4 | Jan95
– States of mind / The key / Switch / Age of panic / What's going on / One touch one bounch / Stubborn / Door game / Peanut game / Peace / Eject / No comply / Worth.
Jul 94. (c-s) *(Topp 027mc)* **AGE OF PANIC. / LOOKING DOWN THE BARREL OF A GUN (live)** | 52 | -
(12"+=/c-s+=/cd-s+=) *(Topp 027 t/mcs/cd)* – ('A'-Sick man mix).

— now without HEITHAM, JOHN MORGAN + HAGGIS who formed LODESTAR with guitarist JULES HODGSON. An eponymous album in September '96, also for 'Ultimate' was another metallic-rap affair. The aforementioned were replaced by **DJ AWE** – scratching

Jul 96. (7"/c-s) *(Topp 045mc)* **CHARMING DEMONS. / HEADCASE** | 42 | -
(cd-s) *(Topp 045cd)* – ('A'-Keep on dreaming vocal mix) / ('A'-DJ Awe mix) / ('A'-Keep on dreaming dub mix).

— **PAUL SODEN** – drums; repl. MORGAN

Feb 98. (7") *(Topp 061)* **ADRENALIN. / ROWS OF PEOPLE** | -
(cd-s) *(Topp 061cd)* – ('A'side) / ('A'-Ladyboy remix) / Spunk.
Mar 98. (7") *(Topp 066)* **BREED. / TRIED AND UNTESTED** | -
(cd-s) *(Topp 066cd)* – ('A'side) / Breed (featuring DJ Awe & Kerstin) / 6's & 7's.
(12"/cd-s) *(Topp 066 t/cdx)* – ('A'side) / ('A'-Anorak mix) / ('A'-De Senser mix).
Apr 98. (cd/c/lp) *(Topp cd/mc/lp 064)* **ASYLUM** | 73 | -
– Book of flies / Charming demons / Adrenalin / Strange asylum / Burn out / Desensitised / Breed / Lizard / Oyster / Weatherman. *(also d-cd; Toppcdx 064)*

SENSURROUND (see under ⇒ MEMBRANES)

SENTRIDOH (see under ⇒ SEBADOH)

Will SERGEANT (see under ⇒ ECHO & THE BUNNYMEN)

SERIOUS DRINKING

Formed: Norwich, England . . . early 1981 by MARTIN SIMON, LANCE, JEM, EUGENE and ANDY. With most of the members having met while studying at the University Of East Anglia, SERIOUS DRINKING set out to celebrate that most famous of student pastimes i.e. getting plastered. A kind of precursor to 90's "lad" culture, the band enjoyed a cult following throughout the 80's via albums such as 'THE REVOLUTION BEGINS AT CLOSING TIME' (1983) and 'THEY MAY BE DRINKERS ROBIN, BUT THEY'RE STILL HUMAN BEINGS' (1984), although with their staunchly socialist outlook and an offbeat sense of humour, they were a world apart from the genuine mob mentality of the 'Oi!' scene. Like their most famous fan, John Peel, the boys' other great love was football, 1990's re-issue of their debut, 'LOVE ON THE TERRACES', released to coincide with that year's World Cup. The same year saw the release of brilliantly titled compilation (complete with free beer mat!), 'STRANGER THAN TANNADICE – THE HITS, MISSES AND OWN GOALS OF SERIOUS DRINKING', 'Tannadice', for the benefit of English readers, being the home of Scottish Premier League stragglers Dundee United (although many might argue that nearby Dundee ground, 'Dens Park', is even stranger!). Said to be the inspiration for HALF MAN HALF BISCUIT and I, LUDICROUS, SERIOUS DRINKING were a little ahead of their time (time? – time gentlemen please!).

Album rating: THE REVOLUTION STARTS AT CLOSING TIME (*5) / THEY MAY BE DRINKERS ROBIN, BUT THEY'RE STILL HUMAN BEINGS (*5)

MARTIN SIMON – vocals (ex-HIGSONS) / **EUGENE** – vocals / **ANDY** – guitar (ex-FARMERS BOYS) / **JEM** – bass / **LANCE** – drums

Upright | not iss.

Sep 82. (7"ep) *(UP 4)* **LOVE ON THE TERRACES EP** ☐ [-]
– Love on the terraces / Hypocrite / Bobby Moore was innocent / Nobody likes him.

Mar 83. (7"m) *(UP 5)* **HANGOVER. / DON'T SHOOT ME DOWN / BABY I'M DYING A DEATH** ☐ [-]

Sep 83. (lp) *(UPLP 3)* **THE REVOLUTION STARTS AT CLOSING TIME** ☐ [-]
– The revolution starts at closing time / Winter's over / Spirit of '66 / Love on the terraces / Bobby Moore was innocent / Hangover / Countdown to Bilko / Really good bloke / 12XU / Am I coming over to yours.

Mar 84. (lp) *(UPLP 7)* **THEY MAY BE DRINKERS ROBIN, BUT THEY'RE ALSO HUMAN BEINGS** ☐ [-]

May 84. (7") *(UP 8)* **COUNTRY GIRL BECAME DRUGS AND SEX PUNK. / GO FOR THE BURN!** ☐ [-]

— **KAREN YARNELL** – drums (ex-GYMSLIPS) repl. LANCE and JEM

— **CARL KENNEDY** – also joined at some stage

— basically, they returned to the pub and the terraces, until . . .

Worker's Playtime | not iss.

Jun 90. (cd/lp) *(PLAY CD/LP 14)* **STRANGER THAN TANNADICE – THE HITS, MISSES AND OWN GOALS** (part compilation) ☐ [-]
– Love on the terraces / Don't shoot me down / Baby I'm dying a death / Hangover / Time is right / World service / Winter's over / Country girl becomes sex and drugs punk / Go for the burn / A nice piece of trout / A day at the races / He's an angry bastard but I like him / 12XU – Bobby Moore was innocent – I'm on drugs. *(cd+=)* – Love on the terraces / Spirit of '66 / Countdown to Bilko / Really good bloke / Pillars of society / Young hearts run free.

— the odd sporadic release still surfaced from the dug-out

Musical Tragedies | not iss.

Jan 93. (7") *(EFA 11366)* **RED SKIES OVER WEMBLEY. /** ☐ [-]

Damaged Goods | not iss.

Jun 96. (7") *(DAMGOOD 101)* **BACK HOME 1996. /** ☐ [-]

SERVANTS

Formed: London, England . . . 1985 by songwriter DAVID WESTLAKE, along with JOHN MOHAN, PHILIP KING and JOHN WILLS. Displaying an obvious SYD BARRETT fetish, WESTLAKE and Co made their vinyl debut with their self-financed 7", 'SHE'S ALWAYS HIDING', consolidated by an appearance on the NME's high-profile C-86 cassette. However, after a second single, 'THE SUN, A SMALL STAR', later in the year, The SERVANTS took early retirement when most of the band became involved in other projects; while WILLS joined LOOP and KING became a FELT member, the latter also moonlighted with JOHN MOHAN in 'Creation' act, APPLE BOUTIQUE, issuing a one-off 12", 'LOVE RESISTANCE', in '88. Meanwhile, WESTLAKE was already carving out his own solo career with a mini-set entitled simply 'WESTLAKE' (1987) before re-employing The SERVANTS moniker alongside newcomers LUKE HAINES, ALICE READMAN and former HOUSEMARTINS drummer, HUGH WHITAKER. A solitary single, 'IT'S MY TURN', appeared on 'Glass' records in 1989, while a long-awaited debut album for 'Paperhouse' (home of The PASTELS), 'DISINTERESTED' appeared almost a year later. Unfortunately, the title proved all too prophetic and the SERVANTS were finally laid to rest; HAINES and READMAN would achieve greater recognition with their own outfit, The AUTEURS.

Album rating: DISINTERESTED (*5)

DAVID WESTLAKE – vocals / **PHILIP KING** – bass, guitar / **JOHN MOHAN** – guitar, keyboards / **JOHN WILLS** – drums (of WISHING STONES)

Head | not iss.

Mar 86. (7") *(HEAD 1)* **SHE'S ALWAYS HIDING. / TRANSPARENT** ☐ [-]

Oct 86. (12"ep) *(HEAD 3)* **THE SUN, A SMALL STAR / MEREDITH. / IT TAKES NO GENTLEMAN / FUNNY BUSINESS** ☐ [-]

— split when WILLS joined LOOP and KING joined FELT (also to BIFF BANG POW!). Early in '88, KING and MOHAN got together as APPLE BOUTIQUE, releasing one-off 12", 'LOVE RESISTANCE' with b-side 'I DON'T BELIEVE IN YOU' & 'BALLAD OF JET HARRIS' on 'Creation' *(CRE 052T)*

DAVID WESTLAKE

Creation | not iss.

Nov 87. (m-lp) *(CRELP 019)* **WESTLAKE** ☐ [-]
– The word around town / Dream come true / Rings on her fingers / Everlasting / She grew and she grew / Talk like that. *(cd-iss. Jul93; CRECD 019)*

SERVANTS

— **WESTLAKE** recruited new line-up **LUKE HAINES** (b. 7 Oct'67, Walton-On-Thames, Surrey, England) – vocals, guitar / **ALICE READMAN** (b.1967, Harrow, Middlesex, England) – bass / **HUGH WHITAKER** – drums (ex-HOUSEMARTINS)

Glass | not iss.

Sep 89. (7") *(GLASS 056)* **IT'S MY TURN. / AFTERGLOW** ☐ [-]
(12"+=) *(GLASS12 056)* – Faithful to 3 lovers / Do or be done.

Paperhouse | not iss.

Jul 90. (cd/lp) *(PAP CD/LP 005)* **DISINTERESTED** ☐ [-]
– Move out / Restless / Thin skinned / Hush now / Hey Mrs. John / Big future / The power of woman / Third wheel / Self destruction / They should make a statue / Look like a girl / Afterglow.

— split for the final time when HAINES and READMAN formed The AUTEURS

7 SECONDS

Formed: Reno, Nevada, USA . . . 1981 by KEVIN SECONDS, STEVE YOUTH and drummer TROY MOWAT, the latter being deposed first by TOM BORHINO and then BIX BIGLER. After completing a couple of self-financed demo cassettes for 'Vicious Scam', the group signed to JELLO BIAFRA's 'Alternative Tentacles' label – then still in its infancy – for a solitary EP, 'SKIN, BRAINS AND GUTS'. Released in summer '82, the record's lyrical concerns were reflected in such archetypal hardcore titles as 'REDNECK SOCIETY', 'ANTI-KLAN' and 'RACISM SUCKS'. Moving on to the 'Better Youth Organisation' (also home YOUTH BRIGADE), 7 SECONDS continued their crusade through the mid-80's with a trio of albums, 'THE CREW' (1984), 'WALK TOGETHER ROCK TOGETHER' (1985) and 'NEW WIND' (1986), the last of which saw the return of TROY. Like many US hardcore bands, they gravitated towards a more accessible punk-metal crossover as the 80's wore on, signing to 'Restless' ('G.W.R.' in the UK) for a further two sets. More independent releases followed in the early 90's, although 7 SECONDS finally hit paydirt with a major label deal courtesy of 'Epic'. Despite criticism that their music had been progressively diluted, the veteran punksters kept the faith with 'THE MUSIC, THE MESSAGE' (1995).

Album rating: THE CREW (*5) / WALK TOGETHER ROCK TOGETHER mini (*4) / NEW WIND (*4) / OLD SCHOOL compilation (*5) / THE MUSIC, THE MESSAGE (*4)

KEVIN SECONDS – vocals, guitar / **STEVE YOUTH** – bass / **BIX BIGLER** – drums; repl. TROY (other early drummer, TOM BORHINO)

— issued 2 cassettes on 'Vicious Scam' US

not iss. | Alternative Tentacles

Jul 82. (7"ep) *<VIRUS 15>* **SKIN, BRAINS AND GUTS** [-] ☐
– Skin, brains and guts / No authority / Redneck society / Baby games / Racism sucks / This is my life / Anti-klan / I hate sports / We're gonna fight.

Better Youth Org'n | Better Youth Org'n

Sep 84. (lp/c) *<(BYO 5/+C)>* **THE CREW** ☐ ☐
– The crew / Clenched fists / Black eyes / Colourblind / Aim to please / Boss / Young 'til I die / Red and black / Die hard / I have a dream / Bully / Trust / Here's your warning / Spread / Not just boys fun / Rock together. *<US cd-iss. 1989 inc. live tracks; BYO 5CD>* – Here's your warning / Definite choice / Not just boys fun / This is the angry (part 2) / Straight on / You lose / What if there's a war in America.

Jun 85. (m-lp/m-c) *<(BYO 10/+C)>* **WALK TOGETHER ROCK TOGETHER** ☐ ☐
– Regress no way / We're gonna fight it / In your face, spread / 99 red balloons / Remains to be seen / Walk together, rock together / How do you think you'd feel / Strength.

— **TROY MOWAT** – drums; returned to repl. BIX

Sep 86. (lp/c) *<(BYO 14/+C)>* **NEW WIND** ☐ ☐

G.W.R. | Restless

1988. (lp) *(GWLP 49)* *<72276-1>* **OURSELVES** ☐ ☐
– Escape and run / Far away friends / Save ourselves / If I abide / Wish I could help / Sleep / Sister / Middleground / When one falls / Some sort of balance / Seven years. *(cd-iss. Jul95 on 'Restless'; same as US)*

1989. (lp) *<72344-1>* **SOULFORCE REVOLUTION** [-] ☐
– Satyagraha / Busy like people / I can sympathise / It makes a lot sense now / Mother's day / Tribute freedom landscape / Copper ledge / Tickets to a better place / 4 a.m. in Texas / Soul to keep. *(UK cd-iss. Jul95 on 'Restless'; same as US)*

not iss. | Headhunter

Jul 93. (cd/c/lp) *<HED 028-2/-4/-1>* **OUT THE SHIZZY** [-] ☐
– Shizzy / His way, go away / Happy rain / Free to space / Weak link / Reuben said / Yet again / G / Widespread / Motionary / Naked / Nate / Some kind of sign.

Epic Epic
Dec 95. (cd/c) <(481454-2/-4)> **THE MUSIC, THE MESSAGE**
– Ghost / Such and such / The music, the message / Kinda future / My gravity / See you tomorrow / Get a different life / Talkbox / My list / First ya told us / Born without a mind / Punk rock teeth / Girl song / I can remember / Even better plan / The kids are united.

– compilations, etc. –

1988. (lp) *Head Hunter;* **OLD SCHOOL** (early material) [-]
Nov 95. (cd) *Headhunter; <053>* **ALT.MUSIC.HARDCORE** [-]
– ('SKINS, BRAINS & GUTS') + 5 years of lies / Drug control / Bottomless pit / Fight your own fight / Committed for life / This is the angry / Aggro / War in the head / The kids are united.

7 YEAR BITCH

Formed: Seattle, Washington, USA . . . 1991 by SELENE VIGIL, STEFANIE SARGENT, ELIZABETH DAVIS and VALERIE AGNEW. Not short of selling points, this all-female Seattle act generated an immediate buzz with their debut single, 'LORNA', the girls' righteously browned off, distortion-drenched racket earning them fawning column inches and a PEARL JAM support slot. Even the shock death of SARGENT wasn't enough to halt the band's momentum and after a period of uncertainty they decided to carry on with new guitarist ROICI DUNNE. In the meantime the ladies released a compilation – dedicated to SARGENT – of their work to date, 'SICK 'EM', on the local 'C/Z' label; despite shying away from any real connection with the militant Riot Grrrl movement, titles like 'DEAD MEN DON'T RAPE' spelled out in black and white exactly where this band was coming from. A debut album proper, 'VIVA ZAPATA!' finally arrived in 1994, its title and subject matter no doubt influenced by sterling politico-rap tourmates RAGE AGAINST THE MACHINE. With encouraging reviews and a further round of high profile touring it was only a matter of time before the girls moved on up to a major, 'Atlantic' clinching their signatures and releasing follow-up set, 'GATO NEGRO' in 1996. • **Covered:** IT'S TOO LATE (Jim Carroll) / GO! (Tones On Tails).

Album rating: SICK 'EM (*6) / VIVA ZAPATA! (*6) / GATO NEGRO (*6)

SELENE VIGIL – guitar / **STEFANIE SARGENT** – guitar / **ELIZABETH DAVIS** – bass / **VALERIE AGNEW** – drums

not iss. unknown
1991. (7") **LORNA. /** [-]
10 Past 12 10 Past 12
Jul 92. (10"pic-ep) <(DUMP 009)>
ANTIDISESTABLISHMENTARIANISM EP
– 8 ball / No fuckin' war / You smell / Lonely / Dead men don't rape.
C/Z C/Z
Oct 92. (lp/cd) <(CZ 048/+CD)> **SICK 'EM**
– Chow down / Tired of nothing / Knot / In lust you trust / Sink / Gun / Lorna / You smell lonely / No fucking war / Dead men don't rape / 8-ball deluxe / Can we laugh now?

—— tragically, STEFANIE died a month before above release date

—— she was repl. by **ROICI DUNNE** – guitar
May 95. (cd) <CZ 078> **VIVA ZAPATA!** [-]
– The scratch / Hip like junk / M.I.A. / Derailed / Cats meow / Rock a bye / It's too late / Damn good and well / Kiss my ass goodbye / Icy blue / Get lit.

—— (mid '96) **LISA FAYE** – guitar (ex-MUDWIMMIN) repl. DUNNE
not iss. Atlantic
Mar 96. (cd/c/lp) <82873-2/-4/-1> **GATO NEGRO** [-]
– The history of my future / Crying shame / Disillusion / Deep in the heart / The midst / 24,900 miles per hour / Whoopie cat / Miss understood / Sore subject / Rest my head / 2nd hand / Jack.
not iss. Man's Ruin
1996. (7") <MR 026> **MISS UNDERSTOOD. / GO!** [-]

disbanded after above

SEX GANG CHILDREN

Formed: London, England . . . 1982 out of PANIC BUTTON by ANDI SEX GANG and DAVE ROBERTS, who in turn recruited TERRY McLEAY and ROB STROUD. Rapidly building up a cult following, this bunch of ghoulish goth-fetish merchants (who took their offensive moniker from a line in a William Burroughs novel) released a self-financed, cassette-only live album, 'NAKED', later the same year. An appearance at Leeds' Futurama festival helped push their debut vinyl release, 'BEASTS!', an EP consisting mainly of reworked material from 'NAKED' and their first release for 'Illuminated'. A follow-up single, 'INTO THE ABYSS' rounded the year off as the band became indie chart favourites with their patented brand of scratchy guitar, shrieking, often unintelligible vocals and general musical chaos. 'SEBASTIANE', the first single from debut album, 'SONG AND LEGEND' (1983) threw grating violin into the already crowded mix courtesy of MARC & THE MAMBAS member, GINI HEWES. 1983 also saw the release of a compilation album put together by ROBERTS; entitled 'THE WHIP', it featured a duet between ANDI and MARC ALMOND, 'THE HUNGRY YEARS'. The subsequent departure of STROUD was temporarily solved by the recruitment of ex-THEATRE OF HATE man, NIGEL PRESTON; he stayed for one single, 'MAURITIA MAYER', released on 'Clay' records after The 'GANG were dropped by 'Illuminated'. Matters became even more confused as another temp sticksman, DEATH CULT's RAY MONDO, was deported as the band returned from an American tour. To add insult to injury, ROBERTS jumped ship for his new band, the catchily monikered CARCRASH INTERNATIONAL, before 1983 was out. ANDI and McLEAY soldiered on briefly with new recruits CAM CAMPBELL and KEVIN MATTHEWS before Mr SEX GANG struck out for a solo career and effectively brought the band to an end. Renewed interest following the release of a retrospective album in 1991 led to a short-lived Stateside reformation, an independently released set of new material, 'MEDEA', surfacing in 1993. • **Trivia:** Produced by NICKY GARRETT (ex-UK SUBS) early on, before TONY JAMES (ex-GENERATION X) took over.

Album rating: THE HUNGRY YEARS: BEST OF THE SEX GANG CHILDREN compilation (*6)

ANDI SEX GANG (b. ANDREW HAYWARD) – vocals, guitar / **TERRY MacLEAY** (b. Scotland) – guitar / **DAVE ROBERTS** – bass, acoustic guitar / **ROB STROUD** – drums

Illuminated not iss.
Jun 82. (12"ep) *(ILL 11-12)* **BEASTS** [-]
– Cannibal queen / Times of our lives / Sense of elation. *(re-iss. Feb85)*
Oct 82. (7") *(ILL 15)* **INTO THE ABYSS. / DEICHE** [-]
Mar 83. (7") *(ILL 20)* **SONG AND LEGEND. / SEBASTIANE** [-]
Mar 83. (lp) *(JAMS 666)* **SONG AND LEGEND** [-]
– The crack-up / German nun / State of mind / Sebastiane / Draconian dream / Shout and scream / Killer K / Cannibal queen / Kill machine / Song and legend. *(re-iss. Apr86 on 'Dojo' lp/cd; DOJO LP/CD 16)*
Jun 83. (12"m) *(ILL 22-12)* **SEBASTIANE / MONGOLIA. / WHO ON EARTH CAN THAT BE** [-]

—— **NIGEL PRESTON** – drummer (ex-THEATRE OF HATE) repl. STROUD who formed Huddersfield outfit AEMOTU CRII, then PINK AND BLACK
Clay not iss.
Sep 83. (7"/ext.12") *(CLAY/12CLAY 27)* **MAURITIA MAYER. / CHILDREN'S PRAYER** [-]

—— **RAY MONDO** – drums (ex-DEATH CULT) repl. PRESTON who was swopped into same band

—— DAVE ROBERTS left late '83 to form CAR CRASH INTERNATIONAL. Trimmed to just ANDI and TERRY with new bassist **CAM CAMPBELL** and drummer **KEVIN MATTHEWS** when RAY was deported back to home country Sierra Leone. They split in 1984, but got the 7-year itch and reformed due to support in the US. **ANDI / DAVE** (now on guitar) / **GERALD SANTANA** (b. USA) – bass / + drummer

– compilations, etc. –

Dec 83. (lp) *Illuminated; (JAMS 34)* **BEASTS** [-]
– Beasts / Cannibal queen / Who on Earth can that be / Sense of elation / Into the abyss / Deiche / Salvation / Mongolia / Times of our lives. *(re-iss. Aug86 on 'Dojo'; DOJOLP 30)*
Jul 84. (12") *Illuminated; (ILL 39-12)* **DEICHE. / DRACONIAN DREAM** [-]
Aug 84. (c) *R.O.I.R.; (A 127)* **ECSTASY AND VENDETTA OVER NEW YORK (live)** [-]
(cd-iss. Aug94 on 'Cleopatra'; CLEO 3833)
Sep 85. (12") *Saderal; (SLS 12-001)* **DEICHE. / BEASTS** [-]
Apr 86. (lp/c) *Dojo; (DOJO LP/TC 13)* **RE-ENTER THE ABYSS** [-]
May 88. (lp) *Arkham House; (AHLP 1001)* **NIGHTLAND USA, 1983 (live)** [-]
May 88. (lp) *Sex; (SEX 2)* **LIVE IN LONDON AND GLASGOW (live)** [-]
Dec 91. (cd/lp) *Receiver; (RR CD/LP 149)* **THE HUNGRY YEARS: THE BEST OF THE SEX GANG CHILDREN** [-]

ANDI SEX GANG

Illuminated not iss.
Sep 84. (7") *(ILL 52)* **LES AMANTS D'UN JOUR. / OH HENRY** [-]
Jan 85. (lp) *(JAMS 48)* **BLIND** [-]
– Welcome to my world / Boss and beauty / Dead metal / Ecstasy and vendetta / Ida-ho / Last chants for the slow dance / The quick gas gang / Dying fall / Immigrant / Oh Henry / I've done it all before / Strike blind / Gas reprise. *(cd-iss. Jun93 on 'Trident'; TMI 1) (re-iss. cd Mar94 on 'Cleopatra'; CLEO 5122-2)*
Mar 85. (7") *(ILL 53)* **IDA-HO. / QUICK GAS GANG** [-]
(12"+=) *(ILL 53-12)* – You don't know me.
Revolver not iss.
Sep 86. (12"m) *(12REV 27)* **THE NAKED AND THE DEAD. / YOU DON'T KNOW ME / THE QUICK AND THE DEAD** [-]

—— below featured MICK RONSON – guitar
Jungle Jungle
Nov 88. (7") *(JUNG 42)* **SEVEN WAYS TO KILL A MAN. /** [-]
(12"+=) *(JUNG 42T)* –
Nov 88. (lp) *(FREUD 24) <51185>* **ARCO VALLEY** Feb89
– 7 ways to kill a man / Queen of broken dreams / Power waits / Jesus phoned / Les amants d'un jour / Rock revo / Station 5 / Christian circus Joe / Assassin years / Belgique blue. *(re-iss. Jul89 c/cd; FREUD/+C/CD 24) (cd re-iss. Aug95 on 'Triple X'; TX 511852CD)*
Mar 89. (7") *(JUNG 48)* **ASSASSIN YEARS. /** [-]
(12"+=) *(JUNG 48T)* –
not iss. Cleopatra
1993. (cd,c) <5861> **GOD ON A ROPE** [-]
– Bormann chain – Victor Jara / Psyche Sara / Pig of a god: Heartless Harvey – Comedy / Captain Careful – Tin house, glass . . . / Almagordo – Miriam pain / Cold hard stone / Atom dance / Patient performers / Violin valley / Egypt's ancient lovers – The last great / God dies.

—— next with **ADRIAN PORTAS** – multi / **KEVIN MATTHEWS** – drums
Triple X Triple X
Aug 95. (m-cd) *(<TX 51186CD>)* **WESTERN SONGS FOR CHILDREN** May95
– Diamond girls / Heaven shines for you / Welcome to my world / Waiting for the assassin / Beauty of lovers.
Oct 95. (cd; by ANDI SEX GANG & MICK ROSSI) *(TX 51195CD)* **GABRIEL AND THE GOLDEN HORN**

SEX PISTOLS

Formed: London, England . . . summer 1975 out of The SWANKERS by PAUL COOK, STEVE JONES and GLEN MATLOCK, the latter two regular faces at MALCOLM McLAREN's 'Sex' boutique on the capital's King's Road. With the NEW YORK DOLLS already on his CV, McLAREN was well qualified to mastermind the rise and fall of The SEX PISTOLS as he dubbed his new plaything, the entrepeneur/svengali installing another 'Sex' customer, the green-haired JOHN LYDON, as a suitably sneering frontman. JONES soon renamed the latter JOHNNY ROTTEN, informing his farting rear-end, "You're rotten, you are"; the tone of the SEX PISTOLS was set. After a few local gigs, the group supported JOE STRUMMER's 101'ers in April '76, their bedraggled, low-rent bondage chic troupe of followers including the likes of SIOUXSIE SIOUX (later of BANSHEES fame) and one SID VICIOUS, allegedly the perpetrator behind the infamous glass-throwing incident at the 100 Club punk all-dayer in which a girl was partially blinded. Controversy, intentional or otherwise, hung around the group like a bad smell and made The SEX PISTOLS into minor legends with barely one single under their belts. Signed to 'E.M.I.' for £40,000, their debut release, 'ANARCHY IN THE U.K.' (having already shocked those of a sensitive disposition after being aired on the 'So It Goes' TV pop show) was finally released in November '76. An inflammatory slice of primal nihilism which surpassed even The STOOGES' finest efforts, the track initially climbed into the Top 40 before being unceremoniously withdrawn following the band's riotous appearance on a local chat/news programme, 'Today'. With JONES swearing copiously at presenter Bill Grundy, the tabloids had a field day, stirring up the moral majority and prompting more "must we subject our pop kids to this filth" editorials than you could shake a snotty stick at. 'E.M.I.' of course, bailed out (writing off the advance as a particularly bad debt) early the following year, MATLOCK was fired around the same time for being, well, er . . . too nice. His replacement was the aforementioned VICIOUS, a suitably violent and abusive character who duly became more of a punk anti-hero/caricature than McLAREN could ever have dreamed. After a short period in label limbo, The 'PISTOLS signed to 'A&M' in March '77 for another six figure sum; the honeymoon period was probably the shortest in recording history as the band's infamous antics at the post-signing party, together with protests from other artists on the label saw the UK's foremost punk band once again minus a recording contract. Once again, the band retained the loot from the advance and once again, a single, 'GOD SAVE THE QUEEN', was withdrawn (some copies did find their way into circulation and now fetch considerably more than the original 50p price tag). Arguably The 'PISTOLS defining moment, this jaw-clenching two-fingured salute to the monarchy and everything it represented was to truly make the band public enemy No.1, its release coinciding sweetly with her highness' silver jubilee year. Re-released by new label 'Virgin' (virtually the only company willing to take the band on-for a meagre £15,000 advance), the single was predictably banned by the BBC, though that didn't prevent it from outselling the official No.1 at the time, Rod Stewart's 'I Don't Want To Talk About It'. That long, hot summer also saw the band hiring a boat and sailing up and down the Thames in a publicity stunt which ended in chaos; cue yet more controversy and howls of derision from the nation's moral guardians. Knuckle-headed English royalists decided to take matters into their own hands, both COOK and ROTTEN attacked in separate incidents as another blankly brilliant single, 'PRETTY VACANT', gatecrashed the Top 10. Previewed by the seething, squalling outrage of 'HOLIDAYS IN THE SUN', the legendary debut album, 'NEVER MIND THE BOLLOCKS, HERE'S THE SEX PISTOLS' was finally released at the end of the year. While the record undeniably contained some filler, it remains the classic punk statement, the blistering 'BODIES' and the gleeful kiss-off to their former employers, 'E.M.I.', almost standing up against the intensity of the singles (included in their entirety). As ever, controversy clouded its release, the album reaching No.1 in spite of the word 'Bollocks' – a near contravention of the 1889 Indecent Advertisements Act(!) – resulting in boycotts from many major outlets. Constantly on the verge of falling apart, the band subsequently flew to America for a string of chaotic dates, the final round of blanks in The 'PISTOLS depleted armoury. Amid sporadic showdowns with Deep South cowboys and SID's ever worsening heroin problem, ROTTEN (bowing out on stage in San Francisco with the immortal phrase "Ever get the feeling you've been cheated") effectively ended the whole sorry affair with his departure after the final gig. While LYDON (the name he now reverted back to) went on to form PUBLIC IMAGE LTD., McLAREN had other ideas for the splintered remains of the band, namely jetting off to Rio De Janeiro to record a single with exiled trainrobber, RONNIE BIGGS. The result, 'NO ONE IS INNOCENT (A PUNK PRAYER BY RONNIE BIGGS)', made the Top 10 in summer '78, although VICIOUS was absent from the recording, holed up in New York with his similarly addicted girlfriend, Nancy Spungeon. He did find time to record a peerless rendition of Paul Anka's 'MY WAY', the single taking on an added poignancy following his untimely but hardly surprising death early the following year; out on bail after being charged with the murder of Spungeon in October, VICIOUS succumbed to a fatal heroin overdose on the 2nd of February '79. The following month saw the belated release of McLAREN's pet project, an artistically licensed celluloid account of The SEX PISTOLS' history entitled 'THE GREAT ROCK'N'ROLL SWINDLE'. Widely criticised for its its blatant exclusion of GLEN MATLOCK, the glaring absence of ROTTEN as an active participant and its paper-thin storyline, the movie was nevertheless an occasionally exhilirating, often hilarious trip through the misspent youth of Britain's best-loved punk band. While a perfunctory cover of Eddie Cochran's 'C'MON EVERYBODY' (a posthumous VICIOUS recording) made the Top 10 later that summer and 'Virgin' continued to flog The SEX PISTOLS' dead corpse with a variety of exploitation jobs, COOK and JONES fomed the short-lived PROFESSIONALS. Although they didn't invent punk, The SEX PISTOLS certainly helped popularise it and while they were at least partly responsible for an avalanche of unlistenably amateurish shit, the band's uncompromising approach permanently altered the machinations of the music industry and took three-chord rock'n'roll to its ultimate conclusion. Despite the fact original fans had long since given up on the UK ever descending into anarchy, the original 'PISTOLS line-up of LYDON, MATLOCK, JONES and COOK reformed in summer '96 for a handful of outdoor gigs and an accompanying live album. Opinion was divided as to whether this blatantly commercial venture (billed as "The Filthy Lucre Tour") was in keeping the original punk spirit; probably not, although few paying punters complained about what was subsequently hailed as one of the events of the summer and it was certainly a safer bet than the new GREEN DAY album . . . • **Songwriters:** Group compositions, until COOK & JONES took over in 1978. They also covered; NO FUN (Stooges) / ROCK AROUND THE CLOCK (Bill Haley) / JOHNNY B. GOODE (Chuck Berry) / STEPPING STONE (Boyce-Hart) / etc. • **Trivia:** In 1979, they took McLAREN to court for unpaid royalties. In 1986, the official receiver, through McLAREN paid a 7-figure out of court settlement to LYDON, JONES, COOK and SID's mother.

Album rating: NEVER MIND THE BOLLOCKS, HERE'S THE SEX PISTOLS (*10) / THE GREAT ROCK'N'ROLL SWINDLE (*8)

JOHNNY ROTTEN (b.JOHN LYDON, 31 Jan'56) – vocals / **STEVE JONES** (b. 3 Sep'55) – guitar / **GLEN MATLOCK** (b.27 Aug'56) – bass / **PAUL COOK** (b.20 Jul'56) – drums

		E.M.I.	not iss.
Nov 76.	(7") *(EMI 2566)* **ANARCHY IN THE U.K. / I WANNA BE ME**	38	-

— (Feb77) **SID VICIOUS** (b.JOHN RITCHIE, 10 May'57) – bass, vocals (ex-SIOUXSIE & THE BANSHEES) repl. MATLOCK who soon formed RICH KIDS

		A&M	not iss.
Mar 77.	(7"w-drawn) *(AMS 7284)* **GOD SAVE THE QUEEN. / NO FEELINGS**	-	-

— Were soon paid off yet again. Above copies filtered through and soon became a collectors item).

		Virgin	Warners
May 77.	(7") *(VS 181)* **GOD SAVE THE QUEEN. / DID YOU NO WRONG**	2	-

— (above was banned by the BBC, and outsold the official No.1 at the time; Rod Stewart's 'I Don't Want To Talk About It'.)

Jul 77. (7") *(VS 184)* **PRETTY VACANT. / NO FUN** [6] [-]
Oct 77. (7") *(VS 191)* **HOLIDAYS IN THE SUN. / SATELLITE** [8] [-]
Nov 77. (7") **PRETTY VACANT. / SUBMISSION** [-] [ ]
Nov 77. (lp/c) *(V/TCV 2086) <3147>* **NEVER MIND THE BOLLOCKS, HERE'S THE SEX PISTOLS** [1] [106]
– Holidays in the sun / Bodies / No feelings / Liar / God save the Queen / Problems / Seventeen / Anarchy in the UK / Submission / Pretty vacant / New York / E.M.I. *(7" free w/some copies of 'Submission'; SPOTS 001)* – **SUBMISSION** (one-sided). *(pic-lp Jan78; VP 2086) (re-iss. Oct86 lp/c; OVED/+C 136) (cd-iss. Oct86; CDV 2086) (re-iss. cd May93; CDVX 2086) (re-iss. 1996 on cd w/ free 'SPUNK' bootleg tracks) <cd-iss. Jul96 on 'Alex'; 5695>*

— ROTTEN left, reverted to JOHN LYDON and created new band PUBLIC IMAGE LTD. His place was temporarily taken by **RONNIE BIGGS** (the Great Train Robber escapee now exiled in Brazil) 'A'-side vocals / **SID VICIOUS** – 'B'side vocals

Jun 78. (7") *(VS 220)* **NO ONE IS INNOCENT (A PUNK PRAYER BY RONNIE BIGGS). / MY WAY** [7] [-]
(12") *(VS 220-12 A1/2)* – The biggest blow (a punk prayer by Ronnie Biggs) / My way.
(12"+=) *(VS 220-12 A3)* – (above listing) / (interview).

— On 11 Oct'78, SID was charged with the murder of girlfriend NANCY SPUNGEN. MALCOLM McLAREN/'Virgin' bailed him out, but he died 2 Feb'79 of drug overdose. The 1979/80 singles were all taken from THE GREAT ROCK'N'ROLL SWINDLE film.

Feb 79. (7") *(VS 240)* **SOMETHING ELSE. / FRIGGIN' IN THE RIGGIN'** [3] [-]
Mar 79. (d-lp/d-c) *(VD/TCV 2510) <45083>* **THE GREAT ROCK'N'ROLL SWINDLE (Film Soundtrack)** [7] [ ]
– God save the Queen symphony / Rock around the clock / Johnny B. Goode / Roadrunner / Black Arabs / Watcha gonna do about it (* on some) / Who killed Bambi? / Silly thing / Substitute / No lip / (I'm not your) Stepping stone / Lonely boy / Somethin' else / Anarchie pour le UK / Einmal war Belsen vortrefflich / No one is innocent / My way / C'mon everybody / E.M.I. / The great rock'n'roll swindle / You need hands / Friggin' in the riggin'. *(re-iss. 1-lp May80; V 2168) (re-iss. Apr89 lp/c; OVED/+C 234) (d-cd iss.Jul86; CDVD 2510) (re-iss. cd May93; CDVDX 2510)*
Apr 79. (7") *(VS 256)* **SILLY THING. / WHO KILLED BAMBI?** [6] [ ]

— (above 'A'vocals – **STEVE JONES**, 'B'vocals – **EDDIE TENPOLE TUDOR**) (below 'A'vocals – **SID VICIOUS**)

Jun 79. (7") *(VS 272)* **C'MON EVERYBODY. / GOD SAVE THE QUEEN SYMPHONY / WATCHA GONNA DO ABOUT IT** [3] [ ]
Aug 79. (lp/c) *(VR/ 2)* **SOME PRODUCT: CARRI ON SEX PISTOLS** [6] [-]
– The very name (the Sex Pistols) / From beyond the grave / Big tits across America / The complex world of Johnny Rotten / Sex Pistols will play / Is the Queen a moron / The fuckin' rotter. *(cd-iss. May93; CDVR 2)*
Oct 79. (7") *(VS 290)* **THE GREAT ROCK'N'ROLL SWINDLE. / ROCK AROUND THE CLOCK** [21] [ ]
Dec 79. (lp/c; by SID VICIOUS) *(V/TCV 2144)* **SID SINGS** [30] [-]
– Born to lose / I wanna be your dog / Take a chance on me / (I'm not your) Stepping stone / My way / Belsen was a gas / Somethin' else / Chatterbox / Search and destroy / Chinese rocks / My way. *(re-iss. Aug88 lp/c; OVED/+C 85)* (cd-iss. Feb89; *CDV 2144)*

— There were other SID VICIOUS exploitation releases later.

Feb 80. (lp/c) *(V/TCV 2142)* **FLOGGING A DEAD HORSE** [23] [-]
– (singles compilation) *(re-iss. Apr86 lp/c; OVED/+C 165) (cd-iss. Oct86; CDV 2142)*
Jun 80. (7") *(VS 339)* **(I'M NOT YOUR) STEPPING STONE. / PISTOLS PROPAGANDA** [21] [-]

— COOK and JONES were now The PROFESSIONALS (see further below)

– compilations, exploitation releases –

Note; on 'Virgin' until mentioned otherwise.

Jan 80. (lp) *Flyover; (YX 7247)* **THE BEST OF . . . AND WE DON'T CARE** [ ] [-]
Dec 80. (6x7"box) *(SEX 1)* **PISTOLS PACK** [ ] [-]
– GOD SAVE THE QUEEN. / PRETTY VACANT / / HOLIDAYS IN THE SUN. / MY WAY / / SOMETHING ELSE. / SILLY THING / / C'MON EVERYBODY. / THE GREAT ROCK'N'ROLL SWINDLE / / STEPPING STONE. / ANARCHY IN THE U.K. / / BLACK LEATHER. / HERE WE GO AGAIN
(below 45 credited EDDIE TENPOLE TUDOR)
Sep 81. (7") *(VS 443)* **WHO KILLED BAMBI?. / ROCK AROUND THE CLOCK** [ ] [-]
1983. (7") *(VS 609)* **ANARCHY IN THE UK. / NO FUN** [ ] [-]
(12"+=) *(VS 609-12)* – E.M.I.
Jan 85. (7"/7"pic-d)(12") *Cherry Red; (PISTOL 76P)(12PISTOL 76)* **LAND OF HOPE AND GLORY. ("EX-PISTOLS") / FLOWERS OF ROMANSK** [69] [-]
Jan 85. (m-lp) *Chaos; (MINI 1)* **THE MINI-ALBUM** [ ] [-]
(pic-m-lp.Jan86; AMPL 37) (cd-iss. Mar89; APOCA 3)
Mar 87. (7",7"yellow,7"pink) *Chaos; (DICK 1)* **SUBMISSION. / NO FEELINGS** [ ] [-]
(12",12"colrd) *(EXPORT 1)* – ('A'side) / Anarchy in the U.K.
Feb 85. (lp) *Receiver; (RRLP 101)* **THE ORIGINAL PISTOLS LIVE (live)** [ ] [-]
(pic-lp Jun86 on 'American Phono.'; APKPD 13) (re-iss. Jan89 on 'Dojo'; DOJOLP 45) (re-iss. May86 on 'Fame' lp/c; FA 41-3149-1/-4) (cd-iss. Jul89; CDFA 3149)
1985. (lp) *Receiver; (RRLP 102)* **AFTER THE STORM** [ ] [-]
(above with tracks by NEW YORK DOLLS) (cd-iss. Jul91; RRCD 102)
Aug 85. (lp) *Konnexion;* **LIVE WORLDWIDE (live)** [ ] [-]
Nov 85. (lp) *Receiver;* **WHERE WERE YOU IN '77** [ ] [-]
Nov 85. (lp/pic-lp) *Bondage;* **BEST OF SEX PISTOLS LIVE (live)** [ ] [-]
Nov 85. (lp) *Hippy;* **NEVER TRUST A HIPPY** [ ] [-]
Nov 85. (lp) *'77 Records;* **POWER OF THE PISTOLS** [ ] [-]
Feb 86. (lp) *McDonald-Lydon; (JOCK 1)* **THE LAST SHOW ON EARTH (live)** [ ] [-]
Apr 86. (12") *McDonald-Lydon; (JOCK 1201)* **ANARCHY IN THE U.K. (live). / FLOGGING A DEAD HORSE** [ ] [-]
Aug 86. (lp) *McDonald-Lydon; (JOCKLP 3)* **THE SEX PISTOLS 10th ANNIVERSARY ALBUM** [ ] [-]
Aug 86. (12"ep) *Archive 4; (TOF 104)* **ANARCHY IN THE UK / I'M A LAZY SOD. / PRETTY VACANT / SUBSTITUTE** [ ] [-]
Jan 87. (6xlp-box) *McDonald-Lydon; (JOCK BOX1)* **THE FILTH AND THE FURY** [ ] [-]
– FILTH & THE FURY / LAST SHOW ON EARTH / 10th ANNIVERSARY ALBUM / ITALIAN DEMOS / NO FUTURE USA / THE REAL SID & NANCY
May 88. (lp/cd) *Restless; <72255-1/-2>* **BETTER LIVE THAN DEAD (live)** [-] [ ]
Jun 88. (cd/lp) *M.B.C.; (JOCK/+LP 12)* **IT SEEMED TO BE THE END UNTIL THE NEXT BEGINNING** [ ] [-]
Jun 88. (3"cd-s) *(CDT 3)* **ANARCHY IN THE U.K. / E.M.I. / NO FUN** [ ] [-]
Oct 88. (m-lp) *Specific; (SPAW 101)* **ANARCHY WORLDWIDE** [ ] [-]
Oct 88. (cd-ep) *Specific; (SPCFC 102)* **CASH FOR CHAOS** [ ] [-]
– Submission (live) / God save the Quen / Liar.
Oct 88. (cd-ep) *Classic Tracks; (CDEP 13C)* **THE ORIGINAL PISTOLS (live)** [ ] [-]
– Anarchy in the U.K. / Pretty vacant / No fun / Substitute.
Dec 88. (3"cd-s) *(CDT 37)* **GOD SAVE THE QUEEN / DID YOU NO WRONG / DON'T GIVE ME NO LIP CHILD** [ ] [-]
Jun 89. (lp,pink-lp,green-lp/c) *Link; (LINK LP/MC 063)* **LIVE AND LOUD (live)** [ ] [-]
(cd-iss. Oct92; LINKCD 063)
Dec 89. (lp/c/cd,pic-cd) *Receiver; (RR LP/MC/CD 117)* **NO FUTURE U.K.?** [ ] [-]
Feb 90. (cd/c) *Action Replay; (CDAR/ARLC 1008)* **THE BEST OF AND THE REST OF THE SEX PISTOLS** [ ] [-]
1990. (12"blue-ep) *Receiver; (REPLAY 3012)* **THE EARLY YEARS LIVE** [ ] [-]
– Anarchy in the U.K. / Pretty vacant / Liar / Dolls (aka 'New York').
Jan 91. (d-lp) *Receiver; (RRLD 004)* **PRETTY VACANT** [ ] [-]
(d-cd-iss. Jul93; RRDCD 004)
Sep 92. (7"/c-s) *(VS/+C 1431)* **ANARCHY IN THE U.K. / I WANNA BE ME** [33] [ ]
(cd-s+=/s-cd-s+=) *(VSCD T/X 1431)* – ('A'demo).
Oct 92. (cd) *Streetlink; (STRCD 019)* **EARLY DAZE – THE STUDIO COLLECTION** [ ] [-]
(re-iss. May93 on 'Dojo'; DOJOCD 119)
Oct 92. (cd/c/d-lp) *(V/TC/CDV 2702) / Alex; <2931>* **KISS THIS** [10] [ ]
– Anarchy in the UK / God save the Queen / Pretty vacant / Holidays in ther Sun / I wanna be me / Did you no wrong / No fun / Satellite / Don't give me no lip child / (I'm not your) Stepping stone / Bodies / No feelings / Liar / Problems / Seventeen / Submission / New York / E.M.I. / My way / Silly thing. // *(cd w/bonus cd+=)* **LIVE IN TRONDHEIM 21st JULY 1977** :- Anarchy in the UK / I wanna be me / Seventeen / New York / E.M.I. / No fun / No feelings / Problems / God save the Queen.
Nov 92. (7") *(VS 1448)* **PRETTY VACANT. / NO FEELINGS (demo)** [56] [-]
(12"+=) *(VST 1448)* – Satellite (demo) / Submission (demo).
(cd-s+=) *(VSCDG 1448)* – E.M.I. (demo) / Satellite (demo).
(cd-s) *(VSCDT 1448)* – ('A'side) / Seventeen (demo) / Submission (demo) / Watcha gonna do about it?
Mar 93. (cd) *Dojo; (DOJOCD 66)* **LIVE AT CHELMSFORD PRISON** [ ] [-]
Nov 93. (cd) *Dojo; (DOJOCD 73)* **BETTER LIVE THAN DEAD** [ ] [-]
Jul 95. (cd) *Dojo; (DOJOCD 216)* **WANTED – THE GOODMAN TAPES** [ ] [-]
Oct 95. (d-cd) *Essential; (ESDCD 321)* **ALIVE** [ ] [-]
Jan 96. (cd) *Dojo; (DOJOCD 222)* **PIRATES OF DESTINY** [ ] [-]
Jan 97. (7") *Man's Ruin; (MR 053)* **split with the UGLYS** [ ] [-]
Mar 97. (7") *Man's Ruin; (MR 056)* **split with the SOPHISTICATES** [ ] [-]
Jun 97. (cd) *Emporio; (EMPRCD 716)* **RAW** [ ] [-]

PROFESSIONALS

STEVE JONES – vocals, guitar / **PAUL COOK** – drums / **ANDY ALLEN** – guitar, vocals / **RAY McVEIGH** – guitar, vocals / **PAUL MYERS** – bass (ex-SUBWAY SECT)

Virgin — not iss.

Jul 80. (7") *(VS 353)* **JUST ANOTHER DREAM. / ACTION MAN** [ ] [-]
Aug 80. (lp/c) *(V/TCV 2167)* **THE PROFESSIONALS** [ ] [-]
– All the way / Are you? / Kick down the doors / Crescendo / Little boys in blue / Does anybody care / Kamikaze / 1-2-3 / Rockin' Mick.
Sep 80. (7"m) *(VS 376)* **1-2-3. / BABY I DON'T CARE / WHITE LIGHT, WHITE HEAT** [43] [-]
May 81. (7") *(VS 426)* **JOIN THE PROFESSIONALS. / HAS ANYBODY GOT AN ALIBI** [ ] [-]
Oct 81. (7") *(VS 456)* **THE MAGNIFICENT. / JUST ANOTHER DREAM** [ ] [-]
Nov 81. (lp/c) *(V/TCV 2220)* **I DIDN'T SEE IT COMING** [ ] [-]
– The magnificent / Payola / Northern slide / Friday night square / Kick down the doors / Little boys / Too far to fall / Crescendo / Madhouse / Too far to fall.

— PROFESSIONALS split early in '82 and COOK subsequently joined CHIEFS OF RELIEF. STEVE JONES augmented IGGY POP and went solo in 1987. He released two albums, 'MERCY' (1987) and 'FIRE AND GASOLINE' (1989).

SEX PISTOLS

— The original SEX PISTOLS re-formed at the back end of '95. Messrs LYDON, JONES, COOK + MATLOCK finally returned live on 24th June 1996, with packed out Finsbury Park concert. Embarked on their 'Filthy Lucre' tour soon after.

Virgin America — Caroline

Jul 96. (7"silver) *(VUS 113)* **PRETTY VACANT – LIVE. /** [18] [-]
(cd-s+=) *(VUSCD 113)* –
Aug 96. (cd/c/lp) *(41926) <7541>* **FILTHY LUCRE LIVE (live)** [26] [ ]
– Seventeen / New York / Did you no wrong / God save the Queen / Liar / Satellite / (I'm not your) Stepping stone / Holidays in the sun / Submission / No feelings / Pretty vacant / E.M.I. / Problems / Anarchy in the UK / No fun.

— JONES was also part-member of trans-Atlantic supergroup, NEUROTIC OUTSIDERS, alongside DUFF McKAGAN and MATT SORUM (Guns n' Roses) and JOHN TAYLOR (Duran Duran). They released an eponymous album for 'Maverick' in August '96 and from it they lifted the single, 'JERK'.

S.F. SEALS (see under ⇒ MANNING, Barbara)

SHACK (see under ⇒ PALE FOUNTAINS)

SHAMEN

Formed: Aberdeen, Scotland ... 1984 as ALONE AGAIN OR (named after a LOVE track from '67) by COLIN ANGUS and McKENZIE brothers DEREK and KEITH. After two singles (one for 'Polydor'; DREAM COME TRUE), they became The SHAMEN, releasing the singles 'YOUNG TILL YESTERDAY' (1986) and 'SOMETHING ABOUT YOU' (1987) on their own 'Moksha' label. The debut album, 'DROP' (1987), followed soon after and at this point the band were touting a fairly derivative indie take on classic West coast psychedelia combined with overtly political/drug orientated lyrics. As Angus became increasingly preoccupied with the nascent dance scene, however, DEREK McKENZIE split ranks and was replaced by WILL SINOTT. After the controversial single, 'JESUS LOVES AMERIKA' (1988), ANGUS and SINOTT relocated to LONDON, immersing themselves in the burgeoning acid house scene. The 'SHAMEN VS BAM BAM' (1988) moved the duo ever further into electronic territory and though the 'IN GORBACHEV WE TRUST' (1989) album fitted with the indie/dance crossover zeitgeist, The SHAMEN were one of the only acts to take the phenomenon to its ultimate conclusion. After a last outing for 'Moksha', the band signed to the 'One Little Indian' label in 1989. Their second single for the label, 'PROGEN' (1990), finally saw The SHAMEN make their mark on the dance scene. Although it barely scraped into the charts, the track was huge on the club scene and climbed to No.4 upon its re-release (in remixed form) the following year. In addition to this pivotal track, the album 'EN-TACT' (1990), contained the liquid psychedelia of 'HYPERREAL' (featuring the velvet tones of Polish singer PLAVKA) and the dancefloor manifesto of 'MAKE IT MINE', both minor hit singles. Having initially had DJ EDDIE RICHARDS play acid house ar their gigs, The SHAMEN had now developed the 'Synergy' live experience, a pioneering integration of live electronica and top flight DJ's (including the likes of MIXMASTER MORRIS and PAUL OKENFOLD) that attmepted to create a cultural fusion between the excitement of live performance and the communal vibe of the party scene. Just as the band were beginning to realise their dreams, WILL SINOTT drowned while swimming off the coast of The Canary Islands in May '91. ANGUS eventually decided to carry on and recruited RICHARD WEST aka Mr C, a veteran of the house scene, having DJ'd at the seminal RIP club. He was a natural choice, having rapped on the revamped 'PROGEN' single and collaborated on the 'Synergy' gigs, his inimitable cockney patois possessing a ragamuffin charm. He was also visually striking and along with SOUL FAMILY SENSATION singer JHELISSA ANDERSON, would become the public face of the The SHAMEN, ANGUS cannily content to communicate with the media via E-mail. The 'L.S.I. (LOVE, SEX, INTELLIGENCE)' (1992) single introduced a more commercial sound to the new look SHAMEN, as did the unashamed pop/dance of controversial hit, 'EBENEEZER GOODE' (1992) (the question of whether Mr C did actually sing 'E's are good' was endlessly debated by those tireless moral guardians of the nation's wellbeing). Many longtime fans couldn't stomach the new sound although the band gained a whole new following of pop kids enamoured with cheeky chappy Mr C. The million selling 'BOSS DRUM' (1992) album combined the aforementioned chart fodder with typically SHAMEN-esque communiques on ~'Archaic Revivals' and the like (i.e.'RE-EVOLUTION', the title track etc.). 1995 saw ex-SOUL II SOUL chanteuse VICTORIA WILSON JAMES replace ANDERSON and a new album in the shops, 'AXIS MUTATIS'. Although the record included the celebratory dance pop of single 'DESTINATION ESCHATON', overall it was more cerebral with a companion ambient album, 'ARBOR BONA/ARBOR MALA', released at the same time. 'HEMPTON MANOR' (1996) carried on The SHAMEN's overriding theme of transformation through mind altering substances and although the media profile of the band has shrunk considerably over the last couple of years, The SHAMEN have kept fans abreast of their activities with a rather fabby self-produced internet web-site, 'Nemeton'. • **Songwriters:** All written by COLIN and DEREK, until latter's departure and replacement by the late WILL SINNOTT. ANGUS & WEST took over in '91. Covered; GRIM REAPER OF LOVE (Turtles) / FIRE ENGINE + SLIP INSIDE THIS HOUSE (13th Floor Elevators) / LONG GONE (Syd Barrett) / SWEET YOUNG THING (Monkees) / PURPLE HAZE (Jimi Hendrix). • **Trivia:** In Apr'88, they were dropped from a McEwans lager TV ad, because of their then anti-commercial approach.

Album rating: IN GORBACHEV WE TRUST (*7) / BOSS DRUM (*8) / EN-TACT (*9) / AXIS MUTATIS (*7) / ARBOR BONA/ARBOR MALA (*7)

ALONE AGAIN OR

COLIN ANGUS (b.24 Aug'61) – keyboards / **DEREK McKENZIE** (b.27 Feb'64) – vocals, guitar / **KEITH McKENZIE** (b.30 Aug'61) – drums

All One / not iss.

Dec 84. (7") *(ALG 1)* **DRUM THE BEAT (IN MY SOUL). / SMARTIE EDIT** [ ] [-]

All One – Polydor / not iss.

Mar 85. (7") *(ALG 2)* **DREAM COME TRUE. / SMARTER THAN THE AVERAGE BEAR** [ ] [-]
(12") *(ALGX 2)* – ('A'-Splintered version) / ('B'-Ursa Major) / Drum the beat (shall we dance?).

SHAMEN

— added **ALISON MORRISON** – bass, keyboards

One Big Guitar / not iss.

Apr 86. (12"ep) *(OBG 003T)* **THEY MAY BE RIGHT . . . BUT THEY'RE CERTAINLY WRONG** [ ] [-]
– Happy days / Velvet box / I don't like the way the world is turning.

— **PETER STEPHENSON** (b. 1 Mar,62, Ayrshire) – keyboards repl. ALISON

Moksha / not iss.

Nov 86. (7"m) *(SOMA 1)* **YOUNG TILL YESTERDAY. / WORLD THEATRE / GOLDEN HAIR** [ ] [-]
(12"m) *(SOMA 1T)* – (first 2 tracks) / It's all around / Strange days dream.

May 87. (7") *(SOMA 2)* **SOMETHING ABOUT YOU. / DO WHAT YOU WILL** [ ] [-]
(12"+=) *(SOMA 2T)* – Grim reaper of love.

Jun 87. (lp/c) *(SOMA LP/C 1)* **DROP** [ ] [-]
– Through with you / Something about you / Four letter girl / The other side / Passing away / Young till yesterday / Happy days / Where do you go / Through my window / I don't like the way the world is turning / World theatre / Velvet box. *(c+=)* – Do what you will. *(cd-iss. Nov88 ++=; SOMACD 1)* – Strange days dream. *(re-iss. Jan92 on 'Mau Mau' lp/c/cd; MAU/+MC/CD 613)*

Sep 87. (7") *(SOMA 3)* **CHRISTOPHER MAYHEW SAYS. / SHITTING ON BRITAIN** [ ] [-]
(12"+=) *(SOMA 3T)* – Fire engine / Christopher Mayhew says a lot.

— **WILL SINNOTT** (b.23 Dec'60, Glasgow, Scotland) – bass repl. DEREK (COLIN now vocals, guitar)

Feb 88. (7") *(SOMA 4)* **KNATURE OF A GIRL. / HAPPY DAYS** [ ] [-]
(12"+=) *(SOMA 4T)* – What's going down / Sub knature of a girl.

Ediesta / not iss.

Jun 88. (7") *(CALC 069)* **JESUS LOVES AMERIKA. / DARKNESS IN ZION** [ ] [-]
(12"+=) *(CALCT 069)* – Do what you will.
(cd-s++=) *(CALCCD 069)* – Sub knatural dub.

— now a duo of **COLIN + WILL**

Desire / not iss.

Nov 88. (12"; as SHAMEN VS BAM BAM) *(WANTX 10)* **TRANSCENDENTAL. / ('A'-housee mix)** [ ] [-]

Demon / Demon

Jan 89. (lp/c/cd) *(<FIEND/+C/CD 666>)* **IN GORBACHEV WE TRUST** [ ] [ ]
– Synergy / Sweet young thing / Raspberry infundibulum / War prayer / Adam Strange / Jesus loves Amerika / Transcendental / Misinformation / Raptyouare / In Gorbachev we trust / (Fundamental). *(c+=)* – Resistance (once again). *(cd+=)* – Yellow cellaphane day / Mayhew speaks out.

— added **SANDRA** – percussion

Moksha / not iss.

Apr 89. (7") *(SOMA 6)* **YOU, ME & EVERYTHING. / RERAPTYOUARE** [ ] [-]
('A'-Evil edits; 12"+=/cd-s+=) *(SOMA 6 T/CD)* – Ed's bonus beats.

May 89. (10"m-lp/c/cd) *(SOMA LP/C/CD 3)* **PHORWARD** [ ] [-]
– You, me & everything (else) / Splash 2 / Negation state / Reraptyouare / SDD 89 / Phorward. *(free 7")* – (The S&N Sessions) *(c+=/cd+=)* – Happy days / Knature of a girl.

— **JOHN DELAFONS** – percussion repl. SANDRA

One Little Indian / Epic

Nov 89. (12"ep/cd-ep) *(30TP 12/7CD)* **OMEGA AMIGO / OMEGA A. / OMEGA PRE-MIX / PH 1** [ ] [-]

Mar 90. (7") *(36 TP7)* **PRO>GEN (Beatmasters mix). / ('A'dub version)** [55] [-]
(12") *(36 TP12L)* – ('A'-C-mix F+) / ('B'side) / Lightspan (Ben Chapman mix).
(c-s++=) *(36 TP7C)* – ('A'-Paul Oakenfold 'Land Of Oz' mix).
(12") *(36 TP12)* – (above mix) / Lightspan (Ben Chapman mix).
(cd-s) *(36 TP7CD)* – (above 2 mixes) / ('A'-Steve Osborne mix).

Sep 90. (7"/c-s) *(46 TP7/+C)* **MAKE IT MINE (Lenny D vox). / ('A'-Evil Ed mix)** [42] [ ] Feb92
(12"/cd-s) *(46TP 12/7CD)* *<742 36/41>* – ('A'-Lenny D mix) / ('A'-Progress mix) / ('A'-Lenny D vox) / Something wonderful.
(12") *(46 TP12L)* – ('A'-Evil Ed mix) / ('A'-Outer Limits mix) / Pro>gen (Land of Oz mix) / ('A'-Micro minimal mix).

Oct 90. (cd)(c)(2x12"lp) *(TPLP 22 CD/MC/SP)* *<48722>* **EN-TACT** [31] [ ]
– Human N.R.G. / Pro>gen (land of Oz) / Possible worlds / Omega amigo / Evil is even / Hypereal / Lightspan / Make it mine V 2.5 / Oxygen restriction / Here are my people (orbital delays expected). *(cd+=)* – (Oxygen reprise (V 2.0 mix) / Human NRG (Massey mix) / Make it mine (pirate radio mix) / (etc.) *(re-iss. Nov90 lp; TPLP 22)*

Mar 91. (7"/c-s) *(48 TP7/+C)* **HYPERREAL (William Orbit mix). / ('A'-lp version)** [29] [-]
(12") *(48 TP12)* – ('A'versions incl. Maguire + dub) / In the bag.
(cd-s) *(48 TP7CD)* – ('A'versions incl. Meatbeat Manifesto mix) / In the bag.
(12") *(48 TP12L)* – ('A'-Meatbeat Manifesto mixes) / ('A'-Maguire + Dirty dubbing mixes).
(above featured **PLAVKA** (b. Poland) – vocals)

— On the 23 May'91, WILL drowned while on holiday in Ibiza.

Jul 91. (7"/c-s) *(52 TP7/+C)* *<74044>* **MOVE ANY MOUNTAIN – PROGEN '91 (Beatmasters edit). / ('A'-The Goat From The Well Hung Parliament mix)** [4] [38] Nov91
(12") *(52 TP12)* *<74043>* – ('A'-mixes; Landslide / Devil / Rude / R.I.P. in the Land Of Oz).
(cd-s) *(52 TP7CD)* *<74044>* – ('A'mixes; Beatmasters / Landslide / F2 Mello / Mountains in the sky).

Sep 91. (3xlp/c/cd) *(TPLP 32/+MC/CD)* **PROGENCY 2(8 versions)** [23] [-]

— New line-up **COLIN** plus **MR.C** – vocals, rhythm / **+ JHELSA ANDERSON** – backing vox (ex-SOUL FAMILY SENSATION) / **BOB BREEKS** – live keyboards / **GAVIN KNIGHT** – live drums / **RICHARD SHARPE** – occasional analogue

Jun 92. (7"/12") *(68 TP 7/12)* *<74437>* **L.S.I. (LOVE SEX INTELLIGENCE). / POSSIBLE WORLDS** [6] [ ]
(c-s+=/cd-s+=) *(68 TP 7 C/CD)* – Make it mine (Moby mix).

Aug 92. (7"/c-s) *(78 TP7/+C)* **EBENEEZER GOODE. / ('A'dub)** [1] [ ]
(12"+=/cd-s+=) *(78 TP 12/7CD)* – ('A'mix) / L.S.I. (mix).

Oct 92. (lp/c/cd) *(TPLP 42/+C/CD) <52925>* **BOSS DRUM** [3] [ ]
– Boss drum / L.S.I.: Love Sex Intelligence / Space time / Librae solidi denari / Ebeneezer Goode (Beatmasters mix) / Comin' on / Phorever people / Fatman / Scientas / Re: evolution.

Oct 92. (7"/c-s) *(88 TP 7/+C) <74953>* **BOSS DRUM. / OMEGA AMIGO** [4] [ ] Apr93
(cd-s+=) *(88 TP7CD)* – (3 'A'mixes).
(12"-2 diff.) *(88 TP12)* – (5 'A'mixes either J.Robertson or Beatmasters).
(cd-s++=) *(88 TP7CDL)* – ('A'-Steve Osbourne mixes & Youth).

Dec 92. (7"ep/c-ep/12"ep/cd-ep) *(98 TP 7/7C/12/CD) <74898>* **PHOREVER PEOPLE. / ('A'dub + 'A'-Hyperreal orbit mix)** [5] [ ]
(cd-s++=) *(98 TP7CDL)* – ('A'mixes).

Feb 93. (c-s; as SHAMEN with TERENCE McKENNA) *(118 TP7C)* **RE:EVOLUTION / ('A'mix)** [18] [ ]
(12"+=/cd-s+=) *(118 TP 12/7CD)* – ('A'mixes).

Oct 93. (c-ep/12"ep/cd-ep) *(108 TP 7C/12/7CD)* **THE S.O.S. EP** [14] [ ]
– Comin' on / Make it mine / Possible worlds.
(cd-ep) *(108 TP7CDL)* – ('A'mixes).

— now with vocalist **VICTORIA WILSON-JAMES**

Aug 95. (c-s) *(128 TP7C) <78038>* **DESTINATION ESCHATON (Beatmasters mix) / ('A'-Deep melodic mix)** [15] [ ]
(cd-s) *(128 TP7CD)* – ('A'-Shamen acid: Escacid) / (2 'A'-Hardfloor mixes).
(cd-s) *(128 TP7CDL)* – (2 'A'-Basement Boys mixes) / (3 'A'-Beatmasters mixes).

Oct 95. (c-s) *(138 TP7C)* **TRANSAMAZONIA (Beatmasters mix) / ('A'-Visnadi mix) / ('A'-Watershed instrumental) / ('A'-LTJ Bukin mix)** [28] [ ]
(12"+=) *(138 TP12)* – ('A'-Deep dish mix).
(cd-s) *(138 TP7CD)* – (6 'A'mixes including; Alex Party Aguirre / Zion Train).
(cd-s+=) *(138 TP7CDL)* – ('A'-Nuv Idol mix).

Oct 95. (d-lp/c/cd) *(TPLP 52/+C/CD) <57796>* **AXIS MUTATIS** [27] [ ]
– Destination Eschaton / Transamazonia / Conquistador / Mauna Kea to Andromeda / Neptune / Prince of Popacatapertl / Heal the separation / Persephone's quest / Moment / Axis mundi / Eschaton omega (deep melodic techno). *(cd/c/d-lp with other cd/c/d-lp) (TPLP 52 CDL/CL/L)* **ARBOR BONA / ARBOR MALA** – Asynptotic Escaton / Sefirotic axis (a)(b)(c) Formation (d) Action / Extraterrestrial / Deneter / Beneath the underworld / Xochipilis return / Rio Negro / Above the underworld / A moment in dub / Pizarro in Paradiso / West of the underworld / Anticipation Escaton (be ready for the storm) / Out in the styx.

Feb 96. (c-s) *(158 TP7C)* **HEAL (THE SEPARATION) / ('A'mix)** [31] [ ]
(cd-s) *(158 TP7CD)* – ('A'mixes; organ / science park / PM Dawn / Steve Osborne ambient – H.E.L.P. breakfast / Beatmasters / foul play vocal).
(cd-s) *(158 TP7CDL)* – ('A'mixes; mighty organ / live '95) / Boss drum (Lionrock dub) / Phorever people (Todd Terry).

Oct 96. (3x12"lp/c/cd) *(TPLP 62/+C/CD)* **HEMPTON MANOR** [ ] [-]
– Freya / Urpflanze / Cannabeo / Khat / Bememe / Indica / Rausch / Kava / El-fin / Monoriff.

Dec 96. (c-s) *(169 TP7C)* **MOVE ANY MOUNTAIN '96 / ('A'mix)** [35] [ ]
(12"/cd-s) *(169 TP 12P/7CD)* – (mixes; Beatmasters radio / Tony De Vit edit) / Indica / L.S.I. (Beat edit).
(cd-s) *(169 TP7CDL)* – (mixes:- Tomka / Tony De Vit / Sneaker Pimps / Beatmasters 12").

Moksha — Moksha

Oct 98. (cd-ep) *(<MOKSHA 3CD>)* **UNIVERSAL (mixes:- 1999 vocal / 187 B.P. metamix (major) / 1999 dance vocal / Sharp trade life dub / Mr.C tech house mix / 187 Lockdown dark dub)** [ ] [ ] Nov98

– compilations, others, etc. –

Aug 88. (lp/c)(cd) *Materiali Sonori; (MASO 33041/+C)(MASOCD 9008)* **STRANGE DAY DREAMS** [-] [-] Italy
(re-iss. cd Oct91 imported) (re-iss. Jan93; same)

Dec 89. (m-lp/cd) *Communion; (COMM 4 LP/CD)* **WHAT'S GOING DOWN** [-] [ ]

Nov 93. (cd/c/lp) *Band Of Joy; (BOJ CD/MC/LP 006)* **ON AIR (live BBC sessions)** [61] [-]
(cd re-iss. Mar98 on 'Strange Fruit'; SFRSCD 055)

Jan 97. (cd/c) *One Little Indian; (TPLP 72 CD/C)* **THE SHAMEN COLLECTION** [ ] [ ]

Jan 97. (cd/c) *One Little Indian; (TPLP 72 CDR/CR)* **THE SHAMEN REMIX COLLECTION – STARS ON 45** [ ] [ ]
(both above re-iss. Apr98 d-cd/d-c; TPLP 72 CDE/CE) – hit UK No.26

Mar 98. (12") *Moksha; (AGC 002)* **U-NATIONS** [ ] [-]

SHAMPOO

Formed: Plumstead, London, England . . . 1994 by schoolgirls JACQUI BLAKE and CARRIE ASKEW. The lucky recipients of an NME Single Of The Week award for a one-off track, 'BLISTERS & BRUISES', on BOB STANLEY's (of ST. ETIENNE fame) 'Icerink' label, SHAMPOO emerged kicking and screaming into the music world as a kind of inverse glam-punk Barbie doll version of Riot Grrl femme-pop. All pigtails, lollipops, vacant lyrics and Smash Hits teen appeal, SHAMPOO were perhaps the most annoying girly band of the pre-SPICE GIRLS era, their self-conscious "attitude" only making the whole package even more unbearable. The truly awful 'TROUBLE' was the first result of their deal with E.M.I. subsidiary, 'Food', while 'VIVA LA MEGABABES' really was as insufferable as its title suggests. A whole album's worth of similar guff, 'WE ARE SHAMPOO', was foisted upon an unsuspecting music world in 1994 although by the time they'd gotten round to releasing a follow-up, 'GIRL POWER' (1996), that self same slogan was being put to far more successful use by The SPICE GIRLS.

Album rating: WE ARE SHAMPOO (*4) / GIRL POWER (*3)

CARRIE ASKEW (b.1975) – vocals / **JACQUI BLAKE** (b.1977) – vocals / with various music writers **LAWRENCE** (of DENIM, ex-FELT)

Icerink — not iss.

May 93. (7"ep) *(DAVO 6)* **BLISTERS AND BRUISES. / PAYDIRT / I LOVE LITTLE PUSSY** [ ] [-]

Food — Capitol

Jul 94. (c-s/7"pink) *(TC+/FOOD 51)* **TROUBLE. / SCHOOL IS BORING** [11] [-]
(cd-s+=) *(CDFOOD 51)* – We don't care.

Oct 94. (c-s/7") *(TC+/FOOD 54) <58444>* **VIVA LA MEGABABES. / HOUSE OF LOVE** [27] [ ] Sep95
(cd-s+=) *(CDFOOD 54)* – Girls 'round here.

Oct 94. (cd/c/lp) *(FOOD CD/TC/LP 12) <35084>* **WE ARE SHAMPOO** [45] [ ]
– Trouble / Delicious / Viva la megababes / Dirty old love song / Skinny white thing / Glimmer globe / Shiny black taxi cab / Me hostage / Game boy / House of love / Shampoo you / Saddo. *(re-iss. Aug95; same)*

Feb 95. (7"pic-d/c-s) *(FOODPD/TCFOOD 58) <58467>* **DELICIOUS. / KINKY KEN** [21] [ ] Sep95
(cd-s) *(CDFOOD 58)* – ('A'side) / Trouble / Outta control / Trouble (mix).

Food — Atlantic

Jul 95. (c-s) *(TCFOOD 66) <87145>* **TROUBLE / SHINY BLACK TAXI CAB** [36] [ ] May95
(cd-s+=) *(CDFOOD 66)* – Excellent.
(cd-s) *(CDFOODS 66)* –

Jul 96. (c-s/7") *(TC+/FOOD 76)* **GIRL POWER. / DON'T CALL ME BABE** [25] [ ]
(cd-s+=) *(CDFOOD 76)* – Cars.

Jul 96. (cd/c/lp) *(FOOD 16 CD/TC/LP)* **GIRL POWER** [ ] [-]
– Girl power / News flash / I know what boys like / Bare knuckle girl / Zap pow / War paint / You love it / Boys are us / We play dumb / I'm gonna scream / Don't call me babe.

Sep 96. (7") *(FOOD 83)* **I KNOW WHAT BOYS LIKE. / BOUFFANT HEADBUTT** [42] [ ]
(cd-s+=) *(CDFOOD 83)* – Blisters and bruises / I love little pussy.
(cd-s) *(CDFOODS 83)* – ('A'side) / ('A'mix) / Top of the pops.

— it looks like the girls were put in the shade by the SPICE GIRLS

SHAM 69

Formed: London, England . . . 1976 by JIMMY PURSEY, ALBIE SLIDER, MARK CAIN and DAVE PARSONS (the latter two replacing original members BILLY BOSTIK and NEIL HARRIS – who himself had replaced the curiously monikered JOHN GOODFORNOTHING – respectively). Inspired by The SEX PISTOLS, PURSEY set out making pogo-friendly, dumbly anthemic punk with a fiercely working class agenda, issuing a statement of intent with an independently released, JOHN CALE-produced single, 'I DON'T WANNA'. Subsequently signing with 'Polydor', the band made their major label debut with the inimitable 'BORSTAL BREAKOUT' in early '77, following it up with a partly live album, 'TELL US THE TRUTH'. What really took their terrace chant appeal to the masses, however, was the subsequent trio of hit singles led by 'ANGELS WITH DIRTY FACES'; 'HURRY UP HARRY' and 'IF THE KIDS ARE UNITED' followed into the Top 10 shortly after, the latter track (complete with hilarious chirpy cockney intro) a well meant but naive call for youthful brotherhood. Which kind of summed up SHAM 69's fate; PURSEY's idealistic working class warrior philosophy backfired as the air-punching punk-by-numbers began attracting more and more face-punching neo-Nazi skinheads. Despite a considered attempt to brush up on the lads-on-the-loose formula with their third set, 'THE ADVENTURES OF THE HERSHAM BOYS' (1979), Top 10 success only seemed to make the situation worse. PURSEY finally disbanded SHAM 69 in the summer of '79 only to reform a couple of months later for a final album, 'THE GAME' (1980). This failed to chart and PURSEY subsequently pursued a low key solo career, initially with 'Polydor' (who released his 1980 debut set, 'IMAGINATION CAMOUFLAGE') then with 'Epic', before going on to record a series of one-off singles for various indie labels. With this going nowhere fast, PURSEY and PARSONS resurrected SHAM 69 in 1987, releasing a largely ignored album, 'VOLUNTEER' the following year. Retreating from view for a further four years, they were back yet again in the 90's, releasing a string of albums for the diehards and playing regular gigs on the punk nostalgia circuit. • **Songwriters:** Penned by PURSEY-PARSONS except; YOU'RE A BETTER MAN THAN I (Yardbirds) / WITH A LITTLE HELP FROM MY FRIENDS (Beatles). The WANDERERS covered THE TIMES THEY ARE A-CHANGIN' (Bob Dylan). • **Trivia:** PURSEY appeared on Various Artists lp, 'The Whip', in '83.

Album rating: THE FIRST, THE BEST AND THE LAST compilation (*7)

JIMMY PURSEY (b. Hersham, Surrey, England) – vocals / **DAVE PARSONS** – guitar repl. NEIL HARRIS who had repl. JOHNNY GOODFORNOTHING / **ALBIE SLIDER** (b. ALBERT MASKAIL) – bass, vocals / **MARK CAIN** – drums repl. BILLY BOSTIK

Step Forward — not iss.

Oct 77. (7"m/12"m) *(SF 4/+12)* **I DON'T WANNA. / RED LONDON / ULSTER** [ ] [-]
(re-iss. 1979; same)

— **DAVE TREGANNA** – bass, vocals repl. ALBIE

Polydor — Sire

Jan 78. (7") *(2058 966)* **BORSTAL BREAKOUT. / HEY LITTLE RICH BOY** [ ] [-]

Feb 78. (lp) *(2383 491) <6060>* **TELL US THE TRUTH** (some live) [25] [ ]
– We gotta fight / Rip off / Ulster / George Davis is innocent / They don't understand / Borstal breakout / Family life / Hey little rich boy / I'm a man, I'm a boy / What about the lonely / Tell us the truth / It's never too late / Whose

generation. *(re-iss. Mar89 on 'Receiver'; RRD 001) (cd-iss. Mar96 on 'Dojo'; DOJOCD 256)*

Apr 78. (7") *(2059 023)* **ANGELS WITH DIRTY FACES. / COCKNEY KIDS ARE INNOCENT** 19 -
Jul 78. (7") *(2059 050)* **IF THE KIDS ARE UNITED. / SUNDAY MORNING NIGHTMARE** 9 -
Oct 78. (7") *(POSP 7)* **HURRY UP HARRY. / NO ENTRY** 10 -
Nov 78. (lp) *(2442 158)* **THAT'S LIFE** 27 -
– Leave me alone / Who gives a damn / Everybody's right, everybody's wrong / That's life / Win or lose / Hurry up Harry / Evil way (live) / Reggae pick up (part 1) / Sunday morning nightmare / Reggae pick up (part 2) / Angels with dirty faces / Is this me or is this you. *(re-iss. Jul88 on 'Skunx'; SHAMX 1) (cd-iss. Mar96 on 'Dojo'; DOJOCD 257)*
Mar 79. (7"m) *(POSP 27)* **QUESTIONS AND ANSWERS. / I GOTTA SURVIVE (live) / WITH A LITTLE HELP FROM MY FRIENDS** 18 -
Jul 79. (7"m) *(POSP 64)* **HERSHAM BOYS. / I DON'T WANNA (live) / TELL US THE TRUTH (live)** 6 -
(12"m+=) *(POSPX 64)* – I'm a man, I'm a boy (live).
Sep 79. (lp) *(POLD/+C 5025)* **THE ADVENTURES OF THE HERSHAM BOYS** 8 -
– Money / Fly dark angel / Joey's on the street / Cold blue in the night / You're a better man than I / Hersham boys / Lost on Highway 46 / Voices / Questions and answers / What have we got. *(free 12") (2812 045)* – IF THE KIDS ARE UNITED. / BORSTAL BREAKOUT *(cd-iss. Mar96 on 'Dojo'; DOJOCD 258)*
Oct 79. (7") *(POSP 82)* **YOU'RE A BETTER MAN THAN I. / GIVE A DOG A BONE** 49 -

— Disbanded for two months Jul'79. **MARK GOLDSTEIN** – drums repl. CAIN

Mar 80. (7") *(POSP 136)* **TELL THE CHILDREN. / JACK** 45 -
May 80. (lp) *(2442 173)* **THE GAME** -
– The game / Human zoo / Lord of the flies / Give a dog a bone / In and out / Tell the children / Spray it on the wall / Dead or alive / Simon / Deja vu / Poor cow / Run wild run free / Unite and win. *(re-iss. Mar89 on 'Receiver'; RRLD 002) (cd-iss. Mar96 on 'Dojo'; DOJOCD 259)*
Jun 80. (7") *(2059 259)* **UNITE AND WIN. / I'M A MAN** -
Nov 80. (lp) *(2383 596)* **THE FIRST, THE BEST AND THE LAST** (compilation) -
– Borstal breakout / Hey little rich boy / Angels with dirty faces / Cockney kids are innocent / If the kids are united / Sunday morning nightmare / Hurry up Harry / Questions and answers / Give the dog a bone / Hersham boys / Tell the children / Unite & win. *(free 7"ep live)(RIOT 1 – 2816 028) (cd-iss. Apr94; 513429-2).*

— Had already splintered, with PURSEY going solo (see further below).

WANDERERS

(**TREGANNA, PARSONS + GOLDSTEIN**) added **STIV BATORS** – vocals (ex-DEAD BOYS)

Polydor | not iss.

Mar 81. (7") *(POSP 237)* **READY TO SNAP. / BEYOND THE LAW** -
May 81. (lp) *(POLS 1028)* **THE ONLY LOVERS LEFT ALIVE** -
– Fanfare for 1984 / No dreams / Dr.Baker / Take them and break them / Little bit frightening / It's all the same / The times they are a-changin' / Ready to snap / Can't take you anymore / Sold your soul for fame / Circles of time / There'll be no end fanfare.
Jun 81. (7") *(POSP 284)* **THE TIMES THEY ARE A-CHANGIN'. / (IT'S A) LITTLE BIT FRIGHTENING** -

— Split Aug'81, TREGANNA followed BATORS into LORDS OF THE NEW CHURCH. PARSONS formed FRAMED later in 1982.

JIMMY PURSEY

Polydor | not iss.

Sep 80. (7") *(POSP 154)* **LUCKY MAN. / BLACK AND WHITE ROCK REGGAE** -
Oct 80. (lp) *(2442 180)* **IMAGINATION CAMOUFLAGE** -
– Moon morning funday / Have a nice day / Lucky man / You never can tell / Situation's vacant / Playground soldier / White trash / Fifty-fifty / Freak show / Your mother should have told you / Just another memory.

Epic | not iss.

Jun 81. (7") *(EPCA 1336)* **ANIMALS HAVE MORE FUN. / SUS** -
Nov 81. (7") *(EPCA 1830)* **NAUGHTY BOYS LIKE NAUGHTY GIRLS. / WHO'S MAKING YOU HAPPY** -
Feb 82. (lp) *(EPC 85235)* **ALIEN ORPHAN** -
– Alien orphan / The first deadly kiss / I'm a human being / One invite only / Why (he shouldn't be here) / Who's making you happy / Spies / Jungle west one / Oh isn't it a weird weird world / One night in Paris / Technical / Naughty boys like naughty girls.
Feb 82. (7") *(EPCA 2118)* **ALIEN ORPHAN. / CONVERSATIONS** -

Code Black | not iss.

Jan 83. (lp) **REVENGE IS NOT THE PASSWORD** -
Feb 83. (7") **MAN WORRIES MAN. / ?** -

An Eskimo | not iss.

May 84. (12"/7"; as JAMES T. PURSEY) *(CODE 02/+7)* **IF ONLY BEFORE. / ABOVE AND BEYOND** -

Videocat | not iss.

Sep 86. (7"/12") *(JIMMY/+T 1)* **ZAP POW. / ('A'-Bass camp mix)** -

SHAM 69

— re-formed in '87. (**PURSEY, PARSONS,** +2)

Legacy | Legacy

Jul 87. (7") *(LGY 69)* **RIP AND TEAR. / THE GREAT AMERICAN SLOWDOWN** -
Feb 88. (7") *(LGY 71)* **OUTSIDE THE WAREHOUSE. / ('A'version)** -
(12"+=) *(LGY/+T 71)* – How the west was won.
Jun 88. (lp/c) *(<LLP/LLK 117>)* **VOLUNTEER**
– Outside the warehouse / Wicked tease / Wallpaper / Mr.Know it all / As black as sheep / How the west was won / That was the day / Rip and tear / Bastard club / Volunteer. *(cd-iss. Dec89; LLCD 117) (cd re-iss. Mar92 on Castle'; CLACD 274)*
Nov 92. (12") **M25. /** -

Rotate | not iss.

Nov 92. (cd/lp) *(ROT CD/LP 006)* **INFORMATION LIBRE** -
– Break on through / Uptown / Planet trash / Information libretaire / Caroline's suitcase / Feel it / King Kong drinks Coca-Cola / Saturdays and Strangeways / Breeding dinosaurs / Wild and wonderful. *(cd re-iss. Nov95 on 'Dojo'; DOJOCD 236)*

C.M.P. | not iss.

Mar 93. (7") **UPTOWN. / BORSTAL BREAKOUT** -
(12"+=) – Flowers / Wild and wonderful.
Nov 93. (cd) **KINGS & QUEENS** -
– Action time vision / I don't wanna / Ulster boy / They don't understand / Tell us the truth / Borstal breakout / Family life / The kids are united / Hurry up Harry / Hey little rich boy / Bosnia / Reggae giro. *(re-iss. Jul95 on 'Dojo')*
Oct 93. (cd-ep) *(CMCCD 002)* **ACTION TIME & VISION / BOSNIA / HEY LITTLE RICH BOY / REGGAE GIRO** -

Red Cat | not iss.

Jul 95. (cd) *(A1Cd 001)* **SOAPY WATER & MR. MARMALADE** -

– compilations, others, etc. –

Oct 82. (12"ep) *Polydor; (POSPX 602)* **ANGELS WITH DIRTY FACES / BORSTAL BREAKOUT. / HURRY UP HARRY / IF THE KIDS ARE UNITED** -
Nov 86. (lp/c) *Receiver; (RRLP/RRLC 104)* **ANGELS WITH DIRTY FACES – THE BEST OF SHAM 69** -
Dec 87. (lp) *Link; (LINKLP 004)* **LIVE AND LOUD (live)** -
Apr 88. (lp) *Link; (LINKLP 025)* **LIVE AND LOUD VOL.2** -
May 89. (lp/cd) *Receiver; (RRLP/CD 112)* **THE BEST OF THE REST OF SHAM 69** -
Oct 89. (cd/c/lp) *Castle; (CLA CD/MC/LP 153)* **COMPLETE LIVE (live)** -
Apr 90. (cd/c) *Action Replay; (CDAR/ARLC 1011)* **SHAM 69 LIVE (live)** -
Aug 90. (cd/lp) *Receiver;* **LIVE AT THE ROXY (live tapes '77)** -
Jul 91. (cd) *Dojo; (DOJOCD 62)* **LIVE AT THE CBGB'S** -
Apr 93. (cd) *Dojo; (DOJOCD 95)* **SHAM'S LAST STAND** -
Oct 93. (cd) *Dojo; (DOJOCD 105)* **LIVE IN JAPAN (live)** -
Nov 93. (cd) *Windsong; (WINCD 049)* **BBC RADIO 1 LIVE IN CONCERT (Live)** -
Mar 95. (cd; shared with 999) *Step-1;* **LIVE AND LOUD** -
Sep 95. (cd) *Emporio; (EMPRCD 582)* **SHAM 69 LIVE** -
Dec 95. (cd) *Essential; (ESDCD 350)* **LIVE / THE BEST OF SHAM 69** -
Jun 96. (cd/c) *Hallmark; (30446-2/-4)* **UNITED** -
Oct 98. (7"; shared with DIE TOTEN HOSEN) *M Tradegy; (MT 385)* **SAWBLADE SERIES #19** -

SHARKBOY

Formed: Brighton, Sussex, England ... early 90's by AVY, ADRIAN OXAAL, ALAN STIRNER and JESSICA FISCHER. Bringing to mind the likes of MY BLOODY VALENTINE, MAZZY STAR, DRUGSTORE and even BLONDIE, SHARKBOY specialise in moody echoe and atmosphere, AVY's breathy vocals draped like an alter cloth over the slow burning musical backdrop. Noted indie label, 'Nude' (home to SUEDE) were quick to recognise their potential, 1994 seeing the release of well received debut album, 'MATINEE'. Personnel changes ensued as JESSICA bailed out, her replacements being not one member but three, GAVIN CHEYENE, DIL DAVIES and NICK WILSON. While the critics weren't so keen to praise follow-up set, 'THE VALENTINE TAPES' (1995), AVY had nevertheless come up with another compelling musical travelogue through rootsy noir and doomed romance, knob twiddling courtesy of Phil Wright and Jem Noble (responsible for GALLON DRUNK's 'From The Heart Of Town' and 'In The Long Still Night' respectively) and violin flourishes from TINDERSTICKS man DICKON HINCHCLIFFE. • **Covers:** SOME MISUNDERSTANDING (Gene Clark) / DIAMONDS ARE FOREVER (John Barry) / WISHING ON A STAR (Candi Staton) / JE T'AIME (Serge Gainbourg).

Album rating: MATINEE (*6) / THE VALENTINE TAPES (*4)

AVY (b. Preston, England) – vocals / **ADRIAN OXAAL** (b. USA) – guitars, cello, keyboards, marimba, vocals / **ALAN STIRNER** – guitars, percussion / **JESSICA FISCHER** – bass, cello

Nude | Tristar

Nov 93. (12"ep/cd-ep) *(NUD 7 T/CD)* **CRYSTALINE /**
Feb 94. (12"ep/cd-ep) *(NUD 8 T/CD)* **RAZOR / BRIGHT THINGS LIE. / DEAR GILDA / SHOW ME NOW**
Apr 94. (cd/c/lp) *(NUDE CD/MC/LP 2) <66638>* **MATINEE**
– Sacramento child / My star / Forest fire / Razor / Don't walk run / Crystaline / Road / Yo yo / Sugar / Carrying some.

— **GAVIN CHEYNE** – bass + **DIL DAVIES** – drums, percussion, marimba + **NICK WILSON** – keyboards, trumpet, percussion; repl. JESSICA

May 95. (7") *(NUD 14S)* **BIG BLACK JAGUAR. / DIAMONDS ARE FOREVER** -
Jun 95. (7") *(NUD 15S)* **LITTLE LEOPARD. / WISHING ON A STAR** -
Jun 95. (7") *(NUD 16S)* **MY MAGNETIC SUSAN. /** -
Jul 95. (7") *(NUD 17S)* **TINY SEISMIC NIGHT. /** -
Sep 95. (cd/c/lp) *(NUDE CD/MC/LP 4)* **THE VALENTINE TAPES** -
– Tiny seismic night / Big black jaguar / Take my hand / Same mother of pearl / From your eye / Blazer / Sugarmanshine / Dean / 3D angelshell / Teenage heart / Maxine.

— disbanded after above

SHED SEVEN

Formed: York, England . . . late 1991 by RICK WITTER, PAUL BANKS, TOM GLADWIN and ALAN LEACH. Signing to 'Polydor' in 1994, the group were initially grouped in with the hopelessly contrived "new wave of new wave" scene alongside run-of-the-mill pseudo-punk revivalists like S*M*A*S*H and THESE ANIMAL MEN. Resisting the lure of the Big Smoke, the lads preferred to stay in their native York, their sound a more glam/mod retro pastiche lying somewhere between SUEDE and The CHARLATANS. A debut single, 'MARK', had certain sections of the music press tipping them for big things and they finally assaulted the Top 30 later that summer with the 'DOLPHIN' and 'SPEAKEASY' singles. While SHED SEVEN's music was no great shakes really, the diminutive WITTER had a remarkable voice, somewhat akin to a sleazy liaison between BRETT ANDERSON and ADAM ANT (!?). They also had attitude in abundance, something which translated well in the live arena, SHED SEVEN becoming a regular attraction in the UK's sweatier venues. A debut album, 'CHANGE GIVER' (1994), wasn't exactly groundbreaking although it consolidated their limited appeal. Only a couple of unremarkable singles followed in the next year and a half, before the band returned with 'GETTING BETTER' in 1996, their biggest hit single to date. While the accompanying album, 'MAXIMUM HIGH' (1996), drew some critical praise it ultimately failed to drag the band out of the indie second division ghetto. • **Songwriters:** WITTER lyrics / group compositions. Covered JUMPING JACK FLASH (Rolling Stones). • **Trivia:** Said to have taken their group name, after it was revealed by ALAN the drummer that he lost his virginity in a shed aged only 7. (eh!)

Album rating: CHANGE GIVER (*7) / A MAXIMUM HIGH (*8)

RICK WITTER (b.1973) – vocals / **PAUL BANKS** (b.1973) – guitar / **TOM GLADWIN** (b.1973) – bass / **ALAN LEACH** (b.1970) – drums

		Polydor	Atlantic
Mar 94.	(7"green) *(YORK 1)* **MARK. / CASINO GIRL**	77	-
	(12"+=/cd-s+=) *(YORK X/CD 1)* – Mobile 10.		
Jun 94.	(7"/c-s) *(YORK/YORCS 2)* **DOLPHIN. / IMMOBILITIES**	28	-
	(12"+=/cd-s+=) *(YORK X/D 2)* – ('A'remix).		
Aug 94.	(7"/c-s) *(YORK/YORCS 3)* **SPEAKEASY. / AROUND YOUR HOUSE**	24	-
	(12"+=/cd-s+=) *(YORKX/YORCD 3)* – Your guess is as good as mine / Dolphin.		
Sep 94.	(cd/c/lp) *(523 615-2/-4/-1) <4063>* **CHANGE GIVER**	16	
	– Dirty soul / Speakeasy / Long time dead / Head and hands / Casino girl / Missing out / Dolphin / Stars in your eyes / Mark / Ocean pie / On an island with you.		
Nov 94.	(7"/c-s) *(YORK/YORCS 4)* **OCEAN PIE. / NEVER AGAIN**	33	-
	(12"+=/cd-s+=) *(YORKX/YORCD 4)* – Sleepeasy / Sensitive.		
Apr 95.	(7"green/c-s) *(YORK/YORCS 5)* **WHERE HAVE YOU BEEN TONIGHT? / SWING MY WAVE**	23	-
	(cd-s+=) *(YORCD 5)* – This is my house.		
		Polydor	Polygram
Jan 96.	(7"/c-s) *(577 890-7/-4)* **GETTING BETTER. /**	14	-
	(cd-s+=) *(577 890-2)* –		
Mar 96.	(7"/c-s) *(576 215-7/-4)* **GOING FOR GOLD. /**	8	-
	(cd-s+=) *(576 215-2)* –		
Apr 96.	(cd/c/lp) *(<531 039-2/-4/-1>)* **A MAXIMUM HIGH**	8	
	– Getting better / Magic streets / Where have you been tonight? / Going for gold / On standby / Out by my side / Lies / This day was ours / Ladyman / Falling from the sky / Bully boy / Parallel lines. *(d-cd re-iss. Sep96; 533 416-2)* – (includes THE B-SIDES).		
May 96.	(7"ep/c-ep) *(576 596-7/-4)* **BULLY BOY / WHERE HAVE YOU BEEN TONIGHT? (live). / DOLPHIN (live) / SPEAKEASY (live)**	22	-
	(cd-ep) *(576 596-2)* – ('A'side) / Mark (live) / Ocean pie (live) / Getting better (live).		
Aug 96.	(7"/c-s) *(575 188-7/-4)* **ON STANDBY. / JUMPING JACK FLASH**	12	-
	(cd-s+=) *(575 273-2)* – Killing time.		
	(cd-s) *(575 188-2)* – ('A'side) / Long time dead (version) / Stepping on hearts.		
Nov 96.	(7"/c-s) *(575 929-7/-4)* **CHASING RAINBOWS /**	17	-
	(cd-s+=) *(575 928-2)* –		
Mar 98.	(7") *(569540-7)* **SHE LEFT ME ON FRIDAY. / BOTTOM UPWARDS**	11	
	(cd-s+=) *(569541-2)* – Melpomene.		
	(cd-s) *(569543-2)* – ('A'side) / Mispent youth / You.		
May 98.	(7"/c-s) *(569916-7/-4)* **HEROES. / SLINKY LOVE THEME**	18	-
	(cd-s+=) *(569917-2)* – She left me on Friday.		
	(cd-s) *(569923-2)* – ('A'side) / She left me on Friday / Forever (isn't such a long time).		
Jun 98.	(cd/c/lp) *(557359-2/-4/-1)* **LET IT RIDE**	9	-
	– Return / Let it ride / Heroes / Halfway home / Devil in your shoes / She left me on Friday / Hole / Drink your love / Stand up and be counted / Chasing rainbows / Goodbye.		
Aug 98.	(7") *(567207-7)* **DEVIL IN YOUR SHOES (WALKING ALL OVER). /**	37	-
	(cd-s+=) *(567207-2)* –		
	(cd-s) *(567205-2)* –		

SHEEP ON DRUGS

Formed: London, England . . . 1991 by KING DUNCAN (X) and LEE (303). Setting out to satirise the blind consumerism of pop culture and the club scene in particular, this dastardly duo took to their task with nihilistic, self-deprecating abandon, making a name for themselves with garish cabaret-style gigs and grinding industrial/neo-goth music (like DEVO or NITZER EBB fused with SOFT CELL or CARTER – KING DUNCAN was prone to wearing a white bra and tutu on stage!); an independenly released debut single, 'CATCH 22', berated the pointlessness of workaday existence while its flip side, 'DRUG MUSIC', mocked the manufactured escapism of the dance scene. Following up the 'MOTORBIKE' single with the 'TV USA' and 'TRACK X' EP's, SHEEP ON DRUGS had soon engineered enough of an, ahem.. buzz, to convince 'Island' of their potential. With just a touch of irony, 'GREATEST HITS' was unveiled as the outfit's debut album in 1993, the accompanying single, '15 MINUTES OF FAME', coming within firing range of mainstream coverage. Realistically, the duo's uncompromising material and anti-populist stance was never really likely to grab the average music fan's attention and following the more ambitious ' . . . ON DRUGS' (1994), SOD were quietly dropped. Since then, messrs. DUNCAN and LEE have formed their own 'Drug Squad' label, carrying out sporadic raids on good taste with EP's such as 'SUCK' and 'STRAPPED FOR CASH'. A subsequent move to industrial label, 'Invisible', saw the band issue a handful of releases including a couple of albums, 'ONE FOR THE MONEY' (1997) and 'TWO FOR THE SHOW' (1998).

Album rating: GREATEST HITS (*6) / ON DRUGS (*4) / ONE FOR THE MONEY (*4)

KING DUNCAN (GIL-RODRIGUEZ) – vocals / **LEE (FRASER)** – keyboards, guitars, drums

		Transglobal	not iss.
Nov 91.	(12"/cd-s) **CATCH-22. / DRUG MUSIC**		-
Mar 92.	(12") **MOTORBIKE. / MARY JANE**		-
	(cd-s+=) – Radio.		
Jun 92.	(12") *(TRAN 8T)* **TV USA. / THE FLAMING CHURCH**		-
	(cd-s+=) *(TRAN 8CD)* – USA / Church.		
Nov 92.	(12"ep) *(TRAN 9T)* **TRACK X. / ACID TEST / DRUG MUSIC**		-
	(cd-ep+=) *(TRAN 9CD)* – Catch.		
		Island	Smash
Mar 93.	(7") *(IS 564)* **15 MINUTES OF FAME (part 1). / (part 2)**	44	-
	(12"+=/cd-s+=) *(12IS/CID 564)* – ('A'-part 3).		
Apr 93.	(cd/c) *(CIS/ICT 8006) <162-888006-2/-4>* **GREATEST HITS**	55	
	– Uberman / Acid test / 15 minutes of fame / Track X / Suzy Q / Catch-22 / Mary Jane / Motorbike / TV USA / Chard / Sheep.		
Oct 93.	(7") *(IS 576)* **FROM A TO H AND BACK AGAIN. / MOTORBIKE**	40	-
	(12"+=/cd-s+=) *(12IS/CID 575)* – Drug music (unplugged).		
	(cd-s) *(CIDX 575)* – ('A'side) / Cathode ray / TV USA.		
May 94.	(7") *(IS 576)* **LET THE GOOD TIMES ROLL. / GOT NOTHING GOOD TO SAY TODAY**	56	-
	(10"etched+=/12"purple+=/cd-s+=) *(10IS/12IS/CID 576)* – ('A'mix).		
Jun 94.	(cd/c/brown-lp) *(CID/ICT/ILPS 8020)* **. . . ON DRUGS**		-
	– Intro / Chasing dreams / English Rose / Let the good times roll / Beefcake / Segway / A 2 H / Clucking / Slap happy / Slim Jim / Lolita / Slow suicide / Hi-fi low-life / Dirtbox blues.		
		Drug Squad	not iss.
Jul 95.	(12"ep) *(DRUG 001)* **SUCK EP**		-
	– Come fly with me / Talk about drugs / Comatose.		
	(cd-ep+=) *(DRUG 001CD)* – Come fly with me (No.2).		
Nov 95.	(12"ep/cd-ep) *(DRUG 002/+CD)* **STRAPPED FOR CASH EP**		-
	– X-lover / Night fever / Here to stay / And more.		
		Invisible	Invisible
Apr 96.	(cd) *(<INV 057CD>)* **DOUBLE TROUBLE**		
	– Come fly with me / Coma / Talk about drugs / Comatose / Come fly with me / X-lover / Night fever / Here to stay / And more.		
Jan 97.	(cd) *(<INV 061CD>)* **ONE FOR THE MONEY**		
	– Crime time / Money machine / Waiting for the man / Strange days / Life is just a game / Come fly with me / She's hot / Joyrider / WCFM / X-lover.		
Oct 97.	(cd) *(<INV 067CD>)* **NEVERMIND THE METHADONE** (remixes by other artists)		
	– WCFM / Life is just a game / Come fly with me / She's hot / Crime time / Money machine / X-lover / Bong track / Strange days / Back in black.		
Sep 98.	(cd) *(<INV 073CD>)* **TWO FOR THE SHOW (live)**		
	– Uberman / Let the good times roll / X-lover / Come fly with me / To H / Motorbike / WCFM / Dirt box blues / 15 minutes of fame / Here to stay.		

SHELLAC (see under ⇒ BIG BLACK)

Pete SHELLEY (see under ⇒ BUZZCOCKS)

SHELLEYAN ORPHAN

Formed: Bournemouth, England . . . 1980 by CAROLINE CRAWLEY and songwriter JEMAUR TAYLE. Sharing an enduring appreciation of the works of famous poet, Shelley, the duo took the group name from one of his works and set about conceiving a romantic musical vision of their own. Teaching themselves the rudiments of their chosen instruments, they subsequently recruited a crew of classical musicians upon their relocation to London in the early 80's. Following an unlikely support to feedback merchants The JESUS & MARY CHAIN, SHELLEYAN ORPHAN were signed up to 'Rough Trade', releasing a debut single, 'CAVALRY OF CLOUD', in '86. This was closely followed by the EVERYTHING BUT THE GIRL-esque vocal surges of 'ANATOMY OF LOVE' and a debut album, 'HELLEBORINE' (1987). Marrying the middle-England pastoral fantasy and string flourishes of NICK DRAKE to airy acoustic pop in the mould of the aforementioned EBTG, the record was an enchanting proposition utilising such classical instrumentation as oboe, cor Anglais, bassoon, cello and viola alongside lightly strummed guitars, violin etc. Two years on, 'CENTURY FLOWER' (1989) displayed a shift towards a more conventional style of songwriting while retaining the exotic flair which was their trademark. Yet despite some favourable noises from certain sections of the press and a high profile support slot to The

CURE, SHELLEYAN ORPHAN never managed to rise above cult status, 'HUMROOT' (1993) being their last recording to date. A shame as current press darlings like The CARDIGANS and BELLE & SEBASTIAN possibly have a SHELLEYAN ORPHAN album tucked away in their collection somehwere.

Album rating: HELLEBORINE (*8) / HUMROOT (*6)

JEMAUR TAYLE – vocals, acoustic guitar / **CAROLINE CRAWLEY** – vocals, clarinet

Rough Trade / Columbia

Sep 86. (7") *(RT 170)* **CAVALRY OF CLOUD. / TANGLED PERPETUAL** [ ] [-]
(12"+=) *(RTT 170)* – One hundred hands (for strings).

Apr 87. (7") *(RT 207)* **ANATOMY OF LOVE. / HARMONY DRONE** [ ] [-]

— duo with **DANNY THOMPSON** – double bass / **NICKY HOLLAND** – cor anglais / **STUART ELLIOT** – percussion / **PADDY BUSH** – mandolin, tambourine / **EMMA COLE** – flute / **BERNARD PARTRIDGE** – violin / **IAN JEWEL** – viola / **STEVEN ORTON** – cello / **THOMAS DAVEY** – oboe / **PRUDENCE WHITTAKER** – clarinet / **NICHOLAS HUNTER** – bassoon / **RUTH HOLDEN** – harp / **ANDREW POWELL** – harpsicord, piano / **RICHARD TOMES** – additional violin

May 87. (lp/c/cd) *(ROUGH/+C/CD 97)* <40545> **HELLEBORINE** [ ] [ ]
– Helleborine / Seeking bread and Heaven / Melody of birth / Jeremiah / Anatomy of love / Midsummer pearls and plume / Epitaph ivy and woe / Blue black grape / One hundred hands / Calvary of cloud / Southern Bess – A field holler.

— duo with **DANNY THOMPSON** – double bass / **CHARLIE MORGAN + JIM RUSSELL** – drums / **JACKIE NORRIE** – violin / **KATIE WILKINSON + ANNETTE HALES** – viola / **MARTIN EVENS** – piano / **TONY ROBERTS** – flute / **GEOFF BLYTHE** – saxophone / **PAUL HOOKHAM** – percussion / **JACK EMBLOW** – accordion / **JEANETTE MURPHY** – French horn / **EMILY BURRIDGE + ROBERT IRVINE + ANNE-LOUISE HYDE** – cello / **MIKE WINFIELD** – oboe, cor anglais / **PAUL GOODEY** – oboe

May 89. (lp/c/cd) *(ROUGH/+C/CD 137)* <45198> **CENTURY FLOWER** [ ] [ ]
– Shatter / Timeblind / Tar baby / Self / Summer flies / The silent day / Century flower / Amanita muscaria / Between two waves / A few small hours.

Jul 89. (7") *(RT 217)* **SCATTER. / TAR BABY (live)** [ ] [-]
(12"+=) *(RTT 217)* – Aanita muscaria / Timeblind.

— with **BORIS WILLIAMS** – drums / **JULES SINGLETON** – violin / **ROBERT SOAVE** – bass / **BRIAN SHIELDS** – double bass / etc

Mar 92. (cd/c/lp) *(R 279 2/4/1)* <46050> **HUMROOT** [ ] [ ]
– Muddied-up / Dead cat / Fishes / Burst / Sick / Little death / Big sun / Dolphins / Mull / Long dead flowers / Swallow / Supernature on a superhighway.

— split after above

SHIRTS

Formed: Brooklyn, New York, USA . . . early 1975 out of The LACKEYS and The SCHEMERS by ANNIE GOLDEN, ARTIE LaMONICA, RONNIE ARDITO, JOHN PICCOLO, ROBERT RACIOPPO and JOHN CRISCIONE. Originally conceived as a pop covers outfit, The SHIRTS fitted right in to the burgeoning New Wave scene after building up a loyal following at clubs such as CBGB's. A major signing to 'Capitol' ('Harvest' in Britain), the sartorial Noo Yoikers found favour on the continent with their summer '78 debut single, 'TELL ME YOUR PLANS'. This was accompanied by a slightly disappointing eponymous debut album that failed to break America, although GOLDEN's voice did shine on standout track, 'TEENAGE CRUTCH' and the aforementioned single. Even a subsequent support slot to the more mainstream PETER GABRIEL failed to raise their profile and despite a further two albums, 'STREET LIGHT SHINE' (1979) and 'INNER SLEEVE' (1980), GOLDEN became more famous for her role in the 1979 movie adaptation of 'Hair' and her work on Broadway.

Album rating: THE SHIRTS (*5) / STREET LIGHT (*4) / INNER SLEEVE (*4) / TELL ME YOUR PLANS compilation (*5)

ANNIE GOLDEN (b.1953) – vocals / **ARTIE LaMONICA** – lead guitar, vocals / **RONNIE ARDITO** – rhythm guitar, vocals / **JOHN PICCOLO** – keyboards / **ROBERT RACIOPPO** – bass / **JOHN CRISCIONI** – drums, percussion

Harvest / Capitol

Jul 78. (7") *(HAR 5165)* **TELL ME YOUR PLANS. / CYRINDA** [ ] [-]

Jul 78. (lp) *(SHSP 4089)* <SW 11791> **THE SHIRTS** [ ] [ ]
– Reduced to a whisper / Tell me your plans / Empty never after / Teenage crutch / Tenth floor clown / The story goes / Lonely android / Running through the night / They say the sun shines / Poe.

Oct 78. (7") *(HAR 5170)* **RUNNING THROUGH THE NIGHT. / LONELY ANDROID** [ ] [-]

Aug 79. (7") *(HAR 5190)* **OUT ON THE ROPES. / MAYBE, MAYBE NOT** [ ] [-]

Oct 79. (lp) *(SHSP 4104)* <ST 11986> **STREET LIGHT SHINE** [ ] [ ]
– Laugh and walk away / Love is a fiction / Don't you hesitate / Milton at the Savoy / Ground zero / Triangulum / Out on the ropes / Starts with a handshake / Can't cry anymore / I feel so nervous / Outside the cathedral door / Kensington gardens.

Oct 79. (7") <4750> **CAN'T CRY ANYMORE. / I'M IN LOVE AGAIN** [-] [ ]

Dec 79. (7") <4783> **DON'T YOU HESITATE (HOLD ME). / GROUND ZERO** [-] [ ]

Feb 80. (7") *(HAR 5195)* **LAUGH AND WALK AWAY. / TRIANGULUM** [ ] [-]

Capitol / Capitol

Aug 80. (7") *(CL 16161)* **ONE LAST CHANCE. / TOO MUCH TROUBLE** [ ] [ ]

Oct 80. (lp) *(EST 12085)* **INNER SLEEVE** [ ] [ ]
– I'm not one of those / One last chance / Can't get it through my head / I've had it / I don't wanna know / Pleasure is the pain / As long as the laughter lasts / Too much trouble / Hanging around / Small talk.

— disbanded the following year, with GOLDEN having a short-lived solo career in '84

– compilations, etc. –

Feb 98. (cd) *Disky; (DC 88608-2)* **TELL ME YOUR PLANS** [ ] [-]
– Tell me your plans / Laugh and walk away / One last chance / Out on the ropes / Running through the night / Triangulum / Too much trouble / Lonely android / Reduced to a whisper / Empty never after / Teenage crutch / Tenth floor clown / The story goes / They say the sun shines / Poe.

SHOCKABILLY (see under ⇒ CHADBOURNE, Eugene)

Michelle SHOCKED

Born: KAREN MICHELLE JOHNSTON, 24 Feb'62, Gilmer, East Texas, USA. After a childhood spent moving around army bases with her stepfather, SHOCKED experienced a turbulent adolescence which included a spell in a psychiatric hospital (committed by her Mormon mother) and a stint as an anarcho-punk squatter in San Francisco, all girst for the songwriting mill (and inspration for her adoption of the SHOCKED moniker) of this radical post-folk singer. Her break came in 1986 when she was talent-spotted at the Kerrville Folk Festival by 'Cooking Vinyl' bod, Pete Lawrence, the eagle eared Englishman recording an informal campfire-side set on a walkman. It was a break which SHOCKED was initially unsure about, however, the singer understandably suspicious of the machinations of the music industry. The recordings were eventually released in late '86 as 'THE TEXAS CAMPFIRE TAPES', MICHELLE no doubt, erm . . . shocked (ouch!) to find herself at the top of the UK indie charts. Once again with much trepidation, the singer eventually relented to a deal with the massive 'Polygram' corporation, signing with 'London' in Britain, 'Mercury' in the States. In keeping with her fiercely held beliefs and constant striving for integrity, SHOCKED reportedly made sure that she retained some creative control, the singer vindicated by the critical and commercial success of her debut album, 'SHORT SHARP SHOCKED' (1988). As the title and cover (SHOCKED in a police stranglehold) might suggest, the record was a defiant rabble of engaging protest songs combining roots folk with rock and pop accessibility. Among the highlights were the lilting 'ANCHORAGE' and the affecting 'GRAFFITI LIMBO', an elegy for murdered street artist, Michael Stewart. While the record made the UK Top 40 and garnered a groundswell of support, a follow-up album, 'CAPTAIN SWING' (1989) was way off the mark, moving away from her lone acoustic approach in favour of more ambitious arrangements. While SHOCKED was criticised in some quarters for political preaching, her more hardcore fans thought the record wasn't radical enough. Casting these complaints aside, SHOCKED went off on a musical pilgrimage of sorts, touring America Woody Guthrie-style and recording with an array of respected roots musicians including TAJ MAHAL, POPS STAPLES, DOC WATSON and the brilliant UNCLE TUPELO. Issued as 'ARKANSAS TRAVELER' (1992), the set reclaimed some of the singer's lost critical ground although it failed to make much of an impact on the charts. Unhappy with the way she was being treated by her record label, SHOCKED subsequently sued the company and self-financed her next album, 'KIND HEARTED WOMAN' (1994), the record receiving a belated UK release two years later. • **Songwriters:** Writes all material and borrows some trad., except ZIP-A-DEE-DOO-DAH (Wrubel-Gilbert) / GOODNIGHT IRENE (Leadbelly).

Album rating: TEXAS CAMPFIRE TAPES (*8) / SHORT SHARP SHOCKED (*7).

MICHELLE SHOCKED – vocals, acoustic guitar

Cooking Vinyl / Mercury

Nov 86. (lp/c) *(COOK/+C 002)* <834581-1/-4> **THE TEXAS CAMPFIRE TAPES** [ ] [ ]
– 5 a.m. in Amsterdam / The secret admirer / The incomplete image / Who cares? / Down on St. Thomas St. / Fogtown / Steppin' out / The hepcat / Necktie / (Don't you mess around with) My little sister / The ballad of Patch eye & Meg / The secret to a long life (is knowing when it's time to go). *(cd-iss. Apr88 += ' COOKCD 002)* – The chain smoker / Stranded in a limousine / Goodnight Irene. *(re-iss. Nov93 cd/c; same as US)*

Jun 87. (7") *(FRY 002)* **DISORIENTATED. / IF LOVE WAS A TRAIN** [ ] [-]
(12"+=) *(FRY 002T)* – Chain smoker / Stranded in a limousine / Goodnight Irene.

— now added numerous session people

London / Mercury

Aug 88. (lp/c)(cd) *(CV LP/MC 1)*<(834924-2)>**SHORT SHARP SHOCKED** [33] [73]
– When I grow up / Hello Hopeville / Memories of East Texas / (Making the run to) Gladewater / Graffiti limbo / If love was a train / Anchorage / The L&N don't stop here anymore / V.F.D. / Black widow.

Sep 88. (7") *(LON 193)* **ANCHORAGE. / FOGTOWN** [60] [-]
(10"+=) *(LONT 193)* – Remodelling the Pentagon / Penny Evans (live).
(12"+=/cd-s+=) *(LON X/CD 193)* – Strawberry jam (live) / Penny Evans (live).

Nov 88. (7") <870611> **ANCHORAGE. / ('A'live)** [-] [66]

Dec 88. (7") *(LON 212)* **IF LOVE WAS A TRAIN. / MEMORIES OF EAST TEXAS** [63] [ ]
(12"+=) *(LONX 212)* – Graffiti limbo (live).
(cd-s+=) *(LONCD 212)* – V.F.D. / Jambouree queen.

Feb 89. (7") *(LON 219)* **WHEN I GROW UP. / 5 A.M. IN AMSTERDAM (live)** [67] [ ]
(12"+=) *(LONX 219)* – Goodnight Irene.
(cd-s+=) *(LONCD 219)* – Camper crusade.

Nov 89. (lp/c/cd) <(838 878-1/-4/-2)> **CAPTAIN SWING** [31] [95]
– God is a real estate developer / On the greener side / Silent ways / Sleep keeps me awake / The cement lament / (You don't mess around with) My little sister / Looks like Mona Lisa / Too little too late / Street corner ambassador / Must be luff.

Nov 89. (7"/c-s) *(LON 245)* **ON THE GREENER SIDE. / RUSSIAN ROULETTE** [ ] [ ]
(12"+=/cd-s+=) *(LON X/CD 245)* – The Titanic / Old paint.

Mar 92. (7"/c-s) **COME A LONG WAY. / OVER THE WATERFALL**
(cd-s+=) – Contest coming / Jump Jim Crow-Zip-a-dee-doo-dah.
(cd-s+=) – Worth the weight / Shaking hands (soldier's toy).

Apr 92. (cd/c/lp) *(512 189-2/-4/-1)* **ARKANSAS TRAVELER** 46
– 33 r.p.m. soul / Come a long way / Secret to a long life / Contest coming (Cripple Creek) / Over the waterfall / Shaking hands (Soldier's joy) / Medley:- Jump Jim crow – Zip-a-dee-doo-dah / Hold me back / Strawberry jam / Prodigal daughter (Cotton-eyed Joe) / Blackberry blossom / Weaving way / Arkansas traveler / Woody's rag.

May 92. (7") **33 R.P.M. SOUL. / BLACKBERRY BOSSOM (live)**
(cd-s+=) – Over the waterfall (live) / ('A'live).

— Independently released an album in 1994.

Private-BMG / Private

Nov 96. (cd/c) *<(01005 82145-2/-4)>* **KIND HEARTED WOMAN**
– Stillborn / Homestead / Winter wheat / Cold comfort / Eddie / Child like Grace / Fever breaks / Silver spoon / Hard way / No sign of rain.

– compilations, etc. –

Nov 96. (cd) *London; (532960-2/-4)* **MERCURY POISED**
– On the greener side / Anchorage / Come along way / Quality of mercy / Street corner ambassador / Too little too late / If love was a train / When I grow up / Prodigal daughter / Over the waterfall / Holy spirit / Stillborn.

SHOCK HEADED PETERS (see under ⇒ BLAKE, Karl)

SHOES

Formed: Zion, Illinois, USA . . . 1974 by GARY KLEBE, JEFF MURPHY, his brother JOHN and SKIP MEYER. Wearing their classic BEATLES influences proudly, The SHOES made their first tentative steps into the music business with a couple of self-financed cassettes before spreading the net wider via debut album proper, 'BLACK VINYL SHOES' (1977). Strangely enough, it was released in Britain by 'Sire' while the band moved on to Greg Shaw's 'Bomp' for a one-off double-A 45, 'OKAY' / 'TOMORROW NIGHT'. With power-pop increasingly in vogue (in the States at least) on the back of the New Wave explosion, The SHOES kicked off their deal with 'Elektra' via the 'PRESENT TENSE' (1979) album. Containing the minor hit, 'TOO LATE', the record scraped into the US Top 50, although the 1981 follow-up, 'TONGUE TWISTER', failed to make the grade. Subsequent releases, 'SILHOUETTE' (1984), 'BOOMERANG' (1987) and 'STOLEN WISHES' (1990), extended their polished legacy and rounded off the first chapter in the career. A mid-90's reformation resulted in the two quickfire sets, 'PROPELLER' and 'FRET BUZZ', proving that these veterans weren't ready to hang up their boots just yet.

Album rating: BLACK VINYL SHOES (*7) / PRESENT TENSE (*6) / TONGUE TWISTER (*6) / SILHOUETTE (*6) / STOLEN WISHES (*5) / BOOMERANG (*6)

GARY KLEBE – vocals, guitar / **JEFF MURPHY** – vocals, bass, guitar / **JOHN MURPHY** – vocals, guitar / **SKIP MEYER** – drums

Sire / Black Vinyl

Dec 77. (lp) *(SRK 6075) <51477>* **BLACK VINYL SHOES**
– Boys don't lie / Do you wanna get lucky / She'll disappear / Tragedy / Writing a postcard / Not me / Someone finer / Capital gain / Fatal running start / Okay it really hurts / Fire for a while / If you'd stay / Nowhere so fast. *<re-iss. 1978 on 'P.V.C.'; 7904> (cd-iss. Sep93 on 'Creation Rev-Ola'; CREV 016CD) (cd re-iss. Nov96 on 'Black Vinyl'; BV 10092-2)*

not iss. / Bomp

Jun 78. (7") *<BMP 116>* **OKAY. / TOMORROW NIGHT** -

Elektra / Elektra

Oct 79. (lp) *(K 52187) <GE 244>* **PRESENT TENSE** 50
– Tomorrow night / Too late / Hangin' around with you / Your very eyes / In my arms again / Somebody has what I had / Now and then / Every girl / I don't miss you / Cruel you / Three times. See me – Say it – Listen / I don't wanna hear it.

Feb 80. (7") *(K 12404) <46557>* **TOO LATE. / NOW AND THEN** 75 Oct79

Feb 80. (7") *<46598>* **I DON'T MISS YOU. /** -

Apr 81. (7") *(K 12520)* **YOUR IMAGINATION. / THE THINGS YOU DO** -

Jun 81. (lp) *(K 52261) <303>* **TONGUE TWISTER** Jan81
– Your imagination / Burned out love / The things you do / Only in my sleep / Karen / She satisfies / Girls of today / Hopin' she's the one / When it hits / Yes or no / Found a girl / Hate to run.

Demon / not iss.

Sep 84. (lp) *(FIEND 19)* **SILHOUETTE** -
– Get my message / Will you spin for me / When push comes to shove / Shining / It's only you / Twist and bend it / I wanna give it to you / Turn around / Running wild / Oh, Angeline / Bound to fade / Suspicion. *(re-iss. 1985 on 'New Rose' lp/c; ROSE 44/+C) (cd-iss. Nov96 on 'Black Vinyl'; BV 15191-2)*

Jan 85. (7") *(D 1029)* **WHEN PUSH COMES TO SHOVE. / DORMANT LOVE** -

New Rose / not iss.

1985. (7") *(NEW 49)* **WILL YOU SPIN FOR ME. /** -

— SKIP MEYER had now departed

Fan Club / not iss.

Jul 87. (lp) *(FC 028)* **BOOMERANG** -
– In her shadow / Curiosity / Mayday / Too soon / Double talk / Summer rain / Under the gun / The tube / What love means / Bound to be a reason / Shake it away / Tested charms.

New Rose / Black Vinyl

May 90. (lp/cd) *(ROSE 202/+CD) <SPV 54012>* **STOLEN WISHES** Dec89
– Feel the way that I do / I'll follow you / Love does / Let it go / Your devotion / I know you'd be mine / Want you bad / Torn in two / She's not the same / Untangled / I don't know why / Inside of you / I can't go wrong / Love is like a bullet / Never had it better. *(cd re-iss. Nov96 on 'Black Vinyl'; BV 10189-2)*

— disbanded in the early 90's but re-formed again later with **GARY KLEBE, JEFF + JOHN MURPHY** plus **RIC MENCK + MIKE ZELENKO** – drums

Black Vinyl / Black Vinyl

Nov 96. (cd) *<(BV 10294-2)>* **PROPELLER** Apr94
– Animal attraction / Treading water / Don't do this to me / Last of you / Slipping through your fingers / Tore a hole / Bittersweet / If all I had was you / In my mind / Silence is deadly / Thing of the past / Never ending.

— **JOHN RICHARDSON** – drums; repl. drummers

Nov 96. (cd) *<(BV 10495-2)>* **FRET BUZZ** May95
– Animal attraction / Mayday / When push comes to shove / Want you bad / I don't wanna hear it / Turnaround / Love is like a bullet / Your devotion / Feel the way I do / Silence is deadly / Tore a hole / In harm's way.

– compilations, etc. –

on 'Black Vinyl' unless mentioned otherwise

Aug 88. (cd) *<(BV 19787-2)>* **SHOES BEST** 1987
– Burned out love / Tomorrow night / Turnaround / Get my message / Love is like a bullet / Karen / Mayday / She satisfies / When push comes to shove / Too late / Your imagination / Now and then / Summer rain / Curiosity / Piece of glass / Will you spin for me? / Too soon / Double talk / Boys don't lie / I don't wanna hear it / I don't miss you / Hate to run. *(re-iss. Nov96; same)*

Nov 96. (cd) *(BV 18190-2)* **BOOMERANG / SHOES ON ICE**

Nov 96. (cd) *(BV 19888-2)* **PRESENT TENSE / TONGUE TWISTER**

Jan 97. (d-cd) *(BV 10596-2)* **AS IS**

SHONEN KNIFE

Formed: Osaka, Japan . . . 1981 by sisters ATSUKO and NAOKO YAMANO with fellow school student MICHIE NAKATANI. Punkette "kewpie-doll" pop heavily influenced by western culture rock and pop (like X-RAY SPEX meeting PHIL SPECTOR's RONETTES), the youthful looking trio released several albums throughout the 80's, finding their way onto many a Stateside turntable. The American interest was down to the efforts of CALVIN JOHNSON (of the BEAT HAPPENING), who had discovered them on their home turf and later distributed 1983's 'BURNING FARM' via his own 'K' label. 1986 saw the band's first bonafide US release in the shape of the album 'PRETTY LITTLE BAKA GUY', an eponymous compilation set following in 1990. KURT COBAIN, for one, was a big fan and the girls actually supported NIRVANA, subsequently moving to America around the same time. The Grunge era also saw a host of bands (including SONIC YOUTH and HOLE) paying tribute to the diminutive threesome via an album, 'Every Band Has A Shonen Knife Who Loves Them'. SHONEN KNIFE rounded off their most successful year to date with the festive frenzy, 'SPACE CHRISTMAS'. Subsequently signing to UK Creation off-shoot label, 'August' ('MCA-Victor' in the States), they issued 'LET'S KNIFE' towards the end of '92. Athough the press hype diminished, the girls kept plugging away with their trademark nursery school lyrics and day-glo buzz-pop via albums such as 'WE ARE VERY HAPPY YOU CAME' (1993), 'ROCK ANIMALS' (1994), 'BRAND NEW KNIFE' (1997) and 'HAPPY HOUR' (1998). • **Covered:** (LIVE IS LIKE A) HEAT WAVE (Martha & The Vandellas) / TOP OF THE WORLD (Carpenters) / PARADISE (Nilsson) / BOYS (Dixon-Farrell) / TILL THE END OF THE DAY (Kinks) / DON'T HURT MY LITTLE SISTER (Beach Boys) / DAYDREAM BELIEVER (hit; Monkees).

Album rating: BURNING FARM mini (*6) / YAMANO ATCHAN mini (*5) / PRETTY LITTLE BAKA GUY (*6) / SHONEN KNIFE compilation (*8) / 712 (*5) / LET'S KNIFE (*4) / WE ARE VERY HAPPY YOU CAME (*5) / ROCK ANIMALS (*4) / BRAND NEW KNIFE (*6) / HAPPY HOUR (*4)

NAOKO YAMANO (b.18 Dec'61) – vocals / **ATSUKO YAMANO** (b.22 Feb'60) – drums / **MICHIE NAKATANI** (b. 8 Oct'61) – bass

X.A. / not iss.

Aug 82. (c) **MINNA TANOSHIKU SHONEN KNIFF** - - Japan

Zero / K

Jul 83. (8"m-lp) **BURNING FARM** - - Japan

May 84. (8"m-lp) **YAMANO ATCHAN** - Jun85

— Dec'84, also released Jap comp 'HUDDLE NO TROUBLE' for 'Balcony'

Zero / Subversive

Jun 86. (8"m-lp) **PRETTY LITTLE BAKA GUY** - Oct86
<US re-iss. Dec90 on 'Rockville' cd+=/c+=; 6053-2/-4> – LIVE IN JAPAN

— Jan 90, another Jap comp 'FLOWER WORLD' was issued on cassette.

not iss. / Giant

May 90. (cd/c/lp) *<6047-2/-4/-1>* **SHONEN KNIFE** (compilation) -

Seminal Twang / Rockville

Mar 91. (7") **LAZYBONE. / BLUE OYSTER CULT (Jap version)** -

Jul 91. (cd/c) *<ROCK 6065-2/-4>* **712** (also on 'Nippon Crown' in Japan) -

Jul 91. (7") **NEON ZEBRA. / BEAR UP BISON** -
(above single issued for 'Sub Pop')

Nov 91. (7") **SPACE CHRISTMAS. / BEAR UP BISON** -
(cd-s+=) – Christmas message '91.

Nov 92. (7") *<6075-7>* **SPACE CHRISTMAS. / CHRISTMAS MESSAGE '91** -

August / Capitol

Oct 92. (cd/c/lp) *(RUST 001 CD/MC/LP) <86638>* **LET'S KNIFE** Jan93
– Riding the rocket / Bear up bison / Twist Barbie / Tortoise theme 2 / Antonio baka guy / Ah Singapore / Flying jelly attack / Black bass / Cycling is fun / Watchin' girl / I am a cat / Tortoise theme 1 / Devil house / Insect collector / Burning farm. *(cd+=)* – Space Christmas / Bear up bison / Mickey Way / Do the Bartman.

Nov 92. (7") *(CAUG 001)* **RIDING ON THE ROCKET. / NEON ZEBRA (English version)** -
(12"/cd-s) *(CAUG 001 T/CD)* – ('A'side) / Milky Way / Burning farm (long version) / ('A'reprise).

Jan 93. (7") *(CAUG 003)* **GET THE WOW. / TWIST BARBIE** [ ] [-]
(12"+=/cd-s+=) *(CAUG 003 T/CD)* – Fruit loop dreams / Don't hurt my little sister.
(cd-s) *(CAUG 003CDL)* – ('A'side) / Animal song / Ice cream city (John Pel session) / Neon zebra (English version).
Apr 93. (cd/lp) *(RUST 004 CD/LP)* **WE ARE VERY HAPPY YOU CAME (live)** [ ] [-]
– Lazybone / Public bath / Goose steppin' mama / I wanna eat choco bars / Suzy is a headbanger / Boys / Red Kross.

August Virgin

Jan 94. (cd-ep) *<38414>* **BROWN MUSHROOMS / BUTTERFLY BOY / STRAWBERRY CREAM PUFF / TILL THE END OF THE DAY** [-] [ ]
Jan 94. (cd/c) *(RUST 009 CD/MC) <39063>* **ROCK ANIMALS** [ ] [ ]
– Quavers / Concrete animals / Butterfly boy / Little tree / Catnip dream / Tomato head / Another day / Brown mushrooms / Johnny, Johnny, Johnny / Cobra versus mongoose / Music square.
May 94. (cd-s) *<38433>* **TOMATO HEAD /** [-] [ ]

M.C.A. Big Deal

Sep 97. (d-cd) *(MCD 80071) <9035>* **BRAND NEW KNIFE** [ ] [ ] Mar97
– Explosion! / Wind your spring / The perfect world / E.S.P. / Loop di loop / Wonder wine / Magic Joe / Fruit & vegetables / Tower of the sun / Keep on rockin' / Frogphobia / Buddha's face / One week.

Big Deal Big Deal

Nov 97. (cd-ep) *<(BD 9047-2)>* **EXPLOSION!** [ ] [ ]
– Explosion! / Explosion! / E.S.P. / Loop-di-loop / Wind your spring / One week.
1998. (cd) *<BD 9055>* **HAPPY HOUR** [-] [ ]
– Shonen Knife planet / Konnichiwa / Cookie day / Hot chocolate / Sushi bar song / Fish eyes / Banana chips / Dolly / Jackalope / Gyoza / Catch your bus / People traps / His pet / Daydream believer.

– compilations, others, etc. –

May 94. (cd) *Tec Tones; (19422)* **KNIFE COLLECTORS** [-] [-] Japan
Mar 96. (cd) *Virgin; <41414>* **THE BIRDS AND THE B-SIDES** [-] [ ]
– (Love is like a) Heat wave / Gomi day / Top of the world / Ice cream city / Paradise / Little tree / Space Christmas / Fruit loop dreams / Boys / Till the end of the day / Elmer elevator / Don't hurt my little sister / Strawberry cream puff / Neon zebra / Lazybone / Public bath / I wanna eat choco bars / Redd Kross.
Apr 96. (cd) *Tec Tones; (SHONEN)* **FAN CLUB CD** [-] [-] Japan

SHOP ASSISTANTS

Formed: Edinburgh, Scotland . . . 1984 originally as BUBA & THE SHOP ASSISTANTS by DAVID KEEGAN, AGGI, SARAH KNEALE, ANN DONALD and LAURA McPHAIL. Following an extremely limited debut single, 'SOMETHING TO DO', on the 'Villa 21' label, the band (now without AGGI who'd been replaced by ALEX TAYLOR) released a more widely distributed follow-up, 'ALL DAY LONG' on the 'Subway Organisation' imprint. Amid increasing critical acclaim from the London-based music press, The SHOP ASSISTANTS topped the indie charts with third single, 'SAFETY NET', the first release on KEEGAN's '53rd & 3rd' label. 1986 proved to be a pivotal year as the band signed to Chrysalis offshoot 'Blue Guitar' and released their eponymous debut album, in addition contributing the delicate strum of 'IT'S UP TO YOU' to the NME's C86 tape and the noisier retro-pop of 'TRAIN FROM KANSAS CITY' to Sounds magazine's 'Showcase' sampler. Despite their ringing, girlish charm, mainstream chart success wasn't on the cards and the band fell apart the following with TAYLOR going off to form MOTORCYCLE BOY. A subsequent reformation in 1990 was decidedly low key, the band releasing material on the capital's 'Avalanche' label. With KEEGAN later joining The PASTELS on a full-time basis, it seems like the band have finally shut up shop for good. In the early 90's, the 1986 line-up sued their management company, 'Globeshire', for being unforthcoming with a 5-figure royality share. Due to neglect, the band had to pay over a fee of £1,000 to the taxman as they weren't registered for VAT.

Album rating: THE SHOP ASSISTANTS (*6)

AGGI – vocals (of JUNIPER BELL BER) / **DAVID KEEGAN** – guitar / **SARAH KNEALE** – bass / **LAURA MacPHAIL** – drums / plus guests **STEPHEN PASTEL** – producer, b.vocals / **ANN DONALD** – drums (later of FIZZBOMBS)

Villa 21 not iss.

Nov 84. (7"; as BUBA & THE SHOP ASSISTANTS) *(002)* **SOMETHING TO DO. / DREAMING BACKWARDS** [ ] [-]

—— **ALEX(ANDRA) TAYLOR** – vocals; repl. AGGI who later joined The SUGARCUBES

Subway not iss.

Aug 85. (7"ep) *(SUBWAY 1)* **ALL DAY LONG / ALL THAT EVER MATTERED. / IT'S UP TO YOU / SWITZERLAND** [ ] [-]

53rd & 3rd not iss.

Feb 86. (7"m/12"m) *(AGAAR 1/+12)* **SAFETY NET. / SOMEWHERE IN CHINA / ALMOST MADE IT** [ ] [-]

Blue Guitar not iss.

Sep 86. (7") *(AZUR 2)* **I DON'T WANNA BE FRIENDS WITH YOU. / LOOK BACK** [ ] [-]
(12"+=) *(AZURX 2)* –
Nov 86. (lp/c) *(AZ/ZAZ LP 2)* **THE SHOP ASSISTANTS** [ ] [-]
– I don't wanna be friends with you/ All day long / Before I wake / Caledonian road / All that ever mattered / Fixed grin / Somewhere in China / Train from Kansas City / Home again / Seems to be / All of the time / What a day to die / Nature lover.

—— Disbanded early 1987. ALEX joined MOTORCYCLE BOY. Reformed late '89, McPHAIL now on bass + **MARGARITA** – drums

Avalanche not iss.

Jan 90. (7"flexi-ep) *(AGAP 001C)* **HERE IT COMES / I'D RATHER BE WITH YOU / YOU TRIP ME UP / THE OTHER ONE** [ ] [-]
(7"flexi-box-ep) *(AGAP 001B)* – (first 2 tracks) / Look out / Adrenalin.
May 90. (7"/c-s) *(AGAP 003/+MC)* **BIG 'E' POWER. / ?** [ ] [-]
(12"+=/cd-s+=) *(AGAP 003 T/CD)* –

—— split after above and KEEGAN joined The PASTELS full-time

SHRIEKBACK

Formed: Kentish Town, London, England . . . 1981 by ex-GANG OF FOUR bassist, DAVE ALLEN and former XTC vocalist/keyboard player, BARRY ANDREWS. Subsequently recruiting CARL MARSH, the trio set about creating sinuous, experimental CAN/POP GROUP-esque white-boy funk, debuting with the 'TENCH' EP on indie label 'Y Records' in 1982. This was followed by 'SEXTHINKONE' and 'MY SPINE (IS THE BASS LINE)', the latter a compelling fix of reverberating, contorting rhythm alchemised from the same uncompromising, instinctive ingredients the RED HOT CHILI PEPPERS would utilise – if not with quite the same complex finesse – a few years later. A further single 'WORKING ON THE GROUND', another version of 'LINED UP' and an album, 'CARE' – picked up by 'Warners' in America – appeared over the next 18 months and 'Arista' were quick to secure their signatures. Now a quartet following the addition of MARTYN BARKER, the resulting 'JAM SCIENCE' (1984) album introduced a more synth-heavy SHRIEKBACK sound together with female backing vocals, losing a bit of the lean hunger of their earlier work but attracting a wider audience for singles 'HAND ON MY HEART' and 'MERCY DASH'. Bonafide chart success remained elusive, however, and after 'OIL AND GOLD' (1985), MARSH jumped ship while the remaining members moved on to 'Island' for the piano-based 'BIG NIGHT MUSIC' (1987). On top of losing the vital MARSH/ALLEN chemistry, the band were dealt a further blow with the departure of the latter to form KING SWAMP. Although they limped on for 1988's 'GO BANG' with TACKHEAD man DOUG WIMBISH, SHRIEKBACK reached its natural conclusion at the turn of the decade, ANDREWS, ALLEN and BARKER later reuniting and resurrecting the SHRIEKBACK name for 1992's 'SACRED CITY'.

Album rating: CARE (*5) / JAM SCIENCE (*5) / OIL AND GOLD (*5) / BIG NIGHT MUSIC (*5) / GO BANG (*4) / THE INFINITE – THE BEST OF SHRIEKBACK compilation (*7) / SCARED CITY (*4)

CARL MARSH – vocals (ex-OUT ON BLUE SIX) / **BARRY ANDREWS** – keyboards, vocals (ex-XTC, ex-LEAGUE OF GENTLEMEN, ex-IGGY POP, ex-RESTAURANT FOR DOGS, ex-Solo Artist) / **DAVE ALLEN** – bass (ex-GANG OF FOUR)

Y Records Warners

Jun 82. (12"ep) *(Y 21T)* **TENCH EP** [ ] [-]
Jun 82. (7") *(Y 22)* **SEXTHINKONE. / HERE COMES MY HANDCLAP** [ ] [-]
Sep 82. (7"/12") *(Y 27/+T)* **MY SPINE (IS THE BASS LINE). / TINY BIRDS** [ ] [-]
Feb 83. (7") *(Y 102)* **LINED UP. / LEPAX LEGOMENA** [ ] [-]
(12"+=) *(YT 102)* – ('A'instrumental).
Mar 83. (lp) *(YLP 502) <23874>* **CARE** [ ] [ ] Jun83
– Lined up / Clear trails / Hapax legomena / Petulant / Lines from the library / Brink of collapse / Sway / Madness into method / Evaporation / Accretions.
May 83. (7") *(Y 104)* **WORKING ON THE GROUND. / CLOSEWORK** [ ] [-]
(12"+=) *(YT 104)* – Nightwork (dance).
Aug 83. (7") *(Y 106)* **LINED UP (remix). / MY SPINE (IS THE BASS LINE)** [ ] [-]
(12"+=) *(YT 106)* – Madness into method (planet mix) / Accretions (monstrous dance mix).

—— added **MARTYN BARKER** – drums / live only **PEDRO ORITZ** – percussion

Arista Island

Jul 84. (7"/7"pic-d) *(SHR K/PD 1)* **HAND ON MY HEART. / NERVE** [ ] [-]
(12"+=) *(SHRK 12-1)* – Suck.
(12"+=) *(SHRK 22-1)* – Cloud of nails / Mistah Linn – he's dead.
Aug 84. (lp/c) *(206/406 416)* **JAM SCIENCE** [85] [-]
– Hand on my heart / Newhome / Achtung / Partyline / Midnight maps / Mercy dash / Under the lights / My careful hands / Suck / Hubris.
Sep 84. (7") *(SHRK 2)* **MERCY DASH. / GATED JOY** [ ] [-]
(12"+=) *(SHRK 12-2)* – Bricks and whistles.
(12"pic-d) *(SHRK 22-2)* – ('A'mix) / Hand on my heart / Jumping on the ribcage with the digital Rasta / Suck / Cloud of nails / Pump up a storm.
May 85. (7") *(SHRK 3)* **NEMESIS. / SUCK (live)** [ ] [-]
(d7"+=) *(FSHRK 3)* – Mothloop (live) / Feelers (live).
(12"+=) *(SHRK 12-3)* – ('A'version).
Jun 85. (lp/c) *(207/407 206) <842882-1/-4>* **OIL AND GOLD** [ ] [ ]
– Malaria / Everything that rises must converge / Fish below the ice / This big hush / Faded flowers / Nemesis / Only thing that shines / Health and knowledge and wealth and power / Hammerheads / Coelacanth.
Sep 85. (7") *(SHRK 4)* **FISH BELOW THE ICE. / COELACANTH** [ ] [-]
(d7"+=/12"+=) *(SHRK D/12-4)* – All lined up / My spine (is the bass line).

—— **MIKE COZZI** – guitars; repl. MARSH who went solo (in April '92, his HAPPYHEAD issued an album, 'GIVE HAPPYHEAD', for 'Atlantic')

—— guests incl. **STEVE HALLIWELL** – keyboards / **WENDY + SARAH PARTRIDGE** – backing vocals

Island Island

Dec 86. (7") *(IS 314)* **GUNNING FOR THE BUDDHA. / BLUDGEONED** [ ] [-]
(12"+=) *(12IS 314)* – Black light trap.
Jan 87. (lp/c/cd) *(ILPS/ICT/CID 9849) <90552>* **BIG NIGHT MUSIC** [ ] [ ]
– Underwaterboys / Exquisite / The reptiles and I / Sticky jazz / Cradle song / Black light trap / Gunning for the buddha / Running on the rocks / Shining path / Pretty little thing.

—— when DAVE ALLEN returned to GANG OF FOUR, the line-up comprised **ANDREWS, BARKER, COZZI and The PATRIDGE sisters**

Jul 88. (7") *(IS 343)* **GET DOWN TONIGHT. / BIG FUN** [ ] [-]
(12"+=) *(12IS 343)* – Big fun (acid house mix).
Nov 88. (lp/c/cd) *(ILPS/ICT/CID 9910) <90949>* **GO BANG!** [ ] [ ]
– Intoxication / Shark walk / Over the wire / New man / Nighttown / Go

bang! / Big fun / Get down tonight / Dust and a shadow. *(cd re-iss. 1989; IMCD 27)*

—— disbanded in the late 80's, ANDREWS worked on a few low-key projects before re-forming the group in 1992

World Domination Capitol

Sep 92. (cd-ep) *<15899>* **BASTARD SONS OF ENOCH** -

Feb 94. (cd) *(SHRIEK 1CD) <98780>* **SACRED CITY** Sep92
– Signs / Psycho drift / The bastard sons of Enoch / (Open up your) Filthy heart (to me) / Exquisite corpse / Below / Beatles zebra crossing / Hymn to the local gods / Every force evolves a form / 3 a.m.

– compilations, etc. –

Mar 84. (lp/c) *Kaz; (KAZLP 1)* **THE INFINITE (THE BEST OF SHRIEKBACK)** -
– Lined up / Clear trails / Accretions / Sway / Into method / My spine (is the bass line) / Mothloop / Sexthinkone / Evaporation / A kind of fascination / Working on the ground. *(c-iss.Oct85; KAZMA 1) (cd-iss. Dec86; KAZCD 1)*

May 88. (lp/c/cd) *Kaz; (KAZ LP/MC/CD 5)* **EVOLUTION – BEST OF SHRIEKBACK VOL.2** -
– Nemesis / Fish below the ice / Hand on my heart / Newhome / Despite dense weed / Midnight maps / Mercy dash / Malaria / Under the lights / My careful hands / Nerve / Lines from the library.

Apr 90. (cd/c/lp) *Island; (CID/ICT/ILPS 9960)* **THE BEST OF SHRIEKBACK** -
– Underwaterboys / Exquisite / The reptiles and I / Sticky jazz / Cradle song / Black light trap / Gunning for the buddha / Running on the rocks / Shining path / Pretty little thing.

Jul 94. (d-cd) *Essential; (ESDCD 217)* **NATURAL HISTORY – THE VERY BEST OF SHRIEKBACK** -
– Lined up / Clear trails / Accretions / Sway / Madness into method / My spine (is the bass line) / Mothloop / Sexthinkone / Evaporation / A kind of fascination / Working on the ground / Nemesis / Hand on my heart / Newhome / Despite dense weed / Midnight maps / Mercy dash / Malaria / Under the lights / My careful hands / Nerve / Lines from the library / Fish below the ice.

Sep 94. (cd) *Arista; (07822 22636-2)* **PRIESTS AND KANNIBALS: THE BEST OF SHRIEKBACK**
– Nemesis / Hammerheads / All lined up / My spine (is the bass line) / Hand on my heart / Achtung / Mercy dash / Suck / Health and knowledge and wealth and power / Nerve / Only thing that shines / Coelacanth / Nemesis (arch deviant) / Cloud of nails (pump up a storm) / Mercy dash (extended) / Fish below the ice.

SHRUBS

Formed: Watford, England . . . mid '85 initially as the KEVIN STAPLES BAND by part-time STUMP "singer", NICK HOBBS, along with JULIAN HATTON, MICHAEL RICKETS, PHIL ROBERTS and JOHN BENTLEY. One of the noisier bands to feature on NME's C-86 V/A compilation, The SHRUBS contributed the track, 'BULLFIGHTER'S BONES', an ear-shredding clatter of loping, discordant fret abuse on the brink of sonic collapse; JOHN LYDON fronting the POP GROUP comes to mind. One of several bands to sign for the 'Ron Johnson' imprint (A WITNESS, MACKENZIES, BIG FLAME, etc), they debuted in their own right with summer '86's appropriately titled 12" EP, 'FULL STEAM INTO BRAINSTORM'. After PHIL moved on to pastures new with The CREEPERS (i.e. MARC RILEY), his position was taken by STEVE BROCKLEY who joined in time for the 'BLACKMAILER' EP and 1987's long-player, 'TAKE A SIDE FOR A MIDNIGHT HARANGUE'. A year later, their own label, 'Public Domain', was home to swansong set, 'VESSELS OF THE HEART'.

Album rating: TAKE A SIDE FOR A MIDNIGHT HARANGUE (*4) / VESSELS OF THE HEART (*4)

NICK HOBBS – vocals (also of STUMP) / **JULIAN HATTON** – guitar / **MICHAEL RICKETS** – guitar / **PHIL ROBERTS** – bass / **JOHN BENTLEY** – drums

Ron Johnson not iss.

Jul 86. (12"ep) *(ZRON 10)* **FULL STEAM INTO BRAINSTORM** -
– Black saloons / The dealer / Bullfighter's bones / Carbreaker / Dead teachers / Warm sea.

—— **STEVE BROCKLEY** – bass; repl. PHIL who joined (MARC RILEY &) THE CREEPERS

Dec 86. (12") *(ZRON 17)* **BLACKMAILER. /** -

Jun 87. (lp) **TAKE A SIDE FOR A MIDNIGHT HARANGUE** -

Public Domain not iss.

Sep 88. (12"ep) *(DOM 001)* **ANOTHER AGE (live)** -

Nov 88. (lp/cd) *(DOM 002/+CD)* **VESSELS OF THE HEART** -
– Papa chaperon / Cole / Resurrection chain / Ballet gorilla / Cash register brain / Mass mental (long abusive rental) / Villa burgher / Shawl blight zone / Myth night / King Urn / Sullen days are over / Mistress of the moral ground.

—— split after above

SHUDDER TO THINK

Formed: Washington DC, USA . . . 1986 by STUART HILL, CHRIS MATTHEWS, MIKE RUSSELL and vocalist, CRAIG WEDREN. Hardly a typical 'Dischord' act, SHUDDER TO THINK began their career with a privately circulated demo, 'CIRSE, SPELLS, VOODOO, MOOSES', in '89, before signing to IAN MacKAYE's operation and releasing 'TEN-SPOT' as their debut album proper at the turn of the decade. Eschewing a straight forward hardcore sound for a more complex, awkwardly melodic approach, the quartet attracted a cult following with albums such as 'FUNERAL AT THE MOVIES' (1991) and 'GET YOUR GOAT' (1992). Personnel ructions resulted in MATTHEWS and RUSSELL departing and being replaced by NATHAN LARSON and ADAM WADE respectively, although things took a turn for the better as 'Epic' saw potential in the band's diverse musical talents. While 'PONY EXPRESS RECORD' (1994) might've made few concessions to their new major label status, the long-awaited '50,000 B.C.' was a far more immediate affair, putting an alternative twist on everything from rootsy rock to harmony- flowing power-pop/rock. A year on, SHUDDER TO THINK made a radical move into soundtrack work, no doubt alienating part of their loyal fanbase with the atmospheric score to 'HIGH ART' and retro-pastiche of 'FIRST LOVE, LAST RITES', the latter featuring guest vocal turns by the likes of BILLY CORGAN, JEFF BUCKLEY, LIZ PHAIR, ROBIN ZANDER and JOHN DOE.

Album rating: TEN-SPOT (*5) / FUNERAL AT THE MOVIES (*5) / GET YOUR GOAT (*6) / PONY EXPRESS RECORD (*7) / 50,000 B.C. (*6) / LIVE (*5) / HIGH ART (*6) / FIRST LOVE, LAST RITES (*6)

CRAIG WEDREN – vocals, guitar / **CHRIS MATTHEWS** – guitar / **STUART HILL** – bass / **MIKE RUSSELL** – drums

Dischord Dischord

Jun 90. (lp/c) *<(DISCHORD 46/+C)>* **TEN-SPOT**
– Heaven here / Jade-dust eyes / Rags / About three dreams / Speak / Corner of my eye / Summertime train / On the rain / Vacation brain / Yes / Tony told me.

Jun 91. (lp/c) *<(DISCHORD 54/+C)>* **FUNERAL AT THE MOVIES**
– Chocolate / Lies about the sky / Day ditty / Crosstown traffic / Red house / Funeral at the movies / I blew away / Ride that sexy horse. *(cd-iss. Jul91 +=; DISCHORD 55)*

May 92. (lp/c/cd) *<(DIS 67/+C/CD)>* **GET YOUR GOAT**
– Love catastrophe / Shake your halo down / White page / Goat / Pebbles / Baby drop / The hair pillow / She wears he-harem / Rain-covered cat / Funny.

Nov 92. (7") *(DIS 76V)* **HIT LIQUOR. / NO ROOM 9, KENTUCKY**

—— **NATHAN LARSON** – guitar; repl. MATTHEWS

Your Choice Your Choice

Aug 94. (cd) *<(YCLS 021)>* **LIVE** May94
– White page / Birthday song / Baby drop / Pebbles / Rain covered cat / I grow cold / Rag / Day ditty / Chocolate / So into you / Shake your halo down.

—— **ADAM WADE** – drums; repl. RUSSELL

Big Cat Epic

Aug 94. (12"ep/cd-ep) *(ABB 72 T/CD) <66415>* **HIT LIQUOR EP**
– Hit liquor / Kissi Penny / Red house / Heaven here / Full body anchor.

Sep 94. (cd) *(ABB 65CD) <57855>* **PONY EXPRESS RECORD**
– Hit liquor / Gang of $ / 9 fingers on you / Sweet year old / Earthquakes come home / Kissi Penny / X-French Tee shirt / No Rm. 9, Kentucky / Chakka / Own me / So into you / Trackstar / Full body anchor. *(re-iss. Aug95; same)*

Big Cat Sub Pop

Jun 95. (7") *(ABB 81SCD) <SP 283>* **X-FRENCH TEE SHIRT. / SHAKE YOUR HALO DOWN** Nov94

Epic Epic

May 97. (cd/c) *(486938-2/-4)* **50,000 BC**
– Call of the playground / Red house / Beauty strike / The saddest day of my life / The man who rolls / All eyes are different / Kissesmack of past action / Resident wine / She's a skull / Survival / You're gonna look fine / Love / Hop on one foot.

Jun 98. (cd) *<79735>* **HIGH ART** (soundtrack) -
– Opening / Dominoes / Cocoa butter / Mom's Mercedes / Photographic ecstasy / Gavial / Noetony / Ph balanced (for a lady) / Battle soaked / That's fat / She gives tone / Last lines / She might be waking up / Fools / End frame.
<above issued on 'Velvel'>

Aug 98. (cd,c) *<69029>* **FIRST LOVE, LAST RITES** -
– I want someone badly / Erecting a movie star / Diamonds, sparks and all / When I was born, I was bored / Apalachian lullaby / Airfield dream / Automatic soup / Lonesome dove / Speed of love / Day ditty / The wedding is over / Jelly on the table / Just really wanna see you / I want someone badly / Final dream.

Jane SIBERRY

Born: 12 Oct '55, Toronto, Canada. She began writing music from an early age and gained a degree in microbiology. She became a waitress to help finance her self-titled album in 1980. This suggested influences of JONI MITCHELL, ANGELA CARTER or even early ELTON JOHN in her piano style. Her next album 'NO BORDERS HERE', included her excellent 'MIMI ON THE BEACH'. Produced by her long-time friend and cohort JOHN SWITZER. She progressed into more experimental territory for fourth 'THE WALKING' which eventually turned up on 'Reprise' in 1987/8. It was even compared with the avant-garde 'Trout Mask Replica' by BEEFHEART. She attempted a more commercial approach for 1989's 'BOUND BY THE BEAUTY'. After a compilation in '92, she made comeback album 'WHEN I WAS A BOY', which was augmented by BRIAN ENO and MICHAEL BROOK. Her song 'IT CAN'T RAIN ALL THE TIME' was then used on the film 'THE CROW', before her last album for the label; 'MARIA' appeared in 1995.

Album rating: THE WALKING (*7) / BOUND BY THE BEAUTY (*7) / WHEN I WAS A BOY (*6) / MARIA (*6)

JANE SIBERRY – vocals, piano, guitar / with **BRUCE FOWLER** – synthesizer / **JOHN SWITZER** – bass / **CARL KEESEE** – bass, clarinet / **DAVID BRADSTREET** – drums, guitar / etc

not iss. Street

Feb 81. (lp) *<SR 002>* **JANE SIBERRY** - - Canada
– Marco Polo / This girl I know / The sky is so blue / Mystery at Ogwen's farm / Magic beads / Writers are a funny breed / Strange well / Above the treeline / In the blue light. *(UK cd-iss. Nov97 on 'Street'; SRCD 002)*

—— now with **JOHN SWITZER** – bass / **ANNE BOURNE** – keyboards / **AL CROSS** – drums / **KEN MYHR** – guitar

Reprise Open Air

Dec 83. (lp/c) <OD/OT 0302> **NO BORDERS HERE** [-] [ ]
– Waitress / I muse aloud / Dancing class / Extra executives / You don't need / Symmetry (the way things have to be) / Follow me / Mimi on the beach / Map of the world (part 1).

Jun 87. (lp/c) *(9-25578-1/-4)* <OD 0305> **THE SPECKLESS SKY** [ ] [ ] May86
– One more colour / Seven steps to the wall / The very large hat / Mien bitte / Vladimir – Vladimir / Map of the world (part 2) / The empty city / The taxi ride. *(UK+=)* – Mimi on the beach. *(cd-iss. Nov97 on 'Duke St.'; DSBD 31019)*

Reprise Reprise

Apr 88. (lp/c/cd) <(25678-1/-4/-2)> **THE WALKING** [ ] [ ] Nov87
– The white tent / The raft / Red high heels / Goodbye / Ingrid (and the footman) / Lena is a white table / The walking (and constantly) / The lobby / The bird in the gravel. *(cd re-iss. Nov97 on 'Duke St.'; DSBD 31040)*

—— **STITCH WYNSTON** – drums repl. CROSS

—— **TEDDY BOROWIECKI** – piano repl. BOURNE

Aug 89. (lp/c)(cd) *(WX 293/+C)*<(K 25942-2)> **BOUND BY THE BEAUTY** [ ] [ ]
– Bound by the beauty / Something about trains / Hockey / Everything reminds me of my dog / The valley / The life is the red wagon / Half angel half eagle / La jalouse / Miss Punta Blanca / Are we dancing now? (Map III).

Apr 92. (7"/c-s) *(W 0097/+C)* **THE LIFE IS THE RED WAGON. / BOUND BY THE BEAUTY** [ ] [ ]
(12"+=/cd-s+=) *(W 0097 T/CD)* – Everything reminds me of my dog.

Apr 92. (cd) <(7599 26936-2)> **SUMMER IN THE YUKON**
(compilation) <US-title 'A COLLECTION 1984-1989> [ ] [ ] 1993
– My life is the red wagon / Miss Punta Blanca / Calling all angels (with k.d. LANG) / Above the treeline / In the blue light / Seven steps to the wall / Mimi on the beach / The walking (and constantly) / The very large hat / The lobby / Red high heels / Map of the world (part II) / The taxi ride.

—— now augmented by MICHAEL BROOK, and session people

Jul 93. (cd/c) <(7599 26824-2/-4)> **WHEN I WAS A BOY** [ ] [ ]
– Calling all angels (with k.d. LANG) / Temple / Love is everything / Sail across the water / All the candles in the world / Sweet incarnadine / The gospel according to darkness / An angel stepped down / The vigil / At the beginning of time / Love is everything 2.

Aug 93. (cd-ep) <41174> **TEMPLE (5 mixes) / ANGEL STEPPED DOWN (AND SLOWLY LOOKED UP)** [-] [ ]

—— **TIM RAY + DAVID TRAVERS-SMITH + GAIL ANN DORSEY**

Aug 95. (cd/c) <(7599 45915-2/-4)> **MARIA** [ ] [ ]
– Maria / See the child / Honey bee / Caravan / Lovin' cup / Begat begat / Goodbye sweet pumpkinhead / Would you go? / Mary had . . . Oh my my.

Oct 95. (cd-s) <17742> **LOVIN' CUP /** [-] [ ]

—— now on her own 'Sheeba' after amicably leaving Reprise

Sheeba Blackbird

Oct 96. (cd) <7939> **TEENAGER** [-] [ ]
– Introduction / Squirrel crossed the road / Let's not talk now / Song to my father / Broken birds / Puppet city / Oh my sister / Long pirouette / Bessie / We should be there by morning / Viking heart / When Spring comes / Angel voyeur / Trumpeter swan.

Nov 97. (d-cd) *(SHEEB 2)* <62156> **CHILD** (music for the Christmas season) [ ] [ ]
– She's playing the taxidriver / Caravan / Wildwood carol / Bitter Christmas / What is this fragerance softly . . . Quio, ma voisine, es-tu fachee? / Shir anami / Mary's lullaby / Angel stepped down / Silent night / You will be born / O holy night / In the bleak midwinter / Christmas mass / Christmas song / Maria wanders through the thorn / What child is this? / Valley / Hockey / Twelve days of Christmas / Are you burning, little candle?

SICK OF IT ALL

Formed: New York City, New York, USA . . . 1986 by brothers LOU and PETE KOLLER, along with EDDIE and E.K. An influential, uncompromising straight-edged band, SOIA were a pivotal part of the late 80's NY hardcore scene, early albums such as 'BLOOD, SWEAT & NO TEARS' (1989) and 'JUST LOOK AROUND' (1991) akin to a more vicious combination of RANCID and The BEASTIE BOYS. Their third (half live) set, 'WE STAND ALONE' (1992), was the last with EDDIE and E.K, the pair being replaced by CRAIG SETARI and ARMIN MAJIDI respectively for their first major label outing, 'SCRATCH THE SURFACE' (1994). Like many bands of their ilk, SOIA were snapped up amid the punk/hardcore revival of the early 90's, the group signing away their particular soul with 'East West'. During this time, a number of exploitation releases flooded the market, the band taking until 1997 to release a follow-up, 'BUILT TO LAST'. SICK OF IT ALL had also helped their roadie, TOBY MORSE, to turn his/their stage party piece act, H2O, get off the ground. • **Covered:** BORSTAL BREAKOUT (Sham 69).

Album rating: BLOOD, SWEAT AND NO TEARS (*6) / WE STAND ALONE (*5) / JUST LOOK AROUND (*6) / SCRATCH THE SURFACE (*6) / BUILT TO LAST (*6)

LOU KOLLER – vocals / **PETE KOLLER** – guitar / **EDDIE** – bass / **E.K.** – drums

not iss. Revelation

1987. (7"ep) <3> **SICK OF IT ALL** [-] [ ]
– It's clobberin' time – Just lies / Pete's sake / Friends like you / Bullshit justice / Pay the price / Pushed too far – Give respect / Deal / N.S. – My revenge. *<cd-iss. Sep97; same>*

not iss. Combat

1989. (lp,c,cd) <3005> **BLOOD, SWEAT AND NO TEARS** [-] [ ]
– The blood and the sweat / Clobberin' time – Pay the price / Give respect / Breeders of hate / Pushed too far / Friends like you / B.S. justice / Rat pack / Pete's sake / Stick together / G.I. Joe head stomp / Alone / My life / World full of hate / My revenge / No labels / Disillusion / Deal / Injustice system!

1992. (cd/c) <88561-3017-2/-4> **JUST LOOK AROUND** [-] [ ]
– We want the truth / Locomotive / Pain strikes / Shut me out / What's goin' on / Never measure up / Just look around / Violent generation / Shield / Now it's gone / We stand alone / Will we survive / Indust. *(UK cd-iss. May95 on 'Roadrunner'; RR 9191-2)*

not iss. In-Effect

1992. (cd) <468100-2> **WE STAND ALONE** (rec.1990/91) [-] [ ]
– What's goin' on / Betray / We stand alone / Disillusion / My revenge – World full of hate / Pete's sake / Injustice system / The deal / G.I. Joe head stomp / Pushed too far / The blood & the sweat / Politics.

—— **CRAIG SETARI** – bass + **ARMIN MAJIDI** – drums; repl. EDDIE + E.K.

East West East West

Nov 94. (cd/c/lp) <(7567 92422-2/-4/-1)> **SCRATCH THE SURFACE** [ ] [ ]
– No cure / Inserrection / Consume / Goatless / Maladjusted / Free spirit / Desperate fool / Force my hand / Cease fire / Farm team / Return to reality / Scratch the surface / Step down / Who sets the rules. *(lp re-iss. Apr97 on 'Equal Vision'; EVR 023)*

Jan 95. (12"etched) *(A 8202X)* **SCRATCH THE SURFACE. / BORSTAL BREAKOUT** [ ] [ ]
(cd-ep+=) *(A 8202EP)* – Consume / Straight ahead.

Mar 97. (cd/c) *(62008-2/-4)* **BUILT TO LAST** [ ] [ ]
– Good lookin' out / Built to last / Closer / One step ahead / Us vs them / Laughingstock / Don't follow / Nice / Busted / Burn 'em down / End the era / Chip away / Too late / Jungle. *(lp-iss.May97 on 'Equal Vision'; EVR 036)*

– compilations, etc. –

on 'Lost & Found' unless mentioned otherwise

Dec 93. (cd) *<(LF 073CD)>* **LIVE IN A WORLD FULL OF HATE** [ ] [ ] Apr95
– Injustice system! / It's clobberin' time / Violent generation / Alone / Pain strikes / Shut me out / Pushed too far / Friends like you / Locomotive / World full of hate / Just look around / What's going on / Give respct / Disillusion / No labels / Pete's sake / G.I. Joe head stomp / We want the truth / Blood and the sweat / Shield / We stand alone / Indist. / My life / Betray.

May 94. (cd) *(LF 083CD)* **THE REVELATION RECORDINGS 1987-89** [ ] [-]

May 94. (m-cd) *(LF 084MCD)* **SPREADING THE HARDCORE REALITY** [ ] [-]

Jan 95. (d-lp) *(LF 121)* **LIVE IN A WORLD FULL OF HATE / BROTHER AGAINST BROTHER (by The Rykers)** [ ] [-]

SIDI BOU SAID

Formed: Greenwich & Lewisham, South London, England . . . 1990 by songwriters CLAIRE LEMMON and LOU HOWTON, alongside GAYL HARRISON and MELANIE WOODS. Named, apparently, after a town in Tunisia, this all-female outfit are definitely not your run-of-the-mill girly band. Consistently compared – much to their collective annoyance – with THROWING MUSES, there's no getting away from the similarities in terms of songwriting complexity, vocal interplay, general quirkiness and decidedly (but subtle) femininist lyrical slant. Nevertheless, SIDI BOU SAID are readily identifiable as being from this side of the pond even if the bulk of their influences – VIOLENT FEMMES, PATTI SMITH, even bluesy doomsters MASTERS OF REALITY – originate across the Atlantic. Signed to the 'Ultimate' label, the band's career got off to a shaky start with the 'BROOCH' (1993) album which met with a lukewarm critical reception. More promising was 1995's 'BODIES' set and the attendant 'ODE TO DRINK' single, adding the influence of LED ZEPPELIN and – in the carefully arranged strings – The BEATLES to the above list. Despite their confident talk of a female revolution in rock, the group have still to make the leap to mainstream acceptance, 1996's 'OBSESSIVE' album merely underlining the fact that their introspective sound and lyrical perspective is perhaps a bit too challenging for the average (male) indie fan.

Album rating: BROOCH (*4) / BODIES (*5) / OBSESSIVE (*5)

CLAIRE LEMMON – vocals, guitar / **LOU HOWTON** – vocals, guitar / **GAYL HARRISON** – bass / **MELANIE WOODS** – drums

Ultimate not iss.

Feb 93. (7") *(TOPP 14)* **TWILIGHT EYES. /** [ ] [-]
(cd-s+=) *(TOPP 14CD)* –

May 93. (7") *(TOPP 17)* **THREE SIDES. / ROMP** [ ] [-]
(12"+=/cd-s+=) *(TOPP 17 T/CD)* – Wild.

Oct 93. (lp) *(TOPPLP 5S)* **BROOCH** [ ] [-]
(re-iss. Jul94 cd/c/lp; TOPP CD/MC/LP 5)

Apr 94. (7") *(TOPP 23)* **THING. /** [ ] [-]
(cd-s+=) *(TOPP 23CD)* –

—— now without HOWTON

Mar 95. (10"/cd-s) *(TOPP 31 K/CD)* **WORMEE. /** [ ] [-]

May 95. (cd/c/lp) *(TOPP CD/MC/LP 34)* **BODIES** [ ] [-]

Jul 95. (7") *(TOPP 37)* **ODE TO DRINK. / FASTER (acoustic)** [ ] [-]
(cd-s+=) *(TOPP 37CD)* – Blood / ('A'mix).

Sep 96. (7") *(TOPP 50)* **FUNNYBODY. /** [ ] [-]
(cd-s+=) *(TOPP 50CD)* –

Jan 97. (cd-s) *(TOPP 57CD)* **LIKE YOU / OBSESSIVE** [ ] [-]
(cd-s+=) *(TOPP 57CDX)* – Obsessive (mix).

Apr 97. (cd/lp) *(TOPP CD/LP 53)* **OBSESSIVE** [ ] [-]
– Obsessive / Like you / Funny body / Zazie / Minotaur / Harold and Maude / 20,000 horses / Seams undone / Rat king / Bella / Bridge song.

Chris SIEVEY / Frank SIDEBOTTOM

(see under ⇒ FRESHIES)

SIGUE SIGUE SPUTNIK

Formed: London, England . . .1985 by punk veteran, TONY JAMES who recruited MARTIN DEGVILLE, NEIL X, RAY MAYHEW and CHRIS KAVANAGH. The epitome of 80's philosophy, SIGUE SIGUE SPUTNIK brazenly favoured style over content, adopting a dayglo, designer chic, sci-fi image. Picked up by 'E.M.I.' for a reputed four million pounds, the group revelled in a hype overload not witnessed since The SEX PISTOLS' heyday. If you managed to get past the pink PVC and fishnet stocking masks (no, seriously!), there was the small matter of the actual music, a surprisingly tame and largely cosmetic amalgam of amateur electronics and glam/punk-pop posturing. The kids loved it though, the debut single, 'LOVE MISSILE F1-11' making the UK Top 3 amid a classic Top Of The Pops appearance. To be fair, it was certainly infectious and a damn sight more exciting than the 80's pop chaff clogging up the charts at the time. '21st CENTURY BOY' continued in the same vein, making the Top 20 and preceeding the debut album later that summer, 'FLAUNT IT' (1986). That record remains something of a fascinating period piece, if only for the between song adverts (real!) and will no doubt become highly sought after come the inevitable 80's revival (noooo!, a nation cries in unison). Still, if any band qualified for the '15 minutes of fame' maxim then it was SIGUE SIGUE SPUTNIK, arguably the ultimate in pop-art music. Sure enough, then, a belated follow-up album, 'DRESS FOR EXCESS' (1989) stiffed and the group folded soon after, JAMES proving that he was actually a sad, frustrated goth all along by briefly joining The SISTERS OF MERCY. While KAVANAGH went on to join BIG AUDIO DYNAMITE, DEGVILLE subsequently recorded an abysmal solo effort, 'WORLD WORLD FAIR' (1991) alongside ex-SLAUGHTER & THE DOGS guitarist, MICK ROSSI. • **Songwriters:** TONY JAMES wrote & produced songs. • **Trivia:** TONY JAMES previously produced for goth band SEX GANG CHILDREN.

Album rating: FLAUNT IT (*5)

TONY JAMES (b.1956) – space guitar, bass, producer (ex-GENERATION X) / **MARTIN DEGVILLE** (b.1957) – vocals / **NEAL X** (b. NEAL WHITMORE, 1962) – guitar / **RAY MAYHEW** (b.1965) – drums / **CHRIS KAVANAGH** (b. 4 Jun'64) – drums / **YANA YA YA** (b. JANE FARRIMOND) – sound mixer

Parlophone Manhattan

Feb 86. (7") *(R 5551)* **LOVE MISSILE F1-11. / HACK ATTACK** [3] [ ]
(12"+=) *(12R 5551)* – ('A'extended dance).
(12") – ('A'side) / ('A'mixes).

May 86. (7") *(SSS 2)* **21st CENTURY BOY. / BUY E.M.I.** [20] [-]

Jul 86. (lp/c)(cd) *(PCS/TCPCS 7305)(CDP 7463422) <53033>* **FLAUNT IT** [11] [96]
– Love missile F1-11 / Atari baby / Sex bomb boogie / Rockit Miss U.S.A. / 21st century boy / Massive retaliation / Teenage thunder / She's my man.

Aug 86. (7") **MASSIVE RETALIATION. / TEENAGE THUNDER** [-] [ ]

Dec 86. (video-single) *(MVW 9900642)* **SEX BOMB BOOGIE / LOVE MISSILE F1-11 (US mix)** [ ] [-]

Nov 88. (7") *(SSS 3)* **SUCCESS. / FRANKENSTEIN CHA CHA CHA** [31] [ ]
(12"+=/12"pic-d+=) *(12SSS 3/+P 3)* – Last temptation of Sputnik.
(cd-s++=) *(CDSSS 3)* – Bodaera city

E.M.I. EMI America

Mar 89. (7") *(SSS 5)* **DANCERAMA. / BARBARANDROID** [50] [ ]
(12"/12"pic-)(cd-s) *(12SSS/+PD 5)(CDSSS 5)* – ('A'club mix) / ('A'extended) / ('A'lp mix).

Apr 89. (cd/c/lp) *(CD/TC+/PCS 7328)* **DRESS FOR EXCESS** [53] [ ]
– Albinoni vs. star wars (part 1 & 2) / Boom boom satellite / Hey Jayne Mansfield superstar! / Super crook blues / Success / Dancerama / Orgasm / M.A.D. (Mutual Assured Destruction) / Is this the future?

May 89. (7") *(SSS 4)* **ALBINONI VS. STAR WARS. / ('A'-part 2)** [75] [ ]
(12"+=/cd-s+=) *(12/CD SSS 4)* – ('A'extended).

Jul 89. (7") *(SSS 6)* **RIO ROCKS. / ALIENS** [ ] [ ]
(12"/cd-s) *(12/CD SSS 6)* – ('A'side) / ('A'-samba mix ext.) / ('A'-acid mix).

Jungle R.O.I.R.

Jun 90. (lp/c/cd)<US-c> *(FREUD/+C/CD 035)* **THE FIRST GENERATION** (demos, rarities, some new) [ ] [ ] 1991

— disbanded when TONY JAMES joined The SISTERS OF MERCY. KAVANAGH later went to BIG AUDIO DYNAMITE II.

MARTIN DEGVILLE

— augmented by **MICK ROSSI** – guitar (ex-SLAUGHTER & THE DOGS)

Receiver not iss.

Feb 91. (cd/c/lp) *(RR CD/LC/LP 138)* **WORLD WORLD FAIR** [ ] [-]
– Nuclear powered sex machine / Judge Dread on a BSA / Only the lonely / Saturn 5 / Sexy robot / Transformer transex / Freak show city / Wild is the wind / Space rider / Planet Mars. *(cd+=)* – Sexy robot (skin job remix) / Sexy lover (safe sex remix).

SILICON TEENS (see under ⇒ NORMAL)

SILKWORM

Formed: Missoula, Montana, USA ... 1987 by co-songwriters/vocalists, JOEL PHELPS, ANDREW COHEN and TIM MIDGETT. Three years on, the trio flitted to Seattle, Washington, recruiting drummer MICHAEL DALQUIST in the process. A number of singles found their way to the public, although it took until early '94 for their debut long-player, 'IN THE WEST', to hit the more disering indie shops. The quartet laid bare their influences (such as the MINUTEMEN and PAVEMENT) on the table, although by the time of follow-up, 'LIBERTINE' (1994), producer STEVE ALBINI (ex-BIG BLACK) had moved their hardcore ideals a little further. Following its release however, PHELPS decided to go it alone, leaving the remaining trio (who subsequently signed to 'Matador') to deliver two further sets, the ALBINI-produced 'FIREWATER' (1996) and 'DEVELOPER' (1997). In 1998, with PHELPS back in the line-up, the indie-rock outfit squeezed out two albums, the double-set, 'EVEN A BLIND CHICKEN FINDS A KERNAL OF CORN NOW AND THEN', and 'BLUEBLOOD', the latter their debut for 'Touch & Go'.

Album rating: IN THE WEST (*6) / LIBERTINE (*7) / FIREWATER (*6) / DEVELOPER (*6) / EVEN A CHICKEN FINDS A KERNAL . . . (*6) / BLUEBLOOD (*7)

TIM MIDGETT – vocals, bass / **JOEL PHELPS** – vocals, guitar / **ANDREW COHEN** – vocals, guitar / **MICHAEL DALQUIST** – drums

not iss. unknown

— a number of us singles

not iss. C/Z

Jan 94. (cd,c) *<71>* **IN THE WEST** [-] [ ]
– Garden city blues / Dust my broom / Into the woods / Punch drunk five / Raised by tigers / Enough is enough / Parsons / Incanduce / Dremate / Pilot.

not iss. El Recordo

Aug 94. (cd) *<1>* **LIBERTINE** [-] [ ]
– There is a party in Warsaw tonight / Grotto of miracles / Cotton girl / Yen + Janet forever / Oh how we laughed / Cigarette lighters / Couldn't you wait? / Tunnel / Written on the wind / Wild in my day / Bloody eyes.

Matador Matador

Sep 95. (d7"ep/cd-ep) *<(OLE 154-7/-2)>* **THE MARCO COLLINS SESSIONS** [ ] [ ]
– Couldn't you wait / Scruffy tutor / Cotton girl / Raised by tigers.

Feb 96. (cd/d-lp) *<(OLE 158-2/-1)>* **FIREWATER** [ ] [ ]
– Nerves / Drink / Wet firecracker / Slow hands / Cannibal cannibal / Tarnished angel / Quicksand / Ticket Tulane / Swings / Severence / Lure of beauty / Miracle mile / The river / Killing my ass / Caricature of a joke / Don't make plans this Friday.

Nov 96. (7") *<(OLE 226-7)>* **I NEVER MET A MAN I DIDN'T LIKE. / YOU AIN'T GOING NOWHERE / BLUE PANIC** [ ] [ ]

Apr 97. (cd/lp) *<(OLE 220-2/-1)>* **DEVELOPER** [ ] [ ]
– Give me some skin / Never met a man I didn't like / City glows / Developer / The Devil is beating his wife / Ice Station Zebra / Waiting on a train / Song with one part / Goodnight Mr. Maugham / It's too bad.

Feb 98. (d-cd) *<(OLE 259-2)>* **EVEN A BLIND CHICKEN FINDS A KERNAL OF CORN NOW AND THEN** [ ] [ ]
– Slipstream / Little sister / Scruffy / St. Patrick's day / Homoactivity / Scrawl / Three beatings / Slow burn / Our secret / Chain / Inside outside / Shithead / Slipstream / Scruffy tumour / No revolution / Eye window / Pearl Harbour / Motel blues / Violet / Around a light / In the bleak midwinter / Incanduce California / Insider / Hangman / Smoochy life.

— trimmed down duo of **COHEN + MIDGETT**

Touch & Go Touch & Go

Jul 98. (cd/lp) *<(TG 191 CD/LP)>* **BLUEBLOOD** [ ] [ ]
– Eff / I must prepare (tablecloth tint) / Said it too late / Redeye / Empty elevator shaft / Beyond repair / Tonight we're meat / Ritz dance / Pearly gates / Clean'd me out.

JOEL R.L. PHELPS

— with The DOWNER TRIO:- **ROBERT MERCER + WILLIAM HERZOG**

not iss. El Recordo

Oct 95. (cd) *<3>* **WARM SPRINGS NIGHT** [-] [ ]
(UK-iss.Nov98 on 'Glitterhouse'; GRCD 394)

Pacifico Pacifico

Jun 98. (cd) *<(PAC 07)>* **THE DOWNER TRIO: 3** [ ] [ ]
– Way down / Rev Robert Irving / Hope's hit / Always glide / Give me back my animal / Who can I burn? / Chaplin's radiotelephone / Fifty / Alita aleta / Lull.

SILOS

Formed: New York City, New York, USA . . . 1985 by WALTER SALAS-HUMARA and BOB RUPE, both veterans of the Florida alt-rock scene with outfits such as the VULGAR BOATMEN and the BOBS respectively. Adding MARY ROWELL and the first in a series of fill-in drummers, JOBS ROSS, the duo completed their self-financed debut album, 'ABOUT HER STEPS', a promising set of retro influenced alternative roots-rock. 1987 saw the band turn the corner critically with the independently released 'CUBA', a much loved collection of earthy Americana that subsequently led to The SILOS being farmed out to 'R.C.A.'. The turn of the decade witnessed their major label debut, an eponymous album that didn't quite harvest any mainstream sales. With RUPE bailing out for GUTTERBALL and CRACKER, WALTER was left to plough his own furrow, alternately recording under his own name, as The SILOS or a combination of both. • **Covered:** I'M STRAIGHT (Jonathan Richman).

Album rating: ABOUT HER STEPS (*5) / CUBA (*7) / THE SILOS (*6) / HASTA LA VICTORIA! (*4) / SUSAN ACROSS THE OCEAN (*5)

WALTER SALAS-HUMARA (b.21 Jun'61, New York City) – vocals, guitar (of VULGAR BOATMEN) / **BOB RUPE** (b.16 Sep'56. Michegan) – vocals, guitar (of the BOBS) / **MARY ROWELL** (b. 6 Sep'58, Newport, Vermont) – violin / **JOBS ROSS** – drums

not iss. Record Collect

Aug 85. (lp) *<RC 21>* **ABOUT HER STEPS** [-] [ ]
(UK-iss.Dec87 on Dead Man's Curve'; DMC 020)

Jan 87. (cd-ep) *<RC 23>* **TENNESSEE FIRE / MAYBE EVERYTHING / GET BACK MY NAME / START THE CLOCK** [-] [ ]

— now without ROSS

Ediesta Watermelon

May 87. (lp) *(CALCLP 021) <1022>* **CUBA** [ ] [ ]
– Tennessee fire / She lives up the street / For always / Margaret / Mary's getting married / Memories / Just this morning / Going round / It's alright / All falls away / Get back my name / Maybe everything / Head party / Hook in my lip / Tennessee fire #2. *(cd-iss. Jan88; CALC 021CD) (cd-iss. Jun94 on 'Normal'; NORMAL 123CD)*

— now without ROWELL, although she did return occasionally after below set

not iss. R.C.A.

Feb 90. (cd/lp) *<2051-2R/-1R>* **THE SILOS** [-] [ ]
– Caroline / Picture of Helen / Commodore Peter / Anyway you choose me / Maybe

everything / I'm over you / Take my country back / Out of town / Don't talk that way / The only story I tell / Porque no / Here's to you.

— now without RUPE who went on to work with GUTTERBALL and CRACKER

— the band was now basically **WALTER** + session people. SALAS-HUMARA also moonlighted with ALEJANDRO ESCOVEDO (ex-RANK & FILE, ex-TRUE BELIEVERS) and MIKE HALL (of WILD SEEDS) in a one-off album project with The SETTERS.

Normal Watermelon

May 93. (cd) *(NORMAL 143CD) <1023>* **HASTA LA VICTORIA!**
– Miles away / All I know is your name / Your last life / My big car / Nobody but you / All night / Henrietta / Sometimes when I come over / Find someone / All Spring all Summer / Try tomorrow / Find a way.

May 94. (cd) *(NORMAL 163CD) <1021>* **DIABLO** <US-title 'SUSAN ACROSS THE OCEAN'> Mar94
– Let's take some drugs and drive . . . Upside down instead / Shaking all over the place / All she wrote / Wanna ride / Susan across the ocean / Change the locks / The sounds next door / Start to burn / Nothing's gonna last / I'm straight / Fallen angel.

Jun 95. (cd; The SILOS / WALTER SALAS-HUMARA) *(NORMAL 166CD) <1024>* **ASK THE DUST**
– Shine it down / 4 wanted signs / Susan / A few hundred thank you's / Now that I've lost you / Seeing blue / Heart + soul / Carol / About her steps / Two voices / September / Cuba / Promises / Bridge / You look like Sheila / Don't go home / Nobody's business / Heartbeat / O' fat bass / Thinking about you tonight.

not iss. Last Call

Jun 97. (cd; WALTER SALAS-HUMARA / The SILOS) *<501833>* **LONG GREEN BOAT** [-]
– All falls away / Commodore Peter / Two voices / Just this morning / I'm over you / You look like Sheila / Margaret / Shine it down / Miles away / Your last life / Tennessee fire / Find a way / September / Let's take some drugs and drive . . .

Normal Chequered Past

Aug 98. (cd) *(NORMAL 218CD) <010>* **HEATER**
– Prison song / Northern lights / Thanks a million / Eleanora / Angels / Front porch / Arms of the sea / I like you / Stoplight / Mom out dancing / Cold hands of fate / Away.

WALTER SALAS-HUMARA

Rough Trade Record Collect

Apr 90. (lp/c/cd) *(ROUGH 144/+C/CD) <51>* **LAGARTIJA** Nov88
– Carol / About her steps / Two voices / September / Cuba / Promises / Bridge / You look like Sheila / Don't go home / Wide open.

Normal Watermelon

Jul 94. (cd) *(RTS 9)* **LEAN** [-]

Oct 95. (cd) *<1044>* **RADAR** [-]
– Three, two, one and more / Be honest with me / Evangeline / Letter to send / Light from the box / Star / One more dance / I won, you won / Rejuvenation / Ride / Get out.

SILVERFISH

Formed: London, England . . . 1988 by ANDREW 'FUZZ' DUPREY, who enlisted the help of CHRIS POWFORTH and STUART WATSON to create SIVERFISH in its earliest incarnation. Subsequently installing wild Scotswoman, LESLEY RANKINE as vocalist, the band began gigging around their local Camden stomping ground. With the support of John Peel and a couple of 'Wiiija' EP's under their belt (the eponymous 'SILVERFISH' and the quaintly titled 'TOTAL FUCKING ASSHOLE'), the group released their debut album, 'FAT AXL' early in 1991, its title a reference to a journalistic comment comparing RANKINE to an overweight AXL ROSE (of GUNS N' ROSES fame). Though the group had been pigeonholed in the extremely dubious 'Camden Lurch' scene along with the likes of TH' FAITH HEALERS, SILVERFISH were clearly in a league of their own as a cursory listen to the album would testify. Over a chainsaw barrage of blues-ish guitar noise, RANKINE howled her way from originals like the self-explanatory 'SHIT OUT OF LUCK' to a sound trashing of GRANDMASTER FLASH's classic 'WHITE LINES'. Picked up by 'Creation', SILVERFISH released the brillianlty titled 'FUCKIN' DRIVIN' OR WHAT . . . EP' later that summer to coincide with their triumphant Reading Festival appearance, 'BIG BAD BABY PIG SQUEAL's clarion call of 'HIPS, LIPS, TITS, POWER..' making a SILVERFISH t-shirt de rigeur. An American tour and a JIM THIRLWELL-produced Top 75 follow-up album, 'ORGAN FAN' (1992), ensued, although RANKINE (now living in New Orleans) subsequently left to form her own outfit, RUBY, alongside co-writer MARK WALK. An album, 'SALT PETER', surfaced in late '95, with RANKINE making a brooding, memorable appearance on JOOLS HOLLAND's 'Later..'. • **Songwriters:** Most by RANKINE-DUPREY or group, except ROCK ON (David Essex). • **Trivia:** Their song, 'DOLLY PARTON', contained the thigh-slapping lyrics 'Jolene, Jolene, oh f . . . off'.

Album rating: FAT AXL (*6) / ORGAN FAN (*7) / COCKEYE compilation (*6) / Ruby: SALT PETER (*6)

ANDREW 'FUZZ' DUPREY (b.14 Jun'63, Kent, England) – guitar / **LESLEY RANKINE** (b.11 Apr'65, Edinburgh, Scotland) – vocals / **CHRIS POWFORTH** (b.30 May'64, Middlesex, England) – bass / **STUART WATSON** (b.10 Nov'62, Northamptonshire, England) – drums

Wiiija Touch & Go

Jul 89. (12"ep) *(WIIIJT 4)* **SILVERFISH EP** [-]
– Weird shit / Don't fuck / Dolly Parton / On the motorway.
(re-iss. Feb93 as 'DOLLY PARTON EP'; same)

Feb 90. (7"ep/12"ep) *(WIJ/12WIJ 5)* **TOTAL FUCKING ASSHOLE. / DIE / DRILLER** [-]

Jan 91. (lp/c/cd) *(WIJ 6/+C/CD) <TG 67/+C/CD>* **FAT AXL**
– Pink and lively / Fat painted carcass / Harry Butcher / Shit out of luck / White lines / Two marines / Spoon / Baby baby baby / Ich bin eih- / Schifttek trauser. *(re-iss. Feb93 on 'Southern' cd/c/lp; 18502-2/-4/-1)*

Creation Chaos-CBS

Aug 91. (12"ep)(cd-ep) **F***IN' DRIVIN' OR WHAT . . . E.P.**
– Big bad baby pig squeal / Puppy truck / Texas tea.

— In Nov 91, LESLEY SILVERFISH was credited on 'Clawfist' collaboration with The ROCKINGBIRDS:- 'Your Good Girl's Gonna Go Bad'.

Mar 92. (12"ep)(cd-ep) *(CRE 118T)(CRESCD 118)* **SILVERFISH WITH SCRAMBLED EGGS** [-]
– Crazy / Jimmy / Vitriola / Jenny.

Jun 92. (cd/lp)(c) *(CRE CD/LP 118)(CCRE 118) <53316>* **ORGAN FAN** [65]
– This bug / Mary Brown / Suckin' gas / Petal / Fuckin' strange way to get attention / Big bad baby pig squeal / Elvis leg / Dechainee / Scrub me mama with that boogie beat / Rock on / Joos. *(lp w/free 7")*

Mar 93. (7") *(CRE 138)* **DAMN FINE WOMAN. / SUCKING GAS** [-]
(12"ep)(cd-ep) **DAMN FINE EP** *(CRE 138T)(CRESCD 138)* – ('A'side) / Scrub me mama / Petal / F.S.W.T.G.A.

Jul 93. (cd-s) *<74923>* **CRAZY** [-]

— disbanded later in '93

– compilations, others, etc. –

Aug 90. (lp/c/cd) *Touch & Go; (T&GLP 56/+C/CD)* **COCKEYE**

RUBY

— **LESLEY RANKINE** – vocals (now living New Orleans) with co-writer **MARK WALK** (named after both grandmothers' name)

Creation Sony

Sep 95. (c-s) *(CRECS 165) <78188>* **PARAFFIN / THE WHOLE IS EQUAL TO THE SUM OF IT'S PARTS** Nov95
(cd-s) *(CRESCD 165)* – ('A'-Red Snapper remix) / ('A'-Wagon Christ remix) / ('A'-Dead Elvis remix) / ('A'-Mark Walk remix).
(cd-s) *(CRESCD 165X)* – ('A'-Harpie mix) / ('A'-album version) / ('A'-Wagon Christ vocal) / ('A'-Richard Fearless dub).
(above also issued as 2 x 12"singles; CTP 165/+X)

Oct 95. (cd/lp)(c) *(CRE CD/LP 166)(CCRE 166) <67458>* **SALT PETER** Nov95
– Flippin' tha bird / Salt water fish / Heidi / Tiny meat / Paraffin / Hoops / Pine / Swallow baby / The whole is equal to the sum of its parts / Bud / Carondelet.

Feb 96. (12")(cd-s) *(CRE 173T)(CRESCD 173)* **TINY MEAT (mixes)** [-]
(cd-s) *(CRESCD 173X)* – ('A'remixes).

Apr 96. (cd) *(CRECD 166RL)* **REVENGE – THE SWEETEST FRUIT (SALT PETER remixed)** [-]

May 96. (12")(cd-s) *(CRE 227T)(CRESCD 227)* **HOOPS (mixes)** [-]
(cd-s) *(CRESCD 227X)* – ('A'remixes).

Oct 96. (m-cd) *<67883>* **STROKING THE FULL LENGTH** (remixes) [-]
– Swallow baby / Hoops / Flippin' tha bird / Salt water fish / Tiny meat / The whole is equal to the sum of its parts.

SILVER JEWS

Formed: Virginia, USA . . . 1990 by DAVID BERMAN, co-writer of songs by ROYAL TRUX and PAVEMENT, in fact the latter outfit provided the back-up on that year's SILVER JEWS' debut release, the 'DIME MAP OF THE REEF' EP. After a long-awaited second EP/mini-set in '93, they finally came up with their first long-player, 'STARLITE WALKER' (1994). Released on the 'Drag City' ('Domino' in the UK) label, the album's off-beat alt-country stylings bore at least a spiritual comparison with the likes of PALACE and SMOG although BERMAN's cryptic lyrics and dry, LOU REED-esque vocal delivery distinguished The SILVER JEWS as backporch pioneers in their own right. With a cult fanbase already established through the PAVEMENT connection, the acclaimed follow-up set was feverishly anticipated in some quarters prior to its release in late '96. Critically acclaimed, the record featured some of BERMAN's most affecting compositions to date, not least the brilliant 'HOW TO RENT A ROOM', equal parts offhand cynicism and pained revelation. More please! was the cry and band supplied yet another masterful work with 1998's 'AMERICAN WATER'.

Album rating: ARIZONA RECORD mini (*6) / STARLITE WALKER (*7) / THE NATURAL BRIDGE (*7) / AMERICAN WATER (*7)

DAVID BERMAN – vocals, guitar / with **PAVEMENT** members

Domino Drag City

1990. (cd-ep) *<DC 18>* **DIME MAP OF THE REEF** [-]

1993. (m-cd) *<DC 29>* **ARIZONA RECORD** [-]
– Secret knowledge of backroads / I love the rights / Jackson nightz / War in apartment 1812 / West S / You can't trust it to remain / Wild palms / Welcome to the house of the bats / Bar scene from Star Wars.

Oct 94. (cd/lp) *(WIG CD/LP 15) <DC 55>* **STARLITE WALKER**
– Introduction II / Trains across the sea / The moon is number 18 / Advice to the graduate / Tide to the oceans / Pan American blues / New Orleans / Country diary of a subway conductor / Living waters / Rebel Jew / Silver pageant.

— **BERMAN** retained **MALKMUS** + **NASTANOVICH** plus members of **SCUD MOUNTAIN BOYS** etc

Oct 96. (cd/lp) *(WIG CD/LP 28) <DC 101>* **THE NATURAL BRIDGE**
– How to rent a room / Pet politics / Black and brown blues / Ballad of Reverend war character / Right to remain silent / Dallas / Inside the golden days of missing you / Albemarle station / Frontier index / Pretty eyes.

— now with **MALKMUS** + **MIKE FELLOWS, CHRIS STROFFOLINO** + **TIM BARNES**

Sep 98. (7") *(RUG 77)* **SEND IN THE CLOUDS. / SELF-IGNITION** [-]
(cd-s+=) *(RUG 77CD)* – Walnut falcon (live in 1990).

Oct 98. (cd,c) *<DC 149>* **AMERICAN WATER** [-]
– Random rules / Smith & Jones forever / Night society / Federal dust / People / Blue arrangements / We are real / Send in the clouds / Like like the the the death / Bukingham rabbit / Honk if you're lonely / The wild kindness.

SILVER SUN

Formed: Camden, London, England . . . 1995 as SUN..! by songwriter JAMES BROAD and RICHARD KANE who met at a record store. The pair soon found RICHARD SAYCE and PAUL SMITH, changing their name to SILVER SUN (a German metal band was already named SUN) and signing to 'Polydor' the same year. Fusing JELLYFISH, WEEZER and the anthemic rush of SLADE with sugar-coated indie glam-pop, these post-pubescent alt-rockers scored a minor hit with 'LAVA' towards the end of '96. Early the following year, they cracked the Top 50 with 'LAST DAY', entering a purple patch as they went on to notch up three further hits and a Top 30 eponymous album. However, a summery 1998 cover of Johnny Mathis' (!!!) 'TOO MUCH, TOO LITTLE, TOO LATE' was more attuned to a teeny-pop audience, no doubt putting off many of their more disserning fans and possibly accounting for the lowly chart position (No.74) afforded sophomore effort, 'NEO WAVE' (1998). • **Covered:** XANADU (Rush) / I'M A DICK (Muffs) / YOU MAKE ME REALISE (My Bloody Valentine).

Album rating: SILVER SUN (*6) / NEO WAVE (*5)

JAMES BROAD – vocals / **PAUL SMITH** – guitar, vocals / **RICHARD KANE** – bass, vocals / **RICHARD SAYCE** – drums, vocals

		Polydor	Polygram
Jul 96.	(7"ep/c-ep; as SUN..!) *(575112-7/-4)* **E.P.** – There will never be another me / etc. (cd-ep+=) *(575113-2)* –		-
Oct 96.	(7"/c-s) *(575686-7/-4)* **LAVA. / CHANGING** (cd-s+=) *(575687-2)* – Streets are paved with tarmac.	54	-
Feb 97.	(7"/c-s) *(573242-7/-4)* **LAST DAY. / TRICKLE DOWN** (cd-s+=) *(cd-s+=) (573243-2)* – Gossip.	48	-
Apr 97.	(7"pink) *(573826-7)* **GOLDEN SKIN. / SHE'LL DO** (cd-s) *(573829-2)* – ('A'side) / 17 times / In nature. (cd-s) *(573827-2)* – ('A'side) / Hight times / It couldn't be you.	32	-
May 97.	(cd/c/lp) *(537208-2/-4/-1)* **SILVER SUN** – Test / Golden skin / Dumb / Julia / Far out / Last day / Service / Yellow light / Lava / 2 digits / This 'n' that / Wonderful / Bad haircut / Nobody / Animals feets.	30	-
Jun 97.	(7"/c-s) *(571174-7/-4)* **JULIA. / REASONS TO LIVE** (cd-s+=) *(571175-2)* – American metal. (cd-s) *(571177-2)* – ('A'side) / Angel eyes / Made for you.	51	-
Oct 97.	(7") *(571422-7)* **LAVA. /** (cd-s) *(571422-2)* – (cd-s) *(571424-2)* –	35	-
Jun 98.	(7"/c-s) *(569968-7/-4)* **TOO MUCH, TOO LITTLE, TOO LATE. / XANADU** (cd-s+=) *(569915-2)* – You made me realise / I'm a dick.	20	-
Sep 98.	(c-s) *(<567452-4>)* **I'LL SEE YOU AROUND / MISSED / ('A'acoustic)** (cd-s) *(<567453-2>)* – (first two tracks) / Jessica. (cd-s) *(567455-2)* – (first & third tracks) / Disguise.	26	Nov98
Oct 98.	(cd/c/lp) *(559085-2/-4/-1)* **NEO WAVE** – Cheerleading / I'll see you around / Would've if I could've / Too much, too little, too late / Scared / There goes summer / Sharks / The prophet of the prairie / Mustard / Pixie, pixie / Hey girl friend / Only a girl / Special powers / Fire & blood / Patients / Dead end.	74	-
Nov 98.	(7") *(563118-7)* **SHARKS. / WAYS OF LOVE** (cd-s+=) *(563118-2)* – Hey girlfriend (live). (cd-s) *(563119-2)* – ('A'side) / I can't wait (live) / Animals feet (live). (cd-s) *(563118-4)* – ('A'side) / Too much too little too late / Lava.		-

SIMPLE MINDS

Formed: Gorbals, Glasgow, Scotland . . . early 1978 after four members (frontman JIM KERR, guitarists CHARLIE BURCHILL and DUNCAN BARNWELL and drummer BRIAN McGEE) had left punk band, JOHNNY & THE SELF ABUSERS. Taking the group name from a line in a BOWIE song, the band gigged constantly at Glasgow's Mars Bar, finally being signed on the strength of a demo tape by local Edinburgh music guru and record store owner, Bruce Findlay. Also becoming the band's manager, Findlay released their debut album, 'LIFE IN A DAY' (1979) on his own 'Zoom' label, the record scoring a Top 30 placing. Its minor success led to a deal with 'Arista' who released the follow-up, 'REEL TO REEL CACOPHONY' (1979), a set of post-punk, electronic experimentation best sampled on the evocative synth spirals of 'FILM THEME'. SIMPLE MINDS took another about turn with 'EMPIRES AND DANCE' (1980), an album heavily influenced by the harder end of the Euro-disco movement, the abrasive electro pulse of the 'I TRAVEL' single becoming a cult dancefloor hit. Initially released as a double set, 'SONS AND FASCINATION' / 'SISTER FEELINGS CALL' (1981), marked the first fruits of a new deal with 'Virgin' and gave the group their first major success, peaking at No.11 in the UK chart on the back of the Top 50 single, 'LOVE SONG'. SIMPLE MINDS were beginning to find their niche, incorporating their artier tendencies into more conventional and melodic song structures. This was fully realised with 'NEW GOLD DREAM (81-82-83-84)' (1982), a record which marked the pinnacle of their early career and one which arguably, they've since failed to better. Constructed with multiple layers of synth, the band crafted a wonderfully evocative and atmospheric series of undulating electronic soundscapes, often married to pop hooks, as with 'GLITTERING PRIZE' and 'PROMISED YOU A MIRACLE' (the group's first Top 20 hits), but more effectively allowed to veer off into dreamier territory on the likes of 'SOMEONE SOMEWHERE IN SUMMERTIME'. While SIMPLE MINDS and U2 were often compared in terms of their anthemic tendencies, a closer comparison could be made, in spirit at least, between 'NEW GOLD..' and U2's mid-80's experimental classic, 'The Unforgettable Fire'. The album reached No.3 in the UK charts, a catalyst for SIMPLE MINDS' gradual transformation from an obscure cult act to stadium candidates, this process helped along nicely by the success of 'SPARKLE IN THE RAIN' (1984), the band's first No.1 album. Though it lacked the compelling mystery of its predecessor, the record featured such memorable SIMPLE MINDS' moments as 'UP ON THE CATWALK', 'SPEED YOUR LOVE TO ME' and an inventive cover of Lou Reed's 'SREET HASSLE'. For better or worse, the album also boasted SIMPLE MINDS' first truly BIG anthem, the sonic bombast of 'WATERFRONT'. But the track that no doubt finally alienated the old faithful was 'DON'T YOU (FORGET ABOUT ME)', the theme tune for quintessentially 80's movie, 'The Breakfast Club' and surely one of the most overplayed records of that decade. The song had stadium-friendly written all over it, subsequently scaling the US charts and paving the way for the transatlantic success of 'ONCE UPON A TIME' (1985). Unashamedly going for the commmercial pop/rock jugular, the album was heady, radio orientated stuff, the likes of 'ALIVE AND KICKING', 'SANCTIFY YOURSELF' and 'OH JUNGLELAND' among the most definitive anthems of the stadium rock genre. Predictably, the critics were unimpressed, although they didn't really stick the knife in until the release of the overblown 'BELFAST CHILD', a UK No.1 despite its snoozeworthy meandering and vague political agenda. The accompanying album, 'STREET FIGHTING YEARS' (1989) brought more of the same, although it cemented SIMPLE MINDS' position among the coffee table elite. Down to a trio of KERR, BURCHILL and and drummer, MEL GAYNOR, the group hired a team of session players for their next album, 'REAL LIFE' (1991), the record almost spawning a Top 5 hit in the celebratory 'LET THERE BE LOVE'. Although the album narrowly missed the UK top spot, it held nothing new, nor did their most recent release, 'GOOD NEWS FROM THE NEXT WORLD' (1995). You can't help feeling a little sorry for JIM KERR, not only does a young pretender like LIAM GALLAGHER hook up with his wife (PATSY KENSIT), but his band have become something of an anachronism in the ever changing world of 90's music. While U2 have at least made an attempt to move with the times, however embaressing, SIMPLE MINDS' sound is so deeply rooted in the 80's that it seems inconceivable they could ever make any kind of relevant departure. • **Songwriters:** All group compositions or KERR-BURCHILL. Covered BIKO (Peter Gabriel) / SIGN O' THE TIMES (Prince) / DON'T YOU FORGET ABOUT ME (Keith Forsey-Steve Chiff). • **Trivia:** On the 5th May'84, JIM KERR married CHRISSIE HYNDE. SIMPLE MINDS have played both LIVE AID and MANDELA DAY concerts in 1985 and 1988 respectively.

Album rating: GLITTERING PRIZE 81-91 (*9) / CELEBRATION (*7) / EMPIRES AND DANCE (*8) / SONS AND FASCINATION (*8) / NEW GOLD DREAM (*8) / ONCE UPON A TIME (*7) / SPARKLE IN THE RAIN (*8) / LIFE IN A DAY (*7)

JOHNNY & THE SELF ABUSERS

JIM KERR (b. 9 Jul'59) – vocals / **CHARLIE BURCHILL** (b.27 Nov'59) – guitar / **DUNCAN BARNWELL** – guitar / **BRIAN McGEE** – drums / + 3 future CUBAN HEELS members.

		Chiswick	not iss.
Nov 77.	(7") *(NS 22)* **SAINTS AND SINNERS. / DEAD VANDALS**		-

SIMPLE MINDS

—— (KERR, BURCHILL, McGEE) recruited **MICK McNEILL** (b.20 Jul'58) – keyboards / **DEREK FORBES** (b.22 Jun'56) – bass

		Zoom	not iss.
Apr 79.	(7") *(ZUM 10)* **LIFE IN A DAY. / SPECIAL VIEW**	62	-
Apr 79.	(lp) *(ZULP 1)* **LIFE IN A DAY** – Someone / Life in a day / Sad affair / All for you / Pleasantly disurbed / No cure / Chelsea girl / Wasteland / Destiny / Murder story. *(re-iss. Oct82 on 'Virgin' lp/c; VM/+C 6) (re-iss. 1985 on 'Virgin' lp/c; OVED/+C 95) (cd-iss. Jul86; VMCD 6)*	30	-
Jun 79.	(7") *(ZUM 11)* **CHELSEA GIRL. / GARDEN OF HATE**		-
		Arista	Arista
Nov 79.	(lp/c) *(SPART/TC-SPART 1109)* **REAL TO REAL CACOPHONY** – Real to real / Naked eye / Citizen (dance of youth) / Carnival (shelter in a suitcase) / Factory / Cacophony / Veldt / Premonition / Changeling / Film theme / Calling your name / Scar. *(re-iss. Oct82 on 'Virgin' lp/c; V/TCV 2246) (re-iss. 1985 on 'Virgin' lp/c; OVED/+C 124) (cd-iss. May88; CDV 2246)*		
Jan 80.	(7") *(ARIST 325)* **CHANGELING. / PREMONITION (live)**		-
Sep 80.	(lp/c) *(SPART/TC-SPART 1140)* **EMPIRES AND DANCE** – I travel / Today I died again / Celebrate / This fear of gods / Capital city / Constantinople line / Twist-run-repulsion / Thirty frames a seconds / Kant-kino / Room. *(re-iss. Oct82 on 'Virgin' lp/c; V/TCV 2247) (cd-iss. May88; CDV 2247)*	41	
Oct 80.	(7") *(ARIST 372)* **I TRAVEL. / NEW WARM SKIN** (w/ free 7"blue flexi) – KALEIDOSCOPE / FILM DUB THEME (12") *(ARIST 12-372)* – ('A'side) / Film dub theme.		
Feb 81.	(7") *(ARIST 394)* **CELEBRATE. / CHANGELING (live)** (12"+=) *(ARIST 12-394)* – I travel (live).		
		Virgin	A&M
May 81.	(7"/remix.12") *(VS 410/+12)* **THE AMERICAN. / LEAGUE OF NATIONS**	59	-

—— **KENNY HYSLOP** (b.14 Feb'51, Helensburgh, Scotland) – drums (ex-SKIDS, ex-ZONES, ex-SLIK) repl. McGEE, who in 1994 became a songwriter for LES McKEOWN (ex-BAY CITY ROLLERS)

Aug 81.	(7"/12") *(VS 434/+12)* **LOVE SONG. / THE EARTH THAT YOU WALK UPON (instrumental)**	47	-
Sep 81.	(2xlp/d-c) *(V/TCV 2207)* **SONS AND FASCINATION / SISTER FEELINGS CALL** – SONS AND FASCINATION – In trance as mission / Sweat in bullet / 70 cities as love brings the fall / Boys from Brazil / Love song / This Earth that you walk upon / Sons and fascination / Seeing out the angels. SISTER FEELINGS CALL – Theme for great cities * / The American / 20th Century promised land / Wonderful in young life / League of nations / Careful in career / Sound in 70 cities. *(issued*	11	

separately Oct81; V 2207 / OVED 2) (cd-iss. Apr86 + Apr90; CDV 2207) – (omits tracks *)

Oct 81. (7") *(VS 451)* **SWEAT IN BULLET. / 20th CENTURY PROMISED LAND** [52] [-]
(d7"+=) *(VSD 451)* – League of nations (live) / Premonition (live).
(12"+=) *(VS 451-12)* – League of nations (live) / In trance as mission (live).

Apr 82. (7") *(VS 488)* **PROMISED YOU A MIRACLE. / THEME FOR GREAT CITIES** [13] [-]
(12"+=) *(VS 488-12)* – Seeing out the angel (instrumental mix).

— **MIKE OGLETREE** – drums repl. HYSLOP who formed SET THE TONE

Aug 82. (7"/12") *(VS 511/+12)* **GLITTERING PRIZE. / GLITTERING THEME** [16] [ ]

— **MEL GAYNOR** (b.29 May'59) – drums (ex-sessions) repl. MIKE who joined FICTION FACTORY

Sep 82. (lp/c)<gold-lp> *(V/TCV 2230)* *<4928>* **NEW GOLD DREAM (81-82-83-84)** [3] [69] Jan83
– Someone, somewhere in summertime / Colours fly and the Catherine wheel / Promised you a miracle / Big sleep / Somebody up there likes you / New gold dream (81-82-83-84) / Glittering prize / Hunter and the hunted / King is white and in the crowd. *(cd-iss. Jul83 & Apr92; CDV 2230) (re-iss. Apr92 lp/c; OVED/+C 393)*

Nov 82. (7"/7"pic-d) *(VS/+Y 538)* **SOMEONE, SOMEWHERE IN SUMMERTIME. / KING IS WHITE AND IN THE CROWD** [36] [ ]
(12"+=) *(VS 538-12)* – Soundtrack for every Heaven.

Nov 82. (7") **PROMISED YOU A MIRACLE. / THE AMERICAN** [-] [ ]

Nov 83. (7"/12") *(VS 636/+12)* **WATERFRONT. / HUNTER AND THE HUNTED (live)** [13] [ ]

Jan 84. (7"/7"pic-d) *(VS/+Y 649)* **SPEED YOUR LOVE TO ME. / BASS LINE** [20] [ ]
(12"+=) *(VS 649-12)* – ('A'extended).

Feb 84. (cd/c/lp,white-lp) *(CD/TC+/V 2300)* *<4981>* **SPARKLE IN THE RAIN** [1] [64]
– Up on the catwalk / Book of brilliant things / Speed your love to me / Waterfront / East at Easter / White hot day / Street hassle / "C" Moon cry like a baby / The kick inside of me / Shake off the ghosts. *(re-iss. cd Mar91; same)*

Mar 84. (7"/7"pic-d)(12") *(VS/+Y 661)(VS 661-12)* **UP ON THE CATWALK. / A BRASS BAND IN AFRICA** [27] [ ]

Apr 85. (7"/7"sha-pic-d)(12") *(VS/+S 749)(VS 749-12)* *<2703>* **DON'T YOU (FORGET ABOUT ME). / A BRASS BAND IN AFRICA** [7] [1] Feb85
(re-iss. Jun88 cd-s; CDT 2)

— **KERR, BURCHILL, McNEILL + GAYNOR** brought in new member **JOHN GIBLING** – bass (ex-PETER GABRIEL sessions) to repl. FORBES

Oct 85. (7"/12") *(VS 817/+12)* **ALIVE AND KICKING. / ('A'instrumental)** [7] [-]
(12"+=) *(VS 817-13)* – Up on the catwalk (live).

Oct 85. (cd/c/lp,pic-lp) *(CD/TC+/V 2364)* *<5092>* **ONCE UPON A TIME** [1] [10]
– Once upon a time / All the things she said / Ghost dancing / Alive and kicking / Oh jungleland / I wish you were here / Sanctify yourself / Come a long way.

Oct 85. (7") *<2783>* **ALIVE AND KICKING. / UP ON THE CATWALK (live)** [-] [3]

Jan 86. (7") *(SM 1)* *<2810>* **SANCTIFY YOURSELF. / ('A'instrumental)** [10] [14]
(d7"+=) *(SMP 1)* – Love song (live) / Street hassle (live).
(12") *(SM 1-12)* – ('A'mix). / ('A'dub instrumental).

Apr 86. (7") *(VS 860)* *<2828>* **ALL THE THINGS SHE SAID. / DON'T YOU (FORGET ABOUT ME)** [9] [28]
(12"+=) *(VS 860-12)* – Promised you a miracle (US mix).

Nov 86. (7") *(VS 907)* **GHOSTDANCING. / JUNGLELAND (instrumental)** [13] [ ]
(12"+=/cd-s+=) *(VS/MIKE 907-12)* – ('A'instrumental) / ('B'instrumental).

May 87. (d-cd/d-c/d-lp) *(CDVSM/SMDCX/SMDLX 1)* *<6850>* **LIVE IN THE CITY OF LIGHT (live)** [1] [96] Jul87
– Ghostdancing / Big sleep / Waterfront / Promised you a miracle / Someone somewhere in summertime / Oh jungleland / Alive and kicking / Don't you (forget about me) / Once upon a time / Book of brilliant things / East at Easter / Sanctify yourself / Love song / Sun City – Dance to the music / New gold dream (81-82-83-84).

Jun 87. (7"/10") *(SM 2/+10)* **PROMISED YOU A MIRACLE (live). / BOOK OF BRILLIANT THINGS (live)** [19] [ ]
(12"+=/c-s+=) *(SM/+C 2-12)* – Glittering prize (live) / Celebrate (live).

— **KERR, BURCHILL + McNEILL** were basic trio, w/other 2 still sessioning.

Feb 89. (7") *(SMX 3)* **BELFAST CHILD. / MANDELA DAY** [1] [ ]
(c-s+=/12"ep+=/12"box-ep+=/cd-ep+=) **BALLAD OF THE STREETS** *(SMX C/T/C/CD 3)* – Biko.

Apr 89. (7") *(SMX 4)* **THIS IS YOUR LAND. / SATURDAY GIRL** [13] [ ]
(c-s+=/12"+=/12"g-f+=/3"cd-s+=) *(SMX C/T/TG/CD 4)* – Year of the dragon.

May 89. (cd/c/lp) *(MIND D/C/S 1)* *<3927>* **STREET FIGHTING YEARS** [1] [70]
– Soul crying out / Wall of love / This is your land / Take a step back / Kick it in / Let it all come down / Biko / Mandela day / Belfast child / Street fighting years. *(re-iss. Dec89 box-cd/c +=; SMBX D/C 1)* – (interview cassettes).

Jul 89. (7"/c-s) *(SMX/+C 5)* **KICK IT IN. / WATERFRONT ('89 mix)** [15] [ ]
(12"+=/cd-s+=) *(SMX T/CD 5)* – Big sleep (live).
(12"g-f+=) *(SMXTG 5)* – ('A'mix).

Dec 89. (7"ep/c-ep/12"ep/cd-ep) *(SMX/+C/T/CD 6)* **THE AMSTERDAM EP** [18] [ ]
– Let it all come down / Sign o' the times / Jerusalem.
(12"ep+=/cd-ep+=) *(SMX TR/X 6)* – Sign o' the times (mix).

— **KERR, BURCHILL + GAYNOR** brought in sessioners **MALCOLM FOSTER** – bass / **PETER JOHN VITESSE** – keyboards / **STEPHEN LIPSON** – bass, keyboards / **ANDY DUNCAN** – percussion / **GAVIN WRIGHT** – string leader / **LISA GERMANO** – violin

Mar 91. (7"/c-s) *(VS/+C 1332)* **LET THERE BE LOVE. / GOODNIGHT** [6] [ ]
(12"+=) *(VST 1332)* – Alive and kicking (live).
(cd-s++=) *(VSCD 1332)* – East at Easter (live).

Apr 91. (cd/c/lp) *(CD/TC+/V 2660)* *<5352>* **REAL LIFE** [2] [74]
– Real life / See the lights / Let there be love / Woman / Stand by love / African skies / Let the children speak / Ghostrider / Banging on the door / Travelling man / Rivers of ice / When two worlds collide.

May 91. (7"/c-s) *(VS/+C 1343)* **SEE THE LIGHTS. / THEME FOR GREAT CITIES ('91 edit)** [20] [-]
(12"+=/cd-s+=) *(VS T/CD 1343)* – Soul crying out (live).

May 91. (c-s,cd-s) *<1553>* **SEE THE LIGHTS / GOODNIGHT** [-] [40]

Aug 91. (7"/c-s) *(VS/+C 1358)* **STAND BY LOVE. / KING IS WHITE AND IN THE CROWD (live)** [13] [ ]
(12"+=/cd-s+=) *(VS T/CD 1358)* – Let there be love (live).

Oct 91. (7"/c-s) *(VS/+C 1382)* **REAL LIFE. / SEE THE LIGHTS** [34] [ ]
(ext.12"+=) *(VST 1382)* – Belfast child (extended).
(cd-s++=) *(VSCD 1382)* – Ghostrider.

Oct 92. (7"/c-s) *(VS/+C 1440)* **LOVE SONG. / ALIVE AND KICKING** [6] [ ]
(ext.cd-s+=) *(VSCDG 1440)* – ('B'instrumental).
(cd-s+=) *(VSCDX 1440)* – Travelling man / Oh jungleland.

Oct 92. (cd/c/lp) *(SMTV D/C/S 1)* **GLITTERING PRIZE – SIMPLE MINDS 81-92** (compilation) [1] [-]
– Waterfront / Don't you (forget about me) / Alive and kicking / Sanctify yourself / Love song / Someone somewhere in summertime / See the lights / Belfast child / The American / All the things she said / Promised you a miracle / Ghostdancing / Speed your love to me / Glittering prize / Let there be love / Mandela Day.

— **KERR + BURCHILL** with guests MARK BROWNE, MALCOLM FOSTER, MARCUS MILLER + LANCE MORRISON – bass / MARK SCHULMAN, TAL BERGMAN + VINNIE COLAIUTA – drums

Virgin Virgin

Jan 95. (7"/c-s/cd-s) *(VS/+C/+DG 1509)* *<38467>* **SHE'S A RIVER. / E55 / ('A'mix)** [9] [52]
(cd-s) *(VSCDX 1509)* – ('A'side) / Celtic strings / ('A'mix).

Jan 95. (cd/c/lp) *(CD/TC+/V 2760)* *<39922>* **GOOD NEWS FROM THE NEXT WORLD** [2] [87]
– She's a river / Night music / Hypnotised / Great leap forward / 7 deadly sins / And the band played on / My life / Criminal world / This time.

Mar 95. (7"/c-s) *(VS/+C 1534)* **HYPNOTISED. / #4** [18] [-]
(cd-s+=) *(VSCDX 1534)* – ('A'-Tim Simenon extended remixes) / ('A'-Malfunction mix).
(cd-s) *(VSCDT 1534)* – ('A'side) / Up on the catwalk (live) / And the band played on (live) / She's a river (live).

— **KERR + BURCHILL** brought back **DEREK FORBES** – bass / **MEL GAYNOR** – drums / also **HAMI LEE** – additional programming

Chrysalis not iss.

Mar 98. (c-s) *(TCCHS 5078)* **GLITTERBALL / WATERFRONT (Union Jack mix)** [18] [-]
(cd-s+=) *(CDCHSS 5078)* – Love song (Philadelphia Bluntz mix).
(cd-s) *(CDCHS 5078)* – ('A'side) / Don't you forget about me (Jam & Spoon mix) / Theme for great cities (Fila Brazillia mix).

Mar 98. (cd/c) *(493712-2/-4)* **NEAPOLIS** [19] [-]
– Song for the tribes / Glitterball / War babies / Tears of a guy / Superman v supersoul / Lightning / If I had wings / Killing Andy Warhol / Androgyny.

May 98. (ext;c-s/7") *(TC+/CHS 5088)* **WAR BABIES. / I TRAVEL (Utah Saints mix)** [43] [-]
('A'-Bascombe mix;cd-s+=) *(CDCHS 5088)* – Theme for great cities '98 (Fluke's Atlantis mix) / ('A'-Johnson Somerset extended mix).

– compilations, others, etc. –

on 'Virgin' unless otherwise mentioned

Jan 82. (7") *Arista; (ARIST 448)* **I TRAVEL. / THIRTY FRAMES A SECOND (live)** [ ] [-]
(12"+=) *(ARIST12 448)* – ('A'live).

Feb 82. (lp/c) *Arista; (SPART/TCSPART 1183)* **CELEBRATION** [45] [ ]
(re-iss. Oct82 on 'Virgin' lp/c; V/TCV 2248) (re-iss. Apr89 on 'Virgin' lp/c; OVED/+C 275) (cd-iss. Aug89; CDV 2248)

Apr 83. (12") *(VS 578-12)* **I TRAVEL (mix). / FILM THEME** [ ] [-]

Aug 90. (5xcd-box-ep) **THEMES – VOLUME ONE** [ ] [ ]
– (Apr79 – LIFE IN A DAY – Apr82 – PROMISED YOU A MIRACLE singles)

Sep 90. (5xcd-box-ep) **THEMES – VOLUME TWO** [ ] [ ]
– (Aug82 – GLITTERING PRIZE – Apr85 – DON'T YOU (FORGET ABOUT ME) singles)

Oct 90. (5xcd-box-ep) **THEMES – VOLUME THREE** [ ] [ ]
– (Oct85 – ALIVE AND KICKING – Jun87 – PROMISED YOU A MIRACLE (live) singles)

Nov 90. (5xcd-box-ep) **THEMES – VOLUME FOUR** [ ] [ ]
– (Feb89 – BELFAST CHILD, Dec89 – THE AMSTERDAM EP)

Nov 90. (3xcd-box) *(TPAK 2)* **COLLECTOR'S EDITION** [ ] [-]
– (LIFE IN A DAY / REEL TO REAL CACOPHONY / EMPIRES AND DANCE)

SINK (see under ⇒ STUPIDS)

SIOUXSIE & THE BANSHEES

Formed: London, England . . . September '76 by SIOUXSIE SIOUX and STEVE SEVERIN, both members of the infamous 'Bromley Contingent' punk troupe who religiously followed The SEX PISTOLS during the turbulent early years of their career; an early incarnation of The BANSHEES even featured future PISTOL, SID VICIOUS on drums, the outfit mangling the Lord's Prayer at the legendary 100 Club punk all-dayer in summer '76. SIOUX gained further notoriety following her appearance (as a fan) on the fateful edition of Bill Grundy's 'Today' programme wherein his tete-a-tete with the 'PISTOLS outraged the country's more upstanding citizens. Cutting a striking dash through the punk scene with her Nazi chic and proto-goth garb, SIOUXSIE and her BANSHEES (who, after much to-ing and fro-ing, were eventually completed by JOHN McKAY amd KENNY MORRIS) toured constantly throughout 1977, eventually signing to 'Polydor' the following year after their original label, 'Track', went bust. A debut single, 'HONG KONG GARDEN' was a sprightly slice of oriental flavoured post-punk which hit the Top 10 with ease and introduced the band outwith the confines of the

London scene. 'THE SCREAM' (1978) was instantly hailed as a classic upon its release a few months later, the record's queasy, churning goth-psychedelia breaking new ground and spearheading a new direction for many bands inspired by a movement already dying on its feet. For many recent converts, then, 'JOIN HANDS' (1979) was a disappointment, a turgid affair which lacked the bite of its predecessor and presaged a band breakdown; McKAY and MORRIS upped sticks and left mid-tour, ROBERT SMITH (The CURE) briefly deputising before a new guitarist was eventually found in erstwhile MAGAZINE man, JOHN McGEOGH. The drum seat, meanwhile, was taken by ex-SLITS man, BUDGIE, who would subsequently become SIOUXSIE's beau and eventual husband. The revamped line-up bounced back in 1980 with the enchanting 'HAPPY HOUSE' (a Top 20 hit that Spring) and an accompanying Top 5 album, 'KALEIDOSCOPE', investing their sound with a newly acquired accessibility and ensuring a degree of crossover success for SIOUXSIE's icy sensuality. 'JU JU' (1981) further refined the group's subtle gothic tapestries, again taking the band into the UK Top 10 and spawning a clutch of minor hits while 'ONCE UPON A TIME – THE SINGLES' neatly rounded up the first instalment in The BANSHEES' career. More overtly experimental was the following year's 'A KISS IN THE DREAMHOUSE', utilising strings and flirting with club sounds. 1983 saw a flurry of side project activity as SIOUXSIE and BUDGIE formed The CREATURES, releasing 'FEAST', the first of two albums together (they also had a major hit with Mel Torme's 'RIGHT NOW'). SEVERIN, meanwhile, formed The GLOVE with SMITH (who had also rejoined the BANSHEES ranks as a part-time, temporary replacement for the departing McGEOGH), releasing the 'BLUE SUNSHINE' album the same year. No new BANSHEES material surfaced, although an atmospheric cover of The Beatles' 'DEAR PRUDENCE' hit No.3 and gave them their biggest selling single to date. The track featured on 1983's live set, 'NOCTURNE', while the following year's 'HYAENA', saw SMITH making his presence felt over the course of a haunting set that was unfairly panned by the critics. With SMITH subsequently finding the demands of a dual lifestyle too tiring, ex-CLOCKDVA man, JOHN CARRUTHERS was drafted in for 'TINDERBOX' (1986), an album which carried on in much the same vein, spawning a sizeable hit with the infectious 'CITIES IN DUST'. Perhaps the band really were running out of ideas as their detractors suggested, a suitably gothic Top 20 rendition of Bob Dylan's 'THIS WHEEL'S ON FIRE' trailing a whole album's worth of competent but hardly inspiring cover versions. Featuring yet another guitarist, JON KLEIN, 1988's 'PEEPSHOW' was a much more compelling proposition, a perversely eclectic selection best sampled on the mutant dancefloor hit, 'PEEK-A-BOO'. Now something of an alternative institution, SIOUXSIE & THE BANSHEES cruised into the 90's with their most chart-friendly original material to date, the swooning 'KISS THEM FOR ME' (the band's first – and to date only – major US hit) single and attendant 'SUPERSTITION' (1991) album. Despite the latter set's commercial and critical success, the group reached the end of its natural lifespan in the mid-90's, bowing out on a high with the majestic 'THE RAPTURE'. Officially splitting in April '96, SIOUXSIE is rumoured to be working on new CREATURES material with spouse BUDGIE, while SEVERIN scored the soundtrack for the movie, 'Visions Of Ecstacy'. • **Songwriters:** All written by SIOUXSIE / SEVERIN except; HELTER SKELTER (Beatles) / 20th CENTURY BOY (T.Rex) / IL EST NE LE DIVIN ENFANT (French festive song) / ALL TOMORROW'S PARTIES (Velvet Underground). THROUGH THE LOOKING GLASS was a covers album containing THE PASSENGER (Iggy Pop) / YOU'RE LOST LITTLE GIRL (Doors) / GUN (John Cale) / THIS TOWN AIN'T BIG ENOUGH FOR THE BOTH OF US (Sparks) / SEA BREEZES (Roxy Music) / STRANGE FRUIT (Billie Holiday) / WALL OF MIRRORS (Kraftwerk) / LITTLE JOHNNY JEWEL (Television) / TRUST IN ME ('Jungle Book' animated film). • **Trivia:** SEVERIN produced ALTERED IMAGES debut 45 'Dead Pop Stars'.

Album rating: THE SCREAM (*9) / JOIN HANDS (*7) / KALEIDOSCOPE (*7) / HYAENA (*8) / JU JU (*7) / ONCE UPON A TIME – THE SINGLES compilation (*9) / TWICE UPON A TIME compilation (*7) / A KISS IN THE DREAMHOUSE (*7)

SIOUXSIE SIOUX (b. SUSAN DALLION, 27 May'57) – vocals / **STEVEN SEVERIN** (b. STEVEN BAILEY, 25 Sep'55) – bass / **JOHN McKAY** – guitar repl. PT FENTON who had repl. MARCO PIRRONI (he joined MODELS and later ADAM & THE ANTS) / **KENNY MORRIS** – drums repl. SID VICIOUS who later became bassman for SEX PISTOLS

Polydor Polydor

Aug 78. (7") *(2059 052)* **HONG KONG GARDEN. / VOICES** [7] [-]

Oct 78. (7") **HONG KONG GARDEN. / OVERGROUND** [-] [ ]

Nov 78. (lp/c) *(POLD/+C 5009) <6207>* **THE SCREAM** [12] [ ]
– Pure / Jigsaw feeling / Overground / Carcass / Helter skelter / Mirage / Metal postcard / Nicotine stain / Suburban relapse / Switch. *(cd-iss. Mar89 & Mar95 on 'Wonderland'; 839 008-2) (cd re-iss. Mar95)*

Mar 79. (7") *(POSP 9)* **THE STAIRCASE (MYSTERY). / 20th CENTURY BOY** [24] [-]

Jun 79. (7") *(POSP 59)* **PLAYGROUND TWIST. / PULLED TO BITS** [28] [-]

Sep 79. (lp/c) *(POLD/+C 5024)* **JOIN HANDS** [13] [-]
– Poppy day / Regal zone / Placebo effect / Icon / Premature burial / Playground twist / Mother / Oh mein papa / The Lord's prayer. *(cd-iss. Mar89 & Mar95 on 'Wonderland'; 839004-2)*

Sep 79. (7") *(2059 151)* **MITTAGEISEN (METAL POSTCARD). / LOVE IN A VOID** [47] [-]

— **BUDGIE** (b.PETER CLARK, 21 Aug'57, St.Helens, England) – drums (ex-SLITS, ex-PLANETS, ex-BIG IN JAPAN, etc.) repl. MORRIS who bailed out (he subsequently released a solo 12", 'LA MAIN MORTE', for 'Temple' records in '86) / **JOHN McGEOGH** (b. 1955, Greenock, Scotland) – guitar (of MAGAZINE) finally repl. ROBERT SMITH (of The CURE) + JOHN CARRUTHERS who repl. McKAY (he finally formed ZOR GABOR in 1986 – with vocalist LINDA CLARK – and released one single, 'TIGHTROPE', for 'In-Tape' early '87)

Mar 80. (7") *(POSP 117)* **HAPPY HOUSE. / DROP DEAD** [17] [-]

May 80. (7") *(2059 249)* **CHRISTINE. / EVE WHITE EVE BLACK** [24] [-]

Aug 80. (lp)(c) *(2442 177)(3184 146)* **KALEIDOSCOPE** [5] [-]
– Happy house / Tenant / Trophy / Hybrid / Lunar camel / Christine / Desert kisses / Red light / Paradise place / Skin. *(cd-iss. Mar89 & Mar95 on 'Wonderland'; 839006-2)*

Nov 80. (7"/dance-12") *(POSP/+X 205)* **ISRAEL. / RED OVER WHITE** [41] [-]

May 81. (7") *(POSP 273)* **SPELLBOUND. / FOLLOW THE SUN** [22] [-]
(12"+=) *(POSPX 273)* – Slap dash snap.

Jun 81. (lp/c) *(POLS/+C 1034)* **JU JU** [7] [-]
– Spellbound / Into the light / Arabian knights / Halloween / Monitor / Night shift / Sin in my heart / Head cut / Voodoo dolly. *(cd-iss. Mar89 & Mar95 on 'Wonderland'; 839005-2)*

Jul 81. (7") *(POSP 309)* **ARABIAN KNIGHTS. / SUPERNATURAL THING** [32] [-]
(12"+=) *(POSPX 309)* – Congo conga.

— SIOUXSIE & BUDGIE as The CREATURES hit Top 30 with WILD THINGS EP.

Dec 81. (lp/c) *(POLS/+C 1056)* **ONCE UPON A TIME – THE SINGLES** [21] [-]
– Hong Kong garden / Mirage / The staircase (mystery) / Playground twist / Happy house / Christine / Israel / Spellbound / Arabian knights / Fireworks. *(cd-iss. Mar89 on 'Wonderland'; 831542-2)*

May 82. (7") *(POSPG 450)* **FIREWORKS. / COAL MIND** [22] [-]
(12"+=) *(POSPX 450)* – We fall.

Sep 82. (7") *(POSP 510)* **SLOWDIVE. / CANNIBAL ROSES** [41] [-]
(12"+=) *(POSPX 510)* – Obsession II.

Nov 82. (lp/c) *(POLD/+C 5064)* **A KISS IN THE DREAMHOUSE** [11] [-]
– Cascade / Green fingers / Obsession / She's a carnival / Circle / Melt! / Painted bird / Cocoon / Slowdive. *(cd-iss. Apr89 & Mar 95 on 'Wonderland'; 839007-2)*

Nov 82. (7") *(POSP 539)* **MELT! / IL EST NE LE DIVIN ENFANT** [49] [ ]
(12"+=) *(POSPX 539)* – A sleeping rain.

— **ROBERT SMITH** – guitar (of The CURE) returned part-time to repl. McGEOGH who later joined The ARMOURY SHOW.

— In 1983, SMITH and SEVERIN had also splintered into The GLOVE, with SIOUXSIE and BUDGIE re-uniting as The CREATURES (see further on).

Wonderland – Polydor Geffen

Sep 83. (7") *(SHEG 4)* **DEAR PRUDENCE. / TATTOO** [3] [-]
(12"+=) *(SHEX 4)* – There's a planet in my kitchen.

Nov 83. (d-lp/c) *(SHAH/+C 1)* **NOCTURNE (live)** [29] [-]
– Intro – The rite of Spring / Israel / Dear Prudence / Paradise place / Melt! / Cascade / Pulled to bits / Night shift / Sin in my heart / Slowdive / Painted bird / Happy house / Switch / Spellbound / Helter skelter / Eve white eve black / Voodoo dolly. *(cd-iss. Apr89 & Mar95; 839009-2)*

Mar 84. (7") *(SHE 6)* **SWIMMING HORSES. / LET GO** [28] [-]
(12"+=) *(SHEX 6)* – The humming wires.

May 84. (7") *(SHE 7)* **DAZZLE. / I PROMISE** [33] [-]
(12"+=) *(SHEX 7)* – Throw them to the lions / ('A'mix).

Jun 84. (lp/c)(cd) *(SHEH P/C 1)(821510-2) <24030>* **HYAENA** [15] [ ]
– Dazzle / We hunger / Take me back / Belladonna / Swimming horses / Bring me the head of the preacher man / Running town / Pointing bone / Blow the house down. *(re-iss. cd Mar95; same)*

— **JOHN CARRUTHERS** – guitar (ex-CLOCKDVA, ex-JEFFREY LEE PIERCE) returned to repl. SMITH who had CURE commitments.

Oct 84. (12"ep) *(SHEEP 8)* **THE THORN (live)** [47] [-]
– Voices / Placebo effect / Red over white / Overground.

Oct 85. (7") *(SHE 9)* **CITIES IN DUST. / AN EXECUTION** [21] [-]
(12"+=) *(SHEX 9)* – Quarter drawing of the dog.

Feb 86. (7") *(SHE 10)* **CANDYMAN. / LULLABY** [34] [-]
(12"+=) *(SHEX 10)* – Umbrella.

Apr 86. (lp/c)(cd) *(SHE LP/MC 3)(829145-2) <24092>* **TINDERBOX** [13] [88]
– Candyman / The sweetest chill / This unrest / Cities in dust / Cannons / Partys fall / 92° / Lands End. *(cd+=)* – An execution / Quarter drawing of the dog / Lullaby / Umbrella / Candyman (extended). *(re-iss. cd Mar95; same)*

Jan 87. (7") *(SHE 11)* **THIS WHEEL'S ON FIRE. / SHOOTING SUN** [14] [-]
(12"+=) *(SHEX 11)* – Sleepwalking (on the high wire).

Feb 87. (lp/c)(cd) *(SHE LP/MC 3)(831474-2) <24134>* **THROUGH THE LOOKING GLASS** [15] [ ]
– Hall of mirrors / Trust in me / This wheel's on fire / Strange fruit / This town ain't big enough for the both of us / You're lost little girl / The passenger / Gun / Sea breezes / Little Johnny Jewel. *(re-iss. cd Mar95; same)*

Mar 87. (7") *(SHE 12)* **THE PASSENGER. / SHE'S CUCKOO** [41] [-]
(12"+=) *(SHEX 12)* – Something blue.

— **JON KLEIN** (b. 9 May'??, Bristol, England) – guitar (ex-SPECIMEN) repl. CARRUTHERS / added **MARTIN McCARRICK** (b.29 Jul'??) – cello, keyboards (ex-MARC ALMOND, ex-The GLOVE) (to SIOUXSIE, SEVERIN, BUDGIE + KLEIN)

Jul 87. (7"/7"pic-d/c-s) *(SHE/+P/+PC 13)* **SONG FROM THE EDGE OF THE WORLD. / THE WHOLE PRICE OF BLOOD** [59] [-]
(12"+=) *(SHEX 13)* – Mechanical eyes.

Jul 88. (7"/7"g-f) *(SHE/+G 14) <27760>* **PEEK-A-BOO. / FALSE FACE** [16] [53]
(c-s+=/cd-s+=) *(SHE CS/CD 14)* – Catwalk / ('A'-Big suspender mix).
(12"+=) *(SHEXR 14)* – ('A'-2 other mixes).

Sep 88. (lp/c)(cd) *(SHE LP/MC 5)(837240-2) <24205>* **PEEPSHOW** [20] [68]
– Peek-a-boo / Killing jar / Scarecrow / Carousel / Burn-up / Ornaments of gold / Turn to stone / Rawhead and bloodybones / The last beat of my heart / Rhapsody. *(re-iss. cd Mar95; same)*

Sep 88. (7"/7"g-f/7"pic-d) *(SHE/+G/P 15)* **KILLING JAR. / SOMETHING WICKED (THIS WAY COMES)** [41] [-]
(12"+=/cd-s+=) *(SHE X/CD 15)* – Are you still dying, darling.

Nov 88. (7"/7"g-f) *(SHE/+G 16)* **THE LAST BEAT OF MY HEART. / EL DIABLO LOS MUERTOS** [44] [ ]
(12"+=) *(SHEX 16)* – Sunless.
(cd-s++=) *(SHECD 16)* – ('B'mix).

— In Autumn'89, The CREATURES issued singles and 'BOOMERANG' album.

May 91. (7"/c-s) *(SHE/+CS 19) <19031>* **KISS THEM FOR ME. / RETURN** [32] [23]

(ext-12"+=/12"pic-d+=) *(SHE X/XD 19)* – Staring back.
(cd-s++=) *(SHECD 19)* – ('A'side).

Jun 91. (cd/c/lp) *(847731-2/-4/-1)) <24387>* **SUPERSTITION** [25] [65]
– Kiss them for me / Fear (of the unknown) / Cry / Drifter / Little sister / Shadowtime / Silly thing / Got to get up / Silver waterfalls / Softly / The ghost in you. *(re-iss. cd Mar95; same)*

Jul 91. (7"/c-s) *(SHE/+CS 20)* **SHADOWTIME. / SPIRAL TWIST** [57] [ ]
(12"+=/cd-s+=) *(SHE X/CD 20)* – Sea of light. / ('A'-Eclipse mix).

— Below single from the film 'Batman Returns'.

Jul 92. (7"/c-s) *(SHE/+CS 21)* **FACE TO FACE. / I COULD BE AGAIN** [21] [ ]
(cd-s+=) *(SHECD 21)* – ('A'-catatonic mix) / Hothead.
(12") *(SHEX 21)* – ('A'side) / ('A'-catatonic mix) / Hothead.

Oct 92. (cd/c/lp) *(517160-2/-4/-1)* **TWICE UPON A TIME – THE THING** [26] [ ]
– Fireworks / Slowdive / Melt / Dear Prudence / Swimming horses / Dazzle / Overground (from The Thorn) / Cities in dust / Candyman / This wheel's on fire / The passenger / Peek-a-boo / The killing jar / The last beat of my heart / Kiss them for me / Shadowtime / Fear (of the unknown) / Face to face. *(re-iss. cd Mar95; same)*

— In Aug 94, SIOUXSIE partnered MORRISSEY on his single, 'INTERLUDE'.

Dec 94. (c-s) *(SHECS 22)* **O BABY. / OURSELVES** [34] [-]
(cd-s+=) *(SHECD 22)* – ('A'-Manhattan mix).
(cd-s) *(SHECDX 22)* – ('A'side) / Swimming horses (live) / All tomorrow's parties (live).

Jan 95. (cd/c/lp) *(523725-2/-4/-1) <24630>* **THE RAPTURE** [33] [ ]
– O baby / Tearing apart / Stargazer / Fall from grace / Not forgotten / Sick child / The lonely one / Falling down / Forever / The rapture / The double life / Love out me.

Feb 95. (7"/c-s) *(SHE/+CS 23)* **STARGAZER. / HANG ME HIGH** [64] [ ]
(cd-s+=) *(SHECD 23)* – Black Sun.
(cd-s) *(SHECDX 23)* – ('A'-Mambo sun) / ('A'-Planet queen mix) / ('A'-Mark Saunders mix).

— Split Apr'96, although SIOUXSIE and BUDGIE recorded a third album as The CREATURES. SEVERIN has written for the film 'Visions Of Ecstacy'.

– compilations, etc. –

Feb 87. (12"ep) *Strange Fruit; (SFPS 012)* **THE PEEL SESSIONS (29.11.77)** [ ] [-]
– Love in a void / Mirage / Suburban relapse / Metal postcard. *(c-ep-iss.Jun87; SFPSC 012) (cd-ep-iss.Mar88; SFPSCD 012)*

Feb 89. (12"ep/cd-ep) *Strange Fruit; (SFPS/+CD 066)* **THE PEEL SESSIONS (Feb78)** [ ] [-]
– Hong Kong garden / Carcass / Helter skelter / Overground.

CREATURES

(SIOUXSIE & BUDGIE)

Polydor / not iss.

Sep 81. (d7"ep/d7"gf-ep) *(POSP D/G 354)* **WILD THINGS** [24] [-]
– Mad-eyed screamer / So unreal / But not them / Wild thing / Thumb.

Wonderland / Geffen

May 83. (7") *(SHE 1)* **MISS THE GIRL. / HOT SPRING IN THE SNOW** [21] [-]

May 83. (lp/c) *(SHE LP/MC 1)* **FEAST** [17] [-]
– Morning dawning / Inoa 'ole / Ice house / Dancing on glass / Gecko / Sky train / Festival of colours / Miss the girl / A strutting rooster / Flesh.

Jul 83. (7") *(SHE 2)* **RIGHT NOW. / WEATHERCADE** [14] [-]
(12"+=) *(SHEX 2)* – Festival of colours.

Oct 89. (7") *(SHEP 17)* **STANDING THERE. / DIVIDED** [53] [-]
(12"+=/cd-s+=) *(SH X/CD 17)* – Solar choir / ('A'-Andalucian mix).
('A'-La Frontera mix-10"+=) *(SHET 17)* – Solar choir.

Nov 89. (lp/c/cd) *(841463-1/-4/-2) <24275>* **BOOMERANG** [ ] [ ]
– Standing there / Manchild / You! / Pity / Killing time / Willow / Pluto drive / Solar choir * / Speeding * / Fury eyes / Fruitman / Untiedundone * / Simoom * / Strolling wolf / Venus sands / Morriha. *(extra tracks on cd= *)*

Feb 90. (7"/7"box) *(SHE/+B 18)* **FURY EYES. / ABSTINENCE** [ ] [-]
(12"/cd-s) *(SHE P/CD 18)* – ('A'-20/20 mix) / ('A'dub) / ('A'-Fever mix).

Sioux / Record Of Substance

Jun 98. (7") *(SIOUX 1)* **SAD CUNT. / SAD CUNT (chix'n'dix mix)** [ ] [-]

Aug 98. (10"ep/cd-ep) *(SIOUX 2 V/CD) <1>* **ERASER CUTS** [ ] [ ]
– Pinned down / Guillotine / Thank you / Slipping away.

Oct 98. (7"green) **(SIOUX 3V) 2ND FLOOR. / TURN IT ON** [ ] [-]
(12"on 'Hydrogen Jukebox'+=)(cd-s+=) *(DUKE 044DJV)(SIOUX 3CD)* – ('A'-Girl eats boy mix) / ('A'-Emperor Sly mix).

The GLOVE

(SEVERIN & ROBERT SMITH) also incl. **MARTIN McCARRICK** – cello / **ANNE STEPHENSON + GINNY HEWES** – strings / **ANDY ANDERSON** – drums / (JEANETTE) **LANDRAY** – dual vocals w/**SMITH**

Wonderland / Rough Trade

Aug 83. (7") *(SHE 3)* **LIKE AN ANIMAL. / MOUTH TO MOUTH** [52] [-]
(12"+=) *(SHEX 3)* – Animal (club mix).

Aug 83. (lp/c) *(SHE LP/MC 2) <ROUGHUS 85>* **BLUE SUNSHINE** [35] [ ]
– Like an animal / Looking glass girl / Sex-eye-make-up / Mr. Alphabet says / A blues in drag / Punish me with kisses / This green city / Orgy / Perfect murder / Relax. *(re-iss. Sep90 lp/c/cd+=; 815019-1/-4/-2)* – Mouth to mouth / The tightrope / Like an animal (club mix).

Nov 83. (7") *(SHE 5)* **PUNISH ME WITH KISSES. / THE TIGHTROPE** [ ] [-]

SISTER DOUBLE HAPPINESS

Formed: San Francisco, California, USA . . . 1986 by two former members of The DICKS, namely LYNN PERKO and GARY FLOYD. This semi-legendary Texan politico-punk act debuted on a shared album, 'LIVE AT RAULS' with The BIG BOYS, before finally unleashing two further sets, 'KILL FROM THE HEART' (1983) and 'THESE PEOPLE' (1985). Having subsequently split, they teamed up with BEN COHEN and MIKEY DONALDSON, SISTER DOUBLE HAPPINESS initiating their crusade in 1988 with an eponymous album on L.A. indie label, 'S.S.T.'. Carrying on the blues/punk spirit of the DICKS, the record's rawhide intensity and bludgeoning, blistering hard rock'n'roll was convincingly carried off by the gravel-gargling vocals of GARY FLOYD, the overall effect sufficiently impressive to attract 'Warners' subsidiary, 'Reprise'. Disappointingly, the band's belated major label debut, 'HEART & MIND' (featuring guests JOHN CALE and RODDY BOTTUM), failed to capture their trademark piledriving power and by the time of the record's 1992 UK release, DONALDSON had been replaced by JEFF PALMER. FLOYD and Co were freed from the constraints of a big budget studio with 'UNCUT' (1993) – released on 'Dutch East India' – and went for broke on the blues wailing, harmonica-huffing 'HORSEY WATER' (1994), released on 'Sub Pop'. FLOYD had already issued a 'Glitterhouse' solo set, 'WORLD OF TROUBLE', a month previously and following the subsequent demise of SISTER DOUBLE HAPPINESS, would go on to release 'BROKEN ANGELS' (1995) as The GARY FLOYD BAND.

Album rating: SISTER DOUBLE HAPPINESS (*7) / HEART AND MIND (*6) / UNCUT (*6) / HORSEY WATER (*6) / Dicks: KILL FROM THE HEART (*5) / THESE PEOPLE (*5)

DICKS

GARY FLOYD – vocals / **GLEN** – guitar, bass / **BUXF** – bass, vocals, guitar / **PAT** – drums

not iss. / Selfless

1981. (m-lp; shared with the BIG BOYS) **LIVE AT RAUL'S (live)** [-] [ ]

S.S.T. / S.S.T.

Oct 83. (lp) *<(SST 017)>* **KILL FROM THE HEART** [ ] [ ]
– Anti-Klan (part 1) / Rich daddy / No Nazi's friend / Marilyn Buck / Kill from the heart / Little boys' feet / Pigs run wild / Bourgeois fascist pig / Anti-Klan (part 2) / Purple haze / Right wing – White wing / Dicks can'd swim: 1. Cock jam – 2. Razor blade dance.

— **LYNN PERKO** – drums; repl. PAT

Alternative Tentacles / Alternative Tentacles

Jul 85. (lp) *<(VIRUS 43)>* **THESE PEOPLE** [ ] [ ]
– The police (force) / Off duty sailor / Executive dive / Sidewalk begging / Lost and divided / Dead in a motel room / Cities are burning / Doctor daddy / Decent and clean / Legacy of man / Little rock'n'roller / George Jackson.

— disbanded the following year and evolved into (see below)

– compilations, etc. –

Jun 93. (7"; shared with the BIG BOYS) *Selfless; (SFLS 10-7)* **LIVE AT RAUL'S** [ ] [ ]

Apr 97. (cd) *Alternative Tentacles; <(VIRUS 200CD)>* **DICKS 1980-1986** [ ] [ ]

SISTER DOUBLE HAPPINESS

GARY FLOYD – vocals / **BEN COHEN (ex-POLKACIDE) – guitar / MIKEY DONALDSON** – bass / **LYNN PERKO** – drums

S.S.T. / S.S.T.

Jul 88. (lp) *<(SST 162)>* **SISTER DOUBLE HAPPINESS** [ ] [ ]
– Sister double happiness / Freight train / Let me in / Cry like a baby / On the beach / Poodle dog / It's our life / I tried / Sweet talker / Get drunk and die / You don't know me. *(re-iss. May93 cd/c; SST 162 CD/C)*

— **JEFF PALMER** – bass; repl. DONALDSON

Reprise / Reprise

Feb 92. (cd-s) *<40356>* **HEY KIDS** [-] [ ]

May 92. (cd/c) *<(7599 26657-2/-4)>* **HEART AND MIND** [ ] [ ] Apr91
– Bobby Shannon / Ain't it a shame / Exposed to you / Sweet talker / You don't know me / The sailor song / Dark heart / Heart and mind / Hey kids / I'm drowning / Don't worry / You for you.

Sub Pop / Dutch East

Dec 92. (7") *<SP 77>* **DON'T WORRY. / WHEELS A' SPINNING** [-] [ ]

Jun 93. (7") *<(SP 104-276)>* **DO WHAT YOU GOTTA DO. /** [ ] [ ]
(cd-s+=) *<(SPCD 104-276)>* –

Jul 93. (lp/cd) *(SP/+CD 105-277) <2029>* **UNCUT** [ ] [ ] Jun93
– San Diego / Will you come / Ashes / Whipping song / Doesn't make sense / Honey don't / Keep the city clean / Do what you gotta do / Where do we run / No good for you / Lightnin' / Louise.

— **MILES MONTALBANO** – bass + **DANNY ROMAN** – guitar; repl. PALMER

Sub Pop / Sub Pop

Nov 94. (lp/cd) *<(SP/+CD 137-337)>* **HORSEY WATER** [ ] [ ] Oct94
– Jack freak / Gurden jail / Bad line / Holly said / Waiting for anyone / A+R man / Heart of ice / Who's been fucking you / Sweet home California / Everything will be alright tomorrow.

— split after above, GARY had already recorded a solo set

GARY FLOYD

Glitterhouse / Glitterhouse

Sep 94. (cd) *<(GRCD 316)>* **WORLD OF TROUBLE** [ ] [ ]

Oct 94. (7") *<(THM 002)>* **MORE THAN A LIFETIME. /** [ ] [ ]
(above issued on 'Tres Hombres')

Jun 95. (cd; as the GARY FLOYD BAND) *<(GRCD 367)>* **BROKEN ANGELS** [ ] [ ]

SISTERS OF MERCY

Formed: Leeds, England ... 1980 by frontman/lyricist extrordinaire, ANDREW ELDRITCH along with guitarist, GARY MARX. The original "goth" combo, ELDRITCH and Co. were among the first acts to define the genre in its lasting image of black clad, po-faced rockers meditating on dark, impenetrable lyrics, decipherable only for those willing to substitute make-up for flour or wear pointy boots (and, more importantly, never to emerge in daylight!). For their early releases, the group employed a drum machine, christened Doktor Avalanche, issuing material on their self-financed label, 'Merciful Release'. Following the debut single, 'DAMAGE DONE', ELDRITCH and MARX recruited guitarist BENN GUNN and bassist CRAIG ADAMS, fleshing out the sound on a further series of 7 and 12's, the 'ALICE' EP drawing widespread interest with its goth/alternative/dance fusion. GUNN was then replaced with ex-DEAD OR ALIVE guitarist, WAYNE HUSSEY, for the piledriving theatrics of 'TEMPLE OF LOVE'. During this time, the group had also built up a live reputation, supporting the likes of The BIRTHDAY PARTY and The PSYCHEDELIC FURS as well as appearing at the Leeds Futurama festival. Word was spreading, and in 1984, The SISTERS OF MERCY and their label were signed to a worldwide deal with 'WEA'. A debut album, 'FIRST AND LAST AND ALWAYS', appeared the following year, a worthwhile effort which saw the group almost break into the UK Top 10. Yet only a month after the record's release, the band announced they were to split, tension between ELDRITCH and MARX resulting in the latter leaving the group first. After a final concert at London's Royal Albert Hall, a bitter legal battle ensued between ELDRITCH and ADAMS/HUSSEY. At stake was the SISTERS OF MERCY moniker, ELDRITCH eventually winning out, though not before he'd hastily released a single and album, 'GIFT' (1986), under The SISTERHOOD, primarily to prevent ADAMS and HUSSEY using the title. The latter two subsequently formed The MISSION while ELDRITCH relocated to Berlin/Hamburg, retaining ex-GUN CLUB bassist, PATRICIA MORRISON (who'd played on 'GIFT') and recording 'FLOODLAND' (1987) with the help of his ever faithful drum machine. The prededing single, 'THIS CORROSION' was suitably grandiose, all ominous vocals and OTT production courtesy of JIM STEINMAN, the single giving ELDRITCH his first UK Top 10 hit. The album achieved a similar feat, incorporating a more overtly rhythmic feel to create a kind of doom-disco sound (perfect for goths who couldn't dance anyway!). MORRISON subsequently left, ELDRITCH recruiting an array of diverse musicians including TIM BREICHENO, ANDREAS BRUHN and punk veteran, TONY JAMES (ex-SIGUE SIGUE SPUTNIK, ex-GENERATION X) to record 'VISION THING' (1990). Employing a more commercial hard rock sound, 'MORE' was one of The SISTERS' most effective singles to date while again the album was a Top 20 success. Further acclaim came in 1992 with the surprisingly consistent retrospective, 'SOME GIRLS WANDER BY MISTAKE' (1992), and its attendant single, a brilliant re-vamp of 'TEMPLE OF LOVE', Israeli warbler, OFRA HAZA, adding that extra mystical touch. After a 1991 joint tour with PUBLIC ENEMY (nice idea, but probably taking the Lollapollooza ethic a bit too far) was abandoned after poor ticket sales, not much has been heard from The SISTERS OF MERCY. ELDRITCH remains an enigmatic figure, any significant activity normally resulting in intense interest from the music press. The odds are that he'll return, though whether in the guise of The SISTERS OF MERCY remains to be seen. • **Covered:** EMMA (Hot Chocolate) / 1969 (Stooges) / GIMME SHELTER (Rolling Stones) / KNOCKIN' ON HEAVEN'S DOOR (Bob Dylan).

Album rating: SOME GIRLS WANDER BY MISTAKE compilation (*9) / FIRST AND LAST AND ALWAYS (*8) / FLOODLAND (*8) / VISION THING (*7) / Sisterhood: GIFT (*7)

ANDREW ELDRITCH (b. ANDREW TAYLOR, 15 May'59, East Anglia, England) – vocals / **GARRY MARX** (b. MARK PEARMAN) – guitar / + drum machine DOKTOR AVALANCHE

Merciful Release — not iss.

1980. (7"m) *(MR 7)* **THE DAMAGE DONE. / WATCH / HOME OF THE HITMAN** [ ] [-]

— added **BEN GUNN** (b. BENJAMIN MATTHEWS) – guitar / **CRAIG ADAMS** (b. 4 Apr'62) – bass (ex-EXPELAIRES)

C.N.T. — not iss.

Feb 82. (7") *(CNT 002)* **BODY ELECTRIC. / ADRENOCHROME** [ ] [-]

Merciful — BrainEater

Nov 82. (7") *(MR 015)* **ALICE. / FLOORSHOW** [ ] [-]
Mar 83. (7") *(MR 019)* **ANACONDA. / PHANTOM** [ ] [-]
Apr 83. (12"ep) *(MR 021)* **ALICE. / FLOORSHOW / 1969 / PHANTOM** [ ] [ ]
May 83. (12"ep) *(MR 023)* **THE REPTILE HOUSE** [ ] [ ]
– Kiss the carpet / Lights / Valentine / Burn / Fix. *(re-iss. Apr94)*

— **WAYNE HUSSEY** (b. JERRY LOVELOCK, 26 May'58, Bristol, England) – guitar (ex-DEAD OR ALIVE, ex-HAMBI & THE DANCE) repl. BEN

Oct 83. (7") *(MR 027)* **TEMPLE OF LOVE. / HEARTLAND** [ ] [-]
(ext.12"+=) *(MRX 027)* – Gimme shelter.
Jun 84. (7"; as The SISTERS) *(MR 029)* **BODY AND SOUL. / TRAIN** [46] [-]
(12"+=) *(MR 029T)* – After hours / Body electric.

Merciful Release — Elektra

Oct 84. (7") *(MR 033)* **WALK AWAY. / POISON DOOR** [45] [-]
(above w/free 7"flexi) *(MR 033 – SAM 218)* – Long Train.
(12"+=) *(MR 033T)* – On the wire.
Feb 85. (7") *(MR 035)* **NO TIME TO CRY. / BLOOD MONEY** [63] [-]
(12"+=) *(MR 035T)* – Bury me deep.
Mar 85. (lp/c) *(MR 337 L/C) <60405>* **FIRST AND LAST AND ALWAYS** [14] [ ]
– Black planet / Walk away / No time to cry / A rock and a hard place / Marian / First and last and always / Possession / Nine while nine / Amphetamine logic / Some kind of stranger. *(cd-iss. Jul88; 240616-2) (re-iss. re-mastered.Jul92 on 'East West' lp/c; MR 571 L/C) (cd re-mast.Jun92; 9031 77379-2)*

— disbanded mid-'85 . . . GARRY MARX helped form GHOST DANCE. HUSSEY and ADAMS formed The MISSION after squabbles with ANDREW over use of group name.

— **ELDRITCH** with ever faithful drum machine adopted

The SISTERHOOD

— recruited **PATRICIA MORRISON** (b.14 Jan'62) – bass, vocals (ex-FUR BIBLE, ex-GUN CLUB) / **JAMES RAY** – guitar / **ALAN VEGA** – synthesizers (ex-SUICIDE) / **LUCAS FOX** – drums (ELDRITCH moved to Berlin, Germany)

Merciful — not iss.

Feb 86. (7") *(SIS 001)* **GIVING GROUND (remix). / GIVING GROUND (album version)** [ ] [-]
Jul 86. (lp/c) *(SIS 020/+C)* **GIFT** [90] [-]
– Jihad / Colours / Giving ground / Finland red, Egypt white / Rain from Heaven. *(cd-iss. Sep89; SIS 020CD) (re-iss. Jul94 cd/c; 1131684-2/-4)*

— JAMES RAY went solo (backed with The PERFORMANCE), subsequently issuing a couple of 45's, 'MEXICO SUNDOWN BLUES' and 'TEXAS', for 'Merciful Release'. At the turn of the decade, he and his new outfit, JAMES RAY'S GANGWAR, issued a few more, 'DUSTBOAT' and 'WITHOUT CONSCIENCE', the former from a part compilation set, 'A NEW KIND OF ASSASSIN' (1989). In 1992 and '93, the band delivered two more, 'DIOS ESTA DE NUESTRO LADO' and 'THIRD GENERATION'.

The SISTERS OF MERCY

— were once again **ELDRITCH + MORRISON** obtaining rights to name

Merciful-WEA — Elektra

Sep 87. (7") *(MR 39)* **THIS CORROSION. / TORCH** [7] [ ]
(c-s+=/12"+=/cd-s+=) *(MR 39 C/T/CD)* – Colours.
Nov 87. (lp/c)(cd) *(MR 441 L/C)(242246-2) <60762>* **FLOODLAND** [9] [ ]
– Dominion / Mother Russia / Flood I / Lucretia my reflection / 1959 / This corrosion / Flood II / Driven like the snow / Neverlan. *(c+=)*– Torch. *(cd-s++=)* – Colours.
Feb 88. (7") *(MR 43)* **DOMINION. / SANDSTORM / UNTITLED** [13] [-]
(d12"+=) *(MR 43TB)* – Emma.
(c-s+=/3"cd-s+=) *(MR 43 C/CD)* – Ozy-Mandias.
May 88. (7"/ext.12"/ext.3"cd-s) *(MR 44/+T/CD)* **LUCRETIA MY REFLECTION. / LONG TRAIN** [20] [ ]

— (Feb'90) **ELDRITCH** w/drum machine, recruited complete new line-up / **TONY JAMES** (b.1956) – bass, vocals (ex-SIGUE SIGUE SPUTNIK, ex-GENERATION X) / **ANDREAS BRUHN** (b. 5 Nov'67, Hamburg, Germany) – guitar / **TIM BRICHENO** (b. 6 Jul'63, Huddersfield, England) – guitar (ex-ALL ABOUT EVE) / guests were **MAGGIE REILLY** – b.vocals (ex-MIKE OLDFIELD) / **JOHN PERRY** – guitar (ex-ONLY ONES)

Oct 90. (7"/c-s) *(MR 47/+C) <66595>* **MORE. / YOU COULD BE THE ONE** [21] [ ]
(cd-s+=/cd-s+=) *(MR 47CD/+X)* – ('A'extended).
Oct 90. (cd)(c/lp) *(9031 72663-2)(MR 449 C/L) <61017>* **VISION THING** [11] [ ]
– Vision thing / Ribons / Destination Boulevard / Something fast / When you don't see me / Doctor Jeep / More / I was wrong.
Dec 90. (7") *(MR 51)* **DOCTOR JEEP. / KNOCKIN' ON HEAVEN'S DOOR (live)** [37] [ ]
(12"+=/cd-s+=) *(MR 51 T/CD)* – ('A'extended).
(ext.12") *(MR 51TX)* – Burn (live) / Amphetamine logic (live).

— (Oct91) **TONY JAMES** split from ELDRITCH amicably.

— Next featured vocals by **OFRA HAZA**

East West — Elektra

Apr 92. (7") *(MR 53)* **TEMPLE OF LOVE (1992). / I WAS WRONG (American fade)** [3] [ ]
(ext.12"+=) *(MR 53T)* – Vision thing (Canadian club mix).
(cd-s+=) *(MR 53CD)* – When you don't see me (German release).
Apr 92. (cd)(c/d-lp) *(9031 76476-2)(MR 449 C/L) <61306>* **SOME GIRLS WANDER BY MISTAKE** (1980-1983 material) [5] [ ]
– Alice / Floorshow / Phantom / 1969 / Kiss the carpet / Lights / Valentine / Fix / Burn / Kiss the carpet (reprise) / Temple of love / Heartland / Gimme shelter / Damage done / Watch / Home of the hitmen / Body electric / Adrenochrome / Anaconda.

— now just **ANDREW ELDRITCH** on own with guests

Aug 93. (7"/c-s) *(MR 59/+C)* **UNDER THE GUN. / ALICE (1993)** [19] [-]
(12"+=/cd-s+=) *(MR 59 T/CD)* – ('A'-Jutland mix).
Aug 93. (cd/c/d-lp) *(4509 93579-2/-4/-1) <61399-2/-4>* **GREATEST HITS VOLUME 1 – A SLIGHT CASE OF OVERBOMBING** (compilation) [14] [ ]
– Under the gun / Temple of love (1992) / Vision thing / Detonation boulevard / Doctor Jeep / More / Lucretia my reflection / Dominion – Mother / This corrosion / No time to cry / Walk away / Body and soul.

— ELDRITCH and his gang seem to have split from music biz

– compilations, etc. –

Jan 94. (cd) *Cleopatra; (CLEO 6642CD)* **FIRST, LAST FOREVER** [ ] [-]

SIX.BY SEVEN

Formed: Nottingham, England . . . 1992 by five hard-working, hard-playing, hard-drinking college lads, CHRIS OLLEY, SAM HEMPTON, JAMES FOWLER, PAUL DOUGLAS and CHRIS DAVIS. Rehearsing night and day to perfect their alternative drone machine, the 12 incher 'EUROPEAN ME', finally hit the shops in the Autumn of '97. A third single for Beggars Banquet's offshoot 'Mantra', 'CANDLELIGHT' (taken from their debut set, 'THE THINGS WE MAKE'), broke into the UK Top 75, its lengthy noisy overtures classic SPACEMEN 3/SONIC YOUTH-esque affairs.

Album rating: THE THINGS WE MAKE (*6 or *7, possibly)

CHRIS OLLEY – vocals, guitar / **SAM HEMPTON** – guitar / **JAMES FOWLER** – Hammond organ, tenor sax / **PAUL DOUGLAS** (b. Irvine, Scotland) / **CHRIS DAVIS** – drums

		Mantra	Interscope
Sep 97.	(12") *(SIX 001)* **EUROPEAN ME. / BRILLIANTLY CUTE**		-
Feb 98.	(12"/cd-s) *(MNT 29 T/CD)* **88-92-96. / YOUR TIME / THIS**		-
Apr 98.	(7") *(MNT 034)* **CANDLELIGHT. / YOUNG MAN'S STRIDE**	70	
	(12"+=/cd-s+=) *(MNT 034 T/CD)* – ('A'-Flaming Lips mix).		
May 98.	(cd/c/lp) *(MNT CD/MC/LP 1011)* <90270> **THE THINGS WE MAKE** – A beautiful shape / European me / Candlelight / For you / Spy song / Something wild / Brilliantly cute / Oh! dear / 88-92-96 / Comedown.		Oct98
Aug 98.	(cd-s) <85001> **SIX.BY SEVEN** – European me / 88-92-96 / Your town.	-	
Aug 98.	(7") *(MNT 037)* **FOR YOU. / GET A REAL TATTOO**		-
	(cd-s+=) *(MNT 037CD)* – Oh dear (John Peel session).		
	(cd-s) *(MNT 037CD2)* – ('A'side) / Something wild / I'm wide open.		

SIX FINGER SATELLITE

Formed: Rhode Island, USA . . . 1992 by J. RYAN, JOHN MacLEAN, RICHARD PELLETIER, along with short-time members PETER PHILLIPS and CHRIS DIXON. An unorthodox signing even by 'Sub Pop' standards, SFS were a breath of fresh air to the guitar-orientated US indie scene. A kind of Stateside precursor to ADD N TO X, if less futuristic, this combo merged elements of SUICIDE, KRAFTWERK and early 80's alt-punk using analogue synths for authenticity and smothering the sound in Dalek-style distortion and noise. Preceded by an EP, 'WEAPON', 1993's debut set, 'THE PIGEON IS THE MOST POPULAR BIRD', received surprisingly little coverage of the band in the press. Whether intentional or not, the band remained one of the most low-key acts on the 'Sub Pop' roster. They subsequently became a quartet with the addition of JAMES APT and, after a further two mini-sets during the mid-90's, delivered the much-improved 'PARANORMALIZED' in 1996. Two of the album's highlights were unusual to say the least, 'SLAVE TRAITOR' was an archetypal SUICIDE dirge while 'PERICO' subjected the listener to a weird reverberating synth sound akin to a cross between a horse snoring and an elephant breaking wind! • **Note:** Not sure of connection with GREEN MAGNET SCHOOL (who issued two albums in Apr+Nov92, 'BLOOD MUSIC' & 'DECLARATION OF TECHNO . . .' for 'Sub Pop' (SP/+CD 191) + (SPCD 55-217).

Album rating: THE PIGEON IS THE MOST POPULAR BIRD (*5) / MACHINE CUISINE (*5) / SEVERE EXPOSURE (*5) / PARANORMALIZED (*6) / LAW OF RUINS (*6)

J. RYAN – vocals, synthesizer / **JOHN MacLEAN** – synthesizers, guitar synthesizer / **RICHARD PELLETIER** – drums, drum machine / with also **PETER PHILLIPS** – guitar, vocals / **CHRIS DIXON** – bass

		Sub Pop	Sub Pop
Mar 92.	(12"ep) <*(SP 143)*> **WEAPON EP**		
——	**ROBERT WESTON** – bass, Moog; repl. CHRIS		
Aug 93.	(lp/cd) *(SP/+CD 268)* <*SP 215*> **THE PIGEON IS THE MOST POPULAR BIRD** – Home for the holy day / Laughing Larry / Funny like a clown / Deadpan / Hi-lo jerk / Love (via satellite) / Save the last dance for Larry / Solitary Hiro / Neuro-harmonic conspiracy / Takes one to know one.		
——	now without PHILLIPS		
Sep 94.	(10"m-lp/m-cd) <*(SP 133-330/-CD)*> **MACHINE CUISINE** – Love (via machine) / Blue melodica / The magic bus / Hans pocketwatch / The well-tempered monkey / Like to get to know you / The Greek arts / White temples.		
——	**JAMES APT** – bass, clarinet; repl. WESTON		
Jul 95.	(lp/cd) <*(SP 299/+B)*> **SEVERE EXPOSURE** – Bad comrade / Parlour games / White Queen to Black Knight / Pulling a train / Simian fever / Cock fight / Dark companion / Where humans go / Rabies (baby's got the) / Board the bus.		
Jun 96.	(c) <*8*> **CLONE THEORY**	-	
	<above issued on 'Load'>		
Jul 96.	(7"m) <*(SP 362)*> **MAN BEHIND THE GLASSES. / WAR CRIMES / DARK COMPANION**		
Sep 96.	(cd) <*(SPCD 366)*> **PARANORMALIZED** – 30 lashes / The greatest hit / Do the suicide / Coke and mirrors / Last transmission / Slave traitor / The white shadow / Paralyzed by normal life / Padded room / Perico / The great depression.		
Aug 98.	(cd) <*(SP 428)*> **LAW OF RUINS** – Race against space / Surveillance house / Fall to pieces / Sea of tranquility / Law of ruins / Lonely grave / New kind of rat / White visitation / Bad aptitude.		

16 HORSEPOWER

Formed: Denver, Colorado, USA . . . 1992 by DAVID EUGENE EDWARDS, plus JEAN YVES TOLA and PASCAL HUMBERT (the latter subsequently replaced by KEVIN SOLL after a spell in LA). Brought up under a strict religious regime, EDWARDS' preoccupation with the fire and brimstone of the Old Testament was channeled through 16 HORSEPOWER's gothic rockabilly/country stylings, the ghost of JEFFREY LEE PIERCE (ex-GUN CLUB) haunting his every phrase. EDWARDS and Co were lucky enough to secure a major label deal for their debut release, 1995's eponymous mini-CD (also known as 'HAW') being issued on A&M's offshoot 'Paradox'. A debut album, 'SACKCLOTH 'N' ASHES' (1996) was released to critical acclaim the following year, hitting the British shops (with the addition of 'HAW') in Spring '97. With HUMBERT returning and the addition of guitarist/fiddle man, JEFFREY PAUL NORLANDER (the 90's alt-country equivalent of CHARLIE DANIELS!), follow-up set, 'LOW ESTATE' (1997) benefitted from the talents of PJ HARVEY collaborator, JOHN PARRISH.

Album rating: 16 HORSEPOWER (*5) / SACKCLOTH 'N' ASHES (*8) / LOW ESTATE (*8)

DAVID EUGENE EDWARDS – vocals / **JEAN YVES TOLA** – drums (ex-PASSION FODDER) / **KEVIN SOLL** – double bass; repl. PASCAL HUMBERT

		Paradox-A&M	Paradox-A&M
Jun 96.	(m-cd) <*(540 436-2)*> **16 HORSEPOWER** – Haw / South Pennsylvania waltz / Shametown / Straight-mouth stomp / Coal black horses / I gotta gal.		Nov95
Apr 97.	(cd) <*(540 591-2)*> **SACKCLOTH 'N' ASHES** – Seen what I saw / Black soul choir / Haw / Scrawled in sap / Horse head / Ruthie Lingle / Harm's way / Black bush / Heel on the shovel / American wheeze / Red neck reel / Prison shoe romp / Neck on the new blade / Strong man. *(UK cd+=)* – 16 HORSEPOWER E.P.		1996
——	**HUMBERT** returned to repl. KEVIN		
——	added **JEFFREY PAUL NORLANDER** – guitar, fiddle (ex-DENVER GENTLEMEN)		
Sep 97.	(cd) <*(540 709-2)*> **LOW ESTATE** – Brimstone rock / My narrow mind / Low estate / For Heaven's sake / Sac of religion / Denver grab / Coal black horses / Pure clob road / Phyllis Ruth / Black rung / Dead run / Golden rope / Hang my teeth on your door.		
Oct 97.	(cd-ep) *(582 395-2)* **COAL BLACK HORSES / FOR HEAVEN'S SAKE / HAW / BRIMSTONE ROCK**		

60 FT DOLLS

Formed: Newport, Gwent, Wales . . . 1993 by son of a preacher man, CARL BEVAN (oh yes he was!), MIKE COLE and RICHARD JOHN PARFITT. Spearheading the Welsh-rock revival in the seismic wake of The MANIC STREET PREACHERS, these self professed "niggers of Europe" (with regards to their place in the good old – and thankfully fast dissipating – United Kingdom) first vented their smalltown spleen with 1994's 'HAPPY SHOPPER' single. Released on their own 'Townhill' label, the single set the band up for a healthy range of major league support slots and incredibly, a Stateside deal with 'Geffen'. Unfortunately, however, the band's domestic deal with 'Rough Trade' came just as the label were on the verge of folding; this, together with the frustration felt by the whole Welsh rock community following the disappearance of The MANICS' RICHEY EDWARDS was fuel for the seething 'WHITE KNUCKLE RIDE'. Subsequently signing with R.C.A.-offshoot, 'Indolent' (home to SLEEPER), the trio began 1996 with the 'STAY' single, the long awaited debut album, 'THE BIG 3', surfacing soon after. Proving that there was more to the band than indie-punk/R&R, the record showcased a few subdued moments alongside the trademark pop-art fusing The MANICS with The JAM or MOTT THE HOOPLE. Two years passed before another single, 'ALISON'S ROOM', surfaced, its disappointing chart performance affecting sales of the "difficult" second album, 'JOYA MAGICA' (1998). • **Songwriters:** PARFITT or COLE or both. Covered; AFTERGLOW (Small Faces) / EVERYBODY'S GOT SOMETHING TO HIDE . . . (Beatles).

Album rating: THE BIG 3 (*7) / JOYA MAGICA (*5)

RICHARD JOHN PARFITT – vocals, guitar / **MIKE COLE** – vocals, bass / **CARL BEVAN** – drums

		Townhill	not iss.
Jul 94.	(7") *(TIDY 001)* **HAPPY SHOPPER. / LONDON BREEDS** *(re iss. Mar95, same)*		-
		Rough Trade	**not iss.**
May 95.	(7") *(R 379-7)* **WHITEKNUCKLE RIDE. / NO.1 PURE ALCOHOL**		-
	(cd-s+=) *(R 379-3)* – Piss funk.		
		Indolent	**D.G.C.**
Oct 95.	(7"/cd-s) *(DOLLS 001/+CD)* **PIG VALENTINE. / BRITISH RACING GREEN / YELLOW CANDLES**		Dec95
Jan 96.	(7"/c-s) *(DOLLS 002/+MC)* **STAY. / THE MAINDEE RUN**	48	-
	(cd-s+=) *(DOLLS 002CD)* – Rosalyn.		
Apr 96.	(7"colrd/c-s) *(DOLLS 003/+MC)* **TALK TO ME. / PONY RIDE**	37	-
	(cd-s+=) *(DOLLS 003CD)* – Angel / Easy.		
May 96.	(cd/c/lp) *(DOLLS CD/MC/LP 004)* **THE BIG 3** – New loafers / Talk to me / Stay / Hair / Happy shopper / The one / Good times / No.1 pure alcohol / Streamlined / Loser / Pig valentine / Terminal crash fear / Buzz. *(lp w/ free 7")* **WHITEKNUCKLE RIDE**	36	-
Jul 96.	(7"tin/c-s) *(DOLLS 005/+MC)* **HAPPY SHOPPER. / AFTERGLOW**	38	-

(cd-s) *(DOLLS 005CD)* – *('A'side) / Everybody's got something to hide (except for me and my monkey) (live) / Dr Rat.*

Sep 96. (cd-ep) <22224> **SUPERNATURAL JOY EP** –
– Happy shopper / White knuckle ride / British racing green / Yellow candles / Rosalyn.

Nov 96. (10"colrd-ep/cd-ep) *(DOLLS 006/+CD)* **HAIR / BALLERINA. / DREAMING / MESS / PRETTY HORSES** –

Apr 98. (7") *(DOLLS 007)* **ALISON'S ROOM. / TWO LANE BLACKTOP** 61 –
(cd-s+=) *(DOLLS 007CD2)* – Time after time / Let the spirit move you.
(cd-s) *(DOLL 007CD1)* – ('A'side) / It's over / I don't miis you / Spirit (Wubble U mix).

Jun 98. (cd/lp) *(DOLLS 008 CD/LP)* **JOYA MAGICA**

SKELETAL FAMILY

Formed: Bingley, Yorkshire, England . . . 1982 by ANNE MARIE HURST, STAN GREENWOOD, TROTWOOD, STEVE CRANE and KARL HEINZ. Following a debut single, 'JUST A FRIEND', on the tiny 'Luggage' label in Spring '83, the band were picked up by influential local independent operation, 'Red Rhino'. A further two singles, 'THE NIGHT' and 'ALONE SHE CRIES' generated press interest prior to the debut album, 'BURNING OIL'. Bracketed with such early 80's goth merchants as BAUHAUS and SISTERS OF MERCY, The SKELETAL FAMILY were actually a more accessible proposition than their name might suggest, the female vocals (like a deeper throated SIOUXSIE SIOUX with the odd POLY STYRENE yelp) framing dark, spiralling guitars as on the impressive 'SO SURE'. The indie success of 1985's 'FUTILE COMBAT' alerted 'Chrysalis' to the band's potential yet by the release of major label debut, 'GHOSTS' (1986), ANNE-MARIE had left to join fellow pop-doomsters, GHOST DANCE. The record showcased new singer, KATRINA HUNTER (once backing vocalist for TERRY HALL's COLOURFIELD) fronting a more mainstream SKELETAL FAMILY sound, one that failed to cross over and ultimately cost them their deal as the band were subsequently dropped amid poor sales.

Album rating: BURNING OIL (*6) / FUTILE COMBAT (*7)

ANNE MARIE HURST – vocals / **STAN GREENWOOD** – guitar / **TROTWOOD** (b. ROGER NOWELL) – bass / **STEVE CRANE** – drums / **KARL HEINZ** – synthesizers

Luggage not iss.

Mar 83. (7") *(RRP 00724)* **JUST A FRIEND. / TREES** –

— **HOWARD DANIELS** – drums repl. CRANE

Red Rhino not iss.

Jul 83. (7") *(RED 36)* **THE NIGHT. / WAITING HERE** –

— **MARTIN HENDERSON** – drums repl. DANIELS (to MY PIERROT DOLLS)

Jan 84. (7") *(RED 41)* **SHE CRIES ALONE. / THE WIND BLOWS** –
(12"+=) *(REDT 41)* – Eternal.

Apr 84. (12"ep) *(REDT 42)* **RECOLLECT** –
– The night / Waiting here / She cries alone / The wind blows / Eternal / Lies.

Jun 84. (7") *(RED 43)* **SO SURE. / BATMAN** –
(12"+=) *(REDT 43)* – Trees / Lies.

Aug 84. (lp) *(REDLP 44)* **BURNING OIL** –

— **GRAHAM PLEETH** – synthesizers repl. KARL HEINZ

Feb 85. (7") *(RED 54)* **PROMISED LAND. / STAND BY ME** –
(12"+=) *(REDT 54)* – Just a friend.

May 85. (lp) *(REDLP 57)* **FUTILE COMBAT** –

— **KATRINA HUNTER** – vocals (ex-COLOUR FIELD) repl. ANNE MARIE who formed GHOST DANCE

— **KEVIN PHILIPS** – drums repl. RICHARD HAWKINS (ex-GENE LOVES JEZEBEL) who repl. MARTIN (to JUNE BRIDES) + GRAHAM

Chrysalis not iss.

Mar 86. (7"/12") *(CHS/+12 2970)* **RESTLESS. / WHAT GOES UP** –

Aug 86. (7"/12") *(CHS/+12 3015)* **JUST A MINUTE. / BIG LOVE** –

— disbanded soon after above. TROTWOOD and HUNTER formed SAY YOU.

– compilations, etc. –

Oct 85. (d-c) *Red Rhino; (REDC 59)* **TOGETHER (BURNING OIL / FUTILE COMBAT)** –

Oct 86. (lp) *Onsala International; (ONS 1)* **GHOSTS** –

Mar 94. (cd) *Anagram; (CDMGRAM 75)* **THE SINGLES PLUS 1983-85** –

SKIDS

Formed: Dunfermline, Scotland . . . Spring 1977 by RICHARD JOBSON and STUART ADAMSON together with BILL SIMPSON and TOM KELLICHAN. Careering into the wreckage of the post-punk music scene with the self-financed 'CHARLES' single, the band soon found themselves with a deal courtesy of the ever eclectic 'Virgin' label. After a couple of minor hit singles, the group hit the UK Top 10 with 'INTO THE VALLEY', a shining example of The SKIDS' anthemic, new wave warriors style. In addition to JOBSON's highly distinctive, affected vocals and ADAMSON's strident axework (which he'd later perfect in BIG COUNTRY), The SKIDS were notable for their clever visual image (i.e. JOBSON's kick-dance and ultra-slick wavey hairdo). A debut album, 'SCARED TO DANCE' (1979), made the UK Top 20 and established the group as a more tasteful Caledonian alternative to The BAY CITY ROLLERS. Later that Spring, The SKIDS scored another Top 20 hit single with 'MASQUERADE', a highlight of the BILL NELSON-produced follow-up album, 'DAYS IN EUROPA' (1979), alongside the almost militaristic clarion call of 'WORKING FOR THE YANKEE DOLLAR'. All wasn't well within The SKIDS camp, however, personnel upheaval (leading to an all-new rhythm section of RUSSELL WEBB and MIKE BAILLIE) adding to criticisms of JOBSON's increasing lyrical complexities and the group's more schitzo pop/experimental sound. Despite all this, a third album, 'THE ABSOLUTE GAME' (1980) saw a return to form of sorts, furnishing the group with their one and only Top 10 set. ADAMSON became increasingly disillusioned, however, and finally departed the following summer. Left to his own devices, JOBSON dominated The SKIDS' final album, 'JOY' (1981), an at times trad/folk concept effort which met with a frosty critical reception and signalled the subsequent demise of the group early in '82. While ADAMSON went on to massive success with "bagpipe"-guitar rockers, BIG COUNTRY, JOBSON concentrated on a solo career which extended to writing (and recording) poetry. He then went on to form the short-lived and critically derided ARMOURY SHOW along with ex-MAGAZINE men, JOHN McGEOGH and JOHN DOYLE, releasing a sole album, 'WAITING FOR THE FLOODS' (1985). More recently, JOBSON's recording career has taken a backseat to his more successful forays into modelling and TV journalism. • **Songwriters:** JOBSON lyrics/group compositions, except ALL THE YOUNG DUDES (hit; Mott The Hoople) / BAND PLAYED WALTZING MATILDA (Australian trad.). • **Trivia:** In 1981, JOBSON published book of poetry, 'A MAN FOR ALL SEASONS'.

Album rating: SCARED TO DANCE (*8) / SWEET SUBURBIA – THE BEST OF THE SKIDS compilation (*8)

RICHARD JOBSON (b. 6 Apr'60) – vocals, guitar / **STUART ADAMSON** (b.WILLIAM STUART ADAMSON, 11 Apr'58, Manchester, England) – lead guitar, vocals / **BILL SIMPSON** – bass / **TOM KELLICHAN** – drums

No-Bad not iss.

Mar 78. (7"m) *(NB 1)* **CHARLES. / REASONS / TEST-TUBE BABIES** –

Virgin not iss.

Sep 78. (7",7"white) *(VS 227)* **SWEET SUBURBIA. / OPEN SOUND** 70 –

Oct 78. (7"red-ep/12"red-ep) *(VS 232/+12)* **WIDE OPEN** 48 –
– The saints are coming / Of one skin / Confusion / Night and day.

Feb 79. (7",7"white) *(VS241)* **INTO THE VALLEY. / T.V. STARS** 10 –

Feb 79. (lp/c) *(V/TCV 2116)* **SCARED TO DANCE** 19 –
– Into the valley / Scared to dance / Of one skin / Dossier (of fallibility) / Melancholy soldiers / Hope and glory / The saints are coming / Six times / Calling the tune / Integral plot / Charles / Scale. *(re-iss. Apr84 lp/c; OVED/+C 41) (cd-iss. Jun90+=; CDV 2116)* – Sweet suburbia / Open sound / TV stars / Night and day / Contusion / Reasons / Test tube babies. *<US cd-iss. 1991 on 'Caroline'; CAROL 1817-2>*

May 79. (7") *(VS 262)* **MASQUERADE. / OUT OF TOWN** 14 –
(d7"+=) *(VS 262-12)* – Another emotion / Aftermath dub.

— **RUSTY EGAN** – drums (ex-RICH KIDS) repl. KELLICHAN

Sep 79. (7") *(VS 288)* **CHARADE. / GREY PARADE** 31 –

Oct 79. (lp/c) *(V/TCV 2138)* **DAYS IN EUROPA** 32 –
– Animation * / Charade / Dulce et decorum (pro patria mor) / Pros and cons / Home of the saved / Working for the Yankee dollar / The olympian / Thanatos / Masquerade / A day in Europa / Peaceful times. *(re-dist.Mar80 += *) (re-iss. Mar84 lp/c; OVED/+C 42)*

Nov 79. (7") *(VS 306)* **WORKING FOR THE YANKEE DOLLAR. / VANGUARD'S CRUSADE** 20 –
(d7"+=) *(VS 306)* – All the young dudes / Hymns from a haunted ballroom.

— **RUSSELL WEBB** – bass, vocals (ex-ZONES, ex-SLIK) repl. SIMPSON / **MIKE BAILLIE** – drums (ex-INSECT BITES) repl. EGAN who joined VISAGE

Feb 80. (7") *(VS 323)* **ANIMATION. / PROS AND CONS** 56 –

Jul 80. (7") *(VS 359)* **CIRCUS GAMES. / ONE DECREE** 32 –

Sep 80. (lp/c) *(V/TCV 2174)* **THE ABSOLUTE GAME** 9 –
– Circus games / Out of town / Goodbye civilian / The children saw the shame / A woman in winter / Hurry on boys / Happy to be with you / The Devil's decade / One decree / Arena. *(free-lp w.a.) (VDJ 333)* **STRENGTH THROUGH JOY** *(re-iss. Mar84 lp/c; OVED/+C 43)*

Oct 80. (7"/7"pic-d) *(VS/+P 373)* **GOODBYE CIVILIAN. / MONKEY McGUIRE MEETS SPECKY POTTER BEHIND THE LOCHORE INSTITUTE** 52 –

Nov 80. (7") *(VSK 101)* **A WOMAN IN WINTER. / WORKING FOR THE YANKEE DOLLAR (live)** 49 –

— **KENNY HYSLOP** (b.14 Feb'51, Helensburgh, Scotland) – drums (ex-ZONES, ex-SLIK) repl. BAILLIE who joined EPSILON.

Aug 81. (7"/12") *(VS 401/+12)* **FIELDS. / BRAVE MAN** –

— **JOBSON + WEBB** recruited **PAUL WISHART** – saxophone, flute to repl. ADAMSON who formed BIG COUNTRY and HYSLOP who joined SIMPLE MINDS. Session people on album incl. **J.J. JOHNSON** – drums / **The ASSOCIATES / VIRGINIA ASTLEY / MIKE OLDFIELD** – guitar / **KEN LOCKIE / TIM CROSS** – piano / **ALAN DARBY** – guitar

Oct 81. (7") *(VS 449)* **IONA. / BLOOD AND SPOIL** –

Nov 81. (lp/c) *(V/TCV 2217)* **JOY** –
– Blood and soil / A challenge, the wanderer / Men of mercy / A memory / Iona / In fear of fire / Brothers / And the band played Waltzing Matilda / The men of the fall / The sound of retreat (instrumental) / Fields. *(re-iss. 1988 lp/c; OVED/+C 200)*

— folded early '82 with JOBSON already concentrating on poetry & solo work

– compilations, etc. –

on 'Virgin' unless mentioned otherwise

May 82. (lp/c) *(VM/+C 2)* **FANFARE** –

May 83. (12"ep) *(VS 591-12)* **INTO THE VALLEY / MASQUERADE. / SCARED TO DANCE / WORKING FOR THE YANKEE DOLLAR** –

Jul 87. (cd) *(CDVM 9022)* **DUNFERMLINE (THE SKIDS' FINEST MOMENTS)** –

Feb 92. (m-cd) *Windsong; (<WINCD 008>)* **BBC RADIO 1 LIVE IN CONCERT (live)**

Jan 95. (cd) *(CDOVD 457)* **SWEET SUBURBIA – THE BEST OF THE SKIDS** –

– Into the valley / Charles / The saints are coming / Scared to dance / Sweet suburbia / Of one skin / Night and day / Animation / Working for the Yankee dollar / Charade / Masquerade / Circus games / Out of town / Goodbye civilin / A woman in winter / Hurry on boys / Iona / Fields.

RICHARD JOBSON

solo with **JOHN McGEOGH** – guitar / **VIRGINIA ASTLEY** – piano, flute / **JOSEPHINE** – wind, piano

Cocteau / not iss.

Oct 81. (lp) *(JC 1)* **THE BALLAD OF ETIQUETTE** (some poetry) [ ] [-]
– India song / Don't ever tell anybody anything / Pavillion pole / Etiquette / Joy / Thomas / Anonymous / The night of crystal / Orphee / Stormy weather. *(re-iss. Jul85)*

Crepescule / not iss.

Feb 83. (lp) **10:30 ON A SUMMER NIGHT** [ ] [-]

— with **VINI REILLY** – guitar (of DURUTTI COLUMN) / **WIM MERTENS** (of SOFT VERDICT) / **BLAINE L. REININGER** (of TUXEDO MOON) / **PAUL HAIG** – synthesizers (ex-JOSEF K) / **STEVEN BROWN** – sax

Jul 84. (lp; as THOMAS THE IMPOSTER) **AN AFTERNOON IN COMPANY** [ ] [-]
– Autumn / The return to England / Auden / The Pyrenees / Verbier / The Rhur Valley / Hollow men / Savannah / Jericho 1 / Meditation / Oran / Aragon / Jericho 2 / Dignity / Mount Fuji / The end of the era.

Feb 86. (d-lp) *(TWI 615)* **THE OTHER MAN** [ ] [-]

Jan 87. (lp) *(TWI 807)* **16 YEARS OF ALCOHOL** [ ] [-]

ARMOURY SHOW

was formed by **RICHARD JOBSON** – vocals + RUSSELL WEBB – bass / plus **JOHN McGEOGH** – guitar (ex-SIOUXSIE & THE BANSHEES, ex-MAGAZINE) / **JOHN DOYLE** – drums (ex-MAGAZINE) / **EVAN CHARLES** – keyboards (ex-COWBOYS INTERNATIONAL)

Parlophone / Capitol

Aug 84. (7") *(R 6109)* **CASTLES IN SPAIN. / INNOCENTS ABROAD** [69] [-]
(12"+=) *(12R 6109)* – Is it a wonder.

Jan 85. (7") *(R 6087)* **WE CAN BE BRAVE AGAIN. / A FEELING** [66] [-]
(12"+=) *(12R 6087)* – Catherine.

Jul 85. (7") *(R 6098)* **GLORY OF LOVE. / HIGHER THAN THE WORLD (instrumental)** [ ] [-]
(12"+=) *(12R 6098)* – ('A'part 2) / ('A'instrumental).

Sep 85. (lp/c) *(ARM/TC-ARM 1)* **WAITING FOR THE FLOODS** [57] [ ]
– Castles in Spain / Kyria / A feeling / Jungle of cities / We can be brave again / Higher than the world / Glory of love / Waiting for the floods / Sense of freedom / Sleep city sleep / Avalanche.

Oct 85. (7") *(R 6079)* **CASTLES IN SPAIN. / A GATHERING** [ ] [-]
(12"+=) *(12R 6079)* – Ring those bells.

Jan 87. (7"/12") *(R/12R 6149)* **LOVE IN ANGER. / TENDER IS THE NIGHT** [63] [-]

Apr 87. (7") *(R 6153)* **NEW YORK CITY. / WHIRLWIND** [ ] [-]
(12"+=) *(12R 6153)* – ('A'versions).

— Crumbled around mid'87, with . . .

RICHARD JOBSON

again trying solo career augmented by co-writer RUSSELL WEBB.

Parlophone / not iss.

Aug 88. (7"/12") *(R/12R 6181)* **BADMAN. / THE HEAT IS ON** [ ] [-]
(cd-s+=) *(CDR 6181)* – Big fat city.

Nov 88. (cd/c/lp) *(CD/TC+/PCS 7321)* **BADMAN** [ ] [-]
– Badman / This thing caled love / Monkey's cry / The heat is on / Uptown – downtown / A boat called Pride / Angel / Fire. *(cd+=)* – Big fat city.

— JOBSON, who was now a successful male model while also taking up TV work mainly interviews. Most people now know of him winning his battle against alcohol and epilepsy. In the late 80's, his marriage to TV presenter, Mariella Frostrup failed, although they remained very good friends. He subsequently went on to present late night TV shows including 'Hollywood Report'.

(WORLD OF) SKIN (see under ⇒ SWANS)

SKINNY PUPPY

Formed: Vancouver, Canada . . . 1983 by NIVEK OGRE (aka DAVID OGILVIE), cEVIN KEY and BILL LEEB. Basically a distorted Industrial electronic dance outfit influenced by THROBBING GRISTLE or CABARET VOLTAIRE, their first release in 1985, 'REMISSION', saw them fuse teutonic electro with an early form of acid-house! Live performances combined footage of vivisection experiments with a splattering of fake stage blood and samples of the voice of killer, Charles Manson. DWAYNE GOETTEL was added during the mid-80's, his debut appearance being on the album, 'CLEANSE, FOLD AND MANIPULATE', a record that brought them critical acclaim. Their credibility was partly lost after signing to 'Capitol', the conglomerate plucking them from the depths of Euro-indie obscurity (i.e. 'Nettwerk'). However, by 1990 their sound had incorporated a new off-kilter beat, highlighted on the album, 'TOO DARK PAR'. In August 1995, tragedy struck when heroin addict, DWAYNE, died of a suspected overdose. A final postscript set, 'THE PROCESS', surfaced in early '96, although members have since splintered into DOWNLOAD and PIGFACE. The former had also released two albums for 'Westcom' prior to DWAYNE's death ('SIDEWINDER', 'FURNACE' and new in 1996, 'EYES OF STANLEY PAIN'). KEY had also been part of TEARGARDEN with LEGENDARY PINK DOTS' mainman, EDWARD KA-SPEL.

Album rating: REMISSION mini (*5) / BITES (*6) / MIND: THE PERPETUAL INTERCOURSE (*6) / CLEANSE, FOLD AND MANIPULATE (*7) / VIVIsectVI (*6) / RABIES (*6) / SPASMOLYTIC (*5) / TOO DARK PARK compilation (*7) / LAST RIGHTS (*6) / BACK AND FORTH 2 (*5) / THE PROCESS (*6)

NIVEK OGRE (b. DAVID OGILVIE, 5 Dec'62) – vocals / **cEVIN KEY** (b. KEVIN CROMPTON, 13 Feb'61) – percussion, synthesizer / **BILL LEEB** –

Scarface / Nettwerk

Jun 85. (m-lp) *(MFACE 010)* <30082> **REMISSION** [ ] [ ]
– Smothered hope / Glass houses / Far too frail / Solvent / Sleeping beast / Brap.

— now without LEEB who formed FRONTLINE ASSEMBLY

Feb 86. (lp) *(FACE 15)* <30002> **BITES** [ ] [ ]
– Assimilate / The choke / Blood on the wall / Church / Deadline / Last call / Basement / Tomorrow. *('REMISSION AND BITES' cd-iss. Jan87 on 'Play It Again Sam'; BIAS 048) <US on 'SPV'; 857100>*

Play It Again Sam / not iss.

1986. (12") *(BIAS 037)* **DIG IT. / THE CHOKE** [ ] [-]

Capitol / Capitol

Feb 87. (cd/c) *<C2/C4 90467>* **MIND: THE PERPETUAL INTERCOURSE** [-] [ ]
– One time one place / God's gift (maggot) / Three blind mice / Love / Stairs and flowers / Antagonism / 200 years / Dig it / Burnt with water. *(cd-iss. 1988 on 'Nettwerk'; NT CD 037)* – Chainsaw / Addiction / Stairs and flowers (dub) / Deep down trauma hounds. *(re-iss. lp Aug89 on 'Play It Again Sam'; BIAS 43)*

— added **DWAYNE GOETTEL** (b. 1 Feb'64) – keyboards, samples

Nettwerk / Nettwerk

May 87. (12"/c-s) *(NTM/+C 6305)* **CHAINSAW. /** [ ] [ ]

Oct 87. (12") *(NT12 3010)* **ADDICTION. /** [ ] [ ]

Capitol / Nettwerk

Jan 88. (lp/c) *(EST/TCEST 2052)* <46922> **CLEANSE FOLD AND MANIPULATE** [ ] [ ]
– First aid / Addiction / Shadow cast / Draining faces / The mourn / Second tooth / Tear or beat / Deep down / Trauma hounds / Anger / Epilogue. *(cd-iss. Sep93; NET 019CD)*

1988. (12") *(12CL 517)* **CENSOR (extended). / PUNK IN PARK ZOO'S / CENSOR** [ ] [ ]

Nov 88. (lp/c)(cd) *(EST/TCEST 2079)(CDP 791 040-2)* <91040> **VIVIsectVI** [ ] [ ] Jul88
– Dogshit / VX gas attack / Harsh stone white / Human disease (S.K.U.M.M.) / Who's laughing now? / Testure? / State aid / Hospital waste / Fritter (Stella's home). *(cd+=)* – Yes he ran / Punk in park zoos / The second opinion / Funguss. *(re-iss. cd Sep93 on 'Nettwerk'; NET 021CD)*

— added guest producer **AL JOURGENSEN** – guitar, vocals (MINISTRY)

Nettwerk / Capitol

Jul 90. (lp/cd) *(NET 023/+CD)* <93007> **RABIES** [ ] [ ] Jan90
– Rodent / Hexonxonx / Two time grime / Fascist Jockitch / Worlock / Rain / Tin omen / Rivers / Choralone / Amputate / Spahn dirge (live).

Nov 90. (cd-ep) *(NET 024CD)* **SPASMOLYTIC** [ ] [-]

Feb 91. (cd) *(NET 026CD)* <94683> **TOO DARK PARK; TWELVE INCH ANTHOLOGY** (compilation) [ ] [ ]
– Convulsion / Tormentor / Sasmolytic / Rash reflection / Natures revenge / Short lived poison / Grave wisdom / T.F.W.O. / Morpheus laughing / Reclamation. *(re-iss. Sep93; same)*

Apr 92. (cd) *(NET 038CD)* <98037> **LAST RIGHTS** [ ] [ ]
– Hinder / Killing game / Cancelled / Xception / Catbowl / Hurtful 2 / Rivers end / Fester / Premonoition / Wrek / Epilogue 2. *(re-iss. Sep93; same)*

— now without OGRE. Tragically on 23 August '95, GOETTEL died of a heroin overdose. They were both featured on below album.

American / Warners

Feb 96. (cd) *(74321 31097-2)* <43057> **THE PROCESS** [ ] [ ]
– Jahya / Death / Candle / Hardset head / Cult / The process / Crucible / Blue Serge / Morter / Amnesia / Cellar heat.

– compilations, etc. –

1990. (cd/lp) *Nettwerk;* <30041> **12" ANTHOLOGY** [-] [ ]

1991. (cd) *Nettwerk;* <30061> **AIN'T IT DEAD YET (live)** [-] [ ]
– Intro / Anger / Choke / Addiction / Assimilate / First aid / Dig it / One time one place / Deep down trauma hounds / Chainsaw / Brap / Smothered hope.

Jan 93. (cd) *Nettwerk;* <30078> **BACK AND FORTH SERIES VOL.2** [-] [ ]
– Intro (live in Winnipeg) / Clanging beast / K-9 / Monster radio man / Quiet solitude / Pit / Sore in a masterpiece – Dead of winter / Unovis on a stick / To a baser nature / A.M. – Meat flavour / My voice sounds like shit / Smothered hope / Explode the P.A. / Assimilate / Edge of insanity.

May 96. (d-cd) *Westcom; (0892240-2) / Nettwerk;* <30103> **BRAP** (rare material) [ ] [ ] Apr96

Oct 98. (cd) *Nettwerk;* <30128> **REMIX DAYS TEMPER** [-] [ ]

TEARGARDEN

KEY / + EDWARD KA-SPEL (of LEGENDARY PINK DOTS) / **DOWNLOAD**

Play It Again Sam / Nettwerk

1986. (12") *(BIAS 031)* **CENTRE BULLET. / OPHELIA / TEAR GARDEN / MY THORNY THORNY CROWN** [ ] [ ]

Nettwerk / Nettwerk

Feb 88. (lp/c)(cd) *<(NTL/NTLC 30019)>(NTCD 034)* **TIRED EYES SLOWLY BURNING** [ ] [ ]
– Deja vu / Room with a view / Coma / Valium / You and me and rainbows (parts 1-6) / Oo ee oo. *(cd+=)* – CENTER BULLET EP

1991. (cd) <30074> **THE LAST MAN TO FLY** [-] [ ]
– Hyperform / Running man / Turn me on, Dean man / Romulus and Venus / Great lie / Empathy with the Devil / Circles in the sand / Love notes and carnations / A ship named despair / White coats and halos / Isis veiled / The last post / 3-D technicolour scrambled egg – Trip etc.

1992. (cd) <6315> **SHEILA LIKED THE RODEO** [-] [ ]
– Blobbo / Sybil the spider consumes himself / Sheila liked the rodeo / The strong and winding toad / Do it yourself from A-Z / Sunev DNA Sulumor / Keep the bomb under your coat.

Aug 93. (cd) *(NET 047CD)* **A BOUQUET OF BLACK ORCHIDS** [ ] [ ]
– Sheila liked the rodeo / Orphelia / Tear garden / My thorny thorny crown / Romulus

and Venus / White coats and haloes / Blobbo / Sybil the spider consumes himself / A ship named Despair / The centre bullet / You and me and rainbows / Oo ee oo.

Oct 96. (cd) *<30107>* **TO BE AN ANGEL BLIND, THE CRIPPLED SOUL DIVIDE** [-] [ ]
– Ascension day / We the people / In search of my rose / Crying from outside / Psycho 9 / With wings / Judgement hour / New Eden / Tasteless / Cyberspider / Malice through the looking glass / Phoenix / Habit.

— KEY + friend ALAN NELSON also recorded an album as HILT in 1990.

SKI PATROL (see under ⇒ LOWERY, Ian)

SKREWDRIVER

Formed: Blackpool, England . . . late '76 by IAN STEWART, RON HARTLEY, KEVIN McKAY and GRINNY. Unashamed white-power skinheads, SKREWDRIVER were part of punk's lower division vanguard alongside the likes of CHELSEA, COCK SPARRER and EATER. Signed to the capital's 'Chiswick' label (once home of JOE STRUMMER's 101'ERS), SKREWDRIVER began their notorious recording career in Spring 1977 with the boorish 'YOU'RE SO DUMB' (a blueprint for the UK "oi" movement no doubt). Half a year on, with the 'PISTOLS riding high at No.1, the lads released the self-explanatory 'ANTI-SOCIAL' single backed by a painfully raw cover of The Rolling Stones' '19th NERVOUS BREAKDOWN'. In November that year, their debut (mini) album, 'ALL SKREWED UP' hit the shops, its 45rpm playing speed something of a novelty for the time; its only redeeming feature being a punked-up version of the Who's 'WON'T GET FOOLED AGAIN'. SKREWDRIVER found it hard to get their message across, the majority of punks now finding the pop/punk-friendly anthems of SHAM 69 and their ilk more palatable. During the early 80's, SKREWDRIVER became media hate figures, presented by the tabloids as the unacceptable face of the far right neo-Nazi's. The music press were just as scathing in their criticism, the music obviously taking a backseat to the so-called message of tracks like 'VOICE OF BRITAIN' and 'RETURN OF ST. GEORGE'. Still beloved of racists and bigots today, SKREWDRIVER continue to ply their ugly trade at one-off gigs and extremist rallies.

Album rating: ALL SKREWED UP (*3)

IAN STEWART – vocals / **RON HARTLEY** – guitar / **KEVIN McKAY** – bass / **GRINNY** – drums

Chiswick / not iss.

Apr 77. (7") *(S 11)* **YOU'RE SO DUMB. / BETTER OFF CRAZY** [ ] [-]

Oct 77. (7") *(NS 18)* **ANTI-SOCIAL. / 19TH NERVOUS BREAKDOWN** [ ] [-]

Nov 77. (m-lp; @45rpm) *(CH 3)* **ALL SKREWED UP** [ ] [-]
– Where's it gonna end / Government action / Back street kids / Gotta be young / I don't need your love / I don't like you / Anti-social / Streetfight / (Too much) Confusion / 9 till 5 / Jailbait / Unbeliever / We don't pose / The only one / Won't get fooled again. *(German-iss.lp @33rpm; WIK 3)* – (3 extra included in above).

Mar 78. (7"; shelved) *(NS 28)* **STREETFIGHT. / UNBELIEVER** [-] [-]

T.J.M. / not iss.

Jan 80. (7"ep) *(TJM 4)* **SKREWDRIVER EP** [ ] [-]
– Built up, knocked down / A case of pride / Breakout.

Skrewdriver / not iss.

Sep 82. (12"ep) *(SKREW 1T)* **BACK WITH A BANG** [ ] [-]

White Noise / not iss.

1983. (7"m) *(WN 1)* **WHITE POWER. / SMASH THE I.R.A. / SHOVE THE DOVE** [ ] [-]

1983. (7") *(WN 2)* **VOICE OF BRITAIN. / SICK SOCIETY** [ ] [-]

1984. (7"m) *(WN 3)* **WHEN THE BOAT COMES IN. / WHITE WORKING CLASS MAN / RETURN OF ST. GEORGE** [ ] [-]

— disbanded as a musical recording unit but still played sporadic live gigs and appeared at a few rallies

SKUNK ANANSIE

Formed: London, England . . . early 1994 by striking, shaven-headed black lesbian frontwoman, SKIN and bassist CASS LEWIS. With ACE and ROBBIE FRANCE completing the line-up, SKUNK ANANSIE kicked up enough of a stink to get themselves signed after only a handful of gigs. Their first single, however, was an unofficial limited edition mail order affair lifted from a BBC Radio One Evening Session, 'LITTLE BABY SWASTIKKKA'. A debut single proper, 'SELLING JESUS' hit the shops and the Top 50 in March '95, its controversial content attracting even more interest than the band's burgeoning live reputation. A further couple of furious indie-metallic missives followed in the shape of 'I CAN DREAM' and 'CHARITY', while the band hooked up with labelmate BJORK on her 'Army Of Me' single. Surely one of the most radical acts to ever be associated with the metal scene, the intense interest surrounding scary SKIN and her uncompromising musical vision/political agenda guarenteed a Top 10 placing for the debut album, 'PARANOID & SUNBURNT' (1995). One of the record's most soul-wrenching tracks, 'WEAK', became their biggest hit to date (Top 20) the following January, SKIN's cathartic howl akin to a more soulful PATTI SMITH. Temporary replacement LOUIS was succeeded in turn by MARK RICHARDSON prior to their next Top 20 hit, 'ALL I WANT', one of the many highlights on their second set, 'STOOSH' (1996). Even more scathing than their debut, this angst-ridden collection saw SKUNK ANANSIE championed by Kerrang!, the lead track, 'YES IT'S FUCKING POLITICAL' summing things up perfectly. Riding high in the end of year polls, the Top 10 album contained a further three hit singles, 'TWISTED (EVERYDAY HURTS)', 'HEDONISM (JUST BECAUSE YOU FEEL GOOD)' and 'BRAZEN (WEEP)'. • **Songwriters:** SKIN – ARRAN, some with other two.

Album rating: PARANOID & SUNBURNT (*7) / STOOSH (*9)

SKIN (b. DEBORAH DYER, 3 Aug'67, Brixton, London) – vocals / **ACE** (b.MARTIN KENT, 30 Mar'67, Cheltenham, England) – guitar / **CASS LEWIS** (b.RICHARD LEWIS, 1 Sep'60) – bass / **ROBBIE FRANCE** – drums

One Little Indian / Sony

Mar 95. (10"white/c-s) *(101 TP10/TP7C)* **SELLING JESUS. / THROUGH RAGE / YOU WANT IT ALL** [46] [-]
(cd-s+=) *(101 TP7CD)* – Skunk song.

Jun 95. (10"lime/c-s) *(121 TP10/TP7C)* **I CAN DREAM. / AESTHETIC ANARCHIST / BLACK SKIN SEXUALITY** [41] [-]
(cd-s+=) *(121 TPCD)* – Little baby Swastikkka.

— **LOUIS** – drums; repl. ROBBIE

Aug 95. (c-s) *(131 TP7C)* **CHARITY / I CAN DREAM (version)** [40] [-]
(cd-s+=) *(131 TP7CD)* – Punk by numbers.
(cd-s+=) *(131 TP7CDL)* – Kept my mouth shut.
(10"colrd) *(131 TP10)* – ('A'side) / Used / Killer's war.

Sep 95. (lp/c/cd) *(TPLP 55/+C/CD)* *<67216>* **PARANOID & SUNBURNT** [8] [ ]
– Selling Jesus / Intellectualise my blackness / I can dream / Little baby swastikkka / All in the name of pity / Charity / It takes blood & guts to be this cool but I'm still just a cliche / Weak / And here I stand / 100 ways to be a good girl / Rise up.

Jan 96. (c-s) *(141 TP7C)* **WEAK / TOUR HYMN** [20] [-]
(cd-s+=) *(141 TP7CD)* – Selling Jesus ('Strange Days' film version).
(cd-s) *(141 TP7CDL)* – ('A'side) / Charity (clit pop mix) / 100 ways to be a good girl (anti matter mix) / Rise up (Banhamoon mix).

Apr 96. (c-s) *(151 TP7C)* **CHARITY / I CAN DREAM (live)** [20] [-]
(cd-s+=) *(151 TP7CD)* – Punk by numbers (live).
(cd-s) *(151 TP7CDL)* – ('A'side) / And here I stand (live) / It takes blood & guts to be this cool but I'm still just a cliche (live) / Intellectualise my blackness (live).

— **MARK RICHARDSON** (b.28 May'70, Leeds, England) – drums; repl. LOUIS

Sep 96. (7") *(161 TP7)* **ALL I WANT. / FRAGILE** [14] [-]
(cd-s+=) *(161 TP7CD)* – Punk by numbers / Your fight.
(cd-s) *(161 TP7CDL)* – ('A'side) / But the sex was good / Every bitch but me / Black skinhead coconut dogfight.

Oct 96. (lp/c/cd) *(TPLP 85/+C/CD)* *<67555>* **STOOSH** [9] [ ]
– Yes it's fucking political / All I want / She's my heroine / Infidelity (only you) / Hedonism (just because you feel good) / Twisted (everyday hurts) / We love your apathy / Brazen (weep) / Pickin on me / Milk is my sugar / Glorious pop song.

Nov 96. (c-s) *(171 TP7C)* **TWISTED (EVERYDAY HURTS) / SHE'S MY HEROINE (polyester & cotton mix)** [26] [-]
(cd-s+=) *(171 TP7CD1)* – Milk in my sugar (cement mix) / Pickin on me (instrumental pick'n'mix).
(cd-s) *(171 TP7CD2)* – ('A'-Cake mix) / Pickin on me (pick'n'mix) / Milk in my sugar (instrumental cement mix) / Yes it's fucking political (comix).

Jan 97. (c-ep/cd-ep) *(181 TP7C/+D)* **HEDONISM (JUST BECAUSE YOU FEEL GOOD) / SO SUBLIME / LET IT GO / STRONG** [13] [-]
(cd-ep) *(181 TP7CDL)* – ('A'side) / Song recovery / Contraband / I don't believe.

Jun 97. (cd-ep) *(191 TP7CD1)* **BRAZEN (WEEP) / TWISTED (EVERYDAY HURTS) (radio 1 session) / ALL I WANT (radio 1 session) / IT TAKES BLOOD & GUTS TO BE THIS COOL BUT I'M STILL JUST A CLICHE (radio 1 session)** [11] [-]
(cd-ep) *(191 TP7CD2)* – ('A'-Dreadzone remix) / ('A'-Hani's Weeping club mix) / ('A'-Ventura's Underworld mix) / ('A'-Stealth Sonic Orchestra remix) / ('A'-Cutfather & Joe electro mix).
(cd-ep) *(191 TP7CD3)* – ('A'-Junior Vasquez's Arena anthem) / ('A'-Paul Oakenfold & Steve Osborne mix) / ('A'-Dreadzone's instrumental mix) / ('A'-Junior Vasquez's riff dub) / ('A'-Hani's Hydro instrumental mix).

SKY CRIES MARY

Formed: Seattle, Washington, USA . . . 1987 out of GRINDERS CEASE by RODERICK ROMERO, KEN STRINGFELLOW and JONATHON AUER. Inspired by JIMI HENDRIX and the Euro industrial scene, the band made their debut in early '89 with 'UNTIL THE GRINDERS CEASE', released on the obscure 'Lively Arts' label. Following the departure of KEN and JOHN (to from The POSIES), ROMERO carried on with a new line-up (ANISA, TODD ROBBINS aka DJ FALLOUT, GORDON RAPHAEL, JOSEPH E. HOWARD, BENNETT JAMES and IVAN KRAL) for the turn-of-the-decade mini-set, 'DON'T EAT THE DIRT'. A subsequent deal with 'World Domination' saw the group jump on the neo-psychedelic bandwagon with the hypnotic 'RETURN TO THE INNNER EXPERIENCE' (1994), ROMERO and Co trancing-out the Stooges' 'WE WILL FALL' and the Rolling Stones' '2,000 LIGHT YEARS FROM HOME'. The mystical schtick continued with further releases, 'THIS TIMELESS TURNING' (1994) and one-off major label effort (for 'Warners'), 'MOONBATHING ON SLEEPING LEAVES' (1997) while the band issued the interestingly titled compilation, 'FRESH FRUITS FOR THE LIBERATION' (1998).

Album rating: UNTIL THE GRINDERS CEASE (*4) / DON'T EAT THE DIRT mini (*6) / RETURN TO THE INNER EXPERIENCE (*6) / THIS TIMELESS TURNING (*6) / MOONBATHING ON SLEEPING LEAVES (*6) / FRESH FRUITS FOR THE LIBERATION compilation (*6)

RODERICK ROMERO – vocals, keyboards, etc / **KEN STRINGFELLOW** – guitar, vocals / **JONATHON AUER** – guitar, vocals

Lively Arts / Lively Arts

Jan 89. (lp/c/cd) *<ARTY 011/C/CD>* **UNTIL THE GRINDERS CEASE** [ ] [ ]
– Progergenda / Bath house / Und die flamen / Shakespeare factory / When the fear stops / 9 nite chant / Desert song / Circus nursery rhyme / Serpent sheds.

— **ROMERO** with complete new band when KEN + JOHN formed the POSIES

Dec 90. (m-lp/m-cd) <*(ARTY 026/+CD)*> **DON'T EAT THE DIRT**

— **RODERICK** now with **ANISA ROMERO** – vocals / **TODD ROBBINS** (aka DJ FALLOUT) – turntables, mixer / **GORDON RAPHAEL** – keyboards / **JOSEPH E. HOWARD** – sitar, mellotron, bass / **BENNETT JAMES** – drums / **MARC OLSEN** – guitar; repl. IVAN KRAL / added **JUANO DAVISON** – bass

World Domination / World Domination

May 94. (12"ep/cd-ep) <*(WDOM 003 T/SCD)*> **GONE EP**
– Moon dream meadow allegory / Back to the sea / Cornerman / The elephant song.

May 94. (cd) <*(WDOM 006CD)*> **RETURN TO THE INNER EXPERIENCE**
– Walla walla / Moving like water / Gone / 2000 light years from home / When the fear stops / Lay down your head / Rain / Ocean which humanity is / Broken down / Rosaleen / Bus to gate / Joey's aria / We will fall.

— added **MIKE COZZI** – guitar (ex-SHRIEKBACK)

Sep 94. (cd-ep) *(WDOMO 13SCD)* **EVERY ICEBERG IS AFRICA EP**

Oct 94. (cd) <*(WDOM 011CD)*> **THIS TIMELESS TURNING**
– Shipwrecked / Vuh / Don't forget the sky / These old bones / Stretched / Every iceburg is afire / Scapegoat / Sister ship twenty three / Deep sunless sea / Slow down time / Objects in the mirror / 4:00 a.m. / Walk of nothingness.

— **BEN IRELAND** – drums; repl. JAMES

not iss. / Warners

Feb 97. (cd,c) <*46464*> **MOONBATHING ON SLEEPING LEAVES** -
– Breathe in / The ant, the stars, an owl and its prey / Moonbathing / Grey eyes / Queen of the slug theater / The ringing / Smoke break / Want / Headless man (another song) / Sister / Deep river / Gliding / Nowhere / Insectoria.

– compilations, etc. –

Jun 98. (cd) *World Domination;* <*(WDM 10076-2)*> **FRESH FRUITS FOR THE LIBERATION** (remixes)
– Bath house / Goodbye house / Where does it end . . . / . . . Well, where does it begin? / 2000 light years from home / Corner man / Movement of water / Every iceberg is afire / Wots . . . uh the deal? / Moonbathing / To the one you love.

SLANT 6

Formed: Washington DC, USA ... mid 1992 by MYRA POWER, CHRISTINA BILLOTTE and MARGE MARSHALL. Taking their unusual moniker from a Dodge engine (c.1960's), this all-female trio began their vinyl career with a sporadic series of 7" singles and V/A compilation appearances. Having signed to local hardcore bastion, 'Dischord', SLANT 6 released their debut long-player, 'SODA POP * RIP OFF', in early '94, more an overview of their progress to date rather than a cohesive body of work in itself. IAN MacKAYE (of FUGAZI) also offered his knob-twiddling skills to the follow-up, 'INZOMBIA' (1995), which developed the group's girly punk guitar assault without offering any real innovation.

Album rating: SODA POP * RIP OFF (*6) / INZOMBIA (*4)

CHRISTINA BILLOTTE – vocals, guitar (ex-AUTOCLAVE) / **MYRA POWER** – bass (ex-LUCKY 13) / **MARGE MARSHALL** – drums, organ

Dischord / Dischord

Jul 93. (7") <*(DIS 85V)*> **WHAT KIND OF MONSTER ARE YOU? /**

Mar 94. (cd/lp) <*(DIS 91 CD/V)*> **SODA POP * RIP OFF**
– Don't you ever? / Nights x9 / Love shock / Double edged knife / Time expired / Invisible footsteps / Poison arrows shot at heroes / Don't censor me / Blood song / Soda pop * rip off / Become your ghost / Blue angel / March 6* / What kind of monster are you? / Semi-ble tile / Thirty-thirty vision.

May 95. (cd/lp) <*(DIS 94 CD/V)*> **INZOMBIA**
– G.F.S. / Babydoll / Click-click / Instrumental / Ladybug superfly / Retro duck / Partner in crime / Victim of your own desires / Eight swimming pools / Insider spider / Mascaria / Inzombia.

— disbanded after above

SLAUGHTER & THE DOGS

Formed: Manchester, England ... 1976 by WAYNE BARRETT, MIKE ROSSI, HOWARD BATES and MAD MUFFET. Emerging from a fertile Manchester punk scene concentrated around the city's Electric Circus venue, SLAUGHTER AND THE DOGS were initially signed to local independent label, 'Rabid', through which they issued a debut single, 'CRANKED UP REALLY HIGH'. Signed to 'Decca' in the wake of the punk explosion, the band issued their one and only album, the provocatively titled 'DO IT DOG STYLE', in 1978. Featuring such enduring aggro anthems as 'WHERE HAVE ALL THE BOOT BOYS GONE' (their major label debut single), the record was a first-wave mini-classic played out with more than a passing nod to the proto-punk glam of The NEW YORK DOLLS (especially with regards to BARRETT's THUNDERS-like vocals!). One famous admirer, of course, was a young STEVEN MORRISSEY, auditioned but not taken on for the vacant role of lead singer after BARRETT's subsequent departure. With ROSSI eventually taking over the post and future CULT man BILLY DUFFY added on guitar, the group re-emerged as SLAUGHTER (nothing to do with the American metal-boys!). When that name didn't work, they rather unadvisedly adopted the STUDIO SWEETHEARTS moniker before finally splitting after a brief period with BARRETT back in the fold. More often mentioned for the big name connections rather than their actual music, SLAUGHTER AND THE DOGS nevertheless remain one of the key players in the early punk scene.
• **Songwriters:** BARRETT-ROSSI except; QUICK JOEY SMALL (Kasenetz-Katz Singing Orchestral Circus) / I'M WAITING FOR THE MAN (Velvet Underground).

Album rating: WHERE HAVE ALL THE BOOT BOYS GONE compilation (*6)

WAYNE BARRETT – vocals / **MIKE ROSSI** – guitar / **HOWARD BATES** – bass / **MAD MUFFET** (b. BRIAN CRANFORD) – drums

Rabid / not iss.

Jun 77. (7") *(TOSH 101)* **CRANKED UP REALLY HIGH. / THE BITCH** -

Decca / not iss.

Sep 77. (7") *(FR/LF 13723)* **WHERE HAVE ALL THE BOOT BOYS GONE. / YOU'RE A BORE** -

Nov 77. (7") *(FR 13743)* **DAME TO BLAME. / JOHNNY T** -

Feb 78. (7") *(FR 13758)* **QUICK JOEY SMALL. / COME ON BACK** -

— above featured **MICK RONSON** – guitar (ex-DAVID BOWIE)

May 78. (lp) *(SKL 5292)* **DO IT DOG STYLE** -
– Where have all the boot boys gone / Victims of the vampire / Boston babies / I'm waiting for the man / I'm mad / You're a bore / Quick Joey Small / Keep on trying / We don't care / Since you went away / Who are the mystery girls / Dame to blame.
(re-iss. 1989 colrd-lp on 'Damaged Goods'; FNARR 2)

Rabid / not iss.

Dec 78. (lp) *(HAT 23)* **LIVE SLAUGHTER RABID DOGS (live)** -
(re-iss. Mar 89 on 'Receiver'; RRLP 109)

— **ED BANGER** (EDDIE GARRITY) – guitar (ex-NOSEBLEEDS) repl. WAYNE

T.J.M. / not iss.

Mar 79. (12"ep) *(TJM 3)* **IT'S ALRIGHT / EDGAR ALLEN POE. / TWIST & TURN / UFO** -

D.J.M. / not iss.

Jun 79. (7") *(DJS 10915)* **I BELIEVE. (as "STUDIO SWEETHEARTS") / IT ISN'T ME** -

Nov 79. (7") *(DJS 10927)* **YOU'RE READY NOW. / RUNAWAY** -

SLAUGHTER

— **PHIL ROWLAND** – drums (ex-EATER) repl. MUFFET

— WAYNE BARRETT also returned to repl. BILLY DUFFY who joined THEATRE OF HATE

Feb 80. (7") *(DJS 10936)* **EAST SIDE OF TOWN. / ONE BY ONE** -

Mar 80. (lp) *(DJF 20566)* **BITE BACK** -
– Now I know / What's wrong boy / Won't let go / All over now / She ain't gonna show / Heel in New York / Crashing out with Lucy / Chasing me / It's in the mind / East side of town / Don't wanna die.

Jun 80. (7") *(DJS 10945)* **I'M THE ONE. / WHAT'S WRONG BOY? (live) / HELL IN NEW YORK** -

SLAUGHTER & THE DOGS

— now without ED BANGER

Thrush / not iss.

Feb 83. (12"ep) *(THRUSH 1)* **HALF ALIVE** -
– Twist and turn / Cranked up really high (live) / Where have all the boot boys gone (live).

— split after above

– compilations, etc. –

Jun 83. (lp) *Thrush; (THRUSHLP 1)* **THE WAY WE WERE** -

Nov 88. (7",7"red or green) *Damaged Goods; (FNARR 1)* **WHERE HAVE ALL THE BOOT BOYS GONE. / YOU'RE A BORE / JOHNNY T** -

May 89. (lp) *Receiver; (RRLP 14)* **LIVE AT THE FACTORY (live 1981)** -
– Now I know / Hell in New York / Runaway / Mystery girls / What's wrong boy? / You're ready now / Johnny T / Boston babies / All over now.

Jun 89. (lp) *Link; (LINKLP 092)* **SLAUGHTERHOUSE TAPES** -

Feb 92. (cd/lp) *Receiver; (RR CD/LP 151)* **SHOCKING** -

Mar 94. (cd) *Receiver; (RRCD 183)* **WHERE HAVE ALL THE BOOT BOYS GONE** -

SLAUGHTER JOE

Formed: Hendon / Newcastle, England . . . 1984 by namesake, JOE FOSTER, a one-time member of the TELEVISION PERSONALITIES in the early 80's and subsequent to that, The MISSING SCIENTISTS. This 4-piece – who also included DAN PAN (aka TREACY), EMPIRE (also of The TVP's) and JAQUI (aka DANIEL MILLER) – only recorded one 'Rough Trade' single in 1980, a cover of Dandy Livingstone's 'BIG CITY, BRIGHT LIGHTS' backed with 'DISCOTHEQUE X', before JOE returned for spells with the TVP's. In 1984, the guitarist helped initiate ALAN McGEE's 'Creation' stable, issuing a few psychedelic 45's himself, 'I'LL FOLLOW YOU DOWN' and 'SHE'S SO OUT OF TOUCH' (the latter B-side a cover of The Byrds' rare 'I KNOW YOU RIDER'). Also in 1986, JOE guested for ex-GUN CLUB leader, JEFFREY LEE PIERCE, and married Helen Fitzgerald of The Melody Maker. The following year, JOE formed his own label, 'Kaleidoscope Sound', releasing SLAUGHTER JOE's debut album, 'ALL AROUND MY HOBBY HORSE'S HEAD' (a play on words of a STEELEYE SPAN track!) soon after. His label became the launching pad for at least one great outfit, MY BLOODY VALENTINE.

Album rating: ALL AROUND MY HOBBY HORSE'S HEAD (*5)

JOE FOSTER – vocals, guitar (ex-TELEVISION PERSONALITIES) / **RICHARD BERLIN** – electric viola / **NATHAN DETROIT** – bass / **MEMPHIS** – drums

Creation / not iss.

Jun 85. (7") *(CRE 019)* **I'LL FOLLOW YOU DOWN. / NAPALM GIRL** -
(12"+=) *(CRE 019T)* – Surely some sort of Slaughter's blues / Fall apart.

Nov 86. (7") *(CRE 035)* **SHE'S SO OUT OF TOUCH. / I KNOW YOU RIDER** [ ] [-]
(12"+=) *(CRE 035T)* – The lonesome death of Thurston Moore.

Kaleidoscope Sound / not iss.

Nov 87. (lp) *(KSLP 003)* **ALL AROUND MY HOBBY HORSE'S HEAD** [ ] [-]
(cd-iss. Jun88; KSC 003)

—— JOE continued with production work

– compilations, etc. –

Nov 90. (cd/lp) *Creation; (CRE CD/LP 084)* **THE PIED PIPER OF FEEDBACK** (all his 'Creation' work) [ ] [-]

SLEATER-KINNEY

Formed: Olympia, Washington, USA . . . 1994 by CARRIE BROWNSTEIN and CORIN TUCKER (ex-HEAVENS TO BETSY). The pair met at a feminist convention and became lesbian lovers for a while, CARRIE leaving her outfit, EXCUSE 17, and forming SLEATER-KINNEY (named after a stretch of highway) with CORIN. The twin-guitar playing punk singers eventually recruited drummer, LORA McFARLANE, the all-girl trio becoming darlings of the underground feminist-rock movement, 'Riot Grrrl'. All-girl outfits including the more well-known (at the time) BIKINI KILL and HUGGY BEAR, were all the rage, having been championed by male! rock journalists, Robert Christgau and Greil Marcus. Raised on a musical diet of Scottish indie bands such as the PASTELS, the VASELINES and BEAT HAPPENING (the latter played their own Washington State in the late 80's), CARRIE and CORIN hung out with up and coming, late 80's grunge acts, most notably, NIRVANA and MUDHONEY! S-K's eponymous debut album crashed out on the radical 'Chainsaw' imprint, TONI GOGIN replacing LORA not long afterwards due to the latter's commitments with several other outfits in her homeland Australia. A second set, 'CALL THE DOCTOR' (1996), fared even better leading to major label corporates banging on their door. Shunning their advances like true punks and replacing TONI with JANET WEISS (of QUASI), SLEATER-KINNEY delivered their finest hour yet, 'DIG ME OUT' (1997). In September '98, they toured Britain heralding a long-awaited single release of 'LITTLE BABIES', while, of course, taking time out to visit their long-time musical chums north of the border.

Album rating: SLEATER-KINNEY (*5) / CALL THE DOCTOR (*6) / DIG ME OUT (*7)

CARRIE BROWNSTEIN (b.1975) – vocals, guitar (ex-HEAVENS TO BETSY) / **CORIN TUCKER** (b.1973) – vocals, guitar / **LORA McFARLANE** – drums

Chainsaw / Chainsaw

Apr 95. (cd) *<CHSW 012>* **SLEATER-KINNEY** [-] [ ]
– Don't think you wanna / The day I went away / Real man / Her again / How to play dead / Be yr mama / Sold out / Slow song / Lora's song / The last song. *(UK-iss.Jun98 on 'Matador'; OLE 267-2)*

—— **TONI GOGIN** – drums; repl. LORA who stayed in Australia

Dec 96. (lp/cd) *<(CHSW 013/+CD)>* **CALL THE DOCTOR** [ ] [ ] Mar96
– Call the doctor / Hubcap / Little mouth / Anonymous / Stay where you are / Good things / I want to be your Joey Ramone / Taking me home / Taste test / My stuff / I'm not waiting / Heart attack. *(lp re-iss. Mar98; same) (cd re-iss. Jun98 on 'Matador'; OLE 268-2)*

Villa Villakula / Villa Villakula

Feb 97. (7") *(VVK 02)* **YOU AIN'T IT. /** [ ] [ ]

Matador / Kill Rock Stars

Oct 97. (cd/lp) *(OLE 269-2/-1) <KRS 279>* **DIG ME OUT** [ ] [ ] Apr97
– Dig me out / One more hour / Turn it on / Drama you've been craving / Heart factory / Words and guitar / It's enough / Little babies / Not what you want / Buy her candy / Things you say / Dance song '97 / Jenny. *(re-iss. Mar98 on 'Kill Rock Stars' lp/cd; KRS 279/+CD)*

Nov 97. (10"pic-d) *(VVK 06P)* **SLEATER-KINNEY EP** [ ] [ ]
(above on 'Villa Villakula' and below released on 'Candy Ass')

Nov 97. (7"; split with CYPHER IN THE SNOW) *(CAR 028)* **split** [ ] [ ]

Apr 98. (7") *(VVK 22)* **YOU'RE NOT IT. /** [ ] [ ]
(above issued on 'Villa Villakula')

Jun 98. (7"yellow/cd-s) *(OLE 321-7/-2)* **ONE MORE HOUR. / I WANNA BE YOUR JOEY RAMONE** [ ] [ ]

Sep 98. (7"blue/cd-s) *(OLE 326-7/-2)* **LITTLE BABIES. / I'M NOT WAITING** [ ] [ ]

SLEEPER

Formed: Ilford, Essex, England . . . 1993 by LOUISE WENER and her boyfriend JOHN STEWART, the pair duly recruiting ANDY McCLURE and DIID OSMAN. Signing to upcoming 'R.C.A.'-offshoot, 'Indolent', SLEEPER released their debut EP in late '93, 'ALICE IN VAIN', WENER causing controversy from the off with an attack on the sacred cow of feminism. If she brought the wrath of the more radical in the female population, then she no doubt scored a few brownie points with the boys, indie lads increasingly besotted by her saucer-eyed cuteness as well as her outspoken personality. Another couple of EP's, 'SWALLOW', and 'DELICIOUS', followed in quick succession, their sexual frankness further endearing WENER to the more hormonal element of her audience. The singer had already acquired a burgeoning reputation for her lippy diatribes by the time the 'INBETWEENER' single broke the Top 20 in early '95 and the attendant interest in all things WENER ensured the debut album, 'SMART', a Top 5 placing. Getting down to the nitty gritty i.e. the music, were SLEEPER actually any good? Well, they could certainly hold their own among the Brit-pop competition although that wasn't saying much; basically they were a competent spiky guitar outfit with the odd ear-catching tune, notably the dreamy bit/noisy bit pop rush of 'VEGAS', arguably their finest moment. Later that year, the group scored a second Top 20 hit with the lightweight indie-pop of 'WHAT DO I DO NOW' followed by 'SALE OF THE CENTURY', their first Top 10 single, though by no means their best. WENER's profile was at an all-time high, her forthright views offending and delighting in equal measure; there was no middle ground with this lass, you either admired her or wished she would sod off (the aptly named SLEEPER also proved that work and pleasure were actually compatible after all). Predictably, then, a follow-up album, 'THE IT GIRL' (1996), met with decidedly mixed reviews although it sold respectably. A backlash was inevitable, however, a third set, 'PLEASED TO MEET YOU' (1997) only produced universal indifference, both critically and commercially. Being ignored is probably one thing which WENER never counted on, although its doubtful such a feisty babe will bow out without a fight, or at least a controversial word or two. • **Songwriters:** Most by WENER or some w/ STEWART. Covered OTHER END OF THE TELESCOPE (Elvis Costello & Aimee Mann) / ATOMIC (Blondie); used on 'Trainspotting' film.

Album rating: SMART (*8) / THE IT GIRL (*6) / PLEASED TO MEET YOU (*6)

LOUISE WENER – vocals, guitar / **JOHN STEWART** – lead guitar / **DIID OSMAN** – bass / **ANDY MacCLURE** – drums, percussion

Indolent / Arista

Nov 93. (7"ep/12"ep/cd-ep) *(SLEEP 001/+T/CD)* **THE ALICE EP** [ ] [-]
– Alice in vain / Ha ha you're dead / Big nurse.

Feb 94. (7"ep/cd-ep) *(SLEEP 002/+CD)* **SWALLOW. / TWISTED / ONE GIRL DREAMING** [ ] [-]

May 94. (7"ep/cd-ep) *(SLEEP 003/+CD)* **DELICIOUS. / LADY LOVE YOUR COUNTRYSIDE / BEDSIDE MANNERS** [75] [-]
(12"ep+=) *(SLEEP 003T)* – Tatty.

Oct 94. (7"mail-order) **BUCKET AND SPADE (live)** [-] [-]
– Bedhead / Alice in vain / Swallow.

Jan 95. (7"/c-s) *(SLEEP 006/+MC)* **INBETWEENER. / LITTLE ANNIE** [16] [-]
(cd-s+=) *(SLEEP 006CD)* – Disco Duncan.
(12"++=) *(SLEEP 006T)* – Bank.

Feb 95. (cd/c/lp) *(SLEEP CD/MC/LP 007) <25825>* **SMART** [5] [ ] Mar95
– Inbetweener / Swallow / Delicious / Hunch / Amuse / Bedhead / Lady love your countryside / Vegas / Poor flying man / Alice in vain / Twisted / Pyrotechnician.

Mar 95. (7"blue/c-s) *(SLEEP 008/+MC)* **VEGAS. / HYMN TO HER** [33] [-]
(12"pic-d/cd-s+=) *(SLEEP 008 T/CD)* – It's wrong to breed / Close.

Sep 95. (7"/c-s) *(SLEEP 009/+MC)* **WHAT DO I DO NOW? / PAINT ME** [14] [-]
(cd-s+=) *(SLEEP 009CD1)* – Room at the top.
(cd-s) *(SLEEP 009CD2)* – ('A'side) / Vegas (live) / Amuse (live) / Disco Duncan (live).

Apr 96. (7"colrd/c-s/cd-s) *(SLEEP 011/+MC/CD1)* **SALE OF THE CENTURY. / ATOMIC** [10] [-]
(cd-s) *(SLEEP 011CD2)* – ('A'side) / Package holiday / Oh well.

May 96. (cd/c/lp) *(SLEEP CD/MC/LP 012) <18824>* **THE IT GIRL** [5] [ ]
– Lie detector / Sale of the century / What do I do now? / Good luck Mr. Gorsky / Feeling peaky / Shrinkwrapped / Dress like your mother / Statuesque / Glue ears / Nice guy Eddie / Stop your crying / Factor 41 / Click . . . off . . . gone.

Jul 96. (7"/c-s) *(SLEEP 013/+MC) <3064>* **NICE GUY EDDIE. / INBETWEENER** [10] [ ]
(cd-s+=) *(SLEEP 013CD)* – Poker face / Blazer sleeves.

Sep 96. (7") *(SLEEP 014)* **STATUESQUE. / SHE'S A SWEETHEART** [17] [-]
(cd-s+=) *(SLEEP 014CD1)* – Spies.
(cd-s) *(SLEEP 014CD2)* – ('A'side) / ('A'-The Boxed Off mix) / Other end of the telescope / Atomic (Wubble U mix).

Sep 97. (7"/c-s) *(SLEEP 015/+MC)* **SHE'S A GOOD GIRL. / COME ON COME ON** [28] [-]
(cd-s+=) *(SLEEP 015CD)* – I'm a man.

Oct 97. (cd/c/lp) *(SLEEP CD/MC/LP 016)* **PLEASED TO MEET YOU** [7] [-]
– Please please please / She's a good girl / Rollercoaster / Miss you / Romeo me / Breathe / You got me / Superclean / Firecracker / Because of you / Nothing is changing / Motorway man / Traffic accident.

Nov 97. (7"clear) *(SLEEP 017)* **ROMEO ME. / C**T LONDON** [39] [-]
(cd-s) *(SLEEP 017CD1)* – ('A'side) / This is the sound of someone else / What do I get? / Nice guy Eddie (Peel session).
(cd-s) *(SLEEP 017CD2)* – ('A'side) / When will you smile? / What do I do now? (radio 1 evening session) / Motorway man (Arctic mix).

SLINT

Formed: Louisville, Kentucky, USA . . . 1988 by former SQUIRREL BAIT partners, BRIAN McMAHON and BRITT WALFORD, who had already teamed up with DAVID PAJO and ETHAN BUCKLER prior to the latter band's division into BASTRO and SLINT. The influential noiseniks made their debut the following year with the self-financed, STEVE ALBINI-produced album, 'TWEEZ', a willfully weird clutch of mainly instrumental guitar/bass-led creations named after their family members (including a dog!). While WALFORD (aka SHANNON DOUGHTY) moonlighted on The BREEDERS first album, 'Pod', BUCKLER would subsequently leave to form KING KONG, replacement TODD BRASHER installed as work commenced on a BRIAN PAULSON-produced follow-up set, 'SPIDERLAND'. Upon its release (on 'Touch & Go') in '91, the album generated a healthy ammount of column inches praising its uncategorisable guitar-scapes, Scotland's own MOGWAI later citing the record as a pivotal reference point. While rumours circulated that the album's recording had almost sent SLINT over the edge, the individual members were obviously sane enough to work on various projects including WILL OLDHAM's PALACE BROTHERS (WALFORD,

McMAHON and BRASHER) and TORTOISE (PAJO). A final postscript to the SLINT story came in 1994 with the release of double-A side single, 'GLENN' / 'RHODA' (the latter a cut from '89). Following PAJO's stint with avant-jazz combo, TORTOISE, the musical Jack-of-all trades followed a similar dusty path to the aforementioned OLDHAM, on his eponymous 1997 debut solo set (released under the AERIAL-M moniker), foregoing vocals in favour of backporch strumming. Licensed from 'Drag City' to 'Domino' in the UK, the rootsy homegrown affair showed a mellower side to the normally uncompromising guitarist and paved the way for two further releases over the course of the following year. Neither single, 'M IS . . .' and 'OCTOBER', featured on the album, although they may well make an appearance on the anticipated follow-up.

Album rating: TWEEZ (*7) / SPIDERLAND (*8) / Aerial-M: AERIAL-M (*7)

BRIAN McMAHON – vocals, guitar (ex-SQUIRREL BAIT) / **DAVID PAJO** – guitar / **ETHAN BUCKLER** – bass / **BRITT WALFORD** – drums (ex-SQUIRREL BAIT)

Jennifer Hartman / Jennifer Hartman

Sep 89. (lp) *<JHR 136>* **TWEEZE** [ ] [ ]
– Ron / Nan ding / Carol / Kent / Charlotte / Darlene / Warren / Pat / Rhoda. *<(re-iss. May93 on 'Touch & Go' lp/cd; TG 138/+D)>*

— **TODD BRASHER** – bass; BUCKLER who formed KING KONG

Touch & Go / Touch & Go

Mar 91. (cd/c/lp) *<(TG CD/MC/LP 64)>* **SPIDERLAND** [ ] [ ]
– Breadcrumb trail / Nosferatu man / Don a man / Washer / For dinner . . . / Good morning, captain. *(re-iss. Sep98; same)*

Sep 94. (10"/cd-s) *<(TG 132/+CD)>* **GLENN. / RHODA** [ ] [ ]

— disbanded when WALFORD + McMAHON joined the PALACE BROTHERS. PAJO subsequently joined TORTOISE before going solo with AERIAL-M

AERIAL-M

DAVID PAJO – guitars

Domino / Drag City

1996. (7") **SAFELESS. /** [-] [ ]

Dec 96. (7"; split with MONADE) **VOL DE NUIT. /** [-] [ ]

Sep 97. (cd/lp) *(WIG CD/LP 037) <DC 114>* **AS PERFORMED BY . . . AERIAL-M** [ ] [ ] Aug97
– Dazed and awake / Aass / Wedding song No.2 / Rachmaninoff / Skrak theme / Compassion for M / Always farewell.

Feb 98. (7"m)<cd-ep> *(RUG 062)<DC 144CD>* **M IS . . . / WEDDING THEME NO.3 / MOUNTAINS HAVE EARS** [ ] [ ] Dec97

Jun 98. (7") *(RUG 070) <DC 155>* **OCTOBER** [ ] [ ] Feb99
– Vivea / Last caress.

SLIPSTREAM

Formed: Rugby, England . . . 1993 by MARK REFOY when he was still a member of SPIRITUALIZED. Early in 1994, SLIPSTREAM (who were completed by IAN ANDERSON, GARY LENNON and STEVE BESWICK) signed to indie label, 'Che', releasing three singles over the course of the following year, the last of which was a version of Kraftwerk's 'COMPUTER LOVE'. Their accompanying eponymous ZION TRAIN-produced album was issued in March '95, featuring some fine acoustic PINK FLOYD/CAN-ish styled songs. Later that year, two more singles preceded a compilation, although all was quiet on the SLIPSTREAM front until 1997's 'BE GROOVY OR LEAVE'.

Album rating: SLIPSTREAM (*6) / BE GROOVY OR LEAVE (*5)

MARK REFOY – vocals, guitar (ex-SPIRITUALIZED) / **IAN ANDERSON** – guitar / **GARY LENNON** – bass / **STEVE BESWICK** – drums

Kinglake / not iss.

Jan 94. (7") *(KLR 006)* **YOUR STAR IS FALLING. /** [ ] [-]

Che / Carrot Top

Jul 94. (7") *(che 14)* **SUNDOWN. / SWEET MERCY / IT'S TRUE SHE SAID** [ ] [-]

Oct 94. (7") *(che 19)* **YOUR PRESENCE. / GIVE IT SOME TIME** [ ] [-]
(cd-s+=) *(che 19cd)* – Kornbus / I saw your face.

Feb 95. (7"one-sided-pink) *(che 21)* **COMPUTER LOVE** [ ] [-]

Mar 95. (cd/c/lp) *(che 22 cd/mc/lp) <7>* **SLIPSTREAM** [ ] [ ]
– Harmony / Riverside / Pulsebeat / One step ahead / Sensurround / Computer love / Sweet mercy / Feel good again / Sundown / She passes by.

Sep 95. (7") *(che 35)* **UP IN HEAVEN. / HEARING VOICES** [ ] [-]

Sep 95. (7") *(che 36)* **COME BACK. / LATE TOO LATE** [ ] [-]

Che / Elektra

Dec 95. (cd) *(che 37cd) <61875>* **SIDE EFFECTS** (singles compilation) [ ] [ ] Oct95
– Up in Heaven / Hearing voices / Come back / Late too late / Do you have an answer? / All for nothing / All the symphonies / Computer love / Your presence / Give it some time / Hometown / I saw your face / Sundown / Sweet mercy / It's true she said.

Urban Culture / not iss.

Jul 96. (12") *(05)* **INTERFERENCE. / THE ABYSS** [ ] [-]

— **STEVE NEW** – bass; repl. LENNON

Che / Che-Warners

Jun 97. (lp/cd) *(che/+cd 69) <62083>* **BE GROOVY OR LEAVE** [ ] [ ]
– Dancing mood / You'll never catch me out again / Scars / Not there with you / There is a love / Come on and listen / Madeleine / Beneath the waves / Say it now / Leave it all behind.

Dec 97. (7") *(che 73)* **MADELEINE. / HEALING HANDS** [ ] [-]

Enraptured / not iss.

Dec 98. (7") *(RAPT 4522)* **EVERYTHING & ANYTHING. /** [ ] [-]

Utopia / not iss.

Dec 98. (lp) *<033>* **UTOPIA** [-] [ ]

SLITS

Formed: London, England . . . early 1977 as the foremost all-girl outfit on the punk scene (until BUDGIE joined that is) and initially comprising ARI UP (aka ARIANNA FOSTER), KATE KORUS, SUZI GUTSY and PALMOLIVE. By the time the group had secured a support slot on The CLASH's Spring 1977 tour, KORUS and GUTSY had been replaced by VIV ALBERTINE and TESSA POLLITT respectively, the band's infamously amateurish approach compensated by their bolshy hardline feminist attitude. Although they had two John Peel sessions under their belts, The SLITS didn't actually sign a deal until 1979, having turned down the 'Real' label (home to The HEARTBREAKERS and PRETENDERS) the previous year. In the event the not-so "TYPICAL GIRLS" signed with 'Island' and set to work on a debut album with reggae producer, Dennis Bovell, the aforementioned BUDGIE (PETER CLARK) coming in as a replacement for PALMOLIVE who departed midway through the recording sessions. A Top 30 hit upon its release in late '79, the seminal 'CUT' showcased ARI's distinctive vocal phrasing against a compelling backdrop of unorthodox tribal rhythms and raw guitar abrasion, the sleeve's cover shot of the lasses getting butt naked and muddy generating almost as much interest as the music. With BUDGIE decamping to SIOUXSIE & THE BANSHEES, BRUCE SMITH was recruited in his place and despite the presence of respected jazz trumpeter, DON CHERRY (father of NENEH), a dreadful untitled bootleg/jam affair did the band no favours. Much more enjoyable was the subsequent cover of John Holt's 'MAN NEXT DOOR', released as a single a couple of months later in the summer of 1980. A further single followed on the 'Human' label before The SLITS signed to 'C.B.S.' for a final disappointing patchy album, 'RETURN OF THE GIANT SLITS' (1981), the group disbanding in early '82. While SMITH joined Bristolian avant-funk collective RIP, RIG & PANIC, the remaining members (minus POLLITT) went on to be part of colossus ensemble, The NEW AGE STEPPERS. • **Songwriters:** Group compositions, except I HEARD IT THROUGH THE GRAPEVINE (Marvin Gaye). • **Trivia:** Early in 1978, they were sighted in the punk film, 'Jubilee'.

Album rating: CUT (*9) / RETURN OF THE GIANT (*6)

ARI UP (b. ARIANNA FOSTER) – vocals / **VIVIEN ALBERTINE** – guitar (ex-FLOWERS OF ROMANCE) repl. KATE KORUS to KLEENEX (Feb77) / **TESSA POLLITT** – bass repl. SUZI GUTSY who formed The FLICKS. / **PALMOLIVE** – drums (ex-FLOWERS OF ROMANCE) was repl. (Oct78) by **BUDGIE** (b. PETER CLARK, 21 Aug'??, St.Helens, England) – percussion, drums (ex-BIG IN JAPAN, ex-SECRETS,etc)

Island / Antilles

Sep 79. (lp/c) *(ILPS/ZCI 9573) <7072>* **CUT** [30] [ ]
– Instant hit / So tough / Spend spend spend / Shoplifting / FM / Newtown / Ping pong affair / Love and romance / Typical girls / Adventures close to home. *(cd-iss. Apr90; IMCD 89)*

Sep 79. (7") *(WIP 6505)* **TYPICAL GIRLS. / I HEARD IT THROUGH THE GRAPEVINE** [60] [ ]
(12"+=) *(12WIP 6505)* – Typical girls (brink style) / Liebe and romanze.

— **BRUCE SMITH** – drums (of POP GROUP) repl. BUDGIE to SIOUXSIE & BANSHEES jazz-trumpeter **DON CHERRY** guested

Y – Rough Trade / not iss.

Mar 80. (7") *(Y1 – RT 039)* **IN THE BEGINNING THERE WAS RHYTHM. / (B-side by the Pop Group)** [ ] [-]

May 80. (lp) *(Y3LP)* **UNTITLED (Y3LP)** (bootleg demo jam) [ ] [-]
– A boring life / Slime / Or what it is / No.1 enemy / Once upon a time in a living room / Bongos on the lawn / Face place / Let's do the split / Mosquitos / Vaseline / No more rock and roll for you.

Jun 80. (7") *(Y4 – RT 044)* **MAN NEXT DOOR. / MAN NEXT DOOR (dub version)** [ ] [-]

— added guest **STEVE BERESFORD** – keyboards, guitar (of FLYING LIZARDS)

Human / not iss.

Nov 80. (7") *(HUM 4)* **ANIMAL SPACE. / ANIMAL SPACIER** [ ] [-]

C.B.S. / Epic

1981. (12"m) **ANIMAL SPACE. / ANIMAL SPACIER / IN THE BEGINNING THERE WAS RHYTHM** [-] [ ]

Aug 81. (7") *(A 1498)* **EARTHBEAT. / BEGIN AGAIN RHYTHM** [ ] [-]
(12"+=) *(A13 1498)* – Earthdub.

Oct 81. (lp/c) *(CBS/40 85269)* **RETURN OF THE GIANT SLITS** [ ] [ ]
– Earthbeat / Or what it is? / Face place / Walkabout / Difficult fun / Animal space – Spacier / Improperly dressed / Life on Earth. *(free-7"w/ lp) (XPS 125)* – AMERICAN RADIO INTERVIEW (Winter 1980). / FACE DUB

Dec 81. (7") *(49-02567>* **EARTHBEAT. / OR WHAT IT IS?** [-] [ ]

— Parted ways early 1982. BRUCE joined RIP, RIG & PANIC. All except TESSA were part of colossus band NEW AGE STEPPERS.

– compilations, others, etc. –

on 'Strange Fruit' unless otherwise mentioned

Feb 87. (12"ep) *(SFPS 021)* **THE PEEL SESSION** (19.9.77) [ ] [-]
– Love and romance / Vindictive / Newtown / Shoplifting.

Nov 88. (m-lp/cd) *(SFPMA/+CD 207)* **DOUBLE PEEL SESSIONS** [ ] [-]

SLOAN

Formed: Halifax, Novia Scotia, Canada . . . 1991 by CHRIS MURPHY, PATRICK PENTLAND, JAY FERGUSON and ANDREW SCOTT. Touting an unrestrained soundclash of melodic grunge and fuzz-pop, SLOAN snagged a deal with 'Geffen' after an unlikely showcase at Canada's predominantly folk orientated East Coast Music Awards. Yet by the time they'd moved on up to major label land, the band had already cut a debut EP, 'PEPPERMINT', releasing it on their own 'Murder' label in Autumn '92. Debut album, 'SMEARED', followed later that year amid positive press reaction praising the band's affecting combination of pointed lyrics and gonzoid RAMONES-style enthusiasm. Despite promising North American sales, the group parted company with 'Geffen' after follow-up set, 'TWICE REMOVED' (1994), subsequently taking time out themselves to rethink their strategy. The SLOAN crew eventually re-emerged with the self-financed 'ONE CHORD TO ANOTHER' in 1997, successfully licensing the record to 'E.M.I.' for worldwide release. • **Covered:** DIGNIFIED AND OLD (Jonathan Richman) / GLITTER AND GOLD (Mann-Weil) / OVER YOU (Roxy Music) / I CAN'T LET GO (Gorgoni-Taylor) / STOOD UP (. . . Grimson) / ON THE ROAD AGAIN – TRANSOMA FIVE (Canned Heat – Stereolab) / I WOULDN'T WANT TO LOSE YOUR LOVE (. . . Goodwyn)

Album rating: SMEARED (*6) / TWICE REMOVED (*6) / ONE CHORD TO ANOTHER (*7) / NAVY BLUES (*7)

JAY FERGUSON – vocals, guitar / **PATRICK PENTLAND** (b. N.Ireland) – guitar, vocals / **CHRIS MURPHY** – bass, vocals / **ANDREW SCOTT** – drums

Murderchords Murderchords

Feb 93. (cd-ep) <(MURCD 001)> **PEPPERMINT EP**

Geffen Geffen

Feb 93. (cd/c/lp) <(GED/GEC/GEF 24498)> **SMEARED**
– Underwhelmed / Raspberry / I am the cancer / Median strip / Take it in / 500 up / Marcus said / Sugartune / Left of centre / Lemonzinger / Two seater / What's there to decide.

Mar 93. (12"ep/cd-ep) (GFST/+D 36) **UNDERWHELMED / WHAT'S THERE TO DECIDE? / AMPED / SLEEPOVER**

Jul 93. (12"ep/cd-ep) (GFST/+D 45) **I AM THE CANCER / TWO SEATER. / RAG DOLL / LAYING BLAME**

Enclave not iss.

1994. (cd) (24711) **TWICE REMOVED** [-]

Murderechords Capitol

Apr 97. (lp/cd) (MUR/+SD 023) <55281> **ONE CHORD TO ANOTHER**
– Good in everyone / Nothing left to make me wanna stay / Autobiography / Junior panthers / G turns to D / Side wins / Everything you've done wrong / Anyone who's anyone / Lines you amend / Take the bench / Can't face up / 400 metres / Let's get the party started / I can feel it. <cd+=>**PARTY** – Dignified and old / Glitter and gold / Over you / I am the cancer / I can't let go / Stood up / One the road again – Transoma five / I wouldn't want to lose your love.

Murderecords Murderecords

May 98. (cd) <(MURCD 36)> **NAVY BLUES**
– She says what she means / C'mon c'mon (we're gonna get it started) / Iggy & Angus / Sinking ships / Keep on thinkin' / Money city maniacs / Seems so heavy / Chester the molester / Stand by me, yeah / Suppose they close the door / On the horizon / I wanna thank you / I'm not through with you yet.

SLOWDIVE

Formed: Thames Valley, Reading, England . . . 1990 by schoolfriends RACHEL GOSWELL and NEIL HALSTEAD. The pair duly recruited NICK CHAPLIN and belatedly accepted a final member, CHRISTIAN SAVILLE, who had been desperate to join them. After only a handful of gigs, SLOWDIVE signed to Alan McGee's 'Creation' label, where they debuted with a self-titled EP. Early the following year, the quartet scored another massive alternative chart hit with 'MORNINGRISE'. Their third EP, 'HOLDING OUR BREATH', nearly cracked the UK Top 50, the debut album, 'JUST FOR A DAY', accomplishing this feat later that year. Immersed in shimmering, distortion-happy guitars and ethereal atmospheric harmonies, their sound lay somewhere between MY BLOODY VALENTINE, The JESUS & MARY CHAIN and other "shoegazers" (RIDE and MOOSE) of that early 90's era. However, emerging grunge acts like NIRVANA were to hasten SLOWDIVE's downfall, well at least in the music press stakes where "shoegazing" bands were now looked down upon. After an 18-month hiatus, they returned with the follow-up, 'SOUVLAKI', although it was clear from their poor sales they had left it too long. An EP entitled '5EP' (their 5th) showed greater promise, using techno acts RELOAD and BANDULU to boost their now ambient direction. After their third and probably best work, 'PYGMALION' (1995), they were dropped amid a fundamental shake-up at their record label. NEIL and RACHEL were promptly snatched up by '4 a.d.', resurfacing later that year with the much underrated MOJAVE 3, actually a 5-piece completed by IAN McCUTCHEON, SIMON ROWE and POPPY (aka AUDREY RILEY). Mapping out entirely different territory from SLOWDIVE, the HALSTEAD – GOSWELL songwriting axis was now geared towards a wistful, heavy-lided amalgam of countrified alt-folk/pop taking in the likes of LEONARD COHEN, NICK DRAKE and MAZZY STAR. This much was evident from even a cursory listen to their inaugural long-player, 'ASK ME TOMORROW'. Unfortunately it would be three long years before a follow-up, the acclaimed but generally ignored 'OUT OF TUNE' (1998). • **SLOWDIVE covered:** GOLDEN HAIR (Syd Barrett).

Album rating: JUST FOR A DAY (*6) / SOUVLAKI (*5) / PYGMALION (*7) / Mojave 5: ASK ME TOMORROW (*7) / OUT OF TUNE (*7)

RACHEL GOSWELL (b.16 May'71, Hampshire, England) – vocals, guitar / **NEIL HALSTEAD** (b. 7 Oct'70, Luton, England) – vocals, guitar / **CHRISTIAN SAVILLE** (b. 6 Dec'70, Bury, England) – guitar / **NICK CHAPLIN** (b.23 Dec'70, Slough, England) – bass / **NEIL CARTER** (ex-COLOUR MARY), who had repl. original ADRIAN SELL

Creation S.B.K.

Nov 90. (12"ep)(cd-ep) (CRE 093T)(CRESCD 093) **SLOWDIVE:- AVALYN I. / SLOWDIVE:- AVALYN II** [-]

— **SIMON SCOTT** (b. 3 Mar'71, Cambridge, England) – drums (ex-CHARLOTTES), repl. NEIL CARTER

Feb 91. (12"ep)(cd-ep) (CRE 098T)(CRESCD 098) **MORNINGRISE. / SHE CALLS / LOSING TODAY** [-]

Jun 91. (7") (CRE 112) **CATCH THE BREEZE. / SHINE** [52] [-]
(12"ep+=)(cd-ep+=) **HOLDING OUR BREATH** (CRE 112T)(CRESCD 112) – Albatross / Golden hair.

Aug 91. (cd/lp)(c) (CRE CD/LP 094)(CCRE 094) <98074> **JUST FOR A DAY** [32]
– Spanish air / Cedlia's dream / Catch the breeze / Ballad of Sister Sue / Erik's song / Waves / Brighter / The sadman / Primal.

1992. (cd/lp) **BLUE DAY** [-]
– Slowdive:- Avalyn I / Morningrise / She calls / Losing today / Shine / Albatross.

— now without CHAPLIN

May 93. (12"ep)(cd-ep) (CRE 119T)(CRESCD 119) **OUTSIDE YOUR ROOM** [69] [-]
– Alison / So tired / Souvlaki space station / Moussaka chaos.

Jun 93. (cd/lp)(c) (CRE CD/LP 139)(CCRE 139) <88263> **SOUVLAKI** [51] Feb94
– Alison / Machine gun / 40 days / Sing / Here she comes / Souvlaki space station / When the Sun hits / Altogether / Melon yellow / Dagger.

Nov 93. (12"ep)(cd-ep) (CRE 157T)(CRESCD 157) **5 EP** [-]
– Bandulu (in mind mix) / (open mind mix) / (in mind mix) / Reload (remix – the 147 take).
(12"ep)(cd-ep) (CRE 157TR)(CRESCD 157R) – ('A'-other mixes).

Feb 95. (cd/lp)(c) (CRE CD/LP 168)(CCRE 168) **PYGMALION** [-]
– Rutty / Crazy for you / Miranda / Trellisaze / Cello / Jay's heaven / Visions of L.A. / Blue skied and clear / All of us.

— split later in the year, SIMON resurfaced in 1998 as frontman for INNER SLEEVE.

MOJAVE 3

— **RACHEL + NEIL** plus **IAN McCUTCHEON** – drums, percussion / **SIMON ROWE** – guitar / **POPPY (AUDREY RILEY)** – cello / with guest **CHRISTOPHER ANDREWS** – piano

4 a.d. 4ad-Reprise

Oct 95. (lp/cd) (CAD 5013/+CD) <46084> **ASK ME TOMORROW** Feb96
– Love songs on the radio / Sarah / Tomorrow's taken / Candle song 3 / You're beautiful / Where is the love / After all / Pictures / Mercy. (cd re-iss. Jul98; GAD 5013CD)

Jun 98. (cd-ep) (BAD 8011CD) **WHO DO YOU LOVE / THIS ROAD I'M TRAVELLING / BETWEEN US / WHO DO YOU LOVE (demo)** [-]

Sep 98. (7") (AD AD 8016) **SOME KINDA ANGEL. / ALL I WANT** [-]
(cd-s+=) (BAD 8016CD) – Go lady go.

Oct 98. (lp/cd) (<CAD 8018/+CD>) **OUT OF TUNE**
– Who do you love / Give what you take / Some kinda angel / All your tears / Yer feet / Caught behind your heel / Keep it all hid / Baby's coming home / To whom should I write.

SMALLER

Formed: Liverpool, England . . . early 90's by drummer/songwriter PETER DEARY, his brother and frontman STEPHEN DEARY, plus PAUL CAVANNAGH and JASON RILEY. Boasting a chequered musical CV including a stint in early 80's popsters COOK DA BOOKS, PETER DEARY (aka DIGSY) had been slogging away at writing songs almost as long as his old mucker NOEL GALLAGHER (a guest on the debut album), the latter giving him a starring role in OASIS favourite, 'Digsy's Dinner' (from 'Definitely Maybe'). Located firmly in the hard-bitten realism school of writing, DEARY spelled out his self-admittedly cynical worldview on SMALLER's debut single, 'GOD I HATE THIS TOWN', issued in Autumn '95 on independent label, 'Better'. Over the course of the next 18 months, SMALLER delivered three singles, the latter two, 'WASTED' and 'IS', hitting the lower regions of the charts. A full length debut album, 'BADLY BADLY' (1997), carried on in the same vein, self-deprecatingly detailing the trials and tribulations of years in the pop wilderness.

Album rating: BADLY BADLY (*6)

STEPHEN DEARY – vocals, lead guitar / **PAUL CAVANNAGH** – bass / **JASON RILEY** – guitar, vocals / **PETER DEARY** – drums (ex-COOK DA BOOKS)

Better not iss.

Sep 95. (7") (betcd 002) **GOD I HATE THIS TOWN. /** [-]
(cd-s+=) (betscd 002) –

Apr 96. (7") (bet 005) **STRAY DOGS AND BIN BAGS. /** [-]
(cd-s+=) (betscd 005) –

Sep 96. (7") (bet 006) **WASTED. / AIMLESS** [72] [-]
(cd-s+=) (betscd 006) – Garden shed / Chain of solitude.

Mar 97. (7") (bet 008) **IS. / ALL THE SAME TO ME** [55] [-]
(cd-s+=) (betscd 008) – The pane.
(cd-s) (betscd 008L) – ('A'album version) / Wasted (live) / ('A'live) / The cross (live).

Apr 97. (cd/c/lp) (bet cd/mc/lp 003) **BADLY BADLY** [-]
– Small time / The biscuit tin / Is / Whenever love lies / Wasted / On your own / God I hate this town / Ticket to Hell / Just as bad / Giz a life / In my livable hole.

S*M*A*S*H

Formed: Welwyn Garden City, Hertfordshire, England . . . 1992 as SMASH AT THE BLUES by ED BORRIE, SALVADOR ALESSI and ROB HAIGH. One of the most fiercely political bands since The CLASH (an obvious influence alongside the ISTOLS and the ANGELIC UPSTARTS), S*M*A*S*H made an immediate impact in summer '93 with the 'REAL SURREAL' single. Issued on their own 'Le Disques De Popcor' label, the track was followed up by early '94's 'SHAME', a double A-sided NME/Melody Maker single of the week and the subject of much controversy due to its flip side, 'LADY LOVE YOUR CUNT' (the title a reference to an essay by Germaine Greer). By this point the band were also being heralded as leaders of the much hyped "New Wave Of New Wave" scene alongside THESE ANIMAL MEN (they had previously shared an album, 1993's 'WHEELERS, DEALERS AND CHRISTINE KEELERS'), the press coverage not exactly harming them as incendiary live performances blazed a trail across the UK. The band subsequently signed to 'Hi-Rise' along with THESE ANIMAL MEN, releasing a mini-set compilation of their work to date, 'S*M*A*S*H SPRING 1994'. It broke the Top 30, as did the controversial '(I WANT TO KILL) SOMEBODY' – which infamously included a hit list of Tory MP's – the subject of censorship from Radio One. The band's political beliefs were further underlined when they played an Anti-Nazi League rally alongside BILLY BRAGG, the fact that they were more effective in a live environment than the studio confirmed with the release of a full length debut album, 'SELF ABUSED' (1994). Criticisms centred around the thin production yet amidst all the buzzsaw bluster were genuinely affecting moments such as 'REFLECTIONS OF YOU (REMEMBER ME)', 'TIME' etc. Whatever, the album failed to sell and the band concentrated on a US tour, supported by a one-off single on 'Sub Pop', 'BARRABAS'. Their return to British shores was marked with the release of mini-set, 'ANOTHER LOVE (SONG)' (1995), although it contained only a handful of genuinely new tracks. With Brit-pop now dominating the music scene, S*M*A*S*H's moment seemed to have passed and following a final single, 'REST OF MY LIFE', they officially split.

Album rating: SELF ABUSED (*6) / ANOTHER LOVE (SONG) mini (*5)

ED BORRIE – vocals, guitar / **SALVADOR ALESSI** – bass / **ROB HAIGH** – drums (ex-NIGHTMARE, ex-ASTRONAUTS)

		Les Disques	not iss.
Jul 93.	(7") *(POPCOR 001)* **REAL SURREAL. / DRUGS AGAIN / REVISITED NO.3**		-
Dec 93.	(c-ep) *(POPCOR 002)* **WHEELERS, DEALERS & CHRISTINE KEELERS** – Self-abused / Kill somebody / Altruism / Bang bang bang / (5 other tracks by THESE ANIMAL MEN)		-
Feb 94.	(7",7"pink/one-sided7"red) *(POPCOR 003/+V)* **LADY LOVE YOUR CUNT. / SHAME**		-
		Hi-Rise	Hut
Mar 94.	(m-cd/m-c/m-lp) *(FLATM CD/TC/LP 2)* *<3>* **S*M*A*S*H SPRING 1994** – Real surreal / Drugs again / Revisited No.3 / Lady love your c*** / Shame.	28	
Jul 94.	(c-ep/12"ep/cd-ep) *(FLATS TC//CD 5)* **(I WANT TO) KILL SOMEBODY (Topper mix). / ('A'-Keith LeBlanc mix) / ('A'Gunshot headhunter mix) / ('A'-Bragg reshuffle mix)**	26	
Sep 94.	(cd/c/lp) *(FLAT CD/MC/LP 6)* *<HUSCD 6>* **SELF ABUSED** – Revisited No.5 / Barrabas / Oh ovary / Altruism / Reflections of you (remember me) / Self abused / Scream silent / Another love / Another shark in the deep end of my swimming pool / Real surreal / Dear Lou / Bang bang bang (granta 25) / Time. *(cd+=)* – A.L.L.Y.C. *(also other lp++=; FLATLPX 6)* – Trainspotter.	59	
Nov 94.	(7") *(SP 276)* **BARRABAS (PILOTED). / TURN ON THE WATER** (above single on 'Sub Pop')		
Feb 95.	(m-cd/m-c/m-lp) *(FLATM CD/TC/LP 10)* **ANOTHER LOVE (SONG) EP** – Another love (Bobbit mix) / Petal buzz / You've got a friend who's a friend of mine / Reflections of you (remember me) (live) / Time (live) / Self abused (live) / Another love (uncut).		-
		Popcor	not iss.
Jan 96.	(7"/cd-s) *(POPCOR 9/+CD)* **THE REST OF MY LIFE. /**		-

— broke up after above

SMASHING ORANGE

Formed: Wilmington, Delaware, USA . . . 1990 by the songwriting siblings, ROB and SARA MONTEJO. Completed by RICK HODGSON, STEVE WAGNER and TIM SUPPLEE, who, together with the MONTEJO's, worked in a local record store, the band were formed after the various members had either dropped out or just left college. While supporting LUSH in New York, SMASHING ORANGE signed to 'Native', releasing their debut single in '91, 'MY DERANGED HEART'. Compared to everyone from GALAXIE 500 to MY BLOODY VALENTINE, the record was a taster for the distorted noise-pop of their much lauded eponymous debut album. Unfortunately, however, the band were dealt a fatal blow with the subsequent collapse of their record company, the fact that their was already a top flight band with a similar name probably not helping any.

Album rating: SMASHING ORANGE (*7) / THE GLASS BEAD GAME (*5) / NO RETURN IN THE END (*5)

ROB MONTEJO – vocals / **SARA MONTEJO** – vocals / **RICK HODGSON** – guitar / **STEVE WAGNER** – bass / **TIM SUPPLEE** – drums

		Native	Ringers Lactate
Apr 91.	(7") **MY DERANGED HEART ./** (cd-s+=) –		
May 91.	(cd/c/lp) **SMASHING ORANGE**		
Nov 91.	(7"/cd-s) *<03>* **NOT VERY MUCH TO SEE. / COLLIDE**	-	
		Native	Chameleon
Mar 93.	(cd) *(CD 7001)* *<61444>* **THE GLASS BEAD GAME**		Feb93
		not iss.	M.C.A.
Oct 94.	(cd) *<11116>* **NO RETURN IN THE END** – God is a woman / The way that I love you / You are the sun / Jaded / Don't have to tell me / Gifted / You're gonna get yours / Fata Morgana / She carries her own weight / Culminate / Early morning love.	-	

— another to be eaten up by the music industry and bad luck

SMASHING PUMPKINS

Formed: Chicago, Illinois, USA . . .late 80's by BILLY CORGAN, JAMES IHA, D'ARCY WRETZKY. The son of a jazz guitarist and former member of local goth band, The MARKED, CORGAN initiated The SMASHING PUMPKINS as a three piece using a drum machine, before the band recruited sticksman, JIMMY CHAMBERLAIN. After a debut single for a local label, 'I AM ONE', and the inclusion of two tracks on a local compilation album, the group came to the attention of influential Seattle label, 'Sub Pop'. After only one single, 'TRISTESSA', The SMASHING PUMPKINS moved once more, signing to Virgin subsidiary, 'Hut', in the UK, 'Caroline' in America. Produced by BUTCH VIG, a debut album, 'GISH', was released in early '92, its grunge pretensions belying a meandering 70's/psychedelic undercurrent which distanced the band from most of their contemporaries. Nevertheless, the group amassed a sizable student/grassroots following which eventually saw the debut go gold in the States, a re-released 'I AM ONE' sneaking into the UK Top 75 later that year. With the masterful 'SIAMESE DREAM' (1993), the band went from underground hopefuls to alternative rock frontrunners, the album fully realising the complex 'PUMPKINS sound in a delicious wash of noise and gentle melody. Influenced by acoustic LED ZEPPELIN fused with slices of 70's PINK FLOYD, CORGAN's croaky but effective voice was at its best on the pastel, NIRVANA-esque classics, 'TODAY' and 'DISARM', while the 'PUMPKINS went for the jugular on the likes of 'CHERUB ROCK', 'ROCKET' and 'GEEK U.S.A.'. The album made the Top 5 in Britain, Top 10 in the States, selling multi-millions and turning the band into a 'grunge' sensation almost overnight, despite the fact that their mellotron stylings and complex arrangements marked them out as closer in spirit to prog-rock than punk. Amidst frantic touring, the band released the outtakes/B-sides compilation, 'PISCES ISCARIOT' (1994), the next album proper surfacing in late '95 as the sprawling double set, 'MELLON COLLIE AND THE INFINITE SADNESS'. Dense and stylistically breathtaking, the album veered from all-out grunge/thrash to acoustic meandering and avant-rock doodlings, a less cohesive whole than its predecessor but much more to get your teeth into. Inevitably, there were criticisms of self-indulgence, though for a two-hour set, there was a surprising, compelling consistency to proceedings; among the highlights were 'BULLET WITH BUTTERFLY WINGS', 'TONIGHT, TONIGHT' and the visceral rage of '1979'. The record scaled the US charts, where The SMASHING PUMPKINS were almost reaching the commercial and critical heights of NIRVANA, the group also taking Britain by storm, headlining the 1995 Reading Festival. Never the most stable of bands, disaster struck the following year when new boy (keyboard player) JONATHAN MELVOIN died of a drugs overdose and heroin addict CHAMBERLAIN was finally kicked out. More recently (early 1998), IHA released an acclaimed solo album of acoustic strumming and the latest news is that the group are currently recording with a drum machine, taking things full circle. • **Songwriters:** CORGAN, except several with IHA. Covered; A GIRL NAMED SANDOZ (Eric Burdon & The Animals) / LANDSLIDE (Fleetwood Mac) / DANCING IN THE MOONLIGHT (Thin Lizzy) / NEVER LET ME DOWN (Depeche Mode) / YOU'RE ALL I'VE GOT TONIGHT (Cars) / CLONES (WE'RE ALL) (Alice Cooper) / DREAMING (Blondie) / A NIGHT LIKE THIS (Cure) / DESTINATION UNKNOWN (Missing Persons) / SAD PETER PAN with Red Red Meat (Vic Chesnutt).

Album rating: GISH (*6) / SIAMESE DREAM (*9) / MELLON COLLIE AND THE INFINITE SADNESS (*9) / PISCES ISCARIOT compilation (*5) / THE AEROPLANE FLIES HIGH boxed set (*6)

BILLY CORGAN (b.17 Mar'67) – vocals, guitar / **JAMES IHA** (b.26 Mar'68, Elk Grove, Illinois) – guitar / **D'ARCY (WRETZKY)** (b. 1 May'68, South Haven, Michigan) – bass, vocals / **JIMMY CHAMBERLIN** (b.10 Jun'64, Joliet, Illinois) – drums

		not iss.	Limited Potential
Apr 90.	(7") *<Limp 006>* **I AM ONE. / NOT WORTH ASKING**	-	
		Glitterhouse	Sub Pop
Dec 90.	(7",7"pink) *<SP 90>* **TRISTESSA. / LA DOLLY VITA** (UK-12"+=; May93) *(SP 10-137)* – Honeyspider.	-	
		Hut	Caroline
Aug 91.	(12") *(HUTT 6)* **SIVA. / WINDOW PAINE**		-
Feb 92.	(12"ep/cd-ep) *(HUTT/CDHUT 10)* **LULL EP** – Rhinoceros / Blue / Slunk / Bye June (demo).		-
Feb 92.	(cd/c/lp) *(HUT CD/MC/LP 002)* *<1705>* **GISH** – I am one / Siva / Rhinoceros / Bury me / Crush / Suffer / Snail / Tristessa / Window paine / Daydream. *(re-iss. May94; diff.versions cd/lp; HUT CDX/LPX 002)*		Aug91
Jun 92.	(c-ep/12"ep/cd-ep) *(HUT C/T/CD 17)* **PEEL SESSIONS** – Siva / A girl named Sandoz / Smiley.		-

Aug 92. (12"ep/cd-ep) *(HUTT/CDHUT 18)* **I AM ONE. / PLUME / STARLA** [73] [-]
(10"ep) *(HUTTEN 18)* – ('A'side) / Terrapin (live) / Bullet train to Osaka.

Jun 93. (7"clear) *(HUT 31)* **CHERUB ROCK. / PURR SNICKETY** [31] [-]
(12"/cd-s) *(HUTT/CDHUT 31)* – ('A'side) / Pissant / French movie theme / (Star spangled banner).

Jul 93. (cd/c/d-lp) *(HUT CD/MC/LP 011) <88267>* **SIAMESE DREAM** [4] [10]
– Cherub rock / Quiet / Today / Hummer / Rocket / Disarm / Soma / Geek U.S.A. / Mayonaise / Spaceboy / Silverfuck / Sweet sweet / Luna.

Sep 93. (7"red) *(HUT 37)* **TODAY. / APATHY'S LAST KISS** [44] [-]
(c-s/12"/cd-s) *(HUTC/HUTT/CDHUT 37)* – ('A'side) / Hello kitty kat / Obscured.

Feb 94. (7"purple) *(HUT 43)* **DISARM. / SIAMESE DREAM** [11] [-]
(12"/cd-s) *(HUT T/CD 43)* – ('A'side) / Soothe (demo) / Blew away.
(cd-s) *(HUTDX 43)* – ('A'side) / Dancing in the moonlight / Landslide.

Oct 94. (cd/c/gold-lp) *<39834>* **PISCES ISCARIOT** (compilation of B-sides & rarities) [-] [4]
– Soothe / Frail and bedazzled / Plume / Whir / Blew away / Pissant / Hello Kitty Kat / Obscured / Landslide / Starla / Blue / A girl named Sandoz / La dolly vita / Spaced. *<w/ free gold-7"; CAR 1767-7>* **NOT WORTH ASKING. / HONEY SPIDER II** *(UK-iss.Oct96 cd/c/lp; HUT CD/MC/LP 41)*

Hut Virgin

Dec 94. (7"peach) *(HUTL 48)* **ROCKET. / NEVER LET ME DOWN** [ ] [-]
(4x7"box-set) *(SPBOX 1)* **SIAMESE SINGLES** – (last 3 singles 1993-94 + above)

Oct 95. (c-s/cd-s) *(HUT C/CD 63) <38522>* **BULLET WITH BUTTERFLY WINGS / . . .SAID SADLY** [20] [25]

Oct 95. (d-cd/d-c) *(CD/TC HUTD 30) <40861>* **MELLON COLLIE AND THE INFINITE SADNESS** [4] [1]
– DAWN TO DUSK:- Mellon Collie and the infinite sadness / Tonight, tonight / Jellybelly / Zero / Here is no why / Bullet with butterfly wings / To forgive / An ode to no one / Love / Cupid de Locke / Galapogos / Muzzle / Porcelina of the vast oceans / Take me down. // TWILIGHT TO STARLIGHT:- Where boys fear to tread / Bodies / Thirty-three / In the arms of sleep / 1979 / Tales of a scorched Earth / Thru the eyes of Ruby / Stumbleine / X.Y.U. / We only come out at night / Beautiful / Lily (my one and only) / By starlight / Farewell and goodnight. *(re-iss. Apr96 as t-lp+=; HUTTLP 30)* – Tonight reprise / Infinite sadness.

— added on tour **JONATHAN MELVOIN** – keyboards (ex-DICKIES) (brother of WENDY; ex-WENDY & LISA, ex-PRINCE)

Jan 96. (c-ep/12"ep/cd-ep) *(HUT C/T/CD 67) <38547>* **1979 / UGLY. / BELIEVE / CHERRY** [16] [12]
(12"ep/cd-ep; Mar96) *(HUT TX/CDX 67)* – 1979 REMIXES: Vocal / Instrumental / Moby / Cement.

May 96. (c-ep) *(HUTC 69) <38547>* **TONIGHT, TONIGHT / MELADORI MAGPIE / ROTTEN APPLES** [7] [36] Jun96
(cd-ep+=) *(HUTCD 69)* – Medellia of the gray skies.
(cd-ep) *(HUTDX 69)* – ('A'side) / Jupiter's lament / Blank / Tonite (reprise).

— On 12th Jul'96, MELVOIN died of a heroin overdose. CHAMBERLIN, who found him dead, was charged with drug offences and sacked by the remaining trio who were said to sick of his long-lasting drug addiction. In August, they were replaced for tour by **DENNIS FLEMION** – keyboards (ex-FROGS) + **MATT WALKER** – drums (of FILTER)

Sep 96. (m-cd) *(HUTCD 73) <38545>* **ZERO EP** [ ] [46] May96
– Zero / God / Mouths of babes / Tribute to Johnny / Marquis in spades / Pennies / Pastichio medley: (excerpts).

Nov 96. (cd-ep) *(HUTCD 78) <38574>* **THIRTY THREE / THE LAST SONG / THE AEROPLANE FLIES HIGH (TURNS LEFT, LOOKS RIGHT) / TRANSFORMER** [21] [39]
(cd-ep) *(HUTDX 78)* – ('A'side) / The bells / My blue Heaven.

Nov 96. (5xcd-ep;box) *<SPBOX 2>* **THE AEROPLANE FLIES HIGH** [-] [42]
– (BULLET WITH BUTTERFLY WINGS / 1979 / TONIGHT, TONIGHT / THIRTY THREE / ZERO)

— early in '97, CORGAN provided six songs for 'RANSOM' film soundtrack credited to conductor JAMES HORNER (Hollywood HR 62086-2)

Jun 97. (c-s) *(W 0404C)* **THE END IS THE BEGINNING IS THE END / THE BEGINNING IS THE END IS THE BEGINNING** [10] [ ]
(cd-s+=) *(W 0404CD)* – The ethers tragic / The guns of love disastrous.
(12"/cd-s) *(W 0410 T/CD)* – ('A'mixes; 2 Fluke mixes / 2 Rabbit in The Moons mixes / Hallucination Gotham mix).
(above from the film 'Batman And Robin' on 'Warners')

May 98. (7") *(HUT 101) <38647>* **AVA ADORE. / CZARINA** [11] [42] Jun98
(c-s+=/cd-s+=) *(HUT C/CD 101)* – Once in a while.

Jun 98. (cd/c/d-lp) *(CDHUT/TCHUT/HUTDLP 51) <45879>* **ADORE** [5] [2]
– To Sheila / Ava adore / Perfect / Daphne decends / Once upon a time / Tear / Crestfallen / Appels + oranjes / Pug / The tale of Dusty and Pistol Pete / Annie-dog / Shame / Behold! the night mare / For Martha / Blank page / 17.

Sep 98. (c-s/cd-s) *(HUT C/CD 106) <38650>* **PERFECT / SUMMER / PERFECT (Nellee Hooper mix)** [24] [54]
(cd-s) *(HUTDX 106)* – ('A'side) / Daphne descends (Oakenfold Perfecto mix) / Daphne descends (Kerry B mix).

JAMES IHA

JAMES IHA – vocals, guitar / **NEAL CASAL** – guitar / **ADAM SCHLESINGER** – piano (of FOUNTAINS OF WAYNE) / **GREG LEISZ** – steel guitar / **JOHN GINTY** – hammond organ / **SOLOMON SNYDER** – bass / **MATT WALKER** – drums / **NINA GORDON** (of VERUCA SALT) also a part of initial basement set-up

Feb 98. (cd/c/lp) *(CDHUT/HUTMC/HUTLP 47) <45411>* **LET IT COME DOWN** [ ] [ ]
– Be strong now / Sound of love / Beauty / See the sun / Country girl / Jealousy / Lover, lover / Silver string / Winter / One and two / No one's gonna hurt you.

Feb 98. (12"ep/cd-ep) *(HUT T/CD 99)* **BE STRONG NOW / MY ADVICE. / TAKE CARE / FALLING** [ ] [ ]

Pat SMEAR (see under ⇒ GERMS)

Elliott SMITH

Born: 1970, Dallas, Texas, USA, although raised from a young age by his father in Portland, Oregon, after his parents divorced. The singer/songwriter relocated to university digs in Brooklyn, New York, playing in mid-90's noisy alternative rock band, HEATMISER. They released four rare albums, 'DEAD AIR' (1993), 'YELLOW NO.5' (1994; a mini-set), 'COP AND SPEEDER' (1995) and 'MIC CITY SONS' (1996), while ELLIOTT, meantime had opted for a more sedate solo career. He delivered three very well received albums for the 'Kill Rock City' imprint', namely 'ROMAN CANDLE' (1994), 'ELLIOTT SMITH' (1995) and 'EITHER/OR' (1997) – all licensed in 1998 to the UK arm of 'Domino' – before he inked a deal with 'DreamWorks'. This was due to the plaudits heaped upon him after appearing on stage alongside CELINE DION and TRISHA YEARWOOD at the "Oscars" ceremony! An unlikely story you may think, although the truth is, he provided part of the soundtrack to one of the best films of the year, 'Good Will Hunting'. His unfashionable (especially his taste in clothing and headgear – sometimes a tammy) approach was slightly reminiscent of SIMON & GARFUNKEL, BIG STAR or the lo-fi RICHARD DAVIES (of CARDINAL). His fourth album, 'XO', hit the shops later in 1998 and ELLIOTT looked certain to make his impact on the music scene.

Album rating: ROMAN CANDLE (*7) / ELLIOTT SMITH (*7) / EITHER/OR (*8) / XO (*7) / Heatmiser: DEAD AIR (*6) / COP AND SPEEDER (*7) / MIC CITY SONS (*6)

HEATMISER

ELLIOTT SMITH – vocals / **NEIL GUST** – guitar, vocals / **SAM COOMES** – bass / **TONY LASH** – drums

Frontier Frontier

Jul 93. (cd/c) *<(31057-2/-4)>* **DEAD AIR** [ ] [ ] Jun93
– Still / Candyland / Mock up / Dirt / Bottle rocket / Blackout / Stray / Can't be touched / Cannibal / Don't look down / Sands hotel / Low life / Buick / Dead air.

Jul 94. (m-cd) *<(31062-2)>* **YELLOW NO.5** [ ] [ ]
– Wake / Fortune 500 / The corner seat / Idler / Junior mint / Yellow No.5.

Apr 95. (cd) *<(31063-2)>* **COP AND SPEEDER** [ ] [ ]
– Disappearing ink / Bastard John / Flamel / Temper / Why did I decide to stay? / Collect to NYC / Hitting on the waiter / Busted lip / Antonio Carlos Jobim / It's not a prop / Something to lose / Sleeping pill / Trap door / Nightcap.

Caroline Cavity Search

Oct 96. (cd) *(CAR 75402) <CSR 35-2>* **MIC CITY SONS** [ ] [ ]
– Get lucky / Plainclothes man / Low flying jets / Rest my head against the wall / Fix is in / Eagle eye / Cruel reminder / You gotta move / Pop in G / Blue highway / See you later.

— split after SMITH was already making a name for himself as a solo act, while COOMES was in a duo with JANET WEISS called QUASI.

ELLIOTT SMITH

- vocals, drums, bass saxophones, etc.

not iss. Suicide Squeeze

1994. (7") *<5>* **DIVISION DAY. / NO NAME #6** [-] [ ]

not iss. Cavity Search

Dec 94. (cd) *<CSR 13-2>* **ROMAN CANDLE** [-] [ ]
– Roman candle / Condor avenue / No name #I / No name #II / No name #III / Drive all over town / No name #IV / The last call / Kiwi mad-dog 20-20. *(UK-iss.Mar98 on 'Cavity Search'; same as US) (re-iss. Aug98 on 'Domino' cd/lp; REWIG CD/LP 002)*

Kill Rock Stars Kill Rock Stars

Feb 95. (7") *(KRS 239)* **NEEDLE IN THE HAY. /** [ ] [ ]

Jul 95. (lp/cd) *<KRS 246/+CD>* **ELLIOTT SMITH** [-] [ ]
– Needle in the hay / Christian brother / Clementine / Southern belle / Single file / Coming up roses / Satellite / Alphabet town / St.Ides heaven / Good to go / White lady loves you more / Biggest lie. *(UK-iss.Mar98; same) (re-iss. Aug98 on 'Domino' cd/lp; REWIG CD/LP 001)*

Oct 96. (7") *<(KRS 266)>* **SPEED TRIALS. /** [ ] [ ]

Mar 97. (lp/cd) *<(KRS 269/+CD)>* **EITHER/OR** [ ] [ ]
– Speed trials / Alameda / Ballad of big nothing / Between the bars / Pictures of me / No name No.5 / Rose parade / Punch and Judy / Angeles / Cupid's trick / 2:45 am / Say yes. *(UK-iss.Jun98 on 'Domino' cd/lp; WIG CD/LP 51)*

Jun 98. (7") *(RUG 74)* **BALLAD OF BIG NOTHING. / SOME SONG / DIVISION DAY** [ ] [ ]
(cd-s+=) *(RUG 74CD)* – Angeles.

— with a plethora of session people + strings

DreamWorks DreamWorks

Aug 98. (cd/c) *<(DRD/DRC 50048)>* **XO** [ ] [ ]
– Sweet Adeline / Tomorrow tomorrow / Waltz #2 (XO) / Baby Britain / Pitseleh / Independence day / Bled white / Waltz #1 / Amity / Oh well, okay / Bottle up and explode! / A question mark / Everybody cares, everybody understands / I didn't understand. *<(lp-iss.on 'Bongload'; BL 35)>*

Dec 98. (c-s/cd-s) *(DRM S/CD 22347)* **WALTZ #2 (XO) /** [52] [ ] Feb99

Patti SMITH

Born: 31 Dec'46, Chicago, Illinois, USA. She started to write for New York magazine 'Rock' in 1969, having earlier being shipped around by her family between Paris and London. In the early 70's, PATTI began writing poetry full-time and met fellow rock-scribe, LENNY KAYE, who provided guitar accompaniment for her beat-poet monologues at readings/gigs. By 1971 she was writing for 'Creem' magazine and soon developed a professional musical partnership with playwright, SAM SHEPHERD. A prolific time for SMITH, come Christmas '72 she had two books of poetry, 'Witt' and '7th Heaven' in the stores and, after contributing to TODD RUNDGREN's 'A WIZARD, A TRUE STAR' album, he credited her for nicknaming him 'Runt'. RICHARD SOHL was recruited alongside SMITH and KAYE for a one-off single in 1974, 'HEY JOE / PISS FACTORY' on the small 'MER' label. A suitably caustic slice of proto-punk, it later gained airplay after being picked up by 'Sire' records. Meanwhile, SMITH completed the line-up of what would become The PATTI SMITH GROUP with IVAN KRAAL and JAY DEE DAUGHERTY, signing to 'Arista' and starting work on the 'HORSES' (1975) album with JOHN CALE producing. From the monochrome androgyny of the cover shot to the DIY three chord thrash which formed the bulk of the musical backing, the album was a blueprint for a generation of both American and British punk/new wave artists. Although SMITH's vocals were something of an acquired taste, her distinctive intonation was a perfect vehicle for the image rich symbolism of her free flowing lyrics. 'GLORIA' and 'LAND OF 1,000 DANCES' were transformed into weird, beat-inspired flashes of nervous energy, while quieter moments like the intro to 'REDONDO BEACH' and 'FREE MONEY' possessed a stark beauty. After this alternative tour de force, the follow-up, 'RADIO ETHIOPIA' (1976), came as something of a departure. Possessing a more straightforward hard-rock approach save for the chaotic feedback-drenched exploration of the title track, the album received mixed reviews. After SMITH survived breaking her neck after falling from the stage at a gig, it was to be another two years before the release of her next album. 'EASTER' (1978) was a confident comeback which moved even further into commercial rock territory without extinguishing the livewire spark that had made 'HORSES' so compelling. The record contained an unlikely collaboration with BRUCE SPRINGSTEEN, 'BECAUSE THE NIGHT', which saw SMITH breach the upper reaches of the singles charts on both sides of the Atlantic and propelled the album to similar success. 'WAVE' (1979) sounded slightly unfocused although it attained a higher chart placing Stateside than its predecessor. After a final tour in 1979, SMITH bowed out of the music business for domestic bliss with her new husband FRED 'SONIC' SMITH (ex-MC5). Together with her spouse, SOHL and DOUGHERTY, she recorded a low-key comeback album in 1988, 'DREAM OF LIFE', although tragedy struck in the 90's when both SOHL and her husband died from heart failure. With many artists namechecking her as an influence, SMITH recorded 'GONE AGAIN' (1996) amid a mini-renaissance. A tribute to FRED, it was filled with a sense of loss and yearning, echoing the intensity of her earlier work. • **Songwriters:** Lyrics PATTI, some music KAYE. Covered HEY JOE (Jimi Hendrix) / LAND OF A THOUSAND DANCES (Cannibal & The Headhunters) / MY GENERATION (The Who) / GLORIA (Them) / SO YOU WANNA BE A ROCK'N'ROLL STAR (Byrds) / 5-4-3-2-1 (Manfred Mann) / DOWNTOWN TRAIN (Tom Waits) / WICKED MESSENGER (Bob Dylan). • **Trivia:** In 1974, she co-wrote with ex-boyfriend ALLEN LANIER, his groups' (BLUE OYSTER CULT) 'Career Of Evil'. Her albums were produced by JOHN CALE (1st) / JACK DOUGLAS (2nd) / JIMMY IOVINE (3rd) / TODD RUNDGREN (4th) / FRED SMITH and JIMMY IOVINE (1988).

Album rating: HORSES (*9) / RADIO ETHIOPIA (*7) / EASTER (*7) / WAVE (*6) / DREAM OF LIFE (*5) / GONE AGAIN (*6) / PEACE AND NOISE (*6)

PATTI SMITH – vocals, poetry / with **LENNY KAYE** – guitar / **RICHARD SOHL** – piano not iss. M.E.R.

Aug 74. (7") *<601>* **HEY JOE. / PISS FACTORY** [-] [ ]
(UK-iss.Mar78 on 'Sire'; SRE 1009)

— added **IVAN KRAL** – bass, guitar, piano / **JAY DEE DAUGHERTY** – drums

Arista Arista

Dec 75. (lp) *(ARTY 122) <4066>* **HORSES** [ ] [47]
– Gloria / Redondo Beach / Birdland / Free money / Kimberly / Break it up / Land: Horses – Land of a thousand dances – La mer (de) / Elegie. *(re-iss. Aug88 lp/c/cd; 201/401/252-112) (cd re-iss. Jul96+=; 18827-2)* – My generation (live).

Apr 76. (7") *(ARIST 47)<AS 0171>* **GLORIA. / MY GENERATION (live)** [ ] [ ]
(re-iss. 12"-Sep77; ARIST 12135)

Oct 76. (lp/c) *(SPARTY/TCSPARTY 1001) <4097>* **RADIO ETHIOPIA** [ ] [ ]
– Ask the angels / Ain't it strange / Poppies / Pissing in the river / Pumping (my heart) / Distant fingers / Radio Ethiopia / Abyssinia. *(re-iss. Aug88 lp/c/cd; 201/401/251-117) (re-iss. cd Jul96; 18825-2)*

— Her tour featured **LEIGH FOXX** – bass repl. SOHL. Others augmenting at the time **ANDY PALEY** (ex-ELLIOT MURPHY) + **BRUCE BRODY** – keyboards (ex-JOHN CALE)

PATTI SMITH GROUP

with **KAYE, KRAAL, DAUGHERTY, BRODY + SOHL**

Mar 78. (7") *(ARIST 181) <AS 0318>* **BECAUSE THE NIGHT. / GOD SPEED** [5] [13]

Mar 78. (lp/c) *(SPARTY/TCSPARTY 1043) <4171>* **EASTER** [16] [20]
– Till victory / Space monkey / Because the night / Ghost dance / Babelogue / Rock'n'roll nigger / Privilege (set me free) / We three / 25th floor / High on rebellion / Easter. *(re-iss. Jan83 on 'Fame' lp/c; FA/TCFA 3058) (re-iss. Aug88 lp/c/cd; 201/401/251-128) (re-iss. cd Jul96; 18826-2)*

Jun 78. (7") *(ARIST 191)* **PRIVILEGE (SET ME FREE). / ASK THE ANGELS** [72] [-]
(12"+=) *(ARIST 12191)* – 25th floor (live) / Bablefield (live).

— **FRED 'Sonic' SMITH** – drums (ex-MC5) repl. DAUGHERTY to TOM VERLAINE

May 79. (7") *(ARIST 264)* **FREDERICK. / FIRE OF UNKNOWN ORIGIN** [63] [-]

May 79. (lp/c) *(SPART/TCART 1086) <4221>* **WAVE** [41] [18]
– Frederick / Dancing barefoot / Citizen ship / Hymn / Revenge / So you want to be a rock'n'roll star / Seven ways of going / Broken flag / Wave. *(re-iss. Aug88 lp/c/cd; 201/401/251-139) (re-iss. cd Jul96; 18829-2)*

Jun 79. (7") *<AS 0427>* **FREDERICK. / FREDERICK (live)** [-] [90]

Jul 79. (7") *(ARIST 281)* **DANCING BAREFOOT. / 5-4-3-2-1 (live)** [ ] [-]

Aug 79. (7"m) *<AS 0453>* **SO YOU WANT TO BE A ROCK'N'ROLL STAR. / 5-4-3-2-1 / FIRE OF UNKNOWN ORIGIN** [-] [ ]

Sep 79. (7") *(ARIST 291)* **SO YOU WANT TO BE A ROCK'N'ROLL STAR. / FREDERICK (live)** [ ] [-]

— PATTI retired Mar'80 with her new husband FRED SMITH to bring up children. BRUCE BRODY was another to join ex-TELEVISION singer TOM VERLAINE's band.

PATTI SMITH

re-appeared in 1988 with still **SOHL, DAUGHERTY & SONIC**

Fierce Fierce

Feb 88. (7"m) *(white label)* **BRIAN JONES. / STOCKINGED FEET / JESUS CHRIST** [ ] [-]

Arista Arista

Jul 88. (7")<US-c-s> *(109877) <AS1/CAS 9689>* **PEOPLE HAVE THE POWER. / WILD LEAVES** [ ] [ ]
(12"+=) *(609877)<AD1 9688>* – Where duty calls.
(cd-s++=) *(659877)* – ('A'-album version).

Jul 88. (lp/c/cd) *(209/409/259-172) <8453>* **DREAM OF LIFE** [70] [65]
– People have the power / Going under / Up there, down there / Paths that cross / Dream of life / Where duty calls / (I was) Looking for you / The Jackson song. *(re-iss. cd.Apr92;) (cd re-iss. Jul96; 18828-2)*

— RICHARD SOHL was to die from a cardiac arrest on 3 Jun'90. PATTI returned to reciting and recording her poetry in 1995. Now with some of her original group (**DAUGHERTY + KAYE**), **TONY SHANAHAN** – bass / **LUIS RESTO** – keyboards and on some **TOM VERLAINE** – guitar (ex-TELEVISION) / **OLIVER RAY** – guitars. Album featured guest spots from JOHN CALE, JEFF BUCKLEY and JANE SCARPANTONI – cello

Jul 96. (cd/c) *(74321 38474-2/-4) <18747>* **GONE AGAIN** [44] [55]
– Gone again / Beneath the Southern Cross / About a boy / My madrigal / Summer cannibals / Dead to the world / Wing / Ravens / Wicked messenger / Fireflies / Farewell reel.

Aug 96. (cd-ep) *(74321 40168-2)* **SUMMER CANNIBALS / COME BACK LITTLE SHEEBA / GONE AGAIN (live) / PEOPLE HAVE THE POWER** [ ] [-]
(cd-ep) *(74321 40299-2)* – ('A'side) / People have the power (live) / Beneath the Southern cross / Come in my kitchen.

— **OLIVER RAY** ; repl. RESTO

Nov 97. (cd/c) *<(07822 18986-2/-4)>* **PEACE AND NOISE** [ ] [ ] Sep97
– Waiting underground / Whirl away / 1959 / Spell / Don't say nothing / Dead city / Blue poles / Death singing / Memento Mori / Last call.

– compilations, others, etc. –

Apr 83. (7") *Arista; (ARIST 513)* **BECAUSE THE NIGHT. / GLORIA** [ ] [-]
(12") *(ARIST 12513)* – ('A'side) / Redondo beach / Dancing barefoot / Free money.

Jul 84. (7") *Old Gold; (OG 9458)* **BECAUSE THE NIGHT. / GLORIA** [ ] [-]

Sep 91. (3xcd-box) *R.C.A.; (354.226)* **BOX SET** [ ] [ ]
– (RADIO ETHIOPIA / HORSES / WAVE albums)

t.v. SMITH (see under ⇒ ADVERTS)

SMITHEREENS

Formed: New Jersey, USA . . . early 1980 by JIM BABJAK and DENNIS DIKEN, who had played together in bands since the early 70's. The pair recruited MIKE MESAROS and frontman/songwriter PAT DiNIZIO, this line-up presiding over their inaugural EP in Xmas 1980, 'GIRLS ABOUT TOWN'. Save for backing up legendary writer and occasional singer, OTIS BLACKWELL (the man behind R&R classics such as 'Don't Be Cruel', 'Fever' and 'Great Balls Of Fire') on a couple of low-key recordings. The SMITHEREENS returned in their own right in '83 with another independent release, the mini-set, 'BEAUTY & SADNESS'. Described as a cross between The BEATLES, The BYRDS and AC/DC!, The SMITHEREENS were the acceptable face of alternative power-pop. Subsequently signing to 'Enigma', the band found a ready-made audience for their first album proper, 'ESPECIALLY FOR YOU' (1986) via college radio, the record's sales further boosted by a collaborative single, 'IN A LONELY PLACE', with rising folk-pop chanteuse, SUZANNE VEGA. During the late 80's, they broke into the US Top 60 a further twice with well-received albums, 'GREEN THOUGHTS' (1988) and '11' (1989). However, with the onset of Grunge in the early 90's and their ill-advised choice to contribute to the soundtrack of teen-movie, 'Class Of Nuke 'Em High', it looked as if the band's golden years had passed. 1991's 'BLOW UP' album was a miserable failure in both critical and commercial terms, the record not even managing to break the US Top 100. Subsequently signing to 'R.C.A.', the new pop-friendly SMITHEREENS suffered a similar fate with 1994's 'A DATE WITH . . .'. • **Covered:** THE SEEKER (Who) / GIRL DON'T TELL ME (Beach Boys) / DON'T BE CRUEL (Elvis Presley) / HANG TEN HIGH (. . . Frontiere) / JUST A LITTLE (Durand-Elliott) / YOU REALLY GOT ME + THE WORLD KEEPS GOING 'ROUND (Kinks) / ONE AFTER 909 (Beatles) / SOMETHING STUPID (. . . Parks) / SHAKIN' ALL OVER (Johnny Kidd) / RUDOLPH THE RED-NOSED REINDEER (Marks-Scott) / RULER OF MY HEART (Aaron Neville) / IT DON'T COME EASY (Ringo Starr) / LUST FOR LIFE (Iggy Pop). • **Note:** Not to be confused with a Dutch band of same name (c. mid-80's) who released a single, 'YOURS IS A GUARANTEE FOR LOVE'.

Album rating: ESPECIALLY FOR YOU (*7) / GREEN THOUGHTS (*8) / 11 (*8) / BLOW UP (*5) / A DATE WITH THE SMITHEREENS (*4) / ATTACK OF THE SMITHEREENS (*4) / BLOWN TO SMITHEREENS compilation (*8)

PAT DiNIZIO – vocals, guitar / **JIM BABJAK** – guitar / **MIKE MESAROS** – bass / **DENNIS DIKEN** – drums

not iss. D-Tone

Dec 80. (7"ep) *<DT 150>* **GIRLS ABOUT TOWN / GIRL DON'T TELL ME. / GOT ME A GIRL / GIRLS ARE LIKE THAT** [-] [ ]

not iss. Little Ricky

1983. (m-lp) *<LR 103>* **BEAUTY & SADNESS** [-] [ ]
– Beauty & sadness / Some other guy / Tracey's world / Much too much / Beauty and sadness (instrumental). *(UK-iss.Jul89 on 'Enigma' lp/cd; ENVLP/CDENV 519)*

Enigma Enigma

Dec 86. (lp) *<(73208-1)>* **ESPECIALLY FOR YOU** [ ] [51] Aug86
– Strangers when we meet / Listen to me girl / Groovy Tuesday / Cigarette / I don't want to lose you / Time and time again / Behind the wall of sleep / In a lonely place / Blood and roses / Crazy mixed-up kid / Hand of glory / Alone at midnight. *(cd-iss. Mar87; CD 73208-2) (pic-lp Nov87; SEAX 73258)*

Jan 87. (7"red; by The SMITHEREENS with SUZANNE VEGA) *(ENIG 1) <50032>* **IN A LONELY PLACE. / BEAUTY AND SADNESS** [ ] [-]
(12"+=) *(ENIGT 1)* – Blood and roses / Mr. Eliminator.

Jan 87. (7"; by The SMITHEREENS with SUZANNE VEGA) *<50032>* **IN A LONELY PLACE. / BLOOD AND ROSES (live)** [-] [ ]

Mar 87. (7") *(ENIG 2)* **BEHIND THE WALL OF SLEEP. / BLOOD AND ROSES** [ ] [ ] Sep86
(12"+=) *(ENIGT 2)* –

Jul 87. (12"m) *(ENIG 3)* **STRANGERS WHEN WE MEET. / THE SEEKER / HANG TEN HIGH** [ ] [ ]

Dec 87. (lp/cd) *<97924-1/-2>* **SMITHEREENS LIVE (live)** [-] [ ]
– Blood and roses / Behind the wall of sleep / Beauty and sadness / Alone at midnight / Strangers when we meet / The seeker.

Enigma Capitol

Mar 88. (7") *(SMIT 1)* **ONLY A MEMORY. / LUST FOR LIFE** [ ] [-]
(12"+=) *(SMITT 1)* – Something new.

May 88. (7") *<44150>* **ONLY A MEMORY. / THE SEEKER** [-] [92]

Apr 88. (lp/c/cd) *(3375 1/4/2) <48375>* **GREEN THOUGHTS** [ ] [60]
– Only a memory / House we used to live in / Something new / The world we knew / Especially for you / Drown in my own tears / Deep black / Elaine / Spellbound / If the Sun doesn't shine / Green thoughts.

Jun 88. (7") **THE HOUSE WE USED TO LIVE IN. / ONLY A MEMORY** [-] [ ]

Oct 88. (7") *(ENV 2)* **THE HOUSE WE USED TO LIVE IN. / RULER OF MY HEART** [ ] [-]
(12"+=) *(ENVT 2)* – Blood and roses (live).
(cd-s++=) *(ENVCD 2)* – ('A'live version).

Dec 88. (7") **DROWN IN MY OWN TEARS. / THE HOUSE WE USED TO LIVE IN** [-] [ ]

Enigma-EMI Capitol

Nov 89. (lp/c/cd) *(ENVLP/TCENV/CDENV 1000) <91194>* **11** [ ] [41]
– Girl like you / Blues before and after / Blue period / Baby be good / Room without a view / Yesterday girl / Cut flowers / Willian Wilson / Maria Elana / Kiss your tears away.

Nov 89. (c-s,cd-s) *<44480>* **A GIRL LIKE YOU (parts I & II) / LIKE SOMEONE IN LOVE** [-] [38]

Feb 90. (7") *(ENV 15)* **A GIRL LIKE YOU. / CUT FLOWERS** [ ] [-]
(12"+=/cd-s+=) *(12/CD ENV 15)* – Like someone in love.
May 90. (7") *(ENV 21)* **BLUE PERIOD. / MARIA ELENA (acoustic)** [ ] [-]
(12"+=/cd-s+=) *(12/CD ENV 21)* – Room without a view.
May 90. (c-s,cd-s) *<44516>* **BLUES BEFORE AND AFTER / MARIA ELENA (acoustic)** [-] [94]

Capitol Capitol

Sep 91. (cd/c/lp) *(CD/TC+/EST 2151) <94963>* **BLOW UP** [ ] [ ]
– Top of the pops / Too much passion / Tell me when did things go so wrong / Evening dress / Get a hold of my heart / Indigo blues / Now and then / Girl in room 12 / Anywhere you are / Over and over again / It's alright / If you want to see to shine.
Feb 92. (c-s,cd-s) *<44784>* **TOO MUCH PASSION / IF YOU WANT THE SUN TO SHINE** [-] [37]

not iss. R.C.A.

May 94. (cd/c) *<66391-2/-4>* **A DATE WITH THE SMITHEREENS** [-] [ ]
– War for my mind / Everything I have is blue / Miles from nowhere / Afternoon tea / Point of no return / Sleep the night away / Love is gone / Wrong way back again / Gotti / Sick of Seattle / Can't go home anymore / Life is so beautiful.
Aug 94. (cd-s) *<62942>* **TIME WON'T LET ME /** [-] [ ]
Jan 98. (cd-s; shared with WOOLDRIDGE BROTHERS & BILLY MANN) *<58691>* **DOWN BOUND TRAIN** [-] [ ]

– compilations, etc. –

Nov 95. (cd,c) *Capitol; <32247>* **ATTACK OF THE SMITHEREENS** (B-sides, etc) [-] [ ]
– Here come the Smithereens / Girl don't tell me / Girls about town / Time and time again / Don't be cruel / Hang ten high / Tracey's world / Blood and roses / Just a little / The seeker / Yesterday girl / Poor little pitiful one / Maria Elena / You really got me / One after 909 / The world keeps going 'round / Behind the wall of sleep / Something stupid / Shakin' all over / Rudolph the red-nosed reindeer / Ruler of my heart / It don't come easy / Lust for life / Like someone in love / A girl like you.
Apr 98. (cd,c) *Cema Special; <19502>* **THE BEST OF THE SMITHEREENS** [-] [ ]
– Strangers when we meet / Only a memory / A girl like you / Behind the wall of sleep / Blood and roses / Yesterday girl / In a lonely place / Too much passion / Drown in my own tears / The house we used to live in.
Aug 98. (cd) *Capitol; <(31481 8 31481-2/-4)* **BLOWN TO SMITHEREENS – BEST OF THE SMITHEREENS** [ ] [ ] Apr95
– Beauty and sadness / Strangers when we meet / Blood and roses / In a lonely place / Behind the wall of sleep / Only a memory / The house we used to live in / Drown in my own tears / A girl like you / Blue period / Blues before and after / Yesterday girl / Top of the pops / Too much passion / Miles from nowhere / Time won't let me.

SMITHS

Formed: Manchester, England . . . late '82 by (STEPHEN PATRICK) MORRISSEY and JOHNNY MARR. An intellectually intense, budding pop scholar and music journalist, MORRISSEY had previously had a book, 'James Dean Isn't Dead', published by 'Babylon' and had served a stint as UK president of The NEW YORK DOLLS fan club. MARR, meanwhile, had cut his six-string teeth in a variety of Manc beat combos, the pair initially forming a songwriting partnership and subsequently bringing in drummer MIKE JOYCE and bassist ANDY ROURKE to realise their vision of The SMITHS. Kicking off at The Ritz in Manchester, the group played a series of debut gigs around the country, earning rave reviews and attracting the interest of indie label, 'Rough Trade'. Turning down a deal with the local 'Factory', The SMITHS recorded a one-off single for 'Rough Trade', 'HAND IN GLOVE', the track championed by John Peel and subsequently topping the indie charts. Wooed by the majors, MORRISSEY and Co. stuck to their principals and inked a long-term contract with 'Rough Trade'. Later that year saw the release of the Top 30 hit, 'THIS CHARMING MAN', the first real glimpse of the The SMITHS' strange allure, MARR's rhythmic exuberance buoying MORRISSEY's morose verbal complexities. This was also the first time the Great British public were treated to the legendary sight of MORRISSEY sashaying and shimmying across the Top Of The Pops stage sporting a hearing aid and a back pocketfull of gladioli. Defiantly original, The SMITHS rapidly amassed a large, fiercely partisan fanbase with MORRISSEY as chief deity, MARR running a close second. A follow-up single, 'WHAT DIFFERENCE DOES IT MAKE', narrowly missed the Top 10 in early '84 with the breathlessly anticipated debut, 'THE SMITHS', hitting the shelves the following month. It didn't disappoint, a darkly ruminating kick in the eye for the tosspot music scene of the mid-80's and a compelling showcase for the unbounded potential of the MORRISSEY/MARR writing partnership. While the album missed the No.1 slot by a whisker, a high profile scrape with the tabloids followed soon after, the press hounds rounding on what they supposed to be ambiguous references to child abuse. The highly articulate MORRISSEY vocally put matters to right, the singer finally vindicated when a mother of one of the Moors murder victims openly supported the 'SUFFER THE LITTLE CHILDREN' track, another target of press speculation. The SMITHS were nothing if not controversial, MORRISSEY's pro-miserablist, anti-royalist and openly celibate stance making him the first real 'bedsit' non-pop star and drawing more and more attention to the group. No bad thing of course, when the music was as good as 'HEAVEN KNOWS I'M MISERABLE NOW' and 'WILLIAM, IT WAS REALLY NOTHING', another couple of fine Top 20 singles released later that summer. Both were included on the brilliant 'HATFUL OF HOLLOW' (1984) set along with a number of BBC session recordings and a few new tracks, notably the haunting 'PLEASE PLEASE PLEASE LET ME GET WHAT I WANT' and one of The SMITHS' trump cards, 'HOW SOON IS NOW' (previously released as a B-side to 'WILLIAM . . .' and subsequently as a single in its own right in early '85), a churning mantra presumably laying bare the depths of MORRISSEY's tortured soul with its bitter lyrical plea; that pop/dance outfit SOHO later managed to incorporate its ominous guitar reverb into a club hit is surely one of the great wonders of modern music. The following month saw the release of the acclaimed 'MEAT IS MURDER', MORRISSEY partly substituting the navel gazing of old for a more socially-pointed stance; slap happy headmasters, teenage thugs, child abusers and of course, those partial to a bit of steak, being the prime targets of the frontman's razor-sharp lyrical barbs. MORRISSEY wasn't hogging all the limelight, however, MARR's nimble fingered genius on the likes of 'THAT JOKE ISN'T FUNNY ANYMORE' seeing him touted as the greatest British guitarist since ERIC CLAPTON. The album gave the group their first No.1, solidifying their position as the biggest "indie" band of the decade, The SMITHS now at the peak of their powers. Next up was the irrepressible 'THE BOY WITH THE THORN IN HIS SIDE' and the scathing wit of 'BIGMOUTH STRIKES AGAIN', both featured on, and acting as preludes to 'THE QUEEN IS DEAD' (1986). Though the album was delayed due to record company hassles, with personnel difficulties (ROURKE briefly kicked out for heroin abuse, the addition of CRAIG GANNON) also arising, it remains The SMITHS' magnum opus and, for many, the album of the decade. Effortlessly segueing from the darkly claustrophobic (the stinging social commentary of the title track and to a lesser extent, the lugubrious 'NEVER HAD NO ONE EVER') to the whimsically witty ('VICAR IN A TUTU') and on to the heartbreakingly poignant ('THERE IS A LIGHT THAT NEVER GOES OUT'), the album was breathtaking in its emotional sweep and musical focus. Though they would never quite reached those heights again, The SMITHS highly prolific recording schedule continued apace with the anthemic 'PANIC' (indie kids delighting in its clarion call of 'Hang the DJ') and the breezy 'ASK', probably The SMITHS most commercial moment. The fact that, like most of their singles, it failed to break the Top 10, led to the group announcing a split with 'Rough Trade' and a new deal with 'E.M.I.'. Further controversy followed around this time as CRAIG GANNON was sacked, the guitarist duly sueing the group. Early '87 saw the release of another semi-compilation of old and new material, 'THE WORLD WON'T LISTEN', essential if only for the classic MORRISSEY angst of 'HALF A PERSON' and the sublime 'OSCILLATE WILDLY'. Though the wellspring of the MORRISSEY/MARR muse was seemingly bottomless, relations between the pair were reaching breaking point and by the release of the 'STRANGEWAYS HERE WE COME' (1987) opus, The SMITHS had already split. The album's morbid, fractured sound apparently confirmed the growing musical differences between the group's main protagonists, an inevitability perhaps, for such a consistently intense and prefectionist band. A posthumous live album, 'RANK' (1988) appeared the following year, documenting the London stop on The SMITHS' final frenzied tour of 1986. Various compilations were released in successive years, especially after 'Warners' secured the rights to The SMITHS back catalogue in 1992, heralding a period when, ironically, most of the material was only available on US import! While MARR sessioned for the likes of The PRETENDERS and BRYAN FERRY before working with THE THE and forming ELECTRONIC with NEW ORDER's BERNARD SUMNER, MORRISSEY went on to a relatively successful, if comparitively drab solo career. As is so often the case, the sum of The SMITHS parts was always greater than the whole, the group's influence on modern rock music incalculable, their unique sound echoing through the strains of countless indie success stories and untold hopefuls alike. • **Songwriters:** Lyrics – MORRISSEY / music – MARR, except HIS LATEST FLAME (Elvis Presley) / GOLDEN LIGHTS (Twinkle).

Album rating: THE SMITHS (*10) / MEAT IS MURDER (*10) / THE QUEEN IS DEAD (*10) / HATFUL OF HOLLOW part compilation (*9) / THE WORLD WON'T LISTEN (*9) part compilation / STRANGEWAYS HERE WE COME (*9) / BEST . . . I (*10) compilation / BEST II compilation (*9) / RANK (*7) / LOUDER THAN BOMBS import (*8)

MORRISSEY (b. STEPHEN PATRICK MORRISSEY, 22 May'59) – vocals (ex-NOSEBLEEDS) / **JOHNNY MARR** (b. JOHN MAHER, 31 Oct'63) – guitar, harmonica, mandolins, piano / **ANDY ROURKE** (b.1963) – bass / **MIKE JOYCE** (b. 1 Jun'63) – drums

Rough Trade Sire

May 83. (7") *(RT 131)* **HAND IN GLOVE. / HANDSOME DEVIL** [ ] [-]
Nov 83. (7") *(RT 136)* **THIS CHARMING MAN. / JEANE** [25] [-]
(12") *(RTT 136)* – ('A'side) / Accept yourself / Wonderful woman.
Jan 84. (7") *(RT 146)* **WHAT DIFFERENCE DOES IT MAKE?. / BACK TO THE OLD HOUSE** [12] [-]
(12"+=) *(RTT 146)* – These things take time.
Feb 84. (lp/c) *(ROUGH/+C 61) <25065>* **THE SMITHS** [2] [ ]
– Reel around the fountain / You've got everything now / Miserable lie / Pretty girls make graves / The hand that rocks the cradle / Still ill / Hand in glove / What difference does it make? / I don't owe you anything / Suffer little children. *(cd-iss. May87; ROUGHCD 61) (cd re-iss. 1989 on 'Line'; LICD 9.00308) (re-iss. cd/c)(ltd-10"lp Nov93 on 'WEA'; 4509 91892-2/-4)(SMITHS 1)*
May 84. (7") *(RT 156)* **HEAVEN KNOWS I'M MISERABLE NOW. / SUFFER LITTLE CHILDREN** [10] [ ]
(12"+=) *(RTT 156)* – Girl afraid.
Aug 84. (7") *(RT 166)* **WILLIAM, IT WAS REALLY NOTHING. / PLEASE PLEASE PLEASE LET ME GET WHAT I WANT** [17] [ ]
(12"+=) *(RTT 166)* – How soon is now?
Nov 84. (lp/c) *(ROUGH/+C 76)* **HATFUL OF HOLLOW** (with BBC sessions *) [7] [-]
– William, it was really nothing / What difference does it make? * / These things take time * / This charming man * / How soon is now? / Handsome devil * / Hand in glove / Still ill * / Heaven knows I'm miserable now / This night has opened my eyes * / You've got everything now * / Accept yourself * / Girl afraid / Back to the old house * / Reel around the fountain * / Please please please let me get what I want. *(cd-iss. May87; ROUGHCD 76) (re-iss. cd/c)(ltd-d10"lp Nov93 on 'WEA'; 4509 91893-2/-4)(SMITHS 2)*

Jan 85. (7") *(RT 176)* **HOW SOON IS NOW?. / WELL I WONDER** [24] [-]
(12"+=) *(RTT 176)* – Oscillate wildly.
Feb 85. (7") **HOW SOON IS NOW?. / THE HEADMASTER RITUAL** [-] [ ]
Feb 85. (lp/c) *(ROUGH/+C 81) <25269>* **MEAT IS MURDER** [1] [ ]
– The headmaster ritual / Barbarism begins at home / Rusholme ruffians / I want the one I can't have / What she said / Nowhere fast / That joke isn't funny anymore / Nowhere fast / Well I wonder / Meat is murder. *(cd-iss. May87; ROUGHCD 81) (re-iss. cd/c)(ltd-d10"lp Nov93 on 'WEA'; 4509 91895-2/-4)(SMITHS 3)*
Mar 85. (7") *(RT 181)* **SHAKESPEARE'S SISTER. / WHAT SHE SAID** [26] [ ]
(12"+=) *(RTT 181)* – Stretch out and wait.
Jul 85. (7") *(RT 186)* **THAT JOKE ISN'T FUNNY ANYMORE. / MEAT IS MURDER (live)** [49] [ ]
(12"+=) *(RTT 186)* – Nowhere fast / Shakespeare's siste / Stretch out and wait (all live).
Sep 85. (7") *(RT 191)* **THE BOY WITH THE THORN IN HIS SIDE. / ASLEEP** [23] [ ]
(12"+=) *(RTT 191)* – Rubber ring.

— added **CRAIG GANNON** – guitar, bass (ex-AZTEC CAMERA, ex-BLUEBELLS)

May 86. (7") *(RT 192)* **BIGMOUTH STRIKES AGAIN. / MONEY CHANGES EVERYTHING** [26] [ ]
(12"+=) *(RTT 192)* – Unloveable.
Jun 86. (lp/c) *(ROUGH/+C 96) <25426>* **THE QUEEN IS DEAD** [2] [70]
– Frankly Mr. Shankly / I know it's over / Never had no one ever / Cemetery gates / Big mouth strikes again / Vicar in a tutu / There is a light that never goes out / Some girls are bigger than others / The queen is dead / The boy with the thorn in his side. *(cd-iss. May87; ROUGHCD 96) (re-iss. cd/c)(ltd-d10"lp Nov93 on 'WEA'; 4509 91896-2/-4)(SMITHS 4)*
Jul 86. (7") *(RT 193)* **PANIC. / VICAR IN A TUTU** [11] [ ]
(12"+=) *(RTT 193)* – The draize train.
Oct 86. (7") *(RT 194)* **ASK. / CEMETRY GATES** [14] [ ]
(12"+=/c-s+=) *(RTT 194/+C)* – Golden lights.

— Reverted to a quartet, when GANNON left to join The CRADLE.

Feb 87. (7") *(RT 195)* **SHOPLIFTERS OF THE WORLD UNITE. / HALF A PERSON** [12] [ ]
(12"+=) *(RTT 195)* – London.
Feb 87. (lp/c/cd) *(ROUGH/+C/CD 101)* **THE WORLD WON'T LISTEN** (part compilation) [7] [-]
– Panic / Ask / London / Big mouth strikes again / Shakespeare's sister / There is a light that never goes out / Shoplifters of the world unite / The boy with the thorn in his side / Asleep / Unloveable / Half a person / Stretch out and wait / That joke isn't funny anymore / Oscillate wildly / You just haven't earned it yet baby / Rubber ring. *(c+=)* – Money changes everything. *(re-iss. cd/c)(ltd-d10"lp Nov93 on 'WEA'; 4509 91898-2/-4)(SMITHS 5)*
Apr 87. (7") *(RT 196)* **SHEILA TAKE A BOW. / IS IT REALLY SO STRANGE?** [10] [ ]
(12"+=) *(RTT 196)* – Sweet and tender hooligan.
Jun 87. (d-lp/d-c/d-cd) *(ROUGH/+C/CD 255) <25569>* **LOUDER THAN BOMBS** (compilation) [38] [62] Apr87
– Is it really so strange? / Sheila take a bow / Sweet and tender hooligan / Shoplifters of the world unite / Half a person / London / Panic / Girl afraid / Shakespeare's sister / William, it was really nothing / You just haven't earned it yet, baby / Golden lights / Ask / Heaven knows I'm miserable now / Unloveable / Asleep / Oscillate wildly / These things take time / Rubber ring / Back to the old house / Hand in glove / Stretch out and wait / This night has opened my eyes / Please, please, please, let me get what I want. *(cd re-iss. Feb95 on 'WEA'; 4509 93833-2)*
Aug 87. (7") *(RT 197)* **GIRLFRIEND IN A COMA. / WORK IS A FOUR-LETTER WORD** [13] [ ]
(12"+=/c-s+=) *(RTT 197/+C)* – I keep mine hidden.
Sep 87. (lp/c/cd) *(ROUGH/+C/CDR 106) <25649>* **STRANGEWAYS HERE WE COME** [2] [55]
– A rush and a push and the land is ours / I started something I couldn't finish / Death of a disco dancer / Girlfriend in a coma / Stop me if you think you've heard this one before / Last night I dreamt that somebody loved me / Unhappy birthday / Paint a vulgar picture / Death at one's elbow / I won't share you. *(re-iss. cd/c)(ltd-d10"lp Nov93 on 'WEA'; 4509 91899-2/-4)(SMITHS 6)*
Oct 87. (7") **STOP ME IF YOU THINK YOU'VE HEARD THIS ONE BEFORE. / I KEEP MINE HIDDEN** [-] [ ]
Nov 87. (7") *(RT 198)* **I STARTED SOMETHING I COULDN'T FINISH. / PRETTY GIRLS MAKE GRAVES** [23] [ ]
(12"+=) *(RTT 198)* – Some girls are bigger than others (live).
(c-s++=) *(RTT 198C)* – What's the world (live).
Dec 87. (7") *(RT 200)* **LAST NIGHT I DREAMT THAT SOMEBODY LOVED ME. / NOWHERE FAST (BBC version)** [30] [ ]
(12"+=) *(RTT 200)* – Rusholme Russians (BBC version).
(cd-s++=) *(RTT 200CD)* – William, it was really nothing (BBC version).

— they broke-up in August '87, ROURKE and JOYCE splintered with ADULT NET before joining MORRISSEY when he went solo.

– compilations, etc. –

Note; on 'Rough Trade' UK / 'Sire' US, unless otherwise mentioned.
Aug 88. (lp/c/cd/dat) *(ROUGH/+C/CD 126) <25786>* **RANK (live October '86)** [2] [77]
– The queen is dead / Panic / Vicar in a tutu / Ask / Rusholme ruffians / The boy with the thorn in his side / What she said / Is it really so strange? / Cemetry gates / London / I know it's over / The draize train / Still ill / Bigmouth strikes again / (Marie's the name) His latest flame – Take me back to dear old blighty. *(re-iss. cd/c)(ltd-d10"lp Nov93 on 'WEA'; 450991900-2/-4)(SMITHS 7)*
Nov 88. (3"cd-ep) *(RTT 215CD)* **THE HEADMASTER RITUAL / NOWHERE FAST (live) / MEAT IS MURDER (live) / STRETCH OUT AND WAIT (live)** [ ] [-]
Nov 88. (3"cd-ep) *(RTT 171CD)* **BARBARISM BEGINS AT HOME / SHAKESPEARE'S SISTER / STRETCH OUT AND WAIT** [ ] [-]

— (Note:- 12"singles from Jan84 / May84 / Sep85 / Jul86 / Oct86 were issued on 3"cd-ep Nov88 – add suffix of CD to cat no.).

Oct 88. (12"ep/cd-ep) *Strange Fruit; (SFPS/+CD 055)* **THE PEEL SESSIONS** (18.5.83) [ ] [-]
– What difference does it make? / Reel around the fountain / Miserable lie / Handsome devil.

— Note; Below on 'WEA' UK/ 'Sire' US unless otherwise mentioned.

Jul 92. (7"/c-s) *(YZ 0001/+C)* **THIS CHARMING MAN. / WONDERFUL WOMAN / ACCEPT YOURSELF** [8] [-]
(cd-s+=) *(YZ 0001CD)* – Jeane.
Aug 92. (cd)(lp/c) *(4509 90044-2)(SMITHS 8/+C) <45042>* **BEST . . . 1** [1] [ ]
– This charming man / William, it was really nothing / What difference does it make / Stop me if you think you've heard it before / Girlfriend in a coma / Half a person / Rubber ring / How soon is now? / Hand in glove / Shoplifters of the world unite / Sheila take a bow / Some girls are bigger than others / Panic / Please please please let me get what I want.
Sep 92. (7"/c-s) *(YZ 0002/+C)* **HOW SOON IS NOW. / HAND IN GLOVE** [16] [-]
(cd-s+=) *(YZ 0002CD1)* – The queen is dead / Handsome devil / I started something I couldn't finish.
(cd-s+=) *(YZ 0002CD2)* – I know it's over / Suffer little children / Back to the old house.
Oct 92. (7"/c-s) *(YZ 0003/+C)* **THERE IS A LIGHT THAT NEVER GOES OUT. / HANDSOME DEVIL (live)** [25] [ ]
(cd-s+=) *(YZ 0003CD1)* – I don't owe you anything / Hand in glove / Jeane.
(cd-s+=) *(YZ 0003CD2)* – Money changes everything (live) / Some girls are bigger than others (live) / Hand in glove (live).
Nov 92. (cd)(lp/c) *(4509 90406-2)(SMITHS 9/+C)* **BEST II** [29] [ ]
– The boy with a thorn in his side / The headmaster ritual / Heaven knows I'm miserable now / Ask / Oscilliate wildly / Nowhere fast / Still ill / That joke isn't funny anymore / Shakespeare's sister / Girl afraid / Reel around the fountain / Last night I dreamt somebody loved me / There is a light that never goes out.
Feb 95. (7"/c-s) *(YZ 0004/+C)* **ASK. / CEMETARY GATES** [62] [-]
(cd-s+=) *(YZ 0004CD)* – Golden lights.
Mar 95. (cd/c) *(4509 99090-2/-4)* **"SINGLES"** [5] [ ]
– Hand in glove / This charming man / What difference does it make? / Heaven knows I'm miserable now / William, it was really nothing / How soon is now? / Shakespeare's sister / That joke isn't funny anymore / The boy with the thorn in his side / Bigmouth strikes again / Panic / Ask / Shoplifters of the world unite / Sheila take a bow / Girlfriend in a coma / I started something I couldn't finish / Last night I dreamt that somebody loved me / There is a light that never goes out.

SMOG

Formed: Silver Springs, Maryland, USA . . . 1988 by sole member, BILL CALLAHAN. The painfully introverted grandaddy of the American lo-fi scene (although he professes to loathe that particular term), CALLAHAN began releasing his bedroom creations in the late 80's as a series of mainly instrumental cassette-only affairs. All issued on his own 'Disaster' imprint, 'MACRAME GUNPLAY' (1988), 'COW' (1989), 'A TABLE SETTING' (1990) and 'TIRED MACHINE' (1990) set the tone for a debut album proper, 'SEWN TO THE SKY' (1991). This was originally released only in the States on the 'Drag City' label and carried on in the same vein as its skeletal predecessors; CALLAHAN only really began taking SMOG in a more conventionally song-structured direction with the 'FORGOTTEN FOUNDATION' (1992) album and only really started whetting critical appetites with 1993's acclaimed 'JULIUS CAESAR'. The latter set was recorded with sometime collaborator CYNTHIA 'CINDY' DALL, boasting sharper, more robust songwriting embellished with string flourishes and synth tinkling although the lyrical misery continued unabated. The mood blackened further on 1994's mini-album, 'BURNING KINGDOM', the reclusive pessimeister making WILL OLDHAM sound like a circus clown. Yet while CALLAHAN's sad-eyed music could be overbearingly claustrophobic, it was more often genuinely moving, the painstakingly recounted tales of everday heartbreak/failure featured on 'WILD LOVE' (1995) and the 'KICKING A COUPLE AROUND' EP offering up an almost voyeuristic view into the man's insular world. The bitter fruit of 'THE DOCTOR CAME AT DAWN' (1996) and 'RED APPLE FALLS' (1997) further confirmed BILL as the crown prince of sad-core, a label he'd no doubt detest even more than lo-fi.

Album rating: SEWN TO THE SKY (*6) / FORGOTTEN FOUNDATION (*7) / JULIUS CAESAR (*8) / BURNING KINGDOM mini (*5) / WILD LOVE (*7) / THE DOCTOR CAME AT DAWN (*8) / RED APPLE FALLS (*7)

BILL CALLAHAN (b.1966) – vocals, guitar, etc

not iss. / Disaster

1988. (c) **MACRAME GUNPLAY** [-] [ ]
1989. (c) **COW** [-] [ ]
1990. (c) **A TABLE SETTING** [-] [ ]
1990. (c) **TIRED MACHINE** [-] [ ]

Matador / Drag City

1991. (lp/cd) *<DC 74/+CD>* **SEWN TO THE SKY** [-] [ ]
– Souped up II / Kings tongue / Garb / Hollow out cakes / Confederate bills and pinball slugs / Coconut cataract / Fruit bats / Peach pit / Disgust / Russian winter / Polio shimmy / Smog / Lost my key / Fried piper / Fables / Puritan work ethic / A jar of sand / I want to tell you about a man / Olive drab spectre / The weightlifter. *(UK-iss.Nov95 on 'Drag City'; same as US)*
1992. (lp/cd) *<DC 13>* **FORGOTTEN FOUNDATION** [-] [ ]
– Burning kingdom / Filament / High school freak / Your dress / Barometric pressure / Guitar innovator / Evil tyrant / Head of stone I / Head of stone II / Long gray hair / Kiss your lips (with LISA CARVER) / Bad ideas for country songs I / Bad ideas for country songs II / Dead river / Bad investment / Brown bag / Let me have that jar back / This insane cop / 97th street / Do the bed / I'm smiling / With a green complexion. *<cd re-iss. Jan96; same>*

— now with **CINDY DALL** – vocals, etc

Jul 94. (cd/lp) *(OLE 097-2/-1) <DC 31>* **JULIUS CAESAR** [ ] [ ] Nov93
– Strawberry rash / Your wedding / 37 push ups / Stalled on the tracks / One less star / Golden / When you talk / I am star wars / Connections / When the power goes out / Chosen one / What kind of angel / Stick in the mud.

City Slang | Drag City

Nov 94. (m-cd/m-lp) *(EFA 04946-2/-1)* <DC 41> **BURNING KINGDOM** — Sep94
– My shell / Renee died 1:45 / My family / Drunk on the stars / Not lonely anymore / Desert.

Mar 95. (7") *(EFA 04951-7)* **A HIT. /** — -

Apr 95. (cd/lp) *(EFA 04952-2/-1)* <DC 60> **WILD LOVE** — Mar95
– Bathysphere / Wild love / Sweet Smog children / Bathroom floor / Emperor / Limited capacity / It's rough / Sleepy Joe / Candle / Be hit / Prince alone in the studio / Goldfish bowl.

Domino | Drag City

May 96. (12"ep/cd-ep) *(RUG 45 T/CD)* <DC 81> **KICKING A COUPLE AROUND EP** — Apr96
– Your new friend / Back in school / I break horses / Orange glow of a stranger's living room

Sep 96. (cd/lp) *(WIG CD/LP 27)* <DC 95> **THE DOCTOR CAME AT DAWN**
– You moved in / Somewhere in the night / Lize / Spread your bloody wings / Carmelite light / Everything you touch becomes a crutch / All your women things / Whistling teapot (rag) / Four hearts in a can / Hangman blues.

Nov 96. (7") *(HM 19)* **CAME BLUE. / SPANISH MOSS** — -
(above issued on 'Hausmusik')

May 97. (cd/lp) *(WIG CD/LP 35)* <DC 116> **RED APPLE FALLS**
– Morning papers / Blood red bird / Red apples / I was a stranger / To be of use / Red apple falls / Ex-con / Inspirational / Finer days.

Oct 97. (7") *(RUG 58)* **EX-CON. / JUST LIKE NAPOLEON** — -
(cd-s+=) *(RUG 58CD)* – Little girl shoes / Duck pond blues.

SNAKES OF SHAKE

Formed: Glasgow, Scotland . . . 1984 by SEORI BURNETTE, SANDY BROWN, ROBERT RENFREW, TZEN VERMILLION and RHOD BURNETT. Country-tinged indie-rockers in the trademark West Of Scotland mould, the SNAKES OF SHAKE issued a mini-set, 'SOUTHERN CROSS', its title track simultaneously released in Spring '85. It wouldn't be the first time the song would surface, although by the time it revamped a year later, both VERMILLION and BURNETT had been substituted with (WILSON) NEIL SCOTT and IAIN SHEDDON respectively. Their one and only full-length set, 'GRACELANDS AND THE NATURAL WOOD' (1987), would again feature what had now become their theme tune although the collapse of their label, 'Making Waves', put paid to any chances they might have had. Getting a foothold once more on the music business ladder, three former SNAKES (SEORI, WILSON and IAIN, together with KEITH GILES and session man extrordinaire, BJ COLE) re-emerged in 1988 as SUMMERHILL. Following a few West Coast/BYRDS-influenced releases including the mini-set, 'LOWDOWN', the line-up was slightly amended when SHEDDON was replaced with MICHAEL STURGIS. Finally rewarded for their years of struggle, SUMMERHILL were snapped up by 'Polydor', the resulting 'WEST OF HERE' set hitting the shops early in 1990. Described (probably unfairly) as a countrified, poor man's DEACON BLUE, the band received a smattering of positive reviews but failed to make their mark on the ever fickle and evolving pop-rock scene. • **Covered:** DO RIGHT WOMAN, DO RIGHT MAN (Dan Penn – Spooner Oldham) / WILD HORSES (Rolling Stones).

Album rating: SOUTHERN CROSS mini (*4) / GRACELANDS AND THE NATURAL WOOD (*6) / Summerhill: LOWDOWN (*5) / WEST OF HERE (*5)

SEORI BURNETTE – vocals, guitar, harmonica / **TZEN VERMILLION** – guitar / **SANDY BROWN** – piano, accordion, vocals / **ROBERT RENFREW** – bass, slide guitar, vocals / **RHOD BURNETT** – drums

Tense But Confident | not iss.

Mar 85. (m-lp) *(TBC 1)* **SOUTHERN CROSS** — -

Mar 85. (12"m) *(GOBS12-1)* **SOUTHERN CROSS. / LIFE'S TOO STRONG / INDISPENSIBLE** — -

— **(WILSON) NEIL SCOTT** – guitar; repl. VERMILLION

— **IAIN SHEDDON** – drums (ex-JOLT) repl. RHOD BURNETT

Making Waves | not iss.

Aug 86. (7") *(SURF 116)* **SOUTHERN CROSS. / YOU WALK** — -
(12"+=) *(SURFT 116)* – ('A'-part 2).

Jul 87. (cd/c/lp) *(CD/C+/SPRAY 106)* **GRACELANDS AND THE NATURAL WOOD** — -
– Southern cross / Make it shine / Gracelands / No reason / Strange affair / Man the man / Sender down / Last resort / Like no ther / Get me out of here.

SUMMERHILL

— were formed by **SEORI, (WILSON) NEIL, IAIN / + KEITH GILES** – bass, vocals / guest **B.J. COLE** – steel guitar (session man extraordinaire)

Rocket 5 | not iss.

Jun 88. (7") *(HUCS 102)* **I WANT YOU. /** — -

Diabolo | not iss.

Oct 88. (m-lp) *(SORCM 4)* **LOWDOWN** — -
– Rosebud / I'll keep you in mind / Lately / Knew I would return / Hold back the heartache / It's gonna be alright / I can't stay / Say goodbye.

— **MICHAEL STURGIS** – drums; repl. IAIN

Polydor | not iss.

Oct 89. (7"/7"g-f) *(TTRC/+G 1)* **HERE I AM. /** — -
(12"+=) *(TTRCX 1)* –

Mar 90. (7"/c-s) *(TTRC/+S 2)* **DON'T LET IT DIE. / KEEP YOU IN MIND** — -
(10"+=/12"+=/cd-s+=) *(TTRC T/X/D 2)* – Do right woman, do right man / It's gonna be alright.

Mar 90. (cd/c/lp) *(843130-2/-4/-1)* **WEST OF HERE** — -
– Don't let it die / Here I am / If you hold a gun / The ballad of Summerhill / I've found a friend / If I knew you better / Somehow, somewhere / Lately / I have a reason / Last to find out. *(cd+=/c+=)* – Wild horses (live in the studio).

Apr 90. (7") *(TTRC 3)* **WILD HORSES. / RIVER BLUE** — -
(12"+=/cd-s+=) *(TTRC X/D 3)* – Please don't go away.

— later that year, two ex-SUMMERHILL members (they had now split) teamed up with singer, SUMISHTA BRAHM, on a one-off 13 FRIGHTENED GIRLS single, 'Lost At Sea'. The following year, WILSON SCOTT joined HORSE LATITUDES, who released a mini-set, 'SEPTEMBER SONGS'. SUMMERHILL re-formed in the mid 90's

Tupelo | unknown

Jan 95. (cd-s) *(TTRCD 4)* **NO MATTER WHAT YOU DO /** — -

SNAPPER

Formed: Dunedin, New Zealand . . . 1988 by songwriter and former CHILLS and CLEAN founder, PETER GUTTERIDGE, along with CHRISTINE VOICE, ALAN HAIG and DOMINIC STONES. An eponymous debut EP emerged on veteran Kiwi label, 'Flying Nun', although it was Edinburgh's 'Avalanche' imprint (an offshoot of their long established indie retail outlet) that later gave it a UK release. The label also issued their 1991 debut set, 'SHOTGUN BLOSSOM', revealing the band to be in the firmly established NZ tradition, if a little noisier and less melodic than their forebears. Employing a garage guitar/organ drone with girl/boy vocals drenched in fuzz-distortion and placed well back in the mix, the band could've been Antipodean cousins of Scotland's own JESUS & MARY CHAIN. With the subsequent establishment of a 'Flying Nun' UK base, the belated 'A.D.M.' (1996) was given a full British release while indie label, 'New Red Archives' issued both 1996's 'IT SMELLS, IT BURNS, IT STINGS' and the following year's 'QUEEN BITCH OF ROCK'N'ROLL'.

Album rating: SHOTGUN BLOSSOM (*5) / A.D.M. (*5) / IT SMELLS, IT BURNS, IT STINGS (*5) / QUEEN BITCH OF ROCK'N'ROLL (*5)

PETER GUTTERIDGE (b.19 May'61) – vocals, guitar, keyboards (ex-CHILLS, ex-CLEAN, ex-GREAT UNWASHED) / **CHRISTINE VOICE** – keyboards, vocals / **DOMINIC STONES** – guitar (ex-BIRDNEST ROYS) / **ALAN HAIG** (b. 5 Aug'61) – drums (ex-CHILLS)

Flying Nun | not iss.

May 89. (7"ep) **SNAPPER** — - | - New Z.
(UK-iss.Dec90 on 'Avalanche';)

Avalanche | not iss.

Jul 91. (cd/c/lp) *(ONLY C.D./M.C./L.P. 010)* **SHOTGUN BLOSSOM** — -
– Pop your top / Can / Telepod fly / Eyes that shine / Dark sensation / Dead pictures / Snapper and the ocean / What are you thinking / Hot sun / I don't know / Emmanuelle / Dry spot / Rain.

Dec 91. (7") **DARK SENSATION. / SNAPPER AND THE OCEAN** — -

Flying Nun | not iss.

1993. (7") *(FN 264)* **VADER. / GENTLE HOUR** — -

Mar 96. (c/cd) *(FN/+CD 294)* **A.D.M.** — -

New Red Archives | not iss.

1996. (cd) **IT SMELLS, IT BURNS, IT STINGS** — -

Dec 97. (cd) *(NRA 67CD)* **QUEEN BITCH OF ROCK'N'ROLL** — -

SNATCH

Formed: Lower East Side, New York, USA . . . 1976 by JUDY NYLON and PATTI PALLADIN, a pair of Noo Yoik proto-punks influenced by the pioneering work of PATTI SMITH. Having cut a number of demos, SNATCH were finally taken on by Bomp's GREG SHAW, who released the double-A sided 7", 'STANLEY' / 'I.R.T.' early the following year. Featuring an intro of which even LYDIA LUNCH would be proud, the former track was typical of the band's barebones, razor-wire R&B-punk with obligatory snotty vocals. UK distributor, 'Lightning', would later re-issue the record and go on to release a follow-up, 'ALL I WANT' / 'WHEN I'M BORED', while English ambient boffin, ENO, invited them to collaborate with him on the B-side ('R.A.F.') of his own 'King's Lead Hat'. British label, 'Fetish', would subsequently issue some unearthed recordings in the summer of 1980 as the 'SHOPPING FOR CLOTHES' EP, PALLADIN having already joined the FLYING LIZARDS. She would go on to work with JOHNNY THUNDERS, while her partner in crime, NYLON delivered her ADRIAN SHERWOOD-produced solo set, 'PAL JUDY', in '82. A belated retrospective of all SNATCH's material surfaced around a year later, an essential listen for anyone interested in the deepest roots of US DIY "No Wave", especially the femme-friendly variation.

Album rating: SNATCH compilation (*6) / Judy Nylon: PAL JUDY (*5)

JUDY NYLON – vocals / **PATTI PALLADIN** – vocals / with **KEITH PAUL** – guitar / **NICK PLYTAS** – piano / **BRUCE DOUGLAS** – bass / **JERRY NOLAN** – drums

Lightning | Bomp

Feb 77. (7") <BP 108> **STANLEY. / I.R.T.** — -
(UK-iss.Jul78 on 'Lightning'; LIG 502)

Jan 78. (7") *(LIG 006)* **ALL I WANT. / WHEN I'M BORED** — -

— Jan'78, were credited on ENO b-side of 'KINGS LEAD HAT' 45 with 'R.A.F.' on 'Polydor'; *2001 762)*

— PATTI PALLADIN moved to England and joined The FLYING LIZARDS. She later teamed up with JOHNNY THUNDERS (ex-Heartbreakers).

Fetish | Fetish

Jul 80. (12"ep) *(FET 004)* **SHOPPING FOR CLOTHES. / JOEY / RED ARMY** — -

— finally split after above. DOUGLAS joined DECLINE AND FALL.

– compilations, etc. –

Nov 83. (lp) *Pandemonium; (WITCH 1)* **SNATCH** (demos & singles, etc) [ ] [-]

JUDY NYLON

with session people incl. GEORGE OBAN, CHRIS JOYCE and SEAN OLIVER

Demon / not iss.

Feb 82. (7") *(D 1011)* **CARLOTTA. / SLEEPLESS NIGHTS** [ ] [-]

On-U-Sound / R.O.I.R.

May 82. (lp) *(ONULP 16) <A-179>* **PAL JUDY** [ ] [ ]
– Information rain / Dateline Miami / Live in a lift / Jailhouse rock / Trial by fire / Slepless nights / Others / The dice / Room without a view. *(cd-iss. Aug91 on 'R.O.I.R.'; same as US)*

— virtually retired from music biz. An album 'BITE YOUR TONGUE' by a different indie SNATCH on Jul'93.

SNFU

Formed: Edmonton, Alberta, Canada . . . early 80's by MISTER CHI PIG (aka MARC BEKLE) and his brother BRENT. A persistant if workmanlike hardcore/punk act that always existed in the shadow of their more critically revered countrymen, D.O.A., SNFU began life on the 'Better Youth Organisation' label (also home to YOUTH BRIGADE) with debut album, ' . . .AND NO ONE ELSE WANTED TO PLAY' (1984). Like many hardcore outfits, they were dogged by numerous personnel changes and weren't particularly prolific although three further albums, 'IF YOU SWEAR, YOU'LL CATCH NO FISH' (1986), 'BETTER THAN A STICK IN THE EYE' (1989) and 'THE LAST OF THE BIG TIME SUSPENDERS' (1991), appeared before MARC completely overhauled the band. Bringing in ROB JOHNSON and DAVID REES, the new SNFU signed to modern punk specialist, 'Epitaph', where they continued to churn out brash, unadulterated hardcore to order throughout the 90's.

Album rating: . . . AND NO ONE ELSE WANTED TO PLAY (*4) / IF YOU SWEAR YOU'LL CATCH NO FISH (*5) / BETTER THAN A STICK IN THE EYE (*4) / LAST OF THE BIG TIME SUSPENDERS (*3) / SOMETHING GREEN AND LEAFY THIS WAY COMES (*3) / ONE VOTED MOST LIKELY TO SUCCEED (*3) / FYULABA (*3)

MISTER CHI PIG (alias MARC BEKLE) – vocals / **BRENT BEKLE** – guitar / **JIMMY SCHMITZ** – bass / **JOHN CARD** – drums

Better YouthOrg'n / Better YouthOrg'n

1984. (lp/c) *<BYO 9/+C>* **. . . AND NO ONE ELSE WANTED TO PLAY** [ ] [ ]
– Broken toy / She's not on the menu / Money matters / I'm real scared / Joy ride / Seeing life through the bottom of a glass / Cannibal cafe / Misfortune / Plastic surgery kept her beautiful / Gravedigger / Bodies in the wall / Get off your ass / Loser at life – Loser at death / This is the end. *(re-iss. Oct96 lp/cd; BYO 9/+CD)*

— CARD joined D.O.A.

1986. (lp/c) *<BYO 17/+C>* **IF YOU SWEAR, YOU'LL CATCH NO FISH** [ ] [ ]
– Devil's voice / Where's my legs? / Better homes and gardens / Scarecrow / Black cloud / I forget / Ceiling / Mind like a door / He's not getting older, he's getting younger / Electric chair / Welcome to my humble life of disarray / Snapping turtle. *(re-iss. Oct96 lp/cd; BYO 17/+CD)*

Cargo / Cargo

1989. (lp/cd) *<CAR 001/+CD>* **BETTER THAN A STICK IN THE EYE** [ ] [ ]
– Time to buy a Futon / G.I. Joe gets angry with humankind / The quest for fun / Tears / In the first place / Postman's pet peeve / What good Hollywood? / The happy switch / Straightening out the shelves / Thee maul that eats peephole / Tour tantram / Wild world. *(re-iss. Jul95 & Oct96 lp/cd; CAR 001/+CD)*

Jan 92. (lp/cd) *<CAR 011/+CD>* **LAST OF THE BIG TIME SUSPENDERS** [-] [ ]
– The kitchen kreeps / Cannibal cafe / Beautiful, unlike you and I / Gimme some water / I know more than you / I'm real scared / I used to write songs / The electric chair / Visiting the bad again / She's not on the menu (Dunce mix) / Appraise the Lord / Wonder what they're thinking / Grunt, groan, rant and rave. *(UK-iss.Jul95 & Oct96; same as US)*

— **MARC BELKE** (aka MISTER CHI PIG) – guitar, vocals / **ROB JOHNSON** – bass / **DAVID REES** – drums

Epitaph / Epitaph

Dec 93. (cd/c/lp) *<(E 86430-2/-4/-1)>* **SOMETHING GREEN AND LEAFY THIS WAY COMES** [ ] [ ]
– All those opposed / Reality is a ride on the bus / Joni Mitchell tapes / Bomb / Tin fish / Painful reminder / Costume trunk / Gladky in gloom / This is a goodbye / Strangely strange / X-creep / Trudging / Great mind eraser / Limping away / Seven minutes closer to death / Watering hole.

May 95. (cd/c/lp) *<(E 86441-2/-4/-1)>* **THE ONE VOTED MOST LIKELY TO SUCCEED** [ ] [ ]
– Rusty rake / A better place / Big thumbs / Drunk on a bike / Manuel / My mold collection / Bumper stickers / Eri's had a bad day / The king of skin / Mutated dog / Bizarre novelties / Lovely little Frankenstein / One last loveshove.

Sep 96. (cd/c/lp) *<(86472-2/-4/-1)>* **FYULABA** [ ] [ ]
– Step stranger / You make me thick / Bobbitt / Better than Eddie Vedder / Don't have the cow / Fate / Dean Martian / Charlie still smirks / Spaceghost, the twins & blip / My pathetic past.

– compilations, etc. –

Sep 98. (cd) *Aquarius; <587>* **LET'S GET IT RIGHT THE FIRST TIME** [-] [ ]
– I forget / Eddie Vedder / Loser at life / Don't have the cow / Bobbitt / Fate / Big thumbs / Painful reminder / Rusty rake / Eric's had a bad day / You make me tick / Drunk on a bike / Charlie still smirks / Reality / Gravedigger / Cannibal cafe / Victims of the womanizer / Watering hole.

SNUFF

Formed: Hendon, London, England . . . 1986 by DUNCAN REDMONDS, SIMON CRIGHTON and ANDY WELLS. Leavening the "straight edge" seriousness of much hardcore from across the pond, SNUFF set out there agenda with 'NOT LISTENING ANYMORE', a debut single that struck a chord with Radio One DJ John Peel. Released on the 'Workers Playtime' label in the spring of '89, it was to feature in the man's final Festive 50 of the 80's. By that time, it had also appeared on first album, 'SNUFF SAID . . .', the comic book funsters introducing their penchant for mind-bogglingly unpronounceable titles, raucous, good-time melodic hardcore/punk and amphetamine party-piece cover trashings of pop hits such as Tiffany's 'I THINK WE'RE ALONE NOW'. Famed for their manic live shows and diehard following, it came as a bit of a surprise when they split in summer '91 after a final gig at Kilburn National Ballroom. With healthy patronage from American practitioners such as GREEN DAY and NOFX, however, the lads were persuaded to re-group in 1994 along with new members, trombonist DAVE and hammond player LEE. Subsequently signing to 'Deceptive', the trio returned in characteristic style at Xmas '95 with a version of the theme from vintage Brit TV sitcom, 'WHATEVER HAPPENED TO THE LIKELY LADS'. A comeback album, 'DEMMAMUSSABEBONK' (1996), meanwhile, saw LOZ replacing SIMON but demonstrated the trio had lost none of their roughneck charm or sense of humour. On the contrary, the trio entered the most prolific period of their career, releasing a mini-covers set, 'POTATOES AND MELONS AT WHOLESALE PRICES (DIRECT TO YOU THE PUBLIC)' in '97 and a further long player, 'TWEET TWEET MY LOVELY', the following year. • **Covers:** CAN'T EXPLAIN (Who) / DO NOTHING + YOU'RE WONDERING NOW (Specials) / REACH OUT I'LL BE THERE (Four Tops) / I CAN SEE CLEARLY NOW (Johnny Nash) / I THINK WE'RE ALONE NOW (Rubinoos) / PURPLE HAZE (Jimi Hendrix) / IN SICKNESS & IN HEALTH (Chas & Dave) / MAGIC MOMENTS (hit. Perry Como) / RIVERS OF BABYLON (hit. Boney M) / SHADOWS OF LOVE (Dozier-Holland-Holland) / SOUL LIMBO (Booker T.) / etc. • **Trivia:** SNUFF also did versions of themes for TV commercials (Bran Flakes + Shake'n'vac + Cadbury's Flake) and more recently 'ANY OLD IRON'.

Album rating: SNUFF SAID (*6) / DEMMAMUSSABEBONK (*7)

SIMON CRIGHTON (b.11 Dec'66) – guitar, vocals / **DUNCAN REDMONDS** (b.22 Aug'64) – drums, vocals / **ANDY WELLS** (b. 4 Jul'63) – bass

Workers Playtime / Aftertan

Apr 89. (7"ep/cd-ep) *(PLAY 008)* **NOT LISTENING ANYMORE EP** [ ] [-]
– Not listening / Dead and buried / That's enough / For both sides – No one home.*(re-iss. Jul96; same)*

Nov 89. (lp/c/cd) *(PLAY-LP/MC/CD 010)* **SNUFF SAID: GORBLIMEYGUVSTONEMEIFHEDIDN'TTHROWA WOBBLERCHACHACHACHACHACHACHACHACHA YOU'REGOINGHOMEINACOSMICAMBULANCE** [ ] [ ]
– Words of wisdom / Some how / Now you don't remember / Not listening / I see – H.M. Trout / Too late / Another girl / I think we're alone now / Win some lose some / Pass me by / Keep the best / Night of the Li's / Purple haze / Little git / What kind of love. *(re-iss. Apr95; same) <US cd-iss. 1996 on 'Fat Wreck Chords'+=; 543>* – NOT LISTENING EP

Apr 90. (12"ep/cd-ep) *(PLAY 011-T/CD)* **FLIBBEDDEDYDIBBIRDDYDOB** [ ] [-]
– Rods and mockers / Do nothing / Shake'n'black / Can't explain / Ecstasy / Reach out / Hazy shade of winter / Do it quick / City attacked by rats / Bran flakes / In sickness & in health. *(12"ep re-iss. Mar95; same) <US cd-iss. Aug96 on 'Fat Wreck Chords'; 544>*

— split August '91 after mail-order final gig lp 'KILBURN NATIONAL BALLROOM 17/11/90'. ANDY joined LEATHERFACE for a few years.

10 Past 12 / not iss.

Jul 91. (12"ep) **THAT'S FINE. / I CAN SEE CLEARLY NOW / YOU'RE WONDERING NOW** [ ] [-]

Apr 92. (lp/cd) *(PARKA 003/+CD)* **REACH** [ ] [-]
– I know what you want / Teabag / The damage is done / Spend, spend, spend / If I tried / Hellbound / Smile (that's fine) / It's you / Bingo / Ichola buddha / Porro / Sweet dreams. *(re-iss. Jun97 on 'K'; KLP 012)*

— **DUNCAN, ANDY + SIMON** re-formed in 1994, although the latter was replaced a year later by **LOZ** – guitar, vocals. Other 2 members were **DAVE** – trombone / **LEE M** – hammond organ, vocals (late bass)

Deceptive / Fat Wreck Chords

Dec 95. (7"one-sided) *(BLUFF 019)* **THEME FROM 'WHATEVER HAPPENED TO THE LIKELY LADS'** [ ] [-]

Feb 96. (cd/c/lp) *(BLUFF 023 CD/MC/LP) <533>* **DEMMAMUSSABEBONK** [ ] [ ]
– Vikings / Defeat / Dick trois / Martin / Nick Northern / Batten down the hatches / G to D / Sunny places / Horse and cart / Squirrels / Cricklewood / B / Punchline / Who.

Mar 96. (7"ep/cd-ep) *(BLUFF 026/+CD)* **LONG BALL TO NO-ONE (EP)** [ ] [-]
– Caught in session / Nick Northern / Walk / Dow dow boof boof.

Aug 96. (7"ep/cd-ep) *(BLUFF 033/+CD)* **DO DO DO (EP)** [ ] [-]
– Standing in the shadows of love / I will survive / Soul limbo / It must be boring being in Snuff.

Jun 97. (10"m-lp/m-cd) *(BLUFF 042 TN/CD) <556>* **POTATOES AND MELONS AT WHOLESALE PRICES (DIRECT TO YOU THE PUBLIC)** [ ] [ ]
– Rivers of Babylon / Whatever happened to the Likely Lads / Shadows of love / Soul limbo / Come and gone / It must be boring being Snuff / Ye olde folke twatte / Magic moments / Russian fields / Time dub / Pink purple.

Apr 98. (7"ep/cd-ep) *(BLUFF 061/+CD) <563>* **SCHMINKIE MINKIE PINKIE EP** [ ] [ ] May98
– Nick Motown / Spicy / Medaka no gakoh / Bit cosy.

May 98. (cd/lp) *(BLUFF 056 CD/LP)* <562> **TWEET TWEET MY LOVELY**
– No reason / Ticket / Timebomb / Lyehf taidu leikh / Nick Motown / Brickwall / Arsehole / Bob / All you need / Etc. / The thief / Verdidn't / Bit cosy / Take me home (piss off).

Nov 98. (7") *(BLUFF 065)* **YUKI. / ROMEO & JULIET** -
(cd-s+=) *(BLUFF 065CD)* – Rockafeller skank.

– compilations, etc. –

Jan 95. (cd) *Vinyl Japan; (ASKCD 048)* **KILBURN NATIONAL 27.11.90 (live)** -
(re-iss. Jan97; same)

Sep 97. (cd/lp) *Vinyl Japan; (MASKCD/ASKLP 073)* **CAUGHT IN SESSION** -

SOCIAL DISTORTION

Formed: Fullerton, Orange County, California, USA . . . summer 1978 by the AGNEW brothers RIKK (vocals) and FRANK, plus MIKE NESS and CASEY ROYER. With the AGNEWS subsequently departing the following year (to form The ADOLESCENTS), NESS took over vocals while DENNIS DANELL came in on bass and CARROT was recruited as the new sticksman. This wholesale personnel upheaval signalled early on that this band's ride was going to be anything but easy. Things got off to a promising start though, the group signing a one-off deal with Robbie Fields' 'Posh Boy' records, the label releasing the 'MAINLINER' 7". In true DIY fashion, SOCIAL DISTORTION then decided to form their own '13th Floor' records, a further line-up change seeing new boys DEREK O'BRIEN (of DI) and BRENT LILES (DANNELL moving to rhythm guitar, a key element in the development of the band's sound) gracing the belated debut album, 'MOMMY'S LITTLE MONSTER' (1983). A record celebrated in hardcore circles, the album nevertheless distinguished itself from the lemming-like pack by dint of its pop nous and freewheeling R&B undertow (critical references to The ROLLING STONES were rife). Despite the acclaim, SOCIAL DISTORTION almost went belly-up as NESS battled with drug problems. After time in a detox unit, NESS returned in 1988 with a new line-up (CHRIS REECE and JOHN MAURER having replaced O'BRIEN and LILES respectively) and equally belated follow-up set, 'PRISON BOUND'. Like The ROLLING STONES themselves had done in the past, NESS attempted to introduce roughshod country (obviously influenced by 'outlaw' artists such as JOHNNY CASH and MERLE HAGGARD) into his band's equation with impressive results. No doubt buffeted by his difficult experiences, NESS' material was now markedly more considered, the band's 1992 major label follow-up (having been snapped up by 'Epic'), 'BETWEEN HEAVEN AND HELL' trawling the personal depths of NESS' drug hell. Musically, the SOCIAL DISTORTION sound was earthier and grittier than ever, combining trad authenticity with righteous anger. Four years in the making and graced by the ubiquitous CHUCK BISCUITS, the wittily titled 'WHITE LIGHT, WHITE HEAT, WHITE TRASH' (1996) was arguably the group's most affecting album to date, the US Top 30 record even including a paint-stripping makeover of their Rolling Stones cover, 'UNDER MY THUMB'.

Album rating: MOMMY'S LITTLE MONSTER (*5) / PRISON BOUND (*6) / SOCIAL DISTORTION (*7) / SOMEWHERE BETWEEN HEAVEN AND HELL (*7) / WHITE LIGHT, WHITE HEAT, WHITE TRASH (*9)

MIKE NESS – vocals, guitar / **DENNIS DANELL** – bass repl. FRANK / **CARROTT** – drums; repl. CASEY who formed The ADOLESCENTS with other early members RIKK and FRANK AGNEW / guitarists **TIM MAG + DANNY FURIOUS** (ex-AVENGERS) were also early members. The former later joined D.I.

not iss. Posh Boy

Nov 81. (7") <PBS 11> **MAINLINER. / PLAYPEN** -

—— **DEREK O'BRIEN** – drums, vocals repl. CARROTT

—— added **BRENT LILES** – bass (DANELL switched to rhythm guitar)

not iss. 13th Story

1982. (7"ep) <SD 4501> **1945 EP** -

1983. (7") <SD 4502> **ANOTHER STATE OF MIND. / MOMMY'S LITTLE MONSTER** -

1984. (lp) **MOMMY'S LITTLE MONSTER** -
– The creeps / Another state of mind / It wasn't a pretty picture / Telling them / Hour of darkness / Mommy's little monster / Anti-fashion / All the answers / Moral threat. *(UK-iss.Dec95 on 'Timebomb' cd/lp; 43500-2/-1) (cd-iss. Sep96 on 'R.C.A.'; 0930 43500-2)*

—— (1985) **JOHN MAURER** – bass repl. LILES who joined AGENT ORANGE

—— **CHRIS REECE** drums (ex-LEWD) repl. O'BRIEN (full-time D.I.)

G.W.R. Enigma

Feb 89. (lp) *(GWLP 43)*-<772251> **PRISON BOUND** 1988
– It's the law / Indulgence / Like an outlaw / Backstreet girl / Prison bound / No pain no gain / On my nerves / I want what I want / Lawless / Lost child. *(re-iss. Dec95 on 'Timebomb' cd/lp; 43501-2/-1) (cd-iss. Sep96 on 'R.C.A.'; 0930 43501-2)*

Epic Epic

May 90. (cd/c/lp) <46055-2/-4/-1> **SOCIAL DISTORTION**
– So far away / Let it be me / Story of my life / Sick boys / Ring of fire / Ball and chain / It coulda been me / She's a knockout / A place in my heart / Drug train.

1990. (cd-ep) <73571> **STORY OF MY LIFE / 1945 (live) / MOMMY'S LITTLE MONSTER (live) / PRETTY THING / SHAME ON ME** -

1992. (7") <74229> **BAD LUCK. / BYE BYE BABY** -

Sep 92. (cd/lp) <471343-2/-1> **SOMEWHERE BETWEEN HEAVEN AND HELL** 76 Feb92
– Cold feelings / Bad luck / Making believe / Born to lose / Bye bye baby / When she begins / 99 to life / King of fools / Sometimes I do / This time darlin'. *(cd+=)* – Ghost town blues.

—— **CHUCK BISCUITS** – drums (ex-DANZIG, etc.) repl. REECE

Sep 96. (cd/c) *(484374-2/-4)* <64380> **WHITE LIGHT, WHITE HEAT, WHITE TRASH** 27
– Dear lover / Don't drag me down / Intitled / I was wrong / Through these eyes / Down on the world again / When the angels sing / Gotta know the rules / Crown of thorns / Pleasure seeker / Down here / Under my thumb.

Nov 96. (7"red) *(663955-7)* **I WAS WRONG. / RING OF FIRE**
(cd-s+=) *(663955-2)* – Born to lose.

Time Bomb Time Bomb

Jul 98. (lp/cd) *(TB 70930/+CD)* <43516> **LIVE AT THE ROXY (live)** Jun98
– Story of my life / Bad luck / Under my thumb / Prisin bound / Mommy's little monster / Mass hysteria / Creeps / Another state of mind / Let it be me / No pain, no gain / Cold feelings / Telling them / I was wrong / 1945 / Don't drag me down / Ball and chain / Ring of fire.

– compilations, etc. –

Dec 95. (cd/lp) *Time Bomb; (43502-2/-1)* **MAINLINER**

SOFA SURFERS

Formed: Vienna, Austria . . . 1997 by WOLFGANG SCHLOGL, MICHAEL HOLZGRUBER, MARKUS KEINZL and WOLFGANG FRISCH, with the addition of live drummer, ROB HOT. After a year of touring Europe, etc., the SOFA's (and their label 'Klein') signed to 'M.C.A.', releasing their debut long-player, 'TRANSIT', early '98. A month later, they were moved along the corridor to 'Universal', issuing a first single, 'THE PLAN', for the label soon after. A pop-promo of the aforementioned track suffered a playlisting ban by MTV for its portrayal of a robbery (with guns!). Their slack-beat rock was best described as techno-TORTOISE with shades of LEE PERRY in a soundclash an' ting.

Album rating: TRANSIT (*6)

WOLFGANG SCHLOGL – / **MICHAEL HOLZGRUBER** – / **MARKUS KEINZL** – / **WOLFGANG FRISCH** – / **ROB HOT** – (live) drums

M.C.A. M.C.A.

Feb 98. (cd) *(<MCD 70053>)* **TRANSIT**
– Bon voyage / Fiaker / Walking ghosts / Flat / The plan / Internacional / Monoscopolis / Lost muchachos / Sofa rockers / Tse Tse fly / Dead men tell no tales / Daktari / Untitled / Lada Taiga / Life in Malmo / No more bon jour.

Universal M.C.A.

Mar 98. (12"/cd-s) *(UMT/UMD 70352)* **THE PLAN. /**

Sep 98. (d12"ep) *(UMT 70396)* **LIFE IN MALMO. /**

SOFT BOYS (see under ⇒ HITCHCOCK, Robyn)

SOFT CELL (see under ⇒ ALMOND, Marc)

SONIC BOOM (see under ⇒ SPACEMEN 3)

SONIC YOUTH

Formed: New York City, New York, USA . . . early 1981 by THURSTON MOORE and KIM GORDON. They replaced an early embryonic rhythm section with LEE RANALDO and RICHARD EDSON. After numerous releases on various US indie labels (notably Glenn Branca's 'Neutral' records), they signed to 'Blast First' in the U.K. First up for the label was 'BAD MOON RISING' in 1985, showing them at their most menacing and disturbing, especially on the glorious 'DEATH VALLEY 69' (a macabre reference to killer Charles Manson) with LYDIA LUNCH providing dual vox. They subsequently secured a US deal with 'S.S.T.', heralding yet another socially passionate thrash effort with 'EVOL'. A sideline project, CICCONE YOUTH, saw KIM and the lads plus MIKE WATT (of fIREHOSE), take off MADONNA's 'INTO THE GROOVE(Y)', which became a surprise dancefloor fave. Two more classic pieces, 'SISTER' (1987) & 'DAYDREAM NATION' (1988), finally secured them a major deal with 'D.G.C.' (David Geffen Company). In the early 90's, they smashed into the UK Top 40 with the album 'GOO', featuring a cameo by CHUCK D (of PUBLIC ENEMY) on the track/single 'KOOL THING'. The album, which sweetened their garage-punk/art-noise collages with melodic hooks, also included their deeply haunting tribute to KAREN CARPENTER, 'TUNIC (SONG FOR KAREN)'. They supported PUBLIC ENEMY that year, also stepping out with NEIL YOUNG on his 'Ragged Glory' tour in '91 (much to the distaste of YOUNG's more conservative fans!). In 1992, many thought 'DIRTY' to be a disappointment, the record being overproduced and overtaken by their new rivals and labelmates NIRVANA. By the mid-90's, they had returned to ground roots with acoustic psychedelia and the albums, 'EXPERIMENTAL JET SET' and 'WASHING MACHINE' were again lauded by the alternative music press. All members had also taken on side solo projects, KIM featuring in all-star punk-grunge affair, FREE KITTEN.

• **Songwriters:** MOORE / RANALDO / GORDON compositions, except I WANNA BE YOUR DOG (Stooges) / TICKET TO RIDE + WITHIN YOU WITHOUT YOU (Beatles) / BEAT ON THE BRAT + others (Ramones) / TOUCH ME, I'M SICK (Mudhoney) / ELECTRICITY (Captain Beefheart) / COMPUTER AGE (Neil Young). Their off-shoot CICCONE YOUTH covered INTO THE GROOVE (Madonna) / ADDICTED TO LOVE (Robert Palmer) / IS IT MY BODY (Alice Cooper) / PERSONALITY CRISIS (New York

Dolls) / CA PLANE POUR MOI (Plastic Bertrand) / MOIST VAGINA = (MV) (Nirvana). FREE KITTEN covered: OH BONDAGE UP YOURS (X-Ray Spex). • **Trivia:** Early in 1989, they were featured on hour-long special TV documentary for Melvyn Bragg's 'The South Bank Show'.

Album rating: CONFUSION IS SEX (*6) / KILL YR IDOLS (*4) / BAD MOON RISING (*8) / EVOL (*8) / SISTER (*9) / DAYDREAM NATION (*9) / GOO (*9) / DIRTY (*7) / EXPERIMENTAL JET SET, TRASH AND NO STAR (*6) / WASHING MACHINE (*8) / Lee Ranaldo: FROM HERE TO INFINITY (*4) / EAST JESUS (*7) / Thurston Moore: PSYCHIC HEARTS (*5)

THURSTON MOORE (b.25 Jul'58, Coral Gables, Florida) – vocals, guitar / **KIM GORDON** (b.28 Apr'53, Rochester, N.Y.) – vocals, bass / **LEE RANALDO** (b. 3 Feb'56, Glen Cove, N.Y.) – vocals, guitar repl. ANN DEMARIS / **RICHARD EDSON** – drums repl. DAVE KEAY

Neutral / not iss.

Feb 84. (m-lp) *(ND 01)* **SONIC YOUTH (live)** [-] [-] German
– The burning spear / I dreamt I dreamed / She's not alone / I don't want to push it / The good and the bad. *(re-iss. cd Oct87 on 'S.S.T.'; SSTCD 097)*

— **JIM SCLAVUNOS** – drums repl. EDSON

Feb 84. (lp) *(ND 02)* **CONFUSION IS SEX** [-] [-] German
– Inhuman / The world looks red / Confusion is next / Making the nature scene / Lee is free / (She's in a) Bad mood / Protect me you / Freezer burn / I wanna be your dog / Shaking Hell. *(re-iss. cd Oct87 on 'S.S.T.'; SSTCD 096)*

— **BOB BERT** – drums repl. SCLAVUNOS (still featured on 2 tracks)

Zensor / not iss.

Oct 83. (m-lp) *(ZENSOR 10)* **KILL YR. IDOLS** [-] [-] German
– Protect me you / Shaking Hell / Kill yr. idols / Brother James / Early American.

not iss. / Ecstatic Peace

1984. (c) *<none>* **SONIC DEATH (SONIC YOUTH LIVE)** [-] [ ]
– Sonic Death (side 1) / Sonic Death (side 2). *(UK cd-iss. Jul88 on 'Blast First'; BFFP 32CD>*

not iss. / Iridescence

Dec 84. (12"; by SONIC YOUTH & LYDIA LUNCH) *<1-12>* **DEATH VALLEY '69. / BRAVE MEN (RUN IN MY FAMILY)** [-] [ ]

Blast First / Homestead

Mar 85. (lp) *(BFFP 1) <HMS 016>* **BAD MOON RISING** [ ] [ ]
– Intro / Brave men rule / Society is a hole / I love her all the time / Ghost bitch / I'm insane / Justice is might / Death valley '69. *(cd-iss. Nov86+=; BFFP 1CD)* – Satan is boring / Flower / Halloween. *<US cd re-iss. 1995 on 'Geffen'; 24512>*

Jun 85. (12"ep; by SONIC YOUTH & LYDIA LUNCH) *(BFFP 2) <HMS 012>* **DEATH VALLEY '69. / I DREAMT I DREAMED / INHUMAN / BROTHER JAMES / SATAN IS BORING** [ ] [ ]

Jan 86. (12",12"yellow) *(BFFP 3)* **HALLOWEEN. / FLOWER** [-] [ ]

Jan 86. (7") *(BFFP 3)* **FLOWER. / REWOLF (censored)** [ ] [-]
(12") – ('A'side) / Satan is boring (live).

Mar 86. (etched-12") *(BFFP 3-B)* **HALLOWEEN II** [ ] [-]

— **STEVE SHELLEY** (b.23 Jun'62, Midland, Michigan) – drums repl. BOB BERT who joined PUSSY GALORE

Blast First / S.S.T.

May 86. (lp/c) *(BFFP 4/+C) <SST/+C/CD 059>* **EVOL** [ ] [ ]
– Green light / Star power / Secret girl / Tom Violence / Death to our friends / Shadow of a doubt / Marilyn Moore / In the kingdom / Madonna, Sean and me. *(cd-iss. Nov86+=; BFFP 4CD)* – Bubblegum. *<US cd re-iss. 1995 on 'Geffen'; 24513>*

Jul 86. (7") *(BFFP 7) <SST 80>* **STAR POWER. / BUBBLEGUM** [ ] [ ]
(12"+=) *(BFFP 7T) <SST 80-12>* – Expressway.

— added guest **MIKE WATT** – bass (of fIREHOSE)

Nov 86. (12"; as CICCONE YOUTH) *(BFFP 8)* **INTO THE GROOVE(Y). / TUFF TITTY RAP / BURNIN' UP** [ ] [ ]

Jun 87. (lp/c/cd) *(BFFP 20/+C/CD) <SST/+C/CD 134>* **SISTER** [ ] [ ]
– White cross / (I got a) Catholic block / Hot wire my heart / Tuff gnarl / Kotton crown / Schizophrenia / Beauty lies in the eye / Stereo sanctity / Pipeline – killtime / PCH. *(cd+=)* – Master-Dik (original). *<US cd re-iss. 1995 on 'Geffen'; 24514>*

Jan 88. (m-lp) *(BFFP 26T)* **MASTER-DIK** [ ] [ ]
– Master-Dik / Beat on the brat / Under the influence of the Jesus & Mary Chain: Ticket to ride / Ringo – He's on fire – Florida oil / Chines jam / Vibrato – Guitar lick – Funky fresh / Our backyard / Traffik.

Blast First / Capitol

Jan 88. (lp/c/cd; as CICCONE YOUTH) *(BFFP 28/+C/CD) <C1/C4/C2 75402>* **THE WHITEY ALBUM** [63] [ ]
– Needle-gun (silence) / G-force / Platoon II / Macbeth / Me & Jill / Hendrix Cosby / Burnin' up / Hi! everybody / Children of Satan / Third fig / Two cool rock chicks / Listening to Neu! / Addicted to love / Moby-Dik / March of the Ciccone robots / Making the nature scene / Tuff titty rap / Into the groovey. *<US cd re-iss. 1995 on 'Geffen'; 24516>*

Feb 88. (d-one-sided-7"on 'Fierce') *(FRIGHT 015-016)* **STICK ME DONNA MAGICK MOMMA / MAKING THE NATURE SCENE (live)** [ ] [-]
(also soon issued as normal-7")

Blast First / Torso

Oct 88. (d-lp/c/cd) *(BFFP 34/+C/CD) <2602339>* **DAYDREAM NATION** [99] [ ]
– Teenage riot / Silver rocket / The sprawl / 'Cross the breeze / Eric's trip / Total trash / Hey Joni / Providence / Candle? / Rain king / Kissability / Trilogy: The wonder – Hyperstation – Eliminator Jr.

— Late in '88, KIM teamed up with LYDIA LUNCH and SADIE MAE to form one-off project HARRY CREWS. Their live appearences were issued in Apr 90 as 'NAKED IN GARDEN HILLS' for 'Big Cat' UK + 'Widowspeak' US.

Feb 89. (12") *(BFFP 46)* **TOUCH ME, I'M SICK. / (Halloween; by MUDHONEY)** [ ] [ ]

W.E.A. / D.G.C.

Jun 90. (cd/c/lp) *<(7599 24297-2/-4/-1)>* **GOO** [32] [96]
– Dirty boots / Tunic (song for Karen) / Mary-Christ / Kool thing / Mote / My friend Goo / Disappearer / Mildred Pierce / Cinderella's big score / Scooter + Jinx / Titanium expose. *(re-iss. cd Oct95 on 'Geffen'; GFLD 19297)*

Sep 90. (7")(c-s) **KOOL THING. / THAT'S ALL I KNOW (RIGHT NOW)** [ ] [-]
(12"+=) – ('A'demo version).
(cd-s++=) – Dirty boots (rock & roll Heaven version).

— In Autumn '90, THURSTON was part of 'Rough Trade' supergroup VELVET MONKEYS.

D.G.C. / D.G.C.

Apr 91. (m-lp/m-c/m-cd) *(DGC/+C/D 21634)* **DIRTY BOOTS** (all live, except the title track) [69] [-]
– Dirty boots / The bedroom / Cinderella's big scene / Eric's trip / White kross. *(re-iss. cd Apr92; DGLD 19060)*

— Early in '92, THURSTON and STEVE also teamed up with RICHARD HELL's off-shoot group The DIM STARS.

Jun 92. (7") *(DGCS 11)* **100%. / CREME BRULEE** [28] [-]
(10"orange+=/12"+=) *(DGC V/T 11)* – Hendrix necro.
(cd-s++=) *(DGCTD 11)* – Genetic.

Jul 92. (d-lp/c/cd) *<(DGC/+C/D 24485)>* **DIRTY** [6] [83]
– 100% / Swimsuit issue / Theresa's sound-world / Drunken butterfly / Shoot / Wish fulfillment / Sugar Kane / Orange rolls, angel's spit / Youth against fascism / Nic fit / On the strip / Chapel Hill / JC / Purr / Creme brulee. *(d-lp+=)* – Stalker. *(re-iss. cd Oct95; GFLD 19296)*

Geffen / D.G.C.

Oct 92. (7") *(GFS 26)* **YOUTH AGAINST FASCISM. / PURR** [52] [-]
(10"colrd+=) *(GFSV 26)* – ('A'version).
(12"++=/cd-s++=) *(GFST/+D 26)* – The destroyed room (radio version)

Apr 93. (7"/c-s) *(GFS/+C 37)* **SUGAR KANE. / THE END OF THE END OF THE UGLY** [26] [-]
(10"blue+=/cd-s+=) *(GFS V/TD 37)* – Is it my body / Personality crisis.

Apr 94. (10"silver/c-s/cd-s) *(GFS V/C/TD 72)* **BULL IN THE HEATHER. / RAZORBLADE** [24] [-]

May 94. (cd/c/blue-lp) *<(GED/GEC/GEF 24632)>* **EXPERIMENTAL JET SET, TRASH AND NO STAR** [10] [34]
– Winner's blues / Bull in the heather / Starfield road / Skink / Self-obsessed and sexxee / Bone / Androgynous mind / Quest for the cup / Waist / Doctor's orders / Tokyo eye / In the mind of the bourgeois reader / Sweet shine.

— In Sep 94; 'A&M' released CARPENTERS tribute album, which contained their single 'SUPERSTAR'. It was combined with also another cover from REDD KROSS, and reached UK No.45.

Oct 95. (cd/c/d-lp) *<(GED/GEC/GEF 24925)>* **WASHING MACHINE** [39] [58]
– Becuz / Junkie's promise / Saucer-like / Washing machine / Unwind / Little trouble girl / No queen blues / Panty lies / Becuz coda * / Skip tracer / The diamond sea. *(cd+= *)*

Apr 96. (12"/cd-s) *(GRS T/D 22132)* **LITTLE TROUBLE GIRL. / MY ARENA / THE DIAMOND SEA (edit)** [ ] [-]

Feb 98. (12"/cd-s; SONIC YOUTH & JIM O'ROURKE) *(SYR 003/+CD)* **INVITO AL CIELO. /** [ ] [ ]
(above issued on own 'Sonic Youth Records')

May 98. (d-cd/d-lp) *<(GED/GEF 25203)>* **A THOUSAND LEAVES** [38] [85]
– Contre le sexisme / Sunday / Female mechanic now on duty / Wildflower soul / Hoarfrost / French tickler / Hits of sunshine (for Allen Ginsberg) / Karen Koltrane / The ineffable me / Snare / Girl / Heather angel.

Jun 98. (7") *(GFS 22332)* **SUNDAY. / MOIST VAGINA** [72] [-]
(cd-s+=) *(GFSTD 22332)* – Silver panties / ('A'edit).

— THURSTON collaborated with DON FLEMING and JIM DUNBAR on the freeform/experimental project, FOOT, releasing 'S/T' for 'God Bless' in Jul'98.

– compilations, others, etc. –

Feb 92. (cd) *Sonic Death; <(SD 13001)>* **GOO DEMOS LIVE AT THE CONTINENTAL CLUB (live)** [ ] [ ] Nov89

Mar 95. (cd/c) *Blast First; (BFFP 113 CD/C)* **CONFUSION IS SEX / KILL YR IDOLS** [ ] [-]

Mar 95. (cd) *Warners-Rhino; (8122 71591-2)* **MADE IN THE U.S.A.** (1986 soundtrack) [ ] [-]

Apr 95. (cd) *Blast First; (BFFP 119CD)* **SCREAMING FIELDS OF SONIC LOVE** [ ] [-]

May 97. (pic-lp) *Sonic Death; (SYLB 1)* **LIVE IN BREMEN (live)** [ ] [-]

Jun 97. (12"ep/cd-ep) *Sonic Youth; (SYR 1/+CD)* **SYR VOL.1** [ ] [ ]
– Anagrama / Improvisation ajout'e / Tremens / Mieux: de corrosion.

Jul 98. (cd) *S.K.R.; (SKR 1)* **SILVER SESSION FOR JASON KNUTH** [ ] [ ]

Aug 98. (cd) *Goofin' (GOO 2CD)* **HOLD THAT TIGER (live 1987)** [ ] [ ]

LEE RANALDO

Blast First / S.S.T.

Jul 87. (m-lp/c) *(BFFP 9/+C) <SST 113>* **FROM HERE ⇒ ETERNITY** [ ] [ ]
– Time stands still / Destruction site / Ouroboron / Slodrown / New groove loop / Florida flower / Hard left / Fuzz-locusts / To Mary / Lathe speaks / The resolution / King's egg. *(re-iss. May93 on 'S.S.T.' lp/c/cd; same as US)*

not iss. / Blast First

Oct 95. (cd) *<BFFPCD 103>* **EAST JESUS** [-] [ ]
– Bridge / Time stands still / Destruction site / Oroboron / Slo drone / Some distortion / Live #1 / New groove loop / Some hammering . . . / Walker grooves / Fuxx – Locusts / To Mary (x2) / Lathe speaks / Deva, Spain / Resolution – King's Ogg.

FREE KITTEN

KIM GORDON – vocals, bass, guitar / **JULIE CAFRITZ** – vocals, guitar (ex-PUSSY GALORE)

Wiiija / Ecstatic Peace

1992. (7") **OH BONDAGE UP YOURS. /** [-] [ ]

— there were other singles collected on their compilation, see below

1992. (m-cd) **CALL NOW** [-] [ ]
– Falling backwards / + 5

— added **MARK IBOLD** – bass (of PAVEMENT) + **YOSHIMI** – drums, trumpet

Jun 94. (cd) *(WIJ 036CD)* **UNBOXED** (compilation) [ ] [ ]
– Skinny butt / Platinumb / Smack / Falling backwards / Oneness / Dick / Yoshimi Vs. Mascis / Oh bondage up yours / 1-2-3 / Party with me punker / John Stark blues / Guilty pleasures / Sex boy / Cleopatra / Loose lips / Oh baby.

Jan 95. (7"one-sided) *(LTD 002)* **HARVEST SPOON** [ ] [-]

Feb 95. (cd/lp) *(WIJ 041 CD/V)* **NICE ASS**
– Harvest sppon / Rock of ages / Proper band / What's fair / Kissing well / Call back / Blindfold test / Greener pastures / Revlon liberation orchestra / The boaster / Scratch the D.J. / Secret sex friend / Royal flush / Feelin' / Alan Licked has ruined music for an entire generation.

Feb 96. (7"ep) *(WIJ 047V)* **PUNKS SUING PUNKS EP** -
– Kitten bossa nova / Punk v. punk / Coco's theme.

Oct 97. (12"ep) *(WIJ 074)* **CHINATOWN EXPRESS. / NEVER GONNA SLEEP / GAA** -

Oct 97. (cd/lp) *(WIJ CD/LP 1076)* **SENTIMENTAL EDUCATION**
– Teenie weenie boppie / Top 40 / Never gonna sleep / Strawberry milk / Played yrself / Dr. Spooky's spatialized Chinatown express / Bouwerie's boys / Records sleep / Picabo who / Sentimental education / One forty five / Eat cake / Gaa / Daddy long legs / Noise doll.

THURSTON MOORE

Geffen D.G.C.

May 95. (cd/c/d-lp;colrd 3-sides) *<(GEF/GEC/GED 24810)>* **PSYCHIC HEARTS**
– Queen bee and her pals / Ono soul / Psychic hearts / Pretty bad / Patti Smith math scratch / Blues from beyond the grave / See-through play-mate / Hang out / Feathers / Tranquilizor / Staring statues / Cindy (rotten tanx) / Cherry's blues / Female cop / Elergy for all dead rock stars.

Victo Victo

Mar 97. (cd) *<(VICTOCD 045)>* **PIECE FOR JETSUN DOLMA**

Corpus Hermeticum Corpus Herme

Apr 97. (cd) *(HERMES 011)* **KLANGFARBENMELODIE**

Father Yod Father Yod

May 97. (cd; THURSTON MOORE & PHIL MILSTEIN) *(HOTYOD 1)* **SONGS WE TAUGHT THE LORD VOL.2** -

SON VOLT (see under ⇒ UNCLE TUPELO)

SOUL ASYLUM

Formed: Minneapolis, Minnesota, USA . . . 1981 as LOUD FAST RULES, by ex-AT LAST guitarist DAN MURPHY and ex-SHITS frontman DAVE PIRNER, who were subsequently joined by KARL MUELLER then PAT MORLEY. Very much in the mould of HUSKER DU and The REPLACEMENTS, SOUL ASYLUM joined the latter at 'Twin Tone' records, while the former's BOB MOULD produced their 1984 debut album, 'SAY WHAT YOU WILL'. Later that year, MORLEY departed while the rest of the band took a break, SOUL ASYLUM subsequently returning in 1986 with GRANT YOUNG on their follow-up, 'MADE TO BE BROKEN'. A fusion of 60's pop and 70's punk, the album (also produced by MOULD) showed PIRNER blossoming into a cuttingly perceptive lyricist. Later that year, the band delivered another fine set, 'WHILE YOU WERE OUT', the record attracting major label attention in the form of 'A&M'. Fulfilling their contract with 'Twin Tone', SOUL ASYLUM cut a covers set, 'CLAM DIP AND OTHER DELIGHTS', displaying their wide range of tastes from Barry Manilow's 'MANDY' to Foreigner's 'JUKEBOX HERO'. In 1988, A&M issued the LENNY KAYE and ED STASIUM produced album, 'HANG TIME', an endearing collection of gleaming power-pop nuggets that occasionally veered off the beaten track into country. Their second and final release for A&M, 'SOUL ASYLUM AND THE HORSE THEY RODE IN ON' (1990), saw PIRNER spiral into despair despite the album's critical acclaim. Disillusioned with the major label inertia, the frontman took a break from amplified noise while his colleagues resumed their day jobs. Staking their chances on yet another major label, SOUL ASLYLUM subsequently signed to 'Columbia' and achieved almost instantaneous success with the album 'GRAVE DANCERS UNION' in 1992. This was mainly due to the massive interest in the TOM PETTY-esque 'RUNAWAY TRAIN', a single that hit the American Top 5 in the summer of '93. The track's radio friendly success paved the way for more typically abrasive numbers as 'SOMEBODY TO SHOVE' and 'BLACK GOLD', PIRNER landing on his feet as he wooed sultry actress, Winona Ryder (he appeared with her in the film, 'Generation X'). SOUL ASYLUM subsequently became MTV darlings and friends of the stars, such luminaries as BOB DYLAN, PETER BUCK and GUNS N' ROSES professing to fan status. In 1995, they returned with a new drummer, STERLING CAMPBELL, and a new album, 'LET YOUR DIM LIGHT SHINE', another worldwide seller which spawned the melancholy Top 30 gem, 'MISERY'. MURPHY and PIRNER (latter part-time) had also moonlighted in the countrified GOLDEN SMOG with among others the JAYHAWKS' GARY LOURIS and MARC PERLMAN. An EP of covers in '92 was finally followed up by an album in '96, 'DOWN BY THE OLD MAINSTREAM'. A few years later y'all supergroup added BIG STAR's JODY STEPHENS to replace the drumming PIRNER, a second set, WEIRD TALES', gaining many plaudits. • **Covers:** MOVE OVER (Janis Joplin) / RHINESTONE COWBOY (Glen Campbell) / BARSTOOL BLUES (Neil Young) / SEXUAL HEALING (Marvin Gaye) / ARE FRIENDS ELECTRIC (Tubeway Army) / SUMMER OF DRUGS (Victoria Williams) / WHEN I RAN OFF AND LEFT HER (Vic Chesnutt).

Album rating: SAY WHAT YOU WILL (*6) / MADE TO BE BROKEN (*6) / WHILE YOU WERE OUT (*6) / HANG TIME (*6) / CLAM DIP AND OTHER DELIGHTS (*5) / SOUL ASYLUM AND THE HORSE THEY RODE IN ON (*8) / GRAVE DANCERS UNION (*7) / LET YOUR DIM LIGHTS SHINE (*6)

DAVE PIRNER (b.16 Apr'64, Green Bay, Wisconsin) – vocals, guitar / **DAN MURPHY** (b.12 Jul'62, Duluth, Minnesota) – guitar, vocals / **KARL MUELLER** (b.27 Jul'63) – bass / **PAT MORLEY** – drums, percussion

Rough Trade Twin Tone

Aug 84. (m-lp) *<TT 8439>* **SAY WHAT YOU WILL** -
– Long day / Voodoo doll / Money talks / Stranger / Sick of that song / Walking / Happy / Black and blue / Religiavision. *<US re-iss. May89+=; same>* – Dragging me down / Do you know / Spacehead / Broken glass / Masquerade. *(UK cd-iss. Mar93 as 'SAY WHAT YOU WILL CLARENCE . . . KARL SOLD THE TRUCK' on 'Roadrunner'; RR 9093-2) (cd re-iss. Mar95 on 'Twin Tone'; TTR 8439-2)*

— **GRANT YOUNG** (b. 5 Jan'64, Iowa City, Iowa) – drums, percussion; repl. MORLEY

Sep 86. (lp) *(ROUGH 102) <TT 8666>* **MADE TO BE BROKEN**
– Tied to the tracks / Ship of fools / Can't go back / Another world another day / Made to be broken / Never really been / Whoa! / New feelings / Growing pain / Lone rider / Ain't that tough / Don't it (make your troubles seem small). *(cd-iss. Mar93 on 'Roadrunner'+=; RR 9094-2)* – Long way home. *(cd re-iss. Sep98 on 'R.C.A.'; 74321 60573-20)*

Sep 86. (7") **TIED TO THE TRACKS. /**

What Goes On Twin Tone

Mar 88. (lp) *(GOES ON 16) <TT 8691>* **WHILE YOU WERE OUT** 1987
– Freaks / Carry on / No man's land / Crashing down / The judge / Sun don't shine / Closer to the stars / Never too soon / Miracles mile / Lap of luxury / Passing sad daydream. *(cd-iss. Mar93 on 'Roadrunner'; RR 9096-2) (cd re-iss. Feb95 on 'Twin Tone'; TTR 8691-2)*

May 88. (m-lp) *(GOES ON 22) <TT 8814>* **CLAM DIP AND OTHER DELIGHTS** 1987
– Just plain evil / Chains / Secret no more / Artificial heart / P-9 / Take it to root / Jukebox hero / Move over / Mandy / Rhinestone cowboy. *(cd-iss. Mar93 on 'Roadrunner'; RR 9097-2) (cd re-iss. Feb95 on 'Twin Tone'; TTR 8814-2)*

— split but re-formed adding guest **CADD** – sax, piano

A&M A&M

Jun 88. (7"/12") *(AM/+Y 447)* **SOMETIME TO RETURN. / PUT THE BOOT IN** -
(12"-iss.Jun91 +=; same) – Marionette.

Jun 88. (lp/c/cd) *(AMA/AMC/CDA 5197) <395197-1/-4/-2>* **HANG TIME**
– Down on up to me / Little too clean / Sometime to return / Cartoon / Beggars and choosers / Endless farewell / Standing in the doorway / Marionette / Ode / Jack of all trades / Twiddly dee / Heavy rotation. *(re-iss. Sep93 cd/c; CD/C MID 189)*

Aug 88. (7") *(AM 463)* **CARTOON. / TWIDDLY DEE** -
(12"+=) *(AMY 463)* – Standing in the doorway.

Sep 90. (cd/c/lp) *(395318-2/-4/-1)* **SOUL ASYLUM & THE HORSE THEY RODE IN ON** 1989
– Spinnin' / Bitter pill / Veil of tears / Nice guys (don't get paid) / Something out of nothing / Gullible's travels / Brand new shine / Grounded / Don't be on your way / We / All the king's friends. *(re-iss. Sep93 cd/c; CD/C MID 190)*

Jan 91. (7") **EASY STREET. / SPINNING**
(12"+=) – All the king's friends / Gullible's travels.

Columbia Columbia

Oct 92. (cd/c/lp) *(472253-2/-4/-1) <48896>* **GRAVE DANCERS UNION** 11
– Somebody to shove / Black gold / Runaway train / Keep it up / Homesick / Get on out / New world / April fool / Without a trace / Growing into you / 99% / The Sun maid. *(re-dist.Jul93; hit UK No.52) (UK No.27 early '94)*

Mar 93. (10"ep/cd-ep) *(659 088-0/-2)* **BLACK GOLD. / BLACK GOLD (live) / THE BREAK / 99%**

May 93. (c-s,cd-s) *<74966>* **RUNAWAY TRAIN / NEVER REALLY BEEN (live)** - 5

Jun 93. (7"/c-s) *(659 390-7/-4)* **RUNAWAY TRAIN. / BLACK GOLD (live)** 37 -
(12"+=) *(659 390-6)* – By the way / Never really been (live).
(cd-s++=) *(659 390-2)* – Everybody loves a winner. (- Black Gold).
(above single returned into UK chart Nov'93 to hit No.7)

Aug 93. (12"ep/cd-ep) *(659 649-6/-2)* **SOMEBODY TO SHOVE / SOMEBODY TO SHOVE (live). / RUNAWAY TRAIN (live) / BY THE WAY (demo)** 34 -
(c-ep) *(659 649-4)* – ('A'side) / Black gold (live) / Runaway train (live).

Jan 94. (7"/c-s) *(659 844-7/-4)* **BLACK GOLD. / SOMEBODY TO SHOVE** 26 -
(cd-s+=) *(659 844-2)* – Closer to the stairs / Square root.
(cd-s+=) *(659 844-5)* – Runaway train (live).

Mar 94. (7"/c-s) *(660 224-7/-4)* **SOMEBODY TO SHOVE. / BY THE WAY** 32 -
(cd-s+=) *(660 224-2)* – Stranger (unplugged) / Without a trace (live).
(cd-s++=) *(660 224-5)* – ('A'mix).

— **STERLING CAMPBELL** – drums; repl. YOUNG

Jun 95. (cd/c) *(480 320-2/-4) <57616>* **LET YOUR DIM LIGHT SHINE** 22 6
– Misery / Shut down / To my own devices / Hopes up / Promises broken / Bittersweetheart / String of pearls / Crawl / Caged rat / Eyes of a child / Just like anyone / Tell me when / Nothing to write home about / I did my best.

Jun 95. (c-s,cd-s) *<77959>* **MISERY / HOPE** - 20

Jul 95. (7"white/c-s) *(662 109-7/-4)* **MISERY. / STRING OF PEARLS** 30 -
(cd-s+=) *(662 109-2)* – Hope (demo) / I did my best.

Nov 95. (c-s) *(662 478-4)* **JUST LIKE ANYONE / DO ANYTHING YOU WANNA DO (live)** 52 -
(cd-s+=) *(662 478-2)* – Get on out (live).
(cd-s) *(662 478-5)* – ('A'side) / You'll live forever (demo) / Fearless leader (demo).

Feb 96. (c-s,cd-s) *<78215>* **PROMISES BROKEN / CAN'T EVEN TELL (live)** - 63

— now a trio of **PIRNER, MURPHY + MUELLER**

May 98. (cd/c) *(487265-2/-4) <67618>* **CANDY FROM A STRANGER**
– Creatures of habit / I will still be laughing / Close / See you later / No time for waiting / Blood into wine / Lies of hate / Draggin' out the lake / Blackout / The game / Cradle chain.

SOUL COUGHING

Formed: New York City, New York, USA . . . 1993 by lyricist M. DOUGHTY, MARK de GLI ANTONI, SEBASTIAN STEINBERG and YUVAL GABAY. All regulars of cult NY club, 'The Knitting Factory', SOUL COUGHING approach their music with a resolutely experimental attitude. 'Slash' were quick to pick up on the band's oddball appeal, releasing their debut set, 'RUBY VROOM', in 1994, and initiating a slew of rave reviews. Two years on, a follow-up, 'IRRESISTIBLE BLISS', gave them their first taste of chart success, although this lasted all of one week at No.136. Things dramatically improved with the release of 1998's 'EL OSO', a hit and miss amalgam of off-kilter time signatures, geek-indie and amphetamine pop/rock which surprised many by hitting the US Top 50.

Album rating: RUBY VROOM (*8) / IRRESISTIBLE BLISS (*6) / EL OSO (*7)

M. DOUGHTY – vocals, guitar / **MARK de GLI ANTONI** – keyboards, samples / **SEBASTIAN STEINBERG** – double bass (ex-MARC RIBOT) / **YUVAL GABAY** (b. Israel) – drums

Slash – London / Slash – Warners

Sep 94. (cd/c) *(828 555-2/-4) <45752>* **RUBY VROOM**
– Is Chicago, is not Chicago / Sugar free jazz / Casiotone / Blue eyed devil / Bus to Beelzebug / True dreams of Wichita / Screenwriter's blues / Moon Sammy / Supra genius / City of motors / Uh zoom zip / Down to this / Mr. Bitterness / Janine. *(cd re-iss. Aug98; same)*

Apr 95. (12"/cd-s) *(43519)* **DOWN TO THIS** –

Dec 95. (12"/cd-s) *(COUP 002) <43582>* **SUGAR FREE JAZZ (remixes). / Collapsed Lung: MACLIFE** Oct95
(above issued on 'Jealous')

Jun 96. (cd/c/lp) *(828 759-2/-4/-1) <46175>* **IRRESISTIBLE BLISS**
– Super bob bon / Soft serve / White girl / Soundtrack to Mary / Lazybones / 4 out of 5 / Paint / Disseminated / Collapse / Sleepless / Idiot kings / How many cans?

Jun 97. (cd-s) *(LASCD 60)* **SUPER BON BON / CASIOTONE NATION**
(12") *(LASHX 60)* – ('A'-Propellerheads Mezzanine mix) / ('A'original) / ('A'-Propellerheads radio edit).

Oct 98. (cd) *(556 049-2) <46800>* **EL OSO** 49
– Rolling / Misinformed / Circles / Blame / St. Louise is listening / Maybe I'll come down / Houston / $300 / Fully retractable / Monster man / Pensacola / I miss the girl / So far I have not found the science / The incumbent.

SOULSIDE (see under ⇒ GIRLS AGAINST BOYS)

SOUND

Formed: Wimbledon, London, England . . . 1978 out of punk act The OUTSIDERS by mainman ADRIAN BORLAND along with GRAHAM GREEN, MICHAEL DUDLEY and initially JAN. After making their vinyl debut in 1979 with the 'PHYSICAL WORLD' EP, the band signed to the 'Korova' label and released a debut album, 'JEOPARDY' (1980). Gloomy, paranoid alternative pop/rock distinguished by its edgy bass and washes of synth, the band's approach generally met with good reviews even if the likes of 'MISSILES' and 'JEOPARDY' sound overly earnest and naive in hindsight. As a darker sideline, BORLAND and GREEN recorded as SECOND LAYER, the album 'WORLD OF RUBBER' surfacing in '82. 'FROM THE LION'S MOUTH' (1982) appeared the same year, The SOUND subsequently securing a major label deal with 'WEA' and releasing 'ALL FALL DOWN' (1982). Despite a glossier production and more commercial material like 'CALLING THE NEW TUNE', sales didn't meet the label's expectations and The SOUND were back on more familiar indie territory – with 'Statik' – for 1984's mini-set, 'SHOCK OF DAYLIGHT'. Its lead track (and accompanying single), 'COUNTING THE DAYS', was one of BORLAND's most accessible and surprisingly affecting compositions to date, akin to a fusion of The COMSAT ANGELS and The PSYCHEDELIC FURS. The rest of the material was equally impressive, especially the shimmering guitar atmospherics of 'LONGEST DAYS'. The following year's full-length 'HEADS AND HEARTS' album was even more refined and embellished the sound with sax, yet the band was reaching the end of its lifespan and BORLAND split for a solo career after 1987's 'THUNDER'. The man later went into production work with Dublin band, INTO PARADISE, while around the same time he (& His Citizens) released their first album, 'ALEXANDRIA' (1989).

Album rating: JEOPARDY (*6) / FROM THE LION'S MOUTH (*5) / ALL FALL DOWN (*4) / HEADS AND HEARTS (*6) / IN THE HOTHOUSE (*6) / THUNDER UP (*5) / Adrian Borland & The Citizens: ALEXANDRIA (*5) / BRITTLE HEAVEN (*5)

OUTSIDERS

ADRIAN BORLAND – vocals, guitar / **BOB LAWRENCE** – bass / **ADRIAN JAMES** – drums

Raw Edge / not iss.

Oct 77. (lp) *(RER 001)* **CALLING ON YOUTH** –

Nov 77. (7"ep) *(RER 002)* **ONE TO INFINITY** –
– One to infinity / New uniform / Freeway / Consequences.

Apr 78. (lp) *(RER 003)* **CLOSE UP** –

Xciting Plastic / not iss.

May 78. (7";w-drawn) *(none)* **VITAL HOURS. / TAKE UP** – –

—— late '78, **GRAHAM GREEN** – bass; repl. BOB

—— **MICHAEL DUDLEY** – drums, percussion; repl. ADRIAN

—— with also initially **JAN** – percussion, they changed name to . . .

SOUND

Tortch / not iss.

Dec 79. (7"ep) *(TOR 003)* **PHYSICAL WORLD EP** –
– Cold beat / Physical world / Unwritten law.

May 80. (lp; shelved) *(TOR 008) THE SOUND* – –

—— added **BI MARSHALL** (b. BENITA) – keyboards

Korova / not iss.

Sep 80. (7") *(KOW 10)* **HEYDAY. / BRUTE FORCE** –

Oct 80. (lp) *(KODE 2)* **JEOPARDY** –
– I can't escape myself / Heartland / Hour of need / Words fail me / Missiles / Heyday / Jeopardy / Night versus day / Resistance / Unwritten law / Desire.

—— **MAX MAYERS** (b. COLVIN) – keyboards; repl. BI

Sep 81. (7") *(KOW 21)* **SENSE OF PURPOSE. / POINT OF NO RETURN** –
(12"+=) *(KOW 21T)* – Cold beat.

Nov 81. (lp) *(KODE 5)* **FROM THE LION'S MOUTH** –
– Winning / Sense of purpose / Contact the fact / Skeletons / Judgement / Fatal flaw / Possession / The fire / Silent air / New dark age.

Mar 82. (7") *(KOW 23)* **HOT HOUSE. / NEW DARK AGE** –

WEA / WEA

Nov 82. (lp) *(240019-1)* **ALL FALL DOWN**
– All fall down / Party of the mind / Monument / In suspense / Where the love is / Song and dance / Calling the new tune / Red paint / Glass and smoke / We could go far.

—— **GRAHAM BAILEY** – bass; repl. GREEN

Statik / not iss.

Mar 84. (m-lp/m-c) *(STAB/+C 1)* **SHOCK OF DAYLIGHT** –
– Golden soldiers / Longest days / Counting the days / Winter / New way of life / Dreams then plans.

May 84. (7") *(TAK 16)* **COUNTING THE DAYS. / NEW WAY OF LIFE** –
(12"+=) *(TAK 16-12)* – Dreams then plans.

Nov 84. (7") *(TAK 28)* **ONE THOUSAND REASONS. / BLOOD AND POISON** –
(12"+=) *(TAK 28-12)* – Steal your air.

Mar 85. (lp/c) *(STAT LP/C 24)* **HEADS AND HEARTS** –
– Whirlpool / Total recall / Under you / Burning part of me / Love is not a ghost / Wildest dreams / One thousand reasons / Restless time / Mining for heart / World as it is / Temperature drop. *(cd-iss. Dec86 as 'COUNTING THE DAYS'+=; CDST 24)* – SHOCK OF DAYLIGHT

Jun 85. (7") *(TAK 34)* **TEMPERATURE DROP. / OILED** –

Nov 85. (d-lp) *(STATDLP 1)* **IN THE HOTHOUSE (live)** –
– Winning / Under you / Total recall / Skeletons / Prove me wrong / Wildest dreams / Burning part of me / Heartland / Hothouse / Judgement / Counting the days / Red paint / Silent air / Sense of purpose / Missiles.

Play It Again Sam / not iss.

May 87. (7") *(BIAS 063)* **HAND OF LOVE. /** –
(12"+=) *(BIAS 063T)* –

May 87. (cd/lp) *(CD+/BIAS 053)* **THUNDER UP** –
– Acceleration group / Hand of love / Barria Alta / Kinetic / Iron years / Prove me wrong / Shot up and shut down / Web of wicked ways / I give you pain / You've got a way.

Oct 87. (7") *(BIAS 049)* **IRON YEARS. /** –
(12"+=) *(BIAS 049T)* –

—— they split at the turn of the year

ADRIAN BORLAND

—— went solo, augmented by The CITIZENS (on first two sets & single)

Sep 89. (lp/cd) *(BIAS 125/+CD)* **ALEXANDRIA** –
– Light the sky / Rogue beauty / Crystalline / Shadow of your grace / Weight if stuff / She's my heroine / Beneath the big wheel / Community call / Other side of the world / Deep deep blue / No ethereal.

Mar 90. (7") *(BIAS 155)* **BENEATH THE BIG WHEEL. /** –

Mar 92. (cd) *(BIAS 215CD)* **BRITTLE HEAVEN** –

Resolve / not iss.

Mar 96. (cd) *(RES 002)* **CINEMATIC** –
– Dreamfuel / Bright white light / When can I be me / Cinematic / Night cascade / Neon and stone / Long dark train / Antartica / Western veil / We are the night / Dreamfuel 2 / I can't stop the world / Heading emotional / The south / Spanish hotel / March.

Earth / not iss.

Sep 97. (cd) *(EAR 001CD)* **5.00 A.M.** –

Sep 97. (cd) *(EAR 002CD)* **OVER THE UNDER** –

SECOND LAYER

—— was a sideline for **BORLAND + GREEN** (augmented by drum machine)

Tortch / not iss.

1979. (7"ep) *(TOR 001)* **FLESH AS PROPERTY** –
– Courts or wars / Metal sheet / Germany. *(re-iss. 1981 on 'Fresh'; FRESH 5) (shelved re-iss. 1980 on 'Cherry Red'; CHERRY 21)*

1980. (7"ep) *(TOR 006)* **STATE OF EMERGENCY. / I NEED NOISE / THE CUTTING MOTION** –

Cherry Red / not iss.

Feb 82. (lp) *(BRED 14)* **WORLD OF RUBBER** –
– Underneath the gloss / Fixation / In bits / Save our souls / Distortion / Zero / Definition of honour / Japanese headset / Black flowers.

Licensed / not iss.

Aug 88. (d-lp) *(LD 8711)* **SECOND LAYER** –

SOUNDGARDEN

Formed: Seattle, Washington, USA . . . 1984 by CHRIS CORNELL, KIM THAYIL and HIRO YAMAMOTO. With the addition of MATT CAMERON in '86, the band became one of the first to record for the fledgling 'Sub Pop' label, releasing the 'HUNTED DOWN' single in summer '87. Two EP's, 'SCREAMING LIFE', and 'FOPP' followed, although the group signed to 'S.S.T.' for their debut album, 'ULTRAMEGA OK' (1988). Despite its lack of focus, the record laid the foundations for what was to follow; a swamp-rich miasma of snail-paced, bass-crunch uber-riffing, wailing vocals and punk attitude shot through with bad-trip psychedelia (i.e. not something to listen to last thing at night). And with the Grammy-nominated 'LOUDER THAN LOVE' (1989), the group's major label debut for 'A&M', SOUNDGARDEN harnessed their devilish wares onto infectious melodies and fuck-off choruses; one listen to the likes of 'HANDS ALL OVER', 'LOUD LOVE' and the tongue-in-cheek brilliance of 'BIG DUMB SEX' was enough to convince you that these hairy post-metallers were destined for big, grunge-type things. Success wasn't immediate however, the album failing to make a dent beyond the Sub-Pop in-crowd and a few adventurous metal fans. YAMAMOTO departed soon after the record's release, his replacement being ex-NIRVANA guitarist JASON EVERMAN, who was succeeded in turn by BEN SHEPHERD. CORNELL and CAMERON subsequently got together with future PEARL JAM mambers, EDDIE VEDDER, STONE GOSSARD and JEFF AMENT to form TEMPLE OF THE DOG, releasing an eponymous album in early '91 to critical acclaim. SOUNDGARDEN, meanwhile, finally got their break later that year when 'BADMOTORFINGER' broke the US/UK Top 40. An even more accessible proposition, the record combined a tighter, more driven sound with pop/grunge hooks and their trademark cerebral lyrics to create such MTV favourites as 'JESUS CHRIST POSE' and 'OUTSHINED'. 'RUSTY CAGE' was another juggernaut riffathon, while 'SEARCHING WITH MY GOOD EYE CLOSED' meted out some of the most brutal psychedelia this side of MONSTER MAGNET. A high profile support slot on GUNS N' ROSES' 'Lose Your Illusion' tour afforded the band valuable exposure in the States, their crossover appeal endearing them to the metal hordes on both sides of the Atlantic. Previewed by the Top 20 'SPOONMAN' single, SOUNDGARDEN's masterful fourth set, 'SUPERUNKNOWN' (1994), finally gave the group long overdue success, scaling the US charts and going Top 5 in Britain. Constructed around a head-spinning foundation of acid-drenched retro-rock and JIM MORRISON-esque doom, this epic album spawned the Grammy-winnning 'BLACK HOLE SUN' while 'FELL ON BLACK DAYS' stands as one of their most realised pieces of warped psychedelia to date. Following a world tour with the likes of The SMASHING PUMPKINS, the group began work on 'DOWN ON THE UPSIDE' (1996). Another marathon set boasting sixteen tracks, the record inevitably failed to garner the plaudits of its predecessor; the claustrophobia of old had given way to a marginally more strightforward melodic grunge sound, evidenced to best effect on the likes of 'BURDEN IN MY HAND'. Subversiveness was still the key word; 'TY COBB's mutant country-punk and gonzoid expletive-filled attitude was reminiscent of MINISTRY's seminal 'Jesus Built My Hotrod'. The album ultimately proved to be their swan song, SOUNDGARDEN subsequently pushing up the daisies as of April '97. • **Songwriters:** Most by CORNELL and group permutations. Covered SWALLOW MY PRIDE (Ramones) / FOPP (Ohio Players) / INTO THE VOID tune only (Black Sabbath) / BIG BOTTOM (Spinal Tap) / EARACHE MY EYE (Cheech & Chong) / I CAN'T GIVE YOU ANYTHING (Ramones) / HOMOCIDAL SUICIDE (Budgie) / I DON'T CARE ABOUT YOU (Fear) / CAN YOU SEE ME (Jimi Hendrix) / COME TOGETHER (Beatles).

Album rating: ULTRAMEGA OK (*7) / LOUDER THAN LOVE (*8) / BADMOTORFINGER (*9) / SUPERUNKNOWN (*9) / DOWN ON THE UPSIDE (*6)

CHRIS CORNELL (b.20 Jul'64) – vocals, guitar / **KIM THAYIL** (b. 4 Sep'60) – lead guitar / **HIRO YAMAMOTO** (b.13 Apr'61) – bass / **MATT CAMERON** (b.28 Nov'62, San Diego, Calif.) – drums, percussion

not iss. Sub Pop

Jun 87. (7"blue) *<SP 12a>* **NOTHING TO SAY. / HUNTED DOWN** –

Oct 87. (12"ep,orange-12"ep) *<SP 12>* **SCREAMING LIFE** –
– Hunted down / Entering / Tears to forget / Nothing to say / Little Joe / Hand of God.

Aug 88. (12"ep) *<SP 17>* **FOPP** –
– Fopp / Fopp (dub) / Kingdom of come / Swallow my pride.

S.S.T. S.S.T.

Nov 88. (m-lp/c/cd) *<SST 201/+C/CD)>* **ULTRAMEGA OK**
– Flower / All your lies / 665 / Beyond the wheel / 667 / Mood for trouble / Circle of power / He didn't / Smokestack lightning / Nazi driver / Head injury / Incessant mace / One minute of silence. *(re-iss. Oct95;)*

May 89. (12"ep/c-ep/cd-ep) *<SST 231/+C/CD)>* **FLOWER. / HEAD INJURY / TOY BOX**

A&M A&M

Sep 89. (lp/c/cd) *<(AMA/AMC/CDA 5252)>* **LOUDER THAN LOVE**
– Ugly truth / Hands all over / Gun / Power trip / Get on the snake / Full on Kevin's mom / Loud love / I awake / No wrong no right / Uncovered / Big dumb sex / Full on (reprise).

Apr 90. (10"ep/cd-ep) *(AM X/CD 560)* **HANDS ALL OVER** –
– Hands all over / Heretic / Come together / Big dumb sex.

Jul 90. (7"ep/12"ep) *(AM/+Y 574)* **THE LOUD LOVE E.P.** –
– Loud love / Fresh deadly roses / Big dumb sex (dub) / Get on the snake.

— **JASON EVERMAN** (b.16 Aug'67) – bass (ex-NIRVANA) repl. HIRO who later formed TRULY after working in a bike shop.

Oct 90. (7",7"purple/green) *<SP 83>* **ROOM A THOUSAND YEARS WIDE. / H.I.V. BABY** –
(above issued on 'Sub Pop')

— **BEN SHEPHERD** (b. HUNTER SHEPHERD, 20 Sep'68, Okinawa, Japan) – bass repl. JASON

Oct 91. (cd/c/lp) *(395374-2/-4/-1) <5374>* **BADMOTORFINGER** 39 39
– Rusty cage / Outshined / Slaves & bulldozers / Jesus Christ pose / Face pollution / Somewhere / Searching with my good eye closed / Room a thousand years wide / Mind riot / Drawing flies / Holy water / New damage.

Mar 92. (7") *(AM 862)* **JESUS CHRIST POSE. / STRAY CAT BLUES** 30 –
(cd-s+=) *(AMCD 862)* – Into the void (stealth).

Jun 92. (7"pic-d) *(AM 874)* **RUSTY CAGE. / TOUCH ME** 41 –
(12"+=/cd-s+=) *(AM Y/CD 874)* – Show me.
(cd-s+=) *(AMCDX 874)* – Big bottom / Earache my eye.

Nov 92. (7") *(AM 0102)* **OUTSHINED. / I CAN'T GIVE YOU ANYTHING** 50 –
(12"+=/cd-s+=) *(AM 0102 T/CD)* – Homocidal suicide.
(cd-s+=) *(AM 0102CDX)* – I don't care about you / Can't you see me.

Feb 94. (7"pic-d/c-s) *(580 538-7/-4)* **SPOONMAN. / FRESH TENDRILS** 20 –
(12"clear+=/cd-s+=) *(580 539-1/-2)* – Cold bitch / Exit Stonehenge.

Mar 94. (cd/c/orange-d-lp) *(540215-2/-4/-1) <0198>* **SUPERUNKNOWN** 4 1
– Let me drown / My wave / Fell on black days / Mailman / Superunknown / Head down / Black hole Sun / Spoonman / Limo wreck / The day I tried to live / Kickstand / Fresh tendrils / 4th of July / Half / Like suicide / She likes surprises.

Apr 94. (7"pic-d/c-s) *(580594-7/-4)* **THE DAY I TRIED TO LIVE. / LIKE SUICIDE (acoustic)** 42 –
(12"etched+=/cd-s+=) *(580595-1/-2)* – Kickstand (live).

Aug 94. (7"pic-d/c-s) *(580736-7/-4)* **BLACK HOLE SUN. / BEYOND THE WHEEL (live) / FELL ON BLACK DAYS (live)** 12 –
(pic-cd-s+=) *(580753-2)* – Birth ritual (demo).
(cd-s) *(580737-2)* – ('A'side) / My wave (live) / Jesus Christ pose (live) / Spoonman (remix).

Jan 95. (7"pic-d/c-s) *(580947-7/-4)* **FELL ON BLACK DAYS. / KYLE PETTY, SON OF RICHARD / MOTORCYCLE LOOP** 24 –
(cd-s) *(580947-2)* – ('A'side) / Kyle Petty, son of Richard / Fell on black days (video version).
(cd-s) *(580947-5)* – ('A'side) / Girl u want / Fell on black days (early demo).

May 96. (7"red/cd-s) *(581620-7/-4)* **PRETTY NOOSE. / JERRY GARCIA'S FINGER** 14 –
(cd-s) *(581620-2)* – ('A'side) / Applebite / An unkind / (interview with Eleven's Alain and Natasha).

May 96. (cd/c/d-lp) *(540526-2/-4/-1) <0526>* **DOWN ON THE UPSIDE** 7 2
– Pretty noose / Rhinosaur / Zero chance / Dusty / Ty Cobb / Blow up the outside world / Burden in my hand / Never named / Applebite / Never the machine forever / Tighter & tighter / No attention / Switch opens / Overfloater / An unkind / Boot camp.

Sep 96. (7"/cd-s) *(581854-7/-2)* **BURDEN IN MY HAND. / KARAOKE** 33 –
(cd-s) *(581855-2)* – ('A'side) / Bleed together / She's a politician / (Chris Cornell interview).

Dec 96. (7") *(581986-7)* **BLOW UP THE OUTSIDE WORLD. / DUSTY** 38 –
(cd-s+=) *(581987-2)* – Gun.
(cd-s) *(581986-2)* – ('A'side) / Get on the snake / Slice of spacejam.

— split on the 9th of April 1997

– compilations, etc –

Oct 93. (cd) *A&M; (CDA 24118)* **LOUDER THAN LOUD / BADMOTORFINGER**

Oct 93. (c/cd) *Sub Pop; (SP/+CD 12)* **SCREAMING LIFE / FOPP**

Nov 97. (cd) *A&M; (540833-2) <0833>* **A-SIDES** 63
– Nothing to say / Flower / Loud love / Hands all over / Get on the snake / Jesus Christ pose / Outshined / Rusty cage / Spoonman / The day I tried to live / Black hole sun / Fell on black days / Pretty noose / Burden in my hand / Blow up the outside world / Ty Cobb / Bleed together.

TEMPLE OF THE DOG

splinter-group feat. **CORNELL + CAMERON** plus **STONE GOSSARD / JEFF AMENT** (both ex-MOTHER LOVE BONE, future PEARL JAM)

A&M A&M

Jun 92. (cd/c/lp) *(395 350-2/-4/-1) <5350>* **TEMPLE OF THE DOG** 5
– Say hello to Heaven / Reach down / Hunger strike / Pushing forward back / Call me a dog / Times of trouble / Wooden Jesus / Your saviour / 4-walled world / All night thing.

Oct 92. (7"pic-d/c-s) *(AM 0091/+C)* **HUNGER STRIKE. / ALL NIGHT THING** 51
(12"+=/cd-s+=) *(AM 0091 T/CD)* – Your saviour.

HATER

MATT + BEN

Sub Pop Sub Pop

Aug 93. (7") *<(SP 233)>* **CIRCLES. / GENOCIDE**

A&M A&M

Sep 93. (cd/c) *(540 137-2/-4) <0137>* **HATER**
– Mona bone jakon / Who do I kill? / Tot finder / Lion and lamb / Roadside / Down undershoe / Circles / Putrid / Blistered / Sad McBain. *(re-iss. cd May95; same)*

SOUNDTRACK OF OUR LIVES

Formed: Gothenberg, Sweden . . . 1986 as UNION CARBIDE PRODUCTIONS by EBBOT LUNDBERG, a loud talking modern Viking, er . . . so to speak. UCP released a number of cranium-shredding STOOGES-esque albums – 'IN THE AIR TONIGHT' (1987), 'FINANCIALLY DISSATISFIED, PHILOSOPHICALLY TRYING' (1989), 'FROM INFLUENCE TO IGNORANCE' (1991) and 'SWING' (1992) –

spread over several years before LUNDBERG started from scratch under the moniker, SOUNDTRACK OF OUR LIVES. Drinkers all, the grisly, growling LUNDBERG and his new recruits issued an album, 'EXTENDED REVELATION' for 'Telegram' records in 1996 before they were scooped up by WEA subsidiary, 'Coalition'. A debut single, 'INSTANT REPEATER '99', showed them at their rawkist, psychedelic best, while their 1997 album, 'WELCOME TO THE INFANT FREEBASE', was loved by at least TIM BURGESS of The CHARLATANS.

Album rating: WELCOME TO THE INFANT FREEBASE (*8) / Union Carbide Productions: IN THE AIR TONIGHT (*7) / FINANCIALLY DISSATISFIED, PHILOSOPHICALLY TRYING (*6) / SWING (*5)

UNION CARBIDE PRODUCTIONS

EBBOT LUNDBERG – vocals, sax / **PATRICK CAGANIS** – guitar / **BJORN OLSSON** – guitar, sax

Ediesta Skyclad

Sep 88. (lp)<cd> *(CALCLP 056) <61>* **IN THE AIR TONIGHT** [ ] [ ] Nov87
– Ring my bell / Financial declaration / Summer holiday camp / Cartoon animal / So long / In the air tonight / Three mile eyes / Teenage bankman / Pour en flirt avec toi / Down on the beach.

1989. (cd) *<71>* **FINANCIALLY DISSATISFIED, PHILOSOPHICALLY TRYING** [-] [ ]
– At dawn / Born in the 60's / San Francisco boogie / 13th trip / Down on the farm / Maximum dogbreath / Here comes God / Another rock'n'roll statement / Glad to have you back / Career opportunities / Swedish meatball revival.

EfA Radium

1991. (cd) *(14365) <226.05>* **FROM INFLUENCE TO IGNORANCE** [ ] [ ]
– Train song / Be myself again / Golden age / Can't hear nothing / Baritone Street / Got my eyes on you / Can't slow down / Sunset trip / Circles / Coda.

Roadrunner Fishpuppet

1992. (7") *<010>* **HIGH SPEED ENERGY. / DOIN' MY TIME** [-] [ ]

Nov 92. (cd) *(RR 9136-2) <014>* **SWING** [ ] [ ]
– Waiting for turns / High speed energy / Mr. Untitled / Right phrase / Solution / Chameleon ride / Turn off the blues / How do you feel today? / Game boy / Beefhead / TV spiders.

SOUNDTRACK OF OUR LIVES

EBBOT LUNDBERG – vocals / **MARTIN HEDROS** – keyboards / **IAN PERSSON** – guitar / **MATTHIAS BARJED** – guitar / **KALLE GUSTAVSSON** – bass / **FREDRIK SANDSTEN** – drums

Telegram not iss.

1996. (cd-s) *(017486-2)* **BLACKSTAR /** [-] [-] Sweden

1996. (cd) *(422786-2)* **EXTENDED REVELATION** [-] [-] Sweden
(all UK-iss.May98; same)

Coalition not iss.

Jun 97. (7"/c-s) *(COLA 018/+C)* **INSTANT REPEATER '99. / RETIRED TEENAGE ANGST / GRAND CANARIA** [ ] [-]
(cd-s+=) *(COLA 018CD)* – ('A'side) / Blow my cool / Mantra slider / Firmament vacation / Endless song.
(re-iss. Jun98; same)

Oct 97. (7"/c-s) *(COLA 029/+C)* **MANTRA SLIDER. /** [ ] [-]
(cd-s+=) *(COLA 029CD)* –

Nov 97. (cd/c) *(0630 18871-2/-4)* **WELCOME TO THE INFANT FREEBASE** [ ] [-]
(re-iss. May98 on 'Telegram'; 16652-2)

Apr 98. (7"/c-s) *(COLA 045/+C)* **FIRMAMENT VACATION. / GREATEST HITS PROVIDERS / CLEANING SESSION RAGA** [ ] [-]
(cd-s+=) *(COLA 045CD)* –

SOUP DRAGONS

Formed: Bellshill, Lanarkshire, Scotland . . . 1985 by SEAN DICKSON, JIM McCULLOCH, ROSS SINCLAIR and SUSHILL K.DADE. Taking their name from cult kids TV show, 'The Clangers', The SOUP DRAGONS were initially signed to the 'Subway' label for whom they released the 'SUN IN THE SKY' EP and a follow-up, 'WHOLE WIDE WORLD'. The band's BUZZCOCKS/UNDERTONES three-chord flurry gained subsequently gained valuable exposure later that summer when the latter single's B-side, 'PLEASANTLY SURPRISED', was featured on the NME's C86 compilation. One unlikely fan was ex-WHAM! manager, Jazz Summers, who masterminded the next phase of their career via the 'Raw TV' label and oversaw the release of a string of singles including their first Top 75 chart entry, 1987's 'CAN'T TAKE NO MORE'. Further singles, 'SOFT AS YOUR FACE' and 'THE MAJESTIC HEAD' found them dabbling with a 60's retro sound, 'Sire' trying and failing to break the band into the mainstream with a long awaited debut album, 'THIS IS OUR ART' (1988). Moving back to 'Raw TV' and re-evaluating their approach, DICKSON & Co. emerged in the second half of 1989 with two singles, 'BACKWARDS DOG' and 'CROTCH DEEP TRASH', critics only too ready to mention the similarities with the latest STOOGES-fixated offering from fellow Glaswegians, PRIMAL SCREAM. Following the replacement of ROSS with PAUL QUINN, detractors were furnished with further ammunition amid accusations of banwagoneering as the 'DRAGONS released the singalong indie/dance crossover, 'MOTHER UNIVERSE', in 1990. The accompanying album, 'LOVEGOD' (1990), confirmed the transformation and The SOUP DRAGONS finally broke big time a few months later with a cover of the Rolling Stones' 'I'M FREE'. Transforming an R&B jangle into a stoned, fringe-shaking anthmem for the baggy generation – complete with reggae toasting courtesy of JUNIOR REID – really didn't do the band much good in retrospect. Despite being a massive worldwide hit and an MTV stalwart, the track's success couldn't prevent The SOUP DRAGONS dying a swift commercial death when the scene came to an abrupt end in the early 90's. Granted, they spun it out with a re-issued 'MOTHER UNIVERSE' but yet another change in direction on 'HOTWIRED' (1992) made no headway with a music buying public who'd simply moved on, the band's chequered career eventually coming to a close after their short-lived tenure with 'Big Life'. • **Songwriters:** DICKSON compositions, except PURPLE HAZE (Jimi Hendrix) / OUR LIPS ARE SEALED (Go-Go's) / I'M NOT YOUR STEPPING STONE (Monkees).

Album rating: LOVEGOD (*7) / THIS IS OUR ART (*6) / HYDROPHONIC (*3)

SEAN DICKSON (b.21 Mar'67) – vox, guitar / **JIM McCULLOCH** (b.19 May'66) – guitar, vocals / **ROSS SINCLAIR** – drums / **SUSHILL K. DADE** (b.15 Jul'66) – bass (ex-WAKE)

Subway not iss.

Feb 86. (ltd.7"ep) *(SUBWAY 2)* **THE SUN IN THE SKY** [ ] [-]
– Quite content / Swirling round the garden with you / Fair's fair / Not for Humbert.

May 86. (7") *(SUBWAY 4)* **WHOLE WIDE WORLD. / I KNOW EVERYTHING** [ ] [-]
(12"+=) *(SUBWAY 4T)* – Pleasantly surprised.

— May 86, SEAN (bass) & JIM (guitar) were part-time auxiliaries of BMX BANDITS who were fronted by DUGLAS and released 'SAD'. / 'E102' on '53rd & 3rd' label. JIM played on their Jan'87 follow-up 'WHAT A WONDERFUL WORLD'. / 'THE DAY BEFORE TOMORROW'.

Raw TV Products not iss.

Sep 86. (7",7"red,7"blue) *(RTV 1)* **HANG TEN!. / SLOW THINGS DOWN** [ ] [-]
(12"+=) *(RTV 12-1)* – Just mind your step girl / Man about town with chairs.

Jan 87. (7") *(RTV 2)* **HEAD GONE ASTRAY. / GIRL IN THE WORLD** [ ] [-]
(12"+=/12"w-poster+=) *(RTV/+P 12-2)* – So sad I feel.

Jun 87. (7") *(RTV 3)* **CAN'T TAKE NO MORE. / WHITEWASH** [65] [-]
(12"+=) *(RTV 12-3)* – A-Ha! experience.
(12"ep) *(RTVL 12-3)* – ('A'&'B'live) / Hang ten! (live) / Purple haze (live).

Aug 87. (7") *(RTV 4)* **SOFT AS YOUR FACE. / IT'S ALWAYS AUTUMN** [66] [-]
(12"+=) *(RTV 12-4)* – Our lips are sealed / Soft as your face – arrangement.
(double-groove 12"+=) *(RTV 12-4D)* – Can't take no more (vocal squad version) / Whole wide world (live).

Mar 88. (7") *(RTV 5)* **THE MAJESTIC HEAD. / 4-WAY BRAIN** [ ] [-]
(12"+=) *(RTV 12-5)* – Them.
(12"pic-d+=) *(RTV 12-5P)* – Corporation headlock.

Sire Sire

Apr 88. (lp/c)(cd) *(WX 169/+C)(K 925702-2) <25702>* **THIS IS OUR ART** [60] [ ]
– Kingdom chairs / Great empty space / The majestic head / Turning stone / Vacate my space / On overhead walkways / Passion protein / King of the castle / Another dream ticket / Soft as your face / Family ways. *(cd re-iss. Jul91; K 925702-2)*

Jun 88. (7") *(W 7820)* **KINGDOM CHAIRS. / WHITE CRUISING** [ ] [ ]
(12") *(W 7820T)* – ('A'side) / I'm not your stepping stone / All because of you.
(10") *(W 7820TE)* – ('A'&'B'live) / Family way (live) / King of the castle (live).

Raw TV Big Life

Jul 89. (7") *(RTV 6)* **BACKWARDS DOG. / BURN OUT** [ ] [-]
(12"+=) *(RTV 6T)* – Supercherry / Kill kill kill me.

Oct 89. (7") *(RTV 7)* **CROTCH DEEP TRASH. / YOU CAN FLY** [ ] [-]
(ext.12"+=) *(RTV 7T)* – Superangel / ('A'dub version).

— **PAUL QUINN** – drums repl. ROSS. / added guest **ALEX McLAREN** – guitar

Mar 90. (7") *(RTV 8)* **MOTHER UNIVERSE. / ('A'-Solar mix)** [ ] [-]
(12"+=) *(RTV 8T)* – ('A'-Love dub mix).
(cd-s++=) *(RTV 8CD)* – 4-way brain.

May 90. (cd/c/lp) *(SOUP CD/MC/LP 2) <842985>* **LOVEGOD** [60] [88] Oct90
– Mother Universe / Backwards dog / Softly / Drive the pain / Lovegod / Dream E-forever / Sweetmeat / Kiss the gun / Love you to death / Beauty freak / Lovegod (dub) / Crotch deep trash. *(cd+=)* – (2 extra mixes) *(re-iss. Aug90 on 'Big Life'+= cd/c/lp; SOUP CD/MC/LP 2R)* – I'm free. *(hit UK No.7)*

Jul 90. (7"/c-s/ext.12") *(RTV 9/+MC/T) <877568>* **I'M FREE (featuring JUNIOR REID). / LOVEGOD (dub)** [5] [79] Sep90
(cd-s+=) *(RTV 9CD)* – ('A'-12"version).
(12") *(RTV 9R)* – ('A'-Terry Farley Boys Own mix) / Backwards dog (remix).

Big Life Big Life

Oct 90. (7"/c-s) *(BLR/+C 30)* **MOTHER UNIVERSE. / BACKWARDS DOG** [26] [ ]
(12"+=/cd-s+=) *(BLR T/CD 30)* – ('A'dub remix) / ('A'-'89 remix).

Aug 91. (7"/c-s) *(BLR 56)* **ELECTRIC BLUES. / UNEARTHED** [ ] [ ]
(12"+=/cd-s+=) *(BLRT/BLC 56)* – Solar rise / ('A'dub version).

Apr 92. (7"/c-s) *(BLR/+C 68) <865764>* **DIVINE THING. / DRIVING** [53] [35]
(12"+=/cd-s+=) *(BLR T/CD 68)* – ('A'revisited) / American sweetmeat.

May 92. (cd/c/lp) *(BLR CD/MC/LP 15) <13178>* **HOTWIRED** [74] [97]
– Pleasure / Divine thing / Running wild / Getting down / Forever yesterday / No more / Understanding / Dream on (Solid gone) / Everlasting / Absolute heaven / Everything / Sweet layabout / Mindless.

Sep 92. (12"ep/c-ep/cd-ep) *<867416>* **PLEASURE / PLEASURE (revisited). / WHAT YOU WANT / DIVE-BOMBER** [ ] [69]
(cd-ep) – ('A'revisited) . . . repl. by 'Man'.
(cd-s+=) – ('A'revisited) / I'm free (original) / Mother universe / Electric blues.

— **DICKSON** virtually solo + a plethora of session people and special guests incl. MICKEY FINN, TINA WEYMOUTH, NEVILLE STAPLES, BOOTSY COLLINS

not iss. Polygram

Jan 95. (cd,c,lp) *<522732>* **HYDROPHONIC** [-] [ ]
– One way street / Don't get down (get down) / Do you care? / May the force be with you / Contact high / All messed up / The time is now / Freeway / Rest in peace / J.F. junkie / Automatic speed queen / Out of here / Motherfunker / Black and blues / Hypersonic re-entry.

SPACE

Formed: Liverpool, England … 1993 by TOMMY SCOTT, JAMIE MURPHY, FRANNY GRIFFITHS and ANDY KOWALSKI, all seasoned campaigners of the local music scene (TOMMY and FRANNY played in The AUSTRALIANS, whose track, 'THE GIRL WHO LOVED HER MAN ENOUGH TO KILL HIM' appeared on the 'Hit The North' various artists compilation). After a one-off single on the independent 'Home', the band were snapped up by 'Gut', a label which brought us the bare-arsed "pop thrills" of RIGHT SAID FRED. Equally camp in a more masculine kind of Scouse way, SPACE were light years removed from the shower of Brit-pop retro merchants doing the rounds in the mid-90's; the 'NEIGHBOURHOOD' single sounded like ENNIO MORRICONE waltzing round the last chance saloon to an acid-fried Mariachi soundtrack, SCOTT's robotic vocal affectations carrying lyrics cut from the same cloth as PETE SHELLEY's (Buzzcocks) creations. For all his little-boy-lost charm, SCOTT sounded pretty damn scary throughout much of the 'SPIDERS' (1996) album, his tales of losers, freaks and paranoid killers balancing black humour with unhinged Liverpudlian menace. Preceded by the voodoo-xylophone pop genius of 'FEMALE OF THE SPECIES' (a Top 20 hit and arguably one of the singles of the year) and the brassy, bouncy life affirming 'ME & YOU VERSUS THE WORLD' (about as commercial as SPACE get and a nod to native forebears, The Fab Four), the debut was released in late '96 to encouraging reviews and a subsequent Top 5 chart placing. Running the gamut of the band's many influences, from SINATRA and KRAFTWERK to 'South Pacific' and 'Midnight Cowboy', the album even catered for MURPHY's avowed love of techno with an acid freakout, 'GROWLER', bolted on as the closing track. Armed with a further two Top 20 hits in a re-released 'NEIGHBOURHOOD' and 'DARK CLOUDS', SPACE were ready to explore the final frontier where no (sensible) band had gone before i.e. the festival circuit. 1997 proved to be an even more hectic year, one that nearly broke them; JAMIE (at only 21, the stress of it all had played havoc with his peace of mind) pulled out on the eve of an American tour in February, TOMMY mysteriously lost his voice for a couple of months as well as being stalked and the general pressures of slogging round the world turned them into emotional wrecks. No doubt the experiences which formed the basis for follow-up Top 3 album, 'TIN PLANET' (1998), the cadets safely back on earth and ready for a new mission that resulted in two Top 10 hits, 'AVENGING ANGEL' and the tongue-in-cheek duet with CATATONIA's CERYS, 'THE BALLAD OF TOM JONES'. • **Songwriters:** Perm any SCOTT / GRIFFITHS / MURPHY and group.

Album rating: SPIDERS (*7) / TIN PLANET (*7)

TOMMY SCOTT – vocals, guitar / **JAMIE MURPHY** – guitar, vocals / **FRANNY GRIFFITHS** – bass / **ANDY KOWALSKI** – drums

Home | not iss.

Oct 95. (c-s) *(CAHOME 1)* **MONEY / KILL ME** [ ] [-]
(cd-s+=) *(CDHOME 1)* – ('A'club) / ('B'club).
(12") *(12HOME 1)* – ('A'-Lost in space remix) / ('A'-Still lost in space & safe bass mix) / ('A'-Space club mix) / ('A'-instrumental).

Gut | Uptown – Universal

Mar 96. (c-s) *(CAGUT 1)* **NEIGHBOURHOOD / REJECTS** [56] [-]
(cd-s+=) *(CDGUT 1)* – Turn me on to spiders.
(12") *(12GUT 1)* – ('A'-Live it! club) / ('A'-Live it! instrumental club) / ('A'-Pissed up stomp) / ('A'-radio).
Jun 96. (c-s) *(CAGUT 2)* **FEMALE OF THE SPECIES / LOONEY TUNE** [14] [-]
(12"+=/cd-s+=) *(12/CD GUT 2)* – ('A'radio) / Give me something.
Aug 96. (c-s) *(CAGUT 4)* **ME & YOU VERSUS THE WORLD / SPIDERS** [9] [-]
(cd-s+=) *(CDGUT 4)* – Life of a miser / Blow your cover.
(cd-s) *(CXGUT 4)* – ('A'mixes).
Sep 96. (cd/c/lp) *(GUT CD/MC/LP 1)* *<53028>* **SPIDERS** [5] [ ] Jan97
– Neighbourhood / Mister Psycho / Female of the species / Money / Me & you vs the world / Lovechild of the queen / No-one understands / Voodoo roller / Drop dead / Dark clouds / Major pager / Kill me / Charlie M. / Growler.
Oct 96. (c-s) *(CAGUT 5)* *<1152>* **NEIGHBOURHOOD / ONLY HALF AN ANGEL** [11] [ ]
(cd-s+=) *(CDGUT 5)* – Crisis / Shut your mouth.
(cd-s) *(CXGUT 5)* – ('A'side) / Welcome to the neighbourhood / Nighthood / Neighbourhood (pissed up stomp mix).
Feb 97. (c-s) *(CAGUT 6)* **DARK CLOUDS / HAD ENOUGH** [14] [-]
(cd-s+=) *(CDGUT 6)* – Children of the night / Influenza.
(cd-s) *(CXGUT 6)* – ('A'side) / Darker clouds / Storm clouds.

Gut | Imprint

Dec 97. (7"blue) *(7GUT 16)* **AVENGING ANGELS. / I AM UNLIKE A LIFEFORM YOU'VE NEVER MET** [6] [-]
(c-s) *(CAGUT 16)* – ('A'side) / Bastard me, bastard you.
(cd-s++=) *(CDGUT 16)* – Theme from "Baretta Vendetta".
(cd-s) *(CXGUT 16)* – ('A'side) / ('A'mixes:- John 'OO' Fleming Theramin mix / Ultra Vegas mix / The Jumping Soundboy mix / Franny's 'Peaceful Devil' mix / Brainbasher's 'Kick Ass Angel' mix / Jonnie Newman's 'Altered State' mix).
Feb 98. (7"red; with CERYS of CATATONIA) *(7GUT 18)* **THE BALLAD OF TOM JONES. / NOW SHE'S GONE** [4] [-]
(c-s+=) *(CAGUT 18)* – Happy endings.
(cd-s++=) *(CDGUT 18)* – Stress transmissions.
(cd-s) *(CXGUT 18)* – ('A'mixes:- Cocktail Lounge mix / Dirty Beatniks mix / Sound 5 mix / Sure Is Pure dub mix / SX Dub Scratching Cuckoo mix / Tom Jones Axe To Your Head mix).
Mar 98. (cd/c/lp) *(GUT CD/MC/LP 5)* *<110683>* **TIN PLANET** [3] [ ] Jul98
– Begin again / Avenging angels / The ballad of Tom Jones / 1 o'clock / Be there / The man / A liddle biddy help from Elvis / The unluckiest man in the world / Piggies / Bad day's / There's no you / Disco dolly / Fran in Japan.
Jun 98. (c-s/cd-s) *(CA/CD GUT 19)* **BEGIN AGAIN / YOU ROMANTIC FOOL / NUMB THE DOUBT / INFLUENZA (flu mix)** [21] [ ]
(cd-s) *(CXGUT 19)* – ('A'side) / The ballad of Tom Jones (live) / Female of the species (live) / Avenging angels (live).
Nov 98. (c-s) *(CAGUT 22)* **BAD DAYS EP** [20] [ ]
– Bad days / We gotta get out of this place / Unluckiest man.
(cd-s) *(CDGUT 22)* –
(cd-s) *(CXGUT 22)* –

SPACEHOG

Formed: Leeds, England …1994 by ROYSTON LANGDON and brother ANTHONY, who hooked up with RICHARD STEEL and JOHNNY CRAGG in New York a year earlier. Signed to Elektra off-shoot, 'Hifi', in 1995, they scored a minor US hit single with 'IN THE MEANTIME' early the folowing year. Enjoyable if not exactly original, SPACEHOG's sound was a Glam retro-rock pastiche fusing the likes of BOWIE and SUEDE with GUNS N' ROSES, a recipe which saw them securing a Top 50 Stateside position for their debut album, 'RESIDENT ALIEN' (1995). Although they failed to make any lasting impression in the UK, the debut did scrape into the Top 40 after it was re-promoted the following year. Nevertheless, the suitably interstellar single, 'SPACE IS THE PLACE', failed to chart despite being re-released within a matter of months. After a quiet '97, the group were scheduled to release an album early '98 (a single 'CARRY ON' will precede it). • **Songwriters:** LANGDON; 'In The Meantime' phone-tone intro/outro sampled from PENGUIN CAFE ORCHESTRA tune, 'Telephone And Rubber Band'.

Album rating: RESIDENT ALIEN (*6)

ROYSTON LANGDON – vocals, bass / **RICHARD STEEL** – lead guitar / **ANTHONY LANGDON** – guitar, vocals / **JONNY CRAGG** – drums

Elektra | Sire

Feb 96. (c-s,cd-s) *<64303>* **IN THE MEANTIME / TO BE A MILLIONAIRE . . . WAS IT LIKELY? (live)** [-] [32]
Apr 96. (c-s/cd-s) *(EKR 218 C/CD)* **IN THE MEANTIME / ZEROES** [ ] [-]
(cd-s+=) *(EKR 218CDX)* – To be a millionaire . . .was it likely (live). *(re-iss. Dec96 hit UK No.27; same)*
May 96. (cd/c) *<(7559 61834-2/-4)>* **RESIDENT ALIEN** [ ] [49] Oct95
– In the meantime / Spacehog / Starside / Candyman / Space is the place / Never coming down (part 1) / Cruel to be kind / Ship wrecked / Only a few / The last dictator / Never coming down (part 2) / Zeroes / To be a millionaire . . . was it likely? *(re-dist.Feb97 hit UK No.40)*
Jul 96. (c-s) *(EKR 225C)* **CRUEL TO BE KIND / THE HORROR** [ ] [-]
(12"+=) *(EKR 225CD)* – Crack city / Starside.
Oct 96. (c-s) *(EKR 230C)* **SPACE IS THE PLACE (blank bar mix) / CRUEL TO BE KIND (live)** [ ] [-]
(cd-s+=) *(EKR 230CD)* – ('A'-lp version) / Candyman (live).
Feb 97. (c-s) *(EKR 234C)* **SPACE IS THE PLACE /** [ ] [-]
(cd-s) *(EKR 234CD1)* –
(cd-s) *(EKR 234CD2)* –

Warners | Warners

Jan 98. (c-s) *(W 0428C)* **CARRY ON / ONE OF THESE DAYS** [43] [-]
(cd-s+=) *(W 0428CD)* – Adam & Steve / Carry on (acoustic).
Mar 98. (cd/c) *<(9362 46851-2/-4)>* **THE CHINESE ALBUM** [ ] [ ]
– One of these days / Goodbye violet race / Lucy's shoe / Mungo city / Skylark / Sand in your eyes / Captain Freeman / 2nd avenue / Almond kisses / Carry on / Anonymous / Beautiful girl.
Apr 98. (7") *(W 0439)* **MUNGO CITY. / ISLE OF MANHATTAN** [ ] [-]
(cd-s+=) *(W 0439CD1)* – Final frontier / Skylark.
(cd-s) *(W 0439CD2)* –

SPACEMEN 3

Formed: Rugby, Warwickshire, England . . . 1983 by SONIC BOOM (PETE KEMBER) and JASON PIERCE. They enlisted PETE BAINES and ROSCO as a rhythm section and through their manager, Gerald Palmer, they signed to indie label, 'Glass'. In 1986, they debuted with 'SOUND OF CONFUSION', a primal embryo for "shoegazers" to come. Their follow-up, 'THE PERFECT PRESCRIPTION', set the world alight (well! the indie world anyway), with some clever pulsating, psychedelic garage-noise intertwined with melancholy bursts of beauty and experimentation, i.e 'WALKIN WITH JESUS' (again!), 'TRANSPARENT RADIATION' and 'TAKE ME TO THE OTHER SIDE'. In 1989, they were back again with a third set, 'PLAYING WITH FIRE', featuring the 10-minute squall of 'SUICIDE', and 'REVOLUTION' (later covered by MUDHONEY). SONIC BOOM's heroin addiction was taking its toll during the early 90's and with JASON having founded SPIRTITUALIZED, the group were heading for their own proverbial rocketship to oblivion. Their final outing, 'RECURRING' (1991), recorded amid escalating tension, was a slight disappointment. By this time, SONIC had gone solo, subsequently going under the guise of SPECTRUM. His debut was followed by two albums of patchy, yet somewhat appealing albums, 'SOUL KISS (GLIDE DIVINE)' (1992) and 'HIGH LOWS AND HEAVENLY BLOWS' (1994). The ever prolific KEMBER went on play with mid 90's outfit, JESSAMINE, who to date have released a string of albums including 1997's 'ANOTHER FICTIONALIZED HISTORY'. Around the same, KEMBER/SONIC simultaneously resurfaced with a SPECTRUM set, 'FOREVER ALIEN', released on the '3rd Stone' imprint. • **Songwriters:** KEMBER or PIERCE material until the 90's when KEMBER penned all. Covered; IT'S ALRIGHT (Bo Diddley) / CHE +

ROCK'N'ROLL IS KILLING MY LIFE (Suicide) / WHEN TOMORROW HITS (Mudhoney) / COME TOGETHER + STARSHIP (MC5) / MARY-ANNE (. . .Campbell) / ROLLER COASTER (13th Floor Elevators).

Album rating: SOUND OF CONFUSION (*7) / THE PERFECT PRESCRIPTION (*8) / PLAYING WITH FIRE (*8) / SPECTRUM (SONIC BOOM; *5) / SOUL KISS (GLIDE DIVINE) (SPECTRUM; *6) / HIGH LOWS AND HEAVENLY BLOWS (SPECTRUM; *6)

SONIC BOOM (b. PETE KEMBER, 19 Nov'65) – vocals / **JASON PIERCE** (b.19 Nov'65) – guitar / **STEWART (ROSCO) ROSSWELL** – keyboards / **PETE (BASSMAN) BAINES** – bass

Glass | not iss.

Jun 86. (lp) *(GLA 018)* **SOUND OF CONFUSION** | | -
– Losing touch with my mind / Hey man / Roller coaster / Mary Anne / Little doll / 2:35 / O.D. catastrophe. *(re-iss. Sep89 on 'Fire' lp/c/cd; REFIRE CD/MC/LP 5) <US cd-iss. 1994 on 'Taan~g!'; 93>*

Dec 86. (12"m) *(GLAEP 105)* **WALKIN' WITH JESUS (SOUND OF CONFUSION). / ROLLERCOASTER / FEEL SO GOOD** | | -

Jul 87. (12"m) *(GLAEP 108)* **TRANSPARENT RADIATION / ECSTASY SYMPHONY / TRANSPARENT RADIATION (FLASHBACK). / THINGS'LL NEVER BE THE SAME / STARSHIP** | | -

Aug 87. (lp/c) *(GLA LP/MC 026)* **THE PERFECT PRESCRIPTION** | | -
– Take me to the other side / Walking with Jesus / Ode to street hassle / Ecstasy – Symphony / Feel so good / Things'll never be the same / Come down easy / Call the doctor / Soul 1 / That's just fine. *(re-iss. Dec89 on 'Fire' lp/c/cd, REFIRE LP/MC/CD 6) <US cd-iss. 1994 on 'Taang!'; 94>*

Mar 88. (12") *(GLASS 12-054)* **TAKE ME TO THE OTHER SIDE. / SOUL 1 / THAT'S JUST FINE** | | -

Jul 88. (lp/cd) *(GLA LP/CD 030)* **PERFORMANCE** (live 1988 Holland) | | -
– Mary-Anne / Come together / Things'll never be the same / Take me to the other side / Roller coaster / Starship / Walkin' with Jesus. *(re-iss. May91 on 'Fire' cd/c/lp; REFIRE CD/MC/LP 11)*

— **WILLIE B. CARRUTHERS** – bass / **JON MATLOCK** – drums repl. ROSCO + BAINES who formed The DARKSIDE

Fire | not iss.

Nov 88. (7") *(BLAZE 29S)* **REVOLUTION. / CHE** | | -
(12"+=/cd-s+=) *(BLAZE 29 T/CD)* – May the circle be unbroken.

Feb 89. (lp/c/cd) *(FIRE LP/MC/CD 16)* **PLAYING WITH FIRE** | | -
– Honey / Come down softly to my soul / How does it feel? / I believe it / Revolution / Let me down gently / So hot (wash away all my tears) / Suicide / Lord can you hear me. *(free-12"ep/cd-ep+=)* – Starship / Revolution / Suicide (live) / Repeater / Live intro theme (xtacy). *<US cd-iss. 1994 on 'Taang~'; 97>*

Jul 89. (7") *(BLAZE 36S)* **HYPNOTIZED. / JUST TO SEE YOU SMILE HONEY (part 2)** | | -
(12"+=/3"cd-s+=) *(BLAZE 36 T/CD)* – The world is dying.
(free 7"flexi w.a) *(CHEREE 5)* – EXTRACTS FROM A CONTEMPORARY SITAR EVENING (with other artists).

Jan 91. (7") *(BLAZE 41)* **BIG CITY. / DRIVE** | | -
(12"+=/cd-s+=) *(BLAZE 41 T/CD)* – Big City (everybody I know can be found here).
(12"w-drawn) *(BLAZE 41TR)* – ('A'remix) / I love you (remix).

Feb 91. (cd/lp)(s-lp) *(FIRE CD/LP 23)(FIRELP 23S)* **RECURRING** | 46 | -
– Big city (everybody I know can be found here) / Just to see you smile (orchestral) / I love you / Set me free – I've got the key / Set me free (reprise) / Feel so bad (reprise) / Hypnotized / Sometimes / Feelin' just fine (head full of shit) / Billy Whizz – blue 1. *(cd+=)* – When tomorrow hits / Why couldn't I see / Just to see you smile (instrumental) / Feel so sad (demo) / Drive.

— Had already folded June '90.

– compilations, etc. –

Dec 90. (cd/d-lp) *Fierce; (FRIGHT 042/+CD)* **DREAM WEAPON / ECSTASY IN SLOW MOTION** | | -
(re-iss. Nov95 on 'Space Age' cd/d-lp; ORBIT 001 CD/LP)

Jun 94. (cd/lp) *Taang!; <TAANG 96 CD/LP>* **THE SINGLES** | - |

Nov 94. (cd) *Bomp; (<BCD 4047>)* **TAKING DRUGS TO MAKE MUSIC TO TAKE DRUGS TO** (demos of 1986) | |

May 95. (cd/lp) *Sympathy For The Record Industry; (<SFTRI 1368 CD/LP>)* **FOR ALL FUCKED UP CHILDREN OF THE WORLD WE GIVE YOU . . .** (debut recording session) | |

May 95. (cd) *Bomp; (<BCD 4044>)* **SPACEMEN ARE GO!** | |

Jun 95. (cd/d-lp) *Fire; (FLIP CD/DLP 003)* **TRANSLUCENT FLASHBACKS** | | -

Sep 95. (cd) *Taang~; <TAANG 95CD>* **LIVE AT THE MILKWEG 6/2/88 (live)** | - |
– Mary Ann / Come together / Things'll never be / Take me to the other side / Rollercoaster / Walking with Jesus / Repeater / Starship / Revolution / Suicide.

Oct 95. (cd) *Fierce; (FRIGHT 063)* **THE CHOICE IS REVOLUTIONORHERION** | | -

Nov 95. (cd/d-lp) *Space Age; (ORBIT 002 CD/LP)* **LIVE IN EUROPE 1989 (live)** | | -

Mar 97. (d-cd) *Nectar; (NTMCDD 534)* **1 + 1 = 3** | | -

SONIC BOOM

(**PETE KEMBER** solo with **WILLIE B. CARRUTHERS** and also **PHIL PARFITT + JO WIGGS** of PERFECT DISASTER)

Silvertone | not iss.

Oct 89. (12"ep/cd-ep) *(ORE/+CD 11)* **ANGEL. / ANGEL (version) / HELP ME PLEASE** | | -

Feb 90. (cd/c/lp) *(ORE CD/MC/LP 506)* **SPECTRUM** | 65 | -
– Pretty baby / If I should die / Lonely avenue / Help me please / Angel / Rock'n'roll is killing my life / You're the one. *(free 10" w-lp) (SONIC 1)* – DRONE DREAM EP: OCTAVES. / TREMELOS *<US-iss.Oct97 as 'WHEN CAME BEFORE AFTER' on 'Sympathy For The Record Industry'; SFTRI 493>*

Apr 91. (7"; gig freebie) *(SONIC 2)* **(I LOVE YOU) TO THE MOON AND BACK. / CAPO WALTZ (live)** | - | -

— SONIC BOOM has now featured in E.A.R. (EXPERIMENTAL AUDIO RESEARCH), who after first low-key album 'MESMERISED' in 1994 on 'Sympathy For The Record Industry), released for 'Big Cat' the 1996 lp/cd 'BEYOND THE PALE' *(ABB 96/+CD)*. It featured KEVIN SHIELDS (of; we still think; MY BLOODY VALENTINE),KEVIN MARTIN (of GOD) and EDDIE PREVOST. SONIC BOOM and E.A.R. released a split 7" in Jul'98 on 'Earworm' (WORM 22)

— In Mar 92, HONEY TONGUE (aka MATTOCK + WIGGS) released lp 'NUDE NUDES' on 'Playtime'; *AMUSE 012CD)*

SPECTRUM

KEMBER, CARRUTHERS, etc

Silvertone | Warners

Jun 92. (7") *(ORE 41)* **HOW YOU SATISFY ME. / DON'T GO (instrumental 2)** | | -
(12"clear+=/cd-s+=) *(ORE 41 T/CD)* – My life spins around your every smile / Don't go (instrumental 1).

Jun 92. (cd/c/lp) *(ORE CD/C/LP 518) <41501>* **SOUL KISS (GLIDE DIVINE)** | |
– How you satisfy me / Lord I don't even know my name / The drunk suite (overture) / Neon sigh / Waves wash over me / (I love you) To the Moon and back / My love for you never died away but my soul gave out and wit / Sweet running water / Touch the stars / Quicksilver glide divine / The drunk suite / Phase me out (gently). *(re-iss. Apr95; same)*

Sep 92. (7") *(ORE 44)* **TRUE LOVE WILL FIND YOU IN THE END. / MY LIFE SPINS AROUND YOUR EVERY SMILE** | 70 | -
(12"/cd-s) *(ORE T/CD 44)* – ('A'side) / To the moon and back / Waves wash over me.

Aug 93. (7") *(ORE 56)* **INDIAN SUMMER. / BABY DON'T YOU WORRY (California lullabye)** | | -
(12"+=/cd-s+=) *(ORE T/CD 56)* – It's alright / True love will find you in the end.

Oct 94. (12"ep/cd-ep) *(ORE T/CD 65)* **UNDO THE TABOO / IN THE FULLNESS OF TIME. / TURN THE TIDE (SUB AQUA) / GO TO SLEEP** | | -

Nov 94. (cd/lp) *(ORE CD/LP 532)* **HIGHS, LOWS AND HEAVENLY BLOWS** | | -
– Undo the taboo / Feedback / Then I just drifted away / Take your time / Soothe me / All night long / Don't pass me by / I know they say / Take me away.

not iss. | Sympathy F

Oct 96. (10"ep) *<SFTRI 278>* **CALIFORNIA LULLABY EP** | - |

— SONIC BOOM also became part of JESSAMINE, an outfit who released a few albums including 'Another Fictionalized History' in '97.

3rd Stone | Warners

Oct 96. (cd-ep) *<46303>* **SONGS FOR OWLSLEY** | - |

Aug 97. (lp/cd) *(ORBIT 008/+CD) <46715>* **FOREVER ALIEN** | |
– Feels like I'm slipping away / The stars are so far (how does it feel?) / Close your eyes and you'll see / Delia Derbyshire / Owsley / Forever alien / Matrix / Like . . . / The new Atlantis / End.

Sep 97. (cd-s) *(ORBIT 010CD)* **FEELS LIKE I'M SLIPPING AWAY** | | -

— Note; Not to be confused with dance outfit, who released 'SKY ABOVE' & 'BRAZIL'.

SPARKLEHORSE

Formed: Richmond, Virginia, USA . . . 1995 by MARK LINKOUS. Early releases on 'Slow River', including 'CHORDS I'VE KNOWN' and 'HAMMERING THE CRAMPS' introduced this drawling southern singer-songwriter. Subsequently securing a deal with 'Capitol', LINKOUS supported labelmates RADIOHEAD in late '95 prior to the release of a debut single, 'SOMEDAY I WILL TREAT YOU GOOD' early the following year. A second single, a re-issue of 'HAMMERING THE CRAMPS', appeared a few months later, both tracks featuring on the tongue twistingly titled debut album, 'VIVADIXIESUBMARINETRANSMISSIONPLOT' (1996). Determinedly lo-fi, melancholic alt-country characterised by LINKOUS' catatonic vocals and influenced by the likes of TOM WAITS, NEIL YOUNG and The AFGHAN WHIGS, the album was an instant hit with the critics and even made a Top 60 showing in the UK charts. A former heroin addict, LINKOUS' health was almost the end of him when he collapsed with a heart attack and badly damaged his legs (he was also confined to a wheelchair for three months) following SPARKLEHORSE's live UK debut. When he eventually resurfaced in 1998 with the acclaimed 'GOOD MORNING SPIDER', several critics suggested that LINKOUS's near-death experience was perhaps a key factor in the vitality of the music. A record of strange beauty, 'GOOD MORNING..' segued from distorted sample-driven noise to passages of forlorn majesty with LINKOUS singing his blues against a lonely acoustic strum. Along with the likes of WILL OLDHAM and SMOG's BILL CALLAHAN, LINKOUS has become an unlikely figurehead for the lo-fi Americana scene with SPARKLEHORSE pushing the genre's boundaries while others are content to recycle. • **Covered:** WISH YOU WERE HERE (Pink Floyd) / WEST OF ROME (Vic Chesnutt).

Album rating: VIVADIXIESUBMARINETRANSMISSIONPLOT (*9) / GOOD MORNING SPIDER (*8)

MARK LINKOUS – vocals, guitar (ex-DANCING HOODS) / **BOB RUPE** or **ARMSTEAD WELLEFORD** – bass / **DAVID BUSH** or **JOHNNY HOTT** – drums / **DAVID CHARLES** – electric guitar, producer

not iss. | Slow River

Apr 95. (7"ep) *<SRR 14>* **CHORDS I'VE KNOWN EP** | - |
– Heart of darkness / Almost lost my mind / Midget in a junkyard / Dead opera star / Hatchet song.

1995. (7") *<SRR 74>* **HAMMERING THE CRAMPS. /** | - |
(UK-iss.Oct96; same)

Capitol | Capitol

Feb 96. (7") *(CL 766)* **SOMEDAY I WILL TREAT YOU GOOD. / LONDON** | |
(cd-s+=) *(CDCL 766)* – In the dry.

Apr 96. (7") *(CL 770)* **HAMMERING THE CRAMPS. / SPIRIT DITCH** [ ] [ ]
(cd-s+=) *(CDCL 770)* – Dead opera star / Midget in a junkyard.
May 96. (cd/c/d-lp) *(CD/TC+/EST 2280)* *<72438 32816-2/-4>*
VIVADIXIESUBMARINETRANSMISSIONPLOT [58] [ ] Nov95
– Homecoming queen / Weird sisters / 850 double pumper Holley / Rainmaker / Spirit ditch / Tears on fresh fruit / Saturday / Cow / Little bastard choo choo / Hammering the cramps / Most beautiful widow in town / Heart of darkness / Ballad of a cold lost marble / Someday I will treat you good / Sad and beautiful world / Gasoline horseys.

— LINKOUS brought in **SCOTT MINOR, PAUL WATSON + SCOTT FITZSIMMONS**

Aug 96. (7") *(CL 777)* **RAINMAKER. / I ALMOST LOST MY MIND** [61] [-]
(cd-s) *(CDCLS 777)* – Intermission.
(cd-s) *(CDCL 777)* – ('A'side) / Homecoming queen (live on KCRW) / Gasoline horseys (live on KCRW).
Feb 98. (7") **COME ON IN. /** [-] [ ]
(above an old release on 'Slow River')

— virtually **LINKOUS** with **MINOR, WATSON + SOFIA MITCHALITSIANOS** – cello / **MELISSA MOORE** – violin / **JOHNNY HOTT** – drums, piano / guests **STEPHEN McCARTHY + DAVID LOWERY + VIC CHESNUTT**

Jul 98. (cd-ep) *(CDCL 806)* **PAINBIRDS / MARIA'S LITTLE ELBOWS / THE DIRT BIKE WRECK (enhanced) / WISH YOU WERE HERE** [ ] [ ]
Jul 98. (cd/lp) *(496014-2/-1)* *<36671>* **GOOD MORNING SPIDER** [30] [ ] Feb99
– Pig / Painbirds / Saint Mary / Good morning spider / Sick of goodbyes / Box of stars (part one) / Sunshine / Chaos of the galaxy – Happy man / Hey, Joe / Come on in / Maria's little elbows / Cruel sun / All night home / Ghost of his smile / Hundreds of sparrows / Box of stars (part two) / Junebug.
Oct 98. (7"clear) *<(CL 808)>* **SICK OF GOODBYES. / GOOD MORNING SPIDER (session version)** [57] [ ]
(cd-s) *<(CDCL 808)>* – ('A'side) / I shot a dog / Gasoline horseys.
(cd-s) *<(CDCLS 808)>* – ('A'side) / Happy place / Happy pig (session version).

SPEAR OF DESTINY

Formed: Westminster, London, England . . . late 1982 by ex-THEATRE OF HATE mainmen, KIRK BRANDON and STAN STAMMERS. The latter outfit initially traded under the name, The PACK, releasing a couple of singles on manager Terry Razor's 'SS' label, before evolving into THEATRE OF HATE in early 1980. By this point, the line-up numbered BRANDON, SIMON WERNER, JONATHAN WERNER and LUKE RANDALL, the group releasing a promising double A-side debut, 'ORIGINAL SIN' / 'LEGION' towards the end of the year. With JAMIE STUART and STEVE GUTHRIE replacing the WERNER brothers, the group released a live set, 'HE WHO DARES WINS' in Spring of the following year. Following a change of name from the controversially monikered ~'SS' to the slightly less controversial 'Burning Rome', the band's label issued a further two singles, 'REBEL WITHOUT A BRAIN' and 'NERO'. Although the group were beginning to develop their pulverising rhythmic assault, BRANDON brought in a whole new line-up (BILLY DUFFY, the aforementioned STAMMERS, NIGEL PRESTON and JOHN BOY LENNARD) prior to the recording of debut album 'WESTWORLD'. Produced by CLASH guitarist MICK JONES and released in early '82, the record was characterised by BRANDON's punk-choirboy vocal bombast and PRESTON's rolling thunder drums, LENNARD's twilight sax lines adding an air of desolation. Although Top 20 success led to intense major label interest, the group chose to remain independent, at least for the final few months of their career. With the implosion of THEATRE OF HATE later that summer, BRANDON and STAMMERS formed SPEAR OF DESTINY with CHRIS BELL and LASCELLES AMES, their 'Burning Rome' label taken on by 'Epic'. Preceded by the 'FLYING SCOTSMAN' single, the keenly anticipated 'GRAPES OF WRATH' (1983) was met with a muted critical reception upon its release in Spring '83, barely scraping into the Top 75. More personnel changes ensued with LENNARD back on sax, DOLPHIN TAYLOR replacing BELL and NEIL PYZER added on keyboards. After a one-off single in early '84, 'PRISONER OF LOVE', MICKEY DONNELLY replaced the departing LENNARD while ALAN ST. CLAIRE was added as a second guitarist. With a fuller sound, the resulting 'ONE-EYED JACKS' (1984) more accurately realised BRANDON's alternative power-rock vision, almost making the Top 20 and ushering in the most creative and commercially fruitful period of the singer's career. 'WORLD SERVICE' (1985) was released amid a hectic bout of touring, the group building up a sizeable fanbase who helped take the album to a near-Top 10 placing. Ironically, however, no Top 40 singles were forthcoming and SPEAR OF DESTINY split with their label, the existing line-up falling apart. Going back to the drawing board, BRANDON surfaced a year later with new recruits, STEVIE BLANCHARD, VOLKER JANSSON and the BARNACLE brothers, PETE and STEVE. Newly signed to '10-Virgin', SPEAR OF DESTINY at last scored the elusive Top 20 hit with 'NEVER TAKE ME ALIVE', while the accompanying album, 'OUTLAND' (1987) became their biggest selling effort to date. Just when it looked as if the group might move up to first division status, BRANDON was incapacitated by illness and the group were forced to lie low for almost a year. By the release of 'THE PRICE YOU PAY' (1988), the momentum seemed to have been irrevocably lost, BRANDON putting the lid on his band for what was conceivably the last time. The early 90's, however, saw BRANDON touring alongside fellow veteran STAMMERS and newcomers MARK THWAITE / BOBBY RAE MAYHEM under both the THEATRE OF HATE and SPEAR OF DESTINY monikers. This regrouping susbequently resulted in a one-off album, 'SOD'S LAW' (1992), for the resurrected 'Burning Rome' label; largely ignored by press and public alike, the record's failure led to BRANDON burying the name for good. The new decade brought further bad luck for the singer (now partly based in Denmark), as he lost a court battle with BOY GEORGE (whom he once played alongside in an early incarnation of CULTURE CLUB) following the latter's claim that he'd had a homosexual relationship with BRANDON. Beleagured but clearly not beaten, he re-emerged in 1995 with KIRK BRANDON's 10:51, releasing an album, 'STONE IN THE RAIN'.

Album rating: S.O.D. – THE EPIC YEARS compilation (*8) / OUTLAND (*7) / Theatre Of Hate: WESTWORLD (*8) / REVOLUTION compilation (*9)

The PACK

KIRK BRANDON (b. 3 Aug'56) – vocals, guitar / **SIMON WERNER** – guitar / **JONATHAN WERNER** – bass / **JIM WALKER** – drums (ex-PUBLIC IMAGE LTD.)

S.S. not iss.

1979. (7") *(PAK 1)* **BRAVE NEW SOLDIERS. / HEATHEN** [ ] [-]

Rough Trade not iss.

Nov 79. (7") *(RT 025)* **KING OF KINGS. / NUMBER 12** [ ] [-]
(re-iss. 1980 as 7"ep; all 4 above on 'S.S.'; SS 1N2- SS 2N1)

— Early 1980, they had evolved into . . .

THEATRE OF HATE

LUKE RANDALL – drums repl. WALKER

S.S. not iss.

Nov 80. (7") *(SS 3)* **ORIGINAL SIN. / LEGION** [ ] [-]

— **JAMIE STUART** – bass + **STEVE GUTHRIE** – guitar repl. both WERNERS

Mar 81. (lp) *(SSSSS 1P)* **HE WHO DARES WINS – LIVE AT THE WAREHOUSE, LEEDS (live)** [ ] [-]
– The original sin / Do you believe in the westworld / The klan / Conquistador / Poppies / Incinarator / Judgement hymn / 63 / Rebel without a brain / Legion.

Burning Rome not iss.

Apr 81. (12") *(BRR 1)* **REBEL WITHOUT A BRAIN. / MY OWN INVENTION** [ ] [-]
Jul 81. (12") *(BRR 1931)* **NERO. / INCINERATOR** [ ] [-]

— **KIRK BRANDON** brought in entire new line-up **BILLY DUFFY** – guitar / **STAN STAMMERS** – bass (ex-STRAPS) repl. JAMIE who joined RITUAL then DEATH CULT / **NIGEL PRESTON** – drums / **JOHN BOY LENNARD** – saxophone

Jan 82. (7") *(BRR 2)* **DO YOU BELIEVE IN THE WESTWORLD?. / PROPAGANDA** [40] [-]
(12"+=) *(BRR T2-2T)* – Original sin (version) / Ministry of broadcast.
Feb 82. (lp) *(TOH 1)* **WESTWORLD** [17] [-]
– Do you believe in the westworld? / Judgement hymn / 63 / Love is a ghost / The wake / Conquistador / The new trail of tears / Freaks / Anniversary / The klan / Poppies. *(re-iss. May91;* **BRR 010LP)** *(with free 7"ep)* **ORIGINAL SIN / LEGION./ / HEATHEN (The PACK) / BRAVE NEW SOLDIERS (The PACK)** (cd+=) – Incinerator / Rebel without a brain / Propaganda / Legion / Nero.
May 82. (7") *(BRR 3)* **THE HOP. / CONQUISTADOR** [70] [-]

— reverted to a quartet, when DUFFY also joined The (DEATH) CULT.

Nov 82. (7") *(BRR 4)* **EASTWORLD. / ASSEGAI** [ ] [-]
(12"+=) *(BBR 4T)* – Poppies.

— Had already disbanded Autumn '82. LENNARD moved to Canada to form DIODES. PRESTON joined The SEX GANG CHILDREN, and was later another to join The CULT.

SPEAR OF DESTINY

— were almost immediately formed by **KIRK + STAN** with **CHRIS BELL** – drums (ex-KING TRIGGER, ex-THOMPSON TWINS) / **LASCELLES AMES** – saxophone (ex-MIGHTY DIAMONDS) ('Burning Rome' was taken over by 'Epic')

Epic C.B.S.

Feb 83. (7") *(SPEAR 1)* **FLYING SCOTSMAN. / THE MAN WHO TUNES THE DRUMS** [ ] [-]
(12"+=) *(SPEAR13 1)* – Africa.
Apr 83. (lp/c) *(EPC/40 25318)* **GRAPES OF WRATH** [62] [-]
– The wheel / Flying Scotsman / Roof of the world / Aria / Solution / Murder of love / The preacher / Omen of the times / The man who tunes the drums / Grapes of wrath. *(re-iss. Apr86 lp/c; EPC/40 32779)*
May 83. (7"/7"pic-d) *(A/WA 3372)* **THE WHEEL. / THE HOP** [59] [-]
(d7"+=) *(DA 3372)* – The preacher (live) / Grapes of wrath (live).
(12"+=) *(TA 3372)* – Solution (live) / Roof of the world (live) / Love is a ghost (live).

— **JOHN LENNARD** – saxophone returned to the fold repl. LASCELLES / **DOLPHIN TAYLOR** – drums (ex-STIFF LITTLE FINGERS, ex-TOM ROBINSON BAND) repl. BELL who joined The SPECIMEN then GENE LOVES JEZEBEL / added **NEIL PYZER** – keyboards, saxophone (ex-HOWARD DEVOTO, ex-The CASE)

Jan 84. (7") *(A 4068)* **PRISONER OF LOVE. / ROSIE** [59] [-]
(12"+=) *(TA 4068)* – Grapes of wrath (1984).
(d7"+=) *(DA 4068)* – Rainmaker (live) / Don't turn away (live).

— **BRANDON, STAMMERS, PYZER + TAYLOR** added **ALAN ST.CLAIRE** – guitar / **MICKEY DONNELLY** – saxophone (ex-The CASE) repl. LENNARD

Apr 84. (7") *(A 4310)* **LIBERATOR. / FORBIDDEN PLANET** [67] [-]
(12"+=) *(TA 4310)* – ('A'dub version) / ('A'extended).
Apr 84. (lp/c) *(EPC/40 25836)* **ONE-EYED JACKS** [22] [ ]
– Rainmaker / Young men / Everything you ever wanted / Don't turn away / Liberator / Prisoner of love / Playground of the rich / Forbidden planet / Attica / These days are gone. *(re-iss. Feb88 lp/c450886-1/-4;)*
May 85. (7") *(A 6333)* **ALL MY LOVE (ASK NOTHING). / LAST CARD** [61] [-]
(12"+=) *(TA 6333)* – Walk in the shadow.
(12"+=) *(QTA 6333)* – The wheel (live) / Prisoner of love (live) / Liberator (live).
Jul 85. (7") *(A 6445)* **COME BACK. / COLE YOUNGER** [55] [-]
(12"+=) *(TA 6445)* – Young men (the return of).
Aug 85. (lp/c) *(EPC/40 26514)* **WORLD SERVICE** [11] [-]

– Rocket ship / Up all night / Come back / World service / I can see / All my love (ask nothing) / Mickey / Somewhere in the east / Once in her lifetime / Harlan County.

— **BRANDON** recruited entire new band when STAMMERS + PYZER formed CRAZY PINK REVOLVERS. Newcomers:- **STEVIE BLANCHARD** – guitar (ex-TOM ROBINSON BAND) / **VOLKER JANSSON** – keyboards (ex-BERLIN) / **STEVE BARNACLE** – bass, keyboards / **PETE BARNACLE** – drums

10-Virgin Virgin

Jan 87. (7") *(TEN 148)* **STRANGERS IN OUR TOWN. / SOMEWHERE OUT THERE** 49 -
(12"+=) *(TENX 148)* – Time of our lives / ('A'&'B'versions).
(d12"++=) *(TENZ 148)* – ('A'&'B'dub versions).

— **MIKE PROCTOR** – guitar repl. STEVIE B.

Mar 87. (7") *(TEN 162)* **NEVER TAKE ME ALIVE. / LAND OF SHAME** 14
(ext.12"+=) *(TENX 162)* – Pumpkin man / Embassy song.
(3"cd-s+=) *(TENZ 162)* – Jack Straw / The man that never was.

— **MARCO PIRRONI** – guitar (ex-ADAM & THE ANTS, ex-MODELS) repl. PROCTOR

Apr 87. (lp/c/cd) *(DIX/CDIX/DIXCD 59) <90579>* **OUTLAND** 16 Oct87
– Outlands / Land of shame / The traveller / Was that you? / Strangers in our town / The whole world's waiting / Tonight / Miami vice / Never take me alive. *(c-ep+=)* – Time of our lives / Pumpkin man / Embassy song / Jack straw / The man that never was. *(re-iss. Mar91)*

Jul 87. (7") *(TEN 173)* **WAS THAT YOU?. / WAS THAT YOU? (live)** 55 -
(12"+=/12"pic-d+=) *(TENT/+P 173)* – Miami vice / Outlands.
(live-12"+=) *(TENR 173)* – Land of shame / Jack Straw. *<US-iss. 5 track cd-ep>*

Sep 87. (7") *(TEN 189)* **THE TRAVELLER. / LATE NIGHT PSYCHO** 44 -
(12"+=) *(TENR 189)* – Strangers in our town (live) / Mickey (live).

— **ALAN ST.CLAIRE** – guitar returned to repl. PIRRONI / **CHRIS BOSTOCK** – bass (ex-JO BOXERS) repl. STEVE

Virgin Virgin

Sep 88. (7") *(VS 1123)* **SO IN LOVE WITH YOU. / MARCH OR DIE** 36 -
(12"+=) *(VST 1123)* – ('A'extended).
(cd-s+=) *(VSCD 1123)* – Junkman.
(10"+=) *(VSA 1123)* – Jungle.

Oct 88. (cd/c/lp) *(CD/TC+/V 2549)* **THE PRICE YOU PAY** 37
– So in love with you / Tinseltown / The price / I remember / Dreamtime / Radio radio / If the guns / View from a tree / Junkman. *(cd+=)* – Soldier soldier / Brave new world. *(re-iss. Mar91)*

Nov 88. (7"/7"g-f) *(VS/+G 1144)* **RADIO RADIO. / LIFE GOES ON** -
(10"+=) *(VSA 1144)* – Made in London.
(cd-s++=) *(VSCD 1144)* – ('A'extended).
(12"+=) *(VST 1144)* – ('A'extended) / Spirits.

— In the 90's, **KIRK** brought back **STAN STAMMERS** – bass / + newcomers **MARK THWAITE** – guitar / **BOBBY RAE MAYHEM** – drums. Toured as TOH & SOD

Burning Rome not iss.

Sep 92. (12"/cd-s) **BLACK COUNTRY GIRL. / BABYLON TALKING** -

Oct 92. (lp/c/cd) *(BRR/+MC/CD 011)* **SOD'S LAW** -
– Goldmine / Into the rising Sun / Black country girl / When the bull comes down / Slow me down / T.C.B. / In the city / Babylon talking / Crystalize / Killing ground. *(c+=)* – Rave on Albion. *(cd++=)* – Captain America.

KIRK BRANDON'S 10:51

Anagram not iss.

Mar 95. (7") *(ANA 55)* **CHILDREN OF THE DAMNED. / SATELLITE** -
(cd-s+=) *(CDANA 55)* – At her majesties request.

Apr 95. (cd) *(CDGRAM 92)* **STONE IN THE RAIN** -
– Stone in the rain / Communication ends / How long? / Satellite / Children of the damned / Europa / Psycho woman / Revolver / Propaganda / Heroes / Future world / Spirit tribe.

– compilations, etc. –

Feb 86. (12"ep) *Old Gold; (OG 4007)* **FLYING SCOTSMAN / THE WHEEL. / PRISONER OF LOVE / LIBERATOR** -

May 87. (lp/c/cd) *Epic; (450872-1/-4/-2)* **S.O.D. – THE EPIC YEARS** 53 -
– The wheel / Rainmaker / Prisoner of love / Playground of the rich / Young men / Up all night / Come back / All my love (ask nothing) / Mickey / Liberator.

Nov 91. (cd/c) *Old Gold; (OG 3/2 303)* **SPEAR OF DESTINY** -

Jul 93. (cd) *Mau Mau; (MAUCD 638)* **LIVE AT THE LYCEUM 22.12.85 (live)** -

Apr 94. (cd) *Windsong; (WINCD 055)* **THE BBC RADIO ONE LIVE IN CONCERT (live)** -

Mar 95. (cd) *Virgin; (CDOVD 049)* **TIME OF OUR LIVES – THE BEST OF SPEAR OF DESTINY** -

– (THEATRE OF HATE) compilations, etc. –

Jun 81. (c) *Strange Music;* **LIVE AT THE LYCEUM (live)** -

Feb 82. (lp) *S.S.;* **HE WHO DARES WINS – LIVE IN BERLIN (live)** -

Aug 84. (lp/d-c) *Burning Rome; (TOH 2)* **REVOLUTION** (The Best Of . . .) -
– Legion / The original sin / Rebel without a brain / My own invention / Nero / Do you believe in the westworld? / Propaganda / The hop / Incinerator / Eastworld / Americanos. *(d-c+=)* – HE WHO DARES WINS *(cd-iss. Feb93 on 'Line')*

Nov 85. (12"ep) *Burning Rome; (BRRT 1985)* **THE HOP / CONQUISTADOR. / ORIGINAL SIN / WESTWORLD?** -

Mar 85. (live-7"ep) *Bliss; (TOH 1EP)* **THE WAKE / LOVE IS A GHOST. / POPPIES / LEGION** -

Dec 85. (lp) *Dojo;* **ORIGINAL SIN LIVE (live)** -

Jul 93. (cd) *Mau Mau; (MAUCD 637)* **THEATRE OF HATE** -

Jun 95. (cd) *Anagram; (CDGRAM 93)* **THE COMPLETE SINGLES COLLECTION** -

– (The PACK) compilations, etc. –

Apr 82. (7"ep) *Cyclops; (CLCLOPS 1)* **LONG LIVE THE PAST (demos from Aug'78)** -
– Thalidomide / King of kings / St.Teresa / Abattoir.

1982. (c) *Donut; (DONUT 2)* **THE PACK LIVE 1979 (live)** -

The SENATE

(**KIRK BRANDON + RUSTY EGAN** ex-SKIDS, ex-VISAGE)

Jul 84. (7") *Burning Rome; (BRR 7)* **THE ORIGINAL SIN. / DO YOU BELIEVE IN THE WESTWORLD?** -

Jul 84. (7") *W.A.R.; (WAR 1)* **THE ORIGINAL SIN. / DO YOU BELIEVE IN THE WESTWORLD? (live)** -
(12"+=) *(12WAR 1)* – ('A'extended).

SPECIAL EFFECT (see under ⇒ MINISTRY)

SPECTRUM (see under ⇒ SPACEMEN 3)

SPEEDBALL BABY

Formed: New York, USA . . . early 1994 when Bostonians RON WARD (ex-drummer of BLOOD ORANGES) and MATT VERTA-RAY (ex-MADDER ROSE) met at a friend's wedding. Completing the line-up with the rhythm section of ALI SMITH and DAVE ROY, the band signed to 'Matador' sub-label, 'P.C.P.', releasing their eponymous EP later that year. Mixing up a Molotov Cocktail of JON SPENCER-esque primal blues and raucous punk, the band served it neat on the following year's mini-set, 'GET STRAIGHT FOR THE LAST SUPPER'. The record even included a clutch of mangled covers, including the Ramones' 'BLITZKREIG BOP' and Van Morrison's 'T.B. SHEETS'. Making a foray into major label land via MCA's 'Fort Apache' subsidiary, SPEEDBALL BABY released their debut album proper, 'CINEM~A!' (1996). Issued a year later in Britain (on 'Konkurrent'), its release coincided with that of a mini-set on 'Sympathy For The Record Industry', 'I'M GONNA STOMP MR. HARRY LEE'.

Album rating: CINEMA! (*6)

RON WARD – vocals (ex-BLOOD ORANGES) / **MATT VERTA-RAY** – guitar (ex-MADDER ROSE) / **ALI SMITH** – bass / **DAVE ROY** – drums

P.C.P. P.C.P.

Dec 94. (7"ep) *<PCP 018-1>* **SPEEDBALL BABY EP**
– Fucked up town / Black eyed girl / Percoset.
(cd-ep+=) *(PCP 018-2)* – Corn river.

Aug 95. (10"m-lp/m-cd) *<PCP 023-1/-2>* **GET STRAIGHT FOR THE LAST SUPPER**
– Phoenix hotel / Five dollar priest / Blitzkreig bop / Ballad of the thin / Pillbilly / Milking stool blues / T.B. sheets / The edge / Phoenix hotel pt.1.

Konkurrent Fort Apache-MCA

Mar 98. (cd) *(K 182CD) <11425>* **CINEMA!** Sep96
– Stranger's skin / Rubber connection / Black cat moan / Suicide girl / Black eyed girl / Dog on fire / Skull poppin', skin tastin', love . . . / Shakin' it loose / Cinema! / Toss my head / Mr. Heat / Dancin' with a fever / Drug owl.

Sympathy F Sympathy F

Apr 98. (10"m-lp/m-cd) *<(SFTRI 531/+CD)>* **I'M GONNA STOMP MR. HARRY LEE**

SPEED THE PLOUGH

Formed: Haledon, New Jersey, USA . . . 1982 as The TRYPES, by JOHN BAUMGARTNER who had been school friends of new wave/psychedelic outfit The FEELIES. When The FEELIES, (BILL MILLION & GLEN MERCER) decided to take a hiatus in 1983/84, they guested on the EP, 'THE EXPLORER'S HOLD'. They also played together on Sunday nights at the local Peanut Gallery bar, a series dubbed, "Music For Neighbors". In 1986 when The FEELIES sorted out their problems, the TRYPES became SPEED THE PLOUGH. Many gigs later, their first album was issued in 1989, a set of avant-garde psychedelia, drawing inspiration from RAVI SHANKAR, BRIAN ENO and PHILIP GLASS. Three more appeared in the first half of the 90's, the best of which was 1995's 'MARINA'.

Album rating: SPEED THE PLOUGH (*6) / WONDER WHEEL (*7) / MASON'S BOX (*4) / MARINA (*7)

JOHN BAUMGARTNER – vocals, keyboards, etc / with **GLEN MERCER + BILL MILLION** (of The FEELIES)

not iss. Coyote

1984. (12"ep; as TRYPES) **THE EXPLORER'S HOLD** -

— now without part-time FEELIES who re-joined said outfit

— **JOHN** enlisted **MILLION + MARC FRANCIA** – guitars, drums / **FRANK O'TOOLE** – guitar / **PETE PEDULLA** – bass, trumpet / **TONI PARUTA** – wind / **JIM DeROGATIS** – percussion, drums

not iss. Twin/Tone

1989. (cd) *<88136>* **SPEED THE PLOUGH** -
– River street / Veszprem / Big bus / Tommy's house / Ella's way / Cardinal rules / No one's alone / Blue bicycle / Fathers and sons / Everyday needs. *<re-iss. 1991 on 'East Side Digital'; ESD 8066-2>*

— now with **MILLION, FRANCIA, O'TOOLE + BRENDA SAUTER** – bass (ex-FEELIES) / **MICHAEL LIPTON** – guitars

East Side Digital / East Side Digital

1991. (cd/c) <*ESD 8053-2/-4*> **WONDER WHEEL** [-] [ ]
– Aeroplane / The tide won't tire / The story of the moon / Coal and courage / Hemlock tree / Cutting branches for a temporary. . . / Final day / Trains / Centerville / One of your friends / The Plough and the stars.

—— added **RICHARD BARNES** – guitars

Jan 94. (cd) <*ESD 8087-2*> **MASON'S BOX** [-] [ ]
– Lock and key / Deepest brown / The roof is off (the stars are there and . . .) / Napoleon / Follow your visions / Oh, the paradise / Wide awake / Book of reasons / Seven stairs / Song / Morrow bay / Screen door.

Jul 96. (cd) <(*ESD 8110-2*)> **MARINA** [ ] [ ] Nov95
– Just a little / Written each day / Said and done / Once in a while / Late birds / A saint restored / High wine / Love song / Bayswater lane / A hard friend to keep / Hourglass / In the atmosphere / Marina.

—— SAUTER was also part of WILD CARNATION, who issued one US album 'TRICYCLE' for 'Delmore' in 1995.

SPELL

Formed: Denver, Colorado, USA . . . 1991 by GARRETT SHAVLIK, CHANIN FLOYD and TIM BECKMAN. All veterans of the American punk/hardcore scene (especially SHAVLIK, a former member of early 'Sub Pop' act The FLUID and friend of the late KURT COBAIN), the trio got together after a drunken, impromptu jam session and set about creating a suitably intense, post-grunge sound. With such an impressive track record, the band were able to bypass the independent sector and secure a deal with 'Island Red', no mean feat. A debut single, 'SUPERSTAR', preceded the 'MISSISSIPPI' album, released in early '95 and drawing comparisons with the likes of The AFGHAN WHIGS, CHANIN's vocal adding a feminine slant reminiscent of The BREEDERS. • **Note:** Not to be confused with the 'Mute' band of the same name who issued the single, 'BIG RED BALLOON'.

Album rating: MISSISSIPPI (*4)

TIM BECKMAN – guitar, vocals (ex-ROPE) / **CHANIN FLOYD** – bass, vocals (ex-57 LESBIANS) / **GARRETT SHAVLIK** – drums, vocals (ex-FLUID)

Island Red / Island Red

Mar 95. (7") (*IR 105*) **SUPERSTAR. / HAZEL MOTES** [ ] [ ]
(cd-s+=) (*CIRD 105*) – Best friend (demo). (*7" w/free 7"*)

Apr 95. (cd/c/lp) (*CIRD/IRCT/IRLP 1003*) **MISSISSIPPI** [ ] [ ]
– Dixie / Seems to me / Superstar / More / Straight to Hell / 4-B / Hazel motes / Safe / Mom / Bring the old man.

—— disbanded after above

Jon SPENCER BLUES EXPLOSION

Formed: New York City, New York, USA . . . 1991 by former PUSSY GALORE namesake, JON SPENCER and ex-HONEYMOON KILLERS, JUDAH BAUER and RUSSELL SIMINS. Hardly blues in the conventional sense, SPENCER rather puts the emphasis on EXPLOSION, grinding out a bass-less groove-noise and howling out lip-curled soundbites. It was a formula that had its roots in the primal sludge of PUSSY GALORE and the first instalment in the JSBX saga carried on where that band left off, kind of. Released by 'Caroline' in the States and Virgin subsidiary, 'Hut', in Britain, the eponymous STEVE ALBINI-produced album surfaced in Spring '92, showcasing SPENCER's newly adopted blues drawl and revelling in defiantly dishevelled guitar abuse. Although some critics argued that SPENCER was all mouth and no trousers, so to speak, the man answered in strutting style on the likes of 'BELLBOTTOMS', one of the highlights from 1994's acclaimed 'ORANGE' album; that record, together with its 1993 predecessor, 'EXTRA WIDTH' (both released on 'Matador') really set out the band's manifesto of fractured 70's groove-funk, semi-detached melodies, hand claps, sweat dripping testimonial and sheer distorted noise. Sure, it might've been a style over substance white trash/noise interpretation of delta blues in the loosest sense but SPENCER's tongue was planted firmly in his cheek and following MTV exposure and a tour with The BEASTIE BOYS, JSBX were suddenly big news. A subsequent remix EP roped in such luminaries as BECK and if a move to 'Mute' seemed a little strange, there was no denying the blistering potential of 'NOW I GOT WORRY' (1996). From the delirious swagger of '2KINDSA LOVE' (surely a companion piece, if there ever was one, to MUDHONEY's 'Touch Me I'm Sick') to the disembodied static of Dub Narcotic's 'FUCK SHIT UP', SPENCER sounded as if he'd finally cut that deal down at the crossroads. Still, the man's recorded work only tells half the story; if you really want a baptism by BLUES EXPLOSION fire then you'll have to catch them live. • **Songwriters:** SPENCER/ group except; LOVIN' UP A STORM (Willie Dixon)

Album rating: JON SPENCER BLUES EXPLOSION (*5) / ORANGE (*7) / NOW I GOT WORRY (*7) / ACME (*7)

JON SPENCER – vocals, guitar / **JUDAH BAUER** – guitar / **RUSSELL SIMINS** – drums

Hut / Caroline

Apr 92. (cd/lp) (*HUT CD/LP 003*) <*CAROL 1719*> **JON SPENCER BLUES EXPLOSION** [ ] [ ]
– Write a song / IEV / Exploder / Rachel / Chicken walk / White tail / '78 style / Changed / What to do / Eye to eye / Eliza Jane / History of sex / Come back / Support-a-man / Maynard Ave. / Feeling of love / Vacuum of loneliness / Intro A / Biological / Water man. (*cd re-iss. Jun97 on 'Caroline'; same as US*)

Matador / Matador

Aug 93. (cd/c/lp) <(*OLE 052-2/-4/-1*)> **EXTRA-WIDTH** [ ] [ ] Nov93
– Afro / History of lies / Black slider / Soul letter / Soul typecast / Pant leg / Hey mom / Big road / Train No.2 / Inside the world of the blues explosion / The world of sex.

Feb 94. (7") (*OLE 077-7*) **AFRO. / RELAX-HER**

Mar 94. (cd/lp) (*EFA 11502-2/-1*) <*29*> **CRYPT-STYLE** (rec.1991 NYC) [ ] [ ]
– Lovin' up a storm / Support a man / White tail / Maynard Ave. / '78 style / Chicken walk / Mo' chicken – Let's get funky / Watermain / Like a hawk / Big headed baby / Write a song / Eye to eye / Feeling of love / Kill a man / Rachel / History of sex / Comeback / The vacuum of loneliness.
(above on 'Crypt' records) (below 2 on 'In The Red')

Oct 94. (7") (*ITR 9*) **TRAIN NO.3. / ?** [ ] [ ] Jun94

Oct 94. (7") (*ITR 11*) **SON OF SAM. / ?** [ ] [ ]

Oct 94. (cd/c/lp) <(*OLE 105-2/-4/-1*)> **ORANGE** [ ] [ ]
– Bellbottoms / Ditch / Dang / Very rare / Sweat / Cowboy / Orange / Brenda / Dissect / Blues x men / Full grown / Flavor / Greyhound.

Feb 95. (7") (*OLE 111-7*) **BELLBOTTOMS. / MISS ELAINE** [ ] [-]
(12") (*OLE 111-1*) – ('A'remix) / Flavor 1 / Flavor 2.
(cd-s+=) (*OLE 111-2*) – Soul typecast / Greyhound.
(*the REMIXES ep of above iss.May95*)

Mute / Matador – Capitol

Sep 96. (cd/c/lp) (*cd/c+/stumm 132*) <*OLE 193 – 53553*> **NOW I GOT WORRY** [50] [ ]
– Skunk / Identify / Wail / Fuck shit up / 2Kindsa love / Love all of me / Chicken dog / Rocketship / Dynamite lover / Hot shot / Can't stop / Firefly child / Eyeballin / R.L. got soul / Get over here / Sticky. (*re-iss. May97; same*)

Oct 96. (7") (*MUTE 202*) **2 KINDSA LOVE. / LET'S SMERF** [ ] [ ]
(cd-s) (*CDMUTE 202*) – ('A'side) / Fish sauce / Cool Ve.

Jan 97. (7") (*ITR 42*) **GET WITH IT. /** [ ] [-]
(above issued on 'In The Red')

Apr 97. (7"m) (*MUTE 204*) **WAIL. / JUDAH LOVE THEME / RADIO SPOT** [66] [ ]
(7"m) (*LMUTE 204*) – ('A'-Mario C remix) / Afro (live) / Flavor (live).
(cd-s) (*CDMUTE 204*) – ('A'video mix) / Yellow eyes / Buscemi / Turn up Greene.

Feb 97. (lp/cd) <*ANDA 166/+CD*> **MO' WIDTH** [ ] [ ] Jan95
– Afro / Out of luck / Cherry lime / Rob K / Ole man trouble / Wet cat blues / Johnson / There stands the glass / Lion cut / Beat of the traps / Memphis soul typecast.

Oct 97. (7") <*ANDA 231*> **ROCKETSHIP. / DOWN LOW** [ ] [ ] Jun98
(cd-s+=) <*ANDA 231CD*> – Dynamite lover / Flavor / Full grown.
(above single and album issued on 'Au Go Go')

Oct 98. (cd/lp) (*CD+/STUMM 154*) <*OLE 322 – 95566*> **ACME** [72] [ ]
– Calvin / Magical colors / Do you wanna get heavy? / High gear / Talk about the blues / I wanna make it all right / Lovin' machine / Bernie / Blue green Olga / Give me a chance / Desperate / Torture / Attack.

Nov 98. (7"colrd) (*MUTE 222*) **MAGICAL COLORS. / CONFUSED** [ ] [-]
(cd-s) (*CDMUTE 222*) – ('A'side) / Bacon / Get down lover.

SP!N (see under ⇒ GENE)

SPINANES

Formed: Portland, Oregon, USA . . . 1991 by singer/songwriter REBECCA GATES and drummer SCOTT PLOUF, brought together through a mutual friend of a friend. Proving that bass players aren't essential in today's anything goes world of Lo-Fi rock'n'roll, The SPINANES drew encouraging support for their beguiling minimalism/miserabalism. After two obscure 45's on a local imprint, the duo became an unlikely signing for 'Sub Pop', releasing their debut long-player, 'MANOS', in the Autumn of '93. Critics commentated on the emotional rawness of GATES' lyrics, while fans voted with their feet by placing it atop the college radio charts. Not persuaded to pack in the day jobs just yet, the fiercely independent pair (they don't even have a roadie!) knuckled down to gigs with labelmates, CODEINE. A follow-up set, the careworn 'STRAND', surfaced early in '96, another collection of harrowing tales of woe set to a picturesque musical backdrop. A subsequent split in the partnership occurred when SCOTT left for BUILT TO SPILL, leaving REBECCA to soldier on towards a third set, 'ARCHES AND AISLES', in 1998.

Album rating: MANOS (*6) / STRAND (*7) / ARCHES AND AISLES (*6)

REBECCA GATES – vocals, guitar / **SCOTT PLOUF** – drums

not iss. / unknown

1992. (7") **SUFFICE. / HALLOWEEN CANDY** [-] [ ]

1993. (7") **HAWAIIAN BABY. / RUMMY** [-] [ ]

Sub Pop / Sub Pop

Sep 93. (7") <(*SP 113-291*)> **SPITFIRE. /** [ ] [ ]

Nov 93. (lp/c/cd) <(*SP/+MC/CD 114-292*)> **MANOS** [ ] [ ] Oct93
– Entire / Noel, Jonah and me / Spitfire / I love that party with the monkey . . . / Uneasy / Epiphany / Manos / Dangle / Basement galaxy / Grand prize / Sunday / Shellburn.

May 94. (cd-ep) <(*SPCD 132-328*)> **NOEL, JONAH AND ME** [ ] [ ]

Oct 94. (7"ep/cd-ep) (*MONTY 1/+CD*) **THE BARE DOLL EP** [ ] [ ]
(above issued on 'Lowlife')

Jan 96. (7") <(*SP 317*)> **MADDING. / 10 METRE PLATFORM** [ ] [ ]

Feb 96. (lp/cd) <(*SP/+CD 345*)> **STRAND** [ ] [ ]
– Madding / Azure / Lines and lines / Meridian / Punchline loser / Valency / Luminous / Oceanwide / Winter on ice / Watch down / For no one else.

—— now just REBECCA after PLOUF joined BUILT TO SPILL

Aug 98. (lp/cd) <(*SP/+CD 417*)> **ARCHES AND AISLES** [ ] [ ] Apr98
– Kid in candy / Greetings from the sugar lick / 72-74 / Leisure run / Love, the lazee / Sucker's trial / Slide your ass / Reach v. speed / Den trawler / Eleganza / Heisman stance.

SPIREA X

Formed: Glasgow, Scotland . . . 1988 by ex-PRIMAL SCREAM member JIM BEATTIE (writer of their classic 'Velocity Girl'), who took the moniker from an old 'SCREAM b-side. Featuring a core line-up comprised of girlfriend JUDITH BOYLE and ANDY KERR, they worked on songs for well over a year before supplying a demo to a plethora of labels, eventually becoming an unlikely signing for '4 a.d.'. In spring '91, they finally unleashed their debut disc, 'CHLORINE DREAM', inspired by the life rather than death of BRIAN JONES. In fact, the single also took its musical cue from The ROLLING STONES, BEATTIE typically arrogant in his praise for the track, although for once the critics agreed. Unfortunately the public weren't so enthusiastic, neither follow-up single, 'SPEED REACTION', nor debut album, 'FIREBLADE SKIES' (named after a volume of Arthur Rimbaud's poetry), making much of an impression outside closeknit Glasgow scene. Nevertheless, the record was a pleasant enough listen, taking in the obligatory BYRDS/LOVE influences (they covered the latter's 'SIGNED D.C.') alongside SLY STONE's style funk and soul. Subsequently reduced to a duo of BEATTIE and BOYLE, SPIREA X were dropped by the label and later split in '93.

Album rating: FIREBLADE SKIES (*6)

JIM BEATTIE – vocals, guitar (ex-PRIMAL SCREAM) / **JUDITH BOYLE** – vocals, guitar / **ANDY KERR** – drums / with also **THOMAS McGURK** – rhythm guitar / **JAMIE O'DONNELL** – bass

4 a.d. 4ad-Warners

Apr 91. (7") *(AD 1004)* **CHLORINE DREAM. / SPIREA RISING** [ ] [-]
(12"+=/cd-s+=) *(BAD 1004/+CD)* – Risk.

Jun 91. (7") *(AD 1006)* **SPEED REACTION. / JET PILOT** [ ] [-]
(12"+=/cd-s+=) *(BAD 1006/+CD)* – What kind of love / Re action.

Oct 91. (lp/cd)(c) *(CAD 1017/+CD)(CADC 1017) <45001>* **FIREBLADE SKIES** [ ] [ ]
– Smile / Nothing happened yesterday / Rollercoaster / Chlorine dream / Fire and light / Spirea 9 / Speed reaction / Confusion in my soul / Signed D.C. / Sisters and brothers / Sunset dawn.

— split in 1993 after being dropped by their label

SPIRITUALIZED

Formed: Rugby, England . . . 1990, initially as a side project for JASON 'SPACEMAN' PIERCE, who was soon to split from SONIC BOOM and SPACEMEN 3. He retained JON MATTOCK and WILLIE B. CARRUTHERS from the latter outfit and set about getting to grips with a new 90's psychedelia. Their first release was a version of The Troggs' 'ANYWAY THAT YOU WANT ME', which squeezed into the UK Top 75. The debut album, 'LAZER GUIDED MELODIES', was awash with VELVET-tones, recycled, and heavily distorted. A three year hiatus did not deter the British buying public, who also assured the follow-up, 'PURE PHASE', of a Top 30 placing in 1995. It was blessed with a more soulful vibe, while the majestic, lo-fi rhythm lifted it from an ambient crypt. In June '97, they returned to the fold (albeit a month after schedule) with their third album, 'LADIES AND GENTLEMEN WE ARE FLOATING IN SPACE B P'. The delay was due to ELVIS PRESLEY's team of whatnots objecting to the sample of 'Can't Help Falling In Love'. Nevertheless, the album, complete with bizarre prescription pill cd packaging, duly floated into the UK Top 5. Described by one reviewer as 'album of the decade', the record met with almost universal praise while its blissful melange of retro-psych, ambient noise and gospel was a heady tonic for the Dad-rock by numbers peddled by most 'indie' bands. • **Songwriters:** PIERCE, except more covers; BORN NEVER ASKED (Laurie Anderson) / WALKING WITH JESUS (Spacemen 3) / OH HAPPY DAY (Edwin Hawkins Singers). • **Trivia:** In the early 90's, they headlined at the ICA Rock Week sponsored by Irn Bru.

Album rating: LAZER GUIDED MELODIES (*8) / PURE PHASE (*8) / LADIES AND GENTLEMEN WE ARE FLOATING IN SPACE B P (*10)

JASON PIERCE – guitar / **WILLIE B. CARRUTHERS** – bass / **JON MATTOCK** – drums plus girlfriend **KATE RADLEY** – organ, keyboards, vocals / **MARK REFOY** – guitar, dulcimer

Dedicated R.C.A.

Jun 90. (7") *(ZB 43783)* **ANYWAY THAT YOU WANT ME. / STEP INTO THE BREEZE** [75] [-]
(12"+=/cd-s+=) *(ZT/ZD 43784)* – ('B'-part 2).
(12") *(ZT 43780)* – ('A'remix) / ('B'-parts 2-3) / ('A'demo).

Jun 91. (7") *(FRIGHT 053)* **FEEL SO SAD. / I WANT YOU** [ ] [-]
(above is a gig freebie given away by 'Fierce' re-iss. Apr97)

Aug 91. (7") *(SPIRIT 002)* **RUN. / I WANT YOU** [59] [-]
(12"+=/cd-s+=) *(SPIRIT 002 T/CD)* – Luminescent (stay with me) / Effervescent.

Nov 91. (7") *(SPIRIT 003)* **WHY DON'T YOU SMILE NOW. / SWAY** [ ] [-]
(12"+=/cd-s+=) *(SPIRIT 003 T/CD)* – ('A'extended).

Apr 92. (cd/c/2x12"lp) *(DED CD/MC/LP 004) <66035-2/-4>* **LAZER GUIDED MELODIES** [27] [ ]
– You know it's true / If I were with her now / I want you / Run / Smiles / Step into the breeze / Symphony space / Take your time / Shine a light / Angel sigh / Sway / 200 bars. *(free-7" at 'Chain With No Name' shops)* – ANY WAY THAT YOU WANT ME / WHY DON'T YOU SMILE NOW *(re-iss. Jul97; same)*

Jul 92. (7"red) *(SPIRIT 005)* **MEDICATION. / SMILES (Peel session)** [55] [-]
(12"+=) *(SPIRIT 005T)* – Feel so sad (Peel session) / Angel sigh.
(cd-s++=) *(SPIRIT 005CD)* – Space (instrumental).

Jun 93. (mail-order cd) *(SPIRIT 006CD)* **F***ED UP INSIDE** [-] [-]

Oct 93. (7") *(SPIRIT 007)* **GOOD TIMES / LAY BACK IN THE SUN** [49] [-]
(12"ep+=/cd-ep+=) *(SPIRIT 008 T/CD)* – Electric Mainline 1 + 2.

— now without REFOY, who formed SLIPSTREAM. They issued two albums for 'Che' in 1995; 'SLIPSTREAM' & 'SIDE EFFECTS'.

SPIRITUALIZED ELECTRIC MAINLINE

— **SPACEMAN (JASON)** + **KATE RADLEY** – keyboards, vox / **SEAN COOK** – bass, harmonica / plus **MARK REFOY** – guitar (guest only) / **JON MATTOCK** – percussion / **LEON HUNT** – banjo / **STEWART GORDON** – violin / **THE BALANESCU QUARTET** – strings / + others on wind instruments

Dedicated Arista

Jan 95. (cd-ep) *(SPIRIT 009CD)* **LET IT FLOW / DON'T GO / STAY WITH ME / DON'T GO / STAY WITH ME (THE INDIVIDUAL)** [30] [-]
(cd-ep) *(SPIRIT 009CD2)* – ('A'side) / Take good care of it / Things will never be the same / Clear rush.
(cd-ep) *(SPIRIT 009CD3)* – ('A'side) / Medication / Take your time / Smile.
(3xbox-cd-ep/10"ep) *(SPIRIT 009BOX/T)* – (all above).

Feb 95. (cd/c/d-lp) *(DED CD/MC/LP 017) <26035>* **PURE PHASE** [20] [ ] Mar95
– Medication / The slide song / Electric phase / All of my tears / These blues / Let it flow / Take good care of it / Born never asked / Electric mainline / Lay back in the sun / Good times / Pure phase / Spread your wings / Feel like goin' home. *(re-iss. Jul97; same)*

Nov 95. (cd-ep) *(74321 31178-2)* **LAY BACK IN THE SUN / THE SLIDE SONG / SPREAD YOUR WINGS / LAY BACK IN THE SUN** [ ] [ ]

SPIRITUALIZED

— **DAMON REECE** – percussion + guests, repl. MATTOCK, HUNT + GORDON

Jun 97. (cd/c/lp) *(DED CD/MC/LP 034) <18974>* **LADIES AND GENTLEMEN WE ARE FLOATING IN SPACE** [4] [ ]
– Ladies and gentlemen we are floating in space / Come together / I think I'm in love / All of my thoughts / Stay with me / Electricity / Home of the brave / The individual / Broken heart / No god only religion / Cool waves / Cop shoot cop . . . *(re-iss. Jan98 as 12xcd-s box; DEDCD 034A)*

Jul 97. (7") *(SPIRIT 012)* **ELECTRICITY. / COOL WAVES (instrumental)** [32] [-]
(cd-s+=) *(SPIRIT 012CD1)* – Take your time (live) / All of my tears (live).
(cd-s) *(SPIRIT 012CD2)* – ('A'album version) / Cop shoot cop (live) / Shine a light (live) / Electric mainline (live).

Feb 98. (7") *(SPIRIT 014)* **I THINK I'M IN LOVE. / ('A'version)** [27] [-]
(12"+=/cd-s+=) *(SPIRIT 014 T/CD)* – ('A'-Chemical Brothers vocal & instrumental mixes).

May 98. (7") *(SPIRIT 015) <13508>* **THE ABBEY ROAD EP** [39] [ ]
– Come together / Broken heart.
(cd-s+=) *(SPIRIT 015CD)* – Broken heart (instrumental).
(12"++=) *(SPIRIT 015T)* – ('A'-Richard Fearless remix) / ('A'-Two Lone Swordsmen remix).

Oct 98. (d-cd/d-lp) *(74321 62285-2/-1) <19032>* **LIVE – ROYAL ALBERT HALL (live 10th October, 1997)** [38] [ ] Nov98
– Intro / Shine a light / Electric mainline / Electricity / Home of the brave / The individual / Medication / Walking with Jesus / Take your time / No God, only religion / Broken heart / Come together / I think I'm in love / Cop shoot cop / Oh happy day.

SPITFIRE

Formed: Crawley, Sussex, England . . . 1990 by JEFF PRITCHER, his brother NICK, STEVE WHITE and SCOTT KENNY and MATT WISE. Signed to the 'Eve' label, this ambitious bunch of retro heads set the controls for the heart of the sun and modelled their latter day retro-indie on the likes of SPACEMEN 3, LOOP and MY BLOODY VALENTINE, with a healthy dose of strutting JIM MORRISON-style cool thrown in for good measure. After witnessing the SPITFIRE space cadets supporting his girlfriend's band, VOICE OF THE BEEHIVE, THAT PETROL EMOTION frontman, STEVE MACK, was sufficiently impressed to proffer his production skills for their debut EP, 'TRANSLUCENT'. The result saw a preponderance of such adjectives as hypnotic, compelling, dizzying etc., SPITFIRE even applying their musical weaponry to a cover of the 'Six Million Dollar Man' theme tune. By the release of follow-up EP, 'SUPERBABY', the band had relocated to Brighton and WHITE had been replaced by SIMON WALKER while JUSTIN WELCH filled the drum stool as KENNY concentrated on his other band, EVER. A bonafide full length album, 'SEX BOMB', finally emerged on 'Paperhouse' records in 1993 although the resulting sales were hardly explosive.

Album rating: FEVERISH compilation (*6) / SEX BOMB (*6)

JEFF PITCHER – vocals / **MATT WISE** – lead guitar / **STEVE WHITE** – guitar / **NICK PITCHER** – bass / **SCOTT KENNY** – drums (of EVER)

Eve Danceteria

Apr 91. (7"ep) **THE TRANSLUCENT. / DIVE / THE SIX MILLION DOLLAR MAN** [ ] [-]

— **SIMON WALKER** – guitar repl. WHITE

— **JUSTIN WELCH** – drums repl. KENNY

Aug 91. (7"ep) **SUPERBABY. / SUNFLOW / WOMBCHILD** [ ] [-]

Feb 92. (cd/lp) **FEVERISH** (compilation of above) [-] [ ]
(UK-iss.Mar95 on 'Danceteria'; DANCD 097)

Mar 92. (7"red-ep) **FREEMACHINE** [ ] [-]

Paperhouse not iss.

Aug 93. (12"ep/cd-ep) *(PAPER 025 T/CD)* **MINIMAL LOVE. / THE BALLAD OF JET HARRIS / FLUID** [ ] [-]

Oct 93. (cd/lp) *(PAP CD/LP 21)* **SEX BOMB** [ ] [-]

Lowlife not iss.

Mar 95. (7"/cd-s) *(MONTY 3/+CD)* **COME ON, GET ON. /** [ ] [-]

— will return with an album in '99

SPIZZ

Formed: London, England . . . August '77 by one-man DIY punk act, SPIZZ (surname, SPIERS), who first entertained an audience at that summer's Barbarellas Punk Festival. A few months later, SPIZZ 77 (his new group name at the time), hired the services of guitarist PETE PETROL and subsequently became the first act to sign for Geoff Travis' 'Rough Trade' label having been playlisted on the John Peel show. In the first of many name changes, the outfit released their first two maxi-singles, '6,000 CRAZY' and 'COLD CITY', towards the end of '78 under the SPIZZ OIL moniker. Both were 2-minute gems, proving that punk-rock was best sampled stripped down to its bare bones, the futuristic lyrics marking SPIZZ out from the bulk of his "New Wave" contemporaries. The following year saw the project expand into a full band set-up (going under the name SPIZZENERGI) with the addition of MARK COALFIELD, JIM SOLAR and BRIAN B. BENZINE. Boasting a beefed-up sound built around bass and plink-plonk keyboards, SPIZZ's third single, 'SOLDIER, SOLDIER' was backed up by a spikey version of Roxy Music's 'VIRGINIA PLAIN'. The space theme continued as the man went "Warp Factor 2" on the classic punk anthem, 'WHERE'S CAPTAIN KIRK?', even putting in his best BUDDY HOLLY on speed impression to fill out the chorus line. The new decade saw the birth of ATHLETICO SPIZZ '80, the band's most successful incarnation to date. A goodbye 45 for 'Rough Trade', the double-A sided 'NO ROOM' / 'SPOCK'S MISSING', suggested that SPIZZ had finally located his vocal chords. Almost immediately, the punk startroopers appeared on 'A&M' with the single, 'HOT DESSERTS' and debut album, 'DO A RUNNER', the latter surprisingly denting the UK Top 30. However, the album fell short of expectations and for many fans the SPIZZ spark had fizzled out. Obviously running out of ideas, the man (alongside SOLAR and SNARE) returned in 1981 as The SPIZZLES, the new moniker displaying almost as much of a lack of imagination as the accompanying album, 'SPIKEY DREAM FLOWERS'. Looking to regain his indie credibility, he resurrected the SPIZZENERGI moniker (Mk.2, that is) and returned to 'Rough Trade', although two singles, 'WORK' and 'JUNGLE FEVER', were woefully short of requirements. SPIZZ sensibly retired from the scene for almost five years, eventually staging another comeback attempt when he revamped his most famous three minutes, 'WHERE'S CAPTAIN KIRK?', as a solo artist in '87.

Album rating: DO A RUNNER (*6) / SPIKEY DREAM FLOWERS (*4) / SPIZZ HISTORY compilation (*7)

SPIZZ OIL

SPIZZ (b. SPIERS) – vocals, keyboards, guitar, etc / **PETE PETROL** (b. HYDE) – guitar

	Rough Trade	not iss.
Oct 78. (7"m) *(RTS 01)* **6,000 CRAZY. / 1989 / FIBRE**		-
Dec 78. (7"m) *(RTS 02)* **COLD CITY / RED AND BLACK. / SOLARISATION (SHUN) / PLATFORM 3**		-

SPIZZENERGI

— added **MARK COALFIELD** – keyboards / **JIM SOLAR** – bass / **BRIAN B. BENZINE** – drums

Sep 79. (7") *(RTS 03)* **SOLDIER, SOLDIER. / VIRGINIA PLAIN**		-
Dec 79. (7") *(RTS 04)* **WHERE'S CAPTAIN KIRK? / AMNESIA**		-

ATHLETICO SPIZZ '80

— **DAVE SCOTT** – guitar (ex-BANK OF DRESDEN) repl. PETROL who joined REPETITION

Jun 80. (7") *(RTS 05)* **NO ROOM. / SPOCK'S MISSING**		-

— **C.P. SNARE** (b. CLIVE PARKER) – drums; repl. BENZINE

	A&M	A&M
Jul 80. (7") *(AMS 7550)* **HOT DESSERTS. / LEGAL PROCEEDINGS**		-
Jul 80. (lp) *(AMLE 68514)* **DO A RUNNER**	27	

– Touched / New species / Intimate / Effortless / European heroes / Energy / Red and black / Rhythm inside / Person impersonator / Clocks are big / Airships.

— **LU EDMUNDS** – drums (ex-DAMNED, etc) repl. SCOTT

Oct 80. (7") *(AMS 7566)* **CENTRAL PARK. / CENTRAL PARK (Dr. & Nurses dub version)**		-

SPIZZLES

— **SPIZZ, SOLAR + SNARE**

Feb 81. (7") *(AMS 8107)* **RISK. / MELANCHOLY**		-
Apr 81. (lp) *(AMLE 68253)* **SPIKEY DREAM FLOWERS**		-

– Brainwashing time / Five year mission / Dangers of living / Robots holiday / Soldier soldier / Downtown / Risk / Central Park / Scared / Melancholy.

Apr 81. (7") *(AMS 8124)* **DANGERS OF LIVING. / SCARED**		-

— CLIVE (C.P.) joined BIG COUNTRY on a temp. basis

SPIZZENERGI 2

	Rough Trade	not iss.
Feb 82. (7") *(RT 096)* **WORK. / MEGACITY III**		-
Jun 82. (7") *(RT 108)* **JUNGLE FEVER. / MEANING**		-

— retired for half a decade

SPIZZ

— returned in solo form 1987 with a re-working of his old classic

— added **MARK FERDA** – guitar

	Hobo Railway	not iss.
Sep 87. (7") *(HOBO 001)* **WHERE'S CAPTAIN KIRK? / LIVING IS BETTER WITH FREEDOM**		-

(12"+=) *(HOBO12 001)* – ('A'extended).

	Plastic Head	not iss.
Nov 88. (12") *(PLASPOP 2)* **LOVE ME LIKE A ROCKET. /**		-

— SPIZZ's career again fizzled out

SPIZZENERGI

— re-formed recorded an album in 1993/94

	Damaged Goods	not iss.
Mar 94. (cd) *(DAMGOOD 36)* **UNHINGED**		-

– compilations, etc. –

(below was scheduled for release in March '82)

Nov 83. (lp) *Rough Trade; (ROUGHSO 1)* **SPIZZ HISTORY** (compilation of singles, etc)		-
Feb 87. (12"ep) *Strange Fruit; (SFPS 022)* **THE PEEL SESSIONS** (7.8.78) (early material)		-

– Cold city / 6,000 crazy / Pure noise / Alien language / Protect from heat / Platform 3 / Switched off.

May 96. (cd) *Cherry Red; (CDMRED 130)* **SPIZZ NOT DEAD SHOCK 1978-1988**		-

S.P.K.

Formed: Sydney, Australia . . . 1978 as SURGICAL PENIS KLINIK, by mental hospice carer, DEREK THOMPSON (aka OBLIVION), with one of his patients, NE/H/IL (er.. NEIL) along with DOMINIK PINKER. Early singles, 'GERMANIK', 'SLOGAN' and 'MEAT PROCESSING SECTION' were Australian-only affairs, as was debut album, 'INFORMATION OVERLOAD UNIT' (1981). Britain was treated to its first taste of the band's uncompromising industrial noise via 1982's 'LEICHENSCHREI', released under the less squeamish moniker of SOZIALISTISCHES PATIENTEN KOLLEKTIV (a German organisation committed to lobbying for the rights of mental patients). A cassette only release, 'FROM SCIENCE TO RITUAL' (1984) – with GRAEME REVELL now replacing NE/H/IL and PINKER – followed in early '84, the same month as a German release, 'AUTO-DA-FE'. As contrary with regards to their moniker as the music itself, SPK subsequently announced that their initials now stood for SYSTEMS PLANNING KORPORATION. They'd also recruited a Chinese female "singer" , SINAN LEONG, replacing THOMPSON, the last remaining founder member. Having incredibly secured a deal with 'Warners', the band made their break for the big time with the 'MACHINE AGE VOODOO' (1984) album. Bracketed with contemporaries TEST DEPT. and EINSTURZENDE NEUBAUTEN, SPK had a similar penchant for ear-crippling live displays of metal-bashing and general sonic mayhem, the memorable screening of the 'METAL DANCE' single on Channel 4's 'The Tube', about as close to mainstream indie fame as SPK came. 'ZAMIA LEHMANNI' (1986) saw them back on indie label, 'Side Effekts', the record a complete departure towards the classical sounds of ancient Greece. A final two albums, 'OCEANIA' (1988) and 'DIGITALES AMBIGUA, GOLD & POISON', followed in 1988 before the band split for good. GRAEME REVELL also released a couple of simultaneous solo sets, 'THE INSECT MUSICIANS' (1987) and 'NECROPOLIS AMPHIBIAN REPTILES' (1988), employing the "music" of insects!

Album rating: OCEANIA (*6)

SURGICAL PENIS KLINIK

OBLIVION (b. DEREK THOMPSON) – synthesizer, tapes, metal percussion, vocals / **NE/H/IL** (b. NEIL LUSTMORE) – synthesizer, tapes, vocals / **PINKER** – drums, metal percussion, vocals

	P.R.S.	not iss.
Apr 79. (7") *(2617)* **GERMANIK. / NO MORE / CONTACT**	-	- Austra
Nov 79. (7"m) *(2655)* **SLOGAN. / MEKANO / CONTACT**	-	- Austra

	Industrial	not iss.
Jun 80. (7") *(IR 0011)* **MEAT PROCESSING SECTION**		-

– Slogan / Mekano. *(different titles on label)*

	Side Effekts	not iss.
Feb 81. (lp) *(SER 01)* **INFORMATION OVERLOAD UNIT**		-

– Emanation machine R. Gie 1916 / Suture / obsession / Macht schrecken / Beruftverbot / Ground zero: infinity dose / Stammheim torturkammer / Retard / Epilept: convulse / Kaltbruchig acideath. *(re-iss. May85 on 'Normal'; NORMAL 09)* *(cd-iss. Sep92 on 'Grey Area-Mute'; SPK 1CD)*

	M Squared	not iss.
Jul 81. (7") *(M 2009)* **SEE SAW. / CHAMBERMUSIK**	-	- Austra

	Sterile	not iss.
Nov 81. (c) *(SRC 4)* **LIVE AT THE CRYPT (live)**	-	- Austra

(UK-iss.Apr85; same)

	Side Effekts	Thermidor
1982. (lp; as SOZIALISTISCHES PATIENTEN KOLLEKTIV) *(SER 002)* <T-9> **LEICHENSCHREI**		

– Genetic transmission / Postmortem / Desolation / Napalm (terminal patient) / Cry from the sanitorium / Baby blue eyes / Israel / Internal bleeding / Chamber music / Despair / The agony of the plasma / Day of pigs / War of Islam / Maladia Europa (the European sickness). *(cd-iss. Sep92 on 'Grey Area-Mute'; SPK 2CD)*

May 83. (12"; as SEPPUKU) *(SER 003)* **DEKOMPOSITIONES** [ ] [-]
– Another dark age / Twilight of the idols / Culturecide.

— **GRAEME REVELL** – synthesizer, electronics, metal bashing; repl. NE/H/IL + PINKER

Plasma / not iss.

Jan 84. (c) *(PLASMA 004)* **FROM SCIENCE TO RITUAL** [ ] [-]

Walter Ulbright / not iss.

Jan 84. (lp) *(WULP 002)* **AUTO-DA-FE** [-] [-] German
– Contakt / Germanik / Mekano / Retard / Slogun / Metal field / Walking on dead steps / A heart that breaks (in no time or place). *(cd-iss. Jan93 on 'Grey Area-Mute'+=; SPK 4CD)* – Another dark age / Twilight of the idols / Culturecide.

S.P.K.

— they claimed it now stood for SYSTEMS PLANNING KORPORATION

— **SINAN (LEONG)** – voice (& many guests); repl. last original DEREK

WEA / Elektra

Sep 84. (7"/12") *(YZ 24/+T)* **JUNK FUNK. / HIGH TENSION** [ ] [ ]

Nov 84. (lp) *(WX 10)* <60386-1> **MACHINE AGE VOODOO** [ ] [ ]
– Junk funk / With love from China / High tension / One world / Flesh and steel / Metropol / Metal dance / Thin ice / Crime of passion.

Desire / not iss.

Apr 85. (7"/12") *(WANT/+X 1)* **METAL DANCE. / WILL TO POWER** [ ] [-]

Side Effekts / not iss.

May 86. (12") *(SFX 01)* **IN FRAGRANTE DELICTO. / INVOCATION (TO SECULAR HERESIES)** [ ] [-]

Oct 86. (lp) *(SER 09)* **ZAMIA LEHMANNI** [ ] [-]
– Invication (to secular heresies) / Palms crossed in sorrow / Romanz in moll (romance in a minor key) / In the dying moments / In fragrante delicto (intro) / In fragrante delicto / Alocasia metallica / Necropolis / The garden of earthy delights. *(re-iss. Nov92 on 'Grey Area-Mute' lp/cd+=; SPK 3/+CD)* – The doctrine of eternal ice.

Jan 88. (lp) *(SER 011)* **OCEANIA** [ ] [-]
– Oceania / The doctrine of eternal ice / Breathless / Mouth to mouth / Kambuja / Crack! / Seduction / Dies Irae. *(cd-iss. Jun88 +=; DFX 01)* – In fragrante delicto / Necropolis / In the dying moments.

Nettwerk / Nettwerk

Sep 87. (12") *(NT12 3008)* **OFF THE DEEP END. /** [ ] [-]

Feb 88. (12") *(NT12 3016)* **BREATHLESS (remix). /** [ ] [-]
(re-iss. May88; NET 002)

Feb 88. (lp/c)(cd) *(NTL/+C 30017)(<NTCD 035>)* **DIGITALES AMBIGUA, GOLD & POISON** [ ] [ ]
– Breathless / Mouth to mouth / Sheer naked aggression / Crack! / The doctrine eternal ice / Invocation (to secular heresies) / White island / Palms crossed in sorrow / Alocasia metallica / The garden of earthly delight.

— disbanded later in the year

– compilations, etc. –

Aug 92. (cd-box) *Grey Area-Mute; (CDSPKBOX 1)* **S.P.K. CD-BOX SET** [ ] [-]

GRAEME REVELL

— also combined a solo career

Musique Brut / not iss.

Jul 87. (lp) *(BRU 001)* **THE INSECT MUSICIANS** [ ] [-]
(cd-iss. Jul94 +=; BRUT 1CD) – NECROPOLIS AMPHIBIAN REPTILES

Jan 88. (lp) *(BRU 002)* **NECROPOLIS AMPHIBIAN REPTILES** [ ] [-]
– Necropolis amphibians & reptiles / Countless saladine / Chimpnas-apes of the union Canada / Allegebrah / Ebony tower in the Orient water / The Balli / St. Adolf's comet / Natural form of the holy light / Rhama margarine / Lea tantaaria / Great God father nieces.

— wrote many film scores from 1993's 'HARD TARGET' onwards

SPLODGENESSABOUNDS

Formed: London, England . . . early 1979 out of The FABER BROTHERS by MAX SPLODGE, PAT THETIC, BABY GREENSLEEVES, MILES FLAT, DONKEY GUT, WHIFFY ARCHER, DESERT ISLAND JOE LURCH SLYTHE and believe it or not, a dog! Briefly infamous in 1980 with their rampaging racket of a one-hit wonder, 'TWO PINTS OF LAGER AND A PACKET OF CRISPS PLEASE' (actually the flip of 'SIMON TEMPLAR'), the band had somehow managed to secure a deal with 'Deram' and further proved their inability to record anything resembling a tune with an eponymous debut album in 1981. Further attempts at infiltrating the mainstream came to little, save for a last gasp Top 30 entry with a demented reading of Rolf Harris' 'TWO LITTLE BOYS', later that summer. Subsequently abbreviating his name to SPLODGE and signing with 'Razor', he resurfaced – alongside a revamped motley crew numbering RONNIE PLONKER, TONE TONE THE GARDEN GNOME, SMACKED ARSE O'REARDON and POODLE – with the tastefully titled 'IN SEARCH OF THE SEVEN GOLDEN GUSSETS' (1982). Whether they actually located the underwear in question is unclear although their extended absence from the recording scene seems to suggest they're still looking.

Album rating: SPLODGENESSABOUNDS (*3) / IN SEARCH OF SEVEN GOLDEN GUSSETS (*3) / LIVE AND LOUD!! (*2)

MAX SPLODGE – vocals / **BABY GREENSLEEVES** – vocals / **ROBERT RODENT** – bass; repl. guitarist MILES FLAT / **DONKEY GUT** (b. WINSTON FORBE) – keyboards / plus **WHIFFY ARCHER + DESERT ISLAND JOE LURCH SLYTHE**

Deram / not iss.

Jun 80. (7") *(BUM 1)* **SIMON TEMPLAR. / MICHAEL BOOTH'S TALKING BUM / TWO PINTS OF LAGER AND A ACKET OF CRISPS PLEASE** [7] [-]

Aug 80. (7") *(ROLF 1)* **TWO LITTLE BOYS. / HORSE** [26] [-]
(12"+=) *(ROLF 12)* – Sex / Butterfly.

Jan 81. (7"; as MAX SPLODGE) *(BUM 2)* **BICYCLE SEAT. / ('A'version)** [ ] [-]

Jan 81. (lp/c) *(SML/KSCM 1121)* **SPLODGENESSABOUNDS** [ ] [-]
– Malcolm opera (course you can, Malcolm etc) / Whimsy zoom zoom / It's that sound / I fell in love with a female plumber from Harlsden, NW10 / Anarchy chaos Stanley Ogden / Blow away like a fart in a thunderstorm / Poison babies vs Batman / Two little boys / Rolf / I've got a lot of famous people living under the floorboards / Porky scratchins / Simon Templar / Desert island Joe / What's that funny noise / Wiffy smells / Two pints (dub).

May 81. (7"m) *(BUM 3)* **COWPUNK MEDLUM. / HAVE YOU GOT A LIGHT BOY? / MORNING MILKY** [69] [-]
(w/ free flexi) *(BUMF 3)* – YARMOUTH 5-0 / BROWN PAPER DUB

Secret / not iss.

Dec 81. (7"; by MAX SPLODGE) *(SHH 126)* **THE 12 DAYS OF CHRISTMAS. /** [ ] [-]

— **MAX** recruited newcomers **RONNIE PLONKER** – guitar / **TONE TONE THE GARDEN GNOME** – guitar / **SMACKED ARSE O'REARDON** – bass / **POODLE** – drums

Razor / not iss.

Nov 82. (7"; as SPLODGE) *(RZS 102)* **MOUTH AND TROUSERS. / IN SEARCH OF THE SEVEN GOLDEN GUSSETS** [ ] [-]

Nov 82. (lp; as SPLODGE) *(RAZ 1)* **IN SEARCH OF THE SEVEN GOLDEN GUSSETS** [ ] [-]
– Pooh oo's trumped / In search of the seven golden gussets / Old ya cherries / Tough shit Wilson / My baked bean / Crabs / Over dramatic songs (in very low voices) / Freefall from Paradise / Grafitti / Renfrew / Very unfunny comedian / What's thru this dooorrrr / Pathetique / Pilchard freak / Mouth and trousers / We luv you / Give it some bollox / No no yeah / Les Splodge / singers / 'Ole in the wall / Slooshshalongamix / Cigarette / Seven golden gussets / Dellar / Lager top / Sandra / My grandma. *(cd-iss. Jun98 on 'Captain Oi'; AHOYCD 089)*

Completely Different / not iss.

1987. (7"; by MAX SPLODGE) *(MAD 003)* **PHUT, PHUT, SPLODGENIK. / '86 – THE YEAR OF THE BEAN** [ ] [-]

Link / not iss.

1988. (lp) **LIVE AND LOUD!! (live)** [ ] [-]
(cd-iss. Mar98 on 'Receiver'; RRCD 237)

Receiver / not iss.

Oct 91. (cd/lp) *(RRCD/RRLP 148)* **A NIGHTMARE ON RUDE STREET** [ ] [-]
– Touch of the rods / Answers on a postcard / Double entendres / Lemmy's mole (wart?) / Lager in the house / Go the whole hog / Dangerous / Not many people know that / Haemorrhoids / Rude boy / They're coming to take me away.

— SPLODGE retired from the er, music biz

SPONGE

Formed: Detroit, Michigan, USA . . . 1994 out of the ashes of LOUDHOUSE, by VINNIE DOMBROWSKI, MIKE CROSS, TIM CROSS, JOEY MAZZOLA and CHARLIE GROVER (the latter being replaced by JIMMY PALUZZI). Following the release of one independent single, 'THE CRASH', SPONGE were soaked up by 'Columbia' as the next great white hope of Grunge. A couple of singles, 'MOLLY (SIXTEEN CANDLES)' and 'PLOWED', along with a debut album, 'ROTTING PINATA' (1995), revealed the band to be firmly in the epic melodic-grunge mould of PEARL JAM, vocalist DOMBROWSKI a throaty dead ringer for EDDIE VEDDER. The album (which made the Top 60 in the States) also had its fair share of 80's-esque guitar solos, no doubt endearing them to the more trad elements of the American metal fraternity (although there were moments of light and shade such as 'FIELDS', what The POLICE might've sounded like had they grown up in L.A.). Accompanying single, 'PLOWED', even scraped into the UK Top 75 although no further success in the British market would be forthcoming. It was a different story in America of course, where their sales approached the half million mark, a follow-up album, 'WAX ECSTATIC' also making the Top 60.

Album rating: ROTTING PINATA (*6) / WAX ECSTATIC (*6)

VINNIE DOMBROWSKI – vocals / **MIKE CROSS** (b. RYGIEL) – guitar / **TIM CROSS** (b. RYGIEL) – bass / **JOE MAZZOLA** – guitar / **JIMMY PALUZZI** – drums, vocals; repl. CHARLIE GROVER

Suburban / Suburban

Feb 95. (12") *(SUBBASE 48)* **THE CRASH. / SHABBUTZ** [ ] [ ]

Columbia / Work

Jul 95. (c-s,cd-s) <77976> **MOLLY (SIXTEEN CANDLES) / I HATE MYSELF** [-] [55]

Aug 95. (7") *(662316-7)* **PLOWED. / WELCOME HOME** [74] [-]
(cd-s+=) *(662316-2)* – Severed hearty mums.

Sep 95. (cd/c) *(476982-2/-4)* <57800> **ROTTING PINATA** [ ] [58] Feb95
– Pennywheels / Rotting pinata / Giants / Neenah Menasha / Miles / Plowed / Drownin' / Molly / Fields / Rainin. *(cd+=)* – Candy corn.

Oct 95. (7"/c-s) *(662547-7/-4)* **MOLLY (SIXTEEN CANDLES) / COWBOY EYES** [ ] [-]
(cd-s+=) *(662547-2)* – ('A'live) / Seventeen.

Columbia / Columbia

Aug 96. (cd/c/lp) *(484186-2/-4/-1)* <67578> **WAX ECSTATIC** [ ] [60] Jun96
– My putty / Got to be a bore / Wax ecstatic (to sell Angelina) / Drag queen of Memphis / I am Anastasia / Silence is their drug / Have you seen Mary / My baby said / Death of a drag queen / Velveteen.

Tobin SPROUT (see under ⇒ GUIDED BY VOICES)

SQUEEZE

Formed: Deptford, South London, England ... March '74 by CHRIS DIFFORD and GLEN TILBROOK, the pair initially forming a writing partnership whereby the former penned the lyrics with the latter writing the music. Their genius was subsequently incorporated into a group format as the pair recruited ace pianist, JOOLS HOLLAND, bassist HARRY KAKOULLI and drummer PAUL GUNN, forming SQUEEZE in the process. Early 1977 saw the group's vinyl debut on the independent 'B.T.M.' label with the mock-Egyptian new wave pop/rock of 'TAKE ME I'M YOURS'. Despite the single being subsequently withdrawn, the group replaced GUNN with GILSON LAVIS and proceeded to release the JOHN CALE-produced 'PACKET OF THREE' EP on the 'Deptford Fun City' label. This duly attracted the attentions of 'A&M', keen to get in on the new wave act after their abortive signing of the SEX PISTOLS earlier that year. Immediate Top 20 chart success came with the re-release of 'TAKE ME..', an eponymous debut surfacing soon after. With the addition of JOHN BENTLEY on bass as a replacement for the departing KAKOULLI, the group narrowly missed No.1 in Spring '79 with the cockney wide-boy rap of 'COOL FOR CATS', a similarly titled follow-up album almost breaking the Top 40. The record consolidated the growing reputation of the DIFFORD/TILBROOK songwriting axis; their sagely observed, often darkly amusing social commentary drew inevitable comparisons with prime RAY DAVIES, definitely more accurate than the fanciful LENNON & McCARTNEY references. 'UP THE JUNCTION' was a perfect example, a compelling, hard-bitten tale of love on the breadline leading to broken-hearted disillusionment, a swooning, deceptively melancholy keyboard refrain holding the whole thing together. The song clearly struck a chord in the populace at large, SQUEEZE once again coming within a whisker of No.1. 'ARGYBARGY' (1980) gave the group their first Top 40 album, although the comparatively lowly placings afforded SQUEEZE's long players never really reflected the enduring quality of the songs contained within. Tracks like 'PULLING MUSSELS (FROM THE SHELL)', a brilliant slice of pop genius featuring a rollicking piano break courtesy of the illustrious HOLLAND. The latter left soon after to follow his boogie-woogie muse with JOOLS HOLLAND AND THE MILLIONAIRES and more famously, to present Channel 4's legendary music show, 'The Tube', alongside a young Paula Yates. Finding a replacement in respected vocalist/pianist, PAUL CARRACK (ex-ACE, ex-FRANKIE MILLER etc.), SQUEEZE cut their most successful album to date, 'EAST SIDE STORY' (1981). Co-produced by ELVIS COSTELLO, the album had a rootsier feel, CARRACK's COCKER-esque vocals gracing the grittily soulful 'TEMPTED', while the poignant 'LABELLED WITH LOVE' proved SQUEEZE could 'do' country better than most country artists. The latter song (Top 5) marked the end of their reign as a singles band, however, with the evocative 'BLACK COFFEE IN BED' not even breaching the Top 40. By this point CARRACK had left for a solo career, DON SNOW brought in for a final, patchy album, 'SWEETS FROM A STRANGER' (1982). Though the group were at the height of their popularity, creatively they were beginning to stall and wisely decided to quit while they were still on top. Later that year, the compilation, 'THE SINGLES – 45 AND UNDER', brought the era neatly to a close, a seminal record (no household is complete without a copy!) illustrating why SQUEEZE have aged better than many "new wave" bands of the era. This wasn't the end, though, and after a solo 'DIFFORD & TILBROOK' (1984) album, the pair reunited with HOLLAND, recruiting KEITH WILKINSON on bass. A new album, 'COSI FAN TUTTI FRUTTI' appeared in summer '85, although they didn't really recapture anything resembling the old magic until 'BABYLON ON AND ON' (1987). That album gave SQUEEZE their first UK Top 20 hit in years with 'HOURGLASS', as well as some belated US chart action, the single reaching No.15 in the States while the album made the Top 40. 'FRANK' (1989) failed to capitalise on the momentum and SQUEEZE were subsequently dealt a double blow when HOLLAND left once again to concentrate on TV work and A&M finally let the band go. The band soldiered on, releasing a sole album, the acclaimed 'PLAY' (1991), for 'Reprise' before eventually regrouping with CARRACK and re-signing with 'A&M' for a further couple of 90's albums, 'SOME FANTASTIC PLACE' (1993) and 'RIDICULOUS' (1995). • **Songwriters:** Mostly DIFFORD & TILBROOK compositions, and some by CARRACK who joined late 1980. Covered END OF THE CENTURY (Blur).

Album rating: ARGYBARGY (*7) / EAST SIDE STORY (*7) / GREATEST HITS compilation (*8)

CHRIS DIFFORD (b. 4 Nov'54) – vocals, guitar / **GLENN TILBROOK** (b.31 Aug'57) – vocals, guitar / **JOOLS HOLLAND** (b.JULIAN, 24 Jan'58) – keyboards / **HARRY KAKOULLI** – bass / **PAUL GUNN** – drums (below 45 withdrawn from release)

B.T.M. — not iss.

Jan 77. (7"; w-drawn) *(SBT 107)* **TAKE ME I'M YOURS. / NO DISCO KID, NO** [-] [-]

— **GILSON LAVIS** (b.27 Jun'51) – drums (ex-MUSTARD) repl. GUNN

Deptford Fun City — not iss.

Aug 77. (7"ep,12"ep) *(DFC 01)* **PACKET OF THREE** [ ] [-]
– Cat on a wall / Back track / Night ride. *(re-iss. Nov79 12"ep; same)*

A&M — A&M

Feb 78. (7"/12") *(AMS/+P 7335)* **TAKE ME, I'M YOURS. / NIGHT NURSE** [19] [ ]

Mar 78. (lp/c) *(AMLH/CAM 68465)* <4687> **SQUEEZE** [ ] [ ]
– Sex master / Bang bang / Strong in reason / Wild sewerage tickles Brazil / Out of control / Take me, I'm yours / The call / Model / Remember what / First thing wrong / Hesitation (rool Britania) / Get smart. *(re-iss. Mar82 lp/c; AMID/CMID 122)*

May 78. (7",7"green) *(AMS 7360)* **BANG BANG. / ALL FED UP** [49] [-]

— **JOHN BENTLEY** (b.16 Apr'51) – bass; repl. KAKOULLI who went solo (he released an album, 'EVEN WHEN I'M NOT', in 1980 and subsequently released a handful of singles in the first half on the 80's)

Nov 78. (7") *(AMS 7398)* **GOODBYE GIRL. / SAINTS ALIVE** [63] [-]

Mar 79. (7",7"pale pink,7"pink,7"red/12"pink) *(AMS/+P 7426)* **COOL FOR CATS. / MODEL** [2] [ ]

Apr 79. (lp/c) *(AMLH/CAM 68503)* <4759> **COOL FOR CATS** [45] [ ]
– Slap and tickle / Revue / Touching me, touching you / It's not cricket / It's so dirty / The knack / Hop, skip and jump / Up the junction / Hard to find / Slightly drunk / Goodbye girl / Cool for cats. *(cd-iss. Mar91; CDMID 131)*

May 79. (7",7"lilac) *(AMS 7444)* **UP THE JUNCTION. / IT'S SO DIRTY** [2] [-]

Jun 79. (7") <2168> **SLIGHTLY DRUNK. / GOODBYE GIRL** [-] [ ]

Aug 79. (7",7"red) *(AMS 7466)* **SLAP AND TICKLE. / ALL'S WELL** [24] [ ]

Nov 79. (7",7"white) *(AMS 7495)* **CHRISTMAS DAY. / GOING CRAZY** [ ] [-]

Jan 80. (7",7"clear) *(AMS 7507)* **ANOTHER NAIL IN MY HEART. / PRETTY THING** [17] [-]

Feb 80. (7") <2229> **IF I DIDN'T LOVE YOU. / PRETTY ONE** [-] [ ]

Feb 80. (lp/c) *(AMLH/CAM 64802)* <4802> **ARGYBARGY** [32] [71]
– Pulling mussels (from the shell) / Another nail in my heart / Seperate beds / Misadventure / I think I'm go go / Farfisa beat / Here comes that feeling / Vicky Verky / If I didn't love you / Wrong side of the Moon / There at the top.

Apr 80. (7",7"red) *(AMS 7523)* **PULLING MUSSELS (FROM THE SHELL). / WHAT THE BUTLER SAW** [44] [-]

Jun 80. (7") <2247> **PULLING MUSSELS (FROM THE SHELL). / PRETTY ONE** [-] [ ]

Sep 80. (7"m) <2263> **ANOTHER NAIL IN MY HEART. / GOING CRAZY / WHAT THE BUTLER SAW** [-] [ ]
<re-iss. Sep82>

— **PAUL CARRACK** (b. Apr'51, Sheffield, England) – keyboards (ex-ACE, ex-FRANKIE MILLER, ex-ROXY MUSIC) repl. JOOLS who formed his own MILLIONAIRES

Apr 81. (7") *(AMS 8129)* **IS THAT LOVE. / TRUST** [35] [-]

May 81. (lp/c) *(AMLH/CAM 64854)* <4854> **EAST SIDE STORY** [19] [44]
– In quintessence / Someone else's heart / Tempted / Piccadilly / There's no tomorrow / A woman's world / Is that love / F-hole / Labelled with love / Someone else's bell / Mumbo jumbo / Vanity fair / Messed around. *(cd-iss. Jan87; CDA 3253) (re-iss. cd Mar91; same)*

Jul 81. (7") *(AMS 8147)* **TEMPTED. / YAP YAP YAP** [40] [-]
(free 5"w.a.) **ANOTHER NAIL IN MY HEART. / IF I DIDN'T LOVE YOU**

Jul 81. (7") <2345> **TEMPTED. / TRUST** [-] [49]

Sep 81. (7") *(AMS 8166)* **LABELLED WITH LOVE. / SQUABS ON FORTY FAB** [4] [ ]

Oct 81. (7") <2377> **MESSED AROUND. / YAP YAP YAP** [-] [ ]

— **DON SNOW** (b.13 Jan'57, Kenya) – keyboards (ex-VIBRATORS, ex-SINCEROS) repl. CARRACK (now solo)

Apr 82. (7",7"pic-d) *(AMS 8219)* <2424> **BLACK COFFEE IN BED. / THE HUNT** [51] [ ] Jul82

Apr 82. (12") <2413> **WHEN THE HANGOVER STRIKES. / I'VE RETURNED** [-] [ ]

May 82. (lp/c) *(AMLH/CAM 64899)* <4899> **SWEETS FROM A STRANGER** [37] [32]
– Out of touch / I can't hold on / Points of view / Stranger than the stranger on the shore / Onto the dance floor / When the hangover strikes / Black coffee in bed / I've returned / Tongue like a knife / His house her home / The very last dance / The elephant ride.

Jul 82. (7",7"pic-d) *(AMS 8237)* **WHEN THE HANGOVER STRIKES. / THE ELEPHANT RIDE** [ ] [-]

Oct 82. (7") *(AMS 8259)* <2518> **ANNIE GET YOUR GUN. / SPANISH GUITAR** [43] [ ] Feb83

Nov 82. (lp/c) *(AMLH/CAM 68552)* <4922> **SINGLES – 45 AND UNDER** (compilation) [3] [47]
– Take me I'm yours / Goodbye girl / Cool for cats / Up the junction / Slap and tickle / Another nail in my heart / Pulling mussels (from the shell) / Tempted / Is that love / Labelled with love / Black coffee in bed / Annie get your gun. *(cd-iss. Dec84; CDA 64922)*

Dec 82. (7") <2534> **ANOTHER NAIL IN MY HEART. / GOING CRAZY – WHAT THE BUTLER SAW** [-] [ ]

— Split at same time of compilation.

DIFFORD & TILBROOK

— carried on as duo, augmented by **KEITH WILKINSON** (b.24 Sep'54, Southfield, England) – bass / other musicians

Jun 84. (7"/ext.12") *(AM/+X 193)* **LOVE'S CRASHING WAVES. / WITHIN THESE WALLS OF WITHOUT YOU** [57] [-]

Jun 84. (lp/c) *(AMLX/CXM 64985)* <4985> **DIFFORD & TILBROOK** [47] [55]
– Action speaks faster / Love's crashing waves / Picking up the pieces / On my mind tonight / Man for all seasons / Hope fell down / Wagon train / You can't hurt the girl / Tears for attention / The apple tree.

Jun 84. (7") <2648> **PICKING UP THE PIECES. / WITHIN THESE WALLS OF WITHOUT YOU** [-] [ ]

Oct 84. (7"/12") *(AM/+X 219)* **HOPE FELL DOWN. / ACTION SPEAKS FASTER** [ ] [-]

SQUEEZE

— reformed '78 line-up except **KEITH WILKINSON** – bass (- HARRY)

Jun 85. (7"/12") *(AM/+Y 255)* **LAST TIME FOREVER. / SUITE FROM FIVE STRANGERS** [45] [ ]

Aug 85. (lp/c/cd) *(AMLH/AMC/CDA 5085)* <5085> **COSI FAN TUTTI FRUTTI** [31] [57]
– Big bang / By your side / King George Street / I learnt how to pray / Last time

forever / No place like home / Heartbreakin' world / Hits of the year / Break my heart / I won't ever go drinking again.

Sep 85. (7") <2776> **HITS OF THE YEAR. / THE FORTNIGHT SAGA** [-] [ ]

Sep 85. (7") *(AM 277)* **NO PLACE LIKE HOME. / THE FORTNIGHT SAGA** [ ] [-]

(12"+=) *(AMY 277)* – Last time forever.

Nov 85. (7") *(AM 291)* **HEARTBREAKING WORLD. / BIG BANG** [ ] [-]

(10"+=) *(AMY 291)* – Tempted (live) / By your side (live).

Apr 86. (7") *(AM 306)* **KING GEORGE STREET. / LOVE'S CRASHING WAVES (live)** [ ] [-]

(12"+=) *(AMY 306)* – Up the junction (live).

— added **ANDY METCALFE** – keyboards (ex-SOFT BOYS)

Aug 87. (7") *(AM 400)* <2967> **HOURGLASS. / WEDDING BELLS** [16] [15]

(12"+=) *(AMY 400)* – Splitting into three.

Sep 87. (lp/c/cd) *(<AMA/AMC/CDA 5161>)* **BABYLON AND ON** [14] [36]

– Hourglass / Footprints / Tough love / The prisoner / 853-5937 / In today's room / Trust me to open my mouth / Striking matches / Cigarette of a single man / Who are you? / The waiting game / Some Americans.

Sep 87. (7") *(AM 412)* **TRUST ME TO OPEN MY MOUTH. / TAKE ME, I'M YOURS (live)** [72] [-]

(12"+=) *(AMY 412)* – Black coffee in bed (live).

Nov 87. (7") *(AM 420)* **THE WAITING GAME. / LAST TIME FOREVER** [ ] [ ]

(12"+=) *(AMY 420)* – The prisoner.

Dec 87. (7") <2994> **853-5937. / TAKE ME I'M YOURS (live)** [-] [32]

Jan 88. (7"/ext.12") *(AM/+Y 426)* **853-5937. / TOUGH LOVE** [ ] [-]

Apr 88. (7") <3021> **FOOTPRINTS. / BLACK COFFEE IN BED (live)** [-] [ ]

Jun 88. (7") *(AM 450)* **FOOTPRINTS. / STRIKING MATCHES (INSTANT BLUFF)** [ ] [-]

(ext.12"+=) *(AMY 450)* – In today's room.

— Reverted back to 5-piece when METCALFE departed.

Sep 89. (7") *(AM 350)* <1457> **IF IT'S LOVE. / FRANK'S BAG** [ ] [-]

(12"+=/cd-s+=) *(AMY/CDEE 350)* – Vanity fair.

Sep 89. (lp/c/cd) *(<AMA/AMC/CDA 5278>)* **FRANK** [58] [ ]

– Frank / If it's love / Peyton Place / Rose I said / Slaughtered, gutted and heartbroken / (This could be) The last time / She doesn't have to shave / Love circles / Melody hotel / Can of worms / Dr. Jazz / Is it too late.

Jan 90. (7") *(AM 535)* **LOVE CIRCLES. / RED LIGHT** [ ] [-]

(12"+=/cd-s+=) *(AMY/CDEE 535)* – Who's that.

Deptford Fun City — I.R.S.

Mar 90. (cd/c/lp) *(DFC CD/MC/LP 1)* <82040> **A ROUND AND A BOUT (live 1974-1989)** [50] [ ]

– Footprints / Pulling mussels (from the shell) / Black coffee in bed / She doesn't have to shave / Is that love / Dr. Jazz / Up the junction / Slaughtered, gutted and heartbroken / Is it too late / Cool for cats / Take me, I'm yours / If it's love / Hourglass / Labelled with love / Annie get your gun / Boogie woogie country girl / Tempted. *(free 7"ep 'PACKET OF THREE')*

— JOOLS left again to go solo and take up more TV work. In 1991 he was repl. by **MATT IRVING + STEVE NIEVE** – keyboards / **TONY BERG** – guitar, keyboards / **BRUCE HORNSBY** – accordion

Reprise — Reprise

Jul 91. (7"/c-s) *(W 0054/+C)* **SUNDAY STREET. / MAIDSTONE** [ ] [-]

(12"+=/cd-s+=) *(W 0054 T/CD)* – Mood swings.

Aug 91. (lp/c)(cd) *(WX 428/+C)(<7599 26644-2>)* **PLAY** [41] [ ]

– Satisfied / Crying in my sleep / Letting go / The day I get home / The truck / House of love / Cupid's toy / Gone to the dogs / Walk a straight line / Sunday street / Wicked and cruel / There is a voice. *(re-iss. cd Feb95; same)*

— **DIFFORD + TILBROOK + WILKINSON** plus returning **PAUL CARRACK** – keyboards / **PETE THOMAS** – drums

A&M — A&M

Jul 93. (7"/c-s) *(580337-7/-4)* **THIRD RAIL. / TAKE ME I'M YOURS (live)** [39] [-]

(cd-s+=) *(580337-2)* – Cool for cats (live medley).

(cd-s) – ('A'side) / The truth (live) / Melody hotel (live) / Walk a straight line (live).

Aug 93. (7"/c-s) *(580379-7/-4)* **SOME FANTASTIC PLACE. / JUMPING** [73] [-]

(cd-s+=) *(580379-2)* – Dark saloons / Discipline.

(cd-s) *(580379-5)* – ('A'side) / Is that the time? / Don't be a stranger / Stark naked.

Sep 93. (cd/c/lp) *(<540140-2/-4/-1>)* **SOME FANTASTIC PLACE** [26] [ ]

– Everything in the world / Some fantastiv place / Third rail / Loving you tonight / It's over / Cold shoulder / Talk to him / Jolly comes home / Images of loving / True colours (the storm) / Pinocchio.

Oct 93. (7"/c-s) *(580412-7/-4)* **LOVING YOU TONIGHT. / ('A'mix)** [ ] [-]

(12"+=/cd-s+=) *(580413-1/-2)* – Tempted / Third rail.

Feb 94. (7"/c-s) *(580506-7/-4)* **IT'S OVER. / IS THAT LOVE? (live)** [ ] [-]

(cd-s+=) *(580507-2)* – Pulling mussels (from the shell) / Goodbye girl (live).

A&M — IRS-Capitol

Aug 95. (c-s) *(581189-4)* **THIS SUMMER / GOODBYE GIRL (live)** [47] [-]

(cd-s+=) *(581189-2)* – All the king's horses.

(cd-s) *(581191-2)* – ('A'side) / End of a century (live) / Periscope.

Nov 95. (c-ep/cd-ep) *(581271-4/-2)* **ELECTRIC TRAINS / CRACKER JACK / FIGHTING FOR PEACE / COLD SHOULDER (live)** [44] [-]

(cd-ep) *(581269-2)* – ('A'side) / Some fantastic place / It's over / Hour glass.

Nov 95. (cd/c) *(540440-2/-4)* <38304> **RIDICULOUS** [50] [ ]

– Electric trains / Heaven knows / Grouch of the day / Walk away / This summer / Got to me / Long face / I want you / Daphne / Lost for words / Great escape / Temptation for love / Sound asleep / Fingertips. *(re-iss. Sep97 cd/c; same)*

Jun 96. (cd-s) *(581605-2)* **HEAVEN KNOWS /** [27] [-]

(cd-s) *(581607-2)* –

(cd-s) *(581609-2)* –

Aug 96. (cd-s) *(581837-2)* **THIS SUMMER (remix) / ELECTRIC TRAINS / HEAVEN KNOWS** [32] [-]

(cd-s) *(581839-2)* – ('A'side) / Cool for cats / Up the junction / Black coffee in bed.

(cd-s) *(581841-2)* – ('A'side) / Sweet as a nut / In another lifetime / Never there.

– compilations, etc. –

1981. (10"m-lp) *A&M;* <SP 3413> **SIX SQUEEZE SONGS CRAMMED ONTO ONE TEN INCH RECORD** [-] [ ]

Oct 83. (7") *Old Gold; (OG 9364)* **TAKE ME, I'M YOURS. / UP THE JUNCTION** [ ] [-]

Sep 85. (7") *Old Gold; (OG 9546)* **COOL FOR CATS. / LABELLED WITH LOVE** [ ] [-]

Apr 92. (7"/c-s) *A&M; (AM/+C 860)* **COOL FOR CATS. / TRUST ME TO OPEN MY MOUTH** [62] [-]

(cd-s+=) *(AMCD 860)* – Squabs on forty fab (medley hits).

May 92. (cd/c/d-lp) *A&M' (397181-2/-4/-1)* **GREATEST HITS** [6] [ ]

– (as THE SINGLES 45 AND UNDER +) Take me, I'm yours / Goodbye girl / Cool for cats / Up the junction / Slap and tickle / Another nail in my heart / Pulling mussels (from the shell) / Tempted / Is that love / Labelled with love / Black coffee in bed / Annie get your gun / King George Street / Last time forever / No place like home / Hourglass / Trust me to open my mouth / Footprints / If it's love / Love circles.

Oct 93. (cd) *A&M; (CDA 24120)* **BABYLON AND ON / EAST SIDE STORY** [ ] [ ]

Nov 96. (d-cd) *A&M; (540651-2)* **EXCESS MODERATION** [ ] [ ]

Oct 97. (6xcd-box) *(540801-2)* **SIX OF ONE** [ ] [ ]

SQUIRREL BAIT

Formed: Louisville, Kentucky, USA . . . 1985 by DAVID GRUBBS, PETER SEARCY, BRIAN McMAHON, BRITT WALFORD and CLARK JOHNSON. A seminal indie hardcore act with a neat line in adolescent humour, SQUIRREL BAIT set their first musical trap in early '86 with an eponymous HUSKER DU-esque album for Steven Joerg's 'Homestead' imprint. Their lifespan was brief however, the band effectively extinct as college captured them following the release of the excellent 'SKAG HEAVEN' (1987). While most of the posse were buried in their books, SEARCY formed The BIG WHEEL and GRUBBS (with JOHNSON) worked on a trio of thrash-metal/noise sets as BASTRO, the latter two surprisingly featuring drummer, JOHN McENTIRE, before he crawled off to form TORTOISE. The most famous by-product of SQUIRREL BAIT, however, was SLINT, an influential indie outfit formed from the ashes of the former band's final line-up (i.e. McMAHON, WALFORD, DAVID PAJO and ETHAN BUCKLER). In 1991, GRUBBS initiated GASTR DEL SOL, a more intelligent, musically complex proposition which originally saw him working with BUNDY K BROWN and the ubiquitous McENTIRE (in a guest capacity) on the 1993 mini-set, 'THE SERPENTINE SIMILAR'. The latter sticksman also featured on the following single, '20 SONGS LESS', a collaboration with GRUBBS and JIM O'ROURKE (BUNDY had already joined TORTOISE). Having been part of the 'TeenBeat' operation, GASTR DEL SOL signed with 'Drag City' for 1994's acclaimed long-player, 'CROOKT, CRACKT, OR FLY', a subtle, spellbinding record that made genuine innovations in the use of dense acoustic guitar textures and traversed the boundaries of standard indie-rock structures. Never one to shirk a challenge, GRUBBS (and some local friends/musicians) took it upon himself to create a mini-orchestral suite scored to the usual freeform rules, the resulting 17-minute long 'HARP FACTORY ON LAKE STREET' (1995), taking the post-rock ethos into uncharted territory. The following year, GASTR DEL SOL returned to a more song-based approach on 'UPGRADE & AFTERLIFE', a slightly disappointing set which featured a cover of John Fahey's 'DRY BONES IN THE VALLEY'. The partnership of GRUBBS and O'ROURKE was tied up with the 'CAMOFLEUR' (1998) album, an impressive swansong that found the pair in a more reflective mood, dabbling in a cinematic mix of folk and avant-jazz influences.

Album rating: SQUIRREL BAIT (*6) / SKAG HEAVEN (*7) / Bastro: RODE HARD AND PUT UP WET (*4) / DIABLO GUAPO (*4) / SING THE TROUBLED BEAST (*5) / Gastr Del Sol: THE SERPENTINE SIMILAR mini (*6) / CROOKT, CRACKT, OR FLY (*7) / UPGRADE & AFTERLIFE (*5) / CAMOFLEUR (*7)

PETER SEARCY – vocals / **BRIAN McMAHON** – guitar, vocals / **DAVID GRUBBS** – guitar / **CLARK JOHNSON** – bass / **BRITT WALFORD** – drums

Homestead — Homestead

Jan 86. (lp) <(HMS 028-1)> **SQUIRREL BAIT** [ ] [ ]

– Hammering so hard / Thursday / Sun god / When I fall / The final chapter / Mixed blessing / Disguise.

Nov 86. (7") **KID DYNAMITE. / SLAKE TRAIN COMING** [ ] [ ]

Mar 87. (lp/cd) <(HMS 072-1/-2)> **SKAG HEAVEN** [ ] [ ]

– Kid Dynamite / Vigil's return / Black light poster child / Choose your poison / Short straw wins / Too close to the fire / Slake train coming / Rose Island road / Tape to California. *(cd-iss. w/ debut)*

— split in 1988 (after BRITT was replaced by BEN DAUGHTRY), singer SEARCY forming BIG WHEEL with guitarist and co-songwriter, GLEN TAYLOR. The duo released only one non-hardcore 1989 album, 'EAST END' for 'Giant' records.

BASTRO

— meanwhile, **GRUBBS + JOHNSON** formed this outfit

Homestead — Homestead

Sep 88. (m-lp/m-c) <(HMS 111/+C)> **RODE HARD AND PUT UP WET** [ ] [ ]

— added **JOHN McENTIRE** – drums

Apr 89. (7") <(HMS 137)> **SHOOT ME A DEAR. /** [ ] [ ]

Jul 89. (lp/c/cd) <(HMS 132-1/-4/-2)> **DIABLO GUAPO** [ ] [ ]

– Tallow waters / Filthy five filthy ten / Guapo / Flesh-coloured house / Short-haired robot / Can of whoopass / Decent skin / Engaging the reverend / Wurlitzer / Pretty smart on my part / Hoosier logic / Shoot me a deer.

1990. (cd/c/lp) <HMS 164-2/-4/-1> **SING THE TROUBLED BEAST** [-] [ ]

– Demons begone / Krakow, Illinois / I come from a long line of ship-builders /

Tobacco in the sink / Recidivist / Floating home / Jefferson-in-drag / The sifter / Noise – Star / Recidivist.

— disbanded after above, McINTIRE later formed TORTOISE

GASTR DEL SOL

DAVID GRUBBS – vocals, guitar, piano / **BUNDY K. BROWN** – bass (of TORTOISE) / with **JOHN McENTIRE** – percussion (of TORTOISE)

not iss. Teenbeat

Aug 93. (m-cd/m-lp) *<TB 95>* **THE SERPENTINE SIMILAR** -
– Watery Kentucky / Easy company / Jar of fat / Ursus arctos wonderfilis / Eye street / For Soren Mueller / The serpentine orbit / Even the odd orbit. *<re-iss. 1997 on 'Drag City'; DC 106> (UK-iss.Jun97 on 'Dexter's Cigar' cd/lp; DEX 13 CD/LP)*

— **GRUBBS** now with **JIM O'ROURKE** – guitar / guests were McENTIRE + STEVE BUTTERS – percussion

Dec 93. (7") *<TB 125>* **20 SONGS LESS. /** -

Drag City Drag City

Nov 94. (cd/c) *<DC 43 CD/C>* **CROOKT, CRACKT, OR FLY** -
– Wedding in the park / Work from smoke / Parenthetically / Every five miles / Thos. Dudley ah old must dye / Is that a rifle when it rains? / C in cake / Wrong soundings. *(UK-iss.Dec96; same as US)*

Jan 95. (12"ep/cd-ep) *<DC 54/+CD>* **MIRROR REPAIR** -
– Photographed yawning / Eight corners / Dictionary of handwriting / Why sleep / Mirror repair.

— below with help from **McENTIRE, JEB BISHOP + BOB WESTON**

Aug 95. (cd-s) *<19>* **HARP FACTORY ON LAKE STREET** -
<above issued on 'Table Of Elements'>

— now the pair had guests **TONY CONRAD + KEVIN DRUMM**

Dec 96. (d-lp/cd) *<DC 90/+CD>* **UPGRADE AND AFTERLIFE** Jun96
– Our exquisite replica of "eternity" / Rebecca Sylvester / Sea incertain / Hello spiral / Relay / Crappie tactics / Dry bones in the valley.

— the duo with past musicians

Domino Drag City

Feb 98. (cd/lp) *(WIG CD/LP 44) <DG 133>* **CAMOFLEUR** Jan98
– Seasons reverse / Blues subtitled no sense of wonder / Black horse / Each dream is an example / Mouth canyon / Puff dew / Bauchredner.

STABBING WESTWARD

Formed: Chicago, Illinois, USA . . . 1990 by CHRISTOPHER HALL and WALTER FLAKUS, who after the release of a self-financed EP, recruited JIM SELLERS and ANDY KUBISZEWSKI. Hard-hitting US alt-rock with base elements of tribal industrial hardcore held together by well-structured melodies, the STABBING WESTWARD sound first hit the shops courtesy of 'Columbia' late in '93. Aired live to British fans via a worthy half hour slot at that year's Reading Festival, the album in question, 'UNGOD', was sufficiently impressive to see the band hired to contribute towards the soundtracks of movies, 'The Cable Guy' and 'Escape From L.A.'. The band's growing reputation was consolidated with the release of follow-up set, 'WITHER, BLISTER, BURN & PEEL' (1996), which steadily headed northward up the US Top 100. Later that year, frontman HALL gave a full, er . . . frontal for the August edition of female top-shelf mag, 'Playgirl'. HALL and Co continued their.. er.. rise to fame with a third set, 'DARKEST DAYS' (1998), nearly poking the Top 50.

Album rating: UNGOD (*6) / WITHER, BLISTER, BURN & PEEL (*6) / DARKEST DAYS (*6)

CHRISTOPHER HALL – vocals, guitar / **WALTER FLAKUS** – keyboards / **JIM SELLERS** – bass / **ANDY KUBISZEWSKI** – drums

Columbia Columbia

May 94. (cd/c/lp) *(475735-2/-4/-1) <CK/CT+/53614>* **UNGOD** Dec93
– Lost / Control / Nothing / ACF / Lies / Ungod / Throw / Violent mood swings / Red on white / Can't happen here.

Sep 94. (12"/cd-s) *(660426-6/-2)* **NOTHING. /**

May 96. (cd/c) *(481580-2/-4) <66152>* **WITHER, BLISTER, BURN & PEEL** 67 Jan96
– I don't believe / Shame / What do I have to do? / Why / Inside you / Falls apart / So wrong / Crushing me / Sleep / Slipping away.

Apr 98. (cd/c) *<68006>* **DARKEST DAYS** - 52
– Darkest day / Everything I touch / How can I hold on / Drugstore / You complete me / Save yourself / Haunting me / Torn apart / Sometimes it hurts / Drowning / Desperate now / Goodbye / When I'm dead / The thing I hate / On your way down / Waking up beside you.

Jun 98. (cd-s) *<3277>* **SAVE YOURSELF / SAVE YOURSELF (longer)** -

Nov 98. (cd-s) *<41803>* **HAUNTING ME (versions)** -
<above from the movie, 'Faculty'>

Chris STAMEY

Born: 6 Dec'54, Chapel Hill, North Carolina, USA. Formerly a member of the RITTENHOUSE SQUARE in 1972 along with with future dB, PETER HOLSAPPLE, STAMEY subsequently founded The SNEAKERS with WILL RIGBY and GENE HOLDER. Following a move to New York in early '77, the singer released a solo single, 'SUMMER FUN' for Alex Chilton's 'Ork' imprint (STAMEY was also helping the former BIG STAR man with his current album project), before HOLSAPPLE, RIGBY, HOLDER and STAMEY adopted the dB's moniker (mid-'78). CHRIS was an integral part of The dB's prior to his departure in 1984, having already begun the process of carving out a respectable solo career for himself. A single, 'IN THE WINTER OF LOVE', preceded a full-length debut album, 'IT'S A WONDERFUL LIFE' (1983), proving that STAMEY's songwriting talent was valid in its own right. He continued to record sporadically throughout the 80's, most notably 1987's 'IT'S ALRIGHT', boasting a star-studded cast of friends including CHILTON, ANTON FIER, BERNIE WORRELL, MITCH EASTER, RICHARD LLOYD and JANE SCARPANTONI. The 90's got off to a relatively prolific start with a STAMEY solo set, 'FIREWORKS' (1991) and a collaborative reunion effort with HOLSAPPLE, 'MAVERICKS' (1991). Another combined effort, this time with KIRK RUSS, was released in 1995 as the snappily-titled, 'THE ROBUST BEAUTY OF IMPROPER LINEAR MODELS IN DECISION MAKING: COMPOSITIONS AND IMPROVISATIONS FOR GUITAR'.

Album rating: CHRISTMAS TIME (*5) / IT'S A WONDERFUL LIFE (*5) / IT'S ALRIGHT (*5) / FIREWORKS (*5)

CHRIS STAMEY – vocals, guitar (ex-SNEAKERS)

not iss. Ork

1977. (7") *<81982>* **SUMMER FUN. / WHERE THE FUN IS** -

— subsequently formed The dB's

Albion Palo Alto

Jun 83. (12") *(12ION 1045)* **IN THE WINTER OF LOVE. / IT'S A WONDERFUL LIFE** -

Jan 84. (lp) *(ALB 114) <PA 8022>* **IT'S A WONDERFUL LIFE** Nov83
– Winter of love / Never enters my mind / Get a job / Oh yeah / Brushfire in Hoboken / It's a wonderful life / Still life #3 / Depth of field / Face of the crowd.

— with **ALEX CHILTON, PETER HOLSAPPLE, WILL RIGBY, TED LYONS, WES LACHOT, GENE HOLDER, JODY STEPHENS, ALAN BEZOZI + JOHN HOWIE**

not iss. Twin/Tone-Coyote

1985. (7"ep) **INSTANT EXCITEMENT EP** -

1986. (lp) *<TTC 8564>* **CHRISTMAS TIME** -
– Christmas time / Christmas is the only time (I think . . .) / Sha la la / O holy night / The only law that Santa Claus understood / Jesus Christ / Silent nocturne / Holiday spirit / (I'm always touched by your) Presence dear / The snow is falling / Occasional shivers / You're what I want (for Christmas) / Santa's moonlight sleighride / Silver bells / I's a wonderful life / Feliz Vavidad.

— next also with a host of session men including; MITCH EASTER, ANTON FIER, RICHARD LLOYD, BERNIE WORRELL, ALEX CHILTON and JANE SCARPANTONI

not iss. A&M

Oct 87. (lp) *<SP 65180>* **IT'S ALRIGHT** -
– From the word go / When we're alone / The seduct / It'a alright / Of time and all she to mind / Big time / In the dark / If you hear my voice / 27 years in a single day / Incredible happiness.

Rhino Rhino

1991. (cd) *(98695-2)* **FIREWORKS**
– The company of light / Something came over me / Glorious delusion / Time is running out / Two places at once / Perfect time / The newlyweds / On the radio / All the heart's desire – Black orchids / Fireworks / The brakeman's consolation / I want you / You don't miss your water.

— In 1991, he collaborated with old mate PETER HOLSAPPLE on album 'MAVERICKS' for 'Rhino'. In 1995, CHRIS did another with KIRK RUSS; 'THE ROBUST BEAUTY OF IMPROPER LINEAR MODELS IN DECISION MAKING: COMPOSITIONS AND IMPROVISATIONS FOR GUITAR' for label 'ESD'.

S.O.L. not iss.

Apr 93. (7") *(SOL 250)* **ALIVE. /** -

STANFORD PRISON EXPERIMENT

Formed: Los Angeles, California, USA . . . early 90's by MARIO JIMINEZ, MIKE STARKEY, MARK FRASER and DAVEY LATTER. Taking their moniker from an infamous 70's experiment gone-wrong at California's Stanford College (wherein students took on the opposing roles of Warders and Prisoners in a mock-up jail scenario), this uncompromising quartet set out to expose societal indoctrination via a basic but intense hardcore assault. Signed to the 'World Domination' imprint, they unleashed their inaugural single, 'MR. TEACHER DAD', in Spring 1994, preceding an eponymous album the following month. In '95, SPE were back to terrorise the establishment with a second set of fierce, no holds barred (oops! sorry) jailhouse rock, 'THE GATO HUNCH'. Of late, the band seem to have gone AWOL.

Album rating: STANFORD PRISON EXPERIMENT (*5) / THE GATO HUNCH (*6)

MARIO JIMINEZ – vocals / **MIKE STARKEY** – guitar, vocals / **MARK FRASER** – bass / **DAVEY LATTER** – drums

World Domination World Domination

May 94. (7") *<(WDOM 008S)>* **MR. TEACHER DAD. / OPEY OF THE MASSES**

Jun 94. (cd) *<(WDOM 009CD)>* **STANFORD PRISON EXPERIMENT**
– Disbelief / Take it / Written apology / Supermonkey / Get on / Course / What's an epidemic / Mr. Teacher dad / It's expected I'm gone / Frozen / Sheepshit / Rob hates.

Oct 94. (7") **SUPERMONKEY. /**

— In July '95, their track, 'YOU'RE THE VULGARIAN', featured on the B-side of a QUICKSAND single for 'Island Red' (IR 107)

Sep 95. (cd) *<(WDOM 020CD)>* **THE GATO HUNCH**
– You're the vulgarian / Repeat removal / (Very) Put out / Cansado / Flap / So far, so good / El nuevo / Accomplice / Harcord idiot / Swoon / Worst case scenario.

— escaped from the music biz after above

STARJETS (see under ⇒ ADVENTURES)

STATE OF PLAY (see under ⇒ CURVE)

STEEL POLE BATH TUB

Formed: Bozeman, Montana, USA . . . late 80's by DALE FLATTUM, MIKE MORASKY and DARREN MOR-X (former MR EPP, an outfit which also featured future MUDHONEY members, MARK ARM and STEVE TURNER). Relocating to San Francisco, they signed to 'Tupelo', where they set about causing maximum aural damage with their particularly twisted brand of industrial grunge-metal, calling up the damned soul of BLACK SABBATH and The STOOGES via the latter day sonic terrorism of MINISTRY. In 1989, SPBT delivered their debut album, 'BUTTERFLY LOVE', although it would the following years' MELVINS collaboration, 'SWEET YOUNG THING' (borrowed from old muckers, MUDHONEY) that would bring them more exposure in the emerging Seattle grunge scene. Around the same time, the lads issued their follow-up set, 'LURCH', which featured an industrial strength remake of 'HEY BO DIDDLEY'. Their busiest year to date, 1991, saw STEEL POLE BATH TUB release another long-player, 'TULIP', while collaborating with fellow SF resident and former DEAD KENNEDYS frontman, JELLO BIAFRA, on the TUMOUR CIRCUS project. Two further SPBT sets, 'THE MIRACLE OF SOUND IN MOTION' (1993) and 'SOME COCKTAIL SUGGESTIONS' (1994), preceded a major label deal with 'Slash'. Although the band had cleaned up their act somewhat, 'SCARS FROM FALLING DOWN' (1995), their slightly watered down sound disappeared through the proverbial corporate plughole. • **Covered:** CHEMICAL WARFARE (Dead Kennedys) / THE GHOST (Willie Nelson).

Album rating: BUTTERFLY LOVE (*6) / LURCH (*6) / TULIP (*6) / THE MIRACLE OF SOUND IN MOTION (*5) / SOME COCKTAIL SUGGESTIONS (*5) / SCARS FROM FALLING DOWN (*5)

DALE FLATTUM – vocals, bass / **MIKE MORASKY** – guitar, vocals / **DARREN MOR-X** – drums

		Tupelo	Tupelo
1989.	(lp) **BUTTERFLY LOVE**	-	
Jul 90.	(7") **SWEET YOUNG THING (w/ MELVINS) /**		
Jul 90.	(cd/lp) <*(TUP CD/LP 15)*> **LURCH**		

– Christine / Hey you / Paranoid / I am Sam I am / Bee sting / Swerve / Heaven on dirt / Lime away / The river / Time to die / Welcome aboard it's love / Hey Bo Diddley / Thru the windshields of love / Tear it apart.

Feb 91.	(cd/lp) <*(TUP CD/LP 27)*> **TULIP**		

– Soul cannon / Sister / Quark / One thick second / Pirate 5 / Mercurochrome / Wonders of dust / The scarlet / Misty Mt. Blowtorch / Myrna Loy / Pause.

May 92.	(7"/cd-s) **BOZEMAN. / BORSTAL**		
Apr 93.	(cd/lp) >*(TUP 47-2/-1)*> **THE MIRACLE OF SOUND IN MOTION**		

– Pseudoephendrine hydrochloride / Train to Miami / Exhale / Thumbnail / Down all the days / Cartoon / Bozeman / Borstal / 594 / Waxl.

Jan 94.	(m-cd/m-c/m-10"lp) <*(TUP 051-2/-4/-1)*> **SOME COCKTAIL SUGGESTIONS**		

– Ray / Living end / Slip / Hit it / Speaker phone / Wasp jar.

		Slash	Slash
Jan 96.	(cd/c) <*(828 685-2/-4)*> **SCARS FROM FALLING DOWN**		Nov95

– 500 club / Population / Home is a rope / Conversation / Twist / Everything / 3 of cups / Four barrels / Decline / Kansas City / Friday.

– compilations, etc. –

1992.	(lp) *Your Choice;* <*(YCR 015)*> **LIVE**		
Jul 94.	(cd) *Your Choice;* <*(YCLS 019)*> **LIVE (live)**		

Martin STEPHENSON

Born: 1965, Durham, England. STEPHENSON began his musical career in 1983 with busking outfit, The DAINTEES. Signed to the local 'Kitchenware' label by boss Keith Armstrong, the band – who at this point were a trio completed by JOHN STEEL and ANTHONY DUNN – made their vinyl debut at Christmas '83 with the sublime (and hopefully titled!) 'ROLL ON SUMMERTIME'. This was followed with the 'TROUBLE TOWN' single and the 'INFERNO' EP before the band recruited a drummer, PAUL SMITH, to anchor the sound and embarked upon recording a debut album, 'BOAT TO BOLIVIA' (1986). Rootsy pop wearing its heart on its sleeve and infused with folk, country and blues, the record saw STEPHENSON draw comparisons with such vintage acoustic balladeers as LEONARD COHEN and AL STEWART. Glowing reviews and a swelling grassroots following – due in no small part to the man's sterling live performances – saw the album graze the lower end of the UK chart. Embellished with violin, flute, dobro etc. courtesy of a sizeable cast of musicians, 1988's 'GLADSOME, HUMOUR & BLUE' was again acclaimed and gave STEPHENSON his first Top 40 hit. As might be expected for a folk singer from the North East, his work had always been at least partly concerned with the plight of the downtrodden and dispossessed and 'SALUTATION ROAD' (1990) contained some of his most openly political statements to date including 'LEFT US TO BURN' (an anti-Thatcher broadside) and 'MIGRANTS'. While not exactly crossing over to a mainstream audience, the album (part of a licensing deal with 'London') proved his most successful to date. The 90's have seen his profile dip somewhat, STEPHENSON roping in punk stalwart, PAULINE MURRAY and FATIMA MANSIONS man, CATHAL COUGHLAN, for 'THE BOY'S HEART' (1992). A best of compilation and previously recorded set, 'HIGH BELLS RING THIN' (1993) wrapped things up with 'Kitchenware' and the man moved to re-issue specialist, 'Demon', for 1995's 'YOGI IN MY HOUSE'. • **Covered:** HIGH COIN (Van Dyke Parks) / LET'S CALL THE WHOLE THING OFF (Ira & George Gershwin) / etc.

Album rating: BOAT TO BOLIVIA (*8) / THERE COMES A TIME (*6)

DAINTEES

MARTIN STEPHENSON – vocals, acoustic guitar / **JOHN STEEL** – piano, organ / **ANTHONY DUNN** – bass

		Kitchenware	not iss.
Dec 83.	(7") *(SK 3)* **ROLL ON SUMMERTIME. / INVOLVED WITH LOVE**		-
Sep 84.	(7") *(SK 13)* **TROUBLE TOWN. / BETTER PLAN**		-

(12"+=) *(SKX 13)* – Jealous mind.
(above re-iss. Jan87 with free ltd.c-s 'DAINTEES LIVE' hit No.58) – Running waters / Crocodile cryer / Boat to Bolivia / Tremelo man.

May 86.	(7"ep) *(SKEP 1)* **INFERNO EP**		-

– Running water / Look down, look down (live) / Synergy.

MARTIN STEPHENSON & THE DAINTEES

— added guest **PAUL SMITH** – drums, percussion

		Kitchenware – London	Capitol
May 86.	(lp/c) *(KWLP/KWC 5)* **BOAT TO BOLIVIA**	85	-

– Crocodile cryer / Coleen / Little red bottle / Tribute to the late Reverand Gary Davis / Running water / Candle in the middle / Piece of the cake / Look down, look down / Slow lovin' / Caroline / Rain. *(re-iss. Mar87; same c+=)* – Boat to Bolivia. *(cd+=; 828045-2)* – Slaughterman / Wholly humble heart.

Jun 86.	(7") *(SK 25)* **CROCODILE CRYER. / LOUIS (acoustic version)**		-

(12") *(SKX 25)* – ('A'full version) / ('B'live version).

Aug 86.	(7") *(SK 26)* **SLOW LOVIN'. / TRIBUTE TO THE LATE REVERAND GARY DAVIS**		-

(12"+=) *(SKX 26)* – Smile on the summertime / Look down, look down (live).

Oct 86.	(7") *(SK 27)* **BOAT TO BOLIVIA. / SLAUGHTERMAN**	70	-

(12"+=) *(SKX 27)* – Wholly humble heart.
(d12"+=) *(SKXD 27)* – Crocodile cryer (full version) / Louis (live).

— **MICK WATSON** – keyboards, percussion, sax, string arr. repl. STEEL / added **GYPSY DAVE SMITH** – dobro guitar / **GARY DUNN** – lead + rhythm guitars Guests inc. **VIRGINIA ASTLEY** – flute / **ANNE STEPHENSON** – violin / **CAROLINE LAVELLE** – cello / **CAROLINE BARNES** – violin / **FAY EVANS** – viola / **D.BREWIS** – guitar, keyboards / **SHEILA & SHERYL PARKER** – backing vocals

Apr 88.	(lp/c)(cd) *(KWLP/KWC 8)(828091-2)* <*91751*> **GLADSOME, HUMOUR AND BLUE**	39	

– There comes a time / Slaughterman / The wait / I can see / The old church is still standing / Even the night / Wholly humble heart / Me and Matthew / Nancy / Goodbye John / I pray.

Jun 88.	(7") *(SK 36)* **WHOLLY HUMBLE HEART. / GET GET GONE**		-

(12"+=) *(SKX 36)* – Come back to me.
(12"+=/cd-s+=) *(SK XR/CD 36)* – I can see (live) / Slow lovin' (live).

Oct 88.	(7") *(SK 34)* **THERE COMES A TIME. / RUNNING WATER**		

(12"+=) *(SKX 34)* – Little red bottle (live) / Coleen (live).
(12"+=) *(SKXR 34)* – Crocodile cryer (live) / Coleen (live).

— **MARTIN** retains **ANTHONY, GARY + MICK** (now bass), plus guests **ANDREA MACKIE** – vocals / **PETE ANDERSON** – producer, guitar, sitar / **JEFF DONOVAN** – **SKIP EDWARDS** – keyboards, organ / **LARRY KNIGHT** – guitar / **LENNY CASTRO** – perc. / **DUSTY WAKEMAN** – bass / **DON REED** – viola / **LEE THORNBERG** – trumpet / **LEN PRICE** – sax / **GREG SMITH** – baritone sax / **BEVERLEY DAHLHE SMITH** – flute / **STEVE GROVE** – tenor sax / **FREEBO** – tuba / **DONNIE GERRARD, SHAUN MURPHY, LAURA CREAMER** – backing vocals

Apr 90.	(7"/c-s) *(SK/+TC 44)* **LEFT US TO BURN. / BIG NORTH LIGHTS**		-

(12"+=/cd-s+=) *(SK X/CD 44)* – Eyot / Kathy (live).

May 90.	(cd/c/lp) *(828198-2/-4/-1)* <*94638*> **SALUTATION ROAD**	35	

– Left us to burn / Endurance / In the heat of the night / Big north lights / Long hard road / Spoke in the weel / Heart of the city / Too much in love / We are storm / Migrants / Morning time / Salutation road.

Jun 90.	(7"/c-s) *(SK 46/+TC)* **ENDURANCE. / MEN CAN BE FLUNG**		-

(12"+=/cd-s+=) *(12SK/SKCD 46)* – Release the first.

— **PAUL SMITH** – drums returned adding also to The **DUNN's; BRENDAN HEALEY** – piano / **FRANKIE GIBBON** – organ, b.vocals / **PAULINE MURRAY, FRED PURSER** (both ex-PENETRATION) and **CATHAL COUGHAN** (of FATIMA MANSIONS) – backing vocals

Jun 92.	(7"/c-s) *(SK/+TC 57)* **BIG SKY NEW LIGHT. / SONG ABOUT THE MEMBER / WAKE ME IN THE MORNING**	71	-

(cd-s) *(SKCD1 57)* – ('A'side) / You really had a heart / Peace of mind / Let's call the whole thing off.
(cd-s) *(SKCD2 57)* – ('A'side) / Far away meadows / Should my friends be gone / Every night.

Jul 92.	(cd/c/lp) *(828324-2/-4/-1)* **THE BOY'S HEART**	68	-

– Big sky new light / The boy's heart / We can roll / Ballad of the English rose / Neon skies / Hollywood fields / Sentimental journey / Sunday halo / 8.30 Mowbray morning / (Least we're a) Map in the world / Him, her and the Moon / Cab attack.

Mar 93.	(cd/c) *(828398-2/-4)* **THERE COMES A TIME – THE BEST OF MARTIN STEPHENSON & THE DAINTEES** (compilation)		-
Apr 93.	(cd/c) *(KWCD/KWC 23)* **HIGH BELLS RING THIN** (rec.1990)		-

– You really had a heart / Looking for some peace of mind / Song about the member / Should my friends be gone / Don't be afraid of the night / Far away meadows / Synergy / Wake me in the morning / I like in the east / Him, her and the Moon / Every night / Music and life / Let's call the whole thing off.

MARTIN STEPHENSON

Demon Demon

Feb 95. (cd) *(<FIENDCD 762>)* **YOGI IN MY HOUSE** [ ] [ ] Oct95
– Solomon / In fire / Take on the globe / Think only of the child / New wave / Spirit child / Bridge of nae hope / Fair company / Gone the gipsy Davey / Always us / Dance the last goodbye.

—— now featured **JOE GUILLEN** – guitar

Oct 95. (cd) *(<FIENDCD 770>)* **SWEET MISDEMEANOUR (THE BEST OF MARTIN STEPHENSON & THE DAINTEES)** (compilation) [ ] [ ]
– Maverick waltz / Can't find the door-knob / Sweet misdemeanour / Candyman / I could never be happy / Rag time groove / Dream of you / South wind / Tremolo man / Talking to the child / Kep this time / Ball of fire / Hold me love me / Smokey mokes.
(above also featured several covers)

Nov 97. (cd) *(<FIENDCD 938>)* **BEYOND THE LEAP, BEYOND THE LAW** [ ] [ ]
– Losing all part of the team / Testing time / Great star of fraternity / Wholly humble heart / Carry my friend / Crying / Song of love and desertion / Great spirit / Out of communion / Waves / Hollow days / Indian summer.

STEREOLAB

Formed: South London, England . . . late 1990, by ex-indie stalwart TIM GANE (mainman for McCARTHY), who invited girlfriend LAETITIA SADIER to join. They soon completed the initial line-up with MARTIN KEAN and JOE DILWORTH (other past indie veterans), subsequently forming their own label, 'Duophonic Super 45s'. The group released three 45's ('SUPER 45', 'SUPER ELECTRIC' & 'STUNNING DEBUT ALBUM') in 1991, the second of which was for the 'Too Pure' label (these have re-instated vinyl as worthy product, whether for limited edition collectors or just vinyl junkies who hate cd's). The following year, the eclectic ambient-boogie machine that was STEREOLAB topped the indie charts with their actual "stunning debut album", 'PENG!'. The record ran the gamut of the band's minimalist influences including VELVET UNDERGROUND, JOHN CAGE, NEU! and SPACEMEN 3. During this period, the couple introduced four new members; MARY HANSEN, SEAN O'HAGAN, DUNCAN BROWN and ANDY RAMSAY, who helped them with a busy touring schedule. In 1993, they signed to 'Elektra' in the States for a 6 figure-sum, while in the UK, they released several more 45's! and an album, 'TRANSIENT RANDOM NOISE BURSTS WITH ANNOUNCEMENTS', which, like the classy single, 'JENNY ONDIOLINE', scraped into the UK charts (the track was premiered on Channel 4's "The Word" programme). 1994 saw them unsurprisingly hit the UK Top 20 with another double album, 'MARS AUDIAC QUINTET'. Two years later, with their best offering to date, 'EMPEROR TOMATO KETCHUP', they had established themselves as leaders of the "Metronomic Underground" scene, as the opening track suggested. Over the course of the last three years, the band's sound had become increasingly characterised by the dreamy French-style vocals of LAETITIA (pronounced Le-ti-seaya), akin to a spacier SARAH CRACKNELL (of SAINT ETIENNE). • **Songwriters:** GANE songs / SADIER lyrics.

Album rating: PENG! (*7) / TRANSIENT RANDOM . . . (*8) / MUSIC FOR THE AMORPHOUS BODY STUDY CENTER (*8) / MARS AUDIO QUINTET (*8) / EMPEROR TOMATO KETCHUP (*9)

TIM GANE (b. 1966) – guitar, vox organ, guitar (ex-McCARTHY) / **LAETITIA SADIER** (b. 1968, Paris, France) – vocals, vox organ, guitar, tambourine, moog / **REBECCA MORRIS** – vocals / **JOE DILWORTH** – drums (of TH' FAITH HEALERS)

Duophonic not iss.

May 91. (10"ep-mail order) *(DS45-01)* **SUPER 45** [ ] [-]
– The light (that will cease to fail) / Au grand jour / Brittle / Au grand jour!.

—— added **MARTIN KEAN** (b.New Zealand) – guitar (ex-CHILLS) / **RUSSELL YATES** – live guitar (of MOOSE). **MICK CONROY** (ex-MOOSE) was also a live member early '92.

Nov 91. (7"clear,7"colrd) *(DS45-02)* **STUNNING DEBUT ALBUM: Doubt / Changer** [ ] [-]

Too Pure Slumberland

Sep 91. (10"ep) *(PURE 4)* **SUPERELECTRIC / HIGH EXPECTATION. / THE WAY WILL BE OPENING / CONTACT** [ ] [-]

Apr 92. (cd-ltd.) *(31022)* *<Slumberland 22>* **SWITCHED ON** (compilation) [ ] [ ]
– Superelectric / Doubt / Au grand jour / The way will be opening / Brittle / Contract / Au grand jour / High expectation / The light that will cease to fail / Changer. *(re-iss. Mar97 on 'Dupophonic' cd/lp; TBC 25/24)*

—— GINA departed after above. (when did she join?)

Too Pure American

May 92. (cd,c,lp) *(PURE 11)* *<43018>* **PENG!** [ ] [ ]
– Super falling star / Orgiastic / Peng! 33 / K-stars / Perversion / You little shits / The seeming and the meaning / Mellotron / Enivrez-vous / Stomach worm / Surrealchemist.

—— added **MARY HANSEN** – vocals, tambourine, guitar / **ANDY RAMSAY** – percussion, vox organ, bazouki repl. DILWORTH

Sep 92. (10"ep,10"clear-ep,cd-ep) *(PURE 14)* **LOW FI** [ ] [-]
– Et de votre coeur endormi / (Varoom!) / Laisser-faire / Elektro – He held the world in his iron grip.

—— added **SEAN O'HAGAN** – vox organ, guitar (ex-MICRODISNEY, ex-HIGH LLAMAS)

Feb 93. (7",7"pink) *<Slumberland 24>* **JOHN CAGE BUBBLEGUM. / ELOGE D'EROS** [-] [ ]

—— added **DUNCAN BROWN** – bass, guitar, vocals

Mar 93. (cd,c,m-lp) *(PURE 19)* *<43013>* **THE GROOP PLAYED "SPACE AGE BACHELOR PAD MUSIC"** [ ] [ ]
– Avant-garde M.O.R. / Space age bachelor pad music (mellow) / The groop play chord X / Space age bachelor pad music (foamy) / Ronco symphony / We're not adult orientated / UHF-MFP / We're not adult orientated (new wave live).

Duophonic Elektra

Aug 93. (10"ep/cd-ep) *(DUHF D/CD 01)* *<8815>* **JENNY ONDIOLINE / FRUCTION / GOLDEN BALL / FRENCH DISCO** [75] [ ]

Sep 93. (cd/c/2xlp) *(DUHF CD/DMC/D 02)* *<61536>* **TRANSIENT RANDOM-NOISE BURSTS WITH ANNOUNCEMENTS** [62] [ ]
– Tone burst / Our trinitone blast / Pack yr romantic mind / I'm going out of my way / Golden ball / Pause / Jenny Ondioline / Analogue rock / Crest / Lock-groove lullaby.

Nov 93. (7") *(DUHF D01P)* **FRENCH DISKO (new version). / JENNY ONDIOLINE** [ ] [-]

—— added **KATHERINE GIFFORD** – synthesizers, keyboards

Jul 94. (7"ltd) *(DUHFD 04S)* **PING PONG. / MOOGIE WONDERLAND** [45] [-]
(10"+=/cd-s+=) *(DUHF D/CD 04)* – Pain et spectacles / Transcoma (live).

Aug 94. (cd/c/d-lp) *(DUHF CD/MC/D 05)* *<61669>* **MARS AUDIAC QUINTET** [16] [ ]
– Three-dee melodie / Wow and flutter / Transona five / Des etoiles electroniques / Ping pong / Anamorphose / Three longers later / Nihilist assault group / International colouring contest / The stars of our destination / Transporte sans bouger / L'enfer des formes / Outer accelerator / New orthophony / Fiery yellow. *(free clear-7" w /d-lp + cd-s on cd) (DUHF D/CD 05X)* – Klang-tang / Ulaan batter.

Oct 94. (7"ltd) *(DUHFD 07S)* **WOW AND FLUTTER. / HEAVY DENIM** [70] [-]
(10"+=/cd-s+=) *(DUHF D/CD 07)* – Nihilist assault group / Narco Martenot.

Apr 95. (10"ep/cd-ep) *(DUHF D/CD 08)* **AMORPHOUS BODY STUDY CENTRE** [59] [-]
– Pop quiz / The extension trip / How to explain your internal organs overnight / The brush descends the length / Melochord seventy five / Space moment.

Sep 95. (cd/c/colrd-d-lp) *(DUHF CD/MC/D 09) / Drag City; <DC 82>* **REFRIED ECTOPLASM (SWITCHED ON – VOLUME II)** (compilation) [30] [ ]
– Harmonium / Lo boob oscillator / Mountain / Revox / French disko / Exploding head movie / Eloge d'eros / Tone burst (country) / Animal or vegetable (a wonderful wooden reason) / John Cage bubblegum / Sadistic / Farfisa / Tempter.

—— **GANE / SADIER / HANSEN / RAMSAY + BROWN** added **MORGANE LHOTE** (guests; SEAN O'HAGAN / JOHN McINTYRE (of TORTOISE) + RAY DICKARTY)

Feb 96. (7") *(DUHFD 10S)* **CYBELE'S REVERIE. / BRIGITTE** [62] [-]
(10"+=/cd-s+=) *(DUHF D/CD 10)* – Les yper yper sound / Young lungs.

Mar 96. (d-lp/c/cd) *(DUHF D/MC/CD 11)* *<61640>* **EMPEROR TOMATO KETCHUP** [27] [ ] Apr96
– Metronomic underground / Cybele's reverie / Percolator / Les ypersound / Spark plug / Olv 26 / The noise of carpet / Tomorrow is already here / Emperor tomato ketchup / Monstre sacre / Motoroller scalatron / Slow fast Hazel / Anonymous collective.

Apr 96. (12"ltd.) *(DS 3311)* **SIMPLE HEADPHONE MIND. / (other track by NURSE WITH WOUND)** [ ] [-]
(re-iss. Jun97; same)

—— now without BROWN, who was repl. by **RICHARD HARRISON**

Sep 96. (7";on 'Lissys') *(LISS 15)* **SHE USED TO CALL ME SADNESS. /** [ ] [-]

Nov 96. (7"ep)(12"ep/cd-ep) *(DUHFD 14S)(DUHF D/CD 14)* **FLUORESCENCES EP** [ ] [-]
– Fluorescences / Pinball / You used to call me sadness / Soop groove *2.

Dec 96. (12"; STEREOLAB & WAGON CHRIST) *(DUHFD 15)* **METROGNOMIC UNDERGROUND. /** [ ] [-]

Sep 97. (7") *(DUHFD 16S)* **MISS MODULAR. / ALLURES** [60] [-]
(12"+=/cd-s+=) *(DUHF D/CD 16)* – Off-on / Spinal column.

Sep 97. (cd/c/d-lp) *(DUHF CD/C/D 17)* *<62065>* **DOTS AND LOOPS** [19] [ ]
– Brakhage / Miss Modular / The flower called Nowhere / Prisoner of Mars / Rainbo conversation / Refractions in the plastic pulse / Parsec / Ticker-tape of the unconscious / Contronatura.

– more very limited singles, etc. –

Jun 92. (7"pink) *B.M.I.; (BMI 025)* **THE LIGHT (THAT WILL CEASE TO FAIL). / AU GRAND JOUR** [ ] [-]

Jul 92. (7"colrd) *Duophonic; (DS45-04)* **HARMONIUM. / FARFISA** [ ] [-]

Oct 93. (10"ep) *Clawfist; (Clawfist 20)* **CRUMB DUCK (with NURSE WITH WOUND)** [ ] [-]
– Animal or vegetable / Exploding head movie.

Oct 93. (7"clear) *Sub Pop; (<SP 107/283>)* **LE BOOB OSCILLATOR. / TEMPTER** [ ] [ ]

Nov 93. (7") *Teenbeat; <Teenbeat 121>* **MOUNTAIN. / ('B'by Unrest)** [-] [ ]

Oct 98. (d-cd/d-lp) *<DC 159>* **ALUMINIUM TUNES: SWITCHED ON VOL.3** [-] [ ]
– Pop quiz – The extension trip / How to play your internal organs / Brush descends the length / Melochord seventy-five / Space moment / Speedy car / Golden atoms / Olan bator / One small step / Iron man / Long hair of death / You used to call me sadness / New orthophony / One note samba – Surfboard / Cadriopo / Klang tone / Get Carter / 1000 miles an hour / Percolations / Seeperbold / Check and double check / Munich madness / Metronumro underground / Incredible He-woman.

STEREOPHONICS

Formed: Cwmaman, South Wales . . . late 80's as The TRAGIC LOVE COMPANY by songwriter KELLY JONES, RICHARD JONES and STUART CABLE, initially treading the boards as a teenage covers band. The trio proved they were more than capable of spearheading Richard Branson's new 'V2' label with the release of debut single, 'LOOKS LIKE CHAPLIN', a melodic riffathon that had more in common with trad 70's rock and Seattle grunge than the still dominant Britpop. A Spring '97 follow-up, 'LOCAL BOY IN THE PHOTOGRAPH', came within breathing distance of the Top 50, a dizzying amalgam of the MANICS, RADIOHEAD, OASIS and BUFFALO TOM that managed to sound simultaneously contemporary and classic. JONES confirmed his newfound status as one of Britain's most promising young songwriters as The STEREOPHONICS embarked on an impressive chart run with the Top 40-breaking 'MORE LIFE IN A TRAMP'S VEST'. Late summer saw them nudge closer to the Top 20 with 'A THOUSAND TREES', the opening track on debut album, 'WORD GETS AROUND'. A massive selling UK Top 10 success, the record featured in the upper reaches of many end-of-year polls, helping to net the band a Brit Award (Best New Group) in early '98. Having seen out '97 with the moody magnificence of 'TRAFFIC', JONES and Co began the new year with a Top 20 reissue of 'LOCAL BOY' prior to a summer of heavy touring. Towards Christmas, The STEREOPHONICS became a household name with Top 3 hit, 'THE BARTENDER & THE THIEF', proving that despite the continued predictions of its imminent demise, good old fashioned guitar-rock and solid songwriting was alive and well in Wales.

Album rating: WORD GETS AROUND (*7)

KELLY JONES – vocals, guitar / **RICHARD JONES** – bass / **STUART CABLE** – drums

V2 V2

Nov 96. (7") *(SPH 1)* **LOOKS LIKE CHAPLIN. / MORE LIFE IN A TRAMP'S VEST** [ ] [-]
(cd-s+=) *(SPHD 1)* –

Mar 97. (7") *(SPH 2)* **LOCAL BOY IN THE PHOTOGRAPH. / TWO SANDWICHES** [51] [ ]
(cd-s+=) *(SPHD 2)* – Buy myself a small plane.

May 97. (7") *(SPH 4)* **MORE LIFE IN A TRAMP'S VEST. / RAYMOND'S SHOP** [33] [-]
(cd-s+=) *(SPHD 4)* – Poppy day.
(cd-s) *(SPHDX 4)* – ('A'side) / Looks like Chaplin (live) / Too many sandwiches (live) / Last of the big time drinkers (live).

Aug 97. (7"/c-s) *(VVR 500044-7/-5)* **A THOUSAND TREES. / CARROT CAKE AND WINE** [22] [-]
(cd-s+=) *(VVR 500044-3)* – ('A'live).
(cd-s) *(VVR 500044-8)* – ('A'acoustic) / Home to me (acoustic) / Looks like Chaplin (acoustic) / Summertime (acoustic).

Aug 97. (cd/c/lp) *(VVR 100043-2/-4/-1) <27006>* **WORD GETS AROUND** [6] [ ]
– A thousand trees / Looks like Chaplin / More life in a tramps vest / Local boy in the photograph / Traffic / Not up to you / Check my eyelids for holes / Same size feet / Last of the big time drinkers / Goldfish bowl / Too many sandwiches / Billy Daveys daughter.

Nov 97. (7"/c-s) *(VVR 500094-7/-5)* **TRAFFIC. / TIE ME UP TIE ME DOWN** [20] [-]
(cd-s+=) *(VVR 500094-3)* – Chris Chambers.
(cd-s) *(VVR 500094-8)* – ('A'side) / More life in a tramps vest (live) / A thousand trees (live) / Local boy in the photograph (live).

Feb 98. (7"/c-s) *(VVR 500126-7/-5)* **LOCAL BOY IN THE PHOTOGRAPH / WHO'LL STOP THE RAIN** [14] [-]
(cd-s+=) *(VVR 500126-3)* – Check my eyelids for holes / ('A'-CD-rom video).
(cd-s) *(VVR 500126-8)* – ('A'side) / Not up to you (live in session) / The last resort / Traffic (CD-rom video live).

Nov 98. (7"/c-s) *(VVR 500467-7/-5)* **THE BARTENDER AND THE THIEF. / SHE TAKES HER CLOTHES OFF** [3] [-]
(cd-s+=) *(VVR 500465-3)* – Fiddler's green.
(cd-s) *(VVR 500466-3)* – ('A'side) / Traffic (live) / Raymonds shop (live).

ST. ETIENNE (see under ⇒ SAINT ETIENNE)

Mark STEWART (see under ⇒ POP GROUP)

STIFF LITTLE FINGERS

Formed: Belfast, N.Ireland . . . 1977 by teenagers JAKE BURNS, HENRY CLUNEY, ALI McMORDIE and GORDON BLAIR, the latter soon being replaced by BRIAN FALOON. Famously taking their name from a line in a VIBRATORS' b-side, the group began life as a CLASH covers band. Taken under the wing of journalist, GORDON OGILVIE (who subsequently became both band manager and BURNS' writing partner), the group began to rely on original material, releasing their incendiary 1978 debut single, 'SUSPECT DEVICE'. / 'WASTED LIFE' on the self-financed 'Rigid Digits' label. Wound tight, both lyrically and musically, with the frustration and anger of living in war-torn Belfast, the record introduced SLF as one of the most visceral and compelling punk bands since The SEX PISTOLS. Championed by the ever vigilant John Peel, the single led to a deal with 'Rough Trade' who jointly released a follow-up single, 'ALTERNATIVE ULSTER', the track rapidly assuming legendary status, although it was originally penned for release as a magazine flexi-disc. A debut album, 'INFLAMMABLE MATERIAL', followed in early '79, a raging, politically barbed howl of punk protest which lined up all the aforementioned tracks alongside such definitive SLF material as 'STATE OF EMERGENCY' and 'JOHNNY WAS'. Storming into the Top 20, the album expanded their already voracious fanbase, the group undertaking their first major headlining tour to promote it. The insistent, bass-heavy pop-punk dynamics of 'GOTTA GETAWAY' marked the debut of JIM REILLY (replacing the departing FALOON on the drum stool) and no doubt fuelled a thousand teenage runaway fantasies while the vicious 'STRAW DOGS' marked the group's major label debut for 'Chrysalis'. Early the following year, SLF scored their sole Top 20 hit with 'AT THE EDGE', another seething account of BURNS' troubled youth in Northern Ireland and arguably one of the group's finest moments. 'NOBODY'S HEROES' (1980) saw a move towards a more varied musical palate and a distinctly melodic feel, notably on the title track although 'TIN SOLDIERS' was as brutal as ever. The seminal live album, 'HANX!' (1980) gave the band their only Top 10 success later that year, surprising given the band's increasingly commercial approach as witnessed on the infectious 'JUST FADE AWAY' (possibly the only song ever written about a woman harassing a man!). A centerpiece of the 'GO FOR IT' (1981) set, the single stood in stark contrast to the insipid cod-reggae that so many punk bands, SLF unfortunately included, were now falling back on. 'NOW THEN' (1982) was an uncomfortable attempt to branch out even further into uncharted pop/rock territory, BURNS' leaving soon after to form JAKE BURNS & THE BIG WHEEL. This effectively spelled the end for the band, and after a farewell tour, they called it a day. The live demand for SLF was so strong, however, that they were able to regroup in 1987, new material eventually surfacing in 1991 following the replacement of the disillusioned McMORDIE with ex-JAM bassist BRUCE FOXTON. The album in question, 'FLAGS AND EMBLEMS', hardly set the rock world alight, gigs predictably characterised by diehard fans shouting for old favourites. 'GET A LIFE' (1994) was similarly formualaic and, without being precious, one can't help but wonder how such a vital, influential band are now reduced to basically retreading past glories for a greying audience. • **Songwriters:** BURNS penned, some with OGILVIE. They also covered JOHNNY WAS (Bob Marley) / RUNNING BEAR (Johnny Preston) / WHITE CHRISTMAS (Bing Crosby) / LOVE OF THE COMMON PEOPLE (Nicky Thomas) / THE MESSAGE (Grandmaster Flash). • **Trivia:** JAKE once applied for a job of a Radio 1 producer.

Album rating: INFLAMMABLE MATERIAL (*9) / NOBODY'S HEROES (*8) / ALL THE BEST compilation (*8)

JAKE BURNS – vocals, lead guitar / **HENRY CLUNEY** – guitar / **ALI McMORDIE** – bass / **BRIAN FALOON** – drums repl. GORDON BLAIR who later joined RUDI

Rigid Digits not iss.

Mar 78. (7") *(SRD-1)* **SUSPECT DEVICE. / WASTED LIFE** [ ] [-]
(re-iss. Jun78) (re-iss. Mar79 on 'Rough Trade'; RT 006)

Rough Trade not iss.

Oct 78. (7") *(RT 004)* **ALTERNATIVE ULSTER. / '78 R.P.M.** [ ] [-]

Feb 79. (lp) *(ROUGH 1)* **INFLAMMABLE MATERIAL** [14] [-]
– Suspect device / State of emergency / Here we are nowhere / Wasted life / No more of that / Barbed wire love / White noise / Breakout / Law and order / Rough trade / Johnny was / Alternative Ulster / Closed groove. *(re-iss. Mar89 on 'E.M.I.' lp/c(cd); EMC/TC-EMC 3554)(CDP 792105-2) <US cd-iss. 1992 on 'Restless'; 72363>*

— **JIM REILLY** – drums repl. FALOON

May 79. (7") *(RT 015)* **GOTTA GETAWAY. / BLOODY SUNDAY** [ ] [-]

Chrysalis Chrysalis

Sep 79. (7") *(CHS 2368)* **STRAW DOGS. / YOU CAN'T SAY CRAP ON THE RADIO** [44] [-]

Feb 80. (7") *(CHS 2406)* **AT THE EDGE. / SILLY ENCORES: RUNNING BEAR – WHITE CHRISTMAS** [15] [-]

Mar 80. (lp/c) *(CHR/ZCHR 1270)* **NOBODY'S HEROES** [8] [ ]
– Gotta getaway / Wait and see / Fly the flag / At the edge / Nobody's hero / Bloody dub / Doesn't make it alright / I don't like you / No change / Suspect device / Tin soldiers. *(re-iss. Mar89 on 'E.M.I.' lp/c(cd); EMC/TC-EMC 3555)(CDP 792106-2) <US cd-iss. 1992 on 'Restless'; 72364>*

May 80. (7") *(CHS 2424)* **TIN SOLDIERS. / NOBODY'S HERO** [36] [-]

Jul 80. (7") *(CHS 2447)* **BACK TO FRONT. / MR FIRE COAL-MAN** [49] [-]

Sep 80. (lp/c) *(CHR/ZCHR 1300)* **HANX! (live)** [9] [-]
– Nobody's hero / Gotta getaway / Wait and see / Barbed wire love / Fly the flag / Alternative Ulster / Johnny was / At the edge / Wasted life / Tin soldiers / Suspect device. *(re-iss. Feb89 on 'Fame-EMI' lp/c/cd; FA/TC-FA/CD-FA 3215) <US cd-iss. 1992 on 'Restless'; 72365>*

Mar 81. (7"m) *(CHS 2510)* **JUST FADE AWAY. / GO FOR IT / DOESN'T MAKE IT ALRIGHT (live)** [47] [-]

Apr 81. (lp/c) *(CHR/ZCHR 1339)* **GO FOR IT** [14] [-]
– Roots, radicals, rockers and reggae / Just fade away / Go for it / The only one / Hits and misses / Kicking up a racket / Safe as houses / Gate 49 / Silver lining / Piccadilly Circus. *(re-iss Feb89 on 'Fame-EMI' lp/c/cd+=; FA/TC-FA/CD-FA 3216)* – Back to front. *<US cd-iss. 1992 on 'Restless'; 72366>*

May 81. (7") *(CHS 2517)* **SILVER LINING. / SAFE AS HOUSES** [68] [-]

— **BRIAN 'DOLPHIN' TAYLOR** – drums (ex-TOM ROBINSON BAND) repl. REILLY

Jan 82. (7"ep) *(CHS 2580)* **R.E.P. PAY 1.10 OR LESS EP** [33] [-]
– Listen / Sad-eyed people / That's when your blood bumps / Two guitars clash.

Apr 82. (7") *(CHS 2601)* **TALK BACK. / GOOD FOR NOTHING** [ ] [-]

Aug 82. (7"/12") *(CHS/+12 2637)* **BITS OF KIDS. / STANDS TO REASON** [73] [-]

Sep 82. (lp/c) *(CHR/ZCHR 1400)* **NOW THEN** [24] [-]
– Falling down / Won't be told / Love of the common people / The price of admission / Touch and go / Stands to reason / Bits of kids / Welcome to the whole week / Big city night / Talkback / Is that what you fought the war for. *(cd-iss. Dec94 on 'Fame'; CDFA 3306) (cd re-iss. Apr97 on 'EMI Gold'; CDGOLD 1090)*

Jan 83. (d-lp/d-c) *(CTY/ZCTY 1414)* **ALL THE BEST** (compilation) [19] [ ]
– Suspect device / Wasted life / Alternative Ulster / '78 R.P.M. / Gotta getaway / Bloody Sunday / Straw dogs / You can't say crap on the radio / At the edge / Running bear / White Christmas / Nobody's hero / Tin soldiers / Back to front / Mr. Fire coal-man / Just fade away / Go for it / Doesn't make it alright / Silver lining / Safe as houses / Sad eyed people / Two guitars clash / Listen / That's when your blood bumps / Good for nothing / Talkback / Stand to reason / Bits of kids / Touch and go / The price of admission / Silly encores *[not on cass]*. *(d-cd-iss. Jun88; CCD 1414) (re-iss. Sep91 on 'E.M.I.' d-cd/d-c; CD/TC EM 1428) <US d-cd-iss. 1995 on 'One Way'; 18429>*

Feb 83. (7") *(CHS 2671)* **THE PRICE OF ADMISSION. / TOUCH AND GO** [ ] [-]

— Had already disbanded late 1982. McMORDIE joined FICTION GROOVE and DOLPHIN joined SPEAR OF DESTINY after stint with GO WEST.

JAKE BURNS & THE BIG WHEEL

— were formed by **JAKE** plus **NICK MUIR** – keyboards / **SEAN MARTIN** – bass / **STEVE GRANTLEY** – drums

Survival / not iss.

Jul 85. (7"/12") *(SRD/+T 2)* **ON FORTUNE STREET. / HERE COMES THAT SONG AGAIN**

Mar 86. (7"/12") *(SRD/+T 3)* **SHE GREW UP. / RACE YOU TO THE GRAVE**

Jive / not iss.

Feb 87. (7"/ext.12") *(JIVE/+T 139)* **BREATHLESS. / VALENTINE'S DAY**

STIFF LITTLE FINGERS

— re-formed in 1987 by **BURNS, TAYLOR, CLUNEY & McMORDIE**

Link / not iss.

Apr 88. (d-lp,green-d-lp) *(LP 026)* **LIVE AND LOUD (live)**
– Alternative Ulster / Roots radicals rockers and reggae / Silver lining / Wait and see / Gotta getaway / Just fade away / Wasted life / The only one / Nobody's hero / At the edge / Listen / Barbed wire love / Fly the flag / Tin soldiers / No sleep till Belfast / Suspect device / Johnny was. *(re-iss. May88 as 'NO SLEEP TILL BELFAST' on 'Kaz' c/cd; KAZ MC/CD 6) (cd-iss. Sep89; CD 026)*

Skunx / not iss.

Jun 88. (12"ep) *(SLFX 1)* **NO SLEEP TILL BELFAST (live)**
– Suspect device / Alternative Ulster / Nobody's hero.

Virgin / Caroline

Mar 89. (12"ep/cd-ep) *(SLF/+CD 1)* **ST.PATRIX** (the covers live)
– The wild rover / Love of the common people / Johnny Was.

Apr 89. (d-lp/d-c/d-cd) *(VGD/+C/CD 3515) <CAROL 1377-1/-4/-2>* **SEE YOU UP THERE! (live)**
– (intro: Go for it) / Alternative Ulster / Silver lining / Love of the common people / Gotta getaway / Just fade away / Piccadilly Circus / Gate 49 / Wasted life / At the edge / Listen / Barbed wire love / Fly the flag / Tin soldiers / The wild rover / Suspect device / Johnny was.

— (Mar91) **BRUCE FOXTON** – bass (ex-JAM, ex-solo) repl. McMORDIE

Essential / Taang!

Oct 91. (cd/c/lp)(pic-lp) *(ESS CD/MC/LP 171)(EPDLP 171)* **FLAGS & EMBLEMS**
– (It's a) Long way to Paradise (from here) / Stand up and shout / Each dollar a bullet / The cosh / Beirut Moon / The game of life / Human shield / Johnny 7 / Dread burn / No surrender. *(cd re-iss. Jul95 on 'Dojo';)*

Oct 91. (cd-ep) *(ESSX 2007)* **BEIRUT MOON / STAND UP AND SHOUT / (JAKE interview)**

Jan 94. (12"ep) *(ESS 2035)* **CAN'T BELIEVE IN YOU. / SILVER LINING (unplugged) / LISTEN (unplugged) / WASTED LIFE (unplugged)**
(cd-ep) *(ESSX 2035)* – ('A'side) / ('A'extended) / Alternative Ulster (featuring RICKY WARWICK of The ALMIGHTY) / Smithers-Jones (live with BRUCE FOXTON vocals).

Feb 94. (cd/c) *(ESS CD/MC 210) <TAANG 100>* **GET A LIFE** — Oct94
– Get a life / Can't believe in you / The road to kingdom come / Walk away / No laughing matter / Harp / Forensic evidence / Baby blue ((what have they been telling you?) / I want you / The night that the wall came down / Cold / When the stars fall from the sky / What if I want more? i(re-iss. Apr97; *ESMCD 488)*

Jun 94. (12"/cd-s) **HARP. / SHAKE IT OFF / NOW WHAT WE WERE (PRO PATRIA MORI)**

— **STEVE GRANTLEY** – drums (ex-JAKE BURNS . . .) repl. TAYLOR

Spitfire / Taang!

Jun 97. (cd/lp) *(SLF 100 CD/LP) <T 137>* **TINDERBOX** — Jul97
– You never hear the one that hits you / (I could) Be happy yesterday / Tinderbox / Dead of night / The message / My ever changing moral stance / Hurricane / You can move mountains / River flowing / You don't believe in me / In your hand / Dust in my eye / Roaring boys (part 1) / Roaring boys (part 2).

– compilations, etc. –

Sep 86. (12"ep) *Strange Fruit; (SFPS 004)* **THE PEEL SESSIONS** (12.9.78)
Johnny was / Law and order / Barbed wire love / Suspect device. *(c-ep-iss.May87; SFPSC 004) (cd-ep-iss.Jul88; SFPCD 004)*

Nov 89. (lp/c/cd) *Strange Fruit; (SFR LP/MC/CD 106) / Dutch East India; <8103>* **THE PEEL SESSIONS**

Oct 89. (12"ep) *Link; (LINK 1203)* **THE LAST TIME. / MR.FIRE-COAL MAN / TWO GUITARS CLASH**

Apr 91. (cd) *Streetlink; (STRCD 010)* **GREATEST HITS LIVE (live)**

Oct 91. (cd) *Link; (AOK 103)* **ALTERNATIVE CHARTBUSTERS**

Oct 89. (cd/green-lp) *Limited Edition; (LTD EDT 2 CD/LP)* **LIVE IN SWEDEN (live)**

Dec 92. (cd) *Dojo; (<DOJOCD 75>)* **FLY THE FLAGS – LIVE AT BRIXTON ACADEMY (27/9/91)** — Oct94

Aug 93. (cd) *Windsong; (<WINCD 037>)* **BBC RADIO 1 LIVE IN CONCERT (live)**

Mar 95. (cd) *Dojo; (DOJOCD 224)* **PURE FINGERS LIVE – ST.PATRIX 1993**

STOCKHOLM MONSTERS

Formed: New York, USA . . . early 80's by brothers TONY and KARL FRANCE, the other half of the indie/dance act comprising JOHN RHODES and SHAN HIRA. Discovered by 'Factory' boss, Anthony Wilson, the band packed their suitcases for Manchester, England and debuted in 1981 with the 12" 'FAIRY TALES'. Akin to a more tribal, airy, pastel-hued NEW ORDER, The STOCKHOLM MONSTERS were readily identifiable as a "Factory" band, the proof of the pudding being further singles, 'HAPPY EVER AFTER' and 'MISS MOONLIGHT'. In 1984, the quartet finally got round to issuing a full-set, 'ALMA MATER', although its lack of sparkle or indeed anything approaching a hookline alienated prospective fans. Although they carried on for another couple of years, they gave up the ghost after a final PETER HOOK-produced single, 'MILITIA', failed to raise their profile.

Album rating: ALMA MATER (*4)

TONY FRANCE – vocals / **KARL FRANCE** – bass / **JOHN RHODES** – keyboards / **SHAN HIRA** – drums

Factory / not iss.

Sep 81. (12") *(FACT 41)* **FAIRY TALES. / DEATH IS SLOWLY COMING**
(7"-iss.Jan82; FAC 41)

Aug 82. (7") *(FAC 58)* **HAPPY EVER AFTER. / SOFT BABIES**

1983. (12") *Factory Benelux;* **MISS MOONLIGHT. /** — Belgian

Mar 84. (lp) *(FACT 80)* **ALMA MATER**

Jun 84. (7") *(FAC 107)* **ALL AT ONCE. / NATIONAL PASTIME**

Oct 85. (12") *Factory Benelux;* **HOW CORRUPT IS ROUGH TRADE? / KAN KILL!** — Belgian

Mar 87. (12"ep) *Materiali Sonori; (MASO 70002)* **GREETINGS TWO** — Italy

Jul 87. (12") *(FAC 146)* **MILITIA. / PARTYLINE**

— disbanded after above

J.J. STONE (see under ⇒ GALLON DRUNK)

STONE ROSES

Formed: Sale & Chorley, Gtr. Manchester, England . . . 1984 by IAN BROWN, JOHN SQUIRE, RENI, ANDY COUZENS and PETER GARNER who took their name from a group called ENGLISH ROSE and The ROLLING STONES. After a MARTIN HANNETT produced 45, they signed a one-off deal with 'Black' records and in 1988, were snapped up by ANDREW LAUDER's 'Jive' subsidiary, 'Silvertone'. They soon became darlings of the music press after the indie success of the single, 'ELEPHANT STONE' (1988), a gloriously uplifting piece of pristine pop. Propelled by RENI's consummate drumming and featuring SQUIRE's dizzy, spiralling guitar, the track was a blueprint for the group's eponymous debut album, released the following year. Surely a contender for album of the decade, the record was flawless, from the ominous opening bass rumble of 'I WANNA BE ADORED' to the orgasmic finale of 'I AM THE RESURRECTION'. This life-affirming hybrid of BYRDS-style psychedelia and shuffling rhythmic flurries remains the definitive indie album, its all-pervading influence more pronounced with each successive crop of guitar bands. Incredibly, the band topped the magic of their debut with the 'FOOL'S GOLD' single, which exploded into the Top 10 later that year. A seminal guitar-funk workout, it was the crowning glory of the 'Baggy' movement with which The STONE ROSES had become so closely affiliated, and marked a creative highpoint in their career. After a few one-off shows (that have since achieved almost mythical status) and a solitary single, 'ONE LOVE', the following year, the band went to ground. In the five years that followed, the band fought a protracted court battle with 'Silvertone', eventually signing with 'Geffen' for a reported record sum of $4,000,000. After much speculation and intrigue into when or if a follow-up would finally appear, the appropriately title 'SECOND COMING' was eventually released in 1994. A month previously, they had enjoyed a return to the singles chart with the ZEPPELIN-esque 'LOVE SPREADS'. On the album, the effervescent pop of old took second place to riff-heavy guitar workouts, alienating many of their original fans. Nevertheless, the blistering funk-rock of 'BEGGING YOU' partly made up for any excess noodling by SQUIRE. As the STONES ROSES faithful dusted down their flares and beany hats in readiness for the band's headlining spot at the 1995 Glastonbury festival, they were again bitterly disappointed. At the last minute the band pulled out, apparently due to SQUIRE breaking his collarbone, young pretenders OASIS stealing the show in their absence. They had failed to seize the moment and from here on in, it was all downhill. Despite an ecstatically received Winter tour, SQUIRE shocked the music world by departing the following Spring (RENI had already quit a year earlier). BROWN and MANI bravely soldiered on for a headlining appearance at the 1996 Reading Festival but were given a critical mauling (particularly by the NME), finally splitting later that year. It was a sorry, messy end for a band that had seemed, at one point, to be on the brink of world domination and it remains a bitter irony that their duller Manchester progeny, OASIS, seem to have inherited the success that tragically eluded the 'ROSES. While SQUIRE has gone on to relative success with The SEAHORSES, their sound pales next to the magic of The STONE ROSES, a band that remain as fondly remembered as any in the history of rock. • **Songwriters:** Mainly SQUIRE but with other members also collaborating. The SEAHORSES was mainly SQUIRE, except a few by HELME. one with FLETCHER. NOEL GALLAGHER (Oasis) co-wrote 'LOVE ME AND LEAVE ME'. • **Trivia:** Their debut album artwork was a pastiche of a Jackson Pollock splatter job painted by the multi-talented SQUIRE.

Album rating: THE STONE ROSES (*10) / SECOND COMING (*8) / SEAHORSES: DO IT YOURSELF (*8)

IAN BROWN (b.20 Feb'63, Ancoats, Manchester) – vocals / **JOHN SQUIRE** (b.24 Nov'62, Broadheath, Manchester) – guitar, vocals / **PETER GARNER** – rhythm guitar / **ANDY COUZENS** – bass / **RENI** (b. ALAN WREN, 10 Apr'64) – drums

Thin Line / not iss.

Sep 85. (12") *(THIN 001)* **SO YOUNG. / TELL ME**

— now a quartet, when PETER departed.

Revolver | not iss.

May 87. (12"m) *(12REV 36)* **SALLY CINNAMON. / HERE IT COMES / ALL ACROSS THE SAND** [ ] [-]
(re-iss. Feb89; same) (re-iss. Dec89 cd-ep+=; CDREV 36); hit No.46) – ('A'demo).

— (1987) **GARY 'Mani' MOUNFIELD** (b.16 Nov'62, Crumpsall, Manchester) – bass, vocals repl. COUZENS who later joined The HIGH.

Silvertone | Silvertone

Oct 88. (7") *(ORE 1)* **ELEPHANT STONE. / THE HARDEST THING IN THE WORLD** [ ] [-]
(12"+=) *(ORE 1T)* – Full fathoms five. *(re-iss. Feb90 c-s/cd-s; ORE 1 C/CD); hit No.8. (cd-s re-iss. Oct96; same)*

Mar 89. (7") *(ORE 2)* **MADE OF STONE. / GOING DOWN** [ ] [-]
(12"+=) *(ORE 2T)* – Guernica. *(re-iss. Mar90 c-s/cd-s; ORE 2 C/CD); hit No.20. (cd-s re-iss. Oct96; same)*

Apr 89. (lp/c/cd) *(ORE LP/MC/CD 502) <1184-1/-4/-2>* **THE STONE ROSES** [19] [86]
– I wanna be adored / She bangs the drum / Waterfall / Don't stop / Bye bye badman / Elizabeth my dear / (Song for my) Sugar spun sister / Made of stone / Shoot you down / This is the one / I am the resurrection. *(re-iss. Aug91 as 2x12"+=; OREZLP 502)* – Elephant stone / Fool's gold. *(cd re-iss. Mar97; same)*

Jul 89. (7"/7"s) *(ORE/+X 6)* **SHE BANGS THE DRUM. / STANDING HERE** [36] [-]
(12"+=/12"s+=) *(ORE T/Z 6)* – Mersey Paradise.
(c-s++=/cd-s++=) *(ORE C/CD 6)* – Simone. *(re-entered chart Mar90; hit No.34) (cd-s re-iss. Oct96; same)*

Silvertone | Jive

Nov 89. (7"/ext.12") *(ORE/+T 13) <1315-1>* **FOOL'S GOLD. / WHAT THE WORLD IS WAITING FOR** [8] [ ] Mar90
(c-s+=/cd-s+=) *(ORE C/CD 13)* – ('A'extended). *(flipped over re-entered chart Sep90; hit No.22) (re-iss. remix May92, hit No.73) (cd-s re-iss. Oct96; same)*
(12") *(ORET 13)* – ('A'-The Top Won mix) / ('A'-The Bottom Won mix).

Nov 89. (12"ep) *<1301>* **I WANNA BE ADORED / (long version) / GOING DOWN / SIMONE** [-] [ ]

Jul 90. (7"/c-s/12"/cd-s) *(ORE/+C/T/CD 17) <1399-1/-2>* **ONE LOVE. / SOMETHING'S BURNING** [4] [ ]
(cd-s re-iss. Oct96; same)

Sep 91. (7"/c-s) *(ORE/+C 31)* **I WANNA BE ADORED. / WHERE ANGELS PLAY** [20] [-]
(12"+=/cd-s+=) *(ORE T/CD 31)* – Sally Cinnamon (live).
(cd-s re-iss. Oct96; same)

Jan 92. (7"/c-s) *(ORE/+C 35)* **WATERFALL (remix). / ONE LOVE (remix)** [27] [ ]
(12"+=/cd-s+=) *(ORE T/CD 35)* – ('A'&'B'extended versions).
(cd-s re-iss. Oct96; same)

Apr 92. (7"/c-s) *(ORE/+C 40)* **I AM THE RESURRECTION. / ('A'-Pan & scan radio version)** [33] [ ]
(12"+=) *(ORET 40)* – Fool's gold (The Bottom Won mix).
(cd-s++=) *(ORECD 40)* – ('A'-5:3 Stoned Out club mix).
(cd-s re-iss. Oct96; same)

Jul 92. (cd/c/lp) *(ORE CD/C/LP 521)* **TURNS INTO STONE** (demos & rare) [32] [-]
– Elephant stone / The hardest thing in the world / Going down / Mersey Paradise / Standing here Where angels play / Simone / Fools gold / What the world is waiting for / One love / Something's burning. *(cd re-iss. Mar97; same)*

Geffen | Geffen

Nov 94. (7"/c-s) *(GFS/+C 84)* **LOVE SPREADS. / YOUR STAR WILL SHINE** [2] [ ]
(cd-s+=) *(GFST 84)* – Breakout.
(12"++=) *(GFSTD 84)* – Groove harder.

Dec 94. (cd/c/lp) *<(GED/GEC/GEF 24503)>* **SECOND COMING** [4] [47] Jan95
– Breaking into Heaven / Driving south / Ten storey love song / Daybreak / Your star will shine / Straight to the man / Begging you / Tightrope / Good times / Tears / How do you sleep? / Love spreads. *(cd+=)* – (untitled hidden track No.90).

Feb 95. (7"/c-s) *(GFS/+C 87)* **TEN STOREY LOVE SONG. / RIDE ON** [11] [ ]
(12"+=/cd-s+=) *(GFST/+D 87)* – Moses.

— In Apr'95, RENI quit and was replaced by **ROBERT MADDIX** (ex-GINA GINA).

Oct 95. (c-s) *(GFSC 22060)* **BEGGING YOU / ('A'-Chic mix)** [15] [ ]
(cd-s+=) *(GFSTD 22060)* – ('A'-Stone Corporation mix) / ('A'-Lakota mix) / ('A'-Young American primitive remix).
(12") *(GFST 22060)* – ('A'-Carl Cox mix) / ('A'-Development Corporation mix).

— Late in March '96, SQUIRE left to pursue new venture, The SEAHORSES. The STONE ROSES continued on and in Aug'96, they recruited **AZIZ IBRAHIM** (ex-SIMPLY RED) / **NIGEL IPPINSON** – keyboards

— They officially split in Nov'96, after MANI joined PRIMAL SCREAM.

– compilations, etc. –

on 'Silvertone' unless mentioned; who else?

Jan 92. (8xcd-s-box-set) *(SRBX 1)* **SINGLES BOX** [ ] [-]

Nov 92. (10x12"box-set) *(SRBX 2)* **SINGLES BOX** [ ] [-]

Apr 95. (c-s) *(OREC 71)* **FOOL'S GOLD '95 / ('A'extended mix)** [23] [ ]
(12"+=/cd-s+=) *(ORE T/CD 71)* – ('A'-Tall Paul remix) / (A'-Cricklewood Ballroom mix).

May 95. (cd/c/lp) *(ORE CD/C/ZLP)* **THE COMPLETE STONE ROSES** [4] [ ]

Nov 96. (cd/c/lp) *(GARAGE CD/C/LP 1)* **GARAGE FLOWER** (early demos) [58] [-]

Jun 97. (7"ep) *Fierce; (FRIGHT 044)* **SPIKE ISLAND EP** (interviews, etc.) [ ] [-]

IAN BROWN

on mostly all vocals/instruments except co-writers **AZIZ IBRAHIM** – guitars, etc / **SIMON MOORE** – drums / **NIGEL IPPINSON** – keyboards, bass / guests **MANI MOUNFIELD + NOEL GALLAGHER + DENISE JOHNSON +** cp-writer/mixer **ROBBIE MADDIX**

Polydor | not iss.

Jan 98. (7"/c-s/cd-s) *(571 987-7/-4/-2)* **MY STAR. / SEE THE DAWN / FOURTEEN** [5] [-]

Feb 98. (cd/c/lp) *(539 565-2/-4/-1)* **UNFINISHED MONKEY BUSINESS** [4] [-]
– Intro under the paving stones: The beach / My star / Can't see me / Ice cold cube / Sunshine / Lions / Corpses in their mouths / What happened to ya part 1 / What happened to ya part 2 / Nah nah / Deep pile dreams / Unfinished monkey business.

Mar 98. (7") *(569 654-7)* **CORPSES. /** [14] [-]
(cd-s+=) *(569 655-2)* –
(cd-s) *(569 657-2)* –

Jun 98. (7") *(567 092-7)* **CAN'T SEE ME (Bacon & Quarmby remix). / CAN'T SEE ME (Bacon & Quarmby vocal dub)** [21] [-]
(cd-s+=) *(044 045-2)* – Under the paving stone: The beach (Gabriel's 13th dream remix).
(cd-s) *(044 047-2)* – ('A'side) / ('A'-Harvey's invisible mix) / Come again part two / My star (CD-ROM video).

STRAITJACKET FITS

Formed: Auckland, New Zealand ... 1985 by songwriters SHAYNE CARTER and ANDREW BROUGH alongside a rhythm section of DAVID WOOD and JOHN COLLIE. Signed to 'Flying Nun', the band followed in the established Kiwi tradition of The CHILLS, The CLEAN etc although they preferred their music with a bit more of a punch then many bands on the NZ scene. Although they debuted in 1987 with the 'LIFE IN ONE CHORD' EP, it would be another two years before the release of their first album, 'HAIL', licensed for UK release by 'Rough Trade'. Despite featuring many songs previously released on the EP, the album also boasted a version of Leonard Cohen's 'SO LONG MARIANNE', a surprising but effective cover sitting comfortably with the band's darkly atmospheric garage drone. Subsequently securing a deal with 'Arista', the band released follow-up set, 'MELT', in 1991, although like the bulk of their musical countrymen, failed to attract a wider crossover audience. Back on 'Flying Nun', for third set, 'BLOW', the band finally gave up the ghost after a final single, 'IF I WERE YOU', in late '93.

Album rating: HAIL (*7) / MELT (*5) / BLOW (*4)

SHAYNE CARTER – vocals, guitar / **ANDREW BROUGH** – vocals, guitar, keyboards / **DAVID WOOD** – bass / **JOHN COLLIE** – drums

Flying Nun Europe | not iss.

1987. (12"ep) *(FNE 25)* **LIFE IN ONE CHORD** [ ] [-]
– Dialling a prayer / All that that brings / Sparkle that shines / She speeds.

Rough Trade | not iss.

Nov 89. (cd/c/lp) *(CDR/ROUGHC/R 147)* **HAIL** [ ] [-]
– Dialling a prayer / All that that brings / Hail / Sparkle that shines / She speeds / So long Marianne / Grate / Fabulous things / Life in one chord / This taste delight. *(cd+=)* – Telling tales / Dead heat / Only you knew / Take from the years.

Arista | Arista

Oct 91. (cd/c) *(261/411 908) <ARCD 8645>* **MELT** [ ] [ ] Jun91
– Bad note for a heart / Missing presumed drowned / Melt against yourself / Head wind / Down in a splendour / A.P.S. / Quiet come / Such a daze / Skin to wear / Hand in mine / Roller ride / Cast stone.

Oct 91. (cd-ep) *<2244>* **MISSING FROM MELT EP** [-] [ ]
– Missing presumed drowned / Bad note for a heart / Skin to wear / In spite of it all / Cave in.

Dec 91. (cd-s) *<2356>* **ROLLER RIDE / DOWN IN SPLENDOUR / BAD NOTE FOR A HEART / A.P.S.** [-] [ ]

Flying Nun | Arista

1992. (7") *<FN 175>* **BAD NOTE FOR A HEART. / IN SPITE OF IT ALL** [-] [ ]

Sep 93. (cd/c) *(FN CD/MC 251) <18697>* **BLOW** [ ] [ ] May93
– Done / Falling / Brother's keeper / Cat inna can / Burn it up / Joyride / Train / Let it blow / If I were you / Turn / Way / Spacing.

Nov 93. (cd-s) *(FNUN 285)* **IF I WERE YOU /** [ ] [ ]

— disbanded after above

Richard STRANGE (see under ⇒ DOCTORS OF MADNESS)

STRANGELOVE

Formed: Bristol, England ... 1991 by PATRICK DUFF and ALEX LEE (ex-BLUE AEROPLANES), who subsequently recruited JULIAN-PRANSKY POOLE, JOE ALLEN and DAVE FRANCOLINI (of LEVITATION), the latter promptly replaced by JOHN LANGLEY. Debuting with the 'VISIONARY' EP on the independent 'Sermon' label and following it up with the acclaimed 'HYSTERIA UNKNOWN' single, the band's portentous, pseudo-goth rumblings combined with DUFF's miserabilist charisma engendered a major label signing rush. 'Food-E.M.I.' were the lucky recipients of the band's signature, releasing the morose debut album, 'TIME FOR THE REST OF YOUR LIFE' in summer '94. Hardly the success they might have hoped for, the album struggled to make the Top 75 despite some favourable reviews, STRANGELOVE's reputation among the media for being humourless and po-faced not helping them any. Previewed by the group's first Top 40 hit, 'BEAUTIFUL ALONE', 1996's follow-up set, 'LOVE AND OTHER DEMONS', continued in much the same vein with mainstream indie success continuing to elude them. Despite the sentiments of the self-loathing 'FREAK' single, a newly rehabilitated (from alcohol that is) DUFF emerged with something approaching a sense of wellbeing on 1997's eponymous 'STRANGELOVE'. Considerably more accessible and upbeat than any of the band's material to date, tracks such as 'RUNAWAY BROTHERS' and 'SOMEDAY SOON' suggested that there'd always been an indie-pop element to STRANGELOVE's goth laments, though this was hardly The BOO RADLEYS. Yet again, the record struggled to make any impact on the charts, STRANGELOVE seemingly destined to be the perpetual outsiders of 'New Grave'. • **Songwriters:** Group penned except MOTORPSYCHO NITEMARE (Bob Dylan) / IF I CAN DREAM (Skunk Anansie). • **Trivia:** Produced by ANGELO BRUSCHINI also ex-BLUE AEROPLANES.

Album rating: TIME OUT FOR THE REST OF YOUR LIFE (*7) / LOVE AND OTHER DEMONS (*6) / STRANGELOVE (*6)

PATRICK DUFF – vocals / **ALEX LEE** – guitar (ex-BLUE AEROPLANES) / **JOHN LANGLEY** – drums (ex-BLUE AEROPLANES) / **JOE ALLEN** – vocals, rhythm guitar (ex-RODNEY ALLEN EXPERIENCE) / **JULIAN PRANSKY-POOLE** – bass (ex-JAZZ BUTCHER)

Sermon / not iss.

Oct 92. (12"ep) *(SERT 001)* **VISIONARY / FRONT. / CHANCES / SNAKES** [ ] [-]

Feb 93. (7") *(SER 002)* **HYSTERIA UNKNOWN. / MY DARK** [ ] [-]
(12"+=/cd-s+=) *(SERT 002/+CD)* – Walls / Sea.

Rough Trade / not iss.

Sep 93. (7") *(45REV 18)* **ZOO'D OUT. / CIRCLES** [ ] [-]

Food-EMI / not iss.

Jun 94. (7") *(FOOD 49)* **TIME FOR THE REST OF YOUR LIFE. / IT'S SO EASY** [ ] [-]
(12"+=/cd-s+=) *(12/CD FOOD 49)* – Motorpsycho nitemare.

Aug 94. (cd/c/d-lp) *(FOOD CD/TC/LP 11)* **TIME FOR THE REST OF YOUR LIFE** [69] [-]
– Sixer / Time for the rest of your life / Quiet day / Sand / I will burn / Low life / World outside / The return of the real me / All because of you / Fire (show me light) / Hopeful / Kite / Is there a place?. *(cd re-iss. Sep97; same)*

Oct 94. (12"ep/cd-ep) *(12/CD FOOD 55)* **IS THERE A PLACE? / SAND. / NOBODY'S THERE / THE KING OF SOMEWHERE ELSE** [ ] [-]

Apr 96. (7") *(FOOD 70)* **LIVING WITH HUMAN MACHINES. / MR. HONEY CATCHER** [53] [-]
(cd-s+=) *(CDFOODS 70)* – Killing time.
(cd-s) *(CDFOOD 70)* – ('A'side) / Hysteria unknown / Chances / My dark.

Jun 96. (7") *(FOOD 81)* **BEAUTIFUL ALONE / VISIONARY** [35] [-]
(cd-s+=) *(CDFOOD 81)* – Zoo'd out / Sea.
(cd-s) *(CDFOODS 81)* – ('A'side) / Wolf's story part I / Wolf's story part II / Wolf's story part III.

Jun 96. (cd/c/lp) *(FOOD CD/TC/LP 15)* **LOVE AND OTHER DEMONS** [44] [-]
– Casualties / Spiders and flies / Living with the human machines / She's everywhere / Sway / Beautiful alone / Elin's photograph / 20th century cold / 1432 / The sea of black.

Oct 96. (7") *(FOOD 82)* **SWAY / HOLD ON** [47] [-]
(cd-s+=) *(CDFOODS 82)* – Nowhere days / Ghost haddock.
(cd-s) *(CDFOOD 82)* – 20th century cold (live acoustic) / Moon river (live acoustic) / She's everywhere (live).

—— added **NICK POWELL** – keyboards

Jul 97. (7"white) *(FOOD 97)* **THE GREATEST SHOW ON EARTH. / LIVING WITH THE HUMAN MACHINES (loop mix)** [36] [-]
(cd-s) *(CDFOODS 97)* – ('A'side) / Couples / Crofters / Ascension day.
(cd-s) *(CDFOOD 97)* – ('A'side) / Elin's photograph (live acoustic) / Spiders and flies (live acoustic) / If I can dream (live acoustic).

Sep 97. (7"clear) *(FOOD 105)* **FREAK. / THE FREAK** [43] [-]
(cd-s) *(CDFOOD 105)* – ('A'side) / The city song / King of the real men.
(cd-s) *(CDFOODS 105)* – ('A'side) / The Devil you know / Bethlehem.

Oct 97. (cd/c/d-lp) *(FOOD CD/TC/LP 24)* **STRANGELOVE** [67] [-]
– Superstar / Freak / Someday soon / Wellington Road / The runaway brothers / Another night in / The greatest show on Earth / Little Queenie / She's on fire / Mona Lisa / Jennifer's song.

Feb 98. (7"red) *(FOOD 110)* **ANOTHER NIGHT IN. / ANOTHER ANOTHER NIGHT IN** [46] [-]
(cd-s) *(CDFOOD 110)* – ('A'side) / The last great rock'n'roll queen / Extract from journal No.17th 1997.
(cd-s) *(CDFOODS 110)* – ('A'side) / The drinker / Measured in blood.

STRANGLERS

Formed: Chiddington, Surrey, England ... Autumn 1974 as The GUILDFORD STRANGLERS by ex-science teacher, HUGH CORNWELL, history graduate JEAN-JACQUES BURNEL and jazz drummer JET BLACK. Augmented by organist DAVE GREENFIELD in the Spring of '75, they commenced gigging around the pub-rock circuit, developing their boorish, black-clad brand of DOORS/ELECTRIC PRUNES/DR.FEELGOOD retro rock with scant encouragement from the press. Late in '76, after supporting the likes of The FLAMIN' GROOVIES and The RAMONES, The STRANGLERS were signed to 'United Artists' and initially lumped in with the fermenting punk/new wave scene. Released early the following year, '(GET A) GRIP (ON YOURSELF)' found the band at their sneering, leering best, GREENFIELD's churning organ characterising a sound with which they'd stick fairly closely over the early part of their career. The single stalled outside the UK Top 40 – reportedly due to a chart mistake – although its controversial follow-up, 'PEACHES', made the Top 10 and immediately brought the band into conflict with feminists and the more liberal contingent of the music press. It was also banned by the BBC (a slightly modified version was later deemed acceptable), the surrounding controversy the first of many throughout the band's career and one which certainly didn't harm sales of the classic debut album, 'STRANGLERS IV – RATTUS NORVEGICUS' (1977). A Top 5 success comprising both singles and the enduring STRANGLERS' favourite, 'HANGING AROUND', the record met with enthusiastic reviews

as the group enjoyed the briefest of honeymoon periods with the press. A not entirely convincing attempt at political comment, 'SOMETHING BETTER CHANGE', gave the band a second Top 10 hit later that summer, closely followed by the vicious momentum of 'NO MORE HEROES'. Also released in '77, the album of the same name narrowly missed No.1, another solid set which armed their detractors with more ammunition in the form of 'BRING ON THE NUBILES'; a notorious, stripper-enhanced gig at Battersea Park didn't help matters and The STRANGLERS' were firmly tarred as sexist yobs. Not that their fans cared, helping put a further two singles, 'FIVE MINUTES' and 'NICE 'N' SLEAZY', into the Top 20, both tracks featuring on the album, 'BLACK AND WHITE' (1978). The latter set came free with a limited edition 7" featuring the lads' interesting cover of the BACHARACH/DAVID standard, 'WALK ON BY' tastefully placed side by side with the inimitable 'TITS'. More promising and certainly more memorable was the surprisingly melodic 'DUCHESS', a Top 20 hit lifted from accompanying album, 'THE RAVEN' (1979). That year also saw the release of solo albums from both J.J. BURNEL and HUGH CORNWELL (with ROBERT WILLIAMS), the former's 'EUROMAN COMETH' barely making the Top 40 while the latter's 'NOSFERATU' failed to make any impression on the charts. Worse was to come for CORNWELL when, on the 7th of January 1980, the singer was found guilty of drug possession and sentenced to three months in prison. Later that year, the whole band fell foul of the law, this time in the South of France where they were accused of inciting a riot; although threatened with serious jail terms, they were susbsequently let off with fines, later claiming it was 'NICE IN NICE' on 1986's 'DREAMTIME' album. The STRANGLERS' commercial fortunes didn't fare much better with 'THE MEN IN BLACK' (1981), a tongue-in-cheek (but critically derided nonetheless) pseudo-concept affair about alien undercover agents. Boasting the exquisite harpsichord stylings of 'GOLDEN BROWN', 'LA FOLIE' (1981) was a considerably more successful album, if somewhat pretentious. In line with the prevailing trend, The STRANGLERS' moved perilously closer to synth-pop as the 80's wore on, 'Epic' albums such as 'FELINE' (1983) and 'AURAL SCULPTURE' (1984) seeing the band's hardcore fanbase dwindle. Even a return to their former stamping ground (and the UK Top 10) with a musclebound run-through of The Kinks' 'ALL DAY AND ALL OF THE NIGHT' couldn't rejuvenate them and the subsequent studio album, '10' (1990) was the last to feature CORNWELL. Deciding to carry on with new frontman, JOHN ELLIS, the band recorded for various indie labels in the 90's and although the likes of 'STRANGLERS IN THE NIGHT' (1992) and 'ABOUT TIME' (1995) made the Top 40, most commentators (and many fans) were agreed that the band's glory days were definitely behind them. • **Songwriters:** Mostly CORNWALL penned except some by BURNEL. They also covered; 96 TEARS (? & The Mysterians).

Album rating: RATTUS NORVEGICUS (*9) / NO MORE HEROES (*8) / BLACK AND WHITE (*8) / LIVE CERT (*8) / AURAL SCULPTURE (*6) / DREAMTIME (*7) / THE STRANGLERS' GREATEST HITS compilation (*9)

HUGH CORNWALL (b.28 Aug'48, London, England) – vocals, guitar / **JEAN-JAQUES BURNEL** (b.21 Feb'52, London; French parents) – bass, vocals / **DAVE GREENFIELD** (b.29 Mar'49, Brighton, England) – keyboards / **JET BLACK** (b. BRIAN DUFFY, 26 Aug'43, Ilford, England) – drums

U.A. A&M

Jan 77. (7") *(UP 36211)* **(GET A) GRIP (ON YOURSELF). / LONDON LADY** [44] [-]

Apr 77. (lp/c) *(UAG/UAC 30045) <4648>* **STRANGLERS IV – RATTUS NORVEGICUS** [4] [ ]
– Sometimes / Goodbye Toulouse / London lady / Princess of the streets / Hanging around / Peaches / (Get a) Grip (on yourself) / Ugly / Down in the sewer: (a) Falling – (b) Down in the sewer – (c) Trying to get out again – (d) Rats rally. *(free ltd.7"w.a.)* **CHOOSEY SUSIE. / IN THE BIG SHITTY (live)** *(re-iss. May82 on 'Fame' lp/c; FA/TC-FA 3001) (cd-iss. Apr88; CDFA 3001) (cd-iss. Feb88 on 'Liberty'; CZ 85)*

May 77. (7") *(UP 36248)* **PEACHES. / GO BUDDY GO** [8] [-]

— Jun77; They backed CELIA & THE MUTATIONS on cover single 'MONY MONY'.

Jul 77. (7") *(UP 36277)* **SOMETHING BETTER CHANGE. / STRAIGHTEN OUT** [9] [-]

Sep 77. (7") *(UP 36300)* **NO MORE HEROES. / IN THE SHADOWS** [8] [-]

Oct 77. (lp/c) *(UAG/UAC 30200) <4659>* **NO MORE HEROES** [2] [ ]
– I feel like a wog / Bitching / Dead ringer / Dagenham Dave / Bring on the nubiles / Something better change / No more heroes / Peasant in the big shitty / Burning up time / Dagenham Dave / English towns / School mam / In the shadows. *(re-iss. 1985 lp/c; ATAK/TC-ATAK 32) (cd-iss. Feb88 on 'E.M.I.'; CDP 746613-2) (re-iss. Sep87 on 'Fame' lp/c; FA/TC-FA 3190) (cd-iss. Aug88; CDFA 3190)*

Nov 77. (7"pink-ep) **SOMETHING BETTER CHANGE / STRAIGHTEN OUT. / GRIP / HANGIN' AROUND** [-] [ ]

Jan 78. (7") *(UP 36350)* **FIVE MINUTES. / ROK IT TO THE MOON** [11] [ ]

Apr 78. (7") *(UP 36379)* **NICE 'N' SLEAZY. / SHUT UP** [18] [ ] Aug78

May 78. (lp/c)<US-grey-lp> *(UAK/TCK 30222) <4706>* **BLACK AND WHITE** [2] [ ]
– Tank / Nice 'n' sleazy / Outside Tokyo / Mean to me / Sweden (all quiet on the Eastern Front) / Hey! (rise of the robots) / Toiler on the sea / Curfew / Threatened / Do you wanna? – Death and night and blood (Yukio) / In the shadows / Enough time / Walk on by. *(free ltd.7"w.a.) (FREE 9)* **WALK ON BY. / TITS / MEAN TO ME** *(re-iss. Jan86 on 'Epic' lp/c; EPC/40 26439) (cd-iss. Jul88 on 'E.M.I.'+=; CZ 109)* – (free 7" tracks).

Jul 78. (7"m) *(UP 36429)* **WALK ON BY. / OLD CODGER / TANK** [21] [-]

U.A. I.R.S.

Mar 79. (lp/c) *(UAG/TCK 30224) <70011>* **X-CERT (live)** [7] [ ]
– (Get a) Grip (on yourself) / Dagenham Dave / Burning up time / Dead ringer / Hanging around / I feel like a wog / Straighten out / Do you wanna – Death and night and blood (Yukio) / Five minutes / Go buddy go. *(re-iss. 1985 lp/c; ATAK/TC-ATACK 33) (cd-iss. Jul88 +=; CZ 110)* – In the shadows / Peasant in the big shitty.

Aug 79. (7") *(BP 308)* **DUCHESS. / FOOLS RUSH OUT** [14] [ ]

Sep 79. (lp/c) *(UAG/TCK 30262)* **THE RAVEN** [4] [-]
– Longships / The raven / Dead Loss Angeles / Ice / Baroque bordello / Nuclear device / Shah shah a go go / Don't bring Harry / Duchess / Meninblack / Genetix. *(re-iss. Sep85 on 'Fame' lp/c; FA/TC-FA 3131) (cd-iss. Aug88; CDFA 3131) (cd-iss. Oct87 on 'EMI'+=; CZ 20)* – Bear cage.

Oct 79. (7") *(BP 318)* **NUCLEAR DEVICE (THE WIZARD OF AUS). / YELLOWCAKE UF6** [36] [-]

Nov 79. (7"ep) *(STR 1)* **DON'T BRING HARRY** [41] [-]
– Don't bring Harry / Wired / Crabs (live) / In the shadows (live).

Liberty I.R.S.

Jan 80. (7") **DUCHESS. / THE RAVEN** [-] [ ]

Jan 80. (lp) *<SP 70011>* **STRANGLERS IV** [-] [ ]
– (5 tracks from 'THE RAVEN', plus recent singles)
(above w/ free 7"ep) – Do The European / Choosie Suzie / Wired / Straighten out.

Mar 80. (7"/12") *(BP/12BP 344)* **BEAR CAGE. / SHAH SHAH A GO GO** [36] [-]

May 80. (7") *(BP 355)* **WHO WANTS THE WORLD. / MENINBLACK** [39] [-]

Jan 81. (7") *(BP 383)* **THROWN AWAY. / TOP SECRET** [42] [-]

Feb 81. (lp/c) *(LBG/TC-LBG 30313)* **THE MEN• IN• BLACK** [8] [-]
– Waltzinblack / Just like nothing on Earth / Second coming / Waiting for the men in black / Turn the centuries, turn / Two sunspots / Four horsemen / Thrown away / Manna machine / Hallo to our men. *(re-iss. 1985 lp/c; ATAK/TC-ATAK 34) (re-iss. Sep88 on 'Fame' lp/c/cd; FA/TCFA/CDFA 3208)* – Top secret / Maninwhite.

Mar 81. (7") *(BP 393)* **JUST LIKE NOTHING ON EARTH. / MANINWHITE** [ ] [-]

Nov 81. (7") *(BP 405)* **LET ME INTRODUCE YOU TO THE FAMILY. / VIETNAMERICA** [42] [-]

Nov 81. (lp/c) *(LBG/TC-LBG 30342)* **LA FOLIE** [11] [-]
– Non stop / Everybody loves you when you're dead / Tramp / Let me introduce you to the family / The man they love to hate / Pin up / It only takes two to tango / Golden brown / How to find true love and happiness in the present day / La folie. *(re-iss. Nov83 on 'Fame' lp/c; FA/TC-FA 3083) (cd-iss. Aug88; CDFA 3083) (cd-iss. Feb88; CZ 86)*

Jan 82. (7") *(BP 407)* **GOLDEN BROWN. / LOVE 30** [2] [-]

Apr 82. (7") *(BP 410)* **LA FOLIE. / WALTZINBLACK** [47] [-]

Jul 82. (7") *(BP 412)* **STRANGE LITTLE GIRL. / CRUEL GARDEN** [7] [-]

Sep 82. (lp/c) *(LBG/TC-LBG 304353)* **THE COLLECTION 1977-1982** (compilation) [12] [-]
– (Get a) Grip (on yourself) / Peaches / Hanging around / No more heroes / Duchess / Walk on by / Waltzinblack / Something better change / Nice'n'sleazy / Bear cage / Who wants the world / Golden brown / Strange little girl / La folie. *(cd-iss. 1985; CDP 746066-2) (re-iss. Aug89 on 'Fame' cd/c/lp; CD/TC+/FA 3230)*

Epic Epic

Nov 82. (7"/7"pic-d) *(EPCA/+11 2893)* **THE EUROPEAN FEMALE. / SAVAGE BEAST** [9] [-]

Jan 83. (lp/c) *(EPC/40 25237) <38542>* **FELINE** [4] [ ]
– Midnight summer dream / It's a small world / Ships that pass in the night / The European female / Let's tango in Paris / Paradise / All roads lead to Rome / Blue sister / Never say goodbye. *(free ltd.one-sided-7"w.a.)* **AURAL SCULPTURE** *(re-iss. Apr86 lp/c; EPC/40 32711) <US lp+=>* – Golden brown. *(cd-iss. Dec92)*

Feb 83. (7"/12") *(A/+13 3167)* **MIDNIGHT SUMMER DREAM. / VLADIMIR AND OLGA** [35] [-]

Jul 83. (7") *(A 3387)* **PARADISE. / PAWSHER** [48] [-]
(12"+=) *(A13 3387)* – Permission.

Jul 83. (12") **MIDNIGHT SUMMER DREAM. / PARADISE** [-] [ ]

Sep84. (7") *(A 4738)* **SKIN DEEP. / HERE AND NOW** [15] [-]
(12"+=) *(TA 4738)* – Vladimir and the beast.

Nov 84. (lp/c) *(EPC/40 26220) <39959>* **AURAL SCULPTURE** [14] [ ]
– Ice queen / Skin deep / Let me down easy / No mercy / North winds / Uptown / Punch & Judy / Spain / Laughing / Souls / Mad Hatter. *(re-iss. May87 lp/c; 450488-1/-4) (cd-iss. 1987; 450488-2) (re-iss. cd Sep93 on 'Sony Collectors') (cd re-iss. Feb97; 474676-2)*

Nov 84. (7"/7"sha-pic-d) *(A/WA 4921)* **NO MERCY. / IN ONE DOOR** [37] [-]
(12"+=) *(TA 4921)* – Hot club (riot mix).
(d7"++=) *(GA 4921)* – Head on the line.

Feb 85. (7") *(A 6045)* **LET ME DOWN EASY. / ACHILLES HEEL** [48] [-]
(12"+=) *(TA 6045)* – Place des victories.
(12"++=) *(QTA 6045)* – Vladimir goes to Havana / The aural sculpture manifesto.

Aug 86. (7"/12"/7"sha-pic-d) *(650055-7/-6/-0)* **NICE IN NICE. / SINCE YOU WENT AWAY** [30] [-]

Oct 86. (7"/7"sha-pic-d) *(SOLAR/+P 1)* **ALWAYS THE SUN. / NORMAN NORMAL** [30] [-]
(12"+=) *(SOLART 1)* – Soul.
(d7"+=) *(SOLARD 1)* – Nice in Nice / Since you went away.

Oct 86. (lp/c/cd/pic-lp) *(EPC/40/CD/11 26648) <40607>* **DREAMTIME** [16] [ ]
– Always the sun / Dreamtime / Was it you? / You'll always reap what you sow / Ghost train / Nice in Nice / Big in America / Shakin' like a leaf / Mayan skies / Too precious. *(re-iss. Feb89 lp/c/cd; 463366-1/-4/-2)*

Dec 86. (7"/7"sha-pic-d) *(HUGE/+P 1)* **BIG IN AMERICA. / DRY DAY** [48] [-]
(12"+=) *(HUGET 1)* – Uptown.
(d7"+=) *(HUGED 1)* – Always the sun / Norman normal.

Feb 87. (7"/7"sha-pic-d) *(SHEIK/+P 1)* **SHAKIN' LIKE A LEAF. / HIT MAN** [58] [-]
('A'-Jelly mix-12"+=) *(SHEIKQ 1)* – Was it you?
('A'live-12") *(SHEIKB 1)* – (an evening with Hugh Cornwall).

Dec 87. (7"/7"sha-pic-d) *(VICE/+P 1)* **ALL DAY AND ALL OF THE NIGHT (live). / VIVA VLAD** [7] [ ]
(12"+=) *(VICET 1)* – Who wants the world (live).
(cd-s+=) *(CDVICE 1)* – Strange little girl.

Feb 88. (lp/c/cd) *(460259-1/-4/-2) <44209>* **ALL LIVE AND ALL OF THE NIGHT (live)** [12] [ ]
– No more heroes / Was it you? / Down in the sewer / Always the sun / Golden brown / North winds / The European female / Strange little girl / Nice 'n' sleazy / Toiler on the sea / Spain / London lady / All day and all of the night.

Feb 90. (7"/c-s) *(TEARS/+M 1)* **96 TEARS. / INSTEAD OF THIS** [17] [-]
(12"+=/cd-s+=) *(TEARS T/C/P 1)* – Poisonality.

Mar 90. (cd/c/lp/pic-lp) *(466483-2/-4/-1/-0)* **10** [15] [-]
– The sweet smell of success / Someone like you / 96 tears / In this place / Let's

celebrate / Man of the Earth / Too many teardrops / Where I live / Out of my mind / Never to look back. *(re-iss. cd Dec92)*

Apr 90. (7"/c-s/7"pic-d) *(TEARS/+M/P 2)* **THE SWEET SMELL OF SUCCESS. / MOTORBIKE** 65 -
(12"+=/cd-s+=) *(TEARS T/C 2)* – Something.

Nov 90. (cd/c/lp/pic-cd) *(467541-2/-4/-1/-9) <47081>* **THE STRANGLERS' GREATEST HITS 1977-1990** (complation) 4
– Something better change / No more heroes / Walk on by / Duchess / Golden brown / Strange little girl / European female / Skin deep / Nice in Nice / Always the Sun / Big in America / All day and all of the night / 96 tears / No mercy / Peaches.

Dec 90. (7"/c-s) *(656 430-7/-4)* **ALWAYS THE SUN. / BURNHAM BEECHES** 29 -
(12"+=) *(656 430-6)* – Straighten out.
(cd-s) *(656 430-2)* – ('A'side) / Nuclear device (live) / All day and all of the night (live) / Punch and Judy (live).

Mar 91. (7"/c-s) *(656 761-7/-4)* **GOLDEN BROWN (re-mix). / YOU** 68 -
(cd-s+=) *(656 761-2)* – Skin deep (extended) / Peaches.

— (late 1990) **JOHN ELLIS** (b. 1 Jun'52, London) – guitar, vocals (once p/t member) (ex-VIBRATORS, etc.) repl. CORNWALL who has already ventured solo.

— (Jan'91) also added **PAUL ROBERTS** (b.31 Dec'59, London) – vocals (ex-SNIFF 'N' THE TEARS)

China Viceroy

Aug 92. (7") *(WOK 2025)* **HEAVEN OR HELL. / DISAPPEAR** 46 -
(12"+=/c-s+=/cd-s+=) *(WOK T/C/CD 2025)* – Brainbox / Hanging around.

Sep 92. (lp/c/cd) *(WOL/+MC/CD 1030) <8007>* **STRANGLERS IN THE NIGHT** 33 Feb93
– Time to die / Sugar bullets / Heaven or Hell / Laughing at the rain / This town / Brainbox / Southern mouintains / Gain entry to your soul / Grand canyon / Wet afternoon / Never see / Leave it to the dogs.

Psycho not iss.

Oct 92. (7"/c-s) *(PSY/+MC 002)* **SUGAR BULLETS. / SO UNCOOL** -
(cd-s+=) *(PSYCD 002)* – ('A'version).

— **TIKAKE TOBE** – drums repl. JET BLACK

Essential Viceroy

Jun 93. (cd/c/lp) *(ESS CD/MC/LP 194) <ESM 388>* **SATURDAY NIGHT SUNDAY MORNING (live)** Mar96
– Toiler on the sea / 96 Tears / Always the sun / No more heroes / Golden brown / Tank / Strange little girl / Something better change / Hanging around / All day and all of the night / Duchess / *Medley / Was it you? / Down in the sewer.

— In Jun'93, old Strangler HUGH CORNWALL released album 'WIRED' on 'Transmission' label. Nearly a year earlier as CCW, he, ROGER COOK & AND WEST issued cd 'CCW FEATURING HUGH CORNWALL • ROGER COOK • ANDY WEST' on 'UFO'.

— **JET BLACK** returned

When! Beacon

May 95. (cd/c/lp) *(WEN CD/MC/LP 001) <51568>* **ABOUT TIME** 31 Jan96
– Golden boy / Money / Sinister / Little blue lies / Still life / Paradise row / She gave it all / Lies and deception / Lucky finger / And the boat sails by.

Jun 95. (12"/cd-s) *(WEN T/X 1007)* **LIES AND DECEPTION. / SWIM / DANNY COOL** -
(cd-s) *(WENX 1008)* – ('A'side) / Kiss the world goodbye / Bed of nails.

Jan 97. (pic-cd/cd/c) *(WEN PD/CD/MC 009)* **WRITTEN IN RED** 52 -

Feb 97. (c-s/cd-s) *(WEN N/X 1018)* **IN HEAVEN SHE WALKS / GOLDEN BROWN (live)** -
(cd-s) *(WENX 1020)* – ('A'side) / Grip (live) / Something better change (live).

Eagle Festival

Oct 98. (cd) *(EAGCD 042) <31965>* **COUP DE GRACE** Mar99
– God is good / You don't think that what you've done is wrong / Tonight / Jump over my shadow / Miss you / Coup de grace (S-O-S) / In the end / No reason / Known only unto God / The light.

– compilations, etc. –

Mar 84. (7") *EMI Gold; (G45 6)* **GOLDEN BROWN. / STRANGE LITTLE GIRL** -

Sep 86. (lp/c) *Liberty; (LBG/TCLBG 5001)* **OFF THE BEATEN TRACK** 80 -

Nov 88. (lp/c) *Liberty; (EMS/TCEMS 1306)* **RARITIES** -

Jan 89. (7"/7"red) *E.M.I.; (EM/+R 84)* **GRIP '89. / WALTZINBLACK** 33
(12"+=) *(12EM 84)* – Tomorrow was thereafter.
(cd-s++=) *(CDEM 84)* – ('A'mix).

Feb 89. (cd/c/lp) *E.M.I.; (CD/TC+/EM 1314)* **THE SINGLES** 57 -

Jun 89. (12"ep) *Nighttracks; (SFNT/+CD 020)* **RADIO 1 SESSION (1982)** -
– The man they love to hate / Nuclear device / Genetix / Down in the sewer.

Dec 90. (3xcd-box) *Epic; (467395-2)* **FELINE / AURAL SCULPTURE / DREAMTIME**

Feb 92. (cd/c/d-lp) *Newspeak; (SPEAK CD/MC/LP 101)* **THE EARLY YEARS 74-75-76, RARE LIVE & UNRELEASED** -

Mar 92. (cd/c) *Epic; (471416-2/-4)* **ALL TWELVE INCHES** -

May 92. (cd/c) *(CDGO/TCGO 2033)* **LIVE AT THE HOPE AND ANCHOR (live)** -
(cd re-iss. Feb95 on 'Fame'; CDFA 3316)

Jul 92. (d-cd) *Epic; (466835-2)* **FELINE / DREAMTIME** -

Dec 92. (4xcd-box) *E.M.I.; CDS 799924-2)* **THE OLD TESTAMENT – THE U.A. STUDIO RECORDINGS (demos)** -

May 94. (cd) *Receiver; (<RRCD 187>)* **DEATH AND NIGHT AND BLOOD**

Jun 94. (cd) *Castle; (CLACD 401)* **THE EARLY YEARS 1974-76** -

Feb 95. (cd) *Receiver; (RRCD 195)* **LIVE IN CONCERT (live w/ FRIENDS)**

Nov 95. (cd) *Essential; <ESM 283>* **RADIO ONE** -

Nov 95. (cd-s) *Old Gold; (12623 6339-2)* **GOLDEN BROWN / NO MORE HEROES** -

Feb 97. (cd/c) *E.M.I.; (CD/TC EMC 3759)* **THE HIT MEN (The Complete Singles 1977-1990)** -

Dec 97. (cd) *Rialto; (<220>)* **LIVE IN LONDON (live)** -

Feb 98. (cd) *Cleopatra; <206>* **FRIDAY THE THIRTEENTH** -

Jul 98. (cd) *Voiceprint; <1>* **ACCESS ALL AREAS (live)** -

J.J. BURNEL

— solo with **BRIAN JAMES** – guitar / **CAREY FORTUNE** – drums / **LEW LEWIS** – harmonica

U.A. not iss.

Mar 79. (7") *(UP 36500)* **FREDDIE LAKER (CONCORDE AND EUROBUS). / OZYMANDIAS** -

Apr 79. (lp/c) *(UAG/TCK 30214)* **EUROMAN COMETH** 40 -
– Euroman / Jellyfish / Freddie Laker (Concorde and Eurobus) / Euroness / Deutschland nicht uber alles / Do the European / Tout comprendre / Triumph (of the good city) / Pretty face / Crabs / Eurospeed (your own speed). *(re-iss. Feb88 on 'Mau Mau' pic-lp/lp; P+/MAU 601) (cd-iss. Jan92 on 'EMI' +=; CDP7 98535-2)* – (9 tracks).

— toured with **ELLIS, PETER HOWELLS & PENNY TOBIN.**

Jul 80. (7"w-drawn) *(BP 361)* **GIRL FROM SNOW COUNTRY. / ODE TO JOY (live) / DO THE EUROPEAN (live)** - -

DAVE GREENFIELD & JEAN-JAQUES BURNEL

Epic Epic

Dec 83. (lp/c) *(EPC/40 25707)* **FIRE AND WATER** -
– Liberation / Rain, dole & tea / Vladimir and Sergei / Le soir / Trois pedophiles pour Eric Sabyr ino rap / Nuclear power (yes please) / Detective privee / Consequences.

Feb 84. (7") *(A 4076)* **RAIN, DOLE & TEA. / CONSEQUENCES** -

— In 1989, they with ALEX GIFFORD, MANNY ELIAS and JOHN ELLIS splintered as The PURPLE HELMUTS. They made an album RIDE AGAIN for 'New Rose' Jan89.

J.J. BURNEL

Epic Epic

1988. (7") *(652836-7)* **LE WHISKEY. / EL WHISKEY** - - French
(12"+=/cd-s+=) *(652836-6/-3)* – Garden of Eden.

1988. (lp/cd) *(462424-1/-4)* **UN JOUR PARFAIT** - - French

1988. (7") *(654576-7)* **REVES. / (SHE DRIVES ME) CRAZY** - - French
(12"+=/cd-s+=) *(654576-6/-3)* – ('A'extended).

HUGH CORNWALL & ROBERT WILLIAMS

— with **ROBERT WILLIAMS** – drums, bass, guitar, vocals, synthesizer / **MARK + BOB MOTHERSBAUGH** – synth + guitar (of DEVO) / **DAVID WALLDROOP** – guitar / **IAN UNDERWOOD** – synth, saxes

U.A. not iss.

Oct 79. (lp) *(UAG 30251)* **NOSFERATU** -
– Nosferatu / Losers in a lost land / White room / Irate caterpillar / Rhythmic itch / Wired / Big bug / Mothra / Wrong way round / Puppets. *(cd-iss. May92 on 'E.M.I.'; CDP 799104-2)*

Nov 79. (7") *(BP 320)* **WHITE ROOM. / LOSERS IN A LOST LAND** -

HUGH CORNWALL

— (solo with session people)

Portrait Portrait

Sep 85. (7"/12") *(A/TX 6509)* **ONE IN A MILLION. / SIREN SONG** -

Sep 85. (lp) **BLEEDING STAR** (various Soundtrack) -

Virgin not iss.

Jan 87. (7"/12") *(VS 922)* **FACTS AND FIGURES. / ('A'version)** -

Apr 88. (7") *(VS 945)* **ANOTHER KIND OF LOVE. / REAL PEOPLE** -
(12"+=)(cd-s+=) *(VS 945-12)(VSCD 945)* – Nothing but the groove / Where is this place . . .

Jun 88. (cd/c/lp) *(CD/TC+/V 2420)* **WOLF** 98 -
– Another kind of love / Cherry rare / Never never / Real slow / Break of dawn / Clubland / Dreaming away / Decadence / All the tea in China / Getting involved.

Jul 88. (7") *(VS 1093)* **DREAMING AWAY. / BLUE NOTE** -
(12"+=) *(VST 1093)* – Getting involved.
(cd-s++=) *(VSCD 1093)* The English walk.

In May92, ex-member HUGH CORNWALL teamed up with COOK & WEST (ex-BLUE MINK) to release single 'Sweet Sister'.

Syd STRAW

Born: Los Angeles, California, USA. The daughter of actor, Jack Straw, SYD headed for New York after leaving school and eventually landed session work for PAT BENATAR. The mid-80's saw her working with the loose alternative collective, The GOLDEN PALAMINOS, appearing on the albums, 'Visions Of Excess' and 'Blast Of Silence', although it wasn't until 1989 that the singer would record an album of her own material. Released on 'Virgin', 'SURPRISE' featured a guestlist that read like a who's who of critical faves including VAN DYKES PARKS, RY COODER, MICHAEL STIPE and RICHARD THOMPSON. Nevertheless, as any Hollywood executive knows, the big names don't always pull in the punters and as the album sank into obscurity, STRAW busied herself with other projects. Seven years went by before the release of 'WAR AND PEACE' (1996), a belated sophomore effort released on the recently reactivated 'Capricorn' label ('Mercury' in the UK) and featuring musical backing from the SKELETONS i.e. DON THOMPSON, LOU WHITNEY, KELLY BROWN and JOE TERRY. Confirming her talents as a painfully honest and insightful singer/songwriter, the record was full of rootsy odes to lost love and missed opportunites that functioned perfectly as a soundtrack for crying into your proverbial beer. When not putting her emotional life under the scalpel, STRAW was as busy as ever with other artists, working with the likes of VIC CHESNUTT and WILCO amongst others.

Album rating: SURPRISE (*7) / WAR AND PEACE (*6)

SYD STRAW – vocals (ex-GOLDEN PALOMINOS) / with a plethora of session people incl. VAN DYKE PARKS, RICHARD THOMPSON, RY COODER, MICHAEL STIPE, ANTON FIER, MARSHALL CRENSHAW, DON WAS, PETER BLEGVAD, PETER HOLSAPPLE, BENMONT TENCH, MARC RIBOT, DAVE ALVIN, MATT IRVING, BERNIE WORRELL, J.D. FOSTER, TONY LEVIN, JOHN DOE, JERRY MAROTTA, JODY HARRIS, PINO PALLADINO, CHRIS STAMEY, MICHAEL BLAIR, JIM KELTNER, ERIC AMBEL, etc

Virgin America / Virgin

Jun 89. (lp/c/cd) *(VUSLP/VUSMC/CDVUS 6)* <260110> **SURPRISE** [ ] [ ]
– Think too hard / Heart of darkness / Chasing vapor trails (his turn to cry) / Almost magic / Crazy American / Hard times / Future 40's (string of pearls) / The unanswered question / Sphinx / Racing the ruins / Golden dreams.

Sep 89. (7") *(VUS 6)* **FUTURE 40'S (STRING OF PEARLS). / TAKEN** [ ] [ ]
(12"+=/3"cd-s+=) *(VUS T/CD 6)* – Learning the game.

Jan 90. (7") *(VUS 16)* **THINK TOO HARD. / HARD TIMES** [ ] [ ]
(12"+=/cd-s+=) *(VUS T/CD 16)* – If you don't want my love / Racing to the ruins.

— during her solo recording hiatus, she helped out VIC CHESNUTT, RICKIE LEE JONES, WILCO, LEMONHEADS, DAVID SANBORN, etc.

— now with The SKELETONS as backing:- **DON THOMPSON** – guitar / **LOU WHITNEY** – bass / **KELLY BROWN + JOE TERRY** – keyboards / **BOBBY HICKS** – drums

Mercury / Capricorn

Oct 96. (cd) <(532457-2)> **WAR AND PEACE** [ ] [ ] May96
– Toughest girl in the world / A million miles / Time has done this / Love, and the lack of it / CBGB's / All things change / Madrid / Almost as blue / Water, please / X-ray / Howl / Static / Black squirrel / Train that takes you away.

STRAWBERRY SWITCHBLADE

Formed: Glasgow, Scotland . . . early 80's by JILL BRYSON and ROSE McDOWELL. This new wave female duo made their debut in 1983 with the introspective 'TREES AND FLOWERS' single, such indie scene notables as KATE ST. JOHN and RODDY FRAME lending their musical expertise. Cult acclaim turned into bonafide Top 5 success the following year when the bewitching pop atmospherics of 'SINCE YESTERDAY' gave the girls a brief period of fame. With no further major hits to support it, an eponymous debut album made a similarly brief appearance in the Top 30, the girls following in Glasgow's long C&W tradition and making a last ditch attempt to breathe some life into their career with a cover of the Dolly Parton classic, 'JOLENE'. Depsite a Top 60 placing, the duo subsequently called it a day with McDOWELL going on to perform with INTO A CIRCLE and various other experimental projects.

Album rating: STRAWBERRY SWITCHBLADE (*4)

ROSE McDOWELL – vocals, guitar / **JILL BRYSON** (b.11 Feb'61) – vocals, guitar / with guests **KATE ST. JOHN** – oboe (ex-RAVISHING BEAUTIES) / **RODDY FRAME** – acoustic guitar (of AZTEC CAMERA) / **MARK 'BEDDERS' BEDFORD** – bass (of MADNESS)

92 Happy Customers / not iss.

Jul 83. (7") *(HAP 001)* **TREES AND FLOWERS. / GO AWAY** [ ] [-]
(12"+=) *(HAPT 001)* – Trees and flowers (just music).

— now with **GARY HITCHINS + ALAN PARK** – keyboards / **BORIS WILLIAMS** – drums / **DAVE MORRIS** – percussion / **BRUCE NOCKLES** – trumpet

Korova / not iss.

Oct 84. (7") *(KOW 38)* **SINCE YESTERDAY. / BY THE SEA** [5] [-]
(12"+=) *(KOW 38T)* – Sunday morning.

Mar 85. (7") *(KOW 39)* **LET HER GO. / BEAUTIFUL END** [59] [-]
(12"+=) *(KOWT 59)* – Michael walks by night.

Apr 85. (lp/c) *(KODE/CODE 11)* **STRAWBERRY SWITCHBLADE** [25] [-]
– Since yesterday / Deep water / Another day / Little river / 10 James Orr Street / Let her go / Who knows what love is / Go away / Secrets / Being cold.

May 85. (7") *(KOW 41)* **WHO KNOWS WHAT LOVE IS. / POOR HEART** [ ] [-]
(12"+=) *(KOW 41T)* – Let her go (mix).

Sep 85. (7") *(KOW 42)* **JOLENE. / BEING COLD** [53] [-]
(12"+=) *(KOW 42T)* – Black taxi.

— split late '85; ROSE subsequently joined INTO A CIRCLE

Joe STRUMMER (see under ⇒ CLASH)

Dan STUART (see under ⇒ GREEN ON RED)

STUMP

Formed: based- London, England . . . 1983 by former MICRODISNEY members MICK LYNCH (who actually replaced SHRUBS-bound original singer NICK HOBBS) and ROB McKAHEY, alongside KEV HOPPER and CHRIS SALMON. The inimitable STUMP made their debut on the ubiquitous 'Ron Johnson' label in early '86 with the acclaimed 'MUD ON A COLON' EP, featuring the madcap indulgence of 'GRAB HANDS'. Championed by Radio 1's John Peel, the band's clanking rhythms, atonal, wobbling guitars and demented vocals/lyrics were brought to an even wider audience via the inclusion of the seminal 'BUFFALO' on the NME C86 compilation. Witnessing LYNCH barking out the "How Much Is The Fish? . . . Does The Fish Have Chips?' refrain on Channel 4's 'The Tube' was surely one of the musical highlights of the 80's, certainly one of the most talked about. For anyone who missed it first time round, the track was duly featured on debut mini-set, 'QUIRK OUT' (1986), released on the 'Stuff' label following the financial collapse of 'Ron Johnson'. A period of furious studio beavering ensued, eventually resulting in a full length debut proper, 'A FIERCE PANCAKE' (1988). The first release of their new major label deal with 'Ensign', the record pleased hardcore fans with such SPLODGE/BEEFHEART-esque behaviour as 'CHARLTON HESTON' (apparently "keeps his vest on!") but received a cold shoulder from a music press keen to distance themselves from anything remotely C86. Criminally ignored, the band took one last shot at success with a re-issued 'BUFFALO' later that year; its failure and the band's subsequent split remain one of indie music's more vexing injustices.

Album rating: QUIRK OUT (*7) / A FIERCE PANCAKE (*8)

MICK LYNCH – vocals (ex-MICRODISNEY) repl. NICK HOBBS who joined SHRUBS / **CHRIS SALMON** – guitar / **KEV HOOPER** – bass / **ROB MacKAHEY** – drums (ex-MICRODISNEY)

Ron Johnson / not iss.

Feb 86. (12"ep) *(ZRON 6)* **MUD ON A COLON** [ ] [-]
– Orgasm way / Grab hands / Ice the leviant / 55-0-55.

Stuff / not iss.

Oct 86. (m-lp) *(STUFF 2)* **QUIRK OUT** [ ] [-]
– Tupperware stripper / Our fathers / Kitchen table / Buffalo / Everything in its place / Bit part actor. *(c-iss.May87; STUFFCU 2)*

Ensign / not iss.

Feb 88. (7") *(ENY 612)* **CHAOS. / ICE THE LEVIANT** [ ] [-]
(12"+=) *(ENYX 612)* – Safe sex.

Mar 88. (cd)(c/lp) *(CCD 1641)(Z+/CHEN 9)* **A FIERCE PANCAKE** [ ] [-]
– Lying it down / In the green / Roll the bodies over / Bone / Eager bereaver / Chaos / Alcohol / Charlton Heston / A fierce pancake / (A visit to the) Doctor / Heartache.

— (the track, 'CHARLTON HESTON', featured The IRRESISTABLE FORCE)

Jun 88. (7") *(ENY 614)* **CHARLTON HESTON. / THE RATS** [72] [-]
(12"+=) *(ENYX 614)* – Angst forecast.

Nov 88. (7") *(ENY 619)* **BUFFALO. / THE SONG REMAINS THE SAME** [ ] [-]
(12"+=) *(ENYX 619)* – Thelma.

— disbanded early 1989 and KEV HOOPER went solo. In May '90, he issued the single, 'THE SOUND OF GYROSCOPES', and album (Jul'90), 'STOLEN JEWELS' for the 'Getty' label. MICK and ROB re-formed STUMP in Sep '91.

– compilation, others, etc. –

Feb 87. (12"ep) *Strange Fruit; (SFPS 019)* **THE PEEL SESSIONS** (5/2/86) [ ] [-]
– Down on the kitchen table / Orgasm way / Grab hands / Buffalo.

STUPIDS

Formed: Ipswich, Suffolk, England . . . December '83 by a loose, pseudonymous crew with a core of TOMMY STUPID, MARTY TUFF, ED WENN and STEVIE SNAX. Inspired by US hardcore icons such as The CIRCLE JERKS and SUICIDAL TENDENCIES, The STUPIDS took their own irreverent approach to slamdiving and skateboarding via a series of albums on their own 'Children Of The Revolution Records'. A precursor to bands like SNUFF and The SENSELESS THINGS, The STUPIDS quickly acquired cult status, a deal with 'Vinyl Solution' ensuring a wider audience for the 'VAN STUPID' (1987) and 'JESUS MEETS THE STUPIDS' (1987) albums (by the release of which MARTY had been substituted with PAULY PIZZA) while the continuing support of John Peel made sure they were heard by a varied cross section of the indie community. Comparisons were often drawn between The STUPIDS and Aussie hardcore pranksters The HARD-ONS, both bands sharing a juvenile sense of humour and a dedication to anarchic live sets. Never the most stable of bands, it came as little surprise when they finally fell apart in 1989. The various band members were also simultaneously involved with their own bands (BAD DRESS SENSE, SCHNOZZER and FRANKFURTER II), ED and PAULY subsequently forming SINK at the turn of the decade.

Album rating: PERUVIAN VACATION (*6) / RETARD PICNIC (*6) / VAN STUPID (*6) / JESUS MEETS THE STUPIDS (*6)

TOMMY STUPID (b. WITHERS) – vocals, guitar, drums / **ED SHRED** (b. WENN) – guitar, bass, vocals / **STEVIE SNAX** – bass / **MARTY TUFF** – guitar

Children Of The Revolution / not iss.

Mar 85. (7"ep) *(COR 3)* **VIOLENT NUN EP** [ ] [-]

May 86. (lp) *(GURT 9)* **PERUVIAN VACATION** [ ] [-]
(cd-iss. Sep93 on 'Clay'+=; CLAYCD 116) – VIOLENT NUN EP / Leave your ears behind / (11 rare tracks).

Oct 86. (lp) *(GURT 15)* **RETARD PICNIC** [ ] [-]
– The memory burns / Sleeping troubles / Terrordome / Heard it all before / Jesus, do what you have to do / Yah dude!! / Something's got to give / Hawaiian vacation / Shaded eyes / Frankfurter / Slumber party massacre / Waltz of the new wavers / Your little world / Killed by a cripple / We suck / Peiople in your neighbourhood / I'm so lazy / Wipe out. *(cd-iss. Nov93 on 'Clay'+=; CLAYCD 117)* – (Stupids flexi / Feedback sessions / Retard Picnic out-takes).

— **PAULY PIZZA** – bass; repl. MARTY

Vinyl Solution / not iss.

May 87. (m-lp) *(SOL 2)* **VAN STUPID** [ ] [-]

Jul 87. (lp; as BAD DRESS SENSE) *(SOL 4)* **GOODBYE . . . IT WAS FUN** [ ] [-]
– G.C.B. / Could I ever / Truth / Cynical smile / Life's demand / Never mine / Always away / Need to love.

— no ED or TOMMY on above

Aug 87. (12"ep) *(FART 1)* **meet (FRANKFURTER) ep** [ ] [-]
– Eat me / etc.

Dec 87. (lp) *(SOL 7)* **JESUS MEETS THE STUPIDS** [ ] [-]
– Skid row / You never win / Do you really have to? / Fridge / Blue blood / Slit your wrists / etc *(w/ free 7"ep)*

— disbanded the following year

– compilations, etc. –

Sep 88. (12"ep) *Strange Fruit; (SFPS 054)* **PEEL SESSIONS** (12.5.87) [ ] [-]
– Life's a drug / Heard it all before / Shaded eyes / Dog bog / Stupid Monday.

SINK

ED SHRED (aka WENN) – vocals, guitar / **PAULY** – bass

Poontang | not iss.

Jan 89. (7"ep) *(POON 1)* **TAKE THE HOSSES WITH THE LOSSES** [ ] [-]
– Diamonds / I hate yourself / Some lilac evening / Mama sink / Birthday song / For what it's worth (acoustic).

Jun 89. (7"ep) *(POON 2)* **ON THE TRACKS, FEELING BLUE** [ ] [-]
– Blue noodles / Slippin' thru my hands / Blues man / Fire and brimstone / If only you were lonely.

Decoy | not iss.

Jan 90. (lp) *(DYL 6)* **ANOTHER LOVE TRIANGLE** [ ] [-]

— new guitarist (ex-PERFECT DAZE)

Jun 90. (lp) **OLD MAN SNAKE AND THE FAT BLACK PIG** [ ] [-]
(above might have been abandoned)

Nov 90. (lp/cd) *Decoy; (DYL 21/+CD)* **MAMA SINK THE FIRST 18 YEARS (1963-1989)** (compilation of first 2 EP's) [ ] [-]

City Slang | unknown

Jan 92. (lp/cd) *(EFA 04072/+CD)* **VEGA-TABLES** [ ] [ ]

X-Mist | not iss.

Oct 92. (7") *(EFA 1548-7)* **100 TONS. /** [ ] [ ]

— disappeared after above

STYLE COUNCIL (see under ⇒ WELLER, Paul)

Poly STYRENE (see under ⇒ X-RAY SPEX)

STYRENES (see under ⇒ ELECTRIC EELS)

SUBCIRCUS

Formed: London, England ... 1995 by North East-born frontman PETER BRADLEY JR, Danish-born guitarist NICOLAJ BLOCH, bassist GEORGE BROWN and drummer TOMMAS ARNBY. Inspired by the success of RADIOHEAD and SUEDE, this angst-rock outfit earned a deal with 'Echo' records (home to JULIAN COPE, BABYBIRD, MOLOKO, etc), releasing their eponymous debut set in late summer '96. The relative success of minor spin off hits such as '86'd' and 'U LOVE U', seemed to bode well for the future and the group looked set to establish themselves in the States courtesy of a deal with 'Dreamworks'. Re-packaged as 'CAROUSEL', the debut album was issued once more a year later, although this strategy proved flawed as many ringside seats lay vacant.

Album rating: SUBCIRCUS (or) CAROUSEL (*6)

PETER BRADLEY JR – vocals / **NICOLAJ BLOCH** – guitar / **GEORGE BROWN** – bass / **TOMMAS ARNBY** – drums

Echo | DreamWorks

Sep 96. (cd/lp) *(ECH CD/LP 013)* **SUBCIRCUS** [ ] [-]
– I want you like an accident / U love U / 20th century bitch / Shelly's on the telephone / Storm fly baby / 86'D / Gravity girl and analogue / Las zoot suit / Article 11 (early departure) / So strange.

Jan 97. (7") *(ECS 030)* **86'D. / ARTICLE 11** [ ] [-]
(cd-s+=) *(ECSCD 030)* – Animals they'll remember you (temporary dream decay) / Gravity girl and analogue.

Apr 97. (7"blue) *(ECS 034)* **U LOVE U. / CENTRAL HEATING BOILER** [61] [-]
(cd-s+=) *(ECSCD 034)* – She ain't heavy.
(cd-s) *(ECSXS 034)* – ('A'session) / 86'd (session) / Article 11 (session) / I want you like an accident (session).

Jun 97. (7"bronze) *(ECS 043)* **86'D. / DISPOSABLE YOUTH** [56] [-]
(gold-cd-s+=) *(ECSCD 043)* – Kill the distraction, kill your reaction / 86'd the video (CD-ROM).
(cd-s) *(ECSCX 043)* – ('A'-LHB's big top mix) / ('A'-Moloko mix) / ('A'-Wide receiver sawn off dub mix).

Aug 97. (7") *(ECS 038)* **SHELLY'S ON THE TELEPHONE. / ('A'live demo)** [ ] [-]
(cd-s+=) *(ECSCD 038)* – Accident (live) / U love u (video).
(cd-s) *(ECSCX 038)* – ('A'side) / ('A'-Fuzz Townshend mix) / ('A'-Beatniks mix) / ('A'video).

Sep 97. (cd/c/lp) *(ECH CD/MC/LP 018) <50026>* **CAROUSEL** [ ] [ ]
– Shelly's on the telephone / 86'd / 20th century bitch / U love U / Stormfly baby / I want you like an accident / Las zoot suit / Gravity girl and analogue / Article 11 (early departure) / So strange / Kill this distraction, kill your reaction.

SUBHUMANS

Formed: Vancouver, Canada ... late 70's by WIMPY BOY, MIKE GRAHAM, GERRY USELESS and GREG DIMWIT. Pioneering the Canadian hardcore/punk scene, they released a series of singles beginning with 'DEATH TO THE SICKOIDS', in late '78. Two further 45's for 'Quintessence', 'DEATH WAS TOO KIND' and 'FIRING SQUAD', displayed the uncompromisingly politically correct stance which would eventually see GERRY end up in jail. Following their debut album, 'INCORRECT THOUGHTS' later in 1980, the bass player was sentenced to ten years for his part in a bombing campaign which took in such targets as a nuclear components factory, a hydro-power station and several sex shops. He was subsequently replaced by bass player, RON, while the band had already found a new drummer, JIM IWAGAMA to fill in for GREG JAMES. The upheaval undoubtedly put a brake on their career and only one further album ('NO WISHES, NO PRAYERS') appeared before WIMPY BOY (BRIAN GOBLE) and GREG joined D.O.A.

Album rating: INCORRECT THOUGHTS (*7) / NO WISHES, NO PRAYERS (*6)

WIMPY BOY (b. BRIAN GOBLE) – vocals (ex-SKULLS) / **MIKE GRAHAM** – guitar / **GERRY USELESS** (b. GERRY HANNAH) – bass / **GREG DIMWIT** (b. GREG JAMES) – drums

not iss. | SI

Dec 78. (7") <A00> **DEATH TO THE SICKOIDS. / OH CANADUH** [-] [ ]

not iss. | Quintessence

Feb 80. (12"ep) *<QEP12 02>* **DEATH WAS TOO KIND / FUCK YOU. / INQUISITION DAY / SLAVE TO MY DICK** [-] [ ]

Jun 80. (7") *<QS 105>* **FIRING SQUAD. / NO PRODUCTIVITY** [-] [ ]

not iss. | Friends

Nov 80. (lp) *<FR 008>* **INCORRECT THOUGHTS** [-] [ ]
– The scheme / New order / Behind my smile / Out of line / Big picture / Dead at birth / Urban gorillas / War in my head / Firing squad / Slave to my dick / Death to the sickoids / Greaser boy / Model of stupidity / We're alive / Refugee / Let's go down to Hollywood and shoot people. *(UK-iss.Apr88 on 'CD Presents'; CD 036)*

— **JIM IWAGAMA** – drums; repl. GREG JAMES who joined POINTED STICKS, although he returned and was joined by **RON** – bass; who had repl. the jail-bound GERRY (see above)

not iss. | S.S.T.

1983. (lp) **NO WISHES, NO PRAYERS** [-] [ ]

— they split when GOBLE and JAMES joined D.O.A. (the latter was the elder brother of their CHUCK BISCUITS).

SUBHUMANS

Formed: Melksham, Wiltshire, England ... 1981 by main writer DICK LUCAS, BRUCE, GRANT and TROTSKY. Inspired by the uncompromising ideology of CRASS, anarcho-punks The SUBHUMANS concerned themselves with human rights, vegetarianism and a hankering for the downfall of the Tories. This much was evident from a series of EP's in the early 80's, namely, 'DEMOLITION WAR', 'REASONS FOR EXISTENCE' and 'RELIGIOUS WARS'. The self-explanatory 'THE DAY THE COUNTRY DIED', was the title of their late 1982 debut album, although this was the last recording to feature GRANT who was replaced by PHIL. The following year, the band set up their own label, 'Bluurg', to release both their own recordings and those of other acts with a similarly militant outlook. Moving towards a more heavyweight punk sound, LUCAS and Co continued to release the odd album or two before they metamorphosised into ska/reggae/punk fusion act, CULTURE SHOCK, in 1987. Towards the end of the decade, by which time they had delivered three albums, DICK broke away to spearhead his own outfit, CITIZEN FISH. Driving home his 90's free spirit message more successfully than ever before, LUCAS continued to command the festival/crusty crowd with a conscientious but ebullient mixture of politico skank-punk beginning with the 'FREE SOULS IN A TRAPPED ENVIRONMENT' set.

Album rating: THE DAY THE COUNTRY DIED (*6) / TIME FLIES ... BUT AEROPLANES CRASH (*5) / FROM THE CRADLE TO THE GRAVE (*5) / WORLDS APART (*5) / EP-LP (*5) / 29:29 SPLIT VISION (*5) / Culture Shock: GO WILD! (*5) / ONWARDS AND UPWARDS (*5) / ALL THE TIME (*5) / Citizen Fish: FREE SOULS IN A TRAPPED ENVIRONMENT (*6) / WIDER THAN A POSTCARD (*5) / MILLENNIA MADNESS (*5)

DICK (b. RICHARD LUCAS) – vocals / **BRUCE** – guitar / **GRANT** – bass / **TROTSKY** – drums

Spiderleg | not iss.

Nov 81. (7"ep) *(SOB 1)* **DEMOLITION WAR** [ ] [-]
– Parasites / Drugs of youth / Animal / Who's gonna fight in the third world war / Society / Human error. *(re-iss. 1988 on 'Bluurg'; XEP 1)*

Apr 82. (7"ep) *(SDL 5)* **REASONS FOR EXISTANCE** [ ] [-]
– Big city / Reason for existance / Cancer / Peroxide. *(re-iss. 1988 on 'Bluurg'; XEP 2)*

Aug 82. (7"ep) *(SDL 7)* **RELIGIOUS WARS** [ ] [-]
– Religious wars / Love is [illegible] / Work experience / It's gonna get worse. *(re-iss. 1988 on 'Bluurg'; XEP 3)*

Dec 82. (lp) *(SDL 9)* **THE DAY THE COUNTRY DIED** [ ] [-]
– All gone dead / Ashtray dirt / Killing / Minority / Nothing I can do / Mickey Mouse is dead / Dying world / Subvert city / Big brother / No / New age / I don't wanna die / Zyklon B-movie / No more gigs / Black and white / 'Til the pigs come round. *(re-iss. 1988 on 'Bluurg' lp/c; XLP 1/+C) (cd-iss. Jun91 lp/c/cd; XLP 1/+C/CD)*

— **PHIL** – bass; repl. GRANT

Bluurg | not iss.

Jun 83. (7"ep) *(FISH 2)* **EVOLUTION / SO MUCH MONEY. / GERM / NOT ME** [ ] [-]

Nov 83. (12"ep) *(FISH 5)* **TIME FLIES . . . BUT AEROPLANES CRASH** [ ] [-]

Jun 84. (lp/c) *(FISH 8/+C)* **FROM THE CRADLE TO THE GRAVE** [ ] [-]
– Forget / Waste of breath / Where's the freedom? / Adversity / Reality is waiting for a bus / Wake up screaming / Rain / From the cradle to the grave. *(cd-iss. Mar92; FISH 8CD)*

Dec 84. (7"ep) *(FISH 10)* **RATS EP** [ ] [-]

Jan 86. (lp/c) *(FISH 12/+C)* **WORLDS APART** [ ] [-]
– 33322 / British disease / Heads of state / Apathy / Fade away / Businessmen /

Someone is lying / Pigman / Can't hear the words / Get to work on time / Carry on laughing / Straightline thinking / Ex teenage rebel / Power games / 33322. *(cd-iss. Nov91; FISH 12CD)*

Oct 86. (lp/c) *(FISH 14/+C)* **EP-LP** -
(cd-iss. Nov91; FISH 14CD)

Oct 87. (lp/c) *(FISH 16/+C)* **29-29 SPLIT VISION** -
(cd-iss. Mar92; FISH 16CD)

—— had already split early '87, and above was postumous

– compilations, others –

Jun 91. (lp/c/cd) *Bluurgh; (FISH 12/+C/CD)* **TIME FLIES . . . BUT AEROPLANES EP / RATS EP** -

CULTURE SHOCK

DICK, BRUCE, PHIL + TROTSKY

Bluurg not iss.

May 87. (lp) *(FISH 18)* **GO WILD** -
(re-iss. Feb93; same)

Apr 88. (lp/c) *(FISH 20/+C)* **ONWARDS AND UPWARDS** -
(cd-iss. Feb93; FISH 20CD)

Nov 89. (lp/c) *(FISH 23/+C)* **ALL THE TIME** -
(re-iss. Feb93; same)

CITIZEN FISH

DICK, PHIL + TROTSKY with **JASPER** – bass

Bluurg Bluurg

Oct 90. (lp/c/cd) *(<FISH 24/+C/CD>)* **FREE SOULS IN A TRAPPED ENVIRONMENT**
– Supermarket song / Break into a run / Rainbows / Possession / Small scale wars / Home economics / Paint / Talk is cheap / Face off / Youth / Flesh and blood / Get off the phone / Experiment Earth / How to write ultimate protest songs / Charity. *(cd-iss. Apr94; (FISH 24CD)*

Mar 92. (lp/c/cd) *(<FISH 26/+C/CD>)* **WIDER THAN A POSTCARD**

Nov 93. (lp/cd) *(FISH 28/+CD)* **LIVE FISH (live)** -

Jan 94. (lp/c/cd) *(<FISH 31/+C/CD>)* **FLINCH**
– TV dinner / Naked / Small talk / Time control / Dividing lines / Media men / Bag lady / First impressions / Wet cement / Circular vision / Social insecurity / Invisible people / Flinch.

Bluurg Lookout

1990's. (7") *<LK 60>* **DISPOSABLE DREAM. / FLESH AND BLOOD II** -

Sep 95. (lp/cd) *(FISH 34/+CD)* *<LK 123>* **MILLENNIA MADNESS** Oct95

Lookout Lookout

Sep 96. (cd/lp) *(<LK 152>)* **THIRST**
– Feeding / Pop songs / City on a river / Used to work / Plasticash / Scene 496: Care in a Melksham / Words on overtime / Talk about the weather / Catholic sex confession / Criminal / What Charlie said / Fill me up.

Nov 98. (7") *(LK 209)* **HABIT. /**

SUBWAY SECT (see under ⇒ GODARD, Vic)

Nikki SUDDEN (see under ⇒ SWELL MAPS)

SUDDEN SWAY

Formed: Peterborough, England . . . 1980 by MIKE McGUIRE and PETE JOSTIN, who were augmented by various personnel during the formative years of their career. Over this period a couple of self-financed singles had the music press raving, the second of which, the 'TO YOU, WITH REGARD' EP, sold well enough to gain a respectable placing in the indie charts. With the addition of SIMON FOREMAN, the SUDDEN SWAY set-up became more stable, the band almost inking a deal with majors 'C.B.S.' and 'Virgin'. Following a further single on their own label ('Chant') however, the ACR/SHRIEKBACK-influenced trio moved on to Warners subsidiary 'Blanco Y Negro', pre-dating the modern craze for remixing by gleefully churning out eight(!) different versions of 'SING SONG', their skewed interpretation of the label's request for a pop song. Confusing if not alienating their small but loyal fanbase, it was followed by another wilfully unconventional attempt to subvert their status as a major label backed "pop" outfit in the shape of 1986's double-12" EP, 'SPACEMATE'. In the wake of the inevitable parting of the ways, 'Rough Trade' would bail the band out and release a 7" EP, 'AUTUMN CUT BACK JOB LOT OFFER', featuring eight 1-minute variations on a single theme. In 1988, they finally delivered their first "normal" LP, '76 KIDS FOREVER', a quasi-concept affair that formed the basis for a pioneering series of shows bordering on interactive performance art. SIMON, quite wisely perhaps, departed soon after, leaving McGUIRE and JOSTINS to go a league beyond with 1990's swansong, 'KO-OPERA'. The pair subsequently channeled their creative powers into 'Klub Londonium', another mischievous adventure which sent its devotees/members on the equivalent of a post-modern orienteering course around the capital!

Album rating: SPACEMATE (*6) / 76 KIDS FOREVER (*5) / KO-OPERA (*6)

MICHAEL McGUIRE – vocals / **PETE JOSTINS** – instruments

Chant not iss.

1980. (7",c-s) *(CHANT 1)* **JANE'S THIRD PARTY. / DON'T GO** -

Aug 81. (12"ep) *(CHANT 2-EJSP 9692)* **TO YOU, WITH REGARD EP** -
– Alleluia! / The psychic sons / Pretty people again / Dance of joy / Tales of talking town.

—— added **SIMON FOREMAN** – guitar

Feb 84. (12"m) *(CHANT 3)* **THE TRAFFIC TAX SCHEME. / SIR SAVOIR HER VALOUR / HE SAYS CONSCIENCE** -

Blanco Y Negro not iss.

Mar 86. (7"ep/12"ep) *(NEG 18 V1/V5)* **SING SONG** -
– A Finepro demonstration (8 different versions).

Sep 86. (2x12"ep) *(BYN 8)* **SPACEMATE** -

Rough Trade not iss.

Jan 87. (7"ep) *(RT 183)* **AUTUMN CUT BACK JOB LOT OFFER** -
– (8 versions).

Dec 87. (12") *(RTT 213)* **SAT'DAY MORNIN' EPISODE** -

May 88. (lp) *(ROUGH 133)* **76 KIDS FOREVER** -

—— now without SIMON

Mar 90. (cd/lp)(c) *(CD+/R 142)(ROUGHC 142)* **KO-OPERA** -
– League of the unfashioned / League of the incomplete / League of the violated / League of the uniformed / League of the delirious / League of the noueveau poore / League of the postal modernists / League of the disappointed.

– compilations, etc. –

Nov 86. (12"ep/c-ep) *Strange Fruit; (SFPS/+C 005)* **PEEL SESSION** (16.11.83) -
– Let's evolve / Relationships.

SUEDE

Formed: London, England . . . 1989 by BRETT ANDERSON, who, by 1992 had put together the final line-up of guitarist BERNARD BUTLER, bassist MATT OSMAN and drummer SIMON GILBERT (ELASTICA prime mover, JUSTINE FRISCHMANN, had also been an early member). After a single, 'BE MY GOD' / 'ART', failed to appear in 1990 on 'RML' (this lost recording was famous for featuring ex-SMITHS drummer, MIKE JOYCE), the band signed to 'Nude', precipitating a storm of media hype and adulation. Featured

on the cover of NME before they had even released their debut single, the band became press darlings of a post-grunge/pre-Brit pop music scene desperate for a bit of cheap glamour. Widely touted as spiritual antecedents of The SMITHS, the group were actually closer in style to the camp affectations of mid-period BOWIE, although there was definitely a MORRISSEY-like archness to the lyrics, the glum one actually taking to covering 'MY INSATIABLE ONE' (the B-side of SUEDE's acclaimed debut effort, 'THE DROWNNERS') live. Another couple of singles followed, 'METAL MICKEY' and 'ANIMAL NITRATE', these scoring successively higher chart positions. The media support, together with ANDERSON's sleazy, androgynous posturing, made him, and his band, instant heroes for a new generation of crazy, mixed up kids, the eponymous 1993 debut album quickly reaching No.1. 'Nude's takeover by 'Sony' in early '93 gave the act a bit of major label muscle, ironically helping them on their way to becoming one of the biggest "indie" bands in Britain. In early '94, the band scored their biggest hit single to date with the epic 'STAY TOGETHER', the track peaking at No.3. Later that Spring, gay drummer SIMON bravely went to the House Of Commons to air his views on the homosexual laws of consent, which were to be lowered from 21 to either 16 (the heterosexual age) or 18, as it finally turned out. Around the same time, more controversy dogged the group when an American jazz singer called SUEDE won her lawsuit against the band in the US, the upshot of the affair being that from that point on, the band were to be known in America as LONDON SUEDE (lucky for them they didn't come from Leatherhead!). Meantime, the group had won the Mercury Music Prize for their acclaimed debut album and were well on the way to releasing a follow-up, 'DOG MAN STAR' (1994). The last album to feature the departing BUTLER (heralded by some as the UK's most promising guitarist since JOHNNY MARR, BUTLER subsequently went on to a successful, if short lived, collaboration with DAVID McALMONT before signing to 'Creation' and embarking on a solo career), it marked something of a departure in the band's sound, a dense, ambitious set which met with a mixed critical reception. Unbowed, SUEDE swaggered on, recruiting the teenage RICHARD OAKES as BUTLER's replacement and providing a welcome diversion from the laddish excesses of Brit-pop. SUEDE's next effort, 'COMING UP' proved to be their most consistent set to date, spawning the brilliant lowlife anthem, 'TRASH' along with the similarly infectious, organic glam of 'FILMSTAR' and the dislocated melancholy of 'SATURDAY NIGHT'. • **Songwriters:** ANDERSON / BUTLER, except; BRASS IN POCKET (Pretenders).

Album rating: SUEDE (*9) / DOG MAN STAR (*8) / COMING UP (*7)

BRETT ANDERSON – vocals / **BERNARD BUTLER** – guitar, piano / **MATT OSMAN** – bass / **SIMON GILBERT** – drums

Nude | not iss.

Apr 92. (7") *(nud 1s)* **THE DROWNERS. / TO THE BIRDS** 49 -
(12"+=/cd-s+=) *(nud 1 t/cd)* – My insatiable one.

Sep 92. (7"/c-s) *(nud 3 s/mc)* **METAL MICKEY. / WHERE THE PIGS DON'T FLY** 17 -
(12"+=/cd-s+=) *(NUD 3 t/cd)* – He's dead.

Nude-Sony | Columbia

Feb 93. (7"/c-s) *(NUD 4 s/mc)* **ANIMAL NITRATE. / THE BIG TIME** 7 -
(12"+=/cd-s+=) *(nud 4 t/cd)* – Painted people.

Apr 93. (cd/c/lp) *(NUDE 1 cd/mc/lp)* <53792> **SUEDE** 1
– So young / Animal nitrate / She's not dead / Moving / Pantomime horse / The drowners / Sleeping pills / Breakdown / Metal Mickey / Animal lover / The next life.

May 93. (7"/c-s) *(nud 5 s/mc)* **SO YOUNG. / HIGH RISING** 22 -
(12"+=/cd-s+=) *(nud 5 t/cd)* – Dolly.

Sep 93. (cd-ep) <44K 77172> **THE DROWNERS / MY INSATIABLE ONE / TO THE BIRDS / THE BIG TIME / HE'S DEAD (live)** -

Feb 94. (7"/c-s) *(nud 9 s/mc)* **STAY TOGETHER. / THE LIVING DEAD** 3 -
(ext;12"+=/cd-s+=) *(nud 9 t/cd)* – *My dark star.*

— In Spring 1994, gay drummer SIMON went to House Of Commons, to air his views on the homosexual laws of consent, which were to be lowered from 21 to either 16 (the heterosexual age) or 18, as it turned out to be. Around the same time, an American jazz singer called SUEDE won her lawsuit against the band in the US. They are now to be called LONDON SUEDE, but thankfully only in the States.

Mar 94. (cd-ep) <CK 64382> **STAY TOGETHER / THE LIVING DEAD / MY DARK STAR / DOLLY HIGH RISING / STAY TOGETHER (extended)** -

Sep 94. (7"/c-s) *(nud 10 s/mc)* **WE ARE THE PIGS. / KILLING OF A FLASH BOY** 18 -
(12"+=/cd-s+=) *(nud 10 t/cd)* – Whipsnade.

Oct 94. (cd/c/d-lp) *(nude 3 cd/mc/lp)* <66769> **DOG MAN STAR** 3
– Introducing the band / We are the pigs / Heroine / The wild ones / Daddy's speeding / The power / New generation / This Hollywood life / The 2 of us / Black or blue / The asphalt world / Still life. *<US-version +=>* Modern boys.

— BUTLER left July '94 and was repl. by 17 year-old **RICHARD OAKES** after recording album.

Nov 94. (c-s) *(nud 11mc)* **THE WILD ONES / MODERN BOYS** 18 -
(cd-s+=) *(nud 11cd1)* – This world needs a father.
(12") *(nud 11t)* – ('A'side) / Eno's introducing the band.
(cd-s) *(nud 11cd2)* – (above 2) / Asda town.

Jan 95. (7"/c-s) *(nud 12mc)* **NEW GENERATION. / TOGETHER** 21 -
(12"+=/cd-s+=) *(nud 12 t/cd1)* – Bentswood boys.
(cd-s) *(nud 12cd2)* – ('A'side) / Animal nitrate (live) / The wild ones (live) / Pantomime horse (live).

— added new member **NEIL CODLING** – keyboards, vocals

Jul 96. (c-s) *(nud 2mc)* **TRASH / EUROPE IS OUR PLAYGROUND** 3 -
(cd-s+=) *(nud 21cd1)* – Every Monday morning comes.
(pic-cd-s) *(nud 21cd2)* – ('A'side) / Have you ever been this low? / Another no one.

Sep 96. (cd/c/lp) *(nude 6 cd/mc/lp)* <67911> **COMING UP** 1
– Trash / Filmstar / Lazy / By the sea / She / Beautiful ones / Starcrazy / Picnic by the motorway / The chemistry between us / Saturday night.

Oct 96. (c-s) *(nud 23mc)* **BEAUTIFUL ONES / BY THE SEA (demo)** 8 -
(cd-s) *(nud 23 cd1)* – ('A'side) / Young men / The sound of the streets.
(cd-s) *(nud 23 cd2)* – ('A'side) / Money / Sam.

Jan 97. (c-s) *(nud 24mc)* **SATURDAY NIGHT / PICNIC BY THE MOTORWAY (live)** 6 -
(cd-s) *(nud 24cd1)* – ('A'side) / W.S.D. / Jumble sale mums.
(cd-s) *(nud 24cd2)* – ('A'side) / This time / ('A'demo).
(d7") *(nud 24s)* – ('A'side) / This time / Beautiful ones / The sound of the streets.

Apr 97. (c-s) *(nud 27mc)* **LAZY / SHE (live)** 9 -
(cd-s) *(nud 27cd1)* – ('A'side) / These are the sad songs / Feel.
(cd-s) *(nud 27cd2)* – ('A'side) / Sadie / Digging a hole.

Aug 97. (7") *(nud 30s)* **FILMSTAR. / ('A'original demo)** 9 -
(cd-s) *(nud 30cd1)* – ('A'side) / Graffiti women / Duchess. *(w/ free video footage; Beautiful ones / Coming up.*
(cd-s) *(nud 30cd2)* – ('A'side) / Rent / Saturday night / Saturday night (cd-rom).

Oct 97. (d-cd) *(nude 9cd)* <68857> **SCI-FI LULLABIES** (flipsides) 9
– My insatiable one / To the birds / Where the pigs don't fly / He's dead / The big time / High rising / The living dead / My star / Killing of a flash boy / Whipsnade / Modern boys / Together / Bentswood boys / Europe is our playground // Every Monday morning comes / Have you ever been this low? / Another no one / Young men / The sound of the streets / Money / W.S.D. / This time / Jumble sale mums / These are the sad songs / Sadie / Graffiti women / Duchess.

SUGAR

Formed: Minneapolis, USA . . . 1992 by former HUSKER DU frontman/co-writer, BOB MOULD. Upon the demise of the latter act in 1987, MOULD signed to 'Virgin America' and subsequently entered PRINCE's 'Paisley Park' studios to lay down his first solo set, 'WORKBOOK' (1989). Augmented by the former PERE UBU rhythm section of ANTON FIER and TONY MAIMONE and employing cellists JANE SCARPANTONI and STEVE HAIGLER, MOULD confounded expectations with a largely acoustic affair trading in melodic distortion for fragments of contemplative melancholy; only the closing 'WHICHEVER WAY THE WIND BLOWS' acknowledged the sonic assault of prime HUSKER DU. Despite the guaranteed critical plaudits and the more accessible nature of the material, 'WORKBOOK's sales were modest. Perhaps as a reaction, the following year's 'BLACK SHEETS OF RAIN' – again recorded with FIER and MAIMONE – was a searing return to bleaker, noisier pastures; 'HANGING TREE' remains among the most tormented work of MOULD's career, while the likes of 'HEAR ME CALLING' and 'IT'S TOO LATE' combined keening melody with blistering soloing/dischordant riffing in patented MOULD fashion. When this album also failed to take off, the singer parted comapny from 'Virgin' and undertook a low-key acoustic tour. His wilderness period was brief, however, the emerging grunge vanguard citing HUSKER DU as a massive influence and inspiring MOULD to form another melodic power trio. Comprising of fellow songwriter/bassist, DAVE BARBE and drummer MALCOLM TRAVIS, SUGAR signed to 'Creation' and proceeded to cut one of the most feted albums of the era in 'COPPER BLUE' (1992). Leaner, tighter and cleaner, the record's bittersweet pop-hardcore crunch finally provided MOULD with a springboard for commercial success; a UK Top 10 hit, the album even spawned a Top 30 hit single in the sublime 'IF I CAN'T CHANGE YOUR MIND'. 'BEASTER', 1993's mini-album follow-up, took tracks from the 'COPPER BLUE' sessions and buried them in a multi-tiered blanket of howling distortion. Unsurprisingly it failed to spawn a hit, although its Top 3 success was no doubt sweet for the ever contrary MOULD, his follow-up proper, 'FILE UNDER EASY LISTENING (F.U.E.L.)' (1994), suggesting that he'd become bored with the whole concept. MOULD eventually disbanded the project in Spring '96, releasing a third solo album the same year, simply titled 'BOB MOULD'. • **Songwriters:** MOULD and now same with others. Covered; SHOOT OUT THE LIGHTS (Richard Thompson).

Album rating: Bob Mould: WORKBOOK (*7) / BLACK SHEETS OF RAIN (*6) / Sugar: COPPER BLUE (*10) / FILE UNDER: EASY LISTENING (*8) / BEASTER (*8) / Bob Mould: BOB MOULD (*8) / THE LAST DOG AND PONY SHOW (*7)

BOB MOULD

BOB MOULD – vocals, guitar, etc (ex-HUSKER DU) / with **ANTON FIER** – drums / **TONY MAIMONE** – bass, (both ex-PERE UBU) / **JANE SCARPANTONI** – cello (of TINY LIGHTS) / **STEVE HAIGLER** – cello

Virgin | Virgin

Jun 89. (7") *(VUS 2)* **SEE A LITTLE LIGHT. / ALL THOSE PEOPLE KNOW** -
(12"+=/cd-s+=) *(VUS 2T/CD2)* – Shoot out the lights / Composition for the young and the old (live).

Jul 89. (lp/cd) *(VUS LP/CD 2)* <91240> **WORKBOOK** Apr89
– Sunspots / Wishing well / Heartbreak a stranger / See a little light / Poison years / Sinners and their repentances / Lonely afternoon / Brasilia crossed the Tranton / Compositions for the young and old / Dreaming, I amd / Whichever way the wind blows. *(re-iss. Sep90; OVED 340)*

Aug 90. (cd/c/lp) *(VUS CD/MC/LP 21)* <91395> **BLACK SHEETS OF RAIN** May90
– Black sheets of rain / Stand guard / It's too late / One good reason / Stop your crying / Hanging tree / The last night / Hear me calling / Out of your life / Disappointed / Sacrifice – let there be peace.

Virgin | Virgin

May 94. (cd) *(CDVM 9030)* <39587> **THE POISON YEARS**
(compilation from first two sets) Jul94

SUGAR

BOB MOULD – vox, guitar, keyboards, percussion / **DAVE BARBE** – bass (ex-MERCYLAND) / **MALCOLM TRAVIS** – drums, percussion (ex-ZULUS)

Creation Rykodisc

Jul 92. (cd-ep) *<1024>* **HELPLESS / NEEDLE HITS E / IF I CAN'T CHANGE YOUR MIND / TRY AGAIN** [-] [ ]

Aug 92. (12"ep)(cd-ep) *(CRE 126T)(CRESCD 126)* **CHANGES / NEEDLE HITS E. / IF I CAN'T CHANGE YOUR MIND / TRY AGAIN** [ ] [-]

Sep 92. (cd/lp)(c) *(CRE CD/LP 129)(C-CRE 129) <RCD/RACS 10239>* **COPPER BLUE** [10] [ ]
– The act we act / A good idea / Changes / Helpless / Hoover dam / The slim / If I can't change your mind / Fortune teller / Slick / Man on the Moon.

Oct 92. (7"ep/c-ep) *(CRE/+CS 143) <1030>* **A GOOD IDEA. / WHERE DIAMONDS ARE HALOS / SLICK** [65] [ ]
(12"ep+=)(cd-ep+=) *(CRE 143T)(CRESCD 143)* – Armenia city in the sky.

Jan 93. (7"/c-s) *(CRE/+CS 149)* **IF I CAN'T CHANGE YOUR MIND. / CLOWN MASTER** [30] [ ]
(12"+=) *(CRE 149T) <1031>* – Anyone (live) / Hoover dam (live).
(cd-s) *(CRESCD 149) <1032>* – ('A'side) / The slim / Where diamonds are halos.

Apr 93. (m-cd/m-lp)(m-c) *(CRE CD/LP 153)(C-CRE 153) <50260>* **BEASTER** [3] [ ]
Come around / Tilted / Judas cradle / JC auto / Feeling better / Walking away.

Aug 93. (7") *(CRE 156)* **TILTED. / JC AUTO (live)** [48] [-]

Aug 94. (7"/c-s) *(CRE/+CS 186)* **YOUR FAVORITE THING. / MIND IS AN ISLAND** [40] [ ]
(12"+=)(cd-s+=) *(CRE 186T)(CRESCD 186) <1038>* – Frustration / And you tell me (T.V. mix).

Sep 94. (cd/lp)(c) *(CRE CD/LP 172)(C-CRE 172) <10300>* **FILE UNDER EASY LISTENING (F.U.E.L.)** [7] [50]
– Gift / Company book / Your favorite thing / What you want it to be / Gee angel / Panama city hotel / Can't help it anymore / Granny cool / Believe what you're saying / Explode and make up.

Oct 94. (7"/c-s) *(CRE/+CS 193)* **BELIEVE WHAT YOU'RE SAYING. / GOING HOME** [73] [ ]
(cd-s+=) *(CRESCD 193) <1039>* – In the eyes of my friends / And you tell me.

Dec 94. (cd-ep) *<RCD5 1040>* **GEE ANGEL / EXPLODE AND MAKE UP / SLIM / AFTER ALL THE ROADS HAVE LED TO . . .** [-] [ ]

Jul 95. (d-cd) *<10321>* **BESIDES** (compilation of b-sides, live, etc) [-] [ ]

— disbanded and BARBE formed BUZZHUNGRY / TRAVIS went to CUSTOMIZED

BOB MOULD

Creation Rykodisc

Apr 96. (cd/lp) *(CRE CD/LP 188) <10342>* **BOB MOULD** [52] [ ]
– Anymore time between / I hate alternative rock / Fort Knox, King Solomon / Next time that you leave / Egoverride / Thumbtack / Hair stew / Hair stew / Deep karma canyon / Art crisis / Roll over and die.

— now with **MATT HAMMON** – drums / **ALISON CHESLEY** – cello

Aug 98. (7") *(CRE 206)* **CLASSIFIEDS. / MOVING TRUCKS** [ ] [-]

Aug 98. (cd/lp) *(CRE CD/LP 215) <10443>* **THE LAST DOG AND PONY SHOW** [58] [ ]
– New #1 / Moving trucks / Taking everything / First drag of the day / Classifieds / Who was around? / Skintrade / Vaporub / Sweet serene / Megamaniac / Reflecting pool / Along the way / (interview).

SUGARCUBES (see under ⇒ BJORK)

SUICIDAL TENDENCIES

Formed: Venice, California, USA . . . 1982 by MIKE MUIR, LOUICHE MAYORFA and AMERY SMITH. Signing to the small frontier label, the group debuted in 1984 with the eponymous 'SUICIDAL TENDENCIES'. Vaguely political hardcore skate-punk, the record was a promising start, the frantic 'INSTITUTIONALIZED' summing up their two-fingered defiance at the "American Dream", complete with a brilliantly surreal video. With RALPH HERRERA and ROCKY GEORGE replacing AMERY and ESTES respectively, they signed to 'Virgin' worldwide, eventually releasing a follow-up effort, 'JOIN THE ARMY' (1987). The album significantly broadened the band's musical framework and when SUICIDAL TENDENCIES were really cooking, there were few acts who could match their compelling mash-up of punk, metal and bass-heavy melodic hardcore. MUIR's drawling vocals were one of the main weapons in their bandana'd, check-shirted armoury, the singer coming on like some streetsmart Godfather of skate-punk. Alongside high-octane wipe-outs like the seminal 'POSSESSED TO SKATE' and the blistering 'WAR INSIDE MY HEAD', more reflective numbers like 'A LITTLE EACH DAY' packed twice the emotional punch with half the bravado. SUICIDAL TENDENCIES also slowed things down on the the title track, its grinding groove and insistent quasi-rapping making it one of the most effective cuts on the album. On the strength of MUIR's lyrics, he's one troubled guy and his depictions of depression and anxiety are certainly more affecting and convincing than many. The dour but honestly titled 'HOW WILL I LAUGH TOMORROW . . . WHEN I CAN'T EVEN SMILE TODAY?' (1988) continued the journey through MUIR's bleak mindset, most effectively on the gonzoid 'TRIP AT THE BRAIN'. The album saw a decidedly more metallic influence creeping in which was even more pronounced on 1989's 'CONTROLLED BY HATRED / FEEL LIKE SHIT . . . DEJA VU', the monster riffing often suffocating the SUICIDAL's natural exuberance. The acclaimed 'LIGHTS . . . CAMERA . . . REVOLUTION' (1990) was an entirely different affair, the group paying heed to the funk/rap-metal revolution (which they arguably had at least something of a hand in starting). The single, 'SEND ME YOUR MONEY', was an upbeat jibe against TV evangelism (a perrenial metal favourite) built on an elasticated bass groove. The whole album was more commercial overall with an unsettling display of positivety in the lyrics, a Top 60 UK chart placing indicating the group's brief firtation with the mainstream. SUICIDAL TENDENCIES promoted the album with an opening slot on the 'Clash Of The Titans' tour alongside such thrash heavyweights as TESTAMENT, MEGADETH and SLAYER, not exactly complimentary company. It was clear MUIR was more into shaking his booty at this stage and together with new SUICIDAL bass player, ROBERT TRUJILLO, the singer took his funk-metal urges to their ultimate and rather unremarkable conclusion with side project INFECTIOUS GROOVES. The group released three albums, 'THE PLAGUE THAT MAKES YOUR BOOTY MOVE, IT'S THE INFECTIOUS GROOVE' (1991), 'SARSIPPIUS' ARK' (1993) and 'GROOVE FAMILY CYCO' (1994), although none threatened the likes of the 'CHILI PEPPERS. SUICIDAL TENDENCIES, meanwhile, returned as angry as ever with 'THE ART OF REBELLION' (1992) and 'SUICIDAL FOR LIFE' (1994), the latter album boasting no less than four tracks with the word 'fuck' in the title. Despite the current vogue for all things snotty, punky and funky, it seems that SUICIDAL TENDENCIES have yet again been shamefully overlooked, many groups aping the style and verve of a band that literally helped to invent the concept of musical cross-fertilisation. • **Trivia:** MUIR appeared on TV show 'Miami Vice' in 1992.

Album rating: SUICIDAL TENDENCIES (*6) / JOIN THE ARMY (*7) / HOW WILL I LAUGH TOMORROW . . . (*6) / CONTROLLED BY HATRED / FEEL LIKE SHIT . . . DEJA VU (*5) / LIGHTS . . . CAMERA . . . REVOLUTION (*7) / THE ART OF REBELLION (*6) / STILL CYCO AFTER ALL THESE YEARS (*6) / SUICIDAL FOR LIFE (*5) / PRIME CUTS compilation (*6) / Infectious Grooves: THE PLAGUE THAT MAKES YOUR BOOTY (*5)

MIKE MUIR – vocals / **GRANT ESTES** – guitar / **LOUICHE MAYOREA** – bass / **AMERY SMITH** – drums

not iss. Frontier

1984. (lp) *<FLP 1011>* **SUICIDAL TENDENCIES** [-] [ ]
– Suicide's an alternative / You'll be sorry / I shot the Devil / Won't fall in love today / Memories of tomorrow / I want more / I saw your mommy . . . / 2 sided politics / Suicidal failure / Sublimal / Institutionalized / Possessed / Fascist pig. *(UK-iss.Jan88 & Sep91 on 'Virgin' cd+=/c/lp; CD/TC+/V 2495)* – Possessed to skate / Human guinea pig / Two wrongs don't make a right. *(re-iss. Apr97 on 'Epitaph' cd/c/lp; 0104-2/-4/-1)*

— **RALPH HERRERA** – drums repl. AMERY / **ROCKY GEORGE** – guitar repl. ESTES

Virgin Caroline

Apr 87. (7") *(VS 967)* **POSSESSED TO SKATE. / HUMAN GUINEA PIG** [ ] [ ]
(12"+=/12"pic-d+=) *(VS 967-12)* – Two wrongs don't make a right (but they make me feel better).

Apr 87. (cd/c/lp) *(CD/TC+/V 2424) <1336>* **JOIN THE ARMY** [81] [100]
– Suicidal maniac / Join the army / You got, I want / A little each day / The prisoner / War inside my head / I feel your pain and I survive / Human guinea pig / Possessed to skate / No name, no words / Cyco / Looking in your eyes / Two wrongs don't make a right (but they make me feel better). *(re-iss. Apr90 lp/c; OVED/+C 307)*

Jan 88. (12"m) *(VST 1039)* **INSTITUTIONALIZED. / WAR INSIDE MY HEAD / CYCO** [ ] [ ]

— added **MIKE CLARK** – rhythm guitar

— **BOB HEATHCOTE** – bass; repl. MAYORGA

Virgin Epic

Aug 88. (12") *(VST 1127)* **TRIP AT THE BRAIN. / SUICYCO MANIA** [ ] [ ]

Sep 88. (cd/c/lp) *(CD/TC+/V 2551) <44288>* **HOW WILL I LAUGH TOMORROW . . . WHEN I CAN'T EVEN SMILE TODAY?** [ ] [ ]
– Trip at the brain / Hearing voices / Pledge your allience / How will I laugh tomorrow . . . when I can't even smile today? / The miracle / Surf and slam / If I don't wake up / Sorry? / One too many times / The feeling's back. *(cd+=)* – Suicyco mania.

Epic Epic

Jun 89. (cd/c/lp) *(465 399-2/-4/-1) <45244>* **CONTROLLED BY HATRED / FEEL LIKE SHIT . . . DEJA VU** [ ] [ ]
– Master of no mercy / How will I laugh tomorrow (video edit) / Just another love song / Walking the dead / Choosing my own way of life / Controlled by hatred / Feel like shit . . . deja vu / It's not easy / How will I laugh tomorrow (heavy emotion mix). *(re-iss. Oct94 cd/c; same)*

Jul 90. (cd/c/lp) *(466 569-2/-4/-1) <45389>* **LIGHTS . . . CAMERA . . . REVOLUTION** [59] [ ]
– You can't bring me down / Lost again / Alone / Lovely / Give it revolution / Get whacked / Send me your money / Emotion No.13 / Disco's out / Murder's in / Go'n breakdown.

Oct 90. (7"ep/7"sha-pic-ep/12"ep/cd-ep) *(656 332-7/-0/-6/-2)* **SEND ME YOUR MONEY / YOU CAN'T BRING ME DOWN. / WAKING THE DEAD / DON'T GIVE ME YOUR NOTHING** [ ] [ ]

— **ROBERT TRUJILLO** – bass / **JOSH FREESE** – drums; repl. BOB + RALPH

Jul 92. (cd/c/lp) *(471 885-2/-4/-1) <48864>* **THE ART OF REBELLION** [ ] [52]
– Can't stop / Accept my sacrifice / Nobody hears / Tap into the power / Monopoly on sorrow / We call this mutha revenge / Medley: I wasn't meant to feel this – Asleep at the wheel / Gotta kill Captain Stupid / I'll hate you better / Which way to free / It's going down / Where's the truth.

Jul 93. (cd/c/lp) *(473749-2/-4/-1) <46230>* **STILL CYCO AFTER ALL THESE YEARS** [ ] [ ]
– Suicide's an alternative / Two sided politics / Subliminal / I shot the Devil / Won't fall in love today / Institutionalized / War inside my head / Don't give me your nothin' / Memories of tomorrow / Possessed / I saw your mommy . . . / Fascist pig / A little each day / I want more / Suicidal failure.

Jun 94. (cd/c/lp) *(476 885-2/-4/-1) <57774>* **SUICIDAL FOR LIFE** [ ] [82]
– Invocation / Don't give a f***! / No f***'n problem / Suicyco muthaf***a / F***ed up just right! / No bullshit / What else could I do? / What you need's a friend / I wouldn't mind / Depression and anguish / Evil / Love vs. loneliness / Benediction.

— line-up: **MIKE MUIR** plus **MIKE CLARK + DEAN PLEASANTS** – guitar / **JOSH PAUL** – bass / **BROOKS WACKERMAN** – drums

Jun 97. (cd/c) *(484123-2/-4)* **PRIME CUTS** (compilation)
– You can't bring me down / Join the new army / Lovely / Institutionalised / Gotta kill Captain Studio / Berserk / I saw your mommy / Pledge your allegiance / Feeding the addiction / I wasn't meant to feel this / Asleep at the wheel / Send me your money / No fuck'n problem / Go skate / Nobody hears / How will I laugh tomorrow.

– compilations, etc. –

Jun 92. (cd/c) *Virgin; (CD/TC VM 9003)* **F.N.G.**

INFECTIOUS GROOVES

were formed by **MUIR + ROBERT TRUJILLO** – bass + **STEPHEN PERKINS** – drums (ex-JANE'S ADDICTION) / **ADAM SIEGAL + DEAN PLEASANTS** – guitar

Epic Epic

Oct 91. (cd/c/lp) *(468 729-2/-4/-1)* <47402> **THE PLAGUE THAT MAKES YOUR BOOTY MOVE, IT'S THE INFECTIOUS GROOVE**
– Punk it up / Therapy / I look funny? / Stop funk'n with my head / I'm gonna be my king / Closed session / Infectious grooves / Infectious blues / Monster skank / Back to the people / Turn your head / You lie . . . and yo breath stank / Do the sinister / Mandatory love song / Infecto groovalistic / Thanx but no thanx.

— **JOSH FREESE** – drums repl. PERKINS

Mar 93. (cd/c/lp) *(473 591-2/-4/-1)* <53131> **SARSIPPIUS' ARK**
– Intro / Turtle wax (funkaholics anonymous) / No cover – 2 drink minimum / Immigrant song / Caca de kick / Don't stop, spread the jam! / Three headed mind pollution / Slo-motion slam / A legend in his own mind (ladies love 'sip) / Infectious Grooves / The man behind the man / Fame / Savor da flavor / No budget – Dust off the 8-track! / Infectious Grooves / You pick me up (just to throw me down) / Therapy / Do the sinister / Big big butt, by infectiphibian / Spreck.

May 94. (cd/c/lp) *(475 929-2/-4/-1)* <57279> **GROOVE FAMILY CYCO**
– Violent & funky / Boom boom boom / Frustrated again / Rules go out the window / Groove family cyco / Die like a pig / Do what I tell ya / Cousin Randy / Why / Made it.

SUICIDE

Formed: New York, USA . . . 1971 by ALAN VEGA and ex-jazz band organist MARTIN REV. After a series of sporadic, performance art-style gigs in the early 70's, the duo laid low until the emergence of the CBGB's punk/new wave scene a few years later. Signed to US independent, 'Red Star' (run by Marty Thau, former manager of The NEW YORK DOLLS), the duo released one of the most influential records of the era in 1977's eponymous 'SUICIDE'. Delivering shock screams and whispered goth-rockabilly vocals over brooding, churning Farfisa organ, the duo laid the foundations for the industrial/electro experimentation of the following decade and in 'ROCKET U.S.A.' and 'FRANKIE TEARDROPS', penned two of the most compelling compositions in the NY avant-garde pantheon. Now almost universally heralded as being ahead of their time, punters of the day weren't always so appreciative; SUICIDE performances were infamous for audience stand-off's, a tour with the CLASH running into trouble while a gig in Belgium ended in a full-on riot (the same gig documented on the 1978 "official bootleg", '24 MINUTES OVER BRUSSELS'). Unperturbed, the pair moved to 'Ze' records ('Island' in the UK) and recorded a follow-up, 'ALAN VEGA / MARTIN REV – SUICIDE' (1980). Produced by CARS mainman, RIC OCASEK, the record presented a slightly more palatable version of SUICIDE's patented synth apocalypse, although sales remained minimal. Subsequently embarking on solo careers, the pair met with little more than cult success, although VEGA's eponymous 1980 solo debut spawned a Top 5 hit in France, 'JUKEBOX BABE'. Following his eponymous 1980 solo debut, REV devoted his time to sculpture with his work exhibited in 1982-83. VEGA continued working with OCASEK, also bringing in a young AL JOURGENSEN (later of MINISTRY fame) for 1983's 'SATURN STRIP' (featuring an unlikely but entertaining cover of Hot Chocolate's 'EVERYONE'S A WINNER') and guesting for SISTERS OF MERCY re-incarnation, The SISTERHOOD in 1986. VEGA and REV eventually reformed SUICIDE in 1988 and recorded 'A WAY OF LIFE' (1989) for 'Wax Trax!' (licensed to 'Chapter 22' in the UK), a label heavily indebted to the duo's pioneering electronics. With the album afforded little interest, VEGA resumed his solo activites on through the 90's, collaborating with STEPHEN LIRONI on his REVOLUTIONARY CORPS OF TEENAGE JESUS project and also ALEX CHILTON on their 1997 set, 'Cubist Blues'. Ironically, there's been something of an upsurge of interest in SUICIDE of late, the duo receiving renewed press attention after their performances with critical darlings SPRITUALIZED.

Album rating: SUICIDE (*8) / A WAY OF LIFE (*7)

ALAN VEGA (b.1948) – vocals / **MARTIN REV** – keyboards, percussion

Bronze Red Star

Nov 77. (lp) *(BRON 508)* <RS 1> **SUICIDE**
– Ghost rider / Rocket U.S.A. / Cheree / Frankie Teardrops / Johnny / Girl / Che. *(re-iss. Sep86 on 'Demon'; FIEND 74) (cd-iss. Jun88; FIENDCD 74)*

Jul 78. (7",12") *(BRO 57)* **CHEREE. / I REMEMBER**
(re-is.Nov86 on 'Demon' 12"; D 1046T)

1978. (lp-ltd; official bootleg) *(FRANKIE 1)* **24 MINUTES OVER BRUSSELS (live)** -

Island Ze

Nov 79. (ext.12"/7") *(12+/WIP 6543)* **DREAM BABY DREAM. / RADIATION**

May 80. (lp) *(ILPS 7007)* <7080> **ALAN VEGA / MARTIN REV – SUICIDE**

– Diamonds, furcoats, champagne / Mr. Ray / Sweetheart / Fast money music / Touch me / Harlem / Be bop kid / Las Vegas man / Shadazz / Dance.

— Split partnership in the early 80's and both went solo.

ALAN VEGA

with **PHIL HAWK** – guitar

not iss. P.V.C.

1980. (lp) <PVC 7915> **ALAN VEGA** -
– Jukebox babe / Fireball / Kung Foo cowboy / Love cry / Speedway / Ice drummer / Bye bye bayou / Lonely.

— w/band 81-83 **MARK KUGH** – guitar / **LARRY CHAPLAN** – bass / **SESU COLEMAN** – drums

Island Island

Nov 81. (lp) <(ILPS 9692)> **COLLISION DRIVE**
– Magdalena 82 / Be bop a lula / Outlaw / Raver / Ghost rider / I believe / Magdalena 83 / Rebel / Viet vet.

Nov 81. (ext.12"/7") *(12+/WIP 6744)* **JUKEBOX BABE. / LONELY** -

— added **AL JOURGENSEN** – keyboards (of MINISTRY) / **STEPHEN GEORGE** – drums / **GREG HAWKES** – synth, sax (of CARS) / **RIC OCASEK** – guitar, producer (of CARS)

Elektra Elektra

Sep 83. (lp) *(K 960259-1)* <60259-1> **SATURN STRIP**
– Saturn drive / Video babe / American dreamer / Wipeout beat / Je t'adore / Angel / Kid Congo / Goodbye darling / Every 1's a winner.

— retained **OCASEK** + added **KENNAN KEATING** – guitar / **CHRIS LORD** – synth

Oct 85. (7") *(EKR 24)* **ON THE RUN. / CRY FIRE** -
(12"+=) *(EKR 24T)* – Rah rah baby.

Dec 85. (lp/c) *(EKT 15/+C)* <60434-1/-4> **JUST A MILLION DREAMS**
– On the run / Shooting for you / Hot fox / Too late / Wild heart / Creation / Cry fire / Ra ra baby.

— In 1986, VEGA guested for SISTERS OF MERCY re-incarnation, SISTERHOOD

MARTIN REV

not iss. Infidelity

Feb 80. (lp) <228> **MARTIN REV** -
– Mari / Baby o baby / Nineteen 86 / Temptation / Jomo / Asia.

New Rose Red Star

Mar 85. (lp) *(ROSE 52)* **CLOUDS OF GLORY**
– Rodeo / Clouds of glory / Metatron / Whisper / Rocking horse / Parade / Island. *(cd-iss. 1997 on 'Mau Mau'; MAUCD 648)*

SUICIDE

re-formed in 1988

Chapter 22 Wax Trax!

Jan 89. (lp/cd) *(CHAP LP/CD 35)* <WAX/+CS/CD 7072> **A WAY OF LIFE**
– Wild in blue / Surrender / Jukebox baby 96 / Rain of ruin / Sufferin' in vain / Dominic Christ / Love so lonely / Devastation.

Feb 89. (12") *(12CHAP 36)* **RAIN OF RUIN. / SURRENDER** -

Brake Out Brake Out

Jun 92. (cd) <(OUT 108-2)> **Y B BLUE**
– Why be blue / Cheat-cheat / Hot ticket / Universe / The last time / Play the dream / Pump it / Flashy love / Chewy-chewy / Mujo.

ALAN VEGA

returned to solo work for the 90's. **LIZ LAMERA** – drums

Chapter 22 Infinite Zero

Feb 90. (cd/lp) *(CHAP CD/LP 45)* <43032> **DEUCE AVENUE**
– Body bop jive / Sneaker gun fire / Jab Gee / Bad scene / La la bola / Deuce avenue / Faster blaster / Sugee / Sweet sweet money / Love on / No tomorrow / Future sex. *(re-iss. Jun90 on 'Musicdisc' cd/c/lp; 10558-2/-4/-1)*

Musidisc Warners

Jul 91. (cd/c/lp) *(10812-2/-4/-1)* <43027> **POWER ON TO ZERO HOUR**
– Bring in the year 2000 / Sucker / Fear / Doomo dance / Automatic terror / Jungle justice / Full force of them nuclear shoes / Believe it / Cry a sea of tears / Quasi.

May 93. (cd/c) *(11012-2/-4)* <43051> **NEW RACEION**
– The pleaser / Christ dice / Gamma pop / Viva the legs / Do the job / Junior's little sister's dropped ta cheap / How many lifetimes / Holy skips / Keep it alive / Go Trane go / Just say.

— next with **LIZ LAMERE** – keyboards, vocals

Thirsty Ear Thirsty Ear

Dec 96. (cd) <(21308)> **DUJANG PRANG** Jul96
– Dujang prang / Hammered / Chennaroka / Saturn drive 2 (subtalk) / Jaxson gnome / Life ain't life / Flowers, candles, crucifixes / Big daddy stat's livin' on Tron / Sacrifice / Kiss.

Last Call Thirsty Ear

May 97. (cd; ALAN VEGA, ALEX CHILTON, BEN VAUGHN) *(422466)* <21314> **CUBIST BLUES** Oct96
– Fat city / Fly away / Freedom / Candyman / Come on Lord / Promised land / Lover of love / Sister / Too late / Do not do not / Werewolf / Dream baby revisited.

– (SUICIDE) compilations, etc. –

Dec 81. (c) *R.O.I.R.;* <(A 103)> **HALF-ALIVE (half studio)**

Oct 86. (c) *R.O.I.R.;* <(A 145)> **GHOST RIDERS (live)**
(cd-iss. Apr90 on 'Danceteria'; DANCD 029) (cd-iss. Feb95 on 'ROIR Europe'; RE 145CD)

1995. (cd; by MARTIN REV) *Alive;* <1006> **CHEYENNE** -

Jan 96. (cd; by MARTIN REV) *R.O.I.R.;* <(RUSCD 8220)> **SEE ME RIDIN'**

Mar 96. (cd; by ALAN VEGA) *Infinite Zero;* <43069> **JUKEBOX BABE / COLLISION DRIVE** -

Jan 98. (12"ep) *Blast First; (BFFP 115)* **CHEREE. / HARLEM / I REMEMBER** -

—— Their classic 'FRANKIE TEARDROP' was used by STEPHEN LIRONI (producer and ex- ALTERED IMAGES guy) on project REVOLUTIONARY CORPS, etc

SUICIDE COMMANDOS (see under ⇒ BEAT RODEO)

SULTANS OF PING F.C.

Formed: Cork, Ireland . . . 1991 by one-time near neighbours of FRANK AND WALTERS, NIALL O'FLAHERTY, PADDY O'CONNELL, ALAN McFEALY and MORTY McCARTHY. Having been caught live in their act by Martin Heath (of trendy dance label, 'Rhythm King'), The SULTANS OF PING F.C. secured an atypical UK distribution deal for their own 'Divine' imprint, kicking off with the fun-tastic 'WHERE'S ME JUMPER'. A surreal tale of a nicked jersey down the local disco, the track hit the Top 75 and briefly secured the band a role as court jesters to the music press. These Irish loonies traced a lineage back to early DAMNED through STUMP and The POGUES, newly shaken 'n' strirred in an eccentric, hard-drinking glam pop-punk cocktail. Two further minor hits, 'STUPID KID' and 'VERONICA', also surfaced in '92, paving the way for 'Rhythm King' to team up with 'Epic' and release Top 30 breaker, 'U TALK TOO MUCH'. A debut album, the brilliantly-titled 'CASUAL SEX IN THE CINEPLEX', was given promising reviews upon its release in early '93, following the single into the Top 30. Now under the aegis of major label paymasters, The SULTANS OF PING mysteriously dropped the F.C. from their name, a ploy that backfired as subsequent singles only managed to scrape into the Top 50; a follow-up album, 'TEENAGE DRUG' (1993), fared even worse. After losing their zing they also lost their PING, abbreviating their moniker even further to simply, The SULTANS. Now back with 'Rhythm King', the lads had one final (doomed) stab at glory with the comeback album, 'GOOD YEAR FOR THE TROUBLE' (1996). • **Songwriters:** O'FLAHERTY, except covers; MIRACLES (Shonen Knife) / SISTERS (Yoko Ono) / RED CADILLAC AND A BLACK MOUSTACHE (Thompson-May) / BLOODSPORTS FOR ALL (Carter The Unstoppable Sex Machine).

Album rating: CASUAL SEX IN THE CINEPLEX (*6) / TEENAGE DRUG (*5) / GOOD YEAR FOR THE TROUBLE (*4)

NIALL O'FLAHERTY – vocals / **PADDY O'CONNELL** – guitar / **ALAN McFEALY** – bass / **MORTY McCARTHY** – drums

Divine-Rhythm King — not iss.

Jan 92. (7"/c-s) *(ATHY 01/+C)* **WHERE'S ME JUMPER. / I SAID I AM I SAID** 67 -
(12"+=/cd-s+=) *(ATHY 01 T/CD)* – Turnip fish.

Apr 92. (7"/c-s) *(ATHY 02/+C)* **STUPID KID (live). / GIVE HIM A BALL (AND A YARD OF GRASS) (live)** 67 -
(12"+=/cd-s+=) *(ATHY 02 T/CD)* – Football hooligan (live) / No more nonsense (live).

Oct 92. (7"/c-s) *(ATHY 03/+C)* **VERONICA. / TEENAGE VAMPIRE** 69 -
(12"+=/cd-s+=) *(ATHY 03 T/CD)* – Riot at the sheepdog trials.

Rhythm King – Epic — not iss.

Dec 92. (7") *(658579-7)* **U TALK TOO MUCH. / JAPANESE GIRLS** 26 -
(12"+=/10"+=/cd-s+=) *(658579-6/-0/-2)* – Armitage Shanks / Turnip fish.

Feb 93. (cd/c/lp) *(472495-2/-4/-1)* **CASUAL SEX IN THE CINEPLEX** 26 -
– Back in a tracksuit / Indeed you are / Veronica / 2 pints of rasa / Stupid kid / You talk too much / Give him a ball (and a yard of grass) / Karaoke queen / Let's go shopping / Kick me with your leather boots / Clitus Clarke.

SULTANS OF PING

Aug 93. (12"ep) *(659579-6)* **TEENAGE PUNKS / HE THOUGHT I WAS YOUR BEST FRIEND. / INDEED YOU ARE / VERONICA (live)** 49 -
(cd-ep) *(659579-2)* – (1st 3 tracks) / Crash pad chick.
(c-ep) *(659579-5)* – (1st 3 tracks) / Back in a tracksuit (live).

Oct 93. (12"pic-d/c-s) *(659822-6/-4)* **MICHIKO / MIRACLES. / XMAS BUBBLEGUM MACHINE / STUPID KID (live)** 43 -
(cd-s) *(659822-2)* – (1st 3 tracks) / Japanese girls (acoustic party mix).

Nov 93. (cd/c/lp) *(474716-2/-4/-1)* **TEENAGE DRUG** -
– Teenage drug / Wake up and scratch me / Teenage punks / Curse / Michiko / Love and understanding / Psychopath / Terrorist angel / Teenage rock and roll girl / Pussycat / Sisters / Pussycat (reprise) / Telephone lover / Red Cadillac and a black moustache.

Feb 94. (c-ep/12"ep/cd-ep) *(660112-4/-6/-2)* **WAKE UP AND SCRATCH ME / DO RE MI. / EVERYTHING YOU DO YOU DO FOR YOU / LET'S GO SHOPPING** 50 -

SULTANS

Rhythm King — not iss.

Mar 96. (7") *(ATHY 04)* **MESCALINE. /** -
(cd-s+=) *(CDATHY 04)* –

Jul 96. (cd/lp) *(ATHY 05 CD/LP)* **GOOD YEAR FOR THE TROUBLE** -

Fantastic Plastic — not iss.

Aug 96. (12") *(FP 001)* **WHAT ABOUT THOSE SULTANS. /** -

SUMMERHILL (see under ⇒ SNAKES OF SHAKE)

SUN AND THE MOON (see under ⇒ CHAMELEONS)

SUNCATCHER

Formed: Sacramento, California, USA . . . mid 90's through a classified ad by singer/songwriter, DOUG HAMMOND, alongside BRIAN KNIGHT and ROY MURRAY; RAYMOND SANCHEZ was a 4th member. Inking a deal with 'Restless', SUNCATCHER found themselves under the glare of the media spotlight with their shiny happy debut album, 'THE GIRL THAT GOOD FORGOT' (1996). Alternately referred to as the "OWLFLOWER" album due to its cover art, the record drew obvious comparisons to STIPE/R.E.M. while recalling the poppier elements of 60's psychedelia.

Album rating: THE GIRL THAT GOOD FORGOT "OWLFLOWER" (*6)

DOUG HAMMOND – vocals, guitar / **RAYMOND SANCHEZ** – guitar / **BRIAN KNIGHT** – bass / **ROY MURRAY** – drums

Restless — Restless

Jul 96. (7") **LITTLE STEVIE WONDER. / STRAWBERRY FIELDS FOREVER** -

Aug 96. (cd) *<72920>* **THE GIRL THAT GOOD FORGOT** (the 'OWLFLOWER' album) -
– The puritan song / To move you / 3 viva / Birds on the wire / Have a nice day / Trouble / The girl that good forgot / Heaven / Dandelion / Juvenelia / Trippin.

SUNDAYS

Formed: London, England . . . 1988 by HARRIET WHEELER, DAVID GAVURIN and PAUL BRINDLEY, initially playing with a drum machine before recruiting sticksman PATRICK 'Patch' HANNAN. Subsequently signing to 'Rough Trade', the band's fawning music press hype was justified with the release of the semi-classic 'CAN'T BE SURE' single in early '89. A luscious slice of sugary indie, the track's reverberating guitar and fragile, bone-china vocals (courtesy of WHEELER) brought comparisons with "shoegazing" forebears The COCTEAU TWINS, some critics also mentioning THROWING MUSES. Yet The SUNDAYS were in seemingly little hurry to follow-up this indie chart topper (and minor Top 40 hit), almost a full year passing before the release of much anticipated debut album, 'READING, WRITING AND ARITHMETIC' (1990). Its glistening jangle-pop didn't disappoint and The SUNDAYS suddenly found themselves in the UK Top 5, the US Top 40 and the glare of the world's media. An ensuing continent-straddling tour together with the collapse of the band's label conspired to slow down the band's already notoriously relaxed attitude to songwriting and it was late '92 before they re-emerged via a new 'Parlophone' deal. The resulting single, 'GOODBYE', displayed a more world-weary sound (the band even covering The Rolling Stones' mournful classic, 'WILD HORSES' on the B-side) and the accompanying album, 'BLIND', sounded frayed at the edges. While the record's Top 20 placing and the success of the attendant tour suggested that The SUNDAYS' fans hadn't lost interest, their patience would be tested with a subsequent five year gap prior to a third album. When 'STATIC & SILENCE' (1997) finally arrived, critics found fault with what they saw as musical stagnation although loyal fans helped put it into the UK Top 10, proving their enduring appeal. • **Trivia:** An instrumental piece was used on the 1993 series for comedy duo, Newman & Baddiel.

Album rating: READING, WRITING AND ARITHMETIC (*8) / BLIND (*7) / STATIC & SILENCE (*6)

HARRIET WHEELER (b.26 Jun'63, Maidenhead, England) – vocals (ex-JIM JIMINEE) / **DAVID GAVURIN** (b. 4 Apr'63) – guitar / **PAUL BRINDLEY** (b. 6 Nov'63, Loughborough, England) – bass / **PATRICK 'Patch' HANNAN** (b. 4 Mar'66) – drums repl. drum machine

Rough Trade — D.G.C.

Feb 89. (7") *(RT 218)* **CAN'T BE SURE. / I KICKED A BOY** 45 -
(12"+=/cd-s+=) *(RT 218 T/CD)* – Don't tell your mother.

Jan 90. (lp/c/cd) *(ROUGH/+C/CD 148)* *<24277>* **READING, WRITING AND ARITHMETIC** 4 39
– Skin & bones / Here's where the story ends / Can't be sure / I won / Hideous towns / You're not the only one I know / A certain someone / I kicked a boy / My finest hour / Joy. *(re-iss. May96 cd/c; CD/TC PCS 7378)*

Jan 90. (7") **HERE'S WHERE THE STORY ENDS. / SKIN AND BONES** -

Parlophone — D.G.C.

Sep 92. (c-s/7") *(TC+/R 6319)* **GOODBYE. / WILD HORSES** 27 -
(cd-s+=) *(CDR 6319)* – Noise.

Oct 92. (cd/c/lp) *(CD/TC+/PCSD 121)* *<24479>* **BLIND** 15
– I feel / Goodbye / Life and soul / Marc / On Earth / God made me / Love / What do you think? / 24 hours / Blood on my hands / Medieval. *(re-iss. Mar94; same)*

Sep 97. (7") *(R 6475)* **SUMMERTIME. / NOTHING SWEET** 15 -
(cd-s+=) *(CDR 6475)* – Gone.
(cd-s) *(CDRS 6475)* – ('A'side) / Skin & bones (live) / Here's where the story ends (live).

Capitol — Geffen

Sep 97. (cd/c/lp) *(CD/TC+/EST 2300)* *<25131>* **STATIC & SILENCE** 10 33
– Summertime / Homeward / Folk song / She / When I'm thinking about you / I can't wait / Another flavour / Leave this city / Your eyes / Cry / Monochrome.

Nov 97. (c-s) *(TCR 6487)* **CRY / THROUGH THE DARK** 43 -
(cd-s+=) *(CDR 6487)* – Life goes on.
(cd-s) *(CDRS 6487)* – ('A'side) / Can't be sure (demo) / You're not the only one I know (demo).

SUN DIAL

Formed: South London, England . . . 1985 out of MODERN ART by GARY RAMON. They/he had issued a few limited edition releases on 'Color Disc', the 1986 single, 'DREAMS TO LIVE' / 'BEAUTIFUL TRUTH', the 1987 lp, 'STEREOLAND', the 1989 one-sided 7"clear-flexi freebie, 'PENNY VALENTINE' & 'ONE-WAY TICKET', released at the same time as German-only lp, 'ALL ABOARD THE MIND TRAIN'. These recordings featured drummers DAVE MORGAN (Weather Prophets) and ED KENT alongside GERALD on guitar and occasional saxophone. SUN DIAL blasted onto the scene in the early 90's when they debuted with 'EXPLODING IN YOUR MIND'. This 12" appeared on 'Tangerine', a label formed by record dealer, Hugo Chavez-Smith. Its very limited release was rectified when Mark Heyward (of Vinyl Experience record store) set up 'UFO' records to create an outlet for future SUN DIAL recordings. The group subsequently expanded into a quartet (briefly a 5-piece) after they released their debut album, 'OTHER WAY OUT' (1991), a neo-psychedelic guitar-noise trip through the musical black hole of SPACEMEN 3 and LOOP via The STOOGES and The JESUS & MARY CHAIN. RAMON then enlisted a new-look crew of JOHN PELECH, CHRIS DALLEY and NIGEL CARPENTER for the 'OVERSPILL' EP and 'REFLECTER' (1992) LP, the former produced by Vic Keary (boss of Mushroom records), the first person to record MARC BOLAN! In 1993, after CRAIG ADRIENNE replaced PELECH, the quartet signed to 'Beggars Banquet', releasing the album, 'LIBERTINE', before RAMON reinstated the original rhythm section of CLOUGH and MORGAN. This line-up completed one further set, 'ACID YANTRA' (1995), before they were eclipsed for good. • **Songwriters:** RAMON except covers; CIRCLE SKY (Monkees) / MAGIC POTION (Open Mind) / ONLY A NORTHERN SONG (Beatles). • **Trivia:** 'OTHER WAY OUT' was voted best album in Italian magazine, 'Rockerilla'.

Album rating: OTHER WAY OUT (*8) / REFLECTER (*6) / LIBERTINE (*6) / ACID YANTRA (*6)

GARY RAMON – guitar with **DAVE MORGAN** – drums / **TONY CLOUGH** – keyboards, flute

UFO | Continuum

Jan 91. (12"ep/cd-ep) *(45002 T/CD)* **EXPLODING IN YOUR MIND (edit). / OTHER SIDE / PLAINS OF NAZCA (edit)** [ ] [-]

— Note: the unreleased test pressing of above was on 'Tangerine' *(TAN111)*

— Below album was also released on 'Tangerine' in 1990.

Apr 91. (pic-cd/c) *(UFO 1 CD/MC) <19107>* **OTHER WAY OUT** [ ] [ ]
– Plains of Nazca / Exploding in your mind / Magic flight / World without time / She's looking all around / Lorne blues. *(cd+=)* – Visitation / Other side. *(re-iss. cd 1994 on 'Acme'++=; AC8003CD)* – Slow motion / Fountain.

— **JOHN PELECH** – drums; repl. MORGAN

— **CHRIS DALLEY** – bass + **NIGEL CARPENTER** – guitar (both ex-BIKINIS) repl. CLOUGH who joined SPIRAL SKY

Sep 91. (12"ep,12"orange-ep/cd-ep) *(45002 T/CD)* **OVERSPILL** [ ] [-]
– Fireball/ Only a northern song / Never fade / Overspill.

UFO | Dutch East

Mar 92. (clear-lp/cd) *(UFO 8/+CD) <2020>* **REFLECTER** [ ] [ ] Apr93
– Reflecter / Easy for you / I don't mind / Slow motion / Tremelo / Never fade / Sunstroke / Mind train. *(ltd-cd+=) (UFO 8XCD)* – Reflecter 2.

UFO | DEI

Jul 92. (12"green-ep/cd-ep) *(45008 T/CD) <2024>* **FAZER** [ ] [ ]
– I don't mind / Let it go / Out of place / Easy fazer.

— above featured **MICKY MANN** (of The SHAMEN)

— **CRAIG ADRIENNE** – drums; repl. PELECH

Beggars Banquet | Beggars Banquet

Jun 93. (lp/c/cd) *(BBQ/+C/CD 138) <92326>* **LIBERTINE** [ ] [ ] Aug93
– Send / Going down / Watch you smile / Deep inside / Everything you see / Dual / Hold on / Around and around / Star baby / Believer.

Oct 93. (7"white-ep/cd-ep) *(BBQ 51/+CD)* **GOING DOWN / WATCH YOU SMILE. / JEWEL / STARBABY (live)** [ ] [-]

— now w/out DALLEY + CARPENTER, they had become a trio (**RAMON, CLOUGH + MORGAN**) adding guest **JAKE HONEYWELL** – bass

May 95. (12"green/cd-s) *(BBQ 54/+CD)* **BAD DRUG. / FAIRGROUND** [ ] [-]

Jun 95. (cd) *(BBQCD 173) <92637>* **ACID YANTRA** [ ] [ ] Oct95
– Red sky / Apollo / 3000 miles / Are you supernatural? / Bad drug / Fly into the sun / Rollercoaster / Nova / Yantra jam.

– compilations, etc. –

1994. (bootleg-cd,lp) *Acme; (AC 8001)* **RETURN JOURNEY** (rec.1991 lost 2nd lp) [ ] [-]

1996. (red-lp,cd) *Acme; (AC 8015 LP/CD)* **LIVE DRUG** [ ] [-]

SUNNY DAY REAL ESTATE

Formed: Seattle, Washington, USA . . . early 90's by JEREMY ENIGK, WILLIAM GOLDSMITH, NATE MENDEL and DAN HOERNER. On the strength of a self-financed debut 45, 'SONG NUMBER 8 – SONG NUMBER 9', they signed to veteran US indie label, 'Sub Pop', who released their debut album, 'DIARY', the following year. As their name might suggest, SDRE offered up a brighter take on the grunge formula of their hometown, even going so far as to package their album in a day-glo pink sleeve. Despite a further promising eponymous release, the band effectively sold up with the sudden departure of ENIGK who'd converted to Christianity. MENDEL and GOLDSMITH in turn, joined ex-NIRVANA drummer DAVE GROHL in his new FOO FIGHTERS project. However, GOLDSMITH broke away from the aforesaid chartbusters to hook up once more with ENIGK and breathe some new life into SDRE in the shape of a comeback album, 'HOW DOES IT FEEL TO BE SOMETHING ON' (1998).

Album rating: DIARY (*7) / SUNNY DAY REAL ESTATE (*6) / HOW IT FEELS TO BE SOMETHING ON (*7)

JEREMY ENIGK (b.16 Jul'74) – vocals, guitar / **DAN HOERNER** (b.13 May'69) – vocals, guitar / **NATE MENDEL** (b. 2 Dec'68) – bass / **WILLIAM GOLDSMITH** (b. 4 Jul'72) – drums

not iss. | One Day I Stopped Breathing

1993. (7") **SONG NUMBER 8 - SONG NUMBER 9. /** [-] [ ]

Sub Pop | Sub Pop

Jun 94. (lp/cd) *(SP/+CD 121-302) <SP 246/+CD>* **DIARY** [ ] [ ]
– Seven / In circles / Song about an angel / Round / 47 / Blankets were the stairs / Pheurton skeurto / Shadows / 48 / Grendel / Sometimes.

Oct 95. (lp/cd) *<(SP/+CD 316)>* **UNTITLED** ("The Pink Album") [ ] [ ]
– Friday / Theo B / Red elephant / 5/4 / Waffle / 8 / Iscarabaid / J'nuh / Rodeo Jones.

— split when JEREMY found God and became a disciple of Jesus. MENDEL and GOLDSMITH were recruited by DAVE GROHL in The FOO FIGHTERS.

— **ENIGK + GOLDSMITH** reformed SDRE in 1998 with a new bassist **J PALMER**

Sep 98. (cd) *<(SP 409)>* **HOW IT FEELS TO BE SOMETHING ON** [ ] [ ]
– Pillars / Roses in water / Every shining time you arrive / Two promises / 100 million / How it feels to be something on / The prophet / Guitar and video games / The hark's own private fuck / Days were golden.

JEREMY ENIGK

with a plethora of session people

1996. (cd) *<SP 323>* **RETURN OF THE FROG QUEEN** [-] [ ]
– Abegail Anne / Return of the frog queen / Lewis hollow / Lizard / Carnival / Call me steam / Explain / Shade and black hat / Fallen heart.

1998. (cd-ep) *<SP 58>* **THE END SESSIONS** (U.S. tour 1997) [-] [ ]
– Abegail Anne / Return of the frog queen / Lizard / Carnival / Explain.

SUNSONIC (see under ⇒ FLOWERPOT MEN)

SUPERCHUNK

Formed: Chapel Hill, North Carolina, USA . . . 1989 as CHUNK by RALPH 'MAC' McCAUGHAN, STEVEN WILBUR, LAURA BALLANCE and CHUCK GARRISON. One of the original Chapel Hill bands, SUPERCHUNK (the new improved moniker implemented at the turn of the decade) kicked up a local storm with feverishly enthusiastic live performances and an eponymous debut EP (which included an unlikely but effective cover of The Shangri-las' 'TRAIN FROM KANSAS CITY') but it was 1990's 'SLACK MOTHERFUCKER' which brought them to wider attention. A brilliant pop-punk anthem for the nascent "slacker" generation, the single preceded an eponymous debut album and a growing surge of cult acclaim. The early promise was finally fulfilled with Steve Albini-produced follow-up album, 'NO POCKY FOR KITTY' (1992), a dizzying, breathless collection of noise-pop gems following a lineage from Brit pioneers like The BUZZCOCKS through FUGAZI, HUSKER DU, DINOSAUR JR., SONIC YOUTH etc. Enduring favourites like 'TOSSING SEEDS' and 'SKIP STEPS 1 & 3' favoured a straightforward, heartfelt rush of bruised melody over the more oblique approach of contemporaries like PAVEMENT; it was exactly this simplicity that earned the band such vociferous support from their fans and criticism from their detractors, as witnessed in the mixed reviews for singles compilation, 'TOSSING SEEDS' (1992). Yet despite all the predictions of imminent world domination, 1993's 'ON THE MOUTH' was met with a decidedly lukewarm reception, attempts at lengthier compositions negating the infectiousness of their best work. 'FOOLISH' (1994) and 'HERE'S WHERE THE STRINGS COME IN' (1995) redressed the balance somewhat yet save for the soaring 'HYPER ENOUGH' there was a distinct lack of the trademark, in-your-face hooks. In the meantime, frontman McCAUGHAN had been working on 'I HOPE YOUR HEART IS NOT BRITTLE' (1994), the debut album for his PORTASTATIC side-project. A further SUPERCHUNK album, 'INDOOR LIVING', surfaced on 'City Slang' in 1997, yet there's no getting away from the feeling that the band's time has come and gone. • **Songwriters:** Group; except GIRL U WANT (Devo) / IT'S SO HARD TO FALL IN LOVE (Sebadoh) / BRAND NEW LOVE (Lou Barlow) / 100,000 FIREFLIES (Magnetic Fields) / LYING IN STATE (Verlaines) / I'LL BE YOUR SISTER (Motorhead) / NIGHT OF THE CHILL BLUE (. . . Phillips) / etc. • **Trivia:** MAC guested in 1992 on SEAM's 'Headsparks' album, alongside BITCH MAGNET members.

Album rating: SUPERCHUNK (*4) / NO POCKY FOR KITTY (*8) / TOSSING SEEDS compilation (*8) / ON THE MOUTH (*6) / FOOLISH (*6) / INCIDENTAL MUSIC compilation (*8) / HERE'S WHERE THE STRINGS COME IN (*5) / INDOOR LIVING (*5)

MAC McCAUGHAN – vocals, guitar / **STEVEN WILBUR** – guitar / **LAURA BALLANCE** – bass / **CHUCK GARRISON** – drums

not iss. | Merge

1989. (7"ep; as CHUNK) **THE CHUNK EP** [-] [ ]
– What do I / My noise / Train from Kansas City.

— **JON WURSTER** – drums repl. CHUCK

City Slang | Matador

May 90. (7") **SLACK MOTHERFUCKER. / NIGHT CREATURES / GARLIC** [-] [ ]

1990. (lp/cd) *<4>* **SUPERCHUNK** [-] [ ]

– Sick to move / My noise / Let it go / Swinging / Slow / Slack motherfucker / Binding / Down the hall / Half a life / Not tomorrow.

—— **JIM** – guitar repl. STEVEN

City Slang Matador

Nov 91. (7") **FISHING. / COOL**

Jan 92. (lp/cd) *(EFA 04073/+CD) <35>* **NO POCKY FOR KITTY**
– Skip steps 1 & 3 / Seed toss / Cast iron / The tower / Punch me harder / Sprung a leal / 30 xtra / Tie a rope to the back of the bus / Press / Sidewalk / Creek / Throwing things.

City Slang Merge

Apr 92. (lp/c/cd) *(EFA 04078/+C/CD) <MRG 20/+C/CD>* **TOSSING SEEDS** (singles 1989-1991)
– What do I / My noise / Train from Kansas City / Slack motherfucker / Night creatures / Garlic / Fishing / Cool / Breadman / Cast iron / Seed toss / It's so hard to fall in love / Brand new love.

Oct 92. (7") *(EFA 04906S)* **MOWER. / ON THE MOUTH**
(12"+=/cd-s+=) *(EFA 04906/+CD)* – Fishing (live).

Jan 93. (7"ep/12"ep/cd-ep) *(EFA 04910-45/-02/-03) <MRG 34CD>* **THE QUESTION IS HOW FAST**
– The question is how fast / Forged it / 100,000 fireflies.

Feb 93. (cd/lp) *(EFA 04915-2/-4) <MRG 49CD>* **ON THE MOUTH**
– Precision auto / From the curve / For tension / Mower package thief / Swallow that / I guess I remembered it wrong / New low / Untied / The question is how fast / Trash heap / Flawless / The only piece that you get.

Oct 93. (7") *(RUG 9)* **RIBBON. / WHO NEEDS LIGHT** –
(above issued on 'Domino')

Mar 94. (7") *(EFA 04937-7) <MRG 59CD>* **THE FIRST PART. / CONNECTICUT**
(cd-s+=) *(EFA 04937-2)* – Foolish.

Apr 94. (cd/lp) *(EFA 04938-2/-1) <MRG 60CD>* **FOOLISH** Dec93
– Like a fool / The first part / Water wings / Driveway to driveway / Saving my ticket / Kicked in / Why do you have to put a date on everything / Without blinking / Keeping track / Revelations / Stretched out / In a stage whisper.

Jan 95. (cd-ep) *(EFA 04948-2) <MRG 69CD>* **DRIVEWAY TO DRIVEWAY** Oct94
– Driveway to driveway / Seed toss / Sick to move / Driveway to driveway.

Jul 95. (cd/d-lp) *(EFA 04959-2/-1) <MRG 85CD>* **INCIDENTAL MUSIC 1991-95** (compilation)
– Shallow end / Mower / On the mouth / Cadmium / Who needs light / Ribbon / Foolish / 100,000 fireflies / Invitation / Makeout bench / Baxter / Connecticut / Lying in state / Throwing things / I'll be your sister / Night of the chill blue / Forged it / Home at dawmn.

Sep 95. (7") *(EFA 04968-7) <MRG 89CD>* **HYPER ENOUGH. / NEVER TOO YOUNG TO SMOKE** Aug95
(cd-s+=) *(EFA 04968-2)* – Detroit has a skyline.

Oct 95. (cd/lp) *(EFA 04966-2/-1) <MRG 90CD>* **HERE'S WHERE THE STRINGS COME IN** Sep95
– Hyper enough / Silverleaf and snowy tears / Yeah, it's beautiful here too / Iron on / Sunshine state / Detroit has a skyline / Eastern terminal / Animated airplanes over Germany / Green flowers, blue fish / Here's where the strings come in / Certain stars.

Dec 96. (cd-ep) *<MRG 118CD>* **LAUGHTER GUNS EP** –

Aug 97. (7"ep/cd-ep) *<(MRG 128/+CD)>* **WATERY HANDS. / WITH BELLS ON / WATERY HANDS (Wet Wurlitzer mix)** Jul97

Sep 97. (cd/lp) *(EFA 04997-2/-1) <MRG 129CD>* **INDOOR LIVING**
– Unbelievable things / Burn last Sunday / Marquee / Watery hands / Nu bruises / Every single instinct / Song for Marion Brown / Popular music / Under our feet / European medicine / Martini's on the roof.

PORTASTATIC

McCAUGHAN – vocals, guitar (side-project) / with various

Elemental Merge

Feb 94. (lp/lp/cd) *(ELM 17/+X/CD) <MRG 51CD>* **I HOPE YOUR HEART IS NOT BRITTLE**
– Mute 2 / Polaroid / Gutter / Naked pilseners / Tree killer / Creeping around / Weird time / Silver screw / Beer and chocolate bars / Had / Memphis / Receiver / Why have you come back / The main thing.

Matador Matador

May 94. (7"/cd-s) *<(OLE 076-7/-2)>* **NAKED PILSENERS. / FEEL BETTER / JOSEPHINE**

Merge Merge

Mar 95. (cd-ep) *<MRG 80CD>* **SCRAPBOOK EP** –
– St. Elmo's fire / Why pinch yourself / Bear that chokes / My favorite sound / Scrapbook X's.

Jun 95. (cd) *<MRG 86CD>* **SLOW NOTE FROM A SINKING SHIP** –
– When you crashed / Skinny glasses girl / San Andreas / Taking you with me / Angels of sleep / Cunning latch / Spooky / Great escape / Running water / You can't win / Isn't that the way / On our hands / Pastime / In the manner of Anne Frank.

Mar 97. (cd) *<MRG 120CD>* **THE NATURE OF SAP** –
– You know where to find me / Lovely Niles / Hurrican warning (ignored) / Reverse Lester / Flare / Jonathan's organ / Before you sailed around the world / Ben's revenge / Impolite cheers / Spying on the spys / BJJT / Landed / If you could sing / The nature of sap.

SUPER DELUXE

Formed: Seattle, Washington, USA . . . 1994 by songwriter/vocalist. guitarist, BRADEN BLAKE, along with JOHN KIRSCH, JAKE NESHEIM and CHRIS LOCKWOOD. Melodic punk-poppers swimming in the slipstream of their hometown Grunge scene, SUPER DELUXE were an adolescent hybrid of NIRVANA, the POSIES and TEENAGE FANCLUB, who initially signed to US indie, 'Tim/Kerr'. Debut album, 'FAMOUS' (1995), confirmed their precocious talent while Indolent offshoot, 'Luminous', gave it a UK release the following year. A period of high profile touring preceded a major label deal with 'Warners', through whom they issued the 1997 sophomore effort, 'VIA SATELLITE'.

Album rating: FAMOUS (*6) / VIA SATELLITE (*5)

BRADEN BLAKE – vocals, guitar / **JOHN KIRSCH** – guitar / **JAKE NESHEIM** – bass / **CHRIS LOCKWOOD** – drums

Luminous Tim/Kerr

Jul 96. (7") *(LUX 001)* **SHE CAME ON. / GIVE A LITTLE BIT** –
(cd-s+=) *(LUX 001CD)* – Years ago / On Lisa.

Aug 96. (7") *(LUX 002)* **FAMOUS. / VIRNANA 1234** –
(cd-s+=) *(LUX 002CD)* – Wilted and faded / Famous #2 (acoustic).

Sep 96. (cd/c) *(LUX CD/MC 003) <TK95CD 106>* **FAMOUS** Oct95
– Lizadrin / Famous / She came on / Love her madly / Flustered / Disappearing / Johnny's gone fishin' / Holly's dream vacation / Smile / Suitcases / Sunshine for now. *(re-iss. Feb98 on 'Tim/Kerr' lp/cd; TK/+95CD 106)*

Dec 96. (7") *(LUX 004)* **ALL I WANTED WAS A SKATEBOARD. / GOD REST YE MERRY GENTLEMEN** –

not iss. Warners

Jul 97. (cd/c) *<24678-2/-4>* **VIA SATELLITE** –
– Your pleasure's mine / Lost in your failures / Farrah Fawcett / Love liquid wraparound / Alright / Commonplace / Divine / What's up with me / One in a million / New variations / Half asleep / I can see / Suicide doll / Years ago.

SUPERDRAG

Formed: Knoxville, Tennessee, USA . . . 1993 out of The USED by JOHN DAVIS, BRENDAN FISHER, TOM PAPPAS and DON COFFEY JNR. As DAVIS assumed the bulk of the songwriting duties and took over as frontman, the quartet coined the new moniker of SUPERDRAG and set about building up a local following. During this period the band circulated a rough demo tape, 'STEREO 360 SOUND', that eventually found its way into the hands of US indie imprint 'Darla'. In 1995, they delivered their first release, the mini-set 'THE FABULOUS 8 TRACK SOUND OF SUPERDRAG', leading to a major record deal with 'Elektra' and an impressive proper album debut, 'REGRETFULLY YOURS' (1996). In your face punk-pop with turbo-charged attitude, the record proved a favourite with the US college crowd and whetted appetites for 1998's meatier follow-up, 'HEAD TRIP IN EVERY KEY'. • **Covered:** SEPTEMBER GURLS (Alex Chilton) / DIANE (Husker Du).

Album rating: THE FABULOUS 8-TRACK SOUND OF SUPERDRAG mini (*6) / REGRETFULLY YOURS (*6) / HEAD TRIP IN EVERY KEY (*6) / STEREO 360 SOUND demo collection (*6)

JOHN DAVIS – vocals, guitar / **BRENDAN FISHER** – guitar / **TOM PAPPAS** – bass / **DON COFFEY JNR.** – drums

not iss. Darla

Oct 95. (m-cd) *<7>* **THE FABULOUS 8-TRACK SOUND OF SUPERDRAG** –
– Sugar / Bloody hell / Really thru / Liquor / 6/8 / Blown away / Load.

Elektra Elektra

Oct 96. (cd-s) *(EKR 229CD)* **SUCKED OUT / SEPTEMBER GURLS** –

Oct 96. (cd) *<(7559 61900-2)>* **REGRETFULLY YOURS**
– Scootin' / Cynicality / Carried / Slot machine / Garmonbozia / Phaser / Rocket / Nothing good is real / What if you don't fly / Truest love / Whitney's theme / N.A. kicker / Destination Ursa Major.

Mar 98. (cd/c) *<62114-2/-4>* **HEAD TRIP IN EVERY KEY** –
– I'm expanding my mind / Hellbent / Sold you an alibi / Do the vampire / Amphetamine / Bankrupt vibration / Mr. Underground / Annetichrist / She is a holy grail / Pine away / Shuck and jive / Wrong vs. right doesn't matter / The art of dying.

– compilations, etc. –

Nov 98. (cd) *Superdrag Sound; <001>* **STEREO 360 SOUND** –
– Whitney's theme / My prayer / Senorita / H.H.T. / Nothing good is real / Cuts and scars / Diane / Sleeping beauty / Take your spectre away/

SUPER FURRY ANIMALS

Formed: Cardiff, Wales . . . 1993 by GRUFF RHYS, DAFYDD IEUAN, CIAN CIARAN, GUTO PRYCE and HUW BUNFORD. Emerging from the Welsh underground scene in the mid-90's with a wholly unpronounceable EP on their native 'Ankst' label, the band whipped up a fair bit of interest from the London-based media and industry insiders alike. Alan McGee's 'Creation' subsequently took them on with the proviso that the bulk of their work be in English, the 'FURRY's famously stipulating that they never be made to work on St. David's day. Their first single for the label, 'HOMETOWN UNICORN' appeared in early '96 and dented the Top 50, while the dayglo rampage of 'GOD! SHOW ME MAGIC' made the Top 40 a couple of months later. Hailed by critics as one of the debuts of the year, the accompanying 'FUZZY LOGIC' (1996) album thrilled jaded Brit-pop fans with its dayglo showcase of deranged prog-retro pop/rock; 'MARIO MAN' was their most definitive slice of pseudo psychedelia to date while 'HANGIN' WITH HOWARD MARKS' gave them instant cool – the record's cover art depicted the various guises of "nice guy" one-time drug smuggler, MARKS. A Top 30 hit, the album spawned a further two singles in 'SOMETHING 4 THE WEEKEND' and 'IF YOU DON'T WANT ME TO DESTROY YOU', while the blase brilliance of 'THE MAN DON'T GIVE A FUCK' (repetitive line from the STEELY DAN number, 'Show Biz Kids') drew a swaggering close to a successful but inevitably controversial year, the group having been earlier banned from the Welsh BAFTA awards after a skirmish in the crowd. 1997's follow-up set, 'RADIATOR', made the Top 10, its less intense but equally compelling shenanigans threatening to take the band into the big league (they played the festival circuit that included a return to the rainy 'T In The Park' – Muddy Waters was not even invited).

Album rating: FUZZY LOGIC (*8) / RADIATOR (*7) / OUTSPACED collection (*6)

GRUFF RHYS (b.18 Jul'70) – vocals, guitars (ex-EMILY, ex-FFA COFFI PAWB) / **CIAN**

CIARAN (b.16 Jun'76) – keyboards / **HUW 'Bumpf' BUNFORD** (b.15 Sep'67, Bath, England) – guitars, vocals / **GUTO PRYCE** (b. 4 Sep'72) – bass / **DAFYDD IEUAN** (b. 1 Mar'69) – drums, percussion, vocals (ex-ANHREFN, ex-FFA COFFI PAWB)

Ankst not iss.

Jun 95. (7"ep/cd-ep) *(ANKST 057/+CD)* **LLANFAIRPWLLGWYNGYLLGOGERYCHWYNDROBW-LLANTYSILIOGOGOGOCHOCYNYGOFOD (IN SPACE) EP** [ ] [-]
– Organ yn dy geg / Fix idris / Crys Ti / Blerwytirhwng? *(re-iss. May97; same)*
Oct 95. (7"ep/cd-ep) *(ANKST 062/+CD)* **MOOG DROOG EP** [ ] [-]
– PamV? / God! show me magic / Sali Mali / Focus pocus – Debiel. *(re-iss. May97; same)*

Creation Sony

Feb 96. (7"/c-s) *(CRE/+CS 222)* **HOMETOWN UNICORN. / DON'T BE A FOOL, BILLY!** [47] [-]
(cd-s+=) *(CRESCD 222)* – Lazy life (of no fixed identity).
Apr 96. (7"/c-s) *(CRE/+CS 231)* **GOD! SHOW ME MAGIC. / DIM BENDITH** [33] [-]
(cd-s+=) *(CRESCD 231)* – Death by melody.
May 96. (cd/lp)(c) *(CRE CD/LP 190)(CCRE 190) <67827>* **FUZZY LOGIC** [23] [ ]
– God! show me magic / Fuzzy birds / Something 4 the weekend / Frisbee / Hometown unicorn / Gathering moss / If you don't want me to destroy you / Bad behaviour / Mario man / Hangin' with Howard Marks / Long gone / For now and ever.
Jul 96. (7"/c-s) *(CRE/+CS 235)* **SOMETHING 4 THE WEEKEND. / WAITING TO HAPPEN** [18] [-]
(cd-s+=) *(CRESCD 235)* – Arnofio / Glow in the dark.
Sep 96. (7"/c-s/cd-s) *(CRE/+CS/SCD 243)* **IF YOU DON'T WANT ME TO DESTROY YOU. / GUACAMOLE** [18] [-]
(cd-s+=) *(CRESCD 243)* – (Nid) Hon yw'r gan sy'n mynd I achub yr iaith (This song will save the Welsh language (not).
Dec 96. (one-sided-7"blue) *(CRE 247)* **THE MAN DON'T GIVE A FUCK** [22] [-]
(cd-s+=) *(CRESCD 247)* – ('A'-Matthew 'Herbert' Herbert mix) / ('A'-Howard Marks mix).
(12"++=) *(CRE 247T)* – ('A'-Darren Price mix).

— In Feb'97, HUW BUNFORD was fined £700 on an earlier drug possession charge

Creation Flydaddy

May 97. (7"/c-s) *(CRE/+CS 252)* **HERMANN LOVES PAULINE. / CALIMERO** [26] [-]
(cd-s+=) *(CRESCD 252)* – Trons Mr. Urdd.
Jul 97. (7"/c-s) *(CRE/+CS 269)* **THE INTERNATIONAL LANGUAGE OF SCREAMING. / WRAP IT UP** [24] [-]
(cd-s+=) *(CRESCD 269)* – Foxy music / nO.K.
Aug 97. (cd/c/lp) *(CRECD/CCRE/CRELP 214) <FLY 34CD>* **RADIATOR** [8] [ ]
– Furryvision / The placid casual / The international language of screaming / Demons / Short painkiller / She's got spies / Play it cool / Hermann love's Pauline / Chupacabras / Torra fy ngwallt yn hir / Bass tuned to D.E.A.D. / Down a different river / Download / Mountain people.
Sep 97. (7"/c-s) *(CRE/+CS 275)* **PLAY IT COOL. / PASS THE TIME** [27] [-]
(cd-s+=) *(CRESCD 275)* – Cryndod yn dy lais.
Nov 97. (7"/c-s) *(CRE/+CS 283)* **DEMONS. / HIT AND RUN** [27] [-]
(cd-s+=) *(CRESCD 283)* – Carry the can.
May 98. (7"/c-s) *(CRE/+CS 288)* **ICE HOCKEY HAIR. / SMOKIN'** [12] [-]
(12"+=)(cd-s+=) *(CRE 288T)(CRESCD 288)* – Mu-tron / Let's quit smokin'.
Nov 98. (cd/lp) *(CRE CD/LP 229)* **OUT SPACED** (rare B-sides, etc) [44] [-]

SUPERGRASS

Formed: Oxford, England . . . 1991 as The JENNIFERS by schoolboy GAZ COOMBES and DANNY GOFFEY along with brother NICK and ANDY DAVIES. After a sole EP on 'Nude' (home to SUEDE), DAVIES went off to university, COOMBES and DANNY subsequently recruiting MICKEY QUINN and forming SUPERGRASS. Their raucous debut single, 'CAUGHT BY THE FUZZ', complete with a STIFF LITTLE FINGERS like intro and a snotty, shouty vocal rampage recounting the teenage trauma of being busted for cannabis, could've conceivably come straight out of 1977. Initially released on the small 'Backbeat' label in 1994, the single was eventually re-released by 'Parlophone' after the label promptly snapped the group up in 1994. Although the track narrowly missed the Top 40, a 1995 follow-up, 'MANSIZE ROOSTER', made the Top 20, the MADNESS comparisons inevitable as SUPERGRASS wore their influences proudly on their retro sleeves. Another couple of singles followed in quick succession, 'LOSE IT' as a limited 'Sub Pop' singles club release and 'LENNY' as the group's first Top 10 hit. Few were surprised, then, when the debut album, 'I SHOULD COCO' (1995) made No.1 the following month, a proverbial grab-bag of musical styles from 60's harmony pop to sneering punk. The record's indisputable highlight was 'ALRIGHT', a perfectly formed BEACH BOYS via The YOUNG ONES' pop romp guaranteed to bring a smile to your face and proving that "Brit-pop" didn't necessarily mean second rate STRANGLERS/BLONDIE rip-offs. The song, and especially the Raleigh Chopper-riding exploits of the video, did much to crystallise The SUPERGRASS image, carefree, fun-loving lads with GAZ's wildly impressive sideburns adding to the cartoon appeal. Steven Spielberg was apparently even moved to offer the band the opportunity of starring in a 90's remake of The MONKEES! This was turned down, as was an offer for GAZ to model for Calvin Klein, the group preferring to concentrate solely on the music and downplay the novelty factor. Instead, there were two gems hidden away at the end of 'I SHOULD..' which indicated the direction SUPERGRASS were headed; the intoxicating, slow rolling 70's groove of 'TIME' and the dreamy psychedelia of 'SOFA (OF MY LETHARGY). Save a few live appearances and a solitary single, 'GOING OUT', SUPERGRASS were notably absent in 1996, tucked away once more at Sawmill Studios crafting their acclaimed follow-up, 'IN IT FOR THE MONEY'. Eventually released in Spring '97, the record was something of a departure to say the least. The impetuous buzzsaw punk-pop of old had been replaced by the dark assault of 'RICHARD III' while the bulk of the album fed off warped neo-psychedelia and stark introspection. Horn flourishes were sighted here and there, most satisfyingly on the lazy chug of the aforementioned 'GOING OUT', while parping organs and acoustic strumming were the order of the day. The enigmatic shadow of The BEATLES' 'White Album' loomed large over proceedings, especially on 'YOU CAN SEE ME' and the oom-pa-pa eccentricity of 'SOMETIMES I MAKE YOU SAD'. In fact, the only glimpse of the old SUPERGRASS came with 'SUN HITS THE SKY', a soaring, handclapping, spirit-lifting celebration of good times and faraway places. No matter though, the record's dark charm ensured the band remained a critical favourite, if not quite consolidating the commercial heights of the debut. Clearly, SUPERGRASS are looking at a long term, albums-based career, and on the strength of 'IN IT..', the future seems promising. • **Covered:** STONE FREE (Jimi Hendrix) / ITCHYCOO PARK (Small Faces) / SOME GIRLS ARE BIGGER THAN OTHERS (Smiths).

Album rating: I SHOULD COCO (*9) / IN IT FOR THE MONEY (*8)

JENNIFERS

GAZ COOMBES (b.1976) – vocals, guitar / **NICK GOFFEY** – guitar / **ANDY DAVIES** – bass / **DANNY GOFFEY** (b.1975) – drums

Nude-Sony not iss.

Aug 92. (12"ep/cd-ep) *(NUD2 T/CD)* **JUST GOT BACK TODAY / ROCKS AND BOULDERS. / DANNY'S SONG / TOMORROW'S RAIN** [ ] [-]

— **MICKEY QUINN** (b.1970) – guitar repl.TARA MILTON who had repl.NICK

SUPERGRASS

— now without DAVIES who went to Bristol University.

Parlophone Capitol

Oct 94. (7"/c-s) *(R/TCR 6396) <81769>* **CAUGHT BY THE FUZZ. / STRANGE ONES** [43] [ ] Feb95
(cd-s+=) *(CDR 6396)* – Caught by the fuzz (acoustic).
Feb 95. (7"/7"red/c-s) *(R/RS/TCR 6402) <81964>* **MANSIZE ROOSTER. / SITTING UP STRAIGHT** [20] [ ] Jun95
(cd-s+=) *(CDR 6402)* – Odd.
Mar 95. (7"yellow) *(<SP 281>)* **LOSE IT. / CAUGHT BY THE FUZZ (acoustic)** [75] [ ]
(above on 'Sub Pop' also feat. on Jul95 box-set 'HELTER SHELTER')
Apr 95. (7"blue/c-s) *(RS/TCR 6401)* **LENNY. / WAIT FOR THE SUN** [9] [-]
(cd-s+=) *(CDR 6410)* – Sex!.
May 95. (cd/c/lp) *(CD/TC+/PCS 7373) <33350>* **I SHOULD COCO** [1] [ ] Jul95
– I'd like to know / Caught by the fuzz / Mansize rooster / Alright / Lose it / Lenny / Strange ones / Sitting up straight / She's so loose / We're not supposed to / Time / Sofa (of my lethargy) / Time to go. *(7"free w/ ltd lp)* **STONE FREE. / ODD?**
Jul 95. (c-s/7"colrd) *(TC+/R 6413) <82277>* **ALRIGHT. / TIME** [2] [ ]
(cd-s+=) *(CDR 6413)* – Condition / Je suis votre papa sucre.
(cd-s+=) *(CDRX 6413)* – Lose it.
Feb 96. (c-s/7"burgundy) *(TC+/R 6428)* **GOING OUT. / MELANIE DAVIS** [5] [-]
(cd-s+=) *(CDR 6428)* – Strange ones (live).
Apr 97. (cd-s/7"yellow) *(CD/+R 6461) <83820>* **RICHARD III. / NOTHING MORE'S GONNA GET IN MY WAY** [2] [ ]
(cd-s+=) *(CDRS 6461)* – 20ft halo.
(cd-s) *(CDRS 6461)* – ('A'side) / Sometimes I make you very sad / Sometimes we're very sad.
Apr 97. (cd/c/lp) *(CD/TC+/PCS 7388) <55228>* **IN IT FOR THE MONEY** [2] [ ] May97
– In it for the money / Richard III / Tonight / Late in the day / G-song / Sun hits the sky / Going out / It's not me / Cheapskate / You can see me / Hollow little reign / Sometimes I make you sad.
Jun 97. (c-s/7") *(TC+/R 6469) <84187>* **SUN HITS THE SKY. / SOME GIRLS ARE BIGGER THAN OTHERS** [10] [ ]
(cd-s+=) *(CDR 6469)* – ('A'extended).
Oct 97. (7"gold) *(R 6484) <84758>* **LATE IN THE DAY. / WE STILL NEED MORE (THAN ANYONE CAN GIVE)** [18] [ ]
(cd-s+=) *(CDRS 6484)* – It's not me (demo).
(cd-s) *(CDR 6484)* – ('A'side) / Don't be cruel / The animal.

— while SUPERGRASS took a deserved break from the biz, DANNY moonlighted with the indie superband, LODGER, who issued a few singles in '98

SUPER J LOUNGE

Formed: Tunbridge Wells, England . . . mid '96 by STUART SMITH and DON BROSNAN, two Anglophiled Tucson-born Americans who had been living in the capital for around a year. Enlisting a couple of locals, TIM HUGHES and STEN STENHOUSE, they wigged-out with their Krautrock-meets-the WHO-type power-pop on a debut single, 'SORRY', in early 1998.

Album rating: awaiting debut album

STUART SMITH – vocals, guitar / **STEN STENHOUSE** – guitar / **TIM HUGHES** – keyboards, samples / **DON BROSNANA** – bass

Fierce Panda not iss.

Feb 98. (7") *(NING 46)* **SORRY. / HOME** [ ] [-]
Jul 98. (7") *(NING 55)* **BILLBOARD. /** [ ] [-]

SUPERMODEL

Formed: Egham, England . . . 1995 by WOLSEY WHITE and LINDSAY JAMIESON, the line-up completed by TRIANI and CHRIS. Courting controversy before they'd even got past their debut release, the band found themselves on the wrong side of parent's indignation after they'd given away free copies of the 'PENIS SIZE AND CARS' EP to kids who put in a cameo appearance in the accompanying homemade video. Fortunately a tabloid furore failed to materialise and SUPERMODEL were free to pursue further their campaign of combining 70's production values and American noise-pop. Dubbed ELO-fi by one imaginative critic, the group followed their idiosyncratic path via a deal with 'Fire' records, licensing out their 'NO SECOND COMING' single and 'CLUMBA MAR' debut album in 1996.

Album rating: CLUMBA MAR (*6)

WOLSEY WHITE – vocals, guitar / **LINDSAY JAMIESON** – drums / with **TRIANI** – / **CHRIS** –

		Fire	not iss.
Oct 95.	(7"; as SUPERMODEL GT) *(BLAZE 96)* **PENIS SIZE AND CARS. /**		-
	(cd-s+=) *(BLAZE 96CD)* –		
Jan 96.	(7") *(BLAZE 99)* **HAIRCUT. /**		-
Mar 96.	(7") *(BLAZE 104)* **NO SECOND COMING. / FLAMENCO KARAOKE**		-
	(cd-s+=) *(BLAZE 014CD)* – Yeah.		
Apr 96.	(cd/lp) *(FIRE CD/LP 56)* **CLUMBA MAR**		-

SUPERNATURALS

Formed: Glasgow, Scotland . . . mid-90's by JAMES McCOLL, KEN McALPINE, DEREK McMANUS, ALAN TILSTON and MARK GUTHRIE. The Scottish equivalent to HERMAN'S HERMITS, The SUPERNATURALS took the softer elements of TEENAGE FANCLUB and smiled their way WET WET WET-style into the hearts of the nation's less discerning retro-pop fans. Although the aforementioned 'SMILE' failed to chart first time round in '96, the frighteningly annoying follow-up, 'LAZY LOVER' gave them their first Top 40 hit. Spookily enough, the band notched up a further series of Top 30 sub-DODGY hits the following year, all included on their debut long-player, 'IT DOESN'T MATTER ANYMORE' (you could well be right, lads!).

Album rating: IT DOESN'T MATTER ANYMORE (*6)

JAMES McCOLL – vocals, guitar / **KEN McALPINE** – keyboards, tambourine / **DEREK McMANUS** – guitar, vocals / **ALAN TILSTON** – drums / **MARK GUTHRIE** – bass

		Food	not iss.
Jul 96.	(7") *(FOOD 79)* **SMILE. / CAN'T GET BACK TO NORMAL**		-
	(cd-s+=) *(CDFOOD 79)* – Mint choc chip.		
Oct 96.	(c-s/7") *(TC+/FOOD 85)* **LAZY LOVER. / JOSEPHINE**	34	-
	(cd-s) *(CDFOOD 85)* – Caterpillar song.		
Jan 97.	(7") *(FOOD 88)* **THE DAY BEFORE YESTERDAY'S MAN. / HONK WILLIAMS**	25	-
	(cd-s+=) *(CDFOOD 88)* – Ken's song.		
	(cd-s) *(CDFOODS 88)* – ('A'side) / Deep in my heart I know I'm a slob / Brontosaurus.		
Apr 97.	(7") *(FOOD 92)* **SMILE. / STALINGRAD**	23	-
	(cd-s+=) *(CDFOODS 92)* – Childhood sweetheart.		
	(cd-s) *(CDFOOD 92)* – ('A'side) / Can't get back to normal / Mint choc chip.		
May 97.	(cd/c) *(FOOD CD/MC/LP 21)* **IT DOESN'T MATTER ANYMORE**	9	-
	– Please be gentle with me / Smile / Glimpse of the light / Lazy lover / Love has passed away / Dung beetle / Stammer / I don't think so / Pie in the sky / The day before yesterday's man / Prepare to land / Trees.		
Jul 97.	(c-s) *(TCFOOD 99)* **LOVE HAS PASSED AWAY / THE DAY BEFORE YESTERDAY'S MAN / LAZY LOVER**	38	-
	(cd-s) *(CDFOODS 99)* – ('A'side) / Scandinavian girlfriend / That's not me.		
	(cd-s) *(CDFOOD 99)* – ('A'side) / Trying too hard / Rupert the bear.		
Oct 97.	(7") *(FOOD 106)* **PREPARE TO LAND. / STUPID LOVESONG**	48	-
	(cd-s+=) *(CDFOOD 106)* – Skyway.		
	(cd-s) *(CDFOODS 106)* – ('A'side) / High tension at Boghead / Take some time out.		
Jul 98.	(c-s/cd-s) *(TCFOOD/CDFOODS 112)* **I WASN'T BUILT TO GET UP / ROBOT SONG / I JUST CAN'T GO ON LIKE THIS**	25	-
	(cd-s) *(CDFOOD 112)* – ('A'side) / Star wars / Bubblegum hill.		
Aug 98.	(cd/c) *(856893-2/-4)* **A TUNE A DAY**	21	-
	– You take yourself too seriously / Monday mornings / Submarine song / I wasn't built to get up / Country music / Motorcycle parts / Sheffield song (I love her more than I love you) / VW song / Idiot / Magnet / Still got that feeling / Let me know / It doesn't matter anymore / Everest.		
Oct 98.	(c-s/cd-s) *(TCFOOD/CDFOODS 115)* **SHEFFIELD SONG (I LOVE HER MORE THAN I LOVE YOU) / I DON'T THINK IT'S OVER / X COUNTRY SONG**	45	-
	(cd-s) *(CDFOOD 115)* – ('A'side) / Boys in the band / Hang out with you.		

SUPERSTAR

Formed: Glasgow, Scotland . . . 1991 by JOE McALINDEN, JIM McCULLOCH, QUENTIN McAFEE and ALAN HUTCHISON. The baby of musical maestro/trained violinist and former ex-BMX BANDIT / EUGENIUS / SOUP DRAGON, JOE McALINDEN, SUPERSTAR signed to 'Creation' in '92, releasing a mini debut confusingly titled, 'GREATEST HITS VOL.1', before inking an ill-advised deal with American label, 'S.B.K.'. A period of five years subsequently elapsed before the band re-emerged on the 'Camp Fabulous' label with the mini-set, '18 CARAT', McALINDEN famously turning down an opportunity to work with BRIAN WILSON along the way. The former BEACH BOYS genius wasn't the only famous muso bod to fall under the SUPERSTAR spell, the likes of PETER BUCK (R.E.M.) and ROD STEWART (who recorded the track 'SUPERSTAR' on his recent covers album) singing the praises of their belated debut album, 'PALM TREE' (1998). Described by one critic as a cross between QUEEN and RADIOHEAD, the Glaswegian quartet tend to draw extreme reactions (usually positive) with their alternately dramatic and heart-rending sound. Beautifully crafted and seemingly wrung from McALINDEN's tortured soul, the likes of 'EVERYDAY I FALL APART' even moved three separate Radio 1 DJ's to name it as their single of the week. Another admirer was novelist Alan Warner, who subsequently recorded a joint single with the band in summer '98.

Album rating: PALM TREE (*7)

JOE McALINDEN – vocals, guitar, piano, vocals (ex-EUGENIUS, ex-BMX BANDITS, ex-SOUP DRAGONS) / **JIM McCULLOCH** – guitar, vocals / **ALAN HUTCHISON** – bass, vocals, euphonium / **QUENTIN McAFEE** – drums, vocals

		Creation	Capitol
Jun 92.	(m-cd/m-lp) *(CRE CD/LP 134)* **GREATEST HITS VOL.1**		-
	– Barfly / The reason why / She's got everything I own / Let's get lost / Taste / After taste.		
1994.	(cd) *<28819>* **SUPERSTAR**	-	
	– Amouricity / Feels like forever / Barfly / Don't wanna die / The reason why / I can't help it / Noise level / Let's get lost / Will I ever see you again / Thought for today / Could it be you.		

—— disappeared for a while after signing a new deal with 'S.B.K.'

		Camp Fabulous	not iss.
Mar 97.	(m-cd/m-lp) *(CFAB 001 CD/LP)* **18 CARAT**		-
Sep 97.	(7") *(CFAB 002)* **BREATHING SPACE. / PALM TREE**		-
	(cd-s) *(CFAB 002CD)* – ('A'side) / Blind spot / Teacher (acoustic) / Disappointed man.		
Jan 98.	(7") *(CFAB 003S)* **EVERY DAY I FALL APART. / EVERY SECOND HURTS**	66	-
	(cd-s+=) *(CFAB 003CD)* – Hum / Lazy bones.		
Apr 98.	(7") *(CFAB 007S)* **SUPERSTAR. / HEY MONTANA SAN**	49	-
	(cd-s+=) *(CFAB 007CD)* – Waiting room.		
	(cd-s) *(CFAB 007ZCD)* – ('A'side) / Monstermind / Everyday I fall apart.		
Apr 98.	(cd/c/lp) *(CFAB 005X CD/MC/LP)* **PALM TREE**		
	– Monstermind / Superstar / Breathing space / Sparkle / Every day I fall apart / Once again / Palm tree / And when the morning comes / Two of a kind / Life is elsewhere / Teacher.		
Aug 98.	(10"ep; SUPERSTAR VS. ALAN WARNER) *(CFAB 009XS)* **SUPERSTAR VS. ALAN WARNER (SOUNDCLASH)**		-
	– Hum (whole new meaning) / One minute story / Introduction / Life is elsewhere / Every second hurts / Little picture.		

SUPERSUCKERS

Formed: Tucson, Arizona . . . late 80's as BLACK SUPERSUCKERS (after a porn mag!) by EDDIE SPAGHETTI, DAN BOLTON, RON HEATHMAN and DAN SIEGAL. Following a series of singles on various US indie labels – collected together on 1992 compilation, 'THE SONGS ALL SOUND THE SAME – the band relocated to Seattle (long before the media circus arrived) in search of work, shortened their name to SUPERSUCKERS, signed to 'Sub Pop' and embarked on a campaign of good-time grunge creation. Debut album proper, the Jack Endino-produced 'THE SMOKE OF HELL' (1992), drew comparisons with Australia's long lost COSMIC PSYCHOS while a subsequent tour with 'Sub Pop' rockabilly preacher The REVEREND HORTON HEAT brought the SUCKER musical punch to British shores for the first time. While never exactly threatening to claim NIRVANA's crown, the band continued to churn out reliably un-challenging, reinforced three-minute grunge-pop over albums such as 'LA MANO CORNUDA' (1994), 'THE SACRILICIOUS SOUNDS OF . . .' (1995) and the self-explanatory 'MUST'VE BEEN HIGH' (1997). • **Covered:** BURNIN' UP (Madonna) / WHAT LOVE IS . . . (Dead Boys) / RAZZAMANAZZ (Nazareth).

Album rating: THE SMOKE OF HELL (*6) / LA MANO CORNUDA (*6) / THE SACRILICIOUS SOUNDS OF . . . (*5) / MUST'VE BEEN HIGH (*5) / THE SONGS ALL SOUND THE SAME compilation (*5)

EDDIE SPAGHETTI – vocals, bass / **RON HEATHMAN** – guitar / **DAN BOLTON** – guitar / **DAN SEIGAL** – drums

—— released a number of 7" singles for Sympathy For The Record Industry

		Musical Tragedies	eMpTy
Jul 92.	(cd) *(EFA 11351)* *<162>* **THE SONGS ALL SOUND THE SAME** (compilation)		Nov91
	– Alright / Saddle tramp / Poor / Burnin' up / Gravity Bill / Sex & outrage / What love is . . . / Junk / 4-stroke / The girl I know / Razzamanazz.		

		Sub Pop	Sub Pop
Sep 92.	(7") **LIKE A BIG FUCKIN' TRAIN. /**	-	
Oct 92.	(cd)(lp) *(SP 212CD)(SP 50-212)* *<SP 164>* **THE SMOKE OF HELL**		Sep92
	– Coattail rider / Luck / I say fuck / Alone and stinking / Caliente / Tasty greens / Hell city, Hell / Hot rod rally / Drink and complain / Mighty Joe Young / Ron's got the cocaine / Sweet'n'sour Jesus / Retarded Bill / Thinking 'bout revenge.		
May 93.	(7") *<(SP 23-265)>* **DEAD HOMIEZ. / HELL CITY HELL**		
	(cd-s+=) *<(SPCD 23-265)>* –		
Apr 94.	(cd/lp) *<(SP CD/LP 120-301)>* **LA MANO CORNUDA**		
	– Creepy jackalope eye / Seventeen poles / High ya! / On the couch / Clueless / Sugie / Mudhead / Gold top / How to maximize your kill count / I was born without a spine / Glad, damn glad / She's my bitch / The schmooze.		
May 94.	(7") *<(SP 125-308)>* **400 BUCKS. / (other track by REVEREND HORTON HEAT)**		

Oct 94. (7") *<(SP 141-345)>* **ON THE COUCH. /**
(cd-s+=) *<(SPCD 141-345)>* –

— **RICK SIMS** – guitar (ex-DIDJITS) repl. HEATHMAN

Jul 95. (7") *<(SP 314)>* **BORN WITH A TAIL. /**
(cd-s+=) *<(SPCD 314)>* –

Sep 95. (7") *<(SP 315)>* **MARIE. /**
(cd-s+=) *<(SPCD 3145)>* –

Sep 95. (lp/c/cd) *<(SP 303/+A/CD)>* **THE SACRILICIOUS SOUNDS OF THE SUPERSUCKERS**
– Bad bad bad / Born with a tail / 19th most powerful woman in rock / Doublewide / Bad dog / Money into sin / Marie / Thing about that / Ozzy / Run like a motherfucker / Hittin' the gravel / Stoned if you want it / My victim / Don't go blue.

Nov 96. (7") *<(SP 384)>* **LEAVE THIS TOWN. / (B-side by TENDERLOIN)**

Sep 97. (lp/cd) *<(SP/+CD 380)>* **MUST'VE BEEN HIGH** Mar97
– Must've been high / Dead in the water / Barricade / Roamin' 'round / Hungover together / Non-addictive marijuana / Captain / Blow you away / Roadworn and weary / Hangin' out with me.

SURGICAL PENIS KLINIK (see under ⇒ S.P.K.)

SWALLOW

Formed: Early 90's . . . by Irish pair, MIKE MASON and LOUISE TREHY in London, England. The former had been a keyboard-player with INTO PARADISE, before he received his marching orders, while the latter's only previous musical background was in a directorial capacity for a SPACEMEN 3 video. After being given a tape of MASON's rough demos, singer TREHY decided to collaborate with the man and together, the duo completed a more polished 3-track demo which they sent to '4 a.d.' supremo, IVO. Bluffing their way into a record deal, SWALLOW glided into pop consciousness with the very 4ad-esque 'BLOW' (1992) album, a dead ringer for MY BLOODY VALENTINE and The COCTEAU TWINS. Later in the year, the record was remixed although their highly derivative sound proved to be an albatross round their neck. Despite a couple more years of experience behind them, MASON and TREHY took flight following a final EP, 'HUSH', on 'Rough Trade'.

Album rating: BLOW (*5)

LOUISE TREHY – vocals / **MIKE MASON** – instruments (ex-INTO PARADISE)

4 a.d. / Reprise

Jul 92. (cd)(lp/c) *(CAD 2010CD)(CAD/+C 2010)* **BLOW**
– Lovesleep / Tastes like honey / Sugar your mind / Mensurral / Peekaboo / Lacuna / Oceans and blue skies / Follow me down / Halo / Cherry stars collide / Head in a cave.

Oct 92. (cd) **BLOWBACK** (remixes) -

Rough Trade / not iss.

Jun 94. (12"ep/cd-ep) *(R 322-0/-3)* **HUSH EP** -
– Hush / Flooded / Watching the sun / Dear Mary.

— disbanded after above

SWAMP CHILDREN (see under ⇒ A CERTAIN RATIO)

SWANS

Formed: New York, USA . . . 1982 as a vehicle for the musical experimentation of MICHAEL GIRA. With an initial line-up of GIRA, ROLI MOSSIMAN, NORMAN WESTBURG, HARRY CROSBY and JONATHAN KANE, SWANS made their less than graceful debut with an EP in 1982, following it up with debut album, 'FILTH' (1983), both releases appearing – in Europe at least – on the German 'Zensor' label. Subsequently signing to British indie imprint, 'K.422', and replacing KANE with IVAN NAHEM, the band unleashed the pulverising 'COP' (1984) album. A harsh lesson in rock deconstruction, the record found GIRA and co. taking a metaphorical pneumatic drill to the form and pounding it till it barely even resembled music. Lyrically, GIRA was also scraping the margins, focusing on the blackest, most violent, paranoid and disturbing elements of life's dark side; 'RAPING A SLAVE' for instance, this controversial track also appearing as the lead track to a subsequent EP. Not music to play to your grandchildren then, but a brutally honest response to what GIRA perceived as the rotten core of human (and certainly American) society. Previewed by the memorably titled 'TIME IS MONEY (BASTARD)', 'GREED' (1986) was the next instalment in SWANS' dismantling of the capitalist rock beast, taking horror-industrial minimalism to new depths via a skeletal soundtrack of stark piano and percussion. Introducing the haunting vocals of JARBOE (MOSSIMAN had decamped to form WISEBLOOD), the 'HOLY MONEY' album continued along the same (production) lines later that year. 1987 proved a turning point as GIRA and JARBOE created SKIN as an outlet for their more fragile, acoustic creations, albums such as 'BLOOD, WOMEN, ROSES' (1987) and 'SHAME, HUMILITY, REVENGE' (1988) representing a more endearing flipside to the brutality of SWANS. Both albums appeared on 'Product Inc.', as did SWANS' 'CHILDREN OF GOD' (1988), a double set which introduced a new rhythm section (TED PARSONS and ALGYS 'AL' KIZYS) and found the band showing definite signs of mellowing. The shift was underlined with a surprise acoustic reading of Joy Division's 'LOVE WILL TEAR US APART', issued as a single in summer '88. incredibly, perhaps, the band signed to corporate giant, 'M.C.A.', in 1989, releasing 'THE BURNING WORLD' as their major label debut. The partnership didn't last long, however, GIRA and JARBOE subsequently forming their own 'Young God' label for the release of '10 SONGS FOR ANOTHER WORLD', a third SKIN project issued under the revamped moniker WORLD OF SKIN (after Brit cock-rockers SKIN claimed the name). 1991's 'WHITE LIGHT FROM THE MOUTH OF INFINTIY' moved even further away from the rampant nihilism of GIRA's earlier work, the man sounding uncannily like NICK CAVE (ironically another former prophet of doom who now seems to have found at least a measure of spiritual redemption) in places; while the brilliantly morose 'FAILURE' was the GIRA we all know and love, 'SONG FOR THE SUN' was positively joyous, suggesting there was indeed some light filtering through to the man's formerly obscured world view. Subsequent 90's albums, 'LOVE OF LIFE' (1992), 'OMNISCENCE' (1992), 'THE GREAT ANNIHILATOR' (1995) and 'SOUNDTRACKS FOR THE BLIND' (1996)- continued in a similarly (relatively) accessible vein although the latter marked their ahem, SWAN(S)-song as GIRA and JARBOE decided the project had reached its natural conclusion. Nevertheless, 1995 had proved a fruitful year for SWANS-related material as GIRA launched a book, 'The Consumer And Other Stories', through HENRY ROLLINS' publishing operation, '21/3/61' as well as his debut solo set, 'DRAINLAND'. JARBOE, meanwhile, also released a debut solo set the same year, 'SACRIFICIAL CAKE'.

Album rating: FILTH (*6) / COP (*7) / GREED (*6) / HOLY MONEY (*6) / CHILDREN OF THE GOD (*7) / FEEL GOOD NOW (*6) / THE BURNING WORLD (*6) / WHITE LIGHT FROM THE MOUTH OF INFINITY (*7) / THE GREAT ANNIHILATOR (*6) /

MICHAEL GIRA – vocals (ex-LITTLE CRIPPLES) / **ROLI MOSSIMAN** – piano, percussion / **NORMAN WESTBURG** – guitar / **HARRY CROSBY** – bass / **JONATHAN KANE** – drums, percussion

Zensor / Labour

1982. (7"ep) **EP #1** -
(UK-iss.Sep90 on 'Young God'; YGEP 001)

Zensor / Neutral

1983. (lp) *<ND 02>* **FILTH** -
– Stay here / Big strong boss / Blackout / Power for power / Freak / Right wrong / Thank you / Weakling / Gang. *(UK-iss.Sep90 on 'Young God' cd+=/c/lp; TG CD/MC/LP 1)* – Speak / Laugh / Sensitive skin / Take advantage. *(re-iss. Sep90 on 'Young God' lp/cd; YG LP/CD 001) (cd re-iss. Aug94 on 'Sky'; SKY 75061CD)*

K.422 / P.V.C.

— **IVAN NAHEM** – drums; repl. JONATHAN who joined The HOOD

Nov 84. (lp) *(KCC 001)* **COP** -
– Half life / Job / Why hide / Clayman / I crawled / Raping a slave / Your property / Cop / Butcher / Thug / Young god / This is mine. *(cd-iss. Jan89 ; KCCCD 001)*

Feb 85. (12"ep) *(KDE 12-1)* **I CRAWLED / RAPING A SLAVE. / YOUNG GOD / THIS IS MINE** -

Jan 86. (12") *(KDE 12-2)* **TIME IS MONEY (BASTARD). / SEALED IN SKIN / TIME IS MONEY (mix)** -

Mar 86. (lp) *(KCC 2)* **GREED**
– Time is money (bastard) / Money is flesh / Another you / Greed.

— **JARBOE** – keyboards, vox; repl. MOSSIMAN who formed WISEBLOOD

Sep 86. (lp) *(KCC 3)* **HOLY MONEY**
– A hanging / You need me / Fool / A screw (holy money) / Another you / Money is flesh / Coward / A screw (mix) / Black mail / A screw . *(cd-iss. Feb88 +=; KCCCD 3)* – GREED

Sep 86. (12") *(KDE 3-12)* **A SCREW (HOLY MONEY). / BLACKMAIL / A SCREW** -

Nov 86. (d-lp) **PUBLIC CASTRATION IS A GOOD IDEA (live)** -
– Money is flesh / Fool / A screw / Anything for you / Coward / A hanging / Stupid child / Another you.

— **TED PARSONS** – drums + **ALGYS 'AL' KIZYS** – bass; repl. NAHEM + CROSBY who both formed OF CABBAGES AND KINGS (they issued a few releases, mainly an eponymouse set plus the 'FACE' album in '88.

Product Inc / Caroline

Aug 87. (7") *(PROD 16)* **NEW MIND. / I'LL SWALLOW YOU** -
(12"+=) *(12PROD 16)* –

Oct 87. (d-lp/c/cd) *(33/C PROD 17)(PRODCD 17) <CAROL 1346-1/-4/-2>* **CHILDREN OF GOD**
– New mind / In my garden / Sex god sex / Blood and honey / Like a drug / You're not real, girl / Beautiful child / Trust me / Blackmail / Real love. *(cd+=)* – Our love lies.

Jun 88. (7"red) *(PROD 23)* **LOVE WILL TEAR US APART. / TRUST ME** -
(12"+=/cd-s+=) *(PROD 23 T/CD)* – ('A'-Black version) / New mind (purple version).
(12"red+=) *(PROD 23B)* – Our love lies.

Love / not iss.

Aug 88. (d-lp) *(LOVE ONE)* **FEEL GOOD NOW** -

— guests incl. **STEVEN** – bass + **VINNY** – drums repl. ALGYS + TED

M.C.A. / not iss.

Apr 89. (7") *(MCA 1322)* **SAVED. / NO CRUEL ANGEL** -
(12"+=/cd-s+=) *(MCAT/DMCAT 1332)* – See you more.

May 89. (lp/c/cd) *(MCG/MCGC/DMCG 6047)* **THE BURNING WORLD** -
– The river that runs with love won't run dry / Let it come down / Can't find my way home / Mona Lisa, Mother Earth / (She's a) Universal emptiness / Saved / I remember who you are / Jane Mary, cry one tear / See no more / God damn the sun.

Aug 89. (7") *(MCA 1347)* **CAN'T FIND MY WAY HOME. / UNIVERSAL EMPTINESS** -
(12"+=/12"g-f+=)(cd-s+=) *(MCAT/+G 1347)(DMCAT 1347)* –

— w/ guests **ANTON FIER** (GOLDEN PALOMINOES) / **CLINTON STEELE** (MARY MY HOPE) / **HAHN ROWE** (HUGO LARGO)

Young God / not iss.

Apr 91. (cd/c/d-lp) *(YG CD/MC/LP 003)* **WHITE LIGHT FROM THE MOUTH OF INFINITY** -
– Better than you / Power and sacrifice / You know nothing / Song for dead time / Will we survive / Love will save you / Failure / Song for the sun / Miracle of love /

When she breathes / Why are we alive? / The most unfortunate lie. *(cd re-iss. Aug94 on 'Sky'; SKY 75060CD)*

Nov 91. (cd/c/lp) *(YG CD/MC/LP 004)* **BODY TO BODY, JOB TO JOB** (compilation of live & out takes from 1982-85) -
– I'll cry for you / Red sheet / Loop 33 / Your game / Seal it over / Whore / We'll hang out for that / Half life / Loop 21 / Get out / Job / Loop 1 / Mother, my body disgusts me / Cop / Only I can hear, only I can touch / Thug. *(cd re-iss. Aug94 on 'Sky'; SKY 75063CD)*

Feb 92. (cd/c/lp) *(YG CD/MC/LP 005)* **LOVE OF LIFE** -
– Love of life / The golden boy that was swallowed by the sea / The other side of the world / Her / The sound of freedom / Amnesia / Identity / In the eyes of nature / She crys / God loves America / No cure for the lonely. *(cd re-iss. Aug94 on 'Sky'; SKY 75064CD)*

Apr 92. (12") **LOVE OF LIFE (M. Gira remix). / AMNESIA (Martin Bisi re mix)** -
(cd-s+=) – Picture of Maryanne.

Young God / Dog Gone

Oct 92. (cd/c/lp) *(YG CD/MC/LP 007)* *<5160>* **OMNISCENCE** Jan93
– Mother's milk / Pow r sac / Will serve / Her / Black eyed dog / Amnesia / Love of life / (----) / The other side of the world / Rutting / God loves America / Omnipotent. *(cd re-iss. Aug94 on 'Sky'; SKY 75160CD)*

Young God / Invisible

Jan 95. (cd/d-lp) *(YG CD/LP 009)* *<INV 35CD>* **THE GREAT ANNIHILATOR**
– In / I am the sun / She lives! / Celebrity lifestyle / Mother, father / Blood promise / Mind / Body / Light / Sound / My buried child / Warm / Alcohol the seed / Killing for company / Mother's milk / Where does a body end / Telepathy / The great annihilator / Out.

Aug 96. (10") *(ART 01)* **ANIMUS. / FAILURE** -
(above issued on 'Arts & Commerce')

Young God / Atavistic

Oct 96. (d-cd) *(YGCD 010)* *<61959>* **SOUNDTRACKS FOR THE BLIND**
– Red velvet corridor / I was a prisoner in your skull / Helpless child / Live through me / Yumyab killers / Beautiful days / Volcano / Mellothumb / All lined up / Surrogate 2 / How they suffer / Animus / Red velvet wound / Sound / Her mouth is filled with honey / Bloodsection / Jypogirl / Minus something / Empathy / I love you this much / YRP / Fans lament / Secret friends / Final sac / YRP 2 / Surrogate drone.

– compilations, etc. –

Nov 92. (cd) *K.422; (KCC 001CD)* **COP / YOUNG GOD** -
(re-iss. Aug94 on 'Sky'; SKY 75068CD)

Nov 92. (cd) *K.422;* **GREED / HOLY MONEY** -
(re-iss. Aug94 on 'Sky'; SKY 75069CD)

Mar 96. (cd) *Atavistic; <57>* **KILL THE CHILD (live)** -

May 96. (cd) *Atavistic; <58>* **REAL LOVE** -

Jun 96. (cd) *World Service; (RTD 1573140-2)* **DIE TUR IST ZU** -
– Liget's breath / Hilfios kind / Ich sehe die alle in einer reihe / Y.R.P. / You know everything / M-F / Sound section.

— disbanded in '97

SKIN

— an off-shoot duo of **MICHAEL GIRA + JARBOE**

Product Inc. / not iss.

Mar 87. (7") *(7PROD 3)* **1000 YEARS. / MY OWN HANDS** -
(12"+=) *(12PROD 3)* –

Mar 87. (lp/cd) *(33/CD PROD 4)* **BLOOD, WOMEN, ROSES** -
– 1000 years / Cry me a river / We'll fall apart / Still a child / The man I loved (with LESTER YOUNG) / Red rose / Blood on your hands. *(re-iss. Jun89 d-lp; PROD 33-025)* – SHAME, HUMILITY, REVENGE *(cd+=)* – My own hands / 1000 years (remix) / Girl: come out (remix).

Jun 87. (7") *(PROD 6)* **GIRL: COME OUT. / ('A'dub version)** -

May 88. (lp/cd) *(33/CD PROD 11)* **SHAME, HUMILITY, REVENGE** -
(cd+=) – I wanna be your dog.

— now w/ **ROLI MOSSIMANN / CLINTON STEELE / TONY MAIMONE**

Young God / not iss.

Oct 90. (cd/lp; as WORLD OF SKIN) *(YG CD/MC/LP 002)* **10 SONGS FOR ANOTHER WORLD** -
– Please remember me / Drink to me only with thine eyes / The child's right / Everything for Maria / I'll go there, take me home / Black eyed dog / A parasite and other memories / Dream dream / You'll never forget / Mystery of faith. *(cd re-iss. Aug94 on 'Sky'; SKY 75062CD)*

JARBOE

Hyperium / not iss.

Sep 92. (cd/lp) *(3910002-2/-1)* **THIRTEEN MASKS** -
(cd re-iss. Aug94 on 'Sky'; SKY 75065CD)

Young God / not iss.

Jul 95. (cd) *(YGCD 008)* **SACRIFICIAL CAKE** -
– Lavender girl / Ode to V / Shimmer 1 / My buried child / Not logical / Spiral staircase / Yum yab / Surgical savior / Cache toi / Tragic seed / Troll lullaby / Deflowered / The body lover / Shimmer 2 / Act 3 / Troll.

Cold Spring / not iss.

Jun 96. (7") *(CSR 11P)* **CACHE TOI. /** -

MICHAEL GIRA

Sub Rosa / not iss.

Jun 95. (cd) *(SR 086)* **DRAINLAND** -
– You see through me / Where does your body begin? / I see them all lined up / Unreal / Fan letter / Your naked body / Low life form / If you . . . / Why I ate my wife / Blind.

SWANS WAY

Formed: Birmingham, England . . . 1982 by singer ROBERT SHAW, who enlisted the help of New Zealanders, MAGGIE DE MONDE (keyboards & vocals) and RICK P. JONES (on double bass!), who had both served their time in Christchurch outfit, The PLAYTHINGS. Although their debut single, '(EXCERPT FROM THE) BALCONY THEME)', didn't do much at all, the trio earned their lucky break via Channel 4's 'The Tube', Jools Holland and Co screening the video for 'SOUL TRAIN'. A slick throwback to the jazzy nightclub sophistication of the 30's complete with period attire, the clip was enough to power the song into the Top 20 in early '84. Aspiring to articulate a similar passion and moodiness to BILLY MacKENZIE (of the ASSOCIATES), SHAW was a compelling focal point, the unique SWANS WAY sound also incorporating the curious glamour of DE MONDE and the reverberating double-bass of JONES. Unfortunately, after a move up to 'Mercury' records, SWANS WAY were found to be treading water on two further singles, 'ILLUMINATIONS' (only Top 60!) and 'WHEN THE WILD CALLS' (a complete flop!). The year (which started off so promisingly) went from bad to worse when their debut long-player, 'THE FUGITIVE KIND', was met with a lukewarm response and didn't even scrape into the Top 75. SHAW subsequently took flight to form POP GUN, while Kiwi duo, DE MONDE and JONES, resurfaced three years later with the frankly embarrassing SCARLET FANTASTIC. A complete change of direction was heralded with the pop-tastic Top 30 hit, 'NO MEMORY', although history was to repeat itself as follow-up, 'PLUG ME IN (TO THE CENTRAL LINE)', barely made the Top 75 and the accompanying album, '24 HOURS' (1988), stiffed.

Album rating: THE FUGITIVE KIND (*5) / Scarlet Fantastic: 24 HOURS (*4)

ROBERT SHAW – vocals / **MAGGIE LE MONDE** – keyboards, vocals (ex-PLAYTHINGS) / **RICK P. JONES** – double bass (ex-PLAYTHINGS)

Exit / not iss.

Aug 82. (7"/ext.12") *(7/12 EXIT 2)* **(EXCERPT FROM THE) BALCONY THEME. / VIBRATION HOIST** -

Jan 84. (7"/ext.12") *(EXT 3/+12)* **SOUL TRAIN. / GLOOMY SUNDAY** 20 -

Balgier-Mercury / Mercury

Apr 84. (7"/12") *(PH 5/+12)* **ILLUMINATIONS. / ('A'-intro mix)** 57 -

Sep 84. (7"/ext-12") *(PH 9/+12)* **WHEN THE WILD CALLS. / HANGOVER** -

Oct 84. (lp)(cd) *(SWAN 1)(818858-2)* **THE FUGITIVE KIND** 88 -
– Soul train / Keeping it strong / Club secrets / In trance / Je joue / The blade / The anchor / When the wild calls / Stay / Illuminations.

Nov 84. (7"/12"; w-drawn) *(PH 30/+12)* **KEEPING IT STRONG. / FIRES WERE STARTED** - -

Nov 84. (7") *(PH 31)* **THE ANCHOR. / ('A'instrumental)** -
(12"+=) *(PH 31/+12)* – Keeping it strong.

— they split the following year when SHAW formed POP GUN and the remaining two formed the short-lived chart act, SCARLET FANTASTIC

Matthew SWEET

Born: 6 Oct'64, Lincoln, Nebraska, USA. While studying at Athens university in Georgia, SWEET made his first tentative steps into the music industry with local outfit, OH-OK, an indie-pop outfit led by MICHAEL STIPE's sister, LYNDA. But it would be SWEET's recordings under the BUZZ OF DELIGHT (a collaboration with OH-OK drummer, DAVID PIERCE) moniker that would get him noticed and subsequently secure him a deal with 'Columbia' in the mid-80's. While boasting an array of guest artists that almost amounted to a who's who of the American underground (BERNIE WORRELL, ANTON FIER and The BANGLES to name but a few), SWEET's debut album, 'INSIDES' (1986), suffered from a heavy-handed 80's production that suffocated the singer/songwriter's latent talent. Dropped by 'Columbia' after the record sank without trace, he was picked up by 'A&M' and began work on the sessions for 1989's follow-up album, 'EARTH'. This marked the beginning of a long term musical partnership with veteran New York guitarists, RICHARD LLOYD and ROBERT QUINE although SWEET's artistic and commercial breakthough was put on hold until 1991's acclaimed 'GIRLFRIEND'. Having switched label once again, this time to 'Zoo'/'BMG', he finally silenced his critics with a classy collection of harmony-sparkling power-pop gems which, while acknowledging a debt to the likes of R.E.M., BIG STAR, The BEACH BOYS and NEIL YOUNG, never laboured under the burden of their influences. Critical raves and a US Top 100 placing saw the record go gold and it looked as if SWEET was headed for major success yet a musical about turn on 'ALTERED BEAST' (1993) precluded much crossover potential. Anchored once more by the guitar duelling of QUINE and LLOYD, the record also featured the likes of NICKY HOPKINS, MICK FLEETWOOD and JODY STEPHENS, a schizophrenic combination that mirrored the album's contents, swinging wildly between brash guitar abuse and heart-piercing ballads. Nevertheless, the record notched up a Top 75 chart placing with heavy MTV rotation for the likes of 'UGLY TRUTH' and the country lilt of 'TIME CAPSULE'. While the darker lyrical turn was still at least partly in evidence on third set, '100% FUN' (1995), the music was kept simple and effective: breezy, feel-good guitar-pop abandon with choruses to match. Its positive critical reception was reflected in a further chart progression (No.65) and another gold award although SWEET's fear of flying (a trait shared with one of his heroes, the late GENE CLARK) has restricted his touring possibilities and the attendant promotional spin-offs. Having parted company with both LLOYD and QUINE prior to the recording of 'BLUE SKY ON MARS' (1997),

SWEET was left without the foil which had served him so well over the bulk of his career. As a result, he was prone to charges that the record sounded too one dimensional and lacked bite, his melodies a mite too sugary for prolonged consumption.

Album rating: INSIDE (*5) / EARTH (*6) / GIRLFRIEND (*8) / ALTERED BEAST (*7) / 100% FUN (*7) / BLUE SKY ON MARS (*6)

MATTHEW SWEET – vocals, multi (ex-OH-OK, ex-BUZZ OF DELIGHT) / with a drum machine plus ANTON FIER, AIMEE MANN, CHRIS STAMEY + FRED MAHER

not iss. Columbia

1986. (lp) **INSIDE** [-] [ ]

— now with DAVE ALVIN, RICHARD LLOYD, ROBERT QUINE + KATE PIERSON, RIC MENCK, GARY LUCAS, FRED MAHER

not iss. A&M

1989. (lp/cd) <395233-1/-2> **EARTH** [-] [ ]
– Easy / When I feel again / Wind and the sun / Children of time (forever) / Love / Vertigo / Underground / The alcohol talking / Vixen / How cool / Having a bad dream.

— added LLOYD COLE, etc

R.C.A. Zoo

Jun 92. (cd/c) *(PD/PK 90644)* <72445 11015-2/-4> **GIRLFRIEND** [-] [100] Feb92
– Divine intervention / I've been waiting / Girlfriend / Looking at the sun / Winona / Evangeline / Day or night / Thought I knew you / You don't love me / I wanted to tell you / Don't go / Your sweet voice / Does she talk? / Holy war / Nothing lasts.

— with QUINE, LLOYD + IVAN JULIAN, PETE THOMAS, NICKY HOPKINS, JODY STEPHENS + MICK FLEETWOOD

Zoo Zoo

Jul 93. (cd) <(72445 11050-2)> **ALTERED BEAST** [ ] [75]
– Dinosaur act / Devil with the green eyes / The ugly truth / Time capsule / Someone to pull the trigger / Knowing people / Life without you / Metro / Ugly truth rock / Do it again / In too deep / Reaching out / Falling / What do you know? / Evergreen.

Mar 95. (cd/c) <(72445 11081-2/-4)> **100% FUN** [ ] [65]
– Sick of myself / Not when I need it / We're the same / Giving it back / Everything changes / Lost my mind / Come to love / Walk out / I almost forgot / Super baby / Get older / Smog moon.

Apr 97. (cd) *(614453113029)* **BLUE SKY ON MARS** [ ] [ ]
– Come back to California / Back to you / Where you get love / Hollow / Behind the smile / Until you break / Over it / Heaven and Earth / All over my head / Into your drug / Make believe / Missing time.

SWEET 75 (see under ⇒ NIRVANA)

SWELL MAPS

Formed: Solihull, Midlands, England . . . 1972 by brothers NIKKI SUDDEN and EPIC SOUNDTRACKS, who, in 1976, were joined by PHONES SPORTSMAN, RICHARD EARL and JOWE HEAD. This loose aggregate of D-I-Y punks (who also included early contributor, JOHN COCKRILL at this time) finally issued their semi-legendary debut 45, 'READ ABOUT SEYMOUR', on their own 'Rather' label early in 1978. Favoured by John Peel for their pared down noise assaults, the band secured many sessions for the man's Radio One show, the cream of these released (jointly by 'Rather' and 'Rough Trade') as singles, 'DRESDEN STYLE' and 'REAL SHOCKS'. These clattering FALL-esque tracks didn't even feature on their 1979 debut set, 'A TRIP TO MARINEVILLE', a love-it-or-hate-it affair which found a vocal supporter in journalist, Paul Morley. Completed on a 4-track in under a week and characterised by SUDDEN's scuzzy guitar freak-outs and his flat larynx, the album placed the energetic nihilism of punk in the context of Kraut-rock experimentalism and, in the sporadic piano interludes of EPIC SOUNDTRACKS, recalled the likes of FAUST and CAN. The 80's got off to a productive start with what has retrospectively come to be regarded as their finest three minutes, 'LET'S BUILD A CAR', a speaker-busting example of the 'MAPS at their off-kilter piano-abusing best. Later in the year, after an ill-starred tour of Italy (where they had found a sizeable fanbase!), they finally fell apart having already completed the bulk of the work for a new album. 'JANE FROM OCCUPIED EUROPE', hit the shelves that summer, a more confident piece of work that threw in everything but the kitchen sink. Despite the split, fans were kept busy with a slew of archive releases including 1981's home-recorded outtakes set, 'WHATEVER HAPPENS NEXT . . .' and the following years' singles collection, 'COLLISION TIME'. PHONES SPORTSMAN had already begun a solo career, having released an EP, 'I REALLY LOVE YOU', in summer 1980, prior to playing alongside solo bound JOWE HEAD in 1982. JOWE released the first of several albums that year, 'PINCER MOVEMENT', while in the mid 80's, he fronted another recording outfit, The PALOOKAS. Meanwhile, EPIC SOUNDTRACKS issued two singles in '81/'82, the solo 'POPULAR, CLASSICAL' and a JOWE HEAD collaboration, 'RAIN RAIN RAIN'. EPIC subsequently joined former BIRTHDAY PARTY members in CRIME & THE CITY SOLUTION, while simultaneously moonlighting with NIKKI SUDDEN's outfit, The JACOBITES. SUDDEN himself had kickstarted his solo career in 1981 with 'BACK TO THE START' trailing it with an album, 'WAITING ON EGYPT' (1982). Following another solo album and two JACOBITES (a trio featuring NIKKI, EPIC and DAVE KUSWORTH) sets, the former SWELL MAPS leader signed to 'Creation', releasing several albums starting with 1986's mini-set, 'TEXAS' (which featured an obscure Neil Young cover, 'CAPTAIN KENNEDY'). • **Trivia:** SONIC YOUTH are known to be admirers of their early attitude and sound.

Album rating: A TRIP TO MARINEVILLE (*6) / JANE FROM OCCUPIED EUROPE (*6) / WHATEVER HAPPENS NEXT . . . (*5) / COLLISION TIME compilation (*8) / TRAIN OUT OF IT (*4) / Nikki Sudden: WAITING ON EGYPT (*6) / THE BIBLE BELT (*6) / JACOBITES (*6) / ROBESPIERRE'S VELVET BASEMENT with the Jacobites (*6) / TEXAS mini (*5) / DEAD MEN TELL NO TAILS mini (*5) / KISS YOU KIDNAPPED CHARABANC with Roland S. Howard (*6) / FORTUNE OF FAME with Dave Kusworth (*5) / GROOVE (*5) / BACK TO THE COAST (*5) / THE JEWEL THIEF (*6) / Jowe Head: PINCER MOVEMENT (*5) / STRAWBERRY DEUTSCHMARK (*5) / THE JOWE HEAD PERSONAL ORGANIZER (*5) / UNHINGED (*5)

NIKKI SUDDEN (b.19 Jul'56) – guitar, vocals / **EPIC SOUNDTRACKS** (b. PAUL GODLEY, 1960) – drums, vocals, some keyboards / **PHONES SPORTSMAN** (b.DAVID BARRINGTON) – vocals / **JOWE HEAD (JOE HENDON)** – bass, vocals / **RICHARD EARL** – vocals / guest on a couple **JOHN** (GOLDEN) **COCKRILL** – vocals

Rather not iss.

Feb 78. (7"m) *(GEAR ONE)* **READ ABOUT SEYMOUR. / RIPPED AND TORN / BLACK VELVET** [ ] [-]
(re-iss. Oct79 on 'Rough Trade-Rather'; RT 10-GEAR ONE MK.2)

— (next releases were jointly issued on own 'Rather')

Rough Trade not iss.

Feb 79. (7"m) *(RT 012 – GEAR 3)* **DRESDEN STYLE / MYSTERY TRACK. / AMMUNITION TRAIN / FULL MOON (dub)** [ ] [-]
(re-iss. Sep80; same) – (new vocal 'A';- mystery track).

Jun 79. (7"m) *(RT 021 – GEAR 6)* **REAL SHOCKS. / AN ENGLISH VERSE / MONOLOGUES** [ ] [-]

Jul 79. (lp) *(ROUGH 2 – TROY 1)* **A TRIP TO MARINEVILLE** [ ] [-]
– H.S. art / Another song / Vertical slum / Spitfire parade / Harmony in your bathroom / Don't throw ashtrays at me / Midget submarines / Bridge head / Full moon in my pocket / Blam!! / Full Moon (reprise) / Gunboats / Adventuring into basketry / My little shops / Ripped and torn / International rescue / Loin of the surf / Shoot the angels. *(free-7"ep) (GEAR FIVE)* **LOIN OF THE SURF / DOCTOR AT CAKE. / STEVEN DOES / BRONZE & BABY SHOES** *(re-iss. Feb90 on 'Mute' cd/lp; CD+/MAPS 1) (+=)* – (8 extra tracks).

Jan 80. (7"m) *(RT 036 – GEAR 7)* **LET'S BUILD A CAR. / BIG MAZ IN THE COUNTRY / . . . THEN POLAND** [ ] [-]

Jul 80. (lp) *(ROUGH 15)* **JANE FROM OCCUPIED EUROPE** [ ] [-]
– Robot factory / Let's buy a bridge / Border country / Cake shop / The helicopter spies / Big Maz in the desert / Big empty field / Mining villages / Collision with a frogman vs. the Mangrove Delta Plan / Secret island / Whatever happens next / Blenheim shots / Raining in my room. *(re-iss. Feb90 on 'Mute' cd/lp; CD+/MAPS 2) (cd+=)* – Let's build a car / Epic's trip / Uh / Secret island (instrumental) / Amphitheatres / Big empty field (No.2) / The stairs are like an avalanche / . . . Then Poland.

— Disbanded later in 1980, with all going off to solo careers, etc.

– compilations, others, etc. –

on 'Rough Trade' unless otherwise mentioned

May 81. (d-lp) *(ROUGH 21)* **WHATEVER HAPPENS NEXT . . .** [ ] [-]
– Read about Seymour / Fashion cult / Armadillo / (I am) The greatest plumming! – Radio ten / Here's the cupboard (thrash) / Terribly insect / Midget submarines / Whatever happens next / Clearasil record (stuck) / Blam / Down with tractors / Amphibious landing craft / Paul's dead / Sheep dip / avoc all ended / The Himalayas / The stairs are like an avalanche / Vertical slum / Forest fire / Midget submarines (II) / Armadillo (II) / Bandits one five. *(cd-iss. Aug91 on 'Mute'; CDMAPS 4)*

May 82. (lp) *(ROUGH 41)* **COLLISION TIME** [ ] [-]
– Read about Seymour / Ammunition train / Full Moon in my pocket / Blam / Real shocks / Midget submarines / Let's build a car / . . .Then Poland / Secret Island / Whatever happens next / Big Maz in the desert from the trolley / Big empty field / Blenheim shots / A raincoat's room. *<US-iss.Jul89 as 'COLLISION TIME REVISITED' d-lp/cd; 7 71421-1/-2>*

May 87. Antar; (lp) *(ANTAR 4)* **TRAIN OUT OF IT** [ ] [-]
(cd-iss. Oct91 on 'Mute'; CDMAPS 3) – (8 extra tracks).

— SWELL MAPS associated releases ('Rather' or 'Rough Trade')

Aug 78. (7"ep; by STEVE TREATMENT) *(GEAR 2)* **5-A-SIDED 45** [ ] [-]
– The hippy posed engrosement / Hooked on a trend / Negative nights / Taste your own medicine / Danger zone.

Jul 79. (7"m; as CULT FIGURES) *(RT 020)(GEAR 4)* **ZIP NOLAN (HIGHWAY PATROLMAN). / PLAYING WITH TOYS / ZIP DUB** [ ] [-]

May 80. (7"ep; as CULT FIGURES) *(GEAR 8)* **IN LOVE EP** [ ] [-]
– I remember / Almost a love song / Laura Kate.

Jun 80. (7"ep; by PHONES SPORTSMAN BAND) *(GEAR 9)* **I REALLY LOVE YOU EP** [ ] [-]
– I realy love you / Get down & get with it / I woke up this morning / Wah wah track / The Olton.

Aug 81. (7"ep; by EPIC SOUNDTRACKS) *(RT 084)* **POPULAR, CLASSICAL** [ ] [-]
– Jelly babies / A 3-acre floor / Pop in packets.

Jun 82. (12"; by EPIC SOUNDTRACKS & JOWE HEAD) *(RTT 104)* **RAIN RAIN RAIN. / GHOST TRAIN** [ ] [-]

— EPIC went on to join CRIME & THE CITY SOLUTION, who later evolved into THESE IMMORTAL SOULS. Returned to solo work in 1992, augmented by LEE RANALDO, KIM GORDON (both SONIC YOUTH), J. MASCIS (DINOSAUR JR), ROWLAND S. HOWARD. In Nov'92 he released album 'RISE ABOVE' and in Sep'95 'SLEEPING STAR' on 'Normal'.

— SWELL MAPS also guested on singles by METROPHASE; 'IN BLACK'. / 'NEO BEAUTY' / 'COLD REBELLION' (Jul79 on 'Neo London', re-iss. 1980 on 'Fresh') & 'NEW AGE'. / 'FRAMES OF LIFE' (Mar89 on 'Neo London').

NIKKI SUDDEN

— now with **PHONES** – bass / **HUGO BURNHAM** – drums (of GANG OF FOUR) / **STEVE TAYTON** – saxophone / **JOHN RIVERS** – keyboards

Rather not iss.

Mar 81. (7") *(GEAR 11)* **BACK TO THE START. / RUNNING ON MY TRAIN** [ ] [-]

1983. (c) *(RATHER 10)* **BEAU GESTE** (rec.1981) [ ] [-]

— now with **EMPIRE** – drums (of TELEVISION PERSONALITIES) / **PHONES** – bass /

RICHARD EARL – guitar / **PAUL PAPYRUS** – bass / **ANTHONY THISTLETWAITE** – saxophone

Abstract not iss.

Apr 82. (7") *(ABS 009)* **CHANNEL STEAMER. / CHELSEA EMBANKMENT** [ ] [-]

May 82. (lp) *(ABT 003)* **WAITING ON EGYPT** [ ] [-]
– Channel steamer / Still full of shreds / Back to the coast / Stuck on China / Knife my next / Fashion cult / Forest fire.

Flicknife not iss.

May 83. (lp) *(SHARP 110)* **THE BIBLE BELT** [ ] [-]
– Gold painted fingernails / English girls / Cathy / Chelsea embankment / Bethlehem castle / The road of broken dreams / Six hip princes / Out of Egypt / The angels are calling / Missionary boy / The only boy in heaven.

JACOBITES

— NIKKI with the ex-RAG DOLLS member & **EPIC SOUNDTRACKS** – drums

Glass not iss.

Apr 84. (lp; as NIKKI SUDDEN & DAVE KUSWORTH) *(GLALP 008)* **JACOBITES** [ ] [-]
– Big store / Kissed you twice / Hurt me more / Jacobites grave / Kings and queens / Silver street / Hanging out the banners / Need a friend / Little bird / Angels in my arms / For the roses. *(cd-iss. Aug88; GLACD 008) (cd re-iss. Jun93 on 'Carlton'; JANIDA 001) <US cd-iss. 1994 on 'Mammoth'; MR 84>*

Sep 84. (12"ep; as NIKKI SUDDEN & DAVE KUSWORTH) *(Pawnhearts; 1747-01)* **THE SHAME OF THE ANGELS EP** [ ] [-]

— added **MARK LEMON** – bass, vocals / **ANDY WICKETT** – organ / **TYLA** – guitar / etc

Aug 85. (lp) *(GLALP 012)* **ROBESPIERRE'S VELVET BASEMENT** [ ] [-]
– I'm just a broken heart / Only children sleeping / Fortune of fame / It'll end up in tears / Ambulance station / Where the rivers end. *(cd-iss. Aug88; GLACD 012) (cd re-iss. Sep93 on 'Carlton'; JANIDA 002)*

Sep 85. (7"ep) *(GLAEP 102)* **PIN YOUR HEART TO ME NIKKI, DAVE + EPIC** [ ] [-]

Feb 86. (7"/12") *(GLASS/+12 045)* **WHEN THE RAIN COMES. / COUNTRY GIRL** [ ] [-]

not iss. What's So Funny About

1985. (lp) **LOST IN A SEA OF SCARVES** [-] [ ]

— In Aug'86, NIKKI teamed up with SIMON CARMODY (of GOLDEN HORDE) & JOHNNY FEAN (ex-HORSLIPS) for album 'THE LAST BANDITS IN THE WORLD' on 'Hotwire'; *(HWLP 8504)*.

NIKKI SUDDEN

— (solo) with **ROWLAND S. HOWARD** – guitar (ex-BIRTHDAY PARTY) / **EPIC SOUNDTRACKS** – drums (the new JACOBITES, who repl. KUSWORTH)

Creation not iss.

Oct 86. (7") *(CRE 033)* **JUNGLE TOWN. / THE LAST BANDIT** [ ] [-]
(12"+=) *(CRE 033T)* – When you're alone / Captain Kennedy.

Oct 86. (m-lp; NIKKI SUDDEN & THE JACOBITES) *(CRELP 012)* **TEXAS** [ ] [-]
– Jungle town / Death is hanging over me / In your room / Glass-such a little girl / Broken tooth / Stuka / Basement tapes / Wedding dress / When I left you / Captain Kennedy / Captain Kennedy (instrumental).

— In Mar'87, he featured on JEREMY GLUCK's lp 'I Knew Buffalo Bill'.

Apr 87. (m-lp) *(CRELP 016)* **DEAD MEN TELL NO TAILS** [ ] [-]
– When I cross the line / Before I leave you / Dog latin / Wooden leg / Dog rose / How many lies / Cupful of change / Kiss at dawn. *(cd-iss. Feb91 +=; CRECD 016)* – TEXAS

— In Jun'87, he was augmented by The TIMES & The NECESSARITARIANS on 12"ep 'LUNACY IS DEAD' on 'Barracuda'; *12UTA 9)*

Aug 87. (12"ep; by NIKKI SUDDEN & ROLAND S. HOWARD) *(CRE 040T)* **WEDDING HOTEL. / GIRL WITHOUT A NAME / HELLO WOLF (LITTLE BABY)** [ ] [-]

Nov 87. (lp; NIKKI SUDDEN & ROLAND S. HOWARD) *(CRELP 022)* **KISS YOU KIDNAPPED CHARABANC** [ ] [-]
– Wedding hotel / Rebel grave / Sob story / Snow plough / Quick thing / Feather beds / French revolution blues / Crossroads / Don't explain / Hello wolf (little baby) / Better blood / Debutante blues / Girl without a name / Wedding hotel (the moose) *(cd-iss. Mar90; CRECD 022)*

Jul 88. (lp/cd; JACOBITES) *(GLA LP/CD 029)* **FORTUNE OF FAME** (compilation) [ ] [-]
– When the rain comes / Country girl / Pin your heart to me / Slave for the angels / Road of broken dreams / Into my arms / The old church steps / Heart of hearts / Ratcliffe highway / Romance / Every girl / Fortune of fame. *(cd+=)* – (7 tracks).

Apr 89. (d-lp/cd; by NIKKI SUDDEN & THE FRENCH REVOLUTION) *(CRELP 041 D/CD)* **GROOVE** [ ] [-]
– See my rider / Murder valley / French revolution blues / Breaking lines / Groove / Sea dog blues / Great pharoah / Poor relation / Wild cathedral / Beethoven's ring / Back to the coast / Too bad for you / Village Green.

Dec 90. (cd/lp) *(CRE CD/LP 083)* **BACK TO THE COAST** [ ] [-]
– Back to the coast / Death is hanging over me / In your life / Jangle town / Feather beds / Flower bed romance / The last bandit / Great pharoah / Crossroads / Broken tooth.

— (solo) with R.E.M. backing (except STIPE)

U.F.O. not iss.

Oct 91. (lp/c/cd) *(UFO 004/+MC/CD)* **THE JEWEL THIEF** [ ] [-]
– I belong to you / The bagman and the twangman / Mountains of New York / Spend a little gold with me / Paying the way / Hotel blues / Failing / Liquor, guns and ammo / Don't let them mess with you / Grevious angel.

Nov 91. (12"/cd-s) **I BELONG TO YOU. / ALLEY OF THE STREET / JIGSAW BLUES** [ ] [-]

JACOBITES

— **NIKKI SUDDEN + DAVE KUSWORTH** (also a solo artist in his own right) + / GLENN TRANTER (b. 7 Jul'62, Dudley, England) – acoustic guitar / **CARL EUGENE PICOT** (b.11 May'64, Weymouth, England) / **MARK WILLIAMS** (b.30 Oct'65, Birmingham, England) – drums

Carlton unknown

Jun 94. (cd/lp) *(JANIDA/+LP 004)* **HOWLING GOOD TIMES** [ ] [-]
– Don't you ever leave me / Can't you see / 100 miles from here / Howling good times / Some people / Ambulance / Chelsea springtime / Older women / Margarita / Flying / Don't ever leave me (reprise).

May 95. (cd) *(JANIDA 003)* **HAWKS GET RELIGION** (compilation) [ ] [ ]

Por Caridad Productions not iss.

Oct 95. (cd) *(PCP 012CD)* **HEART OF HEARTS (THE SPANISH ALBUM)** [ ] [-]

Glitterhouse unknown

Dec 95. (cd) *(GRCD 382)* **OLD SCARLETT** [ ] [ ]

JOWE HEAD

solo with **BARRY** – organ / **PRINCE EMPIRE** – drums / **PHONES** – bass, etc / **JOSEPH** – bass, organ

Hedonics not iss.

Mar 82. (lp) *(HEDON 5)* **PINCER MOVEMENT** [ ] [-]
– Vatican chime / Cake shop girl / Blood bank / Glistening pincers / Curt replies / Leeches / Mermaid / Quartermass & the pulpit / Son of crawfish / Wimoweh / Radio Vatican / Crawfish / Swissair / Diesel loco / Feeding time / Glass animal colony / Cake shop chime / Locotrain / Beergarten / Uncle Mac's revenge / Vatican chime.

— JOWE went off to join The TELEVISION PERSONALITIES for a few years. He had spent some time between 1982-83 in The HEADHUNTERS who issued a few singles 'WIPE OUT THE FUNK' & 'IMPOSSIBLE'.

— w/ **EMPIRE / SPORTSMAN / JOHN RIVERS** – keyboards / **CARMEL** – vocals / **EPIC SOUNDTRACKS** + guest CARMEL

Constrictor not iss.

Feb 86. (lp) *(CON 00001)* **STRAWBERRY DEUTSCHMARK** [-] [-] German
– Cakeshop girl / Crawfish / The lion sleeps tonight / Cold finger / Son of a crawfish / Insect flavour valentine / Shiney black shirt / February / Swissair / Sliding down / Nearest faraway place / Coding fires / Chad valley / Tar babies / Slow babies.

Hollow Planet not iss.

— w/ **TRUDI HOLT + MARTIN GILES** – keyboards / **LUCY THE HOLY GHOST** – sax / **MERCEDES MOLE** – vox

Oct 88. (lp) *(HOLP 002)* **THE JOWE HEAD PERSONAL ORGANIZER** [ ] [ ]
– Sudden shower / For who the bell tolls / Lolita / Shy town / Mosquito / Exhibition / Shoe horn / Nebel werger / Town shy / Crabson land. *(re-iss. Sep89 on 'Constrictor'; CON 00042)*

Oct 88. (7") *(HOP 004)* **SUDDEN SHOWER. /** [ ] [-]

Overground not iss.

Nov 94. (cd) *(OVER 35CD)* **UNHINGED** [ ] [-]

PALOOKAS

— **JOWE** with **PAUL HOLT** – guitar / **TRUDI HOLT** – keyboards / **JAMES ROWBOTTAM** – bass / **RITCHIE PRALINE** – drums

Prophet not iss.

Jul 85. (7"m/12"m) *(PROFIT 11)* **CLEAR DAY. / VIRGINIA'S WOLF / PHANTOM OF THE GAUMONT** [ ] [-]

Constrictor not iss.

Apr 86. (lp) *(CON 00002)* **GIFT** [-] [-] German
– Clear day / Hot tin roof / Cut the rug / Hobby hoss / Saddle in the ground / Raise the Titanic / Anaesthesia / Wooden hills / Hedge hog / Red letter day.

1987. (7") **I WANT TO BE FREE. /** [-] [-] German

1987. (lp) *(CON 00012)* **DUMP** [-] [-] German
– I want to be free / Fondest regards / Only get to heaven / Phantom of the Gaumont / All the will in the world.

Nov 87. (7") *(HOP 001.2)* **RUN RABBIT. / A HAPPY SONG** [ ] [-]
(12"+=) *(HOP 001)* – Hit the bottle.
(above single on 'Hollow Planet'; shared with SPIT LIKE PAINT)

Aug 88. (lp) *(CON 00032)* **HIT THE BOTTLE** [ ] [-]
– Hit the bottle / Quality street / The girl with everything / Leggo land / Chicken in a basket / Dr. No / Run rabbit / Black Peter / Rubber Johnny.

1989. (lp) *(CON 00039)* **CLASSICAL MUSIC** (compilation) [-] [-] German
– Hit the bottle / Clear day / Virginia's wolf / Leggo land / Girl with every thing / Fondest regards / Phantom of the Gaumont / Swim head / Take me back / Quality street / Run rabbit / I want to be free / Only get to Heaven / Dr. No / Cufflinks / Black Peter.

— now w/out ROWBOTTAM

Historia not iss.

1991. (7") *(STAR 9101)* **SCHMALOOKAS** [-] [-] German
– Monopoly / Babysham / Hippy song / Hygiene high / Paint the town / Wandering / Nest egg / Mummy / Piss me off / Country builders.

SWERVEDRIVER

Formed: Oxford to Camden, London, England ... late 1989 initially as SHAKE APPEAL, by ADAM FRANKLIN, JIMMY HARTRIDGE, GRAHAM BONNAR and spokesman ADRIAN VINES. This outfit issued one 7" in 1988, 'GIMME FEVER' for 'No Town'; (NO 002). SWERVEDRIVER signed to 'Creation' in the early 90's and broke through with acclaimed EP's, 'SON OF MUSTANG FORD' and 'RAVE DOWN'. Loosely associated with the 'Shoegazing' scene, SWERVEDRIVER were lent a bit of crusty credibility via FRANKLIN's dreadlocks and stoned vocals while the music was tighter and more melodic than many of their contemporaries. In 1991, they scored a minor UK hit with their third EP, 'SANDBLASTED', which preceded their classy Top 50 debut album, 'RAISE'. Although they supported the likes of

The WONDER STUFF, SWERVEDRIVER were bafflingly lauded as the new UK "great white hopes" of the metal world! A 1992 Stateside tour with SOUNDGARDEN took its toll and eventually led to BONNER quitting. The band subsequently returned home and were soon another member down when VINES decided he couldn't cope. A follow-up album, 'MEZCAL HEAD' (1993), was produced by ALAN MOULDER, who had previously worked with the top-rated SMASHING PUMPKINS. Unfortunately, his midas touch didn't quite turn to gold this time around and by the release of the more solid follow-up, 'EJECTOR SEAT RESERVATION', in 1995, they were dropped by their label. Although FRANKLIN & co. were rumoured to be working out a new deal with 'Geffen', they finally reappeared on 'A&M' in early '97 with 'MAGIC BUS'. Possibly one of the unluckiest indie bands of the 90's, SWERVERIVER found themselves back in obscurity following the surprise collapse of the veteran label founded by Jerry Moss and Herb Alpert. A low-key EP, 'SPACE TRAVEL ROCK'N'ROLL' and album, '99th DREAM' followed in '98, although sadly it seems their moment has passed. • **Songwriters:** HARTRIDGE / FRANKLIN penned except; JESUS (Velvet Underground).

Album rating: RAISE (*8) / MEZCAL HEAD (*6) / EJECTOR SEAT RESERVATION (*7) / 99th DREAM (*5)

ADAM FRANKLIN (b.19 Jul'68, Essex, England) – vocals, guitar / **JIMMY HARTRIDGE** (b.27 Nov'67, Oxfordshire, England) – guitar / **ADRIAN 'ADI' VINES** (b.25 Jan'68, Yorkshire, England) – bass / **GRAHAM BONNAR** (b.28 Apr'67, Glasgow, Scotland) – drums, vocals (ex-UT)

Creation / A&M

Jul 90. (7"ep/12"ep)(cd-ep) *(CRE 079/+T)(CRESCD 079)* **SON OF MUSTANG FORD / VOLCANO TRASH. / KILL THE SUPERHEROES / JUGGERNAUT RIDE** | -

Nov 90. (7"ep/12"ep)(cd-ep) *(CRE 088/+T)(CRESCD 088)* **RAVE DOWN / SHE'S BESIDE HERSELF. / AFTERGLOW / ZED HEAD** | -

Jul 91. (7"ep/12"ep)(cd-ep) *(CRE 102/+T)(CRESCD 102)* **SANDBLASTED / OUT. / FLAWED / LAZE IT UP** 67 | -

Sep 91. (cd/lp)(c) *(CRE CD/LP 093)(C-CRE 093) <5376>* **RAISE** 44
– Sci-flyer / Pole-up / Son of Mustang Ford / Deep seat / Rave down / Sunset / Feel so reel / Sandblasted / Lead me where you dare. *(free-12"w.a.)* – SURF TWANG. / DEEP TWANG

May 92. (7") *(CRE 120)* **NEVER LOSE THAT FEELING. / SCRAWL AND SCREAM** 62 | -
(12"+=)(cd-s+=) *(CRE 120T)(CRESCD 120)* – The watchman's hands / Never learn.

—— ADI left in Sep'92. He was soon replaced by **JEZ** – drums

Aug 93. (7") *(CRE 136)* **DUEL. / PLANES OVER THE SKYLINE** 60 | -
(12"+=)(cd-s+=) *(CRE 136T)(CRESCD 136)* – Year of the girl.

Sep 93. (cd/lp)(c) *(CRE CD/LP 143)(C-CRE 143) <540129>* **MEZCAL HEAD** 55 | Oct93
– For seeking heat / Duel / Blowin' cool / MM abduction / Last train to Satansville / Mary and Maggie / A change is gonna come / Girl on a motorbike / Duress / You find it everywhere.

Feb 94. (12"ep)(cd-ep) *(CRE 174T)(CRESCD 174)* **LAST TRAIN TO SATANSVILLE / JESUS. / SATANSVILLE REVISITED / LAND OF THE LOST**

Jul 94. (7") *(FLOWER 004)* **MY ZEPHYR (SEQUEL). / MARS** | -
(above 45 was a one-off for 'Flower Shop' records)

Jun 95. (12"white-ep)(c-ep/cd-ep) *(CRE 179T)(CRE CS/SCD 179)* **LAST DAY ON EARTH / MAELSTROM / I AM SUPERMAN / THE DIRECTORS CUT OF YOUR LIFE** | -

Aug 95. (cd/lp)(c) *(CRE CD/LP 157)(C-CRE 157)* **EJECTOR SEAT RESERVATION** | -
– Single factor salute / Bring me the head of the fortune teller / The other Jesus / Song of Jaguar E / I am Superman / Bubbling up / Ejector seat reservation / How does it feel to like Candy? / Last day on Earth / The birds. *(c+=/cd+=)* – Untitled / So downhearted. *(w/ free-7")* – FLAMING HEART / PLAN 7 SATELLITE 10.

Echostatic / not iss.

Jan 97. (d7") *(ECHO 09-10)* **SPLIT SINGLE (with SOPHIA)** | -

A&M / A&M

Feb 97. (7"/c-s) *(582130-7/-4)* **MAGIC BUS. /**
(cd-s+=) *(582131 2)* –

Sessions / not iss.

Jun 97. (7") *(7SMS 07)* **93 MILLION MILES FROM THE SUN (AND COUNTING). /** | -

Cortex / Zero Hour

Feb 98. (cd-ep) *(CORX 050CD) <1233>* **SPACE TRAVEL ROCK'N'ROLL EP**
– 99th dream / Good ships / Hate yr kind / Stimulini.

Sonic Waves / Zero Hour

Jul 98. (12"ep/cd-ep) *(SWD 098 EP/CD)* **SPACE TRAVEL ROCK'N'ROLL EP** | -

Aug 98. (cd/lp) *(SWD 099 CD/LP) <1230>* **99th DREAM** | Feb98
– 99th dream / Up from the sea / She weaves a tender trap / These times / Electric 77 / Stellar Caprice / Wrong treats / You've sealed my fate / In my time / Expressway / Behind the scenes of the sound and the . . .

Oct 98. (cd-ep) *(SWD 100CD)* **WRONG TREATS / HOMELESS HOMECOMING / CHATEAU IN VIRGINIA WATER** | -

SWIMMER (see under ⇒ TEN BENSON)

SWIMMING POOL Q'S

Formed: Athens, Georgia, USA . . . 1978 by songwriter JEFF CALDER, guitarist BOB ELSEY, bassist PETE JARKINAS and drummer ROBERT SCHMID, although things really got underway when co-vocalist to-be, ANNE RICHMOND BOSTON, joined (as a joke initially!). Yet another bunch of college friendly folk-jangle pop/rockers to be thrown up by the fertile Athens music scene, the embarrassingly badly named SWIMMING POOL Q'S saw out the 70's with a US-only debut 45, 'RAT BAIT'. Subsequently signing to 'D.B.' (also home to PYLON), the quintet surfaced in summer '81 with a punningly-titled debut long-player, 'THE DEEP END'. After three years in the Southern wilderness, the SPQ's returned with a new rhythm section (J.E. GARNETT and BILLY BURTON) and a major label deal with 'A&M'. The resulting eponymous set was a more polished affair, CALDER's harmonies coming across like a presumably unintentional hybrid of LINDSAY BUCKINGHAM and A-HA backed by a less countrified GUADALCANAL DIARY. A further set, 'BLUE TOMORROW' (1986), met with a less than enthusiastic response, the group immediately dropped as a result. CALDER and Co then altered their gameplan with a 12" EP, 'FIRING SQUAD FOR GOD', before signing off in fine style with a swansong album for 'Capitol', 'WORLD WAR TWO POINT FIVE' (1989). CALDER would re-emerge with his band the SUPREME COURT, while ANNE settled down with her husband, ROB GAL (of The COOLIES).

Album rating: THE DEEP END (*4) / THE SWIMMING POOL Q'S (*7) / BLUE TOMORROW (*5) / WORLD WAR TWO POINT FIVE (*6)

JEFF CALDER – vocals, guitar / **ANNE RICHMOND BOSTON** – vocals, keyboards / **BOB ELSEY** – guitar / **PETE JARKINAS** – bass / **ROBERT SCHMID** – drums

not iss. / Clorinated

1979. (7") *<SPQR 079V>* **RAT BAIT. / THE A-BOMB WOKE ME UP** - |

Armageddon / D.B.

Jun 81. (lp) *(ARM 12) <DB 55>* **THE DEEP END**
– Little misfit / Big fat tractor / Stick in my hand / The A-bomb woke me up / Rat bait / Restless youth / Stock car sin / Walk like a chicken / Black bus / Overheated / I like to take orders from you.

—— **J.E. GARNETT** – bass; repl. PETE

—— **BILLY BURTON** – drums; repl. ROBERT

A&M / A&M

Jul 85. (7") *(AM 263)* **THE BELLS RING. / PURPLE RIVERS**
(12"+=) *(AMY 263)* – Celestion.

Jul 85. (lp/c) *(AMA/AMC 5012)* **THE SWIMMING POOL Q'S** | Nov84
– The bells ring / Pull back my spring / Purple rivers / The knave / Some new highway / Just property / Silver slipper / She's bringing down the poison / Celestion / Sacrificial altar.

Feb 86. (7") *(AM 300)* **PRETTY ON THE INSIDE. / BLUE TOMORROW**
(w/ free 7") – PURPLE RIVERS. / THE BELLS RING

1986. (lp/cd) *<395107-1/-2>* **BLUE TOMORROW** - |
– Now I'm looking about now / She's lookin' real good (when she's lookin') / Pretty on the inside / Laredo radio / Wreck around / More than one Heaven / Corruption / Blue tomorrow / A dream in gray / Big fat tractor.

1987. (12"ep) *<DB 87>* **FIRING SQUAD FOR GOD** - |

not iss. / Capitol

1989. (lp/c/lp) *<C1/C4/C2 91068>* **WORLD WAR TWO POINT FIVE** - |

—— disbanded later in '89; ANNE concentrated on her family life with hubby, ROB GAL (of The COOLIES). She returned to recording in the 90's (aged 36), releasing an album, 'THE BIG HOUSE OF TIME', co-written with CALDER and her husband. It also contained a handful of cover versions:- LEARNING HOW TO LOVE YOU (John Hiatt) / WHEN YOU DANCE I CAN REALLY LOVE (Neil Young) / DARLING BE HOME SOON (Lovin' Spoonful) / BANKS OF THE OHIO (Welsh-Farmer).

SWIRLIES

Formed: Cambridge, Massachusetts, USA . . . 1990 by DAMON TUTUNJIAN, SEANA CARMODY, ANDY BERNICK and BEN DRUCKER. This appropriately monikered pseudo-psychedelic proto "shoegazing" outfit signed to the 'Taang!' label (once home of The LEMONHEADS) and made their debut in '91 with the 'NUMBER ONE' EP. Clearly taking their cue from noise-pop experimentalists MY BLOODY VALENTINE, The SWIRLIES concocted an amorphous, effects driven sound that marked them out as spiritual cousins to UK acts like CHAPTERHOUSE, RIDE, etc. 1992's mini-set, 'WHAT TO DO ABOUT THEM', collected together the cream of the band's work to date alongside a handful of fresh tracks, none of them appearing on their debut album proper, 'BLONDER TONGUE AUDIO BATON' (1993). A solitary EP the following year marked time while the band found their feet again with newcomers CHRISTINA FILES and ANTHONY DeLUCA (replacements for SEANA and BEN), the re-modelled SWIRLIES defying musical gravity once again with 1996's belated comeback set, 'THEY SPENT THEIR WILD YOUTHFUL DAYS IN THE GLITTERING WORLD OF THE SALONS'. Later that year (with ADAM PIERCE having replaced the aforementioned new members), the EP 'SNEAKY FLUTE MUSIC' hit the US indie shops, previewing 1998's full-length sequel, 'STRICTLY EAST COAST SNEAKY FLUTE MUSIC'.

Album rating: WHAT TO DO ABOUT THEM mini (*5) / BLONDER TONGUE AUDIO BATON (*7) / THEY SPENT THEIR WILD YOUTHFUL DAYS IN THE GLITTERING WORLD OF THE SALONS (*6) / STRICTLY EAST COAST SNEAKY FLUTE MUSIC (*9)

DAMON TITUNJIAN – vocals, guitar / **SEANA CARMODY** – vocals, guitar / **ANDY BERNICK** – bass / **BEN DRUCKER** – drums

Taang! / Taang!

1991. (12"ep) **SWIRLIES NUMBER ONE** - |

1992. (7"split with CUDGEL) **FISH DREAMS RED. /** - |

Oct 92. (m-lp/m-cd) *<(TAANG 065/+CD)>* **WHAT TO DO ABOUT THEM**

– Tall ships / Sarah sitting / Her life of artistic freedom / Didn't understand / Upstairs / Chris R. / Cousteau.

Apr 93. (lp/cd) *<(TAANG 067/+CD)>* **BLONDER TONGUE AUDIO BATON** [ ] [ ] Mar93
– Bell / Vigilant always / His love of academic freedom / Pancake / Jeremy Parker / Park the car by the side of the road / Tree chopped down / Wrong tube / Wait forever.

Aug 94. (cd-ep) *<TAANG 078CD>* **BROKEDICK CAR EP** [-] [ ]
– Wrong tube / Labrea tarpit / Pancake cleaner / You're just jealous / House of pancake.

— split a 45 with PITCHBLEND

— **DAMON + ANDY** recruited newcomers **CHRISTINA FILES** – vocals / **ANTHONY DeLUCA** – drums

Apr 96. (cd) *<TAANG 101CD>* **THEY SPENT THEIR WILD YOUTHFUL DAYS IN THE GLITTERING WORLD OF THE SALONS** [-] [ ]
– French radio / In her many new found freedom / No identifier / Sounds of Sebring / San Cristobal de las Casas / You can't be told it, you must behold it / Pony / Do any of you know anything about . . . / Two girls kissing / Sterling Moss / Boys, protect yourselves from aliens / Sunn / Vehicle is invisible.

Oct 96. (cd-ep) *<TAANG 111>* **SNEAKY FLUTE MUSIC EP** [-] [ ]

— **ADAM PIERCE** – drums; repl. DeLUCA + FILES

Apr 98. (d-lp/cd) *<(TAANG 132/+CD)>* **STRICTLY EAST COAST SNEAKY FLUTE MUSIC** [ ] [ ]
– Au revoir / In harmony / Sea wolf / Adams mix / Bobs mix / River of action / Swan / No identifier / Reese's mix / Cotsey's mix / Soulsinger / #1 song / Adagio / Allegro / Finale / Torr empathy jam.

David SYLVIAN (see under ⇒ JAPAN)

SYMPOSIUM

Formed: Kensington, London, England . . . early '96 by fresh-faced youths and former Catholic school choirboys, ROSS CUMMINS, HAGOP TCHAPARIAN (part Armenian), WOJTEK GODZISZ (fully Polish), WILL McGONAGLE and JOSEPH BIRCH. Taking their cue from the noisy pop-punk fusion of GREEN DAY and ASH, these religiously fanatic QPR (a West London football club) fans bounded onto the indie scene in 1996 with the 'DRINK THE SUNSHINE' single. Their debut effort for 'Infectious' (home of ASH), the lads proceeded to gatecrash the Top 30 with their follow-up, 'FAREWELL TO TWILIGHT', a taster from their spunky, CLIVE LANGER/ALAN WINSTANLEY-produced Top 30 debut set, 'ONE DAY AT A TIME' (1997). • **Songwriters:** GODZISZ or CUMMINGS except HARD DAY'S NIGHT (Beatles).

Album rating: ONE DAY AT A TIME mini (*7) / ON THE OUTSIDE (*8)

ROSS CUMMINS – vocals / **HAGOP TCHAPARIAN** – guitar / **WILL McGONAGLE** – guitar / **WOJTEK GODZISZ** – bass / **JOSEPH BIRCH** – drums

Infectious | not iss.

Oct 96. (7") *(infect 30s)* **DRINK THE SUNSHINE. / DISAPPEAR** [ ] [-]
(cd-s+=) *(infect 30cd)* – Smiling.

Mar 97. (7") *(infect 34s)* **FAREWELL TO TWILIGHT. / XANTHEIN** [25] [-]
(7") *(infect 34sx)* – ('A'side) / Song.
(cd-s++=) *(infect 34cd)* – Easily scared.

May 97. (7") *(infect 37s)* **ANSWER TO WHY I HATE YOU. / JIM** [32] [-]
(cd-s+=) *(infect 37cd)* – Natural.
(cd-s) *(infect 37cdx)* – ('A'side) / Torquoise / Keeping the secret.

Aug 97. (7") *(infect 44s)* **FAIRWEATHER FRIEND. / ('A'live)** [25] [-]
(cd-s+=) *(infect 44cd)* – Greeting song / Just so.
(cd-s+=) *(infect 44cdx)* – The answer to why I love you (live) / Disappear (live).

Oct 97. (m-cd/m-c/m-lp) *(infect 49 cd/mc/lp)* **ONE DAY AT A TIME** [29] [-]
– Drink to the sunshine / Farewell to twilight / Puddles / Fairweather friend / One day at a time / Fizzy / Girl with brains in her feet / Smiling.

Nov 97. (7"purple) *(infect 50s)* **DRINK THE SUNSHINE. / FIZZY** [ ] [-]

Mar 98. (7") *(infect 52s)* **AVERAGE MAN. / TWIST** [45] [-]
(cd-s) *(infect 52cd)* – ('A'side) / Journey / Little things / Me.
(cd-s) *(infect 52cdx)* – ('A'side) / Hard day's night (live).

May 98. (7"pic-d) *(infect 55s)* **BURY YOU. / SCHOSTAKOWICH** [41] [-]
(cd-s) *(infect 55cd)* – ('A'side) / Serenade the idiot / Standing honoured / Higher.
(cd-s) *(infect 55cdx)* – ('A'side) / Fluorescent / Mairamout / ('A'-CD-ROM video clip).

May 98. (cd/c/lp) *(infect 56 cd/mc/lp)* **ON THE OUTSIDE** [32] [-]
– Impossible / The answer to why I hate you / Bury you / Blue / The end / Nothing special / Circles squares and lines / Stay on the outside / Paint the stars / Obsessive compulsive disorder / Natural / Way.

Jul 98. (7") *(infect 57s)* **BLUE. / LIFE OF RILEY** [48] [-]
(cd-s+=) *(infect 57cd)* – Carnival.
(cd-s) *(infect 57cdx)* – ('A'side) / Cartwheels / Ode to the frogs.

TAD

Formed: Seattle, Washington, USA . . . 1988 by namesake Idaho-born TAD DOYLE and KURT DANIELSON, both graduates of BUNDLES OF PISS (the group, that is). With STEVE WIED on drums, they subsequently signed to cult US indie label 'Sub Pop' and after one single, 'RITUAL DEVICE', TAD unleashed their classic debut (mini) album 'GOD'S BALLS' (1989). A claustrophobic trawl through the fetid back alleys of grunge, the gargantuan DOYLE laid down the foundations of the genre with a monolithic grind which brought to mind early doom merchants, BLACK SABBATH. Subsequently issuing a cover of Black Flag's 'DAMAGED' and touring with stablemates NIRVANA, the group employed the services of the illustrious STEVE ALBINI to produce a noisier follow-up set, 'SALT LICK' (1990). However, in early '91, the artwork on their third album, '8-WAY SANTA' (featuring a photograph of a hairy man – not TAD – resting his hand on a woman's breast), caused the woman in question to proceed with a lawsuit which resulted in its removal from the shelves. The record saw the grunge behemoths lightening up a little and actually indulging in some melodies/choruses to impressive effect. The brilliant 'JINX' adequately described the band's regular brushes with the fickle hand of fate; amongst other incidents, DOYLE and Co. narrowly missed being blown up by the I.R.A. in a Belfast hotel, survived a lightning strike and miraculously escaped being crushed by a stray boulder! It wasn't all bad, for DOYLE anyway, who subsequently scored a small (not big!) part in the Cameron Crowe film, 'Singles'. Meanwhile, TAD recruited a new drummer, REY WASHAM (to replace JOSH) and, along with the rest of the grunge pack, signed to a major label ('Giant'). The ensuing album, 'INHALER' (1993), saw the band once more throwing their weight around and indicating that commercial compromise was some way off. They moved to 'Music For Nations' for a one-off concert set, 'LIVE ALIEN BROADCAST' (1994), before they majored in 1995 with the 'East West' empire, releasing 'INFRARED RIDING HOOD' the same year. Like fellow instigators MUDHONEY, TAD remain a footnote in the major label grunge rewrite, while acts such as STONE TEMPLE PILOTS, BUSH, etc. coin it in. Oh the irony!

Album rating: GOD'S BALLS (*8) / SALT LICK (*7) / 8-WAY SANTA (*8) / INHALER (*6) / LIVE ALIEN BROADCAST (*4) / INFRARED RIDING HOOD (*6)

TAD DOYLE – vocals, guitar / **KURT DANIELSON** – bass, vocals / **STEVE WIED** – drums

Glitterhouse / Sub Pop

Aug 88. (7",7"clear) <*SP 19*> **RITUAL DEVICE. / DAISY** [-] [ ]

May 89. (m-lp) (*GR 0051*)<*SP 27*> **GOD'S BALL** [ ] [ ] Mar89
– Behemoth / Pork chop / Helot / Tuna car / Cyanide bath / Boiler room / Satan's chainsaw / Hollow man / Nipple belt / Ritual device.

Jun 89. (7") <*SP 37*> **DAMAGED 1. / DAMAGED 2 (by Pussy Galore)** [-] [ ]

—— **GARY THORSTENSEN** – guitar / **JOSH SINDER** – drums repl. WIED

Jan 90. (7",7"green) <*SP 55*> **LOSER. / COOKING WITH GAS** [-] [ ]

Apr 90. (m-lp) (*GR 0076*)<*SP 49*> **SALT LICK** [ ] [ ] Feb90
– Jinx / Giant killer / Wired god / Delinquent / Hedge hog / Flame tavern / Trash truck / Stumblin' man / Jack Pepsi / Candy / 3-D witchhunt / Crane's cafe / Plague years. *(US-cd/c incl. 'GOD'S BALL'; SP49 B/A)*

Sub Pop / Sub Pop

Dec 90. (7",7"yellow) <*SP 80*> **JINX. / SANTA** [-] [ ]

Jan 91. (fan club-cd-s) <*SP 99B*> **JACK PEPSI. / PLAGUE YEARS** [-] [-]

Mar 91. (lp/c/cd) <(*SP 89/+A/B*)> **8-WAY SANTA** [ ] [ ]
– Jinx / Giant killer / Wired god / Delinquent / Hedge hog / Flame tavern / Trash truck / Stumblin' man / Jack Pepsi / Gandi / 3-D witch hunt / Crane's cafe / Plague years.

Feb 93. (12"/cd-s) (*SP/+CD 229*) <*SP 182*> **SALEM. / WELT / LEPER** [ ] [ ]

—— **TEXAS REY WASHAM** – drums (ex-RAPEMAN, ex-SCRATCH ACID) repl. JOSH

Mechanic / Giant

Oct 93. (cd/c/lp) <(*4321 16570-2/-4/-1*)> **INHALER** [ ] [ ]
– Grease box / Throat locust / Leafy incline / Lucimo! / Ulcer lycanthorpe / Just bought the farm / Rotor / Paregoric Pansy / Gouge.

Music For Nations / Futurist

Jan 95. (cd) (*CDMFN 181*) <*11065*> **LIVE ALIEN BROADCASTS** [ ] [ ]
– Throat locust / Just bought the farm / Paregoric / Delinquent / Rotor / Pale corkscrew / Stumblin' man / Demon seed / Sunday drive / Jack.

East West / Atlantic

May 95. (cd/c/lp) <(*7559 61789-2/-4*)> **INFRARED RIDING HOOD** [ ] [ ]
– Ictus / Emotional cockroach / Red eye angel / Dementia / Halycon nights / Tool marks / Mystery copter / Particle accelerator / Weakling / Thistle suit / Bullhorn bludge.

—— **MIKE MONGRAIN** – drums; repl. WASHAM

Amphetam. Reptile / Amphetam. Reptile

May 98. (7") (*SCALE 096*) **OBSCENE HAND. / KEVORKIAN'S HOLIDAY** [ ] [ ]

Up / Up

Jul 98. (7") (*UP 055*) **TAD. /** [ ] [ ]

TALKING HEADS

Formed: Manhattan, New York, USA . . . May'75 by former art & design students DAVID BYRNE, TINA WEYMOUTH and CHRIS FRANTZ. Their first gig was supporting The RAMONES at the CBGB's club in New York, circa mid '75. The band were soon spotted by Seymour Stein, who duly signed them to his new US label, 'Sire' and in late 1976 they released their debut 45, 'LOVE GOES TO A BUILDING ON FIRE'. Although this flopped, the following year's '77' album sold well enough to reach the lower regions of the album chart. The record's centerpiece was the spastic, new wave-funk of 'PSYCHO KILLER', BYRNE's compelling eccentricity making the number a live favourite. By this point the band were well established as one of the leading lights in the New York art-punk scene, firing subversively intelligent broadsides at the overblown rock establishment. The follow-up album, 'MORE SONGS ABOUT BUILDINGS AND FOOD' (1978) was produced by BRIAN ENO whom the band had met on a British tour the previous year. Sharing ENO's disregard for the workmanlike, the band were spurred on to new heights, FRANTZ and WEYMOUTH fashioning intricate but gloriously funky rhythms, BYRNE turning around Al Green's 'TAKE ME TO THE RIVER' with his wonderfully idiosyncratic vocal style. ENO stuck around for 'FEAR OF MUSIC' (1979), an album which saw them experimenting with complex ethnic rythms and instrumentation, an area that was further explored on the BYRNE/ENO collaboration, 'MY LIFE IN THE BUSH OF GHOSTS' (1981). Bolstered by a crew of esteemed session musicians, the band cut 'REMAIN IN LIGHT' (1980). Swathed in giddy funk and rooted by African polyrhythms, the album spawned the wondrous 'ONCE IN A LIFETIME' single. The band had now established themselves as a top live draw and were notching up increasing record sales, although it was to be three years before the next TALKING HEADS studio album as the band divided their time between solo projects and live work. Worth the wait, 'SPEAKING IN TONGUES' (1983) was another classy outing, spawning the trance-rock of the 'SLIPPERY PEOPLE' (1984) single and the jittery 'BURNING DOWN THE HOUSE' (1983) which went top 10 in the UK. The Jonathon Demme-directed concert movie 'STOP MAKING SENSE' contained some of the most innovative live footage ever commited to celluloid and further increased The TALKING HEADS' burgeoning reputation. Another groundbreaking piece of film came with the video for 'ROAD TO NOWHERE' (1985), the band's biggest chart hit to date. Its parent album, 'LITTLE CREATURES' (1985), marked a return to a more basic sound. From this point on, the band began to spend an increasing amount of time on solo projects. 'TRUE STORIES' (1986) was a patchy TALKING HEADS version of the soundtrack to the DAVID BYRNE film of the same name while 'NAKED' (1986) came on like an over-produced version of 'REMAIN IN LIGHT'. Following this album, the various 'HEADS went on to do their own thing, BYRNE concentrating on his solo career. The band officially split in 1991, although The HEADS (as WEYMOUTH, FRANTZ and HARRISON were now known) made a comeback album of sorts in '96 entitled 'NO TALKING, JUST HEAD', a record that utilised an array of vocal talent including SHAUN RYDER on the minor hit single, 'DON'T TAKE MY KINDNESS FOR WEAKNESS'.
• **Songwriters:** Group compositions except; TAKE ME TO THE RIVER (Al Green) / SLIPPERY PEOPLE (Staple Singers). TOM TOM CLUB:- UNDER THE BOARDWALK (Drifters) / FEMME FATALE (Velvet Underground) / YOU SEXY THING (Hot Chocolate). DAVID BYRNE: – GREENBACK DOLLAR (Hoyt Axton) / GIRLS ON MY MIND (Toquinnho Vinicius) / DON'T FENCE ME IN (Cole Porter). • **Trivia:** FRANTZ and WEYMOUTH (later TOM TOM CLUB) married on the 18th of June '77. BYRNE produced The B-52's on their 1982 album, 'Mesopotamia' and FUN BOY THREE on their 1983, 'Waiting' album. HARRISON produced The VIOLENT FEMMES on 1986 album, 'The Blind Leading The Naked'. TOM TOM CLUB started out producing in 1988 with ZIGGY MARLEY, later working with HAPPY MONDAYS.

Album rating: TALKING HEADS '77 (*9) / MORE SONGS ABOUT BUILDINGS AND FOOD (*8) / FEAR OF MUSIC (*9) / REMAIN IN LIGHT (*8) / ONCE IN A LIFETIME – THE BEST OF TALKING HEADS compilation (*9)

DAVID BYRNE (b.14 May'52, Dumbarton, Scotland) – vocals, guitar / **TINA WEYMOUTH** (b.22 Nov'50, Coronado, Calif.) – bass, vocals / **CHRIS FRANTZ** (b. CHARLTON CHRISTOPHER FRANTZ, 8 May'51, Fort Campbell, Kentucky) – drums

		Sire	Sire
Feb 77.	(7") *(6078 604)* <737> **LOVE GOES TO A BUILDING ON FIRE. / NEW FEELING**		

— added **JERRY HARRISON** (b.21 Feb'49, Milwaukee, Wisconsin) – guitar, keyboards (ex-JONATHAN RICHMAN & THE MODERN LOVERS)

Date	Release	UK	US
Sep 77.	(lp) *(9103 328)* <SR 6306> **TALKING HEADS '77** – Uh-oh, love comes to town / New feeling / Tentative decisions / Happy day / Who is it? / No compassion / The book I read / Don't worry about the government / First week – last week . . . carefree / Psycho killer / Pulled up. *(re-iss. Sep78; SR 6036) (cd-iss. Feb87; K2 56647)*	60	97
Oct 77.	(7") *<1002>* **UH-OH, LOVE COMES TO TOWN. / I WISH YOU WOULDN'T SAY THAT**	-	
Dec 77.	(7") *(6078 610)* **PSYCHO KILLER. / I WISH YOU WOULDN'T SAY THAT**		-
	(12"+=) *(same)* – Psycho killer (acoustic).		
Jan 78.	(7") *<1013>* **PSYCHO KILLER. / PSYCHO KILLER (acoustic)**	-	92
May 78.	(7") *(6078 620)* **PULLED UP. / DON'T WORRY ABOUT THE GOVERNMENT**		-
Jul 78.	(lp/c) *(K/K4 56531)* <SR 6058> **MORE SONGS ABOUT BUILDINGS AND FOOD** – Thank you for sending me an angel / With our love / The good thing / Warning sign / Girls want to be with the girls / Found a job / Artists only / I'm not in love / Stay hungry / Take me to the river / The big country. *(double-play cass. includes debut album) (cd-iss. Jan87; K2 56531)*	21	29
Oct 78.	(7") *<1032>* **TAKE ME TO THE RIVER. / THANK YOU FOR SENDING ME AN ANGEL**	-	26
Jun 79.	(7") *(SIR 4004)* **TAKE ME TO THE RIVER. / FOUND A JOB**		-
	(d7"+=) *(SAM 87)* – Love goes to a building on fire / Psycho killer.		
Aug 79.	(lp/c) *(K/K4 56707)* <SRK 6076> **FEAR OF MUSIC** – Air / Animals / Cities / Drugs / Electric guitar / Heaven / I Zimbra / Life during wartime / Memories can't wait / Mind / Paper. *(re-iss. Sep79 lp/c; SRK/SRC 6076) (w/ free 7") – PSYCHO KILLER (live). / NEW FEELING (live) (cd-iss. Jul84; K2 56707)*	33	21
Oct 79.	(7") *(SIR 4027)* <49075> **LIFE DURING WARTIME. / ELECTRIC GUITAR**		80
Feb 80.	(7") *(SIR 4033)* **I ZIMBRA. / PAPER**		-
Jun 80.	(7") *(SIR 4040)* **CITIES. / CITIES (live)**		-
	(12"+=) *(SIR 4040T)* – Artists only.		

— basic 4 added **BUSTA CHERRY JONES** – bass / **ADRIAN BELEW** – guitar / **BERNIE WORRELL** – keyboards / **STEVEN SCALES** – percussion / **DONETTE McDONALD** – backing vox

Date	Release	UK	US
Oct 80.	(lp/c) <(SRK/SRC 6095)> **REMAIN IN LIGHT** – The great curve / Crosseyed and painless / Born under punches / Houses in motion / Once in a lifetime / Listening wind / Seen and not seen / The overlord. *(cd-iss. Mar84; K2 56867)*	21	19

Feb 81. (7"/ext.12") *(SIR 4048/+T)* <40649> **ONCE IN A LIFETIME. / SEEN AND NOT SEEN** [14] [ ]
May 81. (7") <49734> **HOUSES IN MOTION (remix). / THE OVERLORD** [-] [ ]
May 81. (7") *(SIR 4050)* **HOUSES IN MOTION (remix). / AIR** [50] [-]
(ext.12"+=) *(SIR 4050T)* – ('A'live).
—— In 1981, all 4 diversed into own projects
Mar 82. (7") *(SIR 4055)* **LIFE DURING WARTIME (live). / LIFE DURING WARTIME** [ ] [-]
(12"+=) *(SIR 4055T)* – Don't worry about the government (live).
Apr 82. (d-lp/d-c) <(SRK/SRC 23590)> **THE NAME OF THIS BAND IS TALKING HEADS (live)** [22] [31]
– I Zimbra / Drugs / Houses in motion / Life during wartime / Take me to the river / The great curve / Cross-eyed and painless / New feeling / A clean break / Don't worry about the government / Pulled up / Psycho killer / Artists only / Stay hungry / Air / Building on fire / Memories can't wait. *(cd-iss. May87; K2 66112)*
Jun 83. (lp,clear-lp/c/cd) *(923883-1/-4/-2)* <23883> **SPEAKING IN TONGUES** [21] [15]
– Burning down the house / Making flippy floppy / Girlfriend is better / Slippery people / I get wild – Wild gravity / Swamp / Moon rocks / Pull up the roots / This must be the place (naive melody). *(c+=/cd+=)* – (6 extra mixes).
Jul 83. (7") *(W 9565)* <29565> **BURNING DOWN THE HOUSE. / I GET WILD – WILD GRAVITY** [ ] [9]
(12"+=) *(W 9565T)* – Moon rocks.
Jan 84. (7") *(W 9451)* <29451> **THIS MUST BE THE PLACE (NAIVE MELODY). / MOON ROCKS** [51] [62] Oct83
(ext.d12"+=) *(W 9451T / SAM 176)* – Slippery people (remix) / Making flippy floppy (remix).
Feb 84. (7") <29163> **ONCE IN A LIFETIME (live). / THIS MUST BE THE PLACE (live)** [-] [ ]

E.M.I. Sire

Oct 84. (7"/ext.12") *(EMI/12EMI 5504)* **SLIPPERY PEOPLE (live). / THIS MUST BE THE PLACE (NAIVE MELODY) (live)** [68] [-]
Oct 84. (lp/c) *(TAH/+TC 1)* <25121> **STOP MAKING SENSE (live)** [37] [41]
– Psycho killer / Swamp / Slippery people / Burning down the house / Girlfriend is better / Once in a lifetime / What a day that was / Life during wartime / Take me to the river. *(cd-iss. Feb85; CDP 746064-2) (c+=/cd+=)* – (extra tracks) *(re-iss. Mar90 cd)(c/lp; CZ 289)(TC+/ATAK 147) (re-iss. Nov93 on 'Fame' cd/c; CD/TC FA 3302)*
Nov 84. (7"/ext.12") *(EMI/12EMI 5509)* **GIRLFRIEND IS BETTER (live). / ONCE IN A LIFETIME (live)** [ ] [-]
Dec 84. (7") <29080> **STOP MAKING SENSE (GIRLFIRIEND IS BETTER) (live). / HEAVEN** [-] [ ]
May 85. (7"/ext.12") *(EMI/12EMI 5520)* **THE LADY DON'T MIND. / GIVE ME BACK MY NAME** [ ] [-]
(d12"+=) *(12EMID 5520)* – Slippery people (live) / This must be the place (naive melody) (live).
Jun 85. (lp/c)(cd) *(TAH/+TC 2)(CDP 746158-2)* <25035> **LITTLE CREATURES** [10] [20]
– And she was / Give me back my name / Creatures of love / The lady don't mind / Perfect world / Stay up late / Walk it down / Television man / Road to nowhere. *(c+=)* – The lady don't mind (extended). *(re-iss. Mar90 cd)(c/lp; CZ 287)(TC+/ATAK 146) (re-iss. Nov93 on 'Fame' cd/c; CD/TC FA 3301)*
Jun 85. (7") <28987> **ROAD TO NOWHERE. / GIVE ME BACK MY NAME** [-] [ ]
Sep 85. (7") <28917> **AND SHE WAS. / ('A'dub)** [-] [54]
Sep 85. (7"/7"pic-d) *(EMI/+P 5530)* **ROAD TO NOWHERE. / TELEVISION MAN** [6] [-]
(d12"+=) *(12EMID 5530)* – Slippery people (extended live) / This must be the place (naive melody) (live).
Feb 86. (7") *(EMI 5543)* **AND SHE WAS. / PERFECT WORLD** [17] [-]
(12"pic-d+=) *(12EMIP 5543)* – ('A'extended).
Apr 86. (7") <29163> **ONCE IN A LIFETIME (live). / THIS MUST BE THE PLACE (live)** [-] [91]
(above re-generated from 1984 album & taken from 'Down And Out In Beverly Hills')
Aug 86. (7") *(EMI 5567)* <28629> **WILD WILD LIFE. / PEOPLE LIKE US (movie version)** [43] [25]
(12"+=/12"pic-d+=) *(12EMI/+P 5567)* – ('A'extended).
Sep 86. (lp/c)(cd) *(EU/TCEU 3511)(CDP 746345-2)* <25512> **TRUE STORIES** [7] [17]
– Love for sale / Puzzlin' evidence / Hey now / Radio head / Papa Legba / Wild wild life / Radio head / Dream operator / People like us / City of dreams. *(cd+=)* – Wild (ET mix). *(re-iss. Sep89 on 'Fame' cd/c/lp; CD/TC+/FA 3231)*
Nov 86. (7") <28497> **LOVE FOR SALE. / HEY NOW** [-] [ ]
Nov 86. (lp/c) *(ENC/TCENC 3520)* **SONGS FROM 'TRUE STORIES' (Original DAVID BYRNE Film Soundtrack; w/ other artists)** [ ] [ ]
– Cocktail desperado / Road song / Freeway son / Brownie's theme / Mall muzak: Building a highway – Puppy polka – Party girls / Dinner music / Disco hits / City of steel / Love theme from 'True Stories' / Festa para um Rei Negro / Buster's theme / Soy de Tejas / I love metal buildings / Glass operator.
Apr 87. (7") *(EM 1)* **RADIO HEAD. / HEY NOW (movie version)** [52] [-]
(d7"+=)(12"+=/cd-s+=) *(EMD 1)(12/CD EM 1)* – ('A'remix) / ('B'-Milwaukee remix).
Mar 88. (cd/c/lp) *(CD/TC+/EMD 1005)* <26654> **NAKED** [3] [19]
– Blind / Mr. Jones / Totally nude / Ruby dear / (Nothing but) Flowers / The Democratic circus / The facts of life / Mommy daddy you and I / Big daddy / Cool water. *(other cd+=; CDP 790156-2)* – Bill. *(re-iss. Nov93 on 'Fame' cd/c; CD/TC FA 3300)*
Aug 88. (c-s/7") *(TC+/EM 68)* <27948> **BLIND. / BILL** [59] [ ]
(ext.12"+=/cd-s+=) *(12/CD EM 68)* – ('A'-Def, dub & blind mix).
Oct 88. (c-s/7") *(TC+/EM 53)* <27992> **(NOTHING BUT) FLOWERS. / RUBY DEAR** [ ] [ ] Apr88
(10"+=) *(10EM 53)* – Facts of life / Mommy, daddy, you and I.
(12") *(12EM 53)* – ('A'extended) / ('B'-Lillywhite mix).
(cd-s) *(CDEM 53)* – ('A'side) / ('B'-bush mix) / Mommy, daddy, you and I / ('A'-Lillywhite mix).
—— cease to function as a group, after last recording. Officially split 1991.

– compilations, others, etc. –

on 'E.M.I.' UK / 'Sire' US unless mentioned otherwise
Apr 81. (c-s) *WEA; (SPC 9)* **TAKE ME TO THE RIVER / PSYCHO KILLER** [ ] [-]
1989. (3"cd-ep) *Sire; (921 135-2)* **LOVE GOES TO A BUILDING ON FIRE / PSYCHO KILLER / ONCE IN A LIFETIME / BURNING DOWN THE HOUSE** [ ] [-]
Oct 92. (c-s/7") *(TC+/EM 250)* **LIFETIME PILING UP. / ROAD TO NOWHERE** [50] [ ]
(cd-s+=) *(CDEM 250)* – Love for sale / The lady don't mind (extended).
(cd-s) *(250)* – ('A'side) / Stay up late / Radio head / Take me to the river.
Oct 92. (d-cd/d-c/d-lp) *(CD/TC+/EQ 5010)* <26760> **POPULAR FAVOURITES 1976-1992** [7] [ ]
– ONCE IN A LIFETIME:- Psycho killer / Take me to the river / Once in a lifetime / Burning down the house / This must be the place (naive melody) / Slippery people (live) / Life during wartime (live) / And she was / Road to nowhere / Wild wild life / Blind / (Nothing but) Flowers / Sax and violins / Lifetime piling up. // SAND IN MY VASELINE:- Sugar on my tongue / I want to live / Love goes to a building on fire / I wish you wouldn't say that / Don't worry about the government / The big country / No compassion / Warning sign / Heaven / Memories can't wait / I Zimbra / Crosseyed and painless / Swamp / Girlfriend is better (live) / Stay up late / Love for sale / City of dreams / Mr. Jones / Gangster of love / Popsicle.
Nov 95. (3xcd-box) *(CDOMB 003)* **THE ORIGINALS** [ ] [-]
– (STOP MAKING SENSE / LITTLE CREATURES / TRUE STORIES). *(re-iss. Mar97; same)*

DAVID BYRNE

Early in 1981, he had collaborated with BRIAN ENO ⇒ on album 'MY LIFE IN THE BUSH OF GHOSTS'.

Sire Sire

Dec 81. (7") *(SIR 4054)* **BIG BLUE PLYMOUTH (EYES WIDE OPEN). / CLOUD CHAMBER** [ ] [-]
(12") *(SIR 4054T)* – ('A'side) / Leg bells / Light bath.
Jan 82. (lp/c) *(SRK/SRC 3645)* <3645> **SONGS FROM 'THE CATHERINE WHEEL' (Stage score)** [ ] [ ] Dec81
– His wife refused / Two soldiers / The red house / My big hands (fall through the cracks) / Big business / Eggs in a briar patch / Poison / Cloud chamber / What a day that was / Big blue Plymouth (eyes wide open). *<US d-lp+=)* – Ade / Walking / Under the mountain / Dinosaur / Wheezing / Black flag / Combat / Leg bells / The blue flame / Danse beast / Five golden sections. *(cd-iss. Jan93; 7599 27418-2)*
Feb 82. (12"ep) <50034> **THREE BIG SONGS** [-] [ ]
– Big business (remix) / My big hands (fall through the cracks) / Big blue Plymouth (eyes wide open).

E.M.I. ECM

Sep 85. (lp/c) *(EJ 240381-1/-4)* <ECM 25022> **MUSIC FOR THE KNEE PLAYS** [ ] [ ] May 85
– Tree (today is an important occasion) / In the upper room / The sound of business / Social studies / (The gift of sound) Where the sun never goes down / Theadora is dozing / Admiral Perry / I bid you goodnight / I've tried / Winter / Jungle book / In the future.
—— Recorded collaboration with RYUICHI SAKAMOTO on film 'THE LAST EMPEROR'.
—— BYRNE now used a plethora of Brazilian musicians, after compiling various artists BELEZA TROPICAL', 'O SAMBA', etc.

Luaka Bop-Sire Luaka Bop

Oct 89. (lp/c)(cd) *(WX 319/+C)(K 925990-2)* <25990> **REI MOMO** [52] [71]
– Independence day / Make believe mambo / The call of the wild / Dirty old town / The rose tattoo / The dream police / Don't want to be part of your world / Marching through the wilderness / Lie to me / Women vs. men / Carnival eyes / I know sometimes a man is wrong.
Dec 89. (7"/ext.12") **MAKE BELIEVE MAMBO. / LIE TO ME** [ ] [ ]
Jun 91. (cd) *(7599 26584-2)* **THE FOREST (instrumental)** [ ] [ ]
– Ur / Kish / Dura Europus / Nineveh / Ava / Machu picchu / Teotihuaean / Asuka.
Mar 92. (cd)(lp/c) *(7599 26799-2)(WX 464/+C)* <26799> **UH-OH** [26] [ ]
– Now I'm your mom / Girls on my mind / Something ain't right / She's mad / Hanging upside down / Twistin' in the wind / A walk in the dark / The cowboy mambo (hey lookit me now) / Tiny town / Somebody. *(re-iss. Feb95 cd/c;)*
Apr 92. (7"/c-s) **GIRLS ON MY MIND. / MONKEY MAN** [ ] [ ]
(12"+=/cd-s+=) – Cantode oxum.
May 92. (7"/c-s) **HANGING UPSIDE DOWN. / TINY TOWN** [ ] [ ]
(cd-s) – ('A'side) / Dirty old town (live) / (Nothing but) Flowers (live) / Girls on my mind (live).
(cd-s) – ('A'side) / Something ain't right (live) / Who we're thinking of (live) / Rockin' in the free world (live).
Jul 92. (7"/c-s) **SHE'S MAD. / SOMEBODY** [ ] [ ]
(12") – *('A'side) / Butt naked / Greenback dollar.*
(cd-s++=) – ('A'side) / Now I'm your man.
—— with **PAUL SOCOLOW** – bass, vocals / **TODD TURKISHER** – drum, percussion / **VALERIE NARANJO** – percussion, tambourine (live: MAURO REFOSCO – percussion) / **BILL WARE** – marimba / **ARTO LINDSAY** – guitar / **JOHN MEDESKI** – organ / **BASHIRI JOHNSON** – congas, bongos / **BEBEL GILBERTO** – vocals
May 94. (cd/c) *(9362 45558-2/-4)* <45558> **DAVID BYRNE** [44] [ ]
– A long time ago / Angels / Crash / A self-made man / Back in the box / Sad song / Nothing at all / My love is you / Lillies of the valley / You & eye / Strange ritual / Buck naked.
Jun 94. (7"/c-s) *(W 0253/+C)* **ANGELS. / PRINCESS** [ ] [ ]
(12"+=/cd-s+=) *(W 0253 T/CD)* – Ready for this world.
Sep 94. (c-s/cd-s) *(W 0263 C/CD)* **BACK IN THE BOX / GYPSY WOMAN (live) / GIRLS ON MY MIND (live)** [ ] [ ]
May 97. (cd/c) *<(9362 46605-2/-4)>* **FEELINGS** [ ] [ ]
– Fuzzy freaky / Miss America / A soft seduction / Dance on vaseline / The gates of Paradise / Amnesia / You don't know me / Daddy go down / Finite = alright / Wicked little doll / Burnt by the sun / The civil wars / They are in love.
Jun 97. (cd-s) *(W 0401CD)* **MISS AMERICA /** [ ] [-]

TOM TOM CLUB

CHRIS FRANTZ + TINA WEYMOUTH plus her 2 sisters + **STEVE SCALES** – percussion / **ALEX WEIR** – guitar / **TYRON DOWNIE** – keyboards

Island | Sire

Jun 81. (7") *(WIP 6694)* **WORDY RAPPINGHOOD. / YOU DON'T STOP (WORDY RAP)** [7] [ ]
(12"+=) *(12WIP 6694)* – L'elephant.

Sep 81. (7") *(WIP 6735) <49882>* **GENIUS OF LOVE. / LORELEI (instrumental)** [65] [31] Jan82
(12"+=) *(12WIP 6735)* – Rappa rappa rhythm / Yella.
(re-iss. Oct82; same)

Oct 81. (lp/c) *(ILPS/ICT 9686) <SRK 3628>* **TOM TOM CLUB** [78] [23]
– Wordy rappinghood / Genius of love / Tom Tom theme / L'elephant / As above, so below / Lorelei / On, on, on, on . . . / Booming and zooming. *(re-iss. Oct86 lp/c; ILPM/ICM 9686) (cd-iss. May87; CID 9686) (re-iss. cd Apr90; IMCD 103)*

Jul 82. (7") *(WIP 6762)* **UNDER THE BOARDWALK. / ON, ON, ON, ON . . . (remix)** [22] [ ]
(12"+=) *(12WIP 6762)* – Lorelei (remix).

Jul 83. (7"/12") *(IS/12IS 117)* **THE MAN WITH THE 4-WAY HIPS. / ('A'dub version)** [ ] [ ]

Aug 83. (lp/c) *(ILPS/ICT 9738) <23916>* **CLOSE TO THE BONE** [ ] [73]
– Pleasure of love / On the line again / This is a foxy world / Bamboo town / The man with the 4-way hips / Measure up / Never took a penny / Atsababy! (life is great).

Dec 83. (7") **NEVER TOOK A PENNY. / PLEASURE OF LOVE** [-] [ ]

— **TINA + CHRIS** added **GARY POZNER** – keyboards / **MARK ROULE** – guitar, percussion

Fontana | Sire

Sep 88. (7") *(TCB 1)* **DON'T SAY NO. / DEVIL DOES YOUR DOG BITE?** [ ] [ ]
(12"+=) *(TCBX 1)* – ('A'version) / Beats and pieces.
(cd-s+=) *(TCBCD 1)* – Beats and pieces / Percapella.

Oct 88. (lp/c)(cd) *(SF LP/MC 8)(836 416-2) <25888>* **BOOM BOOM CHI BOOM BOOM** [ ] [ ]
– Suboceana / Shock the world / Don't say no / Challenge of the love warriors / Femme fatale / Born for love / Broken promises / She belongs to me / Little Eva / Misty teardrop.

— **KIRSTY MacCOLL** makes a guest vocal appearance

Jan 92. (cd/c) *<2-/4-26951>* **DARK SNEAK LOVE ACTION** [-] [ ]
– Love wave / Sunshine and ecstasy / You sexy thing / Who wants an ugly girl? / Say I am / Irrisistable party dip / Dark sneak love action / Innocent sex kiss / Dogs in the trash / My mama told me / As the disco ball turns / Daddy come home.

JERRY HARRISON

Sire | Sire

Oct 81. (7") *(SIR 4053)* **THINGS FALL APART. / WORLDS IN COLLISION** [ ] [ ]

Oct 81. (lp/c) *<(SRK/SRC 3631)>* **THE RED AND THE BLACK** [ ] [ ]
– Things fall apart / Slink / The new adventure / Magic hymie / Fast karma / No questions / Worlds in collision / The red nights / No more returns / No warning no alarm. *(cd-iss. Apr96 on 'Warners'; 7599 23631-2)*

Fontana | Sire

Feb 88. (7") *(JERRY 1)* **REV IT UP. / BOBBY** [ ] [ ]
(12"+=)(12"pic-d+=)(cd-s+=) *(JERRY 1-12)(JERYP 1-12)(JERCD 1)* – ('A'versions). *(re-iss. Jul88; same)*

Feb 88. (lp/c)(cd) *(SF LP/MC 2)(832992-2) <25663>* **JERRY HARRISON: CASUAL GODS** [ ] [78]
– Rev it up / Songs of angels / Man with a gun / Let it come down / Cherokee chief / A perfect lie / Are you running? / Breakdown in the passing lane / A.K.A. love / We're always talkin' / Bobby. *(cd+=)* – Bobby (12"version).

May 88. (7") *(JERRY 2)* **MAN WITH A GUN. / ('A'radio edit)** [ ] [ ]
(12"+=)(cd-s+=) *(JERRY 2-12)(JERCD 2)* – Breakdown on the passing line / Wire always talking.

— backing incl. **BROOKS, WORRELL, BAILEY, SIEGER + WEIR**

Jun 90. (7") *(JERRY 3)* **WALK ON WATER. / MAN WITH A GUN** [ ] [ ]
(12"+=)(cd-s+=) *(JERRY 3-12)(JERCD 3)* – Racing the fire.

Jun 90. (cd/c/lp) *(846321-2/-4/-1) <25943>* **WALK ON WATER** [ ] [ ]
– Flying under radar / Cowboy's got to go / Kick start / I don't mind / Sleep angel / Confess / I cry for Iran / Never let it slip / If the rain returns / The doctor's lie.

HEADS

HARRISON, WEYMOUTH, FRANTZ + guest vocalists & lyricists (see below)

Radioactive-MCA | M.C.A.

Oct 96. (c-s) *(MCS 48024)* **DON'T TAKE MY KINDNESS FOR WEAKNESS /** [60] [ ]
(cd-s) *(MCSTD 48024)* –

Nov 96. (cd/c) *<(MCD/MCC 11504)>* **NO TALKING, JUST HEAD** [ ] [ ]
– Damage I've done (w/ JOHNETTE NAPOLITANO) / The king is gone (w/ MICHAEL HUTCHENCE) / No talking just head (w/ DEBBIE HARRY) / Never mind (w/ RICHARD HELL) / No big bang (w/ MARIA McKEE) / Don't take my madness for weakness (w/ SHAUN RYDER) / No more lonely nights (w/ MALIN ANNETEG) / Indie hair (w/ ED KOWALCZYK) / Punk lolita (w/ DEBBIE HARRY, JOHNETTE NAPOLITANO & TINA WEYMOUTH) / Only the lonely (w/ GORDON GANO) / Papersnow (w/ ANDY PARTRIDGE) / Blue blue moon (w/ GAVIN FRIDAY).

TALL DWARFS

Formed: Dunedin, New Zealand . . . early 80's by CHRIS KNOX, who had previously initiated what was possibly the first ever NZ punk act, The ENEMY. The latter outfit quickly earned a reputation but never actually released any records, subsequently evolving into TOY LOVE with a line-up of KNOX, ALEC BATHGATE, JANE WALKER, MIKE DOOLEY and PAUL KEAN. A more commercially viable New Wave-biased unit, TOY LOVE were signed to the New Zealand arm of 'WEA' and made their debut with the critically acclaimed 'REBEL' single in summer '79. While generally acknowledged as being a pivotal influence on the coming decade's proliferation of NZ bands, KNOX and Co failed to make much headway outside of their homeland; a further single, 'DON'T ASK ME', and a solitary eponymous album were generally regarded as being disappointing and unrepresentative of the band's infamous live show (wherein KNOX had taken to slashing himself in true masochistic rock'n'roll style). Following a final independently released single, 'BRIDE OF FRANKENSTEIN', TOY LOVE were finally divorced, buckling under the weight of a punishing touring schedule. It didn't take KNOX and BATHGATE long to surface with a new outfit, TALL DWARFS, regularly cited as the grandaddy of all the 'Flying Nun' bands. The latter label became home to the band in 1982, prior to which the duo had released the 'THREE SONGS' EP. While DOOLEY had also initally been part of the set-up, KNOX and BATHGATE soon pared the group down to a two-man operation, working from the most basic of home studios to complete a string of DIY EP's: 'LOUIS LOVES HIS DAILY DIP' (1982), 'CANNED MUSIC' (1983) and the Australian-only 'SLUGBUCKET HAIRY BREATH MONSTER' (1984). These releases established the trademark TALL DWARFS sound, a melange of retro garage, psychedelia and melodic punk buried in droning fuzz guitar with occasional forays into acoustic pop. It served the band well over the course of the 80's although they didn't actually release a full length album until the turn of the decade. 1985 had seen the release of mini-set, 'THAT'S THE SHORT AND LONG OF IT', while two years later, 'HELLO CRUEL WORLD' served as a career retrospective for UK fans. The band's bonafide debut album, 'WEEVILLE' finally arrived in 1990, by which time KNOX's songwriting had begun to take on a less confrontational hue. A true bedroom warrior, KNOX had already completed a string of domestic solo releases including 'SONGS FOR CLEANING GUPPIES' (1983) and 'SEIZURE' (1989). He maintained his prolific release schedule into the 90's with the likes of 'CROAKER' (1991) and 'POLYFOTO, DUCK SHAPED PAIN & GUM' (1994), the latter album one of the few to gain a full UK release. While showcasing his consistently thought-provoking lyrics and sly humour, KNOX's solo material tended, if anything, to be more self-indulgent than TALL DWARFS although the likes of 'FORK SONGS' (1992) and the more recent 'STUMPY: THE ALBUM' (1997) were hardly easy listening.

Album rating: HELLO CRUEL WORLD compilation (*6) / 3 E.P.'s compilation (*6) / STUMPY: THE ALBUM (*5) / Chris Knox: SEIZURE (*6) / NOT GIVEN LIGHTLY (*6) / CROAKER (*6) / POLYFOTO, DUCK SHAPED PAIN & GUM (*6)

TOY LOVE

CHRIS KNOX – vocals, guitar (ex-ENEMY) / **ALEC BATHGATE** – guitar (ex-ENEMY) / **JANE WALKER** – keyboards / **MIKE DOOLEY** – drums (ex-ENEMY) / **PAUL KEAN** – bass

WEA | not iss.

Jul 79. (7") **REBEL. / SQUEEZE** [-] [-] New Z
Jan 80. (7") **DON'T ASK ME. / SHEEP** [-] [-] New Z
Jun 80. (lp) **TOY LOVE** [-] [-] New Z

Deluxe | not iss.

1980. (7") **BRIDE OF FRANKENSTEIN. / GOOD OLD JOE / AMPUTEE SONG** [-] [-] New Z

TALL DWARFS

— **CHRIS KNOX** – vocals, guitar, keyboards, bass, percussion, etc / **ALEC BATHGATE** – guitar, vocals / MIKE DOOLEY (soon repl. by tape)

unknown | not iss.

1981. (12"ep) **THREE SONGS EP** [ ] [-] New Z
– Nothing's going to happen / Luck or loveliness / All my hollowness to you.

Flying Nun | not iss.

1982. (12"ep) **LOUIS LOVES HIS DAILY DIP** [-] [-] New Z
– Louis the first / Maybe / Pictures on the floor / Paul's place / Clover / Song of the silents / Louis the second.

1983. (12"ep) **CANNED MUSIC** [-] [-] New Z
– Canopener / Beauty / This room is wrong / Walking home / Turning brown & torn on two / Woman / Shade for today.

1984. (12"ep) **SLUGBUCKET HAIRYBREATH MONSTER** [-] [-] Austra
– The brain that wouldn't die / I've left memories behind / Phil disease (day 1) / Phil's disease (day 4) / Crush.

— added musicians on various strings, etc

1984. (7") **NOTHING'S GOING TO HAPPEN. /** [-] [-] New Z
1985. (m-lp) *(FNLONG 1)* **THAT'S THE SHORT AND LONG OF IT** [-] [-] New Z
– Nothing's going to happen / Nothing's going to stop it / The hills are alive / Clover / Pretty poison / Sleet / Burning blue / Carpetorabber / Gone to the worms / Woman / Get outta the grange / Scrapbook.

1986. (12"ep) **THROW A SICKIE** [-] [-] New Z
(cd-iss. 1992 as 'THE SHORT AND SICK OF IT'+=;)

Flying Nun | Homestead

Dec 87. (lp) *(FNE 15) <HMS 113>* **HELLO CRUEL WORLD** (compilation 1981-1984) [ ] [ ]
– (see above EP's) *<US cd-iss. 1995; same>*

1989. (m-lp) *(FNE 27)* **DOGMA** [-] [-] German
– Lurlene Bayliss / Waltz of the good husband / The slide / Can't / Dog / Missed again.

1990. (cd) *<HMS 143>* **WEEVILLE** [-] [ ]
– Lag / What more / Breath / Skin of my teeth / Pirovette / Licky / Bodies / Mr. Brocolli / Lie / Winer / Rorschach / Tip of my tongue / Ozone / Hallelujah boy.

1992. (cd) *(FN 218)* **FORK SONGS** [-] [-] New Z

Apr 94. (3x12"lp/cd) *(FN/+CD 296)* **3 E.P.'S** (compilation) [ ] [-]
– For all the waiters in the world / Entropy / What goes up / High rise / Starry eyed and wholly brained / Folding / Neusyland / Two dozen lousy hours / Bob's yer uncle / More 54 / Archaeuptery / Ain't it funny / Senile dementia / Bee to honey /

Post modern deconstructivist blues / Kid stuff / Selfdeluded dreamboy (in a mess) / Our advice to you.

— added **IVAN MUNJAK** – drum loop

Flying Nun Flying Nun

Sep 98. (cd) <(FNCD 384)> **STUMPY: THE ALBUM** Feb97
– Swan song / They like you undone / Green green grass of someone else's home / Severed head of Julio / Crocodile / Macrame / Song of the jealous lover / Honey, I'm home / Jesus the beast / Cruising with Cochran / Things / Mojave / Box of aroma / Ghost town / Deep-fried / Disorientated boogie / And that's not all!! / Pull the thread (and unravel me) / Dessicated / Albumen / Two minds / Up. *(issued 1997 in NZ)*

CHRIS KNOX

Flying Nun not iss.

1983. (m-lp) **SONGS FOR CLEANING GUPPIES** – – New Z
1987. (c) **MONK III-AD 1987** – – New Z
(above issued on 'Walking Monk')
1989. (lp) *(FNE 30)* **SEIZURE** – – German
– The face of fashion / The woman inside of me / Statement of intent / Filling me / Not given lightly / Break! / Uncle Tom's cabin / Wanna! / And I will cry / Rapist / Grand ma! / Voyeur / Honesty's not enough / My dumb luck / Ache.
1989. (m-lp) **NOT GIVEN LIGHTLY / GUPPIPLUS** – – New Z
– Not given lightly / SONGS FOR CLEANING GUPPIES (8 out 10 tracks). *(UK-iss.Nov98 of 'NOT GIVEN LIGHTLY' on 'Curveball' 12"/cd-s; CURVE 3/+CD)*
1990. (cd) **SONG FOR 1990 + OTHER SONGS** – – New Z
1991. (cd) **CROAKER** – – New Z
Apr 93. (cd) <28> **MEAT** –

Flying Nun Communion

Mar 94. (cd) *(FNCD 249)* <34> **POLYFOTO, DUCK-SHAPED PAIN & "GUM"** Dec93
– Polyfoto / Split / Inside story / Replace me / (And you think it all started with) Trim / Glide / Under the influence / Not a victim / Psmosis / Get a life / Heart failure / Letter from L.A. / God sez "No!" to cosmetic surgery / Blameless / Outer skin / Intensive care / Honey stung paws / Mum's the word / View from the bridge / Space / Self pity's just a name for feeling low.
Jul 94. (7") *(FN 266)* **UNDER THE INFLUENCE. / STASIS** –

Flying Nun Caroline

Feb 95. (7"/cd-s) *(FN/+CD 316)* **ONE FELL SWOOP. /** –
Apr 95. (cd/c) *(FNCD/FNMC 313)* <CAROL 1788> **SONGS OF YOU & ME** May95
– Vol au vent / Lamini ol the craslie pool / Song to welcome the onset of maturity / Belly up and grinning / Half man – half mole / Brave / Sympathy for the cripple / Limited liabilty / Giving her away / Chemicals are our friends / Young female caucasian / Rust / Instant mashed potato 2 / Mirror mirror / Open / Hubba-hubba has been hoot / One fell swoop / Nothing comes clear / Dixie / Instant mashed potato.
Sep 97. (cd) *(FN 400)* **YES!!** –
– Joy of sex / Sweaty hide of circumstance / Pibroch / Backstab boogie / Ballad of a victim of the economic . . . / Gold / Tantamount to treasury / Uncoupled / Engaged / Uncertainty people / Penultimatum / Almost tempted / Flaky pastry / Ndidi.

TALULAH GOSH

Formed: Oxford, England . . . early '86 by PETER MOMTCHILOFF, PEBBLES (aka ELIZABETH PRICE), MARIGOLD (aka AMELIA FLETCHER), her brother MATHEW FLETCHER and ROBERT PURSEY, the latter being replaced by CHRIS SCOTT. Named after the headline from a CLARE GROGAN interview in the NME, TALULAH GOSH hit upon the novel idea of simultaneously releasing two singles as their debut. The songs in question, 'BEATNIK BOY' and 'STEAMING TRAIN', appeared in late '86 on Edinburgh label, '53rd & 3rd', both climbing high in the indie charts. Latterly easy pickings for the music press, this asexual looking boy-girl outfit were part of a wider indie anorak brigade reminiscent of a pastel VELVET UNDERGROUND or a moody SHANGRI-LA'S. With PEBBLES forming The CAROUSEL and EITHNE FARRY joining soon after, TG released an eponymous single in Spring '87 as a primer for their ironically titled debut album, 'ROCK LEGENDS VOL.69'. Early the following year, the English version of The PASTELS delivered another two 45's hot on the heels of each other, namely 'BRINGING UP BABY' (from the EP 'WHERE'S THE COUGAR MATEY?') and 'TESTCARD GIRL', although they disbanded soon after. AMELIA re-emerged with a solo single, 'CAN YOU KEEP A SECRET?', subsequently guesting for The WEDDING PRESENT and The POOH STICKS. In the early 90's, the band were to resurface under a different moniker, HEAVENLY, with more or less the same line-up including original TG member, PURSEY. Signed to home of twee, 'Sarah' records, the band released a series of singles which suggested the band had come of age at last. A mini-set, 'HEAVENLY VS. SATAN', appeared in '91, while a debut album proper 'LE JARDIN DE HEAVENLY' arrived in the summer of '92. Not exactly the most ambitious of bands, these perennial underachievers nevertheless warmed the hearts of their fans with further releases throughout the early to mid 90's. • **HEAVENLY covered:** NOUS NE SOMMES PAS DES ANGES (Serge Gainsbourg).

Album rating: ROCK LEGENDS VOL.69 (*5) / THEY'VE SCOFFED THE LOT compilation (*7) / Heavenly: HEAVENLY VS. SATAN mini (*6) / LE JARDIN DE HEAVENLY (*6) / OPERATION HEAVENLY (*6)

PEBBLES (b. ELIZABETH PRICE, 6 Nov'66, Bradford, England) – vocals **MARIGOLD** (b. AMELIA FLETCHER, 1 Jan'66, London, England) – vocals, guitar / **PETER MOMTCHILOFF** – guitar / **CHRIS SCOTT** (b.31 Oct'61, Hemel Hempstead, England) – bass / **MATHEW FLETCHER** (b. 5 Nov'70, London) – drums

53rd & 3rd not iss.

Nov 86. (7") *(AGARR 4)* **BEATNIK BOY. / MY BEST FRIEND** –
Nov 86. (7") *(AGARR 5)* **STEAMING TRAIN. / JUST A DREAM** –
(12"+=) *(AGARR 4-5T)* – Beatnik boy / My best friend.

— **EITHNE FARRY** (b.21 May'65, London) – vocals; repl. PEBBLES who later formed The CAROUSEL

May 87. (7") *(AGARR 8)* **TALULAH GOSH. / DON'T GO AWAY** –
(12"+=) *(AGARR 8T)* – Escalator over the hill.
Oct 87. (clear-lp) *(AGAS 004)* **ROCK LEGENDS VOL.69**
– Beatnik boy / My best friend / Just a dream / Steaming train / Talulah gosh / Don't go away / Escalator over the hill / My boy says / Way of the world / Testcard girl / Bringing up baby / I can't get no satisfaction, thank God / The girl with strawberry hair. *(cd-iss. Jun91 on 'Avalanche'; ONLYCD 011)*
Jan 88. (7") *(AGARR 14)* **BRINGING UP BABY. / THE GIRL WITH STRAWBERRY HAIR** –
(12"+=) *(AGARR 14T)* **WHERE'S THE COUGAR MATEY? EP** – I can't get no satisfaction, thank God / Do you remember? / Sunny inside.
Feb 88. (7") *(AGARR 16)* **TESTCARD GIRL. / WAY OF THE WORLD** –

— split later in 1988. CHRIS and EITHNE formed SATURN 5, while PETER joined The RAZORCUTS. TG later released compilation below.

Mar 91. (lp) *Sarah; (SARAH 604)* **THEY'VE SCOFFED THE LOT** (radio sessions) –

AMELIA

Fierce not iss.

1988. (7") **CAN YOU KEEP A SECRET? / WRAP MY ARMS AROUND HIM** –

HEAVENLY

AMELIA, MATHEW, PETER + ROBERT PURSEY (b.27 May'64, Chipping Sodbury, England) – bass

Sarah K

Feb 90. (7") *(SARAH 030)* **I FELL IN LOVE LAST NIGHT. / OVER AND OVER** –
Jan 91. (7") **OUR LOVE IS HEAVENLY. / WRAP MY ARMS AROUND HIM** –
Feb 91. (m-lp) *(SARAH 603)* **HEAVENLY VS. SATAN** –
– Cool guitar boy / Boyfriend stays the same / Lemonhead boy / Shallow / Wish me gone / Don't be fooled / It's you / Stop before you say it.

— added **CATHY ROGERS** (b.29 May'68, Tatsfield, England) – keyboards, vocals

Aug 91. (7") **SO LITTLE DESERVE. / I'M NOT SCARED OF YOU** –
Feb 92. (7") **SHE SAYS. / ESCORT CRASH ON MARSTON STREET** –
Jun 92. (lp/cd) *(SARAH 610/+CD)* **LE JARDIN DE HEAVENLY**
– Starshy / Tool / Orange corduroy dress / Different day / C is the Heavenly option / Smile / And the birds aren't singing / Sort of mine. <US+=> – So little deserve / I'm not scared of you.
Jul 93. (7") *(SARAH 081)* **P.U.N.K. GIRL. / HEARTS AND CROSSES** –
Aug 93. (7") *(SARAH 082)* **ATTA GIRL. / DIG YOUR OWN GRAVE / SO?** –
(cd-s+=) *(SARAH 082CD)* – P.U.N.K. girl / Hearts and crosses.
Jul 94. (cd-ep) <025> **P.U.N.K. GIRL EP** –
– P.U.N.K. girl / Hearts and crosses / Atta girl / Dig your own grave / So?
Sep 94. (m-lp/m-cd) *(SARAH 623/+CD)* <033> **THE DECLINE AND FALL OF THE HEAVENLY**
– Me and my madness / Modestic / Skipjack / Itchy chin / Sacramento / Three star compartment / Sperm meets egg, so what? / She and me.

Wiiija K

Sep 96. (7"m) *(WIJ 58)* <073> **SPACE MANATEE. / YOU TORE ME DOWN / ART SCHOOL**
Oct 96. (cd/lp) *(WIJ CD/LP 1053)* <059> **OPERATION HEAVENLY**
– Trophy girlfriend / K-klass kisschase / Space manitee / Ben Sherman / By the way / Cut off / Nous ne sommes pas des anges / Mark angel / Fat Lenny / Snail trail / Pet monkey.

– compilations, etc. –

May 96. (d-lp/d-cd; by TALULAH GOSH) *K; (<KLP 44/+CD>)* **BACKWASH** (all material)

Elefant not iss.

Jul 97. (cd) *(ER 1017)* **THIS IS HEAVENLY** (compilation) –

TAPPI TIKARRASS (see under ⇒ BJORK)

TANSADS

Formed: Wigan, Lancashire, England . . . 1990 by the KETTLE brothers, JOHN, ANDREW and BOB, along with JANET ANDERTON, ED JONES, DOMINIC LOWE, SHRUB, BUG and CUDO. Proffering salt-of-the-earth, honest-to-goodness, heart-on-the-sleeve folky indie/rock, The TANSADS (named after a pram, apparently) are Real Ale spiritual Northern cousins to Brighton's LEVELLERS. The self-financed 'SHANDYLAND' (1991) got the band's career off to a frothy start, attracting the attention of LEVELLERS/WATERBOYS producer, Phil Tennant, who worked on the band's follow-up for 'Musidisc', 'UP THE SHIRKERS' (1993). Following the replacement of founding members, DOMINIC, BUG and SHRUB with GUY KEEGAN and LEE GOULDING, a slightly modified TANSADS signed to the reactivated roots label, 'Transatlantic', for third set, 'FLOCK' (1994). A more composed affair taking in the usual lyrical targets (religion, business, suits, etc.), the album's harmony-happy rave-ups were leavened by a couple of fine, string-enhanced ballads, 'SHE'S NOT GONE' and 'SUNLIGHT IN THE MORNING', powerfully carried by ANDERTON. This was followed in '95 by a live set, 'DRAG DOWN THE MOON', capturing the band in their element in Wigan. While never quite managing to fire the average music fan's imagination in the same way as The LEVELLERS, for example, The TANSADS remain an institution for diehard fans.

Album rating: SHANDYLAND (*6) / UP THE SHIRKERS (*6) / FLOCK (*7) / DRAG DOWN THE MOON (*7)

ANDREW KETTLE – vocals / **JANET ANDERTON** – vocals / **JOHN KETTLE** – guitars, banjo / **BOB KETTLE** – mandolin, guitar, harmonica / **ED JONES** – bass, vocals / **DOMINIC LOWE** – accordion / **SHRUB** – keyboards / **BUG** – drums / **CUDO** – percussion

unknown — not iss.

1991. (cd) **SHANDYLAND** –
– Cobbly back yard / Wood in th' hole / Right on / Big Wednesday / Feed me / Horses / Shandyland / Juvenile / No more / London's burning / Spirit move / Big bad Devil. *(cd re-iss. Nov95 on 'Essential'; ESMCD 351)*

— **LEE GOULDING** – keyboards; repl. LOWE

— **GUY KEEGAN** – drums (ex-RAILWAY CHILDREN) repl. BUG + SHRUB

Musidisc — not iss.

Feb 93. (cd/c/lp) *(10985-2/-4/-1)* **UP THE SHIRKERS** –
– Eye of the average / Camelot / Brian Kant / Zig zag / Music down / Waste of space / Chip pan ocean / The English rover / John John / Reason to be / Up the revolution / Turn on, tune up, drop out, be late. *(cd re-iss. Nov95 on 'Essential'; ESMCD 352)*

— now without CUDO

Aug 94. (cd/c) *(11212-2/-4)* **FLOCK**
– A band on the rainbow / Fear of falling / She's not gone / God on a string / Iron man / Waiting for the big one / Dance / Sunlight in the morning / G man / Ship of fools / I know I can (but I won't) / Heading for the heart / Separate fools. *(re-iss. Oct94 & Apr96 on 'Transatlantic' cd/c; TRA CD/MC 101)*

Transatlantic — not iss.

Sep 94. (c-s) *(TRAM 1001)* **A BAND ON THE RAINBOW / THURSDAY'S CHILD** –
(cd-s+=) *(TRAX 1001)* – The English rover (live) / Cobby back yard (live).

Oct 95. (cd/c) *(TRA CD/MC 118)* **DRAG DOWN THE MOON (live)** –

Apr 96. (cd-s) *(TRAX 1006)* **I KNOW I CAN /** –

— seemed to have disbanded

TARNATION

Formed: San Francisco, California, USA . . . 1992 by Sautee Nacoochee, Georgia-born PAULA FRAZER, a veteran of the Bay Area alt-rock acts; all-female FRIGHTWIG the most noteworthy. Prior to this and just into her teens, she had moved with her family to Arkansas, where she honed her multi-ranged soprano voice to perfection; PAULA would subsequently sing in a Bulgarian woman's choir. Having met up with former SF SEALS members, LINCOLN ALLEN and MICHELLE CERNUTO (MATT SULLIVAN would soon make it a quartet), they decided to form their own roots/alt-country group. The haunting prairie laments of TARNATION found FRAZER revisiting her presbyterian upbringing via a trademark cinematic country sound. Following a low-key self-financed debut, 'I'LL GIVE YOU SOMETHING TO CRY ABOUT' (1992), the band were signed to London label, '4 a.d.', through whom they released 1995's 'GENTLE CREATURES'. Delivered in a high, lonesome wail lying somewhere between DOLORES O'RIORDAN, GILLIAN WELCH and TAMMY WYNETTE!, FRAZER's dark narratives were set against a moody soundtrack of vibrato-shimmering guitar, subtle lap steel and shuffling percussion. Not the most immediate of approaches and one which, along with labelmates such as RED HOUSE PAINTERS and MOJAVE 3, has seen TARNATION enjoy critical acclaim without any corresponding rise in their profile. This despite one of their finest efforts to date in 1997's 'MIRADOR' album and the SMITHS-meet-The CRANBERRIES-in-Mexico brilliance of accompanying single, 'YOUR THOUGHTS AND MINE'; FRAZER was now the sole survivor, the other three being replaced by ALEX OROPEZA, BILL CUEVAS and JOE BYRNES. Her most famous moment came later that year when she duetted with TJINDER SINGH on CORNERSHOP's 'Good To Be On The Road Back Home Again'. Still, with a major label deal – courtesy of 'Resprise' – in the bag, TARNATION might yet achieve the same level of recognition as alt-country stalwarts and new labelmates WILCO.

Album rating: I'LL GIVE YOU SOMETHING TO CRY ABOUT (*6) / GENTLE CREATURES (*6) / MIRADOR (*7)

PAULA FRAZER – vocals, guitars, bass, keyboards, accordion, etc / **LINCOLN ALLEN** – guitar (ex-SF SEALS / **MATT SULLIVAN** – guitar / **MICHELLE CERNUTO** – drums (ex-SF SEALS)

not iss. — Nuf Sed

1993. (cd) **I'LL GIVE YOU SOMETHING TO CRY ABOUT** –

— now with **YUMA JOE BYRNES** – drums, percussion / **JAMIE MEAGAN** – bass, guitar (+ lap steel), vocals, percussion, organ / **ALEX OROPEZA** – guitars (+ lap steel), organ, vocals / **SHEILA SCHAT** – cello, violin / **ARCH STANTON** – noise

4 a.d. — 4ad-Reprise

Sep 95. (lp/cd) *(CAD 5010/+CD) <45961>* **GENTLE CREATURES** — Aug95
– Game of broken hearts / Halfway to madness / Well / Big A motel / Tell me it's not so / Two wrongs / Lonely lights / Gentle creatures / Listen to the wind / Hand / Do you fancy me / Yellow birds / Burn again / Stranger in the mirror / It's not easy.

— **FRAZER** now with **OROPEZA** – guitars / **BILL CUEVAS** – bass, lap steel / **JOE BYRNES** – drums

Jan 97. (7"ltd.) *(TAD 7000)* **THERE'S SOMEONE. / I DIDN'T MEAN IT: PALADINA** –

Feb 97. (12"ep)(cd-ep) *(AAD 7001)(BAD 7001CD)* **YOUR THOUGHTS AND MINE / YOU'LL UNDERSTAND. / LEAVE THE SAD THINGS BEHIND / LAND THAT TIME LOST** –

Apr 97. (cd)(d-lp) *(CAD 7004CD)(DAD 7004) <46482>* **MIRADOR**
– An awful shade of blue / Wait / A place where I know / Is she lonesome now? / Your thoughts and mine / Christine / Destiny / There's someone / Like a ghost / Idly / Little black egg / You'll understand.

TARWATER

Formed: East Berlin, Germany . . . 1995 by long-time compatriots and punk rockers, BERND JESTRAM and RONALD LIPPOK (latter of TO ROCOCO ROT). After a number of homeland releases – including, '11/6 12/10', 'RABBIT MOON REVISITED' and the radio theatre play 'JOHN DONNE' – their first official album issued in the UK, 'SILUR' (means 'the Silurian Age when the Earth was underwater), came out in the Autumn of '98. An experimental masterpiece, this textured piece combined elements of CABARET VOLTAIRE and MASSIVE ATTACK, 'THE WATERSAMPLE' being the highlight. • **Covered:** DOWN IN THE SEWER (Stranglers).

Album rating: 11/6 12/10 (*7) / RABBIT MOON REVISITED (*5) / SILUR (*8)

BERND JESTRAM – bass, keyboards / **RONALD LIPPOK** – vocals, keyboards (of TO ROCOCO ROT)

Kitty-Yo — not iss.

1996. (cd) *(96004)* **11/6 12/10** – – German

1996. (m-cd) *(9801)* **RABBIT MOON REVISITED** – – German
(above issued on 'Cap Stack')

1996. (m-cd) **JOHN DONNE** (radio music play) – – German

1997. (cd-s) **DOWN IN THE SEWER /** – – German

Sep 98. (cd/lp) *(EFA 55213-2/-1)* **SILUR** –
– Visit / To maouf / The watersample / Seafrance Cezanne / Silur / No more extra time / Otomo / Ford / Pomps of the subsoil / 20 miles up / To describe you / V-AT.

Troy TATE

Born: Liverpool, England. His formative punk days were spent fronting CLASH-esque, Cheltenham-based outfit, INDEX, who finally got round to issuing their debut single, 'JET LAG' (although only 500 of them hit the small independent shops) in 1978. TROY left RUSSELL ELLIOTT (bass) and DAVE HOUGH (drums) to carry on without him having taken the opportunity to join ex-REZILLOS members in the outfit, SHAKE. He stayed for two 45's, 'INVASION OF THE GAMMA MEN' and 'WOAH YEAH!', the last of which was released around the same time as his summer '81 solo debut, 'THOMAS'. It was for his time with The TEARDROP EXPLODES, however, that TROY TATE would become best known, although his tenure was cut short even before their untimely break-up in 1983. FASHION was the next port of call for this musical mercenary, but that too lasted under a year, the man opting for a more secure solo career. Having signed to 'Rough Trade', a single, 'I DON'T KNOW WHAT LOVE IS', appeared in July '83 while the remixed version of 'THOMAS' that surfaced a year later was his first for 'Sire'. Now seven years in the business, TROY finaly delivered his debut album, 'TICKET TO THE DARK', in 1984, a safe mixture of alternative pop that did little in the sales department. A follow-up, 'LIBERTY', in 1985, was, I suppose, appropriately titled as his record company set him free soon after.

Album rating: TICKET TO THE DARK (*5) / LIBERTY (*4)

TROY TATE – vocals, guitar (ex-INDEX, ex-SHAKE) / with various personnel

Whi-Fi — not iss.

Jun 81. (7") *(WHY 3)* **THOMAS. / LONDON'S SWINGING** –

— he also joined The TEARDROP EXPLODES at this point

Jan 82. (10"ep) *(WHY 6)* **LIFELINE (HOLD ONTO THAT). / KAMIKAZE / THOMAS** –

— after above, he left COPE and Co. to join FASHION, although he subsequently left them to continue his solo career

Rough Trade — not iss.

Jul 83. (7") *(RT 134)* **I DON'T KNOW WHAT LOVE IS ANYMORE. / I'M MAD** –
(12"+=) *(RTT 134)* – Lifeline.

— his band consisted of **JON HURST** – keyboards / **PETE RIZZO** – bass / **ALI PATERSON** – drums

Sire — not iss.

Jul 84. (7") *(W 9222)* **THOMAS. / E 209** –
(12"+=) *(W 9222T)* – What cha gonna do next?

Sep 84. (lp) *(925160-1)* **TICKET TO THE DARK** –
– Party / Thomas / Love is . . . / Winning team / All the way up / Whip crack away / Safety net / House of the new breed / Lifeline / I'm not your toy.

Jun 85. (7"/12") *(U 9043/+T)* **SORROW. / HIGH ALTITUDE** –

Jul 85. (lp) *(925312-1)* **LIBERTY** –
– Sorrow / Girl on a ferry / Merry go round / High altitude / Liberty / All in a row / Tomorrow I'll be gone / Round and round / God's puppet / Airport of silence.

— TROY retired from the music biz

TATEM TOTZ (see under ⇒ REDD KROSS)

James TAYLOR QUARTET (see under ⇒ PRISONERS)

TEARDROP EXPLODES (see under ⇒ COPE, Julian)

TEAR GARDEN (see under ⇒ SKINNY PUPPY)

TECHNO ANIMAL (see under ⇒ ICE)

TEENAGE FANCLUB

Formed: Glasgow, Scotland . . . 1989 although earlier they had posed as The BOY HAIRDRESSERS. After a one-off single, 'GOLDEN SHOWERS' (1988), bassist GERRY LOVE was recruited and BRENDAN O'HARE replaced FRANCIS McDONALD (who went off to join that other Glasgow institution, The PASTELS) on the drums. As TEENAGE FANCLUB, they cut the inspired chaos of the 'EVERYTHING FLOWS' (1990) single and followed it up with the debut album, 'A CATHOLIC EDUCATION' later the same year. The term slacker rock was surely coined with this bunch of cheeky Glaswegian wide boys in mind and if it was lazy to compare their honey-in-the-dirt melodic dischord with DINOSAUR JR., that was nothing compared to the laid back, laissez faire philosophy that fuelled (if that's not too strong a word) TEENAGE FANCLUB's ramshackle racket, both on stage and in the studio. By the release of the DON FLEMING-produced 'BANDWAGONESQUE' (1991), ('THE KING' was a sub-standard effort released to fulfill contractual obligations), the band were sounding more professional, crafting an album of langourous harmonies and chiming guitar that was a thinly veiled homage to BIG STAR as well as taking in such obvious reference points as The BYRDS, The BEACH BOYS, BUFFALO SPRINGFIELD etc. Ironically, rather than propelling TEENAGE FANCLUB into the big league, the album seemed instead to merely rekindle interest in BIG STAR's back catalogue and after a honeymoon period of being indie press darlings, the backlash was sharp and swift. The fact that the self-produced 'THIRTEEN' (1993) lacked their trademark inspired sloppiness didn't help matters any. Not that the band were overly concerned, they crafted modern retro more lovingly than most and had a loyal following to lap it up. The FANNIE's further developed their niche with 'GRAND PRIX' (1995) and if it was that reliably trad, West Coast via Glasgow roots sound you were after then TEENAGE FANCLUB were your band. While they wear their influences more proudly than any other group, (O.K., so I forgot about OASIS . . .) they do it with such verve and style that it'd be churlish to write them off as mere plagiarists and they remain one of Scotland's best loved exports. Their latest effort, 'SONGS FROM NORTHERN BRITAIN' (1997) was their most considered release to date, sharpening up their sound and arrangements to an unprecedented degree. But if that's what it takes to come up with something as engagingly swoonsome as 'I DON'T CARE' or 'IS THAT ENOUGH', no one's going to make much of a fuss. • **Songwriters:** BLAKE or BLAKE-McGINLEY or group compositions except; DON'T CRY NO TEARS (Neil Young) / THE BALLAD OF JOHN AND YOKO (Beatles) / LIKE A VIRGIN (Madonna) / LIFE'S A GAS (T.Rex) / FREE AGAIN + JESUS CHRIST (Alex Chilton) / CHORDS OF FAME (Phil Ochs) / BAD SEEDS (Beat Happening) / HAVE YOU EVER SEEN THE RAIN? (Creedence Clearwater Revival) / BETWEEN US (Neil Innes) / FEMME FATALE (Velvet Underground). • **Trivia:** ALEX CHILTON (ex-BOX TOPS) guested on 1992 sessions and contributed some songs.

Album rating: A CATHOLIC EDUCATION (*6) / BANDWAGONESQUE (*8) / THIRTEEN (*7) / GRAND PRIX (*8) / SONGS FROM NORTHERN BRITAIN (*8)

NORMAN BLAKE (b.20 Oct'65, Bellshill, Scotland) – vocals, guitar (ex-BMX BANDITS) / **RAYMOND McGINLEY** (b. 3 Jan'64, Glasgow) – bass, vocals / **FRANCIS McDONALD** (b.21 Nov'70, Bellshill, Scotland) – drums / **JOE McALINDEN** – violin / **JIM LAMBIE** – vibraphone

53rd & 3rd | not iss.

Jan 88. (12"; as BOY HAIRDRESSERS) *(AGARR 12T)* **GOLDEN SHOWERS. / TIDAL WAVE / THE ASSUMPTION AS AN ELEVATOR** [ ] [-]

— **NORMAN + RAYMOND** – guitars, vocals plus **GERARD LOVE** (b.31 Aug'67, Motherwell, Scotland) – bass, vocals / **BRENDAN O'HARE** (b.16 Jan'70, Bellshill, Scotland) – bass repl. McDONALD who joined The PASTELS

Paperhouse | Matador

Jun 90. (7"m) *(PAPER 003)* **EVERYTHING FLOWS. / PRIMARY EDUCATION / SPEEEDER** [ ] [ ]
(cd-ep+=) *(PAPER 003CD)* – Don't Cry No Tears. *(rel.Feb91)*

Jul 90. (cd/c/lp) *(PAP CD/MC/LP 004) <12>* **A CATHOLIC EDUCATION** [ ] [ ]
– Heavy metal / Everything flows / Catholic education / Too involved / Don't need a drum / Critical mass / Heavy metal II / Catholic education 2 / Eternal light / Every picture I paint / Everybody's fun. *(re-iss. cd Mar95; same)*

Oct 90. (one-sided-7") *(PAPER 005)* **THE BALLAD OF JOHN AND YOKO** [ ] [-]

Nov 90. (7") *(PAPER 007) <23>* **GOD KNOWS IT'S TRUE. / SO FAR GONE** [ ] [ ]
(12"+=/cd-s+=) *(PAPER 007 T/CD)* – Weedbreak / Ghetto blaster.

Creation | Geffen

Aug 91. (cd/lp) *(CRE CD/LP 096)* **THE KING** (instrumental) [53] [-]
– Heavy metal 6 / Mudhoney / Interstellar overdrive / Robot love / Like a virgin / The king / Opal inquest / The ballad of Bow Evil (slow and fast) / Heavy metal 9. (above originally only meant for US ears, deleted after 24 hours)

Aug 91. (7") *(CRE 105)* **STAR SIGN. / HEAVY METAL 6** [44] [-]
(12"+=)(cd-s+=) *(CRE 105T)(CRESCD 105)* – Like a virgin / ('A'demo version).
(7"ltd) *(CRE 105L)* – ('A'side) / Like a virgin.

Oct 91. (7"/c-s) *(CRE/+CS 111) <4370>* **THE CONCEPT. / LONG HAIR** [51] [ ] Jan92
(12"+=)(cd-s+=) *(CRE 111T)(CRESCD 111)* – What you do to me (demo) / Robot love.

Nov 91. (cd)(c/lp) *(CRECD 106)(C+/CRE 106) <24461>* **BANDWAGONESQUE** [22] [ ]
– The concept / Satan / December / What you do to me / I don't know / Star sign / Metal baby / Pet rock / Sidewinder / Alcoholiday / Guiding star / Is this music?.

Jan 92. (7"/c-s) *(CRE/+CS 115) <21708>* **WHAT YOU DO TO ME. / B-SIDE** [31] [ ]
(12"+=)(cd-s+=) *(CRE 115T)(CRESCD 115)* – Life's a gas / Filler.

Jun 93. (7"/c-s) *(CRE/+CS 130)* **RADIO. / DON'S GONE COLUMBIA** [31] [ ]
(12"+=)(cd-s+=) *(CRE 130T)(CRESCD 130)* – Weird horses / Chords of fame.

Sep 93. (7"/c-s) *(CRE/+CS 142)* **NORMAN 3. / OLDER GUYS** [50] [-]
(12"+=)(cd-s+=) *(CRE 142T)(CRESCD 142)* – Golden glades / Genius envy.

Oct 93. (cd)(c/lp) *(CRECD 144)(C+/CRE 144) <24533>* **THIRTEEN** [14] [ ] Nov93
– Hang on / The cabbage / Radio / Norman 3 / Song to the cynic / 120 minutes / Escher / Commercial alternative / Fear of flying / Tears are cool / Ret live dead / Get funky / Gene Clark.

— In Mar'94, they teamed up with DE LA SOUL on single 'FALLIN''. This was from the rock-rap album 'Judgement Day' on 'Epic' records (hit UK 59).

1994. (cd-ep) *<21887>* **AUSTRALIAN TOUR SAMPLER** [-] [ ]

— **PAUL QUINN** – drums (ex-SOUP DRAGONS) repl. O'HARE

Mar 95. (7"/c-s) *(CRE/+CS 175)* **MELLOW DOUBT. / SOME PEOPLE TRY TO FUCK WITH YOU** [34] [-]
(cd-s+=) *(CRESCD 175)* – Getting real / About you.
(cd-s) *(CRESCD 175X)* – ('A'side) / Have you ever seen the rain? / Between us / You're my kind.

May 95. (7"/c-s) *(CRE/+CS 201)* **SPARKY'S DREAM. / BURNED** [40] [-]
(cd-s+=) *(CRESCD 201)* – For you / Headstand.
(cd-s) *(CRESCD 201X)* – ('A'-alternative version) / Try and stop me / That's all I need to know / Who loves the sun.

May 95. (cd)(c/lp) *(CRECD 173)(C+/CRE 173) <24802>* **GRAND PRIX** [7] [ ] Jul95
– About you / Sparky's dream / Mellow doubt / Don't look back / Verisinilitude / Neil Jung / Tears / Discolite / Say no / Going places / I'll make it clear / I gotta know / Hardcore – ballad. *(lp w/free 7")* – DISCOLITE (demo). / I GOTTA KNOW (demo)

Aug 95. (7"/c-s) *(CRE/+CS 210)* **NEIL JUNG. / THE SHADOWS** [62] [-]
(cd-s+=) *(CRESCD 210)* – My life / Every step is a way through love.
(cd-s) *(CRESCD 210X)* – ('A'side) / Traffic jam / Hi-fi / I heard you looking.

Dec 95. (7"ep/c-ep/cd-ep) *(CRE/+CS/SCD 216)* **TEENAGE FANCLUB HAVE LOST IT EP (acoustic)** [53] [-]
– Don't look back / Everything flows / Starsign / 120 mins.

Creation | Sony

Jun 97. (cd-s) *(CRESCD 228)* **AIN'T THAT ENOUGH / KICKABOUT / BROKEN** [17] [-]
(cd-s) *(CRESCD 228X)* – ('A'side) / Femme fatale / Jesus Christ.

Jun 97. (cd/c/lp) *(CRECD/CCRE/CRELP 196) <68202>* **SONGS FROM NORTHERN BRITAIN** [3] [ ]
– Start again / Ain't that enough / Can't feel my soul / I don't want control of you / Planets / It's a bad world / Take the long way round / Winter / I don't care / Mount Everest / Your love is the place where I come from / Speed of light.

Aug 97. (7") *(CRE 238)* **I DON'T WANT CONTROL OF YOU. / THE COUNT** [43] [-]
(cd-s) *(CRESCD 238)* –
(cd-s) *(CRESCD 238X)* –

Nov 97. (7") *(CRE 280)* **START AGAIN. /** [54] [ ]
(cd-s+=) *(CRESCD 280)* –
(cd-s) *(CRESCD 280X)* –

Jun 98. (7") *(CRE 298)* **LONG SHOT. /** [ ] [-]

– compilations, others, etc. –

May 92. (7") *K; <IPU 26>* **FREE AGAIN. / BAD SEEDS** [-] [ ]

Nov 92. (12"ep/cd-ep) *Strange Fruit; (SFPS/+CD 081)* **THE JOHN PEEL SESSION** [ ] [-]
– God knows it's true / Alcoholiday / So far gone / Long hair. *(re-iss. Dec93 & Jul95; same)*

— (in 1995, they backed FRANK BLACK on his PEEL SESSION)

Mar 95. (cd/c) *Fire; (FLIPCD 002)* **DEEP FRIED FANCLUB** [ ] [-]
– Everything flows / Primary education / Speeeder / Critical mass (orig.) / The ballad of John and Yoko / God knows it's true / Weedbreak / So far gone / Ghetto blaster / Don't cry no tears / Free again / Bad seed.

Apr 97. (cd) *Nectar; (NTMCD 543)* **FANDEMONIUM** [ ] [-]

Sep 97. (7"ep) *Radiation; (RARE 033)* **TEENAGE FANCLUB EP** [ ] [-]

TEENAGE FILMSTARS (see under ⇒ BALL, Ed)

TEENAGE JESUS & THE JERKS (see under ⇒ LUNCH, Lydia)

TELESCOPES

Formed: Burton-Upon-Trent, Staffordshire, England . . . 1987 by STEPHEN LAWRIE, JOANNA DORAN, DAVE FITZGERALD, ROBERT BROOKS and DOMINIC DILLON. Their first release in '88 was actually a track on a shared flexidisc with LOOP, 'FOREVER CLOSE YOUR EYES'. The following year, 'Cheree' also issued a further couple, 'KICK THE WALL' and '7th DISASTER', before US label, 'What Goes On' took over the reins. A debut album, 'TASTE' (1989), carried on in their trademark JESUS & MARY CHAIN/RIDE guitar fusion, although their label subsequently went belly up. Left in debt to the tune of a 5-figure sum, ALAN McGEE of 'Creation' duly bailing them out by buying out the rights for their songs. A clutch of singles – including minor hit 'FLYING' – previewed a long-awaited bonafide follow-up album in 1992, 'UNTITLED'; EDWARD BALL (ex-TELEVISION PERSONALITIES) guested on the set which showed them mellowing towards a more harmonious, archetypally 'Creation' outfit. Curiously the band haven't been sighted since.

Album rating: TASTE (*7) / UNTITLED (*6)

STEPHEN LAWRIE (b.28 Mar'69, East Hartford, England) – vocals / **JOANNA DORAN** (b. West Midlands, England) – guitar, vocals / **DAVID FITZGERALD** (b.30 Aug'66, Wellingborough, England) – guitar / **ROBERT BROOKS** (b.11 Apr'69, Burton-Upon-Trent) – bass / **DOMINIC DILLON** (b.26 Sep'64, Bolton, England) – drums

Cheree / not iss.

1988. (7"flexi) *(CHEREE 1)* **FOREVER CLOSE YOUR EYES. / (LOOP: Soundhead)** [ ] [-]

Jan 89. (7") *(CHEREE 2)* **KICK THE WALL. / THIS IS THE LAST OF WHAT'S COMING NOW** [ ] [-]

Apr 89. (12"ep) *(CHEREET 4)* **7th # DISASTER / NOTHING. / THIS PLANET / COLD** [ ] [-]

What Goes On / not iss.

Sep 89. (12"ep) *(WHAT 15T)* **THE PERFECT NEEDLE / SADNESS PALE. / S.H.C. BURN / YOU CANNOT BE SURE** [ ] [-]
(12"+=) *(WHAT12 15)* –

Oct 89. (lp/cd) *(GOES ON 32/+CD)* **TASTE** [ ] [-]
– And let me drift away / I fall, she screams / Oil seed rape / Violence / Threadbare / The perfect needle / There is no floor / Anticipating nowhere / Please, before you go / Suffercation / Silent water / Suicide. *(re-iss. cd Jul90 on 'Cheree'; CHEREE 9 CD)*

Jan 90. (12"ep/cd-ep) *(GOES ON 18 T/CD)* **TO KILL A SLOW GIRL WALKING. /** [ ] [-]

Fierce / not iss.

1990. (lp/cd) *(FRIGHT/+CD 039)* **TRADE MARK OF QUALITY** (compilation) [ ] [-]

Creation / Tristar

Jun 90. (7") *(CRE 081)* **PRECIOUS LITTLE. / NEVER HURT YOU** [ ] [-]
(12"+-)(cd-s+=) *(CRE 81T)(CRESCD 81)* – Deep hole / Sense.

Nov 90. (7") *(CRE 092)* **EVERSO. /** [ ] [-]
(12"+=)(cd-s+=) *(CRE 092T)(CRESCD 092)* –

Feb 91. (7") *(CRE 103)* **CELESTE. /** [ ] [-]
(12"+=)(cd-s+=) *(CRE 103T)(CRESCD 103)* –

Jul 91. (12"ep)(cd-ep) *(CRE 108T)(CRESCD 108)* **FLYING** [79] [-]

May 92. (cd/lp)(c) *(CRE CD/LP 079)(CCRE 079)* <57564> **THE TELESCOPES** [ ] [ ] Mar94
– Splashdown / High on fire / You set my soul / Spaceships / The presence of your grace / And / Flying / Yeah / Ocean drive / Please tell mother / To the shore.

— still looking out for their next release although 'Tristar' in the US released a compilation in '94

TELEVISION

Formed: New York City, New York, USA based . . . late '73 by TOM VERLAINE, RICHARD HELL and BILLY FICCA who had all been members of The NEON BOYS. In 1975, William Terry Ork gave them a deal on his own self-named indie label, for whom they issued a one-off flop single, 'LITTLE JOHNNY JEWEL'. By this point, HELL (who went on to form the equally seminal RICHARD HELL & THE VOID-OIDS) had been replaced by ex-MC5 man, FRED 'SONIC' SMITH, TELEVISION subsequently signing with 'Elektra' and unleashing their classic debut album, 'MARQUEE MOON'. Although virtually ignored in America (more astute British punk/new wave fans placed it in the UK Top 30) upon its 1977 release, the album has since been acknowledged as a landmark release. The hypnotic near-10 minute title track (also a UK Top 30 hit) breathtakingly showcased the driving/free-from cool guitar interplay between LLOYD and virtuoso VERLAINE (the track first debuted at their early CBGB's shows and perfected/modified over the next couple of years), while the album as a whole testified to VERLAINE's barely disguised passion for The ROLLING STONES, PINK FLOYD and the darker moments of The VELVET UNDERGROUND. While VERLAINE's tortured vocals were reminiscent of LOU REED/PATTI SMITH, his molten-spark histrionics resolutely distinguished the band from the more wilfully amateurish new wave pack and TELEVISION remain the most musically adept band of the era. Unsurprisingly, however, they found it difficult following up such a milestone and although 'ADVENTURE' (1978) contained sporadic moments of genius, TELEVISON were beginning to lose clarity. Ironically, as the New York scene was at its height, LLOYD effectively pulled the plug on the group after walking out mid-tour later that year. VERLAINE tried unsuccessfully to translate his distinctive sound into a more mainstream rock setting with his solo career, retaining his characteristic vocals and of course, his trademark guitar alchemy. TELEVISION eventually reformed in the 90's with the classic line-up of VERLAINE, LLOYD, SMITH and FICCA, recording the acclaimed 'TELEVSION' (1992) for 'Capitol' and suggesting that what VERLAINE's solo career was lacking was the anchor and foil of LLOYD's rhythm playing. • **Songwriters:** VERLAINE lyrics / group compositions, except early live material; FIRE ENGINE (13th Floor Elevators) / KNOCKIN' ON HEAVEN'S DOOR (Bob Dylan) / SATISFACTION (Rolling Stones). • **Trivia:** VERLAINE played guitar on PATTI SMITH's 1974 single 'Hey Joe'.

Album rating: MARQUEE MOON (*10) / ADVENTURE (*5) / TELEVISION (*6) / TOM VERLAINE – COVER (*7)

TOM VERLAINE (b. THOMAS MILLER, 13 Dec'49, Mt.Morris, New Jersey) – vocals, lead guitar / **RICHARD LLOYD** – guitar, vocals / **RICHARD HELL** (b. RICHARD MYERS, 2 Oct'49, Lexington, Kentucky) – bass, vocals / **BILLY FICCA** – drums

not iss. / Ork

Oct 75. (7") *<81975>* **LITTLE JOHNNY JEWEL. / (part 2)** [-] [ ]

— **FRED SMITH** (b.10 Apr'48) – bass, vocals (ex-BLONDIE) repl. RICHARD HELL who went solo

Elektra / Elektra

Feb 77. (lp/c) *(K/K4 52046) <7E 1098>* **MARQUEE MOON** [28] [ ]
– See no evil / Venus / Friction / Marquee moon / Elevation / Guiding light / Prove it / Torn curtain. *(cd-iss. 1989; 960616-2)*

Mar 77. (12")(2-part-7") *(K 12252)* **MARQUEE MOON (stereo). / MARQUEE MOON (mono)** [30] [-]

Jul 77. (7"/12",12"green) *(K 12262/+T)* **PROVE IT. / VENUS** [25] [-]

Apr 78. (lp,red-lp/c) *(K/K4 52072) <6E 133>* **ADVENTURE** [7] [ ]
– Glory / Days / Foxhole / Careful / Carried away / The fire / Ain't that nothin' / The dream's a dream. *(cd-iss. Nov93 on 'WEA'; 7559 60523-2)*

Apr 78. (7"/12"red) *(K 12287/+T)* **FOXHOLE. / CAREFUL** [36] [-]

Jul 78. (7") *(K 12306)* **GLORY. / CARRIED AWAY** [ ] [-]

Jul 78. (7") *<45516>* **GLORY. / AIN'T THAT NOTHIN'** [-] [ ]

— Broke ranks in Aug'78. FICCA joined The WAITRESSES, FRED joined The PATTI SMITH GROUP and RICHARD LLOYD went solo.

– compilations, others, etc. –

Jan 83. (c) *R.O.I.R.; <A-114>* **THE BLOW UP (live)** [-] [ ]
(UK cd-iss. Feb90 on 'Danceteria'; DANCD 030) (cd re-iss. Nov94 on 'R.O.I.R.'; RE 114CD)

1979. (12"m) *Ork-WEA; (NYC 1T)* **LITTLE JOHNNY JEWEL (parts 1 & 2). / ('A'live version)** [ ] [-]

TOM VERLAINE

— went solo augmented mainly by **FRED SMITH** – bass / **JAY DEE DAUGHERTY** – drums / **BRUCE BRODY** – keyboards / **ALLAN SCHWARTZBERG** – drums, percussion

Elektra / Elektra

Sep 79. (lp/c) *(K/K4 52156) <2156>* **TOM VERLAINE** [ ] [ ]
– The grip of love / Souvenir from a dream / Kingdom come / Mr. Bingo / Yonki time / Flash lightning / Red leaves / Last night / Breakin' in my heart.

Warners / Warners

Sep 81. (lp/c) *(K/K4 56919)* **DREAMTIME** [ ] [ ]
– There's a reason / Penetration / Always / The blue robe / Without a word / Mr. Blur / Fragile / A future in noise / Down on the farm / Mary Marie.

Sep 81. (7"/12") *(K 17855/+T)* **ALWAYS. / THE BLUE ROBE** [ ] [ ]

— **JIMMY RIPP** – guitar repl. BRODY

Virgin / Warners

May 82. (lp/c) *(V/TCV 2227) <BSK 3685>* **WORDS FROM THE FRONT** [ ] [ ]
– Present arrived / Postcard from Waterloo / True story / Clear it away / Words from the front / Coming apart / Days on the mountain. *(cd-iss. Aug88; OVED 87) (re-iss. cd Jun89; CDV 2227)*

May 82. (7"/12") *(VS 501/+12)* **POSTCARD FROM WATERLOO. / DAYS ON THE MOUNTAIN** [ ] [ ]

Jun 84. (7") *(VS 696)* **LET'S GO TO THE MANSION. / ('A'version)** [ ] [ ]
(12"+=) *(VS 696/+12)* – Lindi Lu.

Aug 84. (7") *(VS 704)* **FIVE MILES OF YOU. / YOUR FINEST HOUR** [ ] [ ]
(12"+=) *(VS 704/+12)* – Dissolve reveal.

Sep 84. (lp/c) *(V/TCV 2314) <25144>* **COVER** [ ] [ ]
– Five miles of you / Let's go the mansion / Travelling / O foolish heart / Dissolve – Reveal / Miss Emily / Rotation / Swim. *(re-iss. Apr86 lp/c; OVED/+C 168) (cd-iss. Jun89; (CDV 2314)*

— **ANDY NEWMARK** – drums repl. JAY DEE

Fontana / Mercury-IRS

Feb 87. (7") *(FTANA 1)* **A TOWN CALLED WALKER. / SMOOTHER THAN JONES** [ ] [ ]
(12"+=) *(FTANA 1-12)* – ('A'version) / Caveman flashlight.

Feb 87. (lp/c)(cd) *(SF LP/MC 1)(830861-2) <42050>* **FLASH LIGHT** [99] [ ]
– Cry mercy, judge / Say a prayer / A town called Walker / Song / The scientist writes a letter / Bomb / 4 a.m. / The funniest thing / Annie's tellin' me / One time at sundown.

Mar 87. (7") *(FTANA 2)* **CRY MERCY JUDGE. / CALL ME THE CIRCLING** [ ] [ ]
(12"+=) *(FTANA 2-12)* – At this moment (live) / Lover of the night (live) / Strange things happening.

Jun 87. (7") *(VLANE 3)* **THE FUNNIEST THING. / ONE TIME AT SUNDOWN** [ ] [ ]
(12"+=) *(VLANE 3-12)* – Marquee Moon ('87 version).

Aug 87. (7") *(VLANE 4)* **THE SCIENTIST WRITES A LETTER. / ('A'-Paris version)** [ ] [ ]

Oct 89. (7") *(VLANE 5)* **SHIMMER. / BOMB** [ ] [ ]
(12"+=)(cd-s+=) *(VLANE 5-12)(VLACD 5)* – The scientist writes a letter.

Mar 90. (7") *(VLANE 6)* **KALEIDOSCOPIN'. / SIXTEEN TULIPS** [ ] [ ]
(12"+=)(cd-s+=) *(VLANE 6-12)(VLACD 6)* – Vanity fair.

Apr 90. (cd/c/lp) *(842420-2/-4/-1)* **THE WONDER** [ ] [ ]
– Kaleidoscopin' / August / Ancient Egypt / Shimmer / Stalingrad / Pillow / Storm / 5 hours from Calais / Cooleridge / Prayer.

Rough Trade / Rykodisc

Apr 92. (cd/lp) *(R 288-2/-1) <10216>* **WARM AND COOL**
– Those harbour lights / Sleepwalkin' / The deep dark clouds / Saucer crash / Depot (1951) / Boulevard / Harley Quinn / Sor Juanna / Depot (1957) / Spiritual / Little dance / Ore.

– compilation –

Apr 96. (cd) *Virgin; (CDVDM 9034)* **A MILLER'S TALE (The Tom Verlaine Story)** [ ] [ ]

RICHARD LLOYD

— solo augmented by **JIM MAESTRO** – guitar (ex-BONGOS) / **MATTHEW MacKENZIE** – guitar, piano / **MICHAEL YOUNG** – guitar, synthesizer / **FRED SMITH** – bass / **VINNY DeNUNZIO** – drums

Elektra / Elektra

Jan 80. (lp) *(K 52196)* **ALCHEMY** [ ] [ ]
– Misty eyes / In the night / Alchemy / Womans ways / Number nine / Should've known better / Blue and grey / Summer rain / Pretend / Dying words.

Apr 80. (7") **BLUE AND GREY. / PRETEND** [-] [ ]

— Enlisted new line-up.

Mistlur / Mistlur

Jan 86. (lp) *(MLR 046)* **FIELD OF FIRE** [ ] [ ]

Celluloid / GrandSlamm

Oct 87. (lp/c/cd) *(CELL 6135/+C/CD)* **REAL TIME (live)** [ ] [ ]
– Fire engine / Misty eyes / Alchemy / Spider talk / Lost child / No.9 / The only

feeling / Soldier blue / Field of fire / Pleading / Watch yourself / Louisianna Anna / Black to white. *(cd+=)* – Watch yourself / Losin' Anne / Black to white.

— LLOYD went onto join JOHN DOE (ex-X)

TELEVISION

— re-formed with **VERLAINE, LLOYD, FICCA + SMITH**

Capitol Capitol

Sep 92. (cd/c/lp) *<(CD/TC+/EST 2181)>* **TELEVISION**
– 1880 or so / Shane, she wrote this / In world / Call Mr. Lee / Rhyme / No glamour for Willi / Beauty trip / The rocket / This fire / Mars.

TELEVISION PERSONALITIES

Formed: Chelsea, London, England . . . 1976 by schoolmates DAN TREACY and EDWARD BALL, who found JOE FOSTER and later added brothers JOHN and GERARD BENNETT. After originally going under the moniker of TEEN 78, they came up with the name TV PERSONALITIES, parading themselves as HUGHIE GREEN, BRUCE FORSYTHE, BOB MONKHOUSE, RUSSELL HARTY and NICHOLAS PARSONS. Their first 45, '14th FLOOR', was released in the early summer of 1978, and with the help of airplay from John Peel, sold out of its 867 print run. The TVP's soon formed their own 'King's Road' label, (distributed initially by 'Rough Trade') and released an EP, 'WHERE'S BILL GRUNDY NOW?', which included the superb title track, alongside another sarcastic gem, 'PART-TIME PUNKS'. Around this time ED and GERARD were also part of The O-LEVEL, who, after one 45, became The TEENAGE FILMSTARS (with DAN and JOE). In 1980, after a short retirement, they gigged for the first time and issued the 'SMASHING TIME' single, a more retro-themed affair as the band moved increasingly towards punk-influenced psychedelic whimsy. Their recordings over the course of the previous year were issued on the album, 'AND DON'T THE KIDS JUST LOVE IT' (1981), a record that paid homage (of sorts!) to one of the band's mentors in the shape of the classic 'I KNOW WHERE SYD BARRETT LIVES' alongside naively charming cockney tales, 'GEOFFREY INGRAM' and 'JACKANORY STORIES'. A year later, DAN and ED set up their own label, 'Whaam!', although they were subsequently forced to fold it after a only few releases (including two TVP albums, 'MUMMY YOU'RE NOT WATCHING ME' and 'THEY COULD HAVE BEEN BIGGER THAN THE BEATLES') due to pressure from pop duo, WHAM. As a result, the proposed 1983 release of 'THE PAINTED WORD', was shelved and the album later released by 'Illuminated', early in '85. Later that year, they chose another name for their recording venture, 'Dreamworld', although this too became defunct, even after signing The MIGHTY LEMON DROPS. The TVP's (now minus BALL who had been replaced with former SWELL MAPS man, JOWE HEAD) broke their long silence in 1989 when 'Fire' records finally issued their remarkable comeback 45, 'SALVADOR DALI'S GARDEN PARTY', soon to be included on the following year's 'PRIVILEGE' set. By 1992's 'CLOSER TO GOD' they had lost their initial impact and TREACY became more heavily into drugs, leading to bouts of depression and little creative output. In the Autumn of '95, he was back to his near best with the sarcastic 'I WAS A MOD BEFORE YOU WERE A MOD'. • **Songwriters:** DAN and ED penned most, until latters' departure. Covered BIKE (Pink Floyd) / NO ONE'S LITTLE GIRL (Raincoats) / SEASONS IN THE SUN (Jacques Brel). • **Trivia:** While in the studio, DAN once tried to decapitate another member at the time, MARK SHEPPARD, although producer, DALE GRIFFIN, reportedly locked him in the cupboard!

Album rating: AND DON'T THE KIDS JUST LOVE IT (*8) / MUMMY YOU'RE NOT WATCHING ME (*6) / THEY COULD HAVE BEEN BIGGER THAN THE BEATLES (*6) / THE PAINTED WORD (*7) / PRIVILEGE (*8) / CLOSER TO GOD (*6) / I WAS A MOD BEFORE YOU WERE A MOD (*6) / YES DARLING, BUT IS IT ART? compilation (*7)

DAN TREACY – vocals / **EDWARD BALL** – organ, vocals / **JOE FOSTER** – guitar / **JOHN BENNETT** – bass / **GERARD BENNETT** – drums

W1 Teen not iss.

May 78. (7"; as TV PERSONALITIES) *(SRTS-CUS 77089)* **14th FLOOR. / OXFORD STREET** [ ] [-]
(re-iss. Aug89 on 'Overground', 7" + yellow or white; OVER 03)

— now as trio (ED, DAN & JOE)

Kings Road not iss.

Nov 78. (7"ep) *(LYN 5976-7)* **WHERE'S BILL GRUNDY NOW?** [ ] [-]
– Part-time punks / Where's Bill Grundy now? / Happy families / Posing at the Roundhouse. *(re-iss. Nov79 on 'Rough Trade', RT 033)*

— disbanded for a year. **MARK 'EMPIRE' SHEPPARD** – drums (of SWELL MAPS)

Rough Trade not iss.

Jul 80. (7") *(RT 051)* **SMASHING TIME. / KING AND COUNTRY** [ ] [-]

— JOE FOSTER left and soon became The MISSING SCIENTISTS who released a 45 in Sep80 'BIG CITY BRIGHT LIGHTS'. / 'DISCOTEQUE X', which featured DAN TREACY and DANIEL MILLER of Mute label.

Jan 81. (lp; as TV PERSONALITIES) *(ROUGH 24)* **AND DON'T THE KIDS JUST LOVE IT** [ ] [-]
– I know where Syd Barrett lives / This angry silence / The glittering prizes / Silly girl / Jackanory stories / Geoffrey Ingram / La grande illusion / Look back in anger. *(re-iss. Jan84; same) (cd-iss. Aug91 on 'Fire'; REFIRECD 7)*

Feb 81. (7") *(RT 063)* **I KNOW WHERE SYD BARRETT LIVES. / ARTHUR THE GARDENER** [ ] [-]

— were now just **DAN + EMPIRE** + new bassman BERNARD COOPER (ED BALL had formed The TIMES.)

Whaam! not iss.

May 81. (7"; as GIFTED CHILDREN) *(WHAAM 001)* **PAINTING BY NUMBERS. / LICHTENSTEIN GIRL** [ ] [-]

— **ED** returned on guitar & bass. SLAUGHTER JOE FOSTER also returned.

Jan 82. (lp) *(WHAAM 3)* **MUMMY YOU'RE NOT WATCHING ME** [ ] [-]
– Adventure playground / A day in heaven / Scream quietly / Mummy you're not watching me / Brians magic ear / Where the rainbow ends / David Hockney's diaries / Painting by numbers / Lichtenstein painting / Magnificent dreams If I could write poetry. *(re-iss. Jun86 on 'Dreamworld'; BIG DREAM 4) (re-iss. Sep91 on 'Fire' cd/lp; REFIRE CD/LP 8)*

Aug 82. (lp) *(BIG 5)* **THEY COULD HAVE BEEN BIGGER THAN THE BEATLES** [ ] [-]
– Three wishes / David Hockney's diary / In a perfumed garden / Flowers for Abigail / King and country / The boy in the Paisley shirt / Games for boys / Painter man / Psychedelic holiday / 14th floor / Sooty's disco party / Makin time / When Emily cries / The glittering prizes / Anxiety block / Mysterious ways.. *(re-iss. Jun86 on 'Dreamworld'; BIG DREAM 2) (re-iss. Sep91 on 'Fire' cd/lp; REFIRE CD/LP 9)*

Sep 82. (7"m) *(WHAAM 4)* **THREE WISHES. / GEOFFREY INGRAM / AND DON'T THE KIDS JUST LOVE IT** [ ] [-]

— **DAN + ED** added **DAVE MUSKER** – organ / **JOE FOSTER** – guitar / **MARK FLUNDER** – bass / (JOWE HEAD repl. MARK who joined ROBYN HITCHCOCK)

Rough Trade not iss.

Dec 83. (7") *(RT 109)* **A SENSE OF BELONGING. / PARADISE ESTATE** [ ] [-]
(below lp should have been issued by 'Whaam!' in Nov83)

Illuminated not iss.

Jan 85. (lp) *(JAMS 37)* **THE PAINTED WORD** [ ] [-]
– Stop and smell the roses / The painted word / A life of her own / Bright sunny smiles / Mentioned in dispatches / A sense of belonging / Say you won't cry / Someone to share my life with / You'll have to scream louder / Happy all the time / The girl who had everything / Paradise estates / Back to Vietnam. *(re-iss. Sep91 on 'Fire' cd/lp; REFIRE CD/LP 10)*

— now with **JOWE HEAD** – bass / **JEFF BLOOM** – drums (FOSTER became SLAUGHTER JOE and MUSKER formed JASMINE MINKS. ED continued with The TIMES and later went solo

Dreamworld not iss.

Feb 86. (12"m) *(DREAM 4)* **HOW I LEARNED TO LOVE THE . . .BOMB! / THEN GOD SNAPS HIS FINGERS. / NO YOU'RE JUST BEING RIDICULOUS** [ ] [-]

Nov 86. (7"m) *(DREAM 10)* **HOW I LEARNED TO LOVE THE BOMB. / GROCER'S DAUGHTER / GIRL CALLED CHARITY** [ ] [-]

— (next album was to have been issued a year earlier on 'Dreamworld')

— **JOWE HEAD** – bass (ex-SWELL MAPS) repl. BALL.

Fire not iss.

Oct 89. (7") *(BLAZE 37S)* **SALVADOR DALI'S GARDEN PARTY. / ROOM AT THE TOP OF THE STAIRS** [ ] [-]
(12"+=) *(BLAZE 37T)* – This time there is no happy ending / Part one: Fulfilling the contractual obligations.

Dec 89. (ltd.7") *(CAFF 5)* **I STILL BELIEVE IN MAGIC. / RESPECTABLE** [ ] [-]
(above single on 'Caff' label)

Feb 90. (cd/c/lp) *(FIRE CD/MC/LP 21)* **PRIVILEGE** [ ] [-]
– Paradise is for the blessed / Conscience tells me no / All my dreams are dead / The man who paints the rainbows / Sad Mona Lisa / Sometimes I think you know me / Privilege / Good and faithful servant / My hedonistic tendencies / Salvador Dali's garden party / What if it's raining? / The engine driver song / Better than I know myself. *(c+=/cd+=)* – (3 tracks).

Sep 91. (12"ep/cd-ep) *(BLAZE 48 T/CD)* **STRANGELY BEAUTIFUL / REACHING FOR THE STARS. / NOT EVEN A MAYBE / ('A'-Chill out mix)** [ ] [-]

Feb 92. (12"ep/cd-ep) *(BLAZE 440/550 49)* **SHE NEVER READ MY POEMS / THE DAY THE DOPLINS LEAVE THE SEA. / CHRIST KNOWS I HAVE TRIED / ('A'extended)** [ ] [-]

Sep 92. (7"/cd-s) *(TWANG 15/+CD)* **WE WILL BE OUR GURUS. / AN EXHIBITION BY JOAN MIRO / LOVE IS BETTER THAN WAR** [ ] [-]
(above on 'Seminal Twang')

Oct 92. (cd/c/d-lp) *(FIRE CD/MC/LP 032)* **CLOSER TO GOD** [ ] [-]
– You don't know how lucky you are / Hard luck story No. 30 / Little works of art / Razorblades and lemonade / Coming home soon / Me and big ideas / Honey for the bears / I see myself in you / Goodnight Mr. Spaceman / My very nervous breakdown / We will be your gurus / You are special and you always will be / Not for the likes of us / You're younger than you know / Very dark today / I hope you have a nice day / Baby you're only as good as you should be / Closer to God.

May 93. (7"/cd-s) *(BLAZE 65)* **GOODNIGHT MR. SPACEMAN. / IF I WAS YOUR GIRLDRIEND** [ ] [-]
(cd-s+=) *(BLAZE 65CD)* – She loves it when he sings like Elvis / ('A'-Lost in space mix).

Vinyl Japan not iss.

May 94. (12"ep/cd-ep) *(TASK 28)* **FAR AWAY AND LOST IN JOY / I DON'T WANT TO LIVE THIS LIFE. / DO YOU KNOW WHAT THEY'RE SAYING ABOUT ME NOW? / I GET FRIGHTENED** [ ] [-]

Oct 95. (12"ep/cd-ep) *(TASK/+CD 048)* **DO YOU THINK IF YOU WERE BEAUTIFUL YOU'D BE HAPPY / HE USED TO PAINT IN COLOURS / WHO WILL BE YOUR PRINCE / I SUPPOSE YOU THINK IT'S FUNNY** [ ] [-]

Overground not iss.

Sep 95. (lp/cd; as TV PERSONALITIES) *(OVER 41/+CD)* **I WAS A MOD BEFORE YOU WAS A MOD** [ ] [-]
– As John Belushi said / I was a mod before you were a mod / A stranger to myself / Little Woody Allen / A long time gone / Evan doesn't ring me anymore / Things have changed since I was girl / Haunted / I can see my whole world crashing down / Something flew over my head / Everything she touches turns to gold. *(re-iss. Jun97; same)*

Twist not iss.

Jan 96. (7"m) *(TWIST 20)* **SEASONS IN THE SUN. / BIKE / NO ONE'S LITTLE GIRL** [ ] [-]

– compilations, etc. –

1985. (lp) *Pastell; (POW 2)* **CHOCOLAT-ART (A TRIBUTE TO JAMES LAST) (live Germany 1984)** [-] [-] German
(re-iss. Jul93 cd/lp; POW 2)

Aug 91. (lp/cd; as TV PERSONALITIES) *Overground; (OVER 21/+CD)* **CAMPING IN FRANCE (live '85)** [ ] [-]

1994. (lp/cd; as TV PERSONALITIES) *Overground; (OVER 30/+CD)* **HOW I LEARNED TO LOVE THE BOMB** [ ] [-]
(re-iss. Jun97; same)

Feb 95. (cd) *Fire; (FLIPCD 001)* **YES DARLING BUT IS IT ART?** [ ] [-]

Mar 96. (cd; as TV PERSONALITIES) *Overground; (OVER 48CD)* **TOP GEAR** [ ] [-]

1996. (7"/cd-s) *Overground; (OVER 50/+CD)* **I WAS A MOD BEFORE YOU WERE A MOD** [ ] [-]

Jun 97. (cd; as TV PERSONALITIES) *Overground; (OVER 52/+CD)* **PAISLEY SHIRTS & MINI SKIRTS** [ ] [-]

TELSTAR PONIES

Formed: Glasgow, Scotland . . . 1994 by ex-18 WHEELER man, DAVID KEENAN and ex-TEENAGE FANCLUB japester, BRENDAN O'HARE. With the intention of moving as far away as possible from the Scots-indie-by-numbers of KEENAN's former band, the pair eventually roped in GAVIN LAIRD and RACHEL DEVINE and set about creating a sound more in tune with cosmic sounds of CAN, FAUST etc. Signed to 'Fire' records, the band released the relatively hummable 'MAPS AND STARCHARTS' as their debut single that year, progressing to the more experimental 'NOT EVEN STARCROSSED' in summer '95. The full extent of their stellar-rock experimentation was revealed later that year on the debut album, 'IN THE SPACE OF A FEW MINUTES', while the subsequent addition of organist RICHARD YOUNGS added a further dimension to the band's sound. Follow-up set, 'VOICES FROM THE NEW MUSIC' (1996), featured some of the band's most adventurous compositions to date, not least the marathon 'DOES YOUR HEART HAVE WINGS'. Yet by the end of the year, O'HARE and LAIRD had broken ranks to form their own outfit, the short-lived MACROCOSMICA, the former later enjoying a brief tenure with fellow Glaswegian sound/noise sculptors, the mighty MOGWAI.

Album rating: IN THE SPACE OF A FEW MINUTES (*8) / VOICES FROM THE NEW MUSIC (*7)

DAVID KEENAN – guitar, vocals (ex-18 WHEELER) / **RACHEL DEVINE** – guitar, piano, vocals / **GAVIN LAIRD** – bass / **BRENDAN O'HARE** – drums (ex-TEENAGE FANCLUB)

Fire / Velvel

Nov 94. (7") *(BLAZE 74)* **MAPS & STARCHARTS. /** [ ] [-]
(cd-s+=) *(BLAZE 74CD)* –

Apr 95. (10"ep/cd-ep) *(BLAZE 85 T/CD)* **NOT EVEN STARCROSSED. /** [ ] [-]

Oct 95. (7") *(BLAZE 94)* **HER NAME. /** [ ] [-]
(cd-s+=) *(BLAZE 94CD)* –

Oct 95. (cd/lp) *(FIRE CD/LP 52)* **IN THE SPACE OF A FEW MINUTES** [ ] [-]

May 96. (12"/cd-s) *(BLAZE 100 T/CD)* **DOES YOUR HEART HAVE WINGS** [ ] [-]

—— added **RICHARD YOUNGS** – keyboards

Sep 96. (7") *(BLAZE 110)* **BREWERY OF EGGSHELLS. /** [ ] [-]
(cd-s+=) *(BLAZE 110CD)* –

Oct 96. (cd/d-lp) *(FIRE CD/LP 60)* <97100> **VOICES FROM THE NEW MUSIC** [ ] [ ] Mar97
– Bells for Albert Ayler / Voices from the new music / The last outpost / Shizuka / Little cloud / Little cloud / Brewery of eggshells / Aegis falling / Sail her on / Feather on the breath / Fall of little summer / Does your heart have wings? / Song of Ansuz / Vienna.

Jan 97. (cd-s) *(BLAZE 112CD)* **VOICES FROM THE NEW MUSIC /** [ ] [-]

—— **KEENAN** + **DEVINE** carried on when LAIRD + O'HARE formed MACROCOSMICA (the latter sunsequently joined MOGWAI in June '97)

TEMPLE OF THE DOG (see under ⇒ SOUNDGARDEN)

TEN BENSON

Formed: London, England-based . . . mid 90's out of various outfits by frontman CHRIS TECKKAM (sole survivor of SWIMMER, an act which delivered one long-player, 'PETITS POIS' in '96), the Oriental NAPOLEON CATILO (former SHIVA EFFECT drummer, a band who had one solitary 1993 single plus a 1994 album, 'YAHWEH' for 'Frog') and bassist DUNCAN LOVATT. Reclusive in nature, these overtly weird, psychedelic hillbillies mix'n'matched a variety of influences including FRANK ZAPPA, MEDICINE HEAD and GORKY'S ZYGOTIC MYNCI. Three 45's appeared between 1997 and '98, the best of which, 'EVIL CLAW', stupified the listener into believing this might be HANK WILLIAMS and ROY ROGERS re-incarnated in some sort of manic duo. A mini-cd, '6 FINGERS OF BENSON' (1998), will surely see the band play a live gig, although a Reading Festival appearance was pencilled in. No doubt there was something far stronger than ten Benson (& Hedges) getting smoked that day.

Album rating: 6 FINGERS OF BENSON mini (*6)

SWIMMER

CHRIS TECKKAM – vocals, guitar / with

Quixotic / Quixotic

Apr 94. (10") *(QX 009-10)* **WHIPPINGS. /** [ ] [ ]

Aug 94. (7") *(QXUK 001-7)* **SHE. /** [ ] [-]
(10"+=/cd-s+=) *(QXUK 001 10/CD)* –

Sweet / not iss.

Jun 95. (7") *(SWEE 001-7)* **BREAKFAST WITH OMAR. /** [ ] [-]
(cd-s+=) *(SWEE 001-CD)* –

Jun 96. (cd) *(SWEE 004CD)* **PETITS POIS** [ ] [-]

—— above not to be confused with another band of the same name, who issued 12" singles for the 'Spirit' imprint.

TEN BENSON

CHRIS TECKKAM – vocals, guitar / **DUNCAN LOVATT** – bass / **NAPOLEON LOVATT** – drums (ex-SHIVA EFFECT)

Sweet / not iss.

Sep 97. (7") *(SWEE 008)* **CITY HOPPERS. / TRANSPORT OVERSEAS** [ ] [-]

Feb 98. (7") *(SWEE 010)* **THE CLAW. / BARDOT STYLE** [ ] [-]

Deceptive / not iss.

Jun 98. (7") *(BLUFF 062)* **EVIL HEAT. / UNCLE BENSON** [ ] [-]

Jul 98. (m-cd) *(BLUFF 063CD)* **6 FINGERS OF BENSON** (compilation) [ ] [-]
– Evil heat / Bardot style / The claw / Transport overseas / Uncle Benson / City hoppers.

Nov 98. (7"ep/cd-ep) *(BLUFF 066/+CD)* **UNITED COLORS OF BENSON EP** [ ] [-]
– Mystery man / Hell this hour / Mad ferret / Luvly guy.

TENPOLE TUDOR

Formed: London, England . . . late 70's by EDDIE TUDOR-POLE, who recruited former VISITORS members GARY LONG, DICK CRIPPEN and BOB KINGSTON. EDDIE enjoyed initial exposure through Malcolm McLaren's SEX PISTOLS' cash-in, 'The Great Rock'n'Roll Swindle', co-writing some of the material and performing the inimitable 'WHO KILLED BAMBI?'. TENPOLE TUDOR the band made their vinyl debut with the 'REAL FUN' single on 'Korova' records. Subsequently signing to New Wave specialists, 'Stiff', the band crashed into the UK Top 10 with tongue-in-cheek, chest-beating anthem, 'SWORDS OF A THOUSAND MEN', hitting the Top 50 a further twice with 'WUNDERBAR' and 'THROWING MY BABY OUT WITH THE BATH WATER'. Two albums, 'EDDIE, OLD BOB, DICK AND GARY' (1981) and 'LET THE FOUR WINDS BLOW' (1981) were released within the space of a year and by 1982, the medieval japery was wearing just a tad thin. The band subsequently split in two with LONG, CRIPPEN and KINGSTON forming the short-lived TUDORS while EDDIE released a hillbilly-influenced novelty record, 'HAYRICK SONG'. TUDOR-POLE would go on to reform TENPOLE TUDOR during breaks in his acting career, the singer appearing in films such as 'Absolute Beginners' and 'Straight To Hell' before landing the position of host for Channel 4's cult gameshow, 'The Crystal Maze'. • **Songwriters:** EDDIE wrote most of material, except; ROCK'N'ROLL MUSIC (Chuck Berry). • **Trivia:** EDDIE is a staunch SNP political supporter.

Album rating: EDDIE, OLD BOB, DICK & GARRY (*5)

EDDIE TENPOLE (b. 6 Dec'55, Scotland) – vocals / **OLD BOB KINGSTON** – guitar, vocals / **DICK CRIPPEN** – bass, vocals / **GARRY LONG** – drums, vocals. Augmented at times by **MUNCH UNIVERSE** – guitar

Korova / not iss.

Feb 80. (7") *(KOW 4)* **REAL FUN. / WHAT'S IN A WORD** [ ] [-]

Stiff / not iss.

Oct 80. (7") *(BUY 98)* **THREE BELLS IN A ROW. / FASHION / ROCK'N'ROLL MUSIC** [ ] [-]

Mar 81. (7") *(BUY 109)* **SWORDS OF A THOUSAND MEN. / LOVE AND FOOD** [6] [-]

Mar 81. (lp/c) *(SEEZ/ZSEEZ 31)* **EDDIE, OLD BOB, DICK & GARRY** [4] [-]
– Swords of a thousand men / Go wilder / I wish / Tell me more / Header now / There are boys / Wunderbar / Judy annual / What else can I do / I can't sleep / Anticipation / Confessions. *(cd-iss. Jan92 on 'Repertoire'; REP 4220WY)*

Jul 81. (7") *(BUY 120)* **WUNDERBAR. / TENPOLE 45** [16] [-]

Oct 81. (7") *(BUY 129)* **THROWING MY BABY OUT WITH THE BATHWATER. / CONGO TRIBE** [49] [-]

Nov 81. (lp/c) *(SEEZ/ZSEEZ 42)* **LET THE FOUR WINDS BLOW** [ ] [-]
– Let the four winds blow / Throwing my baby out with the bathwater / Trumpeters / It's easy to see / Sea of thunder / What you doing in Bombay / Local animal / Her fruit is forbidden / Tonight is the night / The unpaid debt / The King of Siam. *(cd-iss. Feb94 on 'Disky'; STIFFCD 12)*

Feb 82. (7") *(BUY 137)* **LET THE FOUR WINDS BLOW. / SEA OF THUNDER** [ ] [-]

—— disbanded mid-1982

– compilation, etc. –

Dec 92. (cd) *Dojo; (DOJOCD 76)* **WUNDERBAR – THE BEST OF TENPOLE TUDOR** [ ] [-]
– Three bells in a row / Swords of a thousand men / Go wilder / Header now / Wunderbar / What else can I do / I can't sleep / Confessions / Tell me more / Throwing my baby out with the bathwater / Let the four winds blow / Tonight is the night / What you doing in Bombay / Her fruit is forbidden / Sea of thunder / The Hayrick song.

EDDIE TEN POLE

(solo, first single with SEX PISTOLS)

Virgin / not iss.

Sep 81. (7") *(VS 443)* **WHO KILLED BAMBI? / ROCK AROUND THE CLOCK** [ ] [-]

Stiff / not iss.

Apr 83. (7"/12") *(BUY/+IT 177)* **THE HAYRICK SONG. / TAKE YOU TO THE DANCE** [ ] [-]

The TUDORS

went own way.

Stiff / not iss.

Feb 83. (7") *(BUY 172)* **TIED UP WITH LOU COOL. / CRY BABY CRY** [ ] [-]

10,000 MANIACS

Formed: Jamestown, New York, USA . . . 1981 by NATALIE MERCHANT and J.C. LOMBARDO, who had been part of the band, STILL LIFE. Initially a new wave covers outfit, the group (which was completed by ROBERT BUCK, STEVEN GUSTAFSON, DENNIS DREW and JERRY AUGUSTYNAK) debuted on the obscure 'Christian Burial' label in 1982 with the mini-album, 'HUMAN CONFLICT NUMBER FIVE'. After a further full-length set, 'THE SECRETS OF THE I-CHING' (1984), which scaled the UK indie chart and won praise from Radio 1 guru John Peel, the group secured an international deal with 'Elektra'. Produced by veteran folk man, Joe Boyd, 'THE WISHING CHAIR' (1985) saw the band develop their eclectic, rootsy sound, although it wasn't until the release of 'IN MY TRIBE' (1987) that 10,000 MANIACS began to reap some commercial rewards to match their growing critical acclaim. By this point LOMBARDO had departed after the previous years heavy touring alongside R.E.M., the group further changing their strategy by enlisting the services of another seasoned producer, Pte Asher. The result was a sparer sound and sharpened songwriting which emphasised MERCHANT's hypnotically plangent vocals, the group scoring minor US hits with 'LIKE THE WEATHER' and 'WHAT'S THE MATTER HERE'. A cover of Cat Stevens' 'PEACE TRAIN' failed to chart, the band later withdrawing the track from subsequent pressings following hardline Islamic comments made by the former singer/songwriter. Perhaps as a result, the follow-up set, 'BLIND MAN'S ZOO' (1989), took a more political stance, though the enigmatic MERCHANT stopped short of preaching, the album becoming a transatlantic Top 20 hit. Following the accompanying tour, the band took a brief sabbatical, eventually returning in September '92 with another successful set, 'OUR TIME IN EDEN'. The minor hit, 'CANDY EVERYBODY WANTS', was backed with a suitably lugubrious reading of Morrissey's 'EVERYDAY IS LIKE SUNDAY' while CD formats included a MERCHANT/MICHAEL STIPE duet on a version of R.E.M.'s country-tinged classic,~~ 'DON'T GO BACK TO ROCKVILLE'. By the release of the languorous 'MTV UNPLUGGED' (1993) set, however, MERCHANT was disillusioned with the group's attitude and left soon after for a solo career. While 10,000 MANIACS replaced MERCHANT with ex-member, J.C. LOMBARDO and new frontwoman MARY RAMSEY, the group's former focal point almost made the US Top 20 in summer '95 with her debut solo set, 'TIGERLILY'. • **Songwriters:** lyrics – NATALIE / music – JC LOMBARDO until his departure. MERCHANT was then the main writer with DREW or BUCK. Covered: I HOPE THAT I DON'T FALL IN LOVE WITH YOU (Tom Waits) / STARMAN – MOONAGE DAYDREAM (David Bowie) / THESE DAYS (Jackson Browne) / BECAUSE THE NIGHT (Patti Smith Group) / MORE THAN THIS (Bryan Ferry).

Album rating: THE WISHING CHAIR (*8) / IN MY TRIBE (*9) / HOPE CHEST (*8) / BLIND MAN'S ZOO (*8) / OUR TIME IN EDEN (*8)

NATALIE MERCHANT (b.26 Oct'63) – vocals / **ROBERT BUCK** (b. 1 Aug'58) – guitar, synthesizers / **J.C. LOMBARDO** (b. JOHN, 30 Sep'52) – rhythm guitar, bass / **STEVEN GUSTAFSON** (b.10 Apr'57, Madrid, Spain) – bass, guitar / **DENNIS DREW** (b. 8 Aug'57, Buffalo, N.Y.) – organ / **JERRY AUGUSTYNAK** (b. 2 Sep'58, Lackawanna, N.Y.) – drums

not iss. / Christian Burial

1982. (m-lp) *(>* **HUMAN CONFLICT NUMBER FIVE** [-] [ ]
– Orange / Planed obsolescence / Anthem for doomed youth / Groove dub / Tension. *(UK-iss.Jun84 on 'Press'; P 2010)*

Jan 84. (lp) **THE SECRETS OF I-CHING** [-] [ ]
– Grey victory / Pour de Chirico / Death of Manolette / Tension / Daktari / Pit viper / Katrina's fair / The Latin one / My mother the war. *(UK-iss.Aug84 on 'Press'; P 3001)*

Reflex / Reflex

Mar 84. (12"m) *(RE 1)* **MY MOTHER THE WAR (remix). / PLANNED OBSOLESCENCE / NATIONAL EDUCATION WEEK** [ ] [ ]

Elektra / Elektra

Jun 85. (7") *(EKR 11)* **CAN'T IGNORE THE TRAIN. / DAKTARI** [ ] [ ]
(12"+=) *(EKR 11T)* – Grey victory / The colonial wing.

Nov 85. (lp/c) *(EKT 14/+C)* **THE WISHING CHAIR** [ ] [ ]
– Can't ignore the train / Just as the tide was a-flowing / Scorpio rising / Lilydale / Maddox table / Everyone a puzzle lover / Arbor day / Back o' the Moon / Tension takes a tangle / Among the Americans / Grey victory / Cotton alley / My mother the war. *(cd-iss. 1989; 960 428-2)*

Nov 85. (7"w/drawn) *(EKR 19)* **JUST AS THE TIDE WAS A-FLOWING. / AMONG THE AMERICANS** [-] [ ]

Jan 86. (7") *(EKR 28)* **SCORPIO RISING. / ARBOR DAY** [ ] [ ]

—— Depleted to a quintet, when LOMBARDO departed.

Aug 87. (7") *(EKR 61)* **PEACE TRAIN. / THE PAINTED DESERT** [ ] [ ]

Aug 87. (lp/c)(cd) *(EKT 41/+C)(960 738-2)* <60738> **IN MY TRIBE** [ ] [37]
– What's the matter here? / Hey Jack Kerouac / Like the weather / Cherry tree / Painted desert / Don't talk / Peace train / Gun shy / Sister Rose / A campfire song / City of angels / Verdi cries. *(initial copies cont. Elektra sampler with X / The CALL; SAM 390)*

Nov 87. (7") *(EKR 64)* **DON'T TALK. / CITY OF ANGELS** [ ] [ ]
(12"+=) *(EKR 64T)* – Goodbye (Tribal outtake).

Mar 88. (7") *(EKR 71)* **WHAT'S THE MATTER HERE?. / VERDI CRIES** [ ] [-]
(12"+=/cd-s+=) *(EKR 71T)* – Like the weather (live) / Gun shy (live).

Jul 88. (7") *(EKR 77)* <69418> **LIKE THE WEATHER. / A CAMPFIRE SONG** [ ] [68] May88
(12"+=/12"w-poster) *(EKR 77T/+W)* – Poison in the well (live) / Verdi cries (live).

Jul 88. (7") <69388> **WHAT'S THE MATTER HERE? / CHERRY TREE** [-] [80]

May 89. (lp/c)(cd) *(EKT 57/+C)(960 815-2)* <60815> **BLIND MAN'S ZOO** [18] [13]
– Eat for two / Please forgive us / The big parade / Trouble me / You happy puppet / Headstrong / Poison in the well / Dust bowl / The lion's share / Hateful hate / Jubilee.

Jun 89. (7"/c-s) *(EKR 93)* <69298> **TROUBLE ME. / THE LION'S SHARE** [ ] [44]
(12"+=/3"cd-s+=/3"s-cd-s+=) *(EKR 93 T/CD/CDX)* – Party of God.

Sep 89. (7") <69253> **YOU HAPPY PUPPET. / GUNSHY** [-] [ ]

Nov 89. (7"ep) *(EKR 100)* **EAT FOR TWO / WILDWOOD FLOWER. / DON'T CALL US / FROM THE TIME YOU SAY GOODBYE** [ ] [-]
(12"/12"w/poster/3"cd-s) *(EKR 100 T/TW/CD)* – (1st & 2nd track) / Gun shy (acoustic) / Hello in there.
(10") *(EKR 100TE)* – (1st & 4th track) / What's the matter here? (acoustic) / Eat for two (acoustic).

Sep 92. (7"/c-s) *(EKR 156/+C)* <64700> **THESE ARE DAYS. / CIRCLE DREAM** [58] [66]
(cd-s+=) *(EKR 156CD)* – I hope that I don't fall in love with you.
(cd-s) *(EKR 156CDX)* – ('A'side) / Medley:- Starman – Moonage daydream / These days.

Sep 92. (cd/c/lp) <*(7559 61385-2/-4/-1)*> **OUR TIME IN EDEN** [33] [28]
– Noah's dove / These are days / Eden / Few and far between / Stockton gala days / Gold rush brides / Jezebel / How you've grown / Candy everybody wants / Circle dream / If you intend / I'm not the man. *(cd+=)* – Tolerance.

Feb 93. (c-s,cd-s) <64665> **CANDY EVERYBODY WANTS / I HOPE THAT I DON'T FALL IN LOVE WITH YOU** [-] [67]

Mar 93. (7"/c-s) *(EKR 160/+C)* **CANDY EVERYBODY WANTS. / EVERYDAY IS LIKE SUNDAY** [47] [-]
(cd-s+=) *(EKR 160CD1)* – Don't go back to Rockville (with MICHAEL STIPE co-vocals) / Sally Ann.
(cd-s+=) *(EKR 160CD2)* – Don't go back to Rockville (with MICHAEL STIPE) / ('A' MTV version).
(cd-s) *(EKR 160CD3)* – ('A'side) / Eat for two (live) / My sister Rose (live) / Hey Jack Kerouac (live).

Aug 93. (cd-ep) <66296> **FEW AND FAR BETWEEN / CANDY EVERYBODY WANTS / TO SIR WITH LOVE / LET THE MYSTERY BE** [-] [95]

Oct 93. (7"/c-s) *(EKR 175/+C)* **BECAUSE THE NIGHT. / STOCKTON GALA DAYS** [65] [-]
(cd-s+=) *(EKR 175CD)* – Let the mystery be / Sally Ann.

Oct 93. (c-s,cd-s) <64595> **BECAUSE THE NIGHT / EAT FOR TWO** [-] [11]

Oct 93. (cd/c) <*(7559 61569-2/-4)*> **UNPLUGGED (live)** [40] [13]
– These are days / Eat for two / Candy everybody wants (MTV version) / I'm not the man / Don't talk / Hey Jack Kerouac / What's the matter here / Gold rush brides / Like the weather / Trouble me / Jezebel / Because the night / Stockton gala days / Noah's dove.

—— 10,000 MANIACS split when NATALIE went solo. The rest re-formed in 1995 and added ex-original JOHN LOMBARDO and his (JOHN & MARY duo) partner MARY RAMSAY on vocals and violin.

Geffen / Geffen

Sep 97. (c-s) *(GFSC 22284)* <19411> **MORE THAN THIS /** [ ] [25] Jul97
(12"+=/cd-s+=) *(GFST/+D 22284)* –

Oct 97. (cd) <*(GED 25009)*> **LOVE AMONG THE RUINS** [ ] [ ] Jul97
– Rainy day / Love among the ruins / Even with my eyes closed / Girl on a train / Green children / Room for everything / More than this / Big star / You won't find me there / All that never happens / Shining light / Across the fields.

– compilations, others, etc. –

Oct 90. (lp/c)(cd) *Elektra; (EKT 79/+C)(7599 60962-2)* <60962> **HOPE CHEST** [ ] [ ]
– (HUMAN CONFLICT NUMBER FIVE / THE SECRETS OF I-CHING)

TESTCARD-F (see under ⇒ GEE MR. TRACY)

TEST DEPT

Formed: New Cross, London, England . . . 1982 by PAUL JAMROZY, GRAHAM CUNNINGHAM and ANGUS FARQUAR (in 1983, ALISTAIR ADAMS and TOBY CUDLIP replaced original percussionist, BURDON after their vinyl debut on V/A album, 'The Batcave: Young Limbs And Numb Hymns'). Industrial in the true sense of the word, TEST DEPT are possibly the nearest you'll get to having a steel works in your living room this side of Germany's EINSTURZENDE NEUBAUTEN. Defiantly experimental and rooted in performance art, the group stayed true to their original industrial ethic, employing scrap metal, lead pipes, power tools, et al as "instruments" to reflect the mechanisation of "modern man" and society. Setting up their own 'Ministry Of Power' label (which was initially distributed by Stevo's 'Some Bizzare'), they unleashed their first 12" single, 'COMPULSION', prior to a double 12" set, 'BEATING THE RETREAT' (1984). Overtly political from the outset, TEST DEPT showed their solidarity with the striking Welsh miners, hooking up with the South Wales choir on the appropriately titled album, 'SHOULDER TO SHOULDER'. In between releasing the odd groundbreaking, nay earthquaking album, they drew publicity for their sporadic musical performances, one-off affairs culminating in 1990's appearance at a disused railway works in Glasgow as part of that city's Year Of Culture. They subsequently set about creating their ambitious project on British Imperialism past and present, 'PAX BRITANNICA' (1991), a worthy epitaph for the Thatcher years.

Album rating: BEATING THE RETREAT (*6) / SHOULDER TO SHOULDER (*5) / THE UNACCEPTABLE FACE OF FREEDOM (*5) / A GOOD NIGHT OUT (*5) / TERRA FIRMA (*5) / THE GODODDIN (*5) / PAX BRITANNICA (*5) / PROVEN IN ACTION (*5) / TOTALITY (*5)

PAUL JAMROZY (b. 3 Mar'59) – percussion / **GRAHAM CUNNINGHAM** (b.23 Aug'60) – percussion / **TOBY CUDLIP** (b. 9 Sep'59) – percussion; repl. ... BURDON / **ANGUS FARQUAR** – percussion / added **ALISTAIR ADAMS** (b. 5 Oct'59) – percussion

own / not iss.

1982. (c) **THE STRENGTH OF METAL OF MOTION** [ ] [-]

Some Bizzare / not iss.

Dec 83. (12") *(TEST 1-12)* **COMPULSION. / PULSATIONS** [ ] [-]

Jul 84. (lp/c) *(TEST/+C 2-3)* **BEATING THE RETREAT** [ ] [-]
– The fall from light / Kick to kill / Sweet sedation / Spring into action / Beating the retreat / Total state machine / Plastic / Inheritance / Cold witness. *(re-iss. Dec84 as 'SECOND EDITION BOXED SET' 2x12"; TEST 33) (cd-iss. 1988 on 'Polydor'; 818859-2) <cd-iss. 1997 on 'Thirsty Ear'; 57033>*

Ministry Of Power / not iss.

Mar 85. (lp) *(MOP 1)* **SHOULDER TO SHOULDER (with the South Wales Striking Miners' Choir)** [ ] [-]

— above featured **SARAH JANE** – vocals

Apr 86. (m-lp) *(MOP 2)* **THE UNACCEPTABLE FACE OF FREEDOM** [ ] [-]
– Fuckhead / 51st state of America / Comrade enver hoxha / Fist / Statement / The crusher / Victory / Corridor of cells / The unacceptable face of freedom (face 1, 2 & 3). *(cd-iss. May88 + Apr94; MOPCD 2) <cd-iss. 1997 on 'Thirsty Ear'; 57027>*

Dec 87. (7"/12") *(MOP 13/+12)* **VICTORY. / CHA TILL SINN TUILLE (WE SHALL RETURN NO MORE)** [ ] [-]

Dec 87. (lp) *(MOP 3)* **A GOOD NIGHT OUT** [ ] [-]
– A good night out / Generous term / Victory / Cha till sinn tuille / Demonomania / Voice of reason. *(cd-iss. Jan89 + Apr94; MOP 3CD)*

Sub Rosa / Play It Again Sam

May 88. (12") *(SUB 12005-13)* **NATURE VICTUS. / ?** [ ] [-]

Jun 88. (lp/cd) *(SUB 33/CD 009-12) <BIAS 010-2>* **TERRA FIRMA** [ ] [-]
– Nadka / Siege / Current affairs / Dark eyes / Terra firma.

Media City / not iss.

Mar 89. (12"; with BRITH GOF) *(CMC 004)* **GODODDIN** [ ] [-]
(cd-iss. Nov93 on 'Ministry Of Power')

Ministry Of Power / Invisible

Aug 89. (lp/cd; with BRITH GOF) *(MOP 4/+CD)* **THE GODODDIN** [ ] [-]
– Sarff (Entry of the warriors) / Gwyr a aeth gatraeth (prologue) / Arddyledog ganu (Heroic society) / Glasfedd eu hancwyn (Beserking) / Trichant Eurodorchog (Journey) / Yn nydd cadiawr (Battle) / Truan yw gennyffi (Lament). *(cd re-iss. Sep92; same)*

Nov 90. (12") *(MOP 5)* **JIHAD. / PAX AMERICANA** [ ] [-]

— (next with the SCOTTISH CHAMBER ORCHESTRA)

May 91. (lp/c/cd) *(MOP 6/+C/CD)* **PAX BRITANNICA** [ ] [-]
– Movement I: Pledge – Jerusalem – Heaven's command – Characters of light – Agincourt – Accusation / Movement II: Territory (The epic) / Movement III: From the land / Movement IV: God, king & the law – The cracked fascade – Farewell to the trumpets / Movent V: The legacy.

Sep 91. (lp/cd) *(MOP 7/+CD) <83>* **PROVEN IN ACTION (live)** [ ] [ ]
– Jerusalem / Siege (of Quebec) / Agincourt / Empire / Territory / Wojna (War) / Emigrant / Vastness. *(cd re-iss. Apr96 on 'Sub Rosa'; DEPTCD 002)*

Apr 93. (12"/cd-s) *(MOP 8 T/CD)* **BANG ON IT! / ('A'mix)** [ ] [-]

KK / Invisible

Jul 95. (12"/cd-s) *(KK 136/+CDS)* **TOTALITY 1** [ ] [-]

Nov 95. (d-lp/cd) *(KK 140/+CD) <056>* **TOTALITY** [ ] [ ]
– Once the red dust passes (part 1) / Chillo (sunrise) / Hole / Gripper (a lifetime of knowledge) / Genius / Timebomb / Woza Moya Woza (come spirit come) / The point / Gamma ray / Rolihlahla (stirring up trouble) / Chillio (sunset).

Oct 96. (12") *(KK 139)* **TOTALITY 2 (GENIUS REMIXES)** [ ] [ ]

May 97. (cd) *<088>* **TOTALITY VOL.1-2: REMIXES** [-] [ ]
– Zenergy / Zen essence / Tabla rasa / Genius No.7 (magic number) / Tortured genius / Ingenious / Il est un sac de merde / Tabla.

Feb 98. (cd) *<114>* **TACTICS FOR EVOLUTION** [-] [ ]
– Enigma of Doctor Dee / The unforgiven / Voyager / Atlantis / 2 ghettos / Dark light / Motivation / Miotica / Vena cava (Life blood) / Rat.

– compilations, etc. –

Jul 92. (cd) *Dossier; (EFA 9038)* **ATONAL & HAMBURG (live)** [ ] [-]

Oct 94. (lp/cd) *Jungle; (FREUD/+CD 47)* **THE LEGACY (1990-93)** [ ] [-]

Jan 95. (cd) *Sub Rosa; (DEPTCD 001) / Invisible; <84>* **MATERIA PRIMA** (rec.1990) [ ] [ ]

Oct 95. (cd) *R.O.I.R.; (RUSCD 8213)* **ECSTASY UNDER DURESS** [ ] [-]

that dog.

Formed: Los Angeles, California, USA ... 1991 by ANNA WARONKER (daughter of Warner Brothers producer and top man, LENNY WARONKER), along with sisters RACHEL and PETRA HADEN (daughters of jazz giant, CHARLIE HADEN). Completing the line-up with 'Virgin' records employee, TONY MAXWELL, this well connected quartet issued a solitary single for US indie label, 'Magnatone', before securing a prestigious deal with 'D.G.C.' (4 a.d.-offshoot, 'Guernica' in the UK). Surfing on sassy girly harmonies and shot through with pussysure attitude, the band's eponymous debut album was reminiscent of The BREEDERS on uppers, drawing admiring comments from many an alternative publication. Sophomore effort, 'TOTALLY CRUSHED OUT' (1995), was even more impressive, PETRA once again adding her complementary violin touches while the likes of 'ANYMORE' and 'HOLIDAYS' tempered the grungy assault with a lilting acoustic guitar/strings tapestry. Despite never really entering the alternative premier league, the ladies (and lad!) delivered another slab of lusty, guitar-mangling frustration in the shape of 1997's 'RETREAT FROM THE SUN'.

Album rating: that dog. (*6) / TOTALLY CRUSHED OUT! (*8) / RETREAT FROM THE SUN (*7)

ANNA WARONKER – vocals, guitar / **RACHEL HADEN** – bass / **PETRA HADEN** – violin / **TONY MAXWELL** – drums

not iss. / Magnatone

1992. (d7") **unknown** [-] [ ]

Guernica-4ad / D.G.C.

Nov 93. (cd/lp) *(GU 6 CD/LP) <DGC D/C 99999>* **that dog.** [ ] [ ] Mar94
– Old timer / Jump / Raina / You are here / Just like me / She / Angel / Westside angst / She looks at me / Punk rock girl / Zodiac / You Family functions / She looks at me (reprise) / Paid programming / This boy. *(lp w/free 7")* – BUY ME FLOWERS. / (untitled) *(cd re-iss. Jul98; same)*

Jul 95. (cd) *<DGCD 24735>* **TOTALLY CRUSHED OUT!** [-] [ ]
– Ms. Wrong / Silently / In the back of my mind / He's kissing Christian / Anymore / To keep me / Lip gloss / She doesn't know how / Holidays / Side part / One summer night / Michael Jordan / Rockstar.

Apr 97. (cd) *<DGCD 25115>* **RETREAT FROM THE SUN** [-] [ ]
– I'm gonna see you / Never say never / Being with you / Gagged and tied / Retreat from the sun / Minneapolis / Annie / Every time I try / Long Island / Hawthorne / Did you ever / Cowboy hat / Until the day I die.

THAT PETROL EMOTION

Formed: Derry, N.Ireland ... 1984 by the O'NEILL brothers, SEAN and DAMIAN (both ex-UNDERTONES) along with CIARAN McLAUGHLIN, REAMANN O'GORMAN and US-born frontman, STEVE MACK. Basing themselves in London from the mid-80's onwards, the band made their vinyl debut in summer '85 with the independently released 'KEEN'. A further indie single, 'V2' followed a few months later before 'Demon' took them on for a critically acclaimed ROLI MOSSIMAN-produced debut album, 'MANIC POP THRILL' (1986). Strikingly different from The UNDERTONES' three-chord rush, THAT PETROL EMOTION dealt in a more caustic, politicised brand of alternative pop/rock which embraced elements of 60's garage and psychedelia, their potential subsequently recognised by 'Polydor'. The major label backing paid almost immediate dividends as the band narrowly missed the UK Top 40 with their next single, 'BIG DECISION'. A follow-up album, 'BABBLE' (1987) appeared a couple of months later and landed the band their first and only Top 30 success; despite vocal support from the likes of John Peel and the NME, THAT PETROL EMOTION seemed unable to convert their potential into sales. Moving on to 'Virgin', they came up with the more experimental 'END OF THE MILLENIUM PSYCHOSIS BLUES' (1988), featuring O'NEILL's political coup de grace, 'CELLOPHANE'. Yet he was unhappy with the life of a professional musician and subsequently moved back to Derry. A potentially fatal blow was overcome with the recruitment of JOHN MARCHINI and the songwriting development of McLAUGHLIN, the group attempting a final shot at pop glory with the 'SENSITIZE' and 'HEY VENUS' singles. Both were culled from 1990's 'CHEMICRAZY' album and both fell cruelly short of the Top 40 to the exasperation of the band, their label and their many advocates in the media. Dropped by 'Virgin', the band stuck it out for one final set, 'FIREPROOF' (1993) on their own 'Koogat' label before finally throwing in the towel. • **Songwriters:** Most written by O'NEILL's except covers; ME AND BABY BROTHER (War) / FOR WHAT IT'S WORTH (Buffalo Springfield) / NON-ALIGNMENT PACT (Pere Ubu) / ZIGZAG WANDERER (Captain Beefheart) / HEY BULLDOG (Beatles) / CINNAMON GIRL (Neil Young) / FUNTIME (Iggy Pop).

Album rating: MANIC POP THRILL (*7) / BABBLE (*8) / END OF THE MILLENIUM PSYCHOSIS BLUES (*6) / CHEMICRAZY (*5) / FIREPROOF (*6)

STEVE MACK (b.19 May'63, New York City, USA) – vocals / (ex-EAGER SIN BABIES) / **SEAN O'NEILL** (b. JOHN, 26 Aug'57) – guitar (ex-UNDERTONES) / **DAMIAN O'NEILL** (b.15 Jan'61) – bass, keyboards (ex-UNDERTONES) / **REAMANN O'GORMAIN** (b. 7 Jun'61) – guitar / **CIARAN McLAUGHLIN** (b.18 Nov'62) – drums

Pink / not iss.

Jun 85. (7") *(PINKY 004)* **KEEN. / A GREAT DEPRESSION ON SLUM NIGHT** [ ] [-]
(re-iss. Oct86; PINKY 13T)

Noise A Noise / not iss.

Oct 85. (7") *(NAN 1)* **V2. / THE GONEST THING** [ ] [-]
(12"+=) *(NAN 1T)* – Happiness drives me round the bend.

Demon / Demon

Apr 86. (7") *(D 1042)* **IT'S A GOOD THING. / THE DEADBEAT** [ ] [-]
(12"+=) *(D 1042T)* – Mine.

May 86. (lp/c/cd)<US-orange-lp> *(<FIEND/+CASS/+CD 70>)* **MANIC POP THRILL** [84] [ ]
– Fleshprint / Can't stop / Lifeblood / Natural kind of joy / It's a good thing / Circusville / Mouth crazy / Tight lipped / A million miles away / Lettuce / Cheepskate / Blind spot. *(cd+=)* – V2 / Jesus said / The deadbeat. *(cd re-iss. Mar97 on Diabolo'; DIAB 823)*

Jul 86. (7") *(D 1043)* **NATURAL KIND OF JOY. / CAN'T STOP** [ ] [-]
(12"+=) *(D 1043T)* – Non-alignment pact / Jesus said.

Polydor / Polydor

Mar 87. (7"/12") *(TPE/+X 1)* **BIG DECISION. / SOUL DEEP** [43] [-]
(ext.10"+=) *(TPE/+T 1)* – Split!

May 87. (lp/c/cd) *(TPELP/+MC/+CD 1) <833132-1/-4/-2>* **BABBLE** 30
– Swamp / Spin cycle / For what it's worth / Big decision / Static / Split! / Belly bugs / In the playpen / Inside / Chester Burnette / Creeping to the cross.
Jun 87. (7") *(TPE 2)* **SWAMP. / DANCE YOUR ASS OFF** 64 -
(12"+=) *(TPEX 2)* – Creeping to the cross (live).
(7"ep++=) *(TPEE 2)* – Me and baby brother (live).
Virgin Virgin
Oct 87. (7") *(VS 1022)* **GENIUS MOVE. / PARTY GAMES** 65 -
(12"+=) *(VST 1022)* – Mouthcrazy.
Sep 88. (lp/c/cd) *(V/TCV/CDV 2550) <91019-1/-4/-2>* **END OF THE MILLENIUM PSYCHOSIS BLUES** 53
– Sooner or later / Every little bit / Cellophane / Candy love satellite / Here it is . . . take it! / The price of my soul / Groove check / The bottom line / Tension / Tired shattered man / Goggle box / Under the sky.
Oct 88. (7") *(VS 1116)* **CELLOPHANE. / THINK OF A WOMAN** -
(12"+=/cd-s+=) *(VST/VSCD 1116)* – Hot head / Fast 'n' bullbous.

— **JOHN MARCHINI** – bass; repl. SEAN O'NEILL (only temporary until 1989 then full-time)

Feb 89. (10"ep/3"cd-ep) *(VSA/VSCD 1159)* **GROOVE CHECK / CHEMICRAZY. / TENSION (live) / UNDER THE SKY (live)**
Mar 90. (7") *(VS 1242)* **ABANDON. / FAT MOUTH CREED** 73 -
(12"+=) *(VST 1242)* – Jewel.
(cd-s+=) *(VSCD 1242)* – ('A'-Boys own mix) / Headstaggered.
Apr 90. (cd/c/lp) *(CD/TC+/V 2618) <91354-2/-4/-1>* **CHEMICRAZY** 62
– Hey Venus / Blue to black / Mess of words / Sensitize / Another day / Gnaw mark / Scum surfin' / Compulsion / Tingle / Head staggered / Abandon / Sweet shiver burn.
May 90. (7") *(VS 1261)* **SENSITIZE. / CHEMICRAZY (revitalized)** -
(10"+=/12"+=/cd-s+=) *(VSAX/VST/VSCDT 1261)* – Abandon (Boys Own mix) / Groove check this groove.
Aug 90. (7") *(VS 1290)* **HEY VENUS. / ('A'-Mad Thatcher mix)** 49 -
(12"+=/cd-s+=) *(VST/VSCD 1290)* – (2-'A'mixes).

— **FRANK TREISCHLER** – bass (ex-YOUNG GODS) repl. MARCHINI

Jan 91. (7") *(VS 1312)* **TINGLE. / ('A'-Hard bop edit)** 49 -
(12"+=) *(VST 1312)* – ('A'mix).
(cd-s+=) *(VSCD 1312)* – Light and shade / Hey Bulldog.
(12") *(VSTX 1312)* – ('A'-Christmas mix) / 'A'-Jazz tup mix).
Apr 91. (7"ep/12"ep) *(VS/+T 1261)* **SENSITIZE. / ABANDON (mix) / GROOVE CHECK** 55 -
(10"ep+=/c-ep+=/cd-ep+=) *(VS X/C/CD 1261)* – Cinnamon girl.

— **MARCHINI** now returned to substitute TREICHE who went back to the YOUNG GODS

Koogat Rykodisc
Mar 93. (12"ep/cd-ep) *(GAT 1 T/CDS)* **DETONATE MY DREAMS. / BLUE TO BLACK (extended) / BIG HUMAN THING** -
Apr 93. (cd/c/lp) *(GAT 1 CD/MC/LP) <RCD/RAC+/10289>* **FIREPROOF** Feb94
– Detonate my dreams / Catch a fire / Last of the true believers / Too late blues / 7th wave / Infinite thrill / Speed of light / Shangri-la / Heartbeat mosaic / Metal mystery.
Jul 93. (12"ep/cd-ep) *(GAT 2 T/CDS)* **CATCH A FIRE (re-mix). / FUN TIME / LITTLE BIKINI / CHROME** -

— disbanded at the end of April 1994

– compilations, others, etc. –

Oct 87. (12"ep) *Strange Fruit; (SFPS 038)* **THE PEEL SESSIONS** -
– Blind spot / Lettuce / V2 / Can't stop.
Dec 89. (m-lp/m-cd) *Strange Fruit; (SFPMA/+CD 205) / Dutch East India; (8401>* **DOUBLE PEEL SESSIONS II**

THEATRE OF HATE (see under ⇒ SPEAR OF DESTINY)

THEE HYPNOTICS

Formed: High Wycombe, Buckinghamshire, England . . . late 80's by JAMES JONES, RAY HANSON, WILL PEPPER and MARK THOMPSON. After a debut single on the 'Hipsville' label, the band were picked up by 'Beggars Banquet' offshoot, 'Situation 2', releasing the epic 'JUSTICE IN FREEDOM' early the following year. A third single, 'SOUL TRADER', brought further cult acclaim while a live mini-set, 'LIVE'R THAN GOD' (1989) appeared on the fledlging American 'Sub Pop' label as the band were briefly associated with the nascent grunge scene. Certainly, THEE HYPNOTIC's retro sound had more in common with the likes of SOUNDGARDEN, GREEN RIVER etc., than any British indie acts, the distorted mogodon riffing and leadweight vocals of 'COME DOWN HEAVY' (1990) confirming their status as harbingers of stoner rock. Produced by CHRIS ROBINSON of fellow archivists The BLACK CROWES, 'SOUL, GLITTER AND SIN' (1991) received further praise from both the rock and indie press without really making much headway in either scene. Hedonism turned to tragedy the following year, however, as new bassist CRAIG PIKE died of a heroin overdose. It would be another two years before the release of 'THE VERY CRYSTAL SPEED MACHINE' (1995), on 'S.P.V.' and subsequently re-issued after gaining a new deal with Rick Rubin's 'American' label. • **Covered:** ROCK ME BABY (B.B. King).

Album rating: LIVE'R THAN GOD! (*6) / COME DOWN HEAVY (*6) / SOUL, GLITTER AND SIN (*5) / THE VERY CRYSTAL SPEED MACHINE (*6)

JIM JONES – vocals / **RAY HANSON** – guitar / **WILL PEPPER** – bass / **MARK THOMPSON** – drums

Hipsville not iss.
Jul 88. (7"; HYPNOTICS) *(HIP 1)* **LOVE IN A DIFFERENT VEIN. / ALL NIGHT LONG** -
Situation 2 Sub Pop
Mar 89. (12"ep) *(SIT 056T)* **JUSTICE IN FREEDOM. / PREACHIN' & RAMBLIN' / CHOOSE MY OWN WAY** -
Sep 89. (7") *(SIT 062)* **SOUL TRADER. / EARTH BLUES** -
(12"+=) *(SIT 062T)* – Rock me baby (live).
Oct 89. (m-lp/m-c/m-cd) *(SITUM 026/+CD) <SP 54/+B>* **LIVE 'R THAN GOD (live Powerhouse, London)** Jan90
– All night long / Let's get naked / Revolution stone / Rock me baby / Justice in freedom. *(re-dist.Jul91; same)*
Situation 2 Beggars Banquet
May 90. (7") *(SIT 067)* **HALF MAN, HALF BOY. /** -
(12"+=/cd-s=) *(SIT 067 T/CD)* –
Jun 90. (lp/cd) *(SITU 28/+CD) <2320>* **COME DOWN HEAVY**
– Half man, half boy / All messed up / Unearthed / Release the feeling / Resurrection Joe / Let it come down heavy / Bleeding heart / What to do / Sonic lament / Revolution stone.

— recruited **RAT SCABIES** – drums (ex-DAMNED) to repl. THOMPSON

Sep 91. (12"ep/cd-ep) *(SIT T/CD)* **SHAKE DOWN** -
– Loco / etc.
Oct 91. (lp/cd) *(SITU 35/+CD) <61079>* **SOUL, GLITTER & SIN: TARGET FROM THE SONIC UNDERWORLD**
– Shakedown / Kissed by the flame / The big fix / Point blank mystery / Soul accelerator / Black river shuffle / Cold blooded heart / Coast to coast. *(cd+=)* – Samedi's cookbook / Don't let it get you down.
Jan 92. (12"ep/cd-ep) *(SIT T/CD)* **COAST TO COAST** -

— **CRAIG PIKE** – bass (also ex-IGGY POP) repl. PEPPER

— CRAIG died (o.d.) on 30th June '93.

S.P.V. Warners
Mar 95. (cd) *(SPV 084 8906-2) <45600>* **THE VERY CRYSTAL SPEED MACHINE**
– Keep rollin' on / Heavy liquid / Phil's drum acropolis / Goodbye / If the good Lord loves ya / Ray's baudelaire / Caroline inside out / Tie it up / Down in the hole / Peasant song / Fragile / Look what you've done / Broken morning has. *(re-iss. Jul95 on 'American'; 74321 26451-2)*
Rocket not iss.
Nov 98. (7") **EARTH BLUES '99. / THING 4U** -

THELONIOUS MONSTER

Formed: Los Angeles, California, USA . . . 1986 by BOB FORREST, along with K.K., PETE WEISS, JOHN HUCK, BILL STOBAUGH, DIX DENNEY and CHRIS HANDSOME. A freewheeling collective of assorted Cali alternative types, THELONIOUS MONSTER made their vinyl debut on hardcore-punk label, 'Epitaph' with the self explanatory 'BABY . . . YOU'RE BUMMIN' MY LIFE OUT IN A SUPREME FASHION' (1986). The shambolic stylings of this free-for-all ragbag translated to the band's stage show which had already earned a formidable reputation for inspired sloppiness, the whole shebang saved from self-indlulgence by FORREST's emotive lyrics/vocalising. A further couple of albums, 'NEXT SATURDAY AFTERNOON' (1987) and 'STORMY WEATHER' (1989) for metal label, 'Combat', found the 'MONSTER refining their ramshackle brand of blues/country roots and punk, even convincing 'Capitol' to take them on for 1992's 'BEAUTIFUL MESS'. Boasting an array of hip names such as DAN PIRNER, TOM WAITS and BENMONT TENCH, the album benefitted from the major label recording budget, allowing FORREST to exorcise his demons in a more cohesive, polished setting. • **Covered:** SEE THAT MY GRAVE IS KEPT CLEAN (Blind Lemon Jefferson) / FOR MY LOVER (Tracy Chapman) / WEAKNESS IN ME (Joan Armatrading).

Album rating: BABY . . . YOU'RE BUMMIN' MY LIFE OUT IN A SUPREME FASHION (*4) / NEXT SATURDAY AFTERNOON (*5) / STORMY WEATHER (*7) / BEAUTIFUL MESS (*5)

BOB FORREST – vocals / with guitarists **CHRIS HANDSOME, BILL STOBAUGH, DIX DENNEY, K.K.** / bassist **JON HUCK** / drums **PETE WEISS**

not iss. Epitaph
1986. (lp/c) *<EPI/EPC-TM 1>* **BABY . . . YOU'RE BUMMIN' MY LIFE OUT IN A SUPREME FASHION** -
Combat Combat
Aug 87. (lp) *<(88561-8174-1)>* **NEXT SATURDAY AFTERNOON**
Relativity Relativity
1989. (lp) **STORMY WEATHER** -
– Walk on water / Swan song / Colorblind / Lena Horne still sings Stormy Weather / You better run / Oh (no sense at all) / Hang tough / See that my grave is kept clean / Michael Jordan / Pop star / Key to life . . . tonight / Anymore / Real kinda hatred / For my lover / Sammy Hagar weekend / Nuthin's perfect / My boy / Zelda / So what if I did / Low boy (butterflies are free) / Tree n' Sven orbit the planet / Lookin' to the west / Saturday afternoon. *<d-cd-iss. 1989 on 'Combat'+=; >* – NEXT SATURDAY AFTERNOON

— **FORREST** with various guests **TOM WAITS, DAVE PIRNER, DAN MURPHY, BENMONT TENCH, MICHAEL PENN** etc

not iss. Capitol
Oct 92. (cd/c) *<C2/C4 80227>* **BEAUTIFUL MESS** -
– I live in a nice house / Blood is thicker than water / Body and soul? / Adios lounge (with TOM WAITS) / I get so scared / Song for a politically correct girl from the valley / Ain't never been nuthin' for me in this world / Bus with no driver / Weakness in me / The beginning and the end #12 N35.

— above was their last album before breaking up

THERAPY?

Formed: Belfast, N. Ireland . . . summer '89 by ANDY CAIRNS, MICHAEL McKEEGAN and FYFE EWING. After failing to attract major label interest, they took the DIY route and issued a double A-side debut single, 'MEAT ABSTRACT' / 'PUNISHMENT KISS' (1990) on their own bitterly named

'Multifuckingnational' label. With the help of Radio One guru, John Peel and Silverfish's LESLIE RANKINE, the band secured a deal with London indie label, 'Wiiija'. The following year, they released two mini-sets in quick succession, 'BABYTEETH' and 'PLEASURE DEATH', the latter nearly breaking them into the Top 50 (both topping the independent charts). This initial early 90's period was characterised by a vaguely industrial hardcore/proto-grunge sound lying somewhere between American noiseniks, BIG BLACK and HUSKER DU. Their mushrooming street kudos tempted 'A&M' into offering them a deal and in 1992 THERAPY? made their major label debut with the Top 30 single, 'TEETHGRINDER', following it up with their first album proper, 'NURSE'. A Top 40 injection, its blunt combination of metal/punk and ambitious arrangements something of a love it or hate it affair. The following year, they released a trio of Top 20 singles, starting off with the 'SHORTSHARPSHOCK EP' which opened with the classic 'SCREAMAGER' track. In the first few months of '94, THERAPY? once again crashed into the charts with 'NOWHERE', an adrenaline rush of a single, that preceded their Mercury-nominated Top 5 album, 'TROUBLEGUM'. However, by the release of 1995's 'INFERNAL LOVE', the band affected something of a musical departure from their stock-in-trade indie-metal extremity with aching ballads (including a heart rending cover of Husker Du's 'DIANE') and string flourishes courtesy of MARTIN McCARRICK. The cellist (who also appeared on their 1994 set) was made full-time member in early 1996, while EWING was replaced by GRAHAM HOPKINS. • **Songwriters:** Mostly CAIRNS or group penned, except TEENAGE KICKS (Undertones) / INVISIBLE SUN (Police) / WITH OR WITHOUT YOU (U2) / BREAKING THE LAW (Judas Priest) / C.C. RIDER (hit; Elvis Presley) / ISOLATION (Joy Division) / TATTY SEASIDE TOWN (Membranes) / NICE'N'SLEAZY (Stranglers) / REUTERS (Wire) / VICAR IN A TUTU (Smiths). • **Trivia:** In 1994, they featured w/ OZZY OSBOURNE on 'IRON MAN' for a BLACK SABBATH tribute album.

Album rating: BABYTEETH (*5) / PLEASURE DEATH (*7) / NURSE (*7) / TROUBLEGUM (*8) / INFERNAL LOVE (*5)

ANDY CAIRNS (b.22 Sep'65, Antrim, N.Ireland) – vocals, guitar / **MICHAEL McKEEGAN** (b.25 Mar'71, Antrim) – bass / **FYFE EWING** – drums

Multifuck-ingnational / not iss.

Aug 90. (7") *(MFN 1)* **MEAT ABSTRACT. / PUNISHMENT KISS** [ ] [-]

Wiiija / not iss.

Jul 91. (m-lp) *(WIJ 9)* **BABYTEETH** [ ] [-]
– Meat abstract / Skyward / Punishment kiss / Animal bones / Loser cop / Innocent X / Dancin' with Manson. *(re-iss. Mar93 + Jun95 on 'Southern' cd/c/red-m-lp; 18507-2/-4/-1)*

Jan 92. (m-lp) *(WIJ 11)* **PLEASURE DEATH** [52] [-]
– Skinning pit / Fantasy bag / Shitkicker / Prison breaker / D.L.C. / Potato junkie. *(re-iss. Sep92 on 'A&M';) (re-iss. Mar93 + Jun95 on 'Southern' cd/c/m-lp; 18508-2/-4/-1)*

A&M / A&M

Oct 92. (7"purple) *(AM 0097)* **TEETHGRINDER. / SUMMER OF HATE** [30] [-]
(12") *(AMY 0097)* – ('A'side) / Human mechanism / Sky high McKay(e).
(cd-s+=) *(AMCD 0097)* – (all four songs above).
(12") – *(AMX 0097)* – ('A'-Tee hee dub mix) / ('A'-Unsane mix).

Nov 92. (cd/c/lp) *(540044-2/-4/-1)* **NURSE** [38] [-]
– Nausea / Teethgrinder / Disgracelands / Accelerator / Neck freak / Perversonality / Gone / Zipless / Deep skin / Hypermania.

Mar 93. (7"pink-ep/c-ep/12"ep/cd-ep) *(AM/+MC/Y/CD 208)* **SHORTSHARPSHOCK EP** [9] [-]
– Screamager / Auto surgery / Totally random man / Accelerator.

—— In May93, they appeared on the B-side of PEACE TOGETHER single 'BE STILL', covered The Police's 'INVISIBLE SUN' on 'Island' records.

Jun 93. (7"grey-ep/c-ep/12"ep/cd-ep) *(580304-7/-4/-1/-2)* **FACE THE STRANGE EP** [18] [-]
– Turn / Speedball / Bloody blue / Neck freak (re-recording).

Aug 93. (7"clearorblue-ep/c-ep/cd-ep) *(580360-7/-4/-2)* **OPAL MANTRA / INNOCENT X (live). / POTATO JUNKIE (live) / NAUSEA (live)** [13] [-]

Sep 93. (cd) *<POCM 1033>* **HATS OFF TO THE INSANE** (compilation) [-] [ ]
– Screamager / Auto surgery / Totally random man / Turn / Speedball / Opal mantra.

Jan 94. (7"ep/c-ep/cd-ep) *(580504-7/-4/-2)* **NOWHERE / PANTOPON ROSE. / BREAKING THE LAW / C.C. RIDER** [18] [-]
(cd-s) *(580 504-2)* – ('A'side) / ('A'-Sabres Of Paradise mix) / ('A'-Therapeutic Distortion mix).

Feb 94. (cd/c/lp,green-lp) *(540196-2/-4/-1)* **TROUBLEGUM** [5] [-]
– Knives / Screamager / Hellbelly / Stop it you're killing me / Nowhere / Die laughing / Unbeliever / Trigger inside / Lunacy booth / Isolation / Turn / Femtex / Unrequited / Brainsaw.

—— above album guests **PAGE HAMILTON** – lead guitar (of HELMET) / **MARTIN McCARRICK** (b.29 Jul'62, Luton, England) – guitar, cello (of THIS MORTAL COIL) / **LESLEY RANKINE + EILEEN ROSE** – vocals

Feb 94. (7"yellow-ep/c-ep/cd-ep) *(580534-7/-4/-2)* **TRIGGER INSIDE / NICE'N'SLEAZY. / REUTERS / TATTY SEASIDE TOWN** [22] [-]
(12"ep) *(580534-1)* – ('A'side) / ('A'-Terry Bertram mix 1 & 2) / Nowhere (Sabres of Paradise mix 1 & 2).

May 94. (7"red-ep/c-ep/cd-ep) *(580588-7/-4/-2)* **DIE LAUGHING / STOP IT YOU'RE KILLING ME (live). / TRIGGER INSIDE (live) / EVIL ELVIS (the lost demo)** [29] [-]
(12") *(580588-1)* – ('A'-David Holmes mix 1 & 2).

—— In May '95, they hit No.53 UK with remix of 'INNOCENT X', with ORBITAL on the B-side, 'Belfast' / 'Wasted (vocal mix)'.

May 95. (7"orange) *(581504-7)* **STORIES. / STORIES (cello version)** [14] [-]
(c-s+=/cd-s+=) *(581105-4/-2)* – Isolation (Consolidated synth mix).

Jun 95. (cd/c/red-lp) *(540379-2/-4/-1)* **INFERNAL LOVE** [9] [-]
– Epilepsy / Stories / A moment of clarity / Jude the obscene / Bowels of love / Misery / Bad mother / Me vs you / Loose / Diane / 30 seconds.

Jul 95. (c-s/cd-s) *(581163-4/-2)* **LOOSE / OUR LOVE MUST DIE / NICE GUYS / LOOSE (Photek remix)** [25] [-]
(cd-s) *(581165-2)* – ('A'side) / Die laughing (live) / Nowhere (live) / Unbeliever (live).
(7"green/one-sided-12") *(581162-7/-1)* – ('A'side) / ('A'-Photek remix).

Nov 95. (7"red-ep/c-ep/cd-ep) *(581293-7/-4/-2)* **DIANE / JUDE THE OBSCENE (acoustic) / LOOSE (acoustic) / 30 SECONDS (acoustic)** [26] [-]
(cd-ep) *(581291-2)* – ('A'side) / Misery (acoustic) / Die laughing (acoustic) / Screamager (acoustic).

—— Jan 96, **GRAHAM HOPKINS** (b.20 Dec'75, Dublin, Ireland) – drums (ex-MY LITTLE FUNHOUSE) repl. FYFE. Also added full-time **MARTIN McCARRICK**

Mar 98. (7"red) *(582538-7)* **CHURCH OF NOISE. / 60 WATT BULB / ('A'-Messenger mix)** [29] [-]
(cd-s) *(582539-2)* – (first & third tracks) / Suing God / ('A'-CD-Rom video).

Mar 98. (cd/c) *(540891-2/-4)* **SEMI-DETACHED** [21] [-]
– Church of noise / Tightrope walker / Black eye, purple sky / Lonely, cryin', only / Born too soon / Stay happy / Safe / Straight life / Heaven's gate / Don't expect roses / Tramline / The boy's asleep. *(also iss.6x7"box; 582548-7)*

May 98. (7"blue) *(582684-7)* **LONELY, CRYIN', ONLY. / SKYWARD** [32] [-]
(cd-s) *(582685-2)* – ('A'side) / High noon / Diane (new version) / Teethgrinder (new version).
(cd-s) *(044121-2)* – ('A'side) / Kids stuff / Disgracelands / ('A'-CD-Rom video).

– compilations, etc. –

Mar 92. (cd) *1/4 Stick; <QUARTERSTICK 8>* **CAUCASIAN PSYCHOSIS** [-] [ ]
– (BABYTEETH + PLEASURE DEATH)

THERMADORE

Formed: Los Angeles, California, USA . . . 1995 by songwriter ROBBIE ALLEN (a one-time roadie for the RED HOT CHILI PEPPERS) who enlisted ex-MARY'S DANISH members CHRIS WAGNER, DAVID KING and in a guest capacity, JULIE RITTER. Heading straight into major label land via a deal with 'Atlantic', THERMADORE made their debut with the album, 'MONKEY ON RICO' (1996), the freewheeling cast of alt-rock veterans sculpting a brooding post-grunge landscape that concluded with a re-working of 'EVERYTHING'S ALRIGHT' (from 'Jesus Christ Superstar').

Album rating: MONKEY ON RICO (*6)

ROBBIE ALLEN (b. 1964) – vocals, guitar / **CHRIS WAGNER** – bass (ex-MARY'S DANISH) / **DAVID KING** – guitar (ex-MARY'S DANISH) / guest incl. **JULIE RITTER** – vocals (ex-MARY'S DANISH) / **CHAD SMITH + JOSH FREESE + STONE GOSSARD**

Holiday-Atlantic / Holiday-Atlantic

May 96. (cd/c) *<(7567 82874-2/-4)>* **MONKEY ON RICO** [ ] [ ] Mar96
– Three days / Amerasian / Missing / Go / Spinning / Candywrapper / Pushing / Punk rock beating / Santa Rosa / Anton / Everything's alright.

—— probably their last as the group were a loose unit

THESE ANIMAL MEN

Formed: Brighton, England . . . 1991 by JULIAN HOOLIGAN (HEWINGS), BOAG, PATRICK (HUSSEY) and STEVE MURRAY. Hailed as flag bearers for the hopelessly contrived 'New Wave Of New Wave' scene – as well as encouraging a glut of pointless third-rate punk throwbacks, it was also the root cause of Brit-pop – THESE ANIMAL MEN emerged in 1993 with a track on the 6-band 'Fierce Panda' punk compilation EP 'Shaggin' In The Streets'. A debut cassette EP, 'WHEELERS, DEALERS AND CHRISTINE KEELERS' (shared with S*M*A*S*H), featured five tracks, the mini-set later to resurface as 'TOO SUSSED?' in '94. Having reinvented themselves (after rather dodgy beginnings) as a would-be CLASH for the 90's – complete with retro-Adidas-chic image – the band thrived on notoriety rather than any engaging musical talent, the 'SPEEED KING' single predictably baiting the usual suspects (i.e. MP's, local councils etc.) but failing to say anything new, either musically or lyrically. After a further single, 'THIS IS THE SOUND OF YOUTH', a debut album, '(COME ON, JOIN) THE HIGH SOCIETY' surfaced later that year, critics divided over its amateur pop-punk sloganeering but generally agreeing that they'd captured something of the zeitgeist. With the mid-90's onset of the aforementioned Brit-pop, the band found themsleves somewhat sidelined despite a more expansive musical outlook on mini-set, 'TAXI FOR THESE ANIMAL MEN' (1995) and follow-up album for Virgin-offshoot, 'Hut', 'ACCIDENT AND EMERGENCY' (1997).

Album rating: TOO SUSSED? mini (*5) / (COME ON, JOIN) THE HIGH SOCIETY (*6) / TAXI FOR THESE ANIMAL MEN (*5) / ACCIDENT AND EMERGENCY (*5)

BOAG – vocals / **JULIAN HOOLIGAN (HEWINGS)** – guitar / **PATRICK (HUSSEY)** – bass / **STEVE MURRAY** – drums

Les Disques De Popcor / not iss.

Dec 93. (c-ep) **WHEELERS, DEALERS AND CHRISTINE KEELERS** [ ] [-]
– (5 tracks; see TOO SUSSED? m-lp) / (4 tracks by S*M*A*S*H)

Hi-Rise / Vernon Yard

Mar 94. (7") *(FLAT 2)* **SPEEED KING. / JOBS FOR THE BOYS** [ ] [-]

Apr 94. (7") *(FLAT 3)* **YOU'RE NOT MY BABYLON. / WHO'S THE DADDY NOW?** [ ] [-]

Jun 94. (cd/c/m-lp) *(FLAT MCD/MTC/MLP 4) <VUSCD 4>* **TOO SUSSED?** [39] [ ]

– Too sussed? (live) / Speeed king / Jobs for the boys / Who's the daddy now? / You're not my Babylon.

Sep 94. (7"ep;pic-d/c-ep/12"ep/cd-ep) *(FLAT/+C/T/CD 7)* **THIS IS THE SOUND OF YOUTH. / SAIL AROUND THE WORLD / HOOLIGAN'S PROGRESS** 72 -

Sep 94. (cd/c/lp) *(FLAT CD/MC/LP 8)* **(COME ON, JOIN) THE HIGH SOCIETY** 62 -
– Sharp kid / Empire building / Ambulance / This year's model / You're always right / Flawed is beautiful / This is the sound of youth / Sitting tenant / Too sussed? / (Come on, join) The high society / We are living / High society (return).

Mar 95. (m-cd/m-c/m-lp) *(FLAT CD/MC/LP 14)* **TAXI FOR THESE ANIMAL MEN** 64 -
– You're always right / Nowhere faces / My human remains / False identification / Wait for it.

Hut — not iss.

Jan 97. (7"/cd-s) *(HUT/+CD 76)* **LIFE SUPPORT MACHINE. / (MY) MAGAZINE / APRIL 7th** 62 -
(cd-s) *(HUTDX 76)* – ('A'side) / Wichita lineman / Hammond heavy (emptyheads).

Mar 97. (7") *(HUT 81)* **LIGHT EMITTING ELECTRICAL WAVE. / SISTE ANNE** 72 -
(cd-s+=) *(HUTCD 81)* – Seamen's mission lament / Louis Louis. (cd-s) *(HUTDX 81)* – Every bullet's (got my name on it).

Apr 97. (cd)(c/lp) *(CDHUT 40)(HUT MC/LP 40)* **ACCIDENT AND EMERGENCY** -
– Life support machine / So sophisticated / When your hands are tied / Monumental moneymaker / Riverboat captain / New wave girl / 24 hours to live / Going native / Ambulance man / Light emitting electrical wave / April 7th.

THESE IMMORTAL SOULS

Formed: Europe . . . late 1986 by breakaway members of Australian outfit, CRIME & THE CITY SOLUTION: ROWLAND S. HOWARD (also a former sidekick of NICK CAVE in The BIRTHDAY PARTY), his brother HARRY HOWARD and EPIC SOUNDTRACKS (a Brit and one-time member of experimental punks, SWELL MAPS). Expanding the line-up to a quartet with the addition of GENEVIEVE McGUCKIN, THESE IMMORTAL SOULS remained with 'Mute' ('S.S.T.' in America), home to their aforementioned musical progenitors. Stylistically, the group carried on in the same vein as these past masters, recounting tales of damned romanticism through the trademark American gothic lens to a brooding, bluesy musical backing. The single, 'MARRY ME (LIE, LIE)', also opened up their debut long-player, 'GET LOST (DON'T LIE)' (1987), a record that received glowing reviews but appealed to the usual post-goth crowd without crossing over. ROWLAND and Co took their time over a prophetically titled follow-up, 'I'M NEVER GONNA DIE AGAIN' (1992), the band enjoying a critical resurrection after their spell in the musical wilderness. With a third album now seven years in the waiting, it seems THESE IMMORTAL SOULS have finally been laid to rest.

Album rating: GET LOST (DON'T LIE) (*7) / I'M NEVER GONNA DIE AGAIN (*6)

ROWLAND S. HOWARD – guitar (ex-CRIME & THE CITY SOLUTION, ex-BIRTHDAY PARTY) / **GENEVIEVE McGUCKIN** – keyboards / **HARRY HOWARD** – bass (ex-CRIME & THE CITY SOLUTION) / **EPIC SOUNDTRACKS** – drums (ex-CRIME & THE CITY SOLUTION, ex-RED CRAYOLA, ex-SWELL MAPS)

Mute — S.S.T.

Sep 87. (12"ep) *(12MUTE 63)* <SST 183> **MARRY ME (LIE, LIE) / OPEN UP AND BLEED. / BLOOD AND SAND, SHE SAID**

Oct 87. (lp/cd) *(STUMM/CDSTUMM 48)* <SST 164> **GET LOST (DON'T LIE)**
– Marry me (lie, lie) / Hide / Hey! little child / These immortal souls / I ate the knife / Blood and sand, she said / One in shadow, one in sun. *(cd+= alternative versions of)* – Open up and bleed / Blood and sand, she said / I ate the knife / These immortal souls.

Mute — Elektra

Oct 92. (12"ep/cd-ep) *(12/CD MUTE 90)* **KING OF KALIFORNIA E.P.**
– The king of Kalifornia / Bad / My one eyed daughter (live in Las Vegas) / Up on the roof.

Oct 92. (cd) *(CDSTUMM 98)* <61396> **I'M NEVER GONNA DIE AGAIN**
– The king of Kalifornia / Shamed / Black milk / Hyperspace / So the story goes / Insomnicide / All the money's gone / Crowned / Bad / My one eyed daughter / Up on the roof.

— disbanded soon after above set

THE THE

Formed: Swadlincote, Derbyshire, England . . . 1979 as a studio project by MATT JOHNSON who was part of post-punk outfit The GADGETS, at the same time. JOHNSON signed to indie label, '4 a.d.' in 1980, unleashing the poignant single, 'CONTROVERSIAL SUBJECT'. JOHNSON released a further debut album for the label in summer '81, 'BURNING BLUE SOUL', although in effect it was a THE THE recording in all but name, JOHNSON being the sole permanent member of the group. Signing briefly to 'Some Bizzare', THE THE released another three singles, 'COLD SPELL AHEAD', 'PERFECT' and the brilliant 'UNCERTAIN SMILE', before securing a deal with 'Epic'. The long awaited and much anticipated 'SOUL MINING' was eventually released in late '83, JOHNSON's critical favour and cult standing seeing the album reach the UK Top 30. An entrancing, ambitious pop record with a brooding undertow, the keening 'THIS IS THE DAY' stands among the best of JOHNSON's work, the album's claustrophobic lyrics marking out JOHNSON as a bedsit commentator par excellence. For live work, JOHNSON recruited the likes of ex-ORANGE JUICE man, ZEKE MANYIKA, JIM THIRLWELL and JOOLS HOLLAND, the latter actually having guested on the album. Three years in the making, 'INFECTED' (1986) was JOHNSON's tour de force, a scathing attack on the industrial, economic and moral wasteland that was Thatcher's Britain. Nowhere was this better articulated than the malignant power of the album's centrepiece, 'HEARTLAND', JOHNSON berating 80's material gain and America's all-pervasive influence through gritted teeth. The pumping electro-soul of the title track, meanwhile, dealt with sexual obsession and the AIDS crisis, the attendant devil-masturbating video causing a storm of controversy. Other highlights included the tortured 'OUT OF THE BLUE (INTO THE FIRE)' and the breathy duet with NENEH CHERRY, 'SLOW TRAIN TO DAWN', JOHNSON's mastery of mood and atmosphere, together with a crack troupe of guest musicians making this one of the most realised albums of the decade. Accompanied by a full-length video/film (which was aired on Channel 4), the record also gave JOHNSON some belated Top 20 success. Spurred on, the restless maverick subsequently recruited a permanent band to turn THE THE into a group proposition, namely DAVID PALMER, JAMES ELLER and ex-SMITHS guitarist JOHNNY MARR. Though the resulting album, 'MIND BOMB' (1989) was THE THE's most successful to date (Top 5), its caustic barrage of political ranting lacked the twisted pop subtlety of its predecessor and left some critics unimpressed (a guest spot from SINEAD O'CONNOR on 'KINGDOM OF RAIN' made up for the pop tones of 'THE BEAT(EN) GENERATION'). Retaining the same core of musicians while adding keyboard player, D.C. COLLARD, THE THE eventually resurfaced with a full length album in the form of 'DUSK' (1993). Previewed by the harmonica howl of 'DOGS OF LUST', the album saw JOHNSON once again wrestling with his inner demons in his disturbingly insinuating way. A mid-life dark-night-of-the-soul, JOHNSON has rarely bared his soul or expressed his despair as affectingly as on the very SMITHS-esque 'SLOW EMOTION REPLAY', MARR literally wringing the pathos from his chiming guitar. This cathartic collection of urban blues nevertheless ended on something of a more hopeful note with 'LONELY PLANET', JOHNSON coming to some kind of peace with himself and the world. The record deservedly reached No.2, becoming the most successful THE THE release to date and making up the critical and commercial ground lost with 'MIND BOMB'. Of course, the ever restless JOHNSON turned his hand to something completely different, so to speak, for his next full-length release; 'HANKY PANKY' (1995) was a tribute album to his hero, country star HANK WILLIAMS, although only the track 'I SAW THE LIGHT' was of much note. Given short thrift by critics (the same ones probably), the record saw JOHNSON going out on a limb, no doubt alienating many of his long-time fans, although he was distant from them after relocating to Sherman Oaks in California. Then again, anyone familiar with the work of this elusive genius knows to expect the unexpected.

Album rating: SOUL MINING (*8) / INFECTED (*9) / MIND BOMB (*9) / DUSK (*7) / HANKY PANKY (*4) / Matt Johnson: BURNING BLUE SOUL (*7)

GADGETS

MATT JOHNSON / COLIN TUCKER – synthesizers / **JOHN HYDE** – synthesizers (both ex-PLAIN CHARACTERS)

Final Solution — not iss.

Dec 79. (lp) *(FSLP 001)* **GADGETREE** -
– Kyleaking / Making cars / Narpath / UFO import No.1 / Slippery / Singing in the rain / Only one me / Shouting 'Nispers' / There over there / Termite mound / Sleep / Devil's dyke / Six mile bottom / UFO import No.2 / Autumn 80 / Duplicate / Bog track / Thin line. *(re-iss. Jun89 on 'Plastic Head' lp/cd; PLAS LP/CD 013)*

— They continued as a studio set-up with MATT's help.

Dec 80. (lp) *(FSLP 002)* **LOVE, CURIOSITY, FRECKLES & DOUBT** -
– Bodorgan / Gadget speak / Checking to make sure / Aeron / Leave it to Charlie / Prayers / Happy endido / Quatt / Pictures of you / Aaft / Railway line through blubber houses / She's queen of toyland / Sex / It wasn't that way at all / The death and resurrection of Jennifer Gloom / Bill posters will be prosecuted. *(re-iss. Jun89 on 'Plastic Head' lp/cd; PLAS LP/CD 014)*

— next featured **PETER ASHWORTH** dubbed in instead of MATT

Glass — not iss.

Jan 83. (lp/c) *(GLA LP/C 006)* **THE BLUE ALBUM** -
– We had no way of knowing / Space in my heart / Bodies without heads / The boyfriend / Uneasy listening / Juice of love / Discuss the sofa / Long empty train / Bite the sawdust / Broken fall. *(re-iss. Jun89 on 'Plastic Head' lp/cd; PLAS LP/CD 016)*

Jun 83. (7"/12"; unissued) *(GLASS/+12 026)* **WE HAD NO WAY OF KNOWING. / ACID BATH** - -

THE THE

MATT JOHNSON (b.15 Aug'61, Essex, England . . . raised London) – vocals, guitar, etc. (also of The GADGETS) / **KEITH LAWS** – synthesizers, drum machine / **PETER 'Triash' ASHWORTH** – drums / **TOM JOHNSTON** – bass

4 a.d. — not iss.

Jul 80. (7") *(AD 10)* **CONTROVERSIAL SUBJECT. / BLACK AND WHITE** -

— next with guests **GILBERT & LEWIS** (of WIRE) on 2nd last track

Aug 81. (lp; as MATT JOHNSON) *(CAD 113)* **BURNING BLUE SOUL** -
– Red cinders in the sand / Song without an ending / Time again for the golden sunset / Icing up / Like a Sun risin' thru my garden / Out of control / Bugle boy / Delirious / The river flows east in Spring / Another boy drowning. *(re-iss. Sep83; same) (re-iss. credited to THE THE, Jun93 cd)(c; HAD 113CD)(HADC 113); hit UK No.65 <us cd-iss. 1993 on 'Warners'; 45266>*

Some Bizzare | not iss.

Sep 81. (7") *(BZ 4)* **COLD SPELL AHEAD. / HOT ICE** | | -
(re-iss. Aug92, 12"pic-d/cd-s;)

— **MATT JOHNSON** was now virtually **THE THE,** although he was augmented by others on tour.

Epic | Epic

Oct 82. (7") *(EPCA 2787)* **UNCERTAIN SMILE. / THREE ORANGE KISSES FROM KAZAN** | 68 | -
(12"+=,12"yellow+=) *(EPC13 2787)* – Waiting for the upturn.

Dec 82. (7") **UNCERTAIN SMILE. / WAITING FOR THE UPTURN** | - |

Feb 83. (7") *(EPCA 3119)* **PERFECT. / THE NATURE OF VIRTUE** | | -
(12"+=) *(EPCA13 3119)* – The nature of virtue II.

Sep 83. (7") *(A 3710)* **THIS IS THE DAY. / MENTAL HEALING PROCESS** | 71 |
(w/ free-7") *(same)* – Leap into the wind / Absolute liberation.
(12") *(TA 3710)* – ('A'side) / I've been waiting for tomorrow (all of my life).

— added live **ZEKE MANYIKA** – drums (of ORANGE JUICE) / **JIM THIRLWELL / JOOLS HOLLAND** – piano (ex-SQUEEZE) / **THOMAS LEER** – synthesizers, keyboards

Oct 83. (lp/c) *(EPC/40 25525)* *<EK 39266>* **SOUL MINING** | 27 |
– I've been waiting for tomorrow (all of my life) / This is the day / The sinking feeling / Uncertain smile / The twilight hour / Soul mining / Giant. *(free-12"ep.w.a.)* **PERFECT. / SOUP OF MIXED EMOTIONS / FRUIT OF THE HEART** *(c+=)* – Perfect / Three orange kisses from Kazan / Nature of virtue / Fruit of the heart / Soup of mixed emotions / Waiting for the upturn. *(cd-iss. Jun87+=; CD 25525)* – Perfect. *(re-iss. Mar90 cd/c/lp; 466337-2/-4/-1)*

Nov 83. (7") *(A 3588)* **UNCERTAIN SMILE. / DUMB AS DEATH'S HEAD** | | -
(12") *(TA 3588)* – ('A'side) / Soul mining.

— guests for next album **ROLI MOSSIMAN / NENEH CHERRY / DAVID PALMER / STEVE HOGARTH / ANNA DOMINO / JAMIE TALBOT / WAYNE LIVESEY / ZEKE MANYIKA /** etc.

May 86. (12"m) *(TRUTH 1)* **SWEET BIRD OF TRUTH. / HARBOUR LIGHTS / SLEEPING JUICE** | | -

Jul 86. (7") *(TRUTH 2)* **HEARTLAND. / BORN IN THE NEW S.A.** | 29 | -
(12"+=) *(TRUTH T2)* – Flesh and bones.
(d12"++=) *(TRUTH D2)* – Perfect / Fruit of the heart.
(12"+=) *(TRUTH Q2)* – Sweet bird of truth.
(c-s++=) *(TRUTH C2)* – Harbour lights.

Oct 86. (7") *(TRUTH 3)* **INFECTED. / DISTURBED** | 48 |
(12"+=/12"uncensored+=) *(TRUTH T/Q 3)* – ('A'-energy mix).
(d12"++=) *(TRUTH D3)* – Soul mining (remix) / Sinking feeling.
(c-s+=) *(TRUTH C3)* – ('A'-Skull crusher mix) / Soul mining / Sinking feeling.

Nov 86. (lp/c/cd) *(EPC/40/CD 26770)* *<40471>* **INFECTED** | 14 | 89
– Infected / Out of the blue (into the fire) / Heartland / Angels of deception / Sweet bird of truth / Slow train to dawn / Twilight of a champion / The mercy beat. *(cd+=)* – ('A'-INFECTED singles remixed) *(TA 3588)*

Jan 87. (7") *(TENSE 1)* **SLOW TRAIN TO DAWN. / HARBOUR LIGHTS** | 64 |
(12"+=/12"w-stencil+=) *(TENSE T/D 3)* – The nature of virtue.

May 87. (7") *(TENSE 2)* **SWEET BIRD OF TRUTH. / SLEEPING JUICE** | 55 |
(12"+=) *(TENSE T2)* – Harbour lights.
(c-s++=)(cd-s++=) *(TENSE C2)(CDTHE 2)* – Soul mining (12"mix).

— THE THE were again a group when **MATT** with past session man **DAVID PALMER** – drums (ex-ABC) / recruited **JOHNNY MARR** – guitar (ex-SMITHS) / **JAMES ELLER** – bass (ex-JULIAN COPE)

Feb 89. (7") *(EMU 8)* **THE BEAT(EN) GENERATION. / ANGEL** | 18 |
(12"box+=/cd-s+=/3"cd-s+=) *(EMUB/EMUCD/CBEMU 8)* – Soul mining (mix).
(12"+=/pic-cd+=) *(EMUT/CPEMU 8)* – ('A'-Palmer mix) / ('A'-campfire mix).

May 89. (lp/c/cd) *(463319-1/-4/-2)* *<45241>* **MIND BOMB** | 4 |
– Good morning beautiful / Armageddon days are here (again) / The violence of truth / Kingdom of rain / The beat(en) generation / August & September / Gravitate to me / Beyond love.

Jul 89. (7"/c-s) *(EMU/+C 9)* **GRAVITATE TO ME. / THE VIOLENCE OF TRUTH** | 63 |
(12"+=/cd-s+=) *(EMUT/CDEMU 9)* – I've been waiting for tomorrow (all of my life).
(etched-12") *(EMUE 9)* – ('A'dub) / I've been waiting for tomorrow.

Sep 89. (7"/c-s) *(EMU/+C 10)* **ARMAGEDDON DAYS ARE HERE (AGAIN). / ('A'orchestral)** | 70 |
(12"+=) *(EMUT 10)* – The nature of virtue / Perfect.
(cd-s+=) *(CDEMU 10)* – Perfect / Mental healing process.
(10"ep) *(EMUQT 10)* **THE THE V. THE WORLD EP** – ('A'side) / The nature of virtue / Perfect / Mental healing process.
(etched-12") *(EMUE 10)* – ('A'edit) / Perfect.

Feb 91. (12"/c-s) *(655 798-6/-4)* **JEALOUS OF YOUTH. / ANOTHER BOY DROWNING (live)** | 54 |
(cd-s+=) **SHADES OF YOUTH EP** *(655 796-8)* – Solitude / Dolphins.

— added **D.C. COLLARD** – instruments

Jan 93. (7"marble) *(658 457-7)* **DOGS OF LUST. / THE VIOLENCE OF TRUTH** | 25 |
(12"pic-d+=/cd-s+=) *(658 457-6/-2)* – Infected (live).
(cd-s) *(658 457-5)* – ('A'side) / Jealous of youth (live) / Beyond love (live) / Armageddon days are here (again) (D.N.A. remix).

Jan 93. (cd/c/lp) *(472468-2/-4/-1)* *<53164>* **DUSK** | 2 |
– True happiness this way lies / Love is stronger than death / Dogs of lust / This is the night / Slow emotion replay / Helpline operator / Sodium light baby / Lung shadows / Bluer than midnight / Lonely planet.

Apr 93. (12"red-ep/cd-ep) *(659 077-6/-9)* **SLOW MOTION REPLAY. / DOGS OF LUST (3 mixes by Jim Thirlwell)** | 35 |
(cd-ep) *(659077-0)* – ('A'side) / Scenes from Active Twilight (parts I-V).

Jun 93. (12"ep/cd-ep) *(659 371-6/-2)* **LOVE IS STRONGER THAN DEATH. / THE SINKING FEELING (live) / THE MERCY BEAT (live) / ARMAGEDDON DAYS ARE HERE (AGAIN) (live)** | 39 |
(cd-ep) *(659 371-5)* – ('A'side) / Infected / Soul mining / Armageddon days are . . .

Jan 94. (c-ep/12"ep/cd-ep) *(659811-4/-6/-2)* **DIS-INFECTED EP** | 17 |
– This was the day / Dis-infected / Helpline operator (sick boy mix) / Dogs of lust (germicide mix).

Jan 95. (c-ep/10"ep/cd-ep) *(661091-0/-6/-9)* *<61119>* **I SAW THE LIGHT / I'M FREE AT LAST. / SOMEDAY YOU'LL CALL MY NAME / THERE'S NO ROOM IN MY HEART FOR THE BLUES** | 31 | Aug95

Feb 95. (cd/c/10"lp) *(478139-2/-4/-0)* *<66908>* **HANKY PANKY** | 28 |
– Honky tonkin' / Six more miles / My heart would know / If you'll be a baby to me / I'm a long gone daddy / Weary blues from waitin' / I saw the light / Your cheatin' heart / I can't get you off of my mind / There's a tear in my beer / I can't escape from you.

– compilations, others, etc. –

Dec 88. (d-cd) *Epic; (CDTT 241)* **SOUL MINING / INFECTED** | | -

THEY MIGHT BE GIANTS

Formed: Brooklyn, New York . . . 1985 by former Bostonians, JOHN FLANSBURGH and JOHN LINNELL, who poached the group name from an early 70's movie starring George C. Scott. In true DIY fashion, this enterprising duo set up a "Dial-A-Song" service to preview their work, gathering up the cream of the material on offer for an eponymous debut album via NY indie, 'Bar None'. Licensed for the UK by 'Rough Trade', the record introduced British listeners to their quirky folk/punk hybrid and geek-appeal, drawing critical comparisons with everyone from R.E.M. to DEVO and even The RESIDENTS. Rising from relative obscurity to become college radio heroes in the space of a few years, THEY MIGHT BE GIANTS found alternative fame with follow-up set, 'LINCOLN' (1989), the band's offbeat combination of surreal/subversive lyrics and sherbet-laced melodies making them the toast of America's alternative scene. A subsequent transatlantic deal with 'Elektra' saw the duo score an unlikely UK Top 10 hit single with 'BIRDHOUSE IN YOUR SOUL', while the accompanying album, 'FLOOD', made the Top 20 despite its wilful experimentation. Mainstream success was fleeting, however, further singles failing to make the grade and a third album, 'APOLLO 18' (1992), proving too challenging even for many hardened fans. Things improved with the addition of four new band members in time for 'JOHN HENRY' (1994), the album pushing them to new heights back home and even securing them a soundtrack appearance on 1995 kids movie, 'Mighty Morphin Power Rangers'. Of late, the group has released two albums, 'FACTORY SHOWROOM' (1997) and 'SEVERE THE DAMAGE' (1998), the latter a live set which included a new track, 'DOCTOR WORM' and seven untitled songs written on the night! • **Covered:** ONE HERE PARADE (Phil Ochs) / 25 O'CLOCK (Dukes Of Stratosphear) / LADY IS A TRAMP (Hart-Rodgers).

Album rating: THEY MIGHT BE GIANTS (*7) / LINCOLN (*6) / DON'T LET'S START compilation (*6) / FLOOD (*4) / APOLLO 18 (*4) / JOHN HENRY (*6) / FACTORY SHOWROOM (*5)

JOHN FLANSBURGH (b. 6 May'60, Boston) – vocals, guitar, bass drum / **JOHN LINNELL** (b.12 Jun'59, New York City) – vocals, accordion, keyboards

Rough Trade | Bar None

Oct 87. (lp/c) *(ROUGH/+C 15)* *<72603>* **THEY MIGHT BE GIANTS** | |
– Everything right is wrong again / Put your hand inside the puppet head / Number three / Don't let's start / Hide away folk family / 32 footsteps / Toddler hiway / Rabid child / Nothing's gonna change my clothes / (She was a) Hotel detective / She's an angel / Youth culture killed my dog / Boat of car / Chess piece face / Absolutely Bill's mood / I hope that I get old before I die / Alienation's for the rich / The day / Rhythm section want ad. *(cd-iss. Mar89; RTDCD 57) (cd re-iss. Nov90 on 'Elektra'; EKT 80CD)*

Jun 88. (7") *<72605>* **DON'T LET'S START. / WE'RE THE REPLACEMENTS** | |
(12"+=) – When it rains it snows / The famous polka.

One Little Indian | Bar None

Jan 89. (12"ep) *(12TP 22)* **THEY'LL NEED A CRANE / I'VE GOT A MATCH. / KISS ME, SON OF GOD / I'LL SINK MANHATTAN** | |

Feb 89. (lp/c/cd) *(TP LP/C/CD 12)* *<72600>* **LINCOLN** | | 89 Dec88
– The world's address / I've got a match / Santa's beard / You'll miss me / They'll need a crane / Shoehorn with teeth / Stand on your head / Snowball in Hell / Kiss me, son of God / Ana Ng / Cowtown / Lie still, little bottle / Purple toupee / Cage & aquarium / Where your eyes don't go / Piece of dirt / Pencil rain. *(re-iss. Jun91 on 'Elektra' cd)(c; 7559 61145-2)(EKT 89C)*

Mar 89. (12"ep) *(12TP 24)* **ANA NG / NIGHTGOWN OF THE SULLEN MOON. / IT'S NOT MY BIRTHDAY / LIE STILL, LITTLE BOTTLE** | |

Elektra | Elektra

Feb 90. (7") *(EKR 104)* **BIRDHOUSE IN YOUR SOUL. / HOT CHA** | 6 |
(12"+=/cd-s+=) *(EKR 104 T/CD)* – Hearing aid / Ant.

Mar 90. (cd)(lp/c) *<(7559 60907-2/-4)>* **FLOOD** | 14 | 75 Feb90
– Theme from Flood / Birdhouse in your soul / Lucky ball and chain / Istanbul (not Constantinople) / Dead / Your racist friend / Particle man / Twisting / We want a rock / Someone keeps moving my chair / Hearing aid / Minimum wage / Letterbox / Whistling in the dark / Hot cha / Women & men / Sapphire bullets of pure love / They might be giants / Road movie to Berlin.

May 90. (7"/c-s) *(EKR 110/+C)* **ISTANBUL (NOT CONSTANTINOPLE). / JAMES K. POLK** | 61 |
(12"+=) *(EKR 110T)* – Stormy pinkness.
(cd-s++=) *(EKR 110CD)* – ('A'-Brownsville mix).

Sep 90. (7"/c-s) **DON'T LET'S START (remix). / LETTERBOX** | |
(12"+=/cd-s+=) – Your racist friend (remix).

May 91. (7"/c-s) **ANA NG. / THEY'LL NEED A CRANE** | |
(12"+=/cd-s+=) – (She was a) Hotel detective / Don't let's start.

Jan 92. (7"/c-s) **THE STATUE GOT ME HIGH. / SHE'S ACTUAL SIZE** | |

(12"/cd-s) – ('A'side) / I'm def / Which describes how you're feeling (1985 demos).

Mar 92. (cd)(lp/c) *<(7559 61257-2)>(EKT 104/+C)* **APOLLO 18** | | 99
– Dig my grave / I palindrome I / She's actual size / My evil twin / Mammal / The statue got me high / Spider / The guitar (the lion sleeps tonight) / Dinner bell / Narrow your eyes / Hall of heads / Which desribes how you're feeling / See the constellation / If I wasn't shy / Turn around / Hypnotist of ladies / Fingertips / Space suit.

Apr 92. (7"/c-s) **THE GUITAR (THE LION SLEEPS TONIGHT). / ('A'extended)**
(12"+=) – Larger than life (Joshua Fried's remake of 'She's Actual Size') / ('A'outer planet mix) / ('A'other outer planet mix).
(cd-s+=) – Cabbage town / Siftin'.

— The 2 JOHNS added; **TONY MAIMONE** (b.27 Sep'52, Cleveland, Ohio) – bass / **BRIAN DOHERTY** (b. 2 Jul'62, Brooklyn) – drums

Sep 94. (cd/c) *<(7559 61654-2/-4)>* **JOHN HENRY** | | 59
– Subliminal / Snail shell / Sleeping in the flowers / Unrelated thing / AKA driver / I should be allowed to think / Extra saviour faire / Why must I be sad? / Spy / O do not forsake me / No one knows my plan / Dirt bike / Destination Moon / A self called nowhere / Meet James Ensor / Thermostat / Window / Out of jail / Stomp box / The end of the tour.

Oct 94. (7"ep/c-ep/12"ep/cd-ep) *(EKR 194/+C/T/CD)* **BACK TO SKULL EP**
– Snail shell / She was a hotel detective (1994 version) / Mrs. Train / Snail dust (the Dust Brothers remix of Snail shell).

— now with a plethora of backing musicians

Feb 97. (cd/c) *<(7559 61862-2/-4)>* **FACTORY SHOWROOM** | | 89
– S.E.X.X.Y / Till my head falls off / How can I sing like a girl? / Exquisite dead guy / Metal detector / New York City / Your own worst enemy / XTC vs. Adam Ant / Spiraling shape / James K. Polk / Pet name / I can hear you / The bells are ringing.

not iss. | Restless

1998. (cd) *<72965>* **SEVERE TIRE DAMAGE (live)** | - |
– Doctor Worm / Severe tire damage / They got lost / Why does the sun shine? / Birdhouse in your soul / She's an angel / XTC vs. Adam Ant / Istanbul (not Constantinople) / Anang / First kiss / Spider / Particle man / She's actual size / S-E-X-X-Y / Meet James Esnor / Till my head falls off / About me.

– compilations, etc. –

Nov 89. (lp/c/cd) *Rough Trade; (TP LP/C/CD 14)* **DON'T LET'S START** | | -
Jul 91. (cd/c) *Enigma; <72646-2/-4>* **MISCELLANEOUS T** (B-sides, etc) | - |
Mar 97. (d-cd) *Restless; <72931>* **THEN: THE EARLIER YEARS** | - |
– (THEY MIGHT BE GIANTS + LINCOLN + MISCELLANEOUS T)

THIEVES (see under ⇒ McALMONT, David)

THINKING FELLERS UNION LOCAL #282

Formed: San Francisco, California, USA . . . 1987 by HUGH SWARTS, plus BRIAN HAGEMAN, MARK DAVIES and ANNE EICKELBERG. Arty, experimental indie/noise merchants to a man (and woman!), THINKING FELLERS UNION LOCAL #282 liked nothing better than to create stubbornly off-kilter musi-forms by doing strange things with such un-rock'n'roll instruments as banjo, trombone and mandolin. The quirky quartet made their debut in 1988 with the extremely rare cassette-only release, 'WORMED, BY LEONARD'; this, like its follow-up, 'TANGLE', was issued on the 'Thwart' imprint, a label run by the band's own HUGH SWARTS. Moving on to 'Matador' at the turn of the decade, they made at least some concessions to musical convention with 'LOVELYVILLE', flickering melodies clearly discernible through the avant-garde fog. The uninitiated are directed towards 1992's 'MOTHER OF ALL SAINTS', a twenty-plus collection of bonafide "songs" interspersed with snippets of wilfull weirdness. SWARTS and Co moved even further towards relative songwriting "normality" with 1994's low-key 'STRANGERS FROM THE UNIVERSE', their final effort for 'Matador'. A further couple of independently released albums, 'PORCELAIN ENTERTAINMENTS' and 'I HOPE IT LANDS', appeared in the mid-90's although it appears the UNION have since returned to the shop floor.

Album rating: LOVELYVILLE (*5) / MOTHER OF ALL SAINTS (*6) / STRANGERS FROM THE UNIVERSE (*4)

HUGH SWARTS – vocals, guitar / **MARK DAVIES** – guitar, banjo, trombone / **BRIAN HAGEMAN** – guitar, mandolin, viola / **ANNE EICKELBERG** – bass, vocals / **JAY PAGET** – guitar, drums, keyboards

not iss. | Thwart

1988. (c) *<THW 002>* **WORMED, BY LEONARD** | - |
– It's seven / Hell rules / Leaky bag / I don't know / Milva spectre / Nipper / Oregon trail / Misfits park / Coming and going / Mr. Tuna's big old place / Narlus spectre / K.L.T.X. / Truck driving man / Out in the kitchen / Serious matter / Mile wide / Motorin' flarey Henderson / Indigestion. *(UK-iss.Oct95 & Dec96 on 'Thwart' d-lp/cd; THW 002-1/-2)*

1989. (lp) **TANGLE** | - |

Matador | Matador

1991. (cd) *<031>* **LOVELYVILLE** | - |
1992. (cd) *<043>* **MOTHER OF ALL SAINTS** | - |
– Untitled / Gentlemen's lament / Catcher / Hornet's heart / Star Trek / Tell me / Heaven for addled imbeciles / Hive / Hummingbird in a cube of ice / None too fancy / Wide forehead / Infection / Pleasure circle / Tight little thing / Hosanna loud Hosanna / Tuning notes / Shuddering big butter / 1" tall / Raymond H. / Untiled / Cistern / El cerrito / Fishbowl.

Feb 94. (10"ep/cd-ep) *(OLE 068-1/-2)* **ADMONISHING THE BISHOPS**
– Hurricane / Undertaker / Million dollars / Father.

Oct 94. (cd/lp) *<(OLE 109-2/-1)>* **STRANGERS FROM THE UNIVERSE**
– My pal the tortoise / Socket / Bomber pilot WWII / Hundreds of years / Guillotine / Uranium / February / Pull my pants up tight / Cup of dreams / The oxenmaster / The operation / The piston and the shaft / Communication / Noble experiment.

not iss. | Amarillo

1995. (12") **EVERYDAY. / SELECTIONS FROM A FISTFUL OF DOLLARS** | - |

Return To Sender | Return To Sender

Jan 96. (cd) *<(RTS 21)>* **PORCELAIN ENTERTAINMENTS**

Communion | Communion

Dec 96. (lp/cd) *<(COMM 043/+CD)>* **I HOPE IT LANDS** | | 1995
– Poem / Lamb's lullaby / Empty cup / I hope it lands / Lizard's dream / Comad adrift toward Mars / Elgin Miller / Hudson bottom dance / Jagged ambush bug / Brains / Rampaging fuckers of anything on the planet / Cuckoo at the world / Inspector fat ass / Arbeiter / Triple X / Booth delirium / Hills.

— looked to have disbanded after above

– others, etc. –

Mar 94. (cd)/(lp) *Brinkman; (BR 21CD) / Ajax; (AJAX 038-1)* **FUNERAL PUDDING** | | Jan95

THIN WHITE ROPE

Formed: Davis, Sacramento, California, USA . . . 1984 by mainman GUY KYSER. Despite being initially lumped in with the retro psyche/country movement peopled by the likes of RAIN PARADE and The LONG RYDERS, THIN WHITE ROPE's debut album, 'EXPLORING THE AXIS', suggested more in common, spiritually at least, with the parched desert-rock of HOWIE GELB and his GIANT SAND project. The album found its way into the hands of Demon off-shoot label, 'Zippo', who gave it a UK release in late '85 although it wasn't until the release of 1987's acclaimed 'MOONHEAD' that THIN WHITE ROPE (named after William Burrough's memorable description of the male ejaculation) began attracting the recognition they so richly deserved. The twin guitar assault of messrs. KYSER and KUNKEL brought frequent comparisons with NEIL YOUNG/CRAZY HORSE's trademark sonic alchemy while the frontman's twisted lyrics did indeed suggest a love of Burrough's dark surrealism. 'IN THE SPANISH CAVE' followed a year later as their critical standing soared, the band subsequently signing to 'R.C.A.' in 1989. The resulting 'SACK FULL OF SILVER' (1990) was received with slightly less enthusiasm and with diminishing critical and creative returns, the band was amicably wound up in summer '92. A farewell gig was recorded and released the following year as 'THE ONE THAT GOT AWAY'. All the members continued with other projects while KYSER combined songwriting with studying for a degree. • **Covered:** ROADRUNNER (Bo Diddley) / AIN'T THAT LOVIN' YOU BABY (Jimmy Reed) / TOWN WITHOUT PITY (hit; Gene Pitney) / SOME VELVET MORNING (Lee Hazlewood) / MAY THIS BE LOVE (Jimi Hendrix) / YOO DOO RIGHT (Can) / THE MAN WITH THE GOLDEN GUN (John Barry) / BORN TO FLAMES (13th Floor Elevators) / OUTLAW BLUES (Bob Dylan) / EYE (Foster Children) / THEY'RE HANGING ME TONIGHT (Love – Wolpert) / HERE SHE COMES NOW (Velvet Underground) / etc.

Album rating: MOONHEAD (*8) / IN THE SPANISH CAVE (*7)

GUY KYSER – vocals, guitar / **ROGER KUNKEL** – guitar / **STEPHEN TESLUK** – bass; who repl. KEVIN STAYHODOR / **JOZEF BECKER** – drums; repl. FRANK FRENCH (ex-TRUE WEST)

Zippo | Frontier

Sep 85. (lp/c) *(ZONG/+CASS 006) <FRO 1015>* **EXPLORING THE AXIS**
– Down in the desert / Disney girl / Soundtrack / Lithium / Dead grammas on a train / The three song / Eleven / Roger's tongue / The real west / Exploring the axis. *(cd-iss. Jul90; ZONGCD 006) (cd re-iss. Apr97 on 'Diablo'+=; DIAB 824)* – BOTTOM FEEDERS

Jan 87. (lp) *(ZONG 017) <FRO 1020>* **MOONHEAD**
– Not your fault / Wire animals / Take it home / Thing / Moonhead / Wet heart / Mother / Come around / If those tears / Crawl piss freeze. *(w/free-flexi-7"; FRT 104)* – WIRE ANIMALS. / WET HEART *(cd-iss. Jul90 +=; ZONGCD 017)* – Waking up / Valley of the bones / Atomic imagery / Ain't that lovin' you baby. *(cd re-iss. Apr97 on 'Diablo'+=; DIAB 825)*

Sep 87. (m-lp) *(ZANE 005)* **BOTTOM FEEDERS** (rare, etc.) | | -
– Ain't that loving you baby / Macy's window / Waking up / Valley of the bones / Atomic imagery / Rocket U.S.A. (live).

— now without JOZEF who joined GAME THEORY (now full-time)

Demon | Frontier

Mar 88. (lp/cd) *(FIEND/+CD 114) <46151-2>* **IN THE SPANISH CAVE**
– Mr. Limpet / Ring / It's o.k. / Alu-Skidar / Red sun / Elsie crashed the party / Timing / Astronomy / Wand / July. *(cd+=)* – BOTTOM FEEDERS (m-lp) *<US-c++=>* – Munich Eunich.

Oct 88. (m-lp) *(VEX 8)* **RED SUN** | | -
– Red sun / Town without pity / The man with the golden gun / They're hanging me tonight / Some velvet morning / Red sun (original). *(cd-iss. May92;)*

R.C.A. | R.C.A.

May 90. (cd/c/lp) *(PD/PK/PL 90469) <9994-2/-4/-1>* **SACK FULL OF SILVER** | | Feb90
– Hidden lands / Sack full of silver / Yoo do right (can) / The napkin song / Americana – The ghost / Whirling Dervish / The tiggle song / Diesel man / On the floe. *(re-iss. Jul92 on 'Frontier' clear-lp; 34638-1)*

Sub Pop | Sub Pop

Apr 91. (7") *<(SP 94)>* **ANTS ARE CAVEMEN. / LITTLE DOLL (live)**

Frontier | Frontier

May 91. (m-cd/m-lp) *<(FCD/FLP 1035)>* **SQUATTERS RIGHTS**
– Caravan / Roadrunner / Film theme / May this be love / Everybody's been burned / I knew I'd want you.

Aug 91. (cd/c/lp) *<(34632-2/-4/-1)>* **THE RUBY SEA**

– The ruby sea / Tina and Glen / Puppet dog / Bartender's rag / Midwest flower / Dinosaur / The lady vanishes / Up to midnight / Hunter's moon / Christmas skies / The fish song / The clown song.

— Disbanded on 28th June 1992, after their last concert below.

Mar 93. (d-cd/d-c/d-lp) <(34642-2/-4/-1)> **THE ONE THAT GOT AWAY (live)**
– Down in the desert / Disney girl / Eleven / Not your fault / Wire animals / Take it home / Mr. Limpet / Elsie crashed the party / Red sun / Some velvet morning / Triangle song / Yoo doo right / Tina & Glen / Napkin song / Ants are cavemen / Fish song / Bartender's rag / Hunter's moon / Astronomy / Outlaw blues / It's o.k. / Wreck of the ol' 97 / Roadrunner / Munich Eunich / Silver machine / The clown song.

Dec 93. (7"ltd.) *(4678-7)* **MOONHEAD. / THE RUBY SEA** [ ] [-]

Munster Bird Cage

May 94. (cd/lp) *(MR 047 CD/LP)* <11778> **WHEN WORLDS COLLIDE** [ ] [ ] 1996

– compilations, etc. –

Feb 95. (cd/lp) *Frontier-RCA; <(31064-2/-1)>* **SPOOR** [ ] [ ]
– Radio afternoon / Town without pity / Red sun / The man with the golden gun / They're hanging me tonight / Some velvet morning / Ants are caveman / Little doll / Outlaw blues / Born to flames / Eye / Skinhead / Tina and Glen / Munich Eunich / God rest ye merry gentlemen / Here she comes now.

THIRD EYE FOUNDATION

Formed: Bristol, England . . . 1996 solely by drum'n'bass afficianado and ex-FLYING SAUCER ATTACK member, MATT ELLIOT, who admits to having a penchant for the wacky backy. Having travelled the world, ELLIOT kept down a daytime job at his local Revolver records, the dreadlocked spliffhead (he has since cut his locks due to itchyness) released a few mini-cd's in 1996, namely 'SEMTEX' and 'IN VERSION', before signing for 'Domino'. The following Spring, his THIRD EYE FOUNDATION released their debut set, 'GHOST', a largely experimental journey through hip-hop and Eastern sounds. A second album, 'YOU GUYS KILL ME' (1998), was an even darker affair from the travelling man who incidentally dislikes aeroplanes. • **Note:** not to be confused with another outfit, THIRD EYE.

Album rating: SEMTEX (*6) / IN VERSION (*5) / GHOST (*6) / YOU GUYS KILL ME (*7)

MATT ELLIOT (b.1974) – samples, etc (ex-FLYING SAUCER ATTACK)

Planet not iss.

Sep 96. (7") *(PUNK 015)* **UNIVERSAL COOLER. /** [ ] [-]

Linda's Strange Day not iss.

Oct 96. (m-cd) *(LSD 02)* **SEMTEX** [ ] [-]
– Sleep / Still-life / Dreams on his fingers / Next of kin / Once when I was an Indian / Rain. *(re-iss. Nov96 on 'Series 500-Domino' m-lp/m-cd; SER 502/+CD)*

Oct 96. (m-cd) *(LSD 04)* **IN VERSION /** [ ] [-]

Domino Merge

Apr 97. (cd/lp) *(WIG CD/LP 32)* <MRG 119> **GHOST** [ ] [ ]
– What to do but cry / Corpses as bedmates / Star's gone out / Out sound from way in / I've seen the light and it's dark / Ghosts / Donald Crowhurst.

Nov 97. (12"/cd-s) *(RUG 059 T/CD)* <MRG 134CD> **SOUND OF VIOLENCE. / NAME FOR MY PAIN / PAIN / CORPSES** [ ] [ ] Jan98

Oct 98. (12"/cd-s) *(RUG 075 T/CD)* **FEAR OF A WACK PLANET. / A GALAXY OF SCARS (version)** [ ] [ ]

Oct 98. (cd/lp) *(WIG CD/LP 053)* <MRG 149> **YOU GUYS KILL ME** [ ] [ ]
– Galaxy of scars / For all the brothers and sisters / There's a fight at the end of the tunnel / Even harder shade of dark / Lions writing the bible / No dove no covenant / I'm sick and tired of being sick and tired / That would be exhibiting the same weak traits / In Bristol with a pistol.

Sub Rosa not iss.

Nov 98. (12"; shared with BUMP 'N' GRIND) *(QUANTUM 321)* **PAN ODYSSEY** [ ] [-]

THIRST (see under ⇒ BLUE ORCHIDS)

THIS HEAT

Formed: Brixton, London, England . . . late 1975 by CHARLES BULLEN, CHARLES HAYWARD and GARETH WILLIAMS. They were originally called RADAR FAVOURITES, later changing to DOLPHIN LOGIC. Setting up their own studio in a local disused meat factory, their line-up was augmented by tape editor CHRIS BLAKE, the band subsequently sending a demo to John Peel, who gave them airtime on his night time Radio One show in early '77. Going back into the studio with ANTHONY MOORE (Slapp Happy) and DAVID CUNNINGHAM (Flying Lizards), they recorded a self-titled debut album for CUNNINGHAM's label, 'Piano'. Experimental improvisers lying between THROBBING GRISTLE and CAN, THIS HEAT swapped instruments and multi-layered tracks on tape loops. During this period and after the album's release in 1979, they worked with "world music" musicians from India, Ghana (MARIO BOYER DIEKVUROH) and Senegal, branching out on tour the following year. After a further 12" single, the band signed to 'Rough Trade' and in '81, hooked up with reggae mixer, MARTIN FREDERICK on a follow-up album, 'DECEIT', this time around fusing industrial ethnic-folk with dub. However, THIS HEAT later split when WILLIAMS went to study Indian dance, drama and music theory, HAYWARD later surfacing in another trio, The CAMBERWELL NOW.

Album rating: THIS HEAT (*8) / DECEIT (*7)

CHARLES BULLEN (b. Liverpool) – guitar, clarinet, viola, vocals, tapes (also of PEOPLE IN CONTROL) / **CHARLES HAYWARD** (b. 1951) – percussion, keyboards, vocals, tapes (ex-QUIET SUN) / **GARETH WILLIAMS** – keyboards, guitar, bass, vocals, tapes

Piano not iss.

Aug 79. (lp) *(THIS 1)* **THIS HEAT** [ ] [-]
– Testcard / Horizontal hold / Not waving / Water / Twilight furniture / 24 track loop / Diet of worms / Music like escaping gas / Rainforest / The fall of Saigon / Testcard. *(re-iss. Aug84 on 'These'; HEAT 1) (cd-iss. Nov91; HEAT 1CD)*

Sep 80. (12"ep) *(THIS 12-01)* **HEALTH AND EFFICIENCY. / GRAPHIC / VARISPEED** [ ] [-]
(3"cd-ep iss.Sep98 on 'These'; THESE 12)

Rough Trade not iss.

Sep 81. (lp) *(ROUGH 26)* **DECEIT** [ ] [-]
– Sleep / Paper hats / Triumph / S.P.Q.R. / Cenotaph / Shrink wrap / Radio Prague / Makeshift Swahili / Independence / A new kind of water. *(re-iss. Aug84 on 'These'; HEAT 2) (cd-iss. Nov91; HEAT 2CD)*

— split in 1982 when WILLIAMS' place was filled by tour temps **IAN HILL** – keyboards, vocals / **TREVOR GORONWY** – bass, vocals / **STEVE RICKARD** – engineer. BULLEN became a sound engineer and released one rare 'LIFETONES' lp in 1983

— HAYWARD went onto work with Rough Trade outfits LAURA LOGIC (Pedigree Charm) and RAINCOATS (Odyshape)

– compilations, etc. –

1993. (cd) *These; (THESE 6CD)* **REPEAT** [ ] [-]
– Repeat / Metal / Graphic – Varispeed. *(re-mast.Sep98; same)*

Jun 97. (cd) *These; (THESE 010CD)* **MADE AVAILABLE – PEEL SESSIONS** [ ] [-]
(lp-iss.Sep98; THESE 10)

Jul 98. (2x12") *These; (THESE 12-6)* **REPEAT / HEALTH AND EFFICIENCY** [ ] [-]

CAMBERWELL NOW

HAYWARD, GORONWY + RICKARD + guest **BULLEN**

Duplicate not iss.

1983. (12"ep) *(0011)* **MERIDIANS** [ ] [-]
– Cutty Sark / Trade winds / Pearl divers / Spirit of Dunkirk / Splash.

Ink not iss.

May 86. (lp) *(INK 19)* **THE GHOST TRADE** [ ] [-]
– Working nights / Sitcom / Wheat futures / Speculative fiction / Green lantern / The ghost trade.

— added guest **MARIA LANBURN** – saxophone

Feb 87. (12") *(INK 12-24)* **GREENFINGERS. /** [ ] [-]

— HAYWARD's drum trio then recorded 'NOISY CHAMPS' as LES BATTERIES (on 'Ayaa Disques'; *AYAADT 0486*), alongside drummers GUIGOU CHENEBIER and RICK BROWN.

– compilations, etc. –

1992. (cd) *RecDec; (CD 1015)* **ALL'S WELL** [ ] [-]

CHARLES HAYWARD

Ink not iss.

Nov 87. (lp) *(INK 31)* **SURVIVE THE GESTURE** [ ] [-]
– Make believe / Let's pretend / North Southwark / Pretend to believe / Crystal Palace / This misunderstanding / You and me / Time and motion / That distant light / Australia. *(cd-iss. Nov88; INKCD 004)*

Sub Rosa Sub Rosa

1990. (cd) *(<SUBCD 01033>)* **SKEW WHIFF – A TRIBUTE TO MARK ROTHKO** [ ] [ ]
– The actor merges with the crowd / Cold blue sun / Smell of metal / Lopside / Thames water authority (parts 1 & 2).

1992. (cd) *(<SUBCD 01740>)* **SWITCH ON WAR – MUSIC FOR THE ARMCHAIR THEATRE OF WAR** [ ] [ ]
– Crying shame / Strong-arm deadline / Pinpoint / Sweetheart / Never before.

— HAYWARD also drummed in outfits KEEP THE DOG and CAROL, SINGING, which included FRED FRITH (ex-HENRY COW) and NICK DOYNE-DITMUS (ex-PINSKI ZOO) respectively. He also sessioned for EVERYTHING BUT THE GIRL. With NICK DOYNE-IT, he issued cd/lp 'MY SECRET ALPHABET' *(SR 59)*

Marina not iss.

Mar 97. (cd; CHARLES HAYWARD, DAVID SHEA & NUS) *(MAR 21)* **SUB ROSA SESSIONS: BARI OCTOBER 1996** [ ] [ ]

THIS MORTAL COIL

Formed: Wandsworth, London, England . . . 1983 by IVO WATTS-RUSSELL, aided by producer JOHN FRYER. The brainchild of '4 a.d.' mainman, IVO, THIS MORTAL COIL was basically a loose collective of mainly 4ad artists gathered together with the intention of creating atmospheric and inspiring gothic-esque sounds, most effectively through their startling cover versions (see further below). With the COCTEAU TWINS (ELIZABETH FRASER and ROBIN GUTHRIE) initially taking a lead role, THIS MORTAL COIL made their mark with a haunting cover of Tim Buckley's 'SONG TO THE SIREN', wherein LIZ FRASER's lyrical mystical mantra was actually coherant to the unfamiliar ear. Originally intended as a B-side to a version of MODERN ENGLISH's '16 DAYS' (with the latter act's ROBBIE GREY on vocals), the track secured a minor chart place and has since become a cult classic (even providing inspiration for The CHEMICAL BROTHERS, or The DUST BROTHERS as they were known at the time!). Encouraged by the response, IVO took the opportunity to provide a wider platform for the emerging talent on his label, roping in selected personnel from DEAD CAN DANCE, COLOURBOX, WOLFGANG PRESS and X-MAL DEUTSCHLAND alongside vocalists HOWARD DEVOTO (ex-MAGAZINE) and GORDON SHARPE (of CINDYTALK – a non '4ad' act) to record a full-length THIS MORTAL COIL album, 'IT'LL END IN TEARS'. Preceded by the 'KANGAROO' single (from the pen of Alex Chilton), the 1984 set cracked the UK Top 40, its combination of low-key covers (featuring another Chilton number, 'HOLOCAUST') and moody instrumentals receiving lavish praise from the critics. IVO continued to expand his record company with new US acts (i.e. The PIXIES, THROWING MUSES, etc), lending a different flavour to the 1986 follow-up, 'FILIGREE & SHADOW'. Featuring new singer/writer DOMINIC APPLETON (from another non '4ad' act, BREATHLESS), this double-set contained a number of more well-known but just as inventive interpretations including Van Morrison's 'COME HERE MY LOVE', Tim Buckley's 'I MUST HAVE BEEN BLIND' and Talking Heads' 'DRUGS'. It was five years before TMC's third and final album, the UK Top 30 double-set, 'BLOOD' (1991), starring a stripped down cast of musicians including stalwart, APPLETON, alongside KIM DEAL, TANYA DONELLY, CAROLINE CRAWLEY (from SHELLEYAN ORPHAN) and HEIDI BERRY. More accessible than its two predecessors, the record was nevertheless a graceful swansong, featuring as it did engaging renditions of CHRIS BELL classics, 'YOU AND YOUR SISTER' and 'I AM THE COSMOS'. • **Songwriters:** IVO and some 4 a.d. musicians, except; GATHERING DUST (Modern English) / ANOTHER DAY (Roy Harper) / NOT ME (Colin Newman) / THE JEWELLER (Tom Rapp) / HELP ME LIFT YOU UP (Mary Margaret O'Hara) / NATURE'S WAY (Spirit) / STRENGTH OF STRINGS + WITH TOMORROW (Gene Clark) / MY FATHER (. . . Collins) / I WANT TO LIVE (. . . Ogan) / FIRE BROTHERS (. . . Duncan) / MR. SOMEWHERE (. . . Walsh) / SEVERAL TIMES (. . . Nooten) / CAROLYN'S SONG (. . . Roback) / LATE NIGHT + TARANTULA (Syd Barrett) / TILL I GAIN CONTROL AGAIN (. . . Crowell) / I COME AND STAND AT EVERY DOOR (Byrds).

Album rating: IT'LL END IN TEARS (*8) / FILIGREE & SHADOW (*7) / BLOOD (*7)

IVO WATTS-RUSSELL (b.1955) – tapes, loops, etc. / **JOHN FRYER** – instruments, producer with **COCTEAU TWINS:- ELIZABETH FRAZER** – vox / **ROBIN GUTHRIE** – guitar

		4 a.d.	4ad-Reprise
Sep 83.	(7") *(AD 310)* **SONG TO THE SIREN. / 16 DAYS (reprise)**	66	-
	(12"+=) *(BAD 310)* – Gathering dust.		

(above 'B'sides featured **ROBBIE GREY** – vocals (of MODERN ENGLISH)
(below 'A'side featured **MARTIN McCARRICK** – cello, strings (of WILLING SINNERS; MARC ALMOND) / **GORDON SHARPE** – vocals (of CINDYTALK) / **SIMON RAYMONDE** – guitar, tapes (of COCTEAU TWINS)

Aug 84.	(7") *(AD 410)* **KANGAROO. / IT'LL END IN TEARS**		-

— below album featured above musicians, plus **GINI BALL** – violin (of WILLING SINNERS) / DEAD CAN DANCE: **LIZA GERRARD** – accordion, vocals / **BRENDAN PERRY** – bass drone, drum / **PETER ULRICH** – percussion / COLOURBOX: **STEVEN YOUNG** – piano / **MARTYN YOUNG** – sitar, guitar, bass / X-MAL DEUTSCHLAND: **MANUELA RICKERS** – guitar / WOLFGANG PRESS: **MARK COX** – organ / **HOWARD DEVOTO** – vocals (ex-MAGAZINE)

Oct 84.	(lp/c) *(CAD/+C 411) <96269>* **IT'LL END IN TEARS**	38	

– Kangaroo / Song to the siren / Holocaust / FYT / Fond affections / The last ray / Waves become wings / Another day / Barramundi / Dreams made flesh / Not me / A single wish. *(cd-iss. 1986; CAD 411CD) <US cd-iss. 1993 on 'Warners'; 45454>*

— Retained guests **SIMON RAYMONDE / PETER ULRICH / MARK COX / STEVEN YOUNG** plus new BREATHLESS: **DOMINIC APPLETON** – vocals / **RICHENEL** – vocals / DIF JUZ: **DAVID CURTIS** – guitar / **ALAN CURTIS** – guitar / **RICHARD THOMAS** – saxophone / **MODERN ENGLISH: ANDREW GRAY** – guitar / / **JEAN** – vocals / **ALISON LIMERICK** – vocals / **CAROLINE SEAMAN** – vocals / **KEITH MITCHELL** – guitar / **DIERDRE RUTOWSKI** – backing vocals / **LOUISE RUTOWSKI** – backing vocals / **KEITH MITCHELL** – guitar / **NIGEL K.HINE** – guitar / **CHRIS PYE** – guitar / **JOHN TURNER** – organ, keyboards / **TONY WAEREA** – didgeridoo / **ANNE TURNER + LES McKUEN** – choir

Sep 86.	(d-lp/c)(cd) *(DAD/+C 609)(DAD 609CD)* **FILIGREE & SHADOW**	53	-

– Velvet belly / The jeweller / Ivy and neet / Meniscus / Tears / Tarantula / My father / Come here my love / At first, and then / Strength of strings / Morning glory / Inch-blue / I want to live / Mama K I / Filigree & shadow / Firebrothers / Thais I / I must have been blind / A heart of glass / Alone / Mama K II / The horizon bleeds and sucks its thumb / Drugs / Red rain / Thais II. *<US cd-iss. 1993 on 'Warners'; 45453>*

Sep 86.	(ltd-10") *(BAD 608)* **COME HERE MY LOVE. / DRUGS**		-

— They used past musicians, plus **CAROLINE CRAWLEY, KIM DEAL + TANYA DONELLY, DOMINIC APPLETON, HEIDI BERRY + The RUTOWSKI's**, etc.

Apr 91.	(d-lp/c/cd) *(DAD/+C/CD 609)* **BLOOD**	28	-

– The lacemaker / Mr. Somewhere / Ardialu / With tomorrow / Loose joints / You and your sister / Nature's way / I come and steal at every door / Bitter / Baby Ray baby / Several times / The lacemaker II / Late night / Ruddy and wretched / Help me lift you up / Carolyn's song / DD and E / Til I gain control again / Dreams are like water / I am the cosmos / (Nothing but) Blood. *<US cd-iss. 1993 on 'Warners'; 45452>*

— above was their final release

– compilations, etc. –

Dec 89.	(cd) *Alex; <1426>* **THIS MORTAL COIL**	-	
Mar 93.	(cd) *Warners; <45135>* **1983-1991**	-	

David THOMAS (see under ⇒ PERE UBU)

Tracy THORN (see under ⇒ EVERYTHING BUT THE GIRL)

THOSE NAUGHTY LUMPS

Formed: Liverpool, England . . . 1977 by PETER HART, GERRY MULLIGAN, KEVIN WILKINSON, BILL DRUMMOND (from BIG IN JAPAN) and DAVID BALFE, the latter subsequently moving on to The TEARDROP EXPLODES. His replacement, PETE YOUNGER, was in place for the group's long-awaited debut 45, 'IGGY POP'S JACKET', a brilliant indie-pop tribute to the Godfather Of Punk. By the time of their 1980 follow-up, 'DOWN AT THE ZOO', a major upheaval in the ranks left only HART and WILKINSON at the core, the other three including 'Zoo' label boss, DRUMMOND, all went on to better things.

Album rating: never released any

PETER HART – vocals / **BILL DRUMMOND** – lead guitar (ex-BIG IN JAPAN) / **GERRY MULLIGAN** – saxophone / **KEVIN WILKINSON** – drums / **PETE YOUNGER** – bass; repl. DAVID BALFE (to TEARDROP EXPLODES)

		Zoo	not iss.
Jan 79.	(7") *(CAGE 002)* **IGGY POP'S JACKET. / PURE AND INNOCENT**		-

— **BOBBY CARL** – guitar; repl. DRUMMOND who later formed KLF

— **MARTIN COOPER** – saxophone (ex-DALEK I LOVE YOU) repl. MULLIGAN

— **BREAM** – bass; repl. YOUNGER who joined WAH! HEAT

		Open Eye	not iss.
1980.	(7"ep) *(OEEP 1002)* **DOWN AT THE ZOO EP**		-

– Ice cream / Down at the zoo / I'm gonna die / Love is a reflex.

— basically split when WILKINSON joined HOLLY & THE ITALIANS (and later CHINA CRISIS). COOPER went on to ORCHESTRAL MANOEUVRES IN THE DARK.

THOUSAND YARD STARE

Formed: Slough, Berkshire, England . . . 1988 by STEPHEN BARNES, GILES DUFFY, SEAN McDONOUGH, DOMINIC BOSTOCK and a guy called ALEX. Following a self-financed debut EP, 'WEATHERWATCHING' (on 'Stifled Aardvark'), the band accrued sufficient press interest for a major label deal via 'Polydor'. With KEVIN MOXON having replaced ALEX, the quartet embarked upon a long journey to the Shetland Isles, undertaking an island-hopping mini tour to delighted pop-starved locals. Minor players in the shoegazing scene, THOUSAND YARD STARE might've lacked the muso intensity of RIDE or the feminine charm of LUSH but were nevertheless capable of turning out a half-decent slice of chiming guitar-pop when they felt like it. 'COMEUPPANCE' was a prime example, a UK Top 40 hit and a taster for debut album, 'HANDS ON' (1992). Given a bit of a rough ride by the press, especially when the "scene that celebrated itself" rapidly fell out of media favour, the band made little critical or commercial headway with a further two albums, 'FAIR TO MIDDLING' (1993) and 'MAPPAMUNDI' (1993). • **Songwriters:** BARNES lyrics / group penned, except STRANGE (Wire).

Album rating: FAIR TO MIDDLING (*7)

STEPHEN BARNES – vocals / **GILES DUFFY** – lead guitar / **ALEX** – rhythm guitar / **SEAN McDONOUGH** – bass / **DOMINIC BOSTOCK** – drums

		Stifled Aardvark	not iss.
Nov 90.	(12"ep) **WEATHERWATCHING**		-

– Medley: Weatherwatching (live) – Another and on / Buttermouth / Twice times.

— **KEVIN MOXON** – rhythm guitar; repl. ALEX

May 91.	(10"yellow-ep/12"ep) **KEEPSAKE**		-
	– Three doors down / Stonesthrow / Wonderment.		
Oct 91.	(12"ep/10"blue-ep/c-ep/cd-ep) *(AARD 005 T/X/C/CD)* **SEASONSTREAM EP**	65	-
	– O-O A.E.T. / Village end / Keepsake / Worse for wear.		
Nov 91.	(12";one-sided gig freebie) **STRANGE. / TWICE TIMES**		-

— Note; 'Stifled Aardvark' were now licensed to 'Polydor'.

Jan 92.	(7"/10"red) *(AARD 007/+X)* **COMEUPPANCE. / WISH A PERFECT**	37	-
	(12"+=/cd-s+=) *(AARD 007 T/CD)* – Standoffish.		
Feb 92.	(cd/c/lp) *(513001-2/-4/-1)* **HANDS ON**	38	-

– O-O A.E.T. / Thisness / Comeuppance / Cottager / Seasonstream / Junketing / Nonplussed / Absentee / Last up first to go / Buttermouth / Wideshire.*(lp w/ free 10"ep)*

Jun 92.	(12"ep/cd-ep/10"green or clear-ep) *(AAR DT/CD/X 010)* **SPINDRIFT EP**	58	-
	– Wideshire two / Hand, son (live) / Happenstance! (live) / Mocca pune (live).		
May 93.	(7") *(AARD 012)* **VERSION OF ME. / STRANGE**	57	-

(cd-s+=/12"clear+=) *(AAR CD/DT 012)* – Darkness of her eyes / ('A'demo version).
(cd-s) *(AARDD 012)* – ('A'side) / Spacehopper / Happenstance (live) / Comeuppance (live).

May 93.	(cd/c/lp) *(519359-2/-4/-1)* **MAPPAMUNDI**		-

– Version of me / God's P45 / Tragedy No.6 / Debutante / One and all / Snoozer / Half size / Small change / Monsieur Bour and his coat / Naturesway (Earth watching) / What's your level? / Downtown mystic.

— disbanded after above

– compilations, etc. –

Mar 93. (cd)(lp) *Stifled Aardvark; (AAR 11CD)(AARLP 11)* **FAIR TO MIDDLING** (early material) ☐ -

3 COLOURS RED

Formed: London, England . . . 1995 by vocalist/bassist PETE VUCKOVIC and Geordie guitarist CHRIS McCORMACK, who recruited drummer KEITH BAXTER and guitarist BEN HARDING (ex-SENSELESS THINGS). Named after the Kieslowski film of the same name, the band issued their debut 45, 'THIS IS MY HOLLYWOOD' early '97, which immediately led to them signing with 'Creation'. Their first release for the label, the 3-chord pop punk/rock thrash 'NUCLEAR HOLIDAY' homed in on the UK Top 20, narrowly missing its target. 'SIXTY MILE SMILE' however, achieved this feat as did their debut album, 'PURE'. The band subsequently gained a groundswell of support, gigging heavily with the likes of KISS, ANTHRAX and SKUNK ANANSIE, becoming crown princes of the metal press in the process.

Album rating: PURE (*7)

PETE VUCKOVIC (b.16 Feb'71, Tiveton, Devon, England) – vocals, bass (ex-DIAMOND HEAD) / **CHRIS McCORMACK** (b.21 Jun'73, South Shields, England) – guitar, vocals (ex-HONEYCRACK) / **BEN HARDING** (b.31 Jan'65, Stoke-On-Trent, England) – guitar, vocals (ex-SENSELESS THINGS) / **KEITH BAXTER** (b.19 Feb'71, Morcambe, England) – drums

Fierce Panda / not iss.

Mar 96. (7"/cd-s) *(NING 17/+CD)* **THIS IS MY HOLLYWOOD. / HATE SLICK** ☐ -

Creation / Sony

Jan 97. (7"/c-s) *(CRE/+CS 250)* **NUCLEAR HOLIDAY. / HUMAN FACTORY** 22 -
(cd-s+=) *(CRESCD 250)* – My own gauge.

Mar 97. (7") *(CRE 254)* **SIXTY MILE SMILE. / ANISEED (live)** 20 -
(cd-s) *(CRESCD 254)* – ('A'side) / Zip the morals / Till I'm ready.
(cd-s) *(CRESCD 254X)* – ('A'side) / This is my Hollywood (live) / Nerve gas (live).

Apr 97. (7") *(CRE 265)* **PURE. / HATESLICK (live)** 28 -
(cd-s) *(CRESCD 265)* – ('A'side) / Throughbreeze / Fake apology.
(cd-s) *(CRESCD 265X)* – ('A'side) / Mental blocks (live) / Nuclear holiday (live).

May 97. (cd/lp)(c) *(CRE CD/LP 208)(C-CRE 208) <67958>* **PURE** 16 ☐
– This is my Hollywood / Nerve gas / Nuclear holiday / Copper girl / Sixty mile smile / Sunny in England / Alright ma / Mental blocks / Fit boy & faint girl / Halfway up the downs / Hateslick / Love's cradle / Aniseed.

Jun 97. (7") *(CRE 270)* **COPPER GIRL. / SUNNY IN ENGLAND (live)** 30 -
(cd-s) *(CRESCD 270)* – ('A'side) / Inside / This opera.
(cd-s) *(CRESCD 270X)* – ('A'side) / Sixty mile smile (live) / Alright ma (live).

Oct 97. (7") *(CRE 277)* **THIS IS MY HOLLYWOOD. / INSIDE (live)** 48 -
(cd-s) *(CRESCD 277)* – ('A'side) / On no ones side / Sunny in England (demo).
(cd-s) *(CRESCD 277X)* – ('A'side) / ('A'-Ice-T sober mix) / Yellow hair carriage / Pure (live).

Oct 98. (7"ep/cd-ep) *(CRE/+SCD 304)* **PARALYSE EP** ☐ -
– Paralyse / Throwing the world away / Say something / Room with a view.

THREE JOHNS

Formed: Leeds, England . . . 1981 by art-college buddies JOHN HYATT, JON LANGFORD (also of Leeds stalwarts The MEKONS) and JOHN BRENNAN. Socialists to a man (or even a John!), the trio formed against a background of rampant Thatcherism and fervent Rock Against Racism activity, their debut single, 'ENGLISH WHITE BOY ENGINEER' (a MEKONS cover) a damning indictment of South Africa's apartheid system. As much renowned for their manic sense of humour and boozing as for their benefit gigging and community activities, The THREE JOHNS proceeded to infiltrate the indie charts with a string of offbeat singles including 'MEN LIKE MONKEYS' and 'PINK HEADED BUG'. A debut album, 'ATOM DRUM BOP' (1984) found the band casting around for a focus to their drum machine-driven sound, while a subsequent tour of the States inspired 1986's more impressive follow-up, 'THE WORLD BY STORM'. Driving, pulsing indie-rock fuelled by HYATT's strident vocal proclamations, the record featured such singalong anti-US diatribes as 'DEATH OF THE EUROPEAN' and 'TORCHES OF LIBERTY'. Never more than a part-time concern, the band drifted apart following a disastrous American tour and final, patchy album, 'THE DEATH OF EVERYTHING' (1988). While LANGFORD balanced his MEKON activities with record production, HYATT concentrated on his career as a college lecturer.

Album rating: ATOM DROP BOP (*6) / THE WORLD BY STORM (*7) / THE DEATH OF EVERYTHING (*5) / EAT YOUR SONS (*5) / CRIME PAYS compilation (*6)

JON LANGFORD – vocals, guitar (also of MEKONS) / **JOHN HYATT** – vocals, drums (ex-SHEENY AND THE GOYS, ex-ANOTHER COLOUR) / **JOHN BRENNAN** (b. PHIL) – bass (ex-25 RIFLES)

C.N.T. / not iss.

May 82. (7") *(CNT 003)* **ENGLISH WHITE BOY ENGINEER. / SECRET AGENT** ☐ -

Jan 83. (7") *(CNT 011)* **PINK HEADED BUG. / LUCY IN THE RAIN** ☐ -
(above 2 re-iss. Jan84 as 12"ep 'SOME HISTORY' on 'Abstract'; 12ABS 022)

May 83. (12"ep) *(CNT 013)* **MEN LIKE MONKEYS / TWO MINUTE APE? / WINDOLENE / MARX'S WIFE / PARIS 1941** ☐ -

Abstact / not iss.

Sep 83. (7") *(ABS 019)* **A.W.O.L. / ROOSTER BLUES** ☐ -
(12"+=) *(12ABS 019)* – Image or animal / Kick the dog right out.

Mar 84. (7") *(ABS 023)* **DO THE SQUARE THING. / ZOWEE** ☐ -
(12"+=) *(12ABS 023)* – World of the workers / Kinky beat.

Aug 84. (m-lp/c) *(ABT/+C 010)* **ATOM DROP BOP** ☐ -
– Teenage nightingales to wax / 3 junk / Sun of mud / Missing / Do not cross the line / The Devil's music / Dr. Freedom / No place / Class war (!). *(c/ repl.(!) track, w/ +=)* – World of the workers / A.W.O.L. / Do the square thing.

May 85. (7") *(ABS 034)* **DEATH OF THE EUROPEAN. / HEADS LIKE CONVICTS** ☐ -
(12"+=) *(12ABS 034)* – Rabies / 20th century boy.

Nov 85. (7") *(ABS 036)* **BRAINBOX (HE'S SO BRAINBOX). / WATCH IT GO** ☐ -
(12"+=) *(12ABS 036)* – Men without bones.

Apr 86. (7") *(ABS 040)* **SOLD DOWN THE RIVER. / ROSE OF YORKSHIRE** ☐ -
(12"+=) *(12ABS 040)* – Fruitflies.

May 86. (lp/c) *(ABT/+C 012)* **THE WORLD BY STORM** ☐ -
– King car / Sold down the river / The ship that died of shame / Demon drink / Torches of liberty / Death of the European / World by storm / Atom drum bop / The crunge / Johnny was a good man / Coals to Newcastle. *(c+=)* – Watch it go / Brainbox (he's so brainbox). *(free live 7"w/ lp)* – ENGLISH WHITE BOY ENGINEER / DEVIL'S MUSIC. / A.W.O.L. / INDUSTRY

Nov 86. (lp) *(ABT 015)* **CRIME PAYS – ROCK'N'ROLL IN THE . . . DEMONOCRACY (1982-86)** (compilation) ☐ -
– English white boy engineer / Pink headed bug / Men like monkeys / Windolene / Rooster blue / A.W.O.L. / Do the square thing / Zowee / Death of the European / Brainbox (he's so brainbox) / Sold down the river.

Aug 87. (7") *(ABS 043)* **NEVER AND ALWAYS. / TURN UP THOSE DOWN HEARTED BLUES** ☐ -
(12"+=) *(12ABS 043)* –

Mar 88. (7") *(ABS 049)* **TORCHES OF LIBERTY. / BIG WHALES (NEVER LIVE)** ☐ -

T.I.M. / not iss.

Oct 88. (lp/cd) *(MOT LP/CD 20)* **THE DEATH OF EVERYTHING** ☐ -
– The king is dead / Bullshitaco / Moonlight in Vermont / Go ahead bikini / Spin me around / Nonsense spew from my song machine / Humbug / Fast fish / Downhearted blues / Never and always.

Tupelo / not iss.

Oct 90. (cd/c/lp) *(TUP CD/MC/LP 018)* **EAT YOUR SONS** ☐ -

— split after above, LANGFORD continued with the MEKONS and later released a solo album

– compilations, etc. –

May 87. (lp) *Last Time Around; (LAST 001/+C)* **LIVE IN CHICAGO (live)** ☐ -

1992. (c) *ROIR; <A 160>* **DEATHROCKER SCRAPBOOK** (out-takes) - ☐
– Incredible Wendy Frith / Nightmare / Snitch / Burn while you learn / Hello Dickie / Conversation with Freud / Is your brain your own? / Mouths to feed / You're not like Manson, are you? / Mountain man / Buzz be goode / Machinery seeds / Cheap computer / We won't wobble / Peter's advertising agency / One fine day / High standards / Press is a toad / Ballad of Colin Buggers / Compensation / Fill me up / Spider spaceship.

Jun 96. (cd) *Dojo; (DOJOCD 225)* **THE BEST OF THE THREE JOHNS** ☐ -

3 MUSTAPHAS 3

Formed: North London, England via Szegerely, Balkans . . . 1982 as a revolving collective of worldly wise musicians including UNCLE PATREL, HIJAZ, HOUZAM, ISFA'ANI, OUSSAK and NIAVETTI, all, of course, assuming the MUSTAPHA surname. Making their live London debut in summer '82, this bunch of fun loving, cross-fertilising world music connoisseurs soon established themselves as favourites with Radio One DJ's John Peel and Andy Kershaw, issuing an introductory mini-set, 'BAM! MUSTAPHAS PLAY STEREO' (1985) on their own 'Fez-o-Phone' label (a subdivision of world label, 'Globestyle'). By the release of 1987's 'SHOPPING' album, the line-up had been expanded with the addition of SABAH HABAS and KEMO, the record exploring a more eclectic array of styles from the trademark Balkan hoedown to African and Arabic. Self styled Godfathers Of World Music, HABAS urged his band to "take it to the fridge" on the klezmer/rap crossover, 'XAMENH EVTEXIA – FIZ'N (LOST FORTUNE – LOST REFRIDGERATION), clearly more fruit machine than 'Sex Machine!'. Their quintessentially continental humour nevertheless belied a wealth of talent performing on such diverse instrumentation as bouzouki, accordian, slack-key guitar and cello in addition to the standard bass and drums. The MUSTAPHAS also acquired a secret weapon in the shape of vocalist LAVRA TIMA DAVIZ MUSTAPHA, an enchanting songstress capable of singing in a dazzling range of languages and styles. Her impact was felt fully on the more accomplished and widely acclaimed 'HEART OF UNCLE' (1989), the group concocting ingenious combinations of seemingly incongruous styles incorporating everything from Hindu folk to Carribbean calypso. Following the addition of woodwind player, DAOUDI MUSTAPHA, 1990's 'SOUP OF THE CENTURY' received even more widespread praise, the album topping the American Billboard World Music chart. The group were conspicuous by their absence for the 90's, all but SABAH HABAS (he went on to a solo career with one album, 'DENPASAR MOON') disappearing from view although a couple of MUSTAPHAS played on a 1994 tribute album, 'Out On The Rolling Sea', dedicated to Bahamian guitarist, JOSEPH SPENCE.

Album rating: SHOPPING (*6) / HEART OF UNCLE (*6) / FRIENDS, FIENDS & FRONDS compilation (*7)

OUSSACK MUSTAPHA – cello / **NIAVETI MUSTAPHA III** – flute, gajde, etc / **HIJAZ MUSTAPHA** – violin, bouzouki, Hawaiian guitar / **HOUZAM MUSTAPHA** – percussion / **ISFA'ANI MUSTAPHA** – hand drums / **UNCLE PATREL MUSTAPHA** – narrator

Fez-O-Phone — not iss.

Mar 85. (m-lp) *(FEZ 001)* **BAM! MUSTAPHAS PLAY STEREO** – Lebedik un freilach / To tilephone tiszenitias / Bel 2 – Singe tema / A chilling tale pt.4 / Thalasso p'ola ta nera / Mehmeteli.

Feb 86. (7") *(NS 111)* **SI VOUS PASSEZ PAR LA. / STAREHE MUSTAPHA** (12"=Mar89+=) *(NST 111)* – Maldita guajira.

Aug 86. (m-lp) *(FEZ 002)* **L'ORCHESTRE "BAM" DE GRAND MUSTAPHA INT. & PARTY HITS (LOCAL MUSIC FROM THE WORLD)** – Vranjanski ekspres / O Memetis / Hora lui marin / Besarabia / Niska banja / Ainy la la – Ah ya assmar el lawn / Cabra.

— now without OUSSACK who was repl. by **SABAH HABAS MUSTAPHA** – vocals, bass, etc / **KEMO "KEM KEM" MUSTAPHA** – accordion, piano / + flexible members **EXPENSIVE MUSTAPHA** – trumpet / **sister LAVRA TIMA DAVIZ MUSTAPHA** – vocals

Globestyle — Shanachie

Aug 87. (12") *(NST 120)* **SHOUFFI RHIROU. / VOULEZ VOUS DANSER / DARLING, DON'T SAY 'NO'**

Aug 87. (lp/cd) *(ORB/CDORB 022) <64006>* **SHOPPING** – Ljubav krajizvora – Zvezdanova (skupovo) kolo / Shika shika (hold hold) / Xamenh evtexia – Fiz'n (lost fortune – lost refridgeration) / Musafir (oh traveller) / Szegerely farewell / A night off Beirut / Selver / Shouffi Rhirou / Valle e pogradecit. *(cd+=)* – Darling, don't say 'no' / Voulez vous danser.

— guest on next single **OFRA HAZA** – vocals

Feb 88. (7") *(NS 121)* **LINDA LINDA. / KOPANISTA** (12"+=) *(NST 121)* – ('A'-Longer mix) / ('A'-Szegerely mix).

Feb 88. (c) *(ORBC 027)* **THE GOLDEN WORLD OF MUSTAPHA** – Linda Linda / Vranjanski ekspres / A chilling tale / Voulez vous danser / Shika shika / Mehmeteli / Kopanitsa / Besarabia / Si vous passez par la / Shouffi Rhirou / Singe tema / A night off Beirut / Szegerely farewell.

Globestyle — Rykodisc

May 89. (lp/c/cd) *(ORB/ORBC/CDORB 043) <20156>* **HEART OF UNCLE** – Awara moon / Trois fois trois / Sitna Lisa / Mama o / Ovcepolsko oro *[cd-only]* / Kem Kem / Vi bist du geveyzn far prohisish'n? *[cd-only]* / Kaba Mustapha / Valle e gajdes / Trois fois trois (country version) *[cd-only]* / Yeni yoi *[cd-only]* / Taxi driver (I don't care) / Benga taxi / Aj zajdi zajdi jasno sonce / Anapse to tsigaro.

— added **DAOUDI MUSTAPHA** – woodwind (was a guest in '88)

Fez-O-Phone — Rykodisc

Sep 90. (cd/c/lp) *(CDFEZ/FEZC/FEZLP 004) <10195>* **SOUP OF THE CENTURY** – Buke e kripe ne vater tone / Kalaxhojne / Zohar No.2 / Soba song / Golden clarinet / Ti citron / Sadilo mome / Tropnalo oro / This city is very exciting / Madre / Ya habibi, ya ghaybine / Mamo, snezhets navalyalo. *(cd+=/c+=)* – Yogurt koydum dolaba / Televizyon / Upovacko kolo.

— when they disbanded, SABAH HABAS went solo, releasing one album

– compilations, etc. –

May 91. (cd/c) *Globestyle; (CDORB/ORBC 070) / Omnium; <OMM 2003 D/C>* **FRIENDS, FIENDS & FRONDS** – Si vous passez par la / Starehe Mustapha I, II & III / Maldita gujira / Linda Linda / Kopanitsa / Linda Linda (ach ya LInda, ya Linda) / Fiz-n-DJ Trouble Fezz meets 3 Mustaphas 3 / Buke e kripe ne vater tone – Kalaxhojne / Anapse to Tsigaro / Shouffi rhirou / Niska banja / Kac kuzulu Ceylan / Selma.

Apr 97. (cd) *Fez-O-Phone; (CDFEZ 005) / Globestyle; <705>* **"BAM" BIG MUSTAPHAS PLAY STEREO LOCAL MUSIC** (first 2 mini-sets)

THREE O'CLOCK

Formed: Sun Valley, California, USA ... early 80's by MICHAEL QUERCIO, LOUIS GUTIERREZ, MIKE MARIANO and DANNY BENAIR, who were formerly known as The SALVATION ARMY. Their debut, 'BAROQUE HOEDOWN', was released late in 1982 on France's 'Lolita' records, basically a fairly reverential stab at classic psych/bubblegum pop. Gaining exposure via the emerging Paisley Underground movement (RAIN PARADE, DREAM SYNDICATE, etc), The THREE O'CLOCK followed-up with the slightly improved 'SIXTEEN TAMBOURINES', subsequently gaining a contract with Miles Copeland's 'I.R.S.' (now with PATRICK WANINGHAM replacing GUTIERREZ for one album only – STEVEN ALTENBERG deputising thereafter). In 1988, after a further two patchy sets, 'ARRIVE WITHOUT TRAVELING' (1985) and 'EVER AFTER' (1987), the band – now with future JELLYFISH frontman, JASON FALKNER replacing short-lived member STEVEN ALTENBERG – hooked up with PRINCE's 'Paisley Park' label for their swansong set, 'VERMILLION'. • **Songwriters:** QUERCIO and GUTIERREZ, some with MARIANO; except covers SORRY (Easybeats) / IN MY OWN TIME (Bee Gees) / FEEL A WHOLE LOT BETTER (Byrds) / LUCIFER SAM (Pink Floyd) / etc. • **Trivia:** WILL GLENN (Rain Parade) played viola/violin on first two albums and WENDY & LISA guested on their final outing.

Album rating: BAROQUE HOEDOWN (*6) / SIXTEEN TAMBOURINES (*6)

MICHAEL QUERCIO – vocals, bass, percussion / **LOUIS GUTIERREZ** – guitar, vocals, percussion / **MIKE MARIANO** – keyboards, vocals, percussion / **DANNY BENAIR** – drums, vocals, percussion (ex-QUICK)

Lolita — not iss.

Dec 82. (m-lp) *(5003)* **BAROQUE HOEDOWN** — France – With Cantaloupe girlfriend / I go wild / Marjorie tells me / Sorry / As real as real. *(some copies +=)* – Feel a whole lot better / In love in too / Lucifer Sam.

Dec 83. (lp) *(5008)* **SIXTEEN TAMBOURINES** — France – Jetfighter / Stupid Einstein / And so we run / Fall to the ground / A day in Erotica / Tomorrow / In my own time / On my own / When lightning starts / Seeing is believing. *(cd-iss. May86 +=(LOLITA 1101-2)* – BAROQUE HOEDOWN *(re-iss. 1991 on 'Frontier'+=; 4605-2-L)* – BAROQUE HOEDOWN / Around the world.

— **PATRICK WANINGHAM** – guitar, vocals repl. LOUIS

I.R.S. — I.R.S.

Sep 85. (7") *(IRM 101)* **HAND IN HAND. / WATCHING PICTURES** (12"+=) *(IRT 101)* – I go wild.

Oct 85. (lp/c) *(MIRF/+C 1002) <5591>* **ARRIVE WITHOUT TRAVELLING** – Her head's revolving / Each and every lonely heart / Underwater / Mrs. Green / Hand in hand / Knowing when you smile / Half the way there / Simon in the park / Another world / The girl with the guitar / Spun gold.

— **STEVEN ALTENBERG** – guitar, vocals; repl. WANINGHAM

Feb 87. (lp/c) *(MIRF 1016) <5833>* **EVER AFTER** – Suzie's on the ball now / Look into your eyes / When we can / The penny girls / Follow him around / Warm aspirations / Step out of line / We are one / If you could see my way / Songs and gentle hands.

Apr 87. (7") *(IRM 127)* **WARM ASPIRATIONS. / REGINA CAELI** (12"+=) *(IRMT 127)* – Suzie's on the ball.

— **JASON FALKNER** – guitar, vocals; repl. ALTENBERG

Paisley Park — Paisley Park

Jun 88. (lp/c/cd) *<(925717-1/-4/-2)>* **VERMILLION** – Vermillion / To be where you are / When she becomes my girl / World on fire / Neon telephone / On paper / Ways of magic / Time is going slower / Love has no heart / Through the creepy town.

— split in '89 FALKNER later turning up in JELLYFISH and subsequently went solo

– compilations, etc. –

1985. (lp; as The SALVATION ARMY) *Frontier; <FLP 1008>* **BEFOUR THREE O'CLOCK**

1992. (cd/c; as BEFOUR THREE O'CLOCK) *Frontier; <34639-2/-4>* **HAPPEN HAPPENED** – Happen happened / For hours / Fight songs / Mind gardens / She turns to flowers / Grimly forming / Seventeen forever / Going home / Cellophane nirvana / She turns to flowers / Upside down / Seventeen forever / Mind gardens / Grimly forming / While we were in your room talking to / Minuet / Happen happened / I am your guru / Going home.

Sep 96. (cd) *We Bite; (WB 1153CD)* **SONGS & NAILS**

THROBBING GRISTLE

Formed: Manchester, England ... Autumn '75 by GENESIS P-ORRIDGE and girlfriend COSEY FANNI TUTTI, a nude model, the couple having previously met at an art exhibition in Hull. Defiantly unconventional from day one, their early live shows boasted some dubious attractions as COSEY going topless, P-ORRIDGE and other member CHRIS CARTER slashing themselves and a backdrop of stomach-churning slides. In 1977, along with PETER CHRISTOPHERSON, the act set up their own independent label, 'Industrial', as a means of issuing limited edition material. A debut album, '2ND ANNUAL REPORT', was given a low-key release at the height of punk in '77. Although revelling in the genre's subversiveness, P-ORRIDGE & Co. were more interested in monotonic electronic textures than three-chord rock. Beloved of the more arty avant-garde post-punk set, THROBBING GRISTLE were largely a vehicle for the bizarre P-ORRIDGE's psycho-sexual narratives, usually set to pioneering synth-musak (CABARET VOLTAIRE and SUICIDE were mining a similar seam). A doubled-header single, 'UNITED' / 'ZYKLON B ZOMBIE' emerged the following summer, pursued by a second set, 'D.O.A.', at the end of '78. The following year, THROBBING GRISTLE made a vague stab at commerciality with the cynically titled '20 JAZZ FUNK GREATS', unearthing the wild 'PERSUASION' and the tortuously ponderous 'CONVINCING PEOPLE'. The record unsurprisingly failed to win the band any new admirers, especially in the music press, a swansong album, 'HEATHEN EARTH' (1980), paving the way for new ground; the group split two ways, P-ORRIDGE forming PSYCHIC TV, while CHRIS AND COSEY formed their own duo. • **Songwriters:** GENESIS P-ORRIDGE or mainly group compositions. • **Trivia:** Many or all performance / art gigs were recorded on tape and video.

Album rating: GREATEST HITS: ENTERTAINMENT THROUGH PAIN compilation (*7) / 20 JAZZ FUNK GREATS (*7) / D.O.A. (*8)

GENESIS P-ORRIDGE (b. NEIL ANDREW MEGSON, 22 Feb'50) – vox, electric violin, bass (ex-PORK DUKES) / **COSEY FANNI TUTTI** – guitar, cornet, effects / **CHRIS CARTER** – synthesizers, keyboards / **PETER 'Sleazy' CHRISTOPHERSON** – tapes, synthesizers, trumpet

Industrial — not iss.

Dec 76. (ltd-c) *(IR 0001)* **BEST OF VOLUME II** – Slug bait / Very friendly / We hate you / Seers of E / etc. *(cd-iss. Jun91 on 'Grey Area-Mute'; TGCD 1)*

Nov 77. (ltd-lp) *(IR 0002)* **SECOND ANNUAL REPORT** (some live) – Industrial introduction / Slug bait (ICA) / Slug bait (live at Southampton) / Slug bait (live at Brighton) / Maggot death (live at the Rat Club) / Maggot death (live at Southampton) / Maggot death (live at Brighton) / After cease to exist – The original soundtrack of the Coum transmission film. *(re-iss. Nov78 + Apr79; same) (re-iss. Jun81 on 'Fetish'; FET 2001) (re-iss. Apr83 + Nov83 on 'Mute'; MIR 1) (cd-iss. Jul91 on 'Grey Area-Mute'+=; TGCD2)* – Zyklon B Zombie / United. *<US cd-iss. 1993 on 'Mute-Warners'; 61093>*

Jun 78. (7"/7"white) *(IR 0003/+U)* **UNITED. / ZYKLON B ZOMBIE** *(re-iss. Jan80; same)* – B-side longer.

Dec 78. (lp) *(IR 0004)* **D.O.A. – THE THIRD AND FINAL REPORT** – I.B.M. / Hit by a rock / United / The valley of the shadow of death / Dead on arrival / Weeping / Hamburger lady / Hometime / Ab-7a / E-Coli / Death threats / Walls of sound / Blood on the floor. *(re-iss. Nov83 on 'Mute';) (cd-iss. Jul91 on 'Grey Area-Mute'; TGCD 3) <US cd-iss. 1993 on 'Mute-Warners'+=; 61094>* – Five knuckle shuffle / We hate you (little girls).

Jul 79. (7") *<SS45 001>* **WE HATE YOU (LITTLE GIRLS). / FIVE KNUCKLE SHUFFLE** - - French
(above on 'Sordid Sentimentale') *<US-iss.Sep81 on 'Adolescent'; ARTI 010>*

Oct 79. (lp) *(IR 0008)* **20 JAZZ FUNK GREATS** -
– 20 jazz funk greats / Beach Head / Still walking / Tanith / Convincing people / Exotica / Hot on the heels of love / Persuasion / Walkabout / What a day / Six six sixties. *(re-iss. Nov83 on 'Mute'; MIR 3) (cd-iss. Jul91 on 'Grey Area-Mute'+=; TGCD 4)* – Discipline (Berlin) / Discipline (Manchester). *<US cd-iss. 1993 on 'Mute-Warners'; 61095>*

Jun 80. (lp,blue-lp) *(IR 0009)* **HEATHEN EARTH** -
– Heathen Earth (pts 1-8) / Adrenalin / Subhuman *(re-iss. Nov83 on 'Mute'; MIR 004) (cd-iss. Jul91 on 'Grey Area-Mute'; TGCD 5)* – (also on video). *<US cd-iss. 1993 on 'Mute-Warners'; 61696>*

Sep 80. (7") *(IR 0013)* **SUBHUMAN. / SOMETHING CAME OVER ME** -

Sep 80. (7") *(IR 0015)* **ADRENALIN. / DISTANT DREAMS (Part Two)** -
Fetish Fetish

May 81. (12") *(FET 006)* **DISCIPLINE (live in Manchester). / DISCIPLINE (live in Berlin)**

— Dissolved in 1981, when P-ORRIDGE and CHRISTOPHERSON formed PSYCHIC TV. The other two formed duo CHRIS & COSEY.

– compilations, others, etc. –

Oct 81. (lp) *Mute; <61001-2>* **GREATEST HITS: ENTERTAINMENT THROUGH PAIN** -
– Hamburger lady / Hot on the heels of love / Subhuman / Ab 7a / Six six sixties / Blood on the floor / 20 jazz funk greats / Tiab guls / United / What a day / Adrenalin. *(UK-iss.Dec84 on 'Rough Trade'; ROUGHUS 23) (cd-iss. Oct90 & Jul91 on 'Grey Area-Mute'; TGCD 7) (<re-iss. Feb93 on 'Grey Area-Mute' c; 961001-4>)*

Nov 81. (lp) *Zensor; (ZENSOR 1D)* **FUNERAL IN BERLIN** - - Germ'y
– Stained by dead horses / Trained condition of obedience zero's death / Nomon / Raudive bunker experiment / Denial of death / Funeral in Berlin / Trade deficit.

Feb 82. (5xlp-box) *Fetish; (FX 1)* **A BOXED SET** -
– (5 original albums) *(cd's 1988 on 'Mute')*

1982. (ltd-lp) *Death; (01)* **MUSIC FROM THE DEATH FACTORY, MAY '79 (live)** -

1982. (ltd-lp) *Walter Ulbricht; (001)* **JOURNEY THROUGH THE BODY** -
(cd-iss. Oct93 on 'Grey Area-Mute'; TGCD 8)

1982. (ltd-lp) *Power Focus; (001)* **ASSUMING POWER FOCUS** (most rec.1975) - - fanclub
– Debris of murder / Freedom is a sickness / His arm was her leg / What a day! / Dead'd / Last exit / Propaganda yogananga / Sunstroke militia / Heathen earth / Urge to kill / Epping forest / Persuasion / Leeds ripper. *(<cd-iss. Oct95 on 'Paragoric'; PA 016CD>)*

Nov 82. (d-lp) *Karnage; (KILL 1)* **THEE PSYKICK SACRIFICE** -
(re-iss. Aug86 as 'SACRIFICE' on 'Dojo'; DOJOLP 29)

1983. (lp) *Expanded;* **MISSION IS TERMINATED: NICE TRACKS** (free-12"w.a.) **DAMURA SUNRISE. / YOU DON'T KNOW** -

1983. (10"lp) *Phonograph;* **FUHRER DER MEIN SHEAT** -

1983. (lp) *Illuminated; (SJAMS 31S)* **EDITIONS FRANKFURT – BERLIN** -

Nov 83. (lp) *Mute; (MIR 5)* **MISSION OF DEAD SOULS (THE LAST LIVE PERFORMANCE OF THROBBING GRISTLE) (live San Francisco)** -
– Dead souls / Guts on the floor / Circle of animals / Looking for the Oto / Vision and voice / Funeral rites / Spirits flying / Persuasion U.S.A. / Process / Discipline / Distant dreams / Something came over me. *(cd-iss. Jul91 on 'Grey Area-Mute'; TGCD 6) <US cd-iss. Feb93 on 'Mute-Warners'; 61097>*

Feb 84. (lp) *Illuminated; (JAMS 35)* **IN THE SHADOW OF THE SUN (Soundtrack)** -
(cd-iss. Oct93 on 'Grey Area-Mute'; TGCD 9)

Apr 84. (lp) *Casual Abandon; (CAS 1J)* **ONCE UPON A TIME** -

May 84. (c) *Cause For Concern; (CFC 001)* **NOTHING SHORT OF TOTAL WAR** -
(lp-iss.Oct87; CFC 016)

1984. (lp) *Mental Decay; (MD 01-1)* **SPECIAL TREATMENT** -
(re-iss. May88; same)

1980's. (lp) *Sprut; (001)* **VERY FRIENDLY – THE FIRST ANNUAL REPORT OF T.G.** -
(cd-iss. Oct96 on 'New Millenium'; CDTG 23)

1980's. (4xc-box) *Industrial; (IRC 1-IRC 24)* **24 HOURS** -

Mar 93. (4xcd-box/4xc-box) *Grey Area;* **LIVE BOX SET (live)** -

Apr 93. (cd) *Grey Area-Mute; (TGCD 10)* **LIVE – VOLUME 1 (live 1976-1978)** -

Apr 93. (cd) *Grey Area-Mute; (TGCD 11)* **LIVE – VOLUME 2 (live 1977-1978)** -

Apr 93. (cd) *Grey Area-Mute; (TGCD 12)* **LIVE – VOLUME 3 (live 1978-1979)** -

Apr 93. (cd) *Grey Area-Mute; (TGCD 13)* **LIVE – VOLUME 4 (live 1979-1980)** -

Dec 93. (cd) *Dossier; (EFA 08450CD)* **FUNK BEYOND JAZZ** -

Oct 94. (cd) *Dossier; (EFA 08458-2)* **GIFTGAS** -

Dec 95. (cd) *Dossier; (EFA 08448-2)* **BLOOD PRESSURE** -

Oct 96. (cd) *New Millenium; (CDTG 24)* **GRIEF** -

Oct 97. (cd) *EFA; <8490>* **KREEME HORN** -
– Careless idle chatter / Merely nodding / Raw mode of life / Rumour and dishonour / Ugliness is a form of genius.

Sep 98. (cd) *EFA; <8493>* **DIMENSIA IN EXCELSIS (live first US gig)** -

THROWING MUSES

Formed: Boston, Massachusetts, USA . . . 1983 by KRISTIN HERSH and her half-sister, TANYA DONELLY, who duly recruited a rhythm section of ELAINE ADAMEDES and DAVID NARCIZO. After an independently released US-only EP, the group were signed up (alongside fellow Bostonians, The PIXIES) to British indie label, '4 a.d.', the first American band to be bestowed such an honour. Produced by Gil Norton, the band's eponymous debut album (featuring new bassist LESLIE LANGSTON) centred around the emotional anguish of chief writer HERSH; her tortured, BUFFY SAINTE-MARIE-like wailing and oblique lyrics conjured up an air of ill-defined unease on the likes of 'RABBIT'S DYING' and 'SOUL SOLDIER' while the twisting, folk-noir minimalism of the music lent proceedings an umcomfortable unpredictability. Raved over in Britain (John Peel was a particularly vocal fan) but largely ignored at home, the 'MUSES consolidated their cult appeal with a further couple of EP's the following year before 1988's slightly disappointing follow-up proper, 'HOUSE TORNADO'. The record signalled a move towards the more accessible territory staked out in 'HUNKPAPA' (1989), US college radio's increasing influence seeing their native fanbase mushrooming. Feeling creatively stifled by HERSH's lion's share of the songwriting, DONELLY subsequently formed her own outfit, The BREEDERS while simultaneously working on her final 'MUSES album, 'THE REAL RAMONA' (1991). A breakthrough set which contained some of the group's most immediate compositions ('COUNTING BACKWARDS' was perhaps the nearest HERSH has come to writing a pop song), DONELLY's contributions a blueprint for the more straightforward alternative pop she would perfect in BELLY. Taking then 'MUSES bassist, ABONG with her, DONELLY finally left the band in 1992, leaving a core of HERSH and NARCIZO. Welcoming LANGSTON back into the fold, HERSH proved THROWING MUSES was still a going concern with the soft grunge-friendly distortion of 'RED HEAVEN' (1992), the band's highest (UK) charting album to date. Nevertheless, the 'MUSES' muse took time out in 1994 to complete a solo debut, 'HIPS AND MAKERS'. Produced by LENNY KAYE and featuring a guest appearance from MICHAEL STIPE, the album found HERSH probing her troubled psyche through a skewed, childlike lens, distorting the sparse acoustic backing and making for compelling listening. Hailed by critics, the record made the UK Top 10 and saw the singer gaining belated recognition from an often reluctant music press. 1995 saw the release of the sixth THROWING MUSES album, 'UNIVERSITY', another fine set which maintained the hi-octane approach of its predecessor. The following years' 'LIMBO' was exactly that, the group becoming a little directionless and stale, although its highlights were the minor hit, 'SHARK'. • **Songwriters:** KRISTIN lyrics / group compositions except; AMAZING GRACE (trad. hit Judy Collins) / CRY BABY CRY (Beatles) / RIDE INTO THE SUN (Velvet Underground) / MANIC DEPRESSION (Jimi Hendrix) / WHEN THE LEVEE BREAKS (Led Zeppelin). HERSH solo:- PANIC PURE (Vic Chesnutt) / JESUS CHRIST (Alex Chilton) / CAN THE CIRCLE BE UNBROKEN (. . . Carter) / AMAZING GRACE (trad).

Album rating: THROWING MUSES (*8) / HUNKPAPA (*8) / THE REAL RAMONA (*7) / THE RED HEAVEN (*7) / Kristin Hersh: HIPS AND MAKERS (*6)

KRISTIN HERSH (b. 7 Aug'66, Atlanta, Georgia) – vocals, lead guitar, piano / **ELAINE ADAMEDES** – bass / **TANYA DONELLY** (b.14 Jul'66) – rhythm guitar, vocals / **DAVID NARCIZO** (b. 6 May'66) – drums, percussion, vocals

not iss. Throwing Muses

Feb 86. (7"ep) **STAND UP / PARTY. / SANTA CLAUS / DIRT ON THE DANCE FLOOR** -

— **LESLIE LANGSTON** (b. 1 Apr'64) – bass, vocals repl. ELAINE

4 a.d. 4ad-Sire

Sep 86. (lp/c)(cd) *(CAD/+C 607)(CAD 607CD)* **THROWING MUSES** -
– Call me / Green / Hate my way / Vicky's box / Rabbit's dying / America (she can't say no) / Fear / Stand up / Soul soldier / Delicious cutters.

Mar 87. (12"ep/c-ep) *(BAD 701/+C)* **CHAINS CHANGED**
– Cry baby cry / Finished / Reel / Snail head.

Aug 87. (m-lp/c) *(CAD/+C 706) <25640>* **THE FAT SKIER**
– Soul soldier / Garoux des larmes / Pool in eyes / A feeling / You cage / Soap and water / And a she-wolf after the war.

Mar 88. (lp/c)(cd) *(CAD/+C 802)(CAD 802CD) <25710>* **HOUSE TORNADO**
– Colder / Mexican woman / The river / Juno / Marriage tree / Run letter / Saving grace / Drive / Downtown / Giant / Walking in the dark. *(cd+=)* – THE FAT SKIER

Jan 89. (lp/c)(cd) *(CAD/+C 901)(CAD 901CD) <25855>* **HUNKPAPA** 59
– Devil's roof / Bea / Dizzy / No parachutes (say goodbye) / Dragonhead / Fall down / I'm alive / Angel / Mania / The burrow. *(c+=)* – Take. *(cd++=)* – Santa Claus.

Feb 89. (7") *(AD 903)* **DIZZY. / SANTA CLAUS** -
(12"+=/10"+=)(cd-s+=) *(BAD/+D 903)(BAD 903CD)* – Mania (live) / Downtown (live).

— TANYA with DAVID (only in '89) formed off-shoot The BREEDERS. She stayed with the MUSES until next album's completion. **FRED ABONG** – bass repl. her

Jan 91. (7") *(AD 7001) <21833>* **COUNTING BACKWARDS. / AMAZING GRACE** 70
(12"+=/cd-s+=) *(BAD/+CD 1001)* – Some sun / Cotton mouth.

Feb 91. (cd)(lp/c) *(CAD 1002CD)(CAD/+C 1002) <26489>* **THE REAL RAMONA** 26
– Counting backwards / Him dancing / Red shoes / Graffiti / Golden thing / Ellen West / Dylan / Hook in her head / Not too soon / Honey chain / Say goodbye / Two step.

Nov 91. (7") *(AD 1015) <40135>* **NOT TOO SOON. / CRY BABY CRY**
(12"+=/cd-s+=) *(BAD 1015/+CD)* – Dizzy (remix) / Him dancing (remix).

— (Sep91) DONELLY and ABONG had now quit to form BELLY in 1992.

— **KRISTIN + NARCIZO** recruited newcomer **BERNARD GEORGES** (b.29 Mar'65, Gonaive, Haiti) – bass

Jul 92. (12"ep/cd-ep) *(BAD 2012/+CD)* **FIREPILE / MANIC DEPRESSION. / SNAILHEAD / CITY OF THE DEAD** 46 -
(12"ep)(cd-ep) *(BADR 2012)(BAD 2012CDR)* – ('A'remix) / Jack / Ride into the Sun / Handsome woman.

Aug 92. (cd)(lp/c) *(CAD 2013CD)(CAD/+C 2013) <26897>* **RED HEAVEN** 13
– Furious / Firepile / Die / Dirty water / Stroll / Pearl / Summer Street / Vic / Backroad / The visit / Dovey / Rosetta stone / Carnival wig. *(free-lp w.a.)* **LIVE (live)** – Juno / Marriage tree / Pearl / Stand up – Dovey – Mexican woman / Run letter / Soap and water / Rabbit dying / Cry baby cry / Counting backwards – Handsome woman / Take / Soul soldier / Bea / Delicate cutters.

Nov 92. (cd) *(TAD 2019CD)* **THE CURSE (live)** 74 -
– Manic depression / Counting backwards / Fish / Hate my way / Furious / Devil's roof / Snailhead / Firepile / Finished / Take / Say goodbye / Mania / Two step / Delicate cutters / Cottonmouth / Pearl / Vic / Bea.

Dec 94. (7") *(AD 4018)* **BRIGHT YELLOW GUN. / LIKE A DOG** 51 -
(12"+=/cd-s+=) *(BAD 4018/+CD)* – Red eyes / Crayon sun.

Jan 95. (cd)(lp/c) *(CAD 5002CD)(CAD/+C 5002) <45796>* **UNIVERSITY** 10
– Bright yellow gun / Start / Hazing / Shimmer / Calm down, come down / Crabtown / No way in Hell / Surf cowboy / That's all you wanted / Teller / University / Snake face / Fever few.

Jul 96. (7") *(AD 6016)* **SHARK. / TAR MOOCHERS** 53 -
(7") *(ADD 6016)* – ('A'side) / Limbobo.
(cd-s++=) *(BAD 6016CD)* – Serene swing.

4 a.d. Rykodisc

Aug 96. (cd)(lp/c) *(CAD 6014CD)(CAD/+C 6014) <10354>* **LIMBO** 36
– Buzz / Ruthie's knocking / Freefloader / The field / Limbo / Tar kisser / Tango / Serene / Mr. Bones / Night driving / Cowbirds / Shark.

Sep 96. (7"etched) *(TAD 6017) <51052>* **RUTHIE'S KNOCKING**

Jan 97. (cd-s) *<51055>* **FREELOADER /** -

— disbanded later in '97

– compilations, etc. –

Jul 98. (d-cd) *Rykodisc; <8017>* **IN A DOGHOUSE** -
– (THROWING MUSES album tracks) / (CHAINS CHAINED ep tracks) / Call me / Sinkhole / Green / Hate my way / Vicky's box / America (she can't say no) / Fear / Raise the roses / And a she wolf after the war / Fish / Catch / Lizzie Sage / Clear and great / Doghouse / People.

KRISTIN HERSH

first below featured **MICHAEL STIPE** (R.E.M.) / **JANE SCARPANTONI** – cello

4 a.d. Sire

Jan 94. (12"ep/cd-ep) *(BAD 4001/+CD)* **YOUR GHOST / THE KEY. / UNCLE JUNE AND AUNT KIYOTI / WHEN THE LEVEE BREAKS** 45 -

Feb 94. (cd)(lp/c) *(CAD 4002CD)(CAD/+C 4002) <45413>* **HIPS AND MAKERS** 7
– Your ghost / Beestung / Teeth / Sundrops / sparky / Houdini blues / A loon / Velvet days / Close your eyes / Me and my charms / Tuesday night / The letter / Lurch / The cuckoo / Hips and makers. *(cd re-iss. Jul98; same)*

Apr 94. (7"/c-s) *(AD 4006) <45667>* **A LOON. / VELVET DAYS** 60 Jun94
(12"ep+=/cd-ep+=) *(BAD 4006/+CD)* **STRINGS EP** – Sundrops / Me and my charms.

4 a.d. Rykodisc

Dec 95. (cd-ep) *(TAD 5017CD) <1049>* **THE HOLY SINGLE**
– Jesus Christ / Amazing grace / Sinkhole / Can the circle be unbroken.

Feb 98. (cd) *(CAD 8003CD) <10429>* **STRANGE ANGELS** 64
– Home / Like you / Aching for you / Cold water coming / Some catch flies / Stained / Shake / Hope / Pale / Baseball field / Heaven / Gazebo tree / Gut pageant / Rock candy brains / Cartoons.

Mar 98. (cd-ep) *(TAD 8005CD)* **LIKE YOU / SHAKE (live to tape) / YOUR GHOST (live to tape)** -

THROWN UPS (see under ⇒ MUDHONEY)

THRUM

Formed: Bellshill, Glasgow, Scotalnd . . . 1992 by JOHNNY SMILLIE, DAVE McGOWAN, GARY JOHNSTON and singer MONICA QUEEN. Following the established pedigree of homegrown indie bands (TEENAGE FANCLUB, BMX BANDITS etc.), THRUM specialised in updating the classic sounds of West Coast Americana with one ear cocked to the 90's US alternative scene. Released as the first fruits of a deal with 'Fire' records, an eponymous debut EP surfaced in 1993 (containing a tortured version of Roy Orbison's 'CRYING') and confirmed early live evidence of potential Laurel Canyon via Bellshill greatness. Further acclaim was heaped upon singles, 'SO GLAD' and 'HERE I AM', prior to a long awaited debut album, 'RIFFERAMA' (1994). NEIL YOUNG was an obvious and oft-quoted influence with SMILLIE's rootsy guitar workouts complemented by MONICA's powerful MARIA McKEE meets TINA TURNER vocal. Perhaps the timing wasn't right as despite constantly being tipped for big things, THRUM seemed to be forever struggling around the toilet circuit, playing their emotive country-rock to a core of fans but failing to interest the wider music buying public.

Album rating: RIFFERAMA (*6)

MONICA QUEEN – vocals, guitar / **JOHNNY SMILLIE** – guitar, vocals / **DAVE McGOWAN** – bass, vocals / **GARY JOHNSTON** – drums

Fire not iss.

Apr 93. (12"ep/cd-ep) *(BLAZE 64 T/CD)* **THRUM EP** -
– Lullaby / Illegitimate clown (mix) / Does anybody know? / Crying (live).

Sep 93. (12"ep/cd-ep) *(BLAZE 67 T/CD)* **SO GLAD / ?** -

Jun 94. (7") *(BLAZE 70)* **HERE I AM. / WAITING FOR THE SUN** -
(7") *(7SM 3)* – ('A'side) / Get a life.
(cd-s) *(BLAZE 70CD)* – (all 3 tracks).

Sep 94. (cd/c/lp) *(FIRE CD/MC/LP 38)* **RIFFERAMA**
– Rifferama / Purify / So glad / You wish / Lullaby II / Here I am / Hey Joe / Won't be long / Nowhere to run / Almost done.

Dec 94. (7") *(BLAZE 81)* **PURIFY. / IF EVERY DAY WAS LIKE CHRISTMAS DAY** -

— must have split

Johnny THUNDERS

Born: JOHN ANTHONY GENZALE, 15 Jul'52, Leesburg, Florida, USA. Having been an integral part of The NEW YORK DOLLS in the first half of the 70's, vocalist/guitarist THUNDERS formed new wave/punk act, The HEARTBREAKERS alongside ex-'DOLLS drummer, JERRY NOLAN and ex-TELEVISION bassist, RICHARD HELL. After an initial gig as a trio, they picked up extra guitarist, WALTER LURE, although this incarnation was short-lived as RICHARD promptly departed to form his own RICHARD HELL & THE VOID-OIDS. Filling the void with BILLY RATH, they were invited to London by ex-'DOLLS manager, MALCOLM McLAREN, who offered them a support slot with his punk proteges, The SEX PISTOLS (on their 'Anarchy' tour of late '76). The HEARTBREAKERS subsequently signed to UK label, 'Track', issuing their debut 45, 'CHINESE ROCKS' (a tribute to oriental narcotics co-written with DEE DEE RAMONE), in early '77; both the lead track and the B-side, 'BORN TO LOSE', drawled out with inimitably wasted NY cool. In September of that "Jubilee" year, the group released their much-anticipated debut album, 'L.A.M.F.' (New York street slang for 'Like A Mother F***** '), and although it suffered from terrible production provided by SPEEDY KEEN (ex-THUNDERCLAP NEWMAN), the set still managed a Top 60 placing in Britain. So bad was the record's sound that NOLAN left in protest, further calamity befalling the band as they found themselves on the wrong side of the immigration authorities having abandoned their label. Deported back to NY, the band inevitably splintered despite having recruited a replacement drummer, TY STYX. THUNDERS subsequently returned to London where he recorded a solo album, 'SO ALONE' (1978) aided and abetted by the cream of the UK new wave scene including PETER PERRETT (The Only Ones), CHRISSIE HYNDE (Pretenders), PAUL COOK and STEVE JONES (Sex Pistols) and even PHIL LYNOTT (Thin Lizzy)! In the interim, THUNDERS teamed up with SID VICIOUS in the ill-fated, unfortunately named, The LIVING DEAD (SID was to die shortly afterwards). Just prior to the turn of the decade, The HEARTBREAKERS regrouped in New York with THUNDERS masterminding the affair and prefixing the band name with his own; the resulting stage set, 'LIVE AT MAX'S KANSAS CITY' stands as testament to what might have been. In the 80's, THUNDERS released a series of sporadic albums/singles mostly for UK indie label, 'Jungle', although he never managed to shake off the cult legend tag. Sadly, THUNDERS died in New Orleans on the 23rd of April 1991, the circumstances remaining shrouded in mystery until a subsequent autopsy revealed what most people suspected, that he'd overdosed on heroin. • **Covered** CAN'T KEEP MY EYES OFF YOU (Andy Williams) / DO YOU LOVE ME (Brian Poole & The Tremeloes) / DOWNTOWN (Petula Clark) / LIKE A ROLLING STONE (Bob Dylan) / CRAWFISH (Elvis Presley) / QUE SERA SERA (hit; Doris Day). 'COPY CATS' was a complete covers album.

Album rating: L.A.M.F. – REVISITED (*7) / LIVE AT MAX'S KANSAS CITY (*7) / D.T.K. (*6)

HEARTBREAKERS

JOHNNY THUNDERS – vocals, guitar / **JERRY NOLAN** (b. 7 May'46) – drums / **WALTER LURE** (b.22 Apr'49) – guitar, vocals / **BILLY RATH** – bass, vocals repl. RICHARD HELL who formed his own group

Track not iss.

May 77. (7"/12") *(2094 135/+T)* **CHINESE ROCKS. / BORN TO LOSE** -

Sep 77. (lp) *(2409 218)* **L.A.M.F.** 55 -
– Born to lose / Baby talk / All by myself / I wanna be loved / It's not enough / Get off the phone / Chinese rocks / Pirate love / One track mind / I love you / Goin' steady / Let go. *(re-iss. May85 as 'L.A.M.F. – REVISITED' on 'Jungle' lp,pink-lp/pic-lp; FREUD 4/+P) <(re-iss. Sep96 as 'THE LOST '77 MIXES' cd/c/lp; FREUD CD/C/LP 044)>*

Nov 77. (7") *(2094 137)* **ONE TRACK MIND. / CAN'T KEEP MY EYES OFF YOU (live) / DO YOU LOVE ME (live)** -

Mar 78. (7"w-drawn) *(2094 142)* **IT'S NOT ENOUGH. / LET GO** -

— split early '78 after being deported back to New York, NOLAN joined SNATCH, while RATH and LURE disappeared

JOHNNY THUNDERS

— returned to London and went solo using session people

Real-W.E.A. not iss.

May 78. (7") *(ARE 1)* **DEAD OR ALIVE. / DOWNTOWN** -

Sep 78. (7"/12"pink,12"blue) *(ARE 3/+T)* **YOU CAN'T PUT YOUR ARMS AROUND A MEMORY. / HURTIN'** -

Oct 78. (lp) *(RAL 1)* **SO ALONE** -

– Pipeline / You can't put your arms around a memory / Great big kiss / Ask me no questions / Leave me alone / Daddy rolling stone / London boys / Untouchable / Subway train / Downtown. *<re-iss. Jul92 & Feb95 on 'Warners' lp/cd; 7599 26982-2>*

JOHNNY THUNDERS & THE HEARTBREAKERS

—— re-formed '79, with **WALTER, BILLY / + STYX** – drums

Beggars Banquet | Max's Kansas

Jul 79. (7") *(BEG 21)* **GET OFF THE PHONE (live). / I WANNA BE LOVED (live)** [ ] [-]

Sep 79. (lp) *(BEGA 9) <DTK 213>* **LIVE AT MAX'S KANSAS CITY (live)** [ ] [ ]
– (intro) / Milk me / Chinese rocks / Get off the phone / London / Take a chance / One track mind / All by myself / Let go / I love you / Can't keep my eyes on you / I wanna be loved / Do you love me?. *(cd-iss. Jul91; BBL 9CD) <(cd-iss. Dec95 on 'ROIR USA'; RUSCD 8219)>*

—— Split again '79. In 1980, THUNDERS joined WAYNE KRAMER'S GANG WAR.

JOHNNY THUNDERS

solo again with **WALTER LURE** – guitar / **BILLY ROGERS** – drums

New Rose | not iss.

Dec 82. (7") *(NEW 14)* **IN COLD BLOOD / ('A'live)** [-] [-] France

Jan 83. (d-lp) *(NR 18)* **IN COLD BLOOD** (some live) [-] [-] France
– In cold blood / Just another girl / Green onions / Diary of a lover / Look at my eyes / Live: (intro) / Just another girl / Too much junkie business / Sad vacation / Louie Louie / Gloria / Treat me like a nigger / Do you love me / Green onions / 10 commandments. *(re-iss. Apr94 lp/cd; 422367) (re-iss. cdJun95 on 'Dojo'; DOJOCD 221) <(cd re-iss. Aug97 on 'Essential'; ESMCD 589)>*

Jan 84. (7"m) *(NEW 27)* **HURT ME. / IT'S NOT ENOUGH / LIKE A ROLLING STONE** [ ] [-]

Jan 84. (lp) *(ROSE 26)* **HURT ME** [ ] [-]
– So alone / It ain't me babe / Eve of destruction / You can't put your arms round a memory / You're so strange / I'm a boy in a girl / Lonely planet boy / Sad vacation / Hurt me / Diary of a lover / Ask me no questions. *(cd-iss. May94; 422366) (re-iss. cd Jul95 on 'Dojo'; DOJOCD 217) <(cd re-iss. Aug97 on 'Essential'; ESMCD 588)>*

Jungle | not iss.

Oct 85. (7"/7"pic-d; by JOHNNY THUNDERS with PATTI PALLADIN) *(JUNG 23/+P)* **CRAWFISH. / TIE ME UP (LOVE KNOT)** [ ] [-]
(ext.12"+=) *(JUNG 23T)* – ('A'-Bayou mix).

—— (w/ PATTI PALLADIN – vocals (ex-SNATCH, FLYING LIZARDS)

Dec 85. (lp) *(FREUD 9)* **QUE SERA, SERA** [ ] [-]
– Que sera, sera / Short lives / M.I.A. / I only wrote this song for you / Little bit of whore / Cool operator / Blame it on mom / Tie me up / Alone in a crowd / Billy boy / Endless party. *(pic-lp iss.Jun87; FREUDP 09) <(cd-iss. Dec94; FREUDCD 49)>*

Jun 87. (7") *(JUNG 33)* **QUE SERA SERA. / SHORT LIVES** [ ] [-]
(12"+=) *(JUNG 33T)* – I only wrote this song.

JOHNNY THUNDERS & PATTI PALLADIN

May 88. (7") *(JUNG 38)* **SHE WANTS TO MAMBO. / UPTOWN** [ ] [ ]
(12"+=) *(JUNG 38T)* – Love is strange.

Jun 88. (lp/c/cd) *(FREUD/+C/CD 20)* **YEAH, YEAH, I'M A COPY CAT** [ ] [-]
– Can't seem to make you mine / Baby it's you / She wants to mambo / Treat her right / Uptown to Harlem / Crawfish / Alligator wine / Two time loser / Love is strange / (I was) Born to cry / He cried (she cried) / Let me entertain you (part 1 & 2). *(re-iss. cd Nov96; same)*

Jan 89. (7") *(JUNG 43)* **(I WAS) BORN TO CRY. / TREAT HER RIGHT** [ ] [-]
(12"+=) *(JUNG 43T)* – Can't seem to make her mine.

—— THUNDERS died on the 23rd April '91, aged 38. He left three children from his first marriage plus another 3 year-old daughter, Jamie, conceived while he'd lived in Sweden with his girlfriend, Suzanne. JERRY NOLAN died on the 14th January '92 of a stroke (aged 45) after a bout of pneumonia and meningitis. Original drummer, BILLY MURCIA, also died in the 90's.

– compilations, etc. –

on 'Jungle' unless otherwise mentioned

Nov 82. (lp,pink-lp,white-lp/pic-lp) *(FREUD/+P 1)* **D.T.K. – LIVE AT THE SPEAKEASY (live)** [ ] [-]
<(cd-iss. Aug94 on 'Receiver'; R 191)>

May 83. (7"ep) *(JUNG 1)* **VINTAGE '77** [ ] [-]
– Let go / Chinese rocks / Born to lose.

1983. (c) *R.O.I.R.; <A 118>* **TOO MUCH JUNKIE BUSINESS** [-] [ ]
(cd-iss. Feb95 on 'ROIR Europe'; same) <US 'Combat'; 5029>

Mar 84. (7"/7"pic-d) *(JUNG 14/+P)* **GET OFF THE PHONE. / ALL BY MYSELF** [ ] [-]
(12"+=) *(JUNG 14X)* – Pirate love.

Jun 84. (lp) *A.B.C.; (ABCLP 2)* **LIVE AT THE LYCEUM BALLROOM 1984 (live)** [ ] [-]
<(re-iss. Jun91 on 'Receiver' lp/c/cd; RR LP/LC/CD 134)>

Feb 85. (7") *Twins; (T 1702)* **BORN TO LOSE. / IT'S NOT ENOUGH** [ ] [-]

May 85. (7"ep/12"ep) *(JUNG 18/+X)* **CHINESE ROCKS / BORN TO LOSE / ONE TRACK MIND / I WANNA BE LOVED** [ ] [-]

Feb 87. (c) *R.O.I.R.; (A 146) / Combat; <5028>* **STATIONS OF THE CROSS** [-] [ ]
(re-iss. cd Jul94 on 'Receiver'; RRCD 188) (re-iss. cd Feb95 on 'ROIR Europe'; same)

May 88. (box-lp) *(JTBOX 1)* **THE JOHNNY THUNDERS ALBUM COLLECTION** [ ] [-]

Feb 90. (lp/cd) *(FREUD/+CD 30)* **BOOTLEGGIN' THE BOOTLEGGERS** [ ] [-]

Jan 92. (cd) *Fan Club;* **LIVE AT MOTHERS (live)** [ ] [-]

Feb 92. (cd) *Bomp; (BCD 4039)* **WHAT GOES AROUND (live)** [ ] [-]

Oct 92. (cd) *Fan Club; (422365)* **HAVE FAITH (live solo)** [ ] [-]
<(re-iss. Aug96 on 'Mutiny'; MUT 8005CD)>

Dec 93. (cd) *Anagram; (CDGRAM 70)* **CHINESE ROCKS – THE ULTIMATE LIVE COLLECTION (live)** [ ] [-]

Sep 94. (cd) *Skydog; (62251)* **VIVE LE REVOLUTION – LIVE PARIS, 1977 (live JOHNNY THUNDERS & THE HEARTBREAKERS)** [ ] [-]

Nov 94. (cd) *Essential; (ESDCD 226)* **ADD WATER AND STIR – LIVE IN JAPAN 1991 (live)** [ ] [-]

Apr 96. (cd) *Dojo; (DOJOCD 231)* **THE STUDIO BOOTLEGS** [ ] [-]

TIGER

Formed: London, England . . . early '96 by DAN LAIDLER, JULIE SIMS, and 3 others. On the strength of a one-off single, 'SHINING IN THE WOODS', for the 'Fierce Panda' imprint, TIGER signed to Island off-shoot, 'Trade 2', the FALL comparisons abound due to their Moog attacking indie rock. Two further singles, 'RACE' and 'MY PUPPET PAL', were also unleashed that year, although they were minor hits, it was their debut set, 'WE ARE PUPPETS' (1996), that critics took note of. In 1998, they roared back into gear with the 'FRIENDS' single, the much maligned and misunderstood bunch of one-time NME darlings were back. • **Note:** Not to be confused with the late 80's outfit.

Album rating: WE ARE PUPPETS (*7) / ROSARIA (*6)

DAN LAIDLER – vocals / **JULIE SIMS** – guitar, vocals / **DIDO** – bass, Moog / **TINA** – keyboards / – drums

Fierce Panda | not iss.

Jun 96. (7") *(NING 22)* **SHINING IN THE WOOD. / WHERE'S THE LOVE** [ ] [-]
(cd-s+=) *(NING 22CD)* – Bicycle.

Trade 2 | Bar None

Aug 96. (7") *(TRDS 004)* **RACE. / HONEY FRIENDS** [37] [-]
(c-s+=) *(TRDMC 004)* – I'm in love with an RAF nurse.
(cd-s++=) *(TRDCD 004)* – Time tunnel cellar.

Nov 96. (7"/c-s) *(TRD S/MC 005)* **MY PUPPET PAL. / ICICLE** [62] [-]
(cd-s+=) *(TRDCD 005)* – Flea's song.

Nov 96. (cd/c/lp) *(TRD CD/MC/LP 1002)* **WE ARE PUPPETS** [ ] [-]
– My puppet pal / Shamed all over / Race / Bollinger farm / Storm injector / Depot / On the rose / Sorry monkeys / Cateader reddle / She's o.k. / Ray Travey / Keep in touch.

Feb 97. (7") *(TRDS 008)* **ON THE ROSE. / ON SPANISH FARMLAND** [57] [-]
(cd-s+=) *(TRSCD 008)* – Babe.
(cd-s) *(TRDCX 008)* – ('A'side) / Ray Travez (live) / Depot (session) / I am in love with a RAF nurse (session).

Apr 97. (m-cd) *<72>* **SHINING IN THE WOOD** [-] [ ]
– Shining in the wood / Where's the love? / Honey friends / Time tunnel cellar / Bicycle / I'm in love with an RAF nurse.

—— now a quartet

Aug 98. (7") *(TRDS 013)* **FRIENDS. / WENSLEYDALE** [72] [-]
(cd-s+=) *(TRDCD 013)* – Bottle of juice.
(cd-s) *(TRDCX 013)* – ('A'side) / White Saab, dark night / Rouge Robyn.

Sep 98. (7") *(TRDS 014)* **GIRL FROM THE PETROL STATION. / PAUL YOUNG** [ ] [-]
(cd-s+=) *(TRDCD 014)* – Sea shandy.
(cd-s) *(TRDCX 014)* – ('A'side) / God it's good / Rolling Rose.

Oct 98. (cd/lp) *(TRD CD/LP 1006)* **ROSARIA** [ ] [-]

TIMES (see under ⇒ BALL, Ed)

TINDERSTICKS

Formed: Nottingham, England . . . 1988 as ASPHALT RIBBONS, by STUART STAPLES, DAVE BOULTER and DICKON HINCHCLIFFE, the line-up completed by NEIL FRASER, MARK COLWILL and AL McCAULEY. Abandoning their previous TRIFFIDS/GO-BETWEENS-esque indie attempts, the group adopted a darkly brooding hybrid of faded-glamour easy listening and semi-acoustic strumming, incorporating swooning strings, mournful violin, frantic flamenco and hints of country. Surely the heartbroken, doomed romantic to top all doomed romantics, STAPLES' low-key mumblings were somehow utterly compelling, his often barely audible melange of NICK CAVE, LEE HAZLEWOOD and TOM WAITS capable of expressing every nuance in the music regardless of what he was actually saying. The TINDERSTICKS came to critical notice with only their second single, 'MARBLES', a lo-fi STAPLES monologue cosetted by an aching melody. Released on their own 'Tippy Toe' label, the track was unanimously awarded Single Of The Week by both NME and Melody Maker, creating a buzz which would eventually see the group sign to the newly formed 'This Way Up' label. Previewed by the string-drenched melancholy of the 'CITY SICKNESS' single, the eponymous 'TINDERSTICKS' (1993) was released in late '93. A dense, bleakly beautiful, seedily glamourous near 80-minute epic, the record was so strikingly different from anything else around (save for maybe GALLON DRUNK or NICK CAVE) it sounded timeless. From the edgy resignation of 'WHISKEY & WATER' to the lovelorn lament of 'RAINDROPS', this was one of the most luxuriantly dark albums of the 90's, reeking of failed relationships and nicotine-stained despair. With gushing praise from the music press, both for the album and their hypnotic live shows, The TINDERSTICKS even managed to scrape a Top 60 chart placing. Released simultaneously with the album was a cover of John Barry's 'WE HAVE ALL THE TIME IN THE WORLD' alongside

GALLON DRUNK on a 'Clawfist' 7", the latter group's TERRY EDWARDS having guested on the album and subsequently adding string arrangements on their next long player. Preceded by a cover of the late Townes Van Zandt's 'KATHLEEN', 'TINDERSTICKS' (same title, different album) was finally released in Spring '95, its grainy noir narratives and downtrodden country enhanced with exquisite orchestration. There were no great stylistic leaps, just a further exploration and refinement of the blurred shadows and twilit corners that graced the debut. An undisputed highlight was the goose-bump country duet with The WALKABOUTS' CARLA TORGERSON, 'TRAVELLING LIGHT', released as a single that summer. The TINDERSTICKS were also in the process of refining their live sound, or rather expanding it, with the help of a full orchestra; the gorgeous results can be heard on concert set, 'THE BLOOMSBURY THEATRE 12.3.95'. Unable to sustain such a money draining enterprise for too long, The TINDERSTICKS-plus-orchestra phase reached its zenith during a hugely successful week long residency at London's ICA theatre in late '96. The same year also saw the group's first foray into soundtrack work, scoring the music for French art film, 'Nenette et Boni'. Largely instrumental, the piano and bass-led main theme was fleshed out with the moving 'TINY TEARS' (or 'PETITES GOUTTES D'EAU' in French) from the second album; hardly essential but a pleasant listen all the same. Following the group's own fears that the fragile balance of The TINDERSTICKS' muse was becoming unworkable, the difficult third album, 'CURTAINS' was finally completed in a fevered rush of creativity and released in Summer '97. Less sprawling and more cohesive than previous efforts, it was also bolder and more accessible, STAPLES actually singing comprehensibly on the bulk of the tracks. Predictably, there were also more strings than ever, HINCHCLIFFE's orchestral flourishes crescendoing majestically on 'DON'T LOOK DOWN' and achieving a pathos only previously glimpsed before on 'LET'S PRETEND', JESUS ALEMANY's mariachi-style trumpet a bittersweet counterpart. There was even another country duet, 'BURIED BONES', a brilliantly executed NANCY/LEE-style sparring match featuring the velvet tones of BONGWATER's ANNE MAGNUSON. Lyrically, the themes remained reliably unchanged, tales of everyday lust and disillusionment dripping from STAPLES' lips like the honey from his claws as described in the gripping, unsettling 'BEARSUIT'. And, with 'BALLAD OF TINDERSTICKS', STAPLES indicated that they don't take this music business lark TOO seriously. If there was any justice, TINDERSTICKS would be bigger than OASIS, as it is they remain a treasured secret for anyone who's ever glimpsed the universe in the bottom of a wine glass. • **Other covers:** KOOKS (David Bowie) / I'VE BEEN LOVING YOU TOO LONG (Otis Redding & Jerry Butler) / HERE (Pavement). • **Trivia:** JON LANGFORD of The THREE JOHNS, produced early ASPHALT RIBBONS material.

Album rating: TINDERSTICKS (*8) / THE SECOND TINDERSTICKS ALBUM (*7) / THE BLOOMSBURY THEATRE 12.3.95 (*6) / NANETTE ET BONI soundtrack (*6) / CURTAINS (*8)

ASPHALT RIBBONS

STUART STAPLES – vocals / **DICKON HINCHCLIFFE** – violin / **DAVE BOULTER** – keyboards / **BLACKHOUSE** – guitar / **FRASER** – bass / **WATT** – drums

In-Tape / not iss.

Oct 89. (7"ep) *(IT 063)* **THE ORCHARD** [ ] [-]
– Over again / Red sauce / Greyhound / I used to live T.

May 90. (7"m) *(IT 068)* **GOOD LOVE. / LONG LOST UNCLE / THE DAY I TURNED BAD** [ ] [-]

— (Alongside new stablemates MY LIFE WITH PATRICK, their new label below issued a free flexi sampler with 'Zip Code' fanzine; cat no. LILY 001)

Tiger Lily / not iss.

Apr 91. (12"ep) *(LILY 002)* **PASSION, COOLNESS, INDIFFERENCE, BOREDOM, MOCKERY, CONTEMPT, DISGUST** [ ] [-]

E.T.T. / not iss.

Aug 91. (m-lp) *(E 101)* **OLD HORSE & OTHER SONGS** [ ] [-]
(cd-iss. Apr92; E 101-?)

TINDERSTICKS

— were formed by **STUART, DICKON and DAVE**, plus Londoners **NEIL FRASER** – guitar / **MARK COLWILL** – bass / **AL McCAULEY** – drums

Tippy Toe / No.6

Nov 92. (7") *(TIPPY TOE 1)* **PATCHWORK. / MILKY TEETH** [ ] [-]

Mar 93. (10"ep) *(TIPPY TOE – che 2)* **MARBLES / JOE STUMBLE. / FOR THOSE . . . / BENN** [ ] [-]

— Below featured dual vox of **NIKI SIN** of HUGGY BEAR.

Rough Trade Sing. Club / not iss.

Mar 93. (7") *(45REV 16)* **A MARRIAGE MADE IN HEAVEN. / (instrumental)** [ ] [-]

Domino / No.6

Jul 93. (7"ep) *(RUG 6)* **UNWIRED E.P.** [ ] [-]
– Feeling relatively good / Rottweilers and mace / She / Kooks.

Sep 93. (7") *<KAR 028>* **MARBLES. / FOR THOSE NOT BEAUTIFUL** [-] [ ]

This Way Up / Bar None

Sep 93. (7"/cd-s) *(WAY 1811/1833)* **CITY SICKNESS. / UNTITLED / THE BULLRING** [ ] [-]

Oct 93. (cd/c/lp) *(518306-2/-4/-1) <46>* **TINDERSTICKS** [56] [ ]
– Nectar tyed / Sweet, sweet man (pt.1) / Whiskey & water / Blood / City sickness / Patchwork / Marbles / The Walt blues / Milky teeth (pt.2) / Sweet, sweet man (pt.2) / Jism / Piano song / Tie dye / Raindrops / Sweet, sweet man (pt.3) / Her / Tea stain / Drunk tank / Paco de Renaldo's dream / The not knowing. *(lp+=)* – Fruitless. *(re-iss. Jun97; same)*

— In Oct'93, alongside GALLON DRUNK, they issued 'Clawfist' 7" WE HAVE ALL THE TIME IN THE WORLD (XPIG 21). 'Tippy Toe' also gave away 7" 'LIVE IN BERLIN' at gigs.

Jan 94. (7"ep/10"ep/cd-ep) *(WAY 2811/2888/2833)* **KATHLEEN EP** [61] [-]
– Kathleen / Summat Moon / A sweet sweet man / E-type Joe.

— In Aug'94, they appeared on Various Artists EP on 'Blue Eyed Dog'; track 'LOVE BITES', and others by STRANGELOVE / GOD MACHINE + BREED.

This Way Up / London

Mar 95. (7") *(WAY 38-11)* **NO MORE AFFAIRS. / (instrumental)** [58] [-]
(cd-s+=) *(WAY 38-33)* – Fruitless.

Apr 95. (cd/c/d-lp) *(526303-2/-4/-1) <6303>* **THE SECOND TINDERSTICKS ALBUM** [13] [ ] Oct95
– El diablo en el ojo / My sister / Tiny tears / Snowy in F minor / Seaweed / Vertrauen 2 / Talk to me / No more affairs / Singing / Travelling light / Cherry blossoms / She's gone / Mistakes / Vertraven 3 / Sleepy song. *(ltd.lp w/ free one-sided-7")* – PLUS DE LIAISONS

Jun 95. (7") *<SP 297>* **THE SMOOTH SOUNDS OF TINDERSTICKS** [-] [ ]
– Here / Harry's dilemma.
<above issued for 'Sub Pop'>

Jul 95. (7"/cd-s) *(WAY 45-11)* **TRAVELLING LIGHT. / WAITING 'ROUND YOU / I'VE BEEN LOVING YOU TOO LONG** [51] [-]

Oct 95. (cd/d-10"lp) *(528597-2/-1)* **THE BLOOMSBURY THEATRE 12.3.95 (live)** [32] [-]
– El diablo en el ojo / A night in / Talk to me / She's gone / My sister * / No more affairs / City sickness / Vertrauen II / Sleepy song / Jism / Drunk tank / Mistakes / Tiny tears / Raindrops / For those . . . *(d-lp+= *)*

This Way Up / Bar None

Oct 96. (cd/lp) *(524300-2/-1) <99>* **NENETTE ET BONI (Original Soundtrack)** [ ] [ ]
– Ma souer / La passerelle / Les gateaux / Camions / Nenette est la / Petites chiennes / Nosterfrau / Petites gouttes d'eau / Les Cannes a peche / La mort de Felix / Nenette s'en va / Les bebes / Les fleurs / Rumba.

This Way Up / Polygram

May 97. (12"ep/cd-ep) *(WAY 61-22/-33)* **BATHTIME. / MANALOW / SHADOWS / PACO'S THEME** [38] [-]
(cd-ep) *(WAY 61-66)* – ('A'side) / Kathleen / Here / Tyed.

Jun 97. (cd/c/lp) *(<524344-2/-4/-1>)* **CURTAINS** [37] [ ]
– Another night in / Rented rooms / Don't look down / Dick's slow song / Fast one / Ballad of Tindersticks / Dancing / Let's pretend / Desperate man / Buried bones / Bearsuit / (Tonight) Are you trying to fall in love again / I was your man / Bathtime / Walking.

Oct 97. (7") *(WAY 65-22)* **RENTED ROOMS. / ('A'-Swing version)** [56] [ ]
(cd-s+=) *(WAY 65-33)* – Make believe.
(cd-s) *(WAY 65-66)* – ('A'side) / Cherry blossoms (live) / She's gone (live) / Rhumba (live).

Island / Polygram

Sep 98. (cd/lp) *(CID/ILPS 8074) <524588>* **DONKEYS 92-97 (A COLLECTION OF SINGLES ° RARITIES ° UNRELEASED RECORDINGS)** [ ] [ ]
– Patchwork / Marbles / Her / City sickness / Travelling light / I've been loving you too long / Plus de liaisons / Here / Tiny tears / Bathtime / A marriage made in Heaven / For those . . .

TIN HUEY

Formed: Akron, Ohio, USA . . . 1977 by CHRIS BUTLER and RALPH CARNEY, who completed the line-up with HARVEY GOLD, STUART AUSTIN, MICHAEL AYLWARD and MARK PRICE. Following the release of a couple of singles on the indie label, 'Clone', namely 'PUPPETS WIVES' and 'BREAKFAST WITH . . .', TIN HUEY's experimental blend of jazzy ZAPPA-rooted "New Wave" pop/rock was enough to convince 'Warners' of their potential. First up was an avant-pop version of The Monkees' 'I'M A BELIEVER', probably released too soon after ROBERT WYATT's UK Top 30 cover from '74. The resulting album, 'CONTENTS DISLODGED DURING SHIPMENT', proved too challenging for mainstream public consumption even in 1979 and the band split after a final Labor Day gig the following year. While BUTLER initiated The WAITRESSES, CARNEY formed The SWOLLEN MONKEYS (with DAVID BUCK, DAN KLAYMAN, MARS WILLIAMS, DON DAVIS, TED ORR, BILL YLITANO and CHRIS MORGAN), releasing one solitary lp, 'AFTERBIRTH OF THE COOL', for 'Cachelot' <CA 128> early in 1982. CARNEY subsequently teamed up with DAVID HILD and MARK KRAMER, the trio of CARNEY-HILD-KRAMER issuing a 1987 set, 'HAPPINESS FINALLY CAME TO THEM'.

Album rating: CONTENTS DISLODGED DURING SHIPMENT (*6)

CHRIS BUTLER – guitar, percussion, vocals / **RALPH CARNEY** – saxophones, clarinets / **HARVEY GOLD** – synthesizer, keyboards, vocals / **MICHAEL AYLWARD** – guitar + slide, vocals / **MARK PRICE** – bass, vocals / **STUART AUSTIN** – drums, percussion, synthesizer

not iss. / Clone

1977. (7"ep) *<CL 002>* **PUPPET WIVES / CUYAHOGA CREEPING BENT. / POOR ALPHONSO (live) / THE TIN HUEY STORY** [-] [ ]

1978. (7") *<CL 004>* **BREAKFAST WITH THE HUEYS** [-] [ ]
– Robert takes the road to Liebernawash / Squirm you worm.

not iss. / Warners

Jun 79. (7") *<WBS 49001>* **I'M A BELIEVER. / NEW YORK'S FINEST DINING EXPERIENCE** [-] [ ]

Jul 79. (lp) *<BSK 3297>* **CONTENTS DISLODGED DURING SHIPMENT** [-] [ ]
– I'm a believer / Revelations of Dr. Modesto / I could rule the world if only I / Coronation / Slide / Hump day / Pink berets / Squirm, you worm / Chinese circus / Puppet wives / New York's finest dining experience.

not iss. / Clone

1980. (7") *<CL 011>* **ENGLISH KIDS. / SISTER ROSE** [-] [ ]

— CARNEY split the band in 1980

TOADIES

Formed: Fort Worth, Texas, USA . . . 1990 by son of a preacher man, TODD LEWIS alongside DARREL HERBERT, LISA UMBARGER and MARK REZNICEK. Following the release of a self-financed debut EP, 'VELVET', these musical amphibians went on to record a second EP, 'PLEATHER' and single, 'MISTER LOVE', for the independent 'Grass' label. Amid the mid-90's major label goldrush on alternative guitar bands, LEWIS & Co were signed to 'Interscope', exposing their hard hitting, vaguely alternative but ulitmately derivative post-grunge sound to a wider crossover market with 1996's debut album, 'RUBBERNECK'. With no material having surfaced in the latter part of the 90's, it seems as if the TOADIES have finally become extinct.

Album rating: RUBBERNECK (*6)

TODD LEWIS – vocals, guitar / **DARREL HERBERT** – guitar / **LISA UMBARGER** – bass / **MARK REZNICEK** – drums

not iss. indie

1992. (7"ep) **VELVET EP** -

Grass Grass

May 93. (cd-ep) *<ASS 001-2>* **PLEATHER**
– Mister love / Got a heart / Ruth / Happy face / Possum kingdom. *<re-iss. 1997 on 'Interscope'; 90137>*

May 93. (7") *<ASS 002-7>* **MISTER LOVE /**

Revelation Interscope

1995. (cd-ep) **BACKSLIDER** -
Dec 95. (cd-ep) **SANTACIDE / POSSUM KINGDOM** -
Jan 96. (cd)(c) *(IS 2402) <92402>* **RUBBERNECK** 56 Aug95
– Mexican hairless / Mister love / Backslider / Possum kingdom / Quitter / Away / I come from the water / Tyler / Happyface / Velvet / I burn.

TOILING MIDGETS (see under ⇒ AMERICAN MUSIC CLUB)

Russ TOLMAN (see under ⇒ TRUE WEST)

TONES ON TAIL (see under ⇒ BAUHAUS)

Winston TONG (see under ⇒ TUXEDOMOON)

TONIC

Formed: Los Angeles, California, USA . . . 1993 by EMERSON HART along with JEFF RUSSO, DAN ROTHCHILD and KEVIN SHEPARD. After honing their live skills around L.A., the band signed a major label deal straight off with 'A&M' and proceeded to build up a groundswell of media support with a trio of singles: 'OPEN UP YOUR EYES', 'CASUAL AFFAIR' and 'IF YOU COULD ONLY SEE'. These formed the opening sequence of the band's debut album, 'LEMON PARADE' (1997), a JACK JOSEPH PUIG (who had previously worked on The BLACK CROWES' 'Amorica')-produced record that combined a mature, vaguely alternative rock sound with subtle rootsy blues/country touches. DAN LAVERY was drafted in (as a replacement for the departing ROTHCHILD) after its completion and although the band's crossover potential was confirmed with a Top 30 US chart placing, TONIC have yet to deliver a follow-up to remedy their lengthy absence from the music scene.

Album rating: LEMON PARADE (*6)

EMERSON HART – vocals, guitar / **JEFF RUSSO** – guitar / **DAN ROTHCHILD** – bass, slide guitar / **KEVIN SHEPARD** – drums

A&M A&M

1997. (cd-s) **OPEN UP YOUR EYES /** -
1997. (cd-s) **CASUAL AFFAIR /** -
Sep 97. (7") *(571308-7)* **IF YOU COULD ONLY SEE. /** Jun98
(cd-s+=) *(571369-2)* –
Sep 97. (cd) *<531042-2>* **LEMON PARADE** 28 Jul96
– Open up your eyes / Casual affair / If you could only see / Soldier's daughter / Lemon parade / Mountain / Thick / Wicked soldier / Mr. Golden deal / Bigot sunshine / Celtic aggression / My old man.

— **DAN LAVERY** – bass; repl. ROTHCHILD

TOP (see under ⇒ WILD SWANS)

TO ROCOCO ROT

Formed: Berlin, Germany . . . 1994 by KREIDLER bassist, STEFAN SCHNEIDER, along with the LIPPOK brothers, ROBERT and RONALD. Latter day carriers of the experimental electronic flame originally lit by Germanic forebears such as KRAFTWERK and TANGERINE DREAM, the palindromically monikered TO ROCOCO ROT were originally conceived as a multi-media art project. Attempting to align these ideas within the context of post-rock minimalism, the trio made their musical debut in 1996 with an eponymous German-only album, drawing praise from both the alternative-rock and electronic scenes alike. The reception was positive enough for 'Kitty-Yo' to give the album a full UK release as '.CD' (1997), critics comparing the record's undulating grooves to Stateside practioners like TORTOISE, TRANS and ROME. By this point, the group had already begun to make waves in Britain and America with the more trance-Europe-expressive 'VEICULO', released some five months previously.

Album rating: TO ROCOCO ROT / .CD (*5) / VEICULO (*6)

ROBERT LIPPOK – guitar, electronics / **RONALD LIPPOK** – drums, effects / **STEFAN SCHNEIDER** – bass, organ, turntables (of KREIDLER)

EFA not iss.

1996. (cd) *(707120)* **TO ROCOCO ROT** - - German
– Im lilienthal / Kritische masse I / Veramun / Dekothek / Polo star / Susse kuche / National velvet / Tour de repechage / Testfield / Parabola. *(UK-iss.Jul97 as '.CD' on 'Kitty Yo'+=; KITTY 010)* – Weiter / Schon sehr viel telefoniert / Kabine / Autonachmittag.

City Slang Emperor Jones

Feb 97. (cd/lp) *(efa 04990-2/-1) <15>* **VEICULO**
– Micromanaged / He loves me / Modern homes / Moto / Mit dir in der gegend / Leggiero / Geheimnis eines mantels / Extra / Fach / Lips / Merano / Allover dezent / Lift.

Oct 97. (12"ep)<cd-ep> *(efa 049941) <19>* **PARIS 25** Feb98
– Lift (denso) / Mit dir in der gegend (sehr) / Dual use / History on discs / Days between stations.

Fat Cat not iss.

Apr 98. (12"ep) *(12FAT 007)* **SHE UNDERSTANDS THE DYNAMICS. / THINGS HAVE A WAY OF HAPPENING BY THEMSELVES / RUPTURE IN A FINE AND STEADY DAY** -

Soul Static not iss.

Nov 98. (m-cd) *(23)* **TRRD** -

TORTOISE

Formed: Chicago, Illinois, USA . . . 1990 by DOUG McCOMBS and JOHN HERNDON, who started jamming together with JOHN McENTIRE, BUNDY K BROWN and DAN BITNEY. This cult outfit initially crawled out of their collective shell with a series of early 90's EP's before finally unleashing their eponymous debut in '94. Remixed by STEVE ALBINI on the following years' blistering EP, 'RHYTHMS, RESOLUTIONS & CLUSTERS', the record proved TORTOISE to be the foremost purveyors of cut'n'mix avant-jazz. In 1996, their second album, 'MILLIONS NOW LIVING WILL NEVER DIE' (featuring the STEREOLAB trio of TIM, LAETITIA and MARY) was even better, opening with the psychedelic/Krautrock marathon of 'DJED'. This 20-minute track was subsequently given the 'Mo Wax' treatment, the extent of the band's appeal illustrated by their impressive run of collaborations over the course of the next year. The hard-working McENTIRE, who was also a part-time member of RED CRAYOLA and The SEA AND CAKE, returned to the studio at the end of the year, beavering away on what was yet another classic TORTOISE set, 'T.N.T.' (1998). A segued journey from cool avant-jazz rock that unsuspectingly flowed into complex rhythmical landscapes.

Album rating: TORTOISE (*5) / MILLIONS NOW LIVING WILL NEVER DIE (*8) / T.N.T. (*8)

JOHN McENTIRE – synthesizers, drums, vibraphone (ex-BASTRO) / **BUNDY K BROWN** – guitar, bass / **DOUG McCOMBS** – bass (ex-ELEVENTH DREAM DAY) / **JOHNNY HERNDON** – drums, synthesizers, vibraphone / **DAN BITNEY** – synthesizers, percussion / 6th member **CASEY** – soundman

not iss. Torsion

1993. (7") *<003>* **MOSQUITO. / ONIONS WRAPPED IN RUBBER / GOOSENECK** -

not iss. Soul Static

1994. (7") *<SOUL 7>* **WHY WE FIGHT. / WHITEWATER** -
(UK-iss.Jan95; same)

City Slang Thrill Jockey

1994. (12") *<THRILL 006>* **LONESOME SOUND. / RESERVOIR / SHEETS** -
Jan 95. (cd/lp) *(EFA 04950-2/-1) <THRILL 013>* **TORTOISE**
– Magnet pulls through / Night air / Ry Cooder / Onions wrapped in rubber / Tin cans and twine / Spiderwebbed / His second story island / On noble / Flyrod / Cornpole brunch. *(cd-iss. remixed May97; TKCB 71016) (lp re-iss. Jun97 on 'Thrill Jockey'; THRILL 013)*
Apr 95. (12") *(Dodgey Beast; DS 3309)* **GAMERA. / CLIFF DWELLER SOCIETY**
(12") *(DS 3309S)* – ('A'mixes).
Jun 95. (m-cd/m-lp) *(EFA 04957-2/-1) <THRILL 019>* **RHYTHMS, RESOLUTIONS & CLUSTERS: REMIXED AND RARE**
– Alcohall / Your new rod / Cobwebbed / Match incident / Not quite east of the Ryan / Initial gesture protraction.

— **DAVE PAJO** – guitar (ex-SLINT) repl. BROWN who formed DIRECTIONS IN MUSIC. He and McCOMBS were also part of alt-supergroup, PULLMAN.

Jan 96. (cd/lp) *(EFA 04972-2/-1) <THRILL 025>* **MILLIONS NOW LIVING WILL NEVER DIE**
– Djed / Glass museum / A survey / The taut and the tame / Dear grandma and grandpa / Along the banks of rivers. *(cd-iss. Japanese version May97; TKCB 70931)*
Apr 96. (12"; by TORTOISE Vs U.N.K.L.E./JOHN McENTIRE) *(SHELL 001) <TJ 12.1>* **DJED (bruise blood mix). / TJED**
Jul 96. (12"; by TORTOISE Vs BUNDY BROWN) *<TJ 12.2>* **ROME** -
Jul 96. (12"; by TORTOISE Vs OVAL) *(SHELL 002) <TJ 12.3>* **MUSIC FOR WORK GROUPS EP**
– The bubble economy (mix by Marcus Popp) / Learning curve (mix by Marcus Popp).
Sep 96. (12"; by TORTOISE VS SPRING HEEL JACK) *(SHELL 003) <TJ 12.4>* **GALAPAGOS 1 (Spring Heel Jack remix). / REFERENCE RESISTANCE GATE (Jim O'Rourke remix)**
(re-iss. Jun97 on 'Thrill Jockey'; TJ 124)

Oct 96. (12"; by TORTOISE Vs LUKE VIBERT/BUNDY K BROWN) *(SHELL 004)* <*TJ 12.5*> **THE TAUT AND THE TAME. / FIND THE ONE (WAIT, ABSTRACTION NO . . .)**

— In 1996, they also shared a single with STEREOLAB, 'VAUS' / 'SPEEDY CAR', released on 'Duophonic'; *D-UHF-D12)*

— **JEFF PARKER** – guitar; repl. PAJO who formed AERIAL M

Mar 98. (cd/d-lp) *(EFA 08705-2/-1)* <*THRILL 050*> **TNT**
– Swung from the gutters / Ten-day interval / I set my face to the hillside / The equator / A simple way to go faster than light that does not work / The suspension bridge at Iguazu Falls / Four-day interval / In Sarah, Mencken, Christ, and Beethoven there were women and men / Almost always is nearly enough / Jetty / Everglade.

Jul 98. (ltd-12"; TORTOISE VS. DERRICK CARTER) *(087096)* **IN SARAH, MENCKEN, CHRIST, AND BEETHOVEN THERE WERE WOMEN AND MEN** -
– (D's winter crazy mix) / (D's winter outtake).
(above issued on 'Rephlex')

– compilations, others, etc. –

May 97. (cd) *Thrill Jockey;* <*(TKCB 70932)*> **A DIGEST COMPENDIUM OF TORTOISE'S WORLD** 1996
– Tin cans & twine / Alcohall / Night air / Gooseneck / Onions wrapped in rubber / Spiderwebbed / Cobnebbed / Your new rod / Ry Cooder (the beer incident) / Not quite east of the Ryan / Reservoir / Cornpone brunch / Whitewater / Initial gesture protraction.

Apr 98. (cd) *Thrill Jockey;* <*(TKCB 71016)*> **TORTOISE REMIXED** (all the 4 collaboration/Vs singles) 1996

Frank TOVEY (see under ⇒ FAD GADGET)

TOWERING INFERNO

Formed: London, England . . . 1993 by performance artists, RICHARD WOOLFSON and ANDY SAUNDERS. As the name might suggest, TOWERING INFERNO specialise in music of a burning intensity; 'KADDISH' (1995) was an experimental collage informed by the genocide perpetrated against Jews by Nazi Germany during WWII, WOOLFSON and SAUNDERS conjuring up the horror and sorrow of their subject matter through an often disconcerting combination of ambient keyboard textures, guitar riffs, world music and snippets of dialogue, religious ceremonies etc. Released on the ever open minded 'Island' label and raved over by veteran electro-experimentalist, BRIAN ENO, the record won praise from a diverse range of sources; inspired by the critical reception, the TOWERING INFERNO duo subsequently performed the album as a multi-media event in London.

Album rating: KADDISH (*6)

RICHARD WOOLFSON – keyboards, guitar, percussion, etc / **ANDY SAUNDERS** – flute, keyboards, programming, etc / with a plethora of session people incl. ELTON DEAN, CHRIS CUTLER, GASPAR LAWAL, JOHN MARSHALL, JOCELYN POOK, ANDREW DAVIS, MARTA SEBESTYEN etc.

Island Island

Aug 95. (cd/c) *(CID/ICT 8039)* <*531034*> **KADDISH** Feb96
– Rose / Prayer / Dachau / 4 by 2 / Edvard Kiraly / Memory / Not me / Reverse field / Occupation / Sto mondo rotondo / Organ loop / Toll (I) / Toll (II) / Ruin / Juden / Pogrom / Partisans / Modern times / Rose (II) Bell / Kaddish / Weaver.

— unfortunately they've put nothing on record since

TOYAH

Born: TOYAH ANN WILLCOX, 18 May'58, King's Heath, Birmingham. Following a stint in drama school and a bit part in a BBC play, TOYAH'S big break came when the late Derek Jarman offered a her a prestigious role in his influential punk flick, 'Jubilee' (she later starred in his version of 'The Tempest'). Through this, the budding singer met ADAM ANT with whom she played in a short-lived outfit named The MAN EATERS. Soon after, TOYAH formed her own group with the help of JOEL BOGEN, PETE BUSH, MARK HENRY and STEVE BRAY. Securing a deal with burgeoning indie label, 'Safari', they released their debut single, 'VICTIMS OF THE RIDDLE', in the summer of '79. Unsurprisingly for such a cringe-inducingly titled track, it failed to break the chart, with an accompanying album, ahem . . . 'SHEEP FARMING IN BARNET' (1979) meeting a similar fate. Wisely perhaps, TOYAH continued to juggle an acting career simultaneously, scoring roles in TV and film including a part in 'The Corn Is Green' and in PETE TOWNSHEND's seminal mod-revisionist movie, 'Quadrophenia'. Though a follow-up album, 'THE BLUE MEANING', and a live effort, 'TOYAH! TOYAH! TOYAH!' (1981) gave the singer her first Top 40 action, it was only with the release of the 'FOUR FROM TOYAH' EP (1981) that the kids really took to her new wave/goth histrionics. The lead track, 'IT'S A MYSTERY', was infect-t-tious enough to take her into the Top 5, though it was largely her aggressively hyped image (dauntingly flame-haired, quintessentially 80's ice-queen) which turned her into an unlikely pop star. Next up was 'I WANT TO BE FREE', a rebel song up there with Cliff Richard's 'SUMMER HOLIDAY' in terms of anti-establishment ire but naively charming and annoyingly hummable nonetheless. TOYAH's third and final Top 10 single was 'THUNDER IN THE MOUNTAINS', a song as majestically bombastic as the title suggests. The latter two tracks both featured on the 'ANTHEM' (1981) set, TOYAH's most successful album by far, narrowly missing the No.1 spot. The singer continued her mythical/futuristic lyrical musings with 'THE CHANGELING' (1982) the following year, the set spawning two further Top 30 hits, 'BRAVE NEW WORLD' and 'BE LOUD BE PROUD (BE HEARD)'. Though she suffered constant music press jibes about her slight lisp, TOYAH retained a loyal following who put later albums like 'LOVE IS THE LAW' (1983) and 'MINX' (1985) into the Top 30 despite any major hits. Taking a sabbatical in the mid-80's during which she married ex-KING CRIMSON guitar maestro ROBERT FRIPP, TOYAH eventually returned in the summer of '87 with 'DESIRE', an album that followed a co-credited set, 'THE LADY OR THE TIGER' to both her and her new spouse. Though she never sees any chart action these days, TOYAH continues to collaborate with FRIPP, most recently on the 1994 set, 'DREAMCHILD'. The singer has also sidelined into TV presenting of late, living it up on far-flung exotic beaches for BBC 1's 'Holiday' programme, while also presenting videos on Sky channel show, 'VH1'. • **Songwriters:** She and band wrote music, except ECHO BEACH (Martha + The Muffins) / SCHOOL'S OUT (Alice Cooper). • **Trivia:** Her other acting attributions were in 1983's 'TRAFFORD TANZI' and in 1987, she acted in the West End play, 'CABARET'. Amongst other roles, she subsequently appeared in the TV detective series, 'Shoestring'.

Album rating: SHEEP FARMING IN BARNET (*6) / THE BLUE MEANING (*7) / TOYAH TOYAH compilation (*7)

TOYAH – vocals / with band **JOEL BOGEN** – guitar / **PETE BUSH** – keyboards / **MARK HENRY** – bass / **STEVE BRAY** – drums

Safari not iss.

Jun 79. (7") *(SAFE 15)* **VICTIMS OF THE RIDDLE. / VICTIMS OF THE RIDDLE (VIVESECTION)** -

Jul 79. (7"ep) *(SAP 1)* **SHEEP FARMING IN BARNET** -
– Neon womb / Indecision / Waiting / Our movie / Vivisection / Danced.

Dec 79. (lp/c) *(IC 064/264)* **SHEEP FARMING IN BARNET** -
– Neon womb / Indecision / Waiting / Computer / Victims of the riddle / Elusive stranger / Our movie / Danced / Last goodbye / Victims of the riddle (vivisection) / Race through space. *(re-iss. Aug90 on 'Great Expectations' cd/c/lp; PIP MC/CD/LP 014)*

Jan 80. (7") *(SAFE 22)* **BIRD IN FLIGHT. / TRIBAL LOOK** -

— **CHARLIE FRANCIS** – bass; repl. MARK HENRY

May 80. (7"/ext.12"white) *(SAFE/+LS 28)* **IEYA. / SPACE WALKING (HELIUM SONG)** -
(re-iss. Jul82 + 7"pic-d; SAFEX 28) – hit UK No.48.

May 80. (lp/c) *(IEYA/CIEYA 666)* **THE BLUE MEANING** 40 -
– Ieya / Space walking (helium song) / Ghosts / Mummys / Blue meanings / She / Tiger tiger / Insects / Vision / Love me. *(re-iss. Jul90 on 'Great Expectations' cd/c/lp; PIP CD/MC/LP 015)*

Nov 80. (7"m) *(SAFE 32)* **DANCED (live). / GHOSTS (live) / NEON WOMB (live)** -

Jan 81. (lp/c) *(LIVE/CLIVE 2)* **TOYAH! TOYAH! TOYAH! (live)** 22 -
– Victims of the riddle / Indecision / Love me / Vision / Tribal look / Bird in flight / Danced / Insects / Race through space / Ieya. *(re-iss. Aug90 on 'Great Expectations' cd/c/lp; PIP CD/MC/LP 016)*

— **TOYAH** retained only **BOGEN,** and recruited **ADRIAN LEE** – keys / **PHIL SPALDING** – bass (ex-ORIGINAL MIRRORS) / **NIGEL GLOCKER** – drums (ex-ASSOCIATES)

Feb 81. (7"ep) *(TOY 1)* **FOUR FROM TOYAH** 4 -
– It's a mystery / War boys / Angels and demons / Revelations.

May 81. (7"m) *(SAFE 34)* **I WANT TO BE FREE. / WALKIE TALKIE / ALIEN** 8 -

May 81. (pic-lp/c) *(VOOR/+C 1)* **ANTHEM** 2
– I want to be free / Obsolete pop star / Elocution lesson (the door is a whore) / Jungles of Jupiter / I am / It's a mystery / Masai boy / Marionette / Demolition man / We are. *(cd-iss. Nov85 +=; VOORD 1)* – Thunder in the mountains / War boys / Angels and demons / Revelations.

— **SIMON PHILIPS** – drums, percussion; repl GLOCKER who left to join SAXON. **ANDY CLARKE + SIMON DARLOW** – keyboards; repl LEE.

Sep 81. (7"pic-d) *(SAFE 38)* **THUNDER IN THE MOUNTAINS. / STREET ADDICT** 4 -
(w/ free 7"flexi) *(SAFELS 38)* – STAND PROUD

Nov 81. (7"ep) *(TOY 2)* **FOUR MORE FROM TOYAH** 14 -
– Good morning universe / Urban tribesman / In the fairground / The furious futures.

May 82. (7"pic-d) *(SAFE 45)* **BRAVE NEW WORLD. / WARRIOR ROCK** 21 -

Jun 82. (lp/c) *(VOOR/+C 9)* **THE CHANGELING** 6 -
– Creepy room / Street creature / Castaways / The druids / Angel and me / The pact / Life in the trees / Dawn chorus / Run wild run free / Brave new world.

— **KEITH HALE** – keyboards, vocals; repl. CLARKE

Sep 82. (7"pic-d) *(SAFE 52)* **BE LOUD BE PROUD (BE HEARD). / LAUGHING WITH THE FOOLS** 30 -

Nov 82. (d-lp/d-c) *(TNT/CTNT 1)* **WARRIOR ROCK – TOYAH ON TOUR (live)** 20 -
– Good morning universe / Warrior rock / Danced / Jungles of Jupiter / Castaways / Angel and me / Brave new world / The pact / Thunder in the mountains / We are / I want to be free / Dawn chorus / War boy / Ieya / Be loud be proud (be heard).

— **ANDY DUNCAN** – drums repl. PHILIPS

Safari Safari

Sep 83. (7") *(SAFE 56)* **REBEL RUN. / MOUNTAINS HIGH** 24 -

Oct 83. (lp/c) *(VOOR/+C 10)* **LOVE IS THE LAW** 28
– Broken diamonds / I explode / Rebel of love / Rebel run / Martian cowboy / Dream scape / Time is ours / Love is the law / Remember / The vow.

Nov 83. (7") *(SAFE 58)* **THE VOW. / I EXPLODE** 50 -
(12"+=) *(SAFELS 58)* – Haunted.

— now w / **DARLOW / LEE / PETER VAN HOOKE** – drums / **AL HODGE + PHIL PALMER** – guitar / **IAN WHERRY + ANDY BROWN** – bass

Portrait Portrait

Apr 85. (7"/12") *(A/TX 6160)* **DON'T FALL IN LOVE (I SAID). / SNOW COVERS THE KISS** 22

Jun 85. (7"pic-d) *(A 6359)* **SOUL PASSING THROUGH SOUL. / ALL IN A RAGE** 57
(12"+=) *(TA 6359)* – ('A'extended).

Jul 85. (lp/c/cd) *(PRT/40/CD 26415)* **MINX** [24] [ ]
– Soldier of fortune, terrorist of love / Don't fall in love (I said) / Soul passing through soul / Sympathy / I'll serve you well / All in a rage / Space between the sounds / School's out / World in action / America for beginners. *(c+=/cd+=)* – Over twenty-one / Vigilante.

Sep 85. (7"/12") *(A/TA 6545)* **WORLD IN ACTION. / SOLDIERS OF FORTUNE** [ ] [-]

—— in Sep'85, she guested on TONY BANKS (of Genesis) EP track, 'You Call This Victory'.

—— below was credited with her new hubby, ROBERT FRIPP (ex-KING CRIMSON)

E.G. not iss.

Jan 87. (lp/c; TOYAH & FRIPP) *(EGED/+C 44)* **THE LADY OR THE TIGER** [ ] [-]
– The lady or the tiger / Discourager of hesitancy.

Apr 87. (7"/12") *(EGO/+X 31)* **ECHO BEACH. / PLENTY** [54] [-]

Jun 87. (lp/c/cd) *(EG LP/MC/CD 71)* **DESIRE** [ ] [-]
– Echo beach / Moonlight dancing / Revive the world / The view / Moon migration / Love's unkind / Dear diary / Deadly as a woman / Goodbye baby / When a woman cries / Desire.

Jun 87. (7") *(EGO 35)* **MOONLIGHT DANCING. / SUN UP** [ ] [-]
(12"+=) *(EGOX 35)* – R.E.-N.T.R.Y. – Into dance.

—— now w / backing from **STEVE SIDEH** – drums, percussion, keyboards

Nov 88. (lp/c/cd; as TOYAH WILLCOX) *(EGED/EGEDC/EEGCD 59)* **PROSTITUTE** [ ] [ ]
– Hello / Prostitute / Wife / The show / Dream house / Homecraft / Obsession / Let the power bleed / Restless / Falling to Earth / Jazz singers in the trees / Vale of Evesham / Ghosts in the universe.

—— FRIPP appeared on above (their tour was billed as FRIPP & FRIPP)

—— new band:- **GUNN, GEBALLE + BEAVIS** and guest **ROBERT FRIPP**

Feb 91. (cd/c/lp) *(EGCD/EGMC/EGLP 78)* **OPHELIA'S SHADOW** [ ] [-]
– Ophelia's shadow / The shaman says / Brilliant day / Prospect / Turning tide / Take what you will / Ghost light / The woman who had an affair with herself / Homeward / Lords of the never known.

—— now with **MIKE BENNETT** – guitar, producer, main writer / **PAUL MORAN** – keyboards, producer / **JAY STAPLEY** – guitar / **BOB SKEAT** – bass / **SASHA ADAMS** – tape operator

Cryptic not iss.

Nov 93. (12"/cd-s) *(12/CD TOY 1)* **OUT OF THE BLUE (Trancentral mix). / OUT OF THE BLUE (deep ocean mix)** [ ] [-]
(12+=) *(12XTOY 1)* – Out of The Blue (Transcentral radio mix).

Apr 94. (c-s/12"/cd-s) *(12/MC/CD TOY 2)* **NOW AND THEN. / ('A'mixes)** [ ] [-]

May 94. (cd/c) *(TOY CD/MC 1001)* **DREAMCHILD** [ ] [-]
– Now and then / Let me go / Unkind / Out of the blue / Dreamchild / World of tension / Lost and found / Over you / I don't know / Disappear / Tone poem.

—— TOYAH now concentrates on her television work

– compilations, etc. –

Feb 84. (lp/c) *K-Tel; (NE/C1 1268)* **TOYAH TOYAH** [43] [-]
Nov 85. (lp/c) *Safari; (VOOR/+C 77)* **MAYHEM** [ ] [-]
Mar 94. (cd) *Connoisseur; (CSAPCD 115)* **THE BEST OF TOYAH** [ ] [-]
Nov 96. (cd) *Tring; (ANT 012)* **THE ACOUSTIC ALBUM** [ ] [-]
Nov 96. (cd) *Tring; (QED 065)* **LOOKING BACK** [ ] [-]
Apr 97. (cd) *Receiver; (<RRCD 235>)* **PHOENIX** [ ] [ ] May97
Feb 98. (cd) *Reactive; (REMCD 501)* **THE VERY BEST OF TOYAH** [ ] [-]
– It's a mystery / Good morning universe / I want to be free / Be proud be loud be heard / Bird in flight / Rebel run / Brave new world / Thunder in the mountains / Ieya / Street creature / Elusive stranger / Martian cowboy / Love me / Broken diamonds / Castaways / She / Jungles of Jupiter / We are.
Jun 98. (cd) *Connoisseur; (CSAPCD 125)* **LIVE AND MORE (live)** [ ] [-]

—— In Jun'82, a single as "The ANTEATERS", 'NINE TO FIVE', was lifted from the 1977 film, 'Jubilee', in which she appeared with ADAM ANT.

TOY DOLLS

Formed: Sunderland, England . . . early 80's by OLGA, FLIP and HAPY BOB. A punk institution to some, one-hit wonders to most people, The TOY DOLLS moniker will forever conjure up images of drunken conga-chain shindigs and general dancefloor mayhem caused by exposure to their Christmas '84 Top 5 "classic", 'NELLIE THE ELEPHANT'. Part nursery rhyme, part Young Ones-style student humour, the record was shamelessly addictive but thankfully a one-off, at least as far as the charts were concerned. Nevertheless, the band attracted a hardcore of dichard fans eager for more Northern humour – you can't argue with titles like 'YUL BRYNNER WAS A SKINHEAD' and 'DEIRDRE'S A SLAG' (for 'Corry' fans omly!) – and fully prepared to snap up albums such as 'A FAR OUT DISC' (1985), 'BARE FACED CHEEK' (1987), 'DIG THAT GROOVE BABY' (1988), 'IDLE GOSSIP' (1988) and 'WAKEY WAKEY' (1989). The bulk of these were released on the 'Volume' label although the 'DOLLS signed with 'Receiver' at the turn of the decade, issuing concert set, '20 TUNES LIVE IN TOKYO' (1990). While the fact that Japan took the band to their bosom was perhaps not as surprising as the fact that The TOY DOLLS continued releasing albums right up until the late 90's, namely 'ABSURD-DITTIES' (1993), 'ORCASTRATED' (1995) and 'ONE MORE MEGABYTE' (1997). • **Covered"** SABRE DANCE, BLUE SUEDE SHOES, etc. • **Note:** The SHOWBIZ KIDZ isuued a version of 'SHE GOES TO FINOS'.

Album rating: THE HISTORY OF THE TOY DOLLS 79-96 compilation (*3)

OLGA (b. MICHAEL ALGAR) – vocals, guitar / **FLIP** – bass / **HAPPY BOB** – drums

G.B.H. not iss.

Aug 81. (ltd-7") *(SSM 005)* **TOMMY KOWEY'S CAR. / SHE GOES TO FINOS** [ ] [-]

G.R.C. not iss.

Oct 81. (7"ep) *(GRC 104)* **TOMMY KOWEY'S CAR / SHE'S A WORKING TICKET. / EVERYBODY JITTERBUG / TEENAGER IN LOVE / I'VE GOT ASTHMA** [ ] [-]

Zonophone not iss.

Apr 82. (7") *(Z 31)* **EVERYBODY JITTERBUG. / (SHE'S A) WORKING TICKET** [ ] [-]

Volume not iss.

Nov 82. (7") *(VOL 3)* **NELLIE THE ELEPHANT. / DIG THAT GROOVE BABY** [ ] [-]
Aug 83. (7") *(VOL 5)* **CHEERIO AND TOODLE PIP. / H.Q.** [ ] [-]
Nov 83. (7") *(VOL 7)* **ALFIE FROM THE BRONX. / HANKY PANKY** [ ] [-]
Jul 84. (7") *(VOL 10)* **WE'RE MAD. / DEIRDRE'S A SLAG** [ ] [-]
(12"+=) *(VOLT 10)* – Rupert the bear.
Nov 84. (7") *(VOL 11)* **NELLIE THE ELEPHANT. / FISTICUFFS IN FREDERICK STREET** [4] [-]
(12"+=) *(VOLT 11)* – ('A'-1982 version).
Jan 85. (lp/c) *(VOLP/VOMC 1)* **DIG THAT GROOVE BABY** [ ] [-]
– Theme tune / Dig that groove baby / Dougy giro / Spiders in the dressing room / Glenda and the test tube baby / Up the garden path / Nellie the elephant / Poor Davey / Stay mellow / Queen Alexandra road is where she said she'd be, but was she there to meet me . . . no chance / / Worse things happen at sea / Blue suede shoes / Fiery Jack / Theme tune. *(cd-iss. Apr88; VOCD 1) (<cd re-iss. Nov92 on 'Receiver'; RRCD 166>)*

—— **NICK BUCK + FREDDIE** repl. FLIP and HAPPY BOB

Mar 85. (7") *(VOL 12)* **SHE GOES TO FINOS. / SPIDERS IN THE DRESSING ROOM** [ ] [-]
(12"+=) *(VOLT 12)* – Come back Jackie.
May 85. (lp/c) *(VOLP/VOMC 2)* **A FAR OUT DISC** [71] [-]
– A far out theme tune / She goes to Finos / Razzmatazz intro / Modern schools of motoring / Carol Dodds is pregnant / You & a box of handerchiefs / Bless you my son / My girlfriend's dad's a vicar / The "even further out" side / Come back Jackie / Do you want to finish . . . or what? / Commercial break / "Chartbuster" – Razzmatazz outro / We're mad / Wipe out! / Florence is deaf (but there's no need to shout) / A far out theme tune. *(cd-iss. Aug88; VOCD 2) (<cd re-iss. Sep92 on 'Receiver'; RRCD 164>)*
Sep 85. (7") *(VOL 17)* **JAMES BOND (LIVES DOWN OUR STREET). / OLGA I CANNOT** [ ] [-]
(12"+=) *(VOLT 17)* – Griefsville.
Aug 86. (7") *(VOL 21)* **GEORDIES GONES TO JAIL. / IDLE GOSSIP** [ ] [-]
(12"+=) *(VOLT 21)* – ('A'-Japanese version).
Sep 86. (lp/c) *(VOLP/VOMC 3)* **IDLE GOSSIP** [ ] [-]
– Idle gossip / Do you wanna be like Dougy Bell / The Lambrusco kid / You won't be merry on a North Sea ferry / Harry Cross (a tribute to Edna) / Geordie's gone to jail / Silly Billy / If you're in a pop group you'll end up paying a fortune practicing at Peter Practise's practicd place / P.C. Stoker / I tried to trust Tracey / Keith's a thief / I'll get even with Steven (Steve is tender). *(cd-iss. Aug88; VOCD 3) (<cd re-iss. Sep92 on 'Receiver'; (RRCD 165>)*

—— **DEAN** – bass, vocals + **MARTI** – drums, vocals; repl. NICK + FREDDIE

Neat not iss.

Oct 87. (lp/c/cd) *(NIT/+C/CD 001)* **BAREFACED CHEEK** [ ] [-]
– Bare faced cheek / Yul Bryner was a skinhead / How do you deal with Neal / Howza bouta kiss babe / Fisticuffs in Frederick Street / A diamond / Quick to quit the Quentin / Nowt can compare to Sunderland Fine-Fare / The Ashbrooke launderette. *(cd re-iss. Jan97 on 'Receiver'; RRCD 232) <US cd-iss. Oct94 on 'Castle'; CLA 280>*
Oct 88. (lp/c/cd) *(NIT/+C/CD 002)* **TEN YEARS OF TOYS** (compilation) [ ] [-]
– Florence is deaf (but there's no need to shout) / Glenda and the test tube baby / Idle gossip / Carol Dodd's is pregnant / Tommy Kowey's car / Peter practise's practice place / Dierdre's a slag / Blue suede shoes / Dig that groove baby / The Lambrusco kid / Doughy giro / Bless you my son / My girlfriend's dad's a vicar / She goes to Finos / Fiery Jack. *(re-iss. Dec95; same) (<cd re-iss. Mar97 on 'Receiver'; RRCD 234>)*

Receiver Receiver

Dec 89. (lp/c/cd) *(<RRLP/RRLC/RRCD 119>)* **WAKEY WAKEY** [ ] [ ]
– Introduction / Wakey wakey intro / Lester fiddled the tax man / Pot belly Bill / One night in Moscow / Cloughy is a boot boy! / Sabre dance / Davey's took the plunge / There's a trollop up Elmwood Street / No particular place to go / Poverty pleadin' Peter / Blaze of the borough / Wakey wakey outro / Goodnight Irene.
Jul 90. (cd/c/lp) *(<RRCD/RRLC/RRLP 129>)* **TWENTY (TWO) TUNES LIVE FROM TOKYO (live)** [ ] [ ]
– Wakey wakey intro / Dig that groove baby / Cloughy is a boot boy! / The Lambrusco kid / I've got asthma / Peter practises practice place / Deirdre's a slag / Ashbrooke lauderette / Bless you my son / My girlfriend's dad's a vicar / Spiders in the dressing room / Popeye medley / She goes to Finos / Fisticuffs in Frederick Street / Harry Cross / Blenda and the test tube baby / Wakey wakey outro / When the saints go marching in / Wipe out / Nellie the elephant. *(cd+=)* – Sabre dance / Blue suede shoes.
Dec 90. (7") **TURTLE CRAZY. /** [ ] [-]
Mar 91. (cd/c/lp) *(<RRCD/RRLC/RRLP 139>)* **FAT BOB'S FEET** [ ] [ ]
– Gloomy intro – Toy Doll tonic / Fat Bob's feet / We quit the calvary / The sphinx stinks / Rodney's memory / Olga crack corn / Bitten by a bed bug / Kids in Tyne & Wear / Frankie's got the blues / A bunch o' fairies / Yellow Burt / Back in '79 / The coppers copt Ken's cash / Toy Doll tonic – Gloomy outro.
Feb 93. (cd/lp) *(<RRCD/RRLP 172>)* **ABSURD-DITTIES** [ ] [ ]
– Absurd-ditties / I'm a telly addict / Terry talking / Ernie had a hernia / Toccata in Dm / My wife's a psychopath / Sod the neighbours / Melancholy Margaret / Drooling banjos / Alecs gone / When you're Jimmy Saville / Caught up in the peeperbahn / Dez the demon decorator / Absurd-ditties (end bit).
Jan 95. (cd-s) *(RRSCD 1011)* **LAZY SUNDAY AFTERNOON /** [ ] [-]
Jan 95. (cd/lp) *(<RRCD/RRLP 194>)* **ORCASTRATED** [ ] [ ]
– Orcastrated / Poltergeist in the pantry / Please release me – "Darling I loathe you" / Taken for a mug / Any dream will do / Harry Hands / David's XR2 / Pot luck Percy / Ivy's lurid lips / The psychosurgery / Ron Dixon dumped D-D / Lazy Sunday afternoon / Bowling barmy / Orcastrated.

Receiver Rotten

May 97. (cd/lp) *(RRCD/RRLP 236) <3002>* **ONE MORE MEGABYTE**
– Mega intro / One more megabyte / I'm a lonely bastard / She's a leech / Me 'n' John Williams / She'll be back with Keith someday / I'm gonna be (500 miles) / Bachelor boy – When Garry married / Fred Oliver / In Tommy's head / Bored housewife / Memory of Nobby / The Devil went down to Scunthorpe / Mega outro.

– compilations, etc. –

Jul 85. (lp) *Wonderful World; (WOWLP 1)* **THE TOY DOLLS** -
Feb 86. (m-lp) *Dead Vol; (VOLM 020)* **THE SINGLES 1983-84** -
(<cd-iss. Dec92 on 'Receiver'; RRCD 167>)
Aug 93. (4xcd-box) *Receiver; (RRXCD 502)* **THE VOLUME YEARS** -
Sep 95. (4xcd-box) *Receiver; (RRCDX 504)* **THE RECEIVER YEARS** -
Sep 96. (d-cd) *Receiver; (<RDPCD 10>)* **THE HISTORY OF THE TOY DOLLS '79-96**
Sep 98. (d-cd) *Receiver; (<RDPCD 12>)* **THE HISTORY OF THE TOY DOLLS VOL.2** -

TOY LOVE (see under ⇒ TALL DWARFS)

TRANS AM

Formed: Washington DC, USA ... 1990 by college graduates, PHIL MANLEY, NATHAN MEANS and SEBASTIAN THOMPSON. More tongue-in-cheek than many of their supposed post-rock contemporaries, TRANS AM set out to prove that Americans do actually have a sense of irony, using experimental dexterity to exaggerate the cliches of prime 70's FM-friendly ROCK (i.e. YES, JOURNEY, etc) on their eponymous debut mini-set. After a lengthy gestation period, the JOHN McINTIRE (TORTOISE)-produced record eventually emerged on 'Thrill Jockey' early in 1996. Exactly a year later, the band returned with sophomore effort, 'SURRENDER TO THE NIGHT' (1997), its cheesy title(s) belying a more straightforwardly retro outing that paid homage to the likes of KRAFTWERK. The following year, TRANS AM continued their back-to-the-future road trip with 'THE SURVEILLANCE' album, a more sophisticated hybrid of digitally enhanced instrumental rock ambience.

Album rating: TRANS AM (*7) / SURRENDER TO THE NIGHT (*5) / THE SURVEILLANCE (*6)

PHIL MANLEY – electronics / **NATHAN MEANS** – electronics / **SEBASTIAN THOMPSON** – drums, drum programming

City Slang Thrill Jockey

Apr 96. (m-cd/m-lp) *(efa 04977-2/-1) <THRILL 24>* **TRANS AM** Jan96
– Ballbados / Enforcer / Technology corridor / Trans am / Firepoker / Single ray of light on an otherwise . . . / Prowler / Orlando / Love affair / American kooter.
Nov 96. (12"ep) *<HAPPY 06>* **ILLEGAL ASS** -
<issued on 'Happy Go Lucky'> *(UK-iss.Apr98; same as US)*
Feb 97. (cd/lp) *(efa 04988-2/-0) <THRILL 38>* **SURRENDER TO THE NIGHT**
– Motr / Cologne / Illegalize it / Love commander / Rough justice / Zero tolerance / Tough love / Night dreaming / Night dancing / Carboforce.
Mar 98. (cd,lp) *<THRILL 54>* **THE SURVEILLANCE** -
– Armed response / Prowler '97 / The campaign / Access control / Endgame / E.S.I. / Home security / Extreme measures / Shadow boogie / Stereo situation.
Aug 98. (12") *(PM 003)* **INSTICTIVE CODES** -
(above issued on 'Phont Music')

TRANSLATOR

Formed: Los Angeles, California, USA ... 1979 by singer-songwriters STEVE BARTON and ROBERT DARLINGTON, who recruited LARRY DEKKER and DAVE SCHEFF. Moving up the coast to San Francisco, the quartet signed to the 'Columbia'-backed independent label, '415', releasing their debut album, 'HEARTBEATS AND TRIGGERS', in 1982. Opening with their much loved JOHN LENNON tribute, 'EVERYWHERE THAT I'M NOT', the record betrayed BARTON and DARLINGTON's BEATLES fixation while filtering it through a glinting New Wave lens. Sophomore effort, 'NO TIME LIKE NOW' (1983), stands as a transitional affair between 1985's more accomplished eponymous set; the latter would actually prove to be the band's final studio set, a creative peak of sorts that was matched by the more intricate displays of musical dexterity heard on 1986's swansong live set, 'EVENING OF THE HARVEST'. • **Covered:** TODAY (Jefferson Airplane) / CRY ME A SHADOW (Beatles).

Album rating: HEARTBEATS AND TRIGGERS (*6) / NO TIME LIKE NOW (*5) / TRANSLATOR (*6) / EVENING OF THE HARVEST (*7) / TRANSLATION compilation (*6) / EVERYWHERE THAT WE WERE: THE BEST OF TRANSLATOR compilation (*7)

STEVE BARTON – vocals, guitar / **ROBERT DARLINGTON** – vocals, guitar, harmonica / **LARRY DEKKER** – bass / **DAVID SCHEFF** – drums, percussion

C.B.S. 415-Columbia

Nov 82. (lp) *<(CBS 85953)>* **HEARTBEATS AND TRIGGERS**
– Everywhere that I'm not / Necessary spinning / My heart / Everything you see / When I am with you / Nothing is saving me / Dark region / Sleeping snakes / Favourite drug / Everywhere / Your heart.
Oct 83. (lp/c) *(CBS/40 25674) <38927>* **NO TIME LIKE NOW**
– Un-Alone / Beyond today / I hear you follow / Break down barriers / L.A., L.A. / I love you / No time like now / Everything is falling / Simple things / The end of their love / About the truth / Circumstance laughing.
Nov 83. (7") *(A 3715)* **UN-ALONE. / L.A., L.A.**
Jun 85. (lp/c) *(CBS/40 26460) <39984>* **TRANSLATOR**
– Gravity / Fall forever / Come with me / Friends of the future / New song / Another American night / O Lazarus / Inside my mind / Heaven by a string / Breathless agony.
Jul 85. (7") *(A 6377)* **COME WITH ME. / DIZZY MISS LIZZY**
1986. (lp) **EVENING OF THE HARVEST (live)** -
– Standing in line / These old days / Crazier everyday / I need you to love / Is there a Heaven singing / Winter crying / Stony gates of time / Complications / Point of no return / Toiling of the bells / Evening of the harvest.

—— disbanded after above

– compilations, etc. –

Dec 86. (lp) *Columbia; <40529>* **EVERYWHERE THAT I'M NOT: A RETROSPECTIVE** -
– Everywhere that I'm not / Sleeping snakes / O Lazarus / Alone / Gravity / Today / I need you to love / Everywhere / Standing in line / When I am with you / These old days / I hear you follow.
Aug 95. (cd) *Oglio; <81580>* **TRANSLATION** -
– Everywhere that I'm not / Un-alone / Everywhere / I hear you follow / Standing in line / Today / Gravity / Necessary spinning / These old days / O Lazarus / No time like now.
Mar 96. (cd) *Legacy-Columbia; <64778>* **EVERYWHERE THAT WE WERE: THE BEST OF TRANSLATOR** -
– Everywhere that I'm not / O Lazarus / Un-alone / Come with me / Everywhere / No time like now / Gravity / Sleeping snakes / Stony gates of time / Everything is falling / Cry for a shadow / When I am with you / I love you / Favorite drug / Necessary spinning / Circumstance laughing.

TRASH CAN SINATRAS

Formed: Irvine, Scotland ... late 80's by FRANK READ, PAUL LIVINGSTON, GEORGE McDAID, and brothers JOHN and STEPHEN DOUGLAS. Possibly a band out of their time, TRASH CAN SINATRAS early 90's material echoed the sounds of the early 80's 'Postcard' era, particularly AZTEC CAMERA. Signed to 'Go! Discs', the quintet released their debut EP, 'OBSCURITY KNOCKS' (chancing their arm a bit with a title that would later become a self-fulfilling prophecy!), a follow-up track, 'ONLY TONGUE CAN TELL', preceding the band's debut album, 'CAKE' (1990). As well as breaking into the UK Top 75, the record was a surprise success Stateside, eventually spending three months in the US Top 200 after gaining exposure through the influential college radio circuit. With the pressure on to "crack America", transatlantic touring kept the 'SINATRAS' off the domestic scene for almost three years. When they did return, McDAID had been replaced by DAVID HUGHES on UK Top 50 comeback set, 'I'VE SEEN EVERYTHING' (1993), the album's reletive success promoted by the preceding single, 'HAYFEVER'. Marginalised in Britain and overtaken by the grunge scene in the States, TCS went to ground for a further three years, re-emerging with a series of singles in mid '96. An accompanying third album, 'A HAPPY POCKET', failed to win any new support while the old fans appeared to have unceremoniously dumped them, obviously prefering a bit of GARBAGE instead. • **Covered:** LITTLE THINGS (THAT KEEP US TOGETHER) (Scott WAlker) / BORN FREE (hit; Matt Monro) / YOU ONLY LIVE TWICE (John Barry).

Album rating: CAKE (*6) / I'VE SEEN EVERYTHING (*5) / A HAPPY POCKET (*4)

FRANK READ (b.1966) – vocals / **PAUL LIVINGSTON** (b. 1970) – guitar / **JOHN DOUGLAS** (b. 1963) – guitar / **GEORGE McDAID** (b. 1966) – bass / **STEPHEN DOUGLAS** – drums

Go! Discs London

Feb 90. (7"ep/c-ep/12"ep/cd-ep) *(GOD/+MC/X/CD 34)* **OBSCURITY KNOCKS EP** -
May 90. (7"/c-s) *(GOD/+MC 41)* **ONLY TONGUE CAN TELL. /** -
(12"+=/cd-s+=) *(GOD X/CD 41)* –
Jun 90. (cd/c/lp) *(<828 201-2/-4/-1>)* **CAKE** 74 Jan91
– Obscurity knocks / Maybe I should drive / Thrupenny tears / Even the odd / The best man's fall / Circling the circumference / Funny / Only tongue can tell / You made me feel / January's little joke.
Oct 90. (12") **CIRCLING THE CIRCUMFERENCE. /** -

—— **DAVID HUGHES** – bass; repl. McDAID

Apr 93. (7"/c-s) *(GOD/+MC 98)* **HAYFEVER. /** 61 -
(12"+=/cd-s+=) *(GOD X/CD 98)* –
May 93. (cd/c/lp) *(<828 408-2/-4/-1>)* **I'VE SEEN EVERYTHING** 50
– Easy road / Hayfever / Bloodrush / Worked a miracle / Perfect reminder / Killing the cabinet / Orange fall / I'm immortal / Send for Benny / Iceberg / One at a time / I've seen everything / Hairy years / Earlies.
Jun 93. (7"/c-s) *(GOD/+MC 100)* **I'VE SEEN EVERYTHING. / HOUSEPROUD** -
(12"+=/cd-s+=) *(GOD X/CD 100)* – I'm the one who fainted / Ask Davy.
Mar 96. (7"/c-s) *(GOD/+MC 141)* **THE MAIN ATTRACTION. /**
(12"+=/cd-s+=) *(GOD X/CD 141)* –
May 96. (7"/c-s) *(GOD/+MC 147)* **TWISTED AND BENT. / NO GASOLINE**
(cd-s+=) *(GODCD 147)* – Aberration.
Jul 96. (7"/c-s) *(GOD/+MC 151)* **HOW CAN I APPLY. / SAVE ME** -
(cd-s+=) *(GODCD 151)* – A worm with a head / Little things (that keep us together).
Sep 96. (cd/c/lp) *(828 696-2/-4/-1)* **A HAPPY POCKET** -
– Outside / Twisted and bent / Unfortunate age / To sir, with love / Make yourself at home / The main attraction / How can I apply . . .? / The pop place / The genius I was / The sleeping policeman / I must fly / I'll get them in / The safecracker / The therapist.
Dec 96. (7"/c-s) *(GOD/+MC 157)* **TO SIR WITH LOVE. / CLAW** -
(12"+=/cd-s+=) *(GOD X/CD 157)* – A boy and a girl / You only live twice.

TRAVIS

Formed: Glasgow, Scotland . . . 1991 by FRAN HEALY, who brought in former GLASS ONION members ANDY DUNLOP and NEIL PRIMROSE (DOUGLAS PAYNE eventually joining in '96). Following a self-financed debut single, 'ALL I WANT TO DO IS ROCK', the band were taken under the wing of (ex-Go! Discs man) Andy McDonald's 'Independiente' early in '97. Subsequently relocating to London after signing a publishing deal with 'Sony', the band released their controversial follow-up single, 'U16 GIRLS', apparently a peaon to the charms of under age females. A re-vamp of their debut single followed into the Top 40 and suddenly TRAVIS were one of the hippest new names on the block. Though HEALY was a charismatic frontman, the Top 10 debut album, 'GOOD FEELING', illustrated the one-dimensional nature of much of their material. Nevertheless, the record did spawn two further Top 40 hits, 'TIED TO THE 90's' and 'HAPPY', indicating that there was at least some potential for the future.

Album rating: GOOD FEELING (*6)

FRANCIS HEALY – vocals / **ANDY DUNLOP** – guitar / **DOUGIE PAYNE** – bass / **NEIL PRIMROSE** – drums

Red Telephone | not iss.

Oct 96. (10"ep) *(PHONE 001)* **ALL I WANT TO DO IS ROCK. / LINE IS FINE / FUNNY THING** [ ] [-]

Independiente | Sony

Mar 97. (7"pic-d) *(ISOM 1S)* **U16 GIRLS. / HAZY SHADES OF GOLD** [40] [-]
(c-s+=/cd-s+=) *(ISOM 1 MS/CS)* – Good time girls / Good feeling.

Jun 97. (7") *(SOM 3S) <6080>* **ALL I WANT TO DO IS ROCK. / BLUE ON A BLACK WEEKEND** [39] [ ] Apr98
(cd-s+=) *(ISOM 3MS)* – Combing my hair.
(cd-s) *(ISOM 3SMS)* – 20 / 1922.

Aug 97. (7") *(ISOM 5S) <6084>* **TIED TO THE 90'S. / CITY IN THE RAIN** [30] [ ] Apr98
(cd-s+=) *(ISOM 5MS)* – Whenever she comes.
(cd-s+=) *(ISOM 5SMS)* – Standing on my own.

Sep 97. (cd/c/lp) *(ISOM 1 CD/MC/LP) <68239>* **GOOD FEELING** [9] [ ] Oct97
– All I want to do is rock / U16 girls / Line is fine / Good day to die / Good feeling / Midsummer nights dreamin' / Tied to the 90's / I love you anyways / Happy / More than us / Falling down / Funny thing.

Oct 97. (c-s) *(ISOM 6CS) <6081>* **HAPPY. / UNBELIEVERS** [38] [ ] Apr98
(cd-s+=) *(ISOM 6MS)* – Everyday faces.
(cd-s) *(ISOM 6SMS)* – ('A'side) / When I'm feeling blue / Mother.

Mar 98. (c-s) *(ISOM 11CS)* **MORE THAN US / GIVE ME SOME TRUTH / FUNNY THING** [16] [-]
(cd-s) *(ISOM 11MS)* – (first 2 tracks) / All I want to do is rock.
(cd-s) *(ISOM 11SMS)* – (first & third tracks) / Beautiful bird / Reason.

TREEPEOPLE

Formed: Boise, Idaho, USA . . . late 80's by DOUG MARTSCH, SCOTT SCHMALJOHN, PAT BROWN and WAYNE RHINO. Debuting on the 'Toxic Shock' label with 1989's 'GUILT, REGRET, EMBARRASSMENT', this pre-grunge alternative outfit were spiritual cousins to the likes of GREEN RIVER and HUSKER DU, employing a twin-guitar attack that never veered too far from punk primitivism while putting an emphasis on melody. Sticksman, RHINO was replaced by TONY DALLAS REED for 1992's 'C/Z'-released follow-up, 'SOMETHING VICIOUS FOR TOMORROW', a record that mauled The Smiths' 'BIGMOUTH STRIKES AGAIN'. In true Spinal Tap style, yet another drummer, ERIC AKRE, was in place for 'JUST KIDDING' (1993), the band summing up the slacker ethos with 'ANYTHING'S IMPOSSIBLE'. MARTSCH was the next one to climb down, leaving the TREEPEOPLE and later joining BUILT TO SPILL; the gap was subsequently filled with JOHN POLLE and ERIC CARNELL, the line-up on the band's fourth and final album, 'ACTUAL RE-ENACTMENT' (1994).

Album rating: GUILT, REGRET, EMBARRASSMENT (*6) / SOMETHING VICIOUS FOR TOMORROW (*4) / JUST KIDDING (*7) / ACTUAL RE-ENACTMENT (*5)

DOUG MARTSCH – vocals, guitar / **SCOTT SCHMALJOHN** – guitar, vocals / **PAT BROWN** – bass / **WAYNE RHINO** – drums

not iss. | Toxic Shock

1989. (cd) *<23>* **GUILT, REGRET, EMBARRASSMENT** [-] [ ]
– No doubt / Andy Warhol / GRE / Lost / Transitional devices / Pity / (I'm gonna) Miss you (when you're gone) / Wasted on you / Stay / Chunks of milk / Everytime when I fall down and my head . . . / Trailer park.

— **TONY DALLAS REED** – drums; repl. the departing RHINO (on some)

C/Z | C/Z

Mar 92. (lp/cd) *<(CZ 040/+CD)>* **SOMETHING VICIOUS FOR TOMORROW** [ ] [ ]
– Liquid boy / It's alright now ma / Something vicious for tomorrow / Big mouth strikes again / Filter / Ad campaigns / Funnelhead / Party / Tongues on thrones / Lives / Radio man / Size of a quarter / Time whore. *<US cd-iss. w/+=>* – TIME WHORE EP (tracks above)

— **ERIC AKRE** – drums (ex-CHRIST ON A CRUTCH) repl. BROWN (REED took over bass!)

1993. (cd) *<CZ 54>* **JUST KIDDING** [-] [ ]
– Today / In C / Cartoon brew / Ballard bitter / Clouds and faces / Fishbasket / Nod and blink / Anything's impossible / Neil's down / Outside in.

— **SCHMALJOHN + AKRE** recruited newcomers (**JOHN POLLE** – guitar + **ERIC CARNELL** – bass) when MARTSCH left to form BUILT TO SPILL

1994. (cd) *<CZ 80>* **ACTUAL RE-ENACTMENT** [-] [ ]
– Wha'd I mean to think you said / Feed me / Slept through mine / Heinz von Foerster / Boot straps / Liver vs. heart / Better days / Bag of wood / Low / Will we ever / To long.

TRIBUTE TO NOTHING

Formed: London, England . . . early '92 by brothers JIM and BEN TURNER, the pubescent schoolboys subsequently turning it into a family affair and recruiting their younger brother, SAM (two further musicians were used early on). Licensed by their local education authority to prevent charges of truancy while they were gigging, the young scamps were offered a deal with the brand new 'Kinglake' imprint. They debuted with the 'OFFICE JOBS' EP late in '93 (surely a record NOT born of experience!), following it up with '24 HRS', a track reminiscent of early DEAD KENNEDYS, although their overall image was more in line with the prevailing NIRVANA worship. Like HANSON brought up on hardcore, the siblings continued in precocious fashion with a further clutch of singles on the 'Free' label. A long awaited debut set, 'STRAIGHT LINE' (1997), was quickly followed by another album in the same year, 'WRENCH', the trio finally coming of age.

Album rating: STRAIGHT LINE (*6) / WRENCH (*6)

JIM TURNER (b. 1979) – vocals, bass / **SAM TURNER** (b. 1980) – guitar / **BEN TURNER** (b. 1977) – drums

Kinglake | not iss.

Nov 93. (7"ep) *(KLR 001)* **OFFICE JOBS EP** [ ] [-]

Apr 94. (7") *(KLR 003)* **24 HRS. / YET AGAIN** [ ] [-]

Free | not iss.

Nov 94. (7") *(FOC 9)* **CAN'T GET UP. /** [ ] [-]

Jun 95. (7"blue) *(FOC 10)* **THINK YOU SHOULD. / DO SOMETHING** [ ] [-]
(cd-s+=) *(FOCCD 10)* – Lost your mind.

Apr 96. (7") *(FOC 11)* **STRAIGHT LINE. /** [ ] [-]
(cd-s+=) *(FOCCD 11)* –

Lockjaw | not iss.

Jun 97. (cd-ep) *(LJCD 001)* **FINDING MY OWN MIND / R.T.A. / CLAMP / CATCH YOUR GRIP** [ ] [-]

Jun 97. (cd) *(LJCD 002)* **STRAIGHT LINE** [ ] [-]
– Straight line / Find it / Cecil / Could I / Think you should / Do something / How could things / Don't care.

Oct 97. (cd) *(LJCD 004)* **WRENCH** [ ] [-]
– Backdown / Time to see / Finding my own mind / Should the quiet / Two minutes of hate / R.T.A. / Fight for life / Prevention / 212 / Catch your grip / Blue alloy / Timebomb.

Nov 98. (cd-s) *(LJCDS 011)* **ENEMY / SICKNESS / LOSE** [ ] [-]

TRICKY

Born: 1969, Knowle West, Bristol, England. After a troubled youth growing up on one of BRISTOL's poorer housing estates, ADRIAN THAWES began spending less time lawbreaking and more time busying himself with the city's club culture, helping run sound systems and hanging out with The WILD BUNCH, a loose collective of musicians and DJ's that icluded MASSIVE ATTACK and famed producer NELLEE HOOPER. In between trips to court in OXFORD, where he was defending an assault charge, TRICKY KID (as he was nicknamed by his Bristolian cohorts) occasionally collaborated with MASSIVE ATTACK on their seminal 'BLUE LINES' album, contributing stoned raps on several tracks. He also contributed to MASSIVE's follow-up, 'PROTECTION', although his first solo effort was a 'Betty Blue'-sampling track entitled 'LOYALTY IS VALUABLE', engineered by future PORTISHEAD mainman GEOFF BARROWS and featured on the 1991 Sickle Cell charity album, 'HARD SELL', alongside the likes of MASSIVE ATTACK, SMITH & MIGHTY etc. Yet the track that brought him to the attention of a discerning public was the sublime claustrophobia of 'AFTERMATH'. Eventually released in early '94, the track had previously been recorded a couple of years earlier with TRICKY's musical partner, MARTINA, predating the trip-hop scene that TRICKY would later be lumped in with. Next came the jarring loops and nervous paranoia of 'PONDEROSA', another taster for the pioneering debut album, 'MAXINQUAYE' (1994), released later that summmer. A dense, brooding collection of slow motion beat-poetry from the darkside, the record was immediately hailed as a classic. Taking bastardised hip-hop beats as his raw material then suffocating them with layers of samples, disjointed rhythms, freak instrumental lines and obscure noises, TRICKY created music that was wired yet lethargic, with lyrics equally contradictory and ambiguous to match. Collaborating with TERRY HALL, NENEH CHERRY and ALISON MOYET amongst others, TRICKY released his 'NEARLY GOD' project in 1996. The album revisited the dark intensity of 'MAXINQUAYE' without quite the same effect, possibly a case of too many cooks (or too many spliffs) spoiling the broth. 'PRE-MILLENNIUM TENSION', released later the same year, was on a par with 'MAXINQUAYE' and if it didn't exactly break new ground, the album illustrated that TRICKY's wellspring of paranoid psychosis is far from running dry. Tracks like 'BAD THINGS', 'MAKES ME WANNA DIE' and 'MY EVIL IS STRONG' speak for themselves, and though it's a well worn cliche, it would appear that this man really does suffer for his art. Then again, maybe he shouldn't smoke so much. • **Songwriters:** Self-penned & samples except; BLACK STEEL + THE MOMENT I FEARED (Public Enemy) / PONDEROSA (co-with HOWIE B) / HELL IS ROUND THE CORNER (same source that PORTISHEAD found 'Glory Box'?) / SINGING THE BLUES (Mary McReary) / sampled a song by Billie Holiday on 'Carriage For Two'.

Album rating: MAXINQUAYE (*9) / NEARLY GOD (*8)

TRICKY – vocals / with **MARTINE** – vocals / etc

4th & Broadway | 4th & Broadway

Jan 94. (7") *(BRW 288)* *<590>* **AFTERMATH. / ('A'-I could be looking for people mix)** [69] [ ]
(12"+=) *(12BRW 288)* – ('A'mix).
(cd-s++=) *(BRCD 288)* – ('A'mix).

Apr 94. (7") *(BRW 299)* *<595>* **PONDEROSA. / ('A'-Dobie's roll pt.1 mix)** [ ] [ ] Jul94
(12"+=/cd-s+=) *(12BRW/BRCD 299)* – (3 'A'mixes; Ultragelic / Original / Dobie's roll pt.2).

Jan 95. (7"/c-s) *(BR W/CA 304)* **OVERCOME. / ABBA ON FAT TRACKS** [34] [-]
(12"+=/cd-s+=) *(12BRW/BRCD 304)* – ('A'-Zippy & Bungle mix).

— guests on below ALISON GOLDFRAPP + RAGGA – vocals / PETE BRIQUETTE – bass / MARK SAUNDERS – keyboards / FTV – guitar, drums / TONY WRAFTER – flute / JAMES STEVENSON – guitar

Feb 95. (cd/c/lp) *(BR CD/CA/LP 610)* *<524089>* **MAXINQUAYE** [3] [ ] Apr95
– Overcome / Ponderosa / Black steel / Hell is round the corner / Pumpkin / Aftermath / Abbaon fat tracks / Brand new you're retro / Suffocated love / You don't / Strugglin' / Feed me.

Mar 95. (c-s) *(BRCA 320)* **BLACK STEEL. / ('A'-Been caught stealing mix)** [28] [-]
(12"+=/cd-s+=) *(12BRW/BRCD 320)* – ('A'live) / ('A'-In the draw mix).
(cd-s++=) *(BRCDX 320)* – ('A'edit).

Jul 95. (7"pic-d-ep/12"red-ep/cd-ep; as TRICKY VS. THE GRAVEDIGGAZ) *(BRW/12BRW/BRCD 326)* *<383>* **THE HELL E.P.** [12] [ ]
– Hell is round the corner (original) / ('A'-Hell and water mix) / Psychosis / Tonite is a special nite (chaos mass confusion mix).

Nov 95. (c-s) *(BRCA 330)* **PUMPKIN / MOODY BROODY BUDHIST CAMP / NEW KINGDOM** [26] [ ]
(cd-s+=) *(BRCD 330)* – Brand new you're retro (Alex Reece mix).
(12"colrd) *(12BRW 330)* – ('A'side) / (above track) / Slick 66.

NEARLY GOD

TRICKY with **TERRY HALL / MARTINE / BJORK / NENEH CHERRY / ALISON MOYET + CATH COFFEY**

Durban Poison | Island

Apr 96. (7") *(DP 003)* **POEMS / CHILDREN'S STORY** [28] [ ]
(12"+=/cd-s+=) *(DP X/CD 003)* – ('A'extended).

Apr 96. (cd/c/lp) *(DP CD/MC/LP 1001)* *<531064>* **NEARLY GOD** [11] [ ]
– Tattoo / Poems / Together now / Keep your mouth shut / I be the prophet / Make a chane / Black cofee / Bubbles / I sing for you / Yoga.

— above was to have been under his DURBAN POISON project.

— Aug 96, TRICKY PRESENTS GRASS ROOTS 12"ep for 'Ultra'.

TRICKY

— with a plethora of musicians incl. **PATRICE CHEVALIER** – guitar / **JOHN TONKS** – drums / **PAT McMANUS** – piano, violin

4th & Broadway | Island

Oct 96. (7"pic-d) *(BRW 340)* **CHRISTIANSANDS. / FLYNN** [36] [ ]
(12"+=/cd-s+=) *(12BRW/BRCD 340)* – Ghetto youth.

Nov 96. (cd/c/lp) *(BR CD/CA/LP 623)* *<524302>* **PRE-MILLENNIUM TENSION** [30] [ ]
– Vent / Christiansands / Tricky kid / Bad dreams / Makes me wanna die / Ghetto youth / Sex drive / Bad things / Lyrics of fury / My evil is strong / Piano. *(d-cd-iss. ; BRCDX 623)*

— late '96, featured on the hit single by GARBAGE; 'Milk'.

Dec 96. (cd-ep) *(BRCDX 341)* **TRICKY KID. / MAKES ME WANNA DIE (Tricky's extremix) / GRASS ROOTS** [28] [ ]
(12"ep+=) *(12BRW 341)* – Smoking Beagles (Sub Sub vs Tricky).
(cd-ep) *(BRCD 341)* – ('A'side) / Devils helper / Smoking Beagles (Sub Sub vs Tricky) / Suffocated love (live on 'Later with Jools').

Apr 97. (cd-s) *(BRCDX 348)* **MAKES ME WANNA DIE / MAKES ME WANNA DIE (The Weekend mix – remixed by The Stereo MC's) / PIANO (the Green sticky mix remixed by A Guy Called Gerald)** [29] [ ]
(12"clear+=) *(BRX 348)* – Here comes the aliens (AFRIKA IZLAM & TRICKY).
(cd-s) *(BRCD 348)* – ('A'side) / ('A'acoustic) / Here come the aliens (AFRIKA IZLAM & TRICKY).

Island | Island

May 98. (7"; TRICKY featuring POLLY JEAN HARVEY) *(IS 701)* **BROKEN HOMES. / MONEY GREEDY** [25] [ ]
(cd-s+–) *(CID 701)* – Anti histamine / Taxi.
(cd-s+=) *(CIDX 701)* – 360 degrees.

May 98. (cd/c/d-lp) *(CID/ICT/ILPS 8071)* *<524520>* **ANGELS WITH DIRTY FACES** [23] [84] Jun98
– Money greedy / Mellow / Singing the blues / Broken homes / 6 minutes / Analyze me / The moment I feared / Talk to me (angels with dirty faces) / Carriage for two / Demise / Tear out my eyes / Record companies / Peyote sings / Taxi.

Dec 98. (cd-s) *<572515>* **6 MINUTES (mixes)** [-] [ ]

TRIFFIDS

Formed: Perth, Australia . . . 1980 by New Zealand-born DAVID McCOMB, his brother ROBERT, MARTYN CASEY, ALSY McDONALD and PHIL KAKULAS (soon replaced by JILL BIRT). Following a string of domestic singles releases on obscure labels, The TRIFFIDS were signed to appropriately named Aussie independent imprint, 'Hot', making their vinyl debut in 1983 with the eerie, sun-parched sounds of the 'TREELESS PLAIN' album. Screeching violins circled over McCOMB's gloomy intonations like vultures, the atmospheric likes of 'RED PONY' echoed years later in the work of The TINDERSTICKS amongst others. Follow-up set, 'RAINING PLEASURE', surfaced the following year but it was 1986's acclaimed 'BORN SANDY DEVOTIONAL' which saw The TRIFFIDS make their mark on European territory. With the subtle nuances of pedal steel/slide guitar player, 'EVIL' GRAHAM LEE, lending the sound a new depth, the full extent of the band's transatlantic influences were apparent on the awesome 'WIDE OPEN ROAD', while the melancholy sparseness of BIRT's vocal lent proceedings a ghostly hue. Getting er . . ., back to nature, they recorded the hastily released follow-up, 'IN THE PINES' in a sheep-shearing shed in the Australian outback (!), thankfully minus any live bleating. With the subsequent addition of extra guitarist ADAM PETERS and a major label deal courtesy of 'Island', at last The TRIFFIDS looked to be set for major alternative success. The resulting 'CALENTURE' (1987) album didn't disappoint, McCOMB's stark portraits thrown into sharp relief by Gil Norton's superior production. Yet despite a UK Top 75 hit with 'A TRICK OF THE LIGHT', success proved as elusive as ever, the band roping in MORRISSEY producer, Stephen Street, for 1989's 'BLACK SWAN'. The album scraped the lower regions of the chart but failed to score with such potential hit singles as 'GOODBYE LITTLE BOY' and 'BURY ME DEEP IN LOVE'. With recognition seemingly as far off as ever, The TRIFFIDS split at the turn of the decade, the posthumously released live album, 'STOCKHOLM' (1990) serving as a fair epitaph. While McCOMB went on to record a solo album, 'LOVE OF WILL', for 'Mushroom', the brooding spirit of The TRIFFIDS has infused the work of such gothic country luminaries as The WALKABOUTS, WILLARD GRANT CONSPIRACY and The HANDSOME FAMILY. • **Songwriters:** DAVID McCOMB penned except covers; / INTO THE GROOVE (Madonna) / BRIGHT LIGHTS BIG CITY / GOOD MORNING, GOOD MORNING (Beatles)

Album rating: TREELESS PLAIN (*7) / RAINING PLEASURE mini (*8) / BORN SANDY DEVOTIONAL (*7) / IN THE PINES (*6) / CALENTURE (*8) / THE BLACK SWAN (*7) / AUSTRALIAN MELODRAMA compilation (*8) / Dave McComb: LOVE OF WILL (*6)

DAVID McCOMB (b.1962) – vocals, guitar, piano, etc. / **ROBERT McCOMB** – violin, guitar, keyboards, vocals / **JILL BIRT** – keyboards, some vocals repl. PHIL KAKULAS / **MARTIN CASEY** – bass, vocals / **ALSY McDONALD** – drums, percussion, vocals

ShakeSome Action | not iss.

Jul 81. (7") *(SG-MX 57828)* **STAND UP. / FARMERS NEVER VISIT NIGHT CLUBS** [-] [-] Austra

not iss. | Resonant

Dec 81. (7"ep) **REVERIE** [-] [-] Austra
– Reverie / Place in the sun / Joan of Arc / This boy.

not iss. | No Records

1982. (7") **SPANISH BLUE. / TWISTED BRAIN** [-] [-] Austra
1982. (7"ep) **BAD TIMING** [-] [-] Austra
– Bad timing / Left to rot / Being driven / Snake pit.

Hot UK | not iss.

Nov 83. (lp) *(HOT 1003)* **TREELESS PLAIN** [ ] [-]
– Red pony / Branded / My baby thinks she's a train / Roseval / I am a lonesome hobo / Place in the sun / Play thing / Old ghostrider / Hanging shed / Hell of a summer / Madeline / Nothing can take your place. *(cd-iss. Nov91)*

Dec 83. (7") **BEAUTIFUL WASTE. / PROPERTY IS CONDEMNED** [-] [-] Austra

Dec 84. (m-lp) *(MINIHOT 1)* **RAINING PLEASURE** [ ] [-]
– Jesus calling / Embedded / St. James Infirmary / Everybody has to eat / Ballad of Jack Frost / Property is condemned / Raining pleasure. *(re-iss. Jun94; same)*

Apr 85. (12"m) *(HOT12 007)* **FIELD OF GLASS. / BRIGHT LIGHTS BIG CITY / MONKEY ON MY BACK** [ ] [-]

— added **'Evil' GRAHAM LEE** – steel guitar (of The APARTMENTS)

Aug 85. (7") *(HOT7 26)* **YOU DON'T MISS YOUR WATER (TILL YOUR WELL RUNS DRY). / CONVENT WALLS** [ ] [-]
(12"+=) *(HOT12 26)* – Beautiful water / ('A'instrumental).
(re-iss. 7"ep Oct94; HEP7 26)

May 86. (7") *(HOT7 30)* **WIDE OPEN ROAD. / TIME OF WEAKNESS** [ ] [-]
(12"+=) *(HOT12 30)* – Dear Miss Lonely Hearts / Native bride.

Jun 86. (lp) *(HOTLP 1023)* **BORN SANDY DEVOTIONAL** [ ] [-]
– The seabirds / stuary bed / Chicken killer / Tarrilup Bridge / Lonely stretch / Wide open road / Life of crime / Personal things / Stolen property / Tender is the night (the long fidelity). *(cd-iss. Mar95 on 'Mushroom'; D 19457)*

Nov 86. (lp) *(HOTLP 1028)* **IN THE PINES** [ ] [-]
– Suntrapper / In the pines / Kathy knows / 25 to 5 / Do you want me near you? / Once a day / Just might fade away / Better off this way / Only one life / Keep your eyes on the hole / One soul less on your fiery list / Born Sandy Devotional / Love and affection. *(re-iss. Jun94; same) (cd-iss. Mar95 on 'Mushroom'; D 19480)*

— added **ADAM PETERS** – guitar (ex-FLOWERPOT MEN)

Island | not iss.

Oct 87. (7") *(IS 337)* **BURY ME DEEP IN LOVE. / BABY CAN I WALK YOU HOME** [ ] [-]
(12"+=) *(12IS 337)* – Region unknown.
(cd-s++=) *(CID 337)* – Vagabond holes.

Nov 87. (lp/c/cd) *(ILPS/ICT/CID 9885)* **CALENTURE** [ ] [-]
– Bury me deep in love / Kelly's blues / A trick of the light / Hometown farewell kiss / Unmade love / Open for you / Holy water / Blinded by the hour / Vagabond holes / Jerducuttup man / Calenture / Save what you can. *(cd re-iss. Dec89; IMCD 46) (cd-iss. Mar95 on 'Mushroom'; D 19458)*

Jan 88. (7") *(IS 350)* **A TRICK OF THE LIGHT. / LOVE DECEIVER** [73] [-]
(10"+=) *(10IS 350)* – Bad news always reminds me of you.
(12"+=/cd-s+=) *(12IS/CID 350)* – Everything you touch turns to time.

Aug 88. (7") *(IS 367)* **HOLY WATER. / GOOD MORNING, GOOD MORNING** [ ] [-]
(12"+=/cd-s+=) *(12IS/CID 367)* – Raining pleasure / Red pony.

— added guests **PHIL KAKULAS** (who returned) + **RITA MENENDEZ**

Mar 89. (7"; by DAVE McCOMB * ADAM PETERS) *(IS 410)* **I DON'T NEED YOU. / WILLIE THE TORCH** [ ] [-]
(12"+=) *(12IS 410)* – Liberty and a thousand fares.

Apr 89. (lp/c/cd) *(ILPS/ICT/CID 9928)* **THE BLACK SWAN** [63] [-]
– Too hot to move, too hot to think / American sailors / Falling over you / Goodbye little boy / Bottle of love / The spinning top song / Butterflies into worms / The clown prince / Good fortune Rose / New Year's greetings / Blackeyed Susan Brown / Fairytale love. *(re-iss. cd Mar95 on 'Mushroom')*

Apr 89. (7") *(IS 413)* **FALLING OVER YOU. / GO HOME EDDIE** [ ] [-]
(12"+=/cd-s+=) *(12IS/CID 413)* – Shell of a man / You minus me.

May 89. (7") *(IS 420)* **GOODBYE LITTLE BOY. / GO HOME EDDIE** [ ] [-]
(12"+=) *(12IS 420)* – Shell of a man.
(10"++=/cd-s++=) *(10IS/CID 420)* – You minus me.

Aug 89. (7") *(IS 424)* **BURY ME DEEP IN LOVE. / RENT** [ ] [-]
(12"+=/cd-s+=) *(12IS/CID 424)* – Into the groove.

M.N.W. not iss.

Jul 90. (lp/c/cd) *(MNW X/MCX/MCDX 9)* **STOCKHOLM** (live on Swedish radio late 1989) [ ] [-]
– Property is condemned / Hell of a summer / Personal things / Raining pleasure / Lonely stretch / Sure the girl I love / Wide open road / Keep your eyes on the hole / In the pines / Billy / I am a lonesome hobo / How could I help but love you. *(cd-iss. Mar95 on 'Mushroom'; D 30231)*

— disbanded late in 1989

– compilations, etc. –

Oct 87. (12"ep) *Strange Fruit; (SFPS 036) / Dutch East India; <8340>* **THE PEEL SESSIONS** (5/5/85) [ ] [ ]
– Life of crime / Chicken killer / Lonely stretch.

Dec 94. (cd) *Mushroom; (D 31182)* **AUSTRALIAN MELODRAMA (THE BEST OF THE TRIFFIDS)** [ ] [ ]
– Red pony / Hell of a summer / Beautiful waste / Raining pleasure / Bright lights, big city / The seabirds / Wide open road / Lonely stretch / Tender is the night / Bury me deep in love / trick of the light / Hometown farewell kiss / Unmade love / Jerdacuttup man / Save what you can / Falling over you / Goodbye little boy / New Year's greetings / In the pines.

DAVE McCOMB

Foundation not iss.

Sep 91. (12") **THE MESSAGE. / SONG OF NO RETURN / ('A'club version)** [ ] [-]
(cd-s+=) – I've heard things turn out this way.

Mushroom not iss.

Mar 94. (c-ep/cd-ep) *(C/D 11589)* **SETTING YOU FREE / HOME FOR FALLEN ANGELS / YOU'VE GOT A FUNNY WAY OF SHOWING YOU LOVED ME / MY FRIEND SLEEP** [ ] [-]

Mar 94. (cd/c) *(D/C 31071)* **LOVE OF WILL** [ ] [-]
– Clear out my mind / Setting you free / Day of the ascension / Deep in a dream / Nothing good / The Lord burns every clue / Lifelike / Lover sister number one / Heard you had a bed / Inside of me / Leaning / I want to conquer you / Pack up your troubles.

— stop press: DAVE died on the 1st February 1999

TRIPPING DAISY

Formed: Dallas, Texas, USA . . . 1991 by lyricist TIM DeLAUGHTER, WES BERGGREN, MARK PIRRO and BRYAN WAKELAND. Signed to 'Island', the band debuted with the 'BILL' album in 1994. Sporting a psychedelic punk / hard-rock sound similar to JANE'S ADDICTION (DeLAUGHTER's whining vocals a bizarre cross between PERRY FARRELL and LIAM GALLAGHER!), the group soon attracted a growing following on the American alternative scene. With media coverage also gathering strength, the band released a follow-up set, 'i am an ELASTIC FIRECRACKER' (complete with sleevework by deceased artist, Gugliemo Achille Cavellini) in early '96. The record was their most successful to date, scraping into the lower regions of the US Top 100, while the swaggering 'PIRANHA' single made the Top 75.

Album rating: BILL (*5) / i am an ELASTIC FIRECRACKER (*8)

TIM DeLAUGHTER – vocals, guitar / **WES BERGGREN** – guitar / **MARK PIRRO** – bass / **BRYAN WAKELAND** – drums

Island Red Dragon St.

Jul 94. (cd/c/lp) *(CIRD/IRCT/IRLP 1001) <70392>* **BILL** [ ] [ ] Nov92
– My umbrella / One through four / Lost and found / Change of mind / On the ground / The morning / Blown away / Brown-eyed pickle boy / Miles and miles of pain / Triangle. *<cd re-iss. 1997 on 'Polygram'; 555002>*

Jul 94. (12"ep/cd-ep) *(12IR/CIRD 102)* **MY UMBRELLA / IT'S SAFE, IT'S SOCIAL (live). / GET IT ON (live) / WE'RE ONLY GONNA DIE (live)** [ ] [-]

Island Island

Feb 96. (c-s/7") *(C+/IS 636)* **I GOT A GIRL. / MARGARITA TROPENZANDO** [ ] [-]
(12"+=/cd-s+=) *(12IS/CID 636)* – Cause tomb shop / Noose.

Feb 96. (cd/lp) *(CIRD/IRLP 1004) <524112>* **i am an ELASTIC FIRECRACKER** [ ] [95] Aug95
– Rocket pop / Bang / I got a girl / Piranha / Motivation / Same dress new day / Trip along / Raindrop / Step behind / Noose / Prick / High.

Mar 96. (7") *(IS 638)* **PIRANHA. / CREATURE** [72] [-]
(12"+=/cd-s+=) *(12IS/CID 638)* – High.

1997. (m-cd) *<531095>* **TIME CAPSULE** [-] [ ]
– Rise / Cause tomb shop / Creature / Boobie the clown / I'm a fish / Blue train.

— added **ERIC DREW FELDMAN** – producer, multi (ex-CAPTAIN BEEFHEART, ex-FRANK BLACK)

Jul 98. (cd,c) *<524518>* **JESUS HITS US LIKE AN ATOM BOMB** [-] [ ]
– Field day jitters / Waited a light year / Sonic bloom / Bandaids for Mire / Mechanical breakdown / Your socks have no name / Geeareohdoubleyou / New plains medicine / Our drive to the sun – Can a man mark / Human contact / Pillar / 8 ladies / About the movies / Tiny men / Indian poker (pt.2 & 3).

TRUE BELIEVERS

Formed: Austin, Texas, USA . . . 1984 by the ESCOVEDO brothers ALEJANDRO and JAVIER. Both veterans of the local punk/roots scene (ALEJANDRO had previously helped form the influential RANK & FILE), the siblings completed their line-up with DANNY DeGORGIO and JOHN DEE GRAHAM. Signed to the then 'E.M.I.'-backed 'Roots' label, 'Rounder', the group made their debut with an eponymous album in 1986 having already built up a grassroots following through local live work. Impressed by its balls-out, raggedy-assed rock'n'roll pedigree, critics deemed the record a success and the TRUE BELIEVERS subsequently began work on a follow-up. In the event, a breakdown in communications between the band and their label led to the album being shelved; the TRUE BELIEVERS subsequently called it a day with ALEJANDRO going on to a solo career. Nearly a decade on, the long lost recordings were finally made available by 'Rykodisc' as a 2 on 1 package, 'HARD ROAD' (1994), together with the band's debut. • **Note:** Not to be confused with early 80's US indie band, plus a religious outfit who issued, 'Time Ain't Long', in 1990.

Album rating: TRUE BELIEVERS (*6) / HARD ROAD compilation (*6)

ALEJANDRO ESCOVEDO – guitar, vocals (ex-NUNS) / **JAVIER ESCOVEDO** – guitar, vocals / **DANNY DeGORGIO** – bass / added **JON DEE GRAHAM** – guitars / + various drummers

EMI America Rounder

1986. (lp/c) *(AML/TC-AML 3107)* **TRUE BELIEVERS** [ ] [ ]
– Tell her / Ring the bell / So blue about you / Rebel kind / Train around the bend / Lucky moon / We're wrong / I get excited / Sleep enough to dream / Rain won't help you when it's over.

— new drummer **KEVIN FOLEY** – drums

— after recording an album (see tracks below) they were dropped by their label. They split after **HECTOR MUNOZ** – drums; repl. KEVIN

— **J.D. FOSTER** – bass, vocals (ex-DWIGHT YOAKAM) repl. DANNY

– compilations, etc. –

Mar 94. (cd) *Rykodisc; <(RCD 40287)>* **HARD ROAD** [ ] [ ]
– (TRUE BELIEVERS lp tracks) / She's got / All mixed up / One moment to another / Who calls my name / Outside your door / Wild eyed and wound up / Nobody's home / Only a dream / Please don't fade away.

TRUE WEST

Formed: Los Angeles, California, USA . . . 1980 by former SUSPECTS members (with STEVE WYNN), RUSS TOLMAN and GAVIN BLAIR, plus KEN LACEWELL, FRANK FRENCH and last incoming member RICHARD McGRATH. Loosely affiliated with L.A.'s Paisley Underground scene, TRUE WEST made their vinyl debut in early '83 with an eponymous EP on their own 'Bring Out Your Dead' label. French label, 'New Rose', picked them up for mini-set, 'HOLLYWOOD HOLIDAY' a few months later, a record that featured their debut EP in its entirety alongside a handful of new tracks. Among these was a cover of Pink Floyd's 'LUCIFER SAM', an appropriate choice for a band that often sounded like a cross between FLOYD and mid-period BYRDS. Following JOSEF BECKER's (who himself had replaced FRENCH) exit to THIN WHITE ROPE, the band recruited STEVE PACKENHAM and signed to the 'P.V.C.' label (Clapham's 'Zippo' in the UK) for 'THE DRIFTERS'; darkly ruminating, downward spiralling laments such as 'AND THEN THE RAIN' ensured the record ranked as one of the band's finest, TOLMAN's hypnotic guitar work reminscent of TOM VERLAINE or BOB DYLAN. When he himself departed for a solo career soon after the record's release, the group brought in scene stalwarts, MATT PUICCI and CHUCK PROPHET for 1986's 'HAND OF FATE' album. Tragically, the latter proved to be the band's swansong as STAYDOHAR suffered a fatal brain tumour the following year. • **Covered:** HAPPENINGS TEN YEARS TIME AGO (Yardbirds) / LUST FOR LIFE (Iggy Pop) / SUSPICIOUS MINDS (hit; Elvis Presley).

Album rating: HOLLYWOOD HOLIDAY (*5) / DRIFTERS (*5) / HAND OF FATE (*5)

GAVIN BLAIR – vocals / **RUSS TOLMAN** (b.15 Aug'56) – guitar / **RICHARD McGRATH** – guitar / **KEVIN STAYDOHAR** – bass; repl. KEN LACEWELL / **JOSEF BECKER** – drums; repl. FRANK FRENCH

not iss. Bring Out Your Dead

Jan 83. (12"ep) *<1>* **TRUE WEST** [-] [ ]
– (5 tracks from below mini-set)

New Rose not iss.

Apr 83. (m-lp) *(ROSE 23)* **HOLLYWOOD HOLIDAY** [ ] [-]
– Steps to the door / I'm not there / And then the rain / Hollywood holiday / Lucifer Sam / It's about time / Throw away the key / You.

— **STEVE PACKENHAM** – drums; repl. BECKER who joined THIN WHITE ROPE

Zippo P.V.C.

Dec 84. (lp) *(ZONG 004) <PVC 54032>* **DRIFTERS** [ ] [ ]
– Look around / At night they speak / Speak easy / Shot you down / What about you / Hold on / And then the rain / Backroad bridge song (what could I say) / Ain't no hangman / Morning light. *<US+=> – HOLLYWOOD HOLIDAY. (also on 'New Rose' lp/c; ROSE 45/+C) (cd-iss. Sep90; ROSE 23CD)*

Jun 85. (7") **SHOT YOU DOWN. / 1969**

— TOLMAN departed for a solo career in 1985 (see below). The remaining members carried on with guest help from MATT PUICCI + CHUCK PROPHET

not iss. CD Presents

1986. (cd) <041> **HAND OF FATE**
– Falling away / Gunner / Just one chance / Mark time / Trim the fat / Hand of fate / Waved me by / Lost at daybreak / Happening ten years time ago / No comebacks.

— sadly STAYDOHAR died of a brain tumour in '87 and the band split

- compilations, etc. -

1990. (m-cd) *Skyclad;* <62> **TV WESTERN + BEST WESTERN**

1992. (cd) *Skyclad;* <127> **TWO TRUE**
– Steps to the door / I'm not here / And then the rain / Hollywood holiday / Lucifer Sam / It's about time / Throw away the key / You / Look around / At night they speak / Speak easy / Shot you down / What about you / Hold on / And then the rain / Backroad bridge song (what could I say) / Ain't no hangman / Morning light / Throw away the key.

May 98. (cd) *BOYD;* <(1003-2)> **BIG BOOT: LIVE** (live 22 November, 1984)
– Backroad bridge song / Waved me by / Happenings ten years time ago / And then the rain / Hold on / It's about time / Hollywood holiday / Look around / You / Lust for life / Lucifer Sam / Suspicious minds.

RUSS TOLMAN

Zippo Down There

Sep 86. (lp) *(ZONG 012)* <72210> **TOTEM POLES AND GLORY HOLES**
– Lookin' for an angel / Talking Hoover Dam blues / Four winds / Everything you need and everything you want / Galveston mud / Better than before / I am not afraid / Nothin' slowin' me down / Play hard to forget / Waitin' for rain.

Oct 86. (7") **TALKING HOOVER DAM BLUES. / SOLITARY MAN**

Demon Skyclad

Aug 88. (lp) *(FIEND 125)* <54> **DOWN IN EARTHQUAKE TOWN**
– Vegas / Domino / Down in earthquake town / Palm tree land / Midnight / Planes, trains, automobiles / Baby / Face you wear / Jump into the fire / You don't have to say goodbye.

— next with **JON KLAGES** – guitar / **DAVE PROVOST** – bass / **DAVE DREWRY** – drums / + others on session

New Rose Skyclad

Nov 90. (lp/cd; as RUSS TOLMAN & THE TOTEM POLEMEN) <65> **GOODBYE JOE**
– Marla Jane / Portrait of blue / The Devil and the sea / Ragged but righteous / Blame it on the girl / Hollywood holiday / Soul murder / Murphy's barn / God only knows / Bob's house of failure.

May 94. (cd) *(422368)* **ROAD MOVIE** (rec.1992)

not iss. Brilliant

1994. (cd) **SWEET SPOT**

not iss. Blue Rose

1998. (cd) **CITY LIGHTS**

- compilations, etc. -

Nov 93. (cd) *Diablo; (DIAB 802)* **TOTEM POLES AND GLORY HOLES / DOWN IN EARTHQUAKE TOWN**

TRULY

Formed: Seattle, Washington, USA . . . 1995 by former SOUNDGARDEN bassman HIRO YAMAMOTO, who gathered together drummer MARK PICKEREL (from SCREAMING TREES) and ex-STORYBOOK KROOKS singer/guitarist/songwriter ROBERT ROTH. This trio would have been *thee* grunge supergroup but for one thing, they didn't play grunge. TRULY chose to widen their musical horizons with self-indulgent progressive experiments, witnessed at times on the patchy debut set, 'FAST STORIES . . . FROM KID COMA' (1995). A second, more low-key long-player, 'FEELING YOU UP', appeared in '98, although 'Capitol' records were not involved.

Album rating: FAST STORIES . . . FROM KID COMA (*6)

ROBERT ROTH – vocals, guitar (ex-STORYBOOK KROOKS) / **HIRO YAMAMOTO** – bass (ex-SOUNDGARDEN) / **MARK PICKEREL** – drums (ex-SCREAMING TREES)

not iss. Sub Pop

Oct 91. (cd-ep) <SP 118> **TRULY EP**
– Heart and lungs / Color is magic / Truly drowning / Married in the playground.

1993. (7") <SP 201> **LESLIE'S COUGHING UP BLOOD. / VIRTUALLY**

Capitol Capitol

Feb 96. (cd) *(CDEST 2278)* <28414> **FAST STORIES . . . FROM KID COMA** Jun95
– Blue Flame Ford / Four girls / If you don't let it die / Hot summer 1991 / Blue lights / Leslie's coughing up blood / Hurricane dance / Angelhead / Tragic telepathic (soul slasher) / Virtually / So strange / Strangling / Chlorine.

Headhunter Headhunter

Mar 98. (lp/cd) *(HUK 003/+CD)* **FEELING YOU UP**

TRUMANS WATER

Formed: San Diego, California, USA . . . 1991 by ELY MOYAL, GLEN GALLOWAY and brothers KEVIN and KIRK BRANSTETTER. Debuting in 1992 with 'OUR SCARS LIKE BADGES', the band were quick off the mark with a follow-up set, 'OF THICK TUM', initial copies of the latter coming complete with a hand-painted sleeve. Aired in its entirety by DJ, John Peel, the album captured their chaotic disharmony (like BEEFHEART on punk pills fused with lo-fi no wave retro) in full flow. Live on his Radio One show, Peel subsequently offered them a session, which led to a contract with 'Elemental'. First up was a double-album, 'SPASM SMASH XXXOXOX OX & ASS' (1993), a schizoid sprawl of nigh on unintelligible avant-pop/indie-rock. Defying all recognised music business convention, the wacky Californians proceeded to release four lp's in '94, 'GODSPEED THE PUNCHLINE', being the first in the 'GODSPEED' series and perhaps unsurprisingly, their last for 'Elemental'. The band certainly weren't taking the 'MILKTRAIN TO PAYDIRT' (1995), the latter set sending them on a one-way ticket to obscurity after receiving short thrift in the press. Unfortunately the band weren't able to simply 'COUGH FORTH SUCH DILEMMAS' (the name of a US-only cassette in '96), still searching for the 'FRAGMENTS OF A LUCKY BREAK' in '98. • **Trvia:** GLEN was left facing a hefty 5-figure bill after failing to graduate from Naval College in the early 90's.

Album rating: OF THICK TUM (*8) / GODSPEED THE PUNCHLINE (*5) / MILKTRAIN TO PAYDIRT (*5) / FRAGMENTS OF A LUCKY BREAK (*5) /

KEVIN BRANSTETTER – vocals, bass / **KIRK BRANSTETTER** – guitar, vocals / **GLEN GALLOWAY** – guitar, vocals / **ELY MOYAL** – drums

not iss. Homestead

1992. (7"ep) <HMS 190-7> **OUR SCARS LIKE BADGES**
– Apolitix / Mind yer altar / Another movement / Sad sailor story.

not iss. Justice My Eye – Elevated Loin

1992. (lp) **OF THICK TUM**
(UK-iss.Mar93 on 'Homestead' cd/lp; HMS 192-2/-1)

not iss. Way Out

1992. (7"ep) <004> **JUBILEEEEE**

not iss. Drunken Fish

Dec 92. (7"ep,7"clear-ep) <DF 03> **LAUGH LIGHTS LIT**
– Habits are spirits / Silver tongue please / X-ray eyes or.

Apr 93. (7"m) <DF 06> **HEY FISH. / MR. E / EMPTY QUEEN**

Elemental Homestead

Apr 93. (d-lp/cd) *(ELM 9/+CD)* **SPASM SMASH XXXOXOX OX & ASS** Mar93
– Aroma of Gina Arnold / Speeds exceeding / Good blood after bad / Rations / Death to dead things / Sun go out / Bludgeon elites and stagger / Limbs / Athlete who is suck / Top of morning / Lo priest / Soar ossinaxx at long last / Our doctor thinks we're blind / Fingers / Steps ahead of our minds / La jolly my armpit / K-song / Mindstab, forklift to milktruck / Bladder stomp: Krautrack / The sad skinhead.

Sep 93. (10"ep/cd-ep) *(ELM 14/+CD)* **10 X MY AGE**

Jan 94. (lp/s-lp/cd) *(ELM 15/+X/CD)* <209-2> **GODSPEED THE PUNCHLINE**
– Destroy / Long end of a firearm / All wet west of Washington / Hair junk fibre / Ungalaxy / Antsmashes yer star (dead airwaves) / Enflamed / Outpatient lightspeed / Infinity times zero / Sucker mystique / Playboy stabtone bloodbath go / Slander in new slang / No big (wave) star / Theme of blast / Fuller piston vinegar / .22 / Horsesense / Spaceship next door.

Jan 95. (lp) <10> **GODSPEED THE VORTEX**

Jan 95. (lp) **GODSPEED THE HEMORRHAGE**

Jan 95. (lp) **GODSPEED THE STATIC**
<above lp's were released by different small indies & very ltd; first up was on 'Way Out Sound'>

— they also released a few experimental cassettes in the US

Homestead Homestead

Aug 95. (cd/lp) <(HMS 221-2/-1)> **MILKTRAIN TO PAYDIRT**
– Mechanical days safety system / Unitraction bath / Lick observatory spectroheliоscope / Stares from new enemies / Vexation fruits / Sour synapse – St. Job int'l Gore / Concussed / American fat / Irly traitor consent / Mnemonic elflock / Siski you armiger / Asleep sneeze / Off peak arson / Wind and rain over wings.

— <'Union Pole' issued US cassette, 'COUGH FORTH SUCH DILEMMAS' in '96>

Infinite Chug Emperor Jones

Jul 98. (lp)<cd> *(CHUG 10LP)* <EJ 23CD> **FRAGMENTS OF A LUCKY BREAK**
– Obstacle / Lyrical nozzle / Strat-as-fear / Wealth in a flask / Sky landslide / Your courage / Woed world whirlers / Tiny world with the jitters / Mall removal machine / 60 seconds over medium / Worth of wait / Matter smasher / Water for a thirsty city / Someday you'll be king / All eye and movement.

Oct 98. (7") *(CHUG 11)* **split w/ group I'M BEING GOOD**

- compilations, others, etc -

Apr 95. (cd) *Strange Fruit; (SFRCD 133)* **PEEL SESSIONS**

Jun 97. (cd) *Runt; (RUNT 28)* **ACTION ORNAMENTS**

Apr 98. (cd) *Justice My Eye; (JME 006)* **APISTOGRAMMA**

T.S.O.L.

Formed: as TRUE SOUNDS OF LIBERTY, Long Beach, California, USA . . . 1980 by JACK GREGGORS, RON EMORY, MIKE ROCHE and TODD BARNES. They made their eponymous debut (an EP) for 'Posh Boy', an album, 'DANCE WITH ME', following shortly after. Their second set of the year, 'BENEATH THE SHADOWS', moved on from hardcore to basic punk rock, showing signs of British influence (i.e. DAMNED or STRANGLERS), with the addition of keyboard player, BOB KUEHN. In 1983, having recruited a second guitarist, FRANK AGNEW (borrowed from The ADOLESCENTS), T.S.O.L. were involved in a riot with fans and police at a gig on Sunset Boulevard. A year later, they veered off into glam-metal when GREGGORS joined CATHEDRAL OF TEARS then TENDER FURY. Both he, and BARNES were subsequently replaced by JOE WOOD and MITCH DEAN respectively, the resulting album, 'CHANGE TODAY?' (1984), a poor reflection of their passionate early work (another album 'REVENGE' – '86, was just as bad). By 1990's 'STRANGE LOVE' set, all original members had departed, as did any remaining credibility. As an alternative, the initial line-up reformed for some gigs as THE ORIGINAL TSOL. • **Trivia:** JACK GREGGORS changed his name for each release (aka GRISHAM, LLOYD, etc).

Album rating: BENEATH THE SHADOWS (*6) / THOUGHTS OF YESTERDAY compilation (*7)

JACK GREGGORS (b. GRISHAM) – vocals / **RON EMORY** – guitar / **MIKE ROCHE** – bass / **(FRANCIS GERALD) 'TODD' BARNES** – drums

not iss. Posh Boy

1981. (7"ep) <*PBS 1013*> **T.S.O.L.** [-] [ ]
– Superficial love / Property is theft / No way out / Abolish government / Silent majority / World War III.

not iss. Frontier

1981. (lp) <*FLP 1002*> **DANCE WITH ME** [-] [ ]
– Sounds of laughter / Core blue / Triangle / 80 times / I'm tired of life / Love storm / Silent scream / Funeral march / Die for me / Peace thru power / Dance with me. *(UK-iss.Apr88 on 'Weird Systems'; WS 033)*

— added **BOB KUEHN** – keyboards

Alternative Tentacles Alternative Tentacles

Apr 82. (7"ep) <*(VIRUS 10)*> **WEATHERED STATUES** [ ] [ ]
– Man and machine / Weathered statues / Thoughts of yesterday / Word is.

Dec 82. (lp; as TRUE SOUNDS OF LIBERTY) <*(VIRUS 29)*> **BENEATH THE SHADOWS** [ ] [ ]
– Soft focus / Forever old / She'll be saying / Beneath the shadows / Send my thoughts / Glass streets / Other side / Walk alone / Wash away / Waiting for you. *(UK-iss.1989 on 'GWR'; GWLP 52) <re-iss. 1989 on 'Restless'; 72338>*

— **JOE WOOD** – vocals, guitar (ex-HATED) repl. JACK who joined CATHEDRAL OF TEARS, then TENDER FURY

— **MITCH DEAN** – drums (ex-JONESES) repl. BARNES

— BOB KUEHN also departed and turned up backing BOB DYLAN!

Enigma Enigma

1984. (lp) <*ENIG 1076-1*> **CHANGE TODAY?** [-] [ ]
– Blackmagic / Just like me / In time / Red shadows / Flowers by the door / American zone / It's gray / John / Nice guys / How do. *(UK-iss.Nov86; same as US)*

Nov 86. (lp) *(ENIG 3211-1) <US-cd 971203>* **REVENCHE** [ ] [ ]
– No time / Nothin' for you / Memories / Colors / Madhouse / Revenche / Change today / Still the same / Your eyes / Everybody's a cop.

Jun 87. (lp) *(ENIG 3263-1) <US-cd 971263>* **HIT AND RUN** [ ] [ ]
– It's too late / Road and gold / The name is love / Dreamer / Good mornin' blues / Hit and run / Not alone anymore / Sixteen / Stay with me / Where did I go wrong / You can try.

Restless Restless

1988. (lp) <*72249-2*> **TSOL LIVE (live)** [-] [ ]
– Sixteen / Introduction / Red shadows / Hit and run / Nothin' for you / It's gray / It's too late / Colors (take me away) / The name is love / Road house blues / No time / Dreamer / All along the watchtower / Road of gold.

— now without ROCHE and EMORY, who were repl. by 2 unknowns

May 90. (cd/lp) *(LS 939-2/-1) <73541>* **STRANGE LOVE** [ ] [ ]
– Hell on Earth / Strange love / In the wind / Angel / White lightning / One shot away / Blow by blow / Candy / Let me go / Stop me at the edge / Good goodbye.

— split when the originals also made a comeback

Triple X Triple X

Dec 91. (cd) <*TX 51070CD*> **LIVE '91 (live)** [-] [ ]
(UK-iss.Aug95; same as US)

— GRISHAM subsequently formed JOYKILLER, who signed to 'Epitaph'.

– compilations, etc. –

1987. (lp) *Posh Boy; <88150>* **THOUGHTS OF YESTERDAY 1981-1987** [-] [ ]
– Peace thru' power / Poverty is theft / Word is / Abolish government – Silent majority / Weathered statues / Thoughts of yesterday / Superficial love / Man and machine / No way out / World War III / Youths of age / Inside looking out / Blind resistance / etc *(UK-iss.Oct94 on 'Poshboy'; EFA 12214-2)*

Jul 95. (cd) *Restless; (772581-2)* **HELL & BACK TOGETHER 1984-1990** [ ] [ ]

TSUNAMI

Formed: Arlington, Virginia, USA … 1990 by KRISTIN THOMSON, JENNY TOOMEY, ANDREW WEBSTER and JOHN PALMER. Enthusiastic exponents of the original DIY punk ethic, TSUNAMI are that rare example of a band walking it like they talk it. As well as being an outlet for their own product, the THOMSON/TOOMEY-run 'Simple Machines' (Washington DC-based) label has released material by such semi-legendary alternative/hardcore acts as SUPERCHUNK and NATION OF ULYSSES. Following a debut 1991 EP, 'HEADRINGER' and a series of imaginatively packaged singles ('MATCHBOX', for instance, was under the guise of a book of matches), a fully formed debut album, 'DEEP END', surfaced in 1993. Bursting with fizzing guitar-pop tunes written largely from a feminine angle, the record was well received in indie circles where Riot Grrrl was the flavour of the month. A slot on the 1993 Lollapalooza tour – where they also set up a 'Simple Machines' stall – was followed in early '94 by the release of a follow-up set, 'THE HEART'S TREMELO'. TOOMEY's other bands included CHOKE and GEEK. • **Trivia:** TSUNAMI is a type of tidal wave.

Album rating: WORLD TOUR AND OTHER DESTINATIONS compilation (*6)

JENNY TOOMEY – guitar, vocals / **KRISTIN THOMSON** – guitar, vocals / **ANDREW WEBSTER** – bass, vocals / **JOHN PALMER** – drums

Simple Machines Simple Machines

Jan 93. (7") <*(SMR 16)*> **LOAD HOG. /** [ ] [ ]

Jan 93. (7") <*(HMS 179)*> **GENIUSES OF CRACK. / ANSWERMAN** [ ] [ ]
(above issued on 'Homestead', below on 'I.T.Q.')

Mar 93. (7") <*(IVR 1)*> **BEAUTIFUL ARLINGTON. /** [ ] [ ]

Apr 93. (7") <*(SMR 18)*> **MATCHBOOK. /** [ ] [ ]

May 93. (cd/c/lp) <*(SMR 13 CD/C/V)*> **DEEP END** [ ] [ ]

Apr 94. (7") <*(SMR 24)*> **BE LIKE THAT. / NEWSPAPER** [ ] [ ]

May 94. (cd/c/lp) <*(SMR 25 CD/C/V)*> **THE HEART'S TREMOLO** [ ] [ ]
– Loud is as loud does / Quietnova / Be like that / Fast food medicine / Kidding on the square / Slaw / Cowed by the bla bla / The heart's tremolo / Bride d-elegance / Fits and starts.

Apr 95. (cd) <*(SMR 33CD)*> **WORLD TOUR & OTHER DESTINATIONS (live)** [ ] [ ]
– Flameproof suit / World tour / Ski trip / Kickball babe / Candyman / Genius of crack / Answerman / Left behind / Punk means cuddle / Could have been Christmas / Load hog / Goldigger / Beauty (pt.2) / Brick book building / Sometimes a notion / Walking tour / Crackers / Not living / Bossa nova / Kidding on the square / Newspaper / Courage.

Aug 97. (7") <*SMR 52*> **POODLE. / OLD CITY** [-] [ ]

Sep 97. (cd) <*(SMR 53CD)*> **BRILLIANT MISTAKE** [ ] [ ]
– Old gray mare / Great times / Double shift / Enter misguided / Workers are punished / Liar's dice (flight of the chickens) / Match / Poodle / Unbridled / DMFH / David Foster Wallace / Hockey / PBS.

TUBES

Formed: Phoenix, Arizona, USA … 1972 by BILL SPOONER, VINCE WELNICK and ex-drama student FEE WAYBILL, who moved the outfit to the Bay Area, San Francisco, the line-up completed by RICK ANDERSON, MICHAEL COTTEN, ROGER STEEN, PRAIRIE PRINCE and REG STYLES. Coming on like a perverted, pseudo-punk precursor to MEAT LOAF's theatrical overload, the group became infamous for their garish shows which placed scantily clad ladies against such unsavoury stage characters as Dr. Strangekiss and Quay Lude. Signed to 'A&M', their debut single was the legendary 'WHITE PUNKS ON DOPE', a UK Top 30 hit some three years later when Britain was in the grip of three-chord fever. The accompanying AL KOOPER-produced, eponymous debut album narrowly missed the US Top 100, while follow-up, 'YOUNG AND RICH' (produced by KEN SCOTT), broke them into the US Top 50 in 1976. But the music often took second place to the theatrics and in 1979, obviously bored with the limitations of the genre, swapped anthemic punk/new wave for easier going pop/rock on that years' TODD RUNDGREN-produced 'REMOTE CONTROL' album. A proposed 1980 set, 'SUFFER FOR SOUND', was shelved by 'A&M' prior to the band being dropped. Inking a new deal with 'Capitol', the group moved even further towards the mainstream with 'THE COMPLETION BACKWARD PRINCIPLE' (1981), an album which spawed a one-off Top 10 hit in 'SHE'S A BEAUTY'. After a final couple of albums, 'OUTSIDE INSIDE' (1983) and 'LOVE BOMB' (1986), The TUBES realised the joke had run its course and packed it in. Having already released a solo set, 'READ MY LIPS' (1984), WAYBILL went on to write material for RICHARD MARX (!), while SPOONER and WELNICK subsequently went on to work with Bay Area veterans, The GRATEFUL DEAD. • **Songwriters:** WAYBILL penned except I SAW HER STANDING THERE (Beatles) / etc. • **Trivia:** In 1980, they undertook a cameo performance in the film, 'Xanadu', soundtrack courtesy of ELECTRIC LIGHT ORCHESTRA and OLIVIA NEWTON-JOHN.

Album rating: T.R.A.S.H. (TUBES RARITIES AND SMASH HITS) compilation (*7)

FEE WAYBILL (b. JOHN WALDO, 17 Sep'50, Omaha, Nebraska) – vocals / **BILL 'Sputnik' SPOONER** (b.16 Apr'49) – guitar / **VINCE WELNICK** (b.21 Feb'51) – keyboards / **RICK ANDERSON** (b. 1 Aug'47, St. Paul, Minnesota) – bass / **MICHAEL COTTEN** (b.25 Jan'50, Kansas City, Missouri) – synthesizer / **ROGER STEEN** (b.13 Nov'49, Pipestone, Minnesota) – guitar / **PRAIRIE PRINCE** (b. 7 May'50, Charlotte, New Connecticut) – drums / **REG STYLES** (b. 3 Mar'50) – vocals, guitar

A&M A&M

Jul 75. (7") <*1733*> **WHITE PUNKS ON DOPE. / (part 2)** [-] [ ]

Jul 75. (lp/c) *(AMLH/CAM 64534) <4534>* **THE TUBES** [ ] [ ]
– Up from the deep / Haloes / Space baby / Malaguena Salerosa / Mondo bondage / What do you want from life / Boy crazy / White punks on dope. *(re-iss. May83 on 'Fame') (d-cd-iss. Dec85 on 'Mobile Fidelity', incl.next album)*

Nov 75. (7") <> **WHAT DO YOU WANT FROM LIFE. / SPACE BABY** [-] [ ]

Jan 76. (7") *(AMS 7209)* **WHAT DO YOU WANT FROM LIFE. / WHITE PUNKS ON DOPE** [ ] [-]

May 76. (lp/c) *(AMLH/CAM 64580) <4580>* **YOUNG AND RICH** [ ] [46]
– Tubes world tour / Brighter day / Pimp / Stand up and shout / Don't touch me there / Slipped my disco / Proud to be an American / Poland whole / Madam I'm Adam / Young and rich.

Jun 76. (7") *(AMS 7239) <1826>* **DON'T TOUCH ME THERE. / PROUD TO BE AMERICAN** [ ] [61]

Jan 77. (7") **YOUNG AND RICH. / LOVE WILL KEEP US TOGETHER** [-] [ ]

— added **MINGO LEWIS** – percussion

May 77. (lp/c) *(AMLH/CAM 64632) <4632>* **THE TUBES NOW** [ ] [ ]
– Smoke (la vie en fumer) / Hit parade / Strung out on strings / Golden boy / My head is my house (unless it rains) / God-bird-change / I'm just a mess / Cathy's clone / This town / Pound of flesh / You're no fun.

Aug 77. (7") <*1956*> **I'M JUST A MESS. / THIS TOWN** [-] [ ]

Nov 77. (7m)(12"m) *(AMS7323)* **WHITE PUNKS ON DOPE. / DON'T TOUCH ME THERE / WHAT DO YOU WANT FROM LIFE** [28] [-]

Feb 78. (d-lp/d-c) *(AMLM/CLM 68460) <6003>* **WHAT DO YOU WANT FROM LIVE (live)** [38] [82]

– (overture) / Got yourself a deal / Show me a reason / What do you want from life / God-bird-change / Special ballet / Don't touch me there / Mondo bondage / Smoke (la vie en fumer) / Crime medley: (themes from 'Dragnet' – 'Peter Gunn' – 'Perry Mason' – 'The Untouchables') / I was a punk before you were a punk / I saw her standing there / (drum solo) / Boy crazy / You're no fun / Stand up and shout / White punks on dope. *(cd-iss. Apr97; 396003-2)*

Apr 78. (7") *(AMS 7349)* **SHOW ME A REASON (live). / MONDO BONDAGE (live)** [ ] [-]
Jul 78. (7") *<2037>* **SHOW ME A REASON (live). / I SAW HER STANDING THERE (live)** [-] [ ]
Feb 79. (7")(7"colrd-7 diff.) *(AMS 7423,) <2120>* **PRIME TIME. / NO WAY OUT** [ ] [34]
May 79. (lp/c) *(AMLH/CAM 64751) <4751>* **REMOTE CONTROL** [40] [46] Mar 79
– Turn me on / TV is king / Prime time / I want it all / No way out / Getoverture / No mercy / Only the strong survive / Be mine tonight / Love's a mystery (I don't understand) / Telecide.
May 79. (7") *<2149>* **LOVE'S A MYSTERY (I DON'T UNDERSTAND). / TELECIDE** [-] [ ]
Jul 79. (7")(7"yellow) *(AMS 7462,)* **TV IS KING. / TELECIDE** [ ] [ ]

— trimmed slightly when LEWIS + STYLES left.

Capitol Capitol

May 81. (7") *<5016>* **TALK TO YA LATER. / POWER TOOLS** [-] [ ]
May 81. (7") *(CL 201)* **TALK TO YA LATER. / WHAT'S WRONG WITH ME** [ ] [-]
May 81. (lp/c) *(EST/TCEST 26285) <12151>* **THE COMPLETION BACKWARD PRINCIPLE** [ ] [36]
– Talk to ya later / Let's make some noise / Matter of pride / Mr. Hate / Attack of the fifty foot woman / Think about me / Sushi girl / Don't want to wait anymore / Power tools / Amnesia. *(re-iss. +cd.Mar91 on 'B.G.O.')*
Jul 81. (7") *(CL 208) <5007>* **DON'T WANT TO WAIT ANYMORE. / THINK ABOUT ME** [60] [35] Jun81
Oct 81. (7") *(CL 219)* **SUSHI GIRL. / MR. HATE** [ ] [ ]
Apr 83. (7") *(CL 288) <5217>* **SHE'S A BEAUTY. / WHEN YOU'RE READY TO COME** [ ] [10]
(12"+=) *(12CL 288)* – Fantastic delusion.
May 83. (lp/c) *(EST/TCEST 12260) <12260>* **OUTSIDE INSIDE** [77] [18] Apr 83
– She's a beauty / No not again / Out of the business / The monkey time / Glass house / Wild women of Wongo / Tip of my tongue / Fantastic delusion / Drums / Theme park / Outside lookin' inside. *(cd-iss. Jul92 on 'B.G.O.')*

— above feat. guests **MAURICE WHITE** (of EARTH, WIND & FIRE) + **MARTHA DAVIS** – vocals (of MOTELS)

Jul 83. (7") *<5258>* **TIP OF MY TONGUE. / KEYBOARD KIDS** [-] [52]
Sep 83. (7") *<5254>* **THE MONKEY TIME. / SPORTS FAN** [-] [68]

— In 1984, WAYBILL released solo album READ MY LIPS (see further on)

Mar 85. (7") *<5443>* **PIECE BY PIECE. / NIGHT PEOPLE** [-] [87]
Mar 86. (lp/c) *<12381>* **LOVE BOMB** [ ] [87] May85
– Piece by piece / Stella / Come as you are / One good reason / Bora Bora 2000 – Love bomb / Night people / Say hey / Eyes / Muscle girls / Theme from a wooly place – Wolly bully – Theme from a summer place / For a song / Say hey (part 2) / Feel it / Night people (reprise). *(cd-iss. Aug93 on 'B.G.O.')*

— Group disbanded after above album. WAYBILL continued to write and guest on noteably albums by RICHARD MARX (1988). WELNICK joined GRATEFUL DEAD. The TUBES re-formed in 1993; **WAYBILL, STEEN, PRINCE, ANDERSON / + GARY CAMBRA** – vocals, keyboards / **JENNIFER McFEE + AMY FRENCH** – vocals

– compilations, others, etc. –

Nov 81. (lp/c) *A&M; (AMLH/CAM 64870) <4870>* **T.R.A.S.H. (TUBES RARITIES AND SMASH HITS)** [ ] [ ]
– Drivin' all night / What do you want from life / Turn me on / Slipped my disco / Mondo bondage / Love will keep us together / I'm just a mess / Only the strong survive / Don't touch me there / White punks on dope / Prime time.
Sep 85. (7") *Old Gold; (OG 9545)* **PRIME TIME. / ('B'by 'Styx')** [ ] [-]
Jan 87. (7") *Old Gold; ()* **(above tracks)** [ ] [-]
(12"+=) *(OG 4013)* – White punks on dope / (other by 'Styx').
Nov 86. (lp) *Plastic Head; (PLASLP 006)* **PRIME TIME** [ ] [-]
Apr 93. (cd) *Capitol; (C 298359)* **THE BEST OF THE TUBES** [ ] [ ]

FEE WAYBILL

Capitol Capitol

Oct 84. (7") **WHO SAID LIFE WOULD BE PRETTY. / YOU'RE STILL LAUGHING** [-] [ ]
Nov 84. (lp/c) *<12369>* **READ MY LIPS** [-] [ ]
-You're still laughing / Nobody's perfect / Who loves you baby / I don't even know your name (passion play) / Who said life would be pretty / Thrill of the kill / Saved my life / Caribbean sunsets / Star of the show / I could've been somebody.
Dec 84. (7") **STAR OF THE SHOW. / I DON'T EVEN KNOW YOUR NAME** [-] [ ]

TUBEWAY ARMY (see under ⇒ NUMAN, Gary)

TUMOUR CIRCUS (see under ⇒ DEAD KENNEDYS)

TURBINES

Formed: Roxbury, Massachusetts, USA . . . mid 80's by JOHN HOVORKA, JACK HICKEY, DAVID SHIBLER and FRED NAZZARO. Signed to 'Big Time', the band made their debut in 1986 with the 'LAST DANCE BEFORE THE HIGHWAY' album, a raucous blast of brooding, bluesy twisted Americana that saw them loosely associated with the insurgent cowpunk scene. French label, 'New Rose' were to release follow-up, 'MAGIC FINGERS AND HOURLY RATES' (1987), although the TURBINES quickly ran out of steam.

Album rating: LAST DANCE BEFORE THE HIGHWAY (*5) / MAGIC FINGERS AND HOURLY RATES (*5)

JOHN HOVORKA – vocals, guitar / **JACK HICKEY** – guitar / **FRED NAZZARO** – drums / **DAVID SHIBLER** – bass

Big Time Big Time

May 86. (lp) *<(BTA 007)>* **LAST DANCE BEFORE THE HIGHWAY** [ ] [ ]
– Skull & crossbones / That's the way / Highway 51 / Slop / Wah-hey / Throw it down / Rock in my pocket / Hangin' tough.

New Rose unknown

Jun 87. (lp) *(ROSE 118)* **MAGIC FINGERS AND HOURLY RATES** [ ] [ ]
– Rules of the road / Roy's hotel / Eye for an eye / Big motor man / Stray dog / Nowhere fast / Last ride / She's my witch / 1969 / Little pig.

— never quite got into gear and disbanded soon after

TUXEDOMOON

Formed: San Francisco, California, USA . . . mid-'77 by BLAINE REININGER and WINSTON TONG (an early line-up also included VICTORIA LOWE, MIKEL BELFER and PAUL ZAHL). In 1978 they issued their debut single, 'PINHEADS ON THE MOVE', on the self-financed 'Tidal Wave' imprint before the band set up their own 'Time Release' label for 1979's 'NEW MACHINE' EP. Late addition, STEVE BROWN, augmented the already exotic brew of violin-led, avant-garde electro with his sax playing; this four tracker (as 'NO TEARS'), along with a whole batch of TUXEDOMOON material received a UK release in the mid-80's on the 'Cramboy' label). Following the 1979 addition on PETER PRINCIPLE, the band subsequently took up residence at 'Ralph' records ('Pre' in the UK), home of er.. The RESIDENTS. The 'SCREAM WITH A VIEW' EP and full-length debut, 'HALF-MUTE' (1980), the former was recorded in the absence of TONG, who put in some part-time effort on the latter. The man himself could be heard in full monged-out flight on Belgian label, 'Les Disques Du Crepuscule's various artists set, 'The Fruit Of The Original Sin', memorably crawling his way through spoken word effort, 'THE LAST THING TO DEATH'. TONG was back in a full-time capacity for 1981's 'DESIRE' album alongside guest RAINCOAT, VICKY ASPINALL, the group subsequently relocating to Brussels, Belgium after a spell in Rotterdam, Netherlands. From this new base, the free-from space jazz/electro cadets released a clutch of European-only affairs including an album, 'SUITE EN SOUS-SOL' on Italian label, 'Expanded', sung in French (!). Pretentious ? Non! Founding members TONG and REININGER both departed to concentrate on solo careers (the latter had already released two sets, 'BROKEN FINGERS' and 'NIGHT AIR' on the aforementioned 'Crepuscule . . .' label in the mid-80's, TONG taking his leave after 1985's 'HOLY WARS' set. TUXEDOMOON continued with a line-up of PRINCIPLE, BRUCE GEDULDIG, LUC VAN LIESHOUT, JAN D'HAESE and IVAN GEORGIEV for a couple more albums, 'SHIP OF FOOLS' (1986) and 'YOU' (1987) before disbanding. Bizarrely enough, a posthumous live set emerged on 'R.C.A.' at the turn of the decade while a final, mysterious TUXEDOMOON studio set, 'THE GHOST SONATA', appeared in 1991. REININGER continued to record in Belgium for the bulk of the 80's, although only two albums, '(SONGS FROM THE) RAIN PALACE' and 'EXPATRIATE' have appeared in the 90's. TONG's last vinyl appearance, meanwhile, was 1985's 'THEOROETICALLY CHINESE'. • **Covered:** 19th NERVOUS BREAKDOWN (Rolling Stones).

Album rating: 13 + 1 OF THE BEST compilation (*5)

BLAINE L. REININGER – violin, keyboards, guitars / **MIKEL BELFER** – guitar / **PAUL ZAHL** – drums, electronic percussion / **WINSTON TONG** – vocals / **VICTORIA LOWE** – vocals

not iss. Tidal Wave

1978. (7") *<001>* **PINHEADS ON THE MOVE. / JOEBOY** [-] [ ]
<re-iss. 1978 on 'Time Release'; TRR 101>

— **STEVEN BROWN** – vocals, keyboards, saxophone, etc; repl. LOWE

not iss. Time Release

1979. (12"ep) *<TREP 101>* **NEW MACHINE / LITE BULB OVERKILL. / NITE & DAY / NO TEARS** [-] [ ]
(UK-iss.Mar86 as 'NO TEARS EP' on 'Cramboy'; CBOY 7070)

— **PETER PRINCIPLE** (b. DACHERT) – bass, guitar, etc; repl. ZAHL

1979. (7") *<TR 102>* **STRANGER. / LOVE – NO HOPE** [-] [ ]

— now without TONG (he returned for the following album)

Pre Ralph

Dec 79. (12"ep) *(PRE 1-12)* **SCREAM WITH A VIEW** [ ] [-]
– Nervous guy / Where interest lie / Special treatment for the family man / Midnite stroll. *(re-iss. Oct85 on 'Cramboy'; CBOY 4040)*

— now without BELFER

May 80. (7") *<TX 80032>* **WHAT USE? / CRASH** [-] [ ]
Sep 80. (lp) *<TX 8004>* **HALF-MUTE** [-] [ ]
– Nazca / 59 to 1 / Fifth column / Tritone / Loneliness / James Whale / What use? / Volo vivace / 7 years / Km / Seeding the clouds. *(UK-iss.Oct84 on 'Cramboy'; CBOY 1010) (cd-iss. 1988 +=; CBOY 1040)* – SCREAM WITH A VIEW
Oct 80. (7") *(PRE 010) <TX 8054>* **DARK COMPANION. / 59 TO 1 (remix)** [ ] [ ]

— **WINSTON TONG** – vocals (now a full-time member again)

— w/ guests VICKY ASPINALL – vocals (of RAINCOATS) / AL ROBINSON – cello

Mar 81. (lp) *(PREX/PRICS 4) <TX 8104>* **DESIRE** [ ] [ ]
– East – Jinx / Blue suit / Music 1 / Victims of the dance / Incubus / Desire again / In the name of talent / Holiday for plywood. *(re-iss. Oct85 on 'Cramboy'; CBOY 3030) (re-iss. Aug88 on 'Charisma'; CHC 66) (cd-iss. 1989 on 'Cramboy'+=; CBOY 3070)* – NO TEARS EP

— group now moved base to Brussels, Belgium

— added part-timer **BRUCE GEDULDIG** – visuals, films, percussion

Operation Twilight / not iss.

Apr 82. (12") *(TWI 055)* **NINOTCHKA. / AGAIN**
May 82. (lp) *(6399348)* **DIVINE** - - German
– Mata Hari / Anna Christie / Grand hotel / Ninotchka / Conquest / Queen Christina / Camille.
Jul 82. (m-lp) *(TWI 084)* **TIME TO LOSE**
– Time to lose / Music #2 / Blind / Cage / This beast.*(cd-ep iss.Oct88 on 'Cramboy'; CBOY 8081)*
Apr 83. (12") **THE CAGE. /** - - Belgian

Expanded / not iss.

Dec 82. (d-lp) *(EX 38-Y2)* **SUITE EN SOUS-SOL** - - Italian
– Prelude / Allemande bleue / Courante marocaine / Sarabande en bas de l'escalier / Polonaise mecanique / L'etranger.

New Ralph / New Ralph

Jan 84. (lp) <*(TX 8354)*> **A THOUSAND LIVES BY PICTURE (live)**
– What use? / Incubus (blue suit) / 7 years / Tritone (musica diablo) / Desire / Dark companion / Jinx / 59 to 1 / Crash.

Joeboy / not iss.

Jul 84. (7") *(SW 7007)* **SOMA. / HUGGING THE EARTH** - - Belgian

— now without mainman REININGER was already releasing solo material

— **TONG, PRINCIPLE + BROWN** recruited **LUC VAN LIESHOUT** – trumpet, flugelhorn / **ALAIN LeFEBVRE** – congas, percussion / **JAN D'HAESE** – vocals

Cramboy / not iss.

Apr 85. (lp/cd) *(CBOY 2020/+CD)* **HOLY WARS**
– The waltz / St. John / Bonjour tristesse / Hugging the earth / In a manner of speaking / Some guys / Holy wars / Watching the blood flow / Egypt.

— **BRUCE GEDULDIG** – vocals (returned) to repl. TONG who had already initiated his own solo career

— **IVAN GEORGIEV** – keyboards, synths, vocals; repl. LeFEVRE

— **MARCIA BARCELLOS** – vocals; repl. D'HAESE

Jun 86. (m-lp) *(CBOY 6060)* **SHIP OF FOOLS**
– Atlantis / Reeding, righting, phythmatic / Break the rules / A piano solo / Lowlands tone poem / Music for piano & guitar / An afternoon with N / The train.

— now without MARCIA

Sep 87. (lp) *(CBOY 9090)* **YOU**
– Roman P. / The train / 2000 / Never ending story / Boxman (Mr. Niles) / Spirits & ghosts / Boxman (the city) / You / Boxman (home).

— disbanded the following year

R.C.A. / not iss.

Aug 90. (lp/cd) *(PB 5921/+CD)* **TEN YEARS IN ONE NIGHT (live 1985-1988)**
– Michael's theme / Burning trumpet / The waltz / In a manner of speaking / The cage / Everything you want / Courante marocaine / Lite bulb overkill / Desire / Nervous guy / Pinheads on the move / No tears / In Heaven / Nazca. *(was issued 1989 on 'Materiali Sonoro'; MASO 90006) (cd-iss. Jun98; MASOCD 90006)*

Les Tempes Modernes / not iss.

May 91. (cd) *(LTMCD 203)* **THE GHOST SONATA**
– Funeral of a friend / The ghost sonata / Catalyst / Affair at the soiree / Music No.2 / Drowning / Cascade / Mystic death / Basso pomade / Licorice stick ostinado / Laboratory / Les odalisques / Unsigned postcard. *(re-iss. Oct97 on 'Cramboy'; CBOY 1414)*

— above was their final release

– compilations, etc. –

Jan 88. (d-lp/cd) *Cramboy;* <*(CBOY 5050/+CD)*> **PINHEADS ON THE MOVE**
– Pinheads on the move / Joeboy the electronic ghost / Stranger / Jungle 7 / Love – No hope / In Heaven / I heard it through the grapevine / Fifth column / Touched / Waterfront seat / Nuit au fond de la frayere / I left my heart in San Francisco / Everything you want / Next to nothing / Egypt / Over his head / Martial – This land / Straight line forward / Jingle 9 / Pinheads on the move.
Jan 94. (cd) *Cramboy;* <*(CBOY 1313)*> **13 + 1 OF THE BEST**
– What use? / No tears / The cage / Some guys / Dark companion / In a manner of speaking / Atlantis / The waltz / L'etranger / Tritone (music diablo) / East – Jinx / Desire / 59 to 1 / You (Christmas mix).
1997. (cd) *Cramboy;* <*(CBOY 8081)*> **SUITE EN SOUS SOL – TIME TO LOSE**

STEVEN BROWN

— with **REININGER** – violin (on 1st)

Another Side / not iss.

1984. (lp) *(SIDE 8405)* **MUSIC FOR SOLO PIANO** - - Belgian
– Piano No.1 / Waltz / The ball / Hold me while I'm naked / Close little sixes / Fanfare / Egypt / The fall / Fantasie for clarinet & violin / R.W.F. / Rotterdam lullabye. *(UK-iss.Jul88 on 'Crepescule'; TWI 110) (cd-iss. Mar90; TWI 110-2)*

— now with **LEW** – synths, tapes / **MARC HOLLANDER** – clarinet

Crammed Discs / not iss.

1984. (lp; by BENJAMIN LEW & STEVEN BROWN) *(CRAM 020)* **DOUZIEME JOURNEE: LA VERBE, LA PARURE, L'AMOUR**
– Bamako ou ailleurs / Passage / De l'autre cote fleuve / L'ile l'hotel / A veugle, depuis / Elle s'avanca / Dans les jardins / Les autres, tou / Il, les quitta a l'aube. *(re-iss. Mar88 on 'Made To Measure'; MTM 15)*

— added **ALAIN LeFEBVRE** – drums, percussion / + guests **VINI REILLY** – guitar, piano (of DURUTTI COLUMN) / **FORTIS** – vocals

1985. (lp; by BENJAMIN LEW & STEVEN BROWN) *(CRAM 038)* **A PROPOS D'UN PAYSAGE**
– Moments / Les enormes et pourtant l'invisibles / Profondeurs des eaux des laques / Une telle richesse / S'ignorer / Pareseuse aussi / Au sujet d'un paysage / Face a ce qui se derobe / Noubelles observations / La vie aussi / Etendue.

Play It Again Sam / not iss.

Jun 87. (7") *(BIAS 066)* **THE LAST RENDEZVOUS. /**
Jun 87. (cd/lp) *(CD+/BIAS 055)* **SEARCHING FOR CONTACT**
– Habit / Audiences & stages / Does day / In praise of money / Manner of means / This land, scene 1-3 / De hamburger veermaster / Voxcon.

Sub Rosa / not iss.

Jul 87. (12") *(SUB12 002-4)* **ME & YOU & THE LICORICE STICK. /**
Oct 88. (lp/cd; by BENJAMIN LEW & STEVEN BROWN) *(MTM 17/+CD)* **NEBKA**
(above on 'Made To Measure')
1989. (lp/cd) *(SUB 33/CD 00921)* **THE DAY IS GONE**
Jan 90. (12") *(SUB12 007-28)* **LOVE, YES. /**

Les Tempes Modernes / not iss.

Apr 90. (lp/cd) *(LTM/+CD 2304)* **LA GRACE DU TOMBEUR**
– The labyrinth / The flight / The fall.

– (his) compilations, others, etc. –

Nov 88. (lp/c) *Materiali Sonoro; (MASO 33044/+C)* **ZOO STORY** - - Italian
May 89. (lp/cd) *Crepescule; (TWI 872/+2)* **COMPOSES POUR LE THEATRE ET LE CINEMA**

PETER PRINCIPLE

— with **SASHKIA LUPINI** – flute

Made To Measure / not iss.

Mar 84. (lp) *(MTM 2)* **REVAUX AU BONGO**
(cd-iss. Nov88; MTM 2CD)
Mar 85. (lp) *(MTM 4)* **SEDIMENTAL JOURNEY**
– The anvil chorus / Pandemonium / Spring / Friends of extinction / Tippi rider / The eleventh race / Noon / Ain't superstitious / Dnieper / Before the wind. *(cd-iss. Sep88; MTM 4CD)*
Nov 88. (lp/cd) *(MTM 18/+CD)* **TONE POEMS**
– Le maka / Sphinx / Sub-lunar folly / The observatory / Independence day / Pillar of salt / Orfal / Orion's shadow / Dolphins / Riding the silver chord.

BLAINE L. REININGER

— with **PETER PRINCIPLE, STEVEN BROWN, MIKEL BELFER, JJ LaRUE + ALAIN GAUTIER**

Crepescule / not iss.

Jul 82. (lp) *(TWI 068)* **BROKEN FINGERS**
– Broken fingers / Nurr al Hajj / Magic time / Petite piece Chinoise / Right mind / Gigolo grasiento / Spiny doughboys / Sons of the silent age / Uptown / Les nuages / Magnetic life / Playin' your game. *(cd-iss. May88; TWICD 068)*
Oct 83. (12") **MAGNETIC LIFE. /** - - Belgian

— **WINSTON TONG** – vocals; repl. LaRUE

— **MARC HOLLANDER** – clarinet; repl. PRINCIPLE

Dec 83. (lp) *(TWI 267)* **NIGHT AIR** - - Belgian
– Night air / Birthday song / Beak people / Mystery and confusion / Bizarre bizarre / Intermission / Ash and bone / L'entree de l'hierophante / Un cafe au lait for Mr. XYZPTLK / Miraculous absense / El mensajero divino.
Oct 84. (lp; by BLAINE L. REININGER & MIKEL ROUSE) *(MTM 3)* **COLORADO (suite)**
– Side wind / Windy outside / West wind / Sun study / Friendship '84 / Big pine II / Airland 2000 / Hardfall / Winter in Wyoming / The eloquent dissenter / A walk in the woods.
(above issued on 'Made To Measure')

— only retained **GOUTIER** + enlisted **THIERRY PLAS** – guitar / **WERNER PENSAERT** – keyboards / **BOB DI MARCO** – saxophone / **MARC BONNE** – drums

Jul 85. (lp; by BLAINE REININGER & ALAIN GOUTIER) *(TWI 380)* **PARIS EN AUTOMNE**
– Paris en automne / Singular world / Raise your hands / Burn like Rome / The homecoming.

— **KLAUS WANG** – vocals, keyboards; repl. WERNER + THIERRY

— **DANIEL WANG** – drums, trumpet; repl. MARC

May 86. (lp) *(TWICD 637)* **LIVE IN BRUSSELS (live)**
– Volo / Night air / Birthday song / What use indeed? / Uptown (extremely long concert version) / Broken fingers.

— **BLAINE** with **LEON VAN DEN ACKER + ERIC SLEICHIM**

Apr 87. (lp/cd) *(TWI/+CD 767)* **BYZANTIUM**
– Rolf and Florian go Hawaiian / Blood of a poet / Teenage theatre / Some fine day / Japanese dream / Too cool to die / Bird on the wire / Rosebud.
1988. (cd; by STEVEN BROWN & BLAINE L. REININGER) *(TWI 916-2)* **LIVE IN PORTUGAL (live)**
– Iberia / Egypt / The fall / L'arrivee dans le jour / Music number two / Fanfare / The waltz / Piano No.1 / Salad variation / Licorice stick ostinato / Volo vivace / Lite bulb overkill.
Oct 88. (7") *(NORMAL 72)* **EL PASO. /**
(12"+=/3"cd-s+=) *(NORMAL 72 T/CD)* –
(above issued on German label, 'Normal')
1989. (lp/cd) *(TWI 845/+2)* **BOOK OF HOURS**
– Zombie bop / St. Therese / To the green door / Salad days / El Paso / Letter from home / Come the Spring / Software pancake house.
Sep 90. (cd) *(TWI 909-2)* **(SONGS FROM THE) RAIN PALACE**

Giant / not iss.

1990's. (cd/lp) *(GRI 6042-2/-1)* **EXPATRIATE**

– (his) compilations, etc. –

1988. (lp) *Interior Music; (IM 008)* **INSTRUMENTALS 1982-86**
– Contempt / Les chose de la vie / Le dernier amant romantique / Les nuages / Petite piece Chinoise / Travelling / Music Number two / Licorice stick ostinado / Basso pomade – Dogs licking my heart.
May 96. (cd) *Crepescule; (TWI 964-2)* **BRUSSELS / USA – THE BEST OF BLAINE L. REININGER, VOL.1**
– Night air / Gigolo grasiento / Mystery and confusion / Ash and bone / Teenage theatre / Tombee de la nuit / Zen and Lulu / Software pancake house / To the green door / Cafe au lait / Come the Spring / Ralf and Florian go Hawaiian / Right mind / Letter from home / Broken fingers / One-way man / El mensajero divino.

WINSTON TONG

Crepescule not iss.

Jun 83. (lp) *(044)* **LIKE THE OTHERS** [-] [-] Japan

— with guests SUSAN DEHIM – vocals / DAVE FORMULA – keyboards (ex-MAGAZINE) / STEVE MORRIS – drums (of NEW ORDER) / ALAN RANKINE – guitar, synthesizer, percussion (ex-ASSOCIATES) / JAH WOBBLE – bass (Solo Artist) / SIMON TOPPING – trumpet (ex-A CERTAIN RATIO) / ALAIN LeFEBVRE – drums / PIETRO LACRIGINOLA – sax / NIKKI MONO – vocals

Dec 84. (12") *(TWI 310)* **THEORETICAL CHINA. / HUNGER** [ ] [-]

Aug 85. (lp) *(6911)* **REPORTS FROM THE HEART** [-] [-] German
– Phadre slips on her silver girdle / In a white room / What makes the click in me / Now we were misunderstood / Orpheus: The last march of a poet / The other half lives / Thirteenth hour / Silence / China he said / Soulsearch / Lost everywhere.

Operation Afterglow not iss.

Nov 85. (lp) *(LPOPA 004)* **THEORETICALLY CHINESE** [ ] [-]
– Big brother / Yellow peril / Theoretical China / Endgame / The quotidan / The principles of movement / No regrets / Reports from the heart. *(cd-iss. May86 on 'Crepescule'; CDTWI 549)*

TV PERSONALITIES (see under ⇒ TELEVISION PERSONALITIES)

TWANG

Formed: Manchester/Preston, England . . . 1985 by JOHN TWANG, ANDY LADD, DAVE HINDMARSH and LEN. Fusing dancefloor elements of A CERTAIN RATIO and The FIRE ENGINES, TWANG's first record, 'WHAT'S THE RUB', was available on a 'Lyntone' flexidisc towards the end of '85. They subsequently signed to the 'Ron Johnson' imprint the following year, releasing a small handful of 45's, 'SHARP', 'KICK AND COMPLAIN' and 'SNAP BACK', before breaking up.

Album rating: never released any

ANDY LADD – vocals / **DAVE HINDMARSH** – guitar / **JOHN TWANG** – bass / **LEN** – drums

Ron Johnson not iss.

Oct 86. (7") *(ZRON 14)* **SHARP. / EIGHT AT A TIME** [ ] [-]

Mar 87. (7") *(ZRON 22)* **KICK AND COMPLAIN. /** [ ] [-]

Nov 87. (12") *(ZRON 29)* **SNAP BACK. / ('A'-Defence mix)** [ ] [-]

— all returned to their day jobs

12 RODS

Formed: Ohio, USA . . . 1992 (moved to Cincinnati & Minnesota in 1994) by RYAN OLCOTT, his brother EV OLCOTT and CHRISTOPHER McGUIRE. All three were classically-trained, geeky-looking lads on a noisy-pop mission to revive punk and electro at the same time. Signing a worldwide deal with Richard Branson's new imprint, 'V2', 12 RODS unleashed the weird, 'GAY?' mini-set late in '97. The following summer saw the trio make a minor breakthrough with the equally zany, 'SPLIT PERSONALITY'.

Album rating: GAY? mini (*5) / SPLIT PERSONALITIES (*6)

RYAN OLCOTT – vocals, guitar / **EV OLCOTT** – synthesizer, guitar / **CHRISTOPHER McGUIRE** – drums

V2 V2

Nov 97. (m-cd) *(VVR 100098-2) <27509>* **GAY?** [ ] [ ] Oct97
– Red / Make-out music / Gaymo / Mexico / Friend / Revolute.

Jun 98. (7"/cd-s) *(VVR 500230-7/-3)* **SPLIT PERSONALITY. / STELLA / BABIES** [ ] [-]

Jul 98. (cd) *<27015>* **SPLIT PERSONALITIES** [ ] [ ]
– Split personality / Red / I am faster / Chromatically declining me / Part of 2 / Stupidest boy / I wish you were a girl / Lovewaves / Make-out music / Girl sun.

28th DAY (see under ⇒ MANNING, Barbara)

27 VARIOUS (see under ⇒ POLARA)

23 SKIDOO

Formed: London, England . . . 1979 by FRITZ HAAMAN, J.C.M. and A. LIM, taking their name from Aleister Crowley's 'Book Of Lies'. They subsequently issued a debut 45, 'ETHICS', with further sporadic vinyl appearances reaching the shops in the early 80's. These featured artwork by future ('The Face') designer, Neville Brody, the man applying his trade on 'LAST WORDS' and 'THE GOSPEL ACCORDING TO NEW GUINEA'. 1982's 'SEVEN SONGS' mini-set showed more diversity especially on opening tracks, 'KUNDALINI' and 'VEGAS EL BANDITO'. Drawing comparisons with CABARET VOLTAIRE and THROBBING GRISTLE, this percussive/industrial dub unit's originality lay in the use of ethnic African/Indonesian styles (samples/dialogue stemming from Kung Fu movies). During the following two years, they delivered another two studio sets, 'THE CULLING IS COMING' (1983) and the more stripped-down funk of 'URBAN GAMELAN' (1984). The latter featured ANDREW WEATHERALL (later of SABRES OF PARADISE), in one of his earliest vinyl appearances, however, barring a few further EP's (including 1986's 'ASSASSINS OF SOUL'), it was sadly to be their last work.

Album rating: SEVEN SONGS mini (*5) / THE CULLING IS COMING (*5) / URBAN GAMELAN (*7)

J.C.M. (JOHNNY) TURNBULL – guitar, congas, percussion / **A. LIM (ALEX TURNBULL)** – bass, percussion / **FRITZ HAAMAN** – drums, percussion / early members **SAM + TOM**

Pineapple not iss.

Jul 81. (7") *(PULP 23)* **ETHICS. / ANOTHER BABY'S FACE** [ ] [-]

Fetish not iss.

Sep 81. (7"promo) *(FE 10)* **LAST WORDS. / VERSION** [-] [-]

Oct 81. (12"m) *(FE 11)* **THE GOSPEL COMES TO NEW GUINEA. / LAST WORDS** [ ] [-]

Feb 82. (m-lp) *(FM 2008)* **SEVEN SONGS** [ ] [-]
– Kundalini / Vegas el bandito / Mary's operation / Lock groove / New testament IV / Porno base / Quiet pillage. *(re-iss. Feb85 on 'Illuminated'; JAMS 47)*

May 82. (12"m) *(FP 20)* **TEARING UP THE PLANS. / JUST LIKE EVERYBODY / GREGOUKA** [ ] [-]

— added **DAVID TIBET** – instruments (of PSYCHIC TV)

Operation Twilight not iss.

Feb 83. (lp) *(OPT 23)* **THE CULLING IS COMING** [ ] [-]
– Banishing / Invocation / Flashing / Stifling / Healing / 9-2 contemplation / S-matrix / 9-3 insemination / Shrine / Mahakala. *(re-iss. Nov88 on 'Laylah'; LAY 23) (cd-iss. Apr90; LAY 23CD)*

— added **MR. SKETCH** – bass, samples

Illuminated not iss.

Nov 83. (12") *(ILL 28-12)* **COUP. / VERSION (IN THE PALACE)** [ ] [-]

May 84. (12") *(ILL 38-12)* **LANGUAGE. / ('A'version)** [ ] [-]

Jul 84. (lp) *(JAMS 40)* **URBAN GAMELAN** [ ] [-]
– Fuck you G.I. (23 F.P.M.) / Fire / Misr wakening / Jalan Jalan / Urban gamelan / Sirens / Helicopters / Kongo-do / Language dub / Drunken reprisal / Coup de grace.

Mar 85. (12") *(ILL 58-12)* **OOZE. / ('A'version)** [ ] [-]

— early '86, 'GI (AMERICAN EPILOGUE)' was on b-side of 400 BLOWS single

Aug 86. (12"ep) *(12LEV 72)* **ASSASSINS OF SOUL** [ ] [-]
– T.O.Y. (Thoughts Of You) / Assassin / Ooze.

— disbanded after above. TIBET was already part of PSYCHIC TV and he soon joined DEATH IN JUNE and others NURSE WITH WOUND, etc. Some members became BAHALA-NA GANG, who released in 1990 a version of ISLEY BROTHERS' 'Summer Breeze' for 'Ronin' label. FRITZ and SAM were also part of LAST FEW DAYS.

– compilations, etc. –

Apr 87. (lp) *Bleeding Chin; (BC 1)* **JUST LIKE EVERYBODY** [ ] [-]
– Kundalini / Vegas el bandito / I.Y. / Just like everybody / Assassin / Coup / Urban gamelan act 1 / Congo do / Language dub / Drunkards reprise / Shrine / Porno base.

22 PISTEPIRKKO

Formed: North Finland . . . late 70's by P-K KERANEN, his brother ASKO KERANEN and ESPE HAVERINEN. Naming themselves after a type of beetle, they won Helsinki's Battle Of The Bands in '82, quickly spreading their unique RAMONES-meets-CAPTAIN BEEFHEART style. The trio released their first single in '85, finally getting around to a full set of tracks on their 1987 debut, 'THE KINGS OF HONG KONG'. A second album, 'BARE BONE NEST', fused a varied mix'n'match batch of genres, while three years on, their dark and moody major label debut, 'BIG LUPU', now fused A-HA vocals with SMASHING PUMPKINS or VELVET UNDERGROUND. Another lengthy break ensued, until 1996's trip-hop and dub attempt, 'RUMBLE CITY LA LA LAND', failed to achieve its goal.

Album rating: THE KINGS OF HONG KONG (*6) / BARE BONE NEST (*6) / BIG LUPU (*6) / RUMBLE CITY, LA LA LAND (*5) / ELEVEN (*7)

P-K KERANEN – vocals, guitar / **ASKO KERANEN** – bass, keyboards / **SEPE HAVERINEN** – drums, vocals

Pygmi not iss.

1988. (lp) **THE KINGS OF HONG KONG** [-] [-] Finland

Sonet not iss.

Oct 90. (cd) *(SNTCD 1007)* **BARE BONE NEST** [ ] [-]

Sep 91. (m-lp) *(SONL 22)* **22 PISTERPIRKKO** [ ] [-]

Spirit – Polygram not iss.

1992. (cd) **BIG LUPU** [-] [-] Finland

Bare Bone Business not iss.

Mar 96. (cd) *(BBBCD 002)* **RUMBLE CITY, LA LA LAND** [ ] [-]
– Wild Billy / Oo my head / (Just a) Little bit more / Tokyo tiger / Snowy Dave / At the everybody's / I never said / I do do I / Gimme some water / Blue balloon / Nappy king blues / Coffee girl.

Clearspot Clearspot

Oct 98. (cd/lp) *(efa 05409-2/-1) <019>* **ELEVEN** [ ] [ ]
– Taxi 74 / Onion soup / Coma moon / Sad lake city / Boardroom walk / Hey man / Let the Romeo weep / Morning / Frustration / Shadows.

Nov 98. (cd-s) *(efacd 05449) <021>* **ONION SOUP / MILES & NEMO / ROMEO INSTRUMENTAL** [ ] [ ]

TWINKEYZ

Formed: Sacramento, California, USA . . . 1976 by DONNIE JUPITER, KEITH McKEE, TOM DARLING and vocalist HONEY. One of California's first punk-influenced acts, the TWINKEYZ made their debut in 1977 with a single, 'ALIENS IN OUR MIDST', on the tiny 'Grok' label. Bizarrely enough, the band gained a foothold on continental Europe, where Dutch label, 'Plurex', released their one and only album, 'ALPHA JERK'. While the latter was available in the UK, a final single, 'WATCH OUT FOR HER KISS' was released exclusively onto the Dutch market in 1980 prior to the band's final split.

Album rating: ALPHA JERK (*5)

DONNIE JUPITER – vocals, rhythm guitar / **HONEY** – vocals, bass, guitar / **TOM DARLING** – lead guitar, bass, vocals / **KEITH McKEE** – drums, vocals

not iss. Grok

1977. (7"white) <1.00> **ALIENS IN OUR MIDST. / ONE THOUSAND REASONS** [-] [ ]

1978. (7"opalescent) <2.00> **E.S.P. / CARTOON LAND** [-] [ ]

Plurex not iss.

Aug 79. (lp) *(1000)* **ALPHA JERK** [-] [-] Dutch
– Aliens in our midst / Tonight again / Sweet nothing / 1000 reasons / Cartton land / E.S.P. / Twinkeyz theme / That's the way it goes / Alpha jerk / Strange feeling / Wild love.

Oct 80. (7") *(0019)* **WATCH OUT FOR HER KISS. /** [-] [-] Dutch

— after they split, DARLING joined The VEIL (and later GAME THEORY)

TWO NICE GIRLS

Formed: Austin, Texas, USA . . . 1989 by er, actually three nice girls, GRETCHEN PHILLIPS, KATHY KORNILOFF and LAURIE FREELOVE. Signed to 'Rough Trade', this rootsy singing/songwriting-based outfit impressed many critics with their 1989 eponymous debut album, the girls taking a democratic approach to both scripting their songs and performing them; a nod towards their guiding influences, the track 'SWEET JANE (WITH AFFECTION)' was a clever coupling of The Velvet Underground classic and Joan Armatrading's 'Love And Affection'. The turn of the decade saw FREELOVE depart for a solo career (she released the 'SMELLS LIKE TRUTH' album on 'Ensign' in 1991), replacements MEG HENTGES and PAM BARGER making for a fuller, if more cluttered sound on 1991's swansong, 'CHLOE LIKED OLIVIA' (1991).

Album rating: TWO NICE GIRLS (*5) / LIKE A VERSION mini (84) / CHLOE LIKED OLIVIA (*4)

LAURIE FREELOVE – vocals, guitar / **GRETCHEN PHILLIPS** – vocals, mandolin, bass, guitar / **KATHY KORNILOFF** – vocals, guitar, synthesizer / with a plethora of session people

Rough Trade Rough Trade

Jun 89. (lp/c/cd) *(ROUGH/+C/CD 135)* <ROUGHUS 59> **TWO NICE GIRLS** [ ] [ ]
– The sweet postcard / Follow me / Goons / Money / I spent my last $10.00 (on birth control and beer) / Sweet Jane (with affection) / My heart crawls off / Looking out / Heaven on Earth / Kick.

— **MEG HENTGES** – vocals, bass, guitar, piano + **PAM BARGER** – drums, vocals, percussion; repl. FREELOVE who issueed her own solo album, 'SMELLS LIKE TRUTH', for 'Ensign' in 1991

Apr 90. (m-lp/m-cd) *(RTM 235/+CD)* **LIKE A VERSION** [ ] [ ]
– I feel (like makin') love / Bang bang / Top of the world / Speed racer / Cotton crown / I spent my last $10.00 (on birth control and beer).

1991. (lp) **CHLOE LIKED OLIVIA** [-] [ ]

— not surpringly they split after above

UK DECAY

Formed: Luton, Bedfordshire, England . . . 1978 out of The RESISTORS by JOHN ABBOT aka ABBO, MARTYN SMITH aka SEGOVIA and STEVE HARLE. Adopting the UK DECAY moniker at the turn of the decade, the band's first release under the new name came via a limited edition split EP with fellow Luton band, PNEU-MANIA. Further changes came with the recruitment of the latter's guitarist, STEVE SPON, bolstering the sound on early 1980's 'THE BLACK CAT' EP. By this point the group had become one of the prime movers in the fermenting goth scene, the serrated punk, vaguely P.I.L. feel of the music making up for the horsemen-of-the-apocalypse vocals and cod-occult lyrics of tracks like 'SHATTERED' and 'LAST IN THE HOUSE OF FLAMES'. The latter two were featured on the long awaited debut album, 'FOR MADMEN ONLY' (1981), followed up by the 'RISING FROM THE DREAD' EP a year later. Yet even as the band were enjoying indie chart success and the loyal attentions of flour-faced fans, they played their last gig in late '82 – released the following year as 'A NIGHT FOR CELEBRATION' – with SPON going on to form goth outfit IN EXCELSIS and the remaining members carrying on as FURYO.

Album rating: FOR MADMEN ONLY (*6)

ABBO (b. JOHN ABBOTT) – vocals, guitar / **SEGOVIA** (b. MARTYN SMITH) – bass / **STEVE HARLE** – drums

Plastic / not iss.

1979. (7"ep) *(PLAS 001)* **UK DECAY / CARCRASH. / (PNEU-MANIA:- Exhibition / Coming Attack)** [ ] [-]

—— added **STEVE SPON** – guitar, piano (ex-PNEU-MANIA)

Feb 80. (7"ep) *(PLAS 002)* **THE BLACK CAT EP** [ ] [-]
– Black cat / Middle of the road man / Message distortion / Disco romance. *(re-iss. Oct81; same)*

Fresh / not iss.

Sep 80. (7") *(FRESH 12)* **FOR MY COUNTRY. / UNWIND TONIGHT** [ ] [-]
(re-iss. 1982 on 'UK Decay')

Feb 81. (7") *(FRESH 26)* **UNEXPECTED GUEST. / DRESDEN** [ ] [-]
(re-iss. 1982 on 'UK Decay')

Oct 81. (7") *(FRESH 33)* **SEXUAL. / TWIST IN THE TALE** [ ] [-]

Oct 81. (lp) *(FRESHLP 5)* **FOR MADMEN ONLY** [ ] [-]
– Duel / Battle of the elements / Shattered / Stage struck / Last in the house of flames / Unexpected guest / Sexual / Dorian / Decadence / Mayday malady / For madmen only.

—— **TWIGGY** – bass; repl. SEGOVIA

—— **EDDIE BRANCH** – bass; repl. TWIGGY

Corpus Christi / not iss.

Aug 82. (12"ep) *(CHRIST ITS 1)* **RISING FROM THE (D)READ / TESTAMENT. / WEREWOLF / JERUSALEM OVER (THE WHITE CLIFFS OF DOVER)** [ ] [-]

—— split but left behind below cassette

UK Decay / not iss.

Aug 83. (c) *(DK 6)* **A NIGHT FOR CELEBRATION** (last gig) [ ] [-]
– Unwind / Werewolf / Dresden / Barbarian / Barbarians / Sexual / Stage struck / Rising from the dead / Twist in the tale / Unexpected guest / Testament / Black cat / UK Decay / For my country / Unwind.

—— SPON joined IN EXCELSIS with ex-RITUAL members

FURYO

—— stemmed from MEAT OF YOUTH who appeared on 'The BATCAVE' various artists album.

ABBO / STEVE HARLE / EDDIE BRANCH + ALBIE DE LUCA – guitar

Anagram / not iss.

Apr 84. (m-lp) *(MGRAM 12)* **FURYO** [ ] [-]
– The gold of our lives / Vultures / In the arena / Monster of a thousand heads / The opera in the air.

Oct 84. (12") *(12ANA 24)* **LEGACY (ANDANTE). / KING OF HEARTS / CAVALCADE** [ ] [-]

—— ABBO later found and aided EMF.

UKRAINIANS

Formed: Leeds, England . . . initially as a sideline for The WEDDING PRESENT (PETER SOLOWKA's father handed down the tradition of playing the mandolin and balalaika) on a series of John Peel sessions (released as 'UKRAINSKI VISTUPI V JOHNA PEELA' in the Spring of '89). A few years later, after he parted company with DAVID GEDGE & co., PETER formed The UKRAINIANS with other like-minded traditionalists, lyricist LEN LIGGINS and ROMAN REMEYNES. Signed to top roots label, 'Cooking Vinyl', the group unveiled their eponymous debut album in Autumn '91, turning their their impressively authentic Eastern European folk style to The SMITHS. Yes, The SMITHS (!), LIGGINS sounding too close to MORRISSEY for comfort on the likes of 'BATYAR' (i.e. 'Bigmouth Strikes Again') and 'KOROLEVA NE POLERMA' ('The Queen Is Dead'), the 'PISNI IZ THE SMITHS' EP possibly proving that there's alwyas been an er . . . Balkans element to The SMITHS' sound. Following the replacement of REMEYNES with STEPAN PASICZNYK, The UKRAINIANS released a follow-up set, 'VORONY' (1993), this time turning their dolorous charm to a reading of the Velvet Underground's 'VENUS IN FURS' (under the guise of 'CHEKAAANYA'). 1994's 'KULTURA', meanwhile, was a rockier affair (courtesy of mew members DAVE LEE, PAUL DINO and MICHAEL L.B. WEST) combining breakneck stompalongs like 'EUROPA' with more easy going fare in the vein of the countrified 'HORILKA'. Nigh on four years passed before the band inflicted the self explanatory 'PRINCE' EP on an unsuspecting public, SOLOWKA and his minstrels lending a measure of threadbare austerity to the lavish creations of the artist formerly known as.

Album rating: THE UKRAINIANS (*5) / VORONY (*5) / KULTURA (*5)

THE 'Legendary' LEN LIGGINS (b. London, England) – vocals, violin (ex-SINISTER CLEANERS) / **PETER SOLOWKA** – guitars, mandolin, vocals (ex-WEDDING PRESENT) / **ROMAN REMEYNES** – accordion, vocals

Cooking Vinyl / Omnium

Sep 91. (cd/c) *(COOK CD/C 044)* <2002> **THE UKRAINIANS** [ ] [ ]
– Oi divchino / Hopak / Ti moyi radoshchi / Zavtra / Slava kobzarya / Dity plachut / Cherez richku, cherez hal / Pereyidu / Tebe zhdu / Son.

—— **STEPAN PASICZNYK** – accordion, vocals; repl. ROMAN

Jan 93. (cd-ep) *(FRYCD 023)* **PISNI IZ THE SMITHS** [ ] [-]
– Batyar (Bigmouth strikes again) / Koroleva ne Polerma (The Queen is dead) / M'yaso – Ubivstvo (Meat is murder) / Spivaye solovey (What difference does it make?).

Cooking Vinyl / Xenophile

Feb 93. (cd/c) *(COOK CD/C 054)* <4015> **VORONY** [ ] [ ]
– Vorony / Koroleva ne Polerma (The Queen is dead) / Chi skriptsi hrayu / Sche raz / Nadia pishla / Doroha / Rospryahaite / Durak / Sertsem i dusheyu / Dvi lebidky / De ye moya mila? / Teper mi hovorymo / Chekannya (Venus in furs).

—— now with also **DAVE LEE** – drums / **PAUL DINO** – Briggs bass guitar / **MICHAEL L.B. WEST** – mandolin, duda, piano

Cooking Vinyl / Cooking Vinyl

Sep 94. (cd) *(<COOKCD 070>)* **KULTURA** [ ] [ ]
– Polityka / UkrainAmerica / Kievskiy express / Smert / Horilka / Slava / Europa / Kinets / Tycha voda / Zillya zelenenke / Ya / Tsyhanochka / Dyakuyu i dobranich.

—— little was heard from them for just under 4 years

Aug 98. (cd-ep) *(FRYCD 071)* **PRINCE E.P.** [ ] [-]
– Nothing compares 2 U / Sign 'o' the times / Purple rain.

UK SUBS

Formed: London, England . . . Spring '76 by former R&B singer CHARLIE HARPER and guitarist NICKY GARRETT. This hardy punk outfit – completed by PAUL SLACK and PETE DAVIS – made their vinyl debut in early '78 on the various artists lp, 'Farewell To The Roxy' before issuing a debut single on the small 'City' label. Although the band arrived a bit late for the punk party, their subsequent signing to R.C.A. subsidiary, 'Gem', resulted in a string of minor hit singles beginning with the frantic three-chord stomp of 'STRANGLEHOLD' in summer '79. Along with the excellent 'TOMORROW'S GIRLS', the track was featured on debut album, 'ANOTHER KIND OF BLUES' (1979), an amphetamine-fuelled collection of simple but effective hooklines and RAMONES-style lyrics. The following month saw the release of an EP with an unlikely cover of The Zombies' 'SHE'S NOT THERE' as the lead track, the busy schedule continuing apace with the classic 'WARHEAD' single early in 1980. 'BRAND NEW AGE' hit the Top 20 later that year, although its success was outstripped by seminal live set, 'CRASH COURSE'; while the UK SUBS were perhaps a second division outfit in the shadow of The CLASH etc., there was no doubting their onstage power and formidable aura of HARPER in full flight. The record made the Top 10, an all-time best that the 'SUBS would struggle to emulate as their commercial fortunes began to wane in the early 80's. Personnel upheavals dogged the band, SLACK and DAVIS replaced by ALVIN GIBBS and STEVE ROBERTS prior to the band's last charting album, 'DIMINISHED RESPONSIBILITY' (1981). The subsequent departure of co-songwriter GARRETT dealt a blow that the UK SUBS never really recovered from, HARPER continuing to release workmanlike albums such as 'FLOOD OF LIES' (1983) and 'HUNTINGTON BEACH' (1985) to an ever diminishing core of fans. At the dawn of the 90's HARPER was still fronting the latest incarnation of the UK SUBS, 'MAD COW FEVER's hackneyed collection of pub-rock favourites a far cry from the band's late 70's heyday. • **Covered:** SHE'S NOT THERE (Zombies) / I'M WAITING FOR THE MAN (Velvet Underground) / I WALKED WITH A ZOMBIE (13th Floor Elevators) / ROUTE '66 (hit; Nelson Riddle) / BABY PLEASE DON'T GO (hit; Them). • **Trivia:** HARPER had also been part of garage-influenced URBAN DOGS between 1983-85.

Album rating: ANOTHER KIND OF BLUES (*5) / BRAND NEW AGE (*5) / CRASH COURSE (*6) / DIMINISHED RESPONSIBILTY (*5) / DANGEROUS SPECIES (*4) / FLOOD OF LIES (*3) / SCUM OF THE EARTH – THE BEST OF . . . compilation (*6)

CHARLIE HARPER (b. DAVID CHARLES PEREZ, 25 Apr'44) – vocals, rhythm guitar / **NICKY GARRETT** – lead guitar / **PAUL SLACK** – bass / **PETE DAVIS** – drums

City — not iss.

Dec 78. (7"clear,7"blue,7"green,7"orange,7"red) *(NIK 5)* **C.I.D. / I LIVE IN A CAR / B.I.C.** –
(re-iss. Oct79 on 'Pinnacle'; PIN 22)

Gem-RCA — R.C.A.

Jun 79. (7"red) *(GEMS 5)* **STRANGLEHOLD. / WORLD WAR / ROCKERS** 26 –

Aug 79. (7"blue) *(GEMS 10)* <PB 11766> **TOMORROW'S GIRLS. / SCUM OF THE HEART / TELEPHONE NUMBERS** 28

Oct 79. (blue-lp) *(GEMLP 100)* **ANOTHER KIND OF BLUES** 21
– C.I.D. / I couldn't be you / I live in a car / Tomorrow's girl / Killer / World war / Rockers / I.O.D. / T.V. blues / Lady Esquire / All I wanna know / Crash course / Young criminals / B.I.C. / Disease / Stranglehold. *(re-iss. Sep91 on 'Abstract' cd/c; AAB CD/TC 801) (cd-iss. Jul95 on 'Dojo'; DOJOCD 226) (cd re-iss. + Jul98 on 'Diabolo'; DIAB 86-2)*

Nov 79. (7"green-ep) *(GEMS 14)* **SHE'S NOT THERE / KICKS. / VICTIM / THE SAME THING** 36 –

Feb 80. (7"brown) *(GEMS 23)* **WARHEAD. / I'M WAITING FOR THE MAN / THE HARPER** 30 –

Apr 80. (clear-lp) *(GEMLP 106)* **BRAND NEW AGE** 18 –
– You can't take it anymore / Brand new age / Public servant / Warhead / Barbie's dead / Organised crime / Rat race / Emotional blackmail / Kicks / Teenage / Dirty girls / 500 c.c. / Bomb factory. *(re-iss. Sep91 on 'Abstract' cd/c; AAB CD/TC 802) (cd-iss. Jul95 on 'Dojo'; DOJOCD 228)*

May 80. (7"pink,7"orange) *(GEMS 30)* **TEENAGE. / LEFT FOR DEAD / NEW YORK STATE POLICE** 32 –

Sep 80. (purple-lp) *(GEMLP 111)* **CRASH COURSE (live)** 8 –
– C.I.D. / I couldn't be you / I live in a car / Tomorrow's girl / Left for dead / Kicks / Rat race / New York state police / Warhead / Public servant / Telephone numbers / Organised crime / Rockers / Brand new age / Dirty girls / The same thing / Crash course / Teenage / Killer / Emotional blackmail. *(w/ free-12") (re-iss. Sep91 on 'Abstract' cd/c; AAB CD/TC 803) (cd-iss. Jul95 on 'Dojo'; DOJOCD 229)*

— **ALVIN GIBBS** – bass (ex-USERS, ex-HELLIONS) repl. SLACK — **STEVE ROBERTS** – drums; repl. DAVIS

Oct 80. (7"yellow) *(GEMS 42)* **PARTY IN PARIS. / FALL OF THE EMPIRE** 37 –

Feb 81. (red-lp) *(GEMLP 112)* **DIMINISHED RESPONSIBILITY** 18 –
– You don't belong / So what / Confrontation / Fatal / Time and matter / Violent city / Too tired / Party in Paris / Gangster / Face the machine / New order / Just another jungle / Collision cult. *(re-iss. Sep91 on 'Abstract' cd/c; AAB CD/TC 804) (cd-iss. Jul95 on 'Dojo'; DOJOCD 232)*

Apr 81. (7"blue) *(GEMS 45)* **KEEP ON RUNNIN' (TILL YOU BURN). / PERFECT GIRL** 41 –
(7"ep+=) **KEEP RUNNIN' EP** *(GEMEP 45)* – Ice age / Party in Paris (French version).

NEMS — not iss.

Nov 81. (7") *(NES 304)* **COUNTDOWN. / PLAN OF ACTION** –

— **KIM WYLIE** – drums; repl. ROBERTS who joined CYANIDE then LIGOTAGE

Abstract — not iss.

Oct 82. (7"red-ep) *(ABS 012)* **SHAKE UP THE CITY** –
– Self destruct / Police state / War of the roses.

Oct 82. (red-lp) **ENDANGERED SPECIES** –
– Endangered species / Living dead / Countdown / Ambition / Fear of girls / Lay down and die / Down on the farm / Sensitive boys / Divide by 8, multiply by 5 / Ice age / I robot / Flesh wound. *(re-iss. Jun90 on 'Link'; CLINK 4)*

— **CHARLIE HARPER** recruited entire new band **CAPTAIN SCARLET** – guitar repl. GARRETT who formed REBEKKA FRAME / **PAUL SLACK** – bass returned to repl. GIBBS who joined URBAN DOGS / **STEVE JONES** – drums repl. WYLIE

Fall Out — not iss.

Aug 83. (7") *(FALL 017)* **ANOTHER TYPICAL CITY. / STILL LIFE** –
(12"+=) *(FALL12 017)* – Veronique.

Oct 83. (lp/c) *(FALL LP/CLP 018)* **FLOOD OF LIES** –
– Flood of lies / Veronique / Soldiers of fortune / Db's / Tampa Bay / After the war / Vilent revolution / In the red / Dress code / Still life / Revenge of the yellow devils / Another typical city / In the wild / Seas. *(cd-iss. 1995; FALLCD 018)*

Sep 84. (12"ep) *(FALL12 024)* **MAGIC / PRIVATE ARMY. / THE SPELL / MULTIPLE MINDS / PRIMARY STRENGTH** –

— **HARPER** again + new members **JOHN FALLON** – guitar / **JEZZ MONCUR** – bass / **RAB FAE BEITH** – drums (ex-WALL, ex-PATRIK FITZGERALD)

Jan 85. (lp) *(FALLLP 031)* **GROSS OUT U.S.A. (live)** –
– Intro / Emotional blackmail / New barbarians / In the wild / Veronique / Flood of lies / Warhead / Limo life / Disease / Violent revolution / Soldiers of fortune / Ice-age / Dress code / Telephone numbers / Stranglehold / You don't belong / Party in Paris. *(cd-iss. 1995; FALLCD 031)*

Jun 85. (7"red,7"blue) *(FALL 036)* **THIS GUN SAYS. / SPEAK FOR MYSELF / WANTED** –

Red Flame — not iss.

Dec 85. (lp/c) *(RFB LP/CA 1)* **HUNTINGTON BEACH** –
– Rock'n'roll savage / Between the eyes / Suicide taxi / Party animal / The unknown / Miss Tennage USA / Huntington / All the king's horses / Juke box / Sk8 tough / Death row / Bullshitter / Dirty boy / All change for Hollywood / Blinding stories. *(re-iss. Jun90 on 'FM-Revolver' cd/c/lp; REV XD/MC/LP 150)*

Apr 86. (7"ep) *(RFBSIN 1)* **LIVE IN HOLLAND – TENTH ANNIVERSARY (live)** –
– Stranglehold / New barbarians / Tomorrow's girls / Between the eyes.

Apr 86. (lp/c) *(RFB LP/CA 2)* **IN ACTION (10 YEARS)** –
(re-iss. Mar90 on 'FM-Revolver' cd/c/lp; REV XD/MC/LP 142)

Fall Out — New Red Archives

Dec 87. (12") *(FALL12 044)* **HEY SANTA (LEAVE THESE KIDS ALONE). / THUNDERBIRD** –

Dec 87. (lp) *(FALLLP 045)* **JAPAN TODAY (live)** –
– Another Cuba / Funk rap / Streets on fire / Sex object / Warzone / Japan inc. / (interview) / Comin' back / Thunderbird / Hey! Santa / Street legal / Captain Scarlett / Skateboard Billy / Surf bastard / Angel. *(cd-iss. Apr93; FALLCD 045)*

Mar 89. (lp/c/cd) *(FALL LP/C/CD 047)* <06> **KILLING TIME** (reunion album)
– Yellowman / Motivator / Lower East Side / Drag me down / Never say you won't / Magalopolis / Planet I / Killing time / Holy land / American motors / Big Apple / Killing with kindness / Sabre dance / No heart / Fear to go / Nico. *(cd has extra tracks)*

— latest UK SUBS alongside **HARPER** were **ALAN LEE** – guitar / **FLEA DAVE FARRELLY** – bass / **MATTHEW McCOY** – drums

— **DARRELL BARTH** – guitar; repl. LEE

Released Emotions — not iss.

Feb 89. (12"ep) *(REM 004)* **THE MOTIVATOR / COMBAT ZONE / FASCIST REGIME. / AULD LANG SYNE / CYCLE SLUTS FROM HELL** –

Fall Out — Amsterdamned

Feb 91. (cd/c/lp) *(FALL CD/C/LP 048)* **MAD COW FEVER** –
– I walked with a zombie / Mandarins of change / Boneyard / Welfare mother / Saints and sinners / Pearl divers / Roadhouse blues / Talkin' 'bout you / Road runner / Route '66 / Pills / Baby please don't go / Last bus boogie / Ecology blues.

— **DAVIS + CAMPBELL** repl. LEE + FARRELLY

Sep 93. (cd/lp) *(FALL CD/LP 050)* **NORMAL SERVICE RESUMED** –
– Dumfux / Killer time / Jodie Foster / Here comes Alex / Ozone death / Strangeways / Joyride / Believe in yourself / Down on the farm / Mohawk radio / Brixton / Reaper / All the people / Squat the world / Lydia.

Nov 93. (7"ep/cd-ep) *(FALL 051/+CD)* **THE ROAD IS HARD, THE ROAD IS LONG EP** –
– Jodie Foster / Here comes Alex / Killer time / Another Cuba / Lydia.

Apr 96. (cd/lp) *(FALL CD/LP 052)* <5> **OCCUPIED** Mar97
– Let's get drunk / Shove it / DF 118 / Solutions / Public address / Revolving boys / One of the girls / Darkness / Not so secret wars / Infidel / MPRI.

Fall Out — New Red Archives

Apr 97. (cd/lp) *(FALL CD/LP 054)* <69> **QUINTESSENTIALS** May97
– Jump on it / Your ego / War on the Pentagon (parts 1 & 2) / Quintessentials / State of alert / The day of the dead / AK47 / Media man / Mouth on a stick / Outside society / Bitter and twisted / Accident prone / Killer cops / Psychosis.

Apr 98. (7"red) *(FALL 056)* **RIOT '98. /** –

– compilations, etc. –

Jun 82. (c-ep) *Chaos; (LIVE 009)* **LIVE AT GOSSIPS (live)** –
Oct 82. (blue-lp) *Abstract; (AABT 300)* **RECORDED '79-'81** –
Apr 84. (lp/c) *Mausoleum; (AMOK/KOMA 788005)* **DEMONSTRATION TAPES** (rare demos) –
Apr 86. (lp) *Dojo; (DOJOLP 28)* **SUB STANDARDS** –
Jun 86. (c) *R.O.I.R.; (A 142)* **LEFT FOR DEAD (ALIVE IN HOLLYWOOD)** –
(cd-iss. Nov94; RE 412CD)
Jul 86. (lp) *Killerwatt; (KILP 2001)* **RAW MATERIAL** –
Apr 90. (lp) *Released Emotions;* **GREATEST HITS (LIVE IN PARIS)** –
(cd-iss. Jun93 on 'Dojo'; DOJOCD 130)
May 91. (blue-lp) *Abstract; (AABT 800)* **THE SINGLES 1978-1982** –
(cd-iss. Apr93 on 'Get Back'; GBR 001)
Dec 91. (cd) *Streetlink; (STRCD 017)* **DOWN ON THE FARM (A COLLECTION OF THE LESS OBVIOUS)** –
(re-iss. Apr93 on 'Dojo'; DOJOCD 117)
Mar 92. (cd) *Released Emotions; (REM 012CD)* **EUROPE CALLING** –
(re-iss. Jul98 on 'Pinhead'; PINCD 101)
May 93. (cd) *Get Back; (BGR 002)* **ANOTHER KIND OF BLUES / CRASH COURSE** –
May 93. (cd) *Get Back; (BGR 003)* **BRAND NEW AGE / DIMINISHED RESPONSIBILITY** –
Jun 93. (cd/c) *Optima; (OPTM CD/C 016)* **PUNK AND DISORDERLY** –
Jul 93. (cd/lp) *Receiver; (RRCD/RRLP 146)* **LIVE AT THE ROXY (live)** –
Aug 93. (cd/c) *Music Club; (MCCD/MCTC 120)* **SCUM OF THE EARTH – THE BEST OF THE UK SUBS** –
Feb 94. (cd) *Loma; (LOMACD 7)* **ENDANGERED SPECIES / HUNTINGTON BEACH** –
May 95. (cd) *C.A.S.; (CD 43000-2)* **THE PUNK IS BACK** –
Sep 95. (cd) *Anagram; (CDPUNK 66)* **THE PUNK SINGLES COLLECTION** –
Jul 96. (cd) *Cleopatra; (CLP 97032)* **PUNK CAN TAKE IT** –
Oct 96. (cd) *Cleopatra; (CLP 9826)* **SELF DESTRUCT: PUNK CAN TAKE IT VOL.2** –
Nov 96. (4xcd-box) *Abstract; (SUBBOX 1)* **UK SUBS BOX SET** –
Mar 97. (cd/lp) *Fallout; (FALL CD/LP 53)* **THE PEEL SESSIONS (1978-1979)** –
Jun 97. (cd) *Anagram; (CDMGRAM 113) / Cleopatra; <9929>* **RIOT** Mar97

CHARLIE HARPER

Gem — not iss.

Jul 80. (7") *(GEMS 35)* **BARMY LONDON ARMY. / TALK IS CHEAP** 68 –

Ramkup — not iss.

Jul 81. (7") *(CAC 005)* **FREAKED. / JO** –

Flicknife — not iss.

Feb 82. (lp) *(SHARP 100)* **STOLEN PROPERTY** [ ] [-]
– Hoochie coochie man / Femme fatale / Hey Joe / Louie Louie / Pills / Light my fire / I'm waiting for the man / etc.

Fall Out — not iss.

Nov 82. (7"; CHARLIE HARPER'S URBAN DOGS) *(FALL 008)* **NEW BARBARIANS. / SPEED KILLS / COCAINE** [ ] [-]

Mar 83. (7"; CHARLIE HARPER'S URBAN DOGS) *(FALL 011)* **LIMO LIFE. / WARHEAD** [ ] [-]

ULTRAMARINE

Formed: Chelmsford, Essex, England . . . 1984 as A PRIMARY INDUSTRY, an avant-garde noise-merchant troupe formed by IAN COOPER and PAUL HAMMOND, alongside other musicians, JEMMA, GUY and SIMON. In the early 90's, IAN and PAUL became ULTRAMARINE after basing themselves in Leamington Spa. The duo were showered with praise during 1992 after the release of their album, 'EVERY MAN AND WOMAN IS A STAR', a trip into left field Balearic territory complete with distinctive fairground organ and samples. Just prior to this, they had taken a canoe trip with AMERICA's (the band, that is) organist, DEWEY BUNNELL. In the Autumn of '93, they managed to scrape into the UK Top 50 with the SOFT MACHINE/KEVIN AYERS-influenced 'UNITED KINGDOMS' album, which featured veteran Canterbury legend, ROBERT WYATT. They took another about turn in 1995, with the release of the uninspiring US West Coast type album, 'BEL AIR'. • **Songwriters:** Group except HEART OF GLASS (Blondie) / HYMN (Kevin Ayers). • **Trivia:** Another group (foreign?) named ULTRAMARINE issued 2 albums 'DE' & 'E SI MALA' 1990-1993.

Album rating: EVERY MAN AND WOMAN IS A STAR (*8) / UNITED KINGDOMS (*8)

A PRIMARY INDUSTRY

IAN COOPER – acoustic guitar, keyboards, prog. / **PAUL HAMMOND** – bass, keyboards, programming / **JEMMA MELLERIO** – vocals / **GUY** – keyboards / **SIMON HAMMOND** – drums

Les Tempes Modernes — not iss.

Nov 84. (7") *(CSBTV:V)* **AT GUNPOINT. / PERVERSION** [ ] [-]
(re-iss. Feb86 on 'N.I.S.S.' 12"; C88TV)

Sweatbox — not iss.

Nov 85. (12"ep) *(SOX 007)* **7 HERTZ** [ ] [-]
– Cicatrice / Obeah / Biting back / Bled dry.

Oct 86. (lp) *(SAX 015)* **ULTRAMARINE** [ ] [-]
– Body blow / Beacon Hill / Shear / Sans orange / Cicatrice / Watchword weal / Gush / Raw umber / Silesia / Rose madder.

Jul 87. (7") *(OX 22)* **HEART OF GLASS. / WHERE IS YOUR VORTEX** [ ] [-]
(12") *(BOX 25)* – ('A'extended) / ('A'extended).

Mar 88. (m-lp) *(BOX 26)* **WYNDHAM LEWIS** [ ] [-]
– The liquid brown detestable Earth Fokker Bomb shit / The song of the militant romance / If so the man you are / End of enemy interlude / Merde alors!

— changed group name to . . .

ULTRAMARINE

— GUY replaced by **RICHARD HASLAM** – keyboards / **FRANK MICHIELS** – percussion / **STAF VERBEEK** – accordion

Sweatbox — not iss.

Jun 89. (m-lp) *(BOX 28)* **WYNDHAM LEWIS** [ ] [-]
– (the re-issue of A PRIMARY INDUSTRY m-lp)

Crepuscule — not iss.

Mar 90. (lp/cd) *(TWI 894/+CD)* **FOLK** [ ] [-]
– Lobster / Antiseptic / Bronze eye / Bastard folk / Bullprong / Softspot / Vulgar streak / The golden target. *(re-iss. cd Nov94 on 'Offshore'+=; OSHCD 1)* – Stella / Interstellar.

Dancyclopaedia — not iss.

Sep 90. (12"ep) *(DAN 002)* **STELLA. / INTERSTELLAR / ULTRABASS (Eddy De Cierca mix)** [ ] [-]

— basically now duo of **IAN + PAUL**

Brainiak — Dali – Chameleon

May 91. (12") *(BAUBJ 11)* **STELLA CONNECTS. / STELLA BREATHS** [ ] [-]

Oct 91. (12"ep) *(BRAINK 019)* **WEIRD GEAR. / WEIRD GEAR (version) / BRITISH SUMMERTIME** [ ] [-]

Dec 91. (cd/m-lp) *(BRAIN KCD/MKLP 21)* <61443> **EVERY MAN AND WOMAN IS A STAR** [ ] [ ]
– Discovery / Weird gear / Pansy / Money / Stella / Geezer / Panther / British summertime / Lights in my brain / Canoe trip / Skyclad / Gravity. *(re iss. & re-mixed Jul92 on 'Rough Trade' cd)(lp+=; R 292)(RT 896)* – Nova Scotia / Saratoga.

Rough Trade — Dali – Chameleon

May 92. (7"ltd.) *(45REV 7)* **SARATOGA. / NOVA SCOTIA** [ ] [-]

Nov 92. (12"ep/cd-ep) *(R 294-0/-3)* <66324> **NIGHTFALL IN SWEETLEAF** [ ] [ ]
– Panther (Coco Steel remix) / Lights in my brain (Spooky mix) / Geezer (Sweet Exorcist mix).

Mar 93. (12"ep)(cd-ep) *(066324)(PRCD 8737)* **WEIRD GEAR (remix) / LIGHTS IN MY BRAIN (Spooky mix) / GEEZER (Sweet Exorcist mix) / PANTHER (Coco Steel & Lovebomb mix) / OUTRO** [-] [ ]

— now with **ROBERT WYATT** – vocals ('A'above) / **SIMON KAY** – Hammond organ / **JIMMY HASTINGS** – clarinet, flute, piccolo, sax / **JIM RATTIGAN** – accordion / **ROBERT ATCHISON** – violin / **PHIL JAMES** – trumpet, harmonica / **PAUL JOHNSON** – percussion

Blanco Y Negro — Unitary

Jul 93. (7"/c-s) *(NEG 65/+C)* **KINGDOM. / GOLDCREST** [46] [ ]
(12"/cd-s) *(NEG 65 T/CD)* – ('A'side) / ('B'extended) / ('A'extended mix).

Aug 93. (cd/c/lp) *(4509 93425-2/-4/-1)* **UNITED KINGDOMS** [49] [-]
– Source / Kingdom / Queen of the Moon / Prince Rock / Happy land / Urf / English heritage / Instant kitten / The badger / Hooter / Dizzy fox / No time. *(cd re-iss. Jan97; same)*

Jan 94. (c-ep/12"ep/cd-ep) *(NEG 67 C/T/CD)* **THE BAREFOOT EP** [61] [-]
– Hooter / The badger / Urf / Happy land.

Jan 95. (12"/c-s) *(NEG 76 T/C)* **HYMN. / HYMN (mix)** [ ] [-]
(cd-s+=) *(NEG 76CD1)* – Base element.
(cd-s+=) *(NEG 76CD2)* – ('A'mix).

Aug 95. (cd/c/clear-d-lp) *(0603 11206-2/-4/-1)* **BEL AIR** [ ] [-]
– Welcome / Buena vista / Maxine / Pioneer spirit / Mutant / Fantasy filter / 78 / I got sane / Schnaltz / Citizen / Alter ego / Free radical / Harmony Street / K-V / Escape velocity / Rainbow brew / Everyone in Brazil. *(cd re-iss. Jan97; same)*

Apr 96. (c-s; ULTRAMARINE featuring DAVID McALMONT) *(NEG 87C)* <76> **HYMN (David McAlmont mix) / HYMN (Kevin Ayers mix) / BASE ELEMENT** [65] [ ]
(cd-s+=) *(NEG 87CD1)* – (first & last track) / Our love / Love life.
(12") *(NEG 87T)* – Hymn (U-ziq mix) / Hymn (Luke Slater mix) / Our love / Love life.
(cd-s) *(NEG 87CD2)* – Hymn (U-ziq mix) / Hymn (Luke Slater mix) / Hymn (Paul Sampson's lullabye mix) / Hymn (Sugar J mix) / Hymn (Mouse On Mars: a sleep mix) / Hymn (Ultramarine & Kevin Ayers version).

New Electronica — not iss.

Jan 98. (12") *(ELEC 34T)* **ON THE BRINK. / SURFACING / 4U (mix)** [ ] [-]

Feb 98. (cd) **A USER'S GUIDE** [ ] [-]

ULTRASOUND

Formed: Newcastle, England . . . early 90's by the bulky (ex-POSSESSION) singer, TINY and guitarist RICHARD GREEN, whom he had met at a music course at Wakefield College. The pair decided to form wacky CARDIACS-induced outfit, SLEEPY PEOPLE, adding drummer ANDY PEACE in the process. Relocating to London (Acton, actually), they added VANESSA BEST on bass and MATT JONES on keyboards, although times were tough playing gigs for next to nothing and trying to explain that to the dole office the next day. TINY, with a look between EDDIE IZZARD on a very bad night and a chubby MORRISSEY, began to attract the right people to ULTRASOUND gigs. Among the A&R pack was 'Virgin' supremo himself, Richard Branson, who was enticed to go and see them perform by staff at his offshoot imprint, 'V2'. Fortunately, they played at NME's Unsigned Bands Gig early the following year, releasing a debut 45, 'SAME BAND', for 'Fierce Panda' soon after. This in turn, led to 'Nude' records subsequently giving them a deal, their second single, 'BEST WISHES', breaking the hard working quintet into the UK Top 75. In the summer of '98, they cracked the Top 30 with the excellent 'STAY YOUNG', the B-side featuring an unusual cover of Neil Young's 'HEY, HEY, MY, MY (INTO THE BLACK)'.

Album rating: awaiting debut album

TINY (b. ANDREW VICTOR WOOD, 1962, Birkenhead, Liverpool) – vocals / **RICHARD GREEN** – guitar / **MATT JONES** – keyboards / **VANESSA BEST** – bass / **ANDY PEACE** – drums

Fierce Panda — not iss.

Jul 97. (ltd-7"/cd-s) *(NING 35/+CD)* **SAME BAND. / FLOODLIGHT WORLD** [ ] [-]

Nude — not iss.

Feb 98. (ltd;10"/cd-s) *(NUD 33 T/CD)* **BEST WISHES / KURT RUSSELL / BLACK HOLE** [68] [-]

Jun 98. (7") *(NUD 35S)* **STAY YOUNG. /** [30] [-]
(cd-s) *(NUD 35CD1)* – ('A'side) / Football meat / Hey, hey, my, my (into the black).
(cd-s) *(NUD 35CD2)* –

Oct 98. (12"/cd-s) *(NUD 39 T/CD)* **I'LL SHOW YOU MINE. /** [ ] [-]

ULTRA VIVID SCENE

Formed: New York, USA . . . 1988 as a vehicle for singer/songwriter KURT RALSKE, who flitted between the local jazz and hardcore scenes. He then moved to London, England in '86, forming the bands NOTHING BUT HAPPINESS and CRASH. Having gained a contract with the UK label, '4 a.d.', KURT subsequently returned to New York where he formed UVS and it wasn't long before his eponymous HUGH JONES-produced debut set scaled the UK indie charts. Trading in a bubblegum ambient sound influenced by The VELVET UNDERGROUND and latter day noise merchants The JESUS & MARY CHAIN, RALSKE's insinuating vocals and uncompromising subject matter (perversion, suicide, mental illness, etc.) made him a kind of transatlantic spiritual cousin of MOMUS. Previous to this, he'd released the 'SHE SCREAMED' EP, which included his tribute to HANK WILLIAMS and the MARQUIS DE SADE; 'NOT IN LOVE (HIT BY A TRUCK)'. The man's 1990 follow-up album fared even better, attracting considerable interest from the US college circuit. He finally gave up solo/group work, moving into production for singer LIDA HUSIK after 1992's disappointing 'REV' album.

Album rating: ULTRA VIVID SCENE (*8) / JOY 1967-1990 (*7)

NOTHING BUT HAPPINESS

KURT RALSKE (b. 1967) – guitar / **DAVID MAREADY BOWAN / BILL GERSTALL / LYNN CUTHBERTSON**

Remorse Justine

Jun 86. (7") *(LOST 1) <JUS 002>* **COULDN'T MAKE YOU MINE. / NARCOTICS DAY** Feb89

Mar 87. (lp) *(REMLP 1)* **DETOUR**
– For waitress friends / Striped songs / Battle hymn / Buried in the flowers / Facsimile / Don't laugh / Couldn't make you mine / My summer dress / Blue kiss / Narcotics day.

CRASH

had already been formed by **KURT** plus **MARK DUMAIS** – vocals, guitar, main songwriter / **BILL CAREY** – guitar (ex-EXCENTRICKS) / **ADAM WRIGHT** – bass / **BYRON GUTHRIE** – drums

Remorse Justine

Nov 86. (12"ep) *(LOST 2) <JUS 001>* **DON'T LOOK NOW (NOW!). / INTERNATIONAL VELVET / DON'T LOOK NOW (acoustic)** Jun88

Nov 86. (12"ep) *(LOST 4)* **ALMOST. / MY MACHINE / ON AND ON (version)** -

Feb 87. (lp) *(REMLP 2)* **I FEEL FINE** -
– Almost / Craig egg / International velvet / I go round / Superfly / Everything under the sun / I feel fine / My machine / On and on / Rings, chains and groups / Get set / John stood by / What I found.

Aug 87. (7") *(LOSS 6)* **BRIGHT COLOURED LIGHTS. / IN MY HEAD** -

— Disbanded soon after above. BYRON joined JOHN MOORE'S EXPRESSWAY and CAREY joined SOMETHING PRETTY BEAUTIFUL. It was an entirely different CRASH that issued for 'Creation', a single 'SUNBURST' early '89.

ULTRA VIVID SCENE

KURT RALSKE – vocals, everything (solo)

4 a.d. Columbia

Aug 88. (12"ep/cd-ep) *(BAD 806/+CD)* **SHE SCREAMED / WALKIN' AFTER MIDNIGHT / NOT IN LOVE (HIT BY A TRUCK)** -

Oct 88. (lp/c)(cd) *(CAD/+C 809)(CAD 809CD) <47485>* **ULTRA VIVID SCENE**
– She screamed / Crash / You didn't say please / Lynne-Marie 2 / Nausea / Mercy seat / Dream of love / Lynne-Marie / This isn't real / The whore of God / Bloodline / How did it feel / Hail Mary. *(cd+=)* – (1 track).

1989. (7") *<JUS 003>* **SLOW YOU DOWN. / TOTALLY FREE** -

— added **KRISTAN KRAMER** – bass / **MAZORA CREAGER** – cello, vocals / + the returning **BYRON GUTHRIE** – drums

Mar 89. (7") *(AD 906)* **MERCY SEAT. / CODINE** -
(12"+=/cd-s+=) – H like in Heaven / ('A'-lp version).

Jul 89. (7"ltd.shop-freebie) *(AD 908)* **SOMETHING TO EAT. / H LIKE IN HEAVEN** - -

— **KURT** retained **BYRON** + recruited **COLLIN RAE** – rhythm guitar / **ANN HOLLIS** – bass

Apr 90. (7"ep/c-ep/12"ep/cd-ep) *(BAD/+C/T/CD 0004) <73371>* **STARING AT THE SUN / THREE STARS (*** version). / CRASH / SOMETHING BETTER**

Apr 90. (cd)(lp/c) *(CAD 0005CD)(CAD/+C 0005)* **JOY 1967-1990** -
– It happens every time / Staring at the sun / Three stars / Special one / Grey turns white / Poison / Guilty pleasure / Extra ordinary / Beauty No.2 / The kindest cut / Praise the law / Lightning.

Nov 90. (7")<cd-ep> *(AD 0016) <73534>* **SPECIAL ONE. / KIND OF A DRAG** -

— **RALSKE** recruited entire new line-up; **JACK DALEY** – bass / **JULIAN KLEPACZ** – drums

Oct 92. (cd)(lp/c) *(CAD 2017CD)(CAD/+C 2017) <53133>* **REV**
– Candida / Cut-throat / Mirror to mirror / The portion of delight / Thief's love song / How sweet / Medicating angels / Blood and thunder / This is the way.

Feb 93. (12"ep/cd-ep) *(BAD 3003/+CD)* **BLOOD AND THUNDER EP** -
– Blood and thunder (remix) / Don't look now (now!) / Candida (theme from 'Red Pressure Mounting') / Winter song.

— As said, KURT concentrated on production demands.

ULTRAVOX

Formed: London, England . . . mid '76 out of TIGER LILY (whose one and only single was a bizarre cover of Fats Waller's 'AIN'T MISBEHAVIN', subsequently withdrawn from release) comprising frontman JOHN FOXX, CHRIS CROSS, STEVE SHEARS, BILLY CURRIE and WARREN CANN. With the addition of violin (courtesy of CURRIE) and added synth power, the group became ULTRAVOX, initially with a ! at the end!. The fact that the band were picked up by 'Island' records and their eponymous 1977 debut album produced by BRIAN ENO says a lot about where ULTRAVOX! were coming from; artsy avant-pop combining elements of a punked-up ROXY MUSIC, the group were something of a cult live act. This didn't translate into sales, however, and despite an improved second effort, 'HA! HA! HA!' (1977), the group languished in relative obscurity. With ROBIN SIMON replacing SHEARS, they decamped to Germany to begin work on a third set under the auspices of electronic maestro, CONNY PLANK. The underwhelming result, 'SYSTEMS OF ROMANCE' (1978), failed to change the group's fortunes and by the Spring of '79, FOXX had abandoned ship for a solo career while SIMON went on to join MAGAZINE. The ubiquitous MIDGE URE was brought in as lead man, the singer having already cut his music business teeth in such diverse outfits as SLIK, The RICH KIDS and THIN LIZZY. He was also an integral part of moody synth-poppers, VISAGE, co-writing some of their material alongside mainman, STEVE STRANGE. Ironically, all this upheaval seemed to work wonders for all concerned, FOXX going his experimental electronic way and scoring a Top 40 hit almost immediately with the brilliant 'UNDERPASS' (early '80), while the newly revamped ULTRAVOX (now without a ! and signed to 'Chrysalis') broke the Top 30 that summer with 'SLEEPWALK'. 'VIENNA' (1980; again produced by CONNY PLANK) was released later that year, its Top 5 placing indicating that the new-look outfit had effectively cornered the burgeoning new romantic/electropop market. This was confirmed early in '81 when the album's title track narrowly missed the UK No.1 spot, its chilly, grandiose Euro feel and indelible melody managing to combine pretentiousness with mass public appeal. This was a talent which was to serve the group well over over the ensuing five years, ULTRAVOX scoring an impressive run of seven Top 10 albums and a string of Top 30 hits. 'RAGE IN EDEN' (1981) was another Top 5 success, spawning three Top 20 singles including the po-faced 'ALL STOOD STILL'. The album also marked the end of the group's tenure with PLANK, GEORGE MARTIN overseeing production duties on 'QUARTET' (1982). The result was a markedly warmer sound and more commercial appeal, evident on the preceding single, 'REAP THE WILD WIND'. By the release of 'LAMENT' (1984), ULTRAVOX were a fully fledged pop band, the evocative heartbreak of 'DANCING WITH TEARS IN MY EYES' giving the group their biggest hit since 'VIENNA'. A bonus new track on the best selling compilation, 'THE COLLECTION' (1984), 'LOVE'S GREAT ADVENTURE', was another pop odyssey, its rolling synth crescendos a taster for the latest chapter in URE's solo career. Strangely enough, ULTRAVOX's last hit single was the sombre 'ALL FALL DOWN', its subject matter the war-torn Northern Ireland, an almost militaristic rhythm and uillean pipes ultilised for greater effect. The track was lifted from the 'U-VOX' (1986) set, an album featuring the drumming talents of BIG COUNTRY's MARK BRZEZICKI. Realising they'd reached a creative impasse, ULTRAVOX disbanded the following year, URE taking up the solo career that had begun so successfully in 1982 with a Top 10 cover of Tom Rush's 'NO REGRETS' (made famous by the WALKER BROTHERS) and continued with the soaring pop of ~'IF I WAS', a No.1 single in summer '85 (URE had also helped to mastermind the Band Aid single, 'Do They Know It's Christmas). He struggled, however, to resurrect his flagging solo career, the 1988 set, 'ANSWERS TO NOTHING' barely scraping into the Top 40 while a Spring '89 single, 'SISTERS AND BROTHERS' was withdrawn by 'Chrysalis'. Subsequently securing a new contract with 'Arista', URE returned in 1991 with the Top 20 hit, 'COLD COLD HEART' and a Top 40 album, 'PURE'. While ULTRAVOX made a low-key comeback in 1993 with a new singer, TONY FENELLE, and a new album, 'REVELATION', URE has been conspicuous by his absence from the charts for most of the 90's. • **Songwriters:** FOXX and group until URE replaced FOXX. Covered only KING'S LEAD HAT (Brian Eno). MIDGE URE's solo career included THE MAN WHO SOLD THE WORLD (David Bowie) / STRANGE BREW (Cream).

Album rating: THREE INTO ONE early material compilation (*8) / VIENNA (*7) / THE COLLECTION compilation (*7)

TIGER LILY

DENNIS LEIGH (JOHN FOXX) – vocals / **STEVE SHEARS** – guitar / **BILLY CURRIE** (b. 1 Apr'52, Huddersfield, Yorkshire, England) – keyboards / **WARREN CANN** (b.20 May'52, Victoria, Canada) – drums / **CHRIS ST. JOHN** (b. CHRISTOPHER ALLEN, 14 Jul'52) – bass

Gull not iss.

Mar 75. (7") *(GULS 54)* **AIN'T MISBEHAVIN'. / MONKEY JIVE** -

— (w/drawn before release) *(iss.Oct77) (re-iss. Oct80 on 'Dead Good')*

ULTRAVOX!

LEIGH became **JOHN FOXX** and ST.JOHN now **CHRIS CROSS.** (CURRIE now added violin, synthesizers.)

Island Antilles

Feb 77. (7") *(WIP 6375)* **DANGEROUS RHYTHM. / MY SEX** -

Mar 77. (lp/c) *(ILPS/ICT 9449)* **ULTRAVOX!** -
– Saturday night in the city of the dead / Life at Rainbow End (for all the tax exiles on Main Street) / Slip away / I want to be a machine / Wide boys / Dangerous rhythm / The lonely hunter / The wild the beautiful and the damned / My sex.

May 77. (7") *(WIP 6392)* **YOUNG SAVAGE. / SLIPAWAY** -

Oct 77. (7") *(WIP 6404)* **ROCKWROK. / HIROSHIMA MON AMOUR** -
(all 3 ULTRAVOX! singles were re-iss. Jul81)

Oct 77. (lp/c) *(ILPS/ICT 9505)* **HA! HA! HA!** -
– Rockwrok / The frozen ones / Fear in the western world / Distant smile / The man who dies every day / Artificial life / While I'm still alive / Hiroshima mon amour. *(free-7"w.a.)–* **QUIRKS. / MODERN LOVE (live)**

Feb 78. (7"ep) *(IEP 8)* **RETRO E.P. (live)** -
– The wild the beautiful and the damned / Young savage / My sex / The man who dies every day.

— **ROBIN SIMON** – guitar (ex-NEO) repl. SHEARS to COWBOYS INTERNATIONAL

Aug 78. (7"/12"violet) *(WIP/12WIP 6454)* **SLOW MOTION. / DISLOCATION**

Sep 78. (lp/c) *(ILPS/ICT 9555) <7069>* **SYSTEMS OF ROMANCE**
– Slow motion / I can't stay long / Someone else's clothes / Blue light / Some of them / Quiet men / Dislocation / Maximum acceleration / When you walk through me / Just for a moment.

Oct 78. (7"/12"white) *(WIP/12WIP 6459)* **QUIET MEN. / CROSS FADE**

— (Apr79) **MIDGE URE** (b.JAMES, 10 Oct'53, Cambuslang, Scotland) – vocals, guitar (ex-SLIK, ex-RICH KIDS, ex-THIN LIZZY, ex-VISAGE) repl. JOHN FOXX who went solo. ROBIN also departed to MAGAZINE. Now as ULTRAVOX, after dropping the exclamation mark!

Chrysalis Chrysalis

Jun 80. (7",7"clear) *(CHS 2441)* **SLEEPWALK. / WAITING** 29

Sep 80. (7",7"clear/12") *(CHS 2457/122457)* **PASSING STRANGERS. / SOUND ON SOUND** 57

Oct 80. (lp/c) *(CHR/ZCHR 1296)* <1296> **VIENNA** 3
– Astradyne / New Europeans / Private lives / Passing strangers / Sleepwalk / Mr. X / Western promise / Vienna / All stood still. *(cd-iss. 1985) (re-iss. cd Mar94 + Jul94)*

Jan 81. (7",7"clear) *(CHS 2481)* **VIENNA. / PASSIONATE REPLY** 2
(12"+=) *(CHS 122481) - Herr X.*

Apr 81. (7",7"clear) *(CHS 2457)* **PASSING STRANGERS. / FACE TO FACE** -
(12"+=) *(CHA 122457)* – King's lead hat.

May 81. (7",7"clear) *(CHS 2522)* **ALL STOOD STILL. / ALLES KLAR** 8
(12"+=) *(CHS 122522)* – Keep talking.

Aug 81. (7",7"clear/ext-12") *(CHS 2549/122549)* **THE THIN WALL. / I NEVER WANTED TO BEGIN** 14

Sep 81. (lp/c) *(CHR/ZCHR 1338)* <1338> **RAGE IN EDEN** 4
– The voice / We stand alone / Rage in Eden / I remember (death in the afternoon) / The thin wall / Stranger within / Accent on youth / The ascent / Your name has slipped my mind again. *(cd-iss. Jun87)*

Nov 81. (7",7"clear) *(CHS 2559)* **THE VOICE. / PATHS AND ANGELS** 16
(12"+=,12"clear+=) *(CHS 122559)* – All stood still (live) / Private lives (live).

Sep 82. (7",7"clear/c-s/12") *(CHS 2639/122639)* <42682> **REAP THE WILD WIND. / HOSANNA (IN EXCELIS DEO)** 12 71 Mar 83

Oct 82. (lp/c/pic-lp) *(CDL/ZCDL/PCDL 1394)* <1394> **QUARTET** 6 61 Mar83
– Reap the wild wind / Serenade / Mine for life / Hymn / Visions of blue / When the scream subsides / We came to dance / Cut and run / The song (we go).

Nov 82. (7",7"clear) *(CHS 2557)* **HYMN. / MONUMENT** 11
(12"+=,12"clear+=) *(CHS 122557)* – The thin wall.

Mar 83. (7",7"clear,7"pic-d) *(CHS 2676)* **VISIONS IN BLUE. / BREAK YOUR BACK** 15
(12"+=,12"clear+=) *(CHS 122676)* – Reap the wild wind.

May 83. (7",7"pic-d,7"clear/12",12"clear) *(VOX/+X 1)* **WE CAME TO DANCE. / OVERLOOK** 18

Oct 83. (lp/c) *(CUX/ZCUX 1452)* **MONUMENT – THE SOUNDTRACK (live)** 9
– Monument / Reap the wild wind / The voice / Vienna / Mine for life / Hymn.

Feb 84. (7",7"clear/12") *(VOX/+X 2)* **ONE SMALL DAY. / EASTERLY** 27

Apr 84. (lp/c/pic-lp/cd) *(CDL/ZCDL/PCDL/CCD 1459)* <41459> **LAMENT** 8
– White China / One small day * / Dancing with tears in my eyes / Lament * / Man of two worlds / Heart of the country / When the time comes / A friend I called Desire. *(c+cd+=)*– (tracks * remixed).

May 84. (7",7"clear/12") *(UV/+X 1)* **DANCING WITH TEARS IN MY EYES. / BUILDING** 3

Jul 84. (7",7"clear) *(UV 2)* **LAMENT. / HEART OF THE COUNTRY** 22
(12"+=) *(UVX 2)* – ('A'instrumental).

Oct 84. (7",7"clear,7"pic-d/12") *(UV/+X 3)* **LOVE'S GREAT ADVENTURE. / WHITE CHINA** 12

Nov 84. (lp/c/cd) *(UTV/ZUTV 1)(CCD 1490)* **THE COLLECTION** (compilation) 2
– Dancing with tears in my eyes / Hymn / The thin wall / The voice / Vienna / Passing strangers / Sleepwalk / Reap the wild wind / All stood still / Visions in blue / We came to dance / One small day / Love's great adventure / Lament. *(w/ free 12")*

— guest **MARK BRZEZICKI** (b.21 Jun'57) – drums (of BIG COUNTRY) repl. CANN to HELDEN

Sep 86. (7",7"clear,7"pic-d) *(UV 4)* **SAME OLD STORY. / 3** 31
(12",12"clear) *(UVX 4)* – ('A'side) / All in one day.

Oct 86. (lp/c/cd) *(CDL/ZCDL/CCD 1545)* **U-VOX** 9
– Same old story / Sweet surrender / Dream on / The prize / All fall down / Time to kill / Moon madness / Follow your heart / All in one day.

Nov 86. (7",7"clear) *(UV 5)* **ALL FALL DOWN. / DREAM ON** 30
(12"+=) *(UVX 5)* – ('A'version).

May 87. (7",7"clear) *(UV 6)* **ALL IN ONE DAY. / THE PRIZE (live)**
(12"+=) *(UVX 6)* – Stateless.

— Disbanded 1987, although U-VOX was formed by BILLY CURRIE, ROBIN SIMON and MARCUS O'HIGGINS – vocals. They toured 1989 playing ULTRAVOX songs.

— **TONY FENELLE** – vocals repl. MIDGE URE who was by now continuing solo.

D.S.B. not iss.

May 93. (cd/c/lp) *(DSB 3098-2/-4/-1)* **REVELATION** -
– I am alive / Revelation / Systems of love / Perfecting the art of common ground / The great outdoors / The closer I get to you / No turning back / True believer / Unified / The new frontier.

Jun 93. (7"/c-s/7"clear) *(DSB 3097-7/-3/-1)* **I AM ALIVE. / SYSTEMS OF LOVE**
(cd-s+=) *(DSB 30975)* – ('A'extended).

— line-up: **CURRIE / BLUE / BURNS**

Resurgence not iss.

Nov 95. (cd) *(RES 109CD)* **INGENUITY** -
– Ingenuity / There goes a beautiful world / Give it all back / Future picture forever / The silent cries / Distance / Ideals / Who'll save you / A way out, a way through / Majestic.

– compilations, others, etc. –

Jun 80. (lp/c) *Island/ US= Antilles; (ILPS/ICM 9614)* <7079> **THREE INTO ONE**
– Young savage / Rockwrok / Dangerous rhythm / The man who dies every day / The wild the beautiful and the damned / Slow motion / Just for a moment / My sex / Quiet men / Hiroshima mon amour. *(re-iss. Nov86, cd-iss. 1990)*

Mar 81. (12"ep,12"clear-ep) *Island; (DWIP 6691)* **SLOW MOTION / DISLOCATION. / QUIET MEN / HIROSHIMA MON AMOUR** 33 -

Apr 88. (12"ep) *Strange Fruit; (SFPS 047)* **THE PEEL SESSIONS** (21.7.77) -
– My sex / Artificial life / Young savage.

Sep 93. (cd/c) *Spectrum; (550112-2/-4)* **SLOW MOTION** -

Aug 94. (cd) *Chrysalis; (CDCHR 6053)* **RARE VOLUME 2** -

Jun 95. (cd) *Receiver; (RRCD 199)* **FUTURE PICTURE** -

Aug 95. (cd-s) *Old Gold;* **VIENNA / REAP THE WILD WIND** -

Oct 95. (cd) *MFP; (CDMFP 6175)* **DANCING WITH TEARS IN MY EYES** -

Nov 95. (3xcd-box) *Island; (5241522)* **ULTRAVOX! / HA! HA! HA! / SYSTEMS OF ROMANCE** -

– (MIDGE URE & ULTRAVOX) compilations, etc. –

Jan 93. (7"/c-s) *Chrysalis; (TCCHS 3936)* **VIENNA. / WASTELANDS** 13
(cd-s+=) *(CDCHS 3936)* – Answers to nothing / The voice.
(cd-s) *(CDCHSS 3936)* – ('A'side) / Call of the wild / One small day / Hymn.

Feb 93. (cd/c/lp) *Chrysalis; (CD/TC/+CHR 1987)* **IF I WAS: THE VERY BEST OF MIDGE URE & ULTRAVOX** 10
– If I was / No regrets / Love's great adventure / Dear God / Cold cold heart / Vienna / Call of the wild / Dancing with tears in my eyes / All fall down / Yellow pearl / Fade to grey / Reap the wild wind / Answers to nothing / Do they know it's Christmas? (BAND AID). *(cd+=)* After a fashion (with MICK KARN) / That certain smile.

Dec 82. (d-c) *Chrysalis; (ZCDP 109)* **VIENNA / RAGE IN EDEN** -

Feb 87. (7") *Old Gold; (OG 9675)* **VIENNA. / THE VOICE** -

Apr 87. (7") *Old Gold; (OG 9698)* **DANCING WITH TEARS IN MY EYES. / REAP THE WILD WIND** *(12"-iss.Jan88)* -

UNBELIEVABLE TRUTH

Formed: Abingdon, Oxford, England . . . 1993 by school friends JASON MOULSTER, NIGEL POWELL and ANDY YORKE (yes, that YORKE!). Having paid their musical dues in various bands in and around their home town, MOULSTER and POWELL hooked up with YORKE upon his return from Moscow (where he'd completed a degree in Russian literature) and set about forming a band of their own. Of course, any hopes that the group might be able to avoid the inevitable comparisons with elder brother THOM's mighty RADIOHEAD were doomed from the beginning. Especially as their music dealt in a similar vein of melancholic atmospherics (vaguely akin to a cross between latter day TALK TALK and AMERICAN MUSIC CLUB) and soul searching of the long dark night variety. Nevertheless, ANDY's voice was singled out for particular praise by critics, his tonsils possessed of enough individual character to deflect any predictable murmurs of family influence. Similarly, UNBELIEVABLE TRUTH's rise to cult acclaim has apparently been achieved with a dignified determination not to ride on the coat-tails of sibling success, the band attracting the attentions of 'Virgin' records after an early 1997 effort, 'BUILDING' for 'Shifty Disco'. After three further singles over the course of the next year and a bit (most notably Top 40 breakers, 'HIGHER THAN REASON' and 'SOLVED'), their debut album, 'ALMOST HERE', appeared in May '98. Fittingly navel gazing listening for one of the most overcast summers anyone can remember, the record almost made the UK Top 20 despite mixed reviews. Whether they can build upon this and truly emerge from the shadow of big brother remains to be seen; success on the scale of RADIOHEAD really would be unbelievable. • **Trivia:** In 1997, they made an appearance on the quaintly titled 'Fierce Panda' compilation, 'Cry Me A Liver'.

Album rating: ALMOST HERE (*7)

ANDY YORKE – vocals, guitar / **JASON MOULSTER** – bass / **NIGEL POWELL** – drums, keyboards, acoustic guitar

Shifty Disco not iss.

Feb 97. (cd-s) *(DISCO 9702)* **BUILDING /** -

Virgin Virgin

Oct 97. (7"/c-s) *(VS/+C 1657)* **STONE. / FINEST LITTLE SPACE** -
(cd-s+=) *(VSCDT 1657)* – Roadside No.1 / Tyre tracks.

Feb 98. (7"/c-s) *(VS/+C 1676)* **HIGHER THAN REASON. / WHO'S TO KNOW** 38 -
(cd-s+=) *(VSCDT 1676)* – Coming round / Revolution.

Apr 98. (7"/c-s) *(VS/+C 1684)* **SOLVED. / NEVERMIND** 39 -
(cd-s+=) *(VSCDT 1684)* – Yesterday never leaves / There if you want it.

May 98. (cd/c/lp) *(<CDVX/TCV/V 2849>)* **ALMOST HERE** 21
– Solved / Angel / Stone / Same mistakes / Forget about me / Settle down / Finest little space / Building / Almost here / Higher than reason / Be ready.

Jul 98. (7"/c-s) *(VS/+C 1697)* **SETTLE DOWN. / DUNE SEA** 46 -
(cd-s+=) *(VSCDT 1697)* – Circle.

UNCLE TUPELO

Formed: Belleville, Illinois, USA . . . 1987 by schoolmates JEFF TWEEDY and JAY FARRAR (who had played in punk outfit, The PRIMITIVES – US), MIKE HEIDORN completing the line-up. A band that have achieved almost legendary status among alternative country afficionados, UNCLE TUPELO christened a whole movement with the release of their seminal debut album, 'NO DEPRESSION' (1990). Issued on the small 'Rockville' label, the record translated the raw expression and sonic assault of punk into a contemporary country context; the spirit of what TWEEDY and FARRAR were trying to do was best illustrated on the title track, an impressive excavation of an ancient CARTER FAMILY song yearning for the sanctuary of Heaven, performed with as much conviction as any bonafide gospel act. Follow-up set, 'STILL FEEL GONE' (1991) continued in the same vein, developing and updating country in a fashion a damn sight closer to GRAM PARSONS' cosmic vision than the polished dross coming out of Nashville. Yet it was the stark testimony of the PETER BUCK-produced 'MARCH 16-20' (1992) that really cut to the heart of American roots tradition, a breathtaking album of grainy originals and hard-bitten folk covers. While the quality of the songwriting arguably outstripped almost anything released under the banner of country/alt-country in the past twenty years, it was the bruised beauty of the vocals (especially FARRAR) that really brought on the goose-bumps and belied UNCLE TUPELO's relative youthfulness. The likes of 'GRINDSTONE', 'BLACK EYE' and the traditional 'MOONSHINER' resonated with what sounded like the careworn resignation of a lifetime's toil and trouble, the whole album religious in its rawness. Released to rave reviews, it didn't take long for word to spread and with major labels eager for a piece of the action, FARRAR and TWEEDY opted to sign for 'Resprise' (home to spiritual forefathers PARSONS and NEIL YOUNG amongst others). With FARRAR and TWEEDY maintaining a hard-drinking, volatile relationship at the best of times, 'ANODYNE' (1993) proved to be the final product of their mercurial partnership. A return to more upbeat material, the album featured a rousing cover of Doug Sahm's 'GIVE BACK THE KEY TO MY HEART' (featuring the cult Texan roots man on guitar) alongside more reflective fare like the gorgeously plaintive 'SLATE', one of the most perfectly formed compositions in the FARRAR/TWEEDY canon with fiddle arrangements to break the hardest heart. While many mourned the band's passing, fans could look forward to the prospect of two solo projects, FARRAR's SON VOLT and TWEEDY's WILCO. The latter outfit (comprising TWEEDY, JAY BENNETT, JOHN STIRRATT and UNCLE TUPELO veterans MAX JOHNSTON and KEN COOMER) were first off the starting block with 1994's 'A.M.'. An enjoyable enough set of uptempo country-rock, it was nevertheless eclipsed by the 1996 follow-up, 'BEING THERE', a sprawling double set drawing comparisons with The 'STONES 'Exile On Main Street' and hailed as one of the album's of the year. Reaching far beyond TWEEDY's patented musical boundaries to encompass everything from bar-room belters to Spector-esque rock/pop, the record proved conclusively that FARRAR's other half was blessed with his own distinct musical vision. Fans yearning for the down-at-heel spirit of UNCLE TUPELO's moodier moments were comforted by the fact that FARRAR himself was still treading the dirt-road backstreets of country's dark underbelly with SON VOLT, releasing 'TRACE' in 1994 and 'STRAIGHTAWAYS' in late '96. While some critics railed against what they perceived as the unrelenting miserabilism of FARRAR's approach (especially with regards to the SON VOLT live experience), there was no disputing the quality or honesty of the writing. While both camps continue to come up with the goods, the prospect of an UNCLE TUPELO reunion is still tantalisingly within reach. • **Songwriters:** All compositions FARRAR/TWEEDY except arrangements of traditional tunes, plus covers: NO DEPRESSION (A.P.Carter) / JOHN HARDY (Leadbelly) / ATOMIC POWER (Louvin Brothers/B.Bain) / BLUE EYES (Gram Parsons) / EFFIGY (Creedence Clearwater Revival). • **Other info:** TWEEDY was also an integral part of y'allternative supergroup, GOLDEN SMOG, alongside members of the JAYHAWKS, SOUL ASYLUM, RUN WESTY RUN and BIG STAR.

Album rating: NO DEPRESSION (*7) / STILL FEEL GONE (*7) / MARCH 16-20 (*10) / ANODYNE (*8) / Wilco: A.M. (*6) / BEING THERE (*8) / Son Volt: TRACE (*6) / STRAIGHTAWAYS (*7)

JEFF TWEEDY (b.25 Aug'67) – vocals, guitar, bass / **JAY FARRAR** (b.26 Dec'66) – vocals, guitar / **MICHAEL HEIDORN** – drums

Rockville Rockville

1990. (lp) *<ROCK 6050-1>* **NO DEPRESSION** -
– Graveyard shift / That year / Before I break / No depression / Factory belt / Whiskey bottle / Outdone / Train / Life worth livin' / Flatness / So called friend / Screen door / John Hardy. *(UK cd-iss. Sep97; ROCK 6050-2)*

1990. (7") *<ROCK 6055-7>* **I GOT DRUNK. / SIN CITY** -

1991. (7") *<ROCK 6069-7>* **GUN. / I WANNA DESTROY YOU** -

1991. (lp) *<ROCK 6070-1>* **STILL FEEL GONE** -
– Gun / Looking for a way out / Fall down easy / Nothing / Still be around / Watch me fall / Punch drunk / Postcard / D. Boon / True to life / Cold shoulder / Discarded / If that's alright. *(UK-iss.cd Nov92 on 'Yellow Moon'; BUFF 001CD)*

Nov 92. (7") *<(ROCK 6089-7)>* **SAUGET WIND. /**

Mar 93. (cd/c/lp) *<(6110-2/-4/-1)>* **MARCH 16-20, 1992** Aug92
– Grindstone / Coalminers / Wait up / Criminals / Shaky ground / Satan, your kingdom must come down / Black eye / Moonshiner / I wish my baby was born / Atomic power / Lilli Schull / Warfare / Fatal wound / Sandusky / Wipe the clock.

— **KEN COOMER** – drums + **JOHN STIRRATT** – bass repl. HEIDORN

Warners Sire

Oct 93. (cd/c) *(9362 45330-2/-4) <45424>* **ANODYNE**
– Slate / Acuff-Rose / The long cut / Give back the key to my heart / Chickamauga / New Madrid / Anodyne / We've been had / Fifteen keys / High water / No sense in lovin' / Steal the crumbs.

— arguments arose, FARRAR subsequently forming SON VOLT with MICHAEL HEIDORN. They enlisted brothers DAVE and JIM BOQUIST and released album late '95' 'TRACE'.

– compilations, etc. –

May 95. (c) *Dutch East; <6110>* **STILL FEEL GONE / MARCH 16-20, 1992** -

WILCO

TWEEDY with remaining UNCLE TUPELO members (except FARRAR)

Warners Reprise

Apr 95. (cd) *<(9362 45857-2)>* **A.M.**
– I must be high / Casino queen / Box full of letters / Shouldn't be ashamed / Pick up the change / I thought IU held you / That's not the issue / It's just that simple / Should've been in love / Passenger side / Dash 7 / Blue eyed soul / Too far apart.

Jul 95. (c-s) *(W 0306MC)* **BOX FULL OF LETTERS / I AM NOT WILLING**
(cd-s+=) *(W 0306)* – Who were you thinking of (live).

— added **JAY BENNETT** – guitar

Feb 97. (d-cd) *<(9362 46236-2)>* **BEING THERE** 73 Nov96
– Misunderstood / Forget the flowers / I got you (at the end of the century) / Red eyed and blue / (Was I) In your dreams / Dreamer in my dreams / Lonely one / Why would you wanna live / Kingpin / Someone else's song / Outta mind (outta sight) / Someday soon / Sunken treasure / Say you miss me / Hotel Arizona / What's the world got in store / Far far away / Monday.

Apr 97. (cd-ep) *(W 0397CD)* **OUTTA SIGHT (OUTTA MIND) / OUTTA MIND (OUTTA SIGHT) / THIRTEEN / A LASTING FONDER** -

— In the middle of '98, WILCO collaborated with BILLY BRAGG on a tribute album ('MERMAID AVENUE') to WOODY GUTHRIE

SON VOLT

JIM FARRAR – vocals, guitar, organ, harmonica, songwriter / **DAVE BOQUIST** – guitars, fiddle, banjo, lap steel / **JIM BOQUIST** – bass, backing vocals / **MIKE HEIDORN** – drums

Warners Warners

Oct 95. (cd/c) *<(9362-46010-2/-4)>* **TRACE** Sep95
– Windfall / Live free / Tear stained eye / Route / Ten second news / Drown / Loose string / Out of the picture / Catching on / Too early / Mystifies me.

— with guests **ERIC HEYWOOD** – pedal steel, mandolin / **PAULI RYAN** – tambourine

Aug 97. (cd) *<(9362-46518-2/-4)>* **STRAIGHTWAYS** 44 May97
– Caryatid easy / Back into the world / Picking up the signal / Left a slide / Cresote / Cemetery savior / Last minute shakedown / Been set free / No more parades / Way down Watson.

Oct 98. (cd/c) *<(9362 47059-2/-4)>* **WIDE SWING TREMELO** 93
– Straightface / Driving the view / Jodel / Medicine hat / Strands / Flow / Dead man's clothes / Right on through / Chanty / Carry you down / Question / Streets that time walks / Hanging blue side / Blind hope.

UNDERNEATH (see under ⇒ BLAKE, Karl)

UNDERTONES

Formed: Londonderry, N.Ireland ... late '75 by the O'NEILL brothers, DAMIAN and JOHN, alongside FEARGAL SHARKEY, MIKE BRADLEY and BILLY DOHERTY. Taking up the offer of a one-off singles deal with Belfast label, 'Good Vibrations', they released a debut EP in September '78 with the seminal 'TEENAGE KICKS' as the lead track. Immediately championed by DJ John Peel, this compelling slice of adolescent angst reached the collective ear of 'Sire' records leading to a prestigious deal. Their major label debut, 'GET OVER YOU', scraped into the Top 60 although they eventually cracked the chart later that Spring with 'JIMMY JIMMY', a boisterous post-punk stomper reminiscent of a wittier, more laid-back SHAM 69. This was closely followed by an eponymous debut album, establishing The UNDERTONES as one of the most promising and intelligent new-wave punk/pop bands in the UK. Like a more hyperactive KINKS, the band chronicled the nitty gritty, highs and lows of everyday life in such unforgettable pop nuggets as 'HERE COMES THE SUMMER', 'TRUE CONFESSIONS' and 'FAMILY ENTERTAINMENT'. Arguably, 'YOU'VE GOT MY NUMBER (WHY DON'T YOU USE IT), remains The UNDERTONES' finest moment, a jarring, insistent riff marking it out from the group's standard pop rush. While the song barely made the UK Top 40, The UNDERTONES were back in the Top 10 the following year with the sneering 'MY PERFECT COUSIN', a humerous tale of a goody-two shoes relative which obviously struck a chord with more than a few disaffected youngsters. The accompanying album, 'HYPNOTISED' (1980), consolidated the group's standing, critically and commercially, a more assured set which also spawned another classic single in 'WEDNESDAY WEEK'. Inevitably, however, along with many of their contemporaries, The UNDERTONES increasingly moved away from the roughshod charm of old to a more refined sound. This was evident in the group's third album, 'THE POSITIVE TOUCH' (1981), only one track making the Top 20 ('IT'S GOING TO HAPPEN') despite such enduring material as the lovely 'JULIE OCEAN'. By 1983's 'THE SIN OF PRIDE', FEARGAL's quavering vocals and the group's boy-next-door image had been shelved for a blend of "alternative soul". Predictably, this didn't sit well with the group's more traditional fans who were unsurprisingly becoming increasingly critical of The UNDERTONES newfound sophistication. The imminent split eventually came in mid '83 with SHARKEY initially hooking up with VINCE CLARKE in The ASSEMBLY before launching a solo career. Following a minor hit on MADNESS' 'Zarjazz' label, SHARKEY signed to 'Virgin' and scored a massive No.1 hit with Maria McKee's 'A Good Heart'. A fully fledged, if brief, pop star, SHARKEY's eponymous solo debut hit the Top 10 around the same time in late '85, while he scored a follow-up Top 5 hit with 'YOU LITTLE THIEF'. Successive albums failed to chart, however, and SHARKEY moved into A&R work for 'Virgin'. The O'NEILL brothers, meanwhile, formed the critically acclaimed THAT PETROL EMOTION. • **Songwriters:** O'NEILL brothers except UNDER THE BOARDWALK (Drifters). In the mid-80's, FEARGAL, solo, collaborated with DAVE STEWART of The EURYTHMICS. In 1991, he teamed up with writers SHERRILL and DiPIERO. Covered; TAKE ME TO THE RIVER (Al Green). • **More Info:** While spending time in Londonderry in February '86, FEARGAL's mother and sister were abducted by terrorists, although they were thankfully released after a number of hours.

Album rating: UNDERTONES (*9) / HYPNOTISED (*7) / CHER O'BOWLES compilation (*9)

FEARGAL SHARKEY (b.13 Aug'58) – vocals / **DAMIAN O'NEILL** (b.15 Jan'61, Belfast, N.Ireland) – guitar, bass / **JOHN O'NEILL** (b.26 Aug'57) – guitar / **MIKE BRADLEY** (b.13 Aug'59) – bass / **BILLY DOHERTY** (b.10 Jul'58, Larne, N.Ireland) – drums

Good Vibrations — not iss.

Sep 78. (7"ep) *(GOT 4)* **TEENAGE KICKS / TRUE CONFESSIONS. / SMARTER THAN U / EMMERGENCY CASES** [ ] [-]
(re-iss. Oct78 on 'Sire', hit No.31) (re-iss. Jul83 on 'Ardeck', hit 60) (re-iss. 7"ep+cd-ep Apr94 on 'Dojo')

Sire — Sire

Jan 79. (7"m) *(SIR 4010)* **GET OVER YOU. / REALLY REALLY / SHE CAN ONLY SAY NO** [57] [ ]

Apr 79. (7",7"lime green) *(SIR 4015)* **JIMMY JIMMY. / MARS BARS** [16] [ ]

May 79. (lp/c) *(SRK/+C 6071) <6081>* **THE UNDERTONES** [13] [ ] Jan 80
– Family entertainment / Girls don't like it / Male model / I gotta getta / Teenage kicks / Wrong way / Jump boys / Here comes the summer / Get over you / Billy's third / Jimmy Jimmy / True confessions / She's a runaround / I know a girl / Listening in. *(re-iss. Jul83 on 'Ardeck') (re-iss. +cd.Oct87 on 'Fame') (re-iss. cd+c May94 on 'Dojo', with 7 extra tracks)* – Smarter than u / Emergency cases / Top twenty / Really really / Mars Bars / She can only say no / One way love.

Jul 79. (7"m) *(SIR 4022)* **HERE COMES THE SUMMER. / ONE WAY LOVE / TOP TWENTY** [34] [ ]

Sep 79. (7") *(SIR 4024)* **YOU'VE GOT MY NUMBER (WHY DON'T YOU USE IT). / LET'S TALK ABOUT GIRLS** [32] [ ]

Mar 80. (7"m) *(SIR 4038)* **MY PERFECT COUSIN. / HARD LUCK / I DON'T WANNA SEE YOU AGAIN** [9] [ ]
(d7"+=) *(SIR 4038)* – Here comes the summer.

Apr 80. (lp/c) *(SRK/+C 6088) <6088>* **HYPNOTISED** [6] [ ]
– More songs about chocolate and girls / There goes Norman / Hypnotised / See that girl / Whizz kids / Under the boardwalk / The way girls talk / Hard luck / My perfect cousin / Boys will be boys / Tearproof / Wednesday week / Nine times out of ten / Girls that don't talk / What's with Terry?. *(re-iss. Mar86 on 'Fame') (re-iss. cd+c May94 on 'Dojo', with 5 extra tracks)* – You've got my number (why don't you use it?) / Hard luck (again) / Let's talk about girls / I told you so / I don't want to see you again.

Jun80. (7") *(SIR 4042)* **WEDNESDAY WEEK. / I TOLD YOU SO** [11] [ ]

Ardeck-EMI — Rykodisc

Apr 81. (7") *(ARDS 8)* **IT'S GOING TO HAPPEN. / FAIRLY IN THE MONEY NOW** [18] [-]

May 81. (lp/c) *(ARD/TCARD 103) <12159>* **THE POSITIVE TOUCH** [17] [ ]
– Fascination / Life's too easy / You're welcome / The positive touch / Julie Ocean / Crisis of mine / His good looking friend / When Saturday comes / It's going to happen / Sigh and explode / I don't know / Hannah Doot / Boy wonder / Forever Paradise. *(re-iss. May94 on 'Dojo'+=;)* – Kiss in the dark / Beautiful friend / Life's too easy / Fairly in the money now.

Jul 81. (7") *(ARDS 9)* **JULIE OCEAN. / KISS IN THE DARK** [41] [ ]

Feb 82. (7") *(ARDS 10)* **BEAUTIFUL FRIEND. / LIFE'S TOO EASY** [ ] [-]

Jan 83. (7") *(ARDS 11)* **THE LOVE PARADE. / LIKE THAT** [ ] [-]
(12"+=) *(12ARDS 11)* – You're welcome / Family entertainment / Crises of mine.

Mar 83. (7") *(ARDS 12)* **GOT TO HAVE YOU BACK. / TURNING BLUE** [ ] [-]
(12"+=) *(12ARDS 12)* – Bye bye baby blue.

Mar 83. (lp/c) *(ARD/TCARD 104)* **THE SIN OF PRIDE** [43] [-]
– Got to have you back / Valentine's treatment / Luxury / Love before romance / Untouchable / Bye bye baby blue / Conscious / Chain of love / Soul seven / The love parade / Save me / The sin of pride. *(re-iss. cd+c May94 on 'Dojo', with 6 extra tracks)* – Turning blue / Like that / Window shopping for new clothes / Bitter sweet / You stand so close (but you're never there) / I can only dream.

Apr 83. (7") *(ARDS 13)* **CHAIN OF LOVE. / WINDOW SHOPPING FOR NEW CLOTHES** [ ] [-]

— Split mid'83 with FEARGAL SHARKEY joining The ASSEMBLY; (see YAZOO) before going solo. The O'NEILL brothers formed THAT PETROL EMOTION.

– compilations, others, etc. –

Nov 83. (d-lp)(c) *Ardeck-EMI; (ARD 1654283)(1654289)* **ALL WRAPPED UP** [67] [-]
– Teenage kicks / Get over you / Jimmy Jimmy / Here comes the summer / You've got my number (why don't you use it) / My perfect cousin / Wednesday week / It's going to happen / Julie Ocean / Beautiful friend / The love parade / Got to have you back / Chain of love.

— (Note all singles were re-iss. on 'Ardeck-EMI')

May 86. (lp/c) *Ardeck-EMI; (EMS/TCEMS 1172)* **CHER O'BOWLIES – THE PICK OF THE UNDERTONES** [96] [-]
– Teenage kicks / True confessions / Get over you / Family entertainment / Jimmy Jimmy / Here comes the Summer / You got my number (why don't you use it) / My perfect cousin / See that girl / Tearproof / Wednesday week / It's going to happen / Julie Ocean / You're welcome / Forever Paradise / Beautiful friend / Save me / The love parade / Valentine's treatment / Love before romance. *(re-iss. +cd.Oct89 on 'Fame')*

Jun 86. (7") *Ardeck-EMI; (ARDS 14)* **SAVE ME. / TEARPROOF** [ ] [-]
(12"+=) *(12ARDS 14)* – I know a girl.

Dec 86. (12"ep) *Strange Fruit; (SFPS 016)* **THE PEEL SESSIONS** (21.1.79) [ ] [-]
– Listening in / Family entertainment / Here comes the summer / Billy's third. *(cd-ep iss.Mar88)*

Dec 89. (lp/c/cd) *Strange Fruit; (SFR LP/MC/CD 103)* **DOUBLE PEEL SESSIONS** [ ] [-]
(re-iss. cd Mar94 as 'THE PEEL SESSIONS ALBUM')

Sep 93. (cd/c) *Castle / Rykodisc; (CTV CD/MC 121)* **THE BEST OF THE UNDERTONES – TEENAGE KICKS** [45] [ ]

Jul 95. (cd-ep) *Dojo; (TONESCD 1)* **HERE COMES THE SUMMER / GET OVER YOU / JIMMY JIMMY / YOU'VE GOT MY NUMBER (WHY DON'T YOU USE IT)** [ ] [-]

UNDERWORLD

Formed: Romford, London, England ... 1987 by RICK SMITH, KARL HYDE, ALFIE THOMAS and BRYN BURROWS, who had all been in Cardiff outfit FREUR (which was actually a symbol translated into a word!; no, PRINCE wasn't the first!). Even before this, RICK and KARL had played in synth-pop band, The SCREEN GEMS. In 1987, they took on the more conventional moniker, UNDERWORLD and hit America in the late 80's after signing for Seymour Stein's 'Sire' records. After a No.1 smash, 'RADAR', in Australia, they toured the States supporting EURYTHMICS, but it was clear this was not the direction for them. After recruiting DJ DARREN EMERSON, the band signed with the 'Boys Own' label, releasing the seminal techno crescendo of 'REZ' in February '93. They followed this up with the critically acclaimed, early '94 album, 'DUBNOBASSWITHMYHEADMAN', a nouveau-psychedelic classic climaxing with the delirious trance-athon of 'COWGIRL'. However, their big break came with the track 'BORN SLIPPY', a song featured on the 'Trainspotting' soundtrack. When re-released as a single in 1996, the track stormed to No.2, boosting sales of their recently released follow-up album, 'SECOND TOUGHEST IN THE INFANTS'. The band remain one of Britain's best loved techno acts, and with the Stateside success of The PRODIGY, there's still a chance that the band might break in America. • **Songwriters:** SMITH / HYDE / THOMAS then SMITH / HYDE / EMERSON. • **Trivia:** Produced by RUPERT HINES in 1988. HYDE worked on a 1991 'Paisley P.' album with TERRI NUNN (ex-Berlin). GEOFF DUGMORE (ex-ART OF NOISE) was a guest on 1989 album. Also appeared on WILLIAM ORBIT's 'Watch From A Vine Leaf' & ORBITAL's 'Lush 3' and remixed BJORK's 'Human Behaviour'.

Album rating: DUBNOBASSWITHMYHEADMAN (*8) / SECOND TOUGHEST IN THE INFANTS (*8)

FREUR

RICK SMITH – keyboards, vocals / **KARL HYDE** – vocals, guitar / **ALFIE THOMAS** – guitar, vocals / **JOHN WARWICKER LE BRETON** – synthesizers / **BRYN B. BURROWS** – drums

C.B.S. — Epic

Mar 83. (7"pic-d/ext.12") *(WA/A13 3141)* **DOOT DOOT. / HOLD ME MOTHER** [59] [ ]

Jun 83. (7"/7"pic-d) *(A/WA 3456)* **MATTERS OF THE HEART. / YOU'RE A HOOVER** [ ] [ ]
(12"+=) *(TA 3456)* – ('A'extended).

Sep 83. (7")(12") **RUNAWAY. / YOU'RE A HOOVER** [ ] [ ]

Nov 83. (lp/c) *(CBS/40 25522) <81566>* **DOOT DOOT** [ ] [ ]
– Doot doot / Runaway / Riders in the night / Theme from the film of the same name / Tender surrender / Matters of the heart / My room / Steam machine / Whispering / All too much.

Jan 84. (7"/ext.12") *(A/TA 4073)* **DOOT DOOT. / HOLD ME MOTHER** [ ] [ ]

Apr 84. (7") *(A 4333)* **RIDERS IN THE NIGHT. / INNOCENCE** [ ] [ ]
(12"+=) *(TA 4333)* – This is the way I like to live my life.

— added **JAKE BOWIE** – bass

Oct 84. (7") *(A 4726)* **DEVIL AND DARKNESS. / JAZZ 'N' KING** [ ] [ ]
(12"+=) *(TX 4726)* – ('A'extended).

Feb 85. (7") *(A 4983)* **LOOK IN THE BACK FOR ANSWERS. / HEY HO AWAY WE GO** [ ] [ ]
(12"+=) *(TX 4983)* – Uncle Jeff.

Feb 85. (lp/c/cd) **GET US OUT OF HERE** [ ] [ ]
– Look in the back for answers / Emeralds and pearls / Kiss me / A.O.K.O. / The Devil and darkness / The piano song / Happiness / Endless groove / This is the way I'd like to live my life / Bella Donna.

UNDERWORLD

— **BAZ ALLEN** – bass; repl. JOHN

Sire — Sire

Mar 88. (lp/c/cd) *(<925627-1/-4/-2>)* **UNDERNEATH THE RADAR** [ ] [ ]
– Glory! glory! / Call me No.1 / Rubber ball (space kitchen) / Show some emotion / Underneath the radar / Miracle party / I need a doctor / Bright white flame / Pray / The God song.

Jul 88. (7") *(W 7968) <27968>* **UNDERNEATH THE RADAR. / BIG RED X** [ ] [74] Apr88
(12"+=) *(W 7968T)* – ('A'dub version).

Aug 88. (7") **SHOW SOME EMOTION. / SHOCK THE DOCTOR** [-] [ ]

— **PASCAL CONSOLI** – percussion, drums repl. BURROWS who joined WORLDWIDE ELECTRIC

Aug 89. (7"/c-s) *(W 2854/+C) <22852>* **STAND UP. / OUTSKIRTS** [ ] [67]
(12") *(W 2854T)* – Stand up (and dance) / Stand up (ya house) / Outskirts.
(cd-s) *(W 2854CD)* – (all mixes & B-side)

Sep 89. (lp/c)(cd) *(WX 289/+C)(K 925945-2) <25945>* **CHANGE THE WEATHER** [ ] [ ]
– Change the weather / Stand up / Fever / Original song / Mercy / Mr. Universe / Texas / Thrash / Sole survivor / Beach.

Nov 89. (7") **CHANGE THE WEATHER. / TEXAS** [-] [ ]

— ALLEN + CONSOLI became D-INFLUENCE

— **SMITH + HYDE** brought in **DARREN EMERSON** (b.1970, Essex) – keyboards

Boys Own — not iss.

1992. (12"ep/cd-ep) **DIRTY. / DIRTY GUITAR** [ ] [-]

1992. (12"ep/cd-ep) **REZ. / WHY WHY WHY** [ ] [-]

Jan 93. (12"ep/cd-ep) *(BOI X/CD 13)* **MMM . . . SKYSCRAPER I LOVE YOU. / ('A'-Telegraph mix 6.11.92) / ('A'-Jamscraper mix)** [ ] [-]

Sep 93. (12"/12"pink)(cd-s) *(Collect 002/+P)* **REZ. / COWGIRL** [ ] [-]
(re-iss. Aug95 on 'Junior Boys Own'; JBO 1001)

Junior Boys Own | Wax Trax!

1993. (12"; as LEMON INTERRUPT) *(JBO 12-002)* **ECLIPSE. / BIGMOUTH** [ ] [-]
1993. (12"; as LEMON INTERRUPT) *(JBO 7-12)* **DIRTY / MINNEAPOLIS. / MINNEAPOLIS (AIRWAVES)** [ ] [-]
Dec 93. (12"/cd-s) *(JBO 17/+CD)* **SPIKEE. / DOGMAN GO WOOF** [60] [ ]
Feb 94. (cd/c/d-lp) *(JBO CD/CS/LP 1)* <7217> **DUBNOBASSWITHMYHEADMAN** [12] [ ]
– Dark and long / Mmm . . . skyscraper I love you / Surfboy / Spoonman / Tongue / Dirty epic / Cowgirl / River of bass / ME. *(cd re-iss. May97; same)*
Jun 94. (cd-ep) *(JBO 19CDS)* **DARK & LONG (mixes)** [57] [-]
– Hall's mix / Dark train / Most 'ospitable / 215 miles.
(12") *(JB 019)* – ('A'-spoon deep mix) / ('A'-thing in a back mix).
(12") *(JB 019X)* – ('A'-dark train mix) / ('A'-Burt's mix).
Dec 94. (cd-s) <8722> **DIRTY EPIC /** [-] [ ]
May 95. (12") *(JBO 29)* **BORN SLIPPY (telenatic). / COWGIRL (Vinjer mix)** [52] [ ]
(12") *(JBO 29R)* – ('A'side) / ('A'-Nuxx mix).
(cd-s) *(JBO 29CDS)* – (above 2) / ('A'side again).
Mar 96. (cd/c/d-lp) *(JBO CD/MC/LP 4)* <7240> **SECOND TOUGHEST IN THE INFANTS** [9] [ ]
– Juanita – Kiteless – To dream of love / Banstyle – Sappys curry / Confusion the waitress / Rowla / Pearls girl / Air towel / Blueski / Stagger. *(cd re-iss. May97; same)*
May 96. (12"ep) *(JBO 38)* **PEARLS GIRL. / MOSAIC / DEEP ARCH** [24] [-]
(cd ep) *(JBO 38CDS1)* – ('A'-Carp Dreams . . . Koi) / Oich oich / Cherry pie.
(cd-ep) *(JBO 38CDS2)* – ('A'mixes).

Junior Boys Own | TVT

Jun 96. (12") <8737> **ROWLA. / JUANITA** [-] [ ]
Jul 96. (12"/cd-s) *(JBO 44/+CDS1)* <8731> **BORN SLIPPY. / ('A'mixes)** [2] [ ]
(cd-s) *(JBO 38CDS2)* – ('A'side) / ('A'-Deep pan mix) / ('A'-Darren Price mix) / ('A'-Darren Price remix).
Oct 96. (12"/cd-s) *(JBO 45/+CDS1)* <8748> **PEARLS GIRL. / ('A'mixes; Puppies / Oich oich / Cherry Pie)** [22] [ ] Feb97
(cd-s) *(JBO 45CDS2)* – ('A'mixes; Mosaic / Deep arch).
Jan 97. (12") **COWGIRL (mixes)** [-] [ ]
1997. (cd-ep) *(9362 43905-2)* **MOANER (short) / (album) / (relentless legs) / (long)** [ ] [ ]
(above from the Warners movie, 'Batman & Robin')

– compilations, etc. –

Oct 97. (cd) *April;* <002> **DARK & LONG** [-] [ ]

UNION CARBIDE PRODUCTIONS (see under ⇒ SOUNDTRACK OF OUR LIVES)

UNREST

Formed: Washington DC, USA . . . early 80's by school friends MARK ROBINSON, PHIL KRAUTH and DAVE PARK. Inspired by their home city's fertile scene, this melodic hardcore trio issued a couple of early singles and a debut album, 'TINK OF S.E.' (1987) through their own 'Teen Beat' label. Harnessing the energy of punk while still celebrating the diversity of their influences and steering clear of hardcore's inherent singularity, the band indulged in covers of The Troggs' 'WILD THING' and King Crimson's '21st CENTURY SCHIZOID MAN'. Following a further two well received albums, 'MALCOLM X PARK' (1988) and 'KUSTOM KARNAL BLACKXPLOITATION' (1990), PARK was replaced by BRIDGET CROSS, who made her debut on 1992's 'IMPERIAL F.F.R.R.'. A rather unlikely link-up with '4 a.d.' resulted in the 'PERFECT TEETH' (1993) album, an enjoyable set of Amerindie-rock punctuated by the X-files experimentation of 'FOOD & DRINK SYNTHESIZER' and encased in a Robert Mapplethorpe cover shot of 80's goddess, CATH CARROLL. In the event, it proved to be the band's epitaph save for compilation set, 'FUCK PUSSY GALORE (& ALL HER FRIENDS)' (1993), KRAUTH going on to release solo set, 'SILVER EYES' (1995) while ROBINSON concentrated on his 30's retro project, GRENADINE. A trio consisting of ROBINSON, JENNY TOOMEY and ROB CHRISTIANSEN, the latter outfit attempted to pay tribute to the halcyon days of swing and lounge jazz in their own imimitable fashion. Following a debut single, 'TRILOGY', the group released the 'GOYA' (1993) album on 'Shimmy Disc', following it up with '94's 'NOPALITOS' (featuring a cover of Burt Bacharach's 1THIS GIRL'S IN LOVE WITH YOU'). Amid a muted critical reception, ROBINSON increasingly concentrated on AIR MIAMI, along with CROSS and new recruits LAUREN and MIKE. Remaining with '4 a.d.', the band contributed a track to a label sampler before releasing a debut single, 'AIRPLANE RIDER', in Autumn '95. With a new rhythm section of FONTAINE TOUPS and BEN CURRIER in place, the band subsequently recorded an acclaimed debut album, 'ME, ME, ME' (1995).

Album rating: IMPERIAL F.F.R.R. (*6) / PERFECT TEETH (*6) / FUCK PUSSY GALORE compilation (*6) / Air Miami: ME, ME, ME (*6) / Grenadine: GOYA (*6) / NOPALITOS (*6)

MARK ROBINSON – vocals, guitar / **DAVE PARK** – bass / **PHIL KRAUTH** – drums

not iss. | Teen Beat

1985. (7"ep) **. / SO YOU WANNA BE A ROCK AND ROLL STAR** [-] [ ]
1987. (lp) **TINK OF S.E.** [-] [ ]
– 91st century schizoid man / Wild thang / etc.
(UK-iss.1989 on 'Hageland'; HR 015)
1988. (c) **TWISTER** [-] [ ]

not iss. | Caroline

1988. (lp/c) *<CAROL 1366-1/-4>* **MALCOLM X PARK** [-] [ ]
– Malcolm X park / Can't sit still / Strutter / Dago red / Ben's chili bowl / Lucifer rising / The gas chair / Ragged (clthd hsbnd) / Oils / Dalmations / Stranger in my own home town / Oh yeah c'mon / Disko magic / Christ in a Castro '59 / The hill.
1990. (cd) *<CAROL 1399-1/-4>* **KUSTOM KARNAL BLACKXPLOITATION** [-] [ ]
– Invoking the godhead / Shag / Click click / Teenage suicide / Coming hot and proud / The foxey playground / Chick Chelsea delux / She makes me shake like a soul machine / Butch Willis is a psychopath / Konfusion / Kill Whitey / Lord Shiva / Black power dynamo.
1991. (7"; by MARK ROBINSON) **SAMMY SUPREME MY MAN! /** [-] [ ]
1991. (cd; by MARK ROBINSON) **SUPERSTAR** [-] [ ]

—— **BRIDGET CROSS** – bass (ex-VELOCITY GIRL) repl. DAVE

Guernica | No.6

Aug 92. (cd/c/lp) *(GU 1 CD/C/LP)* <KAR 018> **IMPERIAL F.F.R.R.** [ ] [ ] Jul92
– Volume reference tone / Suki / Imperial / I do believe you are blushing / Champion nines / Sugar shack / Isabel / Cherry cream on / Firecracker / June / Loyola. *(lp with free-7")* – Yes, she is my skinhead giel / Hydrofoil No.3 / Full frequency range recording. *(cd++=)* – Wednesday & proud. *(the free 7" was finally issued May97 on 'K'; IPU 17)*

4 a.d. | Warners

May 93. (12"ep/cd-ep) *(BAD 3007/+CD)* **ISABEL BISHOP EP** [ ] [ ]
Jul 93. (cd)(lp/c) *(CAD 3012CD)(CAD/+C 3012)* <45401> **PERFECT TEETH** [ ] [ ]
– Angel I'll walk you home / Cath Carroll / So sick / Light command / Food & drink synthesizer / Soon it is going to rain / Make out club / Breather X.O.X.O. / West Coast love affair / Six layer cake / Stylized ampersand. *(cd re-iss. Jul98; GAD 3012CD)*
Oct 93. (12"/cd-s) *(BAD 3015/+CD)* **CATH CARROLL (remix). / HYDRO** [ ] [ ]

Teenbeat | Teenbeat

Apr 94. (7") *<(TEENBEAT 133)>* **ANIMAL PARK. /** [ ] [ ]

—— split in 1994, PHIL KRAUTH releasing one 'Teen Beat' solo set (cd/lp), 'SILVER EYES' in May '96 (TB 205-2/-1)

– compilations, etc. –

Jan 94. (cd/lp) *Matador;* *<(OLE 024-2/-1)>* **FUCK PUSSY GALORE (& ALL HER FRIENDS)** [ ] [ ]
– So you want to be a rock'n'roll star / Scott and Zelda / The hill / Happy song / Rigormortis / Can't sit still / Cats / Die grunen / Holiday in Berlin / 91st century schizoid man / The hill (part 2) / Picnic at Hanging Rock (the hill 3) / Live on a hot August night / Chastity ballad / Judy says (part 2) / The tundra / Wild thang / Laughter / The 'S' street shuffle (with a beat) / Over the life / Hope / Communist tart / She makes me free to be me / Sammy's mean mustard / Greg Hershley where are you? / Egg cheer.
Aug 95. (cd/lp) *Teen Beat;* *<(TB 175-2/-1)>* **B.P.M. (1991-1994)** [ ] [ ]
– June / Cath Carroll / When it all . . . / So sick / Hydrofoil No.4 / Winina XY / Winina XX / Folklore / Imperial (excerpt) / Cherry cherry / Hey London / Bavarian mods / Vibe out / Hi-tec theme / Wednesday & proud.

GRENADINE

MARK ROBINSON – vocals, guitar / **JENNY TOOMEY** – guitar, vocals (ex-TSUNAMI, etc) / **ROB CHRISTIANSEN** – guitar, trombone (ex-EGGS)

not iss. | Teen Beat

1992. (7") **TRILOGY. /** [-] [ ]

Shimmy Disc | Shimmy Disc

Nov 92. (lp/c/cd) *<(SHIMMY 059/+MC/CD)>* **GOYA** [ ] [ ]
– I only have eyes for you / Decca reprise.

Simple Machines | Teenbeat

1994. (7") **DON'T FORGET THE HALO. /** [-] [ ]
Aug 94. (7"ep) *(SMR 031)* *<TB 166>* **CHRISTIANSEN EP** [ ] [ ]
Oct 94. (cd/lp) *<(SMR 23 CD/V)>* **NOPALITOS** [ ] [ ]
– Mexico big sky / Steely Daniel / Puddle / What on earth has happened to today's / Note in his pocket / Hell over Hickory dew / Speeding / Roundabout on a Tuesday / Drama club / Barnacle / Snik / This girl's in love with you.

AIR MIAMI

MARK ROBINSON – vocals, guitar / **BRIDGET CROSS** – guitar, vocals / with **LAUREN** – bass / **MIKE** – drums

4 a.d. | Warners

Sep 95. (7"ep)(cd-ep) *(AD 5014)(BAD 5014CD)* **FUCK YOU, TIGER EP** [ ] [-]
– I hate milk (remix) / Warm Miami May / Afternoon train (remix) / See-through plastic.
Oct 95. (cd-s) **AIRPLANE RIDER. / STOP SIGN** [-] [ ]

—— **FONTAINE TOUPS** – bass (ex-VERSUS) repl. LAUREN

—— **BEN CURRIER** – drums (ex-EGGS) repl. MIKE

—— both repl. by **GABRIEL STOUT** – drums (now a trio)

Nov 95. (lp/cd) *(CAD 5011/+CD)* <46000> **ME, ME, ME** [ ] [ ] Sep95
– I hate milk / World Cup fever / Seabird / Special angel / Afternoon train / Dolphin expressway / Sweet as a candy bar / You sweet little heartbreaker / Neely / Bubble shield / The event horizon / Definitely beachy / Reprise. *(cd re-iss. Jul98; GAD 5011CD)*

not iss. | Teenbeat

Jul 98. (cd-ep) *<TB 257>* **WORLD CUP FEVER (remixes)** [-] [ ]

URGE OVERKILL

Formed: Chicago, Illinois, USA . . . 1986 by NATIONAL 'NASH' KATO, EDDIE 'KING' ROESSER and BLACKIE 'BLACK CAESAR' ONASSIS. Naming themselves after a FUNKADELIC track and setting out on a mission to resurrect the cream of 70's kitsch in a post-modern punk stylee, URGE

OVERKILL made their debut in 1987 with the self-financed 'STRANGE, I . . .' EP. Chicago's hip 'Touch & Go' label were alert to the possibilities, snatching them up for a debut album, 'JESUS URGE SUPERSTAR' (1989). AC/DC and CHEAP TRICK were the most common reference points, though all in the best possible taste of course, the lads even indulging in a cover of Jimmy Webb's 'WICHITA LINEMAN' to make sure people got the message. The main criticism was the ropey production, BUTCH VIG making sure that 'AMERICRUISER' (1990) didn't head the same way. Another alternative figurehead, STEVE ALBINI, oversaw the graft on the acclaimed 'SUPERSONIC STORYBOOK' (1991), their partnership subsequently turning sour when the former BIG BLACK man publicly chastised them for their defiant decadence (well, that's if you can call touring Chicago in a horse-drawn carriage sipping aperatifs decadence) and concrete commitment to all things kitsch. A stop-gap mini-set, 'STULL', preceded their signing to 'Geffen', a record that featured their peerless take on Neil Diamond's 'GIRL YOU'LL BE A WOMAN SOON'. Later featured as a key inclusion on the soundtrack to Quentin Tarantino's masterful 'Pulp Fiction', the song was also a UK Top 40 hit in its own right without actually drawing in many moviegoers to the weird and wonderful universe of URGE OVERKILL itself, no doubt the name putting them off! Their first major label release, 'SATURATION' (1993) further distanced them from the harsh extremism of their hometown punk scene, the band benefitting from residual interest in the insurgent grunge movement and scoring two minor UK hit singles. Amid the wave of mid-90's publicity following the 'Pulp Fiction' success, URGE OVERKILL were inspired to release their most lovable album to date, 'EXIT THE DRAGON' (1995).

Album rating: JESUS URGE SUPERSTAR (*4) / AMERICRUISER (*4) / THE SUPERSONIC STORYBOOK (*6) / STULL mini (*6) / SATURATION (*7) / EXIT THE DRAGON (*8)

NATIONAL 'Nash' KATO (b.31 Dec'65, Grand Forks, North Dakota) – vocals, guitar / **EDDIE 'King' ROESER** (b.17 Jun'69, Litchfield, Minnesota) – bass / **BLACKIE 'Black Caesar' ONASSIS** (b. JOHNNY ROWAN, 27 Aug'67, Chicago) – vocals, drums

not iss. / Ruthless

1987. (12"ep) **STRANGE, I . . .** [-] [ ]

Touch & Go / Touch & Go

May 89. (lp) *<TGLP 37>* **JESUS URGE SUPERSTAR** [ ] [ ]
– God Flintstone / Very sad trousers / Your friend is insane / Dump dump dump / Last train to Heaven / The Polaroid doll / Head on / Crown of laffs / Dubbledead / Easter '88 / Wichita lineman / Eggs.

Jun 90. (cd/c/lp) *<TG CD/MC/LP 52>* **AMERICRUISER** [ ] [ ]
– Ticket to L.A. / Blow chopper / 76 ball / Empire builder / Faroutski / Viceroyce / Out on the airstrip / Smokehouse. *(cd+=)* – JESUS URGE SUPERSTAR

Mar 91. (cd/c/lp) *<TG CD/MC/LP 70>* **THE SUPERSONIC STORYBOOK** [ ] [ ]
– The kids are insane / The candidate / (Today is) Blackie's birthday / Emmaline / Bionic revolution / What is artane? / Vacation in Tokyo / Henhough: The greatest story ever told / Theme from Navajo.

Roughneck / Touch & Go

Jun 92. (m-cd/m-lp) *(NECKM CD/MC 009) <TG CD/LP 86>* **STULL** [ ] [ ]
– Girl you'll be a woman soon / Stull (part 1) / Stitches / What's this generation coming to / (Now that's) The barclouds / Goodbye to Guyville. *(cd re-iss. Aug96 on 'Nectar'; NTMCD 522)*

Geffen / Geffen

Jun 93. (cd/c/lp) *<(GED/GEC/GEF 24529)>* **SATURATION** [ ] [ ]
– Sister Havana / Tequilla sundae / Positive bleeding / Back on me / Woman 2 woman / Bottle of fur / Crackbabies / The stalker / Dropout / Erica Kane / Nite and grey / Heaven 90210. *(cd+=)* – Operation: Kissinger.

Aug 93. (7"/c-s) *(GFS/+C 51)* **SISTER HAVANA. / WOMAN 2 WOMAN** [67] [ ]
(12"+=/cd-s+=) *(GFST/+D 51)* – Operation: Kissinger.

Oct 93. (7"red/c-s) *(GFS/+C 57)* **POSITIVE BLEEDING. / NITE AND GREY** [61] [ ]
(12"+=/cd-s+=) *(GFST/+D 57)* – Quality love (Hong Kong demo).

Nov 94. (c-s) *(MCSC 2024) <54935>* **GIRL YOU'LL BE A WOMAN SOON / (track by The Tornadoes)** [37] [59]
(cd-s+=) *(MCSTD 2024)* – (tracks by other artists).

—— above from the cult Tarantino film, 'Pulp Fiction', on 'M.C.A.'

Aug 95. (cd/c/lp) *<(GED/GEC/GEF 24818)>* **EXIT THE DRAGON** [ ] [ ]
– Jaywalkin' / The break / Need some air / Somebody else's body / Honesty files / This is no place / The mistake / Take me / View of the rain / Last night – Tomorrow / Tin foil / Monopoly / And you'll say / Digital black epilogue. *(cd re-iss. Feb98; same)*

– compilations, etc. –

Jul 95. (d-cd/t-lp) *Edel; (6613 2/1 RAD)* **10 YEARS OF WRECKING** [ ] [-]

URINALS

Formed: Orange County, California, USA . . . January '78 by L.A. film students, JOHN JONES, KEITH BARRETT and KJEHL JOHANSEN (originally a parody 5-piece). Got serious in '79 and released three 7"er's, although their musical lifespan was mercifully brief. Clearly they became pissed off before their fans did and flushed away their musical ambitions in 1981; despite a second incarnation as 100 FLOWERS, success continued to elude them. • **Songwriters:** JONES with JOHANSEN & BARRETT contributing to others except covers WHY ARE WE SLEEPING? (Soft Machine) / SHAPE OF THINGS TO COME (Mann-Weill) / YOU'RE GONNA MISS ME (13th Floor Elevators) / JETSON MAIN THEME (Barbera-Curtin-Hanna) / RETURN OF JAKE BODDLER (. . . Bludgeon) / GO AWAY GIRL (. . . Nolte).

Album rating: NEGATIVE CAPABILITY compilation (*5)

JOHN JONES – vocals, bass / **KJEHL JOHANSEN** – guitar / **KEITH BARRETT** – drums

not iss. / Happy Squid

Jan 79. (7"ep) *<HS-001>* **THE URINALS EP** [-] [ ]
– Dead flowers / Hologram / The last days of man on Earth / Surfin' with the Shah.

Jul 79. (7"ep) *<HS-002>* **ANOTHER EP** [-] [ ]
– Black holes / I'm white and middle class / I'm a bug / Ack ack ack ack.

Apr 80. (7") *<HS-003>* **SEX. / GO AWAY GIRL** [-] [ ]

—— also the track, 'U', appeared on the label sampler 7"ep; HS-004

—— In 1981, they became 100 FLOWERS, although they only managed to appear on a few various artist compilations, 'Hell Comes To Your House' <Bemis Brain BB 123-124> and 'Keats Rides A Harley' <HS-007>.

– compilations, etc. –

Nov 97. (cd) *Amphetamine Reptile; <(AMREP 045-2)>* **NEGATIVE CAPABILITY** [ ] [ ] Jan97
– Dead flowers / Hologram / The last days of man on Earth / Surfin' with the Shah / Black holes / I'm white and middle class / I'm a bug / Ack ack ack ack / Sex / Go away girl / U / Scholastic attitude / I hate / She's a drone / Male masterbation / Return of Jake Boddler / Presence of mind / Sex / I'm like you / Orange anal sin / Salmonella / I'm a bug / Ack ack ack ack / Mr. Encore / Why are we sleeping? / Shape of things to come / You're gonna miss me / Hologram / Jetsons main theme / Don't make me kill again / You piss me off.

URUSEI YATSURA

Formed: Glasgow, Scotland . . . 1994 by FERGUS LAWRIE, GRAHAM KEMP, plus brother and sister IAN and ELAINE GRAHAM. Part of the US-influenced Glasgow indie scene, their low-key debut release was a very rare mini-lp, 'ALL HAIL URUSEI YATSURA' (1995), a follow-up single, 'PAMPERED ADOLESCENT', receiving airplay from Radio One stalwarts John Peel and Mark Radcliffe. This exposure resulted in an indie Top 30 hit, with London's 'Che' records picking them up for a long-term deal. A handful of singles, including 'SIAMESE', 'PLASTIC ASHTRAY' and 'KEWPIES LIKE WATERMELON', preceded a debut album proper, the self-explanatory 'WE ARE URUSEI YATSURA', in the Spring of '96. Arty bubblegum noise merchants trading in a PAVEMENT meets SONIC YOUTH meets T.REX style, these colourful kitschy characters amassed further critical acclaim with another clutch of three minute gems over the course of the next two years. From 'PHASERS ON STUN' to their first Top 75 entry 'STRATEGIC HAMLETS' to summer '97's 'FAKE FUR', the band were building up to their first Top 40 hit, 'HELLO TIGER', in early '98. URUSEI YATSURA's (YATSURA only in the States!) ultra hip factor was enough to persuade 'Warners' to enter into a part deal with 'Che', the result being a collection of the aforementioned singles, 'SLAIN BY URUSEI YATSURA' (1998). The latter's title track was inspired by their finest moment to date, minor hit single 'SLAIN BY ELF'. • **Trivia:** Their moniker roughly translates as a troublemaking female android in Japanese.

Album rating: WE ARE URUSEI YATSURA (*8) / SLAIN BY URUSEI YATSURA (*8)

FERGUS LAWRIE (b.23 Jan'68, Marlborough, England) – vocals, guitar / **GRAHAM KEMP** (b. 3 Dec'68, Inverness, Scotland) – vocals, guitar / **ELAINE GRAHAM** (b.16 Jun'70) – bass / **IAN GRAHAM** (b.19 Ovt'72) – drums

Hipster / not iss.

Jan 95. (12"ep) *(HIP 001)* **ALL HAIL URUSEI YATSURA** [ ] [-]
(cd-ep iss.Mar98 on 'Tiny Superhero'; SUPERCD 005)

Modern Independent / not iss.

Apr 95. (7") *(MIR 001)* **PAMPERED ADOLESCENT. / (other track by The Blisters)** [ ] [-]

Che / Primary

Sep 95. (7",7"orange) *(che 38)* **SIAMESE. /** [ ] [-]

Nov 95. (7") *(PUBE 08)* **KERNAL. / TEENAGE DREAM** [ ] [-]
(above issued on 'Love Train')

Feb 96. (7",7"pink) *(che 46) <64338>* **PLASTIC ASHTRAY. / GOT THE SUN** [ ] [ ]
(cd-s) *(che 46cd)* – ('A'side) / Miramar / Taster.

Apr 96. (7"ep/cd-ep) *(che 53/+cd) <66077>* **THE STUNRAY EP** [83] [ ]
– Kewpies like watermelon / Majesty / Sucker / Burriko girl.

May 96. (cd/lp,orange-lp) *(che 54 cd/lp) <61957>* **WE ARE URUSEI YATSURA** [ ] [ ]
– Siamese / First day on a new planet / Pow R. Ball / Kewpies like watermelon / Phasers on stun – Sola kola / Black hole love / Velvy blood / Plastic ashtray / Death 2 everyone / Pachinko / Kernel / Road song. *(re-iss. Sep97, same)*

—— (shared a 7" with MOGWAI and BACKWATER) *(che 59)*

Aug 96. (d7"/cd-ep) *(che 62/+cd) <66011>* **PHASERS ON STUN. / THE LOVE THAT BRINGS YOU DOWN // THE POWER OF NEGATIVE THINKING. / SID AND NANCY** [ ] [ ]

Feb 97. (7") *(che 67)* **STRATEGIC HAMLETS. / KOZEE HEART** [64] [-]
(7") *(che 67s)* – ('A'side) / Revir.
(cd-s+=) *(che 67cd)* – Down home Kitty.

Jun 97. (7"white) *(che 73)* **FAKE FUR. / SILVER KREST** [58] [-]
(cd-s+=) *(che 73cd)* – Nova static / Secret crush.
(cd-s) *(che 73cd2)* – ('A'side) / Pampered adolescent / Bewitched / Saki & cremola.

Jun 97. (cd-s) *<62084>* **FAKE FUR / STRATEGIC HAMLETS** [-] [ ]

Feb 98. (7") *(che 75)* **HELLO TIGER. / VANILLA SCARLET** [40] [ ]
(cd-s+=) *(che 75cd1)* – Vent axial.
(cd-s) *(che 75cd2)* – ('A'-Peel session version) / Dice, nae dice (Peel session version) / Everybody hang out.

Che-Warners Sire

Mar 98. (cd) *(che 76cd – <3984-22221-2>)* **SLAIN BY URUSEI YATSURA** [64] [ ]
– Glo starz / Hello tiger / Strategic hamlets / No 1 cheesecake / Superfi / No no girl / Flaming skull / Slain by elf / King of lazy / Exidor / Fake fur / Skull in action / Amber.

May 98. (7") *(che 80)* **SLAIN BY ELF. / HAIL TO THE NEW POOR** [63] [-]
(cd-s+=) *(che 80cd2)* –
(cd-s) *(che 80cd1)* – ('A'side) / Subatomic.

– compilations, etc. –

1997. (cd; as YATSURA) *Che-Sire; <62084>* **PULPO!** [-] [ ]
– Strategic hamlets / Down home Kitty / Pampered adolescent / Kozee heart / Mirimar / Saki and Oremola / Fake fur / Silver krest / Got the sun / Nova static / Revir / Power of negative thinking / Love that brings you down.

U.S. BOMBS

Formed: Orange County, California, USA . . . mid 90's by extrovert skateboarding hero of the late 70's/early 80's, DWAYNE PETERS. Completing the line-up with KERRY MARTINEZ, CHUCK BRIGGS, STEVE REYNOLDS and ALEX GOMEZ, this basic punk rock outfit (not another one!) released the appallingly titled 'NEVER MIND THE OPENED MINDS' track as a debut single in early '97. After an album proper on the 'Disaster' imprint, they hooked up with hardcore nerve centre 'Epitaph' for the 'WAR BIRTH' long player. Their association with the label subsequently led to the group signing with TIM ARMSTRONG's (RANCID) operation, 'Hellcat'. • **Covered:** THAT'S LIFE (hit; Frank Sinatra).

Album rating: WAR BIRTH (*5)

DWAYNE PETERS – vocals / **KERRY MARTINEZ** – guitar / **CHUCK BRIGGS** – guitar / **STEVE REYNOLDS** – bass / **ALEX GOMEZ** – drums

Alive Alive

Jan 96. (cd-ep) *<ALIVE 17>* **U.S. BOMBS EP** [-] [ ]
– Go back home / Retreats / U.S. bombs / Call box.

Apr 96. (cd) *<ALIVE 19>* **GARIBALDI GUARD!** [-] [ ]
– Intro / All the bodies / Deadly kiss / Rumble beach / Spaghetti / Bon voyage / Retreads / Monsters / Don't wanna go / Underdog / No love / Go back home / Not alright / Walkin' blind.

Mar 97. (m-lp/m-cd) *<(ALIVE/+CD 24)>* **NEVER MIND THE OPENED MINDS** [ ] [ ]
– Sex machine / Ballad of Sid / Slow down / Neverland / Outside / Ballad of Sid (reprise).

Disaster Alive

Jun 97. (cd) *(DIS 1) <ALIVECD 033>* **PUT STRENGTH IN FINAL . . .** [ ] [ ]

—— **WADE WALSTON** – bass; repl. REYNOLDS

—— **CHIP** – drums; repl. GOMEZ

Epitaph Epitaph

Oct 97. (cd/c/lp) *<(80404-2/-4/-1)>* **WAR BIRTH** [ ] [ ] Sep97
– That's life / Orange crunch / Jaks / War storyville / 12-25 / Outta touch / U.S. of hate / War birth / The hand me downs / Rocks in Memphis / Beetle boot / Her and me / Don't need you / No company town.

UT

Formed: New York, USA . . . 1978 by NINA CANAL, JACQUI HAM and SALLY YOUNG. Following the demise of their 'Lust-Unlust' imprint in 1980, the girls took flight to London, surfacing a year later with the cassette-only release, 'UT LIVE'. Little was heard from them (bar a few singles) until 1986's 'CONVICTION' album, a more focused affair developing their early experimental "No Wave" sound. Nevertheless, they were still known to indulge in a spot of instrument swopping on stage (basically guitar, bass and drums). Increasingly drifting into SONIC YOUTH-esque territory, they signed to 'Blast First', releasing three albums in the space of three years: an early live set, 'IN GUT'S HOUSE' (1988) and the STEVE ALBINI-produced swansong, 'GRILLER' (1989).

Album rating: UT LIVE (*5) / CONVICTION (*6) / EARLY LIVE LIFE (*5) / IN GUT'S HOUSE (*6) / GRILLER (*6)

SALLY YOUNG – vocals, guitar, bass, violin / **JACQUI HAM** – vocals, bass, guitar / **NINA CANAL** – drums, guitar, bass

not iss. Outtapes

Dec 81. (c) *<C-52>* **UT LIVE (live)** [-] [ ]

not iss. Infidelity

1982. (7") **WHILE I WAIT. / AMPHETA SPEAK** [-] [ ]

Feb 84. (12"ep) **UT EP** [-] [ ]
– Sham shack / This bliss / New colour / Exile goes out.

Outro Outro

Jun 85. (12"ep) *(UTR 01)* **CONFIDENTIAL. / BEDOIN / TELL IT** [ ] [ ]

May 86. (lp) *(OUTRO 3)* **CONVICTION** [ ] [ ]
– Confidential / Sick / Phoenix hotel / Absent farmer / Stain / Prehistory / Bedouin / Kcahsmahs (spare coconut) / Mouse sleep.

Blast First Blast First

May 87. (lp) *<(BFFP 12)>* **EARLY LIVE LIFE (live)** [ ] [ ]
– Fire in Philadelphia / Brink over chicken / Surgery / Ampheta speak / While I wait / Mouse sleep / Sharp's loose / This bliss / No manifesto / Feed / Limbo.

Jan 88. (2x12"ep/cd) *<(BFFP 17/+CD)>* **IN GUT'S HOUSE** [ ] [ ]
– Evangelist / I.D. / Swallow / Big wing / Hotel / Homebled / Shut fog / Mosquito botticelli / Dirty net / Landscape.

—— added **CHARLIE D** – drums

Feb 89. (lp/cd) *<(BFFP 36/+CD)>* **GRILLER** [ ] [ ]
– Safe burning / How it goes / Canker / Rummy / Posse necks / Fuel / Wailhouse / Scrape / Spore / Griller / Doctor No.

—— split soon after above

U2

Formed: Dublin, Ireland . . . 1977 by BONO (b. PAUL HEWSON), THE EDGE (b. DAVID EVANS), ADAM CLAYTON and LARRY MULLEN. Indisputably one of the biggest and the most talked about 'musical phenomenon's of the last two decades, U2 nevertheless graduated from humble beginnings as a covers band. Finally adopting the U2 moniker in 1978, they subsequently attracted the attention of Paul McGuinness, one of the most respected managers in the business. It wasn't long before they found themselves signed to 'C.B.S.' Ireland via A&R man, Jackie Hayden, releasing a debut single, 'U2-3' in late '79. The track scaled the Irish charts, as did a follow-up, 'ANOTHER DAY', the group subsequently snapped up by 'Island' records for a worldwide deal. Initially, U2 made little impact, singles '11 O'CLOCK TICK TOCK' and 'A DAY WITHOUT ME' failing to chart. By the release of the Steve Lillywhite-produced debut album, 'BOY' (1980), however, U2 were already assuming the mantle of cult status. Strikingly original, the group carved out their own plot of fertile territory within the suffocatingly oversubscribed rock format, cultivating a watertight, propulsive minimalism to partner their politically direct lyrics. Carried equally by BONO's crusading vocal theatrics, THE EDGE's serrated guitar cascades and the ryhthmic drive of CLAYTON and MULLEN, the likes of 'I WILL FOLLOW' was a blueprint for the U2 formula. And it was a formula which seemed to command devotion; those who followed the band did so with the same zeal as U2 set out their humanitarian agenda, the group eschewing party politics for a more expansive but no less focused commentary on the world's ills with an overriding religious/spiritual bent. Live, the group were also being hailed as one of the most innovative and exciting act's to emerge from the post-punk morass. Though 'OCTOBER' (1981) almost broke into the Top 10, the album failed to spawn any major hits, the clarion call of 'GLORIA' surprisingly stiffing outside the Top 50. So it was then, that U2 seemed to come out of nowhere in early '83 with a Top 10 single, the highly emotive 'NEW YEAR'S DAY' (inspired by the Lech Walenska's Polish Solidarity Union) and a No.1 album, 'WAR'. U2's first masterstroke, the album was consistently compelling, through the rousing rhythmic militarism of 'SUNDAY BLOODY SUNDAY' (interpreted by many as a republican rebel song, BONO famously declared otherwise when introducing the track live) and the celebratory 'TWO HEARTS BEAT AS ONE' to the more meditative acoustics of 'DROWNING MAN'. The record's anthemic Irish qualities also appealed to the Americans, 'WAR' almost making the US Top 10; from the electric atmosphere of the live 'UNDER A BLOOD RED SKY' (1983), it certainly seemed U2's sound could galvanise a transatlantic audience, probably (and eventually) a world audience. Previewed by perhaps U2's most anthemic, politically pointed song, 'PRIDE (IN THE NAME OF LOVE)' (a tribute to assassinated black civil rights hero, Martin Luther King), 'THE UNFORGETTABLE FIRE' (1984) consolidated the band's commercial and creative maturity. For the most part, however, the record took a completely different approach, BRIAN ENO presiding over a collection of more exploratory, occasionally near-ambient excursions, the highlight arguably being the epic atmospherics of the stunning title track. Equally evocative was 'BAD', an almost hymn-like incantation with which U2 entranced the world at Live Aid in summer '85. One of the key events in the band's career, their celebrated performance undoubtedly won them a massive new audience almost overnight, much in the same way as QUEEN rejuvenated their career through the concert. Understandably, then, the anticipation for U2's forthcoming album, 'THE JOSHUA TREE' (1987), was fevered. Fortunately it was also justified, U2 delivering what was undeniably the most accomplished set of their career and probably one of the greatest rock albums ever released. Like many such masterworks, U2 scaled this pinnacle of creativity by means of a subtle balance, between panoramic euphoria and hushed reflection, between the personal and the political and between insinuation and crystal clarity. The record's undertow of spiritual soul searching evident on the likes of 'I STILL HAVEN'T FOUND WHAT I'M LOOKING FOR' (a US No.1) obviously struck a chord in a decade more concerned with ruthless material gain, while the air of soft-focus melancholy permeating 'WITH OR WITHOUT YOU' and 'RUNNING TO STAND STILL' further enhanced the album's almost tangible warmth. Even the more full-on tracks such as 'WHERE THE STREETS HAVE NO NAME' and 'IN GOD'S COUNTRY' seemed to emanate a deep-seated yearning through the shards of THE EDGE's guitar scree.~ 'THE JOSHUA TREE' was a transatlantic No.1 (a worldwide No.1), facilitating U2's move to the top of the world premier league. As well as being a formidable commercial proposition, U2 were hailed by some commentators as the most 'important' rock group on the planet, both lyrically and musically. Of course, such inflated claims were matched by equally vociferous critics of the group's perceived pomposity and preaching self-importance. Such criticism was nothing new, although it reached its height in the aftermath of 'THE JOSHUA TREE' and its attendant tour, when BONO was being hailed as some kind of messiah. The sight of the singer charging around the stage with a floodlight and a white flag, together with his increasingly politicised between song (or even half-way through) speeches became too much for some, although in a music scene bereft of direction or purpose, BONO probably made up for the prevailing insipidness. Attempting to follow up this musical landmark, U2 released a kind of stop-gap half-live/half-studio affair, 'RATTLE AND HUM' (1988).

A soundtrack to the rockumentary of the same name which marked the culmination of the group's obsession with America, the album was accused of being half-baked in parts. Possibly, but the gut-level punch of 'GOD PART II' and the bleakly beautiful 'VAN DIEMEN'S LAND' were unquestionably full-baked, if oddities nonetheless. Following the poignant love song, 'ALL I WANT IS YOU' (a UK Top 5) in summer '89, U2 went to ground, hard at work on a new strategy. Sporting wraparound shades and skin-tight black leather, BONO finally emerged in late '91 with 'THE FLY', a grinding guitar groove with urgent, hoarsely whispered lyrics. The track entered the UK chart at No.1, paving the way for the massively successful 'ACHTUNG BABY' (1991). Stylistically diverse, the album marked the beginnings of U2's flirtation with dance culture, a sign that the band were wary of falling into the rock dinosaur mould. BONO had also obviously been listening to his critics, changing his persona from earnest poet to lounge lizard sophisticate. Though the likes of 'WHO'S GONNA RIDE YOUR WILD HORSES' and the deeply affecting 'ONE' (probably the most intimate song the group have ever penned) signalled a move into more personal lyrical territory, the album's attendant 'Zoo TV' tour was themed around political events in Europe, albeit with a more post-modern, multi-media stoked irony. Inspired by the tour, 'ZOOROPA' (1993) was U2's most contemporary release to date, a fractured, dance-orientated affair which rather unfairly received a bit of a pasting from more short-sighted critics. Following on from the celebrated dance mixes of 'EVEN BETTER THAN THE REAL THING' (from 'ACHTUNG BABY'), the 12' remix of 'LEMON' was hot property when originally released in limited lemon coloured vinyl. As well as catering for dance trainspotters, U2 even recorded a duet with JOHNNY CASH, the darkly brilliant 'THE WANDERER', in effect kickstarting the aging country star's career. In the ensuing two years, BONO popped up with GAVIN FRIDAY on the theme to the acclaimed 'IN THE NAME OF THE FATHER', while U2 scored a UK No.2 hit with 'HOLD ME, THRILL ME, KISS ME, KILL ME' from the huge box office smash, 'Batman Forever'. This fascination with soundtrack music continued via the PASSENGERS project, a collaboration between U2, BRIAN ENO, italian opera singer PAVAROTTI and Glaswegian beatz guru HOWIE B. Entitled 'ORIGINAL SOUNDTRACKS VOL.1' (1995), a few of the album's tracks (highlight being the hit single, 'MISS SARAJEVO') were actually written as themes to avant-garde films while the remainder were written for imaginary celluloid pieces. As low-key as U2 have ever dared go, the album passed by without much fuss, its ambient noodlings not really indicating a new direction as such but proving that the group were firmly committed to constant experimentation. For their next album proper, U2 retained HOWIE B as co-producer, crafting an album that once again used dance music as a touchstone. Preview single, 'DISCOTHEQUE', sounded like a watered-down 'FLY' although the accompanying VILLAGE PEOPLE-pastiche video showed, shock horror!, U2 having a right old laugh! Despite this newfound sense of humour, the 'POP' (1996) album met with mixed reviews, some hailing it as a bold new dawn, others accusing the band of treading water. The record certainly had its moments, the searing desolation of 'STARING AT THE SUN' and the apocalyptic 'LAST NIGHT ON EARTH' (the video featuring an appearance from counter-culture guru, William Burroughs, just weeks before his death, U2 having previously persuaded the voraciously anti-rock Charles Bukowski to attend a gig, no mean feat!) for example, but there was a feeling of incompleteness to the whole affair. Likewise, the accompanying 'Pop Mart' tour which got off to a shaky start in Las Vegas, its consumerist theme carried by another media extravaganza, albeit downscaled from the Zoo TV era. While U2 undoubtedly lead the way in terms of stadium rock, constantly innovative in new ways to keep the medium fresh, they arguably need to rediscover themselves musically and give up recycling second hand ideas. Whether they have either the willingness or ability to do this is another matter, although being past masters of coming out fighting in the face of adversity, it's highly likely. • **Songwriters:** All written by BONO / THE EDGE, except HELTER SKELTER (Beatles) / ALL ALONG THE WATCHTOWER (Bob Dylan) (hit; Jimi Hendrix) / STAR SPANGLED BANNER (US National anthem) / DANCING BAREFOOT (Patti Smith) / NIGHT AND DAY (Cole Porter) / PAINT IT BLACK (Rolling Stones) / FORTUNATE SON (Creedence Clearwater Revival) / HALLELUJAH (Leonard Cohen) by BONO. • **Trivia:** BONO contributed vox to BAND AID single late '84. That year, the band also started own record label, mainly for other Irish groups and was a starter for HOTHOUSE FLOWERS, CACTUS WORLD NEWS etc. In 1988, BONO and THE EDGE co-wrote for ROY ORBISON on his last living studio album, 'Mystery Girl'. They wrote the theme for the James Bond film 'GOLDEN EYE', which became a hit for TINA TURNER in 1995.

Album rating: BOY (*8) / OCTOBER (*6) / WAR (*9) / UNDER A BLOOD RED SKY (*6) / THE UNFORGETTABLE FIRE (*9) / WIDE AWAKE IN AMERICA (*6) / THE JOSHUA TREE (*10) / RATTLE & HUM (*8) / ACHTUNG BABY (*8) / ZOOROPA (*9) / PASSENGERS: ORIGINAL SOUNDTRACKS 1 (*7)

BONO VOX (b. PAUL HEWSON, 10 May'60) - vocals / **THE EDGE** (b. DAVID EVANS, 8 Aug'61, Barking, Essex) - guitar, keyboards / **ADAM CLAYTON** (b.13 Mar'60, Chinnor, Oxfordshire, England) - bass / **LARRY MULLEN** (b. LAURENCE MULLEN, 31 Oct'61) - drums

		C.B.S.	not iss.
Oct 79.	(7"ep/12"ep) *(CBS/+12 7951)* **U2: THREE**	-	- Irish
	– Out of control / Stories for boys / Boy-girl. *(re-iss.1980 7"orange,yellow,white; same) (re-iss.c-ep 1985; CBS 40-7951)*		
Feb 80.	(7",7"yellow,7"orange,7"white) *(CBS 8306)* **ANOTHER DAY. / TWILIGHT (demo)**	-	- Irish

Island Island

May 80. (7") *(WIP 6601)* **11 O'CLOCK TICK TOCK. / TOUCH** [ ] [-]

Aug 80. (7") *(WIP 6630)* **A DAY WITHOUT ME. / THINGS TO MAKE AND DO** [ ] [-]

Oct 80. (7") *(WIP 6656)* **I WILL FOLLOW. / BOY-GIRL (live)** [ ] [-]

Nov 80. (lp/c) *(ILPS/ICT <9646>)* **BOY** [52] [63] Feb81
– I will follow / Twilight / An cat dubh / Into the heart / Out of control / Stories for boys / The ocean / A day without me / Another time, another place / The Electric Co. / Shadows and tall trees. *(cd-iss.May86; CID 110) (re-iss.May95 cd)(c)(lp; IMCD 211)(ILPM 9646)*

Apr 81. (7") **I WILL FOLLOW. / OUT OF CONTROL** [-] [ ]

Jul 81. (7") *(WIP 6679)* **FIRE. / J. SWALLO** [35] [ ]
(d7"+=) *(U-WIP 6679)* – 11 o'clock tick tock (live) / The ocean (live) / Cry (live) / The Electric Co. (live).

Sep 81. (7") *(WIP 6733)* **GLORIA. / I WILL FOLLOW (live)** [55] [ ]

Oct 81. (lp/c) *(ILPS/ICT <9680>)* **OCTOBER** [11] [ ]
– Gloria / I fall down / I threw a brick through a window / Rejoice / Fire / Tomorrow / October / With a shout / Stranger in a strange land / Scarlet / Is that all?. *(cd-iss.May86; CID 111) (re-dist.Jun92; same) (cd re-iss.Mar96; IMCD 223)*

Mar 82. (7") *(WIP 6770)* **A CELEBRATION. / TRASH, TRAMPOLENE AND THE PARTY GIRL** [47] [ ]

Jan 83. (7") *(WIP 6848)* *<99915>* **NEW YEAR'S DAY. / TREASURE (WHATEVER HAPPENED TO PETE THE CHOP)** [10] [53]
(d7"+=/12"+=) *(U-WIP/12WIP 6848)* – Fire (live) / I threw a brick through the window (live) / A day without me (live).

Feb 83. (lp/c) *(ILPS/ICT 9733)* *<90067>* **WAR** [1] [12]
– Sunday bloody Sunday / Seconds / Like a song / New Year's day / Two hearts beat as one / The refugee / Drowning man / Red light / '40' / Surrender. *(cd-iss.Dec85; CID 112) (re-iss.Aug91 cd/c; IMCD/ICT 141; hit No.51 Jun92, hit UK No.38 Aug93)*

Mar 83. (7") *(IS 109)* *<99861>* **TWO HEARTS BEAT AS ONE. / ENDLESS DEEP** [18] [ ]
(d7"+=) *(ISD 109)* – Two hearts beat as one (U.S. remix) / New Year's day (U.S. remix).
(12") *(12IS 109)* – ('A'-club mix) / New Year's day (U.S. remix) / ('A'-U.S. remix).

Nov 83. (lp/c) *(IMA/IMC 3)* *<90127>* **UNDER A BLOOD RED SKY (live)** [2] [28]
– Gloria / 11 o'clock tick tock / I will follow / Party girl / Sunday bloody Sunday / The Electric Co. / New Year's day / '40'. *(cd-iss.May86; CID 113) (re-dist.Jun92; same)*

Dec 83. (7") *<99789>* **I WILL FOLLOW (live). / TWO HEARTS BEAT AS ONE (live)** [-] [81]

Sep 84. (7"/7"pic-d) *(IS/+P 202)* *<99704>* **PRIDE (IN THE NAME OF LOVE). / BOOMERANG 2** [3] [33]
(d7"+=/c-s+=/12"white+=) *(ISD/CIS/12IS 202)* – 4th of July / Boomerang 1.
(12"blue+=) *(12ISX 202)* – Boomerang 1 / 11 o'clock tick tock (extended) / Touch.

Oct 84. (lp/c)(cd) *(U2/+C 5)(CID 102)* *<90231>* **THE UNFORGETTABLE FIRE** [1] [12]
– A sort of homecoming / Pride (in the name of love) / Wire / The unforgettable fire / Promenade / 4th of July / Bad / Indian summer sky / Elvis Presley and America / MLK. *(re-dist.Jun92 hit No.38 UK; same)*

May 85. (7"/7"sha-pic-d) *(IS/+P 220)* **THE UNFORGETTABLE FIRE. / A SORT OF HOMECOMING (live)** [6] [ ]
(12"+=) *(12IS 220)* – The three sunrises / Bass trap / Love comes tumbling.
(d7"+=) *(ISD 220)* – The three sunrises / Love comes tumbling / 60 seconds in kingdom come.

May 85. (m-lp/c) *(ISSP/+C 22)* *<90279>* **WIDE AWAKE IN AMERICA** [11] [37]
– Bad (live) / A sort of homecoming (live) / The three sunrises / Love comes tumbling. *(cd-iss Oct87; CIDU 22) (cd re-iss.Nov89; IMCD 75)*

— Later in the year, BONO guested for CLANNAD on hit 'IN A LIFETIME'. In Sep'86, THE EDGE issued soundtrack album CAPTIVE (see further below).

Mar 87. (7"/c-s/12"/cd-s) *(IS/CIS/12IS/CID 319)* *<99469>* **WITH OR WITHOUT YOU. / LUMINOUS TIMES (HOLD ON TO LOVE) / WALK TO THE WATER** [4] [1]

Mar 87. (lp/c)(cd) *(U2/+C 6)(CIDU 26)* *<90581>* **THE JOSHUA TREE** [1] [1]
– Where the streets have no name / I still haven't found what I'm looking for / With or without you / Bullet the blue sky / Running to stand still / Red Hill mining town / In God's country / Trip through your wires / One tree hill / Exit / Mothers of the disappeared. *(also on 4x7"box) (re-charted UK Jan92, peaked Jun92 at No.19) (re-iss.Aug93 cd/c/lp, hit UK No.27; same)*

May 87. (7"/c-s/12") *(IS/CIS/12IS 328)* *<99430>* **I STILL HAVEN'T FOUND WHAT I'M LOOKING FOR. / SPANISH EYES / DEEP IN THE HEART** [6] [1]

Sep 87. (7") *(IS 340)* *<99408>* **WHERE THE STREETS HAVE NO NAME. / SILVER AND GOLD / SWEETEST THING** [4] [13]
(c-s+=/12"+=/cd-s+=) *(CIS/12IS/CID 340)* – Race against time.

Jan 88. (7"-US-imp) *<7-99385>* **IN GOD'S COUNTRY. / BULLET THE BLUE SKY / RUNNING TO STAND STILL** [48] [44] Nov87

Sep 88. (7") *(IS 400)* *<99250>* **DESIRE. / HALLELUJAH (HERE SHE COMES)** [1] [3]
(12"+=/12"g-f+=/pic-cd-s+=) *(12IS/12ISG/CIDP 400)* – ('A'-Hollywood remix).

Oct 88. (d-lp/c)(cd) *(U2/+C 7)(CIDU 27)* *<91003>* **RATTLE AND HUM** (some live) [1] [1]
– Helter skelter / Hawkmoon 269 / Van Diemen's land / Desire / Angel of Harlem / I still haven't found what I'm looking for / When love comes to town / God part II / Bullet the blue sky / Silver and gold / Love rescue me / Heartland / Star spangled banner / All I want is you / Freedom for my people / All along the watchtower / Pride (in the name of love). *(re-charted UK No.37 on Jun92) (re-iss.Aug93, hit UK No.34)*

Oct 88. (7") *(IS 402)* *<99254>* **ANGEL OF HARLEM. / A ROOM AT THE HEARTBREAK HOTEL** [9] [14]
(12"+=/pic-cd-s+=/US-3"cd-s+=) *(12IS/CIDP/CIDX 402)* – Love rescue me (live with KEITH RICHARDS & ZIGGY MARLEY).

Apr 89. (7"/c-s; U2 & B.B. KING) *(IS 411)* *<99225>* **WHEN LOVE COMES TO TOWN. / DANCING BAREFOOT** [6] [68]
(12"+=/pic-cd-s+=/US-3"cd-s+=) *(12IS/CIDP/CIDX 411)* – ('A'-live from the kingdom mix) / God part II (the hard metal dance mix).

Jun 89. (7"/7"box/c-s) *(IS/ISB/CIS 422)* *<99199>* **ALL I WANT IS YOU. / UNCHAINED MELODY** [4] [83]
(ext;12"+=/12"box+=) *(12IS/+B 422)* – Everlasting love.
(pic-cd-s++=) *(CIDP 422)* – ('A'extended).

Oct 91. (c-s/7") *(C+/IS 500)* *<868885>* **THE FLY. / ALEX DESCENDS INTO HELL FOR A BOTTLE OF MILK / KOROVA 1** [1] [61]
(12"+=/cd-s+=) *(12IS/CID 500)* – The Lounge Fly mix.

Nov 91. (cd)(lp/c) *(CIDU 28)(U2/+C 8)* *<10347>* **ACHTUNG BABY** [2] [1]
– Zoo station / Even better than the real thing / One / Until the end of the world / Who's gonna ride your wild horses / So cruel / The fly / Mysterious ways / Tryin' to throw your arms around the world / Ultra violet (light my way) / Acrobat / Love is blindness. *(re-iss.Aug93, hit UK No.17; same)*

Dec 91. (c-s/7") *(C+/IS 509)* *<866188>* **MYSTERIOUS WAYS. / ('A'-solar plexus magic hour remix)** [13] [9] Nov91
(12"+=) *(12IS 509)* – ('A'-Apollo 440 remix) / ('A'-Tabla Motown remix).
(pic-cd-s++=) *(CID 509)* – ('A'-Solar Plexus extended club mix).
(12") *(12ISX 509)* – ('A'-Perfecto mix) / ('A'-Ultimatum mix) / ('A'-Apollo 400 Magic Hour remix) / ('A'-Solar Plexus extended club mix).

Feb 92. (c-s/7") *(C+/IS 515)* *<866533>* **ONE. / LADY WITH THE SPINNING HEAD (UVI)** [7] [10]
(12"+=) *(12IS 515)* – Satellite of love.
(cd-s++=) *(CID 515)* – Night and day (steel string remix).

Jun 92. (c-s/7") *(C+/IS 525)* *<866977>* **EVEN BETTER THAN THE REAL THING. / SALOME** [12] [32]
(12"+=/cd-s+=) *(12IS/CID 525)* – Where did it all go wrong (demo) / Lady with the spinning head (UVI) (extended dance mix).

Jul 92. (12") *(REAL U2)* **EVEN BETTER THAN THE REAL THING (the perfecto mix) / ('A'-trance mix) / ('A'-sexy dub mix)** [8] [-]
(cd-s) *(CREAL 2)* – (first 2) / ('A'-Apollo 440 Stealth Sonic remix) / ('A'-V16 Exit Wound remix) / ('A'-Apollo 440 vs. U2 instrumental remix).

Nov 92. (c-s/7") *(C+/IS 550)* *<864521>* **WHO'S GONNA RIDE YOUR WILD HORSES. / PAINT IT BLACK** [14] [35]
(cd-s+=) *(CID 550)* – Fortunate son / ('A'version).
(pic-cd-s+=) *(CIDX 550)* – Salome (Zooromancer remix) / Can't help falling in love (Triple Peaks remix).

Jun 93. (12"ltd) **LEMON. / SALOME (Boys Own Mix)** [-] [-]

Jul 93. (cd)(lp/c) *(CIDU 29)(U2/+C 9)* *<518047>* **ZOOROPA** [1] [1]
– Zooropa / Babyface / Numb / Lemon / Stay (faraway, so close!) / Daddy's gonna pay for your crashed car / Some days are better than others / The first time / Dirty day / The wanderer.

Aug 93. (video-ep) *(088 162-3)* **NUMB / NUMB (video remix) / LOVE IS BLINDNESS** [-] [-]

Nov 93. (c-s/7") *(C+/IS 578)* *<858076>* **STAY (FARAWAY, SO CLOSE!). / FRANK SINATRA WITH BONO: I'VE GOT YOU UNDER MY SKIN** [4] [61]
(cd-s+=) *(CID 578)* – Lemon (Bad Yard club) / Lemon (Perfecto mix).
(pic-cd-s) *(CIDX 578)* – ('A'side) / Slow dancing / Bullet the blue sky (live) / Love is blindness (live).

— In Mar 94, BONO teamed up with GAVIN FRIDAY (Virgin Prunes) on single 'IN THE NAME OF THE FATHER' from the film of the same name. It made No.46 in UK and was taken from soundtrack album. (below from the 'Batman Forever' movie released on 'Atlantic' UK)

Jun 95. (7"red/c-s) *(A 7131/+C)* *<87131>* **HOLD ME, THRILL ME, KISS ME, KILL ME / (themes from 'Batman Forever' by Elliot Goldenthal)** [2] [16]
(cd-s) *(A 7131CD)* – ('Tell Me Now' track by MAZZY STAR).

PASSENGERS

— aka U2, ENO + guests incl. vocalists PAVAROTTI + HOLI

Island Island

Nov 95. (cd/c/lp) *(CID/ICT/ILPS 8043)* **ORIGINAL SOUNDTRACKS 1** [12] [76]
– United colours / Slug / Your blue room / Always forever now / A different kind of blue / Beach sequence / Miss Sarajevo / Ito Okashi / One minute warning / Corpse (these chains are way too long) / Elvis ate America / Plot 180 / Theme from the swan / Theme from let's go native.

Nov 95. (c-s/7") *(C+/IS 625)* **MISS SARAJEVO. / ONE (live)** [6] [ ]
(cd-s+=) *(CID 625)* – Bottoms (Watashitachi No Ookina Yume) (Zoo Station remix) / Viva Davidoff.

U2

Feb 97. (c-s) *(CIS 649)* **DISCOTHEQUE / HOLY JOE (Garage mix)** [1] [10]
(cd-s+=) *(CID 649)* – Holy Joe (Guilty mix).
(cd-s) *(CIDX 649)* – ('A'-DM Deep Club mix) / ('A'-Howie B, hairy mix) / ('A'-Hexidecimal mix) / ('A'-DM Tec radio mix).
(3x12"box) *(12IST 649)* – 1:- (David Morales mixes; 4) // 2:- (12"version & David Holmes mix) // 3:- (Howie B & Steve Osborne's Hexidecimal mix).

Mar 97. (cd/c/d-lp) *(CIDU/UC/U 210)* **POP** [1] [1]
– Discotheque / Do you feel loved / Mofo / If God will send his angels / Staring at the sun / Last night on Earth / Gone / Miami / The Playboy mansion / If you wear that velvet dress / Please / Wake up dead man.

Apr 97. (c-s) *(CIS 658)* **STARING AT THE SUN / NORTH AND SOUTH (OF THE RIVER)** [3] [26]
(cd-s+=) *(CID 658)* – Your blue room.
('A'-Monster Truck mix; cd-s+=) *(CIDX 658)* – ('A'-Sad bastards mix) / ('A'-Lab rat mix).

Jul 97. (c-s) *(CIS 664)* **LAST NIGHT ON EARTH / POP MUZIK (Pop Mart mix)** [10] [57]
(cd-s+=) *(CID 664)* – Happiness is a warm gun (the gun mix).
('First Night In Hell mix; cd-s+=) *(CIDX 664)* – Numb (the Soul Assassins mix) / Happiness is a warm gun (the Danny Saber mix).
(12") *(12IS 664)* –

Sep 97. (c-s) *(CIS 673)* **PLEASE / DIRTY DAY (JUNK DAY)** [7] [ ]
(cd-s+=) *(CID 673)* – Dirty day (bitter kiss) / I'm not your baby (Sky splintered mix).
(cd-ep) **POPHEART EP** *(CIDX 673)* – ('A'live) / Where the streets have no name (live) / With or without you (live) / Staring at the sun (live).

Dec 97. (c-s) *(CIS 684)* **IF GOD WILL SEND HIS ANGELS / MOFO (Romin remix)** [12] [ ]

(cd-s) *(CID 684)* – ('A'side) / Slow dancing (with WILLIE NELSON) / Two shots of happy, one shot of sad / Sunday bloody Sunday (live with THE EDGE on vox).
(cd-s) *(CIDX 684)* – ('A'-The Grand Jury mix) / Mofo (Phunk Phorce mix) / Mofo (Mother's mix).
(12") *(12IS 684)* – Mofo (Funk Force mix) / (Black hole dub) / (Mothers mix) / (House flava mix) / (Roamin' mix).

Oct 98. (c-s) *(CIS 727)* *<radio cut>* **SWEETEST THING / STORIES FOR BOYS (live 1981)** [3] [63]
(cd-s+=) *(CIDX 727)* – Out of control (live 1981).
(cd-s) *(CID 727)* – ('A'side) / Twilight (live 1983) / An cat dubh (live 1983).

Nov 98. (cd/c/d-lp) *(CIDU/UC/U 211)* *<524612>* **THE BEST OF 1980-1990** (compilation) [1] [2]
– Pride (in the name of love) / New years day / With or without you / I still haven't found what I'm looking for / Sunday bloody Sunday / Bad / Where the streets have no name / I will follow / The unforgettable fire / Sweetest thing (new recording) / Desire / When love comes to town / Angel of Harlem / All I want is you. *(also on d-cd; CIDDU 211)<524613>* – (hit UK No.8 & US No.45).

The EDGE

with guest **SINEAD O'CONNOR** - vocals

Virgin Virgin

Sep 86. (cd/c/lp) *(CD/TC+/V 2401)* **CAPTIVE (Soundtrack)** [ ] [ ]
– Rowena's theme / Heroine (theme from 'Captive') / One foot in Heaven / The strange party / Hiro's theme 1 & 2 / Drift / The dream theme / Djinn / Island.

Sep 86. (7"/12") *(VS/+T 897)* **HEROINE. / HEROINE (mix II)** [ ] [-]

— In 1983, The EDGE had collaborated with JAH WOBBLE & HOLGER CZUKAY on m-lp 'SNAKE CHARMER'.

ADAM CLAYTON & LARRY MULLEN

Mother Mother

May 96. (c-s) *(MUMSC 75)* *<576670>* **THEME FROM "MISSION: IMPOSSIBLE" / "MISSION: IMPOSSIBLE" THEME (MISSION ACCOMPLISHED)** [7] [7]
(12"+=/cd-s+=) *('A'-Junior's hard mix) / ('A'-cut the red not the blue mix) / ('A'-Dave Clarke remix).*

VALVES

Formed: Portobello, Edinburgh, Scotland ... 1977 by DEE ROBOT, G. DAIR, RONNIE MacKINNON and GORDON SCOTT. This quirky fun-punk/rock act were the first band to have a record – the double A-sided 'ROBOT LOVE' & 'FOR ADOLFS ONLY' – issued on Bruce Findlay's 'Zoom' label (he subsequently signed SIMPLE MINDS). The VALVES played a number of low-key hotel/venue gigs and managed to squeeze out another 45 before the year was out, namely 'TARZAN OF THE KING'S ROAD'. However, it took all of eighteen months to deliver a third, 'DON'T MEAN NOTHIN' AT ALL', although by this time the punk/new wave scene had gone down the tubes.

Album rating: never released any

DEE ROBOT (b. ROBERTSON) – vocals / **RONNIE MacKINNON** – lead guitar / **GORDON SCOTT** – bass / **G. DAIR** – drums

		Zoom	not iss.
Sep 77.	(7") *(ZUM 1)* **ROBOT LOVE. / FOR ADOLF'S ONLY**		-
Dec 77.	(7") *(ZUM 3)* **TARZAN OF THE KING'S ROAD. / AIN'T NO SURF IN PORTOBELLO**		-
		Albion	not iss.
Jul 79.	(7") *(DEL 5)* **DON'T MEAN NOTHIN' AT ALL. / LINDA VINDALOO**		-

— all retired from the music biz

Cherry VANILLA

Born: Staten Island, New York, USA. This obscure punky looking vocalist formed her first outfit, CHERRY VANILLA & HER STATEN ISLAND BAND in 1976, comprising GARY COHEN (piano), THOMAS MORRONGIELLO (guitar), BUZZY JOHN VIERNO (bass) and FRANK LA ROCCA (drums). They played the infamous Max's Kansas City in the heart of NY, the track 'SHAKE YOUR ASHES' appearing on that year's live Various Artists collection on 'Ram' <1213>; re-issued UK (CBS 82670). VANILLA's innuendo-laden anthemic new wave pop secured her a UK contract with 'R.C.A.' and led to the release of 'THE PUNK' single, a disastrous attempt to jump on the anarchy bandwagon. A debut album, 'BAD GIRL' (released early in '78) was even worse, titles like 'FOXY BITCH' and 'HARD AS A ROCK' left little to the imagination and showed she didn't have much herself. The album also featured (if that's the right word!) a version of Willie Dixon's 'LITTLE RED ROOSTER', conclusive proof of why the Americans shipped her overseas. A year later, VANILLA unleashed that "difficult" second album, 'VENUS DE VINYL', difficult that is, to get rid of once you've bought it.

Album rating: BAD GIRL (*3) / VENUS DE VINYL (*2)

CHERRY VANILLA – vocals / with **LOUIS LEPERE** – guitar / **ZECCA ESQUIBEL** – keyboards / **HOWIE FINKEL** – bass / **STUART ELLIOT** – drums

		R.C.A.	not iss.
Sep 77.	(7") *(PB 5053)* **THE PUNK. / FOXY BITCH**		-
Feb 78.	(lp) *(PL 25217)* **BAD GIRL** – I know how it took / So 1950's / Not so bad / The punk / No more canaries / Hard as a rock / Liverpool / Foxy bitch / Bad girl / Little red rooster.		-

— session bassists **GEORGE FORD + DAVE QUINN + ROY BABBINGTON** repl. FINKEL + ESQUIBEL

Apr 79.	(7") *(PB 5145)* **MOONLIGHT. / MR. SPIDER**		-
Apr 79.	(lp) *(PL 25217)* **VENUS DE VINYL** – Amanda / The young boys / Lover like you / Wayni's sweet / Mr. Spider / You belong to me / California / Tear myself away / The round dance / Moonlight.		-

— CHERRY retired from the music biz until the early 90's

		not iss.	Hot Prod.
Dec 91.	(12") *<12283>* **FONE**	-	
Jun 92.	(12") *<12311>* **TECHNO SEX**	-	

VAPORS

Formed: Guildford, Surrey, England . . . Spring '79 by DAVID FENTON, ED BAZALGETTE, STEVE SMITH and HOWARD SMITH. Essentially one-hit wonders, The VAPORS scored a huge success with the memorable 'TURNING JAPANESE' in 1980. Their second single (after debut effort, 'PRISONERS', failed to chart), the record – released on the 'United Artists' label – was a masterclass in effective power-pop, all breathless melody, buzzsaw guitar and killer chorus complete with cheesy 'Shogun'-style intro. Comparisons with the JAM were inevitable, not least because BRUCE FOXTON was their co-manager, yet even such esteemed patronage couldn't help them build on their early success. Debut album, 'NEW CLEAR DAYS' (1980), was met with little enthusiasm while a third single, 'NEWS AT TEN', failed to capture the popular imagination in quite the same fashion as its predecessor. A more ambitious follow-up set, 'MAGNETS' (1981) was unsuccessful in reversing the downward trend and the band split shortly after.

Album rating: NEW CLEAR DAYS (*5) / MAGNETS (*4) / TURNING JAPANESE (THE BEST OF THE VAPORS) (*5)

DAVID FENTON – vocals, rhythm guitar / **ED BAZALGETTE** – lead guitar / **STEVE SMITH** – bass, vocals / **HOWARD SMITH** – drums

		U.A.	U.A.
Oct 79.	(7") *(BP 321)* **PRISONERS. / SUNSTROKE**		-
Feb 80.	(7") *(BP 334)* **TURNING JAPANESE. / HERE COMES THE JUDGE**	3	-
May 80.	(lp) *(UAG 30300) <LT 1049>* **NEW CLEAR DAYS** – Spring collection / Turning Japanese / Cold war / America / Trains / Bunkers / News at ten / Somehow / Sixty second interval / Waiting for the weekend / Letter from Hiro.	44	62 Aug80
Jun 80.	(7"m) *(BP 345)* **NEWS AT TEN. / WASTED / TALK TALK**	44	
Sep 80.	(7") *<1364>* **TURNING JAPANESE. / TALK TALK**	-	36
		Liberty	Liberty
Sep 80.	(7") *(BP 367)* **WAITING FOR THE WEEKEND. / BILLY**		-
Feb 81.	(7") *(BP 385)* **SPIDERS. / GALLERIES FOR GUNS**		
Mar 81.	(lp/c) *(LBG/TC-LBG 30324) <LT 1090>* **MAGNETS** – Jimmie Jones / Lenina / Spiders / Isolated case / Civic hall / Live at the Marquee / Daylight titans / Johnny's in love again / Can't talk anymore / Silver machines / Magnets.		
Jul 81.	(7") *(BP 401)* **JIMMIE JONES. / DAYLIGHT TITANS**	44	

— disbanded soon after (ED + HOWARD joined ELLERY BOP) STEVE SMITH joined CUT with ex-WORLD DOMINATION ENTERPRISES bass man, STEVE JAMESON

– compilations, etc. –

Nov 96.	(cd) *EMI Gold; (CDGO 2071)* **TURNING JAPANESE (THE BEST OF THE VAPORS)** – Turning Japanese / News at ten / Waiting for the weekend / Spring collection / Sixty second interval / Somehow / Trains / Bunkers / Cold war / America / Letter from Hiro / Jimmie Jones / Daylight titans / Isolated case / Wasted / Billy / Talk talk / Prisoners / Spiders / Here comes the judge.		-

VARNALINE

Formed: New York, USA ... mid 90's as a one-man vehicle for singer-songwriter ANDERS PARKER. 1996's eponymous debut album consisted of songs PARKER had previously recorded on a four-track, initially only as a private project. Picked up by indie label, 'Zero Hour', the tracks introduced PARKER as a man of rootsy introspection even if he was loathe to have his work labelled as 'Lo-fi'. Recruiting his brother JOHN and ex-SCARCE sticksman, JUD EHRBAR, for live work, VARNALINE secured a slot on the 1996 Lollapalooza shindig amid favourable critical comparisons with the likes of BIG STAR. As well as sidelining in experimental sister projects such as SPACE NEEDLE and RESERVOIR, PARKER found time to cut a one-off single, 'PARTY NOW', and work on the second album, 'MAN OF SIN' (1997).

Album rating: VARNALINE (*7) / MAN OF SIN (*4) / A SHOT AND A BEER mini (*4) / SWEET LIFE (*5)

ANDERS PARKER – vocals, guitar / with **BOB MacKAY** – bass

		Rykodisc	Zero Hour
Aug 96.	(cd) *(RCD 10368) <ZERCD 1130>* **MAN OF SIN** – The hammer goes down / Gary's paranoia / Lbs / Thorns and such / Little pills / Dust / No decision, no discipline / Want you / Green again / In the year of dope.		Feb96

— **JOHN PARKER** – bass; repl. MacKAY

— added **JUD EHRBAR** – drums (of SPACE NEEDLE)

		Zero Hour	Zero Hour
May 97.	(cd) *<ZERCD 2130>* **VARNALINE** – Lights / Meet me on the ledge / Sky'd out / Why are you unkind / Empire blues / Really can't say / Velocity / My time / Understanding H / God in your eyes. *(UK-iss.Nov97; same)*	-	
Jan 98.	(m-cd) *<(ZERC 3130)>* **A SHOT AND A BEER** – Hear the birds cry / The only one / In your orbit / Bardust / Judges seventeen / Don't come home.		Oct97
Aug 98.	(cd) *<(ZERC 0413D)>* **SWEET LIFE** – Gulf of Mexico / Northern lights / Now you're dirt / All about love / While you were sleeping / Saviours / This is the river / Underneath the mountain / Fuck and fight / Mare imbrium / Tonight / Sweet life.		

VASELINES

Formed: Bellshill, Lanarkshire, Scotland . . . 1986 by EUGENE KELLY and FRANCES McKEE. A seminal Scottish band which would've earned their place in indie folklore even without the patronage of one KURT COBAIN, The VASELINES released two influential singles in '87/'88 on the small '53rd & 3rd' label, 'SON OF A GUN' (with B-side cover of Divine's 'YOU THINK YOU'RE A MAN') and 'DYING FOR IT'. Lo-fi before lo-fi was even invented, the records sounded as if they'd been recorded in a shed; wonderful bursts of noisy guitar scree and bubblegum melody with McDONALD and McKEE harmonising over sordid, tongue-in-cheek proclamations of lust. Enlisting a rhythm section of JAMES SHEENAN and CHARLIE KELLY, the group finally got round to recording a debut album, 'DUM-DUM' (1989). Opening with the blasphemous rock'n'roll cacophony of 'SEX SUX (AMEN)', the record boasted such tasteful vignettes as 'MONSTER PUSSY' and 'TEENAGE SUPERSTAR'. Perhaps they finally ran out of vaseline, but the group seemed to disappear almost as quickly as they'd burst onto Scotland's insular scene, splitting in 1990. They would no doubt have faded into the annals of Bellshill musical history hadn't NIRVANA released a cover of 'MOLLY'S LIPS' in early '91 (they also covered 'SON OF A GUN' and performed a beautiful version of 'JESUS DOESN'T WANT ME FOR A SUNBEAM' on their 'MTV UNPLUGGED' set), 'Seminal Twang' subsequently re-issuing an EP compilation later that year (interested parties should seek it out, if only for the peerless 'RORY RIDES ME RAW'!). At the Reading festival later that year, EUGENE KELLY joined NIRVANA onstage for 'MOLLY'S LIPS', his new band CAPTAIN AMERICA supporting NIRVANA on their subsequent world tour. With a line-up numbering KELLY, GORDON KEEN, RAYMOND BOYLE and ANDY ROY, CAPTAIN AMERICA released their eponymous debut EP in late '91. KELLY's trademark laconic drawl was still in evidence although, surprise, surprise, their sound was markedly more 'grunge', on lead track 'WOW!' at least. The remaining songs, meanwhile, sounded spookily close to musical cousins TEENAGE FANCLUB, only the driving 'GOD BLESS LES PAUL' retaining the wicked spirit of The VASELINES. After another EP the following Spring (featuring a cover of the Beat Happening's 'INDIAN SUMMER'), the group changed their name to EUGENIUS following legal threats from Marvel comics. An album, 'OOMALAMA' was released later that year, yet despite the interest surrounding KELLY, the record failed to rise above cult status. A similar fate befell 'MARY QUEEN OF SCOTS' (1994), the group now residing at their natural home, 'Creation', alongside fellow under-achievers 18 WHEELER, BMX BANDITS, etc.

Album rating: DUM DUM (*6) / ALL THE STUFF AND MORE . . . compilation (*7) / Eugenius: OOMALAMA (*5) / MARY QUEEN OF SCOTS (*6)

EUGENE KELLY – vocals, guitars / **FRANCES McKEE** – vocals with hired musicians

53rd & 3rd | not iss.

Sep 87. (12"m) *(AGARR 10T)* **SON OF A GUN. / RORY RIDES AWAY / YOU THINK YOU'RE A MAN** ☐ -

Mar 88. (7") *(AGARR 17)* **DYING FOR IT. / MOLLY'S LIPS** ☐ -
(12"+=/cd-s+=) *(AGARR 17 T/CD)* – Teenage superstars / Jesus wants me for a sunbeam. *(re-iss. Aug91 on 'Seminal Twang';)*

— added **JAMES SHEENAN** – bass / **CHARLIE KELLY** (EUGENE's brother) – drums

Jan 90. (lp) *(AGAS 7)* **DUM DUM** ☐ -
– Sex sux / Sloshy / Monster pussy / Teenage superstar / No hope / Oliver twisted / The day I was a horse / Dum-dum / Hairy / Lovecraft. *(cd-iss. + remastered Mar91 on 'Avalanche'; ONLYCD 009)*

— disbanded in 1990 and KELLY briefly joined The PASTELS

– compilations, etc. –

Jun 92. (cd/lp) *Avalanche; (ONLY CD/LP 013)* **ALL THE STUFF AND MORE . . .** ☐ -
(re-iss. Oct95; same)

Feb 94. (lp/cd) *Sub Pop; (<SP/+CD 145>)* **THE WAY OF THE VASELINES – A COMPLETE HISTORY** ☐ ☐ Jul92
– Son of a gun / Rory rides me raw / You think you're a man / Dying for it / Molly's lips / Teenage superstars / Jesus wants me for a sunbeam / Sex sux (amen) / Slushy / Monsterpussy / Bitch / No hope / Oliver twisted / Day I was a horse / Dum-dum / Hairy / Lovecraft / Dying for it (the blues) / Let's get ugly.

CAPTAIN AMERICA

— **EUGENE KELLY** – vocals, guitar / **GORDON KEEN** – lead guitar (of BMX BANDITS) / **JAMES SHEENAN** – bass / **ANDY BOLLEN** – drums; repl. live guest **BRENDAN O'HARE** – drums (of TEENAGE FANCLUB)

Paperhouse | Atlantic

Nov 91. (12"ep/cd-cp) **WOW / BED-IN. / WANNA BEE / GOD BLESS LES PAUL** ☐ -

Apr 92. (12"ep/cd-ep) **FLAME ON. / BUTTERMILK / INDIAN SUMMER** ☐ -

— had to change their moniker after legal threats by Marvel comics

EUGENIUS

— **KELLY + KEEN + RAYMOND BOYLE** – bass; repl. SEENAN

— **ROY LAWRENCE** – drums; repl. BOLLEN + part-time O'HARE

Sep 92. (cd/c/lp) *(PAP CD/MC/LP 011) <82426>* **OOMALAMA** ☐ ☐
– Oomalama / Breakfast / One's too many / Bed-in / Hot dog / Down on me / Flame on / Here I go / I'm the Sun / Buttermilk / Aye aye. *(cd+=)* – Wow! / Wannabee / Indian summer.

Creation-August | Atlantic

Jul 93. (7") *(CAUG 005)* **CAESAR'S VEIN. / GREEN BED** ☐ ☐
(12"+=/cd-s+=) *(CAUG 005 T/CD)* – Mary Queen Of Scots.

Nov 93. (12"ep/cd-ep) *(CAUG 008 T/CD)* **EASTER BUNNY / HOMESICK. / CAESAR'S VEIN / SEX SUX** ☐ ☐

Jan 94. (cd) *(RUST 008CD) <82562>* **MARY QUEEN OF SCOTS** ☐ -
– Pebble-shoe / On the breeze / Blue above the roftops / The Moon's a baloon / Mary Queen of Scots / Easter bunny / Let's hibernate / Friendly high / River Clyde song / Tongue rock / Fake digit / Love, bread and beers.

— McKEE and SHEENAN formed The PAINKILLERS and released a single in 1994; 'TROPICAL ZODIAC' for 'Human Condition' records.

Human Condition | not iss.

Sep 96. (7"/cd-s) *(HC/+CD 0013)* **WOMB BOY RETURNS. /** ☐ -

Alan VEGA (see under ⇒ SUICIDE)

VELDT

Formed: Raleigh, North Carolina, USA . . . 1986 by identical twins DONNY and DANNY CHAVIS, the line-up being completed by MARTIN LEVI and DAVID BURRIS. This multi-racial alt-rock band were heavily influenced by the dark post-punk guitar sound of British acts such as the CURE, PSYCHEDELIC FURS and JAMC, eventually signing to 'Stardog' (home to MOTHER LOVE BONE) for a LINCOLN FONG-produced mini set in '92; officially an eponymous affair, the record was sometimes referred to as 'MARIGOLD' due to its sleeve art. The VELDT furthered developed their loose-limbed rhythmic indie sound over a succession of albums beginning with 1994's 'AFRODISIAC'.

Album rating: THE VELDT (*5) / AFRODISIAC (*6) / UNIVERSE BOAT (*5)

DONNY CHAVIS – vocals, guitar / **DANNY CHAVIS** – guitar, vocals / **DAVID BURRIS** – bass / **MARTIN LEVI** – drums

Mercury | Stardog

Oct 92. (m-cd/m-c) *(864 409-2/-4) <771150-2/-4>* **THE VELDT** ☐ ☐
– CCCP / She stoops to conquer / (untitled) / Pleasure toy / Tinsel town / (untitled) / Chartreuse / Willow tree / Reprise.

Feb 94. (cd/c) *<518349-2/-4>* **AFRODISIAC** - ☐

not iss. | Yesha

1996. (cd) **UNIVERSE BOAT** - ☐

not iss. | End Of The World

May 98. (cd) *<1>* **LOVE AT FIRST HATE** - ☐
– (untitled tracks).

VELOCITY GIRL

Formed: Washington DC, USA . . . 1989 by ARCHIE MOORE and KELLY RILES, who had met at university and only initially intended performing together for a one-off party. Taking their moniker from a PRIMAL SCREAM B-side, they recruited BRIAN NELSON, JIM SPELLMAN and the classically-trained SARAH SHANNON, releasing a handful of singles on obscure labels and making a few apperances via some V/A compilations. These were collected together on the US-only 'MY FORGOTTEN FAVOURITE' mini-set (issued eponymously in the UK in '93). Now signed to grunge bastion, 'Sub Pop', they released 'CRAZY TOWN', although critics noted that their 80's influenced WEATHER PROPHETS/JUNE BRIDES-style jangling was miles apart from NIRVANA et al. VELOCITY GIRL's follow-up, '!SIMPATICO!' (1994), was produced by John Porter (a man more famous for having worked with ROXY MUSIC and The SMITHS), his influence lending the record even more of an Anglicised sheen. Save for a solitary single on 'Heaven' records in '95, all was quiet in the VELOCITY GIRL camp until '96's 'GILDED STARS AND ZEALOUS HEARTS'.

Album rating: COPACETIC (*7) / !SIMPATICO! (*6) / GILDED STARS AND ZEALOUS HEARTS (*6)

SARAH SHANNON (b. 7 Oct'69) – vocals / **ARCHIE MOORE** (b. 3 Jun'68) – guitar, bass, vocals / **KELLY RILES** (b.22 Mar'67, Encino, Calif.) – guitar, bass / **BRIAN NELSON** (b. 2 Nov'67) – guitar / **JIM SPELLMAN** (b. 5 Nov'67) – drums

not iss. | Slumberland

1991. (m-cd) *<SLUM 023CD>* **VELOCITY GIRL** - ☐
– I don't care if you go / Always / Forgotten favorite / Why should I be nice to you? / Not at all / I don't care if you go (acoustic). *(UK-iss.Jun93, same as US)*

Sub Pop | Sub Pop

Nov 92. (7") *<(SP 60-227)>* **CRAZY TOWN. /** ☐ ☐
(12"+=/cd-s+=) *<(SP/+CD 61-228)>* –

Apr 93. (lp/c/cd) *(SP/+MC/CD 75-242) <SP 196/+A/B>* **COPACETIC** ☐ ☐
– Pretty sister / Crazy town / Copacetic / Here comes / Pop loser / Living well / Chang / Audrey's eyes / Lisa librarian / 57 waltz / Cany apples / Catching squirrels.

Jul 93. (7") *<(SP 112-228)>* **AUDREY'S EYES. /** ☐ ☐

May 94. (7") *<SP 257>* **SORRY AGAIN. /** - ☐

Jun 94. (7"/cd-s) *(SP/+CD 130-322)* **I CAN'T STOP SMILING. /** ☐ ☐

Jul 94. (cd/lp) *(SP/+CD 122-303) <SP 247/+A/B>* **!SIMPATICO!** ☐ ☐
– Sorry again / There's only one thing left to say / Tripping wires / I can't stop smiling / All-consumer / Drug girls / Rubble / Labrador / Hey you, get off my moon / Medio core / What you left behind / Wake up, I'm leaving.

Nov 95. (7") *(HV 13)* **SEVEN SEAS. / BREAKING LINES** ☐ -
(above issued on 'Heaven' records)

Feb 96. (7") *<(SP 341)>* **NOTHING. / ANATOMY OF A GUTLESS WONDER** ☐ ☐

Mar 96. (lp/cd) *<(SP/+CD 340)>* **GILDED STARS & ZEALOUS HEARTS** ☐ ☐

– Gilded stars / Nothing / Just like that / Same old city / Go coastal / Lose something / It's not for you / Zealous heart / Only ones / Finest hour / Blue in spite / Formula 1 throwaway / For the record / One word.

—— disbanded later in 1996

Nov 97. (7") *(SHUTE 008)* **split with CHISEL** [ ] [-]
(above issued on 'Shute')

VELVET CRUSH

Formed: Rhode Island, Providence, New York, then settling in Boston, USA . . . 1988 as CHOO CHOO TRAIN by PAUL CHASTAIN, JEFFREY BORCHARDT and RIC MENCK, all having had previous experience in the indie scene. The trio cut a couple of singles, 'THE BRIAR ROSE' and 'HIGH' for the small-ish UK label, 'Subway', before changing the group name to the slightly less childish HONEYBUNCH. In the early 90's, they were back as VELVET CRUSH, a beat/psychedelic fusion of FLAMIN' GROOVIES, BIG STAR and The REPLACEMENTS. First up was a TEENAGE FANCLUB (they also supported the band in late '91) number, 'EVERYTHING FLOWS', a track that led them to sign for Alan McGee's 'Creation' label. That year, they also unleashed their much loved debut album, 'IN THE PRESENCE OF GREATNESS' (apparently recorded on an 8-track at their friend's pad), a companion piece to the 'FANCLUB's 'Bandwagonesque'; BRENDON O'HARE admitted that the towering MENCK was to him, a pillar of inspiration. A few years in the making, the MITCH EASTER-produced 'TEENAGE SYMPHONIES TO GOD' was, appropriately enough, released on American Independence Day, 4th Of July 1994. The lads subsequently worked with STEPHEN DUFFY through the mid to late 90's, eventually surfacing minus 'Creation' with a third VELVET CRUSH set, 'HEAVY CHANGES', in 1998. • **Covered:** ONE HUNDRED YEARS (Gram Parsons) / WHY NOT YOUR BABY (Gene Clark).

Album rating: IN THE PRESENCE OF GREATNESS (*7) / TEENAGE SYMPHONIES TO GOD (*6) / HEAVY CHANGES (*6)

CHOO CHOO TRAIN

PAUL CHASTAIN – vocals, bass / **JEFFREY BORCHARDT** – guitar, vocals / **RIC MENCK** – drums

Subway | not iss.

Jul 88. (12"ep) *(SUBWAY 20T)* **THE BRIAR ROSE** [ ] [-]
– Briar rose / Big blue buzz / Nothing else! / Flower field / Every little knight / Catch another breath.

Nov 88. (7") *(SUBWAY 23)* **HIGH. / WISHING ON A STAR** [ ] [-]
(12"+=) *(SUBWAY 23T)* – My best friend / When Sunday comes / Parasol!

—— they took new name, HONEYBUNCH, before going into a little hibernation

VELVET CRUSH

Seminal Twang | not iss.

Jun 91. (7") **EVERYTHING FLOWS. /** [ ] [-]

Creation | Ringers Lactate

Oct 91. (cd/c) *(CRECD/C-CRE 109)* *<RL 05-2/-4>* **IN THE PRESENCE OF GREATNESS** [ ] [ ]
– Window to the world / Drive me down / Ash and earth / White soul / Superstar / Blind faith / Speedway baby / Stop / Asshole / Die a little every day.

Apr 92. (7") *(CRE 122)* **WINDOW TO THE WORLD. / ATMOSPHERE** [ ] [-]
(12"ep)(cd-ep) **THE POST GREATNESS E.P.** *(CRE 122T)(CRESCD 122)* – The gentle breeze / Butterfly position.

—— added guest **DAVE GIBBS** – guitar (of GIGOLO AUNTS)

Oct 92. (12"ep)(cd-ep) *(CRE 139T)(CRESCD 139)* **DRIVE ME DOWN (SOFTLY). / ATMOSPHERE / SLIP AWAY** [ ] [-]

Creation | Parasol

Jun 94. (7") *<001>* **HOLD ME UP. / MR. SPACEMAN** [-] [ ]

Jun 94. (7") *(CRE 146)* **HOLD ME UP. / DON'T YOU SLIP AWAY FROM ME** [ ] [-]
(12"+=)(cd-s+=) *(CRE 146T)(CRESCD 146)* – One hundred year from now.

Creation | Epic

Jul 94. (cd/lp)(c) *(CRECD/CRELP/C-CRE 130)* *<64442>* **TEENAGE SYMPHONIES TO GOD** [ ] [ ]
– Hold me up / My blank pages / Why not your baby / Time wraps around you / Atmosphere / #10 / Faster days / Somethings goota give / This life is killing me / Weird summer / Star trip / Keep on lingerin'.

—— now worked with (STEPHEN) DUFFY on two sets, 'Duffy' (1995) and 'I Love My Friends' (1998)

—— **CHASTAIN + MENCK** added **JEFF UNDERHILL + PETER PHILLIPS**

Action Musik | Action Musik

Jun 98. (cd/lp) *<(AMCD/AMLP 102)>* **HEAVY CHANGES** [ ] [ ]
– Play for keeps / Standing still / Fear of flying / Think it over / Ever after / Used to believe / Wake up / God speed / White satin bed / Live for now / Seen better days.

– compilations, etc. –

Mar 92. (lp/cd; by CHOO CHOO TRAIN) *Suborg; (SUBORG 015/+CD)* **BRIAR HIGH** (THE 1988 SINGLES) [ ] [-]

VELVET MONKEYS (see under ⇒ B.A.L.L.)

VENT 414 (see under ⇒ WONDER STUFF)

Tom VERLAINE (see under ⇒ TELEVISION)

VERLAINES

Formed: Dunedin, New Zealand . . . 1981 by songwriter GRAEME DOWNES, JANE DODD and CAROLINE EASTER. One of many cult Kiwi acts to sign to NZ's 'Flying Nun' label along with The CHILLS etc. (with whom they recorded the fabled 'DUNDEDIN' EP), The VERLAINES' choppy guitar-pop/rock sound was more contemporary and complex than the retro-fixated approach of the latter act, DOWNES' classical training lending an interesting twist to his material. Debuting with the domestic EP, 'TEN O'CLOCK IN THE AFTERNOON' in 1984, the band (CAROLINE had been replaced by ROBBIE YEATS) issued their debut album, 'HALLELUJAH ALL THE WAY HOME', the following year. Increased American/European interest subsequently led to a deal with 'Homestead', the label releasing 1988's follow-up set, 'BIRD-DOG' and the wittily titled 'SOME DISENCHANTED EVENING' (1990). Having relocated to the States, The VERLAINES were subsequently picked up by established alternative bastion, 'Slash' and following an extended break from the spotlight, the band finally surfaced in 1994 with 'WAY OUT WHERE'. By this point, DOWNES was the only remaining founder member, a line-up of DARREN STEDMAN, MIKE STOOLEY and PAUL WINDERS recording an enjoyable set of frantic indie-rock which stated its point without ever threatening to worry the genre's leading lights. DOWNES was most affecting when he took his foot off the gas, achieving an almost GRANT LEE BUFFALO-style atmosphere on 'BLACK WINGS'.

Album rating: HALLELUJAH ALL THE WAY HOME (*6) / BIRD-DOG (*6) / SOME DISENCHANTED EVENING (*5) / READY TO FLY (*4) / WAY OUT WHERE (*5) / JUVENILIA compilation (*6)

GRAHAM DOWNES – vocals, guitar, piano, oboe / **CAROLINE EASTER** – drums / **JANE DODD** – bass, vocals

Flying Nun | Homestead

Jan 82. (d12"ep) **DUNEDIN EP** [-] [-] New Z
– (2 songs) (others by The CHILLS / STONES / SNEAKY FEELINGS)

1984. (7"ep) **TEN O'CLOCK IN THE AFTERNOON** [-] [-] New Z
– Ten o'clock in the afternoon / etc.

—— CAROLINE joined The CHILLS and was repl. by **ROBBIE YEATS** – drums, xylophone

Sep 86. (lp) *(FN 40)* **HALLELUJAH ALL THE WAY HOME** [ ] [ ]
– It was raining / All laid on / The lady and the lizard / Don't send me away / Lying in state / Phil too? / For the love of Ash Grey / The ballad of Harry Noryb. *(cd-iss. Jul96; FNCD 40)* *<cd-iss. 1990's; HMS 138>*

Oct 86. (7") *(FN)* **DOOMSDAY. / NEW KINDA HERO** [ ] [ ]

Sep 87. (lp) *(FNUK 10)* *<HMS 88>* **JUVENILIA** (compilation) [ ] [ ]
– Death and the maiden / Angela / Baud to tears / Crisis after crisis / Burlesque / Joed out / Pyromaniac / You say you / Windsong / You cheat yourself of everything that moves. *(cd-iss. Jul96; FN 195)*

Oct 87. (7") *(FN 14)* **DEATH AND THE MAIDEN. /** [ ] [-]

Nov 88. (lp)<cd> *(FNE 21)* *<HMS 095CD>* **BIRD-DOG** [ ] [ ]
– Makes no difference / You forget love / Take good care of it / Just mum / Slow sad love song / Only dream left / Dippy's last trip / Bird-dog / Icarus missed / C.D. Jimmy Jazz and me.

1990. (cd) *(FNCD 129)* *<HMS 162>* **SOME DISENCHANTED EVENING** [ ] [ ]
– Jesus what a jerk / The funniest thing / Whatever you run into / Faithfully yours / Damn shame / This train / Down the road / We're all gonna die / Anniversary / Come Sunday / It was. *(re-iss. Jul96; same)*

1991. (7") *(FN 158)* **THE FUNNIEST THING. / YOU FORGET LOVE** [ ] [-]

Slash | Slash

Jul 91. (cd/c) *<2-/4-26771>* **READY TO FLY** [-] [ ]
– Gloom junky / Overdrawn / Tremble / Such as I / Hurricane / War in my head / Inside out / See you tomorrow / Hole in the ground / Ready to fly / Moonlight on snow / Hold on.

—— **DOWNES** with **PAUL WINDERS** – guitars, vocals / **MIKE STOODLEY** – bass (also on last set) / **DARREN STEADMAN** – drums

Dec 93. (cd/c) *(828 388-2/-4)* *<45321>* **WAY OUT WHERE** [ ] [ ] Sep93
– Mission of love / I stare out . . . / This valentine / Blanket over the sky / Cathedrals under the sea / Aches in whisper / Way out where / Lucky in my dreams / Black wings / Stay gone / Incarceration / Dirge.

—— disbanded after above

VERUCA SALT

Formed: Chicago, Illinois, USA . . . early '93 by NINA GORDON and LOUISE POST, who were soon joined by STEVE LACK and NINA's brother JIM SHAPIRO. In mid-94 they enjoyed a minor indie hit with debut single, 'SEETHER' and amid the major label chequebook scramble that followed, opted to remain independent for the 'AMERICAN THIGHS' album later that year. Named after a line in AC/DC's classic track, 'You Shook Me All Night Long', the album was a promising blast of punk-pop directed from a distinctly femme-rock perspective, at times akin to a surreal fusion of a mellow BREEDERS or a heavy PIXIES. Following a further succession of minor US hits including a re-released 'SEETHER' and 'NUMBER ONE BLIND', the band signed to the 'Outpost-MCA' imprint for follow-up set, 'EIGHT ARMS TO HOLD YOU' (1997). Once again taking its title from rock'n'roll history (the original moniker intended for The BEATLES' 'Help' film), the record found the girls utilising a more satisfying sonic palate while retaining the edge that had made their earlier work so compelling. • **Songwriters:** GORDON or POST except; BODIES (Sex Pistols) / STACEY PLEASE (Morris-Felsenthal) / MY SHARONA (Knack). • **Trivia:** Named after a character in Roald Dahl's 'Charlie And The Chocolate Factory'.

Album rating: AMERICAN THIGHS (*7) / EIGHT ARMS TO HOLD YOU (*7)

NINA GORDON – vocals / **LOUISE POST** – vocals, guitar / **STEVE LACK** – bass / **JIM SHAPIRO** – drums

		Scared Hitless	Minty Fresh
Jun 94.	(7") *(FRET 003S)* **SEETHER. / ALL HAIL ME**	61	
	(cd-s+=) *(FRET 003CD)* – Stacey please.		
		Hi-Rise	**Minty Fresh**
Oct 94.	(cd/c/lp) *(FLAT CD/MC/LP 9)* <24732> **AMERICAN THIGHS**		69
	– Get back / All hail me / Seether / Spiderman '79 / Forsythia / Wolf / Celebrate you / Fly / Number one blind / Victrola / Twinstar / 25. *(lp w/free one-sided 12"+=) (FLATLPX 9)* – SLEEPING WHERE I WANT		
Nov 94.	(7"/c-s) *(FLAT/+C 12)* **SEETHER. / STRAIGHT**	73	-
	(12"+=/cd-s+=) *(FLAT T/SDG 12)* – She's a brain.		
Jan 95.	(7"green) *(FLAT 16)* <9> **NUMBER ONE BLIND. / BODIES**	68	
	(12"+=/cd-s+=) *(FLAT T/SCD 16)* – Aurora.		
Jun 95.	(7") *(FLAT 19)* **VICTROLA. / MY SHARONA**		-
	(10"+=/cd-s+=) *(FLAT EN/SCD 19)* – Sundown.		
Apr 96.	(cd) <22212> **BLOW IT OUT YOUR ASS IT'S VERUCA SALT**	-	
	– Shimmer like a girl / I'm taking Europe with me / New York mining disaster 1996 / Disinherit.		
		Outpost	**Outpost**
Feb 97.	(7") *(OPRS 22197)* **VOLCANO GIRLS. / GOOD DISASTER**	56	-
	(cd-s+=) *(OPRCD 22197)* – Sleeper car.		
	(cd-s) *(OPRXD 22197)* – ('A'side) / Pale green / One more page of insincerity please.		
Mar 97.	(cd/c) <(OP CD/C 30001)> **EIGHT ARMS TO HOLD YOU**		55 Feb97
	– Straight / Volcano girls / Don't make me prove it / Awesome / One last time / With David Bowie / Benjamin / Shutterbug / The morning sad / Sound of the bell / Loneliness is worse / Stoneface / Venus man trap / Earthcrosser.		
Aug 97.	(7") *(OPRS 22261)* **BENJAMIN. / THE SPEED OF CANDY (demo)**	75	
	(7") *(OPRSX 22261)* – ('A'side) / Never met her (demo).		
	(cd-s++=) *(OPRCD 22261)* – Swedish fish (demo).		

VERVE

Formed: Wigan, England ... 1990 by local college lads RICHARD ASHCROFT (the main writer), NICK McCABE, SIMON JONES and PETER SALISBURY. They were soon supporting the likes of RIDE and SPIRITUALIZED, signing to 'Hut' in 1991. The following year, they released three singles, the spiralling psychedelia of 'ALL IN THE MIND', 'SHE'S A SUPERSTAR' & 'GRAVITY GRAVE'. In early summer of '93, they had a minor hit with 'BLUE', a taster for the debut album, 'A STORM IN HEAVEN', which made the UK Top 30. The album delivered on the promise of the early singles; an amorphous melange of trippy rock and liquid space-jazz ambience. Ambitious and cocksure, they toured the States, subsequently coming unstuck with US label VERVE, who forced them to slightly change their name to THE VERVE. In 1995, they unleashed a second album, 'A NORTHERN SOUL', a much darker, more intense affair featuring more conventional song structures. Although the album went Top 20, they announced they were splitting several months later, the 'HISTORY' single apparently their swan song. Just when the band were poised to enter the big league, it looked as if they'd missed the boat, McCABE and ASHCROFT's quarreling, together with well documented drug problems, seemingly to blame for the band's demise. By February '97, however, they got it together sufficiently to reform and their first single of the year was to many, their best song yet, the grandiose, string-laden 'BITTER SWEET SYMPHONY' (written by MICK JAGGER and KEITH RICHARDS for The ANDREW LOOG OLDHAM ORCHESTRA). The song crashed into the UK chart at No.2 thanks to a glorious video featuring an angry jaywalking ASHCROFT barging into everyone in sight! • **Songwriters:** Group. • **Trivia:** RICHARD believes in astral travel. His nickname is MAD RICHARD, enough said!

Album rating: A STORM IN HEAVEN (*7) / A NORTHERN SOUL (*8) / URBAN HYMNS (*9)

RICHARD ASHCROFT (b. 1971) – vocals, guitar / **NICK McCABE** – lead guitar / **SIMON JONES** – bass / **PETER SALISBURY** – drums

		Hut	Vernon Yard
Mar 92.	(7") *(HUT 12)* **ALL IN THE MIND. / ONE WAY TO GO**		-
	(12"+=/cd-s+=) *(HUT T/CD 12)* – A man called Sun.		
Jun 92.	(7"/ext-12"/ext-cd-s) *(HUT/+H/CD 16)* **SHE'S A SUPERSTAR. / FEEL**	66	-
Oct 92.	(10"ep) *(HUTEN 21)* **GRAVITY GRAVE EP**		-
	– Gravity grave / Endless life / She's a superstar (live).		
	(12"+=/cd-s++) *(HUT T/CD 21)* – ('A'extended) / Endless life / A man called Sun (live).		
Jan 93.	(m-cd) *(<HUTUS 1>)* **THE VERVE E.P.** (compilation)	-	
	– Gravity grave / A man called Sun / She's a superstar / Endless life / Feel. *(UK-iss.Sep97 on 'Vernon Yard'; YARDCD 001)*		
May 93.	(12"ep) *(HUTT 29)* **BLUE. / TWILIGHT / WHERE THE GEESE GO**	69	-
	(10"ep+=/cd-ep+=) *(HUT EN/CD 29)* – No come down.		
Jun 93.	(cd/c/lp) *(CDHUT/HUTMC/HUTLP 10)* <87950> **A STORM IN HEAVEN**	27	
	– Star sail / Slide away / Already there / Beautiful mind / The sun, the sea / Virtual world / Make it 'til Monday / Blue / Butterfly / See you in the next one (have a good time).		
Sep 93.	(7"pink) *(HUT 35)* **SLIDE AWAY. / 6 O'CLOCK**		-
	(12"/cd-s) *(HUT T/CD 35)* – ('A'side) / Make it 'til Monday (acoustic) / Virtual world (acoustic).		
May 94.	(cd) *(CDHUT 18)* **NO COMEDOWN** (rare / b-sides)		-
	– No come down / Blue (USA mix) / Make it 'til Monday (acoustic) / Butterfly (acoustic) / Where the grease go / 6 o'clock / One way to go / Gravity grave (live) / Twilight. *(re-iss. Sep97 on 'Vernon Yard'; YARDCD 007)*		

THE VERVE

Apr 95.	(7"burgundy) *(HUT 54)* **THIS IS MUSIC. / LET THE DAMAGE BEGIN**	35	-
	(12"+=/cd-s+=) *(HUT T/CD 54)* – You and me.		
Jun 95.	(7"green/c-s) *(HUT/+C 55)* **ON YOUR OWN. / I SEE THE DOOR**	28	-
	(cd-s+=) *(HUTCD 55)* – Little gem / Dance on your bones.		
Jul 95.	(cd/c/d-lp) *(CDHUT/HUTMC/HUTLP 27)* <40437> **A NORTHERN SOUL**	13	
	– A new decade / This is music / On your own / So it goes / A northern soul / Brainstorm interlude / Drive you home / History / No knock on my door / Life's an ocean / Stormy clouds / Stormy clouds (reprise).		
Sep 95.	(c-s) *(HUTC 59)* **HISTORY / BACK ON MY FEET AGAIN**	24	-
	(cd-s+=) *(HUTCD 59)* – On your own (acoustic) / Monkey magic (Brainstorm mix).		
	(cd-s) *(HUTDX 59)* – ('A'extended) / Grey skies / Life's not a rehearsal.		

—— originals re-formed adding **SIMON TONG** – guitar, keyboards

		Hut	Virgin
Jun 97.	(7") *(HUTLH 82)* <38634> **BITTER SWEET SYMPHONY. / SO SISTER**	2	12 Mar98

('A'extended; cd-s+=) *(HUTDX 82)* – Echo bass.
(c-s/cd-s) *(HUT C/DG 82)* – ('A'side) / Lord I guess I'll never know / Country song / ('A'radio version).

Sep 97. (c-s/cd-s) *(HUT C/DG 88)* **THE DRUGS DON'T WORK / THREE STEPS / THE DRUGS DON'T WORK (original demo)** 1 □
(cd-s) *(HUTDX 88)* – ('A'extended) / Bitter sweet symphony (James Lavelle remix) / The crab / Stamped.

Sep 97. (cd/c/lp) *(<44913-2/-4/-1>)* **URBAN HYMNS** 1 23
– Bitter sweet symphony / Sonnet / The rolling people / The drugs don't work / Catching the butterfly / Neon wilderness / Space and time / Weeping willow / Lucky man / One day / This time / Velvet morning / Come on.

Nov 97. (c-s/cd-s) *(HUT C/DG 92)* **LUCKY MAN / NEVER WANNA SEE YOU CRY / HISTORY** 7 □
(cd-s) *(HUT DX 92)* – ('A'side) / MSG / The longest day / Lucky man (happiness more or less).

– compilations, etc. –

Mar 98. (ltd-12"ep) **BITTER SWEET SYMPHONY (original) / LORD I GUESS I'LL NEVER KNOW. / BITTER SWEET SYMPHONY (James Lavelle mix) / COUNTRY SONG** □ -

Mar 98. (ltd-12"ep) **THE DRUGS DON'T WORK / THREE STEPS. / THE DRUGS DON'T WORK (demo) / THE CRAB** □ -

Mar 98. (ltd-12"ep) **LUCKY MAN / NEVER WANNA SEE YOU CRY. / MSG / THE LONGEST DAY** □ -

Mar 98. (ltd-12"ep) **SONNET / STAMPED. / SO SISTER / ECHO BASS** □ -
(the import cd-single version of the above single <895075-2> actually hit UK No.74 in May'98)

VERVE PIPE

Formed: East Lansing, Michigan, USA . . . 1992 out of JOHNNY WITH AN EYE by brothers BRIAN and BRAD VANDER ARK, the pair recruiting former WATER 4 THE POOL members, DONNY BROWN and BRIAN STOUT. Debuting later that year with the mini-set, 'I'VE SUFFERED A HEAD INJURY', The VERVE PIPE began to lay the foundations of a healthy fanbase through a punishing tour schedule. Beefing up their oddball but intelligent alterna-rock sound with the addition of A.J. DUNNING and DOUG CORELLA (to replace STOUT), the hard working quintet delivered a second independent set, 'POP SMEAR' (1993). With acclaim flowing in across the board, 'R.C.A.' were quick to spot their commercial potential, putting them into the studio for 1996's 'VILLAINS' album. Criminally, the band were ignored across the water although obviously the towering profile of Brit-rockers, THE VERVE, didn't help matters. Then again, the guys probably weren't that bothered as the aforementioned record climbed into the US Top 30, spurred on by a massive Stateside Top 5 smash, 'THE FRESHMEN'.

Album rating: I'VE SUFFERED A HEAD INJURY mini (*5) / POP SMEAR (*6) / VILLAINS (*5)

BRIAN VANDER ARK – vocals, guitar / **BRIAN STOUT** – guitar, vocals / **BRAD VANDER ARK** – bass, vocals / **DONNY BROWN** – drums

not iss. Transom

Nov 92. (m-cd) *<VP 001>* **I'VE SUFFERED A HEAD INJURY** - □
– Ark of the envious / Even the score / Acting as your slave / Oceanside / I've suffered a head injury / Clean break / Martyr material. *<re-iss. 1997 on 'R.C.A.'; 67543>*

— **A.J. DUNNING** – guitar / + **DOUG CORELLA** – keyboards; repl. STOUT

not iss. LMNO Pop-!

1993. (cd) **POP SMEAR** - □
– Pretty for you / Spoonful of sugar / Victoria / Honest / River / Sleepy town / Bullies on vacation / What you wanted / Wanna be / Out like a lamb / Senator speak / Is it worth it? *<re-iss. 1997 on 'R.C.A.'; 67544>*

R.C.A. R.C.A.

Nov 96. (7"/cd-s) *(74321 43069-7/-2)* **PHOTOGRAPH. / DRIVE YOU MILD / BLUE BERET** □ □

Nov 96. (cd) *<(07863 66809-2)>* **VILLAINS** □ 24 Mar96
– Barely (if at all) / Drive you mild / Villains / Reverend girl / Cup of tea / Myself / The freshmen / Photograph / Ominous man / Real / Penny is poison / Castle / Veneer.

Jan 97. (cd-s) *<64733>* **THE FRESHMEN /** - 5

Jun 98. (cd-s) *(45351)* **THE FRESHMEN /** □ -

VERY THINGS

Formed: Redditch, Worcestershire, England . . . late 70's by CHRIS SHEND (aka THE SHEND), RICK LONDON, ETHOS YAPP and NIBBS (aka SIR ROBIN RAYMOND). Signed to indie label, 'Small Wonder', the quartet released the sad tale of 'GORDON' as their debut single towards the end of '78. A demented musical cocktail of choppy post-punk guitar, strange bleating sax and Vivien (of 'Young Ones' fame)-style vocal exhortations, The CRAVATS were one of the era's more obscure but interesting propositions. A string of singles ensued including 1979's 'BURNING BRIDGES' EP and 'PRECINCT' single, while a bonafide debut long player, 'THE CRAVATS IN TOYTOWN', emerged in 1980. Although a further handful of singles appeared on various labels over the course of the next few years – including an indie chart hit on the 'Crass' label with 'RUB ME OUT' – The CRAVATS were subsumed under the wider banner of the mysterious 'Dada Cravats Laboratory' organisation. Operating under a Dadaist (influential 1920's French art movement) criterion via various musical endeavours – including The CRAVATS, The BABYMEN and DCL LOCOMOTIVE – the project's most successful venture was The VERY THINGS. Including THE SHEND and SIR ROBIN amongst their number, this outfit debuted with a single, 'THE GONG MAN', on the 'Crass' label before recording a John Peel session and signing to the 'Reflex' label. A suitably bizarre debut album, 'THE BUSHES SCREAM WHILE MY DADDY PRUNES', appeared in 1984 and the band even secured a slot on legendary Channel 4 music show, 'The Tube'. Very reminiscent of BOBBY PICKETT's 'Monster Mash', with a side serving of NICK CAVE/LUX INTERIOR gardening with actor Boris Karloff, the album's comical title track is surely a classic waiting to be unearthed by a new generation. The VERY THINGS re-emerged sporadically over the next few years, a cover of R. Dean Taylor's 'THERE'S A GHOST IN MY HOUSE', withdrawn in May '87 due to The FALL's version being released simultaneously. It was to be a further year, however, before the release of follow-up set, 'MOTORTOWN' (on 'One Little Indian'), by which time the band had folded.

Album rating: THE BUSHES SCREAM WHILE MY DADDY PRUNES (*7) / MOTORTOWN (*5) / Cravats: IN TOYTOWN (*7)

CRAVATS

NIBBS (aka SIR ROBIN RAYMOND) – vocals, guitar / **CHRIS SHENDO** (aka THE SHEND) – bass, vocals / **RICK LONDON** (b. SVOR MANN) – saxophone / **ETHOS YAPP** (b. DAVE BENNETT) – drums

Cravats not iss.

Sep 78. (7") *(CH 004)* **GORDON. / SITUATIONS VACANT** □ -

Small Wonder not iss.

Jun 79. (7") *(SMALL 15)* **THE END. / BURNING BRIDGES / I HATE THE UNIVERSE** □ -

Oct 80. (7") *(SMALL 24)* **PRECINCT. / WHO'S IN HERE WITH ME?** □ -
(w/ free-7"flexi) – Fireman / A FLUX IN 3D: Divide.

Oct 80. (lp) *(CRAVAT 1)* **IN TOYTOWN** □ -
– All around the corner / All on standby / Pressure sellers / Welcome / One in a thousand / X.M.P. / Tears on my machine / Gordon / In your eyes / Still / The hole / Ceasing to be / Live for now / Triplex zone.

Mar 81. (7") *(SMALL 25)* **YOU'RE DRIVING ME. / I AM THE DREG** □ -

Nov 81. (7") *(SMALL 26)* **OFF THE BEACH. / AND THE SUN SHONE** □ -

Glass not iss.

Feb 82. (7") *(GLASS 021)* **TERMINUS. / LITTLE YELLOW FROGGY** □ -

Aug 82. (12"ep) *(GLASS 021/12)* **CRAVATS SING TERMINUS AND OTHER HITS** □ -

Crass not iss.

Jul 82. (7") *(221984/4)* **RUB ME OUT. / WHEN WILL WE FALL** □ -

Corpus Christi not iss.

1983. (12"ep; abandoned) *(none)* **THE COLOSSAL TUNE'S OUT** □ -

— had already disbanded late in '82. SVOR formed The PIG BROS

VERY THINGS

— were formed by **THE SHEND** – lead vocals / **SIR ROBIN** – guitar; plus **GORDON DISNEYTIME** – drums / Horn section – **VINCENT JOHNSON, JOHN GRAHAM, ROBERT HOLARD + PAUL GREEN**

Corpus Christi not iss.

Nov 83. (7") *(CHRIST ITS 2)* **THE GONG MAN. / THE COLOURS (ARE SPEAKING TO ME)** □ -

Reflex not iss.

Jun 84. (7") *(RE 5)* **THE BUSHES SCREAM WHILE MY DADDY PRUNES. / SHEARING MACHINE** □ -

Aug 84. (lp) *(LEX 3)* **THE BUSHES SCREAM WHILE MY DADDY PRUNES** □ -
– The conquerer / The bushes scream while my daddy prunes / Information / Down the final flight / Message from Disney time / Philip's world service / Wall of fir / Shearing machine / World of difference. *(re-iss. Mar94 on 'Fire' cd/lp; REFIRE CD/LP 12)*

— Back to basic trio.

Jul 85. (12"ep) *(12RE 9)* **MUMMY YOU'RE A WRECK. / WHEN FATHER PAPERED THE PARLOUR / THE LIGHT POURS OUT OF MUMMY'S HOUSE** □ -

Feb 86. (12"ep; as The CRAVATS) *(12RE 10)* **IN THE LAND OF THE GIANTS** □ -

DCL Electric not iss.

Sep 86. (7"/12") *(DCL 1/+T)* **THIS IS MOTORTOWN. / MOTORTOWN EPILOGUE (version A)** □ -

One Little Indian not iss.

Sep 88. (7") *(7TP 8)* **LET'S GO OUT. / THE MOTORTOWN TRAILER** □ -
(12"+=) *(12TP 8)* – ('A'version).

Sep 88. (lp) *(TPLP 6)* **MOTORTOWN** □ -
– Let's go out / This is Motortown / There's a ghost in my house / She's standing still / Walking in the sand / Robin Holland is God / Motortown epilogue. *(re-iss. Mar94 on 'Fire' cd/lp; REFIRE CD/LP 14)*

— Had already disbanded. THE SHEND became an actor and appeared in some episodes of 'Eastenders' and 'The Bill'.

– compilations, etc. –

Mar 87. (lp) *B.P.; **LIVE AT THE ZAP CLUB, BRIGHTON (live)*** - - mail-o

Jan 88. (12"ep) *Strange Fruit; (SFPS 046)* **THE PEEL SESSION (17.12.83)** □ -
– Message from Disney Time / Down the final flight / Philip's world service / Wall of fir.

Mar 94. (cd/lp) *Fire; (REFIRE CD/LP 13)* **IT'S A DRUG, IT'S A DRUG** □ -
– Mummy you're a wreck / When father papered the parlour / The gong man /

Where's the rest of me? (link) / Transfusion / The hole / The colours are speaking to me / Motorlogue / (+ other versions).

VIBRATORS

Formed: London, England . . . 1976 by JOHN ELLIS and PAT COLLIER. Both veterans of pub rockers, BAZOOKA JOE, the pair teamed up with KNOX (aka IAN CARNOCHAN) and EDDIE (aka JOHN EDWARDS), turning their talents to the nascent punk scene. A meeting with session whizz, CHRIS SPEDDING, in Oxford Street's 100 Club, subsequently led to a SPEDDING-produced debut single, 'WE VIBRATE', on MICKIE MOST's 'Rak' label at the tail end of '76. Hardly the most auspicious of starts, it nevertheless led to a major label deal with 'Epic' and a debut album, 'PURE MANIA' (1977). More considered, mature and less snotty – the laid-back stomp of 'BABY BABY' would've sounded fine in the hands of TOM PETTY – than the bulk of the safety-pin brigade, the album featured such enduring VIBRATORS favourites as 'INTO THE FUTURE', S&M classic, 'WHIPS & FURS' and the track that inspired one of the era's most vital bands, 'STIFF LITTLE FINGERS'. The predicted success never materialised, however, and COLLIER promptly jumped ship to form new wave outfit, The BOYFRIENDS (later became a renowned producer). His replacement was GARY TIBBS, who played on the bulk of follow-up set, 'V2' (1978), a disappointing promo single, 'LONDON GIRLS' hardly boding well for the record's prospects. A second single, 'AUTOMATIC LOVER', scraped into the Top 40 but the band was already on its last legs; ELLIS left to play with PETER GABRIEL and later The STRANGLERS while the remainder limped on with replacement DAVE BIRCH and keyboard player DON SNOW. They managed a second and final VIBRATORS hit with 'JUDY SAYS (KNOCK YOU IN THE HEAD)' before finally falling apart as TIBBS and SNOW departed. A short-lived reformation featuring a line-up of EDDIE, KNOX, BEN BRIERLEY and GREG VAN COOK was doomed to failure, KNOX eventually going on to a solo career while EDDIE soldiered on as The NEW VIBRATORS. Incredibly, the original line-up re-formed in 1982 and went on to record a series of albums for heavy metal label, 'FM-Revolver', the most recent being 1994's 'HUNTING FOR YOU'. Needless to say, both COLLIER and ELLIS bailed out along the way with the line-up never staying the same for long. • **Songwriters:** Most by KNOX-ELLIS-COLLIER, except covers GIMME SOME LOVIN' (Spencer Davis Group) / RIP IT UP (Little Richard) / JUMPIN' JACK FLASH (Rolling Stones) / HALFWAY TO PARADISE (Billy Fury) / SLOW DEATH (Flamin' Groovies) / etc. • **Trivia:** KNOX teamed up with UK SUBS man, CHARLIE HARPER, to form URBAN DOGS between 1983-85.

Album rating: PURE MANIA (*6) / V2 (*5) / BATTERIES NOT INCLUDED (*6) / GUILTY (*5) / YEAH YEAH YEAH compilation (*6)

KNOX (b. IAN CARNOCHAN) – vocals, guitar / **JOHN ELLIS** – guitar, vocals / **PAT COLLIER** – bass, vocals / **EDDIE** (b.JOHN EDWARDS) – drums

RAK / not iss.

Nov 76. (7") *(RAK 245)* **WE VIBRATE. / WHIPS AND FURS** [ ] [-]

Nov 76. (7"; by The VIBRATORS with CHRIS SPEDDING) *(RAK 246)* **POGO DANCING. / THE POSE** [ ] [-]

Mar 77. (7") *(RAK 253)* **BAD TIMES. / NO HEART** [ ] [-]

Epic / Columbia

May 77. (7") *(EPC 5302)* **BABY BABY. / INTO THE FUTURE** [ ] [-]

Jun 77. (lp) *(EPC 82097) <35038>* **PURE MANIA** [49] [ ]
– Baby baby / London girls / You break my heart / Sweet sweet heart / Yeah yeah yeah / Bad times / Keep it clean / No heart / Into the future / Petrol / Whips and furs / She's bringing you down / Wrecked on you / I need a slave / Stiff little fingers. *(re-iss. Aug91 on 'Repertoire' lp/cd; REP 2001/+TO)*

— **GARY TIBBS** – bass (ex-RED) repl. COLLIER who formed The BOYFRIENDS

Aug 77. (7") *(EPC 5565)* **LONDON GIRLS – LIVE. / STIFF LITTLE FINGERS – LIVE** [ ] [-]

Mar 78. (7") *(EPC 6137)* **AUTOMATIC LOVER. / DESTROY** [35] [-]

Apr 78. (lp) *(EPC 82495)* **V2** [33] [-]
– Automatic lover / 24 hour people / Feel alright / Pure mania / Troops of tomorrow / Wake up / War zone / Flying duck theory / Destroy / Nazi baby / Fall in love / Sulphate / Public enemy number one. *(re-iss. Aug91 on 'Repertoire' lp/cd; REP 2002/+TO) (cd-iss. Aug93; 471408-2)*

— **DAVID BIRCH** – guitar; repl. ELLIS who joined PETER GABRIEL and went solo / added **DON SNOW** – keyboards (ex-RED)

Jun 78. (7") *(EPC 6393)* **JUDY SAYS (KNOCK YOU IN THE HEAD). / PURE MANIA** [ ] [-]

— **GREG VAN COOK** – guitar (ex-ELECTRIC CHAIRS) repl. BIRCH to BRUCE WOOLLEY / **BEN BRIERLEY – bass** repl. TIBBS who joined ROXY MUSIC then ADAM & THE ANTS / SNOW also departed to SINCEROS then SQUEEZE. After a tour they disbanded with KNOX going solo (he released a few singles, 'GIGOLO AUNT' and 'SHE'S SO GOOD LOOKING' and an album in 1983, 'PLUTONIUM EXPRESS'). BRIERLEY joined NAZIS AGAINST RACISM.

— late 1979, The VIBRATORS re-formed with **EDDIE + KIP** – vocals, guitar / **PHIL ABLE** – guitar / + 1

Rat Race / not iss.

Feb 80. (7") *(RAT 2)* **GIMME SOME LOVIN'. / POWER CRY (live)** [ ] [-]

May 80. (7") *(RAT 4)* **DISCO IN MOSCOW. / TAKE A CHANCE** [ ] [-]

— folded again when KIP joins The CHORDS and PHIL forms ABLE RAM. Originals re-united The VIBRATORS. (see above)

Anagram / not iss.

Nov 82. (7") *(ANA 4)* **BABY BABY. / DRAGNET** [ ] [-]

Jan 83. (lp) *(GRAM 02)* **GUILTY** [ ] [-]
– Wolfman howl / Rocket to the moon / Sleeping / Parties / Jumpin' Jack Flash / Watch out baby / Do a runner / We name the guilty / Baby baby / Fighter pilot / The day they caught the killer / Kick it / A dot ain't a lot / Claws in my brain.

May 83. (7") *(ANA 8)* **GUILTY. / HANG TEN** [ ] [-]

Ram / not iss.

Nov 83. (7") *(RAM 7005)* **MR AMERICA. / SHADOW LOVE** [ ] [-]

Mar 84. (12"m) *(RAM 7007T)* **FLYING HOME. / FLASH FLASH FLASH / MX AMERICA** [ ] [-]

Carrere / not iss.

May 84. (7") *(CAR 329)* **FLYING HOME. / PUNISH ME WITH KISSES** [ ] [-]
(12"+=) *(CART 329)* – Mr America.

May 84. (lp) *(CAL 205)* **ALASKA 127** [ ] [-]
– Amphetamine blues / Somnabulist / Baby blue eyes / Peepshow / 4875 / 3-D Jesus / Jesus always lets you down / Flying home / Shadow love / MX America / Flash flash flash / Punish me with kisses.

Jul 84. (7") *(CAR 338)* **BABY BLUE EYES. / AMPHETIMINE BLUES** [ ] [-]
(12"+=) *(CART 338)* – Flying high.

Jun 85. (lp/c) *(CHIPL/ZCCH P002)* **FIFTH AMENDMENT** [ ] [-]
– Blown away by love / Rip up the city / Tomorrow is today / Wipe away / Too late for love / The demolishers / Running right into your heart / Frankenstein stomp / Crazy dream / Criminal.

Revolver / not iss.

Oct 86. (lp) *(REVLP 85)* **VIBRATORS LIVE (live)** [ ] [-]
–

— **KNOX + EDDIE** were joined by **DUNCAN + OWEN**

Jan 88. (lp/c) *(REV LP/MC 101)* **RECHARGED** [ ] [-]
– String him along / Hey little doll / I don't trust you / Too dumb / Go go go / Hey nony no (instrumental) / Everyday I die a little / Picture of you / Rip it up / Someone stole my heart / Electricity / Tight black jeans / Reach for that star.

Mar 88. (7") *(REV 45)* **STRING HIM ALONG. / DISCO IN MOSCOW (live)** [ ] [-]

Nov 88. (lp/c/cd) *(REV LP/MC/CD 121)* **MELTDOWN** [ ] [-]
– Office girls / Don't cha lean on me / So young / Speedtrap / The other side of midnight / Cruel to you / (Na na na) U238 / Dynamite / Letting you go / Danger street / Let's go baby / Sally gardens. *(c+=)* – Wasted life. *(cd++=)* – Don't trust anyone.

— **DONNELLY** ; repl. OWEN

Nov 89. (lp/c/cd; The VIBRATORS & STEVE NUNN) *(REV LP/MC/XD 135)* **VICIOUS CIRCLE** [ ] [-]
– No getting over you / Poll tax blues / I don't wanna fall / Rocket ride to Heaven / Count on me / Slow death / Fire / Halfway to Paradise / Ruby's got a heart / Don't trust anyone / No mercy / Work.

Dec 89. (7") *(REV 52)* **HALFWAY TO PARADISE. / DRIVE** [ ] [-]
(cd-s+=) *(REVXD 52)* – Rocket ride to Heaven / Fire.

Oct 90. (cd/c/lp) *Revolver; (REV XD/MC/LP 159)* **VOLUME 10** [ ] [-]

— **NIGEL BENNETT** – guitar (ex-MEMBERS) repl. DONNELLY

Dojo / not iss.

Oct 94. (cd) *(DOJOCD 179)* **HUNTING FOR YOU** [ ] [-]
– Hunting for you / The kid's a mess / Fever (you gimme) / Please please please / No no no / Modern world / Another day without you / Goodbye you stupid cow / Keep away from me / She's the one you need / Hey hey / Radium city.

Vibes / not iss.

1996. (cd) **UNPUNKED** (acoustic best of) [ ] [-]

Anagram / not iss.

Sep 97. (cd) *(CDGRAM 114)* **FRENCH LESSONS WITH CORRECTION** [ ] [-]
– Tired of living with you / The girl's screwed up / Shiver / Judy's killing herself / Cycle of violence / Cold cold cold / Party on / The rain must fall / A date with disaster / Juice on / The evil that men do / Don't you tell me / Johnny B. Bad / Money money / I hate 'Blind Date'.

– compilations, others, etc. –

Jun 80. (lp) *C.B.S.; (CBS 31840)* **BATTERIES INCLUDED** [ ] [-]

Jan 88. (12"ep) *;* **DISCO IN MOSCOW / RIP UP THE CITY. / AMPHETIMINE BLUES / YEAH YEAH** [ ] [-]

Aug 91. (cd) *Repertoire; (REP 4001WZ)* **YEAH YEAH YEAH** [ ] [-]
– Into the future / Yeah, yeah, yeah / Sweet, sweet heart / Baby, baby / No heart / She's bringing you down / Petrol / London girls / Stiff little fingers / Wrecked on you / I need a slave / Bad time / Pure mania / Automatic lover / Public enemy No.1 / Destroy / Nazi baby / Wake up / Feel alright / War zone / Troops of tomorrow / Wolfman howl / Jumpin' Jack Flash / Disco in Moscow.

Jun 92. (cd/c/lp) *Anagram; (CD/C+/GRAM 52)* **THE POWER OF MONEY (THE BEST OF THE VIBRATORS)** [ ] [-]

Sep 92. (cd) *Released Emotions; (REM 018CD)* **LIVE AT THE MARQUEE 1977 (live)** [ ] [-]

Jul 93. (cd; shared with The BOYS) *Windsong; (WINCD 036)* **BBC RADIO 1 LIVE IN CONCERT (live)** [ ] [-]

Sep 93. (cd) *Anagram; (CDPUNK 16)* **GUILTY / ALASKA 127** [ ] [-]

May 94. (cd) *Anagram; (CDPUNK 34)* **FIFTH AMENDMENT / RECHARGED** [ ] [-]

Jan 95. (cd) *Anagram; (CDPUNK 43)* **THE BEST OF THE VIBRATORS** [ ] [-]

Jun 95. (cd) *Anagram; (CDPUNK 58)* **MELTDOWN / VICIOUS CIRCLE** [ ] [-]

May 96. (cd) *Anagram; (CDPUNK 76)* **THE INDEPENDENT PUNK SINGLES COLLECTION** [ ] [-]

Oct 97. (cd) *Cleopatra; (<CLP 0090>)* **WE VIBRATE (THE BEST OF THE VIBRATORS)** [ ] [ ]
– Automatic lover / 24 hour people / Baby baby / Stiff little fingers / Disco in Moscow / I need a slave / London girls / Judy says (knock you in the head) / We vibrate / Flying home / Dance to the music / Flying duck theory / She's bringing you down / He's a psycho / Whips and furs / Amphetamine blues.

Jan 98. (cd) *Dojo; (DOLECD 102)* **DEMOS 1976-1977** [ ] [-]

Jun 98. (cd) *Overground; (OVER 73CD)* **VOLUME 10 / UNPUNKED** [ ] [-]

Oct 98. (cd-s) *Raw Power; (UKPR 001)* **TROOPS OF TOMORROW /** [ ] [-]

VICE SQUAD

Formed: Bristol, England . . . early 1978 from the ashes of local bands CONTINGENT and TV BRAKES, the line-up featuring 15 year old peroxide blonde bombshell BEKI BONDAGE, DAVE BATEMAN, MARK HAMBLY and SHANE BALDWIN. Issued on their own 'Riot City' label in 1980, 'LAST ROCKERS' was a promising if overwrought debut single. A doom-laden warning set in the aftermath of a nuclear holocaust, the track bordered on SIOUXSIE & THE BANSHEES conceptualism in its distinct three-part musical structure. Following a further EP, 'RESURRECTION', the band – and their label – were picked up by E.M.I. offshoot, 'Zonophone' for a hastily recorded debut album, 'NO CAUSE FOR CONCERN' (1981). Doubters were given plenty of ammunition with what was clearly a rush job, the band subsequently taking more care over, follow-up, 'STAND STRONG STAND PROUD' (1982). Amid increasingly strained band relations, BONDAGE soon opted for a solo career, enjoying a brief hype as BEKI & THE BOMBSHELLS. VICE SQUAD, meanwhile, were still on the case, enlisting a new frontwoman, LIA, and releasing a string of singles and a third album, 'SHOT AWAY' (1985) before finally handing in their badges. • **Trivia:** Rhythm section, HAMBLY and BALDWIN, also moonlighted with oi/punks, CHAOTIC DISCHORD. • **Songwriters:** BOND – BATEMAN penned except THE TIMES THEY ARE A-CHANGIN' (Bob Dylan) / TEENAGE RAMPAGE (Sweet).

Album rating: NO CAUSE FOR CONCERN (*5) / STAND STRONG STAND PROUD (*4) / SHOT AWAY (*4) / LAST ROCKERS – THE SINGLES compilation (*5)

BEKI BONDAGE (b. REBECCA BOND, 3 Jun'63) – vocals (ex-CONTIGENT) / **DAVE BATEMAN** – guitar / **MARK HAMBLY** – bass (ex-TV BRAKES) / **SHANE BALDWIN** – drums

Riot City / not iss.

Jan 81. (7"m) *(RIOT 1)* **LAST ROCKERS. / LATEX LOVE / LIVING ON DREAMS** [ ] [-]

May 81. (7"m) *(RIOT 2)* **RESURRECTION. / YOUNG BLOOD / HUMANE** [ ] [-]

Zonophone / not iss.

Oct 81. (lp) *(ZEM 103)* **NO CAUSE FOR CONCERN** [32] [-]
– Young blood / Coward / Nothing / Summer fashion / 1981 / Saturday night special / Offering / The times they are a-changin' / Evil / Angry youth / It's a sell-out / Still dying / Last rockers. *(cd-iss. Oct93 on 'Dojo'+=; DOJOCD 167)* – (So) What for the 80's / Sterile. *(lp-iss.Jan98; DOJOLP 167)*

Feb 82. (7"m) *(Z 26)* **OUT OF REACH. / (SO) WHAT FOR THE 80'S / STERILE** [68] [-]

Apr 82. (7"m) *(Z 30)* **ROCK'N'ROLL MASSACRE. / STAND STRONG AND PROUD / TOMORROW** [ ] [-]

May 82. (lp) *(ZEM 104)* **STAND STRONG STAND PROUD** [47] [-]
– Stand strong stand proud / Humane / Cheap / Gutterchild / Rock'n'roll massacre / Fist full of dollars / Freedom begins at home / Out of reach / Saviour machine / No right of reply / Death wish / Propaganda. *(cd-iss. Nov93 on 'Dojo'+=; DOJOCD 170)* – Tomorrow's soldier / Darkest hour / Citizen / Scarred for life / Faceless men.

Sep 82. (7"m) *(Z 34)* **CITIZEN. / SCARRED FOR LIFE / FACELESS MEN** [ ] [-]

— **LIA** – vocals; repl. BEKI who formed LIGOTAGE before going solo

— **SOOTY** – guitar; repl. MARK

Anagram / not iss.

Nov 83. (7") *(ANA 16)* **BLACK SHEEP. / NEW BLOOD** [ ] [-]
(12"+=) *(12ANA 16)* – The pledge.

Apr 84. (7") *(ANA 22)* **YOU'LL NEVER KNOW. / WHAT'S GOING ON** [ ] [-]
(12"+=) *(12ANA 22)* – The times they are a-changin'.

Jan 85. (7") *(ANA 26)* **TEENAGE RAMPAGE. / HIGH SPIRITS** [ ] [-]

Feb 85. (lp) **SHOT AWAY** [ ] [-]
– New blood / Take it or leave it / Out in the cold / Nowhere to hide / You'll never know / Rebels and kings / Playground / The rest of your life / What's going on / Killing time / Teenage rampage / Black sheep. *(cd-iss. Feb94 +=; CDPUNK 28)*– The times they are a changin' / High spirits / New blood (version) / The pledge / Nothing.

— they split after above

– compilations, etc. –

1982. (12"ep) *Riot City; (RIOT12 1/2)* **VICE SQUAD SINGLES** [ ] [-]

Feb 92. (cd) *Abstract; (AABT 805CD)* **LAST ROCKERS – THE SINGLES** [ ] [-]
– Last rockers / Living on dreams / Latex love / Young blood / Humane / Resurrection / Out of reach / (So) What for the 80's / Sterile / Stand strong stand proud / Tomorrow's soldier / Rock'n'roll massacre / Darkest hur / Upright citizen / Scarred for life / Faceless men. *(lp-iss.Nov96; DOJOLP 167)*

Apr 95. (cd) *Cleopatra; (<CL 5100>)* **LIVE AND LOUD** [ ] [ ]

Mar 97. (cd) *Anagram; (CDPUNK 89)* **THE PUNK SINGLES COLLECTION** [ ] [-]

Aug 97. (cd) *Anagram; (CDPUNK 99)* **THE BBC SESSIONS** [ ] [-]
(lp-iss.Jun98 on 'Get Back'; GET 29LP)

VICTIMS OF PLEASURE (see under ⇒ ASTLEY, Virginia)

Holly Beth VINCENT (see under ⇒ HOLLY & THE ITALIANS)

VIOLENT FEMMES

Formed: Milwaukee, Wisconsin, USA ... 1982 by GORDON GANO, BRIAN RITCHIE and VICTOR DE LORENZO. Discovered by JAMES HONEYMAN-SCOTT (of The PRETENDERS) and signed to 'Slash' in the States, the group delivered their much-loved eponymous debut in September '83 (licensed to 'Rough Trade' in the UK). With their acoustic cowpunk assault and sarcastic, angst-ridden lyrics, the VIOLENT FEMMES were taken to heart as flagbearers for indie geek-rock; the likes of 'GONE DADDY GONE', 'UGLY' and 'ADD IT UP' were classic slices of adolescent alienation, the album going on to sell more than a million copies with the barest of promotion and no hit singles. Follow-up, 'HALLOWED GROUND' (1984), was met with a more muted response; save the definitive 'COUNTRY DEATH SONG', the record lacked the downtrodden impetus of the debut and disappointed many who had raved over the debut. The 'FEMMES redeemed themsleves somewhat with the JERRY HARRISON-produced 'THE BLIND LEADING THE NAKED' (1986), an exhilirating cover of T.Rex's 'CHILDREN OF THE REVOLUTION' illustrating what they were capable of when they managed to focus some of their schizophrenic zeal. Yet it was too little too late and the band called it a day in 1988. RITCHIE had recorded a solo album for 'S.S.T.' the previous year, while GANO and DE LORENZO worked on separate projects. The trio eventually returned with '3' (1989), another directionless set which failed to add much to the band's legend, likewise 'WHY DO BIRDS SING' (1991). The release of compilation album, 'ADD IT UP' (1993) marked the premature end of their tenure with 'Slash' and the band subsequently signed to 'Elektra' for 1994's 'NEW TIMES'. Neither this or the following year's 'ROCK' (1995) added much to the VIOLENT FEMMES legacy and the band remain victims of the classic first album syndrome. • **Songwriters:** All written by GANO-RITCHIE, except CHINESE ROCKS (Heartbreakers) / DO YOU REALLY WANT TO HURT ME (Culture Club).

Album rating: VIOLENT FEMMES (*7) / HALLOWED GROUND (*6) / THE BLIND LEADING THE NAKED (*6) / 3 (*5) / WHY DO BIRDS SING? (*6) / ADD IT UP (1981-1993) compilation (*8) / NEW TIMES (*5)

GORDON GANO (b. 7 Jun'63, New York, USA) – vocals, guitar / **BRIAN RITCHIE** (b.21 Nov'60) – bass / **VICTOR DE LORENZO** (b.25 Oct'54, Raccine, Wisconsin) – drums

Rough Trade / Slash

Sep 83. (lp) *(ROUGH 55) <23845>* **VIOLENT FEMMES** [ ] [ ]
– Blister in the Sun / Kiss off / Please do not go / Add it up / Confessions / Prove my love / Promise / To the kill / Gone daddy gone / Good feeling. *(re-iss. Mar87 on 'Slash'+=; SLMP 15)* – Ugly / Gimme the car.

Dec 83. (7") *(RT 147)* **UGLY. / GIMME THE CAR** [ ] [ ]
(12"+=) *(RTT 147)* – Good feeling / Gone daddy gone.

Slash – London / Slash – Reprise

Jun 84. (7") *(LASH 1)* **GONE DADDY GONE. / ADD IT UP** [ ] [ ]
(12"+=) *(LASHX 1)* – Jesus walking on the water.

Jul 84. (lp/c) *(SLAP/SMAC 1) <25094>* **HALLOWED GROUND** [ ] [ ]
– Country death song / I hear the rain / Never tell / Jesus walking on the water / I know it's true but I'm sorry to say / Hallowed ground / Sweet misery blues / Black girls / It's gonna rain.

Sep 84. (7") *(LASH 3)* **IT'S GONNA RAIN. / JESUS WALKING ON THE WATER** [ ] [ ]
(12"+=) *(LASHX 3)* – Prove my love.

Feb 86. (7") *(LASH 7)* **CHILDREN OF THE REVOLUTION. / HEARTACHE** [ ] [ ]
(12"+=) *(LASHX 7)* – Good feeling.

Feb 86. (lp/c)(cd) *(SLAP/SMAC 10)(828-130-2) <25340>* **THE BLIND LEADING THE NAKED** [81] [84]
– Old Mother Reagan / No killing / Breakin' hearts / Special / Love and me make three / Candlelight song / I held her in my arms / Children of the revolution / Good friend / Heartache / Cold canyon / Two people. *(cd+=)* – Country death song / Black girls / World without mercy.

Apr 86. (7") *(LASH 7)* **CHILDREN OF THE REVOLUTION. / WORLD WITHOUT MERCY** [-] [ ]
(12"+=) *(LASHX 7)* – Good feeling.

— Disbanded in 1988. GORDON and VICTOR joined EUGENE CHADBOURNE (of SHOCKABILLY). BRIAN RITCHIE went solo (see below).

Jan 89. (lp/c/cd) *(828130-2/-4/-1) <25819>* **3** [ ] [93]
– Nightmares / Just like my father / Dating days / Fat / Fool in the full Moon / Nothing worth living for / World we're living in / Outside the palace / Telephone book / Mother of a girl / See my ships.

— added **MICHAEL BEINHORN** – keyboards, producer

May 91. (7"/c-s) *(LASH/LASCS 29)* **AMERICAN MUSIC. / PROMISE (live)** [ ] [ ]
(ext.12"+=) *(LASHX 29)* – Kiss off (live).
(cd-s++=) *(LASCD 29)* – (all 4 tracks).

May 91. (cd/c/lp) *(828239-2/-4/-1) <26476>* **WHY DO BIRDS SING?** [ ] [ ]
– American music / Out the window / Do you really want to hurt me? / Hey nonny nonny / Polygran used to be / Girl trouble / He likes me / Life is a scream / Flamingo baby / Lack of knowledge / More money tonight / I'm free.

Sep 91. (12"ep/cd-ep) *(LASH/LASCD 31)* **DO YOU REALLY WANT TO HURT ME? / DANCE, MOTHERFUCKER, DANCE / TO THE KILL** [-] [ ]

Oct 93. (cd/c) *<(45403-2/-4)>* **ADD IT UP (1981-1993)** (compilation) [ ] [ ]
– Intro / Waiting for the bus / Blister in the Sun / Gone daddy gone / Gordon's message / Gimme the car / Country death song / Black girls / Jesus walking on the water / 36-24-36 / I held her in my arms / I hate the T.V. / American is / Old mother Reagan / Degradation / Dance, motherfucker, dance / Lies / American / Out the window / Kiss off / Add it up / Vancouver / Johnny.

— **GUY HOFFMAN** – drums (ex-BODEANS) repl. VICTOR + MICHAEL

Elektra / Elektra

May 94. (cd-s) *<66186>* **MACHINE / MACHINE (version) / BALKAN FALCON / CHINESE ROCKS / COLOR ME ONCE** [-] [ ]

May 94. (cd/c/lp) *<(7559 61553-2/-4/-1)>* **NEW TIMES** [ ] [90]
– Don't start me on the liquor / New times / Breakin' up / Key of Z / 4 seasons / Machine / I'm nothing / When everybody's happy / Agememnon / This island life / I saw you in the crowd / Mirror mirror (I see a damsel) / Jesus of Rio.

– others, etc. –

Jun 92. (cd-ep) *Alex; <2742>* **AUSTRALIAN TOUR (live)** [-] [ ]

Jun 98. (cd) *Imprint; <33676>* **ROCK** [-] [ ]

BRIAN RITCHIE

had gone solo in-between breaks.

S.S.T. S.S.T.

Oct 87. (lp/cd) <*(SST/+CD 141)*> **THE BLEND**
– Alphabet / Arab song / Austrian anthill / Days of the blend / Doin' the best we can / Feast of fools / John the revelator / Nuclear war / Song of the highest tower / The toad / Two fat dogs.

1988. (12"ep) <*SST 186*> **NUCLEAR WAR (Deutsch). / ('A'-English version) / ALPHABET** -

1988. (12"ep) <*SST 187*> **ATOMKRIEG. /** -

Feb 89. (lp/cd) <*(SST/+CD 202)*> **SONIC TEMPLE AND THE COURT OF BABYLON**
– Bells / Sonic temple and the court of Babylon / Why did you lie to me? / Sun Ra from Outer Space / Dance*? / Christian for one day / A.D. / Mayerling (let's drink some wine) / No resistin' a Christian / So it goes / Hasan I sabbah / Reach out.

Feb 89. (12"ep/cd-ep) <*(SST/+CD 227)*> **SUN RA MAN FROM OUTER SPACE. /**

not iss. Dali

1990. (cd/c) <*DD/DC 89023*> **I SEE A NOISE** -
– Eva / 2 tongues, 2 minds / Please don't cry for me / Why is that baby's head so big? / Song without any end / Quo Vadis / Animals / The man with the cigarette in his nose / Religion ruined my life / Song of the cricket / I see a noise.

VIRGIN PRUNES

Formed: Dublin, Ireland . . . 1977 by FIONAN HANVEY aka GAVIN FRIDAY, GUGGI, DAVE-ID BUSARAS SCOTT, DIK EVANS (brother of U2's THE EDGE), STRONGMAN and POD. As musical ambassadors of the secretive artistic community known as Lypton Village – PAUL HEWSON aka BONO was also part of the close-knit group which had been inspired by the punk explosion across the water in England – The VIRGIN PRUNES courted controversy with the calculated outrage of their performance-art style gigs. Likely to feature everything from transvestitism to homo-erotic simulation, the band's live reputation continually overshadowed their recorded output. This didn't prevent them signing to 'Rough Trade', though, following on from a split single with The HIGSONS and a self-financed EP, 'TWENTY TENS'. The resulting 'IN THE GREYLIGHT' EP brought further critical acclaim while the band lent new meaning to interactive art by releasing their debut "album", 'NEW FORM OF BEAUTY' in three separate parts and in three different formats. Appropriately enough, The VIRGIN PRUNES' music was as abrasive, schizophrenic and fragmented as their approach to performing with a distinct gothic overtone to proceedings. (WHAT SHOULD WE DO WHEN) BABY TURNS BLUE' and 'PAGAN LOVE SONG' previewed 1982's COLIN NEWMAN (WIRE)-produced 'IF I DIE, I DIE' album, FRIDAY's vocal contortions as demanding as ever in a set which strayed closer to conventional songwriting territory. Inevitably, the band struggled to keep the shock factor intact, the subsequent departure of GUGGI and DIK in 1984 proving a major setback. Produced by SOFT CELL's DAVE BALL, 'THE MOON LOOKED DOWN AND LAUGHED' (1986) failed to halt the decline and FRIDAY struck out on a solo career in 1987 with a cover of The Rolling Stones' 'YOU CAN'T ALWAYS GET WHAT YOU WANT'. Following the release of live set, 'THE HIDDEN LIE – LIVE IN PARIS' (1987), the remains of the band carried on fruitlessly as The PRUNES while FRIDAY pursued his own warped muse via a deal with 'Island'. Having met collaborator, MAURICE ROYCROFT aka THE MAN SEEZER at his recently opened Dublin club, FRIDAY proceeded to indulge his interest in vintage European cabaret-noir with 'EACH MAN KILLS THE THING HE LOVES' (1989). Featuring musicians in the employ of both LOU REED and TOM WAITS, the record found FRIDAY wrestling the usual demons of sex, death, madness etc., in the spirit of KURT WEILL, BERTOLD BRECHT and the like. While some critics hailed it as the best work of his career, they weren't quite so enthusiastic about the more rock-centric 'ADAM 'N' EVE' (1992) upon which FRIDAY forced his 70's glam fantasies. Despite valuable mainstream exposure with contributions to the award-winning 1993 film, 'In The Name Of The Father', FRIDAY remains a cult figure, '95's 'SHAG TOBACCO' album making few concessions to fashion. • **Songwriters:** GAVIN FRIDAY, who also launched solo career in 1989 and covered NEXT (Jacques Brel) / DEATH IS NOT THE END (Bob Dylan) / THE SLIDER (T.Rex). • **Trivia:** GAVIN wrote three songs for model NAOMI CAMPBELL's 'Babywoman' album.

Album rating: IF I DIE, I DIE (*8) / HERESIE (*5) / THE MOON LOOKED DOWN AND LAUGHED (*6) / THE HIDDEN LIE (*6) / Gavin Friday: EACH MAN KILLS THE THING HE LOVES (*6) / ADAM AND EVE (*5) / SHAG TOBACCO (*6)

GAVIN FRIDAY (b. FIONAN HANVEY) – vocals / **GUGGI** (b. DEREK ROWEN) – vocals / **DAVE-ID BUSARAS SCOTT** (b. DAVID WATSON) – narrator / **DIK EVANS** – guitar / **STRONGMAN** (b. TREVOR ROWAN) – bass / **POD** (b. ANTHONY MURPHY) – drums

Baby not iss.

Jan 81. (7"ep) *(BABY 001)* **TWENTY TENS** -
– I've been smoking all night / Revenge / The children are crying.

—— **HAA LACKI BINTTII** – percussion, electronics repl. POD

Rough Trade not iss.

Jul 81. (7"ep) *(RT 072)* **IN THE GREYLIGHT. / WAR / MOMENTS AND MINE (DESPITE STRAIGHT LINES)** -

Oct 81. (7"ep) *(RT 089)* **NEW FORM OF BEAUTY PART ONE** -
– Sandpaper lullaby / Sleep / Fantasy dreams.

Nov 81. (10"ep) *(RT 090)* **NEW FORM OF BEAUTY PART TWO** -
– Come to daddy / Sweet home under white clouds / Sad world.

Dec 81. (12"ep) *(RT 091T)* **NEW FORM OF BEAUTY PART THREE** -
– The beast (seven bastard suck) / The slow children (Abbagal) / Brain damage / No birds to fly.

Dec 81. (7"/10"/12"; box) *(RT 089-91)* **A NEW FORM OF BEAUTY** (compilation) -
(cd-iss. Jan94 on 'New Rose'; NR 452042)

Apr 82. (7") *(RT 106)* **PAGAN LOVE SONG. / DAVE-ID IS DEAD** -
(12"+=) *(RT 106-12)* – Pagan lovesong (vibe akimbo).

—— male **MARY O'NELLON** – drums; repl. HAA LACKI BINTTII who became PRINCESS TINYMEAT and issued three singles for 'Rough Trade' between '85-'87; 'SLOBLANDS', 'BUN IN THE OVEN' and 'DEVILCOCK'.

Oct 82. (7") *(RT 119)* **(WHAT SHOULD WE DO WHEN) BABY TURNS BLUE. / YEO** -
(12"+=) *(RT 119T)* – Chance of a lifetime.

Nov 82. (lp) *(ROUGH 49)* **IF I DIE, I DIE** -
– Ulakennalmloy / Decline and fall / Sweet home under white clouds / Bau-Dachong / Pagan love song / Baby turns blue / Ballad of the man / Walls of Jericho / Caucasian walk / Theme for thought. *(cd-iss. Jun90; LCD 49) (cd re-iss. Jan94 on 'New Rose'; NR 452043)*

—— GUGGI and DIK departed

Baby Touch & Go

Apr 85. (lp/c) *(BABY/+T 002)* **OVER THE RAINBOW (RARITIES 1981-83)** -
– Down the memory lane / Red nettle / Mad bird in the wood / Jigsawmentallama / The king of junk / Just a love song / The happy head / Third secret / Heresie / We love Deirdre / Rhetoric / Man on the corner / Nisam lo / Loved one / Go 'T' away Deirdre. *(cd-iss. Feb88 +=; BABY 002CD)* – HERESIE

—— GAVIN FRIDAY made guest appearances for The FALL on 1984's 'CALL FOR ESCAPE ROUTE' 12", and 'WONDERFUL AND FRIGHTENING WORLD OF . . . ' album.

—— In 1986, The VIRGIN PRUNES were back with **GAVIN, MARY** (now guitar), **DAVE-ID, STRONGMAN** and the returning **POD** – drums

Jan 86. (lp/c/cd) *(BABY 005/+C/+CD)* <*TG 9*> **THE MOON LOOKED DOWN AND LAUGHED**
– Heaven / Love lasts forever / I am God / Sons find devils / Alone / The Moon looked down and laughed / Uncle Arthur's lonely world / Don't look back / Betrayal / Deadly sins. *(cd-iss. Jan94 on 'New Rose'; NR 422474)*

Jun 86. (7") *(BABY 003)* <*TG 15*> **LOVE LASTS FOREVER. / LOVE LORNALIMBO**
(12") *(BABY 004)* – ('A'side) / I like the way you're frightened.

Nov 86. (7") *(BABY 006)* <*TG 16*> **DON'T LOOK BACK. / WHITE HISTORY BOOK**
(12"+=) *(BABY 007)* – Day of ages.

May 87. (lp/c/cd) *(BABY/+C/+CD 008)* **THE HIDDEN LIE – LIVE IN PARIS** (live June '86) -
– Sweet home (under white clouds) / Lady day / God bless the child (with RAY CHARLES) / Never ending story / Pagan love song / Love is danger / The Moon looked down and laughed / Caucasian walk / The blues song. *(cd re-iss. Jan94 on 'New Rose'; NR 422473)*

Jan 88. (2x10"lp) *(BABY 011)* **HERESIE** -
– We love Dierdre / Rhetoric / Down the memory lane / Man on the corner / Nisam Lo / Loved one / Got away Dierdre / LIVE IN PARIS (parts 1 & 2). *(cd-iss. Jan94 on 'New Rose'; (NR 422475)*

—— they altered their moniker slighty to The PRUNES and issued two late 80's albums, 'LITE FANTASTIC' (BABYCD 012) and 'NADA' (BABYCD 013)

– compilations, etc. –

Jan 94. (cd) *New Rose; (NR 453041)* **PAGAN LOVESONG** -
Jan 94. (cd) *New Rose; (NR 422476)* **ARTFUCK** -
Mar 97. (cd) *Burning Airlines; (PILOT 007)* **GREATEST HITS** -
Jan 98. (cd) *Cleopatra; (<CLP 0179>)* **SONS FIND DEVILS (THE BEST OF THE VIRGIN PRUNES)**
– Ulakanakulot / Decline and fall / Pagan love song / New form of beauty / Walls of Jericho / Caucasian walk / Bernie and Attricia sing / Rhetoric / Sweet home under white clouds / Pig children / Come to daddy / Under Arthur's lonely world / Down the memory lane.

GAVIN FRIDAY

went solo augmented by **SIMON CARMODY**

Baby not iss.

Aug 87. (7"colrd) *(BABY 009)* **YOU CAN'T ALWAYS GET WHAT YOU WANT. / BLESSINGS** -

GAVIN FRIDAY & THE MAN SEEZER

with **MAN SEEZER** – keyboards / **MARC RIBOT** – guitar, banjo + **MICHAEL BLAIR** – drums, percussion (both of TOM WAITS' band) / **BILL FRISELL** – guitar / **FERNANDO SAUNDERS** – bass, guitar + **HANK ROBERTS** – cello (both of LOU REED's band)

Island Island

May 89. (7") *(IS 408)* **EACH MAN KILLS THE THINGS HE LOVES. / EXTRACT FROM THE BALLAD OF READING GAOL** -
(12"+=) *(12IS 408)* – ('A'instrumental).

May 89. (lp/c/cd) *(ILPS/ICT/CID 9925)* <*842586*> **EACH MAN KILLS THE THING HE LOVES** Aug89
– Each man kills the thing he loves / He got what he wanted / Tell tale heart / Man of misfortune / Apologia / Dazzle and delight / Rags to riches / The next thing to murder / Love is just a word / You take away the Sun / Another blow on the bruise / Death is not the end.

Aug 89. (7") *(IS 430)* **YOU TAKE AWAY THE SUN. / THE NEXT THING TO MURDER** -
(12"+=) *(12IS 430)* – Love is just a word.
(cd-s++=) *(CID 430)* – ('A'version).

Mar 90. (7") *(IS 455)* **MAN OF MISFORTUNE. / EACH MAN KILLS THE THING HE LOVES** -
(cd-s+=) *(CID 455)* – You take away the sun.

GAVIN FRIDAY

— (solo) with The BIG NO NO: **MAURICE SEEZER / DANNY BLUME** – guitar (ex-KID CREOLE) / **ERIK SANTO** (ex-LOUNGE LIZARDS)

Feb 92. (7") **I WANT TO LIVE. / LAUGH, CLOWN, LAUGH** [ ] [-]
(c-s+=/cd-s+=) – He got what he wanted.

Mar 92. (cd/c/lp) *(CID/ICT/ILPS 9984) <512090>* **ADAM 'N' EVE** [ ] [ ]
– I want to live / Falling off the edge of the world / King of trash / Why say goodbye? / Saint Divine / Melancholy baby / Fun & experience / The big no no / Where in the world? / Wind and rain / Eden.

Apr 92. (7"/c-s) **KING OF TRASH. / REX MORTUS EST** [ ] [-]
(12"+=/cd-s+=) – Geek love.

Sep 92. (7"/c-s) **FALLING OFF THE EDGE OF THE WORLD. / SIBYL VANE'S SUICIDE** [ ] [-]
(12"+=/cd-s+=) – Wake up screaming.

— above A-side featurued a duet with MARIA McKEE

Mar 94. (c-s/7"; by BONO & GAVIN FRIDAY) *(C+/IS 593)* **IN THE NAME OF THE FATHER. / EDEN** [46] [-]
(12"+=/cd-s+=) *(12IS/CID 593)* – (2-'A'mixes).

— above from the film of the same name

Aug 95. (cd/c) *(CID/ICT 8036) <524126>* **SHAG TOBACCO** [ ] [ ] Jan96
– Shag tobacco / Caruso / Angel / Little black dress / The slider / Dolls / Mr. Pussy / You me and World War Three / Kitchen sink drama / My twentieth century / The last song I'll ever sing / Le roi d'amour. *(cd re-iss. Sep96; IMCD 227)*

Oct 95. (c-s) *(CIS 615)* **ANGEL / ('A'-Space hop mix) / A THOUSAND YEARS / MACUSHLA** [ ] [-]
(12") *(12IS 615)* – (first 2 tracks) / ('A'-Space Hop dub) / ('A'-Fallen mix).
(cd-s) *(CID 615)* – ('A'side) / ('A'-Tim Simenon mix) / ('A'-Howie B mix) / ('A'-Danny Gee mix).

Jan 96. (12"ep/c-ep/cd-ep) *(12IS/CIS/CID 621)* **YOU ME AND WORLD WAR THREE (The Grid – Armageddon & Orbiting Planet mixes). / YOU ME AND WORLD WAR THREE (Tim Simenon movie mix) / BILLY BOOLA** [ ] [-]

— GAVIN retained co-writer **MAURICE SEEZER** – instruments / **ANDREW PHILPOTT** – instruments / **BARNES GOULDING** – drums

M.C.A. M.C.A.

Feb 98. (cd) *(<11751>)* **THE BOXER** (original soundtrack) [ ] [ ]
– In the shadow of a gun / Holy family 1 / To the peace line / The boxer / Twelve noon / You broke my heart / Semtex / Night band / Peace / The fight's over / Angus dei / The funeral / Holy family II / End of story, peacemaker / The boxer / Everything's gonna be alright.

VIVA SATELLITE! (see under ⇒ EGGS)

VIVA SATURN (see under ⇒ RAIN PARADE)

VOICE OF THE BEEHIVE

Formed: London, England . . .1985 by Beverly Hill-girlies TRACEY BRYN and MELISSA BROOKE BELLAND (daughters of FOUR PREPS singer BRUCE BELAND). Moving to England in the mid-80's, the girls befriended the likes of grebo metaller ZODIAC MINDWARP, soon starting up their own outfit with the help of guitarist MICK JONES. Taking their name from a Bette Davis movie, the group found themselves with a deal courtesy of the fledgling 'Food' label, subsequently enlisting the additional help of ex-MADNESS players MARK 'Bedders' BEDFORD and DAN 'Woody' WOODGATE. A debut single, 'JUST A CITY', appeared in Spring '87 and while it failed to make a dent in the charts it did lead to a deal with 'London' records. With MARTIN BRETT replacing BEDDERS (who subsequently formed BUTTERFIELD 8), their highly melodic new-wave sparkle-pop finally hit the charts about a year later via the Top 20 'DON'T CALL ME BABY', an earlier couple of singles, 'I SAY NOTHING' and 'I WALK THE EARTH', having stalled outside the Top 40. The debut album, 'LET IT BEE' (1988) appeared later that year, its cringeing title concealing a pandora's box of infectious girly singalongs which grabbed the navel-gazing indie scene squarely by its foppish fringe and manically grinned in its face. Yet these were no bushy-tailed bimbos, their lyrics were as cuttingly intelligent as the archest of guitar-pop commentators. A re-released 'I SAY NOTHING' almost cracked the Top 20 while 'THE MAN IN THE MOON' made the Top 10. After a near-three year sabbatical, the group re-emerged with 'HONEY LINGERS' in the summer of '91. While the pun was marginally funnier this time around, much of the material lacked the fizz-bomb punch of the debut. Undeterred by fair to middling reviews, the group continued apace with their infamous 'Orgy Under The Underworld' gigs in London. An even longer period of silence followed, only punctuated in '95 with the largely ignored 'SEX AND MISERY' set. The first fruits of a new deal with 'East West', the record saw TRACEY and MELISSA striking out on their own, augmented by session musicians. • **Songwriters:** T.BRYN lyrics / music by her, JONES, BROOKE and BRETT. The latter took over from BEDDERS who left 1987. Covers: D'YER MAKER (Led Zeppelin) / INDEPENDENCE DAY (Comsat Angels / IN THE FLESH (Blondie) / I THINK I LOVE YOU (hit; Partridge Family) / LITTLE GODS (Marvin Etzioni) / SAY IT (Jesus Jones) / SIT DOWN (James).

Album rating: LET IT BEE (*7) / HONEY LINGERS (*7)

TRACEY BRYN (b.TRACEY BELLAND, 17 May'62, Encino, Calif.) – vox, guitar / **MELISSA BROOKE BELLAND** (b. 6 Feb'66, Los Angeles, Calif.) – vocals / **MICK JONES** – guitar, vocals, keyboards / **MARK 'Bedders' BEDFORD** (b.24 Aug'61, London) – bass (ex-MADNESS) / **DAN 'Woody' WOODGATE** (b.19 Oct'60, London) – drums (ex-MADNESS)

Food not iss.

Mar 87. (7") *(FOOD 9)* **JUST A CITY. / I WALK THE EARTH** [ ] [-]
(12"+=) *(SNAK 9)* – 7 shocks.

Apr 87. (7") *(FOOD 9)* **JUST A CITY. / 7 SHOCKS** [ ] [ ]
(12"+=) *(FOODX 9)* – D'yer maker.

— **MARTIN BRETT** – bass, piano repl. BEDDERS who formed BUTTERFIELD 8

London London

Sep 87. (7") *(LON 151)* **I SAY NOTHING. / THINGS YOU SEE WHEN YOU DON'T HAVE YOUR GUN (live)** [45] [ ]
(12"+=/12"w-poster+=) *(LONX/+P 151)* – Independence day.
(d12"+=) *(LONXR 151)* – 7 shocks / Any day of the week (live).

Feb 88. (7") *(LON 169)* **I WALK THE EARTH. / THIS WEAK** [42] [ ]
(d7"+=/12"+=/cd-s+=) *(LON B/X/CD 169)* – Jesus / No green blues.

May 88. (7"/7"pic-d) *(LON/+P 175)* **DON'T CALL ME BABY. / JUMP THIS WAY** [15] [ ]
(d7"+=/12"+=) *(LON B/X 175)* – Goodbye tonight.
(10"++=/pic-cd-s++=) *(LON T/CD 175)* – I say nothing.

Jun 88. (lp/c/cd) *(LON LP/MC/CD 57) <828100>* **LET IT BEE** [13] [ ]
– The beat of love / Sorrow floats / Don't call me baby / The man in the Moon / What you have is enough / Oh love / I walk the Earth / Trust me / I say nothing / There's a barbarian in the back of my car / Just a city.

Jul 88. (7"/7"g-f/7"s) *(LON/+H/P 190)* **I SAY NOTHING. / THINGS YOU SEE WHEN YOU DON'T HAVE YOUR GUN (live)** [22] [ ]
(12"+=/12"g-f+=/cd-s+=) *(LON X/F/CD 190)* – Don't call me baby / In the flesh.

Oct 88. (7"/7"w-poster) *(LON/+P 206)* **I WALK THE EARTH. / THIS WEAK** [46] [ ]
(d7"+=) *(LONB 206)* – Don't call me baby / I say nothing.
(10"clear+=/12"+=/cd-s+=) *(LON T/X/CD 206)* – The tattoo song / Everything I had.

Dec 88. (7") *(LON 209)* **THE MAN IN THE MOON. / WHAT YOU HAVE IS ENOUGH** [ ] [ ]
(12"+=/cd-s+=) *(LON X/CD 209)* – 7 shocks (live) / There's a barbarian in the back of my car (live).

Jun 91. (7"/c-s) *(LON/+C 302) <869428>* **MONSTERS AND ANGELS. / ONLY IF YOU WANT TO** [17] [74]
(12"+=/cd-s+=) *(LON X/CD 302)* – Waitress / Pocketsize.

Aug 91. (cd/c/lp) *<(828259-2/-4/-1)>* **HONEY LINGERS** [17] [ ]
– Monsters and angels / Adonis blue / I think I love you / Look at me / Beauty to my eyes / Just like you / Little gods / I'm shooting cupid / Say it / Perfect place. *(cd re-iss. 1996 on 'Spectrum'; 552 111-2)*

Sep 91. (7"/c-s) *(LON/+C 308)* **I THINK I LOVE YOU. / SOMETHING ABOUT GOD** [25] [ ]
(12"/cd-s) *(LON X/CD 308)* – ('A'remix) / Say it / Don't call me baby / VB – Goddess of love / Orgy.

Jan 92. (7"/c-s) *(LON/+C 312)* **PERFECT PLACE. / SIT DOWN (live) / SHINE AWAY** [37] [ ]
(10"pic-d+=) *(LONT 312)* – Trust me (live).
(cd-s) *(LONCD 312)* – (first 2 tracks) / I say nothing (live) / Just a city (live).

East West Discovery

Jul 95. (c-s) *(YZ 973C)* **ANGEL COME DOWN / CARTOON CITY** [ ] [ ]
(cd-s+=) *(YZ 973CD)* – Inconsistencies.

Jan 96. (c-s) *(EW 017C)* **SCARY KISSES / YOU AND YOUR DUMB CLUB** [ ] [-]
(cd-s+=) *(EW 017CD)* – Time on all fours.

Feb 96. (cd/c) *(0630 11004-2/-4) <77036>* **SEX & MISERY** [ ] [ ] Apr96
– Scary kisses / New day / Angel come down / Moon of dust / I'm still in love / Love locked inside / Playing house / Heavenly / Blue in Paradise / So hard / Moonblind.

Apr 96. (c-s,cd-s) *<74528>* **SCARY KISSES / BLUE IN PARADISE** [-] [77]

May 96. (c-s) *(EW 037C)* **HEAVENLY / BLUE IN PARADISE** [ ] [-]
(cd-s+=) *(EW 037CD)* – Moonblind.

Aug 96. (cd-s) *<74542>* **SO HARD /** [-] [ ]

– compilations, etc. –

Feb 89. (12"ep/cd-ep) *Night Tracks; (SFNT/+CD 017)* **THE EVENING SHOW SESSIONS** (26.2.88) [ ] [-]
– No green blues / Jump this way / Independence day / Jesus.

VOWEL MOVEMENT (see under ⇒ CONCRETE BLONDE)

VULGAR BOATMEN

Formed: Gainsville, Florida, USA . . . 1982 by ROBERT RAY, who teamed up alongside ex-GIZMOS frontman DALE LAWRENCE and WALTER SALAS-HUMARA (latter of The SILOS). LAWRENCE (aka KIRKLAND) was actually based in Indianapolis, necessitating a writing process based on correspondance rather than rehearsal! This highly unusual set-up meant that their release schedule was sparse to say the least, only one official album surfacing in the 80's, namely 'YOU AND YOUR SISTER' (1989). The record's warm reception led to a deal with 'Rough Trade', RAY and LAWRENCE augmented this time around by several back-up musicians including MATT SPEAKE, J.D. FOSTER and ALASTAIR GAVIN. The resulting album, 'PLEASE PANIC' (1992), was another critical favourite among retro-pop afficionados which led to belated interest from the world of major labels, 'East West' releasing their swansong set, 'OPPOSITE SEX', in '95.

Album rating: YOU AND YOUR SISTER (*6) / PLEASE PANIC (*6) / OPPOSITE SEX (*7)

ROBERT RAY (b. Memphis, Tennessee) – vocals, guitar / **DALE LAWRENCE** (aka KIRKLAND) (b. Indianapolis, USA) – vocals, guitar / **WALTER SALAS-HUMARA** (b.21 Jun'61, New York City) – guitar, vocals (of The SILOS) / **JEFF BYERS** – bass

not iss. Record Collector

1989. (cd/c) *<RC 1171-2/-4>* **YOU AND YOUR SISTER** [-] [ ]
– Mary Jane / You and your sister / Margaret says / Katie / Drive somewhere /

Decision by the airport / Change the world all around / Fallen down / Hold me tight / Cry real tears / Drink more coffeee / The street where you live.

— **RAY + LAWRENCE** with **MATT SPEAKE** – guitar / **J.D. FOSTER** – bass / **ALASTAIR GAVIN** – organ / **MICHAEL DERRY + JONATHAN ISLEY + ANDY RICHARDS** – drums / **HELEN KIRKLAND + KATHY KOLATA** – viola (WALTER SALAS-HUMARA released a solo album, 'RADAR')

Rough Trade Caroline

Feb 92. (cd/c) *(R 281-2/-4)* <*CAROL 1716-2/-4*> **PLEASE PANIC** ☐ ☐
– Don't mention it / Calling upstairs / We can figure this out / Fool me / You don't love me yet / There's a family / You're the one / Goodnight, Jean-Marie / I'm not stuck on you / Alison says / Stop alternating / The 23rd of September. <*re-iss. 1996 on 'Safe House'; 2102*>

East West East West

Jun 95. (cd/c) <*(0630 10941-2/-4)*> **OPPOSITE SEX** ☐ ☐
– When we talk / Wide awake / Call back instead / In a station / Travelling / Shake / Heartbeat / In a minute / Opposite sex / We can walk / Genie says / Susan, goodnight.

— split after above

WAH!

Formed: Liverpool, England . . . early '79 as WAH! HEAT by ex-CRUCIAL THREE member (alongside JULIAN COPE and IAN McCULLOCH), PETE WYLIE. Roping in ROB JONES and PETE YOUNGER, WYLIE cut a debut single, 'BETTER SCREAM', for the 'Inevitable' label, subsequently recruiting a whole new line-up – the interestingly named KING BLUFF, CARL WASHINGTON, JOE MUSKER – for a follow-up, 'SEVEN MINUTES TO MIDNIGHT' (absolutely no relation to the similarly titled IRON MAIDEN screecher!). The latter track caught the attention of 'WEA' subsidiary, 'Eternal', WYLIE signing up, abbreviating the name to WAH! and replacing MUSKER with ex-IT'S IMMATERIAL man, PAUL BARLOW. Summer '81 saw the release of a flop single, 'FORGET THE DOWN!' and a long awaited debut album, 'NAH! POO! THE ART OF BLUFF' (1981), the sound of the band becoming more focused with the arrival of another ex-IT'S IMMATERIAL musician, HENRY PRIESTMAN. Issued under the moniker of SHAMBEKO! SAY WAH!, Spring '82's 'REMEMBER' indicated a change in direction and by the release of the SPECTOR-esque pop/soul classic, 'THE STORY OF THE BLUES', the transformation was complete. It was also extremely successful, a new line-up centering around the core of WYLIE and a recalled WASHINGTON – PRIESTMAN going on to form white soulboys, The CHRISTIANS – seeing the track make the UK Top 3. At last it seemed as if WYLIE's wayward muse was beginning to pay dividends yet a follow-up, 'HOPE (I WISH YOU'D BELIEVE ME)' barely scraped the Top 40 and ensuing record company problems delayed any further releases for more than a year. WYLIE & Co. eventually returned in summer '84, going Top 20 with the appropriately named 'COME BACK (THE STORY OF THE REDS)' and adopting a harder hitting, more politically abrasive approach. The accompanying album, 'A WORD TO THE WISE GUY' (1984), made the Top 30 although yet again a further single, 'WEEKENDS', stiffed. Compilation set, 'THE WAY WE WAH!' (1984) signalled the end of the line for WAH! in all its multifarious guises, WYLIE later resurfacing in a solo capacity (backing help courtesy of The OEDIPUS WRECKS) with the commercial yet soulful pop favourite, 'SINFUL'. It was a sizeable Top 20 hit yet what was really sinful was the predictable floundering of follow-up single, 'DIAMOND GIRL' and the 'SINFUL' (1987) album. Disappearing for the remainder of the 80's, Liverpool's most dogged pop veteran returned in the early 90's with a remixed 'SINFUL' after his profile had been raised by a guest spot on The FARM's massive 'ALL TOGETHER NOW' single. Despite critical plaudits as ever, both a single, 'DON'T LOSE YOUR DREAMS' and album, 'INFAMY! OR I DIDN'T GET WHERE I AM . . .' (1991), sank without trace. Tragically, it seems that despite WYLIE's continuing penchant for exclamation marks, the man never really got his point across fully to the average pop fan!!!

Album rating: NAH! POO! THE ART OF BLUFF (*5) / A WORD TO THE WISE GUY (*5) / THE WAY WE WAH! compilation (*7) / Pete Wylie: SINFUL (*6)

WAH! HEAT

PETE WYLIE (b.22 Mar'58) – vocals, guitar (ex-CRUCIAL THREE) / **ROB 'Jonie' JONES** – drums (ex-CRASH COURSE, w/Pete Wylie) / **PETE YOUNGER** – bass (ex-THOSE NAUGHTY LUMPS) repl. COLIN WILLIAMS + J.CULT

Inevitable / not iss.

Jan 80. (7") *(INEV 001)* **BETTER SCREAM. / (HEY DISCO) JOE** -

— **WYLIE** recruited **KING BLUFF** – keyboards, synthesizer / **CARL WASHINGTON** – bass; repl. YOUNGER / **JOE MUSKER** – drums (ex-DEAD OR ALIVE) repl. JONES to The HIGH FIVE / + on tour **COLIN REDMOND** – guitar

Nov 80. (7") *(INEV 004)* **SEVEN MINUTES TO MIDNIGHT. / DON'T STEP ON THE CRACKS** -

WAH!

— **PAUL BARLOW** – drums (of IT'S IMMATERIAL) repl. MUSKER

Eternal / not iss.

Jun 81. (7") *(SLATE 1)* **FORGET THE DOWN! / THE CHECKMATE SYNDROME**

Jul 81. (lp) *(CLASSIC 1)* **NAH! POO! THE ART OF BLUFF** 33 -
– The wind-up / Other boys / Why'd you imitate the cut-out / Mission impossible / Somesay / The seven thousand names of Wah! / Sleeep (a lullaby for Josie) / Seven minutes to midnight / The death of Wah!.

— **HENRY PRIESTMAN** – keyboards (of IT'S IMMATERIAL) repl. BLUFF

Oct 81. (7"/12") *(SIMEY 1/+T)* **SOMESAY. / FORGET THE DOWN** -

Apr 82. (7"/12"; as SHAMBEKO! SAY WAH!) *(ZAZU 1/+T)* **REMEMBER. / A CRACK IS A CRACK** -

— **WYLIE + WASHINGTON** enlisted **CHARLIE GRIFFITHS** – synthesizer / **JAY NAUGHTON** – piano / **CHRIS JOYCE** – drums (ex-DURUTTI COLUMN, etc.) / **The SAPPHIRES** – backing vox

Nov 82. (7") *(JF 1)* **THE STORY OF THE BLUES. / TALKIN' BLUES** 3
(12"+=) *(JF 1T)* – Seven minutes to midnight (live).

WEA / Warners

Mar 83. (7") *(X 9880)* **HOPE (I WISH YOU'D BELIEVE ME). / SLEEEP** 37
(12"+=) *(X 9880T)* – You can't put your arms around a memory / Year of decision / Le spwah.

The MIGHTY WAH!

Beggars Banquet / Beggars Banquet

Jul 84. (7"/12") *(BEG 111/+T)* **COME BACK (THE STORY OF THE REDS). / DEVIL IN MISS JONES** 20

Jul 84. (lp) *(BEGA 54)* **A WORD TO THE WISE GUY** 28
– Yuh learn I / Weekends / Everwanna / The lost generation / Yuh learn II / I know there was something / Yuh learn III / In the bleak – (Body and soul) – Midwinter / Papa crack – God's lonely man / What's happening here / Yuh learn IV / Come back (the story of the reds). *(re-iss. Jan89 on 'Beggars Banquet-Lowdown' lp/c)(cd; BBL/+C 54)(BBL 54CD)*

Sep 84. (7") *(BEG 117)* **WEEKENDS. / SHAMBEKO (THE LOST GENERATION)**
(12"+=) *(BEG 117T)* – Body and soul (acoustic) / Something wrong with Eddie / Weekend (original).

— had already split in 1984, CHRIS JOYCE joined SIMPLY RED

– compilations, others, etc. –

Nov 83. (lp) *White Label; (none)* **THE MAVERICK YEARS 80-81 (the official bootleg)** -

Nov 84. (lp/c) *WEA; (WX 11/+C)* **THE WAY WE WAH!** (compilation) -
– Other boys / Somesay / The seven thousand names of Wah! / Seven minutes to midnight / The death of Wah! / The story of the blues parts 1 & 2 / Sleeep (a lullaby for Josie) / You can't put your arms around a memory / Hope (remix) / Remember.

Sep 87. (12"ep) *Strange Fruit; (SFPS 035)* **THE PEEL SESSIONS** (22.8.84) -
– Basement blues / The story of the blues / Better scream / Weekends / Yuh learn.

PETE WYLIE

— (solo, with **The OEDIPUS WRECKS**)

M.D.M. / unknown

Apr 86. (7") *(MDM 7)* **SINFUL. / I WANT THE MOON, MOTHER** 13
(d7"+=) *(MDMD 7)* – Sophie's sinful (for Maurice and Kabelle) / Joy of being booed.
(12"+=)(3"cd-s+=) *(MDM 7-12)(CDT 28)* – Fourelevenfortyfour / ('A'mix) / If I love you.

Sep 86. (7"/12") *(MDM 12/+12)* **DIAMOND GIRL. / SPARE A THOUGHT** 57

Siren / unknown

Jul 87. (7"/12") *(SRN 54/+12)* **IF I LOVE YOU. / NEVER FALL FOR A WHORE**

Aug 87. (lp/c/cd) *(SRNLP/SRNC/CDSRN 10)* **SINFUL**
– Sinful / Shoulder to shoulder / Break out the banners / Fourelevenfortyfour / If I love you / Train to Piranhaville / We can rule the world / All the love. *(re-iss. Apr90 on 'Virgin' lp/c; OVED/+C 290)*

Oct 87. (7") *(SRN 59)* **FOURELEVENFORTYFOUR. / THE MARKSMAN**
(12"+=)(cd-s+=) *(SRN 59-12)(SRNCD 59)* – Sinful (song of the sinful angel).

— late 1990, WYLIE guested for The FARM on their hit single, 'All Together Now'

PETE WYLIE & WAH . . . THE MONGREL

— with The FARM

Siren / Virgin

Apr 91. (7"/c-s) *(SRN 138/+C)* **SINFUL! / FOURELEVENFORTYFOUR** 28
(12") *(SRN 138-12)* – ('A'side) / ('A'-Tribal mix).
(cd-s+=) *(SRNCD 138)* – (all 3 tracks).

Jun 91. (7") **DON'T LOSE YOUR DREAMS (excerpt from A Teenage Opera part 154). / SEAMLESS**
(12"+=)(cd-s+=) – Imperfect.

Aug 91. (cd/c/lp) *(CDSRN/SRNMC/SRNLP 33)* **INFAMY! OR I DIDN'T GET WHERE I AM TODAY**
– Don't lose your dreams (excerpt from a teenage opera part 15) / Never gonna stop: no heshmesh / I didn't get where I am today / Circle of salt / The Kerry baby / John 3:16 – The one tonight / Everything! (a song for Dennis Wilson) / From carpenter to king / Long tall Scally (the ballad thereof) / Getting out of it . . . / Sinful! (tribal mix).

Sep 91. (7") **LONG TALL SCALLY. / . . . AND THE GOOD GUYS DON'T DIE**
(12"+=)(cd-s+=) – Everything (but The Wah!) for Dennis Wilson acappella everything includes orchestrals ultimately.

The MIGHTY WAH!

— re-formed with **WYLIE** and Co.

Columbia Columbia

Nov 98. (c-s/cd-s) *(666720-4/-2)* **HEART AS BIG AS LIVERPOOL /**

WAITRESSES

Formed: Akron & Cleveland, Ohio, USA . . . late '77 by TIN HUEY guitarist, CHRIS BUTLER, alongside vocalist PATTY DONAHUE, TRACY WORMWORTH, session sax man extraordinaire MARS WILLIAMS, STUART AUSTIN and RICK DAILEY. The WAITRESSES first served USA's 'New Wave' clientele with an appearance on the 'Akron' compilation, 'Spirit Of America' and the release of a debut single, 'IN SHORT STACK'. However, it wasn't until 1980 and a deal with Island subsidiary 'Ze', that newly NY-based PATTY and her crew started turning heads with the tongue-in-cheek 'I KNOW WHAT BOYS LIKE'. Following some personnel changes (including former TELEVISION man BILLY FICCA coming in for AUSTIN), the band re-released the song in the States, PATTY's playful DEBBIE HARRY/GO-GO'S style nearly tipping them into the Top 60. This helped their debut set, 'WASN'T TOMORROW WONDERFUL?' (1982), gain a Top 50 booking, although chart success was off the menu for 1982's mini-set, 'I COULD RULE THE WORLD . . .'. Nevertheless, this featured one of their most enduring tracks to date, 'CHRISTMAS WRAPPING', a surprise Yuletide novelty hit in Britain. The following year, the group released their second album proper, 'BRUISEOLOGY', their last effort as PATTY was briefly replaced by HOLLY BETH VINCENT. PATTY was to die of cancer late 1996.

Album rating: WASN'T TOMORROW WONDERFUL (*5) / BRUISEOLOGY (*4)

PATTY DONAHUE – vocals / **CHRIS BUTLER** – guitar (of/ex-TIN HUEY) / **MARS WILLIAMS** – saxophone (of SWOLLEN MONKEYS, of MASSACRE, of TERRORISTS) / **RICK DAILEY** – piano / **TRACY WORMWORTH** – bass / **STUART AUSTIN** – drums

not iss. Clone

1978. (7") *<CL 006>* **IN SHORT STACK. / SLIDE** [-]

Ze-Island Ze-Antilles

Oct 80. (7") *<ANS 105>* **I KNOW WHAT BOYS LIKE. / NO GUILT** [-]
<re-iss. 1982; ANS 4504>

— **DAN KLAYMAN** – keyboards (of SWOLLEN MONKEYS) repl. DAILEY

— **BILLY FICCA** – drums (ex-TELEVISION, etc) repl. AUSTIN

Nov 81. (7") *(WIP 6763)* **CHRISTMAS WRAPPING. / CHRISTMAS FEVER (CHARLELIE COUTURE)**

— **DAVID HOFSTRA** – bass; repl. TRACY

Polydor Polydor

Feb 82. (7") *(POSP 414) <PD 2196>* **I KNOW WHAT BOYS LIKE. / IT'S MY CAR** [62]

Apr 82. (lp) *(POLS 1063) <PD1 6346>* **WASN'T TOMORROW WONDERFUL?** [41] Jan82
– No guilt / Wise up / Quit / It's my car / Wasn't tomorrow wonderful? / I know what boys like / Heat night / Redland / Pussy strut / Go on / Jimmy tomorrow.

— now without KLAYMAN (still a SWOLLEN MONKEY)

Dec 82. (m-lp) *<507>* **I COULD RULE THE WORLD IF I COULD ONLY GET THE PARTS** [-]
– I could rule the world if I could only get the parts / Make the weather / Bread and butter / Square pegs / The smartest person I know / Christmas wrapping.

May 83. (7") *(POSP 582)* **MAKE THE WEATHER. / BREAD AND BUTTER** [-]
(12"+=) *(POSPX 582)* – Square pegs / The smartest person I know.

May 83. (lp/c) *(POLD/+C 5080) <810980>* **BRUISEOLOGY**
– A girl's gotta do / Make the weather / Everything's wrong if my hair is wrong / Luxury / Open city / Thinking about sex again / Bruiseology / Pleasure / Spin / They're all out of liquor, let's find another party.

— **HOLLY BETH VINCENT** – vocals (ex-HOLLY & THE ITALIANS) repl. PATTY (the latter died of cancer on the 9th December, 1996)

— served up their last platter on above album (MARS joined The PSYCHEDELIC FURS)

– compilations, etc. –

Dec 82. (7"/12") *Ze-Island; (WIP/12WIP 6821)* **CHRISTMAS WRAPPING. / HANGOVER (FOR THE 1ST OF THE 1ST '83)** [45] [-]

WAKE

Formed: Glasgow, Scotland . . . early 80's by a mysterious bunch of gloom mongers led by singer, DUNCAN CAMERON (possibly!?). After a one-off self-financed 7", 'ON OUR HONEYMOON', the band joined the black-clad ranks of Tony Wilson's 'Factory' stable, where their blooding blend of NEW ORDER and The CURE fitted in perfectly. A debut LP, 'HARMONY' (1983), showcased their derivative but effective sound, although barring a few sporadic singles, it would be all of three years before a follow-up, 'HERE COMES EVERYBODY' (1986). Of these aforementioned 45's, only 'TALK ABOUT THE PAST' was of any note, featuring as it did DURUTTI COLUMN's VINI REILLY on piano. Subsequently dropped by Factory, The WAKE were resurrected by the infamously fey 'Sarah' label, CAMERON even managing to borrow a couple of ORCHIDS (MATTHEW DRUMMOND and JAMES MOODY) for his 1990 comeback album, 'MAKE IT LOUD'. A tad brighter, if not quite opening the proverbial curtains just yet, the record was an interesting combination of effete vocals, hard-edged jangling, tinkling electric piano and of course that cheap electro drumbeat. Like fellow Glaswegians, the BLUE NILE, The WAKE took their time between albums, 1994's ironically titled 'TIDAL WAVE OF HYPE' their only other release of the decade.

Album rating: HARMONY (*7) / HERE COMES EVERYBODY (*4) / MAKE IT LOUD (*5) / TIDAL WAVE OF HYPE (*4)

DUNCAN CAMERON – vocals / + others unknown

Scan not iss.

1982. (7") *(SCN 01)* **ON OUR HONEYMOON. / GIVE UP** [-]

Factory not iss.

Jan 83. (lp) *(FACT 60)* **HARMONY** [-]
– Judas / Testament / Patrol / The old men / Favour / Heartburn / An immaculate conception.

Nov 83. (c-s) *Factory Benelux; (FBM 24)* **SOMETHING OUTSIDE / HOIST** [-]

Mar 84. (7"/12") *(FAC 88/+12)* **TALK ABOUT THE PAST. / EVERYBODY WORKS SO HARD** [-]

Mar 85. (7") *(FAC 113)* **OF THE MATTER. / (version)** [-]

Jan 86. (lp) *(FACT 130)* **HERE COMES EVERYBODY** [-]
– All I asked you to do / Here comes everybody / World of her own / etc

May 87. (12"ep) *(FAC 177T)* **SOMETHING NO ONE ELSE COULD BRING** [-]
– Gruesome castle /

Sarah not iss.

Dec 89. (7") *(SARAH 021)* **CRUSH THE FLOWERS. /** [-]

— now with **MATTHEW DRUMMOND + JAMES MOODY** (of the ORCHIDS)

Nov 90. (lp) *(SARAH 602)* **MAKE IT LOUD** [-]
– English rain / Glider / Firestone tyres / American grotto / Joke shop / Holy head / Henry's work / Cheer up Ferdinand.

Mar 94. (lp/cd) *(SARAH 618/+CD)* **TIDAL WAVE OF HYPE** [-]
– Shallow end / Obnoxious Kevin / Crasher / Selfish / Provincial disco / I told you so / Britain / Back of beyond / Solo project / Down on your knees / Britain (remix) / Big noise big deal.

WAKE OOLOO (see under ⇒ FEELIES)

WALKABOUTS

Formed: Seattle, Washington, USA . . . 1984 by CHRIS ECKMAN and CARLA TORGERSON, the line-up completed by the former's brothers, GRANT and CURT, although MICHAEL WELLS replaced CURT before any recording. After two EP's on the 'Necessity' label in '85, the group released a debut album, 'SEE BEAUTIFUL RATTLESNAKE GARDENS' (1987), for the obscure 'PopLlama'. Adding GLENN SLATER on keyboards, the group signed to 'Sub Pop', issuing the acclaimed 'CATARACT' (1989). In comparison to the bulk of the grunge acts on the label, the group's rugged folk-rock sound was more reminiscent of the wild scenery of the American North West (Appalachian Mountains to be exact!) than the grimy clubs of Seattle. In that sense, the band were never really part of the 'Sub Pop' phenomenon although they continued to release fine, but generally ignored albums at a prolific pace. Garnering further cult acclaim for the 'SCAVENGER' (1991) and 'NEW WEST MOTEL' (1993) sets (the latter seeing TERRI MOELLER replace GRANT), the group subsequently indulged themselves with a covers album, 'SATISFIED MIND' (1993). Interpreting material by the likes of GENE CLARK, JOHN CALE, NICK CAVE and CHARLIE RICH, the group wore their influences proudly, their subsequent album, 'SETTING THE WOODS ON FIRE' (1994), leaning more towards the rootsy side of things. Strangely, The WALKABOUTS were always more popular in Europe than the States, the group subsequently signing to 'Virgin', for whom they recorded the masterful 'DEVIL'S ROAD' (1996). Among their transatlantic cousins, The WALKABOUTS had most in common with the likes of GALLON DRUNK and TINDERSTICKS, the latter group's DICKON HINCHCLIFFE adding violin flourishes on 'THE LEAVING KIND'. Also, in common with TINDERSTICKS, the group employed the services of an orchestra, more specifically The Warsaw Philharmonic. Their swooning strings were used to stunning effect alongside gorgeous melody and shimmering guitar vibrato on the album's epic lead track, 'THE LIGHT WILL STAY ON'. Ranking as one of the best songs they've ever recorded, the track was partly dedicated to CHARLIE RICH, who passed away the previous year. For now, the group remain a well-kept secret although it's surely only a matter of time before they gain the belated recognition they are deservedly due. • **Covered:** ON THE BEACH + LIKE A HURRICANE (Neil Young) / BIG BLACK CAR (Big Star) / FREE MONEY (Patti Smith) / FEEL LIKE GOING HOME (Charlie Rich) / LOOM OF THE LAND (Nick Cave) / etc.

Album rating: CATARACT (*7) / RAG & BONE (*6) / SCAVENGER (*6) / NEW WEST MOTEL (*6) / SATISFIED MIND (*6) / SETTING THE WOODS ON FIRE (*6) / DEVIL'S ROAD (*5) / NIGHTTOWN (*5)

CHRIS ECKMAN – vocals, guitar / **CARLA TORGERSON** – vocals, guitar / **MICHAEL WELLS** – bass; repl. CURT ECKMAN / **GRANT ECKMAN** – drums / part-time 5th member **LARRY BARRETT** – banjo, mandolin, guitar

not iss. Necessity

Jan 85. (c-ep) **WALKABOUTS** [-]

Nov 85. (12"ep) **22 DISASTERS** [-]

not iss. Pop Llama

1987. (lp/c/cd) *<PL+/C/CD 4129>* **SEE BEAUTIFUL RATTLESNAKE GARDENS** [-]
– Jumping off / Breakneck speed / The wellspring / John Reilly / Robert McFarlane blues / This rotten tree / Laughingstock / Glass palace / Feast or famine / Ballad

of Moss Head / Who-knows-what / Rattlesnake theme / Weights and rivers. *(UK-iss.Jan90 on 'Still Sane'; 089204) (cd-iss. Jun97 on 'Glitterhouse'+=; GRCD 335)* – Linda Evans / Mai Tai time / Cyclone / Gather round / Certain gift.

—— added **GLENN SLATER** – keyboards

Sub Pop Sub Pop

Mar 89. (lp) *<SP 31>* **CATARACT**
– Whiskey XXX / Hell's soup kitchen / Whereabouts unknown / End in tow / Bones of contention / Home as found / Smokestack / The wicked skipper.

Feb 90. (orange.m-lp/m-c/m-cd) *<SP 56/+A/B>* **RAG AND BONE**
– The anvil song / Ahead of the storm / Medicine hut / Wreck of the old #9 / Mr.Clancy / Last ditch. *(m-cd/m-c+=)* – CATARACT *(UK cd-iss. Nov96 on 'Glitterhouse'; GRCD 85)*

Sep 91. (lp/c/cd) *<SP 124/+A/B>* **SCAVENGER**
– Dead man rise / Stir the ashes / The night watch / Hang man / Where the deep water goes / Blown away / Nothing is stranger / Let's burn down the cornfield / River blood / Train to mercy. *(UK cd-iss. Nov96 on 'Glitterhouse'; GRCD 161)*

Oct 91. (cd-ep) *<SP 117>* **WHERE THE DEEP WATER GOES / STIR THE ASHES / BIG BLACK CAR / ON THE BEACH**

—— **TERRI MOELLER** – drums; repl. GRANT

—— added part-time **BRUCE WIRTH** – pedal steel guitar, mandolin

Jul 92. (12"ep/cd-ep) *(SP/+CD 39-197) <SP 150>* **DEAD MAN RISE**
– Dead man rise / Train mercy / (+ 3 live).

Feb 93. (12"ep/cd-ep) *(SP/+CD 251)* **JACK CANDY**

Mar 93. (lp/cd) *(SP/+CD 81-252) <CM 28>* **NEW WEST MOTEL**
– Jack Candy / Sundowner / Grand theft auto / Break it down gently / Your hope shines / Murdering stone / Sweet revenge / Glad nation's death song / Long time here / Wondertown (part 1) / Drag this river / Snake mountain blues / Findlay's motel / Unholy dreams. *(cd re-iss. Nov96 on 'Glitterhouse'; GRCD 70081)*

May 93. (7") *(SP 98-270)* **YOUR HOPE SHINES. /**
(cd-s+=) *(SPCD 98-270)* –

Sub Pop Creative Man

Nov 93. (lp/cd) *(SP/+CD 116-294) <83048>* **SATISFIED MIND**
– Satisfied mind / Loom of the land / River people / Polly / Buffalo ballet / Lovers crime / Shelter for an evening / Dear darling / Poor side of town / Free money / Storms are on the ocean / Feel like going home / Will you miss me when I'm gone? *(cd re-iss. Nov96 on 'Glitterhouse'; GRCD 294)*

Mar 94. (cd-ep) *(SPCD 129-321)* **GOOD LUCK MORNING / NIGHT DRIVE (truck stop version) / FINDLAY'S MOTEL / NOTHING IS A STRANGER**

May 94. (lp/c/cd) *(SP/+MC/CD 128-319) <30>* **SETTING THE WOODS ON FIRE**
– Good luck morning / Firetrap / Bordertown / Feeling no pain / Old crow / Almost wisdom / Sand and gravel / Night drive (truck stop version) / Hole in the mountain / Pass me on over / Up in the graveyard / Promised. *(cd re-iss. Nov96 on 'Glitterhouse'; GRCD 319)*

Dindisc not iss.

Mar 96. (c-s) *(DINSC 152)* **THE LIGHT WILL STAY ON / DEVIL'S ROAD**
(cd-s+=) *(DINSD 152)* – Incognito / Winded.

Virgin Virgin Schallplatter

Apr 96. (cd/c) *(CD/MC VIR 46) <841349>* **DEVIL'S ROAD**
– The light will stay on / Rebecca wild / Stopping off place / Cold eye / Christmas valley / Blue head flame / When fortune smiles / For all this / Fairground blues / Leaving kind / Forgiveness song.

Jun 97. (cd) *(CDVIR 57) <844280>* **NIGHTTOWN**
– Follow me an angel / These proud streets / Tremble (goes the night) / Unwind / Lift your burdens up / Prayer for you / Immaculate / Nocturno / Heartless / Nightbirds / Forever gone / Harbour lights / Slow red dawn.

– compilations, etc. –

Nov 96. (cd) *Glitterhouse; (GRCD 404)* **DEATH VALLEY DAYS (LOST SONGS AND RARITIES 1985-1995)**

WALKING SEEDS

Formed: Liverpool, England . . . 1986 out of the ashes of mid 80's gothabilly noise outfit The MEL-O-TONES (like a serious HALF MAN HALF BISCUIT) by FRANK MARTIN, BOB PARKER and JOHN NEESAM. A three-month spell as CORINTHIANS was put aside with the release of The WALKING SEEDS' debut EP, 'KNOW TOO MUCH' in summer '86. JOHN subsequently dropped out prior to a debut album, 'SKULLFUCK', its title inspired by a GRATEFUL DEAD sleeve. In 1988, the psych/grunge terrorists employed the services of KRAMER, the BONGWATER man producing their follow-up album 'UPWIND OF DISASTER, DOWNWIND OF ATONEMENT'. The band continued to label hop when the 'Glass' imprint dissolved, the 90's beginning with their version of BEVIS FROND's 'REFLECTIONS IN A TALL MIRROR' (available as a mail-order single on 'Clawfist'). Following '91's swansong 'EARTH IS HELL', BOB and TONY went on to form The DEL-BLOODS, who in turn became WHITE BITCH. • **Covered:** SUNSHINE OF YOUR LOVE (Cream) / ASTRONOMY DOMINE (Pink Floyd) / etc. • **Trivia:** Their song MARK CHAPMAN was about the killer of JOHN LENNON, if you didn't know already.

Album rating: SKULLFUCK (*7) / UPWIND OF DISASTER . . . (*6) / SENSORY DEPRIVATION CHAMBER QUARTET DWARF (*5) / BAD ORB . . . WHIRLING BALL (*6) / EARTH IS HELL (*4)

MEL-O-TONES

FRANK MARTIN – vocals / **BOB PARKER** – bass, guitar / **JOHN NEESAM** – drums / were MARTIN DEMPSEY + BOB BELLIS (ex-YACHTS the founders of this lot)

Probe Plus not iss.

Mar 85. (m-lp) *(PROBE 3)* **MEL-O-TONES**
– Bomb sutra / Burton buzz / Lice age / I walked with a Bugs Bunny bendy toy.

Sep 85. (12"ep) *(PP 13)* **MELONHEADED**
– Mad Jesus / Seedy lotion / Happy hour // Happy hour / Melonhead.

WALKING SEEDS

FRANK, BOB + JOHN

Probe Plus not iss.

Jun 86. (12"ep) *(PP 19T)* **KNOW TOO MUCH**
– Tantric wipeout /

—— **BAZ SUTTON** – guitar (ex-MARSHMALLOW OVERCOAT) / **TONY MOGAN** – drums (ex-MARSHMALLOW OVERCOAT) repl. NEESHAM

Mar 87. (12") *(CEDE 2)* **MARK CHAPMAN. / BLATHERING OUT**
(above single released on own 'Moral Burro' label)

Nov 87. (lp) *(PROBE 13)* **SKULLFUCK**
– Iron man / Doom patrol / 666 squadron / When girls the world / Life vs. filth / Blue cheer / Kill kill for inner peace / Obeying the law / St. Alban's / Blathering out.

Glass Communion

Mar 89. (lp/cd) *(GLA LP/CD 034) <9>* **UPWIND OF DISASTER, DOWNWIND OF ATONEMENT**
– 281 f / We rise / Sexorcist / Wreck of the white star / Imperious, vain, selfish and wilful / Louie, Louie, Louie / Help me, mummy's gone / Slow dance of golden lights / Mad river blues.

—— **ANDY ROWAN** – guitar; repl. SUTTON who joined The LA'S

1989. (12"ep) **SHAVED BEATNIK**

—— guest **NICK SALOMAN** (BEVIS FROND) – guitar

—— **LEE WEBSTER** – bass; repl. ROWAN

1989. (12"ep) **SENSORY DEPRIVATION CHAMBER QUARTET DWARF**

Clawfist not iss.

Feb 90. (7"mail-o) *PIS 1)* **REFLECTION IN A TALL MIRROR. / (Bevis Frond: SEXORCIST)**

Paperhouse Shimmy Disc

May 90. (7") *(PAPER 001)* **GATES OF FREEDOM. / ASTRONOMY DOMINE**

May 90. (cd/c/lp) *(PAP CD/MC/LP 001) <SHIMMY 36>* **BAD ORB, WHIRLING BALL**
– Gates of freedom / Weight of the years / Mortal blues / Broken cup / She said she said / Peter's trip / Caged beatnik / World's ok / Skullfuck.

Snakeskin not iss.

1991. (cd/lp) **EARTH IS HELL (live)**

not iss. Fist Puppet

1990's. (7") *<011>* **ROLLIN' MACHINE. / PLAYBOY STOMP**

Dental not iss.

Feb 94. (ltd-7") *(DENT 1)* **BEAT THEM ALL TO DEATH. /**

—— took a hike when BOB and TONY formed DEL-BLOODS who issued 'BLACK RABBIT'. They went onto become WHITE BITCH who released 'ANIMAL WOMAN'. FRANK and the two were part of BATLOAF's 'Meat Out Of Hell' (a parody of MEAT LOAF), while BAZ and LEE joined FROTH.

WALL

Formed: Sunderland, England . . . late '77 by IAN LOWERY, ANDZY GRIFFITHS, JOHN HAMMOND and BRUCE ARCHIBALD. Signed to the local 'Small Wonder' label, this straightahead punk outfit released 'NEW WAY' as their debut single in Spring '79. By the release of their follow-up, 'EXCHANGE', both HAMMOND and ARCHIBALD had been replaced by NICK WARD and RAB FAE BEITH. Following the replacement of LOWERY with KEELY and the addition of new member ANDY HEED FORBES, the band released the 'GHETTO' EP at the turn of the decade, closely followed by a debut album, 'PERSONAL TROUBLES AND PUBLIC ISSUES' (1981) – WARD and KELLY were now absent. Released on indie label, 'Fresh', the album was enough to impress 'Polydor', who – possibly finding a replacement for the recently departed SHAM 69 – issued a new single, 'REMEMBRANCE'. By this point the band had slimmed down to a trio of ANDZY, RAB and HEED, plus former PASSIONS girl CLAIRE BIDWELL, a tour support to STIFF LITTLE FINGERS helping to raise their profile. Yet by the release of 'DIRGES AND ANTHEMS' (1982), the band had fallen out with their major label backers over the usual stumbling block of musical direction. Sticking to their guns, The WALL signed to indie label, 'No Future' and released an EP with The Beatles' 'DAY TRIPPER' as the lead track.

Album rating: PERSONAL TROUBLES & PUBLIC ISSUES (*5) / DIRGES AND ANTHEMS (*5)

IAN LOWERY – vocals / **ANDYZ GRIFFITHS** – bass, vocals / **JOHN HAMMOND** – lead guitar, vocals / **BRUCE ARCHIBALD** – drums

Small Wonder not iss.

Apr 79. (7"m) *(SMALL 13)* **NEW WAY. / SUCKERS / UNIFORMS**

—— **NICK WARD** – guitar; repl. HAMMOND

—— **RAB FAE BEITH** – drums (ex-PATRIK FITZGERALD) repl. ARCHIBALD

Sep 79. (7") *(SMALL 21)* **EXCHANGE. / KISS THE MIRROR**

—— **KELLY** – vocals; repl. LOWERY who formed SKI PATROL, etc.

—— added **ANDY HEED FORBES** – keyboards, guitar (ex-STRAPS)

Fresh not iss.

Apr 80. (7"m) *(FRESH 17)* **GHETTO. / ANOTHER NEW DAY / MERCURY**

—— **PETE WILSON** – keyboards, guitar; repl. KELLY + WARD

Sep 80. (7"m) *(FRESH 27)* **HOBBY FOR A DAY. / REDEEMER / 8334** [ ] [-]

—— now without PETE

Nov 80. (lp) *(FRESHLP 2)* **PERSONAL TROUBLES AND PUBLIC ISSUES** [ ] [-]
– Fight the fright / In nature / Storm / Syndicate / Windows / Delay / Ghetto / Unanswered prayers / Mercury / Cancer / Career mover / One born every day. *(with a free 7"ep)*

Polydor not iss.

Apr 81. (7"m) *(POSP 260)* **REMEMBRANCE. / ILLSI NAO / HOOLIGAN NIGHTS** [ ] [-]

—— **GRIFFITHS, FORBES + BEITH** added **CLAIRE BIDWELL** – sax, vocals (ex-PASSIONS)

Nov 81. (7"m) *(POSP 365)* **EPITAPH. / REWIND / NEW REBEL** [ ] [-]

—— added **BAZ** – guitar

Apr 82. (lp) *(POLS 1048)* **DIRGES AND ANTHEMS** [ ] [-]
– Who are you / Nice to see you / Wunderkind / Epitaph / Money whores / Barriers / Walpurgis night / Only dreaming / Footsteps / Chinese whispers / Anthem / Pete's song / Tyburn / Everybody's ugly / English history.

—— now without BAZ + CLAIRE, the latter forming JU-KAN-JU

No Future not iss.

Nov 82. (7"ep) *(OI 21-7)* **DAY TRIPPER / ANIMAL GRIP. / WHEN I'M DANCING / CASTLES** [ ] [-]
(12"ep+=) *(OI 21-12)* – Ceremony / Industrial nightmare / Hall of miracles / Spirit dance / Funhouse.

—— broke-up after above

WALL OF VOODOO

Formed: Los Angeles, California, USA . . . 1977 by STAN RIDGWAY and the MORELAND brothers, MARC and BRUCE, the line-up completed by JOE NANINI and CHAS T. GRAY. Spotted by Miles Copeland and signed to his 'I.R.S.' label in 1980, they released an eponymous EP later the same year. Filtering a country/folk twang through new wave synths, WALL OF VOODOO had come up with one of the most bizarre takes on American roots music to date. The nearest comparison was DEVO, while RIDGWAY's distinctive, heavily-accented vocal was pitched somewhere between IGGY POP and The B-52's FRED SCHNEIDER. All in all an interesting, often er . . . challenging and occasionally humourous listen – check out the jackboot cover of Johnny Cash's 'RING OF FIRE'. Following on from 1981's debut album, 'DARK CONTINENT', the tongue-in-cheek but patronising dumbness of 'MEXICAN RADIO' gave the band their only hit single (transatlantic Top 75!) and pushed the 'CALL OF THE WEST' (1982) set into the US Top 50. Other highlights included the harmonica-enhanced poke at the 9 to 5 lifestyle of 'FACTORY' and the instrumental piano and theramin travelogue of former single, 'ON INTERSTATE 15'. But the band were subsequently dealt a body blow with the departure of RIDGWAY (readers may recall, or prefer to forget rather, the man's moose-voiced solo yarn, 'CAMOUFLAGE' - a UK Top 5 hit in 1986), recruiting ANDY PRIEBOY in his place and soldiering on with the 'SEVEN DAYS IN SAMMYSTOWN' (1986) album. While they retained a cult following, the new-look WALL OF VOODOO failed to build on the pioneering spirit of their early work and finally split after 1988's live set, 'UGLY AMERICANS IN AUSTRALIA AND BULLSHIT CITY'. • **Songwriters:** RIDGWAY words / group compositions. From the mid-80's, PRIEBOY and group (bar LUEKHARDT) wrote material. They also covered MONA (Bo Diddley) / DO IT AGAIN (Beach Boys) / DARK AS A DUNGEON (M.Travis) / PRETTY BOY FLOYD (Woody Guthrie) / THE GOOD, THE BAD AND THE UGLY (Ennio Morricone).

Album rating: GRANMA'S HOUSE compilation (*8)

STAN RIDGWAY (b. 5 Apr'54) – vocals, harmonica, keyboards / **MARC MORELAND** – guitar / **BRUCE MORELAND** – bass, keyboards / **JOE NANINI** – drums, percussion / **CHAS T. GRAY** – bass, keyboards, synthesizers

Illegal I.R.S.

Sep 80. (12"ep) *<SP 70401>* **WALL OF VOODOO** [-] [ ]
– Long arm / The passenger / Can't make love / Struggle / Ring of fire / Granma's house. *<remix re-iss. Nov81 on 'Index'; EPC 01>*

Oct 81. (lp) *<(SP 70022)>* **DARK CONTINENT** [ ] [ ]
– Red light / Tow minutes till lunch / Animal day / Full of tension / Me and my dad / Back in the flesh / Tsetse fly / Call box (1-2-3) / This way out / Good times / Crack the bell.

—— now a quartet when BRUCE departed

Oct 82. (7") *(ILS 0031)* **ON INTERSTATE 15. / THERE'S NOTHING ON THIS SIDE** [ ] [ ]

Oct 82. (lp) *(ILP 010) <70026>* **CALL OF THE WEST** [ ] [45]
– Tomorrow / Lost weekend / Factory / Look at their way / Hands of love / Mexican radio / Spy world / They don't want me / On Interstate 15 / Call of the west. *(cd-iss. 1986 on 'I.R.S.'; CD 70026)*

Jan 83. (7"/12") *(ILS/ILS12 0036) <9912>* **MEXICAN RADIO. / CALL OF THE WEST** [64] [58]

—— **MARC + CHAS** recruited new members **NED LEUKHARDT** – drums repl. NANINI / **ANDY PRIEBOY** – vocals repl. STAN RIDGWAY who went solo

I.R.S. I.R.S.

Nov 84. (7") *(IRS 116)* **BIG CITY. / ROOM WITH A VIEW** [ ] [-]

—— added the returning **BRUCE MORELAND** – keyboards, bass

Mar 86. (7"/12") *(IRM/IRMT 111)* **FAR SIDE OF CRAZY. / THE WRONG WAY TO HOLLYWOOD** [ ] [-]

May 86. (lp/c) *(MIRF/+C 1006) <5662>* **SEVEN DAYS IN SAMMYSTOWN** [ ] [ ]
– Far side of crazy / Business of love / Faded love / Mona / Room with a view / Blackboard sky / Big city / Dark as the dungeon / Museums / Tragic vaudeville / (Don't spill my) Courage.

May 87. (7") *(IRM 135)* **DO IT AGAIN. / BACK IN THE LAUNDROMAT** [ ] [-]
(12"+=) *(IRMT 135)* – Far side of crazy.

Jun 87. (lp/c) *(MIRF/+C 1022) <5997>* **HAPPY PLANET** [ ] [ ]
– Do it again / Hollywood the second time / Empty room / Chains of luck / When the lights go out / Love is a happy thing – Country of man / Joanne / Elvis bought Dora a Cadillac / The grass is greener / Ain't my day.

—— guest **ROGER MASON** – keyboards; repl. BRUCE who left again

Illegal I.R.S.

Jun 88. (lp) *(ILP 022) <42140>* **UGLY AMERICANS IN AUSTRALIA AND BULLSHIT CITY (live)** [ ] [ ]
– Red light / Crazy, crazy Melbourne / Wrong way to Hollywood / Living in the red / Blackboard sky / Pretty Boy Floyd / The heart never can tell / Far side of crazy / Ring of fire / Mexican radio. *(cd+=)* – The grass is greener.

– compilations, etc. –

Jul 84. (lp) *I.R.S.; (IRSA 7048)* **GRANMA'S HOUSE** [ ] [-]
– Ring of fire / Long arm / The passenger / Can't make love / On interstate 15 / Lost weekend / Mexican radio / Call box / Red light / Tomorrow / Crack the bell / Call of the west / Granma's house.

Jul 92. (cd) *Mau Mau; (MAUCD 619) / Restless; <70111>* **THE INDEX MASTERS** (most live) [ ] [ ]
– Longarm / Passenger / Can't make love / Struggle / Ring of fire / Granma's house / End of an era / Tomorrow / Animal day / Invisible man / Red light / The good, the bad and the ugly / Hang 'em high / Back in flesh / Call box (1-2-3).

—— WALL OF VOODOO tracks appeared on 1992 the STAN RIDGWAY compilation, 'SONGS THAT MADE THIS COUNTRY GREAT, THE BEST OF STAN RIDGWAY'.

WANDERERS (see under ⇒ SHAM 69)

WANNADIES

Formed: Skelleftea, Sweden . . . 1989 by PAR WILKSTEN, CHRISTINA BERGMARK, STEFAN SCHONFELT, FREDERIK SCHONFELT and GUNNAR KARLSSON. Moving to Stockholm, the group secured a deal with independent label, 'Snap', releasing an eponymous debut set the same year. Four years in the making, 'AQUANAUTIC' found the group working with ROXETTE songwriter, PER GESSLE; as might be expected, the results were less than rocking, although 'R.C.A.'-offshoot, 'Indolent', had enough faith in their indie-pop potential to sign them up in 1995. While it missed the chart first time round, the giddy, starry-eyed rush of 'YOU & ME SONG' introduced The WANNADIES as jangling indie fops in the finest tradition of the genre. On the right side of twee, just, the single was a taster for debut album, 'BE A GIRL', released the same month; with the same stilted-English charm as forebears, ABBA, the Swedish popsters traced a time-honoured lineage through the likes of The BYRDS, The DREAM ACADEMY, The GO-BETWEENS etc., right up to modern day practitioners like TEENAGE FANCLUB and served with an extra helping of BLUR-style attitude. After a further couple of minor hits with 'MIGHT BE STARS' and 'HOW DOES IT FEEL', the group finally made the Top 20 in Spring '96 with a re-released 'YOU & ME SONG'. The following year, they continued their steady rise to major league status with the single, 'HIT', a hit! no less from the follow-up set, BAGSY ME'. • **Songwriters:** Group, except; LEE REMICK (Go-Betweens) / NEW LIFE (Depeche Mode) / BLISTER IN THE SUN (Violent Femmes) / I'M A MAN (Spencer Davis Group) / CHILDREN OF THE REVOLUTION (T.Rex) / I GOT A RIGHT (Iggy Pop).

Album rating: WANNADIES (*6) / AQUANAUTIC (*6) / BE A GIRL (*8) / BAGSY ME (*7) / THE WANNADIES (*7)

PAR WILKSTEN – vocals / **CHRISTINA BERGMARK** – keyboards, vocals / **STEFAN SCHONFELT** – guitar / **FREDRIK SCHONFELDT** – bass / **GUNNAR KARLSSON** – drums / **MALMQUIST**

Snap not iss.

1989. (lp) *(SNAP 002)* **WANNADIES** [ ] [-]
– Together / Heaven / My home town / Things that you love / How beautiful is the Moon / Innocent me / So many lies / Smile / Anything / Black waters / The beast cures the lover / Children of the revolution / Lee Remick. *(re-iss. cd Jan94; RESNAP 002)*

Jan 93. (cd) *(SNAP 005)* **AQUANAUTIC** [ ] [-]
– Everything's true / Cherry man / Things that I would love to have undone / ove is dead / So happy now / Lucky you / 1.07 / December days / Something to tell / Suddenly I missed her / God knows / Never killed anyone / I love you love me.

Apr 93. (cd-s) **SO HAPPY NOW / IN THE ALTOGETHER / BIRDS** [ ] [-]

Jul 93. (cd-ep) **CHERRY MAN** [ ] [-]

Jun 94. (cd-s) **LOVE IN JUNE / I GOT A RIGHT** [ ] [-]

—— now without MALMQUIST

Indolent R.C.A.

Aug 95. (7"colrd/c-s) *(DIE 002/+MC)* **YOU & ME SONG. / BLISTER IN THE SUN** [ ] [-]
(cd-s+=) *(DIE 002CD)* – Lift me up (don't let me down).

Aug 95. (cd/c/lp) *(DIE CD/MC/LP 002)* **BE A GIRL** [ ] [-]
– You and me song / Might be stars / Love in June / How does it feel? / Sweet nymphet / New world record / Dying for more / Soon you're dead / Do it all the time / Dreamy Wednesdays / Kid. *(re-dist.Apr96)*

Oct 95. (c-s) *(DIE 003MC)* **MIGHT BE STARS / CHERRY MAN** [51] [-]
(cd-s+=) *(DIE 003CD1)* – Lee Remick / Love is dead.
(cd-s) *(DIE 003CD2)* – ('A'side) / New life / So happy now / Things that I would love to have undone.

Feb 96. (c-s/cd-s) *(DIE 004 MC/CD1)* **HOW DOES IT FEEL? / DYING FOR MORE (live) / LOVE IN JUNE (live) / MIGHT BE STARS (live)** [53] [-]
(cd-s) *(DIE 004CD2)* – ('A'side) / Let go oh oh / I'm a man / Never killed anyone.

Apr 96. (7"colrd/c-s) *(DIE 005/MC)* **YOU & ME SONG. / BLISTER IN THE SUN** [18] [-]
(cd-s) *(DIE 005CD)* – ('A'side) / Everybody loves me / I like you a lalalala lot / You & me song (lounge version).

Aug 96. (7"/c-s) *(DIE 006/+MC)* **SOMEONE SOMEWHERE. / DISAPPOINTED** [38] [-]
(cd-s) *(DIE 006CD)* – ('A'side) / Why / Goodbye.

Oct 96. (7"/c-s) *(DIE 007/+MC)* **FRIENDS. / WE WERE SITTING IN A CAR ON OUR WAY FROM MOLD TO BATH AS A !** [ ] [-]
(cd-s) *(DIE 007CD)* – ('A'side) / Trick me / Can't get enough of that.

Apr 97. (7"colrd) *(DIE 009)* **HIT. / CRUCIFY ME** [20] [-]
(cd-s+=) *(DIE 009CD1)* – Pathetico.
(cd-s) *(DIE 009CD2)* – ('A'side) / As if you care / (Yeah yeah yeah) In your face.

May 97. (cd/c)(lp-box) *(DIE CD/MC 008)(DIELP 008S)* **BAGSY ME** [37] [-]
– Because / Friends / Someone somewhere / Oh yes (it's a mess) / Shorty / Damn it I said / Silent people / What you want / Hit / Bumble bee boy / Combat honey / That's all. *(lp+=)* – What's the fuss.

Jun 97. (7") *(DIE 010)* **SHORTY. / ARE YOU EXCLUSIVE** [41] [-]
(cd-s+=) *(DIE 010CD1)* – Short people.
(cd-s) *(DIE 010CD2)* – ('A'side) / Taking the easy way out / That's all.

Sep 97. (7"/c-s) *(DIE 011/+MC)* **YOU AND ME SONG. / JUST CAN'T GET ENOUGH** [ ] [ ]
(cd-s) *(DIE 011CD)* – ('A'side) / Love in June / How does it feel / Love is dead.

Oct 97. (cd,c) *<67433>* **THE WANNADIES** (compilation) [-] [ ]
– Might be stars / Because / Friends / You and me song / Someone somewhere / Damn it I said / How does it feel / Oh yes (it's a mess) / Shorty / Silent people / What you want / Hit / That's all.

Dean WAREHAM (see under ⇒ GALAXIE 500)

WARM JETS

Formed: Bromley, England . . . 1995 by LOUIS JONES, ED GRIMSHAW, PAUL NOBLE (ex-EAT) and former PALE SAINTS bassist, COLLEEN BROWNE. Driven by JONES' sound-vision of a new-wave futurism taking in such diverse influences as WIRE, TALKING HEADS, KRAFTWERK and BRIAN ENO (whose 'Here Come The Warm Jets' album inspired their name), the band found themselves signed to hip 'Island'-backed indie label, 'This Way Up', after only a few gigs. A debut EP, 'AUTOPIA', appeared in Autumn '96, critics namechecking the likes of The FLAMING LIPS and TIGER (formed by JONES' erstwhile girlfriend, JULIE) in an attempt to come halfway towards describing the JETS' complex sound. Recorded with the help of veteran studio man, Glyn Johns, follow-up EP, 'NEVER NEVER' confirmed the band's mission to explore music's deepest, darkest frontiers, while a much anticipated debut Top 40 album, 'FUTURE SIGNS', saw The WARM JETS hailed as one of the UK's most promising post-Brit-pop bands.

Album rating: FUTURE SIGNS (*6)

LOUIS JONES – vocals / **PAUL NOBLE** – guitar (ex-EAT) / **COLLEEN BROWNE** – bass (ex-PALE SAINTS, ex-PARACHUTE MEN) / **ED GRIMSHAW** – drums

This Way Up / This Way Up

Sep 96. (7") *(WAY 53-11)* **AUTOPIA. / SUNFREEZE** [ ] [-]
(cd-s+=) *(WAY 53-33)* – Wires / Liverpool St.

Apr 97. (7") *(WAY 58-11)* **NEVER NEVER. / SIGNS 2** [ ] [-]
(cd-s+=) *(WAY 58-33)* – Model / In another icture.

Jun 97. (7") *(WAY 63-11)* **MOVE AWAY. / METEORITES** [ ] [-]
(cd-s+=) *(WAY 63-33)* – Dead star boys / Undertow.
(cd-s) *(WAY 63-66)* – ('A'side) / Down down down / 2 shots / Beauty No.3.

Sep 97. (7") *(WAY 66-11)* **HURRICANE. / DESERT CATS / DAKOTA** [ ] [-]
(cd-s+=) *(WAY 66-33)* – Forever.
(cd-s) *(WAY 66-66)* – ('A'side) / Just like you / Never never (live) / Hurricane (home demo).

—— **AKI SHIBAHARA** – bass; repl. COLLEEN

Feb 98. (7"gold) *(WAY 67-11)* **NEVER NEVER. / TOKYO LIMBO** [37] [-]
(cd-s) *(WAY 67-33)* – ('A'side) / On the floor / There is still a mystery.
(cd-s) *(WAY 67-66)* – ('A'side) / Underground / RTZ.

Feb 98. (cd/c/lp) *(<524534-2/-4/-1>)* **FUTURE SIGNS** [40] [ ]
– Move away / Never never / Hurricane / Vapour trails / Future signs / Romero.

Island / not iss.

Apr 98. (7") *(IS 697)* **HURRICANE. / SOFT SONG** [34] [-]
(cd-s+=) *(CID 697)* – Dakota.
(cd-s) *(CISX 697)* – ('A'side) / Faster faster / Just like you.

WATERBOYS

Formed: London, England . . . 1982 by Scots-born MIKE SCOTT, Englishman ANTHONY THISTLETHWAITE and Welshman KARL WALLINGER. SCOTT had previously fronted Edinburgh new wave outfit, ANOTHER PRETTY FACE, along with old Ayr school pals, JOHN CALDWELL and JIM GEDDES. Taking their name from a track on LOU REED's sleaze-noir masterpiece, 'Berlin', The WATERBOYS soon secured a deal with the Irish-run label, 'Ensign', following the release of a self-financed debut single in Spring '83, 'A GIRL CALLED JOHNNY'. A tribute to punk priestess, PATTI SMITH (an obvious early influence), the track received a fair amount of airplay and almost broke into the lower regions of the charts. An eponymous debut album followed later that summer, an esoteric set of avant folk/rock which drew comparisons with TIM BUCKLEY's more ambitious meanderings and introduced SCOTT as a promising singing/songwriting seer. Embellished by additional instrumentation such as horns and violin, 'A PAGAN PLACE' (1984) was a confident follow-up, SCOTT venturing ever further out on his spiritual journey with the likes of 'THE BIG MUSIC' and 'CHURCH NOT MADE WITH HANDS'. A burgeoning live reputation and gushing critical praise saw The WATERBOYS' third set, 'THIS IS THE SEA' (1985) break into the UK Top 40, its centerpiece epic, 'THE WHOLE OF THE MOON', becoming the group's first Top 30 single. Despite this overdue success, WALLINGER subsequently departed to form his own outfit, WORLD PARTY. Relocating to Galway, Ireland for an extended sabbatical at the behest of fiddler, STEVE WICKHAM (who'd played on 'THIS..'), SCOTT and THISTLETHWAITE increasingly infused their music with traditional Irish folk influences. It was an earthier WATERBOYS, then, who eventually emerged in late '88 with the acclaimed 'FISHERMAN'S BLUES', SCOTT seemingly having at last found his true musical calling. From the strident Celtic clarion call of the title track to the soulful cover of Van Morrison's 'SWEET THING', it sounded as if The WATERBOYS had been playing this music for centuries. The record almost made the UK Top 10, an album which established The WATERBOYS as a major league act and which remains their biggest seller. 'ROOM TO ROAM' (1990) continued in the same vein, making the UK Top 5 although it lacked the depth of its predecessor. Bang on cue, 'Ensign' re-released 'THE WHOLE OF THE MOON' to massive success (Top 3), the track being played to death by radio all over again. By this point, however, the original WATERBOYS line-up had splintered following a final UK tour (wherein the group drew criticism for their return to an all-out rock sound), THISTLETHWAITE forming The BLUE STARS while SCOTT eventually moved to New York and gathered together a new group of musicians. Now signed to 'Geffen', he recorded 'DREAM HARDER' (1993), the sixth WATERBOYS album but a SCOTT solo set in all but name. Exploring many familiar themes, the album spawned two Top 30 singles in 'THE RETURN OF PAN' and 'GLASTONBURY SONG', even boasting a brief contribution from Scots comedy legend, BILLY CONNOLLY. All has since been silent on The WATERBOYS front, although SCOTT released a fine solo album in 1995, 'BRING 'EM ALL IN', this highly original musical visionary remaining one of Scotland's most talented exports. • **Covered:** LOST HIGHWAY (Hank Williams) / DEATH IS NOT THE END (Bob Dylan) / WAYWARD WIND (Lebawsky-Newman) / BECAUSE THE NIGHT (Patti Smith – Bruce Springsteen) / PURPLE RAIN (Prince) / and a several traditional renditions.

Album rating: THE WATERBOYS (*6) / A PAGAN PLACE (*6) / THIS IS THE SEA (*7) / FISHERMAN'S BLUES (*6) / ROOM TO ROAM (*6) / THE BEST OF THE WATERBOYS compilation (*9) / DREAM HARDER (*5) / Mike Scott: BRING 'EM ALL IN (*6) / STILL BURNING (*5)

ANOTHER PRETTY FACE

MIKE SCOTT (b.14 Dec'58, Edinburgh, Scotland) – vocals, guitar, piano / **JOHN CALDWELL** – guitar / **JIM GEDDES** – bass / **CRIGG** (b.IAN WALTER GREIG) – drums

New Pleasures / not iss.

May 79. (7") *(Z1)* **ALL THE BOYS LOVE CARRIE. / THAT'S NOT ENOUGH** [ ] [-]

Virgin / not iss.

Feb 80. (7") *(VS 320)* **WHATEVER HAPPENED TO THE WEST?. / GODDBYE 1970's** [ ] [-]

—— trimmed to basic duo of **SCOTT + CALDWELL** plus **MAIRI ROSS** – bass / added **ADRIAN JOHNSON** – drums

Chicken Jazz / not iss.

Dec 80. (7") *(JAZZ 1)* **ONLY HEROES LIVE FOREVER. / HEAVEN GETS CLOSER EVERY DAY** [ ] [-]

Mar 81. (c-ep) *(JAZZ 2)* **I'M SORRY THAT I BEAT YOU, I'M SORRY THAT I SCREAMED, FOR A MOMENT THERE I REALLY LOST CONTROL(live)** [ ] [-]
– This could be Hell / My darkest hour / Lightning that strikes twice / Graduation day / Carrie. *(on most copies, studio tracks +=)* – Another kind of circus / Only heroes live forever / Out of control.

Apr 81. (7") *(JAZZ 3)* **SOUL TO SOUL. / A WOMAN'S PLACE / GOD ON THE SCREEN** [ ] [-]

FUNHOUSE

—— were formed by **SCOTT + CALDWELL**

Ensign / not iss.

Feb 82. (7"/ext.12") *(ENY/+T 222)* **OUT OF CONTROL. / THIS COULD BE HELL** [ ] [-]

The WATERBOYS

MIKE SCOTT plus **ANTHONY THISTLETWAITE** (b. 8 Aug'55, Leicester, England) – saxophone (ex-ROBYN HITCHCOCK / of SOFT BOYS) / **KARL WALLINGER** (b.19 Oct'57, Prestatyn, Wales) – keyboards, bass

Chicken Jazz / not iss.

May 83. (7") *(CJ 1)* **A GIRL CALLED JOHNNY. / THE LATE TRAIN TO HEAVEN** [ ] [-]
(12") *(CJT 1)* – ('A'side) / Ready for the monkey house / Somebody might wave back / Out of control (APF; John Peel session).

Ensign / Chrysalis

Jul 83. (lp/c) *(ENC L/C 1)* **THE WATERBOYS** [ ] [-]
– December / A girl called Johnny / The three day man / Gala / I will not follow / It should have been you / The girl in the swing / Savage Earth heart. *(re-iss. Aug86 on 'Chrysalis-Ensign' lp/c; CHEN/ZCHEN 1) (cd-iss. Feb87; CCD 1541) <US cd-iss. 1987; 21541>*

Sep 83. (7") *(ENY 506)* **DECEMBER. / WHERE ARE YOU NOW WHEN I NEED YOU** [ ] [-]
(12") *(12ENY 506)* – ('A'side) / Red army blues / The three day man (Peter Powell session).

— added **KEVIN WILKINSON** – drums / **RODDY LORIMER** (b. Glasgow, Scotland) – trumpet / **TIM BLANTHORN** – violin

Apr 84. (7") *(ENY 508)* **THE BIG MUSIC. / THE EARTH ONLY ENDURES** [ ] [-]
(12"+=) *(12ENY 508)* – Bury my heart.

May 84. (lp/c) *(ENC L/C 3)* **A PAGAN PLACE** [100] [-]
– Church not made with hands / All the things she gave me / The thrill is gone / Rags / Somebody might wave back / The big music / Red army blues / A pagan place. *(re-iss. Aug86 on 'Chrysalis-Ensign' lp/c; CHEN/ZCHEN 2) (cd-iss. Feb87; CCD 1542) (re-iss. Jul94 cd/c;) <US cd-iss. 1987; 21542>*

— (Oct84) **MIKE + KARL** recruited new people for tour/lp **TERRY MANN** – bass / **CHARLIE WHITTEN** – drums / **STEVE WICKHAM** (b. Dublin, Ireland) – violin / **LORIMER / DELAHAYE** – organ

Sep 85. (lp/c) *(ENC L/C 5)* **THIS IS THE SEA** [37] [-]
– Don't bang the drum / The whole of the Moon / Spirit / The pan within / Medicine bow / Old England / Be my enemy / Trumpets / This is the sea. *(re-iss. Aug86 on 'Chrysalis-Ensign' lp/c; CHEN/ZCHEN 3) (cd-iss. Feb87; CCD CCD 1543) (re-iss. cd Mar94;) <US cd-iss. 1987; 21543>*

Oct 85. (7") *(ENY 502)* **THE WHOLE OF THE MOON. / MEDICINE BOW** [26] [ ]
(ext.12"+=) *(12ENY 520)* – Spirit (extended) / The girl in the swing (live).

— **MIKE SCOTT** now only original survivor (retained THISTLETWAITE + HUTCHISON), when KARL formed WORLD PARTY.

— additional band **STEVE WICKHAM** – violin (ex-IN TUA NUA) / **J.D. DOHERTY** – drums / **COLIN BLAKEY** (b. Falkirk, Scotland) – flute (ex-WE FREE KINGS). /('88) added **SHARON SHANNON** (b. Ireland) – accordion / **NOEL BRIDGEMAN** (b. Dublin, Ireland) – drums repl. DOHERTY

Nov 88. (lp/c)(cd) *(CHEN/ZCHEN 5)(CCD 1589) <41589>* **FISHERMAN'S BLUES** [13] [76]
– Fisherman's blues / We will not be lovers / Strange boat / World party / Sweet thing / And a bang on the ear / Has anybody here seen Hank? / When we will be married? / When ye go away / The stolen child. *(cd+=)* – The lost highway.

Dec 88. (7"/12"/cd-s) *(ENY/+X/CD 621)* **FISHERMAN'S BLUES. / THE LOST HIGHWAY** [32] [-]

Jun 89. (7"/c-s/12"/cd-s) *(ENY/+MC/X/CD 624)* **AND A BANG ON THE EAR. / THE RAGGLE TAGGLE GYPSY** [51] [-]

— **MIKE SCOTT / THISTLETWAITE / HUTCHISON / + KEV BLEVINS** – drums repl. last additional band members

Sep 90. (cd)(c/lp) *(CCD 1768)(Z+/CHEN 16) <21768>* **ROOM TO ROAM** [5] [ ]
– In search of a rose / Songs from the edge of the world / A man is in love / Bigger picture / Natural bridge blues / Something that is gone / The star and the sea / Life on Sundays / Island man / The raggle taggle gypsy / How long will I love you? / Upon the wind and waves / Spring rooms to Spiddal / Further up, further in / Trip to Broadford / Room to roam. *(cd+=)* – The kings of Kerry. *(re-iss. Sep94 cd/c;)*

Mar 91. (7"/c-s) *(ENY/+MC 642) <Alex; 1516>* **THE WHOLE OF THE MOON. / A GOLDEN AGE** [3] [ ]Jul91
(12"+=/cd-s+=) *(ENY X/CD 642)* – Higher in time / High far soon / Soon as I get home.

Apr 91. (cd)(c/lp) *(CCD 1845)(Z+/CHEN 19) <21845>* **THE BEST OF THE WATERBOYS ('81-'90)** (compilation) [2] [ ]
– A girl called Johnny / The big music / All the things she gave me / The whole of the Moon / Spirit / Don't bang the drum / Fisherman's blues / Killing my heart / Strange boat / And a bang on the ear / Old England / A man is in love.

May 91. (7"/c-s) *(ENY/+MC 645) <Alex; 1581>* **FISHERMAN'S BLUES. / LOST HIGHWAY** [75] [ ]Jun91
(12"+=/cd-s+=) *(ENY X/CD 645)* – Medicine bow (live).

— Disbanded soon after last studio album above. In mid'91, MIKE SCOTT re-formed group and signed for US-based label 'Geffen'. THISTLETWAITE formed The BLUE STARS.

— **MIKE SCOTT** with **CHRIS BRUCE** – guitars / **SCOTT THUNES** – bass / **CARLA AZAR** – drums / **BASHIRI JOHNSON** – percussion / **LJUBISA 'Lubi' RISTIC** – sitar / **GEORGE STATHOS** – Greek clarinet / **JAMES CAMPAGNOLA** – saxophone / **JERE PETERS** – rattles / **PAL SHAZAR + JULES SHEAR** – backing vox / **BILLY CONNOLLY**– guest 10 second voiceover

Geffen Geffen

May 93. (7"/c-s) *(GFS/+C 42)* **THE RETURN OF PAN. / KARMA** [24] [ ]
(12"+=/cd-s+=) *(GFS T/CD 42)* – Mister Powers / ('A'demo).

May 93. (cd/c/lp) *(<GED/GEC/GEF 24476>)* **DREAM HARDER** [5] [ ]
– The new life / Glastonbury song / Preparing to fly / The return of Pan / Corn circles / Suffer / Winter winter / Love and death / Spiritual city / Wonders of Lewis / The return of Jimi Hendrix / Good news. *(cd re-iss. Jul96; GFLD 19318)*

Jul 93. (7"/c-s) *(GFS/+C 49)* **GLASTONBURY SONG. / CHALICE HILL** [29] [-]
(12"+=/cd-s+=) *(GFS T/CD 49)* – Burlington Bertie – Accrington Stanley / Corn circle symphony (extended).

– compilations, etc. –

Oct 94. (cd/c) *Ensign; (CD/TC CHEN 35)* **THE SECRET LIFE OF THE WATERBOYS** (81-85 material) [ ] [ ]

Aug 98. (d-cd) *Griffin; <40>* **LIVE ADVENTURES OF THE WATERBOYS (live)** [ ] [ ]
– Death is not the end / Earth only endures / Medicine bow / Fisherman's blues / This is the sea / Meet me at the station / We will not be lovers / Wayward wind / A girl called Johnny / Purple rain / Be my enemy / Old England / The thrill is gone – And the healing has begun / Pain within (including Because the night) / Whole of the moon / Spirit / Savage earth heart / Saints and angels.

MIKE SCOTT

— mostly all solo

Chrysalis Chrysalis

Sep 95. (c-s/7") *(TC+/CHS 5025) <58503>* **BRING 'EM ALL IN. / CITY FULL OF GHOSTS (DUBLIN)** [56] [ ]Nov95
(cd-s+=) *(CDCHS 5025)* – Mother Cluny / Beatles reunion blues.

Sep 95. (cd/c/lp) *(<CD/TC+/CHR 6108>)* **BRING 'EM ALL IN** [23] [ ]
– Bring 'em all in / Iona song / Edinburgh Castle / What do you want me to do? / I know she's in the building / City full of ghosts (Dublin) / Wonderful disguise / Sensitive children / Learning to love him / She is so beautiful / Wonderful disguise (reprise) / Long way to the light / Building the city of light.

Nov 95. (7") *(CHS 5026)* **BUILDING THE CITY OF LIGHT. / WHERE DO YOU WANT THE BOOMBOX, BUDDY** [60] [-]
(cd-s+=) *(CDCHSS 5026)* – Goin' back to Glasters (live) / The whole of the Moon (live).
(cd-s) *(CDCHS 5026)* – ('A'side) / Two great waves / My beautiful guide / Building the city of light (Universal Hall demo).

— now with **CHRIS BRUCE** – lead guitar / **PINO PALLADINO** – bass / **JIM KELTNER** – drums / **JAMRES HALLAWELL** – organ / etc

Sep 97. (c-s) *(TCCHS 5064)* **LOVE ANYWAY / KING OF STARS** [50] [-]
(cd-s) *(CDCHS 5064)* – ('A'side) / King electric (including Moonage Daydream) / Blues is my business.
(cd-s) *(CDCHSS 5064)* – ('A'side) / Big lover / Careful with the mellotron, Eugene / Since I found my school.

Oct 97. (cd/c) *(<CD/TC CHR 6122>)* **STILL BURNING** [34] [ ]
– Questions / My dark side / Open / Love anyway / Rare, precious and gone / Dark man of my dreams / Personal / Strawberry man / Sunrising / Everlasting arms.

Feb 98. (cd-ep) *(CDCHSS 5073)* **RARE, PRECIOUS AND GONE / KISS THE WIND / WHEN WILL WE BE MARRIED (live) / LOVE ANYWAY (demo)** [74] [-]
(cd-ep) *(CDCHS 5073)* – ('A'side) / All things she gave me (live) / She is so beautiful (live) / Nectar (7 days).

Ben WATT (see under ⇒ EVERYTHING BUT THE GIRL)

Mike WATT (see under ⇒ MINUTEMEN)

John WATTS (see under ⇒ FISCHER-Z)

Fee WAYBILL (see under ⇒ TUBES)

WE ARE GOING TO EAT YOU (see under ⇒ HAGAR THE WOMB)

WEATHER PROPHETS

Formed: London, England ... 1980 as THE LOFT by PETER ASTOR, BILL PRINCE and ANDY STRICKLAND. Recruiting sticksman, DAVE MORGAN, the band became one of the first acts to record for 'Creation', releasing the 'WHY DOES THE RAIN' single in Autumn '84. It would be a full year before the appearance of a follow-up, 'UP THE HILL AND DOWN THE SLOPE', by which time the band were on the verge of a split. While BILL went off to form The WISHING STONES and ANDY founded The CARETAKER RACE, ASTOR and MORGAN initiated The WEATHER PROPHETS with OISIN LITTLE and GREENWOOD GOULDING. Remaining with 'Creation', MORGAN & Co. released the 'DIESEL RIVER' (1986) album, benefitting from the cult acclaim that the enigma of The LOFT had generated. ASTOR was still following his BYRDS/VELVET UNDERGROUND fixation, the subsequent near-hit, 'SHE COMES FROM THE RAIN', sounding like a proto-STONE ROSES. Like the accompanying LENNY KAYE-produced album, 'MAYFLOWER' (1987), the track appeared on 'Elevation', Alan McGee's short-lived dalliance with 'Warners'. When the project fell through, the band shifted back to 'Creation', crossover success still tantalisingly out of sight. Giving up the ghost after a final album, 'JUDGES, JURIES AND HORSEMEN' (1988), ASTOR remained with 'Creation' for a solo career, cutting two obscure albums, 'SUBMARINE' (1990) and 'ZOO' (1991). MORGAN, meanwhile, went on to play briefly with fashionable Camden country-rockers, The ROCKINGBIRDS. ASTOR returned in 1997 with his new outfit, The WISDOM OF HARRY. • **Songwriters:** ASTOR main pensmith, except WHO BY FIRE (Leonard Cohen).

Album rating: MAYFLOWER (*8) / Loft: ONCE AROUND THE FAIR (*8)

LOFT

PETE ASTOR (b. ABE SMITH, 1959, Colchester, England) – vocals, guitar / **ANDY STRICKLAND** (b.16 Jul'59, Isle Of Wight) – guitar / **BILL PRINCE** (b.19 Jul'62, Devon, England) – bass / **DAVE MORGAN** – drums

Creation not iss.

Sep 84. (7") *(CRE 009)* **WHY DOES THE RAIN. / LIKE** [ ] [-]

Apr 85. (12") *(CRE 015T)* **UP THE HILL AND DOWN THE SLOPE. / YOUR DOOR SHINES LIKE GOLD / LONELY STREET** [ ] [-]

Jul 85. (7") *(CRE 015)* **UP THE HILL AND DOWN THE SLOPE. / TUESDAY TIME** [ ] [-]

— disbanded in '85 when BILL formed The WISHING STONES and ANDY formed The CARETAKER RACE

WEATHER PROPHETS

— **ASTOR + MORGAN** plus **OISIN LITTLE** – guitar / **GREENWOOD GOULDING** – bass

Creation not iss.

May 86. (7") *(CRE 029)* **ALMOST PRAYED. / YOUR HEARTBEAT BREATHES THE LIFE INTO ME** [ ] [-]
(12"+=) *(CRE 029T)* – Like Frankie Lymon / Wide open arms. (d7"+=) *(CRE 029D)* – Downbound train / Stone in my path way.

Oct 86. (7") *(CRE 031)* **NAKED AS THE DAY YOU WERE BORN. / IN MY ROOM**
(12"+=) *(CRE 031T)* – You're the worst friend I ever had.

Rough Trade not iss.

Nov 86. (lp/cd) *(RT D/CD 2-40)* **DIESEL RIVER**
– Almost prayed / Worm in my brain / Your heartbeat breathes the life into me / Stones in my pathway / Like Frankie Lymon / Wide open arms / Downbound train / Head over heels. *(cd+=)* – In my room / The worst friend I ever had. *(US cd-iss. Apr94 on 'Tristar'; 57785>*

Elevation not iss.

Mar 87. (7") *(ACID 1)* **SHE COMES FROM THE RAIN. / WHO BY FIRE** 62
(12"+=) *(ACID 1T)* – You upset the grade of living when you die / Wide open arms.

Apr 87. (lp/c) *(ELV 1/+C)***MAYFLOWER** 67
– Mayflower / She comes from the rain / Almost prayed / Naked as the day you were born / Why does the rain / The key to my love is green / Can't keep my mind off you / Sleep / Head over heels / Faithfull / Swimming pool blues / Walking under a spell.

Jul 87. (7") *(ACID 2)* **WHY DOES THE RAIN. / MIDNIGHT MILE**
(12"+=) *(ACID 2T)* – Mayflower / Annalea.

— (Apr'88) now a trio when OISIN departed

Creation Combat

Apr 88. (7") *(CRE 054)* **HOLLOW HEART. / JOE SCHMO THE ESKIMO**
(12"+=) *(CRE 054T)* – Sleeping when the sun comes up / Chinese Cadillac.

Jun 88. (cd/lp) *(CRE CD/LP 033) <8244>* **JUDGES, JURIES AND HORSEMEN**
– Always the light / Hollow heart / Poisons mind / Well done Sonny / Born inbetween / Thursday seems a year ago / Bury them deep / You bring the miracles / Never been as good / Ostrich bed.
(free 7" w/ lp) (CREFRE 2) **ODDS AND ENDS:- Sin bin - Get fishy - 1000 hangover's later. / SLEEPING LIGHTLY ON THE ANCIENT PATH**

Aug 88. (7") *(CRE 056)* **ALWAYS THE LIGHT. / BLUE ROOFTOPS**
(12"+=) *(CRE 056T)* – Hill house somersaults.

- compilations, etc. -

on 'Creation' unless mentioned otherwise

Sep 89. (lp/cd; by The LOFT) *(CRE LP/CD 047)* **ONCE AROUND THE FAIR**

Nov 89. (lp/cd) *(CRE LP/CD 050) / Positive; <6046>* **TEMPERANCE HOTEL** (sessions, etc.)
– The key to my love is green / You're my ambulance / Mayflower / Midnight mile / Why does the rain / Can't keep my mind off you / In my room / Odds and ends / Sleep / Chinese Cadillac / Blue rooftop / I saw the light / Stepping lightly on the ancuient path / Joe Shcmo and the Eskimo / Hollow heart (live) / Chinese Cadillac (live).

Jun 91. (cd/c/lp) *(CRECD/C-CRE/CRELP 085)* **WEATHER PROPHETS '87**
– Why does the rain / Head over heels / Poison mind / Like Frankie Lymon / Worm in my brain / She comes from the rain / Mayflower / Your heartbeat breathes the life into me / The key to my love is green / Hollow heart / Almost prayed.

PETER ASTOR

Creation not iss.

Aug 90. (cd/c/lp) *(CRECD/C-CRE/CRELP 065)* **SUBMARINE**
– Beware / Walk into the wind / Firesong / Your Sun leaves the sky / Holy road / I wish I was somewhere else / Emblem / On top above the driver / Submarine / Chevron.

Nov 90. (12"ep)(cd-ep) *(CRE 094T)(CRESCD 094)* **WALK INTO THE WIND (version) / YOUR SUN LEAVES THE SKY. / SUBMARINE / FIRESONG**

Mar 91. (12"ep)(cd-ep) **CHEVRON / BEWARE. / ON TOP ABOVE THE DRIVER / EMBLEM**

May 91. (cd/c/lp) *(CRECD/C-CRE/CRELP 090)* **ZOO**
– Six day weekend / Harvest Moon / We move in an arc whose grace we never see / What was and what could never be / Street of lights / Heart-shaped swimming pool / Ghost sister / Seaplane / Letter to nowhere / The emperor, the dealer and the birthday boy / Blue working nights / Thirteen at seven centuries.

Danceteria not iss.

Apr 92. (cd/c/lp; as PETER ASTOR & THE HOLY ROAD) *(DAN CD/C/LP 105)* **PARADISE**

May 93. (cd) *(DAN 9304CD)* **GOD & OTHER STORIES**
(re-iss. Feb95; same)

WISDOM OF HARRY

— **PETE ASTOR** +

Wurlitzer Jukebox not iss.

Mar 98. (7") *(WJ 33)* **PURE GOLD HENRY. / SPORTS RED**

Lissy's not iss.

Apr 98. (10"ep/cd-ep) *(LISS 28/+CD)* **STAYING IN WITH THE WISDOM OF HARRY**

WEDDING PRESENT

Formed: Leeds, England . . . 1984 by ex-teachers DAVID GEDGE and PETE SOLOWKA (father Ukrainian) along with KEITH GREGORY and SHAUN CHARMAN. They gained a deal with local indie label, 'Reception', in 1985 and, with appearances on John Peel's radio 1 show, quickly grew into a cult act. Debut album, 'GEORGE BEST' (1987) was one of the key 80's indie releases, GEDGE's tunefully challenged monotone combining with the fast and furious punk-jangle racket to somehow create something more than the sum of its parts. Towards the end of the decade, they were finally signed to a major record company, 'R.C.A.', their first release on the label, 'UKRAINSKI . . .', surprising many with its marriage of Ukranian folk styles and indie-rock. GEDGE reverted to his trademark lovelorn lyrical fashion for follow-up proper, 'BIZARRO', a record that disappointed many longtime fans. Nevertheless, The WEDDING PRESENT were nothing if not prolific, even achieving the acolade of a Guinness Book Of Records entry in 1992 when every one of their monthly single (7"only) releases hit the UK Top 30 (The 12 hits also contained an unusual cover version on the B-side, see below). Despite the departure of all founding members save GEDGE (SALOWKA left in the early 90's to form The UKRANIANS), 1994's 'WATUSI' again found the band in favour with the critics if not commanding the fanbase they once had. In 1998, GEDGE re-invented himself as a SERGE GAINSBOURG or BURT BACHARACH-type crooner in the project/duo, CINERAMA, alongside SALLY MURRELL, his sort of JANE BIRKIN, you could say. An album, 'VA VA VOOM', was a marked change of direction from the WEDDOES bust-a-gut blasts, into EDWYN COLLINS glutty vocals. • **Songwriters:** GEDGE compositions, except GETTING NOWHERE FAST (Girls At Our Best) / WHAT BECOME OF THE BROKEN HEARTED (Jimmy Ruffin) / I FOUND THAT ESSENCE RARE (Gang Of Four) / IT'S NOT UNUSUAL (Tom Jones) / FELICITY (Orange Juice) / MAKE ME SMILE (COME UP AND SEE ME) (Steve Harley & Cockney Rebel) / BOX ELDER (Pavement) / SHE'S MY BEST FRIEND (Velvet Underground) / MOTHERS (Jean Michel Satre) / CUMBERLAND GAP (Leadbelly) / CATTLE AND CANE (Go Betweens) / DON'T CRY NO TEARS (Neil Young) / THINK THAT IT MIGHT (Altered Images) / FALLING (Julee Cruise) / PLEASANT VALLEY SUNDAY (Monkees) / LET'S MAKE SOME PLANS (Close Lobsters) / ROCKET (Mud) / THEME FROM SHAFT (Isaac Hayes) / CHANT OF THE EVER CIRCLING SKELETAL FAMILY (Bowie) / GO WILD IN THE COUNTRY (Bow Wow Wow) / U.F.O. (Barry Gray) / STEP INTO CHRISTMAS (Elton John) / JUMPER CLOWN (Marc Riley). • **Trivia:** STEVE ALBINI (ex-BIG BLACK) produced their early 90s material.

Album rating: GEORGE BEST (*9) / TOMMY compilation (*8) / UKRAINSKI VISTUPU V JOHNA PEELA (*5) / BIZARRO (*7) / SEAMONSTERS (*7) / THE HIT PARADE 1 compilation (*7) / THE HIT PARADE 2 compilation (*6) / WATUSI (*5) / MINI (*4) / SATURNALIA (*5) / Cinerama: VA VA VOOM (*6)

DAVID GEDGE (b.23 Apr'60) – vocals, guitar / **PETE SOLOWKA** (b.Manchester) – guitar / **KEITH GREGORY** (b. 2 Jan'63, County Durham) – bass / **SHAUN CHARMAN** (b.Brighton) – drums

Reception not iss.

May 85. (7") *(REC 001)* **GO OUT AND GET 'EM BOY. / (THE MOMENT BEFORE) EVERYTHING'S SPOILED AGAIN**
(re-iss. Sep85 on 'City Slang'; CSL 001)

Feb 86. (7") *(REC 002)* **ONCE MORE. / AT THE EDGE OF THE SEA**

Apr 86. (12"ep) *(REC 002-12)* **DON'T TRY AND STOP ME MOTHER**
– Go out and get 'em boy / (The moment before) Everything's spoiled again / Once more / At the edge of the sea.

Jul 86. (7") *(REC 003)* **THIS BOY CAN'T WAIT. / YOU SHOULD ALWAYS KEEP IN TOUCH WITH YOUR FRIENDS**
(ext.12"+=) *(REC 003-12)* – Living and learning.

Feb 87. (7",7"white/12") *REC 005/+12)* **MY FAVOURITE DRESS. / EVERY MOTHER'S SON / NEVER SAID**
(2,000 copies of above single were also given free with debut lp)

Sep 87. (7") *(REC 006)* **ANYONE CAN MAKE A MISTAKE. / ALL ABOUT EVE**
(c-s+=/12"+=) *(REC 006 C/12)* – Getting nowhere fast.

Oct 87. (lp/c/cd) *(LEEDS 001/+C/CD)* **GEORGE BEST** 47
– Everyone thinks he looks daft / What did your last servant die of? / Don't be so hard / A million miles / All this and more / Getting nowhere fast * / My favourite dress / Shatner / Something and nothing / It's what you want that matters / Give my love to Kevin / Anyone can make a mistake / You can't moan can you / All about Eve *. *(c+=/cd+= * tracks) <US cd-iss. 1997 on 'Cooking Vinyl'+=; COOKCD 134>* – (9 extra).

— **SIMON SMITH** (b. 3 May'65, Lincolnshire) – drums repl. SHAUN to POPGUNS

Feb 88. (7") *(REC 009)* **NOBODY'S TWISTING YOUR ARM. / I'M NOT ALWAYS SO STUPID** 46
(12"+=/cd-s+=) *(REC 009 12/CD)* – Nothing comes easy / Don't laugh.

Jul 88. (lp/c/cd) *(LEEDS 002/+C/CD)* **TOMMY** (compilation 4 singles + Peel sessions) 42
– Go out and get 'em boy / (The moment before) Everything's spoiled again / Once more / At the edge of the sea / Living and learning / This boy can't wait / You should always keep in touch with your friends / Felicity / What becomes of the broken hearted? / Never said / Every mother's son / My favourite dress. *<US cd-iss. 1997 on 'Cooking Vinyl'; COOKCD 135>*

Sep 88. (7") *(REC 011)* **WHY ARE YOU BEING SO REASONABLE NOW?. / NOT FROM WHERE I'M STANDING** 42
(12"+=) *(REC 011-12)* – Give my love to Kevin (acoustic) / Getting better.
(c-s++=/cd-s++=) *(REC 011 C/CD)* – Pourquoi es tu devenue si raisonable?.
(s7") *(REC 011F)* – Pourquoi es tu devenue si raisonable?. / Give my love to Kevin (acoustic).

— added guest **LEN LIGGINS** – vocals, violin (ex-SINISTER CLEANERS, Solo artist) others played assortment of instruments in Ukrainian style.

R.C.A. R.C.A.

Apr 89. (lp/c/cd) *(PL/PK/PD 74104)* **UKRAINSKI VISTUPI V JOHNA PEELA** (Ukrainian style John Peel sessions) 22
– Davny chasy / Yikhav kozak za dunai / Tiutiunyk / Zadmav didochok svitit misyats / Katrusyai Vasya vasyl'ok / Hude dn ipro hude Verkhovyno. *(was to have been issued as 10"m-lp, Nov88 on 'Reception'; REC 010)*

— (Reverted to usual 4-piece & style).

Sep 89. (7"/c-s) *(PB/PK 43117)* **KENNEDY. / UNFAITHFUL** 33
(c-s+=/12"+=/cd-s+=) *(PT/PK/PD 43118)* – One day all this will all be yours / It's not unusual.

Oct 89. (lp/c/cd) *(PL/PK/PD 74302) <2173>* **BIZARRO** 22
– Brassneck / Crushed / No / Thanks / Kennedy / What have I said now /

Granadaland / Bewitched / Take me / Be honest. *(cd+=)* – Brassneck (extended) / Box elder / Don't talk, just kiss / Gone.

Feb 90. (7"/c-s) *(PB/PK 43403)* **BRASSNECK. / DON'T TALK, JUST KISS** 24 -
(c-s+=/12"+=/cd-s+=) *(PK/PT/PD 43404)* – Gone / Box elder.

Sep 90. (7"ep/c-ep)(12"ep/cd-ep) *(PB/PK 44021)(PT/PD 44022)* **THE 3 SONGS EP** 25 -
– Corduroy / Make me smile (come up and see me) / Crawl.
(10"+=) *(PJ 44022)* – Take me (live).

R.C.A. First Warning

Apr 91. (7") *(PB 44495)* **DALLIANCE. / NIAGARA** 29 -
(c-s+=)(12"+=/cd-s+=) *(PK 44495)(PT/PD 44496)* – She's my best friend.
(10"++=) *(PJ 44495)* – What have I said now? (live).

May 91. (cd/c/lp) *(PD/PK/PL 75012)* *<75708>* **SEAMONSTERS** 13
– Dalliance / Dare / Suck / Blonde / Rotterdam / Lovenest / Corduroy / Carolyn / Heather / Octopussy.

Jul 91. (12"ep/cd-ep) *(PT/PD 44750)* **LOVENEST (edit) / MOTHERS. / DAN DARE / FLESHWORLD** 58 -

— **PAUL DORRINGTON** – guitar (ex-AC TEMPLE) repl. SOLOWKA to UKRAINIANS

Jan 92. (7") *(PB 45185)* **BLUE EYES. / CATTLE AND CANE** 26 -
Feb 92. (7") *(PB 45183)* **GO-GO DANCER. / DON'T CRY NO TEARS** 20 -
Mar 92. (7") *(PB 45181)* **THREE. / THINK THAT IT MIGHT** 14 -
Apr 92. (7") *(PB 45311)* **SILVER SHORTS. / FALLING** 14 -
May 92. (7") *(PB 45313)* **COME PLAY WITH ME. / PLEASANT VALLEY SUNDAY** 10 -
Jun 92. (7") *(PB 45313)* **CALIFORNIA. / LET'S MAKE SOME PLANS** 16 -
Jun 92. (cd/c/lp) *(PD/PK/PL 75343)* *<75711>* **THE HIT PARADE 1** 22
– (last 6 singles 'A'&'B')
Jul 92. (7") *(PB 10115)* **FLYING SAUCER. / ROCKET** 22 -
Aug 92. (7") *(PB 10117)* **BOING!. / THEME FROM SHAFT** 19 -
Sep 92. (7") *(PB 10116)* **LOVESLAVE. / CHANT OF THE EVER CIRCLING SKELETAL FAMILY** 17 -
Oct 92. (7") *(PB 11691)* **STICKY. / GO WILD IN THE COUNTRY** 17 -
Nov 92. (7") *(PB 11692)* **THE QUEEN OF OUTER SPACE. / U.F.O.** 23 -
Dec 92. (7"red) *(PB 11693)* **NO CHRISTMAS. / STEP INTO CHRISTMAS** 25 -

— The above 12 singles, were limited to 15,000 copies, and hit peak chart position on its first week of issue.

Jan 93. (cd/c/lp) *(PD/PK/PL 74321)* *<75711>* **THE HIT PARADE 2** 19
– (all last 6 'A'&'B' singles above) (free lp w/lp+=) **BBC SESSIONS** – (all 12 of the years' A-sides).

— **DARREN BELLE** – bass; repl. GREGORY who later formed CHA CHA COHEN

Island Polygram

Sep 94. (c-ep/12"ep/cd-ep) *(CIS/12IS/CID 585)* **YEAH YEAH YEAH YEAH YEAH / THE BIKINI / FLAME ON / HIM OR ME (WHAT'S IT GONNA BE)** 51 -
(cd-ep) *(CIDX 585)* – ('A'side) / Gazebo / So long baby / Spangle.

Sep 94. (cd/c/lp) *(CID/ICT/ILPS 8014)* *<524044>* **WATUSI** 47
– So long, baby / Click click / Yeah yeah yeah yeah yeah / Let him have it / Gazebo / Shake it / Spangle / It's a gas / Swimming pools, movie stars / Big rat / Catwoman / Hot pants.

Nov 94. (c-s/7") *(C+/IS 591)* **IT'S A GAS. / BUBBLES** -
(12"purple+=/cd-s+=) *(12IS/CID 591)* – ('A'acoustic) / Jumper clown.

— SMITH was another to leave and turn up in CHA CHA COHEN

Cooking Vinyl Cooking Vinyl

Jan 96. (10"m-lp/m-cd) *(<COOK/+CD 094>)* **MINI**
– Drive / Love machine / Go, man, go / Mercury / Convertible / Sports car. *(cd+=)* – Sucker / Waiting on the guns / Jet girl.

Aug 96. (7") *(FRY 048)* **2, 3, GO. / UP** 67 -
(cd-s+=) *(FRYCD 048)* – Jet girl / Real thing.

Sep 96. (2x10"lp/c/cd) *(<COOK/+C/CD 099>)* **SATURNALIA** 36
– Snake eyes / Big boots / Spaceman / Skin diving / Real thing / Dreamworld / Kansas / Hula doll / Up / Venus / 50's / Montreal / 2, 3, go.

Jan 97. (7") *(FRY 063)* *<5053>* **MONTREAL. / PROJECT CENZO** 40
(7") *(FRY 053X)* – ('A'side) / Where everybody knows your name.
(cd-s) *(FRYCD 053)* – ('A'side) / Sports car / My favourite dress (live) / Brassneck (live).

Jul 98. (7") *(FRY 072)* **KERRY KERRY. / 7X** -
(7") *(FRY 072X)* – ('A'side) / Mr Kiss Kiss Bang Bang.
(cd-s) *(FRYCD 072)* – ('A'side) / Love / Au pair.

Cooking Vinyl SpinArt

Aug 98. (lp/cd) *(COOK/+CD 150)* *<68>* **VA VA VOOM** Oct98
– Maniac / Comedienne / Hate / Kerry Kerry / Barefoot in the park / You turn me on / Ears / Me next / Hard, fast and beautiful / Dance, girl, dance / Honey rider.

Oct 98. (FRY 077) **DANCE, GIRL, DANCE. / EARS (acoustic version)** -
(cd-s) *(FRYCD 077)* – ('A'side) / Crusoe / Model spy.
(cd-s) *(FRYCD 077X)* – Pacific / King's Cross.

— they officially split after above

– compilations, etc. –

Oct 86. (12"ep) *Strange Fruit; (SFPS 009)* **THE PEEL SESSIONS** (26.2.86) -
– What becomes of the broken hearted / This boy can't wait / Felicity / You should always keep in touch with your friends. *(c-ep iss.Jun87; SFPSC 009) (cd-ep iss.Aug88; SFPSC 009)*

Nov 88. (12"ep/cd-ep) *Nighttracks; (SFNT/+CD 016)* **THE EVENING SHOW SESSIONS** (20.4.86) -
– Everyone thinks he looks daft / I found that essence rare / Shatner / My favourite dress.

Oct 93. (lp/cd) *Strange Fruit; (SFR LP/CD 122)* **JOHN PEEL SESSIONS 1987-1990** -
– Give my regards to Kevin / Getting nowhere fast / A million miles / Something and nothing / Take me I'm yours / Unfaithful / Why are you being so reasonable now? / Happy birthday / Dalliance / Heather Blonde / Niagara.

CINERAMA

DAVID LEWIS GEDGE – vocals, guitar / **SALLY MURRELL** – vocals, programming / with **DARE MASON** – guitar, theremin / **MARTY WILLSON-PIPER** – guitar (of The CHURCH) / **ANTHONY COOTE** – bass (of ANIMALS CAN SWIM) / **DAVEY RAY MOORE** – keyboards (of PUSHA) / **RICHARD MARKANGELO + CHE ALBRIGHTON** – drums, percussion / **JULIA PALMER + ABIGAIL TRUNDLE** – cello / **RACHEL DAVIES** – violin / **DUNCAN BRIDGEMAN** – flute / **THIBAULT DE MONTFORT** – oboe / **DEREK CRABTREE** – trumpet / **EMMA POLLOCK** – vocals (of DELGADOS)

WEEKEND (see under ⇒ YOUNG MARBLE GIANTS)

WEEN

Formed: New Jersey, USA ... early 1985 by 14-year-old MICKEY MELCHIONDO and AARON FREEMAN (alias DEAN and GENE WEEN). They worked together in a farm commune on a 4-track cassette machine for the last half of the 80's, the first fruits of this released as a double album in 1990, 'GOD WEEN SATAN – THE ONENESS'. Its underground cult success led KRAMER of BONGWATER to put out 'THE POD', named after the home they had just been evicted from. After a brief stint on 'Sub Pop', they were signed to 'Elektra' in 1993, Creation off-shoot 'August' subsequently taking up an option on their album, 'PURE GUAVA'. They were later dropped by the label although the UK division of 'Flying Nun' released their next effort, 'CHOCOLATE AND CHEESE'. The duo recruited a full band after a hip-hop attempt as The MOIST BOYZ for The BEASTIE BOYS' 'Grand Royal' label. 1996's '12 GOLDEN COUNTRY GREATS' was psychedelic country of the weirdo variety, shot through with WEEN's inimitable warped humour. Following on from this, the lads completed another set of inspired rock'n'roll piss-taking in 'THE MOLLUSK' (1997). • **Covered:** SHOCKADELICA (Prince).

Album rating: GOD WEEN SATAN – THE ONENESS (*8) / THE POD (*7) / PURE GUAVA (*6) / CHOCOLATE AND CHEESE (*6) / 12 GOLDEN COUNTRY GREATS (*4) / THE MOLLUSK (*6)

DEAN WEEN (b. MICHAEL MELCHIONDO) – vocals, guitar, etc / **GENE WEEN** (b. AARON FREEMAN) – vocals, guitar, etc

Twin/Tone Twin/Tone

1990. (cd/d-lp) *<(TTR 89186-2/-1)>* **GOD WEEN SATAN – THE ONENESS**
– Birthday boy / Blackjack / Quelch the weazel / Marble tulip juicy tree / Puffy cloud / Nan / Lick the palm for Guava / Mushroom festival in Hell / L.M.L.Y.P. / Papa zit / Old man thunder / Up on the hill / Wayne's pet youngin' / Nicole / Common bitch / El camino / Old Queen Cole / You fucked up / Tick / I got a weazel / I'm in the mood / Fat Lenny / Cold + wet / Bumble bee / Don't laugh (I love you) / Never squeal on the pusher. *(re-iss. cd Jul95; same)*

Shimmy Disc Shimmy Disc

1991. (cd/d-lp) *<(SDE 9238 DD/DLP)>* **THE POD**
– Strap on the jammy pack / Dr. Rock / Frank / Sorry Charlie / Pollo Asado / Right to the ways and the rules of the world / Captain Fantasy / emon sweat / Molly / Can u taste the waste / Don't sweat it / Laura / Boing / Oh my dear / Sketches of winkle / Alone / Moving away / She fucks me / Pork roll egg and cheese / The stallion (part 2). *(re-iss. Apr95 on 'Flying Nun' d-lp/cd; FN/+CD 322)*

— 1992, 'SKYCRUISER' was released on 'Sub Pop'

Creation – August Elektra

Jan 93. (cd/lp) *(RUST 002 CD/LP)* *<61428>* **PURE GUAVA** Nov92
– Little Birdy / Tender situation / The stallion (part 3) / Big Jim / Push th' little daisies / The going gets tough from the getgo / Reggaejunkiejew / I play it off legit / Pumpin' 4 the man / Sarah / Springtime / Flies on my dick / I saw Gene cryin' in his sleep / Touch my tooter / Mourning glory / Loving u thru it all / Hey fat boy (asshole) / Don't get 2 close (2 my fantasy) / Poop ship destroyer.

Aug 93. (12"/cd-s) *(CAUG 004 T/CD)* **PUSH TH' LITTLE DAISIES / MANGO WOMAN. / PUERTO RICAN POWER (parts 1 & 2) / ODE TO RON** -

1994. (7"white) **I'M FAT. /**

— above featured **CALVIN CELSIUS** – vocals

Flying Nun Elektra

Jan 95. (7"pic-d) *(FN 321)* **VOODOO LADY. / BUENAS TARDES, AMIGO** -
(cd-s+=) *(FNCD 321)* – There's a pig / Valleso.
(7") *(FNSP 321)* – ('A'side) / Cover it with gas and set it on fire.

Jan 95. (d-lp/cd) *(FN/+CD 314)* *<61639>* **CHOCOLATE AND CHEESE** Sep94
– Take me away / Spinal meningitis / Freedom of '76 / I can't put my finger on it / A tear for eddie / Roses are free / Baby back / Mister, would you please help my pony? / Drifter in the dark / Voodoo lady / Joppa road / Candi / Buenas tardes, amigo / The HIV song / What Deaner was talkin' about / Don't spit when you eat.

Apr 95. (7") *(FN 327)* **FREEDOM OF '76. / POLLO ASADO** -
(cd-s+=) *(FNCD 327)* – ('A'-Shaved dog mix) / Now I'm freaking own.
(7"pic-d) *(FNSP 327)* – ('A'-Shaved dog mix) / Bakersfield.

Jul 96. (7") *(FN 387)* **YOU WERE THE FOOL. /** -
(cd-s+=) *(FNCD 387)* –
(7") *(FNS 387)* –

Aug 96. (lp/s-lp/c/cd) *(FN/+SP/MC/CD 386)* *<61909>* **12 COUNTRY GREATS** Jul96
– I'm holding you / Japanese cowboy / Piss up a rope / I don't want to leave you on the farm / Pretty girl / Powder blue / Mister Richard smoker / Help me scrape the mucus of my brain / You were the fool / Fluffy.

Mushroom Elektra

Sep 97. (cd/lp) *(MUSH 3 CD/LP)* *<62013>* **THE MOLLUSK** Jun97
– I'm dancing in the show tonight / The mollusk / Polka dot tail / I'll be you're Jonny on the spot / Mutilated lips / The Blarney stone / It's gonna be (alright) / The golden

eel / Cold blows the wind / Pink eye (on my leg) / Waving my dick in the wind / Buckingham green / Ocean man / She wanted to leave.

— In Aug'98, WEEN appeared with 'BEACON LIGHT' on the UK Top 20 b-side of a FOO FIGHTERS single.

MOIST BOYZ

DEAN + GENE WEEN (MICKEY MOIST + DICKIE MOIST) alter-ego outfit remixed by The BEASTIE BOYS on their label.

Grand Royal / Grand Royal

Apr 97. (m-lp/m-cd) *<GR 004/+CD)>* **MOISTBOYZ** [ ] [ ] Jan95
– Carjack / I.O. (fuck no) / U blow / Supersoaker Md50 / I am the jury / Adios amigo.

Mar 98. (lp/cd) *<GR 037/+CD)>* **MOISTBOYZ VOL.2** [ ] [ ] Nov96
– It ain't rude / Second hand smoker / Larry and cool / Rock, stock, barrel / Man of the year / American made and duty-free / Crank / Powervice / Keep the fire alive / Good morning America,

WEEZER

Formed: Los Angeles, USA . . .1993 by RIVERS CUOMO, MATT SHARP and PATRICK WILSON. Signing to 'Geffen' and recruiting final member, BRIAN BELL, the group released their eponymous RIC OCASEK-produced debut album in September '94. Helped by the transatlantic success of singles such as 'UNDONE – THE SWEATER SONG' and the pogo-pop of 'BUDDY HOLLY', the album became one of the year's biggest sellers. Often described as The PIXIES meeting The BEACH BOYS, their blaring college 'nerd'-rock saw WEEZER riding the crest of an American 'new wave' triggered by the likes of GREEN DAY and OFFSPRING. Meanwhile, MATT SHARP was also busy with a side project, The RENTALS (comprising CHERIELYNN WESTRICH, ROD CERVERA, PETRA HADEN, PAT WILSON and JIM RICHARDS), releasing an album of New Wave-esque songs in 'RETURN OF THE RENTALS' (1995/96). A second WEEZER album, 'PINKERTON' (1996), was much of the same, although it brought the band a bit of grief when the American security firm of the same name brought legal action; the band have been inactive since. • **Songwriters:** CUOMO, a few w/ WILSON.

Album rating: WEEZER (*7) / PINKERTON (*7) / Rentals: RETURN OF THE RENTALS (*5)

RIVERS CUOMO – vocals / **BRIAN BELL** – guitar, vocals / **MATT SHARP** – bass, vocals / **PATRICK WILSON** – drums

Geffen / D.G.C.

Jan 95. (7"blue) *(GFS 85) <19378>* **UNDONE – THE SWEATER SONG. / HOLIDAY** [35] [57] Sep94
(c-s+=/cd-s+=) *(GFS C/TD 85)* – Mykel & Carli / Susanne.

Feb 95. (cd/c/lp) *<(GED/GEC/GEF 24629)>* **WEEZER** [23] [16] Aug94
– My name is Jonas / No one else / The world has turned and left me here / Buddy Holly / Undone – the sweater song / In the garage / Holiday / Only in dreams.

Apr 95. (7"/c-s) *(GFS/+C 88)* **BUDDY HOLLY. / JAMIE** [12] [-]
(cd-s+=) *(GFSTD 88)* – My name is Jonas / Surf wax America.

Jul 95. (10"ep/c-ep/cd-ep) *(GFS V/C/TD 95)* **SAY IT AIN'T SO (remix). / NO ONE ELSE (live acoustic) / JAMIE (live acoustic)** [37] [ ]

Sep 96. (7"/c-s) *(GFS/+C 22167)* **EL SCORCHO. / YOU GAVE YOUR LOVE TO ME SOFTLY** [50] [-]
(cd-s+=) *(GFSTD 22167)* – Devotion.

Oct 96. (cd/c) *<(GED/GEC 25007)>* **PINKERTON** [43] [19]
– Tired of sex / Getchoo / No other one / Why bother / Across the sea / Good life / El Scorcho / Pink triangle / Falling for you / Butterfly.

RENTALS

MATT SHARP – vocals, bass, Moog synthesizer / plus **CHERIELYNN WESTRICH** – vocals / **ROD CERVERA** – guitar / **PETRA HADEN** – violin, vocals / **JIM RICHARDS** – keyboards / **PAT WILSON** – drums

Warners / Maverick

Jan 96. (cd/c) *<(9362 46093-2/-4)>* **THE RETURN OF THE RENTALS** [ ] [ ] Nov95

Mar 96. (c-s) *(W 0340C)* **FRIENDS OF P / SO SOON** [ ] [ ]
(cd-s+=) *(W 0340CD)* – Love I'm searching for.

WEIRDOS

Formed: Los Angeles, California, USA . . . 1976 initially as The BARBIES then The LUXURIOUS ADULTS by brothers JOHN and DIX DENNEY, with others CLIFF ROMAN, DAVID TROUT and NICKEY BEAT. In 1977, they unleashed first of many cult-punk 45's, 'DESTROY ALL MUSIC', which somehow found its way by import to UK shores. A number of sporadic singles followed, although internal wrangles led to a split in 1981. They did however re-form in the early 90's, and even got round to an album going by the name of 'CONDOR'. Despite their lack of recognition during their short lifespan, this punk/new wave outfit are now regarded by many critics as US pioneers of the movement.

Album rating: WEIRD WORLD 1977-1981 TIME CAPSULE VOLUME ONE compilation (*8)

JOHN DENNEY – vocals / **DIX DENNEY** – guitar / **CLIFF ROMAN** – guitar / **DAVID TROUT** – bass / **NICKEY BEAT** – drums

not iss. / Dangerhouse

1977. (7") **DESTROY ALL MUSIC. /** [-] [ ]

1978. (7") *<SP 1063>* **WE GOT THE NEUTRON BOMB. / SOLITARY CONFINEMENT** [-] [ ]

— **BILLY PERSONS** – bass repl. TROUT

— **DANNY BENAIR** – drums repl. NICKEY

not iss. / Bomp

1979. (12"ep) *<W 3>* **WHO? WHAT? WHEN? WHERE? WHY?** [-] [ ]
– Jungle rock / Happy people / Big shot / Hitman / Idle life / Fort U.S.A.

not iss. / Numbskull

1979. (7") *<none>* **SKATEBOARDS TO HELL. / ADULTHOOD** [-] [ ]

— **WILLY WILLIAMS** – bass; repl. PERSONS

— **ART FOX** – drums; repl. BENAIR

not iss. / Rhino

1980. (12"ep) *<RNEP 508>* **ACTION DESIGN** [-] [ ]
– The hideout / I feel / Break on through / Helium bar.

— split but re-formed nearly a decade later. **DENNEY's + ROMAN**

Frontier / Frontier

1990. (cd/lp) *<(4623-2L/1L)>* **CONDOR** [ ] [ ]

May 91. (cd/lp) *(4630-2L/-4L/-1L)* **WEIRD WORLD 1977-1981 TIME CAPSULE VOLUME ONE** (compilation) [ ] [ ]
– Weird world / Arms race / Pagan / Helium bar / Rhythm syndrome / Fallout / Fort U.S.A. / Happy people / Message from the underworld / Teenage / I'm not like you / We got the neutron bomb / Solitary confinement / Life of crime.

— THE WEIRDOS FEATURING MR. GASSER cd from '95 was from surf band

WE KNOW WHERE YOU LIVE (see under ⇒ WONDER STUFF)

Paul WELLER

Born: 25 May'58, Woking, Surrey, England. (see The JAM for further details). Formed STYLE COUNCIL in early '83 with former MERTON PARKAS keys player, MICK TALBOT, and talented young sticksman, STEVE WHITE. Though it was merely a matter of months since WELLER had folded The JAM, The STYLE COUNCIL followed a radical new direction, taking the agit-soul of CURTIS MAYFIELD as their inspiration and fashioning a very 80's hybrid of cocktail jazz, breezy pop and white funk. Scoring immediately with the Top 5 'SPEAK LIKE A CHILD', the group went Top 3 later that year with the 'LONG HOT SUMMER' EP, its sultry lead track arguably the best the group ever penned and the creative pinnacle of what they were trying to achieve. Previewing The STYLE COUNCIL's debut album, 'CAFE BLEU' (1984), the mellow atmospherics of 'MY EVER CHANGING MOODS' gave the group another huge hit in early '84. The album itself was a lush fusion of summery jazz and easy soul, the keening strum of 'YOU'RE THE BEST THING' making the Top 5. WELLER became increasingly political as the decade wore on, the rousing soul/funk of 'SHOUT TO THE TOP' and 'WALLS COME TUMBLING DOWN' an indication of the direction The JAM may have have taken had they still been in existence. With the miners strike in full effect, politics were very much still an issue in rock/pop and WELLER and Co. released a benefit single, 'SOUL DEEP', at Christmas '84 under the COUNCIL COLLECTIVE banner. With production handled by HEAVEN 17's MARTYN WARE, the project included the likes of JIMMY RUFFIN, JUNIOR (GISCOMBE), VAUGHN TOULOUSE, DIZZY HEIGHTS and DEE C. LEE. The latter became not only WELLER's other half but a full-time backing singer for The STYLE COUNCIL, her sweet soul tones helping make 'OUR FAVOURITE SHOP' (1985) a mid-80's classic. The overall sound was more satisfying and the writing was sharper; 'COME TO MILTON KEYNES' was WELLER's most cutting slice of social commmentary since The JAM heyday. Come 1986, The STYLE COUNCIL became heavily involved in the 'Red Wedge' movement alongside the likes of The COMMUNARDS and BILLY BRAGG, attempting to educate music fans into voting for the right party in the upcoming elections i.e. Labour. Such an openly party political stance was probably doomed to failure from the start, the attendant tour floundering and the Tories of course, predictably romping home. It was the last time WELLER would lay his beliefs on the line and the failure of the project seemed to lie at the heart of the lugubrious meanderings of the double set, 'THE COST OF LOVING' (1987). The following year's 'CONFESSIONS OF A POP GROUP' (1988) was similarly lacking in focus, its string arrangements and classical pretensions seeing The STYLE COUNCIL sinking in a mire of self-indulgence. The record failed to spawn any major hits and didn't even make the Top 10; when 'Polydor' refused to release a proposed fifth set, WELLER finally adjourned the 'COUNCIL and retired to re-evaluate his career. Now without a band or a recording deal, WELLER eventually regained his thirst for music via the low-key PAUL WELLER MOVEMENT, a band comprising STEVE WHITE, JACKO PEAKE, PAUL FRANCIS, MAX BEESLEY, DAMON BROWN, CHRIS LAWRENCE and DJ PAULO HEWITT along with backing singers DEE C.LEE, DR. ROBERT and CAMELLE HINDS. The subsequent '90s/'91s shows saw the singer once again armed with a guitar and suggested that he'd been reacquainting himself with his record collection, more specifically late 60's R&B and psychedelia. The 'MOVEMENT released a sole single, 'INTO TOMORROW' on the DIY 'Freedom High' label. It squeezed into the Top 40 nonetheless and WELLER eventually whittled down the bulk of the group for a more basic sound, signing with 'Go! Discs' and debuting with 'UH HUH OH YEH' in late summer '92. Hailed as the best thing he'd done in years, the single went into the Top 20 and the PAUL WELLER revival was up and running. The music press had given the singer a wide berth since the heyday of The STYLE COUNCIL and as the plaudits began to roll in for his eponymous debut album, were eventually forced to admit that, yes, WELLER was undergoing something of a creative rebirth.

Matching the visceral, emotional punch of the music, the lyrics were of a decidedly more personal nature, eschewing politics for matters of the soul and the heart. With the ebullient 'SUNFLOWER' single and the attendant 'WILD WOOD' (1993) album, WELLER's star was most definately in the ascendant. Characterised by a crisp, uncluttered Brendan Lynch production, the record saw WELLER distill his influences into vintage singer/songwriter maturity. With his voice now sufficiently rough around the edges to complement such material, the likes of the resonating, meditative folkiness of the title track assumed a greater depth. The album reached No.2, featuring in many end of year polls (Mercury Prize), the chino wearing ghost of The STYLE COUNCIL now finally laid to rest. While the UK music press were still largely fixated on US grunge, WELLER was nothing if not instrumental in the upcoming Brit-pop debacle. Cited by the likes of OASIS as a guiding influence, the Modfather, as WELLER came to be known, was everything that the hordes of mop-topped chancers aspired to. It was a role that WELLER fitted into naturally, OCEAN COLOUR SCENE's STEVE CRADDOCK was already a regular musical collaborator, while NOEL GALLAGHER would guest on WELLER's forthcoming No.1 album, 'STANLEY ROAD'. Released in Spring '95 as Brit-pop was reaching its zenith, the album was earthier than anything WELLER had recorded in his career to date. Again produced by LYNCH, the record was previewed by the blistering single, 'THE CHANGINGMAN', its lyrics signalling an even more personal bent to WELLER's writing as the looking-good-for-30-something star even began appearing in the British style press. Elsewhere on the album, WELLER covered Dr. John's 'I WALK ON GILDED SPLINTERS' although it was the spirit of ERIC CLAPTON or NEIL YOUNG that most often came to mind. WELLER was at his most affecting on the ballads, the deeply felt 'YOU DO SOMETHING TO ME', the beautiful gospel-soul of album closer 'WINGS OF SPEED' and the brilliantly evocative hammond/wurlitzer musings of 'BROKEN STONES'. Of course, a backlash was inevitable, and certain sections of the music press derided WELLER's new material as tired 'Dad-rock', an incestuous Brit-pop conspiracy which continually looked to the past instead of breaking new ground. While this may have been true to a certain degree, and WELLER was partly responsible for the vexing success of the terminally workmanlike OCEAN COLOUR SCENE, the man was simply integrating retro influences into his muse as he'd done all the way through his career; it's the fact that these influences changed which seems to annoy some writers. Keeping his profile high with various festival appearances (as well as a predictable guest spot at OASIS' Knebworth show), WELLER (now signed to 'Island' following the demise of 'Go! Discs' eventually returned to the fray in summer '97 with the storming 'BRUSHED' single. Arguably standing among the best of WELLER's work to date, the track was propelled by a stone solid/funky as hell rhythmic thrust (courtesy of WHITE), combining mod, psychedelia and rock in a fashion that he's only previously hinted at. 'Raw' is probably the best word to describe it and the best word to describe the accompanying album, 'HEAVY SOUL' (1997), WELLER's voice as impressive as ever on a set which nevertheless too often relies on 'authentic' sound over songwriting. • **Songwriters:** WELLER penned except for TALBOT's STYLE COUNCIL instrumentals. They also covered MOVE ON UP (Curtis Mayfield) / PROMISED LAND (Joe Smooth) / OHIO (Neil Young). WELLER solo:- FEELIN' ALRIGHT (Traffic) / SEXY SADIE (Beatles) / I'M ONLY DREAMING (Small Faces) / I SHALL BE RELEASED (Bob Dylan).

Album rating: THE SINGULAR ADVENTURES OF THE STYLE COUNCIL (*7) / PAUL WELLER (*6) / WILD WOOD (*9) / STANLEY ROAD (*8) / HEAVY SOUL (*7)

STYLE COUNCIL

PAUL WELLER (b.25 May'58, Woking, Surrey, England) – vocals, guitar (ex-JAM) / **MICK TALBOT** (b.11 Sep'58) – keyboards (ex-MERTON PARKAS) / **STEVE WHITE** – drums / plus various guests.

Polydor Polydor

Mar 83. (7") *(TSC 1)* **SPEAK LIKE A CHILD. / PARTY CHAMBERS** 4

May 83. (7") *(TSC 2)* **MONEY GO ROUND. / (part 2)** 11
(12") *(TSCX 2)* – ('A'side) / Headstart for happiness / Mick's up.

Aug 83. (7"ep/12"ep) *(TSC/+X 3)* **LONG HOT SUMMER / PARTY CHAMBERS. / PARIS MATCH / LE DEPART** 3

Nov 83. (7") *(TSC 4)* **SOLID BOND IN YOUR HEART. / IT JUST CAME TO PIECES IN MY HAND / ('A'instrumental)** 11

Oct 83. (m-lp) *<815277>* **INTRODUCING THE STYLE COUNCIL** –
– (above songs)

Polydor Geffen

Feb 84. (7") *(TSC 5) <29359>* **MY EVER CHANGING MOODS. / MICK'S COMPANY** 5 29
(12"+=) *(TSCX 5)* – Spring, Summer, Autumn.

Mar 84. (lp/c)(cd) *(TSC LP/MC 1)(817535-2) <4029>* **CAFE BLEU** 2 56
<US-title 'MY EVER CHANGING MOODS'>
– Mick's blessings / My ship came in / Blue cafe / The Paris match / My ever changing moods / Dropping bombs on the Whitehouse / A gospel / Strength of your nature / You're the best thing / Here's the one that got away / Headstart for happiness / Council meetin'. *(cd+=)* – The whole point of no return. *(re-iss. cd Sep95; same)*

May 84. (7") *(TSC 6) <29248>* **YOU'RE THE BEST THING. / BIG BOSS GROOVE** 5 76
(12") *(TSCX 6)* – ('A'dub version).

Oct 84. (7") *(TSC 7)* **SHOUT TO THE TOP. / GHOSTS OF DACHAU** 7
(12"+=) *(TSCX 7)* – Piccadilly trail / ('A'instrumental).

Dec 84. (7"; as COUNCIL COLLECTIVE) *(MINE 1)* **SOUL DEEP. / (part 2)** 24 –
(12"+=) *(MINEX 1)* – ('A'version) / (striking miner's interview).
(above single gave proceeds to miner's strike & the deceased miner David Wilkie's widow) The COLLECTIVE featured guests JIMMY RUFFIN, JUNIOR GISCOMBE, VAUGHN TOULOUSE, DEE C.LEE and DIZZY HEIGHTS. Production handled by MARTYN WARE (Heaven 17).

May 85. (7~"ep/12"ep) *(TSC/+X 8)* **WALLS COME TUMBLING DOWN. / THE WHOLE POINT II / BLOODSPORTS** 6 –

Jun 85. (lp/c)(cd) *(TSC LP/MC 2)(825700-2) <24061>* **OUR FAVOURITE SHOP <US title 'INTERNATIONALISTS'>** 1
– Homebreakers / All gone away / Come to Milton Keynes / Internationalists / A stone's throw away / The stand up comic's instructions / Boy who cried wolf / A man of great promise / Down in the Seine / The lodgers / Luck / With everything to lose / Our favourite shop / Walls come tumbling down. *(cd+=)* – Shout to the top. *(c+=)* – (interview). *(cd re-iss. Aug90; same)*

Jun 85. (7") *(TSC 9)* **COME TO MILTON KEYNES. / WHEN YOU CALL ME** 23 –
(12"+=) *(TSCG 9)* – Our favourite shop / ('A'club) / The lodgers (club mix).

Aug 85. (7") *<28941>* **OUR FAVOURITE SHOP. / BOY WHO CRIED WOLF** –

Sep 85. (7") *(TSC 10)* **THE LODGERS (remix). / YOU'RE THE BEST THING (live)** 13
(d7"+=) *(TSCDP 10)* – Big boss groove (live) / Long hot summer (live).
(12"+=) *(TSC?? 10)* – Big boss groove (live) / Move on up (live).
(12"+=) *(TSCX 10)* – Medley: Money go round – Soul deep – Strength of your nature.

Mar 86. (7"ep/12"ep) *(CINEX 1/+12)* **HAVE YOU EVER HAD IT BLUE. / MR. COOL'S DREAM** 14

May 86. (lp/c)(cd) *(TCS LP/MC 3)(829143-2)* **HOME AND ABROAD – LIVE (live)** 8 –
– The big boss groove * / My ever changing moods / The lodgers / Headstart for happiness / (When you) Call me / The whole point of no return / Our favourite shop * / With everything to lose / Homebreakers / Shout to the top / Walls come tumbling down / Internationalists. *(cd+= *) (cd re-iss. Aug90; same)*

Jun 86. (7") *<28674>* **INTERNATIONALISTS. / (WHEN YOU) CALL ME** –

Polydor Polydor

Jan 87. (7"/12") *(TSC/+X 12)* **IT DIDN'T MATTER. / ALL YEAR ROUND** 9

Feb 87. (2x12"lp/c)(cd) *(TSC LP/MC 4)(<831433-2>)* **THE COST OF LOVING** 2
– It didn't matter / Right to go / Waiting / Walking the night / The cost of loving / Heaven's above / Fairy tales / Angel / A woman's song. *(re-iss. Oct90)*

Mar 87. (7") *(TSC 13)* **WAITING. / FRANCOISE** 52
(12"+=) *(TCSX 13)* – Theme from 'Jerusalem'.

Oct 87. (7") *(TSC 14)* **WANTED (FOR WAITER). / THE COST OF LOVING** 20
(12"+=/c-s+=) (TSC X/CS 14) – There's soup in my flies.
(cd-s++=) – The cost.

May 88. (7") *(TSC 15)* **LIFE AT A TOP PEOPLE'S HEALTH FARM. / SWEET LOVING WAYS** 28
(12"+=/cd-s+=) *(TSC X/CD 15)* – Spark (live) / ('A'version).

Jun 88. (lp/c)(cd) *(TSC LP/MC 5)(<835785-2>)* **CONFESSIONS OF A POP GROUP** 15
– It's a very deep sea / The story of someone's shoe / Changing of the guard / The little boy in a castle – A dove flew down from the elephant / The gardener of Eden (a three piece suite):- In the beginning – The gardener of Eden – Mourning the passing of time / Life at a top people's health farm / Why I went missing / How she threw it all away / I was a doledads toyboy / Confessions of a pop group (parts 1, 2 & 3) / Confessions of a pop group. *(cd re-iss. Oct90; same)*

Jul 88. (7"ep/12"ep) *(TSC 16)* **HOW SHE THREW IT ALL AWAY / IN LOVE FOR THE FIRST TIME. / LONG HOT SUMER / I DO LIKE TO BE B-SIDE THE A-SIDE** 41

Feb 89. (7") *(TSC 17)* **PROMISED LAND. / CAN YOU STILL LOVE ME** 27
(12") *(TSCXS 17)* – ('A'-Joe Smooth's alternate club) / ('B'club) / ('B'dub).
(cd-s) *(TSCCD 17)* – ('A'-Juan Atkins mix) / ('A'-Pianopella mix) / ('B'-dub).
(cd-s) *(TSCD 17)* – ('A'side) / ('A'extended) / ('B'vocal) / ('B'dub).
(7"box) *(TSCB 17)* – ('A'-Juan Atkins mix) / ('B'side).

Mar 89. (lp/c)(cd) *(TSC TV/TC 1)(837896-2)* **THE SINGULAR ADVENTURES OF THE STYLE COUNCIL** (compilation) 3 –
– You're the best thing / Have you ever had it blue (extended) / Money go round (parts 1 & 2) / My ever changing moods (extended) / Long hot summer (extended) / The lodgers / Walls come tumbling down / Shout to the top / Wanted / It didn't matter / Speak like a child / A solid bond in your heart / Life at a top people's health farm / Promised land. *(c+=/cd+=)* – How she threw it all away / Waiting.

May 89. (7") *(LHS 1)* **LONG HOT SUMMER ('89 mix). / EVERYBODY'S ON THE RUN** 48 –
(12"+=/cd-s+=) *(LHS X/CD 1)* – ('A'&'B' different mixes).

—— Disbanded Mar'90. WELLER went solo, see below.

– compilations, etc. –

on 'Polydor' unless mentioned otherwise

Nov 87. (cd-ep) *(TSCCD 101)* **CAFE BLEU** –
– Headstart for happiness / Here's one that got away / Blue cafe / Strength of your nature.

Nov 87. (cd-ep) *(TSCCD 102)* **BIRDS AND BEES** –
– Piccadilly trail / It just came to pieces in my hands / Spin drifting / Spring, Summer, Autumn.

Nov 87. (cd-ep) *(TSCCD 103)* **MICK TALBOT IS AGENT '88** –
– Mick's up / Party chambers / Mick's blessing / Mick's company.

Jan 90. (7") *Old Gold; (OG 9924)* **LONG HOT SUMMER. / SPEAK LIKE A CHILD** –

Jan 90. (7") *Old Gold; (OG 9929)* **YOU'RE THE BEST THING. / MY EVER CHANGING MOODS** –

Jul 93. (cd/c) *(519 372-2/-4)* **HERE'S SOME THAT GOT AWAY** 39 –

Feb 96. (cd/c) *(529 483-2/-4)* **THE STYLE COUNCIL COLLECTION** 60

PAUL WELLER

with **STEVE WHITE** – drums, percussion / **JACKO PEAKE** – sax, flute, b.vox / **DEE C.LEE, DR.ROBERT + CAMELLE HINDS** – b.vox

Freedom High | London

May 91. (7"/c-s; as PAUL WELLER MOVEMENT) *(FHP/+C 1)* **INTO TOMORROW. / HERE'S A NEW THING** 36 | 1992
(12"+=/cd-s+=) *(FHP T/CD 1)* – That spiritual feeling / ('A'demo).

Go! Discs | London

Aug 92. (7"/c-s) *(GOD/+MC 86)* **UH HUH OH YEH. / FLY ON THE WALL** 18 | -
(12"+=/cd-s+=) *(GOD X/CD 86)* – Arrival time / Always there to fool you.

Sep 92. (cd/c/lp) *(<828 343-2/-4/-1>)* **PAUL WELLER** 8 | Oct92
– Uh huh oh yeh / I didn't mean to hurt you / Bull-rush / Round and round / Remember how we started / Above the clouds / Clues / Into tomorrow / Amongst butterflies / The strange museum / Bitterness rising / Kosmos. *(re-iss. Apr94; same)*

Oct 92. (7"/c-s) *(GOD/+MC 91)* **ABOVE THE CLOUDS. / EVERYTHING HAS A PRICE TO PAY** 47 | -
(12"+=/cd-s+=) *(GOD X/CD 91)* – All year round (live) / Feelin' alright.

— now with **STEVE WHITE** – drums, percussion / **MARCO NELSON** – bass

Go! Discs | Go! Discs

Jul 93. (7"/c-s) *(GOD/+MC 102)* **SUNFLOWER. / BULL-RUSH – MAGIC BUS (live)** 16 | -
(12"+=/cd-s+=) *(GOD X/CD 102)* – Kosmo's sxdub 2000 / That spiritual feeling (new mix).

Aug 93. (7"/c-s/10"/cd-s) *(<GOD/+MC/T/CD 104>)* **WILD WOOD. / ENDS OF THE EARTH** 14 |

Sep 93. (cd/c/lp) *(<828 435-2/-4/-1>)* **WILD WOOD** 2 | Oct93
– Sunflower / Can you heal us (holy man) / Wild wood – instrumental (pt.1) / All the pictures on the wall / Has my fire really gone out? / Country / 5th season / The weaver – instrumental (pt.2) / Foot of the mountain / Shadow of the Sun – Holy man (reprise) / Moon on your pyjamas. *(re-iss. Apr94 +=; same)* – Hung up.

Nov 93. (7"ep/c-ep/10"ep/cd-ep) *(GOD/+MC/T/CD 107)* **THE WEAVER EP** 18 | -
– The weaver / This is no time / Another new day / Ohio (live).

Mar 94. (7"ep/c-ep/12"ep/cd-ep) *(GOD/+MC/X/CD 111)* **HOME OF THE CLASSIC EP** 11 | -
– Hung up / Foot of the mountain (live from Albert Hall) / The loved / Kosmos (Lynch Mob bonus beats).

Sep 94. (cd/c/lp) *(828 561-2/-4/-1)* *<00601>* **LIVE WOOD (live)** 13 |
– Bull rush – Magic bus / This is no time / All the pictures on the wall / Remember how we started? / Dominoes / Above the clouds / Wild wood / Shadow of the Sun / (Can you hear us) Holy man – War / 5th season / Into tomorrow / Fool of the mountains / Sunflower / Has the fire really gone out?.

Oct 94. (7"ep/c-ep/12"ep/cd-ep) *(GOD/+MC/X/CD 121)* **OUT OF THE SINKING. / SUNFLOWER (Lynch Mob dub) / SEXY SADIE** 20 | -

— with **STEVE WHITE** – drums / **DR.ROBERT** – bass, vocals (ex-BLOW MONKEYS) / **STEVE CRADDOCK** – guitar / **MARK NELSON** – bass / **HELEN TURNER** – strings, organ / **BRENDAN LYNCH** – organ, co-producer / + guests **MICK TALBOT / CARLEEN ANDERSON / STEVE WINWOOD / NOEL GALLAGHER / YOLANDA CHARLES / CONSTANTINE WEIR**

Apr 95. (12"ep/c-ep/cd-ep) *(GOD X/MC/CD 127)* **THE CHANGINGMAN / I'D RATHER GO BLIND / IT'S A NEW DAY, BABY / I DIDNT MEAN TO HURT YOU (live)** 7 |

May 95. (cd/c/lp)(6x7"pack) *(<828 619-2/-4/-1>)(850070-7)* **STANLEY ROAD** 1 |
– The changingman / Porcelain gods / I walk on gilded splinters / You do something to me / Woodcutter's son / Time passes / Stanley Road / Broken stones / Out of the sinking / Pink on white walls / Whirlpool's end / Wings of speed.

Jul 95. (7"ep/c-ep/cd-ep) *(GOD/+MC/CD 130)* **YOU DO SOMETHING TO ME / A YEAR LATE. / MY WHOLE WORLD IS FALLING DOWN / WOODCUTTER'S SON** 9 | -

Sep 95. (7"/c-s) *(GOD/+MC 132)* **BROKEN STONES. / STEAM** 20 |
(cd-s+=) *(GODCD 132)* – Whirlpool's end / Porcelain gods.

— WELLER was also part of one-off supergroup The SMOKIN' MOJO FILTERS alongside PAUL McCARTNEY and NOEL GALLAGHER. They had a Top 20 hit late '95 with 'COME TOGETHER'.

Feb 96. (7"ep/cd-ep) *(GOD/+CD 143)* **OUT OF THE SINKING EP** 16 | -
– Out of the sinking / I shall be released / Porcelain gods / Broken stones.

Aug 96. (7"/c-s) *(GOD/+MC 149)* **PEACOCK SUIT. / EYE OF THE STORM** 5 | -
(cd-s+=) *(GODCD 149)* –

Island | Polygram

Jun 97. (cd/c/lp) *(CID/ICT/ILPS 8058)* *<524277>* **HEAVY SOUL** 2 | Aug97
– Heavy soul / Peacock suit / Up in Suzie's room / Brushed / Driving nowhere / I should have been there to inspire you / Heavy soul (part 2) / Friday Street / Science / Golden sands / As you lean into the light / Mermaids.

Aug 97. (7"ep/c-ep/cd-ep) *(IS/CIS/CID 666)* **BRUSHED EP** 14 | -
– Brushed / Ain't no love in the heart of the city / Shoot the dove / Into the light.

Oct 97. (c-s/7") *(C+/IS 676)* **FRIDAY STREET. /** 21 | -
(cd-s) *(CID 676)* – ('A'side) / Sunflower (live) / Brushed (live) / Mermaids (live).

Nov 97. (c-s/cd-s/7") *(CIS/CID/IS 683)* **MERMAIDS. / EVERYTHING HAS A PRICE TO PAY ('97 version) / SO YOU WANT TO BE A DANCER** 30 | -

Nov 98. (c-s/7") *(C+/IS 711)* **BRAND NEW START. / RIGHT UNDERNEATH IT** 16 |
(cd-s+=) *(CID 711)* – The riverbank (new version).

Nov 98. (cd/c/d-lp) *(CID/ICT/ILPSD 8080)* *<524558>* **MODERN CLASSICS – THE GREATEST HITS** (compilation) 7 |
– Out of the sinking / Peacock suit / Sunflower / The weaver / Wild wood / Above the clouds / Uh huh oh yeh / Brushed / The changingman / Friday Street / You do something to me / Brand new start / Hung up / Mermaids / Broken stones / Into tomorrow. *(lp-box; IBX 8080) (d-cd; CIDD 8080)*

WENDYS

Formed: Edinburgh, Scotland . . . early 1990 by brothers JONATHAN and ARTHUR RENTON, alongside IAN WHITE and JOHNNY MacARTHUR. This all-male outfit were lucky enough to gain an early support slot with The HAPPY MONDAYS, encouraged by SHAUN RYDER's dad Derek to send in a demo their label, 'Factory'. Subsequently signed to Anthony Wilson's imprint through A&R man Phil Sachs, who also became their manager, The WENDYS short career consisted of a couple of singles and an IAN BROUDIE-produced album, 'GOBBLEDYGOOK' (1991). Manchester in approach, despite their Caledonian roots, the band were virtually clones of other 'Factory' outfits; the aforementioned HAPPY MONDAYS, JAMES or even an optimistic JOY DIVISION.

Album rating: GOBBLEDYGOOK (*5)

JONATHAN RENTON – vocals / **IAN WHITE** – guitars / **ARTHUR RENTON** – bass / **JOHNNY MacARTHUR** – drums

Factory | East West

Feb 91. (7"/12"/cd-s) *(FAC 289/T/CD)* **THE SUN'S GOING TO SHINE FOR ME SOON. / EVERYBODY** | -

Apr 91. (7"/c-s) *(FAC 297)* **PULLING MY FINGERS OFF. / I FEEL SLOWLY** | -
(12"+=/cd-s+=) *(FAC 297 T/CD)* – More than enough (instrumental).

May 91. (lp/c/cd) *(FAC 285/+C/CD)* *<91754>* **GOBBLEDYGOOK** |
– Something's wrong somewhere / Pulling my fingers off / Half blind / Suckling / Removal / Gobbledygook / I want you and I want your friend / Soon is fine / Half pie / I feel lovely / The sun's going to shine for me soon.

Sep 91. (12"ep/cd-ep) *(FAC 337 T/CD)* **I INSTRUCT** | -
– Enjoy the things you fear / Newspaper cows / The pop song (live) / The sun's going to shine for me soon (live).

— disappeared from the scene as quick as they came into it

Paul WESTERBERG (see under ⇒ REPLACEMENTS)

David WESTLAKE (see under ⇒ SERVANTS)

WE'VE GOT A FUZZBOX AND WE'RE GONNA USE IT

Formed: Balsall Heath, Birmingham, England . . . 1985 by MAGGIE and JO DUNNE, TINA O'NEILL and VICKIE PERKS. A series of singles on the 'Vindaloo' label helped stamp the trademark FUZZBOX sound (although inspired by KLEENEX and DELTA 5) on the indie nation's consciousness; distorted guitars, frantic drums and girly chants made mini-classics of tracks such as 'XX SEX' and 'RULES AND REGULATIONS', occasional attacks of TONY BASIL-style vocal hiccuping thrown in for good measure. Following the Top 75 success of the 'ROCKIN' WITH RITA (HEAD TO TOE)' Various Artists VINDALOO SUMMER SPECIAL EP, the girls were launched into the heady world of major labeldom courtesy of 'WEA'. The fun-tastic 'LOVE IS THE SLUG' saw the band have a further brush with the charts while a debut album proper, 'BOSTIN' STEVE AUSTIN' (1987) was testament to girl power a full decade before The SPICE GIRLS were foisted upon an unsuspecting nation. By 1989 the group had cracked the Top 20 with the 'INTERNATIONAL RESCUE' single although the dayglo amateurism of old had given way to a cleaner sound and a more consumer-friendly image (they had taken to wearing 'Thunderbirds' clobber!). With their name now abbreviated to FUZZBOX, the gang released what was to be their final Top 5 album, 'BIG BANG!' (1989), many longtime fans lamenting the compromised sound on further hit singles such as 'PINK SUNSHINE' and 'SELF'. It came as little surprise, then, when, in summer 1990, PERKS departed for a solo career and the remaining trio elected to call it a day. • **Songwriters:** Group compositions except; SPIRIT IN THE SKY (Norman Greenbaum) / BOHEMIAN RHAPSODY (Queen) / WALKING ON THIN ICE (Yoko Ono) / TROUBLE (Elvis Presley).

Album rating: BOSTIN' STEVE AUSTIN (*6) / BIG BANG! (*5)

VICKY PERKS (b.9 Oct'68) – vocals / **JO DUNNE** (b.11 Nov'68) – bass, guitar, drums / **MAGS DUNNE** (b. 5 Jun'64) – vocals, percussion / **TINA O'NEILL** (b.20 Jan'69) – sax, drums

Vindaloo | not iss.

Mar 86. (7"ep) *(UGH 11)* **. . .FUZZBOX . . . EP** 41 | -
– X x sex / Do I want to? / Rules and regulations / She.
(12"ep blue or lilac+=) *(UGH 11T)* – Aaarrrggghhh!!!.

Oct 86. (7"/7"pic-d) *(UGH 14/+N)* **LOVE IS THE SLUG. / JUSTINE / SPIRIT IN THE SKY** 31 | -
(12"+=/12"pic-d+=/c-s+=) *(UGH 14 T/TN/C)* – Radio fuzz / Console me.

Vindaloo-WEA | Geffen

Dec 86. (lp/c) *(FBOX/+C 1)* *<24149>* **BOSTIN' STEVE AUSTIN** |
– Love is the slug / Wait and see / Jackie / Spirit in the sky / XX sex / Alive / What's the point / You got me / Hollow girl / Console me / Rules and regulations / Pre-conceptions.

Jan 87. (7") *(YZ 101)* **WHAT'S THE POINT. / FUZZY RAMBLINGS FEVER** 51 | -
(12"+=) *(YZ 101T)* – Bohemian rhapsody.

Feb 87. (7") **LOVE IS THE SLUG. / JUSTINE / CONSOLE ME** - |

WEA | Geffen

Feb 89. (7") *(YZ 347)* **INTERNATIONAL RESCUE. / RAINING CHAMPAGNE** 11 | -
(12"+=) *(YZ 347T)* – Barbarella.
(cd-s++=) *(YZ 347CD)* – Love is the slug.

May 89. (7"/7"box/c-s) *(YZ 401/+B/C)* **PINK SUNSHINE. / WHAT'S THE POINT** 14 -
(12"+=/cd-s+=) *(YZ 401 T/CD)* – ('A'extended) / Spirits in the sky.

Jul 89. (7"/c-s) *(YZ 408/+C)* *<21327>* **SELF! / WAIT AND SEE** 24
(12"+=/cd-s+=) *(YZ 408 T/CD)* – Bohemian rhapsody.

Aug 89. (lp/c)(cd) *(WX 282/+C)(248066-2)* *<24185>* **BIG BANG** 5
– Pink sunshine / Fast forward futurama / Jamaican sunrise / Walking on thin ice / Versatile for discos and parties / Do you know? / International rescue / Self! / Irish bride / Beauty.

Oct 89. (7"/c-s) *(YZ 435/+C)* **WALKING ON THIN ICE. / RULES AND REGULATIONS** -
(12"+=/cd-s+=) *(YZ 435 T/CD)* – ('A'-Fuzz dub mix).

May 90. (7"/c-s) *(YZ 486/+C)* **YOUR LOSS MY GAIN. / PINK SUNSHINE (acoustic)** -
(12"+=/cd-s+=) *(YZ 486 T/CD)* – ('A'version).

— disbanded in August '90. VICKY went solo and others were going to form another group, although this failed to materialise.

WHALE

Formed: Stockholm, Sweden . . . 1993 by former alternative comedian, HENRIK SCHEFFERT along with hip-hop producer, GORDON CYRUS and part-time actress/former punk, CIA BERG. Anthemic debut single, 'HOBO HUMPIN SLOBO BABE', was only intended as a one-off collaboration for 'East West', although WHALE landed a deal with 'Virgin' after its MTV/European success. A further two suitably salacious singles, 'PAY FOR ME' and 'I'LL DO YA' were also given heavy rotation on MTV and WHALE finally came within breathing distance of the Top 40 with mini-album, 'WE CARE' in mid-'95. On the back of this, they re-issued 'HOBO HUMPIN' and had an even bigger smash, especially in Britain, where it made No.15. Hip-hop thrash-punk with knee-trembling, sexual overtones, the WHALE sound was akin to an x-rated fusion of The BEASTIE BOYS and BJORK. After a gap of almost three years, the group (now minus CYRUS) returned in summer '98 with a single, 'FOUR BIG SPEAKERS', released as WHALE featuring BUS 75. A further two singles and an album, 'ALL DISCO DANCE MUST END IN BROKEN BONES' (1998) were all delivered in WHALE's uncompromising style but failed to generate the same fuss they'd been afforded last time round.

Album rating: WE CARE (*7) / ALL DISCO DANCE MUST END IN BROKEN BONES (*5)

HENRIK SCHEFFERT – instruments, etc / **GORDON CYRUS** – DJ, producer / **CIA BERG** – vocals, etc.

East West / Atlantic

Mar 94. (c-s) *(98281)* **HOBO HUMPIN' SLOBO BABE / EYE 242**
(12"+=/cd-s+=) *(98281)* – Lips. *(re-iss. Aug94; same)*

Hut / Virgin

May 95. (m-cd/m-c/m-lp) *(DGHUTM/HUTMMC/HUTMLP 24)* *<1793>* **PAY FOR ME**
– Pay for me / I think no / Darling Nikki / Buzzbox babe / Trying. *<US re-iss. Aug95; 38504>*

Hut / Feedback

Jul 95. (c-s) *(HUTC 51)* *<WH 125>* **I'LL DO YA / THE NOW THING** 53
(ext-12"+=/cd-s+=) *(HUT T/DG 51)* – Sexy MM.

Hut / Virgin

Jul 95. (cd/c/lp) *(CDHUT/HUTMC/HUTLP 25)* *<40560>* **WE CARE** 42
– Kickin' / That's where it's at / Pay for me / Eurodog / I'll do ya / Electricity / Hobo humpin' slobo babe / Tryzasnice / Happy in you / I miss me / Young, dumb & full of c*** / I'm cold / Born to raise hell.

Nov 95. (c-s) *(HUTC 64)* **HOBO HUMPIN' SLOBO BABE / YOU AND YOUR SISTER** 15 -
(cd-s+=) *(HUTCD 64)* – Singer star.
(cd-s) *(HUTDX 64)* – ('A'side) / ('A'-Doggy Style mix) / ('A'-Sniffin' plankton mix) / ('A'-Skorpio mix)

— CYRUS departed and was repl. by **JON** and two others

Hut / Imprint

Jun 98. (cd-s; WHALE featuring BUS 75) *(HUTCD 96)* **FOUR BIG SPEAKERS / 14 ROCK STREET / ANYWHERE BUT HERE** 69 -
(cd-s) *(HUTDX 96)* – ('A'side) / ('A'-Cut La Roc remix) / ('A'-U-ziq remix).

Aug 98. (cd-s) *(HUTCD 102)* **CRYING AT AIRPORTS / HEAVY STICK / SPITTING INDOORS** -
(12"/cd-s) *(HUT T/DX 102)* – ('A'mixes).

Aug 98. (cd) *(CDHUT 52)* *<110718>* **ALL DISCO DANCE MUST END IN BROKEN BONES**
– Crying at airports / Deliver the juice / Roadkill / Smoke / CTRL / Four big speakers / Go where you're feeling free / Into the strobe / Puma gym / You're no better than you feel / 2 cord song.

WHIPPED CREAM

Formed: Gothenburg, Sweden . . . 1989 by ELISABETH PUNZIS, JC (aka JORGEN CREMONESE), LARS ERIK GRIMELUND and JONAS SONESSON. Successfully proving that Scandinavia has more to offer than ABBA clones and Eurocheese, WHIPPED CREAM signed to 'M.N.W.' (in Sweden) and set about reinventing psychedelia Nordic style on their debut album, 'WHIPPED CREAM AND OTHER DELIGHTS' (1990). Although the band disputed the MY BLOODY VALENTINE comparisons, their swirling guitar atmospherics bore at least superficial similarities with the shoegazers while the bizarre dual vocals of ELISABETH and JC lent an exotic slant to proceedings. Critics fell over themselves to praise follow-up, 'TUNE IN THIS CENTURY' (1992), its eddying, churning inventiveness receiving almost universal plaudits, while the choice of Captain Beefheart's 'OBSERVATORY CREST' as a single release suggested the Swedes weren't exactly pandering to any notions of indie convention.

Album rating: WHIPPED CREAM & OTHER DELIGHTS (*6) / TUNE IN THE CENTURY (*7) / HORSEMOUNTAIN (*5)

JORGEN CREMONESE – vocals, guitars / **ELIZABETH PUNZIS** – vocals / **JONAS ONESSON** – bass / **LARS ERIK GRIMELUND** – drums

Snap / Chameleon

1990. (cd) *(SNAP 001)* *<61355>* **WHIPPED CREAM & OTHER DELIGHTS** 1993
– Explosion / Remember / Silver 1 / Let us try it out / Wishing / This time, next time / Theodora wine / I know you're mine / Whatever / Together. *(cd-iss. Jan94 +=; RESNAP 001)* – Come together / Explosion '93.

Sep 92. (cd) *(SNAP 003)* **TUNE IN THE CENTURY** -
– Yes / Tune in the century / Wait for a minute / Lay down beside / Give away / Sensational / Virtuosity / Observatory crest / Up the country / Come and find / Beyond the sun.

Jun 94. (cd-s) *(SNAPC 013)* **YOU AND I / . . . AND I HAVE THIS DREAM** -

Jul 94. (cd) *(SNAP 014)* **HORSEMOUNTAIN** -

— disbanded after above

WHIPPING BOY

Formed: Dublin, Ireland . . . late 80's by FERGHAL McKEE, PAUL PAGE, MYLES McDONNELL and COLM HASSETT. Beginning life as a covers band, WHIPPING BOY signed to Irish indie label, 'Liquid', at the turn of the decade and proceeded to release a single, 'FAVOURITE SISTER' and album, 'SUBMARINE' (1989). A couple of EP's, 'THE WHIPPING BOY' and 'I THINK I MISS YOU', followed on 'Cheree' in 1990/91, the band's growing infamy and cult acclaim leading to a major label deal with 'Columbia'; comparisons with compatriots CATHAL COUGHLAN/FATIMA MANSIONS were inevitable, not least insofar as McKEE had earned himself a well documented reputation for onstage erm, spontaneity. Musically, WHIPPING BOYS' brooding guitar sound encompassed echoes of MY BLOODY VALENTINE and JOY DIVISION, driven by a Celtic boldness, occasional squalls of Seattle-style grunge and a lyrical grit. All these ingredients helped make 'HEARTWORM' (1995) a worthy second album, its cause helped by lavish praise for singles 'TWINKLE', cracked love narrative, 'WE DON'T NEED NOBODY ELSE' and McKEE's vivid portrayal of a rough'n'ready upbringing, 'WHEN WE WERE YOUNG'. The latter was backed by a cover of Lou Reed's 'CAROLINE SAYS II', hardly a sterling choice to deflect accusations of lyrical misogyny from the Irish press. • **Note:** Not the same band from the US who released an lp in 1983, 'The Sound Of No Hands Clapping', and another band on 'Grand Theft Auto'.

Album rating: SUBMARINE (*5) / HEARTWORM (*6)

FERGHAL McKEE – vocals / **PAUL PAGE** – guitar / **MYLES McDONNELL** – bass, vocals / **COLM HASSETT** – drums

Liquid / not iss.

1989. (7") *(LQ 4)* **FAVOURITE SISTER. / SAFARI** - Ire

1989. (lp) *(LQ)* **SUBMARINE** - Ire

Cheree / not iss.

Aug 90. (12"ep) **WHIPPING BOY E.P.** -
– Sugar I swear / Switchblade smile / Valentine '69.

Feb 91. (7"ep) **I THINK I MISS YOU** -
– Daze / Highwayman / I think I miss you / She makes me ill.

Columbia / Sony

Jul 95. (7"/c-s) *(661371-7/-4)* **TWINKLE. / A NATURAL** -
(cd-s) *(661371-2)* – ('A'side) / Plaything / Favourite sister (live).

Oct 95. (cd/c/blue-lp) *(480281-2/-4/-0)* *<67486>* **HEARTWORM**
– Twinkle / When we were young / Tripped / The honeymoon is over / We don't need nobody else / Blinded / Personality / Users / Fiction / Morning rise.

Oct 95. (7"colrd/c-s) *(662220-7/-4)* **WE DON'T NEED NOBODY ELSE. / TWINKLE (acoustic)** 51 -
(cd-s) *(662220-2)* – ('A'side) / Disappointed / Here I am.

Jan 96. (7"red/c-s) *(662806-7/-4)* **WHEN WE WERE YOUNG. / AS THE DAY GOES** 46 -
(cd-s+=) *(662806-2)* – ('A'-Philo version) / Caroline says II.
(above Philo version, sampled PHIL LYNOTT; Thin Lizzy)

May 96. (7") *(663227-7)* **TWINKLE. / THE HONEYMOON IS OVER** 55 -
(cd-s+=) *(663227-2)* – Fiction / Tripped.
(cd-s) *(663227-5)* – ('A'side) / Blinded / Personality / Users.

James WHITE (& THE BLACKS)

(see under ⇒ CHANCE, James)

WHITEOUT

Formed: Greenock, Scotland . . . early 90's by ANDREW JONES and ERIC LINDSAY, along with PAUL CARROLL and STUART SMITH. Hailing squarely from the Bellshill/TEENAGE FANCLUB school of sugary harmonies and retro songwriting, WHITEOUT were nothing if not instantly recognisable as Scottish. Signed to 'Silvertone', the band released 'NOT TIME' as their debut single and, incredibly in retrospect, embarked on a co-headlining tour with OASIS. Further prestigious support slots and festival dates followed along with a further series of singles, 'STARRCLUB', 'DETROIT' and 'JACKIE'S

RACING'. The latter was their most successful release, displaying a healthy affection for 60's West Coast pop a la LOVIN' SPOONFUL and The MAMAS & THE PAPAS. B-side, 'SO CONFUSED', meanwhile, brought to mind the harmonies of 'American Beauty'-era GRATEFUL DEAD. Yet trawling the cobwebbed corridors of America's rock'n'roll hall of fame proved insufficient to elevate WHITEOUT beyond second division status, their debut album, 'BITE IT', released at the tail end of '95 to less than overwhelming reviews. When they were dropped by 'Silvertone', ERIC and PAUL (who had now taken over vocal duties from the departing ANDREW) found drummer MARK FAIRHURST, releasing an EP, 'KICKOUT', and album, 'BIG WOW' (1998) on their own 'YoYo' label. • **Note:** Nothing to do with early 90's Glasgow 4-piece, PERSPEX WHITEOUT.

Album rating: BITE IT (*4) / BIG WOW (*4)

ANDREW JONES – vocals / **ERIC LINDSAY** – guitar / **PAUL CARROLL** – bass / **STUART SMITH** – drums

		Silvertone	not iss.
Apr 94.	(7"/c-s) *(ORE/+C 64)* **STARRCLUB. /** (12"+=/cd-s+=) *(ORE T/CD 64)* –		-
Sep 94.	(7"/c-s) *(ORE/+C 66)* **DETROIT. /** (12"+=/cd-s+=) *(ORE T/CD 66)* –	73	-
Feb 95.	(7"/c-s) *(ORE/+C 68)* **JACKIE'S RACING. / COUSIN JANE** (12"+=/cd-s+=) *(ORE T/CD 68)* – So confused.	72	-
May 95.	(7"/c-s) *(ORE/+C 76)* **NO TIME. / GET ME THROUGH** (cd-s+=) *(ORECD 76)* –		-
Jun 95.	(cd/c/lp) *(ORE CD/C/LP 536)* **BITE IT**	71	-

— **ERIC + PAUL** took over vocal duties from the departing ANDREW

— **MARK FAIRHURST** – drums (a past member) repl. STUART

		YoYo	not iss.
Nov 97.	(cd-ep) *(YOCD 02)* **KICKOUT EP**		-
Jun 98.	(cd) *(YOLP 01)* **BIG WOW**		-

WHITE TOWN

Formed: As a vehicle for DIY singer/songwriter, JYOTI MISHIRA, born Derby, England. After a clutch of 45's (mainly for 'Parasol'), the chubby, bespectacled, one-time DJ was brought mysteriously to the attention of Radio One DJ, MARK RADCLIFFE, who playlisted his 'YOUR WOMAN' single early '97. Stylistically miles apart from fellow Asian acts like FUN-DA-METAL and ADF, JYOTI and his WHITE TOWN pseudonym were picked up by 'Chrysalis', his lo-fi bedroom classic going straight in at No.1 (Top 30 in America!). However, having had a metaphorical five minutes of fame, WHITE TOWN was left to stagnate in musical suburbia as the debut album, 'WOMEN IN TECHNOLOGY', was panned by the critics and hit the bargain bins almost immediately. Subsequent releases have suffered a similar fate, the man and his computer becoming a footnote in pop's cruel history.

Album rating: WOMEN IN TECHNOLOGY (*4)

JYOTI MISHIRA – vocals, etc.

		Lovely	not iss.
Nov 96.	(7") *(LOVELY 006)* **COLD AS HELL. /**		-
		Parasol	**not iss.**
Nov 96.	(7") *(PAR 004)* **ALL SHE SAID. /** (cd-s+=) **SOCIALISM, SEXISM AND SEXUALITY EP** *(PARCD 004)* –		-
Nov 96.	(7") *(PAR 016)* **BEWITCHED. /**		-
Nov 96.	(cd-ep) *(PARCD 021)* **ABORT, RETRY, FAIL EP** – Your woman / Give me some pain / Theme tune for a mid-afternoon game show / Theme for a late-night documentary about the dangers of drugs.		-
		Chrysalis	**Capitol**
Jan 97.	(12"/c-s) *(12/TC CHS 5052)* *<58638>* **YOUR WOMAN / GIVE ME SOME PAIN / ('A'-Fights 2000 mix)** (cd-s+=) *(CDCHS 5052)* – Theme for a mid-afternoon game show / Theme for late night documentary about drug abuse.	1	23 Mar97
Feb 97.	(cd/c) *(CD/TC CHR 6120)* *<56129>* **WOMEN IN TECHNOLOGY** – Undressed / Thursday night at the Blue Note / Week next June / Your woman / White town / Shape of love / Wanted / Function of the orgasm / Going nowhere somehow / Theme for an early evening sitcom / Death of my desire / Once I flew.		84 Apr97
May 97.	(c-s) *(TCCHS 5058)* **UNDRESSED / FAMOUS** (cd-s+=) *(CDCHSS 5058)* – One more day / Your woman. (cd-s) *(CDCHS 5058)* – ('A'mix) / Theme for an early morning romantic mini series / Theme for an early evening American sitcom.	57	-
		Parasol	**not iss.**
Aug 98.	(cd-s) *(PAR 030)* **ANOTHER LOVER /**		May99

WILCO (see under ⇒ UNCLE TUPELO)

WILD ANGELS (see under ⇒ JAZZATEERS)

WILD FLOWERS

Formed: Wolverhampton, Midlands, England . . . 1983 out of the ashes of ANOTHER DREAM by DAVE NEWTON, NEAL COOK and DAVE FISHER (DAVE ATHERTON and PETE WALDRON were also part of the band's first incarnation before MARK ALEXANDER replaced them). After a few early singles and an album, 'THE JOY OF IT ALL' (1984), their frontman NEWTON left to form The MIGHTY LEMON DROPS. With former member ATHERTON returning to the fold, the group signed through owners Craig Jennings and Jem Kemp to the Warwick based indie, 'Chapter 22' in 1985. With their US influenced trad rock sound, they found little favour in the UK indie scene, instead preferring to concentrate on breaking into the lucrative American market. A series of flop singles ensued before the release of a long awaited second set proper (1987's 'DUST' was a compilation), 'SOMEWHERE SOON' (1988). In the late 80's, they upped sticks and left for San Rafael and Burbank, California, the group being the first British act to sign for 'Slash', releasing 'TALES LIKE THESE' at the turn of the decade. However, although they had found a new drummer in SIMON ATKINS by this time, the WILD FLOWERS' recording career was clearly failing to blossom. Opting for a more sympathethic American audience and evolving into a heavy-metal act, The WILD FLOWERS re-surfaced in '97 with a new US-only album, 'BACKWOODS', a 17-track affair that included a cover ELO's 'Livin' Thing'.

Album rating: SOMETIME SOON (*6) / TALES LIKE THESE (*5) / BACKWOODS (*4)

NEAL COOK – vocals, guitar / **DAVE NEWTON** – guitar, vocals (ex-ACTIVE RESTRAINT) / **MARK ALEXANDER** – bass; repl. PETE WALDRON / **DAVE FISHER** – drums

		No Future	not iss.
Jan 84.	(7") *(FS 11)* **MELT LIKE ICE. /**		-
		Reflex	**not iss.**
Mar 84.	(7") *(RE 2)* **THINGS HAVE CHANGED (WHICH SHOULD HAVE STAYED THE SAME). / SECOND THOUGHT**		-
Jun 84.	(lp) *(LEX 2)* **THE JOY OF IT ALL**		-

— **DAVE ATHERTON** – guitar, keyboards returned to repl. NEWTON who formed MIGHTY LEMON DROPS

		Chapter 22	not iss.
Apr 86.	(7"m) *(CHAP 5)* **IT AIN'T SO EASY. / JOSEPH SAID / AT THE CAVE OF MY HEART**		-
Sep 86.	(7") *(CHAP 8)* **A KIND OF KINGDOM. / WHERE MY HEART LIES** (12"+=) *(12CHAP 8)* – Lonesome road.		-
Jun 87.	(7"promo) **NO SURPRISE. / DUST**	-	-
Aug 87.	(lp) *(CHAPLP 15)* **DUST** (compilation)		-
Feb 88.	(7") **(CHAP 24) BROKEN CHAINS. / KEEP ON RUNNING** (12"+=) *(12CHAP 24)* – Something to mention / Glory.		-
Apr 88.	(12"ep) *(12CHAP 29)* **TAKE ME FOR A RIDE / NO SURPRISE. / ('A'version) / DAWN PARADE**		-
May 88.	(lp) *(CHAPLP 25)* **SOMETIME SOON**		-

— **SIMON ATKINS** – drums; repl. FISHER

		London	Slash
Apr 90.	(cd/c/lp) *(828 192-2/-4/-1)* *<26133-2/-4/-1>* **TALES LIKE THESE** – Shakedown / This feeling's gone / Put the blame on me / No holy spirits / Tales like these / Green hotel / Someone's stolen (my dreams) / Love like fire / Fever tree / Hopes crash down. *(cd+=)* – Can't get enough / Await.		

— **COOK, ATHERTON, ATKINS** + bass player **BILL MORRIS**

— relocated to the West Coast and still toured until . . .

		not iss.	Surf
Jul 97.	(cd) *<2401>* **BACKWOODS** – Sideshow / Silently told / Nowhere / Midnight / Good reason / Road to ruin / One step / What happens now / Tattoo / Fall down easy / Livin' thing / Mescalin / Count ten / Getting away / Kings of nowhere / Your barricades / Cheap perfume.	-	

WILD SWANS

Formed: Liverpool, England . . . 1981 by two former TEARDROP EXPLODES members PAUL SIMPSON and GERARD QUINN, alongside JEREMY KELLY (drummer ALAN WILLIS was soon added). Being the last act to sign for Bill Drummond's soon-to-be-wound-up 'Zoo' records, The WILD SWANS only managed to release one 12" single, 'A REVOLUTIONARY SPIRIT', although they managed to assume minor cult status in the process. Obviously influenced by the fresh noises emanating from across the Northern border (i.e. the 'Postcard' label), The WILD SWANS attempted to initiate a parallel "Sound Of Young Mersey" movement. However, by mid '82, the band's dream had fragmented into two separate entities; KELLY and QUINN formed The LOTUS EATERS along with singer PETER COYLE, while SIMPSON found The CARE with the help of local veteran IAN BROUDIE and crew. In the summer of '83, the former outfit scored a soaraway, sunkissed Top 20 hit with 'FIRST PICTURE OF YOU', although SIMPSON and Co. struggled with their debut, 'MY BOYISH DAYS (DRINK TO ME)'. While ironically, The CARE had a Top 50 entry ('FLAMING SWORD') with a follow-up, The LOTUS EATERS failed to build on their early success, a series of singles and even an album, 'NO SENSE OF SIN' (1984), falling wide of the chart mark. The belated release of a (May '82) WILD SWANS John Peel session was sufficient to swing public opinion in favour of a bonafide reformation. The WILD SWANS Mk.II consisted of SIMPSON, KELLY and new bass player, JOSEPH FEARON, the trio signing a prestigious deal with Seymour Stein's 'Sire' label. For most fans, 'BRINGING HOME THE ASHES' (1988) was worth the wait, an impressive set of songs regrettably rendered outdated by dint of their once heralded trademark sound. Now without KELLY but with a feast of Merseyside talent, including IAN BROUDIE, IAN McNABB and CHRIS SHARROCK, the duo of SIMPSON and FEARON completed a WILD SWAN-song in the shape of 1990's 'SPACE FLOWER' set. FEARON later re-emerged with an original WILD SWAN, ALAN WILLIS under the banner of TOP, a pop-tastic baggy combo who managed to deliver a handful of singles and an album, 'EMOTIONAL LOTION' (1991).

Album rating: BRINGING HOME THE ASHES (*7) / SPACE FLOWER (*6) / Lotus Eaters: NO SENSE OF SIN (*5) / Top: EMOTIONAL LOTION (*5)

PAUL SIMPSON – vocals, keyboards (ex-TEARDROP EXPLODES) / **GERARD QUINN** – keyboards (ex-TEARDROP EXPLODES) / **JEREMY KELLY** – guitar (ex-SYSTEMS) / **ALAN WILLIS** – drums; guest **ALAN** – bass

Zoo / not iss.

Jan 82. (12") *(CAGE 009)* **A REVOLUTIONARY SPIRIT. / GOD FORBID** [ ] [-]

— guest **BAZ HUGHES** – bass; repl. ALAN (before they disbanded mid '82). ALAN WILLIS joined The ROOM and later PALE FOUNTAINS (then SHACK).

– compilation, etc. –

Nov 86. (12"ep/c-ep) *Strange Fruit; (SFPS/+C 006)* **THE PEEL SESSIONS** (1.5.82) [ ] [-]
– No bleeding / Enchanted / Thirst.

LOTUS EATERS

GERARD QUINN – keyboards / **JEREMY KELLY** – guitar / **PETER COYLE** – vocals

Sylvan-Arista / Arista

Jun 83. (7",7"pic-d/12") *(SYL/+12 1)* **THE FIRST PICTURE OF YOU. / THE LOTUS EATER** [15] [ ]
Sep 83. (7",7"pic-d/12") *(SYL/+12 2)* **YOU DON'T NEED SOMEONE NOW. / TWO VIRGINS TENDER** [53] [ ]
Mar 84. (7",7"pic-d/12") *(SYL/+12 3)* **SET ME APART. / MY HAPPY DREAM** [ ] [ ]
May 84. (lp/c) *(206/406 263)* **NO SENSE OF SIN** [ ] [ ]
– The first picture of you / Set me apart / German girl / Love still flows / Can you keep a secret / Too young / Out on your own / Put your torch on love / You fill me with need / Alone of all her six / When you look at the boys / Start of the search.
Jun 84. (7") *(SYL 4)* **OUT ON YOUR OWN. / ENDLESS** [ ] [ ]
(12"+=) *(SYL12 4)* – Endless (instrumental).
Feb 85. (7") *(SYL 5)* **IT HURTS. / THE EVIDENCE** [ ] [ ]
(12"+=) *(SYL12 5)* – It hurts – Prestissimo.

— Disbanded in 1985, after record company dropped them. COYLE went solo. In Jan'89, their hit was re-issued by 'Old Gold' (OG 9853); b-side other artist.

CARE

PAUL SIMPSON – vocals, keyboards / **IAN BROUDIE** – vocals, guitar (ex-BIG IN JAPAN, ex-SECRETS) / augmented by **PAUL SANGSTER** – bass / **TONY WHELAN** – drums

Arista / Arista

Jul 83. (7") *(KBIRD 1)* **MY BOYISH DAYS (DRINK TO ME). / AN EVENING IN THE RAIN** [ ] [ ]
(12"+=) *(KBIRD12 1)* – Sad day for England.
Oct 83. (7",7"pic-d) *(KBIRD 2)* **FLAMING SWORD. / MISERICORDE** [48] [ ]
(12"+=) *(KBIRD12 2)* – On the white cloud.
Mar 84. (7") *(KBIRD 3)* **WHATEVER POSSESSED YOU. / BESIDES** [ ] [ ]
(12"+=) *(KBIRD12 3)* – Besides 2.

— Disbanded later in '84, BROUDIE went into production and later formed The LIGHTNING SEEDS.

WILD SWANS

— were reformed by **SIMPSON + KELLY** plus **JOSEPH FEARON** – bass

Sire / Sire

Mar 88. (7") *(W 7973)* **YOUNG MANHOOD. / HOLY HOLY** [ ] [ ]
(12"+=) *(W 7973T)* – The world of milk and blood.
Apr 88. (lp/c/cd) *(925 697-1/-4/-2)* **BRINGING HOME THE ASHES** [ ] [ ]
– Young manhood / Bible dreams / Bitterness / Northern England / Arcangels / Whirlpool heart / Bringing home the ashes / The worst year of my life / Mythical beast / Nomad forever. *(re-dist.Sep88)*
Aug 88. (7") *(W 7765)* **BIBLE DREAMS. / 1982** [ ] [ ]
(12"+=) *(W 7765T)* – Pure evil.

— **SIMPSON + FEARON** added **CHRIS SHARROCK** – guitars, organ (ex-ICICLE WORKS) / **IAN BROUDIE** guitars, organ, producer (of LIGHTNING SEEDS) / **IAN McNABB** – guitars, vocals (ex-ICICLE WORKS)

Nov 90. (cd/c/lp) *(26154-2-4/-1)* **SPACE FLOWER** [ ] [ ]
– Melting blue delicious / Butterfly girl / Tangerine temple / Immaculate / Space flower / Chocolate bubblegum / I'm a lighthouse / Magic hotel / Vanilla melange / Sea of tranquility.

— disbanded again soon after above.

TOP

— were formed by **FEARON** plus the returning **WILLS** and singer **PAUL CAVANAGH** – vocals (ex-IT'S IMMATERIAL)

Island / Island

Oct 90. (12"ep) **SHE'S GOT ALL THE WORLD. / LIFE'S ONLY DREAMING / MAN CAN'T YOU SEE** [ ] [-]
Feb 91. (12") **CHINESE LOLLIPOPS. / TOP** [ ] [-]
Jun 91. (7") *(IS 496)* **NO.1 DOMINATOR. / AS FAR AS I CAN SEE** [67] [ ]
(12"+=/12"pic-d+=/cd-s+=) – Thousand miles away.
Jul 91. (cd/c/lp) *(CID/ICT/ILPS 9978)* **EMOTIONAL LOTION** [ ] [ ]
– No.1 dominator / Buzzin' / Soul magic / Hi baby hi / Goodnight / Feel good / Love by demand / Easy / As far as I can see / She's got all the world / Life's only dreaming / When the summer's gone. *(re-dist.Nov91; ILPSX 9978) (w/free one-sided-7")* – WHEN THE SUMMER'S GONE
Oct 91. (7") **BUZZIN'. / ODE TO LOVE (PART II)** [ ] [-]
(10"+=/12"+=/cd-s+=) – Ode to love / Ode to Marc.
Mar 92. (7") **EASY (LIVIN' ON CLOUD NINE). / CRAZY** [ ] [ ]
(12"+=) – When the summer's gone / Bad luck pt.1.
(10"+=/cd-s+=) – She's got all the world / Life's only dreaming.

Lemon / not iss.

May 93. (7") *(LEM 010)* **I WANT YOU. / THIS IS LOVE** [ ] [-]
(10"+=)(cd-s+=) *(10LEM 010)(LEMON 010CD)* – Space planet.

— dissolved after above

WILLARD GRANT CONSPIRACY

Formed: Boston, Massachusetts, USA ... 1996 out of The FLOWER TAMERS, initially as an informal weekly get together for various local musicians/songwriters. The group (ROBERT FISHER and Co.) eventually took on a more permanent nature for the recording of a self-financed debut album, '3 A.M. SUNDAY AT FORTUNE OTTO'S'. Following in the brooding shadow of such mood masters as NICK CAVE, TINDERSTICKS and The WALKABOUTS, WILLARD GRANT CONSPIRACY revel in detailing life's seedier side to a rootsy, downbeat musical backdrop incorporating such traditional instrumentation as mandolin, bouzouki, etc. Their self-styled 'swamp noir' sound was finally brought to a UK audience via 1998's 'FLYING LOW' on the influential 'Slow River' label. One of last year's finest alt-country releases, highlights included losers anthmem, 'EVENING MASS', a grim meditation on life's hardships also featured on the brilliant 'Uncut' magazine compilation, 'Sounds Of The New West'.

Album rating: FLYING LOW (*6)

ROBERT FISHER – vocals, guitar, etc / and others

Slow River / Slow River

Mar 98. (cd) <(SRRCD 35)> **FLYING LOW** [ ] [ ] Aug98
– The smile at the bottom of the ladder / Evening mass / August list / St.John Street / House is not a home (Palmdale, CA) / Bring the monster inside / No such thing as clean / It doesn't matter / Eephus pitch / Water / Split tender.

Rozz WILLIAMS (see under ⇒ CHRISTIAN DEATH)

Victoria WILLIAMS

Born: 23 Dec'59, Shreveport, Louisiana, USA. A veteran of the US music scene despite still being relatively unknown, this enigmatic singer-songwriter began playing professionally in the late 70's on the LA club circuit. The following decade saw WILLIAMS marry ex-PLIMSOUL man, PETER CASE, before finally signing with 'Geffen' after an earlier recording deal had come to zero. Released in 1987, the record was produced by ANTON FIER and STEPHEN SOLES while VAN DYKE PARKS handled the arrangements, a case of maverick talent nurturing new maverick talent as WILLIAMS showcased her bizarre squealing vocals, pithy, offbeat observations and quirky but enchanting worldview. While her brand of off-kilter folk-pop may have been too much of an acquired taste for the average alternative fan, WILLIAMS attracted an impressive fanclub of fellow artists and songwriters who admired her highly original approach. Moving from major label status back to the independent sector ('Mammoth' in the States, 'Rough Trade' in the UK) for 1990's 'SWING THE STATUE', she again received critical plaudits for what many observers tagged as her best album, co-produced by TOM WAITS and featuring the evocative brilliance of 'SUMMER OF DRUGS'. The latter track was subsequently covered by SOUL ASYLUM for the 1993 tribute album, 'Sweet Relief: A Benefit For Victoria Williams'; the singer had been diagnosed with Multiple Sclerosis the previous year and the album was an attempt to raise funds for her spiralling medical bills, the likes of LOU REED, MATTTHEW SWEET and The JAYHAWKS all pledging their support by interpreting their favourite songs from her back catalogue. WILLIAMS herself returned to the studio for 1994's 'LOOSE', another star-studded collection featuring covers of Sam Cooke's 'WHAT A WONDERFUL WORLD' and Spirit's 'NATURE'S WAY' alongside a duet with future husband, MARK OLSEN (ex-JAYHAWKS). She also duetted with VIC CHESNUTT on a track, 'GOD IS GOOD' for his 1996 tribute album, 'SWEET RELIEF', while her most recent studio set, 'MUSINGS OF A CREEK DIPPER', was written and recorded on the remote desert ranch she now shares with OLSEN.

Album rating: HAPPY COME HOME (*6) / SWING THE STATUE! (*8) / LOOSE (*7) / THIS MOMENT IN TORNADO (*6) / MUSINGS OF A CREEK DIPPER (*7)

VICTORIA WILLIAMS – vocals, piano / with a plethora of session people incl. CARLA BLEY + BERNIE WORRELL – keyboards / T-BONE BURNETT + JODY HARRIS + HUGH McCRACKEN – guitar / STEVE SWALLOW – bass / ANTON FIER – drums / PETER BLEGVAD, RALPH CARNEY, TONY MAIMONE, SYD STRAW

Blanco Y Negro / Geffen

Jun 87. (lp/c) *(BYN/+C 10)* <24140> **HAPPY COME HOME** [ ] [ ]
– Shoes / Frying pan / Merry-go-round / Happy / TC / I'll do his will / Big fish / Main road / Lights / Opalousas / Statue of a bum / Poetry / Animal world. *(cd-iss. Jan94 on 'Geffen'; GFLD 19239)*

— now with WILLIE ARON – guitar, organ / MICHAEL BLAIR – percussion, drums, etc / DON FALZARE – bass / DAVID WILLIAMS – vocals / PHIL SHENALE – keyboards / etc

Rough Trade / Mammoth

Apr 90. (lp/c/cd) *(R 140/+C/CD)* <MR 075> **SWING THE STATUE!** [ ] [ ]
– Why look at the moon / Boogieman / Clothesline / Tarbelly and Featherfoot / On time / Holy spirit / Summer of drugs / I can't cry hard enough / Wobbling / Vieux amis / Weeds / Lift him up. *(re-iss. May94 on 'Mammoth' cd/c; MR 075-2/-4)*

East West / Atlantic

Jan 95. (cd/c/lp) <(7567 92430-2/-4/-1)> **LOOSE** [ ] [ ] Oct94
– Century plant / You R loved / Harry went to Heaven / Crazy Mary / When we sing together / Polish these shoes / Love / What a wonderful world / Waterfall / Nature's

way / Sunshine country / Happy to have known pappy / My ally / Hitchhiker's smile / Get away / Psalms.

Feb 95. (7"/c-s) *(A 8266/+C)* **CRAZY MARY. / POLISH THESE SHOES** [ ] [-]
(cd-s+=) *(A 8266CD)* – ('A'mixes).

— In Aug'95, VICTORIA and SHAWN COLVIN were credited on JULIE MILLER's 'Myrrh' album, 'He Walks Through Walls'.

Jan 96. (cd) *<7567 92642-2>* **THIS MOMENT IN TORONTO WITH VICTORIA WILLIAMS AND THE LOOSE BAND** [ ] [ ] Nov95
– This moment / Graveyard / Harry went to Heaven / Waterfall / Polish these shoes / Hitchhikers smile / Crazy Mary / Summer of drugs / Imagination / Smoke gets in your eyes / Can't cry hard enough / Sunshine country / Love.

Mar 98. (cd) *<7567 83072-2>* **MUSINGS OF A CREEK DIPPER** [ ] [ ] Jan98
– Periwinkle sky / Rainmaker / Kashmir's corn / Train song (demise of the caboose) / The last word / Nature boy / Tree song (eucayptus lullabye) / Let it be so / Allergic boy / Hummingbird / Grandpa in the cornpatch / Blackbird's rise.

Marty WILLSON-PIPER (see under ⇒ CHURCH)

Phil WILSON (see under ⇒ JUNE BRIDES)

WIN (see under ⇒ FIRE ENGINES)

WINDBREAKERS

Formed: Mississippi, USA . . . 1981 by the songwriting duo of TIM LEE and BOBBY SUTLIFF. Another bunch of rootsy Power-poppers to ride out from the American deep south, the unfortunately monikered WINDBREAKERS released a couple of self-financed EP's before becoming one of the first indie acts to release an album for 'Homestead'. The record in question was 'TERMINAL'; issued in the summer of '85, one of its highlights was a collaborative cover of Television's 'GLORY' performed with Paisley underground posse, The RAIN PARADE. After a French-only LP for 'Closer', 1987 saw two albums of impressively varied melodic pop-rock, 'RUN' and 'A DIFFERENT SORT', the latter of which was recorded solely by TIM together with session players. However, the pair were back on song in 1989, releasing 'AT HOME WITH BOBBY & TIM', before finding drummer/producer MITCH EASTER for a final fling with the 'ELECTRIC LANDLADY' (1991). • **Covered:** GLORY (Television) / WALTZING MATILDA (Barber-Barber) / DON'T TAKE HER OUT OF MY WORLD (Katrina & The Waves) / THINGS WE NEVER SAY (Howard Wuefling).

Album rating: TERMINAL (*5) / RUN (*6) / A DIFFERENT SORT (*7) / AT HOME WITH BOBBY & TIM (*6) / ELECTRIC LANDLADY (*6)

BOBBY SUTLIFF – vocals, guitar / **TIM LEE** – vocals, guitar

not iss. — Big Monkey

1983. (7"ep) **MEET THE WINDBREAKERS EP** [-] [ ]
1983. (7"ep) **ANY MONKEY WITH A TYPEWRITER EP** [-] [ ]

Homestead — Homestead

Jun 85. (lp) *<HMS 005>* **TERMINAL** [ ] [ ]
– On and on / Changeless / Stupid idea / A girl and her bible / Can't go on this way / All that stuff / New red shoes / Again / Glory / From a distance / Running out of time.

Closer — not iss.

1985. (lp) *(CL 0029)* **DISCIPLES OF AGRICULTURE** [-] [-] French
– Rerun / Make a fool out of me / You never give up / I never thought / Ya gotta go away / I'll be there / New red shoes / That stupid idea / Again / All that stuff / Lonely beach.

Zippo — D.B.

Jan 87. (lp) *(ZONG 015)* *<DB 79>* **RUN** [ ] [ ]
– Don't wanna know / This time – She said / Visa cards and antique mirrors / Run / You don't know / Ghost town / I'll be back / Voices in my head / Braver on the telephone / Don't say no / Nation of two.

— next was virtually LEE on his own

Nov 87. (lp) *(ZONG 022)* *<DB 85>* **A DIFFERENT SORT** [ ] [ ]
– Knowing me / Fit in / You closed your eyes / Better left unsaid / So far away / A different sort / So much / We never understand / Forget again / Any longer.

— re-united once more **BOBBY + RAPHAEL SEMMES** – bass / **MARK WYATT** – keyboards / **BRUCE GOLDEN** – percussion / etc

1989. (lp,c,cd) *<DB 95>* **AT HOME WITH BOBBY & TIM** [-] [ ]

— **MITCH EASTER** – (now on) drums

1991. (cd,c,lp) *<DB 152>* **ELECTRIC LANDLADY** [-] [ ]
– Colorblind / Big ideas / Keep it on your mind / Elayne lies looking at the sky / Since I last saw you / Girl from Washington / The Devil and the sea / Wall / Do not be afraid / Tell me something / Forever ago / Walting Matilda / Rerun / Make a fool out of me / You never give up / I never thought / You gotta go away / I'll be there.

1991. (12"ep) **I'LL BE BACK EP** [-] [ ]
– I'll be back / Don't take her out of my world / Things we never say.

— disbanded after above

WINDY & CARL

Formed: Dearborn, Michigan, USA . . . 1991 by bassist WINDY WEBER and guitarist CARL HULTGREN. By the time the pair met, HULTGREN had already self-financed a space-fixated, instrumental demo, 'PORTAL', subsequently released in revamped form circa late 1995. In the meantime, WINDY & CARL made their official debut with the 'WATERSONG' single, again released on a self-financed label, 'Blue Flea'. Fleshing out their feedback-droning, cosmic ambient sound, the duo recruited guitarist/keysman RANDALL NIEMAN and percussionist BRENDA MARKOVICH, releasing the 'DRIFTING' EP in early '95 as ONCE DREAMT. Due to the departure of BRENDA and RANDALL (the latter forming FUXA), it would be a few years before the arrival of any fresh material, although fans were treated to a series of singles culminating with early '98's 'Kranky' album, 'DEPTHS'.

Album rating: PORTAL (*5) / DEPTHS (*5)

CARL HULTGREN – guitar / **WINDY WEBER** – bass, vocals

not iss. — Blue Flea

Dec 93. (cd-s) **WATERSONG** [-] [ ]

— added **RANDALL NIEMAN** – guitar, keyboards / **BRENDA MARKOVICH** – percussion

Feb 95. (cd-ep; as ONCE DREAMT) *<BLUEFLEA 05>* **DRIFTING EP** [-] [ ]
(c-ep iss.Apr96)

— now without MARKOVICH + NIEMAN (the latter formed FUXA)

not iss. — Ba Da Bing

Nov 95. (cd) *<BING 004>* **PORTAL** (early + new) [-] [ ]
– Preparation / Awhile / Ode to spaceman / Firebursts / Sound ignition / Approach – Descend / Exploration / Departure / Glowing – Colorful / Gravital loft / Through the portal. *(UK-iss.Nov97; same as US)*

Blue Flea — Blue Flea

Mar 97. (12") *<(BLUEFLEA 07R)>* **DRAWING OF SOUND** [ ] [ ]

Ochre — Ochre

Oct 97. (10") *<(OCH 17)>* **A DREAM OF BLUE** [ ] [ ] Jan99

Darla — Darla

Jan 98. (12"ep/cd-ep) *<(DRL 027/+CD)>* **ANTARTICA. / TRAVELING / SUNRISE** [ ] [ ]

Kranky — Kranky

Feb 98. (cd/d-lp) *<(KRANK 024 CD/LP)>* **DEPTHS** [ ] [ ] Mar98
– Sirens / Undercurrent / Set adrift / Depths / The silent ocean / Aquatica / Surfacing.

WIPERS

Formed: Portland, Oregon, USA . . . 1977 by GREG SAGE, DAVE KOUPAL and SAM HENRY. The former two had begun their musical career in late 60's rock outfit, BEAUREGARDE, named after a professional wrestler (who actually featured on the sleeve of their one and only eponymous album!). The WIPERS debuted in '78 with the EP, 'BETTER OFF DEAD', a full album, 'IS THIS REAL?', emerging at the turn of the decade, the blitzkreig 'D-7' later covered by NIRVANA (KURT COBAIN was only one of a number of alt-rock icons to cite The WIPERS as a seminal influence). After another EP, 'ALIEN BOY', some personnal changes took place, drummer HENRY making way for BRAD DAVIDSON and BRAD NAISH before the subsequent release of their second set, 'YOUTH OF AMERICA' (1982). Following the release of a Canadian-only lp, 'OVER THE EDGE' (1984), GREG signed to rising label 'Enigma' issuing a solo album, 'STRAIGHT AHEAD' (1986) in the process. The WIPERS returned to the fold (STEVE PLOUF replacing NAISH) with a fifth set, 'LAND OF THE LOST' (1986), a dirtier, metallic grunge sound which deserved a lot more success than it achieved. They continued ploughing a singular furrow to the end of the decade, remaining largely unsung until the advent of the Seattle grunge scene. SAGE subsequently went solo in the early '90's with the album 'SACRIFICE (FOR LOVE)', although the resulting surge in interest for all things WIPERS, led to a reformation in 1993. The 'SILVER SAIL' single (their first ever!) and an album of the same name appeared the following year, while 'Tim/Kerr' (the label) also issued another, 'THE HERD', in '96. • **Trivia:** May '94 saw the release of a tribute album, 'SONGS FOR GREG SAGE & THE WIPERS', boasting contributions from the likes of NIRVANA, HOLE, POISON IDEA, etc.

Album rating: IS THIS REAL? (*7) / YOUTH OF AMERICA mini (*6) / OVER THE EDGE (*8) / LAND OF THE LOST (*6) / FOLLOW BLIND (*6) / THE CIRCLE (*6) / SILVER SAIL (*6) / THE HERD (*6) / Greg Sage: STRAIGHT AHEAD (*6)

GREG SAGE – vocals, guitar / **DAVE KOUPAL** – bass / **SAM HENRY** – drums

not iss. — Trap

1978. (7"ep) *<810X44>* **BETTER OFF DEAD. / UP IN FLAMES / DOES IT HURT?** [-] [ ]

not iss. — Park Avenue

Feb 80. (lp) **IS THIS REAL?** [-] [ ]
– Return of the rat / Mystery / Up front / Let's go let's go away / Is this real? / Tragedy / Alien boy / D-7 / Potential suicide / Don't know what I am / Window shop for love / Wait a minute. *<re-iss. Apr84 on 'Psycho'; PSYCHO 22> (UK-iss.Mar87 on 'Weird Systems'; WS 024) (cd-iss. Mar93 on 'Sub Pop'+=; SPCD 82-253)* – ALIEN BOY EP

Aug 80. (7"ep) *<PA 10EP>* **ALIEN BOY** [-] [ ]
– Image of man / Telepathic love / Voices in the rain.

— **BRAD DAVIDSON** – bass + **BRAD NAISH** – drums repl. DAVE (on some) + SAM also departed

Feb 82. (m-lp) *<82802>* **YOUTH OF AMERICA** [-] [ ]
– Taking too long / Can this be / Pushing the extreme / When it's over / No fair / Youth of America. *<re-iss. Apr84 on 'Psycho'; PSYCHO 23> (cd-iss. Dec94 on 'Gift Of Life' lp/cd; GIFT 025/+CD)*

not iss. — Brain Eater

Nov 84. (lp) *<EATER 2>* **OVER THE EDGE** [-] [-] Canada
– Over the edge / Doom town / So young / Messenger / Romeo / Now is the time / What is / No one wants an alien / The lonely one / No generation gap / This time. *(re-iss. Mar87 on 'Enigma'; 2187-1) (UK-iss.Aug94 on 'Gift Of Life' lp/cd; GIFT 020/+CD)*

Enigma — Enigma

Jan 86. (lp; by GREG SAGE) *<2007-1>* **STRAIGHT AHEAD** [-] [ ]
– Straight ahead / Soul's tongue / Blue cowboy / Your empathy / The illusion fades / Seems so clear / On the run / Astro clouds / Lost in space / Let it go / World without fear / Keep on keepin' on. *(UK-iss.Aug94 on 'Gift Of Life' lp/cd; GIFT 022/+CD))*

Mar 86. (lp) *<(2026-1)>* **LIVE: WIPERS (live)** [ ] [ ]
(re-iss. Aug94 & Feb98 on 'Gift Of Life' lp/cd; GIFT 021/+CD)

— **STEVE PLOUF** – drums repl. NAISH

Nov 86. (lp/cd) *<2094-1/-2>* **LAND OF THE LOST**
– Just a dream away / Way of love / Let me know / Fair weather friends / Land of the lost / Nothing left to lose / The search / Different ways / Just say. *(cd re-iss. Aug94 & Feb98 on 'Gift Of Life'; GIFT 023CD)*

Dec 87. (lp) *<971194>* **FOLLOW BLIND** -
– Follow blind / Some place else / Any time you find / The chill remains / Let it slide / Against the wall / No doubt about it / Don't belong to you / Losers town / Coming down / Next time. *(UK-iss.Aug94 & Feb98 on 'Gift Of Life' lp/cd; GIFT 024/+CD)*

Enigma Restless

Dec 88. (lp/c/cd) *(ENVLP/TCENV/CDENV 516) <72339>* **THE CIRCLE**
– I want a way / Time marches on / All the same / True believer / Good thing / Make or break / The circle / Goodbye again / Be there / Blue & red.

Feb 90. (cd/c) *<72378-2/-4>* **BEST OF WIPERS & GREG SAGE** (compilation) -
– Nothing left to lose / The way of love / Some place else / The chill remains / Soul's tongue / Blue cowboy / Taking too long / The circle / Romeo / Messenger / Better off dead / No solution / My vengeance / Just a dream away / Different ways / Losers town.

Roadrunner Restless

Oct 91. (cd; by GREG SAGE) *(LS 9237-2) <772539-2>* **SACRIFICE (FOR LOVE)**
– Stay by me / Sacrifice (for love) / Know by now / Forever (with BOBBY WOMACK) / The same guitar / No turning back / Ready or not / For your love / This planet Earth / Dreams. *(cd re-iss. Jul95 on 'Restess'; same as US)*

— the WIPERS line-up still:- **SAGE / DAVIDSON / KOUPAL**

Tim/Kerr Gift Of Life

Jun 94. (7"/cd-s) **SILVER SAIL. /**

Jun 94. (cd/lp) *<(TK 92 CD/12 031)>* **SILVER SAIL**
– Y I came / Back to the basics / Warning / Mars / Prisoner / Standing there / Sign of the times / Line / On a roll / Never win / Silver sail. *(re-iss. Nov94 on 'Gift Of Life' lp/cd; GIFT 036/+CD)*

Apr 96. (cd) *<(TK 95CD 114)>* **THE HERD** Feb96
– Psychic vampire / No place safe / Last chance / Wind the clock slowly / The herd / Stormy / Green light region / Sinking as a stone / Sunrise / Defiant / Resist / Insane. *(re-iss. Jul97; same)*

Apr 96. (cd-s) *<TK 116>* **INSANE /** -

WIRE

Formed: London, England . . . October '76, by GRAHAM LEWIS, COLIN NEWMAN, BRUCE GILBERT and ROBERT GOTOBED. WIRE made their vinyl debut in April '77 when safety pin-pierced ears were subjected to their punk anthems, '12XU' and 'LOWDOWN' on the seminal Various Artists lp, 'Live At The Roxy'. The EMI backed label 'Harvest', desperate for some hip punk credibility, decided to give WIRE a contract and although unsuccessful with their first single attempt ('MANNEQUIN'), unleashed the Mike Thorne-produced 'PINK FLAG' at the end of '77. The record contained 21 short, sharp shocks of minimalist punk rock/new wave, possessed of a musical intelligence that dwarfed their more retro-fixated contemporaries. Early in 1978, they followed this with the classic 'I AM THE FLY', lyrically a simple piece of what can only be described as progressive punk. After another fruitless stab at the charts with 'DOT DASH', they returned with an even more engaging second set, the oblique, atmospheric 'CHAIRS MISSING'. This record surely deserved better than its Top 50 placing, featuring as it did the classy avant-punk tunes, 'PRACTICE MAKES PERFECT', 'I FEEL MYSTERIOUS TODAY' and the "minor" hit 45, 'OUTDOOR MINER'. In the Autumn of '79, WIRE's third set, '154' hit the Top 40, effectively displaying an even more experimental side to the one-time three-chord wonders. Sadly, however, it was their final outing for 'Harvest', the group moving on to the more appropriate indie label, 'Rough Trade', who released the 1981 single, 'OUR SWIMMER'. An anti-commercial, unproduced live set appeared around the same time, the band members having already taken off for solo projects. One of these, DOME (aka GILBERT & LEWIS), had been in the pipeline for some time, while NEWMAN went onto indie success with several albums. In 1986, the much-in-demand WIRE returned, completing a few EP's for top indie, 'Mute' before the following year's 'THE IDEAL COPY' album. They continued to enjoy cult success, which even spread across the Atlantic, the band signing to US label, 'Enigma'. In 1991, GOTOBED retired (to Bedfordshire, no doubt?!) and the band became WIR, releasing the disappointing 'THE FIRST LETTER' that year. For the remainder of the 90's, each took on individual projects, all fairly obscure of course. • **Songwriters:** Group compositions. • **Trivia:** COLIN NEWMAN produced The VIRGIN PRUNES in 1982 and FAD GADGET in 1984. He moved to India at this time, returning after a few years to live in Belgium, where he founded 'Crammed Discs' records.

Album rating: PINK FLAG (*8) / CHAIRS MISSING (*9) / 154 (*7) / ON RETURNING (*8) / THE IDEAL COPY (*8) / Colin Newman: NOT TO (*6)

COLIN NEWMAN (b.16 Sep'54, Salisbury, England) – vox, guitar, keyboards / **BRUCE GILBERT** (b.18 May'46, Watford, England) – guitar, vocals, synths. / **GRAHAM LEWIS** (b.22 Feb'53, Grantham, England) – bass, vocals, synthesizers / **ROBERT GOTOBED** (b. MARK FIELD, 1951, Leicester, England) – drums, percussion (ex-SNAKES, ex-ART ATTACKS) / **GEORGE GILL** – guitar (left before debut)

Harvest Harvest

Nov 77. (7"m) *(HAR 5144)* **MANNEQUIN. / 12XU / FEELING CALLED LOVE**

Nov 77. (lp/c) *(SHSP/TC-SHSP 4076) <11757>* **PINK FLAG** -
– Reuters / Field day for the Sundays / Three girl rhumba / Ex-lion tamer / Lowdown / Start to move / Brazil / It's so obvious / Surgeon's girl / Pink flag / The commercial / Straight line / 106 beats that / Mr. Suit / Strange / Fragile / Mannequin / Different to me / Champs / Feeling called love / 12XU. *(cd-iss. 1990 on 'Restless'+=; 72360)* – Options R. *(re-iss. cd Aug94 on 'E.M.I.'; CDGO 2063) <cd-iss. 1995 on 'Capitol'; 29857-2>*

Feb 78. (7") *(HAR 5151)* **I AM THE FLY. / EX-LION TAMER** -

Jun 78. (7") *(HAR 5161)* **DOT DASH. / OPTIONS R** -

Sep 78. (lp/c) *(<SHSP/TC-SHSP 4093>)* **CHAIRS MISSING** 48
– Practice makes perfect / French film blurred / Another the letter / Men 2nd / Marooned / Sand in my joints / Being sucked in again / Heartbeat / Mercy / Outdoor miner / I am the fly / I feel mysterious today / From the nursery / Used to / Too late. *(cd-iss. 1990 on 'Restless'+=; 72361)* – Go ahead / A question of degree / Former airline. *(re-iss. cd Aug94 on 'E.M.I.'; CDGO 2065) <cd-iss. 1995 on 'Capitol'; 29858-2>*

Jan 79. (7",7"white) *(HAR 5172)* **OUTDOOR MINER. / PRACTICE MAKES PERFECT** 51 -

Harvest Warners

Jun 79. (7") *(HAR 5187)* **A QUESTION OF DEGREE. / FORMER AIRLINE** -

Sep 79. (lp/c) *(SHSP/TC-SHSP 4105) <3398>* **154** 39
– I should have known better / Two people in a room / The 15th / The other window / Single k.o. / A touching display / On returning / A mutual friend / Blessed state / Once is enough / Map reference 41°N, 93°W / Indirect enquiries / 40 versions. *(free-7"ep w.a) (Dome; PSR 444)* – Song 2 / Get down (parts 1 & 2) / Let's panic / Later / Small electric piece. *(cd-iss. 1990 on 'Restless'+= 72362)* – (7"ep above). *(re-iss. cd Aug94 on 'E.M.I.'; CDGO 2064) <cd-iss. 1995 on 'Capitol'; 39859>*

Oct 79. (7") *(HAR 5192)* **MAP REFERENCE 41°N 93°W. / GO AHEAD** -

— In 1980, WIRE also diversed into own activities; GILBERT & LEWIS became CUPOL and DOME, etc. The pair also joined THE THE. COLIN NEWMAN went solo taking ROBERT GOTOBED with him. The latter also became member of FAD GADGET. (see further on for these activities)

Rough Trade not iss.

May 81. (7") *(RT 079)* **OUR SWIMMER. / MIDNIGHT BAHNHOF CAFE** -

Jul 81. (lp) *(ROUGH 29)* **DOCUMENT AND EYEWITNESS: ELECTRIC BALLROOM (live)** -
– 5 10 / 12XU (fragment) / Underwater experiences / Zegk hoqp / Everything's going to be nice / Instrumental (thrown bottle) / Piano tuner (keep strumming those guitars) / And then . . . / We meet under tables / Revealing trade secrets / Eels sang lino / Eastern standard / Coda. *(free 12"m-lp)* **DOCUMENT AND EYEWITNESS: NOTRE DAME HALL (live) –** Underwater experiences / Go ahead / Ally in exile / Relationship / Our swimmer / Witness to the fact / 2 people in a room / Heartbeat. *(re-iss. 1984 lp/c; same/ COPY 004) (cd-iss. Apr91 on 'Grey Area-Mute'; WIRE 80CD)*

Mar 83. (12"m) *(RTT 123)* **CRAZY ABOUT LOVE. / SECOND LENGTH (OUR SWIMMER) / CATAPULT 30** -

— WIRE were now back to full-time membership.

Mute Enigma

Nov 86. (12"ep) *(12MUTE 53) <72245>* **SNAKEDRILL**
– A serious of snakes / Advantage in height / Up to the sun / Drill.

Mar 87. (7") *(MUTE 57)* **AHEAD. / FEED ME (live)** -
(12"+=) *(12MUTE 57)* – Ambulance chasers (live) / Vivid riot of red (live).

Apr 87. (cd/c/lp) *(CD/C+/STUMM 42) <273270>* **THE IDEAL COPY** 87
– Points of collapse / Ahead / Madman's honey / Feed me / Ambitious / Cheeking tongues / Still shows / Over theirs. *(cd+=)* – Ahead II / SNAKEDRILL EP tracks.

Mar 88. (7") *(MUTE 67)* **KIDNEY BONGOS. / PIETA**
(3"cd-s+=) *(CDMUTE 67)* – Drill (live).
(12"++=) *(12MUTE 67)* – Over theirs (live).

May 88. (cd/c/lp) *(CD/C+/STUMM 54) <73314-1>* **A BELL IS A CUP . . . UNTIL IT IS STRUCK**
– Silk skin paws / The finest drops / The queen of Ur and the king of Um / Free falling divisions / It's a boy / Boiling boy / Kidney bongos / Come back in two halves / Follow the locust / A public place. *(cd+=)* – The queen of Ur and the king of Um (alternate take) / Pieta / Over theirs (live) / Drill (live).

Jun 88. (7") *(MUTE 84)* **SILK SKIN PAWS. / GERMAN SHEPHERDS**
(12"+=) *(12MUTE 84)* – Ambitious (remix).
(3"cd-s+=) *(CDMUTE 84)* – Come back in two halves.

Apr 89. (7"clear; withdrawn) *(MUTE 87)* **EARDRUM BUZZ. / THE OFFER** 68
(12"+=) *(12MUTE 87)* – It's a boy (instrumental).
(cd-s) *(CDMUTE 87)* – ('A'side) / Silk skin paws / A serious of snakes / Ahead (extended).
(live-12") *(LMUTE 87)* – BUZZ BUZZ BUZZ – Eardrum buzz / Ahead / Kidney bongos.

Mute Mute

May 89. (cd/c/lp) *(CD/C+/STUMM 66) <73516-2>* **IT'S BEGINNING TO AND BACK AGAIN (live)**
– Finest drops / Eardrum buzz / German shepherds / Public place / It's a boy / Illuminated / Boiling boy / Over theirs / Eardrum buzz (12"version) / The offer / In vivo.

Jul 89. (7") *(MUTE 98)* **IN VIVO. / ILLUMINATED**
(12"+=/cd-s+=) *(12/CD MUTE 98)* – Finest drops (live).

May 90. (7"; w-drawn) *(MUTE 107)* **LIFE IN THE MANSCAPE. / GRAVITY WORSHIP** -
(12"+=/cd-s+=) *(12/CD MUTE 107)* – Who has wine.

May 90. (cd/c/lp) *(CD/C+/STUMM 80) <73559-2>* **MANSCAPE**
– Patterns of behaviour / Goodbye ploy / Morning bell / Small black reptile / Torch it / Other moments / Sixth sense / What do you see? / Where's the deputation? / You hung your lights in the trees – A craftman's touch. *<US cd+=>* – Life in the manscape / Stampede / Children of groceries.

Apr 91. (cd/c/lp) *(CD/C+/STUMM 74)* **DRILL**
– (7 versions of out-takes from last album)

WIR

Slightly different name when GOTOBED left.

Sep 91. (7") **SO AND SLOW IT GOES. / NICE FROM HERE**
(12") – ('A'side) / ('A'-Orb mix) / Take it (for greedy)
(cd-s+=) – (all 4 tracks).

Oct 91. (cd/c/lp) *(CD/C+/STUMM 87) <61238>* **THE FIRST LETTER**

– Take it (for greedy) / So and slow it goes (extended) / A bargain at 3 and 20 yeah! / Rootsi-rootsy / Ticking mouth / It continues / Looking at me (stop!) / Naked, whooping and such-like / Tailor made / No cows on the ice / A big glue canal.

– compilations, others, etc. –

Mar 86. (m-lp) *Pink; (PINKY 7)* **PLAY POP** ☐ -
Aug 86. (lp) *Dojo; (DOJOLP 36)* **IN THE PINK (live)** ☐ -
Nov 87. (12"ep) *Strange Fruit; (SFPS 041)* **THE PEEL SESSIONS** (18.1.78) ☐ -
– I am the fly / Culture vultures / Practice makes perfect / 106 beats that.
Jul 89. (cd)(c/lp) *Harvest; (CDP 792 535-2)(TC+/SHSP 4127) / Restless; <72358-1>* **ON RETURNING (1977-1979)** ☐ ☐
– 12XU / It's so obvious / Mr. Suit / Three girl rhumba / Ex lion tamer / Lowdown / Strange / Reuters / Feeling called love / I am the fly / Practise makes perfect / French film blurred / I feel mysterious today / Marooned / Sand in my joints / Outdoor miner / A question of degree / I should have known better / The other window / 40 versions / A touching display / On returning. *(cd+=)* – Straight line / 106 beats that / Field day for the Sundays / Champs / Dot dash / Another the letter / Men 2nd / Two people in a room / Blessed state.
Feb 90. (cd/c/lp) *Strange Fruit; (SFR CD/MC/LP 108)* **DOUBLE PEEL SESSIONS** ☐ -
(cd re-iss. May96; same)
May 93. (cd/c/d-lp) *Mute; (CD/C+/STUMM 116)* **1985-1990 THE A LIST** ☐ -
Sep 94. (cd; w/book) *Audioglobe; (SCONC 25)* **EXPLODING VIEWS** ☐ -
May 95. (cd) *E.M.I.; (CDGO 2066)* **BEHIND THE CURTAIN** ☐ -
Dec 95. (12"; WIRE with HAFLER TRIO) *Touch; (TONE 5)* **THE FIRST LETTER / THE LAST LAST NUMBER** ☐ -
May 96. (cd) *W.M.O.; (WMO 004CD)* **TURNS AND STROKES** ☐ -
– Safe / Lorries / Panamanian craze / Remove for improvement / Spare one / Over my head / 12XU / Inventory / Ritual view / Part of our history / Second length (our swimmer) / Catapult 30.
(d-lp-iss.Apr97; same)
Oct 97. (cd) *W.M.O.; (WMO 014CD) / World Domination; <67>* **COATINGS** ☐ ☐
– Ambulance chasers / Series of snakes / Ambitious / Madman's honey / Kidney bongos / It's a boy / German shepherds / Boling boy / Drill / In vivo / Who has nine? / It can't be true can it? / Gravity worship. *(w/ free cd-s)* – AMBITIOUS

COLIN NEWMAN

(solo playing most instruments) **with ROBERT GOTOBED** – drums / **DESMOND SIMMONDS** – bass, guitar / **BRUCE GILBERT** – guitar / **MIKE THORNE** – keyboards

Beggars Banquet / not iss.

Oct 80. (lp) *(BEGA 20)* **A-Z** ☐ -
– I waited for ages / And jury / Alone / Order for order / Image / Life on deck / Troisieme / S-S-S-Star eyes / Seconds to last / Inventory / But no / B. *(re-iss. Sep88 on 'Beggars Banquet-Lowdown' lp/c/cd; (BBL/+C 20/+CD)*
Nov 80. (7"m) *(BEG 48)* **B. / CLASSIC REMAINS / ALONE ON PIANO** ☐ -
Mar 81. (7") *(BEG 52)* **INVENTORY. / THIS PICTURE** ☐ -

—— **COLIN** played everything.

4.a.d. / not iss.

Aug 81. (lp) *(CAD 108)* **PROVISIONALLY TITLED THE SINGING FISH** ☐ -
– Fish 1 / Fish 2 / Fish 3 / Fish 4 / Fish 5 / Fish 6 / Fish 7 / Fish 8 / Fish 9 / Fish 10. *(d-cd-iss. Jan88 +=; CAD 108)* – NOT TO (lp tracks) / Not to (remix) / You and your dog / The grace you know / H.C.T.F.R. / No doubt.

—— added **DES SIMMONDS + SIMON GILHAM** – bass, vocals

Jan 82. (lp) *(CAD 201)* **NOT TO** ☐ -
– Lorries / Don't bring reminders / You me and happy / We meet under tables / Safe / Truculent yet / 5'10 / 1, 2, 3, beep beep / Not to / Indians / Remove for improvement / Blue Jay way.
May 82. (7") *(AD 209)* **WE MEANS WE STARTS. / NOT TO (remix)** ☐ -

Crammed Discs / not iss.

Sep 86. (lp) *(CRAM 045)* **COMMERCIAL SUICIDE** ☐ -
– Their terrain / 2-sixes / Metakest / But I . . . / Commercial suicide / I'm still here / Feigned hearing / Can I explain the delay / I can hear you . . .
Oct 86. (7") *(CRAM 1345-7)* **FEIGNED HEARING. / I CAN'T HEAR YOU . . .** ☐ -
Aug 87. (12") *(CRAM 051)* **INTERVIEW. / INTERVIEW** ☐ -
May 88. (7") *(CRAM 1745-7)* **BETTER LATE THAN NEVER. / AT LAST** ☐ -
May 88. (lp/c/cd) *(CRAM 058/+C/CD)* **IT SEEMS** ☐ -
– Quite unrehearsed / Can't help being / The rite of life / An impressive beginning / It seems / Better late than never / Not being in Warsaw / At rest / Convolutions / Round and round. *(w/ free label 'Various Artists' lp)*

Swim / not iss.

May 95. (12") **VOICE. /** ☐ -

CUPOL

GILBERT & LEWIS under many guises (not initially chronological)

4.a.d. / not iss.

Jul 80. (12"ep) *(BAD 9)* **LIKE THIS FOR AGES. / KLUBA CUPOL** (20min@'33rpm) ☐ -

GILBERT & LEWIS

4 a.d. / not iss.

Nov 80. (m-lp) *(CAD 16)* **3R4** ☐ -
– Barge calm / 3,4 / Barge calm / R.
Aug 81. (7") *(AD 106)* **ENDS WITH THE SEA. / HUNG UP TO DRY WHILE BUILDING AN ARCH** ☐ -

—— In May88, a cd-compilation '8 TIME' was issued by duo on '4 a.d.'; *CAD 16CD)*

DOME

Dome / not iss.

Aug 80. (lp) *(DOME 1)* **DOME 1** ☐ -
– Cancel your order / Cruel when complete / And then . . . / Here we go / Rolling upon my day / Say again / Lina sixup / Airmail / Ampnoise / Madmen. *(free-7")* – SO. / DROP
Feb 81. (lp) *(DOME 2)* **DOME 2** ☐ -
– The red tent 1 + 2 / Long lost life / Breathless / Reading Prof. B / Ritual view / Twist up / Keep it.
Oct 81. (lp) *(DOME 3)* **DOME 3** ☐ -
– Jasz / Ar-gu / An-an-an-d-d-d / Ba-dr / D-o-bo / Na-drm / Dasz / Ur-ur / Danse / Roor-an.
(above with also **RUSSELL MILLS** – percussion / **DANIEL MILLER** – saxophone / **E.C.RADCLIFFE** – guitar / **PETER PRINCE** – drums)

—— (1 & 2 and 3 & 4 were re-issued on 2 cd's for 'Grey Area-Mute' Aug92; *DOME 12CD & DOME 34CD)*

GILBERT, LEWIS & MILLS

Cherry Red / not iss.

May 82. (lp) *(BRED 27)* **MZUI (WATERLOO GALLERY)** ☐ -
– Mzui (part 1) / Mzui (part 2).

W.M.O. / not iss.

Dec 95. (cd) **PACIFIC / SPECIFIC** ☐ -

P'O

Court / not iss.

Jan 83. (lp) *(COURT 1)* **WHILST CLIMBING THIEVES VIE FOR ATTENTION** ☐ -

DUET EMMO

—— **GILBERT & LEWIS** augmented by **DANIEL MILLER** (label boss)

Mute / not iss.

Aug 83. (7") *(MUTE 25)* **OR SO IT SEEMS. / HEART OF HEARTS (OR SO IT SEEMS)** ☐ -
Aug 83. (lp) *(STUMM 11)* **OR SO IT SEEMS** ☐ -
– Hill of men / Or so it seems / Friano / The first person / A.N.C. / Long sledge / Gatemmo / Last's card / Heart of hearts. *(cd-iss. Aug92 on 'Grey Area-Mute'; CDSTUMM 11)*

BRUCE GILBERT

Dome / not iss.

Apr 83. (lp) **TO SPEAK** ☐ -
– To speak / To walk, to run / To duck, to dive / This / Seven year / Atlas. *(iss.Sep84 as 'WILL YOU SPEAK THIS WORD?' on 'Uniton'; U 011)*

Mute / Mute

Sep 84. (m-lp) *(STUMM 18)* **THIS WAY** ☐ -
– Work for do you me / I did / Here visit. *(cd-iss. with next; CDSTUMM 18)*
Mar 87. (lp) *(STUMM 39)* **THE SHIVERING MAN** ☐ -
– Angel food / The shivering man / Not in the feather / There are / Hommage / Eline Court li / Epitaph for Henran Brenlar.
1990. (cd/c) *<71432-2/-4>* **THIS WAY TO THE SHIVERING MAN** - ☐
Jan 91. (cd/lp) *(CD+/STUMM 71) <61030>* **INSIDING (2 excerpts from 'SAVAGE WATER')** ☐ ☐
– Bloodlines (ballet) / Insiding.
Aug 91. (cd/lp) *(CD+/STUMM 91) <61197>* **MUSIC FOR FRUIT** ☐ ☐
– Music for fruit / Push / You might be called.
Oct 95. (7") **BI YO YO. /** ☐ -
(above single on 'Sub Pop')
Mar 96. (cd) *(<CDSTUMM 117>)* **AB OVO** ☐ ☐
May 96. (cd; by GILBERT – HAMPSON – KENDALL) *<1>* **ORR** - ☐
(above issued on the 'Parallel' series)
Dec 97. (cd) *<69050>* **IN ESSE** - ☐
– Soli / Psycho / Eclectic / Extraction.

Sahko / not iss.

Dec 98. (12"; by BRUCE GILBERT & RON WEST) *(efa 620966)* **FREQUENCY VARIATION. /** ☐ -

HE SAID

(aka **GRAHAM LEWIS** solo) aug. by **JOHN FRYER** – drum prog

Mute / Mute

Oct 85. (7"/12") *(7/12 MUTE 41)* **ONLY ONE I. / ONLY ONE I** ☐ -
Apr 86. (7") *(7MUTE 43)* **PUMP. / PUMP (instrumental)** ☐ -
(12"+=) *(12MUTE 43)* – To and fro.
Aug 86. (7") *(7MUTE 48)* **PULLING 3 G's. / PALE FEET** ☐ -
(12"+=) *(12MUTE 48)* – ('A'&'B'extended versions).

—— added **BRUCE GILBERT** – guitar / **NIGEL H. KIND** – guitar / **E.C. RADCLIFFE** – prog. / **ANGELA CONWAY** – backing vocals / **ENO** (guested on 1)

Oct 86. (cd/c/lp) *(CD/C+/STUMM 29)* **HAIL** ☐ -
– Kidnap yourself / Only one I / Pump / I fall in your arms / Do you mean that? / Flagwearing / Shades to escape / Pale feet.
Nov 88. (7"/12") *(MUTE/12MUTE 73)* **COULD YOU?. / HE SAID . . . SHE SAID** ☐ -
Feb 89. (cd/c/lp) *(CD/C+/STUMM 57) <75400>* **TAKE CARE** ☐ -
– Could you? / ABC Dicks love / Watch-take-care / Tongue ties / Not a soul / Halfway house / Get out of that rain / Hole in the sky.

WISEBLOOD (see under ⇒ FOETUS)

WISDOM OF HARRY
(see under ⇒ WEATHER PROPHETS)

WISHPLANTS

Formed: Higham Ferrers, Northampton, England . . . early 90's by ED GILMOUR, PAUL SIMPSON (aka WOLFIE) and JAMES FITZGERALD (aka FRITZ), the line-up completed by SAUL DENTON in Spring '92. Driven to rock'n'roll by small town inertia, The WISHPLANTS enjoyed a brief stint as indie press darlings tipped to follow in the befraggled footsteps of The WONDER STUFF, MEGA CITY FOUR, SENSELESS THINGS etc. Sufficiently impressing WONDER STUFF mainman, MILES HUNT, at their debut London gig, the band netted a support slot with the 'STUFF and soon earned a reputation as an electric live act, dreadlocked frontman SAUL drawing comparisons with charismatic JANE'S ADDICTION genius, PERRY FARRELL. Musically, The WISHPLANTS' alternative "big rock" sound was likened with everything from SONIC YOUTH to BIG COUNTRY (!), 'China' records eventually securing the band's signatures for a debut EP, 'CIRCUS RAIN'. Released in early '93, the record was followed up with a second EP, 'TORTOISESHELL' and full length debut album, 'COMA', later that year. A full-scale UK tour and a series of festival appearances helped maintain the band's profile but a subsequent break of three years didn't exactly realise their lofty ambitions. When 'DADDY LONGLEGS' finally appeared in 1996, the music press had long ago moved on and, ironically, the band seemed something of an anachronism amid the retro-fever of Brit-pop.

Album rating: COMA (*6) / DADDY LONGLEGS (*5)

SAUL STRATFORD – vocals / **ED GILMOUR** – guitar / **PAUL 'WOLFIE' SIMPSON** – bass / **JAMES FITZGERALD** – drums

China — Offbeat

Feb 93. (cd-ep) *(WOKCD 2031)* **CIRCUS RAIN EP** ☐ -

Jul 93. (12"ep/cd-ep) *(WOK T/CD 2035)* **TORTOISESHELL EP** ☐ -

Oct 93. (lp/c/cd) *(<WOL/+MC/CD 1033>)* **COMA** ☐ ☐ Feb95
– Tortoise shell / Lucky me / Over here / Maze / Circus rain / Sepia / Captain Marvel / Reason / Blind / Coma / Move around / Misery.

Mar 94. (c-s) *(WOKMC 2043)* **LUCKY ME /** ☐ ☐
(12"+=/cd-s+=) *(WOK X/CD 2043)* –

Jul 96. (cd) *(WOLCD 1070)* **DADDY LONGLEGS** ☐ ☐

Jah WOBBLE

Born: JOHN WORDLE, 1961, London, England. Having learned to play on SID VICIOUS's bass, he was subsequently invited by JOHN LYDON (the artist formerly known as JOHNNY ROTTEN) to join PUBLIC IMAGE LTD early in 1978. WOBBLE's contributions to albums 'PUBLIC IMAGE' and the excellent 'METAL BOX 1' were a little understated at the time, probably due to LYDON's full-dental attacks. One lasting impression of the bassman's memorable TV appearances was undoubtedly his gap-toothed wide grin on Top Of The Pops' while plucking along to their Top 20 hit 'Death Disco'. JAH's sudden departure in 1980 was due to LYDON's annoyance at his use of PIL rhythm tracks on his awful punk/dub debut, 'THE LEGEND LIVES ON'. Subsequently flying out to Germany, he cut the 'FULL CIRCLE' album with CAN members, HOLGER CZUKAY and JAKI LIEBEZEIT, while in 1983, he was the main thrust behind another collaboration, 'SNAKE CHARMER', with CZUKAY and THE EDGE (of U2). In the mid-80's, WOBBLE was forced to endure the trials of a "real" job when he worked for the London Underground (mind the gap!). Sporadic releases also paid the bills, although it wasn't until 1991's comeback set, 'RISING ABOVE BEDLAM' (which introduced vocalist, NATACHA ATLAS of Transglobal Underground) that WOBBLE became a fully-fledged musician once more. The bassman and his ever-expanding INVADERS OF THE HEART even hit the Top 40 with the beautiful 'VISIONS OF YOU' single featuring vocals by SINEAD O'CONNOR. With WOBBLE's spiritual leanings now looming large over proceedings, 1994's 'TAKE ME TO GOD' album hit the Top 20 following a rapturous appearance at Glastonbury Festival. An accompanying single, 'THE SUN DOES RISE', featured DOLORES O'RIORDAN of The CRANBERRIES, a sublime track which surely should've given him a massive hit. WOBBLE subsequently went on to work with the great BRIAN ENO on Derek Jarman's home film project, 'SPANNERS', more recently the man finding his true vocation as a knowledgable guest on Sunday morning religious TV shows. • **Trivia:** In 1992 he appeared on 12"ers by ONE DOVE and SECRET KNOWLEDGE FEATURING WONDER. Guested on albums by ORB, PRIMAL SCREAM, SINEAD O'CONNOR, JOOLZ, HOLGER CZUKAY, DODGY, SHAMEN, GINGER BAKER + IAN McNABB.

Album rating: INVADERS OF THE HEART (*6) / RISING ABOVE BEDLAM (*8) / TAKE ME TO GOD (*9)

JAH WOBBLE – bass, vocals

Virgin — Caroline

Oct 78. (7"/12") *(VOLE/12VOLE 9)* **DREADLOCK DON'T DEAL IN WEDLOCK. / PTHILIUS PUBIS** ☐ -

Feb 79. (7"/12" by; DON LETTS & JAH WOBBLE) *(VS 239/+12)* **STEEL LEG: STRATETIME & THE WIDE MAN. / ELECTRIC DREAD: HAILE UNLIKELY** ☐ -

Oct 79. (7"ep/12"ep; as DAN McARTHUR) *(VS 275/+12)* **DAN McARTHUR** ☐ -

—— added **MARTIN ATKINS** – drums / **SNOWY WHITE** – vocals

Apr 80. (7"/12") *(VS 337/+12)* **BETRAYAL. / Mr.X: BATTLE OF BRITAIN** ☐ -

May 80. (lp) *(V 2158)* *<CAROL 1669>* **THE LEGEND LIVES ON . . . JAH WOBBLE IN BETRAYAL** ☐ ☐
– Betrayal / Beat the drum for me / Blueberry Hill / Today is the first day of the. . . ? / Not another / Tales from Outer Space / Dan McArthur / Pineapple. *(re-iss. 1988; OVED 205) (cd-iss. 1989 & Mar94 +=; CDV 2158)* – Blueberry hill (computer version) / I need you by my side / Message from Pluto / Seaside special / Something profound / Dreadlock don't deal in wedlock / Mr.X: Battle of Britain.

Jul 80. (12"ep) *(VS 361-12)* **V.I.E.P.** ☐ -
– Blueberry Hill / etc.

Island — not iss.

Jul 81. (12"ep; by JAH WOBBLE, JAKI LIEBEZEIT & HOLGER CZUKAY) *(WIP 6701)* **HOW MUCH ARE THEY? / WHERE'S THE MONEY? / TRENCH WARFARE / TWILIGHT WORLD** ☐ -
(re-iss. May88 on 'Licensed'; LD 8816)

Jah Wobble — not iss.

May 82. (7") *(JAH 1)* **FADING. / NOCTURNAL** ☐ -

Oct 82. (12" by; JAH WOBBLE with ANIMAL) *(JAH 2)* **LONG LONG AWAY. / ROMANY** ☐ -

Virgin — not iss.

Jan 83. (lp) *(none)* **FULL CIRCLE** ☐ -
– (tracks as above +=) / Full circle R.P.S. (No.7) / Mystery R.P.S. (No.8). *(cd-iss. May92; CDOVD 437)*

—— In 1982, formed BARTOK with RAT SCABIES – drums (ex-DAMNED) / SIMON WERBER + JOHN GRANT (both ex-STRAPS). Released 7" on 'On-U-Sound' in Oct82; INSANITY. / I AM THE BOMB.

—— Next with **ANIMAL** – guitar (of MOTORHEAD) / **OLLIE MARLAND** – keyboards / **ANNIE WHITEHEAD** – trombone

Lago — not iss.

May 83. (m-lp) *(LAGO 3)* **JAH WOBBLE'S BEDROOM ALBUM – INVADERS OF THE HEART** ☐ -
– City / Fading / Long long way / Sense of history / Hill in Korea / Journey to death / Invaders of the heart / Sunshine / Concentration camp / Desert song / Heart of the jungle.

Jun 83. (12"ep) *(LAGO 4)* **INVADERS OF THE HEART EP** ☐ -

—— next w / **THE EDGE** – guitar (of U2) / **HOLGER CZUKAY** – percussion, etc (ex-CAN) / **LIEBEZEIT** – (ex-CAN) / **BEN MENDELSON** – (ex-MAGAZINE) / **OLLIE MARTLAND** – keyboards / **JIM WALKER** – drums (ex-PUBLIC IMAGE LTD) / **FRANCOIS KEVORKIAN** – electric drums

Island — Island

Oct 83. (7") *(WOB 1)* **SNAKE CHARMER. / HOLD ON TO YOUR DREAMS** ☐ -

Oct 83. (m-lp/c; by JAH WOBBLE THE EDGE HOLGER CZUKAY) *(IMA/IMC 1)* **SNAKE CHARMER** ☐ -
– Snake charmer / Hold on to your dreams / It was a camel / Sleazy / Snake charmer – reprise.

JAH WOBBLE & OLLIE MARLAND

with sessions **ANIMAL** – guitar / **B.J. COLE** – steel / **HARRY BECKETT** – timpani / **NEVILLE MURRAY** – percussion / **GENERAL SMUTLEY** – drums

Lago — not iss.

Sep 84. (12") *(LAGO 5)* **VOODOO. / EAST** ☐ -

Island — not iss.

Apr 85. (7"/12") *(IS/12IS 9828)* **LOVE MYSTERY. / LOVE MYSTERY (instrumental)** ☐ -

May 85. (lp/c) *(ILPS/ICT 9828)* **NEON MOON** ☐ -
– Love mystery / Love mystery (instrumental) / Running away / Neon Moon / Life on the line / Life on the line (dub) / The beat inside / Despite.

JAH WOBBLE

Lago — not iss.

Nov 85. (12") *(LAGO 6)* **BLOW OUT. / BLOW OUT (instrumental)** ☐ -

May 86. (12" by; JAH WOBBLE with BRETT DICKENS) *(G 2001)* **BETWEEN TWO FREQUENCIES. / 6020** ☐ -
(above issued on 'General Kinetics')

Oct 86. (lp; by JAH WOBBLE & OLLIE MARLAND) *(LAGO 7)* **TRADEWINDS** ☐ -

Wobble — not iss.

Sep 87. (lp) *(WOB 7)* **PSALMS** ☐ -
(re-iss. Aug94 on 'Southern' cd/lp; 18522-2/-1)

Sep 87. (12"ep) *(WOB 8)* **ISLAND PARADISE / ALCOHOL. / JIHAD / ('A'remix)** ☐ -

JAH WOBBLE'S INVADERS OF THE HEART

—— w / **JUSTIN ADAMS** – guitar (ex-sessions FRANK CHICKENS) / **MICK SCHOOTS** – drums / **DAVID HARROW** – keyboards, etc / **NATASHA** – vocals (a Spanish/Belgian belly dancer) of TRANSGLOBAL UNDERGROUND

KK — not iss.

Nov 89. (lp/cd) *(KKUK 001/+CD)* **WITHOUT JUDGEMENT** - - Belgium
– Bungalow park / What the problem is / Anything can happen / A13 / The drowned and the saved / So many years / Message from our sponsor / Coypu / Burger var / What will you say / Spirit / Voodoo / Psyche / Good ghosts / Saracen / Eternal vendor / Invisible cities / Inferno / Location / Uncommercial road / Will the circle be unbroken? *(imported into UK Jun93; same) <US 1994 on 'Restless'; 72750>*

Boys Own — not iss.

Oct 90. (7"/cd-s) *(BOI/+CD 2)* **BOMBA (Miles away mix). / ('A'live)** ☐ -
(12") *(BOIX 2)* – ('A'-Nonsonicus Maximus mix) / ('A'live).

—— Late 1990, he also splintered in MAX with ANDY ROURKE (ex-SMITHS) on 'ZTT'.

Oval-East West — Atlantic

Oct 91. (cd/c/lp) *(9031 75470-2/-4/-1)* *<82386>* **RISING ABOVE BEDLAM** ☐ ☐

– Visions of you / Relight the flame / Bomba / Ungodly kingdom / Rising above bedlam / Erzulie / Everyman's an island / Soledad / Sweet divinity / Wonderful world.

Nov 91. (7") *(OVAL 102)* **ERZULIE. / REMIND ME TO BE NICE TO MYSELF** [ ] [-]
(12"+=/cd-s+=) *(OVAL 102 T/CD)* – ('A'extended dependent mix).

—— Below 'A' + next 'B'-side featured **SINEAD O'CONNOR** – vocals

Jan 92. (7") *(OVAL 103)* **VISIONS OF YOU. / ('A'-Ade phases the parameters of sound mix)** [35] [-]
(12"+=/cd-s+=) *(OVAL 103 T/CD)* – ('A'-Secret love child of Hank & Johnny mix) / ('A'-Pick'n'mix 1 & 2).

Sep 92. (7"ep/12"ep/cd-ep) *(OVAL 107/+T/CD)* **THE UNGODLY KINGDOM EP** [ ] [-]
– Ungodly kingdom (Transformed mix) / Saeta / Josey Walsh / Love life.

—— next with **JUSTIN ADAMS** – guitars, vocals / **MARK FERDA** – guitars, mandolin / **NEVILLE MURRAY** – percussion / **ANNELI DRECKER** (of Norwegian band BEL CANTO) or **XIMENA TADSON** or **ABDEL ALI SLIMANI** or **GAVIN FRIDAY** (ex-VIRGIN PRUNES) or **ANDREA OLIVER** (ex-RIP, RIG & PANIC) or **NAJMA AKHTAR** – vocals / **KRIS NEEDS** – dub (of SECRET KNOWLEDGE) / **JAKI LIEBEZEIT** or **JOHN REYNOLDS** – drums / etc.

Island Polygram

Apr 94. (7") *(IS 571)* **BECOMING MORE LIKE GOD. / WINE, WOMEN AND SONG** [36] [-]
(c-s+=) *(CIS 571)* – Football.
(12"+–) *(12IS 571)* ('A' Secret Knowledge To Hell & Back mix).
(cd-s++=) *(CID 571)* – (all 4 tracks).

May 94. (cd/c/d-lp) *(CID/ICT/ILPSD 8017)* <524000> **TAKE ME TO GOD** [13] [ ]
– God in the beginning / Becoming more like God / Whisky priests / I'm an Algerian / Amor / Amor dub / Take me to God / The Sun does rise / When the storm comes / I love everybody / Yoga of the nightclub / I am the music / The bonds of love / Angels / No change is sexy / Raga / Forever.

—— below featured **DOLORES O'RIORDAN** (of CRANBERRIES)

Jun 94. (c-s/7") *(C+/IS 587)* **THE SUN DOES RISE. / YALILI YA AINI / RAGA** [41] [-]
(12"+=/cd-s+=) *(12IS/CID 587)* – Om namah shiva (tranformation).
(cd-s) *(CIDX 587)* – ('A'side) / A13 / Snake charmer (reprise) / So many years.

Oct 94. (c-s/cd-s) *(CIS/CIDX 602)* **AMOR / ('A'mix)** [ ] [-]
(12"+=) *(12IS 602)* – ('A'-Rockas jungle remix).
(cd-s++=) *(CID 602)* – Sahara.
(cd-s) – (4-'A'mixes).

JAH WOBBLE

Nov 95. (cd/c/d-lp) *(CID/ICT/ILPSD 8044)* <531650> **HEAVEN AND EARTH** [ ] [ ]
– Heaven and Earth / A love song / Dying over Europe / Divine mother / Gone to Croatan / Hit me / Om namah shiva.

—— Had also just collaborated with BRIAN ENO (who hasn't!) on Top 75 album 'SPANNER' on below label; *AS/+C/CD 023)*

All Saints Thirsty Ear

Sep 96. (lp/c/cd) *(AS/+C/CD 029)* <66629> **PRESENTS THE INSPIRATION OF WILLIAM BLAKE** [ ] [ ]
– Songs of innocence / Lonely London / Bananas / Tyger tyger / Holy Thursday / Breathing out the world / Swallow in the world / Kings of Asia / Swallow in the world (reprise) / Bob and Harry / Angel / Gateway / Auguires of innocence.

30 Hertz 30 Hertz

Jun 97. (cd; as JAH WOBBLE'S INVADERS OF THE HEART) *(<30HZCD 001>)* **THE CELTIC POETS** [ ] [ ] Nov98
– Dunes / The man I knew / Market rasen / Thames / Gone in the wind / Saturn / Bagpipe music / Third Heaven / Star of the east / London rain.

Jul 97. (cd) *(<30HZCD 002>)* **REQUIEM** [ ] [ ]
– Requiem I / Requiem II / Requiem III / Father / Mother.

Oct 97. (cd) *(<30HZCD 003>)* **THE LIGHT PROGRAMME** [ ] [ ]
– Veneer / One in 7 / Night / Appearance and thing-it-itself / Nice cop: nasty cop / Magical thought / Maieusia / 15 dohs / Tranquilliser.

Nov 97. (cd-s) *(30HZCD 004)* **MAGICAL THOUGHT (mixes) / 15 DOHS** [ ] [-]

Jun 98. (cd) *(<30HZCD 005>)* **UMBRA SUMUS** [ ] [ ]
– Il jevedro il oblanco / Mehemda jaika bubage / Paternal kindness / Moon slowbeat (part 1) / Moon slowbeat (part 2) / Just a prayer / St. Mary-le-bow / I offer you everything / Organ meditation / Compound / Chela / Umbra sumus (part 1) / Umbra sumus (part 2) / 4 basses an organ jaki and a train / Mount Zion / Limehouse cut.

Jun 98. (cd-s) *(30HZCD 006)* **I OFFER YOU EVERYTHING / IL JEVEDRO IL OBLANCO / TRAIN** [ ] [-]

Jul 98. (cd-s) *(30HZCD 007)* **MOUNT ZION / MOUNT ZION (dance mix) / MOUNT ZION (edited live version)** [ ] [-]

WOLFGANG PRESS

Formed: London, England ... 1980 as REMA REMA by MICK ALEN, MARC COX, GARY ASQUITH and MARCO PIRRONI. Signing to Ivo's '4 a.d.' imprint, they issued a solitary EP before changing their name to MASS and releasing a further single, 'YOU AND I' and album, 'LABOUR OF LOVE' (1981). Subsequently opting for the more complex moniker, WOLFGANG PRESS, COX was by this time the sole survivor, injecting new blood in the shape of ANDREW GRAY and MICHAEL ALLEN. While the name The WOLFGANG PRESS may mean zero to many indie fans, no one could accuse the band of not paying their dues; boasting the longest track record of any '4 a.d.' outfit, this oddball trio have served more than a decade and a half with the label. During that time they've experimented with the whole gamut of popular music styles, beginning life as an angst-ridden avant-garde terrorist proposition with 'THE BURDEN OF MULES' (1983) album before going on to record a series of more adventurous EP's over the next two years, namely 'SCARECROW', 'WATER' and 'SWEATBOX'. A long awaited follow-up album, 'STANDING UP STRAIGHT', finally appeared in 1986, signalling to their growing fanbase that musical compromise wasn't on the agenda. Yet following tentative steps towards a more soulful, CAN meets ROXY MUSIC sound on 'BIRD WOOD CAGE' (1988) – which contained their classic homage to Kennedy & Onassis, 'KANSAS' – The WOLFGANG PRESS embraced the possibilities of the dance scene with 1991's acclaimed 'QUEER' album. Released at the height of indie-dance crossover mania, the album (which featured a cover of Randy Newman's 'MAMA TOLD ME NOT TO COME') nevertheless remained aloof from the pack, ALLEN's semi-detached vocals lending an almost PET SHOP BOYS feel to tracks like 'DARK SIDE OF THE MOON'-sampling 'TIME'. Apparently inspired by hearing DE LA SOUL's classic 'Three Feet High And Rising', the band's move towards a more groovy sound was confirmed with 1995's 'FUNKY LITTLE DEMONS'.
• **Trivia:** ELIZABETH FRASER of The COCTEAU TWINS and MARTIN McCARRICK of MARC ALMOND's WILLING SINNERS guested on the album 'STANDING UP STRAIGHT'.

Album rating: THE LEGENDARY WOLFGANG PRESS ... (*6) / BIRD WOOD CAGE (*7) / QUEER (*6) / FUNKY LITTLE DEMONS (*6)

REMA REMA

MICK ALLEN – vocals, bass (ex-MODELS) / **MARK COX** – keyboards / **GARY ASQUITH** – guitar, vocals / **MARCO PIRRONI** – guitar, vocals (ex-MODELS) / MAX (aka DOROTHY) – drums (ex-B-SIDES)

4 a.d. not iss.

Apr 80. (12"ep) *(BAD 5)* **WHEEL IN THE ROSES** [ ] [-]
– Feedback song / Rema Rema / Fond affections / Instrumental.

—— Had already disbanded Autumn 1979. MARCO joined ADAM & THE ANTS, etc. MAX reverted to real name DOROTHY, and became a solo artist.

MASS

were formed by **MICK, MARK + GARY / + DANNY BRIOTTET** – drums

4 a.d. not iss.

Nov 80. (7") *(AD 14)* **YOU AND I. / CABBAGE** [ ] [-]
May 81. (lp) *(CAD 107)* **LABOUR OF LOVE** [ ] [-]

—— Broke-up after GARY and DANNY left to later become RENEGADE SOUNDWAVE.

WOLFGANG PRESS

were formed by **MICK + MARK / ANDREW GRAY** – guitar

4 a.d. not iss.

Jul 83. (lp) *(CAD 308)* **THE BURDEN OF MULES** [ ] [-]
– Lisa (the passion) / Prostitute I / The burden of mules / Complete and utter / Prostitute II / Slow as a child / Journalists / Give it back / On the hill.

Aug 84. (12"ep) *(BAD 409)* **SCARECROW** [ ] [-]
– Ecstasy / Deserve / Respect.

Mar 85. (12"ep) *(BAD 502)* **WATER** [ ] [-]
– Tremble (my girl doesn't) / My way / The deep Briny / Fire eater.

Aug 85. (12"ep) *(BAD 506)* **SWEATBOX/ MUTED./ HEART OF STONE/ I'M COMING HOME (MAMA)** [ ] [-]

Nov 85. (lp) *(CAD 514)* **THE LEGENDARY WOLFGANG PRESS AND OTHER TALL STORIES** [ ] [-]
– Ecstasy / Deserve / Respect / Tremble (my girl doesn't) / My way / Fire eater / Sweatbox / Heart of stone / I'm coming home (mama). *(cd-iss. Feb87 +=; CAD 514CD)* – THE BURDEN OF MULES (tracks +) / The deep Briny / Muted. *(cd re-iss. Jul98; GAD 514CD)*

—— added guests **MARTIN McCARRICK** – cello / **ELIZABETH FRASER** – vocals

Jul 86. (lp) *(CAD 606)* **STANDING UP STRAIGHT** [ ] [-]
– My life / Hammer the halo / I am the crime / Rotten fodder / Dig a hole / Bless my brother / Fire-fly / Forty days, thirty nights. *(cd-iss. Feb87; CAD 606CD) (cd re-iss. Jul98; GAD 606CD)*

Apr 87. (7"ep/c-ep) *(BAD/+C 702)* **BIG SEX / THE WEDDING. / THE GREAT LEVELLER / THAT HEAT / GOD'S NUMBER** [ ] [-]

Aug 88. (12"ep/cd-ep) *(BAD 804/+CD)* **KING OF SOUL (crowded mix). / KOS (version) / KOS (7"mix)** [ ] [-]

Nov 88. (lp/c)(cd) *(CAD/+C 810)(CAD 810CD)* **BIRD WOOD CAGE** [ ] [-]
– King of soul / Raintime / Bottom drawer / Kansas / Swing like a baby / See my wife / The holy man / Hang on me / Shut that door. *(cd+=)* – BIG SEX EP. *(cd re-iss. Jul98; GAD 810CD)*

Jan 89. (7"ep/12"ep) *(BAD/+12 902)* **ASSASSINATION K – KANSEROUS / KANSAS. / SCRATCH / TWISTER** [ ] [-]

May 89. (12"ep) *(BAD 907)* **RAINTIME (remix). / BOTTOM DRAWER (remix)/ SLOWTIME** [ ] [-]
(cd-ep+=) *(BAD 907CD)* – Longtime ('A'version) / Assassination K – Kanserous.

Apr 91. (12"ep/cd-ep) **TIME. / TIMELESS / DARK TIME** [ ] [-]

May 91. (7") *(AD 1007)* **MAMA TOLD ME NOT TO COME. / ('A'version)** [ ] [-]
(12"/cd-s) *(BAD 1007CD)* – ('A'club mixes; Bad Boy / Inside Out).

Aug 91. (cd)(lp/c) *(CAD 1011CD)(CAD/+C 1011)* **QUEER** [ ] [-]
– Birmingham / Mama told me not to come / Heaven's gate / Riders on the heart / Question of time / Louis XIV / Fakes and liars / Honey tree / The birdy song / Dreams and light / Sucker – Mother Valentine – Sucker / Mamen. *(cd re-iss. Jul98; GAD 1011CD)*

May 92. (7") *(AD 2006)* **A GIRL LIKE YOU. / ANGEL** [ ] [-]
(12"+=/cd-s+=) *(BAD 2006/+CD)* – ('A'-1000 times mix) / ('A'-Born to be kissed mix).

Jan 95. (7") *(AD 5001)* **GOING SOUTH. / GOING SOUTH (country style)** [ ] [-]
(cd-s+=) *(BAD 5001CD)* – Going south (440 mix) / Chains (Wobble mix).
(12") *(BAD 5001)* – Going south (440 mix) / 11 years (Sabres main mix 2) / Christianity (Sherwood mix).

Jan 95. (cd)(lp/c) *(CAD 4016CD)(CAD/+C 4016)* **FUNKY LITTLE DEMONS** [75] [-]

– Going south / 11 years / Blood satisfaction / Chains / Christianity / Derek the confessor / So long dead / Executioner / She's so soft / New glass / Fallen not broken / People say. *(cd w/free cd)* – (remixes by BARRY ADAMSON, ADRIAN SHERWOOD, MICHAEL BROOK & SABRES OF PARADISE). *(cd re-iss. Jul98; GAD 4016CD)*

WOLFHOUNDS

Formed: Romford, Essex, England . . . 1985 out of The CHANGELINGS by DAVID CALLAHAN, PAUL CLARK, ANDY GOULDING, ANDY BOLTON and FRANK STEBBING. Initially signed to the 'Pink' label, The WOLFHOUNDS made an immediate impact with the 'CUT THE CAKE' EP in 1986. It's impressive diversity was enough to secure the band a slot on the famed NME C86 compilation which they filled with the infectious, upbeat archetypal guitar-pop of 'FEELING SO STRANGE AGAIN'. A series of singles, 'THE ANTI-MIDAS TOUCH', 'CRUELTY' and 'ME', ushered in a mediocre debut album, 'UNSEEN RIPPLES FROM A PEBBLE' (1987), while the subsequent replacement of BOLTON and CLARK – with DAVID OLIVER and MATTHEW DEIGHTON respectively – coincided with a move to a denser sound. Previewed on the singles, 'SON OF NOTHING', 'RENT ACT' and anti-consumerist diatribe, 'HAPPY SHOPPER', the new approach was fleshed out on 'BRIGHT AND GUILTY' (1989), a well received album at times vaguely akin to a more listenable WEDDING PRESENT. Later that year, with their melodic instincts still intact, the band went for broke on mini-set, 'BLOWN AWAY', turning up the distortion and giving vent to their noisier impulses. Not exactly in step with the mood of the times, the band bowed out on a low point with 'ATTITUDE' (1990), CALLAHAN relocating to New York where he formed MOONSHAKE (with MARGARET FIEDLER) while GOULDING and STEBBING worked together in CRAWL. MOONSHAKE signed to 'Creation' in 1991 before surfacing on 'Too Pure' records, where they eventually debuted with an album, 'EVA LUNA', a free-form avant-garde jazz odyssey akin to a wailing GALLON DRUNK fused with The POP GROUP or The FALL.

Album rating: THE ESSENTIAL WOLFHOUNDS (*6) / BRIGHT AND GUILTY (*8) / BLOWN AWAY (*7) / Moonshake: DIRTY AND DIVINE (*7)

DAVE CALLAHAN – vocals / **PAUL CLARK** – guitar / **ANDY GOLDING** – guitar / **ANDY BOLTON** – bass / **FRANK STEBBING** – drums

Pink | not iss.

Mar 86. (12"ep) *(PINKY 8)* **CUT THE CAKE / L.A. JUICE. / DEADTHINK / ANOTHER LAZY DAY ON THE LAZY 'A'** | | -

Sep 86. (7") *(PINKY 14)* **THE ANTI-MIDAS TOUCH. / RESTLESS SPELL** | | -
(12"+=) (PINKY 14T) – Midget horror / One foot wrong / Slow lokis.

Apr 87. (7") *(PINKY 18)* **CRUELTY. / I SEE YOU** | | -
(12"+=) *(PINKY 18T)* – Whale on the beach.

May 87. (lp) **UNSEEN RIPPLES FROM A PEBBLE** | | -

Idea | not iss.

Nov 87. (7"/c-s) *(IDEA/ISEACI 10)* **ME. / DISGUSTED** | | -
(12"+=) *(IDEAT 10)* – Hand in the till / Cold shoulder.

—— **DAVID OLIVER** – bass; repl. BOLTON / **MATTHEW DEIGHTON** – guitar; repl. CLARK

September | not iss.

May 88. (12") *(SEPT 07T)* **SON OF NOTHING. / TORTURE** | | -

Midnight | not iss.

Nov 88. (lp)(cd) *(CHIME 0032S)(COLIN 1CD)* **THE ESSENTIAL WOLFHOUNDS** (compilation) | | -

Nov 88. (12") *(DONG 043)* **RENT ACT. /** | | -

Feb 89. (lp/c/cd) *(CHIME 048/+C/CD)* **BRIGHT AND GUILTY** | | -
– Non specific song / Charterhouse / Happy shopper / Useless second cousin / Ex-Cable Street / Tomorrow attacking / Son of nothing / Ropeswing / Rent act / Invisible people / A mess of Paradise / Cottonmouth / Second son / Torture / No soap in a dirty war / Red tape, red light / Natural disasters.

Mar 89. (7") *(DING 046)* **HAPPY SHOPPER. /** | | -
(12"+=) *(DONG 046)* –

Oct 89. (lp/c/cd) *(CHIME 057 F/C/CD)* **BLOWN AWAY** | | -
– Rite of passage / Tropic of Cancer / Living fossil / Dead sea burning / Blown away / Skyscrapers / Personal.

May 90. (lp/c/cd) *(CHIME 1.07/+CC/CD)* **ATTITUDE** | | -

—— split at the start of '90. A year later GOLDING and STEBBING formed CRAWL, while CALLAHAN formed below . . .

MOONSHAKE

DAVE CALLAHAN – vocals, guitar / **MARGARET FIEDLER** (b. New York) – vocals, guitar (ex-ULTRA VIVID SCENE) / **JOHN FRENNETT** – bass / **MIG** – drums

Creation | Matador – Atlantic

May 91. (12"ep)(cd-ep) *(CRE 101T)(CRESCD 101)* **FIRST EP** | | -
– Gravity / etc.

Too Pure | not iss.

Apr 92. (12"ep/cd-ep) *(PURE 9 T/CD)* **SECOND HAND CLOTHES. / BLISTER / DROP IN THE OCEAN** | | -

Oct 92. (12"ep/cd-ep) *(PURE 13 T/CD)* **BEAUTIFUL PIGEON. / BEESIDE / HOME SURVIVAL KIT** | | -

Oct 92. (lp/cd) *(PURE 16/+CD)* *<92274>* **EVA LUNA**
– City poison / Sweetheart / Spaceship earth / Beautiful pigeon / Mugshot heroine / Wanderlust / Tar baby / Seen and not heard / Bleach and salt water / Little thing / Secondhand clothes / Blister / Drop in the ocean.

May 93. (cd-ep) *(PURE 22CD)* *<074>* **BIG GOOD ANGEL**

—— now without MARGARET & JOHN, who formed LAIKA

—— she was replaced by **RAYMOND M. DICKATY** – saxophones, clarinet, flute / guests; **JOHNNY DAWE** – bass (of COLLAPSED LUNG) / **KATHARINE DIFFORD** – vocals (of DUOPHONIC ULTRA HIGH FREQUENCY DISCS) / **POLLY HARVEY** – vocals (of PJ HARVEY) / **ANDREW BLICK** – trumpet / etc

Too Pure | American

May 94. (lp/cd) *(PURE/+CD 33)* *<43014>* **THE SOUND YOUR EYES CAN FOLLOW**
– Joker John / Your last friend in this town / Just a working girl / The sound your eyes can follow / Ghosts of good intention / We're making war / Shadows of tall buildings / Right to fly / The grind / Into deep neutral.

—— **CALLAHAN + DICKATY** hired **MARY HANSEN + KATHERINE GIFFORD** – vocals (of & ex-STEREOLAB) / guest **MICHAEL ROTHER** – drums (ex-NEU!)

not iss. | Cruz

Aug 96. (cd-ep) *<CZ 083>* **CRANES / GAMBLER'S BLUES / NIGHTTRIPPER II** | - |

Oct 96. (cd) *<C/Z 085>* **DIRTY AND DIVINE** | | May96
– Exotic siren song / Cranes / Up for anything / Gambler's blues / Nothing but time / Aqualisa / Hard candy / House on fire / Taboo.

—— disbanded in 1997

– (WOLFHOUNDS) compilations, etc

Apr 96. (cd) *Cherry Red; (CDMRED 126)* **LOST BUT HAPPY** (1986-1990) | | -

WONDER STUFF

Formed: Stourbridge, Midlands, England . . .early 1986 by ex-EDEN drummer turned frontman, MILES HUNT, together with MALCOLM TREECE, THE BASS THING and MARTIN GILKS. After a couple of EP's on their own 'Farout' label, the group signed to 'Polydor' in late '87, initially lumped in with contemporaries like POP WILL EAT ITSELF and CRAZYHEAD under the music press-created 'grebo' banner. It soon became clear, however, that The WONDER STUFF were a unique proposition in their own right, as evidenced on the debut album, 'THE EIGHT LEGGED GROOVE MACHINE' (1988), a diverse collection of sparkling, hard-edged indie pop. HUNT was as bitingly uncompromising in his lyrics as he was in his relations with the media, the sardonic singer ever reliable for a controversial comment. While 'A WISH AWAY' narrowly missed the Top 40, another single, the wry 'IT'S YER MONEY I'M AFTER BABY', just nosed its way into the chart, the track backed by the self-explanatory 'ASTLEY IN THE NOOSE'. 'WHO WANTS TO BE THE DISCO KING?' asked HUNT in his inimitable bad attitude style, taking the WONDER STUFF into the Top 30 for the first time in early '89. A comparatively sensitive side was glimpsed on the jaunty 'DON'T LET ME DOWN' later that year, a Top 20 hit and a taster for the follow-up album, 'HUP' (1989). With the addition of JAMES TAYLOR on organ and MARTIN BELL on banjo/mandolin (no, not THAT JAMES TAYLOR and not THAT MARTIN BELL!), the record combined their high-octane pop/rock with a loose folky feel. It also marked their first major success, reaching the Top 5 and establishing the group as a headlining act. The success brought internal tensions to a head, however, with THE BASS THING (aka ROB JONES) departing for New York where he later formed 8-piece outfit The BRIDGE AND THE TUNNEL CREW (JONES subsequently died from heart problems in 1993). With PAUL CLIFFORD coming in as a replacement, the group entered the most high profile period of their career. Following on from the Top 20 success of the groovy 'CIRCLESQUARE' single, The WONDER STUFF scored a massive hit with the insanely catchy and ultimately annoying 'SIZE OF A COW'. A third set, 'NEVER LOVED ELVIS' (1991), made the Top 3 later that summer, a more mature set which neverthless lacked the raw charm of old. A marriage made in heaven/hell (delete according to taste), The WONDER STUFF teamed up with comedic loonies VIC REEVES & BOB MORTIMER for a cover of TOMMY ROE's 'DIZZY', giving the group their one and only No.1 single later that year. With the help of rootsy chanteuse KIRSTY MacCOLL, the 'WELCOME TO THE CHEAP SEATS' EP (1992) contined the band's folk/indie hybrid, as did the group's final album, 'CONSTRUCTION FOR THE MODERN IDIOT' (1993). Increasingly disillusioned by their failure to break the American market and the direction of the British music scene, The WONDER STUFF finally signed off with the surprisingly ebullient 'HOT LOVE NOW! EP' (1994) and a farewell performance at the 1994 Phoenix festival. While HUNT went on to work as a presenter for MYV before forming VENT 414, the other members subsequently founded the group WEKNOWWHEREYOULIVE.
• **Songwriters:** Group music / HUNT lyrics except; GIMME SOME TRUTH (John Lennon) / THAT'S ENTERTAINMENT (Jam) / INSIDE YOU (Pop Will Eat Itself) / COZ I LUV YOU (Slade).

Album rating: THE EIGHT LEGGED GROOVE MACHINE (*6) / HUP (*6) / NEVER LOVED ELVIS (*7) / IF THE BEATLES HAD READ HUNTER (*8)

MILES HUNT – vocals, guitar / **MALCOLM TREECE** – guitar, vocals / **THE BASS THING** (b.ROB JONES) – bass / **MARTIN GILKS** – drums, percussion (ex-MIGHTY LEMON DROPS)

Farout | not iss.

Feb 87. (7"ep) *(GONE ONE)* **IT'S NOT TRUE . . . / A WONDERFUL DAY. / LIKE A MERRY GO ROUND / DOWN HERE** | | -

Sep 87. (7") *(GONE 002)* **UNBEARABLE. / TEN TRENCHES DEEP** | | -
(12"+=) *(GOBIG 002)* – I am a monster / Frank.

Polydor | Polygram

Apr 88. (7") *(GONE 3)* **GIVE GIVE GIVE ME MORE MORE MORE. / A SONG WITHOUT AN END** | 72 | -
(12"+=/cd-s+=) *(GONE X/CD 3)* – Meaner than mean / See the free world.

Jul 88. (7") *(GONE 4)* **A WISH AWAY. / JEALOUSY** | 43 | -
(12"+=/cd-s+=) *(GONE X/CD 4)* – Happy-sad / Goodbye fatman.

Aug 88. (lp/c)(cd) *(GON LP/MC 1)(837135-2) <837802>* **THE EIGHT LEGGED GROOVE MACHINE** 18 [ ]
– Redbury joy town / No for the 13th time / It's yer money I'm after baby / Rue the day / Give give give me more more more / Like a merry go round / The animals and me / A wish away / Grin / Mother and I / Some sad someone / Ruby horse / Unbearable / Poison. *(cd-iss. Apr95; same)*

Sep 88. (7"ep/12"ep/cd-ep) *(GONE/+X/CD 5)* **IT'S YER MONEY I'M AFTER BABY / ASTLEY IN THE NOOSE. / OOH, SHE SAID / RAVE FROM THE GRAVE** 40 -

Feb 89. (7") *(GONE 6)* **WHO WANTS TO BE THE DISCO KING?. / UNBEARABLE (live)** 28 -
(12"+=/cd-s+=) *(GONEX/GONCD 6)* – Ten trenches deep (live) / No for the 13th time (live).

— added guests **JAMES TAYLOR** – organ (ex-PRISONERS) / **MARTIN BELL** – banjo

Sep 89. (7"/c-s) *(GONE/GONCS 7)* **DON'T LET ME DOWN, GENTLY. / IT WAS ME** 19 -
(12"+=/cd-s+=) *(GONEX/GONCD 7)* – ('A'extended).

Oct 89. (lp/c/cd) *(841 187-1/-4/-2)* **HUP** 5 -
– 30 years in the bathroom / Radio ass kiss / Golden green / Let's be other people / Piece of sky / Can't shape up / Good night though / Don't let me down, gently / Cartoon boyfriend / Unfaithful / Them, big oak trees / Room 410. *(re-iss. cd Apr95; same)*

Nov 89. (7"/c-s) *(GONE/GONCS 8)* **GOLDEN GREEN. / GET TOGETHER** 33 -
(12"+=/cd-s+=) *(GONEX/GONCD 8)* – Gimme some truth.

— (Mar'90) **PAUL CLIFFORD** – bass finally repl. The BASS THING (left '89). He later formed 8-piece The BRIDGE AND THE TUNNEL CREW.

May 90. (7"/c-s) *(GONE/GONCS 10)* **CIRCLESQUARE. / OUR NEW SONG** 20 -
(12"+=/cd-s+=) *(GONEX/GONCD 10)* – ('A'-Paranoia mix).

Mar 91. (7"/c-s) *(GONE/GONCD 11)* **THE SIZE OF A COW. / RADIO ASS KISS (live)** 5 -
(12"+=/cd-s+=) *(GONEX/GONCD 11)* – Give give give me more more more (live).

May 91. (7"/c-s) *(GONE/GONCS 12)* **CAUGHT IN MY SHADOW. / GIMME SOME TRUTH (live)** 18 -
(12"+=/cd-s+=) *(GONEX/GONCD 12)* – ('A'extended).

Jun 91. (cd/c/lp) *(847 252-2/-4/-1)* **NEVER LOVED ELVIS** 3 -
– Mission drive / Play / False start / Welcome to the cheap seats / The size of a cow / Sleep alone / Reaction / Inertia / Maybe / Grotesque / Here come everyone / Caught in my shadow / Line poem. *(re-iss. cd Apr95; same)*

Aug 91. (7"/c-s) *(GONE/GONCS 13)* **SLEEP ALONE. / EL HERMANO DE FRANK** 43 -
(12"+=/cd-s+=) *(GONEX/GONCD 13)* – The takin' is easy.

— In Oct'91, they teamed up with comedian VIC REEVES (& BOB MORTIMER) on No.1 hit cover of Tommy Roe's 'DIZZY'. Next single with guest, KIRSTY MacCOLL

Jan 92. (7"ep/c-ep) *(GONE/GONCS 14)* **WELCOME TO THE CHEAP SEATS** 8 -
– Welcome to the cheap seats / Me, my mum, my dad and my brother / Will the circle be unbroken / That's entertainment.
(cd-ep+=) *(GONECD 14)* – ('A'naked mix) / Caught in my shadw (bare mix) / Circlesque (butt naked mix) / Can't shape up again.

— added **MARTIN BELL** – fiddle, accordion, mandolin, guitar, sitar, keyboards and 6th member **PETE WHITTAKER** – keyboards

Sep 93. (7"ep/c-ep/12"ep/cd-ep) *(GONE/GONCS/GONEX/GONCD 15)* **ON THE ROPES EP** 10 -
– On the ropes / Professional disturber of the peace / Hank and John / Whites.

Oct 93. (cd/c/lp) *(519 894-2/-4/-1)* **CONSTRUCTION FOR THE MODERN IDIOT** 4 -
– Change every light bulb / I wish them all dead / Cabin fever / Hot love now / Full of life (happy now) / Storm drain / On the ropes / Your big assed mother / Swell / A great drinker / Hush / Sing the absurd.

Nov 93. (7") *(GONE 16)* **FULL OF LIFE (HAPPY NOW). / CLOSER TO FINE** 28 -
(cd-s+=) *(GONCD 16)* – Burger standing / A curious weird and ugly scene.
(cd-s) *(GONCDX 16)* – ('A'-Dignity mix) / Change every light bulb (dub mix) / I wish them all dead (dub mix).

— Note: Ex-member ROB JONES (THE BASS THING) died mysteriously on 30 Jul'93 in his New York apartment.

Mar 94. (7"ep/c-ep/cd-ep) *(GONE/GONEX/GONCD 17)* **HOT LOVE NOW! EP** 19 -
– Hot love now! / Just helicopters / I must've had something really useful to say / Room 512, all the news that's fit to print.
(cd-ep) *(GONCDX 17)* – ('A'cardinal error mix) / Unrest song / Flour babies / The Tipperary triangle.

— Disbanded after July Phoenix Festival. MILES went on to work for MTV.

– compilations, etc. –

Sep 94. (7"/c-s/cd-s) *Polydor; (GONE/GONCS/GONCD 18)* **UNBEARABLE. / INSIDE YOU / HIT BY A CAR** 16 -
(cd-s) *(GONCDX 18)* – ('A'original) / Ten trenches deep / I am a monster / Frank.

Sep 94. (cd/c) *Polydor; (521 397-2/-4/-1)* **IF THE BEATLES HAD READ HUNTER . . . THE SINGLES** 8 -
– Welcome to the cheap seats / A wish away / Caught in my shadow / Don't let me gently / Size of a cow / Hot love now! / Dizzy / Unbearable / Circlesquare / Who wants to be the disco king? / Golden green / Give give give me more more more / Sleep alone / Coz I luv you / Full of life / On the ropes / It's yer money I'm after baby / It's not true.

Jul 95. (cd) *Windsong; (WINCD 074)* **LIVE IN MANCHESTER (live)** 74 -

WE KNOW WHERE YOU LIVE

— **TREECE / CLIFFORD / GILKS / + ANGE** – vocals (ex-EAT)

H.M.D. not iss.

Nov 95. (7"ep/cd-ep) *(HMD 0016/0012)* **DON'T BE TOO HONEST. / CONFESSIONS OF A THUG / EXCUSE ME?** [ ] -

Noise Factory not iss.

Jun 96. (7") *(NFRS 002)* **DRAPED. /** [ ] -
(cd-s+=) *(NFRCD 002)* –

VENT 414

— **MILES HUNT** – vocals, guitar / **MORGAN NICHOLLS** – bass (ex-SENSELESS THINGS) / **PETE HOWARD** – drums (ex-EAT)

Polydor not iss.

Sep 96. (7"/c-s) *(575328-7/-4)* **FIXER. / KISSING THE MIRROR** 71 -
(cd-s+=) *(575328-2)* – Give it whole / Dimki pense.
(12"+=) *(575326-6)* – Shimmy.

Oct 96. (cd/c/lp) *(533048-2/-4/-1)* **VENT 414** [ ] -
– Fixer / Fits and starts / At the base of the fire / The last episode / Laying down with / life before you / Correctional / Easy to talk / Night out with a foreign fella / Kissing the mirror / At one / 2113 / Guess my god.

Nov 96. (7"/c-s) *(575534-7/-4)* **LIFE BEFORE YOU. / THE LAST EPISODE** [ ] -
(cd-s+=) *(575535-2)* – Your latest innuendo / Manifold 36 boro.

WOODENTOPS

Formed: Northampton, England . . . 1983 by ROLO McGINTY, SIMON MAWBY, FRANK DE FREITAS, BENNY STAPLES and ALICE THOMPSON. After a one-off debut single, 'PLENTY', for Dave Balfe's 'Food' label, this innovative indie act signed to 'Rough Trade' and released a string of acclaimed singles including 'MOVE ME' and 'IT WILL COME'. A much anticipated debut album, 'GIANT' (1986) brought almost universal praise from the press and The WOODENTOPS' quirky blend of manic drumming, twanging guitar and acoustic punkabilly skiffle attracted a cult fanbase (the skinny bare-chested ROLO proving the object of their affections). The following year's 'LIVE HYPNOBEAT LIVE' (1987) placed the tracks in a more confrontational context and by the release of their swansong, 'WOODEN FOOT COPS ON THE HIGHWAY' (1988), the band had developed into one of the most visionary indie bands of the era. On the back of their adoption by the Balearic dance scene, ROLO and Co returned in 1991 with a house single, 'THE WOODENTOPS VS. BANG THE PARTY' on the 'Hyperactive' label. The rest of the 90's were spent touring Asia and Japan where they had become more popular.

Album rating: GIANT (*7) / LIVE HYPNOBEAT LIVE (*6) / WOODEN FOOT COPS ON THE HIGHWAY (*6)

ROLO McGINTY – vocals, acoustic guitar (ex-INNOCENTS, ex-JAZZ BUTCHER) / **SIMON MAWBY** – guitar / **ALICE THOMPSON** – keyboards / **FRANK DeFREITAS** – bass / **PAUL HOOKHAM** – drums

Food not iss.

Jul 84. (7") *(FOOD 2)* **PLENTY. / HAVE YOU SEEN THE LIGHTS** [ ] -
(12"+=) *(SNAK 2)* – Everybody.

Rough Trade Columbia

Apr 85. (7") *(RT 165)* **MOVE ME. / DO IT ANYWAY** [ ] -
(12"+=) *(RTT 165)* – Steady steady.

— **BENNY STAPLES** (b.New Zealand) – drums; repl. HOOKHAM (to REDSKINS)

Aug 85. (7") *(RT 167)* **WELL WELL WELL. / GET IT ON (John Peel session)** [ ] -
(12"+=) *(RTT 167)* – Cold inside.

Nov 85. (7") *(RT 169)* **IT WILL COME. / SPECIAL FRIEND** [ ] -
(12"+=) *(RTT 169)* – Plutonium rock.

May 86. (7"/12") *(RT/+T 177)* **GOOD THING. / TRAVELLING MAN** [ ] -

Jun 86. (lp/c) *(ROUGH/+C/CD 87) <40468>* **GIANT** 35 [ ]
– Shout / History / Travelling man / Get it on / Love train / Good thing / (Love affair with) Everyday living / Give it time / Hear me James / So good today / Last time / Everything breaks. *(cd-iss. May87 +=; ROUGHCD 87)* – (1 track).

Sep 86. (7") *(RT 178)* **(LOVE AFFAIR WITH) EVERYDAY LIVING. / SO GOOD TODAY** 72 -
(d7"+=) *(RTD 178)* – Move me / Well well well.

Rough Trade Epic

Apr 87. (7") **GIVE IT TIME. / WHY** - [ ]

Apr 87. (lp/c/cd) *(ROUGH/+C/CD 117) <40861>* **LIVE HYPNOBEAT (live in Los Angeles)** [ ] [ ]
– Well well well / Love train / Travelling man / Plenty / Why / Get it on / Everyday living / Good thing / Move me / Everything breaks. *(cd+=)* – (bonus studio tracks).

— **ANNE STEPHENSON** – keyboards, violin (ex-COMMUNARDS) repl. ALICE

Jan 88. (7") *(RT 179)* **YOU MAKE ME FEEL. / STOP THIS CAR** [ ] -
(12"+=) *(RTT 179)* – ('A'&'B'mixes).

Feb 88. (lp/c) *(ROUGH/+C 127)* **WOODEN FOOT COPS ON THE HIGHWAY** 48 -
– Maybe it won't last / They can say what they want / You make me feel / Wheels turning / Stop this car / Heaven / What you give out / Tuesday Wednesday / In a dream.

— After splitting in 1988, **ROLO, BENNY + SIMON** returned.

— BANG PARTY:- **KID BATCHELOR + FRANKIE FONCETT**

Hyperactive not iss.

May 91. (7"ep) **WOODENTOPS VS. BANG THE PARTY** [ ] -
– Tainted world / (+2 other mixes by BANG THE PARTY).

Oct 91. (7") **STAY OUT OF THE LIGHT. / ?** [ ] -

WORLD DOMINATION ENTERPRISES

Formed: London, England . . . 1985 by former HERE & NOW hippie, KEITH 'KIPKIF' DOBSON, STEVE JAMESON and DIGGER. The former set up his own (anti-Band/Live Aid) 'Fuck Off' label, releasing the 'WEIRD NOISE' EP under the pseudonym of DANNY & THE DRESSMAKERS; a cassette, '39 GOLDEN GRATES', followed soon after. Hardware industrial dance pioneers, the trio issued a poisonous debut single for 'Karbon', 'ASBESTOS LEAD ASBESTOS', moving on to 'Product Inc' (home to the SWANS and the YOUNG GODS) where they unleashed a series of equally influential singles. WDE subsequently became involved with the emerging acid-house scene, playing raves organized by the capital's Mutoid Waste Company. These experiences no doubt inspired the band to record a set of remixes, 'LOVE FROM THE CITY', revamped versions of tracks from that year's studio album, 'LET'S PLAY DOMINATION' (1988). Choosing Russia as a starting point for their World Domination, the band's attempts were short-lived as DIGGER opted for a life as a Jehovah's Witness. The other two chose to abandon proceeedings, DOBSON temporarily relocating to Spain while JAMESON formed the group, CUT, with former VAPORS man, STEVE SMITH.

Album rating: LET'S PLAY DOMINATION (*5) / HOT FROM THE CITY (*5)

KEITH DOBSON – vocals, guitar (ex-HERE AND NOW) / **STEVE JAMESON** – bass / **DIGGER** – drums

Karbon | not iss.

Oct 85. (7") *(KAR 008)* **ASBESTOS LEAD ASBESTOS. / BEATS BABY HI** | | -

Product Inc. | Caroline

Oct 86. (12") *(PROD 1.12)* **CATALOGUE CLOTHES. / ST. ETIENNE** | | -

Apr 87. (7"/12") *(7/12 PROD 5)* **HOTSY GIRL. /** | | -

Feb 88. (7"/12") *(7/12 PROD 12)* **I CAN'T LIVE WITHOUT MY RADIO. /** | | -

Apr 88. (cd/c/lp) *(33 CD/C+/PROD 18)* <1357> **LET'S PLAY DOMINATION** | |

Oct 88. (lp/c) *(33PROD/+C 24)* **LOVE FROM THE CITY (HOT FROM THE CITY) (remixes)** | | -

Immaculate | not iss.

Apr 89. (7") *(IMMAC 12)* **COMPANY NEWS. / TUTTI FRUTTI** | | -
(12"+=) *(12IMMAC 12)* – ('A'-Rare mix).

— DIGGER left them to become a Jehovah's Witness and the band split. DOBSON went to the continent in the early 90's. JAMESON subsequently formed CUT with VAPORS man, STEVE SMITH

WORLD OF TWIST

Formed: Manchester, England . . .1989 by GORDON KING, TONY OGDEN, JULIA McSHELLS, ADGE and ANDY HOBSON. One of the many bands skulking in the floppy fringes of the baggy movement, WORLD OF TWIST signed to 'Virgin'-offshoot, 'Circa', scoring a near-Top 40 hit with their debut single, 'THE STORM'. A follow-up track, 'SONS OF THE STAGE', achieved a similar feat in Spring '91, by which point the group had been reduced to a trio of KING, OGDEN and new recruit NICHOLAS SANDERSON. Although a John Peel session helped boost their credibility, the 'SWEETS' single barely nudged into the Top 60 later the same year. Many critics intrigued by the band's colourful, adventurous indie-pop weren't so impressed by the debut album, 'QUALITY STREET' (1991), while a re-released version of their Rolling Stones cover, 'SHE'S A RAINBOW', smacked of last-gasp desperation. • **Songwriters:** Group except: THIS TOO SHALL PASS AWAY (Honeycombs).

Album rating: QUALITY STREET (*5)

GORDON KING – guitar / **TONY OGDEN** – vocals / **JULIA McSHELLS** (MC SHELLS) – synthesizers / **ANDY HOBSON** – keyboards / **ADGE** – visuals

Circa | not iss.

Nov 90. (7") *(YR 55)* **THE STORM. / SHE'S A RAINBOW** | 42 | -
(12"+=/cd-s+=) *(YR/+T/CD 55)* – (2 other 'A'&'B'versions).
(12"+=) *(YRT 55)* – Blackpool Tower suite.

— now reduced to **KING, OGDEN** + new recruit **NICHOLAS SANDERSON** – percussion

Mar 91. (7") *(YR 62)* **SONS OF THE STAGE. / LIFE AND DEATHS (remix)** | 47 | -
(12"+=/cd-s+=) *(YR T/CD 62)* – ('A'version).

Sep 91. (7") *(YR 72)* **SWEETS. / THIS TOO SHALL PASS AWAY** | 58 | -
(cd-s+=) *(YRCD 72)* – The storm / Sons of the stage.

Oct 91. (c/cd/lp) *(CIRC/+D/A 17)* **QUALITY STREET** | 50 | -
– Lose my way / Sons of the stage / This too shall pass away / Jelly baby / Speed wine / The lights / On the scene / Sweets / The spring / The storm. *(cd+=)R* – She's a rainbow / Life and death.

Feb 92. (7") *(YR 82)* **SHE'S A RAINBOW. / LOSE MY WAY** | 62 | -
(12"+=/cd-s+=) *(YR T/CD 82)* –

— disbanded June '92

WORLD SERVICE (see under ⇒ ZOUNDS)

WRECKLESS ERIC

Born: ERIC GOULDEN, 1950, Newhaven, England. Odd-job man turned pub-rock troubadour, GOULDEN took on the WRECKLESS ERIC mantle after netting a deal with 'Stiff' at the height of punk's first wave, causing a stir in 1977 with his anthemic debut single, 'WHOLE WIDE WORLD'. An eponymous debut album appeared the following year as ERIC trooped out alongside the likes of ELVIS COSTELLO and IAN DURY on the riotous 'Stiff' live shindigs. Despite living in the shadow of such talented labelmates, the man turned out a fine follow-up set of more retro-styled, punk-influenced pop/rock, 'THE WONDERFUL WORLD OF WRECKLESS ERIC' (1978). Amid mounting pressure to achieve some kind of breakthrough, he penned his most commercial singles to date in 'HIT AND MISS JUDY' and 'A POP SONG'; chart success remained tantalisingly out of reach, however and WRECKLESS ERIC effectively bowed out of the scene with 1980's sardonically titled 'BIG SMASH'. Reverting back to his real name, GOULDEN eventually resurfaced in 1985 with 'A ROOMFUL OF MONKEYS', musical support coming from members of IAN DURY's BLOCKHEADS. The shortlived LEN BRIGHT COMBO was ERIC's next project before he finally relocated to France and enjoyed a fairly fruitful career with LE BEAT GROUP ELECTRIQUE alongside CATFISH TRUTON and ANDRE BARREAU. Signed to the 'New Rose' label initially, the trio released an eponymous debut in 1989, going on to record a mini-set, 'AT THE SHOP' (1990) and releasing 'THE DONOVAN OF TRASH' in 1991 on the 'Sympathy For The Record Industry' label. • **Songwriters:** GOULDEN compositions except; CRYING, WAITING, HOPING (Buddy Holly) / I WISH IT WOULD RAIN (Temptations) / etc.

Album rating: WRECKLESS ERIC (*5) / THE WONDERFUL WORLD OF . . . (*6) / BIG SMASH (*7) / GREATEST HITS compilation (*7)

ERIC – vocals, guitar with **COLIN FLETCHER** – lead guitar / **WALTER MACON** – guitar / **JOHN BROWN** – bass / **DAVE OTWAY** – drums

Stiff | Stiff

Aug 77. (7") *(BUY 16)* **WHOLE WIDE WORLD. / SEMAPHORE SIGNALS** | | -

Feb 78. (7") *(BUY 25)* **RECONNEZ CHERIE. / RAGS AND TATTERS** | | -

— now with **CHARLIE HART** – keyboards / **STEVE CURRIE** – bass / **JOHN GLYN** – sax / + **DAVE OTWAY, DAVID WHITTON** + **STEVE GOLDING** – drums

Mar 78. (lp/10"brown-lp) *(SEEZ/+B 6)* **WRECKLESS ERIC** | 46 | -
– Reconnez Cherie / Rags and tatters / Waxworks / Telephoning home / Grown ups / Whole wide world / Personal hygiene / Brain thieves / There isn't anything else. *(cd-iss. Aug91 on 'Repertoire'; REP 4217WY)*

— his new band were **MALCOLM MORLEY** + **BRADY** – guitar / **PETE SOLLEY** – keyboards / **JOHN BROWN** – bass / **GIER WADE** – drums

Oct 78. (7") *(BUY 34)* **TAKE THE K.A.S.H. / GIRLFRIEND** | | -

Oct 78. (lp,green-lp,pic-lp) *(SEEZ 9)* **THE WONDERFUL WORLD OF . . .** | | -
– Walking on the surface of the moon / Take the K.A.S.H. / Dizzy / Veronica / Roll over rock-ola / I wish it would rain / Let's go to the pictures / The final taxi / Girlfriend / Crying, waiting, hoping.

Dec 78. (7") *(BUY 40)* **CRYING, WAITING, HOPING. / I WISH IT WOULD RAIN** | | -

Oct 79. (7") *(BUY 49)* **HIT AND MISS JUDY. / LET'S GO TO THE PICTURES** | | -
(12"orange+=) *(BUYIT 49)* – I need a situation.

Oct 79. (7") <OWN 1> **TAKE THE CASH (K.A.S.H.). / LET'S GO TO THE PICTURES** | - |

Dec 79. (lp) <USE 1> **WHOLE WIDE WORLD** (compilation) | - |

Jan 80. (7") *(BUY 64)* **A POPSONG. / RECONNEZ CHERIE** | | -

Stiff | Stiff-Epic

Feb 80. (lp/c) *(SEEZ/ZSEEZ 21)* <36463> **BIG SMASH** | 30 | Apr80
– A popsong / Tonight (is my night) / Too busy / Broken doll / Can I be your hero / Back in my hometown / It'll soon be the weekend / Strange towns / Excuse me / Break my mind / Out of the blue / Good conversation. *(re-iss. Nov80 w/ free GREATEST HITS lp 'WHOLE WIDE WORLD')* – Whole wide world / Take the cash / Let's go to the pictures / Walking on the surface of the Moon / Hit & Miss Judy / I wish it would rain / Reconnez Cherie / Veronica / Brain thieves / Semaphore signals / I need a situation / The final taxi / There isn't anything else. *(cd-iss. Feb94 on 'Disky'; STIFFCD 13)*

Mar 80. (7") *(BUY 75)* **BROKEN DOLL. / I NEED A SITUATION** | | -
(12"+=) *(BUYIT 75)* – A little bit more.

Apr 80. (7") <50870> **BROKEN DOLL. / A LITTLE BIT MORE** | - |

— retired from the music biz in the early 80's.

CAPTAINS OF INDUSTRY

were formed by **ERIC GOULDEN** in 1983 with **MICKEY GALLAGHER** – keyboards + **NORMAN WATT-ROY** – bass (both ex-IAN DURY . . .) / **BAZ MURPHY** – organ / **DAVID ADLAND** – drums (ex-PIRANHAS)

Go! Discs | not iss.

Nov 84. (7") *(GOD 6)* **LIFELINE. / A GIRL IN A MILLION** | | -

— Reduced band to a quartet when BAZ departed

May 85. (lp) *(AGOLP 5)* **A ROOMFUL OF MONKEYS** | | -
– Land of the faint at heart / Our neck of the woods / Julie / Home and away / Lucky ones / Reputation (a serious case of . . .) / Food factory / Lifeline / Lady of the manor / Playtime is over.

— **DAVE CLARKE** – keyboards + **BILL HILL** – bass; repl. MICKEY + NORM who rejoined IAN DURY

LEN BRIGHT COMBO

— were **ERIC** – vocals, guitar plus **RUSS WILKINS** – bass / **BRUCE BRAND** – drums (both ex-MILKSHAKES)

Empire not iss.

Feb 86. (lp) *(NICE 1)* **THE LEN BRIGHT COMBO PRESENTS THE LEN BRIGHT COMBO** [ ] [-]
– You're gonna screw my head off / Shirt without a heart / Selina through the windshield / Lureland / Young, upwardly mobile . . . and stupid / The golden hour of Harry Secombe / Sophie (the dream of Edmund Hirondelle Barnes).

Apr 86. (7") *(LEN 1)* **SOMEONE MUST'VE NAILED US TOGETHER. / MONA** [ ] [-]

Ambassador not iss.

Nov 86. (lp) **IT'S COMBO TIME** [ ] [-]
– Pleasant valley Wednesday / (Swimming against) The tide of reason / Cut off my head / The house burned down / Phasers on stun / The awakening of Edmund Hirondelle Barnes / All charm / Club 18 to 30 / Ticking in my corner.

— In 1988, **ERIC** returned to his old moniker

WRECKLESS ERIC

— with **CATFISH TRUTON + ANDRE BARREAU**

New Rose not iss.

Sep 89. (lp) *(ROSE 179)* **LE BEAT ELECTRIQUE** [ ] [-]
– Tell me I'm the only one / Wishing my life away / Depression / It's a sick sick world / Just for you / Sarah / I'm not going to cry / The Sun is pouring down / You sweet big thing / Fuck by fuck / Parallel bells / True happiness. *(cd-iss. Jun94; 422396)*

Oct 89. (7") *(NEW 100)* **IT'S A SICK SICK WORLD. / RECONNEZ CHERIE** [ ] [-]

May 90. (7") *(NEW 136)* **DEPRESSION. /** [ ] [-]

May 90. (m-lp) *(NR 312)* **AT THE SHOP** (recorded live in a record store 1 day) [ ] [-]
– Big old world / If it makes you happy / (Waiting for the shit) To hit the fan / Semaphore signals / Our neck of the woods / You're the girl for me. *(cd-iss. Jun94; 422395)*

Hangman Sympathy F

Feb 93. (7") <SFTRI 226> **JOE MEEK. / TELL ME I'M THE ONLY ONE** [-] [ ]

Mar 93. (lp) *(HANG 050UP)* <*SFTRI 230*> **THE DONOVAN OF TRASH** [ ] [ ]
– Birthday blues / Duvet fever / Joe Meek / The consolation prize / Semi-porno statuette / Schoo / The nerd / Turkey song / Lureland / Harry's flat / Haunted house / If it makes you happy / Paris in June.

— the wreckless one retired once more

Pete WYLIE (see under ⇒ WAH!)

Steve WYNN (see under ⇒ DREAM SYNDICATE)

X

Formed: Los Angeles, California, USA . . . 1977 by EXENE CERVENKA, BILLY ZOOM, JOHN DOE and original drummer MICK BASHER (the latter subsequently replaced by DJ BONEBRAKE). After a one-off debut in 1978, 'ADULT BOOKS' (for the US 'Dangerhouse' imprint), X marked their spot with the then newly formed indie label, 'Slash'. Pioneers of the cowpunk scene alongside WALL OF VOODOO, The GUN CLUB, etc, the quartet enlisted the help of RAY MANZAREK, the former DOORS organist producing their debut set, 'LOS ANGELES' (1980). A rock hybrid of country and raw punk, X were obviously influenced by 60's garage punks the FUGS and MC5 with a tone of 50's rockabilly, this combination of musical styles used most effectively on follow-up set, 'WILD GIFT' (also recorded with MANZAREK at the helm). The MANZAREK connection continued when X moved to 'Elektra', their third album, 'UNDER THE BIG BLACK SUN' (1982) breaking them into the US Top 100. A fourth set, 'MORE FUN IN THE NEW WORLD' (1983), fared just as well commercially, although the band were in turn accused of selling out. The previous year, EXENE and LYDIA LUNCH had a book of poetry, 'Adulterers Anonymous' (with that title, it's not surprising that EXENE and JOHN were divorced in '84) published in the States, the X frontwoman subsequently teaming up with DOE, DAVE ALVIN (Blasters), HENRY ROLLINS (Black Flag) and JONNY RAY BARTEL to form country-rock outfit, The KNITTERS. The latter project obviously had an effect on X themselves (ALVIN had now replaced ZOOM), who emerged with a more countrified sound on 1985's 'AIN'T LOVE GRAND'. The following year ALVIN was deposed by ex-LONE JUSTICE guitarist, TONY GILKYSON, a fuller heavy sound beginning to manifest itself on 1987's 'SEE HOW WE ARE'. A commercially disastrous double-live set was their last for some time, although the band returned after other solo projects with a disappointing comeback set, 'HEY ZEUS!' (1993). • **Covered:** WILD THING (Troggs) / ALL OR NOTHING (Small Faces) / IT'S IN HIS KISS (Betty Everett) / SOUL KITCHEN (Doors) / POSITIVELY 4th STREET (Bob Dylan) / U.S. MALE (hit; Elvis Presley) / HOME MOTEL (Willie Nelson).

Album rating: LOS ANGELES (*6) / WILD GIFT (*8) / UNDER THE BIG BLACK SUN (*6) / MORE FUN IN THE NEW WORLD (*5) / AIN'T LOVE GRAND (*6) / SEE HOW WE ARE (*5) / HEY ZEUS! (*4) / UNCLOGGED (*4)

EXENE CERVENKA (b. CHRISTINE CERVENKA, 1 Feb'56, Chicago, Illinois) – vocals / **BILLY ZOOM** – guitar / **JOHN DOE** (b.JOHN NOMMENSEN, 25 Feb'53, Decatur, Illinois) – bass, vocals / **D.J. BONEBRAKE** (b. DON, 8 Dec'55, Hollywood, Calif.) – drums repl. MICK BASHER

not iss. / Dangerhouse

Apr 78. (7") *<D 88>* **ADULT BOOKS. / WE'RE DESPERATE** [-] [ ]

not iss. / Slash

Jun 80. (7") **THE WORLD'S A MESS. / IT'S IN MY KISS** [-] [ ]

Jun 80. (lp) *<SR 106>* **LOS ANGELES** [-] [ ]
– Your phone's off the hook, but you're not / Johnny hit and run Pauline / Soul kitchen / Nausea / Sugarlight / Los Angeles / Sex and dying in high society / The unheard music / The world's a mess / It's in my kiss.

May 81. (lp) *<SR 107>* **WILD GIFT** [-] [ ]
– The once over twice / We're desperate / Adult books / Universal corner / I'm coming over / It's who you know / In this house that I call home / Some other time / White girl / Beyond and back / Back 2 the base / When our love passed out on the coach / Year 1.

Jun 81. (7") **WE'RE DESPERATE. / GET USED TO IT** [-] [ ]

Aug 81. (7") *<SRS 106>* **WHITE GIRL. / YOUR PHONE'S OFF THE HOOK** [-] [ ]

Elektra / Elektra

Jul 82. (7") *<69885>* **BLUE SPARK. / DANCING WITH TEARS IN MY EYES** [ ] [ ]

Jul 82. (lp) *(K 52401) <60150>* **UNDER THE BIG BLACK SUN** [ ] [76]
– The hungry wolf / Motel room in my bed / Riding with Mary / Come back to me / Under the big black sun / Because I do / Blue spark / Dancing with tears in my eyes / Real child of Hell / How I (learned my lesson) / The have nots.

Jun 83. (7") *<69825>* **BREATHLESS. / RIDING WITH MARY** [-] [ ]

Sep 83. (lp/c) *(K 960283-1/-4) <60283>* **MORE FUN IN THE NEW WORLD** [ ] [86]
– The new world / We're having much more fun / True love / Poor girl / Make the music go bang / Breathless / I must not think bad thoughts / Devil doll / Painting the town blue / Hot house / Drunk in my past / I see red / True love #2.

Jan 84. (7") *(E 9779)* **THE NEW WORLD. / I MUST NOT THINK BAD THOUGHTS** [ ] [ ]

Jun 84. (12") **WILD THING. / TRUE LOVE (part 2)** [ ] [-]

Jun 84. (7") *<69709>* **WILD THING. / DEVIL DOLL** [-] [ ]

—— In 1985, JOHN DOE splintered with country-western project The KNITTERS. They included HENRY ROLLINS (of BLACK FLAG), DAVE ALVIN (of BLASTERS) + JOHNNY RAY BARTEL and made one album POOR LITTLE CRITTER ON THE ROAD. In fact, X brought in **DAVE ALVIN** – guitar to repl. BILLY

Aug 85. (7") *(EKR 18)* **BURNING HOUSE OF LOVE. / LOVE SHACK** [ ] [ ]
(12"+=) *(EKRT 18)* – Wild thing.

Sep 85. (lp) *(EKT 12) <60430>* **AIN'T LOVE GRAND** [ ] [89] Aug85
– Burning house of love / Love shack / My soul cries your name / My goodness / Around my heart / What's wrong with me . . . / All or nothing / Watch the sun go down / I'll stand up for you / Little honey / Supercharged.

—— **TONY GILKYSON** (b. 6 Aug'52) – guitar (ex-LONE JUSTICE) repl. ALVIN who went solo

Jul 87. (lp/c) *(K 960492-1/-4) <60492>* **SEE HOW WE ARE** [ ] [ ]
– I'm lost / You / 4th of July / In the time it takes / Anyone can fill your shoes / See how we are / Left & right / When it rains . . . / Holiday story / Surprise surprise / Cyrano de Berger's back.

Jul 87. (7") *<69462>* **4th OF JULY. / POSITIVELY 4th STREET** [-] [ ]

May 88. (d-lp/c/cd) *(K 960788-1/-4/-2) <60788>* **LIVE AT THE WHISKEY A GO-GO ON THE FABULOUS SUNSET STRIP (live)** [ ] [ ]
– Los Angeles / House I call home / The new world / Around my heart / Surprise surprise / Because I do / Burning house of love / My goodness / Blue spark / The once over twice / In the time it takes / Devil doll / Hungry wolf / Just another perfect day / Unheard music / Riding with Mary / The world's a mess / True love / White girl / Skin deep town / So long / Call of the wreckin' ball / Year 1 / Johnny hit a run / Pauline.

R.C.A. / D.G.C.

Oct 89. (7") **WILD THING. / (part 2)** [ ] [ ]
(ext;12"+=/cd-s+=) – Oh you angel / U.S. male.

—— split after this final flop, although they re-formed in 1993

Big Life / Mercury

Jun 93. (cd/c) *<519261-2/-4>* **HEY ZEUS!** [-] [ ]
– Someone's watching / Big blue house / Clean like tomorrow / New life / Country at war / Arms for hostages / Into the light / Lettuce and vodka / Everybody / Baby you lied / Drawn in the dark.

Jul 93. (c-s) *(BLRC 94)* **COUNTRY AT WAR /** [ ] [ ]
(12"+=/cd-s+=) *(BLR T/D 94)* –

not iss. / Infidelity

Jun 95. (cd) *<10812>* **UNCLOGGED** (acoustic live) [-] [ ]
– White girl / Because I do / Lying in the road / Unheard music / I must not think bad thoughts / Burning house of love / Stage / See how we are / True love / Have nots / The world's a mess, it's in my kiss / I see red / What's wrong with me.

—— when they finally split, EXENE fronted the band AUNTIE CHRIST who had signed to 'Lookout!'; included in their ranks, MATT FREEMAN (of RANCID).

– compilations, etc. –

Oct 97. (d-cd) *Elektra; <62103>* **BEYOND & BACK: THE X ANTHOLOGY** [-] [ ]
– Los Angeles / The world's a mess, it's in his kiss / Yr ignition / Year one / Hungry wolf / We're desperate / Beyond and back / Back 2 the base / Blue spark / Some other time / Sex and dying in high society / Motel room in my bed / Heater / Once over twice / Because I do / In this house I call home / Soul kitchen / Universal corner / Delta 88 / Real child of hell / I'm coming over / White girl / Nausea / Johnny hit and run Paulene / You phone's off the hook but you're / Riding with Mary / New world / Breathless / Poor girl / What's wrong with me / How I (learned my lesson) / Have nots / Someone like you / Stage / See how we are / Surprise, surprise / 4th of July / Arms for hostages – Country at war / Wild thing / Burning house of love / Devil doll / True love / Call of the wreckin' ball / In the time it takes / I must not think bad thoughts.

JOHN DOE

—— with band; **JOHN DEE GRAHAM** – guitar / **RICHARD LLOYD** – guitar (ex-TELEVISION) /**TONY MARSICO** – bass / **JEFF DONAVAN** – drums

D.G.C. / D.G.C.

Jun 90. (cd/c/lp) *<(7599 24291-2/-4/-1)>* **MEET JOHN DOE** [ ] [ ]
– Let's be mad / A matter of degrees / Dyin' to get home / It's only love / The real one / Take #52 / Worldwide brotherhood / With someone like you / By the light / Knockin' around / Touch me, baby / My offering.

—— next with various session people including EXENE + DJ BONEBRAKE (actress SANDRA BERNHARD also makes an appearance)

Forward / Rhino

1995. (cd) *<72134>* **KISSINGSOHARD** [-] [ ]
– Fallen tears / Safety / Love knows / Mo goodness / Tragedy by definition / Kissing / Hits the ground / Going down fast / TV set / Beer, gas, ride forever / Field of dirt / Williamette / Liar's market.

not iss. / Kill Rock Stars

Jan 98. (cd-ep; as JOHN THING DOE) *<KRS 290>* **FOR THE REST OF US** [-] [ ]
– Step outside / Let's get lost / Unhappy song / Bad, bad feeling / This loving thing.

EXENE CERVENKA

not iss. / Freeway

Jan 86. (lp; EXENE CERVENKA WANDA COLEMAN) *<FRWY 1057>* **TWIN SISTERS: LIVE AT McCABE'S (live poetry)** [-] [ ]

—— with **TONY GILKYSON / STEVE NELSON / JIM CHRISTIE / KEN STRANGE / JULIE CHRISTENSEN / ELIZA GILKYSON** etc not iss. / Rhino

1989. (lp/c/cd) *<R2/R4/R1 70913>* **OLD WIVES' TALES** [-] [ ]
– She wanted / Biggest memory / Here come the crucifiers / Cocktail trees / Famous barmaid / Leave Heaven alone / Good luck / White trash wife / He's got a she / Gravel / Coyote on the town.

1990. (cd/c) *<R2/R4 70757>* **RUNNING SCARED** [-] [ ]
– Slave labor / Clinic / Red dirt / Real estate / Curtains / The boy and his sister / Same denomination / Missing nature / It fell / The ballad of Roberta / Just another perfect day / Will Jesus wash the bloodstains from our souls.

— EXENE also released an album, 'RUDE HIEROGLYPHICS', with LYDIA LUNCH

2.13.61 / Thirsty Ear

Jun 96. (cd) *<(213CD 04)>* **SURFACE TO AIR SERPENTS** [ ] [ ]
– Big stain / Dream bodies / In the year of the ant / Unfortunate / Flies without borders / Living / Closing numbers / Truce / Magdalene / Deep end / Like morning / Three stories / Clay / I want questions / I want answers / I want / Good, then its unanimous/ Being and everythingness / Waiting / Hello / Debate / What is there to be at one with?

X-MAL DEUTSCHLAND

Formed: Hamburg, Germany . . . 1980 by ANJA HUWE, MANUELA RICKERS, FIONA SANGSTER, RITA SIMON and CARO MAY (the latter two were subsequently replaced by MANUELA ZWINGMAN and lone male, WOLFGANG ELLERBROCK). Having issued a couple of 12" singles in their homeland (including the first version of 'INCUBBUS SUCCUBUS'), they were a surprise signing to '4 a.d.' in 1982 after a support slot to the COCTEAU TWINS. Despite refusing to compromise with regards to singing in English, HUWE's vocals were used to startling effect on the band's debut album, 'FETISCH' (1983). Broodingly different in common with all the acts on the label, X-MAL DEUTSCHLAND's gothic post-punk displayed some definite SIOUXSIE-like overtones. However, the departure of ZWINGMANN (for PETER BELLENDIR) seemed to upset the delicate balance of their sound and, although their follow-up set, 'TOCSIN' (1984) briefly entered the Top 75 their dark charm seemed to have deserted them. Disgarded by '4 a.d.', X-MAL took refuge at a Phonogram offshoot 'X-Ile' and delivered (after a couple of singles) an album, 'VIVA', in 1987. This failed to halt the decline, ANJA and WOLFGANG overhauling the band and introducing new blood for the unashamedly poppy set, 'DEVILS' (1989).

Album rating: FETISCH (*7) / TOCSIN (*5) / VIVA (*3) / DEVILS (*2)

ANJA HUWE – vocals / **MANUELA RICKERS** – guitar / **FIONA SANGSTER** – keyboards / **WOLFGANG ELLERBROCK** – bass; repl. RITA SIMON / **MANUELA ZWINGMAN** – drums; repl. CARO MAY

Zick Zack / not iss.

Dec 81. (12") **SCHWARZE WELT. / DIE WOLKEN / GROBSTADTINDIANER** [-] [-] German

Jan 83. (12") *(6060)* **INCUBBUS SUCCUBUS. / BLUT IST LEIBE / ZU JUNG ZU WAN** [-] [-] German

4 a.d. / not iss.

Mar 83. (lp) *(CAD 302)* **FETISCH** [ ] [-]
– Qual / Geheimnis / Young man / In der nacht / Orient / Hand in hand / Kaempfen / Danghem / Boomerang / Stummes kind. *(cd-iss. Jun87 +=; CAD 302CD)* – Qual (remix) / Zeit / Sehnsucht. *(cd re-iss. Jul98; GAD 302CD)*

May 83. (12") *(BAD 305)* **QUAL (remix). / ZEIT / SEHNSUCHT** [ ] [-]

Sep 83. (7"/12") *(AD/BAD 311)* **INCUBBUS SUCCUBUS II. / VITO** [ ] [-]

— **PETER BELLENDIR** – drums; repl. ZWINGMAN

Jun 84. (lp) *(CAD 407)* **TOCSIN** [66] [-]
– Mondlicht / Eiland / Reigen / Tag fur tag / Augen-Blick / Begrab mein herz / Nachtschatten / Xmas's in Australia / Derwisch. *(cd-iss. Jun87 +=; CAD 407CD)* – Incubbus succubbus II / Vito. *(cd re-iss. Jul98; GAD 407CD)*

Red Rhino Europe / not iss.

Oct 85. (12"ep) *(RRET 1)* **SEQUENZ / JAHR UM JAHR. / AUTUMN / POLARLICHT** [ ] [-]

X-Ile – Phonogram / not iss.

Sep 86. (7"/12") *(XMAL 1/+12)* **MATADOR. / PAHO** [ ] [-]
(12") *(XMALR 1-12)* –

Feb 87. (7") *(XMAL 2)* **SICKLE MOON. / ILLUSION** [ ] [-]
(ext.12"+=) *(XMAL 2-12)* – In onyx.

Mar 87. (lp/c)(cd) *(XMA LP/MC 1)(830862-2)* **VIVA** [ ] [-]
– Matador / Eisengrau / Sickle moon / If only / Feuerwerk / Illusion / Morning (will there really be) / Manchmal / Polarlicht / Ozean / Dogma 1. *(cd+=/c+=)* – Illusion four.

— **ANJA + WOLFGANG** recruited new members **FRANK Z + WESLEY PLASS** – guitars / **CURT CRESS** – drums / + producer **HENRY STAROSTE** – keyboards

Metrognome / not iss.

Feb 89. (lp/cd; as X-MAL) *(837940-1/-2)* **DEVILS** [-] [-] German
– I'll be near you / Searchlights / You broke my heart / Sleepwalker / When devils come / Heavens and seas / Dreamhouse / I push it harder / I should have known / All in my hands.

— disbanded after the disaster that was above

– compilations, etc. –

Nov 86. (12"ep) *Strange Fruit; (SFPS 017)* **THE PEEL SESSIONS** (13.5.85) [ ] [-]
– Polarlicht / Der wind / Jahr um jahr / Autumn.

X-RAY SPEX

Formed: Brixton, London, England . . . 1977 by POLY STYRENE, JAK 'AIRPORT' STAFFORD, LORA LOGIC, PAUL DEAN and B.P. HURDING. Fronted by the inimitable STYRENE (a woman who turned metal-braced dentures and figure hugging black bin-liners into a punk fashion statement!), the group secured a residency at the infamous Roxy club, contributing live favourite, 'OH BONDAGE, UP YOURS!' to the club's celebrated v/a compilation. A considerably tamer studio version was released on 'Virgin' in late '77, after which STEVE 'RUDI' THOMPSON relpaced LORA as the band's in-house sax player. Together with STYRENE's banshee wail, the demented sax honking (employed in a STOOGES kinda fashion) marked out X-RAY SPEX from the three-chord hordes and put a groovy spin on such memorable singles as 'THE DAY THE WORLD TURNED DAY-GLO' (the group's first single for 'E.M.I.' and the first of three chart hits), the seething 'IDENTITY' and 'GERMFREE ADOLESCENTS'. The latter track was also the title of the band's one and only album, STYRENE venting her spleen/wondering aloud at the absurdities of a production line society; listen to 'WARRIOR IN WOOLWORTHS' and weep, possibly. Released in late '78, the album made the Top 30 and spawned a further single in 'HIGHLY INFLAMMABLE' the following Spring. In true punk style, however, the group disbanded while their influence was being felt most acutely, only HURDING going on to anything resembling fame with CLASSIX NOUVEAUX. STYRENE, meanwhile, opted for Krishna consciousness, releasing a suitably blissed out solo set, 'TRANSLUCENCE' (1980), before taking an extended sabbatical. Finally, in 1995, STYRENE resurrected the original X-RAY SPEX line-up and released 'CONSCIOUS CONSUMER' on the independent 'Receiver' label.

Album rating: GERMFREE ADOLESCENTS (*8)

POLY STYRENE (b. MARION ELLIOT, 1962) – vocals / **JAK 'AIRPORT' STAFFORD** – guitar / **LORA LOGIC** (b. SUSAN WHITBY, 1961) – saxophone / **PAUL DEAN** – bass / **B.P.HURDING** (b. CHRIS CHRYSLER) – drums

Virgin / not iss.

Oct 77. (7"/12") *(VS 189/+12)* **OH BONDAGE! UP YOURS!. / I AM A CLICHE** [ ] [-]

— **STEVE 'RUDI' THOMPSON** – saxophone repl. LORA who formed ESSENTIAL LOGIC

EMI Internat. / E.M.I.

Mar 78. (7",7"orange) *(INT 553)* **THE DAY THE WORLD TURNED DAY-GLO. / IAMA POSEUR** [23] [ ]

Jul 78. (7",7"pink) *(INT 563)* **IDENTITY. / LET'S SUBMERGE** [24] [ ]

Oct 78. (7") *(INT 573)* **GERMFREE ADOLESCENTS. / AGE** [19] [ ]

Nov 78. (lp/c) *(INS/TCINS 3023)* **GERMFREE ADOLESCENTS** [30] [ ]
– The day the world turned day-glo / Obsessed with you / Genetic engineering / Identity / I live off you / Germfree adolescents / Art-i-ficial / Let's submerge / Warrior in Woolworths / Iama poseur / I can't do anything / Highly inflammable / Age / Plastic bag / I am a cliche / Oh bondage up yours!. *(re-iss. Jun92 on 'Virgin' cd/c; CD/TC VM 9001) <US cd-iss. 1991 on 'Caroline'; CAROL 1813-2>*

Apr 79. (7",7"red) *(INT 583)* **HIGHLY INFLAMMABLE. / WARRIOR IN WOOLWORTHS** [45] [-]

— **JOHN GLIN** – saxophone repl. THOMPSON. Disbanded soon after, GLIN formed The LIVING LEGEND. JAK and PAUL formed AIRPORT & DEAN, while HURDING joined CLASSIX NOUVEAUX.

POLY STYRENE

went solo augmented by **GT MOORE** – guitar / **RICHARD MOORE** – guitar / **KEVIN McALEA** – keyboards / **KUMA KARADA** – bass / **RICHARD BAILEY** – drums / **TED BUNTING** – horns / **DARYLL LEE QUE** – percussion

U.A. / not iss.

Sep 80. (7") *(BP 370)* **TALK IN TOYTOWN. / SUB-TROPICAL** [ ] [-]

Nov 80. (lp) *(UAG 30320)* **TRANSLUCENCE** [ ] [-]
– Dreaming / Talk in Toytown / Sky diver / The day that time forgot / Shades / Essence / Hip city / Bicycle song / Sub-tropical / Translucent / Age / Goodbye. *(re-iss. Mar90 on 'Receiver' cd/c/lp; RRCD/RRLC/RRLP 128)*

— POLY (MARION) took a long sabbatical to bring up her family; she returned to the studio after five years.

Awesome / not iss.

Aug 86. (7"ep/12"ep) *(AOR 7/+T)* **GODS AND GODDESSES** [ ] [-]
– Trick of the witch / Paramatma / Sacred temple / Big boys, big toys.

— In 1990, POLY was part of The DREAM ACADEMY

X-RAY SPEX

— re-formed with **POLY STYRENE / LAURA LOGIC / PAUL DEAN + HURDING**

Receiver / Receiver

Nov 95. (cd) *(<RRCD 205>)* **CONSCIOUS CONSUMER** [ ] [ ]
– Cigarettes / Junk food junkie / Crystal / India / Dog in Sweden / Hi chaperone / Good time girl / Melancholy / Sophia / Peace meal / Prayer for peace / Party.

– compilations, etc. –

Mar 91. (cd/c/lp) *Receiver; (<RR CD/MC/LP 140>)* **LIVE AT THE ROXY CLUB (live)** [ ] [ ]

Jul 91. (cd/lp) *Receiver; (<RR CD/LP 145>)* **OBSESSED WITH YOU** [ ] [ ]

XTC

Formed: Swindon, Wiltshire, England ... 1976 after 3 years of calling themselves The HELIUM KIDZ. Not an early version of acid house as the name might suggest, XTC traded in a quirky blend of pop that owed more to quintessential English psychedelia than the nihilistic three chord assault of their punk peers. Nevertheless, they were picked up by 'Virgin' in the signing scramble that followed The SEX PISTOLS early success in 1977. The debut album, 'WHITE MUSIC' (1978), introduced their tentative art-pop sound, PARTRIDGE's songwriting talent much in evidence even at this early stage. The JOHN LECKIE (STONE ROSES, RADIOHEAD,etc.) produced 'GO 2' (1978) was a more sonically adventurous follow-up, heavily influenced by BRIAN ENO and moulding their pop with quirky electronica. Soon after the record's release, ANDREWS left to join ROBERT FRIPP's 'LEAGUE OF GENTLEMEN' and was replaced by DAVE GREGORY. The new improved unit cut the successful 'DRUMS AND WIRES' (1979) album which spawned a top 20 hit single, the hypnotic, MOULDING-penned 'MAKING PLANS FOR NIGEL'. The rest of the tracks were just as catchy in their distinctive, left-of-centre way. This signalled the onset of a punishing touring/recording schedule during which time the band released a succession of impressive singles, some of which went top 20 and an album, 'BLACK SEA' (1980), that hinted at the psychedelic nostalgia which would characterise their later output. 'ENGLISH SETTLEMENT' (1982) is generally held to be band's finest hour. A double set, the record artfully blended rustic folk, ethnic rhythms and synthesizer pop, all shot through with the spectral hue of psychedelia. Although the stellar single, 'SENSES WORKING OVERTIME' was one of the band's biggest hits and XTC looked to be headed for the big time, PARTRIDGE, never comfortable with live performance, was dreading the inevitable round of touring. In the event, after a few disastrous shows he decided he could suffer it no longer and shortly after, announced that the band would never tour again. CHAMBERS promptly left, unhappy with such a prospect and although PARTRIDGE was now suffering from Agoraphobia, the band struggled on. With no full-time drummer and a string of producers, 'MUMMER' (1983) and 'THE BIG EXPRESS' (1983) were inconsistent and lacking in direction although 'EVERYDAY STORY OF SMALLTOWN' from the latter set was a charming piece of nostalgia-pop. It was clear the band needed some fresh inspiration and with the help of JOHN LECKIE they cut the '25 O'CLOCK' mini-album in 1985 under the pseudonym DUKES OF STRATOSPHERE. More overtly psychedelic than any previous XTC material, PARTRIDGE was given free range to indulge his obvious passions. Re-energised, the band were paired with TODD RUNDGREN for 'SKYLARKING' (1986) and although there were some well documented clashes between PARTRIDGE and the maverick American, the resultant album was a triumphant return to form. Embellishing the gentle hybrid of 'ENGLISH SETTLEMENT' with a 'PET SOUNDS'-like sonic richness, the album spawned the sultry single 'GRASS'. Its B-side, the semi-acoustic sweep of 'DEAR GOD' was picked up by American radio, with the end result that 'SKYLARKING' was a considerable stateside success. After a final DUKES OF STRATOSPHERE album, 'PSONIC PSUNSPOT', XTC began work on the 'ORANGES AND LEMONS' set. Released in 1989, the album was another resounding success, creatively at least, and spawned the charming 'MAYOR OF SIMPLETON' single. While the album was a relative success in America, it failed to make any lasting impact in the U.K. and after 'NONESUCH' (1992) stiffed completely, XTC faded into obscrity. Although sightings are rare, PARTRIDGE has surfaced occasionally, notably on the HAROLD BUDD collaboration, 'THROUGH THE HILL', in 1994. • **Songwriters:** Either penned by PARTRIDGE or MOULDING or both. Covered ALL ALONG THE WATCHTOWER (Bob Dylan) / ELLA GURU (Captain Beefheart).

Album rating: ENGLISH SETTLEMENT (*8) / WHITE MUSIC (*8) / THE COMPACT XTC – THE SINGLES 1978-1985 (*9) / DRUMS AND WIRES (*8) / SKYLARKING (*7) / ORANGES AND LEMONS (*7)

ANDY PARTRIDGE (b.11 Dec'53) – vocals, guitar / **COLIN MOULDING** (b.17 Aug'55) – bass, vocals / **BARRY ANDREWS** (b.12 Sep'56, London) – keyboards repl. JONATHAN PERKINS / **TERRY CHAMBERS** (b.18 Jul'55) – drums

Virgin / Virgin-Epic

Oct 77. (7") *(VS 188)* **SCIENCE FRICTION. / SHE'S SO SQUARE** [ ] [-]
(12"ep+=) *(VS 188-12)* **3-D** – Dance band.

Jan 78. (7") *(VS 201)* **STATUE OF LIBERTY. / HANG ON TO THE NIGHT** [ ] [-]

Feb 78. (lp/c) *(V/TCV 2095)* **WHITE MUSIC** [38] [ ]
– Radios in motion / Cross wires / This is pop? / Do what you do / Statue of liberty / All along the watchtower / Into the atom age / I'll set myself on fire / I'm bugged / New town animal in a furnished cage / Neon shuffle. *(re-iss. Mar84 lp/c; OVED/+C 60) (cd-iss. Mar87 +=; CDV 2095)* – Science friction / She's so square / Dance band / Hang on to the night / Heatwave / Traffic light rock / Instant tunes.

Apr 78. (7") *(VS 209)* **THIS IS POP?. / HEATWAVE** [ ] [-]

Oct 78. (7") *(VS 231)* **ARE YOU RECEIVING ME. / INSTANT TUNES** [ ] [-]

Oct 78. (lp/c) *(V/TCV 2108)* **GO 2** [21] [ ]
– Mekanic dancing (oh we go!) / Battery brides / Buzzcity talking / Crowded room / The rhythm / Beatown / My weapon / Life is good in the greenhouse / Jumping in Gomorrah / My weapon / Super-tuff. *(free-12"ep w/ lp)* **GO +** – Dance with me Germany / Beat the bible / A dictionary of modern marriage / Clap, clap, clap / We kill the beast. *(re-iss. Mar84 lp/c; OVED/+C 61) (cd-iss. Jul87 +=; CDV 2108)* – Are you receiving me.

— **DAVE GREGORY** – synthesizers, guitar repl. ANDREWS who joined LEAGUE OF GENTLEMEN (w/ ROBERT FRIPP). He later went solo and formed SHRIEKBACK

May 79. (7",7"clear) *(VS 259)* **LIFE BEGINS AT THE HOP. / HOMO SAFARI** [54] [-]

Virgin / Virgin Atlantic

Aug 79. (lp/c) *(V/TCV 2129)* *<VA 13134>* **DRUMS AND WIRES** [34] [ ]
– Making plans for Nigel / Helicopter / Life begins at the hop / When you're near me I have difficulty / Ten feet tall / Roads girdle the globe / Reel by reel / Millions / That is the way / Outside world / Scissor man / Complicated game. *(free-7"w/ lp)* – LIMELIGHT. / CHAIN OF COMMAND *(re-iss. 1986 lp/c; OVED/+C 113) (cd-iss. Jun88 +=; CDV 2129)* – Limelight / Chain of command.

Sep 79. (7"m) *(VS 282)* **MAKING PLANS FOR NIGEL. / BUSHMAN PRESIDENT (HSS 2) / PULSING, PULSING** [17] [-]

Nov 79. (7") **TEN FEET TALL. / HELICOPTER / THE SOMNAMBULIST** [-] [ ]

Feb 80. (7"m) *<VA 67009>* **MAKING PLANS FOR NIGEL. / THIS IS POP? / MEKANIC DANCING (OH WE GO!)** [-] [ ]

Mar 80. (7") *(VS 322)* **WAIT TILL YOUR BOAT GOES DOWN. / TEN FEET TALL (U.S. version)** [ ] [ ]

Aug 80. (7") *(VS 365)* **GENERALS AND MAJORS. / DON'T LOSE YOUR TEMPER** [32] [ ]
(d7"+=) *(VS 365)* – Smokeless zone. / The somnambulist.

Sep 80. (lp/c) *(V/TCV 2173)* *<VA 13147>* **BLACK SEA** [16] [41]
– Respectable Street / General and majors / Living through another Cuba / Love at first sight / Rocket from a bottle / No language in our lungs / Towers of London / Paper and iron (notes and coins) / Burning with optimism's flames / Sgt. Rock (is going to help me) / Travels in Nihilon. *(re-iss. 1986 lp/c; OVED/+C 83) (cd-iss. Mar87 +=; CDV 2172)* – Smokeless zone / Don't lose your temper / The somnambulist.

Oct 80. (7") *(VS 372)* **TOWERS OF LONDON. / SET MYSELF ON FIRE (live)** [31] [ ]
(d7"+=) *(VS 372)* – Battery brides (live) / Scissor man.

Oct 80. (7"; as The COLONEL) *(VS 380)* **TOO MANY COOKS IN THE KITCHEN. / I NEED PROTECTION** [ ] [-]
(above by The COLONEL; aka MOULDING + CHAMBERS)

Nov 80. (7") *(RSO 71)* **TAKE THIS TOWN. / (b-side by The Ruts)** [ ] [ ]
(above single was from 'Times Square' film soundtrack on 'R.S.O.')

Dec 80. (7") **LOVE AT FIRST SIGHT. / ROCKET FROM A BOTTLE** [-] [ ]

Jan 81. (7"m) *(VS 384)* **SGT. ROCK (IS GOING TO HELP ME). / LIVING THROUGH ANOTHER CUBA (live) / GENERALS AND MAJORS (live)** [16] [ ]

Mar 81. (7"m) *(VS 407)* **RESPECTABLE STREET. / STRANGE TALES, STRANGE TAILS / OFFICER BLUE** [ ] [ ]

Virgin / Epic

Jan 82. (7"m) *(VS 462)* **SENSES WORKING OVERTIME. / BLAME THE WEATHER / TISSUE TIGERS** [10] [-]
(12"+=) *(VS 462-12)* – Egyptian solution (HSS 3).

Feb 82. (d-lp/c)<US-lp> *(V/TCV 2223)* *<37943>* **ENGLISH SETTLEMENT** [5] [48] Mar82
– Runaways / Ball and chain / Senses working overtime / Jason and the Argonauts / No thugs in our house / Yacht dance / All of a sudden (it's too late) / Melt the guns / ** Leisure * / It's nearly Africa * / Knuckle down * / Fly on the wall * / ** Down in the cockpit * / English roundabout / Snowman. *<US single-lp version omits *>* *(cd-iss. Jun88; CDV 2223)*; omits tracks **)

Mar 82. (7"m) *(VS 482)* **BALL AND CHAIN. / PUNCH AND JUDY / HEAVEN IS PAVED WITH BROKEN GLASS** [58] [ ]
(12"+=) *(VS 482-12)* – Cockpit dance mixture.

May 82. (7"ep,9"ep) *(VS 490)* **NO THUGS IN OUR HOUSE / CHAIN OF COMMAND. / LIMELIGHT / OVER RUSTY WALLS** [ ] [-]

May 82. (7") **SENSES WORKING OVERTIME. / ENGLISH ROUNDABOUT** [-] [ ]

Nov 82. (lp/c) *(V/TCV 2251)* **WAXWORKS** (A-sides compilation) [54] [-]
(free lp w/ above) **BEESWAX** (B-sides) (re-iss. Dec82 lp/c; *OVED/+C 9)*

— Trimmed to basic trio of **PARTRIDGE, MOULDING + GREGORY** plus on session **PETER PHIPPES** – drums (ex-GLITTER BAND) (CHAMBERS emigrated to Australia)

Virgin / Geffen

Apr 83. (7") *(VS 553)* **GREAT FIRE. / GOLD** [ ] [-]
(12"+=) *(VS 553-12)* – Frost circus (HSS 5) / Procession towards learning land (HSS 6).

Jul 83. (7"/7"pic-d) *(VS/+Y 606)* **WONDERLAND. / JUMP** [ ] [ ]

Aug 83. (lp/c) *(V/TCV 2264)* *<4027>* **MUMMER** [51] [ ]
– Beating of hearts / Wonderland / Love on a farmboy's wages / Great fire / Deliver us from the elements / Human alchemy / Ladybird / In loving memory of a name / Me and the wind / Funk pop a roll. *(re-iss. 1986 lp/c; OVED/+C 142) (cd-iss. Mar87 +=; CDV 2264)* – Frost circus (HSS 5) / Jump / Toys / Gold / Procession towards learning land (HSS 6) / Desert island.

Sep 83. (7") *(VS 613)* **LOVE ON A FARMBOY'S WAGES. / IN LOVING MEMORY OF A NAME** [50] [ ]
(d7"+=) *(VS 613)* – Desert island / Toys.
(12") *(VS 613-12)* – ('A'side) / Burning with optimism's flames (live / English roundabout (live) / Cut it out (live).

Nov 83. (7"; as THREE WISE MEN) *(VS 642)* **THANKS FOR CHRISTMAS. / COUNTDOWN TO CHRISTMAS PARTYTIME** [ ] [-]

Sep 84. (7") *(VS 709)* **ALL YOU PRETTY GIRLS. / WASHAWAY** [55] [ ]
(12"+=) *(VS 709-12)* – Red brick dream.

Oct 84. (lp/c) *(V/TCV 2325)* *<24054>* **THE BIG EXPRESS** [38] [ ]
– Wake up / All you pretty girls / Shake you donkey up / Seagulls screaming kiss her, kiss her / This world over / The everyday story of Smalltown / I bought myself a liarbird / Reign of blows / You're the wish you are I had / I remember the sun / Train running low on soul coal. *(cd-iss. 1987 +=; CDV 2325)* – Red brick dreams / Washaway / Blue overall. *(re-iss. 1988 lp/c; OVED/+C 182)*

Oct 84. (7"/12") *(VS 721/+12)* **THIS WORLD OVER. / BLUE OVERALL** [ ] [ ]

Jan 85. (7"m) *(VS 746)* **WAKE UP. / TAKE THIS TOWN / MANTIS ON PAROLE (HSS 4)** [ ] [ ]
(12"+=) *(VS 746-12)* – Making plans for Nigel / Sgt. Rock (is going to help me) / Senses working overtime.

— **IAN GREGORY** (DAVE's brother) – drums repl. PHIPPES

DUKES OF STRATOSPHEAR

Apr 85. (7") *(VS 763)* **THE MOLE FROM THE MINISTRY. / MY LOVE EXPLODES** [ ] [-]
Apr 85. (m-lp/c) *(WOW/+C 1)* **25 O'CLOCK** [ ] [ ]
– 25 o'clock / Bike ride to the Moon / My love explodes / What in the world . . . / Your gold dress / The mole from the ministry.

XTC

Aug 86. (7") *(VS 882)* **GRASS. / DEAR GOD** [ ] [ ]
(12"+=) *(VS 882-12)* – Extrovert.
Oct 86. (lp/c/cd) *(V/TCV/CDV 2399) <24117>* **SKYLARKING** [90] [70]
– Summer's cauldron / Grass / The meeting place / That's really super, Supergirl / Ballet for a rainy day / 1000 umbrellas / Season cycle / Earn enough for us / Big day / Another satellite / Mermaid smiled * / The man who sailed around his soul / Dying / Sacrificial bonfire. *<re-iss. 1987; 'Dear God' repl. *>*
Jan 87. (7"/7"clear) *(VS/+Y 912)* **THE MEETING PLACE. / THE MAN WHO SAILED AROUND HIS SOUL** [ ] [ ]
(12"+=) *(VS 912-12)* – Terrorism.
Jun 87. (7") *(VS 960)* **DEAR GOD. / BIG DAY** [ ] [ ]
(12"+=) *(VS 960-12)* – Another satellite (live).
(cd-s) *(CDEP 3)* – ('A'side) / Homo safari series (HSS 1-6):- Homo safari / Bushman president / Egyptian solution / Mantis on parole / Frost circus / Procession towards learning land.
Jul 87. (7") **DEAR GOD. / MERMAID SMILED** [-] [ ]

DUKES OF STRATOSPHEAR

Jul 87. (7"/7"colrd) *(VS/+Y 982)* **YOU'RE A GOOD MAN ALBERT BROWN (CURSE YOU RED BARREL). / VANISHING GIRL** [ ] [-]
(12"+=) *(VS 982-12)* – The mole from the ministry / My love explodes.
Aug 87. (lp/colrd-lp/c) *(V/VP/TCV 2440)* **PSONIC PSUNSPOT** [ ] [ ]
– Vanishing girl / Have you seen Jackie? / Little lighthouse / You're a good man Albert Brown (curse you red barrel) / Collideascope / You're my drug / Shiny cage / Brainiac's daughter / The affiliated / Pale and precious.
1989. (cd) *(COMCD 11)* **CHIPS FROM THE CHOCOLATE FIREBALL** [ ] [ ]
– (25 O'CLOCK / PSONIC PSUNSPOT)

XTC

— **PAT MASTELOTTO** – drums (of MR. MISTER) repl. IAN
Jan 89. (7") *(VS 1158)* **THE MAYOR OF SIMPLETON. / ONE OF THE MILLIONS** [46] [72]
(12"+=) *(VST 1158)* – Ella guru.
(3"cd-s) *(VSCD 1158)* – ('A'side) / Ella guru / Living in a haunted heart / The good thing.
(12") *(VSR 1158)* – ('A'side) / Dear God / Senses working overtime / Making plans for Nigel.
Feb 89. (d-lp/c/cd) *(V/TCV/CDV 2581) <24218>* **ORANGES AND LEMONS** [28] [44]
– Garden of earthly delights / The Mayor of Simpleton / King for a day / Here comes President Kill again / The loving / Poor skeleton steps out / One of the millions / Scarecrow people / Merely a man / Cynical days / Across this antheap / Hold me my daddy / Pink thing / Miniature sun / Chalkhills and children. *(re-iss. Oct89, 3xcd-ep-box; CDVT 2581)*
Apr 89. (7") *(VS 1177)* **KING FOR A DAY. / HAPPY FAMILIES** [ ] [-]
(12"+=) *(VST 1177)* – ('A'extended).
(c-s+=) *(VSC 1177)* – Generals and majors / Towers of London.
(3"cd-s) *(VSCD 1177)* – ('A'extended) / ('A'side) / My paint heroes (home demo) / Skeletons (home demo).
Aug 89. (7") *(VS 1201)* **THE LOVING. / CYNICAL DAYS** [ ] [ ]
(c-s) *(VSC 1201)* – ('A'side) / The world is full of angry young men.
(12"/cd-s) *(VS T/CD 1201)* – (all 3 tracks).
Sep 89. (cd-ep) *<9-21236-2>* **KING FOR A DAY (Czar mix) / ('A' Versailles mix) / TOYS / DESERT ISLAND** [-] [ ]
Mar 92. (7"/c-s) *(VS/+C 1404)* **THE DISAPPOINTED. / THE SMARTEST MONKEYS** [33] [ ]
(10"+=) *(VST 1404)* – Humble Daisy.
(cd-s++=) *(VSCD 1404)* ('B'demo).
May 92 (cd/c/d-lp) *(CD/TC+/V 2699) <24474>* **NONESUCH** [28] [97]
– The ballad of Peter Pumpkinhead / My bird performs / Dear Madam Barnum / Humble Daisy / The smartest monkeys / The dismal / Holly up on poppy / Crocodile / Rook / Omnibus / That wave / Then she appeared / War dance / Wrapped in grey / The ugly underneath / Bungalow / Books are burning.
Jun 92. (7"/c-s) *(VS/+C 1415)* **THE BALLAD OF PETER PUMPKINHEAD. / WAR DANCE** [71] [ ]
(cd-s+=) *(VSCD1 1415)* – Down a peg (demo) / ('A'demo).
(cd-s+=) *(VSCD2 1415)* – My bird performs (demo) / Always winter never Christmas (demo).

– compilations, others, etc. –

on 'Virgin' unless otherwise mentioned
Jan 87. (cd) *(CDV 2251)* **THE COMPACT XTC – THE SINGLES 1978-1985** [ ] [-]
– Science friction / Statue of liberty / This is pop? / Are you receiving me / Life begins at the hop / Making plans for Nigel / Wait till your boat goes down / Generals and majors / Towers of London / Sgt. Rock (is going to help me) / Senses working overtime / Ball and chain / Great fire / Wonderland / Love on a farmboy's wages / All you pretty girls / This world over / Wake up.
Jul 88. (3"cd-ep) *(VSCDT 9)* **SENSES WORKING OVERTIME / BLAME THE WEATHER / TISSUE TIGERS** [ ] [-]
Nov 88. (7") *Old Gold; (OG 9819)* **MAKING PLANS FOR NIGEL. / SENSES WORKING OVERTIME** [ ] [-]
Aug 90. (cd) *(CDOVD 308)* **EXPLODE TOGETHER (THE DUB EXPERIMENTS 78-80)** [ ] [-]
– (included the ANDY PARTRIDGE album below)
Aug 90. (cd) *(CDOVD 311) / Geffen; <24417>* **RAG & BONE BUFFET** (rare) [ ] [ ]
Nov 94. (cd) *Night Tracks; (CDNT 008)* **DRUMS AND WIRELESS: BBC RADIO SESSIONS 77-89** [ ] [-]
Jun 96. (d-cd) *Geffen; <25137>* **UPSY DAISY ASSORTMENT (A SELECTION OF SWEETEST HITS)** [-] [ ]
Sep 96. (cd/c) *(CD/TC VD 2811)* **FOSSIL FUEL: THE XTC SINGLES 1977-92** [33] [ ]
– (nearly same tracks as 1987 collection + add more recent) *(d-cd; CDVDX 2811)*
Nov 98. (d-cd;box) *TVT; <3240>* **TRANSISTOR BLAST: BEST OF THE BBC SESSIONS** [-] [ ]

MR. PARTRIDGE

Feb 80. (lp/c) *(V/TCV 2145)* **TAKE AWAY (THE LURE OF SALVAGE)** [ ] [-]
– Commerciality / The day the pulled the North Pole down / Cairo / Madhattan / The forgotten language of light / Steam fist futurist / The rotary / Shore leave ornithology (another 1950) / I sit in the snow / Work away Tokyo day / New broom. *(re-iss. Aug88; OVED 130)*

— In Jun'94, ANDY PARTRIDGE co-released with HAROLD BUDD the cd 'THROUGH THE HILL' for 'All Saints' label.

— Also in '94, PARTRIDGE with MARTIN NEWELL, issued album 'THE GREATEST LIVING ENGLISHMAN' for 'Pipeline'.

XYMOX

Formed: Amsterdam, Netherlands . . . 1981 as CLAN OF XYMOX by RONNY MOORINGS, PIETER NOOTEN, FRANK WEYZIG and ANKE WOLBERT. Following the domestic release of debut mini-album, 'SUBSEQUENT PLEASURES', the band were signed to prominent UK indie label, '4 a.d.', releasing an eponymous follow-up set in 1985. Trading in arty electro-rock, the group sat rather uneasily alongside the more COCTEAU-esque experimentation of the label's roster as a whole. This was particularly pronounced when the likes of The PIXIES and The THROWING MUSES began to give the label more of an American slant, 1987's 'MEDUSA' album their parting shot as XYMOX – their newly abbreviated moniker – moved on to 'Polygram'. Although the band had moved toward a more accessible sound by this point, the electro-pop of 1989's 'TWIST OF SHADOWS' album (complete with trademark Vaughan Oliver artwork and string arrangements courtesy of Tony Visconti) sounded decidedly dated. By turns reminscent of ULTRAVOX, DEPECHE MODE and even NEW ORDER (especially 'IMAGINATION'), the record – which strangely made the US charts! – seemed stuck in a mid-80's groove while all the aforementioned artists (well, maybe not ULTRAVOX!) had moved on. And despite moving to England, the band failed to build a sufficient fanbase, leaving 'Polydor' after 'PHOENIX' (1991) and striking out on their own for 'METAMORPHOSIS' (1992) and 'HEADCLOUDS' (1993). • **Songwriters:** MOORINGS except WILD IS THE WIND (Tompkins – Washington). • **Trivia:** MICHAEL BROOK and GAVIN WRIGHT guested on the 1991 album.

Album rating: SUBSEQUENT PLEASURES (*4) / CLAN OF XYMOX (*7) / MEDUSA (*6) / TWIST OF SHADOWS (*5) / PHOENIX (*4) / METAMORPHOSIS (*3) / HEADCLOUDS (*4)

CLAN OF XYMOX

RONNY MOORINGS – vocals, guitar, keyboards / **PIETER NOOTEN** – vocals, keyboards / **FRANK** – guitar, keyboards / **ANKE WOLBERT** – bass, keyboards, vocals

not known / not iss.
1983. (ltd-lp) **SUBSEQUENT PLEASURES** [-] [-] Dutch
– A day (where are you) / Stumble and fall / No words / Stranger / Equal ways / 7th time / Going round / Muscoviet musquito / Strange 9 to 9 / Call it weird / Abysmal thoughts. *<US cd-iss. May94 on 'Alex'; 4419> (cd-iss. Jun97 on 'Pseudonym'; CDP 1013DD)*

4 a.d. / 4 a.d.
May 85. (lp) *(CAD 503)* **CLAN OF XYMOX** [ ] [-]
– A day / No words / Stumble and fall / Cry in the wind / Stranger / Equal ways / Seventh time / No human can drown. *(cd-iss. 1988 +=; CAD 503CD)* – (2- 12"remixes).
May 85. (12") *(BAD 504)* **A DAY. / STRANGER** [ ] [-]
Nov 86. (lp/cd) *(CAD 603/+CD) <941>* **MEDUSA** [ ] [ ]
– Theme I + II / Medusa / Michelle / Louise / Lorrentine / Agonised by love / Masquerade / After the call / Back door.

— **BURT BARTON** – keyboards repl. PIETER / **WILL ANVERS** – drums repl. FRANK / guest **ELISA RICHARDS** – backing vocals
Nov 87. (12"m) *(BAD 711)* **BLIND HEARTS. / A MILLION THINGS/ SCUM** [ ] [-]

XYMOX

MOORINGS + WOLBERT

Wing-Polydor / Atlantic
May 89. (7") *(WING 5)* **OBSESSION. / IN A CITY** [ ] [ ]
(12")(cd-s) *(WINGX 5)(871707-2)* – ('A'side) / ('A'club) / Hitchhiker's dance guide.
May 89. (lp/c/cd) *(839 233-1/-4/-2) <871707-1/-4/-2>* **TWIST OF SHADOWS** [ ] [ ]
– Evelyn / Obsession / Craving / Blind hearts / The river / A million things / Tonight / Imagination / In a city / Clementina.
Feb 90. (12",cd-s) *<873000>* **IMAGINATION. / SENSES COALESCE** [-] [85]

— **RONNY + ANKE** brought back **PIETER**
May 91. (12"/cd-s) *(PZ 146/+CD)* **PHOENIX OF MY HEART. / ('A'-Wild Thing intro-outro mix)** [ ] [ ]
Jun 91. (cd/c/lp) *(848516-2/-4/-1)* **PHOENIX** [ ] [ ]

– Phoenix of my heart / Wild thing outro / At the end of the day / The shore down under / Mar the days / Believe me sometimes / Wonderland / Written in the stars / Dancing barefoot / Smile like Heaven / Crossing the waters.

X-Ult Freestyle

Jul 92. (12"/cd-s) *(12/CD XYM 101)* **DREAM ON. / ('A'instrumental) / SOUL FREE** ☐ ☐

Zok J.R.S.

Oct 92. (cd) *(XYCD 1001) <35826>* **METAMORPHOSIS** ☐ ☐
– Tightrope walker / Dream on / B who U wanna B / Sedated / XDD / Revolve / High and low / Love me / Real / Awakening. *(re-iss. Oct94; ZCDXY 005)*

Mar 93. (12"/cd-s) *(ZCDXY 002)* **REACHING OUT (remix). / THE BEGINNING** ☐ -

May 93. (7") *(XY 003)* **SPIRITUAL HIGH. / WILD IS THE WIND** ☐ -
(12"/cd-s) *(ZVIXYCM/ZCDXY 003)* – (3 'A'mixes).

Zok Off Beat

May 93. (cd/c/lp) *(ZCDXY/ZCSXY/ZVIXY 004) <25004>* **HEADCLOUDS** ☐ ☐ Jan94
– Spiritual high / It's your life / Prophecy / Wild is the wind / A single day / Love thrills / The beginning / Reaching out / Headclouds / January. *(cd re-iss. Apr94; same)*

Koch Int. Koch Int.

Dec 94. (cd) *(34037-2)* **REMIX** ☐ -
– Spiritual high / eaching out / Dream on / Sedated / Awakening / A single day / Soul free / B who U wanna B / Reel / Headclouds / Revolve / January / Tightrope walker / Prophecy / Help your life / Love thrills / XDD / The beginning / High and low / Love me.

Lava Tess

Jun 97. (12"; as CLAN OF XYMOX) *(EFA 064922) <16>* **OUT OF THE RAIN / GOING ROUND '97 / FLATLANDS** ☐ ☐

Oct 97. (cd) *(EFA 06493-2) <15>* **HIDDEN FACES** ☐ ☐

Nov 97. (cd-s) *(EFA 06492-2)* **A DREAM OF BLUE** ☐ -

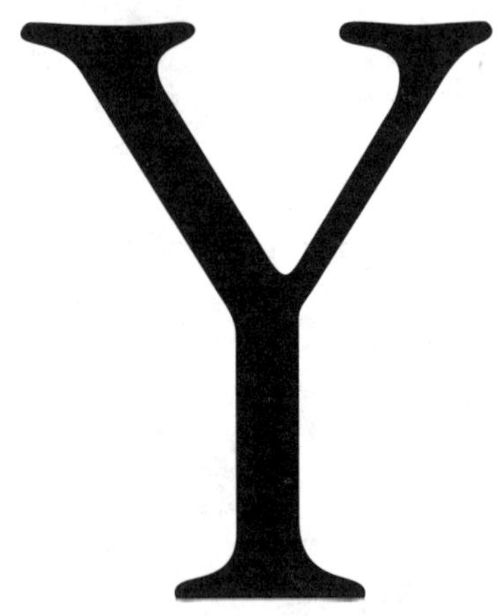

YACHTS

Formed: Liverpool, England . . . 1977 as ALBERT AND THE COD FISH WARRIORS by HENRY PRIESTMAN, J.J. CAMPBELL, MARTIN WATSON, MARTIN DEMPSEY and BOB BELLIS. Adopting the YACHTS moniker, the band cruised on to the New Wave scene via a one-off single, 'SUFFICE TO SAY', launched from the scene's flagship operation, 'Stiff'. Later that year, they almost capsized, unadvisedly issuing a pseudonymous split single (with BIG IN JAPAN) as The CHUDDY NUDDIES, the subsequent departure of CAMPBELL (later to IT'S IMMATERIAL) leaving PRIESTMAN to take the helm (he was also a member of BETTE BRIGHT & THE ILLUMINATIONS). In 1978, The YACHTS charted a different course through a deal with 'Radar', also the home of ELVIS COSTELLO and NICK LOWE (they had supported the former at Eric's in '77). A stream of singles surfaced prior to their 1979 eponymous Richard Gottehrer-produced debut set, a record that revealed The YACHTS to be one of the many outfits jostling for recognition in the overcrowded pop/rock marketplace. With GLYN HAVARD substituting the PINK MILITARY-bound DEMPSEY, the crew turned their hand to an old R.Dean Taylor classic, 'THERE'S A GHOST IN MY HOUSE', although this floundered outside chart waters, as did the follow-up album, 'WITHOUT RADAR' (1980). After a final single on 'Demon', The YACHTS finally sailed off into the sunset, only PRIESTMAN finding mainstream pop fame with The CHRISTIANS.

Album rating: THE YACHTS (*5) / WITHOUT RADAR (*5)

HENRY PRIESTMAN – vocals, keyboards / **J.J. CAMPBELL** – vocals / **MARTIN J. WATSON** – guitar, vocals / **MARTIN DEMPSEY** – bass, vocals / **BOB BELLIS** – drums

		Stiff	not iss.
Sep 77.	(7") *(BUY 19)* **SUFFICE TO SAY. / FREEDOM IS A HEADY WINE**	☐	-
		Eric's	not iss.
Nov 77.	(7"; as CHUDDY NUDDIES) *(0001)* **(A-side by Big In Japan). / DO THE CHUD**	☐	-

— now without CAMPBELL who later formed IT'S IMMATERIAL

		Radar	Polydor
Sep 78.	(7"blue) *(ADA 23)* **LOOK BACK IN LOVE (NOT IN ANGER). / I CAN'T STAY LONG ENOUGH**	☐	-
Nov 78.	(7") *(ADA 25)* **YACHTING TYPES. / HYPNOTISING LIES**	☐	-
Feb 79.	(7") <PD 2027> **YACHTING TYPES. / TANTAMOUNT TO BRIBERY**	-	☐
May 79.	(7") *(ADA 36)* **LOVE YOU, LOVE YOU. / HAZY PEOPLE**	☐	-
Jun 79.	(lp) *(RAD 19)* <PD 6220> **THE YACHTS** – Box 202 / In a second / Love you, love you / Tanytamount to bribery / Easy to please / Mantovani's hits / Then and now / Semaphore love / I can't stay long / Heads will turn / I'll be leaving you / Yachting types. *(w/ free 7"; SAM 98)* – SUFFICE TO SAY (live). / ON AND ON	☐	☐
Jul 79.	(7") *(ADA 42)* **BOX 202. / PERMANENT DAMAGE (live)**	☐	-
Nov 79.	(7") *(ADA 49)* **NOW I'M SPOKEN FOR. / SECRET AGENTS**	☐	-

— **GLYN HAVARD** – bass, vocals; repl. DEMPSEY who joined PINK MILITARY

Apr 80.	(7") *(ADA 52)* **THERE'S A GHOST IN MY HOUSE. / REVERY / YACHTING TYPES**	☐	-
May 80.	(lp) *(RAD 27)* <PD 16270> **WITHOUT RADAR** – Consequences / On the bridge / Trust you / Out of luck / This thing, that thing / March of the moderates / There's a ghost in my house / Live saving's easy / Now I'm spoken for / The lush / Don't call us / Spimosa.	☐	☐
Aug 80.	(7") *(ADA 57)* **I.O.U. / 24 HOURSE FROM TULSA**	☐	-
		Demon	not iss.
Feb 81.	(7") *(D 1005)* **A FOOL LIKE YOU. / DUBMARINE**	☐	-

— after they split, PRIESTMAN joined IT'S IMMATERIAL; he subsequently joined The CHRISTIANS

YARGO

Formed: Manchester, England . . . mid 80's by BASIL CLARKE and PHIL KIRBY, both ex-members of 'Factory' avant-popsters, BITING TONGUES. Hooking up with TONY BURNSIDE and PADDY STEER, YARGO proceeded to shake up a colourful cocktail of modern jazz, soul, blues, reggae and black rock. Memorably described as MARVIN GAYE fronting a dub/reggae outfit, the quartet made their debut on the small 'Skysaw' label with an EP, 'GET HIGH'. A second single followed in '87 before they founded their own label, 'Bodybeat', also the title of their debut album that year. An appearance on Channel 4's 'The Tube', boosted their profile no end, prompting a major label bidding war. 'London' emerged as winners, the company subsequently attempting to take YARGO's eclectic sound to a mainstream audience by repackaging the debut. The group's soundtrack-friendly approach subsequently saw them releasing a theme tune to Tony Wilson's new youth magazine show, 'The Other Side Of Midnight', prior to a follow-up album, 'COMMUNICATE' (1989). Yet YARGO failed to fulfill the commercial potential 'London' had forseen, CLARKE and Co reactivating their own 'Bodybeat' for one last live effort in '91. The frontman later released a solo single and made a guest appearance for The FUTURE SOUND OF LONDON.

Album rating: BODYBEAT (*6) / COMMUNICATE (*6) / LIVE (*5)

BASIL CLARKE – vocals (ex-BITING TONGUES) / **TONY BURNSIDE** – guitar / **PADDY STEER** – bass / **PHIL KIRBY** – drums (ex-BITING TONGUES)

		Skysaw	not iss.
1986.	(12"ep) *(SKY 6)* **GET HIGH / GET HIGH (extended). / GET THERE – GET HIGH**	☐	-
		Racket	not iss.
Feb 87.	(7"/12") *(RTL 2/3)* **CARRYING MINE. /**	☐	-
		Bodybeat	not iss.
Oct 87.	(lp/c/cd) *(BODY 002/+C/CD)* **BODYBEAT** – Carrying mine / Bodybeat blues / Lately / et there / Help / Cocaine / Another Moss side night / Bedtime for Rio.	☐	-
Oct 87.	(12") *(BODY 003)* **HELP. / BODYBEAT BLUES**	☐	-
Feb 88.	(7") *(BODY 004)* **HELP. / CARRYING MINE DUB**	☐	-
		London	London
Jun 88.	(7"/12") *(LON/+X 197)* **HELP. / BODYBEAT BLUES**	☐	-
Jul 88.	(lp/c)(cd) *(LON LP/C 64)(828 114-2)* **BODYBEAT** – (complete re-issue)	☐	☐
Sep 89.	(7"/c-s) *(LON/+CS 230)* **THE OTHER SIDE OF MIDNIGHT. / MARIMBA** (12"+=/cd-s+=) *(LONX/LONCD 230)* –	☐	☐

— guest on below **MALA GHOSH** – vocals

Oct 89.	(lp/c/cd) *(828 171-1/-4/-2)* **COMMUNICATE** *(re-iss. Apr91; same)*	☐	☐
		Bodybeat	not iss.
Sep 90.	(7") **THE LOVE REVOLUTION. /**	☐	-
Feb 91.	(cd/c/lp) *(BODY CD/MC/LP 007)* **LIVE (live)** – The love revolution (live in the studio) / The love revolution (live at the gig) / Train music / Stay / Break my spirit / Riding high / When she's there / What I got / Get high.	☐	-

— disbanded after 7 years. BASIL went solo releasing a single late '91, 'OUT OF MY FACE'. He then made a guest apearance for FUTURE SOUND OF LONDON on their 'Accelerator' album.

YEAH JAZZ

Formed: Uttoxeter, Staffordshire, England . . . 1983 by KEVIN HEAD and MARK 'CHATS' CHATFIELD, who completed the line-up with STU BALLANTYNE and IAN HITCHINS. Debuting unusually with a cassette EP, 'JULIE AND THE SEA LIONS', YEAH JAZZ progressed towards an increasingly folk-orientated sound with the addition of violinist FRANK SWEENEY, a man more used to helping out indie popsters, The JUNE BRIDES. A belated follow-up EP, 'THIS IS NOT LOVE', secured them a minor indie chart hit, although they found this small feat hard to repeat. Ex-HIGSONS man, TERRY EDWARDS joined after a further single, augmenting the sound with his distinctive sax playing on the band's first release for 'Cherry Red', 'SHARON'. The man also had a hand in the production of YEAH JAZZ's debut set, 'SIX LANE ENDS' (1988), the mysterious CHIEF replacing IAN prior to the album's release. Contractual problems dogged the band for the next few years, however, a second long-player, 'APRIL', finally given a release date in 1993. HEAD and CHATS resurfaced in '96 with a new moniker, a new line-up and a new label, 'Scout', releasing the 'SHORT STORIES' album as BIG RED KITE.

Album rating: SIX LANE ENDS (*6) / APRIL (*5) / Big Red Kite: SHORT STORIES (*5)

KEVIN HEAD (b.11 Apr'64) – vocals / **CHATS** (b. MARK CHATFIELD, 1 Apr'62) – guitar / **STU BALLANTYNE** – bass / **IAN HITCHINS** – drums

		Distinctive	not iss.
Jun 84.	(c-ep) **JULIE AND THE SEA LIONS / AMERICAN PLANES. / JULIE AND THE SEA LIONS / ANOTHER SHATTERED DREAM / TOGETHER WE BLEED**	☐	-

— with guest **FRANK SWEENEY** – violin (ex-JUNE BRIDES, ex-RINGING)

		Upright	not iss.
Jun 86.	(12"ep) *(UPT 14)* **THIS IS NOT LOVE. / ANY DAY / CHILDISH GAMES / BOB'S SONG**	☐	-
Oct 86.	(7") *(UP 18)* **SHE SAID. / RAIN** (12"+=) *(UPT 18)* – Travel scrabble.	☐	-

— added **TERRY EDWARDS** – saxophone, guitar, producer (ex-HIGSONS)

Cherry Red | not iss.

Nov 87. (7") **SHARON. / THE GIRL THE YEARS WERE KIND TO** [ ] [-]
(12"+=) – This is not love.

—— **CHIEF** – drums; repl. IAN

Apr 88. (lp) *(BRED 82)* **SIX LANE ENDS** [ ] [-]
– Sharon / Stones / Lee Marvin / All of my days / Freeland / Step into the light / Heaven / The girl the years were kind to / Dirty windows / Make a flat / Stranger than fiction / All the stars.

Oct 88. (12"m) **MORNING O'GRADY. /** [ ] [-]

—— split the following year only to return to the live circuit in '91

Native | not iss.

May 93. (cd) *(NTVCD 76)* **APRIL** [ ] [-]

—— **HEAD + CHATS** recruited **DAVE BLANT** – bass, keyboards, accordion / **LEE BEDDOW** – keyboards, guitar / **FREDDY HOPWOOD** – percussion

Scout | not iss.

May 96. (cd; as BIG RED KITE) *(SR 1010)* **SHORT STORIES** [ ] [-]

YEAH YEAH NOH

Formed: Leicester, England ... early 1984 by former music journalist DEREK HAMMOND on vocals, JOHN GRAYLAND, ADRIAN CROSSAN and SUE DOREY. Signing to MARC RILEY's 'In-Tape' imprint, they released a plethora of singles/EP's over the course of the next few years, including 'COTTAGE INDUSTRY', 'BEWARE THE WEAKLING LINES' and 'PRICK UP YOUR EARS' (collected together as the 'WHEN I AM A BIG GIRL' album). With a vocalist sounding like MORRISSEY on mogadon and a penchant for classic 60's jingle-jangle pop, YEAH YEAH NOH were enjoyable if hardly innovative. Their relatively brief lifespan came to an end in late '85 following the release of the first album proper, 'CUTTING THE HEAVENLY LAWN OF GREATNESS ... LAST RITES FOR THE GOD OF LOVE'. The record featured another version of the accompanying single, 'ANOTHER SIDE TO MRS.QUILL', under the dubiously cryptic title of 'HOME-OWNERSEXUAL'. Slated by critics, YEAH YEAH NOH were perhaps too clever for their own good, the ever evolving indie scene leaving them by the wayside.

Album rating: WHEN I AM A BIG GIRL compilation (*5) / CUTTING THE HEAVENLY LAWN OF GREATNESS ... (5)

DEREK HAMMOND – vocals, acoustic guitar / **JOHN GRAYLAND** – guitars / **ADRIAN CROSSAN** – bass / **SUE DOREY** – drums, vocals

In-Tape | not iss.

Jun 84. (7"m) *(IT 008)* **COTTAGE INDUSTRY. / BIAS BINDING / TOMMY OPPOSITE** [ ] [-]

Oct 84. (7") *(IT 010)* **BEWARE THE WEAKLING LINES. / STARLING PILLOW CASE AND WHY?** [ ] [-]

Jan 85. (book) *(IT 011)* **BUMPER ANNUAL** [-] [-] special

Jan 85. (7"m) *(IT 012)* **PRICK UP YOUR EARS. / BROWN SHIRT / Terry And Gerry: BIAS BINDING** [ ] [-]

May 85. (m-lp) *(IT 016)* **WHEN I AM A BIG GIRL** (compilation) [ ] [-]
– Cottage industry / Brown shirt / 1901 / Starling pillowcase and why? / Prick up your ears / Beware the weakling lines / Tommy opposite / Bias binding.

—— added **TOM SLATER** – guitar

Sep 85. (7") *(IT 020)* **(ANOTHER SIDE TO) MRS. QUILL. / WENDY IN THE WOODS** [ ] [-]
(12"+=) *(ITT 020)* – Penetration.

Oct 85. (lp) *(IT 021)* **CUTTING THE HEAVENLY LAWNS OF GREATNESS ... LAST RITES FOR THE GOD OF LOVE** [ ] [-]
– Home-ownersexual / Crimplene seed lifestyle / Temple of convenience / Starling pillowcase and why? / Married Miss New Jersey / etc

Nov 85. (7") *(IT 023)* **TEMPLE OF CONVENIENCE. / THE TIME BEINGS** [ ] [-]
(12"+=) *(ITT 023)* – Mr. Hammond is out to lunch.

—— split some time '86. HAMMOND formed two groups, The NEW NEW SEEKERS and The TIME BEINGS.

– compilations, etc. –

Jun 86. (lp) *Buggum; (BAAD 2)* **FUN ON THE LAWN LAWN LAWN** [ ] [-]

Apr 87. (12"ep) *Strange Fruit; (SFPS 026)* **THE PEEL SESSIONS** (19.1.86) [ ] [-]
– The superimposed man / Stealing in the name of the Lord / (It's) Easier to suck than to sing.

YELLO

Formed: Zurich, Switzerland .... 1979 by DIETER MEIER and BORIS BLANK. MEIER, who had previously been a member of the Swiss national golf team, was a self-confessed millionaire gambler before joining FRESH COLOUR and going solo. In 1979, they gained a contract with US indie label 'Ralph', which led to UK outlet 'Do-It' signing them in the early 80's. With two electronic, Euro-dance albums behind them ('SOLID PLEASURE' in 1980 and 'CLARO QUE SI' in 1981), UK label 'Stiff' gave them a break into mini-stardom with the Top 75 breaker, 'YOU GOTTA SAY YES TO ANOTHER EXCESS' (1983). This productive early period also saw the duo hitting the Top 75 singles chart with two alternative/dance crossover tracks, 'I LOVE YOU' and 'LOST AGAIN'. YELLO then signed to 'Elektra' and released 'STELLA' in 1985, a turning point featuring such memorable moments as 'DOMINGO', 'DESIRE' and 'VICIOUS GAMES'. 1986 saw the release of a remix set while the following year saw the collaboration with BILLY MacKENZIE on their 'ONE SECOND' long-player. Always forthcoming with diverse ideas, DEITER enticed SHIRLEY BASSEY out of semi-retirement (a pop-tastic tactic that The PROPELLERHEADS would also employ over a decade later!) to sing 'THE RHYTHM DIVINE' on the same album. A steady growth in sales throughout the 80's led to a Top 10 single, 'THE RACE' (from 'THE FLAG') in mid '88, the track subsequently used for many a TV documentary/sports backing theme. They had by this time relocated to London, venturing into movie soundtracks ('Nuns On The Run', etc) while MEIER launched his own label 'Solid Pleasure' in 1991. To date, YELLO have only released one further album this decade, '94's 'ZEBRA', their first new studio set for some time not to chart.

Album rating: SOLID PLEASURE (*5) / CLARO QUE SI (*5) / YOU GOTTA SAY YES TO ANOTHER EXCESS (*6) / STELLA (*6) / ONE SECOND (*6) / THE FLAG (*5) / BABY (*4) / THE ESSENTIAL YELLO compilation (*7) / ZEBRA (*4)

DIETER MEIER

solo with **HEINRICH VOGEL** – guitar / **ROBERT VOGEL** – drums / **ANTHONY MOORE** – keyboards / **MARTIN WALDER** – bass

Periphery Perfume | not iss.

Sep 78. (7") *(PP 00178)* **CRY FOR FAME. / THE SOURCE** [-] [-] Swiss

Mar 79. (7"orange) *(PP 00378)* **JIM FOR TANGO. / MADMAN** [-] [-] Swiss

YELLO

DIETER MEIER – vocals, horns / **BORIS BLANK** – synthesizer, electronics / **CARLOS PERON** – tapes, synthesizers

1979. (7") *(PP 00179)* **I.T. SPLASH. / GLUEHEAD** [-] [ ]

—— added **CHICO HABLAS** – guitar / guest drummers **WALT KAISER / FELIX HAUX**

Do-It | Ralph

Nov 80. (lp) <YL 8059> **SOLID PLEASURE** [-] [ ]
– Bimbo / Night flanger / Reverse lion / Downtown samba / Magneto / Massage / Assistant's cry / Bostich / Rock stop / Coast to polka / Blue green / Eternal legs / Stanztrigger / Bananas to the beat. *(UK-iss.May88 on 'Mercury' lp/c)(cd PRICE/PRIMC 113)(818339-2)*

Apr 81. (7") *(DUN 11)* <YL 8058> **BIMBO. / I.T. SPLASH** [ ] [ ] Dec80

Sep 81. (7") *(DUN 13)* **BOSTICH. / SHE'S GOT A GUN (instrumental)** [ ] [-]
(12") *(DUNIT 13)* – ('A'side) / Downtown samba / Daily disco.

—— new guests were **BEAT ASH** – percussion / **ZINE EL ABADINE** – vocals

Oct 81. (lp) *(RIDE 8)* <YL 8159> **CLARO QUE SI** [ ] [ ]
– Daily disco / No more Roger / Take it all / The evening's young / She's got a gun / Ballet mechanique / Quad el Habib / The lorry / Homer Hossa / Pinball cha-cha. *(re-iss. Feb88 on 'Mercury' lp/c)(cd; PRICE/PRIMC 114)(818340-2)*

Do-It | Stiff

Jan 82. (12"ep) <TEES12-10> **BOSTICH / SHE'S GOT A GUN. / DOWNTOWN SAMBA / DAILY DISCO** [-] [ ]

Feb 82. (7") *(DUN 18)* **SHE'S GOT A GUN. / GLUEHEAD** [ ] [ ]
(12") *(DUNIT 18)* – ('A'side) / Everything's young / There is no reason.

Jun 82. (7"/ext.12") *(DUN/+IT 23)* **PINBALL CHA-CHA. / SMILE ON YOU** [ ] [-]

—— down to duo of **MEIER & BLANK** (HABLAS left + PERON went solo

Stiff | Elektra

Apr 83. (lp) *(SEEZ 40)* <60271> **YOU GOTTA SAY YES TO ANOTHER EXCESS** [65] [ ]
– I love you / Lost again / No more words / Crash dance / Great mission / You gotta say yes to another excess / Swing / Heavy whispers / Smile on you / Pumping velvet / Salut Mayoumba. *(re-iss. Feb88 on 'Mercury' lp/c)(cd; PRICE/PRIMC 115)(812166-2)*

May 83. (7"-3D-pic-d) *(BUY 176)* **I LOVE YOU. / RUBBER VEST** [41] [-]
(12") *(BUYIT 176)* – ('A'extended dance) / Swing / Bostich.

Oct 83. (7") *(BUY 191)* **LOST AGAIN. / BASE FOR ALEC** [73] [-]
(d7"+=) *(DBUY 191)* – Let me cry / She's got a gun.
(12"+=) *(BUYIT 191)* – Pumping velvet / No more words.

—— guests **RUSH WINTERS** – vocals / **ANNIE HOGAN** – piano / **PETIA** – glass harp / plus **BEAT ASH + CHICO HABLAS**

Elektra | Mercury

Mar 85. (lp) *(EKT 1)* <822820> **STELLA** [92] [ ]
– Desire / Vicious games / Oh yeah / Desert Inn / Stalak drama / Koladi-ola (low bow) / Domingo / Sometimes (Dr. Hirsch) / Let me cry / Ciel ouvert / Angel no. *(re-iss. Feb88 on 'Mercury' lp/c)(cd; PRICE/PRIMC 116)(822820-2)*

Mar 85. (7") *(EKR 1)* **VICIOUS GAMES. / BLUE NABOU** [ ] [-]
(ext.12"+=) *(EKR 1T)* – ('A'instrumental).

Aug 85. (7") *(EKR 17)* **DESIRE. / OH YEAH (Indian summer version)** [ ] [-]
(12"+=) *(EKR 17T)* – ('B'-part 2) / XS (first ever version).

Mercury | Mercury

Aug 86. (7") *(MER 218)* **GOLDRUSH. / SHE'S GOT A GUN (live)** [54] [-]
(12"+=) *(MERX 218)* – Goldrush II.
(d12"++=) *(MERXD 218)* – Pinball cha-cha / Vicious games.
(d7"+=) *(MERD 218)* – I love you / Desire.

Oct 86. (lp/c) *(MERD/+C 95)* **1980-1985 THE NEW MIX IN ONE** (remixes) [ ] [-]
– Daily disco / Swing / The evening's young / Pinball cha-cha / I love you / Sometimes (Dr.Hirsch) / Base for Alec / Oh yeah / Lost again / Tub tub / Angel no / Desire / Bananas to the beat / Koladi-ola / domingo / Bostich / Live at the Roxy. *(cd-iss. Jun89; 826773-2)*

Nov 86. (7"/12") *(MER/+X 235)* **VICIOUS GAMES (remix). / LIVE AT THE ROXY (highlights)** [ ] [-]

—— (note: US 12"versions were issued on 'On-U-Sound' & 'Hot Tracks'.)

May 87. (7") *(MER 248)* **CALL IT LOVE. / L HOTEL** [ ] [-]
(12"+=/cd-s+=) *(MER X/CD 248)* – ('A'-Trego snare mix).

Jun 87. (lp/c) *(MERH/+C 100)* <832765> **ONE SECOND** [48] [92] Sep87
– La habanera / Moon on ice / Call it love / Le secret farida / Hawaiian chance / The rhythm divine / Santiago / Goldrush / Dr Van Steiner / Si senor the hairy grill. *(cd-iss. Jun89; 830956-2)*

Aug 87. (7") *<884930>* **OH YEAH. / ('A'remix)** - 51

Aug 87. (7"; as YELLO featuring SHIRLEY BASSEY) *(MER 253)* **THE RHYTHM DIVINE. / DR. VAN STEINER** 54 -
(12"+=/c-s+=) *(MER X/C 253)* – Tool in rose.
(12"+=) *(MERXR 253)* – ('A'mix BILLY McKENZIE – vox).

Jul 88. (7")(ext.12")(cd) *(YELLO 1)(YELLR 1-12)(YELCD 1)* **THE RACE. / LA HABANERA** 7 -
(cd-vid) *(080528-2)* – ('A'side) / ('A'-Sporting mix) / Another race.

Nov 88. (lp/c/cd) *(<836426-1/-4/-2>)* **FLAG** 56
– Tied up / Of course I'm lying / 3rd of June / Blazing saddles / The race / Alhambra / Otto Di Catania / Tied up in red / Tied up in gear. *(re-iss. Aug90 cd/c/lp; 836778-2/-4/-1)*

Nov 88. (7") *(YELLO 2)* **TIED UP (IN LIFE). / ALL STREET BONGO** 60 -
(12"+=) *(YELLR 2-12)* – Tied up in red.
(cd-s+=) *(YELCD 2)* – Oh yeah (Indian summer version).

Mar 89. (7") *(YELLO 3)* **OF COURSE I'M LYING. / OH YEAH** 23 -
(12")(cd-s) *(YELLO 3-12)(YELCD 3)* – ('A'side) / Yello metropolitan mix part 1: – Dakyene intro – The race – Sostich – Call it love (Trego snare) – Santiago – Tied up – Vicious games – I love you – Oh yeah.
(12")(cd-s) *(YELLO 3-22)(YELCD 3-2)* – ('A'side) / Yello metropolitan mix part 2: – Dakyene intro – The rhythm divine – Goldrush – Desire – La Habanera – Blazing saddles – Domingo – Live at the Roxy – Pinball cha cha – wing.

Jul 89. (7") *(YELLO 4)* **BLAZING SADDLES. / I LOVE YOU** 47 -
(12"+=)(c-s+=)(cd-s+=) *(YELLR 4-12)(YELLC 4)(YELCD 4)* – Blue nabou / The rhythm divine.
(12") *(YELLR 4-12)* – ('A'-Latin mix). / ('B'-diff.mix).

—— lp guests **MARCO COLOMBO** – guitar (3) / **BEAT ASH** (4) / **BILLY McKENZIE** (3)

May 91. (7"/c-s) *(YELLO/+C 5)* **RUBBERBANDMAN. / SWEET THUNDER** 58 -
(12"+=)(cd-s+=) *(YELLO 5-12)(YELCD 5)* – ('A'extended).

Jun 91. (cd/c/lp) *(<848791-2/-4/-1>)* **BABY** 37
– Homage to the mountain / Rubberbandman / Jungle Bill / Ocean club / Who's groove / Capri-calling / Drive-driven / On the run / Blender / Sweet thunder.

Aug 92. (7"/c-s) *(MER/+MC 376)* **JUNGLE BILL. / ('A'-Big pig mix)** 61 -
(cd-s+=) *(MERCD 376)* – ('A'-Voodoo mix) / ('A'-Chicken dive mix) / ('A'-Space mix).
(cd-s) *(MERCDX 376)* – ('A'side) / ('A'-shades of Paradise mix 1 & 2) / ('A'-Too tough 4 trego mix 1 & 2).

Sep 92. (cd/c) *(512390-2/-4) / Smash; <888002>* **THE ESSENTIAL YELLO** (compilation)
– Oh yeah / The race / Rubberbandman / Vicious games / Tied up / Lost again / I love you, goodbye / Of course I'm lying / Pinball cha cha / Bostich / Desire / Jungle Bill / Goldrush / The rhythm divine.

Oct 92. (7"/c-s) *(MER/+MC 382)* **THE RACE (Boris Blank remix). / BOSTICH (Kevin Sanderson remix)** 55 -
(12"+=/cd-s+=)*(MER X/CD 382)* – ('A'-Kevin Sanderson remix).

Mercury / 4th & Broadway

Oct 94. (c-s) *(MERMC 414)* **HOW HOW / ('A'instrumental mix)** 59 -
(12"+=) *(MERX 414)* – ('A'-Fluke mix) / ('A'-Plutone mix).
(cd-s++=) *(MERCD 414)* – ('A'mixes).
(cd-s) *(MERCDX 414)* – (4-'A'mixes) / Vicious games (U.S.remix) / Do it (2 mixes).

Oct 94. (cd/c) *(522496-2/-4) <444065>* **ZEBRA**
– Suite 909 / How how / Night train / Do it / I . . . I'm in love / S.A.X. / Fat cry / Tremendous pain / Move dance be born / The premix (how how) / Poom shanka.

not iss. / Mercury

1997. (cd) *<534353>* **POCKET UNIVERSE** -
– Solar driftwood / Celsius / More / On track / Monolith / To the sea / Magnetic / Liquid mountain / Pan blue / Resistor / Beyond mirrors.

– compilations, etc. –

Mar 95. (cd/c) *Urban-Polydor; (<527383-2/-4>)* **HANDS ON YELLO** (remixes)
– best of remixed by The Orb / Westbam / Moby / Jens / The Grid / Hardsequencer / Jam & Spoon / Plutone / Carl Cox / Oliver Lieb / Cosmic Baby / Carl Craig / Isla Gold.

Apr 95. (12"/cd-s; JAM & SPOON'S HANDS ON YELLO) **YOU GOTTA SAY YES TO ANOTHER EXCESS. / (other mixes)** -

YO LA TENGO

Formed: Hoboken, New Jersey, USA . . . 1984 by IRA KAPLAN and GEORGIA HUBLEY, who advertised for musicians. Finally, through much time and varied personnel, they stabilised their line-up with DAVE SCHRAMM and MIKE LEWIS. This configuration recorded the 1986 debut album, 'RIDE THE TIGER', introducing the band's countrified acoustic-rock which drew on the likes of VELVET UNDERGROUND, LOVE and RAIN PARADE. Following the departure of SCHRAMM and LEWIS, KAPLAN assumed writing duties for 'NEW WAVE HOT DOGS', providing the band with their first of many credible and critically acclaimed albums. 1989's 'PRESIDENT YO LA TENGO' was more experimental while 'FAKEBOOK' (1990) was a beguiling album of rootsy covers (see below). Throughout the 90's, the band have released a string of albums for 'City Slang', taking an increasingly left-field direction. • **Songwriters:** SCHRAMM on debut / taken over by KAPLAN. Covered; KICK ME HARD (NBRQ) / YELLOW SARONG (Scene Is Now) / THE ONE TO CRY (Escorts) / HERE COMES MY BABY (Cat Stevens) / EMULSIFIED (Rex Garvin & The Mighty Carvers) / GRISELDA (Peter Stampfel) / SPEEDING MOTORCYCLE (Daniel Johnston) / ANDALUCIA (John Cale) / OKLAHOMA, U.S.A. (Kinks) / TRIED SO HARD (Flying Burrito Brothers) / YOU TORE ME DOWN (Flamin' Groovies) / A HOUSE IS NOT A MOTEL (Love) / I THREW IT ALL AWAY (Bob Dylan) / IT'S ALRIGHT (Velvet Underground) / THE WHOLE OF THE LAW (Only Ones) / DREAMING (Blondie) / etc. • **Trivia:** Duetted with TARA KEY for the film 'I Shot Andy Warhol'. Hip film director Hal Hartley is a big fan, often using the band's music in his movies.

Album rating: NEW WAVE HOT DOGS (*6) / FAKEBOOK (*7) / PRESIDENT YO LA TENGO (*6) / THAT IS YO LA TENGO (*7) / PAINFUL (*7) / ELECTR-O-PURA (*6)

IRA KAPLAN – guitar, vocals / **GEORGIA HUBLEY** – drums, vocals / +2 (guitarist + bassist)

Shigaku / Coyote

Nov 85. (7") **THE RIVER OF WATER. / A HOUSE IS NOT A MOTEL** -

—— **DAVE SHRAMM** – vocals, guitar; repl. unknown

—— **MIKE LEWIS** – bass; repl. unknown

Feb 87. (lp) *(SHIGLP 2) <8676>* **RIDE THE TIGER** 1986
– The cone of silence / The evil that men do / The forest green / The pain of pain / The way some people die / The empty pool / Alrok's bells / Five years / Screaming dead balloons / Living in the country. *(cd-iss. 1995; EFA 0491827) <US cd-iss. Jan98 on 'Matador'; OLE 205>*

—— **STEPHEN WICHNEWSKI** – bass; repl. LEWIS + SCHRAMM

What Goes On / Coyote

Nov 87. (lp) *(GOESON 13) <87125>* **NEW WAVE HOT DOGS**
– Clunk / Did I tell you / House fall down / Lewis / Lost in Bessemer / It's alright / The way that you live / 3 blocks from Groove Street / Let's compromise / Serpentine / A shy dog / No water / The story of jazz.

May 89. (lp) *(GOESON 28) <88142>* **PRESIDENT YO LA TENGO**
– Barnaby, hardly working / Drug test / The evil that men do / Orange song / Alyda / The evil that men do / I threw it all away. *(cd-iss. Aug94 on 'City Slang'+=; EFA 049252-2)* – NEW WAVE NEW DOGS *(d-lp-iss.Jan98 on 'Matador'; OLE 206-1)*

—— **AL GRELLER** – double bass; repl. WICHNEWSKI

Enigma / Bar/None

1990. (lp/cd) *(72641) <20>* **FAKEBOOK**
– Can't forget / Griselda / Here comes my baby / Barnaby, hardly working / Yellow sarong / You tore me down / Emulsified / Speeding motorcycle / Tried so hard / The summer / Oklahoma, U.S.A. / What comes next / The one to cry / Andalucia / Did I tell you / What can I say. *(UK-iss.1990's; EFA 04062-26)*

—— **GENE HOLDER** – producer (also last one), bass repl. STEPHEN

City Slang / City Slang

Jul 91. (lp/cd) *(EFA 04068/+CD) <SLANG 009>* **WHAT IS YO LA TENGO**
– Detouring America with horns / Upside down / Mushroom cloud of hiss / Swing for life / Five cornered drone (crispy duck) / Some kinda fatigue / Always something / 86 second blowout / Out the window / Sleeping pill / Satellite.

—— added **JAMES McNEW** – bass

Alias / City Slang

May 92. (cd-ep) *(A 026CD) <SLANG 021>* **UPSIDE DOWN / (THE) FARMER'S DAUGHTER / OUT OF CONTROL / UPSIDE DOWN (ONE MORE TIME) / SUNSQUASHED**

Jun 92. (lp/cd) *(A 021/+CD) <SLANG 26>* **MAY I SING WITH YOU**
– Out the window / Swing for life / Walking away from you / Five cornered drone (crispy duck) / Fog over Frisco.

City Slang / Matador

Sep 93. (cd/c/lp) *(EFA 04927-2/-4/-1) <92298>* **PAINFUL**
– Big day coming / From a motel 6 / Double dare / Superstar – Watcher / Nowhere near / Sudden organ / A worrying thing / I was the fool beside you far too long / The whole of the law / Big day coming / I heard you looking.

Matador / Matador

Nov 93. (7") *<(OLE 060-7)>* **SHAKER. / FOR SHAME OF DOING WRONG (demo)**
(cd-s+=) *<(OLE 060-2)>* – What she wants.

Apr 94. (cd-s) *<(OLE 080-2)>* **FROM A MOTEL 6 / ASHES ON THE GROUND / NUTRICIA**

City Slang / Matador

Apr 95. (7") *(EFA 04954-7) <OLE 139>* **TOM COURTNEY. / THE BIOSEXUAL BOOGIE**
(cd-s+=) *(EFA 04954-2)* – Treading water / Bad politics / My hearts reflection.

May 95. (cd/lp) *(EFA 04955-2/-1) <92550>* **ELECTR-O-PURA**
– Decora / Flying lesson / The hour grows late / Tom Courtenay / False ending / Pablo and Andrea / Paul is dead / False alarm / The ballad of red buckets / Don't say a word / (Straight down to the) Bitter end / My heart's reflection / Attack on love / Blue line swinger.

Sep 95. (cd-ep) *<OLE 171>* **CAMP YO LA TENGO** -

Matador / Matador

Dec 96. (d-cd) *<(OLE 194-2)>* **GENIUS + LOVE = YO LA TENGO** (compilation)
– Evanescent psychic pez drop / emons / Fog over Frisco / Too late / Hanky panky nohow / Something to do / Ultra-powerful short wave radio picks up music from Venus / Up to you / Somebody's baby / Walking away from you / Artificial heart / Cast a shadow / I'm set free / Barnaby, hardly working / Some kinda fatigue / Speding motorcycle / Her grandmother's gift / From a motel 6 / Gooseneck problem / Surfin' with the Shah / Ecstacy blues / Too much (part 1) / Blitzkreig bop / One self: Fish girl / Enough / Drum solo / From a motel 6 / Too much (part 2) / Sunsquashed.

Feb 97. (7") *(WORM 4)* **BLUE-GREEN ARROW. / WATCHING THE SUN RISE (or) JOHNNY CARSON** -
(above on 'Earworm' / below 45 on 'Planet')

Mar 97. (7"ltd) *(PUNK 016)* **ROCKET NO.9. / ('A'mix)** -

Apr 97. (12"/cd-s) *<(OLE 250-1/-2)>* **AUTUMN SWEATER (4 remixes)**

Apr 97. (cd/lp) *<(OLE 222 2/1)>* **I CAN HEAR THE HEAR BEATING AS ONE**
– Return to hot chicken / Moby octopad / Sugarcube / Damage / Deeper into movies / Shadows / Stockholm syndrome / Autumn sweater / Little Honda / Green arrow / One PM again / Lie and how we told it / Center of gravity / Spec bebop / We're an American band / My little corner of the world.

Aug 97. (7") *<(OLE 272-7)>* **SUGARCUBE. / BUSY WITH MY THOUGHTS**
(cd-s+=) *<(OLE 272-2)>* – Summer / Loony tunes.

Nov 97. (7") *<(OLE 291-7)>* **LITTLE HONDA. / LITTLE HONDA (live)**
(cd-s+=) *<(OLE 291-2)>* – ('A'side) / No return / By the time it gets dark / Black hole.

Feb 98. (cd-ep) *<(OLE 295-2)>* **LITTLE HONDA / NO RETURN / HOW MUCH I LIED / BE THANKFUL / BLACK HOLE / BY THE TIME IT'S GETTING DARK**

YOSSARIAN

Formed: March 1998, by Hackney (London)-born keyboard-player, TIM BRINKHURST, after the man had recently worked on several arty gender-bending films while retaining some dignity keeping down various day jobs to feed his young daughter. Previously to this, TIM was also part of early 90's interracial outfit, SOHO, a twin-fronted trio (nurses, JACQUELINE and PAULINE CUFF) who embarressingly (for him anyway!) scored a massive worldwide hit, 'HIPPYCHICK' (sampling The SMITHS' 'How Soon Is Now'), in 1990. Returning after several years in the proverbial wilderness and taking the name from a character in the book, 'Catch-22', YOSSARIAN debuted with an EP, 'PARIS TRIPTYCH', which included the track, 'CONVERSATION WITH A RACIST'. His trippy Moog-orientated pop psychedelia was again centre stage with the track, 'MY SHY BOY SAINT', taken from the EP, 'SATELLITE QUARTET'.

Album rating: awaiting debut album

TIM BRINKHURST (b.20 Nov'60) – keyboards, guitar, etc.

Satellite — not iss.

Apr 98. (10"ep) *(STL 011)* **PARIS TRIPTYCH EP**
– Conversation with a racist / Reaction overload / Paris London junky express / Seductress 3rd class.

Aug 98. (cd-ep) **SATELLITE QUARTET EP**
– My shy boy saint /

YOUNG FRESH FELLOWS

Formed: Seattle, Washington, USA . . . 1982 by SCOTT McCAUGHEY, CHUCK CARROLL and TAD HUTCHINSON. Coming straight outta the American Northwest a full decade before the area became grunge central, The YOUNG FRESH FELLOWS made a minor stir in 1984 with their debut album, 'THE FABULOUS SOUNDS OF THE PACIFIC NORTHWEST'. Released on indie label, 'PopLlama Products', the record's awkwardly charming guitar pop allure was summed up on 60's girl-group pastiche, 'A HUMBLE GUY', The FELLOWS' student geek appeal setting a precedent for a celebrated lineage of college radio favourites throughout the 80's and into the 90's. Sorting out the self-confessed dodgy bass sound with the addition of JIM SANGSTER, the band conceived a worthwhile follow-up in the acclaimed (at least in Rolling Stone) 'TOPSY TURVY' (1985). From the self-mocking humour and roots flourishes of 'SEARCHIN USA' onwards, the album displayed a fuller, more confident sound without sacrificing the teen-crisis appeal (BEN FOLDS might just have copped an earful of 'THE NEW JOHN AGAR'), eclecticism still the name of the game with the garage-blues hoedown of 'YOU'VE GOT YOUR HEAD ON BACKWARDS' proving an undisputed highlight. The something-for-everyone musical policy and attendant critical praise continued with 'THE MEN WHO LOVED MUSIC' (1987) and the subsequent string of albums for new label, 'Frontier': 'TOTALLY LOST' (1988), 'THIS ONE'S FOR THE LADIES' (1989), 'ELECTRIC BIRD DIGEST' (1991) and 'IT'S LOW BEAT TIME' (1992). The turn-of-the-decade replacement of CARROLL with FASTBACKS man, KURT BLOCH, lent a further dimension to the band's sound and the country roots stylings first introduced on 'TOPSY . . .' became progressively more prominent. While anything more than cult recognition remains unlikely, a mark of the band's peer group admiration was the recruitment of McCAUGHEY for touring services with spiritual compadres R.E.M., the frontman having released his solo debut, 'MY CHARTREUSE OPINION', in 1989. • **Songwriters:** McCAUGHEY except WHERE IS GROOVY TOWN? (. . . Chesterman) / YOU'VE GOT YOUR HEAD ON BACKWARDS (. . . Roslie).

Album rating: THE FABULOUS SOUNDS OF THE PACIFIC NORTHWEST (*7) / TOPSY TURVY (*7) / THIS ONE'S FOR THE LADIES (*7) / THE MEN WHO LOVED MUSIC (*8) / ELECTRIC BIRD DIGEST (*8) / INCLUDES A HELMET (*8)

SCOTT McCAUGHEY – vocals, bass / **CHUCK CARROLL** – guitar / **TAD HUTCHINSON** – drums

not iss. — Walkthrufyre

1984. (lp) *<101>* **THE FABULOUS SOUNDS OF THE PACIFIC NORTHWEST**
– Rock'n'roll pest control / All messed up / Gus theme / Think better of me / Power mowers theme / Empty set takes a vacation / View from above / Big house / This little mystery / A humble guy / Down by the pharmacy / Teenage dogs in trouble / You call that lonely? / That letter / Young Fresh Fellows theme. *(UK-iss.1994 on 'PopLlama'; PLCD 493)*

—— added **JIM SANGSTER** – bass (SCOTT switched to guitar)

not iss. — East Side Digital

Dec 85. (lp) *<ESD 8023>* **TOPSY TURVY**
– Searchin' U.S.A. / How much about last night do you remember? / Where is groovy town? / The new John Agar / Sharing patrol theme / You've got your head on backwards / Two lives / Mr. Salamander's review / Trek to stupidity / Topsy turvy theme / Hang out right / Agar's revenge / Good things go. *<cd-iss. 1993 on 'Pop Llama'; 20>*

not iss. — Frontier

1987. (lp) *<FLP 1021>* **THE MEN WHO LOVED MUSIC**
– Just sit / TV dream / Get outta my cave / Why I oughta / Unimaginable zero summer / When the girls get here / Amy Grant / Hank, Karen and Elvis / My friend Ringo / Two brothers / I got my mojo working (I thought) / I don't let the little things get me down / Ant farm / Where the hell did they go? / Happy death theme / Beer money / Aurora bridge / Broken basket / Three sides to this story / Young Fresh Fellows update theme / Back room of the bar. *<re-iss. 1993 cd/c/lp; 4611-2/-4/-1>*

1987. (m-lp) *<FRT 105>* **REFRESHMENTS**

1988. (lp/c/cd) *<4616-1/-4/-2>* **TOTALLY LOST**

1989. (lp) **BEANS AND INTOLERANCE**

—— **KURT BLOCH** – guitar (ex-FASTBACKS) repl. CARROLL

1989. (lp/c/cd) *<4622-1/-4/-2>* **THIS ONE'S FOR THE LADIES**
– This one's for the ladies / Still there's hope / Carrot head / Middle man of time / Wishing ring / New old song / Family gun / Rotation / Taco wagon / Picture book / Lost track of time / Miss lonely hearts / Deep, down and inbetween / When I'm lonely again – One day you die / Don't you wonder how it ends?

1991. (cd/c/lp) *<4631-2/-4/-1>* **ELECTRIC BIRD DIGEST**
– Telephone tree / Sittin' on a pitchfork / Looking around / Hillbilly drummer girl / Whirlpool / Once in a while / Teen thing / Thirsty / Fear, bitterness and hatred / Hard to mention / Tomorrow's gone (and so are you) / Evening / There's a love / Swiftly but gently.

1992. (7") *(34677)* **DARK CORNER. /**

Munster — Frontier

Apr 92. (cd) *(MR 015CD)* **SOMOS LOS MEJORES**

Oct 92. (cd/c) *<34643-2/-4>* **IT'S LOW BEAT TIME!**
– Low beat jingle / Right here / Snow white / Mr. Anthony's last / Whatever you are / Two headed fight / Minor bird / Faultless / Crafty clerk / Low beat / Love is a beautiful thing / She sees color / Monkey say / 99 girls / She won't budge.

—— after they split in '93, SCOTT McCAUGHEY released a debut solo album in '95.

– compilations, etc. –

Jun 90. (lp/cd) *Utility; (UTIL 010/+CD)* **INCLUDES A HELMET**
– Why I oughta / My friend Ringo / Two lives / Gorilla / Amy Grant / A thing like that / No one realy knows / Young Fresh Fellows theme.

Apr 95. (cd) *Pop Llama; <9117>* **TEMPTATION ON SATURDAY**

YOUNG GODS

Formed: Geneva, Switzerland . . . early 1986 . . .by Fribourg-born FRANZ TREICHLER, CESARE PIZZI and FRANK BAGNOUD. Self-financed debut 45 'ENVOYE', which after follow-up 'DID YOU MISS ME', led to a deal with Belguin indie label 'Play It Again Sam'. An eponymous album gained much critical appraisal due to TREICHLER's Euro-gothic stark delivery sung in French and production techniques of ROLI MOSIMANN (Swans). Second album 'L'EAU ROUGE' continued in the same vein, but it wasn't until 1991's avant-garde 'TV SKY', that they recorded in English, that won over the States. Took a break from the studio until 1995, when awesome 'ONLY HEAVEN' was unleashed. Although it didn't chart, it made new friends from the heavy metal brigade, while retaining industrial, indie rock and techno/ambient fans. The latter style was much in evidence on the excellent 15 minute atmospheric soundscape track 'MOON REVOLUTIONS', while 'KISSING THE SUN' was a hard gut-wrenching explosion of sound. • **Songwriters:** Group (TREICHLER – lyrics), except tribute album to KURT WEILL, which included his SEPTEMBER SONG + ALABAMA SONG. Also covered; HELLO HELLO I'M BACK AGAIN (Gary Glitter).

Album rating: YOUNG GODS (*7) / L'EAU ROUGE (*7) / ONLY HEAVEN (*8)

FRANZ TREICHLER – vocals / **CESARE PIZZI** – tapes, synthesizers / **FRANK BAGNOUD** – drums

Organik — not iss.

May 86. (12") *(ORG 89-6)* **ENVOYE. / SOUL IDIOT / CSCLDF** — Swiss

Feb 87. (12") *(ORG 87-9)* **DID YOU MISS ME. / THE IRRTUM BOYS** — Swiss

Product Inc — Wax Trax!

Apr 87. (12"m) *(12PROD 7)* **DID YOU MISS ME. / HELLO HELLO I'M BACK AGAIN / IRRTUM BOYS**

Jun 87. (lp/cd) *(LD 8821/+CD) <WAX 7135>* **YOUNG GODS**
– Nouse de la lune / Jusqu'au bout / A ciel ouvert / Jimmy / Pais la mouette / Percussione / Feu / Did you miss me / Si tu gardes. *(cd+=)* – The Irrtum boys / Envoye / Soul idiot. *(re-iss. Aug89 lp/cd; 33/CD PROD 10)*

—— **USE HEISTAND** – drums; repl. FRANK

Play It Again Sam — Play It Again Sam

Oct 88. (7"/cd-s) *(BIAS 101/+CD)* **L'AMOURIR. / PAS MAL**
(was to have been issued Aug88; PIAS 99/+CD)

Sep 89. (lp/cd) *(<BIAS/CDBIAS 130>)* **L'EAU ROUGE (THE RED WATER)**
– La fille de la morte / Rue des tempetes / L'eau rouge / Charlotte / Longue route / Crier les chiens. *(cd+ –)* – Ville notre / Les enfants. *<US re-iss. 1995 on 'Interscope'; 92629>*

Apr 90. (12") *(BIAS 158)* **LONGUE ROUTE (remix). / SEPTEMBER SONG**
(cd-s+=) *(BIAS 158CD)* – Envoye (live) / Pas mal (live).

—— **AL MONO** – samples; repl. PIZZI

Apr 91. (lp/cd) *(<BIAS 188/+CD>)* **THE YOUNG GODS PLAY KURT WEILL**
– Prologue / Salomon song / Mackie messer / Speak low / Alabama song / Seerauber Jenny / Ouverture / September song.

Jan 92. (lp/c/cd) *(<BIAS 201/+C/CD>)* **T.V. SKY** — 54
– Our house / Gasoline man / T.V. sky / Skinflowers / Dame chance / The night dance / She rains / Summer eyes.

Mar 92. (7") *(7BIAS 206)* **SKINFLOWERS. / SKINFLOWERS (Brain Forest mix)**
(12"+=/cd-s+=) *(BIAS 206/+CD)* – ('A'-Courtney Speed Love mix) / ('A'edit).

Sep 92. (12"/cd-s) *(BIAS 231/+CD)* **GASOLINE MAN (megadrive mix). / GASOLINE MAN (diesel mix) / ('A'diesel edit)**

Jul 93. (lp/c/cd) *(<BIAS 241/+C/CD>)* **LIVE SKY TOUR (live Melbourne summer 1992)**

– Intro / TV sky / Jimmy / Envoye / Chanson rouge / L'eau rouge / Skinflowers / She rains / Summer eyes / Pas mal / Longue route / September song / Seerauber Jenny.

Jun 95. (lp/c/cd) *(<BIAS 301/+C/CD>)* **ONLY HEAVEN**
– Outside / Strangle / Speed of night / Donnez les espirits / Moon revolutions / Kissing the sun / The dreamhouse / Lointaine / Gardez les espirits / Child in the tree. *(lp re-iss. Jun96 on 'Revelation'; REV 2554)*

Nov 95. (cd-ep) *(BIAS 299CD)* **KISSING THE SUN / (remixes)**

not iss. Paradigm

Jul 97. (cd) *<15>* **HEAVEN DECONSTRUCTION** –
– December / Aoacu / Acid strange! / Improper / Drun / Riversky / F / Borea / Scories / Landing / Messages / Nano pata / Lova / Light residues / Under / Numiere / Windklang.

YOUNG MARBLE GIANTS

Formed: Cardiff, Wales . . . 1978 by the MOXHAM brothers, STUART and PHILIP along with frontwoman, ALISON STATTON. The combination of STUART's highly original songwriting talent, PHILIP's "singing" bass and STATTON's spectral vocals has long been held up as one of the post-punk era's most unique and enchanting musical propositions. 'Rough Trade' supremo, Geoff Travis, for one, was quick to spot their talent, promptly signing the trio and issuing a debut maxi-single in 1980. Minimalist in execution and featuring the sparsest of electronic percussion with occasional primitive organ accompaniment, there really were no musical reference points save for JAYNE CASEY/PINK MILITARY at a pinch. The band's one and only album, 'COLOSSAL YOUTH' (1980) received almost universal acclaim, featuring as it did such quietly considered YMG mini-masterpieces as 'SEARCHING FOR MR RIGHT', 'WURLITZER JUKEBOX' and 'CHOCI LONI'. Following it up with an equally engrossing EP, 'TESTCARD' (1981), the band looked set for major cult success as the record climbed into the upper reaches of the indie chart. Yet The YOUNG MARBLE GIANTS dissolved almost as quickly and mysteriously as they'd formed, STATTON going on to form the lite jazz-influenced WEEKEND with SPIKE, SIMON BOOTH and seasoned jazzmen, HARRY BECKETT and LARRY STABBINS. Sticking with 'Rough Trade', STATTON & Co. released a debut WEEKEND single, 'THE VIEW FROM HER ROOM', in 1982, its bossa-nova swing nevertheless retaining the restraint of her earlier work. Another two singles followed, the jazzier 'PAST MEETS PRESENT' and 'DRUMBEAT FOR BABY', prior to a debut album, 'LA VARIETE' (1982). An eclectic collection ranging from the string-led atmospherics of 'SLEEPY THEORY' to the almost pre-SAINT ETIENNE-esque 'THE END OF THE AFFAIR', the record was the first of only two albums before the outfit again split down the middle. BOOTH and STABBINS subsequently formed WORKING WEEK to indulge their passion for soul-jazz while STATTON moved back to Cardiff. STUART MOXHAM, meanwhile, had founded The GIST upon the break-up of his former band, releasing a debut single, 'YANKS', in late '81. This was followed by the acclaimed 'LOVE AT FIRST SIGHT' in summer '82, a decidedly more conventional slice of atmospheric guitar pop subsequently echoed by The BLUE NILE. Despite the release of a fine accompanying album, 'EMBRACE THE HERD' (1983), the project was once more short-lived and no more was heard from any of the former 'GIANTS until 1987 when Belgian label, 'Crepuscule', persuaded the original trio to reform for a one-off single, 'IT TOOK YOU'. MOXHAM continued to work in both a solo capacity and alongside other artists, balancing his musical endeavours with a career as an animator.

Album rating: COLOSSAL YOUTH (*8) / Various: NIPPED IN THE BUD (*7)

ALISON STATTON (b.?? Mar'58) – vocals / **STUART MOXHAM** – guitar, organ, vocals / **PHILIP MOXHAM** – bass

Rough Trade not iss.

Feb 80. (lp) *(ROUGH 8)* **COLOSSAL YOUTH** –
– Searching for Mr. Right / Include me out / The taxi / Eating Noddemix / Constantly changing / N.I.T.A. / Colossal youth / Music for evening / The man amplifier / Choci Loni / Wurlitzer jukebox / Salad days / Credit in the straight world / Brand-new-life / Wind in the rigging. *(cd-iss. Jun90; ROUGH CD 8) (cd re-iss. Apr94 on 'Crespescule'; TWI 984-2)*

May 80. (7"m/12"m) *(RT/+T 043)* **RADIO SILENTS. / FINAL DAYS / CAKE WALKING** –

Nov 80. (7"/12"; as The GIST) *(RT/+T 053)* **THIS IS LOVE. / YANKS** –

Mar 81. (7"ep/12"ep) *(RT/+T 059)* **TESTCARD EP** –
– Click talk / Zebra trucks / Posed by models / Sporting life / The clock / This way.

—— split two ways; STATTON formed WEEKEND, while the MOXHAM's re-united as . . .

The GIST

STUART MOXHAM – vocals, instruments / **PHIL MOXHAM** – bass / **LEWIS MOTTRAM** – bass (with on lp) **PHILIP LEGG** – bass, guitar, percussion (ex-ESSENTIAL LOGIC + LORA LOGIC) / **DAVE DEARNALEY** – drums (of The LION, THE WITCH & THE WARDROBE) / with guests **EPIC SOUNDTRACKS** – drums / **ALISON STATTON + WENDY SMITH + VIV GOLDMAN + DEBBIE PRITCHARD + NIXON** – vocals / **CHARLES BULLEN + JAKE BOWIE** – percussion

Rough Trade not iss.

Jun 82. (7") *(RT 085)* **LOVE AT FIRST SIGHT. / LIGHT AIRCRAFT** –

Feb 83. (7") *(RT 125)* **FOOL FOR A VALENTINE. / FOOL FOR A DUB** –

Mar 83. (lp) *(ROUGH 25)* **EMBRACE THE HERD** –
– Far concern / Love at first sight / Fretting away / Public girls / Clean bridges / Simian / Embrace the herd / Lambic pentameter / Carnival headache / Concrete slopes / The long run / Dark shots.

WEEKEND

STATTON – vocals, bass / **SIMON BOOTH** (b.12 Mar'56) – guitar, drum machine / **SPIKE** – guitar, viola / + guests **PHIL MOXHAM** – bass / **LARRY STABBINS** (b. 9 Sep'49) – saxes / **ROY DODDS** – drums / **DAVE HARWOOD** – violin, bass / **HARRY BECKETT** – trumpet, flugelhorn / **ANNIE WHITEHEAD** – trombone / **DAWSON MILLER** – percussion

Rough Trade not iss.

May 82. (7"/12") *(RT/+T 097)* **THE VIEW FROM HER ROOM. / LEAVES OF SPRING** –

Jul 82. (7"/12") *(RT/+T 107)* **MIDNIGHT SLOWS. / PAST MEETS PRESENT** –

Oct 82. (7") *(RT 116)* **DRUM BEAT FOR BABY. / SLEEPY THEORY** –
(12"+=) (RTT 116) – Weekend off.

Nov 82. (lp) *(ROUGH 39)* **LA VARIETE** –
– The end of the affair / Weekend stroll / Summerdays / Drum beat for baby / A life in the day of . . . – part 1 & 2 / Sleepy theory / Woman's eyes / Weekend off / Red planes / Nostalgia. *(cd-iss. Jun90; ROUGHCD 39)*

—— **ALISON + SIMON** were joined by **KEITH TIPPETT** – piano

Aug 83. (m-lp) *(RTM 139)* **LIVE AT RONNIE SCOTT'S (live)** –
– Where flamingos fly / Winter Moon / Nostalgia / Weekend off / A day in the life of . . .

—— disbanded; SIMON formed WORKING WEEK with SPIKE + recruited ex-WEEKEND sessioners. They were also part of VIC GODARD's group. ALISON teamed up with (IAN) DEVINE of LUDUS to form DEVINE & STATTON. In Oct'94, ALISON STATTON & SPIKE released a one-off set, 'TIDAL BLUES' for 'Vinyl Japan' (ASKCD 1037).

– compilations, etc. –

1984. (lp) *Rough Trade;* **NIPPED IN THE BUD** –
– (tracks by YOUNG MARBLE GIANTS / GIST / WEEKEND)

Apr 95. (cd-ep) *Vinyl Japan; (TASKCD 047)* **THE '81 DEMOS** –
– Drumbeat / Red planes / Nostalgia / Summerdays (instrumental).

STUART MOXHAM & THE ORIGINAL ARTISTS

Feel Good All Over not iss.

Mar 93. (cd) *(FGAO 015)* **SIGNAL PATH** –
– Over the sea / Between edits / Her shoes (are right) / Knives (always fail) / Broken heart blues / It says here / No one road / That's my love / I wonder why / Remember / It took you / Mutual gaze / Yeah x3 / Unit of desire.

Vinyl Japan not iss.

Mar 95. (cd) *(ASKCD 035)* **CARS IN THE GRASS** –
– My criteria / Hello world / Return to work / The tug of love / Night by night / Soft eject / Against creating war / God knows / The appropriate response / Cars in the grass / Drifting west.

YOUTH BRIGADE

Formed: Washington DC, USA . . . 1980 by NORMAN STREJCEK, TOM CLINTON, BERT QUIEROZ and DANNY INGRAHM. This lot seem to have made only one EP, 1981's '{8 CUTS}', before another group of the same name poached their moniker.

Album rating: er . . . (see below!)

NORMAN STREJCEK – vocals / **TOM CLINTON** – guitar / **BERT QUIEROZ** – bass / **DANNY INGRAHM** – drums

not iss. Dischord

Dec 81. (12"ep) *<DISCHORD 6>* **{8 CUTS}** –

—— must have disbanded

YOUTH BRIGADE

Formed: Hollywood, California, USA . . . 1982, by the STERN brothers, SHAWN, ADAM and MARK. America's answer to SHAM 69, their anthemic barrage of teenage punk rock was first heard on vinyl with their 1984 album, 'SOUND & FURY'. This effort surfaced on their own 'Better Youth Organisation' label, the trio also signing SNFU and The BOUNCING SOULS in the process. From then on, they fought, they split, they reformed, they fought and they didn't conquer.

Album rating: SOUND & FURY / SINK WITH KALIFORNIJA (*5)

SHAWN STERN – vocals, guitar / **ADAM STERN** – bass, vocals / **MARK STERN** – drums, vocals

Better Youth Org. Better Youth Org.

Jul 84. (lp) *<(BYO 002)>* **SOUND & FURY**
– Sink with Kalifornija / Modest proposal / Men in blue (part 1) / Sound & fury / Fight to unite / Jump back / Blown away / Live life / What are you fighting for / Did you wanna die / You don't understand / The circle / Duke of Earl / What will the revolution change. *(cd-iss. Feb91 as 'SINK WITH KALIFORNIJA'; BYO 2CD)*

Nov 84. (12") *<(BYO 6)>* **WHAT PRICE HAPPINESS. /**

—— split but reformed in the 90's

Lost & Found unknown

Jul 93. (7"; split) *(LF 053)* **GIGANTOR split**

EFA EFA

Mar 94. (cd/lp) *(efa 20027-2/-1) <BYO 27 CD/LP>* **HAPPY HOUR**
– All style, no substance / Better without you / Punk rock mom / Guns are for / Let me be / It's not enough / Alive by machine / It just doesn't matter / Wanted / Volare / Sad but true / This is a life / Deep inside of me.

May 94. (7") *(efa 40298-7)* **ALL STYLE AND NO SUBSTANCE. /**
1996. (cd) <*BYO 038*> **TO SELL THE TRUTH** [-]
– It's not my fault / Spies for life / Sick / We're in! / Breakdown / Street dominator / Shrinking / Believe in something / Friends / Not gonna take it / My bartender / Tomorrow / Last day of the year / I hate my life.

– compilations, etc. –

all issued on 'Better Youth Org.'
Nov 93. (cd) <*(BYO 025CD)*> **COME AGAIN**
Apr 94. (cd/lp) *Beri Beri;* <*(efa 11655-2/-1)*> **THE GOOD THE BAD . . .**
Nov 98. (cd) <*(BYO 050CD)*> **OUT OF PRINT**
– Fight to unite / Treachery / Circle / Boys in the brigade / Alienated / You don't understand / Brigade song / Full force / Sound and fury / Confusion / Violence / On the edge / I won't die for you / How can we live like this / Questions / Somebody's gonna get their head kicked in tonight.

YUM-YUM (see under ⇒ HOLMES, Chris)

YUNG WU (see under ⇒ FEELIES)

ZEKE

Formed: Seattle, Washington, USA . . . early 90's by motorbike 'n' girls-fixated songwriter, BLIND MARKY FELCHTONE, along with ABE ZANEUL RIGGS III, DIZZY LEE ROTH and DANNY PAYCHECK. After a handful of rare 45's on numerous labels, these pseudonymous post-grunge sickboys roared into town in 1995 with their turbo-charged debut album, 'SUPER SOUND RACING'. Subsequently moving to their own 'Smooch Pooch' imprint, they delivered their second collection of twisted punk in the shape of 'FLAT TRACKER' (1996), pricking up the ears of 'Epitaph' who issued 1998's 'KICKED IN THE TEETH'.

Album rating: SUPER SOUND RACING (*6) / FLAT TRACKER (*7) / KICKED IN THE TEETH (*5)

BLIND MARKY FELCHTONE – vocals, guitar / **ABE ZANEUL RIGGS III** – guitar / **DIZZY LEE ROTH** – bass / **DANNY PAYCHECK** – drums

I.F.A. I.F.A.

Jul 96. (cd) *<(IFACD 001)>* **SUPER SOUND RACING** Oct95
– Slut / Tuned out / Relapse / Chiva / Quicksand / Runnin' shine / Wreckin' machine / Eroded / Holley 750 / Incest / West Seattle acid party / Action / Mainline / 302 cubic inch V-8 powered blues / Hemicuda / Maybe someday / Galaxie 500 / Highway star / Schmidt value pack / Rid. *(re-iss. Oct96 on 'Smooch Pooch' lp/cd; PO 20/+CD)* *(re-iss. Jul97 on 'Epitaph' cd/lp; 20620-2/-1)*

Junk Junk

Jan 96. (2x7") *<(JR 6)>* **SWPR**

—— **MARK PIERCE** – bass; repl. ROTH

Scooch Pooch Scooch Pooch

Oct 96. (7") *<(PO 11)>* **CHIVA KNIEVEL. /**
(re-iss. Oct97; same)

Oct 96. (lp) *<(PO 16)>* **FLAT TRACKER**
– T-5000 / Eddie Hill / Chiva Knievel / Overkill / Mystery train / Viva agnostini / Hate / Raped / Wanna fuck / Fight in the storeroom / Flat truck / Bitch / Daytona / Super six / Eliminator. *(cd-iss. Jul97 on 'Epitaph'; 20616-2)*

Jan 97. (7") *<(POOW 001)>* **WEST SEATTLE ACID PARTY. /**

not iss. Man's Ruin

Aug 97. (12"ep) *<MR 064>* **HOLLY 75 – OVERKILL – MYSTERY TRAIN – SLUT (live). / WANNA FUCK – CHIVA KNEVEL – T-5000 – RAPED (live)** -

Collective Fruit Collective Fruit

Oct 97. (7") *<(CF 7009)>* **LOVE GUN. /**

Epitaph Epitaph

Mar 98. (cd/c/lp) *<(6513-2/-4/-1)>* **KICKED IN THE TEETH**
– God of G.S.X.R. / Telepath boy / Rodney / Twisted / Dogfight / Kicked in the teeth / Fuck all night / Revolution / Killer inside / Lawson / Revolution reprise / Goggle boy / Zeke you / Porked / Ages high / Shout it out loud / Mert.

ZODIAC MOTEL (see under ⇒ BIRDLAND)

ZOUNDS

Formed: Oxford, England . . . early 80's by STEVE LAKE and LAURENCE WOOD. Emerging from the same post-punk polemic brigade as CRASS, POISON GIRLS, etc, ZOUNDS actually issued a single, 'CAN'T CHEAT KARMA' on the former band's notorious imprint, hot on the heels of a one-side 7", 'MENAGE'. Subsequently signing to 'Rough Trade', the group released a trio of hard-hitting singles which later turned up on the posthumous 'THE CURSE OF THE ZOUNDS!' (1984). By the time of the latter's release, LAKE had already formed another outfit, WORLD SERVICE and was about to embark upon a low-key solo career.

Album rating: THE CURSE OF THE ZOUNDS! (*4)

STEVE LAKE – vocals / **LAURENCE WOOD** – guitar / **LIBERTY KROPOTKIN** (b. JOSEF PORTER) – drums

Recommended not iss.

1980. (one-sided-7") *(RR 14.15)* **MENAGE** -

Crass not iss.

Jan 81. (7") *(421984-3)* **CAN'T CHEAT KARMA. / WAR / SUBVERT** -

Rough Trade not iss.

Apr 81. (7") *(RT 069)* **DEMYSTIFICATION. / GREAT WHITE HUNTER** -
Mar 82. (7") *(RT 094)* **DANCING. / TRUE LOVE** -
May 82. (7") *(RT 098)* **MORE TROUBLE COMING EVERY DAY. / KNIFE** -

NotSoBrave not iss.

Jun 82. (7"ep) *(NSB 001)* **LA VACHE QUI RIT** -

– compilations, etc. –

1984. (lp) *Rough Trade; (ROUGH 31)* **THE CURSE OF ZOUNDS!** -
– Fear / Did he jump / Little bit more / This land / My mummy's gone / New band / Dirty squatters / Loads of noise / Medley – Target / Mr. Disney / The war goes on. *<US cd-iss. 1997 on 'Broken Rekids'+=; 56>* – (extra tracks).

WORLD SERVICE

STEVE + LAURENCE

Rough Trade not iss.

Jun 83. (12"ep) *(RTT 118)* **CELEBRATION TOWN. / TURN OUT THE LIGHTS / CELEBRATION TOWN (NIGHTMARE)** -

STEVE LAKE

NotSoBrave not iss.

Mar 84. (12"ep) *(NSB 5)* **WELCOME TO MONKEY HOUSE EP** -
May 85. (lp) *(NSB 7)* **MURDER VIOLENCE SEX DIVORCE** -
Jun 85. (12"ep) *(NSB 8)* **IN EVERY LIFE** -

Play It Again Sam not iss.

Apr 87. (12") *(BIAS 050)* **RUNNING AWAY. /** -
May 87. (lp) *(BIAS 052)* **SO CRUEL** -

ZUZU'S PETALS

Formed: Minneapolis, USA . . . early 90's by songwriters COLEEN ELWOOD and LAURIE LINDEEN, the all-girl trio being completed by drummer LINDA PITMON. After a few singles including one ('HOW LONG') for Shimmy Disc offshoot, 'Kokopop', ZUZU'S PETALS – who at one point were competing for the ZUZU's moniker with around half a dozen other outfits – signed to 'TwinTone'. Strangely enough, licensed to 'Roadrunner' in Europe, the band's debut set, 'WHEN NO ONE'S LOOKING' (1993), revealed them to be distant cousins of BELLY or The BREEDERS, although critics found their combination of shouty vocals and basic indie-pop difficult to pigeonhole. • **Trivia:** ZUZU'S PETALS stems from Frank Capra's great B&W movie, 'It's A Wonderful Life', as well as being the name of a poem by William Blake.

Album rating: WHEN NO ONE'S LOOKING (*5) / MUSIC OF YOUR LIFE (*4)

LAURIE LINDEEN – vocals, guitar / **COLEEN ELWOOD** – bass, vocals / **LINDA PITMON** – drums, percussion

—— released 2 unknown 45's in 1992

not iss. Kokopop

1992. (7") *<3>* **HOW LONG. /** -

Roadrunner TwinTone

Feb 93. (cd/lp) *(RR 9099-2/-1)* **WHEN NO ONE'S LOOKING**
– Cinderella's daydream / God cries / Madrid / Gypsies cove / Johanne / Psycho tavern / Dork magnet / White trash love / Happy birthday / How long / Rum'n coke / Sisters / Sweat pea / Jackhals.

May 93. (12"ep/cd-ep) *(RR 2384-6/-3)* **CINDERELLA'S DAYDREAM / STANDING BY THE SEA. / GOD CRIES / HUMAN BEING**

Jan 95. (cd/lp) *(RR 8975-2/-1)* *<89260>* **THE MUSIC OF YOUR LIFE**
– Do not / Come true / Chatty chatty / Girl he first met / Remembering why / Don't bother / Feel like going home / Johnny / Slacks / Love bullet / Happy.